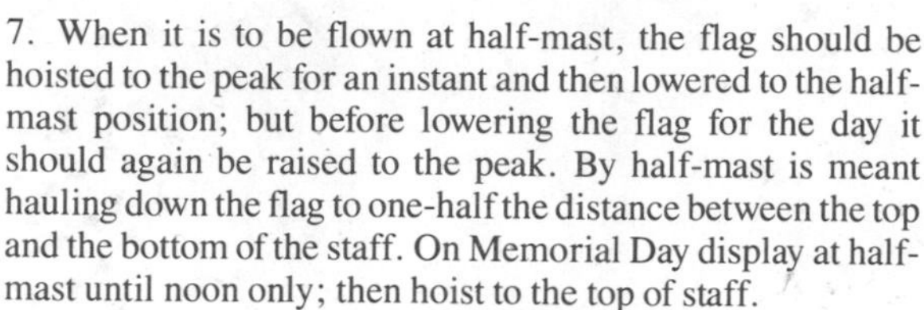

7. When it is to be flown at half-mast, the flag should be hoisted to the peak for an instant and then lowered to the half-mast position; but before lowering the flag for the day it should again be raised to the peak. By half-mast is meant hauling down the flag to one-half the distance between the top and the bottom of the staff. On Memorial Day display at half-mast until noon only; then hoist to the top of staff.

8. When the flag is displayed in a manner other than by being flown from a staff, it should be displayed flat, whether indoors or out. When displayed either horizontally or vertically against a wall, the union should be uppermost and to the flag's own right, that is, to the observer's left. When displayed in a window it should be displayed in the same way, that is, with the union or blue field to the left of the observer in the street. When festoons, rosettes or drapings are desired, bunting of blue, white and red should be used, but never the flag.

9

9. When carried in a procession with another flag or flags, the Stars and Stripes should be either on the marching right, or when there is a line of other flags, in front of the center of that line.

10

11

10. When a number of flags of states or cities or pennants of societies are grouped and displayed from staffs with our National flag, the latter should be at the center and at the highest point of the group.

11. When the flags of two or more nations are displayed they should be flown from separate staffs of the same height, and the flags should be of approximately equal size. International usage forbids the display of the flag of one nation above that of another nation in time of peace.

WEBSTER'S NEW REFERENCE LIBRARY

WEBSTER'S NEW REFERENCE LIBRARY

A NELSON/REGENCY PUBLICATION

THOMAS NELSON PUBLISHERS
Nashville • Camden • New York

Published in Nashville, Tennessee, by Thomas Nelson, Inc., Publishers and distributed in Canada by Lawson Falle, Ltd., Cambridge, Ontario.

Library of Congress Cataloging in Publication Data
Main entry under title:

Webster's new reference library.

Collection of reprints from various dictionaries and encyclopedias.
1. Encyclopedias and dictionaries. I. Thomas Nelson Publishers.
AE6.W43 1984 032.1 84-1117
ISBN 0-8407-4121-9

Manufactured in the United States of America

4 5 6 7 8 9 10 11 12 13 14 15 — 88 87

CONTENTS

DICTIONARY SECTION

ENCYCLOPEDIA SECTION

CREDITS

Webster's New Dictionary of the English Language
- based on the lexical database of the *Concise American Heritage Dictionary.* Copyright 1980 Houghton Mifflin Company. No part of this book may be reproduced or transmitted in any form or by any means, electronic or mechanical, including photocopying and recording, or by any information storage or retrieval system, except as may be expressly permitted by the 1976 Copyright Act or with prior written permission from both Houghton Mifflin Company and Thomas Nelson, Inc.

Words that are believed to be registered trademarks have been checked with authoritative sources. No investigation has been made of common-law trademark rights in any word, because such investigation is impracticable. Words that are known to have current registrations are shown with an initial capital and are also identified as trademarks. The inclusion of any word in this Dictionary is not, however, an expression of the publishers' opinion as to whether or not it is subject to proprietary rights. Indeed, no definition in this Dictionary is to be regarded as affecting the validity of any trademark.

Word Division Dictionary
- based on *Word Division: Supplement to Government Printing Office Style Manual.* Washington, D.C.: U.S. Government Printing Office, 1976.

German/English Dictionary
- based on *German: A Guide to the Spoken Language.* Washington, D.C.: U.S. Government Printing Office, 1975.

Spanish/English Dictionary
- based on *Spanish: A Guide to the Spoken Language.* Washington, D.C.: U.S. Government Printing Office, 1975.

French/English Dictionary
- based on *French: A Guide to the Spoken Language.* Washington, D.C.: U.S. Government Printing Office, 1974.

Medical Dictionary
- based on *Nelson's New Compact Medical Dictionary,* copyright 1978 Thomas Nelson Inc., Publishers.
- illustrations from the *Quick Reference Handbook Set—Basic Health Care and Emergency Aid,* copyright 1984 Thomas Nelson Inc., Publishers and *Medical Aid Encyclopedia for the Home,* copyright 1965, 1972 Stravon Publishers, Inc.

Heart Terms Dictionary
- based on *A Handbook of Heart Terms,* U.S. Department of Health, Education, and Welfare. Washington, D.C.: U.S. Government Printing Office, 1978.

Bible Dictionary
- based on *Nelson's New Compact Illustrated Bible Dictionary,* copyright 1978 Thomas Nelson Inc., Publishers, copyright 1964 Nelson-National.

Roget's Thesaurus
- based on *Nelson's New Compact Roget's Thesaurus,* copyright 1978 Thomas Nelson Inc., Publishers.

Dictionary of Occupational Titles
- based on *Dictionary of Occupational Titles,* U.S. Department of Labor. Washington, D.C.: U.S. Government Printing Office, 1982.

Where to Write for Vital Records
- based on *Where to Write for Vital Records: Births, Deaths, Marriages, and Divorces,* U.S. Department of Health and Human Services. Washington, D.C.: U.S. Government Printing Office, 1982.

World History
- based on *World History Made Simple* copyrighted by Doubleday & Company, Inc., and used by special permission.

The Shuttle Era
- based on *NASA Facts–(100),* National Aeronautics and Space Administration. Washington, D.C.: U.S. Government Printing Office, 1980; *NASA Facts–(127),* National Aeronautics and Space Administration. Washington, D.C.: U.S. Government Printing Office, 1981.

Business Terms Dictionary

Biographical Dictionary

Communication Through Language

Special Compositions

Reading Skills

American History

States and Countries

Math Formulas/Equivalent Measures

Metric Conversions

Four-Year Public Colleges and Universities

Computer Science

Computer Glossary

Music Glossary

Space Glossary
- based on the *Quick Reference Handbook Set—Basic Knowledge and Modern Technology,* copyright 1984 Thomas Nelson, Inc., Publishers; *The Complete Reference Handbook,* copyright 1964 Stravon Publishers; the *Quick Reference Encyclopedia,* copyright 1976 Thomas Nelson, Inc., Publishers; and *The Quick Reference Handbook of Basic Knowledge,* copyright 1979, revised 1982 by Thomas Nelson, Inc., Publishers.

Endsheets (front)
- based on *How To Respect and Display OUR FLAG.* Washington, D.C.: U.S. Government Printing Office, 1973.

Endsheets (back)
- based on *The Great Seal of the United States.* Washington, D.C.: U.S. Government Printing Office, 1980.

PICTURE ACKNOWLEDGMENTS

Air France, 1188; Alaska Travel Division, 1137; American Airlines, 1138(t), 1139, 1146, 1151(t), 1159, 1162, 1172; Arab Information Center, 1207, 1229, 1262; Argosy Gallery, 761, 774, 782; Austrian News and Information Bureau, 1190; Bahamas News Bureau, 1191; BOAC, 988, 989, 990, 1210, 1211, 1217, 1227, 1231, 1232, 1239, 1256, 1258; Brazilian Government Trade Bureau, 1194; British European Airways, 995, 1214, 1222, 1261; Canadian Consulate General, 1197(b), 1198; Chamber of Commerce, 1165; Civic Promotion Division of Commerce of South Bend, 1147; Colorado Department of Public Relations, 1140; Connecticut Development Committee, 1141; Consul General of Chile, 1201; Cram, George F., Co., Inc., maps following page 886; Delaware State Development Department, 1142; Irish Tourist Office, 1005; Italian Tourist Office, 1001, Japan Air Lines, 997; Japan Tourist Association, 1224; Library of Congress, 756, 1088, 1090, Miami Bureau, 1143; Montana Highway Commission, 1157(t); NASA, 1108(t), 1109, 1110; National Park Service, 1138(b), 1144(t), 1144(b), 1145, 1149, 1151(b), 1153, 1155, 1164, 1166, 1171, 1175; Nebraska Game Commission, 1157(b); Netherlands Information Service, 1235; New York-Historical Society, 1084, 1085(t), 1085(b), North Carolina Department of Conservation and Development, 1163; Northwest Orient Airlines, 1169(r); Ontario Department Travel and Publicity, 1197(t); Oregon State Highway Department, 1167; Philippine Tourist and Travel Association, 1240; Rhode Island Development Council, 1169(l); Scandinavian Travel Commission, 1206; "Sni-Yan," 1241; Spanish Ministry of Tourism, 1007; Standard Oil Company, (N.J.), 1150; TWA Airlines, 1152, 1158, 1161; Union Pacific Railroad, 1178; United Nations, 1208, 1219, 1228, 1276(t), 1276(b), 1278, 1279, 1280, 1281, 1283; United Press International, 751, 753, 759, 760, 763, 771, 773, 775, 776, 788, 790, 795, 801, 804, 1108(b.l.), 1108(b.r.), 1113, 1202, 1263, 1264, 1265; U.S. Army, 1096, 1097(t), 1097(b); U.S. Department of State, endsheets (back), 1098, 1099, 1101, 1102, 1103, 1105, 1106, 1107, 1112(t), 1112(b)U.S. Marine Corps, endsheets (front); U.S. Navy, 1083, 1094(b), 1094(t), 1100; Utah Tourist and Publicity Council, 1173(t); Vermont Development Department, 1173(b); Venezuela Ministry of Tourism, 1259; Vilko Zuber, 1003; Virginia Department of Conservation and Economic Development, 1174; West Virginia Department of Commerce, 1176; Wisconsin Conservation Department, 1177

The letters in the parentheses next to the page numbers stand for the following: t = top of page; m = middle of page; b = bottom of page; r = right side of page; l = left side of page; b.l. = bottom left of page; b.r. = bottom right of page; m.l. = middle left of page; m.r. = middle right of page; t.l. = top left of page; t.r. = top right of page.

CONTRIBUTORS AND EDITORS

Titles given below are as of the time of the author's contributions to the book.

Elvin Abeles
Former Associate Editor
Collier's Encyclopedia

Frank Alweis
Director, Honor School
James Monroe High School

Roy O. Billett
Professor of Education, Emeritus
Boston University

Lawrence D. Brennan
Professor, Business Writing and Speaking
New York University

Oscar Cargill
Head, Department of English
Graduate School of Arts and Science
New York University

Bradford Chambers
Author, Editor, *Home Library Press*

Allan Danzig
Assistant Professor,
Department of English
Lafayette College

Mary F. Doherty
Librarian
The Metropolitan Museum of Art

John R. Dugan
Professor of Law
New York Law School

David Ebner
Author, *Elementary Algebra*

Willard Hutcheon
Lecturer, Philosophy
The City University of New York

William Jaber
Geographer

Steele M. Kennedy
Former Education Editor and
Director of Information Services
New Jersey State
Department of Education

Jerome E. Leavitt
Professor of Education
Portland State College

Paul B. Panes
Director, The Reading Institute
New York University

Thomas N. Pappas
Dean of Academic Administration
Warner Pacific College

Ernest D. Partridge, Jr.
Assistant Professor of Philosophy and Education
Paterson State College

Mario Pei
Professor, Romance Languages, Emeritus
Columbia University

Louis M. Pell
Chairman, Department of English
Columbia Grammar School

Gary Ruse
Vice-President, First National Bank
Gordon, Nebraska

Robert M. Segal
Editor
Stravon Educational Press

Clem Stein, Jr.
Merchandising Supervisor
Sears, Roebuck and Co.

Mitchell Weiner
Director
College Entrance Tutoring Service

Consulting Editors

Calvin D. Linton, Ph.D
Dean, Columbian College
The George Washington University

Edward H. Litchfield, Ph.D.
Chancellor
University of Pittsburgh

Editor

Mary Bray Wheeler

Editorial Assistants

Genon Hickerson Neblett
Teri Keas Mitchell

Updating Editors

Alice C. Ewing
John A. Fribley

DICTIONARY SECTION

Webster's New Dictionary of the English Language

Guide to the Dictionary

The Main Entry

The main entry is the word or phrase one looks up in the Dictionary. It is printed in boldface type a little to the left of the rest of the type.

Two or more entries that are identical in spelling but have different etymologies are entered separately; each entry bears a superscript number.

baste[1]

baste[2]

baste[3]

The entry word, whether a solid word, syllabicated word, hyphenated compound, or phrase, is alphabetized as if it were written solid.

wa·ter

Water Bearer

wa·ter·borne

water buffalo

Abbreviations are alphabetized in the same sequence as words.

Syllabication

An entry word is divided into syllables by centered dots.

rep·re·sen·ta·tion

In a phrasal entry, words that appear as separate entries are not syllabicated.

die·sel engine

Engine is a separate entry, **diesel** is not.

However, when principal parts of regular verbs appear as parts of phrasal entries, they are *not* syllabicated.

Variants

If two or more different spellings of a single word are entered, they are set in boldface type and are treated in two ways:

(1) A variant may follow the main entry, separated from it only by a comma. This indicates that the two forms are used almost equally frequently.

ax, axe

(2) When one spelling is distinctly preferred, the variant is introduced by the word "Also."

me·di·e·val . . . Also **me·di·ae·val**.

A large class of variants consists of spellings preferred in British English and sometimes used in American English. Such variants as **colour** and **centre** are labeled *Chiefly Brit.* The variant **-ise**, which occurs in many British spellings where American has **-ize** (for example, **realize, realise**), is not given unless it is also a common American variant.

When a word that has a variant occurs in a compound, the variant is not repeated at the compound; for example, the variant **colour** is given at **color**, but it is not repeated at **colorblind** and other compounds.

A variant spelling that would, if entered, fall within five entries of the preferred spelling is not entered separately.

Apart from variant spellings, which are given at the beginning of an entry, there are often two or more distinct words or phrases that have identical meaning. These alternate names for the same thing are treated as follows:

(1) The alternate name is a main entry, and the preferred form is given in the definition.

ad·ju·tant . . . *n.* **1.** . . . **2.** A stork, the marabou.

darning needle. 1. . . . **2.** A dragonfly.

bi·car·bon·ate of soda. Sodium bicarbonate.

In the last case, because the main entry is a phrasal compound, it is set in boldface type; this indicates that the entry for the preferred form is to be found in its proper alphabetical order in the letter *s*.

(2) The main entry is fully defined; if the alternate name is mentioned, it is treated as a regular synonym, i.e., it appears in lightface roman type.

Sodium bicarbonate. A white . . . ; bicarbonate of soda.

(3) If the alternate name applies only to a single sense of the definition, it is entered just after the proper part-of-speech label or definition number.

mu·si·cal . . . *adj.* . . . —*n.* **musical comedy.** A play . . .

an·ise . . . *n.* **1.** A plant having aromatic licorice-flavored seeds. **2.** Also **an·i·seed** . . . The seeds, used as a flavoring.

In these particular cases, **musical comedy** and **aniseed** will not be entered separately because they would fall within five entries of the main entry.

Inflected Forms

Inflected forms regarded as being irregular or offering possible spelling problems are entered in boldface type, usually in shortened form, immediately following the part-of-speech label or the numbered sense of the definition to which they apply.

base . . . **baser, basest.**

well . . . **better, best.**

fly . . . **flew, flown, flying.**

Regular inflections are normally not entered. For the purposes of this Dictionary, regular inflections include:

1. Plurals formed by suffixing *-s* or *-es*. The regular plural is shown, however, when there is an irregular variant plural or when the spelling of the regular plural might present difficulty, as with words ending in *-o*.

cac·tus . . . *pl.* **-ti** (-tī') or **-tuses.**

to·ma·to . . . *pl.* **-toes.**

pi·an·o . . . *pl.* **-os.**

2. Past tenses and past participles formed by suffixing *-ed* with no other change in the verb form, as **marked, parked,** etc.

3. Present participles formed by suffixing *-ing* with no other change in the verb form, as **marking, parking,** etc.

4. Present-tense forms, with the exception of such highly irregular forms as **is, has,** etc.

5. Comparatives and superlatives formed by suffixing *-er* and *-est* with no other change in the positive form of the adjective and adverb, as **taller, tallest,** etc.

The inflected forms of verbs are given in the following order: past tense, past participle (if it differs from the past tense), and present participle.

fly . . . **flew, flown, flying.**

Alternate inflected forms are given and labeled.

Irregular inflected forms that would fall within five entries of the main entry are not entered separately; in such cases they are pronounced at the main entry. If, however, they fall more than five entries from the main entry (i.e., the infinitive form of a verb, the singular of a noun, etc.), they are separately entered, pronounced, and identified by italicized abbreviations as a part or parts of a verb, comparative of an adjective, plural of a noun, etc.

Order of Definitions

When an entry has multiple numbered definitions, these are ordered by a method of synchronic semantic analysis intended to serve the convenience of the general user of the Dictionary. The numerical order does not indicate the historical sequence in which the senses developed. The first definition, then, is not necessarily the earliest sense of the word, though it may be. Rather, the first definition is the central meaning about which the other senses can most logically be organized. The organization seeks to clarify the fact that, despite its various meanings, the entry is a single "word" and not a number of separate words that happen to be spelled the same way.

Numbers and Letters

When an entry has more than one definition, these are numbered in sequence. In a *combined entry* (one in which the entry word belongs to more than one part of speech), the definitions are numbered in separate sequences beginning with **1.** after each part of speech.

be·hind . . . *adv.* **1.** In, to, or toward the rear . . . **2.** In a place . . . **3.** In arrears; late. —*prep.* **1.** At the back of . . . **2.** On the further side of . . .

When a numbered definition has two or more closely related senses, these are marked **a.**, **b.**, etc.

lat·i·tude . . . *n.* **1.** . . . **2.** . . . **3. a.** The angular distance N or S of the equator, measured in degrees along a meridian. **b.** A region considered in relation to this distance.

When a general definition is further qualified by several specific meanings, the letters **a.**, **b.**, etc., are used.

card[1] . . . *n.* **1.** A small, flat piece of stiff paper or thin pasteboard with numerous uses: **a.** One of a set . . . **b.** A post card. **c.** One bearing . . .

Numbered Boldface Definitions

Plurals

If a noun has, in addition to its ordinary sense, a sense or senses in which it often appears in the plural, this fact is indicated as follows:

ground . . . *n.* 1. . . . 4. Often **grounds.** The foundation or basis . . .

If a noun is *always* used in the plural or if the plural form takes a singular verb, the plural form appears in boldface before the definition and the parenthetical grammatical note.

com•mon . . . *adj.* 1. Belonging equally to all; joint . . . —*n.* 1. A tract of land . . . 2. **Commons.** The lower house of Parliament . . .

gut . . . *n.* 1. . . . 4. **guts.** *Slang.* Courage; fortitude.

a•cous•tic . . . *adj.* Also **a•cous•ti•cal.** Pertaining to sound . . . —*n.* **acoustics.** 1. *(takes sing. v.).* The scientific study of sound. 2. *(takes pl. v.).* The total effect . . .

Combined Upper-case and Lower-case Forms

When upper-case and lower-case words of the same spelling have the same etymology, both forms are usually included in the same entry.

If the lower-case form is a common word with a specific upper-case sense, the lower-case form is the main entry. Most upper-case and lower-case combinations are of this sort.

sav•ior . . . *n.* Also **sav•iour.** 1. One who . . . 2. **the Savior.** Christ.

If, on the other hand, the upper-case form is the original sense and is still current, it is the main entry.

A•pol•lo . . . *n.* 1. Greek sun god, patron of . . . 2. **apollo.** Any young man . . .

The word "Often" immediately following a boldface number indicates that a word is often or usually upper-case (or lower-case) in that sense.

cock•ney . . . *n.* 1. Often **Cockney.** A native of . . . 2. The dialect . . .

Part-of-Speech Labels

The italicized labels below, which follow the pronunciation of the entry word, are used to indicate parts of speech.

n.	noun
adj.	adjective
adv.	adverb
pron.	pronoun
conj.	conjunction
prep.	preposition
v.	verb
interj.	interjection
comb. form.	combining form

The following additional italicized labels are used to indicate inflected forms:

fem.n.	feminine noun
pl.	plural
sing.	singular
pres.p.	present participle
p.t.	past tense
p.p.	past participle
compar.	comparative
superl.	superlative

Part-of-Speech Labels in Combined Entries

In combined entries, the part-of-speech labels that follow the first one are preceded by a dash. Such labels precede all elements that apply to that part of speech, and may be followed by any elements (pronunciation, other labels, etc.) that can appear immediately following the main-entry word, its pronunciation, etc.

ad-lib . . . *v.* **-libbed, -libbing.** To improvise . . . —*n.* Something ad-libbed . . .

If, however, a language, status, or field label applies to a whole entry, the label precedes all part-of-speech labels.

mug[2] . . . *Slang. n.* 1. The face . . . 2. . . . —*v.* **mugged, mugging.** 1. . . .

Verbs

Parentheses are used to indicate a direct object or an intransitive sense in which the object of the verb is included.

ad•min•is•ter . . . *v.* 1. To manage. 2. a. To give (a drug) remedially. b. To dispense (a sacrament) . . .

Parentheses are also used around a final preposition to indicate that a verb can be used either transitively or intransitively in that sense, i.e., that it can be followed by a direct object or that its object may be omitted entirely.

kink . . . *n.* 1. A small, tight . . . —*v.* To form kinks (in).

Idioms

Many entry words are commonly used in phrases the meaning of which is not clear from the meanings of the separate words. Except as noted, such phrases are defined at the entry for the most significant word in the phrase. The phrase is introduced by a boldface dash and is set in boldface type. Phrases such as **water buffalo,** made up of an attributive (adjective or noun) plus a noun, are separate main entries. Verb phrases that form nouns are also separate main entries; for example, **make up** is a separate entry because of the noun **make-up.**

Main Entry Words Having Meaning Only in a Phrase

A certain small class of words has current meaning only in phrasal combinations and is so treated.

a•back . . . *adv.* —**take aback.** To startle; confuse.

re•ly . . . *v.* **-lied, -lying.** —**rely on** (or **upon**). 1. To depend. 2. To trust confidently.

Usage Labels

Usage labels are restrictive labels that serve to warn the reader that a term is not properly available for use in all contexts. A usage label applies only to the definition or definitions that follow it. A single entry may have standard (unlabeled) definitions and any combination of labeled definitions.

Informal signifies "cultivated colloquial," that is, the speech of educated persons when they are more interested in what they are saying than in how they are saying it. *Informal* terms are also used in writing that seeks the effect of speech, but they are not used in formal writing.

Slang does not define a level of speech, as does *Informal,* but a style having features that are usually not hard to identify. Slang may occur in all but the most formal language and remain slang. A primary rule to distinguish it from nonstandard speech is that a slang term may not be used merely to indicate the meaning of a word; it always carries some deliberately informal connotation in addition and suggests some intention—however dully conceived—of rhetorical effect, such as incongruity, hyberbole, irreverence, etc.

Nonstandard, unlike *Informal* and *Slang,* indicates usages that are widespread but not acceptable. It includes forms such as "irregardless" and "ain't."

Obsolete (Obs.) is for obsolete words, few of which are entered; in order to be entered an obsolete term must have appeared in standard literature either frequently or prominently. (A distinction must be made between a term for an obsolete thing and a term that is itself obsolete. The former is not labeled, but the historical situation is explained in the definition, e.g., "An 18th-century hat . . .")

Archaic is used for terms that were once common and continue to have some use, but are now used only to suggest an earlier style. The label does not suggest a date beyond which a word cannot be found, merely that when it is found in a contemporary context, it is readily identifiable as belonging to a style of language no longer in general use.

Rare terms were never common. The label does not imply *Archaic;* a rare term may be of recent coinage. The label is not used for terms whose use is rare because of the limitation of their application, such as abstruse technical terms; it is confined to general terms for which more common synonyms are available.

Poetic is used for such locutions as a shortening *(o'er)* that is or was common in poetry but was never common in prose.

Regional is used for terms that are not common to American speech in general but exist in more than one locality.

Other Labels

Important words belonging to major English dialectal areas of the U.S. or outside the U.S. are so labeled.

Etymologies

Etymologies appear in square brackets following the definitions. [?] indicates "of obscure origin." The symbol < is used to mean "from" and is often an indication that transitional stages have been omitted in order to give a concise history of the word. The etymologies of most basic words are given, with particular emphasis on native words (i.e., words derived from Old English) having their origins in Indo-European. Many of these cross-refer to the Appendix, which begins on page 807.

The abbreviations used in etymologies usually appear as main entries in their proper alphabetical order; they are all listed in "Abbreviations and Symbols used in Etymologies," on page XII.

Field Labels

An italicized word or abbreviation denoting a specific subject and preceding a definition indicates a specialized sense not identical with any other sense the word may have apart from the labeled field.

Abbreviations

Abbreviations are included as main entries in the vocabulary.

Pronunciation

Pronunciation is given for all main entries and for other forms as needed. It is indicated in parentheses following the form to which it applies.

The set of symbols used is designed to enable the reader to reproduce a satisfactory pronunciation with no more than quick reference to the key. All pronunciations given are acceptable in all circumstances. When more than one is given, the first is assumed to be the most common, but the difference in frequency may be insignificant.

It is obvious that Americans do not all speak alike. It is equally obvious, nevertheless, that Americans can understand one another, at least on the level of speech sounds. In fact, the differences among the major regional varieties of American speech are such that for most words a single set of symbols can represent the pronunciation found in each regional variety, provided the symbols are planned for the purpose stated above: to enable the reader to reproduce a satisfactory pronunciation. When a single pronunciation is offered in this Dictionary, the reader will supply those features of his own regional speech that are called forth by his reading of the key. Apart from regional variations in pronunciation, there are variations among social groups. The pronunciations recorded in this Dictionary are exclusively those of educated speech. In every community, educated speech is accepted and understood by everyone, including those who do not themselves use it.

Pronunciation Key

A shorter form of this key appears across the bottom of each pair of facing pages. The symbols marked with an asterisk are discussed in this guide.

spellings	AHD
pat	ă
pay	ā
care	*âr
father	ä
bib	b
church	ch
deed, milled	d
pet	ĕ
bee	ē
fife, phase	f
gag	g
hat	h
which	hw
pit	*ĭ
pie, by	ī
pier	*îr
judge	j
kick, cat, pique	k
lid, needle	*l (nēd′l)
mum	m
no, sudden	*n (sŭd′n)
thing	ng
pot, *horrid	ŏ
toe, *hoarse	ō
caught, paw, *for	ô
noise	oi
took	o͝o
boot	o͞o
out	ou
pop	p
roar	*r
sauce	s
ship, dish	sh
tight, stopped	t
thin	th
this	*th*
cut	ŭ
urge, term, firm, word, heard	*ûr
valve	v
with	w
yes	y
zebra, xylem	z
vision, pleasure, garage	zh
about, item, edible, gallop, circus	*ə
butter	*ər

FOREIGN

French ami	à
French feu, *German* schön	œ
French tu, *German* über	ü
German ich, *Scottish* loch	KH
French bon	N
French compiègne	y' (kôN-pyĕn'y')

STRESS

Primary stress ′	**bi·ol′o·gy** (bī-ŏl′ə-jē)
Secondary stress ′	**bi′o·log′i·cal** (bī′ə-lŏj′ĭ-kəl)

Explanatory Notes

ə: This nonalphabetical symbol is called a *schwa*. The symbol is used in the Dictionary to represent only a reduced vowel, i.e., a vowel that receives the weakest level of stress (which can be thought of as no stress) within a word and therefore nearly always exhibits a change in quality from the quality it would have if it were stressed, as in *telegraph* (tĕl′ə-grăf′) and *telegraphy* (tə-lĕg′rə-fē). Vowels are never reduced to a single exact vowel; the schwa sound will vary, sometimes according to the "full" vowel it is representing and often according to its phonetic environment.

ĭ: This symbol is used to represent the second vowel in **artist** (är′tĭst), a vowel that has been only partially reduced and therefore cannot be represented by the schwa. The choice between schwa (ə) and "breve i" (ĭ) to represent reduced vowels is arrived at through a complex set of considerations. In nearly every case in which (ĭ) appears, there is also a variant pronunciation closer to (ə). As long as reduced vowels receive no stress, the surrounding sounds will lead the reader to produce either (ə) or (ĭ), according to his regional speech pattern.

/y/: The *y* between virgules indicates that the sound is present in the pronunciation of some speakers and absent from the pronunciation of others, as in the word *duty*, where two pronunciations may occur, (do͞o′tē) and (dyo͞o′tē). In this Dictionary both pronunciations are represented in (d/y/o͞o′tē).

âr, îr, ûr, ər: These symbols represent vowels that have been altered by a following *r*. This situation is traditionally exemplified by the words *Mary*, *merry*, and *marry*. In some regional varieties all three are pronounced alike: (mĕr′ē). However, in a broad range of individual American speech patterns cutting across regional boundaries, the three words are distinguished. It is this pattern that the Dictionary represents, thus: *Mary* (mâr′ē), *merry* (mĕr′ē), *marry* (măr′ē). Some words, however, are heard in all three pronunciations, indistinctly grading one into another. For these words the Dictionary represents only (âr), for example, *care* (kâr), *dairy* (dâr′ē).

In words such as *hear*, *beer*, and *dear*, the vowel could be represented by (ē) were it not for the effect of the following *r*, which makes it approach (ĭ) in sound. In this Dictionary a special symbol (îr) is used for this combination, as in *beer* (bîr).

There are regional differences in the distinctions among various pronunciations of the syllable *-or*. In pairs such as *for, four; horse, hoarse;* and *morning, mourning*, the vowel varies between (ô) and (ō). In this Dictionary these vowels are represented as follows: *for* (fôr), *four* (fôr, fōr); *horse* (hôrs), *hoarse* (hôrs, hōrs). Other words for which both forms are shown include those such as *more* (môr, mōr) and *glory* (glôr′ē, glōr′-).

Another group of words with variations for the *-or* syllable includes words such as *forest* and *horrid*, in which the pronunciation of *o* before *r* varies between (ô) and (ŏ). In these words the (ôr) pronunciation is given first: *forest* (fôr′ĭst, fŏr′-).

The symbol (ûr) used in *her* (hûr), *fur* (fûr), etc., has a regular regional variant that is not separately recorded. In one pattern the effect of the *r* is heard simultaneously with the vowel; in the other some, but not all, such syllables are heard with a vowel like ŭ or ə before the onset of the *r*.

Syllabic Consonants

There are two consonants that are represented as complete syllables. These are *l* and *n* (called *syllabics*) following stressed syllables ending in *d* or *t* in such words as *bottle* (bŏt′l), *fatal* (fāt′l), *button* (bŭt′n), *ladle* (lād′l), and *hidden* (hĭd′n). Syllabic *n* is not shown after a syllable ending in *-nd* or *-nt: abandon* (ə-băn′dən), *mountain* (moun′tən); but syllabic *l* is shown in that position: *spindle* (spĭnd′l).

Stress

In this Dictionary, stress, the relative degree of loudness with which the syllables of a word (or phrase) are spoken, is indicated in three different ways. An unmarked syllable has the weakest stress in the word. The strongest stress is marked with a bold mark (**′**). An intermediate level of stress, here called *secondary*, is marked with a similar but lighter mark (′).

Words of one syllable show no stress mark, since there is no other stress level to which the syllable is compared.

The pronunciations are syllabicated for clarity. Syllabication of the pronunciation does not necessarily match the syllabication of the entry word being pronounced. The former follows strict, though not obvious, phonological rules; the latter represents the established practice of printers and editors.

ABBREVIATIONS AND SYMBOLS USED IN ETYMOLOGIES

abbr, abbreviation
abl, ablative
acc, accusative
Afr, African
Afrik, Afrikaans
Algon, Algonquian
aor, aorist
Ar, Arabic
Aram, Aramaic
Assyr, Assyrian
aug, augmentative
Av, Avestan
Brit, British
Bulg, Bulgarian
Cant, Cantonese
Celt, Celtic
Chin, Chinese
Corn, Cornish
CRom, Common Romance
Dan, Danish
dat, dative
dial, dialectal
dim, diminutive
Dravid, Dravidian
Du, Dutch
Egypt, Egyptian
Eng, English
Esk, Eskimo
etym, etymology
expr, expressive
F, French
fem, feminine
Frank, Frankish
freq, frequentative
Fris, Frisian
fut, future
G, German
gen, genitive
Gk, Greek
Gmc, Germanic
Goth, Gothic
Heb, Hebrew
Hitt, Hittite
Hung, Hungarian
Icel, Icelandic
IE, Indo-European
imit, imitative
Ind, Indic
Ir, Irish
Iran, Iranian
It, Italian
Ital, Italic
Jap, Japanese
L, Latin
Latv, Latvian
LG, Low German
LGk, Late Greek
Lith, Lithuanian
LL, Late Latin
Mand, Mandarin
masc, masculine
MDu, Middle Dutch
ME, Middle English
Medit, Mediterranean
Mex, Mexican
MGk, Medieval Greek
MHG, Middle High German
ML, Medieval Latin
MLG, Middle Low German
Nah, Nahuatl
neut, neuter
NF, Norman French
NL, New Latin
nom, nominative
Norw, Norwegian
OCS, Old Church Slavonic
OE, Old English
OF, Old French
OHG, Old High German
OIr, Old Irish
OIt, Old Italian
ON, Old Norse
ONF, Old North French
OP, Old Persian
OProv, Old Provençal
orig, originally
OS, Old Saxon
OSpan, Old Spanish
OSwed, Old Swedish
part, participle
perf, perfect
perh, perhaps
Pers, Persian
Phoen, Phoenician
pl, plural
Pol, Polish
Port, Portuguese
poss, possibly
pp, past participle
pres, present
prob, probably
pron, pronoun
Prov, Provençal
prp, present participle
pt, past tense
redupl, reduplicated
refl, reflexive
Rum, Rumanian
Russ, Russian
Scand, Scandinavian
Scot, Scottish
Sem, Semitic
sing, singular
Sk, Sanskrit
Slav, Slavic
Span, Spanish
superl, superlative
Sw, Swedish
Tag, Tagalog
Tam, Tamil
Tokh, Tokharian
trans, translation
Turk, Turkish
var, variant
VL, Vulgar Latin
W, Welsh
Yidd, Yiddish
< from
[?] Of obscure origin
* unattested

Aa

a, A (ā) *n.* **1.** The 1st letter of the English alphabet. **2.** The 1st in a series. **3.** The highest grade in quality.
a **1.** are (measurement). **2.** *Phys.* atto-.
A **1.** acre. **2.** ammeter. **3.** ampere. **4.** area. **5.** The 6th tone in the scale of C major.
a. **1.** acceleration. **2.** acre. **3.** acreage. **4.** adjective. **5.** anonymous. **6.** answer. **7.** are (measurement).
A. **1.** acre. **2.** alto. **3.** America; American. **4.** answer.
a (ə; *emphatic* ā) *indef. art.* **1. a.** —Used before a noun to indicate nonspecific membership in a class or category: *a generous man.* **b.** —Used before a plural noun with an intervening adjective: *a few phrases.* **2. a.** Similar; like: *birds of a feather.* **b.** Any: *not a drop left.* **3.** —Used prepositionally to indicate *in* or *for each: take one a day.* **4.** —Used before nouns that begin with a consonant sound: *a book.* [< OE *ān,* one. See **oino-.**]
a–¹. *comb. form.* Without, not, or opposite to: **amoral.** [< Gk *an,* not.]
a–². *comb. form.* **1.** On or in: **aboard.** **2.** In the act of: *a-fishing.* **3.** In the direction of, situated at, or toward: **astern.** [< OE *an, on,* ON.]
a–³. *comb. form.* **1.** Up, out, or away: **awake.** **2.** Intensified action: **amaze.** [< OE *ā-.*]
a–⁴. *comb. form.* Of or from: **anew.** [< OE *of,* OF.]
AA Alcoholics Anonymous.
A.A. Associate in Arts.
AAA **1.** American Automobile Association. **2.** antiaircraft artillery.
aard•vark (ärd′värk′) *n.* A burrowing African mammal having large ears and a long snout. [Obs Afrik, "earth-pig."]
ab. about.
A.B. Bachelor of Arts.
a•back (ə-băk′) *adv.* **—take aback.** To startle; confuse.
ab•a•cus (ăb′ə-kəs) *n., pl.* **-cuses** or **-ci** (-sī′). A manual computing device consisting of a frame holding parallel rods strung with movable counters. [< Gk *abax,* slab.]

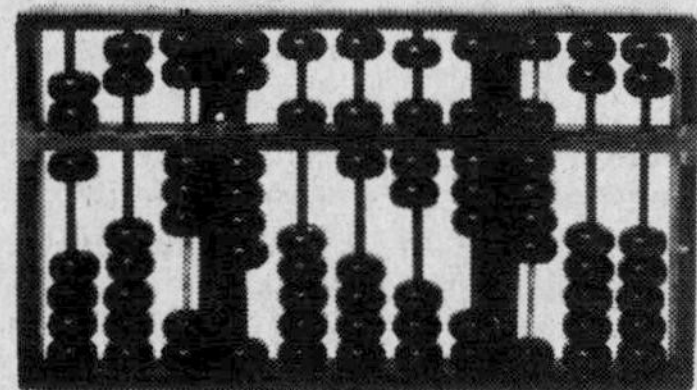

abacus

a•baft (ə-băft′, ə-bäft′) *adv.* Toward the stern. *—prep.* Toward the stern from. [< ON + OE *beæftan,* behind.]
ab•a•lo•ne (ăb′ə-lō′nē) *n.* A marine mollusk having a large, ear-shaped shell. [Amer Span *abulón.*]
a•ban•don (ə-băn′dən) *v.* **1.** To give up; forsake. **2.** To desert. **3.** To desist from. *—n.* A complete surrender of inhibitions. [< OF *(metre) a bandon,* "(to put) in one's power."] **—a•ban′don•er** *n.* **—a•ban′don•ment** *n.*
a•ban•doned (ə-băn′dənd) *adj.* Shameless; immoral. **—a•ban′doned•ly** *adv.*
a•base (ə-bās′) *v.* **abased, abasing.** To humble; humiliate. **—a•base′ment** *n.* **—a•bas′er** *n.*
a•bash (ə-băsh′) *v.* To make ashamed or uneasy; embarrass; disconcert. [< OF *esbahir,* to gape at.] **—a•bash′ment** *n.*
a•bate (ə-bāt′) *v.* **abated, abating.** **1.** To reduce in amount, degree, or intensity; lessen. **2.** To put an end to. [< OF *abattre,* to beat down.] **—a•bat′a•ble** *adj.* **—a•bat′er** *n.*
a•bate•ment (ə-bāt′mənt) *n.* **1.** Diminution in degree or intensity. **2.** The amount abated; reduction.
ab•bé (ăb′ā, ă-bā′) *n.* In France, a title given to a priest.
ab•bess (ăb′ĭs) *n.* The female superior of a convent of nuns.
ab•bey (ăb′ē) *n., pl.* **-beys.** **1.** A monastery or convent. **2.** An abbey church. [< LL *abbātia* < *abbās,* ABBOT.]
ab•bot (ăb′ət) *n.* The superior of a monastery. [< OE *abbod* < LL *abbās* < Aram *abbā,* father.] **—ab′bot•ship′** *n.*
abbr. abbreviation.
ab•bre•vi•ate (ə-brē′vē-āt′) *v.* **-ated, -ating.** To make shorter, esp. to reduce to an abbreviation. [< LL *abbreviāre,* to shorten.] **—ab•bre′vi•a′tor** (-ā′tər) *n.*
ab•bre•vi•a•tion (ə-brē′vē-ā′shən) *n.* **1.** The act or product of abbreviating. **2.** A shortened form of a word or phrase, as *Mass.* for *Massachusetts.*
ab•di•cate (ăb′dĭ-kāt′) *v.* **-cated, -cating.** To relinquish (power or responsibility) formally. [L *abdicāre,* to disclaim.] **—ab′di•ca′tion** *n.*
ab•do•men (ăb′də-mən, ăb-dō′mən) *n.* The part of the mammalian body between the thorax and the pelvis. [L *abdōmen,* belly.] **—ab•dom′i•nal** (-dŏm′ə-nəl) *adj.*
ab•duct (ăb-dŭkt′) *v.* To carry off by force; kidnap. [L *abdūcere.*] **—ab•duc′tion** *n.* **—ab•duc′tor** *n.*
a•beam (ə-bēm′) *adv.* At right angles to the keel of a ship.
a•bed (ə-bĕd′) *adv.* In bed.
ab•er•ra•tion (ăb′ə-rā′shən) *n.* **1.** Deviation or departure from the normal, the typical, or the expected. **2. a.** Blurring or distortion of an image. **b.** A defect, as in a mirror or lens, causing such distortion. [< L *aberrāre,* to go astray.] **—ab•er′rant** *adj.*
a•bet (ə-bĕt′) *v.* **abetted, abetting.** **1.** To encourage; incite. **2.** To assist. [< OF *abeter,* to entice.] **—a•bet′ment** *n.* **—a•bet′tor, a•bet′ter** *n.*
a•bey•ance (ə-bā′əns) *n.* The condition of being temporarily set aside; suspension. [< OF *abeance,* desire < *abaer,* "to gape at."]
ab•hor (ăb-hôr′) *v.* **-horred, -horring.** To dislike intensely; loathe. [< L *abhorrēre,* to shrink from.] **—ab•hor′rence** (-hôr′əns, -hŏr′əns) *n.*
ab•hor•rent (ăb-hôr′ənt, -hŏr′ənt) *adj.* Disgusting; loathsome. **—ab•hor′rent•ly** *adv.*
a•bide (ə-bīd′) *v.* **abode** or **abided, abiding.** **1.** To be in store for; await. **2.** To tolerate; bear. **3.** To remain; last. **—abide by.** To conform to; comply with. [< OE *ābīdan.*]
Ab•i•djan (ăb′ĭ-jän′). The capital of the Ivory Coast. Pop. 258,000.
a•bil•i•ty (ə-bĭl′ə-tē) *n., pl.* **-ties.** **1.** The quality of being able to do something; power to perform. **2.** A skill or talent. [< L *habilitās* < *habilis,* ABLE.]
ab•ject (ăb′jĕkt′, ăb-jĕkt′) *adj.* **1.** Contemptible; mean; base. **2.** Miserable; wretched. [< L *abjicere,* to cast away.] **—ab′jec′tion** *n.* **—ab′ject′ly** *adv.* **—ab′ject′ness** *n.*
ab•jure (ăb-jŏŏr′) *v.* **-jured, -juring.** **1.** To recant solemnly. **2.** To renounce under oath; forswear. [< L *abjūrāre.*] **—ab•jur′er** *n.*
abl. ablative.
ab•la•tion (ă-blā′shən) *n.* A wearing away; erosion. [< L *ablātus,* "removed."]
ab•la•tive (ăb′lə-tĭv) *adj.* Designating a grammatical case indicating separation, direction away from, and sometimes manner or agency, found in some Indo-European languages. [< L *ablātīvus,* "expressing removal."] **—ab′la•ti′val** (ăb′lə-tī′vəl) *adj.* **—ab′la•tive** *n.*
a•blaze (ə-blāz′) *adj.* **1.** On fire. **2.** Radiant with bright color.
a•ble (ā′bəl) *adj.* **abler, ablest.** **1.** Having sufficient ability. **2.** Capable or talented. [< L *habilis,* manageable < *habēre,* to handle.] **—a′bly** *adv.*
–able, –ible. *comb. form.* **1.** Susceptible, capable, or worthy of (the action of a verb or implied verb): **debatable.** **2.** Inclined to (the nature of a noun or implied noun): **knowledgeable.**
a•ble-bod•ied (ā′bəl-bŏd′ēd) *adj.* Physically strong and healthy.
able-bodied seaman. A merchant seaman certified for all seaman's duties.
ab•lu•tion (ă-blōō′shən) *n.* A washing of the body, esp. with religious connotation. [< L *abluere,* to wash away.]
ab•ne•gate (ăb′nĭ-gāt′) *v.* **-gated, -gating.** To deny to oneself; renounce. [L *abnegāre,* to refuse.] **—ab′ne•ga′tion** *n.*
ab•nor•mal (ăb-nôr′məl) *adj.* Not normal; deviant. **—ab•nor′mal•ly** *adv.*
ab•nor•mal•i•ty (ăb′nôr-măl′ə-tē) *n., pl.* **-ties.** **1.** An abnormal state or condition. **2.** An abnormal phenomenon.
a•board (ə-bôrd′, ə-bōrd′) *adv.* On board a ship or other vehicle. *—prep.* On board of.
a•bode (ə-bōd′). *p.t. & p.p.* of **abide.** *—n.* A dwelling place; home.
a•bol•ish (ə-bŏl′ĭsh) *v.* To put an end to; annul. [< L *abolēre,* to destroy.]
ab•o•li•tion (ăb′ə-lĭsh′ən) *n.* **1.** An act of abolishing or the state of being abolished; annulment. **2. Abolition.** The termination of slavery in the U.S. **—ab′o•li′tion•ar′y** *adj.*
ab•o•li•tion•ism (ăb′ə-lĭsh′ən-ĭz′əm) *n.* Advocacy of the abolition of slavery in the U.S. **—ab′o•li′tion•ist** *n.*
A-bomb (ā′bŏm′) *n.* An atomic bomb.
a•bom•i•na•ble (ə-bŏm′ə-nə-bəl) *adj.* Detestable; loathsome. **—a•bom′i•na•bly** *adv.*

a•bom•i•nate (ə-bŏm'ə-nāt') *v.* **-nated, -nating.** To detest; abhor. [L *abōminārī,* "to shun as a bad omen."] **—a•bom'i•na'tor** *n.*

a•bom•i•na•tion (ə-bŏm'ə-nā'shən) *n.* **1.** A great dislike; loathing. **2.** Something that elicits great dislike.

ab•o•rig•i•nal (ăb'ə-rĭj'ə-nəl) *adj.* Native; indigenous. *—n.* An aborigine.

ab•o•rig•i•ne (ăb'ə-rĭj'ə-nē') *n.* One of the original inhabitants of a region. [< L *Aborigines,* name of a pre-Roman people.]

a•bort (ə-bôrt') *v.* To terminate pregnancy or full development prematurely. [L *abortāre,* freq of *aborīrī,* to die, disappear.] **—a•bor'tive** *adj.* **—a•bor'tive•ly** *adj.*

a•bor•tion (ə-bôr'shən) *n.* **1.** Induced premature termination of pregnancy or development. **2.** Something malformed or incompletely developed. **—a•bor'tion•al** *adj.*

a•bor•tion•ist (ə-bôr'shən-ĭst) *n.* One who performs illegal abortions.

a•bound (ə-bound') *v.* **1.** To be great in number or amount. **2.** To be fully supplied; teem. [< L *abundāre,* to overflow.]

a•bout (ə-bout') *adv.* **1.** Approximately; nearly. **2.** Toward a reverse direction. **3.** Aimlessly: *wander about.* **4.** In the vicinity. *—prep.* **1.** On all sides of. **2.** Near to. **3.** Here and there; in or on: *strolled about the grounds.* **4.** Concerning. **5.** Ready to commence: *about to leave.* *—adj.* Astir: *up and about.* [< OE *būtan.* See **ud-**.]

a•bout-face (ə-bout'fās') *n.* A reversal of orientation or attitude.

a•bove (ə-bŭv') *adv.* **1.** Overhead: *the sky above.* **2.** In heaven. **3.** Upstairs. **4.** In a higher place. **5.** In an earlier part of a text. **6.** In a higher rank or position. *—prep.* **1.** Over. **2.** Superior to: *Principles are above expediency.* **3.** Beyond the level or reach of. **4.** In preference to. *—n.* Something that is above. *—adj.* Appearing earlier in the same text. [< OE *abufan.* See **upo.**]

a•bove•board (ə-bŭv'bôrd', -bōrd') *adv.* Without deceit. **—a•bove'board'** *adj.*

abr. abridged; abridgment.

ab•ra•ca•dab•ra (ăb'rə-kə-dăb'rə) *n.* **1.** A word held to possess supernatural powers to ward off disaster. **2.** Jargon; gibberish. [< LGk *abrasadabra,* a magic word.]

a•brade (ə-brād') *v.* **abraded, abrading.** To wear away by friction. [L *abrādere,* to scrape off.] **—a•brad'er** *n.*

A•bra•ham (ā'brə-hăm'). The 1st patriarch and progenitor of the Hebrew people.

ab•ra•sion (ə-brā'zhən) *n.* **1.** A wearing away by friction. **2.** A scraped or worn area.

ab•ra•sive (ə-brā'sĭv, -zĭv) *adj.* Causing abrasion. *—n.* An abrasive substance.

a•breast (ə-brĕst') *adv.* Side by side. **—abreast of (or with).** Keeping up with.

a•bridge (ə-brĭj') *v.* **abridged, abridging.** To reduce the length of; condense; shorten. [< LL *abbreviāre,* ABBREVIATE.] **—a•brid'ger** *n.* **—a•bridg'ment, a•bridge'ment** *n.*

a•broad (ə-brôd') *adv.* **1.** Out of one's own country. **2.** Out of doors. **3.** Broadly; widely. [ME *abro(o)d,* "broadly, widely scattered."]

ab•ro•gate (ăb'rō-gāt') *v.* **-gated, -gating.** To put an end to; abolish; annul. [L *abrogāre.*] **—ab'ro•ga'tion** *n.* **—ab'ro•ga'tor** *n.*

a•brupt (ə-brŭpt') *adj.* **1.** Unexpectedly sudden. **2.** Curt; brusque. **3.** Jerky; disconnected: *abrupt, nervous prose.* **4.** Steeply inclined. [< L *abrumpere,* to break off.] **—a•brupt'ly** *adv.* **—a•brupt'ness** *n.*

abs **1.** absolute; absolutely. **2.** absolute temperature.

ab•scess (ăb'sĕs') *n.* A localized collection of pus surrounded by inflamed tissue. [L *abscēssus,* "a going away."]

ab•scise (ăb-sīz') *v.* **-scised, -scising.** To cut off; remove. [L *abscindere.*] **—ab•scis'sion** (-sĭzh'ən) *n.*

ab•scis•sa (ăb-sĭs'ə) *n., pl.* **-sas** or **-scissae** (-sĭs'ē'). *Math.* The coordinate representing the distance of a point from the *y*-axis in a plane Cartesian coordinate system, measured along a line parallel to the *x*-axis. [< L *abscindere,* ABSCISE.]

ab•scond (ăb-skŏnd') *v.* To leave quickly and secretly and hide oneself. [L *abscondere.*] **—ab•scond'er** *n.*

ab•sence (ăb'səns) *n.* **1.** The state of being away. **2.** The time during which one is away. **3.** Lack: *an absence of curiosity.*

ab•sent (ăb'sənt) *adj.* **1.** Not present. **2.** Not existent; lacking. **3.** Inattentive. *—v.* (ăb-sĕnt'). To keep (oneself) away. [< L *abesse,* to be away.] **—ab'sent•ly** *adv.*

ab•sen•tee (ăb'sən-tē') *n.* One who is absent. *—adj.* Of or pertaining to one who is absent.

ab•sen•tee•ism (ăb'sən-tē'ĭz'əm) *n.* Habitual failure to appear, esp. for work.

ab•sent-mind•ed (ăb'sənt-mīn'dĭd) *adj.* Heedless of one's surroundings; preoccupied. **—ab'sent-mind'ed•ly** *adv.*

ab•sinthe (ăb'sĭnth) *n.* A strong green liqueur made from wormwood. [< L *absinthium,* wormwood.] **—ab•sin'thi•an** *adj.*

ab•so•lute (ăb'sə-lo͞ot') *adj.* **1.** Perfect in quality or nature; complete. **2.** Not mixed; pure. **3. a.** Not limited by restrictions or exceptions; unconditional. **b.** Unqualified in extent or degree; total. **4.** Not to be doubted or questioned; positive. **5.** Lacking a particular grammatical connection with other words in a sentence: *an absolute phrase.* [< L *absolvere,* to free from, complete.] **—ab'so•lute'ly** *adv.* **—ab'so•lute'ness** *n.*

absolute value. The numerical value of a quantity without regard to its sign.

absolute zero. The temperature at which substances possess minimal energy, equal to −273.15°C or −459.67°F.

ab•so•lu•tion (ăb'sə-lo͞o'shən) *n. R.C.Ch.* The formal remission of sin imparted by a priest as part of the sacrament of penance.

ab•so•lut•ism (ăb'sə-lo͞o'tĭz'əm) *n.* **1.** Government in which all power is vested in the ruler. **2.** The political theory reflecting this. **—ab'so•lut'ist** *n. & adj.* **—ab'so•lu•tis'tic** *adj.*

ab•solve (ăb-zŏlv', -sŏlv') *v.* **-solved, -solving.** **1.** To set free from guilt, an obligation, etc.; acquit. **2. a.** To grant a remission of sin to. **b.** To remit (a sin). [< L *absolvere,* to free from.] **—ab•solv'a•ble** *adj.*

ab•sorb (ăb-sôrb', -zôrb') *v.* **1.** To take in through or as through pores or interstices; soak in or up. **2.** To occupy the full attention of; engross. [< L *absorbēre.*]

ab•sorb•ent (ăb-sôr'bənt, ăb-zôr'-) *adj.* Capable of absorbing something. *—n.* A substance that absorbs. **—ab•sorb'en•cy** *n.*

ab•stain (ăb-stān') *v.* To refrain from; forbear. [< L *abstinēre,* to hold (oneself) back.] **—ab•stain'er** *n.*

ab•ste•mi•ous (ăb-stē'mē-əs) *adj.* Eating and drinking in moderation. [L *abstēmius.*]

ab•sti•nence (ăb'stə-nəns) *n.* **1.** Restraint of one's desires. **2.** A refraining from drinking alcoholic beverages or from eating certain foods. **—ab'sti•nent** *adj.*

ab•stract (ăb-străkt', ăb'străkt') *adj.* **1.** Considered apart from concrete existence or a specification thereof. **2.** Theoretical; not applied or practical. **3.** Thought of or stated without reference to a specific instance. **4.** *Fine Arts.* Having nonobjective design, form, or content. *—n.* (ăb'străkt'). **1.** A summary. **2.** Something abstract, as a term. *—v.* (ăb-străkt'). **1.** To take away; remove. **2.** To filch; steal. **3.** (ăb'străkt'). To summarize. [< L *abstractus,* "removed from (concrete reality)."]

ab•strac•tion (ăb-străk'shən) *n.* **1.** The act or process of abstracting. **2.** A product of this process; a general idea or word representing a physical concept. **3.** Preoccupation. **4.** An abstract work of art.

ab•struse (ăb-stro͞os') *adj.* Difficult to understand; recondite. [< L *abstrūdere,* to hide.] **—ab•struse'ly** *adv.* **—ab•struse'ness** *n.*

ab•surd (ăb-sûrd', -zûrd') *adj.* Ridiculously incongruous or unreasonable. [< L *absurdus.*] **—ab•surd'i•ty, ab•surd'ness** *n.* **—ab•surd'ly** *adv.*

A•bu Dha•bi (ä'bo͞o dä'bē). **A sheikdom in E Arabia and capital of the United Arab Emirates. Pop. 46,400.**

a•bun•dance (ə-bŭn'dəns) *n.* Also **a•bun•dan•cy** (-dən-sē). A great quantity; plentiful amount. [< L *abundāre,* ABOUND.] **—a•bun'dant** *adj.* **—a•bun'dant•ly** *adv.*

a•buse (ə-byo͞oz') *v.* **abused, abusing.** **1.** To use wrongly or improperly. **2.** To maltreat. **3.** To berate; insult. *—n.* (ə-byo͞os'). **1.** Misuse. **2.** A corrupt practice or custom. **3.** Maltreatment. **4.** Insulting language. [< L *abūsus,* a using up.] **—a•bu'sive** *adj.* **—a•bu'sive•ly** *adv.*

a•but (ə-bŭt') *v.* **abutted, abutting.** To lie adjacent; border upon. [< OF *abuter,* to buttress, put an end to.] **—a•but'ter** *n.*

a•but•ment (ə-bŭt'mənt) *n.* **1.** The act or process of abutting. **2.** A structure that receives the thrust of an arch or bridge.

a•bysm (ə-bĭz'əm) *n.* An abyss. [< LL *abyssus,* ABYSS.]

a•bys•mal (ə-bĭz'məl) *adj.* **1.** Unfathomable; extreme. **2.** Of or resembling an abyss. **—a•bys'mal•ly** *adv.*

a•byss (ə-bĭs') *n.* **1. a.** The primeval chaos. **b.** The bottomless pit; hell. **2.** Any immeasurably profound depth or void. [LL *abyssus.*]

a•byss•al (ə-bĭs'əl) *adj.* **1.** Abysmal. **2.** Of or pertaining to the great depths of the oceans.

Ab•ys•sin•i•a (ăb'ə-sĭn'ē-ə). Ethiopia. **—Ab'ys•sin'i•an** *adj. & n.*

ac alternating current.

Ac actinium.

a.c. before meals (NL *ante cibum*).

A.C. **1.** alternating current. **2.** before Christ (NL *ante Christum*).

a/c account; account current.

a•ca•cia (ə-kā'shə) *n.* **1.** Any of various trees having tight clusters of small yellow or white flowers. **2.** Any of several related trees. [L.]

acad. academic; academy.

ac•a•dem•ic (ăk'ə-dĕm'ĭk) *adj.* **1.** Of or characteristic of a school. **2.** Liberal or classical rather than technical or vocational, as studies. **3.** Formalistic; conventional. **4.** Theoretical; speculative. **—ac'a•dem'i•cal•ly** *adv.*

ac•a•de•mi•cian (ăk'ə-də-mĭsh'ən) *n.* A member of an association of scholars, artists, etc.

ac•a•dem•i•cism (ăk'ə-dĕm'ə-sĭz'əm) *n.* Also **a•cad•e•mism** (ə-kăd'ə-mĭz'əm). Traditional formalism, especially in art.

a•cad•e•my (ə-kăd'ə-mē) *n., pl.* **-mies.** **1.** An association of scholars. **2.** A school for special instruction. **3.** A private secondary or college-preparatory school. [< Gk *Akadēmia,* name of the place where Plato taught.]

ă pat/ā ate/âr care/ä bar/b **b**i**b**/ch **ch**ew/d **d**ee**d**/ĕ pet/ē be/f **f**it/g **g**a**g**/h **h**at/hw **wh**at/
ĭ pit/ī pie/îr pier/j **j**udge/k **k**ick/l **l**id, fata**l**/m **m**u**m**/n **n**o, sudde**n**/ng si**ng**/ŏ pot/ō go/

A•ca•di•a (ə-kā′dē-ə). **1.** A French colony of E Canada that included Nova Scotia and New Brunswick. **2.** A parish in S Louisiana settled by Acadian exiles. —**A•ca′di•an** *n. & adj.*

a•can•thus (ə-kăn′thəs) *n., pl.* **-thuses** or **-thi** (-thī′). **1.** A plant of the Mediterranean region having large, thistlelike leaves. **2.** An architectural ornament representing these leaves. [< Gk *akantha,* thorn.]

a cap•pel•la (ä kə-pĕl′ə). Without instrumental accompaniment. [It, "in the manner of the chapel (or choir)."]

acc. 1. acceleration. **2.** account; accountant. **3.** accusative.

ac•cede (ăk-sēd′) *v.* **-ceded, -ceding. 1.** To give consent; agree. **2.** To come into an office or dignity. [< L *accēdere,* to approach, agree.] —**ac•ced′ence** (-sēd′əns) *n.* —**ac•ced′er** *n.*

ac•cel•er•ate (ăk-sĕl′ə-rāt′) *v.* **-ated, -ating.** To move or cause to move faster. [L *accelerāre.*] —**ac•cel′er•a•ble** *adj.* —**ac•cel′er•a′tive** *adj.*

ac•cel•er•a•tion (ăk-sĕl′ə-rā′shən) *n.* **1.** The act of accelerating. **2.** The rate of change of velocity with respect to time.

ac•cel•er•a•tor (ăk-sĕl′ə-rā′tər) *n.* Something that causes acceleration: **a.** The gas pedal of an automobile. **b.** A research device that accelerates charged particles.

ac•cel•er•om•e•ter (ăk-sĕl′ə-rŏm′ə-tər) *n.* Any of various devices used to measure acceleration.

ac•cent (ăk′sĕnt′) *n.* **1.** *Ling.* The relative prominence of a syllable of a word by greater intensity, **stress accent,** or by modulation of pitch or tone, **pitch accent. 2.** Vocal emphasis given to a syllable, word, or phrase. **3.** A characteristic pronunciation: *a Southern accent.* **4.** A mark or symbol used to indicate the vocal quality of a particular letter: *an acute accent.* **5.** A mark or symbol used to indicate the stressed syllables of a spoken word. **6.** Rhythmical stress in verse or music. —*v.* (ăk′sĕnt′, ăk-sĕnt′). **1.** To stress the pronunciation of. **2.** To mark with a printed accent. **3.** To call attention to. [< L *accentus,* accentuation, "song added to (speech)."] —**ac•cen′tu•al** *adj.* —**ac•cen′tu•al•ly** *adv.*

ac•cen•tu•ate (ăk-sĕn′chōō-āt′) *v.* **-ated, -ating. 1.** To pronounce or mark with an accent. **2.** To stress; emphasize. —**ac•cen′tu•a′tion** *n.*

ac•cept (ăk-sĕpt′) *v.* **1.** To receive (something offered) willingly or gladly. **2.** To admit to a group or place. **3.** To answer affirmatively. **4.** *Comm.* To consent to pay, as by a signed agreement. [< L *acceptāre,* freq of *accipere,* to receive, "take to oneself."]

ac•cept•a•ble (ăk-sĕp′tə-bəl) *adj.* Satisfactory. —**ac•cept′a•bil′i•ty** *n.* —**ac•cept′a•bly** *adv.*

ac•cep•tance (ăk-sĕp′təns) *n.* **1.** The act of accepting or state of being accepted or acceptable. **2.** An accepted time draft or bill of exchange.

ac•cep•ta•tion (ăk′sĕp-tā′shən) *n.* The usual or accepted meaning, as of a word.

ac•cess (ăk′sĕs′) *n.* **1.** The act or means of approaching. **2.** The right to enter or use. **3.** A sudden outburst. [< L *accēdere,* to near, approach.]

ac•ces•si•ble (ăk-sĕs′ə-bəl) *adj.* **1.** Easily approached or entered. **2.** Easily obtained. —**ac•ces′si•bil′i•ty** *n.*

ac•ces•sion (ăk-sĕsh′ən) *n.* **1.** The attainment of rank or dignity. **2.** An increase by means of something added. **3.** Agreement; assent.

ac•ces•so•ry (ăk-sĕs′ər-ē) *n., pl.* **-ries.** Also **ac•ces•sa•ry. 1.** Something supplementary. **2.** Something nonessential but useful. **3.** One who though absent aids in or contributes to the commission of a crime. [< ML *accessor,* helper, accessory.] —**ac•ces′so•ri•ly** *adv.* —**ac•ces′so•ri•ness** *n.* —**ac•ces′so•ry** *adj.*

ac•ci•dence (ăk′sə-dəns, -dĕns′) *n.* The area of grammar that deals with word inflections.

ac•ci•dent (ăk′sə-dənt, -dĕnt′) *n.* **1.** An unexpected and undesirable event. **2.** Fortune; chance. [< L *(rēs) accidēns,* "(a thing) happening."]

ac•ci•den•tal (ăk′sə-dĕn′təl) *adj.* Occurring unexpectedly or unintentionally. —*n. Mus.* A chromatically altered note not belonging to the key signature. —**ac′ci•den′tal•ly** *adv.*

ac•claim (ə-klām′) *v.* **1.** To applaud. **2.** To salute or hail. —*n.* Enthusiastic applause. [L *acclāmāre,* to shout at.] —**ac•claim′er** *n.*

ac•cla•ma•tion (ăk′lə-mā′shən) *n.* **1.** An enthusiastic oral vote of approval without formal ballot. **2.** Applause of acceptance or welcome.

ac•cli•mate (ə-klī′mĭt, ăk′lə-māt′) *v.* **-mated, -mating.** Also **ac•cli•ma•tize** (ə-klī′mə-tīz′) **-tized, -tizing.** To accustom or become accustomed to a new environment or situation; adapt. —**ac′cli•ma′tion, ac•cli′ma•ti•za′tion** *n.*

ac•cliv•i•ty (ə-klĭv′ə-tē) *n., pl.* **-ties.** An upward slope, as of ground. [< L *acclīvis,* uphill.] —**ac•cliv′i•tous** *adj.*

ac•co•lade (ăk′ə-lād′, ăk′ə-läd′) *n.* **1.** An embrace of greeting or salutation. **2.** Praise; approval: *critics' accolades.* [< Prov *acolada,* an embrace.]

ac•com•mo•date (ə-kŏm′ə-dāt′) *v.* **-dated, -dating. 1.** To do a favor for; oblige. **2.** To supply with. **3.** To contain comfortably or have space for. **4.** To adapt; adjust. **5.** To settle; reconcile. [L *accommodāre,* to make fit.] —**ac•com′mo•da′tive** *adj.*

ac•com•mo•dat•ing (ə-kŏm′ə-dā′tĭng) *adj.* Helpful and obliging. —**ac•com′mo•dat′ing•ly** *adv.*

ac•com•mo•da•tion (ə-kŏm′ə-dā′shən) *n.* **1.** The act or state of accommodating or being accommodated; adaptation. **2.** Anything that meets a need; convenience. **3. accommodations. a.** Lodgings. **b.** A seat, compartment, or room on a public vehicle. **4.** *Comm.* A loan or other financial favor.

ac•com•pa•ni•ment (ə-kŭm′pə-nē-mənt, ə-kŭmp′nē-) *n.* **1.** Something that accompanies; concomitant. **2.** A vocal or instrumental part that supports a solo part.

ac•com•pa•nist (ə-kŭm′pə-nĭst, ə-kŭmp′nĭst) *n.* One who plays an accompaniment.

ac•com•pa•ny (ə-kŭm′pə-nē, ə-kŭmp′nē) *v.* **-nied, -nying. 1.** To go along or occur with. **2.** To perform an accompaniment to. [< OF *accompagner.*] —**ac•com′pa•ni•er** *n.*

ac•com•plice (ə-kŏm′plĭs) *n.* One who aids or abets a lawbreaker in a criminal act. [< ME *a complice,* a COMPLICE.]

ac•com•plish (ə-kŏm′plĭsh) *v.* To succeed in doing; bring to pass. [< OF *accomplir,* to complete.] —**ac•com′plish•er** *n.*

ac•com•plished (ə-kŏm′plĭsht) *adj.* **1.** Completed; done; finished. **2.** Skilled; expert. **3.** Sophisticated.

ac•com•plish•ment (ə-kŏm′plĭsh-mənt) *n.* **1.** The act of accomplishing or of being accomplished; completion. **2.** Something completed successfully. **3.** Social poise.

ac•cord (ə-kôrd′) *v.* To agree or be in agreement. —*n.* **1.** Agreement; harmony. **2.** A settlement, esp. of conflicting opinions between nations. [< VL **accordāre,* "to be heart-to-heart with."] —**ac•cord′a•ble** *adj.*

ac•cord•ance (ə-kôr′dəns) *n.* Agreement; conformity. —**ac•cord′ant** *adj.*

ac•cord•ing•ly (ə-kôr′dĭng-lē) *adv.* **1.** Correspondingly. **2.** Consequently.

ac•cor•di•on (ə-kôr′dē-ən) *n.* A portable, bellows-operated musical instrument with a keyboard and metal reeds. [< G *Akkord,* agreement, "harmony."] —**ac•cor′di•on•ist** *n.*

ac•cost (ə-kôst′, ə-kŏst′) *v.* To approach and speak to first. [< VL **accostāre,* to come alongside someone.] —**ac•cost′a•ble** *adj.*

ac•count (ə-kount′) *n.* **1. a.** A narrative of events. **b.** A written or oral explanation, as of blame. **2. a.** A precise list of monetary transactions. **b.** Any detailed list. **3.** A business relationship involving the exchange of money or credit. **4.** Importance: *a man of some account.* —**on account.** In part payment of. —**on account of.** Because of. —**on no account.** Under no circumstances. —**take into account.** To take into consideration. —*v.* To consider or esteem. —**account for. 1.** To make or render a reckoning, as of funds received. **2.** To be the explanation or cause of. **3.** To be answerable for. [< OF *acompter,* "to count up to," reckon.]

ac•count•a•ble (ə-koun′tə-bəl) *adj.* Answerable. —**ac•count′a•bil′i•ty** *n.* —**ac•count′a•bly** *adv.*

ac•count•ant (ə-koun′tənt) *n.* An expert in accounting. —**ac•count′ant•ship′** *n.*

ac•count•ing (ə-koun′tĭng) *n.* The bookkeeping methods involved in recording the business transactions and preparing the financial statements of a business.

ac•cou•ter (ə-kōō′tər) *v.* Also **ac•cou•tre.** To outfit and equip, as for military duty. [F *accoutrer.*]

ac•cou•ter•ment (ə-kōō′tər-mənt) *n.* Also **ac•cou•tre•ment. 1.** The act of accoutering. **2. accouterments.** Extra equipment, as of a soldier; trappings.

Ac•cra (ə-krä′, ăk′rə). The capital of Ghana. Pop. 338,000.

ac•cred•it (ə-krĕd′ĭt) *v.* **1.** To attribute to. **2.** To authorize. **3.** To certify as meeting a prescribed standard. **4.** To believe. —**ac•cred′i•ta′tion** *n.*

ac•cre•tion (ə-krē′shən) *n.* **1.** Any growth or increase in size, esp. by gradual external addition. **2.** Something added to promote such growth. [< L *accrēscere,* ACCRUE.]

ac•crue (ə-krōō′) *v.* **-crued, -cruing. 1.** To come to someone or something as a gain or increment. **2.** To increase by regular growth, as interest on capital. [< L *accrēscere,* to increase.] —**ac•cru′al** *n.* —**ac•crue′ment** *n.*

acct. account.

ac•cul•tur•a•tion (ə-kŭl′chə-rā′shən) *n.* Modification of a primitive culture by contact with an advanced culture.

ac•cu•mu•late (ə-kyōōm′yə-lāt′) *v.* **-lated, -lating.** To amass or gather; mount up; collect. [L *accumulāre.*] —**ac•cu′mu•la′tion** *n.*

ac•cu•mu•la•tor (ə-kyōōm′yə-lā′tər) *n.* **1.** One that accumulates. **2.** A register or electric circuit that stores figures for computation.

ac•cu•ra•cy (ăk′yər-ə-sē) *n.* Exactness; correctness.

ac•cu•rate (ăk′yər-ĭt) *adj.* Having no errors; correct. [< L *accūrāre,* to attend to carefully.] —**ac′cu•rate•ly** *adv.* —**ac′cu•rate•ness** *n.*

ac•curs•ed (ə-kûr′sĭd, ə-kûrst′) *adj.* Also **ac•curst. 1.** Under a curse. **2.** Abominable. —**ac•curs′ed•ly** *adv.*

ac•cu•sa•tive (ə-kyōō′zə-tĭv) *adj.* Of or pertaining to a grammatical case that indicates the direct object of a verb or the object of certain prepositions. [< L *(cāsus) accūsātīvus,* "(case) indicating accusation."] —**ac•cu'sa•tive** *n.* —**ac•cu'sa•tive•ly** *adv.*

ac•cuse (ə-kyōōz') *v.* **-cused, -cusing. 1.** To charge (someone) with an error. **2.** *Law.* To bring charges against (someone) for a misdeed. [< L *accūsāre,* to accuse, "call to account."] —**ac'cu•sa'tion** *n.* —**ac•cus'er** *n.*

ac•cus•tom (ə-kŭs'təm) *v.* To familiarize or become familiarized, as by constant practice.

ac•cus•tomed (ə-kŭs'təmd) *adj.* **1.** Usual; normal. **2.** In the habit of.

ace (ās) *n.* **1.** A playing card, die, or domino having one spot. **2.** In racket games, a point scored by the failure of one's opponent to return a serve. **3.** A fighter pilot who has shot down five or more enemy planes. **4.** *Informal.* An expert in any field. —*adj. Informal.* First-rate; expert. [< L *ās,* unit.]

ace in the hole. A hidden advantage.

-aceous. *comb. form.* Of, pertaining to, or of the nature of: **farinaceous.** [< L *-āceus,* "of a specific kind or group."]

a•cerb (ə-sûrb') *adj.* **1.** Sour; bitter; astringent. **2.** Acid; sharp. [L *acerbus,* sharp, bitter.] —**a•cer'bi•ty** *n.*

ac•er•bate (ăs'ər-bāt') *v.* **-bated, -bating.** To vex; annoy. [< L *acerbus,* ACERB.]

ac•e•tate (ăs'ə-tāt') *n.* **1.** A durable transparent film derived from cellulose and used esp. in packaging and photography. **2.** Fibers or fabric derived from cellulose acetate.

a•ce•tic acid (ə-sē'tĭk). A clear, colorless, pungent organic acid, $C_2H_4O_2$, used in chemical synthesis and photography. [< L *acētum,* vinegar.]

a•cet•i•fy (ə-sĕt'ə-fī') *v.* **-fied, -fying.** To convert to acetic acid or vinegar.

ac•e•tone (ăs'ə-tōn') *n.* A colorless, extremely flammable liquid, C_3H_6O, used as a solvent.

ac•e•tyl•cho•line (ăs'ə-tĭl-kō'lēn', ə-sĕt'l-) *n.* A white crystalline compound, $C_7H_{17}NO_3$, that transmits nerve impulses across intercellular gaps.

a•cet•y•lene (ə-sĕt'l-ēn', -ən) *n.* A colorless, highly flammable gas, C_2H_2, used for metal welding and cutting.

a•ce•tyl•sal•i•cyl•ic acid (ə-sēt'l-săl'ə-sĭl'ĭk). Aspirin.

ache (āk) *v.* **ached, aching. 1.** To suffer a dull, sustained pain. **2.** *Informal.* To yearn. —*n.* A dull, steady pain. [< OE *ăcan.*]

a•chieve (ə-chēv') *v.* **achieved, achieving. 1.** To accomplish successfully. **2.** To attain with effort. [< OF *achever,* "to bring to a head."] —**a•chieve'ment** *n.* —**a•chiev'er** *n.*

A•chil•les (ə-kĭl'ēz). The hero of Homer's *Iliad.*

Achilles' heel. A small but mortal weakness.

Achilles' tendon. The large tendon running from the heel bone to the calf muscle.

ach•ro•mat•ic (ăk'rə-măt'ĭk) *adj.* **1.** Free of color. **2.** Refracting light without spectral color separation. —**ach'ro•mat'i•cal•ly** *adv.*

ac•id (ăs'ĭd) *n.* **1. a.** Any of a large class of substances in aqueous solution capable of turning litmus indicators red, dissolving certain metals to form salts, reacting with bases or alkalis to form salts, or having a sour taste. **b.** A substance that ionizes in solution to give the positive ion of the solvent. **c.** A substance capable of giving up a proton. **2.** *Slang.* A hallucinogen, LSD. —*adj.* Biting; ill-tempered: *an acid wit.* [L *acidus,* sharp, sour < *acēre,* to be sour.] —**a•cid'i•ty** *n.*

a•cid•i•fy (ə-sĭd'ə-fī') *v.* **-fied, -fying.** To convert to acid. —**a•cid'i•fi'a•ble** *adj.* —**a•cid'i•fi•ca'tion** *n.* —**a•cid'i•fi'er** *n.*

ac•i•do•sis (ăs'ĭ-dō'sĭs) *n.* Pathologically high blood acidity.

acid test. A decisive, critical test of worth.

a•cid•u•lous (ə-sĭj'ōō-ləs) *adj.* Sour in feeling or manner. [< L *acidus,* ACID.]

-acious. *comb. form.* A tendency toward or abundance of something: **fallacious.**

-acity. *comb. form.* A quality or state of being: **tenacity.**

ack. acknowledgment.

ack-ack (ăk'ăk') *n. Mil. Slang.* **1.** Antiaircraft fire. **2.** An antiaircraft gun.

ac•knowl•edge (ăk-nŏl'ĭj) *v.* **-edged, -edging. 1.** To recognize the existence or truth of. **2.** To express gratitude for. **3.** To report the receipt of. **4.** *Law.* To accept or certify as legally binding. —**ac•knowl'edg•er** *n.* —**ac•knowl'edg•ment, ac•knowl'edge•ment** *n.*

ac•me (ăk'mē) *n.* The point of utmost attainment. [Gk *akmē,* point.]

ac•ne (ăk'nē) *n.* An inflammatory disease of the oil glands, characterized by pimples. [< Gk *akmē,* eruption on the face, ACME.]

ac•o•lyte (ăk'ə-līt') *n.* **1.** One who assists a priest at Mass. **2.** An attendant or follower. [< Gk *akolouthos,* follower, following.]

A•con•ca•gua (ä'kōn-kä'gwä). The highest mountain (22,835 ft.) in the W Hemisphere, in Argentina.

ac•o•nite (ăk'ə-nīt') *n.* **1.** A poisonous plant, the monkshood. **2.** A medicinal preparation made from its roots. [< Gk *akoniton.*]

a•corn (ā'kôrn', ā'kərn) *n.* The nut of the oak tree, having a cuplike base. [< OE *æcern.* See **ōg-.**]

a•cous•tic (ə-kōō'stĭk) *adj.* Also **a•cous•ti•cal** (-stĭ-kəl). Pertaining to sound, the sense of hearing, or the science of sound. —*n.* **a•coustics** (ə-kōō'stĭks). **1.** *(takes sing. v.).* The scientific study of sound. **2.** *(takes pl. v.).* The total effect of sound, esp. in an enclosed space. [Gk *akoustikos.*] —**a•cous'ti•cal•ly** *adv.*

acpt. acceptance.

ac•quaint (ə-kwānt') *v.* **1.** To make familiar. **2.** To inform. [< L *accognōscere,* to know perfectly.] —**ac•quaint'ed** *adj.*

ac•quain•tance (ə-kwān'təns) *n.* **1.** Knowledge about someone or something. **2.** A person or persons whom one knows.

ac•qui•esce (ăk'wē-ĕs') *v.* **-esced, -escing.** To consent or comply passively. [L *acquiescere,* to agree tacitly.] —**ac'qui•es'cence** *n.* —**ac'qui•es'cent** *adj.* —**ac'qui•es'cent•ly** *adv.*

ac•quire (ə-kwīr') *v.* **-quired, -quiring.** To gain possession of. [< L *acquīrere,* to add to, get.] —**ac•quire'ment** *n.*

ac•qui•si•tion (ăk'wə-zĭsh'ən) *n.* **1.** The act of acquiring. **2.** Something acquired, esp. as an addition to an established group.

ac•quis•i•tive (ə-kwĭz'ə-tĭv) *adj.* Tending to acquire. —**ac•quis'i•tive•ness** *n.*

ac•quit (ə-kwĭt') *v.* **-quitted, -quitting. 1.** To clear of a charge. **2.** To release from obligation. **3.** To conduct (oneself). [< VL **acquitāre,* "to bring to rest," set free.]

ac•quit•tal (ə-kwĭt'l) *n. Law.* The judgment that a person is not guilty of a crime as charged.

ac•quit•tance (ə-kwĭt'əns) *n.* A release from an obligation.

a•cre (ā'kər) *n.* **1.** A unit of area equal to 4,840 square yards. **2. acres.** Property in the form of land. [< OE *æcer.* See **agro-.**] —**a'cre•age** (ā'kər-ĭj, ā'krĭj) *n.*

ac•rid (ăk'rĭd) *adj.* **1.** Harsh in taste or smell. **2.** Caustic in language. [< L *ācer,* sharp, bitter.] —**a•crid'i•ty** (ə-krĭd'ə-tē) *n.*

ac•ri•mo•ny (ăk'rə-mō'nē) *n.* Animosity in speech or manner. [L *ācrimōnia,* sharpness < *ācer,* sharp.] —**ac'ri•mo'ni•ous** *adj.* —**ac'ri•mo'ni•ous•ness** *n.*

acro-. *comb. form.* A height, tip, or point. [< Gk *akros,* topmost.]

ac•ro•bat (ăk'rə-băt') *n.* One skilled in feats of agility and balance. [< Gk *akrobatēs,* "one who walks on tiptoe."] —**ac'ro•bat'ic** *adj.*

ac•ro•bat•ics (ăk'rə-băt'ĭks) *n. (takes sing. v.).* **1.** The art of an acrobat. **2.** Any manifestation of spectacular agility.

ac•ro•nym (ăk'rə-nĭm') *n.* A word formed from the initial letters of a name, as *WAC* for *W*omen's *A*rmy *C*orps, or by combining initial letters or parts of a series of words, as *radar* for *ra*dio *d*etecting *a*nd *r*anging.

ac•ro•pho•bi•a (ăk'rə-fō'bē-ə) *n.* Abnormal fear of high places.

a•crop•o•lis (ə-krŏp'ə-lĭs) *n.* **1.** The fortified height or citadel of an ancient Greek city. **2. Acropolis.** The citadel of Athens. [Gk *akropolis,* "upper city."]

a•cross (ə-krôs', ə-krŏs') *prep.* **1.** On, at, or from the other side of: *across the road.* **2.** So as to cross; through: *draw lines across the paper.* **3.** From one side of to the other: *a bridge across a river.* —*adv.* **1.** From one side to the other: *The bridge swayed when he ran across.* **2.** On or to the opposite side: *We came across by ferry.* [< OF *a croix,* "in the form of a cross."]

a•cross-the-board (ə-krôs'*th*ə-bôrd', -bōrd', ə-krŏs'-) *adj.* Including all categories or members.

a•cros•tic (ə-krôs'tĭk, ə-krŏs'-) *n.* **1.** A poem or series of lines in which certain letters, usually the first in each line, form a name or message. **2.** A word square. [Gk *akrostikhis,* "end-line."]

a•cryl•ic resin (ə-krĭl'ĭk). Any of numerous polymers used to produce synthetic rubbers and lightweight plastics.

act (ăkt) *n.* **1.** The process of doing something. **2.** Something that is done. **3.** An enactment, as of a legislative body. **4.** A major division of a play or opera. **5.** A performance that forms part of a longer presentation, as in vaudeville. **6.** *Informal.* A pose: *put on an act.* —*v.* **1.** To perform the part of, as in a play. **2.** To behave or comport oneself: *She acts like a lady.* **3.** To be an actor. **4.** To appear to be: *The dog acts friendly.* **5.** To do something. **6.** To function in a specific way. —**act up.** *Informal.* To misbehave or malfunction. [< L *āctus,* pp of *agere,* to drive, do.]

ACTH A pituitary hormone used to stimulate cortisone secretion. [A(DRENO)C(ORTICO)-T(ROPIC) H(ORMONE).]

ac•tin (ăk'tĭn) *n.* A muscle protein, active with myosin in muscular contraction. [< L *āctus,* an ACT.]

act•ing (ăk'tĭng) *adj.* Temporarily assuming the duties of another. —*n.* The occupation or performance of an actor.

ac•ti•nide (ăk'tĭ-nīd') *n.* Any of a series of chemically similar, mostly synthetic, radioactive metallic elements with atomic numbers ranging from 89 (actinium) through 103 (lawrencium).

ac•tin•i•um (ăk-tĭn'ē-əm) *n. Symbol* **Ac** A radioactive metallic element found in uranium ores and used as a source of alpha rays. Atomic number 89, longest-lived isotope Ac 227. [< Gk *aktis,* ray.]

ac•tion (ăk'shən) *n.* **1.** The state or process of doing. **2.** An act or deed. **3.** A movement or manner of movement. **4. actions.** Behavior or conduct. **5.** The operating parts of a mechanism: *the action of a gun.* **6.** The plot of a story or play. **7.** A lawsuit. **8.** Combat.

ac•ti•vate (ăk'tə-vāt') *v.* **-vated, -vating. 1.** To set in motion. **2.** To organize (a military unit). **3.** To make active, reactive, or radioactive.

ac•tive (ăk'tĭv) *adj.* **1.** In action; moving. **2.** Capable of functioning. **3.** Causing action or change. **4.** Participating: *an active member of a club.* **5.** Not passive or quiescent. **6.** Characterized by energetic action. **7.** Denoting that the subject of a sentence is performing or causing the action expressed by the verb: *active voice.* **8.** Producing profit: *active accounts.* **9.** *Mil.* On full duty and full pay. [L *āctīvus* < *āctus,* ACT.]

ac•tiv•ism (ăk'tĭv-ĭz'əm) *n.* A theory or practice based on militant action. **—ac'tiv•ist** *n.*

ac•tiv•i•ty (ăk-tĭv'ə-tē) *n., pl.* **-ties. 1.** The state of being active. **2.** Energetic action. **3.** A specified form of action, esp. one in the area of recreation. **4.** The intensity of a radioactive source.

act of God. *Law.* An unforeseeable or inevitable occurrence, such as a tornado, caused by nature.

ac•to•my•o•sin (ăk'tō-mī'ə-sĭn) *n.* A system of actin and myosin that with other substances constitutes muscle fiber.

ac•tor (ăk'tər) *n.* A theatrical performer. **—ac'tress** (-trĭs) *fem.n.*

Acts of the Apostles. Also **Acts.** The 5th book of the New Testament.

ac•tu•al (ăk'cho͞o-əl) *adj.* **1.** In existence; real. **2.** Existing or acting at the present. [< LL *āctuālis,* "pertaining to acts."] **—ac'tu•al•ly** *adv.*

ac•tu•al•i•ty (ăk'cho͞o-ăl'ə-tē) *n., pl.* **-ties. 1.** The state of being actual. **2. actualities.** Actual conditions or facts.

ac•tu•ar•y (ăk'cho͞o-ĕr'ē) *n., pl.* **-ies.** A statistician who computes insurance risks and premiums. [L *āctuārius,* secretary of accounts.] **—ac'tu•ar'i•al** (-âr'ē-əl) *adj.*

ac•tu•ate (ăk'cho͞o-āt') *v.* **-ated, -ating. 1.** To put into action. **2.** To stimulate; motivate. **—ac'tu•a'tion** *n.*

a•cu•i•ty (ə-kyo͞o'ə-tē) *n.* Keenness; acuteness. [< L *acuere,* to sharpen.]

a•cu•men (ə-kyo͞o'mən) *n.* Keenness of insight. [L *acūmen,* (mental) sharpness.]

a•cute (ə-kyo͞ot') *adj.* **1.** Having a sharp point. **2.** Keenly perceptive. **3.** Sensitive. **4.** Extremely severe or sharp. **5.** *Med.* Reaching a crisis rapidly, as a disease. **6.** Designating angles less than 90°. [L *acūtus,* sharp, pp of *acuere,* to sharpen.] **—a•cute'ness** *n.*

ad (ăd) *n.* An advertisement.

A.D. 1. active duty. **2.** anno Domini.

A.D.A. Americans for Democratic Action.

ad•age (ăd'ĭj) *n.* A short maxim or proverb. [< L *adagium,* proverb.]

a•da•gio (ə-dä'jō, -jē-ō') *adv. Mus.* Slowly. [It *adagio,* "at ease."] **—a•da'gio** *adj.*

Ad•am (ăd'əm). The first man and progenitor of mankind. Genesis 2:7.

ad•a•mant (ăd'ə-mənt, -mănt') *n.* A stone believed to be impenetrable. *—adj.* Unyielding. [< Gk *adamas,* hard metal, diamond, poss "unbreakable."]

Ad•ams (ăd'əmz). **1. John.** 1735–1826. 2nd President of the U.S. (1797–1801). **2. John Quincy.** 1767–1848. 6th President of the U.S. (1825–29).

Adam's apple. The projection of the largest laryngeal cartilage at the front of the throat, esp. in men.

a•dapt (ə-dăpt') *v.* To adjust or become adjusted to new or different conditions. [L *adaptāre,* to fit to.] **—a•dapt'a•bil'i•ty, a•dapt'a•ble•ness** *n.* **—a•dapt'a•ble** *adj.*

ad•ap•ta•tion (ăd'ăp-tā'shən) *n.* **1.** The act or process of adapting. **2.** Adjustment or change.

a•dap•tive (ə-dăp'tĭv) *adj.* Tending to adapt. **—a•dap'tive•ly** *adv.*

add (ăd) *v.* **1.** To join or unite so as to increase in size, quantity, or scope. **2.** To combine to form a sum. **3.** To say or write further. [< L *addere,* to add, "to put to."]

add. 1. addendum. **2.** addition.

ad•den•dum (ə-dĕn'dəm) *n., pl.* **-da** (-də). Something added; a supplement.

ad•der (ăd'ər) *n.* **1.** Any of various venomous Old World snakes. **2.** Any of several nonvenomous snakes popularly believed to be harmful. [< OE *nǣdre,* snake. See **nētr-.**]

ad•dict (ə-dĭkt') *v.* To devote or give (oneself) habitually or compulsively to. *—n.* (ăd'ĭkt). A person who is addicted, esp. to narcotics. [< L *addīcere,* to award to.] **—ad•dic'tion** *n.* **—ad•dic'tive** *adj.*

Ad•dis Ab•a•ba (ăd'ĭs ăb'ə-bə). The capital of Ethiopia. Pop. 505,000.

Ad•di•son's disease (ăd'ə-sənz). A usually fatal disease caused by failure of the adrenal cortex.

ad•di•tion (ə-dĭsh'ən) *n.* **1.** The act, process, or result of adding. **2.** Something added; a supplement or annex. **—ad•di'tion•al** *adj.* **—ad•di'tion•al•ly** *adv.*

ad•di•tive (ăd'ə-tĭv) *adj.* Involving addition. *—n.* A substance added in small amounts to something else to alter it.

ad•dle (ăd'l) *v.* **-dled, -dling. 1.** To make or become confused. **2.** To spoil, as an egg. [< OE *adela,* filth, urine.]

ad•dress (ə-drĕs') *v.* **1.** To speak to. **2.** To mark with a destination. **3.** To direct one's efforts or attention to. *—n.* (ə-drĕs'). **1.** A formal spoken or written communication. **2.** (*also* ăd'rĕs). The indication of destination on mail. **3.** (*also* ăd'rĕs). The location at which an organization or person can be reached. **4.** Skillfulness. [< VL **addrictiāre,* to direct oneself toward.]

ad•dress•ee (ăd'rĕs-ē', ə-drĕs'ē') *n.* One to whom something is addressed.

ad•duce (ə-d/y/o͞os') *v.* **-duced, -ducing.** To cite as an example or means of proof. [L *addūcere,* to bring to (someone).]

Ad•e•laide (ăd'l-ād'). A city of S Australia. Pop. 640,000.

A•den (äd'n, ăd'n). The capital of Southern Yemen, on the Gulf of Aden in the SE part of the country. Pop. 264,300.

Aden, Gulf of. An arm of the Arabian Sea between Somalia and Southern Yemen.

ad•e•nine (ăd'n-ēn', -ĭn) *n.* A constituent of nucleic acid, $C_5H_5N_5$.

ad•e•noids (ăd'n-oidz') *pl.n.* Lymphoid tissue growths above the throat in the nose. [< Gk *adēn,* gland.] **—ad'e•noid'** *adj.*

a•den•o•sine triphosphate (ə-dĕn'ə-sēn'). An organic compound, $C_{10}H_{16}N_5O_{13}P_3$, that provides energy for metabolic reactions.

a•dept (ə-dĕpt') *adj.* Highly skilled. [L *adeptus,* "having attained (knowledge or skill)."] **—ad'ept'** (ăd'ĕpt') *n.* **—a•dept'ly** *adv.* **—a•dept'ness** *n.*

ad•e•quate (ăd'ĭ-kwĭt) *adj.* **1.** Able to satisfy a requirement. **2.** Barely satisfactory or sufficient. [< L *adaequāre,* to make equal to.] **—ad'e•qua•cy** (-kwə-sē) *n.* **—ad'e•quate•ly** *adv.*

ad•here (ăd-hîr') *v.* **-hered, -hering. 1.** To stick to as if glued. **2.** To maintain loyalty, as to a person. **3.** To follow without deviation. [L *adhaerēre,* to stick to.] **—ad•her'ence** *n.* **—ad•her'ent** *adj.* & *n.* **—ad•her'er** *n.*

ad•he•sion (ăd-hē'zhən) *n.* The act or state of adhering.

ad•he•sive (ăd-hē'sĭv) *adj.* **1.** Tending to adhere; sticky. **2.** Gummed so as to adhere. *—n.* An adhesive substance.

ad hoc (ăd hŏk'). For a specific purpose, case, or situation. [L, "toward this."]

ad ho•mi•nem (ăd hŏm'ĭ-nĕm'). Appealing to prejudice rather than reason. [L, "to the man."]

a•dieu (ə-d/y/o͞o') *interj.* Farewell. *—n.* A farewell. [OF *a dieu,* "(I commend you) to God."]

ad in•fi•ni•tum (ăd ĭn'fə-nī'təm). Endlessly. [L, "to infinity."]

ad•i•pose (ăd'ə-pōs') *adj.* Fatty: *adipose tissue.* [< L *adeps,* fat.]

Ad•i•ron•dacks (ăd'ə-rŏn'dăks'). A mountain range in NE New York.

adj. 1. adjacent. **2.** adjective. **3.** adjutant.

ad•ja•cent (ə-jā'sənt) *adj.* Next to; adjoining. [< L *adjacēre,* to lie near.]

ad•jec•tive (ăj'ĭk-tĭv) *n.* Any of a class of words used to modify a noun or other substantive by limiting, qualifying, or specifying. [< L *adjectīvus,* "attributive."] **—ad'jec•ti'val** (-tī'vəl) *adj.* **—ad'jec•ti'val•ly** *adv.*

ad•join (ə-join') *v.* **1.** To be next to. **2.** To unite. [< L *adjungere,* to join to.] **—ad•join'ing** *adj.*

ad•journ (ə-jûrn') *v.* **1.** To suspend until a later stated time. **2.** To move from one place to another. [< OF *ajourner,* "to put off to an appointed day."] **—ad•journ'ment** *n.*

John Adams

John Quincy Adams

ad•judge (ə-jŭj′) *v.* **-judged, -judging. 1.** To determine, rule, or award by judicial procedure. **2.** To judge or deem.

ad•ju•di•cate (ə-jo͞o′dĭ-kāt′) *v.* **-cated, -cating.** To settle by judicial procedure. —**ad•ju′di•ca′tion** *n.* —**ad•ju′di•ca′tive** *adj.* —**ad•ju′di•ca′tor** (-kā′tər) *n.*

ad•junct (ăj′ŭngkt′) *n.* One attached to another in a subordinate relationship. [< L *adjungere,* ADJOIN.] —**ad•junc′tive** *adj.*

ad•ju•ra•tion (ăj′o͞o-rā′shən) *n.* An earnest appeal: *"the tenderest adjurations of a dying friend"* (De Quincey).

ad•jure (ə-jo͝or′) *v.* **-jured, -juring. 1.** To enjoin solemnly, as under oath or penalty: *"and adjuring her in the name of God to declare the truth"* (Increase Mather). **2.** To entreat. [< L *adjūrāre,* to swear to.]

ad•just (ə-jŭst′) *v.* **1.** To regulate or adapt. **2.** To settle (a debt or claim). [< VL **adjuxtāre,* to put close to.] —**ad•just′a•ble** *adj.* —**ad•just′er** *n.* —**ad•just′ment** *n.*

ad•ju•tant (ăj′o͞o-tənt) *n.* **1.** A military officer who is an administrative assistant to a commander. **2.** A stork, the marabou. [< L *adjūtāre,* to aid.]

ad lib (ăd lĭb′). Extemporaneously.

ad-lib (ăd-lĭb′) *v.* **-libbed, -libbing.** To improvise or extemporize. —*n.* Something ad-libbed. [< L *ad libitum,* "to (one's) liking."] —**ad-lib′ber** *n.*

Adm. admiral.

ad•man (ăd′măn′) *n.* One employed in advertising.

ad•min•is•ter (ăd-mĭn′ĭs-tər) *v.* **1.** To manage. **2. a.** To give (a drug) remedially. **b.** To dispense (a sacrament). **3.** To mete out. **4.** To tender (an oath). **5.** To manage or dispose of (an estate). —**ad•min′is•trant** (-trənt) *n.*

ad•min•is•tra•tion (ăd-mĭn′ĭs-trā′shən) *n.* **1.** The act of administering. **2.** Management. **3. a.** The executive body of a government. **b.** Its term of office. **4.** The management and disposal of an estate. —**ad•min′is•tra′tive** *adj.*

ad•min•is•tra•tor (ăd-mĭn′ĭs-trā′tər) *n.* **1.** A business or government executive. **2.** One appointed to administer an estate.

ad•mi•ra•ble (ăd′mər-ə-bəl) *adj.* Deserving admiration; excellent. —**ad′mir•a•bly** *adv.*

ad•mi•ral (ăd′mər-əl) *n.* **1.** The commander in chief of a navy or fleet. **2.** A naval officer of the next-to-the-highest rank. [< Ar *'amīr-al-,* "commander of."]

ad•mi•ral•ty (ăd′mər-əl-tē) *n., pl.* **-ties. 1.** A court exercising jurisdiction over all maritime causes. **2. Admiralty.** The British navy department.

ad•mire (ăd-mīr′) *v.* **-mired, -miring. 1.** To regard with wonder and approval. **2.** To esteem; respect. [L *admīrārī,* to wonder at.] —**ad′mi•ra′tion** (-mə-rā′shən) *n.* —**ad•mir′er** *n.* —**ad•mir′ing•ly** *adv.*

ad•mis•si•ble (ăd-mĭs′ə-bəl) *adj.* Allowable. —**ad•mis′si•bil′i•ty** *n.* —**ad•mis′si•bly** *adv.*

ad•mis•sion (ăd-mĭsh′ən) *n.* **1.** The act or procedure of admitting. **2.** Something admitted, as an acknowledgment or confession. **3.** Appointment to a position or situation. **4.** The right to enter; access. **5.** An entrance fee.

ad•mit (ăd-mĭt′) *v.* **-mitted, -mitting. 1.** To permit to enter or serve as a means of entrance. **2.** To have room for. **3.** To afford possibility; allow; permit (with *of*). **4. a.** To acknowledge; confess. **b.** To concede. [< L *admittere,* to send in to.]

ad•mit•tance (ăd-mĭt′əns) *n.* Right of entrance.

ad•mit•ted•ly (ăd-mĭt′ĭd-lē) *adv.* By general admission.

ad•mix (ăd-mĭks′) *v.* To mix or become mixed. —**ad•mix′ture** *n.*

ad•mon•ish (ăd-mŏn′ĭsh) *v.* **1.** To reprove mildly but seriously. **2.** To counsel against. [< VL **admonestāre,* var of L *admonēre,* to bring to (someone's) mind.] —**ad′mo•ni′tion** (-mə-nĭsh′ən), **ad•mon′ish•ment** *n.* —**ad•mon′i•to′ry** (-ə-tôr′ē, -tōr′ē) *adj.*

ad•nate (ăd′nāt′) *adj. Biol.* Joined to or fused with another part or organ. Said of parts not usually united. [< L *adnāscī,* to be born in addition to.] —**ad•na′tion** *n.*

ad nau•se•am (ăd nô′zē-əm). To a disgusting degree. [L.]

a•do (ə-do͞o′) *n.* Bustle; bother. [ME < *at do,* "to do."]

a•do•be (ə-dō′bē) *n.* **1.** A sun-dried brick of clay and straw. **2.** Clay from which such bricks are made. **3.** A structure built with such bricks. [< Ar *al-ṭōba,* "the brick."] —**a•do′be** *adj.*

ad•o•les•cence (ăd′l-ĕs′əns) *n.* The period or state of development from the onset of puberty to maturity. [< L *adolēscere,* to grow up.] —**ad′o•les′cent** *adj.* & *n.*

Ad•o•nai (ăd′ō-nī′). Lord (spoken substitute for the ineffable name of God). [Heb *adōnāi* < Phoen *adōn,* lord.]

A•don•is (ə-dŏn′ĭs, ə-dō′nĭs) *n.* A beautiful youth. [Gk *Adōnis* (a lover of Aphrodite) < Phoen *adōn,* lord.]

a•dopt (ə-dŏpt′) *v.* **1.** To take (a child) into one's family legally and raise as one's own. **2.** To take and follow by choice or assent. **3.** To take up and use as one's own. [L *adoptāre,* to choose for oneself.] —**a•dopt′er** *n.* —**a•dop′tion** *n.* —**a•dop′tive** *adj.*

a•dor•a•ble (ə-dôr′ə-bəl, ə-dōr′-) *adj. Informal.* Delightful; lovable. —**a•dor′a•bly** *adv.*

a•dore (ə-dôr′, ə-dōr′) *v.* **adored, adoring. 1.** To worship with divine honors. **2.** To love deeply. **3.** *Informal.* To like very much. [< L *adōrāre,* to pray to.] —**ad′o•ra′tion** (ăd′ə-rā′shən) *n.* —**a•dor′er** *n.*

a•dorn (ə-dôrn′) *v.* **1.** To be a decoration to; enhance. **2.** To decorate with or as with ornaments. [< L *adornāre,* to put ornaments on.] —**a•dorn′er** *n.* —**a•dorn′ment** *n.*

ad•re•nal (ə-drē′nəl) *adj.* **1.** At, near, or on the kidneys. **2.** Pertaining to the adrenal glands or their secretions.

adrenal gland. Either of two small endocrine glands, one located above each kidney.

ad•ren•a•lin (ə-drĕn′əl-ĭn) *n.* Also **a•dren•a•line.** Epinephrine.

ad•re•no•cor•ti•co•trop•ic hormone (ə-drē′nō-kôr′tĭ-kō-trŏp′ĭk, -trō′pĭk). A hormone, ACTH.

A•dri•at•ic Sea (ā′drē-ăt′ĭk). An arm of the Mediterranean between Italy and the Balkan Peninsula.

a•drift (ə-drĭft′) *adv.* Without anchor or direction. —**a•drift′** *adj.*

a•droit (ə-droit′) *adj.* **1.** Dexterous. **2.** Skillful under pressing conditions. [F < *a droit,* "rightly."] —**a•droit′ly** *adv.* —**a•droit′ness** *n.*

ad•sorb (ăd-sôrb′, -zôrb′) *v.* To take in (liquid or gas) on the surface of a solid. —**ad•sorp′tion** (-sôrp′shən, -zôrp′-) *n.* —**ad•sorp′tive** *adj.*

ad•u•late (ăj′o͞o-lāt′) *v.* **-lated, -lating.** To praise excessively or fawningly. [< L *adūlārī,* to flatter.] —**ad′u•la′tion** *n.* —**ad′u•la′tor** *n.* —**ad′u•la•to′ry** (-lə-tôr′ē, -tōr′ē) *adj.*

a•dult (ə-dŭlt′, ăd′ŭlt′) *n.* One who has attained maturity or legal age. —*adj.* **1.** Fully developed and mature. **2.** Intended for mature persons. [L *adultus,* pp of *adolescēre,* to grow up.] —**a•dult′hood′** *n.*

a•dul•ter•ate (ə-dŭl′tə-rāt′) *v.* **-ated, -ating.** To make impure or inferior by adding extraneous or improper ingredients. [L *adulterāre,* to pollute, commit adultery.] —**a•dul′ter•ant** *n.* & *adj.*

a•dul•ter•y (ə-dŭl′tər-ē, -trē) *n., pl.* **-ies.** Sexual intercourse between a married person and one other than the lawful spouse. —**a•dul′ter•er** *n.* —**a•dul′ter•ess** (-trĭs, -tər-ĭs) *fem.n.* —**a•dul′ter•ous** *adj.* —**a•dul′ter•ous•ly** *adv.*

ad•um•brate (ăd-ŭm′brāt′, ăd′əm-brāt′) *v.* **-brated, -brating. 1.** To give a sketchy outline. **2.** To foreshadow. [L *adumbrāre,* overshadow.] —**ad′um•bra′tion** *n.*

adv. adverb.

ad•vance (ăd-văns′, -väns′) *v.* **-vanced, -vancing. 1.** To move or bring forward or onward. **2.** To propose. **3.** To aid the growth or progress of. **4.** To make progress. **5.** To raise or rise in rank, amount, or value. **6.** To cause to occur sooner; hasten. **7.** To pay (money) before legally due. —*n.* **1.** The act of moving or going forward. **2.** Improvement; progress. **3.** A rise in price or value. **4. advances.** Personal approaches to secure acquaintance, favor, or agreement. **5.** Payment of money before legally due. —**in advance. 1.** In front. **2.** Ahead of time. —*adj.* **1.** Prior. **2.** Going before. [< L *abante,* "from before."] —**ad•vance′ment** *n.* —**ad•vanc′er** *n.*

ad•van•tage (ăd-văn′tĭj, ăd-vän′-) *n.* **1.** A favorable position or factor. **2.** Benefit or profit; gain. **3.** *Tennis.* The first point scored after deuce. [< OF *avantage,* "the condition of being ahead."] —**ad′van•ta′geous** (ăd′văn-tā′jəs) *adj.* —**ad′van•ta′geous•ly** *adv.*

Ad•vent (ăd′vĕnt′) *n.* **1.** The coming of Christ. **2.** The period including four Sundays before Christmas. **3. advent.** A coming or arrival. [< L *advenīre,* to come to.]

ad•ven•ti•tious (ăd′vĕn-tĭsh′əs) *adj.* Not inherent; accidental. [L *adventīcius,* "arriving (from outside)."] —**ad′ven•ti′tious•ly** *adv.*

ad•ven•ture (ăd-vĕn′chər) *n.* **1.** A risky undertaking. **2.** An unusual or suspenseful experience. **3.** A business venture. [< L *adventūrus,* fut part of *advenīre,* to arrive.] —**ad•ven′tur•ous** *adj.* —**ad•ven′tur•ous•ness** *n.*

ad•ven•tur•er (ăd-vĕn′chər-ər) *n.* **1.** One who undertakes risky ventures. **2.** A soldier of fortune. **3.** One who unscrupulously seeks wealth and social position.

ad•verb (ăd′vûrb′) *n.* **1.** A part of speech comprising a class of words that modify a verb, adjective, or other adverb. **2.** A word belonging to this class, as *rapidly* in *He runs rapidly.* [< L *adverbium,* "added word."] —**ad•ver′bi•al** *adj.* —**ad•ver′bi•al•ly** *adv.*

ad•ver•sar•y (ăd′vər-sĕr′ē) *n., pl.* **-ies.** An opponent; enemy. [< L *adversus,* ADVERSE.]

ad•verse (ăd-vûrs′, ăd′vûrs′) *adj.* **1.** Actively opposed; hostile. **2.** Unfavorable. [< L *adversus,* pp of *advertere,* to turn toward (with hostility).] —**ad•verse′ly** *adv.*

ad•ver•si•ty (ăd-vûr′sə-tē) *n., pl.* **-ties.** Hardship; misfortune.

ad•vert (ăd-vûrt′) *v.* To allude; refer. [< L *advertere,* to turn toward.]

ad•ver•tise (ăd′vər-tīz′) *v.* **-tised, -tising. 1.** To call attention to a product or business so as to promote sales. **2.** To notify. [< OF *a(d)vertir,* to advert.] —**ad′ver•tis′er** *n.*

ad•ver•tise•ment (ăd′vər-tīz′mənt, ăd-vûr′tĭs-mənt, -tĭz-mənt) *n.* A notice designed to attract public attention.

ad•ver•tis•ing (ăd'vər-tī'zĭng) *n.* **1.** The business of preparing and distributing advertisements. **2.** Advertisements collectively.

ad•vice (ăd-vīs') *n.* Opinion about a course of action; counsel. [< VL **advīsum,* opinion.]

ad•vis•a•ble (ăd-vī'zə-bəl) *adj.* Prudent; expedient. **—ad•vis'a•bil'i•ty** *n.*

ad•vise (ăd-vīz') *v.* **-vised, -vising. 1.** To offer advice to. **2.** To recommend. **3.** To inform. [< VL **advīsāre,* to observe.] **—ad•vi'ser, ad•vi'sor** *n.* **—ad•vi'so•ry** *adj.*

ad•vise•ment (ăd-vīz'mənt) *n.* Careful consideration.

ad•vo•cate (ăd'və-kāt') *v.* **-cated, -cating.** To speak in favor of; recommend. *—n.* (ăd'və-kĭt, -kāt'). **1.** One who argues for a cause or person; a supporter or defender. **2.** A lawyer. [< L *advocāre,* to summon to (give evidence).] **—ad'vo•ca•cy** *n.*

adz, adze (ădz) *n.* A tool with an arched blade at right angles to the handle, used for shaping wood. [< OE *adesa.*]

A.E.A. Actors' Equity Association.

AEC Atomic Energy Commission.

Ae•ge•an Sea (ĭ-jē'ən). An arm of the Mediterranean between Greece and Turkey.

ae•gis (ē'jĭs) *n.* **1.** Protection. **2.** Patronage. [< Gk *aigis,* the shield of Zeus.]

Ae•ne•as (ĭ-nē'əs). Trojan hero, reputed ancestor of the Romans.

ae•on. Variant of **eon.**

aer•ate (âr'āt') *v.* **-ated, -ating. 1.** To supply with or expose to gas. **2.** To supply (blood) with oxygen. **—aer•a'tion** *n.*

aer•i•al (âr'ē-əl) *adj.* **1.** Of, in, inhabiting, or caused by the air. **2.** Lofty. **3.** Airy. **4.** Of, for, or by aircraft. *—n.* An antenna. [< Gk *aēr,* air.] **—aer'i•al•ly** *adv.*

aer•i•al•ist (âr'ē-əl-ĭst) *n.* An acrobat who performs on a tightrope, trapeze, or similar apparatus.

aer•ie (âr'ē, ĭr'ē) *n.* A high nest, as of an eagle. [< L *ārea,* open field, AREA.]

aero–. *comb. form.* **1.** Air, gas, or the atmosphere. **2.** Aircraft. [< Gk *aēr,* air.]

aer•o•dy•nam•ics (âr'ō-dī-năm'ĭks) *n. (takes sing. v.).* The dynamics of gases, esp of atmospheric interactions with moving objects. **—aer'o•dy•nam'ic** *adj.*

aer•o•em•bo•lism (âr'ō-ĕm'bə-lĭz'əm) *n.* **1.** The presence of air bubbles in the heart or blood vessels. **2. Caisson disease.**

aer•o•naut (âr'ə-nôt') *n.* A pilot or navigator of a balloon or lighter-than-air craft.

aer•o•nau•tics (âr'ə-nô'tĭks) *n. (takes sing. v.).* **1.** The design and construction of aircraft. **2.** Aircraft navigation. **—aer'o•nau'tic, aer'o•nau'ti•cal** *adj.*

aer•o•plane (âr'ə-plān') *n. Chiefly Brit.* An airplane.

aer•o•sol (âr'ə-sôl', -sŏl', -sōl') *n.* **1.** A gaseous suspension of fine particles. **2.** Detergent, insecticide, or paint packaged under pressure in a dispenser.

aer•o•space (âr'ō-spās') *adj.* **1.** Pertaining to the earth's atmosphere and the space beyond. **2.** Pertaining to the science or technology of flight. **—aer'o•space'** *n.*

Aes•chy•lus (ĕs'kə-ləs, ēs'-). 525–456 B.C. Greek tragic poet.

Aes•cu•la•pi•us (ĕs'kyōō-lā'pē-əs). Roman god of medicine.

Ae•sop (ē'sŏp', ē'səp). Greek fabulist of the late sixth century B.C. **—Ae•so'pi•an** (-sō'pē-ən) *adj.*

aes•thete, es•thete (ĕs'thēt') *n.* One who cultivates or affects a superior appreciation of the beautiful.

aes•thet•ic, es•thet•ic (ĕs-thĕt'ĭk) *adj.* **1.** Of or pertaining to aesthetics. **2.** Of, pertaining to, or sensitive to the beautiful; artistic. *—n.* **aesthetics, esthetics.** *(takes sing. v.).* The branch of philosophy that provides a theory of the beautiful and of the fine arts. [< Gk *aisthētikos,* pertaining to sense perception.] **—aes•thet'i•cal•ly** *adv.*

ae•ther. Variant of **ether.**

AF **1.** air force. **2.** audio frequency.

a.f. audio frequency.

A.F. air force.

a•far (ə-fär') *adv.* From, at, or to a distance; far away.

af•fa•ble (ăf'ə-bəl) *adj.* **1.** Amiable. **2.** Mild; gentle. [< L *affābilis* < *affārī,* to speak to.] **—af'fa•bil'i•ty** *n.* **—af'fa•bly** *adv.*

af•fair (ə-fâr') *n.* **1.** Anything done or to be done; concern. **2. affairs.** Business matters. **3.** A short romantic or sexual involvement. [< OF *a faire,* "to do."]

af•fect[1] (ə-fĕkt') *v.* **1.** To bring about a change in. **2.** To touch the emotions of. [L *afficere* (pp *affectus*), to do something to.]

Usage: *Affect* and *effect* are never interchangeable. *Affect* is now used principally in the senses of influence *(smoking affects health)* and pretense or imitation *(affecting nonchalance to hide fear); effect* refers only to accomplishment or execution *(reductions designed to effect economy).*

af•fect[2] (ə-fĕkt') *v.* **1.** To simulate or imitate so as to impress; feign. **2.** To fancy: *affect big hats.* [< L *affectāre,* to strive after, freq of *afficere,* to AFFECT.] **—af•fect'er** *n.*

af•fec•ta•tion (ăf'ĕk-tā'shən) *n.* Artificial behavior designed to impress others.

af•fect•ed (ə-fĕk'tĭd) *adj.* Assumed or simulated to impress others. **—af•fect'ed•ly** *adv.*

af•fect•ing (ə-fĕk'tĭng) *adj.* Full of pathos; touching; moving.

af•fec•tion (ə-fĕk'shən) *n.* A tender feeling toward another. [< L *affectiō,* (friendly) disposition < *afficere,* to AFFECT.] **—af•fec'tion•ate** *adj.* **—af•fec'tion•ate•ly** *adv.*

af•fer•ent (ăf'ər-ənt) *adj.* Directed toward a central organ or section. [< L *afferre,* to bring toward.]

af•fi•ance (ə-fī'əns) *v.* **-anced, -ancing.** To betroth. [< OF *affier,* to trust to.]

af•fi•da•vit (ăf'ə-dā'vĭt) *n. Law.* A written declaration made under oath. [ML, "he has pledged" < *affīdāre,* to trust to.]

af•fil•i•ate (ə-fĭl'ē-āt') *v.* **-ated, -ating. 1.** To adopt as a subordinate associate. **2.** To associate (with). *—n.* (ə-fĭl'ē-ĭt). An associate or subordinate. [ML *affiliāre,* "to take to oneself as a son."] **—af•fil'i•a'tion** *n.*

af•fin•i•ty (ə-fĭn'ə-tē) *n., pl.* **-ties. 1.** An attraction or attractive force. **2.** Relationship; kinship. [< L *affīnis,* neighboring.]

Usage: *Affinity* may be followed by *of, between,* or *with.* Thus, *affinity of* persons (or things), *between* two persons (or things), *with* another person (or thing).

af•firm (ə-fûrm') *v.* **1.** To declare or maintain to be true. **2.** To confirm. **—af•firm'a•ble** *adj.* **—af'fir•ma'tion** (ăf'ər-mā'shən) *n.*

af•firm•a•tive (ə-fûr'mə-tĭv) *adj.* **1.** Giving assent; responding in a positive manner. **2.** Confirming. *—n.* **1.** A word or phrase signifying assent. **2.** The side in a debate that upholds a proposition.

affirmative action. Action taken to provide equal opportunity, as in hiring, for members of previously disadvantaged groups, such as women and minorities.

af•fix (ə-fĭks') *v.* **1.** To attach: *affix a label to a package.* **2.** To append: *affix a postscript.* *—n.* (ăf'ĭks'). **1.** Something attached or added. **2.** A word element that is attached to a base, stem, or root.

af•fla•tus (ə-flā'təs) *n.* A creative impulse; an inspiration. [< L *afflāre,* to breathe on.]

af•flict (ə-flĭkt') *v.* To inflict suffering upon; cause distress to. [< L *affligere,* to dash against.] **—af•flic'tion** *n.* **—af•flic'tive** *adj.*

af•flu•ence (ăf'lōō-əns) *n.* Wealth; abundance. [< L *affluere,* to flow to.] **—af'flu•ent** *adj.* **—af'flu•ent•ly** *adv.*

af•ford (ə-fôrd', ə-fōrd') *v.* **1.** To have the financial means for. **2.** To be able to spare or give up. **3.** To provide. [< OE *geforthian,* to further.] **—af•ford'a•ble** *adj.*

af•fray (ə-frā') *n.* A quarrel or noisy brawl. [< OF *affreer,* to fight in public.]

af•front (ə-frŭnt') *v.* **1.** To offend. **2.** To confront. *—n.* An insult. [< VL **affrontāre.*]

Af•ghan (ăf'găn', -gən) *n.* **1.** A native of Afghanistan. **2.** Pashto. **3. afghan.** A coverlet knitted or crocheted in colorful geometric designs. *—adj.* Of or pertaining to Afghanistan, its people, or their language.

af•ghan•i (ăf-găn'ē) *n.* The basic monetary unit of Afghanistan.

Af•ghan•i•stan (ăf-găn'ə-stăn'). A kingdom of SW Asia. Pop. 13,800,000. Cap. Kabul.

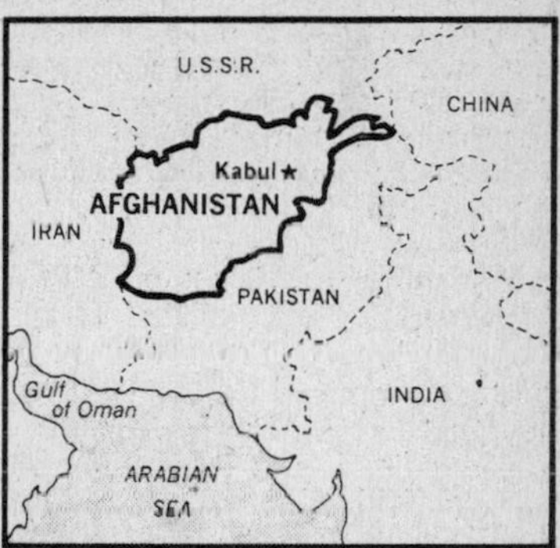

Afghanistan

a•fi•ci•o•na•do (ə-fē'sē-ə-nä'dō, ə-fĭs'ē-ə-) *n., pl.* **-dos.** A devotee. [Span, pp of *aficionar,* to inspire affection.]

a•field (ə-fēld') *adv.* **1.** Off the usual track. **2.** Away from one's home. **3.** To or on a field.

a•fire (ə-fīr') *adj. & adv.* **1.** On fire. **2.** Intensely interested.

a•flame (ə-flām') *adj. & adv.* **1.** On fire. **2.** Keenly interested.

AFL-CIO The American Federation of Labor and Congress of Industrial Organizations.

a•float (ə-flōt') *adj. & adv.* **1.** Floating. **2.** At sea. **3.** Flooded.

a•flut•ter (ə-flŭt'ər) *adj.* Nervous and excited.

a•foot (ə-fōōt') *adj. & adv.* **1.** Walking; on foot. **2.** In progress.

a•fore•said (ə-fôr'sĕd', ə-fōr'-) *adj.* Spoken of earlier.

a•fore•thought (ə-fôr'thôt', ə-fōr'-) *adj.* Premeditated: *malice aforethought.*

a•foul (ə-foul') *adv. & adj.* In an entanglement or collision.

Afr. Africa; African.

a•fraid (ə-frād') *adj.* **1.** Filled with fear. **2.** Reluctant; averse: *afraid of work.* [< OF *affreer,* to AFFRAY.]

a•fresh (ə-frĕsh′) *adv.* Anew; again.
Af•ri•ca (ăf′rĭ-kə). A continent in the E Hemisphere, S of Europe and between the Atlantic and Indian oceans. —**Af′ri•can** *adj. & n.*
Af•ri•kaans (ăf′rĭ-käns′, -känz′) *n.* The language of the Republic of South Africa, developed from 17th-century Dutch.
Af•ri•kan•er (ăf′rĭ-kä′nər) *n.* An Afrikaans-speaking descendant of the Dutch settlers of South Africa.
Af•ro (ăf′rō) *n.* A hair style characterized by dense frizzy hair worn naturally. —*adj.* African in manner or style.
Af•ro-A•mer•i•can (ăf′rō-ə-mĕr′ə-kən) *adj.* Of or pertaining to American Negroes of African ancestry. —*n.* An American Negro of African ancestry.
Af•ro-A•si•at•ic (ăf′rō-ā′zhē-ăt′ĭk) *n.* A language family of SW Asia and N Africa. —**Af′ro-A′si•at′ic** *adj.*
aft (ăft, äft). *Naut. adv.* At, in, toward, or near the stern of a vessel. —*adj.* Situated near or at the stern; after. [Prob short for ABAFT.]
aft. afternoon.
af•ter (ăf′tər, äf′-) *prep.* **1.** Behind in place or order. **2.** In pursuit of: *He runs after girls.* **3.** Concerning: *asked after you.* **4.** At a later time than. **5.** In the style of: *satires after Horace.* **6.** With the same name as: *named after her mother.* **7.** In conformity to: *a man after my own heart.* **8.** Past the hour of: *five minutes after three.* —*adv.* **1.** Behind; in the rear. **2.** At a subsequent time. —*adj.* **1.** Later; following: *afterglow.* **2.** *Naut.* Nearer the stern of a vessel. —*conj.* Subsequent to the time that. [< OE *æfter.* See **apo-**.]
af•ter•birth (ăf′tər-bûrth′, äf′-) *n.* The placenta and fetal membranes expelled from the uterus after childbirth.
af•ter•burn•er (ăf′tər-bûr′nər, äf′-) *n.* A device for augmenting the thrust of a jet engine.
af•ter•care (ăf′tər-kâr′, äf′-) *n.* Treatment or special care given to convalescent patients.
af•ter•ef•fect (ăf′tər-ə-fĕkt′, äf′-) *n.* A delayed or prolonged response to a stimulus.
af•ter•glow (ăf′tər-glō′, äf′-) *n.* **1.** Light emitted or remaining after removal of a source of illumination. **2.** A comfortable feeling following a pleasant experience.
af•ter•im•age (ăf′tər-ĭm′ĭj, äf′-) *n.* A visual image that persists after a visual stimulus ceases.
af•ter•life (ăf′tər-līf′, äf′-) *n.* A life believed to follow death.
af•ter•math (ăf′tər-măth′, äf′-) *n.* **1.** A consequence or result. **2.** A second crop of grass in the same season. [< AFTER + OE *mǣth,* a mowing.]
af•ter•most (ăf′tər-mōst′, äf′-) *adj.* Nearest the end or rear; hindmost; last.
af•ter•noon (ăf′tər-no͞on′, äf′-) *n.* The day from noon until sunset.
af•ter•taste (ăf′tər-tāst′, äf′-) *n.* A taste or feeling persisting after the stimulus causing it is no longer present.
af•ter•thought (ăf′tər-thôt′, äf′-) *n.* An idea, response, or explanation that occurs to one after an event or decision.
af•ter•ward (ăf′tər-wərd, äf′-) *adv.* Also **af•ter•wards** (-wərdz). In or at a later time; subsequently.
Ag silver (L *argentum*).
A.G. 1. adjutant general. **2.** attorney general.
a•gain (ə-gĕn′) *adv.* **1.** Once more; anew. **2.** To a previous place, position, or state. **3.** Furthermore. **4.** On the other hand: *He might go, and again he might not.* **5.** In return; in response. [< OE *ongeagn,* in return, against < Gmc **gagina.*]
a•gainst (ə-gĕnst′) *prep.* **1.** In a direction or course opposite to. **2.** So as to come into contact with: *waves dashing against the shore.* **3.** In hostile opposition or resistance to: *struggle against fate.* **4.** Contrary to; opposed to: *against my better judgment.* **5.** In contrast: *dark colors against a fair skin.* **6.** As a defense or safeguard from. **7.** To the account or debt of. [ME < AGAIN.]
a•gape[1] (ə-găp′, ə-găp′) *adv. & adj.* In a state of wonder or amazement.
a•ga•pe[2] (ä′gə-pā′) *n., pl.* **-pae** (-pē′). The love feast accompanied by Eucharistic celebration in the early Christian church. [Gk *agapē,* love.]
a•gar (ā′gär, ä′gär) *n.* Also **a•gar-a•gar** (ā′-gär′ā′gär′, ä′gär′ä′-). A mucilaginous material prepared from certain seaweeds. [Malay, "jelly, gelatin."]
ag•ate (ăg′ĭt) *n.* **1.** A variety of chalcedony with color banding or irregular clouding. **2.** A child's marble made of this or similar material. **3.** A printer's type size, approx. $5^1/_2$ points. [< Gk *akhātēs.*]
a•ga•ve (ə-gä′vē, ə-gä′-) *n.* Any of various fleshy-leaved tropical American plants. [< Gk *agauos,* noble.]
age (āj) *n.* **1.** The period or amount of time during which someone or something exists. **2.** The time in life when one officially assumes certain rights or responsibilities. **3.** A distinctive period or stage. **4.** The state of being old. **5.** A long time. —*v.* **aged, aging** or **ageing.** To grow or cause to grow old or older. [< L *aetās,* age.] —**ag′er** *n.*
-age. *comb. form.* **1.** Collectively: **leafage. 2.** Relation to or connection with: **parentage. 3.** Condition or position: **marriage. 4.** Charge or fee: **postage. 5.** Residence or place: **orphanage.** [< LL *-āticus.*]
a•ged (ā′jĭd) *adj.* **1.** Old; advanced in years. **2.** (ājd). Of the age of: *aged three.*
age•ism (ā′jĭz′əm) *n.* Discrimination based on age, as against middle-aged and elderly people. —**age′ist** *n. & adj.*
age•less (āj′lĭs) *adj.* **1.** Never seeming to grow old. **2.** Existing forever; eternal.
a•gen•cy (ā′jən-sē) *n., pl.* **-cies. 1.** Action; operation; power. **2.** A mode of action; means. **3.** A business or service acting for others.
a•gen•da (ə-jĕn′də) *pl.n. (takes sing. v.). Sing.* **-dum** (-dəm). A list or program of things to be done. [L, pl of *agendum* < *agere,* to ACT.]
a•gent (ā′jənt) *n.* **1.** One that acts or has power to act. **2.** One that acts as the representative of another. **3.** A means of doing something; instrument. [< L *agere,* to ACT.]
ag•glom•er•ate (ə-glŏm′ə-rāt′) *v.* **-ated, -ating.** To form into a rounded mass. [L *agglomerāre.*] —**ag•glom′er•a′tion** *n.*
ag•glu•ti•nate (ə-glo͞ot′n-āt′) *v.* **-nated, -nating. 1.** To join by adhesion. **2.** To cause (red blood cells or microorganisms) to clump together. [L *agglūtināre.*] —**ag•glu′ti•na′tion** *n.* —**ag•glu′ti•na′tive** *adj.*
ag•glu•ti•nin (ə-glo͞ot′n-ĭn) *n.* A substance that induces agglutination.
ag•gran•dize (ə-grăn′dīz′, ăg′rən-dīz′) *v.* **-dized, -dizing.** To increase; enlarge; extend. —**ag•gran′dize•ment** (ə-grăn′dĭz-mənt, ə-grăn′dīz′-) *n.* —**ag•gran′diz′er** *n.*
ag•gra•vate (ăg′rə-vāt′) *v.* **-vated, -vating. 1.** To make worse. **2.** To annoy; vex. [L *aggravāre,* to make heavier.] —**ag′gra•va′tion** *n.*
ag•gre•gate (ăg′rə-gĭt′) *adj.* Gathered together into a mass constituting a whole. —*n.* (ăg′rə-gĭt). A collective mass or sum; total. —*v.* (ăg′rə-gāt′) **-gated, -gating.** To gather into a mass, sum, or whole. [< L *aggregāre,* to add to (the flock).] —**ag′gre•ga′tion** *n.*
ag•gres•sion (ə-grĕsh′ən) *n.* **1.** The commencing of hostilities; an assault. **2.** Hostile action or behavior. [< L *aggredī,* to attack.] —**ag•gres′sor** (-grĕs′ər) *n.*
ag•gres•sive (ə-grĕs′ĭv) *adj.* **1.** Actively hostile. **2.** Assertive; bold. —**ag•gres′sive•ly** *adv.* —**ag•gres′sive•ness** *n.*
ag•grieve (ə-grēv′) *v.* **-grieved, -grieving. 1.** To distress; afflict. **2.** To injure unjustly; offend. [< L *aggravāre,* to AGGRAVATE.]
a•ghast (ə-găst′, ə-gäst′) *adj.* Horror-stricken; appalled. [< OE *gæstan* < *gāst,* GHOST.]
ag•ile (ăj′əl, ăj′īl) *adj.* Moving quickly and easily; nimble. [< L *agilis,* easily moved < *agere,* to ACT.] —**ag′ile•ly** *adv.* —**a•gil′i•ty** (ə-jĭl′ə-tē), **ag′ile•ness** *n.*
ag•i•tate (ăj′ə-tāt′) *v.* **-tated, -tating. 1.** To stir or move violently. **2.** To upset; disturb. **3.** To arouse or try to arouse public interest. [L *agitāre,* freq of *agere,* to ACT.] —**ag′i•tat′ed•ly** *adv.* —**ag′i•ta′tion** *n.* —**ag′i•ta′tor** *n.*
a•gleam (ə-glēm′) *adj. & adv.* Gleaming.
a•glim•mer (ə-glĭm′ər) *adj. & adv.* Glimmering.
a•glit•ter (ə-glĭt′ər) *adj. & adv.* Glittering.
a•glow (ə-glō′) *adj. & adv.* Glowing.
ag•nos•tic (ăg-nŏs′tĭk) *n.* One who doubts the possibility of knowing the existence of God or absolute truth. —**ag•nos′tic** *adj.* —**ag•nos′ti•cism′** *n.*
Ag•nus De•i (ăg′nəs dē′ī, äg′no͞os dā′ē). **1.** The Lamb of God (emblem of Christ). John 1:29; Isaiah 53:7. **2.** A liturgical prayer to Christ.
a•go (ə-gō′) *adj. & adv.* Gone by; in the past. [< OE *āgān,* to go away.]
a•gog (ə-gŏg′) *adj.* Eagerly expectant; excited. [< OF *en gogues,* "in merriments."] —**a•gog′** *adv.*
-agogue, -agog. *comb. form.* A leader or inciter: **demagogue.** [< Gk *agōgos,* leading, drawing forth.]
ag•o•nize (ăg′ə-nīz′) *v.* **-nized, -nizing.** To suffer or afflict with great anguish. [< Gk *agōnizesthai,* to contend for a prize < *agōnia,* AGONY.] —**ag′o•niz′ing•ly** *adv.*
ag•o•ny (ăg′ə-nē) *n., pl.* **-nies.** Intense physical pain or mental distress. [< Gk *agōnia,* contest, anguish < *agein,* to drive.]
ag•o•ra•pho•bi•a (ăg′ə-rə-fō′bē-ə) *n.* Abnormal fear of open spaces. —**ag′o•ra•pho′bic** (-fō′bĭk, -fŏb′ĭk) *adj.*
agr., agric. agricultural; agriculture.
a•grar•i•an (ə-grâr′ē-ən) *adj.* **1.** Of or pertaining to land and its ownership. **2.** Pertaining to farming; agricultural. [< L *ager,* land, field.]
a•gree (ə-grē′) *v.* **agreed, agreeing. 1.** To consent; give assent. **2.** To be in accord. **3.** To share an opinion or understanding. **4.** To be suitable or beneficial. **5.** To correspond, as in grammatical case or number. [< VL **aggrātāre,* to be pleasing to.]
a•gree•a•ble (ə-grē′ə-bəl) *adj.* **1.** Pleasing; pleasant. **2.** Ready to consent; willing. —**a•gree′a•ble•ness** *n.* —**a•gree′a•bly** *adv.*
a•gree•ment (ə-grē′mənt) *n.* **1.** The act or state of agreeing. **2.** Concord; harmony. **3.** An arrangement between parties; covenant.
ag•ri•busi•ness (ăg′rĭ-bĭz′nĭs) *n.* Farming engaged in as big business, embracing the production, processing, and distribution of

farm products and the manufacture of farm equipment. [AGRI(CULTURE) + BUSINESS.]
ag•ri•cul•ture (ăg'rĭ-kŭl'chər) *n.* Cultivation of crops and the raising of livestock; farming. [< L *agrī cultūra,* "cultivation of land."] —**ag'ri•cul'tur•al** *adj.* —**ag'ri•cul'tur•ist** *n.*
a•ground (ə-ground') *adv. & adj.* Against the ground, as in shallow water: *The ship ran aground.*
a•gue (ā'gyōō) *n.* An attack of fever accompanied by chills or shivering. [< ML *(fēbris) acūta,* "sharp (fever)."]
ah (ä) *interj.* Expressive of surprise, pain, satisfaction, etc.
a•ha (ä-hä') *interj.* Expressive of surprise or triumph.
a•head (ə-hĕd') *adv.* **1.** At or to the front. **2.** Before; in advance. **3.** Onward; forward. —**get** (or **be**) **ahead.** To near or attain success.
a•hoy (ə-hoi') *interj.* Used as a nautical call or greeting.
aid (ād) *v.* To help; assist. —*n.* **1.** The giving of assistance. **2.** One who or that which provides assistance. [< L *adjuvāre,* to give aid to.] —**aid'er** *n.*
aide (ād) *n.* An assistant.
aide-de-camp (ăd'də-kămp') *n., pl.* **aides-de-camp.** A military officer acting as assistant to a superior officer.
ai•grette, ai•gret (ā-grĕt', ā'grĕt) *n.* An ornamental tuft of plumes. [F *aigrette,* "egret."]
ail (āl) *v.* **1.** To feel ill. **2.** To make ill or uneasy. [< OE *eglan.* See **agh-**[1].]
ai•lan•thus (ā-lăn'thəs) *n.* A weedy tree with numerous pointed leaflets. [< NL.]
ai•le•ron (ā'lə-rŏn') *n.* A movable control surface on the trailing edge of an airplane wing. [F, "little wing."]
ail•ment (āl'mənt) *n.* A mild illness.
aim (ām) *v.* **1.** To direct (a weapon, blow, etc.). **2.** To direct one's efforts or purpose. —*n.* **1.** The act of aiming. **2.** The direction of something aimed. **3.** Purpose, intention. [< OF *aesmer,* to guess at < L *aestimāre,* to ESTIMATE.]
aim•less (ām'lĭs) *adj.* Without direction or purpose. —**aim'less•ly** *adv.*
a•in. Variant of **ayin.**
ain't (ānt). *Nonstandard.* Contraction of *am not, are not, is not, has not,* and *have not.* *Usage: Ain't* is acceptable only when used knowingly to provide humor or shock or to reproduce certain speech patterns. Informally, the interrogative construction *aren't I* has somewhat more acceptance as an alternative to *ain't I.*
air (âr) *n.* **1. a.** A colorless, odorless, tasteless gaseous mixture, chiefly nitrogen (78%) and oxygen (21%). **b.** The earth's atmosphere. **2.** A breeze; wind. **3.** An impression; appearance: *an air of fear.* **4. airs.** Affectation. **5.** A melody or tune. —**on the air.** Broadcast; being broadcast. —*v.* **1.** To expose to air. **2.** To give public utterance to. [Blend of senses of several origins: 1. Atmosphere: < Gk *aēr,* breath; 2. Manner: < OF *aire,* "place of origin" < L *ager,* place, field, and L *ārea,* open space, AREA; 3. Melody: It *aria,* ARIA.]
air•borne (âr'bôrn', -bōrn') *adj.* Carried by or through the air.
air•brush (âr'brŭsh') *n.* An atomizer using compressed air to spray paint.
air•burst (âr'bûrst') *n.* An explosion in the atmosphere.
air-con•di•tion (âr'kən-dĭsh'ən) *v.* To control, esp. lower, the temperature and humidity of (an enclosure). —**air conditioner.** —**air conditioning.**
air•craft (âr'krăft', -kräft') *n., pl.* **-craft.** Any machine or device, including airplanes, helicopters, etc., capable of atmospheric flight.
aircraft carrier. A warship carrying aircraft.
air•drome (âr'drōm') *n.* An airport.
air•drop (âr'drŏp') *n.* A delivery, as of supplies or troops, by parachute from aircraft in flight.
Aire•dale (âr'dāl') *n.* A large terrier with a wiry tan and black coat.
air embolism. Aeroembolism.
air•field (âr'fēld') *n.* **1.** An airport having hard-surfaced runways. **2.** A landing strip.
air•foil (âr'foil') *n.* An aircraft control part or surface, such as a wing, propeller blade, or rudder.
air force. The aviation branch of a country's armed forces.
air gun. A gun discharged by compressed air.
air lane. A regular route of travel for aircraft; an airway.
air•lift (âr'lĭft') *n.* A system of transporting troops or supplies by air when surface routes are blocked. —**air'lift'** *v.*
air•line (âr'līn') *n.* **1.** A system for transport of passengers and freight by air. **2.** A business organization providing such a system. **3.** The shortest, most direct distance between two points.
air•lin•er (âr'lī'nər) *n.* A large passenger airplane.
air lock. An airtight chamber between regions of unequal pressure.
air mail. Also **air•mail** (âr'māl'). **1.** The system of conveying mail by aircraft. **2.** Mail thus conveyed. —**air'-mail'** *v.*
air•man (âr'mən) *n.* **1.** An enlisted man in the air force. **2.** An aviator.
air mile. A **nautical mile.**
air•plane (âr'plān') *n.* A winged vehicle capable of flight, heavier than air and propelled by jet engines or propellers.
air•port (âr'pôrt', -pōrt') *n.* A tract of leveled land with cargo and passenger facilities where aircraft take off and land.
air raid. A bombing attack by military aircraft. —**air'-raid'** *adj.*
air•ship (âr'shĭp') *n.* A self-propelled lighter-than-air craft with directional control surfaces; dirigible.
air•sick•ness (âr'sĭk'nĭs) *n.* Nausea resulting from flight in an aircraft. —**air'sick'** *adj.*
air•speed (âr'spēd') *n.* Speed, esp. of an aircraft, relative to the air.
air•strip (âr'strĭp') *n.* A minimally equipped airfield.
air•tight (âr'tīt') *adj.* **1.** Impermeable by air or gas. **2.** Unassailable: *an airtight excuse.*
air•way (âr'wā') *n.* An **air lane.**
air•wor•thy (âr'wûr'thē) *adj.* Fit to fly: *an airworthy old plane.* —**air'wor'thi•ness** *n.*
air•y (âr'ē) *adj.* **-ier, -iest. 1.** Of or like air. **2.** Open to the air; breezy. **3.** Light as air; graceful or delicate. **4.** Insubstantial; unreal. **5.** Nonchalant; carefree. —**air'i•ly** *adv.* —**air'i•ness** *n.*
aisle (īl) *n.* A passageway between rows of seats, as in a church or auditorium. [< OF *aile,* wing of a building.]
a•jar (ə-jär') *adv. & adj.* Partially opened, as a door. [ME *on char,* "in the act of turning."]
a•kim•bo (ə-kĭm'bō) *adj. & adv.* With the hands on the hips and the elbows bowed outward. [ME *in kenebowe,* "in keen bow."]
a•kin (ə-kĭn') *adj.* **1.** Of the same kin; related. **2.** Similar in quality or character.
Ak•ka•di•an (ə-kā'dē-ən) *n.* A Semitic language of a region of ancient Mesopotamia. —**Ak•ka'di•an** *adj.*
Ak•ron (ăk'rən). A city of Ohio. Pop. 290,000.
-al[1]. *comb. form.* A pertinence to or connection with: **adjectival.**
-al[2]. *comb. form.* The act or process of doing or experiencing the action indicated by the verb stem: **denial.**
Al aluminum.
A.L. American Legion.
à la (ä'lä, ä'lə, ăl'ə). In the style or manner of.
ALA American Library Association.
Ala. Alabama.
Al•a•bam•a (ăl'ə-băm'ə). A S state of the U.S. Pop. 3,444,000. Cap. Montgomery. —**Al'a•bam'i•an** (-ē-ən), **Al'a•bam'an** *adj. & n.*
al•a•bas•ter (ăl'ə-băs'tər, -bäs'tər) *n.* A dense, translucent, white or tinted fine-grained gypsum. [< Egypt *'a-la-Baste,* "vessel of (the goddess) *Baste.*"]
à la carte (ä' lä kärt', ăl'ə). With a separate price for each item on the menu. [F, "by the menu."]
a•lac•ri•ty (ə-lăk'rə-tē) *n.* Cheerful eagerness; sprightliness. [< L *alacer,* eager.]
à la king (ä' lə kĭng', ăl'ə). In cream sauce, often with pimiento and mushrooms.
Al•a•mo, the (ăl'ə-mō'). A mission in San Antonio, Texas, site of a defeat of Texans by Mexican forces (1836).
à la mode (ä' lə mōd', ăl'ə). **1.** Fashionable. **2.** Served with ice cream, as pie. [F, "in the fashion."]
a•larm (ə-lärm') *n.* **1.** A sudden feeling of fear. **2.** A warning of danger. **3.** A device that sounds a warning. **4.** The bell or buzzer of a clock. **5.** A call to arms. —*v.* To frighten or warn by an alarm. [< OIt *all'arme,* "to arms!"] —**a•larm'ing•ly** *adv.*
a•larm•ist (ə-lär'mĭst) *n.* A person who needlessly alarms others. —**a•larm'ism'** *n.*
a•las (ə-lăs', ə-läs') *interj.* Expressive of regret or anxiety.
A•las•ka (ə-lăs'kə). The largest state of the U.S., in extreme NW North America. Pop. 302,000. Cap. Juneau. —**A•las'kan** *adj. & n.*
alb (ălb) *n.* A white linen robe worn by the celebrant of a Mass. [< L *albus,* white.]
al•ba•core (ăl'bə-kôr', -kōr') *n.* A large marine fish that is a major source of canned tuna. [< Ar *al-bakrah,* "the young camel."]
Al•ba•ni•a (ăl-bā'nē-ə, -bān'yə, ôl-). A socialist country on the Adriatic. Pop. 2,000,000. Cap. Tirana.

Albania

Al•ba•ni•an (ăl-bā'nē-ən, -bān'yən, ôl-) *n.* **1.** A native or inhabitant of Albania. **2.** The Indo-European language of the Albanians. —**Al•ba'ni•an** *adj.*
Al•ba•ny (ôl'bə-nē). The capital of New York

State. Pop. 115,000.

al•ba•tross (ăl'bə-trôs', -trŏs') *n.* Any of various large, web-footed, long-winged sea birds. [Port *alcatraz,* pelican.]

al•be•it (ôl-bē'ĭt, ăl-) *conj.* Although. [ME *al be it,* "let it be entirely (that)."]

Al•ber•ta (ăl-bûr'tə). A province of W Canada. Pop. 1,332,000. Cap. Edmonton. **—Al•ber'tan** *n.* & *adj.*

al•bi•no (ăl-bī'nō) *n., pl.* **-nos.** A person or animal having abnormally pale skin, very light hair, and lacking normal eye coloring. [< L *albus,* white.] **—al'bin•ism'** (ăl'bə-nĭz'əm) *n.*

al•bum (ăl'bəm) *n.* **1.** A book with blank pages for stamps, photographs, etc. **2.** One or more phonograph records in one binding. [L, blank tablet, neut of *albus,* white.]

al•bu•men (ăl-byo͞o'mən) *n.* **1.** The white of an egg. **2.** Albumin. [L *albūmen* < *albus,* white.]

al•bu•min (ăl-byo͞o'mən) *n.* Any of several proteins found in egg white, blood serum, milk, and plant and animal tissue.

Al•bu•quer•que (ăl'bə-kûr'kē). A city of New Mexico. Pop. 244,000.

al•caz•ar (ăl-kăz'ər, ăl'kə-zär') *n.* A Spanish palace or fortress.

al•che•my (ăl'kə-mē) *n.* **1.** A traditional chemical philosophy concerned primarily with changing base metals into gold. **2.** Any seemingly magical power. [< Ar *al-kīmiyā',* "the art of transmutation."] **—al•chem'i•cal** (-ĭ-kəl) *adj.* **—al'che•mist** *n.*

Al•ci•bi•a•des (ăl'sĭ-bī'ə-dēz'). 450?–404 B.C. Athenian statesman and general.

al•co•hol (ăl'kə-hôl') *n.* **1.** Any of a series of related organic compounds having the general formula $C_nH_{2n+1}OH$. **2.** Ethanol. **3.** Intoxicating liquor containing alcohol. [< ML, fine powder of antimony used to tint the eyelids.]

al•co•hol•ic (ăl'kə-hôl'ĭk, -hŏl'ĭk) *adj.* **1.** Of or resulting from alcohol. **2.** Containing or preserved in alcohol. **3.** Suffering from alcoholism. *—n.* One who suffers from alcoholism.

al•co•hol•ism (ăl'kə-hôl-ĭz'əm) *n.* Habitual excessive alcoholic consumption.

al•cove (ăl'kōv') *n.* A recess or partly enclosed extension of a room. [< Ar *al-qubbah,* "the vault."]

al•de•hyde (ăl'də-hīd') *n.* Any of a class of highly reactive compounds obtained by oxidation of alcohols. [< NL *al(cohol) dehyd(rogenatum),* "dehydrogenized alcohol."]

al•der (ôl'dər) *n.* Any of various shrubs or trees growing in cool, moist places. [< OE *aler.* See **el-²**.]

al•der•man (ôl'dər-mən) *n.* A member of a municipal legislative body. [< OE *(e)aldormann,* viceroy.] **—al'der•man•cy** *n.*

Al•der•ney (ôl'dər-nē) *n., pl.* **-neys.** One of a breed of dairy cattle. [< *Alderney,* island in the English Channel.]

ale (āl) *n.* An alcoholic beverage similar to but more bitter than beer. [< OE *ealu.* See **alu-**.]

a•le•a•to•ry (ā'lē-ə-tôr'ē, -tōr'ē) *adj.* Dependent upon chance. [< L *ālea,* dice.]

a•lee (ə-lē') *adv. Naut.* At, on, or to the leeward side.

a•lem•bic (ə-lĕm'bĭk) *n.* An apparatus formerly used for distilling. [< Ar *al-anbīq.*]

a•leph (ä'lĭf) *n.* Also **a•lef.** The 1st letter of the Hebrew alphabet, representing a glottal stop.

a•lert (ə-lûrt') *adj.* **1.** Vigilantly attentive; watchful. **2.** Mentally responsive; quick. **3.** Brisk; lively. *—n.* **1.** A signal warning of danger. **2.** The period during which such a warning is in effect. *—v.* To warn. [< It *all'erta,* "on the watch."] **—a•lert'ness** *n.*

Al•e•ut (ăl'ē-o͞ot') *n., pl.* **-ut** or **-uts.** Also **A•leu•tian** (ə-lo͞o'shən). An Eskimo native of the Aleutian Islands. **—A•leu'tian** *adj.*

Aleutian Islands. An island chain extending in a westward arc from Alaska.

Al•ex•an•der the Great (ăl'ĭg-zăn'dər, -zän'dər). 356–323 B.C. King of Macedonia; conqueror of Greece, Persia, and Egypt.

Al•ex•an•dri•a (ăl'ĭg-zăn'drē-ə, -zän'drē-ə). A city of Egypt. Pop. 1,513,000.

al•ex•an•drine (ăl'ĭg-zăn'drĭn, -zän'drĭn) *n.* A line of English verse in iambic hexameter.

al•fal•fa (ăl-făl'fə) *n.* A cloverlike plant with purple flowers, widely cultivated for forage. [< Ar *al-fasfaṣah.*]

Al•fred the Great (ăl'frĭd). A.D. 849–899. King of England (A.D. 871–899).

al•fres•co (ăl-frĕs'kō) *adv.* & *adj.* In the fresh air; outdoors. [It, "in the fresh (air)."]

al•gae (ăl'jē) *pl.n. Sing.* **-ga** (-gə). Any of various primitive, chiefly aquatic, one-celled or multicellular plants, as the seaweeds. [< L *alga,* seaweed.] **—al'gal** (-gəl) *adj.*

al•ge•bra (ăl'jə-brə) *n.* A generalization of arithmetic in which symbols represent members of a specified set of numbers and are related by operations that hold for all numbers in the set. [< Ar *al-jebr, al-jabr,* "the (science of) reuniting."] **—al'ge•bra'ic** (-brā'ĭk) *adj.*

algebraic sum. The sum of algebraic quantities produced by arithmetic addition, in which negative quantities are added by the subtraction of corresponding positive quantities.

Al•ge•ri•a (ăl-jĭr'ē-ə). A republic of NW Africa. Pop. 10,454,000. Cap. Algiers. **—Al•ge'ri•an** *adj.* & *n.*

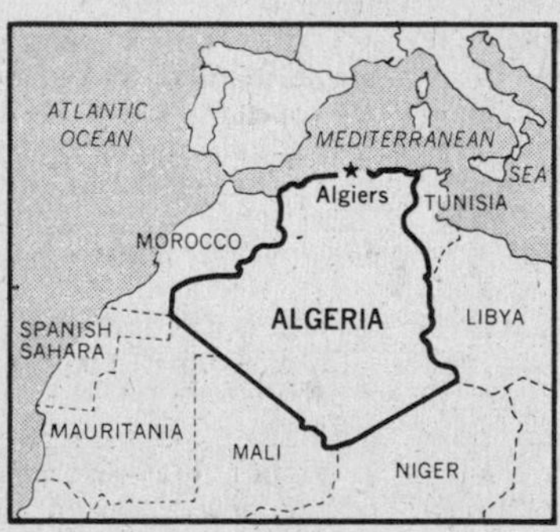

Algeria

-algia. *comb. form.* Pain or disease of: **neuralgia.** [< Gk *algos,* pain.]

Al•giers (ăl-jîrz'). The capital of Algeria. Pop. 884,000.

Al•gon•qui•an (ăl-gŏng'kwē-ən, -kē-ən) *n., pl.* **-an** or **-ans.** Also **Al•gon•ki•an** (-kē-ən). **1.** A family of North American Indian languages spoken in an area from the Atlantic seaboard W to the Rocky Mountains, and from Labrador S to North Carolina and Tennessee. **2.** A member of a tribe using a language of this family. **—Al•gon'qui•an** *adj.*

Al•gon•quin (ăl-gŏng'kwĭn, -kĭn) *n., pl.* **-quin** or **-quins.** Also **Al•gon•kin** (-kĭn). **1.** A member of any of several Algonquian-speaking North American Indian tribes formerly inhabiting a region N of the St. Lawrence River. **2.** The language of these tribes. **3.** Any Indian of these tribes.

al•go•rithm (ăl'gə-rĭth'əm) *n.* Any mechanical or repetitive computational procedure. [< Muhammad ibn-Musa al-Khwarizmi (A.D. 780–850?), Arab mathematician.]

a•li•as (ā'lē-əs, āl'yəs) *n.* An assumed name. *—adv.* Otherwise named: *Johnson, alias Rogers.* [L *aliās,* otherwise < *alius,* other.]

al•i•bi (ăl'ə-bī') *n.* **1.** A form of defense in which a defendant tries to prove he was elsewhere when a crime was committed. **2.** An excuse. [L *alibī,* elsewhere.]

a•li•en (ā'lē-ən, āl'yən) *adj.* **1.** Owing allegiance to another country or government. **2.** Not one's own; unfamiliar: *an alien culture.* **3.** Repugnant; adverse: *Lying is alien to his nature.* *—n.* **1.** An unnaturalized resident of a country. **2.** A member of another people, region, etc. **3.** One excluded from some group; an outsider. [< L *alius,* other.]

al•ien•a•ble (āl'yən-ə-bəl, ā'lē-ən-) *adj. Law.* Able to be transferred to the ownership of another. **—al'ien•a•bil'i•ty** *n.*

al•ien•ate (āl'yən-āt', ā'lē-ən-) *v.* **-ated, -ating.** To cause to become unfriendly or indifferent. [< L *aliēnus,* ALIEN.] **—al'ien•a'tion** *n.*

al•ien•ist (āl'yən-ĭst, ā'lē-ən-) *n.* A physician accepted by a court as an expert on the mental competence of principals or witnesses appearing before it.

a•light¹ (ə-līt') *v.* **alighted** or **alit, alighting. 1.** To come down and settle, as after flight. **2.** To dismount. [< OE *ālīhtan,* to lighten < *līht,* LIGHT (adjective).]

a•light² (ə-līt') *adj.* & *adv.* Burning; lighted.

a•lign (ə-līn') *v.* Also **a•line, alined, alining. 1.** To arrange in a line. **2.** To ally oneself with one side of an argument, cause, etc.

a•lign•ment (ə-līn'mənt) *n.* Also **a•line•ment.** Arrangement or position in a straight line.

a•like (ə-līk') *adj.* Having close resemblance; similar. *—adv.* In the same way, manner, or degree. **—a•like'ness** *n.*

al•i•ment (ăl'ə-mənt) *n.* Food; nourishment. [< L *alimentum* < *alere,* to nourish.]

al•i•men•ta•ry (ăl'ə-mĕn'trē, -tər-ē) *adj.* Pertaining to food or nutrition.

alimentary canal. The mucous-membrane-lined tube of the digestive system, extending from the mouth to the anus and including the pharynx, esophagus, stomach, and intestines.

al•i•mo•ny (ăl'ə-mō'nē) *n., pl.* **-nies.** An allowance for support paid to a divorced person by his former spouse. [L *alimōnia,* support < *alere,* to nourish.]

al•i•phat•ic (ăl'ə-făt'ĭk) *adj.* Pertaining to organic compounds in which the carbon atoms are linked in open chains rather than rings. [< Gk *aleiphar,* oil.]

a•lit (ə-lĭt'). *p.t.* & *p.p.* of **alight.**

a•live (ə-līv') *adj.* **1.** Having life; living. **2.** Not extinct or inactive. **3.** Full of life; lively. **4.** Sensitive. **5.** Teeming. **—a•live'ness** *n.*

al•ka•li (ăl'kə-lī') *n., pl.* **-lis** or **-lies. 1.** A hydroxide or carbonate of an alkali metal, the aqueous solution of which is bitter, slippery, caustic, and basic. **2.** Any of various soluble mineral salts found in natural water and arid soils. [< Ar *al-qalīy,* the ashes (of saltwort, a plant).]

alkali metal. Any of a group of highly reactive metallic elements, including lithium, sodium, potassium, rubidium, cesium, and francium.

al•ka•line (ăl'kə-līn, -lĭn') *adj.* **1.** Relating to or containing an alkali. **2.** Basic. **—al'ka•lin'i•ty** (-lĭn'ə-tē) *n.*

alkaline-earth metal. Any of a group of metallic elements, especially calcium, strontium, and barium, but generally including beryllium, magnesium, and radium.

al•ka•lize (ăl'kə-līz') *v.* **-lized, -lizing.** Also **al•ka•lin•ize** (-lĭn-īz') **-ized, -izing.** To make alkaline or become an alkali. **—al'ka•li•za'tion, al'ka•lin'i•za'tion** *n.*

al•ka•loid (ăl'kə-loid') *n.* Any of various physiologically active nitrogen-containing organic bases derived from plants, including nicotine, quinine, cocaine, atropine, and morphine.

al•ka•lo•sis (ăl'kə-lō'sĭs) *n.* Pathologically high alkali content in the blood and tissues.

al•kyd resin (ăl'kĭd). A widely used durable synthetic resin.

all (ôl) *adj.* **1.** The total extent of: *all Christendom.* **2.** The entire number or quantity of: *all men.* **3.** The utmost of: *in all truth.* **4.** Every: *all kinds.* **5.** Any: *beyond all doubt.* **6.** Nothing but: *all skin and bones.* *—pron.* Each and every one: *All were drowned.* *—n.* **1.** Everything one has: *He gave his all.* **2.** The whole number; totality. *—adv.* **1.** Wholly: *all wrong.* **2.** Each: *a score of five all.* **3.** Exclusively: *The cake is all for him.* **—all but.** Nearly. [< OE *eall* < Gmc **allaz.*]

Al•lah (ăl'ə, ä'lə) *n.* The name of the Deity in Islam.

all-a•round. Variant of **all-round.**

al•lay (ə-lā') *v.* **1.** To lessen; relieve. **2.** To calm; pacify. [< OE *ālecgan.*] **—al•lay'er** *n.*

al•le•ga•tion (ăl'ĭ-gā'shən) *n.* **1.** The act or result of alleging. **2.** An assertion requiring substantiation.

al•lege (ə-lĕj') *v.* **-leged, -leging.** **1.** To assert to be true; affirm. **2.** To assert without proof. [< L *allēgāre,* to dispatch, cite.] **—al•leg'ed•ly** (-ĭd-lē) *adv.* **—al•leg'er** *n.*

Al•le•ghe•ny Mountains (ăl'ə-gā'nē). A section of the Appalachians extending from Pennsylvania to Virginia.

al•le•giance (ə-lē'jəns) *n.* **1.** Loyalty owed to a nation, sovereign, or cause. **2.** The obligations of a vassal to an overlord. [< OF *ligeance* < LIEGE.] **—al•le'giant** *adj.*

al•le•go•ry (ăl'ə-gôr'ē, -gōr'ē) *n., pl.* **-ries.** The symbolic embodiment of generalizations intended to reflect a given aspect of experience. [< Gk *allēgorein,* "to speak in other terms."] **—al'le•gor'ic, al'le•gor'ic•al** *adj.*

al•le•gret•to (ăl'ə-grĕt'ō, ä'lə-) *adv.* *Mus.* Slower than allegro. **—al'le•gret'to** *adj.*

al•le•gro (ə-lĕg'rō, ə-lā'grō) *adv.* *Mus.* At a fast tempo. [It, "lively."] **—al•le'gro** *adj.*

al•lele (ə-lēl') *n.* Any of a group of possible mutational forms of a gene. **—al•le'lic** (ə-lē'lĭk, ə-lĕl'ĭk) *adj.*

al•le•lu•ia (ăl'ə-lōō'yə) *interj.* Expressive of praise to God or of thanksgiving.

Al•len•town (ăl'ən-toun'). A city of Pennsylvania. Pop. 108,000.

al•ler•gen (ăl'ər-jən) *n.* A substance that causes an allergy. **—al'ler•gen'ic** (-jĕn'ĭk) *adj.*

al•ler•gist (ăl'ər-jĭst) *n.* A physician specializing in allergies.

al•ler•gy (ăl'ər-jē) *n., pl.* **-gies.** **1.** Hypersensitive or pathological reaction to environmental factors or substances in amounts that do not affect most people. **2.** An adverse sentiment; dislike. [G *Allergie,* "altered reaction."] **—al•ler'gic** (ə-lûr'jĭk) *adj.*

al•le•vi•ate (ə-lē'vē-āt') *v.* **-ated, -ating.** To make more bearable. [LL *alleviāre,* to lighten.] **—al•le'vi•a'tion** *n.* **—al•le'vi•a'tor** *n.*

al•ley (ăl'ē) *n., pl.* **-leys.** **1.** A narrow passageway between or behind buildings. **2.** A bowling alley. **—up one's alley.** *Slang.* Compatible with one's interests or qualifications. [< OF *alee,* fem pp of *aler,* to go.]

al•li•ance (ə-lī'əns) *n.* **1. a.** A pact of union or confederation between nations. **b.** The nations so conjoined. **2.** A union, relationship, or connection by kinship, marriage, or common interest. **3.** An affinity.

al•li•ga•tor (ăl'ə-gā'tər) *n.* **1.** A large amphibious reptile with sharp teeth, powerful jaws, and a shorter snout than the related crocodiles. **2.** Leather made from alligator hide. [< Span *el lagarto,* the lizard.]

alligator pear. An avocado. [Folk etym, var of AVOCADO.]

al•lit•er•ate (ə-lĭt'ə-rāt') *v.* **-ated, -ating.** To form or arrange with alliteration.

al•lit•er•a•tion (ə-lĭt'ə-rā'shən) *n.* The occurrence of two or more words having the same initial sound, as *wailing in the winter wind.* [< AD- (to) + LETTER.] **—al•lit'er•a'tive** *adj.*

allo–. *comb. form.* Divergence, opposition, or difference. [< Gk *allos,* other.]

al•lo•cate (ăl'ō-kāt', ăl'ə-) *v.* **-cated, -cating.** To allot; assign. [< ML *allocāre,* to place to.] **—al'lo•ca'tion** *n.*

al•lo•morph (ăl'ə-môrf') *n.* *Ling.* Any of the variant forms of a morpheme; for example, the phonetic *s* of *cats, z* of *dogs,* and *iz* of *horses* are allomorphs of the English morpheme *s.* **—al'lo•mor'phic** (-môr'fĭk) *adj.*

al•lo•nym (ăl'ə-nĭm') *n.* The name of one person assumed by another.

al•lo•phone (ăl'ə-fōn') *n.* *Ling.* Any of the variant forms of a phoneme; for example, the *p* of *pit* and the *p* of *spit* are allophones of the English phoneme *p.* **—al'lo•phon'ic** (-fŏn'ĭk) *adj.*

al•lot (ə-lŏt') *v.* **-lotted, -lotting.** **1.** To distribute by lot. **2.** To give or assign. **—al•lot'ment** *n.*

al•lot•ro•py (ə-lŏt'rə-pē) *n.* The existence of two or more crystalline or molecular structural forms of an element. **—al'lo•trope'** (ăl'ə-trōp') *n.* **—al'lo•trop'ic** (ăl'ə-trŏp'ĭk) *adj.*

all-out (ôl'out') *adj.* Wholehearted: *all-out effort.*

al•low (ə-lou') *v.* **1.** To let happen; permit. **2.** To acknowledge or admit. **3.** To permit to have. **4.** To make provision for. **5.** To provide: *allow funds in case of emergency.* **6.** To admit: *allow that to be true.* [< OF *allouer,* to permit, approve.] **—al•low'a•ble** *adj.*

al•low•ance (ə-lou'əns) *n.* **1.** The act of allowing. **2.** A regular provision of money, food, etc. **3.** A price discount.

al•low•ed•ly (ə-lou'ĭd-lē) *adv.* By general admission; admittedly.

al•loy (ăl'oi', ə-loi') *n.* **1.** A macroscopically homogeneous mixture or solid solution, usually of two or more metals. **2.** Anything added that lowers value or purity. [< L *alligāre,* to bind to, ALLY.] **—al•loy'** (ə-loi', ăl'oi') *v.*

all right. **1.** Satisfactory; average. **2.** Correct. **3.** Uninjured. **4.** Very well; yes. **5.** Without a doubt: *He's a fool, all right!*

all-round (ôl'round') *adj.* Also **all-a•round** (ôl'ə-round'). **1.** Comprehensive in extent. **2.** Versatile.

All Saints' Day. November 1, a church festival in honor of all saints.

All Souls' Day. November 2, observed by the Roman Catholic Church as a day of prayer for souls in purgatory.

all•spice (ôl'spīs') *n.* The aromatic berries of a tropical American tree, used as a spice.

all-star (ôl'stär') *adj.* Made up of star performers.

al•lude (ə-lōōd') *v.* **-luded, -luding.** To refer to indirectly. [L *allūdere,* to play with.] **—al•lu'sion** *n.* **—al•lu'sive** *adj.*

al•lure (ə-lŏŏr') *v.* **-lured, -luring.** To entice with something desirable; tempt. *—n.* The power to entice. [< OF *aleurrer.*] **—al•lure'ment** *n.* **—al•lur'ing•ly** *adv.*

al•lu•vi•um (ə-lōō'vē-əm) *n., pl.* **-viums** or **-via** (-vē-ə). Sediment deposited by flowing water, as in a river bed. [L < *alluere,* to wash against.] **—al•lu'vi•al** *adj.*

al•ly (ə-lī', ăl'ī') *v.* **-lied, -lying.** To unite or connect in a formal or close relationship or bond. *—n.* (ăl'ī', ə-lī') *pl.* **-lies.** One united with another in a formal or personal relationship. [< L *alligāre,* to bind to.]

al•ma ma•ter (ăl'mə mä'tər, ăl'mə). **1.** The school, college, or university one has attended. **2.** The anthem of a school, college, or university. [L, "cherishing or fostering mother."]

al•ma•nac (ôl'mə-năk', ăl'-) *n.* An annual publication having calendars with weather forecasts, astronomical information, and often other useful facts. [< ML *almanachus.*]

Al Ma•nam•ah (ăl mə-năm'ə). **The capital of Bahrain. Pop. 89,000.**

al•might•y (ôl-mī'tē) *adj.* **1.** Omnipotent. **2.** *Informal.* Great: *an almighty din.* *—n.* **—the Almighty.** God.

al•mond (ä'mənd, ăm'ənd) *n.* **1.** An oval, edible nut with a soft, light-brown shell. **2.** A tree bearing such nuts. [< LL *amandula* < L *amygdala.*]

al•most (ôl'mōst', ôl-mōst') *adv.* Slightly short of; not quite. [< OE *ealmǣst,* for the most part.]

alms (ämz) *pl.n.* Money or goods given to the poor in charity. [< OE *ælmesse* < Gmc **alemosina* < LL *eleēmosyna.*]

alms•house (ämz'hous') *n.* A poorhouse.

al•oe (ăl'ō) *n.* **1.** Any of various chiefly African plants having fleshy, spiny-toothed leaves. **2. aloes** *(takes sing. v.).* A cathartic drug made from the juice of the leaves of such a plant. [< OE *aluwe* < L *aloē.*] **—al'o•et'ic** (ăl'ō-ĕt'ĭk) *adj.*

a•loft (ə-lôft', ə-lŏft') *adv.* **1.** In or into a high place. **2.** Toward the upper rigging of a ship. [< ON *ā lopt,* "in the sky."]

a•lo•ha (ä-lō'hä') *interj.* *Hawaiian.* Expressive of greeting or farewell.

a•lone (ə-lōn') *adj.* **1.** Apart from other people; single; solitary. **2.** Excluding anything or anyone else; with nothing further; sole; only. [< ME *al one,* "all one."] **—a•lone'** *adv.*

a•long (ə-lông', ə-lŏng') *adv.* **1.** In a line with; following the length or path of. **2.** With a progressive motion. **3.** In association; together. **4.** As a companion: *Bring your son along.* **5.** Advanced: *The evening was well along.* **6.** Approaching: *along about midnight.* *—prep.* Over, through, or by the length of. [< OE *andlang,* "extending opposite."]

a•long•shore (ə-lông'shôr', -shōr', ə-lŏng'-) *adv.* Along, near, or by the shore, either on land or in the water.

a•long•side (ə-lông'sīd', ə-lŏng'-) *adv.* Along, near, at, or to the side of anything. *—prep.* By the side of; side by side with.

a•loof (ə-lōōf') *adj.* Distant; indifferent. [< obs *aloufe!,* "(steer the ship) up into the wind!"] **—a•loof'ness** *n.*

a•loud (ə-loud') *adv.* **1.** Audibly: *afraid to say it aloud.* **2.** Orally: *Read this passage aloud.*

alp (ălp) *n.* A high mountain.

al•pac•a (ăl-păk'ə) *n.* **1.** A South American mammal related to the llama. **2. a.** The fine, soft wool of this animal. **b.** Cloth made from it. [Span.]

al•pen•horn (ăl'pən-hôrn') *n.* A long, curved horn used to call cows to pasture.

al•pen•stock (ăl′pən-stŏk′) *n.* A long staff with an iron point, used by mountain climbers.
al•pha (ăl′fə) *n.* The 1st letter of the Greek alphabet, representing *a.*
al•pha•bet (ăl′fə-bĕt′, -bĭt) *n.* **1.** The letters of a language, arranged in an order fixed by custom. See *Table of Alphabets* on following pages. **2.** Elementary principles; rudiments. [< Gk *alphabētos* : ALPHA + BETA.]
al•pha•bet•i•cal (ăl′fə-bĕt′ĭ-kəl) *adj.* Also **al•pha•bet•ic** (-bĕt′ĭk). **1.** Arranged in the customary order of the letters of a language. **2.** Expressed by an alphabet. **—al′pha•bet′i•cal•ly** *adv.*
al•pha•bet•ize (ăl′fə-bə-tīz′) *v.* **-ized, -izing.** To arrange in alphabetical order.
Alpha Cen•tau•ri (sĕn-tôr′ē). A double star in Centaurus, 4.4 light-years from Earth.
alpha particle. *Symbol* α A positively charged composite particle, indistinguishable from a helium atom nucleus and consisting of two protons and two neutrons.
alpha ray. A stream of alpha particles.
alpha rhythm. Also **alpha wave.** The most common waveform found in electroencephalograms of the adult cerebral cortex, 8–12 smooth, regular oscillations/second in subjects at rest.
Alps (ălps). The major mountain system of south-central Europe, forming an arc from S France to Albania. **—Al′pine′** (ăl′pīn′) *adj.*
al•read•y (ôl-rĕd′ē) *adv.* By this or a specified time. [ME *al redy,* "all ready."]
al•right (ôl-rīt′) *adv. Nonstandard.* All right.
al•so (ôl′sō) *adv.* Besides; in addition; likewise; too. [< OE *ealswā,* even so.]
al•so-ran (ôl′sō-răn′) *n.* One defeated in a competition.
alt. 1. alteration. **2.** alternate. **3.** altitude.
Alta. Alberta.
Al•ta•ic (ăl-tā′ĭk) *n.* A language family of Europe and Asia. **—Al•ta′ic** *adj.*
Al•ta•ir (ăl-tä′ĭr, ăl-târ′) *n.* A very bright, double, variable star in the constellation Aquila, approx. 15.7 light-years from Earth.
al•tar (ôl′tər) *n.* Any elevated structure on which sacrifices may be offered or incense burned or before which religious ceremonies may be enacted. [< OE < L *altāre.*]
al•tar•piece (ôl′tər-pēs′) *n.* A painting, carving, etc., placed above and behind an altar.
al•ter (ôl′tər) *v.* **1.** To change; make or become different; modify. **2.** To castrate or spay. [< ML *alterāre* < L *alter,* other.] **—al′ter•a′tion** *n.*
al•ter•a•tive (ôl′tə-rā′tĭv) *adj.* **1.** Tending to alter or produce alteration. **2.** *Med.* Tending to restore normal health. —*n.* Also **al•ter•ant** (ôl′tər-ənt). *Med.* An alterative treatment or medication.
al•ter•ca•tion (ôl′tər-kā′shən) *n.* A heated and noisy quarrel. [< L *altercāri* < *alter,* another.]
al•ter e•go (ôl′tər ē′gō). **1.** Another aspect of oneself. **2.** An intimate friend. [L, "other I."]
al•ter•nate (ôl′tər-nāt′, ăl′-) *v.* **-nated, -nating. 1.** To occur in successive turns. **2.** To pass from one state, action, or place to a second and back indefinitely. —*adj.* (ôl′tər-nĭt, ăl′-). **1.** Happening or following in turns. **2.** Designating or pertaining to every other one of a series. **3.** Substitute: *an alternate plan.* —*n.* (ôl′tər-nĭt, ăl′-). A person acting in place of another. [L *alternāre* < *alter,* other.] **—al′ter•nate•ly** *adv.* **—al′ter•na′tion** *n.*
alternating current. Electric current that reverses direction at regular intervals.
al•ter•na•tive (ôl-tûr′nə-tĭv, ăl-) *n.* **1.** A choice between two or more than two possibilities.

TABLE OF ALPHABETS

The transliterations shown are those used in the etymologies of this Dictionary.

Arabic

The different forms in the four numbered columns are used when the letters are (1) in isolation; (2) in juncture with a previous letter; (3) in juncture with the letters on both sides; (4) in juncture with a following letter.

Long vowels are represented by the consonant signs *'alif* (for *ā*), *wāw* (for *ū*), and *yā* (for *ī*). Short vowels are not usually written.

Transliterations with subscript dots represent "emphatic" or pharyngeal consonants, which are pronounced in the usual way except that the pharynx is tightly narrowed during articulation.

Hebrew

Vowels are not represented in normal Hebrew writing, but for educational purposes they are indicated by a system of subscript and superscript dots.

The transliterations shown in parentheses apply when the letter falls at the end of a word. The transliterations with subscript dots are pharyngeal consonants, as in Arabic.

The second forms shown are used when the letter falls at the end of a word.

Greek

The superscript ʽ on an initial vowel or *rhō*, called the "rough breathing," represents an aspirate. Lack of aspiration on an initial vowel is indicated by the superscript ʼ, called the "smooth breathing."

When *gamma* precedes *kappa, xi, khi,* or another *gamma,* it has the value *n* and is so transliterated. The second lower-case form of *sigma* is used only in final position.

Russian

[1]This letter, called *tvordiĭ znak,* "hard sign," is very rare in modern Russian. It indicates that the previous consonant remains hard even though followed by a front vowel.

[2]This letter, called *myakiĭ znak,* "soft sign," indicates that the previous consonant is palatalized even when a front vowel does not follow.

ARABIC

Forms 1	2	3	4	Name	Sound
ا	ـا			'alif	'
ب	ـب	ـبـ	بـ	bā	b
ت	ـت	ـتـ	تـ	tā	t
ث	ـث	ـثـ	ثـ	thā	th
ج	ـج	ـجـ	جـ	jīm	j
ح	ـح	ـحـ	حـ	ḥā	ḥ
خ	ـخ	ـخـ	خـ	khā	kh
د	ـد			dāl	d
ذ	ـذ			dhāl	dh
ر	ـر			rā	r
ز	ـز			zāy	z
س	ـس	ـسـ	سـ	sīn	s
ش	ـش	ـشـ	شـ	shīn	sh
ص	ـص	ـصـ	صـ	ṣād	ṣ
ض	ـض	ـضـ	ضـ	ḍād	ḍ
ط	ـط	ـطـ	طـ	ṭā	ṭ
ظ	ـظ	ـظـ	ظـ	ẓā	ẓ
ع	ـع	ـعـ	عـ	'ayn	'
غ	ـغ	ـغـ	غـ	ghayn	gh
ف	ـف	ـفـ	فـ	fā	f
ق	ـق	ـقـ	قـ	qāf	q
ك	ـك	ـكـ	كـ	kāf	k
ل	ـل	ـلـ	لـ	lām	l
م	ـم	ـمـ	مـ	mīm	m
ن	ـن	ـنـ	نـ	nūn	n
ه	ـه	ـهـ	هـ	hā	h
و	ـو			wāw	w
ى	ـى	ـيـ	يـ	yā	y

ă pat/ā ate/âr care/ä bar/b bib/ch chew/d deed/ĕ pet/ē be/f fit/g gag/h hat/hw what/
ĭ pit/ī pie/îr pier/j judge/k kick/l lid, fatal/m mum/n no, sudden/ng sing/ŏ pot/ō go/

HEBREW

Forms	Name	Sound
א	'aleph	
ב	bēth	b (bh)
ג	gimel	g (gh)
ד	dāleth	d (dh)
ה	hē	h
ו	waw	w
ז	zayin	z
ח	ḥeth	ḥ
ט	ṭeth	ṭ
י	yodh	y
כ ך	kāph	k (kh)
ל	lāmedh	l
מ ם	mēm	m
נ ן	nūn	n
ס	samekh	s
ע	'ayin	
פ ף	pē	p (ph)
צ ץ	ṣadhe	ṣ
ק	qōph	q
ר	rēsh	r
שׂ	sin	s
שׁ	shin	sh
ת	tāw	t (th)

GREEK

Forms	Name	Sound
Α α	alpha	a.
Β β	beta	b
Γ γ	gamma	g (n)
Δ δ	delta	d
Ε ϵ	epsilon	e
Ζ ζ	zēta	z
Η η	ēta	ē
Θ θ	thēta	th
Ι ι	iota	i
Κ κ	kappa	k
Λ λ	lambda	l
Μ μ	mu	m
Ν ν	nu	n
Ξ ξ	xi	x
Ο ο	omicron	o
Π π	pi	p
Ρ ρ	rhō	r (rh)
Σ σ ς	sigma	s
Τ τ	tau	t
Υ υ	upsilon	u
Φ φ	phi	ph
Χ χ	khi	kh
Ψ ψ	psi	ps
Ω ω	ōmega	ō

RUSSIAN

Forms	Sound
А а	a
Б б	b
В в	v
Г г	g
Д д	d
Е е	e
Ж ж	zh
З з	z
И и Й й	i, ĭ
К к	k
Л л	l
М м	m
Н н	n
О о	o
П п	p
Р р	r
С с	s
Т т	t
У у	u
Ф ф	f
Х х	kh
Ц ц	ts
Ч ч	ch
Ш ш	sh
Щ щ	shch
Ъ ъ	"¹
Ы ы	y
Ь ь	'²
Э э	e
Ю ю	yu
Я я	ya

2. One of the things to be chosen. *—adj.* Allowing or necessitating a choice. **—al•ter′na•tive•ly** *adv.*

al•though (ôl-*th*ō′) *conj.* Also **al•tho.** Regardless of the fact that; even though.

al•tim•e•ter (ăl-tĭm′ə-tər) *n.* An instrument for determining altitude.

al•ti•tude (ăl′tə-t/y/o͞od′) *n.* **1.** The height of a thing above a reference level, esp. above the earth's surface. **2.** The angular distance of a celestial object above the horizon. **3.** The perpendicular distance from the base of a geometric figure to the opposite vertex, parallel side, or parallel surface. [< L *altitūdō* < *altus,* high.] **—al′ti•tu′di•nal** *adj.*

al•to (ăl′tō) *n., pl.* **-tos. 1.** A low female singing voice. **2.** The range between soprano and tenor. [It, "high."]

al•to•geth•er (ôl′tə-gĕ*th*′ər, ôl′tə-gĕ*th*′ər) *adv.* **1.** Entirely. **2.** With all included or counted: *Altogether 100 people were there.*

al•tru•ism (ăl′tro͞o-ĭz′əm) *n.* Selfless concern for the welfare of others. [F *altruisme* < *autrui,* other.] **—al′tru•ist** *n.* **—al′tru•is′tic** *adj.* **—al′tru•is′ti•cal•ly** *adv.*

al•um (ăl′əm) *n.* Any of several similar double sulfates, esp. $AlK(SO_4)_2 \cdot 12H_2O$, used medicinally as topical astringents and styptics. [< L *alūmen.*]

a•lu•mi•na (ə-lo͞o′mə-nə) *n.* Any of several forms of aluminum oxide, Al_2O_3, used in aluminum production and in abrasives, refractories, and ceramics. [< L *alūmen,* ALUM.]

a•lu•mi•num (ə-lo͞o′mə-nəm) *n.* Also *chiefly Brit.* **al•u•min•i•um** (ăl′yə-mĭn′ē-əm). *Symbol* **Al** A silvery-white, ductile metallic element used to form many hard, light, corrosion-resistant alloys. Atomic number 13, atomic weight 26.98. [< ALUMINA + -IUM.]

a•lum•na (ə-lŭm′nə) *n., pl.* **-nae** (-nē′). A female graduate or former student of a school, college, or university.

a•lum•nus (ə-lŭm′nəs) *n., pl.* **-ni** (-nī′). A male graduate or former student of a school, college, or university. [L, a pupil, foster son.]

al•ways (ôl′wāz, -wĭz) *adv.* **1.** On every occasion. **2.** Continuously; forever. [< OE *ealne weg,* "(along) all the way."]

am (ăm; *unstressed* əm). 1st person sing. present indicative of **be.** [< OE *eam.* See **es-.**]

am amplitude modulation.

Am americium.

AM amplitude modulation.

Am. America; American.

a.m. ante meridiem.

A.M. 1. ante meridiem. **2.** Master of Arts.

AMA American Medical Association.

a•main (ə-mān′) *adv.* With full force.

a•mal•gam (ə-măl′gəm) *n.* **1.** An alloy of mercury with other metals, as with tin or silver. **2.** A blend of diverse elements. [< ML *amalgama.*]

a•mal•ga•mate (ə-măl′gə-māt′) *v.* **-mated, -mating.** To form an amalgam. **—a•mal′ga•ma′tion** *n.* **—a•mal′ga•ma′tor** *n.*

a•man•u•en•sis (ə-măn′yo͞o-ĕn′sĭs) *n., pl.* **-ses** (-sēz). A secretary. [< L *(servus) ā manū,* "(slave) at hand(writing)."]

am•a•ranth (ăm′ə-rănth′) *n.* **1.** Any of various often weedy plants with greenish or purplish flowers. **2.** An imaginary flower that never fades. [< Gk *amarantos,* unfading.] **—am′a•ran′thine** *adj.*

Am•a•ril•lo (ăm′ə-rĭl′ō). A city of Texas. Pop. 138,000.

am•a•ryl•lis (ăm′ə-rĭl′ĭs) *n.* A bulbous plant having large, lilylike reddish or white flowers.

[< L, girl's name.]
a•mass (ə-măs′) *v.* To accumulate. [< OF *amasser.*] —**a•mass′ment** *n.*
am•a•teur (ăm′ə-chŏŏr′, -ə-tər, -ə-tyŏŏr′) *n.* **1.** One who engages in an activity as a pastime rather than as a profession. **2.** One lacking expertise. [< L *amātor,* a lover.] —**am′a•teur′ish** *adj.* —**am′a•teur•ism′** *n.*
am•a•to•ry (ăm′ə-tôr′ē, -tōr′ē) *adj.* Of or expressive of sexual love.
a•maze (ə-māz′) *v.* **amazed, amazing.** To affect with surprise or wonder; astound. [< OE *āmasian,* to bewilder.] —**a•maz′ed•ly** (ə-mā′zĭd-lē) *adv.* —**a•maze′ment** *n.*
Am•a•zon[1] (ăm′ə-zŏn′, -zən) *n.* **1.** *Gk.Myth.* A member of a nation of female warriors in a region near the Black Sea. **2. amazon.** A tall, vigorous, aggressive woman. [< Gk.] —**Am′a•zo′ni•an** (-zō′nē-ən) *adj.*
Am•a•zon[2] (ăm′ə-zŏn′, -zən). A river of South America rising in the Andes and flowing through N Brazil to the Atlantic. —**Am′a•zo′ni•an** (-zō′nē-ən) *adj.*
amb. ambassador.
am•bas•sa•dor (ăm-băs′ə-dər, -dôr′) *n.* An official representative of the highest rank, accredited by one government to another. [< Gmc **ambakhtaz* < L *ambactus,* vassal.] —**am•bas′sa•do′ri•al** (ăm-băs′ə-dôr′ē-əl, -dōr′ē-əl) *adj.* —**am•bas′sa•dor•ship′** *n.*
am•ber (ăm′bər) *n.* **1.** A hard, translucent yellow, orange, or brownish-yellow fossil resin, used for jewelry and ornaments. **2.** Medium to dark orange yellow. [< Ar *'anbar,* ambergris, amber.] —**am′ber** *adj.*
am•ber•gris (ăm′bər-grĭs′, -grēs′) *n.* A waxy, grayish substance produced by sperm whales and used in making perfumes. [< OF *ambre gris,* "amber gray."]
ambi–. *comb. form.* Both. [< L.]
am•bi•ance (ăm′bē-əns) *n.* Environment; atmosphere. [< L *ambiēns,* AMBIENT.]
am•bi•dex•trous (ăm′bĭ-dĕk′strəs) *adj.* Able to use both hands with equal facility.
am•bi•ent (ăm′bē-ənt) *adj.* Surrounding. [< L *ambīre,* to go around.]
am•big•u•ous (ăm-bĭg′yōō-əs) *adj.* **1.** Susceptible of multiple interpretation. **2.** Doubtful; uncertain. [L *ambiguus,* uncertain < *ambigere,* to wander about.] —**am′bi•gu′i•ty** (-gyōō′ə-tē), **am•big′u•ous•ness** *n.*
am•bi•tion (ăm-bĭsh′ən) *n.* **1.** A strong desire to achieve something; will to succeed. **2.** The object or goal desired. [< L *ambitiō,* a going around (for votes).]
am•bi•tious (ăm-bĭsh′əs) *adj.* **1.** Characterized by ambition. **2.** Challenging: *an ambitious plan.* —**am•bi′tious•ly** *adv.*
am•biv•a•lence (ăm-bĭv′ə-ləns) *n.* The existence of mutually conflicting feelings about a person or thing. [Gm *Ambivalenz* (coined by Freud).] —**am•biv′a•lent** *adj.*
am•ble (ăm′bəl) *v.* **-bled, -bling.** To move at an easy gait; saunter. [< L *ambulāre.*] —**am′ble** *n.* —**am′bler** *n.*
am•bro•sia (ăm-brō′zhə, -zhē-ə) *n.* **1.** The food of the Greek gods and immortals. **2.** Something of exquisite flavor or fragrance. [< Gk, "immortality."] —**am•bro′sial** *adj.*
am•bu•lance (ăm′byə-ləns) *n.* A vehicle equipped to transport the sick or wounded. [< F *(hôpital) ambulant,* itinerant (hospital).]
am•bu•la•to•ry (ăm′byə-lə-tôr′ē, -tōr′ē) *adj.* **1.** Of or involving walking. **2.** Capable of walking. **3.** Moving about; movable. [< L *ambulāre,* to go about, walk.]
am•bus•cade (ăm′bə-skād′) *n.* An ambush.
am•bush (ăm′bŏŏsh′) *n.* **1.** Concealment from which a surprise attack is launched: *lie in ambush.* **2.** A surprise attack made from a concealed position. [< VL **imboscāre,* "to hide in the bushes."] —**am′bush′** *v.*
a•me•ba. Variant of **amoeba.**
a•mel•io•rate (ə-mēl′yə-rāt′) *v.* **-rated, -rating.** To make or become better; improve. [< F *améliorer,* to improve.] —**a•me′lio•ra′tion** *n.*
a•men (ā-mĕn′, ä-) *interj.* Used at the end of prayers to express solemn concurrence. [< Heb *āmēn,* certainly, verily.]
a•me•na•ble (ə-mē′nə-bəl, ə-mĕn′ə-) *adj.* **1.** Tractable; responsive: *amenable to reason.* **2.** Responsible; accountable. [< F *amener,* to lead, bring.] —**a•me′na•bil′i•ty** *n.*
a•mend (ə-mĕnd′) *v.* **1.** To improve. **2.** To correct; rectify. **3.** To alter (a law) formally. [< L *ēmendāre,* to free from faults.]
a•mend•ment (ə-mĕnd′mənt) *n.* **1.** Improvement, correction, or reformation. **2. a.** A formal alteration of a law. **b.** The parliamentary process whereby such alteration is made.
a•mends (ə-mĕndz′) *pl.n.* Reparation for insult or injury.
a•men•i•ty (ə-mĕn′ə-tē, ə-mē′nə-) *n., pl.* **-ties.** **1.** Pleasantness; agreeableness. **2.** A means of comfort or convenience. **3. amenities.** Social courtesies; civilities. [< L *amoenus,* pleasant, delightful.]
Amer. America; American.
a•merce (ə-mûrs′) *v.* **amerced, amercing.** **1.** To penalize by an arbitrary fine. **2.** To punish. [< NF *a merci,* at the mercy of.]
A•mer•i•ca (ə-mĕr′ə-kə). **1.** The United States of America. **2.** North America. **3.** South America. **4.** Often **the Americas.** North America, Central America, and South America together. [< *Americus* Vespucius (Latinized form of Amerigo VESPUCCI).]
A•mer•i•can (ə-mĕr′ə-kən) *n.* A native of one of the Americas or a U.S. citizen. —**A•mer′i•can** *adj.*
A•mer•i•ca•na (ə-mĕr′ə-kä′nə, -kăn′ə, -kā′nə) *pl.n.* A collection of things relating to American history, folklore, or geography.
American English. English as spoken in the U.S.
American Indian. A member of any of the aboriginal peoples of North America (except the Eskimos), South America, and the West Indies.
A•mer•i•can•ism (ə-mĕr′ə-kən-ĭz′əm) *n.* **1.** A custom, trait, or tradition originating in the U.S. **2.** A language usage characteristic of American English.
A•mer•i•can•ize (ə-mĕr′ə-kən-īz′) *v.* To make or become American in spirit or methods. —**A•mer′i•can•i•za′tion** *n.*
American Legion. An organization of U.S. veterans of World War I, World War II, and the Korean War, founded in 1919.
American Library Association. An organization of libraries and librarians, founded in 1876.
American Revolution. The war fought between Great Britain and her colonies in North America (1775–83) by which the colonies won independence; Revolutionary War.
American Samoa. A group of U.S. islands in the South Pacific. Pop. 20,000.
American Spanish. The Spanish language of the W Hemisphere.
am•er•ic•i•um (ăm′ə-rĭsh′ē-əm) *n.* *Symbol* **Am** A white metallic radioactive element used as a radiation source in research. Atomic number 95, longest-lived isotope Am 243.
Am•er•ind (ăm′ə-rĭnd′) *n.* An American Indian or an Eskimo. —**Am′er•in′di•an** *adj.* & *n.*
am•e•thyst (ăm′ə-thĭst) *n.* A purple or violet form of transparent quartz or a purple variety of corundum, used as a gemstone. [< Gk *amethustos,* amethyst, "anti-intoxicant."]
a•mi•a•ble (ā′mē-ə-bəl) *adj.* **1.** Good-natured; agreeable. **2.** Cordial; friendly. [< LL *amīcābilis,* AMICABLE.] —**a′mi•a•bil′i•ty, a′mi•a•ble•ness** *n.* —**a′mi•a•bly** *adv.*
am•i•ca•ble (ăm′ĭ-kə-bəl) *adj.* Friendly; peaceable. [< LL *amīcābilis* < L *amīcus,* friend.] —**am′i•ca•bil′i•ty, am′i•ca•ble•ness** *n.* —**am′i•ca•bly** *adv.*
a•mid (ə-mĭd′) *prep.* Also **a•midst** (ə-mĭdst′). In the middle of; among.
a•mid•ships (ə-mĭd′shĭps′) *adv.* Midway between the bow and the stern of a ship.
a•mi•no acid (ə-mē′nō, ăm′ə-nō′). **1.** Any organic compound containing both an amino group (NH_2) and a carboxylic acid group (COOH). **2.** A compound of the form $NH_2CHRCOOH$, found as an essential component of the protein molecule. [< AM(MONIUM) + -INE.]
A•mish (ä′mĭsh, ăm′ĭsh) *pl.n.* Mennonites of a sect founded in the 17th century by Jacob Amman, Swiss religious reformer. —**A′mish** *adj.*
a•miss (ə-mĭs′) *adj.* Out of proper order; wrong. —*adv.* In an improper or faulty way. —**take amiss.** To misunderstand or feel offended by. [< ME *a mis.*]
am•i•ty (ăm′ə-tē) *n.* Friendly relations, as between states. [< L *amīcus,* friend.]
Am•man (ă-măn′). The capital of Jordan. Pop. 296,000.
am•me•ter (ăm′mē′tər) *n.* An instrument that measures electric current.
am•mo (ăm′ō) *n.* *Mil.* Ammunition.
am•mo•nia (ə-mōn′yə) *n.* **1.** A colorless, pungent gas, NH_3, extensively used to manufacture fertilizers and a wide variety of nitrogen-containing organic and inorganic chemicals. **2. Ammonium hydroxide.** [< L *(sal) ammōniăcus,* "(salt) of *Amen*" (Egyptian god of life).]
ammonia water. Ammonium hydroxide.
am•mo•ni•um (ə-mō′nē-əm) *n.* The ion NH_4+. [< AMMON(IA).]
ammonium hydroxide. A colorless basic aqueous solution of ammonia, NH_4OH.
am•mu•ni•tion (ăm′yə-nĭsh′ən) *n.* **1. a.** Projectiles, along with their fuzes and primers, that can be fired from guns. **b.** Explosive materials used in war. **2.** Any means of offense or defense. [< OF *la munition,* the munition.]
am•ne•sia (ăm-nē′zhə) *n.* Loss of memory. [< Gk *amnēsia.*] —**am•ne′si•ac′** (ăm-nē′zē-ăk′, -zhē-ăk′) *n.* & *adj.*
am•nes•ty (ăm′nəs-tē) *n., pl.* **-ties.** A general pardon, esp. for political offenders. [< Gk *amnēstia,* "forgetfulness."]
a•moe•ba, a•me•ba (ə-mē′bə) *n., pl.* **-bas** or **-bae** (-bē). Any of various minute one-celled organisms having an indefinite, changeable form. [< Gk *amoibē,* change.] —**a•moe′bic** (-bĭk) *adj.*
a•mok. Variant of **amuck.**
a•mong (ə-mŭng′) *prep.* Also **a•mongst** (ə-mŭngst′). **1.** In or through the midst of. **2.** In the group, number, or company of. **3.** By the joint action of. **4.** With portions to each of. **5.** Between one another. [< OE *gemang,* a crowd. See **mag-.**]
a•mon•til•la•do (ə-mŏn′tə-lä′dō) *n., pl.* **-dos.** A pale dry sherry. [Span.]

a•mor•al (ā-môr'əl, ā-mŏr'əl) *adj.* Neither moral nor immoral. —**a'mo•ral'i•ty** (ā'mô-răl'ə-tē) *n.* —**a•mor'al•ly** *adv.*

am•o•rous (ăm'ər-əs) *adj.* Of, inclined to, or indicative of sexual love. [< L *amor,* love < *amāre,* to love.] —**am'or•ous•ness** *n.*

a•mor•phous (ə-môr'fəs) *adj.* **1.** Lacking definite form. **2.** Lacking distinct crystalline structure. [< Gk *amorphos.*] —**a•mor'phous•ly** *adv.* —**a•mor'phous•ness** *n.*

am•or•tize (ăm'ər-tīz', ə-môr'tīz') *v.* **-tized, -tizing.** To liquidate (as a debt) by installment payments. [< VL **admortīre,* to deaden.] —**am'or•ti•za'tion** *n.*

a•mount (ə-mount') *n.* **1.** A total, aggregate, or sum. **2.** Principal plus its interest. **3.** Quantity. —*v.* **1.** To reach as a total. **2.** To be equivalent or tantamount. [< OF *amont,* upward, "to the mountain."]

a•mour (ə-mo͞or') *n.* An illicit love affair. [< L *amor,* love.]

a•mour-pro•pre (ə-mo͞or'prôp'r') *n.* Self-respect.

am•per•age (ăm'pər-ĭj, ăm'pîr'ĭj) *n.* The strength of an electric current expressed in amperes.

am•pere (ăm'pîr') *n.* A unit of electric current: the steady current that when flowing in straight parallel wires of infinite length, separated by a distance of one meter in free space, produces a force between the wires of 2×10^{-7} newtons per meter of length. [< A.M. *Ampère* (1775–1836), French mathematician.]

am•per•sand (ăm'pər-sănd') *n.* The character (&) representing *and.* [Contraction of "*and per se and,*" "& (the sign) by itself (equals) *and.*"]

am•phet•a•mine (ăm-fĕt'ə-mēn', -mĭn) *n.* **1.** A colorless volatile liquid, $C_9H_{13}N$, used primarily as a central nervous system stimulant. **2.** A phosphate or sulfate of amphetamine, similarly used.

amphi–. *comb. form.* **1.** On both sides or ends or on all sides. **2.** Around. [< Gk *amphi,* on both sides.]

am•phib•i•an (ăm-fĭb'ē-ən) *n.* **1.** An organism, as a frog or toad, having an aquatic early stage and developing air-breathing lungs as an adult. **2.** An aircraft that can take off and land on either land or water. **3.** A vehicle that can move over land and on water. —*adj.* Amphibious.

am•phib•i•ous (ăm-fĭb'ē-əs) *adj.* **1.** Able to live both on land and in water. **2.** Able to operate on land and water. [Gk *amphibios,* "living a double life."]

am•phi•the•a•ter (ăm'fə-thē'ə-tər) *n.* An oval or round building having tiers of seats rising around an arena.

am•pho•ra (ăm'fə-rə) *n., pl.* **-rae** (-rē') or **-ras.** An ancient Greek jar with two handles and a narrow neck, used to carry wine or oil. [L.]

am•ple (ăm'pəl) *adj.* **-pler, -plest. 1.** Large; capacious. **2.** Sufficient; abundant. [< L *amplus.*] —**am'ple•ness** *n.* —**am'ply** *adv.*

am•pli•fy (ăm'plə-fī') *v.* **-fied, -fying. 1.** To enlarge, extend, or increase. **2.** To make louder. —**am'pli•fi•ca'tion** (-fə-kā'shən) *n.* —**am'pli•fi•ca'tive** (-fĭ-kā'tĭv) *adj.* —**am'pli•fi'er** *n.*

am•pli•tude (ăm'plə-t/y/o͞od') *n.* **1.** Fullness; copiousness. **2.** Breadth, as of mind. **3.** The maximum value of a periodically varying quantity.

amplitude modulation. The encoding of a carrier wave by variation of its amplitude in accordance with an input signal.

am•poule, am•pule (ăm'p/y/o͞ol) *n.* A small sealed vial used as a container for a hypodermic injection solution. [< L *ampulla.*]

am•pu•tate (ăm'pyo͞o-tāt') *v.* **-tated, -tating.** To cut off, as a limb. [L *amputāre,* to cut around.] —**am'pu•ta'tion** *n.*

am•pu•tee (ăm'pyo͞o-tē') *n.* A person who has had one or more limbs amputated.

Am•ster•dam (ăm'stər-dăm'). The constitutional capital of the Netherlands. Pop. 868,000.

amt. amount.

amu *Phys.* atomic mass unit.

a•muck (ə-mŭk') *adv.* Also **a•mok** (ə-mŭk', ə-mŏk'). In a murderous frenzy or in a fit of wildness: *run amuck.* [Malay *amok,* furious attack.]

am•u•let (ăm'yə-lĭt) *n.* Something worn as a charm against evil or injury. [L *amulētum.*]

A•mur (ä-mo͞or'). A river of E Asia.

a•muse (ə-myo͞oz') *v.* **amused, amusing.** To entertain; divert. [< OF *amuser,* "to cause to idle away time."] —**a•muse'ment** *n.*

a•myg•da•lin (ə-mĭg'də-lĭn) *n. Chem.* **Laetrile.**

an (ăn, ən). *indef. art.* A form of *a* used before words beginning with a vowel or with an unpronounced *h: an elephant; an hour.* [< OE *ān,* one. See **oino-.**]

an–. *comb. form.* Not; without. [Gk *an-,* not.]

–an, –n. *comb. form.* **1.** Pertaining to, belonging to, or resembling: **Mexican. 2.** Believing in or adhering to: *Mohammedan.*

ana–. *comb. form.* **1.** Upward progression. **2.** Reversion. **3.** Renewal or intensification. [< Gk *ana,* up.]

a•nach•ro•nism (ə-năk'rə-nĭz'əm) *n.* **1.** The error of placing persons, things, or events in an inappropriate historical period. **2.** One that is chronologically out of place, esp. one that is behind the times. [< Gk *anakhronismos.*] —**a•nach'ro•nis'tic, a•nach'ro•nis'ti•cal** *adj.* —**a•nach'ro•nis'ti•cal•ly** *adv.*

an•a•con•da (ăn'ə-kŏn'də) *n.* A large tropical American snake that constricts its prey in its coils. [Perh < Dravid.]

a•nae•mi•a. Variant of **anemia.**

an•aes•the•sia. Variant of **anesthesia.**

an•a•gram (ăn'ə-grăm') *n.* A word formed by transposing the letters of another word. [< ANA- + -GRAM.]

An•a•heim (ăn'ə-hīm'). A city in SW California. Pop. 104,000.

a•nal (ā'nəl) *adj.* Of or near the anus.

anal. **1.** analogous; analogy. **2.** analysis; analytic.

an•al•ge•si•a (ăn'əl-jē'zē-ə, -zhə) *n.* Inability to feel pain while conscious. [< Gk *analgēsia,* want of feeling.] —**an'al•ge'sic** *adj.* & *n.*

analog computer. A computer in which numerical data are represented by analogous physical magnitudes or electrical signals.

a•nal•o•gous (ə-năl'ə-gəs) *adj.* Similar in a way that permits the drawing of an analogy. [< Gk *analogos,* proportionate.]

an•a•logue (ăn'ə-lôg', -lŏg') *n.* Also **an•a•log. 1.** Something that bears an analogy to something else. **2.** *Biol.* An organ or structure that is similar in function to one in another kind of organism but is of dissimilar evolutionary origin.

a•nal•o•gy (ə-năl'ə-jē) *n., pl.* **-gies. 1.** Correspondence in some respects between things otherwise dissimilar. **2.** An inference that if two things are alike in some respects they must be alike in others.

a•nal•y•sis (ə-năl'ə-sĭs) *n., pl.* **-ses** (-sēz'). **1.** The separation of a whole into constituents with a view to its examination and interpretation. **2.** A statement of the results of such a study. **3.** Psychoanalysis. [< Gk *analusis,* a releasing.] —**an'a•lyst** *n.* —**an'a•lyt'ic** (-ə-lĭt'ĭk), **an'a•lyt'i•cal** *adj.*

an•a•lyze (ăn'ə-līz') *v.* **-lyzed, -lyzing.** To make an analysis of.

an•a•pest (ăn'ə-pĕst') *n.* A metrical foot composed of two short syllables followed by one long one. [< Gk *anapaistos,* "struck back."]

an•ar•chic (ăn-är'kĭk) *adj.* Also **an•ar•chi•cal** (-kĭ-kəl). Lacking order or control; lawless. —**an•ar'chi•cal•ly** *adv.*

an•ar•chism (ăn'ər-kĭz'əm) *n.* The theory that all forms of government are oppressive and should be abolished. —**an'ar•chist** *n.* —**an'ar•chis'tic** *adj.*

an•ar•chy (ăn'ər-kē) *n., pl.* **-chies. 1.** Absence of any form of political authority. **2.** Disorder and confusion. [Gk *anarkhia.*]

anat. anatomical; anatomist; anatomy.

a•nath•e•ma (ə-năth'ə-mə) *n., pl.* **-mas. 1.** A formal ban or curse, as an excommunication. **2.** Someone or something cursed or shunned. [LL, a curse, a person cursed, an offering.] —**a•nath'e•ma•tize'** *v.* **(-tized, -tizing).**

An•a•to•li•a (ăn'ə-tō'lē-ə). Asia Minor.

An•a•to•li•an (ăn'ə-tō'lē-ən) *n.* An extinct group of Indo-European languages of ancient Anatolia, including Hittite. —**An'a•to'li•an** *adj.*

a•nat•o•my (ə-năt'ə-mē) *n., pl.* **-mies. 1.** The structure of an organism or organ. **2.** The science of the structure of organisms and their parts. **3.** A detailed analysis. [< Gk *anatomē,* dissection.] —**an'a•tom'i•cal** (-ə-tŏm'ĭ-kəl), **an'a•tom'ic** *adj.*

anc. ancient.

–ance, –ancy. *comb. form.* An action, quality, or condition: **riddance, compliancy.**

an•ces•tor (ăn'sĕs'tər) *n.* A person or organism from which another or others have descended. [< L *antecessor,* "one that goes before" < *antecēdere,* to go before.]

an•ces•try (ăn'sĕs'trē) *n., pl.* **-tries. 1.** Line of descent; lineage. **2.** Ancestors collectively. —**an•ces'tral** (ăn-sĕs'trəl) *adj.*

an•chor (ăng'kər) *n.* A heavy metal device attached to a vessel and cast overboard to keep the vessel in place. —**at anchor.** Anchored. —*v.* To hold or be held with or as with an anchor. [< OE *ancor* < L *anc(h)ora.*]

an•chor•age (ăng'kər-ĭj) *n.* A place for anchoring a ship.

An•chor•age (ăng'kər-ĭj). A city of Alaska. Pop. 44,000.

an•cho•rite (ăng'kə-rīt') *n.* A religious hermit. [< LGk *anakhōrētēs,* "one who withdraws."] —**an'cho•rit'ic** (-rĭt'ĭk) *adj.*

an•cho•vy (ăn'chō'vē, ăn-chō'vē) *n.* Any of various small, edible, herringlike marine fishes. [Span *anchova.*]

an•cien ré•gime (äN-syăN' rā-zhēm'). **1.** The political and social system in France before the revolution of 1789. **2.** Any former system. [F, "former regime."]

an•cient (ān'shənt) *adj.* **1.** Very old. **2.** Belonging to times long past, esp. to the period before the fall of the Western Roman Empire (A.D. 476). —*n.* **1.** A very old person. **2. ancients.** The ancient Greeks and Romans. [< OF < VL **anteānus,* "going before" < L *ante,* before.] —**an'cient•ness** *n.*

Ancient Chinese. The language of ancient China.

Ancient Greek. See **Greek.**

an•cil•lar•y (ăn'sə-lĕr'ē) *adj.* **1.** Subordinate. **2.** Auxiliary; accessory: *ancillary functions.* [L *ancillāris,* servile.]

–ancy. Variant of **-ance.**

and (ənd, ən; *stressed* ănd) *conj.* **1.** Together with or along with; as well as. **2.** Added to; plus: *Two and two makes four.* **3.** As a result: *Seek, and ye shall find.* **4.** *Informal.* To. Used between finite verbs: *try and find it.* [< OE < Gmc **anda.*]

an•dan•te (ăn-dän'tā, ăn-dăn'tē) *adv. Mus.* Moderately slow in tempo. [It, "walking."] —**an•dan'te** *adj.*

an•dan•ti•no (än'dän-tē'nō, ăn'dăn-tē'nō) *adv. Mus.* Slightly faster in tempo than andante. [It, dim of ANDANTE.] —**an'dan•ti'no** *adj.*

An•des (ăn'dēz). A mountain system stretching the length of W South America from Venezuela to Tierra del Fuego. Highest elevation, Aconcagua (22,835 ft.). —**An'de•an** *adj.*

and•i•ron (ănd'ī'ərn) *n.* One of a pair of metal supports for logs in a fireplace. [< OF *andier,* firedog.]

and/or. Used to indicate that either *and* or *or* may be used to connect words, phrases, or clauses depending upon what meaning is intended.

An•dor•ra (ăn-dôr'ə, -dŏr'ə). A republic in the E Pyrenees. Pop. 13,000. Cap. Andorra la Vella.

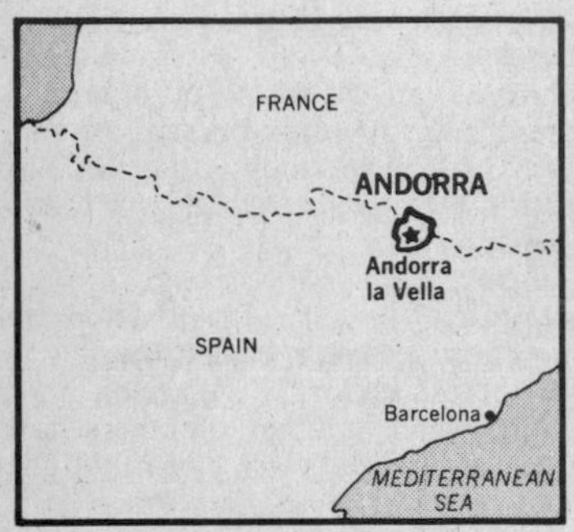

Andorra

andro–. *comb. form.* The male sex or masculine. [< Gk *anēr (andr-),* man.]

an•dro•gen (ăn'drə-jən) *n.* A hormone that develops and maintains masculine characteristics. —**an'dro•gen'ic** (-jĕn'ĭk) *adj.*

an•drog•e•nous (ăn-drŏj'ə-nəs) *adj.* Pertaining to production of male offspring.

an•drog•y•nous (ăn-drŏj'ə-nəs) *adj.* Having female and male characteristics in one. —**an•drog'y•ny** *n.*

an•droid (ăn'droid') *n.* A synthetic man created from biological materials; a humanoid.

An•drom•e•da (ăn-drŏm'ə-də) *n.* A constellation in the N Hemisphere.

–andry. *comb. form.* Number of husbands: **monandry.**

–ane. *comb. form. Chem.* A saturated hydrocarbon: **propane.**

an•ec•dote (ăn'ĭk-dōt') *n.* A short account of an interesting or humorous incident. [< Gk *anekdota,* "things unpublished."] —**an'ec•do'tal** *adj.* —**an'ec•dot'ic** (ăn'ĭk-dŏt'ĭk) *adj.* —**an'ec•dot'ist** (-dō'tĭst) *n.*

an•e•cho•ic (ăn'ĕ-kō'ĭk) *adj.* Neither having nor producing echoes.

a•ne•mi•a (ə-nē'mē-ə) *n.* Also **a•nae•mi•a.** Pathological deficiency in the oxygen-carrying material of the blood. [< Gk *anaimia.*] —**a•ne'mic** *adj.*

an•e•mom•e•ter (ăn'ə-mŏm'ə-tər) *n.* An instrument for measuring wind force and speed. [< Gk *anemos,* wind.]

a•nem•o•ne (ə-nĕm'ə-nē) *n.* **1.** Any of various plants having white, purple, or red cup-shaped flowers. **2.** See **sea anemone.** [< Gk *anemōnē.*]

a•nent (ə-nĕnt') *prep.* Regarding; concerning. [< OE *on efen,* alongside.]

an•es•the•sia (ăn'ĭs-thē'zhə) *n.* Also **an•aes•the•sia.** Total or partial loss of sensation. [< Gk *anaisthēsia,* lack of sensation.]

an•es•the•si•ol•o•gy (ăn'ĭs-thē'zē-ŏl'ə-jē) *n.* Also **an•aes•the•si•ol•o•gy.** The medical study and application of anesthetics. —**an'es•the'si•ol'o•gist** *n.*

an•es•thet•ic (ăn'ĭs-thĕt'ĭk) *adj.* Also **an•aes•thet•ic.** Causing anesthesia. —*n.* An anesthetic agent.

an•es•the•tize (ə-nĕs'thə-tīz') *v.* **-tized, -tizing.** Also **an•aes•the•tize.** To induce anesthesia in. —**an•es'the•tist** *n.* —**an•es'the•ti•za'tion** *n.*

a•new (ə-n/y/ōō') *adv.* **1.** Again. **2.** In a new way.

an•gel (ān'jəl) *n.* **1.** One of the immortal beings attendant upon God. **2.** A kind and lovable person. **3.** A financial backer of an enterprise, esp. a dramatic production. [< Gk *angelos,* messenger.] —**an•gel'ic** (-jĕl'ĭk), **an•gel'i•cal** *adj.* —**an•gel'i•cal•ly** *adv.*

an•gel•fish (ān'jəl-fĭsh') *n.* Any of several tropical fishes having a flattened body.

an•gel•i•ca (ăn-jĕl'ĭ-kə) *n.* A plant having aromatic seeds, leaves, stems, and roots used as flavoring.

an•ger (ăng'gər) *n.* A feeling of extreme hostility, indignation, or exasperation; wrath; rage; ire. —*v.* To make or become angry. [< ON *angr,* grief.]

an•gi•na (ăn-jī'nə) *n.* **1.** Any disease in which spasmodic and painful suffocation or spasms occur. **2. Angina pectoris.** [L, quinsy.]

angina pec•to•ris (pĕk'tə-rĭs). Severe paroxysmal pain in the chest, associated with feelings of suffocation and apprehension. [NL, "angina of the chest."]

Angl. Anglican.

an•gle¹ (ăng'gəl) *v.* **-gled, -gling.** To fish with a hook and line. —**angle for.** To try to get something by using schemes. —*n. Slang.* A scheme. [< OE *angul,* fishhook. See **ank-.**] —**an'gler** *n.*

an•gle² (ăng'gəl) *n.* **1. a.** The figure formed by two lines diverging from a common point. **b.** The rotation required to superimpose either of two such lines or angles on the other. **2. a.** The position or direction from which an object is viewed. **b.** A point of view. —*v.* **-gled, -gling. 1.** To move or turn at an angle or by angles. **2.** To hit (a ball) at an angle. [< L *angulus,* angle, corner.]

An•gles (ăng'gəlz) *pl.n.* A Germanic people that migrated to England in the 5th century A.D. and with the Jutes and Saxons formed the Anglo-Saxon peoples. [L *Anglī, Anglii* (pl) < Gmc.] —**An'gli•an** *adj.* & *n.*

an•gle•worm (ăng'gəl-wûrm') *n.* An earthworm, used as fishing bait.

An•gli•can (ăng'glĭ-kən) *n.* A member of the Church of England or of any of its related churches, esp. the Protestant Episcopal Church. [< ML *Anglicus,* English.] —**An'gli•can** *adj.* —**An'gli•can•ism'** *n.*

An•gli•cism (ăng'glə-sĭz'əm) *n.* Also **an•gli•cism.** An idiom peculiar to the English language, esp. as spoken in England; Briticism.

An•gli•cize (ăng'glə-sīz') *v.* **-cized, -cizing.** Also **an•gli•cize.** To make or become English in form, idiom, or character. —**An'gli•ci•za'tion** *n.*

Anglo–. *comb. form.* English or England.

An•glo•phile (ăng'glə-fīl') *n.* Also **an•glo•phile.** An admirer of England. —**An'glo•phile'** *adj.* —**An'glo•phil'i•a** *n.*

An•glo•phobe (ăng'glə-fōb') *n.* Also **an•glo•phobe.** One who has an aversion to England. —**An'glo•phobe'** *adj.* —**An'glo•pho'bi•a** *n.*

An•glo-Sax•on (ăng'glō-săk'sən) *n.* **1.** A member of one of the Germanic peoples who settled in Britain in the 5th and 6th centuries A.D. **2.** Any of the descendants of these peoples. **3.** See **Old English. 4.** Any person of English ancestry. —**An'glo-Sax'on** *adj.*

An•go•la (ăng-gō'lə). **An independent country occupying 481,351 square miles in SW Africa. Pop. 5,790,000. Cap. Luanda.**

An•go•ra (ăng-gôr'ə, -gōr'ə) *n.* **1.** A goat, rabbit, or cat with long, silky hair. **2. angora.** Yarn or fabric made from the hair of an Angora goat or rabbit. [< *Angora,* former name for *Ankara.*]

an•gry (ăng'grē) *adj.* **-grier, -griest. 1.** Feeling, showing, or resulting from anger. **2.** Having a menacing aspect: *angry clouds.* **3.** Inflamed: *an angry sore.* —**an'gri•ly** (-grə-lē) *adv.*

angst (ängkst) *n.* A feeling of anxiety. [G.]

Ang•ström (ăng'strəm) *n. Symbol* **A** A unit of length equal to one hundred-millionth (10^{-8}) of a centimeter. [< A.J. *Ångström* (1814–1874), Swedish physicist.]

an•guish (ăng'gwĭsh) *n.* An agonizing physical or mental pain. —*v.* To feel or cause to feel anguish. [< L *angustia,* narrowness.] —**an'guished** *adj.*

an•gu•lar (ăng'gyə-lər) *adj.* **1.** Having an angle or angles. **2.** Measured by an angle or degrees of an arc. **3.** Bony and lean. **4.** Awkward: *an angular gait.* —**an'gu•lar'i•ty, an'gu•lar•ness** *n.* —**an'gu•lar•ly** *adv.*

an•hy•dride (ăn-hī'drīd') *n.* A chemical compound formed from another by the removal of water.

an•hy•drous (ăn-hī'drəs) *adj.* Without water. [Gk *anudros,* waterless.]

an•i•line (ăn'ə-līn) *n.* Also **an•i•lin.** A colorless, oily, poisonous liquid, $C_6H_5NH_2$, used to manufacture rubber, dyes, resins, pharmaceuticals, and varnishes.

an•i•mad•vert (ăn'ə-măd-vûrt') *v.* To comment critically, usually with disapproval. [L *animadvertere,* to direct the mind to.] —**an'i•mad•ver'sion** *n.*

an•i•mal (ăn'ə-məl) *n.* **1.** An organism distinguished from a plant by structural and functional characteristics, such as the ability to move. **2.** A nonhuman organism of this kind. **3.** A bestial person; brute. —*adj.* **1.** Of or relating to animals. **2.** Sensual or physical as distinguished from spiritual. [< L *animālis,* living < *animus,* breath, soul.]

an•i•mal•cule (ăn'ə-măl'kyōōl) *n.* A microscopic or minute animal. [NL *animalculum,* dim of ANIMAL.]

animal starch. Glycogen.

an•i•mate (ăn'ə-māt') *v.* **-mated, -mating. 1.** To give life to. **2.** To impart interest to. **3.** To inspire to action. **4.** To make or produce (a cartoon) so as to convey the illusion of motion. —*adj.* (ăn'ə-mĭt). **1.** Possessing life; living. **2.** Of or relating to animal life. **3.** Lively; vivacious. [L *animāre,* to fill with breath.] —**an'i•mat'ed•ly** *adv.* —**an'i•ma'tion** *n.*

a•ni•ma•to (ä'nē-mä'tō) *adv. Mus.* In an animated or lively manner. [It.] —**a'ni•ma'to** *adj.*

an•i•ma•tor (ăn'ə-mā'tər) *n.* One that animates, esp. an artist or technician who produces an animated cartoon.

an•i•mism (ăn'ə-mĭz'əm) *n.* Attribution of an innate soul to natural phenomena and objects.

—an'i•mist *n.* —an'i•mis'tic *adj.*

an•i•mos•i•ty (ăn'ə-mŏs'ə-tē) *n., pl.* **-ties.** Bitter hostility or hatred. [< LL *animōsitās,* vehemence, spirit.]

an•i•mus (ăn'ə-məs) *n.* A feeling of animosity.

an•i•on (ăn'ī'ən) *n.* A negatively charged ion that migrates to an anode, as in electrolysis. [Gk, "that which goes up."] —**an'i•on'ic** (-ŏn'-ĭk) *adj.*

an•ise (ăn'ĭs) *n.* **1.** A plant having aromatic licorice-flavored seeds. **2.** Also **an•i•seed** (ăn'ĭ-sēd'). The seeds, used as flavoring. [< Gk *anison.*]

an•i•sette (ăn'ə-sĕt', -zĕt') *n.* An anise-flavored liqueur.

An•ka•ra (ăng'kə-rə, äng'-). The capital of Turkey. Pop. 650,000.

an•kle (ăng'kəl) *n.* **1.** The joint, consisting of the bones and related structure, that connects the foot with the leg. **2.** The slender section of the leg immediately above the foot. [< ON **ankula* and OE *anclēow.* See **ank-**.]

an•klet (ăng'klĭt) *n.* **1.** An ornament worn around the ankle. **2.** A short sock covering the ankle.

ann. 1. annals. **2.** annual. **3.** annuity.

an•nals (ăn'əlz) *pl.n.* **1.** A chronological record of the events of successive years. **2.** Any descriptive record; history. [L *(lĭbrī) annālēs,* "yearly (books)."] —**an'nal•ist** *n.*

An•nap•o•lis (ə-năp'ə-lĭs). The capital of Maryland. Pop. 30,000.

an•neal (ə-nēl') *v.* **1.** To heat and slowly cool (glass or metal) to toughen and reduce brittleness. **2.** To temper. [< OE *onǣlan.*]

an•nex (ə-nĕks', ăn'ĕks') *v.* **1.** To add or join to, esp. to a larger thing. **2.** To incorporate (territory) into an existing country or state. —*n.* (ăn'ĕks', ăn'ĭks). A building added on to a larger one or situated near the main one. [< L *annectere* (pp *annexus*), to bind to.] —**an'nex•a'tion** *n.*

an•ni•hi•late (ə-nī'ə-lāt') *v.* **-lated, -lating.** To destroy completely. [< LL *annihilāre,* to reduce to nothing.] —**an•ni'hi•la'tor** *n.*

an•ni•hi•la•tion (ə-nī'ə-lā'shən) *n.* **1.** An annihilating or being annihilated. **2.** The phenomenon in which a particle and an antiparticle, such as an electron and a positron, disappear with a resultant release of energy approximately equivalent to the sum of their masses.

an•ni•ver•sa•ry (ăn'ə-vûr'sər-ē) *n., pl.* **-ries.** The annual recurrence of an event that took place in some preceding year or its commemorative celebration on this date. [< L *anniversārius,* "returning yearly."]

an•no Dom•i•ni (ăn'ō dŏm'ə-nī', dŏm'ə-nē). In a specified year of the Christian era. [L, "in the year of the Lord."]

an•no•tate (ăn'ō-tāt') *v.* **-tated, -tating.** To furnish (a literary work) with critical or explanatory notes. [L *annotāre,* to note down.] —**an'no•ta'tion** *n.* —**an'no•ta'tive** *adj.* —**an'no•ta'tor** *n.*

an•nounce (ə-nouns') *v.* **-nounced, -nouncing. 1.** To bring to public notice. **2.** To proclaim the arrival of. **3.** To serve as an announcer. [< L *annuntiāre.*] —**an•nounce'ment** *n.*

an•nounc•er (ə-noun'sər) *n.* A radio or television performer who provides program continuity and gives commercial and other announcements.

an•noy (ə-noi') *v.* **1.** To bother or irritate. **2.** To injure or harm; molest. [< LL *inodiāre,* to make odious.] —**an•noy'ing•ly** *adv.*

an•noy•ance (ə-noi'əns) *n.* **1.** The act of annoying. **2.** A nuisance. **3.** Vexation; irritation.

an•nu•al (ăn'yōō-əl) *adj.* **1.** Recurring or done every year; yearly. **2.** Of or pertaining to a year: *an annual income.* **3.** Living and growing for only one year or season: *annual plants.* —*n.* **1.** A periodical published yearly; yearbook. **2.** An annual plant. [< L *annus,* year.] —**an'nu•al•ly** *adv.*

an•nu•i•tant (ə-n/y/ōō'ə-tənt) *n.* A person who receives an annuity.

an•nu•i•ty (ə-n/y/ōō'ə-tē) *n., pl.* **-ties. 1.** The annual payment of an allowance or income. **2. a.** The interest or dividends paid annually on an investment of money. **b.** The investment made.

an•nul (ə-nŭl') *v.* **-nulled, -nulling.** To nullify or cancel, as a marriage or a law. [< LL *annullāre,* to make into nothing.] —**an•nul'la•ble** *adj.* —**an•nul'ment** *n.*

an•nu•lar (ăn'yə-lər) *adj.* Forming or shaped like a ring. [< L *annulus,* ring.] —**an'nu•lar•ly** *adv.*

an•nu•lus (ăn'yə-ləs) *n., pl.* **-luses** or **-li** (-lī'). A ringlike figure, part, structure, or marking. [L *annulus,* ring.]

an•nun•ci•ate (ə-nŭn'sē-āt') *v.* **-ated, -ating.** To announce; proclaim. [L *annuntiāre,* to ANNOUNCE.]

an•nun•ci•a•tion (ə-nŭn'sē-ā'shən) *n.* **1.** The act of announcing. **2. Annunciation. a.** The angel Gabriel's announcement of the Incarnation. Luke 1:26-38. **b.** The festival, on March 25, celebrating this.

an•ode (ăn'ōd') *n.* A positively charged electrode. [Gk *anodos,* a way up.] —**an•o'dal** (-ō'-dəl), **an•od'ic** (-ŏd'ĭk) *adj.*

an•o•dize (ăn'ə-dīz') *v.* **-dized, -dizing.** To coat (a metallic surface) by electrolysis with a protective oxide.

an•o•dyne (ăn'ə-dīn') *n.* A soothing or pain-relieving agent. [< Gk *anōdunos,* free from pain.]

a•noint (ə-noint') *v.* To apply oil to, esp. in a religious ceremony. [< L *inunguere.*] —**a•noint'er** *n.* —**a•noint'ment** *n.*

a•nom•a•ly (ə-nŏm'ə-lē) *n., pl.* **-lies. 1.** Deviation from the normal order, form, or rule; abnormality. **2.** Anything irregular or abnormal. [< Gk *anōmalos,* uneven.] —**a•nom'a•lis'tic** (-lĭs'tĭk) *adj.* —**a•nom'a•lous** *adj.*

a•non (ə nŏn') *adv.* In a short time; soon. [< OE *on ān,* "into one," at once.]

anon. anonymous.

a•non•y•mous (ə-nŏn'ə-məs) *adj.* Having an unknown or withheld name, authorship, or agency. [< Gk *anōnumos,* nameless.] —**an'o•nym'i•ty** (ăn'ə-nĭm'ə-tē), **a•non'y•mous•ness** *n.* —**a•non'y•mous•ly** *adv.*

an•oth•er (ə-nŭth'ər) *adj.* **1.** Additional; one more. **2.** Distinctly different; some other. **3.** Different but of the same character. —*pron.* **1.** An additional or different one. **2.** One of the same kind. [ME *an other.*]

ans. answer.

an•swer (ăn'sər, än'-) *n.* **1.** A spoken or written reply, as to a question. **2.** A solution or result, as to a problem. —*v.* **1.** To reply to. **2.** To respond correctly to. **3.** To serve (a purpose). **4.** To be responsible for. [< OE *andswaru.* See **swer-**[1].] —**an'swer•a•ble** *adj.* —**an'swer•er** *n.*

ant (ănt) *n.* Any of various usually wingless insects that live in complexly organized colonies. [< OE *ǣmette.* See **mai-**[1].]

-ant. *comb. form.* Performing, promoting, or causing an action: **deodorant.**

ant. 1. antenna. **2.** antonym.

ant•ac•id (ănt-ăs'ĭd) *n.* A substance that neutralizes acid.

an•tag•o•nism (ăn-tăg'ə-nĭz'əm) *n.* Opposition; hostility. —**an•tag'o•nist** *n.* —**an•tag'o•nis'tic** *adj.* —**an•tag'o•nis'ti•cal•ly** *adv.*

an•tag•o•nize (ăn-tăg'ə-nīz') *v.* **-nized, -nizing.** To arouse the hostility of. [Gk *antagōnizesthai,* to struggle against.]

Ant•arc•tic (ănt-ärk'tĭk, -är'tĭk) *adj.* Of or pertaining to the regions surrounding the South Pole. —*n.* **the Antarctic.** Antarctica and its surrounding waters. [< L *antarcticus,* southern.]

Ant•arc•ti•ca (ănt-ärk'tĭ-kə, -är'tĭ-kə). A continent largely contained within the Antarctic Circle, and almost entirely covered by a sheet of ice.

Antarctic Circle. A parallel of latitude, 66° 33′ S, marking the limit of the S Frigid Zone.

Antarctic Ocean. The waters surrounding Antarctica.

An•tar•es (ăn-târ'ēz) *n.* The brightest star in the southern sky, in the constellation Scorpius. [Gk *antarēs,* "opposite Mars."]

an•te (ăn'tē) *n. Poker.* The stake each player must put up before receiving his hand or new cards. —*v.* **-ted** or **-teed, -teing. 1.** *Poker.* To put up (an ante). **2.** *Slang.* To pay (one's share). [< L *ante,* before.]

ante-. *comb. form.* **1.** In front of. **2.** Previous to. [< L *ante,* before, in front of.]

ant•eat•er (ănt'ē'tər) *n.* Any of various long-snouted animals that feed primarily on ants.

an•te•bel•lum (ăn'tē-bĕl'əm) *adj.* Of the period before the Civil War. [L *ante bellum,* before the war.]

an•te•ce•dent (ăn'tə-sēd'ənt) *adj.* Going before; preceding. —*n.* **1.** One that precedes. **2.** An event preceding another. **3. antecedents.** One's ancestry. **4.** The word, phrase, or clause to which a relative pronoun refers. —**an'te•ce'dence** *n.* —**an'te•ce'dent•ly** *adv.*

an•te•cham•ber (ăn'tĭ-chām'bər) *n.* A smaller room leading into a larger one.

an•te•date (ăn'tĭ-dāt') *v.* **-dated, -dating. 1.** To precede in time. **2.** To give a date earlier than the actual date.

an•te•di•lu•vi•an (ăn'tĭ-də-lōō'vē-ən) *adj.* **1.** Of the era before the Flood. **2.** Very old; antiquated.

an•te•lope (ăn'tə-lōp') *n.* Any of various slender, swift-running, long-horned hoofed mammals. [< OF *antelop,* a mythical oriental beast.]

an•te me•rid•i•em (ăn'tē mə-rĭd'ē-əm). Before noon. [L.]

an•ten•na (ăn-tĕn'ə) *n.* **1.** *pl.* **-nae** (-nē). One of the paired, flexible, sensory organs on the head of an insect, crustacean, etc. **2.** *pl.* **-nas.** A metallic apparatus for sending and receiving electromagnetic waves; aerial. [L, sail yard.] —**an•ten'nal** *adj.*

an•te•pe•nult (ăn'tĭ-pē'nŭlt', -pĭ-nŭlt') *n.* The 3rd syllable from the end of a word. —**an'te•pe•nul'ti•mate** (-pĭ-nŭl'tə-mĭt) *adj.* & *n.*

an•te•ri•or (ăn-tîr'ē-ər) *adj.* **1.** Located in front. **2.** Prior in time. [< L *ante,* before.]

an•te•room (ăn'tĭ-rōōm', -rŏŏm') *n.* A waiting room.

an•them (ăn'thəm) *n.* **1.** A hymn of praise or loyalty. **2.** A sacred choral composition. [< OE *antefn,* antiphonal song < ML *antiphōna.*]

an•ther (ăn'thər) *n.* The pollen-bearing organ at the end of a stamen. [< ML *anthēra,* pollen.]

an•thol•o•gy (ăn-thŏl'ə-jē) *n., pl.* **-gies.** A collection of literary pieces. [< Gk *anthologia,* "flower gathering," a collection.] —**an•thol'o•gist** *n.*

an•thra•cite (ăn'thrə-sīt') *n.* Coal having a high carbon content and little volatile matter; hard coal. [< ANTHRAX.]

an•thrax (ăn'thrăks') *n.* An infectious, usually fatal disease of animals, esp. of cattle and sheep, that is transmissible to man. [< Gk, charcoal, carbuncle, pustule.]

anthrop. anthropological; anthropology.

anthropo–. *comb. form.* Man or human. [< Gk *anthrōpos,* man.]

an•thro•po•cen•tric (ăn'thrə-pō-sĕn'trĭk) *adj.* Interpreting reality in terms of human values and experience.

an•thro•poid (ăn'thrə-poid') *adj.* Resembling man, as certain apes. —*n.* An anthropoid ape, such as a gorilla or chimpanzee.

an•thro•pol•o•gy (ăn'thrə-pŏl'ə-jē) *n.* The scientific study of the origin, culture, and development of man. —**an'thro•po•log'ic** (-pə-lŏj'ĭk), **an'thro•po•log'i•cal** *adj.* —**an'thro•po•log'i•cal•ly** *adv.* —**an'thro•pol'o•gist** *n.*

an•thro•po•mor•phism (ăn'thrə-pō-môr'fĭz'əm) *n.* The attribution of human characteristics to nonhuman beings or things. —**an'thro•po•mor'phic** *adj.*

an•ti (ăn'tī', ăn'tē) *n. Informal.* A person who is opposed to a group, policy, proposal, or practice. [< ANTI-.]

anti-. *comb. form.* **1.** Opposition to, effectiveness against, or counteraction. **2.** Reciprocal correspondence to. [< Gk *anti,* opposite, against.]

an•ti•bal•lis•tic missile (ăn'tī-bə-lĭs'tĭk, ăn'tī-). A defensive missile designed to intercept and destroy a ballistic missile in flight.

an•ti•bi•ot•ic (ăn'tĭ-bī-ŏt'ĭk, ăn'tī-) *n.* Any of various substances, such as penicillin and streptomycin, produced by certain fungi, bacteria, and other organisms, that inhibit the growth of or destroy microorganisms, and are widely used to prevent or treat diseases.

an•ti•bod•y (ăn'tĭ-bŏd'ē) *n., pl.* **-ies. 1.** Any of various proteins in the blood that are generated in reaction to foreign proteins or carbohydrates of certain types, neutralize them, and thus produce immunity against certain microorganisms or their toxins. **2.** An object composed of antimatter.

an•tic (ăn'tĭk) *n.* Often **antics.** A ludicrous act or gesture; a caper. [It *antico,* "ancient," "grotesque."] —**an'tic** *adj.*

an•ti•christ (ăn'tĭ-krīst') *n.* **1.** A great enemy of Christ. **2. Antichrist.** Title of Christ's personal antagonist. I John 2:18.

an•tic•i•pate (ăn-tĭs'ə-pāt') *v.* **-pated, -pating. 1.** To realize beforehand; foresee. **2.** To look forward to. **3.** To act in advance to prevent; forestall. [L *anticipāre,* to take before.] —**an•tic'i•pa'tion** *n.* —**an•tic'i•pa'tor** *n.* —**an•tic'i•pa•to'ry** (-pə-tôr'ē, -tōr'ē) *adj.*

an•ti•cli•max (ăn'tĭ-klī'măks') *n.* **1.** A decline in disappointing contrast with a previous rise. **2.** Something commonplace concluding a series of significant events. —**an'ti•cli•mac'tic** *adj.* —**an'ti•cli•mac'ti•cal•ly** *adv.*

an•ti•dote (ăn'tĭ-dōt') *n.* Something that counteracts a poison or injury. [< Gk *antidoton.*] —**an'ti•dot'al** (ăn'tĭ-dōt'l) *adj.*

an•ti•freeze (ăn'tĭ-frēz') *n.* A substance, such as alcohol, mixed with a liquid to lower the freezing point of the latter.

an•ti•gen (ăn'tĭ-jən) *n.* Also **an•ti•gene** (-jēn). Any substance that when introduced into the body stimulates antibody production. —**an'ti•gen'ic** (-jĕn'ĭk) *adj.* —**an'ti•gen'i•cal•ly** *adv.* —**an'ti•ge•nic'i•ty** (-jə-nĭs'ə-tē) *n.*

An•ti•gua (ăn-tē'gwə, -gə). A self-governing island of the West Indies; a former British colony. Pop. 62,000. Cap. Saint Johns.

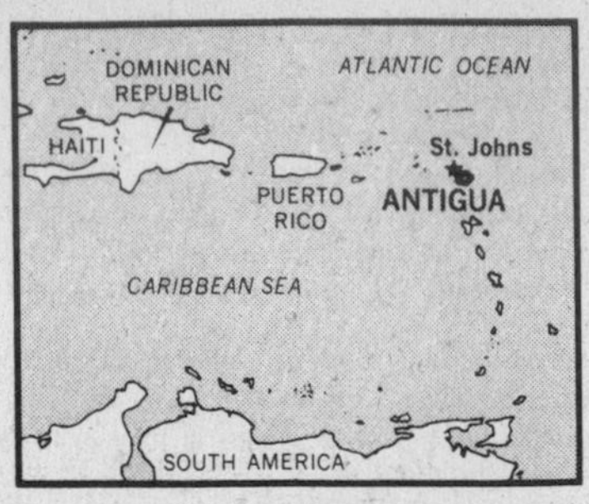

Antigua

an•ti•his•ta•mine (ăn'tĭ-hĭs'tə-mēn', -mĭn) *n.* Any of various drugs used to reduce physiological effects associated with histamine production in allergies and colds.

an•ti•knock (ăn'tĭ-nŏk') *n.* A substance added to gasoline to reduce engine knock.

An•til•les (ăn-tĭl'ēz). The main island group of the West Indies, forming a chain that separates the Caribbean from the Atlantic.

an•ti•log•a•rithm (ăn'tĭ-lôg'ə-rĭth'əm, ăn'tĭ-lŏg'-, ăn'tī-) *n.* The number for which a given logarithm stands; for example, where log *x* equals *y,* the *x* is the antilogarithm of *y.*

an•ti•ma•cas•sar (ăn'tĭ-mə-kăs'ər) *n.* A protective covering for the backs of chairs and sofas.

an•ti•mat•ter (ăn'tĭ-măt'ər) *n.* A hypothetical form of matter consisting of antiparticles and having positron-surrounded nuclei composed of antiprotons and antineutrons.

an•ti•mo•ny (ăn'tə-mō'nē) *n. Symbol* **Sb** A metallic element used in a wide variety of alloys, esp. with lead in battery plates, and in paints, semiconductor devices, and ceramic products. Atomic number 51, atomic weight 121.75. [< ML *antimonium.*]

an•ti•neu•tri•no (ăn'tĭ-n/y/o͞o-trē'nō, ăn'tī-) *n., pl.* **-nos.** The antiparticle of the neutrino.

an•ti•neu•tron (ăn'tĭ-n/y/o͞o'trŏn', ăn'tī-) *n. Symbol* **n** The antiparticle of the neutron.

an•ti•nu•cle•on (ăn'tĭ-n/y/o͞o'klē-ŏn', ăn'tī-) *n.* The antiparticle of a nucleon.

an•ti•ox•i•dant (ăn'tĭ-ŏk'sə-dənt, ăn'tī-) *n.* A chemical compound or substance that inhibits oxidation.

an•ti•par•ti•cle (ăn'tĭ-pär'tĭ-kəl, ăn'tī-) *n.* A subatomic particle, such as a positron or antineutron, having the same mass, average lifetime, magnitude of electric charge, and other properties as the particle to which it corresponds, but having the opposite electric charge, opposite intrinsic parity, and opposite magnetic characteristics.

an•ti•pas•to (än'tē-päs'tō) *n., pl.* **-tos.** An assortment of appetizers often served as a main course. [It.]

an•tip•a•thy (ăn-tĭp'ə-thē) *n., pl.* **-thies. 1.** A feeling of aversion. **2.** The object of aversion. [< Gk *antipathēs,* of opposite feelings.] —**an•tip'a•thet'ic** (-thĕt'ĭk) *adj.*

an•ti•per•son•nel (ăn'tĭ-pûr'sə-nĕl', ăn'tī-) *adj. Mil.* Designed to inflict casualties on personnel.

an•ti•phon (ăn'tə-fŏn', -fən) *n.* **1.** A devotional composition sung responsively as part of a liturgy. **2.** A response: *a resounding antiphon of dissent.* [< Gk *antiphōna,* sung responses.] —**an•tiph'o•nal** (-tĭf'ə-nəl) *adj.*

an•tiph•o•ny (ăn-tĭf'ə-nē) *n., pl.* **-nies. 1.** Antiphonal singing. **2.** A sound or other effect that echoes or answers another.

an•ti•pode (ăn'tĭ-pōd') *n.* A direct or diametrical opposite. [< Gk *antipous,* with the feet opposite.] —**an•tip'o•dal** *adj.*

an•ti•pro•ton (ăn'tĭ-prō'tŏn', ăn'tī-) *n.* The antiparticle of the proton.

an•ti•py•ret•ic (ăn'tĭ-pī-rĕt'ĭk) *adj.* Reducing or tending to reduce fever. —*n.* An antipyretic medicine. —**an'ti•py•re'sis** (-rē'sĭs) *n.*

an•ti•quar•y (ăn'tə-kwĕr'ē) *n., pl.* **-ies.** A student of or dealer in antiquities. —**an'ti•quar'i•an** (ăn'tĭ-kwâr'ē-ən) *adj.* & *n.*

an•ti•quate (ăn'tə-kwāt') *v.* **-quated, -quating.** To make obsolete. —**an'ti•qua'tion** *n.*

an•tique (ăn-tēk') *adj.* **1.** Of or belonging to ancient times, esp. of ancient Greece or Rome. **2.** Belonging to or typical of an earlier period. —*n.* An object having special value because of its age, esp. a work of art or handicraft that is over 100 years old. —*v.* **-tiqued, -tiquing.** To give the appearance of an antique to. [< L *antiquus,* ancient, former.]

an•tiq•ui•ty (ăn-tĭk'wə-tē) *n., pl.* **-ties. 1.** Ancient times, esp. the times preceding the Middle Ages. **2.** The quality of being old or ancient: *a carving of great antiquity.*

an•ti-Sem•ite (ăn'tĭ-sĕm'īt', ăn'tī-) *n.* A person hostile toward Jews. —**an'ti-Se•mit'ic** (-sə-mĭt'ĭk) *adj.* —**an'ti-Sem'i•tism'** *n.*

an•ti•sep•sis (ăn'tə-sĕp'sĭs) *n.* The destruction of microorganisms that cause disease, fermentation, or putrefaction.

an•ti•sep•tic (ăn'tə-sĕp'tĭk) *adj.* **1.** Pertaining to or capable of producing antisepsis. **2.** Thoroughly clean. **3.** Austere; drab. —*n.* An antiseptic drug or agent. —**an'ti•sep'ti•cal•ly** *adj.*

an•ti•so•cial (ăn'tĭ-sō'shəl, ăn'tī-) *adj.* **1.** Unsociable. **2.** Interfering with the social order. —**an'ti•so'cial•ly** *adv.*

an•tith•e•sis (ăn-tĭth'ə-sĭs) *n., pl.* **-ses** (-sēz'). **1.** Direct contrast; opposition. **2.** The direct opposite. **3.** *Rhet.* The juxtaposition of sharply contrasting ideas. [< Gk.] —**an'ti•thet'i•cal** (-tə-thĕt'ĭ-kəl), **an'ti•thet'ic** *adj.*

an•ti•tox•in (ăn'tĭ-tŏk'sĭn) *n.* **1.** An antibody formed in response to, and capable of neutralizing, a poison of biological origin. **2.** An animal serum containing such antibodies.

an•ti•trust (ăn'tĭ-trŭst', ăn'tī-) *adj.* Concerned with the regulation of trusts or similar monopolies.

ant•ler (ănt'lər) *n.* One of the paired, often branched bony growths on the head of a deer. [< VL *anteoculāris.] —**ant'lered** (-lərd) *adj.*

Ant•li•a (ănt'lē-ə) *n.* A constellation in the S Hemisphere.

an•to•nym (ăn'tə-nĭm') *n.* A word having a sense opposite to that of another word. [ANT(I)- + -ONYM.] —**an•ton'y•mous** (ăn-tŏn'ə-məs) *adj.*

Ant•werp (ănt'wûrp). A city of Belgium. Pop. 253,000.

an•u•re•sis (ăn'yo͞o-rē'sĭs) *n.* Inability to urinate. —**an'u•ret'ic** (-rĕt'ĭk) *adj.*

a•nus (ā'nəs) *n., pl.* **anuses.** The excretory opening of the alimentary canal. [L *ānus.*]

an•vil (ăn'vĭl) *n.* A block of iron or steel with a flat top on which metals are shaped by hammering. [< OE *anfealt.* See **pel-**[1].]

anx•i•e•ty (ăng-zī'ə-tē) *n., pl.* **-ties.** A state of uneasiness; apprehension; worry. [L *anxietās* < *anxius,* ANXIOUS.]

anx•ious (ăngk'shəs, ăng'shəs) *adj.* **1.** Worried about some uncertain event or matter. **2.** Eagerly or earnestly desirous. [L *anxius* < *angere,* to torment.] **—anx'ious•ly** *adv.* **—anx'ious•ness** *n.*

an•y (ĕn'ē) *adj.* **1.** One, no matter which, from three or more. **2.** Some, regardless of quantity. *—pron.* **1.** Any one or ones among three or more. **2.** Any quantity or part. [< OE *ǣnig.* See **oino-**.]

an•y•bod•y (ĕn'ē-bŏd'ē, -bəd-ē) *pron.* Anyone. *—n.* A person of some consequence: *everybody who is anybody.*

an•y•how (ĕn'ē-hou') *adv.* **1.** In any way or by any means whatever. **2.** In any case.

an•y•more (ĕn'ē-môr', -mōr') *adv.* From now on.

an•y•one (ĕn'ē-wŭn', -wən) *pron.* Anybody; any person.

an•y•place (ĕn'ē-plās') *adv.* To, in, or at any place; anywhere.

an•y•thing (ĕn'ē-thĭng) *pron.* Any object, occurrence, or matter whatever.

an•y•way (ĕn'ē-wā') *adv.* **1.** In any manner whatever. **2.** Nevertheless.

an•y•where (ĕn'ē-hwâr') *adv.* **1.** To, in, or at any place. **2.** To any extent or degree.

a•or•ta (ā-ôr'tə) *n., pl.* **-tas** or **-tae** (-tē'). The main trunk of the systemic arteries, carrying blood away from the heart. [< Gk *aortē,* aorta, "appendixes (of the heart)."] **—a•or'tic** *adj.*

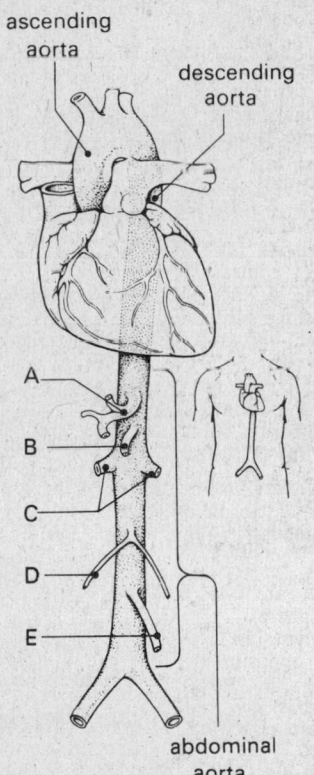

ascending aorta
descending aorta
A
B
C
D
E
abdominal aorta

aorta
A. Celiac artery
B. Superior mesenteric artery
C. Renal arteries
D. Spermatic artery
E. Inferior mesenteric artery

a•ou•dad (ä'o͞o-dăd') *n.* A wild sheep of N Africa with long, curved horns and a beardlike growth of hair on the neck and chest. [F.]

Ap. 1. Apostle. **2.** April.

AP 1. Associated Press. **2.** additional premium. **3.** antipersonnel.

ap. apothecary.

a.p. additional premium.

A.P. Associated Press.

A/P 1. account paid. **2.** accounts payable.

A.P.A. 1. American Philological Association. **2.** American Psychiatric Association.

a•pace (ə-pās') *adv.* At a rapid pace; quickly; swiftly.

A•pach•e (ə-păch'ē) *n., pl.* **Apache** or **-es. 1.** A member of an Athapascan-speaking tribe of North American Indians inhabiting the SW U.S. and N Mexico. **2.** Their languages. [Span.]

ap•a•nage. Variant of **appanage.**

a•part (ə-pärt') *adv.* **1. a.** In pieces. **b.** To pieces. **2. a.** Separately or at a distance in time, place, or position. **b.** To one side; aside. [< OF *a part,* to the side.]

a•part•heid (ə-pärt'hīt', -hāt') *n.* An official policy of racial segregation promulgated in the Republic of South Africa. [Afrik, "apartness."]

a•part•ment (ə-pärt'mənt) *n.* A room or suite of rooms designed for dwelling. [< It *appartare,* to separate.]

ap•a•thy (ăp'ə-thē) *n.* **1.** Lack of emotion or feeling. **2.** Lack of interest in things; indifference. [Gk *apatheia.*] **—ap'a•thet'ic** *adj.* **—ap'a•thet'i•cal•ly** *adv.*

ap•a•tite (ăp'ə-tīt') *n.* A mineral, $Ca_5F(PO_4)_3$, used as a source of phosphorus compounds. [G *Apatit.*]

ape (āp) *n.* **1.** A large primate such as a chimpanzee, gorilla, gibbon, or orang-utan. **2.** Any monkey. **3.** A mimic or imitator. **4.** A clumsy, coarse person. *—v.* **aped, aping.** To mimic. [< OE *apa* < Gmc **apan-.*]

Ap•en•nines (ăp'ə-nīnz'). A mountain range of Italy, extending the length of the peninsula.

a•pé•ri•tif (ä-pĕr'ə-tēf') *n.* A drink of alcoholic liquor taken before a meal. [F.]

ap•er•ture (ăp'ər-cho͝or', -chər) *n.* An opening; orifice. [< L *apertus,* pp of *aperīre,* to open.] **—ap'er•tur'al** *adj.*

a•pex (ā'pĕks') *n., pl.* **apexes** or **apices** (ā'pə-sēz', ăp'ə-). The highest point of anything; culmination; peak. [L, point, summit, top.]

a•pha•sia (ə-fā'zhə) *n.* Loss of the ability to articulate ideas in any form, resulting from brain damage. **—a•pha'si•ac'** (-zē-ăk') *n.* **—a•pha'sic** *adj. & n.*

a•phe•li•on (ə-fē'lē-ən, ə-fēl'yən) *n., pl.* **-lia** (-lē-ə). The orbital point on a planetary orbit farthest from the sun.

a•phid (ā'fĭd, ăf'ĭd) *n.* Any of various small insects that suck sap from plants.

aph•o•rism (ăf'ə-rĭz'əm) *n.* **1.** A brief statement of a principle. **2.** A maxim; an adage. [< Gk *aphorismos,* a distinction.] **—aph'o•ris'tic** *adj.* **—aph'o•ris'ti•cal•ly** *adv.*

a•pho•tic (ā-fō'tĭk) *adj.* Without light.

aph•ro•dis•i•ac (ăf'rə-dĭz'ē-ăk') *adj.* Stimulating or intensifying sexual desire. *—n.* An aphrodisiac drug or food. [< Gk *aphrodisios,* of Aphrodite.]

Aph•ro•di•te (ăf'rə-dī'tē). Greek goddess of love and beauty.

A•pi•a (ä-pē'ä). The capital of Western Samoa. Pop. 22,000.

a•pi•ar•y (ā'pē-ĕr'ē) *n., pl.* **-ies.** A place where bees are raised for their honey. [< L *apis,* bee.] **—a'pi•a•rist** (-ə-rĭst) *n.*

a•pi•ces. Alternate *pl.* of **apex.**

a•piece (ə-pēs') *adv.* To or for each one: *Give them an apple apiece.*

a•plomb (ə-plŏm', ə-plŭm') *n.* Self-confidence; poise. [F, uprightness.]

apmt. appointment.

apo–. *comb. form.* **1.** Being away from. **2.** Lack of. **3.** Separation of. [< Gk *apo,* away from, off.]

APO Army Post Office.

Apoc. 1. Apocalypse. **2.** Apocrypha; Apocryphal.

A•poc•a•lypse (ə-pŏk'ə-lĭps') *n.* **1.** The last book of the New Testament, Revelation. **2. apocalypse.** A prophetic revelation. [< Gk *apokalupsis,* revelation.]

a•poc•a•lyp•tic (ə-pŏk'ə-lĭp'tĭk) *adj.* Also **a•poc•a•lyp•ti•cal** (-tĭ-kəl). Of or pertaining to a prophetic revelation or disclosure. **—a•poc'a•lyp'ti•cal•ly** *adv.*

A•poc•ry•pha (ə-pŏk'rə-fə) *pl.n. (takes sing. v.).* **1.** The 14 books of the Septuagint considered uncanonical by Protestants because they are not part of the Hebrew Scriptures. Eleven of these books are accepted in the Roman Catholic canon. **2. apocrypha.** Writings of questionable authorship or authenticity. [< ML *(scripta) apocrypha,* hidden (writings).]

a•poc•ry•phal (ə-pŏk'rə-fəl) *adj.* **1.** Of questionable authorship or authenticity. **2.** False; counterfeit. **3. Apocryphal.** Of or having to do with the Apocrypha. **—a•poc'ry•phal•ly** *adv.* **—a•poc'ry•phal•ness** *n.*

ap•o•gee (ăp'ə-jē) *n.* **1.** The point in the orbit of the moon or of an artificial satellite most distant from the earth. **2.** The farthest or highest point; apex. [< Gk *apogaios,* "away from the earth."] **—ap'o•ge'an** (-jē'ən), **ap'o•ge'ic** (-jē'ĭk) *adj.*

A•pol•lo (ə-pŏl'ō) *n.* **1.** Greek sun god, patron of prophecy, music, and medicine. **2. apollo.** A young man of great physical beauty.

Apollo

a•pol•o•get•ic (ə-pŏl'ə-jĕt'ĭk) *adj.* Making an apology. *—n.* A formal defense or apology. **—a•pol'o•get'i•cal•ly** *adv.*

ap•o•lo•gi•a (ăp'ə-lō'jē-ə, -jə) *n.* A formal defense or justification.

a•pol•o•gist (ə-pŏl′ə-jĭst) *n.* A person who argues in defense or justification of another person or cause.

a•pol•o•gize (ə-pŏl′ə-jīz′) *v.* **-gized, gizing.** To make an apology. **—a•pol′o•giz′er** *n.*

a•pol•o•gy (ə-pŏl′ə-jē) *n., pl.* **-gies. 1.** A statement expressing regret for a fault or offense. **2.** A formal justification or defense. **3.** An inferior substitute. [< Gk *apologia,* speech in defense.]

ap•o•phthegm. Variant of **apothegm.**

ap•o•plex•y (ăp′ə-plĕk′sē) *n.* Sudden loss of muscular control, sensation, and consciousness, resulting from rupture or blocking of a blood vessel in the brain. [< Gk *apoplēxia.*] **—ap′o•plec′tic** *adj.*

a•port (ə-pôrt′, ə-pōrt′) *adj. Naut.* On or toward the port, or left, side.

a•pos•ta•sy (ə-pŏs′tə-sē) *n., pl.* **-sies.** An abandonment of one's religious faith, political party, or cause. [< Gk *apostasia,* desertion, revolt.]

a•pos•tate (ə-pŏs′tāt′, -tĭt) *n.* One who forsakes his faith or principles.

a pos•te•ri•o•ri (ä pŏs-tîr′ē-ôr′ē, -ōr′ē, ā pŏs-tîr′ē-ôr′ī′, -ōr′ī′). *Logic.* Denoting reasoning from facts or particulars to general principles, or from effects to causes; inductive; empirical. [L, "from the subsequent."]

a•pos•tle (ə-pŏs′əl) *n.* **1. Apostle.** One of a group of disciples chosen by Christ to preach his gospel, esp. one of the original twelve. **2.** One who leads a new cause. [< OE *apostol* < Gk *apostolos,* messenger.]

ap•os•tol•ic (ăp′ə-stŏl′ĭk) *adj.* **1.** Of or pertaining to the Apostles, their faith, teachings, etc. **2.** Of or pertaining to the pope as successor of Saint Peter.

a•pos•tro•phe[1] (ə-pŏs′trə-fē) *n.* The superscript sign (') used to indicate the omission of a letter or letters from a word, the possessive case, and certain plurals. [< Gk *(prosōidia) apostrophos,* "(accent of) turning away."]

a•pos•tro•phe[2] (ə-pŏs′trə-fē) *n.* A digression in discourse, esp. a turning away from an audience to address an absent or imaginary person.

apothecaries' measure. A system of liquid volume measure used in pharmacy.

apothecaries' weight. A system of weights used in pharmacy and based on an ounce equal to 480 grains and a pound equal to 12 ounces.

a•poth•e•car•y (ə-pŏth′ə-kĕr′ē) *n., pl.* **-ies.** A druggist; pharmacist. [< LL *apothecārius,* warehouse man.]

ap•o•thegm (ăp′ə-thĕm′) *n.* Also **ap•o•phthegm.** A maxim; proverb. [Gk *apophthegma,* a pointed saying.]

ap•o•them (ăp′ə-thĕm′) *n.* In a regular polygon, the perpendicular distance from the center to any of the sides. [< APO- + THEME.]

a•poth•e•o•sis (ə-pŏth′ē-ō′sĭs, ăp′ə-thē′ə-sĭs) *n., pl.* **-ses** (-sēz′). **1.** Exaltation to divine rank; deification. **2.** An exalted or glorified ideal. [< Gk *apotheōsis.*]

app. 1. apparatus. **2.** *Lib.Serv.* appendix. **3.** apprentice.

Ap•pa•la•chians (ăp′ə-lā′chənz, -lā′chē-ənz, -lăch′ənz). The major mountain system of E North America, extending from Quebec to Alabama.

ap•pall (ə-pôl′) *v.* To fill with consternation or dismay. [< OF *apalir,* to grow pale.] **—ap•pall′ing** *adj.*

ap•pa•nage (ăp′ə-nĭj) *n.* Also **ap•a•nage. 1.** A source of revenue, as land, given by a king for the maintenance of a member of the ruling family. **2.** A natural adjunct.

ap•pa•ra•tus (ăp′ə-rā′təs, -răt′əs) *n., pl.* **-tus** or **-tuses. 1.** The totality of means by which a designated function is performed or a specific task executed. **2.** A machine or group of machines. **3.** A political organization. [L *apparātus,* pp of *apparāre,* to prepare.]

ap•par•el (ə-păr′əl) *n.* Clothing, esp. outer garments. *—v.* **-eled** or **-elled, -eling** or **-elling.** To clothe; dress. [< OF *apareil,* preparation, apparatus.]

ap•par•ent (ə-păr′ənt, ə-pâr′-) *adj.* **1.** Readily seen; visible. **2.** Readily understood or perceived. [< OF *aparoir,* to appear.] **—ap•par′ent•ly** *adv.*

ap•pa•ri•tion (ăp′ə-rĭsh′ən) *n.* **1.** A ghost; specter. **2.** A sudden or unusual sight. [< LL *apparitiō,* appearance.]

ap•peal (ə-pēl′) *n.* **1.** An earnest request. **2.** An application to some higher authority, as for corroboration. **3.** The power of arousing interest. **4.** *Law.* **a.** The transfer of a case from a lower to a higher court for a new hearing. **b.** A request for a new hearing. *—v.* **1.** To make an earnest request, as for help, corroboration, etc. **2.** To be attractive or interesting. **3.** To transfer or apply to transfer (a case) to a higher court for rehearing. [< L *appellāre,* to apply to, entreat.] **—ap•peal′ing•ly** *adv.*

ap•pear (ə-pîr′) *v.* **1.** To become visible. **2.** To come into existence. **3.** To seem or look. **4.** To come before the public. **5.** *Law.* To present oneself formally before a court. [< L *appārēre.*]

ap•pear•ance (ə-pîr′əns) *n.* **1.** The act or an instance of appearing. **2.** The outward aspect of something. **3.** Something that appears; phenomenon. **4.** A pretense; false show. **5. appearances.** Circumstances; outward indications.

ap•pease (ə-pēz′) *v.* **-peased, -peasing.** To bring peace to or placate, esp. by granting concessions. [< OF *apaisier.*] **—ap•pease′ment** *n.* **—ap•peas′er** *n.*

ap•pel•lant (ə-pĕl′ənt) *n.* One who appeals a court decision.

ap•pel•late (ə-pĕl′ĭt) *adj.* Having the power to hear appeals and to reverse court decisions. [< L *appellāre,* to APPEAL.]

ap•pel•la•tion (ăp′ə-lā′shən) *n.* **1.** A name or title. **2.** The act of naming. [< L *appellāre,* to APPEAL.]

ap•pel•lee (ăp′ə-lē′) *n.* One against whom an appeal is taken.

ap•pend (ə-pĕnd′) *v.* To attach; add as a supplement. [L *appendere.*]

ap•pend•age (ə-pĕn′dĭj) *n.* Something appended, as an attached organ or part.

ap•pen•dec•to•my (ăp′ən-dĕk′tə-mē) *n., pl.* **-mies.** *Surg.* Removal of the vermiform appendix.

ap•pen•di•ci•tis (ə-pĕn′də-sī′tĭs) *n.* Inflammation of the vermiform appendix.

ap•pen•dix (ə-pĕn′dĭks) *n., pl.* **-dixes** or **-dices** (-də-sēz′). **1.** A collection of supplementary material at the end of a book. **2.** The **vermiform appendix.** [L < *appendere,* APPEND.]

ap•per•tain (ăp′ər-tān′) *v.* To belong as a function or part.

ap•pe•tite (ăp′ə-tīt′) *n.* **1.** A desire for food or drink. **2.** Any physical craving or desire. [< L *appetītus* < *appetere,* to strive after.] **—ap′pe•ti′tive** (ap′ə-tī′tĭv, ə-pĕt′ə-tĭv) *adj.*

ap•pe•tiz•er (ăp′ə-tī′zər) *n.* A food or drink served before a meal to stimulate the appetite.

ap•pe•tiz•ing (ăp′ə-tī′zĭng) *adj.* Stimulating the appetite. **—ap′pe•tiz′ing•ly** *adv.*

appl. applied.

ap•plaud (ə-plôd′) *v.* To express approval (of) by clapping the hands. [L *applaudere,* to clap at.] **—ap•plaud′er** *n.*

ap•plause (ə-plôz′) *n.* Approval, esp. when shown by the clapping of hands.

ap•ple (ăp′əl) *n.* **1.** A firm, rounded, often red-skinned edible fruit. **2.** A tree bearing such fruit. [< OE *æppel.* See **abel-.**]

ap•ple•jack (ăp′əl-jăk′) *n.* Brandy distilled from fermented cider.

ap•ple-pol•ish (ăp′əl-pŏl′ĭsh) *v. Informal.* To seek favor by toadying. **—apple polisher.**

ap•ple•sauce (ăp′əl-sôs′) *n.* **1.** Stewed, sweetened apple pulp. **2.** *Slang.* Nonsense; foolishness; rubbish.

ap•pli•ance (ə-plī′əns) *n.* A device or instrument, esp. one operated by electricity and designed for household use. [< APPLY.]

ap•pli•ca•ble (ăp′lĭ-kə-bəl, ə-plĭk′ə-) *adj.* Capable of being applied; appropriate. **—ap′pli•ca•bil′i•ty** *n.* **—ap′pli•ca•bly** *adv.*

ap•pli•cant (ăp′lĭ-kənt) *n.* One who applies, as for a job.

ap•pli•ca•tion (ăp′lĭ-kā′shən) *n.* **1.** The act of applying. **2.** Anything that is applied, such as a cosmetic. **3. a.** A method of applying or using; specific use. **b.** The capacity of being usable; relevance. **4.** Close attention; diligence. **5. a.** A request, as for a job. **b.** The printed form upon which such a request is often made.

ap•pli•ca•tor (ăp′lĭ-kā′tər) *n.* An instrument for applying something, such as medicine.

ap•plied (ə-plīd′) *adj.* Put in practice; used: *applied physics.*

ap•pli•qué (ăp′lĭ-kā′) *n.* Decoration made by sewing or applying cut pieces of material to the surface of another. [F, pp of *appliquer,* to put on, apply.] **—ap′pli•qué′** *v.* **(-quéd, -quéing).**

ap•ply (ə-plī′) *v.* **-plied, -plying. 1.** To bring into contact with something; put on or upon. **2.** To adapt for a special use. **3.** To devote (oneself or one's efforts) to something. **4.** To be pertinent. **5.** To make a request, as for a job. [< OF *aplier* < L *applicāre,* to join to, apply.] **—ap•pli′er** *n.*

ap•pog•gia•tu•ra (ə-pŏj′ə-tŏŏr′ə) *n. Mus.* An embellishing note, usually one step above or below the note it precedes and indicated by a small note or special sign. [It.]

ap•point (ə-point′) *v.* **1.** To name for an office or position. **2.** To fix or set by authority. **3.** To furnish; equip: *a well-appointed room.* [< OF *(rendre) à point,* "(to bring) to a point."]

ap•point•ee (ə-poin′tē′) *n.* A person who is appointed to an office or position.

ap•point•ive (ə-poin′tĭv) *adj.* Pertaining to or filled by appointment: *an appointive office.*

ap•point•ment (ə-point′mənt) *n.* **1.** The act of appointing. **2.** The office or position to which a person has been appointed. **3.** An arrangement to do something or meet someone. **4. appointments.** Fittings or equipment.

Ap•po•mat•tox (ăp′ə-măt′əks). The town in Virginia where Lee surrendered to Grant (April 9, 1865).

ap•por•tion (ə-pôr′shən, ə-pōr′-) *v.* To divide and assign according to some plan or proportion; allot. [OF *apportionner.*] **—ap•por′tion•ment** *n.*

ap•pose (ă-pōz′) *v.* **-posed, -posing. 1.** To apply (one thing) to another. **2.** To arrange (things) near to each other or side by side. [Backformation < APPOSITION.]

ap•po•site (ăp′ə-zĭt) *adj.* Suitable; appropriate. **—ap'po•site•ly** *adv.* **—ap'po•site•ness** *n.*

ap•po•si•tion (ăp'ə-zĭsh'ən) *n.* **1.** *Gram.* A construction in which a noun or noun phrase is placed with another as an explanatory equivalent, as in *Copley, the famous painter, was born in Boston.* **2.** A placing side by side or next to each other. [< L *appōnere* (pp *appositus*), to place near to.] **—ap•pos'i•tive** *adj.* & *n.*

ap•praise (ə-prāz') *v.* **-praised, -praising.** To evaluate, esp. in an official capacity. [< LL *appretiāre,* to set a value on.] **—ap•prais'al** *n.* **—ap•prais'er** *n.*

ap•pre•cia•ble (ə-prē'shə-bəl) *adj.* Capable of being noticed or measured; noticeable. **—ap•pre'cia•bly** *adv.*

ap•pre•ci•ate (ə-prē'shē-āt') *v.* **-ated, -ating. 1.** To estimate the quality or value of. **2.** To value highly. **3.** To be fully aware of; realize. **4.** To be thankful for. **5.** To raise or go up in value or price. [LL *appretiāre,* to set a value on] **—ap•pre'ci•a'tor** (-ā'tər) *n.*

ap•pre•ci•a•tion (ə-prē'shē-ā'shən) *n.* **1.** Gratefulness; gratitude. **2.** Awareness or delicate perception, esp. of aesthetic qualities.

ap•pre•cia•tive (ə-prē'shə-tĭv, -shē-ā'tĭv) *adj.* Capable of or showing appreciation.

ap•pre•hend (ăp'rĭ-hĕnd') *v.* **1.** To arrest. **2.** To grasp mentally; understand. **3.** To anticipate with anxiety. [< L *apprehendere,* to seize.]

ap•pre•hen•sion (ăp'rĭ-hĕn'shən) *n.* **1.** An uneasy anticipation of the future; dread. **2.** An arrest. **3.** The ability to understand.

ap•pre•hen•sive (ăp'rĭ-hĕn'sĭv) *adj.* Anxious about the future; uneasy. **—ap'pre•hen'sive•ly** *adv.* **—ap'pre•hen'sive•ness** *n.*

ap•pren•tice (ə-prĕn'tĭs) *n.* **1.** One who is learning a trade under a skilled craftsman. **2.** Any beginner. *—v.* **-ticed, -ticing.** To place or take on as an apprentice. [< OF *aprendre,* to learn.] **—ap•pren'tice•ship'** *n.*

ap•prise (ə-prīz') *v.* **-prised, -prising.** Also **ap•prize.** To cause to know; inform. [< F *apprendre,* to cause to learn.]

ap•proach (ə-prōch') *v.* **1.** To come near or nearer (to). **2.** To come close to in appearance; approximate. **3.** To make a proposal to; make overtures to. *—n.* **1.** The act of coming near. **2.** A fairly close resemblance; an approximation. **3.** A way of reaching; an access. **4.** Often **approaches.** An advance or overture made by one person to another. [< LL *appropiāre,* to go nearer to.] **—ap•proach'a•bil'i•ty** *n.* **—ap•proach'a•ble** *adj.*

ap•pro•ba•tion (ăp'rə-bā'shən) *n.* Approval; sanction.

ap•pro•pri•ate (ə-prō'prē-ĭt) *adj.* Suitable; proper. *—v.* (ə-prō'prē-āt') **-ated, -ating. 1.** To set apart for a specific use. **2.** To take possession of. [< LL *appropriāre,* to make one's own.] **—ap•pro'pri•ate•ly** *adv.* **—ap•pro'pri•ate•ness** *n.* **—ap•pro'pri•a'tor** *n.*

ap•pro•pri•a•tion (ə-prō'prē-ā'shən) *n.* **1.** The act of appropriating to oneself or to a specific use. **2.** Public funds set aside for a specific purpose.

ap•prov•al (ə-prōō'vəl) *n.* **1.** The act of approving. **2.** An official approbation; a sanction. **—on approval.** For examination by a potential customer without obligation to buy.

ap•prove (ə-prōōv') *v.* **-proved, -proving. 1.** To have a favorable opinion (of); regard favorably. **2.** To consent to. [< L *approbāre,* to make good.] **—ap•prov'ing•ly** *adv.*

approx. approximate; approximately.

ap•prox•i•mate (ə-prŏk'sə-mĭt) *adj.* **1.** Almost exact or correct. **2.** Very similar. **3.** Close together. *—v.* (ə-prŏk'sə-māt') **-mated, -mating.** To come close to; be nearly the same as. [< LL *approximāre,* to come near to.] **—ap•prox'i•mate•ly** *adv.* **—ap•prox'i•ma'tion** *n.*

appt. appoint; appointed; appointment.

ap•pur•te•nance (ə-pûrt'n-əns) *n.* Something added to another, more important thing; an accessory. [< LL *appertinēre,* appertain.]

Apr. April.

a•pri•cot (ā'prĭ-kŏt', ăp'rĭ-) *n.* **1.** A yellow-orange peachlike fruit. **2.** A tree bearing such fruit. [< Ar *al-birqūq,* "the apricot" < LGk *praikokion.*]

A•pril (ā'prəl) *n.* The 4th month of the year. April has 30 days. [< L *aprīlis,* perh "month of Venus."]

a pri•o•ri (ä prē-ōr'ē, ā prī-ōr'ī'). **1.** From a known or assumed cause to a necessarily related effect; deductive. **2.** Based on theory rather than on experience. [L, "from the previous (causes or hypotheses)."]

a•pron (ā'prən, ā'pərn) *n.* **1.** A garment worn over the front of the body to protect one's clothes. **2.** Anything resembling an apron in appearance or function. **3.** The paved strip around airport hangars and terminal buildings. **4.** The part of a stage in a theater extending in front of the curtain. **5.** A continuous conveyor belt. [ME *(an) apron,* orig *(a) napron.*]

ap•ro•pos (ăp'rə-pō') *adj.* Pertinent; opportune. *—adv.* Pertinently. **—apropos of.** With reference to. [F *à propos,* "to the purpose."]

apse (ăps) *n.* A semicircular or polygonal, usually domed, projection of a church. [ML *apsis.*]

apt (ăpt) *adj.* **1.** Exactly suitable; appropriate. **2.** Likely. **3.** Inclined; given. **4.** Quick to learn or understand. [< L *aptus,* pp of *apere,* to fasten.] **—apt'ly** *adv.* **—apt'ness** *n.*

apt. apartment.

ap•ti•tude (ăp'tə-t/y/ōōd') *n.* **1.** A natural talent; inclination. **2.** Quickness in learning. [< LL *aptitūdō,* fitness < *aptus,* APT.]

aq•ua (ăk'wə, ä'kwə) *n., pl.* **aquae** (ăk'wē, ä'kwī') or **-uas. 1.** Water. **2.** Light bluish green. [L, water.] **—aq'ua** *adj.*

aq•ua•ma•rine (ăk'wə-mə-rēn', ä'kwə-) *n.* **1.** A transparent blue-green variety of beryl, used as a gemstone. **2.** Pale blue to light greenish blue.

aq•ua•naut (ăk'wə-nôt', ä'kwə-) *n.* A person trained to live in underwater installations and participate in scientific research.

aq•ua•plane (ăk'wə-plān', ä'kwə-) *n.* A board on which one rides in a standing position while it is towed by a motorboat. **—aq'ua•plane'** *v.* **(-planed, -planing).**

aqua re•gi•a (rē'jē-ə). A corrosive, fuming mixture of hydrochloric and nitric acids, capable of dissolving platinum and gold.

a•quar•i•um (ə-kwâr'ē-əm) *n., pl.* **-ums** or **-ia** (-ē-ə). **1.** A water-filled enclosure in which living aquatic animals and plants are kept. **2.** A place for exhibiting such animals and plants. [< L *aquārius,* of water.]

A•quar•i•us (ə-kwâr'ē-əs) *n.* **1.** A constellation in the equatorial region of the S Hemisphere. **2.** The 11th sign of the zodiac.

a•quat•ic (ə-kwŏt'ĭk, ə-kwăt'-) *adj.* **1.** Living or growing in or on water. **2.** Taking place in or on water.

aqua vi•tae (vī'tē). **1.** Alcohol. **2.** Whiskey, brandy, or other strong liquor.

aq•ue•duct (ăk'wə-dŭkt') *n.* **1.** A conduit designed to transport water from a remote source, usually by gravity. **2.** An elevated structure supporting a conduit or canal passing over a river or low ground. [L *aquae ductus.*]

a•que•ous (ā'kwē-əs, ăk'wē-) *adj.* Of, similar to, containing, or dissolved in water; watery. [< L *aqua,* AQUA.]

aqueous humor. A clear, lymphlike fluid in the chamber of the eye between the cornea and the lens.

Aq•ui•la (ăk'wə-lə) *n.* A constellation in the N Hemisphere and the Milky Way. [L *aquila,* EAGLE.]

aq•ui•line (ăk'wə-līn', -lĭn) *adj.* **1.** Of or similar to an eagle. **2.** Resembling an eagle's beak: *an aquiline nose.* [< L *aquila,* eagle.]

A•qui•nas (ə-kwī'nəs), **Saint Thomas.** 1225–1274. Italian philosopher and theologian.

ar. Variant of **are**[2].

-ar. *comb. form.* Like, pertaining to, or of the nature of: **titular.**

Ar argon.

ar. arrival; arrive.

A/R account receivable.

Ar•ab (ăr'əb) *n.* **1.** A native of Arabia. **2.** Any of a Semitic people of the Near East and North Africa. [< Ar *'arab.*] **—Ar'ab** *adj.*

ar•a•besque (ăr'ə-bĕsk') *n.* An ornate design of intertwined floral, foliate, and geometric figures. [< It *arabesco,* "done in the Arabic fashion."]

A•ra•bi•a (ə-rā'bē-ə). A peninsula of SW Asia between the Red Sea and the Persian Gulf. **—A•ra'bi•an** *adj.* & *n.*

Arabian Sea. The part of the Indian Ocean bounded by E Africa, Arabia, and W India.

Ar•a•bic (ăr'ə-bĭk) *adj.* Of or pertaining to Arabia, the Arabs, their language, or their culture. *—n.* **1.** The SW Semitic language of the Arabs. **2.** The literary language of the Koran, as employed in most formal usage in Arabic-speaking countries.

Arabic numerals. The numerical symbols 1,2,3,4,5,6,7,8,9, and 0.

ar•a•ble (ăr'ə-bəl) *adj.* Fit for cultivation. [< L *arāre,* to plow.]

a•rach•nid (ə-răk'nĭd) *n.* One of a group of eight-legged organisms including the spiders, scorpions, ticks, and mites. [< Gk *arakhnē,* spider.]

Ar•a•ma•ic (ăr'ə-mā'ĭk) *n.* A NW Semitic language. **—Ar'a•ma'ic** *adj.*

Ar•a•wak (ăr'ə-wäk') *n., pl.* **-wak** or **-waks. 1.** A member of an Arawakan-speaking Indian people now living chiefly in certain regions of the Guianas. **2.** Their language.

Ar•a•wa•kan (ăr'ə-wä'kən) *n., pl.* **-kan** or **-kans. 1.** A South American Indian language family spoken in a wide area comprising the Amazon basin in Brazil, Venezuela, Colombia, the Guianas, Peru, Bolivia, and Paraguay. **2.** An Indian or an Indian people of this linguistic stock. **—Ar'a•wa'kan** *adj.*

ar•ba•lest (är'bə-lĭst) *n.* Also **ar•be•list.** A medieval missile launcher designed on the crossbow principle. [< L *arcus,* bow + BALLISTA.]

ar•bi•ter (är'bə-tər) *n.* One who has the power to judge or decide. [< L *arbiter,* judge.]

ar•bit•ra•ment (är-bĭt'rə-mənt) *n.* **1.** The act of arbitrating. **2.** The judgment of an arbiter.

ar•bi•trar•y (är'bə-trĕr'ē) *adj.* **1.** Determined by whim or caprice. **2.** Based on individual judgment. **3.** Not limited by law; despotic. [< L *arbiter,* ARBITER.] **—ar'bi•trar'i•ly** (-ə-lē) *adv.* **—ar'bi•trar'i•ness** *n.*

ar•bi•trate (är'bə-trāt') *v.* **-trated, -trating. 1.** To judge or decide as an arbitrator. **2.** To submit (a dispute) to settlement by an arbitrator.

3. To serve as an arbitrator or arbiter. —**ar'bi•tra'tion** *n.*

ar•bi•tra•tor (är'bə-trā'tər) *n.* A person chosen to settle the issue between parties engaged in a dispute.

ar•bor[1] (är'bər) *n.* Also *chiefly Brit.* **ar•bour.** A shady garden shelter or bower. [< OF *(h)erbier,* herbage, plot of grass.]

ar•bor[2] (är'bər) *n.* **1.** An axis or shaft supporting a rotating part on a lathe. **2.** A bar for supporting cutting tools. **3.** A spindle of a wheel, as in watches and clocks. [L *arbor,* tree.]

ar•bo•re•al (är-bôr'ē-əl, är-bōr'-) *adj.* **1.** Pertaining to or resembling a tree. **2.** Living in trees.

ar•bo•re•tum (är'bə-rē'təm) *n., pl.* **-tums** or **-ta** (-tə). A place for the study and exhibition of trees.

ar•bor•vi•tae (är'bər-vī'tē) *n.* **1.** Any of several evergreen trees with small, scalelike leaves. **2.** *Anat.* The white matter of the cerebellum, in cross section having the appearance of a tree.

ar•bu•tus (är-byo͞o'təs) *n.* A trailing plant with evergreen leaves and pink or white flowers. [< L *arbūtus,* strawberry tree.]

arc (ärk) *n.* **1.** Anything shaped like a bow, curve, or arch. **2.** A segment of a curve. **3.** A luminous discharge of electric current crossing a gap between two electrodes. —*v.* **arced** or **arcked, arcing** or **arcking.** To form an arc. [< L *arcus,* bow, arc.]

A.R.C. American Red Cross.

ar•cade (är-kād') *n.* **1.** A series of arches supported by columns. **2.** A roofed passageway, esp. one with shops on either side. [< It *arcata* < *arco,* arch.]

ar•cane (är-kān') *adj.* Known only by those having secret knowledge; esoteric. [L *arcānus,* closed, secret.]

arch[1] (ärch) *n.* **1.** A curved structural device, esp. of masonry, forming the upper edge of an opening or a support, as in a bridge or doorway. **2.** Any similar structure, as a monument. **3.** Anything curved like an arch. —*v.* **1.** To supply with an arch. **2.** To form or cause to form an arch. [< L *arcus,* arc.] —**arched** (ärcht) *adj.*

arch[2] (ärch) *adj.* **1.** Chief; principal. **2.** Mischievous; roguish: *an arch glance.* —**arch'ly** *adv.* —**arch'ness** *n.*

arch–. *comb. form.* **1.** Highest rank or chief status. **2.** Ultimate of a kind. [< Gk *arkhos,* chief, ruler.]

–arch. *comb. form.* A ruler: **matriarch.** [< Gk *arkhos,* ruler.]

arch. architect; architectural; architecture.

archaeol. archaeology.

ar•chae•ol•o•gy, ar•che•ol•o•gy (är'kē-ŏl'ə-jē) *n.* The systematic recovery and scientific study of material evidence of human life and culture in past ages. [< LL *archaeologia,* "the study of antiquity."] —**ar'chae•o•log'i•cal** (-ə-lŏj'ĭ-kəl), **ar'chae•o•log'ic** *adj.* —**ar'chae•o•log'i•cal•ly** *adv.* —**ar'chae•ol'o•gist** *n.*

Ar•chae•o•zo•ic. Variant of **Archeozoic.**

ar•cha•ic (är-kā'ĭk) *adj.* Also **ar•cha•i•cal** (-ĭ-kəl). **1.** Belonging to a much earlier time. **2.** No longer current or applicable. **3.** Designating words and language that were once common, but are now used chiefly to suggest an earlier style or period. [< Gk *arkhaios,* ancient < *arkhē,* beginning.] —**ar•cha'i•cal•ly** *adv.*

ar•cha•ism (är'kē-ĭz'əm, är'kā-) *n.* An archaic word, phrase, idiom, or expression. —**ar'cha•ist** *n.* —**ar'cha•is'tic** (-ĭs'tĭk) *adj.*

arch•an•gel (ärk'ān'jəl) *n.* A celestial being next in rank above an angel.

arch•bish•op (ärch-bĭsh'əp) *n.* A bishop of the highest rank.

arch•dea•con (ärch-dē'kən) *n.* A church official, chiefly in the Anglican Church, in charge of temporal and other affairs in a diocese.

arch•di•o•cese (ärch-dī'ə-sĭs, -sēs', -sēz') *n.* A diocese under an archbishop's jurisdiction.

arch•duke (ärch-d/y/o͞ok') *n.* In certain royal families, esp. that of imperial Austria, a prince. —**arch•duch'ess** *fem.n.*

arch•en•e•my (ärch-ĕn'ə-mē) *n., pl.* **-mies. 1.** A chief enemy. **2.** Satan.

ar•che•ol•o•gy. Variant of **archaeology.**

Ar•che•o•zo•ic (är'kē-ə-zō'ĭk) *adj.* Also **Ar•chae•o•zo•ic.** Pertaining to the earlier of two generally arbitrary divisions of the Precambrian era. —*n.* The Archeozoic era.

arch•er (är'chər) *n.* **1.** One who shoots with a bow and arrow. **2. Archer.** Sagittarius. [< LL *arcuarius,* "of a bow."]

arch•er•y (är'chər-ē) *n.* The art, sport, or skill of shooting with a bow and arrows.

ar•che•type (är'kə-tīp') *n.* An original model after which other similar things are patterned. [< Gk *arkhetupos,* first molded as a pattern, exemplary.] —**ar'che•typ'al** (-tī'pəl), **ar'che•typ'ic** (-tĭp'ĭk), **ar'che•typ'i•cal** *adj.*

arch•fiend (ärch-fēnd') *n.* **1.** A chief fiend. **2.** Satan.

ar•chi•e•pis•co•pal (är'kē-ĭ-pĭs'kə-pəl) *adj.* Of or pertaining to an archbishop.

ar•chi•man•drite (är'kə-măn'drīt') *n. E.O.Ch.* **1.** A cleric ranking below a bishop. **2.** The head of a monastery and the equivalent of a Western abbot.

Ar•chi•me•des (är'kə-mē'dēz). 287?–212 B.C. Greek mathematician. —**Ar'chi•me'de•an** (är'-kə-mē'dē-ən, -mĭ-) *adj.*

ar•chi•pel•a•go (är'kə-pĕl'ə-gō') *n., pl.* **-goes** or **-gos. 1.** A large group of islands. **2.** A sea containing a large group of islands. [< It *Arcipelago,* "the Chief Sea."]

archit. architecture.

ar•chi•tect (är'kə-tĕkt') *n.* **1.** One who designs and supervises the construction of buildings or other large structures. **2.** Any planner. [< Gk *arkhitektōn,* master builder.]

ar•chi•tec•ton•ics (är'kə-tĕk-tŏn'ĭks) *n. (takes sing. v.).* **1.** The science of architecture. **2.** Structural design, as in a musical work. —**ar'-chi•tec•ton'ic** *adj.*

ar•chi•tec•ture (är'kə-tĕk'chər) *n.* **1.** The art and science of designing and erecting buildings. **2.** A style and method of design and construction: *Byzantine architecture.* —**ar'chi•tec'tur•al** *adj.* —**ar'chi•tec'tur•al•ly** *adv.*

ar•chi•trave (är'kə-trāv') *n.* The lowermost part of an entablature, resting directly on top of a column in classical architecture. [< OIt, "chief beam."]

ar•chives (är'kīvz') *pl.n.* **1.** Public records pertaining to an organization or institution. **2.** A place in which such records are preserved. [< Gk *arkheia,* public records, archives.]

ar•chi•vist (är'kə-vĭst, är'kī'-) *n.* One in charge of archives.

ar•chon (är'kŏn', -kən) *n.* One of the 9 principal magistrates of ancient Athens. [< Gk *arkhōn,* "ruler."] —**ar'chon•ship'** *n.*

arch•way (ärch'wā') *n.* **1.** A passageway under an arch. **2.** An arch covering a passageway.

–archy. *comb. form.* Rule or government: **oligarchy.**

arcked (ärkt). Alternate *p.t.* & *p.p.* of **arc.**

arcking (är'kĭng). Alternate *pres.p.* of **arc.**

arc lamp. An electric lamp in which a current traverses a gas between two incandescent electrodes.

arc•tic (ärk'tĭk, är'tĭk) *adj.* **1.** Of, near, or characteristic of the North Pole or polar regions; frigid. **2. Arctic.** Of or relating to a geographic area extending from the North Pole to the northern timberline. —*n.* A warm, waterproof overshoe. [< Gk *arktikos.*]

Arctic Circle. A parallel of latitude at 66° 33′ N, marking the limit of the N Frigid Zone.

Arctic Ocean. The polar ocean between North America and Eurasia.

Arc•tu•rus (ärk-t/y/o͝or'əs) *n.* The brightest star in the constellation Boötes.

ar•cu•ate (är'kyo͞o-ĭt, -āt') *adj.* Also **ar•cu•at•ed** (-ā'tĭd). Having the form of a bow; curved; arched. [< L *arcus,* ARC.]

–ard, –art. *comb. form.* One who does something to excess: **drunkard.**

ar•den•cy (är'dən-sē) *n.* Strength or intensity of feeling; ardor.

ar•dent (är'dənt) *adj.* **1. a.** Characterized by warmth of passion or desire. **b.** Characterized by strong enthusiasm; zealous. **2.** Glowing; flashing: *ardent eyes.* **3.** Hot as fire; burning. [< L *ardēre,* to burn.] —**ar'dent•ly** *adv.*

ar•dor (är'dər) *n.* Also *Brit.* **ar•dour. 1. a.** Great intensity, as of passion or desire. **b.** Strong enthusiasm; zeal. **2.** Intense heat, as of fire. [< L *ardēre,* to burn.]

ar•du•ous (är'jo͞o-əs) *adj.* Demanding great effort or labor; strenuous; difficult. [L *arduus,* high, steep.] —**ar'du•ous•ly** *adv.* —**ar'du•ous•ness** *n.*

are[1] (är). 2nd person sing. and present tense indicative pl. of **be.** [< OE *earon.*]

are[2] (âr, är) *n.* Also **ar** (är). A metric unit of area equal to 100 square meters.

ar•e•a (âr'ē-ə) *n.* **1.** A flat, open surface or space. **2.** Any specific region, as of a building, city, or geographic entity. **3.** The range or scope of anything. **4.** The measure of a planar region or of the surface of a solid. [L *ārea,* open field.]

Area Code. Also **area code.** A number, often with three digits, assigned to a telephone area, as in the U.S. and Canada, used in calling from one area to another.

ar•e•a•way (âr'ē-ə-wā') *n.* A small sunken area allowing access or light and air to a basement.

a•re•na (ə-rē'nə) *n.* **1.** The area in the center of an ancient Roman amphitheater where contests were held. **2.** A sphere of conflict, activity, etc. [L *(h)arēna,* sand, arena covered with sand.]

aren't (ärnt, är'ənt). Contraction of *are not.* See Usage note at **ain't.**

Ar•e•op•a•gus (ăr'ē-ŏp'ə-gəs) *n.* The highest council of ancient Athens.

Ar•es (âr'ēz). Greek god of war.

ar•gent (är'jənt) *n.* Silver. [< L *argentum.*] —**ar'gent** *adj.*

Ar•gen•ti•na (är'jən-tē'nə). A republic of SE South America. Pop. 22,252,000. Cap. Buenos Aires. —**Ar'gen•tine', Ar•gen•tin'e•an** *adj.* & *n.*

Ar•go (är'gō) *n.* A constellation in the S Hemisphere.

ar•gon (är'gŏn') *n. Symbol* **Ar** A colorless, odorless, inert gaseous element constituting approx. 1% of the earth's atmosphere, used in electric lamps, fluorescent tubes, and radio vacuum tubes. Atomic number 18, atomic weight 39.94. [< Gk *argos,* inert, idle.]

ar•go•sy (är'gə-sē) *n., pl.* **-sies. 1.** A large merchant ship. **2.** A fleet of such ships. [< It

Ragusa, former name of Dubrovnik, Yugoslavia.]

ar•got (är'gō, -gət) *n.* A specialized vocabulary used by a particular group, esp. the jargon of the underworld. [F.]

ar•gue (är'gyōō) *v.* **-gued, -guing. 1.** To put forth reasons for or against something. **2.** To maintain in argument; contend. **3.** To dispute; quarrel. **4.** To persuade or influence, as by presenting reasons. [< L *arguere,* to make clear, assert.] **—ar'gu•a•ble** *adj.*

ar•gu•ment (är'gyə-mənt) *n.* **1. a.** A discussion in which disagreement is expressed; debate. **b.** A quarrel. **2.** A course of reasoning aimed at demonstrating the truth or falsehood of something. [< L *argūmentum* < *arguere,* ARGUE.]

ar•gu•men•ta•tion (är'gyə-mĕn-tā'shən) *n.* The presentation and elaboration of an argument; debate.

ar•gu•men•ta•tive (är'gyə-mĕn'tə-tĭv) *adj.* Given to arguing; disputatious.

ar•gyle (är'gīl') *n.* A knitted design of vari-colored diamonds crossed by contrasting diagonal lines. [< the Scottish clan Campbell of *Argyle.*]

a•ri•a (ä'rē-ə) *n.* A solo vocal piece with instrumental accompaniment, as in an opera. [It, melody, "air."]

-arian. *comb. form.* **1.** Sect: **Unitarian. 2.** A belief: **vegetarian.**

ar•id (ăr'ĭd) *adj.* **1.** Lacking moisture; parched; barren. **2.** Lacking interest; dull. [< L *āridus.*] **—a•rid'i•ty** (ə-rĭd'ə-tē) *n.*

Ar•ies (âr'ēz, âr'ē-ēz') *n.* **1.** A constellation in the N Hemisphere. **2.** The 1st sign of the zodiac. [L *ariēs,* ram.]

a•right (ə-rīt') *adv.* Properly; correctly.

a•rise (ə-rīz') *v.* **arose, arisen** (ə-rĭz'ən), **arising. 1.** To get up, as from a chair. **2.** To move upward. **3.** To come into being. **4.** To result or issue (with *from*). [< OE *ārīsan.*]

ar•is•toc•ra•cy (ăr'ĭs-tŏk'rə-sē) *n., pl.* **-cies. 1.** A hereditary ruling class or nobility. **2.** Government by such a class. **3.** Any group or class considered to be superior. [< Gk *aristokratia,* "rule by the best (citizens)."] **—a•ris'to•crat'** (ə-rĭs'tə-krăt', ăr'ĭs-tə-) *n.* **—a•ris'to•crat'ic** *adj.* **—a•ris'to•crat'i•cal•ly** *adv.*

Ar•is•toph•a•nes (ăr'ĭs-tŏf'ə-nēz'). 448?–380? B.C. Athenian comic poet.

Ar•is•tot•le (ăr'ĭs-tŏt'l). 384–322 B.C. Greek philosopher.

a•rith•me•tic (ə-rĭth'mə-tĭk) *n.* **1.** The mathematics of integers under addition, subtraction, multiplication, division, involution, and evolution. **2.** Computation or problem solving involving real numbers and the arithmetic operations. [< Gk *arithmētikē (tekhnē),* "(the art) of counting."] **—ar'ith•met'ic** (ăr'ĭth-mĕt'ĭk), **ar'ith•met'i•cal** (-ĭ-kəl) *adj.* **—ar'ith•met'i•cal•ly** *adv.*

Argentina

arithmetic mean. The number obtained by dividing the sum of a set of quantities by the number of quantities in the set; average.

-arium. *comb. form.* A place or housing for: **planetarium.**

Ar•i•zo•na (ăr'ə-zō'nə). A SW state of the U.S. Pop. 1,772,000. Cap. Phoenix. **—Ar'i•zo'nan** *adj.* & *n.*

ark (ärk) *n.* **1.** Often **Ark.** The ancient Hebrew chest containing the Ten Commandments on tablets. **2.** The boat built by Noah for the Flood. [< Gmc **ark-* < L *arca,* chest.]

Ar•kan•sas (är'kən-sô'). A S state of the U.S. Pop. 1,923,000. Cap. Little Rock. **—Ar•kan'san** (-kăn'zən) *adj.* & *n.*

Arkansas River (är'kən-sô', är-kăn'zəs). A river of the south-central U.S.

arm¹ (ärm) *n.* **1.** An upper limb of the human body. **2.** A part similar to an arm. **3.** A projecting support on a chair or sofa. **4.** Power; authority: *the arm of the law.* **—with open arms.** Cordially. [< OE *earm* < Gmc **armaz.*]

arm² (ärm) *n.* **1.** A weapon. **2.** A branch of a military force, such as the infantry. *—v.* **1.** To equip with weapons. **2.** To prepare for or as if for war. [< ARMS.] **—armed** *adj.*

ar•ma•da (är-mä'də, -mā'də) *n.* A fleet of warships. [Span < L *armāta,* army, fleet.]

ar•ma•dil•lo (är'mə-dĭl'ō) *n., pl.* **-los.** A burrowing tropical American mammal having a covering of armorlike bony plates. [Span, dim of *armado,* armored.]

Ar•ma•ged•don (är'mə-gĕd'n) *n.* In the Bible, the scene of a final battle between the forces of good and evil, to occur at the end of the world. [< Heb *har megiddōn,* the mountain region of *Megiddo.*]

ar•ma•ment (är'mə-mənt) *n.* **1.** The weapons and supplies of a military unit. **2.** Often **armaments.** All the military forces and war equipment of a country. **3.** The process of arming for war. [< L *armāmenta,* implements < *arma,* ARMS.]

ar•ma•ture (är'mə-chŏŏr') *n.* **1. a.** The rotating part of a dynamo, consisting of copper wire wound around an iron core. **b.** The moving part of a device such as a relay, buzzer, or loud-speaker. **c.** A piece of soft iron connecting the poles of a magnet. **2.** A protective covering; armor. [L *armātūra,* equipment.]

arm•chair (ärm'châr') *n.* A chair with sides for supporting the arms.

armed forces. The military forces of a country.

Ar•me•ni•a (är-mē'nē-ə, -mēn'yə). An ancient country of W Asia, now divided among the Soviet Union, Turkey, and Iran.

Ar•me•ni•an (är-mē'nē-ən, -mēn'yən) *n.* **1.** A native or inhabitant of Armenia. **2.** The Indo-European language of the Armenians. **—Ar•me'ni•an** *adj.*

Armenian Soviet Socialist Republic. A republic of the Soviet Union. Pop. 2,493,000. Cap. Yerevan.

ar•mi•stice (är'mə-stĭs) *n.* A temporary cessation of hostilities by mutual consent; truce. [F.]

arm•let (ärm'lĭt) *n.* A band worn on the arm for ornament or identification.

ar•mor (är'mər) *n.* Also *Brit.* **ar•mour. 1.** A defensive covering, such as chain mail, worn to protect the body against weapons. **2.** Any tough protective covering, such as the metallic plates on tanks. **3.** Any safeguard. **4.** The armored vehicles of an army. [< L *armāre,* to arm.] **—ar'mored** *adj.*

ar•mo•ri•al (är-môr'ē-əl, är-môr'-) *adj.* Of or pertaining to heraldic arms.

ar•mor•y (är'mər-ē) *n., pl.* **-ies. 1.** An arsenal. **2.** An arms factory.

arm•pit (ärm'pĭt') *n.* The hollow under the arm at the shoulder.

arm•rest (ärm'rĕst') *n.* A support for the arm, as on a car door.

arms (ärmz) *pl.n.* **1.** Weapons. **2.** Warfare. **3.** Heraldic bearings. [< L *arma,* weapons, tools.]

ar•my (är'mē) *n., pl.* **-mies. 1.** A large body of men organized for warfare. **2.** The entire military land forces of a country. **3.** Any large group of people organized for a specific cause. **4.** A multitude, as of people or animals. [< L *armāre,* to arm.]

ar•ni•ca (är'nĭ-kə) *n.* **1.** A plant having yellow, daisylike flowers. **2.** A tincture of these flowers. [ML.]

Ar•nold (är'nəld). **1. Benedict.** 1741–1801. American general; attempted to surrender West Point to the British (1780). **2. Matthew.** 1822–1888. English poet and critic.

a•ro•ma (ə-rō'mə) *n.* A pleasant, often spicy, characteristic odor. [< Gk *arōma,* aromatic spice.] **—ar'o•mat'ic** (ăr'ə-măt'ĭk) *adj.*

a•rose (ə-rōz'). *p.t.* of **arise.**

a•round (ə-round') *adv.* **1.** On or to all sides or in all directions. **2.** In a circle or circular motion. **3.** In or toward the opposite direction. **4.** From one place to another: *wander around.* **5.** Close at hand; nearby. *—prep.* **1.** On all sides of. **2.** So as to enclose, surround, or envelop. **3.** About the circumference of; encircling. **4.** About the central point of. **5.** In or to various places within or near. **6.** On or to the farther side of: *the house around the corner.* **7.** *Informal.* Approximately at. [< A- (on) + ROUND (noun).]

a•rouse (ə-rouz') *v.* **aroused, arousing. 1.** To awaken from or as if from sleep. **2.** To stir up; excite; stimulate. **—a•rous'al** *n.*

ar•peg•gi•o (är-pĕj'ē-ō', -pĕj'ō) *n., pl.* **-os.** The playing of the notes of a chord in rapid succession rather than simultaneously. [It, "chord played as on a harp."]

arr. arrival; arrive; arrived.

ar•raign (ə-rān') *v.* **1.** To call before a court to answer to an indictment. **2.** To call to account; accuse. [< VL **adrationāre,* "to call to account."] **—ar•raign'ment** *n.*

ar•range (ə-rānj') *v.* **-ranged, -ranging. 1.** To put into a deliberate order or relation. **2.** To agree about; settle. **3.** To reset (music) for other instruments or voices. [< OF *arangier.*] **—ar•range'ment** *n.* **—ar•rang'er** *n.*

ar•rant (ăr'ənt) *adj.* Unmitigated: *an arrant thief.*

ar•ras (ăr'əs) *n.* **1.** A tapestry. **2.** A wall hanging, esp. of tapestry. [< NF *Arras,* city in N France.]

ar•ray (ə-rā') *v.* **1.** To arrange or draw up, as troops. **2.** To deck in finery; adorn. *—n.* **1.** An orderly arrangement of objects, troops, etc. **2.** An impressive collection. **3.** Splendid attire; finery. [< VL **arrēdāre,* to arrange.]

ar•rear (ə-rîr') *n.* **1.** Often **arrears.** An overdue debt or unfulfilled obligation. **2.** Often **arrears.** The state of being behind in fulfilling obligations or payments: *in arrears.* [< OF *arriere,* behind.]

ar•rest (ə-rĕst′) *v.* **1.** To stop or check. **2.** To seize and hold by legal authority. *—n.* The act of arresting or state of being arrested. **—under arrest.** Detained in legal custody. [< VL **arrestāre,* to cause to stop.] **—ar•rest′er** *n.*

ar•rest•ing (ə-rĕs′tĭng) *adj.* Attracting and holding the attention.

ar•ri•val (ə-rī′vəl) *n.* **1.** The act of arriving. **2.** A person or thing that arrives or has arrived.

ar•rive (ə-rīv′) *v.* **-rived, -riving.** **1.** To reach a destination. **2.** To come at last: *The day of crisis has arrived.* **3.** To achieve success or recognition. [< VL **arripāre,* to land, come to shore.] **—ar•riv′er** *n.*

ar•ro•gant (ăr′ə-gənt) *adj.* Overbearingly proud; haughty. [< L *arrogāre,* ARROGATE.] **—ar′ro•gance** *n.* **—ar′ro•gant•ly** *adv.*

ar•ro•gate (ăr′ə-gāt′) *v.* **-gated, -gating.** To appropriate or claim without right. [L *arrogāre,* to claim for oneself.] **—ar′ro•ga′tion** *n.* **—ar′ro•ga′tive** (-gā′tĭv) *adj.*

ar•row (ăr′ō) *n.* **1.** A straight, thin shaft, shot from a bow and usually having a pointed head and flight-stabilizing feathers at the end. **2.** A symbol shaped like an arrow, used to indicate direction. [< OE *arwe, earh.* See **arkw-.**]

ar•row•head (ăr′ō-hĕd′) *n.* **1.** The striking tip of an arrow. **2.** A marsh plant having arrowhead-shaped leaves.

ar•row•root (ăr′ō-ro͞ot′, -ro͝ot′) *n.* An edible starch made from the root of a tropical American plant.

ar•roy•o (ə-roi′ō) *n., pl.* **-os.** A deep gully cut by an intermittent stream; a dry gulch. [< L *arrugia,* mine shaft.]

ar•se•nal (är′sə-nəl) *n.* **1.** A place for the storing, making, or repairing of munitions. **2.** A stock of weapons. [It *arsenale,* orig naval dockyard.]

ar•se•nate (är′sə-nĭt, -nāt′) *n.* A salt or ester of arsenic acid.

ar•se•nic (är′sə-nĭk) *n.* **1.** *Symbol* **As** A highly poisonous metallic element used in insecticides, weed killers, solid-state devices, and various alloys. Atomic number 33, atomic weight 74.922. **2. Arsenic trioxide.** *—adj.* **ar•sen•ic** (är-sĕn′ĭk). Of or containing arsenic. [< Gk *arsenikon,* yellow orpiment.]

arsenic trioxide. A poisonous white compound, As_2O_3, used in insecticides, rat poison, and weed killers.

ar•son (är′sən) *n.* The crime of burning buildings or other property. [< ML *arsiō,* act of burning.] **—ar′son•ist** *n.*

art¹ (ärt) *n.* **1. a.** The activity of creating beautiful things. **b.** Works, such as paintings or poetry, resulting from such activity. **2.** A branch of artistic activity, as musical composition, using a special medium and technique. **3.** The aesthetic values of an artist as expressed in his works. **4.** Any of various disciplines, as the humanities, that do not rely exclusively on the scientific method. **5.** A craft or trade and its methods. **6.** Any practical skill: *the art of letter writing.* **7.** Cunning; contrivance. **8.** Printed graphic material as distinguished from text. [< L *ars.*]

art² (ärt, ərt). *Archaic.* 2nd person sing. present indicative of **be.** [< OE *eart.*]

-art. Variant of **-ard.**

art. **1.** article. **2.** artificial. **3.** artillery.

Ar•te•mis (är′tə-mĭs). Greek goddess; patroness of women and wild animals.

ar•te•ri•o•scle•ro•sis (är-tîr′ē-ō-sklə-rō′sĭs) *n.* A chronic disease in which thickening and hardening of arterial walls interfere with blood circulation. **—ar•te′ri•o•scle•rot′ic** (-rŏt′ĭk) *adj.*

ar•ter•y (är′tər-ē) *n., pl.* **-ies.** **1.** Any of a branching system of muscular tubes that carry blood away from the heart. **2.** A major transport route into which local routes flow. [< Gk *artēria.*] **—ar•te′ri•al** (-tîr′ē-əl) *adj.*

ar•te•sian well (är-tē′zhən). A drilled well in which water is forced up by internal hydrostatic pressure. [F *(puit) artésien,* (well) of *Artois,* region of France.]

art•ful (ärt′fəl) *adj.* **1.** Skillful; clever. **2.** Cunning; crafty; deceitful. **—art′ful•ly** *adv.* **—art′ful•ness** *n.*

ar•thri•tis (är-thrī′tĭs) *n.* Inflammation of a joint or joints. **—ar•thrit′ic** (-thrĭt′ĭk) *adj. & n.*

arthro-. *comb. form.* Joint. [< Gk *arthron,* joint.]

ar•thro•pod (är′thrə-pŏd′) *n.* Any of a large group of invertebrates, including the insects and crustaceans, having a segmented body and jointed legs.

Ar•thur (är′thər). **1.** Reputed king of the Britons of the 6th century A.D. **2. Chester Alan.** 1830–1886. 21st President of the U.S. (1881–85).

Chester A. Arthur

ar•ti•choke (är′tə-chōk′) *n.* **1.** The unopened flower head of a thistlelike plant, covered with thick, leaflike scales and eaten as a vegetable. **2.** The plant itself. [It *articiocco.*]

ar•ti•cle (är′tĭ-kəl) *n.* **1.** An individual thing in a class, esp. a commodity. **2.** A particular section of a series in a formal document. **3.** A nonfictional composition that forms an independent section of a publication. **4.** Any of a class of words used to signal nouns and specify their application. In English, the articles are *a* and *an* (indefinite articles) and *the* (definite article). [< L *articulus,* small joint, division, dim of *artus,* joint.]

ar•tic•u•lar (är-tĭk′yə-lər) *adj.* Pertaining to a joint or joints. [< L *articulus,* small joint.]

ar•tic•u•late (är-tĭk′yə-lĭt) *adj.* **1.** Having the power of speech. **2.** Able to speak clearly and skillfully. **3.** *Biol.* Jointed. *—v.* (är-tĭk′yə-lāt′) **-lated, -lating.** **1.** To utter (speech sounds). **2.** To pronounce distinctly. **3.** To give voice to, as an emotion. **4.** To unite by or form a joint. [< L *articulāre,* to divide into joints, utter distinctly.] **—ar•tic′u•late•ly** *adv.* **—ar•tic′u•la′tion** *n.* **—ar•tic′u•late•ness** *n.*

ar•ti•fact (är′tə-făkt′) *n.* Also **ar•te•fact.** An object produced or shaped by human workmanship, esp. a simple tool of archaeological interest. [< L *ars,* ART + *factum,* something made.]

ar•ti•fice (är′tə-fĭs) *n.* **1.** A crafty expedient. **2.** Subtle deception. **3.** Ingenuity; skill. [< L *artificium* < *artifex,* craftsman.]

ar•ti•fi•cial (är′tə-fĭsh′əl) *adj.* **1.** Made by man rather than natural forces. **2.** Made in imitation of something natural. **3.** Feigned; pretended. [< L *artificiālis* < *artificium,* ARTIFICE.] **—ar′ti•fi′ci•al′i•ty** (-ē-ăl′ə-tē) *n.* **—ar′ti•fi′cial•ly** *adv.*

artificial respiration. The restoring of normal breathing in an asphyxiated but living person, usually by forcing air into and out of the lungs.

ar•til•ler•y (är-tĭl′ər-ē) *n.* **1.** Large-caliber mounted guns. **2.** The branch of an armed force that specializes in the use of such guns. [< OF *atillier,* to fortify, arm.] **—ar•til′ler•y•man** *n.*

ar•ti•san (är′tə-zən, -sən) *n.* One skilled in making a particular commodity; craftsman. [< L *artītus,* skilled in arts.]

art•ist (är′tĭst) *n.* **1.** One who creates works of art, esp. a painter or sculptor. **2.** A public entertainer. **3.** A practitioner of printed graphics.

ar•tis•tic (är-tĭs′tĭk) *adj.* **1.** Of art or artists. **2.** Skilled. **3.** Appreciative of the fine arts. **—ar•tis′ti•cal•ly** *adv.*

art•ist•ry (är′tĭs-trē) *n.* Artistic ability or quality.

art•less (ärt′lĭs) *adj.* **1.** Without guile; ingenuous. **2.** Natural; simple. **3.** Lacking art; crude. **—art′less•ly** *adv.* **—art′less•ness** *n.*

art•y (är′tē) *adj.* **-ier, -iest.** Affecting artistry. **—art′i•ly** *adv.* **—art′i•ness** *n.*

ar•um (âr′əm) *n.* Any of various plants having small flowers on a clublike spike surrounded by a leaflike part. [< L.]

-ary. *comb. form.* Of, engaged in, or connected with: **reactionary.**

Ar•y•an (âr′ē-ən) *n.* **1.** A member or descendant of the prehistoric people that spoke Proto-Indo-European. **2.** Proto-Indo-European or a language or language group descended from it. **3.** In Nazi ideology, a Caucasian gentile. **—Ar′y•an** *adj.*

as (ăz, əz) *adv.* **1.** To the same extent or degree; equally. **2.** For instance: *large carnivores, as bears.* *—conj.* **1.** To the same degree or quantity that: *as sweet as sugar.* **2.** In the same way that: *Think as I think.* **3.** At the same time that; while. **4.** Since; because. **5.** For the reason that: *Study so as to learn.* **6.** Though: *Pretty as it is, it's worthless.* **7.** That: *I don't know as I can.* **—as for** (or **to**). With regard to; concerning. **—as if** (or **though**). In the same way that it would be if. **—as is.** Just the way it is or appears. *—pron.* **1.** That; which; who: *I received the same grade as you.* **2.** A fact that: *The sun is hot, as everyone knows.* *—prep.* In the role, capacity, or function of: *acting as a mediator.* [< OE *alswā, ealswā,* just as, ALSO.]

As arsenic.

AS antisubmarine.

as•a•fet•i•da (ăs′ə-fĕt′ə-də) *n.* An offensive-smelling plant resin, formerly used in medicine. [< ML *asafoetida.*]

as•bes•tos (ăs-bĕs′təs, ăz-) *n.* Either of two incombustible fibrous mineral forms of impure magnesium silicate, used for fireproofing, building materials, and brake linings. [L, an incombustible fiber.]

as•cend (ə-sĕnd′) *v.* **1.** To move upward; rise. **2.** To climb (a slope). [< L *ascendere.*]

as•cen•dan•cy (ə-sĕn′dən-sē) *n.* Also **as•cen•den•cy.** The state of being dominant.

as•cen•dant (ə-sĕn′dənt) *adj.* Also **as•cen•dent.**

1. Inclining or moving upward; rising. 2. Dominant; superior. *—n.* The state of being dominant or in power: *in the ascendant.*

as•cen•sion (ə-sĕn′shən) *n.* 1. The act or process of ascending. 2. **the Ascension.** The ascent of Christ into heaven, celebrated on the 40th day after Easter.

as•cent (ə-sĕnt′) *n.* 1. The act of ascending. 2. An upward slope.

as•cer•tain (ăs′ər-tān′) *v.* To discover through investigation; find out. [< OF *acertainer.*]

as•cet•ic (ə-sĕt′ĭk) *adj.* Practicing austere self-discipline, esp. from religious motives. [< Gk *askētēs,* hermit.] **—as•cet′ic** *n.* **—as•cet′i•cism′** *n.*

a•scor•bic acid (ə-skôr′bĭk). A vitamin, $C_6H_8O_6$, found in citrus fruits, tomatoes, potatoes, and leafy green vegetables, used to prevent scurvy; vitamin C.

as•cot (ăs′kət, -kŏt′) *n.* A scarf or broad necktie loosely knotted with overlapping ends. [< *Ascot,* a village of S England, site of a famous annual horse race.]

as•cribe (ə-skrīb′) *v.* **-cribed, -cribing.** 1. To attribute to a specified cause or source. 2. To assign as an attribute. [< L *ascrībere,* to add to in writing.] **—as•crip′tion** (ə-skrĭp′shən) *n.*

a•sep•sis (ā-sĕp′sĭs) *n.* The state of being free of pathogenic organisms. **—a•sep′tic** (-sĕp′tĭk) *adj.*

a•sex•u•al (ā-sĕk′shōō-əl) *adj.* 1. Having no evident sex or sex organs. 2. Pertaining to reproduction without male or female gametes, as in binary fission or budding.

ash[1] (ăsh) *n.* 1. The grayish-white to black, soft solid residue of combustion. 2. Pulverized particulate matter ejected by volcanic eruption. 3. **ashes.** Human remains, esp. after cremation. [< OE *asce, æsce.* See **as-.**]

ash[2] (ăsh) *n.* 1. Any of various trees having compound leaves and strong, durable wood. 2. The wood of such a tree. [< OE *æsc.*]

a•shamed (ə-shāmd′) *adj.* 1. Feeling shame. 2. Reluctant through fear of shame. **—a•sham′ed•ly** (ə-shā′mĭd-lē) *adv.*

ash•en (ăsh′ən) *adj.* 1. Of or resembling ashes. 2. Deathly pale.

a•shore (ə-shôr′, ə-shōr′) *adv.* Toward or on the shore.

Ash Wednesday. The 7th Wednesday before Easter and the 1st day of Lent.

A•sia (ā′zhə, ā′shə). The largest of the earth's continents, occupying the E part of the Eurasian land mass and adjacent islands and separated from Europe by the Ural Mountains. Pop. 1,852,946,000. **—A′sian, A′si•at′ic** *adj. & n.*

Asia Minor. The W peninsula of Asia, between the Black Sea and the Mediterranean.

a•side (ə-sīd′) *adv.* 1. On or to one side. 2. Apart; dispensed with: *all joking aside.* **—aside from.** Excluding; excepting. *—n.* 1. A piece of dialogue that other actors on stage are supposed not to hear. 2. A digression.

as•i•nine (ăs′ə-nīn′) *adj.* Stupid or silly. [< L *asinus,* ass.] **—as′i•nin′i•ty** (-nĭn′ə-tē) *n.*

ask (ăsk, äsk) *v.* 1. To put a question to. 2. To inquire (about). 3. To request (of or for). 4. a. To require or call for. b. To expect or demand. 5. To invite. [< OE *āscian, ācsian.* See **ais-.**]

a•skance (ə-skăns′) *adv.* 1. With a side glance. 2. With disapproval or distrust. [< ME *ascaunce,* "as if to say," "so to speak."]

a•skew (ə-skyōō′) *adj.* Crooked. *—adv.* To one side; awry. [A- (on) + SKEW.]

a•slant (ə-slănt′, ə-slänt′) *adj.* Slanting. *—adv.* At a slant. *—prep.* Obliquely over or across.

a•sleep (ə-slēp′) *adj.* 1. Sleeping. 2. Inactive. 3. Numb. *—adv.* Into a condition of sleep.

a•so•cial (ā-sō′shəl) *adj.* 1. Avoiding the society of others. 2. Inconsiderate; self-centered.

asp (ăsp) *n.* Any of several venomous Old World snakes. [< Gk *aspis.*]

as•par•a•gus (ə-spăr′ə-gəs) *n.* 1. The young, edible stalks of a widely cultivated plant. 2. The plant itself. [< Gk *asparagos.*]

A.S.P.C.A. American Society for the Prevention of Cruelty to Animals.

as•pect (ăs′pĕkt′) *n.* 1. A particular facial expression. 2. Appearance to the eye, esp. from a specific view. 3. A particular phase in which something, as an idea, appears as viewed by the mind. 4. A side facing in a particular direction. [< L *aspicere,* look at.]

as•pen (ăs′pən) *n.* Any of several poplar trees having leaves that flutter readily in the wind. [< OE *æspe,* an aspen. See **apsā.**]

as•per•i•ty (ăs-pĕr′ə-tē) *n.* 1. Roughness or harshness. 2. Ill temper. [< L *asper,* rough.]

as•perse (ə-spûrs′, ă-) *v.* **-persed, -persing.** To defame; slander. [L *aspergere,* to sprinkle on.] **—as•per′sion** (-spûr′zhən, -shən) *n.*

as•phalt (ăs′fôlt′) *n.* 1. A brownish-black solid or semisolid mixture of bitumens used in paving, roofing, and waterproofing. 2. Mixed asphalt and crushed stone gravel or sand, used for paving or roofing. [< Gk *asphaltos,* bitumen, pitch, asphalt.]

as•pho•del (ăs′fə-dəl′) *n.* Any of several Old World plants having white or yellow flowers. [< Gk *asphodelos.*]

as•phyx•i•ate (ăs-fĭk′sē-āt′) *v.* **-ated, -ating.** To cause or undergo unconsciousness or death from lack of oxygen. [< Gk *asphuxia,* stopping of the pulse.] **—as•phyx′i•a′tion** *n.*

as•pic (ăs′pĭk) *n.* A jelly made from chilled meat or vegetable juices. [F *(sauce) à l'aspic.*]

as•pi•dis•tra (ăs′pə-dĭs′trə) *n.* A widely grown house plant having long, tough evergreen leaves. [< Gk *aspis,* shield.]

as•pi•ra•tion (ăs′pə-rā′shən) *n.* 1. Expulsion of breath in speech. 2. a. A strong desire for high achievement. b. An object of such desire.

as•pire (ə-spīr′) *v.* **-pired, -piring.** To have a great ambition; strive toward an end. [< L *aspīrāre,* to breathe upon, favor.] **—as′pi•rant** (ăs′pər-ənt, ə-spīr′-) *n. & adj.*

as•pi•rin (ăs′pər-ĭn, -prĭn) *n.* A white crystalline compound of acetylsalicylic acid, $C_9H_8O_4$, used to relieve pain and fever. [AC(ETYL) + *spir(aeic acid),* old name for salicylic acid + -IN.]

ass (ăs) *n.* 1. A hoofed animal, such as the donkey, related to and resembling the horse. 2. A silly or stupid person. [< OE *assa* < OIr *asan* < L *asinus.*]

as•sail (ə-sāl′) *v.* 1. To attack with violent blows. 2. To attack verbally. [< VL **assalīre.*] **—as•sail′a•ble** *adj.* **—as•sail′ant** *n.*

as•sas•sin (ə-săs′ĭn) *n.* A murderer, esp. one who carries out a plot to kill a public official or other prominent person. [< Ar *ḥashshāsh,* "hashish addict."]

as•sas•si•nate (ə-săs′ə-nāt′) *v.* **-nated, -nating.** To murder (a prominent person). **—as•sas′si•na′tion** *n.*

as•sault (ə-sôlt′) *n.* 1. A violent physical or verbal attack. 2. An unlawful attempt or threat to injure another physically. 3. Rape. *—v.* To attack violently. [< VL **assaltus.*]

assault and battery. *Law.* An executed threat to use force upon another.

as•say (ăs′ā′, ă-sā′) *n.* 1. Qualitative or quantitative analysis of a substance, esp. of an ore or drug. 2. The result of such analysis. *—v.* (ă-sā′, ăs′ā′). 1. To subject to or undergo an assay. 2. To evaluate; assess. 3. To attempt. [< OF *assai, essai,* trial, ESSAY.]

as•sem•blage (ə-sĕm′blĭj) *n.* 1. The act or product of assembling. 2. A collection of people or things. 3. A fitting together of parts, as of a machine.

as•sem•ble (ə-sĕm′bəl) *v.* **-bled, -bling.** 1. To bring or gather together into a group; congregate. 2. To fit or join together the parts of. [< VL **assimulāre,* to bring together.]

as•sem•bly (ə-sĕm′blē) *n., pl.* **-blies.** 1. A group of persons gathered for a common purpose. 2. **Assembly.** The lower house of a legislature. 3. a. The putting together of parts to make a completed product. b. A set of parts so assembled. 4. A signal calling troops to assemble.

as•sem•bly•man (ə-sĕm′blē-mən) *n.* A member of a legislative assembly.

as•sent (ə-sĕnt′) *v.* To express agreement (with *to*). *—n.* 1. Agreement. 2. Consent. [< L, "to join in feeling."]

as•sert (ə-sûrt′) *v.* 1. To state or express positively. 2. To defend or maintain, as one's rights. [L *asserere,* "to join to oneself," claim.] **—as•ser′tive** *adj.*

as•ser•tion (ə-sûr′shən) *n.* A positive statement without support of proof.

as•sess (ə-sĕs′) *v.* 1. To estimate the value of (property) for taxation. 2. To charge with a tax, fine, or other special payment. 3. To evaluate. [< L *assidēre,* "to sit beside," be an assistant judge.] **—as•sess′a•ble** *adj.* **—as•sess′ment** *n.* **—as•ses′sor** *n.*

as•set (ăs′ĕt′) *n.* 1. A useful or valuable quality or possession. 2. **assets.** All of a person's or business' properties and claims against others that can be applied to cover liabilities. [< OF *asez,* "enough (to satisfy creditors)."]

as•sid•u•ous (ə-sĭj′ōō-əs) *adj.* Constant in application or attention; diligent. [L *assiduus* < *assidēre,* to sit beside, attend to.] **—as′si•du′i•ty** (ăs′ə-d/y/ōō′ə-tē), **as•sid′u•ous•ness** *n.*

as•sign (ə-sīn′) *v.* 1. To set apart for a particular purpose. 2. To appoint. 3. To give out as a task. 4. To ascribe; attribute. 5. *Law.* To transfer (property, rights, or interests). [< L *assignāre,* to mark out.]

as•sig•na•tion (ăs′ĭg-nā′shən) *n.* An appointment for a meeting between lovers.

as•sign•ment (ə-sīn′mənt) *n.* 1. The act of assigning. 2. Something assigned. 3. *Law.* The transfer of a claim, right, interest, or property.

as•sim•i•late (ə-sĭm′ə-lāt′) *v.* **-lated, -lating.** 1. To consume and incorporate into the body. 2. To absorb or become absorbed, as knowledge. 3. To make or become similar. [< L *assimilāre,* to make similar to.] **—as•sim′i•la•ble** *adj.* **—as•sim′i•la′tion** *n.*

as•sist (ə-sĭst′) *v.* To aid; help. *—n.* 1. An act of giving aid. 2. a. *Baseball.* A handling of the ball that enables a runner to be put out. b. A pass that enables a teammate to score, as in basketball or ice hockey. [< L *assistere,* to stand beside, help.] **—as•sist′er** *n.*

as•sis•tance (ə-sĭs′təns) *n.* Help; aid.

as•sis•tant (ə-sĭs′tənt) *n.* One that assists; a helper.

as•size (ə-sīz′) *n.* 1. A judicial inquest. 2. **assizes.** One of the periodic court sessions held in the counties of England and Wales. [< OF *assis,* pp of *asseior,* to seat.]

assn. association.

assoc. associate; association.

as•so•ci•ate (ə-sō′shē-āt′, -sē-āt′) *v.* **-ated,**

-ating. 1. To join in a relationship. 2. To connect or join together. 3. To connect in the mind. *—n.* (ə-sō'shē-ĭt, -sē-ĭt, -shē-āt', -sē-āt'). 1. A partner; colleague. 2. A companion. *—adj.* (ə-sō'shē-ĭt, -sē-ĭt, -shē-āt', -sē-āt'). Joined with others and having equal or nearly equal status. [< L *associāre,* to join to.]

as•so•ci•a•tion (ə-sō'sē-ā'shən, -shē-ā'shən) *n.* 1. The act of associating. 2. An organized body of people; a society.

as•so•ci•a•tive (ə-sō'shē-ā'tĭv, -sē-ā'tĭv, -shə-tĭv) *adj.* 1. Characterized by association. 2. Mathematically independent of the grouping of elements: *If a + (b + c) = (a + b) + c, the operation indicated by + is associative.*

as•so•nance (ăs'ə-nəns) *n.* Resemblance in sound, esp. in the vowel sounds of words. [< L *assonāre,* to sound in response to.]

as•sort (ə-sôrt') *v.* To separate into groups according to kinds; classify. [OF *assorter.*]

as•sort•ed (ə-sôr'tĭd) *adj.* Of different kinds; various.

as•sort•ment (ə-sôrt'mənt) *n.* 1. The act of assorting. 2. A variety.

asst. assistant.

as•suage (ə-swāj') *v.* **-suaged, -suaging.** 1. To make less severe. 2. To satisfy; appease. [< VL **assuāviāre,* to add sweetness to, sweeten.]

as•sume (ə-so͞om') *v.* **-sumed, -suming.** 1. To undertake. 2. To take on; adopt. 3. To feign; affect. 4. To take for granted; suppose. [< L *assūmere,* to take to oneself.]

as•sump•tion (ə-sŭmp'shən) *n.* 1. The act of assuming. 2. A statement accepted as true without proof. 3. **Assumption.** a. The bodily taking up of the Virgin Mary into heaven after her death. b. A church feast on August 15 celebrating this event.

as•sur•ance (ə-sho͝or'əns) *n.* 1. The act of assuring. 2. A statement or indication that inspires confidence. 3. a. Freedom from doubt. b. Self-confidence.

as•sure (ə-sho͝or') *v.* **-sured, -suring.** 1. To inform confidently. 2. To make certain. 3. To insure, as against loss. [< ML *assēcūrāre,* to make sure.]

as•sured (ə-sho͝ord') *adj.* 1. Undoubted; guaranteed. 2. Confident. 3. Insured. **—as•sur'ed•ly** (-ĭd-lē) *adv.*

As•syr•i•a (ə-sîr'ē-ə). An ancient empire of W Asia. **—As•syr'i•an** *adj.* & *n.*

as•ta•tine (ăs'tə-tēn') *n. Symbol* **At** A highly unstable radioactive element, used in medicine as a radioactive tracer. Atomic number 85, longest-lived isotope At 210. [< Gk *astatos,* unstable.]

as•ter (ăs'tər) *n.* Any of various plants having daisylike, variously colored flowers. [< Gk *astēr,* star.]

as•ter•isk (ăs'tə-rĭsk') *n.* A star-shaped figure (*) used in printing to indicate a reference to a footnote or an omission. [< Gk *asteriskos,* little star.]

as•ter•ism (ăs'tə-rĭz'əm) *n.* 1. a. A cluster of stars. b. A constellation. 2. A six-rayed starlike figure optically produced in some minerals. [< Gk *astēr,* star.]

a•stern (ə-stûrn') *adv. Naut.* 1. Behind a vessel. 2. Toward the rear of a vessel.

as•ter•oid (ăs'tə-roid') *n.* 1. Any of numerous celestial bodies with characteristic diameters between one and several hundred miles and orbits lying chiefly between Mars and Jupiter; planetoid. 2. A starfish. [< Gk *astēr,* star.]

asth•ma (ăz'mə) *n.* A chronic respiratory disease marked by labored breathing, chest constriction, and coughing. [< Gk.] **—asth•mat'ic** (-măt'ĭk) *adj.*

a•stig•ma•tism (ə-stĭg'mə-tĭz'əm) *n.* 1. A refractive defect of a lens that prevents focusing of sharp, distinct images. 2. Faulty vision caused by such a defect in the lens of the eye. [A- + Gk *stigma,* spot, "focus."] **—as'tig•mat'ic** (ăs'tĭg-măt'ĭk) *adj.*

a•stir (ə-stûr') *adj.* Moving about.

a•ston•ish (ə-stŏn'ĭsh) *v.* To fill with sudden wonder or amazement. [< VL **extonāre,* to strike with thunder, stun.] **—a•ston'ish•ment** *n.*

As•tor (ăs'tər), **John Jacob.** 1763–1848. American capitalist.

a•stound (ə-stound') *v.* To strike with sudden wonder. [< ME *astonen,* astonish.]

a•strad•dle (ə-străd'l) *adv.* & *prep.* Astride.

as•tra•khan (ăs'trə-kăn', -kən) *n.* Curly fur made from the skins of young lambs from the region of Astrakhan, on the Volga delta in the U.S.S.R.

as•tral (ăs'trəl) *adj.* Of or resembling the stars. [< Gk *astron,* star.]

a•stray (ə-strā') *adv.* 1. Away from the correct direction. 2. Away from right or good.

a•stride (ə-strīd') *adv.* With the legs separated so that one is on each side of something. *—prep.* Upon or over and with a leg on each side of.

as•trin•gent (ə-strĭn'jənt) *adj.* 1. Tending to draw together or constrict tissue. 2. Harsh. *—n.* An astringent substance or drug. [< L *astringere,* to bind together.] **—as•trin'gen•cy** *n.*

astro–. *comb. form.* 1. Star or star-shaped. 2. Outer space. [< Gk *astron,* star.]

astrol. astrologer; astrological; astrology.

as•tro•labe (ăs'trə-lāb') *n.* A medieval instrument used to determine the altitudes of celestial bodies. [< Gk *(organon) astrolabon,* "(instrument) for taking the stars."]

as•trol•o•gy (ə-strŏl'ə-jē) *n.* The study of the positions and aspects of heavenly bodies with a view to predicting their influence on human affairs. **—as•trol'o•ger** *n.* **—as'tro•log'ic** (ăs'trə-lŏj'ĭk), **as'tro•log'i•cal** *adj.*

astron. astronomer; astronomical; astronomy.

as•tro•naut (ăs'trə-nôt') *n.* A person trained to pilot, navigate, or otherwise participate in the flight of a spacecraft; cosmonaut.

as•tro•nau•tics (ăs'trə-nô'tĭks) *n. (takes sing. v.).* The science and technology of space flight. **—as'tro•nau'tic, as'tro•nau'ti•cal** *adj.*

as•tro•nom•i•cal (ăs'trə-nŏm'ĭ-kəl) *adj.* Also **as•tro•nom•ic** (-nŏm'ĭk). 1. Of or pertaining to astronomy. 2. Inconceivably large; immense.

astronomical unit. A unit of length equal to the mean distance of the earth from the sun, approx. 93 million miles.

as•tron•o•my (ə-strŏn'ə-mē) *n.* The scientific study of the universe beyond the earth. [< Gk *astronomos,* "star-arranger."] **—as•tron'o•mer** *n.*

as•tro•phys•ics (ăs'trō-fĭz'ĭks) *n. (takes sing. v.).* The physics of stellar phenomena. **—as'tro•phys'i•cal** *adj.*

as•tute (ə-st/y/o͞ot') *adj.* Keen in judgment. [< L *astus,* craft.] **—as•tute'ness** *n.*

A•sun•ción (ä'so͞on-syôn'). The capital of Paraguay. Pop. 305,000.

a•sun•der (ə-sŭn'dər) *adv.* 1. Into separate parts. 2. Apart in position or direction. [< OE *onsundran* < ON + *sunder,* apart, separate (see **sen-**).]

a•sy•lum (ə-sī'ləm) *n.* 1. An institution for the mentally ill or aged. 2. A place offering safety. 3. The protection afforded by a sanctuary. [< Gk *asulon,* sanctuary.]

a•sym•met•ric (ā'sĭ-mĕt'rĭk) *adj.* Also **a•sym•met•ri•cal** (-rĭ-kəl). Not symmetrical. **—a'sym•met'ri•cal•ly** *adv.* **—a•sym'me•try** *n.*

as•ymp•tote (ăs'ĭm-tōt', -ĭmp-tōt') *n. Math.* A line considered a limit to a curve in the sense that the perpendicular distance from a moving point on the curve to the line approaches zero as the point moves an infinite distance from the origin. [< Gk *(grammē) asumptōtos,* "(a line) not falling together."] **—as'ymp•tot'ic** (-tŏt'ĭk), **as'ymp•tot'i•cal** (-ĭ-kəl) *adj.* **—as'ymp•tot'i•cal•ly** *adv.*

at (ăt, ət) *prep.* 1. —Used to indicate position, location, or state: *at home; at rest.* 2. —Used to indicate a direction or goal: *look at us; jump at the chance.* 3. —Used to indicate location in time: *at noon.* 4. —Used to indicate manner, means, or cause: *get there at top speed.* [< OE *æt.* See **ad-.**]

At astatine.

at•a•vism (ăt'ə-vĭz'əm) *n.* The reappearance of a characteristic in an organism after several generations of absence. [< L *atavus,* ancestor, great-great-great-grandfather.] **—at'a•vis'tic** *adj.* **—at'a•vis'ti•cal•ly** *adv.*

ate (āt; *Brit.* ĕt). *p.t.* of **eat.**

-ate¹. *comb. form.* 1. a. Possessing: **affectionate.** b. Shaped like or having the general characteristics of: *Latinate.* 2. A substance derived from or a salt or ester of an acid: **sulfate.** 3. Used to form certain verbs: **pollinate.** [< L *-ātus.*]

-ate². *comb. form.* Rank; office: **rabbinate.** [< L *-āt(us)* + *-us,* 4th declension ending.]

at•el•ier (ăt'l-yā') *n.* A workshop or studio, esp. an artist's studio. [< OF *astelier,* woodpile, hence carpenter's shop.]

a tem•po (ä tĕm'pō) *Mus.* In normal time; resuming the original tempo. [It, "in time."]

Ath•a•pas•can (ăth'ə-păs'kən) *n.* Also **Ath•a•bas•can** (-băs'kən). 1. A language family of North American Indians, including languages of Alaska, the Pacific coast of North America, and the Navaho and Apache languages of the SW U.S. 2. A member of an Athapascan-speaking tribe. *—adj.* Of or pertaining to this language family.

a•the•ism (ā'thē-ĭz'əm) *n.* Disbelief in or denial of the existence of God. [< Gk *atheos,* godless.] **—a'the•is'tic, a'the•is'ti•cal** *adj.* **—a'the•is'ti•cal•ly** *adv.*

a•the•ist (ā'thē-ĭst) *n.* One who denies the existence of God.

A•the•na (ə-thē'nə). Greek goddess of wisdom and the arts.

Athena

ath•e•ne•um (ăth'ə-nē'əm) *n.* Also **ath•e•nae•um.** **1.** An institution for the promotion of learning. **2.** A library. [< Gk *Athēnaion,* Athena's temple, where philosophy was taught.]

Ath•ens (ăth'ənz). The capital of Greece. Pop. 1,853,000. —**A•the'ni•an** (ə-thē'nē-ən) *n.* & *adj.*

a•thirst (ə-thûrst') *adj.* Eager (for).

ath•lete (ăth'lēt') *n.* One who takes part in competitive sports. [< Gk *athlētēs,* contestant.]

athlete's foot. A contagious skin infection caused by parasitic fungi, usually affecting the feet, causing itching, cracking, and scaling.

ath•let•ic (ăth-lĕt'ĭk) *adj.* **1.** Of or pertaining to athletics or athletes. **2.** Physically strong; vigorous. —*n.* **athletics.** *(takes pl. v.).* Athletic activities, as competitive sports.

a•thwart (ə-thwôrt') *adv.* Crosswise. —*prep.* **1.** Across. **2.** Contrary to.

a•tilt (ə-tĭlt') *adj.* & *adv.* Tilted; inclined upward.

-ation. *comb. form.* **1.** Action or process of: **pollination. 2.** State, condition, or quality of: **discoloration. 3.** Result or product of: **civilization.** [< L *-ātus,* -ATE.]

-ative. *comb. form.* Relation, nature, or tendency: **illustrative.** [< L *-ātus,* -ATE.]

At•lan•ta (ăt-lăn'tə). The capital of Georgia. Pop. 497,000.

At•lan•tic Ocean (ăt-lăn'tĭk). The second largest of the earth's oceans, lying between the Americas in the W and Europe and Africa in the E.

at•las (ăt'ləs) *n.* **1.** A bound collection of maps. **2.** *Anat.* The top or first cervical vertebra of the neck, which supports the head. [< the Titan ATLAS.]

At•las (ăt'ləs). *Gk.Myth.* A Titan condemned to support the heavens on his shoulders.

Atlas Mountains. A mountain system in NW Africa.

at•mos•phere (ăt'mə-sfîr') *n.* **1.** The gaseous mass or envelope surrounding a celestial body, esp. that surrounding the earth, and retained by the body's gravitational field. **2.** A unit of pressure equal to 1.01325 x 10^5 newtons per square meter. **3.** A psychological environment or effect. [NL *atmosphaera,* "sphere of vapor."] —**at'mos•pher'ic** (-sfîr'ĭk, -sfĕr'ĭk) *adj.*

a•toll (ă'tôl', ă'tŏl', ā'-) *n.* A ringlike coral island that encloses a lagoon. [Malayalam *atoḷu,* "reef."]

at•om (ăt'əm) *n.* **1.** Anything considered an irreducible constituent of a specified system. **2.** The irreducible, indestructible material unit of ancient atomism. **3.** A unit of matter, the smallest unit of an element, consisting of a dense central positively charged nucleus surrounded by a system of electrons, the entire structure characteristically remaining undivided in chemical reactions except for limited removal, transfer, or exchange of certain electrons. **4.** This unit regarded as a source of nuclear energy. [< Gk *atomos,* indivisible.]

a•tom•ic (ə-tŏm'ĭk) *adj.* **1.** Of or relating to an atom or atoms. **2.** Of or employing atomic energy. **3.** Very small.

atomic bomb. **1.** An explosive weapon of great destructive power derived from the rapid release of energy in the fission of heavy atomic nuclei, as of uranium 235. **2.** Any bomb deriving its destructive power from the release of nuclear energy.

atomic clock. An extremely precise timekeeping device regulated in correspondence with a characteristic invariant frequency of an atomic or molecular system.

atomic energy. **1.** The energy released from an atomic nucleus in fission or fusion. **2.** This energy regarded as a source of practical power.

atomic mass unit. A unit of mass equal to 1/12 the mass of the carbon isotope with mass number 12, approx. 1.6604 x 10^{-24} gram.

atomic number. *Symbol* **Z** The number of protons in an atomic nucleus.

atomic pile. A **nuclear reactor.**

atomic reactor. A **nuclear reactor.**

atomic weight. The average weight of an atom of an element, usually expressed relative to 1 atom of the carbon isotope taken to have a standard weight of 12.

at•om•ism (ăt'əm-ĭz'əm) *n.* A Greek philosophical theory of the late 5th century B.C., according to which simple, indivisible, and indestructible atoms are the basic components of the entire universe.

at•om•ize (ăt'əm-īz') *v.* **-ized, -izing.** **1.** To reduce or separate into atoms. **2. a.** To reduce (a liquid) to a spray. **b.** To spray (a liquid) in this form. —**at'om•i•za'tion** *n.*

at•om•iz•er (ăt'əm-ī'zər) *n.* A device for producing a fine spray.

atom smasher. An atomic particle accelerator.

a•to•nal•i•ty (ā'tō-năl'ə-tē) *n. Mus.* A style of composition in which tonal center or key is disregarded. —**a•to'nal** (ā-tō'nəl) *adj.*

a•tone (ə-tōn') *v.* **atoned, atoning.** To make amends (for). [< ME *at one,* of one mind, in accord.] —**a•ton'er** *n.*

a•tone•ment (ə-tōn'mənt) *n.* **1.** Amends or reparation made for an injury or wrong. **2.** Often **Atonement.** The reconciliation of God and man.

a•top (ə-tŏp') *prep.* On top of.

-ator. *comb. form.* One who or that which acts or does: **radiator.**

-atory. *comb. form.* Pertinence to, characteristic of, result or effect of: *perspiratory.*

ATP adenosine triphosphate.

a•tri•um (ā'trē-əm) *n., pl.* **atria** (ā'trē-ə) or **-ums.** A bodily cavity or chamber, as in the heart; auricle. [L *ātrium.*] —**a'tri•al** *adj.*

a•tro•cious (ə-trō'shəs) *adj.* **1.** Extremely evil or cruel. **2.** Exceptionally bad. [< L *ātrōx,* "dark-looking," horrible.]

a•troc•i•ty (ə-trŏs'ə-tē) *n., pl.* **-ties.** An atrocious action, condition, or object.

at•ro•phy (ăt'rə-fē) *n., pl.* **-phies.** Emaciation or wasting of tissues, organs, or the entire body. —*v.* **-phied, -phying.** To cause or undergo atrophy. [< Gk *atrophos,* ill-nourished.]

at•ro•pine (ăt'rə-pēn', -pĭn) *n.* Also **at•ro•pin** (-pĭn). An extremely poisonous alkaloid, $C_{17}H_{23}NO_3$, obtained from belladonna and related plants, used to dilate the pupil of the eye. [G *Atropin.*]

att. attorney.

at•tach (ə-tăch') *v.* **1.** To fasten on or affix; connect. **2.** To adhere. **3.** To affix or append. **4.** To ascribe or assign. **5.** To bind by ties of affection or loyalty. **6.** To seize (persons or property) by legal writ. [< OF *attacher,* to fasten (with a stake).] —**at•tach'er** *n.*

at•ta•ché (ăt'ə-shā', ă-tă'shā') *n.* A person assigned to a diplomatic mission in a particular capacity. [F, "one attached."]

at•tach•ment (ə-tăch'mənt) *n.* **1.** The act of attaching or condition of being attached. **2.** Something that serves to attach one thing to another. **3.** Fond regard. **4.** A supplementary part. **5.** The legal seizure of property.

at•tack (ə-tăk') *v.* **1.** To set upon with force. **2.** To bombard with hostile criticism. **3.** To start work on. **4.** To begin to affect harmfully. —*n.* **1.** An assault. **2.** Seizure by a disease. **3.** The manner in which a musical passage or phrase is begun. [< OIt *attaccare.*]

at•tain (ə-tān') *v.* **1.** To gain or accomplish. **2.** To arrive at. [< OF *ataindre,* to reach to.] —**at•tain'a•ble** *adj.*

at•tain•der (ə-tān'dər) *n.* The loss of civil rights legally consequent to a capital offense. [< OF *ataindre,* to affect, infect, ATTAIN.]

at•tain•ment (ə-tān'mənt) *n.* **1.** The act of attaining. **2.** An acquirement or acquisition.

at•taint (ə-tānt') *v.* To condemn by a sentence of attainder.

at•tar (ăt'ər) *n.* A fragrant oil obtained from flower petals. [Pers *'aṭir,* perfumed.]

at•tempt (ə-tĕmpt') *v.* To try. —*n.* **1.** An effort. **2.** An attack: *an attempt on his life.* [< L *attemptāre.*] —**at•tempt'er** *n.*

at•tend (ə-tĕnd') *v.* **1.** To be present (at). **2.** To accompany. **3.** To take care of. **4.** To heed. [< L *attendere,* to stretch toward, direct attention to.] —**at•tend'er** *n.*

at•ten•dance (ə-tĕn'dəns) *n.* **1.** The act of attending. **2.** The persons or number of persons present, as at a class.

at•ten•dant (ə-tĕn'dənt) *n.* **1.** One who attends or waits on another. **2.** One who is present. **3.** An accompanying circumstance; consequence. —*adj.* Accompanying or consequent. —**at•ten'dant•ly** *adv.*

at•ten•tion (ə-tĕn'shən) *n.* **1.** Concentration of one's mental powers upon an object. **2.** Observant consideration; notice. **3.** Consideration or courtesy. **4.** An erect posture assumed on command by a soldier. —**at•ten'tive** *adj.*

at•ten•u•ate (ə-tĕn'yoo-āt') *v.* **-ated, -ating.** **1.** To make or become slender, fine, or small. **2.** To weaken. **3.** To lessen in density; dilute or rarefy (a liquid or gas). **4.** To make (a pathogenic microorganism) less virulent. [L *attenuāre,* to make thin.]

at•test (ə-tĕst') *v.* **1.** To affirm to be correct, true, or genuine. **2.** To provide evidence of. —**attest to.** To bear witness. [< L *attestārī.*]

Att. Gen. attorney general.

at•tic (ăt'ĭk) *n.* A story or room directly below the roof of a house. [< *Attic story,* a top story having square columns in the ATTIC style.]

At•tic (ăt'ĭk) *adj.* Of or pertaining to ancient Attica, Athens, or the Athenians. —*n.* The Ancient Greek dialect of Athens.

At•ti•ca (ăt'ĭ-kə). The hinterland of ancient Athens.

At•ti•la (ăt'ə-lə, ə-tĭl'ə). A.D. 406?–453. King of the Huns.

at•tire (ə-tīr') *v.* **-tired, -tiring.** To dress; clothe; deck. —*n.* Clothing; array. [< OF *atirier,* to arrange into ranks.]

at•ti•tude (ăt'ə-t/y/ōōd') *n.* **1.** A posture or manner of carrying oneself, indicative of a mood or condition. **2.** A state of mind or feeling. **3.** The orientation of an aircraft's or spacecraft's axes relative to a reference line, plane, or direction of motion. [< L *aptitūdō,* faculty, fitness.] —**at'ti•tu'di•nal** *adj.*

attn. attention.

atto-. *comb. form.* One quintillionth of (a specified unit). [< Norw *atten,* eighteen.]

at•tor•ney (ə-tûr'nē) *n., pl.* **-neys.** A person, esp. a lawyer, legally appointed or empowered to act for another. [< OF *atorner,* to appoint.]

attorney general *pl.* **attorneys general.** The chief law officer and legal counsel of the government of a state or the U.S.

at•tract (ə-trăkt′) *v.* **1.** To cause to draw near or adhere. **2.** To draw or direct to oneself by some quality or action. **3.** To allure or be alluring. [< L *attrahere.*]

at•trac•tion (ə-trăk′shən) *n.* **1.** The act or quality of attracting. **2.** A feature that attracts. **3.** A public spectacle or entertainment.

at•trac•tive (ə-trăk′tĭv) *adj.* **1.** Having the power to attract. **2.** Appealing; charming. **—at•trac′tive•ly** *adv.*

at•trib•ute (ə-trĭb′yo͞ot) *v.* **-uted, -uting.** To regard or assign as belonging to or resulting from someone or something; ascribe. *—n.* (ăt′rə-byo͞ot′). **1.** A distinctive feature of or object associated with a person or thing. **2.** An adjective. [L *attribuĕre.*] **—at•trib′ut•a•ble** *adj.* **—at′tri•bu′tion** *n.*

at•trib•u•tive (ə-trĭb′yə-tĭv) *n.* A word, such as an adjective, or word group that is placed adjacent to the noun it modifies without a linking verb. *—adj.* **1.** Of or functioning as an attributive. **2.** Of or having the nature of an attribute. **—at•trib′u•tive•ly** *adv.*

at•tri•tion (ə-trĭsh′ən) *n.* **1.** A rubbing away or wearing down by friction. **2.** A gradual, natural reduction in membership or personnel, as through retirement, resignation, or death. [< L *atterere,* to rub against.]

at•tune (ə-t/y/o͞on′) *v.* **-tuned, -tuning.** **1.** To tune. **2.** To bring into harmony.

atty. attorney.

Atty. Gen. attorney general.

at wt atomic weight.

a•typ•i•cal (ā-tĭp′ĭ-kəl) *adj.* Not typical.

Au gold (L *aurum*).

au•burn (ô′bərn) *n.* A reddish brown. [< ML *alburnus,* whitish.] **—au′burn** *adj.*

Auck•land (ôk′lənd). A city of New Zealand, on North Island. Pop. 515,100.

au cou•rant (ō ko͞o-räɴ′). Informed on current affairs. [F, "in the current."]

auc•tion (ôk′shən) *n.* A public sale in which items are sold to the highest bidder. *—v.* **—auction off.** To sell at or by an auction. [L *auctiō,* (a sale by) increase (of bids).]

auc•tion•eer (ôk′shə-nîr′) *n.* One who conducts an auction.

auc•to•ri•al (ôk-tôr′ē-əl, ôk-tōr′-) *adj.* Of or pertaining to an author.

aud. audit; auditor.

au•da•cious (ô-dā′shəs) *adj.* **1.** Fearlessly daring; reckless. **2.** Arrogantly insolent. [< L *audāx,* bold.] **—au•da′cious•ly** *adv.* **—au•dac′i•ty** (ô-dăs′ə-tē) *n.*

au•di•ble (ô′də-bəl) *adj.* Capable of being heard. [< L *audīre,* to hear.] **—au′di•bil′i•ty** (ô′də-bĭl′ə-tē) *n.*

au•di•ence (ô′dē-əns) *n.* **1.** A gathering of spectators or listeners. **2.** Those reached by a book, radio broadcast, or television program. **3.** A formal hearing or conference. **4.** An opportunity to be heard. [< L *audīre,* to hear.]

au•di•o (ô′dē-ō′) *adj.* **1.** Pertaining to audible sound or to the broadcasting of sound. **2.** Pertaining to the high-fidelity reproduction of sound. *—n.* **1.** The audio part of television equipment. **2.** Audio broadcasting or reception. **3.** Audible sound.

audio frequency. A range of frequencies usually from 15 cycles per second to 20,000 cycles per second, characteristic of signals audible to the normal human ear.

au•di•o•phile (ô′dē-ō-fīl′) *n.* A high-fidelity audio hobbyist.

au•di•o-vis•u•al (ô′dē-ō-vĭzh′o͞o-əl) *adj.* **1.** Both audible and visible. **2.** Pertaining to educational materials, such as filmed or televised lectures, that present information in both audible and visible form.

au•dit (ô′dĭt) *n.* **1.** An examination, adjustment, or correction of records or accounts. **2.** An examined and verified account. *—v.* **1.** To examine, verify, or correct (accounts, records, or claims). **2.** To attend (a college course) without receiving academic credit. [< L *audītus,* a hearing.]

au•di•tion (ô-dĭsh′ən) *n.* **1.** The act or sense of hearing. **2.** A presentation of something heard; a hearing. **3.** A trial hearing, as of a performer. *—v.* To give or be tested in an audition. [< L *audīre,* to hear.]

au•di•tor (ô′də-tər) *n.* **1.** A listener. **2.** One who audits.

au•di•to•ri•um (ô′də-tôr′ē-əm, -tōr′ē-əm) *n., pl.* **-ums** or **-toria** (-tôr′ē-ə, -tōr′ē-ə). A room or building to accommodate an audience. [< L *audīre,* to hear.]

au•di•to•ry (ô′də-tôr′ē, -tōr′ē) *adj.* Pertaining to the sense, the organs, or the experience of hearing. [< L *audīre,* to hear.]

aug. augmentative.

Aug. August.

au•ger (ô′gər) *n.* A tool for boring. [< OE *nafogār,* "tool for piercing wheel hubs."]

aught (ôt) *n.* Also **ought.** A cipher; the symbol 0; zero. [< *an aught,* orig, a NAUGHT.]

aug•ment (ôg-mĕnt′) *v.* To make or become greater; enlarge; increase. [< LL *augmentāre* < L *augēre,* to increase.] **—aug′men•ta′tion** *n.*

au gra•tin (ō grät′n, grăt′n, ô). Topped with crumbs and/or grated cheese and browned. [F.]

au•gur (ô′gər) *n.* A seer or prophet; soothsayer. *—v.* **1.** To predict, prognosticate, or foretell. **2.** To betoken. [L.]

au•gu•ry (ô′gyə-rē) *n., pl.* **-ries.** **1.** The art, ability, or practice of auguring; divination. **2.** The rite performed by an augur. **3.** A sign or omen.

au•gust (ô-gŭst′) *adj.* Inspiring awe or admiration; majestic; venerable. [L *augustus,* venerable.] **—au•gust′ly** *adv.*

Au•gust (ô′gəst) *n.* The 8th month of the year. August has 31 days. [< AUGUSTUS.]

Au•gus•ta (ô-gŭs′tə). The capital of Maine. Pop. 22,000.

Au•gus•tan (ô-gŭs′tən) *adj.* Of, belonging to, or characteristic of the reign or times of Augustus Caesar.

Au•gus•tine (ô′gə-stēn′, ô-gŭs′tĭn), **Saint.** A.D. 354–430. Latin church father and philosopher. **—Au′gus•tin′i•an** (ô′gə-stĭn′ē-ən) *adj.*

Augustus

Au•gus•tus (ô-gŭs′təs). 63 B.C.–A.D. 14. Founder of the imperial Roman government.

auk (ôk) *n.* A chunky, short-winged sea bird of northern regions. [< ON *ālka.*]

auld (ôld) *adj. Scot.* Old.

aunt (ănt, änt) *n.* **1.** The sister of one's father or mother. **2.** The wife of one's uncle. [< L *amita,* paternal aunt.]

au•ra (ôr′ə) *n., pl.* **-ras** or **aurae** (ôr′ē). **1.** An invisible breath or emanation. **2.** A distinctive air or quality that characterizes a person or thing. [< L, breeze.]

au•ral (ôr′əl) *adj.* Of, pertaining to, or perceived by the ear. [< L *auris,* ear.] **—au′ral•ly** *adv.*

au•re•ate (ôr′ē-ĭt) *adj.* Of a golden color; gilded; ornate. [< L *aureus,* golden.] **—au′re•ate•ly** *adv.* **—au′re•ate•ness** *n.*

au•re•ole (ôr′ē-ōl′) *n.* Also **au•re•o•la** (ô-rē′ə-lə). A halo. [< L *aureolus,* golden.]

Au•re•o•my•cin (ôr′ē-ō-mī′sĭn) *n.* A trademark for an antibiotic.

au•ri•cle (ôr′ĭ-kəl) *n.* Also **au•ric•u•la** (ô-rĭk′yə-lə) *pl.* **-lae** (-lē′) or **-las.** **1. a.** The external part of the ear. **b.** An atrium of the heart. **2.** An earlike part or appendage. [< L *auris,* ear.] **—au′ri•cled** (-kəld) *adj.*

au•ric•u•lar (ô-rĭk′yə-lər) *adj.* **1.** Aural. **2.** Perceived by or spoken into the ear. **3.** Having the shape of an ear. **4.** Of or pertaining to an auricle of the heart. **—au•ric′u•lar•ly** *adv.*

au•rif•er•ous (ô-rĭf′ər-əs) *adj.* Containing gold; gold-bearing.

Au•ri•ga (ô-rī′gə) *n.* A constellation in the N Hemisphere. [L *aurīga,* charioteer.]

au•ro•ra (ô-rôr′ə, ô-rōr′ə, ə-) *n.* High-altitude, many-colored, flashing luminosity, visible in night skies of polar and sometimes temperate zones. [L *aurōra,* dawn.]

aurora aus•tra•lis (ô-strā′lĭs). Aurora occurring in southern regions; southern lights.

aurora bo•re•al•is (bôr′ē-ăl′ĭs, bōr′-). Aurora occurring in northern regions; northern lights.

au•ro•ral (ô-rôr′əl, ô-rōr′-, ə-) *adj.* Of or like an aurora.

aus•cul•ta•tion (ô′skəl-tā′shən) *n.* Diagnostic monitoring of the sounds made by internal organs. [< L *auscultāre,* to listen to.]

aus•pice (ô′spĭs) *n., pl.* **auspices** (ô′spə-sēz′). **1. auspices.** Protection or support; patronage. **2.** A portent or omen. [L *auspicium,* bird divination.]

aus•pi•cious (ô-spĭsh′əs) *adj.* Propitious; fortunate; prosperous. **—aus•pi′cious•ly** *adv.* **—aus•pi′cious•ness** *n.*

Aust. Austria; Austria-Hungary.

aus•tere (ô-stîr′) *adj.* **1.** Severe; stern; somber; grave. **2.** Ascetic; simple; bare. [< Gk *austēros,* harsh, rough, severe.] **—aus•ter′i•ty** (ô-stĕr′ə-tē), **aus•tere′ness** *n.*

Aus•tin (ôs′tən). The capital of Texas. Pop. 252,000.

aus•tral (ôs′trəl) *adj.* Southern. [< L *auster,* south.]

Aus•tra•lia (ô-strāl′yə). **1.** A continent, lying SE of Asia between the Pacific and Indian oceans. **2.** A country comprising this continent and the island of Tasmania. Pop. 11,360,000. Cap. Canberra.

Aus•tra•lian (ô-strāl′yən) *n.* **1.** A native or citizen of Australia. **2.** An aborigine of Australia. **—Aus•tra′lian** *adj.*

Aus•tri•a (ôs′trē-ə). A republic in C Europe. Pop. 7,074,000. Cap. Vienna. **—Aus′tri•an** *adj.* & *n.*

Aus•tri•a-Hun•ga•ry (ôs′trē-ə-hŭng′gə-rē). A former dual monarchy of C Europe.

Aus•tro-A•si•at•ic (ôs′trō-ā′zhē-ăt′ĭk) *n.* A language family of SE Asia. **—Aus′tro-A′si•at′ic** *adj.*

auth. 1. authentic. 2. author. 3. authority. 4. authorized.

au•then•tic (ô-thĕn'tĭk) *adj.* 1. Worthy of trust, reliance, or belief. 2. Genuine; real. [< Gk *authentikos,* genuine, authoritative.] —**au'then•tic'i•ty** (-tĭs'ə-tē) *n.*

au•then•ti•cate (ô-thĕn'tĭ-kāt') *v.* **-cated, -cating.** To establish or confirm as authentic. —**au•then'ti•ca'tion** *n.*

au•thor (ô'thər) *n.* 1. The writer of a literary work; a writer. 2. The beginner, originator, or creator of anything. [< L *auctor,* creator.]

au•thor•i•tar•i•an (ə-thôr'ə-târ'ē-ən, ə-thŏr'-, ô-) *adj.* Characterized by or favoring absolute obedience to authority. —*n.* One who believes in or practices authoritarian policies. —**au•thor'i•tar'i•an•ism'** *n.*

au•thor•i•ta•tive (ə-thôr'ə-tā'tĭv, ə-thŏr'-, ô-) *adj.* 1. Having or arising from proper authority. 2. Wielding authority.

au•thor•i•ty (ə-thôr'ə-tē, ə-thŏr'-, ô-) *n., pl.* **-ties.** 1. The right and power to command, enforce laws, exact obedience, determine, influence, or judge. 2. a. A person or group invested with this right and power. b. **authorities.** Government officials having this right and power. 3. Authorization. 4. a. An accepted source of expert information. b. A citation from such a source. 5. An expert in a given field: *an authority on plants.* [< L *auctōritās* < *auctor,* AUTHOR.]

au•thor•ize (ô'thə-rīz') *v.* **-ized, -izing.** 1. To grant authority or power to. 2. To sanction. 3. To justify. —**au'thor•i•za'tion** *n.*

Authorized Version. The King James Bible.

au•thor•ship (ô'thər-shĭp') *n.* 1. The profession or occupation of writing. 2. A source or origin, as of a book or idea.

au•tism (ô'tĭz'əm) *n.* 1. Abnormal subjectivity; acceptance of fantasy rather than reality. 2. A form of childhood schizophrenia characterized by acting out and withdrawal; infantile autism. [< AUT(O)- + -ISM.]

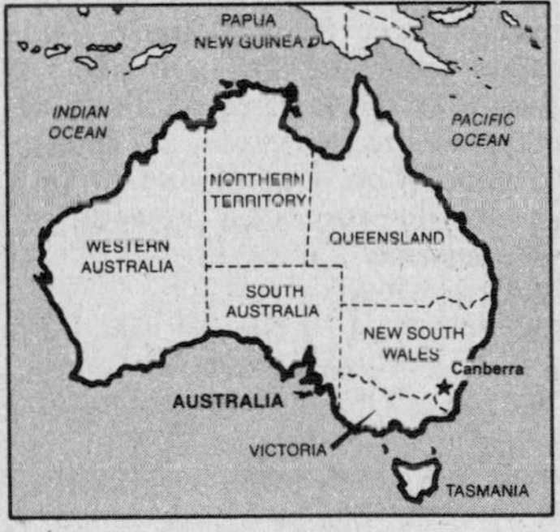

Australia

Austria

au•to (ô'tō) *n., pl.* **-tos.** An automobile.

auto-. *comb. form.* Acting or directed from within; self; same. [< Gk *autos,* self.]

auto. automatic.

au•to•bahn (ou'tō-bän') *n., pl.* **-bahns.** A German superhighway.

au•to•bi•og•ra•phy (ô'tō-bī-ŏg'rə-fē, -bē-ŏg'rə-fē) *n., pl.* **-phies.** The story of a person's life written by himself; memoirs.

au•toch•tho•nous (ô-tŏk'thə-nəs) *adj.* Indigenous; aboriginal.

au•toc•ra•cy (ô-tŏk'rə-sē) *n., pl.* **-cies.** 1. Government by a single person having unlimited power. 2. A country or state having this form of government. —**au'to•crat'** (ô'tə-krăt') *n.* —**au'to•crat'ic** *adj.*

au•to•graph (ô'tə-grăf', -gräf') *n.* 1. A person's own signature or handwriting. 2. A manuscript in the author's handwriting. —*v.* 1. To sign. 2. To write in one's own handwriting.

au•to•mat (ô'tə-măt') *n.* A self-service restaurant in which food is obtained from coin-operated machines.

au•to•mate (ô'tə-māt') *v.* **-mated, -mating.** To convert to, control, or operate by automation.

au•to•mat•ic (ô'tə-măt'ĭk) *adj.* 1. a. Acting or operating in a manner essentially independent of external influence or control. b. Self-regulating. 2. Involuntary; reflex. 3. Capable of firing continuously until ammunition is exhausted. —*n.* An automatic firearm or device [Gk *automatos,* acting by itself.]

au•to•ma•tion (ô'tə-mā'shən) *n.* 1. The automatic operation or control of a process, equipment, or a system. 2. The totality of mechanical and electronic techniques and equipment used to achieve such operation or control. 3. The condition of being automatically controlled or operated. —**au'to•ma'tive** *adj.*

au•tom•a•ton (ô-tŏm'ə-tən, -tŏn') *n., pl.* **-tons** or **-ta** (-tə). 1. A robot. 2. One that behaves in an automatic or mechanical fashion.

au•to•mo•bile (ô'tə-mō-bēl', -mō'bēl', ô'tə-mō-bēl') *n.* A self-propelled land vehicle, esp. a four-wheeled passenger vehicle propelled by an internal-combustion engine. —*adj.* Automotive. —**au'to•mo•bil'ist** *n.*

au•to•mo•tive (ô'tə-mō'tĭv) *adj.* 1. Self-moving; self-propelling. 2. Of or pertaining to automobiles.

au•to•nom•ic nervous system (ô'tə-nŏm'ĭk). The division of the vertebrate nervous system that regulates involuntary action, as of the intestines, heart, and glands, and comprises the sympathetic nervous system and the parasympathetic nervous system.

au•ton•o•mous (ô-tŏn'ə-məs) *adj.* 1. Independent; self-contained. 2. Self-governing. [Gk *autonomos,* self-ruling.] —**au•ton'o•my** *n.*

au•top•sy (ô'tŏp'sē, ô'təp-) *n., pl.* **-sies.** The examination of a dead body to determine the cause of death; post-mortem. [< Gk *autopsia,* a seeing for oneself.]

au•to•sug•ges•tion (ô'tō-səg-jĕs'chən) *n.* The process by which a person induces self-acceptance of an opinion, belief, or plan of action.

au•tumn (ô'təm) *n.* 1. The season of the year between summer and winter. 2. A time or period of maturity verging on decline. [< L *autumnus.*] —**au•tum'nal** (-tŭm'nəl) *adj.*

autumnal equinox. The equinox of September 22 or 23, marking the start of autumn.

aux. auxiliary.

aux•il•ia•ry (ôg-zĭl'yər-ē, -zĭl'ər-ē) *adj.* 1. Giving assistance or support; aiding; helping. 2. Subsidiary; supplementary. —*n., pl.* **-ries.** 1. One that acts in an auxiliary capacity. 2. Also **auxiliary verb.** A verb that accompanies certain verb forms to express tense, mood, voice, or aspect. [< L *auxilium,* help.]

av. 1. avenue. 2. average. 3. avoirdupois.

a•vail (ə-vāl') *v.* To be of use or advantage (to); assist; help. —*n.* Use, benefit: *to* (or *of*) *no avail.* [< L *valēre,* to be strong, be worth.]

a•vail•a•ble (ə-vā'lə-bəl) *adj.* Accessible for use; at hand; usable.

av•a•lanche (ăv'ə-lănch', -länch') *n.* A fall or slide of a large mass of snow, rock, or other material down a mountainside. [F.]

a•vant-garde (ä'vänt-gärd') *n.* 1. A group, as of writers or artists, regarded as the vanguard of a given field. 2. The admirers of such a group and critics acting as its spokesmen —*adj.* 1. Of or belonging to the vanguard, as in the arts. 2. Ahead of the times. [F, vanguard.]

av•a•rice (ăv'ə-rĭs) *n.* Greed for wealth; cupidity. [< L *avēre,* to desire.] —**av'a•ri'cious** (ăv'ə-rĭsh'əs) *adj.*

av•a•tar (ăv'ə-tär') *n.* One regarded as an incarnation. [Sk *avatāra,* descent.]

a•vaunt (ə-vônt', ə-vänt') *interj. Archaic.* Used as a command to be gone. [< OF *avant,* "forward," "go away!"]

avdp. avoirdupois.

ave., Ave. avenue.

A•ve Ma•ri•a (ä'vā mə-rē'ə). Also **A•ve Mar•y** (ā'vē mâr'ē). 1. A Roman Catholic prayer; Hail Mary. Luke 1:28, 42. 2. a. A recitation of this prayer. b. The hour, as at dawn and sunset, when it is customarily said. 3. One of the small beads on a rosary used to count recitations of this prayer. [< ML, "Hail Mary!"]

a•venge (ə-vĕnj') *v.* **avenged, avenging.** 1. To take revenge for (a wrong, injury, etc.). 2. To take vengeance (on behalf of). [< L *vindicāre,* to VINDICATE.] —**a•veng'er** *n.* —**a•veng'ing•ly** *adv.*

av•e•nue (ăv'ə-n/y/o͞o') *n.* 1. A wide street, thoroughfare, or path. 2. A means of approach to a given place, activity, or goal. [< L *advenīre,* to come to.]

a•ver (ə-vûr') *v.* **averred, averring.** To declare in a positive, dogmatic, or formal manner. [< ML *adverāre,* to assert as true.]

av•er•age (ăv'rĭj, ăv'ər-ĭj) *n.* 1. A number that typifies a set of numbers of which it is a function; the arithmetic mean. 2. A relative proportion or degree indicating position or achievement; a representative type. —*adj.* 1. Of, pertaining to, or constituting a mathematical average. 2. Typical; usual. —*v.* **-aged, -aging.** 1. To calculate, obtain, or amount to an average of. 2. To distribute proportionately. [Earlier *averie,* loss on damaged shipping, hence such loss shared equitably among investors.]

a•verse (ə-vûrs') *adj.* —**averse to.** Opposed; reluctant. [< L *āvertere,* AVERT.]

a•vert (ə-vûrt') *v.* 1. To turn away. 2. To ward off or prevent. [< VL **āvertīre.*]

A•ves•ta (ə-vĕs'tə) *n.* The sacred writings of the ancient Persians.

A•ves•tan (ə-vĕs'tən) *n.* The eastern dialect of Old Iranian, which is the oldest attested group in the Indo-Iranian branch of Indo-European.

a•vi•an (ā'vē-ən) *adj.* Of or pertaining to birds. [< L *avis,* bird.]

a•vi•ar•y (ā'vē-ĕr'ē) *n., pl.* **-ies.** A large enclosure for birds, as in a zoo. [< L *avis,* bird.] —**a'vi•a•rist** (ā'vē-ə-rĭst, -ĕr'ĭst) *n.*

a•vi•a•tion (ā'vē-ā'shən, ăv'ē-) *n.* 1. The operation of aircraft. 2. The production of aircraft. 3. Military aircraft. [< L *avis,* bird.]

a•vi•a•tor (ā'vē-ā'tər, ăv'ē-) *n.* A pilot.

av•id (ăv'ĭd) *adj.* 1. Eager; greedy. 2. Enthusiastic; ardent. [< L *avidus* < *avēre,* to long for.] —**av'id•ly** *adv.*

a•vid•i•ty (ə-vĭd'ə-tē) *n.* Eagerness; greed.

a•vi•on•ics (ā'vē-ŏn'ĭks, ăv'ē-) *n.* (*takes sing. v.*). The science and technology of electronics applied to aeronautics and astronautics. —**a'vi•on'ic** *adj.*

av•o•ca•do (ăv'ə-kä'dō) *n., pl.* **-dos.** 1. A tropical fruit with leathery skin and bland, yellow-green pulp. 2. A tree bearing such fruit. [< Nah *ahuacatl,* "testicle" (< the shape of the fruit).]

av•o•ca•tion (ăv'ō-kā'shən) *n.* An activity engaged in, in addition to one's regular work or profession; hobby. [< L *āvocāre,* to call away.]

av•o•cet (ăv'ə-sĕt') *n.* A long-legged shore bird with a long, slender beak. [< It *avocetta.*]

A•vo•ga•dro number (ä'və-gä'drō, ăv'ə-). Also **Avogadro's number, Avogadro constant.** The number of molecules in a mole of a substance, approx. 6.0225 x 10^{23}.

a•void (ə-void') *v.* To keep away from; shun. [< OF *esvuidier,* "to empty out," to leave.] —**a•void'ance** *n.* —**a•void'er** *n.*

av•oir•du•pois (ăv'ər-də-poiz') *n.* 1. **Avoirdupois weight.** 2. Weight; heaviness. [ME *avoir de pois,* "commodities sold by weight."]

avoirdupois weight. A system of weights and measures, used in most English-speaking countries, based on a pound containing 16 ounces or 7,000 grains and equal to 453.59 grams.

a•vouch (ə-vouch') *v.* 1. To guarantee. 2. To affirm. [< L *advocāre,* to call on (as adviser).]

a•vow (ə-vou') *v.* To acknowledge openly; confess. [< L *advocāre,* to call on (as adviser), appeal to.] —**a•vow'al** *n.*

a•vun•cu•lar (ə-vŭng'kyə-lər) *adj.* Of, pertaining to, or resembling an uncle. [< L *avunculus,* maternal uncle.]

A/W actual weight.

a•wait (ə-wāt') *v.* 1. To wait (for). 2. To be in store for. [< ONF *awaitier,* watch for, wait on.]

a•wake (ə-wāk') *v.* **awoke** or *rare* **awaked, awaked** or *rare* **awoke, awaking.** 1. To rouse from sleep; wake up. 2. To excite. 3. To stir up. —See Usage note at **wake.** —*adj.* 1. Not asleep. 2. Alert; vigilant; watchful. [< OE *awacian.*]

a•wak•en (ə-wā'kən) *v.* To wake up; awake. —See Usage note at **wake.** —**a•wak'en•ing** *adj. & n.*

a•ward (ə-wôrd') *v.* 1. To grant or declare as merited or due. 2. To bestow for performance or quality. —*n.* 1. A decision, as one made by a judge or arbitrator. 2. Something awarded. [< ONF *eswarder,* to judge after careful observation.]

a•ware (ə-wâr') *adj.* Conscious; cognizant; alert: *aware of the consequences.* [< OE *gewær.* See **wer-**[4].] —**a•ware'ness** *n.*

a•wash (ə-wŏsh', ə-wôsh') *adj. & adv.* 1. Level with and washed by waves. 2. Flooded.

a•way (ə-wā') *adv.* 1. At or to a distance. 2. In or to a different place or direction. 3. From one's presence or possession. 4. Out of existence: *dwindling away.* 5. Continuously: *working away.* 6. Immediately: *Fire away!* —*adj.* 1. Absent: *while he's away.* 2. At a distance: *He is miles away.* [< OE *aweg, onweg,* "on the way (from)."]

awe (ô) *n.* 1. An emotion of mingled reverence, dread, and wonder. 2. Respect tinged with fear. —*v.* **awed, awing** or **aweing.** To inspire with awe. [< ON *agi.*]

a•wea•ry (ə-wîr'ē) *adj.* Tired; weary.

a•weigh (ə-wā') *adj. Naut.* Hanging just clear of the bottom, as an anchor. [A- (on) + WEIGH.]

awe•some (ô'səm) *adj.* Inspiring awe.

awe-strick•en (ô'strĭk'ən) *adj.* Also **awe-struck** (-strŭk'). Full of awe.

aw•ful (ô'fəl) *adj.* 1. Extremely bad or unpleasant. 2. Dreadful; appalling. 3. Great: *an awful fool.* [ME *aweful* : AWE + -FUL.]

aw•ful•ly (ô'fə-lē, ôf'lē) *adv.* 1. In an awful manner. 2. Very.

a•while (ə-hwīl') *adv.* For a short time.

awk•ward (ôk'wərd) *adj.* 1. Lacking grace or dexterity; clumsy. 2. Hard to handle; unwieldy. 3. Uncomfortable; inconvenient. 4. Embarrassing; trying. [ME *awkeward,* "in the wrong direction," awry.] —**awk'ward•ly** *adv.* —**awk'ward•ness** *n.*

awl (ôl) *n.* A pointed tool for making holes, as in wood or leather. [< OE *eal* < Gmc **āl-.*]

awn (ôn) *n.* One of the bristles on a grass spike. [< ON *ōgn.*]

awn•ing (ô'nĭng) *n.* A structure, as of canvas, stretched over a frame as a shelter from weather. [?]

a•woke (ə-wōk'). *p.t. & rare p.p.* of **awake.**

A.W.O.L., awol (ā'wôl') *Mil.* Absent (or absence) without leave.

a•wry (ə-rī') *adv.* 1. Twisted toward one side; askew. 2. Amiss; wrong. [ME *awrie, on wry* : ON + WRY.] —**a•wry'** *adj.*

ax, axe (ăks) *n., pl.* **axes.** A chopping or cutting tool with a bladed head mounted on a handle. [< OE *æx.* See **agwesi.**] —**ax, axe** *v.* **(axed, axing).**

ax. axiom.

ax•i•al (ăk'sē-əl) *adj.* Of, on, around, or along an axis. —**ax'i•al•ly** *adv.*

ax•i•om (ăk'sē-əm) *n.* 1. An undemonstrated proposition concerning an undefined set of elements, properties, functions, and relationships; postulate. 2. A self-evident or accepted principle. [< Gk *axiōma,* "that which is thought fitting or worthy."] —**ax'i•o•mat'ic** *adj.* —**ax'i•o•mat'i•cal•ly** *adv.*

ax•is (ăk'sĭs) *n., pl.* **axes** (ăk'sēz'). 1. A straight line about which an object rotates or may be conceived to rotate. 2. An unlimited line, half-line, or line segment serving to orient a space or a geometrical object, esp. a line about which the object is symmetrical. 3. A center line or linear part along which parts of a structure or body are arranged. 4. *Fine Arts.* An imaginary line to which elements of the work are referred for measurement or symmetry. 5. **the Axis.** The alliance of Germany and Italy (1936), later including Japan and other nations, that opposed the Allies in World War II. [L, hub, axis.]

ax•le (ăk'səl) *n.* A supporting shaft on which a wheel turns. [< ON *ōxull.*]

ax•o•lotl (ăk'sə-lŏt'l) *n.* Any of several western North American and Mexican salamanders that retain their external gills when mature. [Nah.]

ax•on (ăk'sŏn') *n.* Also **ax•one** (ăk'sōn'). The core of a nerve fiber that generally conducts impulses away from the nerve cell. [< Gk *axōn,* axis.]

aye[1] (ī). Also **ay.** *n.* An affirmative vote. —*adv.* Yes. [Earlier *ay, ei,* orig, *I.*]

aye[2] (ā) *adv.* Also **ay.** *Poetic.* Always; ever. [< ON *ei.*]

a•yin (ä'yĭn) *n.* Also **a•in.** The 16th letter of the Hebrew alphabet, representing a glottal stop.

Ay•ma•ra (ī'mä-rä') *n., pl.* **-ra** or **-ras.** 1. A member of an Indian people inhabiting Bolivia and Peru. 2. Their language or language family. —**Ay'ma•ran'** *adj. & n.*

AZ Arizona (with Zip Code).

az. azimuth.

a•zal•ea (ə-zāl'yə) *n.* Any of several shrubs often cultivated for their showy, variously colored flowers. [NL, "the dry plant" (growing in dry soil).]

A•zer•bai•jan Soviet Socialist Republic (ä'-zər-bī-jän', ăz'ər-). A constituent republic of the Soviet Union on the Caspian Sea. Pop. 5,111,000. Cap. Baku.

az•i•muth (ăz'ə-məth) *n.* 1. The horizontal angular distance from a fixed reference direction to a position, object, or object referent, as to a great circle intersecting a celestial body, usually measured clockwise in degrees along the horizon from a point due south. 2. *Mil.* The lateral deviation of a projectile or bomb. [< Ar *as-sumūt,* pl of *as-samt,* "the way," compass bearing.]

A•zores (ā'zôrz, ə-zôrz'). An island group belonging to Portugal in the N Atlantic.

Az•tec (ăz'tĕk') *n.* 1. A member of an Indian people of Mexico noted for their advanced civilization before the Spanish conquest. 2. Their language, Nahuatl. —*adj.* Also **Az•tec•an** (-ən). Of the Aztecs, their language, culture, or empire.

az•ure (ăzh'ər) *n.* The blue of the clear daytime sky. [< Ar *allāzaward,* lapis lazuli.] —**az'ure** *adj.*

Bb

b, B (bē) *n.* **1.** The 2nd letter of the English alphabet. **2.** The 2nd in a series. **3.** The 2nd highest grade in quality.

b *Phys.* barn.

B **1.** boron. **2.** The 7th tone in the scale of C major.

b. **1.** base. **2.** *Mus.* basso. **3.** breadth.

B. **1.** bachelor. **2.** bacillus. **3.** Bible. **4.** British.

Ba barium.

B.A. **1.** Bachelor of Arts. **2.** British Academy. **3.** British Association (for the Advancement of Science).

baa (bă, bä) *n.* The bleat of a sheep. [Imit.] **—baa** *v.*

Ba•al (bā'əl) *n., pl.* **-alim** (-ə-lĭm). **1.** Any of various local fertility and nature gods of the ancient Semitic peoples. **2.** Any false god or idol.

Bab•bitt (băb'ĭt) *n.* A smug, provincial member of the American middle class. [< the main character in the novel *Babbitt* by Sinclair Lewis (1885–1951).]

bab•ble (băb'əl) *v.* **-bled, -bling.** **1.** To utter incoherent, meaningless sound. **2.** To talk foolishly; chatter. *—n.* The sound or act of babbling. [ME *babelen.*] **—bab'bler** *n.*

babe (bāb) *n.* **1.** A baby. **2.** *Slang.* A girl or young woman. [ME *babe.*]

ba•bel (bā'bəl, băb'əl) *n.,* Also **Ba•bel.** **1.** A confused sound of voices. **2.** A scene of noise and confusion. [< the city of *Babel* (thought to be Babylon), where construction of a tower was interrupted by the confusion of tongues.]

bab•ka (băb'kə) *n.* A yeast-leavened cake made with raisins and almonds. [Pol, "little old woman."]

ba•boon (bă-bo͞on') *n.* A large African monkey with a prominent muzzle. [< OF *babuin,* gaping figure, baboon.]

ba•bush•ka (bə-bo͝osh'kə) *n.* A head scarf folded triangularly and tied under the chin. [Russ, "grandmother."]

ba•by (bā'bē) *n., pl.* **-bies.** **1.** A very young child; infant. **2.** The youngest member of a family or group. **3.** One who acts like an infant. **4.** *Slang.* A girl or young woman. *—v.* **-bied, -bying.** To pamper; coddle. [ME *babie.*] **—ba'by•hood'** *n.* **—ba'by•ish** *adj.*

Bab•y•lon (băb'ə-lən, -lŏn'). The capital of ancient Babylonia.

Bab•y•lo•ni•a (băb'ə-lō'nē-ə). An ancient empire in Mesopotamia.

Bab•y•lo•ni•an (băb'ə-lō'nē-ən) *adj.* Of or pertaining to Babylonia. *—n.* **1.** A native or inhabitant of Babylonia. **2.** The Semitic language of the Babylonians, a form of Akkadian.

ba•by's-breath (bā'bēz-brĕth') *n.* A plant with numerous small white flowers.

ba•by-sit (bā'bē-sĭt') *v.* To care for children when the parents are not at home. **—baby sitter.**

bac•ca•lau•re•ate (băk'ə-lôr'ē-ĭt) *n.* **1.** The degree of bachelor, conferred upon graduates of colleges and universities. **2.** A farewell address delivered to a graduating class, as of a college. [< ML *baccalaureātus,* var of *baccalārius,* BACHELOR.]

bac•cha•nal (băk'ə-năl', -näl', băk'ə-nəl) *n.* **1.** A drunken or riotous celebration, originally in honor of Bacchus. **2.** A participant in such a celebration.

Bac•chus (băk'əs). Greco-Roman god of wine. **—Bac'chic** *adj.*

Bach (bäkн), **Johann Sebastian.** 1685–1750. German composer and organist.

bach•e•lor (băch'ə-lər, băch'lər) *n.* **1.** An unmarried man. **2. a.** A college or university degree signifying completion of the undergraduate curriculum. **b.** A person holding such a degree. [< ML *baccalārius.*] **—bach'e•lor•hood'** *n.* **—bach'e•lor•ship'** *n.*

bach•e•lor's-but•ton (băch'ə-lərz-bŭt'n, băch'lərz-) *n.* The cornflower.

ba•cil•lus (bə-sĭl'əs) *n., pl.* **-cilli** (-sĭl'ī'). Any of various rod-shaped bacteria. [< LL dim of L *baculum,* rod, stick.]

back (băk) *n.* **1. a.** The region of the vertebrate body nearest the spine. **b.** The upper part of the body in invertebrates. **2.** The part farthest from or behind the front; the rear. **3.** The reverse side. **4.** A football player positioned in the backfield. *—v.* **1.** To move backward or in a reverse direction. **2.** To support; strengthen. **3.** To bet on. **4.** To form the back of. **—back down.** To withdraw from a former stand. *—adj.* **1.** At the rear. **2.** Distant; remote. **3.** Of or for a past date or time. **4.** Backward. *—adv.* **1.** To or toward the rear. **2.** To or toward a former place, state, or time. **3.** In reserve, concealment, or check. **4.** In return. [< OE *bæc* < Gmc **bakam.*]

back•bite (băk'bīt') *v.* To speak spitefully or slanderously of a person who is not present. **—back'bit'er** *n.*

back•bone (băk'bōn') *n.* **1.** The vertebrate spine. **2.** A main support. **3.** Strength of character.

back•er (băk'ər) *n.* One who supports or gives aid.

back•field (băk'fēld') *n. Football.* **1.** The players stationed behind the line of scrimmage. **2.** The area occupied by these players.

back•fire (băk'fīr') *n.* An explosion of prematurely ignited fuel or of unburned exhaust. *—v.* **1.** To explode in a backfire. **2.** To produce an unexpected, unwanted result.

back-for•ma•tion (băk'fôr-mā'shən) *n.* The creation of a new word by deletion of what is construed to be an affix from an existing word, as *laze* from *lazy.*

back•gam•mon (băk'găm'ən) *n.* A board game for two, with moves determined by throws of dice. [Prob < BACK + GAME.]

back•ground (băk'ground') *n.* **1.** The area, space, or surface against which objects are seen or represented. **2.** Conditions or events forming a setting. **3.** A place or state of relative obscurity. **4.** One's experience or training.

back•hand (băk'hănd') *n.* **1.** A motion, as of a tennis racket, made with the back of the hand facing outward and moving forward. **2.** Handwriting with letters that slant to the left.

back•hand•ed (băk'hăn'dĭd) *adj.* **1.** With the motion or direction of a backhand. **2.** Containing a disguised insult or rebuke.

back•ing (băk'ĭng) *n.* **1.** Something that supports from the back. **2.** Support or aid. **3.** Supporters; endorsers.

back•lash (băk'lăsh') *n.* **1.** A sudden backward whipping motion. **2.** An antagonistic reaction, as in socio-economic relations.

back•log (băk'lŏg', -lôg') *n.* A reserve supply or accumulation.

back•pack (băk'păk') *n.* A kind of knapsack, often mounted on a lightweight frame. *—v.* **1.** To hike while carrying a backpack. **2.** To carry in a backpack. **—back'pack'er** *n.*

back•side (băk'sīd') *n.* The buttocks; rump.

back•slide (băk'slīd') *v.* To revert to wrongdoing. **—back'slid'er** *n.*

back•spin (băk'spĭn') *n.* A spin that tends to retard, arrest, or reverse the linear motion of an object, esp. of a ball.

back•stop (băk'stŏp') *n.* A screen or fence to prevent a ball from being thrown or hit far out of a playing area.

back•stretch (băk'strĕch') *n.* The part of a racecourse farthest from the spectators and opposite the homestretch.

back•stroke (băk'strōk') *n.* **1.** A backhanded stroke. **2.** A swimming stroke executed with the swimmer on his back and moving the arms upward and backward.

back talk. An insolent retort.

back•track (băk'trăk') *v.* **1.** To retrace one's route. **2.** To reverse one's stand; retreat.

back•ward (băk'wərd) *adv.* Also **back•wards** (-wərdz). **1.** Toward the back. **2.** With the back leading. **3.** In reverse. **4.** Toward a former, often worse, condition. *—adj.* **1.** Reversed. **2.** Reluctant; unwilling. **3.** Retarded in development. **—back'ward•ness** *n.*

back•wash (băk'wŏsh', -wôsh') *n.* A backward flow or motion, as of water or air.

back•wa•ter (băk'wô'tər, -wŏt'ər) *n.* A place of stagnation or arrested progress.

back•woods (băk'wo͝odz', -wo͝odz') *pl.n.* Heavily wooded, thinly settled areas.

ba•con (bā'kən) *n.* Salted and smoked meat from the back and sides of a pig. **—bring home the bacon.** *Informal.* **1.** To provide food and other necessities. **2.** To make good; succeed. [< Frank **bako,* ham.]

Ba•con (bā'kən). **1. Francis.** 1561–1626. English essayist and statesman. **2. Roger.** 1214?–1294. English philosopher and scientist.

bac•te•ri•a (băk-tîr'ē-ə) *pl.n. Sing.* **-terium** (-tîr'ē-əm). Any of numerous sometimes parasitic unicellular organisms having various forms and often causing disease. [< Gk *baktērion,* dim of *baktron,* rod.] **—bac•te'ri•al** *adj.* **—bac•te'ri•al•ly** *adv.*

bac•te•ri•cide (băk-tîr'ə-sīd') *n.* A substance that destroys bacteria. **—bac•te'ri•ci'dal** *adj.*

bac•te•ri•ol•o•gy (băk-tîr'ē-ŏl'ə-jē) *n.* The scientific study of bacteria. **—bac•te'ri•o•log'ic** (-ə-lŏj'ĭk), **bac•te'ri•o•log'i•cal** *adj.* **—bac•te'ri•o•log'i•cal•ly** *adv.* **—bac•te'ri•ol'o•gist** *n.*

bad (băd) *adj.* **worse, worst.** **1.** Having undesirable qualities; not good. **2.** Inferior; poor. **3.** Unfavorable. **4.** Rotten; spoiled. **5.** Severe;

intense: *a bad cold.* **6.** Sorry; regretful. [Perh < OE *bǣdan,* to compel, afflict. See **bheidh-.**] —**bad'ly** *adv.* —**bad'ness** *n.*

Usage: Bad (adj.), not *badly,* is the proper form following linking verbs such as *feel* and *look* when the desired sense is *ill* or *regretful.*

bade (băd). A *p.t.* of **bid.**

badge (băj) *n.* An emblem worn as a sign of rank, membership, or honor. [< NF *bage.*]

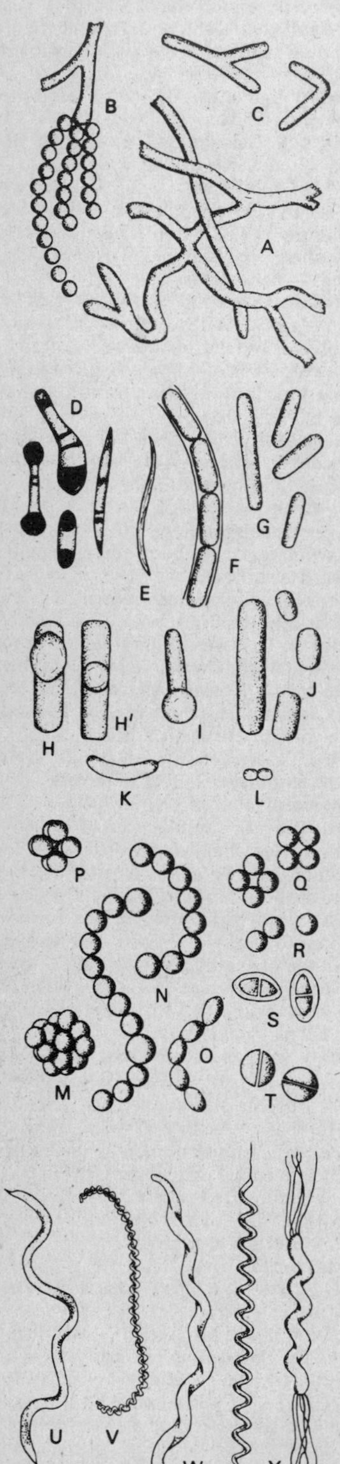

badg•er (băj'ər) *n.* **1.** A burrowing animal with a thick, grizzled coat. **2.** The fur of a badger. —*v.* To harry; pester. [< BADGE.]

bad•i•nage (băd'ə-näzh') *n.* Light, playful banter. [< VL *batāre, to gape.]

bad•min•ton (băd'mĭn'tən) *n.* A net game played with a shuttlecock and long-handled rackets. [< *Badminton,* England.]

baf•fle (băf'əl) *v.* **-fled, -fling. 1.** To foil; thwart. **2.** To make helplessly puzzled. —*n.* Any structure used to impede, regulate, or alter flow direction, as of a gas, of sound, or of a liquid. [?] —**baf'fle•ment** *n.* —**baf'fler** *n.*

bag (băg) *n.* **1.** A nonrigid container, as of cloth or paper. **2.** A suitcase or purse. **3.** An amount of game taken at a time. —*v.* **bagged, bagging. 1.** To hang or bulge loosely. **2.** To capture or kill, as game. [< ON *baggi.*]

bag•a•telle (băg'ə-tĕl') *n.* A trifle. [< L *băca, bacca,* berry.]

ba•gel (bā'gəl) *n.* A tough, chewy ring-shaped roll. [< OHG *boug,* ring.]

bag•gage (băg'ĭj) *n.* **1.** The bags and belongings carried while traveling; luggage. **2.** A wanton or impudent woman. [< OF *bague,* bundle, pack.]

bag•gy (băg'ē) *adj.* **-gier, -giest.** Bulging or hanging loosely. —**bag'gi•ness** *n.*

Bagh•dad (băg'dăd'). Also **Bag•dad.** The capital of Iraq. Pop. 2,124,000.

bag•pipe (băg'pīp') *n.* Often **bagpipes.** A wind instrument with an inflatable bag that produces the different tones.

ba•guette (bă-gĕt') *n.* A gem cut into a narrow rectangle. [F, "small rod."]

Ba•ha•ma Islands (bə-hä'mə). Also **Ba•ha•mas** (-məz). An independent country of over 700 islands SW of Florida in the Atlantic. Pop. 190,000. Cap. Nassau. —**Ba•ha'mi•an** (bə-hā'mē-ən, -hä'mē-ən) *adj. & n.*

bacteria

A. *Actinomyces bovis*
B. *Streptomyces* species
C. *Mycobacterium tuberculosis*
D. *Corynebacterium diphtheriae*
E. *Fusobacterium fusiforme*
F. *Sphaerotilus natans*
G. *Salmonella typhosa*
H, H'. *Bacillus* species
I. *Clostridium tetani*
J. *Bacillus megaterium*
K. *Vibrio comma*
L. *Brucella abortus*
M. *Staphylococcus aureus*
N. *Streptococcus pyogenes*
O. *Streptococcus lactis*
P. *Sarcina homarus*
Q. *Gaffkya tetragena*
R. Single cocci in fission
S. *Diplococcus pneumoniae*
T. *Neisseria gonorrhoeae*
U. *Borrelia recurrentis*
V. *Leptospira icterohaemorrhagae*
W. *Spirochaeta plicatilis*
X. *Treponema pallidum*
Y. *Spirillum minus*

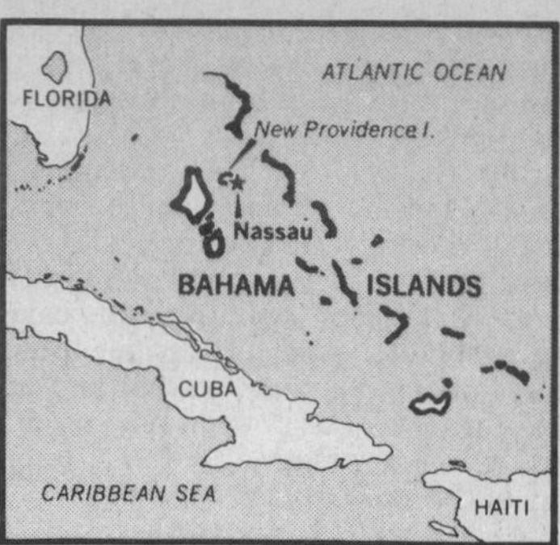

Bahama Islands

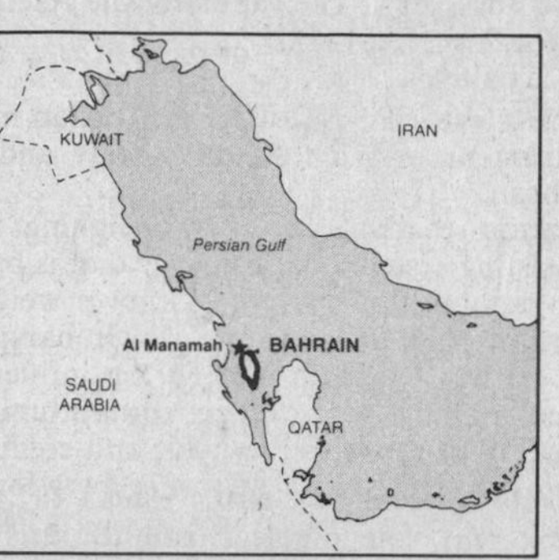

Bahrain

Bah•rain (bä-rān'). An independent sheikdom comprising an archipelago in the Persian Gulf. Pop. 300,000. Cap. Al Manamah.

baht (bät) *n., pl.* **bahts** or **baht.** The basic monetary unit of Thailand.

bail¹ (bāl) *n.* **1.** Money supplied as a guarantee that an arrested person will appear for trial. **2.** Release obtained by such security. **3.** One providing such security. —*v.* To release by providing or taking such security. [< OF *baillier,* to take charge of, carry.] —**bail'er** *n.*

bail² (bāl) *v.* To empty a boat of water by scooping or dipping. —**bail out.** To parachute from an aircraft. —*n.* A container used for bailing. [< VL **bājula,* "carrier (of water)."]

bail³ (bāl) *n.* An arched, hooplike handle, as of a pail. [< ME *baile,* handle.]

bail•iff (bā'lĭf) *n.* **1.** A court attendant who has custody of prisoners and maintains order in a courtroom. **2.** An official who assists a British sheriff by executing writs and making arrests. **3.** *Chiefly Brit.* An overseer of an estate; steward. [< OF *baillif.*]

bail•i•wick (bā'lĭ-wĭk') *n.* **1.** The office or district of a bailiff. **2.** One's field of interest or authority.

Bai•ly's beads (bā'lēz). Bright spots of sunlight that appear briefly around the edge of the moon's disk immediately before and after the central phase in a solar eclipse. [< F. *Baily* (1774–1844), British astronomer.]

bairn (bârn) *n. Scot.* A child; son or daughter. [< OE *bearn.*]

bait (bāt) *n.* **1.** Food or a lure used to catch fish or trap animals. **2.** An enticement; lure. —*v.* **1.** To supply (a fishhook, trap, etc.) with bait. **2.** To lure; entice. **3.** To attack (a captive animal) with dogs for sport. **4.** To harass; persecute. [< ON *beita,* to hunt with dogs, harass, and *beita,* food, fish bait.] —**bait'er** *n.*

baize (bāz) *n.* An often green feltlike fabric. [F *baie* (pl *baies*).]

bake (bāk) *v.* **baked, baking.** 1. To cook with continuous dry heat, esp. in an oven. 2. To harden or dry in or as if in an oven. [< OE *bacan.* See **bhē-.**] —**bak'er** *n.*

Ba•ke•lite (bā'kə-līt') *n.* A trademark for a group of thermosetting plastics with high chemical and electrical resistance.

bak•er•y (bā'kə-rē) *n., pl.* **-ies.** An establishment for baking or selling bread, cake, etc.

baking powder. Any of various powdered mixtures of baking soda, starch, and at least one slightly acidic compound, used as a leavening agent in baking.

baking soda. **Sodium bicarbonate.**

bak•sheesh (băk'shēsh', băk-shēsh') *n.* A gratuity or gift of alms in the Near East. [Pers *bakhshīsh.*]

Ba•ku (bä-ko͞o'). The capital of the Azerbaijan S.S.R. Pop. 1,261,000.

bal. balance.

bal•a•lai•ka (băl'ə-lī'kə) *n.* A Russian musical instrument with a triangular body and three strings.

bal•ance (băl'əns) *n.* 1. A weighing device consisting essentially of a lever that is brought into equilibrium by adding known weights to one end while the unknown weight hangs from the other. 2. Equilibrium. 3. An influence or force tending to produce equilibrium. 4. a. Equality of totals in the debit and credit sides of an account. b. A difference between such totals. 5. Anything that remains or is left over. 6. Equality of symbolic value on each side of an equation. 7. A balance wheel. —*v.* **-anced, -ancing.** 1. To weigh or poise in or as if in a balance. 2. To bring into or be maintained in equilibrium. 3. To counterbalance. 4. To compute the difference between the debits and credits of (an account). [< LL *(lībra) bilanx,* (a balance) having two scales.]

balance of payments. A systematic recording of a nation's total payments to foreign countries, including its total receipts from abroad.

balance wheel. A wheel that regulates rate of movement in machine parts, as in a watch.

bal•bo•a (băl bō'ə) *n.* The basic monetary unit of Panama. [< Vasco de *Balboa* (1475–1517), Spanish explorer.]

bal•brig•gan (băl-brĭg'ən) *n.* A knitted cotton fabric. [< *Balbriggan,* Irish seaport where it was first manufactured.]

bal•co•ny (băl'kə-nē) *n., pl.* **-nies.** 1. A platform projecting from the wall of a building and surrounded by a railing. 2. A gallery projecting over the main floor in a theater or auditorium. [It *balcone.*]

bald (bôld) *adj.* 1. Lacking hair on the top of the head. 2. Lacking natural or usual covering. 3. Having a white head: *bald eagle.* 4. Unadorned. [ME *ballede.*] —**bald'ly** *adv.* —**bald'ness** *n.*

bal•da•chin (bôl'də-kĭn, băl'-) *n.* Also **bal•da•quin, bal•da•chi•no** (băl'də-kē'nō). A canopy over an altar, throne, etc. [< OIt *Baldacco,* BAGHDAD.]

bal•der•dash (bôl'dər-dăsh') *n.* Words without sense; nonsense. [?]

bald•ing (bôld'ĭng) *adj.* Gradually losing one's hair.

bal•dric (bôl'drĭk) *n.* A leather belt worn across the chest to support a sword or bugle. [< OF *baldrei.*]

bale (bāl) *n.* A large bound package of raw or finished material. —*v.* **baled, baling.** To wrap in bales. [ME.] —**bal'er** *n.*

Bal•e•ar•ic Islands (băl'ē-ăr'ĭk, bə-lĭr'ĭk). A Spanish island group in the Mediterranean. Pop. 443,000.

ba•leen (bə-lēn') *n.* Whalebone. [< L *ballaena,* whale.]

bale•ful (bāl'fəl) *adj.* 1. Malignant in intent or effect. 2. Ominous. —**bale'ful•ly** *adv.* —**bale'ful•ness** *n.*

Ba•li (bä'lē). An island of Indonesia, off the E end of Java. Pop. 2,196,000. Cap. Denpasar. —**Ba'li•nese'** *adj.* & *n.*

balk (bôk) *v.* 1. To stop short and refuse to go on. 2. To thwart; check. —*n.* A hindrance; setback. [< OE *balc, balca,* bank, ridge in plowing.] —**balk'er** *n.* —**balk'y** *adj.*

Bal•kan (bôl'kən) *adj.* 1. Of the Balkan Peninsula of SE Europe. 2. Of the Balkans or their inhabitants. —**the Balkans.** The states that occupy the Balkan Peninsula.

Balkan Peninsula. A peninsula in SE Europe, E of Italy.

ball[1] (bôl) *n.* 1. A spherical or almost spherical body or entity. 2. a. Any of various more or less rounded objects used in games. b. A game played with such an object. 3. A pitched baseball that does not pass through the strike zone and is not swung at by the batter. 4. A rounded part or protuberance: *the ball of the foot.* —*v.* To form or become formed into a ball. [< ON *böllr.*]

ball[2] (bôl) *n.* 1. A large formal gathering for social dancing. 2. *Slang.* An enjoyable time. [< OF *baller,* to dance.]

bal•lad (băl'əd) *n.* 1. A narrative poem, often of folk origin and intended to be sung, consisting of simple stanzas and usually having a recurrent refrain. 2. A slow, romantic popular song. [< Prov *balada,* piece to be accompanied by dancing.] —**bal'lad•eer'** (-ə-dîr') *n.* —**bal'lad•ry** *n.*

bal•last (băl'əst) *n.* 1. Any heavy material placed in the hold of a ship or the gondola of a balloon to enhance stability. 2. Coarse gravel or crushed rock laid to form a roadbed. —*v.* To stabilize or provide with ballast. [Perh < OSw *barlast,* "bare load" (cargo carried for its weight).]

ball bearing. 1. A friction-reducing bearing, consisting essentially of a ring-shaped track containing freely revolving hard metal balls. 2. A hard ball used in such a bearing.

bal•le•ri•na (băl'ə-rē'nə) *n.* A female ballet dancer. [< It *ballare,* to dance.]

bal•let (bă-lā', băl'ā') *n.* 1. A dance genre characterized chiefly by a highly formalized technique. 2. A choreographic presentation, usually with music, on a narrative or abstract theme. [< It *ballare,* to dance.]

ballistic missile. A projectile that assumes a free-falling trajectory after an internally guided, self-powered ascent.

bal•lis•tics (bə-lĭs'tĭks) *n. (takes sing. v.).* 1. a. The study of the dynamics of projectiles. b. The study of the flight characteristics of projectiles. 2. a. The study of the functioning of firearms. b. The study of the firing, flight, and effect of ammunition. [< Gk *ballein,* to throw.] —**bal•lis'tic** *adj.* —**bal'lis•ti'cian** (băl'ĭ-stĭsh'ən) *n.*

bal•loon (bə-lo͞on') *n.* 1. A flexible bag inflated with a gas such as helium that causes it to rise in the atmosphere, esp. such a bag with sufficient capacity to lift a suspended gondola. 2. An inflatable toy rubber bag. —*v.* To expand or cause to expand like a balloon. [F *ballon* < It *palla,* ball.]

bal•lot (băl'ət) *n.* 1. A paper or ticket used to cast or register a vote. 2. The act, process, or method of voting. 3. A list of candidates for office. 4. The total of all votes cast in an election. 5. The right to vote; franchise. —*v.* To cast a ballot. [It *ballotta,* small ball or pebble used for voting.]

ball•room (bôl'ro͞om', -ro͝om') *n.* A large room for dancing.

bal•ly•hoo (băl'ē-ho͞o') *n.* Sensational advertising. —*v.* To promote with ballyhoo. [?]

balm (bäm) *n.* 1. An aromatic resin, oil, or ointment used medicinally. 2. Any of various aromatic plants. 3. Something that soothes or comforts. [< L *balsamum,* BALSAM.]

balm•y (bä'mē) *adj.* **-ier, -iest.** 1. Having the quality or fragrance of balm. 2. Mild and pleasant: *a balmy breeze.*

ba•lo•ney (bə-lō'nē) *n. Slang.* Nonsense.

bal•sa (bôl'sə) *n.* 1. A tropical American tree with very light, buoyant wood. 2. The wood of this tree. [Span.]

bal•sam (bôl'səm) *n.* 1. An aromatic resin or ointment obtained from various trees or plants. 2. A tree yielding balsam. 3. A plant cultivated for its colorful flowers. [L *balsamum.*]

Balt (bôlt) *n.* A member of one of the Baltic-speaking peoples.

Bal•tic (bôl'tĭk) *adj.* 1. Pertaining to the Baltic Sea or to the countries on its E coast. 2. Of or designating an Indo-European group of languages consisting of Lithuanian, Latvian, and Old Prussian. —*n.* The Baltic language group.

Baltic Sea. A long arm of the Atlantic Ocean in N Europe, NE of Germany.

Bal•ti•more (bôl'tə-môr', -mōr'). The largest city of Maryland. Pop. 906,000. —**Bal'ti•mo're•an** *adj.* & *n.*

Bal•to-Sla•vic (bôl'tō-slä'vĭk, -slăv'ĭk) *n.* A subfamily of the Indo-European language family, composed of Baltic and Slavic.

bal•us•ter (băl'ə-stər) *n.* One of the upright supports of a handrail. [< It *balaustro.*]

bal•us•trade (băl'ə-strād') *n.* A rail and the row of posts that support it. [< It *balaustrata* < *balaustro,* BALUSTER.]

Ba•ma•ko (băm'ə-kō'). The capital of the Republic of Mali. Pop. 120,000.

bam•boo (băm-bo͞o') *n.* A tall tropical grass with hollow, woody stems having a wide variety of uses. [Prob < Malay *bambū.*]

bam•boo•zle (băm-bo͞o'zəl) *v.* **-zled, -zling.** To trick; deceive. [Perh < a cant var of *bumbazzle.*] —**bam•boo'zler** *n.*

ban (băn) *v.* **banned, banning.** To prohibit, esp. officially. —*n.* A prohibition imposed by law or official decree. [< OE *bannan,* to summon, proclaim, and < ON *banna,* to prohibit, curse. See **bhā-**[2].]

ba•nal (bə-näl', -năl', bā'nəl) *adj.* Completely ordinary. [F, commonplace.] —**ba•nal'i•ty** (bə-năl'ə-tē, bā-) *n.*

ba•nan•a (bə-năn'ə) *n.* 1. The crescent-shaped fruit of a treelike tropical plant, having pulpy flesh and yellow or reddish skin. 2. A plant bearing such fruit. [< native W Afr name.]

band[1] (bănd) *n.* 1. A thin strip of flexible material used to encircle and bind together. 2. A range of numerical values. —*v.* To bind or identify with a band. [< OF *bande,* bond, tie.]

band[2] (bănd) *n.* 1. A group of people or animals. 2. A group of musicians who play together. —*v.* To assemble or unite in a group. [OF *bande,* a troop.]

band•age (băn'dĭj) *n.* A strip of material used to protect a wound or other injury. —*v.* **-aged, -aging.** To apply such a covering to. [F < *bande,* BAND (strip).]

Band-Aid (bănd'ād') *n.* **1.** A trademark for an adhesive bandage. **2.** Any temporary or superficial remedy or solution.

ban•dan•na, ban•dan•a (băn-dăn'ə) *n.* A large scarf for the head. [< Port.]

Ban•dar Se•ri Be•ga•wan (băn'där sĕr'ē bə-gä'wən). The capital of Brunei. Pop. 36,500.

ban•di•coot (băn'dĭ-ko͞ot') *n.* A ratlike Australian marsupial with a long snout. [Telegu *pandikokku.*]

ban•dit (băn'dĭt) *n.* A robber; gangster. [It *bandito.*] **—ban'dit•ry** *n.*

ban•do•leer, ban•do•lier (băn'də-lîr') *n.* A belt with pockets for cartridges, worn across the chest. [F *bandoulière.*]

band saw. A power saw consisting essentially of a continuous, toothed metal band.

band•wag•on (bănd'wăg'ən) *n.* **1.** A decorated wagon carrying musicians in a parade. **2.** An apparently ascendant cause that attracts often cynically opportunistic followers.

ban•dy (băn'dē) *v.* **-died, -dying. 1.** To toss back and forth. **2.** To discuss or exchange in a casual or frivolous manner. *—adj.* Bent in an outward curve: *bandy legs.* [Perh < OF *bander,* to bandy at tennis.]

bane (bān) *n.* **1.** A cause of death or ruin. **2.** A deadly poison. [< OE *bana,* slayer, ruin. See **bhen-.**] **—bane'ful** *adj.*

bang[1] (băng) *n.* **1.** A sudden loud noise or thump. **2.** *Slang.* A sense of excitement; thrill. *—v.* **1.** To hit noisily. **2.** To close or handle noisily or violently. *—adv.* Exactly; precisely. [< Scand.]

bang[2] (băng) *n.* Often **bangs.** Hair cut straight across the forehead. [Perh < ON *banga,* to cut off.]

Bang•kok (băng'kŏk', băng-kŏk'). The capital of Thailand. Pop. 1,669,000.

Ban•gla•desh (băng'glə-dĕsh'). An independent nation bordering on India and Burma. Pop. 50,844,000. Cap. Dacca.

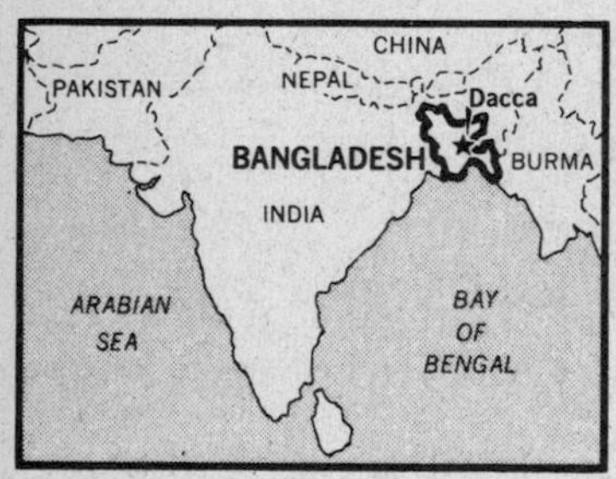

Bangladesh

ban•gle (băng'gəl) *n.* **1.** A rigid bracelet or anklet. **2.** A pendent ornament.

Ban•gui (bäng-gē'). The capital of the Central African Republic. Pop. 187,000.

ban•ish (băn'ĭsh) *v.* **1.** To force to leave a country by official decree; exile. **2.** To drive away; expel. [< OF *banir.*] **—ban'ish•ment** *n.*

ban•is•ter (băn'ĭ-stər) *n.* Also **ban•nis•ter. 1.** A baluster. **2.** The balustrade of a staircase. [Var of BALUSTER.]

ban•jo (băn'jō) *n., pl.* **-jos** or **-joes.** A fretted stringed instrument having a hollow circular body with a stretched diaphragm of vellum. [< L *pandoura,* three-stringed lute.]

Ban•jul (bän-jo͞ol'). The capital of Gambia. Pop. 40,000.

bank[1] (băngk) *n.* **1.** Any piled-up mass, as of snow or clouds. **2.** A steep natural incline. **3.** An artificial embankment. **4.** The slope of land adjoining a lake, river, or sea. **5.** An elevated area of a sea floor. **6.** Lateral tilting of an aircraft in a turn. *—v.* **1.** To border or protect with a bank. **2.** To pile up; amass. **3.** To cover (a fire) with ashes or fuel for low burning. **4.** To construct with a slope rising to the outside edge. **5.** To tilt (an aircraft) laterally in flight. [ME *banke.*]

bank[2] (băngk) *n.* **1.** A business establishment authorized to perform financial transactions, such as receiving and lending money. **2.** The building in which such an establishment is located. **3.** The funds owned by a gambling establishment. **4.** A supply or stock for use in emergencies: *a blood bank.* *—v.* **1.** To deposit (money) in a bank. **2.** To transact business with a bank. **3.** To operate a bank. **—bank on.** To have confidence in. [< It *banca,* bench, moneychanger's table.] **—bank'er** *n.*

bank[3] (băngk) *n.* **1.** A set of similar entities arranged in a row: *a bank of elevators.* **2.** A row of oars in a galley. *—v.* To arrange or set up in a row. [< OF *banc.*]

bank•book (băngk'bo͝ok') *n.* A book held by a depositor in which his deposits and withdrawals are recorded by his bank.

bank•ing (băng'kĭng) *n.* The business of a bank or occupation of a banker.

bank note. A note issued by an authorized bank payable to the bearer on demand and acceptable as money.

bank•roll (băngk'rōl') *n.* **1.** A roll of paper money. **2.** A person's ready cash. *—v.* To underwrite the expense of.

bank•rupt (băngk'rŭpt', -rəpt) *n.* **1.** A debtor who is judged insolvent and whose remaining property is administered for his creditors. **2.** One depleted of some resource or quality. *—adj.* **1.** Legally declared a bankrupt. **2.** Financially ruined. **3.** Depleted; destitute. *—v.* To cause to become bankrupt. [< It *banca rotta,* "broken counter."] **—bank'rupt•cy** *n.*

ban•ner (băn'ər) *n.* **1.** A piece of cloth attached to a staff and used as a standard by a monarch, military commander, etc. **2.** The flag of a nation, state, army, or sovereign. **3.** A headline spanning the width of a newspaper page. *—adj.* Outstanding; superior. [< VL **bandāria.*]

ban•nis•ter. Variant of **banister.**

banns (bănz) *pl.n.* Also **bans.** Announcement in a church of an intended marriage. [ME *banes,* pl of *bane, ban,* proclamation.]

ban•quet (băng'kwĭt) *n.* **1.** An elaborate feast. **2.** A ceremonial dinner honoring a guest or occasion. [OF, dim of *banc,* bench.] **—ban'quet•er** *n.*

ban•quette (băng-kĕt') *n.* **1.** A platform lining a trench or parapet wall where soldiers may stand when firing. **2.** A long upholstered bench, either placed against or built into a wall. [< Prov *banqueta,* dim of *banca,* bench.]

ban•shee (băn'shē) *n.* A female spirit in Gaelic folklore believed to presage a death in a family by wailing. [Ir Gael *bean sidhe,* "woman of the fairies."]

ban•tam (băn'təm) *n.* **1.** One of a breed of small domestic fowl. **2.** A small aggressive person. [< *Bantam,* town in Java.]

ban•ter (băn'tər) *n.* Good-humored teasing. *—v.* To tease or mock gently. [?]

Ban•tu (băn'to͞o) *n., pl.* **-tu** or **-tus. 1.** A member of any of several Negroid peoples of C and S Africa. **2.** A language family, including Swahili and Zulu. [Bantu *Ba-ntu,* "people."] **—Ban'tu** *adj.*

ban•yan (băn'yən) *n.* A tropical tree having many aerial roots that develop into additional trunks. [< Port *banian,* a Hindu merchant.]

Bap., Bapt. Baptist.

bap•tism (băp'tĭz'əm) *n.* **1.** A Christian sacrament of spiritual rebirth by which the recipient is cleansed of original sin through the symbolic application of water. **2.** An ordeal of initiation. [< LL *baptisma.*] **—bap•tis'mal** (-məl) *adj.* **—bap•tis'mal•ly** *adv.*

Bap•tist (băp'tĭst) *n.* A member of any of various Protestant denominations practicing baptism by immersion. **—Bap'tist** *adj.*

bap•tize (băp-tīz', băp'tīz') *v.* **-tized, -tizing. 1.** To dip or immerse in water in a baptismal ceremony. **2.** To cleanse; purify. **3.** To initiate. **4.** To give a first or Christian name to. [< LL *baptizāre.*] **—bap•tiz'er** *n.*

bar (bär) *n.* **1.** A relatively long, rigid piece of solid material. **2. a.** A solid oblong block of a substance, as soap. **b.** A unit of quantity based on such a block. **3.** An obstacle. **4.** A band, as one formed by light. **5.** The nullifying of a claim or action. **6.** The railing in a courtroom enclosing the part of the room where the judges and lawyers sit, witnesses are heard, and prisoners are tried. **7.** A particular system of law courts. **8.** The profession of law. **9.** A vertical line dividing a musical staff into measures. **10.** A counter at which drinks are served. *—v.* **barred, barring.** To fasten or obstruct with or as if with bars. *—prep.* Excluding. [< VL **barra.*]

bar. barometer; barometric.

barb (bärb) *n.* **1.** A sharp backward-pointing projection, as on a weapon or fishhook. **2.** A cutting remark. *—v.* To provide with barbs. [< L *barba,* beard.] **—barbed** *adj.*

Bar•ba•dos (bär-bā'dōs, -dəs). The easternmost island of the West Indies, a former British colony independent since 1966. Pop. 254,000. Cap. Bridgetown.

bar•bar•i•an (bär-bâr'ē-ən) *n.* **1.** One belonging to a people of relatively uncivilized culture and typically destructive tendencies. **2.** A fierce or coarse person. [< L *barbarus,* BARBAROUS.] **—bar•bar'i•an** *adj.*

bar•bar•ic (bär-băr'ĭk) *adj.* Of, pertaining to, or characteristic of a barbarian.

bar•ba•rism (bär'bə-rĭz'əm) *n.* **1.** An act, trait, or custom characterized by brutality or coarseness. **2.** The use of words or forms considered nonstandard in a language.

bar•bar•i•ty (bär-băr'ə-tē) *n., pl.* **-ties. 1.** Harsh or cruel conduct. **2.** An inhuman, brutal act. **3.** Crudity; coarseness.

bar•ba•rous (bär'bər-əs) *adj.* **1.** Uncivilized. **2.** Characterized by savagery or coarseness. [L *barbarus* < Gk *barbaros,* non-Greek, foreign, rude.] **—bar'ba•rous•ly** *adv.*

bar•be•cue (bär'bĭ-kyo͞o') *n.* **1.** A grill, pit, or outdoor fireplace for roasting meat. **2.** Meat roasted over an open fire or on a spit. *—v.* **-cued, -cuing.** To cook (meat) over live coals or an open fire. [Amer Span *barbacoa.*]

barbed wire. Twisted strands of fence wire with barbs at regular intervals.

bar•bell (bär'bĕl') *n.* A bar with adjustable weights at each end, lifted for sport or exercise.

bar•ber (bär'bər) *n.* One whose business is to cut or trim hair or beards. *—v.* To cut the hair or beard of. [< L *barba,* beard.]

bar•ber•ry (bär'bĕr'ē) *n.* Any of various often spiny shrubs with small reddish berries. [< Ar *barbārīs.*]

bar•ber•shop (bär'bər-shŏp') *n.* The place of

business of a barber.

bar•bi•can (bär′bĭ-kən) *n.* A tower or other fortification on the approach to a castle or town. [< ML *barbacana.*]

bar•bi•tu•rate (bär-bĭch′ər-ĭt, -ə-rāt′, bär′bə-t/y/ŏŏr′ĭt, -āt′) *n.* Any of a group of derivatives of **bar•bi•tu•ric acid** (bär′bə-t/y/ŏŏr′ĭk), $C_4H_4N_2O_3$, used as sedatives or hypnotics.

barb•wire (bärb′wīr′) *n.* **Barbed wire.**

bar•ca•role (bär′kə-rōl′) *n.* Also **bar•ca•rolle.** A Venetian gondolier's song with a rhythmic pulse suggestive of rowing. [< It *barcaruolo,* gondolier.]

Bar•ce•lo•na (bär′sə-lō′nə). A city of NE Spain. Pop. 1,696,000.

bar chart. A **bar graph.**

bard (bärd) *n.* **1.** One of an ancient Celtic order of singing, narrative poets. **2.** A poet. [< Ir *bárd* and W *bardd.*] **—bard′ic** *adj.*

bare (bâr) *adj.* **barer, barest. 1.** Without the usual or appropriate covering. **2.** Exposed to view; undisguised. **3.** Lacking the usual equipment or decoration. **4.** Without addition or qualification. **5.** Just sufficient: *bare necessities.* *—v.* **bared, baring.** To make bare. [< OE *bær.* See **bhoso-.**]

bare•back (bâr′băk′) *adj.* Also **bare•backed** (bâr′băkt′). Using no saddle: *a bareback rider.* **—bare′back′** *adv.*

bare•faced (bâr′fāst′) *adj.* **1.** Without covering or beard on the face. **2.** Without disguise; brazen: *a barefaced lie.*

bare•foot (bâr′fŏŏt′) *adj.* Also **bare•foot•ed** (-fŏŏt′ĭd). Wearing nothing on the feet. **—bare′foot′** *adv.*

bare•hand•ed (bâr′hăn′dĭd) *adj.* **1.** Having no covering on the hands. **2.** Unaided by tools or weapons.

bare•head•ed (bâr′hĕd′ĭd) *adj.* Having no head covering.

bare•leg•ged (bâr′lĕg′ĭd, -lĕgd′) *adj.* Having the legs uncovered. **—bare′leg′ged** *adv.*

bare•ly (bâr′lē) *adv.* **1.** By a very little; hardly. **2.** Without disguise; openly.

bar•gain (bär′gĭn) *n.* **1. a.** An agreement or contract, esp. one involving the sale and purchase of goods or services. **b.** The terms or conditions of such an agreement. **c.** The property acquired or services rendered as a result of such an agreement. **2.** Something offered or acquired at a price advantageous to the buyer. *—v.* **1.** To negotiate the terms of a sale, exchange, or other agreement. **2.** To arrive at an agreement. [< OF *bargaignier,* to haggle.] **—bar′gain•er** *n.*

barge (bärj) *n.* **1.** A long, usually flat-bottomed freight boat. **2.** A large pleasure boat used for parties. *—v.* **barged, barging. 1.** To move about clumsily. **2.** To collide (with). **3.** To intrude (with *in* or *into*). [< OF.]

bar graph. A graph consisting of parallel, usually vertical, bars or rectangles with lengths proportional to specified quantities.

bar•ite (bâr′īt′) *n.* A colorless crystalline mineral of barium sulfate that is the chief source of barium chemicals. [< Gk *barus,* heavy.]

bar•i•tone (băr′ə-tōn′) *n.* A male voice having a range higher than a bass and lower than a tenor. [< Gk *barutonos,* deep-sounding.]

bar•i•um (bâr′ē-əm, băr′-) *n. Symbol* **Ba** A soft, silvery-white metal, used to deoxidize copper, in various alloys, and in rat poison. Atomic number 56, atomic weight 137.34. [< earlier form of BARITE.] **—bar′ic** *adj.*

bark[1] (bärk) *n.* The short, harsh sound characteristically made by a dog. *—v.* **1.** To utter or produce such a sound. **2.** To speak sharply; snap. [< OE *beorcan,* to bark. See **bherg-.**]

bark[2] (bärk) *n.* The often rough outer covering of the stems and roots of trees and other woody plants. *—v.* **1.** To remove bark from. **2.** To scrape skin from: *bark one's shins.* [< ON *bǫrkr.*]

bark[3] (bärk) *n.* Also **barque. 1.** A sailing ship with from three to five masts. **2.** Any boat, esp. a small sailing vessel. [< OF *barque,* prob < Gk *baris,* Egyptian barge.]

bar•keep•er (bär′kē′pər) *n.* One who owns or runs a bar selling alcoholic beverages.

bar•ken•tine (bär′kən-tēn′) *n.* Also **bar•quen•tine.** A sailing ship with from three to five masts.

bark•er (bär′kər) *n.* One who stands at the entrance to a show and solicits customers with a loud sales pitch.

bar•ley (bär′lē) *n.* **1.** A cereal grass bearing grain used as food and in making beer and whiskey. **2.** The grain itself. [< OE *bære, bere,* barley. See **bhares-.**]

bar•maid (bär′mād′) *n.* A woman who serves drinks in a bar.

bar•man (bär′mən) *n.* A bartender.

bar mitz•vah (bär mĭts′və). Also **bar miz•vah. 1.** A thirteen-year-old Jewish male who ceremonially assumes the religious responsibilities of an adult. **2.** The ceremony confirming a bar mitzvah. [Heb *bar mitzvāh,* "son of command."]

barn (bärn) *n.* **1.** A large farm building used for storing produce and for sheltering livestock. **2.** A large shed for the housing of vehicles. [< OE *bern, berern,* "barley house."]

bar•na•cle (bär′nə-kəl) *n.* A small, hard-shelled marine crustacean that attaches itself to submerged surfaces. [< ML *bernaca.*] **—bar′na•cled** *adj.*

barn•storm (bärn′stôrm′) *v.* To travel about the countryside presenting plays, lecturing, or making political speeches. **—barn′storm′er** *n.*

barn•yard (bärn′yärd′) *n.* The often enclosed yard adjacent to a barn.

ba•rom•e•ter (bə-rŏm′ə-tər) *n.* **1.** An instrument for measuring atmospheric pressure, used in weather forecasting and in determining elevation. **2.** An indicator of change. [< Gk *baros,* weight.] **—bar′o•met′ric** (băr′ə-mĕt′rĭk), **bar′o•met′ri•cal** *adj.* **—bar′o•met′ri•cal•ly** *adv.* **—ba•rom′e•try** *n.*

bar•on (băr′ən) *n.* **1.** A male member of the lowest rank of nobility in Great Britain, certain European countries, and Japan. **2.** A man with great power in a particular field. [< ML *barō,* man, warrior.] **—bar′on•ess** *fem.n.*

bar•on•et (băr′ə-nĭt, băr′ə-nĕt′) *n.* An Englishman holding a hereditary title of honor next below a baron. **—bar′on•et•cy** *n.*

ba•ro•ni•al (bə-rō′nē-əl) *adj.* **1.** Of or pertaining to a baron. **2.** Stately; imposing.

ba•roque (bə-rōk′) *adj.* **1.** Characteristic of an artistic style current in Europe about 1550–1700 and marked by massive forms and elaborate decoration. **2.** Characteristic of a contrapuntal musical style of composition current in Europe about 1600–1750. **3.** Flamboyant in style. [< It *barocco,* after the founder of the style, Federigo *Barocci* (1528–1612).]

barque. Variant of **bark**[3].

bar•quen•tine. Variant of **barkentine.**

bar•racks (băr′ĭks) *n. (takes sing. v.).* A building or group of buildings used esp. to house soldiers. [< It *baracca,* soldier's tent.]

bar•ra•cu•da (băr′ə-kōō′də) *n.* A narrow-bodied, chiefly tropical marine fish with very sharp teeth. [Span.]

bar•rage[1] (bär′ĭj) *n.* An artificial obstruction in a watercourse. [< F *barrer,* to bar.]

bar•rage[2] (bə-räzh′) *n.* **1.** A heavy curtain of artillery fire directed so as to screen friendly troops. **2.** A rapid outpouring: *a barrage of questions.* [< F *(tir de) barrage,* barrier (fire).] **—bar•rage′** *v.* **(-raged, -raging).**

bar•ra•try (băr′ə-trē) *n., pl.* **-tries. 1.** The offense of exciting quarrels or groundless lawsuits. **2.** An unlawful breach of duty on the part of a ship's master or crew, resulting in injury to the ship's owner. **3.** The sale or purchase of positions in the church or state. [< OF *baraterie,* deception.] **—bar′ra•trous** *adj.*

bar•rel (băr′əl) *n.* **1.** A large cask usually made of curved wooden staves and having a flat top and bottom. **2.** The quantity that a barrel will hold. **3.** A unit of volume or capacity, varying in the U.S. from 31 to 42 gallons as established by law or usage. **4.** The metal, cylindrical part of a firearm through which the bullet travels. **5.** The cylindrical part or hollow shaft of various instruments and mechanisms. *—v.* **-reled** or **-relled, -reling** or **-relling. 1.** To pack in a barrel. **2.** *Slang.* To move at a high speed. [< OF *baril.*]

bar•ren (băr′ən) *adj.* **1. a.** Not producing offspring. **b.** Infertile; sterile. **2.** Lacking vegetation. **3.** Unproductive; unprofitable. **4.** Devoid; lacking: *writing barren of insight.* **5.** Dull. *—n.* A tract of barren land. [< OF *baraigne.*] **—bar′ren•ness** *n.*

bar•rette (bə-rĕt′, bä-) *n.* A small clasp used to hold the hair in place. [F, dim of *barre,* bar.]

bar•ri•cade (băr′ə-kād′, băr′ə-kād′) *n.* A makeshift barrier or fortification set up across a route of access. *—v.* **-caded, -cading.** To block or confine with a barricade. [< OF *barrique,* barrel.] **—bar′ri•cad′er** *n.*

bar•ri•er (băr′ē-ər) *n.* **1.** A fence, wall, or other structure built to bar passage. **2.** Something that restricts or prevents free interchange or movement. **3.** A boundary or limit: *the sound barrier.* [< OF *barriere.*]

bar•ri•o (bä′ryō) *n., pl.* **-os.** A chiefly Spanish-speaking community or neighborhood in a U.S. city. [Ar *barrī,* of an open area.]

bar•ris•ter (băr′ĭ-stər) *n. Chiefly Brit.* A lawyer admitted to plead at the bar in the superior courts. [< BAR (railing).]

bar•room (bär′rōōm′, -rŏŏm′) *n.* A room or building in which alcoholic beverages are sold at a bar.

bar•row (băr′ō) *n.* **1. a.** A flat, rectangular tray or cart having handles at each end. **b.** The load carried on such a tray. **2.** A wheelbarrow. [< OE *bearwe,* basket, wheelbarrow. See **bher-**[1].]

Bart. baronet.

bar•tend•er (bär′tĕn′dər) *n.* One who mixes and serves alcoholic drinks at a bar.

bar•ter (bär′tər) *v.* To exchange (goods or services) without using money. *—n.* The practice of bartering. [< OF *barater,* to barter, cheat.] **—bar′ter•er** *n.*

bas•al (bā′səl, -zəl) *adj.* **1.** Pertaining to, located at, or forming a base. **2.** Of primary importance; basic. **—bas′al•ly** *adv.*

basal metabolism. The least amount of energy required to maintain vital functions in an organism at complete rest.

ba•salt (bə-sôlt′, bā′sôlt′) *n.* A hard, dense, dark volcanic rock. [< L *basaltēs.*] **—ba•sal′tic** (bə-sôl′tĭk) *adj.*

base[1] (bās) *n.* **1.** The lowest or supporting part or layer; bottom. **2.** The fundamental principle or underlying concept of a system or

ô paw, for/oi boy/ou out/ŏŏ took/ōō coo/p pop/r run/s sauce/sh shy/t to/th thin/*th* the/
ŭ cut/ûr fur/v van/w wag/y yes/z size/zh vision/ə ago, item, edible, gallop, circus/

theory. **3.** A chief constituent. **4.** The fact, observation, or premise from which a measurement or reasoning process is begun. **5.** *Sports.* A goal, starting point, or safety area. **6.** A center of organization, supply, or activity. **7. a.** A fortified center of operations. **b.** A supply center for a large force. **8.** *Ling.* A morpheme or morphemes regarded as a form to which affixes or other bases may be added. **9.** A line used as a reference for measurement or computations. **10. a.** Any of a large class of compounds, including the hydroxides and oxides of metals, having a bitter taste, a slippery solution, the ability to turn litmus blue, and the ability to react with acids to form salts. **b.** A molecular or ionic substance capable of combining with a proton to form a new substance. **11.** *Math.* The number that is raised to various powers to generate the principal counting units of a number system. **—off base. 1.** *Baseball.* Not touching the base occupied. **2.** Badly mistaken, inaccurate, or unprepared. *—adj.* Forming or serving as a base. *—v.* **based, basing. 1.** To form or make a base for. **2.** To find a basis for; establish. [< Gk *basis,* pedestal, base.]

base[2] (bās) *adj.* **baser, basest. 1.** *Archaic.* Of low birth, rank, or position. **2.** Servile; menial. **3.** Treacherous; contemptible. **4.** Inferior in quality or value. **5.** Containing inferior substances: *a base metal.* [< LL *bassus,* fat, low.] **—base'ly** *adv.* **—base'ness** *n.*

base•ball (bās'bôl') *n.* **1.** A game played with a wooden bat and hard ball by two opposing teams of nine players, each team playing alternately in the field and at bat, the players at bat having to run a course of four bases laid out in a diamond pattern in order to score. **2.** The ball used in this game.

base•board (bās'bôrd', -bōrd') *n.* A molding that conceals the joint between an interior wall and a floor.

base•born (bās'bôrn') *adj.* **1.** Of humble birth. **2.** Born of unwed parents; illegitimate. **3.** Ignoble; contemptible.

base•less (bās'lĭs) *adj.* Having no basis or foundation.

base•ment (bās'mənt) *n.* **1.** The substructure or foundation of a building. **2.** The lowest habitable story of a building.

ba•ses. *pl.* of **basis.**

bash (băsh) *v.* To strike with a heavy and crushing blow. *—n.* **1.** A heavy, crushing blow. **2.** *Slang.* A celebration; party. [?]

bash•ful (băsh'fəl) *adj.* **1.** Shy; retiring. **2.** Hesitant; unsure. [< ME *baschen,* to abash.] **—bash'ful•ly** *adv.* **—bash'ful•ness** *n.*

ba•sic (bā'sĭk) *adj.* **1.** Of, pertaining to, or constituting a basis. **2.** *Chem.* **a.** Producing or resulting from a base. **b.** Containing a base, esp. in excess of acid. *—n.* Something that is basic. **—ba'si•cal•ly** *adv.*

bas•il (băz'əl, bāz'əl) *n.* An aromatic herb, with leaves used as seasoning. [< Gk *basilikon,* "royal," king.]

bas•i•lar (băs'ə-lər) *adj.* Also **bas•i•lar•y** (-lĕr'ē). Pertaining to or located at or near the base, esp. the base of the skull.

ba•sil•i•ca (bə-sĭl'ĭ-kə) *n.* **1.** An oblong building of ancient Rome used as a court or place of assembly. **2.** Such a building used as a Christian church. **3.** A church accorded certain ceremonial rights by the pope. [< Gk *basilikē (stoa),* "royal (portico, court)."]

bas•i•lisk (băs'ə-lĭsk', băz'-) *n.* A legendary dragon with lethal breath and glance. [< Gk *basiliskos,* "little king."]

ba•sin (bā'sən) *n.* **1.** An open, rounded vessel used esp. for holding liquids. **2.** The amount contained in such a vessel. **3.** A washbowl; a sink. **4.** An artificially enclosed area of a river or harbor. **5.** A small enclosed or partly enclosed body of water. **6.** Any bowl-shaped depression in a land or ocean-floor surface. [< VL **bacca,* water vessel.]

ba•sis (bā'sĭs) *n., pl.* **-ses** (-sēz'). **1.** A foundation upon which something rests. **2.** The chief component of anything. **3.** Principle; criterion. [< Gk, base.]

bask (băsk, bäsk) *v.* **1.** To expose oneself pleasantly to warmth. **2.** To thrive in the presence of an advantageous influence. [ME *basken.*]

bas•ket (băs'kĭt) *n.* **1. a.** A container made of interwoven material. **b.** The amount a basket will hold. **2.** Either of two metal hoops with suspended nets that serve as goals in basketball. [< NF.]

bas•ket•ball (băs'kĭt-bôl') *n.* **1.** A game played between two teams of five players each, the object being to throw the ball through an elevated basket on the opponent's side of the rectangular court. **2.** The ball used in this game.

Basque (băsk) *n.* **1.** One of a people inhabiting the W Pyrenees in France and Spain. **2.** The language of the Basques, having no known linguistic affinities. **—Basque** *adj.*

bas-re•lief (bä'rĭ-lēf') *n.* **Low relief.**

bass[1] (băs) *n., pl.* **bass** or **basses.** Any of several freshwater or marine food fishes. [< OE *bærs.* See **bhar-.**]

bass[2] (bās) *n.* **1.** A low-pitched tone. **2.** The tones in the lowest register of a musical instrument. **3.** The lowest part in vocal or instrumental part music. **4.** A male singing voice of the lowest range. [ME *bas,* low, base.] **—bass** *adj.*

bass drum (bās). A large cylindrical drum having a low, resonant sound when struck.

bas•set (băs'ĭt) *n.* Also **basset hound.** A dog with short legs and long, drooping ears. [< OF, short and low < *bas,* low, base.]

bas•si•net (băs'ə-nĕt') *n.* An oblong basket resting on legs, used as a crib for an infant. [< OF *bacin,* basin.]

bas•so (băs'ō, bä'sō) *n.* A singer with a bass voice. [It.]

bas•soon (bə-so͞on', bă-) *n.* A low-pitched woodwind instrument with a double reed and a long wooden body. [< It *bassone,* aug of BASSO.] **—bas•soon'ist** *n.*

bass viol (bās). A **double bass.**

bass•wood (băs'wo͝od') *n.* A North American linden tree.

bast (băst) *n.* Fibrous plant material. [< OE *bæst* < Gmc **bastaz.*]

bas•tard (băs'tərd) *n.* **1.** An illegitimate child. **2.** Any product of irregular or dubious origin. **3.** *Slang.* An obnoxious or nasty person. **4.** *Slang.* An unfortunate fellow. *—adj.* **1.** Born of unwed parents; illegitimate. **2.** Not genuine. **3.** Of inferior breed or kind. [Perh < OF *(fils de) bast,* "packsaddle (son)."] **—bas'tard•ly** *adj.* **—bas'tard•y** *n.*

bas•tard•ize (băs'tər-dīz') *v.* **-ized, -izing.** To debase; corrupt.

baste[1] (bāst) *v.* **basted, basting.** To sew loosely with large, running, temporary stitches. [< OF *bastir,* to build, prepare, baste.]

baste[2] (bāst) *v.* **basted, basting.** To pour liquid over (meat) while cooking. [?]

baste[3] (bāst) *v.* **basted, basting. 1.** To beat vigorously. **2.** To berate. [Perh < ON *beysta,* to thrash, strike.]

bas•tion (băs'chən, băs'tē-ən) *n.* **1.** A projecting part of a rampart or other fortification. **2.** Any well-fortified position. [< OF *bastille,* a jail.]

bat[1] (băt) *n.* **1.** A stout wooden stick or club; cudgel. **2.** A sharp blow. **3. a.** A rounded, tapered, wooden club used to strike a baseball or softball. **b.** A flat-surfaced wooden club used in cricket. **4.** *Slang.* A binge; spree. *—v.* **batted, batting.** To hit with or as if with a bat. [< OE *batt,* cudgel, club.]

bat[2] (băt) *n.* A mouselike flying mammal with membranous wings. [< Scand.]

bat[3] (băt) *v.* **batted, batting.** To flutter: *bat one's eyelashes.* [Prob < OF *batre,* to beat.]

batch (băch) *n.* **1.** An amount produced or needed for one operation, as baking. **2.** The quantity produced as the result of one operation: *a batch of cement.* **3.** A group of persons or things. [< OE **bæcce* < *bacan,* to BAKE.]

bate (bāt) *v.* **bated, bating. 1.** To lessen the force of: *bate one's breath.* **2.** To take away; subtract. [< ME *abaten,* to abate.]

ba•teau (bă-tō') *n., pl.* **-teaux** (-tōz'). A light, flat-bottomed boat. [< F.]

bath (băth, bäth) *n., pl.* **baths** (bă*thz,* băths, bä*thz,* bäths). **1.** The act of washing or immersing the body in water. **2.** The water used for bathing. **3.** A bathtub. **4.** A liquid or a liquid and its container, used to regulate the temperature of, soak, or otherwise act upon an immersed object. **5.** A bathroom. **6.** Often **baths.** Rooms or a building equipped for bathing. [< OE *bæth.* See **bhē-.**]

bathe (bā*th*) *v.* **bathed, bathing. 1.** To take a bath. **2.** To go swimming. **3.** To immerse or become immersed in or as if in liquid. **4.** To suffuse. [< OE *bathian.*] **—bath'er** *n.*

ba•thet•ic (bə-thĕt'ĭk) *adj.* Characterized by bathos.

bath•house (băth'hous', bäth'-) *n.* **1.** A building equipped for bathing. **2.** A building with dressing rooms for swimmers.

ba•thos (bā'thŏs') *n.* **1.** A ludicrously abrupt transition from an elevated to a commonplace style. **2.** Insincere or grossly sentimental pathos. [Gk, depth.]

bath•robe (băth'rōb', bäth'-) *n.* A loose-fitting robe worn before and after bathing and for lounging.

bath•room (băth'ro͞om', -ro͝om', bäth'-) *n.* A room with a bath or shower and usually a sink and toilet.

bath•tub (băth'tŭb', bäth'-) *n.* A usually oblong tub for bathing.

Bath•urst (băth'ərst). The former name for Banjul.

bath•y•sphere (băth'ĭ-sfîr') *n.* A reinforced, spherical deep-diving chamber, manned, and lowered by cable.

ba•tik (bə-tēk', băt'ĭk) *n.* **1.** A dyeing method in which designs are made by covering fabric parts with removable wax. **2.** Cloth thus dyed. [Malay.] **—ba•tik'** *adj.*

ba•tiste (bə-tēst', bă-) *n.* A fine light fabric of cotton, linen, etc. [Earlier *baptist* cloth, first made in the 13th century by *Baptiste* of Cambrai, France.]

ba•ton (bə-tŏn', băt'n) *n.* A stick, esp. the slender rod used by a conductor to direct an orchestra. [< LL *bastum,* stick.]

Bat•on Rouge (băt'n ro͞ozh'). The capital of Louisiana. Pop. 166,000.

bats (băts) *adj.* *Slang.* Crazy.

bats•man (băts'mən) *n.* *Cricket.* A player at bat.

bat•tal•ion (bə-tăl'yən) *n.* **1.** A tactical military unit, consisting of a headquarters company and four infantry companies or a headquarters battery and four artillery batteries. **2.** An indefinite number of military troops. [< OIt *battaglione,* aug of *battaglia,* troop.]

bat•ten (băt'n) *n.* A flexible wooden strip for covering, fastening, or flattening parts. —*v.* To secure with battens: *batten down the hatches.* [< F *bâton,* baton.]

bat•ter[1] (băt'ər) *v.* To pound or damage with heavy blows. [< OF *battre,* to beat.]

bat•ter[2] (băt'ər) *n. Baseball.* The player whose turn it is to bat.

bat•ter[3] (băt'ər) *n.* A thick, beaten mixture, as of flour and liquid, used in cooking. [ME *bater.*]

bat•ter•ing-ram (băt'ər-ĭng-răm') *n.* A siege engine used to batter down walls and gates.

bat•ter•y (băt'ə-rē) *n., pl.* **-ies. 1.** The unlawful beating of a person. **2. a.** An artillery emplacement. **b.** A set of artillery pieces, as on a warship. **3.** An array: *a battery of lawyers.* **4.** The pitcher and catcher on a baseball team. **5.** The percussion section of an orchestra. **6.** A device for generating an electric current. [< OF *battre,* to BATTER.]

bat•ting (băt'ĭng) *n.* Cotton or wool fiber wadded into a flat mass.

bat•tle (băt'l) *n.* **1.** A large-scale combat between two armed forces. **2.** Any intense or extended struggle. —*v.* **-tled, -tling.** To engage in battle. [< VL **battālia.*]

bat•tle-ax, bat•tle-axe (băt'l-ăks') *n., pl.* **-axes. 1.** An ax formerly used as a weapon. **2.** *Slang.* An overbearing woman.

battle cry. 1. A shout uttered by troops in battle. **2.** A militant slogan.

bat•tle•dore (băt'l-dôr', -dōr') *n.* A flat wooden paddle used in batting a shuttlecock. [ME *batildore.*]

bat•tle•field (băt'l-fēld') *n.* A place where a battle is fought.

bat•tle•ment (băt'l-mənt) *n.* An indented parapet on top of a wall.

bat•tle•ship (băt'l-shĭp') *n.* Any of the most heavily armed and armored class of modern warships.

bat•ty (băt'ē) *adj.* **-tier, -tiest.** *Slang.* Crazy; eccentric.

bau•ble (bô'bəl) *n.* A trinket. [< OF *baubel,* plaything.]

Bau•de•laire (bōd-lâr'), **Charles.** 1821–1867. French poet.

baux•ite (bôk'sīt') *n.* The principal ore of aluminum, 30–75% $Al_2O_3 \cdot nH_2O$, with iron oxide and silica as impurities. [< Les *Baux,* S France.]

bawd (bôd) *n.* A woman of ill repute; a prostitute. [ME *bawde.*]

bawd•y (bô'dē) *adj.* **-ier, -iest.** Humorously coarse; vulgar; lewd. **—bawd'i•ly** *adv.* **—bawd'i•ness** *n.*

bawl (bôl) *v.* To cry out loudly; bellow. **—bawl out.** To scold or reprimand in a loud voice. —*n.* A loud, extended outcry; a wail. [ME *baulen.*] **—bawl'er** *n.*

bay[1] (bā) *n.* A body of water partly enclosed by land, but having a wide outlet to the sea. [< OF *baie.*]

bay[2] (bā) *n.* **1.** A compartment set off from other compartments making up a given structure. **2.** A projecting compartment containing a window. **3.** Any opening or recess in a wall. [< OF *baee,* an opening.]

bay[3] (bā) *adj.* Reddish-brown. —*n.* **1.** A reddish brown. **2.** A reddish-brown animal, esp. a horse. [< L *badius.*]

bay[4] (bā) *v.* To bark with long, deep, howling cries. —*n.* **1.** The position of one cornered by pursuers. **2.** A long, howling bark. [< VL **abbaiāre.*]

bay[5] (bā) *n.* **1.** A laurel. **2.** A similar tree or shrub. **3. bays.** A crown of laurel leaves, given as a sign of honor. **4. bays.** Honor; renown. [ME *baye,* laurel berry.]

bay•ber•ry (bā'bĕr'ē) *n.* **1.** An aromatic shrub bearing waxy berries. **2.** The fruit of such a shrub.

bay leaf. The aromatic leaf of a laurel, used as seasoning.

bay•o•net (bā'ə-nĭt, -nĕt', bā'ə-nĕt') *n.* A sword or knife adapted to be fixed near the muzzle end of a rifle. —*v.* **-neted** or **-netted, -neting** or **-netting.** To stab with a bayonet. [< *Bayonne,* France.]

bay•ou (bī'o͞o, bī'ō) *n., pl.* **-ous.** A marshy, sluggish body of water tributary to a lake or river. [< Choctaw *bayuk.*]

bay rum. An aromatic liquid originally distilled from the leaves of a tropical American tree.

ba•zaar (bə-zär') *n.* Also **ba•zar. 1.** An Oriental market consisting of a street lined with shops and stalls. **2.** A fair for charity. [< Pers *bāzār.*]

ba•zoo•ka (bə-zo͞o'kə) *n.* A rocket launcher consisting of a portable smoothbore tube. [< the *bazooka,* a crude wind instrument made of pipes.]

bb ball bearing.

BB (bē'bē') *n.* A standard size of lead shot that measures 0.18 inch in diameter.

BBB Better Business Bureau.

BBC British Broadcasting Corporation.

BB gun. A small air rifle for firing BB shot.

bbl barrel.

B.C. 1. before Christ. **2.** British Columbia.

bd. 1. board. **2.** bond. **3.** *Bookbinding.* bound.

B.D. 1. bank draft. **2.** bills discounted.

be (bē) *v.*

	1st person	2nd person	3rd person
Present Tense			
singular	**am**	**are**†	**is**
plural	**are**	**are**	**are**
†*Archaic 2nd person singular* **art**			
Past Tense			
singular	**was**	**were**‡	**was**
plural	**were**	**were**	**were**
‡*Archaic 2nd person singular* **wast** *or* **wert**			

Present Participle: **being**
Past Participle: **been**
Present Subjunctive: **be**
Past Subjunctive: **were**

1. To exist in actuality; have reality or life: *I think, therefore I am.* **2.** To exist in a specified place: *"Oh, to be in England,/Now that April's there"* (Robert Browning). **3.** To occupy a specified position: *The food is on the table.* **4.** To take place; occur. **5.** To go. Used chiefly in the past and perfect tenses: *Have you ever been to Italy?* **6.** *Archaic.* To belong; befall. Used in the subjunctive: *Peace be unto you.* **7.** —Used as a copula linking a subject and a predicate nominative, adjective, or pronoun, in such senses as: **a.** To equal in meaning or identity: *"To be a Christian was to be a Roman."* (James Bryce). **b.** To signify; symbolize: *A is excellent, C is passing.* **c.** To belong to a specified class or group: *Man is a primate.* **d.** To have or show a specified quality or characteristic: *She is lovely. All men are mortal.* **8.** —Used as an auxiliary verb in certain constructions, as: **a.** With the past participle of a transitive verb to form the passive voice: *The election is held annually.* **b.** With the present participle of a verb to express a continuing action: *We are working to improve housing conditions.* **c.** With the present participle or the infinitive of a verb to express intention, obligation, or future action: *She is to eat her dinner before she may play. He is leaving next month.* **d.** With the past participle of certain intransitive verbs of motion to form the perfect tense: *"Where be those roses gone which sweetened so our eyes?"* (Philip Sidney). [< OE *bēon,* to come to be. See **bheu-.**]

be–. *comb. form.* **1.** A complete or profuse covering or affecting. **2.** A thorough or excessive degree. **3.** An action that causes a condition to exist. [< OE *be-, bi-,* about, over, on all sides, away, away from.]

Be beryllium.

B.E. Board of Education.

B/E bill of exchange.

beach (bēch) *n.* The shore of a body of water. [Earlier *baich.*]

beach•comb•er (bēch'kō'mər) *n.* One who lives on what he can salvage or earn along the beach.

beach•head (bēch'hĕd') *n.* A position on an enemy shoreline captured by advance troops of an invading force.

bea•con (bē'kən) *n.* **1.** A signal fire. **2.** A lighthouse. **3.** A radio transmitter that emits a signal to guide aircraft. [< OE *bēacen.* See **bhā-**[1]**.**]

bead (bēd) *n.* **1.** A small piece of material pierced for stringing. **2. beads. a.** A necklace made of such pieces. **b.** A rosary. **3.** Any small, round object. **4.** A narrow projecting strip. [< OE *gebed,* prayer (bead). See **bhedh-**[2]**.**] **—bead'y** *adj.*

bea•dle (bēd'l) *n.* A minor parish official in England. [< OE *bydel.* See **bheudh-.**]

bea•gle (bē'gəl) *n.* A small, smooth-coated hound with drooping ears. [Perh < OF *begueule,* noisy person.]

beak (bēk) *n.* **1.** The horny, projecting mouth parts of a bird; bill. **2.** A similar part or structure. [< L *beccus.*]

beak•er (bē'kər) *n.* **1.** A large drinking cup with a wide mouth. **2.** An open glass cylinder with a pouring lip, used as a laboratory vessel. [< ON *bikarr.*]

beam (bēm) *n.* **1.** A length of timber forming a supporting member in construction. **2.** A ship's maximum breadth. **3.** A constant directional radio signal for navigational guidance. **4. a.** A ray of light. **b.** A group of particles traveling together in close parallel trajectories. **—on the beam.** On the right track. —*v.* **1.** To emit or transmit. **2.** To radiate. **3.** To smile radiantly. [< OE *bēam* < Gmc **baumaz.*]

bean (bēn) *n.* **1.** The often edible seed or seed pod of any of various plants. **2.** A plant bearing such seeds or pods. **3.** *Slang.* The head. —*v. Slang.* To hit on the head. [< OE *bēan.* See **bha-bhā-.**]

bear[1] (bâr) *v.* **bore, borne** or **born, bearing. 1.** To carry; support. **2.** To endure. **3.** To conduct (oneself). **4.** To have; show; exhibit. **5.** To transmit: *bear good tidings.* **6.** To render; give: *bear witness.* **7.** *p.p.* **born.** To give birth to. **8.** To yield; produce. **9. a.** To permit of or be liable to: *This will bear investigation.* **b.** To have relevance; apply. **10.** To exert pressure. **11.** To proceed (in a specified direction): *bear right.* **—bear out.** To prove right; confirm. **—bear with.** To be patient with; tolerate. [< OE *beran.* See **bher-**[1]**.**] **—bear'a•ble** *adj.* **—bear'er** *n.*

bear[2] (bâr) *n.* **1.** Any of various usually large

mammals having a shaggy coat and a short tail. **2.** A clumsy or ill-mannered person. **3.** *Stock Market.* An investor or concern that sells shares in the expectation that prices will fall. [< OE *bera.* See **bher-**[3].]

beard (bîrd) *n.* **1.** The hair on the chin and cheeks of a man. **2.** Any similar hairy or hairlike growth, as on an animal or plant. —*v.* To confront boldly. [< OE. See **bhardhā.**]

bear•ing (bâr'ĭng) *n.* **1.** Deportment; mien. **2.** A device that supports, guides, and reduces friction between fixed and moving machine parts. **3.** A supportive element. **4.** Relationship or relevance. **5. a.** Direction measured relative to geographic or celestial reference lines. **b.** A navigational determination of position. **6. bearings.** Grasp of one's situation: *get one's bearings.* **7.** A heraldic emblem.

beast (bēst) *n.* **1.** An animal, esp. a large four-footed animal. **2.** A brutal person. [< L *bēstia.*]

beat (bēt) *v.* **beat, beaten** (bēt'n) or **beat, beating. 1.** To strike repeatedly. **2.** To forge. **3.** To flatten by trampling; tread. **4.** To defeat. **5.** To excel; surpass. **6.** *Slang.* To baffle. **7.** To pulsate; throb. **8.** To mix rapidly: *beat eggs.* **9.** To flap, as wings. —*n.* **1.** A stroke; blow. **2.** A pulsation; throb. **3.** A rhythmic stress. **4.** A regular round: *the night beat.* —*adj.* Tired; exhausted. [< OE *bēatan.* See **bhau-.**] —**beat'er** *n.* —**beat'ing** *n.*

be•a•tif•ic (bē'ə-tĭf'ĭk) *adj.* Showing or producing exalted joy or bliss. [< LL *beātificus.*] —**be'a•tif'i•cal•ly** *adv.*

be•at•i•fy (bē-ăt'ə-fī') *v.* **-fied, -fying. 1.** To make blessedly happy. **2.** To proclaim to be one of the blessed. —**be•at'i•fi•ca'tion** (-fĭ-kā'shən) *n.*

be•at•i•tude (bē-ăt'ə-t/y/o͞od') *n.* Supreme blessedness; exalted joy or happiness. [< L *beātus,* blessed.]

beat•nik (bēt'nĭk) *n.* A young person of the 1950's whose rejection of American mores and dress was associated with a quest for spiritual illumination.

beau (bō) *n., pl.* **beaus** or **beaux** (bōz). **1.** A suitor. **2.** A dandy. [< L *bellus,* handsome, fine.]

Beau Brum•mell (bō brŭm'əl). A dandy; fop. [< *"Beau" Brummell* (1778–1840), British dandy.]

Beau•mont (bō'mŏnt). A city of Texas. Pop. 119,000.

beaut (byo͞ot) *n. Slang.* Something outstanding of its kind: *"When I make a mistake, it's a beaut."* (Fiorello H. La Guardia). [Short for BEAUTY.]

beau•te•ous (byo͞o'tē-əs, -tyəs) *adj.* Beautiful, esp. to the sight.

beau•ti•cian (byo͞o-tĭsh'ən) *n.* A cosmetologist.

beau•ti•ful (byo͞o'tə-fəl) *adj.* Having beauty. —**beau'ti•ful•ly** *adv.*

beau•ti•fy (byo͞o'tə-fī') *v.* **-fied, -fying.** To make beautiful. —**beau'ti•fi•ca'tion** *n.*

beau•ty (byo͞o'tē) *n., pl.* **-ties. 1.** A quality that delights the senses or exalts the mind; loveliness. **2.** One possessing this quality. [< VL **bellitās* < L *bellus,* pretty, handsome, fine.]

beaux. Alternate *pl.* of **beau.**

bea•ver (bē'vər) *n.* **1.** A large aquatic rodent with thick fur, a paddlelike tail, and sharp front teeth with which it fells trees to build dams. **2.** The fur of a beaver. [< OE *beofor.* See **bher-**[3].]

be•calm (bĭ-käm') *v.* To render motionless for lack of wind.

be•came (bĭ-kām'). *p.t.* of **become.**

be•cause (bĭ-kôz', -kŭz') *conj.* For the reason that; since. —**because of.** By reason of; on account of. [ME *bi cause* : BY + CAUSE.]

beck (bĕk) *n.* A summons. —**at one's beck and call.** Very willingly obedient. [< ME *becken,* to beckon.]

beck•on (bĕk'ən) *v.* **1.** To summon, as by nodding or waving. **2.** To attract. [< OE *bēcnan.* See **bhā-**[1].] —**beck'on•er** *n.* —**beck'on•ing•ly** *adv.*

be•cloud (bĭ-kloud') *v.* To obscure.

be•come (bĭ-kŭm') *v.* **-came, -come, -coming. 1.** To grow or come to be. **2.** To be appropriate or suitable to. —**become of.** To be the fate of.

be•com•ing (bĭ-kŭm'ĭng) *adj.* **1.** Appropriate; suitable. **2.** Attractive. —**be•com'ing•ly** *adv.*

bed (bĕd) *n.* **1.** A piece of furniture for reclining and sleeping. **2.** A small plot of cultivated ground: *flower bed.* **3. a.** The surface at the bottom of a body of water. **b.** A horizontally extending layer of earth or rock. **4.** A foundation. —*v.* **bedded, bedding. 1.** To furnish with a bed. **2.** To put to bed. **3. a.** To prepare (soil) for planting. **b.** To plant in a prepared bed of soil. **5.** To lay flat or arrange in layers. **6.** To embed. [< OE *bedd.* See **bhedh-**[1].]

be•daub (bĭ-dôb') *v.* To smear.

be•daz•zle (bĭ-dăz'əl) *v.* **-zled, -zling.** To dazzle so completely as to confuse or blind. —**be•daz'zle•ment** *n.*

bed•bug (bĕd'bŭg') *n.* A wingless, bloodsucking insect that often infests human dwellings.

bed•clothes (bĕd'klōz', -klō*thz*') *pl.n.* Coverings for a bed.

bed•ding (bĕd'ĭng) *n.* **1.** Bedclothes. **2.** A foundation.

be•deck (bĭ-dĕk') *v.* To adorn.

be•dev•il (bĭ-dĕv'əl) *v.* To plague; harass.

be•dew (bĭ-d/y/o͞o') *v.* To wet with or as if with dew.

bed•fel•low (bĕd'fĕl'ō) *n.* **1.** One with whom a bed is shared. **2.** A temporary associate.

be•di•zen (bĭ-dī'zən, -dĭz'ən) *v.* To dress or ornament gaudily.

bed•lam (bĕd'ləm) *n.* **1.** Any place of noisy confusion. **2.** A madhouse. [ME *Bedlem, Bethlem,* Hospital of St. Mary of *Bethlehem.*]

Bed•ling•ton terrier (bĕd'lĭng-tən). A dog of a breed developed in England, having a woolly grayish or brownish coat.

Bed•ou•in (bĕd'o͞o-ĭn) *n.* An Arab of any of the nomadic tribes of the deserts of North Africa, Arabia, and Syria. [< Ar *badāwin.*]

be•drag•gle (bĭ-drăg'əl) *v.* **-gled, -gling.** To make wet and limp.

bed•rid•den (bĕd'rĭd'n) *adj.* Confined to one's bed because of illness or infirmity. [< OE *bedrida,* "one who is bedridden" : BED + *rīdan,* to RIDE.]

bed•rock (bĕd'rŏk') *n.* Solid rock that underlies the earth's surface.

bed•roll (bĕd'rōl') *n.* A portable roll of bedding.

bed•room (bĕd'ro͞om', -ro͝om') *n.* A room for sleeping.

bed•side (bĕd'sīd') *n.* The space alongside a bed, esp. the bed of a sick person. —**bed'side'** *adj.*

bed•sore (bĕd'sôr', -sōr') *n.* A pressure-induced skin ulceration occurring during long confinement to bed.

bed•spread (bĕd'sprĕd') *n.* A decorative bed covering.

bed•stead (bĕd'stĕd') *n.* The frame supporting a bed.

bed•time (bĕd'tīm') *n.* The time when one goes to bed.

bee (bē) *n.* **1.** Any of various winged, often stinging insects that gather nectar and pollen from flowers and in some species produce honey. **2.** A gathering where people work together or compete. [< OE *bēo.* See **bhei-**[1].]

beech (bēch) *n.* A tree having light-colored bark, small, edible nuts, and strong, heavy wood. [< OE *bēce.* See **bhāgo-.**]

beech•nut (bēch'nŭt') *n.* The nut of the beech tree.

beef (bēf) *n.* **1.** The flesh of a full-grown steer, bull, ox, or cow. **2.** *pl.* **beeves** (bēvz). Such an animal raised for meat. **3.** Human strength; brawn. **4.** *pl.* **beefs.** *Slang.* A complaint. —*v.* *Slang.* To complain. —**beef up.** *Slang.* To reinforce; build up. [< L *bōs (bov-),* ox.] —**beef'i•ness** *n.* —**beef'y** *adj.*

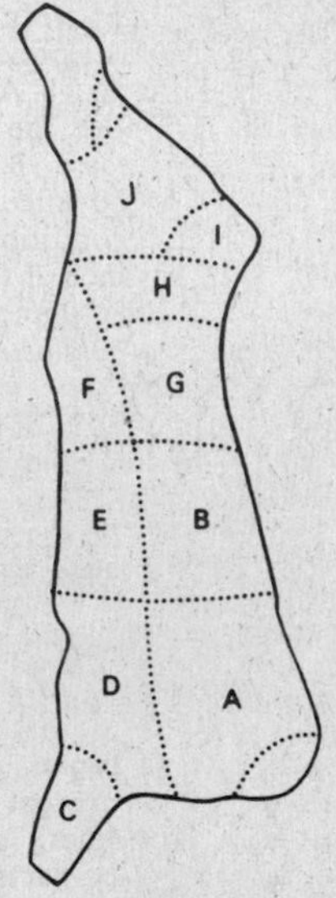

beef
A. Chuck
B. Ribs
C. Shank
D. Brisket
E. Plate
F. Flank
G. Loin (tenderloin and porterhouse)
H. Sirloin
I. Rump
J. Round

bee•hive (bē'hīv') *n.* **1.** A hive for bees. **2.** A very busy place.

bee•keep•er (bē'kē'pər) *n.* One who keeps bees; an apiarist.

bee•line (bē'līn') *n.* A fast, straight course.

Be•el•ze•bub (bē-ĕl'zĭ-bŭb') *n.* The Devil.

been (bĭn). *p.p.* of **be.**

beer (bîr) *n.* **1.** An alcoholic beverage brewed from malt and hops. **2.** Any of various carbonated soft drinks. [< OE *bēor.*]

bees•wax (bēz'wăks') *n.* The wax secreted by bees for making honeycombs and having a variety of commercial uses.

beet (bēt) *n.* **1.** A cultivated plant with a fleshy dark-red or whitish root used as a vegetable or as a source of sugar. **2.** The root of such a plant. [< OE *bēte.*]

Bee•tho•ven (bā'tō-vən), **Ludwig van.** 1770–

1827. German composer.

bee•tle[1] (bēt'l) *n.* An insect with horny front wings that cover the hind wings when not in flight. [< OE *bitela.*]

bee•tle[2] (bēt'l) *adj.* Jutting: *beetle brows.* —*v.* **-tled, -tling.** To project. [< ME *bitel-brouwed,* having shaggy eyebrows.]

bee•tle[3] (bēt'l) *n.* A heavy mallet or similar tool. [< OE *bīetel.*]

beeves. A *pl.* of **beef.**

bef. before.

be•fall (bĭ-fôl') *v.* **-fell, -fallen, -falling. 1.** To come to pass. **2.** To happen to: *"There shall no evil befall thee."* (Psalms 91:10).

be•fit (bĭ-fĭt') *v.* **-fitted, -fitting.** To be suitable to or appropriate for.

be•fog (bĭ-fôg', -fŏg') *v.* **-fogged, -fogging.** To obscure.

be•fore (bĭ-fôr', -fōr') *adv.* **1.** In front; ahead; in advance. **2.** In the past; previously. —*prep.* **1.** In front of. **2.** Prior to. **3.** Awaiting. **4.** In the presence of. **5.** Under the consideration of: *the case before the court.* **6.** In preference to; sooner than. **7.** In advance of or in precedence of, as in rank, condition, or development. —*conj.* **1.** In advance of the time when: *before he went.* **2.** Rather than; sooner than: *He would die before he would betray his country.* [< OE *beforan.* See **per**[1].]

be•fore•hand (bĭ-fôr'hănd', bĭ-fōr'-) *adv.* In advance; early. —**be•fore'hand'** *adj.*

be•foul (bĭ-foul') *v.* To sully.

be•friend (bĭ-frĕnd') *v.* To act as a friend to.

be•fud•dle (bĭ-fŭd'l) *v.* **-dled, -dling.** To confuse. —**be•fud'dle•ment** *n.*

beg (bĕg) *v.* **begged, begging. 1.** To ask for as charity. **2.** To entreat. **3.** To evade: *beg the question.* [ME *beggen.*]

be•gan (bĭ-găn'). *p.t.* of **begin.**

be•get (bĭ-gĕt') *v.* **-got** or *rare* **-gat** (-găt'), **-gotten** or **-got, -getting.** To father; sire. [< OE *begietan.* See **ghend-.**] —**be•get'ter** *n.*

beg•gar (bĕg'ər) *n.* One who solicits alms for a living. —*v.* **1.** To impoverish. **2.** To render impotent.

beg•gar•ly (bĕg'ər-lē) *adj.* Of a beggar; very poor. —**beg'gar•li•ness** *n.*

beg•gar•y (bĕg'ə-rē) *n.* Extreme poverty; penury.

be•gin (bĭ-gĭn') *v.* **-gan, -gun, -ginning. 1.** To commence. **2.** To come into being. [< OE *beginnan* < Gmc **bi-ginnan.*] —**be•gin'ner** *n.*

be•gin•ning (bĭ-gĭn'ĭng) *n.* Commencement, origin, or genesis.

be•gone (bĭ-gôn', -gŏn') *interj.* Expressive of dismissal.

be•go•nia (bĭ-gōn'yə) *n.* Any of various plants cultivated for their showy leaves or flowers. [< M. *Bégon* (1638–1710), governor of Santo Domingo.]

be•got (bĭ-gŏt'). *p.t.* and alternate *p.p.* of **beget.**

be•got•ten (bĭ-gŏt'n). *p.p.* of **beget.**

be•grime (bĭ-grīm') *v.* **-grimed, -griming.** To soil, as with dirt or grime.

be•grudge (bĭ-grŭj') *v.* **-grudged, -grudging. 1.** To envy. **2.** To give with reluctance.

be•guile (bĭ-gīl') *v.* **-guiled, -guiling. 1.** To deceive; cheat. **2.** To divert. **3.** To cause to vanish. —**be•guile'ment** *n.* —**be•guil'er** *n.*

be•gum (bē'gəm, bā'-) *n.* A Moslem lady of rank. [Urdu *begam.*]

be•gun (bĭ-gŭn'). *p.p.* of **begin.**

be•half (bĭ-hăf', -häf') *n.* Interest, support, or benefit: *on his behalf.* [ME *(on min) behalfe,* "on my side."]

be•have (bĭ-hāv') *v.* **-haved, -having. 1.** To act, react, or function in a particular way. **2. a.** To conduct oneself in a specified way. **b.** To conduct oneself in a proper way. [ME *behaven,* "to hold oneself."]

be•hav•ior (bĭ-hāv'yər) *n.* Also *chiefly Brit.* **be•hav•iour. 1.** Deportment; demeanor. **2.** Action, reaction, or function under specified circumstances. —**be•hav'ior•al** *adj.*

be•head (bĭ-hĕd') *v.* To separate the head from; decapitate.

be•he•moth (bĭ-hē'məth, bē'ə-môth') *n.* A huge animal mentioned in the Old Testament. [< Heb *bəhēmāh,* beast.]

be•hest (bĭ-hĕst') *n.* An order or authoritative command. [< OE *behǣs.*]

be•hind (bĭ-hīnd') *adv.* **1.** In, to, or toward the rear: *He walked behind.* **2.** In a place or condition that has been passed or left: *He left his gloves behind.* **3.** In arrears; late. **4.** Slow: *His watch is running behind.* —*prep.* **1.** At the back of or in the rear of. **2.** On the farther side of. **3.** In a former place, time, or situation. **4.** After (a set time): *behind schedule.* **5.** Below, as in rank. **6.** In support of. [< OE *behindan.*]

be•hind•hand (bĭ-hīnd'hănd') *adv.* **1.** In arrears. **2.** Behind the times. —**be•hind'hand'** *adj.*

be•hold (bĭ-hōld') *v.* **-held** (-hĕld'), **-holding.** To gaze at; look upon. —*interj.* Expressive of amazement. [< OE *behealdan,* to possess, hold, observe.] —**be•hold'er** *n.*

be•hold•en (bĭ-hōl'dən) *adj.* Obliged; indebted.

be•hoove (bĭ-ho͞ov') *v.* **-hooved, -hooving.** To be necessary or proper for: *It behooves us to take warning.* [< OE *behōfian,* to require.]

beige (bāzh) *n.* Light grayish brown. [F.] —**beige** *adj.*

be•ing (bē'ĭng) *n.* **1.** Existence. **2.** One that exists. **3.** One's inward nature.

Bei•rut (bā-ro͞ot'). The capital of Lebanon. Pop. 500,000.

be•la•bor (bĭ-lā'bər) *v.* **1.** To beat; thrash. **2.** To insist repeatedly or harp upon: *belabor a point.*

be•lat•ed (bĭ-lā'tĭd) *adj.* Tardy. [BE- + obs *lated* < LATE.] —**be•lat'ed•ly** *adv.*

be•lay (bĭ-lā') *v.* **1.** To make fast; secure. **2.** *Naut.* To stop: *Belay there!* —*n.* A hold in mountain climbing. [< OE *belecgan,* to cover, surround.]

belaying pin. A pin used on shipboard for securing running gear.

belch (bĕlch) *v.* 1. To expel gas from the stomach through the mouth; eruct. 2. To gush forth; erupt. [ME *belchen.*] —belch *n.*

be•lea•guer (bĭ-lē'gər) *v.* **1.** To besiege. **2.** To harass; beset. [Du *belegeren.*]

Bel•fast (bĕl'făst', -fäst', bĕl-făst', -fäst'). The capital of Northern Ireland. Pop. 410,000.

bel•fry (bĕl'frē) *n., pl.* **-fries. 1.** A church bell tower. **2.** The part of a steeple in which the bells are hung. [ME *berfrey,* siege tower, bell tower.] —**bel'fried** *adj.*

Bel•gium (bĕl'jəm). A kingdom of NW Europe. Pop. 9,428,000. Cap. Brussels. —**Bel'gian** (bĕl'jən) *adj.* & *n.*

Bel•grade (bĕl'grăd', bĕl-grăd'). The capital of Yugoslavia. Pop. 598,000.

be•lie (bĭ-lī') *v.* **-lied, -lying. 1.** To misrepresent or disguise. **2.** To show to be false. **3.** To frustrate or disappoint. —**be•li'er** *n.*

be•lief (bĭ-lēf') *n.* **1.** Trust; confidence. **2.** A conviction or opinion. **3.** A tenet or body of tenets; creed.

be•lieve (bĭ-lēv') *v.* **-lieved, -lieving. 1.** To accept as true or real. **2.** To credit with veracity; have confidence in; trust. **3.** To expect or suppose; think. **4.** To hold a religious belief. [< OE *belēfan, gelēfan.* See **leubh-.**] —**be•liev'a•ble** *adj.* —**be•liev'er** *n.*

be•lit•tle (bĭ-lĭt'l) *v.* **-tled, -tling. 1.** To represent or speak of as small or unimportant; depreciate; disparage. **2.** To cause to seem less or little. —**be•lit'tle•ment** *n.* —**be•lit'tler** *n.*

Be•lize (bə-lēz'). A country in Central America. Pop. 122,000. Cap. Belmopan.

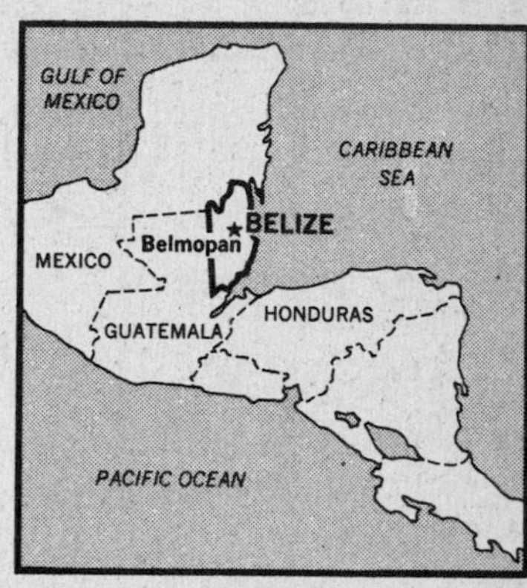

Belize

bell (bĕl) *n.* **1.** A hollow metal instrument that emits a metallic tone when struck. **2.** Something shaped like a bell. **3.** A stroke on a bell to mark the hour on shipboard. —*v.* To furnish with a bell. [< OE *belle.* See **bhel-**[4].]

bel•la•don•na (bĕl'ə-dŏn'ə) *n.* 1. A poisonous plant having small black berries. 2. A medicine derived from this plant, used to treat asthma. [It, "fair lady."]

bell•hop (bĕl'hŏp') *n.* A hotel porter.

bel•li•cose (bĕl'ĭ-kōs') *adj.* Warlike; pugnacious. [< L *bellicus,* of war.] —**bel'li•cos'i•ty** (-kŏs'ə-tē), **bel'li•cose'ness** *n.*

bel•lig•er•ent (bə-lĭj'ər-ənt) *adj.* 1. Aggressively hostile; truculent. 2. Waging war. —*n.* A warring state. [< L *belligerāre,* to wage war.] —bel•lig'er•ence, bel•lig'er•en•cy *n.*

bel•low (bĕl'ō) *v.* **1.** To roar in the manner of a bull. **2.** To shout in a deep loud voice. [< OE **belgan.* See **bhel-**[4].] —**bel'low** *n.*

bel•lows (bĕl'ōz, -əz) *n. (takes pl. v.).* A hand-operated device for directing a strong current of air, as to increase the draft of a fire. [< OE *belig,* bag, bellows. See **belly.**]

bell•weth•er (bĕl'wĕth'ər) *n.* **1.** A male sheep that wears a bell and leads a flock. **2.** One followed as a leader.

Belgium

bel•ly (bĕl'ē) *n., pl.* **-lies.** **1.** The part of the body that contains the intestines; the abdomen. **2.** The underside of the body of an animal. **3.** The stomach. [< OE *belig,* bag, purse, bellows. See **bheigh-**.]

bel•ly•ache (bĕl'ē-āk') *n.* A stomach ache.

bel•ly•but•ton (bĕl'ē-bŭt'n) *n. Informal.* The navel.

Bel•mo•pan (bĕl'mə-păn'). The capital of Belize. Pop. 2,000.

be•long (bĭ-lông', -lŏng') *v.* **1.** To be the property or concern of. **2.** To be part of or in natural association with something. **3.** To be a member of an organization. **4.** To have a proper or suitable place. [ME *belongen.*]

be•long•ing (bĭ-lông'ĭng, bĭ-lŏng'-) *n.* **1. belongings.** Personal possessions. **2.** Close and secure relationship.

be•lov•ed (bĭ-lŭv'ĭd, -lŭvd') *adj.* Greatly loved. —**be•lov'ed** *n.*

be•low (bĭ-lō') *adv.* **1.** In or to a lower place or level. **2.** On earth: *creatures here below.* —*prep.* **1.** Lower than; under. **2.** Inferior to.

belt (bĕlt) *n.* **1.** A supportive or ornamental band of leather worn around the waist. **2.** A continuous moving band used as a machine element. **3.** A geographic region that is distinctive in some specific way. **4.** *Slang.* A powerful blow. —*v.* **1.** To encircle; gird. **2.** To attach with a belt. **3.** To strike with or as if with a belt. [< OE < Gmc **baltjaz.*]

be•ma (bē'mə) *n., pl.* **-mata** (-mə-tə). **1.** Also **bi•mah** (bē'mə). The platform from which services are conducted in a synagogue. **2.** The sanctuary of an Eastern Orthodox church. [< Gk *bēma,* platform.]

be•moan (bĭ-mōn') *v.* To lament.

be•muse (bĭ-myo͞oz') *v.* **-mused, -musing.** To preoccupy; bewilder.

bench (bĕnch) *n.* **1.** A long seat for two or more persons. **2. a.** The judge's seat in court. **b.** The office or position of a judge. **3.** The court or judges. **4.** A craftsman's worktable. [< OE *benc.*]

bend (bĕnd) *v.* **bent, bending.** **1.** To tighten (a bow). **2.** To curve. **3.** To turn or deflect. **4.** To coerce or subdue. **5.** To concentrate; apply. **6.** To fasten. **7.** To yield; submit. —*n.* **1.** The action of bending. **2.** Something bent; a curve; crook. **3.** A knot that joins one rope to another or to some object. **4. bends.** Caisson disease. [< OE *bendan.* See **bhendh-**.]

be•neath (bĭ-nēth') *adv.* **1.** In a lower place; below. **2.** Underneath. —*prep.* **1.** Below; under. **2.** Unworthy of. [< OE *binithan* : *bi,* BY + *nithan,* (from) below (see **ni**).]

ben•e•dic•tion (bĕn'ə-dĭk'shən) *n.* The invocation of blessing, esp. at the end of a worship service. [< L *benedīcere,* to bless, speak well of.]

ben•e•fac•tor (bĕn'ə-făk'tər) *n.* One who gives financial or other aid. —**ben'e•fac'tress** *fem.n.*

be•nef•i•cence (bə-nĕf'ə-səns) *n.* The quality of charity or kindness. [< L *beneficus,* generous.] —**be•nef'i•cent** *adj.*

ben•e•fi•cial (bĕn'ə-fĭsh'əl) *adj.* Helpful; advantageous. [< BENEFICE.] —**ben'e•fi'cial•ly** *adv.* —**ben'e•fi'cial•ness** *n.*

ben•e•fi•ci•ar•y (bĕn'ə-fĭsh'ē-ĕr-ē, -fĭsh'ə-rē) *n., pl.* **-ies.** The recipient of a benefit, as from an insurance policy, will, or trust fund.

ben•e•fit (bĕn'ə-fĭt) *n.* **1.** An advantage. **2.** An aid; help. **3.** A payment or series of payments to one in need. **4.** A fund-raising public entertainment. —*v.* **1.** To be helpful or advantageous to. **2.** To derive advantage; profit. [< L *bene facere,* to do well.]

be•nev•o•lence (bə-nĕv'ə-ləns) *n.* **1.** Charitable good nature. **2.** An act of charity. [< L *benevolēns,* "wishing well."] —**be•nev'o•lent** *adj.*

Ben•gal (bĕn-gôl', bĕng-gôl'). A region of NE India, divided in 1947 into East Bengal, now in Bangladesh, and West Bengal, Republic of India.

Ben•ga•li (bĕn-gô'lē, bĕng-gô'-) *n., pl.* **-li** or **-lis.** **1.** An inhabitant of Bengal. **2.** The Indic language of Bengal. —**Ben•ga'li** *adj.*

Ben•ga•si (bĕn-gä'zē). Also **Ben•gha•zi.** A city of NE Libya. Pop. 170,000.

be•night•ed (bĭ-nī'tĭd) *adj.* Ignorant.

be•nign (bĭ-nīn') *adj.* **1.** Of a kindly disposition; gracious. **2.** Not malignant: *a benign tumor.* [< L *benignus,* "good-natured."]

Be•nin (bĕ-nēn'). A republic of W Africa. Pop. 2,700,000. Cap. Porto-Novo.

bent (bĕnt) *p.t.* & *p.p.* of **bend.** —*adj.* **1.** Deviating from a straight line; crooked. **2.** Determined. **3.** Headed toward. —*n.* **1.** An individual tendency, disposition, or inclination. **2.** A transverse framework used for strengthening a bridge.

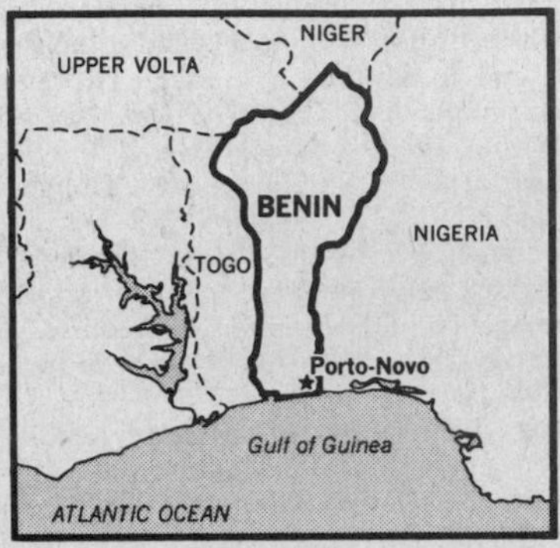

Benin

be•numb (bĭ-nŭm') *v.* **1.** To make numb, esp. by cold. **2.** To make inactive; stupefy.

Ben•ze•drine (bĕn'zə-drēn') *n.* A trademark for an amphetamine.

ben•zene (bĕn'zēn', bĕn-zēn') *n.* A clear, colorless, flammable liquid, C_6H_6, derived from petroleum and used to manufacture DDT, detergents, insecticides, and motor fuels. [BENZ(OIN) + -ENE.]

benzene ring. The hexagonal ring structure in the benzene molecule, each vertex of which is occupied by a carbon atom.

ben•zine (bĕn'zēn', bĕn-zēn') *n.* Also **ben•zin** (bĕn'zĭn). Ligroin.

ben•zol (bĕn'zôl', -zōl') *n.* Benzene. Not in technical use.

be•queath (bĭ-kwēth', -kwēth') *v.* **1.** To leave by will. **2.** To pass on or hand down. [< OE *becwethan,* to say, bequeath. See **gwet-**.]

be•quest (bĭ-kwĕst') *n.* **1.** The act of bequeathing. **2.** Something left by will.

be•rate (bĭ-rāt') *v.* **-rating, -rates.** To rebuke harshly.

Ber•ber (bûr'bər) *n., pl.* **-ber** or **-bers.** **1.** A member of one of several Moslem tribes of North Africa. **2.** The Afro-Asiatic languages of these tribes. —**Ber'ber** *adj.*

be•reave (bĭ-rēv') *v.* **-reaved** or **-reft** (-rĕft'), **-reaving.** To deprive of, as by death. [< OE *berēafian.*] —**be•reave'ment** *n.*

be•ret (bə-rā') *n.* A round, soft, visorless cloth cap. [< LL *birrus,* hooded cape.]

ber•i•ber•i (bĕr'ē-bĕr'ē) *n.* A thiamine deficiency disease characterized by partial paralysis, emaciation, and anemia. [Singhalese.]

Be•ring Sea (bîr'ĭng, bâr'-). The part of the N Pacific between Alaska and Siberia.

Bering time. The time in W Alaska and the Aleutian Islands in the 11th time zone west of Greenwich.

Berke•ley (bûrk'lē). A city of California. Pop. 111,000.

berke•li•um (bûrk'lē-əm) *n. Symbol* **Bk** A synthetic radioactive element. Atomic number 97, longest-lived isotope Bk 247. [< BERKELEY.]

Ber•lin (bĕr-lĭn'). The former capital of Germany, now surrounded by East Germany and divided into **East Berlin** and **West Berlin.** —**Ber•lin'er** *n.*

Ber•mu•da (bər-myo͞o'də). A British colony in the Atlantic Ocean. Pop. 48,000. Cap. Hamilton. —**Ber•mu'di•an** (-dē-ən) *adj.* & *n.*

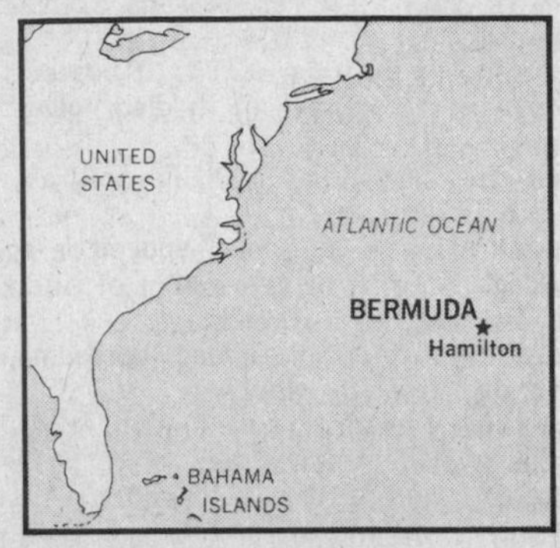

Bermuda

Bern (bûrn, bĕrn). Also **Berne.** The capital of Switzerland. Pop. 167,000.

Ber•noul•li effect (bər-no͞o'lē). The reduction of internal fluid pressure with increased stream velocity. [After D. *Bernoulli* (1700–1782), Swiss mathematician.]

ber•ry (bĕr'ē) *n., pl.* **-ries.** **1.** A usually small, fleshy, many-seeded fruit. **2.** A seed or dried kernel, as of coffee. [< OE *berige.*]

ber•serk (bər-sûrk', -zûrk') *adj.* **1.** Destructively violent. **2.** Deranged. [ON *berserkr,* "bear's skin."] —**ber•serk'** *adv.*

berth (bûrth) *n.* **1.** A built-in bed on a ship or vehicle. **2. a.** A space for a ship to dock or anchor. **b.** Enough space for a ship to maneuver. **3.** A job, esp. on a ship. —*v.* **1.** To bring (a ship) to a berth; dock. **2.** To provide (a ship) with a berth. [Prob < BEAR, "to proceed."]

Ber•til•lon system (bûr'tə-lŏn). A former system for identifying persons by means of a record of various body measurements, coloring, and markings. [< A. *Bertillon* (1853–1914), French criminologist.]

ber•yl (bĕr'əl) *n.* A mineral, essentially $Be_3Al_2Si_6O_{18}$, the chief source of beryllium and used as a gem. [< Gk *bērullos.*] —**ber'yl•line** (-ə-lĭn, -līn') *adj.*

be•ryl•li•um (bə-rĭl'ē-əm) *n. Symbol* **Be** A high-melting, lightweight, corrosion-resistant, rigid, steel-gray metallic element used as an aerospace structural material, as a moderator and reflector in nuclear reactors, and in a copper alloy used for springs, electrical contacts, and nonsparking tools. Atomic number 4, atomic weight 9.0122. [< BERYL.]

be•seech (bĭ-sēch') *v.* **-sought** or **-seeched, -seeching.** To request earnestly; implore. [ME *besechen,* to seek.] —**be•seech'er** *n.*

be•seem (bĭ-sēm') *v. Archaic.* To be appropriate for; befit.

be•set (bĭ-sĕt') *v.* **-set, -setting.** **1.** To attack from all sides. 2. To trouble persistently; harass. —**be•set'ment** *n.*

be•side (bĭ-sīd') *prep.* 1. Next to. 2. In comparison with. 3. Except for. 4. Apart from. —**beside oneself.** Extremely agitated. —*adv.* In addition to.

be•sides (bĭ-sīdz') *adv.* 1. In addition; also. 2. Moreover; furthermore. 3. Otherwise; else. —*prep.* 1. In addition to. 2. Except for.

be•siege (bĭ-sēj') *v.* **-sieged, -sieging.** 1. To lay siege to. 2. To crowd around. 3. To harass or importune, as with requests. —**be•siege'ment** *n.* —**be•sieg'er** *n.*

be•smear (bĭ-smîr') *v.* To smear over.

be•smirch (bĭ-smûrch') *v.* 1. To soil; sully. 2. To dishonor; tarnish. —**be•smirch'er** *n.* —**be•smirch'ment** *n.*

be•sot (bĭ-sŏt') *v.* **-sotted, -sotting.** To muddle or stupefy, esp. with liquor.

be•sought (bĭ-sôt'). *p.t.* & *p.p.* of **beseech.**

be•span•gle (bĭ-spăng'gəl) *v.* **-gled, -gling.** To ornament with spangles.

be•spat•ter (bĭ-spăt'ər) *v.* 1. To soil, as with mud. 2. To defame.

be•speak (bĭ-spēk') *v.* **-spoke, -spoken** or **-spoke, -speaking.** 1. To be or give a sign of; indicate. 2. To reserve. 3. To foretell.

be•spread (bĭ-sprĕd') *v.* **-spread, -spreading.** To spread over, usually thickly.

be•sprin•kle (bĭ-sprĭng'kəl) *v.* **-kled, -kling.** To sprinkle over, as with water.

Bes•se•mer converter (bĕs'ə-mər). A large pear-shaped container used in the Bessemer process. [< Sir Henry *Bessemer* (1813–1898), British metallurgist.]

Bessemer process. A method for making steel by blasting compressed air through molten iron to burn out excess carbon and other impurities.

best (bĕst) *adj. superl.* of **good.** 1. Surpassing all others in quality. 2. Most satisfactory or desirable: *the best solution.* 3. Greatest: *the best part of a week.* —*adv. superl.* of **well.** 1. Most advantageously. 2. To the greatest extent; most. —**had best.** Should. —*n.* 1. The best among several. 2. The best person or persons. 3. The best condition: *look your best.* 4. One's best clothing. 5. The best effort one can make. 6. One's regards: *Give them my best.* —**at best.** Under the most favorable conditions. —**for the best.** For the ultimate good. —**get** (or **have**) **the best of.** To defeat or outwit. —**make the best of.** To do as well as possible under unfavorable conditions. —*v.* To surpass; defeat. [< OE *betest.*]

bes•tial (bĕs'chəl, bĕst'yəl) *adj.* Having the qualities of, or behaving in the manner of, a beast or brute; savage. [< L *bēstia,* BEAST.] —**bes'ti•al'i•ty** *n.* —**bes'tial•ly** *adv.*

be•stir (bĭ-stûr') *v.* **-stirred, -stirring.** To make active; rouse.

best man. A bridegroom's chief attendant.

be•stow (bĭ-stō') *v.* To present as a gift or honor; confer. —**be•stow'al** *n.*

be•strew (bĭ-strōō') *v.* **-strewed, -strewed** or **-strewn, -strewing.** To strew or scatter things profusely.

be•stride (bĭ-strīd') *v.* **-strode, -stridden, -striding.** 1. To sit or stand on with the legs widely spread; straddle. 2. To step over.

bet (bĕt) *n.* 1. A wager. 2. The event on which a wager is made. 3. The amount risked in a wager. —*v.* **bet, betting.** 1. To make or place a bet (with). 2. To make a bet on (a contestant or an outcome). [Perh short for ABET.] —**bet'tor, bet'ter** *n.*

bet. between.

be•ta (bā'tə, bē'-) *n.* The 2nd letter of the Greek alphabet, representing *b.*

be•ta•ine (bē'tə-ēn') *n.* A sweet, crystalline alkaloid, $C_5H_{11}NO_2$, occurring in sugar beets and other plants and used in treatment of muscular degeneration. [< L *bēta,* beet.]

be•take (bĭ-tāk') *v.* **-took, -taken, -taking.** To cause (oneself) to go or move.

beta particle. A high-speed electron or positron.

beta ray. A stream of beta particles, esp. of electrons.

beta rhythm. Also **beta wave.** The second most common waveform occurring in electroencephalograms of the adult brain, having a frequency of 18–30 cycles/second and associated with an alert waking state.

be•tel (bēt'l) *n.* An Asiatic plant, whose leaves are chewed with the **betel nut,** the seed of a palm tree, as a stimulant and narcotic. [Port *betel, betle.*]

bête noire (bĕt nwär'). Someone or something that one esp. dislikes. [F, "black beast."]

beth (bĕt) *n.* The 2nd letter of the Hebrew alphabet, representing *b(bh).*

be•think (bĭ-thĭngk') *v.* **-thought, -thinking.** To remind (oneself).

Beth•le•hem (bĕth'lĭ-hĕm, bĕth'lē-əm). The Palestinian town where David lived and Jesus was born.

be•tide (bĭ-tīd') *v.* **-tided, -tiding.** To happen (to); befall. [< OE *tīdan,* to happen. See **dā-.**]

be•times (bĭ-tīmz') *adv.* In good time; early.

be•to•ken (bĭ-tō'kən) *v.* To give a sign or portent of. [< OE **bitācnian.*]

be•took (bĭ-to͝ok'). *p.t.* of **betake.**

be•tray (bĭ-trā') *v.* 1. To commit treason against or be a traitor to. 2. To be disloyal or faithless to. 3. To show, reveal, or indicate, esp. unintentionally. 4. To seduce and forsake (a woman). [< ME *trayen,* to betray.] —**be•tray'al** *n.* —**be•tray'er** *n.*

be•troth (bĭ-trōth', bĭ-trôth') *v.* To promise to marry. —**be•troth'al** *n.*

be•trothed (bĭ-trōthd', bĭ-trôtht') *n.* A person who is engaged to be married.

bet•ter (bĕt'ər) *adj. compar.* of **good.** 1. Greater in excellence or higher in quality. 2. More useful. 3. Larger; greater: *the better part of a summer.* 4. Healthier. —**better off.** In a better condition. —*adv. compar.* of **well.** 1. In a more useful way. 2. To a greater or higher extent. 3. More: *better than a year.* —**go (someone) one better.** To outdo. —**had better.** Ought to. —**think better of.** To change one's mind. —*n.* 1. Something more useful or suitable. 2. Often **betters.** One's superiors, esp. in social standing or intelligence. —**for the better.** Resulting in an improvement. —**get** (or **have**) **the better of.** To gain an advantage over. —*v.* 1. To make or become better. 2. To surpass or exceed. [< OE *betera.* See **bhad-.**]

bet•ter•ment (bĕt'ər-mənt) *n.* 1. An improvement. 2. Often **betterments.** Any improvement that adds to the value of real property.

be•tween (bĭ-twēn') *prep.* 1. In the space, time, quantity, or degree of comparison separating. 2. In interaction or interrelation of. —**between you and me.** In confidence. —*adv.* In an intermediate space, position, or time; in the interim. —**in between.** In an intermediate situation. [< OE *betwēonum.*]

Usage: *Between (prep.)* is always followed by words in the objective case: *between you and me* (not *you and I*).

be•twixt (bĭ-twĭkst') *adv.* & *prep. Archaic.* Between. [< OE *betwēohs, betwihs.*]

BeV Billion (10^9) electron volts.

bev•el (bĕv'əl) *n.* 1. The angle or inclination of a line or surface that meets another at any angle but 90°. 2. A rule with an adjustable arm, used to measure or draw angles. —*adj.* Inclined at an angle. —*v.* **-eled** or **-elled, -eling** or **-elling.** 1. To cut at an inclination that forms an angle other than a right angle. 2. To be inclined; slope. [OF **bevel.*]

bev•er•age (bĕv'rĭj, bĕv'ə-rĭj) *n.* A liquid refreshment, usually excluding water. [< OF *bevrage.*]

bev•y (bĕv'ē) *n., pl.* **-ies.** A group, esp. of quail or girls.

be•wail (bĭ-wāl') *v.* To express sorrow or regret (over); lament. —**be•wail'er** *n.*

be•ware (bĭ-wâr') *v.* **-wared, -waring.** To be on guard (against); be cautious (of). Used chiefly in the imperative or infinitive.

be•wil•der (bĭ-wĭl'dər) *v.* To confuse or befuddle, esp. with numerous conflicting situations, objects, or statements. [BE- + archaic *wilder,* to stray.] —**be•wil'der•ment** *n.*

be•witch (bĭ-wĭch') *v.* 1. To place under one's power by magic. 2. To fascinate; charm. [< OE *wiccian,* to bewitch.]

bey (bā) *n.* 1. A provincial governor in the Ottoman Empire. 2. A native ruler of the former kingdom of Tunis. [Turk.]

be•yond (bē-ŏnd') *prep.* 1. Farther away than; on the far side of. 2. After (a specified time). 3. Outside the limits, reach, or scope of. —*adv.* Farther along. [OE *begeondan.*]

bez•el (bĕz'əl) *n.* 1. A slanting surface on the edge of various cutting tools. 2. The upper, faceted portion of a cut gem. 3. A groove or flange designed to hold the beveled edge of a watch crystal or a gem. [?]

bf, bf., b.f. boldface.

B/F *Accounting.* brought forward.

B.G. brigadier general.

bhang (băng) *n.* A narcotic made from hemp. [< Sk *bhaṅgā,* hemp.]

bhp, b.hp. brake horsepower.

Bhu•tan (bo͞o-tăn', -tän'). Also **Bho•tan** (bō-). A kingdom in the Himalayas. Pop. 800,000. Cap. Thimphu. —**Bhu'tan•ese'** *n.* & *adj.*

bi-, bin-. *comb. form.* 1. Two. 2. a. Occurrence in intervals of two. b. Occurrence twice during. 3. Occurrence on both sides or directions. 4. *Chem.* a. An element or group in twice the proportion necessary for stability. b. Of organic compounds, a double radical. [< L *bis,* twice.]

Bi bismuth.

bi•a•ly (bē-ä'lē) *n., pl.* **-lys.** A flat roll topped with onion flakes. [< *Bialystok,* Poland.]

bi•an•nu•al (bī-ăn'yo͞o-əl) *adj.* Happening twice each year; semiannual. See Usage note at **bimonthly.** —**bi•an'nu•al•ly** *adv.*

bi•as (bī'əs) *n.* 1. A line cutting diagonally across the grain of fabric. 2. a. Prejudice. b. An instance of this. 3. The fixed voltage applied to an electrode. —*v.* **-ased** or **-assed, -asing** or **-assing.** 1. To prejudice or influence. 2. To apply a small voltage to (a grid). [< OF *biais,* oblique.] —**bi'as** *adj.* & *adv.*

bib (bĭb) *n.* 1. A cloth worn by children to protect clothing during meals. 2. The part of an apron or overalls covering the chest. —*v.* **bibbed, bibbing.** To drink. [< ME *bibben,* to tipple, drink.] —**bib'ber** *n.*

Bib. Bible; Biblical.

bi•be•lot (bĭb'lō) *n.* A trinket. [< OF *beubelet.*]

bibl., Bibl. Biblical.

Bi•ble (bī'bəl) *n.* 1. The sacred book of Christianity, a collection of ancient writings including the books of both the Old Testament and the New Testament. **2.** The Old Testament, the sacred book of Judaism; Hebrew Scriptures. [< Gk *(ta) biblia,* "(the) books."] —**Bib'li•cal** (bĭb'lĭ-kəl) *adj.*

bib•lio–. *comb. form.* Books. [< Gk *biblion,* book.]

bibliog. bibliographer; bibliography.

bib•li•og•ra•phy (bĭb'lē-ŏg'rə-fē) *n., pl.* **-phies.** **1.** A list of the works of an author or publisher or of sources of information in print on a specific subject. **2. a.** The description and identification of the editions, dates of issue, authorship, and typography of books, or other written material. **b.** A compilation of such information. —**bib'li•og'ra•pher** *n.* —**bib'li•o•graph'i•cal** (-lē-ə-grăf'ĭ-kəl), **bib'li•o•graph'ic** *adj.* —**bib'li•o•graph'i•cal•ly** *adv.*

bib•li•o•phile (bĭb'lē-ə-fīl') *n.* A connoisseur of books.

bib•u•lous (bĭb'yə-ləs) *adj.* Given to convivial drinking. [< L *bibere,* to drink.]

bi•cam•er•al (bī-kăm'ər-əl) *adj.* Composed of two branches: *a bicameral legislature.* [BI- + LL *camera,* room, CHAMBER.]

bi•car•bon•ate of soda (bī-kär'bə-nāt', -nĭt). **Sodium bicarbonate.**

bi•cen•ten•ni•al (bī'sĕn-tĕn'ē-əl) *adj.* **1.** Happening once every 200 years. **2.** Lasting for 200 years. **3.** Pertaining to a 200th anniversary. —*n.* A 200th anniversary.

bi•ceps (bī'sĕps') *n., pl.* **-ceps** or **-cepses** (-sĕp'sĭz). A muscle having two points of origin, esp. the large muscle at the front of the upper arm that flexes the elbow joint. [< L, "two-headed."]

bick•er (bĭk'ər) *v.* To engage in a petty quarrel. —*n.* A petty quarrel. [ME *bikeren,* to attack.]

bi•col•or (bī'kŭl'ər) *adj.* Also **bi•col•ored** (-ərd). Having two colors.

bi•cor•po•ral (bī-kôr'pər-əl) *adj.* Also **bi•cor•po•re•al** (bī'kôr-pôr'ē-əl, -pōr'ē-əl). Having two distinct bodies or main parts.

bi•cus•pid (bī-kŭs'pĭd) *adj.* One of the two-pointed teeth located between the canines and molars.

bi•cy•cle (bī'sĭk'əl, -sĭ-kəl) *n.* A vehicle consisting of a metal frame mounted upon two wire-spoked wheels with rubber tires, a seat, handlebars for steering, and two pedals or a small motor by which it is driven. [F.] —**bi'cy'cle** *v.* **(-cled, -cling).** —**bi'cy•clist** *n.*

bid (bĭd) *v.* **I. bade, bidden** (bĭd'n) or **bid, bidding. 1.** To direct; command. **2.** To utter (a greeting). **3.** To invite to attend. **II. bid, bid, bidding. 1.** To seek to win or attain something; strive. **2.** *Card Games.* To state one's intention to take (tricks of a certain number or suit): *bid four hearts.* **3.** To offer (an amount) as a price. —*n.* **1. a.** An offer of a price, as for a contract. **b.** The amount offered. **2.** An invitation. **3.** *Card Games.* **a.** The act of bidding. **b.** The number of tricks or points declared. **c.** The trump declared. **d.** A player's turn to bid. **4.** An earnest effort; a striving. [< OE *biddan* (see **bhedh-**[2]) and < OE *bēodan,* to proclaim, command (see **bheudh-**).] —**bid'der** *n.*

b.i.d. *Med.* twice a day (L *bis in die*).

bide (bīd) *v.* **bided** or **bode, bided, biding. 1.** To remain the same. **2.** To stay: *bide at home.* —**bide one's time.** To await. [< OE *bīdan.* See **bheidh-.**]

bi•en•ni•al (bī-ĕn'ē-əl) *adj.* **1.** Lasting or living for two years. **2.** Happening every second year. —See Usage note at **bimonthly.** —*n.* **1.** An event that occurs once every two years. **2.** A plant that completes its life cycle and dies in its second year. —**bi•en'ni•al•ly** *adv.*

bier (bîr) *n.* A stand on which a coffin is placed to lie in state. [< OE *bēr, bǣr.* See **bher-**[1].]

bi•fo•cal (bī-fō'kəl) *adj.* **1.** Having two different focal lengths. **2.** Correcting for both near and distant vision. —*n.* **bifocals.** Eyeglasses with bifocal lenses.

bi•fur•cate (bī'fər-kāt', bī-fûr'kāt') *v.* **-cated,**

BOOKS OF THE BIBLE

Bible translation is one of the world's oldest scholarly activities; the tradition runs back to the 3rd century B.C. As of the present date, at least some book of the Bible has been translated into more than 1,400 languages. Since there are more than 3,000 languages in the world, it is reasonable to assume that the field will continue to expand. English has an uncommonly rich heritage in this respect; since the metrical paraphrases and Gospels of Anglo-Saxon times, the entire book has been translated again and again. The Jewish Publication Society *Holy Scriptures According to the Masoretic Text,* issued in 1916 by a committee of Jewish scholars, is accepted as standard in American Judaism, and its contents are listed here. For Roman Catholics, both the Douay Version (1582–1610) and the almost completed Confraternity Old and New Testaments have been officially approved for teaching and Church use. The new Revised Standard Version, Catholic Edition (1946–54), is also approved but has as yet gained universal acceptance only among scholars. Protestants may use either the King James Bible (or Authorized Version, as it is often called, especially in Great Britain), which appeared in 1611 under the patronage of James I; or they may use the Revised Standard Version (1946–52). The following table presents the contents as listed in the Douay and King James Versions because they have the longest tradition of general acceptance and the widest range of distribution.

HEBREW SCRIPTURES

Genesis	Micah	II Kings	Song of Songs
Exodus	Nahum	Isaiah	Ruth
Leviticus	Habakkuk	Jeremiah	Lamentations
Numbers	Zephaniah	Ezekiel	Ecclesiastes
Deuteronomy	Haggai	THE TWELVE	Esther
Joshua	Zechariah	Hosea	Daniel
Judges	Malachi	Joel	Ezra
I Samuel	Psalms	Amos	Nehemiah
II Samuel	Proverbs	Obadiah	I Chronicles
I Kings	Job	Jonah	II Chronicles

OLD TESTAMENT

DOUAY VERSION	KING JAMES VERSION	DOUAY VERSION	KING JAMES VERSION
Genesis	Genesis	Canticle of Canticles	Song of Solomon
Exodus	Exodus	Wisdom	
Leviticus	Leviticus	Ecclesiasticus	
Numbers	Numbers	Isaias	Isaiah
Deuteronomy	Deuteronomy	Jeremias	Jeremiah
Josue	Joshua	Lamentations	Lamentations
Judges	Judges	Baruch	
Ruth	Ruth	Ezechiel	Ezekiel
I Kings	I Samuel	Daniel	Daniel
II Kings	II Samuel	Osee	Hosea
III Kings	I Kings	Joel	Joel
IV Kings	II Kings	Amos	Amos
I Paralipomenon	I Chronicles	Abdias	Obadiah
II Paralipomenon	II Chronicles	Jonas	Jonah
I Esdras	Ezra	Micheas	Micah
II Esdras, alias Nehemias	Nehemiah	Nahum	Nahum
Tobias		Habacuc	Habakkuk
Judith		Sophonias	Zephaniah
Esther	Esther	Aggeus	Haggai
Job	Job	Zacharias	Zechariah
Psalms	Psalms	Malachias	Malachi
Proverbs	Proverbs	I Machabees	
Ecclesiastes	Ecclesiastes	II Machabees	

NEW TESTAMENT

Matthew	Matthew	I Timothy	I Timothy
Mark	Mark	II Timothy	II Timothy
Luke	Luke	Titus	Titus
John	John	Philemon	Philemon
The Acts of the Apostles	Acts	To the Hebrews	Hebrews
THE EPISTLES		The Epistle of James	James
Paul to the Romans	Romans	I Peter	I Peter
I Corinthians	I Corinthians	II Peter	II Peter
II Corinthians	II Corinthians	I John	I John
Galatians	Galatians	II John	II John
Ephesians	Ephesians	III John	III John
Philippians	Philippians	Jude	Jude
Colossians	Colossians	The Apocalypse of St. John the Apostle	Revelation
I Thessalonians	I Thessalonians		
II Thessalonians	II Thessalonians		

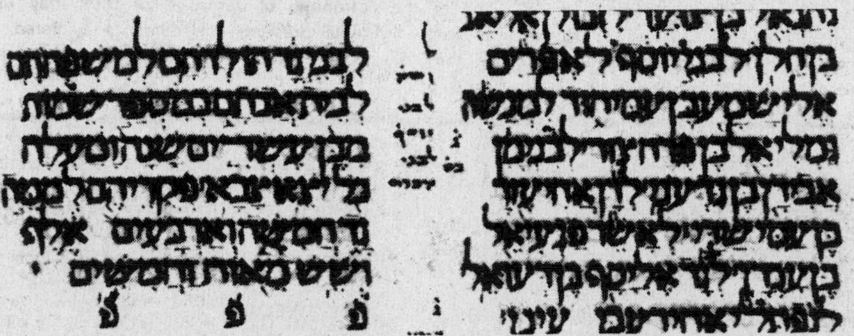

Part of a page from a Spanish Hebrew Bible, 1479

-cating. To divide into two parts or branches. [< L *bifurcus,* two-forked.] —**bi'fur•ca'tion** *n.*

big (bĭg) *adj.* **bigger, biggest. 1.** Of considerable size, number, quantity, magnitude, or extent; large. **2.** Grown-up. **3.** Pregnant. **4.** Important. —*adv.* **1.** Boastfully. **2.** Successfully. [ME, strong, stout, full-grown.] —**big'-gish** *adj.* —**big'ness** *n.*

big•a•my (bĭg'ə-mē) *n., pl.* **-mies.** The crime of marrying one person while still married to another. [< OF *bigame,* bigamous.] —**big'-a•mist** *n.* —**big'a•mous** *adj.*

Big Dipper. An asterism in Ursa Major, consisting of seven stars forming a dipper-shaped configuration.

big•horn (bĭg'hôrn') *n.* A wild mountain sheep of W North America, having large, curved horns.

bight (bīt) *n.* **1.** A loop in a rope. **2.** A curve in a shoreline. **3.** A bay. [< OE *byht,* bend, angle.]

big•ot (bĭg'ət) *n.* An intolerant person, esp. in matters of religion, race, or politics. [< OF, a pejorative term for the Normans.] —**big'ot•ed** *adj.* —**big'ot•ry** *n.*

big•wig (bĭg'wĭg') *n. Informal.* An important person; dignitary.

bike (bīk) *n. Informal.* A bicycle. —**bike** *v.* **(biked, biking).**

bi•ki•ni (bĭ-kē'nē) *n.* A woman's brief two-piece bathing suit. [< *Bikini,* an atoll in the Pacific Ocean.]

bi•lat•er•al (bī-lăt'ər-əl) *adj.* **1.** Of or having two sides. **2.** Affecting two sides or parties equally. —**bi•lat'er•al•ly** *adv.*

bile (bīl) *n.* **1.** A bitter, alkaline, brownish-yellow or greenish-yellow liquid that is secreted by the liver and aids in the digestion of fats. **2.** Irascibility; ill humor. [< L *bīlis.*]

bilge (bĭlj) *n.* **1.** The lowest inner part of a ship's hull. **2.** Water that collects in this part. **3.** *Slang.* Stupid talk; nonsense. [Prob var of BULGE.]

bi•lin•gual (bī-lĭng'gwəl) *adj.* Expressed in or able to speak two languages. [L *bilinguis.*]

bil•ious (bĭl'yəs) *adj.* **1.** Of, pertaining to, or containing bile. **2.** Pertaining to gastric distress caused by sluggishness of the liver or gall bladder. **3.** Irascible.

bil•i•ru•bin (bĭl'ə-ro͞o'bĭn, bĭ'lə-) *n.* A reddish-yellow organic compound, $C_{33}H_{36}O_6N_4$, derived from hemoglobin during normal and pathological destruction of erythrocytes. [< L *bīlis,* BILE + *ruber,* red.]

bilk (bĭlk) *v.* To defraud, cheat, or swindle. [?]

bill¹ (bĭl) *n.* **1.** A statement of charges. **2.** A list of particulars, as a playbill or menu. **3.** An advertising poster or similar public notice. **4.** A piece of paper money. **5.** A bill of exchange. **6.** A draft of a law presented for approval to a legislature. **7.** *Law.* A document containing a formal statement of a case or complaint. —*v.* **1.** To present a statement of costs to. **2.** To enter on a bill. **3.** To advertise by public notice. [< ML *billa.*]

bill² (bĭl) *n.* **1.** The beak of a bird. **2.** A beak-like part. —*v.* To touch beaks together. —**bill and coo.** To kiss and murmur amorously. [< OE *bile.* See **bhei-².**]

bill•board (bĭl'bôrd', -bōrd') *n.* A structure for the display of advertising posters.

bil•let (bĭl'ĭt) *n.* **1.** A lodging for troops. **2.** A written order directing that such quarters be provided. **3.** A position of employment. —*v.* To assign quarters to by billet. [ME *bylett.*]

bil•let-doux (bĭl'ā-do͞o', bĭl'ē-) *n., pl.* **billets-doux** (bĭl'ā-do͞o/z/', bĭl'ē-). A love letter. [F.]

bill•fold (bĭl'fōld') *n.* A wallet.

bil•liards (bĭl'yərdz) *n. (takes sing. v.).* A game in which a cue is used to hit three balls against one another or the side cushions of a rectangular table. [< F *billard,* bent stick, billiard cue.] —**bil'liard** *adj.*

bil•lings•gate (bĭl'ĭngz-gāt') *n.* Foul-mouthed abuse. [< *Billingsgate,* fishmarket of London.]

bil•lion (bĭl'yən) *n.* **1.** The cardinal number represented by 1 followed by 9 zeros. **2.** *Brit.* The cardinal number represented by 1 followed by 12 zeros. [< BI- + (M)ILLION.] —**bil'lion** *adj.*

bil•lionth (bĭl'yənth) *n.* **1.** The ordinal number one billion in a series. **2.** One of a billion equal parts. —**bil'lionth** *adj.* & *adv.*

bill of exchange. A written order directing that a specified sum of money be paid to a specified person.

bill of fare. A menu.

bill of lading. A document listing and acknowledging receipt of goods for shipment.

Bill of Rights. The first ten amendments to the Constitution of the United States.

bil•low (bĭl'ō) *n.* **1.** A large wave. **2.** A great swell or surge, as of smoke. —*v.* To surge, roll, or rise in billows. [< ON *bylgja.*]

bil•ly (bĭl'ē) *n., pl.* **-lies.** *Informal.* A short wooden club. [Prob < the name *Billy.*]

billy goat. A male goat.

bi•mah. Variant of **bema.**

bi•met•al•lism (bī-mĕt'l-ĭz'əm) *n.* The policy of using gold and silver as the monetary standard of currency and value. —**bi•met'al•list** *n.*

bi•month•ly (bī-mŭnth'lē) *adj.* Happening every two months. —*adv.* Once every two months. —*n., pl.* **-lies.** A publication issued bimonthly.

Usage: Bimonthly, in careful usage, means "once in two months"; *biweekly,* "once in two weeks"; and *biyearly,* "once in two years." They are not interchangeable with *semimonthly, semiweekly,* and *semiyearly,* which refer to occurrence twice a month, week, and year, respectively. A similar distinction exists between *biennial* (once in two years, lasting two years) and *biannual* (twice a year).

bin (bĭn) *n.* A storage receptacle or container. [< OE *binne,* basket, crib. See **bhendh-.**]

bin–. Variant of **bi-.**

bi•na•ry (bī'nə-rē) *adj.* **1.** Having two distinct parts. **2.** Having a numerical base of 2. [< L *bīnī,* two by two.]

bin•au•ral (bī-nôr'əl, bĭn-ôr'əl) *adj.* **1.** Hearing with or related to two ears. **2.** Pertaining to sound transmission from two sources.

bind (bīnd) *v.* **bound, binding. 1.** To tie or encircle, as with a rope. **2.** To bandage. **3.** To hold or restrain. **4.** To compel, as with a sense of duty. **5.** To place under legal obligation. **6.** To make or become solid. **7.** To enclose and fasten (a book) between covers. **8.** To reinforce with an edge or border. **9.** To constipate. [< OE *bindan.* See **bhendh-.**] —**bind'a•ble** *adj.* —**bind'er** *n.*

bind•er•y (bīn'də-rē) *n., pl.* **-ies.** A shop where books are bound.

binge (bĭnj) *n. Slang.* A carousal. [Brit dial *binge,* to fill a boat with water, to drink.]

bin•oc•u•lar (bə-nŏk'yə-lər, bī-) *adj.* **1.** Involving both eyes. **2.** Having two eyes arranged to produce stereoscopic vision. —*n.* Often **binoculars.** An optical device, such as field glasses, designed for use by both eyes at once.

bi•no•mi•al (bī-nō′mē-əl) *adj.* Consisting of or pertaining to two names or terms. —*n.* A mathematical expression consisting of two terms connected by a plus or minus sign. [BI- + Gk *nomos,* portion, part.]

bio–. *comb. form.* Life or living organisms. [< Gk *bios,* life.]

bi•o•chem•is•try (bī′ō-kĕm′ĭs-trē) *n.* The chemistry of biological substances and processes. —**bi′o•chem′i•cal** *adj.* —**bi′o•chem′i•cal•ly** *adv.* —**bi′o•chem′ist** *n.*

biog. biographer; biographical; biography.

bi•og•ra•phy (bī-ŏg′rə-fē, bē-) *n., pl.* **-phies.** A written account of a person's life; a life history. —**bi•og′ra•pher** *n.* —**bi′o•graph′ic** (-ə-grăf′ĭk), **bi′o•graph′i•cal** *adj.*

bi•o•de•grad•a•ble (bī′ō-dĭ-grā′də-bəl) *adj.* Capable of being decomposed by natural biological processes: *a biodegradable detergent.*

bi•o•feed•back (bī′ō-fēd′băck′) *n.* A technique whereby one seeks to consciously regulate a bodily function thought to be involuntary, as heartbeat, by using an instrument to monitor the function.

biol. biological; biologist; biology.

bi•ol•o•gy (bī-ŏl′ə-jē) *n.* **1.** The science of life processes and living organisms. **2.** The life processes of any category of living organisms. —**bi′o•log′i•cal** (-lŏj′ĭ-kəl) *adj.* —**bi•ol′o•gist** *n.*

bi•on•ic (bī-ŏn′ĭk) *adj.* Using or containing mechanical equipment to strengthen or replace part of a living creature. [BI(O-) + (ELECTR-)ONIC.]

bi•o•phys•ics (bī′ō-fĭz′ĭks) *n. (takes sing. v.).* The physics of biological processes. —**bi′o•phys′i•cist** *n.*

bi•op•sy (bī′ŏp′sē) *n., pl.* **-sies.** Examination of tissues removed from the body as an aid to medical diagnosis. —**bi•op′sic** (bī-ŏp′sĭk) *adj.*

bi•par•ti•san (bī-pär′tə-zən) *adj.* Consisting of or supported by members of two parties. —**bi•par′ti•san•ship′** *n.*

bi•par•tite (bī-pär′tīt′) *adj.* **1.** Having two parts. **2.** Having two parts, one for each party: *a bipartite treaty.* [< L *bipartire,* to divide into two parts.] —**bi′par•ti′tion** (-tĭsh′ən) *n.*

bi•ped (bī′pĕd′) *n.* A two-footed animal.

bi•plane (bī′plān′) *n.* An airplane with single or paired wings at two different levels.

bi•po•lar (bī-pō′lər) *adj.* **1.** Pertaining to or having two poles. **2.** Relating to or involving both of the earth's poles.

bi•ra•cial (bī-rā′shəl) *adj.* Involving members of two races. —**bi•ra′cial•ism′** *n.*

birch (bûrch) *n.* **1.** Any of several trees with papery, easily peeled bark. **2.** The hard wood of such a tree. **3.** A birch rod used for whipping. —*v.* To whip (someone) with a birch rod. [< OE *birce, beorce.* See **bherəg-.**]

bird (bûrd) *n.* A warm-blooded, egg-laying, feathered vertebrate with forelimbs modified to form wings. [< OE *brid.*]

bird•ie (bûr′dē) *n. Golf.* One stroke under par for any hole.

bird•lime (bûrd′līm′) *n.* A sticky substance smeared on twigs to capture small birds.

bird of paradise. Any of various birds of New Guinea and Australia with characteristically showy plumage.

bird's-eye (bûrdz′ī′) *adj.* **1.** Patterned with small spots: *bird's-eye maple.* **2.** Seen from high above: *a bird's-eye view.*

bi•ret•ta (bə-rĕt′ə) *n.* A square cap worn esp. by Roman Catholic clergymen. [< ML *birretum,* cap.]

Bir•ming•ham (bûr′mĭng-hăm′). **1.** A city in N Alabama. Pop. 301,000. **2.** (bûr′mĭng-əm). The second-largest city in England. Pop. 1,103,000.

birth (bûrth) *n.* **1. a.** The act or condition of being born. **b.** The act or process of bearing young. **2.** Origin; ancestry. **3.** A beginning. [< ON *burdhr.*]

birth•day (bûrth′dā′) *n.* The day or anniversary of one's birth.

birth•mark (bûrth′märk′) *n.* A mark present on the body from birth.

birth•place (bûrth′plās′) *n.* The place where someone is born or where something originates.

birth•rate (bûrth′rāt′) *n.* The number of births in a specified population per unit time, esp. per year.

birth•right (bûrth′rīt′) *n.* Any privilege to which a person is entitled by birth.

birth•stone (bûrth′stōn′) *n.* A jewel associated with the month of one's birth, thought to bring him good luck.

bis•cuit (bĭs′kĭt) *n.* **1.** A small cake of bread leavened with baking powder or soda. **2.** *Chiefly Brit.* A cracker or cooky. [< ML **biscoctus (panis),* "twice-cooked (bread)."]

bi•sect (bī′sĕkt′, bī-sĕkt′) *v.* **1.** To divide or cut into two equal parts. **2.** To split; fork. [BI- + -SECT.] —**bi′sec′tion** *n.* —**bi′sec′tion•al** *adj.* —**bi′sec′tion•al•ly** *adv.*

bi•sec•tor (bī′sĕk′tər, bī-sĕk′-) *n.* A straight line that bisects an angle.

bi•sex•u•al (bī-sĕk′sho͞o-əl) *adj.* **1.** Pertaining to both sexes. **2.** Having both male and female organs. **3.** Sexually attracted to members of both sexes.

bish•op (bĭsh′əp) *n.* **1.** A high-ranking Christian clergyman, usually in charge of a diocese. **2.** A chessman that can move diagonally across any number of unoccupied spaces of the same color. [< VL **biscopus.*]

bish•op•ric (bĭsh′əp-rĭk) *n.* **1.** The office of a bishop. **2.** The diocese of a bishop.

Bis•marck (bĭz′märk). The capital of North Dakota. Pop. 35,000.

Bis•marck (bĭz′märk), **Otto von.** 1815–1898. First chancellor of the German Empire.

bis•muth (bĭz′məth) *n. Symbol* **Bi** A white, crystalline, brittle, metallic element used in alloys to form sharp castings for objects sensitive to high temperatures and in various low-melting alloys for fire-safety devices. Atomic number 83, atomic weight 208.980. [NL *bisemutum.*] —**bis′muth•al** *adj.*

bi•son (bī′sən, -zən) *n.* A shaggy-maned, short-horned bovine mammal of W North America. [L *bisōn.*]

bisque[1] (bĭsk) *n.* **1.** A thick cream soup usually made with shellfish. **2.** Any thick cream soup. **3.** Ice cream mixed with crushed macaroons or nuts. [F.]

bisque[2] (bĭsk) *n.* Fired unglazed pottery. [< BISCUIT.]

bis•tro (bē′strō, bĭs′trō) *n., pl.* **-tros.** A small bar or restaurant. [F.]

bit[1] (bĭt) *n.* **1.** A small piece or amount. **2.** A moment. **3. a.** An entertainment routine. **b.** A short scene or episode in a play or movie. **4.** *Informal.* A particular kind of activity. **5.** *Informal.* An amount equal to $\frac{1}{8}$ of a dollar: *two bits a head.* —**do one's bit.** To make one's contribution. [< OE *bita,* piece bitten off. See **bheid-.**]

bit[2] (bĭt) *n.* **1.** A pointed and threaded tool for drilling and boring. **2.** The metal mouthpiece of a bridle. [< OE *bite,* a sting, bite. See **bheid-.**]

bit[3] (bĭt) *n.* **1.** A single character of a computer language having just two characters, such as either of the binary digits 0 or 1. **2.** A unit of information storage capacity, as of a computer memory. [BI(NARY) (DIGI)T.]

bitch (bĭch) *n.* **1.** A female dog. **2.** *Slang.* A spiteful woman. **3.** *Slang.* A complaint. **4.** *Slang.* A confounding problem. —*v. Slang.* To complain. [< OE *bicce,* female dog < Gmc **bekjōn-.*]

bitch•y (bĭch′ē) *adj.* **-ier, -iest.** *Slang.* Spiteful, malicious, or ill-tempered.

bite (bīt) *v.* **bit, bitten** (bĭt′n) or **bit** (bĭt) (see Usage note below), **biting. 1.** To cut or tear (something) with or as if with the teeth. **2.** To sting, as does a mosquito. **3.** To corrode. **4.** To cause or have a stinging effect or a sharp taste. **5.** To take bait. —**bite the dust.** To fall dead. —*n.* **1.** The act of biting. **2.** An injury resulting from biting. **3. a.** A stinging or smarting sensation. **b.** An incisive, penetrating quality. **4.** A mouthful. **5.** A light meal or snack. **6.** The angle at which the upper and lower teeth meet. [< OE *bītan.* See **bheid-.**]

Usage: Of the two participles *bitten* and *bit,* only *bitten* is now standard in the passive. *The boy was bitten* (not *bit*) *by the dog.*

bit•ter (bĭt′ər) *adj.* **1.** Having a taste that is sharp and unpleasant. **2.** Causing sharp pain to the body or discomfort to the mind. **3.** Exhibiting strong animosity. **4.** Marked by resentfulness. [< OE *biter.* See **bheid-.**] —**bit′ter•ly** *adv.* —**bit′ter•ness** *n.*

bit•tern (bĭt′ərn) *n.* A long-necked, brownish wading bird with a resonant cry. [< VL **būtitaurus,* "bird that bellows like an ox."]

bit•ter•root (bĭt′ər-ro͞ot′, -ro͝ot′) *n.* A plant of W North America with showy pink or white flowers.

bit•ters (bĭt′ərz) *pl.n.* A bitter, usually alcoholic liquid made with herbs or roots and used in cocktails or as a tonic.

bit•ter•sweet (bĭt′ər-swēt′) *n.* **1.** A woody vine having yellowish fruits that split open to expose seeds with fleshy red coverings. **2.** A species of nightshade with purple flowers and poisonous red berries. —*adj.* Bitter and sweet at the same time.

bi•tu•men (bĭ-t/y/o͞o′mən) *n.* Any of various mixtures of hydrocarbons found in asphalt and tar and used for surfacing roads and waterproofing. [< L *bitūmen.*]

bi•tu•mi•nous (bĭ-t/y/o͞o′mə-nəs, bī-) *adj.* **1.** Like or containing bitumen. **2.** Pertaining to a mineral coal that burns with a smoky, yellow flame.

bi•va•lent (bī-vā′lənt) *adj.* Having valence 2.

bi•valve (bī′vălv′) *n.* A mollusk, as an oyster or clam, with a shell having two hinged parts. —**bi′valve′** *adj.*

biv•ou•ac (bĭv′o͞o-ăk, bĭv′wăk) *n.* A temporary encampment made by soldiers in the field. —*v.* **-acked, -acking.** To encamp in a bivouac. [F.]

bi•week•ly (bī-wēk′lē) *adj.* Happening every two weeks. See Usage note at **bimonthly.** —*n., pl.* **-lies.** A publication issued every two weeks. —**bi•week′ly** *adv.*

bi•year•ly (bī-yîr′lē) *adj.* Happening every two years. See Usage note at **bimonthly.** —**bi•year′ly** *adv.*

bi•zarre (bĭ-zär′) *adj.* Strikingly unconventional; odd. [F, orig "handsome," "brave."]

Bi•zet (bē-zā′), **Georges.** 1838–1875. French composer.

Bk berkelium.

bk. **1.** bank. **2.** book.

bkg. banking.
bkpg. bookkeeping.
bl. **1.** black. **2.** blue.
B/L bill of lading.
blab (blăb) *v.* **blabbed, blabbing. 1.** To reveal (a secret), esp. through unreserved talk. **2.** To chatter indiscreetly. [ME *blabben.*] **—blab'ber** *n.* **—blab'by** *adj.*
blab•ber (blăb'ər) *v.* To chatter. [ME *blabberen.*]
black (blăk) *adj.* **1.** Being of the darkest achromatic visual value; producing or reflecting comparatively little light and having no predominant hue. **2.** Having no light whatsoever. **3.** Negroid. **4.** Dark in color. **5.** Evil. **6.** Cheerless. **7.** Sullen. **8.** Calamitous. *—n.* **1.** An achromatic color value of minimum lightness or maximum darkness; one extreme of the neutral gray series of colors, the opposite being white. **2.** A Negro. **—in the black.** Solvent. *—v.* To make black. [< OE *blæc.* See **bhel-**[1].] **—black'ish** *adj.* **—black'ness** *n.*
black-and-blue (blăk'ən-blōō') *adj.* Discolored from a bruise.
black•ball (blăk'bôl') *n.* **1.** A small black ball used as a negative ballot. **2.** A vote against admission of an applicant. **—black'ball'** *v.* **—black'ball'er** *n.*
black•ber•ry (blăk'bĕr'ē, -bər-ē) *n.* **1.** The blackish, glossy, edible berry of a thorny plant. **2.** The plant itself.
black•bird (blăk'bûrd') *n.* Any of various birds having black or predominantly black plumage.
black•board (blăk'bôrd', -bōrd') *n.* A surface for writing on with chalk.
black•en (blăk'ən) *v.* **1.** To make or become black. **2.** To defame. **—black'en•er** *n.*
black eye. A bruised discoloration of the flesh surrounding the eye.
black-eyed Susan. A plant having daisylike flowers with orange-yellow rays and dark-brown centers.
black•guard (blăg'ərd, -ärd) *n.* A scoundrel. [Orig. the menials of a noble household.]
black•head (blăk'hĕd') *n.* A plug of dried fatty matter capped with blackened dust and epithelial debris that clogs a skin pore.
black•jack[1] (blăk'jăk') *n.* A small leather-covered bludgeon with a flexible handle.
black•jack[2] (blăk'jăk') *n.* A card game in which the object is to accumulate cards with a total count nearer to 21 than that of the dealer.
black light. Invisible ultraviolet or infrared radiation.
black•list (blăk'lĭst') *n.* A list of disapproved persons. *—v.* To place (a name) on a blacklist.
black magic. Magic as practiced in league with the Devil; witchcraft.
black•mail (blăk'māl') *n.* Extortion by threat of exposure. [BLACK + ME *maill,* tribute.] **—black'mail'** *v.* **—black'mail'er** *n.*
black market. A market in which goods are sold in violation of restrictions. **—black marketer. —black marketeer.**
Black Muslim. A member of the **Nation of Islam.**
black•out (blăk'out') *n.* **1.** The extinguishing or concealing of lights that might be visible to enemy aircraft during an air raid. **2.** A temporary loss of consciousness. **3.** A stoppage, as of news.
Black Power. A movement among American Negroes to achieve political power without integration.
Black Sea. A large inland sea between Europe and Asia Minor.
black sheep. A person considered disgraceful by his family.
black•smith (blăk'smĭth') *n.* One who forges and shapes iron with an anvil and hammer. [ME *blaksmith,* "a worker in black metal" (iron).]
black•thorn (blăk'thôrn') *n.* A thorny shrub with white flowers and bluish-black, plumlike fruit.
black•top (blăk'tŏp') *n.* A bituminous material, such as asphalt, used to pave roads. **—black'top'** *v.*
black widow. A black and red spider of which the female is extremely venomous.
blad•der (blăd'ər) *n.* **1.** Any of various distensible membranous sacs found in most animals, esp. the urinary bladder. **2.** Anything resembling such a sac. **3.** *Pathol.* A blister, pustule, or cyst filled with fluid or air. [< OE *blǣdre.* See **bhlē-**[2].]
blade (blăd) *n.* **1.** The flat-edged cutting part of a sharpened tool or weapon. **2.** A similar flat, thin part or structure. **3.** A dashing young man. [< OE *blæd,* leaf, blade. See **bhel-**[3].] **—blad'ed** *adj.*
blain (blān) *n.* A skin sore; blister; blotch. [< OE *blegen,* a swelling.]
Blake (blăk), **William.** 1757–1827. English poet and engraver.
blame (blām) *v.* **blamed, blaming. 1.** To hold responsible. **2.** To censure. *—n.* **1.** Responsibility for a fault or error. **2.** Censure. [< OF *blamer, blasmer.*] **—blam'er** *n.*
blame•wor•thy (blām'wûr'*thē*) *adj.* Deserving of blame. **—blame'wor'thi•ness** *n.*
blanch (blănch, blänch) *v.* **1.** To make or become pale or white. **2.** To remove the skin from by immersing in hot water: *blanch almonds.* [< OF *blanc,* white.]
blanc•mange (blə-mänj') *n.* A flavored and sweetened milk pudding, thickened with cornstarch. [< OF *blancmanger,* "white food."]
bland (blănd) *adj.* **1.** Characterized by a moderate or tranquil quality. **2.** Lacking a distinctive character. [L *blandus,* flattering, "soft-spoken."] **—bland'ly** *adv.* **—bland'ness** *n.*
blan•dish (blăn'dĭsh) *v.* To coax by flattery; cajole. [< L *blandīrī* < *blandus,* BLAND.] **—blan'dish•er** *n.* **—blan'dish•ment** *n.*
blank (blăngk) *adj.* **1.** Bearing no writing or marking of any kind. **2.** Not filled in: *a blank questionnaire.* **3.** Having no finishing grooves: *a blank key.* **4.** Expressing nothing; vacant. **5.** Devoid of activity. **6.** Complete: *a blank refusal.* *—n.* **1.** An empty space. **2. a.** A space to be filled in on a document. **b.** A document having one or more such spaces. **3.** An unfinished article, such as a key form. **4.** A gun cartridge with a charge of powder but no bullet. **5.** A dash indicating omission of a word or letter. **6.** The center white circle of a target. **—draw a blank.** *Informal.* To fail utterly. *—v.* **1.** To remove from view. **2.** To prevent (an opponent in a game or sport) from scoring. [ME *blaunk,* white, not written on.] **—blank'ly** *adv.* **—blank'ness** *n.*
blan•ket (blăng'kĭt) *n.* **1.** A piece of wool or other thick cloth used as a covering for warmth, esp. on a bed. **2.** A thick layer that covers. *—adj.* Covering a wide range of conditions. *—v.* To cover with or as if with a blanket. [ME, orig. a white woolen material.]
blank verse. Verse consisting of unrhymed iambic lines.
blare (blâr) *v.* **blared, blaring.** To sound or utter loudly. [ME *bleren,* to bellow.]
blar•ney (blär'nē) *n.* Smooth, flattering talk. [< the *Blarney* Stone, in *Blarney,* Ireland which is said to impart certain skills to those who kiss it.]
bla•sé (blä-zā', blä'zā) *adj.* Having a cynically jaded manner. [< F *blaser,* to blunt, surfeit.]
blas•pheme (blăs-fēm') *v.* **-phemed, -pheming.** To speak of (God or something sacred) in an irreverent or forbidden manner. [< Gk *blasphēmein,* to reproach.] **—blas•phem'er** *n.* **—blas'phe•mous** (blăs'fə-məs) *adj.* **—blas'phe•mous•ly** *adv.* **—blas'phe•my** *n.*
blast (blăst, bläst) *n.* **1.** A strong gust of wind. **2.** A forcible stream of air from an opening, esp. one in a blast furnace to aid combustion. **3.** The sound produced by the blowing of a whistle. **4.** An explosion. **5.** A verbal assault. **6.** *Slang.* A big or wild party. **—(at) full blast.** At full capacity. *—v.* **1.** To explode. **2.** To blight; wither. **3.** To criticize vigorously. **4.** *Slang.* To damn. [< OE *blǣst.* See **bhlē-**[2].]
blas•te•ma (blă-stē'mə) *n., pl.* **-mas** or **-mata** (-mə-tə). A segregated region of embryonic cells from which a specific organ develops. [< Gk *blastēma,* offspring, offshoot.]
blast off. To commence flight, as a rocket or space vehicle.
blast•off (blăst'ŏf', bläst'-) *n.* Also **blast-off.** The launching of a rocket or space vehicle.
bla•tant (blā'tənt) *adj.* **1.** Unpleasantly loud. **2.** Offensively conspicuous; obvious. [< L *blatīre,* to blab, gossip.] **—bla'tant•ly** *adv.*
blath•er (blă*th*'ər) *v.* To speak foolishly or nonsensically. [< ON *bladhra,* to prattle.] **—blath'er** *n.* **—blath'er•er** *n.*
blaze[1] (blāz) *n.* **1.** A burst of fire. **2.** Any bright, hot light. **3.** A destructive fire, esp. one that spreads rapidly. **4.** A sudden outburst, as of emotion. *—v.* **blazed, blazing. 1.** To burn with a bright flame. **2.** To shine brightly. **3.** To be deeply excited, as by emotion. [< OE *blæse,* torch, bright fire. See **bhel-**[1].]
blaze[2] (blāz) *n.* **1.** A white spot, as on the face of a horse. **2.** A mark cut on a tree to indicate a trail. *—v.* **blazed, blazing.** To indicate (a trail) by marking trees with cuts. [Prob < MLG *bles.*]
blaz•er (blā'zər) *n.* An informal sport jacket.
bla•zon (blā'zən) *n.* **1.** A coat of arms. **2.** A splendid display. *—v.* To adorn with or as if with blazons. [< ME *blasoun,* shield, coat of arms.]
bldg. building.
bleach (blēch) *v.* To make or become white or colorless. *—n.* A chemical agent used for bleaching. [< OE *blǣcan.* See **bhel-**[1].]
bleach•ers (blē'chərz) *pl.n.* An unroofed outdoor grandstand.
bleak (blēk) *adj.* **1.** Exposed to the elements; barren. **2.** Cold and cutting. **3.** Gloomy and somber. [< ON *bleikr,* shining, white.]
blear (blîr) *v.* **1.** To blur (the eyes) with or as with tears. **2.** To blur; dim. [ME *bleren.*] **—blear'i•ness** *n.* **—blear'y** *adj.*
bleat (blēt) *n.* The characteristic cry of a goat, sheep, or calf. *—v.* To utter such a sound. [< OE *blǣtan.* See **bhlē-**[1].]
bleed (blēd) *v.* **bled** (blĕd), **bleeding. 1.** To lose or extract blood. **2.** To feel sympathetic grief: *My heart bleeds for you.* **3.** To exude or extract sap. **4.** *Slang.* To pay out or extort money, esp. an exorbitant amount. **5.** To become mixed or run, as dyes in wet cloth. **6.** To draw a fluid from; drain. [< OE *blēdan* < Gmc **blōthjan.*]
bleed•er (blē'dər) *n.* A hemophiliac.
bleed•ing-heart (blē'dĭng-härt') *n.* A garden plant with nodding, pink flowers.
blem•ish (blĕm'ĭsh) *n.* A flaw or disfigure-

ment. [< OF *blemir, blesmir,* to make pale.]

blench[1] (blĕnch) *v.* To draw back or shy away, as from fear; flinch. [< OE *blencan,* to deceive.]

blench[2] (blĕnch) *v.* To turn pale; blanch.

blend (blĕnd) *v.* **1.** To make into or become a uniform mixture. **2.** To become merged into one. *—n.* **1.** That which is blended. **2.** *Ling.* A word produced from parts of other words, as *smog* from *smoke* and *fog.* [< ON *blanda.*] **—blend'er** *n.*

bleph•a•ri•tis (blĕf'ə-rī'tĭs) *n.* Inflammation of the eyelid. [< Gk *blepharon,* eyelid.]

bless (blĕs) *v.* **blessed** or **blest** (blĕst), **blessing. 1.** To make holy; sanctify. **2.** To make the sign of the cross over. **3.** To invoke divine favor upon. **4.** To honor as holy; glorify. **5.** To confer well-being upon. **6.** To favor, as with talent. [< OE *blētsian* < Gmc *blōthisōjan,* "to hallow with blood."] **—bless'ed** (blĕs'ĭd) *adj.* **—bless'ed•ly** *adv.*

Blessed Sacrament. *R.C.Ch.* The consecrated Host.

Blessed Virgin. The Virgin Mary.

bless•ing (blĕs'ĭng) *n.* **1.** The act or words of one who blesses. **2.** An expression of good wishes. **3.** A special favor granted by God. **4.** Anything contributing to happiness. **5.** Approbation. **6.** A short prayer at mealtime.

blew (blo͞o). *p.t.* of **blow.**

blight (blīt) *n.* **1.** A destructive plant disease. **2.** An injurious environmental condition. **3.** One that withers hopes or impairs growth. [?] **—blight** *v.*

blimp (blĭmp) *n.* A buoyant aircraft. [Prob (type) B + LIMP.]

blind (blīnd) *adj.* **1.** Without the sense or use of sight. **2.** Of or for sightless persons. **3.** Performed without preparation: *a blind attempt.* **4.** Not based on reason or evidence: *blind faith.* **5.** Acting without human control: *blind fate.* **6.** Hidden from sight. **7.** Closed at one end. *—n.* **1.** Something that shuts out light. **2.** A shelter for concealing hunters. *—v.* **1.** To deprive of sight. **2.** To dazzle. **3.** To deprive (a person) of his mental powers. [< OE, blind, obscure. See **bhel-[1]**.] **—blind'ness** *n.*

blind date. *Informal.* A social engagement between a man and a woman who have not previously met.

blind•ers (blīn'dərs) *pl.n.* A pair of leather flaps attached to a horse's bridle to curtail side vision.

blind•fold (blīnd'fōld') *v.* **1.** To cover the eyes with or as if with a bandage. **2.** To hamper the sight or comprehension of. *—n.* A bandage over the eyes. *—adj.* **1.** With eyes covered. **2.** Reckless. [< OE *geblindfellian,* "to strike blind."]

blind•man's buff (blīnd'mănz'). A game in which one person, blindfolded, tries to catch and identify one of the other players. [*Buff,* short for BUFFET (a blow).]

blink (blĭngk) *v.* **1.** To close and open (one or both eyes) rapidly. **2.** To flash on and off. **3.** To close the eyes to. *—n.* **1.** The act or an instance of blinking. **2.** A glimpse. **3.** A flash of light; a glimmer. **—on the blink.** *Slang.* Not in working condition. [ME *blinken.*]

blintz (blĭnts) *n.* Also **blin•tze** (blĭn'tsə). A thin, rolled pancake stuffed with various fillings. [Yidd *blintse.*]

blip (blĭp) *n.* A spot of light on a radar screen. [Imit.]

bliss (blĭs) *n.* **1.** Serene happiness. **2.** The ecstasy of salvation. [< OE *bliss, blīths* < Gmc **blithsjo* < **blīthiz,* BLITHE.] **—bliss'ful** *adj.*

blis•ter (blĭs'tər) *n.* **1.** A thin swelling of the skin, containing watery matter, caused by irritation. **2.** Something resembling a blister. [ME *blester, blister.*] **—blis'ter** *v.*

blithe (blīth, blīth) *adj.* Cheerful; carefree. [< OE *blīthe* < Gmc **blīthiz,* gentle, mild.]

blithe•some (blīth'səm, blīth'-) *adj.* Cheerful; merry.

blitz (blĭts) *n.* **1.** A blitzkrieg. **2.** An intensive air raid. **3.** Any intense campaign. **—blitz** *v.* [< BLITZKRIEG.]

blitz•krieg (blĭts'krēg') *n.* A swift, sudden military offensive. [G, "lightning war."]

bliz•zard (blĭz'ərd) *n.* A heavy snowstorm with high winds. [?]

blk. **1.** black. **2.** block. **3.** bulk.

bloat (blōt) *v.* To make or become swollen. [< earlier *blowt,* soft, flabby.]

blob (blŏb) *n.* **1.** A soft, amorphous mass. **2.** A splotch of color. [ME.]

bloc (blŏk) *n.* A group of persons or nations united for common action. [< OF, BLOCK.]

block (blŏk) *n.* **1.** A solid piece of wood or other hard substance having one or more flat sides. **2.** A stand from which articles are displayed at an auction. **3.** A pulley or a system of pulleys set in a casing. **4.** A set of like items. **5. a.** A section of a town bounded on each side by consecutive streets. **b.** A segment of a street bounded by successive cross streets. **6.** An act of obstructing. **7.** An obstacle. **8.** *Med.* An obstruction of a neural, digestive, or other physiological process. **9.** *Psychol.* Sudden cessation of a thought process without an immediate observable cause. **10.** *Slang.* A person's head. *—v.* **1.** To stop or impede the passage of. **2.** *Med.* To interrupt the proper functioning of (a physiological process). **—block out. 1.** To plan with few details. **2.** To obscure from view. [< OF *bloc.*] **—block** *adj.* **—block'age** (blŏk'ĭj) *n.* **—block'er** *n.*

block•ade (blŏ-kād') *n.* The closing off of a city or other area to traffic and communication. [< BLOCK.] **—block•ade'** *v.* **(-aded, -ading). —block•ad'er** *n.*

block and tackle. An apparatus of pulley blocks and cables for hauling.

block•bust•er (blŏk'bŭs'tər) *n. Informal.* **1.** A bomb capable of destroying a city block. **2.** Anything of devastating effect.

block•head (blŏk'hĕd') *n.* A dolt.

bloke (blōk) *n. Brit. Slang.* A man. [?]

blond (blŏnd) *adj.* **1.** Also *fem.* **blonde.** Having fair hair. **2.** Pale or yellowish, as hair. **3.** Light-colored. *—n.* Also *fem.* **blonde.** A blond person. [OF.]

blood (blŭd) *n.* **1.** The red fluid circulated by the heart through the vertebrate vascular system, carrying oxygen and nutrients throughout the body and waste materials to excretory channels. **2.** Loosely, life. **3.** Bloodshed. **4.** Temperament. **5.** Kinship. **6.** Racial or national ancestry. **7.** Personnel. **8.** A dashing young man. [< OE *blōd* < Gmc **blōtham.*]

blood bath. A massacre.

blood•cur•dling (blŭd'kûrd'lĭng) *adj.* Terrifying. **—blood'cur'dling•ly** *adv.*

blood•hound (blŭd'hound') *n.* A hound with drooping ears, sagging jowls, and a keen sense of smell.

blood•less (blŭd'lĭs) *adj.* **1.** Having no blood. **2.** Achieved without bloodshed.

blood•let•ting (blŭd'lĕt'ĭng) *n.* **1.** The bleeding of a vein as a therapeutic measure. **2.** Bloodshed.

blood•line (blŭd'līn') *n.* Direct line of descent.

blood poisoning. **1.** Toxemia. **2.** Septicemia.

blood pressure. The pressure of the blood within the arteries.

blood relation. Also **blood relative.** A person who is related by birth.

blood•shed (blŭd'shĕd') *n.* **1.** The shedding of blood. **2.** Carnage.

blood•shot (blŭd'shŏt') *adj.* Red and irritated: *bloodshot eyes.*

blood stream. The stream of blood flowing through the circulatory system of a living body.

blood•suck•er (blŭd'sŭk'ər) *n.* An animal that sucks blood, as a leech. **—blood'suck'ing** *adj.*

blood•thirst•y (blŭd'thûr'stē) *adj.* Thirsting for bloodshed; murderous; cruel.

blood vessel. Any elastic, tubular canal, such as an artery, vein, or capillary, through which blood circulates.

blood•y (blŭd'ē) *adj.* **-ier, -iest. 1.** Of, containing, or stained with blood. **2.** Giving rise to bloodshed: *a bloody fight.* **3.** Bloodthirsty; cruel. **4.** *Brit. Vulgar.* Used as an intensive: *bloody fool.* *—adv. Brit. Vulgar.* Used as an intensive: *bloody well right.* *—v.* **-ied, -ying.** To stain with or as if with blood. **—blood'i•ly** *adv.* **—blood'i•ness** *n.*

bloody mary. Also **Bloody Mary.** A drink made with vodka and tomato juice.

bloom (blo͞om) *n.* **1.** The flower or blossoms of a plant. **2. a.** The condition or time of flowering. **b.** A condition or time of vigor and beauty; prime. **3.** A fresh, rosy complexion. **4.** A thin, powdery coating on some fruits, leaves, or stems. *—v.* **1.** To bear flowers. **2.** To shine with health and vigor; to glow. **3.** To grow or flourish. [< ON *blōm.*]

bloom•er (blo͞o'mər) *n.* One that blooms.

bloom•ers (blo͞o'mərz) *pl.n.* Women's wide, loose pants or underpants, gathered at or above the knee. [< Amelia *Bloomer* (1818–1894), American social reformer.]

bloom•ing (blo͞o'mĭng) *adj.* **1.** Flowering; blossoming. **2.** Flourishing. **3.** *Slang.* Utter. Used as an intensive: *a blooming idiot.*

bloop•er (blo͞o'pər) *n.* **1.** *Baseball.* A weakly hit fly ball that carries just beyond the infield. **2.** *Informal.* A faux pas. [< *bloop,* sound of such a hit.]

blos•som (blŏs'əm) *n.* **1.** A flower or flowers, esp. of a plant yielding edible fruit. **2.** The condition or time of flowering: *peach trees in blossom.* *—v.* **1.** To flower; bloom. **2.** To develop; flourish. [< OE *blōstma.* See **bhel-[3]**.] **—blos'som•y** *adj.*

blot (blŏt) *n.* **1.** A spot; a stain: *a blot of ink.* **2.** A moral blemish; a disgrace. *—v.* **blotted, blotting. 1.** To spot or stain. **2.** To bring moral disgrace to. **3.** To erase; cancel (with *out*). **4.** To darken; hide. **5.** To dry with absorbent material. **6.** To make a blot. **7.** To become blotted. [ME.]

blotch (blŏch) *n.* **1.** A spot or blot; a splotch. **2.** A discoloration on the skin; blemish. **3.** Any of various plant diseases caused by fungi and resulting in brown or black dead areas on leaves or fruit. [Prob a blend of BLOT and BOTCH.] **—blotch** *v.*

blot•ter (blŏt'ər) *n.* **1.** A piece of blotting paper. **2.** A book containing daily records, as of occurrences or transactions.

blotting paper. Absorbent paper used to blot a surface by soaking up excess ink.

blouse (blous, blouz) *n.* **1.** A loosely fitting shirtlike garment. **2.** The service coat or tunic worn by members of the U.S. Army. *—v.* **bloused, blousing.** To hang or drape loosely around the waist.

blow[1] (blō) *v.* **blew, blown** (blōn), **blowing. 1.** To be in a state of motion, as the wind. **2. a.** To be carried by or as if by the wind. **b.** To cause to move by means of a current of air. **3.** To drive a current of air upon, in, or through. **4.** To expel a current of air, as from a bellows. **5.** To sound or cause to sound by expelling a current of air: *blow a trumpet.* **6.** To pant. **7.** To cause to explode. **8.** To melt (a fuse). **9.** To spout water and air, as a whale. **10.** To shape by forcing air or gas through at the end of a pipe: *blow glass.* **11.** *Slang.* To depart. **12.** *Slang.* To spend (money) freely. **—blow over.** To subside. *—n.* **1. a.** A blast of air or wind. **b.** A storm. **2.** The act of blowing. [< OE *blāwan.* See **bhlē-**[2].] **—blow'er** *n.*

blow[2] (blō) *n.* **1.** A sudden hard stroke, as with the fist. **2.** A sudden shock or calamity. **3.** A sudden attack. **—come to blows.** To begin to fight. [ME *blaw.*]

blow[3] (blō) *v.* **blew, blown** (blōn), **blowing.** To bloom or cause to bloom. [< OE *blōwan,* to blossom.]

blow•gun (blō'gŭn') *n.* A long narrow pipe through which darts or pellets may be blown.

blow out. 1. To extinguish or be extinguished by blowing, as a candle. **2.** To burst suddenly, as a tire. **3.** To melt, as a fuse. **4.** To fail, as an electrical apparatus.

blow•out (blō'out') *n.* **1. a.** A sudden bursting, as of an automobile tire. **b.** The hole so made. **c.** The ruptured object. **2.** A sudden escape of a confined gas. **3.** The burning out of a fuse. **4.** *Slang.* A large party or social affair.

blow•pipe (blō'pīp') *n.* **1.** A metal tube in which a flow of gas is mixed with a controlled flow of air to concentrate the heat of a flame. **2.** A long iron pipe used to blow molten glass.

blow•torch (blō'tôrch') *n.* A gas burner that produces a flame hot enough to melt soft metals.

blow up. 1. To explode. **2.** To lose one's temper. **3.** To enlarge the size of (a photographic print). **4.** To fill with air.

blow•up (blō'ŭp') *n.* **1.** An explosion. **2.** A violent outburst of temper. **3.** A photographic enlargement.

blub•ber[1] (blŭb'ər) *v.* To weep noisily. [ME *blubren,* to bubble, foam.] **—blub'ber** *n.*

blub•ber[2] (blŭb'ər) *n.* **1.** The fat of whales and other marine mammals. **2.** Excessive body fat. [ME *bluber,* bubble, entrails, fish or whale oil.]

blu•cher (blo͞o'chər, -kər) *n.* A laced shoe having the vamp and tongue made of one piece. [< G.L. von *Blücher* (1742–1819), Prussian field marshal.]

bludg•eon (blŭj'ən) *n.* A short club having one end thicker than the other. *—v.* **-eoned, -eoning. 1.** To hit with or as if with a bludgeon. **2.** To threaten or bully. [?]

blue (blo͞o) *n.* **1.** Any of a group of colors whose hue is that of a clear sky. **2.** Anything of this color. **—out of the blue.** Unexpected; unforeseen. **—the blue. 1.** The sea. **2.** The sky. **—the blues. 1.** A state of melancholy. **2.** A style of jazz evolved from Negro folk songs having usually a slow tempo. *—adj.* **bluer, bluest. 1.** Of the color blue. **2.** Having a gray or purplish color, as from cold or contusion. **3.** Gloomy; dreary. **4.** Puritanical; strict. **5.** Aristocratic. **—once in a blue moon.** Rarely. *—v.* **blued, bluing. 1.** To make or become blue. **2.** To use bluing on. [< OF *bleu* < CRom **blāvus.*] **—blu'ish** *adj.*

blue baby. An infant born with bluish skin caused by inadequate oxygenation of the blood.

blue•bell (blo͞o'bĕl') *n.* Any of various plants having blue, bell-shaped flowers.

blue•ber•ry (blo͞o'bĕr'ē, -bər-ē) *n.* **1.** A juicy, edible, blue, or purplish berry. **2.** A shrub bearing such berries.

blue•bird (blo͞o'bûrd') *n.* A North American bird with blue plumage and usually a rust-colored breast.

blue blood. 1. Noble descent. **2.** A member of the aristocracy.

blue•bon•net (blo͞o'bŏn'ĭt) *n.* A plant with compound leaves and clusters of blue flowers.

blue book. Also **blue•book** (blo͞o'bo͝ok'). **1.** A book listing socially prominent people. **2.** A blank notebook with blue covers in which to write college examinations.

blue•bot•tle (blo͞o'bŏt'l) *n.* A fly with a bright metallic-blue body.

blue chip. A stock highly valuable because of public confidence in its long record of steady earnings. **—blue'-chip'** *adj.*

blue-col•lar (blo͞o'kŏl'ər) *adj.* Pertaining to wage earners in jobs involving manual labor.

blue•fish (blo͞o'fĭsh') *n.* A marine food and game fish.

blue•grass (blo͞o'grăs', -gräs') *n.* **1.** A grass with bluish or grayish leaves. **2.** A type of folk music of the southern U.S., marked by fast tempos and the use of banjos and guitars.

blue•ing. Variant of **bluing.**

blue jay. A bird with a crested head and predominantly blue plumage.

blue•nose (blo͞o'nōz') *n.* A puritanical person.

blue-pen•cil (blo͞o'pĕn'səl) *v.* **-ciled, -ciling.** To edit with or as with a blue pencil.

blue point. An edible oyster found chiefly off Blue Point, Long Island, N.Y.

blue•print (blo͞o'prĭnt') *n.* **1.** A photographic reproduction, as of architectural plans, rendered as white lines on a blue background. **2.** Any carefully designed plan.

blue•stock•ing (blo͞o'stŏk'ĭng) *n.* A pedantic or scholarly woman.

bluff[1] (blŭf) *v.* To mislead or intimidate by a false display of confidence *—n.* **1.** The act or practice of bluffing. **2.** One who bluffs. [Du *bluffen,* to boast.] **—bluff'er** *n.*

bluff[2] (blŭf) *n.* A steep headland or bank; cliff. *—adj.* **1.** Presenting a broad, steep front. **2.** Brusque; blunt. [?]

blu•ing (blo͞o'ĭng) *n.* Also **blue•ing.** A rinsing agent used to counteract the yellowing of laundered fabrics.

blun•der (blŭn'dər) *n.* A stupid and grave mistake. *—v.* **1.** To move awkwardly or clumsily. **2.** To make a stupid mistake. [ME *blunderen,* to proceed blindly, bungle.]

blun•der•buss (blŭn'dər-bŭs') *n.* **1.** A short musket of wide bore and flaring muzzle. **2.** A stupid, clumsy person. [Var of Du *donderbus,* "thunder gun."]

blunt (blŭnt) *adj.* **1.** Having a thick, dull edge or end. **2.** Outspoken; brusque. **3.** Slow to understand; dull. *—v.* To make or become blunt. [ME, dull, blunt, stupid.] **—blunt'ly** *adv.*

blur (blûr) *v.* **blurred, blurring. 1.** To make or become indistinct; obscure. **2.** To smear or stain. **3.** To lessen the perception of; dim. *—n.* **1.** A smear; a smudge. **2.** Anything hazy and indistinct. [?] **—blur'ry** *adj.*

blurb (blûrb) *n.* A brief commendatory publicity notice, as on a book jacket.

blurt (blûrt) *v.* To utter impulsively. [Prob imit.]

blush (blŭsh) *n.* A sudden reddening of the face from modesty, embarrassment, or shame. [< OE *blyscan.* See **bhel-**[1].] **—blush** *v.*

blus•ter (blŭs'tər) *v.* **1.** To blow in loud, violent gusts, as wind in a storm. **2.** To speak noisily and boastfully. [ME *blusteren.*] **—blus'ter** *n.* **—blus'ter•er** *n.*

blvd. boulevard.

b.m. bowel movement.

bo•a (bō'ə) *n.* **1.** A large, nonvenomous tropical snake, such as the **boa constrictor,** that coils around and crushes its prey. **2.** A long scarf of feathers, fur, etc. [< L *boa,* a large water snake.]

boar (bôr, bōr) *n.* **1.** An uncastrated male pig. **2.** A wild pig with dense, dark bristles. [< OE *bār* < Gmc **bairoz.*]

board (bôrd, bōrd) *n.* **1.** A long, flat slab of sawed lumber. **2.** A flat piece of wood or similarly rigid material, adapted for a special use. **3.** A table, esp. one for serving food. **4.** Meals collectively: *board and lodging.* **5.** A table at which official meetings are held. **6.** A body of administrators. **7.** An electrical-equipment panel. **8.** A border or edge. **9.** The side of a ship. **—on board.** Aboard. **—the boards.** A theater stage. *—v.* **1.** To cover or close with boards: *board up a door.* **2.** To furnish with or receive meals in return for pay. **3.** To enter or go aboard (a vehicle or ship). [< OE *bord,* plank, border. See **bherdh-.**]

board•er (bôr'dər, bōr'-) *n.* One who pays a homeowner for regular meals or meals and lodging.

boarding house. Also **board•ing•house** (bôr'dĭng-hous', bōr'-). A private home that takes in paying guests and provides meals or meals and lodging.

board•walk (bôrd'wôk', bōrd'-) *n.* A promenade, esp. of planks, along a beach or waterfront.

boast (bōst) *v.* **1.** To talk about or speak with excessive pride. **2.** To take pride in, or be enhanced by, the possession of. *—n.* **1.** An instance of bragging. **2.** That which one brags about. [ME *bosten.*] **—boast'er** *n.*

boast•ful (bōst'fəl) *adj.* Tending to boast. **—boast'ful•ly** *adv.* **—boast'ful•ness** *n.*

boat (bōt) *n.* **1.** A relatively small, usually open water craft. **2.** A ship. Not in nautical usage. **3.** A dish shaped like a boat: *a gravy boat* **—in the same boat.** In the same situation. [< OE *bāt* and ON *bātr.* See **bheid-.**] **—boat'ing** *n.*

boat•man (bōt'mən) *n.* One who works on, deals with, or operates boats.

boat•swain (bō'sən) *n.* A warrant officer or petty officer in charge of a ship's deck crew, rigging, anchors, and cables.

bob[1] (bŏb) *n.* **1.** A short jerking movement. **2.** Any small knoblike pendent object. **3.** A fishing float. **4.** A short haircut on a woman or child. *—v.* **bobbed, bobbing. 1.** To move or jerk up and down. **2.** To cut (hair) short. **—bob up.** To appear suddenly. [< ME *bobbe,* cluster of flowers and *bobben,* to move up and down.] **—bob'ber** *n.*

bob[2] (bŏb) *n., pl.* **bob.** *Brit. Slang.* A shilling. [?]

bob•bin (bŏb'ĭn) *n.* A spool or reel for thread, as on a sewing machine. [F *bobine.*]

bob•by (bŏb'ē) *n., pl.* **-bies.** *Brit. Slang.* A policeman. [After Sir Robert Peel, who was Home Secretary of England when the Metropolitan Police Force was created (1828).]

bobby pin. A ridged, tight metal hair clip. [< BOB (lock of hair).]

bobby socks. Girls' ankle socks.

bob•cat (bŏb'kăt') *n.* A North American wild cat with spotted fur and a short tail.

bob•o•link (bŏb'ə-lĭngk') *n.* An American

songbird. [Imit of its call.]

bob•sled (bŏb'slĕd') *n.* A long racing sled typically made of two shorter sleds joined in tandem. [< BOB (short).] —**bob'sled'** *v.* **(-sledded, -sledding).**

bob•tail (bŏb'tāl') *n.* **1.** A shortened tail. **2.** An animal having such a tail. —**bob'tail', bob'tailed'** *adj.*

bob•white (bŏb-hwīt') *n.* A small North American quail. [Imit of its call.]

Boc•cac•cio (bə-kä'chē-ō'), **Giovanni.** 1313–1375. Italian author.

bock beer (bŏk). A dark spring beer. [G < *Eimbeck,* city in Hanover.]

bode¹ (bōd) *v.* **boded, boding.** To be an omen of: *His ill will bodes no good.* [< OE *boda,* messenger. See **bheudh-.**]

bode² (bōd). Alternate *p.t.* of **bide.**

bod•ice (bŏd'ĭs) *n.* The fitted part of a woman's dress that extends from the waist to the shoulder. [Orig *bodies,* pl of BODY.]

bod•i•ly (bŏd'ə-lē) *adj.* **1.** Of or pertaining to the body. **2.** Physical: *bodily welfare.* —*adv.* **1.** In person. **2.** As a complete physical entity: *He carried her bodily from the room.*

bod•kin (bŏd'kĭn) *n.* **1.** A small pointed instrument for making holes in fabric or leather. **2.** A blunt needle for pulling tape or ribbon through a series of loops or a hem. **3.** *Obs.* A dagger. [ME *boidekyn.*]

bod•y (bŏd'ē) *n., pl.* **-ies. 1. a.** The physical structure of an organism, esp. a human being or animal. **b.** A corpse. **2.** The trunk or torso of a human being or animal. **3.** *Law.* **a.** A person. **b.** A group of individuals regarded as an entity; corporation. **4.** A number of persons or things; a group. **5.** The main or central part of something. **6.** Any bounded aggregate of matter: *a body of water.* **7.** Consistency of substance, as in textiles, wine, etc. [< OE *bodig* < Gmc **bot-,* container.]

bod•y•guard (bŏd'ē-gärd') *n.* A person or persons, usually armed, responsible for the physical safety of someone.

body politic. Collectively, the people of a politically organized nation or state.

Boer (bōr, bôr, bŏŏr) *n.* A Dutch colonist or a descendant of a Dutch colonist in South Africa. [Du, "peasant," "farmer."] —**Boer** *adj.*

bog (bôg, bŏg) *n.* Soft, water-logged ground; a marsh. —*v.* **bogged, bogging.** To hinder or be hindered; slow; impede (with *down).* [Scot Gael *bogach.*]

bo•gey (bō'gē) *n., pl.* **-geys. 1.** Also **bo•gie, bo•gy** *pl.* **-gies.** An evil or mischievous spirit. **2.** *Golf.* One stroke over par on a hole.

Bo•go•tá (bō'gə-tä'). The capital of Colombia. Pop. 1,697,000.

bo•gus (bō'gəs) *adj.* Counterfeit; fake.

Bo•he•mi•an (bō-hē'mē-ən) *n.* Also **bo•he•mi•an.** A writer or artist who disregards conventional standards of behavior. —**Bo•he'mi•an** *adj.*

boil¹ (boil) *v.* **1.** To vaporize a liquid by applying heat. **2.** To cook by boiling. **3.** To be in a state of agitation, as boiling water. **4.** To be greatly excited, as with rage. **5.** To heat to the boiling point. **6.** To separate by evaporation as a result of boiling. —**boil down. 1.** To reduce in bulk or size by boiling. **2.** To summarize. —*n.* The state, condition, or act of boiling. [< OF *bouillir.*]

boil² (boil) *n.* A painful, pus-filled swelling of the skin and subcutaneous tissue caused by bacterial infection. [< OE *b̄yle.* See **beu-.**]

boil•er (boi'lər) *n.* A vessel in which water is heated and circulated, either as hot water or as steam, for heating or power.

boil•er•mak•er (boi'lər-mā'kər) *n. Slang.* A drink of whiskey with beer as a chaser.

Boi•se (boi'zē, -sē). The capital of Idaho. Pop. 75,000.

bois•ter•ous (boi'stər-əs, -strəs) *adj.* **1.** Violent and turbulent. **2.** Noisy and unrestrained. [< ME *boistous,* rude, fierce, stout.] —**bois'ter•ous•ly** *adv.* —**bois'ter•ous•ness** *n.*

Bol. Bolivia.

bold (bōld) *adj.* **1.** Fearless; courageous. **2.** Unduly forward; brazen; impudent. **3.** Clear and distinct to the eye: *a bold handwriting.* **4.** Steep, as a cliff. —**make bold.** To take the liberty; dare. [< OE *beald.*] —**bold'ly** *adv.* —**bold'ness** *n.*

bold•face (bōld'fās') *n.* A typeface that produces a conspicuous black impression. —*v.* **-faced, -facing. 1.** To mark (copy) for printing in boldface. **2.** To print or set in boldface.

bold-faced (bōld'fāst') *adj.* **1.** Impudent. **2.** Set or marked for printing in boldface.

bole (bōl) *n.* The trunk of a tree. [< ON *bolr.*]

bo•le•ro (bō-lâr'ō) *n., pl.* **-ros. 1.** A short jacket, usually with no front fastening. **2. a.** A Spanish dance in triple meter. **b.** The music for this dance. [Span.]

bol•i•var (bŏl'ə-vər) *n.* The basic monetary unit of Venezuela. [< Simón BOLÍVAR.]

Bo•lí•var (bō-lē'vär), **Simón.** 1783–1830. Venezuelan leader in South American struggles for national independence.

Simón Bolívar

Bo•liv•i•a (bə-lĭv'ē-ə). A republic of west-central South America. Pop. 3,520,000. Caps. La Paz and Sucre. —**Bo•liv'i•an** *adj.* & *n.*

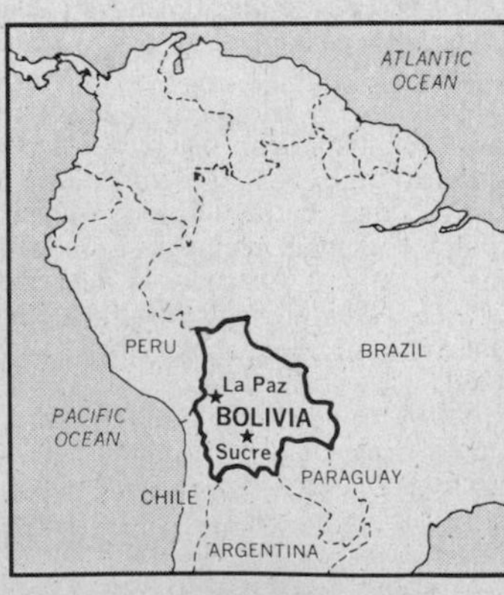

Bolivia

boll (bōl) *n.* A rounded seed pod, as of cotton. [ME *bolle.*]

boll weevil. A long-snouted beetle, having larvae that damage cotton bolls.

bo•lo•gna (bə-lō'nə, -nē, -nyə) *n.* A large sausage made of mixed meats. [< BOLOGNA.]

Bo•lo•gna (bō-lō'nyä). A city of N Italy. Pop. 482,000.

Bol•she•vik (bōl'shə-vĭk', bŏl'-) *n.* A member of the party that seized power and set up a proletarian dictatorship in Russia (1917–22). [Russ *Bol'shevik,* "one of the majority."] —**Bol'she•vik'** *adj.* —**Bol'she•vism'** *n.*

bol•ster (bōl'stər) *n.* A long, narrow pillow or cushion. —*v.* To prop up with or as if with a bolster. [< OE, cushion. See **bhelgh-.**] —**bol'ster•er** *n.*

bolt¹ (bōlt) *n.* **1.** A sliding bar that is used to fasten doors and gates. **2.** A metal bar in a lock thrown or withdrawn by turning the key. **3.** A threaded metal pin used with a nut to hold parts together. **4.** A short, heavy arrow used with a crossbow. **5.** A flash of lightning or a thunderbolt. **6.** A sudden movement; dash. **7.** A large roll of cloth. —*v.* **1.** To secure or lock with a bolt. **2.** To eat hurriedly; gulp. **3.** To desert or withdraw support from (a political party). **4.** To utter impulsively. **5.** To move or spring suddenly; dash. **6.** To flower or produce seeds prematurely. [< OE, heavy arrow. See **bheld-.**]

bolt² (bōlt) *v.* To sift. [< OF *buleter.*]

bo•lus (bō'ləs) *n., pl.* **-luses. 1.** A small round mass. **2.** *Pharm.* A large pill or tablet. [< Gk *bōlos,* lump, clod.]

bomb (bŏm) *n.* **1.** An explosive weapon dropped on or thrown at a target. **2.** A portable, manually operated container that ejects a spray, foam, or gas under pressure. —*v.* To attack or destroy with bombs. [< It *bomba.*]

bom•bard (bŏm-bärd') *v.* **1.** To attack with bombs or missiles. **2.** To attack persistently. **3.** To irradiate (an atom). [< OF *bombarde,* cannon.] —**bom•bard'ment** *n.*

bom•bar•dier (bŏm'bər-dîr') *n.* The member of an aircraft crew who operates the bombing equipment. [< OF *bombarde,* BOMBARD.]

bom•bast (bŏm'băst') *n.* Grandiloquent and pompous speech or writing. [Earlier *bombace,* cotton padding.] —**bom•bas'tic** *adj.*

Bom•bay (bŏm-bā'). A seaport of the W Republic of India. Pop. 2,772,000.

bom•ba•zine (bŏm'bə-zēn') *n.* A fine twilled fabric often dyed black. [< L *bombyx,* silk.]

bomb•er (bŏm'ər) *n.* An aircraft designed to carry and drop bombs.

bomb•shell (bŏm'shĕl') *n.* **1.** A bomb. **2.** A shocking surprise.

bomb•sight (bŏm'sīt') *n.* A device in aircraft for aiming bombs.

bo•na fide (bō'nə fīd', fī'dē, bŏn'ə). **1.** Done or made in good faith: *a bona fide offer.* **2.** Authentic: *a bona fide Rembrandt.* [L, "in good faith."]

bo•nan•za (bə-năn'zə) *n.* **1.** A rich mine or vein of ore. **2.** Any source of great wealth. [Span, fair weather, prosperity.]

bon•bon (bŏn'bŏn') *n.* A candy having a creamy center and often coated with chocolate. [F.]

bond (bŏnd) *n.* **1.** Anything that binds, ties, or fastens together. **2. bonds.** Shackles. **3.** Often **bonds.** A uniting force or tie; a link. **4.** A binding agreement. **5.** The promise or obligation by which one is bound. **6.** A union or cohesion between parts. **7.** *Chem.* A **chemical**

bond. 8. A sum of money paid as bail or surety. **9.** One who acts as bail; bondsman. **10.** A certificate of debt issued by a government or corporation, guaranteeing payment of the original investment plus interest by a specified future date. **11.** The state of storing goods in a warehouse until the taxes or duties due on them are paid. **12.** Surety against losses, theft, etc. **13.** Also **bond paper.** A superior grade of white paper. —*v.* **1.** To mortgage or place a guaranteed bond on. **2.** To furnish bond or surety for. **3.** To place (an employee or merchandise) under bond or guarantee. **4.** To join securely, as with glue. [< ON *band.*]

bond•age (bŏn'dĭj) *n.* The condition of a slave or serf; serfdom. [< OE *bōnda,* householder.]

bonds•man (bŏndz'mən) *n.* **1.** Also **bond•man** (bŏnd'mən). A slave; serf. **2.** One who provides bond or surety for another.

bone (bōn) *n.* **1. a.** The dense, semirigid, porous, calcified connective tissue of the skeleton of most vertebrates. **b.** A skeletal structure made of this material. **2.** A similar material resembling bone, such as ivory. **3.** Something made of bone or similar material. —**have a bone to pick with.** To have grounds for a dispute with. —**make no bones about.** To be frank and candid about. —*v.* **boned, boning.** To remove the bones from. —**bone up on.** To study intensively, usually at the last minute. [< OE *bān* < Gmc **baina-.*]

bone-dry (bōn'drī') *adj.* Very dry.

bone•fish (bōn'fĭsh') *n.* A chiefly tropical marine game fish.

bone meal. Bones crushed and ground to a coarse powder, used as plant fertilizer and animal feed.

bon•er (bō'nər) *n. Slang.* A blunder.

bon•fire (bŏn'fīr') *n.* A large outdoor fire. [ME *banefyre,* a fire in which bones were burned.]

bon•go drum (bŏng'gō). One of a pair of connected and tuned drums. [Amer Span *bongó.*]

bo•ni•to (bə-nē'tō) *n., pl.* **-to** or **-tos.** Also **bo•ni•ta** (-tə). A food and game fish related to the tuna. [Span, "beautiful."]

bon mot (bôɴ' mō') *pl.* **bons mots** (bôɴ' mōz'). A clever saying. [F, "good word."]

Bonn (bŏn). The capital of the German Federal Republic. Pop. 142,000.

bon•net (bŏn'ĭt) *n.* **1.** A hat that is held in place by ribbons tied under the chin. **2.** A feather headdress worn by some American Indians. **3.** A removable metal plate over a valve or other machinery part. **4.** *Brit.* An automobile hood. —*v.* To put a bonnet on. [< OF *bonet.*]

bon•nock. Variant of **bannock.**

bon•ny (bŏn'ē) *adj.* **-nier, -niest.** Also **bon•nie.** *Chiefly Brit.* Cheerful; pleasant. [Perh < OF *bon,* good.] —**bon'ni•ness** *n.*

bon•sai (bŏn-sī') *n., pl.* **-sai. 1.** The growing of dwarfed, ornamental trees in small pots. **2.** A tree thus grown. [Jap, "potted plant."]

bo•nus (bō'nəs) *n., pl.* **-nuses.** Something given or paid in addition to the usual or expected amount. [< L *bonus,* good.]

bon vi•vant (bôɴ vē-väɴ') *pl.* **bons vivants** (bôɴ vē-väɴ'). A person who enjoys life fully.

bon voy•age (bôɴ vwȧ-yȧzh'). A wish for a pleasant journey extended to a departing traveler. [F, "good trip."]

bon•y (bō'nē) *adj.* **-ier, -iest. 1.** Of, resembling, or made of bone. **2.** Having many bones. **3.** Very thin. —**bon'i•ness** *n.*

boo (bo͞o) *n., pl.* **boos.** A shout expressing contempt or disapproval. [Imit.] —**boo** *v.*

boo•by (bo͞o'bē) *n., pl.* **-bies.** Also **boob** (bo͞ob). A stupid person. [< L *balbus,* stammering.]

booby prize. An insignificant or comical award.

booby trap. A device or situation that catches a person off guard.

boo•dle (bo͞od'l) *n. Slang.* **1.** Money accepted as a bribe. **2.** Stolen goods. [< Du *boedel,* estate, effects.]

book (bo͝ok) *n.* **1.** A volume made up of pages fastened along one side and encased between protective covers. **2.** A written or printed literary work. **3.** A volume in which financial transactions are recorded. **4.** A main division of a larger written or printed work. **5.** A libretto. **6. the Book.** The Bible. **7.** A record of bets placed on a race. —*v.* To list, reserve, or schedule by writing in or as if in a book. [< OE *bōc,* written document, composition. See **bhāgo-.**]

book•case (bo͝ok'kās') *n.* A piece of furniture with shelves for holding books.

book end. A prop for keeping a row of books upright.

book•ie (bo͝ok'ē) *n. Slang.* A bookmaker.

book•ing (bo͝ok'ĭng) *n.* A scheduled engagement, as for a performance.

book•ish (bo͝ok'ĭsh) *adj.* **1.** Fond of books; studious. **2.** Relying on book learning.

book•keep•ing (bo͝ok'kē'pĭng) *n.* The recording of the accounts and transactions of a business. —**book'keep'er** *n.*

book learning. Knowledge gained from books rather than from practical experience.

book•let (bo͝ok'lĭt) *n.* A small bound book.

book•mak•er (bo͝ok'mā'kər) *n.* One who accepts and pays off bets.

book•mark (bo͝ok'märk') *n.* A marker, such as a ribbon, placed between the pages of a book.

book•mo•bile (bo͝ok'mō-bēl') *n.* A truck equipped for use as a mobile lending library.

book•plate (bo͝ok'plāt') *n.* A label pasted inside a book and bearing the owner's name.

book•worm (bo͝ok'wûrm') *n.* One who spends much time reading or studying.

boom[1] (bo͞om) *v.* **1.** To make a deep, resonant sound. **2.** To flourish or cause to flourish swiftly or vigorously. —*n.* **1.** A booming sound. **2.** A sudden increase, as in growth, wealth, or popularity. [ME *bomben, bummen* (imit).]

boom[2] (bo͞om) *n.* **1.** A long spar extending from a mast to hold a sail. **2.** A long pole extending upward from the mast of a derrick to support or guide objects lifted. **3.** A chain of floating logs enclosing other free-floating logs. **4.** A long, movable arm used to maneuver a microphone. [Du, tree, pole.]

boo•mer•ang (bo͞o'mə-răng') *n.* **1.** A flat, curved missile that can be hurled so that it returns to the thrower. **2.** An action that rebounds detrimentally. —*v.* To act as a boomerang. [Native Australian word.]

boom town. A town showing sudden growth and prosperity.

boon[1] (bo͞on) *n.* **1.** Something beneficial or pleasant; a blessing. **2.** A favor or request. [< ON *bōn,* prayer, request.]

boon[2] (bo͞on) *adj.* Jolly; convivial: *a boon companion.* [ME *bone,* "good."]

boon•docks (bo͞on'dŏks') *pl.n.* —**the boondocks.** *Slang.* Back country; hinterland. [Tag *bundok,* mountain.]

boon•dog•gle (bo͞on'dôg'əl, -dŏg'əl) *v.* **-gled, -gling.** To waste time on pointless and unnecessary work. —*n.* Time-wasting work. —**boon'dog'gler** *n.*

Boone (bo͞on), **Daniel.** 1734–1820. American pioneer; explored and settled Kentucky.

boor (bo͝or) *n.* A person with rude, clumsy manners and little refinement. [Du *boer,* farmer.]

boor•ish (bo͝or'ĭsh) *adj.* Like a boor; rude; ill-mannered. —**boor'ish•ly** *adv.*

boost (bo͞ost) *v.* **1.** To raise or lift by or as if by pushing up from below. **2.** To increase; raise. **3.** To promote vigorously. —*n.* **1.** A lift or help. **2.** An increase. [?]

boost•er (bo͞o'stər) *n.* **1.** A device for increasing power or effectiveness. **2.** A promoter. **3.** A rocket used to launch a missile or space vehicle. **4.** A supplementary dose of a vaccine.

booster cable. An electric cable used to connect an automobile battery to a power source for charging.

boot[1] (bo͞ot) *n.* **1.** A protective piece of footwear covering the foot and part or all of the leg. **2.** Any protective covering or sheath. **3.** *Brit.* An automobile trunk. **4.** A kick. —**the boot.** *Slang.* A discharge from employment. —*v.* **1.** To put boots on. **2.** To kick. [< OF *bote.*]

boot[2] (bo͞ot) *v. Archaic.* To be of help; avail. —*n.* —**to boot.** In addition. [< OE *bōt,* advantage, addition.]

boot•black (bo͞ot'blăk') *n.* A person who cleans and polishes shoes for a living.

boot camp. A military training camp for recruits.

boo•tee (bo͞o'tē) *n.* Also **boo•tie.** A soft, usually knitted, sock for a baby.

Bo•ö•tes (bō-ō'tēz) *n.* A constellation in the N Hemisphere.

booth (bo͞oth) *n., pl.* **booths** (bo͞o*thz,* bo͞oths). **1.** A small enclosed compartment. **2.** An area in a restaurant with a table and seats whose backs serve as partitions. **3.** A small stall for the display of wares. [ME *bouth.*]

boot•leg (bo͞ot'lĕg') *v.* **-legged, -legging.** To make, sell, or transport illegally, as liquor. —*adj.* Made, sold, or transported illegally. —**boot'leg'ger** *n.*

boot•less (bo͞ot'lĭs) *adj.* Giving no advantage or benefit. —**boot'less•ly** *adv.*

boot•lick (bo͞ot'lĭk') *v.* To behave in a servile manner.

boot tree. A shoetree.

boo•ty (bo͞o'tē) *n., pl.* **-ties. 1.** Plunder taken from an enemy. **2.** Any seized or stolen goods. [< OF *butin.*]

booze (bo͞oz) *n. Informal.* Intoxicating liquor. —*v.* **boozed, boozing.** *Informal.* To drink intoxicating liquor to excess. [ME *bousen,* to carouse.] —**booz'er** *n.* —**booz'y** *adj.*

bor. borough.

bo•rax (bôr'ăks', -əks, bōr'-) *n.* A crystalline compound, **sodium borate,** $Na_2B_4O_7$, used in manufacturing glass, detergents, and pharmaceuticals. [< Ar *būraq.*]

bor•del•lo (bôr-dĕl'ō) *n., pl.* **-los.** A brothel. [< OF *bordel,* "small house," brothel.]

bor•der (bôr'dər) *n.* **1.** A surrounding margin or rim. **2.** A geographic or political boundary. —*v.* **1.** To provide with a border. **2.** To lie on the border of. **3.** To verge; approach. [< OF *border,* to border.]

bor•der•land (bôr'dər-lănd') *n.* **1.** Land on or near a border. **2.** An uncertain area or situation.

bor•der•line (bôr'dər-līn') *n.* **1.** A line that marks a border. **2.** An indefinite line between two qualities or conditions. —*adj.* Marginally certain.

bore[1] (bôr, bōr) *v.* **bored, boring. 1.** To make a hole in or through, as with a drill. **2.** To make by drilling or digging, as a tunnel. *—n.* **1.** A hole made by or as if by drilling. **2.** The interior diameter of a hole, tube, cylinder, etc. **3.** The caliber of a firearm. [< OE *borian.* See **bher-**[2].] **—bor'er** *n.*

bore[2] (bôr, bōr) *v.* **bored, boring.** To tire with repetition or tediousness. *—n.* One arousing boredom. [?]

bore[3] (bôr, bōr). *p.t.* of **bear**[1].

bo•re•al (bôr'ē-əl, bōr'-) *adj.* Pertaining to or located in the north; northern. [< Gk *Boreās,* the north wind.]

bore•dom (bôr'dəm, bōr'-) *n.* The condition of being bored.

bo•ric acid (bôr'ĭk, bōr'-). A white or colorless compound, H_3BO_3, used as an antiseptic and preservative. [< BORON.]

bor•ing[1] (bôr'ĭng, bōr'-) *n.* **1.** The making of a hole by or as if by drilling. **2.** A hole made in this way. **3.** The material produced by such drilling.

bor•ing[2] (bôr'ĭng, bōr'-) *adj.* Uninteresting and tiresome; dull.

born (bôrn). A *p.p.* of **bear**[1]. *—adj.* **1.** Brought into life. **2.** Having an innate talent: *a born artist.*

borne (bôrn, bōrn). A *p.p.* of **bear**[1].

Bor•ne•o (bôr'nē-ō'). An island of the W Pacific Ocean, divided between Indonesia, Malaysia, and Brunei.

bo•ron (bôr'ŏn', bōr'-) *n. Symbol* **B** A soft, brown, amorphous or crystalline, nonmetallic element used in flares, nuclear reactor control elements, abrasives, and hard metallic alloys. Atomic number 5, atomic weight 10.811. [BOR(AX) + (CARB)ON.]

bor•ough (bûr'ō, bûr'ə) *n.* **1.** A self-governing incorporated town, as in certain U.S. states. **2.** One of the five administrative units of New York City. [< OE *burg, burh,* fortress, fortified town. See **bhergh-**[2].]

bor•row (bŏr'ō, bôr'ō) *v.* **1.** To obtain or receive (something) on loan with intent to return. **2.** To adopt or use as one's own: *They borrowed his ideas.* [< OE *borgian.* See **bhergh-**[1].] **—bor'row•er** *n.*

borscht (bôrsht) *n.* Also **borsht, borsch** (bôrsh). A hot or cold beet soup. [Russ *borshch,* "cow parsnip."]

bort (bôrt) *n.* Poorly crystallized diamonds used for industrial cutting and abrasion. [Prob < Du *boort.*]

Bosch (bŏs, bôs), **Hieronymus.** 1450?–1516. Dutch painter.

bos•ky (bŏs'kē) *adj.* Covered with shrubs or trees; wooded. [< ME *bosk, bush,* bush.]

bos•om (bo͝oz'əm, bo͞o'zəm) *n.* **1.** The human chest or breasts. **2.** The center or heart: *in the bosom of one's family.* *—adj.* Intimate: *a bosom friend.* [< OE *bōsm.* See **beu-.**]

Bos•po•rus (bŏs'pər-əs). A strait between European and Asian Turkey.

boss[1] (bôs, bŏs) *n.* **1.** An employer or supervisor. **2.** One who controls a political party or machine. *—v.* **1.** To supervise. **2.** To command in a domineering manner. [Du *baas,* master.]

boss[2] (bôs, bŏs) *n.* A knoblike protuberance or ornament. *—v.* To decorate with bosses. [< OF *boce.*]

boss•y (bô'sē, bŏs'ē) *adj.* **-ier, -iest.** Commanding, domineering, or overbearing. **—boss'i•ly** *adv.* **—boss'i•ness** *n.*

Bos•ton (bô'stən, bŏs'tən). The capital of Massachusetts. Pop. 641,000. **—Bos•to'ni•an** (bô-stō'nē-ən, bŏs-) *adj.* & *n.*

Bos•well (bŏz'wĕl', -wəl), **James.** 1740–1795. Scottish lawyer; biographer of Samuel Johnson.

bot. **1.** botanical; botanist; botany. **2.** bottle.

bot•a•ny (bŏt'n-ē) *n.* The biological science of plants. [< Gk *botanē,* pasture, herb, plant.] **—bo•tan'i•cal** (bə-tăn'ĭ-kəl), **bo•tan'ic** *adj.* **—bot'a•nist** *n.*

botch (bŏch) *v.* **1.** To ruin through clumsiness; bungle. **2.** To repair clumsily. [ME *bocchen,* to patch up.] **—botch** *n.* **—botch'er** *n.*

botch•y (bŏch'ē) *adj.* **-ier, -iest.** Carelessly or clumsily done. **—botch'i•ly** *adv.*

both (bōth) *adj.* Two or two in conjunction: *Both boys arrived.* *—pron.* The one and the other: *Both are patriots.* *—conj.* As well; together; equally: *both Keats and Shelley.* [< ON *bāthir.*]

both•er (bŏth'ər) *v.* **1.** To irritate, particularly by small annoyances; pester; harass. **2.** To trouble or concern oneself. *—n.* A cause or state of disturbance. [Perh < Ir *buaidhrim,* I vex.] **—both'er•some** (-səm) *adj.*

Bot•swa•na (bŏt-swä'nə). A republic in S Africa. Pop. 670,000. Cap. Gaborone.

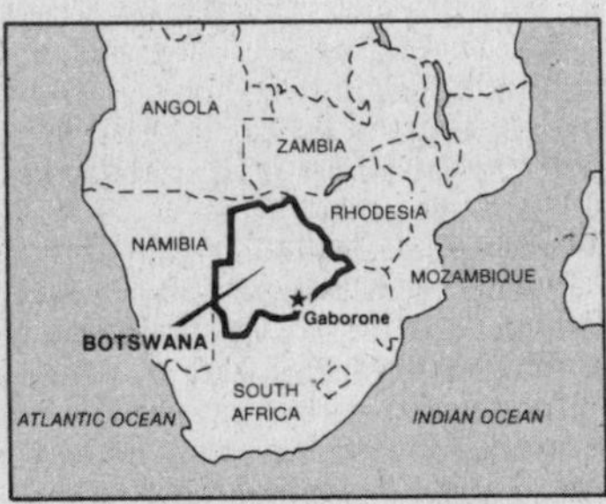

Botswana

Bot•ti•cel•li (bŏt'ĭ-chĕl'ē), **Sandro.** 1444?–1510. Italian painter.

bot•tle (bŏt'l) *n.* **1.** A receptacle, usually glass, having a narrow neck and a mouth that can be corked or capped. **2.** The quantity a bottle contains. **—the bottle. 1.** Intoxicating drink: *addicted to the bottle.* **2.** Milk or formula fed to a baby from a bottle: *brought up on the bottle.* *—v.* **-tled, -tling.** To place in a bottle or bottles. **—bottle up.** To confine as if in a bottle: *bottle up one's emotions.* [< OF *botele, botaille.*] **—bot'tler** *n.*

bot•tle•neck (bŏt'l-nĕk') *n.* **1.** A narrow passage, road, etc. **2.** Any hindrance to production or progress.

bot•tom (bŏt'əm) *n.* **1.** The lowest or deepest part of anything. **2.** The underside. **3.** The supporting part of something; base. **4.** The basic underlying quality; essence. **5.** The land below a body of water: *a river bottom.* **6.** *Informal.* The buttocks. *—adj.* Lowest; undermost; fundamental. [< OE *botm.* See **bhudh-.**] **—bot'tom•less** *adj.*

bottom line. 1. The lowest line in a financial statement, showing net income or loss. 2. The end result of anything.

bot•u•lism (bŏch'o͞o-lĭz'əm) *n.* An often fatal food poisoning caused by bacteria and characterized by vomiting, abdominal pain, coughing, muscular weakness, and visual disturbance. [G *Botulismus,* "sausage-poisoning."]

bou•doir (bo͞o'dwär', -dwôr') *n.* A woman's private room. [F, "place for pouting."]

bouf•fant (bo͞o-fänt') *adj.* Puffed-out; full: *a bouffant hair style.* [< F *bouffer,* to swell, puff up (the cheeks).]

bough (bou) *n.* A large branch of a tree. [< OE *bōg, bōh.* See **bhāghu-.**]

bought (bôt). *p.t.* & *p.p.* of **buy.**

bouil•lon (bo͞ol'yŏn', bo͝ol'yŏn', -yən) *n.* A clear meat broth. [< OF *boulir,* to boil.]

boul•der (bōl'dər) *n.* A large rounded stone block. [< Scand.]

boul•e•vard (bo͝ol'ə-värd', bo͞o'lə-) *n.* A broad city street, often tree-lined. [< OF *boloart,* rampart.]

bounce (bouns) *v.* **bounced, bouncing. 1.** To rebound elastically from a collision. **2.** To cause to collide and rebound. **3.** To bound in a lively and energetic manner. *—n.* **1.** A bound or rebound. **2.** A spring or leap. **3.** Capacity to bounce. **4.** Spirit; vigor. [ME *bunsen,* to beat, thrust.] **—bounc'y** *adj.*

bounc•er (boun'sər) *n.* A person employed to expel disorderly persons from a public place.

bounc•ing (boun'sĭng) *adj.* Vigorous; healthy: *a bouncing baby.* **—bounc'ing•ly** *adv.*

bound[1] (bound) *v.* **1.** To leap or spring. **2.** To progress by bounds. *—n.* **1.** A leap. **2.** A bounce. [F *bondir,* to bounce, orig "to rebound."]

bound[2] (bound) *n.* **1.** Often **bounds.** A boundary. **2. bounds.** The territory on, within, or near limiting lines. **—out of bounds. 1.** Beyond boundaries. **2.** Transgressing conventional limits. *—v.* **1.** To limit. **2.** To constitute the limit of. **3.** To demarcate. [< OF *bunde, bodne.*]

bound[3] (bound). *p.t.* & *p.p.* of **bind.** *—adj.* **1.** Confined by bonds; tied: *muscle-bound.* **2.** Under obligation. **3.** Equipped with a cover or binding. **4.** Predetermined; certain.

bound[4] (bound) *adj.* Headed for: *bound for home.* [ME *boun,* prepared, ready to go.]

bound•a•ry (boun'drē, -də-rē) *n., pl.* **-ries.** A border or limit. [< BOUND (limit).]

bound•en (boun'dən) *adj.* **1.** Under obligation. **2.** Obligatory: *his bounden duty.*

bound•er (boun'dər) *n. Chiefly Brit.* A vulgar man.

bound•less (bound'lĭs) *adj.* Without limit; infinite. **—bound'less•ly** *adv.*

boun•te•ous (boun'tē-əs) *adj.* **1.** Generous. **2.** Plentiful. [< OF *bonte,* bounty.] **—boun'te•ous•ly** *adv.* **—boun'te•ous•ness** *n.*

boun•ti•ful (boun'tĭ-fəl) *adj.* Bounteous. **—boun'ti•ful•ly** *adv.*

boun•ty (boun'tē) *n., pl.* **-ties. 1.** Liberality in giving. **2.** Something that is given liberally. **3.** A reward or inducement, esp. one given by a government. [< L *bonitās,* goodness.]

bou•quet (bō-kā', bo͞o-) *n.* **1.** A bunch of flowers. **2.** (bo͞o-kā'). An aroma, esp. of a wine. [< ONF *bosquet,* clump.]

bour•bon (bûr'bən) *n.* A whiskey distilled from fermented corn mash. [< *Bourbon* County, Ky.]

bour•geois (bo͝or-zhwä', bo͝or'zhwä') *n., pl.* **-geois. 1.** One belonging to the middle class. **2.** *(takes pl. v.).* The bourgeoisie. **3.** In Marxist theory, a capitalist. *—adj.* Of, pertaining to, or typical of the middle class. [< OF *bourg,* fortified town.]

bour•geoi•sie (bo͝or'zhwä-zē') *n.* **1.** The middle class. **2.** In Marxist theory, the capitalist class.

bout (bout) *n.* **1.** A contest; match. **2.** A period of time spent in a particular way: *a drinking bout.* [ME *bought,* bend, turn.]

bou•tique (bōō-tēk') *n.* A small retail shop that specializes in gifts, fashionable clothes, and accessories. [F.]

bou•ton•niere (bōō'tə-nîr', -tən-yâr') *n.* Also **bou•ton•nière.** A flower or small bunch of flowers worn in a buttonhole. [< OF *bouton,* button.]

bo•vine (bō'vīn', -vēn') *adj.* **1.** Of, related to, or resembling a cow or cattle. **2.** Dull; stolid. [< L *bōs (bov-),* ox, cow.] **—bo'vine** *n.*

bow¹ (bou) *n.* The front section of a ship or boat. [< MLG *boog.*]

bow² (bou) *v.* **1.** To bend (the head, knee, or body) in order to express greeting, consent, courtesy, submission, or veneration. **2.** To acquiesce; submit. *—n.* An inclination of the head or body, as in greeting, consent, etc. **—take a bow.** To accept applause. [< OE *būgan.* See **bheug-.**]

bow³ (bō) *n.* **1.** Something that is bent, curved, or arched. **2.** A weapon consisting of a curved stave, strung taut, and used to launch arrows. **3.** A rod strung with horsehair, used in playing violins, violas, etc. **4.** A knot usually having two loops and two ends. *—v.* **1.** To bend into a bow. **2.** To play a stringed instrument with a bow. [< OE *boga,* bow, arch. See **bheug-.**]

bowd•ler•ize (bōd'lə-rīz', boud'-) *v.* **-ized, -izing.** To expurgate prudishly. [< T. *Bowdler* (1754–1825), English editor who published an expurgated edition of Shakespeare's works.] **—bowd'ler•i•za'tion** *n.*

bow•el (bou'əl, boul) *n.* **1.** An intestine, esp. in man. **2.** Often **bowels.** The digestive tract below the stomach. **3. bowels.** The interior of anything. [< OF *bouel.*]

bow•er (bou'ər) *n.* A shaded, leafy recess; arbor. [< OE *būr,* a dwelling. See **bheu-.**]

bowl¹ (bōl) *n.* **1.** A hemispherical vessel for food or fluids. **2.** A bowl-shaped part, as of a spoon. **3.** A bowl-shaped edifice such as a football stadium. [< OE *bolla.* See **bhel-².**]

bowl² (bōl) *n.* **1.** A heavy ball rolled in certain games. **2.** A throw of such a ball. *—v.* To throw or roll a ball in bowling. **—bowl along.** To move smoothly and rapidly. **—bowl over. 1.** To knock over with something rolled. **2.** To overwhelm. [< L *bulla,* ball.]

bow•leg•ged (bō'lĕg'ĭd, -lĕgd') *adj.* Having legs that curve outward at the knee.

bowl•er¹ (bō'lər) *n.* One that bowls.

bowl•er² (bō'lər) *n. Chiefly Brit.* A derby hat. [< J. *Bowler,* 19th-century London hatmaker.]

bowl•ing (bō'lĭng) *n.* A game played by rolling a ball down a wooden alley in order to knock down a triangular group of ten pins.

bowling alley. 1. An alley used in bowling. **2.** A building containing such alleys.

bow•sprit (bou'sprĭt', bō'-) *n.* A spar extending forward from the bow of a ship. [< MLG *bōchsprēt.*]

box¹ (bŏks) *n.* **1.** A rectangular container, often with a lid. **2.** The amount such a container can hold. **3.** A separated compartment for a small group, as in a theater. **4.** A booth. **5.** An awkward situation. *—v.* To place in or as if in a box. [< OE.]

box² (bŏks) *n.* A blow or cuff. *—v.* **1.** To hit with the hand. **2.** To engage in a boxing match with. [ME.]

box³ (bŏks) *n.* **1.** A shrub with small evergreen leaves and hard, yellowish wood. **2.** Also **box•wood** (bŏks'wŏŏd'). The wood of this shrub. [< OE < L *buxus.*]

box•car (bŏks'kär') *n.* An enclosed and covered railway car for the transportation of freight.

box•er¹ (bŏk'sər) *n.* A pugilist.

box•er² (bŏk'sər) *n.* A short-haired dog with a brownish coat and a square-jawed muzzle.

box•ing (bŏk'sĭng) *n.* The sport of fighting with the fists.

box office. A ticket office, as of a theater.

boy (boi) *n.* A male child or youth. *—interj.* Used as a mild exclamation. [ME *boye,* orig "male servant," "knave."] **—boy'hood'** *n.*

boy•cott (boi'kŏt') *v.* To abstain from using, buying, or dealing with, as a means of protest. [< C. *Boycott* (1832–1897), Irish land agent.] **—boy'cott'** *n.*

boy•sen•ber•ry (boi'zən-bĕr'ē) *n.* A large, edible berry hybridized from the loganberry, blackberry, and raspberry. [< R. *Boysen,* 20th-century American horticulturist.]

bp boiling point.

bp. bishop.

B.P. bills payable.

B.P.O.E. Benevolent and Protective Order of Elks.

Br bromine.

Br. 1. Britain; British. **2.** Brother (religious).

B/R bills receivable.

bra (brä) *n.* A brassiere.

brace (brās) *n.* **1.** A clamp. **2.** Any device that steadies or supports something. **3. braces.** A pair of suspenders. **4.** An appliance used to support a bodily part. **5.** Often **braces.** An arrangement of bands and wires fixed to the teeth to correct irregular alignment. **6.** A cranklike device for securing and turning a bit. **7.** One of two symbols, { }, used to connect written or printed lines. **8.** *pl.* **brace.** A pair of like things. *—v.* **braced, bracing. 1.** To support with or as if with a brace. **2.** To prepare so as to be ready for an impact or danger. **3.** To invigorate. **—brace up.** To summon one's strength or endurance. [ME, arm guard, support.]

brace•let (brās'lĭt) *n.* An ornamental band or chain for the wrist. [< OF *bracel,* "little arm," armlet.]

brack•en (brăk'ən) *n.* A large fern with tough stems and branching, finely divided fronds. [ME *braken.*]

brack•et (brăk'ĭt) *n.* **1.** A simple rigid structure fixed to a vertical surface and projecting to support a shelf or other weight. **2.** A shelf supported by brackets. **3. a.** Either of a pair of symbols, [ ], used to enclose written or printed material. **b.** Either of a pair of symbols, < >, similarly used. **4.** A classification, esp. according to income. *—v.* **1.** To support with brackets. **2.** To place within brackets. **3.** To classify or group together. [< OF *braguette,* a pouch.]

brack•ish (brăk'ĭsh) *adj.* Containing some salt; briny. [< Du *brak,* salty.]

bract (brăkt) *n.* A leaflike plant part below a flower or flower cluster. [< L *bractea, brattea,* metal plate or leaf.]

brad (brăd) *n.* A tapered nail with a small head or a side projection instead of a head. [< ON *broddr,* spike.]

brae (brā) *n. Scot.* A hillside. [ME *bra.*]

brag (brăg) *v.* **bragged, bragging.** To talk boastfully. [ME *braggen.*] **—brag'ger** *n.*

brag•ga•do•ci•o (brăg'ə-dō'shē-ō) *n., pl.* **-os. 1.** A braggart. **2. a.** Empty bragging. **b.** Swaggering manner. [< *Braggadocchio,* name coined by Edmund Spenser (1552?–1599), British poet.]

brag•gart (brăg'ərt) *n.* One given to bragging. [< F *braguer,* to brag.]

Brah•ma (brä'mə) *n. Hinduism.* The personification of divine reality in its creative aspect.

Brahma

Brah•man (brä'mən) *n.* Also **Brah•min** (-mĭn). **1.** The single principle comprising all reality, goal of Vedantic mysticism. **2.** A member of the highest Hindu caste, originally composed of priests. [< Sk *brahmán-,* priest.]

Brah•man•ism (brä'mən-ĭz'əm) *n.* Also **Brah•min•ism** (brä'mĭn-). **1.** The religious practices and beliefs of ancient India. **2.** The social caste system of the Brahmans of India. **—Brah'man•ist** *n.*

Brah•ma•pu•tra (brä'mə-pōō'trə). A river of NE India and East Pakistan.

Brahms (brämz), **Johannes.** 1833–1897. German composer.

braid (brād) *v.* **1.** To interweave three or more strands of; plait. **2.** To decorate with an ornamental trim. *—n.* **1.** A narrow length of braided fabric, hair, etc. **2.** An ornamental trim. [< OE *bregdan.* See **bherək-.**] **—braid'er** *n.*

Braille (brāl) *n.* Also **braille.** A system of writing and printing for the blind, in which raised dots represent letters and numerals. [< L. *Braille* (1809–1852), French musician and inventor.]

a,1 ●○ ○○ ○○	b,2 ●○ ●○ ○○	c,3 ●● ○○ ○○	d,4 ●● ○● ○○	e,5 ●○ ○● ○○	f, 6 ●● ●○ ○○
g,7 ●● ●● ○○	h,8 ●○ ●● ○○	i, 9 ○● ●○ ○○	j,0 ○● ●● ○○	k ●○ ○○ ●○	l ●○ ●○ ●○
m ●● ○○ ●○	n ●● ○● ●○	o ●○ ○● ●○	p ●● ●○ ●○	q ●● ●● ●○	r ●○ ●● ●○
s ○● ●○ ●○	t ○● ●● ●○	u ●○ ○○ ●●	v ●○ ●○ ●●	w ○● ●● ○●	x ●● ○○ ●●
y ●● ○● ●●	z ●○ ○● ●●	& ●● ●○ ●●			

Braille alphabet

punctuation

,	;	:	.	!	(	)	" ?	"
○○ ●○ ○○	○○ ●○ ●○	○○ ●● ○○	○○ ●● ○●	○○ ●● ●○	○○ ●● ●●	○○ ●● ●●	○○ ●○ ●●	○○ ○● ●●

apostrophe	numeral	hyphen	capital	numerical positions in the cell
○○ ○○ ●○	○● ○● ●●	○○ ○○ ●●	○○ ○○ ○●	1 ●● 4 2 ●● 5 3 ●● 6

Braille alphabet

brain (brān) *n.* **1.** The portion of the central nervous system in the vertebrate cranium that is responsible for the interpretation of sensory impulses, the coordination and control of bodily activities, and the exercise of emotion and thought. **2.** *Informal.* Often **brains.** Intellectual capacity. —*v.* To smash in the skull of. [< OE *brægen.* See **mregh-mo.**]

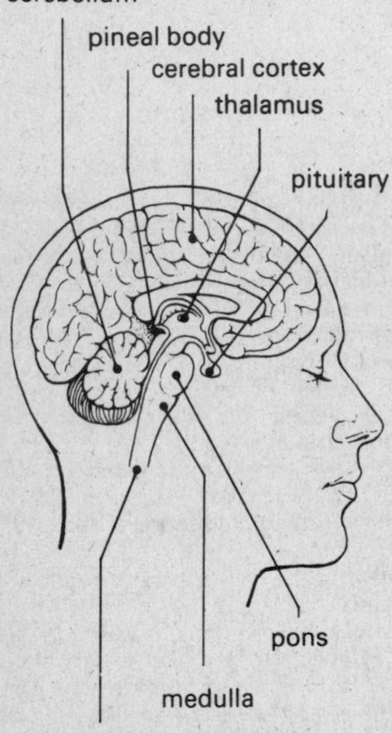

brain

brain child. *Informal.* An original idea or plan.
brain•less (brān'lĭs) *adj.* Stupid.
brain•storm (brān'stôrm') *n.* A sudden inspiration.
brain•wash (brān'wŏsh', -wôsh') *v.* To subject to brainwashing.
brain•wash•ing (brān'wŏsh'ĭng, -wôsh'ĭng) *n.* Intensive indoctrination to change a person's convictions radically.
brain wave. **1.** A rhythmic fluctuation of electric potential between parts of the brain. **2.** A sudden inspiration.
brain•y (brā'nē) *adj.* **-ier, -iest.** *Informal.* Intelligent; learned; smart. —**brain'i•ly** *adv.* —**brain'i•ness** *n.*
braise (brāz) *v.* **braised, braising.** To cook by browning and then simmering in a covered container. [< F *braise,* hot charcoal.]
brake¹ (brāk) *n.* A device for slowing or stopping motion, as of a vehicle or machine. —*v.* **braked, braking.** To reduce the speed of with or as if with a brake. [< ME, crushing instrument.]
brake² (brāk) *n.* A fern such as bracken. [ME, var of BRACKEN.]
brake³ (brāk) *n.* A densely overgrown area; thicket. [< OE *(fearn)braca,* bed of (fern).]
brake•age (brā'kĭj) *n.* The action or capacity of a brake.
brake fluid. The liquid used in a hydraulic brake cylinder.
brake horsepower. The actual or useful horsepower of an engine.
brake•man (brāk'mən) *n.* A railroad employee who assists the conductor and checks on the operation of the train's brakes.
brake shoe. A curved metal block that presses against and thereby arrests the rotation of a wheel.
bram•ble (brăm'bəl) *n.* A prickly plant or shrub such as the blackberry or the raspberry. [< OE *brǣmbel.* See **bhrem-.**] —**bram'bly** *adj.*
bran (brăn) *n.* The outer husks of cereal grains separated from the flour by sifting. [< OF.]
branch (brănch, brānch) *n.* **1.** An extension dividing off from the trunk, main stem, or a limb of a tree or plant. **2.** A similar structure or part. **3.** A limited part of a larger or more complex body. —*v.* **1.** To put forth; spread out in branches. **2.** To separate into subdivisions; diverge. —**branch out.** To enlarge the scope of one's interest or activities. [< LL *branca,* foot, paw.]
brand (brănd) *n.* **1.** A trademark or label. **2.** The make of a product thus marked: *a popular brand of soap.* **3.** A mark indicating ownership, burned on the hide of an animal. **4.** A mark formerly burned into the flesh of criminals. **5.** Any mark of disgrace; stigma. **6.** A piece of burning or charred wood. —*v.* **1.** To mark with or as if with a brand. **2.** To stigmatize. [< OE, piece of burning wood. See **bhreu-².**]
bran•dish (brăn'dĭsh) *v.* **1.** To flourish menacingly, as a weapon. **2.** To display ostentatiously. [< OF *brand,* sword, blade.]
brand-new (brănd'n/y/ōō') *adj.* In fresh and unused condition.
bran•dy (brăn'dē) *n., pl.* **-dies.** An alcoholic liquor distilled from wine or fermented fruit juice. —*v.* **-died, -dying.** To flavor or preserve with brandy. [< Du *brandewijn,* "distilled wine."]
brash (brăsh) *adj.* **1.** Hasty and unthinking; rash. **2.** Impudent; saucy. [Perh imit.] —**brash'ly** *adv.* —**brash'ness** *n.*
Bra•sí•lia (brə-zē'lyə). The capital of Brazil. Pop. 141,000.
brass (brăs, bräs) *n.* **1.** An alloy of copper and zinc with other metals in varying lesser amounts. **2.** Objects made of brass. **3. brasses.** *Mus.* Wind instruments made of brass. **4.** *Informal.* Blatant self-assurance; effrontery. **5.** *Slang.* High-ranking military officers. [< OE *bræs.*] —**brass** *adj.*
bras•siere, bras•sière (brə-zîr') *n.* A woman's undergarment worn to support and shape the breasts. [F *brassière.*]
brass tacks. *Informal.* Essential facts.
brat (brăt) *n.* A child, esp. an unruly one. [Prob < dial *brat,* coarse garment.] —**brat'ti•ness** *n.* —**brat'ty** *adj.*
bra•va•do (brə-vä'dō) *n., pl.* **-does** or **-dos.** **1.** Defiant or swaggering show of courage; false bravery. **2.** An instance of such behavior. [< Span *bravo,* brave.]
brave (brāv) *adj.* **braver, bravest.** **1.** Displaying courage. **2.** Making a fine display; splendid. —*n.* A North American Indian warrior. —*v.* **braved, braving.** **1.** To undergo or face courageously. **2.** To defy; challenge. [< VL **brabus,* wild, savage.] —**brave'ly** *adv.* —**brave'ness** *n.*
brav•er•y (brā'və-rē, brāv'rē) *n., pl.* **-ies.** The state or quality of being brave; courage.
bra•vo (brä'vō, brä-vō') *interj.* Expressive of approval. —*n., pl.* **-vos.** A shout or cry of "bravo." [It, fine, brave.]
bra•vu•ra (brə-vyŏŏr'ə) *n.* **1.** Brilliant musical technique or style. **2.** A showy manner or display. [It, "bravery," spirit.]
brawl (brôl) *n.* A noisy quarrel or fight. —*v.* To quarrel noisily. [ME *brawlen.*]
brawn (brôn) *n.* **1.** Solid and well-developed muscles. **2.** Muscular power. [< OF *braon,* flesh, muscle.] —**brawn'i•ly** *adv.* —**brawn'i•ness** *n.* —**brawn'y** *adj.*
bray (brā) *v.* To utter a loud, harsh cry, as a donkey. —*n.* **1.** The cry of a donkey. **2.** Any sound resembling this. [ME *brayen,* to make noise.]
braze (brāz) *v.* **brazed, brazing.** To solder together using a solder with a high melting point. [Prob < F *braser.*]
bra•zen (brā'zən) *adj.* **1.** Made of brass. **2.** Resembling brass in color, quality, or hardness. **3.** Having a loud, resonant sound. **4.** Impudent; bold. [< OE *bræsen* < *bræs,* BRASS.] —**bra'zen•ly** *adv.* —**bra'zen•ness** *n.*
bra•zier¹ (brā'zhər) *n.* One who works in brass.
bra•zier² (brā'zhər) *n.* A metal pan for holding burning coals or charcoal. [< F *braise,* burning coals.]
Bra•zil (brə-zĭl'). A republic of South America. Pop. 70,967,000. Cap. Brasília. —**Bra•zil'ian** *adj. & n.*

Brazil

Brazil nut. The hard-shelled, edible nut of a tropical American tree.
Braz•za•ville (brăz'ə-vĭl). The capital of the Republic of Congo, on the Congo River. Pop. 200,000.
breach (brēch) *n.* **1.** A violation or infraction,

as of a law. **2.** A gap or rift, esp. in a solid structure such as a dike. **3.** A breaking up of friendly relations. —*v.* To make a hole or gap in; break through. [< OHG *brehhan,* to break, and < OE *brecan,* to break.]

bread (brĕd) *n.* **1.** A foodstuff made from baked, usually leavened dough made with moistened flour. **2.** Food in general, regarded as necessary for life. **3.** The necessities of life; livelihood: *earn one's bread.* —*v.* To coat with bread crumbs, esp. before cooking. [< OE *brēad.* See **bhreu-²**.]

bread and butter. *Informal.* A means of support.

bread•bas•ket (brĕd'băs'kĭt, -bäs'kĭt) *n.* A region serving as a principal source of grain supply.

bread•fruit (brĕd'fro͞ot') *n.* The large, round, edible fruit of a tropical tree.

bread•stuff (brĕd'stŭf') *n.* **1.** Bread. **2.** Flour or grain used in making bread.

breadth (brĕdth) *n.* **1.** The measure or dimension of something from side to side. **2.** Wide extent or scope. **3.** Liberality of views. [< OE *brǣdu* < Gmc **braithaz,* BROAD.]

bread•win•ner (brĕd'wĭn'ər) *n.* One who supports a family by his earnings.

break (brāk) *v.* **broke, broken, breaking. 1. a.** To separate into or reduce to pieces by sudden force; come apart. **b.** To crack without separating into pieces. **2. a.** To render or become unusable by or as if by breaking. **b.** To give way; collapse. **3.** To force or make a way into, through, or out of. **4.** To pierce the surface of. **5.** To disrupt the continuity or unity of: *break ranks.* **6.** To come into being or notice, esp. suddenly: *The news broke.* **7.** To begin suddenly: *breaks into bloom.* **8.** To change suddenly: *His voice broke.* **9.** To overcome or surpass. **10. a.** To ruin or destroy: *"For a hero loves the world till it breaks him"* (Yeats). **b.** To demote. **c.** To train to obey. **11.** To lessen in force: *break a fall.* **12.** To collapse or crash into surf or spray, as waves. **13.** *Informal.* To occur. —**break in. 1.** To train. **2.** To enter forcibly. **3.** To interrupt. —**break off. 1.** To stop suddenly. **2.** To discontinue a relationship. —**break out. 1.** To erupt. **2.** To escape, as from prison. —*n.* **1.** The act of breaking. **2.** The result of breaking; a fracture or crack. **3.** A disruption of continuity. **4.** An emergence: *the break of day.* **5.** *Informal.* A stroke of luck. [< OE *brecan.* See **bhreg-**.]

break•age (brā'kĭj) *n.* **1.** The act or process of breaking. **2.** A quantity broken. **3. a.** Loss as a result of breaking. **b.** An allowance for such a loss.

break•down (brāk'doun') *n.* **1.** The act or process of breaking down and failing to function or the condition resulting from this. **2.** A collapse in physical or mental health. **3.** An analysis, outline, or summary consisting of itemized data or essentials. **4.** Disintegration or decomposition into parts or elements.

break•er (brā'kər) *n.* **1.** One that breaks. **2.** A wave that breaks into foam.

break•fast (brĕk'fəst) *n.* The first meal of the day. [< ME *breken faste,* to break (one's) fasting.] —**break'fast** *v.*

break•neck (brāk'nĕk') *adj.* Heedless of safety.

break•through (brāk'thro͞o') *n.* **1.** An act of breaking through an obstacle or restriction. **2.** A major achievement that permits further progress, as in technology.

break•wa•ter (brāk'wô'tər, -wŏt'ər) *n.* A barrier that protects a harbor or shore from the impact of waves.

breast (brĕst) *n.* **1.** A mammary gland, esp. the human mammary gland. **2.** The surface of the body extending from the neck to the abdomen. —**make a clean breast of.** To make a full confession of. —*v.* To confront boldly. [< OE *brēost.* See **bhreus-¹**.]

breast•bone (brĕst'bōn') *n.* The sternum.

breast•plate (brĕst'plāt') *n.* Armor plate that covers the breast.

breast stroke. A swimming stroke in which one lies face down and extends the arms in front of the head, then sweeps them back laterally while kicking the legs.

breast•work (brĕst'wûrk') *n.* A temporary fortification, usually breast-high.

breath (brĕth) *n.* **1.** The air inhaled and exhaled in respiration. **2.** Respiration. **3.** The capacity to breathe. **4.** A single respiration. **5.** A momentary stirring of air. **6.** A trace. **7.** A soft-spoken sound. [< OE *brǣth,* odor, exhalation. See **bhreu-²**.] —**breath'less** *adj.* —**breath'less•ly** *adv.*

breathe (brēth) *v.* **breathed, breathing. 1.** To inhale and exhale. **2.** To live. **3.** To pause to rest. **4.** To utter, esp. quietly. —**breath'a•ble** *adj.*

breath•er (brē'thər) *n.* **1.** One who breathes in a specified manner. **2.** *Informal.* A strenuous or exhausting task. **3.** *Informal.* A short rest period.

breath•tak•ing (brĕth'tā'kĭng) *adj.* Inspiring awe. —**breath'tak'ing•ly** *adv.*

breech (brēch) *n.* **1.** The buttocks. **2.** The part of a firearm behind the barrel or, in a cannon, behind the bore. [< OE *brēc,* breeches.]

breech•es (brĭch'ĭz) *pl.n.* **1.** Knee-length trousers. **2.** Any trousers. [Pl of BREECH.]

breed (brēd) *v.* **bred** (brĕd), **breeding. 1.** To produce (offspring); reproduce. **2.** To bring about; engender. **3.** To raise (animals). **4.** To rear; bring up. —*n.* **1.** A genetic strain, esp. of a domestic animal developed and maintained by man. **2.** A kind; sort. [< OE *brēdan.* See **bhreu-²**.]

breed•ing (brē'dĭng) *n.* **1.** One's line of descent. **2.** Training in the proper forms of social and personal conduct.

breeze (brēz) *n.* **1.** A gentle wind. **2.** A wind from 4 to 31 miles per hour. [Perh < OSpan *briza,* northeast wind.] —**breez'i•ly** *adv.* —**breez'y** *adj.*

Bre•men (brĕm'ən). A city in West Germany. Pop. 588,000.

Bret•on (brĕt'n) *n.* **1.** A native or inhabitant of Brittany. **2.** The Celtic language of Brittany. —**Bret'on** *adj.*

breve (brĕv, brēv) *n.* **1.** A symbol (˘) placed over a vowel to show that it has a short sound. **2.** A single musical note equivalent to two whole notes. [< ME *bref,* brief.]

bre•vi•ar•y (brē'vē-ĕr-ē, brĕv'-ē-) *n., pl.* **-ies.** A book containing the hymns, offices, and prayers for the canonical hours. [L *breviārium,* abridgment.]

brev•i•ty (brĕv'ə-tē) *n.* **1.** Briefness of duration. **2.** Concise expression; terseness. [< L *brevis,* BRIEF.]

brew (bro͞o) *v.* **1.** To make (ale or beer) from malt and hops by infusion, boiling, and fermentation. **2.** To make (a beverage) by boiling or steeping. **3.** To be imminent; impend. —*n.* A beverage made by brewing. [< OE *brēowan.* See **bhreu-²**.] —**brew'er** *n.*

brew•er•y (bro͞o'ər-ē) *n., pl.* **-ies.** A place where beer or ale is brewed.

Brezh•nev (brĕzh'nĕf), **Leonid Ilyich.** Born 1906. Soviet statesman; general secretary of the Communist Party (since 1966).

Leonid Brezhnev

bri•ar¹ (brī'ər) *n.* Also **bri•er.** A shrub with a hard, woody root used to make tobacco pipes. [F *bruyère,* heath.]

bri•ar². Variant of **brier.**

bribe (brīb) *n.* Anything offered or given to someone in a position of trust to induce him to act dishonestly. —*v.* **bribed, bribing.** To give or offer a bribe (to). [< OF *briber,* to beg.] —**brib'er** *n.* —**brib'er•y** *n.*

bric-a-brac (brĭk'ə-brăk') *n.* Objects collectively, usually small, displayed as ornaments. [F *bric-à-brac.*]

brick (brĭk) *n.* A molded rectangular block of clay, baked until hard and used as a construction material. —*v.* To construct or cover with brick. [ME *brike.*]

brick•bat (brĭk'băt') *n.* **1.** A piece of brick, esp. one used as a weapon. **2.** A blunt criticism or remark.

brick•lay•er (brĭk'lā'ər) *n.* A person skilled in building with bricks. —**brick'lay'ing** *n.*

bri•dal (brīd'l) *n.* A wedding. —*adj.* Of or pertaining to a bride or a wedding. [< OE *brȳdealu,* "bride ale."]

bride (brīd) *n.* A woman recently married or about to be married. [< OE *brȳd* < Gmc **brūdhiz.*]

bride•groom (brīd'gro͞om', -gro͝om') *n.* A man recently married or about to be married. [< OE *brȳdguma,* "bride's man."]

brides•maid (brīdz'mād') *n.* A woman who attends the bride at a wedding.

bridge¹ (brĭj) *n.* **1.** A structure spanning and providing passage over a waterway or other obstacle. **2.** Anything structurally or functionally analogous to a bridge. **3.** The upper bony ridge of the human nose. **4.** *Mus.* **a.** A thin, upright piece of wood in some stringed instruments that supports the strings above the sounding board. **b.** A transitional passage connecting two subjects or movements. **5.** *Dent.* A fixed or removable replacement for one or several, but not all, of the natural teeth, usually anchored at each end to a natural tooth. **6.** A crosswise platform above the main deck of a ship from which the ship is controlled. —*v.* **bridged, bridging. 1.** To build a bridge over. **2.** To cross by or as if by a bridge. [< OE *brycg.*] —**bridge'a•ble** *adj.*

bridge² (brĭj) *n.* Any of several card games for four players, derived from whist. [Earlier *biritch.*]

bridge•head (brĭj'hĕd') *n.* A military position established by advance troops in enemy territory to afford protection for the main attacking force.

Bridge•port (brĭj'pôrt', -pōrt'). A city of Connecticut. Pop. 155,000.

Bridge•town (brĭj'toun'). The capital of Barbados. Pop. 94,000.

bridge•work (brĭj'wûrk') *n. Dent.* **1.** A bridge. **2.** Prosthetics involving bridges.

bri•dle (brīd'l) *n.* **1.** The harness fitted about a horse's head, used to restrain or guide. **2.** Any restraint. —*v.* **-dled, -dling. 1.** To put a bridle on. **2.** To control or restrain. **3.** To display scorn or resentment. [< OE *bridel.* See **bherək-.**] —**bri'dler** *n.*

brief (brēf) *adj.* **1.** Short in time or extent. **2.** Condensed in expression. —*n.* **1.** A short or condensed statement or summary. **2.** A summary of a legal case or argument. —*v.* **1.** To summarize. **2.** To give concise information or instructions to. [< L *brevis,* short.] —**brief'ly** *adv.* —**brief'ness** *n.*

brief•case (brēf'kās') *n.* A portable rectangular case.

bri•er[1] (brī'ər) *n.* Also **bri•ar.** A thorny plant, such as a rosebush. [< OE *brǣr, brēr.*]

bri•er[2]. Variant of **briar**[1].

brig[1] (brĭg) *n.* A two-masted sailing ship, square-rigged on both masts. [Short for BRIGANTINE.]

brig[2] (brĭg) *n.* A ship's prison. [Prob < BRIG[1].]

bri•gade (brĭ-gād') *n.* **1.** A military unit consisting of a variable number of combat battalions, with supporting services. **2.** Any group of persons organized for a specific purpose. [< OIt *brigata,* troop, company.]

brig•a•dier general (brĭg'ə-dîr') *pl.* **brigadier generals.** An officer ranking above a colonel in the U.S. Army, Air Force, and Marine Corps. [F < BRIGADE.]

brig•and (brĭg'ənd) *n.* A robber, esp. one of a band. [ME *brigaunt,* foot soldier, bandit.]

brig•an•tine (brĭg'ən-tēn') *n.* A two-masted, square-rigged sailing ship having a fore-and-aft mainsail. [< It *brigantino,* "pirate ship."]

Brig. Gen. brigadier general.

bright (brīt) *adj.* **1.** Emitting or reflecting light; shining. **2.** Brilliant in color; vivid. **3.** Glorious; splendid. **4.** Auspicious. **5.** Happy; cheerful. **6.** Intelligent. [< OE *beorht.* See **bherəg-.**] —**bright'ly** *adv.* —**bright'ness** *n.*

bright•en (brīt'n) *v.* **1.** To make or become bright or brighter. **2.** To make or become more cheerful.

bril•liant (brĭl'yənt) *adj.* **1.** Shining. **2.** Brightly vivid in color. **3.** Glorious; splendid. **4.** Marked by extraordinary intellect. [< F *briller,* to shine.] —**bril'liance, bril'lian•cy** *n.* —**bril'liant•ly** *adv.*

bril•lian•tine (brĭl'yən-tēn') *n.* An oily, perfumed hairdressing. [< F *brillant,* brilliant.]

brim (brĭm) *n.* **1.** The rim or uppermost edge of a cup or other vessel. **2.** A projecting rim or edge. [ME *brimme.*]

brim•ful (brĭm'fo͝ol') *adj.* Also **brim•full.** Completely full.

brim•stone (brĭm'stōn') *n. Obs.* Sulfur. [< OE *brynstān.*]

brin•dle (brĭnd'l) *adj.* Also **brin•dled** (brĭnd'əld). Tawny or grayish with darker streaks or spots, as an animal's coat. [ME *brende.*]

brine (brīn) *n.* **1.** Water containing large amounts of a salt, esp. of sodium chloride. **2.** The ocean. [< OE *brȳne.*]

bring (brĭng) *v.* **brought, bringing. 1.** To take with oneself to a place. **2.** To carry as an attribute. **3.** To lead into a specified state or situation. **4.** To induce. **5.** To cause to occur. **6.** To sell for. —**bring about.** To cause to happen. —**bring forth.** To produce. —**bring off.** To accomplish successfully. —**bring out. 1.** To reveal. **2.** To produce. —**bring up. 1.** To rear (a child). **2.** To mention. [< OE *bringan.* See **bher-**[1].]

brin (brĭn) *n.* One of the ribs of a fan. [Fr *brin.*]

bring•ing-up (brĭng'ĭng-ŭp') *n.* The care, training, and education of a child.

brink (brĭngk) *n.* **1.** The upper edge of a steep or vertical declivity. **2.** The verge of something. [ME *brinke.*]

brin•y (brī'nē) *adj.* **-ier, -iest.** Of, pertaining to, or resembling brine; salty. —*n. Slang.* The sea. —**brin'i•ness** *n.*

bri•o (brē'ō) *n.* Vigor; vivacity. [It, "vivacity."]

bri•oche (brē-ôsh', -ōsh') *n.* A rich, rounded, soft roll or bun. [< OF.]

bri•quette, bri•quet (brĭ-kĕt') *n.* A block of compressed coal dust or charcoal. [< F *brique,* brick.]

Bris•bane (brĭz'bən, -bān). A city of SE Australia. Pop. 664,000.

brisk (brĭsk) *adj.* **1.** Moving or acting quickly. **2.** Keen or sharp. **3.** Invigorating. [Prob var of BRUSQUE.] —**brisk'ly** *adv.* —**brisk'ness** *n.*

bris•ket (brĭs'kĭt) *n.* **1.** The chest of an animal. **2.** Meat from this part. [ME *brusket.*]

bris•ling (brĭz'lĭng, brĭs'-) *n.* A small sardine. [Norw.]

bris•tle (brĭs'əl) *n.* A short, stiff hair. —*v.* **-tled, -tling. 1.** To erect the bristles, as an animal. **2.** To react with agitation. **3.** To stand out stiffly. **4.** To be covered with bristlelike growth. [< OE *byrst,* bristle. See **bhar-.**] —**bris'tly** *adj.*

Bris•tol (brĭs'təl). A port in SW England. Pop. 431,000.

Brit. Britain; British.

Brit•ain (brĭt'n). Great Britain.

britch•es (brĭch'ĭz) *pl.n. Informal.* Breeches.

Brit•i•cism (brĭt'ə-sĭz'əm) *n.* A word or phrase peculiar to English as spoken in Great Britain.

Brit•ish (brĭt'ĭsh) *adj.* Of or pertaining to Great Britain, the United Kingdom, or its people. —*n.* **1.** The people of Great Britain. **2.** The language spoken in Great Britain; British English. **3.** The language spoken by the ancient Britons.

British Co•lum•bi•a (kə-lŭm'bē-ə). The westernmost province of Canada. Pop. 1,789,000. Cap. Victoria.

British Commonwealth of Nations. The former name for the **Commonwealth of Nations.**

British Empire. The former British Commonwealth of Nations and all British colonies, dependencies, etc.

British English. The English language as spoken, pronounced, and written in England.

Brit•ish•er (brĭt'ĭ-shər) *n. Informal.* A native of Great Britain.

British Guiana. The former name for Guyana.

British Hon•du•ras (hŏn-d/y/o͝or'əs). The former name for Belize.

British Isles. A group of islands off the coast of Europe, comprising Great Britain, Ireland, and adjacent smaller islands.

British thermal unit. The quantity of heat required to raise the temperature of 1 pound of water by 1°F.

British warm. A short, double-breasted overcoat originally worn by British army officers.

Brit•on (brĭt'n) *n.* **1.** A native of Britain. **2.** One of a Celtic people who inhabited ancient Britain.

brit•tle (brĭt'l) *adj.* Likely to break; fragile: *brittle porcelain.* [< OE **brytel.* See **bhreu-**[1].] —**brit'tle•ness** *n.*

bro. brother.

broach (brōch) *n.* **1.** A tapered, serrated tool used to shape or enlarge a hole. **2.** A gimlet for tapping casks. **3.** Variant of **brooch.** —*v.* **1.** To begin to talk about. **2.** To pierce in order to draw off liquid. [< OF *broche,* a spit.] —**broach'er** *n.*

broad (brôd) *adj.* **1.** Wide from side to side. **2.** Spacious. **3.** Widely diffused. **4.** Covering a wide scope. **5.** Liberal; tolerant. **6.** Plain and clear; not subtle. **7.** Indicating a vowel that is pronounced as it is when the *a* in *bath* is pronounced like the *a* in *bard.* [< OE *brād* < Gmc **braithaz.*] —**broad'ly** *adv.*

broad arrow. 1. An arrow with a wide, barbed head. **2.** A wide arrowhead mark identifying British government property.

broad•ax, broad•axe (brôd'ăks') *n., pl.* **-axes.** An ax with a wide, flat head and a short handle; a battle-ax.

broad•bill (brôd'bĭl') *n.* Any of various birds having a short, wide bill and brightly colored plumage.

broad•brim (brôd'brĭm') *n.* A hat with a broad, flat brim, as those worn by Quakers.

broad•cast (brôd'kăst', -käst') *v.* **-cast** or **-casted, -casting. 1.** To transmit (a program) by radio or television. **2.** To make known widely. **3.** To sow (seed). —*n.* **1.** Transmission of a radio or television program or signal. **2.** A radio or television program. —*adj.* **1.** Of or pertaining to transmission by radio or television. **2.** Scattered over a wide area. —*adv.* In a scattered manner; far and wide. —**broad'cast'er** *n.*

broad•cloth (brôd'klôth', -klŏth') *n.* **1.** A thickly textured woolen cloth. **2.** A fine, closely woven cotton, silk, or synthetic fabric.

broad•en (brôd'n) *v.* To make or become broad or broader.

broad jump. In track events, a jump made for distance rather than height.

broad•loom (brôd'lo͞om') *n.* Carpet woven on a loom from 4½ feet to 18 feet wide. —**broad'loom'** *adj.*

broad-mind•ed (brôd'mīn'dĭd) *adj.* Liberal; tolerant. —**broad'-mind'ed•ness** *n.*

broad•side (brôd'sīd') *n.* **1.** The side of a ship above the water line. **2.** Simultaneous discharge of all the guns on one side of a warship. **3.** An explosive verbal attack.

broad•sword (brôd'sôrd', -sōrd') *n.* A sword with a wide blade.

broad•tail (brôd'tāl') *n.* The flat, rippled fur of a prematurely born Asian sheep.

bro•cade (brō-kād') *n.* A fabric with a raised interwoven design. [< It *broccato,* embossed fabric.] —**bro•cad'ed** *adj.*

broc•co•li (brŏk'ə-lē) *n.* A plant with a green, densely clustered flower head eaten as a vegetable before the buds open. [< It *broccolo,* cabbage sprout.]

bro•chure (brō-sho͝or') *n.* A pamphlet or booklet. [F, "a stitching."]

bro•gan (brō'gən) *n.* A heavy, ankle-high shoe. [< Ir Gael *brōg,* BROGUE[2].]

brogue[1] (brōg) *n.* A strong dialectal accent, esp. an Irish accent. [< BROGUE[2].]

brogue[2] (brōg) *n.* A sturdy oxford shoe. [Ir Gael *brōg.*]

broil (broil) *v.* To cook by direct radiant heat. [< OF *bruller, brusler,* to burn.]

broil•er (broi'lər) *n.* **1.** A device or compartment used for broiling. **2.** A young chicken suitable for broiling.

broke (brōk). *p.t.* of **break.** *—adj. Informal.* Lacking funds.

bro•ken (brō'kən). *p.p.* of **break.** *—adj.* **1.** Fractured; shattered. **2.** Violated, as promises. **3.** Discontinuous. **4.** Spoken imperfectly. **5.** Defeated; humbled. **6.** Tamed. **7.** Not functioning.

bro•ken•heart•ed (brō'kən-här'tĭd) *adj.* Grievously sad.

bro•ker (brō'kər) *n.* One who acts as an agent in negotiating contracts, purchases, or sales in return for a fee. [ME, peddler, go-between.]

bro•ker•age (brō'kər-ĭj) *n.* **1.** The business of a broker. **2.** A fee or commission paid to a broker.

bro•mide (brō'mīd') *n.* **1.** A binary compound of bromine. **2.** A sedative, **potassium bromide. 3.** A commonplace remark or notion. **—bro•mid'ic** (-mĭd'ĭk) *adj.*

bro•mine (brō'mēn') *n. Symbol* **Br** A heavy, corrosive, reddish-brown, nonmetallic liquid element used in producing gasoline antiknock mixtures, fumigants, and photographic chemicals. Atomic weight 79.904, atomic number 35. [< Gk *brōmos,* stench.]

bron•chi•al (brŏng'kē-əl) *adj.* Of or pertaining to the bronchi or any of their extensions. **—bron'chi•al•ly** *adv.*

bron•chi•tis (brŏng-kī'tĭs) *n.* Chronic or acute inflammation of the mucous membrane of the bronchial tubes.

broncho–. *comb. form.* Bronchi.

bron•chus (brŏng'kəs) *n., pl.* **-chi** (-kī', -kē'). Either of two main branches of the trachea, leading directly to the lungs. [< Gk *bronkhos,* trachea, windpipe, throat.]

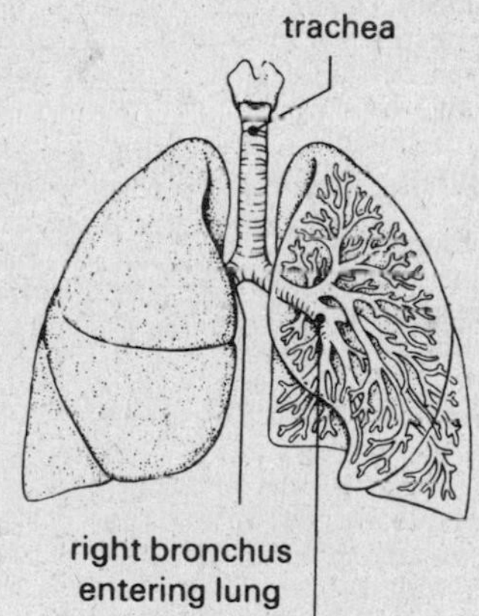

bronchus

bron•co (brŏng'kō) *n., pl.* **-cos.** A wild or semiwild horse of W North America. [< Span, rough, wild.]

bron•to•saur (brŏn'tə-sôr') *n.* Also **bron•to•sau•rus** (brŏn'tə-sôr'əs). A very large, herbivorous dinosaur. [< Gk *brontē,* thunder.]

Bronx, the (brŏngks). A borough of New York City. Pop. 1,425,000.

bronze (brŏnz) *n.* **1.** Any of various alloys principally of copper and tin. **2.** A work of art made of bronze. **3.** Moderate yellowish to olive brown. *—v.* **bronzed, bronzing.** To give the appearance of bronze to. [< It *bronzo.*] **—bronze** *adj.*

Bronze Age. A period of human culture between the Stone Age and the Iron Age, characterized by weapons and implements made of bronze.

brooch (brôch, bro͞och) *n.* Also **broach.** A large decorative pin or clasp. [ME *broche,* brooch, broach (tool).]

brood (bro͞od) *n.* A group of young animals, esp. of young birds hatched at one time. *—v.* **1.** To sit on or cover (eggs or newly hatched young). **2.** To ponder moodily. *—adj.* Kept for breeding: *a brood mare.* [< OE *brōd.* See **bhreu-**[2].]

brood•er (bro͞o'dər) *n.* **1.** One that broods. **2.** A heated enclosure for raising young chickens.

brood•y (bro͞o'dē) *adj.* **-ier, -iest.** Inclined to brood; moody; meditative.

brook[1] (bro͝ok) *n.* A small freshwater stream. [< OE *brōc* < Gmc **brōka.*]

brook[2] (bro͝ok) *v.* To put up with. [< OE *brūcan,* to enjoy.]

Brook•lyn (bro͝ok'lĭn). A borough of New York City. Pop. 2,627,000.

broom (bro͞om, bro͝om) *n.* **1.** A long-handled brushlike implement used for sweeping. **2.** A shrub with yellow flowers and small leaves. [< OE *brōm,* broom plant. See **bhrem-.**] **—broom'y** *adj.*

bros. brothers.

broth (brôth, brŏth) *n.* Soup consisting of the water in which meat, fish, or vegetables have been boiled. [< OE. See **bhreu-**[2].]

broth•el (brŏth'əl, brŏ*th*'-, brô'thəl, *-th*əl) *n.* A house of prostitution. [< OE *brēothan,* to deteriorate. See **bhreu-**[1].]

broth•er (brŭ*th*'ər) *n.* **1.** A male having the same mother and father as another, **full brother,** or one parent in common with another, **half brother. 2.** One who has a close bond with another or others. **3.** A member of a men's religious order who is not in holy orders. [< OE *brōthor.* See **bhrāter-.**] **—broth'er•ly** *adj.* **—broth'er•li•ness** *n.*

broth•er•hood (brŭ*th*'ər-ho͝od') *n.* **1.** The state of being a brother or brothers. **2.** An association of men united for common purposes. **3.** All the members of a specific profession or trade.

broth•er-in-law (brŭ*th*'ər-ĭn-lô') *n., pl.* **broth•ers-in-law. 1.** The brother of one's spouse. **2.** The husband of one's sister. **3.** The husband of the sister of one's spouse.

brougham (bro͞om, bro͞o'əm, brō'əm) *n.* **1.** A closed carriage with an open driver's seat in front. **2.** An automobile with an open driver's seat. [< H.P. *Brougham* (1778–1868), Scottish jurist.]

brought (brôt). *p.t. & p.p.* of **bring.**

brou•ha•ha (bro͞o'hä-hä') *n.* An uproar. [F.]

brow (brou) *n.* **1. a.** The ridge over the eyes. **b.** An eyebrow. **c.** The forehead. **2.** The edge of a steep place. [< OE *brū,* eyelash, eyelid, eyebrow. See **bhrū-.**]

brow•beat (brou'bēt') *v.* To intimidate; domineer; bully.

brown (broun) *n.* Any of a group of colors between red and yellow in hue. *—adj.* **1.** Of the color brown. **2.** Deeply suntanned. *—v.* To make or become brown, esp. to cook until brown. [< OE *brūn.* See **bher-**[3].] **—brown'ish** *adj.*

brown•ie (brou'nē) *n.* **1.** A small, helpful elf of folklore. **2.** A square of flat, moist chocolate cake.

Brown•ing (brou'nĭng), **Robert.** 1812–1889. English poet.

brown•stone (broun'stōn') *n.* **1.** A brownish-red sandstone. **2.** A house built or faced with such stone.

browse (brouz) *v.* **browsed, browsing. 1.** To inspect in a leisurely and casual way. **2.** To feed on leaves, young shoots, and other vegetation; graze (on). [< OF *broust,* shoot, twig.]

Brue•ghel (brœ'gəl), **Pieter.** 1525?–1569. Flemish painter.

bru•in (bro͞o'ĭn) *n.* A bear. [Du, BRUIN, "brown."]

bruise (bro͞oz) *v.* **bruised, bruising. 1. a.** To injure the skin without rupture. **b.** To suffer such injury. **2.** To dent or mar. **3.** To pound into fragments. *—n.* An injury in which the skin is not broken; contusion. [< OE *brȳsan,* to crush (see **bhreus-**[2]) and OF *bruisier,* to break, crush.]

bruit (bro͞ot) *v.* To spread news of; repeat. [< OF, noise.]

brunch (brŭnch) *n.* A combination of breakfast and lunch. [BR(EAKFAST) + (L)UNCH.]

Bru•nei (bro͞o-nī'). A British-protected sultanate of NW Borneo, on the South China Sea. Pop. 135,600. Cap. Bandar Seri Begawan.

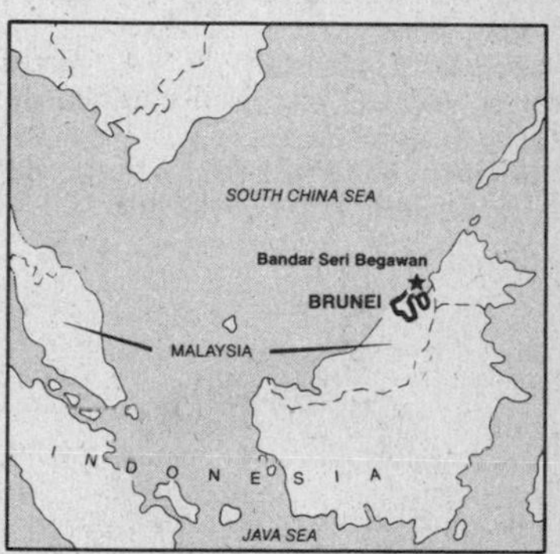

Brunei

bru•net (bro͞o-nĕt'). Also *fem.* **brunette.** *adj.* Dark or brown in color, as hair. *—n.* A person with brown hair. [< OF *brun,* brown.]

brunt (brŭnt) *n.* The main impact, force, or burden, as of a blow. [ME *brunt.*]

brush[1] (brŭsh) *n.* **1.** A device consisting of bristles or other flexible material fastened into a handle, for scrubbing, applying paint, grooming the hair, etc. **2.** A light touch in passing. **3.** A brief encounter. **4.** The bushy tail of a fox or other animal. **5.** A sliding connection completing a circuit between a fixed and a moving conductor. *—v.* **1.** To use a brush (on). **2.** To apply or remove with or as if with motions of a brush. **3.** To touch lightly in passing; graze against. [< OF *broisse.*]

brush[2] (brŭsh) *n.* Also **brush•wood** (brŭsh'wo͝od'). **1.** A dense growth of bushes. **2.** Cut or broken branches. [< OF *broce.*]

brush-off (brŭsh'ôf', -ŏf') *n. Slang.* An abrupt dismissal.

brusque (brŭsk) *adj.* Also **brusk.** Abrupt and curt; discourteously blunt. [< It *brusco,* sour, sharp.] **—brusque'ness** *n.*

Brus•sels (brŭs'əlz). The capital of Belgium. Pop. 1,066,000.

Brussels sprouts. The small, budlike heads of a variety of cabbage, eaten as a vegetable.

bru•tal (bro͞ot'l) *adj.* Characteristic of a brute; cruel; harsh; crude. **—bru•tal'i•ty** (bro͞o-tăl'ə-tē) *n.* **—bru'tal•ly** *adv.*

bru•tal•ize (brōōt'l-īz') *v.* **-ized, -izing. 1.** To render brutal. **2.** To treat in a brutal manner.
brute (brōōt) *n.* **1.** An animal; beast. **2.** A brutal person. *—adj.* **1.** Of or relating to beasts. **2.** Characterized by physical power or instinct rather than intelligence: *brute force.* [< L *brūtus,* heavy.] **—brut'ish** *adj.*
B.S. 1. Bachelor of Science. **2.** balance sheet. **3.** bill of sale.
B.S.A. Boy Scouts of America.
bsh. bushel.
bsk. basket.
Bt. baronet.
Btu British thermal unit.
bu. 1. bureau. **2.** bushel.
bub•ble (bŭb'əl) *n.* A rounded, generally spherical, hollow, or sometimes solid, object, esp. a small globule of gas trapped in a liquid. *—v.* **-bled, -bling.** To form or give off bubbles. [ME *bobelen.*] **—bub'bly** *adj.*
bu•bo (b/y/ōō'bō) *n., pl.* **-boes.** An inflamed swelling of a lymphatic gland, esp. near the armpit or groin. [< Gk *boubōn,* groin, swollen gland.] **—bu•bon'ic** (-bŏn'ĭk) *adj.*
bubonic plague. A contagious, usually fatal epidemic disease transmitted by fleas from infected rats and characterized by chills, fever, vomiting, diarrhea, and buboes.
buc•ca•neer (bŭk'ə-nîr') *n.* A pirate. [F *boucanier,* pirate, "one who cures meat on a barbecue frame."]
Bu•chan•an (byōō-kăn'ən, bə-), **James.** 1791–1868. 15th President of the U.S. (1857–61).

James Buchanan

Bu•cha•rest (b/y/ōō'kə-rĕst'). The capital of Rumania. Pop. 1,372,000.
buck¹ (bŭk) *n.* **1.** An adult male animal, as the deer. **2.** A spirited or dandified young man. *—adj.* Lowest in rank: *buck private.* [< OE *buc,* stag, and *bucca,* he-goat. See **bhugo-.**]
buck² (bŭk) *v.* **1.** To leap forward and upward suddenly; rear up. **2.** To butt (against). **3.** To jolt. **4.** To throw (a rider or burden) by bucking. **5.** To oppose directly and stubbornly. [< BUCK¹.] **—buck** *n.* **—buck'er** *n.*
buck³ (bŭk) *n. Slang.* A dollar. [Short for BUCKSKIN.]
buck•board (bŭk'bôrd', -bōrd') *n.* A four-wheeled open carriage with the seat attached to a flexible board. [< obs *buck,* body of a wagon.]
buck•et (bŭk'ĭt) *n.* **1.** A cylindrical vessel used for holding or carrying liquids or solids; pail. **2.** Any of various machine compartments that receive and convey material, as the scoop of a steam shovel. **3.** The amount that a bucket will hold. [< NF *buket,* bucket, tub.]
bucket seat. A seat with a rounded or molded back, as in sports cars.
buck•eye (bŭk'ī') *n.* **1.** A North American tree with upright flower clusters and glossy brown nuts. **2.** The nut of this tree.
buck fever. *Informal.* Nervous excitement felt by a novice hunter at the first sight of game.
buck•hound (bŭk'hound') *n.* A hound used for hunting deer.
buck•ish (bŭk'ĭsh) *adj.* **1.** Characteristic of a fop; dandified. **2.** Impetuous; dashing. **—buck'ish•ly** *adv.*
buck•le¹ (bŭk'əl) *n.* **1.** A clasp, esp. a frame with movable tongues for fastening two strap or belt ends. **2.** An ornament resembling such a clasp. *—v.* **-led, -ling.** To fasten or secure with a buckle. [< OF *boucle,* metal ring, buckle.]
buck•le² (bŭk'əl) *v.* **-led, -ling. 1.** To bend, warp, or crumple under pressure or heat. **2.** To collapse or yield. *—n.* A bend, bulge, or other distortion. [< OF *boucler,* "to fasten with a buckle."]
buck•ler (bŭk'lər) *n.* A small round shield carried or worn on the arm. [< OF *boucle,* boss on a shield.]
buck•ram (bŭk'rəm) *n.* A coarse cotton fabric, heavily sized with glue, used for stiffening garments and in bookbinding. [ME *bokram,* a fine linen.]
buck•saw (bŭk'sô') *n.* A wood-cutting saw, usually set in an H-shaped frame. [< SAWBUCK.]
buck•shot (bŭk'shŏt') *n.* A large lead shot for shotgun shells.
buck•skin (bŭk'skĭn') *n.* Strong, soft leather originally made from deerskin.
buck•tooth (bŭk'tōōth') *n.* A prominent, projecting upper front tooth. [< BUCK¹.] **—buck'-toothed'** (bŭk'tōōtht') *adj.*
buck•wheat (bŭk'hwēt') *n.* **1.** A plant having small, edible triangular seeds often ground into flour. **2.** The seeds of this plant. [Partial trans of MDu *boecweite,* "beech wheat."]
bu•col•ic (byōō-kŏl'ĭk) *adj.* Pastoral; rustic. [< Gk *boukolos,* cattle herder.]
bud (bŭd) *n.* **1.** A small, protuberant plant structure containing undeveloped flowers, leaves, etc. **2.** A budlike part, as an asexually produced reproductive structure. **3.** An undeveloped or incipient stage. *—v.* **budded, budding. 1.** To form or produce a bud or buds. **2.** To develop as from a bud. [ME *budde.*] **—bud'der** *n.*
Bu•da•pest (bōō'də-pĕst'). The capital of Hungary. Pop. 1,900,000.
Bud•dha (bōō'də, bŏŏd'ə). Title of Gautama Siddhartha. 563?–483? B.C. Indian philosopher; founder of Buddhism. [Sk, "awakened."]
Bud•dhism (bōō'dĭz'əm, bŏŏd'ĭz'-) *n.* Buddha's doctrine that suffering is inseparable from existence but that inward extinction of the self and the senses culminates in a state of illumination beyond both suffering and existence. **—Bud'dhist** *n.* & *adj.*
bud•dy (bŭd'ē) *n., pl.* **-dies.** A good friend; comrade; pal; chum. [Prob a baby-talk var of BROTHER.]
budge (bŭj) *v.* **budged, budging. 1.** To move or cause to move slightly. **2.** To alter or cause to alter a position or attitude. [< OF *bouger.*]
budg•er•i•gar (bŭj'ə-rē-gär') *n.* Also **budg•ie** (bŭj'ē). A small, colorful parakeet popular as a cage bird. [Native Australian name.]
budg•et (bŭj'ĭt) *n.* **1.** An itemized summary of probable expenditures and income for a given period, usually with a plan for meeting expenses. **2.** The total sum of money allocated for a particular purpose or time period. *—v.* **1.** To make a budget. **2.** To enter or plan for in a budget. [ME *bouget,* wallet.]
Bue•nos Ai•res (bwā'nəs âr'ēz, ir'ēz, bō'nəs). The capital of Argentina. Pop. 3,876,000.
buff¹ (bŭf) *n.* **1.** A soft, thick, undyed leather made chiefly from the skins of buffalo, elk, or oxen. **2.** The color of this leather; light yellowish brown. *—adj.* Made of or the color of buff. *—v.* To polish or shine with a soft cloth. [Orig, "buffalo."]
buff² (bŭf) *n.* One who is enthusiastic and knowledgeable about a given subject. [Orig a New York volunteer fireman < their buff uniforms.]
buf•fa•lo (bŭf'ə-lō') *n., pl.* **-loes** or **-los** or **buffalo. 1.** Any of several oxlike African or Asian mammals. **2.** The American bison. *—v. Slang.* To intimidate. [< Gk *boubalos,* African antelope, buffalo.]
Buf•fa•lo (bŭf'ə-lō'). A city of New York State. Pop. 463,000.
buff•er¹ (bŭf'ər) *n.* An implement used to shine or polish, as a soft cloth.
buff•er² (bŭf'ər) *n.* **1.** One that lessens, absorbs, or protects against the shock of an impact. **2.** A substance capable of maintaining the relative acid-base concentration in a solution by neutralizing, within limits, added acids or bases. [Prob < ME *buffe,* a blow.]
buf•fet¹ (bə-fā', bōō-) *n.* **1.** A sideboard. **2.** A counter for meals or refreshments. **3.** A meal at which guests serve themselves from dishes displayed on a table or sideboard. [F.]
buf•fet² (bŭf'ĭt) *n.* A blow or cuff with or as if with the hand. *—v.* **1.** To hit or strike against repeatedly. **2.** To force (one's way). [< OF.] **—buf'fet•er** *n.*
buf•foon (bə-fōōn') *n.* A clown; jester; fool. [< It *buffare,* to puff.] **—buf•foon'er•y** *n.*
bug (bŭg) *n.* **1.** Any of various often harmful insects. **2.** Any insect, spider, etc. **3.** *Informal.* A disease-producing microorganism. **4.** A mechanical, electrical, or other systemic defect

Buddha

or difficulty. **5.** *Slang.* An enthusiast; buff. **6.** A small hidden microphone or other device used for eavesdropping. *—v.* **bugged, bugging. 1.** *Slang.* To annoy; pester. **2.** To eavesdrop on, esp. with electronic devices. [?]

bug•a•boo (bŭg'ə-bo͞o') *n., pl.* **-boos.** A steady source of annoyance or concern. [Perh < Celt.]

bug•bear (bŭg'bâr') *n.* An object of obsessive dread. [< ME *bugge* + BEAR.]

bug-eyed (bŭg'īd') *adj. Slang.* Agog.

bug•gy (bŭg'ē) *n., pl.* **-gies.** A small light carriage. [?]

bu•gle (byo͞o'gəl) *n.* A trumpetlike instrument without keys or valves. [ME, buffalo, horn, bugle.] **—bu'gle** *v.* **(-gled, -gling). —bu'gler** *n.*

build (bĭld) *v.* **built** (bĭlt) or *archaic* **builded, building. 1.** To erect; construct. **2.** To fashion; create. **3.** To add to; develop. **4.** To establish a basis for. **—build up.** To construct or develop in stages. *—n.* The physical make-up of a person or thing. [< OE *byldan* < *bold,* a dwelling. See **bheu-.**] **—build'er** *n.*

build•ing (bĭl'dĭng) *n.* **1.** A structure; edifice. **2.** The act, process, or occupation of constructing.

built-in (bĭlt'ĭn') *adj.* Constructed as part of a larger unit; not detachable; permanent: *a built-in cabinet.*

Bu•jum•bu•ra (bo͞o'jəm-bo͝or'ə, bo͞o-jo͞om'-bo͝or'ə). The capital of Burundi. Pop. 47,000.

bulb (bŭlb) *n.* **1.** A rounded underground plant part, as of a tulip or onion, from which a new plant develops. **2.** A rounded object, projection, or part. **3.** An incandescent lamp or its glass housing. [L *bulbus,* bulb, onion.] **—bul'bar** *adj.*

bul•bous (bŭl'bəs) *adj.* **1.** Bulb-shaped. **2.** Growing from a bulb, as a tulip.

Bulg. Bulgaria; Bulgarian.

Bul•gar•i•a (bŭl-gâr'ē-ə, bo͝ol-). A Balkan republic on the Black Sea. Pop. 8,211,000. Cap. Sofia.

Bulgaria

Bul•gar•i•an (bŭl-gâr'ē-ən, bo͝ol-) *adj.* Of or pertaining to Bulgaria, its people, or their language. *—n.* **1.** Also **Bulgar** (bŭl'gər, bo͝ol'-gär'). A native of Bulgaria. **2.** The Slavic language spoken by Bulgarians.

bulge (bŭlj) *n.* A protruding part; an outward curve or a swelling. *—v.* **bulged, bulging.** To cause to curve outward; swell up. [< L *bulga,* leather bag.] **—bulg'y** *adj.*

bulk (bŭlk) *n.* **1.** Great size, mass, or volume. **2.** The major portion of something. *—v.* To be or appear to be massive in size; loom. [< ON *bulki,* cargo.] **—bulk'y** *adj.*

bulk•age (bŭl'kĭj) *n.* Any substance that stimulates peristalsis by increasing the bulk of material in the intestine.

bulk•head (bŭlk'hĕd') *n.* **1.** An upright partition dividing a ship into compartments. **2.** A wall or embankment constructed in a mine or tunnel. [< BULK.]

bull¹ (bo͝ol) *n.* **1. a.** The adult male of cattle or certain other large mammals. **b.** The uncastrated adult male of domestic cattle. **2.** One who buys commodities or securities in anticipation of a rise in prices. **3. Bull.** Taurus. **4.** *Slang.* Empty talk; nonsense. *—adj.* **1.** Male. **2.** Larger than others. **3.** Characterized by rising prices: *a bull market.* [< OE *bula* < ON *boli.*]

bull² (bo͝ol) *n.* A papal document. [< L *bulla,* bubble, seal.]

bull. bulletin.

bull•dog (bo͝ol'dôg', -dŏg') *n.* A stocky, short-haired dog with a large, square-jawed head. *—v.* **-dogged, -dogging.** To throw (a steer) by seizing its horns and twisting its neck.

bull•doze (bo͝ol'dōz') *v.* **-dozed, -dozing. 1.** To dig up or move with a bulldozer. **2.** *Slang.* To bully.

bull•doz•er (bo͝ol'dō'zər) *n.* A tractor having a metal scoop in front for moving earth and rocks.

bul•let (bo͝ol'ĭt) *n.* A cylindrical metallic projectile that is fired from a gun. [< L *bulla,* bubble, ball.]

bul•le•tin (bo͝ol'ə-tən, -tĭn) *n.* **1.** A printed or broadcast statement on a matter of public interest. **2.** A periodical published by an organization or society.

bull•fight (bo͝ol'fīt') *n.* A public spectacle, esp. in Spain and Mexico, in which a matador engages and usually executes a fighting bull. **—bull'fight'er** *n.* **—bull'fight'ing** *n.*

bull•finch (bo͝ol'fĭnch') *n.* A European bird with a short, thick bill and a red breast.

bull•frog (bo͝ol'frôg', -frŏg') *n.* A large frog with a deep, resonant croak.

bull•head (bo͝ol'hĕd') *n.* A North American freshwater catfish.

bull•head•ed (bo͝ol'hĕd'ĭd) *adj.* Stubborn; headstrong. **—bull'head'ed•ness** *n.*

bul•lion (bo͝ol'yən) *n.* Gold or silver metal. [< NF, "mint."]

bull•ish (bo͝ol'ĭsh) *adj.* **1.** Like a bull. **2.** Stubborn. **3.** Expecting a rise in stock-market prices. **—bull'ish•ness** *n.*

bul•lock (bo͝ol'ək) *n.* A steer or young bull. [< OE *bulluc,* dim of *bula,* BULL.]

bull•pen (bo͝ol'pĕn') *n.* **1.** A pen for confining bulls. **2.** An area where relief pitchers warm up during a baseball game.

bull's eye. Also **bull's-eye** (bo͝olz'ī'). The small central circle on a target or a shot that hits this circle.

bul•ly (bo͝ol'ē) *n., pl.* **-lies.** One who is habitually cruel to smaller or weaker people. *—v.* **-lied, -lying.** To behave like a bully. *—adj.* Excellent; splendid. [Orig "sweetheart."]

bul•rush (bo͝ol'rŭsh') *n.* Any of various tall grasslike sedges or similar marsh plants. [ME *bulrish.*]

bul•wark (bo͝ol'wərk, bŭl'-, -wôrk') *n.* **1.** A wall or wall-like structure for defense; rampart. **2.** Anything serving as a defense against attack or encroachment. [< MHG *bolwerc.*]

bum (bŭm) *n.* **1.** A tramp; hobo. **2.** One who seeks to live off others. *—v.* **bummed, bumming.** *Informal.* **1.** To live or acquire by begging and scavenging. **2.** To loaf. *—adj. Slang.* **1.** Of poor quality. **2.** Disabled; malfunctioning. [< earlier *bummer,* a loafer.]

bum•ble•bee (bŭm'bəl-bē') *n.* Any of various large, hairy bees.

bump (bŭmp) *v.* **1.** To strike or collide with. **2.** To knock. **3.** To displace; oust. *—n.* **1.** A light blow, collision, or jolt. **2.** A slight swelling or lump. [Imit.]

bump•er¹ (bŭm'pər) *n.* A device used to absorb the impact of a collision, esp. a horizontal metal bar attached to the front or rear of an automobile.

bump•er² (bŭm'pər) *n.* **1.** A drinking vessel filled to the brim. **2.** Something unusually large or full. *—adj.* Unusually abundant: *a bumper crop.* [Perh < BUMP.]

bump•kin (bŭmp'kĭn, bŭm'-) *n.* An awkward, untutored rustic. [Perh orig "Dutchman."]

bump•tious (bŭmp'shəs) *adj.* Crudely forward and self-assertive in behavior; pushy. [Perh a blend of BUMP and FRACTIOUS.]

bun (bŭn) *n.* **1.** A rounded, often sweetened roll. **2.** A tight roll of hair resembling this. [ME *bunne.*]

bunch (bŭnch) *n.* A group, cluster, or tuft. [ME *bunche.*] **—bunch** *v.* **—bunch'y** *adj.*

bun•co (bŭng'kō) *n., pl.* **-cos.** A swindle; confidence game. [Span *banca,* name of a card game, "bank."]

bun•dle (bŭnd'l) *n.* **1.** Anything bound, wrapped, or otherwise held together; package. **2.** *Slang.* A large sum of money. *—v.* **-dled, -dling.** To tie, wrap, fold, or otherwise secure together. **—bundle up.** To dress warmly. [ME *bundel.*] **—bun'dler** *n.*

bung (bŭng) *n.* A stopper for a bunghole. [< MDu *bonghe.*]

bun•ga•low (bŭng'gə-lō') *n.* A small cottage, usually of one story. [Perh < Hindi *banglā,* "of Bengal."]

bung•hole (bŭng'hōl') *n.* The hole in a cask, keg, or barrel through which liquid is poured in or drained out.

bun•gle (bŭng'gəl) *v.* **-gled, -gling.** To work, manage, or act ineptly or inefficiently. [Perh < Scand.] **—bun'gler** *n.*

bun•ion (bŭn'yən) *n.* A painful, inflamed swelling at the bursa of the big toe. [Prob < earlier dial *bunny, bony,* swelling.]

bunk¹ (bŭngk) *n.* A narrow bed attached like a shelf against a wall. [Poss short for BUNKER.]

bunk² (bŭngk) *n. Slang.* Bunkum.

bun•ker (bŭng'kər) *n.* **1.** A bin or tank for fuel storage, as on a ship. **2.** A sand trap serving as an obstacle on a golf course. **3.** A fortified earthwork. [Earlier Scot *bonker.*]

bun•kum (bŭng'kəm) *n.* Empty or meaningless talk. [< *Buncombe* County, North Carolina.]

bun•ny (bŭn'ē) *n., pl.* **-nies.** *Informal.* A rabbit. [< dial *bun,* squirrel.]

Bun•sen burner (bŭn'sən). A small, adjustable gas-burning laboratory burner. [< R.W. *Bunsen* (1811–1899), German chemist.]

bunt (bŭnt) *v.* **1.** To butt (something) with the head. **2.** *Baseball.* To tap (a pitched ball) with a half swing so that the ball rolls slowly in front of the infielders. *—n.* **1.** A butt. **2.** *Baseball.* **a.** The act of bunting. **b.** A bunted ball. [Prob < Celt.]

bunt•ing¹ (bŭn'tĭng) *n.* **1.** A light cloth used for making flags. **2.** Flags collectively. [?]

bunt•ing² (bŭn'tĭng) *n.* Any of various birds with short, cone-shaped bills. [ME *buntynge.*]

bunt•ing³ (bŭn'tĭng) *n.* A hooded sleeping bag for infants. [?]

buoy (bo͞o'ē, boi) *n.* **1.** A float moored in water as a warning of danger or as a marker for a channel. **2.** A device made of buoyant material for keeping a person afloat. *—v.* **1.** To mark (a water hazard or a channel) with a buoy. **2.** To keep afloat. **3.** To uplift the spirits of. [ME *boye.*]

buoy•an•cy (boi'ən-sē, bo͞o'yən-) *n.* **1.** The tendency to remain afloat in a liquid or to rise in air or gas. **2.** The upward force of a fluid. **3.** The ability to recover quickly from setbacks. **4.** Cheerfulness. —**buoy'ant** *adj.*

bur[1] (bûr) *n.* Also **burr. 1.** A seed, fruit, etc., encased in a rough, prickly covering. **2.** Any of various rotary cutting tools designed to be attached to a drill. [ME *burre.*]

bur[2]. Variant of **burr.**

Bur. 1. bureau. **2.** Burma.

bur•den (bûrd'n) *n.* **1. a.** Something that is carried. **b.** Something that is difficult to bear. **2.** A responsibility or duty. **3.** The amount of cargo a vessel can carry. —*v.* To load or overload; weigh down; oppress. [< OE *byrthen.* See **bher-**[1].] —**bur'den•some** *adj.*

bur•dock (bûr'dŏk') *n.* A coarse, weedy plant with bristly purplish flowers.

bu•reau (byo͝or'ō) *n., pl.* **-reaus** or **bureaux** (byo͝or'ōz). **1.** A chest of drawers. **2.** A government department or subdivision of a department. **3.** An office or business that performs a specific duty. [F.]

bu•reauc•ra•cy (byo͝o-rŏk'rə-sē) *n., pl.* **-cies. 1. a.** Administration of a government chiefly through bureaus. **b.** The nonelective officials staffing such bureaus. **2.** Government marked by diffusion of authority among numerous offices and adherence to inflexible rules of operation. **3.** Any unwieldy administration. [BUREAU + -CRACY.] —**bu'reau•crat'** (byo͝or'ə-krăt') *n.* —**bu'reau•crat'ic** *adj.*

burg (bûrg) *n.* A city or town. [< OE. See **bhergh-**[2].]

bur•geon (bûr'jən) *v.* **1.** To put forth new buds, leaves, etc.; begin to sprout or grow. **2.** To develop rapidly; flourish. [< ME *burjon,* a bud.]

burg•er (bûr'gər) *n. Informal.* A hamburger.

bur•gess (bûr'jĭs) *n.* A freeman, citizen, or representative of an English borough. [< OF *burgeis.*]

burgh (bûrg) *n.* A chartered town in Scotland. [Scot, var of BOROUGH.]

burgh•er (bûr'gər) *n.* A solid citizen; bourgeois. [G *Bürger* or Du *burger.*]

bur•glar (bûr'glər) *n.* One who commits burglary; housebreaker. [< ML *burgulator.*]

bur•glar•i•ous (bər-glâr'ē-əs) *adj.* Of or pertaining to burglary.

bur•glar•ize (bûr'glə-rīz') *v.* **-ized, -izing.** To commit burglary in.

bur•glar•proof (bûr'glər-pro͞of') *adj.* Secure against burglary.

bur•gla•ry (bûr'glə-rē) *n., pl.* **-ries.** The crime of breaking into and entering a house with intent to commit a felony.

bur•go•mas•ter (bûr'gə-măs'tər, -mäs'tər) *n.* The principal magistrate of some European cities, comparable to a mayor. [Partial trans of Du *burgemeester.*]

Bur•gun•dy (bûr'gən-dē) *n., pl.* **-dies. 1.** A red or white wine produced in Burgundy, a region of SE France. **2. burgundy.** Dark red.

bur•i•al (bĕr'ē-əl) *n.* The interment of a dead body. [< OE *byrgels* (pl). See **bhergh-**[1].]

burl (bûrl) *n.* **1.** A rounded excrescence on a tree trunk or branch. **2.** The wood from such an excrescence. [< OF *bourle.*]

bur•lap (bûr'lăp') *n.* A coarsely woven cloth of jute, hemp, etc. [?]

bur•lesque (bər-lĕsk') *n.* **1.** Any ludicrous or mocking imitation. **2.** Vaudeville entertainment characterized by ribald comedy and display of nudity. —*v.* **-lesqued, -lesquing.** To imitate mockingly. [< It *burlesco.*]

bur•ly (bûr'lē) *adj.* **-lier, -liest.** Heavy and strong. [ME *burli, borlich,* stately, big.]

Bur•ma (bûr'mə). A republic of SE Asia. Pop. 24,229,000. Cap. Rangoon.

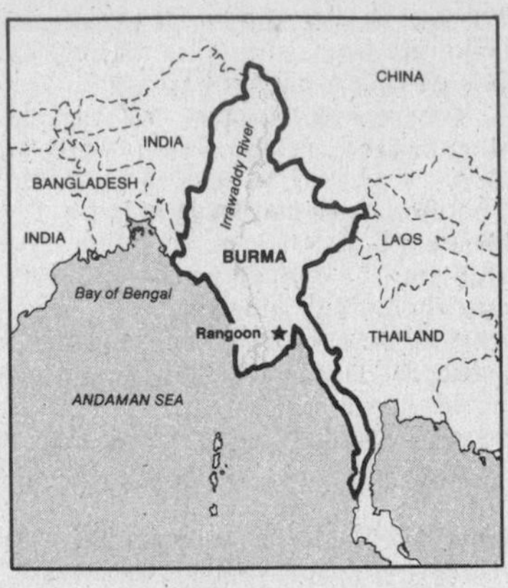

Burma

Bur•mese (bər-mēz', -mēs') *adj.* Of or pertaining to Burma, its people, or their language. —*n., pl.* **-mese. 1.** A native of Burma. **2.** The Sino-Tibetan language of Burma.

burn (bûrn) *v.* **burned** or **burnt, burning. 1.** To undergo or cause to undergo combustion. **2. a.** To destroy or be destroyed by fire. **b.** To damage or be damaged by fire or heat. **3.** To produce by fire or heat: *burn a clearing in the brush.* **4.** To use as a fuel. **5.** To impart a sensation of intense heat to: *The chili burned his mouth.* **6.** To emit heat or light by or as if by means of fire. **7.** To feel or look hot. **8.** To be consumed with strong emotion. —*n.* **1.** An injury produced by fire, heat, or a heat-producing agent. **2.** *Aerospace.* One firing of a rocket. [< OE *beornan, byrnan* and *bærnan.* See **bhreu-**[2].]

burn•er (bûr'nər) *n.* **1.** The part of a stove that produces heat. **2.** A device in which something is burned: *an oil burner.*

bur•nish (bûr'nĭsh) *v.* To polish or become polished by or as if by rubbing. [< OF *burnir, brunir,* "to make brown."] —**bur'nish** *n.*

bur•noose (bər-no͞os') *n.* A hooded cloak worn by Arabs. [< Ar *bournous.*]

Burns (bûrnz), **Robert.** 1759–1796. Scottish poet.

burnt (bûrnt). Alternate *p.t.* & *p.p.* of **burn.** —*adj.* Affected by or as if by burning.

burp (bûrp) *n.* A belch. [Imit.] —**burp** *v.*

burr[1] (bûr) *n.* Also **bur. 1.** A rough trilling of the letter *r,* as in Scottish pronunciation. **2.** A whirring sound.

burr[2]. Variant of **bur.**

bur•ro (bûr'ō, bo͝or'ō) *n., pl.* **-ros.** A small donkey. [Span.]

bur•row (bûr'ō) *n.* A hole or tunnel dug in the ground by an animal, such as a rabbit or mole. —*v.* **1.** To dig a burrow. **2.** To move or form by or as if by tunneling. [ME *borow.*]

bur•sa (bûr'sə) *n., pl.* **-sae** (-sē) or **-sas.** A saclike bodily cavity, esp. one located between joints. [< Gk, bag, purse.]

bur•sar (bûr'sər, -sär') *n.* An official in charge of funds, as at a college. [< Gk *bursa,* purse.]

bur•si•tis (bər-sī'tĭs) *n.* Inflammation of a bursa, esp. of the shoulder, elbow, or knee joints.

burst (bûrst) *v.* **burst, bursting. 1.** To force open or fly apart suddenly, esp. from internal pressure. **2.** To be full to the breaking point. **3.** To emerge suddenly and in full force. **4.** To become audible or visible suddenly. **5.** To give sudden utterance or expression: *burst into song.* —*n.* **1.** The act or result of bursting; a rupture or explosion. **2.** A sudden outbreak. [< OE *berstan.* See **bhres-.**]

Bu•run•di (bo͞o-ro͞on'dē). A country of C Africa. Pop. 3,274,000. Cap. Bujumbura.

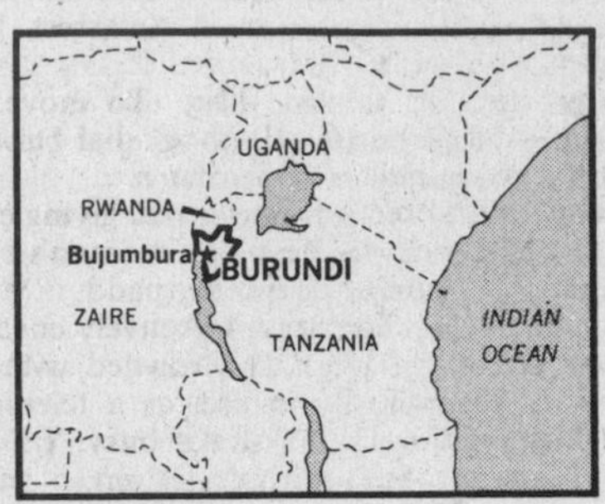

Burundi

bur•y (bĕr'ē) *v.* **-ied, -ying. 1.** To place in the ground and cover with earth. **2.** To place (a dead body) in a grave or tomb. **3.** To hide; conceal. [< OE *byrgan.* See **bhergh-**[1].]

bus (bŭs) *n., pl.* **buses** or **busses.** A large motor vehicle for carrying passengers. —*v.* **bused** or **bussed, busing** or **bussing.** *Informal.* To transport in a bus. [Short for OMNIBUS.]

bus. business.

bus boy. A waiter's assistant.

bus•by (bŭz'bē) *n., pl.* **-bies.** A tall fur hat worn in certain regiments of the British Army. [?]

bush (bo͝osh) *n.* **1.** A low, branching, woody plant; shrub. **2.** Land covered with dense shrubby growth. **3.** A dense growth or tuft. —*v.* To form a dense, tufted growth. [ME *busshe.*] —**bush'y** *adj.*

bushed (bo͝osht) *adj. Informal.* Extremely tired; exhausted.

bush•el (bo͝osh'əl) *n.* **1.** A U.S. Customary System unit of volume or capacity, used in dry measure and equal to 4 pecks or 2,150.42 cubic inches. **2.** A corresponding British Imperial System unit, used in dry and liquid measure, equal to 2,219.36 cubic inches. [< OF *boissiel.*]

bush•ing (bo͝osh'ĭng) *n.* A fixed or removable metal lining used to constrain, guide, or reduce friction. [< earlier *bush.*]

Bush•man (bo͝osh'mən) *n.* A member of a nomadic Negroid people of SW Africa.

bush•mas•ter (bo͝osh'măs'tər, -mäs'tər) *n.* A large, venomous tropical American snake.

bush•whack (bo͝osh'hwăk') *v.* **1.** To make one's way through thick woods by cutting away bushes and branches. **2.** To ambush. —**bush'whack'er** *n.*

busi•ness (bĭz'nĭs) *n.* **1.** The occupation in which a person is engaged. **2.** Commercial, industrial, or professional dealings. **3.** Any commercial establishment. **4.** Volume of commercial trade. **5.** Commercial policy or practice. **6.** One's concern or interest: *"The business of America is business."* (Calvin Coolidge). **7.** An affair or matter: *a peculiar business.* —**mean business.** To be in earnest. [< OE *bisignis,* care, solicitude < *bisig,* BUSY.]

busi•ness•like (bĭz'nĭs-līk') *adj.* Methodical; efficient.

bus•kin (bŭs'kĭn) *n.* 1. A laced half boot worn by actors of Greek and Roman tragedies. 2. Tragedy. [< OF *bouzequin.*]

bus•ses. Alternate *pl.* of **bus.**

bust[1] (bŭst) *n.* 1. A woman's bosom. 2. A piece of sculpture representing a person's head, shoulders, and upper chest. [< It *busto,* piece of sculpture.]

bust[2] (bŭst). *Slang. v.* 1. To burst or break. 2. To make or become short of money. 3. To demote. 4. To punch. 5. To place under arrest. *—n.* 1. A failure. 2. A time of widespread financial depression. 3. An arrest. [Var of BURST.]

bus•tle[1] (bŭs'əl) *v.* **-tled, -tling.** To move energetically and busily. [Prob < dial *busk,* to prepare.] **—bus'tle** *n.* **—bus'tler** *n.*

bus•tle[2] (bŭs'əl) *n.* A frame or pad giving extra fullness at the upper back of a woman's skirt. [Perh < G *Buschel,* a bunch, pad.]

bus•y (bĭz'ē) *adj.* **-ier, -iest.** 1. Actively engaged in some form of work. 2. Crowded with activity. 3. Temporarily in use, as a telephone line. *—v.* **-ied, -ying.** To make busy. [< OE *bysig, bisig.*] **—bus'i•ly** (bĭz'ə-lē) *adv.* **—bus'y•ness** *n.*

bus•y•bod•y (bĭz'ē-bŏd'ē) *n.* One who pries into the affairs of others.

but (bŭt; *unstressed* bət) *conj.* 1. On the contrary. 2. Contrary to expectation; however. 3. Except; save. 4. Except that: *They should have resisted but that they lacked courage.* 5. Without the result that: *It never rains but it pours.* 6. Other than: *I have no goal but to end war.* 7. That. Often used after a negative. 8. That . . . not. Used after a negative or question: *There never is a tax law presented but someone will oppose it.* 9. Who . . . not; which . . . not: *None came to him but were treated well.* *—prep.* With the exception of; barring; save. **—but for.** Were it not for. *—adv.* No more than; only; just. **—all but.** Nearly; almost: *His poem is all but finished.* *—n.* An objection, restriction, or exception: *no ifs, ands, or buts.* [< OE *būtan.* See **ud-.**]

bu•tane (byo͞o'tān') *n.* Either of two isomers of a gaseous hydrocarbon, C_4H_{10}, produced synthetically from petroleum and used as a household fuel, refrigerant, and aerosol propellant.

butch•er (bo͝och'ər) *n.* 1. One who slaughters and dresses animals for food. 2. One who sells meat. 3. A cruel or wanton killer. *—v.* 1. To slaughter or dress (animals). 2. To kill cruelly or wantonly. 3. To botch; bungle. [< OF *bouchier.*]

but•ler (bŭt'lər) *n.* A chief male servant in a household. [< OF *bouteillier,* a bottle bearer.]

butt[1] (bŭt) *v.* To hit with the head or horns. **—butt in** (or **into**). *Informal.* To meddle. [< NF *buter, boter.*]

butt[2] (bŭt) *n.* A person or thing serving as an object of ridicule. [ME *butte,* target.]

butt[3] (bŭt) *n.* 1. The larger end of something: *the butt of a rifle.* 2. A short or broken remnant. [ME *butte,* thicker end.]

butte (byo͞ot) *n.* A hill rising abruptly above the surrounding area and having sloping sides and a flat top. [F.]

but•ter (bŭt'ər) *n.* 1. A soft, yellowish, fatty substance churned from milk or cream and used as a food. 2. A similar substance. *—v.* 1. To put butter on. 2. *Informal.* To flatter. [< OE *butere* < Gmc < Gk *bouturon,* "cow cheese."]

but•ter•cup (bŭt'ər-kŭp') *n.* A plant with glossy yellow flowers.

but•ter•fat (bŭt'ər-făt') *n.* The oily content of milk, from which butter is made.

but•ter•fin•gers (bŭt'ər-fĭng'gərz) *n.* *(takes sing. v.).* A clumsy or awkward person who drops things. **—but'ter•fin'gered** *adj.*

but•ter•fly (bŭt'ər-flī') *n., pl.* **-flies.** Any of various narrow-bodied insects with four broad, usually colorful wings.

but•ter•milk (bŭt'ər-mĭlk') *n.* The sour liquid that remains after the butter has been churned from milk.

but•ter•nut (bŭt'ər-nŭt') *n.* 1. The oily, edible nut of a North American tree. 2. A tree bearing such nuts.

but•ter•scotch (bŭt'ər-skŏch') *n.* A candy or flavoring made from melted butter and brown sugar. [Perh orig made in Scotland.]

butt joint. A joint formed by two abutting surfaces.

but•tocks (bŭt'əks) *pl.n.* The two rounded parts of the lower back. [ME.]

but•ton (bŭt'n) *n.* 1. A small knob, disk, etc., esp. one sewn on a garment as a fastener or trimming. 2. Any of various objects of similar appearance. **—on the button.** *Informal.* Exactly. *—v.* To fasten with a button or buttons. [< OF *bouton,* bud, button.]

but•ton•hole (bŭt'n-hōl') *n.* A slit or loop through which a button is inserted. *—v.* **-holed, -holing.** To accost and detain in conversation.

but•tress (bŭt'rĭs) *n.* 1. A structure, usually brick or stone, built against a wall for support. 2. Anything that serves to support. [< OF *(ars) bouterez,* thrusting (arch).] **—but'tress** *v.*

bux•om (bŭk'səm) *adj.* Ample of figure: *a buxom woman.* [Earlier flexible, gay < OE *būgan,* to bend. See **bheug-.**]

buy (bī) *v.* **bought, buying.** 1. To acquire in exchange for money; purchase. 2. To be capable of purchasing. 3. To acquire by sacrifice or exchange. 4. To bribe. *—n.* 1. Anything bought. 2. *Informal.* A bargain. [< OE *bycgan* < Gmc **bugjan.*]

buy•er (bī'ər) *n.* 1. One who buys; a customer. 2. One who buys for a retail store.

buzz (bŭz) *v.* 1. To make a low droning or vibrating sound like that of a bee. 2. To talk excitedly in low tones. [ME *bussen,* to drone (imit).] **—buzz** *n.*

buz•zard (bŭz'ərd) *n.* 1. Any of various North American vultures. 2. *Chiefly Brit.* Any of various broad-winged hawks. [< OF *busard.*]

buzz•er (bŭz'ər) *n.* Any of various electric signaling devices that make a buzzing sound.

B.V. Blessed Virgin.

bx. box.

by (bī) *prep.* 1. Next to. 2. With the use of; through. 3. Up to and beyond; past. 4. In the period of; during: *sleeping by day.* 5. Not later than: *by 5:00 P.M.* 6. In the amount of: *letters by the thousands.* 7. To the extent of: *shorter by two inches.* 8. According to: *by his own account.* 9. In the presence or name of. 10. Through the agency or action of: *killed by a bullet.* 11. In succession to; after: *day by day.* 12. In behalf of; for: *He does well by his employees.* 13. —Used to link certain expressions to be taken together and indicating: a. multiplication of quantities. b. coordination of measurements: *a room 12 by 18 feet.* *—adv.* 1. On hand; nearby: *stand by.* 2. Aside; away: *He put it by for later.* 3. Up to, alongside, and past: *The car raced by.* 4. Into the past: *as years go by.* **—by and large.** On the whole; for the most part. [OE *bī, bi, be.* See **ambhi.**]

bye (bī) *n.* The position of one who draws no opponent for a round in a tournament and so advances to the next round. [< BY (aside, hence "secondary").]

Bye•lo•rus•sian (byĕl'ō-rŭsh'ən) *n.* 1. A native of the Byelorussian S.S.R. 2. The language of the Byelorussians. **—Bye'lo•rus'sian** *adj.*

Byelorussian Soviet Socialist Republic. Also **Bye•lo•rus•sia** (byĕl'ō-rŭsh'ə). A constituent republic of the Soviet Union, in the W, in Europe. Pop. 9,003,000. Cap. Minsk.

by•gone (bī'gôn', -gŏn') *adj.* Past: *bygone days.* *—n.* **—let bygones be bygones.** To let past differences be forgotten.

by•law (bī'lô') *n.* A law or rule governing the internal affairs of an organization. [ME *bilawe, bylawe,* "village law."]

by-line (bī'līn') *n.* A line at the head of a newspaper or magazine article with the author's name. **—by'-lin'er** *n.*

by-pass (bī'păs', -päs') *n.* 1. A road or highway that passes around or to one side of an obstructed area. 2. *Elec.* A shunt. *—v.* To go around instead of through.

by-path (bī'păth', -päth') *n.* An indirect or little-used path.

by-prod•uct (bī'prŏd'əkt) *n.* Something produced in the making of something else.

By•ron (bī'rən), **George Gordon, Lord.** 1788–1824. English poet. **—By•ron'ic** *adj.*

by•stand•er (bī'stăn'dər) *n.* One who is present at some event without participating in it.

by•street (bī'strēt') *n.* A side street.

by•way (bī'wā') *n.* 1. A side road. 2. A secondary or overlooked field of study.

by•word (bī'wûrd') *n.* 1. A proverb. 2. One that proverbially represents a type, class, or quality. [< OE *bīword* : BY + WORD.]

Byz•an•tine Empire (bĭz'ən-tēn', -tīn', bĭ-zăn'-tĭn). The eastern part of the later Roman Empire, continuing after the fall of Rome as its successor until 1453.

By•zan•ti•um (bĭ-zăn'shē-əm, -tē-əm). 1. A Greek city on the site of which the city of Constantinople (now Istanbul) was founded in A.D. 330. 2. The Byzantine Empire and its culture.

Cc

c, C (sē) *n.* **1.** The 3rd letter of the English alphabet. **2.** The 3rd in a series. **3.** The 3rd highest in quality.
c **1.** carat. **2.** centi-. **3.** cubic.
C **1.** *Elec.* capacitance. **2.** carbon. **3.** centigrade. **4.** coulomb. **5.** *Mus.* The 1st tone in the scale of C major. **6.** The Roman numeral for 100 (L *centum*).
c. **1.** cape. **2.** cent. **3.** century. **4.** chapter. **5.** circa. **6.** copy. **7.** copyright. **8.** cup.
C. **1.** cape. **2.** Catholic. **3.** cent. **4.** century. **5.** chapter. **6.** church. **7.** circa. **8.** city. **9.** copyright. **10.** corps. **11.** court.
ca circa.
Ca calcium.
CAA Civil Aeronautics Authority.
cab (kăb) *n.* **1.** A taxicab. **2.** The compartment of a heavy vehicle, in which the operator sits. [Short for TAXICAB and CABIN.]
ca•bal (kə-băl′) *n.* **1.** A conspiratorial group. **2.** A conspiracy. [F *cabale.*]
ca•ban•a (kə-băn′ə, -băn′yə) *n.* A shelter on a beach used as a bathhouse. [Span *cabaña.*]
cab•a•ret (kăb′ə-rā′) *n.* A restaurant providing short programs of live entertainment. [F.]
cab•bage (kăb′ĭj) *n.* A plant having a compact, rounded head of leaves eaten as a vegetable. [< ONF *caboche.*]
cab•in (kăb′ĭn) *n.* **1.** A small, roughly built house. **2. a.** Living quarters on a ship. **b.** An enclosed compartment on a boat or airplane. [< LL *capanna,* hut, cabin.]
cab•i•net (kăb′ə-nĭt) *n.* **1.** A cupboardlike repository with shelves, drawers, or compartments for the safekeeping or display of objects. **2.** Often **Cabinet.** The body of persons appointed by a chief of state or prime minister to head departments of the government and act as his advisers. [< ONF *cabine,* a gambling house.] **—cab′i•net** *adj.*
ca•ble (kā′bəl) *n.* **1.** A large-diameter steel or fiber rope. **2.** A bound or sheathed group of mutually insulated conductors. **3.** A cablegram. *—v.* **-bled, -bling.** To send a cablegram to. [< ML *capulum,* rope for fastening cattle.]
ca•ble•gram (kā′bəl-grăm′) *n.* A telegram sent by submarine cable.
ca•boose (kə-bōōs′) *n.* The last car on a freight train, having kitchen and sleeping facilities for the crew. [Prob < Du *kabuis.*]
ca•ca•o (kə-kä′ō, -kā′ō) *n.* **1.** The seed of a tropical American tree, used in making chocolate and cocoa. **2.** The tree itself. [< Nah *cacahuatl,* cacao beans.]
cache (kăsh) *n.* **1.** A hiding place used for storage. **2.** A place for concealment and safekeeping. **3.** A store of goods hidden in a cache. [< F *cacher,* to hide.] **—cache** *v.* **(cached, caching).**
ca•chet (kă-shā′) *n.* **1.** A seal on a letter or document. **2.** A mark of distinction, individuality, or authenticity. [< OF *cacher,* to hide, press together.]
cack•le (kăk′əl) *v.* **-led, -ling.** **1.** To make the shrill cry characteristic of a hen after laying an egg. **2.** To laugh or talk in a similar manner. *—n.* The act or sound of cackling. [ME *cakelen.*] **—cack′ler** *n.*
ca•coph•o•ny (kă-kŏf′ə-nē) *n., pl.* **-nies.** Jarring, discordant sound. [< Gk *kakophōnos,* having a bad sound.] **—ca•coph′o•nous** *adj.* **—ca•coph′o•nous•ly** *adv.*
cac•tus (kăk′təs) *n., pl.* **-ti** (-tī′) or **-tuses.** Any of various leafless, fleshy-stemmed, often spiny plants of arid regions. [< Gk *kaktos,* the *cardoon* (a thistlelike plant).]
cad (kăd) *n.* An ungentlemanly man. [Short for CADDIE.] **—cad′dish** *adj.*
ca•dav•er (kə-dăv′ər) *n.* A dead body. [L.] **—ca•dav′er•ic** *adj.*
ca•dav•er•ous (kə-dăv′ər-əs) *adj.* Corpselike; gaunt or pallid.
cad•die (kăd′ē). Also **cad•dy.** *n., pl.* **-dies.** One hired to assist a golfer, esp. by carrying his clubs. *—v.* **-died, -dying.** To serve as a caddie. [F *cadet,* CADET.]
Cad•do•an (kăd′ō-ən) *n.* A family of North American Indian languages formerly spoken in areas W of the Mississippi.
cad•dy (kăd′ē) *n., pl.* **-dies.** A small boxlike container, esp. for tea. [< Malay *kati,* a unit of weight.]
-cade. *comb. form.* Procession or parade: **motorcade.**
ca•dence (kād′əns) *n.* **1.** Rhythmic flow or movement. **2.** Vocal inflection or modulation. **3.** A progression of chords moving to a harmonic close. [< OIt *cadenza.*] **—ca′denced** *adj.*
ca•den•za (kə-dĕn′zə) *n.* An ornamental flourish or section, as near the end of a movement of a concerto. [< OIt, CADENCE.]
ca•det (kə-dĕt′) *n.* **1.** A student training to be a military officer. **2.** A younger son or brother. [F.] **—ca•det′ship′** *n.*
cadge (kăj) *v.* **cadged, cadging.** To get by begging; mooch. [< ME *cadgear,* carrier.] **—cadg′er** *n.*
cad•mi•um (kăd′mē-əm) *n. Symbol* **Cd** A soft, bluish-white metallic element used in low-friction alloys, solders, dental amalgams, and nickel-cadmium storage batteries. Atomic number 48, atomic weight 112.40. [< L *cadmia,* zinc ore.] **—cad′mic** (-mĭk) *adj.*
cad•re (kăd′rē) *n.* A group of trained personnel forming the nucleus of an organization. [< L *quādrum,* a square.]
ca•du•ce•us (kə-d/y/ōō′sē-əs) *n., pl.* **-cei** (-sē-ī′). The winged, snake-entwined staff of Hermes, used as the symbol of the medical profession. [L *cādūceus.*]
cae•cum. Variant of **cecum.**
Cae•sar (sē′zər), **Gaius Julius.** 100–44 B.C. Roman statesman and general.
Cae•sar•e•an (sĭ-zâr′ē-ən). Also **Cae•sar•i•an, Ce•sar•e•an, Ce•sar•i•an.** *adj.* Pertaining to Caesar. *—n.* A **Caesarean section.**
Caesarean section. Also **caesarean section.** A surgical incision through the abdominal wall and uterus, performed to extract a fetus. [< a tradition that Julius *Caesar* was born by this operation and named *ā caesō mātris ūterē,* "from the *incised* womb of his mother."]
Cae•sar•ism (sē′zə-rĭz′əm) *n.* Military dictatorship or absolute government. **—Cae′sar•ist** *n.* **—Cae′sar•is′tic** *adj.*
cae•si•um. Variant of **cesium.**
cae•su•ra (sĭ-zhŏŏr′ə, -z/y/ŏŏr′ə) *n.* A pause in phrasing a metrical line. [L, "a cutting off."] **—cae•su′ral, cae•su′ric** *adj.*
C.A.F. cost and freight.
ca•fé (kă-fā′, kə-) *n.* A restaurant, bar, etc. [F, coffee.]
ca•fé au lait (kă-fā′ ō lā′). **1.** Coffee diluted with hot milk. **2.** A light coffee color. [F, "coffee with milk."]
caf•e•te•ri•a (kăf′ə-tîr′ē-ə) *n.* A restaurant in which customers carry their meals from a service counter to tables. [< Span *cafetero,* coffee maker or seller.]
caf•feine (kă-fēn′, kăf′ē-ĭn) *n.* Also **caf•fein.** A bitter white alkaloid, $C_8H_{10}N_4O_2 \cdot H_2O$, derived from coffee, tea, and cola nuts, and used as a stimulant and diuretic. [< G *Kaffee,* coffee.]
caf•tan (kăf′tən, kăf-tăn′) *n.* A long, coatlike garment worn in the Near East. [Russ *kaftan.*]
cage (kāj) *n.* **1.** A barred or grated enclosure for confining birds or animals. **2.** A similar enclosure or structure. *—v.* **caged, caging.** To confine in or as in a cage. [< L *cavea,* a hollow, enclosure.]
cag•ey (kā′jē) *adj.* **-ier, -iest.** Also **cag•y.** Wary; shrewd; careful; cautious. [?] **—cag′i•ly** *adv.* **—cag′i•ness** *n.*
ca•hoots (kə-hōōts′) *pl.n.* **—in cahoots.** In questionable collaboration. [Perh < F *cahute,* cabin, hut.]
Cain (kān). Eldest son of Adam and Eve, who killed his brother Abel. Genesis 4. **—raise Cain.** To create a disturbance; make trouble.
cairn (kârn) *n.* A mound of stones erected as a landmark or memorial. [ME *carne.*]
Cai•ro (kī′rō). The capital of Egypt. Pop. 3,346,000.
cais•son (kā′sŏn′, -sən) *n.* **1.** A watertight structure within which construction work is carried on. **2. a.** A large box used to hold ammunition. **b.** A horse-drawn vehicle, usu-

Julius Caesar

ă pat/ā ate/âr care/ä bar/b bib/ch chew/d deed/ĕ pet/ē be/f fit/g gag/h hat/hw what/
ĭ pit/ī pie/îr pier/j judge/k kick/l lid, fatal/m mum/n no, sudden/ng sing/ŏ pot/ō go/

ally two-wheeled, once used to carry ammunition. [< OF *casson.*]

cais•son disease. A disorder caused by too rapid return from high pressure to atmospheric pressure, characterized by cramps, paralysis, and eventual death unless treated by gradual decompression.

cai•tiff (kā′tĭf) *n.* A base coward; wretch. [< L *captīvus,* CAPTIVE.]

ca•jole (kə-jōl′) *v.* **-joled, -joling.** To coax; wheedle. [F *cajoler,* "to chatter like a caged jay."] **—ca•jol′er** *n.* **—ca•jol′er•y** *n.*

Ca•jun (kā′jən) *n.* A native of Louisiana descended from French exiles from Acadia.

cake (kāk) *n.* **1.** A sweet food made from baked batter or dough. **2.** A thin baked or fried portion of batter or other food. **3.** A shaped mass, as of soap. *—v.* **caked, caking.** To make or become a hard or compact mass. [< ON *kaka.*]

cal calorie.

cal. **1.** calendar. **2.** caliber.

Cal. California (unofficial).

cal•a•bash (kăl′ə-băsh′) *n.* A large, hard-shelled gourd often used as a utensil. [< Span *calabaza.*]

cal•a•boose (kăl′ə-bōōs′) *n. Slang.* A jail. [< Span *calabozo,* a dungeon.]

cal•a•mine (kăl′ə-mīn′, -mĭn) *n.* A pink powder of zinc oxide with a small amount of ferric oxide, dissolved in mineral oils and used in skin lotions. [< ML *calamīna.*]

ca•lam•i•ty (kə-lăm′ə-tē) *n., pl.* **-ties.** A cause of great distress; disaster. [< L *calamitās.*] **—ca•lam′i•tous** *adj.* **—ca•lam′i•tous•ly** *adv.* **—ca•lam′i•tous•ness** *n.*

cal•car•e•ous (kăl-kâr′ē-əs) *adj.* Of or containing calcium carbonate, calcium, or limestone; chalky.

calci–. *comb. form.* Lime or calcium. [< L *calx,* lime, limestone.]

cal•cif•er•ous (kăl sĭf′ər-əs) *adj* Of or containing calcium or calcium carbonate.

cal•ci•fy (kăl′sə-fī′) *v.* **-fied, -fying.** To make or become stony or chalky by deposition of calcium salts. **—cal′ci•fi•ca′tion** *n.*

cal•ci•mine (kăl′sə-mīn′) *n.* A white or tinted liquid containing zinc oxide, water, glue, and coloring matter, used as a wash for walls and ceilings.

cal•cine (kăl′sīn′, kăl-sīn′) *v.* **-cined, -cining.** To heat to a high temperature but below the melting or fusing point, causing loss of moisture, reduction, or oxidation. [< L *calx,* lime.] **—cal′ci•na′tion** *n.*

cal•cite (kăl′sīt′) *n.* A common crystalline form of natural calcium carbonate. **—cal•cit′ic** (-sĭt′ĭk) *adj.*

cal•ci•um (kăl′sē-əm) *n. Symbol* **Ca** A silvery metallic element that occurs in bone, shells, limestone, and gypsum, and forms compounds used to make plaster, quicklime, cement, and metallurgic and electronic materials. Atomic number 20, atomic weight 40.08. [< L *calx,* lime, limestone < Gk *khalix,* pebble.]

calcium carbonate. A colorless or white crystalline compound, $CaCO_3$, occurring naturally in chalk, limestone, and marble, and used in manufactured products including commercial chalk, medicines, and dentifrices.

calcium chloride. A white deliquescent compound, $CaCl_2$, used chiefly as a drying agent, refrigerant, and preservative.

calcium hydroxide. A soft white powder, $Ca(OH)_2$, used in making cements, paints, hard rubber products, and petrochemicals.

calcium oxide. A white, caustic, lumpy powder, CaO, used in manufacturing steel, glassmaking, waste treatment, and insecticides.

cal•cu•late (kăl′kyə-lāt′) *v.* **-lated, -lating. 1.** To compute mathematically. **2.** To estimate; reckon. **3.** To intend; plan. [< L *calculus,* small stone (used in reckoning).] **—cal′cu•la•ble** *adj.* **—cal′cu•la•bly** *adv.*

cal•cu•lat•ed (kăl′kyə-lā′tĭd) *adj.* Estimated with forethought: *a calculated risk.* **—cal′cu•lat′ed•ly** *adv.*

cal•cu•lat•ing (kăl′kyə-lā′tĭng) *adj.* Shrewd; scheming; conniving.

cal•cu•la•tion (kăl′kyə-lā′shən) *n.* **1.** The act, process, or result of calculating. **2.** Deliberation; foresight.

cal•cu•la•tor (kăl′kyə-lā′tər) *n.* A keyboard machine for the automatic performance of arithmetic operations.

cal•cu•lus (kăl′kyə-ləs) *n., pl.* **-li** (-lī′) or **-luses. 1.** An abnormal mineral concretion in the body, such as a stone in the gallbladder or kidney. **2.** The combined mathematics of differential and integral calculus. [L, small stone used in reckoning.]

Cal•cut•ta (kăl-kŭt′ə). A city of NE India. Pop. 2,927,000.

cal•dron (kôl′drən) *n.* Also **caul•dron.** A large kettle or vat. [< L *caldāria,* warm bath.]

cal•en•dar (kăl′ən-dər) *n.* **1.** A system of reckoning time divisions, esp. in years, months, weeks, and days. **2.** A table showing such divisions, usually for a year. **3.** A chronological list or schedule. *—v.* To enter on a calendar; schedule. [< L *kalendārium,* a moneylender's account book.]

cal•ends (kăl′əndz) *n., pl.* **-ends.** The first day of the month in the ancient Roman calendar. [< L *kalendae.*]

calf[1] (kăf, käf) *n., pl.* **calves** (kăvz, kävz). **1.** The young of cattle or certain other large mammals, as the elephant. **2.** Also **calf•skin** (kăf′skĭn′, käf′-). **a.** The hide of a calf. **b.** Fine leather made from it. [< OE *cealf* < Gmc **kalbam.*]

MONTHS OF THREE PRINCIPAL CALENDARS

GREGORIAN		HEBREW		MOSLEM	
		Months correspond approximately to those in parentheses		Beginning of year retrogresses through the solar year of the Gregorian calendar	
name	**number of days**	**name**	**number of days**	**name**	**number of days**
January	31	Tishri (September–October)	30	Muharram	30
February in leap year	28 29	Heshvan in some years (October–November)	29 30	Safar	29
March	31	Kislev in some years (November–December)	29 30	Rabi I	30
April	30	Tevet (December–January)	29	Rabi II	29
May	31	Shevat (January–February)	30	Jumada I	30
June	30	Adar* in leap year (February–March)	29 30	Jumada II	29
July	31	Nisan (March–April)	30	Rajab	30
August	31	Iyar (April–May)	29	Sha'ban	29
September	30	Sivan (May–June)	30	Ramadan	30
October	31	Tammuz (June–July)	29	Shawwal	29
November	30	Av (July–August)	30	Dhu'l-Qa dah	30
December	31	Elul (August–September)	29	Dhu'l-Hijja in leap year	29 30

*Adar is followed in leap year by the intercalary month Veadar, or Adar Sheni, having 29 days.

calf² (kăf, käf) *n., pl.* **calves** (kăvz, kävz). The fleshy back part of the leg, between the knee and ankle. [< ON *kalfi.*]

Cal•ga•ry (kăl'gə-rē). A city of SW Alberta, Canada. Pop. 311,000.

cal•i•ber (kăl'ə-bər) *n.* Also *chiefly Brit.* **cal•i•bre. 1.** The diameter of the inside of a tube, as the bore of a gun. **2.** The diameter of a bullet or shell. **3.** Quality; worth. [< Ar *qālib,* shoemaker's last.]

cal•i•brate (kăl'ə-brāt') *v.* **-brated, -brating. 1.** To check or adjust the graduations of a quantitative measuring instrument. **2.** To measure the caliber of. —**cal'i•bra'tion** *n.* —**cal'i•bra'tor** (-brā'tər) *n.*

cal•i•co (kăl'ĭ-kō) *n., pl.* **-coes** or **-cos.** A cotton cloth printed with an all-over pattern. [< *Calicut,* former name for Kozhikode, India.]

Calif. California.

Cal•i•for•nia (kăl'ə-fôrn'yə, -fôr'nē-ə). A W state of the U.S. Pop. 19,953,000. Cap. Sacramento. —**Cal'i•for'nian** *adj.* & *n.*

cal•i•for•ni•um (kăl'ə-fôr'nē-əm) *n. Symbol* **Cf** A synthetic radioactive element produced in trace quantities by helium isotope bombardment of curium. Atomic number 98, longest-lived isotope Cf 251.

cal•i•per (kăl'ə-pər) *n.* **1.** Often **calipers.** An instrument having two curved hinged legs used to measure internal and external dimensions. **2.** A **vernier caliper.** [Var of CALIBER.]

ca•liph (kā'lĭf, kăl'ĭf) *n.* Also **ca•lif.** A Moslem chief of state regarded as a successor to Mohammed. [< Ar *khalīfa,* "successor."] —**ca'liph•ate'** *n.*

cal•is•then•ics (kăl'əs-thĕn'ĭks) *pl.n.* Simple gymnastic exercises to promote physical well-being. [CAL(L)I- + Gk *sthenos,* strength.] —**cal'is•then'ic** *adj.*

calk. Variant of **caulk.**

call (kôl) *v.* **1.** To cry or utter loudly or clearly. **2.** To summon. **3.** To telephone. **4.** To name; designate. **5.** To consider; estimate. **6.** To pay a brief visit. **7.** To demand payment of (a loan or bond issue). **8.** To stop (a baseball game) officially. **9.** *Poker.* To demand that an opponent show his cards. —**call down.** To rebuke; scold. —**call for. 1.** To require or demand. **2.** To come and get. —**call off.** To cancel or postpone. —*n.* **1. a.** A shout or loud cry. **b.** A characteristic cry, esp. of a bird. **2.** A summons or invitation. **3.** Demand; need. **4.** A short visit. **5.** A communication by telephone. [< OE *ceallian,* to call, shout < ON *kalla.*] —**call'er** *n.*

cal•la (kăl'ə) *n.* Also **calla lily.** A plant with a showy, usually white petallike leaf enclosing a clublike flower stalk. [< Gk *kallaia,* wattle of a cock.]

calli-. *comb. form.* Beauty. [< Gk *kallos,* beauty.]

cal•lig•ra•phy (kə-lĭg'rə-fē) *n.* **1.** The art of fine handwriting. **2.** Penmanship; handwriting. —**cal•lig'ra•pher** *n.* —**cal'li•graph'ic** (kăl'ə-grăf'ĭk) *adj.*

call•ing (kô'lĭng) *n.* **1.** A vocation, occupation, or profession. **2.** An inner urge; strong impulse.

cal•li•o•pe (kăl'ē-ōp', kə-lī'ə-pē') *n.* An organlike musical instrument fitted with steam whistles. [< *Calliope,* Gk muse of epic poetry.]

Cal•lis•to (kə-lĭs'tō) *n.* One of the 12 moons of Jupiter, the largest known moon of any planet.

cal•lous (kăl'əs) *adj.* **1.** Having calluses; toughened. **2.** Emotionally hardened; unfeeling. —*v.* To make or become callous. —**cal'lous•ly** *adv.* —**cal'lous•ness** *n.*

cal•low (kăl'ō) *adj.* Immature; inexperienced: *a callow youth.* [< OE *calu,* bald. See **gal-¹.**] —**cal'low•ness** *n.*

cal•lus (kăl'əs) *n., pl.* **-luses.** A localized thickening and enlargement of the horny layer of the skin. —*v.* To form or develop a callus. [L.]

calm (käm) *adj.* Not agitated or tumultuous; quiet; serene. —*n.* **1.** Absence of motion or turmoil; serenity. **2.** A condition of little or no wind. —*v.* To make or become calm. [< OIt *calma.*] —**calm'ly** *adv.* —**calm'ness** *n.*

cal•o•mel (kăl'ə-mĕl', -məl) *n.* A white, tasteless compound, Hg_2Cl_2, used as a purgative. [< NL *calomelas,* "beautiful black."]

ca•lor•ic (kə-lôr'ĭk, -lŏr'ĭk) *adj.* Pertaining to heat or calories. —*n.* A hypothetically indestructible all-pervading fluid, formerly postulated to explain the properties of heat.

cal•o•rie (kăl'ər-ē) *n.* **1.** The amount of heat required to raise the temperature of 1 gram of water by 1°C at 1 atmosphere pressure; small calorie. **2.** The amount of heat required to raise the temperature of 1 kilogram of water by 1°C at 1 atmosphere pressure; large calorie. [< L *calor,* heat.]

cal•o•rif•ic (kăl'ə-rĭf'ĭk) *adj.* Pertaining to or generating heat.

cal•o•rim•e•ter (kăl'ə-rĭm'ə-tər) *n.* An apparatus for measuring heat.

cal•u•met (kăl'yə-mĕt', -mət, kăl'yə-mĕt') *n.* A long-stemmed pipe used by North American Indians for ceremonial purposes. [< F *chalumeau,* a straw.]

ca•lum•ni•ate (kə-lŭm'nē-āt') *v.* **-ated, -ating.** To speak falsely and maliciously of; slander. [< L *calumnia,* CALUMNY.] —**ca•lum'ni•a'tion** *n.* —**ca•lum'ni•a'tor** *n.*

cal•um•ny (kăl'əm-nē) *n., pl.* **-nies.** A maliciously false and injurious statement; slander. [< L *calumnia,* "trickery," "deception."] —**ca•lum'ni•ous** (kə-lŭm'nē-əs) *adj.*

Cal•va•ry (kăl'vər-ē). The hill near Jerusalem where Jesus was crucified. [< LL *Calvāria.*]

calve (kăv, käv) *v.* **calved, calving.** To give birth to a calf.

calves. *pl.* of **calf.**

Cal•vin (kăl'vĭn), **John.** 1509–1564. French theologian.

Cal•vin•ism (kăl'vĭn-ĭz'əm) *n.* The doctrine of Calvin, esp. his affirmation of predestination and redemption by grace alone. —**Cal'vin•ist** *n.* & *adj.* —**Cal'vin•is'tic** *adj.*

ca•lyp•so (kə-lĭp'sō) *n.* A type of West Indian music with improvised lyrics on topical or humorous subjects.

ca•lyx (kā'lĭks, kăl'ĭks) *n., pl.* **-lyxes** or **calyces** (kā'lə-sēz', kăl'ə-). The usually green segmented outer envelope of a flower. [L.]

cam (kăm) *n.* A multiply curved wheel mounted on a rotating shaft and used to produce reciprocating motion. [Perh < G *Kamm,* "comb."]

ca•ma•ra•de•rie (kä'mə-rä'də-rē, kăm'ə-) *n.* Comradely good will among friends. [< F *camarade,* comrade.]

cam•ber (kăm'bər) *n.* **1.** A slight arching, as of a road surface. **2.** A setting of automobile wheels closer together at the bottom than at the top. [< L *camurus,* bent or curved inward.]

Cam•bo•di•a (kăm-bō'dē-ə). A country of SE Asia. Pop. 8,110,000. Cap. Phnom Penh. —**Cam•bo'di•an** *n.* & *adj.*

Cam•bri•an (kăm'brē-ən) *adj.* Of or belonging to the geologic time, rock system, or sedimentary deposits of the first period of the Paleozoic era. —*n.* The Cambrian period. [< *Cambria,* Wales.]

cam•bric (kăm'brĭk) *n.* A fine white linen or cotton fabric.

Cam•bridge (kăm'brĭj). **1.** A city in E England; site of Cambridge Univ. Pop. 167,000. **2.** A city in E Massachusetts; site of Harvard Univ. Pop. 108,000.

Cam•den (kăm'dən). A city in SW New Jersey. Pop. 117,000.

came¹ (kām) *n.* A slender, grooved lead bar used to hold together the panes in stained glass or latticework windows.

came² (kām). *p.t.* of **come.**

cam•el (kăm'əl) *n.* A humped, long-necked animal used in Old World desert regions as a beast of burden. [< Gk *kamēlos* < Sem.]

ca•mel•lia (kə-mĕl'yə) *n.* **1.** The showy, many-petaled flower of an evergreen shrub. **2.** The shrub itself. [< G.J. *Kamel* (1661–1706), Czech Jesuit missionary.]

ca•mel•o•pard (kə-mĕl'ə-pärd') *n. Archaic.* A giraffe. [< Gk *kamēlopardalis.*]

Cam•em•bert (kăm'əm-bâr') *n.* A creamy, mold-ripened cheese that softens on the inside as it matures. [< *Camembert,* village in Normandy.]

cam•e•o (kăm'ē-ō') *n., pl.* **-os.** A gem, medallion, etc., with a design cut in raised relief, usually of a contrasting color. [ME *cameu.*]

cam•er•a (kăm'ər-ə, kăm'rə) *n.* **1.** An apparatus consisting of a lightproof enclosure having an aperture with a shuttered lens through which the image of an object is focused and recorded on a photosensitive film or plate. **2.** The part of a television transmitting apparatus that receives the primary image and transforms it into electrical impulses. [LL, room.]

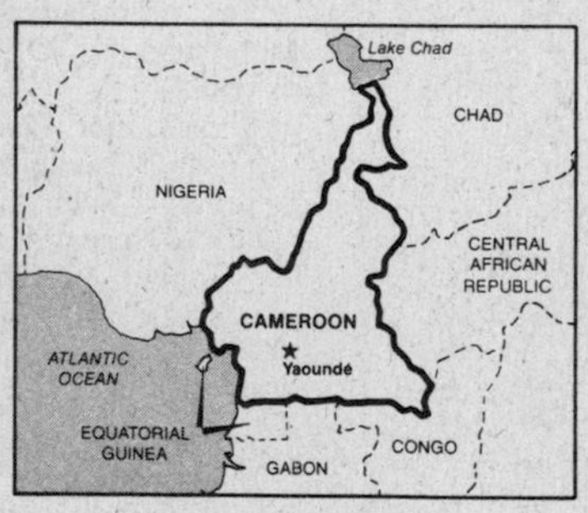

Cameroon

Cam•e•roon (kăm'ə-ro͞on'). Also **Cam•e•roun.** A republic of C Africa. Pop. 6,575,000. Cap. Yaoundé.

cam•i•sole (kăm'ə-sōl') *n.* A woman's short sleeveless undergarment. [< OProv *camisa,* shirt.]

cam•o•mile. Variant of **chamomile.**

cam•ou•flage (kăm'ə-fläzh', -fläj') *n.* A means of concealment that creates the effect of being part of the natural surroundings. —*v.* **-flaged, -flaging.** To conceal by such means. [F.] —**cam'ou•flag'er** *n.*

camp¹ (kămp) *n.* **1. a.** A place where a group of people is temporarily lodged in makeshift shelters. **b.** The shelters in such a place or the persons using them. **2.** A place consisting of more or less permanent vacation cabins. **3.** A group favorable to a common cause, doctrine, or political system. —*v.* To shelter or lodge in a camp; encamp. [< L *campus,* open field.]

camp² (kămp) *n.* Something, as a form of

decorative art, felt to be so banal or dated as to be intrinsically entertaining. [?] —**camp'y** *adj.*

cam•paign (kăm-pān') *n.* **1.** A series of military operations undertaken as one stage in a war. **2.** An operation undertaken to attain some political, social, or commercial goal. —*v.* To engage in a campaign. [< LL *campānia,* countryside.] —**cam•paign'er** *n.*

cam•pa•ni•le (kăm'pə-nē'lē) *n., pl.* **-les** (-lēz) or **-li** (-lē). A bell tower, esp. one freestanding but associated with a church. [< LL *campāna,* bell.]

camp•er (kăm'pər) *n.* **1.** A person who camps outdoors or who attends a camp for recreation. **2. a.** A compact, vanlike vehicle resembling an automobile-and-trailer combination, designed to serve as a dwelling and used for camping or on long motor trips. **b.** A portable shelter resembling the top part of a trailer, made to be mounted on a pickup truck to form such a vehicle.

camp•fire (kămp'fīr') *n.* **1.** An outdoor fire in a camp, used for warmth or cooking. **2.** A meeting held around such a fire.

camp•ground (kămp'ground') *n.* An area used for setting up a camp.

cam•phor (kăm'fər) *n.* A volatile crystalline compound, $C_{10}H_{16}O$, used as an insect repellent. [< ML *camphora.*] —**cam'phor•at'ed** (-āt'ĭd) *adj.* —**cam•phor'ic** *adj.*

camp•site (kămp'sīt') *n.* An area used or suitable for camping.

cam•pus (kăm'pəs) *n., pl.* **-puses.** The grounds of a school, college, or university. [L *campus,* field, plain.]

cam•shaft (kăm'shăft', -shäft') *n.* An engine shaft fitted with a cam or cams.

can[1] (kăn; *unstressed* kən) *v.* Past tense **could,** present tense **can.** —Used as an auxiliary indicating ability, power or prerogative, capacity, or possible contingency. [< OE *cunnan,* to know how. See **gnō-.**]

can[2] (kăn) *n.* **1.** A metal container. **2. a.** An airtight storage container usually made of tin-coated iron. **b.** The contents of such a container. —*v.* **canned, canning. 1.** To seal in a can or jar. **2.** *Slang.* **a.** To dismiss; fire. **b.** To dispense with: *can the chatter.* [< OE *canne* < Gmc **kannōn-.*] —**can'ner** *n.*

can. 1. canceled. **2.** canon. **3.** canto.

Can. Canada; Canadian.

Ca•naan (kā'nən). In Biblical times, Palestine between the Jordan and the Mediterranean; the Promised Land. —**Ca'naan•ite'** *n.*

Can•a•da (kăn'ə-də). A Commonwealth nation occupying the N half of North America. Pop. 19,785,000. Cap. Ottawa. —**Ca•na'di•an** (kə-nā'dē-ən) *adj.* & *n.*

Canadian French. French as used in Canada.

ca•naille (kə-nī', -nāl') *n.* The masses; mob. [< It *canaglia,* "pack of dogs."]

ca•nal (kə-năl') *n.* **1.** A man-made channel filled with water. **2.** *Anat.* A tube or duct. [< L *canālis,* channel.]

ca•nal•ize (kə-năl'īz', kăn'əl-) *v.* **-ized, -izing. 1.** To furnish with or convert into canals. **2.** To provide an outlet for. —**ca•nal'i•za'tion** *n.*

Canal Zone. A strip of territory across the Isthmus of Panama, under lease to the U.S. for the Panama Canal.

can•a•pé (kăn'ə-pā', -pē) *n.* A cracker, piece of toast, etc., topped with a spread or tidbit. [F, "couch" ("seat" for the relish).]

ca•nard (kə-närd') *n.* A false or unfounded story. [F, "duck."]

ca•nar•y (kə-nâr'ē) *n., pl.* **-ies.** A usually yellow songbird popular as a cage bird. [< the CANARY ISLANDS.]

Canary Islands. An island group of Spain off the NW coast of Africa.

ca•nas•ta (kə-năs'tə) *n.* A card game related to rummy and requiring two decks of cards. [Span, "basket" (< the use of two decks, or a "basketful," of cards).]

Can•ber•ra (kăn'bĕr'ə, -bər-ə). The capital of Australia. Pop. 89,000.

can•can (kăn'kăn') *n.* An exuberant exhibition dance characterized by high kicking. [F.]

can•cel (kăn'səl) *v.* **1.** To cross out with lines or other markings. **2.** To annul or invalidate. **3.** To mark or perforate (a postage stamp, check, etc.) to insure against its further use. **4.** To neutralize; offset. **5. a.** To remove a common factor from the numerator and denominator of a fraction. **b.** To remove a common factor or term from both members of an equation or inequality. [< L *cancellāre,* to make like a lattice, cross out.] —**can'cel•a•ble** *adj.* —**can'cel•er** *n.* —**can'cel•la'tion** *n.*

can•cer (kăn'sər) *n.* **1. a.** A malignant tumor that tends to invade healthy tissue and spread to new sites. **b.** The pathological condition characterized by such growths. **2.** A pernicious, spreading evil. [L, crab, creeping ulcer.] —**can'cer•ous** *adj.*

Can•cer (kăn'sər) *n.* **1.** A constellation in the N Hemisphere. **2.** The 4th sign of the zodiac.

can•de•la•brum (kăn'də-lä'brəm, -lăb'rəm, -lā'brəm) *n., pl.* **-bra** (-brə) or **-brums.** Also **can•de•la•bra** *pl.* **-bras.** A decorative candlestick with several branches. [< L *candēla,* CANDLE.]

can•did (kăn'dĭd) *adj.* **1.** Impartial; fair. **2.** Straightforward; open. **3.** Not posed: *a candid picture.* [< L *candidus,* glowing, white, pure.] —**can'did•ly** *adv.* —**can'did•ness** *n.*

can•di•date (kăn'də-dāt', -dĭt) *n.* A person who seeks or is nominated for an office, prize, honor, or the like. [L *candidātus,* "(Roman candidate) clothed in a white toga."] —**can'di•da•cy** (-də-sē), **can'di•da•ture'** (-də-cho͝or', -chər) *n.*

can•dle (kăn'dəl) *n.* A solid, usually cylindrical mass of tallow, wax, or other fatty substance with an axially embedded wick that is burned to provide light. [< L *candēla.*]

can•dle•light (kăn'dəl-līt') *n.* Also **can•dle•light•ing** (-ĭng). **1.** Illumination from a candle or candles. **2.** Dusk; twilight.

can•dle•pin (kăn'dəl-pĭn') *n.* A slender bowling pin used in a variation of the game of tenpins.

can•dle•stick (kăn'dəl-stĭk') *n.* A holder for a candle.

can•dor (kăn'dər) *n.* Also *chiefly Brit.* **can•dour.** Frankness of expression; sincerity; straightforwardness. [L, whiteness, purity.]

can•dy (kăn'dē) *n., pl.* **-dies.** A sweet confection made with sugar and a variety of other ingredients. —*v.* **-died, -dying.** To cook or coat with sugar or syrup. [Short for sugar candy < Ar *qandi,* candied.]

cane (kān) *n.* **1.** A slender, often hollow or flexible woody or pithy stem. **2.** A plant with such stems. **3.** Interwoven strips of such stems, esp. rattan. **4.** A walking stick or similar rod. —*v.* **caned, caning. 1.** To beat with a cane. **2.** To weave with cane. [< Gk *kanna,* reed, cane.] —**can'er** *n.*

cane•brake (kān'brāk') *n.* A dense thicket of cane.

cane sugar. Sugar obtained from sugar cane.

ca•nine (kā'nīn') *adj.* Of or pertaining to dogs or related animals; doglike. —*n.* **1.** One of the conical teeth between the incisors and the bicuspids. **2.** A canine animal. [< L *canis,* dog.]

Ca•nis Ma•jor (kā'nĭs mā'jər). A constellation

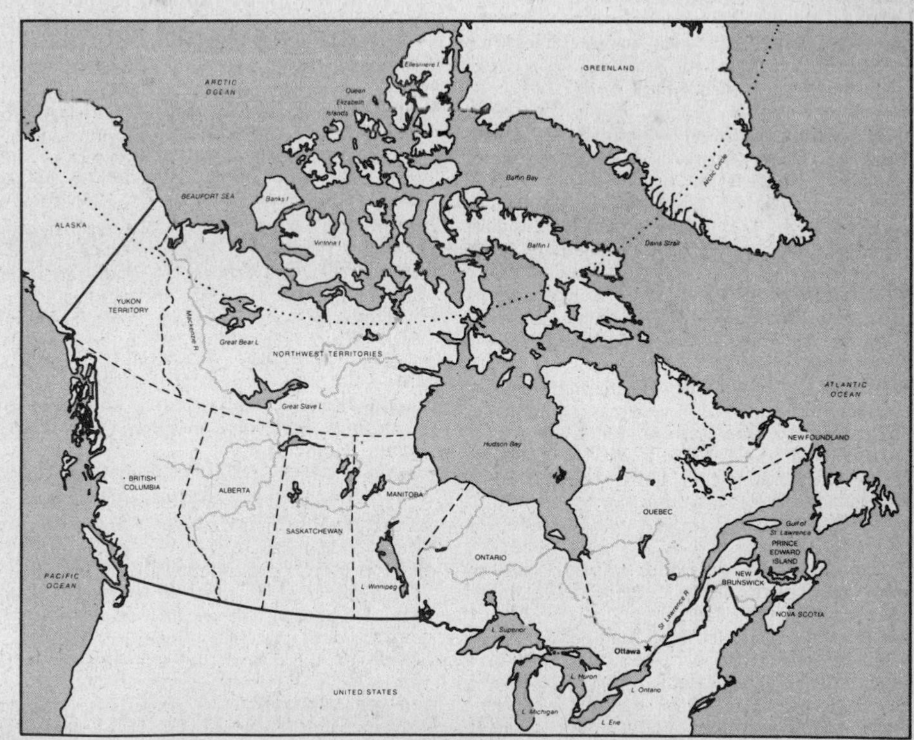

Canada

in the S Hemisphere.

Canis Mi•nor (mī'nər). A constellation in the equatorial region of the S Hemisphere.

can•is•ter (kăn'ĭs-tər) *n.* **1.** A container, usually of thin metal, for holding dry foods. **2.** A metallic cylinder that, when fired from a gun, bursts and scatters the shot packed inside it. **3.** The part of a gas mask containing a filter for poison gas. [L *canistrum,* reed basket.]

can•ker (kăng'kər) *n.* An ulcerous sore of the mouth and lips. [< L *cancer,* CANCER.] **—can'ker•ous** *adj.*

canned (kănd) *adj.* **1.** Preserved and sealed in a can or jar. **2.** Recorded or taped.

can•ner•y (kăn'ər-ē) *n., pl.* **-ies.** An establishment where meat, vegetables, and other foods are canned.

can•ni•bal (kăn'ə-bəl) *n.* **1.** A person who eats the flesh of human beings. **2.** Any animal that feeds on others of its own kind. [< Span *Canibalis, Caribales,* name (recorded by Columbus) of the man-eating Caribs of Cuba and Haiti.] **—can'ni•bal•ism'** *n.* **—can'ni•bal•is'tic** *adj.*

can•ni•bal•ize (kăn'ə-bə-līz') *v.* **-ized, -izing.** To remove serviceable parts from (damaged airplanes, tanks, etc.) for use in the repair of other equipment. **—can'ni•bal•i•za'tion** *n.*

can•non (kăn'ən) *n., pl.* **-non** or **-nons. 1.** A weapon for firing projectiles, consisting of a heavy metal tube mounted on a carriage. **2.** Any heavy firearm larger than 0.60 caliber. **3.** *Brit.* A carom made in billiards. [< It *cannone,* "large tube, barrel."]

can•non•ade (kăn'ə-nād') *v.* **-aded, -ading.** To bombard with cannon fire. *—n.* An extended discharge of artillery.

can•non•ball (kăn'ən-bôl') *n.* A round projectile fired from a cannon. *—v.* To travel rapidly in the manner of a cannonball.

can•non•eer (kăn'ə-nîr') *n.* A gunner or artilleryman.

can•not (kăn'ŏt, kă-nŏt') *v.* The negative form of **can.**

can•ny (kăn'ē) *adj.* **-nier, -niest. 1.** Skillful; competent. **2.** Shrewd; prudent. [< CAN[1].] **—can'ni•ly** *adv.* **—can'ni•ness** *n.*

ca•noe (kə-nōō') *n.* A light, slender boat with pointed ends, propelled by paddles. *—v.* **-noed, -noeing.** To carry or travel by canoe. [< Span *canoa.*] **—ca•noe'ist** *n.*

can•on[1] (kăn'ən) *n.* **1.** A law or code of laws established by a church council. **2.** A secular code of law. **3.** A basis for judgment; standard. **4. a.** The books of the Bible officially recognized by the Church. **b.** The calendar of saints accepted by the Roman Catholic Church. **5.** *Mus.* A round. [< L *canōn,* measuring line, rule.]

can•on[2] (kăn'ən) *n.* One of a chapter of priests serving in a cathedral or collegiate church. [< LL *canōnicus,* one living under a rule.]

ca•non•i•cal (kə-nŏn'ĭ-kəl) *adj.* Also **ca•non•ic** (-ĭk). **1.** Pertaining to, required by, or abiding by canon law. **2.** Authoritative; orthodox. **—ca•non'i•cal•ly** *adv.* **—can'on•ic'i•ty** (kăn'ə-nĭs'ə-tē) *n.*

canonical hours. A form of prayer, prescribed by canon law, normally to be recited at specified times of the day.

can•on•ize (kăn'ə-nīz') *v.* **-ized, -izing. 1.** To declare officially (a deceased person) to be a saint. **2.** To glorify; exalt. **—can'on•i•za'tion** *n.*

can•o•py (kăn'ə-pē) *n., pl.* **-pies. 1.** A covering fastened or held horizontally above a person or an object for protection or ornamentation. **2.** An ornamental, rooflike structure. *—v.* **-pied, -pying.** To form or place a canopy over. [< ML *canapeum, canopeum,* (couch with a) mosquito net.]

canst (kănst). *Archaic.* 2nd person sing. present tense of **can.** Used with *thou.*

cant[1] (kănt) *n.* **1.** Angular deviation from a vertical or horizontal plane or surface. **2.** The tilt caused by such a motion. **3.** A slanted edge or surface. *—v.* To cause to slant or tilt. [< L *canthus,* iron tire, rim of a wheel.]

cant[2] (kănt) *n.* **1.** Wheedling speech. **2.** Discourse recited mechanically. **3.** Hypocritically pious language. **4.** The special vocabulary peculiar to the members of a group. *—v.* **1.** To speak in a whining, pleading tone. **2.** To speak sententiously; moralize. [Prob < NF, singing, jargon.] **—cant'ing•ly** *adv.*

can't (kănt, känt). Contraction of *cannot.*

Cant. Cantonese.

can•ta•bi•le (kän-tä'bē-lā') *adj. Mus.* In a smooth, lyrical, flowing style. [< LL *cantābilis,* singable.] **—can•ta'bi•le'** *adv.*

can•ta•loupe (kăn'tə-lōp') *n.* A melon with a ribbed, rough rind and orange flesh. [< *Cantalupo,* a papal villa near Rome.]

can•tank•er•ous (kăn-tăng'kər-əs) *adj.* Ill-tempered and quarrelsome. [Prob < ME *contekour,* rioter, brawler.]

can•ta•ta (kən-tä'tə) *n.* A vocal and instrumental composition comprising choruses, solos, and recitatives. [It *(aria) cantata,* "sung (aria)."]

can•teen (kăn-tēn') *n.* **1. a.** A store for on-base military personnel. **b.** *Brit.* A club for soldiers. **2.** An institutional recreation hall or cafeteria. [< It *cantina,* a wine cellar.]

can•ter (kăn'tər) *n.* A gait slower than the gallop but faster than the trot. [Short for *Canterbury gallop.*] **—can'ter** *v.*

Can•ter•bur•y (kăn'tər-bĕr'ē). A cathedral city of SE England. Pop. 33,000.

can•thus (kăn'thəs) *n., pl.* **-thi** (-thī'). The corner at either side of the eye, formed by the meeting of the upper and lower eyelids. [< Gk *kanthos.*]

can•ti•cle (kăn'tĭ-kəl) *n.* A liturgical chant. [< L *cantus,* song.]

can•ti•le•ver (kăn'tə-lē'vər, -lĕv'ər) *n.* A projecting beam or other structure supported only at one end. [Poss CANT[1] + LEVER.]

can•tle (kăn'təl) *n.* The rear part of a saddle. [< NF *cantel.*]

can•to (kăn'tō) *n., pl.* **-tos.** A principal division of a long poem. [< L *cantus,* song.]

can•ton (kăn'tən, -tŏn') *n.* A small territorial division of a country, esp. one of the states of Switzerland. *—v.* **1.** (kăn'tən, -tŏn'). To divide into parts. **2.** (kăn-tŏn', -tōn'). To assign quarters to. [F, corner, subdivision.] **—can'ton•al** *adj.*

Can•ton (kăn'tŏn', kăn-tŏn'). **1.** A port in SE China. Pop. 1,840,000. **2.** A city in NE Ohio. Pop. 114,000.

Can•ton•ese (kăn'tə-nēz', -nēs') *n., pl.* **-ese. 1.** The Chinese dialect spoken in S China. **2.** A native or inhabitant of the Canton region. **—Can'ton•ese'** *adj.*

can•ton•ment (kăn-tōn'mənt, kăn-tŏn'-) *n.* **1.** The assignment of troops to temporary quarters. **2.** The quarters assigned.

can•tor (kăn'tər) *n.* The official soloist or chief singer of the liturgy in a synagogue. [L, singer.]

can•vas (kăn'vəs) *n.* **1.** A heavy, closely woven fabric of cotton, hemp, etc., used for making tents and sails. **2.** A piece of such material used as the surface for a painting. **3.** Sailcloth. **4.** Sails. **5.** The floor of a boxing or wrestling ring. [< VL **cannabāceus,* "made of hemp."]

can•vas•back (kăn'vəs-băk') *n.* A North American duck with a reddish head and neck and a whitish back.

can•vass (kăn'vəs) *v.* **1.** To scrutinize. **2. a.** To go through or to solicit votes, orders, subscriptions, etc. **b.** To conduct a survey. *—n.* **1.** An examination or discussion. **2.** A solicitation of votes, sales orders, or opinions. [< CANVAS.] **—can'vass•er** *n.*

can•yon (kăn'yən) *n.* A narrow chasm with steep cliff walls eroded by running water. [< Span *cañon,* pipe, tube, conduit.]

cap (kăp) *n.* **1.** A usually close-fitting covering for the head, with or without a visor. **2.** Any of numerous objects similar to a head covering in form, use, or position: *a bottle cap.* *—v.* **capped, capping. 1.** To put a cap on. **2.** To lie over or on top of: *Snow capped the hills.* [< LL *cappa,* hood.]

cap. **1.** capacity. **2.** capital (city). **3.** capital letter.

C.A.P. Civil Air Patrol.

ca•pa•ble (kā'pə-bəl) *adj.* Having capacity or ability; competent. **—capable of. 1.** Qualified for. **2.** Open to: *an error capable of remedy.* [< LL *capābilis,* "able to hold."] **—ca'pa•bil'i•ty** *n.* **—ca'pa•ble•ness** *n.* **—ca'pa•bly** *adv.*

ca•pa•cious (kə-pā'shəs) *adj.* Able to contain a large quantity; spacious; roomy. [< L *capāx,* able to hold.] **—ca•pa'cious•ly** *adv.* **—ca•pa'cious•ness** *n.*

ca•pac•i•tance (kə-păs'ə-təns) *n.* **1.** The ratio of charge to potential on an electrically charged, isolated conductor. **2.** The ratio of the electric charge transferred from one to the other of a pair of conductors to the resulting potential difference between them. **—ca•pac'i•tive** *adj.* **—ca•pac'i•tive•ly** *adv.*

ca•pac•i•tate (kə-păs'ə-tāt') *v.* **-tated, -tating.** To render fit; make qualified; enable. **—ca•pac'i•ta'tion** *n.*

ca•pac•i•tor (kə-păs'ə-tər) *n.* An electric circuit element used to store charge temporarily, consisting in general of two metallic plates separated by a dielectric.

ca•pac•i•ty (kə-păs'ə-tē) *n., pl.* **-ties. 1.** The ability to receive, hold, or absorb. **2.** A measure of this ability; volume. **3.** The maximum amount that can be contained. **4.** The maximum amount of production: *factories operating below capacity.* **5.** The ability to learn or retain knowledge. **6.** The quality of being suitable for or receptive to specified treatment: *the capacity of elastic to be stretched.* **7.** The position in which one functions; role: *his capacity as host.* **8.** *Elec.* **a.** *Obs.* Capacitance. **b.** A measure of the output of a generator. *—adj.* As numerous as possible: *a capacity crowd.* [< L *capāx,* CAPACIOUS.]

ca•par•i•son (kə-păr'ə-sən) *n.* An ornamental covering for a horse's saddle or harness. [OF *caparaçon.*]

cape[1] (kāp) *n.* A sleeveless garment worn hanging over the shoulders. [< LL *cappa,* hood, cloak.]

cape[2] (kāp) *n.* A point or head of land projecting into a sea or other body of water; promontory. [< L *caput,* head.]

ca•per[1] (kā'pər) *n.* **1.** A playful leap or hop. **2.** A wild escapade. *—v.* To leap or frisk about. [Short for CAPRIOLE.]

ca•per[2] (kā'pər) *n.* A pickled flower bud of a Mediterranean shrub, used as a condiment. [< L *capparis.*]

cape•skin (kāp'skĭn') *n.* Soft leather made

from sheepskin.

Cape Town. Also **Cape•town** (kăp'toun'). The legislative capital of the Republic of South Africa. Pop. 508,000.

caph. Variant of **kaph.**

cap•il•lar•i•ty (kăp'ə-lăr'ə-tē) *n., pl.* **-ties.** The interaction between contacting surfaces of a liquid and a solid that distorts the liquid surface from a planar shape.

cap•il•lar•y (kăp'ə-lĕr'ē) *adj.* **1.** Pertaining to or resembling a hair; fine and slender. **2.** Having a very small internal diameter, as a tube. **3.** In or pertaining to the capillaries. **4.** Pertaining to capillarity. *—n., pl.* **-ies. 1.** One of the minute blood vessels that connect the arteries and veins. **2.** Any tube with a small internal diameter. [< L *capillus,* hair.]

capillary attraction. The force that causes a liquid to be raised against a vertical surface, as is water in a clean glass tube.

cap•i•tal[1] (kăp'ə-təl) *n.* **1.** A town or city that is the official seat of government in a political entity. **2.** Wealth in the form of money or property. **3. a.** The net worth of a business. **b.** The funds invested in a business by the owners or stockholders. **4.** Capitalists considered as a class. **5.** Any asset or advantage. **6.** A capital letter. *—adj.* **1.** First and foremost; chief. **2.** Pertaining to a political capital. **3.** First-rate; excellent: *a capital fellow.* **4.** Extremely serious: *a capital blunder.* **5.** Punishable by or involving death: *capital punishment.* **6.** Pertaining to capital. [< L *capitālis,* "of the head," important.]

cap•i•tal[2] (kăp'ə-təl) *n.* The top of a column. [< LL *capitellum,* "small head."]

capital goods. Goods used in the production of commodities.

cap•i•tal•ism (kăp'ə-təl-ĭz'əm) *n.* An economic system characterized by freedom of the market with private and corporate ownership of the means of production and distribution that are operated for profit.

cap•i•tal•ist (kăp'ə-təl-ĭst) *n.* **1.** An investor of capital in business. **2.** Any person of great wealth. *—adj.* Of or pertaining to capitalism or capitalists. **—cap'i•tal•is'tic** *adj.* **—cap'i•tal•is'ti•cal•ly** *adv.*

cap•i•tal•i•za•tion (kăp'ə-təl-ə-zā'shən) *n.* **1.** The act, practice, or result of capitalizing. **2.** The total investment of owners in a business.

cap•i•tal•ize (kăp'ə-təl-īz') *v.* **-ized, -izing. 1.** To utilize as or convert into capital. **2.** To supply with capital. **3.** To begin a word with an upper-case letter. **4.** To turn to advantage; profit by; exploit: *capitalize on an opponent's error.*

capital letter. A letter of a size larger than and often in a form differing from its corresponding smaller letter; an upper-case letter.

capital punishment. The death penalty.

capital stock. The total amount of stock authorized for issue by a corporation.

cap•i•ta•tion (kăp'ə-tā'shən) *n.* A tax fixed at an equal sum per person; a per capita tax. [< LL *caput,* head, person.]

cap•i•tol (kăp'ə-təl) *n.* A building in which a legislature assembles.

ca•pit•u•late (kə-pĭch'o͞o-lāt') *v.* **-lated, -lating. 1.** To surrender under specified conditions. **2.** To give up all resistance; acquiesce. [< ML *capitulāre,* to draw up under heads or chapters.] **—ca•pit'u•la'tion** *n.*

ca•pon (kā'pŏn', -pən) *n.* A castrated rooster raised for eating. [< L *capō.*]

ca•pric•cio (kə-prē'chō, -chē-ō') *n., pl.* **-cios.** An instrumental work with a whimsical style and a free form. [It, caprice.]

ca•price (kə-prēs') *n.* **1.** An impulsive change of mind. **2.** An inclination to make such a change. [< It *capriccio,* "head with hair standing on end."]

ca•pri•cious (kə-prĭsh'əs, -prē'shəs) *adj.* Characterized by or subject to whim; fickle.

Cap•ri•corn (kăp'rĭ-kôrn') *n.* **1.** Capricornus. **2. Tropic of Capricorn.**

Cap•ri•cor•nus (kăp'rĭ-kôr'nəs) *n.* Also **Cap•ri•corn. 1.** A constellation in the equatorial region of the S Hemisphere. **2.** The 10th sign of the zodiac. [L, "goat-horned."]

cap•ri•ole (kăp'rē-ōl') *n.* **1.** An upward leap made by a trained horse without going forward. **2.** A leap or jump. [< It *capriola,* "leap of a goat."]

caps. capsule.

cap•size (kăp'sīz', kăp-sīz') *v.* **-sized, -sizing.** To overturn or cause to turn over. [?]

cap•stan (kăp'stən) *n.* **1.** A vertical revolving cylinder for hoisting weights by winding in a cable. **2.** A small cylindrical pulley used to regulate the speed of magnetic tape in a tape recorder. [< L *capistrum,* halter.]

cap•su•lar (kăp'sə-lər, -syo͞o-lər) *adj.* Of or like a capsule.

cap•su•late (kăp'sə-lāt', -syo͞o-lāt', -lĭt) *adj.* In or formed into a capsule.

cap•sule (kăp'səl, -syo͞ol) *n.* **1.** A soluble gelatinous sheath enclosing a dose of an oral medicine. **2.** A fibrous, membranous, or fatty envelope enclosing an organ or part. **3.** A seed case that dries and spilts open. **4.** A pressurized modular compartment of an aircraft or spacecraft. [< L *capsula,* dim of *capsa,* box.]

cap•tain (kăp'tən) *n.* **1.** One who commands, leads, or guides. **2.** The officer in command of a ship. **3.** A commissioned officer, as in the army, who ranks above a first lieutenant. **4.** A commissioned officer in the navy who ranks above a commander. *—v.* To command or direct. [< LL *capitāneus,* chief.] **—cap'tain•cy** *n.* **—cap'tain•ship'** *n.*

cap•tion (kăp'shən) *n.* **1.** A short legend or description, as of an illustration or photograph. **2.** A subtitle in a motion picture. **3.** A title, as of a document or chapter. [Orig "arrest," record of execution of a commission < L *capere,* to seize.]

cap•tious (kăp'shəs) *adj.* **1.** Marked by a disposition to find fault. **2.** Intended to entrap or confuse. [< L *captiōsus,* "ensnaring."]

cap•ti•vate (kăp'tə-vāt') *v.* **-vated, -vating.** To fascinate by special charm or beauty. [LL *captivāre,* to capture.] **—cap'ti•va'tion** *n.*

cap•tive (kăp'tĭv) *n.* **1.** A prisoner. **2.** One who is enslaved by a strong emotion or passion. *—adj.* **1.** Held as prisoner. **2.** Obliged to be present: *a captive audience.* [< L *captīvus* < *capere,* to seize.] **—cap•tiv'i•ty** *n.*

cap•tor (kăp'tər, -tôr') *n.* One who captures. [< L *capere,* to seize.]

cap•ture (kăp'chər) *v.* **-tured, -turing. 1.** To take captive. **2.** To win possession or control of. *—n.* **1.** The act of capturing; seizure. **2.** One that is seized, caught, or won. [< L *capere,* to seize.]

car (kär) *n.* **1.** An automobile. **2.** A conveyance with wheels that runs along tracks, as a streetcar or railroad car. [< L *carrus,* two-wheeled wagon.]

car. carat.

Ca•ra•cas (kə-rä'kəs, -răk'əs). The capital of Venezuela. Pop. 1,639,000.

car•a•cul. Variant of **karakul.**

ca•rafe (kə-răf') *n.* A glass bottle for serving water or wine at the table; decanter. [< Ar *gharrāf.*]

car•a•mel (kăr'ə-məl, kär'məl) *n.* **1.** A chewy candy made with sugar, butter, cream or milk, and flavoring. **2.** Burnt sugar, used for coloring and sweetening. [F.]

car•a•pace (kăr'ə-pās') *n.* A hard outer covering, as the upper shell of a turtle. [< Span *carapacho.*]

car•at (kăr'ət) *n.* **1.** A unit of weight for precious stones, equal to 200 milligrams. **2.** Variant of **karat.** [< Ar *qīrāt,* small weight, carat.]

car•a•van (kăr'ə-văn') *n.* **1.** A company of travelers journeying together, esp. across a desert. **2.** A single file of vehicles or pack animals. **3.** A large covered vehicle; van. [< Pers *kārwān.*]

car•a•van•sa•ry (kăr'ə-văn'sə-rē) *n., pl.* **-ries.** Also **car•a•van•se•rai** (-rī'). **1.** In the Near or Far East, an inn for caravans. **2.** Any large inn.

car•a•vel (kăr'ə-vĕl') *n.* A small, light sailing ship of the kind used by the Spanish and Portuguese in the 15th and 16th centuries. [< OF *caravelle.*]

car•a•way (kăr'ə-wā') *n.* **1.** A plant with pungent, aromatic seeds used in cooking. **2.** The seeds of this plant. [ME.]

car•bide (kär'bīd') *n.* A binary compound of carbon with a more electropositive element.

car•bine (kär'bīn', -bēn') *n.* A light shoulder rifle with a short barrel. [F *carabine.*]

carbo–. *comb. form.* Carbon. [< CARBON.]

car•bo•hy•drate (kär'bō-hī'drāt') *n.* Any of a group of chemical compounds, including sugars, starches, and cellulose, containing carbon, hydrogen, and oxygen only, with the ratio of hydrogen to oxygen atoms usually 2:1.

car•bol•ic acid (kär-bŏl'ĭk). Phenol.

car•bon (kär'bən) *n. Symbol* **C 1.** A naturally abundant nonmetallic element that occurs in many inorganic and in all organic compounds, exists in amorphous, graphitic, and diamond allotropes, and is capable of chemical self-bonding to form an enormous number of chemically, biologically, and commercially important long-chain molecules. Atomic number 6, atomic weight 12.01115. **2. a.** A sheet of carbon paper. **b.** A copy made by using carbon paper. [< L *carbō,* charcoal.]

carbon 14. A naturally radioactive carbon isotope with atomic mass 14 and half-life 5,700 years, used in dating ancient carbon-containing objects.

car•bon•ate (kär'bə-nāt') *v.* **-ated, -ating.** To charge with carbon dioxide gas. **—car'bon•a'tion** *n.* **—car'bon•a'tor** *n.*

carbon dioxide. A colorless, odorless, incombustible gas, CO_2, formed during respiration, combustion, and organic decomposition.

car•bon•ic acid (kär-bŏn'ĭk). A weak, unstable acid, H_2CO_3, present in solutions of carbon dioxide in water.

car•bon•if•er•ous (kär'bə-nĭf'ər-əs) *adj.* Producing, containing, or pertaining to carbon or coal.

Car•bon•if•er•ous (kär'bə-nĭf'ər-əs) *adj.* Of, designating, or belonging to a division of the Paleozoic era including the Mississippian and Pennsylvanian periods, characterized by swamp formation and deposition of plant remains later hardened into coal. *—n.* The Carboniferous period.

carbon monoxide. A colorless, odorless, highly poisonous gas, CO, formed by the incomplete combustion of carbon or carbon compounds.

carbon paper. A lightweight paper faced on one side with a dark pigment that is transferred by the impact of typewriter keys or by writing pressure to a copying surface.

carbon tetrachloride. A poisonous, nonflammable, colorless liquid, CCl_4, used in fire extinguishers and as a solvent.

Car•bo•run•dum (kär′bə-rŭn′dəm) *n.* A trademark for a silicon carbide abrasive.

car•boy (kär′boi′) *n.* A large container usually encased in a protective covering and often used to hold corrosive liquids. [< Ar *qarrābah.*]

car•bun•cle (kär′bŭng′kəl) *n.* A painful, localized, pus-producing, sometimes fatal infection of the skin. [< L *carbunculus,* small glowing ember, tumor.] —**car•bun′cu•lar** (-kyə-lər) *adj.*

car•bu•re•tor (kär′bə-rā′tər, kär′byə-) *n.* A device used in gasoline engines to produce an efficient explosive vapor of fuel and air. [< F *carbure,* carbide.]

car•cass (kär′kəs) *n.* A dead body, esp. of an animal. [F *carcasse.*]

car•cin•o•gen (kär-sĭn′ə-jən, kär′sĭn-ə-jĕn′) *n.* A cancer-causing substance. [<Gk *karkinos,* cancer, crab.] —**car′cin•o•gen′ic** *adj.*

card[1] (kärd) *n.* **1.** A small, flat piece of stiff paper or thin pasteboard with numerous uses: **a.** One of a set of playing cards. **b.** A **post card.** **c.** One bearing a greeting or a person's name and other information, as a Christmas or business card. **2.** A program of events, as at horse races. **3.** *Informal.* An amusing or eccentric person. [< L *charta,* leaf of papyrus.]

card[2] (kärd) *n.* A wire-toothed brush used to disentangle textile fibers or raise the nap on a fabric. [< L *cārere,* to card.] —**card** *v.* —**card′er** *n.*

card•board (kärd′bôrd′, -bōrd′) *n.* A stiff pasteboard made of paper pulp.

car•di•ac (kär′dē-ăk′) *adj.* Of or near the heart.

Car•diff (kär′dĭf). The major city of Wales. Pop. 260,000.

car•di•gan (kär′dĭ-gən) *n.* A sweater or collarless jacket opening down the front. [< J.T. Brudenell, 7th Earl of *Cardigan* (1797–1868), British army officer.]

car•di•nal (kärd′n-əl, kärd′nəl) *adj.* **1.** Of foremost importance. **2.** Of a dark to vivid red color. —*n.* **1.** *R.C.Ch.* One of the highest-ranking dignitaries, below papal rank, appointed by the pope to assist him in governing the church. **2.** Dark to vivid red. **3.** A crested, bright-red North American bird. [< LL *cardinālis,* principal, of a hinge.]

car•di•nal•ate (kärd′n-əl-ĭt, kärd′nəl-, -āt′) *n.* *R.C.Ch.* **1.** The body comprising all the cardinals. **2.** The rank, dignity, or term of a cardinal.

cardinal number. A number, such as 3 or 11 or 412, used to indicate quantity but not order.

cardio–. *comb. form.* The heart. [< Gk *kardia,* heart.]

car•di•o•gram (kär′dē-ə-grăm′) *n.* The curve traced by a cardiograph, used to diagnose heart defects.

car•di•o•graph (kär′dē-ə-grăf′, -gräf′) *n.* An instrument used to record the movements of the heart.

car•di•ol•o•gy (kär′dē-ŏl′ə-jē) *n.* The medical study of the diseases and functioning of the heart. —**car′di•ol′o•gist** *n.*

car•di•o•vas•cu•lar (kär′dē-ō-văs′kyə-lər) *adj.* Involving the heart and the blood vessels.

cards (kärdz) *pl.n.* *(Often takes sing. v.).* A game played usually with a deck of 52 cards.

care (kâr) *n.* **1.** Mental distress and grief. **2.** An object or source of attention or solicitude. **3.** Caution: *handle with care.* **4.** Supervision; charge: *in the care of a nurse.* —**(in) care of.** At the address of. —*v.* **cared, caring. 1.** To be concerned or interested. **2.** To object; mind. [< OE *caru, cearu.*]

ca•reen (kə-rēn′) *v.* **1.** To move rapidly and in an uncontrolled manner. **2.** To cause (a ship) to lean to one side; tilt. [< F *(en) carène,* "(on) the keel."] —**ca•reen′er** *n.*

ca•reer (kə-rîr′) *n.* **1.** A chosen pursuit; lifework. **2.** A person's progress in his occupation. —*v.* To move or run at full speed. [F *carrière,* racecourse, course, career.]

care•free (kâr′frē′) *adj.* Free of worries and responsibilities.

care•ful (kâr′fəl) *adj.* **1.** Cautious in thought, speech, or action. **2.** Thorough; painstaking. —**care′ful•ly** *adv.* —**care′ful•ness** *n.*

care•less (kâr′lĭs) *adj.* **1.** Inattentive; negligent. **2.** Marked by or resulting from lack of thought. **3.** Inconsiderate: *a careless remark.* **4.** Free from cares; cheerful. —**care′less•ly** *adv.* —**care′less•ness** *n.*

ca•ress (kə-rĕs′) *n.* A gentle touch or gesture of fondness. —*v.* To touch or treat in an affectionate or loving manner. [< It *carezza,* endearment.] —**ca•ress′er** *n.*

car•et (kăr′ĭt) *n.* A proofreading symbol used to indicate where something is to be inserted in a line of printed or written matter. [L, "there is lacking."]

care•tak•er (kâr′tā′kər) *n.* One employed to look after or take charge of goods, property, or a person; custodian.

care•worn (kâr′wôrn′, -wōrn′) *adj.* Showing the effects of worry or grief.

car•fare (kär′fâr′) *n.* Fare charged a passenger.

car•go (kär′gō) *n., pl.* **-goes** or **-gos.** The freight carried by a ship, airplane, or other vehicle. [Span, load, cargo.]

car•hop (kär′hŏp′) *n.* A waiter at a drive-in restaurant.

Car•ib (kăr′ĭb) *n., pl.* **-ib** or **-ibs. 1.** Also **Car•i•ban** (-ə-bən, kə-rē′-). **a.** A member of a group of American Indian peoples of N South America and the Lesser Antilles. **b.** A member of one of these peoples. **2.** Any of the languages of these peoples. —**Car′ib** *adj.*

Car•i•ban (kăr′ə-bən, kə-rē′bən) *n., pl.* **-ban** or **-bans. 1.** Carib. **2.** A language family of the Lesser Antilles and N South America, comprising the languages spoken by the Caribs. —**Car′i•ban** *adj.*

Car•ib•be•an Sea (kăr′ə-bē′ən, kə-rĭb′ē-ən). An extension of the Atlantic bounded by Central and South America and the West Indies. —**Car′ib•be′an** *adj.*

car•i•bou (kăr′ə-bo͞o′) *n., pl.* **-bou** or **-bous.** A New World arctic deer, considered identical to the reindeer. [< Algon.]

car•i•ca•ture (kăr′ĭ-kə-cho͝or′) *n.* **1.** A representation, esp. pictorial, in which a subject's distinctive features or peculiarities are exaggerated for comic or grotesque effect. **2.** An imitation so inferior as to be absurd. —*v.* **-tured, -turing.** To represent or imitate in or as in a caricature. [< It *caricatura,* caricature, "exaggeration."] —**car′i•ca•tur′ist** *n.*

car•ies (kâr′ēz) *n.* Decay of a bone or tooth. [L *cariēs,* caries, decay.]

car•il•lon (kăr′ə-lŏn′, kə-rĭl′yən) *n.* A set of bells played chiefly on a keyboard. [F.]

ca•ri•na (kə-rī′nə) *n., pl.* **-nae** (-nē′). *Biol.* A keel-shaped ridge, such as that on the breastbone of a bird or in the petals of certain flowers. [< L *carīna,* keel.]

Ca•ri•na (kə-rī′nə) *n.* A constellation in the S Hemisphere.

car•load (kär′lōd′) *n.* The amount a car carries or is able to carry.

car•mine (kär′mĭn, -mīn′) *n.* A strong to vivid red color. [< ML *carminium.*] —**car′mine** *adj.*

car•nage (kär′nĭj) *n.* Massive slaughter, as in war. [< ML *carnāticum,* slaughter of animals.]

car•nal (kär′nəl) *adj.* **1.** Relating to the desires of the flesh; sensual. **2.** Not spiritual. [< L *carō,* flesh.] —**car•nal′i•ty** (kär-năl′ə-tē) *n.*

car•na•tion (kär-nā′shən) *n.* **1.** A plant cultivated for its fragrant many-petaled flowers. **2.** A flower of this plant. [< OF, flesh-colored, carnation.]

car•nel•ian (kär-nēl′yən) *n.* A pale to deep red or reddish-brown variety of clear chalcedony, used in jewelry. [< OF *corneline.*]

car•ni•val (kär′nə-vəl) *n.* **1.** The season just before Lent, marked by merrymaking and feasting. **2.** A traveling amusement show. [OIt *carnelevare,* "the putting away of flesh," Shrovetide.]

car•ni•vore (kär′nə-vôr′, -vōr′) *n.* A flesh-eating animal, esp. one of a group including dogs, cats, bears, and weasels.

car•niv•o•rous (kär-nĭv′ər-əs) *adj.* Flesh-eating or predatory. [L *carnivorus.*] —**car•niv′o•rous•ly** *adv.*

car•ol (kăr′əl) *v.* **-oled** or **-olled, -oling** or **-olling. 1.** To celebrate or praise in song. **2.** To sing joyously. —*n.* A song or hymn of praise or joy, esp. for Christmas. [< OF *carole,* a carol.] —**car′ol•er** *n.*

car•om (kăr′əm) *n.* **1.** A billiards shot in which the cue ball successively strikes two other balls. **2.** A collision followed by a rebound. —*v.* **1.** To collide with and rebound. **2.** To make a carom in billiards. [< Span *carambola,* a kind of fruit.]

car•o•tene (kăr′ə-tēn′) *n.* An orange-yellow to red hydrocarbon, $C_{40}H_{56}$, occurring in many plants and converted to vitamin A in the animal liver. [< L *carōta,* carrot.]

ca•rot•id (kə-rŏt′ĭd) *n.* Either of the two major arteries in the neck that carry blood to the head. [< Gk *karoun,* to stupefy.] —**ca•rot′id•al** *adj.*

ca•rous•al (kə-rou′zəl) *n.* A jovial, riotous drinking party.

ca•rouse (kə-rouz′) *n.* Boisterous, drunken merrymaking; a carousal. —*v.* **-roused, -rousing.** To go on a drinking spree. [< OF *(boire) carous,* (to drink) all out.] —**ca•rous′er** *n.*

car•ou•sel, car•rou•sel (kăr′ə-sĕl′, -zĕl′) *n.* A merry-go-round. [F *carrousel.*]

carp[1] (kärp) *v.* To find fault and complain constantly; nag or fuss. [< ON *karpa,* to boast.] —**carp′er** *n.*

carp[2] (kärp) *n., pl.* **carp** or **carps.** An edible freshwater fish of ponds and lakes. [< LL *carpa.*]

car•pal (kär′pəl) *adj.* *Anat.* Of, pertaining to, or near the carpus: *the carpal joint.* —*n.* Any bone of the carpus.

Car•pa•thi•an Mountains (kär-pā′thē-ən). Also **Car•pa•thi•ans** (-ənz). A mountain system of E Europe.

car•pen•ter (kär′pən-tər) *n.* One whose occupation is constructing, finishing, and repairing wooden objects and structures. [< L *carpentārius (artifex),* carriage(-maker).] —**car′pen•ter** *v.* —**car′pen•try** *n.*

car•pet (kär′pĭt) *n.* **1.** A thick, heavy covering for a floor, usually made of wool or synthetic fibers. **2.** The fabric used for this. —*v.* To cover with or as with a carpet. [< OIt *carpita.*]

car•pet•bag (kär′pĭt-băg′) *n.* A traveling bag made of carpet fabric.

car•pet•bag•ger (kär′pĭt-băg′ər) *n.* A Northerner who went to the South after the Civil War for political or financial advantage. —**car′pet•bag′ger•y** *n.*

car•port (kär′pôrt′, -pōrt′) *n.* A roof projecting from the side of a building, used as a shelter for an automobile.

car•pus (kär′pəs) *n., pl.* **-pi** (-pī′). **1. a.** The wrist. **b.** The bones of the wrist. **2.** Any joint corresponding to the wrist in quadrupeds. [< Gk *karpos,* wrist.]

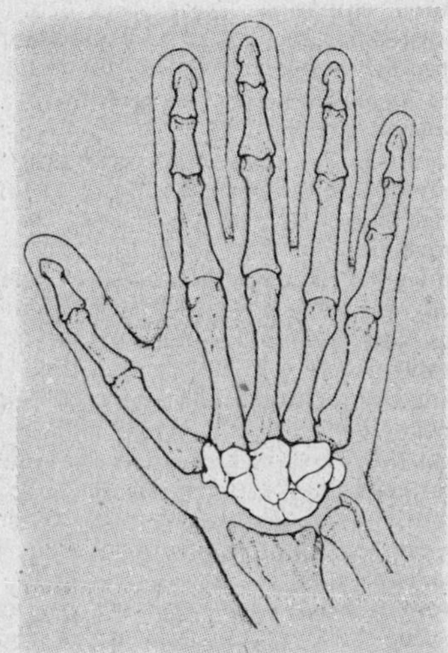

carpus

car•rel (kăr′əl) *n.* A nook in the stacks of a library, designed for individual use. [Perh < OF *carole,* CAROL.]

car•riage (kăr′ĭj) *n.* **1.** A four-wheeled, horse-drawn passenger vehicle. **2.** A movable machine part for holding or shifting another part. **3.** Conveyance of goods; transport. **4.** Manner of carrying oneself; bearing. [< ONF *carier,* to transport in a vehicle, carry.]

car•ri•er (kăr′ē-ər) *n.* **1.** One that carries or conveys. **2.** A person or corporation engaged in transporting passengers or goods. **3.** An immune organism that transmits a pathogen to others. **4.** An **aircraft carrier.**

carrier wave. An electromagnetic wave that can be modulated to transmit sound or images.

car•ri•on (kăr′ē-ən) *n.* Dead and decaying flesh. —*adj.* **1.** Of or similar to carrion. **2.** Carrion-eating. [< L *carō,* flesh.]

car•rot (kăr′ət) *n.* The edible, yellow-orange root of a widely cultivated plant. [< Gk *karōton.*]

car•rou•sel. Variant of **carousel.**

car•ry (kăr′ē) *v.* **-ried, -rying. 1.** To bear; convey; transport. **2.** To win over. **3.** To take; seize; capture. **4.** To keep or have on one's person. **5.** To involve; imply. **6.** To conduct (oneself) in a specified manner. **7.** To sustain; support. **8.** To offer for sale or keep in stock. **9.** To cover a range; reach. **10.** To secure the adoption of. **11.** To win most of the votes of. **12.** To keep in one's accounts. —**carry away.** To excite greatly; transport. —**carry on. 1.** To manage; conduct. **2.** To continue despite hindrance. **3.** To act in a foolish or overwrought manner. —**carry out. 1.** To put into practice. **2.** To obey. —**carry through. 1.** To complete. **2.** To sustain. —*n., pl.* **-ries. 1.** An act or manner of carrying. **2.** A portage, as between two navigable rivers. **3.** The range of a gun or projectile. [< ONF *carier,* to transport in a vehicle.]

Car•son City (kär′sən). The capital of Nevada. Pop. 15,000.

cart (kärt) *n.* **1.** A two-wheeled vehicle. **2.** Any small vehicle. —*v.* **1. a.** To convey in a cart. **b.** To convey laboriously; lug. **2.** To remove or transport unceremoniously: *He was carted off to jail.* [< OE *cræt* and ON *kartr.*] —**cart′a•ble** *adj.* —**cart′er** *n.*

carte blanche (kärt blänsh′). Unrestricted discretion. [F, "blank card."]

car•tel (kär-tĕl′) *n.* A monopolistic combination of independent business enterprises. [< OIt *carta,* card.]

Car•ter (kär′tər), **James Earl ("Jimmy").** Born 1924. 39th President of the U.S. (since 1977).

Car•te•sian (kär-tē′zhən) *adj.* Belonging to the system of Descartes. —**Car•te′sian•ism′** *n.*

Cartesian coordinate. A coordinate in a Cartesian coordinate system.

Cartesian coordinate system. 1. A two-dimensional coordinate system in which the coordinates of a point are its distances from two intersecting, often perpendicular, straight lines, the distance from each being measured along a straight line parallel to the other. **2.** A three-dimensional coordinate system in which the coordinates of a point are its distances from each of three intersecting, often mutually perpendicular, planes along lines parallel to the intersection of the other two.

Car•thage (kär′thĭj). An ancient city on the N coast of Africa. —**Car′tha•gin′i•an** (kär′*thə*-jĭn′ē-ən) *adj.* & *n.*

car•ti•lage (kär′tə-lĭj) *n.* A tough white fibrous connective tissue attached to the articular surfaces of bones. [L *cartilāgo.*] —**car′ti•lag′i•nous** (-lăj′ə-nəs) *adj.*

car•tog•ra•phy (kär-tŏg′rə-fē) *n.* The making of maps. [< F *carte,* map, card + -GRAPHY.] —**car•tog′ra•pher** *n.* —**car′to•graph′ic** (kär′tə-grăf′ĭk) *adj.*

car•ton (kärt′n) *n.* A cardboard box or container. [< It *cartone,* pasteboard.]

car•toon (kär-tōōn′) *n.* **1.** A satirical drawing or caricature. **2.** A painter's preliminary sketch. **3.** A comic strip. [It *cartone,* pasteboard, CARTON.] —**car•toon′ist** *n.*

car•tridge (kär′trĭj) *n.* **1.** A tubular case containing the propellant powder and primer of small arms ammunition or shotgun shells. **2.** A small modular unit of a larger apparatus containing such equipment as a phonograph stylus, photographic film, magnetic tape, or writing ink. [< F *cartouche,* cartridge.]

cart•wheel (kärt′hwēl′) *n.* **1.** The wheel of a cart. **2.** A somersault or handspring with the arms and legs extended. **3.** *Slang.* A silver dollar.

carve (kärv) *v.* **carved, carving. 1.** To divide into pieces by cutting; slice. **2.** To cut and serve meat at table. **3.** To fashion by cutting. [< OE *ceorfan.* See **gerebh-.**] —**carv′er** *n.*

car•y•at•id (kăr′ē-ăt′ĭd) *n., pl.* **-ids** or **-atides** (-ăt′ə-dēz′). A supporting column sculptured in the form of a woman.

ca•sa•ba (kə-sä′bə) *n.* A melon with a yellow rind and sweet, whitish flesh. [< *Kassaba,* former name of Turgutlu, Turkey.]

Cas•a•blan•ca (kăs′ə-blăng′kə, kä′sə-bläng′kə). A seaport of Morocco. Pop. 1,085,000.

Cas•a•no•va (kăs′ə-nō′və, kăz′-) *n.* A philanderer. [< G.J. *Casanova* de Seingalt (1725–1798), Italian adventurer.]

cas•cade (kăs-kād′) *n.* **1.** A waterfall or a series of small waterfalls. **2.** An analogous structure or phenomenon. —*v.* **-caded, -cading.** To fall in or as a cascade. [< It *cascare,* to fall.]

Cascade Range. The N section of the Sierra Nevada Mountains.

cas•car•a (kăs-kăr′ə) *n.* Also **cas•car•a sa•gra•da** (sə-grä′də). The dried bark of a tree of NW North America, used as a laxative. [Span *cáscara,* bark.]

case¹ (kās) *n.* **1.** A specified instance; example. **2.** A question or problem; matter. **3.** A persuasive argument, demonstration, or justification. **4.** An inflectional pattern or form, esp. of a noun or pronoun, expressing syntactic function or relation. **5.** An action or suit in law. **6. a.** An instance of sickness or injury. **b.** A patient. —*v.* **cased, casing.** *Slang.* To inspect (premises), as with intent to rob. [< L *cāsus,* fall, event, occurrence.]

case² (kās) *n.* **1.** A container or receptacle. **2.** A covering. **3.** A set or pair. **4.** The frame of a window or door. **5.** A tray with compartments for storing printing type. —*v.* **cased, casing.** To put into or cover with a case. [< L *capsa,* chest, case.]

case•hard•en (kās′härd′n) *v.* To harden the surface of (iron or steel) by high-temperature shallow infusion of carbon followed by quenching. [< CASE (covering).]

case history. The facts relevant to the development of an individual or group condition under study or treatment.

ca•se•in (kā′sē-ĭn, kā′sēn′) *n.* A white, tasteless, odorless milk and cheese protein, used to make plastics, adhesives, paints, and foods. [< L *cāseus,* cheese.]

case•ment (kās′mənt) *n.* **1.** A window sash that opens outward by means of hinges. **2.** A window with such sashes. **3.** A case or covering. [ME.] —**case′ment•ed** *adj.*

case study. A detailed analysis of an individual or group.

cash (kăsh) *n.* **1.** Ready money. **2.** Immediate money payment for goods or services. —*v.* To exchange for or convert into ready money. [OF *casse,* money box.]

cash•ew (kăsh′ōō, kə-shōō′) *n.* **1.** A tropical American tree bearing kidney-shaped nuts. **2.** The nut of this tree. [< Tupi *acajú.*]

cash•ier¹ (kă-shîr′) *n.* **1.** The officer of a bank or business concern in charge of paying and receiving money. **2.** A business employee responsible for cash transactions. [< F *caisse,* money box.]

cash•ier² (kă-shîr′) *v.* To dismiss in disgrace from a position of responsibility. [Du *casseren.*]

cash•mere (kăzh′mîr′, kăsh′-) *n.* **1.** Fine wool from an Asian goat. **2.** A soft fabric made from this wool. [< *Kashmir,* India.]

cas•ing (kā′sĭng) *n.* An outer cover; case.

ca•si•no (kə-sē′nō) *n., pl.* **-nos.** A gambling house. [It, dim of *casa,* house.]

cask (kăsk, käsk) *n.* A barrel for holding liquids. [Span *casco,* helmet, cask.]

cas•ket (kăs′kĭt, käs′-) *n.* **1.** A small case for jewels or other valuables. **2.** A coffin. [< OF *cassette.*]

Cas•pi•an Sea (kăs′pē-ən). The largest inland

body of water in the world, in SW Asia.

casque (käsk) *n.* A helmet. [< Span *casco*, CASK.]

Cas•san•dra (kə-săn'drə) *n.* One who utters unheeded prophecies. [< *Cassandra*, Trojan prophetess.]

cas•sa•va (kə-sä'və) *n.* A tropical American plant with a starchy root from which tapioca is derived. [Span *cazabe*, cassava bread.]

cas•se•role (kăs'ə-rōl') *n.* **1.** A baking dish in which food is cooked and served. **2.** Food served in such a dish. [< OF, saucepan.]

cas•sette (kă-sĕt') *n.* A cartridge for film or magnetic tape. [F, small box.]

cas•sia (kăsh'ə) *n.* **1. a.** A tropical Asian tree with cinnamonlike bark. **b.** The bark, used as a spice. **2.** Any of various related trees and plants, some of which yield senna. [< Gk *kassia*, a kind of plant.]

Cas•si•o•pe•ia (kăs'ē-ə-pē'ə) *n.* A W-shaped constellation in the N Hemisphere.

cas•sock (kăs'ək) *n.* A long garment worn by clergymen. [< Pers *kazagand*, padded jacket.]

cast (kăst, käst) *v.* **cast, casting. 1.** To throw; hurl; fling. **2.** To turn; direct; aim: *cast an eye.* **3.** To give or deposit (a ballot). **4.** To shed; discard. **5.** To add up (a column of figures); compute. **6.** To assign, as an actor's part. **7.** To form by molding. *—n.* **1.** A throw. **2.** A throw of the dice. **3. a.** A mold. **b.** A rigid plaster dressing, as for immobilizing and protecting a broken bone. **4.** Type; stamp; hue. **5.** A twist, warp, or squint. **6.** Something thrown off or shed. **7.** The actors in a play. [< ON *kasta*, to throw.]

cas•ta•nets (kăs'tə-nĕts') *pl.n.* A pair of concave shells of ivory or hardwood held in the hand and clicked in accompaniment to music and dancing. [< Span *castaña*, chestnut.]

cast•a•way (kăst'ə-wā', käst'-) *adj.* **1.** Shipwrecked; cast adrift or ashore. **2.** Discarded; thrown away. **—cast'a•way'** *n.*

caste (kăst, käst) *n.* **1.** One of the four major hereditary classes into which Hindu society is divided. **2. a.** Any rigidly exclusive social class. **b.** A social system based on such exclusivity. **3.** Social status: *lose caste.* [Port *casta*, caste, race, breed.]

cas•tel•lan (kăs'tə-lən) *n.* The governor of a castle. [< L *castellum*, CASTLE.]

cas•tel•lat•ed (kăs'tə-lā'tĭd) *adj.* Furnished with battlements like a castle.

cast•er (kăs'tər, käs'-) *n.* Also **cas•tor. 1.** A small wheel on a swivel under a piece of furniture or other heavy object, to make it easier to move. **2.** A small bottle or cruet for condiments.

cas•ti•gate (kăs'tə-gāt') *v.* **-gated, -gating.** To punish or criticize severely. [L *castīgāre*, to correct, punish.] **—cas'ti•ga'tion** *n.*

Cas•tile (kăs-tēl'). A region and former kingdom of Spain.

Cas•til•ian (kăs-tĭl'yən) *n.* **1.** Originally, the dialect of Castile, now the standard form of Spanish as spoken in Spain. **2.** A native or inhabitant of Castile. **—Cas•til'ian** *adj.*

cast•ing (kăs'tĭng, käs'-) *n.* **1.** Something cast off or out. **2.** Something cast in a mold. **3.** The selection of actors or performers.

cast iron. A hard, brittle nonmalleable iron-carbon alloy containing 2.0–4.5% carbon and 0.5–3% silicon.

cas•tle (kăs'əl, käs'-) *n.* **1.** A fortified group of buildings. **2.** The rook in chess. *—v.* **-tled, -tling.** *Chess.* To move the king from his own square two squares to one side and then, in the same move, bring the rook from that side to the square immediately past the new position of the king. [< L *castellum*, castle.]

cast off. 1. To discard or reject. **2.** To let go; set loose. **3.** To estimate the space a manuscript will occupy when set into type.

cast-off (kăst'ôf', -ŏf', käst'-) *adj.* Discarded.

cast•off (kăst'ôf', -ŏf', käst'-) *n.* Someone or something that has been discarded.

cas•tor. Variant of **caster.**

cas•tor oil (kăs'tər). A colorless or yellowish oil extracted from the seeds of a tropical plant and used as a cathartic and a fine lubricant.

cas•trate (kăs'trāt') *v.* **-trated, -trating.** To remove the testicles of; geld. [L *castrāre.*] **—cas'tra'tion** *n.*

cas•u•al (kăzh'o͞o-əl) *adj.* **1.** Occurring by chance. **2.** Occasional. **3. a.** Informal. **b.** Designed for informal wear. **4.** Careless; negligent. [< L *cāsus*, fall, chance.] **—cas'u•al•ly** *adv.* **—cas'u•al•ness** *n.*

cas•u•al•ty (kăzh'o͞o-əl-tē) *n., pl.* **-ties. 1.** One injured or killed in an accident. **2.** One injured, killed, captured, or missing in action against an enemy. **3.** A disastrous accident. [< CASUAL.]

cas•u•ist (kăzh'o͞o-ĭst) *n.* One given to adroit rationalization. [< L *cāsus*, chance, case.] **—cas'u•is'tic** *adj.* **—cas'u•is'ti•cal•ly** *adv.* **—cas'u•ist•ry** *n.*

ca•sus bel•li (kā'səs bĕl'ī', kä'səs bĕl'ē'). An act that justifies a declaration of war. [L, "occasion of war."]

cat (kăt) *n.* **1.** A carnivorous mammal domesticated as a catcher of rats and mice and as a pet. **2.** A related animal, as the lion, tiger, or leopard. [< OE *catt* < Gmc **kattuz.*]

cat. catalogue.

cata–. *comb. form.* **1.** Reversing of a process. **2.** Lower in position or down from. [< Gk *kata*, down, down from, according to.]

cat•a•clysm (kăt'ə-klĭz'əm) *n.* A violent and sudden upheaval. [< Gk *katakluzein*, to deluge, inundate.] **—cat'a•clys'mic** (-klĭz'mĭk), **cat'a•clys'mal** (-klĭz'məl) *adj.*

cat•a•combs (kăt'ə-kōmz') *pl.n.* A series of underground tunnels with recesses for graves. [< OF *catacombe*, a subterranean chamber.]

cat•a•falque (kăt'ə-făk', -fôlk', -fôk') *n.* The platform on which a coffin rests during a state funeral. [< VL **catafalicum*, scaffold.]

Cat•a•lan (kăt'l-ăn', -ən) *n.* **1.** A native of Catalonia. **2.** The Romance language of Catalonia. **—Cat'a•lan'** *adj.*

cat•a•lep•sy (kăt'l-ĕp'sē) *n.* Muscular rigidity, lack of awareness of environment, and lack of response to external stimuli. [< Gk *katalēpsis*, "a seizing."] **—cat'a•lep'tic** *adj.*

cat•a•logue (kăt'l-ôg'). Also **cat•a•log.** *n.* An itemized, sometimes descriptive list. *—v.* **-logued, -loguing. 1.** To make a catalogue of. **2.** To list in a catalogue. [< Gk *katalegein*, to recount, enumerate.] **—cat'a•logu'er** *n.*

Cat•a•lo•ni•a (kăt'l-ō'nē-ə, -nyə). A region and former republic of NE Spain.

ca•tal•pa (kə-tăl'pə, -tôl'pə) *n.* A tree with large leaves, showy flower clusters, and long, slender pods. [< Muskhogean.]

cat•a•lyst (kăt'l-ĭst) *n.* A substance that modifies, esp. increases, the rate of a chemical reaction without being consumed in the process. [< Gk *katalusis*, dissolution.] **—ca•tal'y•sis** (kə-tăl'ə-sĭs) *n.* **—cat'a•lyt'ic** *adj.*

cat•a•lyze (kăt'l-īz') *v.* **-lyzed, -lyzing.** To act on (a reaction) as a catalyst.

cat•a•ma•ran (kăt'ə-mə-răn') *n.* A boat with two parallel hulls. [Tamil *kaṭṭumaram.*]

cat•a•mount (kăt'ə-mount') *n.* A mountain lion or lynx. [Short for catamountain, var of earlier *cat of the mountain.*]

cat•a•pult (kăt'ə-pŭlt') *n.* **1.** An ancient military engine for hurling large missiles. **2.** A mechanism for launching aircraft from the deck of a ship. *—v.* To hurl or spring up, as from a catapult. [< Gk *katapaltēs.*]

cat•a•ract (kăt'ə-răkt') *n.* **1.** A great waterfall or downpour. **2.** Opacity of the lens or capsule of the eye, causing partial or total blindness. [< Gk *katar(rh)aktēs*, "a down-swooping."]

ca•tarrh (kə-tär') *n.* Inflammation of mucous membranes, esp. of the nose and throat. [< Gk *katarrhous*, a flowing down.] **—ca•tarrh'al, ca•tarrh'ous** *adj.*

ca•tas•tro•phe (kə-tăs'trə-fē) *n.* A great and sudden calamity; disaster. [< Gk *katastrephein*, to turn down.] **—cat'a•stroph'ic** (kăt'ə-strŏf'ĭk) *adj.* **—cat'a•stroph'i•cal•ly** *adv.*

cat•a•to•ni•a (kăt'ə-tō'nē-ə) *n.* A schizophrenic disorder characterized by immobility, stupor, negativism, and silence. **—cat'a•ton'ic** (-tŏn'ĭk) *adj.* & *n.*

cat•bird (kăt'bûrd') *n.* A dark-gray North American songbird with a call like the mewing of a cat.

cat•boat (kăt'bōt') *n.* A broad-beamed sailboat carrying a single sail on a mast stepped well forward.

cat•call (kăt'kôl') *n.* A shrill cry of derision. **—cat'call'** *v.*

catch (kăch) *v.* **caught, catching. 1.** To capture, esp. after a chase. **2.** To snare or trap. **3.** To surprise. **4.** To take or apprehend suddenly. **5.** To grasp. **6.** To snatch; grab. **7.** To intercept. **8.** To become ensnared. **9.** To become subject to; contract, as by contagion. **10.** To fasten. **11.** To take in and retain. **12.** To get to in time: *catch the plane.* **13.** To watch: *catch a late movie.* *—n.* **1. a.** The act of catching, as a ball. **b.** A game of throwing and catching a ball. **2.** A fastening or checking device. **3.** Something caught. **4.** One worth catching. **5.** A snatch or fragment. **6.** An unsuspected drawback. [< L *captāre*, to chase, strive to seize.]

catch•all (kăch'ôl') *n.* A receptacle for odds and ends. **—catch'all'** *adj.*

catch•er (kăch'ər) *n.* **1.** One that catches. **2.** The baseball player whose position is behind home plate.

catch•ing (kăch'ĭng) *adj.* **1.** Infectious. **2.** Attractive; alluring.

catch•up. A variant of **ketchup.**

catch•y (kăch'ē) *adj.* **-ier, -iest. 1.** Easily remembered: *a catchy melody.* **2.** Tricky; deceptive: *a catchy question.*

cat•e•chism (kăt'ə-kĭz'əm) *n.* An instructional summary of the basic principles of a religion in question-and-answer form. [< LGk *katēkhizein*, to teach orally.] **—cat'e•chist** *n.* **—cat'e•chize'** *v.* **(-chized, -chizing).**

cat•e•chu•men (kăt'ə-kyo͞o'mən) *n.* A convert receiving religious instruction before baptism. [< LGk *katēkhein*, to teach orally.]

cat•e•gor•i•cal (kăt'ə-gôr'ĭ-kəl, -gŏr'ĭ-kəl) *adj.* Also **cat•e•gor•ic.** Absolute; certain. **—cat'e•gor'i•cal•ly** *adv.* **—cat'e•gor'i•cal•ness** *n.*

cat•e•go•rize (kăt'ə-gə-rīz') *v.* **-rized, -rizing.** To put into categories; classify. **—cat'e•go•ri•za'tion** *n.*

cat•e•go•ry (kăt'ə-gôr'ē, -gōr'ē) *n., pl.* **-ries.** A specifically defined division in a system of classification; a class. [< LL *catēgoria*, accusation, predicament, category of predicables.]

cat•e•nar•y (kăt'ə-nĕr'ē, kə-tē'nər-ē) *n., pl.* **-ies.**

The curve theoretically formed by a perfectly flexible, uniform, inextensible cable suspended from two points. [< L *catēna,* chain.]

cat•e•nate (kăt'ə-nāt') *v.* **-nated, -nating.** To connect in a series of ties or links; form into a chain. **—cat'e•na'tion** *n.*

ca•ter (kā'tər) *v.* **1.** To provide food or entertainment. **2.** To provide anything wished for or needed. [< ME *catour,* a caterer.] **—ca'ter•er** *n.*

cat•er-cor•nered (kăt'ər-kôr'nərd, kăt'ē-). Also **cat•er-cor•ner** (-nər), **cat•ty-cor•nered** (kăt'ē-kôr'nərd). *adj.* Diagonal. *—adv.* Diagonally. [< obs *cater,* four at dice.]

cat•er•pil•lar (kăt'ər-pĭl'ər, kăt'ə-) *n.* The wormlike, often hairy larva of a butterfly or moth. [< OF *catepelose,* "hairy cat."]

cat•er•waul (kăt'ər-wôl') *v.* To make a discordant sound or shriek. [< ME *caterwrawen.*] **—cat'er•waul'** *n.*

cat•fish (kăt'fĭsh') *n.* Any of various scaleless fishes with whiskerlike feelers near the mouth.

cat•gut (kăt'gŭt') *n.* A tough cord made from the dried intestines of certain animals.

ca•thar•sis (kə-thär'sĭs) *n., pl.* **-ses** (-sēz'). **1.** Purgation, esp. for the digestive system. **2.** A purifying or figurative cleansing of the emotions. [< Gk *katharsis.*]

ca•thar•tic (kə-thär'tĭk) *adj.* Purgative; cleansing. *—n.* A cathartic agent, as a laxative. **—ca•thar'ti•cal•ly** *adv.*

ca•the•dral (kə-thē'drəl) *n.* The principal church of a bishop's see. [< LL *cathedrālis.*]

cath•e•ter (kăth'ə-tər) *n.* A slender, flexible tube inserted into a body channel to distend or maintain an opening to an internal cavity. [< Gk *kathetēr,* something inserted.]

cath•ode (kăth'ōd') *n.* A negatively charged electrode. [Gk *kathodos,* way down, descent.]

cath•ode-ray tube (kăth'ōd-rā'). A vacuum tube in which a hot cathode emits electrons that are accelerated as a beam, further focused, and allowed to fall on a fluorescent screen.

cath•o•lic (kăth'lĭk, kăth'ə-lĭk) *adj.* **1.** Universal; comprehensive. **2. Catholic.** Of or pertaining to Catholics or to the Roman Catholic Church. *—n.* **Catholic.** A member of the Roman Catholic Church. [< Gk *katholou,* in general.] **—ca•thol'i•cal•ly** (kə-thŏl'ĭk-lē) *adv.*

Ca•thol•i•cism (kə-thŏl'ə-sĭz'əm) *n.* The faith, doctrine, system, and practice of the Roman Catholic Church.

cath•o•lic•i•ty (kăth'ə-lĭs'ə-tē) *n.* **1.** Broadmindedness. **2.** Comprehensiveness; universality. **3. Catholicity.** Roman Catholicism.

cat•i•on (kăt'ī'ən) *n.* An ion having a positive charge and, in electrolytes, characteristically moving toward a negative electrode. [< Gk *katienai,* to go down.] **—cat'i•on'ic** (-ŏn'ĭk) *adj.*

cat•kin (kăt'kĭn') *n. Bot.* A dense cluster of scalelike flowers, as of a birch.

cat nap. A short nap.

cat•nip (kăt'nĭp') *n.* An aromatic plant to which cats are strongly attracted.

cat-o'-nine-tails (kăt'ə-nīn'tālz') *n.* A whip consisting of nine knotted cords fastened to a handle.

cat's cradle. A game in which an intricately looped string is transferred from the hands of one player to another.

Cats•kills (kăts'kĭlz'). A mountain range in SE New York State.

cat's-paw (kăts'pô') *n.* Also **cats•paw.** A dupe or tool.

cat•sup. A variant of **ketchup.**

cat•tail (kăt'tāl') *n.* A tall-stemmed, long-leaved marsh plant with a dense, brown, cylindrical flower head.

cat•tle (kăt'l) *pl.n.* Horned, hoofed mammals, as cows, bulls, and oxen, esp. those domesticated for beef, dairy products, etc. [ME *catel,* personal property, livestock < ML *capitāle,* property.]

cat•ty (kăt'ē) *adj.* **-tier, -tiest.** Malicious; spiteful. **—cat'ti•ly** *adv.* **—cat'ti•ness** *n.*

cat•ty-cor•nered. Variant of **cater-cornered.**

cat•walk (kăt'wôk') *n.* A narrow walk, as on the sides of a bridge.

Cau•ca•sian (kô-kā'zhən, -kăzh'ən, -kā'shən, -kăsh'ən) *n.* **1.** A native of the Caucasus. **2.** A member of the Caucasoid ethnic division. **3.** The group of languages spoken in the area of the Caucasus that are neither Indo-European nor Altaic. [< the CAUCASUS.] **—Cau•ca'sian** *adj.*

Cau•ca•soid (kô'kə-soid') *adj.* Pertaining to a major ethnic division of the human species having skin color varying from very light to brown. *—n.* A Caucasoid individual.

Cau•ca•sus (kô'kə-səs). A region and range of mountains in the SW Soviet Union.

cau•cus (kô'kəs) *n., pl.* **-cuses** or **-cusses.** A meeting of the members of a political party to decide upon questions of policy and the selection of candidates for office. [Prob < Algon.] **—cau'cus** *v.* **(-cused** or **-cussed, -cusing** or **-cussing).**

cau•dal (kôd'l) *adj.* Of the tail or hind parts. [< L *cauda,* tail.] **—cau'dal•ly** *adv.*

caught (kôt). *p.t.* & *p.p.* of **catch.**

caul•dron. Variant of **caldron.**

cau•li•flow•er (kô'lĭ-flou'ər, kŏl'ĭ-) *n.* **1.** A cabbagelike plant with a large, compact, whitish flower head, eaten as a vegetable. **2.** The head itself. [Prob < It *cavolofiore,* "flowered cabbage."]

cauliflower ear. An ear deformed by repeated blows.

caulk (kôk) *v.* Also **calk.** **1.** To make (a boat) watertight by packing seams with oakum or tar. **2.** To make (pipes) tight against leakage by sealing. [< ONF *cauquer,* to trample, tread.] **—caulk'er** *n.*

caus•al (kô'zəl) *adj.* **1.** Pertaining to or involving a cause. **2.** Constituting or expressing a cause. **—cau•sal'i•ty** (-zăl'ə-tē) *n.* **—caus'al•ly** *adv.*

cau•sa•tion (kô-zā'shən) *n.* **1.** The act or process of causing. **2.** A causal agency.

cause (kôz) *n.* **1.** A person or thing responsible for an action or result. **2.** A reason; motive. **3.** Good or sufficient reason. **4.** A goal or principle. **5.** *Law.* **a.** The ground for legal action. **b.** A lawsuit. *—v.* **caused, causing.** To make happen; bring about. [< L *causa,* reason, purpose, motive.] **—caus'er** *n.*

cause cé•lè•bre (kōz sā-lĕb'r'). *French.* **1.** A celebrated legal case. **2.** An issue arousing heated debate.

cause•way (kôz'wā') *n.* A raised roadway across water or marshland. [< VL *calciāta, paved + WAY.]

caus•tic (kôs'tĭk) *adj.* **1.** Able to burn, corrode, or dissolve. **2.** Biting or cutting: *caustic comment.* [< Gk *kaustikos.*]

cau•ter•ize (kô'tə-rīz') *v.* **-ized, -izing.** To burn or sear so as to destroy aberrant tissue. [< Gk *kautēriazein,* to brand.] **—cau'ter•i•za'tion** *n.*

cau•tion (kô'shən) *n.* **1.** Forethought to avoid danger or harm. **2.** A warning. **3.** *Informal.* Someone or something that is striking. *—v.* To warn against danger; put on guard. [< L *cautiō,* a guarding.] **—cau'tion•ar'y** *adj.*

cau•tious (kô'shəs) *adj.* Practicing caution; wary; careful. **—cau'tious•ly** *adv.*

cav•al•cade (kăv'əl-kād', kăv'əl-kād') *n.* **1.** A ceremonial procession, esp. of horsemen. **2.** A colorful procession or pageant. [< OIt *cavalcare,* to ride on horseback.]

cav•a•lier (kăv'ə-lĭr') *n.* **1.** A gentleman accomplished in arms. **2.** A gallant. **3.** A lady's dancing partner. *—adj.* **1.** Haughty; arrogant. **2.** Carefree and gay; offhand. [< LL *caballārius,* horseman.] **—cav'a•lier'ly** *adv.*

cav•al•ry (kăv'əl-rē) *n., pl.* **-ries.** Troops mounted on horseback or riding in armored vehicles. [< OIt *cavaliere,* cavalier.] **—cav'al•ry•man** *n.*

cave (kāv) *n.* A hollow beneath the earth's surface, often having an opening in the side of a hill or cliff. [< L *cavus,* hollow.]

ca•ve•at (kā'vē-ăt', kăv'ē-, kä'vē-) *n.* A warning. [L, let him beware.]

cave in. To collapse.

cave-in (kāv'ĭn') *n.* **1.** An action of caving in. **2.** A place where the ground has caved in.

cave man. **1.** A prehistoric man who lived in caves. **2.** One who is crude or brutal, esp. toward women.

cav•ern (kăv'ərn) *n.* A large cave. [< L *cavus,* hollow.] **—cav'ern•ous** *adj.*

cav•i•ar (kăv'ē-är') *n.* Also **cav•i•are.** The salted roe of a sturgeon or other large fish, eaten as a relish. [Prob < Turk *havyār.*]

cav•il (kăv'əl) *v.* **-iled** or **-illed, -iling** or **-illing.** To quibble or carp. *—n.* A trivial objection. [< L *cavillārī,* to satirize, criticize.]

cav•i•ty (kăv'ə-tē) *n., pl.* **-ties.** **1.** A hollow or hole. **2.** A pitted area in a tooth, caused by caries. [< LL *cavitās,* hollowness.]

ca•vort (kə-vôrt') *v.* To prance; caper; frolic.

caw (kô) *n.* The hoarse, raucous call of a crow or similar bird. [Imit.] **—caw** *v.*

cay (kē, kā) *n.* An islet of coral or sand; key. [Prob < OF *quai,* quay.]

cay•enne pepper (kī-ĕn', kā-). Also **cay•enne.** A very pungent condiment made from the fruit of a variety of the pepper plant. [< Tupi *kyinha.*]

Cb columbium.

C.B.D. cash before delivery.

cc cubic centimeter.

cc. chapters.

c.c. carbon copy.

CCC Civilian Conservation Corps.

Cd cadmium.

c.d. cash discount.

Cdr. commander.

Ce cerium.

C.E. **1.** chemical engineer. **2.** civil engineer.

cease (sēs) *v.* **ceased, ceasing.** To discontinue; stop. *—n.* Cessation. [< L *cessāre,* to delay, stop.] **—cease'less** *adj.* **—cease'less•ly** *adv.*

cease-fire (sēs'fīr') *n.* A suspension of active hostilities; truce.

ce•cum (sē'kəm) *n., pl.* **-ca** (-kə). Also **cae•cum.** **1.** A cavity with only one opening. **2.** The large pouch forming the beginning of the large intestine. [< L *(intestinum) caecum,* blind (intestine).] **—ce'cal** (sē'kəl) *adj.*

ce•dar (sē'dər) *n.* **1.** Any of various evergreen trees with durable, aromatic, often reddish wood. **2.** The wood of such a tree. [< L *cedrus,* cedar, juniper.]

cede (sēd) *v.* **ceded, ceding.** **1.** To relinquish, as by treaty. **2.** To transfer; assign. [< L *cēdere,* withdraw.]

ceil•ing (sē'lĭng) *n.* **1.** The interior upper surface of a room. **2.** A maximum limit. **3.** A vertical boundary, as of operable aircraft altitude. [ME *celing*.]

cel•a•don (sĕl'ə-dŏn') *n.* **1.** Pale to very pale green. **2.** Pale to very pale blue. [< *Céladon,* wan character in d'Urfé's *"Astrée"* (1610).] **—cel'a•don'** *adj.*

cel•e•brant (sĕl'ə-brənt) *n.* **1.** The priest officiating at the celebration of the Eucharist. **2.** One who participates in a celebration.

cel•e•brate (sĕl'ə-brāt') *v.* **-brated, -brating. 1.** To observe (a day or event) with ceremonies of respect or festivity. **2.** To perform (a religious ceremony). **3.** To extol; praise. [L *celebrāre,* to frequent, fill, celebrate.] **—cel'e•bra'tion** *n.* **—cel'e•bra'tor** *n.*

cel•e•brat•ed (sĕl'ə-brā'tĭd) *adj.* Famous.

ce•leb•ri•ty (sə-lĕb'rə-tē) *n., pl.* **-ties. 1.** A famous person. **2.** Renown; fame. [L *celebritās.*]

ce•ler•i•ty (sə-lĕr'ə-tē) *n.* Swiftness; speed. [< L *celer,* swift.]

cel•er•y (sĕl'ər-ē) *n.* A plant cultivated for its succulent, edible stalks and its small seeds, used as seasoning. [< Gk *selinon.*]

ce•les•tial (sə-lĕs'chəl) *adj.* **1.** Pertaining to the sky or the heavens. **2.** Heavenly; divine. [< L *caelestis* < *caelum,* sky, heaven.]

celestial equator. A great circle on the celestial sphere in the same plane as the earth's equator.

celestial navigation. Ship or aircraft navigation based on the positions of celestial bodies.

celestial pole. Either of two points at which the earth's axis intersects the celestial sphere.

celestial sphere. An imaginary sphere of infinite extent with the earth at its center.

ce•li•ac (sē'lē-ăk') *adj.* Of or relating to the abdomen.

cel•i•ba•cy (sĕl'ə-bə-sē) *n.* The condition of being unmarried, esp. because of religious vows. [< L *caelebs,* unmarried.]

cel•i•bate (sĕl'ə-bĭt) *n.* One who remains unmarried. *—adj.* Unmarried.

cell (sĕl) *n.* **1.** A narrow, confining room, as in a prison or convent. **2.** The basic organizational unit of some revolutionary parties. **3.** *Biol.* The smallest structural unit of an organism that is capable of independent functioning, consisting of nuclei, cytoplasm, various organelles, and inanimate matter, all surrounded by a membrane. **4.** A small enclosed cavity or space, as in a honeycomb. **5.** *Elec.* **a.** A single unit for electrolysis or for conversion of chemical into electric energy, usually consisting of a container with electrodes and an electrolyte. **b.** A single unit that converts radiant energy into electric energy. [< L *cella,* storeroom, chamber.]

cel•lar (sĕl'ər) *n.* **1.** An underground storage room. **2.** A stock of wines. [< L *cella,* storeroom, CELL.]

cel•lo (chĕl'ō) *n., pl.* **-los.** Also **'cel•lo.** An instrument of the violin family, pitched lower than the viola but higher than the double bass. [Short for VIOLONCELLO.] **—cel'list** *n.*

cel•lo•phane (sĕl'ə-fān') *n.* A thin, flexible, transparent cellulose material used as a moistureproof wrapping. [< CELLULOSE.]

cel•lu•lar (sĕl'yə-lər) *adj.* **1.** Of or resembling a cell. **2.** Consisting of cells.

Cel•lu•loid (sĕl'yə-loid') *n.* A trademark for a colorless, flammable material used for toys, toilet articles, and photographic film.

cel•lu•lose (sĕl'yə-lōs', -lōz') *n.* An amorphous polymer, $(C_6H_{10}O_5)_x$, the main constituent of all plant tissues and fibers, used in the manufacture of paper, textiles, and explosives. [< F *cellule,* biological cell.]

Cel•o•tex (sĕl'ə-tĕks) *n.* A trademark for a building board used for insulation and soundproofing.

Cel•si•us (sĕl'sē-əs, -shəs) *adj.* Pertaining to a temperature scale that registers the freezing point of water as 0°C and the boiling point as 100°C under normal atmospheric pressure; centigrade. [< A. *Celsius* (1701–1744), Swedish astronomer.]

Celt (kĕlt, sĕlt) *n.* Also **Kelt** (kĕlt). **1.** One of an ancient people of W and C Europe, including the Britons and the Gauls. **2.** A speaker of a Celtic language.

Celt•ic (kĕl'tĭk, sĕl'-). Also **Kelt•ic** (kĕl'tĭk) *n.* A subfamily of the Indo-European family of languages, including Welsh, Irish Gaelic, and Scottish Gaelic. **—Celt'ic** *adj.*

cem•ba•lo (chĕm'bə-lō') *n., pl.* **-los.** A harpsichord. [It.]

ce•ment (sĭ-mĕnt') *n.* **1.** A construction adhesive, essentially powdered, calcined rock and clay materials that form a paste with water and set as a solid mass. **2.** Any adhesive; glue. **3.** Also **ce•ment•um** (sĭ-mĕn'təm). A bony substance covering the roots of teeth. *—v.* To bind with or as if with cement. [< L *caementum,* rough quarried stone.] **—ce•ment'er** *n.*

cem•e•ter•y (sĕm'ə-tĕr'ē) *n., pl.* **-ies.** A graveyard. [< Gk *koimētērion,* sleeping room, burial place.]

cen. **1.** central. **2.** century.

—cene. *comb. form.* A recent geologic period: **Eocene.** [< Gk *kainos,* new, fresh.]

cen•o•bite (sĕn'ə-bīt', sē'nə-) *n.* A member of a religious convent or community. [< Gk *koinobion,* life in community.] **—cen'o•bit'ic** (-bĭt'ĭk), **cen'o•bit'i•cal** *adj.*

cen•o•taph (sĕn'ə-tăf', -täf') *n.* A monument erected in honor of a dead person whose remains lie elsewhere. [< Gk *kenotaphion,* empty tomb.] **—cen'o•taph'ic** *adj.*

Ce•no•zo•ic (sē'nə-zō'ĭk, sĕn'ə-) *adj.* Pertaining to the most recent era of geologic time, which includes the Tertiary and Quaternary periods and is characterized by the evolution of mammals, birds, plants, modern continents, and glaciation. *—n.* The Cenozoic era.

cen•sor (sĕn'sər) *n.* **1.** An official examiner of printed or other materials, who may prohibit what he considers objectionable. **2.** One of two Roman magistrates responsible for supervising the census. *—v.* To examine and expurgate. [< L *cēnsēre,* to assess, estimate, judge.] **—cen•so'ri•al** (sĕn-sôr'ē-əl, sĕn-sōr'-) *adj.*

cen•so•ri•ous (sĕn-sôr'ē-əs, sĕn-sōr'-) *adj.* Faultfinding or critical. **—cen•so'ri•ous•ly** *adv.*

cen•sor•ship (sĕn'sər-shĭp') *n.* **1.** The action or a policy of censoring. **2.** The office of a Roman censor.

cen•sure (sĕn'shər) *n.* An expression of blame or disapproval. *—v.* **-sured, -suring.** To criticize severely; blame. [< L *cēnsor,* censor.] **—cen'sur•a•ble** *adj.* **—cen'sur•er** *n.*

cen•sus (sĕn'səs) *n., pl.* **-suses.** A periodic official enumeration of population. [< L *cēnsēre,* to assess, tax.]

cent (sĕnt) *n.* **1.** A subdivision of the dollar of the U.S. **2.** A subdivision of the dollar of Australia, Canada, Ethiopia, Guyana, Jamaica, Liberia, Malaysia, New Zealand, Trinidad and Tobago, Western Samoa, Hong Kong, and Singapore. **3.** A subdivision of the guilder of the Netherlands, Surinam, and the Netherland Antilles, the leone of Sierra Leone, the piaster of South Vietnam, the rand of the Republic of South Africa, the rupee of Ceylon and Mauritius, and the yuan of the Republic of China. **4.** A subdivision of the shilling of Kenya, Tanzania, Uganda, and the Somali Republic. [OF, "hundred."]

cent. **1.** central. **2.** century.

cen•taur (sĕn'tôr') *n.* One of a race of mythological monsters having the head, arms, and trunk of a man and the body and legs of a horse.

Cen•tau•rus (sĕn-tôr'əs) *n.* Also **Cen•taur** (sĕn'tôr'). A constellation in the S Hemisphere.

cen•ta•vo (sĕn-tä'vō) *n., pl.* **-vos.** A monetary unit equal to 1/100 of the colon of El Salvador, the cordoba of Nicaragua, the escudo of Portugal, the lempira of Honduras, the cruzeiro of Brazil, the peso of Argentina, Bolivia, Colombia, Cuba, the Dominican Republic, Mexico, and the Philippines, the quetzal of Guatemala, the sol of Peru, and the sucre of Ecuador. [Span, "a hundredth."]

cen•te•nar•i•an (sĕn'tə-nâr'ē-ən) *n.* A person one hundred years old or older. **—cen'te•nar'i•an** *adj.*

cen•ten•a•ry (sĕn-tĕn'ə-rē, sĕn'tə-nĕr'ē) *adj. & n.* Centennial. [L *centēnārius,* of a hundred.]

cen•ten•ni•al (sĕn-tĕn'ē-əl) *adj.* **1.** Of or pertaining to an age or period of 100 years. **2.** Of or pertaining to a 100th anniversary. *—n.* A 100th anniversary or its celebration. [L *centum,* hundred + (BI)ENNIAL.] **—cen•ten'ni•al•ly** *adv.*

cen•ter (sĕn'tər). Also *chiefly Brit.* **cen•tre.** *n.* **1.** A point equidistant or at the average distance from all points on the sides or outer boundaries of anything; middle. **2. a.** A point equidistant from the vertexes of a regular polygon. **b.** A point equidistant from all points on the circumference of a circle or on the surface of a sphere. **3.** A point around which something revolves; axis. **4.** A part of an object that is surrounded by the rest; core. **5.** A place of concentrated activity or influence. **6.** A group whose political views and practice are midway between liberal and conservative positions. **7.** A player who holds a middle position. *—v.* **1.** To place in or on a center. **2.** To concentrate or cluster. **3.** To have a center. [< L *centrum.*]

cen•ter•board (sĕn'tər-bôrd', -bōrd') *n.* A flat board or metal plate that can be lowered through the bottom of a sailboat as a keel.

cen•ter•piece (sĕn'tər-pēs') *n.* A decorative object or arrangement placed at the center of a dining table.

centi–. *comb. form.* A hundredth. [< L *centum,* hundred.]

cen•ti•grade (sĕn'tĭ-grād') *adj.* **1.** Divided into 100°. **2.** Celsius.

cen•ti•gram (sĕn'tĭ-grăm) *n.* One hundredth of a gram.

cen•ti•li•ter (sĕn'tə-lē'tər) *n.* One hundredth of a liter.

cen•time (sän'tēm') *n.* **1.** A subdivision of the franc of France, Belgium, Burundi, Cameroun, Central African Republic, Chad, Congo (Brazzaville), Dahomey, Gabon, Guinea, Ivory Coast, Luxembourg, Malagasy Republic, Mali, Mauritania, Niger, Rwanda, Senegal, Switzerland, Togo, Upper Volta, and of various overseas departments and territories of France. **2. a.** A subdivision of the dinar of Algeria. **b.** A subdivision of the gourde of Haiti.

cen•ti•me•ter (sĕn'tə-mē'tər, sän'-) *n.* Also **cen•ti•me•tre.** A unit of length equal to 1/100 of a meter or 0.3937 inch.

cen•ti•pede (sĕn'tə-pēd') *n.* A wormlike arthropod with many legs and body segments.
cen•tral (sĕn'trəl) *adj.* **1.** At, near, or being the center. **2.** Principal; essential. *—n.* **1.** A telephone exchange. **2.** A telephone-exchange operator. **—cen'tral•ly** *adv.*
Central African Republic. A country of C Africa. Pop. 1,800,000. Cap. Bangui.

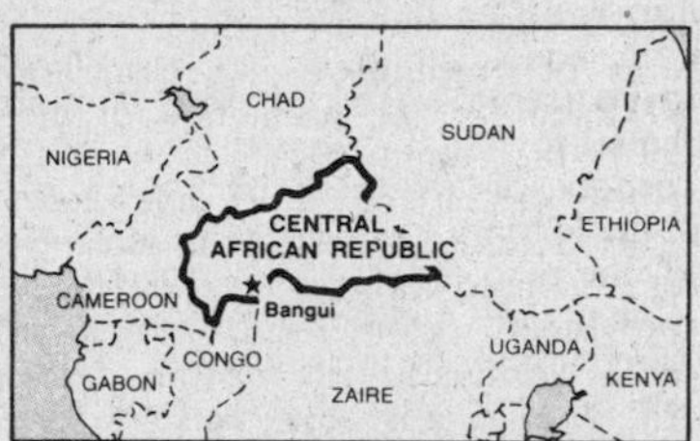

Central African Republic

Central America. The region extending from the S border of Mexico to the N border of Colombia. **—Central American.**
cen•tral•ism (sĕn'trəl-ĭz'əm) *n.* The assignment of authority to a central leadership, as in an organization. **—cen'tral•ist** *n.* & *adj.* **—cen'tral•is'tic** (sĕn'trəl-ĭs'tĭk) *adj.*
cen•tral•i•ty (sĕn-trăl'ə-tē) *n.* The state or quality of being central.
cen•tral•ize (sĕn'trəl-īz') *v.* **-ized, -izing.** To draw toward the center or under central authority. **—cen'tral•i•za'tion** *n.*
central nervous system. The portion of the vertebrate nervous system consisting of the brain and spinal cord.
Central Standard Time. The local civil time of the 90th meridian W of Greenwich, England, six hours earlier than Greenwich time, observed in the C United States.
cen•tre. *Chiefly Brit.* Variant of **center.**
cen•trif•u•gal (sĕn-trĭf'yə-gəl, -trĭf'ə-gəl) *adj.* **1.** Moving or directed away from a center or axis. **2.** Operated by means of centrifugal force. **—cen•trif'u•gal•ly** *adv.*
centrifugal force. The component of apparent force on a body in nonlinear motion, as observed from that body, that is directed away from the center of curvature or axis of rotation.
cen•tri•fuge (sĕn'trə-fyōōj') *n.* A compartment spun about a central axis to separate contained materials of different density or to simulate gravity with centrifugal force. **—cen•trif'u•ga'tion** (sĕn-trĭf'yə-gā'shən, sĕn-trĭf'ə-) *n.*
cen•trip•e•tal (sĕn-trĭp'ə-təl) *adj.* Directed or moving toward a center or axis. **—cen•trip'e•tal•ly** *adv.*
cen•trist (sĕn'trĭst) *n.* One taking a position in the political center.
cen•tro•some (sĕn'trə-sōm') *n.* A small mass of differentiated cytoplasm.
cen•tu•ri•on (sĕn-t/y/ōōr'ē-ən) *n.* An officer commanding a century in the Roman army. [< L *centuriō.*]
cen•tu•ry (sĕn'chə-rē) *n., pl.* **-ries. 1.** A period of 100 years. **2.** A unit of the Roman army. [L *centuria,* a group of a hundred.]
ce•phal•ic (sə-făl'ĭk) *adj.* In, on, or relating to the head or skull. [< Gk *kephalē,* head.]
-cephalic. *comb. form.* Head or skull: *orthocephalic.*
cephalic index. The ratio of the maximum width of the head to its maximum length, multiplied by 100.
ceph•a•li•za•tion (sĕf'ə-lə-zā'shən) *n. Zool.* The gradually increasing concentration of the brain and sensory organs in the head during animal evolution.
-cephalus. *comb. form.* A head: **hydrocephalous.**
ce•ram•ic (sə-răm'ĭk) *n.* **1.** Any of various hard, brittle, heat-resistant and corrosion-resistant materials made by firing clay or other minerals. **2. ceramics.** *(takes sing. v.).* **a.** Objects made of such materials. **b.** The art or technique of making objects of such materials, esp. from fired clay or porcelain. [< Gk *keramos,* potter's clay, earthenware.] **—ce•ram'ic** *adj.* **—ce•ram'ist** *n.*
ce•re•al (sîr'ē-əl) *n.* **1.** An edible grain, as wheat or corn. **2.** A food prepared from such grain. [L *cereālis,* of grain.] **—ce're•al** *adj.*
cer•e•bel•lum (sĕr'ə-bĕl'əm) *n., pl.* **-lums** or **-bella** (-bĕl'ə). The structure of the brain responsible for regulation of complex voluntary muscular movement. [< L *cerebrum,* brain.] **—cer'e•bel'lar** (-bĕl'ər) *adj.*
ce•re•bral (sə-rē'brəl, sĕr'ə-brəl) *adj.* **1.** Of or pertaining to the brain or cerebrum. **2.** Appealing to or marked by the intellect. **—ce•re'bral•ly** *adv.*
cerebral cortex. The extensive outer layer of gray tissue of the cerebral hemispheres, largely responsible for higher nervous functions.
cerebral palsy. Impaired muscular power and coordination from brain damage usually occurring at or before birth.
ce•re•bro•spi•nal (sə-rē'brō-spī'nəl, sĕr'ə-brō-) *adj.* Pertaining to the brain and spinal cord.
cerebrospinal fluid. The serumlike fluid that bathes the lateral ventricles of the brain and the cavity of the spinal cord.
cerebrospinal meningitis. An acute, infectious, often fatal epidemic meningitis.
ce•re•brum (sə-rē'brəm, sĕr'ə-brəm) *n., pl.* **-brums** or **-bra** (-brə). The large rounded structure of the brain occupying most of the cranial cavity, divided into two cerebral hemispheres. [L, brain.]
cere•cloth (sîr'klôth', -klŏth') *n.* Cloth coated with wax, formerly used for wrapping the dead.
cere•ment (sîr'mənt) *n.* A shroud.
cer•e•mo•ni•al (sĕr'ə-mō'nē-əl) *adj.* Characterized by ceremony; formal. *—n.* A set of ceremonies for an occasion; a rite. **—cer'e•mo'ni•al•ist** *n.* **—cer'e•mo'ni•al•ly** *adv.*
cer•e•mo•ni•ous (sĕr'ə-mō'nē-əs) *adj.* **1.** Fond of ceremony. **2.** Rigidly formal. **—cer'e•mo'ni•ous•ly** *adv.* **—cer'e•mo'ni•ous•ness** *n.*
cer•e•mo•ny (sĕr'ə-mō'nē) *n., pl.* **-nies. 1.** A formal act or set of acts as prescribed by ritual, custom, or etiquette. **2.** Strict observance of formalities or etiquette. [< L *caerimōnia,* sacredness, religious rite.]
ce•re•us (sîr'ē-əs) *n.* Any of several tall tropical American cacti. [< L *cēra,* wax.]
cer•iph. *Chiefly Brit.* Variant of **serif.**
ce•rise (sə-rēs', -rēz') *n.* Purplish red. [< OF, cherry.]
ce•ri•um (sîr'ē-əm) *n. Symbol* **Ce** A lustrous, iron-gray, malleable metallic element, used in various metallurgic and nuclear applications. Atomic number 58, atomic weight 140.12. [< *Ceres,* an asteroid between Mars and Saturn.]
ce•rous (sîr'əs) *adj.* Of, pertaining to, or containing cerium. [CER(IUM) + -OUS.]
cert. certificate; certification; certified.
cer•tain (sûrt'n) *adj.* **1.** Definite. **2.** Inevitable. **3.** Indisputable. **4.** Dependable. **5.** Not identified but assumed to be known: *a certain woman.* **6.** Limited: *to a certain degree. —pron.* An indefinite but limited number; some. **—for certain.** Surely. [< VL **certānus.*] **—cer'tain•ly** *adv.*
cer•tain•ty (sûrt'n-tē) *n., pl.* **-ties. 1.** The state of being certain. **2.** An established fact.
certif. certificate.
cer•tif•i•cate (sər-tĭf'ĭ-kĭt) *n.* **1.** A document testifying to a fact, qualification, or promise. **2.** A written statement legally authenticated. *—v.* (sər-tĭf'ə-kāt') **-cated, -cating.** To authorize by a certificate. [< LL *certificāre,* CERTIFY.] **—cer'ti•fi•ca'tion** *n.*
cer•ti•fied (sûr'tə-fīd') *adj.* **1.** Guaranteed in writing. **2.** Holding a certificate. **3.** Committed to a mental institution.
certified check. A check guaranteed by a bank.
certified mail. Uninsured first-class mail whose delivery is recorded by having the addressee sign for it.
certified public accountant. An accountant who has met a state's legal requirements.
cer•ti•fy (sûr'tə-fī') *v.* **-fied, -fying. 1.** To confirm formally as true, accurate, or genuine. **2.** To acknowledge on (a check) that the depositor has funds for its payment. **3.** To declare legally insane. [< LL *certificāre,* to make certain.] **—cer'ti•fi'a•ble** *adj.* **—cer'ti•fi'a•bly** *adv.* **—cer'ti•fi'er** *n.*
cer•ti•tude (sûr'tə-t/y/ōōd') *n.* Complete assurance.
ce•ru•le•an (sə-rōō'lē-ən) *adj.* Sky-blue; azure. [< L *caeruleus,* dark-blue, azure.]
ce•ru•men (sə-rōō'mən) *n.* A yellowish, waxy secretion of the external ear; earwax. [< L *cēra,* wax.]
Cer•van•tes Sa•a•ve•dra (sər-văn'tēz sä'-ä-vē'drä), **Miguel de.** 1547–1616. Spanish author.
cer•vi•cal (sûr'vĭ-kəl) *adj.* Pertaining to a neck or a cervix.
cer•vine (sûr'vīn') *adj.* Pertaining to, resembling, or characteristic of a deer. [< L *cervus,* deer. See **ker-¹.**]
cer•vix (sûr'vĭks) *n., pl.* **-vixes** or **-vices** (-və-sēz', -vī'sēz). A neck-shaped anatomical structure, as the narrow outer end of the uterus. [L *cervix,* neck.]
Ce•sar•e•an, Ce•sar•i•an. Variants of **Caesarean.**
ce•si•um (sē'zē-əm) *n.* Also **cae•si•um.** *Symbol* **Cs** A soft, silvery-white ductile metal, liquid at room temperature, used in photoelectric cells. Atomic number 55, atomic weight 132.905. [< L *caesius,* bluish-gray.]
ces•sa•tion (sĕ-sā'shən) *n.* A ceasing; a temporary or complete halt.
ces•sion (sĕsh'ən) *n.* **1.** A surrendering, as of territory to another country by treaty. **2.** A ceded territory. [< L *cessiō.*]
cess•pool (sĕs'pōōl') *n.* A covered hole or pit for receiving sewage. [Var of earlier *cesperalle,* drainpipe.]
ce•ta•ce•an (sĭ-tā'shən) *n.* A whale or related aquatic mammal. [< L *cētus,* whale.]
Ce•tus (sē'təs) *n.* A constellation in the equatorial region of the S Hemisphere.
Cey•lon (sĭ-lŏn'). The former name for Sri Lanka. **—Cey'lo•nese'** (sĕ'lə-nēz', -nēs') *adj.* & *n.*
Ceylon lily. A large, bulbous plant of the amaryllis family, native to S Asia, having red-striped white flowers.
Cf californium.
cf. compare (L *confer*).
c.f. cost and freight.
C.F. cost and freight.

C/F *Acct.* carried forward.
c.f.i. cost, freight, and insurance.
cg centigram.
c.g. center of gravity.
C.G. **1.** coast guard. **2.** commanding general. **3.** consul general.
ch chain (measurement).
ch. **1.** chaplain. **2.** chapter. **3.** check. **4.** chief. **5.** child; children. **6.** church.
C.H. **1.** clearing-house. **2.** courthouse. **3.** customhouse.
Cha•blis (shă-blē′) *n.* A dry white wine made in Chablis, France.
Chad (chăd). A republic in north-central Africa. Pop. 3,800,000. Cap. N'Djamena.

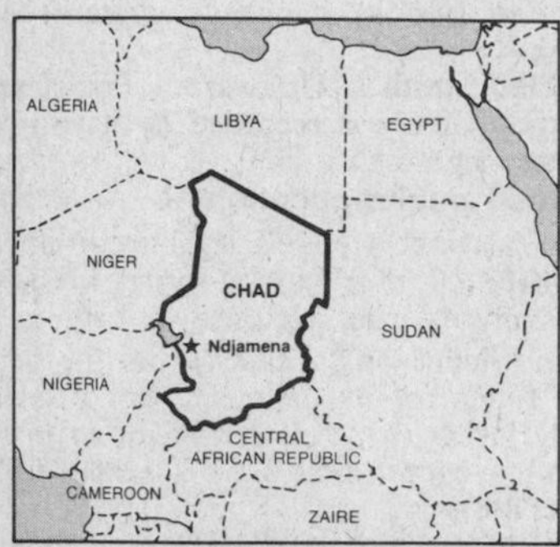

Chad

chafe (chāf) *v.* **chafed, chafing. 1.** To make or become worn or sore from rubbing. **2.** To make or become annoyed. **3.** To warm by rubbing. [< OF *chauffer,* to warm (by rubbing).]
chaff[1] (chăf) *n.* **1.** Grain husks separated from the seed, as by threshing. **2.** Trivial or worthless matter. **3.** Strips of metal foil released in the atmosphere to inhibit radar. [< OE *ceaf.*]
chaff[2] (chăf) *v.* To make fun of good-naturedly; tease. —*n.* Good-natured teasing; banter. [Prob a blend of CHAFF and CHAFE.] —**chaff′er** *n.*
chaf•fer (chăf′ər) *v.* To bargain or haggle. [ME *cheapfare,* trade, merchandise.] —**chaf′fer•er** *n.*
chaf•finch (chăf′ĭnch) *n.* A small European songbird with reddish-brown plumage. [< CHAFF[1] + FINCH.]
chafing dish. A dish or pan heated from below, used to cook food at the table.
cha•grin (shə-grĭn′) *n.* Embarrassment or humiliation. —*v.* To humiliate. [F, sadness.]
chain (chān) *n.* **1.** A connected, flexible series of links, usually of metal, used for binding or connecting. **2.** Anything that restrains. **3. chains.** Bonds, fetters, or shackles. **4.** Any series of related things. **5.** A number of commercial establishments, under common ownership. **6. a.** A measuring instrument for surveying, consisting of 100 linked pieces of iron or steel. **b.** A unit of length, equal to 100 links or 66 feet. **7. a.** A similar instrument used in engineering. **b.** A unit of length equal to 100 feet. —*v.* **1.** To bind or make fast with a chain or chains. **2.** To confine. [< L *catēna.*]
chain gang. A group of convicts chained together to labor outdoors.
chain mail. Flexible armor of joined metal links or scales.
chain•man (chān′mən) *n. Surveying.* Either of the two persons who hold the measuring chain.
chain-re•act (chān′rē-ăkt′) *v.* To undergo a chain reaction.
chain reaction. 1. A series of events, each of which induces or otherwise influences its successor. **2.** A multistage nuclear reaction so constituted, esp. a self-sustaining series of fissions in which the average number of neutrons produced per unit of time exceeds the number absorbed or lost. **3.** A series of chemical reactions in which one product of a reacting set is a reactant in the following set.
chain saw. A power saw with teeth linked in an endless chain.
chair (châr) *n.* **1.** A piece of furniture consisting of a seat, legs, and back, and often arms, designed for one person. **2. a.** A seat of office, authority, or dignity, as that of a bishop, judge, or chairman. **b.** One who holds such an office. **3.** *Slang.* The electric chair. [< L *cathedra,* chair.]
chair lift. A cable-suspended, power-driven chair assembly used to transport people up or down mountains.
chair•man (châr′mən) *n.* One who presides over an assembly, meeting, etc. —**chair′man•ship′** *n.* —**chair′wom′an** *fem.n.*
chaise longue (shāz′ lông′) *pl.* **chaise longues** or **chaises longues** (shāz′ lông′). A chair with a seat long enough to support the sitter's outstretched legs. [F, "long chair."]
chal•ced•o•ny (kăl-sĕd′n-ē) *n., pl.* **-nies.** A translucent to transparent milky or grayish quartz. [< Gk *khalkēdōn,* a mystical stone.] —**chal′ce•don′ic** *adj.*
cha•let (shă-lā′) *n.* **1.** A house with an overhanging roof, common in Switzerland. **2.** The hut of a herdsman in the Alps. [F.]
chal•ice (chăl′ĭs) *n.* **1.** A goblet. **2.** A cup for the consecrated wine of the Eucharist. [< L *calix,* cup, goblet.]
chalk (chôk) *n.* **1.** A soft, compact calcium carbonate with varying amounts of silica, quartz, feldspar, or other mineral impurities. **2.** A piece of chalk used for marking on a blackboard. —*v.* **1.** To mark, draw, or write with chalk. **2.** To treat (soil) with chalk. —**chalk up.** To earn, score, or credit. —*adj.* Made with chalk. [< L *calx,* stone, pebble.] —**chalk′i•ness** *n.* —**chalk′y** *adj.*
chalk•board (chôk′bôrd′, -bōrd′) *n.* A blackboard.
chal•lah (KHä′lə) *n.* Also **hal•lah** (KHä′lə, hä′lə). A usually braided loaf of white egg bread traditionally eaten by Jews on the Sabbath. [Heb *ḥallāh.*]
chal•lenge (chăl′ənj) *n.* **1.** A call to engage in a contest. **2.** A demand for an explanation. **3.** A sentry's call for identification. **4.** The quality of requiring full use of one's abilities: *a career that offers a challenge.* **5.** A formal objection, esp. to the qualifications of a juror or voter. —*v.* **-lenged, -lenging. 1.** To call to engage in a contest. **2.** To dispute. **3.** To order to halt and be identified. **4.** To object formally to (a juror or voter). **5.** To have due claim to; call for. **6.** To stimulate. [< L *calumnia,* trickery, false accusation.] —**chal′lenge•a•ble** *adj.* —**chal′leng•er** *n.*
chal•lis (shăl′ē) *n.* A light, usually printed fabric of wool, cotton, etc. [Poss < the English surname *Challis.*]
cham•ber (chām′bər) *n.* **1.** A room, esp. a bedroom. **2.** A judge's office. **3.** A hall, esp. for the meeting of a legislative assembly. **4.** A legislative, judicial, or deliberative assembly. **5.** Any enclosed space; cavity. **6.** An enclosed space at the bore of a gun that holds the charge. [< LL *camera.*]
cham•ber•lain (chām′bər-lĭn) *n.* **1.** An official who manages a sovereign's household. **2.** A high-ranking officer in a royal court. **3.** A treasurer. [< Frank **kamerling,* bedchamber servant.]
cham•ber•maid (chām′bər-mād′) *n.* A servant who cleans bedrooms, esp. in hotels.
chamber music. Music composed for trios, quartets, etc., and appropriate for performance in a small concert hall.
chamber of commerce. An association of businessmen for the promotion of their interests in the community.
cham•bray (shăm′brā′) *n.* A lightweight usually cotton fabric woven with white threads across a colored warp. [< *Cambrai,* France.]
cha•me•leon (kə-mēl′yən, -mē′lē-ən) *n.* **1.** Any of various lizards capable of changing color. **2.** A changeable person. [< Gk *khamaileōn,* "ground lion."]
cham•ois (shăm′ē) *n., pl.* **chamois** (shăm′ēz). **1.** A goatlike mammal of mountainous regions of Europe. **2.** Also **cham•my, sham•my** *pl.* **-mies.** Soft leather made originally from the hide of this animal. [OF.]
cham•o•mile, cam•o•mile (kăm′ə-mīl′) *n.* An aromatic plant with daisylike white flowers. [< Gk *khamaemēlon,* "earth-apple."]
champ[1] (chămp) *v.* To chew upon noisily. [Poss imit.]
champ[2] (chămp) *n. Informal.* A champion.
cham•pagne (shăm-pān′) *n.* **1.** A sparkling white wine originally produced in Champagne, France. **2.** Pale yellow.
cham•paign (shăm-pān′) *n.* Level and open country. [< LL *campānia.*]
cham•pi•on (chăm′pē-ən) *n.* **1.** One that holds first place or wins first prize in a contest, esp. in sports. **2.** One who defends a cause or another person. **3.** One who fights; a warrior. —*v.* To fight as champion of; support. —*adj.* Holding first place or prize; superior to all others. [< OF.]
cham•pi•on•ship (chăm′pē-ən-shĭp′) *n.* **1.** The position of a champion. **2.** Defense or support. **3.** A competition held to determine a winner.
Chanc. **1.** chancellor. **2.** chancery.
chance (chăns, chäns) *n.* **1. a.** The abstract nature shared by unexpected, random, or unpredictable events. **b.** This quality regarded as a cause of such events; luck. **2.** The likelihood of occurrence of an event; probability. **3.** An opportunity. **4.** A risk. **5.** A raffle ticket. **6.** An unexpected or fortuitous event. —*v.* **chanced, chancing. 1.** To happen by chance. **2.** To risk. —**chance on** (or **upon**). To find or meet accidentally. [< VL **cadentia,* "a fall," happening.] —**chance** *adj.*
chan•cel (chăn′səl, chän′-) *n.* The space around the altar of a church for the clergy and choir. [< LL *cancellus,* altar.]
chan•cel•ler•y (chăn′səl-ər-ē, -slər-ē, chän′-) *n., pl.* **-ies. 1.** The position or office of a chancellor. **2.** The office of an embassy, consulate, or legation.
chan•cel•lor (chăn′səl-ər, -slər, chän′-) *n.* **1.** A state official of high rank. **2.** The chief minister of state in some countries. **3.** The head of certain universities. **4.** The judge of a chancery court in some U.S. states. [< LL *cancellārius,* secretary, doorkeeper.] —**chan′cel•lor•ship′** *n.*
chan•cer•y (chăn′sər-ē, chän′-) *n., pl.* **-ies. 1.** A court with jurisdiction in equity. **2.** An office of archives. **3.** A chancellery. [< ME *chancelerie,* chancellery.]

chan•cre (shăng'kər) *n.* A dull-red, hard, insensitive lesion that is the first manifestation of syphilis. [< L *cancer,* ulcer, CANCER.]

chanc•y (chăn'sē, chän'-) *adj.* **-ier, -iest.** Uncertain or hazardous.

chan•de•lier (shăn'də-lîr') *n.* A branched fixture for lights, usually suspended from a ceiling. [< L *candēlābrum,* candelabrum.]

chan•dler (chăn'dlər, chän'-) *n.* **1.** One who makes or sells candles. **2.** A dealer in specified goods or equipment. **—chan'dler•y** *n.*

change (chānj) *v.* **changed, changing. 1.** To be or cause to become different; alter. **2.** To exchange for or replace by another. **3.** To give or receive an equivalent sum of money in lower denominations or foreign currency. **4.** To put fresh clothes or coverings on. **—***n.* **1.** The process or condition of changing. **2.** Money given in exchange for money of higher denomination. **3.** Any small coins. **4.** A fresh set of clothing. [< LL *cambiāre.*] **—change'a•ble** *adj.* **—chang'er** *n.*

change•less (chānj'lĭs) *adj.* Enduring; unchanging. **—change'less•ly** *adv.*

change•ling (chānj'lĭng) *n.* A child secretly exchanged for another.

change of life. The menopause.

chan•nel (chăn'əl) *n.* **1.** The bed of a stream. **2.** The deeper part of a river or harbor. **3.** A strait. **4.** A tubular passage. **5.** A means of passage. **6. channels.** Official routes of communication. **7.** A specified frequency band for the transmission and reception of electromagnetic signals. **8.** A trench, furrow, or groove. **—***v.* **1.** To make or form channels in. **2.** To direct or guide along a channel. [< L *canālis,* CANAL.]

Channel Islands. A group of nine British islands in the English Channel.

chan•son (shăn'sən) *n.* A song. [F.]

chant (chănt, chänt) *n.* **1.** A melody in which a number of words are sung on each note. **2.** A canticle sung thus. **3.** A monotonous rhythmic voice. **—***v.* **1.** To sing (a chant). **2.** To say or sing in the manner of a chant. **3.** To celebrate in song. [Prob < OF *chanter,* to sing.] **—chant'er** *n.*

chan•teuse (shäN-tœz') *n.* A woman singer, esp. a nightclub singer.

chant•ey (shăn'tē, chăn'-) *n., pl.* **-eys.** A song sailors sing in rhythm with their work. [Prob < F *chanter,* to sing, CHANT.]

chan•ti•cleer (chăn'tə-klîr', shăn'-) *n.* A rooster. [< OF *chanter,* to CHANT + *cler,* clear.]

chan•try (chăn'trē, chän'-) *n., pl.* **-tries. 1.** An endowment for the saying of masses and prayers. **2.** An altar or chapel endowed for this purpose. [< OF *chanter,* to CHANT.]

Cha•nu•kah (KHä'no͞o-kə) *n.* Also **Ha•nuk•kah, Ha•nu•kah.** An eight-day Jewish festival commemorating a victory over the Syrians and the rededication of the Temple at Jerusalem. [Heb *ḥanukkāh,* "dedication."]

cha•os (kā'ŏs') *n.* **1.** Total disorder or confusion. **2.** Often **Chaos.** The amorphous void supposed to have existed before the Creation. [< Gk *khaos,* empty space, chaos.] **—cha•ot'ic** (kā-ŏt'ĭk) *adj.* **—cha•ot'i•cal•ly** *adv.*

chap¹ (chăp) *v.* **chapped, chapping.** To split or roughen, esp. from cold or exposure. [ME *chappen.*]

chap² (chăp) *n. Informal.* A man; fellow. [Short for CHAPMAN.]

chap. chapter.

chap•ar•ral (shăp'ə-răl') *n. Southwestern U.S.* A dense thicket of shrubs. [< Span *chaparro,* evergreen oak.]

cha•peau (shă-pō') *n., pl.* **-peaux** (-pōz') or **-peaus.** A hat. [F.]

chap•el (chăp'əl) *n.* **1.** A place of worship subordinate to a church, esp. in a college, hospital, etc. **2.** The services held at a chapel. [< OF *chapele.*]

chap•er•on (shăp'ə-rōn') *n.* Also **chap•er•one.** One, esp. an older woman, who for propriety accompanies young unmarried people in public. **—***v.* To act as chaperon to or for. [F, "hood," protection.]

chap•lain (chăp'lĭn) *n.* A clergyman attached to a chapel, military unit, or other organization. [< ML *capella,* chapel.]

chap•let (chăp'lĭt) *n.* **1.** A wreath for the head. **2.** *R.C.Ch.* **a.** A string of prayer beads having one third the number of a rosary's beads. **b.** The prayers counted on such beads. **3.** Any string of beads. [< OF *chapelet.*]

Chap•lin (chăp'lĭn), **Charles ("Charlie").** 1889-1977. British motion-picture actor.

chap•man (chăp'mən) *n. Brit.* A peddler; a hawker. [< OE *cēapman* : *cēap,* trade (see **cheap**) + MAN.]

chaps (chăps, shăps) *pl.n.* Trouserlike leather leg coverings worn by cowboys. [Short for Mexican Span *chaparreras.*]

chap•ter (chăp'tər) *n.* **1.** A main division of a book. **2.** A local branch of a club, fraternity, etc. **3.** An assembly of members, as of a religious order. [< L *capitulum,* "small head."]

char¹ (chär) *v.* **charred, charring. 1.** To scorch or become scorched. **2.** To reduce or be reduced to charcoal by incomplete combustion. [Back-formation < CHARCOAL.]

char² (chär) *n.* Any of several fishes related to the trout. [?]

char•ac•ter (kăr'ĭk-tər) *n.* **1.** A distinguishing feature or attribute; a characteristic. **2.** The moral or ethical structure of a person or group. **3.** Moral strength; integrity. **4.** Reputation. **5.** *Informal.* An eccentric person. **6.** A person portrayed in a drama, novel, etc. **7.** A symbol in a writing system. **8.** Any structure, function, or attribute determined by a gene or group of genes. [< Gk *kharaktēr,* engraved mark, brand.]

char•ac•ter•is•tic (kăr'ĭk-tə-rĭs'tĭk) *adj.* Distinctive; typical. **—***n.* A distinguishing feature or attribute. **—char'ac•ter•is'ti•cal•ly** *adv.*

char•ac•ter•ize (kăr'ĭk-tə-rīz') *v.* **-ized, -izing. 1.** To describe the qualities of. **2.** To be a distinguishing trait of. **3.** To give character to, as on the stage. **—char'ac•ter•i•za'tion** *n.*

cha•rades (shə-rādz') *pl.n.* A game in which words are represented in pantomime until guessed by the other players. [< Prov *charra,* to chat.]

char•coal (chär'kōl') *n.* **1.** A black, porous carbon-containing material, produced by the destructive distillation of wood and used as a fuel, filter, and absorbent. **2.** A drawing pencil made from this substance. **3.** Dark gray. [Perh < L *carbo,* CARBON + COAL.]

chard (chärd) *n.* A variety of beet with large, succulent leaves used as a vegetable. [F *carde.*]

charge (chärj) *v.* **charged, charging. 1.** To entrust with a duty, responsibility, etc. **2.** To command. **3.** To blame or accuse. **4.** To set as a price. **5.** To demand payment from. **6.** To record as a debt. **7.** To attack violently. **8.** To load or fill with; impregnate. **9. a.** To cause formation of a net electric charge on or in (a conductor). **b.** To energize (a storage battery). **—***n.* **1.** Care, custody, or responsibility. **2.** A person or thing entrusted to one's care. **3.** A command or injunction. **4.** An accusation or indictment. **5.** Cost; price. **6.** A debit in an account. **7.** An attack. **8.** A load; burden. **9.** The quantity needed to fill an apparatus or container. **10. a.** The intrinsic property of matter responsible for all electric phenomena, occurring in two forms arbitrarily designated *negative* and *positive.* **b.** A measure of this property. [< LL *carricāre,* to load.]

char•gé d'af•faires (shär-zhā' də-fâr') *pl.* **chargés d'affaires** (shär-zhā', shär-zhāz'). An official temporarily in charge of an embassy or legation.

charg•er (chär'jər) *n.* **1.** One that charges. **2.** A cavalry horse.

Cha•ri-Nile (shä'rē-nīl') *n.* A family of languages spoken in E and C Africa.

char•i•ot (chăr'ē-ət) *n.* An ancient two-wheeled vehicle used in war, races, and processions. [< L *carrus,* vehicle.] **—char'i•o•teer'** *n.*

cha•ris•ma (kə-rĭz'mə) *n.* A quality attributed to those with exceptional ability to secure the devotion of large numbers of people. [Gk *kharisma,* favor, divine gift.] **—char'is•mat'ic** (kăr'ĭz-măt'ĭk) *adj.*

char•i•ta•ble (chăr'ə-tə-bəl) *adj.* **1.** Generous to the needy. **2.** Tolerant in judging others. **3.** Of or for charity. **—char'i•ta•bly** *adv.*

char•i•ty (chăr'ə-tē) *n., pl.* **-ties. 1.** Help or alms given to the poor. **2.** An organization or fund that helps the poor. **3.** An act or feeling of benevolence. **4.** Forbearance in judging others. **5.** *Theol.* **a.** The benevolence of God toward man. **b.** The love of man for his fellow men. [< L *cāritās,* love, regard.]

char•la•tan (shär'lə-tən) *n.* One claiming knowledge or skill that he does not have. [< It *cerretano,* inhabitant of *Cerreto,* village near Spoleto, Italy.] **—char'la•tan•ism'** *n.*

Char•le•magne (shar'lə-mān'). A.D. 742–814. King of the Franks; first Holy Roman Emperor.

Charles•ton (chärl'stən). **1.** A seaport of South Carolina. Pop. 67,000. **2.** The capital of West Virginia. Pop. 72,000.

char•ley horse (chär'lē). *Informal.* A muscular cramp or stiffness, esp. of the leg or arm, caused by excessive exertion. [Prob < the use of *Charley* as a name for lame horses.]

Char•lotte (shär'lət). A city of SW North Carolina. Pop. 202,000.

Char•lotte•town (shär'lət-toun'). The capital of Prince Edward Island Province, Canada. Pop. 19,000.

charm (chärm) *n.* **1.** The power or quality of pleasing or attracting. **2.** A small ornament worn on a bracelet. **3.** Anything worn for its supposed magical effect; an amulet. **4.** Any action or formula thought to have magical power. **—***v.* **1.** To attract; be alluring or pleasing. **2.** To act upon as if with magic; bewitch. [< L *carmen,* song, incantation.] **—charm'er** *n.* **—charm'ing** *adj.*

char•nel (chär'nəl) *n.* Also **char•nel house.** A building or room in which bones or bodies are placed. [< LL *carnālis,* carnal.]

Char•on (kâr'ən). *Gk.Myth.* The ferryman of Hades.

chart (chärt) *n.* **1.** A map. **2.** A sheet with information in the form of graphs or tables. **—***v.* **1.** To make a chart of. **2.** To plan. [< L *charta,* papyrus leaf, paper.]

char•ter (chär'tər) *n.* **1.** A document issued by a governmental authority, creating a corporation and defining its rights and privileges. **2.** A document outlining the organization of a corporate body. **3.** An authorization from an organization to establish a local chapter. **4.** The hiring or leasing of an aircraft, vessel, etc. —*v.* **1.** To grant a charter to. **2.** To hire or lease by charter. [< L *charta,* papyrus leaf.]

charter member. An original member of an organization.

char•treuse (shär-trōōz′, -trōōs′) *n.* **1.** A yellow or pale-green liqueur. **2.** Brilliant yellowish green. [< *la Grande Chartreuse,* Carthusian monastery near Grenoble, France.]

char•wom•an (chär′wŏŏm′ən) *n. Brit.* A woman hired to do cleaning.

char•y (chãr′ē) *adj.* **-ier, -iest. 1.** Careful; wary. **2.** Sparing. [< OE *cearig,* sorrowful.] —**char′i•ly** *adv.* —**char′i•ness** *n.*

chase[1] (chās) *v.* **chased, chasing. 1.** To pursue; follow. **2.** To hunt. **3.** To put to flight; drive away. **4.** *Informal.* To rush. —*n.* **1.** The act of chasing. **2. the chase.** The sport of hunting. **3.** That which is hunted. [< L *captāre,* to seize.]

chase[2] (chās) *n.* A groove cut in an object; a slot. —*v.* **chased, chasing.** To decorate (metal) by engraving or embossing. [< OF *chas,* "enclosure."]

chas•er (chā′sər) *n.* **1.** One that chases. **2.** *Informal.* A drink of water, beer, etc., taken after hard liquor.

chasm (kăz′əm) *n.* **1.** A deep cleft in the earth's surface; a narrow gorge. **2.** A gap; hiatus. [< Gk *khasma.*] —**chas′mal** *adj.*

Chas•si•dim (KHä-sē′dĭm) *pl.n. Sing.* **Chas•sid** (KHä′sĭd). Also **Has•si•dim, Ha•si•dim.** A sect of orthodox Jewish mystics founded in Poland (about 1750). [Heb *ḥasīdhīm,* "pious ones."] —**Chas•si′dic** *adj.*

chas•sis (shăs′ē, chăs′ē) *n., pl.* **-sis** (shăs′ēz, chăs′ēz). **1.** The rectangular steel frame that holds the body and motor of an automotive vehicle. **2.** The landing gear of an aircraft, including the wheels, floats, and other structures. **3.** The framework that holds the functioning parts of a radio, television set, etc. [< L *capsa,* box.]

chaste (chāst) *adj.* **1.** Morally pure; modest. **2.** Abstaining from unlawful sexual intercourse. **3.** Celibate. **4.** Simple in style; not ornate. [< L *castus,* morally pure.] —**chaste′ly** *adv.* —**chaste′ness** *n.*

chas•ten (chā′sən) *v.* **1.** To punish; discipline. **2.** To restrain; moderate. **3.** To purify: *chasten one's style.* [< L *castigāre,* to CASTIGATE.]

chas•tise (chăs-tīz′) *v.* **-tised, -tising. 1.** To punish, usually by beating. **2.** To criticize severely. [< ME *chastien,* chasten.] —**chas•tise′ment** (chăs-tīz′mənt, chăs′tĭz-mənt) *n.*

chas•ti•ty (chăs′tə-tē) *n.* The state or quality of being chaste.

chat (chăt) *v.* **chatted, chatting.** To converse in an easy or informal manner. —*n.* An informal conversation. [< ME *chatteren,* to chatter.]

cha•teau, châ•teau (shă-tō′) *n., pl.* **-teaux** (chă-tōz′). **1.** A French castle. **2.** A large country house.

chat•e•laine (shăt′ə-lān′) *n.* **1.** The mistress of a chateau. **2.** A clasp or chain worn at a woman's waist to hold keys, a watch, etc.

Chat•ta•noo•ga (chăt′ə-nōō′gə). A city of SE Tennessee. Pop. 130,000.

chat•tel (chăt′l) *n.* **1.** An article of movable property. **2.** A slave. [ME *chatel,* property, goods.]

chat•ter (chăt′ər) *v.* **1.** To utter inarticulate speechlike sounds. **2.** To talk rapidly, incessantly, and inanely. **3.** To click together quickly, as the teeth from cold. [ME *chatteren.*] —**chat′ter** *n.* —**chat′ter•er** *n.*

chat•ter•box (chăt′ər-bŏks′) *n.* An extremely talkative person.

chat•ty (chăt′ē) *adj.* **-tier, -tiest.** Given to informal conversation. —**chat′ti•ly** *adv.* —**chat′ti•ness** *n.*

Chau•cer (chô′sər), **Geoffrey.** 1340?–1400. English poet.

chauf•feur (shō′fər, shō-fûr′) *n.* One employed to drive a private automobile. [F, stoker.] —**chauf′feur** *v.*

chau•vin•ism (shō′vən-ĭz′əm) *n.* **1.** Fanatical patriotism. **2.** Prejudiced belief in the superiority of one's own group: *male chauvinism.* [< N. *Chauvin,* legendary French soldier extremely devoted to Napoleon.] —**chau′vin•ist** *n.* —**chau′vin•is′tic** *adj.*

cheap (chēp) *adj.* **1.** Inexpensive. **2.** Charging low prices. **3.** Costing little effort: *a cheap victory.* **4.** Of low value or quality. **5.** Not worthy of respect. **6.** Stingy. —*adv.* Inexpensively. [< OE *cēap,* purchase, bargain < Gmc **kaupaz,* trader.] —**cheap′ly** *adv.* —**cheap′ness** *n.*

cheap•en (chē′pən) *v.* To make or become cheap or cheaper. —**cheap′en•er** *n.*

cheap•skate (chēp′skāt′) *n. Slang.* A stingy person.

cheat (chēt) *v.* **1.** To deceive by trickery; swindle. **2.** To act dishonestly. —*n.* **1.** A fraud or swindle. **2.** One guilty of swindle or dishonesty. [ME *cheten,* to revert.] —**cheat′er** *n.* —**cheat′ing•ly** *adv.*

check (chĕk) *n.* **1.** An abrupt halt or stop. **2.** A restraint. **3.** A standard of comparison to verify accuracy. **4.** A mark to show verification. **5.** A slip for identification: *a baggage check.* **6.** A bill at a restaurant. **7.** Also *chiefly Brit.* **cheque.** A written order to a bank to pay an amount from funds on deposit. **8. a.** A pattern of small squares. **b.** A fabric with such a pattern. **9.** *Chess.* A move in which an opponent's king is attacked. —*v.* **1.** To arrest the motion of abruptly. **2.** To hold in restraint. **3.** To examine, as for accuracy. **4.** To make a check mark on. **5.** To deposit for temporary safekeeping: *check one's hat.* **6.** To have item-for-item correspondence. —**check in.** To register, as at a hotel. —**check out. 1.** To pay one's bill and leave, as from a hotel. **2.** To investigate; confirm. **3.** To correspond to what is expected. [< Ar *shāh,* king, check at chess.] —**check′a•ble** *adj.*

check•er (chĕk′ər) *n.* **1.** One of the disks used in the game of checkers. **2.** One who checks. —*v.* To mark with a checked pattern. [< ME *cheker,* chessboard.]

check•er•board (chĕk′ər-bôrd′, -bōrd′) *n.* A game board divided into 64 squares of two alternating colors on which chess and checkers are played.

check•ered (chĕk′ərd) *adj.* **1.** Divided into squares. **2.** Marked by light and dark patches. **3.** Marked by changes in fortune: *a checkered career.*

check•ers (chĕk′ərz) *n. (takes sing. v.).* A game played on a checkerboard by two persons, each with 12 disks.

check•mate (chĕk′māt′) *v.* **-mated, -mating. 1.** *Chess.* To attack (an opponent's king) so that no escape or defense is possible, thus ending the game. **2.** To defeat completely. [< Ar *shāh māt,* the king is perplexed or dead.] —**check′mate′** *n.*

check•room (chĕk′rōōm′, -rŏŏm′) *n.* A place where hats, coats, etc., may be stored temporarily.

check•up (chĕk′ŭp′) *n.* **1.** A thorough examination, as for accuracy. **2.** A physical examination.

Ched•dar (chĕd′ər) *n.* Also **ched•dar.** Any of several types of smooth, hard cheese. [< *Cheddar,* village in Somerset, England.]

cheek (chēk) *n.* **1.** The fleshy part of either side of the face below the eye and between the nose and ear. **2.** Something resembling this. **3.** Impudence; sauciness. [< OE *cēace* < Gmc **kēkōn.*]

cheek•bone (chēk′bōn′) *n.* A bone in the upper cheek, the zygomatic bone.

cheek•y (chē′kē) *adj.* **-ier, -iest.** Impudent. —**cheek′i•ly** *adv.* —**cheek′i•ness** *n.*

cheep (chēp) *n.* A faint, shrill chirp, as of a young bird. [Imit.] —**cheep** *v.*

cheer (chîr) *n.* **1.** Gaiety; happiness. **2.** Anything that gives happiness or comfort. **3.** A shout of encouragement or congratulation. —*v.* **1.** To fill with happiness. **2. a.** To encourage or acclaim with cheers. **b.** To shout cheers. [ME *chere,* cheer, disposition, face.]

cheer•ful (chîr′fəl) *adj.* **1.** In good spirits. **2.** Promoting cheer. —**cheer′ful•ly** *adv.* —**cheer′ful•ness** *n.*

cheers (chîrz) *interj.* Used as a toast.

cheer•y (chîr′ē) *adj.* **-ier, -iest.** Cheerful. —**cheer′i•ly** *adv.* —**cheer′i•ness** *n.*

cheese (chēz) *n.* A solid food prepared from the pressed curd of milk. [< OE *cēse* < Gmc **kasjus* < L *cāseus.*]

cheese•cloth (chēz′klôth′, -klŏth′) *n.* A coarse, loosely woven cotton gauze.

chee•tah (chē′tə) *n.* A spotted, swift-running wild cat of Africa and SW Asia. [Hindi *cītā.*]

chef (shĕf) *n.* A cook, esp. a chief cook. [< OF *chief, chef,* chief.]

Che•khov (chĕk′ôf′), **Anton Pavlovich.** 1860–1904. Russian author.

chem. chemical; chemist; chemistry.

chem•i•cal (kĕm′ĭ-kəl) *adj.* **1.** Pertaining to chemistry. **2.** Involving or produced by chemicals. —*n.* A substance produced by or used in a chemical process. [< ML *alchimia,* alchemy.] —**chem′i•cal•ly** *adv.*

chemical bond. Any of several forces or mechanisms, esp. the ionic bond, covalent bond, and metallic bond, by which atoms or ions are bound in a molecule or crystal.

chemical engineering. The technology of large-scale chemical production. —**chemical engineer.**

Chemical Mace. A trademark for a mixture of organic chemicals used in aerosol form as a disabling weapon.

chemical warfare. Warfare using chemicals other than explosives as weapons.

chem•i•lu•mi•nes•cence (kĕm′ĭ-lōō′mə-nĕs′əns) *n.* The emission of light as a result of a chemical reaction at environmental temperatures.

che•mise (shə-mēz′) *n.* **1.** A woman's loose, shirtlike undergarment. **2.** A dress that hangs straight from the shoulders. [< LL *camīsia,* linen shirt, nightgown.]

chem•ist (kĕm′ĭst) *n.* **1.** A scientist specializing in chemistry. **2.** *Chiefly Brit.* A pharmacist.

chem•is•try (kĕm′ĭs-trē) *n., pl.* **-tries. 1.** The science of the composition, structure, properties, and reactions of matter, esp. of atomic and molecular systems. **2.** The composition, structure, properties, and reactions of a substance.

chemo–. *comb. form.* Chemicals or chemical reactions.

chem•o•ther•a•py (kĕm′ō-thĕr′ə-pē, kē′mō-) *n.* The treatment of disease with chemicals.

chem•ur•gy (kĕm'ər-jē, kĕ-mûr'-) *n.* The development of new industrial chemical products from organic raw materials, esp. from those of agricultural origin.

che•nille (shə-nēl') *n.* **1.** A soft, tufted cord of silk, cotton, or worsted. **2.** Fabric made of this cord. [F, "caterpillar."]

cheque. *Chiefly Brit.* Variant of **check.**

cher•ish (chĕr'ĭsh) *v.* To hold dear. [< OF *cher,* dear.] **—cher'ish•er** *n.*

Cher•o•kee (chĕr'ə-kē', chĕr'ə-kē') *n., pl.* **-kee** or **-kees. 1.** A member of an Iroquoian-speaking tribe of North American Indians, formerly inhabiting SE North America. **2.** The language of this tribe.

cher•ry (chĕr'ē) *n., pl.* **-ries. 1.** A small, fleshy, rounded fruit with a hard stone. **2.** A tree bearing such fruit. **3.** The wood of such a tree. **4.** Deep or purplish red. [< VL **ceresia.*]

cher•ub (chĕr'əb) *n.* **1.** *pl.* **-ubim** (-/y/ə-bĭm'). A winged celestial being. **2.** *pl.* **-ubs.** A representation of such an angel as a winged child with a chubby, rosy face. [Heb *kərūbh.*] **—che•ru'bic** (chə-rōō'bĭk) *adj.*

Ches•a•peake Bay (chĕs'ə-pēk'). An inlet of the Atlantic Ocean, in Virginia and Maryland.

chess (chĕs) *n.* A board game for two players, each possessing an initial force of a king, a queen, two bishops, two knights, two rooks, and eight pawns, all maneuvered following individual rules of movement with the objective of checkmating the opposite king. [< OF *eschec,* check.]

chess•board (chĕs'bôrd', -bōrd') *n.* A checkerboard.

chess•man (chĕs'măn', -mən) *n.* A piece used in playing chess.

chest (chĕst) *n.* **1.** The part of the body between the neck and abdomen. **2.** A sturdy box with a lid, used for storage. **3.** A bureau or dresser. [< OE *cest,* box < Gmc **kistā* < L *cista.*] **—chest'ed** *adj.*

ches•ter•field (chĕs'tər-fēld') *n.* An overcoat with a velvet collar. [< an Earl of *Chesterfield* of the 19th century.]

chest•nut (chĕs'nŭt', -nət) *n.* **1.** An edible nut enclosed in a prickly bur. **2.** A tree bearing such nuts. **3.** The wood of such a tree. **4.** Reddish brown. **5.** An old, stale joke, story, etc. [< Gk *kastenea* + NUT.] **—chest'nut** *adj.*

cheth. Variant of **heth.**

chev•a•lier (shĕv'ə-lîr') *n.* A member of certain orders of knighthood or merit. [< LL *caballārius,* horseman.]

chev•i•ot (shĕv'ē-ət) *n.* A heavy, twilled woolen fabric used chiefly for suits and overcoats.

chev•ron (shĕv'rən) *n.* An insignia consisting of stripes meeting at an angle, worn on the sleeve of a uniform to indicate rank or length of service.

chew (chōō) *v.* To grind (something) with the teeth. **—chew out.** *Slang.* To scold or reprimand. **—chew the rag.** *Slang.* To chat. [< OE *cēowan.* See **gyeu-.**] **—chew'er** *n.*

Chey•enne[1] (shī-ăn', -ĕn') *n., pl.* **-enne** or **-ennes. 1.** A member of a tribe of Algonquian-speaking North American Indians, formerly inhabiting C Minnesota and the Dakotas. **2.** The language of this tribe.

Chey•enne[2] (shī-ăn', -ĕn'). The capital of Wyoming. Pop. 41,000.

chi (kī) *n.* Also **khi.** The 22nd letter of the Greek alphabet, representing *kh* or *ch.*.

Chiang Kai-shek (jyäng' kī'shĕk', chyäng', chăng'). Born 1887. Chinese statesman and general.

chi•a•ro•scu•ro (kē-är'ə-sk/y/ŏŏr'ō) *n., pl.* **-ros.** The technique of using light and shade in pictorial representation.

chic (shēk) *adj.* Sophisticated; elegant; modish. [< G *Schick,* skill.] **—chic** *n.* **—chic'ly** *adv.*

Chi•ca•go (shə-kä'gō, -kô'gō, -kä'gə). A city in NE Illinois, second-largest in the U.S. Pop. 3,367,000. **—Chi•ca'go•an** *n.*

chi•can•er•y (shĭ-kā'nər-ē) *n., pl.* **-ies.** Deception by trickery. [< OF *chicaner,* to quibble.]

Chi•ca•no (shĭ-kä'nō, chĭ-) *n. pl.* **-nos.** A Mexican-American. *—adj.* Of or pertaining to Mexican-Americans. [< American Span *Chicano* < Span *Mejicano,* a Mexican.]

chick (chĭk) *n.* **1.** A young bird, esp. a chicken. **2.** *Slang.* A girl; young woman.

chick•a•dee (chĭk'ə-dē') *n.* A small, gray, dark-crowned North American bird. [Imit.]

chick•en (chĭk'ən) *n.* **1.** The common domestic fowl or its young. **2.** The edible flesh of a chicken. *—adj. Slang.* Afraid. *—v.* **—chicken out.** To lose one's nerve. [< OE *cicen.*]

chicken feed. *Slang.* A trifling amount of money.

chick•en-heart•ed (chĭk'ən-här'tĭd) *adj.* Cowardly; timid.

chick•en-liv•ered (chĭk'ən-lĭv'ərd) *adj.* Cowardly; timid.

chicken pox. A viral disease, usually of young children, characterized by skin eruption and slight fever.

chick•pea (chĭk'pē') *n.* The edible, pealike seed of a bushy Old World plant. [< L *cicer* + PEA.]

chick•weed (chĭk'wēd') *n.* A low, weedy plant with small white flowers.

chic•le (chĭk'əl) *n.* The coagulated milky juice of a tropical American tree, used in making chewing gum. [< Nah *chictli.*]

chic•o•ry (chĭk'ər-ē) *n.* **1.** A plant with blue, daisylike flowers and leaves used as salad. **2.** The ground, roasted root of this plant, used as a coffee admixture or substitute. [< Gk *kikhora.*]

chide (chīd) *v.* **chided** or **chid** (chĭd), **chided** or **chid** or **chidden** (chĭd'n), **chiding.** To scold; reprimand. [< OE *cīd,* strife.] **—chid'er** *n.*

chief (chēf) *n.* One who is highest in rank or authority. *—adj.* **1.** Highest in rank, authority, or office. **2.** Principal; most important. [< L *caput,* head.] **—chief'ly** *adv.*

chief•tain (chēf'tən) *n.* The leader of a clan or tribe.

chif•fon (shĭ-fŏn', shĭf'ŏn') *n.* A fabric of sheer silk or rayon. *—adj.* **1.** Of or relating to chiffon. **2.** *Cooking.* Having a light and fluffy consistency. [F, "rag."]

chig•ger (chĭg'ər) *n.* **1.** A mite that lodges on the skin and causes intense itching. **2.** Also **chig•oe** (chĭg'ō, chē'gō). A tropical flea that causes similar itching. [< Cariban.]

chi•gnon (shēn-yŏn', shēn'yŏn') *n.* A knot of hair worn at the back of the head. [< OF *chaignon,* chain.]

Chi•hua•hua (chĭ-wä'wä, -wə) *n.* A very small smooth-coated dog. [< *Chihuahua,* Mexico.]

chil•blain (chĭl'blān') *n.* An inflammation followed by itchy irritation on the hands, feet, or ears, resulting from exposure to moist cold. [CHIL(L) + BLAIN.]

child (chīld) *n., pl.* **children** (chĭl'drən). **1.** Any person between birth and puberty. **2.** One who is childish or immature. **3.** A son or daughter; an offspring. **—with child.** Pregnant. [< OE *cild* < Gmc **kiltham.*] **—child'hood'** *n.* **—child'less** *adj.*

child•birth (chīld'bûrth') *n.* Parturition.

child•ish (chīl'dĭsh) *adj.* **1.** Of, similar to, or suitable for a child. **2.** Immature in behavior. **—child'ish•ly** *adv.* **—child'ish•ness** *n.*

child•like (chīld'līk') *adj.* Like or befitting a child, as in innocence.

chil•dren. *pl.* of child.

Chil•e (chĭl'ē). A republic of W South America. Pop. 8,515,000. Cap. Santiago. **—Chil'e•an** (chĭl'ē-ən) *adj.* & *n.*

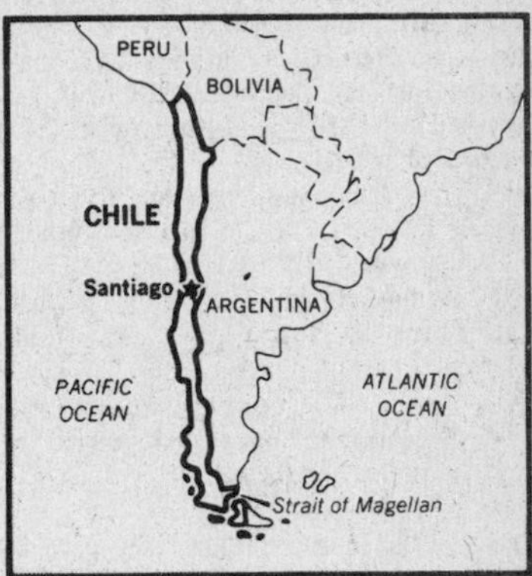

Chile

chil•e con car•ne (chĭl'ē kŏn kär'nē). A highly spiced dish of red peppers, meat, and sometimes beans. [Span, "chili with meat."]

chil•i (chĭl'ē) *n., pl.* **-ies. 1.** The very pungent pod of a variety of red pepper. **2.** Chile con carne. [< Nah *chilli.*]

chill (chĭl) *n.* **1.** A moderate but penetrating coldness. **2.** A sensation of coldness or a similar feeling, as from fever or fear. **3.** A dampening of enthusiasm or spirit. *—adj.* chilly. *—v.* **1.** To make or become cold. **2.** To dispirit. [< OE *ciele.* See **gel-**[3].]

chill•y (chĭl'ē) *adj.* **-ier, -iest. 1.** Cold enough to cause shivering. **2.** Seized with cold. **3.** Unfriendly. **—chill'i•ly** *adv.* **—chill'i•ness** *n.*

chime (chīm) *n.* **1.** Often **chimes.** A set of bells tuned to the musical scale. **2.** The musical sound produced by a bell or bells. *—v.* **chimed, chiming. 1.** To sound with a harmonious ring when struck. **2.** To agree; harmonize. **3.** To make (the hour) known by ringing bells. **—chime in. 1.** To interrupt, as a conversation. **2.** To join in harmoniously. [ME, cymbal, chime.] **—chim'er** *n.*

chi•me•ra (kī-mîr'ə, kə-) *n.* **1. Chimera.** *Gk.Myth.* A fire-breathing monster with the head of a lion, the body of a goat, and the tail of a serpent. **2.** An impossible or foolish fancy. [< Gk *khimaira,* chimera, "she-goat."]

chi•mer•i•cal (kī-mĕr'ĭ-kəl, -mîr'ĭ-kəl, kə-) *adj.* Unrealistic; fantastic.

chim•ney (chĭm'nē) *n.* **1.** A usually vertical passage through which smoke and gases escape from a fire or furnace. **2.** A glass tube for enclosing the flame of a lamp. [< L *caminus,* furnace.]

chim•pan•zee (chĭm'păn-zē', chĭm-păn'zē) *n.* A dark-haired, gregarious African ape. [Native African name.]

chin (chĭn) *n.* The central forward portion of the lower jaw. *—v.* **chinned, chinning. 1.** To grasp an overhead horizontal bar and pull oneself up until one's chin is level with it. **2.** *Informal.* To chat. [< OE *cinn.* See **genu-**[2].]

Chin. China; Chinese.

chi•na (chī'nə) *n.* Pottery, esp. high-quality porcelain.

Chi•na (chī'nə). 1. Officially, People's Republic of China. A republic in east-central Asia, occupying the territory of China proper. Pop. 800,000,000. Cap. Peking. 2. Officially, Republic of China. A republic occupying Taiwan and nearby smaller islands. Pop. 12,429,000. Cap. Taipei.

China

China Sea. A portion of the Pacific Ocean along the E coast of Asia.

chinch bug (chĭnch). A small black and white insect very destructive to grains and grasses.

chin•chil•la (chĭn-chĭl'ə) *n.* 1. A squirrellike South American rodent with soft pale-gray fur. 2. The fur of this animal. 3. A thick wool cloth used for overcoats. [Span.]

chin•cough (chĭn'kôf', -kŏf') *n.* **Whooping cough.**

Chi•nese (chi-nēz', -nēs') *adj.* Of or pertaining to China, its people, or its languages. —*n., pl.* **-nese.** 1. A native of China or one of Chinese ancestry. 2. One of a group of Sino-Tibetan languages and dialects spoken in China. 3. Mandarin, the standard language of China.

chink[1] (chĭngk) *n.* A crack or narrow fissure. [Perh < OE *cinu,* crack.] —**chink'y** *adj.*

chink[2] (chĭngk) *n.* A short, metallic sound. —*v.* To make this sound. [Imit.]

chi•no (chē'nō, shē'-) *n., pl.* **-nos.** 1. A twilled cotton fabric. 2. **chinos.** Trousers made of this material. [Amer Span *chino,* "toasted."]

Chi•nook (shə-nŏŏk', chə-) *n., pl.* **-nook** or **-nooks.** 1. A member of a tribe of North American Indians formerly inhabiting Oregon. 2. The language of this tribe.

Chi•nook•an (shə-nŏŏk'ən, chə-) *n.* A North American Indian language family of Washington and Oregon. —*adj.* Of or pertaining to the Chinook.

chintz (chĭnts) *n.* A printed, usually glazed cotton fabric. [< Hindi *chīṇt.*]

chintz•y (chĭnt'sē) *adj.* **-ier, -iest.** 1. Of or decorated with chintz. 2. Gaudy; trashy; cheap.

chip (chĭp) *n.* 1. A small piece broken or cut off. 2. A mark made by the breaking of such a piece. 3. A coinlike disk used as a counter, as in poker. 4. A thin, crisp piece of food. —*v.* **chipped, chipping.** To break or cut so as to form a chip or chips. —**chip in.** To contribute, as money or a comment. [< OE *cipp,* beam, piece cut off a beam.]

chip•munk (chĭp'mŭngk') *n.* A small squirrellike rodent with a striped back. [< Algon.]

chipped beef. Dried beef sliced very thin.

chip•per (chĭp'ər) *adj.* Cheerful; brisk. [?]

Chip•pe•wa (chĭp'ə-wô', -wä', -wā') *n., pl.* **-wa** or **-was.** Also **Chip•pe•way** (-wā'). Ojibwa.

chip•py (chĭp'ē) *n., pl.* **-pies.** *Slang.* A prostitute.

chiro–. *comb. form.* Hand. [< Gk *kheir.*]

chi•rop•o•dy (kə-rŏp'ə-dē, shə-) *n.* Podiatry. —**chi•rop'o•dist** *n.*

chi•ro•prac•tic (kī'rə-prăk'tĭk) *n.* A system of therapy in which manipulation of the spinal column and other bodily structures is the preferred method of treatment. —**chi'ro•prac'tor** *n.*

chirp (chûrp) *v.* To utter a short, high-pitched sound, as of a small bird. [ME *chirpen.*] —**chirp** *n.*

chir•rup (chûr'əp, chĭr'-) *v.* To utter a series of chirps or similar sounds.

chis•el (chĭz'əl) *n.* A metallic cutting and shaping tool with a sharp, beveled edge. —*v.* **-eled** or **-elled, -eling** or **-elling.** 1. To shape or cut with a chisel. 2. *Slang.* To swindle or obtain by swindling. [< VL **caesellus.*] —**chis'el•er** *n.*

chit[1] (chĭt) *n.* 1. A voucher for an amount owed for food and drink. 2. *Chiefly Brit.* A note; memo. [< Hindi *ciṭṭha,* note, pass.]

chit[2] (chĭt) *n.* A pert girl. [ME *chitte,* young animal.]

chit•chat (chĭt'chăt') *n.* Casual conversation or gossip. [Redupl of CHAT.]

chit•ter•lings (chĭt'lĭnz) *pl.n.* Also **chit•lins, chit•lings.** The intestines of pigs, prepared as food. [ME *chiterling.*]

chiv•al•rous (shĭv'əl-rəs) *adj.* Also **chiv•al•ric** (shĭ-văl'rĭk, shĭv'əl-). 1. Having the qualities attributed to an ideal knight. 2. Of or pertaining to chivalry. —**chiv'al•rous•ly** *adv.*

chiv•al•ry (shĭv'əl-rē) *n., pl.* **-ries.** 1. The medieval institution of knighthood. 2. The qualities, as bravery and courtesy, idealized by knighthood. 3. A chivalrous act. [< LL *caballārius,* horseman, cavalier.]

chive (chīv) *n.* A plant with grasslike, onion-flavored leaves used as seasoning. [< L *cēpa,* onion.]

chiv•vy (chĭv'ē) *v.* **-vied, -vying.** Also **chiv•y.** *Brit.* To chase or harass. [< dial *chevy chase,* pursuit.]

chlo•ral (klôr'əl, klōr'-) *n.* A colorless, mobile oily liquid, CCl_3CHO, used to manufacture DDT and chloral hydrate.

chloral hydrate. A colorless crystalline compound, $CCl_3CH(OH)_2$, used as a sedative.

chlo•ride (klôr'īd', klōr'-) *n.* Any binary compound of chlorine. [CHLOR(O)- + -IDE.]

chlo•rin•ate (klôr'ə-nāt', klōr'-) *v.* **-ated, -ating.** To treat or combine with chlorine or a chlorine compound. —**chlo'ri•na'tion** *n.*

chlo•rine (klôr'ēn', klōr'-, -ĭn) *n. Symbol* **Cl** A highly irritating, greenish-yellow gaseous element, used to purify water, as a disinfectant, a bleaching agent, and in the manufacture of chloroform and carbon tetrachloride. Atomic number 17, atomic weight 35.45. [CHLOR(O)- + -INE.]

chloro–. *comb. form.* 1. The color green. 2. The presence of chlorine. [< Gk *khlōros,* greenish yellow.]

chlo•ro•form (klôr'ə-fôrm', klōr'-) *n.* A clear, colorless liquid, $CHCl_3$, used in refrigerants and propellants and as an anesthetic. —*v.* 1. To anesthetize or kill with chloroform. 2. To apply chloroform to.

chlo•ro•phyll (klôr'ə-fĭl, klōr'-) *n.* A green plant pigment essential in photosynthesis.

chock (chŏk) *n.* A block or wedge placed under a boat, barrel, or wheel to keep it from moving. —*v.* To secure by a chock or chocks. —*adv.* Completely; fully. [?]

chock-a-block (chŏk'ə-blŏk') *adj.* Squeezed or crowded together.

chock-full (chŏk'fŏŏl', chŭk'-) *adj.* Completely filled.

choc•o•late (chôk'lĭt, chô'kə-lĭt, chŏk'-) *n.* 1. Husked, roasted, and ground cacao seeds. 2. A candy or beverage made from this. 3. Deep reddish or grayish brown. [Span.] —**choc'o•late** *adj.*

choice (chois) *n.* 1. The act of choosing; selection. 2. The power or right to choose; option. 3. Something chosen. 4. A number or variety from which to choose. 5. The best part. —*adj.* **choicer, choicest.** 1. Of fine quality. 2. Selected with care. [< OF *choisir,* to choose.]

choir (kwīr) *n.* 1. An organized group of singers, esp. one singing in a church. 2. The part of a church used by such singers. 3. A group or section of orchestral instruments. [< L *chorus,* dance, chorus.]

choke (chōk) *v.* **choked, choking.** 1. To terminate, interfere with, or have difficulty in breathing, as by constricting the windpipe; suffocate. 2. To repress or check forcefully. 3. To block up; obstruct; clog. 4. To reduce the air intake of (a carburetor), thereby enriching the fuel mixture. —*n.* 1. The act or sound of choking. 2. A device used to choke an internal-combustion engine. [< OE *ācēocian* < Gmc **kēkōn-.*]

chok•er (chō'kər) *n.* A short, close-fitting necklace.

chol•er•a (kŏl'ər-ə) *n.* An acute, infectious, often fatal epidemic disease characterized by watery diarrhea, vomiting, cramps, suppression of urine, and collapse. [L, bilious diarrhea.]

chol•er•ic (kŏl'ə-rĭk, kə-lĕr'ĭk) *adj.* Bad-tempered; irritable.

cho•les•ter•ol (kə-lĕs'tə-rôl', -rōl') *n.* A glistening white soapy crystalline substance, $C_{27}H_{45}OH$, occurring notably in bile, gallstones, the brain, blood cells, plasma, egg yolk, and seeds. [< Gk *kholē,* bile + *stereos,* hard, solid.]

choose (chōōz) *v.* **chose, chosen, choosing.** 1. To decide upon and pick out; select. 2. To prefer; desire: *choose to go.* [< OE *cēosan.* See **geus-.**] —**choos'er** *n.*

choos•y (chōō'zē) *adj.* **-ier, -iest.** Also **choos•ey.** Fastidious in choosing; particular. —**choos'i•ness** *n.*

chop (chŏp) *v.* **chopped, chopping.** 1. To cut by striking with a heavy, sharp tool. 2. To cut into bits; mince. 3. To hit with a short downward stroke. —*n.* 1. A swift, short blow or stroke. 2. A small cut of meat, usually from the rib, shoulder, or loin and containing a bone. 3. A short, irregular motion of waves. [ME *choppen.*] —**chop'per** *n.*

Cho•pin (shō'păn'), **Frédéric.** 1810–1849. Polish composer.

chop•py (chŏp'ē) *adj.* **-pier, -piest.** Shifting abruptly, as waves. —**chop'pi•ness** *n.*

chops (chŏps) *pl.n.* The jaws, cheeks, or jowls. [?]

chop•stick (chŏp'stĭk') *n.* One of a pair of slender sticks used as eating implements in China and Japan. [< Pidgin English *chop.*]

chop su•ey (chŏp sōō'ē). A Chinese-American dish made with small pieces of meat, bean sprouts, and other vegetables, served with rice. [Cant *tsap sui.*]

cho•ral (kôr'əl, kōr'-) *adj.* Of or for a chorus or choir. —**cho'ral•ly** *adv.*

cho•rale (kə-răl', -räl') *n.* Also **cho•ral.** 1. A hymn, esp. one harmonized for four voices. 2. A chorus or choir. [G *Choral(gesang),* "choral (song)."]

ă pat/ā ate/âr care/ä bar/b bib/ch chew/d deed/ĕ pet/ē be/f fit/g gag/h hat/hw what/
ĭ pit/ī pie/îr pier/j judge/k kick/l lid, fatal/m mum/n no, sudden/ng sing/ŏ pot/ō go/

chord[1] (kôrd, kōrd) *n.* A combination of three or more usually concordant tones sounded simultaneously. [< ME *cord,* agreement, harmony, short for ACCORD.]

chord[2] (kôrd, kōrd) *n.* **1.** A line segment that joins two points on a curve. **2.** A string or cord, esp. a cordlike anatomical structure. [< CORD.]

chore (chôr, chōr) *n.* A task, esp. a routine or troublesome one. [< OE *cierr,* piece of work < Gmc **karzi.*]

cho•re•a (kô-rē'ə, kō-) *n.* A nervous disorder, esp. of children, marked by uncontrollable movements of the arms, legs, and face; St. Vitus' dance. [< Gk *khoreia,* choral dance.]

cho•re•og•ra•phy (kôr'ē-ŏg'rə-fē, kōr'-) *n.* Also **cho•reg•ra•phy** (kə-rĕg'rə-fē). The creation or arrangement of ballets or dances. [< Gk *khoros,* dance + -GRAPHY.] **—cho're•o•graph'** (kôr'ē-ə-grăf', -gräf', kōr'-) *v.* **—cho'-re•og'ra•pher** *n.* **—cho're•o•graph'ic** *adj.*

cho•rine (kôr'ēn', kōr'-) *n. Slang.* A chorus girl; a show girl.

chor•is•ter (kôr'ĭs-tər, kōr'-, kŏr'-) *n.* A singer in a choir.

cho•roid (kôr'oid', kōr'-) *n.* Also **cho•roi•de•a** (kô-roi'dē-ə, kō-). The dark-brown vascular coat of the eye between the sclera and the retina.

chor•tle (chôrt'l) *v.* **-tled, -tling.** To chuckle loudly and throatily. [Blend of CHUCKLE and SNORT, coined by Lewis Carroll.] **—chor'tle** *n.*

cho•rus (kôr'əs, kōr'-) *n., pl.* **-ruses. 1.** A group of singers who perform together. **2.** Music for such a group. **3.** A group of dancers in a musical comedy, revue, etc. **4.** A group speaking or reciting together. **5.** The simultaneous utterance of several voices. **6.** A repeated refrain or melodic section of a song. **—*v.* -rused** or **-russed, -rusing** or **-russing.** To sing or utter in chorus. [< Gk *khoros,* dance, chorus.]

chose (chōz). *p.t.* of **choose.**

cho•sen (chō'zən). *p.p.* of **choose.** *—adj.* Selected from or preferred above others. *—n., pl.* **chosen. 1.** One of the elect. **2.** The elect collectively.

chow[1] (chou) *n.* A dog with a long, dense reddish-brown or black coat. [Perh < Pidgin English < Cant *kao.*]

chow[2] (chou) *n. Slang.* Food; victuals. [Pidgin English.]

chow•der (chou'dər) *n.* A thick seafood soup, often in a milk base. [F *chaudière,* stew pot.]

chow mein (chou' mān'). A Chinese-American dish of stewed vegetables and meat served over fried noodles. [< Mand *ch'ao*[3] *mien*[4], "fried noodles."]

Chr. Christ; Christian.

chres•ard (krĕs'ərd) *n.* Water present in soil and available for plant absorption. [Gk *khrēsis,* use + *ardein,* to water.]

Christ (krīst) *n.* The title given to Jesus of Nazareth. [< Gk *Khristos,* "the anointed (one)."]

chris•ten (krĭs'ən) *v.* **1.** To baptize. **2.** To give a name to at baptism. **3.** To name and dedicate ceremonially: *christen a ship.* [< CHRISTIAN.] **—chris'ten•er** *n.*

Chris•ten•dom (krĭs'ən-dəm) *n.* **1.** Christians collectively. **2.** The Christian world.

chris•ten•ing (krĭs'ə-nĭng) *n.* The Christian sacrament of baptism.

Chris•tian (krĭs'chən) *adj.* **1.** Professing belief in Christianity. **2.** Pertaining to Jesus or his teachings. **3.** Pertaining to Christianity or its adherents. *—n.* One who professes belief in Christianity.

Chris•ti•an•i•ty (krĭs'chē-ăn'ə-tē) *n.* **1.** The Christian religion, founded on the teachings of Jesus. **2.** Christendom. **3.** The state or fact of being a Christian.

Christian Science. A church and religious system emphasizing healing through spiritual means. Officially, Church of Christ, Scientist. **—Christian Scientist.**

Christ•mas (krĭs'məs) *n.* December 25, a holiday celebrated by Christians as the anniversary of the birth of Jesus.

chro•mat•ic (krō-măt'ĭk) *adj.* **1.** Pertaining to colors or color. **2.** *Mus.* Proceeding by half tones: *a chromatic scale.* [< Gk *khrōma,* color, modification of musical tone.] **—chro•mat'i•cal•ly** *adv.* **—chro•mat'i•cism'** *n.*

chrome (krōm) *n.* **1.** Chromium. **2.** Anything plated with a chromium alloy. [< Gk *khrōma,* color.]

chro•mi•um (krō'mē-əm) *n. Symbol* **Cr** A lustrous, hard, steel-gray metallic element used to harden steel alloys, to produce stainless steels, and in corrosion-resistant decorative platings. Atomic number 24, atomic weight 51.996. [< CHROME.]

chro•mo•some (krō'mə-sōm') *n.* A DNA-containing linear body of the cell nuclei of plants and animals, responsible for the determination and transmission of hereditary characteristics. [Gk *khrōma,* color + -SOME[2].] **—chro'mo•so'mal** (-sō'məl).

chron. chronological; chronology.

Chron. Chronicles (Old Testament).

chron•ic (krŏn'ĭk) *adj.* Of long duration; prolonged; lingering. [< Gk *khronos,* time.] **—chron'i•cal•ly** *adv.*

chron•i•cle (krŏn'ĭ-kəl) *n.* A chronological record of historical events. **—*v.* -cled, -cling.** To record in or as if in a chronicle. [< Gk *(biblia) khronika,* "chronological (books)."] **—chron'i•cler** (-klər) *n.*

chrono–. *comb. form.* Time. [< Gk *khronos,* time.]

chron•o•graph (krŏn'ə-grăf', -gräf', krō'nə-) *n.* An instrument that records time intervals.

chronol. chronological; chronology.

chron•o•log•i•cal (krŏn'ə-lŏj'ĭ-kəl, krō'nə-) *adj.* Also **chron•o•log•ic** (-lŏj'ĭk). Arranged in order of occurrence. **—chron'o•log'i•cal•ly** *adv.*

chro•nol•o•gy (krə-nŏl'ə-jē) *n., pl.* **-gies. 1.** The determination of dates and sequences of events. **2.** The arrangement of events in time. **3.** A chronological list or table. **—chro•nol'o•gist** *n.*

chro•nom•e•ter (krə-nŏm'ə-tər) *n.* An exceptionally precise timepiece.

chrys•a•lis (krĭs'ə-lĭs) *n.* **1.** The pupa of an insect, esp. a moth or butterfly, enclosed in a firm case or cocoon. **2.** Anything still in the process of development. [< Gk *khrusallis,* golden pupa of a butterfly.]

chry•san•the•mum (krĭ-săn'thə-məm) *n.* A plant cultivated in various forms for its showy flowers. [< Gk *khrusanthemon,* "gold flower."]

chub•by (chŭb'ē) *adj.* **-bier, -biest.** Rounded and plump. [Prob < Scand.] **—chub'bi•ly** *adv.* **—chub'bi•ness** *n.*

chuck[1] (chŭk) *v.* **1.** To pat or squeeze playfully, esp. under the chin. **2.** To toss. **3.** *Informal.* To throw out. *—n.* **1.** An affectionate pat or squeeze under the chin. **2.** A toss. [Perh < OF *choquer,* to strike, shock.]

chuck[2] (chŭk) *n.* **1.** A cut of beef extending from the neck to the ribs. **2.** A clamp that holds a tool, or the material being worked, in a machine such as a drill or lathe. [Var of CHOCK.]

chuck•le (chŭk'əl) *v.* **-led, -ling.** To laugh quietly. **—chuck'le** *n.* **—chuck'ler** *n.*

chuck wagon. A wagon equipped with food and cooking utensils, as in a lumber camp.

chug (chŭg) *n.* A brief dull, explosive sound made by or as if by a laboring engine. *—v.* **chugged, chugging. 1.** To make such sounds. **2.** To move while making such sounds: *a train chugging along.* [Imit.]

chuk•ka (chŭk'ə) *n.* A short, ankle-length boot with two pairs of eyelets.

chum (chŭm) *n.* A close friend. *—v.* **chummed, chumming. 1.** To be a close friend. **2.** To share a room. [Oxford University slang, said to be < *chamber fellow,* "roommate."]

chum•my (chŭm'ē) *adj.* **-mier, -miest.** *Informal.* Intimate; friendly. **—chum'mi•ly** *adv.* **—chum'-mi•ness** *n.*

chump (chŭmp) *n.* A blockhead; dolt. [Prob a blend of CHUNK and LUMP or STUMP.]

Chung•king (chŏŏng'kĭng'). A city in south-central China. Pop. 2,121,000.

chunk (chŭngk) *n.* **1.** A thick piece of something. **2.** A substantial amount. [Prob a var of CHOCK.]

chunk•y (chŭng'kē) *adj.* **-ier, -iest.** Short and thick; stocky; thickset. **—chunk'i•ly** *adv.* **—chunk'i•ness** *n.*

church (chûrch) *n.* **1.** All Christians regarded as a spiritual body. **2.** A building for public worship. **3.** A congregation. **4.** A religious service. **5.** Often **Church.** Any Christian denomination. **6.** Ecclesiastical power as distinguished from the secular: *the separation of church and state.* [< LGk *(dōma) kuriakon,* the Lord's (house).]

church•go•er (chûrch'gō'ər) *n.* One who attends church regularly.

Church•ill (chûr'chĭl). A river in north-central Canada.

Church•ill (chûr'chĭl), Sir **Winston.** 1874–1965. British statesman.

Winston Churchill

church•man (chûrch'mən) *n.* **1.** A clergyman. **2.** A member of a church.

Church of Christ, Scientist. See **Christian Science.**

Church of England. The episcopal and liturgical national church of England.

church•war•den (chûrch'wôrd'n) *n. Ang.& Epis.Ch.* A lay officer who handles the secular affairs of a church.

church•yard (chûrch'yärd') *n.* A yard adjacent to a church, often used as a burial ground.

churl (chûrl) *n.* **1.** A rude, boorish person. **2.** A medieval English peasant. [< OE *ceorl,* man, freeman of the lowest rank < Gmc **karlaz.*] **—churl'ish** *adj.* **—churl'ish•ly** *adv.*

churn (chûrn) *n.* A vessel in which cream or milk is agitated to make butter. —*v.* **1.** To stir or agitate (milk or cream) in a churn. **2.** To make (butter) by churning. **3.** To move or be moved with great agitation. [< OE *cyrin* < Gmc **kernjōn.*] —**churn'er** *n.*

chute (sho͞ot) *n.* **1.** An inclined trough or passage down which things can pass. **2.** *Informal.* A parachute. [< OF *cheoir,* to fall.]

chut•ney (chŭt'nē) *n.* Also **chut•nee.** A pungent relish made of fruits, spices, and herbs. [Hindi *caṭnī.*]

chutz•pah (KHo͝ots'pə) *n. Slang.* Brazenness; gall. [Yidd.]

Chu•vash (cho͞o-väsh') *n., pl.* **-vash** or **-vashes. 1.** One of a Tatar people living chiefly in east-central Soviet Russia, in Europe. **2.** The Turkic language of these people.

Ci curie.

CIA Central Intelligence Agency.

ci•ca•da (sĭ-kā'də, -kä'də) *n.* A large insect with membranous wings and specialized organs producing a shrill, droning sound. [L *cicāda.*]

cic•a•trix (sĭk'ə-trĭks', sĭ-kā'trĭks) *n., pl.* **-trices** (sĭk'ə-trī'sēz, sĭ-kā'trə-sēz'). Recently formed connective tissue on a healing wound. [< L *cicātrix.*]

Cic•e•ro (sĭs'ə-rō'), **Marcus Tullius.** 106–43 B.C. Roman statesman and orator.

-cide *comb. form.* **1.** Killer of: **insecticide. 2.** Murder or killing of: **genocide.** [< LL *caedere,* to kill.]

ci•der (sī'dər) *n.* The juice pressed from apples, used to produce vinegar or as a beverage. [< Gk *sikera,* strong drink.]

ci•gar (sĭ-gär') *n.* Tobacco leaves rolled into a cylinder for smoking. [Span *cigarro.*]

cig•a•rette (sĭg'ə-rĕt', sĭg'ə-rĕt') *n.* Also **cig•a•ret.** A small roll of finely cut tobacco enclosed in paper for smoking. [< F *cigare,* cigar.]

cig•a•ril•lo (sĭg'ə-rĭl'ō) *n., pl.* **-los.** A small, narrow cigar.

cil•i•a (sĭl'ē-ə) *pl.n. Sing.* **-ium** (-ē-əm). *Biol.* Microscopic hairlike processes. [< L *cilium,* the lower eyelid.] —**cil'i•ate** (sĭl'ē-ĭt, -āt') *adj.*

cil•i•ar•y (sĭl'ē-ĕr'ē) *adj.* **1.** Of or like cilia. **2.** Of or pertaining to the ciliary body.

ciliary body. The thickened part of the vascular tunic of the eye that connects the choroid with the iris.

cinch (sĭnch) *n.* **1.** A strap that holds a pack or saddle in place. **2.** *Slang.* Something easy to accomplish —*v.* **1.** To tighten a saddle girth on. **2.** *Slang.* To make certain of: *cinch a victory.* [< L *cingere,* to gird.]

cin•cho•na (sĭng-kō'nə, sĭn-chō'nə) *n.* **1.** A South American tree whose bark yields quinine and other medicinal alkaloids. **2.** The dried bark of such a tree. [< F. H. de Ribera, countess of *Cinchón* (1576–1639).]

Cin•cin•nat•i (sĭn'sə-năt'ē, -năt'ə). A city of SW Ohio. Pop. 453,000.

cinc•ture (sĭngk'chər) *n.* A belt; girdle. [L *cinctūra,* girdle.] —**cinc'ture** *v.* **(-tured, -turing).**

cin•der (sĭn'dər) *n.* **1.** A burned substance that is not reduced to ashes, but is incapable of further combustion. **2.** A partly charred substance that can burn further, but without flame. **3. cinders.** Ashes. [< OE *sinder,* (iron) slag, dross. See **sendhro-.**]

cin•e•ma (sĭn'ə-mə) *n.* **1. A motion picture. 2.** A motion-picture theater. **3. the cinema. a.** Motion pictures collectively. **b.** The motion-picture industry.. **c.** The art of making motion pictures. [< Gk *kinēma,* motion.] —**cin'e•mat'ic** (sĭn'ə-măt'ĭk) *adj.* —**cin'e•mat'i•cal•ly** *adv.*

cin•e•ma•tog•ra•phy (sĭn'ə-mə-tŏg'rə-fē) *n.* The technique of making motion pictures.

cin•na•bar (sĭn'ə-bär') *n.* A heavy reddish compound, HgS, that is the principal ore of mercury. [< L *cinnābaris.*]

cin•na•mon (sĭn'ə-mən) *n.* **1.** The aromatic reddish or yellowish-brown bark of a tropical Asian tree, dried and often ground for use as a spice. **2.** Reddish or light yellowish brown. [< Heb *qinnâmown.*]

CIO, C.I.O. Congress of Industrial Organizations.

ci•pher (sī'fər) *n.* **1.** The mathematical symbol (0) denoting absence of quantity; zero. **2.** Any Arabic numeral or figure. **3. a.** Any system of secret writing in which units of plain text are substituted according to a predetermined key. **b.** The key to such a system. **c.** A message in cipher. —*v.* To compute arithmetically. [< Ar *ṣifr.*]

cir., circ. 1. circular. **2.** circumference.

cir•ca (sûr'kə) *prep.* About. Used before approximate dates or figures. [< L *circum,* round about.]

cir•cle (sûr'kəl) *n.* **1.** A plane curve everywhere equidistant from a given fixed point, the center. **2.** A planar region bounded by such a curve. **3.** Anything shaped like a circle. **4.** A group of people sharing an interest, activity, or achievement. —*v.* **-cled, -cling. 1.** To make a circle around. **2.** To move in a circle or circles. [< L *circus,* ring.] —**cir'cler** *n.*

cir•clet (sûr'klĭt) *n.* A small circle, esp. a circular ornament.

cir•cuit (sûr'kĭt) *n.* **1. a.** A closed, usually circular, curve. **b.** The region enclosed by such a curve. **2.** Any closed path or route. **3. a.** A closed path followed by an electric current. **b.** A configuration of electrically or electromagnetically connected components or devices. **4.** A territory under the jurisdiction of a judge, in which he holds periodic court sessions. [< L *circuire, circumīre,* to go around.]

circuit breaker. An automatic switch that stops the flow of current in an overloaded electric circuit.

cir•cu•i•tous (sər-kyo͞o'ə-təs) *adj.* Being or taking a roundabout, lengthy course.

cir•cuit•ry (sûr'kə-trē) *n.* **1.** The plan for an electric circuit. **2.** Electric circuits collectively.

cir•cu•lar (sûr'kyə-lər) *adj.* **1.** Pertaining to a circle. **2. a.** Having the shape of a circle. **b.** Round. **3.** Moving in or forming a circle. —*n.* A printed notice intended for mass distribution. —**cir'cu•lar'i•ty** *n.*

cir•cu•lar•ize (sûr'kyə-lə-rīz') *v.* **-ized, -izing.** To publicize with circulars.

circular saw. An electric saw consisting of a toothed disk rotated at high speed.

cir•cu•late (sûr'kyə-lāt') *v.* **-lated, -lating. 1.** To move in or flow through a circle or circuit. **2.** To move around, as from person to person or place to place. **3.** To move or cause to move, as air. —**cir'cu•la'tor** *n.*

cir•cu•la•tion (sûr'kyə-lā'shən) *n.* **1.** Movement in a circle or circuit. **2.** The movement of blood through bodily vessels as a result of the heart's pumping action. **3. a.** The distribution of a periodical publication. **b.** The number of copies sold or distributed.

cir•cu•la•tor•y system (sûr'kyə-lə-tôr'ē, -tōr'-ē). The system of structures by which blood and lymph are circulated throughout the body.

circum-. *comb. form.* Around or on all sides. [< L *circum,* around.]

circum. circumference.

cir•cum•cise (sûr'kəm-sīz') *v.* **-cised, -cising. 1.** To remove the prepuce of (a male). **2.** To remove the clitoris of (a female). [< L *circumcīdere,* "to cut around."] —**cir'cum•ci'sion** (-sĭzh'ən) *n.*

cir•cum•fer•ence (sər-kŭm'fər-əns) *n.* **1. a.** The boundary line of a circle. **b.** Any perimeter. **2.** The length of such a boundary or perimeter. [< L *circumferre,* to carry around.]

cir•cum•flex (sûr'kəm-flĕks') *n.* A mark (ˆ) used over a vowel to indicate quality of pronunciation. [L *circumflexus,* "a bending around."]

cir•cum•lo•cu•tion (sûr'kəm-lō-kyo͞o'shən) *n.* A roundabout expression, as in speech or writing. [< L *circumloquī,* "to speak in a roundabout way."] —**cir'cum•loc'u•to'ry** (-lŏk'-yə-tôr'ē, -tōr'ē) *adj.*

cir•cum•lu•nar (sûr'kəm-lo͞o'nər) *adj.* Around the moon.

cir•cum•nav•i•gate (sûr'kəm-năv'ī-gāt') *v.* **-gated, -gating.** To sail completely around.

cir•cum•scribe (sûr'kəm-skrīb') *v.* **-scribed, -scribing. 1.** To draw a line around. **2.** To confine within bounds; restrict. —**cir'cum•scrip'tion** (-skrĭp'shən) *n.*

cir•cum•so•lar (sûr'kəm-sō'lər) *adj.* Around the sun.

cir•cum•spect (sûr'kəm-spĕkt') *adj.* Heedful of consequences. [< L *circumspicere,* to look around, take heed.] —**cir'cum•spec'tion** *n.*

cir•cum•stance (sûr'kəm-stăns') *n.* **1.** One of the conditions or facts attending an event and having some bearing upon it. **2.** The sum of determining factors beyond willful control. **3.** Often **circumstances.** Financial status or means. **4.** Formal display; ceremony: *pomp and circumstance.* —**under no circumstances.** Never. —**under** (or **in**) **the circumstances.** Given these conditions. [< L *circumstāre,* to stand around.]

cir•cum•stan•tial (sûr'kəm-stăn'shəl) *adj.* **1.** Of or dependent upon circumstances. **2.** Of no primary significance; incidental. **3.** Complete and full of detail.

cir•cum•stan•ti•ate (sûr'kəm-stăn'shē-āt') *v.* **-ated, -ating.** To give detailed proof or description of. —**cir'cum•stan'ti•a'tion** *n.*

cir•cum•vent (sûr'kəm-vĕnt') *v.* To entrap or overcome by craft. [L *circumvenīre,* to come around.] —**cir'cum•ven'tion** *n.*

cir•cus (sûr'kəs) *n.* **1.** A traveling show of acrobats, clowns, trained animals, etc., often performing under a tent. **2.** *Informal.* Any humorous or rowdy occurrence. [L *circus,* ring, CIRCLE.]

cirque (sûrk) *n.* A steep hollow, often containing a small lake, at the upper end of a mountain valley. [< L *circus,* ring, CIRCLE.]

cir•rho•sis (sĭ-rō'sĭs) *n.* A chronic disease of the liver that ultimately results in liver failure and death. [< NL, "orange-colored disease."] —**cir•rhot'ic** (sĭ-rŏt'ĭk) *adj.*

cir•ro•cu•mu•lus (sĭr'ō-kyo͞om'yə-ləs) *n.* A high-altitude cloud composed of a series of small, regularly arranged cloudlets in the form of ripples or grains.

cir•ro•stra•tus (sĭr'ō-strā'təs, -străt'əs) *n.* A high-altitude, thin hazy cloud, usually covering the sky and often producing a halo effect.

cir•rus (sĭr'əs) *n., pl.* **cirri** (sĭr'ī'). A high-altitude cloud composed of narrow bands or patches of thin, generally white, fleecy parts. [< L *cirrus,* curl, filament, tuft.]

cis•tern (sĭs'tərn) *n.* A receptacle for holding water, esp. rainwater. [< L *cisterna,* water tank.] —**cis•ter'nal** *adj.*

cit. 1. citation; cited. 2. citizen.

cit•a•del (sĭt'ə-dəl, -dĕl') *n.* 1. A fortress in a commanding position in or near a city. 2. Any stronghold. [< L *cīvitās,* CITY.]

cite (sīt) *v.* **cited, citing.** 1. To quote as an authority or example. 2. To mention as support, illustration, or proof. 3. To commend for meritorious action, esp. in military service. 4. To summon before a court of law. [< L *citāre,* freq of *ciēre,* to set in motion, summon.] —**ci•ta'tion** *n.*

cit•i•fy (sĭt'ĭ-fī') *v.* **-fied, -fying.** 1. To make urban. 2. To mark with the styles and manners of the city. —**cit'i•fi•ca'tion** *n.* —**cit'i•fied'** *adj.*

cit•i•zen (sĭt'ə-zən) *n.* 1. A person owing loyalty to and entitled by birth or naturalization to the protection of a given state. 2. An inhabitant of a city or town. [< OF *cite,* city.]

cit•i•zen•ry (sĭt'ə-zən-rē) *n., pl.* **-ries.** Citizens collectively.

cit•i•zen•ship (sĭt'ə-zən-shĭp') *n.* The status of a citizen with its attendant duties, rights, and privileges.

cit•rate (sĭt'rāt') *n.* A salt or ester of citric acid.

cit•ric acid (sĭt'rĭk). A colorless acid, $C_6H_8O_7{\bullet}H_2O$, occurring in lemon, lime, and pineapple juices.

cit•ron (sĭt'rən) *n.* 1. The aromatic, thick-skinned, lemonlike fruit of an Asiatic tree. 2. A melon with a thick, hard rind. 3. The preserved rind of either of these fruits, used in cooking. [< L *citrus,* citron tree.]

cit•ron•el•la (sĭt'rə-nĕl'ə) *n.* A light-yellow, aromatic oil obtained from a tropical grass and used in insect repellents and perfumery. [< F *citron,* citron.]

cit•rus (sĭt'rəs) *adj.* Also **cit•rous.** Of or pertaining to related trees or fruit such as the orange, lemon, lime, and grapefruit. —*n., pl.* **-ruses.** A citrus tree. [< L, citron tree, citrus tree.]

cit•y (sĭt'ē) *n., pl.* **-ies.** 1. A town of significant size. 2. An incorporated municipality with definite boundaries and legal powers set forth in a state charter. 3. The inhabitants of a city as a group. —*adj.* Of or in a city. [< L *cīvitās,* citizenry, state, (later) city.]

city hall. 1. The building housing the offices of a municipal government. 2. The municipal government itself.

cit•y-state (sĭt'ē-stāt') *n.* A sovereign state consisting of a city and its surrounding territory.

civ. civil; civilian.

civ•et (sĭv'ĭt) *n.* 1. Also **civet cat.** A catlike African mammal that secretes a musky fluid. 2. This fluid, used in making perfumes. [< Ar *zabād.*]

civ•ic (sĭv'ĭk) *adj.* Of a city, citizens, or citizenship. —*n.* **civics** *(takes sing. v.).* The study of civic affairs, esp. the rights and duties of citizenship. [< L *cīvis,* citizen.]

civ•ies. Variant of **civvies.**

civ•il (sĭv'əl) *adj.* 1. Of a citizen or citizens. 2. Of ordinary community life, as distinct from the military or ecclesiastical. 3. Civilized. 4. Polite. [< L *cīvis,* citizen.] —**civ'il•ly** *adv.* —**civ'il•ness** *n.*

civil engineer. An engineer trained in the design and construction of public works.

ci•vil•ian (sə-vĭl'yən) *n.* A person in civil life, as distinguished from one in the armed forces.

ci•vil•i•ty (sə-vĭl'ə-tē) *n., pl.* **-ties.** 1. Politeness. 2. A courteous act or utterance.

civ•i•li•za•tion (sĭv'ə-lə-zā'shən) *n.* 1. Any human society having an advanced stage of development in the arts and sciences and social, political, and cultural complexity. 2. The type of culture developed by a particular people or epoch.

civ•i•lize (sĭv'ə-līz') *v.* **-lized, -lizing.** To bring out of a primitive or savage state. —**civ'i•liz'a•ble** *adj.* —**civ'i•liz'er** *n.*

civ•i•lized (sĭv'ə-līzd') *adj.* 1. Having a highly developed society. 2. Of a people or nation so developed. 3. Cultured; refined.

civil law. The body of law dealing with the rights of private citizens.

civil liberty. Legal guarantees of an individual's right to free speech, thought, and action.

civil rights. Rights belonging to a person by virtue of his status as a citizen or as a member of civil society.

civil service. All branches of public service that are not legislative, judicial, or military.

civil war. 1. A war between factions or regions of one country. 2. **Civil War.** The war between the Union and the Confederacy (1861–65); War Between the States.

civ•vies (sĭv'ēz) *pl.n.* Also **civ•ies.** *Slang.* Civilian clothes.

ck. 1. cask. 2. check. 3. cook.

cl centiliter.

Cl chlorine.

cl. 1. class; classification. 2. clause. 3. clearance. 4. clerk.

c.l. 1. carload. 2. *Sports.* center line. 3. common law.

clab•ber (klăb'ər) *n.* Sour, curdled milk. —*v.* To curdle. [< Ir *clabair,* thick sour milk.]

clack (klăk) *v.* 1. To make or cause to make an abrupt, dry sound, as by the collision of hard surfaces. 2. To chatter. —*n.* A clacking sound. [< ON *klaka.*] —**clack'er** *n.*

clad (klăd). Alternate *p.t.* & *p.p.* of **clothe.**

claim (klām) *v.* 1. To demand as one's due. 2. To state to be true. 3. To call for; require. —*n.* 1. A demand for something as one's rightful due. 2. Title or right. 3. Something claimed. 4. A statement of something as a fact. [< L *clāmāre,* to call.]

claim•ant (klā'mənt) *n.* A person making a claim.

clair•voy•ance (klâr-voi'əns) *n.* The supposed power to perceive things that are out of the natural range of human senses. [F, "clear-seeing."] —**clair•voy'ant** *n.* & *adj.*

clam (klăm) *n.* Any of various bivalve mollusks, many of which are edible. —*v.* **clammed, clamming.** To hunt for clams. —**clam up.** To refuse to talk. [Short for *clamshell,* "bivalve that shuts tight like a clamp."]

clam•bake (klăm'bāk') *n.* A picnic where clams and other foods are baked.

clam•ber (klăm'ər, klăm'bər) *v.* To climb with difficulty. [< ON *klembra,* orig "to grip."]

clam•my (klăm'ē) *adj.* **-mier, -miest.** Disagreeably moist and cold. [< OE *clǣman,* to stick, smear.] —**clam'mi•ly** *adv.* —**clam'mi•ness** *n.*

clam•or (klăm'ər). Also *chiefly Brit.* **clam•our.** *n.* 1. A loud outcry; hubbub. 2. A vehement expression of protest. —*v.* To make a clamor. [< L *clāmāre,* to cry out.] —**clam'or•ous** *adj.*

clamp (klămp) *n.* A device used to join, grip, support, or compress mechanical parts. —*v.* To fasten or support with or as if with a clamp. [< MDu *clampe.*] —**clamp'er** *n.*

clan (klăn) *n.* 1. A number of families, as in the Scottish Highlands, claiming a common ancestor. 2. Any group of numerous relatives or associates. [< Scot Gael *clann,* children, family.] —**clan'nish** *adj.* —**clan'nish•ly** *adv.* —**clans'man** (klănz'mən) *n.*

clan•des•tine (klăn-dĕs'tən) *adj.* Concealed; secret. [< L *clandestīnus.*]

clang (klăng) *v.* To make or cause to make a loud, metallic sound. —*n.* A clanging sound. [L *clangere,* to sound.]

clan•gor (klăng'ər, klăng'gər) *n.* Also *chiefly Brit.* **clan•gour.** A clang or repeated clanging.

clank (klăngk) *n.* A metallic sound, sharp but not as resonant as a clang. —*v.* To make this sound. [Imit.]

clap (klăp) *v.* **clapped, clapping.** 1. To strike (the palms of the hands) together, as in applauding. 2. To come together with a sharp noise. 3. To tap with the open hand, as in greeting. 4. To put or send suddenly: *clap in jail.* —*n.* 1. The act or sound of clapping the hands. 2. A loud or explosive noise. 3. A slap. [< OE *clappian,* to throb, beat.]

clap•board (klăb'ərd, klăp'bôrd', -bōrd') *n.* A board with one edge thicker than the other, overlapped to cover the outer walls of frame houses.

clap•per (klăp'ər) *n.* A person or thing that claps, esp., the tongue of a bell.

clap•trap (klăp'trăp') *n.* Pretentious, insincere, or empty language.

claque (klăk) *n.* A group of persons hired to applaud at a performance. [< F *claquer,* to clap.]

clar•et (klăr'ət) *n.* A dry red table wine. [< ML *(vīnum) clārātum,* "clarified (wine)."]

clar•i•fy (klăr'ə-fī') *v.* **-fied, -fying.** To make or become clear. —**clar'i•fi•ca'tion** *n.*

clar•i•net (klăr'ə-nĕt') *n.* A woodwind instrument having a straight, cylindrical tube with a flaring bell and a single-reed mouthpiece, played by means of finger holes and keys. [< L *clārus,* CLEAR.] —**clar'i•net'ist** *n.*

clar•i•on (klăr'ē-ən) *adj.* Shrill and clear. [< L *clārus,* CLEAR.]

clar•i•ty (klăr'ə-tē) *n.* Clearness; lucidity.

clash (klăsh) *v.* 1. To collide or strike together with a loud, harsh noise. 2. To conflict; disagree. —*n.* 1. A loud metallic noise. 2. A conflict. [Imit.]

clasp (klăsp, kläsp) *n.* 1. A fastening, such as a hook, used to hold two objects or parts together. 2. a. An embrace. b. A grip of the hand. —*v.* 1. To fasten with or as if with a clasp. 2. To hold in a tight grasp. [< ME *claspen,* to grip, grasp.] —**clasp'er** *n.*

class (klăs, kläs) *n.* 1. A group whose members have at least one attribute in common; kind; sort. 2. Any division by quality or grade. 3. A social stratum whose members share similar characteristics. 4. a. A group of students graduated in the same year. b. A group of students meeting to study the same subject. 5. *Slang.* High style in manner or dress. —*v.* To classify. [< L *classis,* one of the six divisions of the Roman people, army, fleet.]

class action. A lawsuit in which the plaintiff or plaintiffs bring suit both on their own behalf and on behalf of many others who have the same claim against the defendant.

clas•sic (klăs'ĭk) *adj.* 1. Of the highest rank. 2. Serving as a model of its kind. 3. Pertaining to ancient Greek or Roman literature or art. 4. In accordance with established principles and methods. —*n.* 1. An artist, author, or work of the highest rank. 2. **classics.** The literature of ancient Greece and Rome.

clas•si•cal (klăs'ĭ-kəl) *adj.* 1. Often **Classical.** Of, pertaining to, or in accordance with the precedents of ancient Greek and Roman art and literature. **2.** Pertaining to or versed in studies of antiquity. **3.** *Mus.* **a.** Pertaining to or designating the European music of the latter half of the 18th century. **b.** Designating any music in the educated European tradition, distinguished from popular or folk music. **4.** Standard and authoritative. [< CLASSIC.]

clas•si•cism (klăs′ə-sĭz′əm) *n.* **1.** Aesthetic principles based on the culture, art, and literature of ancient Greece and Rome and characterized by emphasis on form, simplicity, proportion, and restrained emotion. **2.** Classical scholarship. **—clas′si•cist** *n.*

clas•si•fy (klăs′ə-fī′) *v.* **-fied, -fying. 1.** To arrange according to class or category. **2.** To designate as secret or restricted, as a document. **—clas′si•fi•ca′tion** (-fĭ-kā′shən) *n.* **—clas′si•fi′er** *n.*

class•mate (klăs′māt′, kläs′-) *n.* A member of the same academic class.

class•room (klăs′ro͞om′, -ro͝om′, kläs′-) *n.* A room in which academic classes are conducted.

class•y (klăs′ē, kläs′ē) *adj.* **-ier, -iest.** *Slang.* Stylish; elegant.

clat•ter (klăt′ər) *v.* To make or cause to make a rattling sound. *—n.* **1.** A rattling sound. **2.** A loud disturbance. [< OE **clatrian.* See **gel-[2]**.]

clause (klôz) *n.* **1.** A group of words containing a subject and a predicate that forms part of a compound or complex sentence. **2.** A distinct article or provision in a document. [< ML *clausa,* close of a rhetorical period.]

claus•tro•pho•bi•a (klôs′trə-fō′bē-ə) *n.* Pathological fear of confined spaces. [< L *claustrum,* enclosed place + -PHOBIA.] **—claus′tro•pho′bic** *adj.*

clav•i•chord (klăv′ĭ-kôrd′) *n.* An early musical keyboard instrument. [< L *clāvis,* key + CHORD.]

clav•i•cle (klăv′ĭ-kəl) *n.* A bone that links the sternum and the scapula. [< L *clāvis,* key.] **—cla•vic′u•lar** (klă-vĭk′yə-lər) *adj.*

cla•vier (klə-vîr′, klā′vē-ər, klăv′ē-ər) *n.* **1.** A keyboard. **2.** Any stringed keyboard instrument. [< F *clavier,* keyboard.]

claw (klô) *n.* **1.** A sharp, often curved nail on the toe of an animal. **2.** A pincerlike part, as of a lobster. **3.** Anything resembling a claw, as the cleft end of the head of a hammer. *—v.* To scratch or dig with or as if with claws. [< OE *clawu.*]

clay (klā) *n.* **1.** A fine-grained, firm natural material, plastic when wet, that is used in making bricks, tiles, and pottery. **2.** Moist earth; mud. [< OE *clǣg.*] **—clay′ey** (klā′ē), **clay′ish** *adj.*

clean (klēn) *adj.* **1.** Free from impurities; unsoiled. **2.** Thorough; complete. **3.** Morally pure. *—adv.* **1.** In a clean manner. **2.** *Informal.* Entirely. **—come clean.** *Slang.* To admit the truth. *—v.* To rid of dirt or other impurities. **—clean up. 1.** To rid of dirt. **2.** *Informal.* To make a large profit. [< OE *clǣne.* See **gel-[2]**.] **—clean′ness** *n.*

clean-cut (klēn′kŭt′) *adj.* **1.** Clearly defined. **2.** Wholesome; neat.

clean•ly (klĕn′lē) *adj.* **-lier, -liest.** Habitually neat and clean. *—adv.* (klēn′lē). In a clean manner. **—clean′li•ness** (klĕn′lē-nĭs) *n.*

cleanse (klĕnz) *v.* **cleansed, cleansing.** To free from dirt, defilement, or guilt. [< OE *clǣnsian.*] **—cleans′er** *n.*

clear (klîr) *adj.* **1.** Free from anything that dims or obscures. **2.** Free from impediment; open. **3.** Easily perceptible; distinct. **4.** Discerning or perceiving easily: *a clear mind.* **5.** Free from doubt or confusion. **6.** Free from qualification or limitation. **7.** Freed from contact or connection; disengaged: *clear of danger.* **8.** Freed from burden or obligation. *—adv.* **1.** Distinctly. **2.** *Informal.* Entirely. *—v.* **1.** To make or become clear, light, or bright. **2.** To rid of impurities or blemishes. **3.** To rid of obstructions. **4.** To free from a charge of guilt. **5.** To pass by, under, or over without contact. **6.** To gain as net profit or earnings. **7.** To pass through a clearing-house, as a check. **8.** To free (the throat) of phlegm. **—clear out.** *Informal.* To go away. **—clear up. 1.** To make or become understandable. **2.** To become fair, as the weather. *—n.* A clear or open space. [< L *clārus,* bright, clear.] **—clear′a•ble** *adj.* **—clear′er** *n.* **—clear′ly** *adv.* **—clear′ness** *n.*

clear•ance (klîr′əns) *n.* **1.** The act of clearing. **2.** The amount by which a moving object clears something. **3.** Permission to proceed.

clear-cut (klîr′kŭt′) *adj.* **1.** Distinctly defined. **2.** Evident.

clear•ing (klîr′ĭng) *n.* A tract of land from which trees have been removed.

clear•ing-house (klîr′ĭng-hous′) *n.* Also **clear•ing•house.** An office where banks exchange checks and drafts and settle accounts.

cleat (klēt) *n.* A wooden or metallic projection used to grip, provide support, or prevent slipping. [< OE **clēat,* lump, wedge.]

cleav•age (klē′vĭj) *n.* **1.** The act, process, or result of splitting. **2.** A fissure or division.

cleave[1] (klēv) *v.* **cleft** or **cleaved** or **clove, cleft** or **cleaved** or **cloven, cleaving. 1.** To split or separate. **2.** To pierce or penetrate. [< OE *clēofan.* See **gleubh-**.]

cleave[2] (klēv) *v.* **cleaved** or **clove, cleaved, cleaving.** To adhere or cling (to). [< OE *cleofian.*]

cleav•er (klē′vər) *n.* A heavy knife or hatchet used by butchers.

clef (klĕf) *n.* A symbol on a musical staff, indicating the pitch of the notes. [F, key, musical key.]

cleft (klĕft). A *p.t.* & *p.p.* of **cleave[1]**. *—adj.* Divided; split. *—n.* A crack; crevice.

clem•a•tis (klĕm′ə-tĭs) *n.* Any of various vines with white or purplish flowers and plumelike seeds. [< L *clēmatis.*]

clem•en•cy (klĕm′ən-sē) *n.* **1.** Mercy; leniency. **2.** Mildness of weather.

Clem•ens (klĕm′ənz), **Samuel Langhorne.** Pen name, Mark Twain. 1835–1910. American novelist and essayist.

clem•ent (klĕm′ənt) *adj.* **1.** Lenient or merciful. **2.** Mild, as the weather. [< L *clēmēns,* mild, gentle.] **—clem′ent•ly** *adv.*

clench (klĕnch) *v.* **1.** To bring together (hands or teeth) tightly. **2.** To grasp or grip tightly. **3.** To clinch. *—n.* **1.** A tight grip or grasp. **2.** Anything that clenches. [< OE *beclencan.*]

Cle•o•pat•ra (klē′ə-păt′rə, -pā′trə, -pä′trə). 69–30 B.C. Queen of Egypt.

cler•gy (klûr′jē) *n., pl.* **-gies.** The body of men ordained for religious service. [< OF *clerc,* ecclesiastic, clerk.]

cler•gy•man (klûr′jē-mən) *n.* A member of the clergy.

cler•ic (klĕr′ĭk) *n.* A member of the clergy.

cler•i•cal (klĕr′ĭ-kəl) *adj.* **1.** Of or pertaining to clerks or office workers. **2.** Of, relating to, or characteristic of the clergy or a clergyman.

cler•i•cal•ism (klĕr′ĭ-kəl-ĭz′əm) *n.* A policy of supporting the influence of the clergy in political or secular matters.

clerk (klûrk) *n.* **1.** A person who performs such business functions as keeping records and attending to correspondence. **2.** A salesman in a store. *—v.* To work as a clerk. [< LL *clēricus,* a cleric.] **—clerk′ship′** *n.*

Cleve•land (klēv′lənd). A city of NE Ohio. Pop. 751,000.

Cleve•land (klēv′lənd), **(Stephen) Grover.** 1837–1908. 22nd and 24th President of the U.S. (1885–89; 1893–97).

Grover Cleveland

clev•er (klĕv′ər) *adj.* **1.** Showing mental quickness and originality. **2.** Dexterous. [Prob < ME *cliver,* expert to seize, dexterous.] **—clev′er•ly** *adv.* **—clev′er•ness** *n.*

clew. Variant of **clue.**

cli•ché (klē-shā′) *n.* A trite expression or idea. [F, "stereotyped."]

click (klĭk) *n.* A brief, sharp, nonresonant sound. *—v.* **1.** To make or cause to make one or a series of clicks. **2.** *Slang.* **a.** To become a success. **b.** To function well together. [Imit.] **—click′er** *n.*

cli•ent (klī′ənt) *n.* **1.** One for whom professional services are rendered. **2.** A customer or patron. [< L *cliēns,* dependent, follower.]

cli•en•tele (klī′ən-tĕl′) *n.* **1.** The clients of a professional person. **2.** A body of customers or patrons.

cliff (klĭf) *n.* A high, steep, or overhanging face of rock. [< OE *clif* < Gmc **klibam.*]

cli•mac•ter•ic (klī-măk′tər-ĭk, klī′măk-tĕr′ĭk) *n.* **1.** A period or year of major physiological changes. **2.** Menopause. [< Gk *klimaktēr,* rung of a ladder, crisis.]

cli•mac•tic (klī-măk′tĭk) *adj.* Pertaining to or constituting a climax.

cli•mate (klī′mĭt) *n.* **1.** The prevailing weather in a particular region. **2.** A region manifesting particular meteorological conditions. **3.** A prevailing condition in human affairs. [< LL *clīma,* climate, zone of latitude.] **—cli•mat′ic** (klī-măt′ĭk), **cli•mat′i•cal, cli′ma•tal** (-mə-təl) *adj.* **—cli•mat′i•cal•ly** *adv.*

cli•max (klī′măks′) *n.* **1.** The point of greatest intensity in a series or progression of events or statements; culmination. **2.** Orgasm. *—v.* To reach or bring to a climax. [L, rhetorical climax.]

climb (klīm) *v.* **1.** To move up or ascend, esp. by using the hands and feet. **2.** To rise in rank or fortune. **3.** To slope upward. **4.** To grow upward. **—climb down.** To move downward; descend. *—n.* **1.** The act of climbing; ascent. **2.** A place to be climbed. [< OE *climban.*] **—climb′a•ble** *adj.* **—climb′er** *n.*

clime (klīm) *n. Poetic.* Climate.

clinch (klĭnch) *v.* **1.** To fasten securely, as with a nail or bolt. **2.** To settle decisively. **3.** To embrace so as to immobilize an opponent's arms. *—n.* **1.** The act, process, or result of clinching. **2.** *Slang.* An amorous embrace. [Var of CLENCH.]

clinch•er (klĭn'chər) *n.* One that clinches, esp. a decisive point, fact, or remark.

–cline. *comb. form.* Slope: **syncline.** [< Gk *klinein,* to lean.]

cling (klĭng) *v.* **clung, clinging.** To hold fast or adhere to something physically or emotionally. [< OE *clingan.*] **—cling'er** *n.*

clin•ic (klĭn'ĭk) *n.* **1.** A medical lecture in which patients are examined and treated in the presence of students. **2.** An institution associated with a hospital and dealing chiefly with outpatients. **3.** A center that offers counsel or instruction. [< Gk *klinikē,* medical treatment at sickbed.]

clin•i•cal (klĭn'ĭ-kəl) *adj.* **1.** Pertaining to a clinic. **2.** Pertaining to direct observation and treatment of patients. **3.** Analytical; highly objective. **—clin'i•cal•ly** *adv.*

clink¹ (klĭngk) *v.* To make or cause to make a soft, sharp, ringing sound. *—n.* Such a sound. [< MDu *clinken.*]

clink² (klĭngk) *n. Slang.* A prison. [< *The Clink,* a prison in London.]

clink•er (klĭng'kər) *n.* The incombustible, fused residue that remains after the combustion of certain coal. [< obs Du *klinckaerd,* "one that clinks."]

clip¹ (klĭp) *v.* **1.** To cut off or out with shears. **2.** To cut short; curtail. **3.** *Informal.* To hit with a sharp blow. **4.** *Slang.* To cheat or overcharge. *—n. Informal.* A brisk pace. [< ON *klippa,* to cut short.]

clip² (klĭp) *n.* **1.** A device for fastening; clasp. **2.** A container for holding cartridges. *—v.* **1.** To grip securely; fasten. **2.** *Football.* To block (an opponent not carrying the ball) illegally from the rear. [< OE *clyppan.*]

clip•per (klĭp'ər) *n.* **1.** Often **clippers.** An instrument for cutting, clipping, or shearing. **2.** A sailing vessel built for great speed.

clip•ping (klĭp'ĭng) *n.* Something cut off or out, esp. an item from a newspaper.

clique (klēk, klĭk) *n.* An exclusive group of people. [F.]

clit•o•ris (klĭt'ə-rĭs, klī'tə-) *n.* A small erectile organ at the upper end of the vulva. [< Gk *kleitoris,* "small hill."] **—clit'o•ral** (-rəl) *adj.*

clk. clerk.

cloak (klōk) *n.* **1.** A loose outer garment. **2.** Anything that covers or conceals. *—v.* **1.** To cover with a cloak. **2.** To conceal. [ME *cloke.*]

clob•ber (klŏb'ər) *v. Slang.* To batter; defeat completely. [?]

cloche (klōsh) *n.* A close-fitting woman's hat. [F, bell.]

clock¹ (klŏk) *n.* Any instrument for measuring or indicating time. *—v.* To record the time or speed of. [< MDu *clocke,* bell, clock.]

clock² (klŏk) *n.* An embroidered or woven decoration on a stocking or sock.

clock•wise (klŏk'wīz') *adv.* In the same direction as the rotating hands of a clock. **—clock'-wise'** *adj.*

clock•work (klŏk'wûrk') *n.* The mechanism of a clock or similar mechanism.

clod (klŏd) *n.* **1.** A lump, esp. of earth or clay. **2.** An ignorant or stupid person. [< OE *clott,* lump, CLOT.] **—clod'dish** *adj.*

clod•hop•per (klŏd'hŏp'ər) *n.* **1.** A clumsy, coarse person. **2. clodhoppers.** Big, heavy shoes.

clog (klŏg) *n.* **1.** An obstacle. **2.** A weight attached to an animal's leg to hinder movement. **3.** A heavy, usually wooden-soled shoe. *—v.* **clogged, clogging. 1.** To impede or encumber. **2.** To make or become obstructed. [ME *clogge,* block of wood.] **—clog'gy** *adj.*

cloi•son•né (kloi'zə-nā') *n.* Enamelware in which the surface decoration is formed by different colors of enamel separated by thin strips of metal. [< F *cloisonner,* to partition.]

clois•ter (klois'tər) *n.* **1.** A covered walk with an open colonnade on one side, running along the inside wall of a building. **2.** A place of religious seclusion, esp. a monastery or convent. *—v.* To confine in or as if in a cloister; seclude. [< L *claustrum,* enclosed place.]

clop (klŏp) *v.* **clopped, clopping.** To make the sound of a horse's hoofs against pavement. *—n.* Such a sound. [Imit.]

close (klōs) *adj.* **closer, closest. 1.** Proximate in time, space, or relation; near. **2.** Compact: *a close weave.* **3.** Near a surface, as of the skin: *a close shave.* **4.** Nearly equivalent or even, as a contest. **5.** Fitting tightly. **6.** Not deviating from an original: *a close copy.* **7.** Precise. **8.** Complete; thorough: *close attention.* **9.** Bound by mutual interests or affections; intimate. **10.** Shut or shut in. **11.** Confined in space. **12.** Confined to specific persons; restricted. **13.** Hidden; secluded. **14.** Secretive. **15.** Miserly. **16.** Lacking fresh or circulating air. *—v.* (klōz) **closed, closing. 1.** To shut or become shut. **2.** To fill up. **3.** To end; finish. **4.** To join or unite; bring into contact. **5.** To enclose; shut in. **6.** To reach an agreement. **—close down** (or **up**). To stop or cease entirely. **—close in.** To surround and advance upon. *—n.* (klōz). A conclusion. *—adv.* (klōs). In a close manner. [< L *clausus,* pp of *claudere,* to close.] **—close'ly** (klōs'lē) *adv.* **—close'ness** (klōs'nĭs) *n.*

closed circuit. A television transmission circuit with a limited number of reception stations and no broadcasting facilities.

closed shop. A **union shop.**

close-fist•ed (klōs'fĭs'tĭd) *adj.* Stingy; miserly; penurious.

close-mouthed (klōs'mouthd', -moutht') *adj.* Not disposed to talking; reticent.

clos•et (klŏz'ĭt, klō'zĭt) *n.* **1.** A small room or compartment for storage of supplies and clothes. **2.** A small private chamber. *—v.* To shut up in a private room, as for discussion. [< OF *clos,* enclosure.]

close-up (klōs'ŭp') *n.* A picture taken at close range.

clo•sure (klō'zhər) *n.* **1.** The act of closing or condition of being closed. **2.** Something that closes. **3.** Cloture.

clot (klŏt) *n.* A thick, viscous, or coagulated mass. [< OE *clott,* lump. See **gel-¹.**] **—clot** *v.* **(clotted, clotting).**

cloth (klôth, klŏth) *n., pl.* **cloths** (klôths, klôthz, klŏths, klŏthz). **1.** Fabric formed by weaving, knitting, or pressing natural or synthetic fibers. **2.** A piece of fabric used for a specific purpose, as a tablecloth. **3.** Professional mode of dress. **4. the cloth.** The clergy. [< OE *clāth.*]

clothe (klōth) *v.* **clothed** or **clad, clothing. 1.** To put clothes on; dress. **2.** To cover as with clothes; invest. [< OE *clāthian* < *clāth,* CLOTH.]

clothes (klōz, klōthz) *pl.n.* Articles of dress; wearing apparel.

clothes•horse (klōz'hôrs', klōthz'-) *n.* **1.** A frame on which clothes are hung. **2.** A person considered excessively concerned with dress.

clothes•pin (klōz'pĭn, klōthz'-) *n.* A clip of wood or plastic for fastening clothes to a line, as for drying.

cloth•ier (klōth'yər, klō'thē-ər) *n.* One who makes or sells clothing or cloth.

cloth•ing (klō'thĭng) *n.* Clothes collectively.

clo•ture (klō'chər) *n.* Also **clo•sure** (-zhər). A parliamentary procedure by which debate is ended and an immediate vote taken. [< OF *closure,* closure.]

cloud (kloud) *n.* **1.** A visible body of fine water droplets or ice particles in the earth's atmosphere. **2.** Any visible mass in the air, as of dust. **3.** A swarm. **4.** Anything that darkens or fills with gloom. **—under a cloud.** Under suspicion. *—v.* **1.** To cover with or as if with clouds. **2.** To become overcast. **3.** To make or become gloomy or troubled. **4.** To cast aspersions on. [< OE *clūd,* rock, hill. See **gel-¹.**] **—cloud'less** *adj.*

cloud•burst (kloud'bûrst') *n.* A sudden rainstorm; downpour.

cloud seeding. The distributing of dry ice crystals or silver iodide smoke through clouds to stimulate rainfall.

cloud•y (klou'dē) *adj.* **-ier, -iest. 1.** Full of or covered with clouds. **2.** Of or like clouds. **3.** Not transparent. **4.** Obscure; vague. **—cloud'i•ly** *adv.* **—cloud'i•ness** *n.*

clout (klout) *n.* A blow, esp. with the fist. *—v.* To hit with the fist. [< OE *clūt,* patch.]

clove¹ (klōv) *n.* The dried aromatic flower bud of a tropical Asian tree, used as a spice. [ME *clowe (of gilofre),* "nail-shaped bud (of clove)."]

clove² (klōv) *n.* A separable section of a bulb, as of garlic. [< OE *clufu.* See **gleubh-.**]

clove³ (klōv). Alternate *p.t.* of **cleave¹** and **cleave².**

clo•ven (klō'vən). Alternate *p.p.* of **cleave¹.** *—adj.* Split; divided.

clo•ver (klō'vər) *n.* Any of various plants having compound leaves with three leaflets and tight heads of small flowers. [< OE *clǣfre* < Gmc *klaibrōn.]

clown (kloun) *n.* **1.** A buffoon or jester who entertains in a circus or other presentation. **2.** A rude, vulgar person; boor. *—v.* To behave like a clown. [Prob < Scand.] **—clown'-ish** *adj.* **—clown'ish•ly** *adv.*

cloy (kloi) *v.* To surfeit, esp. with something too rich or sweet. [Short for obs *accloy,* to nail, hence to clog, satiate.]

C.L.U. chartered life underwriter.

club¹ (klŭb) *n.* **1.** A heavy stick suitable for use as a weapon; cudgel. **2.** A stick used in certain games, such as golf and hockey, to drive a ball. **3.** Any of a suit of playing cards marked with a black symbol shaped like a cloverleaf. *—v.* **clubbed, clubbing.** To strike or beat with or as with a club. [< ON *klubba,* club.]

club² (klŭb) *n.* **1.** A group of people organized for a common purpose. **2.** The meeting place of such a group. *—v.* **clubbed, clubbing.** To contribute or combine for a common purpose. [Prob archaic *club,* to gather into a mass.]

club•foot (klŭb'fo͝ot') *n.* **1.** Congenital deformity of the foot, marked by a misshapen appearance. **2.** A foot so deformed. **—club'-foot'ed** *adj.*

club sandwich. A sandwich, usually of three slices of toast with various fillings.

cluck (klŭk) *v.* To utter a sound characteristic of a brooding hen. *—n.* **1.** Such a sound. **2.** A stupid or foolish person. [Imit.]

clue (klo͞o) *n.* Also **clew.** Anything that guides or directs in the solution of a problem or mystery. —*v.* **clued, clueing** or **cluing.** To give (someone) guiding information. [< OE *cliewen,* ball of yarn.]

clump (klŭmp) *n.* **1.** A clustered mass or thick grouping; lump. **2.** A heavy dull sound. —*v.* **1.** To walk with a heavy dull sound. **2.** To form clumps (of). [< MLG *klumpe.*]

clum•sy (klŭm'zē) *adj.* **-sier, -siest. 1.** Lacking physical coordination, skill, or grace; awkward; unwieldy. **2.** Gauche; inept. [< obs *clumse,* to be numb with cold.] —**clum'si•ly** *adv.* —**clum'si•ness** *n.*

clung (klŭng). *p.t. & p.p.* of **cling.**

clus•ter (klŭs'tər) *n.* Any configuration of elements occurring close together; group; bunch. —*v.* To gather, grow, or form into clusters. [< OE.]

clutch[1] (klŭch) *v.* To grasp or attempt to grasp and hold tightly. —*n.* **1.** A tight grasp or a device for grasping. **2. clutches.** Control or power. **3.** A device for engaging and disengaging two working parts of a shaft or of a shaft and a driving mechanism. [< OE *clyccan* < Gmc **klukjan.*]

clutch[2] (klŭch) *n.* The eggs or chicks produced or hatched at one time. [< ON *klekja,* to hatch.]

clut•ter (klŭt'ər) *n.* A confused or disordered state; litter; jumble. —*v.* To litter or pile in a disordered state. [< ME *clot,* lump, clot.]

clys•ter (klĭs'tər) *n. Rare.* An enema. [< Gk *klustēr,* "liquid for washing out."]

cm centimeter.

Cm curium.

Cmdr. commander.

cml. commercial.

C/N credit note.

co–. *comb. form.* **1.** Joint, together, or mutually. **2.** Same, similar. **3.** Complement of an angle. [< L.]

Co cobalt.

CO conscientious objector.

co. 1. company. **2.** county.

Co. company.

c.o. 1. care of. **2.** *Accounting.* carried over. **3.** cash order.

C.O. 1. commanding officer. **2.** conscientious objector.

c/o care of.

coach (kōch) *n.* **1.** A closed carriage with four wheels. **2.** A bus. **3.** A railroad passenger car. **4.** One who trains athletes or athletic teams. **5.** A private tutor who prepares a student for an examination. —*v.* To teach or train; tutor. [< *Kocs,* town in Györ, Hungary, where such carriages originated.] —**coach'er** *n.*

coach•man (kōch'mən) *n.* One who drives a coach.

co•ad•ju•tor (kō'ə-jōō'tər, kō-ăj'ə-tər) *n.* A coworker; assistant, esp. to a bishop. [< L *coadjūtor.*]

co•ag•u•lant (kō-ăg'yə-lənt) *n.* An agent that causes coagulation. —**co•ag'u•lant** *adj.*

co•ag•u•late (kō-ăg'yə-lāt') *v.* **-lated, -lating.** To form a soft, semisolid, or solid mass. [< L *coāgulāre,* to curdle.] —**co•ag'u•la'tion** *n.*

coal (kōl) *n.* A natural dark-brown to black, carbon-containing solid used as a fuel. [< OE *col.* See **geulo-.**]

co•a•lesce (kō'ə-lĕs') *v.* **-lesced, -lescing.** To grow or come together; fuse; unite. [L *coalēscere,* to grow together.] —**co'a•les'cence** *n.* —**co'a•les'cent** *adj.*

co•a•li•tion (kō'ə-lĭsh'ən) *n.* An alliance or union, esp. a temporary one. [< L *coalēscere,* COALESCE.] —**co'a•li'tion•ist** *n.*

coal oil. Kerosene.

coal tar. A viscous black liquid obtained by the destructive distillation of coal, used in paints, roofing, and insulation materials.

coarse (kôrs, kōrs) *adj.* **coarser, coarsest. 1.** Of inferior quality. **2.** Lacking in delicacy or refinement. **3.** Not fine in texture; rough. [ME *coars,* ordinary, coarse.] —**coarse'ly** *adv.* —**coarse'ness** *n.*

coars•en (kôr'sən, kōr'-) *v.* To make or become coarse. —**coars'en•er** *n.*

coast (kōst) *n.* **1.** The seashore. **2.** A slope down which one may coast, as on a sled. **3.** The act of sliding or coasting. —*v.* **1.** To slide down an inclined slope. **2.** To move without further acceleration. **3.** To sail near or along a coast. **4.** To move aimlessly. [< L *costa,* rib, side.] —**coast'al** (kōs'təl) *adj.*

coast•er (kōs'tər) *n.* **1.** One that coasts. **2.** A disk placed under a drinking glass to protect a surface beneath.

coast guard. Also **Coast Guard.** The military coastal patrol of a nation.

coast•line (kōst'līn') *n.* The shape or boundary of a coast.

coat (kōt) *n.* **1.** An outer garment covering the body from the shoulders to the waist or below. **2.** A natural outer covering, as the fur of an animal. **3.** Also **coating.** A layer of some material covering something else. —*v.* To provide or cover with a coat or layer. [< Frank **kotta.*] —**coat'ed** *adj.*

coat of arms. A shield blazoned with heraldic bearings or the insignia itself.

coat of mail *pl.* **coats of mail.** An armored coat made of chain mail.

co-au•thor (kō-ô'thər) *n.* A collaborating or joint author.

coax (kōks) *v.* To urge, persuade, or try to persuade by pleading or flattery; wheedle. [Earlier *coaks, cokes,* to fool.] —**coax'er** *n.* —**coax'ing•ly** *adv.*

co•ax•i•al (kō-ăk'sē-əl) *adj.* Having a common axis.

coaxial cable. A transmission cable consisting of a conducting outer metal tube enclosing and insulated from a central conducting core.

cob (kŏb) *n.* **1.** The central core of an ear of corn. **2.** A male swan. **3.** A stocky, short-legged horse. [ME *cobbe,* lump, round object.]

co•balt (kō'bôlt') *n. Symbol* **Co** A hard, brittle metallic element, used for magnetic alloys, high-temperature alloys, and glass and ceramic pigments. Atomic number 27, atomic weight 58.9332. [G *Kobalt, Kobold.*]

cob•ble (kŏb'əl) *v.* **-bled, -bling. 1.** To mend (boots or shoes). **2.** To put together clumsily. [Prob < COBBLER[1].]

cob•bler[1] (kŏb'lər) *n.* One who mends boots and shoes. [ME *cobelere.*]

cob•bler[2] (kŏb'lər) *n.* A fruit pie having only a thick top crust.

cob•ble•stone (kŏb'əl-stōn') *n.* A naturally rounded stone, formerly used for paving streets. [Perh < ME *cobbe,* lump, COB + STONE.]

co•bra (kō'brə) *n.* A venomous Asian or African snake that expands the skin of the neck to form a flattened hood. [< Port *cobra (de capello),* "snake (with a hood)."]

cob•web (kŏb'wĕb') *n.* **1.** The web spun by a spider or a strand of such a web. **2.** Something resembling a cobweb in gauziness or flimsiness. [< OE *āttorcoppe,* spider + WEB.]

co•caine (kō-kān', kō'kān') *n.* Also **co•cain.** A narcotic alkaloid, $C_{17}H_{21}NO_4$, extracted from the leaves of a South American tree and used as a surface anesthetic. [Span *coca,* the tree + -INE.]

coc•cus (kŏk'əs) *n., pl.* **-ci** (-sī', kŏk'ī'). A bacterium with a spherical shape. [< Gk *kokkos,* pit.]

coc•cyx (kŏk'sĭks) *n., pl.* **coccyges** (kŏk-sī'jēz, kŏk'sə-jēz'). A small bone at the base of the spinal column. [< Gk *kokkux,* cuckoo, coccyx.] —**coc•cyg'e•al** (kŏk-sĭj'ē-əl) *adj.*

coch•i•neal (kŏch'ə-nēl', kŏch'ə-nēl') *n.* **1.** A brilliant red dye. **2.** Vivid red. [< L *coccinus,* scarlet.]

coch•le•a (kŏk'lē-ə) *n., pl.* **-leae** (-lē-ē'). A spiral tube of the inner ear containing nerve endings essential for hearing. [< Gk *kokhlos,* land snail.] —**coch'le•ar** *adj.*

cock[1] (kŏk) *n.* **1.** A male bird, esp. the adult male of the domestic fowl. **2.** A faucet or valve. **3. a.** The hammer in a firearm. **b.** Its position when ready for firing. —*v.* **1.** To set the hammer of (a firearm) in position for firing. **2.** To tilt or turn up or to one side. [< LL *coccus.*]

cock[2] (kŏk) *n.* A cone-shaped pile of straw or hay. [ME *cok.*]

cock•ade (kŏk-ād') *n.* A rosette or knot of ribbon worn esp. on the hat as a badge. [< F *cocarde,* jauntily tilted hat.]

cock•a•ma•mie (kŏk'ə-mā'mē) *adj.* Also **cock•a•ma•my.** *Slang.* **1.** Trifling; second-rate. **2.** Ludicrous; nonsensical.

cock•a•too (kŏk'ə-tōō') *n.* A crested Australian parrot. [< Malay *kakatua.*]

cock•a•trice (kŏk'ə-trĭs, -trīs') *n.* A mythical serpent with the power to kill with its glance. [< LL *calcātrix,* "the tracker."]

cock•crow (kŏk'krō') *n.* The time of day when the cock crows; dawn.

cock•er•el (kŏk'ər-əl) *n.* A young rooster. [< COCK[1].]

cock•er spaniel (kŏk'ər). A dog with long, drooping ears and a silky coat. [Orig used for hunting woodcocks.]

cock•eye (kŏk'ī') *n.* A squinting eye.

cock-eyed (kŏk'īd') *adj.* **1.** Cross-eyed. **2.** Crooked; askew.

cock•fight (kŏk'fīt') *n.* A fight between gamecocks that are often fitted with metal spurs.

cock•horse (kŏk'hôrs') *n.* A wooden toy horse.

cock•le[1] (kŏk'əl) *n.* A bivalve mollusk with a ribbed, heart-shaped shell. [< OF *coquille,* shell.]

cock•le[2] (kŏk'əl) *n.* Any of several weedy plants growing in grain fields. [< L *coccus,* a kind of berry.]

cock•ney (kŏk'nē) *n., pl.* **-neys. 1.** Often **Cockney.** A native of the East End, a section of London. **2.** The dialect or accent of cockneys. [ME *cokeney,* "cock's egg," pampered brat.] —**cock'ney** *adj.*

cock•pit (kŏk'pĭt') *n.* **1.** A pit or enclosed space for cockfights. **2.** The space in an airplane for the pilot and crew.

cock•roach (kŏk'rōch') *n.* A flat-bodied brownish insect common as a household pest. [< Span *cucaracha.*]

cocks•comb (kŏks'kōm') *n.* **1.** The comb of a rooster. **2.** The cap of a jester, decorated to resemble a rooster's comb. **3.** Also **coxcomb.** A pretentious fop.

cock•sure (kŏk'shōōr') *adj.* Completely sure; overconfident. —**cock'sure'ly** *adv.*

cock•tail (kŏk'tāl') *n.* **1.** A mixed alcoholic drink. **2.** An appetizer, as of seafood. —*adj.* **1.** Of or pertaining to cocktails. **2.** Suitable for wear on semiformal occasions. [?]

cock•y (kŏk'ē) *adj.* **-ier, -iest.** *Informal.* Cheer-

fully self-confident; conceited.
co•co (kō'kō) *n., pl.* **-cos.** The coconut or the coconut palm. [< Port *coco,* "goblin," coconut shell.]
co•coa (kō'kō) *n.* **1.** Roasted powdered cacao seeds with most of the fat removed. **2.** A beverage made from this powder and milk or water. [Var of CACAO.]
co•co•nut (kō'kə-nŭt', -nət) *n.* Also **co•coa•nut.** The large, hard-shelled, edible nut of a tropical palm tree, the **coconut palm,** having a hollow center filled with milky fluid. [coco + NUT.]
co•coon (kə-kōōn') *n.* **1.** The silky or fibrous pupal case spun by the larva of a moth or other insect. **2.** A similar protective covering or structure. [< Prov *coco,* eggshell, hence cocoon.]
cod (kŏd) *n., pl.* **cod** or **cods.** Also **cod•fish** (kŏd'fĭsh'). A commercially important food fish of N Atlantic waters. [ME.]
COD 1. cash on delivery. **2.** collect on delivery.
co•da (kō'də) *n. Mus.* The final passage of a movement or composition. [It, "tail."]
cod•dle (kŏd'l) *v.* **-dled, -dling. 1.** To cook in water just below the boiling point. **2.** To treat indulgently; baby. **—cod'dler** *n.*
code (kōd) *n.* **1.** A systematically arranged and comprehensive collection of laws or rules and regulations. **2.** A system of signals used in transmitting messages. **3.** An arbitrary system of symbols, letters, or words used for transmitting brief or secret messages. **—***v.* **coded, coding.** To systematize, arrange, or convert into a code. [< L *cōdex,* CODEX.]
co•deine (kō'dēn', kō'dē-ĭn) *n.* A narcotic alkaloid, $C_{18}H_{21}NO_3$, derived from opium or morphine. [< Gk *kōdeia,* capsule of the poppy.]
co•dex (kō'dĕks') *n., pl.* **codices** (kō'də-sēz', kŏd'ə-). A manuscript volume, esp. of a classic work or of the Scriptures. [L *cōdex,* tree trunk, board, writing tablet, book (of laws).]
codg•er (kŏj'ər) *n.* An old man. [Poss < earlier *cadger,* carrier, peddler.]
cod•i•cil (kŏd'ə-sĭl) *n.* A supplement or appendix to a will. [< L *cōdex,* CODEX.]
cod•i•fy (kŏd'ə-fī', kō'də-) *v.* **-fied, -fying. 1.** To arrange or systematize. **2.** To code. **—cod'i•fi•ca'tion** *n.* **—cod'i•fi'er** *n.*
co-ed, co•ed (kō'ĕd') *n.* A female college student. **—***adj.* Co-educational. [Short for *co-educational student.*]
co-ed•u•ca•tion (kō'ĕj-ōō-kā'shən) *n.* The education of both men and women at the same institution. **—co'-ed•u•ca'tion•al** *adj.*
co•ef•fi•cient (kō'ə-fĭsh'ənt) *n.* **1. a.** A numerical factor of an elementary algebraic term, as 4 in the term 4x. **b.** The product of all but one of the factors of a mathematical expression. **2.** A numerical measure of a physical or chemical property that is constant for a specified system. [< CO- + EFFICIENT.]
co•en•zyme (kō-ĕn'zīm') *n.* A heat-stable organic molecule that must be loosely associated with an enzyme for the enzyme to function.
co•e•qual (kō-ē'kwəl) *adj.* Equal with one another. **—***n.* An equal. **—co'e•qual'i•ty** (-kwŏl'ə-tē) *n.* **—co•e'qual•ly** *adv.*
co•erce (kō-ûrs') *v.* **-erced, -ercing. 1.** To compel to act or think in a given manner. **2.** To dominate; restrain. [< L *coercēre,* to enclose together, constrain.] **—co•erc'er** *n.* **—co•er'cion** *n.* **—co•er'cive** *adj.*
co•e•val (kō-ē'vəl) *adj.* Of the same period of time. [L *coaevus.*] **—co•e'val•ly** *adv.*
co•ex•ist (kō'ĭg-zĭst') *v.* To exist together, at the same time, or in the same place. **—co'ex•is'tence** *n.*
co•ex•tend (kō'ĭk-stĕnd') *v.* To extend through the same space or duration. **—co'ex•ten'sive** *adj.*
cof•fee (kô'fē, kŏf'ē) *n.* **1.** An aromatic brown beverage prepared from the beanlike seeds of a tropical tree. **2.** The seeds of this tree. **3.** The tree itself. [< Ar *qahwah.*]
coffee house. Also **cof•fee•house** (kô'fē-hous', kŏf'ē-). A restaurant where coffee and other refreshments are served.
cof•fee•pot (kô'fē-pŏt', kŏf'ē-) *n.* A pot for brewing or serving coffee.
coffee shop. A small restaurant in which light meals are served.
coffee table. A long, low table, often placed before a sofa.
cof•fer (kô'fər, kŏf'ər) *n.* **1.** A strongbox. **2. coffers.** Funds; treasury. [< L *cophinus,* basket.]
cof•fer•dam (kô'fər-dăm', kŏf'ər-) *n.* A temporary watertight enclosure built in the water and pumped dry so that construction, as of piers, can be undertaken.
cof•fin (kô'fən, kŏf'ən) *n.* A box in which a corpse is buried. [< Gk *kophinus,* basket, measure of capacity.]
C. of S. chief of staff.
cog (kŏg) *n.* **1.** A tooth on the rim of a wheel. **2.** A subordinate member of an organization. [ME *cogge.*]
cog. cognate.
co•gent (kō'jənt) *adj.* Forcibly convincing. [< L *cōgere,* to force, drive together.] **—co'gen•cy** (-jən-sē) *n.* **—co'gent•ly** *adv.*
cog•i•tate (kŏj'ə-tāt') *v.* **-tated, -tating. 1.** To meditate; ponder. **2.** To think carefully about. [L *cōgitāre.*] **—cog'i•ta'tion** *n.*
co•gnac (kōn'yăk', kōn'-, kôn'-) *n.* A fine French brandy. [< *Cognac,* France.]
cog•nate (kŏg'nāt') *adj.* **1.** Having a common ancestor or origin, esp. culturally or linguistically akin. **2.** Analogous in nature. **—***n.* One that is cognate with another. [L *cognātus.*]
cog•ni•tion (kŏg-nĭsh'ən) *n.* **1.** The mental process or faculty by which knowledge is acquired. **2.** Knowledge. [< L *cognōscere* (pp *cognitus*), to get to know, learn.] **—cog'ni•tive** (kŏg'nə-tĭv) *adj.*
cog•ni•zance (kŏg'nə-zəns) *n.* Conscious knowledge or recognition; awareness. [< L *cognōscere,* to learn.] **—cog'ni•zant** *adj.*
cog•no•men (kŏg-nō'mən) *n., pl.* **-mens** or **-nomina** (-nŏm'ə-nə). **1.** A family name; surname. **2.** Any name, esp. a descriptive nickname. [L *cognōmen,* "additional name."]
co•hab•it (kō-hăb'ĭt) *v.* To live together in a sexual relationship when not legally married. [LL *cohabitāre.*] **—co•hab'i•ta'tion** *n.*
co•heir (kō-âr') *n.* A joint heir.
co•here (kō-hîr') *v.* **-hered, -hering. 1.** To stick or hold together. **2.** To be logically connected. [L *cohaerēre.*]
co•her•ent (kō-hîr'ənt, kō-hĕr'-) *adj.* **1.** Sticking together; cohering. **2.** Orderly or logical. **—co•her'ence, co•her'en•cy** *n.*
co•he•sion (kō-hē'zhən) *n.* **1.** The process or condition of cohering. **2.** The mutual attraction by which the elements of a body are held together. **—co•he'sive** (-sĭv) *adj.* **—co•he'sive•ly** *adv.* **—co•he'sive•ness** *n.*
co•hort (kō'hôrt') *n.* **1.** A group or band united in some struggle. **2.** A companion or associate. [< L *cohors,* enclosed yard, company of soldiers.]
coif (koif) *n.* A tight-fitting cap. [< LL *cofia.*]
coif•feur (kwä-fœr') *n. Fem.* **coif•feuse** (kwä-fœz'). A hairdresser. [F.]
coif•fure (kwä-fyŏŏr') *n.* A style of arranging the hair. [F.]
coil (koil) *n.* **1.** A series of connected spirals or concentric rings formed by gathering or winding. **2.** A spiral or ring. **3.** *Elec.* **a.** A wound spiral of insulated wire. **b.** Any device of which such a spiral is the major component. **—***v.* To wind in coils. [< L *colligere,* to collect.] **—coil'er** *n.*
coin (koin) *n.* **1.** A piece of metal issued and authorized by a government for use as money. **2.** Metal money collectively. **—***v.* **1.** To make (coins) from metal. **2.** To invent (a word or phrase). [< L *cuneus,* wedge.]
coin•age (koi'nĭj) *n.* **1.** The process of coining. **2.** Coins collectively.
co•in•cide (kō'ĭn-sīd') *v.* **-cided, -ciding. 1.** To occupy the same position simultaneously. **2.** To happen at the same time. **3.** To correspond exactly. [ML *coincidere.*]
co•in•ci•dence (kō-ĭn'sə-dəns, -dĕns') *n.* The state or fact of coinciding. **—co•in'ci•den'tal, co•in'ci•dent** *adj.* **—co•in'ci•den'tal•ly** *adv.*
co•i•tus (kō'ə-təs) *n.* Also **co•i•tion** (kō-ĭsh'ən). Sexual intercourse. [L, "meeting."]
coke[1] (kōk) *n.* The solid residue of coal after removal of volatile material, used as fuel. [ME *coke.*]
coke[2] (kōk) *n. Slang.* Cocaine.
Coke (kōk) *n.* A trademark for Coca-Cola, a soft drink.
col. 1. collect. **2.** college; collegiate. **3.** colony. **4.** column.
Col. 1. colonel. **2.** Colorado (unofficial). **3.** Colossians (New Testament).
co•la[1] (kō'lə) *n.* **1.** A carbonated drink made with an extract from the nuts of a tropical tree. **2.** Also **ko•la.** A tree bearing such nuts.
co•la[2]**.** Alternate *pl.* of **colon.**
col•an•der (kŭl'ən-dər, kŏl'-) *n.* A perforated bowl-shaped kitchen utensil used for draining. [< L *cōlāre,* to strain.]
cold (kōld) *adj.* **1.** Having a low temperature. **2.** Uncomfortably chilled. **3.** Unconscious; insensible: *knocked cold.* **4.** Not affected by emotion; objective. **5.** Sexually frigid. **—***n.* **1.** Relative lack of warmth. **2.** A chilly sensation. **3.** A viral infection of the mucous membranes of the respiratory passages. [< OE *ceald.* See **gel-**[3]**.**] **—cold'ly** *adv.* **—cold'ness** *n.*
cold-blood•ed (kōld'blŭd'ĭd) *adj.* **1.** Ruthless; heartless. **2.** Having a body temperature that varies with the environment, as a fish or reptile. **—cold'-blood'ed•ness** *n.*
cold cream. An emulsion for cleansing and softening the skin.
cold cuts. Slices of assorted cold meats.
cold feet. *Slang.* Failure of nerve.
cold front. The leading portion of a cold atmospheric air mass moving against, and eventually replacing, a warm air mass.
cold sore. A small sore on the lips that often accompanies a fever or cold.
Cole•ridge (kōl'rĭj), **Samuel Taylor.** 1772–1834. English poet and critic.
cole•slaw (kōl'slô') *n.* Also **cole slaw.** A salad of shredded raw cabbage. [Du *koolsla.*]
co•le•us (kō'lē-əs) *n., pl.* **-uses.** A plant cultivated for its showy, varicolored leaves. [< Gk *koleos, koleon,* sheath.]
col•ic (kŏl'ĭk) *n.* Acute paroxysmal pain in the abdomen. [< Gk *kōlikos,* suffering in the colon.] **—col'ick•y** *adj.*
col•i•se•um (kŏl'ə-sē'əm) *n.* A large public amphitheater. [< the *Colosseum* at Rome.]

co•li•tis (kō-lī'tĭs) *n.* Inflammation of the mucous membrane of the colon.

coll. college; collegiate.

col•lab•o•rate (kə-lăb'ə-rāt') *v.* **-rated, -rating.** 1. To work together, esp. in a joint intellectual effort. 2. To cooperate treasonably. [< LL *collabōrāre.*] —**col•lab'o•ra'tion** *n.* —**col•lab'o•ra'tive** *adj.* —**col•lab'o•ra'tor** *n.*

col•lage (kō-läzh') *n.* An artistic composition of materials and objects pasted on a surface. [< F *coller,* to glue, paste.]

col•lapse (kə-lăps') *v.* **-lapsed, -lapsing.** 1. To fall down or inward suddenly; cave in. 2. To cease to function; break down suddenly. 3. To fold compactly. [< L *collāpsus,* pp of *collābī,* to fall together.] —**col•lapse'** *n.* —**col•laps'i•ble** *adj.*

col•lar (kŏl'ər) *n.* 1. The part of a garment that encircles the neck. 2. An encircling bandlike part or structure suggestive of a collar. 3. A ringlike device used to limit, guide, or secure a part. —*v.* To seize or detain. [< L *collāre,* necklace, collar.]

col•lar•bone (kŏl'ər-bōn') *n.* The clavicle.

col•lard (kŏl'ərd) *n.* Often **collards.** A leafy, cabbagelike vegetable.

col•late (kə-lāt', kŏl'āt', kō'lāt') *v.* **-lated, -lating.** 1. To examine and compare (texts) carefully. 2. To assemble in proper numerical sequence. [L *collātus.*] —**col•la'tor** *n.*

col•lat•er•al (kə-lăt'ər-əl) *adj.* 1. Situated or running side by side. 2. Serving to corroborate. 3. Of a secondary nature. 4. Of, designating, or guaranteed by property acceptable as security for a loan or other obligation. 5. Having an ancestor in common but descended from a different line. —*n.* A collateral security. [< ML *collaterālis.*]

col•la•tion (kə-lā'shən, kō-, kō-) *n.* 1. The act or process of collating. 2. A light meal.

col•league (kŏl'ēg') *n.* A fellow member; associate, esp. in a profession. [< L *collēga,* one chosen to serve with another.]

col•lect (kə-lĕkt') *v.* 1. To bring together in a group; assemble; accumulate. 2. To call for and obtain payment of: *collect taxes.* —*adj.* With payment to be made by the receiver. —*adv.* So that the receiver is charged. [< L *colligere,* to gather together.] —**col•lec'tion** *n.* —**col•lec'tor** *n.*

col•lect•ed (kə-lĕk'tĭd) *adj.* Self-possessed; composed. —**col•lect'ed•ly** *adv.*

col•lect•i•bles (kə-lĕk'tə-bəlz) *pl.n.* Objects that are collected because they are novel, rare, or bizarre.

col•lec•tive (kə-lĕk'tĭv) *adj.* 1. Formed by collecting. 2. Of, pertaining to, or made by a number of individuals acting as a group: *a collective decision.* —*n.* A collective enterprise or those working in it. —**col•lec'tive•ly** *adv.*

col•lec•tiv•ism (kə-lĕk'tə-vĭz'əm) *n.* The principle or system of collective ownership and control of the means of production and distribution.

col•lege (kŏl'ĭj) *n.* 1. A school of higher learning that grants a bachelor's degree. 2. Any of the undergraduate divisions or schools of a university. 3. A technical or professional school, often affiliated with a university. 4. A body of persons having a common purpose or common duties. [< L *collēga,* COLLEAGUE.] —**col•le'giate** (kə-lē'jĭt, -jē-ĭt) *adj.*

col•le•gian (kə-lē'jən, -jē-ən) *n.* A college student.

col•lide (kə-līd') *v.* **-lided, -liding.** 1. To come together with violent, direct impact. 2. To meet in opposition. [L *collīdere.*] —**col•li'sion** (kə-lĭsh'ən) *n.*

col•lie (kŏl'ē) *n.* A large, long-haired dog originally used to herd sheep. [Scot.]

col•lier (kŏl'yər) *n. Brit.* 1. A coal miner. 2. A coal ship.

col•lier•y (kŏl'yər-ē) *n., pl.* **-ies.** *Brit.* A coal mine.

col•lin•e•ar (kō'lĭn'ē-ər, kə-) *adj.* 1. Lying on the same line. 2. Containing a common line.

col•lo•di•on (kə-lō'dē-ən) *n.* Also **col•lo•di•um** (-dē-əm). A highly flammable colorless or yellowish syrupy solution, used to hold surgical dressings and for making photographic plates. [< Gk *kolla,* glue.]

col•loid (kŏl'oid', kō'loid') *n.* 1. A suspension of finely divided particles that do not settle out of, and cannot be readily filtered from, the uniform medium in which they are suspended. 2. The particulate matter so suspended. —*adj.* Also **col•loi•dal** (kə-loid'l, kō-). Of, relating to, or having the nature of a colloid. [< Gk *kolla,* glue.]

col•lo•qui•al (kə-lō'kwē-əl) *adj.* Characteristic of or appropriate to conversation but not formal writing. [< COLLOQUY.] —**col•lo'qui•al•ism'** *n.* —**col•lo'qui•al•ly** *adv.*

col•lo•qui•um (kə-lō'kwē-əm) *n., pl.* **-ums** or **-quia** (-kwē-ə). A seminar, usually led by a different lecturer at each meeting.

col•lo•quy (kŏl'ə-kwē) *n., pl.* **-quies.** A conversation, esp. a formal one. [< L *colloquium,* conversation.]

col•lu•sion (kə-lōō'zhən) *n.* A secret agreement for a deceitful or fraudulent purpose. [< L *collūdere,* to play together.] —**col•lu'sive** *adj.*

Colo. Colorado.

co•logne (kə-lōn') *n.* A liquid made of alcohol and fragrant oils. [F *eau de cologne,* "water of COLOGNE."]

Co•logne (kə-lōn'). A city of west-central West Germany. Pop. 848,000.

Co•lom•bi•a (kə-lŭm'bē-ə). A republic of NW South America. Pop. 17,432,000. Cap. Bogotá. —**Co•lom'bi•an** *adj.* & *n.*

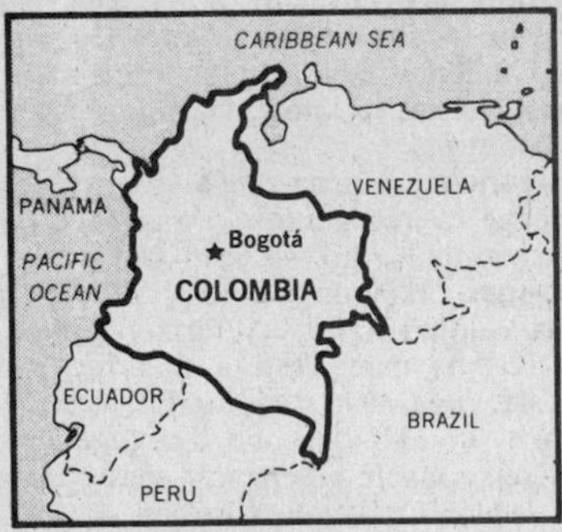

Colombia

Co•lom•bo (kə-lŭm'bō). The capital of Sri Lanka. Pop. 561,000.

co•lon¹ (kō'lən) *n.* A punctuation mark (:) used to introduce a quotation, explanation, example, etc. [L *cōlon,* unit of verses.]

co•lon² (kō'lən) *n., pl.* **-lons** or **-la** (-lə). The section of the large intestine from the cecum to the rectum. [< Gk *kolon,* large intestine.] —**co•lon'ic** (kə-lŏn'ĭk) *adj.*

co•lon³ (kō-lōn') *n., pl.* **-lons** (-lōnz'). 1. The basic monetary unit of Costa Rica. 2. The basic monetary unit of El Salvador. [Span *colón.*]

colo•nel (kûr'nəl) *n.* An officer, as in the army, ranking immediately above a lieutenant colonel. [< OIt *colonnello,* "commander of a column."] —**colo'nel•cy, colo'nel•ship'** *n.*

co•lo•ni•al (kə-lō'nē-əl) *adj.* 1. Of or pertaining to a colony or colonies. 2. Often **Colonial.** a. Of or relating to the 13 British colonies that became the original United States of America. b. Of or relating to the colonial period in the U.S. —*n.* An inhabitant of a colony.

co•lo•ni•al•ism (kə-lō'nē-ə-lĭz'əm) *n.* A policy by which a nation maintains or extends its control over foreign dependencies. —**co•lo'ni•al•ist** *n.* & *adj.*

col•o•nist (kŏl'ə-nĭst) *n.* 1. An original settler of a colony. 2. An inhabitant of a colony.

col•o•nize (kŏl'ə-nīz') *v.* **-nized, -nizing.** 1. To establish a colony in. 2. To settle in a colony. —**col'o•ni•za'tion** (kŏl'ə-nə-zā'shən) *n.* —**col'o•niz'er** *n.*

col•on•nade (kŏl'ə-nād') *n. Archit.* A series of regularly spaced columns. [< L *columna,* column.] —**col'on•nad'ed** *adj.*

col•o•ny (kŏl'ə-nē) *n., pl.* **-nies.** 1. A group of emigrants settled in a distant land but subject to a parent country. 2. A territory thus settled. 3. Any region politically controlled by another country. 4. **Colony.** Any of the 13 British colonies that became the original United States of America. 5. A group with the same interests, concentrated in a particular area. 6. A group of the same kind of animals or plants living or growing together. [< L *colōnia,* farm, settlement.]

col•or (kŭl'ər). Also *chiefly Brit.* **col•our.** *n.* 1. That aspect of things that is caused by differing qualities of the light reflected or emitted by them. 2. A dye, paint, etc., that imparts color. 3. Skin tone. 4. **colors.** A flag or banner, as of a country or military unit. 5. Outward, often deceptive, appearance. 6. Vividness or picturesqueness. —**with flying colors.** With great success. —*v.* 1. To impart color to; change the color of. 2. To give a distinctive character to; influence. 3. To misrepresent. 4. To blush. [< L.]

Col•o•ra•do (kŏl'ə-rä'dō, -răd'ə). A state of the W U.S. Pop. 2,207,000. Cap. Denver. —**Col'o•ra'dan** *adj.* & *n.*

Colorado River. A river of the W U.S.

col•or•a•tion (kŭl'ə-rā'shən) *n.* Arrangement of colors.

col•or•a•tu•ra (kŭl'ər-ə-t/y/ōōr'ə) *n.* 1. Florid ornamentation in vocal music. 2. A singer specializing in this.

col•or•blind (kŭl'ər-blīnd') *adj.* Unable to distinguish certain colors. —**col'or•blind'ness** *n.*

col•ored (kŭl'ərd) *adj.* 1. Having color. 2. Often **Colored.** Designating a dark-skinned people, esp. Negroes. 3. Distorted or biased.

col•or•fast (kŭl'ər-făst', -fäst') *adj.* Having color that will not run or fade, as fabrics. —**col'or•fast'ness** *n.*

col•or•ful (kŭl'ər-fəl) *adj.* 1. Abounding in colors. 2. Vivid. —**col'or•ful•ly** *adv.*

col•or•less (kŭl'ər-lĭs) *adj.* 1. Without color. 2. Weak in color; pallid. 3. Lacking vividness. —**col'or•less•ly** *adv.* —**col'or•less•ness** *n.*

co•los•sal (kə-lŏs'əl) *adj.* Enormous; gigantic. [< L *colossus,* COLOSSUS.] —**co•los'sal•ly** *adv.*

co•los•sus (kə-lŏs'əs) *n., pl.* **-lossi** (-lŏs'ī') or **-suses.** Anything of enormous size or importance. [L.]

col•our. *Chiefly Brit.* Variant of **color.**

colt (kōlt) *n.* A young male horse, zebra, etc. [< OE, young ass or camel.]

Co•lum•bi•a (kə-lŭm'bē-ə). 1. The capital of

South Carolina. Pop. 114,000. **2.** A river of the NW U.S.

col•um•bine (kŏl'əm-bīn') *n.* Any of several plants with variously colored, conspicuously spurred flowers.

co•lum•bi•um (kə-lŭm'bē-əm) *n.* *Symbol* **Cb** Niobium. —**co•lum'bic** *adj.*

Co•lum•bus (kə-lŭm'bəs). **1.** The capital of Ohio. Pop. 540,000. **2.** A city of W Georgia. Pop. 154,000.

Co•lum•bus (kə-lŭm'bəs), **Christopher.** 1451–1506. Italian navigator.

col•umn (kŏl'əm) *n.* **1.** A supporting pillar consisting of a base, shaft, and capital. **2.** Anything resembling a column. **3.** One of two or more vertical sections of printed lines on a page. **4.** A feature article that appears regularly in a periodical. **5.** A long row, as of troops. [< L *columna.*] —**co•lum'nar** (kə-lŭm'nər), **col'umned** *adj.*

col•um•nist (kŏl'əm-nĭst, -ə-mĭst) *n.* A writer of a newspaper column.

com–. *comb. form.* Together; jointly. [< L *cum,* with.]

com. **1.** comma. **2.** commerce; commercial. **3.** commissioner. **4.** committee. **5.** common.

co•ma (kō'mə) *n., pl.* **-mas.** A deep, prolonged unconsciousness. [< Gk *kōma,* deep sleep, lethargy.]

Co•man•che (kə-măn'chē) *n., pl.* **-che** or **-ches.** **1.** A member of a tribe of Uto-Aztecan-speaking North American Indians, formerly ranging over the W plains. **2.** The language of this tribe. —**Co•man'che** *adj.*

co•ma•tose (kō'mə-tōs', kŏm'ə-) *adj.* **1.** Unconscious. **2.** Lethargic; torpid.

comb (kōm) *n.* **1.** A thin, toothed strip of plastic or other material, used to arrange the hair. **2.** Something resembling a comb, as a card for processing wool. **3.** A fleshy crest on the crown of the head of domestic fowl and other birds. **4.** A honeycomb. —*v.* **1.** To arrange with or as if with a comb. **2.** To card (wool or other fiber). **3.** To search thoroughly. [< OE *camb.* See **gembh-.**]

comb. **1.** combination. **2.** combining

com•bat (kəm-băt', kŏm'băt') *v.* **1.** To fight against; contend. **2.** To oppose vigorously. —*n.* (kŏm'băt'). Fighting, esp. armed battle. [< VL **combattere,* to fight with.] —**com•bat'ive** *adj.*

com•bat•ant (kəm-băt'ənt, kŏm'bə-tənt) *n.* One taking part in armed combat.

combat fatigue. A nervous disorder involving anxiety, depression, and irritability, induced by combat.

comb•er (kō'mər) *n.* A long, cresting wave of the sea.

com•bi•na•tion (kŏm'bə-nā'shən) *n.* **1.** The act of combining or state of being combined. **2.** Something resulting from combining; an aggregate. **3.** A sequence of numbers or letters used to open certain locks.

com•bine (kəm-bīn') *v.* **-bined, -bining.** **1.** To make or become united; merge; blend. **2.** To form a chemical compound. —*n.* (kŏm'bīn'). **1.** A machine that harvests and threshes grain. **2.** A group of persons united for commercial or political advantage. [< LL *combināre.*] —**com•bin'er** *n.*

combining form. *Gram.* A word element that combines with other word forms to create compounds.

com•bo (kŏm'bō) *n., pl.* **-bos.** *Informal.* A small band, usually of jazz musicians. [Short for COMBINATION.]

com•bus•ti•ble (kəm-bŭs'tə-bəl) *adj.* Capable of burning. —*n.* A combustible substance. [< L *combūrere,* to burn up.] —**com•bus'ti•bil'i•ty** *n.* —**com•bus'ti•bly** *adv.*

com•bus•tion (kəm-bŭs'chən) *n.* **1.** A burning. **2.** A chemical change, esp. oxidation, accompanied by the production of heat and light. —**com•bus'tive** *adj.*

comd. commanding.

comdg. commanding.

Comdr. commander.

Comdt. commandant.

come (kŭm) *v.* **came, coming. 1.** To advance; approach. **2.** To arrive. **3.** To reach a particular result, state, or position. **4.** To move into view. **5.** To exist at a particular point or place: *The letter* T *comes before* U. **6.** To happen: *How did you come to know that?* **7.** To issue from; originate. **8.** To be obtainable: *It comes in two sizes.* —**come about.** To occur. —**come across.** To meet by chance. —**come around** (or **round**). **1.** To recover. **2.** To change opinion. —**come between.** To cause estrangement. —**come by.** To acquire. —**come down with.** To become ill. —**come off.** **1.** To become detached. **2.** To occur. —**come out. 1.** To be disclosed. **2.** To make a formal social debut. —**come through.** To succeed. —**come to.** To recover consciousness. —**come up with.** *Informal.* To propose; produce. —**how come?** *Informal.* Why? —*interj.* Expressive of anger or impatience: *Come now, that's enough.* [< OE *cuman.* See **gwā-.**]

come•back (kŭm'băk') *n.* **1.** A return to a former position or status. **2.** A retort; repartee.

co•me•di•an (kə-mē'dē-ən) *n.* **1.** A professional entertainer who performs various comic acts. **2.** An actor in comedy. —**co•me'di•enne'** (-mē'dē-ĕn') *fem.n.*

com•e•do (kŏm'ə-dō') *n., pl.* **-dos** or **comedones** (kŏm'ə-dō'nēz). A blackhead. [< L *comedere,* to eat up.]

come•down (kŭm'doun') *n.* A decline in status.

com•e•dy (kŏm'ə-dē) *n., pl.* **-dies. 1. a.** A play, motion picture, etc., that is humorous in its treatment of theme and character. **b.** A comic element in such a work. **2.** A comic occurrence or situation in life. [< Gk *kōmōidia.*] —**co•me'dic** (kə-mē'dĭk) *adj.*

come•ly (kŭm'lē) *adj.* **-lier, -liest.** Having a pleasing appearance; attractive; handsome; graceful. [< OE *cȳmlic,* lovely, splendid.] —**come'li•ness** *n.*

co•mes•ti•ble (kə-mĕs'tə-bəl) *adj.* Edible. —*n.* Anything edible. [< L *comedere,* to eat up.]

com•et (kŏm'ĭt) *n.* A celestial body having a solid head surrounded by a nebulous luminescent cloud and an elongated curved vapor tail arising when the head approaches the sun. [< Gk *(astēr) komētēs,* "long-haired (star)."]

come•up•pance (kŭm'ŭp'əns) *n.* *Informal.* Punishment that one deserves.

com•fort (kŭm'fərt) *v.* To soothe in time of grief or fear; console. —*n.* **1.** A state of ease or well-being. **2.** Consolation; solace. **3.** One that brings ease. **4.** Capacity to give physical ease: *the comfort of his favorite chair.* [< LL *confortāre,* to strengthen.]

com•fort•a•ble (kŭm'fər-tə-bəl, kŭmf'tər-bəl) *adj.* **1.** Providing comfort. **2.** Being in a state of comfort. **3.** *Informal.* Adequate: *comfortable earnings.* —**com'fort•a•ble•ness** *n.* —**com'fort•a•bly** *adv.*

com•fort•er (kŭm'fər-tər) *n.* **1.** One that comforts. **2.** A quilt.

com•ic (kŏm'ĭk) *adj.* Also **com•i•cal. 1.** Of or pertaining to comedy. **2.** Amusing; humorous. —*n.* **1.** One who is comical. **2. comics.** *Informal.* Comic strips. [< Gk *kōmos,* revel, merrymaking.] —**com'i•cal•ly** *adv.*

comic strip. A narrative series of cartoons, as in Sunday newspapers.

com•ing (kŭm'ĭng) *adj.* **1.** Approaching next. **2.** Showing promise of success.

Com•in•tern (kŏm'ĭn-tûrn) *n.* The Third International, esp. its Moscow executive committee. [Communist International.]

comm. **1.** commission; commissioner. **2.** commonwealth.

com•ma (kŏm'ə) *n.* A punctuation mark (,) used to indicate a separation of ideas or elements within the structure of a sentence. [< Gk *komma,* a cut, section, clause.]

com•mand (kə-mănd', -mänd') *v.* **1.** To give orders (to). **2.** To exercise authority (over); rule. **3.** To dominate by location; overlook. —*n.* **1. a.** The act of giving orders. **b.** An order so given. **2.** The authority to command. **3.** Ability to control; mastery. **4.** A unit or post under the command of one officer. [< VL **commandāre.*]

com•man•dant (kŏm'ən-dănt', -dänt') *n.* A commanding officer.

com•man•deer (kŏm'ən-dîr') *v.* To seize arbitrarily, esp. for public use.

com•mand•er (kə-măn'dər, kə-män'-) *n.* **1.** One who commands. **2.** An officer in the navy who ranks next above a lieutenant commander.

commander in chief *pl.* **commanders in chief.** The supreme commander of all the armed forces of a nation.

com•mand•ing (kə-măn'dĭng, kə-män'-) *adj.* **1.** In command. **2.** Impressive. **3.** Dominating. —**com•mand'ing•ly** *adv.*

commanding officer. An officer in charge of a military unit.

com•mand•ment (kə-mănd'mənt, kə-mänd'-)

comet
Comet Alcock, photographed September 1, 1959

n. 1. A command; edict. 2. Often **Commandment.** Any of the Ten Commandments.

com•man•do (kə-măn'dō, kə-män'-) *n., pl.* **-dos** or **-does.** A member of a small military unit trained to make quick raids.

com•mem•o•rate (kə-mĕm'ə-rāt') *v.* **-rated, -rating.** 1. To honor the memory of. 2. To serve as a memorial to. [L *commemorāre,* to call to mind clearly.] —**com•mem'o•ra'tion** *n.* —**com•mem'o•ra•tive** (-ər-ə-tĭv) *adj.*

com•mence (kə-mĕns') *v.* **-menced, -mencing.** To begin; start. [< VL **cominitiāre.*]

com•mence•ment (kə-mĕns'mənt) *n.* 1. A beginning; start. 2. A graduation ceremony, as in a college.

com•mend (kə-mĕnd') *v.* 1. To represent as worthy; recommend. 2. To praise. 3. To commit to the care of another. [< L *commendāre,* to commit to one's charge, commend.] —**com•mend'a•ble** *adj.* —**com•mend'a•bly** *adv.* —**com'men•da'tion** (kŏm'ən-dā'shən) *n.*

com•men•su•ra•ble (kə-mĕn'sər-ə-bəl, -shər-ə-bəl) *adj.* Able to be measured by a common standard. [< LL *commēnsūrābilis.*]

com•men•su•rate (kə-mĕn'sə-rĭt, -shə-rĭt) *adj.* 1. Of the same size, extent, or duration. 2. Corresponding in scale; proportionate. 3. Commensurable. [LL *commēnsūrātus.*]

com•ment (kŏm'ĕnt') *n.* 1. An expression of criticism, analysis, or observation. 2. A statement of opinion. —*v.* To make a comment or comments (on). [< L *commentum,* contrivance, interpretation.]

com•men•tar•y (kŏm'ən-tĕr'ē) *n., pl.* **-ies.** A series of explanations or interpretations.

com•men•ta•tor (kŏm'ən-tā'tər) *n.* A radio or television reporter.

com•merce (kŏm'ərs) *n.* 1. The buying and selling of goods; trade. 2. Social intercourse. [< L *commercium.*]

com•mer•cial (kə-mûr'shəl) *adj.* 1. Of, pertaining to, or engaged in commerce. 2. Having profit as a major aim. —*n.* An advertisement on radio or television.

com•mer•cial•ism (kə-mûr'shə-lĭz'əm) *n.* Commercial practices, aims, and attitudes.

com•mer•cial•ize (kə-mûr'shə-līz') *v.* **-ized, -izing.** To make commercial, esp. for financial gain. —**com•mer'cial•i•za'tion** *n.*

com•min•gle (kə-mĭng'gəl) *v.* **-gled, -gling.** To mix.

com•mis•er•ate (kə-mĭz'ə-rāt') *v.* **-ated, -ating.** To feel or express sorrow or pity; sympathize. [L *commiserārī.*] —**com•mis'er•a'tion** *n.*

com•mis•sar (kŏm'ə-sär') *n.* A Communist Party official in charge of political indoctrination and enforcement of party loyalty. [Russ *komissar.*]

com•mis•sar•i•at (kŏm'ə-sâr'ē-ĭt) *n.* An army department in charge of food and supplies.

com•mis•sar•y (kŏm'ə-sĕr'ē, -sâr'ē) *n., pl.* **-ies.** A store where food or equipment is sold, esp. one on a military post. [< ML *commissārius,* commissioner, agent.]

com•mis•sion (kə-mĭsh'ən) *n.* 1. a. Authorization to carry out a task. b. The authority so granted. c. The task so entrusted. d. A document conferring such authorization. 2. A group authorized to perform certain duties or functions. 3. A committing; perpetration: *commission of a crime.* 4. An allowance to a salesman or agent for his services. 5. A document conferring the rank of a military officer. —*v.* 1. To grant a commission to. 2. To place an order for. [< L *committere,* COMMIT.]

commissioned officer. Any officer who holds a commission and ranks above an enlisted man or warrant officer.

com•mis•sion•er (kə-mĭsh'ən-ər) *n.* 1. A member of a commission. 2. A departmental official in charge of a public service.

com•mit (kə-mĭt') *v.* **-mitted, -mitting.** 1. To do, perform, or perpetrate: *commit a murder.* 2. To consign; entrust. 3. To place in confinement or custody. 4. To pledge (oneself) to a position on some issue. [< L *committere,* to join, connect, entrust.] —**com•mit'ment** *n.*

com•mit•tee (kə-mĭt'ē) *n.* A group officially delegated to perform a function, as reporting or acting on a matter. [ME *committe,* trustee.] —**com•mit'tee•man** *n.*

com•mode (kə-mōd') *n.* 1. A low cabinet or chest of drawers. 2. A movable cupboard containing a washbowl. 3. A toilet. [F, "convenient."]

com•mo•di•ous (kə-mō'dē-əs) *adj.* Spacious; roomy. [< L *commodus,* convenient.]

com•mod•i•ty (kə-mŏd'ə-tē) *n., pl.* **-ties.** Anything useful, esp. a transportable agricultural or mining product. [< L *commoditās,* advantage, convenience.]

com•mo•dore (kŏm'ə-dôr', -dōr') *n.* 1. A naval officer ranking below a rear admiral. 2. a. The senior captain of a naval squadron or merchant fleet. b. The presiding officer of a yacht club. [< Du *komandeur,* commander.]

com•mon (kŏm'ən) *adj.* 1. Belonging equally to all; joint. 2. Pertaining to the whole community; public: *the common good.* 3. Widespread; prevalent; general. 4. Usual; ordinary. 5. Most widely known; occurring most frequently. 6. Without special characteristics; average; standard. 7. Unrefined; coarse. —*n.* 1. A tract of land belonging to a whole community. 2. **Commons.** The lower house of Parliament in Great Britain and Canada. —**in common.** Equally; jointly. [< L *commūnis.*] —**com'mon•ly** *adv.* —**com'mon•ness** *n.*

Common Celtic. The vocabulary of the reconstructed ancestor of the Celtic languages that is attested in the major Celtic subdivisions.

common denominator. A quantity into which all the denominators of a set of fractions can be evenly divided.

com•mon•er (kŏm'ə-nər) *n.* A person without noble rank.

common fraction. A fraction having an integer as a numerator and an integer as a denominator.

Common Germanic. The vocabulary of the prehistoric ancestor of the Germanic languages that is attested in all its major subdivisions.

common law. Any unwritten, generally applied system of law based on court decisions, usages, and customs. —**com'mon-law'** *adj.*

common logarithm. A logarithm to the base 10.

common market. 1. Any customs union. 2. **Common Market.** An economic union established in 1958, originally including Belgium, France, Italy, Luxembourg, the Netherlands, and West Germany.

com•mon•place (kŏm'ən-plās') *adj.* Ordinary; common. —*n.* Something ordinary or common, esp. a trite or obvious remark.

Common Romance. The vocabulary of the reconstructed ancestor of the Romance languages that is attested in all the major Romance subdivisions and that developed from Vulgar Latin in the first century A.D.

common sense. Native good judgment.

com•mon•weal (kŏm'ən-wēl') *n.* 1. The public good. 2. *Archaic.* A commonwealth.

com•mon•wealth (kŏm'ən-wĕlth') *n.* 1. The people of a nation or state. 2. A nation or state governed by the people; republic. 3. A union or federation of self-governing states. [ME *commun welthe,* "public welfare."]

Commonwealth of Nations. Formerly **British Commonwealth of Nations.** The political community constituted by the former British Empire.

com•mo•tion (kə-mō'shən) *n.* Violent or turbulent motion; agitation. [< L *commovēre,* to move violently.]

com•mu•nal (kə-myōō'nəl, kŏm'yə-nəl) *adj.* 1. Of or pertaining to a commune or community. 2. Public. —**com'mu•nal'i•ty** *n.* —**com•mu'nal•ly** *adv.*

com•mune[1] (kə-myōōn') *v.* **-muned, -muning.** To converse intimately. —*n.* (kŏm'yōōn'). Intimate conversation. [< OF *comun, commun,* common.]

com•mune[2] (kŏm'yōōn') *n.* 1. The smallest local political division of various European countries. 2. A place used for group living. 3. The group of people engaged in such living. [< L *commūnis,* public, COMMON.]

com•mu•ni•ca•ble (kə-myōō'nĭ-kə-bəl) *adj.* 1. Able to be communicated or transmitted. 2. Talkative. —**com•mu'ni•ca•bil'i•ty, com•mu'ni•ca•ble•ness** *n.* —**com•mu'ni•ca•bly** *adv.*

com•mu•ni•cant (kə-myōō'nĭ-kənt) *n.* 1. One who receives Communion. 2. One who communicates.

com•mu•ni•cate (kə-myōō'nə-kāt') *v.* **-cated, -cating.** 1. To make known; impart. 2. To transmit, as a disease. 3. To receive Communion. [L *commūnicāre,* "to make common."] —**com•mu'ni•ca'tor** *n.*

com•mu•ni•ca•tion (kə-myōō'nə-kā'shən) *n.* 1. The act of communicating; transmission. 2. The exchange of thoughts, messages, etc. 3. Something communicated. 4. **communications.** A means of communicating.

communications satellite. An artificial satellite used to aid communications, as by reflecting or relaying a radio signal.

com•mu•ni•ca•tive (kə-myōō'nə-kā'tĭv, -nĭ-kə-tĭv) *adj.* 1. Talkative. 2. Pertaining to communication. —**com•mu'ni•ca'tive•ness** *n.*

com•mun•ion (kə-myōōn'yən) *n.* 1. A sharing, as of thoughts or feelings. 2. a. A religious or spiritual fellowship. b. A Christian denomination. 3. **Communion.** a. The Eucharist. b. The consecrated elements of the Eucharist. [< L *commūniō,* participation by all.]

com•mu•ni•qué (kə-myōō'nə-kā', kə-myōō'nə-kā') *n.* An official communication. [< L *commūnicāre,* COMMUNICATE.]

com•mu•nism (kŏm'yə-nĭz'əm) *n.* 1. A system characterized by the absence of social classes and by common ownership of production means. 2. **Communism.** a. The theory of revolutionary struggle toward this system. b. Socialism as exemplified in countries ruled by Communist parties. [< OF *commun,* common.] —**com'mu•nist** *n.* & *adj.* —**com'mu•nis'tic** *adj.* —**com'mu•nis'ti•cal•ly** *adv.*

com•mu•ni•ty (kə-myōō'nə-tē) *n., pl.* **-ties.** 1. a. A group of people living in the same locality and under the same government. b. The locality in which they live. 2. A social group or class. 3. Similarity: *a community of interests.* 4. Society as a whole. [< L *commūnis,* COMMON.]

com•mu•ta•tion (kŏm'yə-tā'shən) *n.* 1. A substitution, exchange, or interchange. 2. The travel of a commuter. 3. *Law.* A reduction of a penalty to a less severe one. [< L *commutāre,* COMMUTE.]

com•mu•ta•tive (kŏm′yə-tā′tĭv, kə-myōō′-tə-tĭv) *adj.* **1.** Pertaining to, involving, or characterized by substitution, interchange, or exchange. **2.** Logically or mathematically independent of order.

com•mu•ta•tor (kŏm′yə-tā′tər) *n.* A device connected to the coils of an electric motor or generator to provide a unidirectional current from the generator or a reversal of current into the coils of the motor.

com•mute (kə-myōōt′) *v.* **-muted, -muting. 1.** To substitute; interchange. **2.** To change (a penalty or payment) to a less severe one. **3.** To travel as a commuter. *—n. Informal.* The distance traveled by a commuter. [<L *commutāre,* to exchange.]

com•mut•er (kə-myōō′tər) *n.* One who travels regularly between his home in one community and his work in another.

comp. 1. comparative. **2.** compilation. **3.** complete. **4.** compositon; compositor.

com•pact[1] (kəm-păkt′, kŏm-, kŏm′păkt′) *adj.* **1.** Closely and firmly united or packed. **2.** Expressed briefly. *—v.* (kəm-păkt′). To press, join, or pack firmly together. *—n.* (kŏm′păkt′). **1.** A small cosmetic case. **2.** A relatively small automobile. [< L *compactus,* pp of *compingere,* to join together.] **—com•pact′ly** *adv.* **—com•pact′ness** *n.*

com•pact[2] (kŏm′păkt′) *n.* An agreement or covenant. [< L *compactus,* pp of *compacīscī,* to agree together.]

com•pac•ter (kəm-păk′tər, kŏm′păk′-) *n.* An apparatus that compresses refuse into relatively small packs for handy disposal.

com•pan•ion (kəm-păn′yən) *n.* **1.** A comrade; associate. **2.** A person employed to live or travel with another. **3.** One of a pair or set of things. [< VL **compāniō,* "one who eats bread with another"] **—com•pan′ion•ship′** *n.*

com•pan•ion•a•ble (kəm-păn′yə-nə-bəl) *adj.* Sociable; friendly. **—com•pan′ion•a•bly** *adv.*

com•pa•ny (kŭm′pə-nē) *n., pl.* **-nies. 1.** A group of people. **2.** People assembled for a social purpose. **3.** A guest or guests. **4.** Companionship; fellowship. **5.** A business enterprise; firm. **6.** A troupe of dramatic or musical performers: *a repertory company.* **7.** A subdivision of a regiment or battalion. [< VL **compāniō,* COMPANION.]

compar. comparative.

com•pa•ra•ble (kŏm′pər-ə-bəl) *adj.* **1.** Able to be compared. **2.** Worthy of comparison. **—com′pa•ra•bly** *adv.*

com•par•a•tive (kəm-păr′ə-tĭv) *adj.* **1.** Pertaining to or involving comparison. **2.** Relative. **3.** Designating a degree of comparison of adjectives and adverbs higher than positive and lower than superlative. *—n.* The comparative degree or an adjective or adverb expressing the comparative degree. **—com•par′a•tive•ly** *adv.*

com•pare (kəm-pâr′) *v.* **-pared, -paring. 1.** To represent as similar, equal, or analogous (with *to*). **2.** To examine in order to note the similarities or differences of (with *with*). **3.** To form the positive, comparative, or superlative degree of (an adjective or adverb). *—n.* **—beyond** (or **without**) **compare.** Without comparison; unequaled. [< L *comparāre,* to pair, match.] **—com•par′er** *n.*

com•par•i•son (kəm-păr′ə-sən) *n.* **1.** The act of comparing. **2.** Similarity. **3.** The modification or inflection of an adjective or adverb to denote the positive, comparative, or superlative degree.

com•part•ment (kəm-pärt′mənt) *n.* One of the parts or spaces into which an area is subdivided.

com•part•men•tal•ize (kŏm′pärt-mĕn′təl-īz′, kəm-pärt′-) *v.* **-ized, -izing.** To divide into compartments.

com•pass (kŭm′pəs, kŏm′-) *n.* **1.** A device used to determine geographical direction, esp. a magnetic needle horizontally mounted and free to pivot until aligned with the magnetic field of the earth. **2.** Often **compasses.** A V-shaped device for drawing circles or circular arcs. **3.** An enclosing line or boundary. **4.** An enclosed space or area. **5.** A range or scope; extent. *—v.* **1.** To make a circuit of; circle. **2.** To surround. **3.** To accomplish. **4.** To scheme; plot. [< VL **compassāre,* "to measure off by steps."]

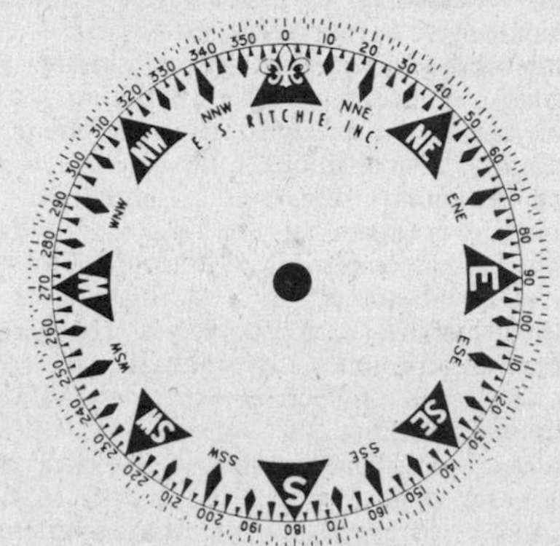

compass
Compass card

com•pas•sion (kəm-păsh′ən) *n.* A deep feeling of sharing the suffering of another; mercy. [< LL *compatī* (pp *compassus*), to sympathize with.] **—com•pas′sion•ate** *adj.*

com•pat•i•ble (kəm-păt′ə-bəl) *adj.* **1.** Capable of living or performing in harmonious combination with others. **2.** Capable of orderly, efficient integration and operation with other elements in a system. [< LL *compatī,* to sympathize with.] **—com•pat′i•bil′i•ty, com•pat′i•ble•ness** *n.* **—com•pat′i•bly** *adv.*

com•pa•tri•ot (kəm-pā′trē-ət, -ŏt′) *n.* A fellow countryman.

com•peer (kəm-pîr′, kŏm′pîr′) *n.* **1.** A peer; equal. **2.** A comrade.

com•pel (kəm-pĕl′) *v.* **-pelled, -pelling. 1.** To force; constrain. **2.** To obtain by force. [< L *compellere,* "to drive (cattle) together," force.]

com•pen•di•um (kəm-pĕn′dē-əm) *n., pl.* **-ums** or **-dia** (-dē-ə). A short, complete summary. [L, "that which is weighed together," gain.]

com•pen•sate (kŏm′pən-sāt′) *v.* **-sated, -sating. 1.** To make up for or offset. **2.** To recompense or reimburse. [L *compensāre,* to weigh one thing against another, counterbalance.] **—com•pen•sa′tion** *n.* **—com•pen′sa•to′ry** (kəm-pĕn′sə-tôr′ē, -tōr′ē) *adj.*

com•pete (kəm-pēt′) *v.* **-peted, -peting.** To contend with another; vie. [L *competere,* "to strive together."]

com•pe•tence (kŏm′pə-təns) *n.* Also **com•pe•ten•cy** (-tən-sē). **1.** The state or quality of being competent. **2.** Sufficient means for a comfortable existence.

com•pe•tent (kŏm′pə-tənt) *adj.* **1.** Properly qualified; capable. **2.** Adequate for a purpose. [< L *competere,* to be competent, COMPETE.] **—com′pe•tent•ly** *adv.*

com•pe•ti•tion (kŏm′pə-tĭsh′ən) *n.* **1.** A vying with others for profit, prize, or position. **2.** A contest of skill. **—com•pet′i•tive** (kəm-pĕt′ə-tĭv) *adj.* **—com•pet′i•tive•ness** *n.*

com•pet•i•tor (kəm-pĕt′ə-tər) *n.* One who competes, as in sports or business; rival.

com•pile (kəm-pīl′) *v.* **-piled, -piling. 1.** To gather into one book or corpus. **2.** To compose from materials gathered from several sources. [< L *compīlāre,* "to heap together," plunder.] **—com′pi•la′tion** (kŏm′pə-lā′shən) *n.* **—com•pil′er** *n.*

com•pla•cen•cy (kəm-plā′sən-sē) *n.* Also **com•pla•cence** (-səns). **1.** A feeling of contentment. **2.** Smugness. [< L *complacēre,* to please.] **—com•pla′cent** *adj.* **—com•pla′cent•ly** *adv.*

com•plain (kəm-plān′) *v.* **1.** To express feelings of pain, dissatisfaction, or resentment. **2.** To make a formal accusation or bring a formal charge. [< OF *complaindre.*] **—com•plain′er** *n.*

com•plain•ant (kəm-plā′nənt) *n.* One who makes a complaint, as in a court of law; plaintiff.

com•plaint (kəm-plānt′) *n.* **1.** An expression of pain, dissatisfaction, or resentment. **2.** A reason for complaining; grievance. **3.** A cause of physical pain. **4.** *Law.* A formal accusation or charge.

com•plai•sance (kəm-plā′səns, -zəns) *n.* Willing compliance.

com•plai•sant (kəm-plā′sənt, -zənt, kŏm′-plā-zănt′) *adj.* Cheerfully obliging. [< L *complacēre,* to please.] **—com•plai′sant•ly** *adv.*

com•ple•ment (kŏm′plə-mənt) *n.* **1.** Something that completes, perfects, or makes up a whole. **2.** The quantity or number needed to make up a whole. **3.** Full quantity, allowance, or amount. **4.** An angle related to another so that the sum of their measures is 90°. **5.** A word or words used after a verb to complete a predicate. *—v.* (kŏm′plə-mĕnt′). To add or serve as a complement to. [< L *complēre,* to COMPLETE.] **—com′ple•men′ta•ry** (-mĕn′tə-rē, -mĕn′trē) *adj.*

com•plete (kəm-plēt′) *adj.* **1.** Having all necessary or normal parts. **2.** Concluded; ended. **3.** Thorough; perfect. *—v.* **-pleted, -pleting. 1.** To make whole. **2.** To finish; end. [< L *complēre,* to fill up.] **—com•plete′ly** *adv.* **—com•ple′tion** (-plē′shən) *n.*

com•plex (kəm-plĕks′, kŏm′plĕks′) *adj.* **1.** Consisting of interconnected parts. **2.** Intricate; complicated. *—n.* (kŏm′plĕks′). **1.** A whole composed of interconnected parts. **2.** A connected group of repressed ideas that compel characteristic or habitual patterns of thought, feeling, and action. [L *complexus,* pp of *complectere,* to entwine.] **—com•plex′i•ty** *n.*

com•plex•ion (kəm-plĕk′shən) *n.* **1.** The natural hue, texture, and appearance of the skin. **2.** General character or appearance. [< ML *complexiō,* "combination of corporeal humors."] **—com•plex′ion•al** *adj.*

complex number. A number of the form $a + bi$, where a and b are real numbers and $i^2 = -1$.

com•pli•ance (kəm-plī′əns) *n.* Also **com•pli•an•cy** (-ən-sē). **1.** A yielding to a wish or demand. **2.** A disposition to yield to others. **—com•pli′ant** *adj.* **—com•pli′ant•ly** *adv.*

com•pli•cate (kŏm′plĭ-kāt′) *v.* **-cated, -cating.** To make or become complex, intricate, or perplexing. [L *complicāre,* to fold together.] **—com′pli•ca′tion** *n.*

com•plic•i•ty (kəm-plĭs′ə-tē) *n.* The state of being an accomplice, as in wrongdoing.

com•pli•ment (kŏm'plə-mənt) *n.* **1.** An expression of praise or admiration. **2.** A formal act of civility, courtesy, or respect. —*v.* To pay a compliment to. [< L *complēre,* to fill up.]
com•pli•men•ta•ry (kŏm'plə-mĕn'tər-ē, -trē) *adj.* **1.** Expressing a compliment. **2.** Given free as a courtesy.
com•ply (kəm-plī') *v.* **-plied, -plying.** To agree; acquiesce, as to a command. [< L *complēre,* to fill up.]
com•po•nent (kəm-pō'nənt) *n.* A relatively simple part of a complex entity; element; constituent. [< L *compōnere,* to place together.] —**com•po'nent** *adj.*
com•port (kəm-pôrt') *v.* **1.** To conduct oneself in a particular manner. **2.** To agree; harmonize. [< L *comportāre,* to bring together, support.]
com•port•ment (kəm-pôrt'mənt) *n.* Bearing; deportment.
com•pose (kəm-pōz') *v.* **-posed, -posing.** **1.** To make up the constituent parts of. See Usage note at **comprise.** **2.** To make by putting together parts or elements. **3.** To create, as a piece of music. **4.** To make calm or tranquil. **5.** To arrange or set (type or matter to be printed). [< OF *composer.*]
com•posed (kəm-pōzd') *adj.* Calm; serene. —**com•pos'ed•ly** (-pō'zĭd-lē) *adv.*
com•pos•er (kəm-pō'zər) *n.* One who composes music.
com•pos•ite (kəm-pŏz'ĭt) *adj.* **1.** Made up of distinct components; compound. **2.** Of or belonging to a large plant family with flower heads consisting of small, densely clustered flowers, often of different kinds, as the daisy. —*n.* **1.** A composite structure or entity. **2.** A composite plant. [L *compositus,* pp of *compōnere,* to put together.] —**com•pos'ite•ly** *adv.*
com•po•si•tion (kŏm'pə-zĭsh'ən) *n.* **1.** The act or result of composing. **2.** The arrangement of parts composed. **3.** Process or technique in structuring music or art. **4.** A short school essay. **5.** Typesetting. [< L *compōnere,* to put together, arrange.]
com•pos•i•tor (kəm-pŏz'ə-tər) *n.* A typesetter.
com•post (kŏm'pōst) *n.* A mixture of decaying organic matter used as fertilizer. [< L *compositus,* put together, COMPOSITE.]
com•po•sure (kəm-pō'zhər) *n.* Self-possession; calm. [< COMPOSE.]
com•pote (kŏm'pōt) *n.* **1.** Fruit stewed in syrup. **2.** A long-stemmed dish for fruit or nuts. [< OF *composte,* stewed fruit.]
com•pound[1] (kŏm-pound', kəm-) *v.* **1.** To combine; mix. **2.** To produce by combining. **3.** To compute (interest) on principal and accrued interest. **4.** To make greater; increase. —*adj.* (kŏm'pound, kŏm-pound'). Consisting of two or more parts. —*n.* (kŏm'pound). **1.** A compound entity. **2.** A combination of words or word elements regarded as a unit. **3.** A pure, macroscopically homogeneous substance consisting of atoms or ions of different elements in definite proportions, usually having properties unlike those of its constituent elements. [< L *compōnere,* to put together.]
com•pound[2] (kŏm'pound) *n.* A group of residences enclosed by a barrier. [< Malay *kampong,* village, cluster of buildings.]
compound eye. An eye, as of insects, composed of many light-sensitive elements.
compound flower. A flower head of a composite plant, consisting of numerous small flowers appearing as a single bloom.
compound fracture. A fracture in which broken bone lacerates soft tissue.
com•pre•hend (kŏm'prĭ-hĕnd') *v.* **1.** To understand. **2.** To include; comprise. [< L *comprehendere,* to grasp mentally.] —**com'pre•hen'sion** (-shən) *n.*
com•pre•hen•si•ble (kŏm'prĭ-hĕn'sə-bəl) *adj.* Also **com•pre•hend•i•ble** (-hĕn'də-bəl). Capable of being comprehended. —**com'pre•hen'si•bil'i•ty** *n.* —**com'pre•hen'si•bly** *adv.*
com•pre•hen•sive (kŏm'prĭ-hĕn'sĭv) *adj.* **1.** Totally inclusive. **2.** Comprehensible. —**com'pre•hen'sive•ly** *adv.*
com•press (kəm-prĕs') *v.* To press together or force into a smaller space; condense. —*n.* (kŏm'prĕs'). A pad applied to control bleeding or reduce pain or infection. [< L *comprimere* (pp *compressus*), to press together.] —**com•press'i•bil'i•ty** *n.* —**com•press'i•ble** *adj.* —**com•pres'sion** *n.* —**com•pres'sive** *adj.*
com•pres•sor (kəm-prĕs'ər) *n.* A machine that compresses gases.
com•prise (kəm-prīz') *v.* **-prised, -prising.** **1.** To consist of. **2.** To include; contain. [< OF *comprendre* (pp *compris*), to comprehend.]
Usage: By definition, the whole *comprises* the parts or *is composed of* them; the parts *compose* or *make up* the whole: *The Union comprises (is composed of) 50 states. Fifty states compose the Union.*
com•pro•mise (kŏm'prə-mīz') *n.* **1. a.** A settlement of differences by mutual concessions. **b.** The result of such a settlement. **2.** Something combining the qualities of different things. —*v.* **-mised, -mising.** **1.** To settle by or agree to concessions. **2.** To expose to suspicion or disrepute. [< L *comprōmittere,* to promise mutually.] —**com'pro•mis'er** *n.*
comp•trol•ler. Variant of **controller.**
com•pul•sion (kəm-pŭl'shən) *n.* **1.** The act of compelling or forcing. **2.** The state of being compelled. **3.** An irresistible impulse to act. [< L *compellere* (pp *compulsus*), COMPEL.] —**com•pul'sive** *adj.* —**com•pul'sive•ly** *adv.*
com•pul•so•ry (kəm-pŭl'sə-rē) *adj.* **1.** Employing or exerting compulsion; coercive. **2.** Obligatory; required. —**com•pul'so•ri•ly** *adv.*
com•punc•tion (kəm-pŭngk'shən) *n.* Uneasiness caused by guilt; remorse. [< LL *compunctiō,* "prick of conscience."]
com•pute (kəm-pyo͞ot') *v.* **-puted, -puting.** To determine by mathematics, esp. by numerical methods. [L *computāre,* to reckon together.] —**com•put'a•ble** *adj.* —**com'pu•ta'tion** *n.*
com•put•er (kəm-pyo͞o'tər) *n.* **1.** A person who computes. **2.** A device that computes, esp. an electronic machine that performs high-speed mathematical or logical calculations or assembles, stores, correlates, or otherwise processes and prints information derived from coded data in accordance with a predetermined program.
com•put•er•ize (kəm-pyo͞o'tə-rīz') *v.* **-ized, -izing.** **1.** To process or store (information) with or in an electronic computer or system of computers. **2.** To furnish with a computer or computer system.
com•rade (kŏm'răd, -rĭd, kŭm'-) *n.* A friend or associate. [< OF *camarade,* roommate, soldier sharing the same room.] —**com'rade•ship'** *n.*
con[1] (kŏn) *adv.* Against; in opposition to. —*n.* That which weighs against, as evidence. [< L *contrā,* against.]
con[2] (kŏn) *v.* **conned, conning.** To study, peruse, or examine carefully. [< OE *cunnan,* to know how. See **gnō-.**] —**con'ner** *n.*
con[3] (kŏn). *Slang.* *v.* **conned, conning.** To swindle or defraud. —*n.* A swindle. [Short for CONFIDENCE.]
con[4] (kŏn) *n. Slang.* A convict.
Con•a•kry (kăn'ə-krē). The capital of the Republic of Guinea. Pop. 112,000.
con•cat•e•nate (kŏn-kăt'ə-nāt') *v.* **-nated, -nating.** To connect in a series. [< LL *concatēnāre.*] —**con•cat'e•nate** (-nĭt, -nāt') *adj.* —**con•cat'e•na'tion** *n.*
con•cave (kŏn-kāv') *adj.* Curved like the inner surface of a sphere. [< L *concavus,* vaulted, hollow.] —**con•cav'i•ty** (-kăv'ə-tē) *n.*
con•ceal (kən-sēl') *v.* To keep from observation, discovery, or understanding. [< L *concēlāre.*] —**con•ceal'er** *n.* —**con•ceal'ment** *n.*
con•cede (kən-sēd') *v.* **-ceded, -ceding.** **1.** To acknowledge as true, just, or proper. **2.** To yield, as a right. [< L *concēdere,* to yield.]
con•ceit (kən-sēt') *n.* **1.** Too high an opinion of one's abilities or worth. **2.** An ingenious or witty thought. **3.** An elaborate or exaggerated metaphor. [< CONCEIVE.]
con•ceit•ed (kən-sē'tĭd) *adj.* Vain.
con•ceive (kən-sēv') *v.* **-ceived, -ceiving.** **1.** To become pregnant (with). **2.** To imagine; understand. **3.** To express in particular words. [< L *concipere,* to take to oneself, be impregnated.] —**con•ceiv'a•bil'i•ty** *n.* —**con•ceiv'a•ble** *adj.* —**con•ceiv'a•bly** *adv.* —**con•ceiv'er** *n.*
con•cen•trate (kŏn'sən-trāt') *v.* **-trated, -trating.** **1.** To direct or draw toward a common center; focus. **2.** *Chem.* To increase the concentration of. —*n. Chem.* A product of concentration. [Prob < L *com-,* same + CENTER.] —**con'cen•tra'tive** *adj.* —**con'cen•tra'tor** *n.*
con•cen•tra•tion (kŏn'sən-trā'shən) *n.* **1.** The act of concentrating or state of being concentrated. **2.** Something concentrated. **3.** The amount of a specified substance in a unit amount of another substance.
concentration camp. A camp where prisoners of war, enemy aliens, or political prisoners are confined.
con•cen•tric (kən-sĕn'trĭk) *adj.* Having a common center. —**con•cen'tri•cal•ly** *adv.* —**con'cen•tric'i•ty** *n.*
con•cept (kŏn'sĕpt) *n.* An idea, esp. an abstraction drawn from the specific. [< LL *conceptus,* a thing conceived, thought.]
con•cep•tion (kən-sĕp'shən) *n.* **1.** The formation of a zygote capable of survival and maturation in normal conditions. **2.** A beginning; start. **3.** The ability to form mental concepts; invention. **4.** A concept, plan, or thought. [< L *concipere,* to take to oneself, CONCEIVE.]
con•cep•tu•al•ize (kən-sĕp'cho͞o-əl-īz') *v.* **-ized, -izing.** To form concepts.
con•cern (kən-sûrn') *v.* **1.** To pertain or relate to; affect. **2.** To engage the interests of. **3.** To cause anxiety or uneasiness in. —*n.* **1.** Something of interest or importance. **2.** Earnest regard: *concern for one's well-being.* **3.** Relation; reference. **4.** Anxiety; worry. **5.** A business establishment. [< ML *concernere,* to relate to, involve with.]
con•cerned (kən-sûrnd') *adj.* Anxious; disturbed.
con•cern•ing (kən-sûr'nĭng) *prep.* In reference to.
con•cert (kŏn'sûrt) *n.* **1.** A public musical performance. **2.** Agreement in purpose, feeling, or action. —**in concert.** All together; in agreement. —*v.* (kən-sûrt'). **1.** To plan or arrange by mutual agreement. **2.** To contrive or devise. [< OIt *concertare,* to bring into agreement, harmonize.]
con•cert•ed (kən-sûr'tĭd) *adj.* Planned or ac-

complished together; combined.

con•cer•ti•na (kŏn'sər-tē'nə) *n.* A small, hexagonal accordion with buttons for keys.

con•cer•tize (kŏn'sər-tīz') *v.* **-tized, -tizing.** To perform in concerts.

con•cert•mas•ter (kŏn'sərt-măs'tər, -mäs'tər) *n.* The first violinist and assistant conductor in a symphony orchestra.

con•cer•to (kən-chĕr'tō) *n., pl.* **-tos.** A composition for an orchestra and one or more solo instruments. [It, concert.]

con•ces•sion (kən-sĕsh'ən) *n.* **1.** The act of conceding. **2.** Something conceded. **3.** Something granted by a government to be used for a specific purpose. **4.** The privilege of maintaining a subsidiary business within certain premises.

con•ces•sion•aire (kən-sĕsh'ən-âr') *n.* The holder of a concession.

con•ces•sive (kən-sĕs'ĭv) *adj.* Tending to concede.

conch (kŏngk, kŏnch) *n., pl.* **conchs** or **conches** (kŏn'chĭz). A tropical marine mollusk with a large, often brightly colored spiral shell. [< Gk *konkhē.*]

con•cil•i•ate (kən-sĭl'ē-āt') *v.* **-ated, -ating. 1.** To overcome the animosity of. **2.** To win, as favor. [L *conciliāre,* to bring together, unite.] **—con•cil'i•a'tion** *n.* **—con•cil'i•a'tor** *n.* **—con•cil'i•a•to'ry** (-ə-tôr'ē, -tōr'ē) *adj.*

con•cise (kən-sīs') *adj.* Expressing much in few words; succinct. [< L *concīdere,* to cut up.] **—con•cise'ly** *adv.* **—con•cise'ness** *n.*

con•clave (kŏn'klāv, kŏng'-) *n.* A secret meeting. [< L *conclāve,* "room locked with a key."]

con•clude (kən-klōōd') *v.* **-cluded, -cluding. 1.** To bring to an end. **2.** To agree. **3.** To reach a decision about. **4.** To determine; decide; resolve. [< L *conclūdere,* to shut up closely.] **—con•clu'sion** *n.*

con•clu•sive (kən-klōō'sĭv) *adj.* Decisive; final.

con•coct (kən-kŏkt') *v.* **1.** To prepare by mixing ingredients. **2.** To invent; contrive. [L *concoquere,* to cook together.] **—con•coc'tion** *n.*

con•com•i•tant (kən-kŏm'ə-tənt) *adj.* Existing or occurring concurrently. *—n.* An accompanying state or thing. [< L *concomitārī,* to accompany.]

con•cord (kŏn'kôrd, kŏng'-) *n.* Harmony; accord; concurrence. [< L *concors,* "of the same mind."]

Con•cord (kŏng'kərd). **1.** A town in Massachusetts; site of a battle (April 19, 1775) of the Revolutionary War. Pop. 13,000. **2.** The capital of New Hampshire. Pop. 30,000.

con•cor•dance (kən-kôr'dəns) *n.* **1.** A state of agreement. **2.** An alphabetical index of the words in a book with their contextual occurrence.

con•cor•dant (kən-kôr'dənt) *adj.* Harmonious; agreeing.

con•cor•dat (kən-kôr'dăt') *n.* A formal agreement; compact.

con•course (kŏn'kôrs, -kōrs, kŏng'-) *n.* **1.** A crowd; throng. **2.** A moving or flowing together. **3.** A large open space for the gathering or passage of crowds. [< L *concurrere,* to run together.]

con•cres•cence (kən-krĕs'əns) *n.* The uniting, esp. the growing together, of related parts, as of physical particles or anatomical structures. [< L *concrēscere,* to grow together.]

con•crete (kŏn-krēt', kŏn'krēt) *adj.* **1.** Relating to an actual, specific thing or instance; not general; particular. **2.** Existing in reality or in real experience. **3.** Formed by the coalescence of separate particles or parts into one mass; solid. **4.** Made of concrete. *—n.* (kŏn'krēt, kŏn-krēt'). **1.** A construction material consisting of conglomerate gravel, pebbles, broken stone, or slag in a mortar or cement matrix. **2.** A mass formed by the coalescence of particles. *—v.* (kŏn'krēt, kŏn-krēt') **-creted, -creting. 1.** To form into a mass by coalescence or cohesion of particles. **2.** To build, treat, or cover with concrete. [< L *concrētus,* pp of *concrēscere,* to grow together, harden.]

con•cre•tion (kən-krē'shən) *n.* **1.** A hard, solid mass. **2.** The process of forming such a mass.

con•cu•bine (kŏng'kyə-bīn', kŏn'-) *n.* A woman who cohabits with a man without being married to him. [< L *concubīna,* "one to sleep with."]

con•cu•pis•cence (kŏn-kyōō'pə-səns) *n.* Sexual desire; lust; sensuality. [< L *concupere,* to have a strong desire for.]

con•cur (kən-kûr') *v.* **-curred, -curring. 1.** To have the same opinion; agree. **2.** To act together. **3.** To coincide. [< L *concurrere,* to run together.] **—con•cur'rence** *n.*

con•cur•rent (kən-kûr'ənt) *adj.* **1.** Happening at the same time or place. **2.** Operating in conjunction. **3.** Meeting or tending to meet at the same point. **—con•cur'rent•ly** *adv.*

con•cus•sion (kən-kŭsh'ən) *n.* **1.** A violent jarring; shock. **2.** An injury of a soft structure, esp. of the brain, resulting from a violent blow.

con•demn (kən-dĕm') *v.* **1.** To express disapproval of; censure; criticize. **2.** To pronounce judgment against; sentence. [< L *condemnāre.*] **—con'dem•na'tion** (kŏn'dĕm-nā'shən) *n.*

con•dense (kən-dĕns') *v.* **-densed, -densing. 1.** To compress. **2.** To abridge. **3.** To form a liquid from a vapor. [< L *condēnsāre.*] **—con•den'sa•ble** *adj.* **—con'den•sa'tion** (kŏn'dən sā'shən) *n.* **—con•den'ser** *n.*

con•de•scend (kŏn'dĭ-sĕnd') *v.* To deal with others in a patronizing manner. [< ML *condescendere,* to stoop to.] **—con'de•scen'sion** *n.*

con•dign (kən-dīn') *adj.* Deserved; adequate: *condign censure.* [< L *condignus,* wholly worthy.] **—con•dign'ly** *adv.*

con•di•ment (kŏn'də-mənt) *n.* A seasoning for food, such as mustard. [< L *condīre,* to season, preserve by pickling.]

con•di•tion (kən-dĭsh'ən) *n.* **1.** The particular state of being of a person or thing. **2.** State of health. **3.** A disease or ailment: *a heart condition.* **4.** A prerequisite. **5.** A qualification. **6.** Often **conditions.** The existing circumstances: *poor driving conditions.* **7.** *Gram.* The dependent clause of a conditional sentence. *—v.* **1.** To make conditional. **2.** To put into a proper condition. [< L *conditio, condicio,* agreement, stipulation.]

con•di•tion•al (kən-dĭsh'ən-əl) *adj.* **1.** Imposing, depending on, or containing a condition or conditions. **2.** Not certain; tentative. **3.** *Gram.* Stating or implying a condition or prerequisite. *—n. Gram.* A mood, tense, clause, or word expressing a condition.

con•di•tioned (kən-dĭsh'ənd) *adj.* **1.** Subject to stipulations. **2.** Prepared for a specific action. **3.** Exhibiting or trained to exhibit a new or modified response.

con•di•tion•ing (kən-dĭsh'ən-ĭng) *n.* The process or result of inducing new or modified behavioral responses.

con•dole (kən-dōl') *v.* **-doled, -doling.** To express sympathy to one in pain, grief, or misfortune. [< LL *condolēre,* to feel another's pain.] **—con•do'lence** *n.* **—con•dol'er** *n.*

con•dom (kŏn'dəm) *n.* Also **cun•dum** (kŭn'dəm). A rubber sheath for covering the penis to prevent disease or conception. [Said to have been invented by Dr. *Condom,* 18th-century English physician.]

con•do•min•i•um (kŏn'də-mĭn'ē-əm) *n.* **1. a.** Joint sovereignty, esp. joint rule of a territory by two or more states. **b.** The territory so governed. **2.** An apartment building in which the apartments are owned individually.

con•done (kən-dōn') *v.* **-doned, -doning.** To forgive or disregard (an offense) without protest or censure. [L *condōnāre,* to give up, forgive.] **—con'do•na'tion** (kŏn'dō-nā'shən) *n.*

con•dor (kŏn'dôr, -dər) *n.* A very large vulture of the Andes or the mountains of California. [Span *cóndor.*]

con•duce (kən-d/y/ōōs') *v.* **-duced, -ducing.** To contribute or lead to. [< L *condūcere,* to lead together, contribute.] **—con•du'cive** *adj.*

con•duct (kən-dŭkt') *v.* **1.** To direct the course of; manage. **2.** To lead or guide. **3.** To serve as a medium or channel for conveying; transmit. **4.** To behave oneself. *—n.* (kŏn'dŭkt). **1.** The way a person acts. **2.** Management; administration. **3.** The act of leading or guiding. [< L *condūcerė,* to lead together.] **—con•duc'tion** *n.* **—con•duc'tive** *adj.*

con•duc•tor (kən-dŭk'tər) *n.* **1.** One who conducts or leads. **2.** The person in charge of a train, bus, etc. **3.** The director of a musical ensemble. **4.** A substance or medium that conducts heat, light, sound, or esp., an electric charge.

con•duit (kŏn'dĭt, -dōō-ĭt) *n.* **1.** A channel or pipe for conveying fluids. **2.** A tube or duct for enclosing electric wires or cable. [< L *condūcere,* to lead together, CONDUCT.]

cone (kōn) *n.* **1.** A surface generated by a straight line passing through a fixed point and moving along the intersection with a fixed curve. **2.** The figure formed by such a surface bound by its vertex and an intersecting plane. **3.** A scaly, rounded or cylindrical seed-bearing structure, as of a pine. **4.** A photoreceptor in the retina of the eye. [< Gk *kōnos.*]

Con•el•rad (kŏn'əl-răd) *n.* A U.S. defense system requiring termination of all broadcasting except for official emergency messages, to prevent enemy navigation with commercial signals.

Con•es•to•ga wagon (kŏn'ĭs-tō'gə). A covered wagon with broad wheels, used by American pioneers. [< *Conestoga,* Pennsylvania.]

co•ney. Variant of **cony.**

conf. conference.

con•fab•u•late (kən-făb'yə-lāt') *v.* **-lated, -lating. 1.** To talk informally; chat. **2.** To replace fact with fantasy in memory. [L *confābulārī.*] **—con•fab'u•la'tion** *n.*

con•fec•tion (kən-fĕk'shən) *n.* A sweet preparation, such as candy or preserves. [< L *conficere* (pp *confectus*), to prepare.]

con•fec•tion•er (kən-fĕk'shən-ər) *n.* One who makes or sells confections.

con•fec•tion•er•y (kən-fĕk'shən-ĕr'ē) *n., pl.* **-ies. 1.** Confections collectively. **2.** A confectioner's shop.

confed. confederation.

con•fed•er•a•cy (kən-fĕd'ər-ə-sē) *n., pl.* **-cies.** An alliance; league. [< L *confoederāre,* to unite.]

con•fed•er•ate (kən-fĕd'ər-ĭt) *n.* **1.** An ally. **2.** An accomplice. **3. Confederate.** A supporter of the Confederate States of America. *—adj.* **1.** United in a confederacy; allied. **2. Confederate.** Of or pertaining to the Confederate States of America. *—v.* (kən-fĕd'ə-rāt') **-ated,**

-ating. To form into or become part of a confederacy. [< L *confoederāre,* to unite in a league.] **—con·fed'er·a'tive** *adj.*

Confederate States of America. The confederation of 11 Southern states that seceded from the U.S. in 1860 and 1861.

con·fed·er·a·tion (kən-fĕd'ə-rā'shən) *n.* **1.** An act of confederating. **2.** An alliance, esp. of states and nations.

con·fer (kən-fûr') *v.* **-ferred, -ferring. 1.** To bestow, as an honor. **2.** To hold a conference. [L *conferre,* to bring together, contribute.]

con·fer·ence (kŏn'fə-rəns, -frəns) *n.* **1.** A meeting for consultation or discussion. **2.** An association, as of schools, for mutual benefit; league. [< L *conferre,* CONFER.]

con·fess (kən-fĕs') *v.* **1.** To disclose or acknowledge one's misdeed or fault. **2.** To concede the truth or validity of. **3. a.** To make known (one's sins), esp. to a priest for absolution. **b.** To hear the confession of. [< LL *confitēri* (pp *confessus*), to acknowledge.] **—con·fess'ed·ly** (-ĭd-lē) *adv.*

con·fes·sion (kən-fĕsh'ən) *n.* **1.** An act of confessing. **2.** Something confessed. **3.** A formal declaration of guilt. **4.** The disclosure of sins to a priest for absolution. **5.** A Christian denomination.

con·fes·sion·al (kən-fĕsh'ən-əl) *n.* An enclosure in which a priest hears confessions.

con·fes·sor (kən-fĕs'ər) *n.* **1.** A priest who hears confession. **2.** One who confesses.

con·fet·ti (kən-fĕt'ē) *n. (takes sing. v.).* Bits of colored paper scattered at festive celebrations. [< It *confetto,* confection, candy.]

con·fi·dant (kŏn'fə-dănt', -dänt', kŏn'fə-dănt, -dänt) *n.* One to whom secrets are confided.

con·fide (kən-fīd') *v.* **-fided, -fiding. 1.** To tell in confidence. **2.** To put into another's keeping. [< L *confīdere.*] **—con·fid'er** *n.*

con·fi·dence (kŏn'fə-dəns) *n.* **1.** Trust in a person or thing. **2.** An intimate and trusting relationship. **3.** Something confided. **4.** A feeling of assurance or certainty. **—con'fi·dent** *adj.* **—con'fi·dent·ly** *adv.*

con·fi·den·tial (kŏn'fə-dĕn'shəl) *adj.* **1.** Done or communicated in confidence. **2.** Entrusted with the confidence of another. **—con'fi·den'tial·ly** *adv.*

con·fig·u·ra·tion (kən-fĭg'yə-rā'shən) *n.* The arrangement of the parts or elements of something. [< L *configūrāre,* "to form together."] **—con·fig'u·ra'tive, con·fig'u·ra'tion·al** *adj.*

con·fine (kən-fīn') *v.* **-fined, -fining. 1.** To keep within bounds; restrict. **2.** To imprison. [< L *confīnis,* having the same border.] **—con·fine'ment** *n.* **—con·fin'er** *n.*

con·firm (kən-fûrm') *v.* **1.** To corroborate; verify. **2.** To strengthen; establish. **3.** To ratify. **4.** To administer the religious rite of confirmation. [< L *confirmāre.*]

con·fir·ma·tion (kŏn'fər-mā'shən) *n.* **1.** An act of confirming. **2.** A verification. **3.** A rite admitting a baptized person to full membership in a church.

con·firmed (kən-fûrmd') *adj.* **1.** Verified. **2.** Inveterate: *a confirmed bachelor.* **3.** Having received the rite of confirmation.

con·fis·cate (kŏn'fĭs-kāt') *v.* **-cated, -cating. 1.** To seize (private property) for a public treasury. **2.** To seize by or as by authority. [L *confiscāre,* to lay up in a chest, confiscate.] **—con'fis·ca'tion** *n.* **—con'fis·ca'tor** *n.*

con·flict (kŏn'flĭkt) *n.* **1.** A prolonged battle. **2.** A controversy; disagreement. **3.** The opposition of mutually exclusive impulses, desires, or tendencies. **—***v.* (kən-flĭkt'). To come into opposition; collide; differ. [< L *conflictus,* pp of *confligere,* to clash together, contend.] **—con·flic'tive** *adj.*

con·flu·ence (kŏn'flōō-əns) *n.* Also **con·flux** (-flŭks). **1.** A flowing together of two or more streams. **2.** The point of juncture of such streams. **3.** A gathering together. [< L *confluere,* to flow together.] **—con'flu·ent** *adj.*

con·form (kən-fôrm') *v.* **1.** To make or become similar. **2.** To act or be in agreement; comply. **3.** To act in accordance with customs or rules. [< L *conformāre,* "to have the same form," shape after.] **—con·form'er** *n.*

con·for·ma·tion (kŏn'fər-mā'shən) *n.* **1.** The structure of something as determined by the arrangement of its parts. **2.** A symmetrical arrangement of the parts of a thing.

con·form·ist (kən-fôr'mĭst) *n.* One who conforms to current usages.

con·form·i·ty (kən-fôr'mə-tē) *n.* Also **con·for·mance** (-fôr'məns). **1.** Similarity in form or character; correspondence. **2.** Action or behavior in correspondence with current customs, rules, or styles.

con·found (kən-found', kŏn-) *v.* **1.** To confuse or cause to become confused. **2.** To fail to distinguish. [< L *confundere,* to pour together, mix up.] **—con·found'er** *n.*

con·front (kən-frŭnt') *v.* **1.** To come face to face with. **2.** To face with hostility; oppose. [< ML *confrontāre,* to have a common border.] **—con'fron·ta'tion** *n.*

Con·fu·cian·ism (kən-fyōō'shən-ĭz'əm) *n.* The ethical system based on the teachings of Confucius. **—Con·fu'cian** *adj. & n.*

Con·fu·cius (kən-fyōō'shəs). 551–479 B.C. Chinese philosopher.

con·fuse (kən-fyōōz') *v.* **-fused, -fusing. 1.** To perplex or bewilder. **2.** To assemble without order or sense. **3.** To mistake one thing for another. [< L *confūsus,* pp of *confundere,* to pour together, mix, confound.] **—con·fus'ed·ly** (-fyōō'zĭd-lē) *adv.* **—con·fus'ing·ly** *adv.*

con·fu·sion (kən-fyōō'zhən) *n.* **1.** The act of confusing or state of being confused. **2.** Disorder; jumble.

con·fute (kən-fyōōt') *v.* **-futed, -futing.** To prove to be wrong or in error. [L *confūtāre,* to check, suppress, restrain.] **—con'fu·ta'tion** *n.*

Cong. Congress; Congressional.

con·geal (kən-jēl') *v.* **1.** To solidify or cause to solidify, as by freezing. **2.** To coagulate; jell. [< L *congelāre,* to freeze solid.]

con·gen·ial (kən-jēn'yəl) *adj.* **1.** Having the same tastes or temperament; sympathetic. **2.** Suited to one's needs; agreeable. [CON- + GENIAL.] **—con·ge'ni·al'i·ty** (-jē'nē-ăl'ə-tē) *n.* **—con·gen'ial·ly** *adv.*

con·gen·i·tal (kən-jĕn'ə-təl) *adj.* **1.** Existing at birth but not hereditary. **2.** Characteristic, as if by nature: *a congenital liar.* [< L *congenitus,* born together with.] **—con·gen'i·tal·ly** *adv.*

con·ger (kŏng'gər) *n.* Also **conger eel.** A large, scaleless marine eel. [< Gk *gongros.*]

con·ge·ries (kən-jîr'ēz) *n. (takes sing. v.)* A collection of things heaped together; an aggregate. [< L *congeriēs,* heap, pile.]

con·gest (kən-jĕst') *v.* **1.** To overfill. **2.** To accumulate excessive blood in (a vessel or organ). [L *congerere* (pp *congestus*), to bring together, heap up.] **—con·ges'tion** *n.* **—con·ges'tive** *adj.*

con·glo·bate (kŏn-glō'bāt', kŏng'glō-) *v.* **-bated, -bating.** To gather into or become a globe or ball. **—***adj.* Shaped like or formed into a ball. [< L *conglobāre,* to make into a globe.] **—con'glo·ba'tion** *n.*

con·glom·er·ate (kən-glŏm'ə-rāt') *v.* **-ated, -ating.** To form or collect into an adhering or rounded mass. **—***n.* (kən-glŏm'ə-rĭt). **1.** A collected heterogeneous mass; a cluster. **2.** *Geol.* A rock consisting of pebbles and gravel embedded in a loosely cementing material. **3.** A business corporation made up of a number of different companies that operate in widely diversified fields. **—***adj.* (kən-glŏm'ə-rĭt). **1.** Gathered into a mass; clustered. **2.** *Geol.* Made up of loosely cemented heterogeneous material. [< L *conglomerāre,* to roll together.]

con·glom·er·a·tion (kən-glŏm'ə-rā'shən) *n.* **1.** The process of conglomerating or state of being conglomerated. **2.** A collection or mass of miscellaneous things; a cluster. **3.** A coherent mass.

Con·go (kŏng'gō). A river of C Africa.

Congo, Democratic Republic of the. A former name for **Zaire. —Con·go·lese'** *adj. & n.*

Congo, Republic of. A republic and former French colony in west-central Africa. Pop. 915,000. Cap. Brazzaville. **—Con'go·lese'** (kŏng'gə-lēz', -lēs') *adj. & n.*

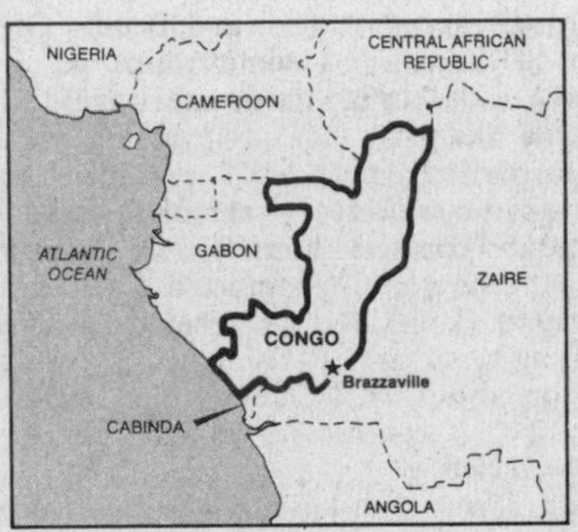

Republic of Congo

con·grat·u·late (kən-grăch'ōō-lāt') *v.* **-lated, -lating.** To express pleasure at the achievement or good fortune of. [L *congrātulārī,* to rejoice with someone.] **—con·grat'u·la'tion** *n.* **—con·grat'u·la·to'ry** (-lə-tôr'ē, -tōr'ē) *adj.*

con·gre·gate (kŏng'grə-gāt') *v.* **-gated, -gating.** To come together in a crowd; assemble. [< L *congregāre,* to assemble.]

con·gre·ga·tion (kŏng'grə-gā'shən) *n.* **1.** An act of congregating. **2.** An assemblage; gathering. **3.** A group of people gathered for religious worship.

con·gre·ga·tion·al (kŏng'grə-gā'shən-əl) *adj.* **1.** Of or pertaining to a congregation. **2. Congregational.** Of or pertaining to a Protestant denomination in which each member church is self-governing.

Con·gre·ga·tion·al·ist (kŏng'grə-gā'shən-əl-ĭst) *n.* A member of a Congregational Christian church. **—Con'gre·ga'tion·al·ism'** *n.*

con·gress (kŏng'grĭs) *n.* **1.** A formal assembly or meeting for the discussion of problems. **2.** A national legislature, esp. of a republic. **3. Congress.** The legislature of the U.S., consisting of the Senate and the House of Representatives. [< L *congressus* < *congredī,* to come together.]

con·gres·sion·al (kən-grĕsh'ən-əl) *adj.* **1.** Of or pertaining to a congress. **2. Congressional.** Of or pertaining to the Congress of the U.S.

con·gress·man (kŏng'grĭs-mən) *n.* Also **Con·gress·man.** A member of the U.S. Congress.

con•gress•wom•an (kŏng'grĭs-wo͝om'ən) *n.* Also **Con•gress•wom•an.** A female member of the U.S. Congress.

con•gru•ent (kŏng'gro͞o-ənt, kən-gro͞o'ənt) *adj.* **1.** Corresponding; congruous. **2.** Coinciding exactly when superimposed: *congruent triangles.* [< L *congruere,* to meet together, agree.] **—con'gru•ence** *n.* **—con'gru•ent•ly** *adv.*

con•gru•ous (kŏng'gro͞o-əs) *adj.* **1.** Corresponding in character or kind; harmonious. **2.** Congruent. **—con•gru'i•ty** (kən-gro͞o'ə-tē) *n.* **—con'gru•ous•ly** *adv.*

con•ic (kŏn'ĭk) *adj.* Also **con•i•cal** (-ĭ-kəl). Of or shaped like a cone.

con•i•fer (kŏn'ə-fər, kō'nə-) *n.* A cone-bearing tree, as a pine or hemlock. **—co•nif'er•ous** (kō-nĭf'ər-əs) *adj.*

conj. **1.** conjugation. **2.** conjunction.

con•jec•ture (kən-jĕk'chər) *v.* **-tured, -turing.** To infer from inconclusive evidence; guess. *—n.* Inference based on inconclusive evidence; guesswork. [< L *conjicere,* "to throw together," put together mentally.] **—con•jec'tur•a•ble** *adj.* **—con•jec'tur•al** *adj.*

con•join (kən-join') *v.* To join together; connect; unite. **—con•join'er** *n.* **—con•joint'** (-joint') *adj.* **—con•joint'ly** *adv.*

con•ju•gal (kŏn'jo͞o-gəl, -jə-gəl) *adj.* Of marriage or the marital relationship. [< L *conjungere,* to join together (in marriage).] **—con'ju•gal•ly** *adv.*

con•ju•gate (kŏn'jo͞o-gāt', -jə-gāt') *v.* **-gated, -gating.** To inflect (a verb). *—adj.* (kŏn'jo͞o-gĭt). **1.** Joined together, esp. in pairs. **2.** Inversely or oppositely related with respect to one of a group of otherwise identical properties. *—n.* (kŏn'jo͞o-gĭt). Either of a pair of conjugate quantities. [< L *conjugāre,* to yoke or join together.] **—con'ju•ga'tor** *n.*

con•ju•ga•tion (kŏn'jo͞o-gā'shən, kŏn'jə-) *n.* **1.** The act of conjugating or state of being conjugated. **2.** The inflection of a verb. **3.** An act or process of sexual joining in reproduction. **—con'ju•ga'tion•al** *adj.*

con•junct (kən-jŭngkt', kŏn'jŭngkt) *adj.* Joined together; united. [< L *conjunctus,* pp of *conjungere,* to join together.]

con•junc•tion (kən-jŭngk'shən) *n.* **1.** A joining together; combination. **2.** Simultaneous occurrence. **3.** A word connecting other words, phrases, clauses, or sentences.

con•junc•ti•va (kŏn'jŭngk-tī'və, kən-jŭngk'tĭ-və) *n., pl.* **-vas** or **-vae** (-vē). The mucous membrane that lines the inner surface of the eyelid and the exposed surface of the eyeball. [< ML *(membrāna) conjunctīva,* "the connective (membrane)."] **—con'junc•ti'val** *adj.*

con•junc•tive (kən-jŭngk'tĭv) *adj.* **1.** Connective. **2.** Combined; conjunct. **3.** *Gram.* Used as a conjunction. [< L *conjunctus,* CONJUNCT.]

con•junc•ti•vi•tis (kən-jŭngk'tə-vī'tĭs) *n.* Inflammation of the conjunctiva.

con•junc•ture (kən-jŭngk'chər) *n.* **1.** A combination of circumstances or events. **2.** A critical set of circumstances.

con•jure (kŏn'jər, kən-jo͞or') *v.* **-jured, -juring.** **1.** To entreat solemnly, esp. by an oath. **2.** To summon (a devil) by sorcery. **3.** To effect by magic or legerdemain. **—conjure up.** To contrive, imagine, or evoke. [< L *conjūrāre,* to swear together, conspire.] **—con'ju•ra'tion** (-rā'shən) *n.* **—con'jur•er** *n.*

conk (kŏngk) *v. Slang.* To hit, esp. on the head. **—conk out.** To fail suddenly. [Prob var of CONCH.]

Conn. Connecticut.

con•nect (kə-nĕkt') *v.* **1.** To join; link; unite. **2.** To associate or consider as related. [< L *connectere.*] **—con•nect'ed•ly** *adv.*

Con•nect•i•cut (kə-nĕt'ə-kət). A state of the NE U.S. Pop. 3,032,000. Cap. Hartford.

con•nec•tion (kə-nĕk'shən) *n.* **1.** Union; junction. **2.** A bond; link. **3.** An association or relation. **4.** Logical ordering of words or ideas; coherence. **5.** The relation of a word to its context. **6. connections.** People with whom one is associated.

con•nec•tive (kə-nĕk'tĭv) *adj.* Serving or tending to connect. *—n.* A connecting word, such as a conjunction.

con•nip•tion (kə-nĭp'shən) *n. Informal.* A fit of violent emotion. [?]

con•nive (kə-nīv') *v.* **-nived, -niving.** **1.** To feign ignorance of a wrong, thus implying consent. **2.** To cooperate secretly; conspire. [< L *connīvēre,* to close the eyes, be indulgent.] **—con•niv'ance** *n.* **—con•niv'er** *n.*

con•nois•seur (kŏn'ə-sûr') *n.* An informed and astute judge in matters of taste. [< L *cognōscere,* to get acquainted with.]

con•no•ta•tion (kŏn'ə-tā'shən) *n.* The configuration of associative implications constituting the general sense of an abstract expression beyond its explicit sense. **—con'no•ta'tive** *adj.*

con•note (kə-nōt') *v.* **-noted, -noting.** **1.** To suggest or imply in addition to literal meaning. **2.** To involve as a condition or consequence. [ML *connotāre,* "to mark in addition."]

con•nu•bi•al (kə-no͞o'bē-əl) *adj.* Of marriage or the married state; conjugal. [L *connūbiālis.*]

con•quer (kŏng'kər) *v.* **1.** To defeat or subdue, as by force of arms. **2.** To overcome. [< L *conquīrere,* to search for, procure, win.] **—con'quer•a•ble** *adj.* **—con'quer•or** *n.*

con•quest (kŏn'kwĕst, kŏng'-) *n.* **1.** The act or process of conquering. **2.** Something acquired by conquering.

con•quis•ta•dor (kŏn-kwĭs'tə-dôr) *n.* One of the Spanish conquerors of Mexico and Peru in the 16th century.

Cons. **1.** constable. **2.** consul.

con•san•guin•e•ous (kŏn'săng-gwĭn'ē-əs) *adj.* Related by blood. [L *consanguineus.*]

con•san•guin•i•ty (kŏn'săng-gwĭn'ə-tē) *n.* **1.** Blood relationship. **2.** Close affinity.

con•science (kŏn'shəns) *n.* **1.** The faculty of recognizing the distinction between right and wrong in regard to one's own conduct. **2.** Conformity to one's own sense of right conduct. [<L *conscīre,* to be conscious.]

con•sci•en•tious (kŏn'shē-ĕn'shəs) *adj.* **1.** Scrupulous; honest. **2.** Painstaking and thorough; careful. **—con'sci•en'tious•ly** *adv.* **—con'sci•en'tious•ness** *n.*

conscientious objector. One who on the basis of religious and moral principles refuses to bear arms or participate in military service.

con•scious (kŏn'shəs) *adj.* **1. a.** Having an awareness of one's own existence and environment. **b.** Capable of complex response to environment. **c.** Not asleep; awake. **2.** Subjectively known: *conscious remorse.* **3.** Intentional; deliberate: *a conscious insult.* [L *conscius,* knowing with others, aware of.] **—con'scious•ly** *adv.* **—con'scious•ness** *n.*

con•scious•ness-rais•ing (kŏn'shəs-nĭs-rā'zĭng) *n.* **1.** A technique whereby one learns to analyze one's own life situation and then to transform it so as to achieve liberation from oppression. **2.** A technique whereby one is made aware of discrimination against a particular class of people who have been oppressed. **—con'scious•ness-rais'er** *n.*

con•script (kŏn'skrĭpt) *n.* One who is compulsorily enrolled for military service. *—v.* (kən-skrĭpt'). To draft for military service. [< L *conscriptus,* pp of *conscrībere,* to write together.] **—con•scrip'tion** *n.*

con•se•crate (kŏn'sə-krāt') *v.* **-crated, -crating.** **1.** To make or declare sacred; hallow. **2.** *R.C.Ch.* To change (the elements of bread and wine) into the body and blood of Christ. **3.** To initiate (a priest) into the order of bishops. **4.** To dedicate to some service or goal. [< L *consecrāre.*] **—con'se•cra'tion** *n.*

con•sec•u•tive (kən-sĕk'yə-tĭv) *adj.* Following successively without interruption. [< L *consequī,* to follow up.] **—con•sec'u•tive•ly** *adv.*

con•sen•sus (kən-sĕn'səs) *n.* Collective opinion or agreement. [< L *consentīre,* to agree, CONSENT.]

Usage: Consensus is preferable to the stock expression *consensus of opinion,* which is redundant.

con•sent (kən-sĕnt') *v.* To give assent; accede; agree. *—n.* Acceptance, agreement, or approval. [< L *consentīre,* to feel together, agree.] **—con•sent'er** *n.*

con•se•quence (kŏn'sə-kwĕns) *n.* **1.** An effect; result. **2.** Importance or significance.

con•se•quent (kŏn'sə-kwĕnt, -kwənt) *adj.* Following as a result. [< L *consequī,* to follow up, accompany.] **—con'se•quent'ly** *adv.*

con•se•quen•tial (kŏn'sə-kwĕn'shəl) *adj.* **1.** Having important consequences. **2.** Conceited; pompous. **—con'se•quen'tial•ly** *adv.*

con•ser•va•tion (kŏn'sûr-vā'shən) *n.* Preservation from loss, waste, or harm, esp. the official preservation of natural resources. **—con'ser•va'tion•al** *adj.* **—con'ser•va'tion•ist** *n.*

con•ser•va•tism (kən-sûr'və-tĭz'əm) *n.* Disposition to maintain existing order.

con•ser•va•tive (kən-sûr'və-tĭv) *adj.* **1.** Favoring preservation of the existing order. **2.** Moderate; prudent; cautious. **3.** Traditional in manner or style. **4.** Tending to conserve; preservative. *—n.* A conservative person.

con•ser•va•tor (kən-sûr'və-tər) *n.* **1.** A protector. **2.** *Law.* A guardian.

con•ser•va•to•ry (kən-sûr'və-tôr'ē, -tōr'ē) *n., pl.* **-ries.** **1.** A glass-enclosed room or greenhouse in which plants are grown. **2.** A school of music or dramatic art.

con•serve (kən-sûrv') *v.* **-served, -serving.** **1.** To protect from loss or depletion; preserve. **2.** To preserve (fruits). *—n.* (kŏn'sûrv). A jam made of two or more fruits stewed in sugar. [< L *conservāre.*] **—con•serv'a•ble** *adj.*

con•sid•er (kən-sĭd'ər) *v.* **1.** To deliberate upon; examine. **2.** To think or deem. **3.** To believe; judge. [< L *considerāre,* to observe.]

con•sid•er•a•ble (kən-sĭd'ər-ə-bəl) *adj.* **1.** Fairly large in amount, extent, or degree. **2.** Worthy of consideration; important; significant. **—con•sid'er•a•bly** *adv.*

con•sid•er•ate (kən-sĭd'ər-ĭt) *adj.* Having regard for the needs or feelings of others. [< L *considerāre,* to be considerate, CONSIDER.]

con•sid•er•a•tion (kən-sĭd'ə-rā'shən) *n.* **1.** Deliberation. **2.** A factor in forming a judgment. **3.** Thoughtfulness; solicitude. **4.** Recompense.

con•sid•ered (kən-sĭd'ərd) *adj.* **1.** Reached after deliberation. **2.** Esteemed.

con•sid•er•ing (kən-sĭd'ər-ĭng) *prep.* In view of. *—adv. Informal.* All things considered.

con•sign (kən-sīn') *v.* **1.** To give over to the care of another; entrust. **2.** To turn over formally to another's charge. **3.** To deliver for custody or sale, as merchandise. **4.** To allot or assign. [< L *consignāre,* to seal, sign.] **—con'sign•ee'** *n.* **—con•sign'or** *n.*

con•sign•ment (kən-sīn'mənt) *n.* A shipment of goods or a cargo to an agent for sale or custody.

con•sist (kən-sĭst') *v.* **1.** To be made up or composed (with *of*). **2.** To be inherent; lie. [< L *consistere,* to stand still, exist.]

con•sis•ten•cy (kən-sĭs'tən-sē) *n., pl.* **-cies.** Also **con•sis•tence** (-təns). **1.** Agreement or compatibility among things or parts. **2.** Uniformity. **3.** Degree of texture or firmness. **—con•sis'tent** *adj.* **—con•sis'tent•ly** *adv.*

con•sis•to•ry (kən-sĭs'tər-ē) *n., pl.* **-ries.** A gathering of Roman Catholic cardinals presided over by the pope. [< L *consistere,* to take one's place (at a meeting), stand, CONSIST.] **—con'sis•to'ri•al** (kŏn'sĭs-tôr'ē-əl, -tōr'ē-əl) *adj.*

consol. consolidated.

con•sole¹ (kən-sōl') *v.* **-soled, -soling.** To comfort; solace. [< L *consōlārī.*] **—con'so•la'tion** (kŏn'sə-lā'shən) *n.* **—con•sol'er** *n.*

con•sole² (kŏn'sōl) *n.* **1.** The desklike part of an organ that contains the keyboard, stops, and pedals. **2.** A cabinet for a radio, television set, or phonograph, designed to stand on the floor. **3.** A control panel. [< L *consōlārī,* CONSOLE.]

con•sol•i•date (kən-sŏl'ə-dāt') *v.* **-dated, -dating.** **1.** To form into a compact mass; solidify. **2.** To unite into one system or body; combine. [L *consolidāre.*] **—con•sol'i•da'tion** *n.* **—con•sol'i•da'tor** *n.*

con•som•mé (kŏn'sə-mā') *n.* A clear soup made of meat or vegetable stock or both. [F, "concentrate."]

con•so•nance (kŏn'sə-nəns) *n.* **1.** Agreement; harmony. **2.** Repetition of terminal consonants as an alternative to full rhyme.

con•so•nant (kŏn'sə-nənt) *adj.* In agreement or accord. *—n.* **1.** A speech sound produced by a partial or complete obstruction of the air stream. **2.** A letter or character representing such a sound. [< L *(littera) consonāns,* "(letter) sounded with (a vowel)."]

con•so•nan•tal (kŏn'sə-năn'təl) *adj.* Of, relating to, or being a consonant. **—con'so•nan'tal•ly** *adv.*

con•sort (kŏn'sôrt) *n.* A husband or wife, esp. the spouse of a monarch. *—v.* (kən-sôrt'). **1.** To keep company; associate. **2.** To be in agreement. [< L *consors,* "one who shares the same fate."]

con•sor•ti•um (kən-sôr'shē-əm) *n., pl.* **-tia** (-shē-ə). An international combination of capitalists and financiers. [< L *consors,* companion, CONSORT.]

con•spic•u•ous (kən-spĭk'yōō-əs) *adj.* Prominent; remarkable. [< L *conspicere,* to look at closely, observe.] **—con•spic'u•ous•ly** *adv.* **—con•spic'u•ous•ness** *n.*

con•spir•a•cy (kən-spîr'ə-sē) *n., pl.* **-cies.** A plot, esp. an illegal one. [< L *conspīrāre,* CONSPIRE.]

con•spire (kən-spīr') *v.* **-spired, -spiring.** **1.** To plan secretly, esp. to commit an illegal act; plot. **2.** To combine or act together. [< L *conspīrāre,* "to breathe together," agree, unite.] **—con•spir'a•tor** (-spîr'ə-tər) *n.* **—con•spir'a•to'ri•al** *adj.* **—con•spir'er** *n.*

const. **1.** constable. **2.** constant. **3.** constitution.

Const. **1.** constable. **2.** constitution.

con•sta•ble (kŏn'stə-bəl, kŭn'-) *n.* A peace officer or policeman. [< LL *comes stabulī,* "count of the stable."]

con•stab•u•lar•y (kən-stăb'yə-lĕr'ē) *n., pl.* **-ies.** **1.** The body of constables of a district or city. **2.** An armed police force organized like a military unit.

con•stan•cy (kŏn'stən-sē) *n.* **1.** Steadfastness; loyalty. **2.** Stability.

con•stant (kŏn'stənt) *adj.* **1.** Continually recurring; persistent. **2.** Unchanging; invariable. **3.** Steadfast. *—n.* **1.** A thing that is unchanging or invariable. **2.** A condition, factor, or quantity that is invariant in specified circumstances. [< L *constāre,* to stand together, remain steadfast.] **—con'stant•ly** *adv.*

Con•stan•ti•no•ple (kŏn'stăn-tə-nō'pəl). The former name for Istanbul.

con•stel•la•tion (kŏn'stə-lā'shən) *n.* **1.** Any of various stellar groups considered to resemble and named after various mythological characters, inanimate objects, and animals. **2.** The position of the stars at the time of one's birth, regarded as determining one's character or fate. **3.** A grouping or configuration. [< LL *constellātiō,* group of stars.]

con•ster•na•tion (kŏn'stər-nā'shən) *n.* Sudden confusion or dismay.

con•sti•pa•tion (kŏn'stə-pā'shən) *n.* Difficult, incomplete, or infrequent evacuation of the bowels. [< L *constīpāre,* to press together.]

con•stit•u•en•cy (kən-stĭch'ōō-ən-sē) *n., pl.* **-cies.** **1.** The body of voters represented by an elected legislator. **2.** An electoral district.

con•stit•u•ent (kən-stĭch'ōō-ənt) *adj.* **1.** Serving as part of a whole; component. **2.** Empowered to elect. **3.** Authorized to make or amend a constitution. *—n.* **1.** One represented by an elected official. **2.** A component. [< L *constituere,* CONSTITUTE.]

con•sti•tute (kŏn'stə-t/y/ōōt') *v.* **-tuted, -tuting.** **1.** To make up; compose. **2.** To establish formally. **3.** To appoint to an office; designate. [< L *constituere,* to cause to stand, set, fix.]

con•sti•tu•tion (kŏn'stə-t/y/ōō'shən) *n.* **1.** The act or process of constituting. **2.** The composition of something; make-up. **3.** A person's prevailing state of health. **4. a.** The basic law of a politically organized body. **b.** The document setting forth such law. **5. the Constitution.** The Constitution of the U.S., adopted in 1787 and put into effect in 1789.

con•sti•tu•tion•al (kŏn'stə-t/y/ōō'shən-əl) *adj.* **1.** Basic; essential. **2.** Contained in, consistent with, or operating under a constitution. *—n.* A walk taken regularly for one's health. **—con'sti•tu•tion•al'i•ty** *n.*

constr. construction.

con•strain (kən-strān') *v.* **1.** To compel; oblige. **2.** To confine. **3.** To restrain. [< L *constringere,* to draw or bind tightly together.] **—con•strain'a•ble** *adj.* **—con•strain'er** *n.*

con•strained (kən-strānd') *adj.* **1.** Resulting from constraint; restrained. **2.** Forced; unnatural. **—con•strain'ed•ly** (-strān'ĭd-lē) *adv.*

con•straint (kən-strānt') *n.* **1.** Compulsion; restraint. **2.** Lack of ease; embarrassment.

con•strict (kən-strĭkt') *v.* To compress, contract, or squeeze. [L *constringere* (pp *constrictus*), to CONSTRAIN.] **—con•stric'tion** *n.* **—con•stric'tive** *adj.* **—con•stric'tor** *n.*

con•struct (kən-strŭkt') *v.* To make or build. [L *construere* (pp *constructus*), to pile up together, build.] **—con•struc'tor** *n.*

con•struc•tion (kən-strŭk'shən) *n.* **1.** The action or business of building. **2.** A structure. **3.** An interpretation. **4.** A meaningful syntax-bound string of words in a sentence.

con•struc•tive (kən-strŭk'tĭv) *adj.* **1.** Useful; helpful. **2.** Structural. **—con•struc'tive•ly** *adv.*

con•strue (kən-strōō') *v.* **-strued, -struing.** **1.** To explain syntactic relations within a sentence. **2.** To interpret. **3.** To translate. [< L *construere,* to CONSTRUCT.] **—con•stru'er** *n.*

con•sul (kŏn'səl) *n.* **1.** Either of the two chief magistrates of the Roman Republic, elected for a term of one year. **2.** An official appointed by a government to reside in a foreign city and represent its citizens there. [< L.] **—con'su•lar** *adj.*

con•su•late (kŏn'sə-lĭt) *n.* The premises occupied by a consul.

con•sult (kən-sŭlt') *v.* **1.** To seek the advice of. **2.** To exchange views; confer. [< L *consulere,* to take counsel.] **—con•sult'ant** *n.* **—con'sul•ta'tion** *n.* **—con•sult'a•tive** (-sŭl'tə-tĭv) *adj.*

con•sume (kən-s/y/ōōm') *v.* **-sumed, -suming.** **1.** To eat up; devour. **2.** To use up; expend. **3.** To waste; squander. **4.** To destroy. **5.** To absorb; engross. [< L *consūmere,* to take completely.] **—con•sum'a•ble** *adj.*

con•sum•er (kən-s/y/ōō'mər) *n.* **1.** One that consumes. **2.** A buyer.

con•sum•er•ism (kən-sōō'mə-rĭz'əm) *n.* The movement seeking to protect the rights of consumers, as by requiring honest advertising and improved safety standards.

con•sum•mate (kŏn'sə-māt') *v.* **-mated, -mating.** **1.** To complete; achieve. **2.** To fulfill (a marriage) with the first act of sexual intercourse. *—adj.* (kən-sŭm'ĭt). **1.** Perfect.. **2.** Complete; utter. [< L *consummāre,* to bring together, sum up.] **—con•sum'mate•ly** *adv.*

con•sump•tion (kən-sŭmp'shən) *n.* **1.** The act or process of consuming. **2.** The amount consumed. **3.** The use of consumer goods. **4. a.** A wasting of tissue. **b.** Tuberculosis. [< L *consūmere,* CONSUME.]

con•sump•tive (kən-sŭmp'tĭv) *adj.* **1.** Wasteful; destructive. **2.** Of or afflicted with consumption. **—con•sump'tive•ly** *adv.*

cont. **1.** containing. **2.** contents. **3.** continent. **4.** continue; continued. **5.** contract. **6.** contraction. **7.** control.

con•tact (kŏn'tăkt') *n.* **1.** A coming together or touching of objects or surfaces. **2.** A relationship; association. **3.** Connection. **4.** A conducting connection between two electric conductors. *—v.* (kŏn'tăkt, kən-tăkt'). **1.** To come or put into contact. **2.** To get in touch with. *—adj.* (kŏn'tăkt'). **1.** Of or making contact. **2.** Caused or transmitted by touching. [L *contāctus,* pp of *contingere,* to touch, border upon.]

contact lens. A thin corrective lens fitted over the cornea.

con•ta•gion (kən-tā'jən) *n.* **1. a.** Disease transmission by contact. **b.** A disease so transmitted. **c.** The causative agent of such a disease. **2.** Transmission of an influence or emotional state. [< L *contingere,* to touch, CONTACT.]

con•ta•gious (kən-tā'jəs) *adj.* **1.** Transmissible by contact. **2.** Carrying or capable of carrying disease. **3.** Tending to spread; catching.

con•tain (kən-tān') *v.* **1.** To enclose. **2.** To comprise; include. **3.** To be able to hold. **4.** To restrict. [< L *continēre,* to hold together, enclose.] **—con•tain'ment** *n.*

con•tain•er (kən-tā'nər) *n.* A receptacle.

con•tam•i•nant (kən-tăm'ə-nənt) *n.* Something that contaminates.

con•tam•i•nate (kən-tăm'ə-nāt') *v.* **-nated, -nating.** To make impure by contact or mixture. [< L *contāmināre.*] **—con•tam'i•na'tion** *n.* **—con•tam'i•na'tive** *adj.*

contd. continued.

con•temn (kən-tĕm') *v.* To view with contempt; despise. [< L *contemnere.*]

contemp. contemporary.

con•tem•plate (kŏn'təm-plāt') *v.* **-plated, -plating.** **1.** To ponder or consider. **2.** To intend; expect. [L *contemplārī,* to observe carefully.] **—con'tem•pla'tion** *n.* **—con•tem'pla•tive** (kən-tĕm'plə-tĭv) *adj.* **—con'tem•pla'tor** *n.*

con•tem•po•ra•ne•ous (kən-tĕm'pə-rā'nē-əs) *adj.* Contemporary. [L *contemporāneus.*]

con•tem•po•rar•y (kən-tĕm'pə-rĕr'ē) *adj.* **1.** Belonging to the same period of time. **2.** Of about the same age. **3.** Current; modern. *—n., pl.* **-ies.** **1.** One of the same time or age. **2.** A person of the present time. [ML *contemporārius.*] **—con•tem'po•rar'i•ly** *adv.*

con•tempt (kən-tĕmpt') *n.* **1.** Bitter scorn, as for something vile; disdain. **2.** Open disrespect or willful disobedience to a court, legislature, etc. [< L *contemptus,* pp of *contemnere,* CONTEMN.]

con•tempt•i•ble (kən-tĕmp'tə-bəl) *adj.* Deserving contempt; despicable.

con•temp•tu•ous (kən-tĕmp'cho͞o-əs) *adj.* Manifesting contempt; scornful. **—con•temp'tu•ous•ly** *adv.* **—con•temp'tu•ous•ness** *n.*

con•tend (kən-tĕnd') *v.* **1.** To strive, vie, or dispute. **2.** To maintain or assert. [< L *contendere,* to strain, strive with.] **—con•tend'er** *n.*

con•tent¹ (kŏn'tĕnt) *n.* **1.** Often **contents.** That which is contained in something. **2.** Often **contents.** Subject matter, as of a book. **3.** Meaning or significance. **4.** The proportion of a specified substance. [< L *contentus,* pp of *continēre,* CONTAIN.]

con•tent² (kən-tĕnt') *adj.* Satisfied. *—v.* To satisfy. *—n.* Satisfaction; contentment. [< L *contentus,* pp of *continēre,* to restrain, CONTAIN.]

con•tent•ed (kən-tĕn'tĭd) *adj.* Satisfied. **—con•tent'ed•ly** *adv.* **—con•tent'ed•ness** *n.*

con•ten•tion (kən-tĕn'shən) *n.* Dispute; controversy. [< L *contendere,* CONTEND.] **—con•ten'tious** *adj.* **—con•ten'tious•ness** *n.*

con•tent•ment (kən-tĕnt'mənt) *n.* The state of being contented.

con•ter•mi•nous (kən-tûr'mə-nəs) *adj.* Having a boundary in common; contiguous. [L *conterminus.*] **—con•ter'mi•nous•ness** *n.*

con•test (kŏn'tĕst') *n.* **1.** A struggle; fight. **2.** A competition. *—v.* (kən-tĕst', kŏn'tĕst'). **1.** To compete or strive for. **2.** To dispute; challenge. [< L *contestārī,* bring in (a lawsuit) by calling witnesses.] **—con•test'a•ble** *adj.*

con•test•ant (kən-tĕs'tənt, kŏn'tĕs'tənt) *n.* A competitor or challenger.

con•text (kŏn'tĕkst) *n.* **1.** The verbal or written environment in which a word or group of words occurs. **2.** The overall situation in which an event occurs. [< L *contextus,* coherence, sequence of words.] **—con•tex'tu•al** (kən-tĕks'cho͞o-əl) *adj.* **—con•tex'tu•al•ly** *adv.*

con•tig•u•ous (kən-tĭg'yo͞o-əs) *adj.* **1.** Touching. **2.** Next or adjacent to. [< L *contingere,* to touch on all sides, CONTACT.] **—con'ti•gu'i•ty** (kŏn'tə-gyo͞o'ə-tē) *n.*

con•ti•nence (kŏn'tə-nəns) *n.* **1.** Self-restraint. **2.** Abstention from sexual activity. **3.** Ability to control bladder or bowel functions. [< L *continēre,* to contain.] **—con'ti•nent** *adj.*

con•ti•nent (kŏn'tə-nənt) *n.* **1.** One of the principal land masses of the earth. **2. the Continent.** The mainland of Europe. [L *(terra) continēns,* "continuous (land)."]

con•ti•nen•tal (kŏn'tə-nĕn'təl) *adj.* **1.** Of or like a continent. **2.** Often **Continental.** European. **3. Continental.** Of or pertaining to the American colonies during the Revolutionary War. *—n.* **Continental.** A soldier in the Continental Army. **—con'ti•nen'tal•ly** *adv.*

continental shelf. A generally shallow, flat submerged portion of a continent.

con•tin•gen•cy (kən-tĭn'jən-sē) *n., pl.* **-cies.** A fortuitous or possible event.

con•tin•gent (kən-tĭn'jənt) *adj.* **1.** Possible. **2.** Conditional. **3.** Fortuitous. *—n.* **1.** A quota, as of troops. **2.** A representative group. [< L *contingere,* to touch on all sides, CONTACT.]

con•tin•u•al (kən-tĭn'yo͞o-əl) *adj.* **1.** Recurring often. **2.** Continuous; incessant. **—con•tin'u•al•ly** *adv.*

con•tin•u•ance (kən-tĭn'yo͞o-əns) *n.* **1.** The act or fact of continuing. **2.** Duration. **3.** Unbroken sequence. **4.** Postponement or adjournment of legal proceedings.

con•tin•u•a•tion (kən-tĭn'yo͞o-ā'shən) *n.* **1.** The act or fact of continuing or state of being continued. **2.** A supplement; sequel.

con•tin•ue (kən-tĭn'yo͞o) *v.* **-ued, -uing.** **1.** To persist. **2.** To endure; last. **3.** To remain in a state, capacity, or place; abide. **4.** To go on after an interruption; resume. **5.** To extend. **6.** To retain. **7.** *Law.* To postpone or adjourn. [< L *continēre,* to hold together, be continuous, CONTAIN.] **—con•tin'u•er** *n.*

con•ti•nu•i•ty (kŏn'tə-n/y/o͞o'ə-tē) *n., pl.* **-ties.** **1.** The state or quality of being continuous. **2.** An uninterrupted succession.

con•tin•u•ous (kən-tĭn'yo͞o-əs) *adj.* Extending or prolonged without interruption; unbroken. **—con•tin'u•ous•ly** *adv.* **—con•tin'u•ous•ness** *n.*

con•tin•u•um (kən-tĭn'yo͞o-əm) *n., pl.* **-tinua** (-tĭn'yo͞o-ə) or **-ums.** Something in which no part can be distinguished from neighboring parts except by arbitrary division.

con•tort (kən-tôrt') *v.* To twist or wrench out of shape. [L *contorquēre* (pp *contortus*), to twist together.] **—con•tor'tion** *n.* **—con•tor'tive** *adj.*

con•tor•tion•ist (kən-tôr'shən-ĭst) *n.* An acrobat who can twist his body into extraordinary postures. **—con•tor'tion•is'tic** *adj.*

con•tour (kŏn'to͝or) *n.* **1.** The outline of a figure, body, or mass. **2. contours.** A surface, esp. of a curving form. *—adj.* Following the contour lines of uneven terrain to limit erosion of topsoil. [< It *contornare,* to go around.]

contour line. A line, as on a map, joining points of equal elevation.

contour map. A map showing elevations and surface configuration by means of contour lines.

contr. **1.** contract. **2.** contraction.

contra–. *comb. form.* Against, opposing, or contrary. [< L *contrā,* against.]

con•tra•band (kŏn'trə-bănd') *n.* **1.** Goods prohibited in trade. **2.** Smuggled goods. **3.** Smuggling. [< It *contrabbando.*]

con•tra•cep•tion (kŏn'trə-sĕp'shən) *n.* Prevention of conception. **—con'tra•cep'tive** (-sĕp'tĭv) *adj. & n.*

con•tract (kŏn'trăkt') *n.* An enforceable agreement; covenant. *—v.* (kən-trăkt', kŏn'trăkt'). **1.** To enter into or establish by contract. **2.** To catch (a disease). **3.** To shrink by drawing together. **4.** To shorten (a word or words) by omitting or combining some of the letters. [< L *contractus,* pp of *contrahere,* to draw together, bring about.] **—con•tract'i•ble** *adj.* **—con•trac'tion** *n.* **—con'trac'tor** *n.*

con•trac•tile (kən-trăk'təl) *adj.* Capable of contracting.

con•tra•dict (kŏn'trə-dĭkt') *v.* **1.** To assert the opposite of. **2.** To deny the statement of. **3.** To be contrary to or inconsistent with. [L *contrādīcere,* to speak against.] **—con'tra•dic'tion** *n.* **—con'tra•dic'to•ry** *adj.*

con•tra•dis•tinc•tion (kŏn'trə-dĭ-stĭngk'shən) *n.* Distinction by contrast.

con•trail (kŏn'trāl') *n.* A visible trail of water droplets or ice crystals formed in the wake of an aircraft. [CON(DENSATION) + TRAIL.]

con•tra•in•di•cate (kŏn'trə-ĭn'də-kāt') *v.* **-cated, -cating.** To indicate the inadvisability of. **—con'tra•in'di•ca'tion** *n.*

con•tral•to (kən-trăl'tō) *n., pl.* **-tos.** **1.** The lowest female voice or voice part. **2.** A singer having such a voice. [It.]

con•trap•tion (kən-trăp'shən) *n.* An elaborate device. [< CONTRIVE and TRAP + -TION.]

con•tra•pun•tal (kŏn'trə-pŭnt'l) *adj.* Of or incorporating counterpoint.

con•tra•ri•e•ty (kŏn'trə-rī'ə-tē) *n., pl.* **-ties.** The condition of being contrary.

con•trar•i•wise (kŏn'trĕr'ē-wīz') *adv.* **1.** Oppositely. **2.** On the contrary.

con•tra•ry (kŏn'trĕr'ē) *adj.* **1.** Opposite, as in character or direction. **2.** Adverse; unfavorable. **3.** Perverse; willful. **4.** Opposed; counter. *—n., pl.* **-ries.** That which is contrary; the opposite. *—adv.* In opposition; contrariwise. [< L *contrā,* against.] **—con'tra'ri•ly** *adv.*

con•trast (kən-trăst') *v.* **1.** To set in opposition in order to show differences. **2.** To show differences when compared. *—n.* (kŏn'trăst'). **1.** Dissimilarity between things compared. **2.** Something showing such dissimilarity. [< ML *contrāstāre.*] **—con•trast'ing•ly** *adv.*

con•tra•vene (kŏn'trə-vēn') *v.* **-vened, -vening.** **1.** To act or go contrary to. **2.** To contradict. [< LL *contrāvenīre,* to come against, oppose.]

con•tre•temps (kŏn'trə-täɴ') *n.* An inopportune or embarrassing occurrence. [F.]

contrib. contribution; contributor.

con•trib•ute (kən-trĭb'yo͞ot) *v.* **-uted, -uting.** To give a share to or participate in. [L *contribuere,* to bring together, unite, collect.] **—con'tri•bu'tion** *n.* **—con•trib'u•tor** *n.* **—con•trib'u•to'ry** (-tôr'ē, tōr'ē) *adj.*

con•trite (kən-trīt') *adj.* Repentant. [< ML *contrītus,* "broken in spirit," repentant.] **—con•trite'ly** *adv.* **—con•tri'tion** (-trĭsh'ən) *n.*

con•tri•vance (kən-trī'vəns) *n.* **1.** A scheme; plan. **2.** A mechanical device.

con•trive (kən-trīv') *v.* **-trived, -triving.** **1.** To plan; devise. **2.** To make or fabricate. **3.** To manage or effect. [< LL *contropāre,* to represent figuratively, compare.] **—con•triv'ed•ly** *adv.* **—con•triv'er** *n.*

con•trol (kən-trōl') *v.* **-trolled, -trolling.** **1.** To exercise a regulating influence over; direct. **2.** To verify or regulate by systematic comparison. *—n.* **1.** Power to regulate, direct, or dominate. **2.** Restraint; reserve. **3.** A standard of comparison for verifying the results of an experiment. **4.** Often **controls.** A set of instruments for regulating a machine. [< ML *contrārotulāre,* to check by a counter roll or duplicate register.] **—con•trol'la•ble** *adj.*

con•trol•ler (kən-trō'lər) *n.* **1.** One who controls. **2.** Also **comp•trol•ler.** The chief accountant of a corporation.

con•tro•ver•sy (kŏn'trə-vûr'sē) *n., pl.* **-sies.** A protracted public dispute. [< L *contrōversus,* turned against, disputed.] **—con'tro•ver'sial** (-vûr'shəl) *adj.* **—con'tro•ver'sial•ly** *adv.*

con•tro•vert (kŏn'trə-vûrt') *v.* To deny. [< CONTROVERSY.] **—con'tro•vert'i•ble** *adj.*

con•tu•ma•cious (kŏn't/y/o͞o-mā'shəs) *adj.* Obstinately rebellious; insubordinate. **—con'tu•ma•cy** (kŏn't/y/o͞o-mə-sē) *n.*

con•tu•me•ly (kŏn't/y/o͞o-mə-lē) *n.* Insulting treatment. [< L *contumēlia,* insult, reproach.]

—con'tu•me'li•ous (-mē'lē-əs) *adj.*

con•tuse (kən-t/y/o͞oz') *v.* **-tused, -tusing.** To injure without breaking the skin; bruise. [< L *contundere* (pp *contūsus*), to beat, pound.] —**con•tu'sion** *n.*

co•nun•drum (kə-nŭn'drəm) *n.* A riddle.

con•va•lesce (kŏn'və-lĕs') *v.* **-lesced, -lescing.** To recuperate from an illness. [L *convalēscere.*] —**con'va•les'cence** *n.* —**con'va•les'cent** *adj.* & *n.*

con•vec•tion (kən-vĕk'shən) *n.* Heat transfer by fluid motion between regions of unequal density that result from nonuniform heating. [< L *convehere,* to carry together, bring along.]

con•vene (kən-vēn') *v.* **-vened, -vening.** To assemble, meet, or convoke. [< L *convenīre.*]

con•ven•ience (kən-vēn'yəns) *n.* **1.** Suitability. **2.** Personal comfort. **3.** Anything that increases comfort or makes work easier.

con•ven•ient (kən-vēn'yənt) *adj.* **1.** Suited to one's comfort or needs. **2.** Easy to reach; accessible. [< L *convenīre,* to be suitable, CONVENE.] —**con•ven'ient•ly** *adv.*

con•vent (kŏn'vənt, -vĕnt') *n.* A monastic community or house, esp. of nuns. [< L *conventus,* a coming together, assembly.] —**con•ven'tu•al** (kən-vĕn'cho͞o-əl) *adj.*

con•ven•tion (kən-vĕn'shən) *n.* **1. a.** A formal assembly, as of a political party. **b.** The delegates attending such an assembly. **2.** An international agreement or compact. **3.** General usage or custom. **4.** An accepted or prescribed practice. [< L *convenīre,* to come together, CONVENE.]

con•ven•tion•al (kən-vĕn'shən-əl) *adj.* **1.** Approved by or following general usage; customary. **2.** Commonplace or ordinary. —**con•ven'tion•al•ism'** *n.* —**con•ven'tion•al'i•ty** *n.* —**con•ven'tion•al•ly** *adv.*

con•verge (kən-vûrj') *v.* **-verged, -verging. 1.** To tend toward a common point or result. **2.** *Math.* To approach a limit. [< LL *convergere,* to incline together.] —**con•ver'gence, con•ver'gen•cy** *n.* —**con•ver'gent** *adj.*

con•ver•sant (kŏn'vər-sənt, kən-vûr'-) *adj.* Familiar, as by experience. [< L *conversārī,* to associate with, CONVERSE.]

con•ver•sa•tion (kŏn'vər-sā'shən) *n.* An informal spoken exchange; a familiar talk. —**con'ver•sa'tion•al** *adj.* —**con'ver•sa'tion•al•ly** *adv.*

con•ver•sa•tion•al•ist (kŏn'vər-sā'shən-əl-ĭst) *n.* One given to or skilled at conversation.

con•verse¹ (kən-vûrs') *v.* **-versed, -versing.** To engage in conversation; talk informally. —*n.* (kŏn'vûrs'). Conversation. [< L *conversārī,* to associate with.]

con•verse² (kən-vûrs', kŏn'vûrs') *adj.* Reversed, as in relation or order. —*n.* (kŏn'-vûrs'). Something that has been reversed; the opposite. [L *conversus,* pp of *convertere,* to turn around.] —**con•verse'ly** *adv.*

con•ver•sion (kən-vûr'zhən, -shən) *n.* **1.** The act of converting or state of being converted. **2.** A change in which one adopts a new religion. **3.** The unlawful appropriation of another's property. **4.** The exchange of one type of security or currency for another.

con•vert (kən-vûrt') *v.* **1.** To change into another form, substance, etc.; transform. **2.** To persuade or be persuaded to adopt a given religion or belief. **3.** To adapt to a new or different purpose. **4.** To exchange for something of equal value. **5.** To misappropriate. —*n.* (kŏn'vûrt'). One who has accepted religious conversion. [< L *convertere,* to turn around, transform.] —**con•vert'er, con•ver'tor** *n.*

con•vert•i•ble (kən-vûr'tə-bəl) *adj.* Capable of being converted. —*n.* An automobile with a top that can be folded back or taken off.

con•vex (kŏn'vĕks, kən-vĕks') *adj.* Curved outward, as the exterior of a sphere. [L *convexus,* arched, convex.] —**con•vex'i•ty** *n.*

con•vey (kən-vā') *v.* **1.** To carry; transport. **2.** To transmit. **3.** To communicate; impart. [< ML *conviāre,* to go with, escort.] —**con•vey'er, con•vey'or** *n.*

con•vey•ance (kən-vā'əns) *n.* **1.** The act of transporting. **2.** A vehicle. **3.** A legal document effecting the transfer of title to property.

con•vict (kən-vĭkt') *v.* To find or prove guilty of an offense. —*n.* (kŏn'vĭkt'). A person found guilty of a crime, esp. one serving a prison sentence. [< L *convincere* (pp *convictus*), to prove guilty, CONVINCE.]

con•vic•tion (kən-vĭk'shən) *n.* **1.** The act of convicting or state of being convicted. **2.** A fixed or strong belief.

con•vince (kən-vĭns') *v.* **-vinced, -vincing.** To bring to belief by argument and evidence; persuade. [L *convincere,* to overcome, refute, prove guilty.] —**con•vinc'er** *n.* —**con•vinc'ing** *adj.* —**con•vinc'ing•ly** *adv.*

Usage: Convince is regularly followed by *of* or a clause introduced by *that,* but not by an infinitive with *to. Persuade,* however, can be used with all three constructions. Thus: *He convinced me* (or *I was convinced*) *of his good intentions. He convinced me* (or *I was convinced*) *that I should go. He persuaded* (not *convinced*) *me to go.*

con•viv•i•al (kən-vĭv'ē-əl) *adj.* Sociable; jovial. [< L *convīvium,* "a living together," banquet.] —**con•viv'i•al'i•ty** *n.* —**con•viv'i•al•ly** *adv.*

con•vo•ca•tion (kŏn'vō-kā'shən) *n.* **1.** The act of convoking. **2.** A formal assembly.

con•voke (kən-vōk') *v.* **-voked, -voking.** To cause to assemble; convene. [< L *convocāre,* to call together, summon.]

con•vo•lut•ed (kŏn'və-lo͞o'tĭd) *adj.* **1.** Coiled; twisted. **2.** Intricate; complicated. [< L *convolvere,* to interweave.]

con•vo•lu•tion (kŏn'və-lo͞o'shən) *n.* **1.** A coiling or twisting together. **2.** An intricacy. **3.** One of the convex folds of the surface of the brain.

con•voy (kŏn'voi', kən-voi') *v.* To escort for protection. —*n.* (kŏn'voi'). An accompanying and protecting force. [< OF *convoier, conveier,* convey.]

con•vulse (kən-vŭls') *v.* **-vulsed, -vulsing. 1.** To shake or agitate violently. **2.** To cause irregular and involuntary muscular contractions. [L *convellere* (pp *convulsus*), to pull violently, wrest.]

con•vul•sion (kən-vŭl'shən) *n.* **1.** An intense paroxysmal involuntary muscular contraction. **2.** A violent disturbance. —**con•vul'sive** *adj.* —**con•vul'sive•ly** *adv.*

co•ny (kō'nē, kŭn'ē) *n., pl.* **-nies.** Also **co•ney** *pl.* **-neys. 1.** A rabbit or similar animal. **2.** The fur of a rabbit. [< L *cunīculus.*]

coo (ko͞o) *v.* To utter the murmuring sound of a dove or pigeon. —*n.* The murmuring call of a dove or a similar sound. [Imit.]

cook (ko͝ok) *v.* **1.** To prepare food for eating by applying heat. **2.** To prepare or treat by heating. —*n.* One who prepares food for eating. [< L *coquere,* to cook.]

cook•book (ko͝ok'bo͝ok') *n.* A book of cooking recipes.

cook•er•y (ko͝ok'ər-ē) *n.* The art or practice of cooking.

cook•out (ko͝ok'out') *n.* A meal cooked and served outdoors.

cook•y, cook•ie (ko͝ok'ē) *n., pl.* **-ies.** Also **cook•ey** *pl.* **-eys.** A small, sweet, usually flat cake. [< Du *koek,* cake.]

cool (ko͞ol) *adj.* **1.** Moderately cold. **2.** Reducing discomfort in hot weather: *a cool blouse.* **3.** Calm; controlled. **4.** Showing dislike or indifference. **5.** Impudent. **6.** *Slang.* Excellent. —*v.* **1.** To make or become less warm. **2.** To make or become less intense. —*n.* **1.** Moderate cold. **2.** *Slang.* Composure. [< OE *cōl.* See **gel-³**.] —**cool'ly** *adv.* —**cool'ness** *n.*

cool•ant (ko͞o'lənt) *n.* A fluid that draws off heat by circulating through a machine or bathing a mechanical part.

cool•er (ko͞o'lər) *n.* **1.** A refrigerator. **2.** *Slang.* Jail.

Coo•lidge (ko͞o'lĭj), **(John) Calvin.** 1872–1933. 30th President of the U.S. (1923–29).

Calvin Coolidge

coo•lie (ko͞o'lē) *n.* Also **coo•ly** *pl.* **-lies.** An unskilled Oriental laborer. [Hindi *kulī, qulī.*]

coon (ko͞on) *n.* A raccoon. [Short for RACCOON.]

coon•hound (ko͞on'hound') *n.* A smooth-coated black and tan hound of a breed developed in the SE U.S. to hunt raccoons.

coon's age. *Slang.* A long time.

coon•skin (ko͞on'skĭn') *n.* **1.** The pelt of the raccoon. **2.** An article made of coonskin, such as a hat. —**coon'skin'** *adj.*

coop (ko͞op) *n.* A cage, as for poultry. —*v.* To confine in or as in a coop. [ME *coupe,* wicker basket, chicken coop.]

co-op (kō-ŏp', kō'ŏp') *n.* A cooperative.

coop. cooperative.

coop•er (ko͞o'pər) *n.* One who makes wooden tubs and casks. [ME *couper.*]

Coop•er (ko͞o'pər), **James Fenimore.** 1789–1851. American novelist.

coop•er•age (ko͞o'pər-ĭj) *n.* **1.** A cooper's work or products. **2.** A cooper's workshop.

co•op•er•ate (kō-ŏp'ə-rāt') *v.* **-ated, -ating.** To work together toward a common end. [L *cooperārī.*] —**co•op'er•a'tion** (kō-ŏp'ər-ā'shən) *n.*

co•op•er•a•tive (kō-ŏp'rə-tĭv, -ə-rā'tĭv) *adj.* **1.** Willing to cooperate. **2.** Engaged in joint economic activity. —*n.* An enterprise collectively owned and operated for mutual benefit: *a farmers' cooperative.* —**co•op'er•a•tive•ly** *adv.* —**co•op'er•a•tive•ness** *n.*

co-opt (kō-ŏpt') *v.* To elect as a fellow member or colleague. [L *cooptāre.*]

co•or•di•nate (kō-ôr'də-nāt', -nĭt) *n.* **1.** One equal in rank or order. **2.** One of a set of numbers that determines the location of a point in a space of a given dimension. *—adj.* (kō-ôr'də-nĭt, -nāt'). **1.** Of equal rank or order. **2.** Of or involving coordination. **3.** Of or based on coordinates. *—v.* (kō-ôr'də-nāt') **-nated, -nating. 1.** To place in the same rank or order. **2.** To arrange in proper relative position. **3.** To harmonize in a common action. [Back-formation < COORDINATION.] **—co•or'di•nate•ly** *adv.* **—co•or'di•na'tor** *n.*

co•or•di•na•tion (kō-ôr'də-nā'shən) *n.* **1.** The act of coordinating or state of being coordinate. **2.** The coordinated functioning of muscles in the execution of a complex task. [< LL *coōrdĭnātiō,* arrangement in the same order.]

coot (ko͞ot) *n.* **1.** A short-billed dark-gray water bird. **2.** *Informal.* A foolish old man. [ME *cote.*]

cop (kŏp) *n. Informal.* A policeman. *—v.* **copped, copping.** *Slang.* To steal or take. [Short for *copper,* policeman, "catcher."]

cop. copyright.

cope[1] (kōp) *v.* **coped, coping.** To contend, esp. on even terms or with success. [< OF *couper,* to strike.]

cope[2] (kōp) *n.* A long ecclesiastical vestment. [< LL *cappa,* cloak, hood.]

Co•pen•ha•gen (kō'pən-hā'gən). The capital of Denmark. Pop. 924,000.

Co•per•ni•cus (kō-pûr'nə-kəs), **Nicolaus.** 1473–1543. Polish astronomer.

co•pi•lot (kō'pī'lət) *n.* The second or relief pilot of an aircraft.

cop•ing (kō'pĭng) *n.* The top part of a wall. [< COPE[2].]

co•pi•ous (kō'pē-əs) *adj.* Ample; abundant. [< L *cōpia,* abundance.] **—co'pi•ous•ly** *adv.* **—co'pi•ous•ness** *n.*

co•pla•nar (kō-plā'nər) *adj.* Lying or occurring in the same plane.

co•pol•y•mer (kō-pŏl'ə-mər) *n.* A polymer of two or more different monomers.

cop•per[1] (kŏp'ər) *n.* **1.** *Symbol* **Cu** A ductile, malleable, reddish-brown metallic element that is an excellent conductor of heat and electricity and is used for electrical wiring, water piping, and corrosion-resistant parts. Atomic number 29, atomic weight 63.54. **2.** A copper object or coin. [< L *Cyprium (aes),* "(copper) of Cyprus."]

cop•per[2] (kŏp'ər) *n. Slang.* A policeman. [< COP.]

cop•per•as (kŏp'ər-əs) *n.* A greenish crystalline compound, $FeSO_4 \cdot 7H_2O$, used in fertilizers and inks and in water purification. [< ML *cup(e)rosa.*]

cop•per•head (kŏp'ər-hĕd') *n.* A venomous reddish-brown snake of E U.S.

cop•pice (kŏp'ĭs) *n. Chiefly Brit.* A thicket. [< OF *coupeiz,* "thicket for cutting."]

cop•ra (kŏp'rə) *n.* Dried coconut meat from which coconut oil is extracted. [Port.]

copse (kŏps) *n.* A thicket. [Short for COPPICE.]

Copt (kŏpt) *n.* A native of Egypt descended from ancient Egyptian stock, esp. one belonging to the Christian church.

Cop•tic (kŏp'tĭk) *n.* The Afro-Asiatic language of the Copts. **—Cop'tic** *adj.*

cop•u•la (kŏp'yə-lə) *n.* A verb, usually a form of *be,* that identifies the predicate of a sentence with the subject. [L *cōpula,* link. bond.] **—cop'u•lar** *adj.*

cop•u•late (kŏp'yə-lāt') *v.* **-lated, -lating.** To engage in coitus. [< L *cōpula,* link, bond.] **—cop'u•la'tion** *n.*

cop•u•la•tive (kŏp'yə-lā'tĭv, -lə-tĭv) *adj.* **1.** Joining or uniting. **2.** Serving to connect coordinate words or clauses, as the conjunction *and.*

cop•y (kŏp'ē) *n., pl.* **-ies. 1.** An imitation or reproduction of something original; duplicate. **2.** One specimen of a printed text or picture. **3.** A manuscript or other material to be set in type. *—v.* **-ied, -ying. 1.** To make a copy of. **2.** To follow as a model; imitate. [< ML *cōpia,* transcript, right of reproduction.]

cop•y•book (kŏp'ē-bo͝ok') *n.* A book of models of penmanship for imitation.

copy boy. A boy in a newspaper office who carries copy and runs errands.

cop•y•cat (kŏp'ē-kăt') *n.* An imitator.

copy desk. The desk in a newspaper office where copy is edited and prepared for typesetting.

cop•y•ist (kŏp'ē-ĭst) *n.* One who makes written copies.

cop•y•read•er (kŏp'ē-rē'dər) *n.* One who edits and corrects newspaper copy for publication.

cop•y•right (kŏp'ē-rīt') *n.* The exclusive right granted by law to publish, sell, or distribute a literary or artistic work. *—adj.* Also **cop•y•right•ed** (-rī'tĭd). Protected by copyright. **—cop'y•right'** *v.*

cop•y•writ•er (kŏp'ē-rī'tər) *n.* One who writes advertising copy.

co•quette (kō-kĕt') *n.* A woman who flirts. [< F *coquet,* flirtatious man.] **—co•quet'tish** *adj.*

cor. 1. corner. **2.** corpus.

Cor. Corinthians (New Testament).

cor•a•cle (kôr'ə-kəl, kŏr'-) *n.* A boat made of waterproof material stretched over wicker or wooden hoops. [< W *corwgl, cwrwgl.*]

cor•al (kôr'əl, kŏr'əl) *n.* **1.** A hard, stony substance, often used for jewelry, formed from the massed skeletons of minute marine organisms. **2.** Such an organism or a structure formed by such organisms. **3.** Yellowish red or pink. [< Gk *korallion.*] **—cor'al** *adj.*

Coral Sea. A portion of the SW Pacific Ocean, NE of Australia.

cor•bel (kôr'bəl, -bĕl) *n.* A bracket of stone or other building material, projecting from a wall and used to support a cornice or an arch. [< OF.]

cord (kôrd) *n.* **1.** A string or small rope of twisted strands or fibers. **2.** An insulated, flexible electric wire fitted with a plug. **3. a.** A raised rib on the surface of a cloth. **b.** A fabric or cloth with such ribs. **4.** A unit of cut fuel wood, equal to 128 cubic feet in a stack measuring 4 by 4 by 8 feet. *—v.* **1.** To fasten with a cord. **2.** To pile (wood) in cords. [< L *chorda,* catgut, cord.] **—cord'er** *n.*

cor•dial (kôr'jəl) *adj.* Hearty; warm; sincere. *—n.* **1.** A stimulant. **2.** A liqueur. [< L *cor (cord-),* heart.] **—cor'dial'i•ty** (kôr'jăl'ə-tē, -jē-ăl'-, -dē-ăl'-) *n.* **—cor'dial•ly** *adv.*

cor•dil•le•ra (kôr'dĭl-yâr'ə, kôr-dĭl'ər-ə) *n.* A chain of mountains. [< Span *cuerda,* cord, chain.] **—cor'dil•ler'an** *adj.*

cord•ite (kôr'dīt') *n.* A smokeless explosive powder dissolved in acetone, dried, and extruded in cords. [< CORD.]

cor•do•ba (kôr'də-bə) *n.* The basic monetary unit of Nicaragua. [< F. de *Córdoba* (1475–1526), Spanish explorer.]

cor•don (kôr'dən) *n.* **1.** A line of people, military posts, ships, etc., stationed around an area to enclose or guard it. **2.** A cord or ribbon worn as an ornament or decoration. [< OF *corde,* cord.]

cor•do•van (kôr'də-vən) *n.* A fine leather made originally at Córdoba, Spain. [Span *cordobán.*]

cor•du•roy (kôr'də-roi, kôr'də-roi') *n.* **1.** A durable, ribbed cotton fabric. **2. corduroys.** Corduroy trousers. [Prob < CORD + obs *deroy,* a coarse woolen fabric.]

core (kôr, kōr) *n.* **1.** The hard or fibrous central part of certain fruits, as an apple. **2.** The most important part of anything. *—v.* **cored, coring.** To remove the core of: *core apples.* [ME.] **—cor'er** *n.*

CORE (kôr, kōr) Congress of Racial Equality.

co•re•spon•dent (kō'rĭ-spŏn'dənt) *n.* A person charged with having committed adultery with the defendant in a suit for divorce. [CO- + RESPONDENT.]

Cor•fam (kôr'făm) *n.* A trademark for a synthetic leather.

co•ri•an•der (kôr'ē-ăn'dər, kōr'ē-) *n.* An herb with aromatic seeds used as a condiment. [< Gk *koriandron.*]

Co•rin•thi•an order (kə-rĭn'thē-ən). One of the three classical orders of architecture, characterized by a fluted column having a capital decorated with acanthus leaves.

co•ri•um (kôr'ē-əm, kōr'-) *n., pl.* **coria** (kôr'ē-ə, kōr'-). The skin layer beneath the epithelium, containing nerve endings, sweat glands, and blood and lymph vessels. [< L, skin, hide.]

cork (kôrk) *n.* **1.** The light, porous outer bark of a Mediterranean tree, the **cork oak. 2.** A bottle stopper or other object made from this. *—v.* To stop or seal with or as with a cork. [< Span *alcorque,* cork sole or shoe.]

cork•er (kôr'kər) *n. Slang.* Someone or something that is remarkable.

cork•screw (kôrk'skro͞o') *n.* A spiral-shaped device for drawing corks from bottles. *—adj.* Like a corkscrew in shape; spiral.

corm (kôrm) *n.* An underground plant stem similar to a bulb. [< Gk *kormos,* a trimmed tree trunk.]

cor•mo•rant (kôr'mər-ənt) *n.* A water bird with dark plumage, webbed feet, and a hooked bill. *—adj.* Greedy; gluttonous; rapacious. [< OF *cormoran.*]

corn[1] (kôrn) *n.* **1.** A tall, widely cultivated cereal grass bearing seeds on large ears; maize. **2.** The seeds or ears of this plant. **3.** *Brit.* Any of various widely grown cereal plants or their grain. **4.** *Slang.* Something trite or dated. *—v.* **1.** To preserve in brine: *corned beef.* **2.** To feed (animals) with corn or grain. [< OE *corn.* See **gra-no-.**]

corn[2] (kôrn) *n.* A horny thickening of the skin, usually on or near a toe, resulting from pressure or friction. [< L *cornū,* horn.]

corn•cob (kôrn'kŏb') *n.* The woody core of an ear of corn.

cor•ne•a (kôr'nē-ə) *n.* A uniformly thick, transparent, nearly circular convex structure covering the lens of the eye. [ML *cornea (tēla),* "horny (tissue)."] **—cor'ne•al** *adj.*

cor•ne•ous (kôr'nē-əs) *adj.* Made of horn or a hornlike substance; horny. [< L *cornū,* horn.]

cor•ner (kôr'nər) *n.* **1. a.** The position at which two lines or surfaces meet. **b.** The immediate interior or exterior region of the angle formed at this position, bounded by the two lines or surfaces. **2.** The place where two streets meet. **3.** A position from which escape is difficult. **4.** Any part or region. **5.** A remote or secret place or area. **6.** Speculation in a stock or commodity by controlling the available supply so as to raise its price. **—cut corners.** *Informal.* To reduce expenses, care in execution, etc.

—*v.* **1.** To place or drive into a corner. **2.** To form a corner in (a stock or commodity). —*adj.* On, at, or used in a corner. [< L *cornū,* horn, extremity.]

cor•ner•stone (kôr′nər-stōn′) *n.* **1.** A stone at the corner of a building uniting two intersecting walls; quoin. **2.** Such a stone laid at a ceremony. **3.** The essential or main basis of something.

cor•net (kôr-nĕt′) *n.* A three-valved instrument of the trumpet class. [< L *cornū,* horn.] —**cor•net′ist** *n.*

corn•flow•er (kôrn′flou′ər) *n.* A garden plant with usually deep-blue flowers.

cor•nice (kôr′nĭs) *n.* A horizontal molded projection that crowns or completes a building or wall. [< It.]

Cor•nish (kôr′nĭsh) *n.* The Celtic language formerly spoken in Cornwall. —**Cor′nish** *adj.*

corn•meal (kôrn′mēl′) *n.* Meal made from corn.

corn•stalk (kôrn′stôk′) *n.* Also **corn stalk.** A stalk or stem of corn, esp. maize.

corn•starch (kôrn′stärch′) *n.* A purified starchy flour made from corn, used as a thickener in cooking.

corn sugar. A sugar, dextrose.

corn syrup. A syrup prepared from corn and containing glucose.

cor•nu•co•pi•a (kôr′nə-kō′pē-ə) *n.* A cone-shaped horn overflowing with fruit, flowers, and corn, signifying prosperity. [L *cornūcōpia,* horn of plenty.] —**cor′nu•co′pi•an, cor′nu•co′pi•ate′** *adj.*

Corn•wall (kôrn′wôl). A region in the extreme SW of England.

corn•y (kôr′nē) *adj.* **-ier, -iest.** *Slang.* Trite, dated, or mawkishly sentimental.

co•rol•la (kə-rŏl′ə) *n.* The structure formed by the petals of a flower. [< L *corōna,* garland, CORONA.]

cor•ol•lar•y (kôr′ə-lĕr-ē, kŏr′-) *n., pl.* **-ies. 1.** A proposition that follows with little or no proof from one already proven. **2.** A natural consequence; result. [< L *corolla,* small garland.]

co•ro•na (kə-rō′nə) *n., pl.* **-nas** or **-nae** (-nē). A faintly colored luminous ring around a celestial body visible through a haze or thin cloud. [L *corōna,* garland, crown.]

Co•ro•na•do (kŏr′ā-nä′dō), **Francisco Vásquez de.** 1510–1554. Spanish explorer.

cor•o•nar•y (kôr′ə-nĕr-ē, kŏr′-) *adj.* **1.** Pertaining to either of two arteries that originate in the aorta and supply blood directly to the heart tissues. **2.** Pertaining to the heart. —*n., pl.* **-ies.** A **coronary thrombosis.** [< L *corōna,* garland, crown, CORONA.]

coronary thrombosis. The occlusion of a coronary artery by a blood clot, often leading to destruction of heart muscle.

cor•o•na•tion (kôr′ə-nā′shən, kŏr′-) *n.* The act or ceremony of crowning a sovereign or his consort. [< L *corōna,* crown, CORONA.]

cor•o•ner (kôr′ə-nər, kŏr′-) *n.* A public officer whose function is to investigate any death thought to be of other than natural causes. [ME, officer charged with maintaining the record of the crown's pleas.]

cor•o•net (kôr′ə-nĕt′, -nĭt′, kŏr′-) *n.* **1.** A small crown worn by nobles below the rank of sovereign. **2.** A jeweled chaplet or headband. [< L *corōna,* crown, CORONA.]

corp. corporation.

cor•po•ra. *pl.* of **corpus.**

cor•po•ral¹ (kôr′pə-rəl) *adj.* Of the body; bodily. [< L *corpus (corpor-),* body.]

cor•po•ral² (kôr′pə-rəl, -prəl) *n.* A noncommissioned officer of the lowest rank, as in the army. [Obs F.]

cor•po•rate (kôr′pə-rĭt) *adj.* **1.** Formed into a corporation; incorporated. **2.** Of a corporation. **3.** United or combined into one body; collective. [< L *corporāre,* to make into a body.]

cor•po•ra•tion (kôr′pə-rā′shən) *n.* **1.** A body of persons granted a charter legally recognizing them as a separate entity having its own rights, privileges, and liabilities. **2.** Such a body created for purposes of government.

cor•po•re•al (kôr-pôr′ē-əl, -pō′rē-əl) *adj.* **1.** Characteristic of the body. **2.** Of a material nature; tangible. [< L *corpus,* CORPUS.]

corps (kôr, kōr) *n., pl.* **corps** (kôrz, kōrz). **1.** A specialized branch or department of the armed forces. **2.** A tactical unit of ground combat forces between a division and an army. **3.** A body of persons under common direction. [< L *corpus,* body, CORPUS.]

corpse (kôrps) *n.* A dead body, esp. of a human being. [< L *corpus,* body, CORPUS.]

cor•pu•lence (kôr′pyə-ləns) *n.* Fatness; obesity. [< L *corpulentus* < *corpus,* CORPUS.] —**cor′pu•lent** *adj.* —**cor′pu•lent•ly** *adv.*

cor•pus (kôr′pəs) *n., pl.* **-pora** (-pə-rə). **1.** A human or animal body, esp. when dead. **2.** A structure constituting the main part of an organ. **3.** A large collection of writings. [L, body, substance.]

Cor•pus Chris•ti (kôr′pəs krĭs′tē). A city of SW Texas. Pop. 168,000.

cor•pus•cle (kôr′pəs-əl, -pŭs-əl) *n.* Also **cor•pus•cule** (kôr-pŭs′kyo͞ol). **1.** A cell capable of free movement in a fluid or matrix as distinguished from a cell fixed in tissue. **2.** A small, discrete particle. [< L *corpus,* CORPUS.] —**cor•pus′cu•lar** (-kyə-lər) *adj.*

corpus de•lic•ti (dĭl-ĭk′tī). **1.** *Law.* The material evidence of the fact that a crime has been committed. **2.** Loosely, the victim's corpse in a murder case. [NL, "body of the crime."]

corr. **1.** correction. **2.** correspondence; correspondent.

cor•ral (kə-răl′) *n.* An enclosure for confining livestock. —*v.* **-ralled, -ralling. 1.** To drive into and hold in a corral. **2.** *Informal.* To seize; capture. [Span.]

cor•rect (kə-rĕkt′) *v.* **1.** To remove the errors or mistakes from. **2.** To mark the errors in. **3.** To admonish or punish. **4.** To remove or counteract, as a malfunction. —*adj.* **1.** Accurate or true. **2.** Conforming to standards; proper. [< L *corrigere* (pp *correctus*), to make straight, correct.] —**cor•rec′tive** *adj.* & *n.* —**cor•rect′ly** *adv.* —**cor•rect′ness** *n.*

cor•rec•tion (kə-rĕk′shən) *n.* **1.** The act or process of correcting. **2.** That which is substituted for a mistake or fault. **3.** Punishment. **4.** A quantity added or subtracted to improve accuracy. —**cor•rec′tion•al** *adj.*

correl. correlative.

cor•re•la•tion (kôr′ə-lā′shən, kŏr′-) *n.* A causal, complementary, parallel, or reciprocal relationship, esp. a structural, functional, or qualitative correspondence between two comparable entities. [ML *correlātiō.*] —**cor′re•late′** *v.* **(-lated, -lating).** —**cor′re•late′** *adj.*

cor•rel•a•tive (kə-rĕl′ə-tĭv) *adj.* **1.** Reciprocally related. **2.** Indicating a reciprocal or complementary grammatical relation, as the conjunctions *neither* and *nor.* —*n.* **1.** Either of two correlative entities. **2.** *Gram.* A correlative word or expression.

cor•re•spond (kôr′ə-spŏnd′, kŏr′-) *v.* **1.** To be in agreement, harmony, or conformity. **2.** To be similar or equal (with *to*). **3.** To communicate by letter.

cor•re•spon•dence (kôr′rə-spŏn′dəns, kŏr′-) *n.* **1.** The act, fact, or state of agreeing or conforming. **2.** Similarity or analogy. **3. a.** Communication by the exchange of letters. **b.** The letters written or received.

cor•re•spon•dent (kôr′ə-spŏn′dənt, kŏr′-) *n.* **1.** One who communicates by means of letters. **2.** One employed, as by a newspaper, to supply news from a distant place. **3.** A thing that corresponds; a correlative. —*adj.* Corresponding; consistent.

cor•ri•dor (kôr′ĭ-dər, -dôr, kŏr′-) *n.* **1.** A narrow passageway, generally with rooms or apartments opening onto it. **2.** A tract of land forming a passageway. [< OIt *corridore,* "a run."]

cor•ri•gen•dum (kôr′ə-jĕn′dəm, kŏr′-) *n., pl.* **-da** (-də). **1.** An error in a book. **2. corrigenda.** A list of errors with their corrections, in a book. [< L *corrigere,* to CORRECT.]

cor•rob•o•rate (kə-rŏb′ə-rāt′) *v.* **-rated, -rating.** To strengthen or support (other evidence). [L *corrōborāre.*] —**cor•rob′o•ra′tion** *n.* —**cor•rob′o•ra′tive** *adj.* —**cor•rob′o•ra′tor** *n.* —**cor•rob′o•ra•to′ry** (-ər-ə-tôr′ē, -tōr′ē) *adj.*

cor•rode (kə-rōd′) *v.* **-roded, -roding.** To wear away gradually, esp. by chemical action. [< L *corrōdere,* to gnaw to pieces.] —**cor•ro′sion** *n.* —**cor•ro′sive** *adj.* —**cor•ro′sive•ly** *adv.*

cor•ru•gate (kôr′ə-gāt′, kôr′yə-, kŏr′-) *v.* **-gated, -gating.** To make folds or parallel and alternating ridges and grooves (in). [L *corrūgāre,* to make full of wrinkles.] —**cor′ru•gate′, cor′ru•gat′ed** (-gā′tĭd) *adj.* —**cor′ru•ga′tion** *n.* —**cor′ru•ga′tor** *n.*

corrugated iron. A structural sheet iron, usually galvanized, shaped in parallel furrows and ridges for rigidity.

cor•rupt (kə-rŭpt′) *adj.* **1.** Immoral; perverted. **2.** Marked by venality. **3.** Decaying; putrid. —*v.* To make or become corrupt. [< L *corruptus,* pp of *corrumpere,* break to pieces, destroy.] —**cor•rupt′i•ble** *adj.* —**cor•rup′tion** *n.* —**cor•rup′tive** *adj.* —**cor•rupt′ly** *adv.*

cor•sage (kôr-säzh′) *n.* A small bouquet worn by a woman, as at the shoulder. [OF, torso, bust.]

cor•sair (kôr′sâr) *n.* **1.** A pirate. **2.** A swift pirate ship. [< ML *cursus,* plunder.]

cor•set (kôr′sĭt) *n.* A close-fitting undergarment, often reinforced by stays, worn to support and shape the waistline, hips, and breasts. [< OF.]

Cor•si•ca (kôr′sĭ-kə). An island of France, in the Mediterranean. —**Cor′si•can** *adj.* & *n.*

cor•tege (kôr-tĕzh′, -tāzh′) *n.* **1.** A train of attendants; retinue. **2.** A ceremonial procession. [< It *corteggiare,* to pay honor, court.]

Cor•tés (kôr-tĕz′), **Hernando.** 1485–1547. Spanish explorer, conqueror of the Aztecs.

cor•tex (kôr′tĕks) *n., pl.* **-tices** (-tə-sēz′) or **-texes. 1.** The outer layer of an organ or part. **2.** *Bot.* **a.** A layer of tissue in roots and stems lying between the epidermis and vascular tissue. **b.** An external layer such as bark or rind. [L, bark, shell, rind.] —**cor′ti•cal** *adj.* —**cor′ti•cal•ly** *adv.*

cor•ti•sone (kôr′tə-sōn, -zōn) *n.* An adrenal hormone, $C_{21}H_{28}O_5$, active in carbohydrate metabolism and used to treat rheumatoid arthritis, adrenal insufficiency, and gout.

co•run•dum (kə-rŭn′dəm) *n.* An extremely hard aluminum oxide mineral, occurring in gem varieties and in a common form used chiefly in abrasives. [Tamil *kuruntam.*]

cor•us•cate (kôr'əs-kāt', kŏr'-) *v.* **-cated, -cating.** To sparkle; glitter; scintillate. [L *coruscāre,* to thrust, vibrate, glitter.] —**cor'us•ca'tion** *n.*

cor•vette (kôr-vĕt') *n.* **1.** A lightly armed warship, smaller than a destroyer. **2.** An armed sailing vessel smaller than a frigate. [< OF.]

co•ry•za (kə-rī'zə) *n.* An acute inflammation of the nasal mucous membrane, marked by discharge of mucus, sneezing, and watering of the eyes. [< Gk *koruza,* catarrh.]

cos•met•ic (kŏz-mĕt'ĭk) *n.* A preparation, such as face powder or skin cream, designed to beautify the body. [< Gk *kosmein,* to arrange, order.] —**cos•met'ic** *adj.*

cos•mic (kŏz'mĭk) *adj.* Also **cos•mi•cal** (-mĭ-kəl). **1.** Pertaining to the universe, esp. as distinct from the earth or, sometimes, from the solar system. **2.** Vast. [Gk *kosmikos,* of the universe.] —**cos'mi•cal•ly** *adv.*

cosmic ray. A stream of ionizing radiation of extraterrestrial origin, chiefly of protons, alpha particles, and other atomic nuclei but including some high-energy electrons and photons.

cosmo–. *comb. form.* World or universe. [< COSMOS.]

cos•mog•o•ny (kŏz-mŏg'ə-nē) *n., pl.* **-nies.** The astrophysical study of the evolution of the universe.

cos•mol•o•gy (kŏz-mŏl'ə-jē) *n.* **1.** A branch of philosophy dealing with the origin, processes, and structure of the universe. **2.** The astrophysical study of the structure and constituent dynamics of the universe. —**cos'mo•log'i•cal** (-mə-lŏg'ĭ-kəl) *adj.* —**cos•mol'o•gist** *n.*

cos•mo•naut (kŏz'mə-nôt) *n.* An astronaut.

cos•mo•pol•i•tan (kŏz'mə-pŏl'ə-tən) *adj.* **1.** Common to the whole world. **2.** At home in all places or in many spheres of interest. —*n.* A cosmopolitan person. [< Gk *kosmopolitēs,* citizen of the world.]

cos•mos (kŏz'məs, -mōs) *n.* **1.** The universe regarded as an orderly, harmonious whole. **2.** Any system regarded as ordered, harmonious, and whole. **3.** Harmony and order as distinct from chaos. **4.** A garden plant with variously colored, daisylike flowers. [Gk *kosmos,* order, the universe, the world.]

Cos•sack (kŏs'ăk) *n.* A member of a people of the S Soviet Union, noted as cavalrymen. [Russ *kazak.*] —**Cos'sack** *adj.*

cost (kôst) *n.* **1.** An amount paid or required in payment for a purchase. **2.** A loss or penalty; detriment. —*v.* To require a specified payment, expenditure, effort, or loss. [< L *constāre,* to stand with or at a particular price.]

Cos•ta Ri•ca (kōs'tə rē'kə, kôs'-). A republic of Central America, between Panama and Nicaragua. Pop. 1,414,000. Cap. San José. —**Costa Rican.**

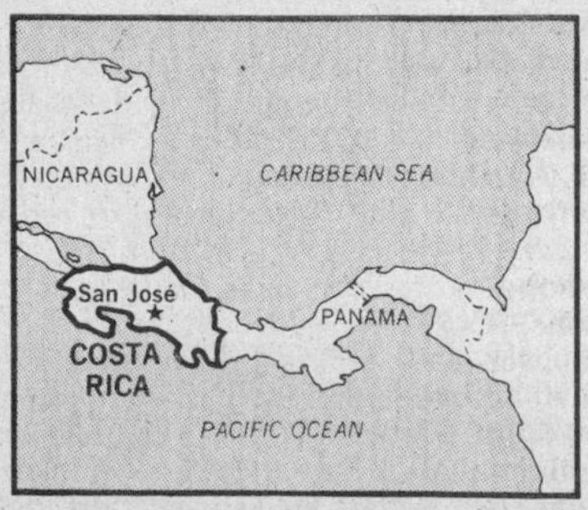

Costa Rica

cost•ly (kôst'lē) *adj.* **-lier, -liest.** **1.** Of high price or value; expensive. **2.** Entailing loss or sacrifice. —**cost'li•ness** *n.*

cost-plus (kôst'plŭs', kŏst'-) *n.* Cost of production plus a fixed rate of profit. Often used as a basis for government contracts.

cos•tume (kŏs't/y/ōōm, kŏs-t/y/ōōm') *n.* **1.** A style of dress, esp. one characteristic of a particular country or period. **2.** A set of clothes for a particular occasion or season. [< L *consuētūdō,* CUSTOM.]

co•sy. Variant of **cozy.**

cot (kŏt) *n.* A narrow bed, esp. one made of canvas stretched on a collapsible frame. [Hindi *khāṭ,* bedstead, couch.]

cote (kōt) *n.* A small shed or shelter for sheep or birds. [< OE.]

co•te•rie (kō'tə-rē) *n.* A small group of persons who associate frequently. [< OF, an association of peasant tenants.]

co•til•lion (kō-tĭl'yən, kə-) *n.* **1.** A lively dance of the 18th century, with intricate patterns and steps. **2.** A formal debutante ball. [F *cotillon,* peasant dress, country dance.]

cot•tage (kŏt'ĭj) *n.* **1.** A small, single-storied country house. **2.** A small summer house. [< OE *cot,* cottage.]

cottage cheese. An extremely soft, mild white cheese made of strained and seasoned curds of skim milk.

cot•ter (kŏt'ər) *n.* A bolt, wedge, key, or pin inserted through a slot in order to hold parts together. [< dial *cotterel.*]

cotter pin. A split cotter inserted through holes in two or more pieces and bent at the ends to fasten them together.

cot•ton (kŏt'n) *n.* **1.** The downy white fiber surrounding the seeds of a plant cultivated in warm regions. **2.** The plant itself. **3.** Thread or cloth made from cotton fiber. —*v.* To take a liking to; become friendly [< Ar *quṭn.*] —**cot'ton•y** *adj.*

cotton gin. See **gin²**.

cot•ton•mouth (kŏt'n-mouth') *n.* A snake, the **water moccasin.**

cot•ton•seed (kŏt'n-sēd') *n.* The seed of cotton, used as a source of an oil used in cooking and in the manufacture of paints, soaps, and other products.

cot•ton•tail (kŏt'n-tāl') *n.* A New World rabbit having a tail with a white underside.

cot•ton•wood (kŏt'n-wŏŏd') *n.* A poplar tree having seeds with cottonlike tufts.

cot•y•le•don (kŏt'ə-lēd'n) *n.* An embryonic plant leaf, the first to appear from a sprouting seed. [< Gk *kotulē,* anything hollow, cup.] —**cot'y•le'don•al, cot'y•le'do•nous** *adj.*

couch (kouch) *n.* An article of furniture, commonly upholstered, on which one can sit or recline; a sofa. —*v.* To place in a certain verbal context. [< OF *coucher,* to lay down.] —**couch'er** *n.*

couch•ant (kou'chənt) *adj. Her.* Lying down with the head raised.

cou•gar (kōō'gər) *n.* The **mountain lion.** [< Tupi *suasuarana,* "like a deer."]

cough (kôf, kŏf) *v.* **1.** To expel air from the lungs suddenly and noisily. **2.** To expel by coughing (with *up* or *out*). [< OE **cohhian.*] —**cough** *n.*

could (kŏŏd). *p.t.* of **can.**

could•n't (kŏŏd'ənt). Contraction of *could not.*

cou•lomb (kōō'lŏm', -lōm') *n.* A unit of electrical charge equal to the quantity of charge transferred in one second by a steady current of one ampere. [< C.A. de *Coulomb* (1736–1806), French physicist.]

coun•cil (koun'səl) *n.* **1.** An assembly called together for consultation, deliberation, etc. **2.** An administrative, legislative, or advisory body. [< L *concilium,* meeting, assembly.]

coun•cil•man (koun'səl-mən) *n.* A member of a council, esp. of a city council.

coun•cil•or (koun'sə-lər) *n.* Also **coun•cil•lor.** A member of a council.

coun•sel (koun'səl) *n.* **1.** An exchanging of opinions and ideas; discussion. **2.** Advice or guidance. **3.** A deliberate resolution; plan. **4.** *pl.* **counsel.** A lawyer or group of lawyers. —*v.* **-seled** or **-selled, -seling** or **-selling.** **1.** To give counsel to; advise. **2.** To urge the adoption of; recommend. [< L *consilium,* deliberation, consultation.]

coun•sel•or (koun'sə-lər) *n.* Also **coun•sel•lor.** **1.** An adviser. **2.** An attorney, esp. a trial lawyer.

count¹ (kount) *v.* **1.** To name or list one by one in order to determine a total. **2.** To recite numerals in ascending order. **3.** To include in a reckoning: *ten dogs, counting the puppies.* **4.** To believe or consider to be. **5.** To merit consideration. **6.** To be of value or importance: *His opinions count for little.* —**count on.** To rely. —*n.* **1.** The act of counting. **2.** A number reached by counting. **3.** A reckoning. **4.** *Law.* Any of the charges in an indictment. [< L *computāre,* to sum up, reckon.] —**count'a•ble** *adj.*

count² (kount) *n.* In some European countries, a nobleman whose rank corresponds to that of an English earl. [< LL *comes (comit-),* occupant of any state office.]

count•down (kount'doun') *n.* The act of counting backward aloud to indicate the time elapsing before an event or operation.

coun•te•nance (koun'tə-nəns) *n.* **1.** Appearance, esp. the expression of the face. **2.** The face. **3.** Support or approval. —*v.* **-nanced, -nancing** To approve; condone. [< OF *contenir,* to behave, contain.]

count•er¹ (koun'tər) *adj.* Contrary; opposing. —*n.* One that is counter; an opposite. —*v.* To move, do, or act in opposition to. —*adv.* In a contrary manner or direction. [< L *contrā,* contrary to, against.]

count•er² (koun'tər) *n.* **1.** A table or similar flat surface on which money is counted, business transacted, or food served. **2.** A piece, as of wood or ivory, used for keeping a count or a place in games. [< L *computāre,* to COUNT.]

count•er³ (koun'tər) *n.* A person or device that counts.

counter–. *comb. form.* **1.** Opposition, as in direction or purpose. **2.** Reciprocation. [< L *contrā,* opposite to, COUNTER.]

coun•ter•act (koun'tər-ăkt') *v.* To oppose and mitigate the effects of by contrary action. —**coun'ter•ac'tion** *n.*

coun•ter•at•tack (koun'tər-ə-tăk') *n.* A return attack. —**coun'ter•at•tack'** *v.*

coun•ter•bal•ance (koun'tər-băl'əns, koun'-tər-băl'əns) *n.* **1.** Any force or influence equally counteracting another. **2.** A weight that balances another. —**coun'ter•bal'ance** *v.* **(-anced, -ancing).**

coun•ter•clock•wise (koun'tər-klŏk'wīz') *adv.* In a direction opposite to that of the movement of the hands of a clock. —**coun'ter•clock'wise'** *adj.*

coun•ter•cul•ture (koun'tər-kŭl'chər) *n.* A culture created by or for the alienated young in opposition to traditional values.

coun•ter•feit (koun'tər-fĭt) *v.* **1.** To make a copy of, usually with intent to defraud; forge.

2. To feign; pretend. —*adj.* 1. Made in imitation of what is genuine with intent to defraud. 2. Feigned; pretended; simulated. —*n.* A fraudulent imitation or facsimile. [< ML *contrāfacere,* to make in contrast to.] —**coun'ter·feit·er** *n.*

coun·ter·in·tel·li·gence (koun'tər-ĭn-tĕl'ə-jəns) *n.* The branch of an intelligence service charged with keeping information from an enemy and preventing subversion and sabotage.

coun·ter·mand (koun'tər-mănd', -mänd') *v.* 1. To reverse (a command or order). 2. To recall by a contrary order. [< COUNTER- + OF *mander,* to command.]

coun·ter·mea·sure (koun'tər-mĕzh'ər) *n.* A measure or action taken in opposition to another.

coun·ter·of·fen·sive (koun'tər-ə-fĕn'sĭv) *n.* A large-scale attack by an army, designed to stop the offensive of an enemy.

coun·ter·pane (koun'tər-pān') *n.* A bedspread. [< ML *culcita puncta,* "stitched quilt."]

coun·ter·part (koun'tər-pärt') *n.* One that closely or exactly resembles another, as in function or relation.

coun·ter·point (koun'tər-point') *n.* 1. The technique of combining two or more melodic lines so that they establish a harmonic relationship while retaining their linear individuality. 2. A contrasting but parallel theme.

coun·ter·poise (koun'tər-poiz') *n.* 1. A counterbalancing weight. 2. A force or influence that balances or counteracts another. 3. The state of being balanced or in equilibrium. —*v.* (koun'tər-poiz') **-poised, -poising.** To oppose with an equal weight.

coun·ter·rev·o·lu·tion (koun'tər-rĕv'ə-lōō'shən) *n.* A movement arising in opposition to a revolution.

coun·ter·sign (koun'tər-sīn') *v.* To sign (a previously signed document), as for authentication. —*n.* A second or confirming signature, as on a previously signed document.

coun·ter·sink (koun'tər-sĭngk') *v.* **-sunk, -sinking.** 1. To enlarge the top part of (a drilled hole) so that a screw or bolthead will lie flush with or below the surface. 2. To drive a screw or bolt into (such a hole). —*n.* 1. A tool for making such a hole. 2. A hole so made.

coun·ter·ten·or (koun'tər-tĕn'ər) *n.* A male singer with a range above that of tenor.

coun·ter·weight (koun'tər-wāt') *n.* A weight used as a counterbalance.

count·ess (koun'tĭs) *n.* 1. The wife or widow of a count or earl. 2. A woman holding the title of count or earl in her own right.

count·less (kount'lĭs) *adj.* Innumerable.

coun·try (kŭn'trē) *n., pl.* **-tries.** 1. A large tract of land distinguishable by features of topography, biology, or culture. 2. A rural area. 3. The territory of a nation or state. 4. The land of a person's birth or citizenship or to which a person owes allegiance. —*adj.* Of or pertaining to rural areas. [< ML *(terra) contrāta,* "(land) lying opposite or before one."]

country club. A suburban club with facilities for golf, other outdoor sports, and social activities.

coun·try·man (kŭn'trē-mən) *n.* 1. A man from one's own country. 2. A rustic.

coun·try·side (kŭn'trē-sīd') *n.* 1. A rural region. 2. Its inhabitants.

coun·ty (koun'tē) *n., pl.* **-ties.** An administrative subdivision of a state or country. [< ML *comitātus,* territory of a count.]

coup (kōō) *n.* 1. A brilliantly executed stratagem. 2. A **coup d'état.** [< L *colaphus,* blow.]

coup de grâce (kōō' də gräs'). 1. The finishing stroke, as given to someone mortally wounded. 2. Any decisive or finishing stroke. [F, "stroke of mercy."]

coup d'é·tat (kōō' dā-tä'). A sudden, deliberate violation of constitutional forms by a group of persons in authority. [F, "stroke of state."]

cou·pé (kōō-pā') *n.* Also **coupe** (kōōp). A closed two-door automobile. [< F *(carrosse) coupé,* "cut-off (carriage)."]

coup·le (kŭp'əl) *n.* 1. Two items of the same kind. 2. Something that joins two things. 3. A man and woman united in some way, as by marriage. 4. *Informal.* A few; several: *a couple of days.* —*v.* **-led, -ling.** 1. To link together. 2. To form pairs. 3. To marry. 4. To copulate. [< L *cōpula,* bond, link.]

coup·let (kŭp'lĭt) *n.* Two successive lines of verse with the same rhyme scheme and meter.

cou·pon (k/y/ōō'pŏn') *n.* 1. A certificate attached to a bond that represents a sum of interest due at a stated maturity. 2. A certificate entitling the bearer to certain benefits, such as a cash refund. [< OF *colpon,* "a piece cut off."]

cour·age (kûr'ĭj) *n.* The quality of mind that enables one to face danger with self-possession or confidence; bravery. [ME *corage,* heart as the seat of feeling, courage < L *cor,* heart.] —**cou·ra'geous** (kə-rā'jəs) *adj.* —**cou·ra'geous·ly** *adv.* —**cou·ra'geous·ness** *n.*

cou·ri·er (kŏŏr'ē-ər, kûr'-) *n.* A messenger, esp. one on urgent or official business. [< L *currere,* to run.]

course (kôrs, kōrs, kŏŏrs) *n.* 1. Onward movement in a particular direction. 2. The route taken by something that moves, as a stream. 3. Duration: *in the course of a year.* 4. A mode of action or behavior. 5. Regular development: *The fad ran its course.* 6. *Ed.* a. A complete body of prescribed studies. b. A unit of such studies. 7. A part of a meal served as a unit at one time. —**in due course.** At the right time. —**of course.** Without any doubt; certainly. —*v.* **coursed, coursing.** 1. To move swiftly (through or over); traverse. 2. To hunt (game) with hounds. 3. To follow a direction. 4. To flow. [< L *cursus,* pp of *currere,* to run.]

cours·er (kôr'sər, kōr'-, kŏŏr'-) *n. Poetic.* A swift horse.

court (kôrt, kōrt) *n.* 1. A courtyard. 2. A short street. 3. A royal mansion or palace. 4. The retinue of a sovereign. 5. A sovereign's governing body, including ministers and state advisers. 6. a. A person or body of persons appointed to hear and submit a decision on legal cases. b. The room in which such cases are heard. c. The regular session of a judicial assembly. 7. An open, level area, marked with lines, upon which tennis, handball, basketball, etc., are played. —**out of court.** Without a trial. —*v.* 1. To attempt to gain the favor of by flattery or attention. 2. To attempt to gain the love of; woo. 3. To invite, often unwittingly or foolishly: *court disaster.* [< L *cohors (cohort-),* enclosure, court, cohort.] —**court'li·ness** *n.* —**court'ly** *adj.* & *adv.*

cour·te·ous (kûr'tē-əs) *adj.* Considerate toward others. [< OF *cort,* court.] —**cour'te·ous·ly** *adv.* —**cour'te·ous·ness** *n.*

cour·te·san (kôr'tə-zən, kōr'-) *n.* Also **cour·te·zan.** A prostitute, esp. one associating with men of rank. [< L *cohors,* COURT.]

cour·te·sy (kûr'tə-sē) *n., pl.* **-sies.** 1. Gracious manner or manners. 2. A polite gesture or remark.

court·house (kôrt'hous', kōrt'-) *n.* A building housing judicial courts.

court·i·er (kôr'tē-ər, kōr'-, -tyər) *n.* An attendant at a sovereign's court.

court-mar·tial (kôrt'mär'shəl, kōrt'-) *n., pl.* **courts-martial.** 1. A military court of officers to try persons for offenses under military law. 2. A trial by court-martial. —*v.* **-tialed** or **-tialled, -tialing** or **-tialling.** To try by court-martial.

court·room (kôrt'rōōm', kōrt'-, -rŏŏm') *n.* A room for court proceedings.

court·ship (kôrt'shĭp', kōrt'-) *n.* The act or period of wooing a woman.

court·yard (kôrt'yärd', kōrt'-) *n.* An open space surrounded by walls or buildings.

cous·in (kŭz'ən) *n.* 1. A child of one's aunt or uncle. 2. A relative descended from a common ancestor. [< L *consōbrinus,* maternal first cousin.]

co·va·lent bond (kō-vā'lənt). A chemical bond formed by the sharing of one or more electrons, esp. pairs of electrons, between atoms.

cove (kōv) *n.* A small, sheltered bay. [< OE *cofa,* chamber, cave.]

cov·en (kŭv'ən, kō'vən) *n.* An assembly of witches. [< ME *covent,* a gathering, convent.]

cov·e·nant (kŭv'ə-nənt) *n.* 1. A binding agreement; contract. 2. God's promises to man, as recorded in the Old and New Testaments. —*v.* To promise by or enter into a covenant. [< OF *co(n)venir,* to agree, convene.]

cov·er (kŭv'ər) *v.* 1. To place upon, over, or in front of (something) so as to protect, shut in, or conceal. 2. To clothe. 3. To occupy the surface of: *Dust covered the table.* 4. To extend over: *a farm covering 100 acres.* 5. To hide or conceal, as a fact or crime. 6. To protect by insurance. 7. To defray (an expense). 8. To deal with; treat of. 9. To travel or pass over. 10. To hold within the range and aim of a firearm. 11. *Jour.* To report the details of (an event or situation). 12. *Informal.* To act as a substitute during someone's absence. —*n.* 1. Something that covers. 2. Shelter of any kind. 3. Something that conceals or disguises. 4. A table setting for one person. 5. An envelope or wrapper for mail. —**take cover.** To seek protection, as from enemy fire. —**under cover.** Operating secretly. [< L *cooperīre,* to cover completely.] —**cov'er·er** *n.*

cov·er·age (kŭv'ər-ĭj) *n.* 1. *Jour.* The extent to which something is reported. 2. The protection afforded by insurance.

cov·er·alls (kŭv'ər-ôlz') *pl.n.* A loose-fitting one-piece garment worn by workmen to protect their clothes.

covered wagon. A wagon with an arched canvas top, used by American pioneers.

cov·er·let (kŭv'ər-lĭt) *n.* A bedspread.

cov·ert (kŭv'ərt, kō'vərt) *adj.* 1. Sheltered. 2. Concealed; hidden; secret. —*n.* 1. A covering or cover. 2. A shelter or hiding place. 3. Thick underbrush affording cover for game. 4. Also **covert cloth.** A sturdy twilled woolen cloth. [< OF *covrir,* to cover.] —**cov'ert·ly** *adv.* —**cov'ert·ness** *n.*

cov·er-up (kŭv'ər-ŭp') *n.* Also **Also cov·er·up.** 1. An effort or strategy designed to conceal something, such as a crime or scandal. 2. An enveloping garment. —**cov'er-up'** *adj.*

cov·et (kŭv'ĭt) *v.* To desire (that which is another's); crave. [< L *cupiditās,* desire.] —**cov'et·er** *n.*

cov•et•ous (kŭv'ə-təs) *adj.* Excessively desirous; avaricious; greedy: *covetous of learning.* —**cov'et•ous•ly** *adv.* —**cov'et•ous•ness** *n.*

cov•ey (kŭv'ē) *n., pl.* **-eys.** A small flock or group, as of partridges. [< OF *covee,* a brood.]

cow[1] (kou) *n.* **1.** The mature female of cattle or of other animals as the whale or elephant. **2.** Broadly, any domesticated bovine. [< OE *cū.* See **gwou-.**]

cow[2] (kou) *v.* To frighten with threats or a show of force. [Perh < ON *kūga,* to oppress.]

cow•ard (kou'ərd) *n.* One who lacks courage in the face of danger or pain. [< OF *couard.*] —**cow'ard•ly** *adj. & adv.*

cow•ard•ice (kou'ər-dĭs) *n.* Lack of courage in the face of danger, pain, etc.

cow•bird (kou'bûrd') *n.* A blackbird of a species that lays its eggs in the nests of other birds.

cow•boy (kou'boi') *n.* **1.** A hired man, esp. in the U.S., who tends cattle and performs many of his duties on horseback. **2.** A performer of feats of horsemanship, calf roping, etc., at a rodeo.

cow•catch•er (kou'kăch'ər) *n.* An iron frame on the front of a locomotive or streetcar that clears the track.

cow•er (kou'ər) *v.* To cringe or shrink away in fear. [Prob < Scand.]

cow•hide (kou'hīd') *n.* **1.** The hide of a cow or leather made from it. **2.** A strong, heavy, flexible whip, usually made of braided leather. —*v.* **-hided, -hiding.** To whip with a cowhide.

cowl (koul) *n.* **1.** The hood worn by monks. **2.** A hood-shaped covering used to increase the draft of a chimney. **3.** The top portion of the front part of an automobile body, supporting the windshield and dashboard. **4.** Also **cowl•ing** (kou'lĭng). A removable metal covering for an aircraft engine. [< L *cucullus,* hood.]

cow•lick (kou'lĭk') *n.* A projecting tuft of hair on the head that will not lie flat.

co•work•er (kō'wûrk'ər) *n.* A fellow worker.

cow•poke (kou'pōk') *n. Informal.* A cowboy, as at a cattle ranch.

cow•pox (kou'pŏks') *n.* A contagious skin disease of cattle, caused by a virus that is isolated and used to vaccinate humans against smallpox.

cow•punch•er (kou'pŭn'chər) *n. Informal.* A cowboy.

cow•ry (kou'rē) *n., pl.* **-ries.** Also **cow•rie.** Any of various tropical marine mollusks with glossy, often brightly marked shells. [Hindi *kauṛī.*]

cow•slip (kou'slĭp') *n.* **1.** An Old World primrose with yellow flowers. **2.** The **marsh marigold.** [< OE *cūslyppe,* "cow dung."]

cox•comb. Variant of **cockscomb.**

cox•swain (kŏk'sən, kŏk'swān') *n.* A person who steers a boat or racing shell.

coy (koi) *adj.* Affectedly shy or devious. [< L *quiētus,* quiet.] —**coy'ly** *adv.* —**coy'ness** *n.*

coy•o•te (kī-ō'tē, kī'ō-tē') *n.* A wolflike animal, common in W North America. [< Nah *coyotl.*]

coz•en (kŭz'ən) *v.* To deceive; cheat. [Poss < obs It *cozzonare,* "to be a horse trader," cheat.] —**coz'en•er** *n.*

co•zy (kō'zē) *adj.* **-zier, -ziest.** Also **co•sy.** Snug and comfortable. —*n., pl.* **-zies.** A padded covering to keep a teapot hot. [Scot *cosie.*] —**co'zi•ly** *adv.* —**co'zi•ness** *n.*

cp. compare.

C.P. Communist Party.

C.P.A. certified public accountant.

cpd. compound.

Cpl. corporal.

C.P.O. chief petty officer.

cps cycles per second.

Cr chromium.

cr. **1.** credit; creditor. **2.** crown.

crab[1] (krăb) *n.* **1.** Any of various chiefly marine crustaceans having a broad body with a shell-like covering. **2. Crab.** The constellation and sign of the zodiac Cancer. [< OE *crabba.* See **gerebh-.**]

crab[2] (krăb) *n.* **1.** A **crab apple.** **2.** A quarrelsome, ill-tempered person. —*v.* **crabbed** (krăbd), **crabbing.** *Informal.* To criticize. [Prob < Scand.]

crab apple. **1.** A small, tart applelike fruit. **2.** A tree bearing such fruit.

crab•bed (krăb'ĭd) *adj.* **1.** Ill-tempered. **2.** Difficult to read: *crabbed handwriting.*

crab•by (krăb'ē) *adj.* **-bier, -biest.** Grouchy; ill-tempered.

crab•grass (krăb'grăs', -gräs') *n.* A coarse grass that spreads and displaces other grasses in lawns.

crack (krăk) *v.* **1.** To break or cause to break with a sharp sound; snap. **2.** To break or cause to break without dividing into parts. **3.** To change sharply in pitch or timbre, as the voice from emotion. **4.** To strike. **5.** To break open or into. **6.** To discover the solution to, esp. after considerable effort. **7.** *Informal.* To tell (a joke). **8.** To decompose (petroleum) into simpler compounds by cracking. —*n.* **1.** A sharp, snapping sound, such as gunfire. **2.** A partial split or break; flaw; fissure. **3.** A narrow space: *The window was open a crack.* **4.** A sharp, resounding blow. **5.** A cracking vocal tone or sound. **6.** A chance: *gave him a crack at the job.* **7.** A sarcastic remark. **8.** A moment; instant: *at the crack of dawn.* —*adj.* Superior; first-rate: *a crack marksman.* [< OE *cracian.* See **ger-[2].**]

crack down. To become demanding, severe, or strict: *crack down on student absences.*

crack•down (krăk'doun') *n.* Sudden punitive action.

crack•er (krăk'ər) *n.* **1.** A thin, crisp wafer or biscuit, usually made of unleavened, unsweetened dough. **2.** A firecracker. **3.** A poor white person of the rural SE U.S. Used disparagingly.

crack•er•jack (krăk'ər-jăk') *adj. Slang.* Of excellent quality or ability; remarkably fine. —**crack'er•jack'** *n.*

crack•ing (krăk'ĭng) *n.* Thermal decomposition, sometimes with catalysis, of a complex substance, esp. of petroleum.

crack•le (krăk'əl) *v.* **-led, -ling.** **1.** To make or cause to make a succession of sharp, snapping noises. **2.** To cause (china) to become covered with a network of fine cracks. [Freq of CRACK.] —**crack'le** *n.*

crack•pot (krăk'pŏt') *n.* An eccentric person. —**crack'pot'** *adj.*

crack up. *Informal.* **1.** To crash; collide. **2.** To have a mental breakdown. **3.** To laugh or cause to laugh boisterously.

crack•up (krăk'ŭp') *n. Informal.* **1.** A collision, as of an airplane or automobile. **2.** A mental breakdown.

-cracy. *comb. form.* Government or rule: **bureaucracy.** [< Gk *kratos,* power.]

cra•dle (krād'l) *n.* **1.** An infant's low bed with rockers. **2.** A place of origin. **3.** A framework of wood or metal used to support something, such as a ship on land. —*v.* **-dled, -dling.** To place into, rock, hold, or lie in or as if in a cradle. [< OE *cradol, cradel.*]

cra•dle•song (krād'l-sông', -sŏng') *n.* A lullaby.

craft (krăft, kräft) *n.* **1.** Skill or ability, esp. in handwork or the arts. **2.** Skill in evasion or deception. **3. a.** A trade, esp. one requiring manual dexterity. **b.** The membership of such a trade; a guild. **4.** *pl.* **craft.** A boat, ship, or aircraft. [< OE *cræft* < Gmc **kraftaz, *krab-taz,* strength.]

crafts•man (krăfts'mən, kräfts'-) *n.* **1.** A skilled worker in a craft. **2.** An artist as considered with regard to technique. —**crafts'man•ly** *adj.* —**crafts'man•ship'** *n.*

craft•y (krăf'tē, kräf'-) *adj.* **-ier, -iest.** Skilled in deception; shrewd; cunning. —**craft'i•ly** *adv.* —**craft'i•ness** *n.*

crag (krăg) *n.* A steeply projecting rock mass. [< Celt.]

crag•gy (krăg'ē) *adj.* **-gier, -giest.** Having crags; steep and rugged. —**crag'gi•ness** *n.*

cram (krăm) *v.* **crammed, cramming.** **1.** To squeeze into an insufficient space; stuff. **2.** To fill too tightly. **3.** To gorge (oneself) with food. **4.** *Informal.* To make a concentrated last-minute review of a subject in studying for an examination. [< OE *crammian.* See **ger-[1].**] —**cram'mer** *n.*

cramp[1] (krămp) *n.* **1.** A sudden, involuntary, severely painful muscular contraction, the result of strain or chill. **2.** A temporary partial paralysis of habitually or excessively used muscles: *writer's cramp.* **3. cramps.** Sharp, persistent pains in the abdomen. —*v.* To cause or have a cramp. [< OF *crampe.*]

cramp[2] (krămp) *v.* To confine; restrict; hamper. [MDu *crampe,* hook.]

cran•ber•ry (krăn'bĕr'ē, -bər-ē) *n.* **1.** The tart red, edible berry of a trailing North American plant. **2.** The plant itself. [Part trans of LG *kraanbere,* "craneberry."]

crane (krān) *n.* **1.** A large wading bird with a long neck, long legs, and a long bill. **2.** A machine for hoisting heavy objects. —*v.* **craned, craning.** To stretch one's neck for a better view. [< OE *cran.* See **ger-[2].**]

cra•ni•um (krā'nē-əm) *n., pl.* **ums** or **-nia** (-nē-ə). **1.** The skull of a vertebrate. **2.** The portion of the skull enclosing the brain. [< Gk *kranion.*] —**cra'ni•al** *adj.*

crank (krăngk) *n.* **1.** A device for transmitting rotary motion, consisting of a handle attached at right angles to a shaft. **2.** *Informal.* An eccentric idea or person. —*v.* To start or operate (an engine) by turning a crank. [< OE *cranc.*]

crank•case (krăngk'kās') *n.* The metal case enclosing the crankshaft and associated parts in a reciprocating engine.

crank•shaft (krăngk'shăft', -shäft') *n.* A shaft that turns or is turned by a crank.

crank•y (krăng'kē) *adj.* **-ier, -iest.** **1.** Ill-tempered; peevish. **2.** Odd; eccentric. —**crank'i•ly** *adv.* —**crank'i•ness** *n.*

cran•ny (krăn'ē) *n., pl.* **-nies.** A small crevice; fissure. [< OF *cran, cren,* notch.]

craps (krăps) *n. (takes sing. v.).* A gambling game played by throwing two dice. [< F *crabs, craps.*]

crap•shoot•er (krăp'sho͞o'tər) *n.* One who plays craps.

crash[1] (krăsh) *v.* **1.** To fall, break, or collide noisily. **2.** To make a sudden loud noise. **3.** To fail suddenly, as a business. —*n.* **1.** A sudden loud noise. **2.** A collision. **3.** A sudden business failure. [< ME *crasen,* to shatter, craze, and *dashen,* to dash.]

crash[2] (krăsh) *n.* A coarse cotton or linen fabric used for towels and curtains. [Russ *krashenina,* a kind of colored linen.]

crass (krăs) *adj.* Grossly ignorant; coarse; stupid. [L *crassus,* fat, gross, dense.] **—crass'ly** *adv.* **—crass'ness** *n.*

-crat. *comb. form.* A member or supporter of a class or form of government: **bureaucrat.**

crate (krāt) *n.* A slatted wooden container for storing or shipping things. *—v.* **crated, crating.** To pack into a crate. [L *cratis,* wickerwork.]

cra•ter (krā'tər) *n.* **1.** A bowl-shaped depression at the mouth of a volcano. **2.** A similar depression or pit. [L *crātēr,* bowl, crater.]

cra•vat (krə-văt') *n.* A necktie. [F *cravate.*]

crave (krāv) *v.* **craved, craving. 1.** To have an intense desire for. **2.** To beg earnestly for. [< OE *crafian,* to beg, demand < Gmc **krabjan.*] **—crav'er** *n.* **—crav'ing•ly** *adv.*

cra•ven (krā'vən) *adj.* Cowardly. *—n.* A coward. [ME *cravant.*] **—cra'ven•ly** *adv.*

crav•ing (krā'vĭng) *n.* A consuming desire; yearning.

craw (krô) *n.* The crop of a bird or the stomach of an animal. [< OE *craga.*]

craw•fish (krô'fĭsh') *n.* A crayfish.

crawl (krôl) *v.* **1.** To move slowly by dragging the body along the ground; creep. **2.** To advance slowly. **3.** To be or feel as if covered with crawling things. **4.** To swim the crawl. *—n.* **1.** The act of crawling. **2.** A rapid swimming stroke. [< ON *krafla,* to crawl, creep.]

cray•fish (krā'fĭsh') *n.* A small, lobsterlike freshwater crustacean. [< OF *crevise.*]

cray•on (krā'ən, -ŏn') *n.* A stick of colored wax, charcoal, or chalk, used for drawing. [< L *crēta,* chalk.]

craze (krāz) *v.* **crazed, crazing.** To be or cause to become insane. *—n.* A short-lived fashion; fad. [< ON **krasa,* to shatter.]

cra•zy (krā'zē) *adj.* **-zier, -ziest. 1.** Unbalanced mentally; insane. **2.** *Informal.* Immoderately fond. **3.** *Informal.* Impractical. **—cra'zi•ly** *adv.* **—cra'zi•ness** *n.*

creak (krēk) *v.* To make or move with a grating or squeaking sound. *—n.* A grating or squeaking sound. [ME *creken* (imit).]

cream (krēm) *n.* **1.** The fatty component of milk. **2.** Yellowish white. **3.** A substance resembling cream, as certain foods or cosmetics. **4.** The choicest part. *—v.* **1.** To beat (butter) to a creamy consistency. **2.** To prepare in a cream sauce. [< LL *chrisma,* ointment, and *crāmum,* cream.] **—cream** *adj.* **—cream'y** *adj.*

cream cheese. A soft white cheese made of cream and milk.

cream•er•y (krē'mə-rē) *n., pl.* **-ies.** An establishment where dairy products are prepared or sold.

crease (krēs) *n.* A line made by pressing, folding, or wrinkling. *—v.* **creased, creasing.** To fold; be or become wrinkled. [< ME *crest,* ridge, crest.] **—creas'er** *n.*

cre•ate (krē-āt') *v.* **-ated, -ating. 1.** To cause to exist; originate. **2.** To bring about; produce. [< L *creāre.*]

cre•a•tion (krē-ā'shən) *n.* **1.** The act of creating. **2.** The world and all things in it. **3.** A product of human invention. **4. the Creation.** God's primal act of bringing the world into existence.

cre•a•tive (krē-ā'tĭv) *adj.* Characterized by originality; imaginative. **—cre'a•tiv'i•ty** *n.*

cre•a•tor (krē-ā'tər) *n.* **1.** One that creates. **2. Creator.** God.

crea•ture (krē'chər) *n.* **1.** An animal. **2.** A person, esp. one regarded with pity or contempt. **3.** One subservient to another.

crèche (krĕsh) *n.* A representation of the Nativity scene. [< OF *creche,* manger, crib.]

cre•dence (krēd'əns) *n.* **1.** Acceptance as true; belief. **2.** The quality of being trustworthy. [< L *crēdere,* to believe.]

cre•den•tial (krĭ-dĕn'shəl) *n.* **1.** That which entitles one to credit or authority. **2.** Often **credentials.** Written evidence of qualification.

cred•i•ble (krĕd'ə-bəl) *adj.* **1.** Believable; plausible. **2.** Reliable. [< L *crēdere,* to believe, entrust.] **—cred'i•bil'i•ty, cred'i•ble•ness** *n.* **—cred'i•bly** *adv.*

cred•it (krĕd'ĭt) *n.* **1.** Belief; trust. **2.** The quality of being trustworthy. **3.** A good reputation. **4.** A source of honor: *a credit to his family.* **5.** Approval; respect. **6.** Certification of completion of a course of study. **7.** Reputation for financial solvency and integrity. **8.** Time allowed for payment for anything sold on trust. **9.** Entry in an account of payment received. **10.** The balance in a person's bank account. *—v.* **1.** To believe; trust. **2.** To give credit to. [< L *crēdere,* to believe, entrust.]

cred•it•a•ble (krĕd'ĭ-tə-bəl) *adj.* Deserving commendation. **—cred'it•a•bil'i•ty, cred'it•a•ble•ness** *n.* **—cred'it•a•bly** *adv.*

cred•i•tor (krĕd'ə-tər) *n.* A person or firm to whom money is owed.

cre•do (krē'dō, krā'-) *n., pl.* **-dos.** A statement of belief; creed. [L *crēdo,* "I believe."]

cred•u•lous (krĕj'o͞o-ləs, krĕd'yo͞o-) *adj.* Disposed to believe too readily; gullible. [< L *crēdere,* to believe.] **—cre•du'li•ty** (krĭ-d/y/o͞o'-lə-tē) *n.* **—cred'u•lous•ly** *adv.*

Cree (krē) *n., pl.* **Cree** or **Crees. 1.** A member of a tribe of Algonquian-speaking Indians formerly living in C Canada. **2.** The language of this tribe.

creed (krēd) *n.* **1.** A statement of the essential articles of a religious belief. **2.** Any statement of conviction, principles, etc. [< L *crēdo,* "I believe."]

creek (krēk, krĭk) *n.* A small stream, often a tributary to a river. [ME *creke, crike.*]

Creek (krēk) *n., pl.* **Creek** or **Creeks. 1.** A member of a confederacy of several Muskhogean-speaking Indian tribes, formerly inhabiting the SE U.S. **2.** The language of these tribes.

creel (krēl) *n.* A wicker basket, esp. one used for carrying fish. [ME (Scot) *crel, crelle.*]

creep (krēp) *v.* **crept, creeping. 1.** To move on hands and knees with the body close to the ground. **2.** To move furtively or slowly. **3.** To grow along the ground or other surface, as a vine. **4.** To have a tingling sensation. [< OE *crēopan.*] **—creep'er** *n.*

creep•y (krē'pē) *adj.* **-ier, -iest.** *Informal.* Causing or having a sensation of repugnance or fear. **—creep'i•ness** *n.*

cre•mate (krē'māt', krĭ-māt') *v.* **-mated, -mating.** To incinerate (a corpse). [L *cremāre,* to burn, consume by fire.] **—cre•ma'tion** (krĭ-mā'shən) *n.* **—cre'ma'tor** *n.*

cre•ma•to•ry (krē'mə-tôr'ē, -tōr'ē, krĕm'ə-) *n., pl.* **-ries.** A furnace or place for cremating corpses.

cren•e•lat•ed (krĕn'ə-lā'tĭd) *adj.* Having battlements. [< OF *crenel,* a crenelation.] **—cren'e•la'tion** *n.*

Cre•ole (krē'ōl') *n.* **1.** Any person of European descent born in the West Indies or Spanish America. **2.** A person descended from the original French settlers of Louisiana. **3.** The French patois spoken by these people. **4.** Any person of mixed European and Negro ancestry. [< Port *crioulo,* Negro born in his master's house.] **—Cre'ole** *adj.*

cre•o•sote (krē'ə-sōt') *n.* **1.** A colorless to yellowish oily liquid, obtained by the destructive distillation of wood tar and formerly used to treat tuberculosis and chronic bronchitis. **2.** A yellowish to greenish-brown oily liquid obtained from coal tar and used as a wood preservative and disinfectant. [G *Kreosot,* "flesh preserver."]

crepe (krāp) *n.* A thin, crinkled fabric of silk, wool, etc. [< OF *crespe,* crisp, curly.]

crept (krĕpt). *p.t.* & *p.p.* of **creep.**

cre•pus•cu•lar (krĭ-pŭs'kyə-lər) *adj.* Of or like twilight; dim. [< L *crepusculum,* twilight.]

cres•cen•do (krə-shĕn'dō, -sĕn'dō) *n., pl.* **-dos. 1.** A gradual increase in the volume or intensity of sound. **2.** A musical passage played in a crescendo. *—adj.* Gradually increasing in volume or intensity. [It, "increasing."] **—cres•cen'do** *adv.*

cres•cent (krĕs'ənt) *n.* **1.** The figure of the moon in its first quarter, with concave and convex edges ending in points. **2.** Something shaped like this. [< L *crēscere,* to increase, grow.]

cress (krĕs) *n.* Any of various related plants with pungent leaves often used in salads. [< OE *cresse, cærse.* See **gras-.**]

crest (krĕst) *n.* **1.** A tuft or similar projection on the head of a bird or other animal. **2.** A heraldic device used on seals, stationery, etc. **3.** The top of something, as a wave; summit. *—v.* **1.** To reach the crest of (a hill). **2.** To form into a crest, as a wave. [< L *crista,* crest, plume.]

crest•fall•en (krĕst'fô'lən) *adj.* Dejected; dispirited. **—crest'fall'en•ly** *adv.*

Cre•ta•ceous (krĭ-tā'shəs) *adj.* Of or belonging to the geologic time, system of rocks, or sedimentary deposits of the most recent period of the Mesozoic era, characterized by the development of flowering plants and the disappearance of dinosaurs. *—n.* The Cretaceous period. [< L *crēta,* chalk, white earth, clay + -ACEOUS.]

Crete (krēt). A Greek island in the Mediterranean. **—Cre'tan** (krē'tən) *adj.* & *n.*

cre•tin•ism (krē'tĭn-ĭz'əm) *n.* A thyroid deficiency causing arrested mental and physical development. [< F *crétin,* idiot.] **—cre'tin** *n.*

cre•tonne (krĭ-tŏn', krē'tŏn') *n.* A heavy unglazed cotton or linen fabric used for draperies and slipcovers. [< *Creton,* village in Normandy.]

cre•vasse (krə-văs') *n.* A deep fissure, as in a glacier. [< OF *crevace,* crevice.]

crev•ice (krĕv'ĭs) *n.* A narrow crack; fissure. [< L *crepāre,* to rattle, crack.]

crew[1] (kro͞o) *n.* **1.** A group of people working together. **2.** The personnel manning a ship or an aircraft. [ME *creue,* military reinforcement.]

crew[2] (kro͞o). A *p.t.* of **crow**[2].

crib (krĭb) *n.* **1.** A child's bed with high sides. **2.** A small building for storing corn. **3.** A rack or trough for fodder. **4.** *Informal.* A translation or synopsis used dishonestly as an aid in doing schoolwork. *—v.* **cribbed, cribbing. 1.** To confine in or as in a crib. **2.** *Informal.* To use a crib in examinations; cheat. [< OE *cribb,* manger.] **—crib'ber** *n.*

crib•bage (krĭb'ĭj) *n.* A card game scored by inserting pegs into holes on a board. [Poss < CRIB.]

crick (krĭk) *n.* A painful cramp, as in the back or neck. [ME *crike.*]

crick•et[1] (krĭk'ĭt) *n.* A leaping insect of which the male produces a shrill, chirping sound. [< OE *criquer,* to click, creak.]
crick•et[2] (krĭk'ĭt) *n.* A game played with bats, a ball, and wickets by two teams of 11 players each. [Prob < OF *criquet,* wicket or bat in a ball game.]
cri•er (krī'ər) *n.* One who shouts out public announcements.
crime (krīm) *n.* An act committed or omitted in violation of the law. [< L *crimen,* verdict, judgment, crime.]
Cri•me•a (krī-mē'ə). A peninsula of the Soviet Union, extending into the Black Sea. —**Cri•me'an** *adj.*
crim•i•nal (krĭm'ə-nəl) *adj.* **1.** Of or pertaining to crime. **2.** Guilty of crime. —*n.* One who has committed a crime. —**crim'i•nal'i•ty** *n.* —**crim'i•nal•ly** *adv.*
crim•i•nol•o•gy (krĭm'ə-nŏl'ə-jē) *n.* The study of crime and criminals. —**crim'i•nol'o•gist** *n.*
crimp (krĭmp) *v.* **1.** To press into small folds or ridges; corrugate. **2.** To curl (hair). —*n.* **1.** The act of crimping. **2.** Something that has been crimped. [< OE *gecrympan,* to curl.] —**crimp'er** *n.*
crim•son (krĭm'zən) *n.* A deep red. —*v.* To make or become crimson. [< Ar *qirmizī.*]
cringe (krĭnj) *v.* **cringed, cringing.** To shrink back, as with fear; cower. [ME *crengen.*]
crin•kle (krĭng'kəl) *v.* **-kled, -kling.** To wrinkle; ripple. —*n.* A wrinkle or ripple. [ME *crinkelen.*] —**crin'kly** *adj.*
crin•o•line (krĭn'ə-lĭn) *n.* **1.** A fabric used to line and stiffen garments. **2.** A hoop skirt. [< It *crinolino.*] —**crin'o•line** *adj.*
crip•ple (krĭp'əl) *n.* One who is partly disabled, lame, or otherwise deficient. —*v.* **-pled, -pling.** To disable or damage. [< OE *crypel.*]
cri•sis (krī'sĭs) *n., pl.* **-ses** (-sēz'). A crucial situation; turning point. [< Gk *krisis,* turning point.]
crisp (krĭsp) *adj.* **1.** Firm but easily broken; brittle. **2.** Firm and fresh: *crisp celery.* **3.** Brisk; invigorating. **4.** Having small curls or waves. —*v.* To make or become crisp. [< OE < L *crispus,* crisped, curly.] —**crisp'i•ness** *n.* —**crisp'ly** *adv.* —**crisp'y** *adj.*
criss•cross (krĭs'krôs', -krŏs') *v.* **1.** To mark with crossing lines. **2.** To move crosswise through or over. —*n.* A pattern made of crossing lines. [Var of *christcross.*]
crit. critic; critical; criticism.
cri•te•ri•on (krī-tîr'ē-ən) *n., pl.* **-teria** (-tîr'ē-ə) or **-ons.** A standard on which a judgment can be based. [Gk *kritērion,* a means for judging, standard.]
crit•ic (krĭt'ĭk) *n.* **1.** One who judges anything, esp. literary or artistic works. **2.** One who finds fault. [< Gk *kritikos,* able to discern, critical.]
crit•i•cal (krĭt'ĭ-kəl) *adj.* **1.** Tending to criticize. **2.** Characterized by careful evaluation. **3.** Pertaining to critics or criticism. **4.** Forming or of the nature of a crisis. —**crit'i•cal•ly** *adv.* —**crit'i•cal•ness** *n.*
critical mass. The smallest mass of a fissionable material that will sustain a nuclear chain reaction.
crit•i•cism (krĭt'ə-sĭz'əm) *n.* **1.** The act of making judgments or evaluations. **2.** A review or article expressing the judgments of a critic. **3.** Censure; disapproval.
crit•i•cize (krĭt'ə-sīz') *v.* **-cized, -cizing.** **1.** To judge the merits and faults of; analyze and evaluate. **2.** To find fault with.
cri•tique (krĭ-tēk') *n.* A critical review or commentary.
crit•ter (krĭt'ər) *n. Regional.* A creature, esp. a domestic animal. [Var of CREATURE.]
croak (krōk) *v.* **1.** To utter a low, hoarse sound, as a frog or crow. **2.** To speak with a low, hoarse voice. **3.** *Slang.* To die. —*n.* A croaking sound. [ME *croken* (imit).] —**croak'er** *n.* —**croak'i•ly** *adv.* —**croak'y** *adj.*
cro•chet (krō-shā') *v.* **-cheted** (-shād'), **-cheting** (-shā'ĭng). To make (a piece of needlework) by looping thread with a hooked needle. —*n.* Needlework made by crocheting. [< OF *croc(he),* a hook.]
crock (krŏk) *n.* An earthenware vessel. [< OE *crocca.*]
crock•er•y (krŏk'ə-rē) *n.* Earthenware.
croc•o•dile (krŏk'ə-dīl') *n.* A large tropical aquatic reptile with armorlike skin, sharp teeth, and long, narrow jaws. [< Gk *krokodilos,* "worm of the pebbles."]
cro•cus (krō'kəs) *n., pl.* **-cuses** or **-ci** (-sī'). A garden plant with showy, variously colored early-blooming flowers. [< Gk *krokos,* saffron.]
crois•sant (krwä-säɴ') *n.* A rich crescent-shaped roll. [< OF, crescent.]
Crom•well (krŏm'wĕl', -wəl, krŭm'-), **Oliver.** 1599–1658. English statesman and general; Lord Protector of the Commonwealth (1653–58).
crone (krōn) *n.* A withered old woman. [< MDu *caroonje,* old ewe, dead body.]
cro•ny (krō'nē) *n., pl.* **-nies.** A close friend or companion. [Earlier *chrony,* "old companion."]
crook (krŏŏk) *n.* **1.** Something bent or curved; a hooked part. **2.** A bent or curved implement. **3.** A swindler; thief. —*v.* To curve; bend. [< ON *krōkr,* a hook.]
crook•ed (krŏŏk'ĭd) *adj.* **1.** Having bends or curves. **2.** Dishonest; fraudulent. **3.** Misshapen. —**crook'ed•ly** *adv.*
croon (krōōn) *v.* To sing or hum (a song) softly. —*n.* A crooning sound. [< MDu *krōnen,* to groan, lament.] —**croon'er** *n.*
crop (krŏp) *n.* **1. a.** Agricultural produce. **b.** A specific yield of such produce. **2.** A short haircut. **3.** A short riding whip. **4.** A pouchlike enlargement of a bird's esophagus, in which food is partially digested. —*v.* **cropped, cropping.** **1.** To cut off the ends of. **2.** To cut very short. **3.** To reap; harvest. —**crop up** (or **out**). To appear unexpectedly. [< OE *cropp,* cluster, bunch, ear of corn.]
cro•quet (krō-kā') *n.* An outdoor game in which wooden balls are driven through a series of wickets. [Perh < F *crochet,* a hook.]
cro•quette (krō-kĕt') *n.* A small cake of minced food fried in deep fat. [< F *croquer,* to crunch, crack (imit).]
cro•sier (krō'zhər) *n.* Also **cro•zier.** A bishop's staff. [< OF *crosse,* bishop's staff.]
cross (krôs, krŏs) *n.* **1.** An upright post with a transverse piece near the top. **2.** A symbolic representation of the cross on which Jesus was crucified. **3.** A trial or affliction. **4.** A pattern formed by two intersecting lines. **5. a.** A hybrid plant or animal. **b.** The process of hybridization. —*v.* **1.** To go or extend across. **2.** To intersect. **3.** To draw a line across. **4.** To place crosswise. **5.** To thwart or obstruct. **6.** To breed by hybridizing. —*adj.* **1.** Lying crosswise. **2.** Contrary or opposing. **3.** Irritable; annoyed. **4.** Crossbred; hybrid. [< L *crux (cruc-).*] —**cross'ness** *n.*
cross•bar (krôs'bär', krŏs'-) *n.* A horizontal bar or line.
cross•beam (krôs'bēm', krŏs'-) *n.* A transverse beam, as a joist.
cross•bones (krôs'bōnz', krŏs'-) *n.* A representation of two bones placed crosswise, usually under a skull.
cross•bow (krôs'bō', krŏs'-) *n.* A medieval weapon consisting of a bow fixed crosswise on a stock.
cross•breed (krôs'brēd', krŏs'-) *v.* To hybridize. —*n.* A hybrid.
cross-coun•try (krôs'kŭn'trē, krŏs'-) *adj.* **1.** Moving across open country rather than roads. **2.** From one side of a country to the opposite side.
cross•cur•rent (krôs'kûr'ənt, krŏs'-) *n.* **1.** A current flowing across another. **2.** A conflicting tendency.
cross•cut (krôs'kŭt', krŏs'-) *v.* To cut or run crosswise. —*adj.* **1.** Used for cutting crosswise: *a crosscut saw.* **2.** Cut across the grain. —*n.* A transverse course or cut.
cross-ex•am•ine (krôs'ĭg-zăm'ĭn, krŏs'-) *v.* To question (someone) closely, esp. to compare the resulting answers with previous responses. —**cross'-ex•am'i•na'tion** *n.*
cross-eye (krôs'ī', krŏs'ī') *n.* A form of strabismus in which one or both eyes deviate toward the nose. —**cross'-eyed'** *adj.*
cross•hatch (krôs'hăch', krŏs'-) *v.* To shade with sets of intersecting parallel lines.
cross•ing (krôs'ĭng, krŏs'-) *n.* **1.** An intersection, as of roads. **2.** The place at which something, as a river, can be crossed.
cross•piece (krôs'pēs', krŏs'-) *n.* A transverse piece, as of a structure.
cross-pol•li•nate (krôs'pŏl'ə-nāt', krŏs'-) *v.* To fertilize (a plant or flower) with pollen from another. —**cross'-pol'li•na'tion** *n.*
cross-re•fer (krôs'rĭ-fûr', krŏs'-) *v.* To refer from one part of a book, index, etc., to another. —**cross'-ref'er•ence** *n.*
cross•road (krôs'rōd', krŏs'-) *n.* **1.** A road that intersects another. **2. crossroads.** A place where roads meet.
cross section. **1.** A section formed by a plane cutting through an object, usually at right angles to an axis. **2.** A piece so cut or a graphic representation of it. **3.** A representative sample. —**cross'-sec'tion•al** *adj.*
cross•talk (krôs'tôk', krŏs'-) *n.* Interference noise on a telephone or other electronic receiver.
cross•walk (krôs'wôk', krŏs'-) *n.* A street crossing marked for pedestrians.
cross•wise (krôs'wīz', krŏs'-) *adv.* Also **cross•ways** (-wāz'). Across; running transversely.
crotch (krŏch) *n.* The angle or fork formed by the junction of parts, as by two branches or legs. [Poss a var of CRUTCH.] —**crotched** (krŏcht) *adj.*
crotch•et (krŏch'ĭt) *n.* An odd or whimsical notion. [< OF *crochet,* small hook.] —**crotch'et•i•ness** *n.* —**crotch'et•y** *adj.*
crouch (krouch) *v.* **1.** To stoop with the limbs close to the body. **2.** To cringe. [< OF *crochir,* to be bent.] —**crouch** *n.*
croup (krōōp) *n.* A pathological condition affecting the larynx in children, characterized by respiratory difficulty and a harsh cough. [Prob imit of coughing.]
crou•pi•er (krōō'pē-ər, -pē-ā') *n.* An attendant at a gaming table who collects and pays bets. [F, orig "rider on the rump (behind another rider)."]
crou•ton (krōō'tŏn', krōō-tŏn') *n.* A cube of toasted bread. [< L *crusta,* CRUST.]
crow[1] (krō) *n.* A large, glossy black bird with a

raucous call. [< OE *crāwe.* See **ger-²**.]

crow² (krō) *v.* **1. crowed** or **crew.** To utter the shrill cry of a rooster. **2.** To boast; exult. **3.** To make a sound expressive of pleasure. —*n.* **1.** The cry of a rooster. **2.** An inarticulate sound expressive of pleasure or delight. [< OE *crāwan.* See **ger-²**.]

Crow (krō) *n., pl.* **Crow** or **Crows. 1.** A member of a tribe of Siouan-speaking Indians of SE Montana. **2.** The language of this tribe.

crow•bar (krō'bär') *n.* A metal bar used as a lever.

crowd (kroud) *n.* **1.** A large number of persons or things gathered together; throng. **2.** A clique. —*v.* **1.** To gather in numbers. **2.** To press or shove; push. **3.** To cram tightly together. [< OE *crūdan,* to hasten. See **greut-**.] —**crowd'er** *n.*

crow•foot (krō'fo͝ot') *n., pl.* **-foots.** Any of various plants of the family that includes the buttercups.

crown (kroun) *n.* **1.** A head covering worn as a symbol of sovereignty. **2.** The power of a monarch. **3.** A wreath worn on the head as a symbol of victory. **4.** Anything resembling a crown in shape or position. **5.** The top of the head. **6.** A former British coin. **7.** The highest point of anything. **8.** The part of a tooth that is covered by enamel and projects beyond the gum line. —*v.* **1.** To put a crown upon. **2.** To invest with regal power. **3.** To confer honor upon. **4.** To surmount or be the highest part of. [< L *corōna,* garland, wreath.]

crown colony. A British colony, usually having an appointed governor, in which the sovereign has complete control of legislation.

crown prince. The heir apparent to a throne.

crow's-nest (krōz'nĕst') *n.* A lookout platform near the top of a ship's mast.

cro•zier. Variant of **crosier.**

cru•ces. Alternate *pl.* of **crux.**

cru•cial (kro͞o'shəl) *adj.* **1.** Of decisive importance. **2.** Difficult; trying. [< L *crux (cruc-),* CROSS.] —**cru'cial•ly** *adv.*

cru•ci•ble (kro͞o'sə-bəl) *n.* A vessel made of a refractory substance, used for melting materials at high temperatures. [ME *crusible.*]

cru•ci•fix (kro͞o'sə-fĭks') *n.* An image of Christ on the cross. [< LL *crucifigere,* CRUCIFY.]

cru•ci•fix•ion (kro͞o'sə-fĭk'shən) *n.* **1.** The act of crucifying. **2.** A representation of Christ on the cross. **3. the Crucifixion.** The crucifying of Christ.

cru•ci•form (kro͞o'sə-fôrm') *adj.* Cross-shaped.

cru•ci•fy (kro͞o'sə-fī') *v.* **-fied, -fying. 1.** To put to death by nailing or binding to a cross. **2.** To torment; torture. [< LL *crucifigere.*]

crude (kro͞od) *adj.* **cruder, crudest. 1.** In an unrefined or natural state; raw. **2.** Lacking finish, tact, or taste. **3.** Roughly made. [< L *crūdus,* bloody, raw.] —**crude'ly** *adv.* —**cru'di•ty, crude'ness** *n.*

crude oil. Petroleum.

cru•el (kro͞o'əl) *adj.* Causing pain or suffering; merciless. [< L *crūdēlis,* morally unfeeling, cruel.] —**cru'el•ly** *adv.* —**cru'el•ty** *n.*

cru•et (kro͞o'ĭt) *n.* A glass bottle for holding vinegar or oil at the table. [< OF *crue,* flask.]

cruise (kro͞oz) *v.* **cruised, cruising. 1.** To sail or travel over or about, as for pleasure. **2.** To travel at a speed providing maximum operating efficiency. —*n.* A sea voyage for pleasure. [Perh < Du *kruisen,* to sail to and fro.]

cruis•er (kro͞o'zər) *n.* **1.** One of a class of fast warships of medium tonnage. **2.** A large motorboat whose cabin has living facilities. **3.** A police squad car.

crul•ler (krŭl'ər) *n.* A small cake of twisted sweet dough fried in deep fat. [< Du *krullen,* to curl.]

crumb (krŭm) *n.* **1.** A small piece broken or fallen, as from bread. **2.** Any fragment or scrap. —*v.* **1.** To break into crumbs. **2.** To cover with bread crumbs. [< OE *cruma.*]

crum•ble (krŭm'bəl) *v.* **-bled, -bling.** To break or fall into small parts or crumbs.

crum•pet (krŭm'pĭt) *n. Chiefly Brit.* A soft, muffinlike bread baked on a griddle. [Prob < ME *crompid (cake),* "curled cake."]

crum•ple (krŭm'pəl) *v.* **-pled, -pling. 1.** To crush together into wrinkles. **2.** To collapse.

crunch (krŭnch) *v.* **1.** To chew with a noisy, grinding sound. **2.** To crush noisily. [Imit.] —**crunch** *n.*

cru•sade (kro͞o-sād') *n.* **1.** Often **Crusade.** Any of the Christian military expeditions in the 11th, 12th, and 13th centuries to recover the Holy Land. **2.** Any zealous movement for a cause. —*v.* **-saded, -sading.** To engage in a crusade. [< L *crux,* CROSS.] —**cru•sad'er** *n.*

crush (krŭsh) *v.* **1.** To mash or squeeze so as to break or injure. **2.** To break, pound, or grind. **3.** To extract or obtain by pressure. **4.** To shove or crowd. **5.** To overwhelm; subdue. —*n.* **1.** The act of crushing. **2.** A great crowd. **3.** *Informal.* An infatuation. [< OF *croissir.*]

crust (krŭst) *n.* **1.** The hard outer part of bread. **2.** A piece of bread consisting mostly of this part. **3.** Any hard, crisp covering or surface. —*v.* To cover or become covered with a crust. [< L *crusta,* shell.] —**crust'y** *adj.*

crus•ta•cean (krŭ-stā'shən) *n.* Any of various chiefly aquatic arthropods having a segmented body with a hard outer covering, as a lobster, crab, or shrimp. [< NL *crustacea,* "the shelled ones."]

crutch (krŭch) *n.* **1.** A support used as an aid in walking, usually having a crosspiece to fit under the armpit. **2.** Anything depended upon for support. [< OE *crycc.*]

crux (krŭks, kro͝oks) *n., pl.* **cruxes** or **cruces** (kro͞o'sēz). **1.** A critical or crucial point. **2.** A puzzling problem. [L, CROSS.]

Crux (krŭks) *n.* A constellation in the S Hemisphere; Southern Cross.

cru•zei•ro (kro͞o-zâ'rō, -ro͞o) *n., pl.* **-ros.** The basic monetary unit of Brazil.

cry (krī) *v.* **cried, crying. 1.** To make inarticulate sobbing sounds; weep. **2.** To utter loudly; shout. **3.** To utter a characteristic sound or call, as an animal does. **4.** To proclaim in public. —*n., pl.* **cries. 1.** A loud utterance of emotion. **2.** Any loud utterance; shout. **3.** A fit of weeping. **4.** An urgent appeal. **5.** The characteristic call of an animal. —**a far cry.** A long way. [< OF *crier.*]

cry•ba•by (krī'bā'bē) *n.* One who cries or complains frequently with little cause.

cry•ing (krī'ĭng) *adj.* Demanding immediate action: *a crying need.*

cry•o•gen•ics (krī'ō-jĕn'ĭks) *n. (takes sing. v.).* The science of low-temperature phenomena. [< Gk *kruos,* frost.] —**cry'o•gen'ic** *adj.*

crypt (krĭpt) *n.* **1.** An underground chamber, esp. one used as a burial place. **2.** *Anat.* Any of various small pits, recesses, glandular cavities, or follicles in the body. [< Gk *kruptos,* hidden.]

cryp•tic (krĭp'tĭk) *adj.* Secret; enigmatic; mystifying. [< Gk *kruptos,* hidden.]

crypto–. *comb. form.* Hidden or secret. [< Gk *kruptos,* hidden.]

cryp•to•gram (krĭp'tə-grăm') *n.* Something written in code or cipher.

cryp•tog•ra•phy (krĭp-tŏg'rə-fē) *n.* The art of writing in or deciphering secret code. —**cryp•tog'ra•pher** *n.*

crys•tal (krĭs'təl) *n.* **1. a.** A three-dimensional atomic, ionic, or molecular structure of periodically repeated, identically constituted, congruent unit cells. **b.** The unit cell of such a structure. **2.** A body, as a piece of quartz, having such a structure. **3.** Anything similar to crystal, as in transparency. [< Gk *krustallos.*] —**crys'tal•line** *adj.*

crys•tal•lize (krĭs'tə-līz') *v.* **-lized, -lizing. 1.** To form or cause to form a crystalline structure. **2.** To assume or cause to assume a definite and permanent form. —**crys'tal•li•za'tion** *n.*

crys•tal•log•ra•phy (krĭs'tə-lŏg'rə-fē) *n.* The science of crystal structure and phenomena. —**crys'tal•log'ra•pher** *n.*

Cs cesium.

C.S. 1. chief of staff. **2.** Christian Science; Christian Scientist. **3.** civil service.

CST, C.S.T. Central Standard Time.

C.T. Central Time.

ct. 1. cent. **2.** court.

ctf. certificate.

ctn. carton.

ctr. center.

Cu copper (L *cuprum*).

cu. cubic.

cub (kŭb) *n.* **1.** A young bear, wolf, lion, etc. **2.** A novice, as in newspaper reporting. [?]

Cu•ba (kyo͞o'bə). An island republic in the Caribbean. Pop. 7,256,000. Cap. Havana. —**Cu'ban** *adj.* & *n.*

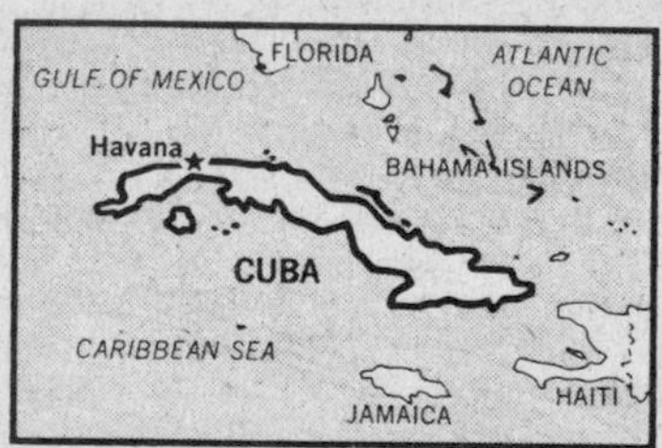

Cuba

cub•by•hole (kŭb'ē-hōl') *n.* A small compartment. [< Du *kubbe,* basket.]

cube (kyo͞ob) *n.* **1.** A regular solid having six congruent square faces. **2.** The third power of a number or quantity. —*v.* **cubed, cubing. 1.** To raise to the third power, as a number or quantity. **2.** To form or cut into cubes or the shape of a cube. [< L *cubus* < Gk *kubos.*]

cu•bic (kyo͞o'bĭk) *adj.* **1.** Having the shape of a cube. **2. a.** Having three dimensions. **b.** Having volume equal to a cube whose edge is of a stated length. **3.** Of the third power, order, or degree.

cu•bi•cle (kyo͞o'bĭ-kəl) *n.* A small compartment. [L *cubiculum,* sleeping chamber.]

cub•ism (kyo͞o'bĭz'əm) *n.* An early 20th-century school of painting and sculpture tending through geometrical reduction of natural forms to establish independence of all imitative intention. —**cub'ist** *adj.* & *n.*

cu•bit (kyo͞o'bĭt) *n.* An ancient unit of linear measure, approx. 17 to 22 inches. [< L *cubitum,* cubit, elbow.]

cuck•old (kŭk'əld) *n.* A man whose wife has committed adultery. —*v.* To make a cuckold of. [< OF *cucu,* cuckoo.]

cuck•oo (ko͞o'ko͞o, ko͝ok'o͞o) *n.* **1.** An Old

World bird with grayish plumage and a characteristic two-note call. **2.** Any of various related birds. *—adj. Slang.* Demented; foolish. [ME *cuccu* (imit).]

cu•cum•ber (kyōō'kŭm'bər) *n.* The long, green-skinned, white-fleshed fruit of a sprawling vine, used in salads and for pickling. [< L *cucumis.*]

cud (kŭd) *n.* Food regurgitated from the first stomach to the mouth of a ruminant and chewed again. [< OE *cwudu, cudu.*]

cud•dle (kŭd'l) *v.* **-dled, -dling. 1.** To fondle; hug. **2.** To nestle; snuggle. [?]

cudg•el (kŭj'əl) *n.* A short, heavy club. *—v.* To beat with a cudgel. [< OE *cycgel.*]

cue[1] (kyōō) *n.* The long, tapered rod used to propel a billiard ball. [F *queue,* "tail."]

cue[2] (kyōō) *n.* **1.** A signal to begin or enter, as in a play. **2.** A reminder. [?] **—cue** *v.* **(cued, cuing).**

cuff[1] (kŭf) *n.* **1.** A fold at the bottom of a sleeve. **2.** The turned-up fold at the bottom of a trouser leg. **—off the cuff.** *Informal.* Extemporaneously. [ME *cuffe,* glove, mitten.]

cuff[2] (kŭf) *v.* To strike with the hand; slap. [?] **—cuff** *n.*

cuff links. A pair of linked buttons used to fasten shirt cuffs.

cui•rass (kwĭ-răs') *n.* A piece of armor for the breast and back. [< VL **coriāca,* "leather buckler."]

cui•sine (kwĭ-zēn') *n.* A characteristic style of preparing food. [< LL *coquīna,* a kitchen, cookery.]

cul-de-sac (kŭl'dĭ-săk', kōōl'-) *n., pl.* **cul-de-sacs. 1.** A dead-end street. **2.** An impasse. [F, "bottom of the sack," blind alley.]

-cule. *comb. form.* Smallness: **molecule.** [< L *-culus, -cula, -culum.*]

cu•li•nar•y (kyōō'lə-nĕr'ē, kŭl'ə-) *adj.* Of kitchens or cookery. [< L *culīna,* kitchen.]

cull (kŭl) *v.* **1.** To pick out from others; select. **2.** To gather; collect. [< L *colligere,* to COLLECT.] **—cull'er** *n.*

cul•mi•nate (kŭl'mə-nāt') *v.* **-nated, -nating.** To reach the highest point or degree; climax. [< L *culmen (culmin-),* top, summit.] **—cul'mi•na'tion** *n.*

cul•pa•ble (kŭl'pə-bəl) *adj.* Responsible for wrong or error; blameworthy. [< L *culpāre,* to blame.] **—cul'pa•bil'i•ty** *n.* **—cul'pa•bly** *adv.*

cul•prit (kŭl'prĭt) *n.* A person charged with or found guilty of a crime. [< the 17th-century legal phrase *"Culprit,* how will you be tryed?"]

cult (kŭlt) *n.* **1.** A system or community of religious worship. **2.** Obsessive devotion to a person or ideal. [< L *cultus,* cultivation, a laboring, worship.] **—cul'tic** *adj.*

cul•ti•vate (kŭl'tə-vāt') *v.* **-vated, -vating. 1.** To improve and prepare (land) for raising crops. **2.** To grow or tend, as a plant or crop. **3.** To form and refine, as by education. **4.** To seek the acquaintance or good will of. [< L *cultus,* pp of *colere,* to till, cultivate.] **—cul'ti•va'tion** *n.* **—cul'ti•va'tor** *n.*

cul•ture (kŭl'chər) *n.* **1.** Cultivation of the soil. **2.** The raising of animals or growing of plants, esp. to improve stock. **3.** A growth or colony of microorganisms in a nutrient medium. **4.** The totality of socially transmitted behavior patterns characteristic of a people. **5.** A style of social and artistic expression peculiar to a society or class. **6.** Intellectual and artistic activity. *—v.* **-tured, -turing. 1.** To cultivate. **2.** To develop in a culture medium, as microorganisms or tissues. [< L *cultus,* cultivation.] **—cul'tur•al** *adj.* **—cul'tur•al•ly** *adv.*

cul•vert (kŭl'vərt) *n.* A drain crossing under a road or embankment. [?]

cum•ber (kŭm'bər) *v.* To weigh down; hamper. [Perh < OF *combre,* hindrance.]

cum•ber•some (kŭm'bər-səm) *adj.* Unwieldy; burdensome. **—cum'ber•some•ness** *n.*

cum•in (kŭm'ĭn) *n.* **1.** The aromatic seeds of an Old World plant, used as a condiment. **2.** The plant itself. [< Gk *kuminon.*]

cum lau•de (kōōm lou'də, lou'dē, kŭm lô'dē). With honor. [NL, "with praise."]

cum•mer•bund (kŭm'ər-bŭnd') *n.* A broad, pleated sash worn as a waistband, esp. by men. [Hindi *kamarband.*]

cu•mu•la•tive (kyōōm'yə-lā'tĭv, -yə-lə-tĭv) *adj.* Increasing by successive addition. [< L *cumulus,* heap.] **—cu'mu•la'tive•ly** *adv.*

cu•mu•lo•nim•bus (kyōōm'yə-lō-nĭm'bəs) *n., pl.* **-buses** or **-bi** (-bī'). An extremely dense, vertically developed cumulus with a relatively hazy outline and a glaciated top, usually producing heavy rains, thunderstorms, or hailstorms.

cu•mu•lus (kyōōm'yə-ləs) *n., pl.* **-li** (-lī'). A dense white, fluffy, flat-based cloud with a multiple rounded top and a well-defined outline. [< L, heap, mass.]

cun•dum. Variant of **condom.**

cu•ne•i•form (kyōō'nē-ə-fôrm', kyōō-nē'-) *adj.* Wedge-shaped, as the characters used in ancient Mesopotamian writings. *—n.* Cuneiform writing. [< L *cuneus,* wedge + -FORM.]

cun•ning (kŭn'ĭng) *adj.* **1.** Shrewd; crafty. **2.** Exhibiting ingenuity. *—n.* **1.** Skill in deception. **2.** Expertness; dexterity. [Perh < OE *cunnan,* to know. See **gnō-.**] **—cun'ning•ly** *adv.*

cup (kŭp) *n.* **1.** A small, open container used for drinking. **2.** A measure of capacity equal to $1/2$ pint, 8 ounces, or 16 tablespoons. **3.** Anything resembling a cup. *—v.* **cupped, cupping.** To shape like a cup: *cup one's hand.* [< OE *cuppe* < LL *cuppa,* drinking vessel.]

cup•board (kŭb'ərd) *n.* A closet or cabinet, usually with shelves for storing food, crockery, etc.

cup•cake (kŭp'kāk') *n.* A small, cup-shaped cake.

cu•pid•i•ty (kyōō-pĭd'ə-tē) *n.* Avarice; greed. [< L *cupere,* to desire.]

cu•po•la (kyōō'pə-lə) *n.* A small, usually domed structure surmounting a roof. [< L *cūpa,* tub, vat.]

cur (kûr) *n.* **1.** A mongrel dog. **2.** A base person. [Perh < ON *kurra,* to growl.]

cur. 1. currency. **2.** current.

cu•ra•çao (kyŏŏr'ə-sō') *n.* A liqueur flavored with orange peel. [< *Curaçao,* island in the Caribbean.]

cu•ra•re (kōō-rär'ē, kyōō-) *n.* Also **cu•ra•ri, u•ra•ri** (ōō-rär'ē, yōō-). A resinous extract obtained from various South American trees, used medicinally as a muscle relaxant and by some South American Indians as an arrow poison. [< Cariban *kurari.*]

cu•rate (kyŏŏr'ĭt) *n.* **1.** A clergyman who has charge of a parish. **2.** A clergyman who assists a rector or vicar. [< ML *cūrātus,* "one having a (spiritual) cure."]

cur•a•tive (kyŏŏr'ə-tĭv) *adj.* Serving or tending to cure. *—n.* A remedy.

cu•ra•tor (kyōō-rā'tər, kyŏŏr'ə-tər) *n.* The director of a museum, library, or similar institution. [< L *cūrāre,* to take care of.]

curb (kûrb) *n.* **1.** Anything that checks or restrains. **2.** Also *Brit.* **kerb.** A concrete or stone edging along a sidewalk. **3.** A chain or strap serving in conjunction with the bit to restrain a horse. *—v.* **1.** To check or restrain. **2.** To furnish with a curb. [< OF *courbe,* a curved object, horse's bit.] **—curb'er** *n.*

curb•stone (kûrb'stōn') *n.* A row of stones that constitutes a curb.

curd (kûrd) *n.* Often **curds.** The coagulated part of milk, used to make cheese. [ME *curd, crudde.*]

cur•dle (kûrd'l) *v.* **-dled, -dling.** To become or cause to become curd; coagulate; thicken. [Freq of CURD.]

cure (kyŏŏr) *n.* **1.** Restoration of health. **2.** A medical treatment or drug used to restore health. *—v.* **cured, curing. 1.** To restore to health. **2.** To rid of (disease). **3.** To process so as to prepare, preserve, or finish (a substance). [< L *cūra,* care, charge, healing.] **—cur'a•ble** *adj.* **—cure'less** *adj.* **—cur'er** *n.*

cure-all (kyŏŏr'ôl') *n.* Something that cures all diseases or evils; panacea.

cu•ret•tage (kyŏŏr'ə-täzh', kyōō-rĕt'ĭj) *n.* Surgical scraping of a bodily cavity. [< F *curer,* to cure.]

cur•few (kûr'fyōō) *n.* A regulation enjoining specified classes of the population to retire from the streets at a prescribed hour. [< OF *cuevrefeu,* "a covering of the fire."]

cu•ri•a (kyŏŏr'ē-ə) *n., pl.* **curiae** (kyŏŏr'ē-ē'). Often **Curia.** The central administration of the Roman Catholic Church. [L *cūria,* curia, council.]

cu•rie (kyŏŏr'ē, kyōō-rē') *n.* A unit of radioactivity, the amount of any nuclide that undergoes exactly 3.7 x 10^{10} radioactive disintegrations per second. [< M. *Curie* (1867–1934), Polish-born French chemist.]

cu•ri•o (kyŏŏr'ē-ō') *n., pl.* **-os.** An unusual object of art or bric-a-brac. [Short for CURIOSITY.]

cu•ri•os•i•ty (kyŏŏr'ē-ŏs'ə-tē) *n., pl.* **-ties. 1.** A desire to know or learn. **2.** That which arouses interest, as by being novel.

cu•ri•ous (kyŏŏr'ē-əs) *adj.* **1.** Eager to know or learn. **2.** Prying; nosy. **3.** Singular; odd. [< L *cūriōsus,* careful, diligent, inquisitive.] **—cu'ri•ous•ly** *adv.* **—cu'ri•ous•ness** *n.*

cu•ri•um (kyŏŏr'ē-əm) *n. Symbol* **Cm** A silvery, metallic synthetic radioactive element. Atomic number 96, longest-lived isotope Cm 247. [< M. *Curie* and her husband Pierre. See **curie.**]

curl (kûrl) *v.* **1.** To form or be twisted into ringlets, as the hair. **2.** To assume or be formed into any curved or coiled shape. *—n.* **1.** Something with a spiral or coiled shape. **2.** A ringlet of hair. [< MDu *crulle,* curly.] **—curl'i•ness** *n.* **—curl'y** *adj.*

cur•lew (kûrl'yōō, kûr'lōō) *n.* A long-billed brownish, long-legged shore bird. [< OF *courlieu.*]

curl•i•cue (kûr'lĭ-kyōō') *n.* A fancy twist or flourish, as in a signature. [CURLY + CUE[1].]

cur•rant (kûr'ənt) *n.* **1. a.** The small, sour fruit of various prickly shrubs. **b.** A shrub bearing such fruit. **2.** A small, seedless raisin. [ME *(raysons of) coraunte,* (raisins of) *Corinth,* city of Greece.]

cur•ren•cy (kûr'ən-sē) *n., pl.* **-cies. 1.** Any form of money in circulation. See *Table of Currency* on following pages. **2.** Common acceptance; prevalence.

cur•rent (kûr'ənt) *adj.* **1.** Belonging to the time now passing; now in progress. **2.** Commonly accepted; prevalent. *—n.* **1.** A steady and smooth onward movement, as of water. **2.** The part of any body of liquid or gas that has a continuous onward movement. **3.** A general tendency. **4. a.** A flow of electric charge. **b.**

The amount of electric charge flowing past a specified circuit point per unit time. [< L *currere,* to run.] —**cur'rent•ly** *adv.*

cur•ric•u•lum (kə-rĭk'yə-ləm) *n., pl.* **-la** (-lə) or **-lums. 1.** All the courses of study offered by a school. **2.** A particular course of study. [< L, a running, course.] —**cur•ric'u•lar** *adj.*

cur•ry[1] (kûr'ē) *v.* **-ried, -rying.** To groom (a horse) with a comb or brush. —**curry favor.** To seek favor by fawning or flattery. [< OF *conreer,* to prepare, equip.]

cur•ry[2] (kûr'ē) *n., pl.* **-ries. 1.** A pungent condiment made from a powdered blend of spices. **2.** A sauce or dish seasoned with this. —*v.* **-ried, -rying.** To season with curry. [Tamil *kari,* relish, sauce.]

curse (kûrs) *n.* **1. a.** An appeal to a supernatural power for evil to befall someone or something. **b.** The evil thus invoked. **2.** A scourge. **3.** Any profane oath. —*v.* **cursed** or **curst, cursing. 1.** To invoke evil upon; damn. **2.** To bring evil upon; afflict. **3.** To utter curses (at someone or something). [< OE *curs.*] —**curs'er** *n.*

curs•ed (kûr'sĭd, kûrst) *adj.* Also **curst** (kûrst). Deserving to be cursed; detestable.

cur•sive (kûr'sĭv) *adj.* Designating writing or printing in which the letters are joined together. [ML *(scripta) cursīva,* "flowing (script)."]

cur•so•ry (kûr'sə-rē) *adj.* Hasty and superficial. [LL *cursōrius,* of running.]

curt (kûrt) *adj.* **1.** Rudely brief or abrupt. **2.** Terse; concise. [L *curtus,* cut short.] —**curt'ly** *adv.* —**curt'ness** *adj.*

cur•tail (kər-tāl') *v.* To cut short; abbreviate. [< L *curtus,* shortened.] —**cur•tail'ment** *n.*

cur•tain (kûrt'n) *n.* A piece of material hanging in a window or other opening as a decoration, shade, or screen. —*v.* To provide or shut off with or as with a curtain. [< LL *cortīna,* enclosure, curtain.]

curt•sy (kûrt'sē) *n., pl.* **-sies.** A gesture of respect made by women by bending the knees with one foot forward. [Var of COURTESY.] —**curt'sy** *v.* **(-sied, -sying).**

cur•va•ceous (kûr-vā'shəs) *adj.* Having a voluptuous figure. —**cur•va'ceous•ly** *adv.*

cur•va•ture (kûr'və-chŏŏr) *n.* A measure, amount, act, or instance of curving.

curve (kûrv) *n.* **1. a.** A line that deviates from straightness in a smooth, continuous fashion. **b.** A surface that deviates from planarity in a smooth, continuous fashion. **2.** Any relatively smooth bend in the shape or course of something. —*v.* **curved, curving.** To move in, form, or cause to form a curve. [< L *curvus,* curved.] —**curv'ed•ly** (-ĭd-lē) *adv.*

cush•ion (kŏŏsh'ən) *n.* **1.** A pad or pillow. **2.** Anything that absorbs shock. —*v.* **1.** To provide with a cushion. **2.** To protect against or absorb the shock of. [< VL **coxīnus,* "hip rest," cushion.] —**cush'ion•y** *adj.*

Cush•it•ic (kŏŏ-shĭt'ĭk) *n.* A group of Hamitic languages, including Somali. —**Cush•it'ic** *adj.*

cusp (kŭsp) *n.* A point or pointed end. [L *cuspis,* a point, spear.]

cus•pid (kŭs'pĭd) *n.* A tooth having one point; canine tooth. [Back-formation < BICUSPID.]

cus•pi•dor (kŭs'pə-dôr') *n.* A spittoon. [< L *conspuere,* to spit upon.]

cuss (kŭs) *v. Informal.* To curse. —*n.* **1.** A curse. **2.** An odd or perverse creature. [Var of CURSE.]

cus•tard (kŭs'tərd) *n.* A dessert of milk, sugar, eggs, and flavoring, cooked until set. [< L *crusta,* CRUST.]

CURRENCY

TABLE OF EXCHANGE RATES

Country	Basic Unit	Standard Subdivision	†	††
Afghanistan	afghani	100 puls	Af.	0.017
Albania	lek	100 quintars	L	0.244
Algeria	dinar	100 centimes	DA	0.256
Argentina	peso	100 centavos	$a	0.018
Australia	dollar	100 cents	$A	1.330
Austria	schilling	100 groschen	S	0.062
Bangladesh	taka	100 paise	T	0.120
Barbados	dollar	100 cents	B$	0.480
Belgium	franc	100 centimes	BF	0.029
Bolivia	peso	100 centavos	Bs	0.050
Brazil	cruzeiro	100 centavos	Cr$	0.108
Bulgaria	lev	100 stotinki	LV	0.600
Burma	kyat	100 pyas	K	0.210
Burundi	franc	100 centimes	FBu	0.013
Cambodia*				
Cameroun	franc	100 centimes	CFAF	0.004
Canada	dollar	100 cents	Can$	0.975
Central African Republic	franc	100 centimes	CFAF	0.004
Ceylon	rupee	100 cents	Cey R	0.170
Chad	franc	100 centimes	CFAF	0.004
Chile	escudo	100 centesimos	E°	0.0002
China, People's Republic of	yuan	10 chiao, 100 fen	$	0.550
China, Republic of (Taiwan)	yuan	100 cents	N.T.$	0.025
Colombia	peso	100 centavos	Col$	0.035
Congo, Republic of	franc	100 centimes	CFAF	0.004
Costa Rica	colon	100 centimos	₡	0.122
Cuba	peso	100 centavos	$	1.200
Cyprus	pound	1000 mils	£C	2.800
Czechoslovakia	koruna	100 halers	Kč	0.008
Dahomey	franc	100 centimes	CFAF	0.004
Denmark	krone	100 öre	DKr	0.187
Dominican Republic	peso	100 centavos	RD$	1.000
East Germany	ostmark	100 pfennigs	OM	0.445
Ecuador	sucre	100 centavos	S/	0.040
Egypt	pound	100 piasters	LE	2.300
El Salvador	colon	100 centavos	₡	0.400
Ethiopia	dollar	100 cents	Eth$	0.480
Finland	markka	100 pennis	Fmk	0.282
France	franc	100 centimes	Fr	0.250
Gabon	franc	100 centimes	CFAF	0.004
Gambia	dalasi	100 butut	£G	0.590
Ghana	cedi	100 pesewa	N₡	0.880
Greece	drachma	100 lepta	Dr	0.033
Guatemala	quetzal	100 centavos	Q	1.000
Guinea	syli	100 cory	S	0.048
Guyana	dollar	100 cents	G$	0.460
Haiti	gourde	100 centimes	G	0.200
Honduras	lempira	100 centavos	L	0.500
Hong Kong	dollar	100 cents	HK$	0.210
Hungary	forint	100 fillér	Ft	0.047
Iceland	krona	100 aurar	IKr	0.008
India	rupee	100 paise	R	0.120
Indonesia	rupiah	100 sen	Rp	0.002
Iran	rial	100 dinars	Rl	0.015
Iraq	dinar	1000 fils	ID	3.410
Ireland, Republic of	pound	100 pence	£Ir.	2.250
Israel	pound	100 agorot	I£	0.160
Italy	lira	100 centesimi	Lit	0.0016
Ivory Coast	franc	100 centimes	CFAF	0.004
Jamaica	dollar	100 cents	J$	1.100
Japan	yen	100 sen	¥	0.003
Jordan	dinar	1000 fils	JD	3.220
Kenya	shilling	100 cents	K Sh.	0.140
Khmer Republic	riel	100 sen	CR	0.250
Kuwait	dinar	10 dirhams	KD	3.490
Laos	kip	100 at	K	0.002
Lebanon	pound	100 piasters	L£	0.440
Liberia	dollar	100 cents	$	1.000
Libya	dinar	1000 dirhams	Din	3.380

**See* Khmer Republic †Abbreviation or Symbol ††Equivalence in U.S. Dollars, August 1975

Country	Basic Unit	Standard Subdivision	†	††
Luxembourg	franc	100 centimes	Lux. F.	0.029
Malagasy Republic	franc	100 centimes	FMG	0.004
Malawi, Republic of	kwacha	100 tambala	KW	1.200
Malaysia	dollar	100 cents	M$	0.420
Maldive Islands	rupee	100 larees	MRp	0.250
Mali	franc	100 centimes	MF	0.002
Malta	pound	100 cents	£M	2.500
Mauritania	ouguya	100 khoums	Oug	0.023
Mauritius	rupee	100 cents	MRp	0.170
Mexico	peso	100 centavos	Mex$	0.080
Mongolian People's Republic	tughrik	100 mongo	Tu.	0.297
Morocco	dirham	100 centimes	DH	0.249
Nepal	rupee	100 pice	NR	0.090
Netherlands	guilder	100 cents	Fls.	0.413
Netherlands Antilles	guilder	100 cents	C. Fls.	0.563
New Zealand	dollar	100 cents	$NZ	1.320
Nicaragua	cordoba	100 centavos	C$	0.144
Niger	franc	100 centimes	CFAF	0.004
Nigeria	niara	100 kobes	N	1.620
North Korea	won	100 jun	W	0.330
North Vietnam	dong	100 sau	D	0.339
Norway	krone	100 öre	NKr	0.205
Oman	riyal-omani	1000 baiza	R.S.	2.870
Pakistan	rupee	100 paisas	PR	0.100
Panama	balboa	100 centesimos	B	1.000
Paraguay	guarani	100 centimos	G	0.008
Peru	sol	100 centavos	S/	0.023
Philippines, Republic of the	peso	100 centavos	₱	0.140
Poland	zloty	100 groszy	Zl	0.050
Portugal	escudo	100 centavos	Esc	0.041
Qatar	riyal	100 dirhams	R	0.250
Rhodesia	dollar	100 cents	R$	0.870
Rumania	leu	100 bani	L	0.097
Rwanda	franc	100 centimes	RF	0.011
Saudi Arabia	riyal	100 halalas	SRl	0.283
Senegal	franc	100 centimes	CFAF	0.004
Sierra Leone	leone	100 cents	Le	1.180
Singapore	dollar	100 cents	S$	0.420
Somali Republic	shilling	100 cents	So. Sh.	0.160
South Africa, Republic of	rand	100 cents	R	1.400
South Korea	won	100 chon	W	0.002
South Vietnam	piaster	100 cents	VN$	0.001
Spain	peseta	100 centimos	Pta or Pts (plural)	0.179
Sudan	pound	100 piasters, 1000 milliemes	SdL	2.790
Surinam	guilder	100 cents	Sur. Fls.	0.563
Sweden	krona	100 öre	SKr	0.254
Switzerland	franc	100 centimes	SwF	0.400
Syria	pound	100 piasters	S£	0.270
Tanzania	shilling	100 cents	T. Sh.	0.140
Thailand	baht	100 satangs	B	0.050
Togo	franc	100 centimes	CFAF	0.004
Trinidad and Tobago	dollar	100 cents	TT$	0.480
Tunisia	dinar	1000 milliemes	D	2.520
Turkey	lira	100 kurus	T£	0.073
Uganda	shilling	100 cents	U. Sh.	0.140
Union of Soviet Socialist Republics	rouble	100 kopecks	R	1.449
United Kingdom of Great Britain and Northern Ireland	pound	100 pence	£	2.130
United States of America	dollar	100 cents	$	1.000
Upper Volta	franc	100 centimes	CFAF	0.004
Uruguay	peso	100 centesimos	UR$	0.0004
Venezuela	bolivar	100 centimos	B	0.232
Western Samoa	tala	100 cents	Tala	1.200
West Germany	Deutsche mark	100 pfennigs	DM	0.426
Yemen	riyal	40 bugshas	R	0.220
Yemen Democratic People's Republic	dinar	1000 fils	SYD	2.950
Yugoslavia	dinar	100 paras	Din	0.059
Zaire	zaire	100 makuta	Z	2.000
Zambia	kwacha	100 ngwee	KW	1.570

U.S.A.
50 cents

U.S.S.R.
10 kopecks

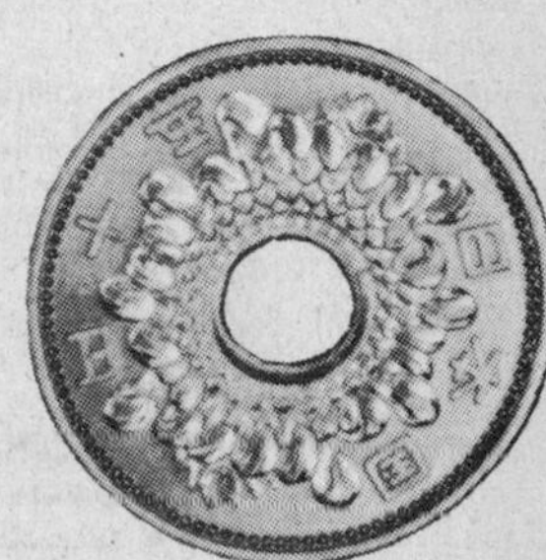
Japan
50 yen

Sweden
10 öre

Netherlands Antilles
5 cents

Spain
25 centimos

cus•to•di•an (kŭs-tō'dē-ən) *n.* **1.** One who has charge of something. **2.** A janitor.

cus•to•dy (kŭs'tə-dē) *n., pl.* **-dies. 1.** The act or right of guarding. **2.** Any state of being kept or guarded, esp. imprisonment. [< L *custōdia.*] **—cus•to'di•al** (-tō'dē-əl) *adj.*

cus•tom (kŭs'təm) *n.* **1.** A practice followed as a matter of course; a convention. **2.** A habit of an individual. **3. customs.** A duty or tax on imported goods. *—adj.* **1.** Made to order. **2.** Specializing in made-to-order goods. [< L *consuēscere,* to accustom.]

cus•tom•ar•y (kŭs'tə-mĕr'ē) *adj.* Commonly practiced or used as a matter of course; usual. **—cus'tom•ar'i•ly** *adv.*

cus•tom•er (kŭs'təm-ər) *n.* **1.** One who buys goods or services, esp. on a regular basis. **2.** *Informal.* One with whom one must deal: *a tough customer.*

cus•tom•house (kŭs'təm-hous') *n.* A building where customs are collected.

cus•tom-made (kŭs'təm-mād') *adj.* Made to the specifications of an individual buyer.

cut (kŭt) *v.* **cut, cutting. 1. a.** To penetrate with a sharp edge. **b.** To penetrate injuriously. **2.** To separate into parts with or as if with a sharp-edged instrument; sever. **3.** To have (a new tooth) grow through the gums. **4.** To fell by sawing; hew. **5.** To harvest. **6.** To form or shape by severing or incising. **7.** To intersect; cross. **8.** To reduce: *cut prices.* **9.** To shorten, trim, or pare. **10.** To allow incision: *Butter cuts easily.* **11.** To go directly or change direction abruptly. **12.** *Informal.* To fail to attend purposely: *cut a class.* **13.** *Informal.* To cease; stop. *—n.* **1.** The act or result of incising, severing, or separating. **2.** A part that has been severed from a main body: *a cut of beef.* **3.** A passage resulting from excavating or probing, as a channel. **4.** A reduction: *a salary cut.* **5.** The style in which a garment is cut. **6.** *Informal.* A share, as of earnings. **7.** *Informal.* An insult. **8.** *Informal.* An unexcused absence, as from school. **9. a.** An engraved block or plate. **b.** A print made from such a block. **—a cut above.** A little better than. [Prob < OE **cyttan.*]

cut-and-dried (kŭt'ən-drīd') *adj.* **1.** Prepared in advance. **2.** Ordinary; routine.

cu•ta•ne•ous (kyo͞o-tā'nē-əs) *adj.* Of or affecting the skin. [< L *cutis,* skin.]

cut•back (kŭt'băk') *n.* A decrease; curtailment: *a cutback in production.*

cute (kyo͞ot) *adj.* **cuter, cutest.** Delightfully pretty or dainty. [Short for ACUTE.] **—cute'ly** *adv.* **—cute'ness** *n.*

cu•ti•cle (kyo͞o'tĭ-kəl) *n.* **1.** The epidermis. **2.** The strip of hardened skin at the base of a fingernail or toenail. [< L *cutis,* skin.]

cut•lass (kŭt'ləs) *n.* A short, heavy sword with a curved blade. [< L *culter,* knife.]

cut•ler•y (kŭt'lĕr-ē) *n.* **1.** Cutting instruments. **2.** Implements used as tableware.

cut•let (kŭt'lĭt) *n.* **1.** A thin slice of meat, as of veal, from the leg or ribs. **2.** A flat croquette of chopped meat or fish. [< L *costa,* rib.]

cut•off (kŭt'ôf', -ŏf') *n.* **1.** A designated limit or point of termination. **2.** A short cut or bypass. **3.** A device for cutting off a flow of steam, water, etc.

cut-rate (kŭt'rāt') *adj.* Sold or on sale at a reduced price.

cut•ter (kŭt'ər) *n.* **1.** One who cuts, esp. in tailoring. **2.** A device that cuts. **3.** A ship's boat for transporting stores or passengers. **4.** A small, lightly armed motorboat. **5.** A small sleigh.

cut•throat (kŭt'thrōt') *n.* A murderer. *—adj.* **1.** Murderous. **2.** Relentless; merciless.

cut•ting (kŭt'ĭng) *adj.* **1.** Capable of incising or severing; sharp. **2.** Piercing and cold: *a cutting wind.* **3.** Sarcastic: *a cutting remark.* *—n.* A part cut off from a main body, esp. a shoot removed from a plant for rooting or grafting.

cut•tle•bone (kŭt'l-bōn') *n.* The chalky internal shell of a cuttlefish, used for feeding cage birds or ground into powder for use as a polishing agent.

cut•tle•fish (kŭt'l-fĭsh') *n.* A ten-armed, squidlike marine mollusk that has a chalky internal shell and secretes a dark, inky fluid. [< OE *cudele,* a cuttlefish.]

cut•up (kŭt'ŭp') *n. Informal.* A mischievous person.

c.w.o. 1. cash with order. **2.** chief warrant officer.

cwt. hundredweight.

-cy. *comb. form.* **1.** A quality or condition: **bankruptcy. 2.** Office or rank: **baronetcy.** [< L *-cia, -tia,* and Gk *-kiā, -tiā.*]

cy•a•nide (sī'ə-nīd') *n.* Also **cy•an•id** (-nĭd). Any of various compounds containing a CN group, esp. the extremely poisonous compounds potassium cyanide and sodium cyanide.

cyano-. *comb. form.* **1.** Blue or dark-blue. **2.** *Chem.* Cyanide or cyanogen. [< Gk *kuanos,* dark-blue enamel, the color blue.]

cy•an•o•gen (sī-ăn'ə-jən) *n.* A colorless, flammable, highly poisonous gas, C_2N_2, used as a rocket propellant, fumigant, and military weapon.

cy•a•no•sis (sī'ə-nō'sĭs) *n. Path.* A bluish discoloration of the skin, resulting from inadequate oxygenation of the blood. **—cy'a•not'ic** (-nŏt'ĭk) *adj.*

cy•an•o•type (sī-ăn'ə-tīp') *n.* A blueprint.

cy•ber•net•ics (sī'bər-nĕt'ĭks) *n. (takes sing. v.).* The theoretical study of control processes in electronic, mechanical, and biological systems. [< Gk *kubernan,* to steer, guide, govern.] **—cy'ber•net'ic** *adj.*

cyc•la•men (sī'klə-mən, sĭk'lə-, -mĕn) *n.* A plant with showy white, pink, or red flowers. [< Gk *kuklaminos.*]

cy•cle (sī'kəl) *n.* **1.** A time interval in which a characteristic, esp. a regularly repeated, event or sequence of events occurs. **2. a.** A single complete execution of a periodically repeated phenomenon. **b.** A periodically repeated sequence of events. **3.** A group of literary or musical works on a single theme. **4.** A bicycle or motorcycle. *—v.* **-cled, -cling. 1.** To occur in or pass through a cycle. **2.** To ride a bicycle or motorcycle. [< Gk *kuklos,* circle.]

cy•clic (sī'klĭk, sĭk'lĭk) *adj.* Also **cy•cli•cal** (-kəl). **1.** Of, relating to, or moving in cycles. **2.** Pertaining to compounds having atoms arranged in a ring or closed-chain structure. **—cy'cli•cal•ly** *adv.*

cy•clist (sī'klĭst) *n.* Also **cy•cler** (-klər). One who rides a bicycle, motorcycle, or similar vehicle.

cyclo-. *comb. form.* **1.** Circle. **2.** A cyclic compound.

cy•clo•hex•ane (sī'klō-hĕk'sān') *n.* An extremely flammable, colorless, mobile liquid, C_6H_{12}, used as a solvent, paint remover, and in making nylon.

cy•cloid (sī'kloid') *adj.* Resembling a circle. **—cy•cloi'dal** *adj.*

cy•clone (sī'klōn') *n.* **1.** A type of atmospheric disturbance characterized by masses of air rapidly circulating about a low-pressure center, usually accompanied by stormy, often destructive, weather. **2.** Loosely, any violent, rotating windstorm, such as a tornado. [Prob < Gk *kuklos,* circle, CYCLE.] **—cy•clon'ic** (-klŏn'ĭk) *adj.*

cy•clo•pe•di•a (sī'klə-pē'dē-ə) *n.* Also **cy•clo•pae•di•a.** An encyclopedia. [Short for ENCYCLOPEDIA.]

cy•clo•tron (sī'klə-trŏn') *n.* A circular accelerator in which charged particles generated at a central source are accelerated spirally outward in a plane at right angles to a fixed magnetic field by an alternating electric field.

cyg•net (sĭg'nĭt) *n.* A young swan. [< Gk *kuknos,* swan.]

Cyg•nus (sĭg'nəs) *n.* A constellation in the N Hemisphere.

cyl•in•der (sĭl'ən-dər) *n.* **1. a.** A surface generated by a straight line moving parallel to a fixed straight line and intersecting a plane curve. **b.** A solid bounded by two parallel planes and such a surface having a closed curve, esp. a circle. **2.** A chamber in which a piston moves. **3.** The rotating chamber of a revolver that holds the cartridges. [< Gk *kulindros,* roller, cylinder.] **—cy•lin'dri•cal** (sə-lĭn'drĭ-kəl) *adj.*

cym•bal (sĭm'bəl) *n.* **1.** One of a pair of brass plates struck together as percussion instruments. **2.** A single brass plate, sounded by hitting with a drumstick. [< Gk *kumbē,* hollow of a vessel, a cup.]

cyn•ic (sĭn'ĭk) *n.* One who believes all men are motivated by selfishness. [< Gk *kunikos,* "doglike," currish.] **—cyn'i•cal** *adj.* **—cyn'i•cal•ly** *adv.* **—cyn'i•cism'** (sĭn'ə-sĭz'əm) *n.*

cy•no•sure (sī'nə-sho͝or', sĭn'ə-) *n.* A center of interest, attraction, or admiration. [< Gk *kunosoura,* "the dog's tail," Ursa Minor.]

cy•press (sī'prəs) *n.* Any of various chiefly evergreen trees with small, scalelike needles. [< Gk *kuparissos.*]

Cy•prus (sī'prəs). An island republic in the E Mediterranean. Pop. 588,000. Cap. Nicosia. **—Cyp'ri•ot** (sĭp'rē-ōt), **Cyp'ri•ote** *n. & adj.*

Cyprus

Cy•ril•lic alphabet (sə-rĭl'ĭk). An old Slavic alphabet presently used in modified form for Russian and other languages.

cyst (sĭst) *n.* A pathological fluid-containing membranous sac. [< Gk *kustis,* bladder, pouch.] **—cys'tic** *adj.*

cystic fibrosis. A congenital disease of mucous glands throughout the body, usually developing during childhood and causing pancreatic insufficiency and pulmonary disorders.

-cyte. *comb. form.* A cell: **leukocyte.** [< Gk

kutos, hollow vessel.]
cyto–. *comb. form.* Cell.
cy•tol•o•gy (sī-tŏl'ə-jē) *n.* The biology of the formation, structure, and function of cells. **—cy'to•log'i•cal** *adj.* **—cy•tol'o•gist** *n.*
cy•to•plasm (sī'tə-plăz'əm) *n.* The protoplasm outside a cell nucleus. **—cy'to•plas'mic** *adj.*
cy•to•sine (sī'tō-sēn') *n.* A pyrimidine base, $C_4H_5N_3O$, that is an essential constituent of both ribonucleic and deoxyribonucleic acids.
C.Z. Canal Zone.
czar (zär) *n.* Also **tsar, tzar. 1.** A king or emperor, esp. one of the former emperors of Russia. **2.** A tyrant. **3.** *Informal.* One in authority; leader. [< Russ *tsar'.*]
cza•ri•na (zä-rē'nə) *n.* The wife of a czar; an empress of Russia.
Czech (chĕk) *n.* **1.** A native or inhabitant of Czechoslovakia. **2.** The Slavic language of these people. **—Czech** *adj.*
Czech•o•slo•va•ki•a (chĕk'ə-slō-vä'kē-ə, -văk'ē-ə). A republic of C Europe. Pop. 14,107,000. Cap. Prague. **—Czech'o•slo'vak, Czech'o•slo•vak'i•an** *adj.* & *n.*

Czechoslovakia

Dd

d, D (dē) *n.* **1.** The 4th letter of the English alphabet. **2.** The 4th in a series. **3. D** The lowest passing grade given to a student.
d deci-.
D 1. democrat; democratic. **2.** deuterium. **3.** The Roman numeral for 500. **4.** *Mus.* The 2nd tone in the scale of C major.
d. 1. date. **2.** daughter. **3.** deputy. **4.** died. **5.** dose. **6.** *Brit.* penny (L *denarius*).
D. 1. December. **2.** democrat; democratic. **3.** deputy. **4.** doctor (in academic degrees). **5.** dose. **6.** drachma. **7.** Dutch.
da deca-; deka-.
Da. Danish.
D.A. district attorney.
dab (dăb) *v.* **dabbed, dabbing. 1.** To apply with short, light strokes. **2.** To strike or hit lightly; pat. *—n.* **1.** A small amount. **2.** A quick, light pat. [ME *dabben.*]
D.A.B. Dictionary of American Biography.
dab•ble (dăb'əl) *v.* **-bled, -bling. 1.** To splash or spatter, as with liquid. **2.** To splash in liquid gently and playfully. **3.** To undertake something superficially or without serious intent. [< DAB¹.] **—dab'bler** *n.*
da ca•po (dä kä'pō, də). *Mus.* From the beginning Used as a direction to repeat a passage. [It.]
dace (dās) *n., pl.* **dace** or **daces.** A small freshwater fish related to the minnows. [< DART (< its swift motion).]
da•cha (dä'chə) *n.* A Russian country house.
dachs•hund (däks'ho͝ont', däks'ho͝ond') *n.* A small dog with a long body, drooping ears, and very short legs. [G.]
Da•cron (dā'krŏn', dăk'rŏn') *n.* A trademark for a synthetic polyester textile fiber.
dac•tyl (dăk'təl) *n.* A metrical foot of one accented syllable followed by two unaccented ones. [< Gk *daktulos,* finger.] **—dac•tyl'ic** *adj.*
dad (dăd) *n. Informal.* Father. [Of baby-talk origin.]
dad•dy (dăd'ē) *n., pl.* **-dies.** Diminutive of **dad.**
daddy long•legs (lông'lĕgz', lŏng'-) *pl.* **daddy longlegs.** A spiderlike arachnid with a small, rounded body and long, slender legs.
da•do (dā'dō) *n., pl.* **-does. 1.** The section of a pedestal between the base and crown. **2.** The lower portion of a wall, decorated differently from the upper section. [It, a die, cube.]
daf•fo•dil (dăf'ə-dĭl) *n.* A plant cultivated for its showy, usually yellow flowers with a trumpet-shaped central part. [Prob < Du *de affodil,* the asphodel.]
daf•fy (dăf'ē) *adj.* **-fier, -fiest.** *Informal.* Silly; zany. [< obs Eng *daff,* fool.]
daft (dăft, däft) *adj.* **1.** Mad; crazy. **2.** Foolish. [< OE *gedæfte,* mild, meek.]
dag decagram.
dag•ger (dăg'ər) *n.* **1.** A short, pointed weapon with sharp edges. **2.** *Ptg.* A reference mark (†). [< OF *dague.*]
dagger fern. An evergreen N American fern having dense clusters of lance-shaped fronds.
da•guerre•o•type (də-gâr'ə-tīp') *n.* A photograph made by an early process on a light sensitive silver-coated metallic plate and developed by mercury vapor. [< L. *Daguerre* (1787–1851), French artist.]
dahl•ia (dăl'yə, däl', dāl'-) *n.* A plant cultivated for its showy, variously colored flowers. [< A. *Dahl,* 18th-century Swedish botanist.]
Da•ho•mey (də-hō'mē). The former name for Benin.
da•hoon (də-ho͞on') *n.* An evergreen tree or shrub of the SE U.S., having red fruit. [?]
dai•ly (dā'lē) *adj.* Of, pertaining to, occurring, or published every day. *—n., pl.* **-lies.** A daily publication, esp. a newspaper. *—adv.* Each day. [< OE *dæg,* DAY.]
dain•ty (dān'tē) *adj.* **-tier, -tiest. 1.** Delicately beautiful. **2.** Delicious; choice. **3.** Of refined taste. **4.** Too fastidious; squeamish. *—n., pl.* **-ties.** Something delicious; a delicacy. [< L *dīgnitās,* dignity, worth.] **—dain'ti•ly** *adv.*
dair•y (dâr'ē) *n., pl.* **-ies. 1.** An establishment that processes or sells milk and milk products. **2.** A farm where milk and milk products are produced. [< OE *dæge,* female breadmaker. See **dheigh-.**] **—dair'y** *adj.*
dairy cattle. Cows bred and raised for milk rather than for meat.
dairy farm. A farm for producing milk and milk products.
dair•y•ing (dâr'ē-ĭng) *n.* The business of running or operating a dairy.
dairy lunch. Also **dairy bar.** A restaurant that serves simple dishes that are made from dairy products.
dair•y•maid (dâr'ē-mād') *n.* A female dairy worker.
da•is (dā'ĭs, dās) *n., pl.* **-ises** (-ĭ-sĭz). A raised platform, as in a lecture hall, for honored guests. [< L *discus,* dish, quoit, DISK.]
dai•sy (dā'zē) *n., pl.* **-sies.** Any of several related plants having flowers with petallike rays surrounding a central disk, esp. a common species with white rays and a yellow center. [< OE *dægesēage,* "day's eye."]
Da•kar (dä-kär', də-). The capital of Senegal. Pop. 298,000.
Da•ko•ta (də-kō'tə) *n., pl.* **-ta** or **-tas. 1.** A member of a large group of tribes of North American Plains Indians, commonly called Sioux. **2.** Their language.
Da•lai La•ma (dä-lī' lä'mə). Title of the former theocratic rulers of Tibet.
dale (dāl) *n.* A valley. [< OE *dæl.* See **dhel-.**]
da•leth (dä'ləth) *n.* The 4th letter of the Hebrew alphabet, representing *d(dh).*
Dal•las (dăl'əs). A city of NE Texas. Pop. 844,000.
dal•ly (dăl'ē) *v.* **-lied, -lying. 1.** To play amorously; flirt. **2.** To trifle; toy. **3.** To waste time. [< NF *dalier.*] **—dal'li•ance** *n.* **—dal'li•er** *n.*
Dal•ma•tian (dăl-mā'shən) *n.* A dog having a short, smooth white coat with black spots. [< *Dalmatia,* region of Yugoslavia.]
dam¹ (dăm) *n.* A barrier, esp. one constructed across a waterway to control the flow of water. *—v.* **dammed, damming. 1.** To construct a dam across. **2.** To obstruct or restrain. [ME.]
dam² (dăm) *n.* A female parent, esp. of a quadruped. [< DAME.]
dam•age (dăm'ĭj) *n.* **1.** Impairment of the usefulness or value of person or property; loss; harm. **2. damages.** *Law.* Money to be paid as compensation for injury or loss. *—v.* **-aged, -aging.** To cause injury to. [< L *damnum,* loss, harm, fine.] **—dam'ag•ing•ly** *adv.*
Da•mas•cus (də-măs'kəs). The capital of Syria. Pop. 545,000.
Damascus steel. An early form of steel having wavy markings and used chiefly in sword blades; damask steel.
dam•ask (dăm'əsk) *n.* **1.** A rich patterned fabric of cotton, silk, etc. **2.** A fine twilled table linen. **3. Damascus steel.** *—adj.* Made from damask or Damascus steel. [< ML *(pannus*

de) damasco, "(cloth of) Damascus."]

dame (dām) *n.* **1.** *Brit.* A woman's title, equivalent to that of a knight. **2.** *Slang.* A woman. [< L *dominus,* master, lord.]

damn (dăm) *v.* **1.** To criticize adversely; condemn. **2.** *Theol.* To condemn to everlasting punishment or a similar fate. **3.** To swear at by saying "damn." *—interj.* Expressive of anger or disappointment. *—n.* The saying of "damn" as a curse. *—adj.* Damned. *—adv.* Damned. [< L *damnum,* loss, damage.]

dam•na•tion (dăm-nā'shən) *n.* The act of damning or condition of being damned. *—interj.* Expressive of anger.

damned (dămd) *adj.* *Superl.* **damndest** or **damnedest.** **1.** Condemned; doomed. **2.** *Informal.* **a.** Detestable: *this damned weather.* **b.** Absolute; utter: *a damned fool.* *—adv. Informal.* Very: *a damned poor excuse.*

Dam•o•cles (dăm'ə-klēz'). A courtier forced by Dionysius the Elder, tyrant of Syracuse, to sit under a sword suspended by a single hair, to demonstrate the precariousness of a king's fortunes.

damp (dămp) *adj.* Slightly wet; moist. *—n.* **1.** Moisture; humidity. **2.** Foul or poisonous gas. *—v.* **1.** To dampen. **2.** To restrain or check. **3.** To decrease the amplitude of. [< MDu, smoke, vapor.] **—damp'ness** *n.*

damp•en (dăm'pən) *v.* **1.** To moisten or become moist. **2.** To depress.

damp•er (dăm'pər) *n.* **1.** One that restrains or depresses. **2.** An adjustable plate in a flue for controlling the draft.

dam•sel (dăm'zəl) *n.* A girl; maiden. [< L *domina,* lady, dame.]

dam•sel•fly (dăm'zəl-flī') *n.* A slender-bodied insect related to the dragonflies.

dam•son (dăm'zən, -sən) *n.* A small, oval, bluish-black plum. [< L *(prūnum) Damascēnum,* "(plum) of Damascus."]

Dan. Daniel (Old Testament).

dance (dăns, däns) *v.* **danced, dancing.** **1.** To move rhythmically to music. **2.** To leap or skip about. **3.** To bob up and down. *—n.* **1.** A series of rhythmical motions and steps, usually to music. **2.** The art of dancing. **3.** A gathering of people for dancing. **4.** Music composed for dancing. [< OF *danser, dancier.*] **—danc'er** *n.* **—danc'ing•ly** *adv.*

dan•de•li•on (dăn'də-lī'ən) *n.* A common weedy plant with many-rayed yellow flowers. [< OF *dent-de-lion,* "lion's tooth."]

dan•der (dăn'dər) *n.* *Informal.* Temper. [?]

dan•di•fy (dăn'də-fī') *v.* **-fied, -fying.** To make resemble a dandy. **—dan'di•fi•ca'tion** *n.*

dan•dle (dănd'l) *v.* **-dled, -dling.** To move (a small child) up and down on one's knees.

dan•druff (dăn'drəf) *n.* A scaly scurf formed on and shed from the scalp. [?]

dan•dy (dăn'dē) *n., pl.* **-dies.** **1.** A man who affects extreme elegance. **2.** *Informal.* Something very good or agreeable. *—adj.* **-dier, -diest.** **1.** Like or dressed like a dandy. **2.** *Informal.* Fine; good. [Perh short for *jack-a-dandy,* pert person, fop.]

Dane (dān) *n.* A native or inhabitant of Denmark or a person of Danish ancestry.

dan•ger (dān'jər) *n.* **1.** Exposure or vulnerability to harm or evil. **2.** A source or instance of peril. [ME *daunger,* power, dominion, peril, damage.]

dan•ger•ous (dān'jər-əs) *adj.* **1.** Involving danger. **2.** Able or apt to do harm. **—dan'ger•ous•ly** *adv.* **—dan'ger•ous•ness** *n.*

dan•gle (dăng'gəl) *v.* **-gled, -gling.** To hang or cause to hang loosely and swing or sway. [Perh < Dan *dangle* or Swed *dangla.*]

dangling participle. *Gram.* A participle that lacks clear connection with the word it modifies. In the sentence *Working at my desk, the sudden noise startled me, Working at my desk* is a dangling participle.

Dan•iel (dăn'yəl). Hebrew prophet during the Babylonian captivity.

Dan•ish (dā'nĭsh) *adj.* Of or pertaining to Denmark, the Danes, or their language. *—n.* The North Germanic language of the Danes.

dank (dăngk) *adj.* Uncomfortably damp; chilly and wet. [ME.] **—dank'ness** *n.*

Dan•te A•li•ghie•ri (dän'tā ä'lē-gyâ'rē). 1265–1321. Italian poet.

Dan•ube (dăn'yo͞ob). The major river of SE Europe. **—Dan•u'bi•an** (dăn-yo͞o'bē-ən) *adj.*

dap•per (dăp'ər) *adj.* **1.** Neatly dressed; trim. **2.** Small and active. [ME *dapyr,* elegant.]

dap•ple (dăp'əl) *v.* **-pled, -pling.** To mark or mottle with spots.

dare (dâr) *v.* **dared, daring.** **1.** To have the courage required for. **2.** To challenge (someone) to do something requiring boldness. **—dare say.** Also **dare•say.** To consider (it) very likely. *—n.* A challenge. [< OE *durran,* to venture, dare. See **dhers-.**]

Usage: Dare (v.) is uninflected in the third person singular in interrogative and negative sentences: *Dare he speak up? He dare not.*

dare•dev•il (dâr'dĕv'əl) *n.* One who is recklessly bold. **—dare'dev'il** *adj.*

Dar es Sa•laam (där' ĕs sə-läm'). The capital of Tanzania. Pop. 129,000.

dar•ing (dâr'ĭng) *adj.* Fearless; bold.

dark (därk) *adj.* **1.** Lacking light or brightness. **2.** Somber in color. **3.** Gloomy; threatening. **4.** Obscure; cryptic. **5.** Ignorant; uncivilized: *a dark era.* **6.** Evil; sinister. *—n.* **1.** Absence of light. **2.** Night; nightfall. **—in the dark.** **1.** Secretly. **2.** Uninformed. [< OE *deorc.* See **dher-¹.**] **—dark'ly** *adv.* **—dark'ness** *n.*

dark•en (där'kən) *v.* **1.** To make or become dark or darker. **2.** To make or become sad. **—dark'en•er** *n.*

dark horse. A little-known entrant or unexpected winner in a race or contest.

dark•room (därk'ro͞om', -ro͝om') *n.* A darkened or specially illuminated room in which photographic materials are processed.

dar•ling (där'lĭng) *n.* **1.** One who is beloved. **2.** A favorite. *—adj.* **1.** Beloved. **2.** Favorite. **3.** Charming; pleasing. [< OE *dēorling* : DEAR + -LING.]

darn¹ (därn) *v.* To mend by weaving thread across a hole. *—n.* A place repaired by darning. [F *darner.*] **—darn'er** *n.*

darn² (därn). Euphemism for **damn.**

dar•nel (där'nəl) *n.* Any of several weedy grasses.

darning needle. **1.** A long needle for darning. **2.** A dragonfly.

dart (därt) *n.* **1.** A slender, pointed missile to be thrown or shot. **2. darts** (*takes sing. v.*). A game in which darts are thrown at a target. **3.** Something dartlike in sharpness. **4.** A sudden movement. **5.** A tapered tuck, as in a garment. *—v.* To move or shoot suddenly. [< Gmc **darōdhaz,* spear.] **—dart'er** *n.*

Dar•win (där'wĭn), **Charles Robert.** 1809–1882. British naturalist; expounded theory of evolution by natural selection. **—Dar•win'i•an** *adj.* **—Dar'win•ism'** *n.*

dash (dăsh) *v.* **1.** To break; smash; destroy. **2.** To hurl, knock, or thrust violently. **3.** To splash. **4.** To perform or complete hastily (with *off*). **5.** To move with haste; rush. *—n.* **1.** A swift blow or stroke. **2.** A splash. **3.** A small amount of an ingredient. **4.** A sudden movement; rush. **5.** A short foot race. **6.** Vigor; verve. **7.** A punctuation mark (—) used to indicate a break or omission. **8.** A long sound or signal used in combination with the dot, a shorter sound, and silent intervals to represent letters or numbers. [< Scand.]

dash•board (dăsh'bôrd', -bōrd') *n.* A panel under the windshield of a car, containing indicator dials and control instruments.

dash•er (dăsh'ər) *n.* The plunger of a churn or ice-cream freezer.

dash•ing (dăsh'ĭng) *adj.* **1.** Audacious; spirited. **2.** Marked by showy elegance.

das•tard (dăs'tərd) *n.* A base, sneaking coward. [Perh < ON *dæsa,* to languish, decay.] **—das'tard•li•ness** *n.* **—das'tard•ly** *adj.*

dat. dative.

da•ta (dā'tə, dăt'ə, dä'tə) *pl.n.* *Sing.* **datum** (dā'təm, dăt'əm, dä'təm). Information, esp. information organized for analysis or computation. [< L *datum,* "something given."]

Usage: Data is now used both as a plural and as a singular collective: *These data are inconclusive. This data is inconclusive.* The plural is more appropriate in formal usage.

data processing. The processing of data by a computer.

date¹ (dāt) *n.* **1.** The particular time at which something happens. **2.** The period to which something belongs. **3.** The day of the month. **4.** An inscription or statement indicating when a thing was made or written. **5.** *Informal.* **a.** An appointment to meet socially. **b.** A person so met, esp. one of the opposite sex. **—to date.** Up to the present time. *—v.* **dated, dating.** **1.** To mark with a date, as a letter. **2.** To determine the date of. **3.** To betray the age of. **4.** To originate in a particular time in the past (with *from*). **5.** *Informal.* To make or have social engagements with (persons of the opposite sex). [< L *datus,* pp of *dare,* to give.]

date² (dāt) *n.* The sweet, oblong, edible fruit of a tropical palm tree. [< Gk *daktulos,* "finger."]

dat•ed (dā'tĭd) *adj.* **1.** Marked with a date. **2.** Old-fashioned. **—dat'ed•ness** *n.*

date•line (dāt'līn') *n.* A phrase in a newspaper or magazine article that gives the date and place of its origin.

da•tive (dā'tĭv) *adj.* Designating or belonging to a grammatical case that principally marks the indirect object of a verb. *—n.* The dative case. [< L *(cāsus) datīvus,* "(case) of giving."]

da•tum. *sing.* of **data.**

daub (dôb) *v.* **1.** To cover or smear with an adhesive substance. **2.** To paint crudely. *—n.*

Charles Darwin

1. The act or a stroke of daubing. 2. A soft adhesive coating. 3. A crude painting. [< L *dēalbāre,* to whitewash.] —**daub'er** *n.*

daugh•ter (dô'tər) *n.* 1. One's female child. 2. A female descendant. [< OE *dohtor.* See **dhughəter-**.] —**daugh'ter•ly** *adj.*

daugh•ter-in-law (dô'tər-ĭn-lô') *n., pl.* **daugh-ters-in-law.** The wife of one's son.

daunt (dônt, dänt) *v.* 1. To intimidate. 2. To discourage. [< L *domāre,* to tame, subdue.]

daunt•less (dônt'lĭs, dänt'-) *adj.* Not easily intimidated or discouraged.

dau•phin (dô'fĭn) *n.* The eldest son of a king of France.

dav•en•port (dăv'ən-pôrt', -pōrt') *n.* A large sofa.

Da•vid (dā'vĭd). Second king of Judah and Israel.

Da•vis (dā'vĭs), **Jefferson.** 1808–1889. President of the Confederate States of America (1861–65).

Jefferson Davis

day•light-sav•ing time (dā'līt'sā'vĭng). Time during which clocks are set one hour or more ahead of standard time.

Day of Atonement. Yom Kippur.

day•time (dā'tīm') *n.* The time between dawn and dark. —**day'time'** *adj.*

Day•ton (dāt'n). A city of SW Ohio. Pop. 262,000.

daze (dāz) *v.* **dazed, dazing.** 1. To stun, as with a blow or shock; stupefy. 2. To dazzle, as with strong light. —*n.* A stunned or bewildered condition. [< ON *dasa.*]

daz•zle (dăz'əl) *v.* **-zled, -zling.** 1. To overpower or be overpowered with intense light. 2. To bewilder or amaze with a spectacular display. [Freq of DAZE.] —**daz'zle** *n.*

dB decibel.

dbl. double.

dc direct current.

D.C. District of Columbia.

D.C.M. Distinguished Conduct Medal.

D.D. 1. demand draft. 2. dishonorable discharge. 3. Doctor of Divinity (Latin *Divinitatis Doctor*).

D.D.S. Doctor of Dental Science; Doctor of Dental Surgery.

DDT A colorless contact insecticide, $C_{14}H_9Cl_5$, toxic to man and animals when swallowed or absorbed through the skin. [Abbr of *d(ichloro)d(iphenyl)t(richloroethane).*]

de-. *comb. form.* 1. Reversal or undoing. 2. Removal. 3. Degradation; reduction. 4. Disparagement. [< L *dē,* from.]

dea•con (dē'kən) *n.* 1. A clergyman ranking just below a priest. 2. A lay assistant to a minister. [< Gk *diakonos,* "servant."] —**dea'-con•ess** *fem.n.*

de•ac•ti•vate (dē-ăk'tə-vāt') *v.* **-vated, -vating.** To render inactive. —**de•ac'ti•va'tion** *n.*

dead (dĕd) *adj.* 1. No longer alive; lifeless. 2. Inanimate. 3. Lacking feeling; unresponsive. 4. No longer in existence or use. 5. Devoid of animation or interest. 6. Not productive. 7. Weary and worn-out. 8. Lacking some important or previously evident quality. 9. Suggestive of the finality of death. 10. Exact; unerring: *dead center.* 11. a. Lacking connection to a source of electric current. b. Discharged, as a battery. —*n.* A period of greatest intensity: *the dead of winter.* —*adv.* 1. Absolutely; altogether. 2. Directly; exactly. [< OE *dēad.* See **dheu-³**.]

dead•beat (dĕd'bēt') *n. Slang.* 1. One who does not pay his debts. 2. A lazy or lethargic person.

dead•en (dĕd'n) *v.* 1. To render less sensitive, intense, or vigorous. 2. To make soundproof.

dead heat. A race in which two or more contestants finish at the same time; a tie.

dead letter. An unclaimed or undelivered letter.

dead•line (dĕd'līn') *n.* A time limit, as for completion of an assignment.

dead•lock (dĕd'lŏk') *n.* A standstill resulting from the opposition of two unrelenting forces. —*v.* To bring or come to a deadlock.

dead•ly (dĕd'lē) *adj.* **-lier, -liest.** 1. Causing or tending to cause death. 2. Suggestive of death. 3. Implacable; mortal. 4. Destructive in effect. 5. Absolute; unqualified. —*adv.* 1. So as to

dav•it (dăv'ĭt, dā'vĭt) *n.* Any of various small cranes used on ships to hoist boats, anchors, and cargo. [< OF *daviot.*]

daw (dô) *n.* A jackdaw. [ME *dawe.*]

daw•dle (dôd'l) *v.* **-dled, -dling.** To waste time by trifling or loitering. —**daw'dler** *n.*

dawn (dôn) *n.* 1. The first appearance of daylight in the morning. 2. A first appearance; beginning. —*v.* 1. To begin to become light in the morning. 2. To begin to appear or develop. 3. To begin to be perceived or understood (with *on* or *upon*). [< OE *dagian,* to dawn. See **agh-²**.]

day (dā) *n.* 1. The period of light between dawn and nightfall. 2. The 24-hour period during which the earth completes one rotation on its axis. 3. The portion of a day devoted to work. 4. A period of activity or prominence: *a writer who has had his day.* 5. Often **days.** A period of time; age; era. 6. The contest or issue at hand: *carry the day.* —**call it a day.** *Informal.* To stop one's work for the day. —**day in, day out.** Continuously. [< OE *dæg.* See **agh-²**.]

day•break (dā'brāk') *n.* The time each morning when light first appears; dawn.

day care. The providing of daytime supervision, training, medical services, and the like for children of preschool age or for the elderly. —**day'-care'** *adj.*

day•dream (dā'drēm') *n.* A dreamlike musing or fantasy. —*v.* To have daydreams.

day•light (dā'līt') *n.* 1. a. The light of day. b. The direct light of the sun. 2. Understanding of what was formerly obscure.

day•lights (dā'līts') *pl.n. Slang.* Life; wits: *scare the daylights out of him.*

Note: Many compounds are formed with *de-.* Normally, *de-* combines with a second element without an intervening hyphen. Exceptions include: a. a second element beginning with *e,* as *de-escalate;* b. a second element beginning with two vowels, as *de-aerate;* c. a second element beginning with a capital letter, as *de-Americanize.* The following is a list of common *de-* compounds.

de•a•cid'i•fy' *v.*
de•aer'ate' *v.*
de-'aer•a'tion *n.*
de'-A•mer'i•can•i•za'tion *n.*
de'-A•mer'i•can•ize' *v.*
de•ash' *v.*
de'as•sim'i•la'tion *n.*
de•car'bon•ate' *v.*
de•cer'ti•fi•ca'tion *n.*
de•cer'ti•fy' *v.*
de•chlor'i•nate' *v.*
de•col'or *v.*
de'col'or•a'tion *n.*
de'com•mis'sion *n.*
de•com'pen•sate' *v.*
de'com•pound' *v.*
de'con•di'tion *n.*
de'con•ges'tion *n.*
de'con•ges'tive *adj.*
de•con'se•crate' *v.*
de•em'pha•size' *v.*
de•en'er•gize' *v.*
de•es'ca•late' *v.*
de•es'ca•la'tion *n.*
de•for'est *v.*
de•horn' *v.*
de•hull' *v.*
de•hy'dro•gen•ate' *v.*
de•hy'dro•ge•na'tion *n.*
de•lam'i•na'tion *n.*
de•lam'i•nate' *v.*
de•lead' *v.*
de•lime' *v.*
de•lint' *v.*
de•lo'cal•ize' *v.*
de•louse' *v.*
de•lus'ter *v.*
de•mast' *v.*
de'ma•te'ri•al•i•za'tion *n.*
de'ma•te'ri•al•ize' *v.*
de•mes'mer•ize' *v.*
de•mount' *v.*
de•na'tion•al•i•za'tion *n.*
de•na'tion•al•ize' *v.*
de•nat'u•ral•i•za'tion *n.*
de•nat'u•ral•ize' *v.*
de•ni'trate' *v.*
de•pas'ture *v.*
de•pig'ment *v.*
de•plume' *v.*
de•po'lar•i•za'tion *n.*
de•po'lar•ize' *v.*
de•pol'ish *v.*
de•ra'tion *v.*
de•req'ui•si'tion *v.*
de're•strict' *v.*
de•salt' *v.*
de•sanc'ti•fy' *v.*
de•sat'u•rate' *v.*
de•scale' *v.*
de•sil'ver *v.*
de•size' *v.*
de•so'cial•ize' *v.*
de•soil' *v.*
de•sug'ar *v.*
de•sul'fur•i•za'tion *n.*
de•sul'fur•ize' *v.*
de•vow' *v.*
de•wool' *v.*
de•worm' *v.*

suggest death. **2.** To an extreme: *deadly earnest.* **—dead'li•ness** *n.*

dead reckoning. Essentially nonobservational navigation by computations of position based on course and distance traveled from a known position.

Dead Sea. A salt lake between Israel and Jordan, 1,302 ft. below sea level.

dead weight. **1.** The unrelieved weight of a heavy, motionless mass. **2.** An oppressive burden or difficulty.

dead•wood (dĕd'wo͝od') *n.* Anything burdensome or superfluous.

deaf (dĕf) *adj.* **1.** Partially or completely unable to hear. **2.** Unwilling or refusing to listen; heedless. [< OE *dēaf.* See **dheu-**[1].] **—deaf'ly** *adv.* **—deaf'ness** *n.*

deaf•en (dĕf'ən) *v.* To make deaf.

deaf-mute (dĕf'myo͞ot') *n.* Also **deaf mute.** One who can neither speak nor hear. **—deaf'-mute'** *adj.*

deal[1] (dēl) *v.* **dealt** (dĕlt), **dealing.** **1.** To apportion or distribute. **2.** To administer; deliver. **3.** To distribute (playing cards) among players. **4.** To be occupied or concerned; treat. **5.** To behave in a specified way toward another or others. **6.** To take action. **7.** To do business; trade. *—n.* **1.** The act of dealing. **2. a.** Cards dealt in a card game; a hand. **b.** The right or turn of a player to distribute cards. **3.** An indefinite quantity, extent, or degree. **4.** *Informal.* A secret agreement, as in politics. **5.** Any agreement or business transaction. **6.** A bargain or favorable sale. **7.** *Informal.* Treatment received, esp. as the result of an agreement. **8.** *Slang.* An important issue: *big deal.* [< OE *dǣlan,* to divide, distribute. See **dail-.**]

deal[2] (dēl) *n.* Fir or pine wood. [< MDu *dele.*]

deal•er (dē'lər) *n.* **1.** One engaged in buying and selling. **2.** One who deals the cards in a card game.

deal•ing (dē'lĭng) *n.* **1.** Often **dealings.** Transactions or relations with others. **2.** Method or manner of conduct in relation to others.

dean (dēn) *n.* **1.** An administrative officer in a university, college, or high school. **2.** The head of the chapter of canons governing a cathedral. **3.** The senior member of any body. [< LL *decānus,* "(one) set over ten."]

dean•er•y (dē'nə-rē) *n., pl.* **-ies.** The office, official residence, jurisdiction, or authority of a dean.

dear (dîr) *adj.* **1.** Beloved; precious. **2.** Highly esteemed or regarded. **3.** High-priced. *—n.* A greatly loved person; a darling. *—interj.* Expressive of surprise or distress. [< OE *dēore* < Gmc **deuriaz.*] **—dear'ly** *adj.*

Dear•born (dîr'bôrn'). A city of SE Michigan. Pop. 112,000.

dearth (dûrth) *n.* Scarcity; paucity; famine. [< DEAR.]

death (dĕth) *n.* **1.** The act of dying or state of being dead. **2.** Termination; extinction. **3.** A cause or manner of dying. [< OE *dēath.*]

death•bed (dĕth'bĕd') *n.* **1.** The bed on which a person dies. **2.** The last hours before death.

death•blow (dĕth'blō') *n.* A fatal blow or occurrence.

death•less (dĕth'lĭs) *adj.* Not subject to death; immortal. **—death'less•ness** *n.*

death•ly (dĕth'lē) *adj.* Resembling or characteristic of death; fatal. *—adv.* **1.** In the manner of death. **2.** Extremely; very.

Death Valley. A desert basin in E California and W Nevada.

death•watch (dĕth'wŏch') *n.* A vigil kept beside a dying or dead person.

de•ba•cle (dĭ-bä'kəl, -băk'əl) *n.* A sudden, disastrous overthrow or collapse; ruin. [< F *débâcler,* to unbar.]

de•bar (dē-bär') *v.* **-barred, -barring.** To exclude, forbid, or prevent. [< OF *desbarrer,* to unbar.] **—de•bar'ment** *n.*

de•bark (dĭ-bärk') *v.* To unload; disembark. [F *débarquer.*] **—de'bar•ka'tion** *n.*

de•base (dĭ-bās') *v.* **-based, -basing.** To lower in character, quality, or value; degrade.

de•bate (dĭ-bāt') *v.* **-bated, -bating.** **1.** To deliberate; consider. **2.** To discuss opposing points. **3.** To discuss or argue formally. *—n.* **1.** The act of debating. **2.** A formal contest in which two opposing teams defend and attack a given proposition. [< OF *debattre.*] **—de•bat'a•ble** *adj.* **—de•bat'er** *n.*

de•bauch (dĭ-bôch') *v.* To corrupt morally. [< OF *desbaucher,* "to roughhew (timber) into a beam," separate.] **—de•bauch'er•y** *n.*

de•ben•ture (dĭ-bĕn'chər) *n.* A certificate acknowledging a debt, esp. a bond issued by a civil or governmental agency. [< L *dēbentur,* "they are due."]

de•bil•i•tate (dĭ-bĭl'ə-tāt') *v.* **-tated, -tating.** To make feeble; weaken. [< L *dēbilis,* weak.] **—de•bil'i•ta'tion** *n.* **—de•bil'i•ta'tive** *adj.*

de•bil•i•ty (dĭ-bĭl'ə-tē) *n., pl.* **-ties.** Feebleness.

deb•it (dĕb'ĭt) *n.* An item of debt, esp. one recorded in an account. *—v.* **1.** To enter a debit in an account. **2.** To charge with a debt. [< L *dēbitum,* DEBT.]

deb•o•nair (dĕb'ə-nâr') *adj.* **1.** Suave; urbane; gracious. **2.** Carefree; gay. [< F *de bon aire,* "of good disposition."] **—deb'o•nair'ly** *adv.*

de•brief (dē'brēf') *v.* To question to obtain knowledge gathered on a military mission. **—de'brief'ing** *n.*

de•bris (də-brē', dā'brē') *n.* Also **dé•bris** (dā'brē'). The scattered remains of something broken or destroyed. [< OF *debrisier,* to break to pieces.]

debt (dĕt) *n.* **1.** Something owed, as money, goods, or services. **2.** *Theol.* A sin; trespass. [< L *dēbitum.*] **—debt'or** *n.*

de•bunk (dĭ-bŭngk') *v.* To expose the falseness or exaggerated claims of.

De•bus•sy (də-byo͞o'sē), **Claude.** 1862–1918. French composer.

de•but (dĭ-byo͞o', dā-, dā'byo͞o') *n.* Also **dé•but.** **1.** A first public appearance. **2.** The formal presentation of a girl to society. **3.** The beginning of a career. [F *début.*]

deb•u•tante (dĕb'yo͝o-tänt', dĕb'yo͝o-tänt', dā'byo͞o-) *n.* Also **dé•bu•tante.** A young woman making a debut into society.

dec. deceased.

Dec. December.

deca–, deka–. *comb. form.* Ten. [< Gk *deka,* ten.]

de•cade (dĕk'ād', dĕ-kād') *n.* A period of 10 years.

dec•a•dence (dĕk'ə-dəns, dĭ-kā'dəns) *n.* A process, condition, or period of deterioration; decay. [< VL **dēcadere,* to decay.] **—dec'a•dent** *adj.* **—dec'a•dent•ly** *adv.*

dec•a•gon (dĕk'ə-gŏn') *n.* A polygon with 10 sides. [< Gk *dekagōnon,* "(one) having 10 angles."]

dec•a•he•dron (dĕk'ə-hē'drən) *n., pl.* **-drons** or **-dra** (-drə). A polyhedron with 10 faces.

de•cal (dē'kăl') *n.* A picture or design transferred by decalcomania.

de•cal•ci•fy (dē-kăl'sə-fī') *v.* **-fied, -fying.** To remove calcium or calcareous matter, as from bones or teeth.

de•cal•co•ma•ni•a (dē'kăl-kə-mā'nē-ə) *n.* **1.** The process of transferring designs printed on specially prepared paper to glass, metal, etc. **2.** A decal. [F *décalcomanie.*]

Dec•a•logue (dĕk'ə-lôg', -lŏg') *n.* The **Ten Commandments.**

de•camp (dĭ-kămp') *v.* **1.** To break camp. **2.** To depart secretly or suddenly.

de•cant (dĭ-kănt') *v.* To pour off without disturbing the sediment, as wine. [ML *dēcanthāre.*] **—de'can•ta'tion** *n.*

de•cant•er (dĭ-kăn'tər) *n.* A decorative bottle used for serving liquids, as wine.

de•cap•i•tate (dĭ-kăp'ə-tāt') *v.* **-tated, -tating.** To behead. [< LL *dēcapitāre.*]

de•cath•lon (dĭ-kăth'lən, -lŏn') *n.* An athletic contest in which each contestant participates in 10 events. [< DECA- + Gk *athlon,* contest.]

de•cay (dĭ-kā') *v.* **1.** To decompose; rot. **2.** To decrease or decline in quality or quantity. *—n.* **1.** Decomposition. **2.** Deterioration. [< VL **dēcadere,* to fall down, decay.]

de•cease (dĭ-sēs') *v.* **-ceased, -ceasing.** To die. *—n.* Death. [< L *dēcēdere,* to depart.]

de•ceit (dĭ-sēt') *n.* **1.** Misrepresentation; deception. **2.** A stratagem; trick. [< L *dēcipere,* DECEIVE.] **—de•ceit'ful** *adj.*

de•ceive (dĭ-sēv') *v.* **-ceived, -ceiving.** To delude; mislead. [< L *dēcipere,* to take in, deceive.] **—de•ceiv'er** *n.*

de•cel•er•ate (dē-sĕl'ə-rāt') *v.* **-ated, -ating.** To decrease in velocity. [DE- + (AC)CELERATE.] **—de•cel'er•a'tion** *n.*

De•cem•ber (dĭ-sĕm'bər) *n.* The 12th month of the year. December has 31 days. [< L, "the tenth month."]

de•cent (dē'sənt) *adj.* **1.** Characterized by conformity to recognized standards of propriety. **2.** Free from indelicacy; modest. **3.** Adequate; passable. **4.** Kind; generous. **5.** Properly dressed. [< L *decēre,* to be fitting, suit.] **—de'cen•cy** (-sən-sē) *n.*

de•cen•tral•ize (dē-sĕn'trə-līz') *v.* **-ized, -izing.** **1.** To distribute the administrative functions of (a central authority) among local authorities. **2.** To cause to withdraw from an area of concentration. **—de•cen'tral•i•za'tion** *n.*

de•cep•tion (dĭ-sĕp'shən) *n.* **1.** The use of deceit. **2.** The fact or state of being deceived.

de•cep•tive (dĭ-sĕp'tĭv) *adj.* Intended or tending to deceive. **—de•cep'tive•ly** *adv.*

deci–. *comb. form.* One-tenth. [< L *decimus,* tenth.]

de•ci•bel (dĕs'ĭ-bəl, -bĕl') *n.* A unit used to express relative difference in power, usually between acoustic or electric signals, equal to one-tenth the common logarithm of the ratio of the two levels.

de•cide (dĭ-sīd') *v.* **-cided, -ciding.** **1.** To conclude, settle, or announce a verdict. **2.** To influence or determine the conclusion of. **3.** To make up one's mind. [< L *dēcīdere,* to cut off, determine.] **—de•cid'er** *n.*

de•cid•ed (dĭ-sī'dĭd) *adj.* **1.** Unquestionable. **2.** Resolute. **—de•cid'ed•ly** *adv.*

de•cid•u•ate (dĭ-sĭj'o͞o-ĭt, -sĭd'yo͞o-) *adj.* Characterized by shedding.

de•cid•u•ous (dĭ-sĭj'o͞o-əs, -sĭd'yo͞o-) *adj.* **1.** Falling off at a specific season or stage of growth: *deciduous leaves.* **2.** Shedding foliage at the end of the growing season: *deciduous trees.* [< L *dēcidere,* to fall off.]

dec•i•gram (dĕs'ĭ-grăm') *n.* One-tenth of a gram.

dec•i•li•ter (dĕs'ə-lē'tər) *n.* One-tenth of a liter.

de•cil•lion (dĭ-sĭl'yən) *n.* **1.** The cardinal num-

ă pat/ā ate/âr care/ä bar/b bib/ch chew/d deed/ĕ pet/ē be/f fit/g gag/h hat/hw what/
ĭ pit/ī pie/îr pier/j judge/k kick/l lid, fatal/m mum/n no, sudden/ng sing/ŏ pot/ō go/

ber represented by 1 followed by 33 zeros. 2. *Brit.* The cardinal number represented by 1 followed by 60 zeros. [L *decem,* ten + (M)ILLION.] —**de•cil'lion** *adj.*

de•cil•lionth (dĭ-sĭl'yənth) *n.* **1.** The ordinal number decillion in a series. **2.** One of a decillion equal parts. —**de•cil'lionth** *adj.* & *adv.*

dec•i•mal (dĕs'ə-məl) *n.* **1.** A linear array of integers that represents a fraction, every decimal place indicating a multiple of a positive or negative power of 10. For example, the decimal .1 = 1/10, .12 = 12/100, .003 = 3/1000. **2.** Any number written using base 10; a number containing a decimal point. —*adj.* **1.** Expressed or expressible as a decimal. **2. a.** Based on 10. **b.** Numbered or ordered by 10's. **3.** Loosely, not integral; fractional. [< L *decimus,* tenth.] —**dec'i•mal•ly** *adv.*

decimal place. The position of a digit to the right of a decimal point, usually identified by successive ascending ordinal numbers with the digit immediately to the right of the decimal point being first.

decimal point. A period placed to the left of a decimal.

dec•i•mate (dĕs'ĭ-māt') *v.* **-mated, -mating.** To destroy or kill a large part of. [L *decimāre.*] —**dec'i•ma'tion** *n.*

dec•i•me•ter (dĕs'ə-mē'tər) *n.* One-tenth of a meter.

de•ci•pher (dĭ-sī'fər) *v.* **1.** To read or interpret (something ambiguous or obscure). **2.** To decode. [DE- + CIPHER.] —**de•ci'pher•a•ble** *adj.*

de•ci•sion (dĭ-sĭzh'ən) *n.* **1.** The passing of judgment on an issue under consideration. **2.** The act of making up one's mind. **3.** A conclusion or judgment reached; verdict. **4.** Firmness of character or action. [< L *dēcīdere,* DECIDE.]

de•ci•sive (dĭ-sī'sĭv) *adj.* **1.** Conclusive. **2.** Resolute; determined. **3.** Beyond doubt; unquestionable. —**de•ci'sive•ly** *adv.* —**de•ci'sive•ness** *n.*

deck¹ (dĕk) *n.* **1. a.** A platform extending horizontally from one side of a ship to the other. **b.** Any similar platform or surface. **2.** A pack of playing cards. [< MDu *decke,* roof, covering.]

deck² (dĕk) *v.* To clothe with finery; adorn. [MDu *dekken,* to cover.]

deck hand. A member of a ship's crew who works on deck.

decl. declension.

de•claim (dĭ-klām') *v.* To speak loudly and with rhetorical effect. —**de•claim'er** *n.* —**dec'la•ma'tion** (dĕk'lə-mā'shən) *n.*

Declaration of Independence. A proclamation issued in 1776, declaring the independence of the 13 American colonies from Great Britain.

de•clar•a•tive (dĭ-klâr'ə-tĭv) *adj.* Serving to declare or state.

de•clare (dĭ-klâr') *v.* **-clared, -claring. 1.** To state officially, formally, or authoritatively. **2.** *Bridge.* To make the final bid that establishes trump or no-trump. [< L *dēclārāre,* to make clear.] —**dec'la•ra'tion** (dĕk'lə-rā'shən) *n.* —**de•clar'er** *n.*

de•clas•si•fy (dē-klăs'ə-fī') *v.* To remove official security classification from (a document). —**de•clas'si•fi•ca'tion** *n.*

de•clen•sion (dĭ-klĕn'shən) *n.* **1.** *Ling.* **a.** The systematic inflection of nouns, pronouns, and adjectives. **b.** A class of such words with similar inflections. **2.** A descent. **3.** A decline or deterioration. [< L *dēclīnāre,* DECLINE.]

de•cline (dĭ-klīn') *v.* **-clined, -clining. 1.** To refuse to do or accept (something). **2.** To slope downward. **3.** To deteriorate gradually; wane. **4.** *Ling.* To give the declension of. —*n.* **1.** The process or result of declining. **2.** A downward slope. **3.** A disease that gradually weakens the body. [< L *dēclīnāre,* to turn aside, go down.]

de•cliv•i•ty (dĭ-klĭv'ə-tē) *n., pl.* **-ties.** A steeply descending slope. [< L *dēclīvis,* sloping down.]

de•code (dē-kōd') *v.* To convert from code into plain text. —**de•cod'er** *n.*

dé•colle•té (dā'kôl-tā') *adj.* Having a low neckline. [< F *décolleter,* to uncover the neck.]

de•com•pose (dē'kəm-pōz') *v.* **1.** To separate or break down into component parts or basic elements. **2.** To rot. —**de'com•po•si'tion** (-kŏm-pə-zĭsh'ən) *n.*

de•com•press (dē'kəm-prĕs') *v.* To relieve of pressure. —**de'com•pres'sion** *n.*

de•con•ges•tant (dē'kən-jĕs'tənt) *n.* Something, as a drug, that relieves congestion.

de•con•tam•i•nate (dē'kən-tăm'ə-nāt') *v.* To remove the contaminants or dangerous elements from.

de•con•trol (dē'kən-trōl') *v.* To free from control.

dé•cor (dā'kôr', dā'kôr') *n.* Also **de•cor.** A decorative style, as of a room, home, stage setting, etc. [< F *décorer,* to decorate.]

dec•o•rate (dĕk'ə-rāt') *v.* **-rated, -rating. 1.** To furnish or adorn with fashionable or beautiful things. **2.** To confer a medal or other honor upon. [L *decorāre.*] —**dec'o•ra'tion** *n.*

dec•o•ra•tive (dĕk'ər-ə-tĭv) *adj.* Ornamental. —**dec'o•ra•tive•ly** *adv.* —**dec'o•ra•tive•ness** *n.*

dec•o•ra•tor (dĕk'ə-rā'tər) *n.* One who decorates architectural interiors; interior decorator.

dec•o•rous (dĕk'ər-əs, dĭ-kôr'əs) *adj.* Characterized by decorum. [< L *decor,* seemliness.]

de•co•rum (dĭ-kôr'əm, dĭ-kōr'əm) *n.* Conformity to social conventions; propriety. [L *decōrum.*]

de•coy (dē'koi', dĭ-koi') *n.* **1.** A living or artificial animal used to entice game. **2.** One who leads another into danger, deception, or a trap. —*v.* (dĭ-koi'). To lure or entrap by or as by a decoy. [Poss < Du *de kooi,* "the cage."]

de•crease (dĭ-krēs') *v.* **-creased, -creasing.** To diminish gradually; reduce. —*n.* (dē'krēs'). The act or process of decreasing or the resulting condition. [< L *dēcrēscere.*]

de•cree (dĭ-krē') *n.* **1.** An authoritative order; edict. **2.** The judgment of a court. —*v.* **-creed, -creeing.** To ordain, establish, or decide by decree. [< L *dēcrētus,* pp of *dēcernere,* to decide.] —**de•cre'er** *n.*

dec•re•ment (dĕk'rə-mənt) *n.* **1.** A decrease. **2.** The amount by which something decreases.

de•crep•it (dĭ-krĕp'ĭt) *adj.* Weakened by old age, illness, or hard use; broken-down. [< L *dēcrepitus.*] —**de•crep'i•tude'** (-ĭ-t/y/o͞od') *n.*

de•cre•scen•do (dē'krə-shĕn'dō) *n., pl.* **-dos. 1.** A gradual decrease in force or loudness. **2.** A musical passage played in a decrescendo. —*adj.* Gradually decreasing in volume or intensity. [It, "decreasing."] —**de'cre•scen'do** *adv.*

de•cry (dĭ-krī') *v.* **-cried, -crying.** To belittle openly; censure. [< OF *descrier,* "to cry down."] —**de•cri'er** *n.*

ded•i•cate (dĕd'ə-kāt') *v.* **-cated, -cating. 1.** To set apart for a deity or for religious purposes. **2.** To set apart for some special use. **3.** To inscribe (a literary work or artistic performance) to someone. **4.** To commit (oneself) to a particular course of thought or action. [< L *dēdicāre,* to give out tidings, proclaim.] —**ded'i•ca'tion** *n.* —**ded'i•ca'tor** *n.*

de•duce (dĭ-d/y/o͞os') *v.* **-duced, -ducing. 1.** To reach (a conclusion) by reasoning. **2.** To trace the origin of. [< L *dēdūcere,* to lead away, infer logically.] —**de•duc'i•ble** *adj.*

de•duct (dĭ-dŭkt') *v.* To subtract. [L *dēdūcere* (pp *dēductus*), to DEDUCE.] —**de•duct'i•ble** *adj.*

de•duc•tion (dĭ-dŭk'shən) *n.* **1.** The act, process, or result of deducing. **2.** That which is or can be deducted.

deed (dēd) *n.* **1.** An act; feat; exploit. **2.** Action or performance in general: *in word and deed.* **3.** A document sealed as an instrument of bond, contract, or conveyance, esp. pertaining to property. —*v.* To transfer by means of a deed. [< OE *dǣd.* See **dhē-.**]

deem (dēm) *v.* To judge; consider; think. [< OE *dēman.* See **dhē-.**]

deep (dēp) *adj.* **1.** Extending to or located at a distance below a surface. **2.** Extending from front to rear or inward from the outside. **3.** Arising from or penetrating to a depth. **4.** Far distant; obscure. **5.** Learned; profound. **6.** Intense; extreme. **7.** Dark rather than pale in shade. **8.** Low in pitch; resonant. —*n.* **1.** Any deep place on land or in a body of water, esp. in the ocean and over 3,000 fathoms in depth. **2.** The most intense or extreme part. **3. the deep.** The ocean. —*adv.* **1.** Profoundly. **2.** Well on in time; late. [< OE *dēop.* See **dheub-.**] —**deep'ly** *adv.* —**deep'ness** *n.*

deep•en (dē'pən) *v.* To make or become deep or deeper. —**deep'en•er** *n.*

deep-root•ed (dēp'ro͞o'tĭd, -ro͝ot'ĭd) *adj.* Firmly implanted.

deep-seat•ed (dēp'sē'tĭd) *adj.* Deeply rooted; ingrained.

Deep South. The southeasternmost part of the U.S.

deer (dîr) *n., pl.* **deer.** Any of various hoofed mammals of which the males characteristically have seasonally shed antlers. [< OE *dēor.* See **dheu-¹.**]

deer•skin (dîr'skĭn') *n.* **1.** Leather made from the hide of a deer. **2.** A garment made from such leather.

de-es•ca•late (dē'ĕs'kə-lāt') *v.* To decrease or reduce the scope or intensity of (a war). —**de'-es'ca•la'tion** *n.*

def. **1.** defense. **2.** definition.

de•face (dĭ-fās') *v.* **-faced, -facing.** To spoil or mar the surface or appearance of; disfigure.

de fac•to (dē făk'tō). In reality or fact; actually. [L, "from the fact."]

de•fal•cate (dĭ-făl'kāt', dĭ-fôl'kāt', dĕf'əl-kāt') *v.* **-cated, -cating.** To misuse funds; embezzle. [ML *dēfalcāre,* to cut off.] —**de'fal•ca'tion** *n.*

de•fame (dĭ-fām') *v.* **-famed, -faming.** To attack the good name of by slander or libel. [< L *diffāmāre.*] —**def'a•ma'tion** (dĕf'ə-mā'shən) *n.* —**de•fam'er** *n.*

de•fault (dĭ-fôlt') *n.* **1.** A failure to perform a task or fulfill an obligation. **2.** Loss by failure to appear. —*v.* **1.** To fail to do what is required. **2.** To lose by not appearing. [< VL **dēfallire,* to fail.] —**de•fault'er** *n.*

de•feat (dĭ-fēt') *v.* **1.** To win victory over; vanquish. **2.** To prevent the success of; thwart. —*n.* The act of defeating or state of being defeated. [< ML *disfacere,* to undo, destroy.] —**de•feat'er** *n.*

de•feat•ism (dĭ-fē'tĭz'əm) *n.* Acceptance of the prospect of defeat. —**de•feat'ist** *n.*

def•e•cate (dĕf'ə-kāt') *v.* **-cated, -cating.** To void feces from the bowels. [L *dēfaecāre.*] —**def'e•ca'tion** *n.* —**def'e•ca'tor** *n.*

de•fect (dē'fĕkt', dĭ-fĕkt') *n.* **1.** The lack of something necessary or desirable. **2.** An imperfection; fault. —*v.* (dĭ-fĕkt'). To abandon an allegiance that one had previously espoused. [< L *dēficere,* to remove from, desert, fail.] **—de•fec'tion** *n.* **—de•fec'tor** *n.*

de•fec•tive (dĭ-fĕk'tĭv) *adj.* Having a defect; lacking perfection; faulty. **—de•fec'tive•ly** *adv.* **—de•fec'tive•ness** *n.*

de•fend (dĭ-fĕnd') *v.* **1.** To protect from danger; shield; guard. **2.** To support or maintain; justify. **3. a.** To represent (the defendant) in a civil or criminal case. **b.** To contest (a legal action or claim). [< L *dēfendere,* to ward off.] **—de•fend'a•ble** *adj.* **—de•fend'er** *n.*

de•fen•dant (dĭ-fĕn'dənt) *n. Law.* A person against whom an action is brought.

de•fense (dĭ-fĕns') *n.* Also *chiefly Brit.* **de•fence. 1.** The act of defending. **2.** One that defends or protects. **3.** An argument in support or justification of something. **4.** A defendant and his legal counsel. **—de•fense'less** *adj.* **—de•fense'less•ly** *adv.* **—de•fen'si•ble** *adj.* **—de•fen'sive** *adj.*

de•fer[1] (dĭ-fûr') *v.* **-ferred, -ferring.** To put off until a future time; postpone; delay. [< L *differre.*] **—de•fer'rer** *n.*

de•fer[2] (dĭ-fûr') *v.* **-ferred, -ferring.** To comply with or submit to the opinion or decision of another. [< L *dēferre,* to carry away, bring to, submit.] **—de•fer'rer** *n.*

def•er•ence (dĕf'ər-əns) *n.* **1.** Courteous yielding to the opinion or wishes of another. **2.** Courteous respect. **—def'er•en'tial** *adj.* **—def'er•en'tial•ly** *adv.*

de•fer•ment (dĭ-fûr'mənt) *n.* Also **de•fer•ral** (-fûr'əl). Postponement.

de•fi•ant (dĭ-fī'ənt) *adj.* **1.** Marked by resistance to authority. **2.** Intentionally provocative. **—de•fi'ance** *n.* **—de•fi'ant•ly** *adv.*

de•fi•cient (dĭ-fĭsh'ənt) *adj.* **1.** Lacking an essential element; incomplete. **2.** Inadequate in amount or degree; insufficient. [< L *dēficere,* to remove from, desert.] **—de•fi'cien•cy** *n.* **—de•fi'cient•ly** *adv.*

def•i•cit (dĕf'ə-sĭt) *n.* The amount by which a sum of money falls short of a required or expected amount; a shortage. [< L *dēficit,* it is lacking.]

deficit spending. The spending of money obtained by borrowing.

de•file[1] (dĭ-fīl') *v.* **-filed, -filing. 1.** To make filthy or dirty. **2.** To corrupt. **3.** To profane, as a good name. **4.** To violate the chastity of. [Prob < OF *defouler.*] **—de•file'ment** *n.* **—de•fil'er** *n.* **—de•fil'ing•ly** *adv.*

de•file[2] (dĭ-fīl') *v.* **-filed, -filing.** To march in single file or in columns. —*n.* A narrow gorge, valley, etc. [F *défiler.*]

de•fine (dĭ-fīn') *v.* **-fined, -fining. 1.** To state the precise meaning of (a word). **2.** To describe the basic qualities of. **3.** To delineate. **4.** To specify distinctly; fix definitely. [< L *dēfinīre,* to set bounds to.] **—de•fin'a•ble** *adj.* **—de•fin'a•bly** *adv.* **—de•fin'er** *n.*

def•i•nite (dĕf'ə-nĭt) *adj.* **1.** Having distinct limits. **2.** Known positively. **3.** Clearly defined; precise. [< L *dēfinīre,* to determine, DEFINE.] **—def'i•nite•ly** *adv.*

definite article. *Gram.* The article *the,* which restricts or particularizes the noun or noun phrase following it.

def•i•ni•tion (dĕf'ə-nĭsh'ən) *n.* **1. a.** The act of defining a word, phrase, or term. **b.** The statement of the meaning of a word, phrase, or term. **2.** The act of making clear and distinct. **3.** A determining of outline, extent, or limits. [< L *dēfinīre,* DEFINE.]

de•fin•i•tive (dĭ-fĭn'ə-tĭv) *adj.* **1.** Precisely defining or outlining. **2.** Determining finally; decisive. **3.** Designating a work that can stand as the most authoritative on its subject. **—de•fin'i•tive•ly** *adv.* **—de•fin'i•tive•ness** *n.*

de•flate (dĭ-flāt') *v.* **-flated, -flating. 1. a.** To release contained air or gas from. **b.** To collapse by such a release. **2.** To lessen the confidence, pride, or certainty of. **3.** *Econ.* To reduce the value or amount of (currency), effecting a decline in prices. [DE- + (IN)FLATE.] **—de•fla'tion** *n.* **—de•fla'tor** *n.*

de•flect (dĭ-flĕkt') *v.* To cause to swerve; turn aside. [L *dēflectere.*] **—de•flec'ta•ble** *adj.* **—de•flec'tion** *n.* **—de•flec'tive** *adj.*

de•fo•li•ate (dĭ-fō'lē-āt') *v.* **-ated, -ating. 1.** To strip (a tree or other plant) of leaves. **2.** To cause the leaves of (a tree or other plant) to fall off, esp. by the use of a chemical spray. [< LL *dēfoliāre.*] **—de•fo'li•a'tion** *n.*

de•form (dĭ-fôrm') *v.* **1.** To spoil the natural form of; misshape. **2.** To deface; disfigure. **—de•form'a•ble** *adj.* **—de•for•ma'tion** (dĭ-fôr'mā'shən, dĕf'ər-) *n.*

de•formed (dĭ-fôrmd') *adj.* Misshapen.

de•form•i•ty (dĭ-fôr'mĭ-tē) *n., pl.* **-ties.** The state or condition of being deformed.

de•fraud (dĭ-frôd') *v.* To swindle. **—de'fraud•a'tion** *n.* **—de•fraud'er** *n.*

de•fray (dĭ-frā') *v.* To meet or satisfy by payment; pay. [< OF *desfrayer.*] **—de•fray'a•ble** *adj.* **—de•fray'al** *n.*

de•frock (dē-frŏk') *v.* To unfrock.

de•frost (dē-frôst', -frŏst') *v.* **1.** To remove ice or frost from. **2.** To become free of ice or frost. **—de•frost'er** *n.*

deft (dĕft) *adj.* Skillful; adroit. [ME *defte,* orig "gentle," "meek."] **—deft'ly** *adv.*

de•funct (dĭ-fŭngkt') *adj.* Having ceased to live or exist. [L *dēfungī,* to discharge.]

de•fuse (dē-fyōōz') *v.* **-fused, -fusing. 1.** To remove the fuse from (an explosive device). **2.** To make less dangerous or tense.

de•fy (dĭ-fī') *v.* **-fied, -fying. 1.** To confront or stand up to; challenge. **2.** To resist successfully; withstand. **3.** To dare (someone) to perform something deemed impossible. [< VL **disfīdāre,* to renounce one's faith.]

deg, deg. degree (thermometric).

De Gaulle (də gōl'), **Charles.** 1890–1970. French general and statesman; president (1945–46; 1959–69).

Charles De Gaulle

de•gauss (dē'gous') *v.* To neutralize the magnetic field of.

de•gen•er•a•cy (dĭ-jĕn'ər-ə-sē) *n.* **1.** The state or condition of being degenerate. **2.** The process of degenerating.

de•gen•er•ate (dĭ-jĕn'ə-rāt') *v.* **-ated, -ating.** To deteriorate or decay. —*adj.* (dĭ-jĕn'ər-ĭt). Morally degraded or sexually deviant. —*n.* (dĭ-jĕn'ər-ĭt). A morally degraded or sexually deviant person. [L *dēgenerāre,* to fall from one's ancestral quality.] **—de•gen'er•ate•ly** *adv.* **—de•gen'er•ate•ness** *n.* **—de•gen'er•a'tion** *n.* **—de•gen'er•a•tive** (-ə-tĭv) *adj.*

de•glu•ti•nate (dĭ-glōōt'n-āt') *v.* **-nated, -nating.** To extract the gluten from: *deglutinate wheat flour.* [L *dēglūtināre.*] **—de•glu'ti•na'tion** *n.*

de•glu•ti•tion (dē'glōō-tĭsh'ən) *n.* The process or act of swallowing. [< L *dēglūtīre,* to swallow down.] **—de'glu•ti'tious** *adj.*

de•grade (dĭ-grād') *v.* **-graded, -grading. 1.** To reduce in grade, rank, or status. **2.** To debase; corrupt. [< LL *dēgradāre.*] **—deg'ra•da'tion** (dĕg'rə-dā'shən) *n.* **—de•grad'ed•ly** *adv.* **—de•grad'ed•ness** *n.* **—de•grad'er** *n.*

de•gree (dĭ-grē') *n.* **1.** One of a series of steps or stages. **2.** Relative social or official rank or position. **3.** Relative intensity. **4.** Relative condition or extent; capacity; manner. **5.** The extent or measure of a state of being, action, etc. **6.** A unit division of a temperature scale. **7.** A unit of angular measure equal in magnitude to the central angle subtended by 1/360 of the circumference of a circle. **8.** A unit of latitude or longitude, 1/360 of a great circle. **9.** The greatest sum of the exponents of the variables in a term of a polynomial or polynomial equation. **10.** An academic title given to one who has completed a course of study or as an honorary distinction. **11.** *Law.* A classification of a crime according to its seriousness. **12.** *Gram.* One of the forms used in the comparison of adjectives and adverbs. **13.** *Mus.* One of the seven notes of a diatonic scale. [< VL **dēgradus,* "a step down."]

de•hu•man•ize (dē-hyōō'mə-nīz') *v.* **-ized, -izing. 1.** To deprive of human qualities or attributes. **2.** To render mechanical and routine. **—de•hu'man•i•za'tion** *n.*

de•hu•mid•i•fy (dē'hyōō-mĭd'ə-fī') *v.* **-fied, -fying.** To decrease the humidity of. **—de'hu•mid'i•fi•ca'tion** *n.* **—de•hu•mid'i•fi'er** *n.*

de•hy•drate (dē-hī'drāt') *v.* **-drated, -drating.** To remove or lose water. **—de'hy•dra'tion** *n.*

de•ice (dē-īs') *v.* **-iced, -icing. 1.** To remove the ice from, esp. by melting. **2.** To prevent the formation of ice on. **—de•ic'er** *n.*

de•i•fy (dē'ə-fī') *v.* **-fied, -fying. 1.** To raise to divine rank. **2.** To worship; idealize. [< LL *deificāre.*] **—de'i•fi•ca'tion** *n.*

deign (dān) *v.* **1.** To think it suitable to one's dignity to do something. **2.** To condescend to give or grant. [< L *dignus,* worthy.]

de•ism (dē'ĭz'əm) *n.* An 18th-century system of natural religion affirming the existence of God while denying the validity of revelation. [< L *deus,* god.] **—de'ist** *n.* **—de•is'tic** *adj.*

de•i•ty (dē'ə-tē) *n., pl.* **-ties. 1.** A god or goddess. **2.** Divinity. [< L *deus,* god.]

de•ject•ed (dĭ-jĕk'tĭd) *adj.* Depressed; disheartened. [< L *dējectus,* pp of *dējicere,* to cast down.] **—de•ject'ed•ly** *adv.*

de•jec•tion (dĭ-jĕk'shən) *n.* A state of depression; melancholy.

de ju•re (dē jŏŏr'ē, dā yōō'rā). According to law; by right. [L.]

deka–. Variant of **deca-.**

del. delegate; delegation.

Del. Delaware.

Del•a•ware[1] (dĕl'ə-wâr') *n., pl.* **-ware** or **-wares.**

1. A member of a group of Algonquian-speaking North American Indian tribes, formerly inhabiting the Delaware River valley. 2. Their language.

Del•a•ware² (dĕl'ə-wâr'). A state of the E U.S. Pop. 548,000. Cap. Dover.

de•lay (dĭ-lā') *v.* 1. To cause to be late. 2. To procrastinate; linger. —*n.* 1. The act of delaying or condition of being delayed. 2. The period of time during which one is delayed. [< OF *deslaier.*] —**de•lay'er** *n.*

de•lec•ta•ble (dĭ-lĕk'tə-bəl) *adj.* 1. Delightful. 2. Delicious. [< L *dēlectāre,* to please.] —**de•lec'ta•bil'i•ty** *n.* —**de•lec'ta•bly** *adv.*

de•lec•ta•tion (dē'lĕk-tā'shən) *n.* Pleasure; delight.

del•e•gate (dĕl'ə-gāt', -gĭt) *n.* One authorized to act as a representative for another or others. —*v.* (dĕl'ə-gāt') **-gated, -gating.** 1. To authorize and send (a person) as one's representative. 2. To commit to one's representative. [< L *dēlēgāre,* to send away, dispatch.]

del•e•ga•tion (dĕl'ə-gā'shən) *n.* 1. The act of delegating or condition of being delegated. 2. A group of persons authorized to represent another or others.

de•lete (dĭ-lēt') *v.* **-leted, -leting.** To strike out; omit. [L *dēlēre,* to wipe out, efface.] —**de•le'tion** *n.*

del•e•te•ri•ous (dĕl'ə-tîr'ē-əs) *adj.* Injurious; harmful. [< Gk *dēleisthai,* to harm, injure.] —**del'e•te'ri•ous•ly** *adv.* —**del'e•te'ri•ous•ness** *n.*

Del•hi (dĕl'ē). A city of NE India. Pop. 2,299,000.

de•lib•er•ate (dĭ-lĭb'ə-rāt') *v.* **-ated, -ating.** 1. To consider or discuss (a matter) carefully. 2. To take careful thought; reflect. —*adj.* (dĭ-lĭb'ər-ĭt). 1. Intentional. 2. a. Careful in deciding. b. Not hastily determined: *a deliberate choice.* 3. Slow; not hurried. [L *dēliberāre,* to weigh well, ponder.] —**de•lib'er•ate•ly** *adv.* —**de•lib'er•ate•ness** *n.*

de•lib•er•a•tion (dĭ-lĭb'ə-rā'shən) *n.* 1. Careful consideration. 2. Often **deliberations.** Careful discussion of an issue. —**de•lib'er•a'tive** (-lĭb'ə-rā'tĭv, -ər-ə-tĭv) *adj.*

del•i•ca•cy (dĕl'ĭ-kə-sē) *n., pl.* **-cies.** 1. The quality of being delicate. 2. A choice food.

del•i•cate (dĕl'ĭ-kĭt) *adj.* 1. Pleasingly small, subtle, etc. 2. Frail in constitution. 3. Easily damaged. 4. Requiring or marked by tact. 5. Keenly sensitive or accurate. 6. Requiring or showing careful skill. [< L *dēlicātus,* alluring, charming, dainty.] —**del'i•cate•ly** *adv.*

del•i•ca•tes•sen (dĕl'ĭ-kə-tĕs'ən) *n.* A shop that sells freshly prepared foods ready for serving. [< G *Delikatesse,* delicacy.]

de•li•cious (dĭ-lĭsh'əs) *adj.* Highly pleasing to the sense of taste. [< L *dēlicere,* to entice away, DELIGHT.] —**de•li'cious•ly** *adv.* —**de•li'cious•ness** *n.*

de•light (dĭ-līt') *n.* 1. Great pleasure; joy. 2. Something that gives great pleasure or enjoyment. —*v.* 1. To take great pleasure or joy. 2. To give (someone) great pleasure or joy. [< L *dēlectāre,* freq of *dēlicere,* to allure.]

de•light•ful (dĭ-līt'fəl) *adj.* Greatly pleasing. —**de•light'ful•ly** *adv.* —**de•light'ful•ness** *n.*

de•lin•e•ate (dĭ-lĭn'ē-āt') *v.* **-ated, -ating.** 1. To draw or outline accurately. 2. To describe broadly but accurately. [L *dēlīneāre.*] —**de•lin'e•a'tion** *n.* —**de•lin'e•a'tive** *adj.*

de•lin•quent (dĭ-lĭng'kwənt) *adj.* 1. Failing to do what is required. 2. Overdue in payment: *a delinquent account.* —*n.* One who fails to do what is required. [< L *dēlinquere,* to fail in duty, "leave undone."] —**de•lin'quen•cy** *n.*

del•i•quesce (dĕl'ə-kwĕs') *v.* **-quesced, -quescing.** To dissolve and become liquid by absorbing moisture from the air. [L *dēliquēscere.*] —**del'i•ques'cent** *adj.*

de•lir•i•um (dĭ-lîr'ē-əm) *n., pl.* **-ums** or **-ia** (-ē-ə). A state of temporary mental confusion and clouded consciousness resulting from high fever, intoxication, or shock, and characterized by anxiety, tremors, hallucinations, delusions, and incoherence. [< L *dēlīrāre,* to deviate from a straight line.] —**de•lir'i•ous** *adj.* —**de•lir'i•ous•ly** *adv.* —**de•lir'i•ous•ness** *n.*

delirium tre•mens (trē'mənz). An acute delirium caused by alcohol poisoning.

de•liv•er (dĭ-lĭv'ər) *v.* 1. To set free. 2. a. To assist (a female) in giving birth. b. To assist in the birth of. 3. To take to an intended recipient. 4. To send forth by discharging or throwing, as a blow. 5. To utter (a lecture). [< LL *dēliberāre.*] —**de•liv'er•er** *n.*

de•liv•er•ance (dĭ-lĭv'ər-əns) *n.* Rescue from bondage or danger.

de•liv•er•y (dĭ-lĭv'ə-rē) *n., pl.* **-ies.** 1. The act of delivering. 2. That which is delivered. 3. Childbirth. 4. Manner of speaking or singing. 5. Manner of throwing or discharging.

dell (dĕl) *n.* A small, secluded valley. [< OE. See **dhel-.**]

del•phin•i•um (dĕl-fĭn'ē-əm) *n.* A tall cultivated plant with spikes of showy, variously colored spurred flowers. [< Gk *delphinion,* larkspur.]

del•ta (dĕl'tə) *n.* 1. The 4th letter of the Greek alphabet, representing *d.* 2. A usually triangular alluvial deposit, as at the mouth of a river. —**del•ta'ic** (-tā'ĭk) *adj.*

del•toid (dĕl'toid') *n.* A thick, triangular muscle covering the shoulder joint, used to raise the arm from the side. [< Gk *deltoeidēs,* triangular : DELTA + -OID.]

de•lude (dĭ-lo͞od') *v.* **-luded, -luding.** To mislead the mind or judgment of; deceive. [< L *dēlūdere,* to play false, deceive.]

del•uge (dĕl'yo͞oj) *v.* **-uged, -uging.** To overrun with or as with water; flood. —*n.* 1. A flood; downpour. 2. Anything that overwhelms as if by a flood. [< L *dīluvium,* flood.]

de•lu•sion (dĭ-l/y/o͞o'zhən) *n.* 1. The state of being deluded. 2. A false belief held in spite of invalidating evidence. [< L *dēlūdere,* DELUDE.] —**de•lu'sive, de•lu'sion•al** *adj.*

de luxe (dĭ lo͝oks', dĭ lŭks'). Luxurious; elaborate; sumptuous: *a de luxe model.* [F, "of luxury."]

delve (dĕlv) *v.* **delved, delving.** To search deeply and laboriously. [< OE *delfan.* See **dhelbh-.**] —**delv'er** *n.*

Dem. Democrat; Democratic.

de•mag•net•ize (dē-măg'nə-tīz') *v.* **-ized, -izing.** To remove magnetic properties from. —**de•mag'net•i•za'tion** *n.*

dem•a•gogue (dĕm'ə-gôg', -gŏg') *n.* A leader who obtains power by means of appeals to emotions and prejudices. [Gk *dēmagōgos,* popular leader.] —**dem'a•gog'ic** (dĕm'ə-gŏj'ĭk) *adj.* —**dem'a•gogu'er•y** *n.*

de•mand (dĭ-mănd', -mänd') *v.* 1. To ask for, leaving no chance for refusal. 2. To claim as just or due. 3. To need or require. —*n.* 1. The act of demanding. 2. Something demanded. 3. a. The state of being sought after. b. An urgent need. [< L *dēmandāre,* to give in charge, entrust.] —**de•mand'er** *n.*

de•mand•ing (dĭ-măn'dĭng, dĭ-män'-) *adj.* 1. Making rigorous demands. 2. Requiring careful attention or constant effort. —**de•mand'ing•ly** *adv.*

de•mar•cate (dĭ-mär'kāt', dē'mär-kāt') *v.* **-cated, -cating.** To mark with or as with boundaries. —**de•mar'ca'tor** *n.*

de•mar•ca•tion (dē'mär-kā'shən) *n.* 1. The setting or marking of boundaries or limits. 2. A separation.

de•mean (dĭ-mēn') *v.* 1. To debase in dignity or stature. 2. To humble (oneself).

de•mean•or (dĭ-mē'nər) *n.* A person's manner toward others.

de•ment•ed (dĭ-mĕn'tĭd) *adj.* 1. Insane. 2. Afflicted with dementia.

de•men•tia (dĭ-mĕn'shə, -shē-ə) *n.* Irreversible deterioration of intellectual faculties with concomitant emotional disturbance resulting from organic brain disorder. [< L *dēmēns,* mad.]

dementia prae•cox (prē'kŏks'). Schizophrenia.

de•mer•it (dĭ-mĕr'ĭt) *n.* A mark against one's record for bad conduct or failure. [Prob < L *dēmerēre,* to deserve.]

Dem•e•rol (dĕm'ə-rōl', -rôl') *n.* A trademark for a synthetic morphine.

de•mesne (dĭ-mān', -mēn') *n.* 1. The grounds belonging to a mansion. 2. An extensive piece of landed property. 3. Any territory; realm. [< OF *demaine,* domain.]

De•me•ter (dĭ-mē'tər). Greek goddess of agriculture.

demi–. *comb. form.* 1. Half. 2. Less than full status. [< L *dīmidius,* half.]

dem•i•god (dĕm'ē-gŏd') *n.* A mythological semidivine being, as the offspring of a god and a mortal.

dem•i•john (dĕm'ē-jŏn') *n.* A large bottle encased in wickerwork.

de•mil•i•ta•rize (dē-mĭl'ə-tə-rīz') *v.* **-rized, -rizing.** To eliminate or prohibit military forces in. —**de•mil'i•ta•ri•za'tion** *n.*

dem•i•monde (dĕm'ē-mŏnd, dĕm'ē-mŏnd') *n.* Any group of doubtful respectability. [F *demi-monde,* "half-world."]

de•mise (dĭ-mīz') *n.* Death. [< L *dīmittere,* to dismiss.]

dem•i•tasse (dĕm'ē-tăs', -täs') *n.* A small cup of strong black coffee. [F.]

de•mo•bil•ize (dē-mō'bə-līz') *v.* **-ized, -izing.** To discharge from military service or use. —**de•mo'bil•i•za'tion** *n.*

de•moc•ra•cy (dĭ-mŏk'rə-sē) *n., pl.* **-cies.** 1. Government by the people, exercised either directly or through elected representatives. 2. A political unit based on this form of rule. [< Gk *dēmos,* common people + -CRACY.]

dem•o•crat (dĕm'ə-krăt') *n.* An advocate of democracy.

dem•o•crat•ic (dĕm'ə-krăt'ĭk) *adj.* 1. Of, characterized by, or advocating democracy. 2. Pertaining to or promoting the interests of the people. 3. Believing in social equality; not snobbish. —**dem'o•crat'i•cal•ly** *adv.*

Democratic Party. One of the two major political parties in the U.S.

de•mog•ra•phy (dĭ-mŏg'rə-fē) *n.* The statistical study of human populations. [< Gk *dēmos,* people + -GRAPHY.] —**dem'o•graph'ic** (dĕm'ə-grăf'ĭk) *adj.* —**dem'o•graph'i•cal•ly** *adv.*

de•mol•ish (dĭ-mŏl'ĭsh) *v.* To tear down completely; destroy. [< L *dēmolīrī,* to throw down, demolish.]

dem•o•li•tion (dĕm'ə-lĭsh'ən) *n.* The act or process of demolishing, esp. destruction by explosives in warfare.

de•mon (dē'mən) *n.* 1. A devil or evil spirit. 2. One who is extremely zealous or skillful in a given activity. [< Gk *daimōn,* divine power, fate, god.]

de•mo•ni•ac (dĭ-mō'nē-ăk') *adj.* Also **de•mo•ni•a•cal** (dē'mə-nī'ə-kəl). **1.** Possessed by or as by a demon. **2.** Devilish; fiendish.

de•mon•stra•ble (dĭ-mŏn'strə-bəl) *adj.* Capable of being shown or proved. —**de•mon'stra•bly** *adv.*

dem•on•strate (dĕm'ən-strāt') *v.* **-strated, -strating.** **1.** To prove or make manifest by reasoning or evidence. **2.** To manifest or reveal. **3.** To display, operate, and explain (a product). **4.** To make a public display of opinion. [L *dēmonstrāre,* to point out.] —**dem'on•stra'tion** *n.* —**dem'on•stra'tor** *n.*

de•mon•stra•tive (dĭ-mŏn'strə-tĭv) *adj.* **1.** Serving to manifest or prove. **2.** Expressive of emotion, esp. affection. **3.** *Gram.* Specifying the person or thing referred to, as the pronoun *these.* —*n. Gram.* A demonstrative pronoun or adjective. —**de•mon'stra•tive•ly** *adv.* —**de•mon'stra•tive•ness** *n.*

de•mor•al•ize (dĭ-môr'əl-īz', dĭ-mŏr'-) *v.* **-ized, -izing.** **1.** To corrupt the morals of. **2.** To undermine the morale of; dishearten. —**de•mor'al•i•za'tion** *n.* —**de•mor'al•iz'er** *n.*

De•mos•the•nes (dĭ-mŏs'thə-nēz'). 384?–322 B.C. Athenian orator and statesman.

de•mote (dĭ-mōt') *v.* **-moted, -moting.** To lower in rank or grade. [DE- + (PRO)MOTE.] —**de•mo'tion** *n.*

de•mul•cent (dĭ-mŭl'sənt) *n.* A soothing, usually mucilaginous or oily medication. [< L *dēmulcēre,* to stroke down, caress.]

de•mur (dĭ-mûr') *v.* **-murred, -murring.** To take exception; raise objections. [< L *dēmorārī,* to delay.] —**de•mur'ra•ble** *adj.*

de•mure (dĭ-myŏŏr') *adj.* **-murer, -murest.** **1.** Modest in manner; reserved. **2.** Affectedly modest. [< OF *demorer,* to stay, delay, demur.] —**de•mure'ly** *adv.* —**de•mure'ness** *n.*

den (dĕn) *n.* **1.** The shelter of a wild animal; lair. **2.** A residence or refuge, esp. if hidden or squalid. **3.** A small room for study or relaxation. [< OE *denn* < Gmc **dan-,* low ground.]

Den. Denmark.

de•na•ture (dē-nā'chər) *v.* **-tured, -turing.** Also **de•na•tur•ize** (-chə-rīz') **-ized, -izing.** To render unfit to eat or drink, esp. to add methanol to for this purpose. —**de•na'tur•ant** *n.*

den•drite (dĕn'drīt') *n.* A branched part of a nerve cell that transmits impulses toward the cell body. [< Gk *dendron,* tree.] —**den•drit'ic** (-drĭt'ĭk) *adj.*

den•gue (dĕng'gē, dĕng'gā) *n.* An infectious tropical epidemic disease transmitted by mosquitoes and marked by fever and severe pains in the joints. [Of African origin.]

de•ni•al (dĭ-nī'əl) *n.* **1.** A negative reply, as to a request. **2.** Refusal to grant the truth of a statement. **3.** A disavowal; repudiation. **4.** Self-denial. [< DENY.]

de•nic•o•tin•ize (dē-nĭk'ə-tĭ-nīz') *v.* **-ized, -izing.** To remove nicotine from.

den•ier (də-nyā', dĕn'yər) *n.* A unit of fineness for rayon, nylon, and silk yarns. [ME *denere,* a small coin.]

den•i•grate (dĕn'ĭ-grāt') *v.* **-grated, -grating.** To belittle maliciously; defame. [L *dēnigrāre,* to blacken.] —**den'i•gra'tion** *n.*

den•im (dĕn'əm) *n.* **1.** A coarse twilled cloth used for work clothes. **2. denims.** Garments made of denim. [F *(serge) de Nîmes,* serge of *Nîmes,* city in France.]

den•i•zen (dĕn'ə-zən) *n.* An inhabitant; resident. [< LL *dēintus,* from within.]

Den•mark (dĕn'märk'). A kingdom of NW Europe. Pop. 4,684,000. Cap. Copenhagen.

de•nom•i•na•tion (dĭ-nŏm'ə-nā'shən) *n.* **1.** A name, esp. the name of a class or group. **2.** A unit having a specified value in a system of currency or weights. **3.** An organized group of religious congregations. —**de•nom'i•na'tion•al** *adj.* —**de•nom'i•na'tion•al•ly** *adv.*

de•nom•i•na•tor (dĭ-nŏm'ə-nā'tər) *n.* The quantity below the line indicating division in a fraction; the quantity that divides the numerator.

de•no•ta•tion (dē'nō-tā'shən) *n.* **1.** The act of denoting. **2.** The explicit meaning of a word as opposed to its connotation.

de•note (dĭ-nōt') *v.* **-noted, -noting.** **1.** To reveal or indicate plainly. **2.** To refer to specifically; mean explicitly.

dé•noue•ment (dā-nōō-mäN') *n.* The outcome or solution of the plot of a play or novel. [F, "an untying."]

de•nounce (dĭ-nouns') *v.* **-nounced, -nouncing.** **1.** To express vehement disapproval of openly. **2.** To accuse formally; inform against. [< L *dēnūntiāre,* make an official announcement of.] —**de•nounce'ment** *n.* —**de•nounc'er** *n.*

Den•pa•sar (dən-pä'sär'). Also **Den Pasar.** The capital of Bali. Pop. 56,000.

dense (dĕns) *adj.* **denser, densest.** **1. a.** Having relatively high density. **b.** Crowded together; compact. **2.** Thick; impenetrable. **3.** Dull; stupid. [L *dēnsus.*] —**dense'ly** *adv.*

den•si•ty (dĕn'sə-tē) *n., pl.* **-ties.** **1. a.** The amount of something per unit measure, esp. per unit length, area, or volume. **b.** The mass per unit volume of a substance under specified conditions of pressure and temperature. **2.** Thickness of consistency; impenetrability. **3.** Stupidity; dullness.

dent (dĕnt) *n.* A depression in a surface made by pressure or a blow. [< OE *dynt,* strike < Gmc **dunti-.*] —**dent** *v.*

dent. dental; dentist; dentistry.

den•tal (dĕnt'l) *adj.* **1.** Of or pertaining to the teeth. **2.** Of or pertaining to dentistry. [< L *dēns (dent-),* tooth.]

denti-. *comb. form.* Tooth.

den•ti•frice (dĕn'tə-frĭs) *n.* A substance for cleaning the teeth.

den•tine (dĕn'tēn') *n.* Also **den•tin** (-tĭn). The part of a tooth between the enamel and pulp. —**den'ti•nal** *adj.*

den•tist (dĕn'tĭst) *n.* One whose profession is dentistry.

den•tist•ry (dĕn'tĭ-strē) *n.* The diagnosis, prevention, and treatment of diseases of the teeth.

den•ti•tion (dĕn-tĭsh'ən) *n.* **1.** The type, number, and arrangement of teeth. **2.** The cutting of teeth. [< L *dēns (dent-),* tooth.]

den•ture (dĕn'chər) *n.* A set of artificial teeth.

de•nude (dĭ-n/y/ōōd') *v.* **-nuded, -nuding.** To divest of covering; make bare. —**den'u•da'tion** (dĕn'yōō-dā'shən) *n.*

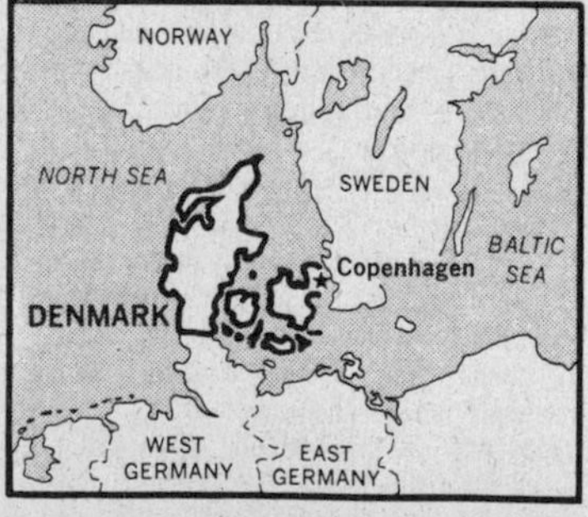

Denmark

de•nu•mer•a•ble (dĭ-n/y/ōō'mər-ə-bəl) *adj.* Capable of being put into one-to-one correspondence with the positive integers; countable. —**de•nu'mer•a•bly** *adv.*

de•nun•ci•a•tion (dĭ-nŭn'sē-ā'shən, -shē-ā'shən) *n.* The act of denouncing.

Den•ver (dĕn'vər). The capital of Colorado. Pop. 515,000.

de•ny (dĭ-nī') *v.* **-nied, -nying.** **1.** To declare untrue; contradict. **2.** To refuse to recognize or acknowledge. **3.** To refuse to grant. [< L *dēnegāre.*] —**de•ni'er** *n.*

de•o•dor•ant (dē-ō'dər-ənt) *n.* A substance used to counteract undesirable odors. [DE- + ODOR + -ANT.]

de•ox•y•ri•bo•nu•cle•ic acid (dē-ŏk'sē-rī-bō-n/y/ōō-klē'ĭk). A complex chromosomal constituent of living cell nuclei, the structural components of which are bonded in a sequence that determines individual hereditary characteristics.

dep. **1.** depart; departure. **2.** department. **3.** deposit. **4.** deputy.

Dep. dependency (territorial).

de•part (dĭ-pärt') *v.* **1.** To go away; leave. **2.** To vary, as from a regular course; deviate: *depart from custom.* [< OF *departir.*] —**de•par'ture** *n.*

de•part•ment (dĭ-pärt'mənt) *n.* **1.** A distinct division of a large organization, as a government, company, or college, having a specialized function. **2.** An area of special knowledge or activity; sphere. [< OF *departir,* divide, DEPART.] —**de'part•men'tal** *adj.*

de•pend (dĭ-pĕnd') *v.* **1.** To rely, as for support or aid (with *on* or *upon*). **2.** To place trust. **3.** To be determined by (with *on* or *upon*): *depends on your taste.* [< OF *dependre,* hang down.]

de•pend•a•ble (dĭ-pĕn'də-bəl) *adj.* Reliable; trustworthy. —**de•pend'a•bil'i•ty, de•pend'a•ble•ness** *n.* —**de•pend'a•bly** *adv.*

de•pen•dence (dĭ-pĕn'dəns) *n.* Also **de•pen•dance.** **1.** The state of being dependent, as for support. **2.** The state of being influenced or controlled by something else. **3.** Trust; reliance.

de•pen•den•cy (dĭ-pĕn'dən-sē) *n., pl.* **-cies.** Also **de•pen•dan•cy.** **1.** Dependence. **2.** A territory or state under the jurisdiction of another country from which it is separated geographically.

de•pen•dent (dĭ-pĕn'dənt). Also **de•pen•dant.** *adj.* **1.** Determined by something or someone else. **2.** Subordinate. **3.** Unable to exist or function satisfactorily without the aid of another. —*n.* One who relies on another, as for support. —**de•pen'dent•ly** *adv.*

de•pict (dĭ-pĭkt') *v.* **1.** To represent in a picture or sculpture. **2.** To describe. [L *dēpingere* (pp *dēpictus*).] —**de•pic'tion** *n.*

de•pil•a•to•ry (dĭ-pĭl'ə-tôr'ē, -tōr'ē) *n., pl.* **-ries.** A substance used to remove hair from the body.

de•plete (dĭ-plēt') *v.* **-pleted, -pleting.** To use up or exhaust. [L *dēplēre* (pp *dēplētus*), to empty.] —**de•plet'a•ble** *adj.* —**de•ple'tion** *n.*

de•plore (dĭ-plôr', -plōr') *v.* **-plored, -ploring.** **1.** To feel or express sorrow over. **2.** To regard as very unfortunate or wrong. [<L *dēplōrāre.*] —**de•plor'a•ble** *adj.* —**de•plor'a•bly** *adv.* —**de•plor'a•ble•ness** *n.*

de•ploy (dĭ-ploi') *v.* To spread out (persons or forces) systematically over an area. [< L *displicāre,* to scatter.] —**de•ploy'ment** *n.*

de•po•nent (dĭ-pō'nənt) *n.* One who testifies under oath, esp. in writing.

de•pop•u•late (dē-pŏp′yə-lāt′) *v.* **-lated, -lating.** To reduce sharply the population of. —**de•pop′u•la′tion** *n.* —**de•pop′u•la′tor** *n.*

de•port (dĭ-pôrt′, -pōrt′) *v.* **1.** To expel from a country. **2.** To behave or conduct (oneself). [< L *dēportāre,* carry off, carry away.]

de•por•ta•tion (dē′pôr-tā′shən, dē′pōr-) *n.* Expulsion from a country.

de•port•ment (dĭ-pôrt′mənt, dĭ-pōrt′-) *n.* Conduct, esp. correct conduct.

de•pose (dĭ-pōz′) *v.* **-posed, -posing. 1.** To remove from office or a position of power. **2.** *Law.* To testify, esp. in writing. [< OF *deposer.*] —**de•pos′a•ble** *adj.*

de•pos•it (dĭ-pŏz′ĭt) *v.* **1.** To place for safekeeping, as money in a bank. **2.** To put down in layers by a natural process. **3.** To give (money) as partial payment or security. —*n.* **1.** Something placed for safekeeping, as money in a bank. **2.** Money given as partial payment or security. **3.** Something, esp. a mineral or sediment, deposited by a natural process. [L *dēpōnere* (pp *dēpositus*), to put aside.] —**de•pos′i•tor** *n.*

dep•o•si•tion (dĕp′ə-zĭsh′ən) *n.* **1.** The act of deposing, as from office. **2.** The act of depositing. **3.** Something deposited. **4.** Testimony under oath.

de•pos•i•to•ry (dĭ-pŏz′ə-tôr′ē, -tōr′ē) *n., pl.* **-ries.** A place where something is deposited for safekeeping.

de•pot (dē′pō) *n.* **1.** A railroad or bus station. **2.** A warehouse. **3.** A place for the storage of military supplies. [< L *dēpositum,* deposit.]

de•prave (dĭ-prāv′) *v.* **-praved, -praving.** To debase morally; corrupt. [< L *dēprāvāre,* to pervert.] —**de•praved′** *adj.* —**de•prav′i•ty** (-prăv′ə-tē) *n.*

dep•re•cate (dĕp′rĭ-kāt′) *v.* **-cated, -cating. 1.** To express disapproval of. **2.** To depreciate; belittle. [L *dēprecārī,* to ward off by prayer.] —**dep′re•ca′tion** *n.* —**dep′re•ca′tor** *n.*

dep•re•ca•to•ry (dĕp′rə-kə-tôr′ē, -tōr′ē) *adj.* Also **dep•re•ca•tive** (-kā′tĭv). Expressing deprecation.

de•pre•ci•ate (dĭ-prē′shē-āt′) *v.* **-ated, -ating. 1.** To make or become less in price or value. **2.** To belittle. [< LL *dēpretiāre.*] —**de•pre′ci•a′tion** *n.* —**de•pre′ci•a′tor** *n.*

dep•re•date (dĕp′rə-dāt′) *v.* **-dated, -dating.** To prey upon; plunder. [LL *dēpraedārī.*] —**dep′re•da′tion** *n.*

de•press (dĭ-prĕs′) *v.* **1.** To dispirit; sadden. **2.** To press down; lower: *depress a pedal.* **3.** To lower or lessen in value, price, etc. [< L *deprimere,* to press down.] —**de•pres′sive** *adj.* —**de•pres′sive•ly** *adv.* —**de•pres′sor** *n.*

de•pres•sant (dĭ-prĕs′ənt) *adj.* Serving to lower the rate of vital activities. —*n.* A depressant drug.

de•pres•sion (dĭ-prĕsh′ən) *n.* **1.** The act of depressing or condition of being depressed. **2.** An area sunk below its surroundings; hollow. **3.** A period of drastic decline in the national economy. **4.** Melancholy; dejection.

de•prive (dĭ-prīv′) *v.* **-prived, -priving. 1.** To take something away from; divest. **2.** To keep from the possession or enjoyment of something to which one has a right. [< ML *dēprīvāre.*] —**dep′ri•va′tion** (dĕp′rə-vā′shən) *n.*

de•pro•gram (dē-prō′grăm′, -grəm) *v.* **-grammed** or **-gramed, -gramming** or **-graming.** To counteract the effect of a previous indoctrination based on sectarian, unusual, or esoteric notions. —**de•pro′gram′mer, de•pro′gram′er** *n.*

dept. department.

depth (dĕpth) *n.* **1.** The condition of being deep. **2.** The distance downward. **3.** Often **depths.** The deepest or most remote part of something. **4.** The most intense or worst part: *the depth of winter.* **5.** Intellectual penetration. **6.** The range of one's understanding: *beyond one's depth.* **7.** Intensity: *depth of color.*

depth charge. An explosive designed for use under water, esp. one used against submarines.

dep•u•ta•tion (dĕp′yə-tā′shən) *n.* A group appointed to represent others; delegation.

dep•u•tize (dĕp′yə-tīz′) *v.* **-tized, -tizing.** To appoint as a deputy.

dep•u•ty (dĕp′yə-tē) *n., pl.* **-ties.** A person empowered to act for another. [< LL *dēputāre,* to allot.] —**dep′u•ty** *adj.*

der. derivation; derivative.

de•rail (dē-rāl′) *v.* To run off or cause to run off the rails. —**de•rail′ment** *n.*

de•range (dĭ-rānj′) *v.* **-ranged, -ranging. 1.** To disturb the arrangement or functioning of. **2.** To make insane. [F *déranger.*] —**de•range′ment** *n.*

der•by (dûr′bē) *n., pl.* **-bies. 1.** A stiff felt hat with a round crown. **2. Derby.** Any of various annual horse races. **3.** Any race with an open field of contestants. [< the 12th Earl of *Derby* (died 1834).]

der•e•lict (dĕr′ə-lĭkt) *adj.* **1.** Neglectful of duty; delinquent. **2.** Abandoned by an owner. —*n.* **1.** Abandoned property, esp. an abandoned ship. **2.** A social outcast; vagrant. [L *dērelictus,* pp of *dērelinquere,* abandon.]

der•e•lic•tion (dĕr′ə-lĭk′shən) *n.* **1.** Willful neglect, as of duty. **2.** Abandonment.

de•ride (dĭ-rīd′) *v.* **-rided, -riding.** To speak of or treat with contemptuous mirth; scoff at. [L *dērīdēre.*] —**de•ri′sion** (dĭ-rĭzh′ən) *n.* —**de•ri′sive** (dĭ-rī′sĭv) *adj.* —**de•ri′sive•ly** *adv.*

der•i•va•tion (dĕr′ə-vā′shən) *n.* **1.** The act or process of deriving or condition of being derived. **2.** The source or origin of something. **3.** The origin and development of a word. **4.** A logical or mathematical sequence of statements indicating that a result necessarily follows from the initial assumptions.

de•riv•a•tive (dĭ-rĭv′ə-tĭv) *adj.* Resulting from derivation; derived. —*n.* Something, such as a word, derived from another.

de•rive (dĭ-rīv′) *v.* **-rived, -riving. 1.** To obtain or issue from a source. **2.** To deduce; infer. **3.** To trace the origin and development of something, as a word. [< L *dērīvāre,* draw off, derive.] —**de•riv′er** *n.*

-derm. *comb. form.* Skin: *endoderm.* [< Gk *derma,* skin.]

der•ma (dûr′mə) *n.* Also **derm** (dûrm), **der•mis** (dûr′mĭs). A layer of skin, the corium. [< Gk *derma,* skin.] —**der′mal** *adj.*

der•ma•ti•tis (dûr′mə-tī′tĭs) *n.* Inflammation of the skin.

dermato–. *comb. form.* Skin. [< Gk *derma,* skin.]

der•ma•tol•o•gy (dûr′mə-tŏl′ə-jē) *n.* The medical study of the physiology and pathology of the skin. —**der′ma•tol′o•gist** *n.*

der•o•gate (dĕr′ə-gāt′) *v.* **-gated, -gating.** To detract or disparage. [L *dērogāre,* repeal, restrict, disparage.] —**der′o•ga′tion** *n.*

de•rog•a•to•ry (dĭ-rŏg′ə-tôr′ē, -tōr′ē) *adj.* Detracting; disparaging.

der•rick (dĕr′ĭk) *n.* **1.** A large crane for hoisting and moving heavy objects. **2.** A framework over the opening of an oil well, used to support equipment.

der•ri•ère (dĕr′ē-âr′) *n.* The buttocks. [F, "the rear."]

der•ring-do (dĕr′ĭng-do͞o′) *n.* Daring spirit and action. [ME *durring don,* daring to do.]

der•rin•ger (dĕr′ĭn-jər) *n.* A small pistol. [< H. *Deringer,* 19th-century American gunsmith.]

der•vish (dûr′vĭsh) *n.* A member of any of various Moslem ascetic orders. [Turk *derviş,* mendicant.]

de•sal•i•nate (dē-săl′ə-nāt′) *v.* **-nated, -nating.** To desalinize. —**de•sal′i•na′tion** *n.*

de•sal•in•ize (dē-săl′ə-nīz′) *v.* **-ized, -izing.** To remove salts and other chemicals from (sea water). —**de•sal′i•ni•za′tion** *n.*

Des•cartes (dā-kärt′), **René.** 1596–1650. French philosopher and mathematician.

de•scend (dĭ-sĕnd′) *v.* **1.** To move to a lower level; come or go down. **2.** To slope or incline downward. **3.** To be derived from ancestors. [< L *dēscendere.*]

de•scen•dant (dĭ-sĕn′dənt) *n.* An immediate or remote offspring. —*adj.* Descendent.

de•scen•dent (dĭ-sĕn′dənt) *adj.* Also **de•scen•dant. 1.** Moving downward; descending. **2.** Proceeding from an ancestor.

de•scent (dĭ-sĕnt′) *n.* **1.** The act or an instance of descending. **2.** A downward incline. **3.** Ancestral extraction; lineage. **4.** A lowering or decline.

de•scribe (dĭ-skrīb′) *v.* **-scribed, -scribing. 1.** To tell about in detail; picture verbally. **2.** To trace or draw the figure of. [L *dēscrībere,* to copy off, write down.] —**de•scrib′er** *n.*

de•scrip•tion (dĭ-skrĭp′shən) *n.* **1.** The act, process, or technique of describing. **2.** An account describing something. **3.** A kind; sort: *costumes of every description.* [< L *dēscrībere,* DESCRIBE.] —**de•scrip′tive adj.**

de•scry (dĭ-skrī′) *v.* **-scried, -scrying.** To discern (something difficult to catch sight of). [ME *descrien,* cry out, proclaim, catch sight of.]

des•e•crate (dĕs′ə-krāt′) *v.* **-crated, -crating.** To subject to sacrilege; profane. [DE- + (CON)-SECRATE.] —**des′e•cra′tion** *n.*

de•seg•re•gate (dē-sĕg′rə-gāt′) *v.* **-grated, -grating.** To abolish racial segregation in. —**de′seg•re•ga′tion** *n.*

de•sen•si•tize (dē-sĕn′sə-tīz′) *v.* **-tized, -tizing.** To render insensitive. —**de•sen′si•ti•za′tion** *n.*

des•ert¹ (dĕz′ərt) *n.* A region rendered barren or partially barren by environmental extremes, esp. by low rainfall. [< L *dēserere,* to DESERT.] —**des′ert** *adj.*

de•sert² (dĭ-zûrt′) *n.* Often **deserts.** That which is deserved, esp. a punishment: *received his just deserts.*

de•sert³ (dĭ-zûrt′) *v.* **1.** To forsake or leave; abandon. **2.** To abandon one's duty or post. [< L *dēserere,* to abandon.] —**de•sert′er** *n.* —**de•ser′tion** *n.*

de•serve (dĭ-zûrv′) *v.* **-served, -serving.** To be worthy of; merit. [< L *dēservire,* serve well.]

de•served (dĭ-zûrvd′) *adj.* Merited or earned. —**de•serv′ed•ly** (-vĭd-lē) *adv.*

de•serv•ing (dĭ-zûr′vĭng) *adj.* Worthy; meritorious. —**de•serv′ing•ly** *adv.*

des•ic•cant (dĕs′ĭ-kənt) *n.* A substance used to absorb moisture. [< L *dēsiccāre,* DESICCATE.]

des•ic•cate (dĕs′ĭ-kāt′) *v.* **-cated, -cating.** To make or become thoroughly dry. [L *dēsiccāre.*] —**des′ic•ca′tion** *n.* —**des′ic•ca′tive** *adj.*

de•sid•er•a•tum (dĭ-sĭd′ə-rā′təm) *n., pl.* **-ta** (-tə). Something needed and desired. [< L *dēsīderāre,* DESIRE.]

de•sign (dĭ-zīn′) *v.* **1.** To conceive; invent. **2.** To form a plan for. **3.** To draw a sketch of. **4.** To have as or make for a purpose; intend. —*n.* **1.** The arrangement of the parts or details of something according to a plan. **2.** A visual composition; pattern. **3.** A purpose; intention; plan. **4.** Often **designs.** A sinister scheme. [< L *dēsignāre,* DESIGNATE.] —**de·sign′er** *n.*

des·ig·nate (dĕz′ĭg-nāt′) *v.* **-nated, -nating. 1.** To indicate or specify. **2.** To give a name to. **3.** To appoint. —*adj.* (dĕz′ĭg-nĭt). Appointed but not yet installed in office. [L *dēsignāre,* designate, mark out.] —**des′ig·na′tion** *n.*

de·sign·ing (dĭ-zī′nĭng) *adj.* Conniving.

de·sir·a·ble (dĭ-zīr′ə-bəl) *adj.* **1.** Worth seeking or having. **2.** Arousing desire. **3.** Advantageous; advisable. —**de·sir′a·bil′i·ty** *n.*

de·sire (dĭ-zīr′) *v.* **-sired, -siring. 1.** To wish or long for; crave. **2.** To express a wish for. —*n.* **1.** A wish, longing, or craving. **2.** A request. **3.** Something longed for. **4.** Sexual appetite. [< L *dēsiderāre.*] —**de·sir′er** *n.*

de·sir·ous (dĭ-zīr′əs) *adj.* Desiring.

de·sist (dĭ-zĭst′) *v.* To cease doing something; stop. [< L *dēsistere,* cease, stand off.]

desk (dĕsk) *n.* A piece of furniture with a flat top for writing. [< L *discus,* quoit, DISK.]

Des Moines (də moin′, moinz′). The capital of Iowa. Pop. 200,000.

des·o·late (dĕs′ə-lĭt) *adj.* **1.** Devoid of inhabitants; deserted. **2.** Unfit for habitation; laid waste. **3.** Cheerless; dismal; gloomy. **4.** Forlorn; lonely. —*v.* (dĕs′ə-lāt′) **-lated, -lating.** To make desolate. [< L *dēsōlāre,* abandon.] —**des′o·late·ly** *adv.*

des·o·la·tion (dĕs′ə-lā′shən) *n.* **1.** The act of rendering desolate. **2.** A wasteland. **3.** Loneliness; wretchedness.

de·spair (dĭ-spâr′) *v.* To lose all hope. —*n.* **1.** Utter lack of hope. **2.** That which destroys all hope. [< L *dēspērāre.*] —**de·spair′ing·ly** *adv.*

des·patch. Variant of **dispatch.**

des·per·a·do (dĕs′pə-rä′dō, -rā′dō) *n., pl.* **-does** or **-dos.** A desperate, dangerous criminal. [Pseudo-Span var of DESPERATE.]

des·per·ate (dĕs′pər-ĭt) *adj.* **1.** Reckless or violent because of despair. **2.** Nearly hopeless; causing despair. **3.** Extreme; very great: *desperate need.* [< L *dēspērāre,* to DESPAIR.] —**des′per·ate·ly** *adv.* —**des′per·ate·ness** *n.*

des·per·a·tion (dĕs′pə-rā′shən) *n.* **1.** The condition of being desperate. **2.** Recklessness arising from despair.

des·pi·ca·ble (dĕs′pĭ-kə-bəl, dĭ-spĭk′-) *adj.* Deserving of contempt or disdain. [< L *dēspicārī,* despise.] —**des′pi·ca·bly** *adv.*

de·spise (dĭ-spīz′) *v.* **-spised, -spising.** To regard with contempt or disdain. [< L *dēspicere,* to look down on.] —**de·spis′er** *n.*

de·spite (dĭ-spīt′) *prep.* In spite of. [< OF *despit,* spite.]

de·spoil (dĭ-spoil′) *v.* To deprive of possessions by force; plunder. [< L *dēspoliāre.*] —**de·spoil′er** *n.* —**de·spoil′ment** *n.*

de·spo·li·a·tion (dĭ-spō′lē-ā′shən) *n.* The act of despoiling or condition of being despoiled; plunder.

de·spond (dĭ-spŏnd′) *v.* To become disheartened. [L *dēspondēre,* despond, promise to give, give up.] —**de·spond′ing·ly** *adv.*

de·spon·den·cy (dĭ-spŏn′dən-sē) *n., pl.* **-cies.** Also **de·spon·dence** (-dəns). Depression of spirits from loss of hope or courage; dejection. —**de·spon′dent** *adj.* —**de·spon′dent·ly** *adv.*

des·pot (dĕs′pət) *n.* An autocratic ruler; tyrant. [< Gk *despotēs.*] —**des·pot′ic** (dĭ-spŏt′ĭk) *adj.* —**des·pot′i·cal·ly** *adv.* —**des′pot·ism′** *n.*

des·sert (dĭ-zûrt′) *n.* A usually sweet food served as the last course of a meal. [< OF *desservir,* clear the table.]

des·ti·na·tion (dĕs′tə-nā′shən) *n.* **1.** The place or point to which someone or something is going. **2.** An ultimate goal or purpose.

des·tine (dĕs′tĭn) *v.* **-tined, -tining. 1.** To determine beforehand; preordain. **2.** To intend for or direct toward a specific end or place. [< L *dēstināre,* determine, destine, make firm.]

des·ti·ny (dĕs′tə-nē) *n., pl.* **-nies. 1.** The preordained or inevitable course of events. **2.** One's fate; lot.

des·ti·tute (dĕs′tə-t/y/ōōt′) *adj.* **1.** Altogether lacking; devoid: *destitute of courage.* **2.** Very poor; penniless. [< L *dēstituere,* to set down, desert.] —**des′ti·tu′tion** *n.*

de·stroy (dĭ-stroi′) *v.* **1.** To put an end to; ruin completely. **2.** To tear down; demolish. **3.** To kill. [< L *dēstruere* (pp *dēstructus*).]

de·stroy·er (dĭ-stroi′ər) *n.* **1.** One that destroys. **2.** A small, fast warship.

de·struct (dĭ-strŭkt′) *n.* The intentional destruction of a space vehicle, rocket, or missile after launching.

de·struc·ti·ble (dĭ-strŭk′tə-bəl) *adj.* Capable of being destroyed. —**de·struc′ti·bil′i·ty** *n.*

de·struc·tion (dĭ-strŭk′shən) *n.* **1.** The act of destroying or state of being destroyed. **2.** A means of destroying. —**de·struc′tive** *adj.* —**de·struc′tive·ly** *adv.* —**de·struc′tive·ness** *n.*

destructive distillation. The simultaneous decomposition by heat and distillation of substances such as wood and coal to produce useful by-products.

des·ue·tude (dĕs′wə-t/y/ōōd′) *n.* A state of disuse. [< L *dēsuēcere,* to put out of use, become unaccustomed.]

des·ul·to·ry (dĕs′əl-tôr′ē, -tōr′ē) *adj.* Progressing aimlessly; disconnected; haphazard. [L *dēsultōrius,* of a leaper.]

det. **1.** *Mil.* detachment. **2.** detail.

de·tach (dĭ-tăch′) *v.* To separate; remove; disconnect. [< OF *destachier.*] —**de·tach′a·ble** *adj.* —**de·tach′a·bly** *adv.*

de·tached (dĭ-tăcht′) *adj.* **1.** Apart from others; separate: *a detached house.* **2.** Free from emotional involvement; disinterested.

de·tach·ment (dĭ-tăch′mənt) *n.* **1.** The act of detaching or condition of being detached; separation. **2.** Disinterest; aloofness. **3.** A military unit dispatched or organized for special duty.

de·tail (dĭ-tāl′, dē′tāl) *n.* **1.** An individual part or item. **2.** Itemized or minute treatment of particulars. **3. a.** A group of military personnel selected to do a specified task. **b.** The task assigned. —*v.* **1.** To relate item by item. **2.** To assign (military personnel) to a specified task. [< OF, piece cut off.]

de·tain (dĭ-tān′) *v.* **1.** To keep from proceeding; delay or retard. **2.** To keep in custody; confine. [< L *dētinēre,* to keep back.] —**de·tain′ment** *n.*

de·tect (dĭ-tĕkt′) *v.* To discover or discern the existence, presence, or fact of. [< L *dētegere* (pp *dētectus*), uncover.] —**de·tect′a·ble, de·tect′i·ble** *adj.* —**de·tec′tion** *n.* —**de·tec′tor** *n.*

de·tec·tive (dĭ-tĕk′tĭv) *n.* One whose work is obtaining evidence or concealed information, as in investigating crimes.

dé·tente (dā-tänt′) *n.* A relaxing of tension, as between nations. [F, a loosening.]

de·ten·tion (dĭ-tĕn′shən) *n.* **1.** The act of detaining or state of being detained. **2.** A period of being kept in confinement or temporary custody. [< L *dētinēre,* DETAIN.]

de·ter (dĭ-tûr′) *v.* **-terred, -terring.** To prevent or discourage (someone) from acting, as through doubt or fear. [L *dēterrēre,* frighten from.] —**de·ter′ment** *n.*

de·ter·gent (dĭ-tûr′jənt) *n.* A cleansing substance, esp. one made from chemical compounds other than fats and lye. [< L *dētergēre,* to wipe off.]

de·te·ri·o·rate (dĭ-tîr′ē-ə-rāt′) *v.* **-rated, -rating.** To become or make worse. [< L *dēterior,* worse.] —**de·te′ri·o·ra′tion** *n.*

de·ter·mi·nant (dĭ-tûr′mə-nənt) *adj.* Serving to determine. —*n.* An influencing or determining factor.

de·ter·mi·nate (dĭ-tûr′mə-nĭt) *adj.* Precisely limited or defined.

de·ter·mi·na·tion (dĭ-tûr′mə-nā′shən) *n.* **1. a.** The act or process of determining or being determined. **b.** A decision or result thus arrived at. **2.** Firmness of purpose; resoluteness.

de·ter·mine (dĭ-tûr′mĭn) *v.* **-mined, -mining. 1.** To decide, establish, or ascertain authoritatively or conclusively. **2.** To limit or regulate. **3.** To affect as a causative factor; influence. **4.** To resolve firmly. [< L *dētermināre,* to limit.] —**de·ter′mi·na·ble** *adj.* —**de·ter′mi·na·bly** *adv.*

de·ter·mined (dĭ-tûr′mĭnd) *adj.* Fixed in purpose; resolute; firm. —**de·ter′mined·ly** *adv.*

de·ter·min·ism (dĭ-tûr′mə-nĭz′əm) *n.* Any philosophical doctrine asserting a mechanical correspondence between determining causes and effects.

de·ter·rent (dĭ-tûr′ənt) *adj.* Serving to deter. —*n.* That which deters. —**de·ter′rence** *n.*

de·test (dĭ-tĕst′) *v.* To dislike intensely; loathe; hate. [L *dētestārī,* curse, execrate.] —**de·test′a·ble** *adj.* —**de′tes·ta′tion** *n.*

de·throne (dē-thrōn′) *v.* **-throned, -throning.** To depose from a throne. —**de·throne′ment** *n.*

det·o·nate (dĕt′n-āt′) *v.* **-nated, -nating.** To explode or cause to explode. [L *dētonāre,* to thunder down.] —**det′o·na·ble** *adj.* —**det′o·na′tion** *n.* —**det′o·na′tor** *n.*

de·tour (dē′tŏŏr′, dĭ-tŏŏr′) *n.* A roundabout way, esp. one used temporarily instead of a main route. —*v.* To go or cause to go by a detour. [< OF *destorner,* to turn away.]

de·tract (dĭ-trăkt′) *v.* To reduce by taking away (from); diminish. [< L *dētrahere,* to pull down, draw away.] —**de·trac′tion** *n.* —**de·trac′tive** *adj.* —**de·trac′tor** *n.*

de·train (dē-trān′) *v.* To leave or cause to leave a railroad train.

det·ri·ment (dĕt′rə-mənt) *n.* **1.** Harm; disadvantage. **2.** A cause of this. [< L *dēterere,* to wear away.] —**det′ri·men′tal** *adj.* —**det′ri·men′tal·ly** *adv.*

de·tri·tus (dĭ-trī′təs) *n.* Fragments formed by disintegration, as of rocks. [< L *dēterere,* to wear away.]

De·troit (dĭ-troit′). A city in SE Michigan. Pop. 1,511,000.

deuce (d/y/ōōs) *n.* **1.** A two in playing cards or dice. **2.** A tied tennis score necessitating the scoring of two successive points by one side to win. **3.** Euphemism for the devil. [< L *duo,* two.]

Deut. Deuteronomy (Old Testament).

deu·te·ri·um (dōō-tîr′ē-əm) *n.* An isotope of hydrogen having an atomic weight of 2.0141. [< Gk *deuteros,* second.]

deuterium oxide. An isotopic form of water with composition D_2O, present in natural water as approximately one part in 6,500.

deu·ter·on (d/y/ōō′tə-rŏn) *n.* The nucleus of a deuterium atom, a composite of a proton and a neutron, regarded as a single subatomic particle. [DEUTER(IUM) + -ON.]

Deut·sche mark (doi′chə märk′). Also **deut·sche·mark.** The basic monetary unit of West

Germany.

de•val•u•ate (dē-văl′yo͞o-āt′) *v.* **-ated, -ating.** Also **de•val•ue** (-văl′yo͞o) **-ued, -uing. 1.** To lower the exchange value of (currency). **2.** To lessen the value of. **—de•val′u•a′tion** *n.*

dev•as•tate (dĕv′ə-stāt′) *v.* **-tated, -tating. 1.** To lay waste. **2.** To overwhelm; confound. [L *dēvāstāre.*] **—dev′as•ta′tion** *n.*

de•vel•op (dĭ-vĕl′əp) *v.* **1.** To bring, grow, or evolve to a more complete, complex, or desirable state. **2.** To appear, disclose, or acquire gradually. **3.** To elaborate; expand. **4.** To make available or usable. **5.** To process (a photosensitive material) chemically in order to render a recorded image visible. [< OF *desveloper.*] **—de•vel′op•er** *n.*

de•vel•op•ment (dĭ-vĕl′əp-mənt) *n.* **1.** The process or result of developing. **2.** An event; occurrence: *await new developments.* **3.** A group of dwellings built by the same contractor.

de•vi•ant (dē′vē-ənt) *adj.* Differing from a norm or accepted standard. *—n.* A deviant individual. **—de′vi•ance** *n.*

de•vi•ate (dē′vē-āt′) *v.* **-ated, -ating.** To move or turn away from a normal or accepted course or standard. *—n.* (dē′vē-ĭt). A deviant, esp. a sexual pervert. [LL *dēviāre.*] **—de′vi•a′tion** *n.* **—de′vi•a′tor** *n.*

de•vice (dĭ-vīs′) *n.* **1.** Something, as a mechanical contrivance, made for a particular purpose. **2.** A scheme; trick; artifice. **3.** A decorative figure or symbol. **—leave to one's own devices.** To allow to do as one pleases. [< OF *deviser,* to divide, devise.]

dev•il (dĕv′əl) *n.* **1. a.** Often **Devil.** The major spirit of evil, esp. in Christian theology. **b.** A demon or similar evil spirit. **2.** A wicked or destructively mischievous person. **3.** A dashing or daring person. **4.** An unfortunate person; wretch. **5.** A printer's apprentice. *—v.* **-iled** or **-illed, -iling** or **-illing. 1.** To annoy; torment. **2.** To prepare (food) with pungent seasonings. [< Gk *diabolos,* slanderer.]

dev•il•ish (dĕv′ə-lĭsh) *adj.* **1.** Of or like a devil; fiendish. **2.** Excessive; extreme. *—adv. Informal.* Extremely; very.

dev•il-may-care (dĕv′əl-mā-kâr′) *adj.* Reckless; careless.

dev•il•ment (dĕv′əl-mənt) *n.* Mischief.

dev•il•try (dĕv′əl-trē) *n.* Also **dev•il•ry** (-əl-rē). Reckless mischief.

de•vi•ous (dē′vē-əs) *adj.* **1.** Deviating from a straight or direct course; roundabout. **2.** Not straightforward; deceitful: *a devious person.* [L *dēvius,* off the main road.] **—de′vi•ous•ly** *adv.* **—de′vi•ous•ness** *n.*

de•vise (dĭ-vīz′) *v.* **-vised, -vising. 1.** To plan; invent; contrive. **2.** To transmit (real property) by will. [< L *dīvidere* (pp *dīvīsus*), to divide.] **—de•vis′er** *n.*

de•vi•tal•ize (dē-vīt′l-īz′) *v.* **-ized, -izing.** To lower or destroy the vitality of.

de•void (dĭ-void′) *adj.* **—devoid of.** Completely lacking; empty. [< OF *desvuidier.*]

de•volve (dĭ-vŏlv′) *v.* **-volved, -volving.** To pass or be transmitted (on) to another person, as duty or authority. [< L *dēvolvere,* to roll down.] **—de•volve′ment** *n.*

De•vo•ni•an (dĭ-vō′nē-ən) *adj.* Of or belonging to the geologic time, system of rocks, or sedimentary deposits of the 4th period of the Paleozoic era, characterized by the appearance of forests and amphibians. *—n.* The Devonian period.

de•vote (dĭ-vōt′) *v.* **-voted, -voting. 1.** To give or apply (oneself, one's time, etc.) entirely. **2.** To dedicate; consecrate. [L *dēvovēre,* to vow, devote.]

de•vot•ed (dĭ-vō′tĭd) *adj.* **1.** Loving; faithful. **2.** Dedicated; zealous. **—de•vot′ed•ly** *adv.*

dev•o•tee (dĕv′ə-tē′, -tā′) *n.* An ardent enthusiast.

de•vo•tion (dĭ-vō′shən) *n.* **1.** Ardent attachment or affection; loyalty. **2.** Religious zeal. **3. Devotions.** Prayers, esp. personal prayers. **—de•vo′tion•al** *adj.* **—de•vo′tion•al•ly** *adv.*

de•vour (dĭ-vour′) *v.* **1.** To eat up greedily. **2.** To consume or destroy; swallow up. **3.** To take in greedily with the senses or mind. [< L *dēvorāre.*] **—de•vour′er** *n.*

de•vout (dĭ-vout′) *adj.* **1.** Deeply religious; reverent; pious. **2.** Sincere; earnest. [< L *dēvovēre,* to vow, DEVOTE.] **—de•vout′ly** *adv.* **—de•vout′ness** *n.*

dew (d/y/o͞o) *n.* **1.** Water droplets condensed from the air, usually at night, onto cool surfaces. **2.** Something resembling or suggestive of dew. [< OE *dēaw.* See **dheu-**[2].] **—dew′i•ly** *adv.* **—dew′i•ness** *n.* **—dew′y** *adj.*

dew•lap (d/y/o͞o′lăp′) *n.* A fold of skin hanging from the neck of certain animals.

dew point. The temperature at which air becomes saturated and produces dew.

dex•ter•i•ty (dĕk-stĕr′ə-tē) *n.* Manual or mental skill; adroitness. [< L *dexter,* skillful, on the right side.]

dex•ter•ous (dĕk′strəs) *adj.* Also **dex•trous.** Skillful, as in manipulation; adroit. **—dex′ter•ous•ly** *adv.* **—dex′ter•ous•ness** *n.*

dex•trose (dĕk′strōs′) *n.* A sugar, $C_6H_{12}O_6 \cdot H_2O$, found in animal and plant tissue and derived synthetically from starch. [< L *dexter,* on the right side.]

dg decigram.

di–. *comb. form.* Twice, double, or two. [< Gk *di-,* two, twice.]

Di didymium.

dia–, di–. *comb. form.* **1.** Through or throughout. **2.** Across or by transmission. **3.** In opposite or different directions. [< Gk *dia,* through.]

dia. diameter.

di•a•be•tes (dī′ə-bē′tĭs, -tēz) *n.* Any of several metabolic disorders marked by excessive discharge of urine and persistent thirst, esp. diabetes mellitus. [< Gk *diabētēs,* "a crossing over or passing through."] **—di′a•bet′ic** (-bĕt′ĭk) *adj.* & *n.*

diabetes mel•li•tus (mə-lī′təs). A chronic disease of pancreatic origin, characterized by insulin deficiency, subsequent inability to utilize carbohydrates, excess sugar in the blood and urine, weakness, emaciation, and, without injection of insulin, eventual coma and death. [NL, "honey-sweet diabetes."]

di•a•bol•ic (dī′ə-bŏl′ĭk) *adj.* Also **di•a•bol•i•cal** (-ĭ-kəl). Devilish; wicked; fiendish. [< LL *diabolus,* devil.] **—di′a•bol′i•cal•ly** *adv.*

di•a•crit•i•cal (dī′ə-krĭt′ĭ-kəl). Also **di•a•crit•ic** (-ĭk). *adj.* Marking a distinction; distinguishing. *—n.* Also **diacritical mark.** A mark added to a letter to indicate a special phonetic value. [G *diakritikos,* distinguishing.]

di•a•dem (dī′ə-dĕm′) *n.* A crown or headband indicative of royalty. [< Gk *diadein,* to bind on either side.]

di•aer•e•sis. Variant of **dieresis.**

diag. 1. diagonal. **2.** diagram.

di•ag•no•sis (dī′əg-nō′sĭs) *n., pl.* **-ses** (-sēz). Identification, esp. of a disease, by examination or analysis. [< Gk *diagnōsis,* discernment.] **—di′ag•nose′** *v.* **(-nosed, -nosing). —di′ag•nos′tic** (-nŏs′tĭk) *adj.* **—di′ag•nos′ti•cal•ly** *adv.* **—di′ag•nos•ti′cian** *n.*

di•ag•o•nal (dī-ăg′ə-nəl) *adj.* **1.** Joining two nonadjacent vertices. **2.** Slanted or oblique in direction. *—n.* A diagonal line or plane. [< Gk *diagōnios,* from angle to angle.] **—di•ag′o•nal•ly** *adv.*

di•a•gram (dī′ə-grăm′) *n.* **1.** A schematic drawing or plan devised as a graphic representation of relationships between parts of a whole. **2.** *Math.* A graphic representation of an algebraic or geometric relationship. *—v.* **-grammed** or **-gramed, -gramming** or **-graming.** To represent by a diagram. [< Gk *diagramma.*] **—di′a•gram•mat′ic, di′a•gram•mat′i•cal** *adj.* **—di′a•gram•mat′i•cal•ly** *adv.*

di•al (dī′əl) *n.* **1.** A marked disk or plate on which a measurement, as of time, speed, or temperature, is indicated by a moving pointer. **2.** A rotatable disk, as of a telephone or radio, for making connections, changing frequency, etc. *—v.* **-aled** or **-alled, -aling** or **-alling. 1.** To indicate or select by means of a dial. **2.** To call on a telephone with a dial. [< ML *diālis,* daily.] **—di′al•er, di′al•ler** *n.*

dial. dialect; dialectal.

di•a•lect (dī′ə-lĕkt′) *n.* **1.** A regional variety of a spoken language. **2.** A jargon. **3.** A language considered as part of a larger group of languages: *Spanish and French are Romance dialects.* [< Gk *dialektos,* speech, language, dialect.] **—di′a•lec′tal** *adj.*

di•a•lec•tic (dī′ə-lĕk′tĭk) *n.* Also **di•a•lec•tics** (-tĭks) *(takes sing. or pl. v.).* The art or process whereby contradictions are disclosed and synthetically resolved. **—di′a•lec′ti•cal, di′a•lec′tic** *adj.*

di•a•logue (dī′ə-lôg′, -lŏg′) *n.* Also **di•a•log. 1.** A conversation between two or more people. **2.** Conversation material in a play or narrative. **3.** An exchange of ideas or opinions. [< Gk *dialegesthai,* to converse.]

di•al•y•sis (dī-ăl′ə-sĭs) *n., pl.* **-ses** (-sēz′). The separation of molecular or particulate constituents in a solution by selective diffusion through a semipermeable membrane. [< Gk *dialuein,* to tear apart.]

di•am•e•ter (dī-ăm′ə-tər) *n.* **1. a.** A straight line segment passing through the center of a figure, esp. of a circle or sphere, and terminating at the periphery. **b.** The length of such a segment. **2.** Thickness or width as a dimension. [< Gk *diametros (grammē),* "(line) that measures through."] **—di′a•met′ri•cal** (-ə-mĕt′rĭ-kəl), **di′a•met′ric** *adj.* **—di′a•met′ri•cal•ly** *adv.*

dia•mond (dī′mənd, dī′ə-) *n.* **1.** An extremely hard, highly refractive colorless or white crystalline allotrope of carbon, used as a gemstone when pure and chiefly in abrasives otherwise. **2.** A rhombus or lozenge. **3.** Any of a suit of playing cards marked with a red, diamond-shaped symbol. **4.** A baseball infield or playing field. [< LL *diamas (diamant-).*]

Di•an•a (dī-ăn′ə). Roman goddess; patroness of women and wild animals.

di•a•pa•son (dī′ə-pā′sən, -zən) *n.* **1.** A full tonal range, as of an instrument or voices. **2.** One of two organ stops that establish tonal range. [< Gk *(hē) dia pasōn (khordōn sumphonia),* (concord) through all (the notes).]

di•a•per (dī′ə-pər, dī′pər) *n.* A folded cloth or similar piece of absorbent material, used to cover the genital and anal areas of a baby. *—v.* To put a diaper on (a baby). [ME *diapre,* linen cloth with diamond pattern.]

di•aph•a•nous (dī-ăf′ə-nəs) *adj.* Delicately transparent or translucent; gauzy. [< Gk *di-*

aphanein, to show through.]

di•a•pho•ret•ic (dī′ə-fə-rĕt′ĭk) *adj.* Producing perspiration. —*n.* A diaphoretic medicine or agent.

di•a•phragm (dī′ə-frăm′) *n.* **1.** A muscular membranous partition separating the abdominal and thoracic cavities and functioning in respiration. **2.** Any similar membranous part that divides or separates. **3.** A thin disk, esp. in a microphone or telephone receiver, the vibrations of which convert electric to acoustic signals or acoustic to electric signals. **4.** A contraceptive consisting of a flexible disk that covers the uterine cervix. **5.** A disk having a fixed or variable opening used to restrict the amount of light traversing a lens or optical system. [< Gk *diaphrassein,* to barricade.]

di•ar•rhe•a (dī′ə-rē′ə) *n.* Also **di•ar•rhoe•a.** Pathologically excessive evacuation of watery feces. [< Gk *diarrhoia,* "a flowing through."]

di•a•ry (dī′ə-rē) *n., pl.* **-ries. 1.** A daily record, esp. of personal experiences and observations. **2.** A book for keeping such a record. [L *diārium,* daily allowance, journal.] —**di′a•rist** *n.*

di•as•to•le (dī-ăs′tə-lē) *n.* The normal rhythmically occurring relaxation and dilatation of the heart cavities during which the cavities are filled with blood. [Gk *diastolē,* dilatation, separation.] —**di′a•stol′ic** (dī′ə-stŏl′ĭk) *adj.*

di•a•ther•my (dī′ə-thûr′mē) *n.* The therapeutic generation of local heat in body tissues by high-frequency electromagnetic waves. —**di′a•ther′mic** *adj.*

di•a•tom (dī′ə-tŏm′, -təm) *n.* Any of various minute, unicellular algae with hard, glasslike cell walls. [< Gk *diatomos,* cut in half.]

di•a•tom•ic (dī′ə-tŏm′ĭk) *adj.* **1.** Made up of two atoms. **2.** Having two replaceable atoms or radicals.

di•a•ton•ic (dī′ə-tŏn′ĭk) *adj.* Of or pertaining to the eight tones of a standard major or minor scale. —**di′a•ton′i•cal•ly** *adv.*

di•a•tribe (dī′ə-trīb′) *n.* A bitter and abusive verbal attack. [< Gk *diatribē,* "a wearing away," "pastime."]

dib•ble (dĭb′əl) *n.* A pointed implement used to make holes in soil, as for planting bulbs. [ME *debylle.*]

dice (dīs) *pl.n. Sing.* **die** (dī). Small cubes marked on each side with from one to six dots, used in gambling games. —*v.* **diced, dicing. 1.** To cut into small cubes. **2.** To gamble with dice. [Pl of DIE[2].] —**dic′er** *n.*

di•chot•o•my (dī-kŏt′ə-mē) *n., pl.* **-mies.** Division into two usually contradictory parts or categories. [< Gk *dikhotomos,* divided.] —**di•chot′o•mous** *adj.* —**di•chot′o•mous•ly** *adv.*

dick (dĭk) *n. Slang.* A detective.

dick•ens (dĭk′ənz). Euphemism for the devil.

Dick•ens (dĭk′ənz), **Charles.** 1812–1870. English novelist.

dick•er (dĭk′ər) *v.* To bargain; haggle. [Prob < earlier *dicker,* ten, ten hides.]

dick•ey (dĭk′ē) *n., pl.* **-eys.** Also **dick•y** *pl.* **-ies. 1.** A detachable blouse or shirt front. **2.** Often **dickeybird.** Any small bird. [< *Dick,* nickname for Richard.]

Dick test (dĭk). A test of susceptibility to scarlet fever. [< G. *Dick* (born 1881), American physician.]

di•cot•y•le•don (dī′kŏt′l-ēd′n) *n.* Also **di•cot** (dī′kŏt). A plant with a pair of embryonic seed leaves that appear at germination. [DI- + COTYLEDON.] —**di′cot•y•le′don•ous** *adj.*

dict. dictionary.

dic•tate (dĭk′tāt′, dĭk-tāt′) *v.* **-tated, -tating. 1.** To say or read aloud for recording or transcription. **2.** To issue (a command, order, etc.) authoritatively. —*n.* (dĭk′tāt′). A directive or command. [L *dictāre,* freq of *dīcere,* to say, tell.] —**dic•ta′tion** *n.*

dic•ta•tor (dĭk′tā-tər) *n.* **1.** A ruler having absolute governmental authority, esp. one considered tyrannical or oppressive. **2.** One who dictates. —**dic•ta′tor•ship′** *n.*

dic•ta•to•ri•al (dĭk′tə-tôr′ē-əl, -tōr′ē-əl) *adj.* Characteristic of or pertaining to a dictator; autocratic; highhanded. —**dic′ta•to′ri•al•ly** *adv.* —**dic′ta•to′ri•al•ness** *n.*

dic•tion (dĭk′shən) *n.* **1.** Choice and use of words in speech or writing. **2.** Distinctness of speech; enunciation. [< L *dīcere,* to say.]

dic•tion•ar•y (dĭk′shə-nĕr′ē) *n., pl.* **-ies.** A reference book containing an alphabetical list of words with definitions or equivalent translations into another language. [< L *dictiō,* diction.]

dic•tum (dĭk′təm) *n., pl.* **-ta** (-tə) or **-tums.** An authoritatively stated pronouncement or opinion. [< L *dīcere,* say.]

did (dĭd). *p.t.* of **do.**

di•dac•tic (dī-dăk′tĭk) *adj.* **1.** Intended to provide instruction, esp. moral instruction. **2.** Inclined to moralize. [Gk *didaktikos,* skillful in teaching.] —**di•dac′ti•cal•ly** *adv.*

did•dle (dĭd′l) *v.* **-dled, -dling. 1.** To cheat; swindle. **2.** To waste time; dawdle. [Prob < Jeremy *Diddler,* a dawdling character in *Raising the Wind* (1803), a farce by J. Kenney.]

did•n't (dĭd′ənt). Contraction of *did not.*

di•do (dī′dō) *n., pl.* **-dos** or **-does.** A mischievous prank; caper. [?]

Di•do (dī′dō). Princess of Tyre; reputed founder of Carthage.

didst (dĭdst). *Archaic.* 2nd person sing. *p.t.* of **do.**

di•dym•i•um (dī-dĭm′ē-əm) *n. Symbol* **Di 1.** A metallic mixture, once considered an element, composed of neodymium and praseodymium. **2.** A mixture of rare-earth elements and oxides used chiefly in manufacturing and coloring various forms of glass. [< Gk *didumos,* twin.]

die[1] (dī) *v.* **died, dying. 1.** To cease living; expire. **2.** To pass out of existence. **3.** To become faint, weak, or inoperative; subside. **4.** To desire greatly; long: *dying to go.* [< ON *deyja.*]

die[2] (dī) *n.* **1.** A device used for cutting out, forming, or stamping material. **2.** *Sing.* of **dice.** [< VL **datum,* "playing piece."]

die-hard (dī′härd′) *n.* Also **die•hard.** One who stubbornly resists change.

di•e•lec•tric (dī′ə-lĕk′trĭk) *n.* A nonconductor of electricity. [DI(A)- + ELECTRIC.] —**di′e•lec′tric** *adj.* —**di′e•lec′tri•cal•ly** *adv.*

di•er•e•sis (dī-ĕr′ə-sĭs, dī-ĭr′-) *n., pl.* **-ses** (-sēz′). Also **di•aer•e•sis. 1.** The pronunciation of adjacent vowels as separate syllables. **2.** A mark (¨) placed over a vowel to indicate this. [< Gk *diairesis,* separation.]

die•sel engine (dē′zəl, -səl). An internal-combustion engine that uses the heat of highly compressed air to ignite a spray of fuel introduced after the start of the compression stroke. [< R. *Diesel* (1858–1913), German inventor.]

di•et[1] (dī′ət) *n.* **1.** One's usual food and drink; sustenance. **2.** A restricted, often medically prescribed selection of food, as for controlling weight. —*v.* To eat according to a prescribed regimen. [< Gk *diaita,* mode of life, regimen, diet.] —**di′e•tar′y** (dī′ə-tĕr′ē) *adj.* —**di′et•er** *n.*

di•et[2] (dī′ət) *n.* A legislative assembly. [ME *diete,* day's journey, day for meeting.]

di•e•tet•ic (dī′ə-tĕt′ĭk) *adj.* Of or for a restricted nutritional diet. —*n.* **dietetics** *(takes sing. v.).* The study of diet and nutrition.

di•e•ti•tian (dī′ə-tĭsh′ən) *n.* Also **di•e•ti•cian.** A specialist in dietetics.

diff. difference; different.

dif•fer (dĭf′ər) *v.* **1.** To be unlike; show dissimilarity. **2.** To disagree; dissent. [< L *differre,* to be different.]

dif•fer•ence (dĭf′ər-əns, dĭf′rəns) *n.* **1.** The fact, condition, or degree of being different; dissimilarity. **2.** Distinction in choosing. **3.** A disagreement; quarrel. **4. a.** The amount by which one quantity is greater or less than another. **b.** The amount that remains after one quantity is subtracted from another; remainder.

dif•fer•ent (dĭf′ə-rənt, dĭf′rənt) *adj.* **1.** Unlike; dissimilar. **2.** Not the same; another. **3.** Unusual; distinctive. —**dif′fer•ent•ly** *adv.*

Usage: Different from is considered preferable to *different than,* especially when what follows it is a single word or a short phrase or clause: *This exhibit is different from that* (or *different from what we expected*). *Different than* is appropriate, as an aid to conciseness, where *different from* would be clumsy: *How different things seem now than yesterday.*

dif•fer•en•tial (dĭf′ə-rĕn′shəl) *adj.* **1.** Pertaining to, showing, or constituting a difference; distinctive. **2.** Dependent on or making use of a difference. —*n. Math.* **1.** An infinitesimal increment in a variable. **2.** The product of the derivative of a function of one variable multiplied by the independent variable increment. —**dif′fer•en′tial•ly** *adv.*

differential gear. An arrangement of gears permitting the rotation of two shafts at different speeds, used on the rear axle of automotive vehicles to allow different rates of wheel rotation on curves.

dif•fer•en•ti•ate (dĭf′ə-rĕn′shē-āt′) *v.* **-ated, -ating. 1.** To constitute or perceive a difference; distinguish. **2.** To make or become different or distinct, as by modification. —**dif′fer•en′ti•a′tion** *n.*

dif•fi•cult (dĭf′ĭ-kŭlt′, -kəlt) *adj.* **1.** Hard to do, achieve, or comprehend; not easy. **2.** Hard to manage or satisfy. —**dif′fi•cult′ly** *adv.*

dif•fi•cul•ty (dĭf′ĭ-kŭl′tē, -kəl-tē) *n., pl.* **-ties. 1.** The fact or condition of being difficult. **2.** Arduous effort or trouble. **3.** A cause or state of trouble. [< L *difficultās.*]

dif•fi•dent (dĭf′ə-dənt, -dĕnt′) *adj.* Lacking self-confidence; timid. [< L *diffidere,* to mistrust.] —**dif′fi•dence** *n.* —**dif′fi•dent•ly** *adv.*

dif•fract (dĭ-frăkt′) *v.* To cause or undergo diffraction. —**dif•frac′tive** *adj.*

dif•frac•tion (dĭ-frăk′shən) *n.* Modification of the behavior of light or of other waves resulting from limitation of their lateral extent, as by an obstacle or aperture. [< L *diffringere,* to break to pieces.]

dif•fuse (dĭ-fyōōz′) *v.* **-fused, -fusing. 1.** To pour out, spread, and disperse. **2.** To be or cause to be widely dispersed. [< L *diffūsus,* pp of *diffundere,* to pour out, spread.] —**dif•fuse′** (-fyōōs′) *adj.* —**dif•fu′sion** *n.*

dig (dĭg) *v.* **dug, digging. 1.** To break up, turn over, or remove (soil or something similar) with a tool. **2.** *Slang.* To understand or enjoy. —**dig in. 1.** To entrench. **2.** To begin to work. —**dig up.** To extract or reveal by digging or searching. —*n.* **1.** A poke: *a dig in the ribs.* **2.** A gibe. **3.** An archaeological excavation. **4. digs.** *Chiefly Brit.* Lodgings. [< OF *diguer,* "to make a dike or ditch."]

dig. digest (compilation).

di•gam•ma (dī-găm'ə) *n.* A rare Greek letter, representing *w.*

di•gest (dĭ-jĕst', dī-) *v.* **1.** To transform food into an assimilable condition, as by chemical and muscular action in the alimentary canal. **2.** To absorb mentally. **3.** To organize summarily. —*n.* (dī'jĕst'). A synopsis of textual materials or data. [< L *dīgerere* (pp *dīgestus*), to divide, distribute, digest.] —**di•gest'i•ble** *adj.* —**di•ges'tion** *n.* —**di•ges'tive** *adj.*

digestive system. The alimentary canal together with accessory glands including the salivary glands, liver, and pancreas, regarded as an integrated system responsible for digestion.

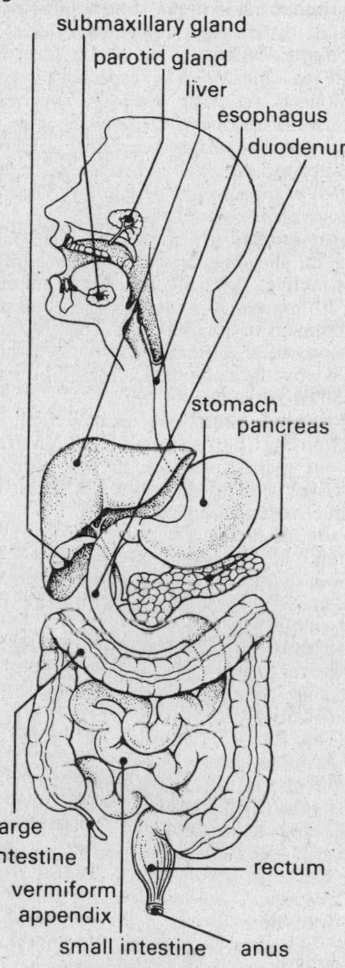

digestive system

dig•ger (dĭg'ər) *n.* **1.** One that digs. **2.** *Informal.* An Australian or New Zealander.

dig•gings (dĭg'ĭngz) *pl.n.* **1.** An excavation site. **2.** *Chiefly Brit.* Lodgings.

dig•it (dĭj'ĭt) *n.* **1.** A finger or toe. **2.** The breadth of a finger, used as a unit of length, equal to about ¾ inch. **3.** Any one of the ten Arabic number symbols, 0 through 9. [< L *digitus,* finger.] —**dig'i•tal** (dĭj'ə-təl) *adj.*

digital computer. A computer that performs operations with quantities represented electronically as digits.

dig•i•tal•is (dĭj'ə-tăl'ĭs) *n.* A drug prepared from the seeds and leaves of the foxglove, used as a cardiac stimulant. [< L *digitus,* DIGIT.]

dig•ni•fied (dĭg'nə-fīd') *adj.* Having or expressing dignity. —**dig'ni•fied'ly** *adv.*

dig•ni•fy (dĭg'nə-fī') *v.* **-fied, -fying.** To give dignity to. [< LL *dignificāre.*]

dig•ni•tar•y (dĭg'nə-tĕr'ē) *n., pl.* **-ies.** A person of high rank.

dig•ni•ty (dĭg'nə-tē) *n., pl.* **-ties. 1. a.** Impressively honorable or appropriate behavior, manner, or quality. **b.** Inherent nobility and worth: *the dignity of labor.* **2.** A high rank. [< L *dignus,* worthy.]

di•graph (dī'grăf') *n.* A pair of letters, sometimes run together, representing a single speech sound, as *ph* in *pheasant* or *œ* in Old English *œfre,* "ever." [DI- + -GRAPH.]

di•gress (dĭ-grĕs', dī-) *v.* To stray from the main subject. [L *dīgredī* (pp *dīgressus*), to go aside.] —**di•gres'sion** *n.* —**di•gres'sive** *adj.*

dike (dīk) *n.* Also **dyke. 1.** An embankment, such as a levee. **2.** A ditch or channel. [< OE *dīc,* moat, ditch. See **dhīgw-.**] —**dik'er** *n.*

dil. dilute (weak).

Di•lan•tin (dī-lăn'tĭn) *n.* A trademark for a drug used to treat epilepsy.

di•lap•i•dat•ed (dĭ-lăp'ə-dā'tĭd) *adj.* Fallen into a state of disrepair; broken-down. [< L *dīlapidāre,* to throw away.] —**di•lap'i•da'tion** *n.*

di•late (dī-lāt', dī'lāt', dĭ-lāt') *v.* **-lated, -lating.** To make or become wider or larger; expand. [< L *dīlātāre,* to enlarge, extend.] —**di•la'tion, dil'a•ta'tion** *n.* —**di•la'tive** *adj.*

dil•a•to•ry (dĭl'ə-tôr'ē, -tōr'ē) *adj.* Tending to delay. [< L *dīlātor,* delayer.]

di•lem•ma (dĭ-lĕm'ə) *n.* A choice between two equal alternatives. [< Gk *dilēmma,* ambiguous proposition.]

dil•et•tante (dĭl'ə-tänt', -tän'tē, -tănt', -tăn'tē, dĭl'ə-tänt') *n., pl.* **-tantes** or **-tanti** (-tän'tē, -tăn'tē). A dabbler in the arts. [It *dilettante,* "amateur."] **dil'et•tan'tish** *adj.*

dil•i•gence (dĭl'ə-jəns) *n.* Persistent, attentive, and energetic application to a task. [< L *dīligere,* "to single out," esteem highly.] —**dil'i•gent** *adj.* —**dil'i•gent•ly** *adv.*

dill (dĭl) *n.* An herb with aromatic leaves and seeds used as seasoning. [< OE *dile* < Gmc *dilja.]

dil•ly (dĭl'ē) *n., pl.* **-lies.** *Slang.* Something remarkable. [Poss < DELIGHTFUL.]

dil•ly-dal•ly (dĭl'ē-dăl'ē) *v.* **-lied, -lying. 1.** To waste time; dawdle. **2.** To vacillate. [Redupl of DALLY.]

di•lute (dĭ-lo͞ot', dī-) *v.* **-luted, -luting.** To reduce the concentration of. —*adj.* Weakened; diluted. [L *dīluere,* to wash away, dilute.] —**di•lut'er** *n.* —**di•lu'tion** *n.*

dim (dĭm) *adj.* **dimmer, dimmest. 1. a.** Faintly lighted. **b.** Shedding a small amount of light. **2. a.** Gloomy. **b.** Lacking luster; dull. **3.** Indistinct; obscure. **4.** Lacking keenness or vigor. —*v.* **dimmed, dimming.** To make or become dim. [< OE *dimm* < Gmc **dim-.*] —**dim'ly** *adv.* —**dim'ness** *n.*

dim. 1. dimension. **2.** diminished. **3.** diminutive.

dime (dīm) *n.* A U.S. or Canadian coin worth ten cents. [< L *decima (pars),* tenth (part), tithe.]

di•men•sion (dĭ-mĕn'shən) *n.* **1.** A measure of spatial extent, esp. width, height, or length. **2.** Often **dimensions.** Extent; magnitude; size; scope. **3. a.** Any of the least number of independent coordinates required to specify a point in space uniquely. **b.** A physical property, often mass, length, time, or some combination thereof, regarded as a fundamental measure. [< L *dīmēnsiō,* "a measuring."] —**di•men'sion•al** *adj.*

di•min•ish (dĭ-mĭn'ĭsh) *v.* **1.** To make or become smaller or less important. **2.** To taper. [< L *dē-,* from + *minuere,* to lessen.] —**di•min'ish•ment** *n.*

di•min•u•en•do (dĭ-mĭn'yo͞o-ĕn'dō) *n., pl.* **-dos** or **-does.** *Mus.* Decrescendo. [It, "diminishing."] —**di•min'u•en'do** *adj.* & *adv.*

dim•i•nu•tion (dĭm'ə-n/y/o͞o'shən) *n.* The act, process, or result of diminishing.

di•min•u•tive (dĭ-mĭn'yə-tĭv) *adj.* **1.** Small. **2.** Denoting smallness or endearment, as the diminutive suffix *-let* in the word *booklet.* [< L *dēminuere,* diminish.]

dim•i•ty (dĭm'ə-tē) *n., pl.* **-ties.** A sheer, crisp cotton fabric, usually corded or checked. [< MGk *dimitos,* double-threaded.]

dim•mer (dĭm'ər) *n.* A rheostat or other device used to reduce the intensity of illumination continuously.

dim•ple (dĭm'pəl) *n.* **1.** A small natural indentation in the flesh, esp. on a chin or cheek. **2.** Any slight depression in a surface. —*v.* **-pled, -pling.** To form dimples, as by smiling. [< OE **dympel,* pool, dimple.]

dim•wit (dĭm'wĭt') *n.* *Slang.* A fool. —**dim'wit'ted** *adj.* —**dim'wit'ted•ness** *n.*

din (dĭn) *n.* A medley of resounding and discordant noises. —*v.* **dinned, dinning.** —**din into.** To impress by wearying repetition: *din an idea into one's head.* [< OE *dyne.* See **dhwen-.**]

di•nar (dĭ-när', dē'när') *n.* The basic monetary unit of Iraq, Jordan, Kuwait, Southern Yemen, Algeria, Tunisia, and Yugoslavia. [Ar *dīnār.*]

dine (dīn) *v.* **dined, dining. 1.** To eat dinner. **2.** To give dinner to. [< VL **disjējūnāre,* to break one's fast.]

din•er (dī'nər) *n.* **1.** A person eating dinner. **2.** A railroad dining car. **3.** A restaurant like a railroad dining car.

di•nette (dī-nĕt') *n.* A nook or alcove for meals.

din•ghy (dĭng'ē) *n., pl.* **-ghies.** Any small rowboat. [Hindi *ḍiṅgī.*]

din•gy (dĭn'jē) *adj.* **-gier, -giest. 1.** Darkened with smoke and grime; dirty. **2.** Drab in color or appearance. **3.** Shabby; worn. —**din'gi•ly** *adv.* —**din'gi•ness** *n.*

dink•y (dĭng'kē) *adj.* **-ier, -iest. 1.** *Informal.* Of small size or consequence; insignificant. **2.** *Brit. Informal.* Dainty; cute. [Prob < Scot *dink,* trim, neat.]

din•ner (dĭn'ər) *n.* **1.** The chief meal of the day, eaten at the noon hour or in the evening. **2.** A banquet. [< OF *disner,* dine.]

dinner jacket. A tuxedo.

di•no•saur (dī'nə-sôr') *n.* Any of various extinct, often gigantic reptiles of the Mesozoic era. [< Gk *deinos,* fearful, monstrous + -SAUR.]

dint (dĭnt) *n.* **1.** Force or effort; power; exertion: *by dint of hard work.* **2.** A dent. —*v.* To dent. [< OE *dynt.*]

di•o•cese (dī'ə-sĭs, -sēs', -sēz') *n.* The district or churches under the jurisdiction of a bishop. [< Gk *dioikēsis,* "housekeeping," administration.] —**di•oc'e•san** (dī-ŏs'ə-sən) *adj.*

di•ode (dī'ōd') *n.* Any electronic device that restricts current flow chiefly to one direction. [DI- + -ODE.]

Di•o•nys•i•an (dī'ə-nĭsh'ən, -nĭzh'ən, -nĭs'ē-ən) *adj.* **1.** Of or relating to Dionysus. **2.** Often **dionysian.** Of an ecstatic, orgiastic, or irrational character.

Di•o•ny•sus (dī'ə-nī'səs). Greek god of wine and of an orgiastic nature cult.

di•o•ram•a (dī'ə-răm'ə, -rä'mə) *n.* A three-dimensional miniature scene.

di•ox•ide (dī-ŏk'sīd') *n.* An oxide with two oxygen atoms per molecule.

dip (dĭp) *v.* **dipped, dipping. 1.** To plunge briefly into a liquid. **2.** To immerse in a disinfectant solution, as cattle or sheep. **3.** To scoop up (liquid). **4.** To lower and raise (a flag) in salute. **5.** To drop or sink suddenly. **6.** To slope downward; decline. **7.** To look casually into a subject or source of information. *—n.* **1.** A brief plunge or immersion. **2.** A smooth creamed preparation, as of softened cheese, into which crackers, potato chips, etc., can be dipped. **3.** An amount taken up by dipping. **4.** A candle made by repeated dipping in tallow or wax. **5.** A downward slope or sloping; a decline. **6.** A hollow; depression. [< OE *dyppan.* See **dheub-**.]

diph•the•ri•a (dĭf-thîr'ē-ə, dĭp-) *n.* An acute contagious disease characterized by the formation of false membranes in the throat and other air passages, causing difficulty in breathing, high fever, and weakness. [< Gk *diphthera,* piece of leather (< the rough false membrane).] **—diph'the•rit'ic** (-thə-rĭt'ĭk), **diph•ther'ic** (-thĕr'ĭk), **diph•the'ri•al** *adj.*

diph•thong (dĭf'thông', -thŏng', dĭp'-) *n.* **1.** A speech sound beginning with one vowel sound and moving to another vowel or semivowel position within the same syllable, as *oy* in the word *boy.* **2.** Either of the two Latin ligatures *æ* or *œ.* [< Gk *diphthongos.*]

dipl. diplomat; diplomatic.

dip•loid (dĭp'loid') *adj.* **1.** Double or twofold. **2.** Having a homologous pair of chromosomes for each characteristic except sex, the total number of chromosomes being twice that of a gamete. [< Gk *diploos,* double.]

di•plo•ma (dĭ-plō'mə) *n.* **1.** A document issued by a university or other school testifying that a student has earned a degree or completed a course of study. **2.** A certificate conferring an honor. [< Gk *diplōma,* something doubled, folded paper.]

di•plo•ma•cy (dĭ-plō'mə-sē) *n., pl.* **-cies. 1.** The art, practice, or profession of conducting international relations. **2.** Tact or skill in dealing with people.

dip•lo•mat (dĭp'lə-măt') *n.* **1.** One appointed to represent his government in its relations with other governments. **2.** One who possesses skill in dealing with others.

dip•lo•mat•ic (dĭp'lə-măt'ĭk) *adj.* **1.** Of or relating to diplomacy. **2.** Characterized by tact in dealing with people. [< L *diplōma,* document.] **—dip'lo•mat'i•cal•ly** *adv.*

di•plo•ma•tist (dĭ-plō'mə-tĭst) *n.* A diplomat.

di•pole (dī'pōl') *n.* **1.** A pair of electric charges or magnetic poles, of equal magnitude but of opposite sign or polarity, separated by a small distance. **2.** An antenna, usually fed from the center, consisting of two equal rods extending outward in a straight line.

dip•per (dĭp'ər) *n.* **1.** One that dips. **2.** A container used for dipping, such as a long-handled cup for taking up water.

dip•py (dĭp'ē) *adj.* **-pier, -piest.** *Slang.* Foolish. [?]

dip•so•ma•ni•a (dĭp'sə-mā'nē-ə, -măn'yə) *n.* An insatiable craving for alcoholic liquors. [< Gk *dipsa,* thirst + -MANIA.] **—dip'so•ma'ni•ac** *adj.* & *n.*

dip•tych (dĭp'tĭk) *n.* A pair of painted or carved panels hinged together. [< Gk *diptukhos,* double-folded.]

dir. director.

dire (dīr) *adj.* **direr, direst. 1.** Dreadful and threatening. **2.** Disastrous. **3.** Ominous. [L *dīrus,* fearful, ill-omened.] **—dire'ly** *adv.*

di•rect (dĭ-rĕkt', dī-) *v.* **1.** To conduct the affairs of; manage. **2.** To take charge of with authority; control. **3.** To conduct (musicians) in a rehearsal or performance. **4.** To aim, guide, or address (something or someone) toward a goal. **5.** To give interpretative dramatic supervision to the actors in a play or film. *—adj.* **1.** Proceeding or lying in a straight course or line. **2.** Straightforward. **3.** Without intervening persons, conditions, or agencies; immediate. **4.** By action of voters, rather than through elected delegates. **5.** Absolute; total: *direct opposites.* **6.** Receiving the action of a transitive verb: *direct object.* **7.** Varying in the same manner as another quantity, [...] creasing if another quantity increases [...] creasing if it decreases. *—adv.* In a[...] manner; straight; directly. [< L *dīrig*[...] *dīrectus*), to arrange in distinct lines, [...]

direct current. An electric current flow[...] one direction.

di•rec•tion (dĭ-rĕk'shən, dī-) *n.* **1.** The a[...] function of directing. **2.** Often **directions**[...] instruction or series of instructions for d[...] something. **3.** A command. **4. a.** The [...] tance-independent relationship between [...] points that specifies the angular position[...] either with respect to the other. **b.** A posit[...] to which motion or another position is [...] ferred. **c.** The line or course along which[...] person or thing moves. **5.** Tendency toward[...] particular end or goal.

di•rec•tion•al (dĭ-rĕk'shən-əl, dī-) *adj.* Of [...]

dis'ac•com'mo•date' *v.*
dis'ac•cord' *n.* & *v.*
dis'ac•cred'it *v.*
dis'ac•cus'tom *v.*
dis'a•cid'i•fy' *v.*
dis'ac•knowl'edge *v.*
dis'ac•knowl'edg•ment *n.*
dis'ac•quain'tance *n.*
dis'ac•quaint'ed *adj.*
dis•ad'van•ta'geous *adj.*
dis'ad•vise' *v.*
dis'af•fil'i•ate' *v.*
dis'af•fil'i•a'tion *n.*
dis'af•firm' *v.*
dis'af•fir•ma'tion *n.*
dis•ag'gre•gate' *v.*
dis•ag'gre•ga'tion *n.*
dis'al•ly' *v.*
dis'a•men'i•ty *n.*
dis•an'chor *v.*
dis'an•nex' *v.*
dis'a•noint' *v.*
dis'as•sem'ble *v.*
dis'as•sem'bly *n.*
dis•bal'ance *n.*
dis•branch' *v.*
dis•bud' *v.*
dis•bur'den *v.*
dis'com•mend' *v.*
dis'com•mend'a•ble *adj.*
dis'com•mod'i•ty *n.*
dis'con•firm' *v.*
dis'con'fir•ma'tion *n.*
dis'con•gru'i•ty *n.*
dis'con'gru•ous *adj.*
dis'con•sid'er *v.*
dis•con'so•nant *adj.*
dis•crown' *v.*
dis'e•con'o•my *n.*
dis•edge' *v.*
dis•ed'i•fy' *v.*
dis'em•balm' *v.*
dis'em•bar'rass *v.*
dis'em•bar'rass•ment *n.*
dis'em•bel'lish *v.*
dis'em•bel'lish•ment *n.*
dis'em•broil' *v.*
dis'em•broil'ment *n.*
dis'em•ploy' *v.*
dis'em•ploy'ment *n.*
dis'en•a'ble *n.*
dis'en•cour'age *v.*
dis'en•cour'age•ment *n.*
dis'en•dow' *v.*
dis'en•dow'ment *n.*
dis'en•joy' *v.*
dis'en•joy'ment *n.*
dis'en•roll' *v.*
dis'en•roll'ment *n.*
dis'en•tail' *v.*
dis'en•thrall' *v.*
dis'en•thrall'ment *n.*
dis'en•ti'tle *v.*
dis'en•tomb' *v.*
dis'en•tomb'ment *n.*
dis'en•trance' *v.*
dis'en•twine' *v.*
dis•e'qui•lib'ri•um *n.*
dis•fea'ture *v.*
dis•fel'low•ship' *n.*
dis•for'est *v.*
dis•gar'ri•son *n.* & *v.*
dis•hal'low *v.*
dis•horn' *v.*
dis'im•ag'ine *v.*
dis'im•pas'sioned *adj.*
dis'im•pris'on *v.*
dis'im•pris'on•ment *n.*
dis'im•prove' *v.*
dis'im•prove'ment *n.*
dis'in•car'nate *adj.*
dis•in'car•na'tion *n.*
dis'in•cen'tive *n.*
dis'in•cor'po•rate' *v.*
dis'in•cor'po•ra'tion *n.*
dis'in•fest' *v.*
dis'in•fes•ta'tion *n.*
dis'in•flate' *v.*
dis'in•fla'tion *n.*
dis'in•fla'tion•ar'y *adj.*
dis'in•hib'i•to'ry *adj.*
dis'in•tox'i•ca'tion *n.*
dis'in•vest' *v.*
dis'in•vest'ment *n.*
dis'in•vite' *v.*
dis'in•volve' *v.*
dis•lus'ter *v.*
dis•mast' *v.*
dis'o•blige' *v.*
dis'o•blig'ing•ly *adv.*
dis•oc'cu•pa'tion *n.*
dis•pau'per•ize' *v.*
dis•peace' *n.*
dis•peo'ple *v.*
dis'per•son'i•fy' *v.*
dis•pet'al *v.*
dis•pope' *v.*
dis•priv'i•lege *v.*
dis•rate' *v.*
dis're•late' *v.*
dis're•la'tion *n.*
dis•rel'ish *v.* & *n.*
dis're•mem'ber *v.*
dis're•spect'a•ble *adj.*
dis•roof' *v.*
dis•root' *v.*
dis•seat' *v.*
dis•serve' *v.*
dis•so'cia•bil'i•ty *n.*
dis•so'cia•ble *adj.*
dis•so'cia•bly *adv.*
dis'sym•met'ri•cal *adj.*
dis•sym'me•try *n.*
dis•throne' *v.*
dis•un'i•fi•ca'tion *n.*
dis•u'ni•form' *adj.*
dis•u'ni•fy' *v.*
dis•un'ion *n.*
dis'u•til'i•ty *n.*
dis•weap'on *v.*
dis•yoke' *v.*

pertaining to spatial direction. **—di•rec'tion•al'i•ty** *n.*

di•rec•tive (dĭ-rĕk'tĭv, dī-) *n.* An order or instruction.

di•rect•ly (dĭ-rĕkt'lē, dī-) *adv.* **1.** In a direct line or manner. **2.** Without anyone or anything intervening. **3.** Exactly; totally. **4.** Instantly.

di•rec•tor (dĭ-rĕk'tər, dī-) *n.* **1.** A manager. **2.** The interpretative supervisor of actors in a play or film or musicians in an orchestra or chorus. **—di•rec'tor•ship'** *n.*

di•rec•to•ry (dĭ-rĕk'tə-rē, dī-) *n., pl.* **-ries.** A book listing names and addresses.

dirge (dûrj) *n.* A funeral hymn or lament. [ME *dirige.*]

dir•ham (də-răm') *n.* The basic monetary unit of Morocco. [Ar.]

dir•i•gi•ble (dĭr'ə-jə-bəl, dĭ-rĭj'ə-bəl) *n.* A steerable lighter-than-air craft. [< L *dīrigere,* to guide, DIRECT.]

dirk (dûrk) *n.* A kind of dagger. [Earlier *durk, dork.*]

dirn•dl (dûrnd'l) *n.* A full-skirted dress with a tight bodice. [G.]

dirt (dûrt) *n.* **1.** Earth or soil. **2.** A soiling substance, such as mud, dust, or excrement. **3.** Something contemptible or vile. **4.** *Informal.* Malicious or scandalous gossip. **5.** Gravel, slag, or other material from which metal is extracted in mining. *—adj.* Made of dirt. [< ON *drit* < Gmc **drit-.*]

dirt•y (dûr'tē) *adj.* **-ier, -iest. 1.** Soiled, as with dirt. **2.** Obscene. **3.** Contemptibly contrary to honor or rules. **4.** Of a clouded or muddy appearance. **5.** Producing an excessive amount of radioactive fallout. **6.** Stormy: *dirty weather.* *—v.* **-ied, -ying.** To make or become soiled. **—dirt'i•ly** *adv.* **—dirt'i•ness** *n.*

dis–. *comb. form.* **1.** Negation, lack, invalidation, or deprivation. **2.** Reversal. **3.** Removal or rejection. [< L *dis,* apart, asunder.]

dis•a•bil•i•ty (dĭs'ə-bĭl'ə-tē) *n., pl.* **-ties. 1.** A disabled condition; incapacity. **2.** Something that disables or disqualifies.

dis•a•ble (dĭs-ā'bəl) *v.* **-bled, -bling. 1.** To weaken or cripple. **2.** To disqualify legally.

dis•a•buse (dĭs'ə-byōōz') *v.* **-bused, -busing.** To free from a misconception; undeceive.

dis•ad•van•tage (dĭs'əd-văn'tĭj, -vän'tĭj) *n.* **1.** An unfavorable condition or circumstance; handicap. **2.** Detriment. **—dis•ad'van•ta'geous** *adj.* **—dis•ad'van•ta'geous•ly** *adv.*

dis•ad•van•taged (dĭs'əd-văn'tĭjd, -vän'tĭjd) *adj.* Poor.

dis•af•fect (dĭs'ə-fĕkt') *v.* To cause to lose affection or loyalty; alienate. **—dis'af•fect'ed** *adj.* **—dis'af•fect'ed•ly** *adv.* **—dis'af•fec'tion** *n.*

dis•a•gree (dĭs'ə-grē') *v.* **-greed, -greeing. 1.** To be different or inconsistent; fail to correspond. **2.** To have a different opinion; dissent. **3.** To dispute. **4.** To cause adverse effects. **—dis'a•gree'ment** *n.*

dis•a•gree•a•ble (dĭs'ə-grē'ə-bəl) *adj.* **1.** Unpleasant; offensive. **2.** Bad-tempered. **—dis'a•gree'a•bly** *adv.*

dis•al•low (dĭs'ə-lou') *v.* **1.** To refuse to allow. **2.** To reject as invalid, untrue, or improper.

dis•ap•pear (dĭs'ə-pîr') *v.* **1.** To pass out of sight either suddenly or gradually; vanish. **2.** To become extinct. **—dis'ap•pear'ance** *n.*

dis•ap•point (dĭs'ə-point') *v.* **1.** To fail to satisfy the hope, desire, or expectation of. **2.** To thwart. [ME *disappointen,* to remove from office, dispossess.] **—dis'ap•point'ing•ly** *adv.*

dis•ap•point•ment (dĭs'ə-point'mənt) *n.* **1. a.** The act of disappointing. **b.** The condition or feeling of being disappointed. **2.** One that disappoints.

dis•ap•pro•ba•tion (dĭs-ăp'rə-bā'shən) *n.* Disapproval.

dis•ap•prov•al (dĭs'ə-prōō'vəl) *n.* The act of disapproving; censure.

dis•ap•prove (dĭs'ə-prōōv') *v.* **-proved, -proving. 1.** To have an unfavorable opinion (of). **2.** To refuse to approve.

dis•arm (dĭs-ärm') *v.* **1.** To deprive of weapons. **2.** To render helpless or harmless. **3.** To overcome the hostility of. **4.** To reduce one's armaments or armed forces.

dis•ar•ma•ment (dĭs-är'mə-mənt) *n.* The reduction of armaments and armed forces by a government.

dis•arm•ing (dĭs-är'mĭng) *adj.* Tending to remove hostility; winning. **—dis•arm'ing•ly** *adv.*

dis•ar•range (dĭs'ə-rānj') *v.* **-ranged, -ranging.** To upset the arrangement of. **—dis'ar•range'ment** *n.*

dis•ar•ray (dĭs'ə-rā') *n.* **1.** A state of disorder; confusion. **2.** Disordered or insufficient dress. *—v.* To throw into confusion.

dis•as•so•ci•ate (dĭs'ə-sō'shē-āt', -sē-āt') *v.* **-ated, -ating.** To dissociate.

dis•as•ter (dĭ-zăs'tər, -zäs'tər) *n.* **1. a.** An occurrence inflicting widespread destruction and distress. **b.** A grave misfortune. **2.** A total failure. [< It *disastrato,* "ill-starred."]

dis•as•trous (dĭ-zăs'trəs, -zäs'trəs) *adj.* Calamitous; ruinous. **—dis•as'trous•ly** *adv.*

dis•a•vow (dĭs'ə-vou') *v.* To disclaim knowledge of, responsibility for, or association with; disown. **—dis'a•vow'al** *n.*

dis•band (dĭs-bănd') *v.* To disperse or be dispersed. **—dis•band'ment** *n.*

dis•bar (dĭs-bär') *v.* **-barred, -barring.** To expel (a lawyer) from the legal profession. **—dis•bar'ment** *n.*

dis•be•lief (dĭs'bĭ-lēf') *n.* Refusal or reluctance to believe.

dis•be•lieve (dĭs'bĭ-lēv') *v.* **-lieved, -lieving.** To refuse to believe (in). **—dis'be•liev'er** *n.*

dis•burse (dĭs-bûrs') *v.* **-bursed, -bursing.** To pay out, as from a fund. [OF *desbourser.*] **—dis•burse'ment, dis•bur'sal** *n.*

disc (dĭsk) *n.* **1.** Also **disk.** A phonograph record. **2.** Variant of **disk.**

disc. discount.

dis•card (dĭs-kärd') *v.* To throw away; reject; dismiss. *—n.* (dĭs'kärd'). **1.** The act of discarding. **2.** A person or thing discarded.

dis•cern (dĭ-sûrn', -zûrn') *v.* **1.** To perceive (something obscure or concealed); detect. **2.** To perceive the distinctions of; discriminate. [< L *discernere,* "to separate by sifting," distinguish between.] **—dis•cern'i•ble** *adj.* **—dis•cern'ing** *adj.* **—dis•cern'ment** *n.*

dis•charge (dĭs-chärj') *v.* **-charged, -charging. 1.** To relieve or be relieved of a burden or contents. **2.** To unload or empty (contents). **3.** To release or dismiss, as from employment. **4.** To send or pour forth; emit. **5.** To shoot (a projectile or weapon). **6.** To perform the obligations or demands of (a duty). **7.** To acquit oneself of (an obligation). **8.** To cause or undergo electrical discharge. *—n.* (dĭs'chärj', dĭs-chärj'). **1.** The act of removing a load or burden. **2.** The act of shooting a projectile or weapon. **3.** A pouring forth; emission. **4.** The amount or rate of emission or ejection. **5.** Something that is discharged. **6.** A relieving from an obligation. **7. a.** Dismissal or release from employment, service, etc. **b.** A document certifying such release, esp. from military service. **8. a.** The release of stored energy in a capacitor by the flow of electric current between its terminals. **b.** The conversion of chemical energy to electric energy in a storage battery. **c.** A flow of electricity in a dielectric, esp. in a rarefied gas.

dis•ci. (dĭs'ī). Alternate *pl.* of **discus.**

dis•ci•ple (dĭ-sī'pəl) *n.* **1. a.** One who subscribes to the teachings of a master and assists in spreading them. **b.** Any active adherent, as of a movement. **2.** One of the companions of Christ. [< L *discere,* to learn, to know.]

dis•ci•pli•nar•i•an (dĭs'ə-plə-nâr'ē-ən) *n.* One who enforces or believes in strict discipline. *—adj.* Disciplinary.

dis•ci•pli•nar•y (dĭs'ə-plə-nĕr'ē) *adj.* Pertaining to or used for discipline.

dis•ci•pline (dĭs'ə-plĭn) *n.* **1.** Training intended to produce a specified character or pattern of behavior. **2.** Controlled behavior resulting from such training. **3.** A state of order based upon submission to rules and authority. **4.** Punishment intended to correct or train. **5.** A set of rules or methods. **6.** A branch of knowledge or of teaching. *—v.* **-plined, -plining. 1.** To train by instruction and control. **2.** To punish. [< L *disciplīna,* instruction, knowledge.] **—dis'ci•plin'er** *n.*

disc jockey. Also **disk jockey.** A radio announcer who presents and comments on phonograph records.

dis•claim (dĭs-klām') *v.* **1.** To deny or renounce claim to or connection with; disown. **2.** To deny the validity of; repudiate. **3.** To renounce a legal right or claim (to).

dis•claim•er (dĭs-klā'mər) *n.* A repudiation of a claim.

dis•close (dĭs-klōz') *v.* **-closed, -closing. 1.** To expose to view, as by removing a cover; uncover. **2.** To divulge. **—dis•clos'er** *n.* **—dis•clo'sure** (-zhər) *n.*

dis•co (dĭs'kō) *n., pl.* **-cos.** *Informal.* A discothèque.

disco–. *comb. form.* A phonograph record. [< DISK.]

dis•cob•o•lus (dĭs-kŏb'ə-ləs) *n., pl.* **-li** (-lī'). A discus thrower. [< Gk *diskobolos.*]

dis•coid (dĭs'koid') *adj.* Also **dis•coi•dal** (dĭs-koid'l). Having the shape of a disk. *—n.* A disk or an object shaped like a disk.

dis•col•or (dĭs-kŭl'ər) *v.* **1.** To alter or spoil the color of. **2.** To become changed or spoiled in color. **—dis•col'or•a'tion** *n.*

dis•com•bob•u•late (dĭs'kəm-bŏb'yə-lāt') *v.* **-lated, -lating.** *Slang.* To throw into a state of confusion.

dis•com•fit (dĭs-kŭm'fĭt) *v.* **1.** To thwart the plans or purposes of; frustrate. **2.** To defeat in battle. **3.** To disconcert. [< VL **disconficere,* to defeat.] **—dis•com'fi•ture'** *n.*

dis•com•fort (dĭs-kŭm'fərt) *n.* **1.** The condition of being uncomfortable in body or mind. **2.** Something that disturbs one's comfort. *—v.* To make uncomfortable.

dis•com•mode (dĭs'kə-mōd') *v.* **-moded, -moding.** To put to inconvenience; disturb. [F *discommoder.*]

dis•com•pose (dĭs'kəm-pōz') *v.* **-posed, -posing. 1.** To disturb the composure of. **2.** To put into a state of disorder. **—dis'com•po'sure** (-zhər) *n.*

dis•con•nect (dĭs'kə-nĕkt') *v.* To sever the connection of or between. **—dis'con•nect'ed** *adj.* **—dis'con•nec'tion** *n.*

dis•con•cert (dĭs'kən-sûrt') *v.* To upset the self-possession of. [< OF *desconcerter.*]

dis•con•so•late (dĭs-kŏn'sə-lĭt) *adj.* **1.** Hopelessly sad. **2.** Gloomy; dismal. **—dis•con'so•late•ly** *adv.* **—dis•con'so•late•ness** *n.*

dis•con•tent (dĭs'kən-tĕnt') *n.* Absence of contentment; dissatisfaction. —*adj.* Discontented. —*v.* To make discontented.

dis•con•tent•ed (dĭs'kən-tĕn'tĭd) *adj.* Restlessly unhappy; dissatisfied. —**dis'con•tent'ed•ly** *adv.* —**dis'con•tent'ed•ness** *n.*

dis•con•tin•ue (dĭs'kən-tĭn'yo͞o) *v.* **-ued, -uing.** **1.** To cause to cease. **2.** To give up; abandon. **3.** To come to an end. —**dis'con•tin'u•ance, dis'con•tin'u•a'tion** *n.*

dis•con•ti•nu•i•ty (dĭs'kŏn-tĭ-n/y/o͞o'ə-tē) *n., pl.* **-ties.** **1.** A lack of continuity, logical sequence, or cohesion. **2.** A break or gap.

dis•con•tin•u•ous (dĭs'kən-tĭn'yo͞o-əs) *adj.* Marked by breaks or interruptions; intermittent. —**dis'con•tin'u•ous•ly** *adv.*

dis•cord (dĭs'kôrd') *n.* **1.** Lack of agreement; dissension. **2.** A harsh mingling of sounds; din. **3.** *Mus.* A harsh or disagreeable combination of sounds; dissonance. —*v.* (dĭs-kôrd'). To fail to agree or harmonize; clash. [< L *discors,* disagreeing.] —**dis•cor'dant** *adj.* —**dis•cor'dant•ly** *adv.*

dis•co•theque (dĭs'kə-tĕk') *n.* Also **dis•co•thèque.** A nightclub featuring dancing to amplified recorded music.

dis•count (dĭs'kount', dĭs-kount') *v.* **1.** To deduct, as from a cost or price. **2. a.** To purchase or sell (a commercial paper) after deducting the interest. **b.** To lend money after deducting the interest. **3.** To disregard as being untrustworthy or exaggerated. **4.** To anticipate and make allowance for. —*n.* (dĭs'kount). **1.** A reduction from the full amount of a price or debt. **2.** The interest deducted in advance in purchasing or selling a commercial paper. **3.** The rate of interest so deducted. **4.** The act or an instance of discounting. —*adj.* Selling at prices below those set by manufacturers: *discount store.* [< ML *discomputāre.*]

dis•coun•te•nance (dĭs-koun'tə-nəns) *v.* **-nanced, -nancing.** **1.** To view with disfavor. **2.** To disconcert.

dis•cour•age (dĭs-kûr'ĭj) *v.* **-aged, -aging.** **1.** To deprive of confidence, hope, or spirit; dishearten. **2.** To dissuade or deter. **3.** To hamper; hinder. —**dis•cour'age•ment** *n.*

dis•course (dĭs'kôrs', -kōrs') *n.* **1.** Verbal expression in speech or writing. **2.** Conversation. **3.** A formal and lengthy discussion of a subject, either written or spoken. —*v.* (dĭs-kôrs', -kōrs') **-coursed, -coursing.** To speak or write formally and at length. [< LL *discursus,* conversation.] —**dis•cours'er** *n.*

dis•cour•te•ous (dĭs-kûr'tē-əs) *adj.* Lacking courtesy; impolite. —**dis•cour'te•ous•ly** *adv.* —**dis•cour'te•sy** *n.*

dis•cov•er (dĭs-kŭv'ər) *v.* **1.** To arrive at through search or study. **2.** To be the first to find, learn of, or observe. —**dis•cov'er•a•ble** *adj.* —**dis•cov'er•er** *n.*

dis•cov•er•y (dĭs-kŭv'ə-rē) *n., pl.* **-ies.** **1.** The act or an instance of discovering. **2.** Something that has been discovered.

dis•cred•it (dĭs-krĕd'ĭt) *v.* **1.** To disgrace; dishonor. **2.** To cast doubt on. **3.** To disbelieve. —*n.* **1.** Damage to one's reputation. **2.** Loss of trust or belief. —**dis•cred'it•a•ble** *adj.*

dis•creet (dĭs-krēt') *adj.* **1.** Having a judicious reserve in speech or behavior. **2.** Unpretentious. [< ML *discrētus,* "showing good judgment."] —**dis•creet'ly** *adv.*

dis•crep•an•cy (dĭs-krĕp'ən-sē) *n., pl.* **-cies.** Divergence or disagreement, as between facts or claims. [< L *discrepāre,* to sound different.] —**dis•crep'ant** *adj.* —**dis•crep'ant•ly** *adv.*

dis•crete (dĭs-krēt') *adj.* **1.** Constituting a separate thing; individual. **2.** Consisting of unconnected distinct parts. [< L *discrētus,* separate.] —**dis•crete'ly** *adv.*

dis•cre•tion (dĭs-krĕsh'ən) *n.* **1.** The quality of being discreet. **2.** Permission given to an individual to make decisions by his own judgment. —**dis•cre'tion•ar'y, dis•cre'tion•al** *adj.*

dis•crim•i•nate (dĭs-krĭm'ə-nāt') *v.* **-nated, -nating.** **1.** To make a clear distinction; differentiate. **2.** To act on the basis of prejudice. [L *discrīmināre,* to divide, distinguish.] —**dis•crim'i•nate•ly** *adv.* —**dis•crim'i•na'tion** *n.* —**dis•crim'i•na'tive, dis•crim'i•na•to'ry** (dĭs-krĭm'ə-nə-tôr'ē, -tōr'ē) *adj.*

dis•crim•i•nat•ing (dĭs-krĭm'ə-nā'tĭng) *adj.* **1.** Able or tending to discriminate. **2.** Fastidiously selective.

dis•cur•sive (dĭs-kûr'sĭv) *adj.* **1.** Moving from subject to subject in a rambling way. **2.** Proceeding to a conclusion through reason rather than intuition. [< L *discursus,* "a running back and forth."] —**dis•cur'sive•ly** *adv.*

dis•cus (dĭs'kəs) *n., pl.* **-cuses** or **disci** (dĭs'ī). A disk, typically wooden with a metal rim, thrown for distance in athletic competitions. [L, DISK.]

dis•cuss (dĭs-kŭs') *v.* **1.** To speak or write about; treat of. **2.** To speak together about; talk over. [< LL *discutere* (pp *discussus*), to investigate, discuss.] —**dis•cus'sion** *n.*

dis•dain (dĭs-dān') *v.* **1.** To regard or treat with contempt. **2.** To consider unworthy of oneself. —*n.* Scornful superiority. [< L *dēdignārī,* to scorn.] —**dis•dain'ful** *adj.*

dis•ease (dĭ-zēz') *n.* **1.** An abnormal condition of an organism or part, esp. as a consequence of infection, inherent weakness, or environmental stress, that impairs normal physiological functioning. **2.** A condition or tendency, as of society, regarded as abnormal and pernicious. [< OF *desaise,* discomfort.] —**dis•eased'** *adj.*

dis•em•bark (dĭs'ĭm-bärk') *v.* To put, go, or cause to go ashore from a ship. —**dis•em'bar'ka'tion** *n.*

dis•em•bod•y (dĭs'ĭm-bŏd'ē) *v.* **-ied, -ying.** To free (a spirit) from the body.

dis•em•bow•el (dĭs'ĭm-bou'əl) *v.* To remove the entrails from.

dis•en•chant (dĭs'ĭn-chănt', -chänt') *v.* To free from enchantment or illusion.

dis•en•cum•ber (dĭs'ĭn-kŭm'bər) *v.* To relieve of encumbrances.

dis•en•gage (dĭs'ĭn-gāj') *v.* **-gaged, -gaging.** **1.** To release from something that holds, connects, or obliges. **2.** To free oneself. —**dis'en•gage'ment** *n.*

dis•en•tan•gle (dĭs'ĭn-tăng'gəl) *v.* **-gled, -gling.** To extricate or be extricated from entanglement. —**dis'en•tan'gle•ment** *n.*

dis•es•tab•lish (dĭs'ĭ-stăb'lĭsh) *v.* To remove the established status of, esp. of a nationally established church. —**dis'es•tab'lish•ment** *n.*

dis•es•teem (dĭs'ĭ-stēm') *n.* Lack of esteem.

dis•fa•vor (dĭs-fā'vər) *n.* **1.** Disapproval. **2.** The condition of being out of favor.

dis•fig•ure (dĭs-fĭg'yər) *v.* **-ured, -uring.** To spoil the appearance or shape of; deform. —**dis•fig'ur•er** *n.* —**dis•fig'ure•ment** *n.*

dis•fran•chise (dĭs-frăn'chīz') *v.* **-chised, -chising.** Also **dis•en•fran•chise** (dĭs'ĕn-frăn'chīz'). **1.** To deprive (an individual) of a right of citizenship, esp. of the right to vote. **2.** To deprive (an institution) of a privilege or franchise. —**dis•fran'chise'ment** (-chīz'mənt, -chĭz-mənt) *n.* —**dis•fran'chis'er** *n.*

dis•gorge (dĭs-gôrj') *v.* **-gorged, -gorging.** **1.** To bring up and expel from the throat or stomach. **2.** To discharge violently; spew.

dis•grace (dĭs-grās') *n.* **1.** Loss of honor, respect, or reputation; shame. **2.** The condition of being out of favor. **3.** Something that brings shame, dishonor, or disfavor. —*v.* **-graced, -gracing.** **1.** To bring shame or dishonor upon. **2.** To put (someone) out of favor. [< It *disgrazia.*] —**dis•grac'er** *n.*

dis•grace•ful (dĭs-grās'fəl) *adj.* Bringing or warranting disgrace; shameful.

dis•grun•tle (dĭs-grŭnt'l) *v.* **-tled, -tling.** To make discontented, resentful, or disappointed.

dis•guise (dĭs-gīz') *v.* **-guised, -guising.** **1.** To modify the manner or appearance of in order to prevent recognition. **2.** To dissemble: *disguise one's interest.* —*n.* **1.** The condition of being disguised. **2.** Something that serves to disguise, as a pretense. [< OF *desguisier.*]

dis•gust (dĭs-gŭst') *v.* **1.** To excite nausea or loathing in; sicken. **2.** To offend the taste or moral sense of; repel. —*n.* Profound aversion or repugnance. [OF *desgouster.*] —**dis•gust'ed** *adj.* —**dis•gust'ed•ly** *adv.*

dis•gust•ing (dĭs-gŭs'tĭng) *adj.* Acutely repugnant; loathsome. —**dis•gust'ing•ly** *adv.*

dish (dĭsh) *n.* **1.** An open container, generally shallow and concave, for holding or serving food. **2. a.** The food contained in a dish. **b.** A particular preparation of food. **3.** A dishlike depression. **4.** *Slang.* An attractive girl or woman. —*v.* —**dish out.** **1.** To serve (food). **2.** *Informal.* To give out; distribute. —**dish up.** To serve (food). [< L *discus,* DISK.]

dis•ha•bille (dĭs'ə-bēl', -bē') *n.* Also **des•ha•bille** (dĕs'-). **1.** The state of being partially or very casually dressed. **2.** Casual or lounging attire. [< F *déshabiller,* to undress.]

dis•har•mo•ny (dĭs-här'mə-nē) *n.* Lack of harmony. —**dis'har•mo'ni•ous** *adj.*

dis•heart•en (dĭs-härt'n) *v.* To diminish or destroy the courage or resolution of. —**dis•heart'en•ing•ly** *adv.*

di•shev•el (dĭ-shĕv'əl) *v.* **-eled** or **-elled, -eling** or **-elling.** **1.** To loosen and let fall (hair or clothing) in disarray. **2.** To disarrange the hair or clothing of (a person). [< OF *descheveler,* to disarrange the hair.] —**di•shev'el•ment** *n.*

dis•hon•est (dĭs-ŏn'ĭst) *adj.* **1.** Lacking honesty; untrustworthy. **2.** Proceeding from or gained by falseness or lack of probity. —**dis•hon'est•ly** *adv.* —**dis•hon'es•ty** *n.*

dis•hon•or (dĭs-ŏn'ər) *n.* **1.** Loss of honor, respect, or reputation; disgrace. **2.** A cause of this. —*v.* **1.** To deprive of honor; disgrace. **2.** To fail to pay, as a note. —**dis•hon'or•a•ble** *adj.* —**dis•hon'or•a•bly** *adv.*

dish•wash•er (dĭsh'wŏsh'ər, -wô'shər) *n.* One who or a machine that washes dishes.

dis•il•lu•sion (dĭs'ĭ-lo͞o'zhən) *v.* To free or deprive of illusion; disenchant. —*n.* **1.** The act of disenchanting. **2.** The condition of being disenchanted. —**dis'il•lu'sion•ment** *n.*

dis•in•cli•na•tion (dĭs-ĭn'klə-nā'shən) *n.* Lack of willingness or disposition.

dis•in•cline (dĭs'ĭn-klīn') *v.* **-clined, -clining.** To make or be reluctant or averse.

dis•in•fect (dĭs'ĭn-fĕkt') *v.* To cleanse of pathogenic microorganisms. —**dis'in•fec'tant** *n.*

dis•in•gen•u•ous (dĭs'ĭn-jĕn'yo͞o-əs) *adj.* Not straightforward; crafty.

dis•in•her•it (dĭs'ĭn-hĕr'ĭt) *v.* To prevent from inheriting.

dis•in•te•grate (dĭs-ĭn'tə-grāt') *v.* **-grated, -grating.** To separate into fragments. —**dis•in'te•gra'tor** *n.* —**dis•in'te•gra'tion** *n.*

dis•in•ter (dĭs'ĭn-tûr') *v.* **-terred, -terring.** To

remove from a grave or tomb.

dis•in•ter•est•ed (dĭs-ĭn′trĭ-stĭd, -ĭn′tə-rĕs′tĭd) *adj.* **1.** Impartial. **2.** *Nonstandard.* Uninterested; indifferent. —**dis•in′ter•est•ed•ly** *adv.*

Usage: *Disinterested* differs from *uninterested* to the degree that lack of self-interest differs from lack of any interest. *Disinterested* is synonymous with *impartial, unbiased. Uninterested* has the sense of *indifferent, not interested.*

dis•join (dĭs-join′) *v.* To undo; separate.

dis•joint (dĭs-joint′) *v.* **1.** To disconnect; separate. **2.** To take apart at the joints. —*adj. Math.* Having no elements in common.

dis•joint•ed (dĭs-join′tĭd) *adj.* **1.** Separated. **2.** Lacking order or coherence. —**dis•joint′ed•ly** *adv.* —**dis•joint′ed•ness** *n.*

disk (dĭsk) *n.* **1.** Also **disc.** Any thin, flat, circular plate. **2.** The central part of a flower head, as of the daisy, consisting of small, densely clustered flowers. **3.** Variant of **disc.** [L *discus,* quoit < Gk *diskos.*]

disk brake. A brake in which the retarding friction is generated by contact between fixed and rotating disks.

dis•like (dĭs-līk′) *n.* An attitude or feeling of distaste or aversion. —**dis•like′** *v.* **(-liked, -liking).**

dis•lo•cate (dĭs′lō-kāt′, dĭs-lō′kāt′) *v.* **-cated, -cating. 1.** To remove from the usual or proper relationship. **2.** To displace from the normal position. **3.** To throw into confusion; upset; disturb. —**dis′lo•ca′tion** *n.*

dis•lodge (dĭs-lŏj′) *v.* **-lodged, -lodging.** To remove forcibly from a dwelling or position.

dis•loy•al (dĭs-loi′əl) *adj.* Lacking in loyalty. —**dis•loy′al•ly** *adv.* —**dis•loy′al•ty** *n.*

dis•mal (dĭz′məl) *adj.* Causing gloom or depression. [< ML *diēs malī,* "bad days."] —**dis′mal•ly** *adv.* —**dis′mal•ness** *n.*

dis•man•tle (dĭs-măn′tl) *v.* **-tled, -tling. 1.** To strip of furnishings or equipment, as a house. **2.** To take apart. —**dis•man′tle•ment** *n.*

dis•may (dĭs-mā′) *v.* **1.** To make anxious or afraid. **2.** To discourage or dishearten. —*n.* Apprehension; consternation. [< OF *desmayer.*]

dis•mem•ber (dĭs-mĕm′bər) *v.* **1.** To cut, tear, or pull off the limbs of. **2.** To separate into pieces. —**dis•mem′ber•ment** *n.*

dis•miss (dĭs-mĭs′) *v.* **1.** To discharge, as from employment. **2.** To direct or allow to leave. **3.** To reject; repudiate. **4.** To put (a claim or action) out of court without further hearing. [< L *dīmittere,* to send away.] —**dis•miss′al** *n.* —**dis•miss′i•ble** *adj.*

dis•mount (dĭs-mount′) *v.* **1.** To get off or down, as from a horse or bicycle. **2.** To remove (a rider) from a horse. **3.** To remove (an apparatus) from its mounting. **4.** To disassemble. —**dis•mount′a•ble** *adj.*

dis•o•be•di•ence (dĭs′ə-bē′dē-əns) *n.* Failure or refusal to obey. —**dis′o•be′di•ent** *adj.* —**dis′o•be′di•ent•ly** *adv.*

dis•o•bey (dĭs′ə-bā′) *v.* To fail or refuse to obey. —**dis′o•bey′er** *n.*

dis•or•der (dĭs-ôr′dər) *n.* **1.** Lack of order. **2.** A public disturbance. **3.** An illness. —*v.* To cause disorder.

dis•or•der•ly (dĭs-ôr′dər-lē) *adj.* **1.** Lacking order. **2.** Disturbing the public peace. —**dis•or′der•li•ness** *n.*

dis•or•gan•ize (dĭs-ôr′gə-nīz′) *v.* **-ized, -izing.** To disrupt the organization of. —**dis•or′gan•i•za′tion** *n.* —**dis•or′gan•iz′er** *n.*

dis•o•ri•ent (dĭs-ôr′ē-ĕnt′, dĭs-ōr′-) *v.* To cause to lose orientation. —**dis•o′ri•en•ta′tion** *n.*

dis•own (dĭs-ōn′) *v.* To refuse responsibility or relationship to; repudiate.

dis•par•age (dĭs-păr′ĭj) *v.* **-aged, -aging. 1.** To belittle. **2.** To reduce in esteem or rank. [< OF *desparager,* "to deprive one of his rank."] —**dis•par′age•ment** *n.* —**dis•par′ag•ing•ly** *adv.*

dis•pa•rate (dĭs′pər-ĭt, dĭs-păr′ĭt) *adj.* Different and distinct; dissimilar. [< L *disparāre,* to separate.] —**dis′pa•rate•ly** *adv.* —**dis•par′i•ty** (dĭs-păr′ə-tē) *n.*

dis•pas•sion•ate (dĭs-păsh′ən-ĭt) *adj.* Devoid of or unaffected by emotion. —**dis•pas′sion•ate•ly** *adv.*

dis•patch (dĭs-păch′). Also **des•patch.** *v.* **1.** To send. **2.** To perform promptly. **3.** To kill. —*n.* **1.** The act of dispatching. **2.** Efficient, expeditious performance. **3.** A message. **4.** A shipment. **5.** A news item sent to a newspaper by a correspondent. [< OF *despeechier,* to set free, unshackle.] —**dis•patch′er** *n.*

dis•pel (dĭs-pĕl′) *v.* **-pelled, -pelling.** To drive away or scatter. [< L *dispellere.*]

dis•pen•sa•ble (dĭs-pĕn′sə-bəl) *adj.* **1.** Capable of being dispensed with; unimportant. **2.** Capable of being administered or distributed.

dis•pen•sa•ry (dĭs-pĕn′sə-rē) *n., pl.* **-ries.** A place at which medical supplies are dispensed.

dis•pen•sa•tion (dĭs′pən-sā′shən, dĭs′pĕn-) *n.* **1.** The act of dispensing. **2.** Something dispensed. **3.** A system by which something is dispensed. **4.** Exemption or release from obligation or rule. **5.** Divine ordering of worldly affairs. **6.** A religious system or code of commands: *the Moslem dispensation.*

dis•pense (dĭs-pĕns′) *v.* **-pensed, -pensing. 1.** To distribute in portions. **2.** To prepare and give out (medicines). **3.** To administer, as laws. **4.** To exempt. [< L *dispensāre,* to pay out, distribute.] —**dis•pens′er** *n.*

dis•perse (dĭs-pûrs′) *v.* **-persed, -persing. 1.** To scatter. **2.** To disseminate or distribute. [< L *dispergere,* to scatter on all sides.] —**dis•per′sion, dis•per′sal** *n.*

dis•pir•it (dĭs-pĭr′ĭt) *v.* To discourage.

dis•place (dĭs-plās′) *v.* **-placed, -placing. 1.** To remove from a place or position. **2.** To take the place of. **3.** To cause displacement of.

dis•place•ment (dĭs-plās′mənt) *n.* **1.** The act of displacing. **2.** The weight or volume of a fluid displaced by a floating body. **3.** The distance from an initial position to a subsequent position assumed by a body.

dis•play (dĭs-plā′) *v.* To place in view; show. —*n.* **1.** An act of displaying. **2.** Something displayed. [< L *displicāre,* to scatter.]

dis•please (dĭs-plēz′) *v.* **-pleased, -pleasing.** To annoy or irritate. —**dis•pleas′ure** (-plĕzh′ər) *n.*

dis•port (dĭs-pôrt′, -pōrt′) *v.* To engage in an activity for diversion or amusement. [< OF *desporter,* "to carry away," divert.]

dis•pos•a•ble (dĭs-pō′zə-bəl) *adj.* **1.** Designed to be discarded after use. **2.** Subject to use; available. —**dis•pos′a•bil′i•ty** *n.*

dis•pos•al (dĭs-pō′zəl) *n.* **1.** Order; arrangement. **2.** A manner or method of disposing. **3.** A throwing out or away. **4.** An apparatus for disposing of something. **5.** Ability or authority to dispose of something.

dis•pose (dĭs-pōz′) *v.* **-posed, -posing. 1.** To place in order; arrange. **2.** To settle; conclude. **3.** To incline: *disposed to laughter.* —**dispose of. 1.** To attend to. **2.** To transfer or part with, as by selling. **3.** To get rid of. [< L *dispōnere,* to place here and there, arrange.]

dis•po•si•tion (dĭs′pə-zĭsh′ən) *n.* **1.** Temperament. **2.** A tendency or inclination. **3.** The act or manner of disposing. **4.** The authority to dispose.

dis•pos•sess (dĭs′pə-zĕs′) *v.* To deprive of the possession of, as a house. —**dis′pos•ses′sion** *n.*

dis•pro•por•tion•ate (dĭs′prə-pôr′shən-ĭt, -pōr′shən-ĭt) *adj.* Out of proportion. —**dis′pro•por′tion** *n.* —**dis′pro•por′tion•ate•ly** *adv.*

dis•prove (dĭs-pro͞ov′) *v.* **-proved, -proving.** To prove to be false, invalid, or in error; refute. —**dis•proof′** (-pro͞of′) *n.*

dis•pu•ta•tious (dĭs′pyo͞o-tā′shəs) *adj.* Inclined to dispute; contentious.

dis•pute (dĭs-pyo͞ot′) *v.* **-puted, -puting. 1.** To argue; debate. **2.** To question the truth or validity of. **3.** To strive against; oppose. —*n.* **1.** An argument; debate. **2.** A quarrel. [< L *disputāre,* to reckon, discuss.] —**dis•put′a•ble** *adj.* —**dis•pu′tant** *adj.* & *n.* —**dis′pu•ta′tion** *n.*

dis•qual•i•fy (dĭs-kwŏl′ə-fī′) *v.* **-fied, -fying.** To declare or render unqualified. —**dis•qual′i•fi•ca′tion** *n.*

dis•qui•et (dĭs-kwī′ĭt) *v.* To disturb or trouble. —*n.* Lack of peace or quiet. —**dis•qui′et•ing•ly** *adv.*

dis•qui•e•tude (dĭs-kwī′ə-t/y/o͞od′) *n.* A state of worry or uneasiness.

dis•qui•si•tion (dĭs′kwə-zĭsh′ən) *n.* A formal discourse. [< L *disquīrere,* to inquire diligently.]

Dis•rae•li (dĭz-rā′lē), **Benjamin.** 1804–1881. British statesman; prime minister (1868 and 1874–80).

dis•re•gard (dĭs′rĭ-gärd′) *v.* To ignore. —*n.* Willful lack of regard.

dis•re•pair (dĭs′rĭ-pâr′) *n.* A condition of needing repairs; dilapidation.

dis•rep•u•ta•ble (dĭs-rĕp′yə-tə-bəl) *adj.* **1.** Not respectable. **2.** Disgraceful; discreditable.

dis•re•pute (dĭs′rĭ-pyo͞ot′) *n.* Discredit; disgrace.

dis•re•spect (dĭs′rĭ-spĕkt′) *n.* Lack of respect; rudeness. —**dis′re•spect′ful** *adj.*

dis•robe (dĭs-rōb′) *v.* **-robed, -robing.** To undress. —**dis•rob′er** *n.*

dis•rupt (dĭs-rŭpt′) *v.* To throw into confusion. [L *disrumpere* (pp *disruptus*), to break asunder.] —**dis•rup′tion** *n.* —**dis•rup′tive** *adj.*

dis•sat•is•fac•tion (dĭs-săt′ĭs-făk′shən) *n.* The feeling of being displeased; discontent.

dis•sat•is•fy (dĭs-săt′ĭs-fī′) *v.* **-fied, -fying.** To make discontented; displease.

dis•sect (dĭ-sĕkt′, dī-, dī′sĕkt′) *v.* **1.** To cut apart or separate (tissue) for anatomical study. **2.** To analyze in minute detail. [L *dissecāre,* to cut apart.] —**dis•sec′tion** *n.*

dis•sem•ble (dĭ-sĕm′bəl) *v.* **-bled, -bling. 1.** To disguise the real nature of. **2.** To simulate; feign. [< OF *dessembler,* to be different.] —**dis•sem′bler** *n.*

dis•sem•i•nate (dĭ-sĕm′ə-nāt′) *v.* **-nated, -nating.** To scatter or spread widely. [L *dissēmināre.*] —**dis•sem′i•na′tion** *n.*

dis•sen•sion (dĭ-sĕn′shən) *n.* Discord; contention. [< L *dissentīre,* to DISSENT.]

dis•sent (dĭ-sĕnt′) *v.* **1.** To disagree; differ. **2.** To withhold assent. —*n.* **1.** Disagreement. **2.** Political or religious nonconformity. [< L *dissentīre,* to feel apart.] —**dis•sent′er** *n.*

dis•ser•ta•tion (dĭs′ər-tā′shən) *n.* A treatise, esp. one written as a doctoral thesis. [< L *disserere,* to discuss.]

dis•ser•vice (dĭs-sûr′vĭs) *n.* A harmful action.

dis•sev•er (dĭ-sĕv′ər) *v.* To separate; break up. [< LL *dissēparāre.*]

dis•si•dent (dĭs′ə-dənt) *adj.* Publicly or violently dissenting. —*n.* A dissenter. [< L *dissidēre,* "to sit apart," dissent.] —**dis′si•dence** *n.* —**dis′si•dent•ly** *adv.*

dis•sim•i•lar (dĭ-sĭm′ə-lər) *adj.* Unlike. —**dis•sim′i•lar′i•ty** (-sĭm′ə-lăr′ə-tē) *n.*

dis•si•mil•i•tude (dĭs'ĭ-mĭl'ə-t/y/o͞od') *n.* **1.** Lack of resemblance. **2.** A point of difference. [< L *dissimilis,* different.]

dis•sim•u•late (dĭ-sĭm'yə-lāt') *v.* **-lated, -lating.** To disguise under a feigned appearance; dissemble. **—dis•sim'u•la'tion** *n.*

dis•si•pate (dĭs'ə-pāt') *v.* **-pated, -pating. 1.** To dispel or scatter. **2.** To waste; squander. **3.** To vanish; disappear. **4.** To indulge in intemperate drinking. [< L *dissipāre,* to disperse, squander.] **—dis'si•pa'tion** *n.*

dis•so•ci•ate (dĭ-sō'shē-āt', -sē-āt') *v.* **-ated, -ating.** To separate. [L *dissociāre.*] **—dis•so'ci•a'tion** *n.* **—dis•so'ci•a'tive** *adj.*

dis•so•lute (dĭs'ə-lo͞ot') *adj.* Lacking in moral restraint; debauched; abandoned. [< L *dissolūtus,* pp of *dissolvere,* DISSOLVE.] **—dis'so•lute'ly** *adv.* **—dis'so•lute'ness** *n.*

dis•so•lu•tion (dĭs'ə-lo͞o'shən) *n.* **1.** Decomposition; disintegration. **2.** Termination or extinction by deconcentration or dispersion. **3.** Death. **4.** Termination of a legal bond. **5.** Formal dismissal of an assembly. **6.** Reduction to a liquid form; liquefaction.

dis•solve (dĭ-zŏlv') *v.* **-solved, -solving. 1.** To enter or cause to enter into solution. **2.** To melt. **3.** To dispel. **4.** To break into component parts. **5.** To terminate or dismiss. **6.** To collapse emotionally. [< L *dissolvere.*]

dis•so•nance (dĭs'ə-nəns) *n.* **1.** Discord. **2.** *Mus.* A combination of tones conventionally considered to suggest unrelieved tension and to require resolution. **—dis'so•nant** *adj.* **—dis'so•nant•ly** *adv.*

dis•suade (dĭ-swād') *v.* **-suaded, -suading.** To discourage from a purpose or course of action by persuasion. [L *dissuādēre.*] **—dis•sua'sion** (-swā'zhən) *n.* **—dis•sua'sive** *adj.*

dist. 1. distance; distant. **2.** district.

dis•taff (dĭs'tăf', -täf') *n.* **1.** A staff that holds on its cleft end the unspun flax, wool, etc., in spinning. **2.** Also **distaff side.** The maternal branch of a family. [< OE *distæf*: *dis-,* bunch of flax + STAFF.]

dis•tal (dĭs'təl) *adj.* Anatomically located far from the origin or line of attachment. [DIST(ANT) + -AL.] **—dis'tal•ly** *adv.*

dis•tance (dĭs'təns) *n.* **1.** Separation in space or time. **2.** The length of a line segment joining two points. **3.** The interval separating any two specified instants in time. **4. a.** The degree of deviation or difference that separates two things in relationship. **b.** The degree of progress between two points in a trend or course. **5.** Coldness; aloofness. **6.** The whole way: *go the distance.* —*v.* **-tanced, -tancing.** To outrun; outstrip.

dis•tant (dĭs'tənt) *adj.* **1.** Separate in space or time. **2.** Far removed. **3.** Located at, coming from, or going to a distance. **4.** Remote in relationship: *a distant cousin.* **5.** Aloof; cold. [< L *distāre,* to be remote.] **—dis'tant•ly** *adv.*

dis•taste (dĭs-tāst') *n.* Dislike or aversion.

dis•taste•ful (dĭs-tāst'fəl) *adj.* Unpleasant; disagreeable. **—dis•taste'ful•ly** *adv.*

dis•tem•per (dĭs-tĕm'pər) *n.* An infectious, often fatal virus disease of certain mammals, esp. dogs.

dis•tend (dĭs-tĕnd') *v.* To expand or swell. [< L *distendere.*] **—dis•ten'si•ble** *adj.* **—dis•ten'tion, dis•ten'sion** *n.*

dis•till (dĭs-tĭl') *v.* **1.** To subject to, or derive by means of, distillation. **2.** To separate from. **3.** To exude in drops. [< L *dēstillāre.*] **—dis•till'er** *n.* **—dis•till'er•y** *n.*

dis•til•late (dĭs'tə-lāt', dĭs-tĭl'ĭt) *n.* The liquid condensed from vapor in distillation.

dis•til•la•tion (dĭs'tə-lā'shən) *n.* Any of various heat-dependent processes used to purify or separate a fraction of a relatively complex substance, esp. the vaporization of a liquid mixture with subsequent collection of components by differential cooling to condensation.

dis•tinct (dĭs-tĭngkt') *adj.* **1.** Individual; discrete. **2.** Different; unlike. **3.** Readily perceived. **4.** Explicit; unquestionable. [< L *distinguere,* DISTINGUISH.] **—dis•tinct'ly** *adv.*

dis•tinc•tion (dĭs-tĭngk'shən) *n.* **1.** The act of distinguishing; differentiation. **2.** A difference. **3.** A distinguishing factor or characteristic. **4.** Personal excellence. **5.** Honor.

dis•tinc•tive (dĭs-tĭngk'tĭv) *adj.* **1.** Serving to identify; distinguishing. **2.** Characteristic. **—dis•tinc'tive•ly** *adv.* **—dis•tinc'tive•ness** *n.*

dis•tin•guish (dĭs-tĭng'gwĭsh) *v.* **1.** To recognize as being distinct. **2.** To perceive distinctly; discern. **3.** To discriminate. **4.** To set apart. **5.** To make eminent. [< L *distinguere,* to separate, distinguish.] **—dis•tin'guish•a•ble** *adj.* **—dis•tin'guish•a•bly** *adv.*

dis•tin•guished (dĭs-tĭng'gwĭsht) *adj.* **1.** Characterized by excellence or distinction; eminent. **2.** Dignified in conduct or appearance.

dis•tort (dĭs-tôrt') *v.* **1.** To twist out of a proper or natural shape. **2.** To alter misleadingly; misrepresent. **3.** To reproduce (sound) improperly. [L *distorquēre* (pp *distortus*).] **—dis•tort'er** *n.* **—dis•tor'tion** *n.*

distr. distributor.

dis•tract (dĭs-trăkt') *v.* **1.** To sidetrack; divert. **2.** To stir up; unsettle emotionally. [< L *distrahere* (pp *distractus*), to pull apart, draw away.] **—dis•trac'tion** *n.* **—dis•trac'tive** *adj.*

dis•traught (dĭs-trôt') *adj.* **1.** Confused and agitated; harried. **2.** Crazed; mad. [< L *distrahere,* to DISTRACT.]

dis•tress (dĭs-trĕs') *v.* To cause anxiety or suffering to. —*n.* **1.** Anxiety or suffering. **2.** Misfortune. **3.** Need of immediate assistance: *a ship in distress.* [< L *districtus,* pp of *distringere,* "to draw tight," hinder.]

dis•trib•ute (dĭs-trĭb'yo͞ot) *v.* **-uted, -uting. 1.** To divide and dispense in portions. **2.** To deliver or parcel out. **3.** To spread through an area or range. **4.** To classify. [< L *distribuere.*] **—dis'tri•bu'tion** *n.* **—dis•trib'u•tive** *adj.*

dis•trib•u•tor (dĭs-trĭb'yə-tər) *n.* Also **dis•trib•ut•er. 1.** One that distributes. **2.** One that markets or sells merchandise, esp. a wholesaler. **3.** A device for applying electric current in proper sequence to spark plugs.

dis•trict (dĭs'trĭkt) *n.* A territorial division created for governmental or other purposes or existing by virtue of a characteristic. [< L *districtus,* pp of *distringere,* to detain, hinder.]

district attorney. The prosecuting officer of a given judicial district.

District of Columbia. The Federal District of the U.S., coextensive with the capital city of Washington. Pop. 764,000.

dis•trust (dĭs-trŭst') *n.* Lack of trust; suspicion. —*v.* To lack confidence in; suspect. **—dis•trust'ful** *adj.* **—dis•trust'ful•ly** *adv.*

dis•turb (dĭs-tûrb') *v.* **1.** To upset the tranquillity or settled state of. **2.** To intrude upon; interrupt. **3.** To disarrange. [< L *disturbāre.*] **—dis•tur'bance** *n.* **—dis•turb'ing•ly** *adv.*

dis•u•nite (dĭs'yo͞o-nīt') *v.* To separate; divide.

dis•u•ni•ty (dĭs-yo͞o'nə-tē) *n.* Lack of unity; dissension.

dis•use (dĭs-yo͞os') *n.* The state of being no longer in use; desuetude.

ditch (dĭch) *n.* A trench dug in the ground. —*v. Slang.* To discard; desert. [< OE *dīc,* moat, ditch. See **dhīgw-.**]

dith•er (dĭth'ər) *n.* A state of agitation or indecision. [ME *didderen.*]

dit•to (dĭt'ō) *n., pl.* **-tos. 1.** The same as before or another of the same. **2.** The pair of small marks (″) used as a symbol for the word *ditto.* [< L *dīcere,* to say.]

dit•ty (dĭt'ē) *n., pl.* **-ties.** A simple short song. [< L *dictātum,* "thing dictated."]

di•u•ret•ic (dī'yo͞o-rĕt'ĭk) *adj.* Tending to increase the discharge of urine. —*n.* A diuretic drug. [< Gk *diourein,* to pass urine.]

di•ur•nal (dī-ûr'nəl) *adj.* **1.** Pertaining to or occurring in daytime. **2.** Daily. [< L *diurnus,* of a day, daily.] **—di•ur'nal•ly** *adv.*

div. 1. divided; division; divisor. **2.** dividend. **3.** divorced.

di•va (dē'və) *n.* An operatic prima donna. [It, "goddess."]

di•va•lent (dī-vā'lənt) *adj.* Having a valence of 2; bivalent.

di•van (dĭ-văn', dī'văn') *n.* A couch; sofa. [< Turk *dīvān.*]

dive (dīv) *v.* **dived** or **dove, dived, diving. 1. a.** To plunge headfirst into water. **b.** To go toward the bottom of a body of water: *dive for pearls.* **2.** To submerge under power, as a submarine. **3.** To drop precipitously; plummet. **4.** To descend in an airplane at an acceleration exceeding that of free fall. **5.** To rush headlong. **6.** To plunge, as into an activity. —*n.* **1.** An act or instance of diving. **2.** *Slang.* A disreputable or run-down bar or nightclub. [< OE *dȳfan,* to dip, immerse, and *dūfan,* to sink, dive. See **dheub-.**] **—div'er** *n.*

di•verge (dĭ-vûrj', dī-) *v.* **-verged, -verging. 1.** To tend in different directions from a common point. **2.** To differ, as in opinion. **3.** To deviate, as from a set course or norm. **4.** *Math.* To fail to approach a limit. [LL *dīvergere,* to turn aside.] **—di•ver'gence** *n.* **—di•ver'gent** *adj.* **—di•ver'gent•ly** *adv.*

di•vers (dī'vərz) *adj.* Various.

di•verse (dĭ-vûrs', dī-, dī'vûrs') *adj.* **1.** Unlike. **2.** Having variety in form; diversified. [< L *dīvertere,* to turn aside, DIVERT.] **—di•verse'ly** *adv.* **—di•verse'ness** *n.*

di•ver•si•fy (dĭ-vûr'sə-fī', dī-) *v.* **-fied, -fying. 1.** To make diverse; vary. **2.** To spread out business activities or investments. **—di•ver'si•fi•ca'tion** (-fĭ-kā'shən) *n.*

di•ver•sion (dĭ-vûr'zhən, -shən, dī-) *n.* **1.** A turning aside. **2.** A pastime or distraction. **3.** A military maneuver that draws the enemy away from a planned point of attack. **—di•ver'sion•ar'y** *adj.*

di•ver•si•ty (dĭ-vûr'sə-tē, dī-) *n., pl.* **-ties. 1.** The quality of being diverse or different; variety. **2.** A point in which things differ.

di•vert (dĭ-vûrt', dī-) *v.* **1.** To turn aside from a course or direction; deflect. **2.** To distract. **3.** To amuse or entertain. [< L *dīvertere,* to turn aside.] **—di•vert'er** *n.*

di•vest (dĭ-vĕst', dī-) *v.* **1.** To strip, as of clothes. **2.** To deprive, as of rights; dispossess. [< OF *desvestir,* to undress.]

di•vide (dĭ-vīd') *v.* **-vided, -viding. 1. a.** To separate or become separated into parts, sections, or groups. **b.** To classify. **2.** To set at odds; disunite. **3.** To cut off; part. **4.** To apportion or share. **5. a.** To subject to mathematical division. **b.** To be an exact divisor of. **6.** To branch out. —*n.* A watershed. [< L *dīvidere.*] **—di•vid'a•ble** *adj.*

div•i•dend (dĭv'ə-dĕnd') *n.* **1.** A quantity to be

divided. 2. A share of profits received by a stockholder. 3. *Informal.* A bonus.
di•vid•er (dĭ-vī'dər) *n.* 1. a. One that divides. b. A partition. 2. **dividers.** A device resembling a compass, used for dividing lines and transferring measurements.
div•i•na•tion (dĭv'ə-nā'shən) *n.* 1. The art or practice of foretelling future events or revealing occult knowledge by means of augury or alleged supernatural agency. 2. Inspired insight or intuition.
di•vine[1] (dĭ-vīn') *adj.* **-viner, -vinest.** 1. a. Being or having the nature of a deity. b. Of or relating to a deity. 2. Supremely good; magnificent. 3. *Informal.* Heavenly; perfect. —*n.* 1. A clergyman. 2. A theologian. [< L *dīvus,* divine, god.] —**di•vine'ly** *adv.*
di•vine[2] (dĭ-vīn') *v.* **-vined, -vining.** 1. To foretell or prophesy. 2. To guess, infer, or conjecture. —**di•vin'er** *n.*
di•vin•i•ty (dĭ-vĭn'ə-tē) *n.* 1. The state or quality of being divine. 2. **Divinity.** God; the godhead. 3. Theology.
di•vis•i•ble (dĭ-vĭz'ə-bəl) *adj.* Capable of being divided, esp. of being divided evenly with no remainder. —**di•vis'i•bil'i•ty** *n.*
di•vi•sion (dĭ-vĭzh'ən) *n.* 1. The act or process of dividing or state of being divided. 2. The proportional distribution of a quantity or entity. 3. A boundary or partition. 4. One of the parts into which something is divided. 5. a. An area of activity organized as a functional unit. b. A territorial section marked off for administrative purposes. 6. A large self-contained tactical unit, as of an army. 7. a. Disagreement. b. Disunion. 8. The operation of determining how many times one quantity is contained in another. —**di•vi'sion•al** *adj.*
di•vi•sive (dĭ-vī'sĭv) *adj.* Creating dissension. —**di•vi'sive•ly** *adv.* —**di•vi'sive•ness** *n.*
di•vi•sor (dĭ-vī'zər) *n.* The quantity by which another, the dividend, is to be divided.
di•vorce (dĭ-vôrs', -vōrs') *n.* 1. The dissolution of a marriage by law. 2. A radical separation. [< L *dīvortere, dīvertere,* to turn aside, separate, DIVERT.] —**di•vorce'** *v.* **(-vorced, -vorcing).**
di•vor•cée (dĭ-vôr-sā', -vôr'sā', -vōr'sā', -vōr'-sā') *n.* A divorced woman.
div•ot (dĭv'ət) *n.* A piece of turf torn up by a golf club in striking a ball. [Scot *devait.*]
di•vulge (dĭ-vŭlj') *v.* **-vulged, -vulging.** To disclose; reveal. [< L *dīvulgāre,* to spread abroad among the people.] —**di•vulg'er** *n.*
div•vy (dĭv'ē) *v.* **-vied, -vying.** —**divvy up.** *Slang.* To divide.
Dix•ie (dĭk'sē). The Southern states. [Orig, a ten-dollar bill issued in New Orleans.]
diz•zy (dĭz'ē) *adj.* **-zier, -ziest.** 1. Having a sensation of whirling or feeling a tendency to fall; giddy. 2. Producing or produced by giddiness. 3. Precipitate. [< OE *dysig,* foolish, stupid. See **dheu-**[1].] —**diz'zi•ly** *adv.* —**diz'zi•ness** *n.* —**diz'zy** *v.* **(-zied, -zying).**
DJ disc jockey.
Dja•kar•ta (jə-kär'tə). The capital of Indonesia, on the NW coast of Java. Pop. 2,907,000.
Dji•bou•ti (jĭ-bo͞o'tē). 1. Officially, Djibouti Republic. A country of E Africa. Pop. 250,000. 2. The capital of this country. Pop. 62,000.
djin•ni, djin•ny. Variants of **jinni.**
dk. 1. dark. 2. deck. 3. dock.
dlr. dealer.
dlvy. delivery.
DM Deutsche mark.
DMZ demilitarized zone.
DNA deoxyribonucleic acid.
Dnie•per (nē'pər). A river of the W Soviet Union.
do (do͞o) *v.* **did, done, doing, does.** 1. To perform or execute. 2. To fulfill; complete. 3. To create, compose, or make. 4. To bring about; effect. 5. To put into action; exert. 6. To deal with as is necessary. 7. To render: *do equal justice.* 8. To work at. 9. To solve (a problem). 10. To present (a play). 11. To have the role of; play. 12. To cover (a specified distance): *do a mile in a minute.* 13. To tour: *do Europe.* 14. To be adequate; suffice. 15. To set or style (the hair). 16. To cheat: *do someone out of his inheritance.* 17. To get along; fare: *do well at school.* 18. —Used as an auxiliary: a. In questions, negative statements, and inverted phrases: *Do you understand? I did not sleep well. Little did he suspect.* b. For emphasis: *I do want to be sure.* c. As a substitute for an antecedent verb: *She tries as hard as they do.* —**do away with.** 1. To eliminate. 2. To kill. —**do for.** To take care of. —**do in.** *Slang.* 1. To exhaust. 2. To kill. —**do over.** *Informal.* To redecorate. —*n., pl.* **do's** or **dos.** 1. *Informal.* A party. 2. A statement of what should be done: *do's and don'ts.* [< OE *dōn.* See **dhē-.**]
do. ditto.
D.O. 1. Doctor of Optometry. 2. Doctor of Osteopathy.
D.O.A. dead on arrival.
doc. document.
doc•ile (dŏs'əl; *Brit.* dō'sīl') *adj.* Tractable; submissive. [L *docilis.*] —**doc'ile•ly** *adv.* —**do•cil'i•ty** (dō-sĭl'ə-tē) *n.*
dock[1] (dŏk) *n.* 1. A slip between two piers that receives a ship. 2. A pier or wharf. 3. A wharflike loading platform. —*v.* 1. To maneuver into or next to a dock. 2. To couple (two or more spacecraft) in space. [< VL **ductia,* conduit, aqueduct.]
dock[2] (dŏk) *v.* 1. To clip or cut off, as an animal's tail. 2. a. To withhold a part of (a salary). b. To penalize (a worker) by such deduction. [Perh < OE **docca* < Gmc **dukk-,* bundle.]
dock[3] (dŏk) *n.* The place where the defendant stands or sits in a criminal court. [Flem *docke,* cage, pen.]
dock[4] (dŏk) *n.* A weedy plant with clusters of small, usually greenish flowers. [< OE *docce.*]
dock•age (dŏk'ĭj) *n.* 1. Facilities for docking vessels. 2. The charge for docking privileges.
dock•et (dŏk'ĭt) *n.* 1. a. A brief entry of the proceedings in a court of justice. b. The book containing such entries. c. A calendar of cases awaiting court action. 2. An agenda. 3. A label on a package listing the contents or directions for use. [ME *doggette.*] —**dock'et** *v.*
dock•hand (dŏk'hănd') *n.* A dock worker; longshoreman.
dock•yard (dŏk'yärd') *n.* A place with facilities for building, repairing, or dry-docking ships.
doc•tor (dŏk'tər) *n.* 1. One who holds the highest academic degree awarded by a university in any specified discipline. 2. One trained in the healing arts, esp. a physician, surgeon, dentist, or veterinarian. —*v.* 1. a. To give medical treatment to. b. To practice medicine. 2. To repair, esp. in a makeshift manner. 3. To alter or falsify. 4. To add ingredients to. [< L, teacher.] —**doc'tor•al** *adj.*
doc•tor•ate (dŏk'tər-ĭt) *n.* The degree or status of a doctor as conferred by a university.
doc•tri•naire (dŏk'trə-nâr') *n.* One inflexibly committed to the application of a given theory regardless of its practicality. —**doc'tri•naire'** *adj.*
doc•trine (dŏk'trĭn) *n.* 1. Something that is taught as a body of principles. 2. A tenet; dogma. [< L *doctrīna,* teaching, learning.] —**doc'tri•nal** *adj.* —**doc'tri•nal•ly** *adv.*
doc•u•ment (dŏk'yə-mənt) *n.* A paper bearing evidence, proof, or information. —*v.* To furnish with or support by a document or documents. [< L *docēre,* to teach.] —**doc'u•men•ta'tion** *n.*
doc•u•men•ta•ry (dŏk'yə-mĕn'tə-rē) *adj.* 1. Of or concerning documents. 2. Presenting facts objectively in artistic form. —*n., pl.* **-ries.** A documentary film or television presentation.
dod•der (dŏd'ər) *v.* To shake or move shakily, as from old age. [Perh < Scand.]
dodge (dŏj) *v.* **dodged, dodging.** 1. To avoid by moving aside. 2. To evade by cunning or deceit. 3. To shift suddenly. —*n.* 1. A quick move or shift. 2. A clever or evasive trick; stratagem. 3. A method or technique. [?] —**dodg'er** *n.*
do•do (dō'dō) *n., pl.* **-does** or **-dos.** A large flightless bird extinct since the 17th century. [Port *doudo.*]
doe (dō) *n.* The female of a deer or of certain other animals, such as the hare. [< OE *dā.*]
do•er (do͞o'ər) *n.* 1. The agent of something. 2. An active, energetic person.
does (dŭz). 3rd person sing. present tense of **do.**
doe•skin (dō'skĭn') *n.* 1. Soft leather made originally from the skin of a doe. 2. A soft, napped woolen fabric.
does•n't (dŭz'ənt). Contraction of *does not.*
doest (do͞o'əst). *Archaic.* 2nd person sing. present tense of **do.**
doeth (do͞o'əth). *Archaic.* 3rd person sing. present tense of **do.**
doff (dôf, dŏf) *v.* 1. To take off: *doff one's clothes.* 2. To tip (one's hat). 3. To discard. [< ME *don off* : *don,* to do + OFF.]
dog (dôg, dŏg) *n.* 1. A domesticated carnivorous mammal related to wolves and foxes. 2. The male of such an animal. —*v.* **dogged, dogging.** 1. To track or trail persistently. 2. To hound; harry. [< OE *docga.*]
dog•catch•er (dôg'kăch'ər, dŏg'-) *n.* One appointed to impound stray dogs.
doge (dōj) *n.* The chief magistrate of the former republics of Venice and Genoa. [< L *dūcere,* to lead.]
dog-ear (dôg'îr', dŏg'-) *n.* A turned-down corner of a page of a book. —**dog'-eared'** *adj.*
dog•fight (dôg'fīt', dŏg'-) *n.* A battle involving two or more fighter planes at close quarters.
dog•fish (dôg'fĭsh', dŏg'-) *n.* Any of various small sharks.
dog•ged (dô'gĭd, dŏg'ĭd) *adj.* Stubborn; tenacious. —**dog'ged•ly** *adv.* —**dog'ged•ness** *n.*
dog•ger•el (dô'gər-əl, dŏg'ər-) *n.* Light verse of a loose, irregular measure. [Perh < DOG.]
dog•house (dôg'hous', dŏg'-) *n.* A house for a dog. —**in the doghouse.** *Slang.* In disgrace; in trouble.
dog•ma (dôg'mə, dŏg'-) *n.* 1. A system of doctrines proclaimed by a church. 2. A tenet or body of tenets. [< Gk, decree.]
dog•mat•ic (dôg-măt'ĭk, dŏg-) *adj.* Marked by an authoritarian assertion of principles. —**dog•mat'i•cal•ly** *adv.*
dog•ma•tism (dôg'mə-tĭz'əm, dŏg'-) *n.* Dogmatic assertion of opinion or belief.
Dog Star. 1. The star Sirius. 2. The star Pro-

cyon.

dog•trot (dôg'trŏt', dŏg'-) *n.* A steady trot.

dog•wood (dôg'wo͝od', dŏg'-) *n.* A tree with small greenish flowers surrounded by showy white or pink petallike bracts.

doi•ly (doi'lē) *n., pl.* **-lies.** A small ornamental mat. [< *Doily,* a London draper, circa 1712.]

dol. dollar.

dol•drums (dōl'drəmz', dôl'-, dŏl'-) *n. (takes sing. v.).* **1.** Ocean regions near the equator, characterized by calms. **2.** A period of inactivity, listlessness, or depression. [Perh < OE *dol,* dull.]

dole (dōl) *n.* **1. a.** The distribution of necessities to the needy. **b.** Something so distributed. **2.** *Chiefly Brit.* Government distribution of relief payments to the unemployed. *—v.* **doled, doling. —dole out.** To distribute in small portions. [< OE *dāl,* share, portion. See **dail-.**]

dole•ful (dōl'fəl) *adj.* Mournful; sad. **—dole'ful•ly** *adv.* **—dole'ful•ness** *n.*

doll (dŏl) *n.* **1.** A figure representing a baby or other human being, used as a child's toy. **2.** *Slang.* An attractive young woman. *—v.* **—doll up.** To dress up smartly. [< *Doll,* pet name for Dorothea.]

dol•lar (dŏl'ər) *n.* The basic monetary unit of the United States, Australia, Canada, Ethiopia, Guyana, Jamaica, Liberia, Malaysia, New Zealand, Trinidad and Tobago, Western Samoa, and Hong Kong and Singapore, equal to 100 cents. [< G *Taler.*]

dol•lop (dŏl'əp) *n.* A lump, helping, or portion, as of ice cream. [?]

dol•ly (dŏl'ē) *n., pl.* **-lies. 1.** A doll. **2.** A low mobile platform that rolls on casters. **3.** A wheeled apparatus used to move a motion-picture or television camera. **4.** A small locomotive for use in a railroad yard, construction site, etc.

dol•men (dŏl'mən) *n.* A prehistoric structure consisting of two or more upright stones with a topstone, forming a chamber. [F.]

do•lor (dō'lər) *n.* Anguish; sorrow. [< L *dolēre,* to feel pain, grieve.] **—do'lor•ous** *adj.* **—do'lor•ous•ness** *n.*

dol•phin (dŏl'fĭn, dôl'-) *n.* **1.** A marine mammal related to the whales but generally smaller and with a beaklike snout. **2.** A marine fish with iridescent coloring. [< Gk *delphis (delphin-).*]

dolt (dōlt) *n.* A blockhead. [Perh a var of DULL.] **—dolt'ish** *adj.* **—dolt'ish•ly** *adv.*

-dom. *comb. form.* **1.** The condition of being: **boredom. 2.** The domain, position, or rank of: **saintdom.** [< OE *-dōm.*]

dom. 1. domestic. **2.** dominant. **3.** dominion.

Dom. Dominican.

do•main (dō-mān') *n.* **1.** A territory or range of rule or control. **2.** A sphere of action or interest; field. [< L *dominium,* property, ownership rights.]

dome (dōm) *n.* A hemispheric roof or vault. [< It *duomo,* (domed) cathedral.]

do•mes•tic (də-mĕs'tĭk) *adj.* **1.** Of or pertaining to the family or household. **2.** Fond of home. **3.** Tame; domesticated. **4.** Of or pertaining to a country's internal affairs. **5.** Indigenous: *domestic wine. —n.* A household servant. [< L *domus,* house.] **—do•mes'ti•cal•ly** *adv.*

do•mes•ti•cate (də-mĕs'tĭ-kāt') *v.* **-cated, -cating.** To adapt to human living conditions and practical uses; tame: *domesticate animals.* **—do•mes'ti•ca'tion** *n.*

do•mes•tic•i•ty (dō'mĕ-stĭs'ə-tē) *n.* Home life or devotion to it.

dom•i•cile (dŏm'ə-sīl') *n.* A home, dwelling place, or legal residence. [< L *domicilium,* habitation, abode.] **—dom'i•cile'** *v.* **(-ciled, -ciling).**

dom•i•nance (dŏm'ə-nəns) *n.* Authority; ascendancy.

dom•i•nant (dŏm'ə-nənt) *adj.* **1.** Exercising the most influence. **2.** Pre-eminent in position. **3.** Producing the same phenotypic effect whether paired with an identical or a dissimilar gene. **—dom'i•nant•ly** *adv.*

dom•i•nate (dŏm'ə-nāt') *v.* **-nated, -nating. 1.** To control, govern, or rule. **2.** To occupy the pre-eminent position in or over. **3.** To overlook from a height. [L *dominārī,* to be lord and master.] **—dom'i•na'tion** *n.* **—dom'i•na'tor** *n.*

dom•i•neer (dŏm'ə-nîr') *v.* **1.** To rule arrogantly; tyrannize. **2.** To be overbearing.

Do•min•i•can Republic (də-mĭn'ĭ-kən). A country occupying E Hispaniola in the Caribbean. Pop. 3,573,000. Cap. Santo Domingo. **—Do•min'i•can** *adj.* & *n.*

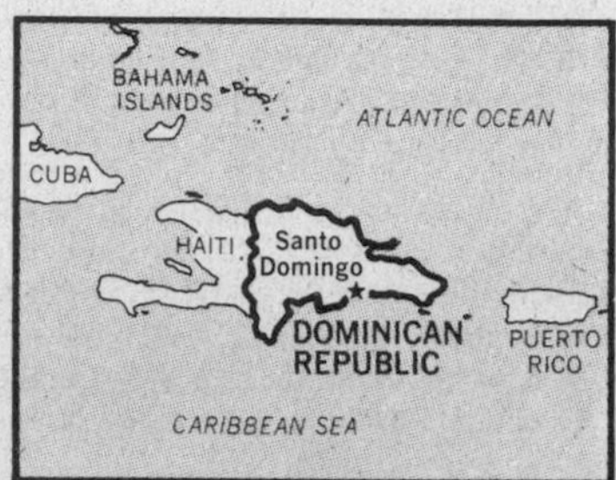

Dominican Republic

do•min•ion (də-mĭn'yən) *n.* **1.** Control or the exercise of control; sovereignty. **2.** A sphere of influence or control; realm; domain. **3.** Often **Dominion.** Formerly, one of the self-governing nations within the British Commonwealth of Nations. [< L *dominium,* property, rights, lordship.]

dom•i•no¹ (dŏm'ə-nō') *n., pl.* **-noes** or **-nos. 1. a.** A hooded robe worn with an eye mask at a masquerade. **b.** The mask itself. **2.** A person wearing this costume. [< L *(benedicamos) domino,* "(let us bless) the Lord."]

dom•i•no² (dŏm'ə-nō') *n., pl.* **-noes** or **-nos. 1.** A small, rectangular block marked with dots. **2. dominoes.** The game played with a set of these pieces. [F.]

don¹ (dŏn) *n.* A head, tutor, or fellow at a college of Oxford or Cambridge. [< L *dominus,* lord, master.]

don² (dŏn) *v.* **donned, donning.** To put on (an article of clothing). [Contraction of *do on.*]

Don (dŏn). A river of the SW Soviet Union.

do•nate (dō'nāt', dō-nāt') *v.* **-nated, -nating.** To give to a fund or cause; contribute. [< L *dōnum,* gift.] **—do•na'tion** *n.*

done (dŭn). *p.p.* of **do.** *—adj.* **1.** Finished. **2.** Cooked adequately. **3.** Socially acceptable: *not done in polite society.*

Do•netsk (də-nĕtsk'). A city of the Ukrainian S.S.R. Pop. 774,000.

dong (dŏng) *n.* The basic monetary unit of North Vietnam.

don•jon (dŏn'jən, dŭn'-) *n.* The main tower of a castle. [Var of DUNGEON.]

Don Juan (dŏn' wän'). A legendary Spanish nobleman and libertine.

don•key (dŏng'kē, dŭng'-, dông'-) *n., pl.* **-keys. 1.** The domesticated ass. **2.** An obstinate or stupid person.

don•ny•brook (dŏn'ē-bro͝ok') *n.* A free-for-all. [< *Donnybrook,* near Dublin, Ireland.]

do•nor (dō'nər) *n.* **1.** One who contributes something. **2.** One who donates blood, tissue, or an organ for use in a transfusion or transplant.

Don Qui•xo•te (dŏn' kē-hō'tē, kwĭk'sət). An idealist bent on righting incorrigible wrongs. [< Cervantes' *Don Quixote* (1605–15).]

don't (dōnt). Contraction of *do not.*

do•nut. Variant of **doughnut.**

doo•dad (do͞o'dăd') *n.* An unnamed or nondescript gadget or trinket.

doo•dle (do͞od'l) *v.* **-dled, -dling.** To draw or scribble while preoccupied. [< dial *doodle,* to trifle, fritter away time.] **—doo'dle** *n.*

doom (do͞om) *n.* **1.** Condemnation to a severe penalty. **2.** A terrible fate. **3.** Disaster; ruin. *—v.* To condemn to ruination or death. [< OE *dōm.* See **dhē-.**]

dooms•day (do͞omz'dā') *n.* The day of the Last Judgment.

door (dôr, dōr) *n.* **1.** A movable, usually hinged, panel used to open or close an entranceway. **2.** An entranceway or passage. **3.** A means of access. [< OE *dor, duru,* gate, door. See **dhwer-.**]

door•jamb (dôr'jăm', dōr'-) *n.* Either of the two vertical pieces framing a doorway.

door•knob (dôr'nŏb', dōr'-) *n.* A handle for opening and closing a door.

door•man (dôr'măn', -mən, dōr'-) *n.* One employed to tend the entrance of a hotel or apartment house.

door•mat (dôr'măt', dōr'-) *n.* A mat placed before a doorway for wiping the shoes.

door•way (dôr'wā', dōr'-) *n.* An entranceway.

dope (dōp) *n.* **1.** Any of various viscous liquids. **2.** *Informal.* A narcotic. **3.** *Slang.* A very stupid person. **4.** *Slang.* Factual information. *—v.* **doped, doping. 1.** To add or apply dope to. **2.** To drug, as a horse. [Du *doop,* sauce.] **—dop'er** *n.*

Dopp•ler effect (dŏp'lər). An apparent change in the frequency of waves, as of sound or light, occurring when the source and observer are in motion relative to one another. [< C. *Doppler* (1803–1853), Austrian physicist.]

Do•ri•an (dôr'ē-ən, dōr'-) *n.* One of a Hellenic people that invaded Greece around 1100 B.C. and settled in the region of Sparta and Corinth. **—Do'ri•an** *adj.*

Dor•ic (dôr'ĭk, dŏr'-) *n.* The Greek dialect of the Dorians. *—adj.* **1.** Belonging to, characteristic of, or designating this dialect. **2.** In the style of the Doric order.

Doric order. One of the three classical orders of architecture, characterized by heavy, fluted columns with a bold, simple cornice.

dorm (dôrm) *n. Informal.* A dormitory.

dor•mant (dôr'mənt) *adj.* **1.** In a state resembling sleep. **2.** In a state of suspended activity or development; inactive. [< L *dormīre,* to sleep.] **—dor'man•cy** *n.*

dor•mer (dôr'mər) *n.* A window set vertically in a gable projecting from a sloping roof. [OF *dormeor,* "bedroom window."]

dor•mi•to•ry (dôr'mə-tôr'ē, -tōr'ē) *n., pl.* **-ries. 1.** A large bedroom for a number of people. **2.** A school residence hall. [< L *dormīre,* to sleep.]

dor•mouse (dôr'mous') *n., pl.* **-mice** (-mīs'). A small, squirrellike Old World rodent. [ME *dormowse,* "sleeping mouse."]

dor•sal (dôr'səl) *adj. Anat.* In, on, or toward the back. [< L *dorsum,* back.]

Dort•mund (dôrt′mənd). A city in NW West Germany. Pop. 650,000.

dose (dōs) *n.* A specified quantity of a therapeutic agent prescribed to be taken at one time or at stated intervals. [< Gk *dosis,* a giving, dose.] **—dos′age** (dō′sĭj) *n.* **—dose** *v.* **(dosed, dosing).** **—dos′er** *n.*

dos•si•er (dŏs′ē-ā′, dôs′yā′) *n.* A file of documents pertaining to a particular person or subject. [< OF, bundle of papers having a label on the back.]

dost (dŭst). *Archaic.* 2nd person sing. present tense of **do.**

Dos•to•yev•sky (dôs′tô-yĕf′skē), **Fyodor.** 1821–1881. Russian novelist.

dot (dŏt) *n.* **1.** A spot; point. **2.** Such a mark used in orthography, as the one over an *i.* **3.** A short sound or signal used in combination with the dash and written as a dot to represent letters, numbers, or punctuation. **4. a.** A decimal point. **b.** A symbol of multiplication. **—on the dot.** Absolutely punctual. *—v.* **dotted, dotting. 1.** To mark with a dot. **2.** To cover with or as with dots: *"Campfires, like red, peculiar blossoms, dotted the night."* (Stephen Crane). [< OE *dott,* head of a boil.] **—dot′ter** *n.*

do•tage (dō′tĭj) *n.* Senility. [< DOTE.]

dote (dōt) *v.* **doted, doting. 1.** To lavish excessive love or fondness. **2.** To be senile. [< MDu *doten,* to be silly.] **—dot′er** *n.*

doth (dŭth). *Archaic.* 3rd person sing. present tense of **do.**

dot•tle (dŏt′l) *n.* The plug of ash left in the bowl of a pipe after it has been smoked. [< DOT.]

dot•ty (dŏt′ē) *adj.* **-tier, -tiest.** Crazy: *a dotty old lady.* [< DOTE.]

Dou•ay Version (do͞o′ā). A translation of the Bible for use by Roman Catholics.

dou•ble (dŭb′əl) *adj.* **1.** Twice as much in size, strength, number, or amount. **2.** Composed of two parts or members. **3.** Twofold; dual. **4.** Designed for two: *a double bed.* **5. a.** Acting two parts: *a double agent.* **b.** Deceitful: *double talk.* **6.** Having numerous overlapping petals. *—n.* **1.** Something increased twofold. **2.** A duplicate; counterpart. **3.** An actor's understudy. **4.** A sharp turn; reversal. **5. doubles.** A game, such as tennis, having two players on each side. **6.** *Baseball.* A two-base hit. **7.** *Bridge.* A bid doubling one's opponent's bid. **—on (or at) the double.** *Informal.* Immediately. *—v.* **-bled, -bling. 1.** To make twice as great. **2.** To be twice as much as. **3.** To fold in two. **4.** To duplicate; repeat. **5.** *Bridge.* To challenge with a double. **6.** To turn sharply backward; reverse: *double back.* **7.** To serve in an additional capacity. **8.** *Baseball.* To make a two-base hit. *—adv.* **1. a.** To twice the extent; doubly. **b.** To twice the amount: *double your money back.* **2.** Two together: *sleeping double.* **3.** In two: *bent double in pain.* [< L *duplus,* twofold, double.] **—doub′ly** *adv.* **—dou′ble•ness** *n.* **—dou′bler** *n.*

double bass. The largest member of the violin family, having a low range.

dou•ble-cross (dŭb′əl-krôs′, -krŏs′) *v. Slang.* To betray; deceive. **—dou′ble-cross′** *n.* **—dou′ble-cross′er** *n.*

dou•ble-deal•ing (dŭb′əl-dē′lĭng) *adj.* Characterized by duplicity; deceitful. *—n.* Duplicity. **—doub′le-deal′er** *n.*

dou•ble-deck•er (dŭb′əl-dĕk′ər) *n.* **1.** A vehicle having two tiers for passengers. **2.** Two beds, one built above the other. **3.** A sandwich having two layers.

double knit. A jerseylike fabric knitted on a machine equipped with two sets of needles so that a double thickness of fabric is produced in which the two sides of the fabric are interlocked.

dou•ble-knit (dŭb′əl-nĭt′) *adj.* Of or made of double knit.

double play. *Baseball.* A play in which two players are put out.

doub•let (dŭb′lĭt) *n.* **1.** A close-fitting jacket formerly worn by men. **2. a.** A pair of similar things. **b.** One of a pair. **3.** *Ling.* One of two words derived from the same source by different routes of transmission.

double take. A delayed reaction to the unexpected.

dou•bloon (dŭ-blo͞on′) *n.* An obsolete Spanish gold coin.

doubt (dout) *v.* **1.** To be uncertain or skeptical (about). **2.** To distrust. *—n.* **1.** A lack of conviction or certainty. **2.** An uncertain condition; uncertainty. **3. doubts.** Lack of trust; suspicion. **—no doubt. 1.** Certainly. **2.** Probably. [< L *dubitāre,* to waver, vibrate.] **—doubt′er** *n.*

doubt•ful (dout′fəl) *adj.* **1.** Causing doubt; uncertain. **2.** Having doubt; undecided. **3.** Questionable; suspicious. **—doubt′ful•ly** *adv.*

doubt•less (dout′lĭs) *adj.* Certain; assured. *—adv.* **1.** Certainly. **2.** Presumably. **—doubt′less•ly** *adv.*

douche (do͞osh) *n.* **1.** A stream of water or air applied to a bodily part or cavity for cleansing or medicinal purposes. **2.** The application of a douche. **3.** A syringe or other instrument for applying a douche. *—v.* **douched, douching.** To cleanse or treat by a douche. [< It *doccia,* conduit pipe, shower, douche.]

dough (dō) *n.* **1.** A thick, pliable mixture of flour and other ingredients baked as bread, pastry, etc. **2.** *Slang.* Money. [< OE *dāg.* See **dheigh-.**] **—dough′y** *adj.*

dough•boy (dō′boi′) *n.* An infantryman in World War I.

dough•nut (dō′nŭt′, -nət) *n.* Also **do•nut.** A small, ring-shaped cake made of light dough that is fried in deep fat.

dough•ty (dou′tē) *adj.* **-tier, -tiest.** Courageous. [< OE *dohtig, dyhtig.*]

Doug•lass (dŭg′ləs), **Frederick,** 1817?–1895. American Negro abolitionist.

Frederick Douglass

dour (do͝or, dour) *adj.* **1.** Stern; forbidding. **2.** Glum; gloomy. [Perh < L *dūrus,* hard.] **—dour′ly** *adv.* **—dour′ness** *n.*

douse¹ (dous) *v.* **doused, dousing.** Also **dowse. 1.** To plunge into liquid; immerse. **2.** To wet thoroughly; drench; soak. [Perh < earlier *douse,* to strike, smite.]

douse² (dous) *v.* **doused, dousing.** To put out (a light or fire); extinguish. [Perh < DOUSE¹.]

dove¹ (dŭv) *n.* **1.** A pigeon or related bird, esp. an undomesticated species. **2.** A member of a group advocating peace. [< OE **dūfe.* See **dheu-¹.**]

dove² (dōv). Alternate *p.t.* of **dive.**

Do•ver (dō′vər). **1.** The capital of Delaware. Pop. 17,000. **2.** A port city of England. Pop. 36,000.

dove•tail (dŭv′tāl′) *n.* **1.** A fan-shaped tenon that forms a tight interlocking joint when fitted into a corresponding mortise. **2.** A joint so formed. *—v.* **1.** To join by means of dovetails. **2.** To combine or interlock into a unified whole.

dow•a•ger (dou′ə-jər) *n.* **1.** A widow with a title derived from her husband. **2.** An elderly woman of high social station. [< L *dōs (dōt-),* dowry.]

dow•dy (dou′dē) *adj.* **-dier, -diest.** Lacking style; shabby. [< ME *doude,* slut.]

dow•el (dou′əl) *n.* A usually round pin that fits into a corresponding hole to fasten or align two adjacent pieces. *—v.* **-eled** or **-elled, -eling** or **-elling.** To fasten or align with dowels. [< MLG *dōvel,* peg, block, nail.]

dow•er (dou′ər) *n.* **1.** The part of a man's real estate allotted by law to his widow for her lifetime. **2.** A dowry. *—v.* To assign a dower to; endow.

down¹ (doun) *adv.* **1.** From a higher to a lower place. **2.** In or to a lower position, point, or condition. **3.** From an earlier to a later time. **4.** Seriously; intensely: *get down to work.* **5.** In partial payment at the time of purchase: *five dollars down.* **6.** In writing: *take down a statement.* **7.** To the source: *track down a rumor.* *—adj.* **1. a.** Moving or directed downward. **b.** In a low position; not up. **2. a.** Sick. **b.** Low in spirit; depressed. **3.** In a competition, trailing an opponent by a specified number: *down one.* **4.** Being the first installment. **—down and out.** Lacking resources; destitute. **—down on.** *Informal.* Hostile toward. *—prep.* In a descending direction along, upon, into, or through. *—n.* **1.** A downward movement; descent. **2.** *Football.* One of four plays during which a team must advance at least ten yards to retain the ball. *—v.* **1.** To bring, put, strike, or throw down. **2.** To descend. [< OE *ofdūne,* "from the hill" < Gmc **dunaz.*]

down² (doun) *n.* **1.** Fine, soft, fluffy feathers. **2.** A similar soft covering or substance. [< ON *dūnn.*] **—down′y** *adj.*

down³ (doun) *n.* Often **downs.** A rolling, grassy upland area. [< OE *dūn,* hill.]

down•cast (doun′kăst′, -käst′) *adj.* **1.** Directed downward. **2.** Dejected; sad.

down•er (dou′nər) *n. Slang.* 1. A depressant or sedative drug, as a barbiturate. 2. A depressing experience.

down•fall (doun′fôl′) *n.* **1.** A sudden loss of wealth, reputation, etc.; ruin. **2.** A heavy or unexpected fall of rain or snow.

down•grade (doun′grād′) *n.* A descending slope. **—on the downgrade.** Declining, as in influence or wealth. *—v.* To lower or minimize the importance of.

down•heart•ed (doun′här′tĭd) *adj.* Depressed; discouraged. **—down′heart′ed•ly** *adv.*

down•hill (doun′hĭl′) *adv.* Down the slope of a hill; in a downward direction.

down•pour (doun′pôr′, -pōr′) *n.* A drenching rain.

down•right (doun′rīt′) *adj.* **1.** Thorough; unequivocal. **2.** Plain; candid. *—adv.* Thoroughly; absolutely.

down•stairs (doun'stârz') *adv.* **1.** Down the stairs. **2.** To or on a lower floor. *—adj.* (doun'stârz'). Also **down•stair** (-stâr'). Located on a lower floor.

down•stream (doun'strēm') *adj.* In the direction of a stream's current. *—adv.* (doun'strēm'). Down a stream.

down-to-earth (doun'tə-ûrth') *adj.* Realistic; sensible.

down•town (doun'toun') *adv.* To, toward, or in the business center of a city or town. *—adj.* (doun'toun'). Of, relating to, or located downtown.

down•trod•den (doun'trŏd'n) *adj.* Oppressed; tyrannized.

down•ward (doun'wərd) *adv.* Also **down•wards** (-wərdz). From a higher to a lower place, level, condition, etc. **—down'ward** *adj.*

down•wind (doun'wĭnd') *adv.* In the direction in which the wind blows. **—down'wind'** *adj.*

dow•ry (dour'ē) *n., pl.* **-ries. 1.** Money or property brought by a bride to her husband. **2.** A natural endowment or gift. [Var of DOWER.]

dowse[1] (douz) *v.* **dowsed, dowsing.** To use a divining rod, esp. to search for underground water. [?] **—dows'er** *n.*

dowse[2]**.** Variant of **douse**[1]**.**

doz. dozen.

doze (dōz) *v.* **dozed, dozing.** To sleep lightly; nap. [Prob < Scand.] **—doze** *n.* **—doz'er** *n.*

doz•en (dŭz'ən) *n.* **1.** *pl.* **-en.** A set of 12. **2.** *pl.* **-ens.** An indefinite number; a great many. *—adj.* Twelve. [< L *duodecim,* twelve.] **—doz'enth** *adj.*

dpt. department.

dr dram.

dr. **1.** debit. **2.** debtor.

Dr. **1.** doctor. **2.** drive (in street names).

drab (drăb) *adj.* **drabber, drabbest. 1.** Of a light grayish or olive brown color. **2.** Dull; dreary. *—n.* Light grayish or olive brown. [Var of obs *drap,* cloth.] **—drab'ly** *adv.*

drach•ma (drăk'mə) *n., pl.* **-mas** or **-mae** (-mē). The basic monetary unit of Greece. [< Gk *drakhmē.*]

Dra•co (drā'kō) *n.* A constellation in the polar region of the N Hemisphere.

draft (drăft, dräft). Also *chiefly Brit.* **draught** (drăft). *n.* **1. a.** A current of air. **b.** A device in a flue controlling air circulation. **2. a.** A pull or traction of a load. **b.** That which is pulled or drawn. **3.** The depth of a vessel's keel below the water line. **4.** A heavy demand upon resources. **5.** A document for transferring money. **6. a.** A gulp, swallow, or inhalation. **b.** The amount taken in by such an act. **7.** The drawing of a liquid, as from a keg. **8. a.** A selection of personnel from a group, esp. conscription for military service. **b.** The body of people so selected. **9. a.** The drawing in of a fishnet. **b.** The catch. **10.** A preliminary outline, version, design, etc. **—on draft.** Tapped from a keg; not bottled. *—v.* **1.** To select from a group for an assignment, as military service. **2.** To draw up a preliminary version of or plan for. *—adj.* **1.** Used for drawing heavy loads. **2.** Drawn from a cask. [ME *draught,* a pulling, a drawing.]

draft•ee (drăf-tē', dräf-) *n.* One drafted for military service.

draft•ing (drăf'tĭng, dräf'-) *n.* The systematic representation and dimensional specification of mechanical and architectural structures.

drafts•man (drăfts'mən, dräfts'-) *n.* One who draws plans or designs.

draft•y (drăf'tē, dräf'-) *adj.* **-ier, -iest.** Having or exposed to drafts of air. **—draft'i•ly** *adv.* **—draft'i•ness** *n.*

drag (drăg) *v.* **dragged, dragging. 1.** To pull or draw along the ground, esp. by force. **2.** To search the bottom of (a body of water), as with a grappling hook. **3.** To bring forcibly to or into. **4.** To move with reluctance, difficulty, etc. **5.** To prolong tediously (with *out*). *—n.* **1.** The act of dragging. **2.** Something dragged along the ground, as a harrow, or under water, as a grappling hook. **3.** Something that retards motion or progress. **4.** The degree of resistance involved in dragging or hauling. **5.** *Slang.* Something obnoxiously tiresome. **6.** *Slang.* A puff, as on a cigarette. [< OE *dragan* or ON *draga.* See **dhragh-.**]

drag•net (drăg'nĕt') *n.* **1.** A net, esp. one for trawling. **2.** A network of procedures used to apprehend criminal suspects.

drag•on (drăg'ən) *n.* **1.** A fabulous monster represented as a gigantic winged reptile with a lion's claws. **2.** A representation of this creature. [< Gk *drakōn,* serpent.]

drag•on•fly (drăg'ən-flī') *n.* A large, narrow-bodied, four-winged insect.

dra•goon (drə-gōōn', dră-) *n.* A heavily armed mounted trooper. *—v.* To force by the use of troops or other harsh means. [F *dragon,* carbine, "fire-breather."]

drain (drān) *v.* **1.** To draw or flow off by a gradual process. **2.** To cause liquid substance to go out from; empty. **3.** To consume totally; exhaust. *—n.* **1.** A pipe or channel by which liquid is drawn off. **2.** An act or instance of draining. [< OE *drēahnian.*]

drain•age (drā'nĭj) *n.* **1.** The action or a method of draining. **2.** A system of drains. **3.** That which is drained off.

drain•pipe (drān'pīp') *n.* A pipe for carrying off rainwater or sewage.

drake (drāk) *n.* A male duck. [Perh < Gmc **drako,* male.]

dram (drăm) *n.* **1. a.** A unit of weight in the U.S. Customary System, an avoirdupois unit equal to 27.344 grains or 0.0625 ounce. **b.** A unit of apothecary weight, equal to 60 grains. **2.** A small draft: *a dram of cordial.* [ME *dragme,* dram, drachma.]

dra•ma (drä'mə, drăm'ə) *n.* **1. a.** A literary composition to be presented before an audience; a play. **b.** Such literature as an art. **2.** A situation of interesting, often exaggerated, conflict or emotion. [< Gk, deed, action on the stage.] **—dra•mat'ic** (drə-măt'ĭk) *adj.*

Dram•a•mine (drăm'ə-mēn') *n.* A trademark for a drug used to treat motion sickness.

dram•a•tist (drăm'ə-tĭst, drä'mə-) *n.* A playwright.

dram•a•tize (drăm'ə-tīz', drä'mə-) *v.* **-tized, -tizing. 1.** To adapt for presentation as a drama. **2.** To present or view in a dramatic way. **—dram'a•ti•za'tion** *n.*

drank (drăngk). *p.t.* of **drink.**

drape (drāp) *v.* **draped, draping. 1.** To dress or hang with or as with cloth in loose folds. **2.** To arrange in loose folds. **3.** To hang or rest loosely. *—n.* **1.** Often **drapes.** A drapery. **2.** The way in which cloth falls or hangs. [< LL *drappus,* cloth.]

drap•er (drā'pər) *n. Brit.* A dealer in cloth or dry goods.

drap•er•y (drā'pə-rē) *n., pl.* **-ies. 1.** Cloth arranged in loose folds. **2.** Often **draperies.** Curtains that hang straight in loose folds. **3.** *Brit.* The business of a draper.

dras•tic (drăs'tĭk) *adj.* **1.** Violently effective. **2.** Severe; extreme. [Gk *drastikos,* active, efficient.] **—dras'ti•cal•ly** *adv.*

draught. *Chiefly Brit.* Variant of **draft.**

draughts (drăfts, dräfts) *n. (takes sing. v.). Chiefly Brit.* The game of checkers.

Dra•vid•i•an (drə-vĭd'ē-ən) *n.* **1.** A large non-Indo-European family of languages, including Tamil and Malayalam. **2.** One who speaks a Dravidian language. **—Dra•vid'i•an** *adj.*

draw (drô) *v.* **drew, drawn, drawing. 1.** To pull (something) toward or after one. **2.** To pull or move (something) in a given direction or to a given position. **3.** To take or pull out, as from a holster. **4.** To suck or take in (air). **5.** To displace (a specified depth of water) in floating. **6.** To induce to act. **7.** To attract. **8.** To extract from evidence; formulate: *draw conclusions.* **9. a.** To earn; bring in: *draw interest.* **b.** To withdraw (money). **10.** To evoke; elicit. **11.** To take or accept as a chance: *draw lots.* **12.** To distort; contract. **13.** To stretch taut. **14.** To eviscerate. **15.** To draft or sketch. **—draw out. 1.** To cause to converse easily. **2.** To prolong. **—draw up. 1.** To draft; compose (a document). **2.** To pull up to a halt. *—n.* **1.** The act or result of drawing. **2.** A special advantage. **3.** A contest ending in a tie. [< OE *dragan.* See **dhragh-.**]

draw•back (drô'băk') *n.* A disadvantage; hindrance.

draw•bridge (drô'brĭj') *n.* A bridge that can be raised or drawn aside.

draw•er. *n.* **1.** (drô'ər). One who draws. **2.** (drôr). A boxlike compartment in furniture that can be drawn on slides. **3. drawers** (drôrz). Underpants.

draw•ing (drô'ĭng) *n.* **1.** The act or an instance of drawing. **2.** The art of depicting forms or figures on a surface by lines. **3.** A portrayal in lines on a surface of a form or figure.

drawing card. An attraction drawing large audiences.

drawing room. 1. A formal reception room. **2.** A private room on a railroad sleeping car. [< *withdrawing room.*]

drawl (drôl) *v.* To speak with lengthened or drawn-out vowels. [Poss a freq of DRAW.] **—drawl** *n.*

drawn (drôn). *p.p.* of **draw.** *—adj.* **1.** Pulled out of a sheath. **2.** Haggard, as from ill health. **3.** Eviscerated.

draw•string (drô'strĭng') *n.* A cord, ribbon, etc., run through a hem or casing and pulled to tighten.

dray (drā) *n.* A low cart used for heavy loads. [< OE *dræge,* dragnet. See **dhragh-.**]

dread (drĕd) *v.* **1.** To be in terror of; fear greatly. **2.** To hold in awe or reverence. **3.** To anticipate with anxiety or reluctance. *—n.* **1.** Profound fear; terror. **2.** Awe; reverence. **3.** Anxious or fearful anticipation. *—adj.* **1.** Terrifying; fearsome. **2.** Awesome; revered. [< OE *drǣdan.*]

dread•ful (drĕd'fəl) *adj.* **1.** Inspiring dread; terrible. **2.** Extremely unpleasant. **—dread'ful•ly** *adv.* **—dread'ful•ness** *n.*

dread•nought (drĕd'nôt') *n.* A heavily armed battleship.

dream (drēm) *n.* **1.** A series of images, ideas, etc., occurring in certain stages of sleep. **2.** A daydream; reverie. **3.** A wild fancy or hope. **4.** Anything extremely beautiful, fine, or pleasant. *—v.* **dreamed** or **dreamt** (drĕmt), **dreaming. 1.** To experience a dream or dreams. **2.** To aspire or hope (with *of*). **3.** To conceive of; imagine. **4.** To pass idly or in reverie, as time. **—dream up.** To invent; concoct. [< OE *drēam,* joy, gladness, music. See **dhreugh-.**]

—dream'er *n.*

dream•y (drē'mē) *adj.* -ier, -iest. 1. Resembling a dream; vague. 2. Given to daydreams or reverie. 3. Soothing; quiet. —dream'i•ly *adv.* —dream'i•ness *n.*

drear•y (drîr'ē) *adj.* -ier, -iest. Also *poetic* **drear** (drîr). 1. Gloomy; dismal. 2. Boring; dull. [< OE *drēor,* blood. See **dhreu-**.] —drear'i•ly *adv.* —drear'i•ness *n.*

dredge[1] (drĕj) *n.* 1. A machine or implement used to scoop or remove dirt, sand, etc., from under water, as in deepening harbors. 2. A boat equipped with such a device. —*v.* dredged, dredging. To deepen, scoop, etc., with a dredge. [?]

dredge[2] (drĕj) *v.* dredged, dredging. To coat (food) with flour, sugar, etc. [?]

dregs (drĕgz) *pl.n.* 1. The sediment of a liquid; lees. 2. The basest or least desirable portion. [< ON *dregg* (sing.).]

drench (drĕnch) *v.* To wet thoroughly; saturate. [< OE *drencan,* to give to drink, to soak. See **dhreg-**.] —drench'er *n.*

dress (drĕs) *v.* 1. To put on clothing; clothe. 2. To adorn or arrange. 3. To wear formal clothes. 4. To put (troops) in ranks; align. 5. To apply therapeutic materials to (a wound). 6. To groom (an animal); curry. 7. To clean (fish or fowl), as for cooking. 8. To put a finish on. —**dress up.** To wear formal clothes or finery. —*n.* 1. Clothing; apparel. 2. A one-piece skirted outer garment for women. —*adj.* 1. Suitable for a formal occasion: *a dress uniform.* 2. Requiring formal clothing: *a dress dinner.* [< VL *dīrectiāre.]

dress•er[1] (drĕs'ər) *n.* One that dresses or assists in dressing.

dress•er[2] (drĕs'ər) *n.* A chest of drawers. [ME *dressour,* kitchen sideboard on which food was prepared.]

dress•ing (drĕs'ĭng) *n.* 1. Therapeutic material applied to a wound. 2. A sauce, as for a salad. 3. A stuffing, as for poultry.

dress•ing-down (drĕs'ĭng-doun') *n.* A severe scolding.

dressing gown. A robe worn informally at home.

dress•mak•er (drĕs'mā'kər) *n.* One who makes women's clothes. —dress'mak'ing *n.*

dress rehearsal. A final, uninterrupted run-through, as of a play with costumes and stage properties.

dress•y (drĕs'ē) *adj.* -ier, -iest. 1. Wearing fancy or elegant clothing. 2. Smart; stylish.

drew (dro͞o). *p.t.* of **draw.**

drib•ble (drĭb'əl) *v.* -bled, -bling. 1. To flow or fall unsteadily; trickle. 2. To drool. 3. To move (a ball) by repeated light bounces or kicks, as in basketball or soccer. —*n.* 1. A trickle. 2. A small quantity; a bit. [< DRIP.]

drib•let (drĭb'lĭt) *n.* 1. A falling drop of liquid. 2. A small amount or portion.

dri•er[1] (drī'ər) *n.* Also **dry•er.** 1. One that dries. 2. A substance added to paint, ink, etc., to speed drying. 3. Variant of **dryer.**

dri•er[2]. *compar.* of **dry.**

drift (drĭft) *v.* 1. To carry or be carried along by or as by a current. 2. To move about without a goal; wander. 3. To pile up in banks or heaps, as by the force of the wind. —*n.* 1. The act or condition of drifting. 2. Drifting material. 3. A bank or pile, as of snow, heaped up by the wind. 4. A trend or general meaning. 5. a. Lateral displacement or deviation of an object or vehicle from a planned course. b. Variation or random oscillation about a fixed setting. 6. The rate of flow of a water current. [< ON, snowdrift, and MDu, herd, course.] —drift'y *adj.*

drift•er (drĭf'tər) *n.* One that drifts, esp. one who moves from place to place or job to job.

drift•wood (drĭft'wo͝od') *n.* Wood floating in or washed up by water.

drill[1] (drĭl) *n.* 1. a. An implement with cutting edges or a pointed end for boring holes in hard materials, usually by a rotating abrasion or repeated blows. b. The hand-operated or hand-powered holder for this tool. 2. Disciplined, repetitious exercise as a means of training. 3. A specific task or exercise designed to develop a skill. —*v.* 1. To make a hole in with a drill. 2. To train by repetition. [< MDu *drillen,* to drill.]

drill[2] (drĭl) *n.* 1. A trench or furrow in which seeds are planted. 2. A device for planting seeds in holes or furrows. [?]

drill[3] (drĭl) *n.* Strong cotton or linen twill. [< L *trilix,* triple-twilled.]

drill press. A powered vertical drilling machine, used mainly on metals.

drink (drĭngk) *v.* drank, drunk, drinking. 1. To swallow (a liquid). 2. To soak up (liquid or moisture); absorb. 3. To take in eagerly through the senses or intellect (with *in*). 4. To give or make (a toast). 5. To imbibe alcoholic liquors, esp. to excess. —*n.* 1. Any liquid for drinking; a beverage. 2. An amount of liquid swallowed. 3. Alcoholic liquor. 4. Excessive indulgence in alcoholic liquor. [< OE *drincan.* See **dhreg-**.] —drink'a•ble *adj.* —drink'er *n.*

drip (drĭp) *v.* dripped, dripping. To fall or allow to fall in drops. —*n.* 1. The process of falling in drops. 2. Liquid that falls in drops. 3. The sound made by dripping liquid. 4. *Slang.* An unpleasant or tiresomely boring person. [ME *drippen.*]

drip•pings (drĭp'ĭngz) *pl.n.* The fat and juice exuded from roasting meat.

drive (drīv) *v.* drove, driven (drĭv'ən), driving. 1. To push, propel, or press forcibly. 2. To force to work or overwork. 3. To force or thrust into or from a particular act or state. 4. To propel (a ball) quickly and forcefully. 5. To force to go through or penetrate. 6. To operate (a vehicle). 7. To cause to function; motivate. 8. To carry through vigorously to a conclusion. —**drive at.** To mean; intend. —*n.* 1. The act of driving. 2. A road, esp. a driveway or highway. 3. A trip in a vehicle. 4. The means or apparatus for transmitting motion to a machine or machine part. 5. An organized effort to accomplish a purpose; a campaign. 6. Energy; initiative. 7. A strong motivating tendency or instinct, esp. of sexual or aggressive origin, that prompts activity toward a particular end. 8. A massive and sustained military offensive. 9. a. A quick, forceful propelling of a ball. b. The propelling stroke or thrust. 10. a. A rounding up of cattle, as for slaughter. b. A driving of logs down a river. [< OE *drīfan.* See **dhreibh-**.]

drive-in (drīv'ĭn') *n.* An establishment, as a restaurant or motion-picture theater, accommodating customers who remain in their automobiles. —drive'-in *adj.*

driv•el (drĭv'əl) *v.* -eled or -elled, -eling or -elling. 1. To slobber; drool. 2. To flow like spittle or saliva. 3. To talk stupidly or childishly. —*n.* 1. Saliva flowing from the mouth. 2. Stupid or senseless talk. [< OE *dreflian.* See **dher-**[1].] —driv'el•er *n.*

driv•er (drī'vər) *n.* 1. One who drives, as a chauffeur. 2. *Golf.* A wooden-headed club with a long shaft, used for making long shots from the tee.

drive•way (drīv'wā') *n.* An often short private road.

driz•zle (drĭz'əl) *v.* -zled, -zling. To rain gently in fine drops. [Perh < OE *drēosan,* to fall. See **dhreu-**.] —driz'zle *n.* —driz'zly *adj.*

drogue (drōg) *n.* A small parachute used to slow down a re-entering spacecraft or satellite prior to deployment of the main parachute. [Perh < OE *dragan,* to DRAW.]

droll (drōl) *adj.* Amusingly odd; whimsically comical. [< MDu *drol,* "little man."] —droll'er•y (drō'lə-rē) *n.*

-drome. *comb. form.* A place or arena, esp. a racecourse: **airdrome.** [< Gk *dromos,* race, course.]

drom•e•dar•y (drŏm'ə-dĕr'ē, drŭm'-) *n., pl.* -ies. The one-humped domesticated camel of N Africa and E Asia. [< Gk *dromas (dromad-),* dromedary, runner.]

drone[1] (drōn) *n.* 1. A male bee, esp. a honeybee. 2. A loafer; sluggard. 3. A pilotless, remote-control aircraft. [< OE *drān, drǣn.* See **dher-**[2].]

drone[2] (drōn) *v.* droned, droning. 1. To make a continuous low, dull humming sound. 2. To speak in a monotonous tone. —*n.* A low humming or buzzing sound.

drool (dro͞ol) *v.* 1. To let saliva run from the mouth; drivel. 2. *Informal.* To make an extravagant show of appreciation. 3. *Informal.* To talk nonsense. —*n.* 1. Saliva; drivel. 2. *Informal.* Silly talk. [Perh var of DRIVEL.]

droop (dro͞op) *v.* 1. To bend or hang downward. 2. To appear dejected or listless: *The roses drooped in the heat.* —*n.* The act or condition of drooping. [< ON *drūpa.*]

drop (drŏp) *n.* 1. The smallest quantity of liquid heavy enough to fall in a spherical or pear-shaped mass. 2. A minute quantity. 3. **drops.** Liquid medicine administered in such quantity. 4. Something that resembles a drop. 5. The act of falling. 6. A swift decline or decrease, as in quality, quantity, etc. 7. The vertical distance from a higher to a lower level. 8. Men and equipment landed by parachute. 9. Something arranged to be lowered, as a stage curtain. —*v.* dropped, dropping. 1. To fall or let fall in drops. 2. To fall or let fall from a higher to a lower place. 3. To become less in number, intensity, etc.; decrease. 4. To descend. 5. To sink into a state of exhaustion. 6. To pass into some specified state or condition. 7. To cease; come to an end. 8. To say or offer casually. 9. To lower the level of (the voice). —**drop by** (or **in**). To stop in for a short visit. —**drop off.** 1. To fall asleep. 2. To decrease. [< OE *dropa.* See **dhreu-**.]

drop kick. A kick made by dropping a football and kicking it just as it starts to rebound. —drop'-kick' (drŏp'kĭk') *v.*

drop•let (drŏp'lĭt) *n.* A tiny drop.

drop out. To withdraw from school, organized society, etc.

drop•out (drŏp'out') *n.* One who has withdrawn, esp. one who leaves school before graduating.

drop•per (drŏp'ər) *n.* A small tube with a suction bulb at one end for drawing in a liquid and releasing it in drops.

drop•sy (drŏp'sē) *n.* Pathological accumulation of diluted lymph in body tissues and cavities. [< Gk *hudrōpisis.*]

dross (drôs, drŏs) *n.* 1. Waste products or impurities formed on the surface of molten metal during smelting. 2. Worthless material; rubbish. [< OE *drōs,* dregs. See **dher-**[1].]

—**dross'i•ness** *n.* —**dross'y** *adj.*

drought (drout) *n.* Also **drouth** (drouth). A long period with no rain. [< OE *drūgath.*]

drove[1] (drōv). *p.t.* of **drive.**

drove[2] (drōv) *n.* A flock, herd, or large group driven or moving in a body. [< OE *drāf* < *drīfan,* to DRIVE.]

drov•er (drō'vər) *n.* A driver of cattle or sheep.

drown (droun) *v.* **1.** To kill or die by suffocating in water or other liquid. **2.** To drench or cover with a liquid. **3.** To overwhelm or muffle (a sound, noise, etc). [< Scand.]

drowse (drouz) *v.* **drowsed, drowsing.** To be half-asleep; doze. —*n.* The condition of being sleepy. [Perh < OE *drūsian,* to be sluggish. See **dhreu-.**]

drow•sy (drou'zē) *adj.* **-sier, -siest.** Having or causing a sleepy feeling. —**drow'si•ly** *adv.* —**drow'si•ness** *n.*

drub (drŭb) *v.* **drubbed, drubbing. 1.** To thrash or beat with a stick. **2.** To defeat emphatically. [Ar *dáraba,* to beat.]

drudge (drŭj) *n.* One who does tedious, menial, or unpleasant work. —*v.* **drudged, drudging.** To do the work of a drudge. [?] —**drudg'er•y** *n.*

drug (drŭg) *n.* **1.** A substance used as medicine in the treatment of disease. **2.** A narcotic, esp. one that is addictive. —**drug on the market.** A commodity for which there is little demand. —*v.* **drugged, drugging. 1.** To administer a drug to. **2.** To poison or mix (food or drink) with drugs. **3.** To stupefy or dull with or as if with a drug. [< OF *drogue,* chemical material.]

drug•gist (drŭg'ĭst) *n.* **1.** A pharmacist. **2.** One who sells drugs.

drug•store (drŭg'stôr', -stōr') *n.* A store where drugs, medical supplies, and other articles are sold.

dru•id (drōō'ĭd) *n.* Also **Dru•id.** A member of an order of priests in ancient Gaul and Britain.

drum (drŭm) *n.* **1.** A percussion instrument consisting of a hollow cylinder or hemisphere with a membrane stretched tightly over one or both ends. **2.** A sound produced by beating such an instrument. **3. a.** A metal cylinder or spool, wound with cable, wire, or heavy rope. **b.** A cylindrical or barrellike metal container. —*v.* **drummed, drumming. 1.** To beat a drum. **2.** To thump or tap rhythmically or continually. —**drum into.** To instruct by constant repetition. —**drum up.** To summon or obtain by soliciting, advertising, etc.: *drum up business.* [< MDu *tromme.*]

drum major. A person who leads a marching band.

drum•mer (drŭm'ər) *n.* **1.** One who plays a drum. **2.** A traveling salesman.

drum•stick (drŭm'stĭk') *n.* **1.** A stick for beating a drum. **2.** The lower part of the leg of a cooked fowl.

drunk (drŭngk). *p.p.* & *p.t.* of **drink.** —*adj.* **1.** Intoxicated with alcoholic liquor; inebriated. **2.** Overcome by strong feeling. —*n.* **1.** A drunken person. **2.** A bout of drinking.

Usage: Drunk (adj.) is chiefly used predicatively after a verb: *He was drunk. Drunken* is preferable to *drunk* as an attributive (before a noun): *a drunken driver; drunken driving.*

drunk•ard (drŭng'kərd) *n.* One who is habitually drunk.

drunk•en (drŭng'kən). Alternate *p.p.* of **drink.** —*adj.* **1.** Intoxicated. **2.** Pertaining to or occurring during intoxication: *drunken driving.* —See Usage note at **drunk.** —**drunk'en•ly** *adv.* —**drunk'en•ness** *n.*

dry (drī) *adj.* **drier** or **dryer, driest** or **dryest. 1.** Free from liquid or moisture. **2.** Having or characterized by little or no rain. **3.** Not under water: *dry land.* **4.** No longer yielding milk: *a dry cow.* **5.** Needing drink; thirsty. **6.** Pertaining to solid rather than liquid substances or commodities. **7.** Not sweet: *a dry wine.* **8.** Dull; boring. **9.** Matter-of-fact; impersonal. **10.** Prohibiting the sale or consumption of alcoholic beverages. —*v.* **dried, drying.** To make or become dry. —**dry up. 1.** To become dry. **2.** *Slang.* To stop talking; shut up. [< OE *drȳge* < Gmc *driug-.] —**dry'ly, dri'ly** *adv.* —**dry'ness** *n.*

dry•ad (drī'əd, -ăd') *n.* A wood nymph.

dry cell. A primary battery cell having an electrolyte in the form of moist paste.

dry-clean (drī'klēn') *v.* To clean (clothing or fabrics) with chemical solvents having little or no water. —**dry cleaning.**

dry dock. A large floating or stationary dock used for maintaining, repairing, and altering ships.

dry•er. 1. Alternate *compar.* of **dry. 2.** Variant of **drier.** —*n.* Also **drier.** An appliance for removing moisture, esp. by heating.

dry•est. Alternate *superl.* of **dry.**

dry farming. A type of farming practiced in arid areas without irrigation by maintaining a fine surface tillage or mulch that protects the natural moisture of the soil from evaporation. —**dry farm.** —**dry farmer.**

dry goods. Textiles, clothing, and related articles of trade.

Dry Ice. A trademark for solid carbon dioxide, used primarily as a refrigerant.

dry run. A trial run or rehearsal, as a military exercise without the use of live ammunition.

d.s. 1. *Commerce.* days after sight. **2.** document signed.

DSC, D.S.C. Distinguished Service Cross.

DSM Distinguished Service Medal.

D.S.O. Distinguished Service Order.

d.s.p. died without issue (L *decessit sine prole*).

DST, D.S.T. daylight-saving time.

D.T.'s (dē'tēz') *pl.n.* **Delirium tremens.**

Du. Dutch.

du•al (d/y/ōō'əl) *adj.* Composed of two parts; double: *dual controls.* [< L *duo,* two.] —**du•al'i•ty** (-ăl'ə-tē) *n.* —**du'al•ly** *adv.*

du•al•ism (d/y/ōō'ə-lĭz'əm) *n.* Any doctrine viewing reality as the product of two conflicting cosmic forces. —**du'al•ist** *n.* & *adj.* —**du'al•is'tic** (-ə-lĭs'tĭk) *adj.*

dub[1] (dŭb) *v.* **dubbed, dubbing. 1.** To tap lightly on the shoulder in conferring knighthood. **2.** To name playfully; nickname. **3.** To cut, rub, etc., so as to make even or smooth. **4.** *Slang.* To execute (a golf stroke) poorly; bungle. [< OE *dubbian.* See **dheubh-.**]

dub[2] (dŭb) *v.* **dubbed, dubbing. 1.** To insert a new sound track, such as a translation of the original dialogue, into (a film). **2.** To insert (sound) into a film or tape (often with *in*). [Short for DOUBLE.]

dub•bin (dŭb'ĭn) *n.* Also **dub•bing** (-ĭng). An application of tallow and oil for dressing leather. [< DUB.]

du•bi•e•ty (d/y/ōō-bī'ə-tē) *n., pl.* **-ties.** A matter of doubt; an uncertainty.

du•bi•ous (d/y/ōō'bē-əs) *adj.* **1.** Fraught with uncertainty or doubt; undecided. **2.** Arousing doubt; questionable. **3.** Skeptical; doubtful. [L *dubius,* dubious, fluctuating.] —**du'bi•ous•ly** *adv.* —**du'bi•ous•ness** *n.*

Dub•lin (dŭb'lĭn). The capital of the Republic of Ireland. Pop. 537,000.

du•cal (d/y/ōō'kəl) *adj.* Pertaining to a duke or dukedom. —**du'cal•ly** *adv.*

duc•at (dŭk'ət) *n.* Any of various gold coins formerly used in Europe. [< ML *ducātus,* duchy.]

duch•ess (dŭch'ĭs) *n.* **1.** The wife or widow of a duke. **2.** A woman holding title to a duchy.

duch•y (dŭch'ē) *n., pl.* **-ies.** The territory ruled by a duke or duchess; a dukedom.

duck[1] (dŭk) *n.* Any of various water birds with a broad, flat bill, short legs, and webbed feet. [< OE **dūcan,* to dive, DUCK.]

duck[2] (dŭk) *v.* **1.** To lower quickly, esp. so as to avoid something. **2.** To evade; dodge. **3.** To submerge briefly in water. [< OE **dūcan,* to dive < Gmc **dukjan.*]

duck[3] (dŭk) *n.* **1.** A durable, closely woven heavy cotton or linen fabric. **2. ducks.** Clothing made of this fabric. [< MDu *doek.*]

duck•bill (dŭk'bĭl') *n.* A platypus.

duck•board (dŭk'bôrd', -bōrd') *n.* A board or boardwalk laid across a wet or muddy surface.

duck•ling (dŭk'lĭng) *n.* A young duck.

duck•pin (dŭk'pĭn') *n.* **1.** A bowling pin, shorter and squatter than a tenpin. **2. duckpins** *(takes sing. v.).* A bowling game played with these pins.

duck•y (dŭk'ē) *adj.* **-ier, -iest.** *Slang.* Excellent; fine. —*n., pl.* **duckies.** Dear. Used as a term of familiarity.

duct (dŭkt) *n.* **1.** Any tubular passage through which a substance, esp. a fluid, is conveyed. **2.** A tube or pipe for electrical cables or wires. [L *ductus,* pp *dūcere,* to lead.]

duc•tile (dŭk'tĭl) *adj.* **1.** Capable of being drawn into wire or hammered thin, as metal. **2.** Readily influenced; tractable. [< L *ductus,* DUCT.] —**duc•til'i•ty** *n.*

duct•less gland (dŭkt'lĭs). An endocrine gland.

dud (dŭd) *n. Informal.* **1.** A bomb, shell, etc., that fails to explode. **2.** One that is disappointingly unsuccessful. [ME *dudde,* article of clothing, thing.]

dude (d/y/ōōd) *n.* **1.** *Informal.* An Easterner or city person staying in the West. **2.** *Informal.* A dandy. [?]

dudg•eon (dŭj'ən) *n.* A sullen or indignant anger. [?]

due (d/y/ōō) *adj.* **1.** Payable immediately or on demand. **2.** Owed as a debt; owing. **3.** Owed by right; fitting or appropriate. **4.** Sufficient; adequate. **5.** Expected or scheduled. —**due to. 1.** Attributable to; caused by. **2.** Because of. —*n.* **1.** Something that is owed or deserved. **2. dues.** A charge or fee for membership. —*adv.* Straight; directly: *due west.* [< VL **dēbūtus,* "owed."]

Usage: Due to is preferably restricted to sentences in which *due* functions as an adjective following a linking verb: *His hesitancy was due to fear.* In formal usage, *due to* is not appropriate when it introduces an adverbial phrase that directly modifies a nonlinking verb: *He hesitated due to fear* (preferably *because of* or *owing to fear*).

du•el (d/y/ōōl) *n.* **1.** A prearranged combat between two persons, fought to settle a point of honor. **2.** Any struggle between two persons, groups, etc. —*v.* **-eled** or **-elled, -eling** or **-elling.** To fight in a duel. [< L *duellum,* war.] —**du'el•er, du'el•ist** *n.*

du•et (d/y/ōō-ĕt') *n.* **1.** A musical composition written for two voices or two instruments. **2.** The two performers of such a composition. [< L *duo,* two.]

duf•fel bag (dŭf'əl). A large cloth bag for carrying personal belongings.

duf•fer (dŭf'ər) *n. Informal.* An incompetent or dull-witted person. [?]
dug¹ (dŭg) *n.* An udder, breast, or teat of a female animal. [?]
dug². *p.t. & p.p.* of **dig.**
dug•out (dŭg'out') *n.* **1.** A boat or canoe made by hollowing out a log. **2.** A shelter dug into the ground or hillside. **3.** A long sunken shelter for the players at the side of a baseball field.
Duis•burg (düs'bŏŏrKH'). A city of West Germany. Pop. 501,000.
duke (d/y/ōōk) *n.* **1.** A nobleman with the highest rank, esp. a man of the highest grade of the British peerage. **2.** A prince who rules an independent duchy. [< L *dux (duc-),* leader.] —**duke'dom** *n.*
dul•cet (dŭl'sĭt) *adj.* Pleasing to the ear; gently melodious. [< L *dulcis,* sweet.]
dul•ci•mer (dŭl'sə-mər) *n.* A musical instrument with wire strings of graduated lengths, played with two padded hammers. [< OF *doulcemer,* perh "sweet song."]
dull (dŭl) *adj.* **1.** Lacking mental agility; slow to learn. **2.** Not brisk; sluggish. **3.** Not sharp; blunt. **4.** Not intensely or keenly felt. **5.** Unexciting; boring. **6.** Not bright or vivid. **7.** Cloudy; gloomy. **8.** Muffled; indistinct. —*v.* To make or become dull. [< MLG *dul.*] —**dul'ly** *adv.* —**dull'ness, dul'ness** *n.*
dull•ard (dŭl'ərd) *n.* A mentally dull person; dolt.
Du•luth (də-lōōth', dōō-). A city of NE Minnesota. Pop. 107,000.
du•ly (d/y/ōō'lē) *adv.* **1.** In a proper manner; fittingly; properly. **2.** At the expected time; punctually. [< DUE.]
dumb (dŭm) *adj.* **1.** Lacking the power or faculty of speech; mute. **2.** Temporarily speechless from shock. **3.** *Informal.* Ignorant or stupid. [< OE. See **dheu-¹.**] —**dumb'ly** *adv.* —**dumb'ness** *n.*
dumb•bell (dŭm'bĕl') *n.* **1.** A weight lifted for muscular exercise, consisting of a short bar with a metal ball at each end. **2.** *Slang.* A stupid person; dolt.
dumb•wait•er (dŭm'wā'tər) *n.* A small elevator for conveying food or other goods from one floor to another.
dum•found (dŭm'found') *v.* Also **dumb•found.** To strike dumb with astonishment; stun; nonplus. [DUM(B) + (CON)FOUND.]
dum•my (dŭm'ē) *n., pl.* **-mies. 1.** An imitation of a real object, used as a substitute. **2.** A figure imitating the human form, used for displaying clothes, as a target, etc. **3.** A blockhead; dolt. **4.** A model page to be reproduced by printing. **5.** In bridge: **a.** The partner whose exposed hand is played by the declarer. **b.** The hand thus exposed. —*adj.* Artificial; imitation. [< DUMB.]
dump (dŭmp) *v.* **1.** To drop in a large mass. **2.** To empty (material) out of a container or vehicle. **3.** To discard or foist (a problem) unceremoniously. **4.** To place (large quantities of goods) on the market at a low price. —*n.* **1.** A place where refuse is dumped. **2.** A storage place; depot. **3.** *Slang.* A dilapidated or disreputable place. [< Scand.]
dump•ling (dŭmp'lĭng) *n.* **1.** A small ball of dough cooked with stew or soup. **2.** Sweetened dough wrapped around fruit, baked, and served as a dessert. [?]
dumps (dŭmps) *pl.n. Informal.* A gloomy, melancholy state of mind: *in the dumps.* [< Du *domp,* haze, exhalation.]
dump•y (dŭm'pē) *adj.* **-ier, -iest.** Short and stout; squat. —**dump'i•ness** *n.*
dun¹ (dŭn) *v.* **dunned, dunning.** To ask (a debtor) persistently for payment. [?]
dun² (dŭn) *n.* A dull grayish brown color. [< OE *dunn.*] —**dun** *adj.*
dunce (dŭns) *n.* A dull-witted or stupid person; numskull.
dun•der•head (dŭn'dər-hĕd') *n.* A numskull; dunce. [Perh "one stunned by a thunderstroke."]
dune (d/y/ōōn) *n.* A hill or ridge of wind-blown sand. [< MDu *dūne.*]
dung (dŭng) *n.* Animal excrement; manure. [< OE < Gmc **dung-.*]
dun•ga•ree (dŭng'gə-rē') *n.* **1.** A sturdy, usually blue denim fabric. **2. dungarees.** Overalls or trousers of this fabric. [Hindi *dungrī.*]
dun•geon (dŭn'jən) *n.* A dark cell used to confine prisoners. [< OF *donjon,* "keep of the lord's castle."]
dunk (dŭngk) *v.* **1.** To plunge into liquid. **2.** To dip (as a doughnut) into coffee or other liquid before eating it. **3.** To submerge oneself briefly in water. [< OHG *dunkōn.*]
du•o (d/y/ōō'ō) *n., pl.* **-os. 1.** A duet. **2.** A pair. [It, "two."]
du•o•dec•i•mal (d/y/ōō'ō-dĕs'ə-məl) *adj.* **1.** Pertaining to or based on the number 12. **2.** Of or pertaining to twelfths. —*n.* A twelfth. [< L *duodecimus,* twelfth.]
du•o•de•num (d/y/ōō'ə-dē'nəm, d/y/ōō-ŏd'-n-əm) *n., pl.* **-odena** (-ŏd'n-ə). The beginning portion of the small intestine, starting at the lower end of the stomach and extending to the jejunum. [< ML *intestinum duodenum digitōrum,* "intestine of twelve digits."] —**du'o•de'nal** (d/y/ōō'ə-dē'nəl, d/y/ōō-ŏd'n-əl) *adj.*
dup. duplicate.
dupe (d/y/ōōp) *n.* One who is easily deceived or used. —*v.* To make a dupe of. [F.] —**dup'er•y** *n.*
du•plex (d/y/ōō'plĕks') *n.* A house divided into two living units. [L, double.]
du•pli•cate (d/y/ōō'plĭ-kĭt) *adj.* **1.** Identically copied from an original. **2.** Existing in two corresponding parts; double. —*n.* An identical copy; facsimile. —*v.* (d/y/ōō'plĭ-kāt') **-cated, -cating. 1.** To make an exact copy of. **2.** To make or perform again. [< L *duplicāre,* to make twofold.] —**du'pli•ca'tion** *n.*
du•pli•ca•tor (d/y/ōō'plĭ-kā'tər) *n.* A machine that reproduces printed or written material.
du•plic•i•ty (d/y/ōō-plĭs'ə-tē) *n., pl.* **-ties.** Deliberate deceptiveness; double-dealing. [< L *duplex,* twofold, DUPLEX.]
du•ra•ble (d/y/ōōr'ə-bəl) *adj.* Able to withstand wear and tear; lasting. [< L *dūrāre,* to last, endure.] —**du'ra•bil'i•ty** *n.*
du•ra ma•ter (d/y/ōōr'ə mā'tər). A tough fibrous membrane that covers the brain and spinal cord. [< ML *dūra mater (cerebrī),* "hard mother (of the brain)."]
dur•ance (d/y/ōōr'əns) *n.* Forced confinement. [< L *dūrāre,* to last.]
du•ra•tion (d/y/ōō-rā'shən) *n.* **1.** Continuance in time. **2.** The time during which something exists. [< L *dūrāre,* to last.]
du•ress (d/y/ōō-rĕs', d/y/ōōr'ĭs) *n.* **1.** Compulsion by threat; coercion: *confessed under duress.* **2.** Forcible confinement; durance. [< L *dūrus,* hard.]
dur•ing (d/y/ōōr'ĭng) *prep.* **1.** Throughout the course of. **2.** Within the time of; at some time in. [< L *dūrāre,* to last.]
durst (dûrst). *Archaic. p.t.* of **dare.**
dusk (dŭsk) *n.* The darker stage of twilight. [< OE *dox,* dark, dusky. See **dheu-¹.**] —**dusk'y** *adj.*
Düs•sel•dorf (dü'səl-dôrf'). A city of W West Germany. Pop. 704,000.
dust (dŭst) *n.* **1.** Fine particulate matter. **2.** The earthy remains of a human body. **3.** The surface of the ground. **4.** Something of no worth. —*v.* **1.** To remove dust (from). **2.** To sprinkle with a powdery substance. [< OE *dūst.* See **dheu-¹.**]
dust bowl. A region reduced to aridity by drought and dust storms.
dust•er (dŭs'tər) *n.* **1.** One that dusts. **2.** A cloth or brush used to remove dust. **3.** A smock worn to protect one's clothing from dust. **4.** A woman's dress-length housecoat.
dust•pan (dŭst'păn') *n.* A short-handled, shovellike pan into which dust is swept.
dust•y (dŭs'tē) *adj.* **-ier, -iest. 1.** Covered with dust. **2.** Like dust; powdery. **3.** Tinged with gray. —**dust'i•ly** *adv.* —**dust'i•ness** *n.*
Dutch (dŭch) *adj.* Of or pertaining to the Netherlands. —*n.* **1. the Dutch** (*takes pl. v.*). The people of the Netherlands. **2.** The Germanic language of the Netherlands. —*adv.* So that each person pays his own way: *go Dutch.* —**in Dutch.** *Informal.* In trouble.
Dutch door. A door divided in half horizontally so that either part may be left open or closed.
Dutch•man (dŭch'mən) *n.* A native or inhabitant of the Netherlands, or a person of Dutch descent.
Dutch oven. An iron kettle with a tight lid, used for slow cooking.
Dutch treat. *Informal.* An outing in which each person pays his own expenses.
du•te•ous (d/y/ōō'tē-əs) *adj.* Obedient; dutiful. —**du'te•ous•ly** *adv.*
du•ti•a•ble (d/y/ōō'tē-ə-bəl) *adj.* Subject to import tax.
du•ti•ful (d/y/ōō'tĭ-fəl) *adj.* **1.** Careful to perform duties. **2.** Expressing a sense of duty. —**du'ti•ful•ly** *adv.* **du'ti•ful•ness** *n.*
du•ty (d/y/ōō'tē) *n., pl.* **-ties. 1.** A course of action required by one's position. **2. a.** Moral obligation. **b.** The compulsion felt to meet such obligation. **3.** A service assigned or demanded of one; function; work. **4.** A tax charged by a government, esp. on imports. **5.** The work capability of a machine under specified conditions. —**off duty.** Not engaged in one's assigned work. —**on duty.** At one's post or work. [< DUE.]
D.V. Douay Version (of the Bible).
D.V.M. Doctor of Veterinary Medicine.
Dvoř•ák (dvôr'zhäk), **Anton.** 1841–1904. Czech composer.
dwarf (dwôrf) *n., pl.* **dwarfs** or **dwarves** (dwôrvz). An atypically small person, animal, or plant. —*v.* **1.** To check the growth of; stunt. **2.** To cause to appear small by comparison. —*adj.* Diminutive; undersized. [< OE *dweorh* < Gmc **dwerg-.*] —**dwarf'ism'** *n.*
dwarf star. A star such as the sun having relatively low mass and average or below average luminosity.
dwell (dwĕl) *v.* **dwelt** (dwĕlt) or **dwelled, dwelling. 1.** To live; reside. **2.** To linger over; emphasize (with *on* or *upon*). [< OE *dwellan,* deceive, hinder. See **dheu-¹.**] —**dwell'er** *n.*
dwell•ing (dwĕl'ĭng) *n.* A place to live in; residence; abode.
dwin•dle (dwĭnd'l) *v.* **-dled, -dling.** To make or become gradually less until little remains. [< OE *dwīnan,* to diminish. See **dheu-³.**]
dwt. pennyweight.
Dy dysprosium.

dy•ad (dī'ăd') *n.* Two units regarded as a pair. [< Gk *duas,* pair.] —**dy•ad'ic** *adj.*

dye (dī) *n.* **1.** Any substance used to color materials. **2.** A color imparted by dyeing. —*v.* **dyed, dyeing. 1.** To color (a material) with a dye. **2.** To take on or impart color. [< OE *dēah, dēag,* hue, tinge.] —**dy'er** *n.*

dyed-in-the-wool (dīd'ĭn-*th*ə-wŏŏl') *adj.* Thoroughgoing; out-and-out.

dy•ing (dī'ĭng) *adj.* **1.** About to die. **2.** Drawing to an end. **3.** Done or uttered just before death.

dyke. Variant of **dike.**

dyn *Phys.* dyne.

dy•nam•ic (dī-năm'ĭk) *adj.* Also **dy•nam•i•cal** (-ĭ-kəl). **1.** Pertaining to energy, force, or motion in relation to force. **2.** Energetic; vigorous; forceful. —*n.* **dynamics** *(takes sing. v.).* **1. a.** The study of the relationship between motion and the forces affecting motion. **b.** The combined study of kinetics and kinematics. **2.** The physical or moral forces that produce motion and change in any field or system. **3.** Variation in force or intensity, esp. in musical sound. [< Gk *dunamis,* power.]

dy•na•mism (dī'nə-mĭz'əm) *n.* **1.** Any of various theories or philosophical systems that explain the universe in terms of force or energy. **2.** A process or mechanism responsible for the development or motion of a system. **3.** The quality of being dynamic. —**dy'na•mist** *n.* —**dy'na•mis'tic** *adj.*

dy•na•mite (dī'nə-mīt') *n.* A powerful explosive composed of nitroglycerin or another explosive compound dispersed in an absorbent medium with a combustible dope such as wood pulp and an antacid such as calcium carbonate. —*v.* **-mited, -miting.** To blow up or destroy with dynamite.

dy•na•mo (dī'nə-mō') *n., pl.* **-mos. 1.** A generator, esp. one for producing direct current. **2.** *Informal.* An extremely energetic and forceful person.

dy•na•mom•e•ter (dī'nə-mŏm'ə-tər) *n.* Any of several instruments used to measure force or power.

dy•nas•ty (dī'nə-stē) *n., pl.* **-ties. 1.** A succession of rulers from the same family or line. **2.** A family or group that maintains power for several generations. [< Gk *dunastēs,* ruler.] —**dy•nas'tic** (dī-năs'tĭk) *adj.*

dyne (dīn) *n.* A unit of force equal to the force required to impart an acceleration of one centimeter per second per second to a mass of one gram. [< Gk *dunamis,* power.]

Dy•nel (dī-nĕl') *n.* A trademark for a polymeric compound used to make a fire-resistant, insect-resistant, and easily dyed textile fiber.

dys–. *comb. form.* Diseased, difficult, faulty, or bad. [< Gk *dus-.*]

dys•en•ter•y (dĭs'ən-tĕr'ē) *n.* An infection of the lower intestinal tract producing pain, fever, and severe diarrhea, often with blood and mucus. [< Gk *dusenteria.*] —**dys'en•ter'ic** *adj.*

dys•lex•i•a (dĭs-lĕk'sē-ə) *n.* Impairment of the ability to read. [< DYS- + Gk *lexis,* speech.] —**dys•lec'tic** (-lĕk'tĭk) *adj.* & *n.*

dys•pep•sia (dĭs-pĕp'shə, -sē-ə) *n.* Indigestion. —**dys•pep'tic** *adj.*

dys•pro•si•um (dĭs-prō'zē-əm) *n. Symbol* **Dy** A soft, silvery metal used in nuclear research. Atomic number 66, atomic weight 162.50. [< Gk *dusprositos,* difficult to approach.]

dys•tro•phy (dĭs'trə-fē) *n.* Also **dys•tro•phi•a** (dĭs-trō'fē-ə). **1.** Defective nutrition. **2.** Any disorder caused by defective nutrition. —**dys•troph'ic** (-trŏf'ĭk, -trō'fĭk) *adj.*

dz. dozen.

Ee

e, E (ē) *n.* **1.** The 5th letter of the English alphabet. **2.** The 5th in a series.

e 1. east; eastern. **2.** electron. **3.** The base of the natural system of logarithms, approx. 2.718.

E 1. Earth. **2.** east; eastern. **3.** English. **4.** *Mus.* The 3rd tone in the scale of C major.

e. 1. east; eastern. **2.** engineer; engineering.

E. 1. east; eastern. **2.** engineer; engineering. **3.** English.

each (ēch) *adj.* One of two or more considered individually; every. —*pron.* Every one of a group considered individually; each one. —*adv.* For or to each one; apiece. [< OE *ǣlc* < Gmc **aiwo galīkaz,* "ever alike."]

ea•ger (ē'gər) *adj.* Impatiently desirous; anxious. [< L *ācer,* sharp.] —**ea'ger•ly** *adv.* —**ea'ger•ness** *n.*

ea•gle (ē'gəl) *n.* **1.** A large bird of prey with a hooked bill and strong, soaring flight. **2.** A former gold coin of the U.S. worth ten dollars. **3.** *Golf.* A score of two below par on any hole. [< L *aquila.*]

ea•glet (ē'glĭt) *n.* A young eagle.

–ean. *comb. form.* Of or pertaining to or derived from: **Caesarean.** [Var of -IAN.]

ear¹ (ĭr) *n.* **1.** The organ of hearing in vertebrates responsible, in general, for maintaining equilibrium as well as sensing sound. **2.** The sense of hearing. **3.** Aural sensitivity, as to differences in musical pitch. **4.** Attention; heed. **5.** Anything resembling an ear. [< OE *ēare.* See **ous-.**] —**ear'less** *adj.*

ear² (ĭr) *n.* The seed-bearing spike of a cereal plant, as corn. [< OE *ēar.* See **ak-.**]

ear•ache (ĭr'āk') *n.* A pain in the ear.

ear•drum (ĭr'drŭm') *n.* The **tympanic membrane.**

ear•flap (ĭr'flăp') *n.* Also **ear•lap** (-lăp'). Either of two appendages to a cap that may be turned down over the ears.

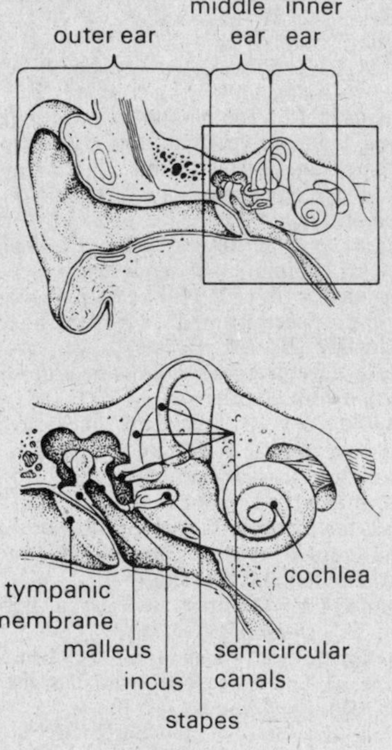

ear¹
The human ear

earl (ûrl) *n.* A British peer ranking above a viscount and below a marquis. [< OE *eorl,* warrior, chief, nobleman < Gmc **erilaz.*] —**earl'dom** *n.*

ear lobe. The soft, fleshy tissue at the lowest portion of the external ear.

ear•ly (ûr'lē) *adj.* **-lier, -liest. 1.** Near the beginning of a given period of time. **2.** In a period far back in time; primitive. **3.** Occurring before the usual time. **4.** Occurring in the near future. —*adv.* **1.** Near the beginning of a given period of time. **2.** Far back in time. **3.** Before the expected or arranged time: *They left early.* [< OE *ǣr,* before. See **ayer-.**] —**ear'li•ness** *n.*

ear•mark (ĭr'märk') *n.* An identifying mark or characteristic. —*v.* **1.** To mark distinctively for identification. **2.** To set aside for some purpose.

ear•muff (ĭr'mŭf') *n.* Either of a pair of ear coverings worn to protect against the cold.

earn (ûrn) *v.* **1.** To gain or deserve (salary, wages, etc.) for one's labor. **2.** To gain or acquire as a result of one's behavior. **3.** To produce (interest or return) as profit. [< OE *earnian.* See **esen-.**] —**earn'er** *n.*

ear•nest¹ (ûr'nĭst) *adj.* **1.** Determined; serious. **2.** Showing deep sincerity or feeling. **3.** Of an important or vital nature. —**in earnest.** With a purposeful or serious intent. [< OE *eornost,* zeal, seriousness. See **er-¹.**] —**ear'nest•ly** *adv.* —**ear'nest•ness** *n.*

ear•nest² (ûr'nĭst) *n.* **1.** Money paid in advance to bind a contract. **2.** A token or assurance of something to come. [< Heb *'ērābhōn,* security, pledge.]

earn•ings (ûr'nĭngz) *pl.n.* Something earned, esp. salary, wages, or profits.

ear•phone (ĭr'fōn') *n.* A device that converts electric signals, as from a radio receiver, to audible sound and is worn in contact with the ear.

ear•ring (îr'rĭng, -ĭng) *n.* An ornament worn on the ear lobe.
ear•shot (îr'shŏt') *n.* The range within which sound can be heard.
earth (ûrth) *n.* **1.** The land surface of the world, as distinguished from the oceans and air. **2.** The softer part of land; soil. **3. Earth.** The 3rd planet from the sun, having a sidereal period of revolution about the sun of 365.26 days at a mean distance of 92.96 million miles, an axial rotation period of 23 hours 56.07 minutes, an average radius of 3,959 miles, and a mass of 13.17×10^{24} pounds. **—down to earth.** Realistic. [< OE *eorthe.* See **er-**[2].]
earth•en (ûr'thən) *adj.* Made of earth or baked clay.
earth•en•ware (ûr'thən-wâr') *n.* Pottery made from baked clay.
earth•ly (ûrth'lē) *adj.* **1.** Of the earth; terrestrial. **2.** Conceivable; possible: *no earthly meaning whatever.* **—earth'li•ness** *n.*
earth•quake (ûrth'kwāk') *n.* A trembling movement of the earth's surface.
earth science. Any of several essentially geologic sciences concerned with the origin, structure, and physical phenomena of the earth.
earth•work (ûrth'wûrk') *n.* An earthen embankment, esp. when used as a military fortification.
earth•worm (ûrth'wûrm') *n.* A round-bodied segmented worm that burrows into soil.
earth•y (ûr'thē) *adj.* **-ier, -iest. 1.** Of or like earth or soil. **2.** Crude or coarse; unrefined. **—earth'i•ness** *n.*
ear•wax (îr'wăks') *n.* The waxlike secretion of certain glands lining the canal of the outer ear.
ear•wig (îr'wĭg') *n.* An insect with pincerlike appendages protruding from the rear.
ease (ēz) *n.* **1.** Freedom from pain, worry, or agitation. **2.** Freedom from constraint or awkwardness; naturalness. **3.** Freedom from difficulty; facility. **—*v.* eased, easing. 1.** To free from pain or trouble; comfort. **2.** To alleviate or lighten (discomfort); mitigate; lessen. **3.** To slacken; loosen. **4.** To move into place slowly and carefully. **5.** To diminish in discomfort, stress, pressure, etc. [< OF *aise,* comfort, convenience.] **—ease'ment** *n.*
ea•sel (ē'zəl) *n.* An upright frame used to support an artist's canvas. [Du *ezel,* "ass."]
east (ēst) *n.* **1. a.** The direction of the earth's rotation. **b.** The point on the mariner's compass 90° clockwise from north, directly opposite west. **2.** Often **East. a.** The E part of any country or region. **b.** The E part of the earth, esp. Asia; the Orient. **—the East.** In the U.S.: **1.** The region E of the Mississippi and N of the Mason-Dixon line. **2.** The region E of the Alleghenies and N of the Mason-Dixon line. *—adj.* **1.** To or from the east. **2. East.** Officially designating the E part of a country, continent, or other geographic area: *East Germany.* *—adv.* In, from, or toward the east. [< OE *ēast.* See **awes-**.]
East Ber•lin (bûr-lĭn'). The capital of the German Democratic Republic. Pop. 1,071,000.
East Chi•na Sea (chī'nə). An arm of the Pacific Ocean off the China coast.
East•er (ē'stər) *n.* A festival in the Christian church commemorating the Resurrection of Christ. [< OE *ēastre.* See **awes-**.]
east•er•ly (ē'stər-lē) *adj.* **1.** Toward the east. **2.** From the east. **—east'er•ly** *adv.*
east•ern (ē'stərn) *adj.* **1.** Toward, in, or facing the east. **2.** Coming from the east. **3.** Often **Eastern.** Of or characteristic of eastern regions or the East, esp. Asia; Oriental.
east•ern•er (ē'stər-nər) *n.* **1.** A native or inhabitant of the East. **2.** Often **Easterner.** A native or inhabitant of the E U.S.
Eastern Hemisphere. The part of the earth including Europe, Africa, Asia, and Australia.
Eastern Orthodox Church. The body of modern Christian churches, including the Greek and Russian Orthodox, derived from the church of the Byzantine Empire.
East Germany. The unofficial name for the German Democratic Republic.
East In•dies (ĭn'dēz). Historically, India, SE Asia, and the Malay Archipelago. **—East Indian.**
east•ward (ēst'wərd) *adv.* Also **east•wards** (-wərdz), **east•ward•ly** (-wərd-lē). Toward the east. *—adj.* Toward, facing, or in the east.
eas•y (ē'zē) *adj.* **-ier, -iest. 1.** Capable of being accomplished without difficulty. **2.** Free from worry, anxiety, or pain. **3.** Pleasant and relaxing. **4.** Relaxed; easygoing; informal. **5.** Not strict; lenient. **6.** Not hurried; moderate. *—adv.* In a cautious, restrained manner. **—take it easy.** *Informal.* **1.** To relax. **2.** To remain calm. [< OF *aise,* EASE.] **—eas'i•ly** *adv.* **—eas'i•ness** *n.*
eas•y•go•ing (ē'zē-gō'ĭng) *adj.* Also **eas•y-go•ing.** Living in a carefree way.
eat (ēt) *v.* **ate, eaten, eating. 1.** To consume (food). **2.** To consume or ravage as if by eating. **3.** To erode or corrode. [< OE *etan.* See **ed-**.] **—eat'er** *n.*
eaves (ēvz) *pl.n.* The projecting overhang at the edge of a roof. [< OE *yfes,* eaves, edge, border. See **upo.**]
eaves•drop (ēvz'drŏp') *v.* **-dropped, -dropping.** To listen secretly to a private conversation. [< ME *evesdrop,* water from the eaves.] **—eaves'drop'per** *n.*
ebb (ĕb) *n.* **1.** Ebb tide. **2.** A period of declining or diminishing. *—v.* **1.** To fall back or recede. **2.** To waste or fall away. [< OE *ebba,* low tide. See **apo-**.]
ebb tide. The period of a tide between high tide and a succeeding low tide.
eb•on•ite (ĕb'ə-nīt') *n.* A hard rubber, esp. when black. [< Gk *ebenos,* EBONY.]
eb•on•y (ĕb'ə-nē) *n.* The hard, dark wood of a tropical Asian tree. *—adj.* **1.** Made of ebony. **2.** Black. [< Gk *ebenos,* ebony tree < Egypt *hebni.*]
e•bul•lient (ĭ-bŭl'yənt) *adj.* **1.** Boiling, as a liquid. **2.** Filled with excitement; exuberant. [< L *ēbullīre,* to boil over.] **—e•bul'lience** *n.* **—e•bul'lient•ly** *adv.*
eb•ul•li•tion (ĕb'ə-lĭsh'ən) *n.* **1.** The bubbling or effervescence of a liquid; a boiling. **2.** A sudden, violent outpouring, as of emotion or violence.
ec•cen•tric (ĕk-sĕn'trĭk, ĭk-) *adj.* **1.** Deviating from a conventional or established pattern. **2.** Deviating from a circular form, as in an elliptical orbit. **3.** Not situated at or in the center. **4.** Not having the same center, as a circle, cylinder, or sphere. *—n.* **1.** An odd or erratic person. **2.** A disk or wheel having its axis of revolution displaced from its center so that it is capable of imparting reciprocating motion. [< Gk *ekkentros,* not having the earth as its center.] **—ec•cen'tri•cal•ly** *adv.* **—ec'cen•tric'i•ty** (-trĭs'ə-tē) *n.*
eccles. ecclesiastic; ecclesiastical.
Eccles. Ecclesiastes (Old Testament).
ec•cle•si•as•tic (ĭ-klē'zē-ăs'tĭk) *adj.* Ecclesiastical. *—n.* A clergyman; priest. [< Gk *ekklēsia,* duly summoned assembly.]
ec•cle•si•as•ti•cal (ĭ-klē'zē-ăs'tĭ-kəl) *adj.* Of or pertaining to a church, esp. as an organized institution.
ech•e•lon (ĕsh'ə-lŏn') *n.* **1.** A steplike formation of troops, vessels, etc. **2.** A subdivision of a military force. **3.** A level of authority in a hierarchy. [F *échelon,* "rung of a ladder."]
ech•o (ĕk'ō) *n., pl.* **-oes. 1.** Repetition of a sound by reflection of sound waves from a surface. **2.** A sound so produced. **3.** Any repetition or imitation. **4.** A reflected wave received by a radio or radar. *—v.* **1.** To repeat by or as by an echo. **2.** To resound with or emit an echo; reverberate. **3.** To imitate: *echo the teacher's ideas.* [< Gk *ēkhō.*]
é•clair (ā'klâr', ĭ-klâr') *n.* A light, tubular, usually iced pastry filled with cream or custard. [< OF *esclairier,* to light, flash.]
é•clat (ā-klä') *n.* **1.** Great brilliance, as of achievement; conspicuous success. **2.** Acclaim. [< F *éclater,* to burst, explode.]
ec•lec•tic (ĭ-klĕk'tĭk) *adj.* Choosing or consisting of what appears to be the best from diverse sources. [< Gk *eklegein,* to single out.] **—ec•lec'ti•cal•ly** *adv.*
e•clipse (ĭ-klĭps') *n.* **1. a.** The partial or complete obscuring, relative to a designated observer, of one celestial body by another. **b.** The period of time during which such an obscuring occurs. **2.** A falling into obscurity or disuse; decline. *—v.* **eclipsed, eclipsing.** To cause an eclipse or obscuring of. [< Gk *ekleipsis,* cessation, abandonment.]

eclipse
Total solar eclipse

e•clip•tic (ĭ-klĭp'tĭk) *n.* The apparent path of the sun among the stars; the intersection plane of the earth's solar orbit with the celestial sphere. [< Gk *ekleipein,* to abandon.]
ec•logue (ĕk'lôg', -lŏg') *n.* A pastoral poem. [< L *ecloga,* "selection."]
ecol. ecological; ecology.
e•col•o•gy (ĭ-kŏl'ə-jē) *n.* The science of the relationships between organisms and their environments. [< Gk *oikos,* house + -LOGY.] **—ec'o•log'i•cal** (ĕk'ə-lŏj'ĭ-kəl) *adj.* **—ec'o•log'i•cal•ly** *adv.* **—e•col'o•gist** *n.*
econ. economics; economist; economy.
ec•o•nom•ic (ĕk'ə-nŏm'ĭk, ē'kə-) *adj.* **1.** Of or pertaining to the production, development, and management of material wealth, as of a country or business enterprise. **2.** Of or pertaining to the necessities of life. *—n.* **economics** *(takes sing. v.).* The science of the production, distribution, and consumption of commodities. **—e•con'o•mist** (ĭ-kŏn'ə-mĭst) *n.*
ec•o•nom•i•cal (ĕk'ə-nŏm'ĭ-kəl, ē'kə-) *adj.*

Not wasteful; prudent; sparing. —ec'o•nom'i•cal•ly *adv.*

e•con•o•mize (ĭ-kŏn'ə-mīz') *v.* **-mized, -mizing.** To be frugal; reduce expenses; practice economy. —**e•con'o•miz'er** *n.*

e•con•o•my (ĭ-kŏn'ə-mē) *n., pl.* **-mies. 1. a.** The careful or thrifty management of resources. **b.** An instance of this. **2.** A system for the management and development of resources: *an agricultural economy.* [< Gk *oikonomos,* manager of a household.]

ec•sta•sy (ĕk'stə-sē) *n., pl.* **-sies. 1.** A state of overwhelming delight; rapture. **2.** An extreme or intense state of any emotion: *an ecstasy of anger.* [< Gk *existanai,* to displace, drive out of one's senses.] —**ec•stat'ic** (ĕk-stăt'ĭk) *adj.* —**ec•stat'i•cal•ly** *adv.*

ecto–. *comb. form.* Outside or external part. [< Gk *ektos,* outside.]

–ectomy. *comb. form.* Removal of a part by surgery: **tonsillectomy.**

ec•to•plasm (ĕk'tə-plăz'əm) *n.* A portion of the continuous phase of cytoplasm distinguishable in some cells as a relatively rigidly jelled cortex limited on the outside by the cell membrane.

Ec•ua•dor (ĕk'wə-dôr'). A republic of NW South America. Pop. 4,485,000. Cap. Quito.

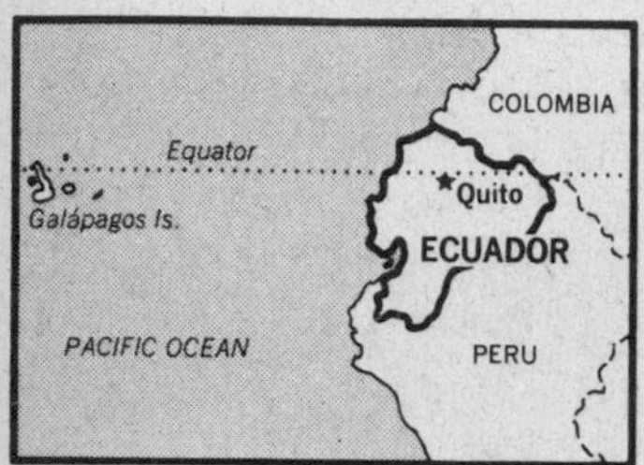

Ecuador

ec•u•men•i•cal (ĕk'yŏŏ-mĕn'ĭ-kəl) *adj.* Pertaining to the general unity of Christians above sectarian differences. [< Gk *oikoumenikos,* of the whole world.]

ec•u•men•ism (ĕk'yŏŏ-mĕn'ĭz'əm) *n.* A movement seeking to achieve worldwide unity among religions through greater cooperation and improved understanding.

ec•ze•ma (ĕk'sə-mə, ĕg'zə-, ĕg-zē'-, ĭg-zē'-) *n.* A noncontagious skin inflammation, marked by redness, itching, and the outbreak of lesions that become encrusted and scaly. [< Gk *ekzema,* eruption.] —**ec•zem'a•tous** (ĕg-zĕm'ə-təs, -zē'mə-təs, ĭg-) *adj.*

–ed¹. *comb. form.* Used to form the past tense of most verbs: **removed.** [< OE *-ode, -ede, -ade.*]

–ed². *comb. form.* Used to form past participles of most verbs: **hoped.** [< OE *-od, -ed, -ad.*]

–ed³. *comb. form.* Used to form adjectives from nouns and phrases: *gray-haired; thick-skinned.* [< OE *-ede.*]

ed. 1. edition; editor. **2.** education.

ed•dy (ĕd'ē) *n., pl.* **-dies.** A current, as of water or air, moving contrary to the direction of a main current, esp. in a circular motion. [< ON *idha,* "that which flows back," whirlpool.] —**ed'dy** *v.* **(-died, -dying).**

Ed•dy (ĕd'ē), **Mary Baker.** 1821–1910. American religious leader; founder of the Church of Christ, Scientist.

e•del•weiss (ā'dəl-vīs') *n.* An Alpine plant with whitish flowers and downy leaves. [G *Edelweiss,* "noble white."]

e•de•ma (ĭ-dē'mə) *n., pl.* **-mas** or **-mata** (-mə-tə). An excessive accumulation of serous fluid in the tissues. [< Gk *oidēma,* tumor, swelling.]

E•den (ēd'n) *n.* The first home of Adam and Eve; Paradise.

edge (ĕj) *n.* **1.** The sharp side of a cutting blade. **2.** Keenness; zest. **3.** A rim, brink, etc., as of a cliff. **4.** A margin; border. **5.** An advantage. —**on edge. 1.** Highly tense; irritable. **2.** Impatient. —*v.* **edged, edging. 1.** To give an edge to. **2.** To move gradually. [< OE *ecg,* edge, point, sword. See **ak-.**]

edge•wise (ĕj'wīz') *adv.* Also **edge•ways** (-wāz'). With the edge foremost.

edg•ing (ĕj'ĭng) *n.* Something that forms an edge or border.

edg•y (ĕj'ē) *adj.* **-ier, -iest.** Tense; nervous. —**edg'i•ness** *n.*

edh (ĕth) *n.* Also **eth.** An old Germanic letter representing *dh* in Scandinavian languages and *th* in Old English.

ed•i•ble (ĕd'ə-bəl) *adj.* Fit to be eaten. —*n.* Often **edibles.** Food. [< L *edere,* to eat.] —**ed'i•bil'i•ty, ed'i•ble•ness** *n.*

e•dict (ē'dĭkt') *n.* A proclamation; decree. [< L *ēdīcere,* to speak out, proclaim.]

ed•i•fi•ca•tion (ĕd'ĭ-fə-kā'shən) *n.* Intellectual, moral, or spiritual improvement.

ed•i•fice (ĕd'ə-fĭs) *n.* A building, esp. one of imposing size. [< L *aedificāre,* to build.]

ed•i•fy (ĕd'ə-fī') *v.* **-fied, -fying.** To instruct, esp. so as to encourage moral improvement. [< L *aedificāre,* to build, instruct.]

Ed•in•burgh (ĕd'n-bûr'ə). The capital of Scotland. Pop. 472,000.

Ed•i•son (ĕd'ə-sən), **Thomas Alva.** 1847–1931. American inventor.

ed•it (ĕd'ĭt) *v.* To prepare something for publication or presentation by revising, selecting, etc. [Back-formation < EDITOR.]

edit. edition; editor.

e•di•tion (ĭ-dĭsh'ən) *n.* **1.** The form in which a book is published. **2.** The entire number of copies of a publication printed at one time. **3.** One similar to an original; version.

ed•i•tor (ĕd'ə-tər) *n.* **1.** One who edits. **2.** One who supervises the policies of a publication. [< L *ēdere,* to bring forth, publish.]

ed•i•to•ri•al (ĕd'ə-tôr'ē-əl, -tōr'ē-əl) *n.* An article in a publication expressing the opinion of its editors or publishers. —*adj.* **1.** Of or pertaining to an editor. **2.** Characteristic of an editorial. —**ed'i•to'ri•al•ly** *adv.*

ed•i•to•ri•al•ize (ĕd'ə-tôr'ē-ə-līz', -tōr'ē-ə-līz') *v.* **-ized, -izing.** To express an opinion in or as if in an editorial.

Ed•mon•ton (ĕd'mən-tən). The capital of Alberta, Canada. Pop. 372,000.

EDP electronic data processing.

E.D.T. Eastern Daylight Time.

educ. education; educational.

ed•u•ca•ble (ĕj'ŏŏ-kə-bəl) *adj.* Capable of being educated.

ed•u•cate (ĕj'ŏŏ-kāt') *v.* **-cated, -cating.** To provide with and develop knowledge, training, or skill, esp. through formal schooling; teach. [< L *ēducāre,* to bring up, educate.] —**ed'u•ca'tor** *n.*

ed•u•ca•tion (ĕj'ŏŏ-kā'shən) *n.* **1. a.** The process of educating. **b.** The skills or knowledge so developed. **2.** The study of the teaching and learning processes; pedagogy. —**ed'u•ca'tion•al** *adj.* —**ed'u•ca'tion•al•ly** *adv.*

e•duce (ĭ-d/y/ŏŏs') *v.* **educed, educing. 1.** To draw out; elicit; evoke. **2.** To work out from given facts; deduce. [L *ēdūcere.*]

–ee¹. *comb. form.* **1.** The recipient of an action: **addressee. 2.** One who is in a specified condition: *standee.* [< L *-ātus,* -ATE¹.]

–ee². *comb. form.* **1.** A particular type of: **bootee. 2.** Something resembling or suggestive of: **goatee.**

EEG electroencephalogram.

eel (ēl) *n.* Any of various long, snakelike marine or freshwater fishes. [< OE *ǣl* < Gmc **ǣlaz.*]

–eer. *comb. form.* **1.** One who works with or is concerned with: **auctioneer, racketeer. 2.** One who makes or composes: **profiteer.** [< L *-ārius,* -ARY.]

ee•rie (ĭr'ē) *adj.* **-rier, -riest.** Also **ee•ry. 1.** Inspiring fear or dread. **2.** Weird; uncanny. [< OE *earg,* cowardly, timid < Gmc **arg-.*]

eff. efficiency.

ef•face (ĭ-fās') *v.* **-faced, -facing. 1.** To obliterate or make indistinct by or as by rubbing out. **2.** To make (oneself) inconspicuous. [OF *effacer,* "to remove the face."] —**ef•face'ment** *n.* —**ef•fac'er** *n.*

ef•fect (ĭ-fĕkt') *n.* **1.** Something brought about by a cause or agent; result. **2.** The capacity to achieve a desired result; influence. **3.** The condition of being operative or in full force. **4.** Basic meaning; purport: *He said something to that effect.* **5. effects.** Possessions; belongings. —**in effect. 1.** Actually. **2.** Virtually. **3.** In operation. —**take effect.** To become operative. —*v.* **1.** To produce as a result; bring about. **2.** To execute; make. —See Usage note at **affect.** [< L *effectus,* pp of *efficere,* to accomplish, perform.] —**ef•fect'er** *n.*

ef•fec•tive (ĭ-fĕk'tĭv) *adj.* **1.** Having an intended effect. **2.** Producing a desired impression; striking. **3.** Operative; in effect. —**ef•fec'tive•ly** *adv.* —**ef•fec'tive•ness** *n.*

ef•fec•tor (ĭ-fĕk'tər) *n.* An organ at the end of a nerve that activates either gland secretion or muscular contraction.

ef•fec•tu•al (ĭ-fĕk'chŏŏ-əl) *adj.* **1.** Producing a desired effect; fully adequate. **2.** Valid; legally binding. —**ef•fec'tu•al•ly** *adv.*

ef•fem•i•nate (ĭ-fĕm'ə-nĭt) *adj.* Having qualities associated with women rather than men; unmanly. [< L *effēmināre,* "to make a woman out of."] —**ef•fem'i•na•cy** (-nə-sē) *n.*

ef•fer•ent (ĕf'ər-ənt) *adj.* Directed away from a central organ or section, esp. carrying impulses from the central nervous system to an effector. [< L *efferre,* to carry away.]

ef•fer•vesce (ĕf'ər-vĕs') *v.* **-vesced, -vescing. 1.** To emit small bubbles of gas, as a carbonated liquid. **2.** To be lively or vivacious. [L *effervēscere,* to boil over.] —**ef'fer•ves'cence** *n.* —**ef'fer•ves'cent** *adj.*

ef•fete (ĭ-fēt') *adj.* **1.** Exhausted of vitality or effectiveness; worn-out; spent. **2.** Decadent. [L *effētus,* worn out by childbearing.]

ef•fi•ca•cious (ĕf'ə-kā'shəs) *adj.* Capable of producing a desired effect. —**ef'fi•ca'cious•ly** *adv.* —**ef'fi•ca•cy** (-kə-sē) *n.*

ef•fi•cien•cy (ĭ-fĭsh'ən-sē) *n., pl.* **-cies. 1.** The quality of being efficient. **2.** The ratio of the effective or useful output to the total input in any system. **3.** A small apartment.

ef•fi•cient (ĭ-fĭsh'ənt) *adj.* **1.** Acting or producing effectively with a minimum of waste or effort. **2.** Exhibiting a high ratio of output to input. —**ef•fi'cient•ly** *adv.*

ef•fi•gy (ĕf'ə-jē) *n., pl.* **-gies.** An image of a person, esp. a crude image of a despised person. [< L *effigiēs,* likeness, image.]

ef•flu•vi•um (ĭ-flŏŏ'vē-əm) *n., pl.* **-via** (-vē-ə) or **-ums.** An often foul-smelling emanation or vapor. [< L *effluere,* to flow out.]

ef•fort (ĕf'ərt) *n.* **1.** The applied use of physical or mental energy. **2.** Exertion. **3.** An attempt. **4.** An achievement; work: *early literary efforts.* [< VL **exfortiāre,* to show strength.]

ef•front•er•y (ĭ-frŭn'tə-rē) *n., pl.* **-ies.** Impudent boldness; audacity. [< LL *effrōns,* shameless, "barefaced."]

ef•ful•gent (ĭ-fŭl'jənt) *adj.* Radiant; resplendent. [< L *effulgēre,* to shine out.] **—ef•ful'gence** *n.* **—ef•ful'gent•ly** *adv.*

ef•fu•sion (ĭ-fyōō'zhən) *n.* **1.** A pouring forth. **2.** An unrestrained outpouring. [< L *effundere,* to pour out.]

ef•fu•sive (ĭ-fyōō'sĭv) *adj.* Unrestrained in emotional expression; gushy. **—ef•fu'sive•ly** *adv.* **—ef•fu'sive•ness** *n.*

eft (ĕft) *n.* A newt, esp. a small reddish form. [< OE *efeta,* lizard.]

e.g. for example (L *exempli gratia*).

e•gad (ĭ-găd', ē-găd') *interj.* By God! [Euphemism for *oh God.*]

e•gal•i•tar•i•an (ĭ-găl'ə-târ'ē-ən) *adj.* Favoring absolute political and social equality. [< L *aequālis,* equal.] **—e•gal'i•tar'i•an** *n.* **—e•gal'i•tar'i•an•ism'** *n.*

egg¹ (ĕg) *n.* **1.** A female reproductive cell; ovum. **2.** The thin-shelled ovum of a bird, esp. that of a domestic fowl, used as food. **3.** *Slang.* A fellow; person: *a bad egg.* [< ON.]

egg² (ĕg) *v.* **—egg on.** To urge or incite. [< ON *eggja.*]

egg•head (ĕg'hĕd') *n. Slang.* An intellectual; highbrow.

egg•nog (ĕg'nŏg') *n.* A drink made with milk, beaten eggs, and often liquor.

egg•plant (ĕg'plănt', -plänt') *n.* **1.** A plant cultivated for its large, ovoid, purple-skinned fruit. **2.** The fruit, eaten as a vegetable.

eg•lan•tine (ĕg'lən-tīn', -tēn') *n.* The sweetbrier. [< VL **aquilentum,* "prickly."]

e•go (ē'gō, ĕg'ō) *n.* **1.** The self as distinguished from all others. **2.** The personality component that is conscious, most immediately controls behavior, and is most in touch with external reality. **3.** Conceit; egotism. [< L, I.]

e•go•cen•tric (ē'gō-sĕn'trĭk, ĕg'ō-) *adj.* Thinking or acting with one's self as the major concern; self-centered.

e•go•ism (ē'gō-ĭz'əm, ĕg'ō-) *n.* **1.** The belief that self-interest is the just and proper motive force. **2.** Preoccupation with one's own interests; egotism. **—e'go•ist** *n.* **—e'go•is'tic, e'go•is'ti•cal** *adj.* **—e'go•is'ti•cal•ly** *adv.*

e•go•tism (ē'gə-tĭz'əm, ĕg'ə-) *n.* **1.** The tendency to speak or write excessively about oneself. **2.** An exaggerated sense of self-importance; conceit. **—e'go•tist** *n.* **—e'go•tis'tic, e'go•tis'ti•cal** *adj.* **—e'go•tis'ti•cal•ly** *adv.*

e•gre•gious (ĭ-grē'jəs, -jē-əs) *adj.* Outstandingly bad; blatant; outrageous. [L *ēgregius,* "standing out from the herd."] **—e•gre'gious•ly** *adv.* **—e•gre'gious•ness** *n.*

e•gress (ē'grĕs) *n.* The way by which one goes out; exit. [< L *ēgredī,* to go out.]

e•gret (ē'grĭt, ĕg'rĭt) *n.* A heronlike, usually white wading bird with long, showy, drooping plumes. [< OProv *aigron,* heron.]

E•gypt (ē'jĭpt). Officially, United Arab Republic. A country of NE Africa. Pop. 29,059,000. Cap. Cairo.

E•gyp•tian (ĭ-jĭp'shən) *n.* **1.** A native or inhabitant of Egypt. **2.** The extinct Hamitic language spoken by the ancient Egyptians. **—E•gyp'tian** *adj.*

E•gyp•tol•o•gy (ē'jĭp-tŏl'ə-jē) *n.* The study of the culture and artifacts of the ancient Egyptian civilization. **—E•gyp'to•log'i•cal** (ĭ-jĭp'tə-lŏj'ĭ-kəl) *adj.*

eh (ā, ĕ) *interj.* **1.** Used interrogatively. **2.** Used in asking for confirmation: *She's a flirt, eh?*

EHF extremely high frequency.

ei•der (ī'dər) *n.* A sea duck of northern regions, having soft down, **ei•der•down** (ī'dər-doun'), used to stuff quilts and pillows. [< ON *ædhr.*]

eight (āt) *n.* The cardinal number written 8 or in Roman numerals VIII. [< OE *eahta.* See **oktō.**] **—eight** *adj. & pron.*

eight•een (ā-tēn') *n.* The cardinal number written 18 or in Roman numerals XVIII. **—eight•een'** *adj. & pron.*

eight•eenth (ā-tēnth') *n.* **1.** The ordinal number 18 in a series. **2.** One of 18 equal parts. **—eight•eenth'** *adj. & adv.*

eighth (ātth, āth) *n.* **1.** The ordinal number 8 in a series. **2.** One of 8 equal parts. **—eighth** *adj. & adv.*

eight•i•eth (ā'tē-ĭth) *n.* **1.** The ordinal number 80 in a series. **2.** One of 80 equal parts. **—eight'i•eth** *adj. & adv.*

eight•y (ā'tē) *n.* The cardinal number written 80 or in Roman numerals LXXX. **—eight'y** *adj. & pron.*

Ein•stein (īn'stīn'), **Albert.** 1879–1955. German-born American theoretical physicist.

Albert Einstein

ein•stein•i•um (īn-stī'nē-əm) *n. Symbol* **Es** A synthetic element first produced by neutron irradiation of uranium in a thermonuclear explosion. Atomic number 99, longest-lived isotope Es 254.

Eir•e (âr'ə). The Gaelic name for the Republic of Ireland.

Ei•sen•how•er (ī'zən-hou'ər), **Dwight David.** 1890–1969. American general; 34th President of the U.S. (1953–61).

ei•ther (ē'thər, ī'thər) *pron.* One or the other: *Choose either.* —*conj.* —Used before the first of two or more stated alternatives, the following alternatives being signaled by *or: Either we go now or remain here forever.* —*adj.* **1.** Any one (of two): *Wear either coat.* **2.** One and the other; each: *She wore rings on either hand.* —*adv.* Likewise; also. Used as an intensifier following negative statements: *If you don't order a dessert, I won't either.* —See Usage note at **neither.** [< OE *ǣgther, ǣghwæther.* See **kwo-.**]

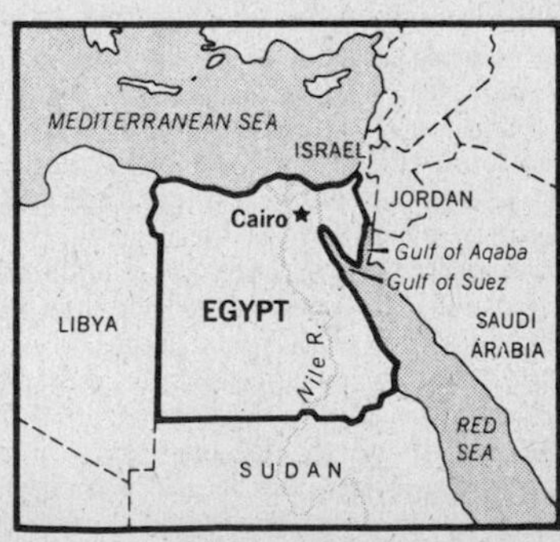

Egypt

e•jac•u•late (ĭ-jăk'yə-lāt') *v.* **-lated, -lating. 1.** To eject abruptly, esp. to discharge (semen). **2.** To utter suddenly and passionately; exclaim. [L *ējaculārī.*] **—e•jac'u•la'tion** *n.* **—e•jac'u•la'tor** *n.*

e•ject (ĭ-jĕkt') *v.* To throw out forcefully; expel; evict. [< L *ēicere* (pp *ējectus*).] **—e•jec'tion** *n.*

eke (ēk) *v.* **eked, eking.** To make or supplement with great effort or strain (with *out*): *eke out a living.* [< OE *ēacan,* to increase. See **aug-.**]

EKG electrocardiogram; electrocardiograph.

el. elevation.

e•lab•o•rate (ĭ-lăb'ər-ĭt) *adj.* Planned or executed with attention to detail; complicated. —*v.* (-ə-rāt') **-rated, -rating. 1.** To work out with care and in detail; develop thoroughly. **2.** To express oneself in greater detail. [< L *ēlabōrāre,* "to work out."] **—e•lab'o•rate•ly** *adv.* **—e•lab'o•rate•ness** *n.* **—e•lab'o•ra'tion** *n.*

é•lan (ā-läɴ') *n.* Enthusiasm; ardor. [< OF *eslancer,* to throw out.]

e•land (ē'lənd) *n.* A large African antelope with spirally twisted horns. [Afrik.]

Dwight David Eisenhower

e•lapse (ĭ-lăps') *v.* **elapsed, elapsing.** To pass; slip by, as time. [L *ēlābī* (pp *ēlapsus*).]

e•las•tic (ĭ-lăs'tĭk) *adj.* **1.** Returning or capable of returning to an initial form or state after deformation. **2.** Adaptable to change; flexible. **3.** Quick to recover or revive. —*n.* **1.** An elastic fabric. **2.** A rubber band. [< Gk *elastos, elatos,* beaten.] **—e•las'ti•cal•ly** *adv.* **—e•las'tic'i•ty** (-tĭs'ə-tē) *n.*

e•late (ĭ-lāt') *v.* **elated, elating.** To raise the spirits of; make happy or proud. [L *ēlātus,* "carried away."] **—e•la'tion** *n.*

El•be (ĕl'bə). A river of C Europe.

el•bow (ĕl'bō) *n.* **1. a.** The joint or bend of the arm between the forearm and upper arm. **b.** The bony outer projection of this joint. **2.** Something having a bend similar to an elbow. —*v.* **1.** To push or shove, as with the elbows. **2.** To make one's way by such pushing or shoving. [< OE *elnboga,* "bow of the forearm." See **el-¹.**]

elbow grease. *Informal.* Strenuous physical effort.

el•bow•room (ĕl'bō-rōōm', -rōōm') *n.* Room enough to move around or function in; ample space.

El•brus, Mount (ĕl'brōōs). The highest (18,480 ft.) mountain of Europe, in the Caucasus Mountains of the Soviet Union.

eld•er¹ (ĕl'dər). Alternate *compar.* of **old.** —*n.* **1.** An older person. **2.** An older, influential man of a family, tribe, etc. **3.** One of the governing officers of a church. [< OE *ieldra, eldra.*]

el•der² (ĕl'dər) *n.* A shrub with clusters of small white flowers and red or blackish berries. [< OE *ellærn, ellen.*]

el•der•ber•ry (ĕl'dər-bĕr'ē) *n.* **1.** The small, edible fruit of an elder. **2.** A shrub, the elder.

eld•er•ly (ĕl'dər-lē) *adj.* Approaching old age.

eld•est (ĕl'dĭst). Alternate *superl.* of **old.**

El Do•ra•do (ĕl də-rä'dō). A place of fabulous wealth.

elec. electric; electrical; electrician; electricity.

e•lect (ĭ-lĕkt') *v.* **1.** To select by vote for an office. **2.** To choose, esp. after deliberation. —*adj.* **1.** Chosen. **2.** Elected but not yet installed in office: *the governor-elect.* [< L *ēligere* (pp *ēlectus*), to pick out, select.]

e•lec•tion (ĭ-lĕk'shən) *n.* **1.** The act or process of electing. **2.** The fact of being elected.

e•lec•tion•eer (ĭ-lĕk'shə-nîr') *v.* To work actively for a candidate or political party.

e•lec•tive (ĭ-lĕk'tĭv) *adj.* **1.** Filled or chosen by election. **2.** Having the power to elect. **3.** Optional. —*n.* An optional course in an academic curriculum. —**e•lec'tive•ly** *adv.*

e•lec•tor (ĭ-lĕk'tər) *n.* **1.** One who elects; a qualified voter. **2.** A member of a special group chosen to elect a person to high office. —**e•lec'tor•al** *adj.*

e•lec•tor•ate (ĭ-lĕk'tər-ĭt) *n.* The body of qualified voters.

e•lec•tric (ĭ-lĕk'trĭk) *adj.* Also **e•lec•tri•cal** (-trĭ-kəl). **1.** Of, pertaining to, producing, derived from, produced, powered, or operated by electricity. **2.** Exciting; thrilling. [< NL *electricus,* "like amber" (amber produces sparks when rubbed).] —**e•lec'tri•cal•ly** *adv.*

electrical engineering. The scientific technology of electricity, esp. the design and application of circuitry and equipment for power generation and distribution, machine control, and communications. —**electrical engineer.**

electric chair. A chair used to electrocute those sentenced to death.

electric eye. A photoelectric cell, esp. when used as a sensor for an automatic switch.

e•lec•tri•cian (ĭ-lĕk'trĭsh'ən) *n.* One whose occupation is the installation, repair, or operation of electric equipment and circuitry.

e•lec•tric•i•ty (ĭ-lĕk'trĭs'ə-tē, ē'lĕk-) *n.* **1.** The class of physical phenomena arising from the existence and interactions of electric charge. **2.** The physical science of such phenomena. **3.** Electric current used or regarded as a source of power.

e•lec•tri•fy (ĭ-lĕk'trə-fī') *v.* **-fied, -fying. 1.** To produce electric charge on or in. **2. a.** To wire or otherwise equip for the use of electric power. **b.** To provide with electric power. **3.** To thrill, startle, or shock. —**e•lec'tri•fi•ca'tion** *n.*

electro–. *comb. form.* **1.** Electric. **2.** Electrically. **3.** Electrolysis.

e•lec•tro•car•di•o•gram (ĭ-lĕk'trō-kär'dē-ə-grăm') *n.* The curve traced by an electrocardiograph, used to diagnose heart disease.

e•lec•tro•car•di•o•graph (ĭ-lĕk'trō-kär'dē-ə-grăf', -gräf') *n.* An instrument used to record electric potentials associated with the electric currents that traverse the heart.

e•lec•tro•chem•is•try (ĭ-lĕk'trō-kĕm'ĭs-trē) *n.* The science of the interaction or interconversion of electric and chemical phenomena. —**e•lec'tro•chem'i•cal** *adj.*

e•lec•tro•cute (ĭ-lĕk'trə-kyōōt') *v.* **-cuted, -cuting.** To kill or execute with electricity. —**e•lec'tro•cu'tion** *n.*

e•lec•trode (ĭ-lĕk'trōd') *n.* A solid electric conductor through which an electric current enters or leaves a medium such as an electrolyte, a nonmetallic solid, a molten metal, a gas, or a vacuum.

e•lec•tro•en•ceph•a•lo•gram (ĭ-lĕk'trō-ĕn-sĕf'ə-lə-grăm) *n.* A graphic record of the electrical activity of the brain as recorded by the electroencephalograph.

e•lec•tro•en•ceph•a•lo•graph (ĭ-lĕk'trō-ĕn-sĕf'ə-lə-grăf', -gräf') *n.* An instrument that records the electrical activity of the brain. —**e•lec'tro•en•ceph'a•lo•graph'ic** *adj.*

e•lec•trol•y•sis (ĭ-lĕk'trŏl'ə-sĭs, ē'lĕk-) *n.* **1.** Chemical change, esp. decomposition, produced in an electrolyte by an electric current. **2.** Destruction of living tissue, as hair roots, by an electric current.

e•lec•tro•lyte (ĭ-lĕk'trə-līt') *n.* A substance that dissociates into ions in solution or when fused, thereby becoming electrically conducting.

e•lec•tro•lyt•ic (ĭ-lĕk'trə-lĭt'ĭk) *adj.* **1. a.** Pertaining to electrolysis. **b.** Produced by electrolysis. **2.** Pertaining to an electrolyte. —**e•lec'tro•lyt'i•cal•ly** *adv.*

e•lec•tro•mag•net (ĭ-lĕk'trō-măg'nĭt) *n.* A magnet consisting essentially of a soft-iron core wound with a current-carrying coil of insulated wire.

e•lec•tro•mag•net•ism (ĭ-lĕk'trō-măg'nə-tĭz'-əm) *n.* Magnetism arising from electric charge in motion. —**e•lec'tro•mag'net'ic** *adj.*

e•lec•tro•mo•tive (ĭ-lĕk'trō-mō'tĭv) *adj.* Pertaining to or producing electric current.

electromotive force. The energy per unit charge that is converted reversibly from chemical, mechanical, or other forms of energy into electrical energy in a conversion device such as a battery or dynamo.

e•lec•tron (ĭ-lĕk'trŏn') *n.* A subatomic particle having a rest mass of 9.1066×10^{-28} gram and a unit negative electric charge of approx. 1.602×10^{-19} coulomb.

e•lec•tro•neg•a•tive (ĭ-lĕk'trō-nĕg'ə-tĭv) *adj.* **1.** Having a negative electric charge. **2.** Tending to attract electrons to form a chemical bond.

e•lec•tron•ic (ĭ-lĕk'trŏn'ĭk, ē'lĕk-) *adj.* **1.** Pertaining to electrons or electronics. **2.** Based on, operated by, or otherwise involving the controlled conduction of electrons or other charge carriers, esp. in a vacuum, gas, or semiconducting material. —*n.* **electronics** *(takes sing. v.).* **1.** The science and technology of electronic phenomena. **2.** The commercial industry of electronic devices and systems. —**e•lec'tron'i•cal•ly** *adv.*

electron microscope. Any of a class of microscopes that use electrons rather than visible light to produce magnified images.

electron tube. A sealed enclosure, either highly evacuated or containing a controlled quantity of gas, in which electrons can be made sufficiently mobile to act as the principal carriers of current between at least one pair of electrodes.

electron volt. A unit of energy equal to the energy acquired by an electron falling through a potential difference of one volt, approx. 1.602×10^{-19} joule.

e•lec•tro•plate (ĭ-lĕk'trə-plāt') *v.* To coat or cover electrolytically with a thin layer of metal.

e•lec•tro•pos•i•tive (ĭ-lĕk'trō-pŏz'ə-tĭv) *adj.* **1.** Having a positive electric charge. **2.** Tending to release electrons to form a chemical bond.

e•lec•tro•scope (ĭ-lĕk'trə-skōp') *n.* An instrument used to detect the presence, sign, and in some configurations the magnitude of an electric charge by the mutual attraction or repulsion of metal foils or pith balls.

e•lec•tro•stat•ic (ĭ-lĕk'trō-stăt'ĭk) *adj.* **1.** Pertaining to stationary electric charges. **2.** Produced or caused by such charges.

electrostatic generator. Any of various devices, esp. the Van de Graaff generator, that generate high voltages by accumulating large quantities of electric charge.

e•lec•tro•ther•a•py (ĭ-lĕk'trō-thĕr'ə-pē) *n.* Medical therapy using electric currents.

e•lec•tro•type (ĭ-lĕk'trə-tīp') *n.* A duplicate metal plate used in letterpress printing, made by electroplating a lead or plastic mold of the original.

e•lec•tro•va•lence (ĭ-lĕk'trō-vā'ləns) *n.* Also **e•lec•tro•va•len•cy** (-lən-sē). **1.** Valence characterized by the transfer of electrons from atoms of one element to atoms of another. **2.** The number of electric charges lost or gained by an atom in such a transfer. —**e•lec'tro•va'lent** *adj.*

el•e•gance (ĕl'ə-gəns) *n.* **1.** Refinement and grace. **2.** Tasteful opulence, as in design. [< L *ēligere,* to choose out.] —**el'e•gant** *adj.* —**el'e•gant•ly** *adv.*

el•e•gi•ac (ĕl'ə-jī'ək, ĭ-lē'jē-ăk') *adj.* **1.** Of or pertaining to an elegy or elegies. **2.** Expressing sorrow; mournful.

el•e•gy (ĕl'ə-jē) *n., pl.* **-gies.** A mournful poem, esp. one that laments the dead. [< Gk *elegos,* lament.]

el•e•ment (ĕl'ə-mənt) *n.* **1.** A fundamental constituent or principle of something. **2.** *Math.* **a.** A member of a set. **b.** A point, line, or plane. **c.** A part of a geometric configuration, as an angle in a triangle. **3.** *Chem. & Phys.* A substance composed of atoms having an identical number of protons in each nucleus. See *Table of Elements* on following pages. **4. elements.** The forces that collectively constitute the weather. **5.** An environment natural to or preferred by an individual. [< L *elementum,* rudiment, first principle.]

el•e•men•tal (ĕl'ə-mĕnt'l) *adj.* **1.** Of an element. **2.** Fundamental or essential. **3.** Resembling a force of nature in power or effect.

el•e•men•ta•ry (ĕl'ə-mĕn'tə-rē, -trē) *adj.* **1.** Fundamental, essential, or irreducible. **2.** Involving or introducing the fundamental aspects of a subject.

elementary particle. A subatomic particle hypothesized or regarded as an irreducible constituent of matter.

elementary school. A school for the first six to eight years of a child's formal education.

el•e•phant (ĕl'ə-fənt) *n.* A very large Asian or African mammal with a long, flexible trunk and long tusks. [< Gk *elephas (elephant-).*]

el•e•phan•ti•a•sis (ĕl'ə-fən-tī'ə-sĭs) *n.* A chronic, often extreme enlargement and hardening of the cutaneous and subcutaneous tissue, esp. of the legs and scrotum.

el•e•phan•tine (ĕl'ə-făn'tĭn, -tēn', -tīn') *adj.*

1. Of or pertaining to an elephant. 2. Ponderous; clumsy; heavy-footed.

elev. elevation.

el•e•vate (ĕl'ə-vāt') *v.* **-vated, -vating. 1.** To raise to a higher place; lift up. **2.** To promote to a higher rank. **3.** To raise to a higher moral or cultural level. **4.** To lift the spirits of; elate. [< L *ēlevāre.*]

el•e•vat•ed (ĕl'ə-vā'tĭd) *adj.* **1.** Raised above a given level: *an elevated scaffold.* **2.** Exalted; lofty: *elevated praise.* —*n. Informal.* An elevated railway.

elevated railway. A railway that operates on a raised structure in order to permit passage of traffic beneath it.

el•e•va•tion (ĕl'ə-vā'shən) *n.* **1.** The act of elevating or condition of being elevated. **2.** An elevated place or position. **3.** The height to which something is elevated, as above sea level.

el•e•va•tor (ĕl'ə-vā'tər) *n.* **1.** A platform or enclosure raised and lowered to transport freight or people. **2.** A granary with devices for hoisting and discharging grain. **3.** A movable control surface used to make an aircraft go up or down.

e•lev•en (ĭ-lĕv'ən) *n.* The cardinal number written 11 or in Roman numerals XI. [< OE *endleofan.* See **oino-.**] —**e•lev'en** *adj.* & *pron.*

e•lev•enth (ĭ-lĕv'ənth) *n.* **1.** The ordinal number 11 in a series. **2.** One of 11 equal parts. —**e•lev'enth** *adj.* & *adv.*

elf (ĕlf) *n., pl.* **elves** (ĕlvz). A small mischievous fairy. [< OE *ælf.*] —**elf'in** *adj.* —**elf'ish** *adj.* —**elf'ish•ly** *adv.* —**elf'ish•ness** *n.*

El Gre•co (ĕl grĕk'ō, grā'kō). 1548?–1614? Spanish painter born in Crete.

el•hi (ĕl'hī') *adj.* Elementary and high school.

e•lic•it (ĭ-lĭs'ĭt) *v.* **1.** To bring out; draw forth; evoke. **2.** To bring to light. [L *ēlicere.*] —**e•lic'i•ta'tion** *n.* —**e•lic'i•tor** *n.*

e•lide (ĭ-līd') *v.* **elided, eliding. 1.** To omit or slur over, as a vowel or syllable in pronunciation. **2.** To leave out or suppress. [L *ēlīdere,* to strike out.] —**e•li'sion** (-lĭzh'ən) *n.*

el•i•gi•ble (ĕl'ə-jə-bəl) *adj.* Qualified; worthy of choice. [< L *ēligere,* to choose, ELECT.] —**el'i•gi•ble** *n.* —**el'i•gi•bil'i•ty** *n.*

E•li•jah (ĭ-lī'jə). Hebrew prophet of the 9th century B.C.

e•lim•i•nate (ĭ-lĭm'ə-nāt') *v.* **-nated, -nating. 1.** To get rid of; remove. **2.** To leave out or omit from consideration. **3.** To excrete (waste products). [L *ēlīmināre,* "to drive outside of the threshold."] —**e•lim'i•na'tion** *n.* —**e•lim'i•na•to'ry** (-nə-tôr'ē, -tōr'ē) *adj.*

e•lite (ĭ-lēt') *n.* Also **é•lite** (ā-lēt'). **1.** *(takes pl. v.).* The superior members of a given social group. **2.** A narrow and powerful clique. [< OF *eslire,* to choose.]

e•lit•ism (ĭ-lē'tĭz'əm) *n.* Also **é•lit•ism** (ā-lē'tĭz'əm). **1.** Rule or domination by an elite. **2.** Belief in such rule or domination. —**e•lit'ist** *adj.* & *n.*

e•lix•ir (ĭ-lĭk'sər) *n.* A sweetened solution of alcohol and water, containing medicine. [< Ar *al-iksīr.*]

E•liz•a•beth I (ĭ-lĭz'ə-bəth). 1533–1603. Queen of England and Ireland (1558–1603). —**E•liz'a•be'than** (-bē'thən, -bĕth'ən) *adj.*

Elizabeth I

E•liz•a•beth II (ĭ-lĭz'ə-bəth). Born 1926.

PERIODIC TABLE OF THE ELEMENTS

KEY

Atomic Number — 1
H — *Symbol*
Hydrogen
1.00797 — *Atomic Weight (or Mass Number of most stable isotope if in parentheses)*

1a	2a	3b	4b	5b	6b	7b	8	8	8	1b	2b	3a	4a	5a	6a	7a	0
1 H Hydrogen 1.00797																	2 He Helium 4.0026
3 Li Lithium 6.939	4 Be Beryllium 9.0122											5 B Boron 10.811	6 C Carbon 12.01115	7 N Nitrogen 14.0067	8 O Oxygen 15.9994	9 F Fluorine 18.9984	10 Ne Neon 20.183
11 Na Sodium 22.9898	12 Mg Magnesium 24.312											13 Al Aluminum 26.9815	14 Si Silicon 28.086	15 P Phosphorus 30.9738	16 S Sulfur 32.064	17 Cl Chlorine 35.453	18 Ar Argon 39.948
19 K Potassium 39.102	20 Ca Calcium 40.08	21 Sc Scandium 44.956	22 Ti Titanium 47.90	23 V Vanadium 50.942	24 Cr Chromium 51.996	25 Mn Manganese 54.9380	26 Fe Iron 55.847	27 Co Cobalt 58.9332	28 Ni Nickel 58.71	29 Cu Copper 63.546	30 Zn Zinc 65.37	31 Ga Gallium 69.72	32 Ge Germanium 72.59	33 As Arsenic 74.9216	34 Se Selenium 78.96	35 Br Bromine 79.904	36 Kr Krypton 83.80
37 Rb Rubidium 85.47	38 Sr Strontium 87.62	39 Y Yttrium 88.905	40 Zr Zirconium 91.22	41 Nb Niobium 92.906	42 Mo Molybdenum 95.94	43 Tc Technetium (97)	44 Ru Ruthenium 101.07	45 Rh Rhodium 102.905	46 Pd Palladium 106.4	47 Ag Silver 107.868	48 Cd Cadmium 112.40	49 In Indium 114.82	50 Sn Tin 118.69	51 Sb Antimony 121.75	52 Te Tellurium 127.60	53 I Iodine 126.9044	54 Xe Xenon 131.30
55 Cs Cesium 132.905	56 Ba Barium 137.34	57–71* Lanthanides	72 Hf Hafnium 178.49	73 Ta Tantalum 180.948	74 W Tungsten 183.85	75 Re Rhenium 186.2	76 Os Osmium 190.2	77 Ir Iridium 192.2	78 Pt Platinum 195.09	79 Au Gold 196.967	80 Hg Mercury 200.59	81 Tl Thallium 204.37	82 Pb Lead 207.19	83 Bi Bismuth 208.980	84 Po Polonium (210)	85 At Astatine (210)	86 Rn Radon (222)
87 Fr Francium (223)	88 Ra Radium (226)	89–103** **Actinides															

**Lanthanides*	57 La Lanthanum 138.91	58 Ce Cerium 140.12	59 Pr Praseodymium 140.907	60 Nd Neodymium 144.24	61 Pm Promethium (145)	62 Sm Samarium 150.35	63 Eu Europium 151.96	64 Gd Gadolinium 157.25	65 Tb Terbium 158.924	66 Dy Dysprosium 162.50	67 Ho Holmium 164.930	68 Er Erbium 167.26	69 Tm Thulium 168.934	70 Yb Ytterbium 173.04	71 Lu Lutetium 174.97
***Actinides*	89 Ac Actinium (227)	90 Th Thorium 232.038	91 Pa Protactinium (231)	92 U Uranium 238.03	93 Np Neptunium (237)	94 Pu Plutonium (244)	95 Am Americium (243)	96 Cm Curium (247)	97 Bk Berkelium (247)	98 Cf Californium (251)	99 Es Einsteinium (254)	100 Fm Fermium (257)	101 Md Mendelevium (256)	102 No Nobelium (254)	103 Lw Lawrencium (257)

Queen of Great Britain and Northern Ireland (since 1952).

elk (ĕlk) *n., pl.* **elks** or **elk.** Either of two large deer, the wapiti or the European moose. [< ON *elgr.*]

ell (ĕl) *n.* A wing of a building at right angles to the main structure.

el•lipse (ĭ-lĭps′) *n.* A plane curve formed by the locus of points the sum of the distances of each of which from two fixed points is the same constant. [Back-formation < ELLIPSIS.]

el•lip•sis (ĭ-lĭp′sĭs) *n., pl.* **-ses** (-sēz′). **1.** The omission of a word or words not necessary for the comprehension of a sentence, as *Stop laughing* for *You stop laughing.* **2.** Marks (... or ***) used to indicate an omission. [< Gk *elleipsis,* a falling short.]

el•lip•soid (ĭ-lĭp′soid′) *n.* A geometric surface whose plane sections are all either ellipses or circles. **—el′lip•soi′dal** *adj.*

el•lip•tic (ĭ-lĭp′tĭk) *adj.* Also **el•lip•ti•cal** (-tĭ-kəl). **1. a.** Pertaining to or having the shape of an ellipse. **b.** Resembling an ellipse. **2.** *Gram.* Containing or characterized by ellipsis. **—el•lip′ti•cal•ly** *adv.*

elm (ĕlm) *n.* A shade tree with arching or curving branches. [< OE. See **el-**[2].]

el•o•cu•tion (ĕl′ə-kyōō′shən) *n.* The art of public speaking. [< L *ēloquī,* to speak out.] **—el′o•cu′tion•ist** *n.*

e•lon•gate (ĭ-lông′gāt′, ĭ-lŏng′-) *v.* **-gated, -gating.** To lengthen; grow in length. **—e•lon′ga′tion** *n.*

e•lope (ĭ-lōp′) *v.* **eloped, eloping.** To run away with a lover, esp. to get married. [< ME **alepen,* to run away.] **—e•lope′ment** *n.*

el•o•quent (ĕl′ə-kwənt) *adj.* Persuasive and fluent in discourse. [< L *ēloquī,* to speak out.] **—el′o•quence** *n.* **—el′o•quent•ly** *adv.*

El Pas•o (ĕl păs′ō). A city of SW Texas. Pop. 277,000.

El Sal•va•dor (ĕl săl′və-dôr′). A republic of Central America. Pop. 2,859,000. Cap. San Salvador.

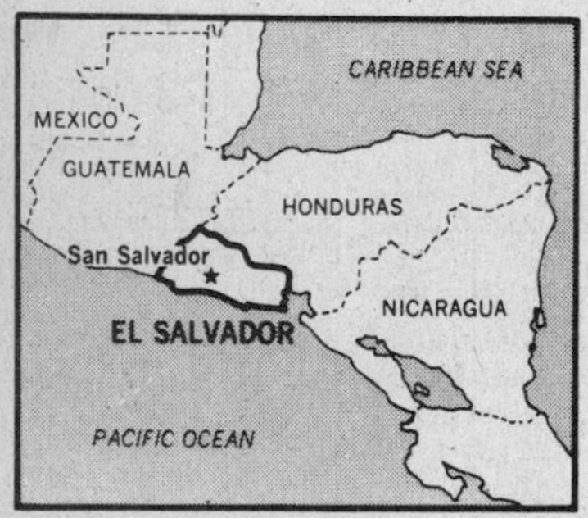

El Salvador

else (ĕls) *adj.* **1.** Other; different: *somebody else.* **2.** In addition; additional; more: *Would you like anything else?* *—adv.* **1.** In a different time, place, or manner; differently: *How else could it be done?* **2.** If not; otherwise: *Be careful, else you will make a mistake.* [< OE *elles,* otherwise, else. See **al-**[1].]

Usage: The possessive forms of combinations employing *else* are now usually written *anyone* (or *anybody*) *else's, everyone* (or *everybody*) *else's, no one* (or *nobody*) *else's, someone* (or *somebody*) *else's.* Both *who else's* (followed by a noun) and *whose else* are used but not *whose else's.*

else•where (ĕls′hwâr′) *adv.* Somewhere or anywhere else.

e•lu•ci•date (ĭ-lōō′sə-dāt′) *v.* **-dated, -dating.** To make clear or plain; clarify. [LL *ēlūcidāre.*] **—e•lu′ci•da′tion** *n.* **—e•lu′ci•da′tor** *n.*

e•lude (ĭ-lōōd′) *v.* **eluded, eluding. 1.** To avoid or escape from; evade. **2.** To escape understanding or detection by; baffle. [L *ēlūdere,* "to take away from at play."]

e•lu•sive (ĭ-lōō′sĭv) *adj.* Tending to elude grasp, perception, or mental retention. **—e•lu′sive•ly** *adv.* **—e•lu′sive•ness** *n.*

el•ver (ĕl′vər) *n.* A young or immature eel.

elves. *pl.* of **elf.**

E•ly•si•um (ĭ-lĭzh′ē-əm, ĭ-lĭz′-) *n.* **1.** *Gk. Myth.* The abode of the blessed after death. **2.** A place or condition of ideal happiness. **—E•ly′sian** (-lĭzh′ən, -ē-ən) *adj.*

'em (əm) *pron. Informal.* Them.

em-[1]. Variant of **en-**[1] (put into).

em-[2]. Variant of **en-**[2] (into).

EM enlisted man.

e•ma•ci•ate (ĭ-mā′shē-āt′) *v.* **-ated, -ating.** To make thin, as by starvation or illness. [L *ēmaciāre.*] **—e•ma′ci•a′tion** *n.*

em•a•nate (ĕm′ə-nāt′) *v.* **-nated, -nating.** To come forth, as from a source; issue; originate. [L *ēmānāre,* flow out.] **—em′a•na′tion** *n.* **—em′a•na′tive** *adj.*

e•man•ci•pate (ĭ-măn′sə-pāt′) *v.* **-pated, -pating. 1.** To free from oppression or bondage. **2.** To free from any restraint. [L *ēmancipāre,* "to release from slavery or tutelage."] **—e•man′ci•pa′tion** *n.* **—e•man′ci•pa′tor** *n.*

e•mas•cu•late (ĭ-măs′kyə-lāt′) *v.* **-lated, -lating. 1.** To castrate. **2.** To make weak. **—e•mas′cu•la′tion** *n.* **—e•mas′cu•la′tor** *n.*

em•balm (ĕm-bäm′, ĭm-) *v.* To prevent the decay of (a corpse) by treatment with preservatives. **—em•balm′er** *n.*

em•bank (ĕm-băngk′, ĭm-) *v.* To confine, support, or protect with a bank or banks. **—em•bank′ment** *n.*

em•bar•go (ĕm-bär′gō, ĭm-) *n., pl.* **-goes. 1.** A government order prohibiting the movement of merchant ships into or out of its ports. **2.** Any prohibition. *—v.* To impose an embargo upon. [< VL **imbarricāre,* "to place behind bars."]

em•bark (ĕm-bärk′, ĭm-) *v.* **1.** To board or cause to board a vessel, esp. at the start of a journey. **2.** To set out on a venture; commence. [< LL *imbarcāre.*] **—em′bar•ka′tion, em•bark′ment** *n.*

em•bar•rass (ĕm-băr′əs, ĭm-) *v.* **1.** To cause to feel ill at ease. **2.** To hamper with financial difficulties. **3.** To impede. [< It *imbarrare,* "to put in bars," impede.] **—em•bar′rass•ing•ly** *adv.* **—em•bar′rass•ment** *n.*

em•bas•sy (ĕm′bə-sē) *n., pl.* **-sies. 1.** The position of an ambassador. **2.** A mission to a foreign government. **3.** An ambassador and his staff. **4.** The headquarters of an ambassador. [< OProv *ambaissada.*]

em•bat•tle (ĕm-băt′l, ĭm-) *v.* **-tled, -tling.** To prepare or array for battle.

em•bed (ĕm-bĕd′, ĭm-) *v.* **-bedded, -bedding.** Also **im•bed** (ĭm-). To fix or become fixed firmly in a surrounding mass.

em•bel•lish (ĕm-bĕl′ĭsh, ĭm-) *v.* **1.** To make more beautiful; adorn. **2.** To add fictitious details to (a statement). [< OF *embellir.*] **—em•bel′lish•ment** *n.*

em•ber (ĕm′bər) *n.* **1.** A piece of live coal or wood, as in a fire. **2. embers.** The smoldering remains of a fire. [< OE *æmerge,* embers, ashes.]

em•bez•zle (ĕm-bĕz′əl, ĭm-) *v.* **-zled, -zling.** To take (money or property) for one's own use in breach of trust. [< NF *enbesiler.*] **—em•bez′zle•ment** *n.* **—em•bez′zler** *n.*

em•bit•ter (ĕm-bĭt′ər, ĭm-) *v.* **1.** To make bitter. **2.** To arouse bitter feelings in. **—em•bit′ter•ment** *n.*

em•blaze (ĕm-blāz′, ĭm-) *v.* **-blazed, -blazing. 1.** To set on fire. **2.** To cause to glow or glitter.

em•bla•zon (ĕm-blā′zən, ĭm-) *v.* **1.** To ornament richly, esp. with heraldic devices. **2.** To make resplendent with colors. **3.** To exalt. **—em•bla′zon•ment** *n.*

em•blem (ĕm′bləm) *n.* **1.** An object or picture that comes to represent something else; a symbol. **2.** A distinctive badge, design, etc. [< Gk *emballein,* to throw in, insert.] **—em′blem•at′ic** (-blə-măt′ĭk) *adj.*

em•bod•y (ĕm-bŏd′ē, ĭm-) *v.* **-ied, -ying. 1.** To invest with or as with bodily form; make corporeal. **2.** To personify. **3.** To make part of a united whole. **—em•bod′i•ment** *n.*

em•bold•en (ĕm-bōl′dən, ĭm-) *v.* To foster boldness in; encourage.

em•bo•lism (ĕm′bə-lĭz′əm) *n.* Obstruction or occlusion of a blood vessel by an air bubble, detached clot, bacterial mass, or other foreign body. [< Gk *emballein,* "to throw in," insert.] **—em•bol′ic** (ĕm-bŏl′ĭk, ĭm-) *adj.*

em•boss (ĕm-bôs′, -bŏs′, ĭm-) *v.* **1.** To represent (a design) in relief. **2.** To cover with or as with a raised design. [< OF *embocer,* "to put a knob in."] **—em•boss′er** *n.*

em•bow•er (ĕm-bou′ər, ĭm-) *v.* To enclose in a bower.

em•brace (ĕm-brās′, ĭm-) *v.* **-braced, -bracing. 1.** To clasp in or hold with the arms, usually in affection; hug. **2.** To encircle. **3.** To include. **4.** To take up; adopt, as a cause. **5.** To accept eagerly. *—n.* An act of embracing; an affectionate hug. [< VL **imbracchiāre.*]

em•bra•sure (ĕm-brā′zhər, ĭm-) *n.* **1.** A window or door recess. **2.** An opening for a gun in a wall or parapet.

em•broi•der (ĕm-broi′dər, ĭm-) *v.* **1.** To ornament (fabric) with needlework; make embroidery. **2.** To embellish (a narrative). [< NF *enbrouder.*]

em•broi•der•y (ĕm-broi′də-rē, ĭm-) *n., pl.* **-ies. 1.** The art or act of embroidering. **2.** A piece of embroidered fabric. **3.** An embellishment.

em•broil (ĕm-broil′, ĭm-) *v.* **1.** To involve in argument or hostile actions. **2.** To throw into disorder; entangle. **—em•broil′ment** *n.*

em•bry•o (ĕm′brē-ō′) *n., pl.* **-os. 1.** An organism in its earliest stages of development, as before birth or hatching. **2.** A rudimentary or beginning stage. *—adj.* Incipient; rudimentary. [< Gk *embroun,* "something that grows in the body."] **—em′bry•on′ic** (-ŏn′ĭk) *adj.*

em•bry•ol•o•gy (ĕm′brē-ŏl′ə-jē) *n.* The science of the formation, early growth, and development of living organisms. **—em′bry•o•log′ic** (-ə-lŏj′ĭk), **em′bry•o•log′i•cal** *adj.* **—em′bry•o•log′i•cal•ly** *adv.* **—em′bry•ol′o•gist** *n.*

em•cee (ĕm′sē′) *n. Informal.* A master of ceremonies. [Short for M(ASTER OF) C(EREMONIES).] **—em′cee′** *v.* **(-ceed, -ceeing).**

e•meer. Variant of **emir.**

e•mend (ĭ-mĕnd′) *v.* To improve (a text) by critical editing. [< L *ēmendāre.*] **—e•men′da′tion** *n.*

em•er•ald (ĕm′ər-əld, ĕm′rəld) *n.* **1.** A brilliant, transparent green beryl used as a gemstone. **2.** Strong yellowish green. [< OF *esmeraude.*] **—em′er•ald** *adj.*

e•merge (ĭ-mûrj′) *v.* **emerged, emerging. 1.** To rise up or come forth from or as from im-

mersion; come into sight. 2. To become obvious. 3. To come into existence. [L *ēmergere.*] —**e•mer'gence** *n.* —**e•mer'gent** *adj.*
e•mer•gen•cy (ĭ-mûr'jən-sē) *n., pl.* **-cies.** A sudden, unexpected occurrence demanding immediate action.
e•mer•i•tus (ĭ-mĕr'ə-təs) *adj.* Retired but retaining an honorary title: *a professor emeritus.* [< L *ēmerēri,* to earn by service.]
Em•er•son (ĕm'ər-sən), **Ralph Waldo.** 1803–1882. American essayist and poet.
em•er•y (ĕm'ə-rē, ĕm'rē) *n.* A fine-grained impure corundum used for grinding and polishing. [< Gk *smuris,* emery powder.]
e•met•ic (ĭ-mĕt'ĭk) *adj.* Causing vomiting. —*n.* An emetic agent or medicine. [< Gk *emein,* to vomit.] —**e•met'i•cal•ly** *adv.*
e•meu. Variant of **emu.**
emf, EMF electromotive force.
–emia, –hemia. *comb. form.* Blood: **leukemia.** [< Gk *haima,* blood.]
em•i•grate (ĕm'ĭ-grāt') *v.* **-grated, -grating.** To leave one country or region to settle in another. [L *ēmigrāre,* to move away from.] —**em'i•grant** (-grənt) *n.* —**em'i•gra'tion** *n.*
é•mi•gré (ĕm'ĭ-grā') *n.* An emigrant, esp. a refugee from a revolution.
em•i•nence (ĕm'ə-nəns) *n.* 1. A position of superiority in achievement, position, etc. 2. A rise of ground; hill.
em•i•nent (ĕm'ə-nənt) *adj.* 1. Towering above others; projecting. 2. Distinguished, as in reputation. [< L *ēminēre,* to stand out.] —**em'i•nent•ly** *adv.*
e•mir (ĕ-mîr') *n.* Also **e•meer.** A prince, chieftain, or governor, esp. in Arabia. [< Ar *'amīr,* commander.]
em•is•sar•y (ĕm'ə-sĕr'ē) *n., pl.* **-ies.** A messenger or agent. [< L *ēmittere,* to send out, EMIT.]
e•mit (ĭ-mĭt') *v.* **emitted, emitting.** 1. To release or send forth, as radiation. 2. To utter or express. 3. To issue with authority, esp. currency or shares of stock. [L *ēmittere,* to send out.] —**e•mis'sion** *n.* —**e•mit'ter** *n.*
e•mol•lient (ĭ-mŏl'yənt, -ē-ənt) *adj.* Having softening and soothing qualities, esp. for the skin. [< L *ēmollīre,* to soften, soothe.] —**e•mol'lient** *n.*
e•mol•u•ment (ĭ-mŏl'yə-mənt) *n.* Profit derived from one's office or employment. [< L *ēmolumentum,* orig "miller's fee for grinding grain."]
e•mote (ĭ-mōt') *v.* **emoted, emoting.** *Informal.* To express emotion or sentiment in an effusive and theatrical manner. [Back-formation < EMOTION.]
e•mo•tion (ĭ-mō'shən) *n.* 1. Agitation of the passions or sensibilities. 2. Any strong subjective feeling, as of joy, sorrow, reverence, hate, or love. [< L *ēmovēre,* to move out, stir up, excite.] —**e•mo'tion•al** *adj.* —**e•mo'tion•al•ism'** *n.* —**e•mo'tion•al•ly** *adv.*
em•pa•thy (ĕm'pə-thē) *n.* Understanding so intimate that the feelings, thoughts, and motives of one are readily comprehended by another. —**em'pa•thize'** *v.* **(-thized, -thizing).**
em•per•or (ĕm'pər-ər) *n.* The ruler of an empire. [< L *imperātor,* emperor, commander.]
em•pha•sis (ĕm'fə-sĭs) *n., pl.* **-ses** (sēz'). 1. Special importance placed upon or imparted to something. 2. Stress given to a syllable, word, or phrase. [< Gk *emphainein,* to exhibit, indicate.]
em•pha•size (ĕm'fə-sīz') *v.* **-sized, -sizing.** To give emphasis to; stress.
em•phat•ic (ĕm-făt'ĭk) *adj.* 1. Expressed or performed with emphasis. 2. Bold and definite. —**em•phat'i•cal•ly** *adv.*
em•phy•se•ma (ĕm'fə-sē'mə) *n.* A pathological condition of the lungs marked by labored breathing and increased susceptibility to infection. [< Gk *emphusan,* to blow in.]
em•pire (ĕm'pīr') *n.* 1. A political unit, usually larger than a kingdom and often comprising a number of territories or nations, ruled by a single authority. 2. Imperial rule. 3. An extensive enterprise. [< L *imperium,* dominion, empire.]
em•pir•i•cal (ĕm-pîr'ĭ-kəl, ĭm-) *adj.* 1. Relying on observation or experiment. 2. Guided by experience rather than theory. [< Gk *empeira,* experience.] —**em•pir'i•cal•ly** *adv.*
em•pir•i•cism (ĕm-pîr'ə-sĭz'əm, ĭm-) *n.* 1. The view that experience, esp. of the senses, is the only source of knowledge. 2. The employment of empirical methods, as in science. —**em•pir'i•cist** *n.*
em•place•ment (ĕm-plās'mənt, ĭm-) *n.* A prepared position for guns within a fortification.
em•ploy (ĕm-ploi', ĭm-) *v.* 1. To use; put to service. 2. To devote or apply (one's time or energies) to some activity. 3. To engage the services of; provide with a job. —*n.* Employment. [< L *implicāre,* to infold, involve.]
em•ploy•ee (ĕm-ploi'ē, ĭm-, ĕm'ploi-ē') *n.* A person who works for another in return for financial compensation.
em•ploy•er (ĕm-ploi'ər, ĭm-) *n.* A person or concern that employs persons for wages or salary.
em•ploy•ment (ĕm-ploi'mənt, ĭm-) *n.* 1. The act of employing or state of being employed. 2. An occupation or activity.
em•po•ri•um (ĕm-pôr'ē-əm, ĕm-pōr'-, ĭm-) *n., pl.* **-ums** or **-poria** (-pôr'ē-ə, -pōr'ē-ə). A store carrying a wide variety of merchandise. [< Gk *emporos,* merchant, traveler.]
em•pow•er (ĕm-pou'ər, ĭm-) *v.* 1. To invest with legal power; authorize. 2. To enable or permit.
em•press (ĕm'prĭs) *n.* 1. A female sovereign of an empire. 2. The wife or widow of an emperor.
emp•ty (ĕmp'tē) *adj.* **-tier, -tiest.** 1. Void of content; containing nothing. 2. Having no occupants or inhabitants; vacant. 3. Lacking purpose or substance; meaningless. —*v.* **-tied, -tying.** 1. To remove the contents of; make or become empty. 2. To discharge or flow into: *The river empties into a bay.* [< OE *ǣmtig* < *ǣmetta,* rest, leisure.] —**emp'ti•ness** *n.*
emp•ty-hand•ed (ĕmp'tē-hăn'dĭd) *adj.* 1. Bearing no gifts or possessions. 2. Having gained nothing.
em•py•re•an (ĕm'pī-rē'ən) *n.* 1. The highest reaches of heaven. 2. The sky; firmament. [< Gk *empuros,* fiery.]
e•mu (ē'myōō) *n.* Also **e•meu.** A large, ostrich-like Australian bird. [Port *ema.*]
em•u•late (ĕm'yə-lāt') *v.* **-lated, -lating.** To strive to equal or excel, esp. through imitation. [< L *aemulus,* imitating.] —**em'u•la'tion** *n.*
e•mul•si•fy (ĭ-mŭl'sə-fī') *v.* **-fied, -fying.** To make into an emulsion. —**e•mul'si•fi•ca'tion** *n.* —**e•mul'si•fi'er** *n.*
e•mul•sion (ĭ-mŭl'shən) *n.* 1. A suspension of small globules of one liquid in a second liquid with which the first will not mix, such as milk fats in milk. 2. A light-sensitive coating, usually of silver halide grains in a thin gelatin layer, on photographic film, paper, or glass. [< L *ēmulgēre,* to drain out, milk out.]
en–¹. Also **em-.** *comb. form.* 1. Used to form verbs from nouns: a. To put or go into or on. b. To cover or imbue with. c. To provide with. 2. Used to form verbs from nouns and adjectives to indicate causing to become or resemble. [< L *in-, im-.*]
en–². Also **em-.** *comb. form.* Used to form nouns and adjectives to indicate in, into, or within. [< Gk.]
–en¹. *comb. form.* 1. Used to form verbs from adjectives to indicate being, becoming, or causing to be: **redden.** 2. Used to form verbs from nouns to indicate causing to have or gain: **lengthen.** [< OE *-nian.*]
–en². *comb. form.* Used to form adjectives from nouns to indicate made of, composed of, or resembling: **earthen.** [< OE.]
en•a•ble (ĕn-ā'bəl) *v.* **-bled, -bling.** To supply with the means, knowledge, or opportunity to do something; make possible.
en•act (ĕn-ăkt') *v.* 1. To pass (a bill); decree by legislative process. 2. To act out as on a stage. —**en•act'ment** *n.* —**en•ac'tor** *n.*
en•am•el (ĭ-năm'əl) *n.* 1. A vitreous, usually opaque coating baked on metal, ceramic ware, etc. 2. A paint that dries to a hard, glossy surface. 3. The hard substance covering the exposed portion of a tooth. —*v.* **-eled** or **-elled, -eling** or **-elling.** To coat or decorate with enamel. [< NF *enameler.*]
en•am•el•ware (ĭ-năm'əl-wâr') *n.* Metal utensils coated with enamel.
en•am•or (ĭ-năm'ər) *v.* Also *chiefly Brit.* **en•am•our.** To inspire with love; captivate. [< L *amāre,* to love.]
enc. enclosed; enclosure.
en•camp (ĕn-kămp', ĭn-) *v.* To set up or live in a camp. —**en•camp'ment** *n.*
en•cap•su•late (ĕn-kăp'sə-lāt', ĭn-) *v.* **-lated, -lating.** Also **in•cap•su•late** (ĭn-). To encase in or as in a capsule. —**en•cap'su•la'tion** *n.*
en•case (ĕn-kās', ĭn-) *v.* **-cased, -casing.** Also **in•case** (ĭn-). To enclose in or as in a case.
–ence, –ency. *comb. form.* Used to form nouns from adjectives ending in *-ent* to indicate action, state, quality, or condition: **reference.** [< L *-entia.*]
en•ce•phal•ic (ĕn'sə-făl'ĭk) *adj.* Pertaining to the brain.
en•ceph•a•li•tis (ĕn-sĕf'ə-lī'tĭs, ĕn'sĕf-) *n.* Inflammation of the brain. —**en•ceph'a•lit'ic** (-lĭt'ĭk) *adj.*
encephalo–. *comb. form.* The brain. [< Gk *(muelos) enkephalos,* "(marrow) in the head," the brain.]
en•ceph•a•lo•gram (ĕn-sĕf'ə-lō-grăm') *n.* 1. An x-ray picture of the brain. 2. An electroencephalogram.
en•ceph•a•lon (ĕn-sĕf'ə-lŏn') *n., pl.* **-la** (-lə). The brain of a vertebrate.
en•chain (ĕn-chān', ĭn-) *v.* To bind with or as with chains; fetter. —**en•chain'ment** *n.*
en•chant (ĕn-chănt', -chänt', ĭn-) *v.* 1. To cast under a spell; bewitch. 2. To delight completely; enrapture. [< L *incantāre.*] —**en•chant'er** *n.* —**en•chant'ment** *n.*
en•ci•pher (ĕn-sī'fər, ĭn-) *v.* To put (a message) into cipher.
en•cir•cle (ĕn-sûr'kəl, ĭn-) *v.* **-cled, -cling.** 1. To surround. 2. To move or go around. —**en•cir'cle•ment** *n.*
encl. enclosed; enclosure.
en•clave (ĕn'klāv', än'-) *n.* A country or part of a country lying wholly within the boundaries of another. [< VL **inclāvāre,* to lock in with a key.]
en•close (ĕn-klōz', ĭn-) *v.* **-closed, -closing.** Also **in•close** (ĭn-). 1. To surround on all sides; fence in. 2. To insert in the same container

with a letter or package. —**en•clo'sure** *n.*

en•code (ĕn-kōd', ĭn-) *v.* **-coded, -coding.** To put (a message) into code. —**en•cod'er** *n.*

en•co•mi•um (ĕn-kō'mē-əm) *n., pl.* **-ums** or **-mia** (-mē-ə). Lofty praise; a eulogy. [< Gk *enkōmion (epos),* "(speech) in praise of a conqueror."]

en•com•pass (ĕn-kŭm'pəs, ĭn-) *v.* **1.** To surround. **2.** To envelop. **3.** To include; contain.

en•core (äng'kôr', -kōr', än'-) *n.* **1.** A demand by an audience for an additional performance. **2.** A performance in response to such a demand. [F, still, yet, again.]

en•coun•ter (ĕn-koun'tər, ĭn-) *n.* **1.** A meeting, esp. when unplanned. **2.** A hostile confrontation. —*v.* **1.** To meet, esp. unexpectedly. **2.** To confront in battle. [< OF *encontrer,* to meet.]

en•cour•age (ĕn-kûr'ĭj, ĭn-) *v.* **-aged, -aging.** **1.** To impart courage or confidence to. **2.** To give support to; foster. —**en•cour'age•ment** *n.* —**en•cour'ag•er** *n.*

en•croach (ĕn-krōch', ĭn-) *v.* To intrude gradually on the possessions or rights of another; trespass. [< OF *encrochier,* "to catch in a hook."] —**en•croach'ment** *n.*

en•crust (ĕn-krŭst', ĭn-) *v.* Also **in•crust** (ĭn-). To cover or surmount with a crust. —**en'crust•a'tion** *n.*

en•cum•ber (ĕn-kŭm'bər, ĭn-) *v.* **1.** To weigh down unduly; handicap. **2.** To hinder; impede. [< OF *encombrer,* to block up.] —**en•cum'brance** (-brəns) *n.*

ency., encyc. encyclopedia.

en•cyc•li•cal (ĕn-sĭk'lĭ-kəl, ĭn-) *n. R.C.Ch.* A papal letter on a grave or timely subject. [< Gk *enkuklios,* circular.]

en•cy•clo•pe•di•a (ĕn-sī'klə-pē'dē-ə, ĭn-) *n.* Also **en•cy•clo•pae•di•a.** A reference work with articles on many subjects or numerous aspects of a particular field. [< Gk *enkuklios paideia,* general education.] —**en•cy'clo•pe'dic, en•cy'clo•pae'dic** *adj.* —**en•cy'clo•pe'di•cal•ly** *adv.*

end (ĕnd) *n.* **1.** An extremity; tip. **2.** A boundary; limit. **3.** The point at which something ceases or is completed; conclusion. **4.** A result; outcome. **5.** Death. **6.** A purpose; goal. **7.** A share of a responsibility: *your end of the bargain.* **8.** *Football.* Either of the players in the outermost position at the line of scrimmage. —**make (both) ends meet.** To manage to live within one's means. —**no end.** *Informal.* A great deal: *no end of trouble.* —*v.* **1.** To bring or come to an end. **2.** To be at or form the end of. [< OE *ende.* See **anti.**]

en•dan•ger (ĕn-dān'jər, ĭn-) *v.* To expose to danger; imperil. —**en•dan'ger•ment** *n.*

endangered species. A species in danger of extinction.

en•dear (ĕn-dîr', ĭn-) *v.* To cause to be held dear; make beloved.

en•dear•ment (ĕn-dîr'mənt, ĭn-) *n.* An expression of affection.

en•deav•or (ĕn-dĕv'ər, ĭn-). Also *chiefly Brit.* **en•deav•our.** *v.* To make an earnest attempt; strive. [< ME *putten in dever,* to put in duty.] —**en•deav'or** *n.*

en•dem•ic (ĕn-dĕm'ĭk) *adj.* Prevalent in or peculiar to a particular locality or people. [< Gk *endēmios,* dwelling in a place.]

en•dive (ĕn'dīv', än'dēv') *n.* **1.** A plant with crisp, succulent leaves used in salads. **2.** A related plant with a narrow, pointed cluster of whitish leaves. [< Gk *entubioi,* chicory.]

end•less (ĕnd'lĭs) *adj.* **1.** Having no end; infinite. **2.** Formed with the ends joined; continuous. —**end'less•ly** *adv.* —**end'less•ness** *n.*

end•most (ĕnd'mōst') *adj.* Being at or closest to the end.

endo–. *comb. form.* Inside or within. [< Gk *endon,* within.]

en•do•crine (ĕn'də-krĭn, -krēn', -krīn') *adj.* **1.** Secreting internally. **2.** Pertaining to any of the endocrine glands.

endocrine gland. Any of the ductless glands, such as the thyroid or adrenal, the secretions of which pass directly into the blood stream from the cells of the gland.

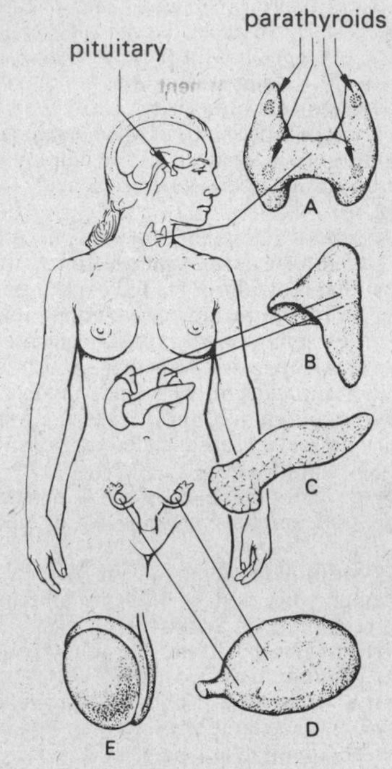

endocrine gland
A. Thyroid
B. Adrenal gland
C. Islands of Langerhans in pancreas
D. Ovary (in female)
E. Testis (in male)

en•do•me•tri•um (ĕn'dō-mē'trē-əm) *n., pl.* **-tria** (-trē-ə). The mucous membrane lining the uterus.

en•do•plasm (ĕn'dō-plăz'əm) *n.* A low-viscosity portion of the continuous phase of cytoplasm distinguishable within some cells. —**en'do•plas'mic** *adj.*

end organ. The expanded functional termination of a sensory nerve or a motor nerve in tissue.

en•dorse (ĕn-dôrs', ĭn-) *v.* **-dorsed, -dorsing.** Also **in•dorse** (ĭn-). **1.** To write one's signature on the back of (a check, stock certificate, etc.) in return for the cash or credit indicated on its face. **2.** To give approval of; sanction. [< OF *endosser,* "to put on the back of."] —**en•dorse'ment** *n.* —**en•dors'er, en•dors'or** *n.*

en•do•the•li•um (ĕn'dō-thē'lē-əm) *n., pl.* **-lia** (-lē-ə). A thin layer of flat cells that lines serous cavities, lymph vessels, and blood vessels. —**en'do•the'li•al** *adj.*

en•do•ther•mic (ĕn'dō-thûr'mĭk) *adj.* Absorbing heat.

en•dow (ĕn-dou', ĭn-) *v.* **1.** To provide with property or income. **2.** To equip with a talent or quality. [< NF *endouer.*] —**en•dow'ment** *n.*

end•plate (ĕnd'plāt') *n.* A terminal that transmits nerve impulses to a muscle.

en•due (ĕn-d/y/ōō', ĭn-) *v.* **-dued, -duing.** Also **in•due** (ĭn-). To provide with some quality or trait. [< L *indūcere,* INDUCE, and *induere,* to don.]

en•dur•a•ble (ĕn-d/y/ŏŏr'ə-bəl, ĭn-) *adj.* Capable of being endured; bearable; tolerable.

en•dur•ance (ĕn-d/y/ŏŏr'əns, ĭn-) *n.* **1.** The power to withstand hardship or stress. **2.** The state or fact of persevering.

en•dure (ĕn-d/y/ŏŏr', ĭn-) *v.* **-dured, -during.** **1.** To bear with tolerance; put up with. **2.** To continue in existence; last. [< LL *indūrāre,* "to harden one's heart against."]

en•dur•ing (ĕn-d/y/ŏŏr'ĭng, ĭn-) *adj.* Lasting; durable.

end•wise (ĕnd'wīz') *adv.* Also **end•ways** (-wāz'). **1.** On end. **2.** With the end foremost. **3.** Lengthwise.

–ene. *comb. form. Chem.* Unsaturation of an organic compound, esp. one having a double bond: **ethylene.** [< Gk *-ēnē.*]

en•e•ma (ĕn'ə-mə) *n.* The injection of liquid into the rectum for laxative or other therapeutic purposes. [< Gk *enienai,* to throw in, inject.]

en•e•my (ĕn'ə-mē) *n., pl.* **-mies.** **1.** One who manifests hostility toward another; a foe; an opponent. **2.** A hostile power, as a nation. [< L *inimīcus.*]

en•er•get•ic (ĕn'ər-jĕt'ĭk) *adj.* Possessing, exerting, or displaying energy; vigorous. —**en'er•get'i•cal•ly** *adv.*

en•er•get•ics (ĕn'ər-jĕt'ĭks) *n. (takes sing. v.).* The physics of energy and its transformations.

en•er•gize (ĕn'ər-jīz') *v.* **-gized, -gizing.** To give energy to. —**en'er•giz'er** *n.*

en•er•gy (ĕn'ər-jē) *n., pl.* **-gies.** **1.** Vigor or power in action. **2.** Capacity for action or accomplishment. **3.** *Phys.* The work that a physical system is capable of doing in changing from its actual state to a specified reference state, the total including, in general, contributions of potential energy, kinetic energy, and rest energy. [< Gk *energos,* active, at work.]

en•er•vate (ĕn'ər-vāt') *v.* **-vated, -vating.** To deprive of strength or vitality; weaken. [L *ēnervāre,* "to remove the sinews from."] —**en'er•va'tion** *n.* —**en'er•va'tor** *n.*

en•fee•ble (ĕn-fē'bəl, ĭn-) *v.* **-bled, -bling.** To make feeble. —**en•fee'ble•ment** *n.*

en•fi•lade (ĕn'fə-lād') *n.* Gunfire that sweeps the length of a target, such as a column of troops. [< F *enfiler,* to thread.]

en•fold (ĕn-fōld', ĭn-) *v.* Also **in•fold** (ĭn-). **1.** To cover with or as if with folds; envelop. **2.** To embrace. —**en•fold'er** *n.*

en•force (ĕn-fôrs', -fōrs', ĭn-) *v.* **-forced, -forcing.** **1.** To compel obedience to. **2.** To impose (specified action or behavior); compel. —**en•force'a•ble** *adj.* —**en•force'ment** *n.*

en•fran•chise (ĕn-frăn'chīz', ĭn-) *v.* **-chised, -chising.** **1.** To endow with the rights of citizenship, esp. the right to vote. **2.** To free, as from bondage.

eng. **1.** engine. **2.** engineer; engineering.

Eng. England; English.

en•gage (ĕn-gāj', ĭn-) *v.* **-gaged, -gaging.** **1.** To employ; hire. **2.** To attract and hold the attention of. **3.** To pledge (oneself), esp. by a promise to marry. **4.** To enter or bring into conflict with. **5.** To interlock or cause to interlock. **6.** To involve oneself or become occupied. [< OF *engager.*] —**en•gag'er** *n.*

en•gage•ment (ĕn-gāj'mənt, ĭn-) *n.* **1.** An act

of engaging or the state of being engaged. **2.** Betrothal. **3.** A commitment to appear at a certain time; appointment. **4.** Employment. **5.** A battle or encounter.

en•gag•ing (ĕn-gā′jĭng, ĭn-) *adj.* Attractive; charming. —**en•gag′ing•ly** *adv.*

Eng•els (ĕng′əls), **Friedrich.** 1820–1895. German socialist; collaborated with Marx.

en•gen•der (ĕn-jĕn′dər, ĭn-) *v.* To bring into existence; give rise to; beget. [< L *ingenerāre.*]

en•gine (ĕn′jən) *n.* **1. a.** A machine, esp. one powered by a fuel, that converts energy into mechanical motion. **b.** Any mechanical appliance, instrument, or tool. **2.** A locomotive. [< L *ingenium,* inborn talent, skill.]

engine block. The cast metal block containing the cylinders of an internal-combustion engine.

en•gi•neer (ĕn′jə-nîr′) *n.* 1. One skilled at or engaged in a branch of engineering. **2.** One who operates an engine. —*v.* **1.** To act as engineer. **2.** To plan or accomplish by skillful acts or contrivance.

en•gi•neer•ing (ĕn′jə-nîr′ĭng) *n.* **1.** The application of scientific principles to practical ends as the design, construction, and operation of efficient and economical structures, equipment, and systems. **2.** The profession of or work performed by an engineer.

Eng•land (ĭng′glənd). The largest division of the United Kingdom of Great Britain and Northern Ireland, in S Great Britain. **2.** Popularly, Great Britain.

Eng•lish (ĭng′glĭsh) *adj.* **1.** Of, pertaining to, or characteristic of England and its inhabitants. **2.** Of, belonging to, or spoken or written in the English language. —*n.* **1. the English** *(takes pl. v.).* The people of England. **2.** The West Germanic language of the English divided historically into Old English, Middle English, and Modern English and now spoken in the British Isles, the United States, and numerous other countries.

English Channel. An arm of the Atlantic between England and France.

English horn. A double-reed woodwind instrument.

Eng•lish•man (ĭng′glĭsh-mən) *n.* A native or inhabitant of England.

engr. **1.** engineer. **2.** engraved; engraving.

en•graft (ĕn-grăft′, -gräft′, ĭn-) *v.* To graft (a shoot) onto a plant. —**en•graft′ment** *n.*

en•gram (ĕn′grăm′) *n.* A persistent protoplasmic alteration hypothesized to occur on stimulation of living neural tissue and to account for memory.

en•grave (ĕn-grāv′, ĭn-) *v.* **-graved, -graving. 1.** To carve, cut, or etch (a design or letters) into a material. **2. a.** To carve, cut, or etch (a design or letters) into a block or surface used for printing. **b.** To print from a block or plate thus made. [EN- + GRAVE[3].] —**en•grav′er** *n.*

en•grav•ing (ĕn-grā′vĭng, ĭn-) *n.* **1.** The technique of one that engraves. **2.** An engraved surface for printing. **3.** A print made from an engraved plate or block.

en•gross (ĕn-grōs′, ĭn-) *v.* **1.** To occupy the complete attentions of. **2. a.** To write or transcribe in a large, clear hand. **b.** To prepare the text of (an official document). [< OF *en gros,* in large quantity.] —**en•gross′er** *n.*

en•gross•ing (ĕn-grō′sĭng, ĭn-) *adj.* Occupying one's complete attention.

en•gulf (ĕn-gŭlf′, ĭn-) *v.* **1.** To surround completely. **2.** To swallow up.

en•hance (ĕn-hăns′, -häns′, ĭn-) *v.* **-hanced, -hancing.** To increase, as in value or beauty. [< VL **inaltiāre,* to raise.] —**en•hance′ment** *n.*

e•nig•ma (ĭ-nĭg′mə) *n.* **1.** An obscure riddle. **2.** A person or thing that is puzzling or inexplicable. [< Gk *ainissesthai,* to speak in riddles, hint.]

en•ig•mat•ic (ĕn′ĭg-măt′ĭk) *adj.* Also **en•ig•mat•i•cal** (-ĭ-kəl). Like an enigma; puzzling. —**en′ig•mat′i•cal•ly** *adv.*

en•join (ĕn-join′, ĭn-) *v.* **1.** To direct; command. **2.** To forbid, esp. by legal action. [< L *injungere,* to join to, impose.] —**en•join′der** *n.*

en•joy (ĕn-joi′, ĭn-) *v.* **1.** To experience joy in. **2.** To have as one's lot. [< OF *enjoïr.*] —**en•joy′a•ble** *adj.* —**en•joy′ment** *n.*

enl. **1.** enlarged. **2.** enlisted.

en•large (ĕn-lärj′, ĭn-) *v.* **-larged, -larging.** To make or become larger in size, scope, or detail. —**en•large′ment** *n.* —**en•larg′er** *n.*

en•light•en (ĕn-līt′n, ĭn-) *v.* **1.** To give knowledge, truth, or understanding to. **2.** To inform. —**en•light′en•er** *n.* —**en•light′en•ment** *n.*

en•list (ĕn-list′, ĭn-) *v.* **1.** To engage the assistance or cooperation of. **2.** To enter the armed forces voluntarily. **3.** To participate in a cause or enterprise. —**en•list′ment** *n.*

enlisted man. A man who has enlisted in the armed forces without an officer's commission or warrant.

en•li•ven (ĕn-lī′vən, ĭn-) *v.* To make lively; animate. —**en•liv′en•ment** *n.*

en masse (ĕn măs′). In one group; all together.

en•mesh (ĕn-mĕsh′, ĭn-) *v.* To entangle or involve in or as if in a mesh.

en•mi•ty (ĕn′mə-tē) *n., pl.* **-ties.** Deep-seated hatred, as between rivals or opponents. [< L *inimīcus,* ENEMY.]

en•no•ble (ĕn-nō′bəl, ĭn-) *v.* **-bled, -bling.** To invest with nobility; add to the honor of. —**en•no′ble•ment** *n.* —**en•no′bler** *n.*

en•nui (än′wē′) *n.* Boredom. [< L *in odiō,* "in hate," odious.]

e•nor•mi•ty (ĕ-nôr′mə-tē) *n., pl.* **-ties. 1.** Extreme wickedness. **2.** A monstrous offense or evil.

e•nor•mous (ĕ-nôr′məs) *adj.* Very great in size, number, or degree; immense. [< L *ēnormis,* unusual, immense.] —**e•nor′mous•ly** *adv.*

e•nough (ĭ-nŭf′) *adj.* Sufficient to meet a need or satisfy a desire. —*n.* An adequate quantity. —*adv.* **1.** To a satisfactory amount or degree. **2.** Very; quite: *glad enough to leave.* [< OE *genōg.* See **nek-**.]

en•plane (ĕn-plān′) *v.* **-planed, -planing.** To board an airplane.

en•rage (ĕn-rāj′, ĭn-) *v.* **-raged, -raging.** To put in a rage; infuriate.

en•rap•ture (ĕn-răp′chər, ĭn-) *v.* **-tured, -turing.** To move to delight.

en•rich (ĕn-rĭch′, ĭn-) *v.* To make rich or richer; add to the quality, value, beauty, or enjoyment of. —**en•rich′ment** *n.* —**en•rich′er** *n.*

en•roll (ĕn-rōl′, ĭn-) *v.* Also **en•rol, -rolled, -rolling. 1.** To enter the name of in a register, record, or roll. **2.** To place one's name on a roll or register. —**en•roll′ment** *n.*

en route (än rōōt′). On the way.

en•sconce (ĕn-skŏns′, ĭn-) *v.* **-sconced, -sconcing. 1.** To settle (oneself) securely or comfortably. **2.** To place or conceal in a secure place.

en•sem•ble (än-säm′bəl) *n.* **1.** A group of parts that contribute to a single effect, as: **a.** A coordinated outfit or costume. **b.** A group of musicians or other players who perform together. **2. a.** Music for two or more performers. **b.** The quality of performance by a group of actors or musicians, with respect to unity and balance of style. [< L *insimul,* at the same time.]

en•shrine (ĕn-shrīn′, ĭn-) *v.* **-shrined, -shrining. 1.** To enclose in or as if in a shrine. **2.** To cherish as sacred. —**en•shrine′ment** *n.*

en•shroud (ĕn-shroud′, ĭn-) *v.* To shroud; veil or conceal.

en•sign (ĕn′sən) *n.* **1.** (also ĕn′sīn′). A flag or banner. **2.** A commissioned officer of the lowest rank in the U.S. Navy or Coast Guard. [< L *insignia,* insignia.]

en•si•lage (ĕn′sə-lĭj) *n.* Green fodder in a silo.

en•sile (ĕn-sīl′, ĭn-) *v.* **-siled, -siling. 1.** To store (fodder) in a silo. **2.** To convert (green fodder) into silage.

en•slave (ĕn-slāv′, ĭn-) *v.* **-slaved, -slaving.** To make a slave of. —**en•slave′ment** *n.*

en•snare (ĕn-snâr′, ĭn-) *v.* **-snared, -snaring.** To catch in or as if in a snare. —**en•snare′ment** *n.*

en•sue (ĕn-sōō′, ĭn-) *v.* **-sued, -suing. 1.** To follow immediately afterward. **2.** To follow as a consequence; result. [< L *insequī,* to follow after or on.]

en•sure. Variant of **insure.**

-ent. *comb. form.* **1.** Used to form adjectives: **effervescent. 2.** Used to form nouns of agency: **referent.** [< L *-ens.*]

en•tail (ĕn-tāl′, ĭn-) *v.* **1.** To have as a necessary accompaniment or consequence. **2.** To limit the inheritance of (property) to a specified, unalterable succession of heirs. —**en•tail′er** *n.* —**en•tail′ment** *n.*

en•tan•gle (ĕn-tăng′gəl, ĭn-) *v.* **-gled, -gling. 1.** To twist together so that disengagement is difficult; snarl. **2.** To complicate; confuse. **3.** To involve inextricably, as in difficulties. —**en•tan′gle•ment** *n.* —**en•tan′gler** *n.*

en•tente (än tänt′) *n.* **1.** An agreement between two or more governments for cooperative action. **2.** The parties to such an agreement. [F, "understanding."]

en•ter (ĕn′tər) *v.* **1.** To come or go into. **2.** To penetrate; pierce. **3.** To introduce; insert. **4.** To become a part or member of. **5.** To begin; embark upon. **6.** To enroll. **7.** To become a participant in. **8.** *Law* **a.** To place formally on record. **b.** To go upon or into (real property) as a trespasser or with felonious intent. **c.** To go upon (land) to take possession of it. [< L *intrā,* within.] —**en′ter•er** *n.*

en•ter•i•tis (ĕn′tə-rī′tĭs) *n.* Inflammation of the intestinal tract. [< Gk *enteron,* intestines.]

en•ter•prise (ĕn′tər-prīz′) *n.* **1.** An undertaking, esp. one of some scope and risk. **2.** A business. **3.** Readiness to venture; initiative. [< OF *entreprendre,* to undertake.]

en•ter•pris•ing (ĕn′tər-prī′zĭng) *adj.* Showing imagination, initiative, and boldness in action. —**en′ter•pris′ing•ly** *adv.*

en•ter•tain (ĕn′tər-tān′) *v.* **1.** To hold the attention of; amuse. **2.** To extend hospitality toward. **3.** To hold in mind. [< VL **intertenēre,* "to hold between."] —**en′ter•tain′er** *n.*

en•ter•tain•ing (ĕn′tər-tā′nĭng) *adj.* Diverting; amusing. —**en′ter•tain′ing•ly** *adv.*

en•ter•tain•ment (ĕn′tər-tān′mənt) *n.* **1.** The act of entertaining. **2.** Something that entertains, esp. a show designed to amuse. **3.** The pleasure afforded by being entertained; amusement.

en•thrall (ĕn-thrôl′, ĭn-) *v.* Also **en•thral. 1.** To hold spellbound; charm. **2.** To enslave. —**en•thrall′ing•ly** *adv.* —**en•thrall′ment** *n.*

en•throne (ĕn-thrōn′, ĭn-) *v.* **-throned, -throning. 1. a.** To seat on a throne. **b.** To invest with sovereign power. **2.** To exalt; revere. —**en•**

throne'ment *n.*

en•thuse (ĕn-thōōz', ĭn-) *v.* **-thused, -thusing.** *Informal.* **1.** To stimulate enthusiasm in. **2.** To show enthusiasm.

en•thu•si•asm (ĕn-thōō'zē-ăz'əm, ĭn-) *n.* **1. a.** Rapturous interest or excitement. **b.** Ardent fondness. **2.** Something that inspires a lively interest. [< Gk *enthousiazein,* to be inspired by a god.]

en•thu•si•ast (ĕn-thōō'zē-ăst', ĭn-) *n.* A person filled with enthusiasm. **—en•thu'si•as'tic** *adj.* **—en•thu'si•as'ti•cal•ly** *adv.*

en•tice (ĕn-tīs') *v.* **-ticed, -ticing.** To attract by arousing hope or desire; lure. [< VL **intītiāre,* to set on fire.] **—en•tice'ment** *n.*

en•tire (ĕn-tīr', ĭn-) *adj.* Having no part missing or excepted; whole; complete. [< L *integer,* intact.] **—en•tire'ly** *adv.*

en•tire•ty (ĕn-tī'rə-tē, ĭn-) *n., pl.* **-ties. 1.** The state or condition of being entire; completeness. **2.** Something that is entire; a whole.

en•ti•tle (ĕn-tīt'l, ĭn-) *v.* **-tled, -tling. 1.** To give a name to. **2.** To give (one) a right.

en•ti•ty (ĕn'tə-tē) *n., pl.* **-ties. 1.** The fact of existence. **2.** Something that exists independently. [< L *ēns,* prp of *esse,* to be.]

entom. entomological; entomology.

en•tomb (ĕn-tōōm', ĭn-) *v.* To place in or as if in a tomb; bury. **—en•tomb'ment** *n.*

en•to•mol•o•gy (ĕn'tə-mŏl'ə-jē) *n.* The scientific study of insects. [< Gk *entomon,* insect + -LOGY.] **—en'to•mo•log'i•cal** *adj.* **—en'to•mo•log'i•cal•ly** *adv.* **—en'to•mol'o•gist** *n.*

en•tou•rage (än'tōō-räzh') *n.* A train of attendants, followers, or associates. [< OF *entour,* surroundings.]

en•tr'acte (än-trăkt') *n.* **1.** The interval between the acts of a theatrical performance. **2.** An entertainment during this interval.

en•trails (ĕn'trālz', -trəlz) *pl.n.* The internal organs, esp. the intestines. [< L *interāneus,* internal.]

en•train (ĕn-trān', ĭn-) *v.* To board a train.

en•trance¹ (ĕn'trəns) *n.* **1.** The act or an instance of entering. **2.** Any passage or opening that affords entry. **3.** Permission or liberty to enter; admission. [< OF *entrer,* enter.]

en•trance² (ĕn-trăns', -träns', ĭn-) *v.* **-tranced, -trancing.** To fill with wonder or enchantment; fascinate. **—en•trance'ment** *n.*

en•trant (ĕn'trənt) *n.* One who enters, esp. one who enters a competition.

en•trap (ĕn-trăp', ĭn-) *v.* **-trapped, -trapping.** To catch in or as if in a trap. **—en•trap'ment** *n.*

en•treat (ĕn-trēt', ĭn-) *v.* To ask earnestly; beseech; beg. [< OF *entraitier.*]

en•treat•y (ĕn-trē'tē, ĭn-) *n., pl.* **-ies.** An earnest request; plea.

en•trée (än'trā) *n.* Also **en•tree. 1.** Power or permission to enter; admittance; access. **2. a.** The main course of an ordinary meal. **b.** A dish served immediately before the main course or between principal courses.

en•trench (ĕn-trĕnch', ĭn-) *v.* **1.** To provide with a trench or trenches. **2.** To establish securely. **—en•trench'ment** *n.*

en•tre•pre•neur (än'trə-prə-nûr') *n.* A person who organizes, operates, and assumes the risk for business ventures. [< OF *entreprendre,* to undertake.]

en•tro•py (ĕn'trə-pē) *n.* **1.** A measure of the capacity of a system to undergo spontaneous change. **2.** A measure of the randomness, disorder, or chaos in a system. [G *Entropie.*]

en•trust (ĕn-trŭst', ĭn-) *v.* Also **in•trust** (ĭn-). **1.** To give over to another for care or performance. **2.** To commit something trustfully to. **—en•trust'ment** *n.*

en•try (ĕn'trē) *n., pl.* **-tries. 1.** The act or right of entering. **2.** A passage affording entrance. **3. a.** The inclusion of an item in a list or record. **b.** An item thus entered. **4.** A word, term, or phrase defined or treated in a dictionary or other reference book. **5.** A participant in a competition.

en•twine (ĕn-twīn', ĭn-) *v.* **-twined, -twining.** To twine or twist around or together.

e•nu•mer•ate (ĭ-n/y/ōō'mə-rāt') *v.* **-ated, -ating. 1.** To name one by one; to list. **2.** To count. [L *ēnumerāre,* to count out.] **—e•nu'mer•a'tion** *n.* **—e•nu'mer•a'tor** *n.*

e•nun•ci•ate (ĭ-nŭn'sē-āt', -shē-āt') *v.* **-ated, -ating. 1.** To pronounce or articulate (speech sounds). **2.** To state precisely or systematically. **3.** To announce; proclaim. [L *ēnunciāre.*] **—e•nun'ci•a'tion** *n.*

en•u•re•sis (ĕn'yə-rē'sĭs) *n.* Involuntary urination. [< Gk *enourein,* to urinate in.]

env. envelope.

en•vel•op (ĕn-vĕl'əp, ĭn-) *v.* **-oped, -oping. 1.** To enclose with or as if with a covering. **2.** To surround. [< OF *enveloper.*] **—en•vel'op•er** *n.* **—en•vel'op•ment** *n.*

en•ve•lope (ĕn'və-lōp', än'-) *n.* **1.** Something that envelopes; cover. **2.** A flat paper container for a letter or similar object. [< OF *enveloper,* ENVELOP.]

en•vi•a•ble (ĕn'vē-ə-bəl) *adj.* Highly desirable. **—en'vi•a•ble•ness** *n.* **—en'vi•a•bly** *adv.*

en•vi•ous (ĕn'vē-əs) *adj.* Feeling or expressing envy. **—en'vi•ous•ly** *adv.* **—en'vi•ous•ness** *n.*

en•vi•ron•ment (ĕn-vī'rən-mənt, ĭn-) *n.* **1.** Something that surrounds; surroundings. **2.** The combination of external or extrinsic conditions that affect the growth and development of organisms. [< OF *environ,* around.] **—en•vi'ron•men'tal** (-mĕnt'l) *adj.*

en•vi•rons (ĕn-vī'rənz, ĭn-) *pl.n.* A surrounding area, esp. of a city; suburbs.

en•vis•age (ĕn-vĭz'ĭj, ĭn-) *v.* **-aged, -aging.** To have an image of; conceive of.

en•vi•sion (ĕn-vĭzh'ən) *v.* To picture in the mind.

en•voy (ĕn'voi, än'-) *n.* **1.** A messenger or other agent. **2.** A diplomatic representative of a government. [< F *envoyer,* to send.]

en•vy (ĕn'vē) *n., pl.* **-vies. 1.** A feeling of discontent and resentment aroused by another's desirable possessions or qualities, with a strong desire to have them for oneself. **2. a.** A possession of another that is strongly desired. **b.** One who possesses what another strongly desires. *—v.* **-vied, -vying.** To feel envy for. [< L *invidēre,* to look at with malice.]

en•zyme (ĕn'zīm') *n.* Any of numerous proteins produced by living organisms and functioning as biochemical catalysts in living organisms. [< MGk *enzumos,* leavened.] **—en'zy•mat'ic** (-zə-măt'ĭk) *adj.*

eo–. *comb. form.* Early. [< Gk *ēos,* dawn, light of day.]

E•o•cene (ē'ə-sēn') *adj.* Of or belonging to the geologic time, rock series, or sedimentary deposits of the second epoch of the Cenozoic era, characterized by the rise of mammals. *—n.* The Eocene epoch. [EO- + -CENE.]

E•o•lith•ic (ē'ə-lĭth'ĭk) *adj.* Relating to the postulated earliest period of human culture preceding the Lower Paleolithic. *—n.* The Eolithic period.

e•on (ē'ŏn', ē'ən) *n.* Also **ae•on. 1.** An indefinitely long period of time; an age. **2.** The longest division of geologic time, containing two or more eras. [< Gk *aiōn.*]

–eous. *comb. form.* Having the nature of or akin to: **beauteous.** [L *-eus.*]

ep•au•let (ĕp'ə-lĕt', ĕp'ə-lĕt') *n.* Also **ep•au•lette.** A shoulder ornament, esp. on a uniform. [< F *épaule,* shoulder.]

é•pée (ā-pā') *n.* Also **e•pee.** A fencing sword with a blade that has no cutting edge and tapers to a blunted point. [< L *spatha,* sword, blade.] **—é•pée'ist** *n.*

Eph. Ephesians (New Testament).

e•phem•er•al (ĭ-fĕm'ər-əl) *adj.* Lasting for a brief time; transitory. [Gk *ephēmeros.*]

epi–. *comb. form.* **1.** On, upon. **2.** Over, above. **3.** Around, covering. **4.** To, toward, close to, next to. **5.** Besides, in addition. **6.** After. **7.** Among. [Gk *epi,* upon, over, at, after.]

ep•ic (ĕp'ĭk) *n.* **1.** A long narrative poem celebrating episodes of a people's heroic tradition. **2.** A literary or dramatic composition likened to epic poetry. *—adj.* Designating or resembling an epic; grand; heroic. [< Gk *epos,* song, word.]

ep•i•cene (ĕp'ə-sēn') *adj.* **1.** Having the characteristics of both the male and the female. **2.** Effeminate. **3.** Sexless. *—n.* An epicene person or object. [< Gk *epikoinos,* common to many, promiscuous.]

ep•i•cen•ter (ĕp'ə-sĕn'tər) *n.* **1.** The part of the earth's surface directly above the origin of an earthquake. **2.** A focal point.

ep•i•cure (ĕp'ĭ-kyŏŏr') *n.* A person with refined taste in food and wine. [< *Epicurus* (died 270 B.C.), Greek philosopher.]

Ep•i•cu•re•an (ĕp'ĭ-kyōō-rē'ən) *adj.* **1.** Devoted to the pursuit of pleasure. **2.** Suited to the tastes of an epicure.

ep•i•dem•ic (ĕp'ə-dĕm'ĭk) *adj.* Spreading rapidly among many individuals in an area. *—n.* **1.** A contagious disease that spreads rapidly. **2.** A rapid spread or development. [< Gk *epidēmos,* prevalent, common.] **—ep'i•dem'i•cal•ly** *adv.*

ep•i•der•mis (ĕp'ə-dûr'mĭs) *n.* The outer, protective layer of the skin. **—ep'i•der'mal** *adj.*

ep•i•glot•tis (ĕp'ĭ-glŏt'ĭs) *n., pl.* **-tises.** An elastic cartilage at the root of the tongue that prevents food from entering the windpipe in swallowing.

ep•i•gram (ĕp'ĭ-grăm') *n.* A statement or short poem expressing a single thought with terseness and wit. [< Gk *epigramma,* inscription.] **—ep'i•gram•mat'ic** (-grə-măt'ĭk) *adj.* **—ep'i•gram•mat'i•cal•ly** *adv.*

ep•i•lep•sy (ĕp'ə-lĕp'sē) *n.* A nervous disorder characterized by recurring attacks of motor, sensory, or psychic malfunction with or without unconsciousness or convulsive movements. [< Gk *epilēpsia.*] **—ep'i•lep'tic** *adj. & n.* **—ep'i•lep'toid'** (-lĕp'toid') *adj.*

ep•i•logue (ĕp'ə-lôg', -lŏg') *n.* Also **ep•i•log. 1.** A short poem or speech spoken directly to the audience following the conclusion of a play. **2.** A short section at the end of any literary work. [< Gk *epilegein,* to say more.]

ep•i•neph•rine (ĕp'ə-nĕf'rēn', -rĭn) *n.* Also **ep•i•neph•rin** (-rĭn). **1.** An adrenal hormone that stimulates autonomic nerve action. **2.** A crystalline compound, $C_9H_{13}NO_3$, isolated from adrenal glands of certain mammals or synthesized, and used as a heart stimulant and in the treatment of asthma.

e•pis•co•pa•cy (ĭ-pĭs'kə-pə-sē) *n., pl.* **-cies. 1.** An episcopate. **2.** Church government in which bishops are the chief ministers.

e•pis•co•pal (ĭ-pĭs'kə-pəl) *adj.* **1.** Of or pertaining to a bishop or bishops. **2.** Of or advocating church government by bishops. **3. Epis-**

ă pat/ā ate/âr care/ä bar/b bib/ch chew/d deed/ĕ pet/ē be/f fit/g gag/h hat/hw what/
ĭ pit/ī pie/îr pier/j judge/k kick/l lid, fatal/m mum/n no, sudden/ng sing/ŏ pot/ō go/

copal. Designating or pertaining to the Anglican Church or a branch of it. [< Gk *episkopos,* overseer.] —**e•pis'co•pal•ly** *adv.*

Episcopal Church. The **Protestant Episcopal Church.**

E•pis•co•pa•li•an (ĭ-pĭs'kə-pā'lē-ən, -pāl'yən) *adj.* Pertaining to or belonging to the Protestant Episcopal Church. —*n.* A member or adherent of the Protestant Episcopal Church. —**E•pis'co•pa'li•an•ism'** *n.*

e•pis•co•pate (ĭ-pĭs'kə-pĭt, -pāt') *n.* **1.** The position or term of a bishop. **2.** The area of jurisdiction of a bishop; a bishopric. **3.** Bishops collectively.

ep•i•sode (ĕp'ə-sōd') *n.* **1.** An incident or series of related events in the course of a continuous experience. **2.** A portion of a narrative that relates an event or connected events and forms a coherent story in itself. [Gk *epeisodion,* "addition."] —**ep'i•sod'ic** (-sŏd'ĭk) *adj.*

Epist. Epistle.

e•pis•tle (ĭ-pĭs'əl) *n.* **1.** A letter, esp. a formal one. **2.** Often **Epistle.** One of the letters written by an Apostle and included in the New Testament. [< Gk *epistellein,* to send to.] —**e•pis'to•lar•y** (ĭ-pĭs'tə-lăr'ē) *adj.*

ep•i•taph (ĕp'ə-tăf', -täf') *n.* An inscription, esp. on a tombstone, in memory of a deceased person. [< Gk *epitaphios,* "over a tomb."]

ep•i•the•li•um (ĕp'ə-thē'lē-əm) *n., pl.* **-ums** or **-lia** (-lē-ə). Membranous tissue composed of closely arranged cells and forming the covering of most internal surfaces and organs and the outer surface of an animal body. —**ep'i•the'li•al** *adj.*

ep•i•thet (ĕp'ə-thĕt') *n.* A term used to characterize the nature of a person or thing. [< Gk *epitheton,* "an addition."]

e•pit•o•me (ĭ-pĭt'ə-mē) *n.* **1.** A summary; abridgment. **2.** One that is consummately representative of an entire class. [< Gk *epitemnein,* to cut short.]

e•pit•o•mize (ĭ-pĭt'ə-mīz') *v.* **-mized, -mizing. 1.** To summarize. **2.** To typify eminently a class, type, or quality.

e plu•ri•bus u•num (ē ploor'ə-bəs yoo'nəm). *Latin.* One out of many. The motto of the U.S.

ep•och (ĕp'ək) *n.* **1.** A particular period of history, esp. one that is characteristic or memorable; an era. **2.** A point in time or progress that marks the beginning of such a period. **3.** A unit of geologic time that is a division of a period. **4.** An instant in time arbitrarily selected as a reference datum. [< Gk *epokhē,* pause.] —**ep'och•al** *adj.* —**ep'och•al•ly** *adv.*

ep•ox•y (ĭ-pŏk'sē) *n., pl.* **-ies.** Any of various resins capable of forming tight cross-linked polymer structures characterized by toughness, strong adhesion, and high corrosion resistance. [EP(I)- + OXY-]

ep•si•lon (ĕp'sə-lŏn') *n.* The 5th letter of the Greek alphabet, representing *e.*

Ep•som salts (ĕp'səm). Hydrated magnesium sulfate used as a cathartic. [< the mineral springs in *Epsom,* England.]

eq. **1.** equal. **2.** equation.

eq•ua•ble (ĕk'wə-bəl, ē'kwə-) *adj.* **1.** Unvarying; even. **2.** Even-tempered. [< L *aequus,* EQUAL.] —**eq'ua•bil'i•ty** *n.* —**eq'ua•bly** *adv.*

e•qual (ē'kwəl) *adj.* **1.** Having the same capability, quantity, or effect as another. **2.** Mathematically related by a reflexive, symmetric, and transitive relationship; broadly, alike or in agreement in a specified sense with respect to specified properties. **3.** Having the same privileges, status, or rights. **4. a.** Having the requisite strength, ability, determination, etc.; qualified or disposed. **b.** Adequate in extent, amount, or degree. —*n.* One that is equal to another. —*v.* **equaled** or **equalled, equaling** or **equalling. 1.** To be equal to, esp. in value. **2.** To do, make, or produce something equal to. [< L *aequus,* even, level.] —**e'qual•ly** *adv.*

e•qual•i•ty (ĭ-kwŏl'ə-tē) *n., pl.* **-ties. 1.** The state or instance of being equal. **2.** A mathematical statement, usually an equation, that one thing equals another.

e•qual•ize (ē'kwə-līz') *v.* **-ized, -izing.** To make equal or uniform. —**e'qual•iz'er** *n.*

e•qua•nim•i•ty (ē'kwə-nĭm'ə-tē, ĕk'wə-) *n.* The quality or characteristic of being even-tempered. [< L *aequanimis,* even-tempered.]

e•quate (ĭ-kwāt') *v.* **equated, equating. 1.** To make, treat, or regard as equal or equivalent. **2.** To reduce to a standard or average; stabilize; balance. **3.** To show or state the equality of. —**e•quat'a•ble** *adj.*

e•qua•tion (ĭ-kwā'zhən, -shən) *n.* **1.** The process or act of equating or of being equated. **2.** The state of being equal; equilibrium. **3.** A linear array of mathematical symbols separated into left and right sides that are designated at least conditionally equal. —**e•qua'tion•al** *adj.* —**e•qua'tion•al•ly** *adv.*

e•qua•tor (ĭ-kwā'tər) *n.* The great circle circumscribing the earth's surface, the reckoning datum of latitudes and dividing boundary of N and S Hemispheres, formed by the intersection of a plane passing through the earth's center perpendicular to its axis of rotation. [ML *(circulus) aequator (diei et nocis),* (circle) equalizing (day and night).] —**e'qua•to'ri•al** (-tôr'ē-əl, -tōr'-) *adj.*

Equatorial Guinea. A country of W Africa. Pop. 300,000. Cap. Malabo.

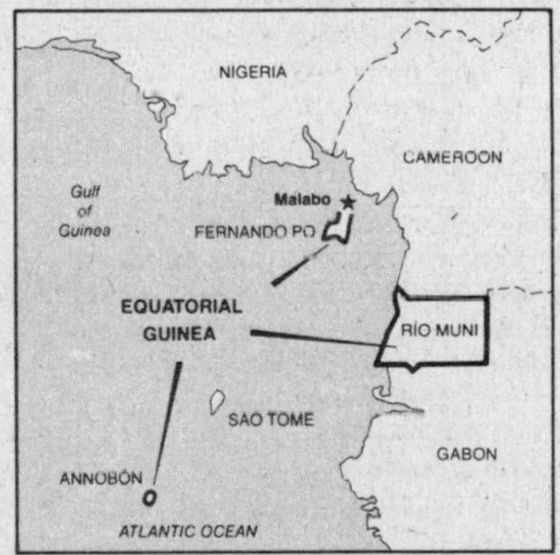

Equatorial Guinea

eq•uer•ry (ĕk'wə-rē) *n., pl.* **-ries. 1.** An officer who supervises the horses of a noble household. **2.** An attendant to the English royal household. [< OF *escuier,* riding master, squire.]

e•ques•tri•an (ĭ-kwĕs'trē-ən) *adj.* **1.** Of or pertaining to horsemanship. **2.** Depicted or represented on horseback. —*n.* One who rides a horse or performs on horseback. [< L *equus,* horse.] —**e•ques'tri•an•ism'** *n.*

e•ques•tri•enne (ĭ-kwĕs'trē-ĕn') *n.* A female equestrian.

equi–. *comb. form.* Equality.

e•qui•an•gu•lar (ē'kwē-ăng'gyə-lər) *adj.* Having all angles equal.

e•qui•dis•tant (ē'kwə-dĭs'tənt) *adj.* Equally distant. —**e'qui•dis'tant•ly** *adv.*

e•qui•lat•er•al (ē'kwə-lăt'ər-əl) *adj.* Having all sides or faces equal.

e•qui•lib•ri•um (ē'kwə-lĭb'rē-əm) *n.* Any condition in which all acting influences are cancelled by others resulting in a stable, balanced, or unchanging system. [L *aequilibrium,* even balance.]

e•quine (ē'kwīn') *adj.* Of, pertaining to, or characteristic of a horse. [< L *equus,* horse.]

e•qui•noc•tial (ē'kwə-nŏk'shəl, ĕk'wə-) *adj.* Pertaining to an equinox.

e•qui•nox (ē'kwə-nŏks', ĕk'wə-) *n.* Either of the two times during a year when the sun crosses the celestial equator and when the length of day and night are approx. equal. [< L *aequinoctium,* "equal night."]

e•quip (ĭ-kwĭp') *v.* **equipped, equipping. 1.** To supply with material necessities. **2.** To supply with intellectual, emotional, or spiritual essentials. [< OF *esquipper,* to put to sea, embark.]

equip. equipment.

eq•ui•page (ĕk'wə-pĭj) *n.* An elegantly equipped carriage.

e•quip•ment (ĭ-kwĭp'mənt) *n.* **1.** The act of equipping or the state of being equipped. **2.** That with which a person, organization, or thing is equipped; furnishings.

e•qui•poise (ē'kwə-poiz', ĕk'wə-) *n.* **1.** Balance; equilibrium. **2.** A counterbalance.

eq•ui•ta•ble (ĕk'wə-tə-bəl) *adj.* Exhibiting equity; impartial; just. —**eq'ui•ta•bly** *adv.*

eq•ui•ta•tion (ĕk'wə-tā'shən) *n.* The learning and practice of riding a horse; horsemanship.

eq•ui•ty (ĕk'wə-tē) *n., pl.* **-ties. 1.** The state, ideal, or quality of being just, impartial, and fair. **2.** The residual value of a business or property beyond any liability therein. **3.** A system of jurisprudence supplementing common law. [< L *aequitās* < *aequus,* EQUAL.]

equiv. equivalent.

e•quiv•a•lence (ĭ-kwĭv'ə-ləns) *n.* Also **e•quiv•a•len•cy** (-lən-sē) *pl.* **-cies.** The state or condition of being equivalent; equality.

e•quiv•a•lent (ĭ-kwĭv'ə-lənt) *adj.* Equal; similar in effects; practically equal; tantamount. —*n.* That which is equivalent. [< LL *aequivalēre,* to be equal in value.] —**e•quiv'a•lent•ly** *adv.*

equivalent weight. The number of parts by weight of any element combining with or replacing the equivalent of half the atomic weight of oxygen or with one atomic weight of hydrogen.

e•quiv•o•cal (ĭ-kwĭv'ə-kəl) *adj.* **1.** Capable of two interpretations; ambiguous. **2.** Of uncertain outcome; indeterminate. **3.** Questionable; not genuine. [< LL *aequivocus.*] —**e•quiv'o•cal•ly** *adv.* —**e•quiv'o•cal•ness** *n.*

e•quiv•o•cate (ĭ-kwĭv'ə-kāt') *v.* **-cated, -cating.** To speak in ambiguities; hedge. —**e•quiv'o•ca'tion** *n.* —**e•quiv'o•ca'tor** *n.*

–er¹. *comb. form.* **1.** One that performs the action indicated by the root verb: **blender. 2.** Geographic origin or residence: **westerner.** [< L *-ārius.*]

–er², –r. *comb. form.* Used to form the comparative degree of adjectives and adverbs: *slower.* [< OE *-re, -ra.*]

Er erbium.

e•ra (ĭr'ə, ĕr'ə) *n.* **1.** A period of time that utilizes a specific point in history as the basis of its chronology. **2.** A distinctive or notable period of time. **3.** The longest division of geologic time comprising one or more periods. [< L *aera,* "counters for calculating."]

ERA Equal Rights Amendment.

e•rad•i•cate (ĭ-răd'ĭ-kāt') *v.* **-cated, -cating. 1.** To uproot; destroy. **2.** To remove all traces of; erase. **3.** To pull or tear up by the roots. [L *ērādicāre,* to pluck up by the roots.] —**e•rad'i•ca'tion** *n.* —**e•rad'i•ca'tor** *n.*

e•rase (ĭ-rās') *v.* **erased, erasing. 1.** To remove; rub, wipe, scrape, or blot out; efface. **2.** To remove all traces of. [L *ērādere* (pp *ērāsus*), to scrape out.] —**e•ras'er** *n.* —**e•ra'sure** *n.*

E•ras•mus (ĭ-răz'məs), **Desiderius.** 1466?–1536. Dutch humanist.

er•bi•um (ûr'bē-əm) *n. Symbol* **Er** A soft, malleable, silvery element, used in metallurgy, nuclear research, and to color glass and porcelain. Atomic number 68, atomic weight 167.26. [< *Ytterby,* Sweden.]

ere (âr). *Archaic. prep.* Previous to; before. —*conj.* **1.** Before. **2.** Rather than. [< OE *ǣr,* before. See **ayer-.**]

e•rect (ĭ-rĕkt') *adj.* Directed or pointing upward; standing upright; vertical. —*v.* **1.** To raise, as a building; construct. **2.** To raise upright; set on end. **3.** To put together; assemble. **4.** To set up; establish. **5.** *Physiol.* To become rigid and upright. [< L *ērectus,* pp of *ērigere,* to raise up, set up.] —**e•rec'tion** *n.*

er•e•mite (ĕr'ə-mīt') *n.* A hermit, esp. a religious recluse. [ME *(h)ermite,* hermit.]

erg (ûrg) *n.* A unit of energy or work equal to the work done by a force of one dyne acting over a distance of one centimeter. [Gk *ergon,* work.]

er•go (ûr'gō, âr'-) *conj. & adv.* Consequently. [L *ergō,* therefore.]

er•gos•ter•ol (ûr'gŏs'tə-rôl', -rōl', -rŏl') *n.* A crystalline compound, $C_{28}H_{14}O$, synthesized by yeast from sugars or derived from ergot.

er•got (ûr'gət, -gŏt') *n.* **1.** A fungus that infects cereal plants. **2.** The dried black filaments of such a fungus, used medicinally. [F, "cock's spur."]

E•rie, Lake (îr'ē). The fourth largest of the Great Lakes.

er•mine (ûr'mĭn) *n.* **1.** A weasel with fur that turns white in winter. **2.** The white fur of this animal. [< ML *(mūs) Armenius,* "Armenian (mouse)."]

e•rode (ĭ-rōd') *v.* **eroded, eroding.** To wear away by or as if by erosion. [L *ērōdere,* to gnaw off, eat away.] —**e•ro'dent** *adj.*

Er•os (îr'ŏs', ĕr'-). Greek god of love, son of Aphrodite.

e•ro•sion (ĭ-rō'zhən) *n.* The group of natural processes including weathering, dissolution, abrasion, corrosion, and transportation by which earthy or rock material is removed from any part of the earth's surface.

e•rot•ic (ĭ-rŏt'ĭk) *adj.* Of or concerning sexual love and desire; amatory. [Gk *erōtikos,* of or caused by love.] —**e•rot'i•cal•ly** *adv.*

err (ûr, ĕr) *v.* **1.** To deviate from proper course or aim. **2.** To make an error. **3.** To sin. [< L *errāre,* to wander.]

er•rand (ĕr'ənd) *n.* **1.** A short trip taken for a specific purpose. **2.** The purpose of such a trip. [< OE *ǣrende,* message < Gmc **arundjam.*]

er•rant (ĕr'ənt) *adj.* **1.** Roving, esp. in search of adventure. **2.** Straying from a proper course or standard; erring. [< OF *errer,* to travel, and *errer,* to err.] —**er'rant•ly** *adv.*

er•ra•ta (ĭ-rä'tə, ĭ-rā'-) *pl.n. Sing.* **-tum** (-təm). A list of corrections appended to a book. [< L *errāre,* to wander, ERR.]

er•rat•ic (ĭ-răt'ĭk) *adj.* **1.** Without a fixed or regular course; inconsistent. **2.** Unconventional; eccentric. [< L *errāticus,* wandering, straying.] —**er•rat'i•cal•ly** *adv.*

er•ro•ne•ous (ĭ-rō'nē-əs) *adj.* Mistaken; false. —**er•ro'ne•ous•ly** *adv.* —**er•ro'ne•ous•ness** *n.*

er•ror (ĕr'ər) *n.* **1.** An unintentional deviation from what is correct, right, or true; mistake. **2.** The condition of having incorrect or false knowledge. **3.** A transgression; wrongdoing. **4.** *Baseball.* A defensive or fielding misplay. [< L *errāre,* to ERR.]

er•satz (ĕr-zäts', ĕr'zäts') *adj.* Substitute; artificial. —*n.* A substitute, esp. an inferior imitation. [< G, compensation, replacement.]

erst (ûrst) *adv. Archaic.* **1.** At first. **2.** Formerly. [< OE *ǣrest.* See **ayer-.**]

erst•while (ûrst'hwīl') *adj.* Former. —*adv. Archaic.* Formerly.

e•ruct (ĭ-rŭkt') *v.* **1.** To belch. **2.** To emit violently, as a volcano. [L *ēructāre.*] —**e•ruc'ta'tion** *n.*

er•u•dite (ĕr'/y/o͞o-dīt') *adj.* Deeply learned. [< L *ērudīre,* "to take the roughness out of," teach.] —**er'u•dite'ly** *adv.* —**er'u•di'tion** *n.*

e•rupt (ĭ-rŭpt') *v.* **1.** To emerge or eject violently. **2.** To become violently active. **3. a.** To pierce the gum, as a tooth. **b.** To appear on the skin, as a blemish. [L *ērumpere* (pp *ēruptus*), to break out.] —**e•rup'tion** *n.* —**e•rup'tive** *adj.* —**e•rup'tive•ly** *adv.*

–ery, –ry. *comb. form.* Used to form nouns from verbs or other nouns to indicate: **1.** A certain activity: **hatchery. 2.** Certain things or persons: **nunnery. 3.** A collection or class of objects: **finery. 4.** A craft, study, or practice: **husbandry. 5. a.** Certain characteristics: **snobbery. b.** A kind of behavior: **knavery. 6.** Condition or status: **slavery.** [< L *-ārius.*]

er•y•the•ma (ĕr'ə-thē'mə) *n.* A redness of the skin, as caused by chemical poisoning or sunburn. [< Gk *eruthros,* red.]

erythro–. *comb. form.* Red. [< Gk *eruthros,* red.]

e•ryth•ro•cyte (ĭ-rĭth'rə-sīt') *n.* The yellowish, nonnucleated, disk-shaped blood cell that contains hemoglobin and is responsible for the color of blood.

Es einsteinium.

–es¹. *comb. form.* The plural form: **trusses, Negroes, ladies.**

–es². *comb. form.* The 3rd person sing. form of the present indicative: **guesses, does.**

es•ca•late (ĕs'kə-lāt') *v.* **-lated, -lating.** To increase, enlarge, or intensify. —**es'ca•la'tion** *n.*

es•ca•la•tor (ĕs'kə-lā'tər) *n.* A moving stairway consisting of steps attached to a continuously circulating belt. [Poss F *escalade,* a scaling + (ELEV)ATOR.]

es•cal•lop. Variant of **scallop.**

es•ca•pade (ĕs'kə-pād') *n.* A carefree or reckless adventure. [< OIt *scappare,* to escape.]

es•cape (ĕ-skāp', ĭ-skāp') *v.* **-caped, -caping. 1.** To break from confinement; get free. **2.** To succeed in avoiding (capture, danger, or harm). **3.** To elude: *The meaning escaped him.* —*n.* **1.** The act, an instance, or a means of escaping. **2.** Temporary freedom from trouble. —*adj.* Affording a means of escape: *an escape clause.* [< ONF *escaper,* "to take off one's cloak."] —**es•cap'a•ble** *adj.*

es•cap•ee (ĕs-kā'pē', ĕ-skā'pē, ĭ-skā'pē) *n.* One that has escaped, esp. a prisoner.

es•cape•ment (ĕ-skāp'mənt, ĭ-skāp'-) *n.* A mechanism used esp. in timepieces to control the wheel movement and provide periodic energy impulses to a pendulum or balance.

escape velocity. The minimum velocity that a body must attain to overcome the gravitational attraction of another body, such as the earth.

es•cap•ism (ĕ-skā'pĭz'əm, ĭ-skā'-) *n.* The habit or tendency of escaping from unpleasant realities through fantasy or entertainment. —**es•cap'ist** *n.*

es•ca•role (ĕs'kə-rōl') *n.* A salad plant having leaves with irregular, frilled edges. [< L *esca,* food.]

es•carp•ment (ĕ-skärp'mənt, ĭ-skärp'-) *n.* A steep slope or long cliff.

–escence. *comb. form.* A beginning or continuing state: **luminescence.** [< -ESCENT.]

–escent. *comb. form.* Beginning to be or exhibit: **phosphorescent.** [< L *-ēscēns.*]

es•chew (ĕs-cho͞o') *v.* To take care to avoid; shun. [< OF *eschiuver,* to shun, avoid.]

es•cort (ĕs'kôrt') *n.* **1.** One or more persons or vehicles accompanying another to give guidance or protection or to pay honor. **2.** A male companion of a woman in public. —*v.* (ĕs-kôrt'). To accompany as an escort. [< VL **excorrigere,* to conduct, escort.]

es•crow (ĕs'krō, ĕ-skrō', ĭ-skrō') *n.* The state of a written agreement, such as a deed, put into the custody of a third party until certain conditions are fulfilled. [< OF *escroe,* strip of parchment, scroll.]

es•cu•do (ĕ-sko͞o'dō, ĭ-sko͞o'-) *n., pl.* **-dos. 1.** The basic monetary unit of Portugal. **2.** The basic monetary unit of Chile.

es•cutch•eon (ĕ-skŭch'ən, ĭ-) *n.* A shield or shield-shaped emblem bearing a coat of arms. [< L *scūtum,* shield.]

–ese. *comb. form.* **1.** A native or inhabitant: **Sudanese. 2.** A language or dialect: **Japanese. 3.** A literary style or diction: **journalese.** [< L *-ēnsis,* "originating in."]

Es•ki•mo (ĕs'kə-mō') *n., pl.* **-mo** or **-mos. 1.** One of a people native to the Arctic coastal regions of North America and parts of Greenland and NE Siberia. **2.** The language spoken by these people. —**Es'ki•mo'** *adj.*

Es•ki•mo-Al•e•ut (ĕs'kə-mō'ăl'ē-o͞ot') *n.* A family of languages spoken chiefly among the Eskimos and the people of the Aleutian Islands.

e•soph•a•gus (ĭ-sŏf'ə-gəs) *n., pl.* **-gi** (-jī'). A muscular, membranous tube for the passage of food from the pharynx to the stomach. [< Gk *oisophagos,* gullet.] —**e'so•phag'e•al** (ē'sō-făj'ē-əl, ĭ-sŏf'ə-jē'əl) *adj.*

es•o•ter•ic (ĕs'ə-tĕr'ĭk) *adj.* **1.** Intended for or understood by only a small group. **2.** Confidential; private. [< Gk *esōterikos.*]

ESP extrasensory perception.

esp. especially.

es•pa•drille (ĕs'pə-drĭl') *n.* A sandal with a rope sole and a canvas upper. [< Prov *espardilho.*]

es•pal•ier (ĕ-spăl'yər, -yā', ĭ-spăl'-) *n.* A fruit tree or shrub trained to grow flat against a wall, often in a symmetrical pattern. [< It *spalliera,* applied to shoulder supports.] —**es•pal'ier** *v.*

es•pe•cial (ĕ-spĕsh'əl, ĭ-spĕsh'-) *adj.* Special; exceptional; particular. —**es•pe'cial•ly** *adv.*

Es•pe•ran•to (ĕs'pə-răn'tō, -rän'tō) *n.* An artificial international language based on word roots common to many European languages. [< Dr. L.L. Zamenhof (died 1917), Polish philologist who wrote under the name of Dr. *Esperanto,* "one who hopes."]

es•pi•o•nage (ĕs'pē-ə-näzh', -nĭj) *n.* The act or practice of spying. [< OIt *spia,* spy.]

es•pla•nade (ĕs'plə-nād', -näd') *n.* A flat, open stretch of pavement or grass used as a promenade. [< It *spianare,* to level.]

es•pouse (ĕ-spouz', ĭ-spouz') *v.* **-poused, -pousing. 1.** To marry. **2.** To give one's loyalty or support to; adopt. [< L *spondēre,* to promise

solemnly.] —**es•pou'sal** *n.* —**es•pous'er** *n.*
es•prit (ĕ-sprē') *n.* **1.** Spirit. **2.** Liveliness of mind and expression. [< L *spiritus,* SPIRIT.]
esprit de corps (də kôr'). A common spirit of devotion and enthusiasm among members of a group.
es•py (ĕ-spī', ĭ-spī') *v.* **-pied, -pying.** To catch sight of; glimpse. [< OF *espier,* to spy.]
-esque. *comb. form.* Possession of a specified manner or quality: **statuesque.** [< Gmc **-iskaz.*]
es•quire (ĕs'kwīr') *n.* **1.** A candidate for knighthood serving as attendant to a knight. **2.** A member of the English gentry ranking just below a knight. **3. Esquire.** A title of courtesy placed after a man's full name. [< OF *esquier, escuier,* squire, "shield-carrier."]
-ess. *comb. form.* A female: **lioness.** [< Gk *-issa.*]
es•say (ĕs'ā, ĕ-sā') *v.* To make an attempt at; try; try out. —*n.* (ĕs'ā, ĕ-sā'). **1.** An attempt; endeavor. **2.** A short literary composition on a single subject, usually presenting the author's personal views. [< OF *essai,* a trial.]
es•say•ist (ĕs'ā'ĭst) *n.* A writer of essays.
Es•sen (ĕs'ən). A city of NW West Germany. Pop. 728,000.
es•sence (ĕs'əns) *n.* **1.** The intrinsic or indispensable properties of a thing. **2.** A concentrated extract of a substance that retains its fundamental properties. **3.** A perfume. [< L *esse,* to be.]
es•sen•tial (ĭ-sĕn'shəl) *adj.* **1.** Constituting or part of the essence of something; basic. **2.** Of the greatest importance; indispensable. —*n.* An essential thing. —**es•sen'tial•ly** *adv.*
-est[1]. *comb. form.* The superlative degree of adjectives and adverbs: **earliest.** [< Gmc **-istaz.*]
-est[2], -st. *comb. form.* The archaic 2nd person sing. form of the present and past indicative tenses: **comest.** [< OE.]
EST Eastern Standard Time.
est. **1.** established. **2.** estimate.
es•tab•lish (ĕ-stăb'lĭsh, ĭ-stăb'-) *v.* **1.** To make firm or secure. **2.** To settle securely in a position. **3.** To cause to be recognized and accepted. **4.** To found or create. **5.** To prove the truth of. [< L *stabilire,* to make firm.]
es•tab•lish•ment (ĕ-stăb'lĭsh-mənt, ĭ-stăb'-) *n.* **1.** The act of establishing or condition of being established. **2.** A business firm or residence, including its members, staff, and possessions. **3. the Establishment.** An exclusive or powerful group in control of society or a field of activity.
es•tate (ĕ-stāt', ĭ-stāt') *n.* **1.** A sizable piece of land with a large house. **2.** All of one's possessions, esp. those left by a deceased person. **3.** A stage, condition, or status of life. [< OF *estat,* state.]
es•teem (ĕ-stēm', ĭ-stēm') *v.* **1.** To regard favorably; respect; prize. **2.** To judge to be; consider. —*n.* Favorable regard; respect. [< L *aestimāre,* to ESTIMATE.]
es•ter (ĕs'tər) *n.* Any of a class of organic compounds chemically corresponding to inorganic salts. [< G *Essigäther,* "vinegar ether."]
es•thet•ics (ĕs-thĕt'ĭks) *n.* Aesthetics. —**es'thete'** (-thēt') *n.* —**es•thet'ic** *adj.*
es•ti•mate (ĕs'tə-māt') *v.* **-mated, -mating.** **1.** To make a judgment as to the likely cost, quantity, or extent of; calculate approximately. **2.** To evaluate. —*n.* (ĕs'tə-mĭt). **1.** A tentative evaluation or rough calculation. **2. a.** A preliminary calculation of the cost of work to be undertaken. **b.** The written statement of such a calculation. **3.** An opinion. [L *aestimāre.*] —**es'ti•ma•ble** (-tə-mə-bəl) *adj.* —**es'ti•ma'tion** *n.* —**es'ti•ma'tor** *n.*
Es•to•ni•a (ĕs-tō'nē-ə). A constituent republic of the Soviet Union, on the Baltic. Pop. 1,357,000. Cap. Tallinn.
Es•to•ni•an (ĕs-tō'nē-ən) *n.* **1.** A native or inhabitant of Estonia. **2.** The Finno-Ugric language of Estonia. —**Es•to'ni•an** *adj.*
es•trange (ĕs-trānj') *v.* **-tranged, -tranging.** **1.** To remove from an accustomed place or relation. **2.** To alienate the affections of. [< L *extrāneus,* STRANGE.] —**es•trange'ment** *n.*
es•tro•gen (ĕs'trə-jən) *n.* Any of several steroid hormones produced chiefly by the ovary and responsible for the development and maintenance of female secondary sex characteristics. —**es'tro•gen'ic** (-jĕn'ĭk) *adj.*
es•tu•ar•y (ĕs'cho͞o-ĕr'ē) *n., pl.* **-ies.** **1.** The wide lower course of a river where its current is met by the tides. **2.** An inland arm of the sea that meets the mouth of a river. [L *aestuārium,* estuary, tidal channel.]
ET Eastern Time.
e•ta (ā'tə, ē'tə) *n.* The 7th letter of the Greek alphabet, representing *ē.*
e.t.a. estimated time of arrival.
et al. and others (L *et alii*).
etc. et cetera.
et cet•er•a (ĕt sĕt'ər-ə, -sĕt'rə). Also **et•cet•er•a, et caet•er•a.** And other unspecified things of the same class; and so forth. [L, "and other (things)."]
etch (ĕch) *v.* **1.** To wear away with or as if with acid. **2.** To make (a pattern) on a surface with acid. **3.** To impress or imprint clearly. [< G *ätzen,* to etch, bite.] —**etch'er** *n.*
etch•ing (ĕch'ĭng) *n.* **1.** The art of preparing etched metal plates. **2.** A design etched on a plate. **3.** An impression made from an etched plate.
e•ter•nal (ĭ-tûr'nəl) *adj.* **1.** Without beginning or end. **2.** Lasting; timeless. **3.** Seemingly endless; interminable. **4.** Of or relating to existence after death. [< L *aeternus,* eternal.] —**e•ter'nal•ly** *adv.*
e•ter•ni•ty (ĭ-tûr'nə-tē) *n.* **1.** The totality of time without beginning or end. **2.** The state or quality of being eternal. **3.** Afterlife; immortality.
eth. Variant of **edh.**
-eth[1], -th. *comb. form.* The archaic 3rd person sing. form of the present indicative tense: *praiseth.* [< OE.]
-eth[2]. Variant of **-th[2].**
eth•ane (ĕth'ān') *n.* A colorless, odorless gas, C_2H_6, occurring as a constituent of natural gas and used as a fuel and refrigerant. [ETH(YL) + -ANE.]
eth•a•nol (ĕth'ə-nôl', -nōl', -nŏl') *n.* A colorless flammable liquid, C_2H_5OH, obtained from fermentation of sugars and starches, and used as a solvent, in drugs, and in intoxicating beverages.
e•ther (ē'thər) *n.* Also **ae•ther.** **1.** Any of a class of organic compounds in which two hydrocarbon groups are linked by an oxygen atom. **2.** A highly flammable liquid, $C_4H_{10}O$, widely used in industry and as an anesthetic. **3.** The regions of space beyond the earth's atmosphere; the clear sky; the heavens. **4.** An all-pervading, infinitely elastic, massless medium formerly postulated as the medium of propagation of electromagnetic waves. [< L *aethēr,* the upper or bright air, ether.]
e•the•re•al (ĭ-thîr'ē-əl) *adj.* **1.** Highly refined; delicate. **2.** Heavenly; spiritual.
eth•ic (ĕth'ĭk) *n.* A principle of right or good conduct, or a body of such principles. —*n.* **ethics.** **1.** *(takes sing. v.).* The study of the general nature of morals and of specific moral choices. **2.** *(takes pl. v.).* **a.** The rules or standards governing the conduct of the members of a profession. **b.** Any set of moral principles or values. **c.** The moral quality of a course of action; propriety. [< Gk *ēthikos,* ethical.]
eth•i•cal (ĕth'ĭ-kəl) *adj.* **1.** Of or dealing with ethics. **2.** In accordance with the accepted principles governing the conduct of a group. —**eth'i•cal•ly** *adv.*
E•thi•o•pi•a (ē'thē-ō'pē-ə). An independent country in E Africa. Pop. 27,000,000. Cap. Addis Ababa. —**E'thi•o'pi•an** *adj.* & *n.*

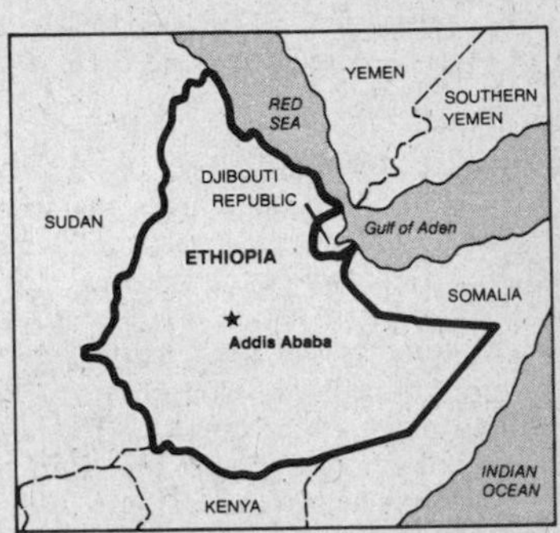

Ethiopia

eth•nic (ĕth'nĭk) *adj.* Of or pertaining to a social group that claims or is accorded special status on the basis of complex, often variable traits including religious, linguistic, ancestral, or physical characteristics. [< Gk *ethnikos,* of a national group, foreign.]
eth•nic•i•ty (ĕth-nĭs'ĭ-tē) *n.* **1.** The condition of belonging to a particular ethnic group. **2.** Ethnic pride.
eth•nol•o•gy (ĕth-nŏl'ə-jē) *n.* The anthropological study of socio-economic systems and cultural heritage, esp. of cultural origins and factors influencing cultural growth and change, in technologically primitive societies. —**eth'no•log'ic** (ĕth'nə-lŏj'ĭk), **eth'no•log'i•cal** *adj.* —**eth•nol'o•gist** *n.*
eth•yl (ĕth'əl) *n.* **1.** An organic radical, C_2H_5. **2. Ethyl.** **a.** A trademark for a gasoline containing an antiknock substance, tetraethyl lead. **b.** A trademark for any of various additives for hydrocarbon fuels and lubricants. [ETH(ER) + -YL.]
ethyl alcohol. Ethanol.
eth•yl•ene (ĕth'ə-lēn') *n.* **1.** A colorless, flammable gas, C_2H_4, derived from natural gas and petroleum. **2.** An organic radical, C_2H_4.
ethylene glycol. A colorless, syrupy alcohol, $C_2H_6O_2$, used as an antifreeze in cooling and heating systems.
e•ti•ol•o•gy (ē'tē-ŏl'ə-jē) *n., pl.* **-gies.** **1.** The study of causes, origins, or reasons. **2.** The cause of a disease or disorder as determined by medical diagnosis. [< Gk *aitiologia,* a giving the cause of.] —**e'ti•o•log'i•cal** (-ə-lŏj'ĭ-kəl) *adj.* —**e'ti•o•log'i•cal•ly** *adv.*
et•i•quette (ĕt'ə-kĕt', -kĭt) *n.* **1.** The body of prescribed social usages. **2.** Any special code of behavior or courtesy. [F *étiquette,* prescribed routine.]
E•tru•ri•a (ĭ-tro͝or'ē-ə). An ancient country of west-central Italy.

E•trus•can (ĭ-trŭs′kən) *n.* **1.** One of a people of ancient Etruria. **2.** The extinct ancient language of the Etruscans, of undetermined linguistic affiliation. —**E•trus′can** *adj.*

-ette. *comb. form.* **1.** Small or diminutive: **kitchenette. 2.** An imitation of: *leatherette.* **3.** Female or feminine: **usherette.** [< OF.]

e•tude (ā′t/y/o͞od′) *n.* A musical piece for the development of a given point of technique. [< OF *estudie,* study.]

etym. etymology.

et•y•mol•o•gy (ĕt′ə-mŏl′ə-jē) *n., pl.* **-gies. 1.** The origin and historical development of a word. **2.** An account of the history of a specific word. **3.** The branch of linguistics that studies the derivation of words. [< Gk *etumologiā.*] —**et′y•mo•log′i•cal** (-mə-lŏj′ĭ-kəl) *adj.* —**et′y•mol′o•gist** *n.*

eu–. *comb. form.* **1.** Well or beneficial. **2.** Derivative of a specified substance. [< Gk *eus,* good.]

Eu europium.

eu•ca•lyp•tus (yo͞o′kə-lĭp′təs) *n., pl.* **-tuses.** Any of various Australian trees yielding valuable timber and an aromatic medicinal oil: [< EU- + Gk *kaluptos,* covered.]

Eu•cha•rist (yo͞o′kər-ĭst) *n.* **1.** The Christian sacrament commemorating Christ's Last Supper; Communion; Holy Communion. **2.** The consecrated elements of bread and wine used in this sacrament. [< Gk *eukharistos,* grateful.] —**Eu′cha•ris′tic, Eu′cha•ris′ti•cal** *adj.*

eu•chre (yo͞o′kər) *n.* A card game played with the 32 highest cards of the deck. [?]

Eu•clid (yo͞o′klĭd). Greek mathematician of the 3rd century B.C. —**Eu•clid′e•an** *adj.*

eu•gen•ics (yo͞o-jĕn′ĭks) *n. (takes sing. v.).* The study of hereditary improvement, esp. of human improvement by genetic control. [< Gk *eugenēs,* well-born.] —**eu•gen′ic** *adj.*

eu•lo•gy (yo͞o′lə-jē) *n., pl.* **-gies. 1.** A public tribute to a person or thing, esp. an oration honoring one recently deceased. **2.** Great praise or commendation. [Prob < Gk *eulogia,* praise.] —**eu′lo•gis′tic** *adj.*

eu•nuch (yo͞o′nək) *n.* A castrated man. [< Gk *eunoukhos,* "bed-watcher," eunuch.]

eu•phe•mism (yo͞o′fə-mĭz′əm) *n.* An inoffensive term substituted for one considered offensively explicit. [< Gk *euphēmia,* use of good words.] —**eu′phe•mis′tic** (-mĭs′tĭk) *adj.*

eu•pho•ny (yo͞o′fə-nē) *n., pl.* **-nies.** Agreeable sound, esp. in the phonetic quality of words. —**eu•pho′ni•ous** (-fō′nē-əs) *adj.*

eu•pho•ri•a (yo͞o-fôr′ē-ə, -fōr′ē-ə) *n.* A feeling of great happiness or well-being. [< Gk *euphoros,* easy to bear, well-borne.] —**eu•phor′ic** *adj.* —**eu•phor′i•cal•ly** *adv.*

Eu•phra•tes (yo͞o-frā′tēz). A river of SW Asia.

Eur. Europe; European.

Eur•a•sia (yo͞o-rā′zhə). The continents of Europe and Asia.

Eur•a•sian (yo͞o-rā′zhən) *adj.* **1.** Of or pertaining to Eurasia. **2.** Of mixed European and Asian ancestry. —*n.* A person of Eurasian ancestry.

eu•re•ka (yo͞o-rē′kə) *interj.* Expressive of triumphant discovery. [Gk *heurēka,* "I have found (it)."]

Eu•rip•i•des (yo͞o-rĭp′ə-dēz′). 480?–406 B.C. Greek tragic poet.

Eu•rope (yo͞or′əp). A continent consisting of the section of Eurasia that extends westward from the Urals. —**Eu′ro•pe′an** *adj. & n.*

European Economic Community. The official name for the **Common Market.**

eu•ro•pi•um (yo͞o-rō′pē-əm) *n. Symbol* **Eu** A soft, silvery-white element used to absorb neutrons in research. Atomic number 63, atomic weight 151.96.

Eu•sta•chian tube (yo͞o-stā′shən, -stā′kē-ən, -stā′shē-ən). A bony and cartilaginous tube through which the tympanic cavity communicates with the nasal part of the pharynx. [< B. *Eustachio* (died 1517), Italian anatomist.]

eu•tha•na•sia (yo͞o′thə-nā′zhə, -shə) *n.* **1.** The act of killing a person painlessly for reasons of mercy. **2.** A painless death. [Gk.]

eu•then•ics (yo͞o-thĕn′ĭks) *n. (often takes sing. v.).* The study of the improvement of human functioning and well-being by adjustment of environment. [< Gk *euthenein,* to flourish, thrive.] —**eu•then′ist** *n.*

eV electron volt.

EVA extravehicular activity.

e•vac•u•ate (ĭ-văk′yo͞o-āt′) *v.* **-ated, -ating. 1. a.** To remove the contents of. **b.** To create a vacuum in. **2.** To excrete or discharge waste matter from (the bowels). **3.** To withdraw, esp. from a threatened area. [L *ēvacuāre,* to empty out.] —**e•vac′u•a′tion** *n.* —**e•vac′u•a′tor** *n.*

e•vac•u•ee (ĭ-văk′yo͞o-ē′) *n.* One evacuated from a threatened area.

e•vade (ĭ-vād′) *v.* **evaded, evading.** To escape or avoid by cleverness or deceit. [< L *ēvādere,* to evade, go out.] —**e•vad′er** *n.*

e•val•u•ate (ĭ-văl′yo͞o-āt′) *v.* **-ated, -ating.** To ascertain, judge, or fix the value or worth of. —**e•val′u•a′tion** *n.* —**e•val′u•a′tor** *n.*

ev•a•nes•cent (ĕv′ə-nĕs′ənt) *adj.* Vanishing or likely to vanish; transitory; fleeting. —**ev′a•nes′cence** *n.* —**ev′a•nes′cent•ly** *adv.*

e•van•gel•i•cal (ē′văn-jĕl′ĭ-kəl) *adj.* Also **e•van•gel•ic** (-jĕl′ĭk). **1.** Pertaining to the Christian Gospel, esp. the Gospels of the New Testament. **2.** Of or pertaining to a Protestant group emphasizing the authority of the Gospel. [< Gk *evangelos,* bringing good news.]

e•van•gel•ism (ĭ-văn′jə-lĭz′əm) *n.* The zealous preaching and dissemination of the Gospel, as through missionary work.

e•van•gel•ist (ĭ-văn′jə-lĭst) *n.* **1.** Often **Evangelist.** Any of the authors of the New Testament Gospels, Matthew, Mark, Luke, or John. **2.** A Protestant who practices evangelism. —**e•van′gel•is′tic** *adj.*

Ev•ans•ville (ĕv′ənz-vĭl, -vəl). A city of SW Indiana. Pop. 102,000.

e•vap•o•rate (ĭ-văp′ə-rāt′) *v.* **-rated, -rating. 1. a.** To change into a vapor. **b.** To remove or be removed in, or as, a vapor. **2.** To vanish. —**e•vap′o•ra′tion** *n.* —**e•vap′o•ra′tor** *n.*

e•va•sion (ĭ-vā′zhən) *n.* **1.** The act of evading. **2.** A means of evading.

e•va•sive (ĭ-vā′sĭv) *adj.* **1.** Characterized by evasion. **2.** Intentionally vague: *an evasive statement.* —**e•va′sive•ness** *n.*

eve (ēv) *n.* **1.** The evening or day preceding a holiday. **2.** The period immediately preceding a certain event: *the eve of war.* **3.** *Poetic.* Evening.

Eve (ēv). The first woman; wife of Adam. Genesis 3:20.

e•ven (ē′vən) *adj.* **1. a.** Flat: *an even floor.* **b.** Smooth. **c.** Level: *The picture is even with the window.* **2.** Uniform; steady; regular: *an even rate of speed.* **3.** Tranquil; calm: *an even temper.* **4.** Equal in degree, extent, or amount; balanced. **5. a.** *Math.* Exactly divisible by 2. **b.** Characterized by a number exactly divisible by 2. **6. a.** Having an even number in a series. **b.** Having an even number of members. **7.** Exact: *an even pound.* —*adv.* **1.** To a higher degree: *an even worse condition.* **2.** At the same time as: *Even as we watched, the building collapsed.* **3.** In spite of: *Even with his head start, I overtook him.* **4.** In fact: *unhappy, even weeping.* —**break even.** To have neither losses nor gains. —**get even.** To exact revenge. —*v.* To make or become even. [< OE *efen* < Gmc **ibnaz.*] —**e′ven•ly** *adv.* —**e′ven•ness** *n.*

eve•ning (ēv′nĭng) *n.* Late afternoon and early night. [< OE *ǣfen,* evening. See **apo-.**]

evening star. Any planet that crosses the local meridian before midnight, esp. Mercury or Venus when either is prominent in the west shortly after sunset.

e•vent (ĭ-vĕnt′) *n.* **1.** An occurrence or incident, esp. a significant one. **2.** One of the items in a sports program. [< L *ēvenīre,* to come out, happen.]

e•vent•ful (ĭ-vĕnt′fəl) *adj.* **1.** Full of or abounding in events. **2.** Important; momentous. —**e•vent′ful•ly** *adv.* —**e•vent′ful•ness** *n.*

e•ven•tu•al (ĭ-vĕn′cho͞o-əl) *adj.* Occurring at an unspecified time in the future: *his eventual death.* [< EVENT.] —**e•ven′tu•al•ly** *adv.*

e•ven•tu•al•i•ty (ĭ-vĕn′cho͞o-ăl′ə-tē) *n., pl.* **-ties.** Something that may occur.

ev•er (ĕv′ər) *adv.* **1.** At all times: *He is ever courteous.* **2.** At any time: *Have you ever seen him?* **3.** In any way: *How could you ever treat him so?* [< OE *ǣfre.* See **aiw-.**]

Ev•er•est, Mount (ĕv′ər-ĭst, ĕv′rĭst). The highest mountain (29,028 ft.) in the world, in the Himalayas.

ev•er•glade (ĕv′ər-glād′) *n.* A tract of usually submerged swampland.

ev•er•green (ĕv′ər-grēn′) *adj.* Having or characterizing foliage that remains green throughout the year. —*n.* An evergreen tree or plant.

ev•er•last•ing (ĕv′ər-lăs′tĭng, -läs′tĭng) *adj.* Lasting forever; eternal.

ev•er•more (ĕv′ər-môr′, -mōr′) *adv.* Forever; always.

eve•ry (ĕv′rē, -ə-rē) *adj.* **1.** Each without exception: *every student in the class.* **2.** Not lacking anything necessary; complete. —*adv.* —Used as an intensifier: *every once in a while.* —**every other.** Each second: *Every other door is unmarked.* [< OE *ǣfre ǣlc,* "ever each," every.]

eve•ry•bod•y (ĕv′rē-bŏd′ē) *pron.* Every person; everyone.

eve•ry•day (ĕv′rē-dā′) *adj.* **1.** Suitable for ordinary days. **2.** Commonplace; usual.

eve•ry•one (ĕv′rē-wŭn′) *pron.* Every person; everybody.

eve•ry•place (ĕv′rē-plās′) *adv.* Everywhere.

eve•ry•thing (ĕv′rē-thĭng′) *pron.* All things that exist or are relevant.

eve•ry•where (ĕv′rē-hwâr′) *adv.* In every place.

e•vict (ĭ-vĭkt′) *v.* To expel (a tenant) by legal process; force out. [< L *ēvincere,* to conquer, overcome.] —**e•vic′tion** *n.* —**e•vic′tor** *n.*

ev•i•dence (ĕv′ə-dəns) *n.* **1.** The data on which a judgment can be based or proof established. **2.** That which serves to indicate: *His reaction was evidence of guilt.* —*v.* **-denced, -dencing.** To indicate clearly.

ev•i•dent (ĕv′ə-dənt) *adj.* Easily recognized or perceived; obvious. [< L *ēvidēns,* evident, clear.] —**ev′i•dent•ly** *adv.* —**ev′i•dent•ness** *n.*

e•vil (ē′vəl) *adj.* **1.** Morally bad or wrong; wicked. **2.** Injurious; harmful. —*n.* **1.** That which is morally bad or wrong; wickedness. **2.** That which causes misfortune, suffering, etc. [< OE *yfel.* See **upo.**] —**e′vil•ly** *adv.*

e•vince (ĭ-vĭns′) *v.* **evinced, evincing.** To show or demonstrate; manifest. [L *ēvincere,* to conquer, prove.] —**e•vin'ci•ble** *adj.*

e•vis•cer•ate (ĭ-vĭs'ə-rāt') *v.* **-ated, -ating. 1.** To remove the entrails of. **2.** To take away a vital part of. [L *ēviscerāre.*] —**e•vis'cer•a'tion** *n.*

e•voke (ĭ-vōk') *v.* **evoked, evoking.** To summon or call forth, as memories; elicit. [L *ēvocāre,* to call forth, summon.] —**ev'o•ca'tion** (ĕv'ə-kā'shən) *n.* —**e•vok'er** *n.*

ev•o•lu•tion (ĕv'ə-lōō'shən) *n.* **1.** A gradual process in which something changes, esp. into a more complex form. **2.** The biological theory or process whereby organisms change with passage of time so that descendants differ from their ancestors. **3.** The extraction of a root of a mathematical quantity. [< L *ēvolvere,* EVOLVE.] —**ev'o•lu'tion•ar•y** *adj.* —**ev'o•lu'tion•ism'** *n.* —**ev'o•lu'tion•ist** *n.*

e•volve (ĭ-vŏlv') *v.* **evolved, evolving. 1.** To develop or achieve gradually. **2.** To develop biologically by evolutionary processes. [L *ē-volvere,* to roll out, unfold.]

ewe (yōō) *n.* A female sheep. [< OE *ēowu.* See **owi-**.]

E•we (ā'vā, ā'wā) *n.* The Niger-Congo language of Togo, Ghana, and parts of Dahomey.

ew•er (yōō'ər) *n.* A wide-mouthed pitcher. [< VL **aquāria.*]

ex-[1]. *comb. form.* **1.** Removal out of or from. **2.** Former. [< L *ex,* out, out of.]

ex-[2]. *comb. form.* Out of. [< Gk *ex.*]

ex. **1.** example. **2.** express. **3.** extra.

Ex. Exodus (Old Testament).

ex•ac•er•bate (ĕg-zăs'ər-bāt', ĭg-, ĕk-săs'-, ĭk-) *v.* **-bated, -bating.** To increase the severity of; aggravate, as a pain, emotion, etc. [L *exacerbāre,* aggravate, make harsh.] —**ex•ac'er•bat'ing•ly** *adv.* —**ex•ac'er•ba'tion** *n.*

ex•act (ĕg-zăkt', ĭg-) *adj.* Strictly accurate; precise. —*v.* **1.** To force the payment of; extort. **2.** To call for; require. [L *exactus,* pp of *exigere,* "to drive out," require.] —**ex•act'ly** *adv.* —**ex•act'ness** *n.*

ex•act•ing (ĕg-zăk'tĭng, ĭg-) *adj.* **1.** Making great demands. **2.** Requiring great effort or attention. —**ex•act'ing•ly** *adv.*

ex•act•i•tude (ĕg-zăk'tə-t/y/ōōd', ĭg-) *n.* The state or quality of being exact.

ex•ag•ger•ate (ĕg-zăj'ə-rāt', ĭg-) *v.* **-ated, -ating.** To enlarge (something) disproportionately; overstate. [L *exaggerāre,* to pile up, exaggerate.] —**ex•ag'ger•a'tion** *n.*

ex•alt (ĕg-zôlt', ĭg-) *v.* **1.** To raise in position, status, etc.; elevate. **2.** To glorify; praise. **3.** To fill with pride, delight, etc.; elate. [< L *exaltāre,* to lift up, exalt.] —**ex'al•ta'tion** *n.*

ex•am (ĕg-zăm', ĭg-) *n. Informal.* An examination.

exam. examination.

ex•am•i•na•tion (ĕg-zăm'ə-nā'shən, ĭg-) *n.* **1.** The act of examining. **2.** A set of questions testing knowledge.

ex•am•ine (ĕg-zăm'ĭn, ĭg-) *v.* **-ined, -ining. 1.** To inspect or analyze (a person, thing, or situation) in detail. **2.** To test knowledge or skills by questioning. **3.** To interrogate formally to elicit facts. [< L *exāmen,* a weighing, consideration.] —**ex•am'in•er** *n.*

ex•am•ple (ĕg-zăm'pəl, -zäm'pəl, ĭg-) *n.* **1.** One representative of a group; a sample. **2.** Something worthy of imitation; a model. **3.** Something that serves as a warning. **4.** Something that illustrates a principle. [< L *exemplum,* "(something) taken out," example.]

ex•as•per•ate (ĕg-zăs'pə-rāt', ĭg-) *v.* **-ated, -ating.** To make angry or irritated; tax the patience of. [L *exasperāre,* to exasperate, make rough.] —**ex•as'per•a'tion** *n.*

exc. **1.** excellent. **2.** except.

ex•ca•vate (ĕk'skə-vāt') *v.* **-vated, -vating. 1.** To dig out; hollow out. **2.** To remove (soil) by digging or scooping out. **3.** To uncover by digging. [L *excavāre,* to hollow out.] —**ex'ca•va'tion** *n.* —**ex'ca•va'tor** *n.*

ex•ceed (ĕk-sēd', ĭk-) *v.* **1.** To be greater than; surpass. **2.** To go or be beyond the limits of. [< L *excēdere,* to depart, go out.]

ex•ceed•ing (ĕk-sē'dĭng, ĭk-) *adj.* Extreme; extraordinary. —**ex•ceed'ing•ly** *adv.*

ex•cel (ĕk-sĕl', ĭk-) *v.* **-celled, -celling.** To be better than (others); surpass; outdo. [< L *excellere.*]

ex•cel•lence (ĕk'sə-ləns) *n.* **1.** The state or quality of excelling. **2.** Something in which a person or thing excels.

Ex•cel•len•cy (ĕk'sə-lən-sē) *n., pl.* **-cies.** A title of honor for certain high officials.

ex•cel•lent (ĕk'sə-lənt) *adj.* Of the highest quality; exceptionally good; superb. —**ex'cel•lent•ly** *adv.*

ex•cel•si•or (ĕk-sĕl'sē-ər, ĭk-) *n.* Wood shavings used for packing, stuffing, etc.

ex•cept (ĕk-sĕpt', ĭk-) *prep.* With the exclusion of; but. —*conj.* Were it not for the fact that; only. —*v.* To leave out; exclude. [< L *excipere,* to take out.]

ex•cept•ing (ĕk-sĕp'tĭng, ĭk-) *prep.* Excluding; except.

ex•cep•tion (ĕk-sĕp'shən, ĭk-) *n.* **1.** The act of excepting. **2.** A case that does not conform to normal rules. **3.** An objection.

ex•cep•tion•a•ble (ĕk-sĕp'shən-ə-bəl, ĭk-) *adj.* Open to exception; objectionable.

ex•cep•tion•al (ĕk-sĕp'shən-əl, ĭk-) *adj.* Uncommon; extraordinary. —**ex•cep'tion•al'i•ty** *n.* —**ex•cep'tion•al•ly** *adv.*

ex•cerpt (ĕk'sûrpt') *n.* A passage selected or quoted from a speech, book, etc. [L *excerptum,* "something picked out," excerpt.]

ex•cess (ĕk-sĕs', ĭk-, ĕk'sĕs') *n.* **1.** An amount beyond what is required; superfluity. **2.** Intemperance; overindulgence. —*adj.* Being more than is required. [< L *excessus,* pp of *excēdere,* to EXCEED.]

ex•ces•sive (ĕk-sĕs'ĭv, ĭk-) *adj.* Exceeding a reasonable degree or amount. —**ex•ces'sive•ly** *adv.* —**ex•ces'sive•ness** *n.*

exch. exchange.

ex•change (ĕks-chānj', ĭks-) *v.* **-changed, -changing. 1.** To give and receive reciprocally; trade. **2.** To replace (one thing by another). —*n.* **1.** An act or instance of exchanging. **2.** A place where things are exchanged, esp. a center where securities are traded. **3.** A central system that establishes connections between individual telephones. [< VL **excambiāre.*]

ex•cheq•uer (ĕks-chĕk'ər, ĭks-, ĕks'chĕk'ər) *n.* A treasury, as of a nation or organization. [< OF *eschequier,* chessboard, counting table.]

ex•cise[1] (ĕk'sīz', ĕk-sīz', ĭk-) *n.* A tax on the production, sale, or consumption of certain commodities within a country. [Obs Du *excijs.*] —**ex'cise'** *v.* **(-cised, -cising).**

ex•cise[2] (ĕk-sīz', ĭk-) *v.* **-cised, -cising.** To remove by cutting. [L *excīdere* (pp *excīsus*), to cut out.] —**ex•ci'sion** (ĕk-sĭzh'ən, ĭk-) *n.*

ex•cite (ĕk-sīt', ĭk-) *v.* **-cited, -citing. 1.** To stimulate; stir to activity. **2.** To arouse strong feeling in (a person); provoke. **3.** *Phys.* To increase the energy of. [< L *excitāre.*] —**ex•cit'ed•ly** *adv.* —**ex•cite'ment** *n.*

ex•claim (ĕks-klām', ĭks-) *v.* To cry out or speak suddenly or vehemently. [< L *exclāmāre,* to call out.] —**ex•claim'er** *n.* —**ex'cla•ma'tion** (-klə-mā'shən) *n.* —**ex•clam'a•tor'y** (-klăm'ə-tôr'ē, -tōr'ē) *adj.*

exclamation point. A punctuation mark (!) used after an exclamation.

ex•clude (ĕks-klōōd', ĭks-) *v.* **-cluded, -cluding. 1.** To prevent from entering a place, group, etc.; bar. **2.** To force out; expel. [< L *exclūdere.*] —**ex•clud'er** *n.* —**ex•clu'sion** *n.*

ex•clu•sive (ĕks-klōō'sĭv, ĭks-) *adj.* **1.** Not divided or shared with others. **2.** Admitting only certain people; select. **3.** Expensive; chic: *exclusive shops.* —**ex•clu'sive•ly** *adv.* —**ex•clu'sive•ness, ex'clu•siv'i•ty** (-sĭv'ĭ-tē) *n.*

ex•com•mu•ni•cate (ĕks'kə-myōō'nĭ-kāt') *v.* **-cated, -cating.** To cut off from the church by ecclesiastical authority. —**ex'com•mu'ni•ca'tion** *n.* —**ex'com•mu'ni•ca'tor** *n.*

ex•co•ri•ate (ĕk-skôr'ē-āt', ĕk-skōr'-, ĭk-) *v.* **-ated, -ating. 1.** To tear or wear off the skin of. **2.** To censure strongly; denounce. [< L *excoriāre,* to strip of skin.] —**ex•co'ri•a'tion** *n.*

ex•cre•ment (ĕk'skrə-mənt) *n.* Bodily waste, esp. fecal matter. [< L *excernere,* to sift out.] —**ex'cre•ment'al** (-mĕn'təl) *adj.*

ex•cres•cence (ĕk-skrĕs'əns, ĭk-) *n.* An abnormal outgrowth or enlargement. [< L *excrēscere,* to grow out.]

ex•cre•ta (ĕk-skrē'tə, ĭk-) *pl.n.* Wastes excreted from the body. —**ex•cre'tal** *adj.*

ex•crete (ĕk-skrēt', ĭk-) *v.* **-creted, -creting.** To eliminate (waste matter) from the blood, tissues, or organs. [L *excernere* (pp *excrētus*), to sift out.] —**ex•cre'tion** *n.* —**ex'cre•tor'y** (ĕk'skrə-tôr'ē, -tōr'ē) *adj.*

ex•cru•ci•at•ing (ĕk-skrōō'shē-ā'tĭng, ĭk-) *adj.* Intensely painful. [< L *excruciāre,* to torment.] —**ex•cru'ci•at'ing•ly** *adv.*

ex•cul•pate (ĕk'skŭl-pāt', ĕk-skŭl'-, ĭk-) *v.* **-pated, -pating.** To clear of a charge; exonerate. [ML *exculpāre.*] —**ex'cul•pa'tion** *n.*

ex•cur•sion (ĕk-skûr'zhən, ĭk-) *n.* **1.** A short journey; outing. **2.** A short, inexpensive pleasure tour. **3.** Movement from an average position or axis. [< L *excurrere,* to run out.]

ex•cuse (ĕk-skyōōz', ĭk-) *v.* **-cused, -cusing. 1.** To grant pardon to; forgive. **2.** To overlook; condone. **3.** To justify. **4.** To free, as from an obligation. —*n.* (ĕk-skyōōs', ĭk-). **1.** An explanation to elicit pardon. **2.** A ground for being excused. [< L *excūsāre.*] —**ex•cus'a•ble** *adj.* —**ex•cus'a•ble•ness** *n.*

exec. **1.** executive. **2.** executor.

ex•e•cra•ble (ĕk'sĭ-krə-bəl) *adj.* **1.** Abominable; detestable. **2.** Extremely inferior. [< L *exsecrārī,* to EXECRATE.] —**ex'e•cra•bly** *adv.*

ex•e•crate (ĕk'sĭ-krāt') *v.* **-crated, -crating. 1.** To inveigh against; denounce. **2.** To abominate; abhor. [L *exsecrārī,* to curse, execrate.] —**ex'e•cra'tion** *n.* —**ex'e•cra'tor** *n.*

ex•e•cute (ĕk'sĭ-kyōōt') *v.* **-cuted, -cuting. 1.** To carry out; perform. **2.** To legalize, as by signing and sealing: *execute a deed.* **3.** To carry out what is required by: *execute a will.* **4.** To subject to capital punishment. [< L *exsequī,* execute, follow to the end.] —**ex'e•cu'tion** *n.*

ex•e•cu•tion•er (ĕk'sĭ-kyōō'shən-ər) *n.* One who administers capital punishment.

ex•ec•u•tive (ĕg-zĕk'yə-tĭv, ĭg-) *n.* **1.** One having administrative authority in an organization. **2.** The branch of government charged with putting into effect a country's laws. —*adj.* **1.** Pertaining to or suited for carrying out plans, duties, etc. **2.** Of or pertaining to the executive branch of a government.

ex•ec•u•tor (ĕg-zĕk'yə-tər, ĭg-) *n.* One appointed by a testator to execute his will. —**ex•ec'u•trix'** (-trĭks') *fem.n.*

ex•e•ge•sis (ĕk'sə-jē'sĭs) *n., pl.* **-ses** (-sēz).

Critical explanation or analysis of a text. [< Gk *exēgeisthai,* to show the way.]

ex•em•plar (ĕg-zĕm′plär′, -plər, ĭg-) *n.* One that is worthy of being copied; a model. [< L *exemplum,* example.] **—ex•em′pla•ry** (-plə-rē) *adj.*

ex•em•pli•fy (ĕg-zĕm′plə-fī′, ĭg-) *v.* **-fied, -fying.** **1.** To illustrate by example. **2.** To serve as an example of. **—ex•em′pli•fi•ca′tion** *n.*

ex•empt (ĕg-zĕmpt′, ĭg-) *v.* To free from an obligation or duty required of others. [< L *eximere,* to take out.] **—ex•empt′** *adj.* **—ex•empt′i•ble** *adj.* **—ex•emp′tion** *n.*

ex•er•cise (ĕk′sər-sīz′) *n.* **1.** An act of employing or putting into use. **2.** Physical activity to develop fitness. **3.** A lesson, problem, etc., designed to increase some skill. **4.** Often **exercises.** A public ceremony with speeches and other formalities: *graduation exercises.* —*v.* **-cised, -cising.** **1.** To put into operation; employ. **2.** To subject to or engage in exercises for physical fitness. **3.** To worry or upset: *exercised by his wife's illness.* [< L *exercēre,* to drive on; practice.]

ex•ert (ĕg-zûrt′, ĭg-) *v.* **1.** To put into vigorous action. **2.** To bring to bear: *exert influence.* [L *exserere,* to stretch out.] **—ex•er′tion** *n.*

ex•hale (ĕks-hāl′, ĕk-sāl′, ĭk-sāl′) *v.* **-haled, -haling.** **1.** To breathe out. **2.** To emit (vapor, smoke, etc.). [< L *exhālāre,* to breathe out.] **—ex′ha•la′tion** (ĕks′hə-lā′shən) *n.*

ex•haust (ĕg-zôst′, ĭg-) *v.* **1.** To let out or draw off (air or fumes). **2.** To use up; expend. **3.** To wear out completely; tire. **4.** To deal with comprehensively: *exhaust a topic.* —*n.* **1.** Vapor or fumes exhausted. **2.** An apparatus or channel for exhausting gases. [< L *exhaurīre,* to draw out.] **—ex•haust′i•ble** *adj.* **—ex•haus′tion** (ĕg-zôs′chən, ĭg-) *n.*

ex•haus•tive (ĕg-zôs′tĭv, ĭg-) *adj.* Comprehensive; thorough: *an exhaustive survey.*

ex•hib•it (ĕg-zĭb′ĭt, ĭg-) *v.* To show; display, esp. to public view. —*n.* **1.** An act of exhibiting. **2.** That which is exhibited. **3.** Something formally introduced as evidence in court. [< L *exhibēre,* to hold forth.] **—ex′hi•bi′tion** (ĕk′sə-bĭsh′ən) *n.*

ex•hi•bi•tion•ism (ĕk′sə-bĭsh′ə-nĭz′əm) *n.* The practice of behaving so as to attract attention. **—ex′hi•bi′tion•ist** *n.* **—ex′hi•bi′tion•is′tic** *adj.*

ex•hil•a•rate (ĕg-zĭl′ə-rāt′, ĭg-) *v.* **-rated, -rating.** **1.** To make cheerful; elate. **2.** To invigorate. [L *exhilarāre.*] **—ex•hil′a•ra′tion** *n.*

ex•hort (ĕg-zôrt′, ĭg-) *v.* To urge by strong argument or appeal; admonish earnestly. [< L *exhortārī.*] **—ex′hor•ta′tion** *n.*

ex•hume (ĕg-zyo͞om′, ĭg-, ĕks-hyo͞om′) *v.* **-humed, -huming.** To remove from a grave. [< ML *exhumāre.*] **—ex′hu•ma′tion** *n.*

ex•i•gen•cy (ĕk′sə-jən-sē) *n., pl.* **-cies.** Also **ex•i•gence** (-jəns). **1.** A situation demanding immediate attention. **2.** Often **exigencies.** Urgent requirements; pressing needs. [< L *exigere,* to demand.] **—ex′i•gent** *adj.*

ex•ile (ĕg′zīl′, ĕk′sīl′) *n.* **1.** Enforced removal from one's native country by decree; banishment. **2.** One who has been separated from his country. —*v.* **-iled, -iling.** To send (someone) into exile. [< L *exilium.*]

ex•ist (ĕg-zĭst′, ĭg-) *v.* **1.** To have being or life; be or live. **2.** To occur. [L *exsistere,* to exist, emerge.] **—ex•is′tence** *n.* **—ex•is′tent** *adj.*

ex•is•ten•tial•ism (ĕg′zĭ-stĕn′shə-lĭz′əm, ĕk′-sĭ-) *n.* A body of ethical thought based on the philosophical analysis of existence and an affirmation of the freedom and responsibility of the individual. **—ex′is•ten′tial•ist** *adj.* & *n.*

ex•it (ĕg′zĭt, ĕk′sĭt) *n.* **1.** The departure of a performer from the stage. **2.** The act of going out. **3.** A way out. [< L *exīre,* to go out.]

exo–. *comb. form.* Outside of, external, or beyond. [Gk *exō,* outside of.]

ex•o•bi•ol•o•gy (ĕk′sō-bī-ŏl′ə-jē) *n.* Extraterrestrial biology.

ex•o•crine (ĕk′sə-krĭn′, -krēn′, -krīn′) *adj.* Involving a glandular secretion through a duct. [EXO- + Gk *krinein,* to separate.]

Exod. Exodus (Old Testament).

ex•o•dus (ĕk′sə-dəs) *n.* **1.** A departure, usually of a large number of people. **2. the Exodus.** The departure of the Israelites from Egypt. [< Gk *exodos,* a going out.]

ex of•fi•ci•o (ĕks′ ə-fĭsh′ē-ō′). By virtue of office or position.

ex•on•er•ate (ĕg-zŏn′ə-rāt′, ĭg-) *v.* **-ated, -ating.** To free from a charge; declare blameless. [< L *exonerāre,* to free from a burden.] **—ex•on′er•a′tion** *n.* **—ex•on′er•a′tor** *n.*

ex•or•bi•tant (ĕg-zôr′bə-tənt, ĭg-) *adj.* Out of all bounds; excessive; immoderate. [< LL *exorbitāre,* to deviate.] **—ex•or′bi•tance** *n.* **—ex•or′bi•tant•ly** *adv.*

ex•or•cise (ĕk′sôr-sīz′, ĕk′sər-) *v.* **-cised, -cising.** Also **ex•or•cize.** **1.** To expel (an evil spirit) by or as by incantation. **2.** To free from evil spirits. [< Gk *exorkizein.*] **—ex′or•cis′er** *n.* **—ex′or•cism′** (-sĭz′əm) *n.*

ex•o•ther•mic (ĕk′sō-thûr′mĭk) *adj.* Releasing heat.

ex•ot•ic (ĕg-zŏt′ĭk, ĭg-) *adj.* **1.** Not indigenous; foreign. **2.** Having the charm of the unfamiliar. [< Gk *exōtikos.*] **—ex•ot′ic** *n.*

exp. **1.** expenses. **2.** export; exported; exporter. **3.** express.

ex•pand (ĕk-spănd′, ĭk-) *v.* **1.** To unfold; spread out. **2.** To increase in size, extent, etc. **3.** To express more fully; expatiate. [< L *expandere.*] **—ex•pand′er** *n.*

ex•panse (ĕk-spăns′, ĭk-) *n.* A wide and open extent, as of land or sky.

ex•pan•sion (ĕk-spăn′shən, ĭk-) *n.* **1.** The act or process of expanding or state of being expanded. **2.** A part produced by expanding. **3.** The extent to which something has expanded.

ex•pan•sive (ĕk-spăn′sĭv, ĭk-) *adj.* **1.** Capable of expanding. **2.** Wide; sweeping. **3.** Open and generous; outgoing. **—ex•pan′sive•ly** *adv.*

ex•pa•ti•ate (ĕk-spā′shē-āt′, ĭk-) *v.* **-ated, -ating.** To speak or write at length on a subject. [L *exspatiārī,* to spread out, expatiate.] **—ex•pa′ti•a′tion** *n.* **—ex•pa′ti•a′tor** *n.*

ex•pa•tri•ate (ĕks-pā′trē-āt′) *v.* **-ated, -ating.** **1.** To banish; exile. **2.** To leave one's own country to reside in another. —*n.* (ĕks-pā′trē-ĭt, -āt′). An expatriated person. [ML *expatriāre.*] **—ex•pa′tri•a′tion** *n.*

ex•pect (ĕk-spĕkt′, ĭk-) *v.* **1.** To look forward to the probable occurrence of. **2.** To consider reasonable or due. [L *exspectāre,* to look out (for), expect.] **—ex•pect′er** *n.*

ex•pec•tan•cy (ĕk-spĕk′tən-sē, ĭk-) *n., pl.* **-cies.** **1.** Expectation. **2.** Something expected: *a life expectancy of seventy years.*

ex•pec•tant (ĕk-spĕk′tənt, ĭk-) *adj.* Expecting. **—ex•pec′tant•ly** *adv.*

ex•pec•ta•tion (ĕk′spĕk-tā′shən) *n.* **1.** The act or state of expecting. **2.** Eager anticipation. **3. expectations.** Prospects of success, profit, etc. **4.** Something expected.

ex•pec•to•rate (ĕk-spĕk′tə-rāt′, ĭk-) *v.* **-rated, -rating.** To eject from the mouth; spit. [L *expectorāre,* to drive from the breast.] **—ex•pec′to•ra′tion** *n.* **—ex•pec′to•ra′tor** *n.*

ex•pe•di•en•cy (ĕk-spē′dē-ən-sē) *n., pl.* **-cies.** Also **ex•pe•di•ence** (-dē-əns). **1.** Appropriateness to a purpose. **2.** Adherence to self-serving means. **3.** An expedient.

ex•pe•di•ent (ĕk-spē′dē-ənt) *adj.* **1.** Appropriate to a particular purpose. **2.** Serving to promote one's interest without regard for principle. —*n.* Something expedient. [< L *expedīre,* to free, make ready.] **—ex•pe′di•en′tial** (-ĕn′shəl) *adj.* **—ex•pe′di•ent•ly** *adv.*

ex•pe•dite (ĕk′spə-dīt′) *v.* **-dited, -diting.** **1.** To speed the progress of; facilitate. **2.** To perform quickly. [< L *expedīre,* to free the feet.] **—ex′pe•dit′er, ex′pe•di′tor** *n.*

ex•pe•di•tion (ĕk′spə-dĭsh′ən) *n.* **1. a.** A trip, march, etc., made by an organized group, as for investigation or military action. **b.** The group thus engaged. **2.** Speed in performance; promptness. [< L *expedīre,* to extricate.]

ex•pe•di•tion•ar•y (ĕk′spə-dĭsh′ə-nĕr′ē) *adj.* Constituting a military expedition.

ex•pe•di•tious (ĕk′spə-dĭsh′əs) *adj.* Acting or done with speed and efficiency. **—ex′pe•di′tious•ly** *adv.* **—ex′pe•di′tious•ness** *n.*

ex•pel (ĕk-spĕl′, ĭk-) *v.* **-pelled, -pelling.** **1.** To force or drive out; eject forcefully. **2.** To dismiss by official decision. [< L *expellere.*]

ex•pend (ĕk-spĕnd′, ĭk-) *v.* To pay out; spend; use up; consume. [< L *expendere,* to pay out.]

ex•pend•a•ble (ĕk-spĕn′də-bəl, ĭk-) *adj.* **1.** Capable of being expended. **2.** Subject to discard or sacrifice; not essential.

ex•pen•di•ture (ĕk-spĕn′də-chər, ĭk-) *n.* **1.** The act or process of expending. **2.** An amount expended, esp. of money.

ex•pense (ĕk-spĕns′, ĭk-) *n.* **1.** An expending; expenditure. **2.** Often **expenses.** Money paid, needed, or provided for a purpose. **3.** Cost; sacrifice.

ex•pen•sive (ĕk-spĕn′sĭv, ĭk-) *adj.* High-priced; costly. **—ex•pen′sive•ly** *adv.*

ex•pe•ri•ence (ĕk-spĭr′ē-əns, ĭk-) *n.* **1.** Apprehension through the mind, senses, or emotions. **2. a.** Activity or practice through which knowledge or skill is gained. **b.** Knowledge or skill thus gained. **3. a.** An event, circumstance, etc., undergone or lived through. **b.** The sum or cumulative effect of such events. —*v.* **-enced, -encing.** To have as an experience; undergo. [< L *experīrī,* to try, test.]

ex•pe•ri•enced (ĕk-spĭr′ē-ənst, ĭk-) *adj.* Skilled through frequent experience.

ex•per•i•ment (ĕk-spĕr′ə-mənt, -mĕnt′, ĭk-) *n.* A test made to demonstrate a known truth, examine the validity of a hypothesis, or determine the efficacy of something previously untried. —*v.* To conduct an experiment; try or test. [< L *experīrī,* to try, test.] **—ex•per′i•men′tal** *adj.* **—ex•per′i•men′tal•ly** *adv.* **—ex•per′i•men•ta′tion** *n.*

ex•pert (ĕk′spûrt′) *n.* A person with a high degree of skill or specialized knowledge. —*adj.* (ĭk-spûrt′, ĕk′spûrt). Highly skilled or knowledgeable. [< L *expertus,* pp of *experīrī,* to try.] **—ex•pert′ly** *adv.* **—ex•pert′ness** *n.*

ex•per•tise (ĕk′spûr-tēz′) *n.* Specialized knowledge or skill.

ex•pi•ate (ĕk′spē-āt′) *v.* **-ated, -ating.** To make atonement for. [L *expiāre.*] **—ex′pi•a′tion** *n.*

ex•pire (ĕk-spīr′, ĭk-) *v.* **-pired, -piring.** **1.** To die. **2.** To come to an end; terminate. **3.** To exhale; breathe out. [< L *exspīrāre,* to breathe out, expire.] **—ex′pi•ra′tion** *n.*

ex•plain (ĕk-splān′, ĭk-) *v.* **1.** To make plain or comprehensible. **2.** To offer reasons for; account for. [< L *explānāre,* to explain, to spread out.] **—ex•plain′a•ble** *adj.* **—ex′pla•na′-**

tion (-splə-nā'shən) *n.* —**ex•plan'a•to'ry** (-splăn'ə-tôr'ē, -tōr'ē) *adj.*

ex•ple•tive (ĕks'plə-tĭv) *n.* An exclamation or oath. [< L *explētus,* pp of *explēre,* to fill out.]

ex•pli•ca•ble (ĕks'plĭ-kə-bəl) *adj.* Capable of being explained.

ex•pli•cate (ĕks'plĭ-kāt') *v.* **-cated, -cating.** To explain, esp. in detail. [L *explicāre,* to unfold, explicate.] —**ex'pli•ca'tion** *n.*

ex•plic•it (ĕk-splĭs'ĭt, ĭk-) *adj.* Precisely expressed; clear and specific. [< L *explicāre,* to EXPLICATE.] —**ex•plic'it•ly** *adv.*

ex•plode (ĕk-splōd', ĭk-) *v.* **-ploded, -ploding.** **1.** To cause or undergo an explosion. **2.** To burst or cause to burst by explosion. **3.** To burst forth or break out suddenly. **4.** To expose as false or unreliable: *explode a hypothesis.* [L *explōdere,* drive out by clapping.]

ex•ploit (ĕks'ploit') *n.* A noteworthy act or deed; feat. —*v.* (ĕk-sploit', ĭk-). **1.** To utilize fully or advantageously. **2.** To make selfish or unethical use of. [< OF, achievement.] —**ex•ploit'a•ble, ex•ploit'a•tive** *adj.* —**ex'ploi•ta'tion** *n.* —**ex•ploit'er** *n.*

ex•plore (ĕk-splôr', -splōr', ĭk-) *v.* **-plored, -ploring.** **1.** To investigate systematically. **2.** To travel into or range over (an area) for the purpose of discovery. [L *explōrāre,* to search out.] —**ex'plo•ra'tion** *n.* —**ex•plor'a•to'ry** (-ə-tôr'ē, -tōr'ē) *adj.* —**ex•plor'er** *n.*

ex•plo•sion (ĕk-splō'zhən, ĭk-) *n.* **1. a.** A sudden rapid, violent release of mechanical, chemical, or nuclear energy. **b.** The loud sound accompanying such a release. **2.** A sudden outburst, increase, etc. [< L *explōdere,* to EXPLODE.]

ex•plo•sive (ĕk-splō'sĭv, ĭk-) *adj.* **1.** Of, pertaining to, or causing an explosion. **2.** Tending to explode. —*n.* A substance that explodes or causes explosion. —**ex•plo'sive•ly** *adv.* —**ex•plo'sive•ness** *n.*

ex•po•nent (ĕk-spō'nənt, ĭk-) *n.* **1.** One that expounds, interprets, or advocates. **2.** A number or symbol, as *3* in $(x+y)^3$, placed to the right of and above another number, symbol, or expression, denoting the power to which the latter is to be raised. —**ex'po•nen'tial** (-nĕn'shəl) *adj.* —**ex'po•nen'tial•ly** *adv.*

ex•port (ĕk-spôrt', -spōrt', ĭk-, ĕks'pôrt', -pōrt') *v.* To send abroad, esp. for trade or sale. —*n.* (ĕks'pôrt, -pōrt). **1.** The act of exporting. **2.** Something exported. [L *exportāre,* to carry out.] —**ex'por•ta'tion** *n.* —**ex•port'er** *n.*

ex•pose (ĕk-spōz', ĭk-) *v.* **-posed, -posing.** **1.** To make visible or known; reveal. **2.** To subject; lay open, as to an influence or danger. **3.** To subject (a photographic film) to the action of light. [< L *expōnere,* to expose, EXPOUND.] —**ex•pos'er** *n.*

ex•po•sé (ĕk'spō-zā') *n.* A public revelation of something discreditable.

ex•po•si•tion (ĕk'spə-zĭsh'ən) *n.* **1.** A setting forth of meaning or intent. **2.** The presentation of information in clear, precise form. **3.** A public exhibition of broad scope. [< L *expōnere,* to EXPOUND.] —**ex•pos'i•tor** *n.* —**ex•pos'i•to'ry** (-tôr'ē, -tōr'ē) *adj.*

ex post fac•to (ĕks' pōst' făk'tō). Formulated or operating retroactively. [L.]

ex•pos•tu•late (ĕk-spŏs'chōō-lāt', ĭk-) *v.* **-lated, -lating.** To reason earnestly with someone, esp. to dissuade. [L *expostulāre,* to demand strongly.] —**ex•pos'tu•la'tion** *n.*

ex•po•sure (ĕk-spō'zhər, ĭk-) *n.* **1.** An act or instance of exposing or being exposed. **2.** A position in relation to direction or weather conditions: *a southern exposure.* **3.** The act or time of exposing a photographic film or plate.

ex•pound (ĕk-spound', ĭk-) *v.* To give a detailed statement (of); explain; elucidate; hold forth. [< L *expōnere,* to put forth, expose.] —**ex•pound'er** *n.*

ex•press (ĕk-sprĕs', ĭk-) *v.* **1.** To make known or indicate, as by words, facial aspect, or symbols. **2.** To press out, as juice. **3.** To send by rapid transport. —*adj.* **1.** Clearly stated or intended; explicit. **2.** Used or adapted for speedy, direct transportation. —*adv.* By express transportation. —*n.* **1.** Transportation by express. **2.** An express train, bus, etc. [< VL **expressāre,* to press out, express.] —**ex•press'i•ble** *adj.* —**ex•press'ly** *adv.*

ex•pres•sion (ĕk-sprĕsh'ən, ĭk-) *n.* **1.** Communication of an idea, emotion, etc., esp. by words. **2.** A symbol; sign; indication. **3.** A manner of expressing, esp. in speaking or performing. **4.** A facial aspect or tone of voice conveying feeling. **5.** A word or phrase. **6.** A symbolic mathematical form, such as an equation. —**ex•pres'sion•ist** *n.* & *adj.* —**ex•pres'sion•is'tic** *adj.* —**ex•pres'sion•is'ti•cal•ly** *adv.*

ex•pres•sive (ĕk-sprĕs'ĭv, ĭk-) *adj.* **1.** Expressing or tending to express. **2.** Eloquent or forceful in expression. —**ex•pres'sive•ly** *adv.* —**ex•pres'sive•ness** *n.*

ex•press•way (ĕk-sprĕs'wā', ĭk-) *n.* A major divided highway designed for fast travel.

ex•pro•pri•ate (ĕks-prō'prē-āt') *v.* **-ated, -ating.** To acquire or take (property) from another, as for public use. [ML *expropriāre.*] —**ex•pro'pri•a'tion** *n.* —**ex•pro'pri•a'tor** *n.*

ex•pul•sion (ĕk-spŭl'shən, ĭk-) *n.* The act of expelling or state of being expelled.

ex•punge (ĕk-spŭnj', ĭk-) *v.* **-punged, -punging.** To erase; strike out. [L *expungere,* to prick out, erase.] —**ex•pung'er** *n.*

ex•pur•gate (ĕks'pər-gāt', -pûr-) *v.* **-gated, -gating.** To amend by removing obscene or objectionable parts, esp. from a text. [L *expurgāre,* to purge out, purify.] —**ex'pur•ga'tion** *n.* —**ex'pur•ga'tor** *n.*

ex•qui•site (ĕks'kwĭ-zĭt) *adj.* **1.** Showing a high degree of craft or excellence. **2.** Delicately or poignantly beautiful. **3.** Acutely discriminating, as in taste. **4.** Keen; intense. [< L *exquīrere,* to search out.] —**ex'qui•site•ly** *adv.*

ext. 1. extension. **2.** external. **3.** extinct. **4.** extra. **5.** extract.

ex•tant (ĕk'stənt, ĕk-stănt', ĭk-) *adj.* Still in existence; not destroyed or extinct. [< L *exstāre,* to stand out, exist.]

ex•tem•po•ra•ne•ous (ĕk-stĕm'pə-rā'nē-əs, ĭk-) *adj.* Not rehearsed or prepared in advance; impromptu. [< L *ex tempore,* EXTEMPORE.] —**ex•tem'po•ra'ne•ous•ly** *adv.*

ex•tem•po•re (ĕk-stĕm'pə-rē, ĭk-) *adj.* Extemporaneous. —*adv.* Extemporaneously. [L *ex tempore.*]

ex•tem•po•rize (ĕk-stĕm'pə-rīz', ĭk-) *v.* **-rized, -rizing.** To do or perform (something) extemporaneously; improvise.

ex•tend (ĕk-stĕnd', ĭk-) *v.* **1.** To spread, stretch, or enlarge to greater length, area, or scope. **2.** To exert to full capacity. **3.** To offer; tender. [< L *extendere.*] —**ex•tend'i•bil'i•ty** *n.* —**ex•tend'i•ble, ex•ten'si•ble** *adj.*

ex•ten•sion (ĕk-stĕn'shən, ĭk-) *n.* **1.** The act of extending or condition of being extended. **2.** The degree or range to which something can be extended. **3.** An extended or added part.

ex•ten•sive (ĕk-stĕn'sĭv, ĭk-) *adj.* Great in extent, range, or amount. —**ex•ten'sive•ly** *adv.*

ex•tent (ĕk-stĕnt', ĭk-) *n.* **1.** The distance or area over which something extends; size or space. **2.** Range or degree to which something extends; scope.

ex•ten•u•ate (ĕk-stĕn'yōō-āt', ĭk-) *v.* **-ated, -ating.** To excuse by minimizing the seriousness of: *extenuate his guilt.* [L *extenuāre,* to thin out, lessen.] —**ex•ten'u•a'tion** *n.*

ex•te•ri•or (ĕk-stîr'ē-ər, ĭk-) *adj.* Outer; external. —*n.* An outer part, surface, or aspect. [< L *exterus,* outward, outside.]

ex•ter•mi•nate (ĕk-stûr'mə-nāt', ĭk-) *v.* **-nated, -nating.** To destroy completely; wipe out. [L *extermināre,* to drive out.] —**ex•ter'mi•na'tion** *n.* —**ex•ter'mi•na'tor** *n.*

ex•ter•nal (ĕk-stûr'nəl, ĭk-) *adj.* **1.** Of or on the outside or an outer part. **2.** Acting or coming from the outside. **3.** Having material existence; not imaginary. **4.** Outward; superficial. **5.** Not internal or domestic; foreign. —*n.* **externals.** External parts or aspects. [< L *exterus,* outward.] —**ex•ter'nal•ly** *adv.*

ex•tinct (ĕk-stĭngkt', ĭk-) *adj.* **1.** No longer existing in living or active form; having died out. **2.** Completely gone or destroyed; extinguished. [< L *exstinguere,* to EXTINGUISH.] —**ex•tinc'tion** *n.*

ex•tin•guish (ĕk-stĭng'gwĭsh, ĭk-) *v.* **1.** To put out (a fire, light, etc.). **2.** To put an end to, as hope; destroy. [L *exstinguere.*]

ex•tin•guish•er (ĕk-stĭng'gwĭ-shər, ĭk-) *n.* One that extinguishes, esp. a device for spraying fire-extinguishing chemicals.

ex•tir•pate (ĕk'stər-pāt', ĕk-stûr'-, ĭk-) *v.* **-pated, -pating.** **1.** To root up or out. **2.** To destroy wholly; exterminate. [L *exstirpāre,* to pluck up by the roots.] —**ex'tir•pa'tion** *n.*

ex•tol (ĕk-stōl', ĭk-) *v.* **-tolled, -tolling.** Also **ex•toll.** To praise highly; eulogize. [< L *extollere,* to lift up.] —**ex•tol'ler** *n.*

ex•tort (ĕk-stôrt', ĭk-) *v.* To obtain (money, information, etc.) by coercion or intimidation. [< L *extorquēre,* to twist out.] —**ex•tor'tion** *n.* —**ex•tor'tion•ist, ex•tor'tion•er** *n.*

ex•tra (ĕk'strə) *adj.* More than what is usual, expected, etc.; additional. —*n.* **1.** Something additional, as an accessory for which an added charge is made. **2.** A special edition of a newspaper. **3.** An additional worker, esp. an actor hired to play a minor part. —*adv.* Very; unusually. [Prob short for EXTRAORDINARY.]

extra–. *comb. form.* Outside a boundary or scope. [< L *extrā,* outside, beyond.]

ex•tract (ĕk-străkt', ĭk-) *v.* **1.** To draw forth or pull out by or as by force. **2.** To obtain by chemical or mechanical action, as by pressure, distillation, etc. **3.** To pick out, as a literary passage, for separate mention or publication. **4.** *Math.* To determine or calculate (a root). —*n.* (ĕk'străkt). **1.** A literary excerpt. **2.** An extracted substance or concentrated preparation, as of a food. [< L *extrahere* (pp *extractus*), to draw out.] —**ex•trac'tor** *n.*

ex•trac•tion (ĕk-străk'shən, ĭk-) *n.* **1.** The act of extracting or condition of being extracted. **2.** Something obtained by extracting. **3.** Descent; lineage.

ex•tra•cur•ric•u•lar (ĕk'strə-kə-rĭk'yə-lər) *adj.* Not part of the regular curriculum, esp. of a school.

ex•tra•dite (ĕk'strə-dīt') *v.* **-dited, -diting.** To surrender or obtain the surrender of (an alleged criminal) for trial by another authority. [< L *ex-,* out + *trāditiō,* a surrendering.] —**ex'tra•di'tion** (-dĭsh'ən) *n.*

ex•tra•ga•lac•tic (ĕk'strə-gə-lăk'tĭk) *adj.* Located or originating beyond the Galaxy.

ex•tra•mar•i•tal (ĕk'strə-măr'ə-təl) *adj.* Adulterous.

ex•tra•ne•ous (ĕk-strā'nē-əs, ĭk-) *adj.* **1.** Coming from without; foreign. **2.** Not essential or relevant. [L *extrāneus,* strange.] **—ex•tra'ne•ous•ly** *adv.* **—ex•tra'ne•ous•ness** *n.*

ex•traor•di•nar•y (ĕk-strôr'də-nĕr'ē, ĭk-, ĕk'-strə-ôr'-) *adj.* Beyond what is ordinary or usual; exceptional; remarkable. **—ex•traor'di•nar'i•ly** *adv.*

ex•trap•o•late (ĕk-străp'ə-lāt', ĭk-) *v.* **-lated, -lating.** To infer (unknown information) from known information. **—ex•trap'o•la'tion** *n.*

ex•tra•sen•so•ry (ĕk'strə-sĕn'sə-rē) *adj.* Not perceptible by or beyond the range of the normal senses.

ex•tra•ter•res•tri•al (ĕk'strə-tə-rĕs'trē-əl) *adj.* Outside the earth or its atmosphere.

ex•trav•a•gant (ĕk-străv'ə-gənt, ĭk-) *adj.* **1.** Spending too much; wasteful; prodigal. **2.** Immoderate; excessive. [< ML *extrāvagārī,* to wander beyond.] **—ex•trav'a•gance, ex•trav'a•gant•ness** *n.* **—ex•trav'a•gant•ly** *adv.*

ex•trav•a•gan•za (ĕk-străv'ə-găn'zə, ĭk-) *n.* An elaborate, spectacular entertainment.

ex•tra•ve•hic•u•lar activity (ĕk'strə-vē-hĭk'-yə-lər). Activity or maneuvers performed by an astronaut outside a spacecraft in space.

ex•treme (ĕk-strēm', ĭk-) *adj.* **1.** Outermost or farthest; most remote. **2.** Final; last. **3.** Very great; intense. **4.** To the utmost degree; radical. **5.** Drastic; severe. **—*n.*** **1.** The greatest or utmost degree. **2.** Either of the two ends of a scale, series, or range. **3.** An extreme condition. **4.** A drastic expedient. [< L *extrēmus.*] **—ex•treme'ly** *adv.* **—ex•treme'ness** *n.*

ex•trem•ist (ĕk-strē'mĭst, ĭk-) *n.* One who advocates or resorts to extreme measures.

ex•trem•i•ty (ĕk-strĕm'ə-tē, ĭk-) *n., pl.* **-ties.** **1.** The outermost or farthest point or part. **2.** The utmost degree. **3.** Grave danger, necessity, or distress. **4.** An extreme or severe measure. **5.** A bodily limb or appendage, esp. a hand or foot.

ex•tri•cate (ĕk'strĭ-kāt') *v.* **-cated, -cating.** To release from entanglement or difficulty; disengage. [L *extricāre.*] **—ex'tri•ca'tion** *n.*

ex•trin•sic (ĕk-strĭn'sĭk, -zĭk, ĭk-) *adj.* **1.** Not inherent or essential. **2.** Originating from without; external. [LL *extrinsecus,* outer.] **—ex•trin'si•cal•ly** *adv.*

ex•tro•vert (ĕk'strə-vûrt') *n.* One interested in others or in the environment as opposed to, or to the exclusion of, self. [< EXTRA- + L *vertere,* to turn.] **—ex'tro•ver'sion** *n.* **—ex'tro•ver'sive** *adj.* **—ex'tro•vert'ed** *adj.*

ex•trude (ĕk-stro͞od', ĭk-) *v.* **-truded, -truding.** **1.** To push or thrust out. **2.** To shape (metal, plastic, etc.) by forcing through a die. [L *extrūdere,* to thrust out.] **—ex•tru'sion** *n.*

ex•u•ber•ant (ĕg-zo͞o'bər-ənt, ĭg-) *adj.* **1.** Full of unrestrained high spirits. **2.** Lavish; profuse. **3.** Growing abundantly; luxuriant. [< L *exūberāre,* to overflow.] **—ex•u'ber•ance** *n.* **—ex•u'ber•ant•ly** *adv.*

ex•u•date (ĕks'yo͞o-dāt') *n.* An exuded substance; exudation.

ex•ude (ĕg-zo͞od', ĭg-, ĕk-so͞od', ĭk-) *v.* **-uded, -uding.** **1.** To ooze or pour forth gradually. **2.** To emit; give off. [L *exsūdāre,* to sweat out, exude.] **—ex'u•da'tion** *n.*

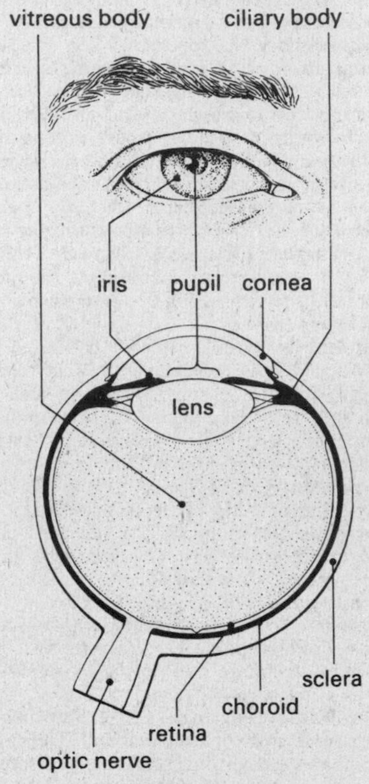

eye
Anterior view and cross section of the human eye

ex•ult (ĕg-zŭlt', ĭg-) *v.* To rejoice greatly, as in triumph. [L *exsultāre,* freq of *exsilīre,* to leap up, rejoice.] **—ex•ul'tant** *adj.* **—ex'ul•ta'tion** *n.*

ex•ur•bi•a (ĕk-sûr'bē-ə, ĕg-zûr'-) *n.* A usually prosperous residential area beyond the suburbs of a city. **—ex•ur'ban•ite** (-bə-nīt) *n.*

—ey[1]. Variant of **-y[1].**

—ey[2]. Variant of **-y[3].**

eye (ī) *n.* **1.** An organ of vision or of light sensitivity. **2.** Sight; vision. **3.** A look; gaze. **4.** Ability to perceive or discern. **5.** Viewpoint; opinion. **6.** Something suggestive of an eye. **—make eyes at.** To gaze at flirtatiously. **—see eye to eye.** To be in agreement. **—*v.* eyed, eyeing** or **eying.** To look at; regard. [< OE *ēage.* See **okw-.**] **—ey'er** *n.*

eye•ball (ī'bôl') *n.* The ball-shaped portion of the eye enclosed by the socket and eyelids.

eye•brow (ī'brou') *n.* The hairs covering the bony ridge over the eye.

eye•ful (ī'fo͝ol') *n.* **1.** An amount that fills an eye. **2.** A close or revealing look. **3.** A pleasing or striking sight.

eye•glass (ī'glăs', -gläs') *n.* **1.** A lens used to aid vision. **2. eyeglasses.** A pair of mounted lenses worn to correct faulty vision.

eye•lash (ī'lăsh') *n.* One of the hairs fringing the edge of an eyelid.

eye•let (ī'lĭt) *n.* **1.** A small, often edged or rimmed hole used for fastening with a cord or hook or to decorate fabric. **2.** A metal ring designed to reinforce such a hole. [< OF *oillet,* dim of *oil,* eye.]

eye•lid (ī'lĭd') *n.* Either of two folds of skin and muscle that can be closed over an eye.

eye•piece (ī'pēs') *n.* The lens or lens group closest to the eye, as in a microscope.

eye shadow. A tinted cosmetic applied to the eyelids.

eye•sight (ī'sīt') *n.* The faculty or range of sight; vision.

eye•sore (ī'sôr', -sōr') *n.* Something offensive to look at.

eye•strain (ī'strān') *n.* Fatigue of the ciliary muscle or of the extrinsic muscles of the eyeball.

eye•tooth (ī'to͞oth') *n.* A canine tooth of the upper jaw. [Perh because it lies immediately under the eye.]

eye•wit•ness (ī'wĭt'nəs) *n.* One who has personally seen something and can bear witness to the fact.

Ff

f, F (ĕf) *n.* **1.** The 6th letter of the English alphabet. **2.** The 6th in a series. **3. F** A failing grade.

f *Mus.* forte.

F **1.** Fahrenheit. **2.** farad. **3.** fluorine. **4.** *Mus.* forte. **5.** *Mus.* The 4th tone in the scale of C major.

F. French.

fa•ble (fā'bəl) *n.* **1.** A fictitious story, often with animal characters, designed to teach a lesson. **2.** A story about legendary persons and exploits. **3.** A falsehood. [< L *fābula,* narration, account.] **—fab'u•list** (făb'yə-lĭst) *n.*

fa•bled (fā'bəld) *adj.* **1.** Made known by fable; legendary. **2.** Existing only in fable; fictitious.

fab•ric (făb'rĭk) *n.* **1.** A structure; framework. **2.** Cloth made by joining fibers, as by weaving, knitting, etc. [< L *fabrica,* workshop, a trade.]

fab•ri•cate (făb'rĭ-kāt') *v.* **-cated, -cating.** **1.** To make or fashion. **2.** To construct; assemble; manufacture. **3.** To make up (a deception). [< L *fabrica,* workshop.] **—fab'ri•ca'tion** *n.*

fab•u•lous (făb'yə-ləs) *adj.* **1.** Of the nature of a fable; legendary. **2.** Told of or celebrated in fables. **3.** Barely credible; astonishing.

fac. **1.** facsimile. **2.** *Ed.* faculty.

fa•çade (fə-säd') *n.* Also **fa•cade.** **1.** The main face or front of a building. **2.** A superficial or false outward appearance. [< VL **facia,* face.]

face (fās) *n.* **1.** The surface of the front of the head. **2.** A facial expression; countenance. **3.** A grimace. **4.** An outward appearance; aspect. **5.** Dignity; prestige. **6.** Effrontery; impudence. **7.** A planar surface bounding a solid. **8.** The appearance and geological surface features of an area of land; topography. **—face to face. 1.** In each other's presence. **2.** Directly confronting: *face to face with death.* —*v.* **faced, facing. 1.** To turn or be turned in the direction of. **2.** To front upon: *a window facing the south.* **3. a.** To meet; encounter. **b.** To confront; meet boldly. **4.** To furnish with a surface or cover of a different material. **5.** To provide the edges of (a cloth or garment) with finishing or trimming. **—face up to. 1.** To recognize the existence or importance of. **2.** To confront bravely. [< L *faciēs,* form, shape, face.] **—face'less** *adj.*

face lifting. Also **face-lift** (fās'lĭft'). Plastic surgery for tightening facial tissues.

fac•et (făs'ĭt) *n.* **1.** One of the flat surfaces cut on a gemstone. **2.** A small planar or rounded smooth surface on a bone or tooth. **3.** An aspect; phase. [< F *face,* face.]

fa•ce•tious (fə-sē'shəs) *adj.* Playfully jocular; flippant. [< L *facētus,* elegant, facetious.] **—fa•ce'tious•ly** *adv.* **—fa•ce'tious•ness** *n.*

face value. 1. The value printed on a bill, bond, etc. **2.** Apparent value or significance.

fa•cial (fā'shəl) *adj.* Of or concerning the face. —*n.* A cosmetic treatment for the face. **—fa'cial•ly** *adv.*

fac•ile (făs'əl, -īl) *adj.* **1.** Achieved with little effort. **2.** Effortlessly fluent. **3.** Arrived at without due care or examination; superficial. [< L *facilis.*] **—fac'ile•ly** *adv.*

fa•cil•i•tate (fə-sĭl'ə-tāt') *v.* **-tated, -tating.** To make easier; aid; assist. [< L *facilis,* FACILE.] **—fa•cil'i•ta'tion** *n.*

fa•cil•i•ty (fə-sĭl'ə-tē) *n., pl.* **-ties. 1.** Ease in doing; aptitude. **2.** Ready skill; fluency. **3.** Often **facilities.** The means used to facilitate an action or process: *the facilities of a library.*

fac•ing (fā'sĭng) *n.* **1. a.** A piece of material sewn to the edge of a garment as lining or decoration. **b.** Fabric used for this. **2.** A coating of different material applied to a surface.

fac•sim•i•le (făk-sĭm'ə-lē) *n.* **1.** An exact copy or reproduction. **2. a.** A method of transmitting images or printed matter electronically. **b.** An image so transmitted. [L *fac simile,* make (it) similar.]

fact (făkt) *n.* **1.** Something having existence supported by evidence; an actuality. **2.** Truth; reality. **3.** An act considered with regard to its legality: *after the fact.* [< L *factus,* pp of *facere,* to do.]

fac•tion (făk'shən) *n.* **1.** A group forming a cohesive, usually contentious, minority within a larger group. **2.** Internal dissension. [< L *factiō,* an acting (together).] **—fac'tion•al** *adj.* **—fac'tion•al•ism'** *n.*

fac•tious (făk'shəs) *adj.* **1.** Produced or characterized by faction. **2.** Creating or promoting faction. **—fac'tious•ness** *n.*

fac•ti•tious (făk-tĭsh'əs) *adj.* Artificial; false. [L *factīcius,* made by art.] **—fac•ti'tious•ly** *adv.* **—fac•ti'tious•ness** *n.*

fac•tor (făk'tər) *n.* **1.** One who acts for another; an agent. **2.** One that actively contributes to a result or process. **3.** One of two or more quantities having a designated product: *2 and 3 are factors of 6.* —*v. Math.* To determine the factors of. [< L *factus,* FACT.] **—fac'tor•ship'** *n.*

fac•to•ry (făk'tə-rē) *n., pl.* **-ries.** A building or buildings in which goods are manufactured. [< FACTOR.]

fac•to•tum (făk-tō'təm) *n.* An employee with a wide range of duties. [< L *fac tōtum,* do everything.]

fac•tu•al (făk'cho͞o-əl) *adj.* **1.** Of the nature of fact; actual. **2.** Of or containing facts. **—fac'tu•al•ly** *adv.*

fac•ul•ty (făk'əl-tē) *n., pl.* **-ties. 1.** An inherent power or ability. **2.** A special aptitude. **3.** A division of learning at a college or university. **4.** The teachers in a college or school. [< L *facultās,* power, capability.]

fad (făd) *n.* A briefly popular fashion. [?] **—fad'dish** *adj.*

fade (fād) *v.* **faded, fading. 1.** To lose or cause to lose brightness or brilliance; dim. **2.** To lose strength or freshness; wither. **3.** To disappear gradually; vanish. [< VL **fatidus,* faded.] **—fad'ed•ly** *adv.*

fad•ing (fā'dĭng) *n.* Fluctuation in the strength of received radio signals because of variations in the transmission medium.

fae•ces. Variant of **feces.**

fa•er•ie (fā'ə-rē, fâr'ē) *n.* Also **fa•er•y** *pl.* **-ies.** *Archaic.* **1.** A fairy. **2.** Fairyland.

fag[1] (făg) *v.* **fagged, fagging.** To work to exhaustion; weary or become weary from toil or long work. [?]

fag[2] (făg) *n. Slang.* A cigarette. [< ME *fagge.*]

fag•ot (făg'ət) *n.* Also **fag•got.** A bundle of twigs or sticks. [< Gk *phakelos.*]

fag•ot•ing (făg'ə-tĭng) *n.* Also **fag•got•ing.** Openwork stitching in which threads are tied in clusters or crisscrossed between two edges.

Fahr•en•heit (făr'ən-hīt') *adj.* Pertaining to a temperature scale that registers the freezing point of water as 32°F and the boiling point as 212°F under standard atmospheric pressure. [< G. *Fahrenheit* (1686–1736), German physicist.]

fa•ience (fī-äns', fā-) *n.* Also **fa•ïence.** Earthenware decorated with opaque, colorful glazes.

fail (fāl) *v.* **1.** To be deficient or unsuccessful. **2.** To decline, weaken, or cease to function. **3.** To disappoint or forsake. **4.** To omit or neglect: *failed to appear.* **5.** To give or receive an unacceptable grade (in a test, course, etc.). [< L *fallere,* to deceive, disappoint, fail.]

fail•ing (fā'lĭng) *n.* A fault or weakness; shortcoming. —*prep.* In the absence of.

faille (fāl, fīl) *n.* A ribbed fabric of silk, rayon, etc. [< OF.]

fail-safe (fāl'sāf') *adj.* **1.** Capable of compensating automatically for a failure. **2.** Acting to stop a military attack on the occurrence of a predetermined condition.

fail•ure (fāl'yər) *n.* **1.** The act, condition, or fact of failing: *the failure of an experiment.* **2.** One that has failed.

fain (fān) *adv. Archaic.* Preferably; gladly. [< OE *fægen,* joyful.]

faint (fānt) *adj.* **1.** Lacking strength or vigor; feeble. **2.** Indistinct; dim. **3.** Suddenly dizzy and weak. —*n.* An abrupt, usually brief loss of consciousness. —*v.* To fall into a faint. [< OF *feindre, faindre,* feign.] **—faint'er** *n.* **—faint'ly** *adv.* **—faint'ness** *n.*

faint-heart•ed (fānt'här'tĭd) *adj.* Lacking conviction or courage; timid. **—faint'heart'ed•ly** *adv.* **—faint'heart'ed•ness** *n.*

fair[1] (fâr) *adj.* **1.** Beautiful; lovely. **2.** Clear and sunny. **3.** Light in color, as hair. **4.** Just; equitable. **5.** Consistent with rules; permissible. **6.** Moderately good. **7.** Unblemished; clean. **8.** Favorable; propitious. —*adv.* **1.** In a fair manner; properly. **2.** Directly; squarely. [< OE *fæger.*] **—fair'ness** *n.*

fair[2] (fâr) *n.* **1.** A regularly held gathering for buying and selling goods. **2.** A public exhibition at which various products, handicrafts, etc., are displayed or judged competitively. **3.** A fund-raising sale or bazaar, as for charity. [< L *fēriæ,* holidays.]

fair-haired (fâr'hârd') *adj.* **1.** Having blond hair. **2.** Favorite: *mother's fair-haired boy.*

fair•ly (fâr'lē) *adv.* **1.** In a fair or just manner. **2.** Moderately; rather. **3.** Completely; altogether.

fair-trade (fâr'trād') *adj.* Of or designating an agreement under which distributors sell products at no less than a minimum price set by the manufacturer.

fair•way (fâr'wā') *n.* The mowed part of a golf course between each tee and putting green.

fair•y (fâr'ē) *n., pl.* **-ies.** A supernatural being of folklore often represented as a tiny person with magical powers. [< L *fāta,* the Fates, pl of *fātum,* FATE.]

fair•y•land (fâr'ē-lănd') *n.* **1.** The imaginary land of the fairies. **2.** Any charming, enchanting place.

fairy tale. 1. A story about fairies. **2.** A fictitious, fanciful story or explanation.

fait ac•com•pli (fĕ'tȧ-kôN-plē') *pl.* **faits accomplis** (fĕ'tȧ-kôN-plē'). An accomplished fact. [F.]

faith (fāth) *n.* **1. a.** Confident belief; trust. **b.** Belief in God; religious conviction. **2.** Loyalty; allegiance. **3.** A system of religious beliefs. **—bad faith.** Deceit; insincerity. **—good faith.** Sincerity; honesty. **—in faith.** *Archaic.* Indeed; truly. [< L *fidēs.*]

faith•ful (fāth'fəl) *adj.* **1.** Loyal. **2.** Truthful; accurate. **—faith'ful•ly** *adv.* **—faith'ful•ness** *n.*

faith•less (fāth'lĭs) *adj.* Failing in faith or loyalty; untrue. **—faith'less•ly** *adv.* **—faith'less•ness** *n.*

fake (fāk) *adj.* Not genuine; false; fraudulent. —*n.* **1.** Something not genuine or authentic; a counterfeit. **2.** An impostor; fraud. —*v.* **faked, faking. 1.** To contrive and present as genuine; counterfeit. **2.** To pretend; feign. [?] **—fak'er** *n.* **—fak'er•y** *n.*

fa•kir (fə-kîr', fā'kər) *n.* A Moslem or Hindu religious mendicant, esp. one who performs feats of magic or endurance. [Ar *faqīr.*]

fal•con (făl'kən, fôl'-, fô'-) *n.* A long-winged, swift-flying hawk, esp. one trained to hunt small game. [< LL *falcō.*]

fal•con•er (făl'kə-nər, fôl'-, fô'-) *n.* One who trains or hunts with falcons. **—fal'con•ry** *n.*

fall (fôl) *v.* **fell, fallen, falling. 1.** To move under the influence of gravity, esp. to drop without restraint. **2.** To come down from an erect position; collapse. **3.** To be killed or severely wounded in battle. **4.** To hang down: *Her hair fell in ringlets.* **5.** To assume an expression of disappointment: *Her face fell.* **6.** To be conquered or overthrown. **7.** To slope. **8.** To diminish. **9.** To decline in rank, status, or importance. **10.** To err or sin. **11.** To pass into a less active condition: *The crowd fell silent.* **12.** To arrive and pervade: *A hush fell on the crowd.* **13.** To occur at a specified time or place. **14.** To be allotted: *The task fell to him.* **15.** To divide naturally: *They fall into three categories.* **16.** To be directed by chance: *His gaze fell on a book.* **17.** To be uttered as if involuntarily. **—fall back on.** To resort to. **—fall for. 1.** To become infatuated with. **2.** To be deceived by. **—fall off.** To decline. **—fall short.** To fail to attain a specified level. **—fall through.** To fail; miscarry. *—n.* **1.** The act or an instance of falling. **2.** That which has fallen: *a fall of hail.* **3. a.** The amount of what has fallen: *a light fall of rain.* **b.** The distance that something falls. **4.** Often **Fall.** Autumn. **5.** Often **falls.** A waterfall. **6.** A woman's hair piece with long, free-hanging hair. **7.** An overthrow or collapse: *the fall of a government.* **8.** A decline or reduction. **9.** A loss of moral innocence. [< OE *feallan.* See **phol-**.]

fal•la•cious (fə-lā'shəs) *adj.* **1.** Containing or based on a fallacy. **2.** Deceptive in appearance or meaning. **—fal•la'cious•ly** *adv.*

fal•la•cy (făl'ə-sē) *n., pl.* **-cies.** **1.** An erroneous idea or opinion. **2.** Incorrectness of reasoning or belief. [< L *fallere,* to deceive.]

fal•li•ble (făl'ə-bəl) *adj.* Capable of erring. [< L *fallere,* to deceive.] **—fal'li•bly** *adv.*

fall•ing-out (fôl'ĭng-out') *n., pl.* **fallings-out** or **falling-outs.** A disagreement or quarrel.

falling sickness. Epilepsy.

falling star. A meteor.

Fal•lo•pi•an tube (fə-lō'pē-ən). Either of a pair of slender ducts that connect the uterus to the region of each of the ovaries in the female reproductive system of humans and higher vertebrates. [< G. *Fallopio* (1523–1562), Italian anatomist.]

fall out. **1.** To quarrel; become estranged. **2.** To happen; occur.

fall•out (fôl'out') *n.* **1. a.** The slow descent of minute particles of radioactive debris in the atmosphere following a nuclear explosion. **b.** The particles so descending. **c.** Such particles collectively. **2.** Any incidental results or side effects: *the technological fallout of the space program; political fallout.*

fal•low (făl'ō) *adj.* Plowed and tilled but left unseeded during a growing season. **—lie fallow.** To remain unused or inactive. [< OE *fealh,* arable land.] **—fal'low•ness** *n.*

fallow deer. An Old World deer with a white-spotted summer coat and broad, flat antlers. [< OE *fealo,* sallow. See **pel-[2]**.]

false (fôls) *adj.* **falser, falsest.** **1.** Contrary to fact or truth. **2.** Insincere: *false promises.* **3.** Not faithful: *a false lover.* **4.** Not real or natural; artificial. **5.** *Mus.* Of incorrect pitch. **—play** (a person) **false.** To betray. [< L *falsus,* pp of *fallere,* to deceive.] **—false'ly** *adv.* **—false'ness** *n.*

false•hood (fôls'ho͝od') *n.* **1.** Contradiction to or disparity with truth or fact. **2.** An untrue statement; lie.

fal•set•to (fôl-sĕt'ō) *n., pl.* **-tos.** A typically male singing voice when artificially producing tones in an upper register beyond its normal range. **—fal•set'to** *adj & adv.*

fal•si•fy (fôl'sə-fī') *v.* **-fied, -fying.** **1.** To state untruthfully. **2.** To alter (a document) in order to deceive. **—fal'si•fi•ca'tion** *n.*

fal•si•ty (fôl'sə-tē) *n., pl.* **-ties.** **1.** The condition of being false. **2.** A lie.

fal•ter (fôl'tər) *v.* **1.** To waver or weaken in purpose, force, etc. **2.** To stammer. **3.** To stumble. [ME *falteren.*] **—fal'ter•ing•ly** *adv.*

fame (fām) *n.* Great reputation and recognition; public esteem; renown. [< L *fāma,* talk, reputation.] **—famed** *adj.*

fa•mil•ial (fə-mĭl'yəl) *adj.* Of, pertaining to, or passed on in a family: *a familial trait.*

fa•mil•iar (fə-mĭl'yər) *adj.* **1.** Of frequent instance or occurrence; common. **2.** Having knowledge of something: *familiar with those roads.* **3.** Friendly; intimate: *on familiar terms.* **4.** Taking undue liberties. [< L *familia,* FAMILY.] **—fa•mil'iar•ly** *adv.*

fa•mil•i•ar•i•ty (fə-mĭl'yăr'ə-tē, -ē-ăr'ə-tē) *n., pl.* **-ties.** **1.** Substantial acquaintance with something. **2.** Close friendship. **3.** Undue liberty; boldness.

fa•mil•iar•ize (fə-mĭl'yə-rīz') *v.* **-ized, -izing.** To make (oneself or another) acquainted with.

fam•i•ly (făm'ə-lē, făm'lē) *n., pl.* **-lies.** **1.** Parents and their children. **2.** A group of persons related by blood or marriage. **3.** Lineage; ancestry. **4.** A group or category of like things, as related organisms. *—adj.* Pertaining to family: *a family reunion.* [< L *familia,* family, household.]

family tree. A genealogical diagram of a family.

fam•ine (făm'ĭn) *n.* **1.** A drastic and wide-reaching shortage of food. **2.** A drastic shortage of anything. [< L *fames,* hunger.]

fam•ished (făm'ĭsht) *adj.* Extremely hungry; starving.

fa•mous (fā'məs) *adj.* **1.** Widely known; publicly acclaimed. **2.** *Informal.* Excellent. [< L *fāma,* FAME.] **—fa'mous•ly** *adv.*

fan[1] (făn) *n.* **1.** A hand-waved implement for creating a cooling breeze. **2. a.** An array of thin, rigid blades attached to a central hub. **b.** A machine that rotates one or more such arrays on electrically powered shafts in order to move air. *—v.* **fanned, fanning.** **1.** To direct a current of air upon. **2.** To stir up: *fan resentment.* **3.** *Baseball.* To strike out. **4.** To spread like a fan (with *out*). [< L *vannus.*]

fan[2] (făn) *n.* *Informal.* An ardent admirer. [Short for FANATIC.]

fa•nat•ic (fə-năt'ĭk) *n.* A person possessed by an excessive or irrational zeal. *—adj.* Variant of **fanatical.** [< L *fānāticus,* of a temple, inspired by a god, mad.]

fa•nat•i•cal (fə-năt'ĭ-kəl) *adj.* Also **fa•nat•ic.** **1.** Driven by fanaticism. **2.** Characteristic of a fanatic. **—fa•nat'i cal•ly** *adv.*

fa•nat•i•cism (fə-năt'ə-sĭz'əm) *n.* Excessive or irrational zeal.

fan•ci•er (făn'sē-ər) *n.* One who has a special enthusiasm, as raising a specific kind of plant or animal.

fan•ci•ful (făn'sĭ-fəl) *adj.* **1.** Created in the fancy; unreal. **2.** Showing invention or whimsy in design. **—fan'ci•ful•ly** *adv.*

fan•cy (făn'sē) *n., pl.* **-cies.** **1.** The light invention or play of the mind through which whims, images, etc., are summoned up. **2.** An associative image. **3.** An unfounded opinion. **4.** A capricious idea. **5.** Capricious or sudden liking. **6.** Taste or preference. *—adj.* **-cier, -ciest.** **1.** Decorative; elegant: *a fancy hat.* **2.** Illusory: *fancy notions.* **3.** Executed with great skill. **4.** Of superior grade: *fancy preserves.* **5.** Excessive or exorbitant: *a fancy bid.* *—v.* **-cied, -cying.** **1.** To visualize; imagine. **2.** To take to or like. **3.** To suppose; guess. [< FANTASY.] **—fan'ci•ly** *adv.* **—fan'ci•ness** *n.*

fan•cy-free (făn'sē-frē') *adj.* Without commitment; unattached.

fan•cy•work (făn'sē-wûrk') *n.* Decorative needlework.

fan•dan•go (făn-dăng'gō) *n., pl.* **-gos.** An animated Spanish dance. [Span.]

fan•fare (făn'fâr') *n.* **1.** A flourish of trumpets. **2.** Spectacular display. [F.]

fang (făng) *n.* A long, pointed tooth, as one with which a venomous snake injects its venom. [< OE, plunder. See **pag-**.] **—fanged** *adj.*

fan•light (făn'līt') *n.* A half-circle window with sash bars arranged like the ribs of a fan.

fan•ta•sia (făn-tā'zhə, -zhē-ə, făn'tə-zē'ə) *n.* A free-form musical composition. [< FANTASY.]

fan•tas•tic (făn-tăs'tĭk) *adj.* **1.** Bizarre; grotesque. **2.** Unreal; illusory. **3.** Capricious or eccentric: *a fantastic old person.* **4.** *Informal.* Wonderful or superb. [< LL *phantasticus,* imaginary.] **—fan•tas'ti•cal•ly** *adv.*

fan•ta•sy (făn'tə-sē, -zē) *n., pl.* **-sies.** **1.** Imagination. **2.** A product of the imagination; illusion. **3.** A delusion. **4.** A capricious or whimsical notion or idea; conceit. **5.** A daydream. **6.** A fantasia. [< Gk *phantasia,* appearance, faculty of imagination.]

far (fär) *adv.* **farther** or **further, farthest** or **furthest.** **1.** To, from, or at considerable distance. **2.** To or at a specific distance or degree. **3.** To a considerable degree; much: *far better.* **4.** Not at all: *far from happy.* **—as far as.** To the extent that: *as far as I know.* **—by far.** To a considerable or evident degree. **—far and away.** Definitely. **—far and wide.** Everywhere. **—far be it from me.** I neither hope nor dare. **—go far.** **1.** To be successful. **2.** To last a long time. **3.** To tend strongly. **—in so far** (or **insofar**) **as.** To the degree or extent that. **—so far.** **1.** Up to now. **2.** To a limited extent. **—so far as.** To the extent that: *so far as I can tell.* *—adj.* **farther** or **further, farthest** or **furthest.** **1.** Distant: *a far country.* **2.** More distant; opposite: *the far corner.* **3.** Long: *a far trek.* [< OE *feor.* See **per[1]**.]

fa•rad (făr'əd, -ăd') *n.* A unit of capacitance, equal to the capacitance of a capacitor having a charge of 1 coulomb on each plate and a potential difference of 1 volt between the plates. [< M. *Faraday* (1791–1867), British scientist.]

far•a•way (fär'ə-wā') *adj.* **1.** Distant; remote. **2.** Abstracted.

farce (färs) *n.* **1.** A play marked by slapstick humor and wild improbabilities of plot. **2.** An empty show; mockery. [< L *farcīre,* to stuff.] **—far'ci•cal** *adj.*

fare (fâr) *v.* **fared, faring.** **1.** To get along. **2.** To turn out; go: *How does it fare with you?* *—n.* **1.** A transportation charge. **2.** A passenger transported for a fee. **3.** Food and drink; diet. [< OE *faran,* to go. See **per-[2]**.]

Far East. An area including China, Japan, and Korea.

fare•well (fâr'wĕl') *interj.* Good-by. *—n.* (fâr-wĕl'). **1.** A good-by. **2.** A leave-taking. *—adj.* (fâr'wĕl'). Parting: *a farewell party.* [< FARE + WELL.]

far-fetched (fär'fĕcht') *adj.* Improbable.

far-flung (fär'flŭng') *adj.* **1.** Wide-ranging. **2.** Remote; distant.

fa•ri•na (fə-rē'nə) *n.* Fine meal, as of cereal grain, often used as a cooked cereal or in puddings. [L *farīna,* ground corn, meal.]

far•i•na•ceous (făr'ə-nā'shəs) *adj.* **1.** Made from, rich in, or consisting of starch. **2.** Having a mealy or powdery texture.

farm (färm) *n.* A tract of land for producing crops or raising livestock. *—v.* **1.** To raise crops or livestock as a business. **2.** To use (land) for this purpose. **—farm out.** To send out (work) to be done elsewhere. [ME *ferme,* lease, rent.]

farm•er (fär'mər) *n.* One who operates a farm.

farm hand. A hired farm laborer.

farm•house (färm'hous') *n.* The farmer's dwelling on a farm.

farm•stead (färm'stĕd') *n.* A farm, including its land and buildings.

far-off (fär'ôf', -ŏf') *adj.* Remote in space or time; distant.

far-out (fär′out′) *adj. Slang.* Extremely unconventional.

far•ra•go (fə-rā′gō, -rä′gō) *n., pl.* **-goes.** A medley; conglomeration. [L *farrāgo,* mixed fodder for cattle.]

far-reach•ing (fär′rē′ching) *adj.* Having a wide range or effect.

far•row (făr′ō) *n.* A litter of pigs. *—v.* To give birth to (a farrow). [Perh < OE *fearh,* little pig.]

far•see•ing (fär′sē′ĭng) *adj.* Foresighted; prudent.

far-sight•ed (fär′sī′tĭd) *adj.* **1.** Able to see objects better from a distance than from short range. **2.** Planning prudently for the future; foresighted. **—far′sight′ed•ness** *n.*

far•ther (fär′*th*ər) *adv.* **1.** To a greater distance. **2.** Further. *—adj.* **1.** More distant. **2.** Additional. [< FURTHER.]

far•thest (fär′*th*ĭst) *adj.* Most remote or distant. *—adv.* To or at the most distant or remote point in space or time.

f.a.s., F.A.S. free alongside ship.

fas•ci•cle (făs′ĭ-kəl) *n.* Also **fas•ci•cule** (-kyo͞ol′). One of the separately published installments of a book. [< L *fascis,* a bundle.]

fas•ci•nate (făs′ə-nāt′) *v.* **-nated, -nating. 1.** To attract irresistibly. **2.** To spellbind or mesmerize. [L *fascināre,* to enchant, bewitch.] **—fas′ci•nat′ing•ly** *adv.* **—fas′ci•na′tion** *n.*

fas•cism (făsh′ĭz′əm) *n.* A system of government that exercises a dictatorship of the extreme right, typically through the merging of state and business leadership, together with a belligerent nationalism. [< It *fascio,* bundle, group.] **—fas′cist** *n.* & *adj.*

fash•ion (făsh′ən) *n.* **1.** The configuration or aspect of something. **2.** Kind; sort. **3.** Manner; way. **4.** The current style. **—after** (or **in**) **a fashion.** In some way or other. *—v.* **1.** To make into a particular shape or form. **2.** To make suitable; adapt. [< L *factiō,* "a making."] **—fash′ion•er** *n.*

fash•ion•a•ble (făsh′ən-ə-bəl) *adj.* **1.** Currently stylish. **2.** Associated with the world of fashion. **—fash′ion•a•bly** *adv.*

fast[1] (făst, fäst) *adj.* **1.** Swift; rapid. **2.** Accomplished in little time: *a fast visit.* **3.** Indicating a time ahead of the correct time: *a fast clock.* **4.** Adapted to rapid travel: *a fast turnpike.* **5.** Flouting conventional mores, esp. in sexual matters. **6.** Resistant: *acid-fast.* **7.** Firmly fixed or fastened. **8.** Secure. **9.** Loyal; constant: *fast friends.* **10.** Proof against fading. **11.** Deep; sound: *a fast sleep.* **12.** *Photog.* **a.** Compatible with a high shutter speed: *a fast lens.* **b.** Designed for short exposure; highly sensitive: *fast film.* *—adv.* **1.** Firmly; securely; tightly. **2.** Deeply; soundly: *fast asleep.* **3.** Quickly; rapidly. **4.** In a dissipated way: *living fast.* [< OE *fæst.* See **past-.**]

fast[2] (făst, fäst) *v.* To abstain from eating all or certain foods. *—n.* The act or a period of fasting. [< OE *fæstan,* to hold fast, abstain from food. See **past-.**]

fas•ten (făs′ən, fäs′-) *v.* **1.** To attach or become attached to something else; join; connect. **2. a.** To make fast or secure. **b.** To close, as by shutting. **3.** To fix or direct steadily, as the gaze. [< OE *fastnian,* to settle, establish, make fast. See **past-.**] **—fas′ten•er** *n.*

fast-food (făst′fo͞od′, fäst′-) *adj.* Specializing in foods prepared and served quickly: *a fast-food restaurant.*

fas•tid•i•ous (fă-stĭd′ē-əs, fə-) *adj.* **1.** Careful in all details; exacting; meticulous. **2.** Difficult to please. **3.** Easily disgusted. [< L *fastīdium,* a loathing.] **—fas•tid′i•ous•ness** *n.*

fast•ness (făst′nĭs, fäst′-) *n.* **1. a.** A fortified place. **b.** A secret place. **2.** The condition or quality of being fast.

fat (făt) *n.* **1. a.** Any of various energy-rich semisolid organic compounds occurring widely in animal and plant tissue. **b.** Organic tissue containing such substances. **c.** A solidified animal or vegetable oil. **2.** Plumpness; obesity. **3.** The best part of something: *the fat of the land.* *—adj.* **1.** Plump; obese. **2.** Oily; greasy. **3.** Abounding in desirable elements. **4.** Fertile or productive; rich. **5.** Ample; well-stocked: *a fat larder.* **6.** Thick; broad; large: *a fat plank.* [< OE *fǣtt.* See **peyə-.**] **—fat′ly** *adv.* **—fat′ness** *n.* **—fat′ty** *adj.*

fa•tal (fāt′l) *adj.* **1.** Deadly; mortal. **2.** Ruinous; disastrous. **3.** Most decisive; fateful. **4.** Controlling destiny. [< L *fātum,* FATE.] **—fa′tal•ly** *adv.* **—fa′tal•ness** *n.*

fa•tal•ism (fāt′l-ĭz′əm) *n.* The belief that all events are predetermined by fate. **—fa′tal•ist** *n.* **—fa′tal•is′tic** *adj.* **—fa′tal•is′ti•cal•ly** *adv.*

fa•tal•i•ty (fā-tăl′ə-tē, fə-) *n., pl.* **-ties. 1.** An accidental death. **2.** Liability to disaster.

fat•back (făt′băk′) *n.* A dried and salt-cured strip of fat taken from the upper part of a side of pork.

fate (fāt) *n.* **1.** The supposed force, principle, or power that predetermines events. **2.** Lot; fortune. **3.** A final result; outcome. **4.** Doom or ruin. **5. the Fates.** *Gk.&Rom.Myth.* The three goddesses who govern human destiny. [< L *fātum,* neut pp of *fārī,* to speak.]

fat•ed (fā′tĭd) *adj.* Governed or condemned by fate.

fate•ful (fāt′fəl) *adj.* **1.** Affecting one's future. **2.** Controlled by fate. **3.** Ruinous; fatal. **4.** Portentous; ominous. **—fate′ful•ly** *adv.*

fath. fathom.

fa•ther (fä′*th*ər) *n.* **1.** A male parent. **2.** A male ancestor; forefather. **3.** An originator. **4. Father.** God, esp. as the first member of the Trinity. **5.** Any elderly or venerable man. **6.** Often **Father.** One of the authoritative early codifiers of Christian doctrines and observances. **7.** A title for a Roman Catholic or Anglican priest. **8.** A leading citizen: *town fathers.* *—v.* **1.** To beget. **2.** To act or serve as a father to. [< OE *fæder.* See **pəter.**] **—fa′ther•less** *adj.* **—fa′ther•ly** *adj.* & *adv.*

fa•ther•hood (fä′*th*ər-ho͝od′) *n.* The condition of being a father; paternity.

fa•ther-in-law (fä′*th*ər-ĭn-lô′) *n., pl.* **fathers-in-law.** The father of one's husband or wife.

fath•om (fă*th*′əm) *n., pl.* **-oms** or **-om.** A unit of length equal to 6 feet, used principally in the measurement of marine depths. *—v.* **1.** To determine the depth of; sound. **2.** To understand. [< OE *fæthm,* a measure of length. See **pet-[2].**] **—fath′om•a•ble** *adj.*

fath•om•less (fă*th*′əm-lĭs) *adj.* Too deep to be fathomed.

fa•tigue (fə-tēg′) *n.* **1.** Weakness or weariness resulting from exertion or prolonged stress. **2.** Manual or menial labor assigned to soldiers. **3. fatigues.** Military dress for work and field duty. *—v.* **-tigued, -tiguing.** To tire out; weary. [< L *fatīgāre,* to fatigue.]

fat•ten (făt′n) *v.* To make or become fat.

fatty acid. Any of a large group of organic acids having the general formula $C_nH_{2n+1}CO$-OH, esp. any of a commercially important subgroup obtained from animals and plants.

fa•tu•i•ty (fə-t/y/o͞o′ə-tē) *n.* Stupidity or foolishness. [< L *fatuus,* FATUOUS.]

fat•u•ous (făch′o͞o-əs) *adj.* Stupid; asinine; inane. [L *fatuus.*] **—fat′u•ous•ly** *adv.*

fau•cet (fô′sĭt) *n.* A device for drawing a flow of a liquid, as from a pipe. [< OF *fausser,* damage, break into, make false.]

Faulkner (fôk′nər), **William Cuthbert.** 1897–1962. American author.

fault (fôlt) *n.* **1.** A failing, defect, or impairment. **2.** A mistake or minor transgression. **3.** Responsibility for something wrong. **4.** A break in the continuity of a rock formation, caused by a shifting or dislodging of the earth's crust, in which adjacent surfaces are differentially displaced parallel to the plane of fracture. **5.** A bad service, as in tennis. **—at fault.** Guilty. **—find fault.** To carp. **—to a fault.** Excessively. *—v.* **1.** To find a fault in. **2.** To produce a geological fault in. **3.** To commit a fault; err. [< L *fallere,* to fail, deceive.] **—fault′i•ly** *adv.* **—fault′less** *adj.* **—fault′less•ly** *adv.* **—fault′y** *adj.*

faun (fôn) *n.* One of a group of ancient Italian rural deities represented as part man and part goat.

fau•na (fô′nə) *n., pl.* **-nas** or **-nae** (-nē′). Animals, esp. of a region or time. [< L *Faunus,* Roman god of nature.]

Faust (foust). A legendary magician who sold his soul to the devil in exchange for power and knowledge. **—Faust′i•an** *adj.*

faux pas (fō pä′) *pl.* **faux pas** (fō päz′). A social blunder. [F, "false step."]

fa•vor (fā′vər) *n.* **1.** A friendly attitude. **2.** An act of kindness. **3.** An indulgence. **4. a.** Friendly regard shown by a superior. **b.** A state of being held in such regard. **5.** Approval or support. **6. favors.** Sexual privileges. **7.** A token of love. **8.** A small, decorative gift handed out at a party. **9.** Advantage; benefit. *—v.* **1.** To oblige. **2.** To like. **3.** To support. **4.** To aid or facilitate. **5.** To resemble: *She favors her father.* **6.** To be gentle with; spare: *favor a sore foot.* [< L *favēre,* to favor.]

fa•vor•a•ble (fā′vər-ə-bəl, fāv′rə-) *adj.* **1.** Advantageous; helpful. **2.** Propitious; encouraging. **3.** Manifesting approval. **—fa′vor•a•ble•ness** *n.* **—fa′vor•a•bly** *adv.*

fa•vor•ite (fā′vər-ĭt, fāv′rĭt) *n.* **1. a.** A person or thing liked above all others. **b.** A person esp. indulged by a superior: *a favorite of the king.* **2.** A contestant regarded as most likely to win. **—fa′vor•ite** *adj.*

fa•vor•it•ism (fā′vər-ə-tĭz′əm, fāv′rə-) *n.* Partiality.

fawn[1] (fôn) *v.* **1.** To exhibit affection, as a dog. **2.** To seek favor by obsequious behavior. [< OE *fægen,* FAIN.]

fawn[2] (fôn) *n.* **1.** A young deer. **2.** Grayish or yellowish brown. [< L *fētus,* offspring, a giving birth.]

fay (fā) *n.* A fairy or sprite. [< L *fāta,* the Fates, pl of *fātum,* FATE.]

faze (fāz) *v.* **fazed, fazing.** To daunt or disconcert. [< OE *fēsian,* to drive off.]

FBI, F.B.I. Federal Bureau of Investigation.

fcap., fcp. foolscap.

FCC Federal Communications Commission.

FDA Food and Drug Administration.

Fe iron (L *ferrum*).

fe•al•ty (fē′əl-tē) *n., pl.* **-ties. 1.** Loyalty. **2.** The obligation of feudal allegiance. [< L *fidēlitās,* faithfulness.]

fear (fîr) *n.* **1.** A feeling of alarm or disquiet caused by awareness or expectation of danger. **2.** An instance or manifestation of such a feeling. **3.** A state of dread. **4.** Concern; solicitude. *—v.* **1.** To be afraid of. **2.** To be apprehensive. **3.** To be in awe of. **4.** To suspect:

I fear you are wrong. [< OE *fǣr,* danger, sudden calamity. See **per-**[3].] **—fear'ful** *adj.* **—fear'ful•ly** *adv.* **—fear'ful•ness** *n.* **—fear'less** *adj.* **—fear'less•ly** *adv.* **—fear'less•ness** *n.*

fear•some (fîr'səm) *adj.* **1.** Frightening; awesome. **2.** Frightened; timid.

fea•si•ble (fē'zə-bəl) *adj.* **1.** Capable of being accomplished or brought about; practicable. **2.** Suitable. **3.** Likely or reasonable: *a feasible excuse.* [< L *facere,* to do.] **—fea'si•bil'i•ty, fea'si•ble•ness** *n.* **—fea'si•bly** *adv.*

feast (fēst) *n.* **1.** A large and elaborate meal; banquet. **2.** A religious festival. *—v.* **1.** To entertain or feed sumptuously. **2.** To delight; gratify. **3.** To partake of a feast. [< L *fēstus,* joyous, festal.] **—feast'er** *n.*

feat (fēt) *n.* A particularly remarkable exploit or achievement. [< L *factum,* something done.]

feath•er (fĕth'ər) *n.* **1.** One of the light, hollow-shafted structures forming the external covering of birds. **2. feathers.** Clothing; attire. **3.** Character; kind: *birds of a feather.* **—in fine** (or **good**) **feather.** In fine fettle. *—v.* **1.** To cover, dress, or line with feathers. **2.** To fit (an arrow) with a feather. [< OE *fether.* See **pet-**[1].] **—feath'er•i•ness** *n.* **—feath'er•y** *adj.*

feather bed. A mattress stuffed with feathers or down.

feath•er•bed (fĕth'ər-bĕd') *v.* **-bedded, -bedding.** **1.** To employ more workers than are actually needed for a given purpose or to limit their production. **2.** To be so employed.

feath•er•weight (fĕth'ər-wāt') *n.* **1.** A boxer weighing between 118 and 127 pounds. **2.** One that weighs very little.

fea•ture (fē'chər) *n.* **1. a.** The shape or aspect of the face: *hard of feature.* **b. features.** The face or its lineaments: *regular features.* **2.** Any prominent or distinctive characteristic. **3.** The main presentation at a motion-picture theater. **4.** A prominent article in a newspaper or periodical. **5.** Anything advertised as a sales inducement. *—v.* **-tured, -turing.** **1.** To make prominent; publicize. **2.** To be a prominent part of. **3.** To draw the features of. [< L *factūra,* a making, formation < *facere,* to do.]

Feb. February.

feb•rile (fĕb'rəl, fē'brəl) *adj.* Of or having fever. [< L *febris,* FEVER.]

Feb•ru•ar•y (fĕb'rōō-ĕr'ē, fĕb'yōō-) *n., pl.* **-ies** or **-ys.** The 2nd month of the year. February has 28 days, 29 in leap years. [< L *februa,* festival of purification held on February 15.]

fe•ces (fē'sēz) *pl.n.* Also **fae•ces.** Waste excreted from the bowels; excrement. [< L *faex (faec-),* dregs.] **—fe'cal** *adj.*

feck•less (fĕk'lĭs) *adj.* **1.** Feeble; ineffectual. **2.** Careless; irresponsible. [< EFFECT + -LESS.]

fe•cund (fē'kənd, fĕk'ənd) *adj.* Fertile; productive; prolific. [< L *fēcundus.*] **—fe•cun'di•ty** (fĭ-kŭn'də-tē) *n.*

fe•cun•date (fē'kən-dāt', fĕk'ən-) *v.* **-dated, -dating.** To impregnate; fertilize.

fed (fĕd). *p.t.* & *p.p.* of **feed.**

fed. federal; federated; federation.

fed•er•al (fĕd'ər-əl) *adj.* **1.** Of or constituting a union of states recognizing the sovereignty of a central authority while retaining certain residual powers. **2.** Of or pertaining to the central government of a federation. **3. Federal. a.** Of or pertaining to the central government of the U.S. **b.** Of or supporting the Federal government during the Civil War; pro-Union. *—n.* A supporter of federation or federal government. [< L *foedus (foeder-),* league, treaty.]

fed•er•al•ism (fĕd'ər-ə-lĭz'əm) *n.* **1.** The doctrine or system of federal government. **2.** The advocacy of such a government.

fed•er•al•ist (fĕd'ər-ə-lĭst) *n.* **1.** An advocate of federalism. **2. Federalist.** A member of a U.S. political party of the 1790's, advocating a strong federal government.

fed•er•al•ize (fĕd'ər-ə-līz') *v.* **-ized, -izing.** **1.** To unite in a federal union. **2.** To put under federal control. **—fed'er•al•i•za'tion** *n.*

fed•er•ate (fĕd'ə-rāt') *v.* **-ated, -ating.** To join or unite in a league, federal union, or similar association. **—fed'e•ra'tion** *n.*

fe•do•ra (fĭ-dôr'ə, -dōr'ə) *n.* A soft felt hat with a crown creased lengthwise and a brim. [< *Fédora,* play by Victorien Sardou (1831–1908), French playwright.]

fee (fē) *n.* **1.** A fixed charge. **2.** A payment for professional services. **3.** *Law.* An inherited or heritable estate in land. **4.** An estate in land held from a feudal lord. [< Frank **fehu-ōd,* payment.]

fee•ble (fē'bəl) *adj.* **-bler, -blest.** **1.** Frail or infirm. **2.** Lacking vigor or force; ineffective. **3.** Faint; slight: *a feeble cry.* [< L *flēbilis,* to be wept over, lamentable.] **—fee'ble•ness** *n.* **—fee'bly** *adv.*

fee•ble-mind•ed (fē'bəl-mīn'dĭd) *adj.* Mentally deficient. **—fee'ble•mind'ed•ness** *n.*

feed (fēd) *v.* **fed, feeding.** **1.** To give food to or provide as food or nourishment. **2.** To eat. **3.** To supply a flow of (a material to be consumed or utilized). **—be fed up.** To be out of patience and disgusted. *—n.* **1.** Food for animals. **2.** *Informal.* A meal. **3. a.** Material supplied, as to a machine. **b.** An apparatus that supplies such material. [< OE *fēdan.* See **pā-.**] **—feed'a•ble** *adj.* **—feed'er** *n.*

feed•back (fēd'băk') *n.* The return of a portion of the output of any process or system to the input.

feel (fēl) *v.* **felt, feeling.** **1.** To perceive, give, or produce through the sense of touch. **2. a.** To touch. **b.** To examine by touching. **3. a.** To experience (an emotion). **b.** To be aware of; sense. **c.** To suffer from. **4.** To believe or consider. **5.** To have compassion or sympathy. *—n.* **1.** Perception by touching or feeling. **2.** The sense of touch. **3.** The nature or quality of something perceived. [< OE *fēlan.* See **pōl-.**]

feel•er (fē'lər) *n.* **1.** An exploratory suggestion or remark. **2.** A sensory organ such as an antenna or tentacle.

feel•ing (fē'lĭng) *n.* **1. a.** The sensation involving perception by touch. **b.** A sensation perceived by touch. **c.** Any physical sensation. **2. a.** Any affective state or disposition. **b.** Emotion: *a deep feeling.* **3.** An awareness; impression. **4. feelings.** Sensibilities. **5.** Opinion. **6.** Sympathy. **7.** A bent; aptitude. *—adj.* **1. a.** Sensitive. **b.** Easily moved emotionally. **2.** Sympathetic. **—feel'ing•ly** *adv.*

feet. *pl.* of **foot.**

feign (fān) *v.* To give a false appearance (of); pretend; sham. [< OF *feindre* < L *fingere,* to form, shape.] **—feign'er** *n.*

feint (fānt) *n.* A feigned attack designed to draw defensive action away from an intended target. **—feint** *v.*

feld•spar (fĕld'spär', fĕl'-) *n.* Any of a group of abundant rock-forming minerals consisting of silicates of aluminum with potassium, sodium, calcium, and rarely barium. [Part trans of obs G *Feldspath,* "field spar."]

fe•lic•i•tate (fĭ-lĭs'ə-tāt') *v.* **-tated, -tating.** To congratulate. [< L *fēlix,* happy.] **—fe•lic'i•ta'tion** *n.* **—fe•lic'i•ta'tor** *n.*

fe•lic•i•tous (fĭ-lĭs'ə-təs) *adj.* **1.** Well-chosen; apt. **2.** Having an appropriate and agreeable manner or style. **—fe•lic'i•tous•ly** *adv.*

fe•lic•i•ty (fĭ-lĭs'ə-tē) *n., pl.* **-ties.** **1.** Great happiness. **2.** Something that causes or produces happiness. **3. a.** Aptness of expression. **b.** An instance of this.

fe•line (fē'līn') *adj.* **1.** Of or pertaining to cats or related animals, such as lions and tigers. **2.** Catlike, as in slyness or suppleness. *—n.* A feline animal. [< L *fēlēs,* cat.]

fell[1] (fĕl) *v.* **1.** To cut or knock down. **2.** To sew or finish (a seam) with the raw edges flattened and turned under. [< OE *fellan, fyllan,* strike down, fell. See **phol-.**]

fell[2] (fĕl) *adj.* **1.** Cruel; fierce; unsparing. **2.** Deadly; lethal. [< ML *fellō,* wicked person, felon.] **—fell'ness** *n.*

fell[3] (fĕl). *p.t.* of **fall.**

fel•lah (fĕl'ə, fə-lä') *n.* A peasant or agricultural laborer in Arab countries. [Ar *fellāh.*]

fel•low (fĕl'ō) *n.* **1.** A man or boy. **2.** Any human being. **3.** A comrade; associate. **4. a.** An equal; peer. **b.** One of a pair; mate. **5.** A member of a learned society. **6.** A recipient of a grant for advanced study. [< ON *fēlagi,* fellow, one who lays down money.]

fel•low•ship (fĕl'ō-shĭp') *n.* **1.** Companionship, comradeship, or friendship. **2.** A union of friends or equals. **3. a.** A graduate stipend. **b.** A foundation awarding such grants.

fellow traveler. One who sympathizes with an organized group, as the Communist Party, without actually joining it.

fel•ly (fĕl'ē) *n., pl.* **-lies.** Also **fel•loe** (fĕl'ō). The rim of a wheel supported by spokes. [< OE *felg* < Gmc **felgam.*]

fel•on[1] (fĕl'ən) *n.* One who has committed a felony. [< VL **fellō.*]

fel•on[2] (fĕl'ən) *n.* An infection at the end of a finger near the nail. [Poss < L *fel,* bile, venom.]

fel•o•ny (fĕl'ə-nē) *n., pl.* **-nies.** Any of several crimes, such as murder, rape, or burglary. **—fe•lo'ni•ous** (fə-lō'nē-əs) *adj.*

felt[1] (fĕlt) *n.* **1.** A fabric of matted, compressed fibers, as wool or fur. **2.** Any material resembling this. [< OE. See **pel-**[1].]

felt[2] (fĕlt). *p.t.* & *p.p.* of **feel.**

fem. feminine.

fe•male (fē'māl') *adj.* **1.** Of, pertaining to, or designating the sex that produces ova or bears young. **2.** Characteristic of or appropriate to this sex; feminine. **3.** Consisting of members of this sex. *—n.* A female person, plant, or animal. [< L *fēmina,* woman, female.] **—fe'male'ness** *n.*

fem•i•nine (fĕm'ə-nĭn) *adj.* **1.** Of or belonging to the female sex. **2.** Characterized by qualities attributed to women. **3.** Indicating or belonging to the gender of words or grammatical forms that are classified as female. *—n.* **1.** The feminine gender. **2.** A word or form belonging to that gender. [< L *fēmina,* FEMALE.] **—fem'i•nin'i•ty** *n.*

fem•i•nism (fĕm'ə-nĭz'əm) *n.* Militant advocacy of equal rights and status for women.

fe•mur (fē'mər) *n., pl.* **-murs** or **femora** (fĕm'ər-ə). **1.** The proximal bone of the lower or hind limb in vertebrates, situated between the pelvis and knee in humans. **2.** The thigh. [L, thigh.] **—fem'o•ral** (fĕm'ər-əl) *adj.*

fen (fĕn) *n.* Low, flat, swampy land; bog; marsh. [< OE *fenn.*]

fe•na•gle. Variant of **finagle.**

fence (fĕns) *n.* **1.** An enclosure, barrier, or boundary made of posts, boards, wire, stakes, or rails. **2. a.** A receiver of stolen goods. **b.** A place where such goods are received and sold. **—on the fence.** *Informal.* Undecided as to which of two sides to support; neutral. *—v.* **fenced, fencing. 1.** To surround, close in, or close off by means of a fence. **2.** To practice the art of fencing. **3.** To avoid giving direct answers; be evasive. **4.** To act as a fence for stolen goods. [< DEFENSE.]

fenc•er (fĕn′sər) *n.* One who fences, as with a foil.

fenc•ing (fĕn′sĭng) *n.* **1.** The art or practice of using a foil or saber. **2.** Material used in the construction of fences.

fend (fĕnd) *v.* To ward off, deflect, or repel. **—fend for oneself.** To provide for oneself. [< DEFEND.]

fend•er (fĕn′dər) *n.* **1.** A guard device over the wheel of an automobile. **2.** A screen in front of a fireplace.

fen•nel (fĕn′əl) *n.* **1.** A plant with aromatic seeds used as flavoring. **2.** The seeds or edible stalks of this plant. [< L *fēnum,* hay.]

-fer. *comb. form.* Agency, bearing, or production: *aquifer.* [< L *ferre,* to carry, bear.]

fer•ment (fûr′mĕnt′) *n.* **1.** Something that causes fermentation, as a yeast or enzyme. **2.** A state of agitation or unrest. *—v.* (fər-mĕnt′). **1.** To produce by or as if by fermentation. **2.** To undergo or cause to undergo fermentation. **3.** To be turbulent; seethe. [< L *fermentum.*] **—fer•ment′a•ble** *adj.*

fer•men•ta•tion (fûr′mĕn-tā′shən) *n.* **1.** Chemical splitting of complex organic compounds into relatively simple substances, esp. the conversion of sugar to carbon dioxide and alcohol by yeast. **2.** Unrest; commotion.

fer•mi•um (fûr′mē-əm) *n. Symbol* **Fm** A synthetic metallic element. Atomic number 100, longest-lived isotope Fm 257. [< E. *Fermi* (1901–1954), Italian-born American physicist.]

fern (fûrn) *n.* Any of numerous flowerless plants characteristically having fronds with divided leaflets and reproducing by means of spores. [< OE *fearn.*]

fe•ro•cious (fə-rō′shəs) *adj.* **1.** Extremely savage; fierce. **2.** Extreme; relentless. [< L *ferōx,* wild, fierce.] **—fe•ro′cious•ly** *adv.*

fe•roc•i•ty (fə-rŏs′ə-tē) *n., pl.* **-ties.** The condition or quality of being ferocious.

-ferous. *comb. form.* Bearing, producing, or containing: *crystalliferous.* [< -FER + -OUS.]

fer•ret[1] (fĕr′ĭt) *n.* **1.** A domesticated, usually white form of the Old World polecat, often trained to hunt rats or rabbits. **2.** A related weasellike North American mammal. *—v.* **1.** To hunt with a ferret. **2.** To drive out; expel. **3.** To uncover and bring to light by searching (with *out*). [< VL **fūrittus,* little thief.] **—fer′ret•er** *n.* **—fer′ret•y** *adj.*

fer•ret[2] (fĕr′ĭt) *n.* Also **fer•ret•ing** (-ĭng). A narrow piece of tape used to bind or edge fabric. [Prob < It *fioretti,* floss silk.]

fer•ric (fĕr′ĭk) *adj.* Of or containing iron, esp. with valence 3. [FERR(O)- + -IC.]

ferric oxide. A dark compound, Fe_2O_3, occurring naturally as hematite ore and rust.

Fer•ris wheel (fĕr′ĭs). Also **fer•ris wheel.** A large upright, rotating wheel having suspended cars in which passengers ride for amusement. [< G. *Ferris* (1859–1896), American engineer.]

fer•rite (fĕr′īt′) *n.* Any of a group of nonmetallic, ceramiclike, usually ferromagnetic compounds of ferric oxide with other oxides.

ferro-. *comb. form.* Iron. [< L *ferrum,* iron.]

fer•ro•mag•net•ic (fĕr′ō-măg-nĕt′ĭk) *adj.* Pertaining to or characteristic of substances, such as iron, nickel, cobalt, and various alloys, that acquire high magnetization in relatively weak magnetic fields. **—fer′ro•mag′net** *n.* **—fer′ro•mag′ne•tism′** *n.*

fer•ro•type (fĕr′ə-tīp′) *n.* **1.** A positive photograph made directly on an iron plate varnished with a thin sensitized film. **2.** The process by which such photographs are made.

fer•rous (fĕr′əs) *adj.* Of or containing iron, esp. with valence 2.

ferrous oxide. A black powdery compound, FeO, used in the manufacture of steel.

fer•rule (fĕr′əl, -ōōl′) *n.* A metal ring or cap attached to or near the end of a cane or wooden handle to prevent splitting. [< L *viriola,* little bracelet.]

fer•ry (fĕr′ē) *n., pl.* **-ries. 1.** A service for transport across a body of water. **2.** A ferryboat. **3.** The place of embarkation of a ferryboat. **4.** A service for transporting people or goods by aircraft, usually over short distances. *—v.* **-ried, -rying. 1.** To transport across a body of water. **2.** To cross on a ferry. **3.** To transport from one place to another. [Prob < ON *ferja.*]

fer•ry•boat (fĕr′ē-bōt′) *n.* A boat used to ferry passengers or goods.

fer•ry•man (fĕr′ē-mən) *n.* One who operates a ferry.

fer•tile (fûrt′l) *adj.* **1.** Capable of initiating, sustaining, or supporting reproduction. **2.** Rich in material needed to sustain plant growth: *fertile soil.* **3.** Highly or continuously productive; prolific: *a fertile imagination.* [< L *ferre,* to bear, carry, produce.] **—fer′tile•ly** *adv.* **—fer•til′i•ty, fer′tile•ness** *n.*

fer•til•ize (fûrt′l-īz′) *v.* **-ized, -izing. 1.** To initiate biological reproduction, esp. to provide with sperm or pollen. **2.** To make fertile, as by spreading fertilizer. **—fer′til•i•za′tion** *n.*

fer•til•iz•er (fûrt′l-ī′zər) *n.* **1.** One that fertilizes. **2.** Any of a large number of natural and synthetic materials, including manure and nitrogen, phosphorus, and potassium compounds, spread on or worked into soil to increase its fertility.

fer•ule (fĕr′əl, -ōōl′) *n.* A baton, cane, or stick used in punishing children. [L *ferula,* giant fennel.]

fer•ven•cy (fûr′vən-sē) *n.* Fervor.

fer•vent (fûr′vənt) *adj.* **1.** Passionate; ardent. **2.** Extremely hot; glowing. [< L *fervēre,* to boil, glow.] **—fer′vent•ly** *adv.*

fer•vid (fûr′vĭd) *adj.* **1.** Zealous; impassioned. **2.** Extremely hot; burning. [< L *fervēre,* to glow, boil.] **—fer′vid•ly** *adv.*

fer•vor (fûr′vər) *n.* **1.** Ardor; enthusiasm. **2.** Intense heat. [< L *fervēre,* to boil.]

fes•tal (fĕs′təl) *adj.* Festive. [< L *fēsta,* FEAST.]

fes•ter (fĕs′tər) *v.* **1.** To generate pus; suppurate. **2.** To form an ulcer. **3.** To be or become a source of irritation; rankle. [< L *fistula,* FISTULA.]

fes•ti•val (fĕs′tə-vəl) *n.* **1.** A day of religious feasting or special observances. **2.** A programmed series of related cultural events: *a film festival.* **3.** Conviviality; revelry. [< L *fēstīvus,* FESTIVE.]

fes•tive (fĕs′tĭv) *adj.* **1.** Of or appropriate to a feast or festival. **2.** Merry; joyous. [L *fēstīvus* < *fēstus,* joyous.] **—fes′tive•ly** *adv.*

fes•tiv•i•ty (fĕs-tĭv′ə-tē) *n., pl.* **-ties. 1.** A joyous feast, holiday, or celebration; festival. **2.** The joy or gaiety of a festival. **3. festivities.** Festive activities.

fes•toon (fĕs-tōōn′) *n.* **1.** A decorative garland suspended in a curve between two points. **2.** A sculptured representation of this. *—v.* **1.** To decorate with or as with festoons. **2.** To form festoons. [< It *festone,* festal ornament.]

fe•tal (fēt′l) *adj.* Also **foe•tal** (fēt′l). Pertaining to the nature of a fetus.

fetch (fĕch) *v.* **1.** To go after and return with. **2.** To cause to come forth. **3. a.** To draw in (breath); inhale. **b.** To heave (a sigh). **4.** To strike or deal (a blow). [< OE *feccan.*] **—fetch′er** *n.*

fetch•ing (fĕch′ĭng) *adj.* Attractive; captivating. **—fetch′ing•ly** *adv.*

fete (fāt) *n.* Also **fête. 1.** A festival. **2.** An elaborate outdoor party. **3.** Any elaborate party. *—v.* **feted, feting. 1.** To honor or celebrate with a fete. **2.** To pay honor to. [< OF *feste,* feast.]

fet•id (fĕt′ĭd, fē′tĭd) *adj.* Foul-smelling; stinking. [< L *fētēre,* to stink.]

fet•ish (fĕt′ĭsh) *n.* **1.** An object believed to have magical power. **2.** An object of obsessive attention or reverence. [< L *factītius,* made by art.] **—fet′ish•ism′** *n.* **—fet′ish•ist** *n.* & *adj.*

fet•lock (fĕt′lŏk′) *n.* A projection above and behind the hoof of a horse or related animal. [ME *fitlok.*]

fet•ter (fĕt′ər) *n.* **1.** A chain or shackle attached to the ankles. **2. fetters.** Anything that serves to restrict; restraint. *—v.* **1.** To shackle. **2.** To restrict or confine. [< OE *feter.* See **ped-**[1].]

fet•tle (fĕt′l) *n.* Condition: *in fine fettle.* [< ME *fetlen,* to shape, make ready.]

fe•tus (fē′təs) *n., pl.* **-tuses.** Also **foe•tus.** The unborn young of a viviparous vertebrate; in humans, the unborn young from the end of the eighth week to the moment of birth as distinguished from the earlier embryo. [L *fētus,* pregnancy, fetus.]

feud (fyōōd) *n.* A protracted quarrel; vendetta. [< OHG *fēhida.*] **—feud** *v.*

feu•dal (fyōōd′l) *adj.* **1.** Pertaining to or characteristic of feudalism. **2.** Of or pertaining to a medieval fee. [< ML *feudum,* a feudal estate.] **—feu′dal•ly** *adv.*

feu•dal•ism (fyōōd′l-ĭz′əm) *n.* The political system of Europe from the 9th to about the 15th century A.D., based on the relation of lord to vassal as a result of land being held on condition of homage and service. **—feu′dal•ist** *n.* **—feu′dal•is′tic** *adj.*

feu•da•to•ry (fyōō′də-tôr′ē, -tōr′ē) *n., pl.* **-ries. 1.** A vassal. **2.** A feudal fee. *—adj.* **1.** Of or characteristic of a feudal relationship. **2.** Owing feudal allegiance.

fe•ver (fē′vər) *n.* **1.** Abnormally high body temperature. **2.** A disease characterized by abnormally high body temperatures. **3.** Heightened activity or excitement; agitation. **4.** A contagious, short-lived enthusiasm; craze. [< L *febris.*] **—fe′ver•ish** *adj.* **—fe′ver•ish•ly** *adv.* **—fe′ver•ish•ness** *n.*

few (fyōō) *adj.* **fewer, fewest.** Amounting to or consisting of a small number. *—n. (takes pl. v.).* **1.** A small number of persons or things. **2.** A select group or elite: *the happy few.* *—pron. (takes pl. v.).* A small number. [< OE *fēa, fēawe.* See **pōu-.**] **—few′ness** *n.*

Usage: Fewer, in contrast to *less,* is the preferred term in most examples involving reference to numbers or units considered individually and therefore capable of being counted or enumerated. *Less* refers to collective quantity or to something abstract: *fewer people, less noise; fewer chances, less opportunity.*

fey (fā) *adj.* **1.** *Scot.* **a.** Fated to die soon. **b.** Marked by a sense of approaching death. **2.** Clairvoyant. **3.** Enchanted; elfin. [< OE *fǣge.* See **peig-**[2].]

fez (fěz) *n., pl.* **fezzes.** A man's felt cap in the shape of a truncated cone, usually red with a black tassel, worn chiefly in the E Mediterranean region. [< *Fez,* Morocco.]

ff. 1. folios. **2.** following.

FHA Federal Housing Administration.

fi•an•cé (fē'än-sā', fē-än'sā') *n.* A man engaged to be married. [< OF *fier,* to trust.]

fi•an•cée (fē'än-sā', fē-än'sā') *n.* A woman engaged to be married.

fi•as•co (fē-ăs'kō) *n., pl.* **-coes** or **-cos.** A complete failure. [< It *(far) fiasco,* "(to make) a bottle."]

fi•at (fī'ăt', -ət, fē'ät') *n.* An arbitrary order or decree. [L *fiat,* "let it be done."]

fib (fĭb) *n.* An inconsequential lie. *—v.* **fibbed, fibbing.** To tell a fib. [?] **—fib'ber** *n.*

fi•ber (fī'bər) *n.* Also *chiefly Brit.* **fi•bre. 1.** Any slender, elongated structure; a filament or strand, as of plant, muscle, or nerve tissue, or a synthetic substance. **2.** Internal strength; toughness: *moral fiber.* [< L *fibra.*]

fi•ber•board (fī'bər-bôrd', -bōrd') *n.* A building material composed of wood or other plant fibers compressed into rigid sheets.

fiber glass. A composite material consisting of glass fibers in resin.

fi•broid (fī'broid') *adj.* Resembling or composed of fibrous tissue.

fi•bro•sis (fī-brō'sĭs) *n.* The formation of fibrous tissue, as in a reparative or reactive process, in excess of amounts normally present.

fi•brous (fī'brəs) *adj.* Consisting of or resembling fibers.

fib•u•la (fĭb'yə-lə) *n., pl.* **-lae** (-lē') or **-las.** The outer and smaller of two bones of the leg. [L *fibula.*]

–fic. *comb. form.* The making, causing, or creating of: **terrific.** [< L *-ficus* < *facere,* to do, make.]

fi•chu (fĭsh'o͞o) *n.* A woman's triangular scarf worn over the shoulders and crossed or tied in front. [F.]

fick•le (fĭk'əl) *adj.* Changeable; inconstant; capricious. [< OE *ficol,* false. See **peig-[2].**] **—fick'le•ness** *n.*

fic•tion (fĭk'shən) *n.* **1.** Something invented or imagined. **2. a.** The category of literature with imaginary characters and events, including novels, short stories, etc. **b.** A work of this category. [< L *fictiō,* a making, fashioning.] **—fic'tion•al** *adj.* **—fic'tion•al•ly** *adv.*

fic•ti•tious (fĭk-tĭsh'əs) *adj.* **1.** Nonexistent; imaginary; unreal. **2.** Purposefully deceptive; false: *a fictitious name.*

fid•dle (fĭd'l) *n.* A violin. *—v.* **1.** *Informal.* To play a violin. **2.** To fidget. [< L *vītulārī,* to celebrate a victory.] **—fid'dler** *n.*

fid•dle•sticks (fĭd'l-stĭks') *interj.* Expressive of mild annoyance or impatience.

fi•del•i•ty (fĭ-dĕl'ə-tē, fī-) *n., pl.* **-ties. 1.** Faithfulness; loyalty. **2.** Truthfulness; accuracy. **3.** The degree to which an electronic system accurately reproduces at its output the essential characteristics of its input signal. [< L *fidēs,* faith.]

fidg•et (fĭj'ĭt) *v.* **1.** To move nervously or restlessly. **2.** To play or fuss; fiddle (with *with*). *—n.* **1.** Often **fidgets.** A condition of restlessness. **2.** One who fidgets. [Prob < ON *fikjast.*] **—fidg'et•i•ness** *n.* **—fidg'et•y** *adj.*

fi•du•ci•ar•y (fĭ-d/y/o͞o'shē-ĕr'ē, fī-) *adj.* **1.** Pertaining to the holding of something in trust. **2.** Held in trust. *—n., pl.* **-ies.** A trustee. [< L *fidūcia,* trust.]

fie (fī) *interj.* Expressive of distaste or shock. [< L *fi.*]

fief (fēf) *n.* A feudal estate. [< OF *fief,* fee.]

field (fēld) *n.* **1.** A broad, level expanse of open land. **2.** A piece of land devoted to a particular crop. **3.** A portion of land containing a specified natural resource: *an oil field.* **4.** An airfield or airport. **5.** A background area, as on a flag. **6.** *Sports.* **a.** An area in which a sports event takes place; ground; stadium. **b.** All the contestants in an event. **7.** An area of activity or knowledge. **8.** A battlefield. **9.** A region of space characterized by a physical property, such as gravitational force, having a determinable value at every point in the region. *—v.* *Sports.* **1.** To retrieve (a ball) and perform the required maneuver. **2.** To put (a team) into a contest. [< OE *feld.* See **pele-.**] **—field'er** *n.*

field glass. Often **field glasses.** A portable binocular instrument used esp. for viewing distant objects.

field goal. 1. *Football.* A score worth three points made by kicking the ball over the crossbar and between the goal posts. **2.** *Basketball.* A score worth two points made by throwing the ball through the basket in regulation play.

field magnet. A magnet used to provide a magnetic field in an electrical device such as a generator or motor.

field marshal. An officer ranking just below the commander in chief in some European armies.

field of force. A region of space throughout which the force produced by a single agent, such as an electric current, is operative.

fiend (fēnd) *n.* **1.** An evil spirit; demon. **2.** A diabolically evil or wicked person. **3.** *Informal.* An addict: *a dope fiend; a crossword-puzzle fiend.* [< OE *fēond.*] **—fiend'ish** *adj.* **—fiend'ish•ly** *adv.* **—fiend'ish•ness** *n.*

fierce (fîrs) *adj.* **1.** Having a savage and violent nature; ferocious. **2.** Extremely severe or violent; terrible. [< L *ferus,* wild.] **—fierce'ly** *adv.* **—fierce'ness** *n.*

fier•y (fīr'ē, fī'ə-rē) *adj.* **-ier, -iest. 1.** Consisting of or containing fire. **2.** Of or like fire. **3.** Charged with emotion; fervent. **4.** Emotionally volatile; tempestuous. **—fier'i•ly** *adv.* **—fier'i•ness** *n.*

fi•es•ta (fē-ĕs'tə) *n.* **1.** A religious feast or holiday. **2.** Any celebration or festival. [< L *fēstus,* joyous, festive.]

fife (fīf) *n.* A musical instrument similar to a flute but higher in range, used primarily to accompany drums. [< OHG *pfiffa.*]

fif•teen (fĭf-tēn') *n.* The cardinal number written 15 or in Roman numerals XV. [< OE *fīftēne.* See **penkwe.**] **—fif•teen'** *adj.* & *pron.*

fif•teenth (fĭf-tēnth') *n.* **1.** The ordinal number 15 in a series. **2.** One of 15 equal parts. **—fif•teenth'** *adj.* & *adv.*

fifth (fĭfth) *n.* **1.** The ordinal number 5 in a series. **2.** One of 5 equal parts. **3.** One-fifth of a gallon of liquor; four-fifths of a quart. [< OE *fīfta.* See **penkwe.**] **—fifth** *adj.* & *adv.*

fif•ti•eth (fĭf'tē-ĭth) *n.* **1.** The ordinal number 50 in a series. **2.** One of 50 equal parts. **—fif'ti•eth** *adj.* & *adv.*

fif•ty (fĭf'tē) *n.* The cardinal number written 50 or in Roman numerals L. [< OE *fīftig.* See **penkwe.**] **—fif'ty** *adj.* & *pron.*

fif•ty-fif•ty (fĭf'tē-fĭf'tē) *adj.* *Informal.* Divided or shared in two equal portions. **—fif'ty-fif'ty** *adv.*

fig (fĭg) *n.* **1.** The pear-shaped, many-seeded, edible fruit of a widely cultivated tree. **2.** A tree bearing such fruit. **3.** A trivial amount; whit: *not care a fig.* [< L *ficus.*]

fig. figurative; figuratively; figure.

fight (fīt) *v.* **fought, fighting. 1.** To participate in combat or battle. **2.** To struggle; contend (with). **3.** To quarrel; argue. **4.** To box or wrestle (against) in a ring. **5.** To try to prevent; oppose. **6.** To wage (a battle). **7.** To make (one's way), as by combat. **—fight off. 1.** To defend against or drive back (a hostile force). **2.** To struggle to avoid: *fight off temptation.* *—n.* **1.** A battle; combat. **2.** A struggle, quarrel, or conflict. **3.** A boxing match; a bout. **4.** Inclination to fight; pugnacity. [< OE *feohtan.*]

fight•er (fī'tər) *n.* **1.** One engaged in fighting; a combatant. **2.** A pugilist. **3.** A pugnacious or determined person. **4.** A fast, maneuverable combat aircraft.

fig•ment (fĭg'mənt) *n.* **1.** Something imagined. **2.** An arbitrary notion. [< L *fingere,* to mold, fashion.]

fig•ur•a•tive (fĭg'yər-ə-tĭv) *adj.* **1.** Based on figures of speech; not literal; metaphorical. **2.** Represented by a figure; emblematic. **—fig'ur•a•tive•ly** *adv.* **—fig'ur•a•tive•ness** *n.*

fig•ure (fĭg'yər) *n.* **1.** A written symbol representing anything other than a letter, esp. a number. **2. figures.** Mathematical calculation involving the use of such symbols. **3.** An amount represented in numbers. **4.** The outline, form, or silhouette of a thing, esp. of a human body. **5.** An individual, esp. a well-known personage. **6.** The impression an individual makes: *He cuts a dashing figure.* **7.** A diagram, design, or pattern. **8.** A group of steps in a dance. **9.** An expression, as a simile. *—v.* **1.** To calculate with numbers; compute. **2.** To make a likeness of; represent. **3.** To adorn with a design. **4.** *Informal.* To conclude, believe, or predict. **5.** To be an element; have mention, pertinence, or importance. **—figure on** (or **upon**). *Informal.* **1.** To depend on. **2.** To plan on; expect. **—figure out.** *Informal.* To solve, decipher, or comprehend. [< L *figūra,* form, shape, figure.]

fig•ure•head (fĭg'yər-hĕd') *n.* **1.** A person holding nominal leadership but having no actual authority. **2.** A carved figure on the prow of a ship.

fig•u•rine (fĭg'yə-rēn') *n.* A small sculptured figure; statuette.

Fi•ji (fē'jē). A British colony in the SW Pacific Ocean. Pop. 456,000.

fil•a•gree. Variant of **filigree.**

fil•a•ment (fĭl'ə-mənt) *n.* **1.** A fine, thin thread or threadlike structure. **2.** A fine wire heated electrically to incandescence in an electric lamp. [< L *filum,* thread.] **—fil'a•men'ta•ry** *adj.* **—fil'a•men'tous** *adj.*

fil•bert (fĭl'bərt) *n.* The rounded, smooth-shelled edible nut of an Old World hazel. [< NF *(noix de) filbert,* "nut of Saint *Philibert*" (died A.D. 684), Frankish abbot.]

filch (fĭlch) *v.* To steal; pilfer. [ME *filchen.*] **—filch'er** *n.*

file[1] (fīl) *n.* **1.** A receptacle for keeping papers, cards, etc., in useful order. **2.** A collection of objects kept thus: *the accounts-due file.* **3.** A line of persons, animals, or things positioned one behind another. **—on file.** Catalogued in a file; on hand. *—v.* **1.** To put in useful order; catalogue. **2.** To enter (as a legal document) on public record. **3.** To transmit (copy) to a newspaper. **4.** To march or walk in a line. [< L *filum,* thread.] **—fil'er** *n.*

file[2] (fīl) *n.* **1.** A tool with hardened ridged

surfaces, used in smoothing, polishing, grinding, or boring. **2.** *Brit. Slang.* A deceitful, cunning person. —*v.* **filed, filing.** To work with or as if with a file. [< OE *fēol, fīl.* See **peig-**[1].] —**fil'er** *n.*

file clerk. One who is employed to maintain the files of an office.

fi•let mi•gnon (fĭ-lā' mĭn-yŏn'). A small, round, very choice cut of beef from the loin. [F, "small or dainty fillet."]

fil•i•al (fĭl'ē-əl) *adj.* Of, pertaining to, or befitting a son or daughter: *filial obedience.* [< L *filius,* son.]

fil•i•bus•ter (fĭl'ə-bŭs'tər) *n.* **1.** Obstructionist tactics, such as the making of prolonged speeches, for the purpose of delaying legislative action. **2.** An adventurer who engages in a private military action in a foreign country. [Orig "freebooter."] —**fil'i•bus'ter** *v.* —**fil'i•bus'ter•er** *n.*

fil•i•gree (fĭl'ə-grē') *n.* Also **fil•a•gree, fil•la•gree.** Delicate ornamental work made from gold, silver, or other fine twisted wire. —*adj.* Made of or resembling filigree. [< F *filigrane.*]

fil•ing (fī'lĭng) *n.* Often **filings.** A particle or shaving removed by a file.

Fil•i•pi•no (fĭl'ə-pē'nō) *n., pl.* **-nos.** A native, citizen, or inhabitant of the Philippines. —*adj.* Of, relating to, or pertaining to the Philippines or Filipinos.

fill (fĭl) *v.* **1.** To make or become full. **2.** To stop or plug up. **3.** To satisfy; fulfill: *fill the requirements.* **4.** To supply the necessary materials for: *fill a prescription.* **5.** To supply (an empty space) with material.. **6.** To put someone into (a specific office or position). **7.** To occupy (a specific office or position). —**fill in. 1.** To write in. **2.** To act as a substitute. —**fill out. 1.** To complete (a document). **2.** To become fuller or rounder. —**fill up.** To make or become full. —*n.* **1.** A full supply: *eat one's fill.* **2.** A built-up piece of land; embankment. —**have one's fill.** To have enough or too much; be thoroughly sated or weary. [< OE *fyllan.* See **pel-**[5].] —**fill'er** *n.*

fil•let (fĭl'ĭt) *n.* **1.** A narrow strip of ribbon or similar material. **2.** (*often* fĭ-lā', fĭl'ā). Also **fi•let.** A strip or slice of boneless meat or fish. —*v.* **1.** (fĭl'ĭt), **filleted** (fĭl'ĭt-ĭd), **filleting** (fĭl'ĭt-ĭng). To bind or decorate with or as with a fillet. **2.** (fĭ-lā', fĭl'ā'), **filleted** (fĭ-lād', fĭl'ād'), **filleting** (fĭ-lā'ĭng, fĭl'ā'ĭng). Also **fi•let.** To slice, bone, or make into a fillet or fillets. [< L *filum,* thread.]

fill•ing (fĭl'ĭng) *n.* **1.** Something used to fill a space, cavity, or container. **2.** The threads that cross the warp in weaving; weft.

fil•lip (fĭl'əp) *n.* **1.** A snap of the fingers. **2.** An incentive; stimulus. [Imit.] —**fil'lip** *v.*

Fill•more (fĭl'môr', -mōr'), **Millard.** 1800–1874. 13th President of the U.S. (1850–53).

fil•ly (fĭl'ē) *n., pl.* **-lies.** A young female horse. [< ON *fylja.*]

film (fĭlm) *n.* **1.** A thin skin or membrane. **2.** Any thin covering or coating. **3.** A thin sheet or strip of flexible cellulose material coated with a photosensitive emulsion, used to make photographic negatives or transparencies. **4. a.** A motion picture. **b.** Motion pictures collectively regarded as an art. —*v.* **1.** To cover with a film. **2.** To make a motion picture of. [< OE *filmen.* See **pel-**[4].] —**film'i•ly** *adv.* —**film'i•ness** *n.* —**film'y** *adj.*

film•dom (fĭlm'dəm) *n.* The motion picture industry or those in it.

film•go•er (fĭlm'gō'ər) *n.* One who goes to see motion pictures.

fil•ter (fĭl'tər) *n.* **1.** Any porous substance through which a liquid or gas is passed in order to remove certain constituents. **2.** A device containing or consisting of such a substance so used. **3.** Any of various electric, electronic, acoustic, or optical devices used to reject signals, vibrations, or radiations of certain frequencies while passing others. —*v.* **1.** To pass through a filter. **2.** To remove by passing through a filter. [< Frank **filtir.*] —**fil•tra'tion** *n.*

fil•ter•a•ble (fĭl'tər-ə-bəl, fĭl'trə-) *adj.* Also **fil•tra•ble. 1.** Capable of being filtered, esp. capable of being removed by filtering. **2.** Sufficiently minute to pass through a fine filter, thereby maintaining the infectivity of the filtrate, as certain viruses and some bacteria. —**fil'ter•a•bil'i•ty** *n.*

filth (fĭlth) *n.* **1.** Foul or dirty matter. **2.** A dirty or foul condition. **3.** Obscene material or language. [< OE *fylth,* putrid matter. See **pu-.**] —**filth'i•ness** *n.* —**filth'y** *adj.*

fil•trate (fĭl'trāt') *n.* The portion of the material subjected to filtration that passes through the filter.

fin (fĭn) *n.* **1.** One of the membranous swimming and balancing appendages extending from the body of a fish, whale, etc. **2.** Something resembling a fin in shape or function. [< OE *finn.*]

fin. 1. finance; financial. **2.** finish.

Fin. Finland; Finnish.

fi•na•gle (fĭ-nā'gəl) *v.* **-gled, -gling.** Also **fe•na•gle.** *Informal.* To use or achieve by dubious or crafty methods. [?] —**fi•na'gler** *n.*

fi•nal (fī'nəl) *adj.* **1.** Concluding; last; ultimate. **2.** Decisive; conclusive; unalterable. —*n.* **1.** The last of a series of athletic contests. **2.** The last examination of an academic course. [< L *finis,* end.] —**fi•nal'i•ty** (fī-năl'ə-tē, fĭ-) *n.* —**fi'nal•ly** *adv.*

fi•na•le (fĭ-năl'ē, -nä'lē) *n.* The concluding part, esp. of a musical composition. [It, "final."]

Millard Fillmore

fi•nal•ist (fī'nəl-ĭst) *n.* A contestant in the final session of a competition.

fi•nal•ize (fī'nə-līz') *v.* **-ized, -izing.** To put into final form; complete.

fi•nance (fĭ-năns', fī'năns', fī'năns') *n.* **1.** The science of the management of money. **2. finances.** Monetary resources. —*v.* To supply the funds or capital for. [< OF *finer,* to end, settle.] —**fi•nan'cial** *adj.* —**fi•nan'cial•ly** *adv.*

fin•an•cier (fĭn'ən-sîr', fī-năn'-, fī'năn-) *n.* One who is occupied with or expert in large-scale financial affairs.

finch (fĭnch) *n.* Any of various small related birds with a short, stout bill, such as a goldfinch, cardinal, or canary. [< OE *finc.* See **sping-.**]

find (fīnd) *v.* **found, finding. 1.** To come upon by accident or after a search. **2.** To attain: *found contentment at last.* **3.** To determine; ascertain. **4.** To consider; regard. **5.** To recover; regain. **6.** To declare as a verdict or conclusion. —*n.* **1.** An act of finding. **2.** That which is found, esp. a rare or valuable discovery. [< OE *findan.* See **pent-.**]

find•er (fīn'dər) *n.* **1.** One that finds. **2.** A device on a camera that indicates what will appear in the field of view of the lens.

find•ing (fīn'dĭng) *n.* **1.** The discovery of something. **2.** Often **findings.** A conclusion reached after investigation.

fine[1] (fīn) *adj.* **finer, finest. 1.** Of superior quality, skill, or appearance. **2.** Most enjoyable; pleasant. **3.** Sharp: *a blade with a fine edge.* **4.** Consisting of extremely small particles: *fine dust.* **5.** Subtle or precise: *a fine shade of meaning.* **6.** Of refined manners; elegant. **7.** Having no clouds; clear: *a fine day.* **8.** *Informal.* Quite well; in satisfactory health. —*adv. Informal.* Very well: *doing fine.* [< L *finis,* the end.] —**fine'ly** *adv.* —**fine'ness** *n.*

fine[2] (fīn) *n.* A sum of money imposed as a penalty for an offense. —*v.* **fined, fining.** To impose a fine on. [< L *finis,* limit, end.]

fine art. Often **fine arts.** Art produced primarily for beauty rather than utility.

fin•er•y (fī'nə-rē) *n.* Elaborate adornment; fine clothing and accessories.

fi•nesse (fĭ-nĕs') *n.* **1.** Artful delicacy of performance or behavior. **2.** Subtlety; tact. [< OF *fin,* fine.]

fin•ger (fĭng'gər) *n.* **1.** One of the five digits of the hand. **2.** Something resembling a finger. —*v.* To touch with the fingers; handle. [< OE. See **penkwe.**]

fin•ger•board (fĭng'gər-bôrd', -bōrd') *n.* The part of a stringed instrument against which the strings are pressed in playing.

finger bowl. A small basin to hold water for rinsing the fingers at table.

fin•ger•ing (fĭng'gər-ĭng) *n.* The indication on a musical score of which fingers are to be used in playing.

fin•ger•ling (fĭng'gər-lĭng) *n.* A young or small fish.

fin•ger•nail (fĭng'gər-nāl') *n.* A thin, horny, transparent plate on the tip of each finger.

fin•ger•print (fĭng'gər-prĭnt') *n.* An ink impression of the pattern of ridges on the surface of a finger. —*v.* To take the fingerprints of.

fin•ick•y (fĭn'ĭ-kē) *adj.* Highly fastidious; difficult to please; very fussy.

fi•nis (fĭn'ĭs, fī'nĭs) *n.* The end. [< L *finis.*]

fin•ish (fĭn'ĭsh) *v.* **1.** To attain the end of; terminate; complete. **2.** To reach the end of a task or undertaking. **3.** To consume all of; use up: *finish a pie.* **4.** To give (as wood or cloth) a desired surface texture. —*n.* **1.** The conclusion of something; end. **2.** Surface texture. **3.** The material used in surfacing or finishing something. **4.** Smoothness of execution; perfection. **5.** Polish or refinement in speech, manners, etc. [< L *finis,* end.] —**fin'ish•er** *n.*

fi•nite (fī'nīt') *adj.* **1.** Having boundaries; limited. **2.** Neither infinite nor infinitesimal. [< L *finīre,* to limit, finish.] —**fi'nite'ly** *adv.* —**fi'nite'ness** *n.*

Fin•land (fĭn′lənd). A republic of north-central Europe. Pop. 4,598,000. Cap. Helsinki.

Finland

Finn (fĭn) *n.* A native or inhabitant of Finland.
Finn•ish (fĭn′ĭsh) *adj.* Of or pertaining to Finland, its language, or its people. —*n.* The Uralic language spoken by the Finns.
Fin•no-U•gric (fĭn′ō-/y/o͞o′grĭk) *n.* Also **Fin•no-U•gri•an** (-/y/o͞o′grē-ən). A subfamily of Uralic, including Hungarian and Finnish. —**Fin′no-U′gric** *adj.*
fin•ny (fĭn′ē) *adj.* **1.** Having fins, as a fish. **2.** Finlike.
fiord. Variant of **fjord.**
fir (fûr) *n.* **1.** An evergreen tree with somewhat flattened needles. **2.** The wood of such a tree. [< OE *fyrh, furh.* See **perkwu-.**]
fire (fīr) *n.* **1.** A rapid, persistent chemical reaction that releases heat and light, esp. the exothermic combination of a combustible substance with oxygen. **2.** A destructive burning: *a forest fire.* **3.** Ardor; enthusiasm. **4.** The discharge of firearms; firing. —**catch fire.** To become ignited. —**hang fire. 1.** To fail to fire, as a gun. **2.** To be delayed, as an event or decision. —**on fire.** Burning; ablaze. —**open fire.** To commence shooting. —**under fire.** Under attack. —*v.* **fired, firing. 1.** To ignite. **2.** To maintain a fire in. **3.** To bake in a kiln. **4.** To arouse; stimulate. **5.** To detonate or shoot (a weapon). **6.** *Informal.* To hurl suddenly and forcefully: *fire a ball.* **7.** *Informal.* To discharge from a position; dismiss. [< OE *fȳr.* See **pūr-.**]
fire•arm (fīr′ärm′) *n.* Any weapon capable of firing a missile, esp. a pistol or rifle.
fire•ball (fīr′bôl′) *n.* **1.** A ball of fire. **2.** A highly luminous, intensely hot cloud generated by a nuclear explosion.
fire•brand (fīr′brănd′) *n.* **1.** A piece of burning wood. **2.** A person who stirs up trouble.
fire•bug (fīr′bŭg′) *n. Informal.* One who deliberately sets fires; pyromaniac.
fire•crack•er (fīr′krăk′ər) *n.* A small explosive charge in a cylinder of heavy paper, used to make noise, as at celebrations.
fire•damp (fīr′dămp′) *n.* **1.** A combustible gas, chiefly methane, occurring naturally in coal mines and forming explosive mixtures with air. **2.** The explosive mixture itself.
fire drill. A practice exercise in the exit procedure to be followed in case of fire.
fire engine. A motor truck that carries firemen and equipment to fight a fire.
fire escape. An outside stairway attached to a building, used for emergency exit in the event of fire.
fire extinguisher. A portable apparatus containing chemicals used to extinguish a small fire.
fire•fly (fīr′flī′) *n.* A night-flying beetle with luminous abdominal organs that produce a flashing light.
fire irons. The equipment used to tend a fireplace, including tongs, a shovel, etc.
fire•man (fīr′mən) *n.* **1.** A man employed to fight fires. **2.** A man who tends fires; stoker.
fire•place (fīr′plās′) *n.* **1.** An open recess for holding a fire at the base of a chimney; hearth. **2.** A structure, usually of stone or brick, for holding an outdoor fire.
fire•plug (fīr′plŭg′) *n.* A pipe from which water can be drawn for extinguishing a fire; a hydrant.
fire•pow•er (fīr′pou′ər) *n.* The capacity, as of a military unit, for discharging fire.
fire•proof (fīr′pro͞of′) *adj.* Capable of withstanding damage by fire. —*v.* To make fireproof.
fire•side (fīr′sīd′) *n.* **1.** The area around a fireplace. **2.** Home.
fire•trap (fīr′trăp′) *n.* A building susceptible to catching fire or difficult to escape from in the event of fire.
fire•wood (fīr′wo͝od′) *n.* Wood used as fuel.
fire•work (fīr′wûrk′) *n.* Often **fireworks.** An explosive used to generate colored lights, smoke, and noise for amusement.
firing line. The line of positions from which fire is directed against a target.
firing pin. The part of the bolt of a firearm that strikes the primer and explodes the charge of the projectile.
firing squad. A detachment assigned to execute condemned persons.
firm¹ (fûrm) *adj.* **1.** Unyielding to pressure; solid. **2.** Securely fixed in place. **3.** Indicating determination or resolution. **4.** Constant; steadfast: *a firm ally.* **5.** Definite; final: *a firm bargain.* **6.** Unfluctuating; steady, as prices. —*v.* To make or become firm. —*adv.* Resolutely; unwaveringly: *stand firm.* [< L *firmus.*] —**firm′ly** *adv.* —**firm′ness** *n.*
firm² (fûrm) *n.* A commercial partnership of two or more persons. [< It, *firmare,* "to confirm by signature."]
fir•ma•ment (fûr′mə-mənt) *n.* The vault or expanse of the heavens; sky. [< L *firmāmentum,* a strengthening, support.]
first (fûrst) *adj.* **1.** Coming or located before all others. **2.** Prior to all others; earliest. **3.** Foremost in importance or quality. —**in the first place.** To begin with. —*adv.* **1.** Before or above all others in time or rank. **2.** For the first time. **3.** Preferably; rather. —*n.* **1.** The ordinal number one in a series. **2.** The one coming, occurring, or ranking first. **3.** The beginning; outset: *from the first.* **4.** The lowest forward gear in an automotive vehicle. **5.** The winning position in a contest. [< OE *fyrst.* See **per¹.**]
first aid. Emergency treatment administered before professional medical care is available.
first-born (fûrst′bôrn′) *adj.* First in order of birth. —*n.* The first-born child.
first class. 1. The most expensive class of accommodations on a train, passenger ship, or airplane. **2.** A class of mail sealed against inspection.
first-class (fûrst′klăs′) *adj.* **1.** The most expensive; preferential, as accommodations. **2.** Of the highest quality; first-rate. —**first′-class′** *adv.*
first•hand (fûrst′hănd′) *adj.* Received from the original source: *firsthand information.* —**first′-hand′** *adv.*
first•ly (fûrst′lē) *adv.* In the first place; to begin with.
first mate. A ship's officer ranking immediately below the captain.
first person. A set of grammatical forms designating the speaker or writer of the sentence in which they appear.
first-rate (fûrst′rāt′) *adj.* Foremost in quality or rank. —*adv. Informal.* Excellently.
first sergeant. In the U.S. Army, the highest ranking noncommissioned officer of a company or other military unit.
firth (fûrth) *n. Chiefly Scot.* A narrow inlet of the sea. [< ON *fjördhr.*]
fis•cal (fĭs′kəl) *adj.* **1.** Of or pertaining to the public treasury or finances. **2.** Of or pertaining to finances in general. [< L *fiscus,* treasury, basket.] —**fis′cal•ly** *adv.*
fish (fĭsh) *n., pl.* **fish** or **fishes. 1.** Any of numerous cold-blooded aquatic vertebrates characteristically having fins, gills, and a streamlined body. **2.** The edible flesh of a fish. **3.** Often **the Fish** or **the Fishes.** Pisces. —*v.* **1.** To catch or try to catch fish. **2.** To draw or pull up, as by fishing (with *out*). **3.** To seek something indirectly: *fish for compliments.* [< OE *fisc.* See **peisk-.**]

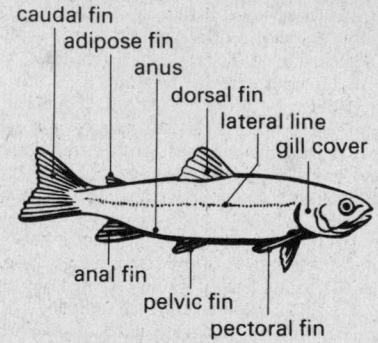

caudal fin
adipose fin
anus
dorsal fin
lateral line
gill cover
anal fin
pelvic fin
pectoral fin

fish

fish•bowl (fĭsh′bōl′) *n.* **1.** A bowl in which live fish are kept. **2.** Something that can be seen through on all sides or at all points.
fish•er•man (fĭsh′ər-mən) *n.* One who fishes as an occupation or sport.
fish•er•y (fĭsh′ə-rē) *n., pl.* **-ies. 1.** The industry of catching fish. **2.** A fishing ground. **3.** A hatchery for fish.
fish•hook (fĭsh′ho͝ok′) *n.* A barbed hook for catching fish.
fish•ing (fĭsh′ĭng) *n.* The business or sport of catching fish.
fishing rod. A rod used with a line for catching fish.
fish story. *Informal.* An implausible and boastful story.
fish•wife (fĭsh′wīf′) *n.* **1.** A woman who sells fish. **2.** A coarse, abusive woman.
fish•y (fĭsh′ē) *adj.* **-ier, -iest. 1.** Resembling or suggestive of fish. **2.** Cold or expressionless: *a fishy stare.* **3.** *Informal.* Questionable; inspiring suspicion. —**fish′i•ness** *n.*
fis•sile (fĭs′əl, fĭs′īl′) *adj.* **1.** Capable of being split. **2.** *Phys.* Fissionable, esp. by neutrons of all energies. —**fis•sil′i•ty** (fĭ-sĭl′ə-tē) *n.*

fis•sion (fĭsh'ən) *n.* **1.** The act or process of splitting into parts. **2.** A nuclear reaction in which an atomic nucleus splits into fragments, usually two fragments of comparable mass, with the evolution of approx. 100 million to several hundred million electron volts of energy. **3.** An asexual reproductive process in which a unicellular organism splits into two or more independently maturing daughter cells. [< L *fissus,* pp of *findere,* to split.] **—fis'sion•a•ble** *adj.*

fis•sure (fĭsh'ər) *n.* A narrow groove, crack, or cleft. [< L *fissus,* split.]

fist (fĭst) *n.* The hand closed tightly, with the fingers bent against the palm. [< OE *fȳst.* See **penkwe.**]

fist•i•cuffs (fĭs'tĭ-kŭfs') *pl.n.* **1.** A fist fight. **2.** Boxing. [< FIST + CUFF².]

fis•tu•la (fĭs'cho͞o-lə) *n., pl.* **-las** or **-lae** (-lē'). An abnormal bodily duct or passage from an abscess, cavity, or hollow organ. [< L.] **—fis'tu•lous** *adj.*

fit¹ (fĭt) *v.* **fitted** or **fit, fitted, fitting. 1.** To be the proper size and shape (for). **2.** To be suitable (to). **3.** To adjust; adapt. **4.** To equip; outfit (with *up* or *out*). **5.** To provide a place or time for (with *in* or *into*). *—adj.* **fitter, fittest. 1.** Suited or adequate to a given circumstance. **2.** Appropriate; proper. **3.** Physically sound; healthy. *—n.* **1.** Adjustment or alteration to a given pattern or standard. **2.** The manner in which clothing fits. [< ME *fitten,* to arrange.] **—fit'ly** *adv.* **—fit'ness** *n.*

fit² (fĭt) *n.* **1.** A sudden violent attack, as of coughing. **2.** A sudden, violent outburst of emotion. **3.** A sudden period of vigorous activity. [< OE *fitt,* conflict.]

fitch (fĭch) *n.* The fur of the Old World polecat. [Prob < MDu *vitsau.*]

fit•ful (fĭt'fəl) *adj.* Occurring in or characterized by fits; intermittent; irregular. **—fit'ful•ly** *adv.* **—fit'ful•ness** *n.*

fit•ting (fĭt'ĭng) *adj.* Suitable; appropriate. *—n.* **1.** A trying on for fit, as of clothes. **2.** Often **fittings.** Furnishings or accessories. **—fit'ting•ly** *adv.* **—fit'ting•ness** *n.*

five (fīv) *n.* The cardinal number written 5 or in Roman numerals V. [< OE *fīf.* See **penkwe.**] **—five** *adj.* & *pron.*

fix (fĭks) *v.* **1.** To place or fasten securely. **2.** To put into a stable or unalterable form, as: **a.** To make a substance nonvolatile or solid. **b.** To convert (nitrogen) into stable, biologically assimilable compounds. **c.** To prevent discoloration of (a photographic image) by washing or coating with a chemical preservative. **3.** To direct (as the gaze) steadily. **4.** To establish definitely; specify: *fix a time.* **5.** To ascribe; place: *fix blame.* **6.** To rectify; adjust. **7.** To set right; repair. **8.** To make ready; put together; prepare. **9.** *Informal.* To take revenge upon; get even with. **10.** To prearrange the outcome of (a contest) by unlawful means. **—fix up.** *Informal.* **1.** To set in order. **2.** To provide with; furnish. *—n.* **1.** A predicament; dilemma. **2.** A position, as of a ship or aircraft, as determined by observations or radio. **3.** An instance of collusion to predetermine a result. **4.** *Slang.* An intravenous injection of heroin. [< L *fixus,* pp of *figere,* to fasten.] **—fix'a•ble** *adj.* **—fix'er** *n.*

fix•a•tion (fĭk-sā'shən) *n.* A strong attachment to a person or thing, esp. such an attachment formed in childhood or infancy and persisting in immature or neurotic behavior.

fix•a•tive (fĭk'sə-tĭv) *adj.* Tending to render permanent, firm, or stable. *—n.* Something that fixes or preserves, esp. a liquid preservative applied to art work, such as charcoal drawings.

fixed (fĭkst) *adj.* **1.** Firmly in position; stationary. **2. a.** Nonvolatile: *fixed oils.* **b.** In a stable combined form. **3.** Not subject to variation; constant. **4.** Stubbornly held to: *a fixed notion.* **—fix'ed•ly** (fĭk'sĭd-lē) *adv.*

fix•ings (fĭk'sĭngz) *pl.n. Informal.* Accessories; trimmings.

fix•ture (fĭks'chər) *n.* **1.** Something attached as a permanent appendage, apparatus, or appliance. **2.** One long established in a place, position, or function.

fizz (fĭz) *v.* To make a hissing or bubbling sound. *—n.* **1.** A hissing or bubbling sound. **2.** An effervescent beverage. [Imit.]

fiz•zle (fĭz'əl) *v.* **-zled, -zling. 1.** To fizz. **2.** To fail or die out, esp. after a hopeful beginning. *—n.* A failure; fiasco. [Prob freq of obs *fist,* to break wind.]

fjord, fiord (fyôrd, fyōrd) *n.* A long, narrow inlet from the sea between steep cliffs or slopes. [< ON *fjördhr.*]

fl fluid.

fl. 1. floor. **2.** fluid.

Fla. Florida.

flab•ber•gast (flăb'ər-găst') *v.* To overwhelm with astonishment; astound. [?]

flab•by (flăb'ē) *adj.* **-bier, -biest. 1.** Lacking firmness; flaccid: *flabby skin.* **2.** Lacking force; feeble. [< FLAP.] **—flab'bi•ly** *adv.* **—flab'bi•ness** *n.*

flac•cid (flăk'sĭd) *adj.* Lacking firmness; flabby. [< L *flaccus,* hanging, flabby.]

fla•con (flăk'ən, -ŏn') *n.* A small stoppered bottle. [< LL *flascō,* FLASK.]

flag¹ (flăg) *n.* **1.** An often rectangular piece of fabric used as a symbol, signal, etc. **2.** Something resembling a flag in appearance or function. *—v.* **flagged, flagging. 1.** To mark with a flag. **2.** To signal with or as with a flag. [?]

flag² (flăg) *n.* A wild iris or similar plant. [ME *flagge,* rush, reed.]

flag³ (flăg) *v.* **flagged, flagging. 1.** To hang limply; droop. **2.** To become languid; tire. **3.** To decline in interest; grow dull. [?]

flag⁴ (flăg) *n.* Flagstone. [Prob < ON *flaga,* slab of stone.]

flag•el•late (flăj'ə-lāt') *v.* **-lated, -lating.** To whip or flog; scourge. [L *flagellāre.*] **—flag'el•la'tion** *n.* **—flag'el•la'tor** *n.*

flag•on (flăg'ən) *n.* A vessel for liquids, usually having a handle and spout. [< LL *flascō,* bottle, FLASK.]

flag•pole (flăg'pōl') *n.* A pole on which a flag is hoisted; flagstaff.

fla•grant (flā'grənt) *adj.* Extremely or deliberately conspicuous; shocking. [< L *flagrāre,* to burn, blaze.] **—fla'gran•cy, fla'grance** *n.* **—fla'grant•ly** *adv.*

flag•ship (flăg'shĭp') *n.* A ship bearing the flag of a fleet or squadron commander.

flag•staff (flăg'stăf', -stäf') *n.* A flagpole.

flag•stone (flăg'stōn') *n.* A flat, evenly layered paving stone.

flail (flāl) *n.* A manual threshing device. *—v.* To beat, thrash, or strike with or as with a flail. [< L *flagrum,* whip.]

flair (flâr) *n.* **1.** A natural talent or aptitude; bent; knack. **2.** Instinctive discernment; keenness. [< L *frāgrāre,* to emit a smell.]

flak (flăk) *n.* **1.** Antiaircraft artillery. **2.** The bursting shells fired from such artillery. [G.]

flake (flāk) *n.* **1.** A flat, thin piece or layer; chip. **2.** A small loose fragment; bit. *—v.* **flaked, flaking.** To form into or come off in flakes. [< Scand.] **—flak'y** *adj.*

flam•boy•ant (flăm-boi'ənt) *adj.* **1.** Highly elaborate; showy. **2.** Richly colored; vivid; resplendent. [< OF *flamboyer,* to blaze.] **—flam•boy'ance** *n.* **—flam•boy'ant•ly** *adv.*

flame (flām) *n.* **1.** The zone of burning gases

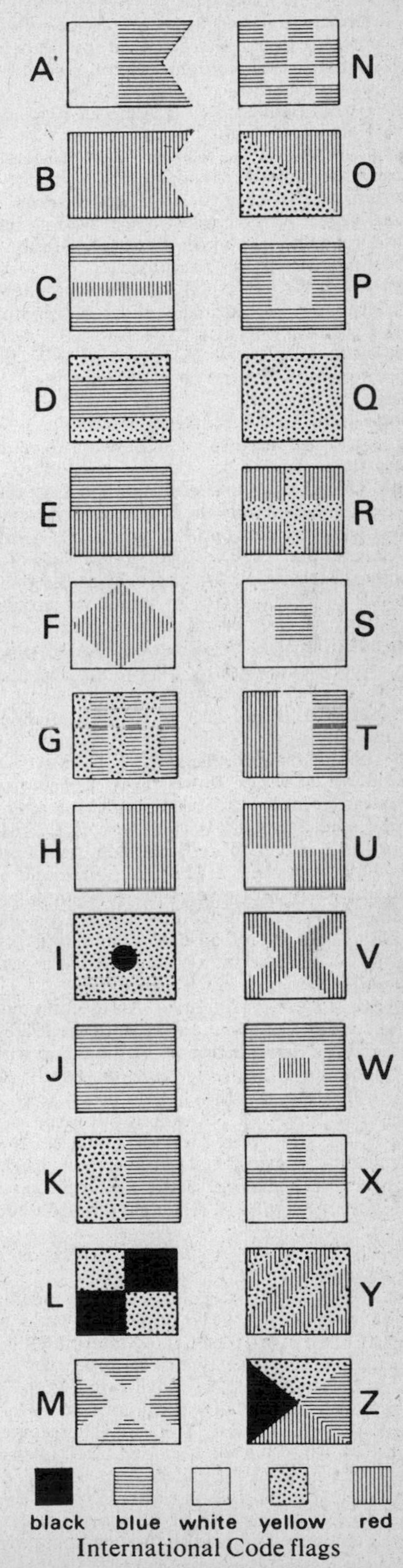

International Code flags

and fine suspended matter associated with the combustion of a substance. **2.** The condition of active, blazing combustion. **3.** Something flamelike in appearance. **4.** A violent or intense passion; a burning emotion. **5.** *Informal.* A sweetheart. —*v.* **flamed, flaming. 1.** To burn brightly; blaze. **2.** To burst into or as into flame. [< L *flamma.*]

fla•men•co (flə-mĕng'kō) *n.* A dance style of Spanish Gypsies, characterized by forceful, often improvised rhythms. [Span, resembling a Gypsy, Flemish.]

flame•out (flām'out') *n.* Failure of a jet aircraft engine in flight.

flame thrower. A weapon that projects a stream of ignited incendiary fuel.

fla•min•go (flə-mĭng'gō) *n., pl.* **-gos** or **-goes.** A long-legged, long-necked tropical wading bird with reddish or pinkish plumage. [Prob < Prov *flamenc,* prob "fire bird."]

flam•ma•ble (flăm'ə-bəl) *adj.* Easily ignitable and capable of burning with great rapidity. [< L *flamma,* FLAME.]

Flan•ders (flăn'dərz). A region of NW Europe, including part of N France and W Belgium.

flange (flănj) *n.* A protruding rim, edge, etc., as on a wheel, used to strengthen an object or hold it in place. [?]

flank (flăngk) *n.* **1.** The section of flesh between the last rib and the hip; side. **2.** A cut of meat from this section of an animal. **3.** A side or lateral part. **4.** The right or left side of a military formation. —*v.* **1.** To be at the flank or side of. **2.** To attack or maneuver around the flank of. [< Frank **hlanca,* side.]

flan•nel (flăn'əl) *n.* A soft woven cloth of wool or a wool blend. [Prob < W *gwlanen,* "woolen cloth."] —**flan'nel•ly** *adj.*

flan•nel•ette (flăn'ə-lĕt') *n.* A soft, napped cotton cloth.

flap (flăp) *v.* **flapped, flapping. 1.** To wave up and down, as wings; flutter; beat. **2.** To swing or sway loosely. **3.** To hit with something broad and flat; slap. —*n.* **1.** A flat, loose appendage attached on one side, as of an envelope or pocket. **2.** The action or sound of flapping. **3.** A blow given with something flat; a slap. **4.** A variable control surface on the trailing edge of an aircraft wing, used primarily to increase lift or drag. [ME *flappen.*]

flap•jack (flăp'jăk') *n.* A pancake.

flap•per (flăp'ər) *n. Informal.* An ostentatiously unconventional young woman of the 1920's.

flare (flâr) *v.* **flared, flaring. 1.** To flame up with a bright, wavering light; blaze unsteadily. **2.** To erupt into emphatic emotion or activity (with *out* or *up*). **3.** To expand outward, as a bell. —*n.* **1.** A brief, wavering blaze. **2.** A pyrotechnic device that produces a bright light, as for signaling. **3.** An outbreak, as of emotion or activity. **4.** An expanding contour. [?]

flare-up (flâr'ŭp') *n.* A sudden outbreak, as of flame, emotion, etc.

flash (flăsh) *v.* **1.** To occur or emerge suddenly in or as in flame. **2.** To appear or cause to appear briefly. **3.** To be lighted intermittently; sparkle. **4.** To cause (light) to appear in intermittent bursts. **5.** To move rapidly. **6.** To signal with light. **7.** To communicate (information) at great speed. **8.** To display ostentatiously; flaunt. —*n.* **1.** A sudden brief, intense display of light. **2.** A sudden, brief display, as of a mental faculty. **3.** An instant: *in a flash.* **4.** A brief news dispatch or transmission. **5. a.** Instantaneous illumination for photography. **b.** Any equipment or device used to produce such illumination. [ME *flashen,* to splash, burst into flame.]

flash•back (flăsh'băk') *n.* A reversion to an event occurring earlier in a narrative.

flash bulb. A glass bulb filled with finely shredded aluminum or magnesium foil that is ignited by electricity to produce a short-duration high-intensity light flash for taking photographs.

flash flood. A sudden flood.

flash gun. A dry-cell-powered photographic apparatus that holds and electrically triggers a flash bulb.

flash•ing (flăsh'ĭng) *n.* Sheet metal used to weatherproof the joints and angles of a roof.

flash lamp. An electric lamp for producing a high-intensity light of very short duration for use in photography.

flash•light (flăsh'līt') *n.* **1.** A small, portable lamp having a bulb and dry batteries. **2.** A brief, brilliant flood of light, as from a photographic lamp.

flash point. The lowest temperature at which the vapor of a combustible liquid can be made to ignite momentarily in air.

flash tube. A gas discharge tube used in an electronic flash to produce a brief, intense pulse of light.

flash unit. 1. An electronic flash system containing both power supply and flash tube in a single compact unit. **2. a.** A flash gun. **b.** A flash gun and reflector.

flash•y (flăsh'ē) *adj.* **-ier, -iest. 1.** Momentarily brilliant. **2.** Showy; gaudy.

flask (flăsk, fläsk) *n.* A small bottle-shaped container. [< LL *flascō.*]

flat¹ (flăt) *adj.* **flatter, flattest. 1. a.** Having no curves. **b.** Having a smooth, even, level surface. **2.** Shallow; low: *a flat box.* **3.** Lying prone; prostrate. **4.** Unequivocal; absolute: *a flat refusal.* **5.** Fixed: *a flat rate.* **6.** Uninteresting; dull; vapid. **7.** Lacking zest; flavorless. **8.** Deflated, as a tire. **9.** *Mus.* **a.** Being one half step lower than the corresponding natural key. **b.** Being below the intended pitch. —*adv.* **1. a.** Horizontally; level with the ground. **b.** Prostrate. **2.** So as to be flat. **3.** Directly; completely. **4.** *Mus.* Below the intended pitch. —*n.* **1.** A flat object, surface, or part. **2.** Often **flats.** A stretch of level ground. **3.** A shallow frame or box for seeds or seedlings. **4.** A deflated tire. **5. flats.** Women's shoes with flat heels. **6.** *Mus.* **a.** A sign (♭) affixed to a note to indicate that it is to be lowered by a half step. **b.** A note that is lowered a half step. —*v.* **flatted, flatting. 1.** To make flat; flatten. **2.** *Mus.* **a.** To lower (a note) a half step. **b.** To sing or play below the proper pitch. [< ON *flatr.*] —**flat'ly** *adv.* —**flat'ness** *n.*

flat² (flăt) *n.* An apartment on one floor of a building. [< OE *flett,* floor, ground, hall. See **plat-.**]

flat•boat (flăt'bōt') *n.* A flat-bottomed boat used for transporting freight.

flat•car (flăt'kär') *n.* A railroad car without sides or roof.

flat•fish (flăt'fĭsh') *n.* A fish, as a flounder or sole, having a flattened body with the eyes on the upper side.

flat•foot (flăt'fo͝ot') *n.* **1.** *pl.* **-feet.** A condition in which the arch of the foot is broken down so that the entire sole makes contact with the ground. **2.** *pl.* **-foots.** *Slang.* A policeman. —**flat'-foot'ed** *adj.*

flat•i•ron (flăt'ī'ərn) *n.* An externally heated iron for pressing clothes.

flat•ten (flăt'n) *v.* To make or become flat or flatter. —**flat'ten•er** *n.*

flat•ter (flăt'ər) *v.* **1.** To compliment excessively and often insincerely. **2.** To please or gratify the vanity of. **3.** To portray favorably. [< Frank **flat,* flat part of a person's hand.] —**flat'ter•er** *n.* —**flat'ter•ing** *adj.*

flat•ter•y (flăt'ə-rē) *n., pl.* **-ies. 1.** The act or practice of flattering. **2.** Insincere praise.

flat•u•lent (flăch'o͞o-lənt) *adj.* **1.** Having or causing excessive gas in the digestive tract. **2.** Inflated with self-importance; pompous. [< L *flātus,* a breaking wind.] —**flat'u•lence** *n.* —**flat'u•lent•ly** *adv.*

flat•ware (flăt'wâr') *n.* Tableware that is fairly flat and fashioned usually of a single piece.

Flau•bert (flō-bâr'), **Gustave.** 1821–1880. French novelist.

flaunt (flônt) *v.* To exhibit ostentatiously; show off. [?] —**flaunt'er** *n.*

fla•vor (flā'vər) *n.* Also *chiefly Brit.* **fla•vour.** *n.* **1.** Distinctive taste; savor. **2.** A characteristic quality. **3.** A seasoning. —*v.* To give flavor to. [< L *flātus,* a blowing, breeze.]

fla•vor•ing (flā'vər-ĭng) *n.* A substance that imparts flavor, as an extract.

flaw (flô) *n.* **1.** An imperfection; defect. **2.** A small fissure; crack. [< ON *flaga,* slab or layer of stone.] —**flaw'less** *adj.*

flax (flăks) *n.* **1.** A widely cultivated plant with blue flowers, seeds that yield linseed oil, and slender stems that yield a fine, light-colored textile fiber. **2.** The fiber obtained from this plant. [< OE *fleax, flæx.* See **plek-.**]

flax•en (flăk'sən) *adj.* **1.** Made of flax. **2.** Having the pale-yellow color of flax fiber.

flay (flā) *v.* **1.** To strip off the skin of. **2.** To assail with stinging criticism. [< OE *flēan.* See **plēk-.**] —**flay'er** *n.*

flea (flē) *n.* Any of various small, wingless, leaping, bloodsucking insects that are parasitic on warm-blooded animals. [< OE *flēah.* See **plou-.**]

fleck (flĕk) *n.* **1.** A tiny mark or spot. **2.** A small bit or flake. **3.** A small patch of color or light. —*v.* To spot or streak. [Prob < ON *flekkr,* spot, stain.] —**fleck'y** *adj.*

fledg•ling (flĕj'lĭng) *n.* Also **fledge•ling. 1.** A young bird with newly developed flight feathers. **2.** One that is young and inexperienced.

flee (flē) *v.* **fled, fleeing. 1.** To run away, as from trouble or danger. **2.** To pass swiftly away; vanish. [< OE *flēon.*] —**fle'er** *n.*

fleece (flēs) *n.* **1.** The coat of wool of a sheep or similar animal. **2.** Any soft, woolly covering or mass. —*v.* **fleeced, fleecing. 1.** To shear the fleece from. **2.** To swindle. [< OE *flēos.* See **pleus-.**] —**fleec'i•ness** *n.* —**fleec'y** *adj.*

fleet¹ (flēt) *n.* **1.** A number of warships operating together under one command. **2.** Any group of vehicles owned or operated as a unit. [< OE *flēotan,* to float. See **pleu-.**]

fleet² (flēt) *adj.* Moving swiftly; rapid or nimble. [Prob < OE *flēotan,* to float.] —**fleet'ing** *adj.* —**fleet'ly** *adv.* —**fleet'ness** *n.*

Flem. Flemish.

Flem•ish (flĕm'ĭsh) *n.* **1.** The people of Flanders. **2.** Their Germanic language, related to Dutch. —**Flem'ish** *adj.*

flesh (flĕsh) *n.* **1.** The soft tissue of the body, esp. skeletal muscle distinguished from bone and viscera. **2.** Meat. **3.** The pulpy part of a fruit or vegetable. **4.** Excess tissue; fat. **5.** The physical being as distinguished from the mind or soul. **6.** One's family; kin. [< OE *flǣsc.* See **plēk-.**]

flesh•ly (flĕsh'lē) *adj.* **-lier, -liest. 1.** Of or pertaining to the body; corporeal. **2.** Carnal; sensual. **3.** Not spiritual; worldly.

flesh•y (flĕsh'ē) *adj.* **-ier, -iest. 1.** Consisting of or like flesh. **2.** Corpulent; plump. **3.** Firm and pulpy, as fruit. **—flesh'i•ness** *n.*

fleur-de-lis, fleur-de-lys (flûr'də-lē', flo͝or'-) *n., pl.* **fleurs-de-lis, fleurs-de-lys** (flûr'də-lēz', flo͝or'-). A stylized three-petaled representation of an iris flower. [< OF *flor de lis,* lily flower.]

flew (flo͞o). *p.t.* of **fly**[1].

flex (flĕks) *v.* **1.** To bend (something pliant). **2.** To contract (a muscle). [L *flectere* (pp *flexus*), to bend.]

flex•i•ble (flĕk'sə-bəl) *adj.* **1.** Capable of being flexed. **2.** Capable of or responsive to change; adaptable. **—flex'i•bil'i•ty** *n.* **—flex'i•bly** *adv.*

flex•time (flĕks'tīm') *n.* Also **flex•i•time** (flĕk'sə-tīm'). An arrangement by which employees set their own work schedule whenever possible.

flib•ber•ti•gib•bet (flĭb'ər-tē-jĭb'ĭt) *n.* A scatterbrained person. [?]

flick (flĭk) *n.* **1.** A light, quick motion or touch. **2.** A light splash or daub. *—v.* **1.** To touch or move with a light, quick motion. **2.** To flutter or dart. [Perh imit.]

flick•er (flĭk'ər) *v.* **1.** To move waveringly; flutter. **2.** To yield irregular, intermittent light. *—n.* **1.** A tremor or flutter. **2.** A brief or wavering light. **3.** A brief sensation. [< OE *flicorian,* to flutter, hover.]

flied. *Baseball. p.t. & p.p.* of **fly**[1].

fli•er (flī'ər) *n.* Also **fly•er. 1.** One that flies. **2.** A daring financial venture. **3.** A circular for mass distribution.

flight[1] (flīt) *n.* **1.** Motion through the earth's atmosphere or through space. **2.** Locomotion through the air by means of wings. **3.** A group flying together, as of birds or aircraft. **4.** A scheduled airline run. **5.** A soaring, as of the imagination. **6. a.** A series of stairs. **b.** Stairs between landings. [< OE *flyht.* See **pleu-.**]

flight[2] (flīt) *n.* A running away. [< OE **flyht.* See **pleu-.**]

flight•y (flī'tē) *adj.* **-ier, -iest.** Capriciously unstable; skittish. **—flight'i•ness** *n.*

flim•flam (flĭm'flăm') *n. Informal.* Humbug; deception. [< Scand.] **—flim'flam'** *v.* **(-flammed, -flamming).**

flim•sy (flĭm'zē) *adj.* **-sier, -siest. 1.** Not strong or substantial. **2.** Implausible; unconvincing. [?] **—flim'si•ly** *adv.* **—flim'si•ness** *n.*

flinch (flĭnch) *v.* To shrink or wince, as from pain or fear. [OF *flenchir* < Gmc.]

fling (flĭng) *v.* **flung, flinging. 1.** To throw or move suddenly and forcefully. **2.** To put or abandon energetically. *—n.* **1.** A toss; a throw. **2.** A short period of indulging one's impulses; a spree. **3.** *Informal.* A brief attempt. [< Scand.] **—fling'er** *n.*

flint (flĭnt) *n.* **1.** A very hard quartz that sparks when struck with steel. **2.** A small solid cylinder of a spark-producing alloy. [< OE. See **splei-.**]

Flint (flĭnt). A city of SE Michigan. Pop. 197,000.

flint•lock (flĭnt'lŏk') *n.* **1.** An obsolete gunlock in which a flint sparks the charge. **2.** A gun with such a gunlock.

flip (flĭp) *v.* **flipped, flipping. 1.** To toss or turn with a light quick motion. **2.** *Slang.* To be delighted or crazed. *—n.* A quick turn or motion. *—adj.* Flippant; pert. [?]

flip•pant (flĭp'ənt) *adj.* Marked by disrespectful levity; pert; saucy. **—flip'pan•cy** *n.* **—flip'pant•ly** *adv.*

flip•per (flĭp'ər) *n.* **1.** A wide, flat limb, as of a seal, adapted for swimming. **2.** A flattened rubber foot covering used in swimming.

flirt (flûrt) *v.* **1.** To amuse oneself in light, playful courtship. **2.** To deal triflingly; toy: *flirt with danger.* **3.** To move jerkily; dart. *—n.* **1.** One given to flirting. **2.** An abrupt jerking movement. [?] **—flir•ta'tion** (-tā'shən) *n.* **—flir•ta'tious** *adj.* **—flir•ta'tious•ly** *adv.*

flit (flĭt) *v.* **flitted, flitting.** To move about rapidly and nimbly; dart. [< ON *flytja,* to convey.]

float (flōt) *v.* **1. a.** To remain or cause to remain suspended within or on the surface of a fluid without sinking. **b.** To be or cause to be suspended unsupported in space. **2.** To move from position to position at random; drift. **3.** To move easily and lightly as if suspended. **4.** To release (a security) for sale. *—n.* **1.** Something that floats. **2.** A small floating object on a fishing line. **3.** A large, flat vehicle bearing an exhibit in a parade. [< OE *flotian.* See **pleu-.**] **—float'er** *n.*

float•ing rib (flō'tĭng). One of the four lower ribs that, unlike the other ribs, are not attached at the front.

flock (flŏk) *n.* **1.** A group of animals, as birds or sheep, that live, travel, or feed together. **2.** A group of people under the leadership of one person. **3.** A large crowd or number. *—v.* To congregate or travel in a flock or crowd. [< OE *flocc* < Gmc **flugnaz.*]

floe (flō) *n.* **1.** A large, flat mass of ice formed on the surface of a body of water. **2.** A segment separated from such an ice mass. [Prob < ON *flō,* stratum, coating.]

flog (flŏg, flôg) *v.* **flogged, flogging.** To beat harshly with a whip or rod. [Perh short for L *flagellāre,* to whip.] **—flog'ger** *n.*

flood (flŭd) *n.* **1.** An overflowing of water onto land that is normally dry. **2.** Also **flood tide.** The rising tide. **3.** Any abundant flow or outpouring. **4. the Flood.** The universal deluge recorded in the Bible. Genesis 7. *—v.* **1.** To cover or submerge with a flood; inundate. **2.** To fill with an abundance or excess. [< OE *flōd.* See **pleu-.**]

flood•gate (flŭd'gāt') *n.* A gate used to control the flow of a body of water.

flood•light (flŭd'līt') *n.* **1.** Artificial light in an intensely bright and broad beam. **2.** A unit that produces such a beam. *—v.* To illuminate with a floodlight.

flood plain. A plain bordering a river, subject to flooding.

floor (flôr, flōr) *n.* **1.** The surface of a room on which one stands. **2.** The ground or lowermost surface, as of a forest or ocean. **3.** The lower part of a room, as a legislative chamber, where business is conducted. **4.** The right to address an assembly. **5.** A story of a building. *—v.* **1.** To provide with a floor. **2.** To knock down. **3.** To stun; overwhelm. [< OE *flōr.* See **pelə-.**] **—floor'er** *n.*

floor•ing (flôr'ĭng, flōr'-) *n.* **1. a.** Floors collectively. **b.** A floor. **2.** Material used in making floors.

floor show. The entertainment presented in a nightclub.

floor•walk•er (flôr'wô'kər, flōr'-) *n.* An employee of a department store who supervises sales personnel.

floo•zy (flo͞o'zē) *n., pl.* **-zies.** Also **floo•zie.** *Slang.* A cheap prostitute. [?]

flop (flŏp) *v.* **flopped, flopping. 1.** To fall down heavily and noisily; plop. **2.** To move about in a clumsy, noisy way. **3.** *Informal.* To fail utterly. *—n.* **1.** The action or sound of flopping. **2.** *Informal.* An utter failure. [Var of FLAP.]

flop•house (flŏp'hous') *n.* A cheap hotel.

flo•ra (flôr'ə, flōr'ə) *n., pl.* **-ras** or **-rae** (flôr'ē', flōr'ē'). Plants, esp. of a region or time. [< L *flōs (flōr-),* flower.]

flo•ral (flôr'əl, flōr'-) *adj.* Of or pertaining to flowers. **—flo'ral•ly** *adv.*

Flor•ence (flôr'əns, flōr'-). A city of N Italy. Pop. 456,000. **—Flor'en•tine'** (-ən-tēn', -tīn') *adj. & n.*

flo•ret (flôr'ĭt, flōr'-) *n.* A small flower, usually part of a dense cluster.

flor•id (flôr'ĭd, flōr'-) *adj.* **1.** Flushed with rosy color; ruddy. **2.** Heavily embellished; flowery. [< L *flōs (flōr-),* FLOWER.]

Flor•i•da (flôr'ə-də, flōr'-). A state of the SE U.S. Pop. 6,789,000. Cap. Tallahassee.

flor•in (flôr'ĭn, flōr'-) *n.* **1.** A guilder. **2.** A British coin worth two shillings. [< It *fiore,* flower.]

flo•rist (flôr'ĭst, flōr'-, flŏr'-) *n.* One whose business is the raising or selling of flowers.

floss (flôs, flŏs) *n.* **1.** Short fibers or waste silk from the cocoon of a silkworm. **2.** A soft, loosely twisted thread. **3.** Any soft, silky, fibrous substance. [Poss < OF *flosche,* down.]

floss•y (flô'sē, flŏs'ē) *adj.* **-ier, -iest. 1.** Made of or resembling floss; silky. **2.** *Slang.* Ostentatiously stylish; flashy.

flo•ta•tion (flō-tā'shən) *n.* Any of several processes in which different pulverized materials, notably minerals, are separated from a fluid mixture by agitation.

flo•til•la (flō-tĭl'ə) *n.* **1.** A fleet of small ships. **2.** A small fleet. [< ON *floti,* raft, fleet.]

flot•sam (flŏt'səm) *n.* Floating wreckage or cargo from a ship. [< VL **flottāre,* to float.]

flounce[1] (flouns) *n.* A strip of gathered or pleated material secured on its upper edge to another surface, such as a garment. [< OF *froncir,* to wrinkle.]

flounce[2] (flouns) *v.* **flounced, flouncing. 1.** To move with exaggerated motions expressive of displeasure or impatience. **2.** To flounder. *—n.* The act or motion of flouncing. [?]

floun•der[1] (floun'dər) *v.* **1.** To move clumsily or awkwardly. **2.** To proceed clumsily and in confusion. [Prob blend of FOUNDER and BLUNDER.] **—floun'der** *n.*

floun•der[2] (floun'dər) *n.* Any of various marine flatfishes used as food. [Prob < Scand.]

flour (flour) *n.* **1.** A fine, powdery substance obtained by grinding grain, esp. wheat. **2.** Any similar soft, fine powder. *—v.* To cover or coat with flour. [ME, finer meal, farina, flower.] **—flour'y** *adj.*

flour•ish (flûr'ĭsh) *v.* **1.** To grow well or abundantly; thrive. **2.** To fare well; succeed. **3.** To be in one's prime. **4.** To make bold, sweeping movements. *—n.* **1.** An embellishment or ornamentation. **2.** A dramatic action or gesture. [< L *flōrēre,* to bloom.]

flout (flout) *v.* To show contempt for; scoff at. *—n.* A contemptuous action or remark. [Prob < ME *flouten,* to play the flute.]

flow (flō) *v.* **1.** To move or run freely in or as in a stream. **2.** To circulate, as the blood in the body. **3.** To proceed steadily and continuously. **4.** To appear smooth, harmonious, or graceful. **5.** To rise, as the tide. **6.** To arise; derive. **7.** To abound or be plentiful. **8.** To hang loosely and gracefully. *—n.* **1. a.** The smooth motion characteristic of fluids. **b.** The act of flowing. **2.** A stream. **3. a.** A continuous outpouring: *a flow of ideas.* **b.** A continuous movement or circulation: *the flow of traffic.* **4.** The amount that flows in a given period of time. **5.** The rising of the tide. [< OE *flōwan.* See **pleu-**.]

flow•er (flou'ər) *n.* **1.** The reproductive structure of a seed-bearing plant, characteristically having specialized male and female organs and often colorful petals. **2.** A plant conspicuous for its blossoms. **3.** The period or an example of highest development; peak. **4.** Often **flowers.** *Chem.* A fine powder produced by condensation or sublimation. —*v.* **1.** To produce flowers; bloom. **2.** To develop fully; reach a peak. [< L *flōs (flōr-).*]

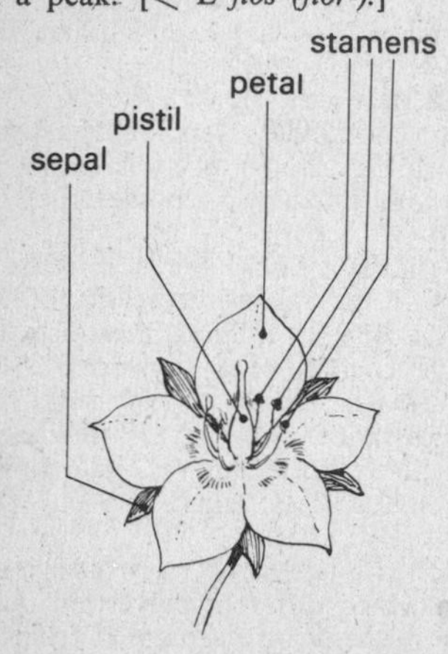

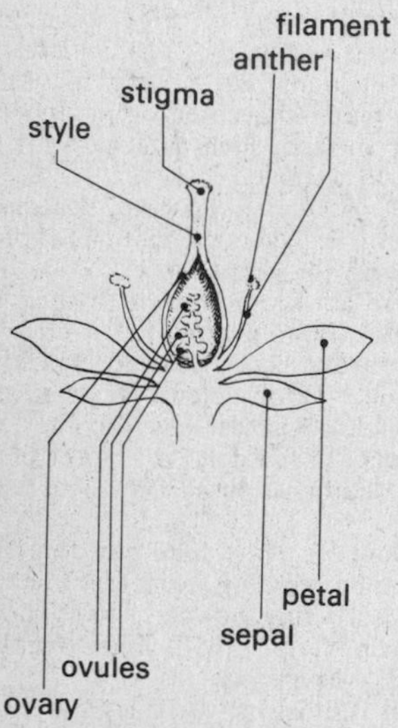

flower
Flower *(above)* and cross section showing details

flow•er•y (flou'ə-rē) *adj.* **-ier, -iest. 1.** Abounding in or suggestive of flowers. **2.** Full of ornate expressions: *a flowery speech.*

flown (flōn). *p.p.* of **fly¹**.

flu (flo͞o) *n. Informal.* Influenza.

fluc•tu•ate (flŭk'cho͞o-āt') *v.* **-ated, -ating. 1.** To vary irregularly. **2.** To rise and fall like waves. [L *fluctuāre.*] —**fluc'tu•a'tion** *n.*

flue (flo͞o) *n.* A pipe, tube, or channel through which air, gas, steam, or smoke can pass, as in a chimney. [?]

flu•ent (flo͞o'ənt) *adj.* **1.** Having facility in the use of a language. **2.** Effortless; polished. **3.** Flowing or capable of flowing; fluid. [< L *fluere,* to flow.] —**flu'en•cy** *n.* —**flu'ent•ly** *adv.*

fluff (flŭf) *n.* **1.** Light down or nap. **2.** Something having a light, soft, or frothy consistency or appearance. **3.** Something of little consequence. **4.** *Informal.* An error or blunder, as by an actor. —*v.* **1.** To make light and puffy by shaking or patting into a soft, loose mass: *fluff a pillow.* **2.** *Informal.* To misread or blunder. [< F *velu,* velvety.] —**fluff'y** *adj.*

flu•id (flo͞o'ĭd) *n.* A substance that exists, or is regarded as existing, as a continuum characterized by low resistance to flow and the tendency to assume the shape of its container. —*adj.* **1.** Characteristic of a fluid, esp. flowing easily. **2.** Used in the measurement of fluids. **3.** Smooth and effortless. **4.** Easily changed or tending to change. **5.** Convertible into cash: *fluid assets.* [< L *fluere,* to flow.] —**flu•id'i•ty, flu'id•ness** *n.* —**flu'id•ly** *adv.*

fluid dram. One-eighth of a fluid ounce.

flu•id•ics (flo͞o-ĭd'ĭks) *n. (takes sing. v.).* The technology of fluids used as nonmoving, nonelectrical components of control and sensing systems.

fluid ounce. 1. A U.S. Customary System unit of volume or capacity, used in liquid measure, equal to 1.804 cubic inches. **2.** A corresponding British Imperial System unit, used in liquid and dry measure, equal to 1.734 cubic inches.

fluke¹ (flo͞ok) *n., pl.* **fluke** or **flukes.** Any of various flatfishes. [< OE *flōc.*]

fluke² (flo͞ok) *n.* **1.** The triangular blade at the end of either arm of an anchor. **2.** A barb or barbed head, as on a harpoon. **3.** One of the two flattened divisions of a whale's tail. [Prob < FLUKE¹.]

fluke³ (flo͞ok) *n.* An accidental stroke of good luck. [?] —**fluk'i•ness** *n.* —**fluk'y** *adj.*

flume (flo͞om) *n.* **1.** A narrow gorge, usually with a stream flowing through it. **2.** An artificial channel for a stream of water, as for conveying logs. [< L *fluere,* to flow.]

flung (flŭng). *p.t.* & *p.p.* of **fling.**

flunk (flŭngk) *v. Informal.* To fail an examination, course, etc. [?]

flun•ky (flŭng'kē) *n., pl.* **-kies.** Also **flun•key** *pl.* **-keys. 1.** A lackey. **2.** An obsequious or fawning person; a toady. [?]

flu•o•resce (flo͞o-ər-ĕs', flo͝or-ĕs') *v.* **-resced, -rescing.** To undergo, produce, or show fluorescence.

flu•o•res•cence (flo͞o-ər-ĕs'əns, flo͝or-ĕs'-) *n.* **1.** The emission of electromagnetic radiation, esp. of visible light, resulting from the absorption of incident radiation and persisting only as long as the stimulating radiation is continued. **2.** The radiation emitted during fluorescence. [< L *fluere,* to flow + -ESCENCE.] —**flu•o•res'cent** *adj.*

fluorescent lamp. A lamp consisting of a glass tube, the inner wall of which is coated with a material that fluoresces when bombarded with secondary radiation generated within the tube.

flu•o•ri•date (flo͝or'ə-dāt', flo͞o'ər-ə-) *v.* **-dated, -dating.** To add a fluorine compound to (a water supply) for the purpose of preventing tooth decay. —**flu'o•ri•da'tion** *n.*

flu•o•ride (flo͞o'ə-rīd', flo͝or'īd') *n.* Any binary compound of fluorine with another element.

flu•o•rine (flo͞o'ə-rēn', flo͝or'ēn', -ĭn) *n. Symbol* **F** A pale-yellow, highly corrosive, highly poisonous gaseous element, the most electronegative and most reactive of all the elements. Atomic number 9, atomic weight 18.9984. [< L *fluor,* fluid, flowing.]

flu•o•ro•scope (flo͝or'ə-skōp', flo͞o'ər-ə-) *n.* A mounted fluorescent screen on which the contents or internal structure of an optically opaque object may be continuously viewed as shadows formed by differential transmission of x rays through the object.

flur•ry (flûr'ē) *n., pl.* **-ries. 1.** A sudden gust of wind. **2.** A light snowfall. **3.** A sudden burst of bustling activity; a stir. —*v.* **-ried, -rying. 1.** To agitate or confuse; fluster. **2.** To move or come down in a flurry. [< obs *flurr,* to whirl up, scatter.] —**flur'ried•ly** *adv.*

flush¹ (flŭsh) *v.* **1.** To flow suddenly and abundantly. **2.** To redden; blush. **3.** To glow, esp. with a reddish color. **4.** To wash out or clean by a rapid, brief gush of water. **5.** To excite or elate. —*n.* **1.** A brief but copious flow or gushing, as of water. **2.** A reddish tinge; a blush. **3.** A feeling of animation or exhilaration. **4.** A sudden freshness, development, or growth. —*adj.* **1.** Having a reddish color; blushing. **2.** Abundant; plentiful. **3.** Prosperous; affluent. **4. a.** Having surfaces in the same plane; even. **b.** Arranged with adjacent sides, surfaces, or edges close together. **5.** Direct; straightforward. —*adv.* **1.** So as to be even, in one plane, or aligned with a margin. **2.** Squarely; solidly: *a hit flush on the face.* [Prob < FLUSH³.]

flush² (flŭsh) *n.* A hand in certain card games in which all the cards are of the same suit. [< L *fluxus,* a flow, FLUX.]

flush³ (flŭsh) *v.* To cause to fly from cover, as a game bird. [Poss < OE **flyscan.*]

flus•ter (flŭs'tər) *v.* To make confused or agitated; upset. —*n.* A state of agitation or confusion. [Poss < Scand.]

flute (flo͞ot) *n.* **1.** A high-pitched tubular woodwind instrument. **2.** One of the long parallel grooves incised on the shaft of a column. **3.** A groove in cloth, as a pleat. [< OF *flaute.*]

flut•ist (flo͞o'tĭst) *n.* One who plays the flute.

flut•ter (flŭt'ər) *v.* **1.** To wave or flap lightly, rapidly, and irregularly. **2.** To fly with a quick, light flapping of the wings. **3.** To vibrate or beat rapidly or erratically. **4.** To move quickly or behave in a restless or excited manner. —*n.* **1.** An act of fluttering; a quick flapping. **2.** A condition of nervous excitement or agitation. **3.** A commotion; flurry. [< OE *floterian.* See **pleu-**.] —**flut'ter•er** *n.* —**flut'ter•y** *adj.*

flux (flŭks) *n.* **1. a.** A flow or flowing. **b.** A continued flow or flood. **2.** Change regarded as an abstract influence or condition persisting in time. **3.** A substance applied to prevent oxide formation and facilitate flowing, as of solder. —*v.* **1.** To melt; fuse. **2.** To apply a flux to. **3.** To flow; stream. [< L *fluxus,* pp of *fluere,* to flow.]

fly¹ (flī) *v.* **flew, flown, flying. 1.** To engage in flight, esp.: **a.** To move through the air with the aid of wings or winglike parts. **b.** To travel by air. **c.** To pilot an aircraft. **2.** To rise, float, or cause to float in the air. **3.** To flee; try to escape. **4.** To hasten; rush. **5.** To pass by swiftly. **6.** To disappear rapidly; vanish. **7.** *p.t.* & *p.p.* **flied.** To bat a baseball in a high arc. —*n., pl.* **flies. 1.** An overlapping fold of cloth that hides the fastening on a garment. **2.** A cloth flap that covers an entrance, as of a tent. **3.** A baseball batted in a high arc. **4. flies.** The area directly over the stage and behind the proscenium of a theater. **5.** *Brit.* A one-horse carriage. [< OE *flēogan.* See **pleu-**.]

fly² (flī) *n., pl.* **flies. 1.** Any of numerous winged insects, esp. one of the family that includes the housefly. **2.** A fishing lure simulating a fly.

[< OE *flēoge.* See **pleu-.**]

fly•blown (flī'blōn') *adj.* Contaminated by or as by flies.

fly•by (flī'bī') *n., pl.* **-bys.** A flight passing close to a specified target or position, esp. a maneuver in which a spacecraft passes close to a planet to make observations without landing.

fly-by-night (flī'bī-nīt') *adj.* **1.** Of unreliable business character. **2.** Dubious and temporary.

fly•catch•er (flī'kăch'ər) *n.* Any of various birds that fly after and catch flying insects.

fly•er. Variant of **flier.**

flying buttress. A free-standing buttress that resists thrust and supports another part of the structure.

flying fish. A marine fish with enlarged, winglike fins that aid in flightlike leaps from the water.

flying saucer. Any of various unidentified flying objects typically reported and described as luminous disks.

fly•leaf (flī'lēf') *n.* A blank leaf at the beginning or end of a book.

fly•pa•per (flī'pā'pər) *n.* Paper coated with a sticky substance, used to catch flies.

fly•speck (flī'spĕk') *n.* A small, dark speck or stain of fly excrement.

fly•weight (flī'wāt') *n.* A boxer weighing 112 pounds or less.

fly•wheel (flī'hwēl') *n.* A heavy-rimmed rotating wheel used to minimize speed variation in a machine subject to fluctuation in drive and load.

Fm fermium.

FM frequency modulation.

fm. fathom.

fn. footnote.

f-num•ber (ĕf'nŭm'bər) *n.* The ratio of focal length to the effective aperture diameter in a lens or lens system.

foal (fōl) *n.* The young offspring of a horse or other equine animal, esp. when under a year old. *—v.* To give birth to (a foal). [< OE *fola.* See **pōu-.**]

foam (fōm) *n.* **1.** A mass of gas bubbles in a liquid-film matrix. **2.** Any of various light, bulky, more or less rigid materials used as thermal or mechanical insulators, esp. in packaging and containers. *—v.* To form or come forth in foam. [< OE *fām.* See **spoimo-.**] **—foam'i•ness** *n.* **—foam'y** *adj.*

foam rubber. A light, firm, spongy rubber containing several times the volume of air ordinarily found in rubber.

fob¹ (fŏb) *n.* **1.** A short chain or ribbon attached to a pocket watch. **2.** An ornament attached to such a chain or ribbon. [Prob < Gmc.]

fob² (fŏb) *v.* **fobbed, fobbing. —fob off. 1.** To dispose of (goods) by fraud. **2.** To put off or appease by deceitful or evasive means. [ME *fobben.*]

f.o.b., F.O.B. free on board.

focal length. The distance of the focal point from the surface of a lens or mirror.

focal point. A point on the axis of symmetry of an optical system to which parallel incident rays converge or from which they appear to diverge after passing through the system.

fo•cus (fō'kəs) *n., pl.* **-cuses** or **-ci** (-sī'). **1.** A point to which something converges or from which it diverges. **2.** *Opt.* **a. Focal point. b. Focal length. c.** The distinctness or clarity with which an optical system renders an image. **d.** Adjustment for distinctness or clarity. **3.** A center of interest or activity. *—v.* **-cused** or **-cussed, -cusing** or **-cussing. 1. a.** To produce a clear image of. **b.** To adjust the setting of (a lens) to produce a clear image. **2.** To concentrate on. **3.** To converge at a focus. [L, fireplace, hearth (the center of the home).] **—fo'cal** *adj.* **—fo'cal•ly** *adv.*

fod•der (fŏd'ər) *n.* Feed for livestock, as coarsely chopped stalks and leaves of corn. [< OE *fōdor.* See **pā-.**]

foe (fō) *n.* **1. a.** A personal enemy. **b.** An enemy in war. **2.** An adversary; opponent. [< OE *gefāh,* hostile. See **peig-².**]

foe•tal. Variant of **fetal.**

foe•tus. Variant of **fetus.**

fog (fôg, fŏg) *n.* **1.** Condensed water vapor in cloudlike masses close to the ground, limiting visibility. **2.** Confusion or bewilderment. **3.** A dark blur on a developed photographic negative. *—v.* **fogged, fogging.** To cover or be obscured by or as by fog. **—fog'gi•ly** *adv.* **—fog'gi•ness** *n.* **—fog'gy** *adj.*

fog•horn (fôg'hôrn', fŏg'-) *n.* A horn used by ships and coastal installations to sound warning signals in fog or darkness.

fo•gy (fō'gē) *n., pl.* **-gies.** Also **fo•gey** *pl.* **-geys.** A person of old-fashioned habits and attitudes. [?] **—fo'gy•ish** *adj.*

foi•ble (foi'bəl) *n.* A minor weakness of character. [< OF *feble,* feeble.]

foil¹ (foil) *v.* To prevent from being successful; thwart. [< ME *foilen,* to trample.]

foil² (foil) *n.* **1.** A thin, flexible leaf or sheet of metal. **2.** Any person or thing that, by contrast, enhances the characteristics of another. [< L *folium,* leaf.]

foil³ (foil) *n.* A fencing sword with a thin, flexible blade tipped with a blunt point. [?]

foist (foist) *v.* **1.** To pass off (something inferior) as genuine, valuable, or worthy. **2.** To impose (something or someone unwanted) upon another, as by coercion. **3.** To insert fraudulently or deceitfully. [< Du *vuist,* fist.]

fol. 1. folio. **2.** following.

fold¹ (fōld) *v.* **1.** To bend over or double up so that one part lies on another. **2.** To bring from an extended to a closed position. **3.** To place together and intertwine: *fold one's arms.* **4.** To wrap; envelop. **5.** To mix in (an ingredient) by slowly and gently turning one part over another, as in cooking. **6.** *Informal.* To fail or collapse. *—n.* **1.** The act or an instance of folding. **2.** The junction of two folded parts. [< OE *fealdan.* See **pel-³.**]

fold² (fōld) *n.* **1.** A fenced enclosure for domestic animals, esp. sheep. **2.** A flock of sheep. **3.** Any group of people with common beliefs, aims, or loyalties. *—v.* To place or keep (sheep) in a fold. [< OE *fald.*]

-fold. *comb. form.* A specified number of parts: *fivefold.* [< OE *-feald.* See **pel-³.**]

fold•er (fōl'dər) *n.* **1.** A group of folded, printed sheets gathered together but not fastened. **2.** A folded piece of cardboard or thick paper used as a container.

fol•de•rol (fŏl'də-rŏl') *n.* **1.** Foolish talk or procedure; nonsense. **2.** A trifle; gewgaw.

fo•li•age (fō'lē-ĭj) *n.* Plant leaves collectively. [< L *folium,* leaf.]

fo•li•ar (fō'lē-ər) *adj.* Of or pertaining to a leaf or leaves.

fo•li•o (fō'lē-ō') *n., pl.* **-os. 1.** A large sheet of paper folded once in the middle. **2.** A book of the largest common size having such folded sheets. **3.** A page number in a book. [< L *folium,* leaf.]

folk (fōk) *n., pl.* **folk** or *informal* **folks. 1.** A people; a nation. **2.** People of a specified group or kind: *city folk.* **3. folks.** *Informal.* The members of one's family. **4. folks.** *Informal.* People in general. *—adj.* Of, occurring in, or originating among the common people: *folk music.* [< OE *folc,* the people, nation < Gmc **folkam.*]

folk•lore (fōk'lôr', -lōr') *n.* The body of orally preserved traditions, beliefs, tales, etc., of a people. **—folk'lor'ist** *n.*

folk•sy (fōk'sē) *adj.* **-sier, -siest.** *Informal.* **1.** Casual; unpretentious. **2.** Sociable; congenial.

fol•li•cle (fŏl'ĭ-kəl) *n.* **1.** An approximately spherical group of cells containing a cavity. **2.** A vascular body in the ovary containing ova. [< L *follis,* bellows.]

fol•low (fŏl'ō) *v.* **1.** To come or go after. **2.** To pursue. **3.** To accompany; attend. **4.** To move along the course of. **5.** To obey; comply with. **6.** To succeed to the place or position of. **7.** To engage in. **8.** To result; ensue. **9.** To be attentive to. **10.** To grasp the meaning or logic of; understand. [< OE *folgian* and *fylgan* < Gmc **fulg-.*]

fol•low•er (fŏl'ō-ər) *n.* **1.** One that follows another. **2.** An attendant or subordinate. **3.** One who subscribes to the teachings of another; an adherent.

fol•low•ing (fŏl'ō-ĭng) *adj.* **1.** Coming next in time or order. **2.** Now to be enumerated. *—n.* A group or gathering of followers.

fol•ly (fŏl'ē) *n., pl.* **-lies. 1.** Lack of good judgment. **2. a.** An act or instance of foolishness. **b.** A costly undertaking having an absurd or ruinous outcome. [< OF *fol,* foolish.]

fo•ment (fō-mĕnt') *v.* **1.** To arouse; stir up; instigate. **2.** To treat with heat and moisture. [< L *fōmentum,* warm application.]

fond (fŏnd) *adj.* **1.** Affectionate; tender. **2.** Having a tender interest or affection (with *of*). **3.** Foolishly affectionate; doting. **4.** Cherished; dear. [Prob < ME *fon,* a fool.] **—fond'ly** *adv.* **—fond'ness** *n.*

fon•dle (fŏnd'l) *v.* **-dled, -dling.** To handle or stroke affectionately; caress.

font¹ (fŏnt) *n.* **1.** A receptacle for holy or baptismal water. **2.** *Archaic.* A fountain or spring. **3.** Any source of abundance. [< L *fons (font-),* spring, fountain.]

font² (fŏnt) *n.* A complete set of printing type of one size and face. [< OF *fondre,* to melt, cast.]

food (fo͞od) *n.* **1.** Any material, usually of plant or animal origin, that is taken in and assimilated by an organism to maintain life and growth. **2.** A specified kind of nourishment. **3.** Solid nourishment as distinguished from liquid nourishment. **4.** Anything that nourishes or sustains. [< OE *fōda.* See **pā-.**]

food stamp. A stamp issued by the government and sold or given to low-income persons to be redeemed for food.

food•stuff (fo͞od'stŭf') *n.* Any substance suitable for food, esp. after processing.

fool (fo͞ol) *n.* **1.** One deficient in judgment, sense, or understanding. **2.** A jester; buffoon. **3.** One who can be easily deceived; a dupe. *—v.* **1.** To deceive or misinform; trick; dupe. **2.** To act or speak in jest; play; joke. **—fool around.** To engage in useless or trifling activity. **—fool with.** To toy or tamper with. [< L *follis,* "bellows," windbag.]

fool•er•y (fo͞o'lə-rē) *n., pl.* **-ies. 1.** Foolish behavior or speech. **2.** A prank or trick.

fool•har•dy (fo͞ol'här'dē) *adj.* **-dier, -diest.** Unwisely bold; rash. **—fool'har'di•ness** *n.*

fool•ish (fo͞o'lĭsh) *adj.* **1.** Having or resulting from poor judgment; unwise. **2.** Silly; ridiculous; inane. **3.** Abashed; embarrassed. —**fool'ish•ly** *adv.* —**fool'ish•ness** *n.*

fool•proof (fo͞ol'pro͞of') *adj.* Designed to be proof against human error or misuse.

fools•cap (fo͞olz'kăp') *n.* A sheet of paper approx. 13×16 inches.

fool's gold. Pyrite or any similar mineral found in gold-colored veins or nuggets, sometimes mistaken for gold.

foot (fo͝ot) *n., pl.* **feet** (fēt). **1.** The lower extremity of the leg that is in direct contact with the ground in standing or walking. **2.** Something resembling or suggestive of a foot in position or function, as the bottom or lowest part or the end opposite the head. **3.** *Pros.* A metric unit consisting of a stressed or unstressed syllable or syllables. **4.** A unit of length equal to ⅓ yard or 12 inches. —**on foot.** Walking or standing; not riding. —**under foot.** Obstructing free movement; in the way. —*v.* **1.** To go on foot; walk. **2.** To dance. **3.** To move steadily; proceed. **4.** To add up; total: *Foot up the bill.* **5.** *Informal.* To pay. [< OE *fōt.* See **ped-**[1].]

Usage: Foot and *feet,* as units of measure, are employed typically in the following: *a four-foot plank; a plank four feet long* (or *four feet in length*); *a man six feet tall; a ledge two feet below.*

foot•age (fo͝ot'ĭj) *n.* **1.** The length of something expressed in feet. **2.** A portion of motion-picture film.

foot•ball (fo͝ot'bôl') *n.* **1. a.** A game played with a ball on a rectangular field by opposing teams of 11 players each. **b.** The ball used in this game, an inflated ellipsoid. **2.** *Chiefly Brit.* **a.** **Rugby football. b.** Soccer.

foot•board (fo͝ot'bôrd', -bōrd') *n.* **1.** A board or small raised platform on which to support the feet. **2.** An upright board across the foot of a bedstead.

foot•bridge (fo͝ot'brĭj') *n.* A narrow bridge for pedestrians.

foot•ed (fo͝ot'ĭd) *adj.* **1.** Having a foot or feet. **2.** Having a specified kind or number of feet: *web-footed.*

foot•fall (fo͝ot'fôl') *n.* **1.** A footstep. **2.** The sound made by a footstep or footsteps.

foot•hill (fo͝ot'hĭl') *n.* A low hill near the base of a mountain.

foot•hold (fo͝ot'hōld') *n.* **1.** A place affording support for the foot in climbing or standing. **2.** A firm or secure position enabling one to advance.

foot•ing (fo͝ot'ĭng) *n.* **1.** A secure placement of the feet. **2.** A place on which one can stand or move securely. **3.** A basis; foundation. **4. a.** The totaling up of a column of figures. **b.** The sum of such a column.

foot•less (fo͝ot'lĭs) *adj.* **1.** Without feet. **2.** Without a firm support or basis. **3.** Clumsy; inept. —**foot'less•ness** *n.*

foot•lights (fo͝ot'līts') *pl.n.* **1.** A row of lights along the front of a stage floor. **2.** The theater as a profession.

foot•lock•er (fo͝ot'lŏk'ər) *n.* A small trunk for storing personal belongings.

foot•loose (fo͝ot'lo͞os') *adj.* Having no attachments or ties; free.

foot•man (fo͝ot'mən) *n.* A male servant employed to wait on table, attend the door, and run errands.

foot•note (fo͝ot'nōt') *n.* A note of comment or reference, often placed at the bottom of a page.

foot•path (fo͝ot'păth', -päth') *n., pl.* **-paths** (-păthz', -päthz', -păths', -päths'). A narrow path for people on foot.

foot-pound (fo͝ot'pound') *n.* A unit of work equal to the work done by a force of one pound acting through a distance of one foot in the direction of the force.

foot•print (fo͝ot'prĭnt') *n.* An outline or indentation of a foot.

foot•rest (fo͝ot'rĕst') *n.* A support on which to rest the feet.

foot soldier. A soldier who fights on foot; infantryman.

foot•step (fo͝ot'stĕp') *n.* **1.** A step with the foot. **2.** The distance covered by one step. **3.** The sound of a foot stepping. **4.** A footprint. **5.** A step up or down.

foot•stool (fo͝ot'sto͞ol') *n.* A low stool for supporting the feet.

foot•wear (fo͝ot'wâr') *n.* Anything worn on the feet, as shoes.

foot•work (fo͝ot'wûrk') *n.* The manner in which the feet are employed, as in boxing.

fop (fŏp) *n.* A man who is preoccupied with clothes and manners; a dandy. [ME, a fool.] —**fop'per•y** *n.* —**fop'pish** *adj.*

for (fôr, *unstressed* fər) *prep.* **1.** —Used to indicate a recipient: *a letter for me.* **2.** As a result of: *weep for joy.* **3.** To the extent or through the duration of. **4.** In order to go to or reach: *start for home.* **5. a.** With an aim or view to: *swim for fun.* **b.** So as to find, get, have, keep, or save. **6.** In preparation toward: *study for the ministry.* **7.** In the amount or at the price of. **8.** In response to or requital of. **9.** In view of the normal character of: *short for a novel.* **10.** At a stated time: *a date for 6 o'clock.* **11.** In the service or hire of. **12.** In honor or behalf of. **13.** In favor, defense, or support of. **14.** In place of. **15.** With effect on or by way of affecting. **16.** In coincidence or conjunction with: *one bad egg for every good one.* **17.** As against: *pound for pound.* **18.** As being: *took him for a fool.* **19.** As the duty or task of; up to: *It's for him to decide.* **20.** —Used with an infinitive preceded by its subject as an equivalent for a corresponding noun clause: *a job for us to do.* **21.** Despite (with *all*): *For all his learning he's a bore.* —*conj.* For this reason; namely. [< OE. See **per**[1].]

for. **1.** foreign. **2.** forestry.

fo•ra. Alternate *pl.* of **forum.**

for•age (fôr'ĭj, fŏr'-) *n.* **1.** Food for animals, as that obtained by grazing. **2.** A search for food or supplies. —*v.* **-aged, -aging. 1.** To search for food or supplies. **2.** To raid; plunder. **3.** To rummage through, esp. in search of provisions. [< OF *feurre,* fodder.]

fo•ra•men (fə-rā'mən) *n., pl.* **-ramina** (-răm'ə-nə) or **-mens.** An anatomical aperture or perforation. [< L *forāmen,* an opening.]

for•ay (fôr'ā') *n.* **1.** A raid, as for plunder. **2.** A venture in some field. [< OF *forrier,* plunderer.] —**for'ay'** *v.*

for•bear[1] (fôr-bâr') *v.* **-bore, -borne, -bearing. 1.** To refrain or desist from. **2.** To be tolerant or patient. [< OE *forberan,* to bear, endure.] —**for•bear'ance** *n.* —**for•bear'er** *n.*

for•bear[2]. Variant of **forebear.**

for•bid (fər-bĭd', fôr-) *v.* **-bade** (-băd', -bād') or **-bad** (-băd'), **-bidden** (-bĭd'n) or **-bid, -bidding. 1.** To command (someone) not to do something. **2.** To prohibit; interdict. **3.** To preclude. [< OE *forbēodan.*]

for•bid•ding (fər-bĭd'ĭng, fôr-) *adj.* **1.** Unfriendly; disagreeable: *a desolate and forbidding landscape.* **2.** Grim; ominous.

force (fôrs, fōrs) *n.* **1.** Strength; power. **2.** The exertion of such power. **3.** Intellectual vigor or persuasiveness, as of a statement. **4.** A body of persons organized for a certain purpose, esp. for the use of military power. **5.** A vector quantity that tends to produce an acceleration of a body in the direction of its application. —**in force. 1.** In full strength. **2.** In effect; operative. —*v.* **forced, forcing. 1.** To compel to perform an action. **2.** To obtain by force; extort. **3.** To produce by effort: *force a tear from one's eye.* **4.** To move (something) against resistance. **5.** To break down or open by force: *force a lock.* **6.** To inflict or impose. **7.** To cause to grow rapidly by artificial means. [< L *fortis,* strong.]

force field. Field of force.

force•ful (fôrs'fəl, fōrs'-) *adj.* Effective; persuasive. —**force'ful•ly** *adv.*

for•ceps (fôr'səps) *n., pl.* **-ceps.** An instrument used for grasping, manipulating, or extracting. [L *forceps,* fire tongs, pincers.]

for•ci•ble (fôr'sə-bəl, fōr'-) *adj.* Effected through or characterized by force. —**for'ci•ble•ness** *n.* —**for'ci•bly** *adv.*

ford (fôrd, fōrd) *n.* A shallow place in a body of water where a crossing can be made on foot or on horseback. —*v.* To cross at such a shallow place. [< OE. See **per-**[2].]

Ford (fôrd, fōrd), **Gerald Rudolph. Original name, Leslie Lynch King, Jr. Born 1913. 38th President of the U.S. (1974–77).**

Ford (fôrd, fōrd), **Henry.** 1863–1947. American automobile designer and manufacturer.

fore (fôr, fōr) *adj.* Located at or toward the front; anterior. —*n.* The front part. —*adv.* Toward or at the bow of a ship; forward. —*interj.* Expressive of a warning to those ahead that a golf ball is about to be driven in their direction. [< OE, beforehand. See **per**[1].]

fore–. *comb. form.* **1.** Before in time. **2.** The front or first part.

fore-and-aft (fôr'ən-ăft', -äft', fōr'-) *adj.* Parallel with the keel of a ship.

fore•arm[1] (fôr-ärm', fōr-) *v.* To prepare in advance for some conflict.

fore•arm[2] (fôr'ärm', fōr'-) *n.* The part of the arm between the wrist and elbow.

fore•bear (fôr'bâr', fōr'-) *n.* Also **for•bear.** An ancestor; forefather. [< FORE- + ME *bear,* "be-er."]

fore•bode (fôr-bōd', fōr-) *v.* **-boded, -boding. 1.** To indicate the threatening likelihood of; portend. **2.** To have a premonition of (a future misfortune). —**fore•bod'ing** *n. & adj.*

fore•cast (fôr'kăst', -käst', fōr'-) *v.* **-cast** or **-casted, -casting. 1.** To estimate or calculate in advance, esp. to predict the weather. **2.** To serve as an advance indication of; foreshadow. —*n.* A prediction. —**fore'cast'er** *n.*

fore•cas•tle (fōk'səl, fôr'kăs'əl, -käs'əl, fōr'-) *n.* **1.** The section of the upper deck of a ship located at the bow. **2.** A superstructure at the bow of a merchant ship, where the crew is housed.

fore•close (fôr-klōz', fōr-) *v.* **-closed, -closing. 1.** To deprive (a mortgagor) of possession of mortgaged property, as when he has failed in his payments. **2.** To shut out; bar.

fore•clo•sure (fôr-klō'zhər, fōr-) *n.* The act of foreclosing, esp. a legal proceeding by which a mortgage is foreclosed.

fore•fa•ther (fôr'fä'*th*ər, fōr'-) *n.* An ancestor.

fore•fin•ger (fôr'fĭng'gər, fōr'-) *n.* The index finger.

fore•foot (fôr'fo͝ot', fōr'-) *n.* One of the front feet of an animal.

fore•front (fôr'frŭnt', fōr'-) *n.* **1.** The foremost part or area of something. **2.** The position of most importance.

fore•go¹ (fôr-gō′, fōr-) *v.* To precede.

fore•go². Variant of **forgo.**

fore•go•ing (fôr-gō′ĭng, fōr-, fôr′gō′ĭng, fōr′-) *adj.* Just past; preceding.

fore•gone (fôr′gôn′, -gŏn′, fōr′-) *adj.* Having gone or been completed previously. [pp of FOREGO¹.]

fore•ground (fôr′ground′, fōr′-) *n.* **1.** The part of a view or picture that is nearest to the viewer. **2.** The most important position.

fore•hand (fôr′hănd′, fōr′-) *adj.* Made with the hand moving palm forward: *a forehand tennis stroke.* —**fore′hand** *n.*

fore•head (fôr′ĭd, fŏr′-, fôr′hĕd′, fōr′-) *n.* The part of the face between the eyebrows and the normal hairline.

for•eign (fôr′ĭn, fŏr′-) *adj.* **1.** Located away from one's native country: *foreign parts.* **2.** Of a country other than one's own: *a foreign custom.* **3.** Conducted or involved with other nations: *foreign trade.* **4.** Situated in an abnormal or improper place. **5.** Not germane; extraneous. [< L *forās,* out of doors, abroad.] —**for′eign•ness** *n.*

for•eign•er (fôr′ə-nər, fŏr′-) *n.* A person from a foreign country.

Foreign Office. The official name, in several countries, of the department in charge of foreign affairs.

fore•knowl•edge (fôr-nŏl′ĭj, fōr-) *n.* Knowledge of something prior to its occurrence.

fore•leg (fôr′lĕg′, fōr′-) *n.* One of the front legs of an animal.

fore•limb (fôr′lĭm′, fōr′-) *n.* An anterior appendage such as a leg, wing, or flipper.

fore•lock (fôr′lŏk′, fōr′-) *n.* A lock of hair that falls on the forehead.

fore•man (fôr′mən, fōr′-) *n.* **1.** A man who has charge of a group of workers. **2.** The spokesman for a jury.

fore•mast (fôr′məst, -măst′, -mäst′, fōr′-) *n.* The forward mast on a sailing vessel.

fore•most (fôr′mōst′, fōr′-) *adj.* Ahead of all others, esp. in position or rank. [< OE *formest,* superl of *forma,* first. See **per¹**.] —**fore′most** *adv.*

fore•noon (fôr′no͞on′, fōr′-, fôr-no͞on′, fōr-) *n.* The period of time between sunrise and noon.

fo•ren•sic (fə-rĕn′sĭk) *adj.* **1.** Of or employed in legal proceedings: *forensic medicine.* **2.** Of debate or argument; rhetorical. —*n.* **forensics.** *(takes sing. v.).* The art of formal debate. [< L *forēnsis,* of a market or forum.]

fore•or•dain (fôr′ôr-dān′, fōr′-) *v.* To appoint or ordain beforehand; predestine.

fore•quar•ter (fôr′kwôr′tər, fōr′-) *n.* The region including the front leg and shoulder of an animal or side of meat.

fore•run•ner (fôr′rŭn′ər, fōr′-) *n.* **1.** A predecessor. **2.** One that provides advance notice of the coming of others; harbinger.

fore•sail (fôr′səl, -sāl′, fōr′-) *n. Naut.* The principal sail hung to the foremast.

fore•see (fôr-sē′, fōr-) *v.* To see or know beforehand. —**fore•see′a•ble** *adj.*

fore•shad•ow (fôr-shăd′ō, fōr-) *v.* To present an indication or suggestion of beforehand.

fore•shore (fôr′shôr′, fōr′shōr′) *n.* The part of a shore covered at high tide.

fore•short•en (fôr-shôrt′n, fōr-) *v.* To represent the long axis of (an object) by contracting its lines so as to produce an illusion of projection or extension in space.

fore•sight (fôr′sīt′, fōr′-) *n.* **1.** The act or ability of foreseeing. **2.** The act of looking forward. **3.** Concern or prudence with respect to the future. —**fore′sight′ed** *adj.*

fore•skin (fôr′skĭn′, fōr′-) *n.* The prepuce.

for•est (fôr′ĭst, fŏr′-) *n.* A dense growth of trees covering a large area. [< LL *forestis (silva),* outside (forest).]

fore•stall (fôr-stôl′, fōr-) *v.* **1.** To prevent or take precautionary measures against beforehand. **2.** To deal with beforehand; anticipate. [< OE *foresteall,* waylaying, interception.]

for•est•ry (fôr′ĭ-strē, fŏr′-) *n.* The science of maintaining and developing forests. —**for′est•er** *n.*

fore•taste (fôr′tāst′, fōr′-) *n.* An advance realization. —**fore′taste′** *v.*

fore•tell (fôr-tĕl′, fōr-) *v.* To tell of or indicate beforehand; predict.

fore•thought (fôr′thôt′, fōr′-) *n.* **1.** Deliberation or planning beforehand. **2.** Preparation for the future.

for•ev•er (fôr-ĕv′ər, fər-) *adv.* **1.** Eternally. **2.** Incessantly.

for•ev•er•more (fôr-ĕv′ər-môr′, -mōr′, fər-) *adv.* Forever.

fore•warn (fôr-wôrn′, fōr-) *v.* To warn in advance.

fore•word (fôr′wûrd′, -wərd, fōr′-) *n.* A preface or introductory note.

for•feit (fôr′fĭt) *n.* **1.** Something surrendered as punishment; a penalty or fine. **2.** Something placed in escrow and then redeemed after payment of a fine. **3.** A forfeiture. —*v.* To surrender or be forced to surrender as a forfeit. [< OF *forsfaire,* to commit a crime.]

for•fei•ture (fôr′fĭ-cho͝or′) *n.* **1.** The act of forfeiting. **2.** Something forfeited.

for•gath•er (fôr-găth′ər, fōr-) *v.* To gather together; assemble.

for•gave (fər-gāv′, fôr-). *p.t.* of **forgive.**

forge¹ (fôrj, fōrj) *n.* A furnace or hearth where metals are heated or wrought; smithy. —*v.* **forged, forging. 1.** To form (metal) by heating and hammering. **2.** To give form or shape to: *forge a treaty.* **3.** To fashion or reproduce for fraudulent purposes: *forge a signature.* [< L *fabrica,* smithy, artisan's workshop.] —**forge′a•ble** *adj.* —**forg′er** *n.*

forge² (fôrj, fōrj) *v.* **forged, forging. 1.** To advance gradually but firmly. **2.** To advance with an abrupt increase of speed. [Perh a var of FORCE.]

for•ger•y (fôr′jə-rē, fōr′-) *n., pl.* **-ies. 1.** The production of something counterfeit or forged. **2.** Something forged.

for•get (fər-gĕt′, fôr-) *v.* **-got** (-gŏt′), **-gotten** (-gŏt′n) or **-got, -getting. 1.** To be unable to remember or call to mind. **2.** To treat with inattention; neglect. **3.** To fail or neglect to become aware at the proper moment. —**forget oneself.** To lose one's reserve or self-restraint. [< OE *forgietan.* See **ghend-.**] —**for•get′ful** *adj.* —**for•get′ful•ness** *n.*

for•get-me-not (fər-gĕt′mē-nŏt′, fôr-) *n.* A low-growing plant with small blue flowers.

for•give (fər-gĭv′, fôr-) *v.* **-gave, -given, -giving. 1.** To excuse for a fault or offense. **2.** To renounce resentment against. **3.** To absolve from payment of. [< OE *forgiefan.*] —**for•giv′a•ble** *adj.* —**for•give′ness** *n.*

for•go (fôr-gō′) *v.* **-went, -gone** (-gôn′, -gŏn′), **-going.** Also **forego.** To relinquish; abstain from; forsake. —**for•go′er** *n.*

fo•rint (fôr′ĭnt) *n.* The basic monetary unit of Hungary.

fork (fôrk) *n.* **1.** An implement with two or more prongs used for raising, carrying, piercing, etc. **2.** A pronged utensil for serving or eating food. **3. a.** A bifurcation into branches. **b.** The point at which this occurs. **c.** One of the branches. —*v.* **1.** To raise, carry, etc., with a fork. **2.** To give the shape of a fork to. **3.** To divide into branches. [< L *furca,* two-pronged fork.]

forked (fôrkt, fôr′kĭd) *adj.* Containing or shaped like a fork.

fork lift. A vehicle with a power-operated pronged platform for lifting and carrying loads.

for•lorn (fôr-lôrn′, fər-) *adj.* **1.** Deserted; abandoned. **2.** Wretched or pitiful. **3.** Nearly hopeless. [< OE *forlēosan,* to abandon. See **leu-.**] —**for•lorn′ly** *adv.*

form (fôrm) *n.* **1.** The contour and structure of something. **2.** The body, esp. of a person. **3.** The essence of something. **4.** The mode in which a thing exists; kind; variety: *a form of animal life.* **5.** Procedure as determined by regulation or custom. **6.** Manners as governed by etiquette. **7.** Performance according to recognized criteria. **8.** Fitness with regard to health or training. **9.** A fixed order of words or procedures, as in a ceremony. **10.** A document with blanks for the insertion of requested information. **11.** Style or manner in literary or musical composition. **12.** The structure of a work of art. **13.** A model for making a mold. **14.** A grade in a British school or in some American private schools. —*v.* **1.** To shape or become shaped. **2.** To shape into or assume a particular form. **3.** To develop by instruction or precept: *form the mind.* **4.** To develop; acquire: *form a habit.* **5.** To constitute a part of. **6.** To develop in the mind: *form an opinion.* **7.** To draw up; arrange. [< L *fōrma,* form, contour, shape.]

-form. *comb. form.* Having the form of: **cuneiform.**

for•mal (fôr′məl) *adj.* **1.** Pertaining to the extrinsic aspect of something. **2.** Pertaining to the essential form of something: *a formal principle.* **3.** Following accepted conventions or proper form. **4.** Characterized by strict observation of forms. **5.** Stiff or cold: *a formal manner.* **6.** Done for the sake of form only: *a purely formal greeting.* —*n.* An occasion requiring formal attire. [< L *fōrmālis,* of or for form.] —**for′mal•ly** *adv.*

for•mal•de•hyde (fôr-măl′də-hīd′) *n.* A colorless, gaseous compound, HCHO, used in aqueous solution as a preservative and disinfectant. [< FORM(IC ACID) + ALDEHYDE.]

for•mal•ism (fôr′mə-lĭz′əm) *n.* Rigorous or excessive adherence to recognized forms.

for•mal•i•ty (fôr-măl′ə-tē) *n., pl.* **-ties. 1.** The quality or condition of being formal. **2.** Rigorous or ceremonious adherence to established rules. **3.** An established rule.

for•mal•ize (fôr′mə-līz′) *v.* **-ized, -izing. 1.** To give a definite form or shape to. **2.** To render formal. **3.** To give formal endorsement to.

for•mat (fôr′măt′) *n.* **1.** A plan for the organization and arrangement of something. **2.** The layout of a publication. [< L *fōrma,* FORM.]

for•ma•tion (fôr-mā′shən) *n.* **1.** The process of forming. **2.** Something that is formed. **3.** The manner in which something is formed. **4.** A specified arrangement, as of troops.

for•ma•tive (fôr′mə-tĭv) *adj.* **1.** Forming or capable of forming. **2.** Pertaining to growth or development: *a formative stage.*

for•mer (fôr′mər) *adj.* **1.** Occurring earlier in time. **2.** Coming before in place or order. **3.** Of the first or first mentioned of two. —See Usage note at **latter.** [< OE *forma,* first. See **per¹.**]

for•mer•ly (fôr′mər-lē) *adv.* At a former time; once.

form•fit•ting (fôrm′fĭt′ĭng) *adj.* Closely fitted to the body.

For•mi•ca (fôr-mī′kə) *n.* A trademark for any of various high-pressure laminated plastic sheets, used esp. for chemical and heat-resistant surfaces.

for•mic acid (fôr′mĭk). A colorless caustic fuming liquid, HCOOH, used in fumigants, insecticides, and refrigerants. [< L *formīca,* ant.]

for•mi•da•ble (fôr′mə-də-bəl) *adj.* **1.** Arousing dread or awe. **2.** Difficult to surmount. [< L *formīdō,* fright, fear.] **—for′mi•da•bly** *adv.*

For•mo•sa (fôr-mō′sə). The former name for **Taiwan.**

for•mu•la (fôr′myə-lə) *n., pl.* **-las** or **-lae** (-lē′). **1.** A set form of words or symbols for use in a ceremony. **2.** A hackneyed expression; a cliché. **3.** A symbolic representation of the composition, or of the composition and structure, of a chemical compound. **4.** A recipe. **5.** A liquid food prescribed for an infant. **6.** A mathematical statement, as an equation, of some logical relation. [< L *fōrma,* FORM.] **—for′mu•la′ic** (fôr′myə-lā′ĭk) *adj.*

for•mu•late (fôr′myə-lāt′) *v.* **-lated, -lating. 1.** To state as a formula. **2.** To express in systematic terms. **3.** To prepare according to a formula. **—for′mu•la′tion** *n.*

for•ni•ca•tion (fôr′nĭ-kā′shən) *n.* Sexual intercourse between a man and woman not married to each other. **—for′ni•cate** *v.* **(-cated, -cating).**

for•sake (fôr-sāk′, fər-) *v.* **-sook** (-so͝ok′), **-saken** (-sā′kən), **-saking. 1.** To give up; renounce. **2.** To leave altogether; abandon. [< OE *forsacan.* See **sāg-**.] **—for•sak′er** *n.*

for•sooth (fôr-so͞oth′, fər-) *adv. Archaic.* In truth; indeed.

for•swear (fôr-swâr′) *v.* **-swore** (-swôr′, -swōr′), **-sworn** (-swôrn′, -swōrn′), **-swearing. 1.** To renounce or forsake unalterably. **2.** To repudiate unalterably. **3.** To commit perjury.

for•syth•i•a (fôr-sĭth′ē-ə, fər-) *n.* A widely cultivated shrub with early-blooming yellow flowers. [< W. *Forsyth* (1737–1804), English botanist.]

fort (fôrt, fōrt) *n.* A fortified place, esp. a permanent post. [< L *fortis,* strong.]

forte[1] (fôrt, fōrt, fôr′tā) *n.* Something in which a person excels. [< OF *fort,* "strong."]

for•te[2] (fôr′tā) *adv. Mus.* Loudly; forcefully. [It, "strongly."] **—for′te** *adj.*

forth (fôrth, fōrth) *adv.* **1.** Forward; onward. **2.** Out into view. [< OE. See **per[1]**.]

forth•com•ing (fôrth-kŭm′ĭng, fōrth-) *adj.* **1.** About to appear: *the forthcoming elections.* **2.** Available when required.

forth•right (fôrth′rīt′, fōrth′-) *adj.* Straightforward; frank; candid.

forth•with (fôrth′wĭ*th*′, -wĭth′, fōrth′-) *adv.* At once; immediately.

for•ti•eth (fôr′tē-ĭth) *n.* **1.** The ordinal number 40 in a series. **2.** One of 40 equal parts. **—for′ti•eth** *adj. & adv.*

for•ti•fy (fôr′tə-fī′) *v.* **-fied, -fying. 1.** To strengthen and secure (a position) with military defenses. **2.** To impart physical strength to. **3.** To give moral or mental strength to; encourage. **4.** To strengthen or increase the content of (a substance), as by adding vitamins to food or alcohol to wine. [< L *fortis,* strong.] **—for′ti•fi•ca′tion** *n.* **—for′ti•fi′er** *n.*

for•tis•si•mo (fôr-tĭs′ə-mō′) *adv. Mus.* Very loudly. [It.] **—for•tis′si•mo′** *adj.*

for•ti•tude (fôr′tə-t/y/o͞od′) *n.* Strength of mind that allows one to endure adversity with courage. [< L *fortis,* strong.]

Fort-La•my (fôr′lə-mē′). The former name for **N'Djamena.**

fort•night (fôrt′nīt′, -nĭt) *n.* A period of 14 days; two weeks. [< OE *fēowertīene niht* : FOURTEEN + NIGHT.]

fort•night•ly (fôrt′nīt′lē) *adj.* Happening or appearing once in every two weeks. **—fort′night′ly** *adv.*

for•tress (fôr′trĭs) *n.* A fort. [< L *fortis,* strong.]

for•tu•i•tous (fôr-t/y/o͞o′ə-təs) *adj.* Happening by accident or chance. [< L *forte,* by chance.]

for•tu•i•ty (fôr-t/y/o͞o′ə-tē) *n., pl.* **-ties. 1.** An accidental occurrence; chance. **2.** The quality or condition of being fortuitous.

for•tu•nate (fôr′chə-nĭt) *adj.* **1.** Occurring by good fortune. **2.** Lucky.

for•tune (fôr′chən) *n.* **1.** A hypothetical force that governs the events of one's life. **2.** Good or bad luck. **3.** Luck, esp. when good; success. **4.** Wealth or riches. [< L *fors,* chance, luck.]

for•tune•tell•er (fôr′chən-tĕl′ər) *n.* A person who, usually for a fee, will undertake to predict one's future. **—for′tune•tell′ing** *n. & adj.*

Fort Wayne (wān). A city in NE Indiana. Pop. 162,000.

Fort Worth (wûrth). A city in NE Texas. Pop. 356,000.

for•ty (fôr′tē) *n.* The cardinal number written 40 or in Roman numerals XL. [< OE *fēowertig.* See **kwetwer-**.] **—for′ty** *adj. & pron.*

fo•rum (fôr′əm, fōr′-) *n., pl.* **-rums** or **fora** (fôr′ə, fōr′ə). **1.** The public square or marketplace of an ancient Roman city. **2.** Any public place or medium for open discussion. **3.** A court of law. [< L, forum, place out-of-doors.]

for•ward (fôr′wərd) *adj.* **1. a.** At, near, or belonging to the front. **b.** Going, tending, or moving toward the front. **2.** Ardently inclined; eager. **3.** Bold; fresh: *a forward woman.* **4.** Progressive: *a forward new nation.* **5.** Advanced in development. **6.** For the future; completed or made in advance. *—adv.* **1.** Also **for•wards** (-wərdz). Toward or tending to the front; frontward: *step forward.* **2.** In or toward the future: *I look forward to seeing you.* **3.** Into view or prominence; forth: *Come forward out of the shadows so I can see you. —n.* A player in the front lines, as in basketball. *—v.* **1.** To send on to a subsequent destination: *forward mail.* **2.** To advance; promote. [< FORE- + -WARD.] **—for′ward•er** *n.*

for•went (fôr-wĕnt′, fōr-). *p.t.* of **forgo.**

fos•sil (fŏs′əl) *n.* **1.** A remnant or trace of an organism of a past geological age embedded in the earth's crust. **2.** One that is outdated. *—adj.* **1.** Of or pertaining to fossils. **2.** Derived from fossils: *Coal is a fossil fuel.* [< L *fossilis,* dug up.]

fos•sil•ize (fŏs′ə-līz′) *v.* **-ized, -izing.** To convert into or become a fossil.

fos•ter (fôs′tər, fŏs′-) *v.* **1.** To bring up; rear. **2.** To encourage; cultivate. *—adj.* Receiving, sharing, or affording parental care although not related through legal or blood ties: *a foster child.* [< OE *fōstor,* food. See **pā-**.]

fought (fôt). *p.t. & p.p.* of **fight.**

foul (foul) *adj.* **1.** Offensive to the senses; disgusting. **2.** Having an offensive odor. **3.** Spoiled; rotten. **4.** Dirty; filthy. **5.** Immoral; wicked. **6.** Vulgar; obscene. **7.** Unpleasant: *a foul day.* **8.** Unfair; dishonorable: *win by foul means.* **9.** *Sports.* **a.** Designating lines that limit the playing area: *foul lines.* **b.** Contrary to the rules or outside the limits set. **10.** Entangled, as a rope. *—n.* **1.** *Sports.* **a.** A foul ball, hit, move, etc. **b.** An infraction of the rules. **2.** An entanglement or collision. *—adv.* In a foul manner. *—v.* **1.** To make or become foul; soil. **2.** To bring into dishonor. **3.** To clog or obstruct. **4.** To entangle or become entangled, as a rope. **5.** *Sports.* To commit a foul. [< OE *fūl.* See **pu-**.] **—foul′ly** *adv.* **—foul′ness** *n.*

fou•lard (fo͞o-lärd′) *n.* A lightweight twill or plain-woven fabric of silk usually having a printed design. [F.]

foul-mouthed (foul′mou*th*d′, -moutht′) *adj.* Using obscene language.

foul play. Unfair action, esp. when involving violence.

found[1] (found) *v.* **1.** To originate or establish; set up, as a college. **2.** To establish the foundation of. **3.** To have a foundation or base (with *on* or *upon*). [< L *fundāre,* to lay the foundation for.] **—found′er** *n.*

found[2] (found) *v.* **1.** To melt (a metal) and pour into a mold. **2.** To make (objects) in this fashion; cast. [< L *fundere,* to pour, melt.] **—found′er** *n.*

found[3] (found). *p.t. & p.p.* of **find.**

foun•da•tion (foun-dā′shən) *n.* **1.** The act of founding or state of being founded. **2.** The basis on which a thing stands; an underlying support. **3.** An endowment. **4.** An endowed institution. **—foun•da′tion•al** *adj.*

foun•der (foun′dər) *v.* **1.** To go lame, as a horse. **2.** To fail utterly; collapse or break down. **3.** To sink below the water. [< VL **fundorāre,* to submerge.]

found•ling (found′lĭng) *n.* A child abandoned by unknown parents. [Prob < ME *finden,* to find.]

foun•dry (foun′drē) *n., pl.* **-dries.** An establishment in which the founding of metals is done.

fount (fount) *n.* **1.** A fountain. **2.** Any source. [Prob < FOUNTAIN.]

foun•tain (foun′tən) *n.* **1.** A spring, esp. the source of a stream. **2.** Any source. **3. a.** An artificially created jet of water. **b.** A device that produces such a jet: *a drinking fountain.* **4.** A container for liquid that can be siphoned off as needed. [< L *fons (font-),* spring.]

foun•tain•head (foun′tən-hĕd′) *n.* A principal source or origin.

fountain pen. A pen containing an ink reservoir that feeds the writing point.

four (fôr, fōr) *n.* The cardinal number written 4 or in Roman numerals IV. [< OE *fēower.* See **kwetwer-**.] **—four** *adj & pron.*

four-flush•er (fôr′flŭsh′ər, fōr′-) *n. Slang.* A bluffer; faker.

four-in-hand (fôr′ĭn-hănd′, fōr′-) *n.* **1.** A team of four horses driven by one person. **2.** A necktie tied in a slipknot with the ends left hanging and overlapping.

four-post•er (fôr′pō′stər, fōr′-) *n.* A bed having tall corner posts originally intended to support curtains or a canopy.

four•score (fôr′skôr′, fōr′skōr′) *adj.* Four times 20; 80.

four•some (fôr′səm, fōr′-) *n.* **1.** Any group of four persons. **2.** Any game played by four persons, two on each side.

four•square (fôr′skwâr′, fōr′-) *adj.* **1.** Square. **2.** Unyielding; firm. **3.** Forthright; frank. **—four′square′** *adv.*

four•teen (fôr-tēn′, fōr-) *n.* The cardinal number written 14 or in Roman numerals XIV. [< OE *fēowertīene.*] **—four•teen′** *adj. & pron.*

four•teenth (fôr-tēnth′, fôr-) *n.* **1.** The ordinal number 14 in a series. **2.** One of 14 equal parts. —**four•teenth′** *adj. & adv.*

fourth (fôrth, fōrth) *n.* **1.** The ordinal number 4 in a series. **2.** One of 4 equal parts. [< OE *fēowertha.*] —**fourth** *adj. & adv.*

fourth dimension. Time regarded as a coordinate dimension and required by geometry, along with three spatial dimensions, to specify completely the location of any event.

Fourth of July. **Independence Day.**

fowl (foul) *n., pl.* **fowl** or **fowls. 1.** A bird used as food or hunted as game, esp. the common domesticated chicken. **2.** The edible flesh of such a bird. —*v.* To hunt wild fowl. [< OE *fugol.* See **pleu-.**] —**fowl′er** *n.*

fox (fŏks) *n.* **1.** A mammal related to the dogs and wolves, having a pointed snout and a long, bushy tail. **2.** The fur of a fox. **3.** A crafty or sly person. —*v.* To trick by ingenuity or cunning. [< OE. See **puk-.**]

foxed (fŏkst) *adj.* Discolored with yellowish-brown stains, as an old book.

fox•glove (fŏks′glŭv′) *n.* A plant with a long cluster of large, tubular, pinkish-purple flowers, and leaves that are the source of the medicinal drug digitalis.

fox•hole (fŏks′hōl′) *n.* A pit dug for refuge against enemy fire.

fox terrier. A small dog with a smooth or wire-haired white coat with dark markings.

fox trot. A ballroom dance in 2/4 or 4/4 time. —**fox′-trot′** *v.*

fox•y (fŏk′sē) *adj.* **-ier, -iest.** Suggestive of a fox; sly; clever. —**fox′i•ness** *n.*

foy•er (foi′ər, foi′ā′) *n.* **1.** The lobby of a public building. **2.** The entrance hall of a private dwelling. [< L *focus,* hearth, fireplace.]

fp freezing point.

fp. foolscap.

Fr francium.

fr. from.

Fr. **1.** father (clergyman). **2.** France; French. **3.** friar. **4.** Friday (unofficial).

fra•cas (frā′kəs) *n.* A brawl. [< It *fracasso.*]

frac•tion (frăk′shən) *n.* **1.** A small part of something. **2.** A disconnected piece of something. **3.** *Math.* An indicated quotient of two quantities. **4.** *Chem.* A component separated by distillation, crystallization, etc. [< L *fractus,* pp of *frangere,* to break.] —**frac′tion•al** *adj.*

frac•tious (frăk′shəs) *adj.* **1.** Inclined to make trouble; unruly. **2.** Cranky; irritable.

frac•ture (frăk′chər) *n.* **1. a.** An act, process, or manner of breaking. **b.** The condition of being broken. **2.** A break, rupture, or crack, as in bone or cartilage. —*v.* **-tured, -turing.** To break; crack. [< L *fractus,* broken.]

frag•ile (frăj′əl, -īl′) *adj.* **1.** Easily broken or damaged; brittle. **2.** Physically weak; frail. **3.** Suggesting fragility; light. **4.** Tenuous; flimsy. [< L *fragilis* < *frangere,* to break.] —**frag′ile•ly** *adv.* —**fra•gil′i•ty** (frə-jĭl′ə-tē), **frag′ile•ness** *n.*

frag•ment (frăg′mənt) *n.* **1.** A part broken off. **2.** Something incomplete, as a manuscript. [< L *frangere,* to break.] —**frag′men•ta′tion** *n.*

frag•men•tar•y (frăg′mən-tĕr′ē) *adj.* Consisting of fragments. —**frag′men•tar′i•ly** *adv.*

fra•grant (frā′grənt) *adj.* Having a pleasing odor. [< L *fragrāre,* to emit an odor.] —**fra′grance** *n.* —**fra′grant•ly** *adv.*

frail (frāl) *adj.* **1.** Having a delicate constitution. **2.** Slight; weak. **3.** Easily broken. **4.** Morally weak. [< L *fragilis,* FRAGILE.]

frail•ty (frāl′tē) *n., pl.* **-ties. 1.** The condition or quality of being frail. **2.** Often **frailties.** A fault arising from human weakness.

frame (frām) *v.* **framed, framing. 1.** To construct; build. **2.** To design; draw up. **3.** To arrange or adjust for a purpose: *The question was framed to draw only one answer.* **4.** To put into words; compose. **5.** To provide with a frame; enclose. **6.** *Slang.* To rig evidence or events so as to incriminate (a person) falsely. —*n.* **1.** Something composed of parts fitted and joined together; a structure, such as: **a.** A skeletal structure: *the frame of a house.* **b.** An open structure or rim: *a window frame.* **c.** The human body. **2.** A machine built upon or utilizing a frame. **3.** The general structure of something: *the frame of government.* **4.** A single exposure on a roll of motion-picture film. [< OE *framian,* to benefit, avail. See **per**[1].] —**fram′er** *n.*

frame-up (frām′ŭp′) *n.* A fraudulent scheme, esp. one involving falsified charges or evidence.

frame•work (frām′wûrk′) *n.* **1.** A structure for supporting or enclosing something. **2.** A basic system or design.

franc (frăngk) *n.* The basic monetary unit of France, Belgium, Burundi, Cameroun, Central African Empire, Chad, Congo, Benin, Gabon, Guinea, Ivory Coast, Luxembourg, Malagasy Republic, Mali, Mauritania, Niger, Rwanda, Senegal, Switzerland, Togo, Upper Volta, and of various overseas departments and territories of France. [OF.]

France (frăns, fräns). A republic of W Europe. Pop. 48,700,000. Cap. Paris.

France

fran•chise (frăn′chīz′) *n.* **1.** A privilege granted a person or group; a charter. **2.** A constitutional or statutory right, as the suffrage. **3.** Authorization granted by a manufacturer to a distributor or dealer. [< OF *franc,* free, FRANK.]

Fran•cis of As•si•si (frăn′sĭs, frän′-; ə-sē′zē), **Saint.** 1182?–1226. Italian monk; founder of a religious order.

fran•ci•um (frăn′sē-əm) *n. Symbol* **Fr** An extremely unstable radioactive metallic element. Atomic number 87, longest-lived isotope Fr 223. [< FRANCE.]

Fran•co (frăng′kō, frăng′-), **Francisco.** 1892–1975. Spanish statesman (1939–75).

Franco–. *comb. form.* French.

frank (frăngk) *adj.* Open and sincere in expression; straightforward. —*v.* **1.** To put an official mark (on a piece of mail) so that it can be sent and delivered free. **2.** To send (mail) free of charge. —*n.* **1.** A mark or signature on a piece of mail indicating the right to send it free. **2.** The right to send mail free. [< OF *franc,* free.]

Frank•en•stein monster (frăng′kən-stīn′). Also **Frank•en•stein's monster** (-stīnz′). A creation that slips from the control of and destroys its creator. [< Mary Shelley's novel *Frankenstein* (1818).]

Frank•fort (frăngk′fərt). The capital of Kentucky. Pop. 21,000.

Frank•furt am Main (frängk′fo͝ort′ äm mīn′). A city of West Germany. Pop. 692,000.

frank•furt•er (frăngk′fər-tər) *n.* A smoked sausage of beef or beef and pork made in long, reddish links. [< FRANKFURT.]

frank•in•cense (frăngk′ĭn-sĕns′) *n.* An aromatic gum resin used chiefly as incense. [< OF *franc encens.*]

Frank•lin (frăngk′lĭn), **Benjamin.** 1706–1790. American statesman, author, and scientist.

Benjamin Franklin

frank•ly (frăngk′lē) *adv.* **1.** In a frank manner. **2.** In truth: *Frankly, I don't care.*

frank•ness (frăngk′nĭs) *n.* Openness and directness of speech; candor.

fran•tic (frăn′tĭk) *adj.* Emotionally distraught; frenzied. [< FRENETIC.] —**fran′ti•cal•ly** *adv.*

frap•pé (fră-pā′, frăp) *n.* **1.** A frozen mixture similar to sherbet. **2.** A beverage poured over shaved ice. **3.** A milk shake with ice cream. [< OF *fraper,* to strike.]

fra•ter•nal (frə-tûr′nəl) *adj.* **1.** Pertaining to brothers; brotherly. **2.** Pertaining to or constituting a fraternity. **3.** Pertaining to a twin or twins developed from separately fertilized ova. [< L *frāter,* brother. See **bhrāter-.**] —**fra•ter′nal•ism′** *n.* —**fra•ter′nal•ly** *adv.*

fra•ter•ni•ty (frə-tûr′nə-tē) *n., pl.* **-ties. 1.** A body of men linked together by similar interests or professions. **2.** A chiefly social organization of male college students. **3.** Brotherhood; brotherliness.

frat•er•nize (frăt′ər-nīz′) *v.* **-nized, -nizing. 1.** To associate with others in a congenial way. **2.** To associate with the people of an enemy or conquered country. —**frat′er•ni•za′tion** *n.*

frat•ri•cide (frăt′rə-sīd′) *n.* **1.** The killing of one's brother or sister. **2.** One who has killed his brother or sister. [< L *frāter,* brother + -CIDE.] —**frat′ri•ci′dal** *adj.*

fraud (frôd) *n.* **1.** A deliberate deception for unfair or unlawful gain. **2.** A swindle; trick. **3.** One who practices deception; an impostor. [< L *fraus.*]

fraud•u•lent (frô′jə-lənt) *adj.* **1.** Engaging in

fraud; deceitful. **2.** Constituting or gained by fraud. —**fraud'u·lence** *n.* —**fraud'u·lent·ly** *adv.*

fraught (frôt) *adj.* Attended; accompanied: *an occasion fraught with peril.* [< MDu *vracht,* freight.]

fray[1] (frā) *n.* **1.** A fight; brawl. **2.** A heated dispute. [< ME *fraien,* to frighten.]

fray[2] (frā) *v.* **1.** To unravel, wear away, or tatter by or through rubbing. **2.** To strain; chafe. [< L *fricāre,* to rub.]

fraz·zle (frăz'əl) *v.* **-zled, -zling.** *Informal.* **1.** To fray; wear out. **2.** To wear out the nerves of.

freak (frēk) *n.* **1.** A person, thing, or occurrence that is abnormal or very unusual. **2.** A whim; vagary. [?] —**freak'ish** *adj.*

freck·le (frĕk'əl) *n.* A small precipitation of pigment in the skin. —*v.* **-led, -ling.** To make or become dotted with freckles. [< ON *freknur* (pl).] —**freck'ly** *adv.*

Fred·er·ic·ton (frĕd'rĭk-tən). The capital of New Brunswick, Canada. Pop. 20,000.

free (frē) *adj.* **freer, freest. 1.** At liberty; not bound or constrained. **2.** Not under obligation or necessity. **3. a.** Politically independent. **b.** Governed by consent and possessing civil liberties. **4. a.** Not affected by a given condition or circumstance. **b.** Exempt: *duty-free.* **5.** Not literal: *a free translation.* **6.** Costing nothing; gratuitous. **7. a.** Unoccupied. **b.** Unobstructed. **8.** Guileless; frank. **9.** Taking undue liberties. **10.** Liberal or lavish. —*adv.* **1.** In a free manner. **2.** Without charge. —*v.* **freed, freeing. 1.** To set at liberty. **2.** To rid or release. **3.** To disengage; untangle. [< OE *frēo.* See **prī-**.] —**free'ly** *adv.* —**free'ness** *n.*

free·boot·er (frē'bōō'tər) *n.* One who plunders; pirate.

freed·man (frēd'mən) *n.* A man freed from bondage.

free·dom (frē'dəm) *n.* **1.** The condition of being free. **2.** Political independence. **3.** Facility, as of motion. **4.** Frankness. **5.** Unrestricted use or access.

free enterprise. The freedom to operate businesses competitively with minimal government regulation.

free fall. The fall of a body within the atmosphere without a drag-producing device such as a parachute.

free-for-all (frē'fər-ôl') *n.* A brawl in which many take part.

free·hand (frē'hănd') *adj.* Drawn without the aid of mechanical devices.

free·hold (frē'hōld') *n.* **1.** An estate held in fee or for life. **2.** The tenure by which such an estate is held. —**free'hold'er** *n.*

free lance. One who sells his services without a long-term commitment to any employer. —**free'-lance'** *v.* **(-lanced, -lancing).** —**free'-lance'** *adj.*

free·man (frē'mən) *n.* **1.** One not in slavery or serfdom. **2.** One having the rights or privileges of a citizen.

Free·ma·son (frē'mā'sən) *n.* A member of the Free and Accepted Masons, an international secret fraternity. —**Free'ma'son·ry** *n.*

fre·er (frē'ər). *comp.* of **free.**

fre·est (frē'ĭst). *superl.* of **free.**

free·stand·ing (frē'stăn'dĭng) *adj.* Standing without support or attachment.

free·stone (frē'stōn') *n.* **1.** A stone soft enough to be cut easily without shattering. **2.** A fruit, esp. a peach, with a stone that does not adhere to the pulp.

free·think·er (frē'thĭng'kər) *n.* One who has rejected authority and dogma, esp. in his religious thinking. —**free'think'ing** *adj.* & *n.*

Free·town (frē'toun'). The capital of Sierra Leone. Pop. 128,000.

free trade. Trade without protective customs tariffs between nations.

free verse. Verse without a conventional metrical pattern and with an irregular rhyme or none.

free·way (frē'wā') *n.* A highway with several lanes; expressway.

free·wheel·ing (frē'hwē'lĭng) *adj.* **1.** Free of restraints or rules in organization, methods, or procedure. **2.** Heedless; carefree.

free will. **1.** Free choice. **2.** The belief that man's choices are or can be voluntary.

freeze (frēz) *v.* **froze, frozen, freezing. 1. a.** To pass or cause to pass from liquid to solid by loss of heat. **b.** To acquire a surface of ice from cold. **2.** To preserve by subjecting to cold. **3.** To make or become inoperative through the formation of frost or ice. **4.** To damage or be damaged by cold. **5. a.** To be at that degree of temperature at which ice forms. **b.** To be uncomfortably cold. **6.** To make or become rigid or inflexible. **7.** To become paralyzed through fear or shyness. **8.** To become icily silent. **9.** To fix (prices or wages) at a current level. **10.** To prohibit further manufacture or use of. **11.** To prevent or restrict the exchange, liquidation, or granting of by law. **12.** To anesthetize by freezing. —*n.* **1.** An act of freezing. **2.** A spell of cold weather; frost. [< OE *frēosan.* See **preus-**.]

freeze-dry (frēz'drī') *v.* To preserve by rapid freezing and drying in a high vacuum.

freez·er (frē'zər) *n.* One that freezes, esp. an insulated cabinet or room for the rapid freezing and storing of perishable food.

freezing point. **1.** The temperature at which a liquid of specified composition solidifies under a specified pressure. **2.** The temperature at which the liquid and solid phases of a substance of specified composition are in equilibrium at atmospheric pressure.

freight (frāt) *n.* **1.** Goods carried by a vessel or vehicle; cargo. **2.** The commercial transportation of goods. **3.** The charge for transporting goods by cargo carrier. **4.** A railway train carrying goods only. —*v.* **1.** To convey commercially as cargo. **2.** To load with cargo. [< MDu *vrecht,* cargo.]

freight·er (frā'tər) *n.* A ship for carrying freight.

French (frĕnch) *n.* **1.** The Romance language spoken by the people of France, W Switzerland, and S Belgium. **2. the French** *(takes pl. v.).* The people of France. —**French** *adj.* —**French'man** *n.*

French dressing. A seasoned oil and vinegar salad dressing.

French fry. To fry in deep fat.

French Gui·an·a (gē-ăn'ə, -ä'nə). An overseas department of France in N South America between Surinam and Brazil. Pop. 34,000. Cap. Cayenne.

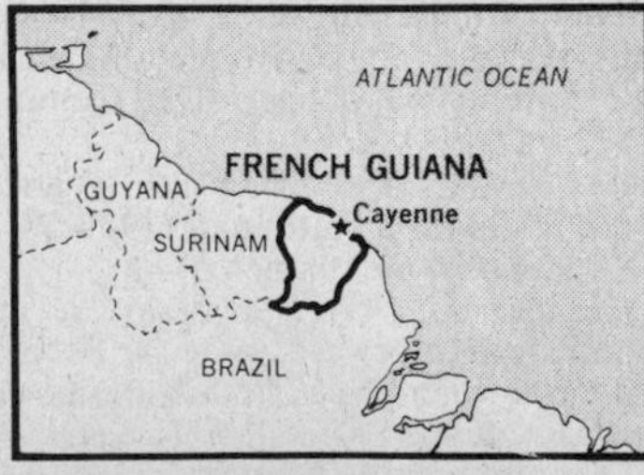

French Guiana

French horn. A brass wind instrument that tapers from a narrow mouthpiece to a flaring bell.

French leave. An unauthorized departure.

French toast. Sliced bread soaked in a milk and egg batter and lightly fried.

fre·net·ic (frə-nĕt'ĭk) *adj.* Also **fre·net·i·cal** (-ĭ-kəl), **phre·net·ic, phre·net·i·cal.** Frantic; frenzied. [< Gk *phrenitis,* brain disease, insanity.] —**fre·net'i·cal·ly** *adv.*

fren·zy (frĕn'zē) *n., pl.* **-zies. 1.** A seizure of violent agitation. **2.** Temporary madness. [< L *phrenēsis.*] —**fren'zied** *adj.*

Fre·on (frē'ŏn') *n.* A trademark for a gas or liquid used as a working fluid in refrigeration and air conditioning and as an aerosol propellant.

freq. **1.** frequentative. **2.** frequently.

fre·quen·cy (frē'kwən-sē) *n., pl.* **-cies. 1.** The number of times a phenomenon occurs within a specified interval, esp. the number of repetitions per unit time of a complete waveform, as of an electric current. **2.** The property or condition of occurring repeatedly in short intervals.

frequency modulation. The encoding of a carrier wave by variation of its frequency in accordance with an input signal.

fre·quent (frē'kwənt) *adj.* Occurring or appearing often or at close intervals. —*v.* (frē-kwĕnt', frē'kwənt). To pay frequent visits to. [< L *frēquens,* full, frequent.] —**fre·quent'er** *n.* —**fre'quent·ly** *adv.* —**fre'quent·ness** *n.*

fre·quen·ta·tive (frē-kwĕn'tə-tĭv) *n.* A verb that denotes repeated action, such as *flicker.* —**fre·quen'ta·tive** *adj.*

fres·co (frĕs'kō) *n., pl.* **-coes** or **-cos. 1.** The art of painting with earth colors on wet plaster. **2.** A painting thus executed. [< It *fresco,* fresh.] —**fres'co·er, fres'co·ist** *n.*

fresh (frĕsh) *adj.* **1.** New to one's experience; novel; original. **2.** Recently made, produced, or harvested; not stale: *fresh bread.* **3.** Not preserved, as by canning or freezing. **4.** Not saline: *fresh water.* **5.** Not yet used; clean. **6.** Additional: *a fresh start.* **7.** Bright and clear; not dull or faded. **8.** Inexperienced: *fresh recruits.* **9.** Having just arrived: *fresh from Paris.* **10.** Refreshed. **11.** Cool and invigorating: *fresh morning air.* **12.** Fairly strong; brisk: *a fresh wind.* **13.** *Informal.* Bold and saucy; impudent. —*adv.* Recently; newly: *fresh-baked bread.* [< Gmc **friskaz.*] —**fresh'ly** *adv.* —**fresh'ness** *n.*

fresh·en (frĕsh'ən) *v.* To make or become fresh. —**fresh'en·er** *n.*

fresh·et (frĕsh'ĭt) *n.* **1.** A sudden overflow of a stream from heavy rain or a thaw. **2.** A stream of fresh water that empties into a body of salt water.

fresh·man (frĕsh'mən) *n.* **1.** A student in the first year of high school or college. **2.** Any beginner.

fresh·wa·ter (frĕsh'wô'tər, -wŏt'ər) *adj.* Of, pertaining to, living in, or consisting of water that is not salty.

Fres·no (frĕz'nō). A city of C California. Pop. 134,000.

fret[1] (frĕt) *v.* **fretted, fretting. 1.** To be or cause to be uneasy or vexed; worry. **2. a.** To gnaw or wear away. **b.** To become worn or corroded. **3.** To disturb the surface of (water); agitate. —*n.* **1.** A hole, worn spot, or path made by abrasion or erosion. **2.** Irritation; annoyance. [< OE *fretan,* to irritate < Gmc **fraitan,* to eat up.]

fret[2] (frĕt) *n.* A ridge set across the fingerboard

of a stringed instrument. [?]

fret³ (frĕt) *n.* A design within a band or border, consisting esp. of a geometrical pattern. [< OF *frete,* embossed work.]

fret•ful (frĕt'fəl) *adj.* Inclined to fret; peevish; troubled. —**fret'ful•ly** *adv.* —**fret'ful•ness** *n.*

fret•work (frĕt'wûrk') *n.* Ornamental work consisting of three-dimensional frets; geometric openwork.

Freud (froid), **Sigmund.** 1856–1939. Austrian physician; founder of psychoanalysis. —**Freu'di•an** (froi'dē-ən) *adj.* & *n.*

Sigmund Freud

Fri. Friday.

fri•a•ble (frī'ə-bəl) *adj.* Readily crumbled; brittle. [< L *friāre,* to crumble.] —**fri'a•bil'i•ty, fri'a•ble•ness** *n.*

fri•ar (frī'ər) *n.* A member of a Roman Catholic order, usually mendicant. [< L *frāter,* brother.]

fric•as•see (frĭk'ə-sē') *n.* Poultry cut into pieces, stewed, and served with a gravy. —*v.* **-seed, -seeing.** To prepare as a fricassee. [< F *fricasser,* to fry.]

fric•tion (frĭk'shən) *n.* **1.** The rubbing of one object or surface against another. **2.** A conflict; a clashing. **3.** *Phys.* A force tangential to the common boundary of two bodies in contact that resists the motion or tendency to motion of one relative to the other. [< L *fricāre,* to rub.] —**fric'tion•al** *adj.*

friction tape. A moisture-resistant adhesive tape, used chiefly to insulate electrical conductors.

Fri•day (frī'dē, -dā') *n.* The 6th day of the week. [< OE *frīgedæg.* See **pri-**.]

fried (frīd). *p.t.* & *p.p.* of **fry¹**.

friend (frĕnd) *n.* **1.** A person one knows, likes, and trusts. **2.** A favored companion; comrade. **3.** One who supports a group or cause. **4. Friend.** A member of the Society of Friends; Quaker. [< OE *frēond.* See **pri-**.] —**friend'less** *adj.* —**friend'ship'** *n.*

friend•ly (frĕnd'lē) *adj.* **-lier, -liest. 1.** Of or befitting a friend. **2.** Favorably disposed; not antagonistic. **3.** Warm; comforting. —**friend'li•ness** *n.*

fri•er. Variant of **fryer.**

frieze (frēz) *n.* A decorative horizontal band, as along the upper part of a wall in a room [< ML *frisium, frigium,* fringe.]

frig•ate (frĭg'ĭt) *n.* **1.** A sailing war vessel of the 17th, 18th, and 19th centuries. **2.** A U.S. warship of approx. 5,000 to 7,000 tons. [< It *fregata.*]

fright (frīt) *n.* **1.** Sudden, intense fear. **2.** *Informal.* Something extremely unsightly or distressing. [< OE *fryhto* < Gmc **furht-*.]

fright•en (frīt'n) *v.* **1.** To make suddenly afraid. **2.** To drive or force by arousing fear: *frightened into confessing.*

fright•ful (frīt'fəl) *adj.* **1.** Causing disgust or shock. **2.** Causing fright. **3.** *Informal.* Excessive; extreme. —**fright'ful•ly** *adv.*

frig•id (frĭj'ĭd) *adj.* **1.** Extremely cold. **2.** Lacking warmth of feeling; cold in manner. [< L *frigus,* cold.] —**fri•gid'i•ty** (frĭ-jĭd'ə-tē) *n.*

Frigid Zone. The area within the Arctic Circle or that within the Antarctic Circle.

frill (frĭl) *n.* **1.** A ruffled, gathered, or pleated border or edging. **2.** *Informal.* Anything superfluous. [?] —**frill'i•ness** *n.* —**frill'y** *adj.*

fringe (frĭnj) *n.* **1.** A decorative border or edging of hanging threads, cords, or strips. **2.** A marginal or peripheral part; edge. —*v.* **fringed, fringing. 1.** To decorate with a fringe. **2.** To grow or occur along the edge of. [< LL *fimbria.*] —**fringe'less** *adj.*

fringe benefit. An employment benefit given in addition to one's wages.

frip•per•y (frĭp'ə-rē) *n., pl.* **-ies. 1.** Excessively ornamented dress. **2.** Pretentious elegance. [< OF *frepe, felpe,* frill.]

Fris. Frisian.

Fri•sian (frĭzh'ən, frē'zhən) *n.* **1.** A native or inhabitant of the Frisian Islands. **2.** The Germanic language spoken by the Frisian people. —**Fri'sian** *adj.*

Frisian Islands. A chain of islands in the North Sea, belonging to the Netherlands, West Germany, and Denmark.

frisk (frĭsk) *v.* **1.** To move about briskly and playfully. **2.** To search (a person) for concealed weapons by passing the hands over clothes or through pockets. [< Gmc **friskaz,* FRESH.] —**frisk'er** *n.*

frisk•y (frĭs'kē) *adj.* **-ier, -iest.** Lively and playful. —**frisk'i•ly** *adv.* —**frisk'i•ness** *n.*

frit•ter¹ (frĭt'ər) *v.* —**fritter away.** To reduce or squander little by little. [Prob < obs *fritter,* to break in pieces.]

frit•ter² (frĭt'ər) *n.* A small cake made of batter, often containing fruit, vegetables, or fish, fried in deep fat. [< L *frigere,* to FRY.]

friv•o•lous (frĭv'ə-ləs) *adj.* **1.** Unworthy of serious attention. **2.** Marked by flippancy. [< L *frivolus.*] —**fri•vol'i•ty** (-vŏl'ə-tē) *n.*

frizz (frĭz) *v.* Also **friz.** To form or be formed into small, tight curls or tufts. —*n.* Hair or fabric in tight curls. [F *friser,* to curl.] —**friz'zi•ly** *adv.* —**friz'zi•ness** *n.* —**friz'zy** *adj.*

friz•zle¹ (frĭz'əl) *v.* **-zled, -zling. 1.** To fry until crisp and curled. **2.** To fry or sear with a sizzling noise. [Perh blend of FRY and SIZZLE.]

friz•zle² (frĭz'əl) *v.* **-zled, -zling.** To frizz. —*n.* A small, tight curl. —**friz'zly** *adj.*

fro (frō) *adv.* Away; back: *to and fro.* [< ON *frā.*]

frock (frŏk) *n.* **1.** A long, loose outer garment; smock. **2.** A robe worn by monks and other clerics. **3.** A woman's dress. [< Gmc **hrok-*.]

frog (frôg, frŏg) *n.* **1.** Any of various tailless, chiefly aquatic amphibians with a smooth, moist skin and long hind legs adapted for leaping. **2.** An ornamental looped braid or cord with a button or knot for fastening a garment. **3.** *Informal.* Hoarseness in the throat. [< OE *frogga.* See **preu-**.]

frog•man (frôg'măn', -mən, frŏg'-) *n.* A swimmer equipped to execute extended underwater, esp. military, maneuvers.

frol•ic (frŏl'ĭk) *n.* **1.** Gaiety; merriment. **2.** A prank or trick. —*v.* **-icked, -icking.** To engage in merrymaking, joking, or teasing. [< MDu *vrolijc.*] —**frol'ick•er** *n.*

frol•ic•some (frŏl'ĭk-səm) *adj.* Full of high-spirited fun; playful.

from (frŭm, frŏm) *prep.* **1.** Beginning at a specified place or time. **2.** With a specified point as the first of two limits. **3.** With a person, place, or thing as the source or instrument. **4.** Out of. **5.** Out of the control or possession of. **6.** So as not to be engaged in: *keep him from making a mistake.* **7.** Measured by reference to: *far from home.* **8.** As opposed to: *know right from wrong.* —See Usage note at **different.** [< OE *from, fram.* See **per¹**.]

frond (frŏnd) *n.* The usually divided leaf of a fern, palm, etc. [L *frōns.*]

front (frŭnt) *n.* **1.** The forward part or surface. **2.** The location or position directly ahead: *in front of the fountain.* **3.** The position of leadership or superiority. **4.** The first part. **5.** Demeanor or bearing: *a brave front.* **6.** A false appearance or manner. **7.** Land bordering a lake, river, or street: *on the lake front.* **8.** *Mil.* **a.** The most forward line of combat force. **b.** The area of contact between opposing combat forces. **9.** *Meteorol.* The interface between air masses at different temperatures. **10.** An apparently respectable person under whose cover secret or illegal business is carried on. —*adj.* Of, pertaining to, aimed at, or located in the front. —*v.* **1.** To face; have a front (on). **2.** To serve as a front for. [< L *frōns.*] —**fron'tal** *adj.*

front•age (frŭn'tĭj) *n.* **1.** The front part of a piece of property. **2.** The dimensions of such a part. **3.** The direction in which something faces. **4.** Land adjacent to something.

frontal bone. A cranial bone with a vertical portion corresponding to the forehead and a horizontal portion that partially forms the roofs of the orbital and nasal cavities.

fron•tier (frŭn-tîr') *n.* **1.** An international border or the area along it. **2.** A region just beyond or at the edge of a settled area. **3.** Any underdeveloped area or field, as of scientific research. [< OF *front,* front.] —**fron•tier'** *adj.* —**fron•tiers'man** *n.*

fron•tis•piece (frŭn'tĭs-pēs') *n.* An illustration that faces or immediately precedes the title page of a book. [< LL *frontispicium,* "examination of the front."]

frost (frôst, frŏst) *n.* **1.** A covering of minute ice crystals formed from frozen water vapor. **2.** The atmospheric conditions when the temperature is below the freezing point of water. —*v.* **1.** To cover or become covered with frost. **2.** To damage or kill by frost. **3.** To cover or decorate with icing. [< OE *frost, forst.* See **preus-**.] —**frost'i•ness** *n.* —**frost'y** *adj.*

Frost (frôst, frŏst), **Robert.** 1875–1963. American poet.

frost•bite (frôst'bīt', frŏst'-) *n.* Local tissue destruction resulting from freezing. —*v.* To injure or damage by freezing.

frost•ing (frôs'tĭng, frŏs'-) *n.* **1.** Icing. **2.** A roughened or speckled surface on glass or metal.

froth (frôth, frŏth) *n.* **1.** A mass of bubbles in or on a liquid; foam. **2.** A salivary foam released as a result of disease or exhaustion. **3.** Anything unsubstantial; triviality. —*v.* To exude or expel froth; to foam. [< ON *frodha.*] —**froth'i•ly** *adv.* —**froth'i•ness** *n.* —**froth'y** *adj.*

frou-frou (fro͞o'fro͞o) *n.* **1.** A rustling sound, as of silk. **2.** Fussy or showy dress or ornamentation. [F.]

fro•ward (frō'wərd, frō'ərd) *adj.* Stubbornly

contrary and disobedient. [< FRO + -WARD.]

frown (froun) *v.* **1.** To wrinkle the brow, as in thought or displeasure. **2.** To regard with disapproval or distaste (with *on* or *upon*). *—n.* A wrinkling of the brow in thought or displeasure. [< OF *froigner.*] **—frown'er** *n.*

frow•zy (frou'zē) *adj.* **-zier, -ziest.** Also **frou•zy, frow•sy.** Unkempt in appearance; slovenly. [?] **—frow'zi•ness** *n.*

froze (frōz). *p.t.* of **freeze.**

fro•zen (frō'zən). *p.p.* of **freeze.** *—adj.* **1.** Made into, covered with, or surrounded by ice. **2.** Very cold. **3.** Preserved by freezing. **4.** Rendered immobile. **5.** Expressive of cold unfriendliness or disdain. **6. a.** Kept at an arbitrary level. **b.** Incapable of being withdrawn, sold, or liquidated: *frozen assets.*

FRS Federal Reserve System.

frt. freight.

fruc•tose (frŭk'tōs', frŏŏk'-) *n.* A very sweet sugar, $C_6H_{12}O_6$, occurring in many fruits and honey. [L *frūctus,* FRUIT + -OSE.]

fru•gal (frōō'gəl) *adj.* Avoiding unnecessary expenditure of money; thrifty. [< L *frūgī,* useful, worthy.] **—fru•gal'i•ty** (-găl'ə-tē) *n.* **—fru'gal•ly** *adv.*

fruit (frōōt) *n., pl.* **fruit** or **fruits. 1.** The ripened seed-bearing structure of a plant, esp. when fleshy and edible. **2.** A plant crop or product. **3.** Result; issue; outcome: *the fruit of labor.* *—v.* To produce fruit. [< L *frūctus,* enjoyment, use, fruit < pp of *fruī,* to enjoy, to eat fruit.]

fruit•ful (frōōt'fəl) *adj.* **1.** Producing fruit. **2.** Producing results; profitable.

fru•i•tion (frōō-ĭsh'ən) *n.* **1.** Enjoyment from use or possession. **2. a.** The condition of bearing fruit. **b.** The achievement of something desired or worked for. [< L *fruī,* to enjoy, eat fruit.]

fruit•less (frōōt'lĭs) *adj.* **1.** Producing no fruit. **2.** Having negligible or no results.

fruit•y (frōō'tē) *adj.* **-ier, -iest.** Tasting or smelling of fruit. **—fruit'i•ness** *n.*

frus•trate (frŭs'trāt') *v.* **-trated, -trating. 1. a.** To prevent from accomplishing a purpose or fulfilling a desire. **b.** To cause feelings of discouragement or bafflement in. **2.** To nullify. [< L *frūstrāre,* to disappoint.] **—frus•tra'tion** *n.*

fry¹ (frī) *v.* **fried, frying.** To cook over direct heat in hot oil or fat. *—n., pl.* **fries. 1.** A dish of any fried food. **2.** A social gathering featuring fried food: *a fish fry.* [< L *frīgere.*]

fry² (frī) *pl.n.* **1.** Young, recently hatched fish. **2.** Young individuals. [Perh < OF *freier,* to spawn, to rub.]

fry•er (frī'ər) *n.* Also **fri•er.** One that fries.

f-stop (ĕf'stŏp') *n.* **1.** A camera lens aperture setting calibrated to a corresponding f-number. **2.** An f-number.

ft foot.

ft. fort.

FTC Federal Trade Commission.

ft-lb foot-pound.

fuch•sia (fyōō'shə) *n.* A widely cultivated plant with showy, drooping, usually red and purple flowers. [< L. *Fuchs* (1501–1566), German botanist.]

fud•dle (fŭd'l) *v.* **-dled, -dling.** To muddle with or as if with liquor. [?]

fudge (fŭj) *n.* **1.** A soft rich candy made of sugar, butter, and flavoring. **2.** Nonsense; humbug. *—v.* **fudged, fudging.** To fake or falsify. [Prob var of archaic *fadge.*]

fueh•rer. Variant of **führer.**

fu•el (fyōō'əl) *n.* **1.** Anything consumed to produce energy, as: **a.** A material such as wood, coal, gas, or oil burned to produce heat. **b.** Fissionable material used in a nuclear reactor. **2.** Anything that maintains or heightens an activity or an emotion. *—v.* **-eled** or **-elled, -eling** or **-elling.** To provide with or take in fuel. [< L *focus,* fire, hearth.]

fuel cell. An electrochemical cell in which the energy of a reaction between a fuel such as liquid hydrogen and an oxidant such as liquid oxygen is converted directly and continuously into the energy of direct electric current.

fuel injection. Any of several methods or mechanical systems by which a fuel is vaporized and sprayed into the cylinders of a diesel or other internal-combustion engine.

fu•gi•tive (fyōō'jə-tĭv) *adj.* **1.** Running or having run away; fleeing, as from justice. **2.** Passing quickly; fleeting: *fugitive hours.* *—n.* One who flees; a runaway. [< L *fugere,* to flee.] **—fu'gi•tive•ly** *adv.*

fugue (fyōōg) *n.* A polyphonic musical form in which a theme stated sequentially and in imitation is developed in contrapuntal form. [< L *fuga,* flight.] **—fu'gal** *adj.*

füh•rer (fyŏŏr'ər) *n.* Also **fueh•rer.** A leader, esp. one exercising the powers of a tyrant, as Adolf Hitler. [G.]

–ful. *comb. form.* **1.** Fullness or abundance: **playful. 2.** Having the characteristics of: **masterful. 3.** Tendency or ability: **useful. 4.** The amount or number that will fill: *armful.* [< OE *full,* FULL.]

Usage: The plurals of nouns that end in *-ful* are most often indicated, esp. in writing, by the addition of the letter *s: glassfuls; spoonfuls; tablespoonfuls; teaspoonfuls.*

ful•crum (fŏŏl'krəm, fŭl'-) *n., pl.* **-crums** or **-cra** (-krə). **1.** The point or support on which a lever turns. **2.** Something through or by means of which vital powers are exercised. [L, bedpost, support.]

ful•fill (fŏŏl-fĭl') *v.* Also **ful•fil. -filled, -filling. 1.** To bring into actuality; effect. **2.** To satisfy. **3.** To go to the end of (a period of time); complete. [< OE *fullfyllan,* to fill full.] **—ful•fill'er** *n.* **—ful•fill'ment** *n.*

full¹ (fŏŏl) *adj.* **1.** Containing all that is normal or possible; complete. **2.** Of maximum or highest degree. **3.** Having a great deal or many: *full of errors.* **4.** Totally qualified or unanimously accepted: *a full member.* **5. a.** Rounded in shape. **b.** Of generous proportions; wide. **6.** Satiated, esp. with food or drink. **7.** Having depth and body. *—adv.* **1.** To a complete extent; entirely: *full well.* **2.** Directly: *full in the path of the moon.* *—n.* The maximum or complete size, amount, or development. [< OE. See **pel-⁵.**]

full² (fŏŏl) *v.* To increase or cause to increase the weight and bulk of (cloth) by shrinking and beating or pressing. [< VL **fullāre.*]

full•back (fŏŏl'băk') *n. Football.* A backfield player whose position is usually behind the quarterback and halfbacks.

full-blood•ed (fŏŏl'blŭd'ĭd) *adj.* **1.** Of unmixed breed or ancestry. **2.** Not pale or anemic. **3.** Vigorous and virile.

full-blown (fŏŏl'blōn') *adj.* **1.** In full blossom. **2.** Fully developed or matured.

full-bod•ied (fŏŏl'bŏd'ēd) *adj.* Having richness of flavor.

full dress. The attire appropriate for formal events.

full-fledged (fŏŏl'flĕjd') *adj.* **1.** Having fully developed adult plumage. **2.** Having full status or rank.

full moon. 1. The phase of the moon when it is visible as a fully illuminated disk. **2.** The period of the month when this occurs.

full-scale (fŏŏl'skāl') *adj.* **1.** Of the actual or full size. **2.** Employing all resources.

ful•ly (fŏŏl'ē) *adv.* **1.** Totally. **2.** Adequately; sufficiently. **3.** At least.

ful•mi•nate (fŭl'mə-nāt', fŏŏl'-) *v.* **-nated, -nating. 1.** To denounce severely. **2.** To explode. [< L *fulmināre,* to strike with lightning.] **—ful'mi•na'tion** *n.*

ful•some (fŏŏl'səm) *adj.* **1.** Offensively excessive or insincere. **2.** Loathsome; disgusting. [< FULL + -SOME.] **—ful'some•ly** *adv.* **—ful'some•ness** *n.*

fum•ble (fŭm'bəl) *v.* **-bled, -bling. 1.** To touch or handle nervously or idly. **2.** To grope awkwardly and uncertainly; blunder. **3.** *Sports.* To mishandle or drop a ball. *—n.* **1.** The act or instance of fumbling. **2.** *Sports.* A ball that has been fumbled. [Perh < Scand.]

fume (fyōōm) *n.* **1.** An exhalation of smoke, vapor, or gas, esp. an irritating or disagreeable exhalation. **2.** A strong or acrid odor. *—v.* **fumed, fuming. 1.** To subject to or treat with fumes. **2.** To give off in or as in fumes. **3.** To feel or show agitation or anger. [< L *fūmus,* smoke, steam.]

fu•mi•gate (fyōō'mĭ-gāt') *v.* **-gated, -gating.** To subject to smoke or fumes, usually in order to exterminate vermin or insects. **—fu'mi•ga'tion** *n.* **—fu'mi•ga'tor** *n.*

fun (fŭn) *n.* **1.** A source of enjoyment or pleasure. **2.** Enjoyment; amusement. **—make fun of.** To ridicule. [Perh < ME *fonnen,* to make fun of.]

func•tion (fŭngk'shən) *n.* **1.** The natural or proper action for which a person, office, mechanism, or organ is fitted or employed. **2. a.** Assigned duty or activity. **b.** Specific occupation or role. **3.** An official ceremony or elaborate social occasion. **4.** *Math.* **a.** A variable so related to another that for each value assumed by one there is a value determined for the other. **b.** A rule of correspondence between two sets such that there is a unique element in one set assigned to each element in the other. *—v.* To have or perform a function; serve. [< L *functus,* pp of *fungī,* to perform.]

func•tion•al (fŭngk'shən-əl) *adj.* **1.** Of or pertaining to a function or functions. **2.** Designed for or adapted to a particular function. **3.** Capable of performing; operative. **4.** Pertaining to a disease having no apparent physiological or structural cause.

func•tion•ar•y (fŭngk'shə-nĕr'ē) *n., pl.* **-ies.** One who holds an office or trust; an official.

fund (fŭnd) *n.* **1.** A source of supply; a stock. **2.** A sum of money set aside for a specific purpose. **3. funds.** Available money; ready cash. **4.** An organization established to administer a fund. *—v.* **1.** To provide funds for. **2.** To convert (a debt), as into a long-term debt, with fixed interest payments. [< L *fundus,* bottom, landed property.]

fun•da•men•tal (fŭn'də-mĕnt'l) *adj.* **1. a.** Elemental; basic. **b.** Central; key. **2.** Generative; primary. **3.** *Phys.* **a.** Of or pertaining to the component of lowest frequency of a periodic wave or quantity. **b.** Of or pertaining to the lowest possible frequency of a vibrating element or system. [< L *fundus,* bottom.] **—fun'da•men'tal** *n.* **—fun'da•men'tal•ly** *adv.*

fun•da•men•tal•ism (fŭn'də-mĕnt'l-ĭz'əm) *n.* A Protestant movement holding the Bible to be the sole historical and prophetic authority. **—fun'da•men'tal•ist** *n.* & *adj.*

fu•ner•al (fyōō'nər-əl) *n.* **1.** The ceremonies

held in connection with the burial or cremation of the dead. **2.** A group accompanying a body to the grave. [< L *fūnus (fūner-),* funeral, death.] —**fu'ner•al** *adj.*

fu•ner•ar•y (fyo͞o'nə-rĕr'ē) *adj.* Of or suitable for a funeral.

fu•ne•re•al (fyo͞o-nîr'ē-əl) *adj.* **1.** Of or suitable for a funeral. **2.** Mournful.

fun•gal (fŭng'gəl) *adj.* Of or pertaining to a fungus; fungous.

fun•gus (fŭng'gəs) *n., pl.* **fungi** (fŭn'jī') or **-guses.** Any of a large group of plants without chlorophyll, including the yeasts, molds, smuts, and mushrooms. [L.] —**fun'goid'** (-goid') *adj.* —**fun'gous** *adj.*

fu•nic•u•lar (fyo͞o-nĭk'yə-lər, fə-) *n.* A cable railway on a steep incline, esp. one with simultaneously ascending and descending cars. [< L *fūnis,* rope.]

fun•nel (fŭn'əl) *n.* **1.** A conical utensil with a small hole or narrow tube at the apex used to channel a substance into a small-mouthed container. **2.** A shaft or flue; smokestack. —*v.* To move or cause to move through or as through a funnel. [< L *infundere,* to pour in.]

fun•ny (fŭn'ē) *adj.* **-nier, -niest. 1.** Causing laughter or amusement; mirthful. **2.** Strange; odd; curious. —*n.* **funnies.** Comic strips.

fur (fûr) *n.* **1.** The thick, soft hair covering the body of various animals, as a fox, beaver, or cat. **2.** The pelt or pelts of such an animal, used for garments or trimming. **3.** A furlike coating. —*adj.* Made of fur. [< OF *forre,* lining.] —**furred** *adj.*

fur•be•low (fûr'bə-lō') *n.* **1.** A ruffle on a garment. **2.** Any small piece of showy ornamentation. [< F *falbala.*]

fur•bish (fûr'bĭsh) *v.* **1.** To brighten by cleaning or rubbing. **2.** To renovate. [< OF *fourbir.*]

fur•cu•la (fûr'kyə-lə) *n., pl.* **-lae** (-lē'). Also **fur•cu•lum** (fûr'kyə-ləm) *pl.* **-la** (-lə). A forked process or bone, esp. the wishbone of a bird. [< L *furca,* FORK.]

fu•ri•ous (fyo͝or'ē-əs) *adj.* Extremely angry; raging; fierce. [< L *furia,* FURY.]

furl (fûrl) *v.* **1.** To roll up and secure (a flag or sail) to a pole, yard, or mast. **2.** To fold. [< OF *ferlier.*] —**furl'er** *n.*

fur•long (fûr'lông', -lŏng') *n.* A unit of length, equal to 1/8 mile or 220 yards. [< OE *furlang,* "a furrow long."]

fur•lough (fûr'lō) *n.* A leave of absence; a vacation, esp. one granted to enlisted personnel of the armed forces. [Du *verlof,* leave, permission.] —**fur'lough** *v.*

fur•nace (fûr'nĭs) *n.* An enclosure in which heat is generated by the combustion of a suitable fuel. [< L *fornāx.*]

fur•nish (fûr'nĭsh) *v.* **1.** To provide furniture for. **2.** To supply; give. [< OF *furnir.*]

fur•nish•ings (fûr'nĭsh-ĭngz) *pl.n.* **1.** The furniture in a home or office. **2.** Wearing apparel and accessories.

fur•ni•ture (fûr'nə-chər) *n.* Movable articles in a room or establishment. [< OF *furnir,* to FURNISH.]

fu•ror (fyo͝or'ôr', -ōr') *n.* **1.** Violent anger; frenzy. **2.** A state of intense excitement. **3.** A public disorder or uproar. [< L *furere,* to rage.]

fur•ri•er (fûr'ē-ər) *n.* One who dresses, designs, sells, or repairs furs.

fur•ring (fûr'ĭng) *n.* Strips of wood or metal applied to a wall to provide a level surface.

fur•row (fûr'ō) *n.* **1.** A trench or similar depression made in the ground by a plow or other implement. **2.** A deep wrinkle in the skin, as on the forehead. [< OE *furh.* See **perk-.**] —**fur'row** *v.* —**fur'row•y** *adj.*

fur•ry (fûr'ē) *adj.* **-rier, -riest. 1.** Consisting of or covered with fur. **2.** Resembling fur.

fur•ther (fûr'*th*ər) *adj.* **1.** More distant in time, degree, or space. **2.** Additional. —*adv.* **1.** To a great extent; more. **2.** In addition; furthermore. **3.** At or to a more distant point in space or time. —*v.* To help the progress of; advance. [< OE *furthor.* See **per**[1].] —**fur'ther•ance** *n.*

fur•ther•more (fûr'*th*ər-môr', -mōr') *adv.* Moreover; in addition.

fur•ther•most (fûr'*th*ər-mōst') *adj.* Most distant or remote.

fur•thest (fûr'*th*ĭst) *adj.* Most distant in time, degree, or space. —*adv.* **1.** To the greatest extent or degree. **2.** At or to the most distant point in space or time.

fur•tive (fûr'tĭv) *adj.* Characterized by stealth; surreptitious; sly. [< L *fūr,* thief.] —**fur'tive•ly** *adv.* —**fur'tive•ness** *n.*

fu•ry (fyo͝or'ē) *n., pl.* **-ries. 1.** Violent anger; rage. **2.** Uncontrolled action; turbulence. [< L *furere,* to rage.]

furze (fûrz) *n.* Gorse. [< OE *fyrs.* See **pûro-.**]

fuse[1] (fyo͞oz) *n.* **1.** A length of readily combustible material that is lighted at one end to detonate an explosive at the other. **2.** Variant of **fuze.** [< L *fūsus,* spindle.]

fuse[2] (fyo͞oz) *v.* **fused, fusing. 1.** To liquefy by heating; melt. **2.** To mix together by or as by melting; blend. —*n.* A device containing an element that protects an electric circuit by melting when overloaded, thereby opening the circuit. [L *fundere* (pp *fūsus*), to pour, melt.] —**fu'si•ble** *adj.* —**fu'si•ble•ness** *n.*

fu•see (fyo͞o-zē') *n.* Also **fu•zee. 1.** A friction match with a large head capable of burning in a wind. **2.** A colored flare used as a railway warning signal. **3.** A fuse for detonating explosives. [< L *fūsus,* FUSE.]

fu•se•lage (fyo͞o'sə-läzh', fyo͞o'zə-) *n.* The central body of an airplane to which the wings and tail assembly are attached. [< F *fuseau,* spindle.]

fu•sil•lade (fyo͞o'sə-lād', -läd', fyo͞o'zə-) *n.* **1.** A simultaneous or rapid discharge of many firearms. **2.** Any rapid outburst. [< F *fusiller,* to shoot.]

fu•sion (fyo͞o'zhən) *n.* **1.** Liquefying or melting together by heat. **2.** A union resulting from fusing. **3.** The merging of different elements into a union. **4.** A nuclear reaction in which nuclei combine to form more massive nuclei with the simultaneous release of energy. [< L *fūsus,* pp of *fundere,* to pour, melt.]

fuss (fŭs) *n.* **1.** Needlessly nervous or useless activity; commotion. **2.** Needless worry. **3.** Objection; protest. **4.** A quarrel. —*v.* **1.** To trouble or worry over trifles. **2.** To be excessively careful or solicitous. [?]

fuss-budg•et (fŭs'bŭj'ĭt) *n.* One who fusses over trifles.

fuss•y (fŭs'ē) *adj.* **-ier, -iest. 1.** Given to fussing; easily upset. **2.** Fastidious; meticulous. **3.** Full of superfluous details or trimmings.

fus•tian (fŭs'chən) *n.* **1.** A coarse, sturdy cloth. **2.** Pretentious or pompous language. [< ML *fustāneus,* cloth.]

fus•ty (fŭs'tē) *adj.* **-tier, -tiest. 1.** Smelling of mildew or decay. **2.** Old-fashioned; antique. [< OF *fuste,* barrel, stale odor of a barrel.]

fut. *Gram.* future.

fu•tile (fyo͞ot'l, fyo͞o'tīl') *adj.* **1.** Having no useful result; ineffectual. **2.** Unproductive; frivolous. [< L *fūtilis,* untrustworthy, useless.] —**fu'tile•ly** *adv.* —**fu•til'i•ty** (-tĭl'ə-tē) *n.*

fu•ture (fyo͞o'chər) *n.* **1.** The indefinite period of time yet to be. **2.** That which will happen in time to come. **3.** The prospective condition of a person or thing. **4.** Prospects of advancement; chances of success. **5.** *Gram.* **a.** A verb tense used to express action in the future. **b.** A verb in this tense. [< L *futūrus.*] —**fu'ture** *adj.*

future shock. The dizzying disorientation suffered by people and brought on by the overwhelmingly rapid changes of modern society.

fu•tu•ri•ty (fyo͞o-t/y/o͞or'ə-tē, fyo͞o-cho͝or'-) *n., pl.* **-ties. 1.** The future. **2.** A future event or possibility.

fuze (fyo͞oz) *n.* Also **fuse.** A mechanical or electrical mechanism used to detonate an explosive. [Var of FUSE[1].]

fu•zee. Variant of **fusee.**

fuzz[1] (fŭz) *n.* A mass of fine, light particles, fibers, or hairs. [Perh < FUZZY.]

fuzz[2] (fŭz) *n. Slang.* The police. [?]

fuzz•y (fŭz'ē) *adj.* **-ier, -iest. 1.** Covered with or resembling fuzz. **2.** Indistinct; blurred; confused. [Perh < LG *fussig,* spongy.]

-fy. *comb. form.* A making or forming into: **nitrify.** [< L *-ficus,* -FIC.]

Gg

g, G (jē) *n.* **1.** The 7th letter of the English alphabet. **2.** The 7th in a series.

g 1. acceleration of gravity. **2.** gram.

G 1. giga-. **2.** gravitation constant. **3.** *Mus.* The 5th tone in the scale of C major. **4.** *Slang.* grand.

G. gulf.

Ga gallium.

Ga. Georgia.

G.A. general assembly.

gab (găb) *v.* **gabbed, gabbing.** To talk easily or excessively about trivial matters; chatter. —*n.*

Chatter; prattle. **—gift of gab.** A talent for speaking easily or well. [Perh < Scot *gab,* mouthful, lump.] **—gab'ber** *n.*

gab•ar•dine (găb'ər-dēn', găb'ər-dēn') *n.* A worsted cotton, wool, or rayon twill, used in making dresses, suits, and coats. [Var of earlier *gaberdine* < OF *gallevardine,* "pilgrim's frock."]

gab•ble (găb'əl) *v.* **-bled, -bling. 1.** To speak rapidly or incoherently. **2.** To make rapid, repeated cackling noises, as a goose or duck. [MDu *gabbelen.*] **—gab'ble** *n.*

gab•by (găb'ē) *adj.* **-bier, -biest.** Tending to talk excessively.

ga•ble (gā'bəl) *n.* A triangular wall section at the ends of a pitched roof. [< OF.] **—ga'bled** *adj.*

Ga•bon (gȧ-bôɴ'). A republic of west-central Africa. Pop. 462,000. Cap. Libreville.

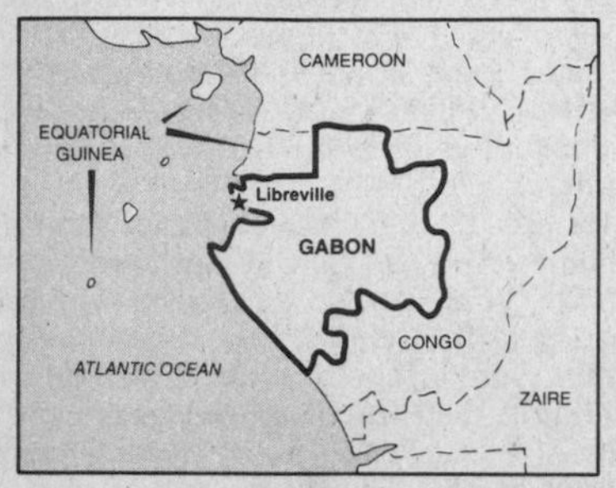

Gabon

Gab•o•ro•ne (găb'ə-rō'nə). The capital of Botswana. Pop. 18,000.

Ga•bri•el (gā'brē-əl). Biblical archangel who acted as the messenger of God.

gad (găd) *v.* **gadded, gadding.** To roam about restlessly or excitedly; rove. [ME *gadden.*] **—gad'der** *n.*

gad•a•bout (găd'ə-bout') *n.* One who gads, esp. one who goes about seeking gossip or excitement.

gad•fly (găd'flī') *n.* **1.** A fly that bites or annoys livestock and other animals. **2.** One that acts as a provocative stimulus. [GAD + FLY.]

gadg•et (găj'ĭt) *n. Informal.* A small specialized mechanical device. [Poss < F *gâchette,* catch (of a lock).] **—gadg'et•ry** *n.*

gad•o•lin•i•um (găd'l-ĭn'ē-əm) *n. Symbol* **Gd** A silvery-white malleable, ductile metallic element, used to improve the high-temperature characteristics of iron, chromium, and related metallic alloys. Atomic number 64, atomic weight 157.25. [< J. *Gadolin* (1760–1852), Finnish chemist.]

Gael (gāl) *n.* A Gaelic-speaking Celt of Scotland, Ireland, or the Isle of Man.

Gael. Gaelic.

Gael•ic (gā'lĭk) *n.* **1.** The Goidelic family of the Celtic languages. **2.** One of the languages of the Gaels. *—adj.* Of or pertaining to the Gaels or their languages.

gaff (găf) *n.* **1.** An iron hook attached to a pole and used to land and maneuver large fish. **2.** A spar used to extend the top edge of a fore-and-aft sail. **3.** Harshness of treatment; abuse. [< OProv *gaf.*]

gaffe (găf) *n.* A clumsy social error; a faux pas. [< F *gaffer,* to hook, hence to blunder.]

gaf•fer (găf'ər) *n.* An old man or rustic. [< GODFATHER.]

gag (găg) *n.* **1.** Something forced into or put over the mouth to prevent the utterance of sound. **2.** Any obstacle to free speech. **3.** A device placed in the mouth to keep it open, as in dentistry. **4. a.** A practical joke. **b.** A comic remark. *—v.* **gagged, gagging. 1.** To prevent from uttering sounds by using a gag. **2.** To repress (free speech). **3.** To keep (the mouth) open by using a gag. **4.** To block off or stop up, as a pipe or valve. **5.** To choke or retch. [ME *gaggen,* to suffocate.]

gage (gāj) *n.* **1.** Something deposited or given as security; a pledge. **2.** Something, as a glove, thrown down as a challenge to fight. **3.** Any test or challenge. [< Frank **wadi.*]

gag•gle (găg'əl) *n.* **1.** A flock of geese. **2.** A gabbling or cackling sound. [ME *gagelen.*]

gai•e•ty (gā'ə-tē) *n.* **1.** A state of being gay or merry. **2.** Festivity; merriment.

gai•ly (gā'lē) *adv.* **1.** In a joyful or cheerful manner. **2.** Colorfully; showily.

gain (gān) *v.* **1.** To become the owner of; acquire; get. **2.** To win. **3.** To earn. **4.** To build up an increase of, as weight. **5.** To arrive at. **6.** To advance or progress. *—n.* Something gained; a profit; advantage; increase. [< OF *gaaignier.*]

gain•ful (gān'fəl) *adj.* Profitable; lucrative. **—gain'ful•ly** *adv.* **—gain'ful•ness** *n.*

gain•say (gān-sā') *v.* **-said** (-sĕd'), **-saying. 1.** To deny. **2.** To contradict. [ME *gaynsayen,* "to say against."] **—gain•say'er** *n.*

gait (gāt) *n.* A way of moving on foot; a manner of walking or running; specifically, such a motion of a horse, as a canter, trot, or walk. [< ON *gata,* path, street.] **—gait'ed** *adj.*

gai•ter (gā'tər) *n.* **1.** A leather or heavy cloth covering for the ankle or legs; a legging; spat. **2.** An ankle-high shoe with elastic sides. **3.** An overshoe with a cloth top. [< OF *guestre.*]

gal (găl) *n. Informal.* A girl.

gal. gallon.

Gal. Galatians (New Testament).

ga•la (gā'lə, găl'ə, gä'lə) *n.* A festive occasion or celebration. *—adj.* Festive. [It.]

Gal•a•had (găl'ə-hăd') *n.* A model of chivalrous virtue. [< Sir *Galahad,* knight of Arthurian legend who achieved the quest of the Holy Grail.]

gal•ax•y (găl'ək-sē) *n., pl.* **-ies. 1. a.** Any of numerous large-scale aggregates of stars, gas, and dust, containing an average of 100 billion solar masses and ranging in diameter from 1,500 to 300,000 light-years. **b. The Galaxy.** The galaxy of which the earth's sun is a part, the **Milky Way. 2.** An assembly of brilliant, beautiful, or distinguished persons or things. [< Gk *galaxias (kuklos),* "milky (circle)."] **—ga•lac'tic** *adj.*

gale (gāl) *n.* **1. a.** A very strong wind. **b.** A wind having a speed between 32 and 63 miles per hour. **2.** A forceful outburst, as of laughter. [Prob short for *gale wind,* "bad wind."]

ga•le•na (gə-lē'nə) *n.* A gray mineral, essentially PbS, the principal ore of lead. [L *galēna,* lead ore.]

Gal•i•le•o (găl'ə-lā'ō). 1564–1642. Italian scientist and astronomer.

gall[1] (gôl) *n.* **1. a.** Liver bile. **b.** The gallbladder. **2.** Rancor; bitterness; resentment. **3.** Something bitter to endure. **4.** Impudence; effrontery. [< OE *gealla.*]

gall[2] (gôl) *n.* **1.** A skin sore caused by friction and abrasion. **2.** Exasperation; irritation. *—v.* **1.** To chafe; abrade. **2.** To exasperate; vex. [< OE *gealla,* sore place.]

gall[3] (gôl) *n.* An abnormal swelling of plant tissue, caused by insects, microorganisms, etc. [< L *galla.*]

gal•lant (găl'ənt) *adj.* **1.** Showy and gay in appearance; dashing. **2.** Stately; majestic; noble. **3.** High-spirited and courageous; daring. **4.** (*also* gə-lănt', -länt'). **a.** Chivalrous; courteous. **b.** Flirtatious. *—n.* (gə-lănt', -länt', găl'ənt). **1.** A fashionable young man. **2. a.** A man courteously attentive to women. **b.** A paramour. [< OF *galant,* gorgeous, showy, brave.] **—gal'lant•ly** *adv.*

gal•lant•ry (găl'ən-trē) *n., pl.* **-ries. 1.** Nobility of spirit or action; courage. **2.** Courtliness;

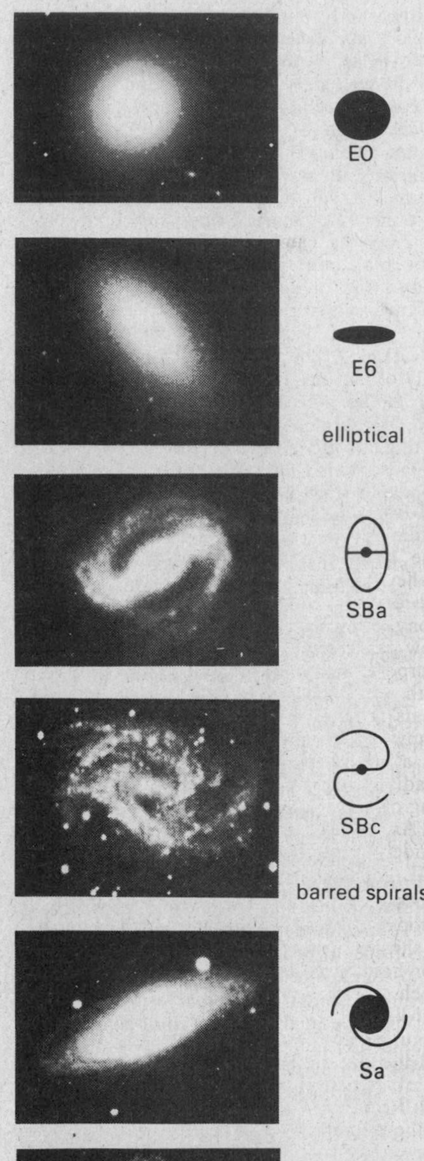

galaxy
Diagrams and letter codes beneath each group identify galactic types

courteousness. **3.** An act or instance of gallantry in speech or behavior.

gall•blad•der (gôl′blăd′ər) *n.* Also **gall bladder.** A small, pear-shaped muscular sac located under the right lobe of the liver, in which bile secreted by the liver is stored.

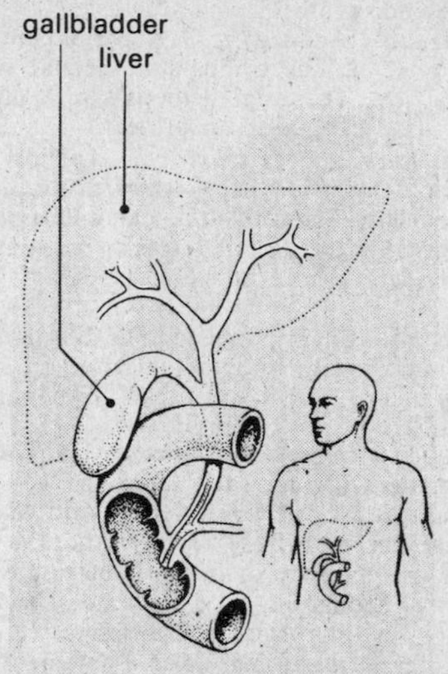

gallbladder

gal•le•on (găl′ē-ən) *n.* A large three-masted sailing ship used by Spain as a warship during the 15th and 16th centuries. [< OF *galie,* galley.]

gal•ler•y (găl′ə-rē) *n., pl.* **-ies.** **1.** A long balcony, often with a roof. **2.** Any enclosed narrow passageway, esp. one used for a specified purpose: *a shooting gallery.* **3.** A porch; verandah. **4. a.** The balcony of a theater. **b.** The seats in such a section. **c.** The audience occupying these seats. **d.** Any similar balcony, as in a church. **5.** Any large audience, as in a stadium or legislative assembly. **6. a.** A building or hall in which artistic work is displayed. **b.** An institution that sells works of art. **7.** An underground tunnel or other passageway. [< ML *galeria.*]

gal•ley (găl′ē) *n.* **1.** A large medieval ship propelled by sails and oars. **2.** The kitchen of a ship or airliner. **3.** *Ptg.* **a.** A long tray used for holding composed type. **b.** A proof from such a tray. [< MGk *galea.*]

Gal•lic (găl′ĭk) *adj.* Of or pertaining to ancient Gaul or modern France; French.

gal•li•mau•fry (găl′ə-mô′frē) *n., pl.* **-fries.** A jumble; hodgepodge. [F *galimafrée.*]

gal•li•um (găl′ē-əm) *n. Symbol* **Ga** A rare metallic element used in semiconductor technology and as a component of various low-melting alloys. Atomic number 31, atomic weight 69.72. [< L *gallus,* cock.]

gal•li•vant (găl′ə-vănt′, găl′ə-vănt′) *v.* **1.** To roam about aimlessly or frivolously; traipse. **2.** To flirt. [Perh var of GALLANT.]

gal•lon (găl′ən) *n.* **1.** A U.S. Customary System unit of volume or capacity, used in liquid measure, equal to 4 quarts or 231 cubic inches. **2.** A British Imperial System unit of volume, used in liquid and dry measure, equal to 277.420 cubic inches. [< ML *gallēta,* jug, measure for wine.]

gal•lop (găl′əp) *n.* A three-beat gait of a horse or other quadruped, faster than a canter and slower than a run. —*v.* **1.** To move or ride at a gallop. **2.** To move or progress rapidly. [< Frank **walahlaupan,* "to run well."]

Gal•lo-Ro•man (găl′ō-rō′mən) *n.* **1.** A native or inhabitant of Roman Gaul. **2.** The Vulgar Latin spoken by the Romanized inhabitants of Gaul. —**Gal′lo-Ro′man** *adj.*

gal•lows (găl′ōz) *n., pl.* **-lowses** or **-lows.** **1.** A frame having two upright beams and a crossbeam from which condemned prisoners are hanged. **2.** Any similar structure used for supporting or suspending. [< OE *gealga,* cross, gallows. See **ghalgh-.**]

gall•stone (gôl′stōn′) *n.* A small, hard concretion, chiefly cholesterol crystals, formed in the gallbladder or in a bile duct.

ga•lore (gə-lôr′, -lōr′) *adj.* In great numbers; in abundance: *opportunites galore.* [Ir Gael *go leór.*]

ga•losh•es (gə-lŏsh′ĭz) *pl.n.* Waterproof overshoes. [Prob < L *gallica (solea),* "Gaulish (sandal)."]

galv. galvanized.

gal•van•ic (găl-văn′ĭk) *adj.* **1.** Of direct-current electricity, esp. when produced chemically. **2.** Having the effect of or produced as if by an electric shock. [F *galvanique.*] —**gal•van′i•cal•ly** *adv.* —**gal′va•nism′** *n.*

gal•va•nize (găl′və-nīz′) *v.* **-nized, -nizing.** **1.** To stimulate or shock with an electric current. **2.** To arouse to awareness or action; spur; startle. **3.** To coat (iron or steel) with rust-resistant zinc. —**gal′va•ni•za′tion** *n.* —**gal′va•niz′er** *n.*

gal•va•nom•e•ter (găl′və-nŏm′ə-tər) *n.* A device for detecting or measuring small electric currents by means of mechanical effects produced by the current to be measured.

Ga•ma (găm′ə), **Vasco da.** 1469?–1524. Portuguese navigator.

Gam•bi•a (găm′bē-ə). A republic of W Africa. Pop. 357,000. Cap. Banjul.

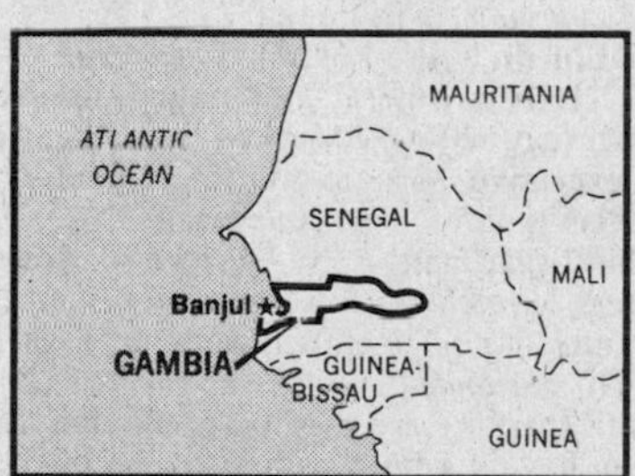

Gambia

gam•bit (găm′bĭt) *n.* **1.** *Chess.* An opening move in which one or more pieces are sacrificed in order to gain a favorable position. **2.** An opening remark or stratagem. [< It *gambetto,* "a tripping up."]

gam•ble (găm′bəl) *v.* **-bled, -bling.** **1. a.** To wager; bet money on the outcome of a game, contest, or other event. **b.** To play a game of chance. **2.** To speculate. **3.** To expose to hazard; risk. —*n.* **1.** A bet, wager, or other gambling venture. **2.** A risk. [< OE *gamen,* amusement, GAME.] —**gam′bler** *n.*

gam•bol (găm′bəl) *v.* **-boled** or **-bolled, -boling** or **-bolling.** To leap about playfully; frolic; skip. [< It *gamba,* leg.] —**gam′bol** *n.*

game¹ (gām) *n.* **1.** A way of amusing oneself; a pastime; diversion. **2.** A sport or other competitive activity. **3.** A single instance of such an activity. **4.** The total number of points required to win a game. **5.** The equipment needed for playing certain games. **6.** A particular style of playing a game. **7.** A scheme; plan. **8.** Animals, birds, or fish hunted for food or sport. **9.** An object of ridicule or scorn. **10.** A vocation or business, esp. a competitive one. —*adj.* **gamer, gamest.** **1.** Plucky and unyielding; resolute. **2.** Ready and willing. [< OE *gamen,* amusement, sport < Gmc **gam-,* to enjoy.]

game² (gām) *adj.* Lame. [Perh < F *gambi,* crooked.]

game•cock (gām′kŏk′) *n.* A rooster trained for cockfighting.

game•some (gām′səm) *adj.* Frolicsome; playful; merry. —**game′some•ly** *adv.*

game•ster (gām′stər) *n.* A habitual gambler.

gam•ete (găm′ēt, gə-mēt′) *n.* A germ cell, esp. a mature sperm or egg, capable of participating in fertilization. [< Gk *gametē,* wife, and *gametēs,* husband.]

game theory. The mathematical analysis of abstract models of strategic competition.

gam•in (găm′ĭn) *n.* A boy who roams the streets; street urchin; waif. [F.]

ga•mine (gă-mēn′) *n.* A girl or woman having elfin appeal. [< GAMIN.]

gam•ma (găm′ə) *n.* **1.** The 3rd letter of the Greek alphabet, representing *g(n).* **2.** A **gamma ray.**

gamma globulin. Any of several globulin fractions of blood serum associated with immune bodies and used to treat measles, poliomyelitis, infectious hepatitis, and other infectious diseases.

gamma ray. Any electromagnetic radiation with energy greater than several hundred thousand electron volts.

gam•mon (găm′ən) *n.* **1.** A cured or smoked ham. **2.** The lower part of a side of bacon. [ONF *gambon.*]

gam•ut (găm′ət) *n.* The complete range of anything; extent. [< ML *gamma ut,* notes named after syllables in a Latin hymn.]

gam•y (gā′mē) *adj.* **-ier, -iest.** **1.** Having the flavor or odor of game, esp. game that has been hung too long. **2.** Plucky; hardy.

-gamy. *comb. form.* Marriage or sexual union: *allogamy.* [< Gk *gamos,* marriage.]

gan•der (găn′dər) *n.* **1.** A male goose. **2.** *Slang.* A quick look; glance. [< OE *gandra, ganra.* See **ghans-.**]

Gan•dhi (gän′dē, găn′-), **Mohandas Karamchand.** Called "Mahatma." 1869–1948. Hindu nationalist and spiritual leader.

Mahatma Gandhi

gang (găng) *n.* **1.** A group of people who associate or work together. **2.** A set, esp. of matched tools. —*v.* To band together as a group or gang. —**gang up (on).** To harass or attack as a group. [< OE *gang,* a going. See **ghengh-.**]

Gan·ges (găn′jēz′). A river in N India and Bangladesh.

gan·gling (găng′glĭng) *adj.* Also **gang·ly** (-glē), **-lier, -liest.** Tall, thin, and ungraceful; lanky. [< dial *gang,* to go, straggle.]

gan·gli·on (găng′glē-ən) *n., pl.* **-glia** (-glē-ə) or **-ons.** A group of nerve cells, such as one located outside the brain or spinal cord, in vertebrates. [Gk, cystlike tumor, nerve bundle, ganglion.] —**gan′gli·on′ic** (-ŏn′ĭk) *adj.*

gang·plank (găng′plăngk′) *n.* A removable bridgelike structure between a ship and a pier.

gan·grene (găng′grēn′, găng-grēn′) *n.* Death and decay of bodily tissue caused by failure of blood supply, injury, or disease. [< Gk *gangraina.*] —**gan′gre·nous** (-grə-nəs) *adj.*

gang·ster (găng′stər) *n.* A member of an organized group of criminals; racketeer.

Gang·tok (gŭng′tŏk). The capital of Sikkim. Pop. 7,000.

gang·way (găng′wā′) *n.* **1.** A passageway, as through a crowd or an obstructed area. **2.** A gangplank.

gan·net (găn′ĭt) *n.* A large sea bird of northern coastal regions with white plumage and black wing tips. [< OE *ganot.* See **ghans-.**]

gan·try (găn′trē) *n., pl.* **-tries.** A frame or support, esp. a large vertical structure used in assembling or servicing rockets. [< L *canthērius,* rafter.]

GAO General Accounting Office.

gaol. *Chiefly Brit.* Variant of **jail.**

gap (găp) *n.* **1.** An opening, as in a partition or wall; fissure; cleft. **2.** A break or pass through mountains. **3.** An interval; hiatus: *a gap in his report.* **4.** A conspicuous difference; disparity. [< ON, chasm.]

gape (gāp, găp) *v.* **gaped, gaping. 1.** To open the mouth wide; yawn. **2.** To stare wonderingly, as with the mouth open. **3.** To open widely. —*n.* **1.** An act or instance of gaping. **2.** A large opening. [< ON *gapa,* to open the mouth.] —**gap′er** *n.*

gap·ing (gā′pĭng) *adj.* Deep and wide open: *a gaping wound.* —**gap′ing·ly** *adv.*

gar (gär) *n.* Also **gar·fish** (gär′fĭsh′). A fish having an elongated body covered with bony plates and a long snout. [< OE *gār,* spear.]

GAR, G.A.R. Grand Army of the Republic.

ga·rage (gə-räzh′, -räj′) *n.* **1.** A structure for housing cars. **2.** A commercial establishment where cars are repaired and serviced. [< OF *garer,* to protect, guard.] —**ga·rage′** *v.* **(-raged, -raging).**

garb (gärb) *n.* Clothing, esp. the distinctive attire of one's occupation or station. —*v.* To clothe; dress; array. [< It *garbo,* grace, elegance of dress.]

gar·bage (gär′bĭj) *n.* **1.** Food wastes, as from a kitchen. **2.** Refuse; rubbish. [ME, offal of an animal.]

gar·ble (gär′bəl) *v.* **-bled, -bling.** To distort or scramble (an account or message) so as to be unintelligible; jumble. [< Ar *gharbala,* to sift.] —**gar′bler** *n.*

gar·den (gärd′n) *n.* **1.** A plot of land used for growing flowers, vegetables, or fruit. **2.** A planted tract used for public enjoyment. **3.** A yard; lawn. **4.** A fertile, well-cultivated region. —*adj.* Of, pertaining to, or found in a garden. —*v.* To work in a garden. [< VL **(hortus) gardīnus,* "enclosed (garden)."]

gar·den·er (gärd′nər, gärd′n-ər) *n.* A person who works in or tends a garden.

gar·de·ni·a (gär-dēn′yə, -dē′nē-ə) *n.* **1.** A shrub with glossy, evergreen leaves and large, fragrant white flowers. **2.** The flower of this shrub. [< Dr. A. *Garden* (1731–1790), Scottish naturalist.]

Gar·field (gär′fēld′), **James Abram.** 1831–1881. 20th President of the U.S. (1881).

James A. Garfield

gar·gan·tu·an (gär-găn′cho͞o-ən) *adj.* Of immense size or volume. [< the hero of Rabelais' *Gargantua and Pantagruel.*]

gar·gle (gär′gəl) *v.* **-gled, -gling. 1.** To exhale through a soothing or medicated liquid held in the back of the mouth, with the head tilted back. **2.** To produce the sound of gargling when speaking or singing. —*n.* A medicated solution for gargling. [< OF *gargouille,* throat, gargoyle.]

gar·goyle (gär′goil′) *n.* A roof spout carved to represent a grotesque human or animal figure. [< L *gurguliō,* windpipe.]

Gar·i·bal·di (găr′ə-bôl′dē), **Giuseppe.** 1807–1882. Italian general and nationalist leader.

gar·ish (gâr′ĭsh) *adj.* Marked by strident color or excessive ornamentation; gaudy. [?] —**gar′ish·ly** *adv.* —**gar′ish·ness** *n.*

gar·land (gär′lənd) *n.* **1.** A crown or wreath of flowers, leaves, etc. **2.** Something resembling a garland. —*v.* To embellish with a garland. [< OF *garlande.*]

gar·lic (gär′lĭk) *n.* **1.** A plant related to the onion, having a bulb with a strong, distinctive odor and flavor. **2.** The bulb of this plant used as a seasoning. [< OE *gārlēac,* "spear leek."]

gar·lick·y (gär′lĭ-kē) *adj.* Containing, tasting of, or redolent of garlic, esp. too much garlic: *a garlicky dish.*

gar·ment (gär′mənt) *n.* An article of clothing, esp. of outer clothing. [< OF *garnement,* "equipment."]

gar·ner (gär′nər) *v.* To amass; acquire. [< L *grānārium,* granary.]

gar·net (gär′nĭt) *n.* **1.** Any of several common, widespread silicate minerals, colored red, brown, black, green, yellow, or white, and used as gemstones and abrasives. **2.** Dark to very dark red. [< OF *grenat,* garnet, pomegranate-colored.]

gar·nish (gär′nĭsh) *v.* To embellish; adorn. —*n.* An embellishment, usually savory, for a dish of food or a drink. [< OF *guarnir,* to adorn.]

gar·nish·ee (gär′nĭ-shē′) *v.* **-eed, -eeing.** *Law.* To attach (a debtor's pay) by garnishment.

gar·nish·ment (gär′nĭsh-mənt) *n. Law.* A proceeding whereby money or property due or belonging to a debtor but in the possession of another is applied to the payment of the debt to the plaintiff.

gar·ret (găr′ĭt) *n.* An attic; loft. [< OF *guarir,* to defend, protect.]

gar·ri·son (găr′ĭ-sən) *n.* **1.** A permanent military post. **2.** The troops stationed at such a post. —*v.* To assign (troops) to a military post. [< OF *guarir,* to protect.]

gar·ru·lous (găr′/y/ə-ləs) *adj.* Talkative; loquacious; wordy. [< L *garrīre,* to chatter.] —**gar·ru′li·ty** (gə-ro͞o′lə-tē), **gar′ru·lous·ness** *n.*

gar·ter (gär′tər) *n.* An elasticized band or suspender to hold up hose. [< Gaul **garr-,* leg.]

garter snake. A nonvenomous North American snake with longitudinal stripes.

Gar·y (gâr′ē). A city of NW Indiana. Pop. 178,000.

gas (găs) *n., pl.* **gases** or **gasses. 1. a.** The state of matter distinguished from the solid and liquid states by very low density and viscosity, the ability to diffuse readily, and the spontaneous tendency to become distributed uniformly throughout any container. **b.** A substance in this state. **2.** Gasoline. **3.** *Slang.* Something providing great excitement. —*v.* **gassed, gassing. 1.** To supply with gas or gasoline. **2.** To treat with gas. **3.** To poison with gas. [Du.]

gas chamber. A sealed enclosure in which prisoners are executed by a poisonous gas.

gas·e·ous (găs′ē-əs, -yəs, găsh′əs) *adj.* Of, pertaining to, or existing as a gas.

gash (găsh) *n.* A long, deep cut or wound; a slash. [Prob < Gk *kharassein,* to carve, cut.] —**gash** *v.*

gas·ket (găs′kĭt) *n.* Any of a wide variety of seals or packings used between matched machine parts or around pipe joints to prevent the escape of a gas or fluid. [F *garcette,* "little girl," rope.]

gas·light (găs′līt′) *n.* **1.** Light produced by burning illuminating gas. **2.** A gas-burning lamp.

gas mask. A respirator covering the face and having a chemical air filter to protect against poisonous gases.

gas·o·line (găs′ə-lēn′, găs′ə-lēn′) *n.* A volatile mixture of flammable liquid hydrocarbons derived chiefly from crude petroleum and used principally as a fuel for internal-combustion engines, and as a solvent, illuminant, and thinner.

gasp (găsp, gäsp) *v.* **1.** To draw in the breath sharply, as from shock. **2.** To breathe convulsively or laboriously. [< ON *geispa.*] —**gasp** *n.*

gas·sy (găs′ē) *adj.* **-sier, -siest.** Containing, full of, or resembling gas.

gas·tric (găs′trĭk) *adj.* Pertaining to the stomach. [< Gk *gastēr,* belly, womb.]

gastric juice. The colorless, watery, acidic digestive fluid secreted by the stomach glands.

gas·tri·tis (găs-trī′tĭs) *n.* Chronic or acute inflammation of the stomach.

gastro–. *comb. form.* The stomach.

gas·tro·en·ter·i·tis (găs′trō-ĕn′tə-rī′tĭs) *n.* Inflammation of the mucous membrane of the stomach and intestine.

gas·tro·in·tes·ti·nal (găs′trō-ĭn-tĕs′tə-nəl) *adj.* Of or pertaining to the stomach and intestines.

gas·tron·o·my (găs-trŏn′ə-mē) *n.* **1.** The art of good eating. **2.** Cooking, as of a particular region. —**gas'tro·nom'ic** (găs'trə-nŏm'ĭk) *adj.* —**gas'tro·nom'i·cal·ly** *adv.*

gas·tro·pod (găs'trə-pŏd') *n.* Also *rare* **gas·ter·o·pod** (-tər-ə-pŏd'). A snail or related mollusk having a single, usually coiled shell and a broad, muscular organ of locomotion. [< NL *Gastropoda,* "belly-footed creatures."]

gas·works (găs'wûrks') *n. (takes sing. v.).* A factory where gas for heating and lighting is produced.

gat (găt). *Archaic. p.t.* of **get.**

gate (gāt) *n.* **1.** A structure, usually hinged, that serves as a door in a wall or fence. **2.** The total admission receipts or attendance at a public spectacle. **3.** A circuit extensively used in computers that has an output dependent on some function of its input. [< OE *geat* < Gmc **gatam.*]

gate·crash·er (gāt'krăsh'ər) *n. Slang.* One who gains admittance without being invited or enters without paying admission.

gate·keep·er (gāt'kē'pər) *n.* A person in charge of a gate.

gate·way (gāt'wā') *n.* **1.** A structure, as an arch, framing an entrance that may be closed by a gate. **2.** Something that serves as an entrance or means of access.

gath·er (găth'ər) *v.* **1.** To bring or come together. **2.** To accumulate gradually; collect. **3.** To harvest or pick. **4.** To increase by degrees: *gather velocity.* **5.** To pull (cloth) along a thread to create small folds. **6.** To draw (a garment) about or closer to something. **7.** To infer: *I gather he's ready.* —*n.* **1.** An act or instance of gathering. **2.** Often **gathers.** A small tuck or pucker in cloth. [< OE *gaderian,* to come together. See **ghedh-.**] —**gath'er·er** *n.* —**gath'er·ing** *n.*

gauche (gōsh) *adj.* Lacking social grace; awkward. [F, "left," "askew."]

gau·che·rie (gō'shə-rē') *n.* An awkward or graceless action.

Gau·cho (gou'chō) *n., pl.* **-chos.** A cowboy of the South American pampas.

gaud·y (gô'dē) *adj.* **-ier, -iest.** Characterized by tasteless or showy colors. [< L *gaudēre,* to delight in.] —**gaud'i·ly** *adv.*

gauge (gāj) *n.* **1. a.** A standard or scale of measurement. **b.** A standard dimension, quantity, or capacity. **2.** An instrument for measuring or testing. **3.** A means of evaluating: *a gauge of character.* —*v.* **gauged, gauging. 1.** To measure precisely. **2.** To determine the capacity or contents of. **3.** To evaluate: *gauge ability.* [< Frank **galga,* cross, perch, windlass.] —**gaug'er** *n.*

Gau·guin (gō-găN'), **Paul.** 1848–1903. French painter.

Gaul[1] (gôl). A region of the Roman Empire in W Europe.

Gaul[2] (gôl) *n.* **1.** A Celt of ancient Gaul. **2.** A Frenchman.

Gaul·ish (gô'lĭsh) *n.* The Celtic language of ancient Gaul.

gaunt (gônt) *adj.* **1.** Very thin and bony; emaciated. **2.** Bleak; desolate. [Prob < Scand.] —**gaunt'ly** *adv.* —**gaunt'ness** *n.*

gaunt·let[1] (gônt'lĭt, gänt'-) *n.* **1.** A protective glove. **2.** A challenge: *fling down the gauntlet.* [< Frank **want,* mitten.]

gaunt·let[2] (gônt'lĭt, gänt'-) *n.* **1.** A double line of men armed with clubs with which to beat a person forced to run between them. **2.** An ordeal in which one comes under fire from several quarters: *run the gauntlet.* [< OSwed *gatulop,* "passageway."]

gauze (gôz) *n.* A thin, transparent fabric with a loose open weave. [< OF *gaze.*] —**gauz'i·ly** *adv.* —**gauz'i·ness** *n.* —**gauz'y** *adj.*

gave (gāv). *p.t.* of **give.**

gav·el (găv'əl) *n.* The mallet used by a presiding officer or auctioneer to signal for attention or order. [?]

gawk (gôk) *n.* An awkward, stupid person. —*v.* To stare stupidly. —**gawk'y** *adj.*

gay (gā) *adj.* **1.** Light-hearted; lively. **2.** Given to social pleasures. **3.** *Slang.* Homosexual. —*n.* A homosexual. [<OF *gai.*]

gaze (gāz) *v.* **gazed, gazing.** To look with fixed attention; stare. [Prob < Scand.] —**gaze** *n.*

ga·zelle (gə-zĕl') *n.* Any of various slender, swift-running horned mammals of Africa and Asia. [Prob < Ar *ghazāl.*]

ga·zette (gə-zĕt') *n.* **1.** A newspaper. **2.** An official journal. [< It *gazetta.*]

gaz·et·teer (găz'ə-tîr') *n.* A geographic dictionary or index.

G.B. Great Britain.

G clef. The **treble clef.**

Gd gadolinium.

gds. goods.

Ge germanium.

gear (gîr) *n.* **1. a.** A toothed wheel or other machine element that meshes with another toothed element to transmit motion or change speed or direction. **b.** A transmission configuration for a specific ratio of engine to axle torque in a motor vehicle. **2.** Equipment, as tools or clothing, required for a particular activity. —*v.* **1. a.** To provide with or connect by gears. **b.** To put into gear. **2.** To adjust or adapt. [< ON *gervi.*]

gear·box (gîr'bŏks') *n.* An automotive transmission.

gear·ing (gîr'ĭng) *n.* A system of gears and associated machine elements.

gear·shift (gîr'shĭft') *n.* A mechanism for changing from one gear to another in a transmission.

gee (jē) *interj.* Expressive of mild surprise. [Euphemistic shortening of JESUS.]

geese. *pl.* of **goose.**

gee·zer (gē'zər) *n. Slang.* An eccentric old man.

Gei·ger counter (gī'gər). An electronic instrument used to detect, measure, and record nuclear emanations, cosmic rays, and artificially produced subatomic particles. [< H. *Geiger* (1882–1945), German physicist.]

gei·sha (gā'shə, gē'-) *n., pl.* **-sha** or **-shas.** A Japanese girl trained to provide entertainment, as singing or dancing, for men. [Jap, "artist."]

gel (jĕl) *n.* A colloid in which the disperse phase has combined with the continuous phase to produce a semisolid such as a jelly. [Short for GELATIN.]

gel·a·tin (jĕl'ə-tən) *n.* Also **gel·a·tine.** A transparent, brittle protein formed by boiling the specially prepared skin, bones, and connective tissue of animals, and used in foods, drugs, and photographic film. [< L *gelāre,* to freeze, congeal.] —**ge·lat'i·nous** (jə-lăt'n-əs) *adj.*

geld (gĕld) *v.* To castrate (a horse or other animal). [< ON *gelda.*]

geld·ing (gĕl'dĭng) *n.* A castrated animal, esp. a horse.

gel·id (jĕl'ĭd) *adj.* Very cold; icy. [< L *gelū,* cold, frost.] —**gel'id·ly** *adv.*

gem (jĕm) *n.* **1.** A precious or semiprecious stone, esp. one that has been cut and polished. **2.** Something that is valued highly. [< L *gemma,* bud, precious stone.]

Gem·i·ni (jĕm'ə-nī', -nē') *n.* **1.** A constellation in the N Hemisphere. **2.** The 3rd sign of the zodiac. [< L *geminus,* twin.]

gem·stone (jĕm'stōn') *n.* A precious or semiprecious stone that can be used as a jewel when cut and polished.

–gen, –gene. *comb. form.* **1.** That which produces: **oxygen. 2.** Something produced: **antigen.** [< Gk *-genēs,* born.]

gen. **1.** gender. **2.** genitive. **3.** genus.

Gen. **1.** general (military rank). **2.** Genesis (Old Testament).

gen·darme (zhän'därm') *n.* A member of the French national police. [< F *gens d'armes,* "men of arms."]

gen·der (jĕn'dər) *n. Gram.* Any of two or more categories, as masculine, feminine, and neuter, into which words are divided and that determine agreement with or selection of modifiers or grammatical forms. [< L *genus (gener-),* race, kind.]

gene (jēn) *n.* A functional hereditary unit that occupies a fixed location on a chromosome, has a specific influence on phenotype, and is capable of mutation to various allelic forms. [< -GEN.]

–gene. Variant of **-gen.**

ge·ne·al·o·gy (jē'nē-ăl'ə-jē, -ŏl'ə-jē, jĕn'ē-) *n., pl.* **-gies. 1.** A record or table of ancestry. **2.** The study of ancestry. [< Gk *genea,* race, generation + -LOGY.] —**ge'ne·a·log'i·cal** (-ə-lŏj'ĭ-kəl) *adj.* —**ge'ne·al'o·gist** *n.*

gen·e·ra. *pl.* of **genus.**

gen·er·al (jĕn'ər-əl) *adj.* **1.** Of, pertaining to, or applicable to the whole or every member of a group. **2.** Widespread; prevalent. **3.** Being usually the case; true in most instances. **4.** Diversified: *general studies.* **5.** Lacking detail or precision: *a general grasp of a subject.* **6.** Chief within a particular sphere: *the general manager.* —*n.* **1.** An officer of the second-highest rank in the U.S. Army or Air Force and the highest rank in the Marine Corps. **2.** A military officer, as in England or Canada, holding a rank just below field marshal. —**in general.** For the most part. [< L *generālis,* relating to all.] —**gen'er·al·ly** *adv.*

gen·er·al·is·si·mo (jĕn'ər-ə-lĭs'ə-mō') *n., pl.* **-mos.** The commander in chief of all the armed forces in certain countries.

gen·er·al·i·ty (jĕn'ə-răl'ə-tē) *n., pl.* **-ties. 1.** The condition or quality of being general. **2.** An observation or principle having general application. **3.** An imprecise or vague statement or idea.

gen·er·al·ize (jĕn'ər-ə-līz') *v.* **-ized, -izing. 1.** To render general rather than specific. **2.** To draw inferences or a general conclusion from. **3.** To speak or think in generalities. —**gen'er·al·i·za'tion** *n.*

General of the Air Force. An officer having the highest rank in the U.S. Air Force.

General of the Army. An officer having the highest rank in the U.S. Army.

general relativity. The geometric theory of gravitation developed by Albert Einstein, incorporating and extending the special theory of relativity to accelerated frames of reference and introducing the principle that gravitational and inertial forces are equivalent.

gen·er·ate (jĕn'ə-rāt') *v.* **-ated, -ating.** To bring into existence; produce. [L *generāre.*] —**gen'er·a'tive** (-ə-rā'tĭv, -ə-rə-tĭv) *adj.*

gen·er·a·tion (jĕn'ə-rā'shən) *n.* **1.** The act or process of generating. **2.** Offspring having common parentage and constituting a stage of descent. **3.** A group of contemporaneous individuals. **4.** The average time interval between the birth of parents and the birth of their offspring.

gen•er•a•tor (jĕn'ə-rā'tər) *n.* One that generates, esp. a machine that converts mechanical energy into electrical energy.

ge•ner•ic (jĭ-nĕr'ĭk) *adj.* **1.** Of or descriptive of an entire group or class. **2.** *Biol.* Of or relating to a genus. [< L *genus (gener-),* race, kind.] **—ge•ner'i•cal•ly** *adv.*

gen•er•ous (jĕn'ər-əs) *adj.* **1.** Liberal in giving; munificent. **2.** Abundant; ample. **3.** Lacking pettiness; magnanimous. [< L *generōsus,* of noble birth, magnanimous.] **—gen'er•os'i•ty** (-ə-rŏs'ə-tē) *n.* **—gen'er•ous•ly** *adv.*

gen•e•sis (jĕn'ə-sĭs) *n., pl.* **-ses** (-sēz'). The coming into being of anything; origin. [< Gk, generation, origin.]

-genesis. *comb. form.* Generation: **parthenogenesis.**

ge•net•i•cist (jə-nĕt'ə-sĭst) *n.* One who specializes in genetics.

ge•net•ics (jə-nĕt'ĭks) *n. (takes sing. v.).* The biology of heredity, esp. the study of hereditary transmission and variation. **—ge•net'ic** *adj.* **—ge•net'i•cal•ly** *adv.*

Ge•ne•va (jə-nē'və). A city of SW Switzerland. Pop. 174,000.

Gen•ghis Khan (jĕn'gĭz kän', jĕng'gĭs, gĕng'gĭs). 1162?–1227. Founder of the Mongol empire.

gen•ial (jēn'yəl, jē'nē-əl) *adj.* **1.** Cheerful and friendly; kindly. **2.** Giving warmth; mild: *a genial climate.* [L *geniālis,* of generation or birth, nuptial, festive.] **—ge'ni•al'i•ty** (jē'nē-ăl'ə-tē) *n.* **—gen'ial•ly** *adv.*

ge•nie (jē'nē) *n.* A supernatural creature who does one's bidding. [< L *genius,* GENIUS.]

gen•i•tal (jĕn'ə-təl) *adj.* **1.** Of or relating to biological reproduction. **2.** Of or pertaining to the genitals.

gen•i•ta•li•a (jĕn'ə-tā'lē-ə, -tāl'yə) *pl.n.* The reproductive organs, esp. the external sex organs. [L *genitālia (membra),* genital (members).]

gen•i•tals (jĕn'ə-təlz) *pl.n.* Genitalia.

gen•i•tive (jĕn'ə-tĭv) *Gram. adj.* Of or pertaining to a case that expresses possession or source. *—n.* The genitive case. [< L *(casus) genitīvus,* "case of origin."]

gen•i•to•u•ri•nar•y (jĕn'ə-tō-yŏŏr'ə-nĕr'ē) *adj.* Of or pertaining to the genital and urinary organs or their functions.

gen•ius (jēn'yəs) *n., pl.* **-iuses. 1. a.** Exceptional intellectual and creative power. **b.** One who possesses such power. **2.** The prevailing spirit or character, as of a place, time, or group. [L, deity of generation and birth.]

genl. general.

Gen•o•a (jĕn'ō-ə). A city of NW Italy. Pop. 784,000.

gen•o•cide (jĕn'ə-sīd') *n.* The systematic annihilation of a racial, political, or cultural group. [Gk *genos,* race + -CIDE.] **—gen'o•ci'dal** (-sīd'l) *adj.*

gen•o•type (jĕn'ə-tīp') *n.* **1.** The genetic constitution of an organism, esp. as distinguished from its physical appearance. **2.** A group or class of organisms having the same genetic constitution. **—gen'o•typ'ic** (-tĭp'ĭk) *adj.*

-genous. *comb. form.* Generating or generated by: **androgenous.** [< -GEN.]

gen•re (zhän'rə) *n.* **1.** Type; class. **2.** A style of painting in which scenes and subjects of everyday life are depicted. **3.** A distinctive class or category of literary composition. [< L *genus (gener-),* race, kind.]

gent (jĕnt) *n. Informal.* A man; fellow. [< GENTLEMAN.]

gen•teel (jĕn-tēl') *adj.* **1.** Refined in manner; polite. **2.** Fashionable; elegant. **3.** Striving to convey an appearance of respectability. **4.** Marked by affected and somewhat prudish refinement. [OF *gentil,* gentle.]

gen•tian (jĕn'shən) *n.* Any of various plants characteristically having showy blue flowers. [< L *gentiāna.*]

gentian violet. A purple dye used chiefly as a biological stain and bactericide.

Gen•tile (jĕn'tīl) *n.* A Christian as distinguished from a Jew. [< LL *gentīlis,* pagan.]

gen•til•i•ty (jĕn-tĭl'ə-tē) *n.* **1.** The condition of being genteel. **2.** Gentle birth.

gen•tle (jĕnt'l) *adj.* **-tler, -tlest. 1.** Considerate or kindly. **2.** Not harsh, severe, or violent; soft.

GEOLOGIC TIME SCALE

ERA	PERIOD		EPOCH	YEARS BEFORE THE PRESENT
Cenozoic	Quarternary		Holocene (Recent)	11,000
			Pleistocene (Glacial)	500,000 to 2,000,000
	Tertiary		Pliocene	13,000,000
			Miocene	25,000,000
			Oligocene	36,000,000
			Eocene	58,000,000
			Paleocene	63,000,000
Mesozoic	Cretaceous			135,000,000
	Jurassic			180,000,000
	Triassic			230,000,000
Paleozoic	Permian			280,000,000
	Carboniferous	Pennsylvanian (Upper Carboniferous)		310,000,000
		Mississippian (Lower Carboniferous)		345,000,000
	Devonian			405,000,000
	Silurian			425,000,000
	Ordovician			500,000,000
	Cambrian			600,000,000
Precambrian				

3. Easily managed or handled: *a gentle horse.* 4. Not steep: *a gentle incline.* 5. Of good family; well-born. —*v.* **-tled, -tling.** To make gentle. [< L *gentīlis,* of the same clan, of noble birth.] —**gen'tle•ness** *n.*

gen•tle•man (jĕnt'l-mən) *n.* 1. A polite or considerate man. 2. **gentlemen.** A form of address for a group of men. [GENTLE + MAN.] —**gen'tle•man•ly** *adj.*

gen•try (jĕn'trē) *n.* 1. People of good birth and superior social position. 2. The upper middle classes in England. [< OF *gentil,* gentle.]

gen•u•flect (jĕn'yə-flĕkt') *v.* To bend the knee in a kneeling or half-kneeling position, as in worship. [LL *genuflectere.*] —**gen'u•flec'tion** *n.*

gen•u•ine (jĕn'yo͞o-ĭn) *adj.* 1. Not artificial; real. 2. Sincere; frank. [L *genuīnus.*]

ge•nus (jē'nəs) *n., pl.* **genera** (jĕn'ə-rə). 1. A category of related organisms usually including several species. 2. Any class or kind with common attributes. [L, birth, race, kind.]

geo–. *comb. form.* The earth. [< Gk *gē,* earth.]

ge•o•cen•tric (jē'ō-sĕn'trĭk) *adj.* 1. Of or from the center of the earth. 2. Having the earth as a center. —**ge'o•cen'tri•cal•ly** *adv.*

ge•o•des•ic dome (jē'ə-dĕs'ĭk). A domed or vaulted structure of lightweight straight elements that form interlocking polygons.

geog. geographer; geographic; geography.

ge•og•ra•phy (jē-ŏg'rə-fē) *n., pl.* **-phies.** 1. The study of the earth and its features and of the distribution on the earth of life, including human life and the effects of human activity. 2. The geographic characteristics of any area. —**ge•og'ra•pher** *n.* —**ge'o•graph'ic** (-ə-grăf'ĭk), **ge'o•graph'i•cal** *adj.* —**ge'o•graph'i•cal•ly** *adv.*

geol. geologic; geologist; geology.

ge•ol•o•gy (jē-ŏl'ə-jē) *n., pl.* **-gies.** 1. The scientific study of the origin, history, and structure of the earth. 2. The structure of a specific region of the earth's surface. —**ge'o•log'ic** (jē'ə-lŏj'ĭk), **ge'o•log'i•cal** *adj.* —**ge'o•log'i•cal•ly** *adv.* —**ge•ol'o•gist** *n.*

geom. geometric; geometry.

geometric progression. A sequence of terms, such as 1, 3, 9, 27, 81, each of which is a constant multiple of the immediately preceding term.

ge•om•e•try (jē-ŏm'ə-trē) *n., pl.* **-tries.** 1. The mathematics of the properties, measurement, and relationships of points, lines, angles, surfaces, and solids. 2. Configuration; arrangement. 3. A surface shape. [< Gk *geōmetrein,* to measure land.] —**ge'o•met'ric** (jē'ə-mĕt'rĭk) *adj.* —**ge'o•met'ri•cal•ly** *adv.* —**ge•om'e•tri'cian** (jē-ŏm'ə-trĭsh'ən, jē'ə-mə-), **ge•om'e•ter** *n.*

George III (jôrj). King of Great Britain and Ireland (1760–1820).

George•town (jôrj'toun). The capital of Guyana. Pop. 78,000.

Geor•gia (jôr'jə). 1. A S state of the U.S. Pop. 4,560,000. Cap. Atlanta. 2. The Georgian S.S.R. —**Geor'gian** *adj.* & *n.*

Georgian Soviet Socialist Republic. A constituent republic of the U.S.S.R., S of the Caucasus Mountains. Pop. 4,638,000. Cap. Tbilisi.

ge•o•stroph•ic (jē'ō-strŏf'ĭk) *adj.* Of or pertaining to force caused by the earth's rotation.

ge•o•ther•mal (jē'ō-thûr'məl) *adj.* Also **ge•o•ther•mic** (-mĭk). Pertaining to the internal heat of the earth.

ger. gerund.

Ger. German; Germany.

ge•ra•ni•um (jĭ-rā'nē-əm) *n.* 1. A widely cultivated plant with rounded leaves and showy clusters of red, pink, or white flowers. 2. A related plant with divided leaves and pink or purplish flowers. [< Gk *geranion,* "small crane."]

ger•bil (jûr'bĭl) *n.* A mouselike rodent of desert regions of Africa and Asia Minor. [< Ar *yerbō',* flesh of the loins.]

ger•i•at•rics (jĕr'ē-ăt'rĭks) *n. (takes sing. v.).* The medical study of the physiology and pathology of old age. —**ger'i•at'ric** *adj.* & *n.*

germ (jûrm) *n.* 1. A small organic structure or cell from which a new organism may develop. 2. Something that may serve as the basis of further development. 3. A microorganism, esp. a pathogen. [< L *germen,* offshoot, sprout, fetus.]

Ger•man (jûr'mən) *n.* 1. A native or citizen of Germany. 2. The West Germanic language spoken in Germany, Austria, and part of Switzerland. —**Ger'man** *adj.*

German Democratic Republic. See **Germany.**

ger•mane (jər-mān') *adj.* Significantly related; pertinent. [< L *germānus,* "of the same race."] —**ger•mane'ly** *adv.* —**ger•mane'ness** *n.*

German Federal Republic. See **Germany.**

Ger•man•ic (jûr-măn'ĭk) *adj.* 1. Of, pertaining to, or characteristic of Germany, the German people, or their culture. 2. Of or pertaining to Germanic or to people who speak a Germanic language. —*n.* A branch of the Indo-European language family, divided into North Germanic (including Scandinavian), West Germanic (including German, Dutch, Flemish, Frisian, English, and Yiddish), and East Germanic (including Gothic).

ger•ma•ni•um (jər-mā'nē-əm) *n. Symbol* **Ge** A brittle, crystalline, gray-white semi-conducting element, widely used as a semiconductor and as an alloying agent and catalyst. Atomic number 32, atomic weight 72.59. [< L *germānus,* germane.]

German measles. A mild, contagious, eruptive disease caused by a virus spread in droplet sprays from the nose and throat.

German silver. Formerly, an alloy, **nickel silver.**

Ger•ma•ny (jûr'mə-nē). A nation of C Europe divided since 1949 into two states: **a. German Democratic Republic** (East Germany). Pop. 17,136,000. Cap. East Berlin. **b. German Federal Republic** (West Germany). Pop. 57,974,000. Cap. Bonn.

Germany

germ cell. A cell having reproduction as its principal function, esp. an egg or sperm cell.

ger•mi•cide (jûr'mə-sīd') *n.* Any agent that kills germs. —**ger'mi•ci'dal** (-sīd'l) *adj.*

ger•mi•nal (jûr'mə-nəl) *adj.* 1. Pertaining to a germ cell. 2. Pertaining to the earliest stage of development.

ger•mi•nate (jûr'mə-nāt') *v.* **-nated, -nating.** To begin to grow; sprout. [< L *germen,* sprout, GERM.] —**ger'mi•na'tion** *n.*

Ge•ron•i•mo (jə-rŏn'ə-mō'). 1829–1909. American Indian leader; chief of the Apaches.

Geronimo

ger•ry•man•der (jĕr'ē-măn'dər, gĕr'-) *v.* To divide into voting districts that give unfair advantage to one political party.

Gersh•win (gûrsh'wĭn), **George.** 1898–1937. American composer.

ger•und (jĕr'ənd) *n.* A verbal form that can be used as a noun, in English ending in *-ing,* as *cooking* in *I don't like cooking.* [< L *gerundum,* acting, carrying.]

ge•stalt, Ge•stalt (gə-shtält', -shtôlt') *n., pl.* **-stalts** or **-stalten** (-shtält'n, -shtôlt'n). A unified physical, psychological, or symbolic configuration having properties that cannot be derived from its parts. [G, form, shape.]

Ge•sta•po (gə-stä'pō) *n.* The German internal security police under the Nazi regime.

ges•ta•tion (jĕ-stā'shən) *n.* The development and carrying of offspring in the uterus. [< L *gerere,* to carry, bear.]

ges•tic•u•late (jĕ-stĭk'yə-lāt') *v.* **-lated, -lating.** To make gestures, esp. while speaking. [L *gesticulārī.*] —**ges•tic'u•la'tion** *n.*

ges•ture (jĕs'chər) *n.* 1. A motion of the limbs or body made as an expression of thought or emphasis. 2. An action or statement made as an indication of intention or attitude. —*v.* **-tured, -turing.** To make or signal by gestures. [ML *gestūra,* bearing, carriage.]

get (gĕt) *v.* **got, got** or **gotten, getting.** 1. To obtain or acquire. 2. To procure; secure. 3. To go after; fetch. 4. To make contact with by or as if by radio or telephone. 5. To earn: *get a reward.* 6. To receive: *get a present.* 7. To buy. 8. To catch; contract: *get chicken pox.* 9. To reach by calculation: *If you add them, you'll get 1,000.* 10. To have obtained or received and now have: *I've got a large collection of books.* 11. To understand: *Do you get his point?* 12. *Informal.* To register, as by eye or ear: *I didn't get your name.* 13. To cause to become or to be in a specific condition: *He can't get the hook loose.* 14. To cause to move, come, or go: *Get that dog out of here!* 15. To bring or take: *I'll get him in here.* 16. To prevail upon: *I'll get my friend to agree.* 17. To capture: *The police got him.* 18. *Slang.* To reciprocate by causing harm: *I'll get you for that remark.* 19. *Informal.* To strike or hit: *That blow got him on the chin.* 20. *Slang.* To puzzle: *Her attitude gets me.*

21. To have the obligation: *I have got to go.* 22. To become or grow. —Used as a linking verb: *I got well again.* 23. To arrive: *When will we get to New York?* 24. To betake oneself: *Get out!* 25. *Informal.* To start: *Get going!* —**get across.** To make or be understandable or clear: *Am I getting this across to you?* —**get ahead.** To be successful. —**get along.** 1. To be mutually congenial. 2. To manage with reasonable success. 3. To advance in years. —**get around.** 1. To avoid doing or encountering; circumvent. 2. *Informal.* To convince or gain the favor of by flattering or cajoling. —**get at.** 1. To determine; ascertain: *I'm trying to get at his point.* 2. To reach: *It's under the desk and I can't get at it.* 3. To lead up to or arrive at, as a conclusion or meaning: *Do you understand what I'm getting at?* —**get away with.** *Informal.* To be successful in avoiding retribution or the discovery of something done. —**get back at.** *Informal.* To retaliate or have revenge against. —**get by.** To manage; survive: *We'll get by.* —**get down to.** To concentrate on. —**get in.** 1. To enter or be allowed to enter. 2. To arrive. —**get it.** 1. To comprehend; understand. 2. *Informal.* To be punished or scolded. —**get nowhere.** To make no progress; have no success. —**get off.** 1. To get down from or out of. 2. To leave; depart. 3. To write and send, as a letter. —**get on.** 1. To climb up onto or into; enter. 2. To get along. 3. To advance: *He's getting on in years.* —**get out of.** 1. To derive or draw: *He gets out of it what he can.* 2. To avoid or get around. —**get over.** To recover from (a sorrow, illness, etc.). —**get there.** *Informal.* To attain one's goal. —**get through to.** 1. To make contact with. 2. To make understandable to. —**get to.** 1. To be able to: *I hope I get to go.* 2. To reach: *We never got to that point.* 3. *Informal.* To happen to start: *Then we got to remembering good times.* [< ON *geta.*] —**get'a•ble, get'ta•ble** *adj.*

get•a•way (gĕt'ə-wā') *n.* 1. An act or instance of escaping. 2. A start, as of a race. —*adj.* Used for escape: *a getaway car.*

get-to•geth•er (gĕt'tə-gĕth'ər) *n.* An informal social gathering.

Get•tys•burg (gĕt'ĭz-bûrg). A town in S Pennsylvania, the site of a major Civil War battle. Pop. 8,000.

get-up (gĕt'ŭp') *n.* An outfit or costume, esp. one remarkable in some way.

GeV *Phys.* Giga (10^9) electron volts.

gew•gaw (gyo͞o'gô') *n.* A trinket; bauble. [?]

gey•ser (gī'zər) *n.* A natural hot spring that intermittently ejects a column of water and steam. [< ON *geysa,* to gush.]

Gha•na (gä'nə). A republic in W Africa. Pop. 7,600,000. Cap. Accra. —**Gha•na'ian, Gha'ni•an** (gə-nā'ən) *adj.* & *n.*

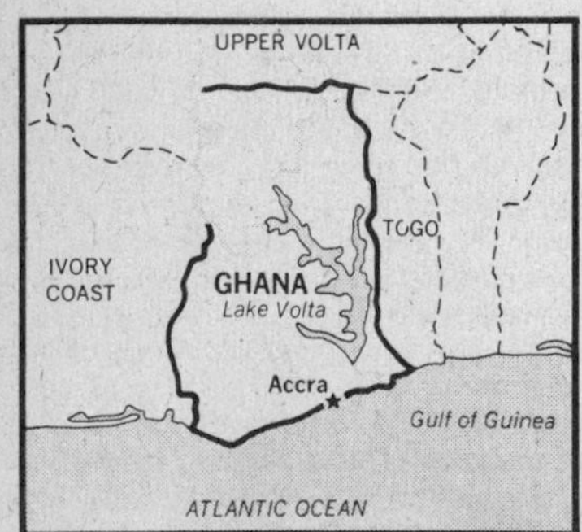

Ghana

ghast•ly (găst'lē, gäst'-) *adj.* -**lier,** -**liest.** 1. Terrifying; dreadful. 2. Deathly pale. 3. Extremely unpleasant. [< OE *gāst,* soul, ghost.]

gher•kin (gûr'kĭn) *n.* A small cucumber, esp. one used for pickling. [Du *agurkje.*]

ghet•to (gĕt'ō) *n., pl.* -**tos** or -**toes.** A section of a city to which an ethnic or economically depressed minority group is restricted, as by poverty or social pressure. [It.]

ghost (gōst) *n.* 1. The disembodied spirit of a dead person, supposed to haunt living persons or former habitats. 2. A slight trace or vestige. 3. A faint secondary photographic or television image. —**give up the ghost.** To die. [< OE *gāst.* See **gheis-.**] —**ghost'ly** *adj.*

ghost•writ•er (gōst'rī'tər) *n.* A person who writes for another who is credited with authorship. —**ghost'write'** *v.*

ghoul (go͞ol) *n.* 1. An evil spirit supposed to plunder graves and feed on corpses. 2. A grave robber. [Ar *ghūl.*] —**ghoul'ish** *adj.*

GHQ general headquarters.

gi gill².

GI (jē'ī') *n., pl.* **GIs** or **GI's.** An enlisted man in the U.S. armed forces. —*adj.* 1. Pertaining to or characteristic of a GI or U.S. military procedures. 2. Issued by an official U.S. military supply department.

GI Government Issue.

gi•ant (jī'ənt) *n.* 1. A legendary manlike being of enormous size and strength. 2. One of unusually great size or importance. —*adj.* Gigantic; huge. [< L *gigās (gigant-).*] —**gi'ant•ess** *fem.n.*

gib•ber (jĭb'ər, gĭb'-) *v.* To chatter unintelligibly. [Imit.]

gib•ber•ish (jĭb'ər-ĭsh, gĭb'-) *n.* Rapid, meaningless talk.

gib•bet (jĭb'ĭt) *n.* A gallows. —*v.* 1. To hang on a gibbet. 2. To expose to public ridicule. [< OF *gibe,* staff, club.]

gib•bon (gĭb'ən) *n.* An ape of tropical Asia with a slender body and long arms.

gib•bous (gĭb'əs) *adj.* More than half but less than fully illuminated: *the gibbous moon.* [< LL *gibbus,* hump.]

gibe (jīb) *v.* **gibed, gibing.** Also **jibe.** To make mocking remarks; taunt. —*n.* Also **jibe.** A taunt. —**gib'er** *n.* —**gib'ing•ly** *adv.*

gib•let (jĭb'lĭt) *n.* Often **giblets.** The edible heart, liver, or gizzard of a fowl. [< OF *gibelet.*]

Gib•ral•tar, Strait of (jĭ-brôl'tər). A waterway connecting the Mediterranean with the Atlantic Ocean.

gid•dy (gĭd'ē) *adj.* -**dier,** -**diest.** 1. a. Lightheaded; dizzy. b. Causing dizziness: *giddy heights.* 2. Frivolous; flighty. [< OE *gydig,* possessed by a god, insane. See **gheu(ə)-.**] —**gid'di•ly** *adv.* —**gid'di•ness** *n.*

gift (gĭft) *n.* 1. Something given; a present. 2. The act or power of giving. 3. A natural ability; talent. [< ON.]

gift•ed (gĭf'tĭd) *adj.* Having or showing great natural ability; talented.

gig¹ (gĭg) *n.* 1. A light, two-wheeled horse-drawn carriage. 2. A long, light ship's boat. [ME *gigg,* giddy girl, something that whirls.]

gig² (gĭg) *n.* A pronged spear for fishing. —*v.* **gigged, gigging.** To fish or catch with a gig.

gig³ (gĭg) *n. Slang.* A job, esp. a booking for a jazz musician.

giga–. *comb. form.* Indicates one billion (10^9); for example, *gigavolt,* or one billion volts. [< Gk *gigas,* giant.]

gi•gan•tic (jī-găn'tĭk) *adj.* Unusually large; enormous; huge. [< L *gigās (gigant-),* GIANT.] —**gi•gan'ti•cal•ly** *adv.*

gi•gan•tism (jī-găn'tĭz'əm) *n.* Excessive growth of the body or any of its parts as a result of oversecretion of the pituitary growth hormone.

gig•gle (gĭg'əl) *v.* -**gled,** -**gling.** To laugh with high-pitched, convulsive sounds. —*n.* A high-pitched, spasmodic laugh. [Imit.] —**gig'gler** *n.* —**gig'gling•ly** *adv.* —**gig'gly** *adj.*

gig•o•lo (jĭg'ə-lō', zhĭg'-) *n., pl.* -**los.** A man paid to be a woman's escort or lover. [< F *gigolette,* dance-hall pickup.]

Gi•la monster (hē'lə). A venomous lizard of the SW U.S.

gild (gĭld) *v.* **gilded** or **gilt, gilding.** 1. To cover with or as with a thin layer of gold. 2. To give a deceptively attractive appearance to. [< OE *gyldan.*] —**gild'er** *n.*

gill¹ (gĭl) *n.* The respiratory organ of fishes and various aquatic invertebrates. [ME *gille.*]

gill² (jĭl) *n.* 1. A U.S. Customary System unit of volume or capacity used in liquid measure, equal to 4 fluid ounces (¼ pint) or 7.216 cubic inches. 2. A corresponding British Imperial System unit used in dry and liquid measure, equal to 5 fluid ounces (¼ pint) or 8.670 cubic inches. [< LL *gillo,* water pot.]

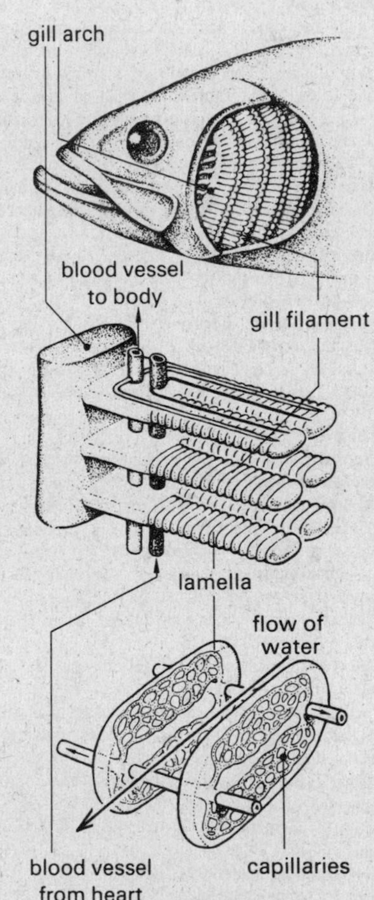

gill¹
Gill of a fish with gill cover removed and enlarged portions showing structural details

gil•ly•flow•er (gĭl'ē-flou'ər) *n.* Also **gil•li•flow•er.** A carnation or other plant with fragrant flowers. [< Gk *karuophullon,* "leaf nut."]
gilt (gĭlt). Alternate *p.t.* & *p.p.* of **gild.** —*adj.* Gilded. —*n.* A thin layer of gold or similar material applied in gilding.
gim•crack (jĭm'krăk') *n.* A cheap, showy, useless object. —**gim'crack'** *adj.*
gim•el (gĭm'əl) *n.* The 3rd letter of the Hebrew alphabet, representing *g(gh).*
gim•let (gĭm'lĭt) *n.* A small screw-tipped hand tool for boring holes. [< OF *guimbelet.*] —**gim'let** *v.*
gim•mick (gĭm'ĭk) *n.* **1.** A tricky, deceptive, often dishonest device. **2.** A concealed disadvantage; catch. **3.** An attention-getting stratagem or inducement. **4.** A gadget. [?] —**gim'mick•ry** *n.* —**gim'mick•y** *adj.*
gin¹ (jĭn) *n.* An alcoholic liquor distilled from grain and flavored with juniper berries. [< L *jūniperus,* JUNIPER.]
gin² (jĭn) *n.* A mechanical device, esp. one used to remove the seeds from cotton fibers. —*v.* **ginned, ginning.** To remove seeds from (cotton) with such a gin. [< ENGINE.]
gin•ger (jĭn'jər) *n.* **1.** The pungent, aromatic root of a tropical Asian plant, used as flavoring. **2.** The plant itself. **3.** *Informal.* Liveliness; pep. —*v.* —**ginger up.** *Informal.* To make more lively. [< Sk *śṛṅgaveram.*]
ginger ale. An effervescent soft drink flavored with ginger.
gin•ger•bread (jĭn'jər-brĕd') *n.* **1.** A dark molasses cake flavored with ginger. **2.** Elaborate, often tasteless ornamentation. [< ML *gingiber,* ginger.]
gin•ger•ly (jĭn'jər-lē) *adj.* Cautiously or timidly careful. —*adv.* Cautiously; carefully; timidly. [Orig "daintily."]
gin•ger•y (jĭn'jə-rē) *adj.* **1.** Having the spicy flavor of ginger. **2.** Sharp; biting.
ging•ham (gĭng'əm) *n.* A cotton fabric with a woven, often checked pattern. [Du *gingang.*]
gin•gi•va (jĭn-jī'və, jĭn'jə-) *n. Anat.* The gum. [< L *gingīva,* gum.]
gin•gi•val (jĭn-jī'vəl, jĭn'jə-) *adj.* Pertaining to the gums.
gin•gi•vi•tis (jĭn'jə-vī'tĭs) *n.* Inflammation of the gums.
gink•go (gĭng'kō) *n., pl.* **-goes.** A widely planted Chinese tree with fan-shaped leaves. [Jap *ginkyō.*]
gin mill. *Slang.* A saloon.
gip. Variant of **gyp.**
Gip•sy. Variant of **Gypsy.**
gi•raffe (jĭ-răf', -räf') *n.* An African mammal with a very long neck and legs and a distinctively marked coat. [< Ar *zirāfah.*]
gird (gûrd) *v.* **girded** or **girt** (gûrt), **girding. 1.** To encircle with or as with a belt or band. **2.** To equip or prepare for action. [< OE *gyrdan.* See **gher-².**]
gird•er (gûr'dər) *n.* A strong horizontal beam used as a main support in building.
gir•dle (gûrd'l) *n.* **1.** A belt, sash, or similar encircling band. **2.** A supporting undergarment worn over the waist and hips. —*v.* **-dled, -dling.** To encircle with or as with a belt. [< OE *gyrdel.* See **gher-².**]
girl (gûrl) *n.* **1.** A female child or young unmarried woman. **2.** *Informal.* Any woman. **3.** A sweetheart. **4.** A female servant. [ME *girle.*] —**girl'hood** *n.* —**girl'ish** *adj.*
girth (gûrth) *n.* **1.** Size measured by encircling something; circumference. **2.** A strap encircling an animal's body to secure a load or saddle. [< ON *györdh,* girdle.]
gist (jĭst) *n.* The central idea, as of an argument or speech. [< OF *(cest action) gist,* (this action) lies.]
give (gĭv) *v.* **gave, given, giving. 1. a.** To make a present of: *give flowers.* **b.** To make gifts: *give generously to charity.* **c.** To deliver in exchange or in recompense: *give five dollars for the book.* **2.** To entrust to or to place in the hands of: *Give me the scissors.* **3.** To convey: *Give him my best wishes.* **4.** To grant: *give permission.* **5.** To expose or subject one to: *She gave him the measles.* **6.** To produce: *This cow gives three gallons of milk per day.* **7.** To provide (something required or expected): *give one's name and address.* **8.** To administer: *give a spanking.* **9.** To accord; concede: *give the benefit of the doubt to.* **10.** To relinquish; yield: *give ground.* **11.** To emit or issue: *give a sigh.* **12.** To allot; assign: *give her five minutes to finish.* **13.** To award: *give first prize to.* **14.** To submit for consideration or acceptance; tender: *give an opinion.* **15.** To stage: *give a dinner party.* **16.** To afford a view of or access to; open: *The French doors give onto a terrace.* —**give back.** To return. —**give in. 1.** To cease opposition; concede. **2.** To hand in; submit: *give in a report.* —**give it to.** *Informal.* To scold or thrash soundly. —**give out. 1.** To distribute. **2.** To break down; fail. —**give rise to.** To cause; occasion. —**give up. 1.** To surrender: *give yourself up.* **2.** To stop: *give up smoking.* **3.** To relinquish: *give up hope.* **4.** To abandon hope for: *give her up as lost.* —**give way. 1.** To make room for: *give way to an oncoming car.* **2.** To collapse: *The ladder gave way.* **3.** To abandon oneself: *give way to hysteria.* —*n. Informal.* Resilient springiness: *The mattress has lots of give.* [< OE *giefan.* See **ghabh-.**] —**give'a•ble** *adj.* —**giv'er** *n.*
give-and-take (gĭv'ən-tāk') *n.* Lively exchange of ideas or conversation.
give•a•way (gĭv'ə-wā') *n. Informal.* **1.** Something given away at no charge. **2.** Something that betrays or exposes, often accidentally or unintentionally.
giv•en (gĭv'ən) *adj.* **1.** Specified: *a given date.* **2.** Accepted as a fact; acknowledged. **3.** Habitually inclined: *given to shyness.* **4.** Bestowed; presented.
giz•zard (gĭz'ərd) *n.* A muscular enlargement of the digestive tract in birds. [< L *gigeria,* cooked entrails of poultry.]
Gk. Greek.
gl. gloss.
gla•cial (glā'shəl) *adj.* **1.** Of or pertaining to a glacier. **2.** Often **Glacial.** Characterized or dominated by the existence of glaciers, as the Pleistocene epoch. **3.** Extremely cold. —**gla'cial•ly** *adv.*
gla•cier (glā'shər) *n.* A huge mass of laterally limited, moving ice originating from compacted snow. [< L *glaciēs,* ice.]
glad (glăd) *adj.* **gladder, gladdest. 1.** Feeling, showing, or giving joy and pleasure; happy. **2.** Pleased; willing: *glad to help.* [< OE *glæd.*] —**glad'ly** *adv.* —**glad'ness** *n.*
glad•den (glăd'n) *v.* To make or become glad.
glade (glād) *n.* An open space in a forest. [Perh < GLAD.]
glad•i•a•tor (glăd'ē-ā'tər) *n.* **1.** A professional combatant, slave, etc., who engaged in mortal combat for public entertainment in ancient Rome. **2.** One engaged in fighting or controversy. [< L *gladius,* sword.] —**glad'i•a•to'ri•al** (-ə-tôr'ē-əl, -tōr'ē-əl) *adj.*
glad•i•o•lus (glăd'ē-ō'ləs) *n., pl.* **-li** (-lī', -lē') or **-luses.** A widely cultivated plant with sword-shaped leaves and a spike of showy, variously colored flowers. [< L *gladius,* sword.]
glad•some (glăd'səm) *adj.* Glad; joyful.
glam•or•ize (glăm'ə-rīz') *v.* **-ized, -izing.** Also **glam•our•ize.** To make or portray as glamorous. —**glam'or•i•za'tion** *n.*
glam•our (glăm'ər) *n.* Also **glam•or.** Alluring charm and excitement. [Scot var of GRAMMAR.] —**glam'or•ous, glam'our•ous** *adj.*
glance (glăns, gläns) *v.* **glanced, glancing. 1.** To strike and be deflected. **2.** To look briefly. **3.** To shine briefly; glint. —*n.* **1.** A quick look. **2.** A flash; gleam. **3.** A glancing impact or motion. [< OF *glacier,* to slide.]
gland (glănd) *n.* An organ or structure that secretes a substance, esp. one that extracts specific substances from the blood for subsequent secretion. [< L *glāns (gland-),* acorn.] —**glan'du•lar** (glăn'jə-lər) *adj.*
glans cli•tor•i•dis (glănz klī-tôr'ə-dĭs, klĭ-). The small mass of erectile tissue at the tip of the clitoris.
glans penis. The head or tip of the penis.
glare (glâr) *v.* **glared, glaring. 1.** To stare fixedly and angrily. **2.** To shine intensely and blindingly. —*n.* **1.** A fixed, angry stare. **2.** An intense and blinding light. [ME *glaren.*]
glar•ing (glâr'ĭng) *adj.* **1.** Staring fixedly and angrily. **2.** Blindingly bright; dazzling. **3.** Obtrusively conspicuous. —**glar'ing•ly** *adv.*
Glas•gow (glăs'gō, -kō, gläs'-). A city of SW Scotland. Pop. 1,796,000.
glass (glăs, gläs) *n.* **1.** Any of a large class of materials that solidify from the molten state without crystallization, are generally transparent or translucent, and are regarded physically as supercooled liquids rather than true solids. **2.** Also **glass•ware** (glăs'wâr', gläs'-). Objects made of glass. **3.** Something made of glass, as a drinking vessel or mirror. **4.** Often **glasses.** A device containing a lens or lenses and used as an aid to vision. **5.** Also **glass•ful** (glăs'fo͝ol', gläs'-). The quantity contained by a drinking glass. [< OE *glæs.*]
glass•y (glăs'ē, gläs'ē) *adj.* **-ier, -iest. 1.** Of or like glass. **2.** Lifeless; expressionless: *a glassy grin.* —**glass'i•ly** *adv.* —**glass'i•ness** *n.*
glau•co•ma (glô-kō'mə, glou-) *n.* A disease of the eye characterized by high intraocular pressure, damaged optic disk, hardening of the eyeball, and partial or complete loss of vision. [L *glaucōma,* cataract.] —**glau•co'ma•tous** *adj.*
glaze (glāz) *n.* A thin, smooth, glassy coating, as on ceramics or ice. —*v.* **glazed, glazing. 1.** To furnish with glass, as a window. **2.** To apply a glaze to. **3.** To become glassy. [< ME *glas,* glass.] —**glaz'er** *n.*
gla•zier (glā'zhər) *n.* One who cuts and fits window glass.
gleam (glēm) *n.* **1.** A brief flash or subdued glow of light. **2.** A brief or dim indication: *a gleam of intelligence.* —*v.* **1.** To flash or glow. **2.** To show briefly or faintly. [< OE *glǣm.*]
glean (glēn) *v.* **1.** To gather (grain) left behind by reapers. **2.** To collect bit by bit, as knowledge. [< LL *glennāre.*] —**glean'er** *n.*
glee (glē) *n.* **1.** Merriment; joy. **2.** An unaccompanied part song for three or more voices. [< OE *glēo.*] —**glee'ful** *adj.* —**glee'ful•ly** *adv.*
glee club. A group of singers who perform part songs or choral music.
glen (glĕn) *n.* A narrow, high-walled valley. [< Scot Gael *gleann.*]
Glen•dale (glĕn'dāl'). A city in SW California. Pop. 119,000.
glib (glĭb) *adj.* **glibber, glibbest.** Easy, fluent, and often superficial, as in speech. [Prob <

MLG *glibberich,* slippery.] **—glib'ly** *adv.* **—glib'ness** *n.*

glide (glīd) *v.* **glided, gliding. 1.** To move or pass smoothly and easily. **2.** To fly without propulsion. *—n.* **1.** A smooth, effortless movement. **2.** An act of flying without propulsion. [< OE *glīdan.*]

glid•er (glī'dər) *n.* **1.** One that glides. **2.** A light, engineless aircraft designed for long periods of gliding. **3.** A swinging couch suspended from a vertical frame.

glim•mer (glĭm'ər) *v.* To emit a dim, flickering light. *—n.* **1.** A dim, flickering light. **2.** A faint indication. [Prob < Scand.]

glimpse (glĭmps) *n.* A brief, hasty look. *—v.* **glimpsed, glimpsing.** To catch a brief, hasty view of. [< Gmc.]

glint (glĭnt) *n.* A brief flash of light; a sparkle. *—v.* To gleam; sparkle. [< Scand.]

glis•ten (glĭs'ən) *v.* To shine or reflect lustrously; gleam. [< OE *glisnian.*] **—glis'ten** *n.*

glit•ter (glĭt'ər) *v.* To sparkle brilliantly. *—n.* **1.** A sparkling light or brightness. **2.** Brilliant or showy splendor. **3.** Small pieces of decorative material. [< ON *glitra.*]

gloam•ing (glō'mĭng) *n.* Twilight. [< OE *glōm,* dusk.]

gloat (glōt) *v.* To show smug, triumphant, or malicious pleasure or satisfaction. [Perh < Scand.]

glob (glŏb) *n.* A small drop or rounded mass. [< L *globus,* GLOBE.]

glob•al (glō'bəl) *adj.* Of or pertaining to the entire earth; worldwide. **—glob'al•ly** *adv.*

globe (glōb) *n.* **1.** A spherical object, as a representation of the earth. **2.** The earth. **3.** A globelike article, as a fishbowl. [< L *globus.*]

globe•trot•ter (glōb'trŏt'ər) *n.* One who travels widely.

glob•ule (glŏb'yōōl) *n.* A very small spherical mass, esp. of liquid. [< L *globus,* GLOBE.] **—glob'u•lar** (-yə-lər) *adj.*

glob•u•lin (glŏb'yə-lən) *n.* Any of a class of simple proteins that are found extensively in blood, milk, muscle, and plant seeds.

glock•en•spiel (glŏk'ən-spēl', -shpēl') *n.* A musical instrument having a series of metal bars played with two light hammers. [G, "play of bells."]

gloom (glōōm) *n.* **1.** Partial or total darkness. **2.** A melancholy or dejected state or atmosphere. [ME *gloumben,* to look glum, become dark.] **—gloom'i•ly** *adv.* **—gloom'y** *adj.*

glo•ri•fy (glôr'ə-fī', glōr'-) *v.* **-fied, -fying. 1.** To invest with glory; make glorious. **2.** To offer glory to; worship; extol. **3.** To exaggerate or overestimate the glory or excellence of. **—glo'ri•fi•ca'tion** *n.* **—glo'ri•fi'er** *n.*

glo•ri•ous (glôr'ē-əs, glōr'-) *adj.* **1.** Having, deserving, or imparting glory; illustrious. **2.** Magnificent; resplendent. **3.** Delightful. **—glo'ri•ous•ly** *adv.* **—glo'ri•ous•ness** *n.*

glo•ry (glôr'ē, glōr'ē) *n., pl.* **-ries. 1.** Great honor or distinction; renown. **2.** Adoration and praise offered in worship. **3.** Magnificent splendor. **4.** A praiseworthy attribute. **5.** The height of achievement, triumph, etc. *—v.* **-ried, -rying.** To rejoice triumphantly; exult. [< L *glōria.*]

gloss[1] (glôs, glŏs) *n.* **1.** Surface shine; luster. **2.** A superficially attractive appearance. *—v.* **—gloss over.** To attempt to excuse or ignore, as a fault or error. [Prob < Scand.] **—gloss'i•ness** *n.* **—gloss'y** *adj.*

gloss[2] (glôs, glŏs) *n.* **1.** A brief explanatory note or translation of a difficult or technical expression. **2.** A translation or commentary accompanying a text. *—v.* To annotate or translate briefly. [< Gk *glōssa,* tongue, language.] **—gloss'er** *n.*

glos•sa•ry (glôs'ə-rē, glŏs'-) *n., pl.* **-ries.** A collection of specialized terms with accompanying definitions. [< L *glōssa,* GLOSS[2].]

glottal stop. A speech sound produced by a momentary closure of the glottis, followed by an explosive release.

glot•tis (glŏt'ĭs) *n., pl.* **-tises** or **glottides** (glŏt'ə-dēz'). The space between the vocal cords at the upper part of the larynx. [< Gk *glōtta, glōssa,* tongue, language.] **—glot'tal** *adj.*

glove (glŭv) *n.* **1.** A fitted covering for the hand, having a separate sheath for each finger. **2.** An oversized padded leather covering for the hand, as one used by a baseball player or boxer. [< OE *glōf.* See **lep-.**] **—gloved** *adj.*

glow (glō) *v.* **1.** To shine brightly and steadily, esp. without a flame. **2.** To have a bright or ruddy color. **3.** To be exuberant or radiant, as with pride. *—n.* **1.** A light produced by or as by a body heated to luminosity. **2.** Brilliance or warmth of color, esp. redness. **3.** A sensation of physical warmth. **4.** A warm feeling of emotion. [< OE *glōwan.*]

glow•er (glou'ər) *v.* To look or stare angrily or sullenly. *—n.* An angry, sullen, or threatening stare. [Prob < Scand.]

glow•ing (glō'ĭng) *adj.* **1.** Incandescent; luminous. **2.** Having a warm or ruddy color. **3.** Ardently enthusiastic or favorable.

glow•worm (glō'wûrm') *n.* The luminous larva or grublike female of a firefly.

glu•cose (glōō'kōs') *n.* **1.** A sugar, dextrose. **2.** A colorless to yellowish syrupy mixture of dextrose and maltose with about 20% water, used in confectionery, alcoholic fermentation, tanning, and treating tobacco. [< Gk *gleukos,* sweet new wine, must.]

glue (glōō) *n.* An adhesive substance or solution used to join or bond. *—v.* **glued, gluing.** To stick or fasten with or as with glue. [< L *glūten.*]

glum (glŭm) *adj.* **glummer, glummest.** Dejected; gloomy. [< GLOOM.] **—glum'ly** *adv.* **—glum'ness** *n.*

glut (glŭt) *v.* **glutted, glutting. 1.** To eat or fill to excess; satiate. **2.** To flood (a market) with a supply that exceeds demand. *—n.* An excessive amount or supply; an oversupply. [Prob < L *gluttīre,* to swallow.]

glu•ten (glōōt'n) *n.* A glutinous, nutritious mixture of plant proteins occurring in cereal grains. [L *glūten,* glue.]

glu•te•us (glōō'tē-əs, glōō-tē'-) *n., pl.* **-tei** (-tē-ī', tē'ī'). Any of three large muscles of the buttocks. [< Gk *gloutos,* buttock.]

glu•ti•nous (glōōt'n-əs) *adj.* Sticky; adhesive. [< L *glūten,* glue.] **—glu'ti•nous•ly** *adv.*

glut•ton (glŭt'n) *n.* One that eats or consumes to excess. [< L *gluttō.*] **—glut'ton•ous** *adj.* **—glut'ton•ous•ly** *adv.* **—glut'ton•y** *n.*

glyc•er•ol (glĭs'ə-rôl', -rōl', -rŏl') *n.* A syrupy liquid, $C_3H_8O_3$, obtained from fats and oils and used as a solvent, antifreeze, and sweetener, and in making dynamite, liquid soaps, and lubricants. [< Gk *glukeros,* sweet.]

gly•co•gen (glī'kə-jən) *n.* A white powder, $(C_6H_{10}O_5)_n$, occurring as the chief animal storage carbohydrate, primarily in the liver. [< Gk *glukus,* sweet + -GEN.] **—gly'co•gen'ic** *adj.*

gm gram.

gnarl (närl) *n.* A protruding knot on a tree. **—gnarled** *adj.*

gnash (năsh) *v.* To grind (the teeth) together. [Prob < Scand.]

gnat (năt) *n.* Any of various small, winged, biting insects. [< OE *gnæt.*]

gnaw (nô) *v.* **gnawed, gnawed** or **gnawn, gnawing. 1.** To consume, wear away, or produce by nibbling: *gnaw a hole.* **2.** To afflict or irritate. [< OE *gnagan.*] **—gnaw'er** *n.* **—gnaw'ing•ly** *adv.*

gneiss (nīs) *n.* A banded metamorphic rock, usually of the same composition as granite. [G *Gneis.*]

gnome (nōm) *n.* One of a race of dwarfs said to live underground and guard treasure hoards. [F.]

GNP gross national product.

gnu (n/y/ōō) *n.* A large bearded African antelope, with curved horns.

go (gō) *v.* **went, gone, going. 1.** To proceed. **2.** To move or start to move. **3.** To move to or from a given place, or out of someone's presence. **4.** —Used in the form *be going* followed by an infinitive to indicate the indefinite future: *He's going to go home.* **5.** To engage in a specified activity: *go riding.* **6.** To function. **7.** To make a specified sound: *The glass went crack.* **8.** To belong (somewhere). **9.** To extend or spread. **10.** To be allotted. **11.** To serve: *It all goes to show.* **12.** To harmonize: *The rug goes well with this room.* **13.** To die. **14.** To come apart or cave in. **15.** To fail: *Her eyes are going.* **16.** To be used up. **17.** To disappear. **18.** To be abolished: *War must go.* **19.** To pass, as time. **20.** To become: *go crazy.* **21.** To be or continue to be: *go unchallenged.* **22.** To fare. **23.** To hold out or endure: *go without water.* **24.** To wager; bid. **25.** To furnish: *go bail for a client.* **26.** To participate to the extent of: *go halves on a deal.* *—n., pl.* **goes.** *Informal.* **1.** A try. **2.** Bargain; deal: *no go.* **—on the go.** Constantly busy. [< OE *gān.* See **ghē-.**]

GO general order.

goad (gōd) *n.* **1.** A pointed stick used for prodding animals. **2.** A stimulus; spur. [< OE *gād.*] **—goad** *v.*

goal (gōl) *n.* **1.** An end; objective. **2.** The finish line of a race. **3.** *Sports.* **a.** A specified place into which players endeavor to advance a ball or puck. **b.** The score awarded for such an act. [Prob < OE *gāl,* obstacle.]

goal•keep•er (gōl'kē'pər) *n.* Also **goal•ie** (gōl'ē). A player assigned to protect the goal in various sports.

goal post. One of a pair of posts joined with a crossbar forming the goal at each end of a football field.

goat (gōt) *n.* **1.** A horned, bearded mammal originally of mountainous regions and now widely domesticated. **2. Goat.** Capricornus. [< OE *gāt.* See **ghaido-.**]

goat•ee (gō-tē') *n.* A small pointed chin beard. [< GOAT + -EE.]

goat•skin (gōt'skĭn') *n.* The skin of a goat, used for leather.

gob[1] (gŏb) *n.* A lump or mass. [< OF *gobe,* mouthful, lump.]

gob[2] (gŏb) *n. Slang.* A sailor. [?]

gob•bet (gŏb'ĭt) *n.* A chunk, morsel, or lump. [< OF *gobe,* GOB[1].]

gob•ble[1] (gŏb'əl) *v.* **-bled, -bling. 1.** To devour greedily. **2.** To snatch; grab. [Freq of ME *gobben,* to drink greedily.]

gob•ble[2] (gŏb'əl) *v.* **-bled, -bling.** To make the guttural sound of a male turkey.

gob•ble•dy•gook (gŏb'əl-dē-gōōk') *n.* Also **gob•ble•de•gook.** Unintelligible jargon. [< GOBBLE.]

gob•bler (gŏb'lər) *n.* A male turkey.

go-be•tween (gō'bĭ-twēn') *n.* An intermediary.

Go•bi Desert (gō'bē). A desert in east-central Asia.

gob•let (gŏb'lĭt) *n.* A drinking glass with a stem and base. [< OF *gobel,* cup.]

gob•lin (gŏb'lən) *n.* A grotesque elf or sprite said to work mischief or evil. [< MHG *kobolt,* goblin.]

go-cart (gō'kärt') *n.* A small toy wagon.

god (gŏd) *n.* **1.** A being of supernatural powers or attributes, believed in and worshiped by a people. **2.** One that is worshiped or idealized as a god. **3. God.** A being conceived as the perfect, omnipotent, omniscient originator and ruler of the universe, the principal object of faith and worship in monotheistic religions. [< OE. See **gheu(ə)-**.]

god•child (gŏd'chīld') *n.* One for whom another serves as sponsor at baptism.

god•daugh•ter (gŏd'dô'tər) *n.* A female godchild.

god•dess (gŏd'ĭs) *n.* **1.** A female deity. **2.** A woman of great beauty.

god•fa•ther (gŏd'fä'*th*ər) *n.* A man who sponsors a child at its baptism.

god•head (gŏd'hĕd') *n.* **1.** Divinity. **2. Godhead.** The essential and divine nature of God.

god•less (gŏd'lĭs) *adj.* **1.** Recognizing or worshiping no god. **2.** Irreverent; wicked. **—god'less•ly** *adv.* **—god'less•ness** *n.*

god•like (gŏd'līk') *adj.* Resembling a god or God.

god•ly (gŏd'lē) *adj.* **-lier, -liest. 1.** Having reverence for God; pious; devout. **2.** Divine. **—god'li•ness** *n.*

god•moth•er (gŏd'mŭ*th*'ər) *n.* A woman who sponsors a child at its baptism.

god•par•ent (gŏd'pâr'ənt) *n.* A godfather or godmother.

god•send (gŏd'sĕnd') *n.* An unexpected boon or stroke of luck. [ME *goddes sand,* God's message.]

god•son (gŏd'sŭn') *n.* A male godchild.

God•speed (gŏd'spēd') *n.* Success or good fortune.

Godt•haab (gôt'hôp'). The capital of Greenland. Pop. 1,400.

Goe•the (gœ'tə), **Johann Wolfgang von.** 1749–1832. German poet.

go-get•ter (gō'gĕt'ər) *n. Informal.* An enterprising, hustling person.

gog•gle (gŏg'əl) *v.* **-gled, -gling.** To stare with wide and bulging eyes. *—n.* **goggles.** A pair of large eyeglasses worn as a protection against wind, dust, or glare. [ME *gogelen,* to roll the eyes.] **—gog'gly** *adj.*

Goi•del•ic (goi-dĕl'ĭk) *n.* A group of Celtic languages, including Irish Gaelic and Scottish Gaelic. **—Goi•del'ic** *adj.*

goi•ter (goi'tər) *n.* Also **goi•tre.** A chronic, noncancerous enlargement of the thyroid gland, visible as a swelling at the front of the neck. [< L *guttur,* throat.] **—goi'trous** (-trəs) *adj.*

gold (gōld) *n.* **1.** *Symbol* **Au** A soft, yellow, corrosion-resistant, highly malleable and ductile metallic element that is used as an international monetary standard, in jewelry, for decoration, and as a plated coating on a wide variety of electrical and mechanical components. Atomic number 79, atomic weight 196.967. **2. a.** Coinage made of gold. **b.** A gold standard. **3.** Money; riches. **4.** Moderate to vivid yellow. [< OE. See **ghel-²**.]

gold•brick (gōld'brĭk') *n.* Also **gold•brick•er** (-ər). *Slang.* One who avoids assigned duties or work; a shirker. **—gold'brick'** *v.*

gold•en (gōl'dən) *adj.* **1.** Made of or containing gold. **2. a.** Having the color of gold. **b.** Lustrous; radiant. **c.** Suggestive of gold: *a golden voice.* **3.** Of the greatest value or importance; precious. **4.** Marked by prosperity. **5.** Very favorable or advantageous; excellent: *a golden opportunity.* **—gold'en•ly** *adv.*

gold•en•rod (gōl'dən-rŏd') *n.* A North American plant with branching clusters of small yellow flowers.

gold•finch (gōld'fĭnch') *n.* A small New World bird having yellow plumage with a black forehead, wings, and tail.

gold•fish (gōld'fĭsh') *n.* A reddish or brass-colored freshwater fish often kept in home aquariums.

gold•smith (gōld'smĭth') *n.* One who fashions or deals in gold articles.

golf (gōlf, gôf) *n.* A game played on a course having nine or eighteen holes, the object being to propel a small ball with the use of a club into each hole with as few strokes as possible. [ME.] **—golf** *v.* **—golf'er** *n.*

Go•li•ath (gə-lī'əth). The Philistine giant slain by David. I Samuel 17:4–51.

-gon. *comb. form.* Having a designated number of angles: **pentagon.** [< Gk *gōnia,* angle.]

go•nad (gō'năd', gŏn'ăd') *n.* The organ that produces gametes; a testis or ovary. [< Gk *gonos,* offspring, genitals.]

gon•do•la (gŏnd'l-ə, gŏn-dō'lə) *n.* **1.** A narrow barge used on the canals of Venice. **2.** Also **gondola car.** An open, shallow freight car. **3.** A structure suspended from and carried aloft by a balloon. [It, roll, rock.]

gon•do•lier (gŏnd'l-îr') *n.* The boatman of a gondola.

gone (gôn, gŏn) *adj.* **1.** Past; bygone. **2. a.** Advanced. **b.** Pregnant. **3.** Dying or dead. **4.** Ruined; lost. **5.** Carried away; absorbed. **6.** Used up; exhausted. **7.** *Slang.* Infatuated: *gone on the girl.*

gon•er (gôn'ər, gŏn'-) *n. Slang.* One who is ruined or doomed.

gon•fa•lon (gŏn'fə-lən) *n.* A banner suspended from a crosspiece. [It *gonfalone,* standard.]

gong (gông, gŏng) *n.* A rimmed metal disk that produces a loud, sonorous tone when struck. [Malay *gōng* (imit).]

gon•or•rhe•a (gŏn'ə-rē'ə) *n.* An infectious disease of the genitourinary tract, rectum, and cervix, caused by a bacterium and transmitted chiefly by sexual intercourse. [< Gk *gonorrhoia.*]

goo (go͞o) *n. Informal.* **1.** A sticky wet substance. **2.** Sentimental drivel. **—goo'ey** *adj.*

goo•ber (go͞o'bər) *n.* A peanut.

good (go͝od) *adj.* **better, best. 1.** Having positive or desirable qualities. **2.** Suitable; serviceable. **3. a.** Not spoiled. **b.** Whole; sound. **4.** Superior to the average: *a good student.* **5. a.** Of high quality. **b.** Discriminating: *good taste.* **6.** Suitable for formal occasions: *good clothes.* **7.** Beneficial; salutary: *a good night's rest.* **8.** Competent; skilled. **9.** Complete; thorough. **10. a.** Safe; sure. **b.** Valid or sound. **c.** Genuine; real. **11. a.** Ample; substantial. **b.** Bountiful. **12.** Full: *a good mile from here.* **13. a.** Pleasant; enjoyable. **b.** Propitious; favorable. **14. a.** Virtuous; upright. **b.** Benevolent; cheerful. **c.** Loyal; staunch. **15. a.** Well-behaved; obedient. **b.** Socially correct; proper. **—as good as.** Practically; virtually; nearly. **—make good. 1.** To fulfill a commitment. **2.** To compensate for or replace. **3.** To prove; verify. **4.** *Informal.* To succeed; do well. *—n.* **1. a.** That which is good. **b.** The valuable or useful part. **2.** Welfare; benefit: *the common good.* **3.** Goodness; virtue; merit. **—for good.** Forever; permanently. *—adv. Informal.* Well. [< OE *gōd.* See **ghedh-**.]

Usage: *Good* occurs frequently after linking verbs such as *be, feel, seem, smell, sound,* and *taste: The news sounds good.* In such usage, acceptable on all levels, *good* is an adjective that qualifies the subject of the verb. Except in distinctly informal usage, *good* does not function as an adverb by qualifying verbs directly; instead, *well* is used: *He dances well* (not *good*). *Things are not going well.*

good-by, good-bye (go͝od'bī') *interj.* Farewell. [Contraction of *God be with you.*] **—good'-by', good'-bye'** *n.*

Good Friday. The Friday before Easter, observed in commemoration of the Crucifixion.

Good Hope, Cape of. A promontory on the SW coast of South Africa.

good•ly (go͝od'lē) *adj.* **-lier, -liest. 1.** Of pleasing appearance. **2.** Somewhat large; considerable. **—good'li•ness** *n.*

good•man (go͝od'mən) *n. Archaic.* **1.** The male head of a household; husband. **2. Goodman.** Mister: *Goodman Jones.*

good•ness (go͝od'nĭs) *n.* **1.** The state or quality of being good. **2.** Virtuousness; rectitude. **3.** Kindness; benevolence. **4.** A euphemism for God: *Thank goodness!*

goods (go͝odz) *pl.n.* **1.** Merchandise; wares. **2.** Portable personal property. **3.** Cloth. [Pl of GOOD.]

Good Sa•mar•i•tan (sə-măr'ĭ-tən). A compassionate person. [< the parable of the *good Samaritan.* Luke 10:30–37.]

Good•wife (go͝od'wīf') *n. Archaic.* Mrs.: *Goodwife Jones.*

good will. Also **good•will** (go͝od'wĭl'). **1.** Benevolence. **2.** Cheerful willingness. **3.** The favorable disposition of clients or customers, reckoned as an intangible asset.

good•y¹ (go͝od'ē) *n., pl.* **-ies.** Something delectable or attractive.

good•y² (go͝od'ē) *n.* Also **Good•y.** *Obs.* Goodwife; Mrs.: *Goody Garlick.*

good•y-good•y (go͝od'ē-go͝od'ē) *adj.* Affectedly sweet or good. **—good'y-good'y** *n.*

goof (go͞of) *Slang. v.* To blunder. **—goof off.** To waste or kill time. **—goof up.** To bungle. *—n.* **1.** A blunder. **2.** A ludicrously incompetent or stupid person. [< OF *goffe,* awkward.] **—goof'i•ness** *n.* **—goof'y** *adj.*

gook (go͝ok, go͞ok) *n. Slang.* A sludgy or slimy substance. [Perh < ME *gowke,* cuckoo.]

goon (go͞on) *n.* **1.** A thug hired for purposes of intimidation. **2.** *Slang.* **a.** An oaf. **b.** A dullard; bore. [?]

goose (go͞os) *n., pl.* **geese** (gēs). **1.** A water bird related to the ducks and swans. **2.** The female of such a bird. **3.** The edible flesh of such a bird. **4.** *Informal.* A silly person. [< OE *gōs.* See **ghans-**.]

goose•ber•ry (go͞os'bĕr'ē, -bə-rē, go͞oz'-) *n.* **1.** The edible greenish berry of a spiny shrub. **2.** A shrub bearing such berries.

goose flesh. Momentary roughness of skin in response to cold or fear.

G.O.P. Grand Old Party (Republican Party of the U.S.).

go•pher (gō'fər) *n.* Any of various burrowing North American rodents with pocketlike cheek pouches. [< earlier *magopher.*]

gore¹ (gôr) *v.* **gored, goring.** To stab with a horn or tusk. [< OE *gār,* spear.]

gore² (gôr) *n.* A triangular or tapering piece of cloth, as in a skirt, umbrella, or sail. [< OE

gāra, triangular piece of land.]
gore[3] (gôr) *n.* Blood, esp. from a wound. [< OE *gor,* dung, dirt.]
gorge (gôrj) *n.* **1.** A deep, narrow ravine. **2.** The throat; gullet. **3.** A mass obstructing a narrow passage: *an ice gorge.* —*v.* **gorged, gorging. 1.** To stuff; satiate; glut. **2.** To eat greedily. [< L *gurges,* whirlpool, throat.]
gor•geous (gôr'jəs) *adj.* **1.** Resplendent; magnificent. **2.** Strikingly beautiful. [< OF *gorgias,* stylish, fine.] —**gor'geous•ly** *adv.* —**gor'geous•ness** *n.*
go•ril•la (gə-rĭl'ə) *n.* A large African ape with a stocky body and dark hair. [< Gk *Gorillai,* African tribe of hairy men.]
Gor•ki (gôr'kē), **Maxim.** 1868–1936. Russian novelist and playwright.
Gor•kiy (gôr'kē). Also **Gor•ki, Gor•ky.** A city of the U.S.S.R., on the Volga. Pop. 1,170,000.
gorse (gôrs) *n.* A spiny European shrub with fragrant yellow flowers. [< OE *gorst, gors.*]
go•ry (gôr'ē, gōr'ē) *adj.* **-rier, -riest. 1.** Bloody; bloodstained. **2.** Bloodcurdling; sensational: *the gory details.* —**gor'i•ly** *adv.*
gos•hawk (gŏs'hôk') *n.* A large hawk with broad, rounded wings and gray or brownish plumage. [< OE *gōs,* GOOSE + *heafoc,* HAWK.]
gos•ling (gŏz'lĭng) *n.* A young goose.
gos•pel (gŏs'pəl) *n.* **1.** Often **Gospel.** The teachings of Christ and the Apostles. **2. Gospel.** Any of the first four books of the New Testament. **3.** Something accepted as unquestionably true. [< OE *godspell,* "good news."]
gos•sa•mer (gŏs'ə-mər) *n.* **1.** A fine film of floating cobwebs. **2.** A sheer gauzy fabric. **3.** Anything delicate, light, or insubstantial. [ME *gossomer.*] —**gos'sa•mer** *adj.*
gos•sip (gŏs'əp) *n.* **1.** Trivial rumor of a personal nature. **2.** One who habitually engages in such talk. **3.** Casual, chatty talk. —*v.* To engage in or spread gossip. [< OE *god,* GOD + *sibb,* kinsman.] —**gos'sip•y** *adj.*
got (gŏt). *p.t.* & *p.p.* of **get.**
Goth (gŏth) *n.* **1.** One of a Germanic people that settled near the Elbe River and invaded the Roman Empire in the early centuries of the Christian era. **2.** An uncultured or uncivilized person; barbarian.
Goth. Gothic.
Goth•ic (gŏth'ĭk) *adj.* **1. a.** Of or pertaining to the Goths or their language. **b.** Germanic. **2.** Of or pertaining to an architectural style of W Europe from the 12th through the 15th century. —*n.* **1.** The extinct East Germanic language of the Goths. **2.** Gothic art or architecture.
got•ten (gŏt'n). Alternate *p.p.* of **get.**
gouge (gouj) *n.* **1.** A chisel with a rounded, troughlike blade. **2.** A groove or hole scooped with or as if with a gouge. —*v.* **gouged, gouging. 1.** To cut or scoop out with or as if with a gouge. **2.** *Slang.* To extort or cheat. [< LL *gubia.*] —**goug'er** *n.*
gou•lash (gōō'läsh, -lăsh) *n.* A meat and vegetable stew seasoned mainly with paprika. [Hung *gulyás (hus),* "herdsman's meat."]
gourd (gôrd, gōrd, gŏŏrd) *n.* **1.** A vine related to the pumpkin, squash, and cucumber, bearing fruits with a hard rind. **2.** The fruit of such a vine. **3.** The dried, hollowed-out shell of such a fruit, used as a utensil. [< L *cucurbita.*]
gourde (gŏŏrd) *n.* The basic monetary unit of Haiti. [< L *gurdus,* heavy, dull.]
gour•mand (gŏŏr'mənd) *n.* **1.** A glutton. **2.** A gourmet. [< OF, glutton.]
gour•met (gŏŏr-mā') *n.* A connoisseur of fine food and drink; epicure. [F.]
gout (gout) *n.* **1.** A disturbance of the uric-acid metabolism occurring predominantly in males and marked by arthritic attacks. **2.** A blob, clot, or splash: *bleeding great gouts of blood.* [< L *gutta,* drop.] —**gout'y** *adj.*
gov. 1. government. **2.** governor.
gov•ern (gŭv'ərn) *v.* **1.** To control; guide; direct. **2.** To rule by exercise of sovereign authority. **3.** To regulate or determine. **4.** To restrain. [< L *gubernāre,* to direct, steer < Gk *kubernan.*] —**gov'ern•a•bil'i•ty, gov'ern•a•ble•ness** *n.* —**gov'ern•a•ble** *adj.* —**gov'ern•ance** *n.*
gov•ern•ess (gŭv'ər-nĭs) *n.* A woman who supervises and trains the children of a private household.
gov•ern•ment (gŭv'ərn-mənt) *n.* **1.** The administration of public policy in a political unit. **2.** The office, function, or authority whereby political power is exercised. **3.** A prevailing political system or policy. **4.** A governing body. —**gov'ern•ment'al** (-mĕnt'l) *adj.*
gov•er•nor (gŭv'ər-nər) *n.* **1.** The chief executive of a state in the U.S. or of some analogous political unit. **2.** A manager or administrative head in certain institutions or organizations. **3.** A military commandant. **4.** A feedback device providing automatic control on a machine. —**gov'er•nor•ship'** *n.*
govt. government.
gown (goun) *n.* **1.** A loose, flowing garment, as a robe or nightgown. **2.** A woman's formal dress. **3.** A distinctive outer robe worn on official or ceremonial occasions, as by a judge or clergyman. **4.** Students and professors as distinguished from townspeople: *town and gown.* [< LL *gunna,* robe, fur.]
G.P. general practitioner.
GPO general post office.
GQ general quarters.
gr. 1. grade. **2.** gross.
Gr. Greece; Greek.
Graaf•i•an follicle (grä'fē-ən). Any of the follicles in the mammalian ovary, containing a maturing ovum. [< R. de *Graaf* (1641–1673), Dutch anatomist.]
grab (grăb) *v.* **grabbed, grabbing. 1.** To grasp suddenly; snatch; seize. **2.** To obtain or appropriate unscrupulously. [MDu and MLG *grabben.*] —**grab** *n.* —**grab'ber** *n.*
grace (grās) *n.* **1.** Beauty or charm of movement, form, or proportion. **2.** Fitness or propriety. **3. a.** Good will. **b.** Mercy; clemency. **4.** Temporary immunity or respite: *a period of grace.* **5. a.** Divine love and protection bestowed freely upon mankind. **b.** The state of being thus protected or sanctified. **c.** A virtue or gift granted by God. **6.** A short prayer at mealtime. **7.** Often **Grace.** A title of courtesy for a duke, duchess, or archbishop: *His Grace the Duke of Leeds.* —**in the good** (or **bad**) **graces of.** In (or out) of favor with. —**with good** (or **bad**) **grace.** In a willing (or grudging) manner. —*v.* **graced, gracing. 1.** To honor or favor. **2.** To embellish. [< L *grātia,* pleasure, favor.] —**grace'ful** *adj.* —**grace'ful•ly** *adv.* —**grace'ful•ness** *n.* —**grace'less** *adj.*
gra•cious (grā'shəs) *adj.* **1.** Generous, tactful, and courteous. **2.** Merciful; compassionate. **3.** Marked by qualities associated with taste and breeding. **4.** Graceful. —*interj.* Expressive of surprise or mild emotion. —**gra'cious•ly** *adv.* —**gra'cious•ness** *n.*
grack•le (grăk'əl) *n.* Any of several New World blackbirds with iridescent blackish plumage. [< L *grāculus,* jackdaw.]
grad (grăd) *n. Informal.* A graduate of a school or college.
gra•da•tion (grā-dā'shən) *n.* **1. a.** A progression of successive stages. **b.** A degree or stage in such a progression. **2.** Advancement by regular stages. **3.** The act of arranging in grades. —**gra•da'tion•al** *adj.*
grade (grād) *n.* **1.** A stage or degree in a process. **2.** A position in a scale. **3.** A homogeneously ranked group or class. **4. a.** An elementary school class. **b. the grades.** Elementary school. **5.** A mark indicating a student's level of accomplishment. **6.** A military, naval, or civil-service rank. **7.** A degree of slope. **8.** A slope or gradual inclination, esp. of a road or railroad track. —*v.* **graded, grading. 1.** To arrange in degrees; rank; sort. **2.** To assign an academic grade to. **3.** To level or smooth to a desired gradient: *grade a road.* [< L *gradus,* step.]
-grade. *comb. form.* Progression or movement: **retrograde.** [< L *gradī,* to step, go.]
gra•di•ent (grā'dē-ənt) *n.* **1.** A rate of inclination. **2.** An incline. **3.** The maximum rate at which a variable physical quantity changes in value per unit change in position.
grad•u•al (grăj'ōō-əl) *adj.* Occurring or proceeding by stages or degrees. [< L *gradus,* GRADE.] —**grad'u•al•ly** *adv.*
grad•u•al•ism (grăj'ōō-ə-lĭz'əm) *n.* The policy of advancing toward a goal by gradual stages.
grad•u•ate (grăj'ōō-āt') *v.* **-ated, -ating. 1.** To grant or be granted an academic degree or diploma. **2.** To divide into categories, steps, or grades. **3.** To divide into marked intervals, esp. for use in measurement. —*n.* (grăj'ōō-ĭt). **1.** A recipient of an academic degree or diploma. **2.** A graduated container. —*adj.* (grăj'ōō-ĭt). **1.** Possessing an academic degree or diploma. **2.** Of or relating to studies beyond a bachelor's degree. [< L *gradus,* GRADE.]
Usage: Either *graduated* or *was graduated* is possible in sentences such as *She graduated* (or *was graduated*) *from college. From* is necessary in either case. *She graduated college* is not acceptable usage.
grad•u•a•tion (grăj'ōō-ā'shən) *n.* **1.** The conferring or receipt of an academic degree or diploma. **2.** A commencement ceremony. **3.** A division mark or interval on a graduated scale. **4.** Division into stages or degrees.
graf•fi•to (grə-fē'tō) *n., pl.* **-ti** (-tē). A crude drawing or inscription, as on a wall. [< It *graffiare,* to scratch.]
graft[1] (grăft, gräft) *v.* **1.** To unite (a shoot, bud, or plant) with a growing plant by insertion or placing in close contact. **2.** To transplant or implant (tissue) into a bodily part. —*n.* **1. a.** A detached shoot or bud grafted onto a growing plant. **b.** The point of union of such plant parts. **2.** Material, esp. tissue or an organ, grafted onto a bodily part. [< OF *grafe,* pencil, shoot for grafting.]
graft[2] (grăft, gräft) *n.* **1.** The unscrupulous use of one's position to derive profit or advantages. **2.** Money or advantage thus gained. —**graft** *v.* —**graft'er** *n.*
gra•ham (grā'əm) *adj.* Made from or consisting of whole-wheat flour. [< S. *Graham* (1794–1851), American vegetarian.]
Grail (grāl) *n.* The cup or dish assertedly used by Christ at the Last Supper, thereafter constituting an object of chivalrous quests. [< ML *gradālis,* dish.]
grain (grān) *n.* **1.** A small, hard seed, esp. of a cereal grass, as wheat, rice, etc. **2.** The seeds of such plants. **3.** Cereal grasses collectively. **4.** A relatively small discrete mass of particles or crystals: *a grain of sand.* **5.** A tiny quantity:

a grain of truth. **6.** A U.S. Customary System avoirdupois unit of weight equal to 0.002285 ounce or 0.036 dram. **7.** The arrangement of the fibrous tissue in wood. **8.** Texture. **9.** Temperament; nature. [< L *grānum,* seed.] **—grain'i•ness** *n.* **—grain'y** *adj.*

grain alcohol. Ethanol.

gram (grăm) *n.* Also *chiefly Brit.* **gramme.** A metric unit of mass and weight equal to one-thousandth of a kilogram. [< LL *gramma,* a small unit.]

-gram[1]. *comb. form.* Something written or drawn: **telegram.** [< Gk *gramma,* letter, and *grammē,* line.]

-gram[2]. *comb. form.* A gram: **kilogram.**

gram. grammar.

gram-at•om (grăm'ăt'əm) *n.* The mass in grams of an element numerically equal to the atomic weight.

gram•mar (grăm'ər) *n.* **1.** The study of syntax and word inflection. **2.** A book containing the syntactic and inflectional rules for a given language. **3. a.** A normative system of usage rules for pedagogical or reference purposes. **b.** Writing or speech judged with regard to such rules: *bad grammar.* [< Gk *gramma,* letter.] **—gram•mar'i•an** (grə-mâr'ē-ən) *n.* **—gram•mat'i•cal** (grə-măt'ĭ-kəl) *adj.* **—gram•mat'i•cal•ly** *adv.*

grammar school. **1.** An elementary school. **2.** A British secondary or preparatory school.

gramme. *Chiefly Brit.* Variant of **gram.**

gram-mo•lec•u•lar weight (grăm'mə-lĕk'yə-lər). *Chem.* A mole.

gram molecule. *Chem.* A mole.

Gram-neg•a•tive (grăm'nĕg'ə-tĭv) *adj.* Of or being a microorganism that does not retain the purple dye used in Gram's method.

gram•o•phone (grăm'ə-fōn') *n.* A phonograph.

Gram-pos•i•tive (grăm'pŏz'ə-tĭv) *adj.* Of or being a microorganism that retains the purple dye used in Gram's method.

gram•pus (grăm'pəs) *n., pl.* **-puses.** A whalelike marine mammal. [< OF *graspois, craspois,* fat fish.]

Gram's method (grămz). A differential staining technique using the retention or lack of retention of a purple dye to classify bacteria. [< H. *Gram* (1855–1938), Danish physician.]

gran•a•ry (grăn'ə-rē, grā'nə-) *n., pl.* **-ries.** A building for storing threshed grain.

grand (grănd) *adj.* **1.** Large and impressive in size, scope, or extent. **2.** Magnificent; sumptuous. **3.** Having higher rank than others of the same category. **4.** Principal; main: *grand ballroom.* **5.** Illustrious. **6. a.** Pretentious. **b.** Calculated to impress: *a grand manner.* **7.** Dignified and admirable. **8.** Stately; regal. **9.** Lofty; noble. **10.** Inclusive; complete: *grand total.* —*n.* **1.** A grand piano. **2.** *Slang.* A thousand dollars. [< L *grandis,* grand, full-grown.] **—grand'ly** *adv.* **—grand'ness** *n.*

gran•dam (grăn'dăm', -dəm) *n.* **1.** A grandmother. **2.** An old woman.

Grand Canyon. A gorge formed by the Colorado River in NW Arizona.

grand•child (grănd'chīld') *n.* A child of one's son or daughter.

grand•daugh•ter (grăn'dô'tər) *n.* The daughter of one's son or daughter.

gran•dee (grăn-dē') *n.* A nobleman of the highest rank in Spain or Portugal. [< Port *grande,* "great (one)."]

gran•deur (grăn'jər, -jŏŏr) *n.* Greatness; splendor; majesty.

grand•fa•ther (grănd'fä'*th*ər) *n.* **1.** The father of one's mother or father. **2.** An ancestor.

gran•dil•o•quence (grăn-dĭl'ə-kwəns) *n.* Pompous or bombastic eloquence. **—gran•dil'o•quent** *adj.* **—gran•dil'o•quent•ly** *adv.*

gran•di•ose (grăn'dē-ōs', grăn'dē-ōs') *adj.* **1.** Grand and imposing. **2.** Affectedly grand. **—gran'di•ose'ly** *adv.* **—gran'di•os'i•ty** (-ŏs'ə-tē), **gran'di•ose'ness** *n.*

grand•ma (grănd'mä', grăn'mä', grăm'mä', grăm'ə) *n. Informal.* Grandmother.

grand mal (gräɴ mäl'). A form of epilepsy characterized by severe seizures involving spasms and loss of consciousness.

grand•moth•er (grănd'mŭ*th*'ər) *n.* **1.** The mother of one's father or mother. **2.** A female ancestor.

grand•pa (grănd'pä', grăm'pä', grăm'pə) *n. Informal.* Grandfather.

grand•par•ent (grănd'pâr'ənt, grăn'-) *n.* A parent of one's mother or father.

grand piano. A piano having the strings strung in a horizontal harp-shaped frame.

Grand Rapids (răp'ĭdz). A city of S Michigan. Pop. 177,000.

grand•son (grănd'sŭn', grăn'-) *n.* The son of one's son or daughter.

grand•stand (grănd'stănd', grăn'-) *n.* A roofed stand for spectators at a stadium or racetrack.

grange (grānj) *n.* **1. Grange. a.** The Patrons of Husbandry, a U.S. farmers' association. **b.** One of its branch lodges. **2.** *Archaic.* A manor house. [< L *grānum,* GRAIN.]

gran•ite (grăn'ĭt) *n.* A common, coarse-grained, light-colored, hard igneous rock consisting chiefly of quartz, orthoclase, and mica, used in monuments and for building. [It *granito,* "grained."] **—gra•nit'ic** (grə-nĭt'ĭk) *adj.*

gran•ny (grăn'ē) *n., pl.* **-nies.** **1.** A grandmother. **2.** A fuss-budget. **3.** *Southern U.S.* A midwife.

grant (grănt, gränt) *v.* **1.** To allow; consent to. **2.** To accord, as a favor. **3. a.** To bestow; confer. **b.** To transfer (property) by a deed. **4.** To concede; acknowledge. —*n.* **1.** The act of granting. **2.** Something granted. **3. a.** A transfer of property by deed. **b.** The instrument of such transfer. **c.** Land thus bestowed. [< OF *greanter, creanter,* to insure, guarantee.]

Grant (grănt), **Ulysses S(impson).** 1822–1885. American general; 18th President of the U.S. (1869–77).

Ulysses S. Grant

gran•u•lar (grăn'yə-lər) *adj.* **1.** Composed of granules or grains. **2.** Grainy. **—gran'u•lar'i•ty** *n.* **—gran'u•lar•ly** *adv.*

gran•u•late (grăn'yə-lāt') *v.* **-lated, -lating.** **1.** To form into grains or granules. **2.** To make rough and grainy. **—gran'u•la'tion** *n.*

gran•ule (grăn'yo͞ol) *n.* A small grain or pellet; particle.

grape (grāp) *n.* **1.** A juicy, smooth-skinned, edible fruit borne in clusters on a woody vine. **2.** A vine bearing such fruit. **3.** Grapeshot. [< OF, bunch of grapes, hook.]

grape•fruit (grāp'fro͞ot') *n.* **1.** A large, round, yellow-skinned, acid-flavored citrus fruit. **2.** A tree bearing such fruit.

grape•shot (grāp'shŏt') *n.* A cluster of iron balls formerly used as a cannon charge.

grape sugar. Dextrose.

grape•vine (grāp'vīn') *n.* **1.** A vine on which grapes grow. **2.** An informal means of transmitting information or rumor. **3.** Gossip; rumor.

graph (grăf, gräf) *n.* **1.** A drawing that exhibits a relationship between two sets of numbers. **2.** Any pictorial device, as a bar graph, used to display numerical relationships. —*v.* **1.** To represent by a graph. **2.** To plot (a function) on a graph.

-graph. *comb. form.* **1.** An apparatus that writes or records: **seismograph. 2.** Something drawn or written: **monograph.** [< Gk *graphein,* to write.]

graph•ic (grăf'ĭk) *adj.* Also **graph•i•cal** (-ĭ-kəl). **1.** Written, printed, drawn, or engraved. **2.** Vividly outlined or set forth: *a graphic account.* **3.** Of or pertaining to the graphic arts. [< Gk *graphein,* to write.] **—graph'i•cal•ly** *adv.*

graphic arts. Any of the fine or applied visual arts, as painting, drawing, etc.

graph•ite (grăf'īt') *n.* The soft, steel-gray to black, hexagonally crystallized allotrope of carbon, used in lead pencils, lubricants, paints, and coatings. [< Gk *graphein,* to write.] **—gra•phit'ic** (-fĭt'ĭk) *adj.*

-graphy. *comb. form.* **1.** A method of graphic representation: **stenography. 2.** A descriptive science of a specific subject or field: **oceanography.**

grap•nel (grăp'nəl) *n.* A small anchor with three or more flukes. [< OF *grapon,* anchor, hook.]

grap•ple (grăp'əl) *n.* **1. a.** A clawed implement formerly used to hold an enemy ship alongside for boarding. **b.** A grapnel. **2.** Hand-to-hand combat. —*v.* **-pled, -pling.** **1.** To lay hold on, make fast, or drag with or as if with a grapple. **2.** To seize firmly with the hands. **3. a.** To come to grips; wrestle. **b.** To attempt to cope: *grapple with a problem.* [< OProv *grapa,* hook.] **—grap'pler** *n.*

grasp (grăsp) *v.* **1.** To take hold of or seize. **2.** To hold with the hand; clasp. **3.** To comprehend. —*n.* **1.** Hold; control; grip. **2.** The ability to seize or reach. **3.** Comprehension. [< OE **grapsan.*]

grasp•ing (grăs'pĭng) *adj.* Greedy; avaricious. **—grasp'ing•ly** *adv.* **—grasp'ing•ness** *n.*

grass (grăs, gräs) *n.* **1.** Any of numerous plants with narrow leaves, jointed stems, and spikes or clusters of inconspicuous flowers. **2.** Such plants collectively. **3.** Ground, as a lawn or pasture, covered with such plants. **4.** *Slang.* Marijuana. [< OE *græs.* See **ghrē-.**] **—grass'y** *adj.*

grass•hop•per (grăs'hŏp'ər, gräs'-) *n.* Any of various related insects with long hind legs adapted for jumping.

grass•land (grăs'lănd', gräs'-) *n.* An area, such as a prairie, of grass or grasslike vegetation.

grass•roots (grăs'ro͞ots', -ro͝ots', gräs'-) *pl.n.*

1. The rural electorate. 2. The groundwork or source of something. —**grass'roots'** *adj.*

grate¹ (grāt) *v.* **grated, grating.** 1. To shred or pulverize by rubbing. 2. To make or cause to make a rasping sound. 3. To irritate. —*n.* A rasping noise. [< OF *grater,* to scrape.] —**grat'er** *n.* —**grat'ing·ly** *adv.*

grate² (grāt) *n.* 1. A framework of parallel bars over an opening. 2. Such a framework of metal, used to hold burning fuel. [< L *crātis,* frame, wicker basket.]

grate·ful (grāt'fəl) *adj.* 1. Appreciative; thankful. 2. Expressing gratitude. 3. Agreeable; pleasing. [< L *grātus,* pleasing, favorable.] —**grate'ful·ly** *adv.* —**grate'ful·ness** *n.*

grat·i·fy (grăt'ə-fī') *v.* **-fied, -fying.** To please, favor, or indulge. —**grat'i·fi·ca'tion** *n.*

grat·ing¹ (grā'tĭng) *adj.* 1. Rasping. 2. Irritating. —**grat'ing·ly** *adv.*

grat·ing² (grā'tĭng) *n.* A grill; grate.

gra·tis (grā'tĭs, grăt'ĭs) *adv.* Without charge; free. [< L *grātus,* favorable.] —**gra'tis** *adj.*

grat·i·tude (grăt'ə-t/y/o͞od') *n.* Thankfulness. [< L *grātus,* favorable.]

gra·tu·i·tous (gră-t/y/o͞o'ə-təs) *adj.* 1. Free; gratis. 2. Unnecessary or unwarranted: *gratuitous criticism.* [L *grātuītus,* given as a favor.] —**gra·tu'i·tous·ly** *adv.*

gra·tu·i·ty (grə-t/y/o͞o'ə-tē) *n., pl.* **-ties.** A tip for service.

grau·pel (grou'pəl) *n.* Precipitation consisting of pellets of snow. [< G *Graupe,* hulled grain.]

grave¹ (grāv) *n.* An excavation for the interment of a corpse; burial place. [< OE *græf.* See **ghrebh-.**]

grave² (grāv) *adj.* **graver, gravest.** 1. Extremely serious; important; weighty. 2. Fraught with danger; critical. [< L *gravis,* heavy, weighty.] —**grave'ly** *adv.* —**grave'ness** *n.*

grave³ (grāv) *v.* **graved, graven** (grā'vən), **graving.** To sculpt or carve; engrave. [< OE *grafan.* See **ghrebh-.**] —**grav'er** *n.*

grav·el (grăv'əl) *n.* Any unconsolidated mixture of rock or rocklike fragments. [< OF *grave.*]

grave·stone (grāv'stōn') *n.* A tombstone.

grave·yard (grāv'yärd') *n.* A cemetery.

grav·id (grăv'ĭd) *adj.* Pregnant. [< L *gravidus.*]

grav·i·met·ric (grăv'ə-mĕt'rĭk) *adj.* Pertaining to measurement by weight.

grav·i·tate (grăv'ə-tāt') *v.* **-tated, -tating.** 1. To move in response to the force of gravity. 2. To be attracted by or toward.

grav·i·ta·tion (grăv'ə-tā'shən) *n.* 1. a. The natural phenomenon of attraction between massive bodies. b. The degree of such attraction; broadly, gravity. 2. A movement toward a source of attraction: *the gravitation of the middle class to the suburbs.* —**grav'i·ta'tion·al** *adj.*

grav·i·ton (grăv'ə-tŏn') *n.* A particle postulated to be the quantum of gravitational interaction, and presumed to have zero electric charge and zero rest mass.

grav·i·ty (grăv'ə-tē) *n.* 1. a. The force of gravitation, being, for any two sufficiently massive bodies, directly proportional to the product of their masses and inversely proportional to the square of the distance between them; esp. the attractive central gravitational force exerted by a celestial body such as the earth. b. Loosely, gravitation. c. *Rare.* Weight. 2. Graveness; seriousness. [< L *gravis,* heavy, GRAVE.]

gra·vure (grə-vyo͝or') *n.* A method of printing using photomechanically prepared plates or cylinders; photogravure. [< F *graver,* to engrave, dig into.]

gra·vy (grā'vē) *n., pl.* **-vies.** 1. The juices that drip from cooking meat. 2. A sauce made from these juices. [< OF *grain,* spice, grain.]

gravy boat. An elongated dish or pitcher for serving gravy.

gray (grā). Also **grey.** *adj.* 1. Of a neutral color ranging between black and white. 2. Dull or dark; gloomy. 3. Having gray hair. —*n.* 1. A neutral color ranging between black and white. 2. An object or animal of this color. [< OE *grǣg.* See **gher-⁴.**] —**gray'ish** *adj.*

gray matter. The brownish-gray nerve tissue of the brain and spinal cord.

graze¹ (grāz) *v.* **grazed, grazing.** 1. To feed on growing grass and herbage. 2. To put (livestock) out to graze. [< OE *grasian,* GRASS.]

graze² (grāz) *v.* **grazed, grazing.** To touch or scrape lightly in passing. —**graz'ing·ly** *adv.*

grease (grēs) *n.* 1. Melted animal fat. 2. Any thick oil or viscous lubricant. —*v.* **greased, greasing.** To coat, smear, lubricate, or soil with grease. [< L *crassus,* fat.]

grease paint. Theatrical make-up.

greas·y (grē'sē, -zē) *adj.* **-ier, -iest.** 1. Coated or soiled with grease. 2. Containing grease; oily.

great (grāt) *adj.* 1. Extremely large; bulky; big. 2. Remarkable; outstanding: *a great work of art.* 3. Eminent; distinguished: *a great leader.* 4. *Informal.* First-rate; very good: *a great book.* 5. Being one generation removed from the relative specified: *a great-grandfather.* —*adv. Informal.* Very well. [< OE *grēat,* thick, coarse. See **ghrēu-.**] —**great'ness.** *n.*

Great Bear. **Ursa Major.**

Great Brit·ain (brĭt'n). An island off the W coast of Europe, comprising England, Scotland, and Wales.

great circle. A circle that is the intersection of the surface of a sphere with a plane passing through the center of the sphere.

Great Dane. A large, powerful dog with a smooth, short coat.

Greater An·til·les (ăn-tĭl'ēz). An island group of the West Indies, including Cuba, Jamaica, Hispaniola, and Puerto Rico.

great-grand·child (grāt'grănd'chīld') *n.* Any of the children of a grandchild.

great-grand·par·ent (grāt'grănd'pâr'ənt) *n.* Either of the parents of any grandparent.

great·heart·ed (grāt'här'tĭd) *adj.* 1. Courageous in spirit; stouthearted. 2. Unselfish; magnanimous.

Great Lakes. The largest group of freshwater lakes in the world, in C North America.

great·ly (grāt'lē) *adv.* To a great degree.

Great Salt Lake. A highly saline lake in N Utah.

Great Smoky Mountains. A range of the S Appalachians.

grebe (grēb) *n.* A diving bird with lobed, fleshy membranes along each toe. [F *grèbe.*]

Gre·cian (grē'shən) *adj.* Greek. —*n.* A native of Greece.

Gre·co-Ro·man (grē'kō-rō'mən, grĕk'ō-) *adj.* Of or pertaining to both Greece and Rome.

Greece (grēs). A nation of SE Europe. Pop. 8,550,000. Cap. Athens.

greed (grēd) *n.* A rapacious desire for more than one needs or deserves; avarice.

greed·y (grē'dē) *adj.* **-ier, -iest.** Excessively eager to acquire; covetous; avaricious. [< OE *grǣdig.*] —**greed'i·ly** *adv.* —**greed'i·ness** *n.*

Greek (grēk) *n.* 1. The language of the Hellenes, constituting the Hellenic group of Indo-European. (In the etymologies of this Dictionary, *Greek* is used to mean **Ancient Greek.**) 2. An indigenous inhabitant of Greece. —*adj.* Of or pertaining to Greece, the Hellenes, their language, or their culture.

Greece

Greek Church. A branch of the Eastern Orthodox Church that is the national church of Greece.

green (grēn) *n.* 1. Any of a group of colors whose hue is that of the emerald or somewhat less yellow than that of growing grass. 2. Leafy plants or plant parts used as food or for decoration. 3. A grassy lawn or plot: *a putting green.* —*adj.* 1. Of the color green. 2. Abounding in green growth or foliage. 3. Not ripe; immature. 4. Lacking experience. —*v.* To make or become green. [< OE *grēne.* See **ghrē-.**] —**green'ish** *adj.* —**green'ness** *n.*

green·back (grēn'băk') *n.* Any official note of U.S. currency.

green·er·y (grē'nə-rē) *n.* Green plants or foliage.

green-eyed (grēn'īd') *adj.* 1. Having green eyes. 2. Jealous; envious.

green·horn (grēn'hôrn') *n.* An inexperienced or immature person. [Orig, a young animal with immature horns.]

green·house (grēn'hous') *n.* A usually glass-enclosed structure in which plants requiring controlled temperature are grown.

Green·land (grēn'lənd, -lănd'). An island in the N Atlantic and Arctic, constituting an integral part of Denmark. Pop. 36,000. Cap. Godthaab.

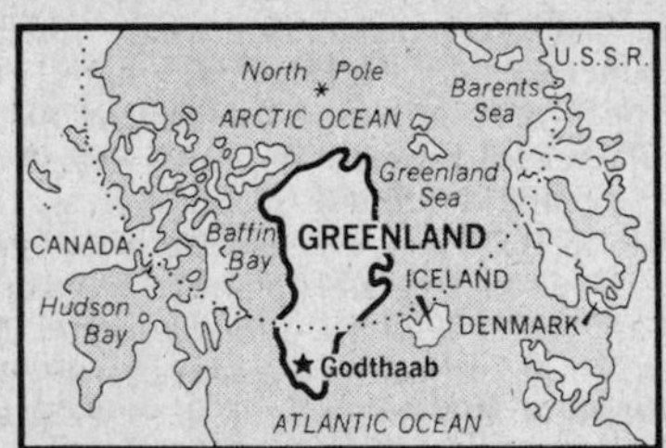

Greenland

Greens·bo·ro (grēnz'bûr'ō). A city of north-central North Carolina. Pop. 120,000.

green·sward (grēn'swôrd') *n.* Turf on which the grass is green.

green thumb. A knack for making plants thrive.

green turtle. A large marine turtle having edible flesh.

Green·wich time (grĭn'ĭj, -ĭch, grĕn'-). Mean solar time for the meridian at Greenwich,

England, used as a basis for calculating time throughout most of the world; Greenwich mean time.

green•wood (grēn'wŏŏd') *n.* A leafy wood or forest.

greet (grēt) *v.* **1.** To address in a friendly way; welcome. **2.** To receive: *greet a joke with laughter.* **3.** To present itself to: *A din greeted our ears.* [< OE *grētan.* See **gher-³**.]

greet•ing (grē'tĭng) *n.* A gesture or word of welcome or salutation.

gre•gar•i•ous (grĭ-gâr'ē-əs) *adj.* **1.** Tending to live or move in herds. **2.** Seeking and enjoying the company of others; sociable. [< L *grex,* herd, flock.] **—gre•gar'i•ous•ly** *adv.*

Gre•go•ri•an calendar (grĭ-gôr'ē-ən, grĭ-gōr'-). The calendar now in use throughout most of the world, introduced by Pope Gregory XIII in 1582.

gre•nade (grə-nād') *n.* A missile containing priming and bursting charges, usually thrown by hand. [< POMEGRANATE.]

gren•a•dier (grĕn'ə-dîr') *n.* A member of a regiment formerly armed with grenades.

gren•a•dine (grĕn'ə-dēn', grĕn'ə-dēn') *n.* A thick, sweet syrup made from pomegranates.

grew (grōō). *p.t.* of **grow.**

grew•some. Variant of **gruesome.**

grey. Variant of **gray.**

grey•hound (grā'hound') *n.* A large, slender, swift-running dog with a smooth coat and a narrow head. [< OE *grīghund.*]

grid (grĭd) *n.* **1.** A grating or gridiron. **2.** A pattern of lines forming squares on a map, used as a reference for locating points. **3. a.** A system of electric cables and power stations over a large area. **b.** A corrugated or perforated conducting plate in a storage battery. **c.** A structure of fine wires located between the plate and filament in an electron tube. [Short for GRIDIRON.]

grid•dle (grĭd'l) *n.* A flat pan used for cooking by dry heat. [< L *crātis,* wickerwork.]

grid•dle•cake (grĭd'l-kāk') *n.* A pancake.

grid•i•ron (grĭd'ī'ərn) *n.* **1.** A framework of parallel metal bars used for broiling. **2.** Any framework or network suggestive of a gridiron. **3.** A football field. [Perh < GRIDDLE.]

grief (grēf) *n.* **1.** Intense mental anguish; acute sorrow. **2.** A source of grief.

griev•ance (grē'vəns) *n.* **1.** A circumstance regarded as just cause for protest. **2.** A complaint based on such a circumstance.

grieve (grēv) *v.* **grieved, grieving.** **1.** To cause grief to; distress. **2.** To be sorrowful; lament; mourn. [< L *gravāre,* to oppress, weigh upon.]

griev•ous (grē'vəs) *adj.* **1.** Causing or expressing grief, pain, or anguish. **2.** Serious or dire; grave. **—griev'ous•ly** *adv.*

grif•fin (grĭf'ən) *n.* Also **grif•fon, gry•phon.** A mythical beast with the head and wings of an eagle and the body of a lion. [< Gk *grups.*]

grill (grĭl) *n.* **1.** A cooking utensil containing metal bars; gridiron. **2.** Food cooked on a grill. **3.** A grillroom. **4.** Variant of **grille.** —*v.* **1.** To broil on a grill. **2.** *Informal.* To question relentlessly; cross-examine. [< L *crātis,* wickerwork.]

grille (grĭl) *n.* Also **grill.** A metal grating used as a screen, as in a window or gate.

grill•room (grĭl'rōōm', -rŏŏm') *n.* A restaurant or room in a restaurant where grilled foods are served.

grim (grĭm) *adj.* **grimmer, grimmest.** **1.** Unrelenting; rigid; stern. **2.** Uninviting in aspect; forbidding; terrible. **3.** Ghastly; sinister. **4.** Ferocious; savage. [< OE, fierce, severe. See **ghrem-.**] **—grim'ly** *adv.* **—grim'ness** *n.*

gri•mace (grĭ-mās', grĭm'ĭs) *n.* A contortion of the face expressing grimace, pain, contempt, or disgust. [< Frank **grīma,* mask.] **—gri•mace'** *v.* **(-maced, -macing).**

grime (grīm) *n.* Black dirt or soot clinging to or ingrained in a surface. [< MDu *grīme.*] **—grim'y** *adj.*

grin (grĭn) *v.* **grinned, grinning.** To smile broadly, showing the teeth. —*n.* The expression produced by grinning. [< OE *grennian,* to grimace.] **—grin'ner** *n.*

grind (grīnd) *v.* **ground, grinding.** **1.** To crush into fine particles. **2.** To shape, sharpen, or refine with friction: *grind a lens.* **3.** To rub together; gnash: *grind the teeth.* **4.** To move with noisy friction: *grind to a halt.* **5.** To bear down on harshly; crush. **6.** To operate or produce by turning a crank. **7.** To produce mechanically or without inspiration (with *out*). **8.** *Informal.* To devote oneself to study or work. —*n.* **1.** The act of grinding. **2.** A specific degree of pulverization, as of coffee beans. **3.** *Informal.* **a.** A laborious task, routine, or study. **b.** One who works or studies excessively. [< OE *grindan.* See **ghren-.**] **—grind'er** *n.* **—grind'ing•ly** *adv.*

grind•stone (grīnd'stōn') *n.* A revolving stone disk used for grinding, polishing, or sharpening tools.

grip¹ (grĭp) *n.* **1.** A tight hold; a firm grasp. **2.** A manner of grasping and holding. **3.** A part to be grasped and held; handle. **4.** A suitcase or valise. **—come to grips.** **1.** To fight in hand-to-hand combat. **2.** To deal actively and conclusively, as with a problem. —*v.* **gripped, gripping.** **1.** To grasp and maintain a tight hold on. **2.** To hold the attention of. [< OE *gripa,* grasp, and *gripa,* handful. See **ghreib-.**] **—grip'ping•ly** *adv.*

grip². Variant of **grippe.**

gripe (grīp) *v.* **griped, griping.** **1.** To cause or suffer sharp pain in the bowels. **2.** *Informal.* To irritate; annoy. **3.** *Informal.* To complain naggingly; grumble. —*n.* **1.** *Informal.* A complaint. **2. gripes.** Sharp, repeated pains in the bowels. [< OE *grīpan.* See **ghreib-.**]

grippe (grĭp) *n.* Also **grip.** Influenza. [< Frank **grīpan.*] **—grip'py** *adj.*

gris•ly (grĭz'lē) *adj.* **-lier, -liest.** Horrifying; repugnant; gruesome. [< OE *grislīc.*]

grist (grĭst) *n.* Grain to be ground or already ground. [< OE *grist.* See **ghren-.**]

gris•tle (grĭs'əl) *n.* Cartilage, esp. in meat. [< OE < Gmc **gristil-.*] **—gris'tly** *adj.*

grit (grĭt) *n.* **1. a.** Minute rough granules, as of sand or stone. **b.** A material composed of such granules. **c.** The texture of such a material. **2.** *Informal.* Indomitable spirit; pluck. —*v.* **gritted, gritting.** To clamp (the teeth) together. [< OE *grēot.* See **ghrēu-.**] **—grit'ty** *adj.*

grits (grĭts) *pl.n.* Coarsely ground grain, esp. corn. [< OE *grytt,* bran.]

griz•zle (grĭz'əl) *v.* **-zled, -zling.** To make or become gray. [< Frank **gris,* gray.]

griz•zly (grĭz'lē) *adj.* **-zlier, -zliest.** Grayish or flecked with gray. —*n., pl.* **-zlies.** Also **grizzly bear.** A large grayish bear of NW North America.

groan (grōn) *v.* To voice a deep, wordless, prolonged sound expressive of pain, grief, annoyance, or disapproval. —*n.* The sound made in groaning; a moan. [< OE *grānian.*]

groats (grōts) *pl.n.* Hulled, usually crushed grain, esp. oats. [< OE *grotan.*]

gro•cer (grō'sər) *n.* A storekeeper who sells foodstuffs and sundry household supplies. [< OF *grossier,* wholesale dealer.]

gro•cer•y (grō'sə-rē) *n., pl.* **-ies.** **1.** A store selling foodstuffs and household supplies. **2. groceries.** Commodities sold by a grocer.

grog (grŏg) *n.* Alcoholic liquor, esp. rum diluted with water.

grog•gy (grŏg'ē) *adj.* **-gier, -giest.** Unsteady and dazed; shaky. **—grog'gi•ly** *adv.*

groin (groin) *n.* **1.** The crease at the junction of the thigh with the trunk, together with the adjacent region. **2.** *Archit.* The curved edge at the junction of two intersecting vaults. [Perh < OE *grynde,* abyss, depression.]

grom•met (grŏm'ĭt) *n.* A reinforced eyelet in cloth, leather, etc., through which a fastener can be passed. [Obs F *grommette,* bridle ring.]

groom (grōōm) *n.* **1.** A man or boy employed to take care of horses. **2.** A bridegroom. —*v.* **1.** To make neat and trim. **2.** To clean and brush (an animal). **3.** To train, as for a specific position.

groove (grōōv) *n.* **1.** A long, narrow furrow or channel. **2.** A settled, humdrum routine; rut. —*v.* **grooved, grooving.** To cut a groove in. [< MDu *groeve,* ditch.]

grope (grōp) *v.* **groped, groping.** **1.** To reach about uncertainly; feel one's way. **2.** To search blindly or uncertainly. [< OE *grāpian.* See **ghreib-.**] **—grop'ing•ly** *adv.*

gros•beak (grōs'bēk') *n.* Any of several often colorful birds with a thick, rounded bill.

gross (grōs) *adj.* **1.** Exclusive of deductions: *gross profits.* **2.** Glaringly obvious; flagrant. **3.** Coarse; vulgar. **4.** Overweight; corpulent. —*n., pl.* **gross.** **1.** Twelve dozen. **2.** A group of 12 dozen items. —*v.* To earn a total of before deductions. [< L *grossus,* thick.] **—gross'ly** *adv.* **—gross'ness** *n.*

gro•tesque (grō-tĕsk') *adj.* **1.** Characterized by ludicrous or incongruous distortion. **2.** Extravagant; outlandish; bizarre. [< OIt *(pittura) grottesca,* "grottolike (painting)."] **—gro•tesque'ly** *adv.* **—gro•tesque'ness** *n.*

grot•to (grŏt'ō) *n., pl.* **-toes** or **-tos.** **1.** A small cave or cavern. **2.** An artificial cavelike structure or excavation. [< L *crypta,* vault, CRYPT.]

grouch (grouch) *v.* To grumble or sulk. —*n.* **1.** A grumbling or sulky mood. **2.** A habitually complaining or irritable person. [ME *grutchen,* to grudge.] **—grouch'y** *adj.*

ground¹ (ground) *n.* **1.** The solid surface of the earth. **2.** Soil; earth. **3.** Often **grounds.** An area of land designated for a particular purpose. **4. grounds.** The land surrounding a building. **5.** Often **grounds.** The foundation or basis for an argument, belief, or action. **6.** A background. **7. grounds.** The sediment at the bottom of a liquid, esp. coffee. **8. a.** The position or portion of an electric circuit that is at zero potential with respect to the earth. **b.** A conducting connection to such a position or to the earth. **c.** A large conducting body, such as the earth, used as a return for electric currents and as an arbitrary zero of potential. —*v.* **1.** To place or set on the ground. **2.** To provide a basis for; substantiate; justify. **3.** To instruct in fundamentals; school. **4.** To prevent (an aircraft, pilot, or crew) from flying. **5.** To connect (an electric circuit) to a ground. **6.** To run (a vessel) aground. [< OE *grund* < Gmc **grunduz.*]

ground² (ground). *p.t.* & *p.p.* of **grind.**

ground hog. A woodchuck.

ground•less (ground'lĭs) *adj.* Having no ground or foundation; unsubstantiated. **—ground'less•ly** *adv.* **—ground'less•ness** *n.*

ground water. Water beneath the earth's surface between saturated soil and rock that supplies wells and springs.

ground•work (ground'wûrk') *n.* A foundation; basis; preliminary work.

group (gro͞op) *n.* A number of individuals or things considered together because of certain similarities. —*v.* To place in or form a group or groups. [< It *gruppo,* "knot."]

group•er (gro͞o'pər) *n.* Any of various large, chiefly tropical marine fishes. [Port *garoupa.*]

grouse[1] (grous) *n., pl.* **grouse.** A plump, chickenlike bird with mottled brown or grayish plumage. [?]

grouse[2] (grous) *v.* **groused, grousing.** *Informal.* To complain; grumble. [?]

grove (grōv) *n.* A small group of trees lacking dense undergrowth. [< OE *grāf.*]

grov•el (grŭv'əl, grŏv'-) *v.* To humble oneself in a servile manner; cringe. [< ON *ā grūfu,* prone.] —**grov'el•er** *n.*

grow (grō) *v.* **grew, grown** (grōn), **growing. 1.** To increase in size by natural processes. **2.** To cultivate; raise: *grow tulips.* **3.** To develop and reach maturity. **4.** To be capable of growth; thrive; flourish. **5.** To become: *grow angry; grow cold.* —**grow up. 1.** To reach maturity; become an adult. **2.** To come into being; develop. [< OE *grōwan.* See **ghrē-.**]

growl (groul) *n.* A low, guttural, menacing sound, as of an angry dog. —*v.* To utter or express by such a sound. [Perh imit.]

grown (grōn) *adj.* Mature; adult.

grown-up (grōn'ŭp') *adj.* Characteristic of or suitable for an adult. —**grown'up'** *n.*

growth (grōth) *n.* **1. a.** The process of growing or developing. **b.** A stage in the process of growing. **2.** An increase, as in size or number. **3.** Something that has grown: *a new growth of grass.* **4.** An abnormal tissue formation.

grub (grŭb) *v.* **grubbed, grubbing. 1.** To clear of roots. **2.** To dig up by the roots. **3. a.** To search laboriously; rummage. **b.** To toil arduously; drudge: *grub for a living.* **4.** *Slang.* To obtain by importunity: *grub a cigarette.* —*n.* **1.** The thick, wormlike larva of certain insects. **2.** *Slang.* Food. [< OE **grybban.* See **ghrebh-.**] —**grub'ber** *n.*

grub•by (grŭb'ē) *adj.* **-bier, -biest.** Dirty; unkempt. —**grub'bi•ness** *n.*

grub•stake (grŭb'stāk') *n.* Supplies or funds advanced to a mining prospector in return for a promised share of the profits.

grudge (grŭj) *v.* **grudged, grudging.** To be reluctant to give or admit. —*n.* A deep-seated feeling of resentment or rancor. [Prob < MHG *grunzen,* to grunt.] —**grudg'ing•ly** *adv.*

gru•el (gro͞o'əl) *n.* A thin, watery porridge. —*v.* To exhaust. [< OF *gru,* groats, oatmeal.] —**gru'el•ing** *adj.* —**gru'el•ing•ly** *adv.*

grue•some (gro͞o'səm) *adj.* Also **grew•some.** Causing horror and repugnance; frightful and shocking. [< obs *grue,* to shiver.] —**grue'-some•ly** *adv.* —**grue'some•ness** *n.*

gruff (grŭf) *adj.* **1.** Brusque and stern in speech or manner. **2.** Harsh; hoarse. [Du *grof.*] —**gruff'ly** *adv.* —**gruff'ness** *n.*

grum•ble (grŭm'bəl) *v.* **-bled, -bling.** To mumble in discontent. —*n.* A grumbling utterance. [< ME *grummen.*] —**grum'bler** *n.*

grump•y (grŭm'pē) *adj.* **-ier, -iest.** Fretful and peevish; irritable; cranky. [< dial *grump,* ill-tempered.] —**grump'i•ness** *n.*

grun•ion (grŭn'yən) *n.* A small fish of California coastal waters that spawns along beaches during high tides at the time of the full moon. [Perh < L *grunnire,* to grunt.]

grunt (grŭnt) *v.* To utter (with) a low, guttural sound, as does a hog. —*n.* A low, guttural sound. [< OE *grunnettan.*]

gry•phon. Variant of **griffin.**

gtd. guaranteed.

GU genitourinary.

Gua•da•la•ja•ra (gwŏd'l-ə-här'ə). A city of west-central Mexico. Pop. 978,000.

Guam (gwŏm). An island of the U.S. in the W Pacific. Pop. 72,000.

gua•nine (gwä'nēn') *n.* A purine, $C_5H_5N_5O$, that is a constituent of both ribonucleic and deoxyribonucleic acids. [< GUANO.]

gua•no (gwä'nō) *n.* A substance composed chiefly of the dung of sea birds or bats, used as fertilizer. [< Quechua *huanu,* dung.]

guar. guaranteed.

gua•ra•ni (gwär'ə-nē') *n., pl.* **-ni** or **-nis.** The basic monetary unit of Paraguay.

Gua•ra•ni (gwär'ə-nē') *n.* **1.** A group of South American Indians of Paraguay, Bolivia, and S Brazil. **2.** The Tupi-Guarani language of these people.

guar•an•tee (găr'ən-tē') *n.* **1.** A formal assurance that something is as represented or that a specified act will be performed. **2.** A guaranty. **3.** A guarantor. —*v.* **-teed, -teeing. 1.** To assume responsibility for the debt or default of. **2.** To undertake to accomplish something. **3.** To furnish security for. [Perh < Frank **wārjan,* to vouch for the truth of.]

guar•an•tor (găr'ən-tər, -tôr') *n.* One that gives a guarantee or guaranty.

guar•an•ty (găr'ən-tē) *n., pl.* **-ties. 1.** An undertaking to answer for another's debts or obligations in the event of default. **2. a.** Anything held as security for something. **b.** The act of providing such security. **3.** A guarantor.

guard (gärd) *v.* **1.** To protect from harm; watch over. **2.** To watch over to prevent escape. **3.** To keep watch at (a door or gate). **4.** To take precautions: *guard against infection.* —*n.* **1.** One that guards. **2.** A body of persons who serve on ceremonial occasions: *an honor guard.* **3.** Watchful care: *under close guard.* **4.** A defensive posture or stance. **5.** *Football.* One of the two players on either side of the center. **6.** *Basketball.* Either of the two defensive players. **7.** Any device that prevents injury, damage, or loss. [< OF *garder, guarder.*] —**guard'er** *n.*

guard•ed (gär'dĭd) *adj.* **1.** Kept safe; protected. **2.** Cautious; restrained: *guarded words.* —**guard'ed•ly** *adv.*

guard•house (gärd'hous') *n.* **1.** A building occupied by a guard. **2.** A military detention house.

guard•i•an (gär'dē-ən) *n.* **1.** One who guards; a custodian. **2.** A person legally responsible for the care of one incompetent to manage his own affairs, as a child during its minority. —**guard'i•an•ship'** *n.*

guards•man (gärdz'mən) *n.* A member of a regiment of guards.

Gua•te•ma•la (gwä'tə-mä'lə). **1.** A republic in Central America. Pop. 4,343,000. **2.** Also **Guatemala City.** The capital of this republic. Pop. 573,000. —**Gua'te•ma'lan** *adj.* & *n.*

gua•va (gwä'və) *n.* The yellow-skinned fruit of a tropical American tree, used for jellies and preserves. [Span.]

gu•ber•na•to•ri•al (g/y/o͞o'bər-nə-tôr'ē-əl, -tōr'ē-əl) *adj.* Of or relating to a governor.

guer•don (gûrd'n) *n. Poetic.* A reward; requital. [< OF.]

guer•ril•la, gue•ril•la (gə-rĭl'ə) *n.* A member of an irregular military force that seeks to immobilize and isolate the superior forces of an occupying enemy. —*adj.* Of or by guerrillas: *guerrilla warfare.* [< Span *guerra,* war.]

guess (gĕs) *v.* **1.** To predict (a result or event) or assume (a fact) without sufficient information. **2.** To estimate or judge correctly. **3.** To suppose. —*n.* **1.** An instance of guessing. **2.** A conjecture arrived at by guessing. [Prob < Scand.] —**guess'er** *n.*

guess•work (gĕs'wûrk') *n.* **1.** The process of making guesses. **2.** An instance of inference by guessing.

guest (gĕst) *n.* **1.** A recipient of hospitality at the home or table of another. **2.** A patron of a restaurant, hotel, etc. [< ON *gestr.*]

guf•faw (gə-fô') *n.* A hearty or coarse burst of laughter. [Imit.] —**guf•faw'** *v.*

Gui•an•a (gē-ăn'ə, -ä'nə). A region of NE South America, including SE Venezuela, part of N Brazil, and French Guiana, Surinam, and Guyana.

gui•dance (gī'dəns) *n.* **1.** An act or instance of guiding. **2.** Counseling, as on vocational, educational, or marital problems.

guide (gīd) *n.* **1.** One who shows the way by leading or directing, esp. a person employed to guide a tour, group, etc. **2.** Any sign or mark that serves to direct. **3.** An example or model to be followed. **4.** A book or manual that serves to instruct or direct. **5.** Any device that acts as an indicator or regulates the motion of something. —*v.* **guided, guiding. 1.** To show the way to; conduct; lead; direct. **2.** To direct the course of; steer. **3.** To manage the affairs of; govern. [< OProv *guidar,* to show the way.] —**guid'er** *n.*

guide•book (gīd'bo͝ok') *n.* A handbook of information for travelers.

guide•line (gīd'līn') *n.* **1.** A mark used as a guide in lettering or drawing. **2.** A statement of general policy.

guided missile. Any missile capable of being guided while in flight.

guide•post (gīd'pōst') *n.* A post with a directional sign.

gui•don (gī'dŏn', gīd'n) *n.* A small flag carried as a standard by a military unit. [< It *guida,* guide.]

guild (gĭld) *n.* An association of persons of the same trade for the furtherance of some purpose, esp. in medieval times, a society of merchants or artisans. [< ON *gildi,* payment, fraternity.]

guil•der (gĭl'dər) *n.* The basic monetary unit of the Netherlands, Surinam, and the Netherlands Antilles.

guile (gīl) *n.* Insidious, treacherous cunning; craftiness. [< OF.] —**guile'ful** *adj.*

guile•less (gīl'lĭs) *adj.* Free of guile; simple; artless. —**guile'less•ness** *n.*

guil•lo•tine (gĭl'ə-tēn', gē'ə-) *n.* A machine with a heavy blade that falls between upright

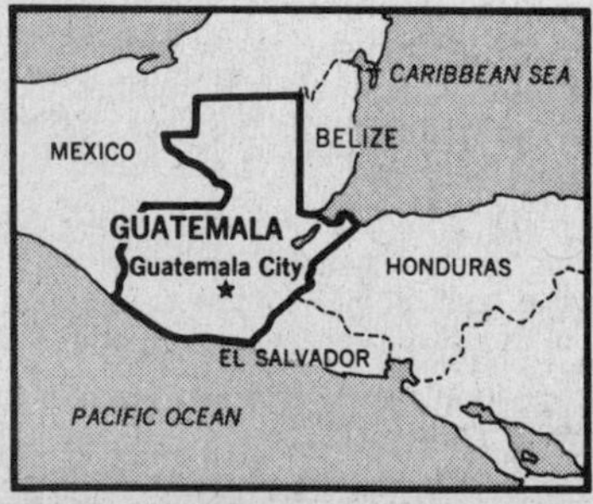

Guatemala

ă pat/ā ate/âr care/ä bar/b bib/ch chew/d deed/ĕ pet/ē be/f fit/g gag/h hat/hw what/
ĭ pit/ī pie/îr pier/j judge/k kick/l lid, fatal/m mum/n no, sudden/ng sing/ŏ pot/ō go/

guides to behead a condemned prisoner. —*v.* (gĭl'ə-tēn') **-tined, -tining.** To behead with a guillotine. [< J. *Guillotin* (1738–1814), French doctor.]

guilt (gĭlt) *n.* **1.** The fact of being responsible for an offense or wrongdoing. **2.** Remorseful awareness of having done something wrong. [< OE *gylt.*] —**guilt'less** *adj.*

guilt•y (gĭl'tē) *adj.* **-ier, -iest. 1.** Responsible for some reprehensible act. **2.** At fault; delinquent; culpable. **3.** Prompted by or showing a sense of guilt: *a guilty conscience.* —**guilt'i•ly** *adv.* —**guilt'i•ness** *n.*

guin•ea (gĭn'ē) *n. Brit.* The sum of one pound and one shilling.

Guin•ea, Republic of (gĭn'ē). A country of W Africa. Pop. 3,420,000. Cap. Conakry.

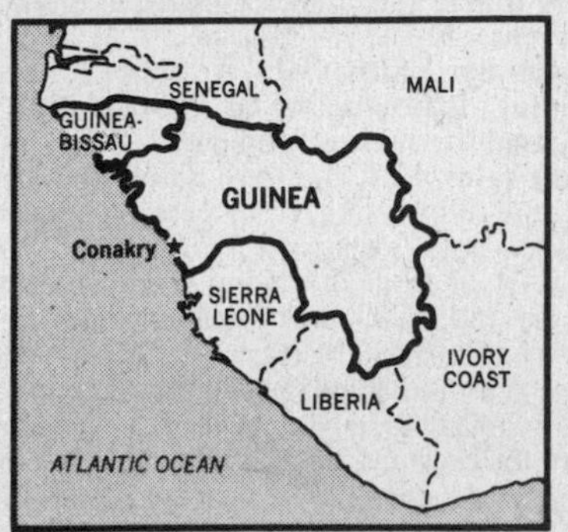

Guinea
Guinea-Bissau

Guin•ea-Bis•sau (gĭn'ē-bĭ-sou'). A country of W Africa. Pop. 535,000. Cap. Bissau.

guinea fowl. Also **guinea hen.** A domesticated pheasantlike bird having blackish plumage marked with many small white spots.

guinea pig. 1. A variously colored, seemingly tailless rodent often kept as a pet or used for biological experiments. **2.** A subject for experimentation.

guise (gīz) *n.* **1.** Outward appearance; aspect. **2.** False appearance; pretense. **3.** Mode of dress; garb. [< OF, manner.]

gui•tar (gĭ-tär') *n.* A stringed musical instrument, generally shaped like a violin, played by strumming or plucking. [< Ar *qītār.*] —**gui•tar'ist** *n.*

gulch (gŭlch) *n.* A small, shallow canyon with smoothly inclined slopes and steep sides; a small ravine. [?]

gul•den (go͝ol'dən) *n.* A guilder.

gulf (gŭlf) *n.* **1.** A large area of a sea or ocean partially enclosed by land. **2.** A deep, wide chasm; abyss. **3.** A separating distance; wide gap. —*v.* To swallow; engulf. [< Gk *kolphos,* bosom, fold, bay.]

gull¹ (gŭl) *n.* Any of various chiefly coastal water birds with long wings, webbed feet, and usually gray and white plumage. [ME.]

gull² (gŭl) *n.* A gullible person; dupe. —*v.* To deceive; dupe.

gul•let (gŭl'ĭt) *n.* **1.** The esophagus. **2.** The throat. [< L *gula,* throat.]

gul•li•ble (gŭl'ə-bəl) *adj.* Easily deceived or duped; credulous. —**gul'li•bil'i•ty** *n.*

Gul•li•ver (gŭl'ə-vər), **Lemuel.** Hero of Swift's *Gulliver's Travels* (1726).

gul•ly (gŭl'ē) *n., pl.* **-lies.** A deep channel cut in the earth by running water. [< GULLET.]

gulp (gŭlp) *v.* **1.** To choke or gasp, as in nervousness. **2.** To swallow in large amounts. —*n.* **1.** The act of gulping. **2.** A large mouthful. **3.** A convulsive attempt to swallow. [< MDu *gulpen.*] —**gulp'er** *n.*

gum¹ (gŭm) *n.* **1.** Any of various viscous plant substances that dry into water-soluble, noncrystalline, brittle solids. **2.** Also **gum tree.** Any of various trees yielding gum. **3.** Chewing gum. —*v.* **gummed, gumming. 1.** To cover, seal, or fill with gum. **2.** To become sticky or clogged with gum. [< Gk *kommi.*] —**gum'my** *adj.*

gum² (gŭm) *n.* The firm connective tissue that surrounds the bases of the teeth. [< OE *gōma,* palate, jaw. See **ghēu-.**]

gum arabic. A gum exuded by various African trees and used esp. in the manufacture of mucilage and candies.

gum•bo (gŭm'bō) *n., pl.* **-bos.** A soup thickened with okra pods. [< Bantu.]

gum•drop (gŭm'drŏp') *n.* A small candy made of sweetened gum arabic or gelatin.

gump•tion (gŭmp'shən) *n. Informal.* **1.** Shrewdness. **2.** Boldness of enterprise; initiative. [?]

gum•shoe (gŭm'sho͞o') *n.* **1.** A rubber overshoe. **2.** *Slang.* A detective.

gun (gŭn) *n.* **1.** A weapon consisting essentially of a metal tube from which a projectile is fired. **2.** A portable firearm. **3.** A device that shoots a projectile. —*v.* **gunned, gunning. 1.** To shoot (with *down*). **2.** To open the throttle of: *gun an engine.* —**gun for.** To seek to catch or obtain. [ME *gunne.*] —**gun'ner** *n.*

gun•boat (gŭn'bōt') *n.* A small armed vessel.

gun•cot•ton (gŭn'kŏt'n) *n.* Nitrocellulose.

gun•fire (gŭn'fīr') *n.* The firing of guns.

gun•lock (gŭn'lŏk') *n.* A device for igniting the charge of a firearm.

gun•man (gŭn'mən) *n.* A professional killer.

gun•nel. Variant of **gunwale.**

gun•ner•y (gŭn'ə-rē) *n.* The science of constructing and operating guns.

gun•ny (gŭn'ē) *n.* **1.** A coarse fabric made of jute or hemp. **2.** Burlap. [< Sk *goṇī,* sack.]

gunny sack. A sack made of burlap or gunny.

gun•pow•der (gŭn'pou'dər) *n.* An explosive powder used to propel projectiles from guns.

gun•shot (gŭn'shŏt') *n.* **1.** Shot fired from a gun. **2.** The range of a gun: *within gunshot.*

gun-shy (gŭn'shī') *adj.* Afraid of gunfire.

gun•smith (gŭn'smĭth') *n.* One who makes or repairs firearms.

gun•wale (gŭn'əl) *n.* Also **gun•nel.** The upper edge of a ship's side.

gup•py (gŭp'ē) *n., pl.* **-pies.** A small, brightly colored tropical freshwater fish. [< R.J.L. *Guppy* of Trinidad.]

gur•gle (gûr'gəl) *v.* **-gled, -gling. 1.** To flow in a broken, uneven current making intermittent low sounds. **2.** To make such sounds. [< L *gurguliō,* gullet.] —**gur'gle** *n.*

gu•ru (go͞o-ro͞o', go͞o'ro͞o') *n.* Also **Gu•ru.** *Hinduism.* A spiritual teacher.

gush (gŭsh) *v.* **1.** To emit or flow forth suddenly and violently. **2.** To make an effusive display of sentiment or enthusiasm. —*n.* A sudden, violent, or copious outflow. [Perh < Scand.]

gush•er (gŭsh'ər) *n.* **1.** One that gushes. **2.** A gas or oil well with an abundant flow.

gush•y (gŭsh'ē) *adj.* **-ier, -iest.** Characterized by excessive sentiment. —**gush'i•ly** *adv.*

gus•set (gŭs'ĭt) *n.* A triangular insert for strengthening or enlarging a garment. [< OF *gousset,* armpit, piece of armor.]

gust (gŭst) *n.* **1.** A violent, abrupt rush of wind. **2.** An abrupt outburst of emotion. [< ON *gustr.*] —**gust'i•ly** *adv.* —**gust'y** *adj.*

gus•ta•to•ry (gŭs'tə-tôr'ē, -tōr'ē) *adj.* Pertaining to the sense of taste.

gus•to (gŭs'tō) *n.* Vigorous enjoyment; relish; zest. [< L *gustus,* taste.]

gut (gŭt) *n.* **1.** The alimentary canal or a portion thereof, esp. the intestine or stomach. **2. guts.** The bowels; entrails; viscera. **3. guts.** The essential contents of something. **4. guts.** *Slang.* Courage; fortitude. —*v.* **gutted, gutting. 1.** To eviscerate; disembowel. **2.** To destroy the interior of: *gut a house.* [< OE *guttas.*]

Gu•ten•berg (go͞ot'n-bûrg'), **Johann.** 1400?–1468? German inventor of movable type.

Johann Gutenberg

gut•ta-per•cha (gŭt'ə-pûr'chə) *n.* A rubbery substance derived from the latex of certain tropical trees, used as electrical insulation and for waterproofing. [Malay *gĕtah percha.*]

gut•ter (gŭt'ər) *n.* A channel for draining off water, as at the edge of a street or under the border of a roof. [< L *gutta,* drop.]

gut•ter•snipe (gŭt'ər-snīp') *n.* A street urchin.

gut•tur•al (gŭt'ər-əl) *adj.* **1.** Of or pertaining to the throat. **2.** Produced in the throat. [< L *guttur,* throat.] —**gut'tur•al•ly** *adv.*

guy¹ (gī) *n.* A rope, cord, or cable used to steady or guide something. —*v.* To steady or guide with a guy. [Prob < LG.]

guy² (gī) *n. Informal.* A man; fellow.

Guy•a•na (gī-ăn'ə). A republic of N South America. Pop. 628,000. Cap. Georgetown.

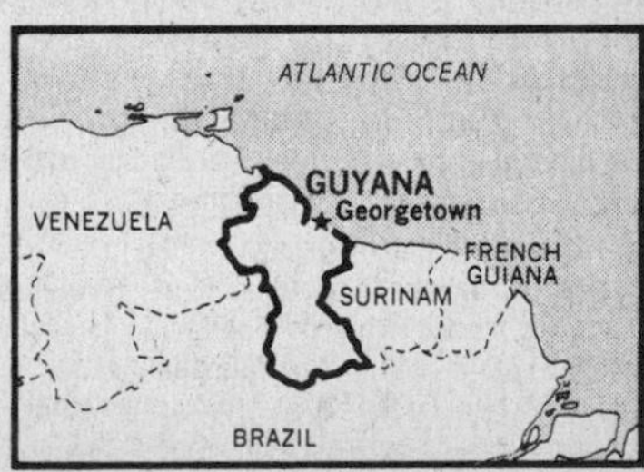

Guyana

guz•zle (gŭz'əl) *v.* **-zled, -zling.** To drink greedily or inordinately. [Poss < OF *gosier,* throat.]
gym (jĭm) *n. Informal.* A gymnasium.
gym•na•si•um. *n.* **1.** (jĭm-nā'zē-əm). *pl.* **-ums** or **-sia** (-zē-ə). A room or building equipped for gymnastics and sports. **2.** (gĭm-nä'zē-o͞om'). *pl.* **-ums** or **-sia.** An academic high school in various C European countries. [< Gk *gumnazein,* "to train naked," practice gymnastics.]
gym•nas•tics (jĭm-năs'tĭks) *pl.n.* Body-building exercises, esp. those performed with special apparatus in a gymnasium. **—gym'nast'** *n.* **—gym•nas'tic** *adj.* **—gym•nas'ti•cal•ly** *adv.*
gyn. gynecology.
gy•ne•col•o•gy (gī'nə-kŏl'ə-jē, jī'-, jĭn'ə-) *n.* The medical science of disease, reproductive physiology, and endocrinology in females. [Gk *gunē,* woman + -LOGY.] **—gy'ne•co•log'i•cal** (-kə-lŏj'ĭ-kəl) *adj.* **—gy'ne•col'o•gist** *n.*
gyp (jĭp) *v.* **gypped, gypping.** Also **gip.** *Informal.* To swindle, cheat, or defraud. *—n.* **1.** A swindle. **2.** A swindler. [Prob short for GYPSY.] **—gyp'per** *n.*
gyp•sum (jĭp'səm) *n.* A white mineral, $CaSO_4$•$2H_2O$, used in the manufacture of plaster of Paris, plaster, and some cements. [< Gk *gupsos.*]
Gyp•sy (jĭp'sē) *n., pl.* **-sies.** Also **Gip•sy. 1.** One of a nomadic people originally migrating to Europe from the border region between Iran and India in the 14th or 15th century. **2.** The Indic language spoken by this people; Romany. **3. gypsy.** One that resembles a Gypsy in appearance or behavior.
gy•rate (jī'rāt') *v.* **-rated, -rating. 1.** To revolve on or around a center or axis. **2.** To circle or spiral. [< L *gȳrus,* circle.] **—gy•ra'tion** *n.* **—gy'ra'tor** *n.*
gyr•fal•con (jûr'făl'kən, -fôl'kən, -fô'kən) *n.* A large falcon of northern regions, with white or grayish plumage. [< ON *geirfalki.*]
gy•ro (jī'rō) *n., pl.* **-ros.** A gyroscope.
gyro–. *comb. form.* **1.** Gyrating. **2.** Spiral. [< Gk *guros,* circle.]
gy•ro•com•pass (jī'rō-kŭm'pəs, -kŏm'pəs) *n.* A navigational device in which a north-south orientation of a gyroscope's spin axis is maintained.
gy•ro•scope (jī'rə-skōp') *n.* A spinning mass, typically a disk or wheel, suspended so that its spin axis maintains a fixed angular orientation when not subjected to external torques. **—gy'ro•scop'ic** (-skŏp'ĭk) *adj.* **—gy'ro•scop'i•cal•ly** *adv.*
gyve (jīv) *n.* Often **gyves.** A shackle or fetter, esp. for the leg. *—v.* **gyved, gyving.** To shackle or fetter. [ME.]

Hh

h, H (āch) *n.* **1.** The 8th letter of the English alphabet. **2.** The 8th in a series. **3. H** Anything shaped like the letter **H.**
h 1. hecto-. **2.** hour.
H 1. henry. **2.** hydrogen.
h. height.
H. height.
ha (hä) *interj.* Also **hah.** Expressive of surprise, wonder, triumph, etc.
ha hectare.
Hab. Habakkuk (Old Testament).
ha•be•as cor•pus (hā'bē-əs kôr'pəs). A writ issued to bring a party before a court to prevent unlawful restraint. [< ML *habēas corpus,* "you shall have the body."]
hab•er•dash•er (hăb'ər-dăsh'ər) *n.* A dealer in men's furnishings, as hats, shirts, etc. [< NF *hapertas,* fabric, cloth.]
hab•er•dash•er•y (hăb'ər-dăsh'ə-rē) *n., pl.* **-ies.** A haberdasher's shop.
hab•it (hăb'ĭt) *n.* **1.** A pattern of behavior acquired by frequent repetition. **2.** Customary manner or practice. **3.** An addiction. **4.** A distinctive dress or costume. [< L *habitus,* pp of *habēre,* to hold, have.]
hab•it•a•ble (hăb'ə-tə-bəl) *adj.* Suitable to live in. [< L *habitāre,* to inhabit.] **—hab'i•ta•bil'i•ty, hab'i•ta•ble•ness** *n.*
hab•i•tat (hăb'ə-tăt') *n.* **1.** The area or type of environment in which a plant or animal normally lives or occurs. **2.** The place where a person or thing is most likely to be found. [< L *habitāre,* to inhabit.]
hab•i•ta•tion (hăb'ə-tā'shən) *n.* **1.** The act of inhabiting. **2. a.** Natural environment or locality. **b.** Place of abode.
hab•it-form•ing (hăb'ĭt-fôr'mĭng) *adj.* Leading to physiological addiction.
ha•bit•u•al (hə-bĭch'o͞o-əl) *adj.* **1.** Established by or acting according to habit. **2.** Inveterate. **3.** Customary; usual. **—ha•bit'u•al•ly** *adv.*
ha•bit•u•ate (hə-bĭch'o͞o-āt') *v.* **-ated, -ating.** To accustom by repetition or exposure. **—ha•bit'u•a'tion** *n.*
hab•i•tude (hăb'ə-t/y/o͞od') *n.* A customary behavior or manner.
ha•bit•u•é (hə-bĭch'o͞o-ā', hə-bĭch'o͞o-ā') *n.* One who frequents a certain place.
ha•ci•en•da (hä'sē-ĕn'də) *n.* **1.** In Spanish-speaking countries, a large estate. **2.** The main house of such an estate. [Span, domestic work, landed property.]
hack¹ (hăk) *v.* **1.** To cut with irregular and heavy blows; chop roughly. **2.** To cough in short, dry-throated spasms. *—n.* **1.** A notch made by hacking. **2.** A tool used for hacking. **3.** A rough, dry cough. [< OE *(tō)haccian,* to cut to pieces.]
hack² (hăk) *n.* **1.** A horse for hire. **2.** A worn-out horse. **3.** A vehicle for hire. **4.** One hired to do routine writing. **5.** A taxicab. *—v.* To employ or work as a hack. *—adj.* **1.** For or by a hack. **2.** Banal; trite. [Short for HACKNEY.]
hack•le (hăk'əl) *n.* **1.** One of the long, slender feathers on the neck of a bird, esp. a rooster. **2. hackles.** Hairs at the back of the neck, as on a dog, that can rise with anger, fear, etc. [ME *hakell.*]
hack•ney (hăk'nē) *n., pl.* **-neys. 1.** A horse for riding or driving. **2.** A coach or carriage for hire. *—v.* To cause to become banal and trite. [< *Hackney,* England.]
hack•neyed (hăk'nēd) *adj.* Overused; trite; banal.
hack•saw (hăk'sô') *n.* A saw with a tough, fine-toothed blade stretched taut in a frame, used for cutting metal.
had (hăd). *p.t. & p.p.* of **have.**
had•dock (hăd'ək) *n., pl.* **-dock** or **-docks.** A food fish of Atlantic waters, related to and resembling the cod. [< OF *hadot.*]
Ha•des (hā'dēz). **1.** The nether world of Greek mythology. **2.** Often **hades.** Hell.
had•n't (hăd'ənt). Contraction of *had not.*
hadst (hădst). *Archaic. p.t. & p.p.* of **have.**
haf•ni•um (hăf'nē-əm) *n. Symbol* **Hf** A brilliant, silvery metallic element used in nuclear reactor control rods and in the manufacture of tungsten filaments. Atomic number 72, atomic weight 178.49. [< *Hafnia,* L name for Copenhagen.]
haft (hăft, häft) *n.* A handle or hilt, as of a sword or knife. [< OE *hæft.*]
hag (hăg) *n.* **1.** An ugly old woman. **2.** A witch; sorceress. [Prob < OE *hægtesse,* witch.]
hag•gard (hăg'ərd) *adj.* Appearing worn and exhausted; emaciated; gaunt. [OF *hagard,* untamed hawk.]
hag•gle (hăg'əl) *v.* **-gled, -gling.** To argue or dispute in an attempt to bargain. [< ON *höggva,* to cut.] **—hag'gler** *n.*
Hag•i•og•ra•pha (hăg'ē-ŏg'rə-fə, hā'jē-) *n.* The third of the three ancient Jewish divisions of the Old Testament, including those books not in the Torah or the Prophets.
hag•i•og•ra•phy (hăg'ē-ŏg'rə-fē, hā'jē-) *n.* Biography of saints. [Gk *hagios,* holy + -GRAPHY.]
Hague, The (hāg). The de facto capital of the Netherlands. Pop. 602,000.
hah. Variant of **ha.**
hail¹ (hāl) *n.* **1. a.** Precipitation in the form of pellets of ice and hard snow. **b.** A hailstone. **2.** Something with the effect of a shower of hail. *—v.* **1.** To precipitate hail. **2.** To pour down or forth. [< OE *hagol.* See **kaghlo-.**]
hail² (hāl) *v.* **1. a.** To salute or greet. **b.** To acclaim enthusiastically. **2.** To signal or call out to. *—n.* **1.** A greeting or expression of acclaim. **2.** Hailing distance. *—interj.* Expressive of greeting or tribute. [< ON *heill,* whole, healthy.]
Hai•le Se•las•sie (hī'lē sə-lăs'ē, sə-lä'sē). 1891–1975. Emperor of Ethiopia (1930–74); deposed.
hail•stone (hāl'stōn') *n.* A hard pellet of snow and ice.
hair (hâr) *n.* **1.** A fine, threadlike outgrowth, esp. from the skin of a mammal. **2.** A covering of such outgrowth, as on the human head. **3.** A minute distance or narrow margin. *—adj.* **1.** Made of or with hair. **2.** For the hair: *a hair dryer.* [< OE *hǣr* < Gmc **hēram.*] **—haired** (hârd) *adj.*

hair•breadth (hâr'brĕdth') *adj.* Extremely close. —*n.* Variant of **hairsbreadth.**

hair•brush (hâr'brŭsh') *n.* A brush for grooming the hair.

hair•cloth (hâr'klôth', -klŏth') *n.* A stiff, wiry fabric usually having a cotton or linen warp with a horsehair filler.

hair•cut (hâr'kŭt') *n.* **1.** A cutting of the hair. **2.** The style in which hair is cut.

hair•do (hâr'do͞o') *n., pl.* **-dos.** A hair style; coiffure.

hair•dress•er (hâr'drĕs'ər) *n.* A person who cuts or arranges women's hair.

hair•line (hâr'līn') *n.* **1.** The outline of the growth of hair on the head. **2.** A very slender line.

hair•pin (hâr'pĭn') *n.* A thin U-shaped pin used to keep the hair in place. —*adj.* Doubled back in a deep U: *a hairpin curve.*

hair-rais•ing (hâr'rā'zĭng) *adj.* Horrifying.

hairs•breadth, hair's-breadth (hârz'brĕdth') *n.* Also **hair•breadth** (hâr'brĕdth'). A small space or distance; narrow margin.

hair•split•ting (hâr'splĭt'ĭng) *n.* The making of unreasonably fine distinctions; quibbling. —*adj.* Concerned with petty distinctions. —**hair'split'ter** *n.*

hair•spring (hâr'sprĭng') *n.* A fine coiled spring that regulates the movement of the balance wheel in a watch or clock.

hair•y (hâr'ē) *adj.* **-ier, -iest. 1.** Covered with hair. **2.** Of or like hair. —**hair'i•ness** *n.*

Hai•ti (hā'tē). A republic of the West Indies. Pop. 4,660,000. Cap. Port-au-Prince. —**Hai'ti•an** *adj.* & *n.*

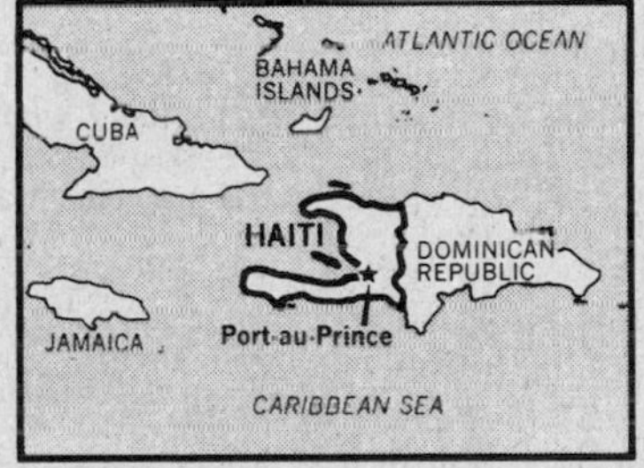

Haiti

hake (hāk) *n., pl.* **hake** or **hakes.** A marine food fish related to and resembling the cod. [ME.]

hal•berd (hăl'bərd) *n.* A weapon of the 15th and 16th centuries having an axlike blade and a steel spike mounted on the end of a long shaft. [< MHG *helmbarde,* "handle ax."]

hal•cy•on (hăl'sē-ən) *adj.* Calm and peaceful; tranquil. [< Gk *halkuōn,* a mythical bird.]

hale[1] (hāl) *adj.* **haler, halest.** Sound in health; robust. [< OE *hāl.* See **kailo-.**]

hale[2] (hāl) *v.* **haled, haling.** To compel to go; force. [< MLG *halen,* to pull.]

Hale (hāl), **Nathan.** 1755–1776. American army officer; hanged by the British for spying.

half (hăf, häf) *n., pl.* **halves** (hăvz, hävz). **1.** One of two equal parts. **2.** A part of something approximately equal to the remainder. —*adj.* **1.** Being a half. **2.** Being approximately a half. **3.** Partial; incomplete. —*adv.* **1.** To the extent of exactly or nearly 50%. **2.** Not completely; partly. —**go halves.** To share equally. [< OE *healf.*]

half•back (hăf'băk', häf'-) *n. Football.* One of the two players positioned near the flanks behind the line of scrimmage.

half-breed (hăf'brēd', häf'-) *n.* A person having parents of different ethnic types.

half brother. A brother related through one parent only.

half-caste (hăf'kăst', häf'käst') *n.* A person of mixed racial descent.

half•heart•ed (hăf'här'tĭd, häf'-) *adj.* Lacking interest or enthusiasm; uninspired. —**half'heart'ed•ly** *adv.*

half-life (hăf'līf', häf'-) *n.* The time required for half the nuclei in a sample of a specific isotopic species to undergo **radioactive decay.**

half-line (hăf'līn', häf'-) *n.* A straight line extending in just one direction from a given point.

half-mast (hăf'măst', häf'mäst') *n.* The position about halfway up a mast or pole at which a flag is flown as a sign of mourning or distress.

half-moon (hăf'mo͞on', häf'-) *n.* **1.** The moon when only half its disk is illuminated. **2.** Something shaped like a crescent. —**half'moon'** *adj.*

half-plane (hăf'plān', häf'-) *n.* The part of a plane lying to one side of a line in the plane.

half sister. A sister related through one parent only.

half step. *Mus.* An interval equal to half a tone in the diatonic scale.

half tide. The tide at a time halfway between high tide and low tide.

half-track (hăf'trăk', häf'-) *n.* A military motor vehicle with caterpillar treads.

half-truth (hăf'tro͞oth', häf'-) *n.* A statement that is only partially true, usually intended to deceive.

half•way (hăf'wā', häf'-) *adj.* **1.** Midway between two points or conditions; in the middle. **2.** Partial; *halfway measures for solving the problem.* —**half'way'** *adv.*

half-wit (hăf'wĭt', häf'-) *n.* **1.** A mentally retarded person. **2.** A stupid, foolish, or frivolous person. —**half'wit'ted** *adj.*

hal•i•but (hăl'ə-bət, hŏl'-) *n., pl.* **-but** or **-buts.** A large, edible flatfish of northern marine waters. [ME *halybutte.*]

hal•ide (hăl'īd', -ĭd, hā'līd', -lĭd) *n.* A binary chemical compound of a halogen with a more electropositive element or group.

Hal•i•fax (hăl'ə-făks). The capital of Nova Scotia. Pop. 93,000.

hal•i•to•sis (hăl'ə-tō'sĭs) *n.* Foul-smelling breath. [< L *hālitus,* breath + -OSIS.]

hall (hôl) *n.* **1. a.** A corridor; hallway. **b.** A large entrance room; lobby. **2.** A large public building. **3.** A large room for meetings, meals, etc. **4.** A college or university building. **5. a.** The main house on a landed estate. **b.** The main residence of a medieval nobleman. [< OE *heall.* See **kel-**[4].]

hal•lah. Variant of **challah.**

hal•le•lu•jah (hăl'ə-lo͞o'yə) *interj.* Expressive of praise or joy. —*n.* An expression or exclamation of "hallelujah." [Heb *hallelūyāh,* praise the Lord.]

hall•mark (hôl'märk') *n.* **1.** A mark placed on an article to indicate purity, quality, etc. **2.** Any indication of quality or excellence.

hal•loo (hə-lo͞o') *interj.* Used to attract attention. —*n.* A shout or call of "halloo." [Perh < OF *halloer.*]

hal•low (hăl'ō) *v.* **1.** To make or set apart as holy; consecrate. **2.** To honor as being holy; revere. [< OE *hālgian.* See **kailo-.**] —**hal'lowed** *adj.*

Hal•low•een (hăl'ō-ēn') *n.* The eve of All Saints' Day, falling on October 31. [Short for *All Hallow E'en.*]

hal•lu•ci•na•tion (hə-lo͞o'sə-nā'shən) *n.* **1.** False perception with a characteristically compelling sense of the reality of objects or events perceived in the absence of relevant and adequate stimuli. **2.** The complex of material so perceived. **3.** Any false or mistaken idea; delusion. [< L *hallūcinārī,* to wander in mind.] —**hal•lu'ci•nate'** *v.* **(-nated, -nating).** —**hal•lu'ci•na•to'ry** (-tôr'ē, -tōr'ē) *adj.*

hal•lu•cin•o•gen (hə-lo͞o'sə-nə-jən) *n.* A drug that induces hallucination. —**hal•lu'cin•o•gen'ic** *adj.*

hall•way (hôl'wā') *n.* **1.** A corridor or passageway. **2.** An entrance hall.

ha•lo (hā'lō) *n., pl.* **-los** or **-loes. 1.** A disk or ring of light surrounding the head, as in a representation of a holy person. **2.** A circular band of colored light around a light source, as around the sun or moon. [< Gk *halōs.*]

hal•o•gen (hăl'ə-jən) *n.* Any of a group of five chemically related nonmetallic elements that includes fluorine, chlorine, bromine, iodine, and astatine. [< Gk *hals,* salt + -GEN.]

halt[1] (hôlt) *n.* A suspension of movement or progress; a stop. [< OHG *haltan,* to stop.]

halt[2] (hôlt) *v.* To limp or hobble. —*adj. Archaic.* Lame; crippled. [< OE *healtian.* See **kel-**[2].]

hal•ter (hôl'tər) *n.* **1.** A rope or leather strap that fits around the head or neck of an animal, such as a horse, used to lead or secure it. **2.** A noose used for execution by hanging. **3.** A bodice for women held in place by ties behind the neck and across the back. —*v.* To put a halter on; control with a halter. [< OE *hælftre.* See **kelp-.**]

halt•ing (hôl'tĭng) *adj.* **1.** Limping; lame. **2.** Uncertain or faltering. —**halt'ing•ly** *adv.*

halve (hăv, häv) *v.* **halved, halving. 1.** To separate or divide into two equal parts. **2.** To lessen or reduce by half. **3.** *Informal.* To share equally.

halves. *pl.* of **half.**

hal•yard (hăl'yərd) *n.* A rope used to raise or lower a sail, flag, or yard. [< ME *halen,* to pull.]

ham (hăm) *n.* **1.** A cut of meat consisting of the thigh of the hind leg of a hog. **2.** The back of the knee. **3.** The back of the thigh. **4. hams.** The buttocks. **5.** *Slang.* An actor who overacts or exaggerates excessively. **6.** *Informal.* A licensed amateur radio operator. —*v.* **hammed, hamming.** To exaggerate or overdo. [< OE *hamm.*]

Ham•burg (hăm'bûrg). A port of N West Germany. Pop. 1,851,000.

ham•burg•er (hăm'bûr'gər) *n.* **1.** Ground or chopped meat, usually beef. **2.** A cooked patty of such meat. **3.** A sandwich made with such a patty. [< HAMBURG.]

Ham•il•ton (hăm'əl-tən), **Alexander.** 1755–1804. American statesman.

Ham•ite (hăm'īt') *n.* A member of a group of related peoples of N and NE Africa, including the Berbers and the descendants of the ancient Egyptians.

Ha•mit•ic (hă-mĭt'ĭk) *adj.* Of or relating to the Hamites or the language of the Hamites. —*n.* A group of North African languages related to Semitic, including the Berber dialects and ancient Egyptian.

Ham•i•to-Se•mit•ic (hăm'ə-tō-sə-mĭt'ĭk) *n.* Afro-Asiatic.

ham•let (hăm'lĭt) *n.* A small village. [< OF *hamelet.*]

Ham•mar•skjöld (hăm'är-shœld'), **Dag.** 1905–1961. Swedish diplomat; secretary-general of the UN (1953–61).

Dag Hammarskjöld

ham•mer (hăm'ər) *n.* **1.** A hand tool used to exert an impulsive force by striking. **2.** Any tool or device of analogous function or action, as: **a.** The part of a gunlock that hits the primer or firing pin or explodes the percussion cap. **b.** One of the padded wooden pieces of a piano that strike the strings. **c.** Any part of an apparatus that strikes a gong or bell, as in a clock. —*v.* **1.** To strike; pound. **2.** To shape or flatten with a hammer. [< OE *hamor.*]

ham•mer•head (hăm'ər-hĕd') *n.* **1.** A large shark having the sides of the head elongated into large extensions with the eyes at the ends. **2.** The head of a hammer.

ham•mer•toe (hăm'ər-tō') *n.* A toe, usually the second, that is congenitally bent downward.

ham•mock (hăm'ək) *n.* A hanging, easily swung cot or bed, suspended by cords between two supports. [Span *hamaca.*]

ham•per¹ (hăm'pər) *v.* To restrain movement, action, etc.; impede. [ME *hamperen.*]

ham•per² (hăm'pər) *n.* A large, usually covered basket. [< ME *hanaper.*]

ham•ster (hăm'stər) *n.* A rodent with large cheek pouches and a short tail, often kept as a pet or used in laboratory research. [< OHG *hamustro* < Slav.]

ham•string (hăm'strĭng') *n.* **1.** Either of two tendons at the rear hollow of the human knee. **2.** The large sinew in the back of the hock of a quadruped. —*v.* **-strung** (-strŭng'), **-stringing.** **1.** To cut the hamstring of (an animal or person) and thereby cripple. **2.** To hinder the efficiency of.

ham•u•lus (hăm'yə-ləs) *n., pl.* **-li** (-lī'). A small hooklike projection or process, as at the end of a bone. [< L *hāmus,* hook.]

hand (hănd) *n.* **1.** The terminal part of the arm below the wrist. **2.** A unit of length equal to 4 in., used esp. to specify the height of a horse. **3.** Something suggesting the shape or function of the human hand. **4.** A pointer on a clock or instrument. **5.** A lateral direction: *at my right hand.* **6.** Handwriting; penmanship. **7.** A round of applause. **8.** Physical assistance; help. **9.** *Card Games.* **a.** The cards held by or dealt to a player. **b.** A round of play. **10.** A laborer. **11.** A person who is part of a group or crew. **12.** A participant; contributor. **13.** Skill; ability. **14.** Often **hands.** **a.** Possession or keeping. **b.** Control. **15.** A source of information: *at first hand.* **16.** A pledge to marry. **—at hand.** **1.** Close by; near; easily accessible. **2.** Soon in time. **—by hand.** Performed by using the hands as opposed to mechanical means. **—hands down.** With no trouble; easily. **—in hand.** **1.** Under control. **2.** Presently accessible. **3.** In preparation. **—on hand.** Available. **—on the other hand.** As another point of view. **—out of hand.** Out of control. —*adj.* **1.** Of or pertaining to the hand. **2.** Made to be transported in one's hand. **3.** Performed, operated, or made by hand; manual. —*v.* **1.** To give or pass with or as with the hands. **2.** To aid, direct, or conduct with the hands. **3.** *Naut.* To roll up and secure (a sail); furl. **—hand down.** **1.** To give as an inheritance. **2.** To pronounce a court decision. **—hand it to.** *Slang.* To give credit to. [< OE < Gmc **handuz.*]

hand•bag (hănd'băg') *n.* A woman's bag for carrying articles such as money, keys, etc.

hand•ball (hănd'bôl') *n.* **1.** A game played by batting a ball against the wall with the hands. **2.** The small rubber ball used in this game.

hand•bill (hănd'bĭl') *n.* A printed sheet or pamphlet distributed by hand.

hand•book (hănd'bo͝ok') *n.* A manual or small reference book providing specific information or instruction.

hand•car (hănd'kär') *n.* A small open hand-propelled railroad car.

hand•cart (hănd'kärt') *n.* A small, usually two-wheeled, cart pulled or pushed by hand.

hand•clasp (hănd'klăsp', -kläsp') *n.* The act of clasping the hand of another person.

hand•cuff (hănd'kŭf') *n.* Often **handcuffs.** A restraining device consisting of a pair of strong, connected hoops that can be locked about the wrist. —*v.* To restrain with handcuffs.

hand•ed (hăn'dĭd) *adj.* **1.** Of or pertaining to dexterity or preference as regards a hand or hands: *one-handed; left-handed.* **2.** Pertaining to a specified number of people: *a four-handed card game.*

Han•del (hănd'l), **George Frederick.** 1685–1759. German-born British composer.

hand•ful (hănd'fo͝ol') *n., pl.* **-fuls.** **1.** The quantity or number that can be held in the hand. **2.** A small but undefined quantity or number. **3.** *Informal.* A person or thing difficult to control.

hand grenade. A small grenade to be thrown by the hand.

hand•i•cap (hăn'dē-kăp') *n.* **1.** A race or contest in which advantages or compensations are given different contestants to equalize the chances of winning. **2.** Such an advantage or penalty. **3.** An anatomical, physiological, or mental deficiency that prevents or restricts normal achievement. —*v.* **-capped, -capping.** **1.** To assign a handicap or handicaps to (a contestant). **2.** To hinder. [< earlier *hand in cap.*] **—hand'i•cap'per** *n.*

hand•i•craft (hăn'dē-krăft', -kräft') *n.* **1.** Skill with the hands. **2.** A trade, craft, or occupation requiring such skill. **3.** The work so produced.

hand•i•work (hăn'dē-wûrk') *n.* **1.** Work performed by hand. **2.** Work accomplished by a single person. **3.** The results of one's efforts.

hand•ker•chief (hăng'kər-chĭf) *n.* A small square of cloth used in wiping the nose, mouth, etc.

han•dle (hănd'l) *v.* **-dled, -dling.** **1.** To touch, lift, or turn with the hands. **2.** To operate with the hands; manipulate. **3.** To manage; deal with or in: *handle corporation law.* —*n.* A part that is held or manipulated with the hand. [< OE *handlian.*]

han•dle•bar (hănd'l-bär') *n.* Often **handlebars.** A curved metal steering bar, as on a bicycle.

hand•made (hănd'mād') *adj.* Made or prepared by hand rather than by machine.

hand•maid (hănd'mād') *n.* A female attendant.

hand•out (hănd'out') *n.* Food, clothing, or money donated to a beggar or destitute person.

hand-pick (hănd'pĭk') *v.* To select carefully or personally.

hand•rail (hănd'rāl') *n.* A narrow rail to be grasped for support.

hand•shake (hănd'shāk') *n.* The grasping of right hands by two people as a gesture of greeting, leave-taking, etc.

hand•some (hăn'səm) *adj.* **1.** Pleasing and dignified in appearance. **2.** Generous; liberal: *a handsome reward.* **3.** Marked by great skill: *a handsome piece of work.* [ME *handsom,* easy to handle.] **—hand'some•ly** *adv.*

hand•spring (hănd'sprĭng') *n.* A gymnastic feat in which the body is flipped forward or backward, landing first on the hands, then on the feet.

hand-to-hand (hănd'tə-hănd') *adj.* At close quarters.

hand•writ•ing (hănd'rī'tĭng) *n.* **1.** Writing done with the hand. **2.** The writing characteristic of a particular person.

hand•y (hăn'dē) *adj.* **-ier, -iest.** **1.** Manually adroit. **2.** Readily accessible. **3.** Easy to use. [< HAND.] **—hand'i•ly** *adv.* **—hand'i•ness** *n.*

hand•y•man (hăn'dē-măn') *n.,* One who does odd jobs.

hang (hăng) *v.* **hung** or **hanged, hanging.** **1.** To fasten or be fastened from above with no support from below. **2.** To suspend or be suspended so as to allow free movement at or about the point of suspension. **3.** To execute or be executed by suspending by the neck. **4.** To attach at an appropriate angle. **5.** **a.** To furnish by suspending objects about: *hang the room with curtains.* **b.** To attach to a wall: *hang wallpaper.* **6.** To hold downward. **7.** To deadlock (a jury). **—hang around.** To loiter. **—hang back.** To lag or hold back. **—hang on.** **1.** To cling to something. **2.** To persevere. —*n.* **1.** The way in which something hangs. **2.** *Informal.* The proper method for doing something. [< OE *hōn,* to hang, suspend, and *hangian,* to hang, be hung, and < ON *hanga,* to cause to hang. See **konk-.**]

Usage: *Hanged* is preferable to *hung* as the past tense and past participle when the verb is used in the sense of capital punishment. In other senses of the verb, *hung* is the customary form as past tense and past participle.

han•gar (hăng'ər) *n.* A shed or shelter, esp. for aircraft. [< OF.]

hang•dog (hăng'dôg', -dŏg') *adj.* **1.** Shamefaced or guilty. **2.** Downcast; intimidated.

hang•er (hăng'ər) *n.* **1.** One that hangs. **2.** A contrivance to which something hangs or by which something is hung.

hang•er-on (hăng'ər-ŏn', -ôn') *n., pl.* **hangers-on** (hăng'ərz-). A sycophant.

hang•ing (hăng'ĭng) *n.* **1.** An execution on a gallows. **2.** Something hung, as drapery. **—hang'ing** *adj.*

hang•man (hăng'mən) *n.* One employed to execute prisoners by hanging.

hang•nail (hăng'nāl') *n.* A small, partly detached piece of dead skin at the side or base of a fingernail.

hang•out (hăng'out') *n.* A frequently visited place.

hang•o•ver (hăng'ō'vər) *n.* **1.** Unpleasant physical effects following the heavy use of alcohol. **2.** A vestige; holdover.

hang up. **1.** To suspend on a hook or hanger. **2.** To replace (a telephone receiver) on its cradle. **3.** To end a telephone conversation.

hang-up (hăng'ŭp') *n. Informal.* An inhibition.

hank (hăngk) *n.* A coil or loop. [< Scand.]

han•ker (hăng'kər) *v.* To have a longing; crave. [< dial *hank.*]

han•ky-pan•ky (hăng'kē-păng'kē) *n. Slang.* Devious or mischievous activity.

Ha•noi (hä-noi', hă-). The capital of Vietnam. Pop. 415,000.

Han•o•ver (hăn'ō'vər). A city of N West Germany. Pop. 571,000.

han•som (hăn'səm) *n.* A two-wheeled covered carriage with the driver's seat above and behind. [< English architect J.A. *Hansom* (1803–1882).]

Ha•nuk•kah, Ha•nu•kah. Variants of **Chanukah.**

hap•haz•ard (hăp-hăz'ərd) *adj.* Dependent upon or characterized by mere chance. —*n.* Mere chance; fortuity. [HAP + HAZARD.] —**hap•haz'ard•ly** *adv.* —**hap•haz'ard•ness** *n.*

hap•less (hăp'lĭs) *adj.* Luckless; unfortunate.

hap•loid (hăp'loid') *adj.* Having the number of chromosomes present in the normal germ cell, equal to half the number in the normal somatic cell. [Gk *haploeidēs,* single.]

hap•ly (hăp'lē) *adv. Archaic.* By chance; perhaps.

hap•pen (hăp'ən) *v.* **1.** To take place. **2.** To take place by chance. **3.** To come upon something by chance. **4.** To appear by chance; turn up. [< HAP.]

hap•pen•ing (hăp'ə-nĭng) *n.* **1.** An event. **2.** An improvised spectacle.

hap•py (hăp'ē) *adj.* **-pier, -piest.** **1.** Characterized by good fortune; prosperous. **2.** Having or demonstrating pleasure; gratified. **3.** Appropriate: *a happy turn of phrase.* [< HAP.] —**hap'pi•ly** *adv.* —**hap'pi•ness** *n.*

hap•py-go-luck•y (hăp'ē-gō-lŭk'ē) *adj.* Carefree.

ha•ra-ki•ri (hăr'ə-kîr'ē) *n.* Ritual suicide by disembowelment. [Jap.]

ha•rangue (hə-răng') *n.* **1.** A long, pompous speech. **2.** A speech characterized by strong feeling or vehement expression. [< ML *harenga.*] —**ha•rangue'** *v.* **(-rangued, -ranguing).** —**ha•rangu'er** *n.*

har•ass (hăr'əs, hə-răs') *v.* **1.** To disturb or irritate persistently. **2.** To wear out; exhaust. **3.** To enervate (an enemy) by repeated raids. [< OF *harer,* to set a dog on.] —**har'ass•er** *n.* —**har'ass•ment** *n.*

Har•bin (här'bən). A city of NE China, in Manchuria. Pop. 1,595,000.

har•bin•ger (här'bən-jər) *n.* A forerunner. [< OS *heriberga,* lodging.]

har•bor (här'bər). Also *chiefly Brit.* **har•bour.** *n.* **1.** A sheltered part of a body of water deep enough to provide anchorage for ships; a port. **2.** Any protected place; a refuge. —*v.* **1.** To give shelter to; protect; keep. **2.** To hold a thought or feeling about. [< OE *herebeorg.*]

hard (härd) *adj.* **1.** Resistant to pressure; not easily penetrated; rigid. **2.** Physically or mentally toughened. **3.** Difficult to do, understand, or endure. **4.** Powerful; intense: *a hard blow.* **5.** Energetic. **6.** Bitter; severe; harsh. **7.** Callous; unfeeling. **8.** Cruel; unjust. **9.** Real: *hard facts.* **10.** Having a high alcoholic content. **11.** Containing salts that interfere with the lathering of soap. **12.** Backed by bullion rather than by credit: *hard currency.* —**hard and fast.** Defined and invariable: *hard and fast rules.* —**hard of hearing.** Deaf to some degree. —**hard up.** In need; poor. [< OE. See **kar-.**] —**hard** *adv.*

hard-bit•ten (härd'bĭt'n) *adj.* Obdurate; toughened.

hard-boiled (härd'boild') *adj.* **1.** Cooked by boiling to a solid consistency, as eggs. **2.** Callous; unfeeling.

hard cash. Available money; cash.

hard cider. Fermented cider.

hard-core (härd'kôr') *adj.* Also **hard•core.** **1.** Stubbornly resistant or inveterate: *a hard-core criminal.* **2.** Held to constitute an intractable social problem: *hard-core poverty.*

hard drug. Any dangerously addictive drug, such as heroin.

hard•en (härd'n) *v.* **1.** To make or become firm or firmer. **2.** To toughen mentally or physically. **3.** To make unfeeling or cold in spirit. —**hard'en•er** *n.*

hard•head•ed (härd'hĕd'ĭd) *adj.* **1.** Stubborn; willful. **2.** Realistic; practical —**hard'head'ed•ly** *adv.* —**hard'head'ed•ness** *n.*

hard•heart•ed (härd'här'tĭd) *adj.* Unfeeling; cold; pitiless. —**hard'heart'ed•ly** *adv.*

har•di•hood (här'dē-hŏŏd') *n.* Boldness and daring; audacity.

Har•ding (här'dĭng), **Warren Gamaliel.** 1865–1923. 29th President of the U.S. (1921–23).

Warren G. Harding

hard•ly (härd'lē) *adv.* **1.** Barely; just. **2.** To almost no degree. **3.** Probably or almost surely not.

Usage: Hardly has the force of a negative; therefore it is not used with another negative: *I could hardly see* (not *couldn't hardly*). *Hardly* is idiomatically followed by clauses introduced by *when* or, less often, *before,* but not by *than* or *until: We were hardly seated when* (or *before*) *the fire broke out.*

hard•ness (härd'nĭs) *n.* **1.** The quality or condition of being hard. **2.** The relative resistance of a substance to denting, scratching, or bending.

hard palate. The relatively hard, bony anterior portion of the palate.

hard•pan (härd'păn') *n.* A layer of hard subsoil or clay.

hard rubber. A relatively inelastic rubber made with 30 to 50% sulfur.

hard-shell (härd'shĕl') *adj.* Unyieldingly orthodox; uncompromising; confirmed.

hard•ship (härd'shĭp') *n.* **1.** Extreme privation; suffering. **2.** A cause of privation or difficulty.

hard•tack (härd'tăk') *n.* A hard biscuit made only with flour and water.

hard•top (härd'tŏp') *n.* An automobile with a fixed hard top, designed to look like a convertible.

hard•ware (härd'wâr') *n.* **1.** Metal goods and utensils. **2. a.** A computer and the associated physical equipment directly involved in communications or data processing. **b.** Broadly, machines and other physical equipment directly involved in performing an industrial, technological, or military function.

hard•wood (härd'wŏŏd') *n.* The wood of a broad-leaved flowering tree as distinguished from that of a conifer.

har•dy (här'dē) *adj.* **-dier, -diest.** **1.** Stalwart and rugged; strong. **2.** Capable of surviving severe cold, drought, etc., as a plant. **3.** Courageous; stouthearted. **4.** Audacious; hotheaded. [< OF *hardir,* to become bold, make hard.] —**har'di•ly** *adv.* —**har'di•ness** *n.*

hare (hâr) *n.* A mammal related to and resembling the rabbits but usually larger and with longer ears and legs. [< OE *hara.* See **kas-.**]

hare•brained (hâr'brānd') *adj.* Giddy; flighty.

hare•lip (hâr'lĭp') *n.* A congenital fissure or pair of fissures in the upper lip.

har•em (hâr'əm, hăr'-) *n.* **1.** A house or section of a house reserved for women in a Moslem household. **2.** The women occupying a harem. [Ar *ḥarīm,* sacred, forbidden place.]

hark (härk) *v.* To listen attentively. [< OE **heorcian.* See **keu-.**]

har•le•quin (här'lə-kwən, -kən) *n.* **1. Harlequin.** A character in comedy, traditionally presented in a mask and parti-colored tights. **2.** A clown; buffoon. [Prob < OE *Herla cyning,* King *Herla,* a mythical figure.]

har•lot (här'lət) *n.* A prostitute. [< OF, young fellow, vagabond.]

harm (härm) *n.* **1.** Injury or damage. **2.** Wrong; evil. —*v.* To damage; injure; impair. [< OE *hearm.* See **kormo-.**] —**harm'ful** *adj.* —**harm'less** *adj.*

har•mon•ic (här-mŏn'ĭk) *adj.* Of or pertaining to musical harmony or harmonics. —*n.* **1.** A musical overtone. **2. harmonics** (*takes sing. v.*). The study of the physical properties of musical sound. —**har•mon'i•cal•ly** *adv.*

har•mon•i•ca (här-mŏn'ĭ-kə) *n.* A small musical instrument played by exhaling or inhaling through a row of reeds.

har•mo•ni•ous (här-mō'nē-əs) *adj.* **1.** Characterized by agreement or accord. **2.** Consisting of pleasingly combined elements. **3.** Marked by harmony of sound.

har•mo•ni•um (här-mō'nē-əm) *n.* An organ-like keyboard instrument with metal reeds.

har•mo•nize (här'mə-nīz') *v.* **-nized, -nizing.** **1.** To be in or bring into agreement or harmony. **2.** To sing or play in harmony.

har•mo•ny (här'mə-nē) *n., pl.* **-nies.** **1.** Agreement or accord, as of feeling. **2.** A pleasing combination of parts or elements. **3.** Combination and progression of chords in musical structure. [< Gk *harmonia.*]

har•ness (här'nĭs) *n.* Gear by which a draft animal pulls a vehicle or implement. —**in harness.** Engaged in one's usual work. —*v.* **1.** To put a harness on. **2.** To control and direct the force of. [< OF *harneis,* military gear.] —**har'ness•er** *n.*

harp (härp) *n.* A musical instrument having an upright frame with strings played by plucking. —*v.* To play a harp. —**harp on.** To discourse tediously on. [< OE *hearpe* < Gmc **harpōn-.*] —**harp'er** *n.* —**harp'ist** *n.*

har•poon (här-pōōn') *n.* A spearlike weapon with a barbed head, used esp. in whaling. —*v.* To strike with or as if with a harpoon. [< L *harpē,* sickle.]

harp•si•chord (härp'sĭ-kôrd', -kōrd') *n.* A keyboard instrument in which the strings are sounded by means of a plucking mechanism. [< It *arpicordo,* "harp string."]

har•py (här'pē) *n., pl.* **-pies. 1.** A shrewish woman. **2.** A predatory person. **3. Harpy.** A voracious monster having a woman's head and a bird's body. [< Gk *harpuiai,* "snatchers."]

har•que•bus (här'kə-bəs, -kwĭ-bŭs') *n.* A heavy 16th-century gun.

har•ri•dan (hăr'ə-dən) *n.* A disagreeable old woman.

har•ri•er[1] (hăr'ē-ər) *n.* **1.** One that harries. **2.** A slender, narrow-winged hawk.

har•ri•er[2] (hăr'ē-ər) *n.* A small hound formerly used to hunt hares. [< HARE.]

Har•ris•burg (hăr'ĭs-bûrg, hâr'-). The capital of Pennsylvania. Pop. 66,000.

Har•ri•son (hăr'ĭ-sən). **1. Benjamin.** 1833–1901. 23rd President of the U.S. (1889–93). **2. William Henry.** 1773–1841. 9th President of the U.S. (1841).

Benjamin Harrison

William Henry Harrison

har•row (hăr'ō) *n.* An implement having a heavy frame with teeth or upright disks, used to break up plowed ground. —*v.* **1.** To break up (soil) with a harrow. **2.** To distress greatly; torment. [ME *harwe.*]

har•ry (hăr'ē) *v.* **-ried, -rying. 1.** To raid; sack; pillage. **2.** To distress by constant attacks; harass. [< OE *hergian.*]

harsh (härsh) *adj.* **1.** Severe; stern. **2.** Unpleasant; irritating. [ME *harsk.*] —**harsh'ly** *adv.* —**harsh'ness** *n.*

hart (härt) *n.* An adult male deer. [< OE *heorot.* See **ker-**[1].]

Hart•ford (härt'fərd). The capital of Connecticut. Pop. 156,000.

har•um-scar•um (hâr'əm-skâr'əm) *adv.* Recklessly. —*adj.* Rash; irresponsible. —*n.* A scatterbrain.

har•vest (här'vĭst) *n.* **1.** The gathering in of a crop. **2.** A gathered crop. —*v.* **1.** To gather (a crop). **2.** To gain, win, or acquire as by gathering; reap. [< OE *hærfest,* autumn. See **kerp-.**] —**har'vest•er** *n.*

harvest moon. The full moon that occurs nearest the autumnal equinox.

has (hăz). 3rd person sing. present indicative of **have.**

has-been (hăz'bĭn') *n.* One no longer popular or successful.

ha•sen•pfef•fer (hä'sən-fĕf'ər) *n.* A highly seasoned rabbit stew. [G, "rabbit pepper."]

hash[1] (hăsh) *n.* **1.** Chopped meat and potatoes mixed together and browned. **2.** A jumble; hodgepodge. —*v.* **1.** To chop up; mince. **2.** To discuss; go over: *hash over future plans.* [< F *hacher,* to mince.]

hash[2] (hăsh) *n. Informal.* Hashish.

hash•ish (hăsh'ēsh', -ish) *n.* A narcotic extract prepared from the flowers of the hemp plant; hash. [Ar *ḥashīsh,* hemp.]

hash mark. *Mil. Slang.* A service stripe on the sleeve of an enlisted man's uniform.

Has•i•dim. Variant of **Chassidim.**

has•n't (hăz'ənt). Contraction of *has not.*

hasp (hăsp, häsp) *n.* A hinged metal fastener that fits over a staple and is secured by a pin, bolt, or padlock. [< OE *hæspe,* fastening, hinge.]

Has•si•dim. Variant of **Chassidim.**

has•sle (hăs'əl) *n.* **1.** An argument or fight. **2.** Trouble; bother. [Perh blend of HAGGLE + TUSSLE.]

has•sock (hăs'ək) *n.* A cushion used as a footstool or for kneeling. [< OE *hassuc,* clump of matted vegetation.]

hast (hăst). *Archaic.* 2nd person sing. present indicative of **have.**

haste (hāst) *n.* **1.** Swiftness; rapidity. **2.** Eagerness or necessity to move swiftly; urgency. **3.** Careless or headlong hurrying. [< OF < Gmc **haifsti-.*]

has•ten (hā'sən) *v.* To move or cause to move swiftly; hurry.

hast•y (hā'stē) *adj.* **-ier, -iest. 1.** Characterized by speed; swift. **2.** Done too quickly to be accurate or wise; rash. —**hast'i•ly** *adv.* —**hast'i•ness** *n.*

hat (hăt) *n.* A covering for the head, esp. one with a shaped crown and brim. [< OE *hæt.* See **kadh-.**]

hatch[1] (hăch) *n.* **1. a.** An opening in the deck of a ship leading to the hold. **b.** A hatchway. **2.** Any small door or opening. [< OE *hæcc,* hatch, wicket < Gmc **khak-.*]

hatch[2] (hăch) *v.* **1.** To emerge from or cause to emerge from an egg. **2.** To cause (an egg or eggs) to produce young. **3.** To originate or formulate. [< OE **hæccan.*]

hatch•er•y (hăch'ə-rē) *n., pl.* **-ies.** A place where eggs, as of fish or domestic fowl, are hatched.

hatch•et (hăch'ĭt) *n.* **1.** A short-handled ax. **2.** A tomahawk. [< OF *hache,* ax.]

hatch•way (hăch'wā') *n.* **1.** An opening in the deck of a ship leading to a hold or lower deck. **2.** A ladder within such an opening.

hate (hāt) *v.* **hated, hating. 1.** To loathe; detest. **2.** To dislike; wish to shun. —*n.* **1.** Strong dislike; animosity. **2.** An object of hatred. [< OE *hatian.* See **kād-.**] —**hate'ful** *adj.*

hath (hăth). *Archaic.* 3rd person sing. present indicative of **have.**

ha•tred (hā'trĭd) *n.* Violent dislike or animosity; abhorrence. [< OE *hete,* hate.]

hat•ter (hăt'ər) *n.* One who makes, repairs, or sells hats.

hau•berk (hô'bûrk) *n.* A tunic of chain mail. [< OF *hauberc.*]

haugh•ty (hô'tē) *adj.* **-tier, -tiest.** Proud and vain to the point of arrogance. [< OF *haut,* "high."] —**haugh'ti•ly** *adv.* —**haugh'ti•ness** *n.*

haul (hôl) *v.* **1.** To pull or drag; tug. **2.** To provide transportation; cart. —*n.* **1.** The act of hauling. **2. a.** The distance over which something is carted. **b.** The load carted. **3.** An amount collected or acquired; take: *a haul of fish.* [< OF *haler,* to pull.]

haul•age (hô'lĭj) *n.* **1.** The act or process of hauling. **2.** The charge made for hauling.

haunch (hônch, hänch) *n.* The hip, buttock, and upper thigh. [< OF *hanche* < Gmc **hanka.*]

haunt (hônt, hänt) *v.* **1.** To visit or appear to in the form of a ghost. **2.** To frequent. **3.** To recur to continually. **4.** To linger or remain in profusion; pervade. —*n.* A place much frequented. [< OF *hanter.*]

Hau•sa (hou'sə, -zə) *n., pl.* **-sa.** Also **Haus•sa. 1.** One of a Negroid people of the Sudan and Nigeria. **2.** Their language.

hau•teur (hō-tûr') *n.* Haughtiness; arrogance. [< F *haut,* high, pious.]

Ha•van•a (hə-văn'ə). The capital of Cuba. Pop. 800,000.

have (hăv) *v.* **had, having, has.** —Used as an auxiliary before a past participle to form the past, present, and future perfect tenses. **1.** To possess; own. **2.** To stand in relationship to. **3.** To be obliged to. **4.** To hold in one's mind; entertain. **5. a.** To win a victory over. **b.** To cheat or trick. **6.** To possess sexually. **7.** To keep in a specified place. **8.** To accept or take. **9.** To partake of; consume. **10.** To be made of, consist of, or contain. **11.** To exercise or exhibit: *have mercy.* **12.** To allow; permit. **13.** To cause to. **14.** To carry out or stage. **15.** To experience: *have a good summer.* **16.** To beget or give birth to. **17.** To be in command of: *have the necessary technique.* **18.** To receive as a guest. —*n.* One of a class enjoying material comforts: *the haves and the have-nots.* [< OE *habban.* See **kap-.**]

ha•ven (hā'vən) *n.* **1.** A harbor or port. **2.** A place of sanctuary. [< OE *hæfen.*]

have-not (hăv'nŏt') *n.* One having little or no property.

have•n't (hăv'ənt). Contraction of *have not.*

hav•er•sack (hăv'ər-săk') *n.* A canvas bag worn over one shoulder to transport supplies on a hike. [< G *Habersack,* "bag for oats."]

hav•oc (hăv'ək) *n.* Widespread destruction or confusion. [< OF *havot,* plunder.]

haw (hô) *n.* **1.** The fruit of a hawthorn. **2.** A hawthorn. [< OE *haga,* hawthorn, hedge.]

Ha•wai•i (hə-wä'ē, -wä'yə). A state of the U.S.; an island group in the C Pacific. Pop.

770,000. Cap. Honolulu.

Ha•wai•ian (hə-wä'yən) *n.* **1.** A native or inhabitant of Hawaii. **2.** The Polynesian language of Hawaii. —**Ha•wai'ian** *adj.*

hawk[1] (hôk) *n.* **1.** Any of various day-flying birds of prey characteristically having a short, hooked bill and strong claws adapted for seizing. **2.** A member of a group advocating a militaristic foreign policy. [< OE *heafoc.* See **kap-**.]

hawk[2] (hôk) *v.* To peddle (wares), esp. in the streets. [Prob < MLG *höken,* to peddle.] —**hawk'er** *n.*

haw•ser (hô'zər) *n. Naut.* A rope or cable used in mooring or towing a ship. [< OF *haucier,* to lift.]

haw•thorn (hô'thôrn') *n.* A thorny tree or shrub with white or pinkish flowers and reddish fruit. [< HAW + THORN.]

Haw•thorne (hô'thôrn'), **Nathaniel.** 1804–1864. American novelist.

hay (hā) *n.* Grass or other forage plants cut and dried for fodder. —*v.* To cut and process grass and herbage to make hay. [< OE *hieg.* See **kau-**.]

hay•cock (hā'kŏk') *n.* A conical mound of hay.

Hay•dn (hīd'n), **Franz Joseph.** 1732–1809. Austrian composer.

Hayes (hāz), **Rutherford B(irchard).** 1822–1893. 19th President of the U.S. (1877–81).

Rutherford B. Hayes

hay fever. An acute allergic condition of the mucous membranes of the upper respiratory tract and the eyes, caused by abnormal sensitivity to certain airborne pollens, esp. of the ragweed and related plants.

hay•fork (hā'fôrk') *n.* **1.** A hand tool for pitching hay. **2.** A machine-operated fork for moving hay.

hay•loft (hā'lôft', -lŏft') *n.* A loft for storing hay.

hay•mow (hā'mou') *n.* A hayloft.

hay•seed (hā'sēd') *n. Slang.* A country bumpkin.

hay•stack (hā'stăk') *n.* Hay piled into a stack for outdoor storage.

hay•wire (hā'wīr') *adj. Informal.* **1.** Not functioning properly; broken. **2.** Crazy.

haz•ard (hăz'ərd) *n.* **1.** A chance or accident. **2.** A danger; risk. **3.** An obstacle on a golf course. —*v.* To run the risk of; venture. [< Span *azar,* unlucky throw of the dice.] —**haz'ard•ous** *adj.* —**haz'ard•ous•ly** *adv.*

haze[1] (hāz) *n.* **1.** Atmospheric moisture, dust, smoke, and vapor suspended to form a partially opaque condition. **2.** A vague state of mind. [< HAZY.]

haze[2] (hāz) *v.* **hazed, hazing.** To persecute or harass with humiliating tasks or practical jokes. [?]

ha•zel (hā'zəl) *n.* **1.** A shrub or small tree bearing smooth-shelled edible nuts enclosed in a leafy husk. **2.** Light or yellowish brown. [< OE *hæsel.* See **koselo-**.] —**ha'zel** *adj.*

ha•zel•nut (hā'zəl-nŭt') *n.* The nut of a hazel.

haz•y (hā'zē) *adj.* **-ier, -iest. 1.** Marked by the presence of haze. **2.** Vague; confused. [?] —**haz'i•ly** *adv.* —**haz'i•ness** *n.*

H-bomb (āch'bŏm') *n.* A **hydrogen bomb.**

hdqrs. headquarters.

he[1] (hē) *pron.* The 3rd person sing. pronoun in the nominative case, masculine gender. **1.** —Used to represent the male person last mentioned. **2.** —Used to represent any person whose sex is not specified: *He who hesitates is lost.* —*n.* A male animal or person: *Is the cat a he?* [< OE *hē, he.* See **ko-**.]

he[2] (hā) *n.* The 5th letter of the Hebrew alphabet, representing *h.*

He helium.

head (hĕd) *n.* **1.** The upper or anterior bodily extremity, containing the brain or the principal ganglia and in vertebrates the eyes, ears, nose, mouth, and jaws. **2. a.** Intellect; mind. **b.** Aptitude. **3.** Self-control. **4.** Freedom of choice or action: *Give him his head.* **5.** The obverse side of a coin. **6. a.** Each individual within a group. **b.** *pl.* **head.** A single animal within a herd. **7.** A leader; chief. **8.** The foremost position: *the head of the line.* **9.** A turning point; crisis. **10.** A projecting or striking part of something. **11.** The upper or higher end of something. **12.** Either end, as of a drum. **13.** Pressure: *a head of steam.* **14.** A rounded, compact mass of leaves, as of cabbage, or flowers, as of clover. —**go to one's head. 1.** To make one lightheaded. **2.** To increase one's conceit. —*adj.* **1.** Foremost in importance. **2.** Placed at the top or front. **3.** Coming from the front: *head winds.* —*v.* **1.** To be chief of; command. **2.** To assume or be placed in the first or foremost position of. **3.** To aim: *head the horse for home.* **4.** To proceed or set out: *head for town.* [< OE *hēafod.* See **kaput.**]

head•ache (hĕd'āk') *n.* **1.** A pain in the head. **2.** *Informal.* Something that bothers.

head•band (hĕd'bănd') *n.* A band worn around the head.

head•dress (hĕd'drĕs') *n.* Something worn on the head, as a covering or ornament.

head•first (hĕd'fûrst') *adv.* **1.** With the head leading; headlong. **2.** Impetuously.

head•gear (hĕd'gîr') *n.* A covering for the head, such as a hat or helmet.

head•ing (hĕd'ĭng) *n.* **1.** A word or words at the beginning of a chapter, paragraph, etc. **2.** The course or direction of movement of a ship or aircraft.

head•land (hĕd'lənd, -lănd') *n.* A point of land extending out into a body of water; promontory.

head•light (hĕd'līt') *n.* A lamp mounted on the front of a vehicle.

head•line (hĕd'līn') *n.* The title or caption of a newspaper article, set in large type.

head•lock (hĕd'lŏk') *n.* A wrestling hold in which the head of one wrestler is locked under the arm of the other.

head•long (hĕd'lông', -lŏng') *adv.* **1.** With the head leading; headfirst. **2.** Impetuously. **3.** At breakneck speed. —**head'long'** *adj.*

head•mas•ter (hĕd'măs'tər, -mäs'tər) *n.* A male principal of a private school.

head•mis•tress (hĕd'mĭs'trĭs) *n.* A woman principal of a private school.

head•phone (hĕd'fōn') *n.* A receiver, as for a radio, held to the ear by a headband.

head•quar•ters (hĕd'kwôr'tərz) *pl.n. (often takes sing. v.).* The command center, as of a military unit.

head•rest (hĕd'rĕst') *n.* A support for the head.

head•set (hĕd'sĕt') *n.* A pair of headphones.

head•stall (hĕd'stôl') *n.* The section of a bridle that fits over the horse's head.

head•stone (hĕd'stōn') *n.* A stone set at the head of a grave.

head•strong (hĕd'strông', -strŏng') *adj.* Willful; obstinate.

head•wait•er (hĕd'wā'tər) *n.* A waiter in charge of other waiters in a restaurant.

head•wa•ters (hĕd'wô'tərz, -wŏt'ərz) *pl.n.* The waters from which a river rises.

head•way (hĕd'wā') *n.* **1.** Movement forward. **2.** Progress. **3.** Clearance overhead.

head•y (hĕd'ē) *adj.* **-ier, -iest. 1.** Intoxicating. **2.** Headstrong; obstinate. —**head'i•ly** *adv.*

heal (hēl) *v.* **1.** To restore or return to health; cure. **2.** To set right; amend. [< OE *hǣlen.* See **kailo-**.] —**heal'er** *n.*

health (hĕlth) *n.* **1.** The state of an organism with respect to functioning, disease, and abnormality at any given time. **2.** Optimal functioning with freedom from disease and abnormality. **3.** A wish for someone's good health, expressed as a toast. **4.** Flourishing condition; vitality. [< OE *hǣlth.* See **kailo-**.]

health•ful (hĕlth'fəl) *adj.* **1.** Conducive to good health. **2.** Healthy. —**health'ful•ly** *adv.*

health•y (hĕl'thē) *adj.* **-ier, -iest. 1.** Possessing good health. **2.** Conducive to good health; healthful. **3.** Indicative of a constructive frame of mind: *a healthy attitude.* **4.** Sizable; considerable: *a healthy portion.* —**health'i•ly** *adv.* —**health'i•ness** *n.*

heap (hēp) *n.* **1.** A group of things haphazardly gathered; a pile. **2.** Often **heaps.** A great deal; lots. —*v.* **1.** To put or throw in a heap. **2.** To fill to overflowing. [< OE *hēap.*]

hear (hîr) *v.* **heard** (hûrd), **hearing. 1.** To perceive by the ear. **2.** To listen attentively. **3.** To learn. **4.** To listen to in an official capacity, as in a court. [< OE *hieran.* See **keu-**.]

hear•ing (hîr'ĭng) *n.* **1.** The capacity to hear. **2.** The range of audibility. **3.** An opportunity to be heard. **4.** A preliminary examination of an accused person. **5.** A session, as of an investigative committee, at which testimony is taken.

heark•en (här'kən) *v. Poetic.* To listen attentively; give heed. [< OE **heorcian,* to hark, hear. See **keu-**.]

hear•say (hîr'sā') *n.* Information or a rumor heard from another.

hearse (hûrs) *n.* A vehicle for conveying a dead body to a cemetery. [ME *herse,* frame for holding candles.]

heart (härt) *n.* **1.** *Anat.* The hollow muscular organ that pumps blood received from the veins into the arteries, thereby supplying the entire circulatory system. **2.** The heart regarded as the seat of emotions, as: **a.** Mood. **b.** Compassion. **c.** Affection. **d.** Character or fortitude. **3. a.** The innermost area or part. **b.** The essence: *the heart of the problem.* **4.** Any of a suit of playing cards marked with a red, heart-shaped symbol. —**at heart.** Essentially;

fundamentally. —**by heart.** By rote. [< OE *heorte.* See **kerd-**.]

heart•ache (härt′āk′) *n.* Emotional anguish; deep sorrow.

heart attack. **1.** Partial failure of the pumping action of the heart. **2.** Any seizure of abnormal heart functioning, as a coronary thrombosis.

heart•beat (härt′bēt′) *n.* A single complete pulsation of the heart.

heart•break (härt′brāk′) *n.* Intense grief or disappointment. —**heart′break′ing** *adj.*

heart•burn (härt′bûrn′) *n.* A burning sensation in the stomach and esophagus, caused by excess acidity of stomach fluids.

heart•en (härt′n) *v.* To give strength or hope to; encourage.

heart•felt (härt′fĕlt′) *adj.* Deeply or sincerely felt.

hearth (härth) *n.* **1.** The floor of a fireplace, usually extending into a room. **2.** The fireside; family life. **3.** The lowest part of a blast furnace or cupola, from which the molten metal flows. [< OE *heorth.* See **ker-³**.]

hearth•stone (härth′stōn′) *n.* **1.** Stone used in constructing a hearth. **2.** The fireside; home.

heart•less (härt′lĭs) *adj.* Without compassion; pitiless; cruel. —**heart′less•ly** *adv.*

heart-rend•ing (härt′rĕn′dĭng) *adj.* Causing anguish or deep sympathy.

heart•sick (härt′sĭk′) *adj.* Profoundly disappointed; despondent; unhappy.

heart•strings (härt′strĭngz′) *pl.n.* The deepest feelings or affections.

heart-to-heart (härt′tə-härt′) *adj.* Personal and candid.

heart•y (här′tē) *adj.* **-ier, -iest. 1.** Expressed with warmth of feeling; exuberant. **2.** Complete or thorough. **3.** Vigorous; robust. **4.** Nourishing. —**heart′i•ly** *adv.*

heat (hēt) *n.* **1.** Energy associated with the motion of atoms or molecules in solids and capable of being transmitted through solid and fluid media by conduction, through fluid media by convection, and through empty space by radiation. **2.** The perceptible, sensible, or measurable effect of such energy so transmitted, esp. a physiological sensation of being hot. **3.** A recurrent condition of sexual activity in female mammals. **4.** One of a series of efforts. **5.** *Slang.* Pressure, as from police pursuing criminals. —*v.* **1.** To make or become warm or hot. **2.** To excite the feelings of. [< OE *hǣtu.* See **kai-**.]

heat•er (hē′tər) *n.* An apparatus that provides heat.

heath (hēth) *n.* **1.** An open, uncultivated tract of land covered with heather or similar plants. **2.** A plant, as heather, that grows on such land. [< OE *hǣth.* See **kaito-**.]

hea•then (hē′*th*ən) *n., pl.* **-thens** or **-then. 1.** One who adheres to a religion that does not acknowledge the God of Judaism, Christianity, or Islam. **2.** One who is regarded as irreligious, uncivilized, or unenlightened. [< OE *hǣthen.* See **kaito-**.] —**hea′then, hea′then•ish** *adj.* —**hea′then•dom** (-dəm) *n.*

heath•er (hĕ*th*′ər) *n.* A low-growing evergreen shrub having small purplish flowers and forming dense masses. [Prob < HEATH.]

heave (hēv) *v.* **heaved** or *chiefly naut.* **hove, heaving. 1.** To raise or lift. **2.** To throw, esp. with great effort. **3.** *Naut.* **a.** To pull on or haul. **b.** To push. **4.** *Naut.* To come to be in a specified position: *The ship hove alongside.* **5.** To breathe or emit: *heaved a sigh.* **6.** To rise up or swell. **7.** *Informal.* To vomit. —*n.* **1.** The act or strain of heaving. **2.** *Informal.* A throw. **3. heaves** *(takes sing. or pl. v.).* A respiratory disease of horses characterized by coughing and irregular breathing. [< OE *hebban.* See **kap-**.]

heav•en (hĕv′ən) *n.* **1.** *Often* **heavens.** The sky or universe as seen from the earth. **2.** The abode of God, the angels, and the souls granted salvation. **3. a. Heaven.** The divine providence. **b.** Often **heavens.** A euphemism for God: *Good heavens!* **4. heavens.** The celestial powers; the gods: *The heavens favored our plan.* **5.** A place or thing that affords supreme happiness. [< OE *heofon.*] —**heav′en•ly** *adj.* —**heav′en•ward** *adv.* & *adj.*

heav•y (hĕv′ē) *adj.* **-ier, -iest. 1.** Having relatively great weight. **2.** Having relatively high density. **3. a.** Large in number or volume: *heavy rainfall; a heavy turnout.* **b.** Intense or sustained: *heavy activity.* **4.** Dense or thick: *heavy fog; a heavy coat.* **5. a.** Concerted or powerful; severe: *a heavy blow.* **b.** Rough; violent: *heavy seas.* **6. a.** To a great or habitual degree. **b.** On a large scale. **7.** Of great import or seriousness. **8. a.** Hard to do. **b.** Oppressive: *heavy taxes.* **9. a.** Copious: *a heavy breakfast.* **b.** Not easily or quickly digested. **10.** Having large or marked physical features. **11.** Weighed with concern or sadness: *a heavy heart.* **12.** Ponderous. **13. a.** Weighed down; laden. **b.** Showing weariness. **14.** Involving large-scale manufacturing: *heavy industry.* **15.** Bearing heavy arms or armor. —*adv.* Heavily. —*n., pl.* **-ies. 1.** A villain in a story or play. **2.** An actor who portrays villains or scoundrels in plays. [< OE *hefig.* See **kap-**.] —**heav′i•ly** *adv.* —**heav′i•ness** *n.*

heav•y-dut•y (hĕv′ē-d/y/ōō′tē) *adj.* Made for hard use: *heavy-duty equipment.*

heav•y-hand•ed (hĕv′ē-hăn′dĭd) *adj.* **1.** Clumsy. **2.** Tactless. **3.** Oppressive.

heav•y•set (hĕv′ē-sĕt′) *adj.* Having a heavy, compact build.

heavy water. Any of several isotopic varieties of water, esp. **deuterium oxide.**

heav•y•weight (hĕv′ē-wāt′) *n.* **1.** One of above average weight. **2.** One that competes in the heaviest class, esp. a boxer weighing more than 175 pounds.

Heb. **1.** Hebrew. **2.** Hebrews (New Testament).

Hebr. Hebrew.

He•bra•ic (hĭ-brā′ĭk) *adj.* Also **He•bra•i•cal** (-ĭ-kəl). Of or characteristic of the Hebrews or their language or culture. —**He′bra•ism′** (hē′brā-ĭz′əm, hē′brə-) *n.*

He•brew (hē′brōō) *n.* **1.** One of the Semitic people claiming descent from Abraham, Isaac, and Jacob; an Israelite. **2. a.** The Semitic language of the ancient Hebrews, used in most of the Old Testament. **b.** Any of various later forms of this language, esp. the form now spoken in Israel. —*adj.* Relating or pertaining to Hebrews.

Hebrew Scriptures. The Pentateuch, the Prophets, and the Hagiographa, forming the convenant between God and the Jewish people that is the foundation and Bible of Judaism.

heck (hĕk). Euphemism for hell.

heck•le (hĕk′əl) *v.* **-led, -ling.** To harass persistently, as with questions or objections. [< OE **hǣcel,* "comb for flax."] —**heck′ler** *n.*

hec•tare (hĕk′târ′) *n.* A metric unit of area equal to 100 ares or 2.471 acres. [< Gk *hekaton,* hundred.]

hec•tic (hĕk′tĭk) *adj.* **1.** Characterized by feverish activity, confusion, or haste. **2.** Of or having an undulating fever, as in diseases such as tuberculosis or septicemia. **3.** Flushed. [< Gk *hektikos,* formed by habit, consumptive, hectic.] —**hec′ti•cal•ly, hec′tic•ly** *adv.*

hec•tor (hĕk′tər) *v.* To intimidate or dominate in a blustering way.

Hec•tor (hĕk′tər). Trojan prince and champion slain by Achilles in Homer's *Iliad.*

he'd (hēd). **1.** Contraction of *he had.* **2.** Contraction of *he would.*

hedge (hĕj) *n.* A row of closely planted shrubs forming a boundary. —*v.* **hedged, hedging. 1.** To enclose or bound with or as if with hedges. **2.** To counterbalance (a bet) with other transactions, so as to limit risk. **3.** To avoid committing oneself, as by making evasive statements. [< OE *hecg.* See **kagh-**.]

hedge•hog (hĕj′hôg′, -hŏg′) *n.* A small Old World mammal having the back covered with dense spines.

hedge•hop (hĕj′hŏp′) *v.* To fly an airplane close to the ground.

he•don•ism (hēd′n-ĭz′əm) *n.* **1.** Pursuit of or devotion to pleasure. **2.** The ethical doctrine that only that which is pleasant is intrinsically good. [< Gk *hēdonē,* pleasure.] —**he′don•ist** *n.* —**he′don•is′tic** *adj.*

heed (hēd) *v.* To pay attention (to). —*n.* Close attention or consideration. [< OE *hēdan.* See **kadh-**.] —**heed′ful** *adj.* —**heed′ful•ly** *adv.* —**heed′less** *adj.* —**heed′less•ly** *adv.*

heel¹ (hēl) *n.* **1.** The rounded posterior portion of the human foot under and behind the ankle. **2.** A similar or corresponding part, as in animals. **3.** That part of footwear which covers the heel. **4.** A lower, rearward surface of a thing. **5.** *Slang.* A dishonorable man. —*v.* **1.** To furnish with a heel or heels. **2.** *Slang.* To furnish (a person) with something, esp. money. **3.** To follow at the heels of. [< OE *hēla.* See **kenk-¹**.] —**heel′less** *adj.*

heel² (hēl) *v.* To tip or cause to tip to one side, esp. a ship. —*n.* A tilting to one side; list. [Prob < OE *hieldan.*]

heft (hĕft) *n. Informal.* Weight; heaviness. —*v.* **1.** To determine the weight of by lifting. **2.** To hoist; heave. [< HEAVE.]

heft•y (hĕf′tē) *adj.* **-ier, -iest. 1.** Heavy. **2.** Large and powerful.

He•gel (hā′gəl), **Georg Wilhelm Friedrich.** 1770–1831. German philosopher.

he•gem•o•ny (hĭ-jĕm′ə-nē, hĕj′ə-mō′nē) *n., pl.* **-nies.** Predominance, esp. that of one state over others. [Gk *hēgemonia,* authority, rule.]

he•gi•ra (hĭ-jī′rə, hĕj′ər-ə) *n.* A flight, as from danger. [Ar *(al)hijrah,* abandonment of Mecca, flight.]

heif•er (hĕf′ər) *n.* A young cow, esp. one that has not borne a calf. [< OE *hēahfore,* young ox.]

height (hīt) *n.* **1.** The highest or uppermost point. **2.** The most advanced degree; point of highest intensity. **3. a.** The distance from the base to the top of something. **b.** The elevation of something above a given level; altitude. **4.** Stature, esp. of the human body. **5.** An eminence. [< OE *hēhthu, hīehthu.*]

height•en (hīt′n) *v.* **1.** To make or become greater in quantity or degree; intensify. **2.** To make or become high or higher.

Hei•ne (hī′nə), **Heinrich.** 1797–1856. German poet and critic.

hei•nous (hā′nəs) *adj.* Grossly wicked or reprehensible. [< OF *haïr,* to hate.]

heir (âr) *n.* A person who inherits or is entitled by law to inherit the property, title, or office of another. [< L *hērēs.*]

heir apparent. An heir whose right to inheritance is indefeasible by law provided he survives his ancestor.

heir•ess (âr'ĭs) *n.* A female heir.

heir•loom (âr'lo͞om') *n.* **1.** A possession passed down in a family through succeeding generations. **2.** *Law.* An article of personal property included in an inherited estate.

heist (hīst) *v. Slang.* To rob; steal. —*n. Slang.* A robbery. [Dial var of HOIST.]

held (hĕld). *p.t.* & *p.p.* of **hold.**

Hel•e•na (hĕl'ə-nə). The capital of Montana. Pop. 20,000.

Helen of Troy. *Gk.Myth.* A daughter of Zeus and queen of Sparta whose abduction by Paris caused the Trojan War.

hel•i•cal (hĕl'ĭ-kəl) *adj.* Shaped like a helix.

hel•i•cop•ter (hĕl'ĭ-kŏp'tər) *n.* An aircraft that derives its lift from blades that rotate about an approximately vertical central axis. [F *hélicoptère,* "spiral wing."]

helio–. *comb. form.* The sun. [< Gk *hēlios,* the sun.]

he•li•o•cen•tric (hē'lē-ō-sĕn'trĭk) *adj.* Having the sun as a center. —**he'li•o•cen•tric'i•ty** (-sĕn-trĭs'ə-tē) *n.*

he•li•o•graph (hē'lē-ə-grăf', -gräf') *n.* A signaling apparatus that reflects sunlight with a movable mirror.

he•li•o•trope (hē'lē-ə-trōp') *n.* A cultivated plant with small, fragrant, purplish flowers.

hel•i•port (hĕl'ə-pôrt', -pōrt') *n.* An airport for helicopters.

he•li•um (hē'lē-əm) *n. Symbol* **He** A colorless, odorless, tasteless, inert gaseous element used to provide lift for balloons and as an inert component of various artificial atmospheres. Atomic number 2, atomic weight 4.0026. [< Gk *hēlios,* the sun.]

he•lix (hē'lĭks) *n., pl.* **-lixes** or **helices** (hĕl'ə-sēz', hē'lə-). **1.** A three-dimensional curve that lies on a cylinder or cone and cuts the elements at a constant angle. **2.** Any spiral or helical object. [< Gk, spiral.]

hell (hĕl) *n.* **1.** The abode of the dead; the underworld where departed souls were believed to dwell. **2.** The place or state of torture and punishment for the wicked after death. **3.** The infernal powers of evil and darkness. **4. a.** Torment; anguish. **b.** Something that causes agony. —**a** (or **one**) **hell of a.** *Informal.* Unusually (bad, good, hard, etc.). —**raise hell.** *Slang.* To cause a disturbance or trouble. —*interj. Slang.* Expressive of acute anger, disgust, or impatience. [< OE. See **kel-⁴.**]

he'll (hēl). **1.** Contraction of *he will.* **2.** Contraction of *he shall.*

hell-bent (hĕl'bĕnt') *adj.* Impetuously bent on doing something.

hell•cat (hĕl'kăt') *n.* A furious and evil woman.

hel•le•bore (hĕl'ə-bôr', -bōr') *n.* Any of several chiefly poisonous plants with white or greenish flowers. [< Gk *helleboros,* perh "eaten by fawns."]

Hel•lene (hĕl'ēn') *n.* Also **Hel•le•ni•an** (hĕ-lē'nē-ən). A Greek. [< Gk *Hellēn.*]

Hel•len•ic (hĕ-lĕn'ĭk) *adj.* Of or relating to the ancient Greeks or their language.

hell•gram•mite (hĕl'grə-mīt') *n.* A large, brownish aquatic insect larva, often used as fishing bait. [?]

hell•hole (hĕl'hōl') *n.* A place of extreme wretchedness and squalor.

hel•lion (hĕl'yən) *n. Informal.* A mischievous, unrestrainable person. [?]

hell•ish (hĕl'ĭsh) *adj.* **1.** Of or relating to hell. **2.** *Informal.* Like hell; devilish. —**hell'ish•ly** *adv.* —**hell'ish•ness** *n.*

hel•lo (hĕ-lō', hə-) *interj.* **1.** Used to greet another or summon attention. **2.** Expressive of surprise. —*n., pl.* **-loes.** A calling or greeting of "hello." [Var of earlier *holla,* stop!]

helm (hĕlm) *n.* **1.** The tiller, wheel, or whole steering gear of a ship. **2.** A position of leadership or control. [< OE *helma.* See **kelp-.**]

hel•met (hĕl'mĭt) *n.* **1.** A protective head covering of metal, used in combat or warfare. **2.** A protective head covering of hard material, as leather or plastic, worn by policemen, firemen, etc. [< Frank **helm.*]

helms•man (hĕlmz'mən) *n.* One who steers a ship.

hel•ot (hĕl'ət, hē'lət) *n.* A serf; bondsman. [< Gk *Heilōtes,* a class of Spartan serfs.]

help (hĕlp) *v.* **1.** To give assistance (to); aid. **2.** To contribute to; further. **3.** To give relief to. **4.** To improve; benefit. **5.** To be able to prevent, change, or rectify: *I cannot help her laziness.* **6.** To refrain from; avoid: *He cannot help laughing.* **7.** To wait on; serve. —**cannot help but.** To be compelled to. —*n.* **1.** Aid; assistance. **2.** Relief; remedy. **3.** One that helps. **4. a.** A person employed to assist. **b.** Such employees collectively. [< OE *helpan.* See **kelb-.**] —**help'er** *n.*

Usage: The construction *cannot help but* is a less formal variant of *cannot help* plus gerund and of *cannot but* plus infinitive without *to.* All three express substantially the same idea: *One cannot help but admire his courage. One cannot help admiring his courage. One cannot but admire his courage.*

help•ful (hĕlp'fəl) *adj.* Providing help; useful; beneficial. —**help'ful•ly** *adv.* —**help'ful•ness** *n.*

help•ing (hĕl'pĭng) *n.* A portion of food for one person.

help•less (hĕlp'lĭs) *adj.* **1.** Unable to manage by oneself; defenseless; dependent. **2.** Lacking power to help; impotent. —**help'less•ly** *adv.* —**help'less•ness** *n.*

help•mate (hĕlp'māt') *n.* A helper, esp. a spouse.

help•meet (hĕlp'mēt') *n.* A helpmate.

Hel•sin•ki (hĕl'sĭng'kē). The capital of Finland. Pop. 470,000.

hel•ter-skel•ter (hĕl'tər-skĕl'tər) *adv.* **1.** In disorderly haste. **2.** Haphazardly. **3.** In confusion. —*adj.* **1.** Carelessly hurried and confused. **2.** Haphazard. [?]

helve (hĕlv) *n.* A handle of a wagon or tool. [< OE *hielfe.*]

hem¹ (hĕm) *n.* An edge or border of a piece of cloth, esp. a finished edge made by folding under and stitching down the selvage or raw edge. —*v.* **hemmed, hemming.** **1.** To fold back and stitch down the edge of. **2.** To encircle and confine; shut in; enclose. [<OE *hemm.* See **kem-².**] —**hem'mer** *n.*

hem² (hĕm) *n.* A short cough or clearing of the throat made to gain attention, fill a pause, etc. —*v.* **hemmed, hemming.** To utter this sound. —**hem and haw.** To be hesitant and indecisive in speech. [Imit.]

he-man (hē'măn') *n. Informal.* A strong, virile man.

hem•a•tite (hĕm'ə-tīt', hē'mə-) *n.* A blackish-red to brick-red mineral, essentially Fe_2O_3, the chief ore of iron. [< Gk *(lithos) haimatitēs,* "bloodlike (stone)."]

hemato–. *comb. form.* Blood. [< Gk *haima,* blood.]

he•ma•tol•o•gy (hē'mə-tŏl'ə-jē, hĕm'ə-) *n.* The science encompassing the generation, anatomy, physiology, pathology, and therapeutics of blood. —**he'ma•tol'o•gist** *n.*

heme (hēm) *n.* The nonprotein, ferrous-iron-containing component of hemoglobin, having composition $C_{34}H_{32}FeN_4O_4$.

hemi–. *comb. form.* Half. [< Gk *hēmi-.*]

–hemia. Variant of **-emia.**

Hem•ing•way (hĕm'ĭng-wā'), **Ernest.** 1899–1961. American novelist.

hem•i•sphere (hĕm'ə-sfîr') *n.* **1. a.** A half of a sphere bounded by a great circle. **b.** A symmetric half of an approximately symmetrical object. **2.** Either the N or S half of the earth as divided by the equator or the E or W half as divided by a meridian. —**hem'i•spher'ic** (-sfîr'ĭk, -sfĕr'ĭk), **hem'i•spher'i•cal** *adj.*

hem•lock (hĕm'lŏk') *n.* **1. a.** An evergreen tree with short, flat needles and small cones. **b.** The wood of such a tree. **2. a.** A poisonous plant with compound leaves and small whitish flowers. **b.** A poison obtained from this plant. [< OE *hemlic.*]

hemo–. *comb. form.* Blood. [< Gk *haima,* blood.]

he•mo•glo•bin (hē'mə-glō'bən, hĕm'ə-) *n.* The oxygen-bearing, iron-containing protein in vertebrate red blood cells, consisting of about 6% heme and 94% globin. [< HEMATO- + GLOBULIN.]

he•mo•phil•i•a (hē'mə-fĭl'ē-ə, hĕm'ə-) *n.* A hereditary plasma-coagulation disorder, principally affecting males but transmitted by females and characterized by excessive, sometimes spontaneous, bleeding. —**he'mo•phil'i•ac'** (-ăk') *adj.* & *n.*

hem•or•rhage (hĕm'ə-rĭj) *n.* Bleeding, esp. copious discharge of blood from the vessels. —*v.* **-rhaged, -rhaging.** To bleed copiously. —**hem'or•rhag'ic** (-răj'ĭk) *adj.*

hem•or•rhoid (hĕm'ə-roid') *n.* **1.** An itching or painful mass of dilated veins in swollen anal tissue. **2. hemorrhoids.** The pathological condition in which such swollen masses occur. [< Gk *haimorrhoos,* flowing with blood.]

he•mo•stat (hē'mə-stăt') *n.* Any agent that stops bleeding, esp. a clamplike instrument used in surgery.

hemp (hĕmp) *n.* **1.** A tall Asian plant with stems that yield a coarse fiber used in cordage. **2.** The fiber of this plant. [< OE *hænep.*] —**hemp'en** *adj.*

hem•stitch (hĕm'stĭch') *n.* A decorative stitch made by drawing out several parallel threads and catching together the cross threads in uniform groups, thus creating an open design. —*v.* To ornament with this stitch.

hen (hĕn) *n.* A female bird, esp. the adult female of the domestic fowl. [< OE. See **kan-.**]

hence (hĕns) *adv.* **1. a.** For this reason; therefore. **b.** From this source. **2.** From now. **3.** Forth from this place. [< OE *heonane,* from here, away. See **ko-.**]

hence•forth (hĕns'fôrth') *adv.* Also **hence•for•ward** (hĕns'fôr'wərd). From now on; from this time forth.

hench•man (hĕnch'mən) *n.* **1.** A loyal and trusted follower or subordinate. **2.** One who supports a political figure chiefly out of self-seeking interests. [ME *hengestman,* prob groom.]

hen•na (hĕn'ə) *n.* **1. a.** A cosmetic dyestuff obtained from the leaves of a Middle Eastern shrub. **b.** The shrub itself. **2.** Strong reddish brown. —*v.* To dye or rinse (hair) with henna. [Ar *ḥinnā'.*]

hen•peck (hĕn'pĕk') *v. Informal.* To afflict (one's husband) with persistent nagging.

ô paw, for/oi boy/ou out/o͝o took/o͞o coo/p pop/r run/s sauce/sh shy/t to/th thin/*th* the/
ŭ cut/ûr fur/v van/w wag/y yes/z size/zh vision/ə ago, item, edible, gallop, circus/

hen•ry (hĕn′rē) *n., pl.* **-ries** or **-rys.** The unit of inductance in which an induced electromotive force of one volt is produced when the current is varied at the rate of one ampere per second. [< J. *Henry* (1797–1878), American physicist.]

Hen•ry VIII (hĕn′rē). 1491–1547. King of England (1509–47); broke with Rome (1533).

Hen•ry (hĕn′rē), **Patrick.** 1736–1799. American Revolutionary leader and orator.

hep. Variant of **hip²**.

he•pat•i•ca (hĭ-păt′ĭ-kə) *n.* A North American woodland plant with three-lobed leaves and lavender or white flowers. [< ML *hēpatica,* liverwort.]

hep•a•ti•tis (hĕp′ə-tī′tĭs) *n.* Inflammation of the liver characterized by jaundice and usually accompanied by fever and other systemic manifestations. [< Gk *hēpar (hēpat-),* liver + -ITIS.]

her (hûr; *unstressed* hər, ər). **I.** *—pron.* The objective case of the 3rd person pronoun *she,* used as the direct or indirect object of a verb or as the object of a preposition. **II.** The possessive form of the pronoun *she,* used attributively: *her umbrella.* [< OE *hire.* See **ko-.**]

He•ra (hîr′ə). *Gk.Myth.* The sister and wife of Zeus.

her•ald (hĕr′əld) *n.* **1.** One who proclaims important news. **2.** One that announces or gives indication of something to come. **3.** An official formerly charged with making royal proclamations. *—v.* To proclaim; usher in. [< OF *herault* < Gmc.]

he•ral•dic (hə-răl′dĭk) *adj.* Of or pertaining to heralds or heraldry.

her•ald•ry (hĕr′əl-drē) *n., pl.* **-ries. 1. a.** The profession of devising, granting, and blazoning arms and tracing pedigrees. **b.** The history and description of armorial bearings. **2.** Armorial ensigns. **3.** Pomp and ceremony.

herb (ûrb, hûrb) *n.* **1.** A plant that has a fleshy rather than woody stem and that generally dies back at the end of each growing season. **2.** An often aromatic plant used in medicine or as seasoning. [< L *herba.*]

her•ba•ceous (hûr-bā′shəs) *adj.* Of herbs as distinguished from woody plants.

herb•age (ûr′bĭj, hûr′-) *n.* **1.** Grass or leafy plants used esp. for pasturage. **2.** The fleshy, often edible parts of plants.

herb•al (hûr′bəl, ûr′-) *adj.* Of or relating to medicinal or culinary herbs.

her•bi•vore (hûr′bə-vôr′, -vōr′) *n.* A herbivorous animal.

her•biv•o•rous (hûr-bĭv′ər-əs) *adj.* Feeding on plants.

Her•cu•les (hûr′kyə-lēz′) *n.* **1.** Often **hercules.** A man of prodigious strength. **2.** A constellation in the N Hemisphere. [< *Hercules,* Greco-Roman mythological hero noted for his strength.] **—Her′cu•le′an** *adj.*

herd (hûrd) *n.* **1.** A group of animals, as domestic cattle or elephants, that remain or are kept together. **2.** A number of people banded together. *—v.* **1.** To congregate in a herd. **2.** To gather, keep, or drive (animals) in a herd. [< OE *heord.* See **kerdh-.**]

herd•er (hûr′dər) *n.* **1.** One who tends or drives a herd. **2.** Also **herds•man** (hûrdz′mən). One who owns or breeds livestock.

here (hîr) *adv.* **1.** At or in this place. **2.** At this time. **3.** At or on this point or detail. **4.** In the present life or condition. **5.** To this place; hither. *—interj.* Used as a response to a roll call or summons. [< OE *hēr.* See **ko-.**]

here•a•bout (hîr′ə-bout′) *adv.* Also **here•a•bouts** (-bouts′). In this general vicinity; around here.

here•af•ter (hîr-ăf′tər, -äf′tər) *adv.* **1.** After this; henceforth. **2.** In the afterlife. *—n.* Life after death.

here•by (hîr-bī′) *adv.* By this means.

he•red•i•tar•y (hə-rĕd′ə-tĕr′ē) *adj.* **1.** *Law.* **a.** Passing down by inheritance. **b.** Having title or possession through inheritance. **2.** Genetically transmitted or transmissible. **3.** Derived from or fostered by one's ancestors; traditional. **—he•red′i•tar′i•ly** *adv.*

he•red•i•ty (hə-rĕd′ə-tē) *n., pl.* **-ties. 1.** The genetic transmission of characteristics from parents to offspring. **2.** The totality of characteristics and associated potentialities so transmitted to an individual organism. [< L *hērēs (hērēd-),* heir.]

here•in (hîr-ĭn′) *adv.* In or into this.

here•of (hîr-ŭv′, -ŏv′) *adv.* Pertaining to this.

here•on (hîr-ŏn′, -ôn′) *adv.* Hereupon.

her•e•sy (hĕr′ə-sē) *n., pl.* **-sies. 1.** An opinion or doctrine at variance with established beliefs, esp. dissension from or denial of Roman Catholic dogma by a professed believer or baptized church member. **2.** Adherence to such dissenting opinion. [< Gk *hairesis,* "a taking," faction.]

her•e•tic (hĕr′ə-tĭk) *n.* One who holds controversial opinions, esp. one who publicly dissents from the officially accepted dogma of the Roman Catholic Church. [< Gk *hairetikos,* able to choose, factious.] **—he•ret′i•cal** (hə-rĕt′ĭ-kəl) *adj.* **—he•ret′i•cal•ly** *adv.*

here•to (hîr-to͞o′) *adv.* To this place or matter.

here•to•fore (hîr′tə-fôr′, -fōr′) *adv.* Up to the present time; before this.

here•un•to (hîr-ŭn′to͞o) *adv.* Hereto.

here•up•on (hîr′ə-pŏn′, -pôn′) *adv.* **1.** Following instantly upon this. **2.** On this point or matter.

here•with (hîr-wĭth′, -wĭth′) *adv.* **1.** Along with this. **2.** By this means; hereby.

her•i•ta•ble (hĕr′ə-tə-bəl) *adj.* Capable of being inherited.

her•i•tage (hĕr′ə-tĭj) *n.* **1.** Property that is or can be inherited. **2.** Something other than property passed down from preceding generations; legacy; tradition. **3.** Birthright. [< L *hērēs (hērēd-),* heir.]

her•maph•ro•dite (hər-măf′rə-dīt′) *n.* One having the sex organs and often the secondary sex characteristics of both male and female. [< Gk *Hermaphroditos,* the son of Hermes and Aphrodite, who became united in one body with a nymph.] **—her•maph′ro•dit′ic** (-dĭt′ĭk) *adj.* **—her•maph′ro•dit′i•cal•ly** *adv.*

Her•mes (hûr′mēz′). Greek god of commerce, invention, cunning, and theft.

her•met•ic (hər-mĕt′ĭk) *adj.* Also **her•met•i•cal** (-ĭ-kəl). **1.** Completely sealed, esp. against the escape or entry of air. **2.** Impervious to outside interference or influence. **—her•met′i•cal•ly** *adv.*

her•mit (hûr′mĭt) *n.* One who has withdrawn from society and lives a solitary existence. [< Gk *erēmitēs,* "(one) of the desert."]

her•mit•age (hûr′mə-tĭj) *n.* **1.** The habitation of a hermit. **2.** A retreat; hideaway.

her•ni•a (hûr′nē-ə) *n., pl.* **-as** or **-niae** (-nē-ē′). Protrusion of an organ, organic part, or any bodily structure through the wall that normally contains it. [< L.]

her•ni•ate (hûr′nē-āt′) *v.* **-ated, -ating.** To protrude through an abnormal bodily opening. [HERNI(A) + -ATE¹.]

he•ro (hîr′ō) *n., pl.* **-roes. 1.** In mythology and legend, a man celebrated for his strength and bold exploits. **2.** Any man noted for his special achievements. **3.** The principal male character in a novel, poem, or dramatic work. [< Gk *hērōs.*]

He•rod•o•tus (hĭ-rŏd′ə-təs). Greek historian of the 5th century B.C.

he•ro•ic (hĭ-rō′ĭk) *adj.* Also **he•ro•i•cal** (-ĭ-kəl). **1.** Of or appropriate to a hero or heroes; courageous; noble. **2.** Calling for heroism; involving risk. **3.** Impressive in size or scope; on a grand or grandiose scale. *—n.* **heroics.** Melodramatic behavior or language. **—he•ro′i•cal•ly** *adv.* **—he•ro′i•cal•ness** *n.*

her•o•in (hĕr′ō-ən) *n.* A highly addictive narcotic, $C_{17}H_{17}NO(C_2H_3O_2)_2$, derived from morphine.

her•o•ine (hĕr′ō-ĭn) *n.* **1.** The female counterpart of a hero. **2.** The principal female character in a literary or dramatic work.

her•o•ism (hĕr′ō-ĭz′əm) *n.* **1.** The condition or quality of being a hero. **2.** Courage; gallantry.

he•ron (hĕr′ən) *n.* A wading bird with a long neck, long legs, and a long, pointed bill. [< OF *hairon.*]

her•pes zos•ter (hûr′pēz′ zŏs′tər, zōs′-). A viral infection with eruption of vesicles along a nerve path on one side of the body, often involving severe neuralgia. [NL, "girdle herpes."]

her•ring (hĕr′ĭng) *n., pl.* **-ring** or **-rings.** A commercially important food fish of Atlantic and Pacific waters. [< OE *hæring* < Gmc **hēringaz.*]

her•ring•bone (hĕr′ĭng-bōn′) *n.* **1.** A pattern consisting of rows of slanted parallel lines, with the direction of the slant alternating row by row. **2.** A fabric woven in this pattern.

hers (hûrz). The possessive form of the pronoun *she,* used as a predicate adjective or as a substantive: *The gloves are hers. My husband is a doctor and hers is a lawyer.* **—of hers.** Belonging to her: *a friend of hers.*

her•self (hûr-sĕlf′) *pron.* A form of the 3rd person sing. feminine pronoun: **1.** —Used reflexively: *She hurt herself.* **2.** —Used for emphasis: *She did it herself.* **3.** —Used to indicate one's normal or proper state: *She hasn't been herself lately.* **—by herself. 1.** Alone. **2.** Without help.

hertz (hûrts) *n.* A unit of frequency equal to one cycle per second. [< H. *Hertz* (1857–1894), German physicist.]

he's (hēz). **1.** Contraction of *he is.* **2.** Contraction of *he has.*

hes•i•tant (hĕz′ə-tənt) *adj.* Inclined or tending to hesitate. **—hes′i•tan•cy** *n.*

hes•i•tate (hĕz′ə-tāt′) *v.* **-tated, -tating. 1.** To be slow or reluctant to act or decide; waver; demur. **2.** To pause briefly, as in uncertainty. **3.** To falter. [L *haesitāre,* to stick fast, hesitate.] **—hes′i•tat′er** *n.* **—hes′i•tat′ing•ly** *adv.* **—hes′i•ta′tion** *n.*

hetero–. *comb. form.* Other, another, or different. [< Gk *heteros,* other.]

het•er•o•cy•clic (hĕt′ə-rō-sī′klĭk, -sĭk′lĭk) *adj.* *Chem.* Containing more than one kind of atom joined in a ring.

het•er•o•dox (hĕt′ər-ə-dŏks′) *adj.* **1.** Not in agreement with accepted beliefs, esp. departing from church doctrine or dogma. **2.** Holding unorthodox opinions. [< Gk *heterodoxos,* differing in opinion.] **—het′er•o•dox′y** *n.*

het•er•o•ge•ne•ous (hĕt′ər-ə-jē′nē-əs, -jēn′yəs) *adj.* Also **het•er•og•e•nous** (hĕt′ə-rŏj′ə-nəs). Consisting of or involving parts that are unlike or without interrelation; having dissimilar elements; not homogeneous. [<

HETERO- + Gk *genos*, kind, sex.] —**het'er·o·ge·ne'i·ty** (-ə-rō-jə-nē'ə-tē) *n.*

het·er·o·sex·u·al (hĕt'ə-rō-sĕk'sho͞o-əl) *adj.* **1.** Characterized by attraction to the opposite sex. **2.** Pertaining to different sexes. —*n.* A heterosexual person.

heth (KHĕt, KHĕth, KHĕs) *n.* Also **cheth.** The 8th letter in the Hebrew alphabet, representing *ḥ*.

hew (hyo͞o) *v.* **hewed, hewn** (hyo͞on) or **hewed, hewing. 1.** To make or shape with or as with an ax, knife, etc. **2.** To cut down with an ax. **3.** To adhere or conform; hold. [< OE *hēawan.* See **kau-.**] —**hew'er** *n.*

HEW Department of Health, Education, and Welfare.

hex (hĕks) *n.* **1.** An evil spell; curse. **2.** A bad influence on or dominating control over someone or something. —*v.* **1.** To bewitch. **2.** To wish or bring bad luck to. [< G *Hexe*, witch.]

hex. hexagon; hexagonal.

hexa–. *comb. form.* Six. [< Gk *hex*, six.]

hex·a·chlo·ro·phene (hĕk'sə-klôr'ə-fēn', -klōr'ə-fēn') *n.* A white powder, $(C_6HCl_3OH)_2$-CH_2, used as a bactericidal agent in soaps, cosmetics, and skin medications.

hex·a·gon (hĕk'sə-gŏn') *n.* A polygon having six sides. —**hex·ag'o·nal** (-săg'ə-nəl) *adj.*

hex·a·he·dron (hĕk'sə-hē'drən) *n., pl.* **-drons** or **-dra** (-drə). A polyhedron with six faces. —**hex'a·he'dral** *adj.*

hex·am·e·ter (hĕk-săm'ə-tər) *n.* A verse line consisting of six feet.

hey (hā) *interj.* **1.** Expressive of surprise, appreciation, etc. **2.** Used to attract attention: *Hey, you!* [ME *hei, hay.*]

hey·day (hā'dā') *n.* The period of greatest popularity, success, fashion, power, etc.; prime. [Prob < HEY.]

hf high frequency.

Hf hafnium.

Hg mercury (L *hydrargyrum*).

HG High German.

hgt. height.

hi (hī) *interj.* Expressive of greeting. [ME *hy.*]

H.I. Hawaiian Islands.

hi·a·tus (hī-ā'təs) *n., pl.* **-tuses** or **-tus. 1.** A gap or missing section. **2.** An interruption in time; break. **3.** *Anat.* A separation, aperture, or fissure. [L *hiātus*, a gaping, gap.]

hi·ba·chi (hĭ-bä'chē) *n., pl.* **-chis.** A portable charcoal-burning brazier. [Jap.]

hi·ber·nate (hī'bər-nāt') *v.* **-nated, -nating.** To pass the winter in a dormant or torpid state. [L *hībernāre.*] —**hi'ber·na'tion** *n.*

hi·bis·cus (hī-bĭs'kəs) *n.* Any of various chiefly tropical plants or shrubs with large, showy, variously colored flowers. [< Gk *hibiskos*, marshmallow.]

hic·cup (hĭk'ŭp). Also **hic·cough.** *n.* **1.** A spasm of the diaphragm resulting in a sudden, abortive inhalation that is stopped by a spasmodic glottal closure. **2. the hiccups.** An attack of such spasms. —*v.* **-cupped, -cupping.** To have the hiccups. [Earlier *hicket, hickop.*]

hick (hĭk) *n. Informal.* A gullible, provincial person; yokel. —*adj.* Rural. [< *Hick*, pet form of *Richard.*]

hick·o·ry (hĭk'ə-rē) *n., pl.* **-ries. 1.** Any of several North American trees having smooth or shaggy bark, compound leaves, hard-shelled, edible nuts, and hard wood. **2.** The wood of such a tree. [< Virginian native name.]

hi·dal·go (hĭ-dăl'gō) *n., pl.* **-gos.** A member of the minor nobility in Spain. [Span.]

hide[1] (hīd) *v.* **hid** (hĭd), **hidden** (hĭd'n) or **hid, hiding. 1.** To put or keep out of sight; secrete; conceal. **2.** To avert (one's gaze) in shame or grief. **3.** To seek refuge. [< OE *hȳdan.* See **skeu-.**] —**hid'er** *n.*

hide[2] (hīd) *n.* The skin of an animal, esp. the thick, tough skin of a large animal. [< OE *hȳd.* See **skeu-.**]

hide-and-seek (hīd'n-sēk') *n.* A children's game in which one player tries to find and catch others who are hiding.

hide·a·way (hīd'ə-wā') *n.* **1.** A place of concealment; hide-out. **2.** A secluded place.

hide·bound (hīd'bound') *adj.* Bigoted.

hid·e·ous (hĭd'ē-əs) *adj.* **1.** Physically repulsive; ugly. **2.** Repugnant to the moral sense; despicable. [< OF *hisde*, fear, horror.]

hide-out (hīd'out') *n.* A place of shelter or concealment.

hie (hī) *v.* **hied, hieing** or **hying.** To go quickly; hasten. [< OE *hīgian*, to strive, hurry.]

hi·er·ar·chy (hī'ə-rär'kē, hī'rär'-) *n., pl.* **-chies. 1.** A body of persons, esp. clergy, classified according to rank or authority. **2.** A body of entities arranged in a graded series. [< Gk *hierarkhēs*, high priest.] —**hi'er·ar'chi·cal, hi'er·ar'chic** *adj.* —**hi'er·ar'chi·cal·ly** *adv.*

hi·er·o·glyph·ic (hī'ər-ə-glĭf'ĭk, hī'rə-) *n.* **1.** A picture or symbol used in writing, esp. in the writing system of ancient Egypt. **2. hieroglyphics.** Illegible or undecipherable symbols. [< Gk *hierogluphikos*, written in hieroglyphics.]

hi-fi (hī'fī') *n.* **1. High fidelity. 2.** An electronic system for reproducing high-fidelity sound. [HI(GH) FI(DELITY).]

hig·gle·dy-pig·gle·dy (hĭg'əl-dē-pĭg'əl-dē) *adv.* In utter disorder or confusion. [Rhyming and jingling formation prob based on PIG.]

high (hī) *adj.* **1.** Tall; elevated. **2.** Being at or near a peak or culmination. **3.** Far removed in time; remote. **4.** Piercing in tone or sound. **5.** Situated far from the equator. **6.** Of great moment or importance; serious; weighty: *high treason.* **7.** Lofty or exalted in quality. **8.** Of great quantity, magnitude, or degree. **9.** Costly; expensive. **10.** In a state of excitement or euphoria. **11.** *Slang.* Intoxicated. —*n.* **1.** A high place or region. **2.** The transmission gear of an automotive vehicle producing maximum speed. **3.** A center of high atmospheric pressure. **4.** *Slang.* Intoxication or euphoria. [< OE *hēah.*] —**high'ly** *adv.*

high·ball (hī'bôl') *n.* A mixed alcoholic beverage served in a tall glass.

high·born (hī'bôrn') *adj.* Of noble birth.

high·boy (hī'boi') *n.* A tall chest of drawers supported on four legs.

high·bred (hī'brĕd') *adj.* Of superior breed or stock.

high·brow (hī'brou') *n.* One who has or affects superior learning or culture. —**high'brow'** *adj.*

high-class (hī'klăs', -kläs') *adj.* First-class.

high·er-up (hī'ər-ŭp') *n. Informal.* One who has a higher rank, position, or status.

high·fa·lu·tin, hi·fa·lu·tin (hī'fə-lo͞ot'n) *adj. Informal.* Pompous or pretentious.

high fidelity. The electronic reproduction of sound, esp. from broadcast, recorded, or taped sources, with minimal distortion. —**high'-fi·del'i·ty** *adj.*

high-flown (hī'flōn') *adj.* **1.** Lofty; exalted. **2.** Pretentious; inflated.

high frequency. A radio frequency in the range between 3 and 30 megacycles per second.

High German. 1. German as spoken and written in S Germany. **2.** German.

high·hand·ed (hī'hăn'dĭd) *adj.* In an arrogant or arbitrary manner. —**high'hand'ed·ly** *adv.* —**high'hand'ed·ness** *n.*

high·land (hī'lənd) *n.* **1.** Elevated land. **2. highlands.** A mountainous or hilly region or part of a country.

high·land·er (hī'lən-dər) *n.* **1.** One who lives in a highland area. **2. Highlander.** An inhabitant of The Highlands.

High·lands, The (hī'ləndz). A mountainous region of N and W Scotland.

high·light (hī'līt') *n.* An outstanding event or prominent detail. —*v.* **1.** To give prominence to. **2.** To be the highlight of.

high-mind·ed (hī'mīn'dĭd) *adj.* Characterized by morally lofty ideals or conduct; magnanimous. —**high'-mind'ed·ly** *adv.*

high·ness (hī'nĭs) *n.* **1.** Tallness; height. **2. Highness.** A title of honor for royalty.

high profile. *Informal.* A conspicuous, well-publicized presence or stance.

high-rise (hī'rīz') *adj.* Designating a building with many stories.

high·road (hī'rōd') *n.* **1.** *Chiefly Brit.* A main road; highway. **2.** A direct or sure path.

high school. A school that usually includes grades 9 through 12. —**high'-school'** *adj.*

high seas. The open waters of an ocean or sea beyond the limits of national territorial jurisdiction.

high-sound·ing (hī'soun'dĭng) *adj.* Pompous.

high-spir·it·ed (hī'spĭr'ə-tĭd) *adj.* **1.** Brave. **2.** Vivacious. —**high'-spir'it·ed·ness** *n.*

high-strung (hī'strŭng') *adj.* Acutely nervous and sensitive.

high-ten·sion (hī'tĕn'shən) *adj.* Having a high voltage.

high tide. 1. The tide when the water reaches its highest level. **2.** The time at which this occurs.

high-toned (hī'tōnd') *adj.* **1.** Intellectually or socially superior. **2.** Elegant or slick.

high·way (hī'wā') *n.* A main public road.

high·way·man (hī'wā'mən) *n.* A robber who holds up travelers on a highway.

hi·jack (hī'jăk') *v.* **1.** To rob (a vehicle) by stopping it in transit. **2.** To seize forcibly or commandeer (a moving vehicle). —**hi'jack'er** *n.*

hike (hīk) *v.* **hiked, hiking. 1.** To go on an extended walk, esp. for pleasure. **2.** To raise or go up, as prices. **3.** To be raised, caught up, or uneven. **4.** To raise with a sudden motion; hitch. —*n.* **1.** A walk or march. **2.** A rise as in prices. [?] —**hik'er** *n.*

hi·lar·i·ous (hĭ-lâr'ē-əs, hī-) *adj.* Boisterously funny or merry. [< L *hilaris.*]

hi·lar·i·ty (hĭ-lăr'ə-tē, hī-) *n.* Boisterous merriment. [< Gk *hilaros*, cheerful.]

hill (hĭl) *n.* **1.** A well-defined, naturally elevated area of land smaller than a mountain. **2.** A heap, pile, or mound. [< OE *hyll.* See **kel-**[6].] —**hill'i·ness** *n.* —**hill'y** *adj.*

hill·bil·ly (hĭl'bĭl'ē) *n., pl.* **-lies.** *Informal.* A person from a rural mountainous area. —**hill'bil'ly** *adj.*

hill·ock (hĭl'ək) *n.* A small hill.

hill·side (hĭl'sīd') *n.* The side or slope of a hill.

hill·top (hĭl'tŏp') *n.* The crest or top of a hill.

hilt (hĭlt) *n.* The handle of a weapon or tool, esp. of a sword or dagger. —**to the hilt.** Completely. [< OE < Gmc *hilt-.]

him (hĭm) *pron.* The objective case of the 3rd person pronoun *he*, used as the direct or indirect object of a verb or as the object of a preposition. [< OE. See **ko-.**]

Hi·ma·la·yas (hĭm'ə-lā'əz, hĭ-mäl'yəz). A mountain range of south-central Asia. Highest elevation, Mount Everest (29,028 ft.).

him·self (hĭm-sĕlf') *pron.* A form of the 3rd

person sing. masculine pronoun: **1.** —Used reflexively: *He hurt himself.* **2.** —Used for emphasis: *He did it himself.* **3.** —Used to indicate one's normal or proper state: *He hasn't been himself lately.* **—by himself.** **1.** Alone. **2.** Without help.

hind[1] (hīnd) *adj.* Located at the rear; posterior: *hind legs.* [Perh < OE *hinder,* behind, or *hindan,* from behind.]

hind[2] (hīnd) *n.* The female of the Old World deer. [< OE. See **kem-[1]**.]

hin•der (hĭn'dər) *v.* **1.** To hold back; hamper. **2.** To obstruct or delay the progress of; prevent. [< OE *hindrian.*] **—hin'der•er** *n.*

Hin•di (hĭn'dē) *n.* **1. a.** A group of Indic dialects spoken in N India. **b.** A literary language based upon these dialects. **2.** One who speaks a Hindi dialect. **—Hin'di** *adj.*

hind•most (hīnd'mōst') *adj.* Also **hin•der•most** (hĭn'dər-). Farthest to the rear; most remote; last.

hind•quar•ter (hīnd'kwôr'tər) *n.* **1.** The hind leg and posterior part of a side of meat. **2.** The rump of a four-footed animal.

hin•drance (hĭn'drəns) *n.* **1.** The act of hindering. **2.** One that hinders.

hind•sight (hīnd'sīt') *n.* Perception of events after they have occurred.

Hin•du (hĭn'do͞o) *n.* **1.** A native of India, esp. N India. **2.** A believer in Hinduism. **—Hin'du** *adj.*

Hin•du•ism (hĭn'do͞o-ĭz'əm) *n.* A syncretistic body of religious, philosophical, and social doctrines native to India.

Hindu Kush (ko͝osh). A mountain range of C Asia.

Hin•du•sta•ni (hĭn'do͞o-stä'nē, -stăn'ē) *n.* **1.** A subdivision of Indic, including Urdu and Hindi. **2.** One who speaks a Hindustani language. **—Hin'du•sta'ni** *adj.*

hinge (hĭnj) *n.* **1.** A flexible device permitting pivoting of a part, as a door, on a stationary frame. **2.** A similar structure or part. *—v.* **hinged, hinging.** **1.** To attach by or equip with a hinge or hinges. **2.** To depend; be contingent. [ME *heng.*] **—hinge'less** *adj.*

hint (hĭnt) *n.* **1.** A subtle suggestion or slight indication; clue. **2.** A barely perceptible amount. *—v.* **1.** To make known by a hint. **2.** To give a hint or hints. [?] **—hint'er** *n.*

hin•ter•land (hĭn'tər-lănd') *n.* **1.** The land directly adjacent to a coast. **2.** A region remote from urban areas. [G.]

hip[1] (hĭp) *n.* **1.** The laterally projecting prominence of the pelvis or pelvic region from the waist to the thigh. **2.** The **hip joint.** [< OE *hype.*] **—hip'py** *adj.*

hip[2] (hĭp) *adj.* **hipper, hippest.** Also **hep** (hĕp). *Slang.* **1.** Aware of advanced tastes and attitudes. **2.** Cognizant; wise. [?]

hip[3] (hĭp) *n.* The berrylike fruit of a rose. [< OE *hēope.*]

hip•bone (hĭp'bōn') *n.* The **innominate bone.**

hip joint. The joint between the innominate bone and the femur.

hip•pie (hĭp'ē) *n.* Also **hippy** *pl.* **-pies.** A member of a loosely knit nonconformist group, esp. one that rejects conventional social mores. [< HIP[2].] **—hip'pie** *adj.*

Hip•poc•ra•tes (hĭ-pŏk'rə-tēz'). 460?–377? B.C. Greek physician.

hip•po•drome (hĭp'ə-drōm') *n.* An arena, esp. for horse shows. [< Gk *hippodromos.*]

hip•po•pot•a•mus (hĭp'ə-pŏt'ə-məs) *n., pl.* **-muses** or **-mi** (-mī'). A large African river mammal with dark, almost hairless skin and a broad, wide-mouthed muzzle. [< Gk *hippos ho potamios,* "horse of the river."]

hip•py. Variant of **hippie.**

hire (hīr) *v.* **hired, hiring.** **1.** To engage the services of (a person) for a fee; employ. **2.** To rent. **3.** To rent out. *—n.* **1.** The payment for services or use of something. **2.** The act of hiring. **3.** The condition or fact of being hired. [< OE *hȳrian* < Gmc **khūrjan.*]

hire•ling (hīr'lĭng) *n.* A mercenary.

Hi•ro•shi•ma (hîr'ə-shē'mə, hĭ-rō'shĭ-mə). A city of SW Honshu, Japan. Pop. 485,000.

hir•sute (hûr'so͞ot', hûr'so͞ot') *adj.* Hairy. [L *hirsūtus.*] **—hir'sute'ness** *n.*

his (hĭz). The possessive form of the pronoun *he:* **1.** —Used attributively: *his wallet.* **2.** —Used as a predicate adjective or as a substantive: *The boots are his. If you can't find your hat, take his.* **—of his.** Belonging to him: *a friend of his.* [< OE. See **ko-.**]

His•pa•nio•la (hĭs'pən-yō'lə). An island of the West Indies, occupied in the W by Haiti and in the E by the Dominican Republic.

hiss (hĭs) *n.* **1.** A sharp, sibilant sound similar to a sustained *s.* **2.** This sound as an expression of disapproval or contempt. *—v.* **1.** To make a hiss. **2.** To direct hisses at in disapproval. [ME *hissen* (imit).] **—hiss'er** *n.*

hist. historian; historical; history.

his•ta•mine (hĭs'tə-mēn', -mĭn) *n.* A white crystalline compound, $C_5H_9N_3$, found in plant and animal tissue, a stimulant of gastric secretion. **—his'ta•min'ic** (-mĭn'ĭk) *adj.*

histo–. *comb. form.* Bodily tissue. [< Gk *histos,* web, beam, mast.]

his•to•gram (hĭs'tə-grăm') *n.* A graphic representation of a frequency distribution in which the widths of contiguous vertical bars are proportional to the class widths of the variable and the heights of the bars are proportional to the class frequencies. [HISTO(RY) + -GRAM.]

his•tol•o•gy (hĭ-stŏl'ə-jē) *n.* **1.** The study of the microscopic structure of animal and plant tissues. **2.** The microscopic structure of tissue.

his•tol•y•sis (hĭ-stŏl'ə-sĭs) *n.* The breakdown and disintegration of organic tissue. **—his'to•lyt'ic** (hĭs'tə-lĭt'ĭk) *adj.* **—his'to•lyt'i•cal•ly** *adv.*

his•to•ri•an (hĭ-stôr'ē-ən, hĭ-stōr'-) *n.* A writer or student of history.

his•tor•ic (hĭ-stôr'ĭk, hĭ-stŏr'-) *adj.* Having importance in or influence on history; famous.

his•tor•i•cal (hĭ-stôr'ĭ-kəl, hĭ-stŏr'-) *adj.* **1.** Of or relating to history. **2.** Based on or concerned with events in history. **3.** Historic. **—his•tor'i•cal•ly** *adv.*

his•to•ry (hĭs'tə-rē) *n., pl.* **-ries.** **1.** A narrative of events; a story; chronicle. **2.** A chronological record of events. **3.** The branch of knowledge that records and analyzes past events. **4.** The events of the past. **5.** An interesting past. **6.** That which is not of current concern. **7.** A record of a patient's medical background. [< Gk *histōr,* learned man.]

his•tri•on•ic (hĭs'trē-ŏn'ĭk) *adj.* **1.** Of or pertaining to actors or acting. **2.** Overemotional or dramatic; theatrical; affected. *—n.* **histrionics** *(takes pl. v.).* Exaggerated emotional behavior calculated for effect. [< LL *histriō,* actor.] **—his'tri•on'i•cal•ly** *adv.*

hit (hĭt) *v.* **hit, hitting.** **1.** To come or cause to come in contact with forcefully; strike. **2.** To affect adversely. **3.** To arrive at. **4.** To appeal. **5.** To propel with a blow. **6.** *Baseball.* To bat; succeed in getting (a base hit). *—n.* **1.** A collision or impact. **2.** A successfully executed shot, blow, or throw. **3.** A successful or popular venture. **4.** *Baseball.* A base hit. [< ON *hitta,* to hit.] **—hit'ter** *n.*

hit-and-run (hĭt'n-rŭn') *adj.* Designating or involving the driver of a motor vehicle who drives on after striking a pedestrian or another vehicle.

hitch (hĭch) *v.* **1.** To fasten with a loop, hook, or noose; tie. **2.** To connect or attach. **3.** *Informal.* To join or be united in marriage. **4.** To raise by pulling or jerking. **5.** To hitchhike (a ride). *—n.* **1.** A kind of knot. **2.** A short jerking motion. **3.** An impediment or delay. **4.** A term of military service. [ME *hytchen,* to lift with a jerk.] **—hitch'er** *n.*

hitch•hike (hĭch'hīk') *v.* To solicit or get (a free ride) along a road. **—hitch'hik'er** *n.*

hith•er (hĭth'ər) *adv.* To or toward this place. *—adj.* Located toward this side; nearer. [< OE *hider.* See **ko-.**]

hith•er•to (hĭth'ər-to͞o') *adv.* Until this time.

Hit•ler (hĭt'lər), **Adolf.** 1889–1945. Austrian-born Nazi leader; dictator of German Reich (1933–45).

Adolf Hitler

Hit•tite (hĭt'īt') *n.* **1.** One of an ancient people living in Asia Minor and N Syria about 2000–1200 B.C. **2.** An extinct Indo-European language spoken by these people. *—adj.* Of or pertaining to the Hittites, their culture, or their language.

hive (hīv) *n.* **1.** A structure for housing bees, esp. honeybees. **2.** A colony of bees. **3.** A place swarming with active people. *—v.* **hived, hiving.** To collect or go into a hive. [< OE *hȳf.*]

hives (hīvz) *n.* Urticaria. [?]

H.M. His (or Her) Majesty.

H.M.S. His (or Her) Majesty's Ship.

Ho holmium.

ho. house.

hoard (hôrd, hōrd) *n.* A hidden or stored fund or supply guarded for future use; a cache. *—v.* To accumulate a hoard. [< OE *hord.* See **skeu-.**] **—hoard'er** *n.*

hoar•frost (hôr'frôst', -frŏst', hōr'-) *n.* Frozen dew that forms a white coating on a surface. [< OE *hār.* See **kei-[2]**.]

hoarse (hôrs, hōrs) *adj.* **hoarser, hoarsest.** Low and grating in sound; husky; croaking. [< ON *hās* < Gmc **hairsa-.*] **—hoarse'ly** *adv.*

hoars•en (hôr'sən, hōr'-) *v.* To cause to be or become hoarse.

hoar•y (hôr'ē, hōr'ē) *adj.* **-ier, -iest.** **1.** Gray or white with or as with age. **2.** Very old; ancient. **—hoar'i•ness** *n.*

hoax (hōks) *n.* An act intended to deceive or trick. *—v.* To deceive, cheat, or trick by using a hoax. [Perh short for HOCUS-POCUS.] **—hoax'er** n.

hob (hŏb) *n.* A hobgoblin. **—play** (or **raise**) **hob.** To make mischief or trouble.

hob•ble (hŏb′əl) *v.* **-bled, -bling. 1.** To walk or move awkwardly or with difficulty; limp. **2.** To fetter; restrain; impede. —*n.* **1.** An awkward, clumsy, or irregular walk or gait. **2.** A device used to hobble an animal. [ME *hoblen.*] —**hob′bler** *n.*

hob•ble•de•hoy (hŏb′əl-dē-hoi′) *n.* A gawky adolescent. [?]

hobble skirt. A type of long skirt, popular between 1910 and 1914, that was so narrow below the knees that it restricted the wearer's normal stride.

hob•by (hŏb′ē) *n., pl.* **-bies.** An activity or interest engaged in primarily for pleasure; a pastime. [ME *hoby,* a hobbyhorse, something one pursues.] —**hob′by•ist** *n.*

hob•by•horse (hŏb′ē-hôrs′) *n.* **1.** A child's toy consisting of a long stick with an imitation horse's head on one end. **2.** A rocking horse. **3.** A favorite topic or hobby.

hob•gob•lin (hŏb′gŏb′lən) *n.* **1.** A mischievous or evil goblin. **2.** A bugbear.

hob•nail (hŏb′nāl′) *n.* A short nail used to protect the soles of shoes or boots.

hob•nob (hŏb′nŏb′) *v.* **-nobbed, -nobbing.** To associate familiarly (with *with*). [< earlier *hab or nab,* hit or miss.]

ho•bo (hō′bō) *n., pl.* **-boes** or **-bos.** A tramp; vagrant. [?]

Ho Chi Minh (hō′ chē′ mĭn′). 1890?–1969. President of Vietnam (1945–54) and of North Vietnam (1954–69).

Ho Chi Minh

Ho Chi Minh City. The official name for Saigon.

hock¹ (hŏk) *n.* The joint of the hind leg of a horse or other four-footed animal that corresponds to the human ankle. [< OE *hōh,* heel. See **kenk-¹**.]

hock² (hŏk) *v.* To pawn. —*n.* The state of being pawned. [< Du *hok,* prison.]

hock•ey (hŏk′ē) *n.* A game played on ice in which two opposing teams of skaters, using curved sticks, try to drive a puck into the opponents' goal. [?]

ho•cus-po•cus (hō′kəs-pō′kəs) *n.* **1.** Nonsense words or phrases used as a formula by conjurers. **2.** Deception or chicanery.

hod (hŏd) *n.* **1.** A trough carried over the shoulder for transporting loads, as of bricks. **2.** A coal scuttle. [Perh < OF *hotte.*]

hodge•podge (hŏj′pŏj′) *n.* A mixture of dissimilar ingredients. [< OF *hochepot,* "a gathering."]

Hodg•kin's disease (hŏj′kĭnz). A usually chronic, progressive, ultimately fatal disease of unknown etiology, marked by inflammatory enlargement of the lymph nodes, spleen, liver, and kidneys, and occurring approximately twice as often in adult males as females. [< T. *Hodgkin* (1798–1866), English physician.]

hoe (hō) *n.* A tool with a flat blade and a long handle, used for weeding, cultivating, and gardening. [< Frank **hauwa.*] —**hoe** *v.* **(hoed, hoeing).** —**ho′er** *n.*

hog (hôg, hŏg) *n.* **1.** A pig, esp. a full-grown domesticated pig. **2.** A self-indulgent, gluttonous, or vulgar person. —*v.* **hogged, hogging.** To take more than one's share of. [< OE *hogg* < Celt. See **su-**.] —**hog′gish** *adj.*

hogs•head (hôgz′hĕd′, hŏgz′-) *n.* **1.** Any of various units of volume or capacity ranging from 62.5 to 140 gallons, esp. a unit used in the U.S., equal to 63 gallons. **2.** A barrel or cask with such capacity.

hog-tie (hôg′tī′, hŏg′-) *v.* Also **hog•tie. 1.** To tie together the legs of. **2.** To impede in movement or action.

hog•wash (hôg′wŏsh′, -wôsh′, hŏg′-) *n.* **1.** Garbage fed to hogs; swill. **2.** Worthless, false, or ridiculous speech or writing.

hoi pol•loi (hoi′ pə-loi′). The common people. [Gk *hoi polloi,* the many, the masses.]

hoist (hoist) *v.* To raise or haul up. —*n.* **1.** An apparatus for lifting heavy or cumbersome objects. **2.** A pull; lift. **3.** The height or vertical dimension of a raised flag. [Var of dial *hoise.*] —**hoist′er** *n.*

Hok•kai•do (hō-kī′dō). The second-largest island of Japan, situated N of Honshu.

ho•kum (hō′kəm) *n.* Nonsense; fakery. [Perh < HOCUS-POCUS.]

hold¹ (hōld) *v.* **held, holding. 1.** To have and keep in possession; grasp; clasp. **2.** To support; keep up; maintain in a certain position or relationship. **3.** To contain; be filled by. **4.** To own. **5.** To maintain for use; wield. **6.** To restrain. **7.** To retain the attention or interest of. **8.** To detain; delay. **9.** To have the position of; occupy. **10.** To cause to keep; obligate. **11.** To keep in one's mind or heart. **12. a.** To believe; regard. **b.** To assert; affirm. **13.** To cause to take place; put on. **14.** To assemble; convene. **15.** To stand up under stress; last. **16.** To be valid, applicable, or true. —*n.* **1.** The act or a means of grasping; a grip; clasp. **2.** A means of obtaining or controlling something. **3.** Something held onto, as for support. **4.** A container. **5.** A strong influence or power. **6.** A prison cell. **7.** A temporary halt, as in a countdown; pause. [< OE *healdan.*] —**hold′er** *n.*

hold² (hōld) *n.* The interior of a ship below decks where cargo is stored. [Var of ME *hole,* hole.]

hold•ing (hōl′dĭng) *n.* **1.** Land rented or leased from another. **2.** Often **holdings.** Legally possessed property.

hold•up (hōld′ŭp′) *n.* **1.** A suspension of activity; delay. **2.** A robbery, esp. an armed robbery.

hole (hōl) *n.* **1.** A cavity in a solid. **2.** An opening or perforation through something; a gap; aperture. **3.** A hollow place. **4.** An animal's burrow or similar dwelling place. **5.** An ugly, squalid, or depressing dwelling. **6.** A fault or flaw. **7.** A bad situation; predicament. **8.** *Golf.* The small pit lined with a cup into which the ball must be hit. **9.** A vacant electron energy state manifested as a positive charge carrier with magnitude equal to that of the electron. [< OE *hol,* hollow place. See **kel-⁴**.] —**hole** *v.* **(holed, holing).**

hol•i•day (hŏl′ə-dā′) *n.* **1.** A day on which a particular event is celebrated. **2.** A religious feast day. **3.** A day off. **4.** *Chiefly Brit.* A vacation. [< OE *hālig,* HOLY + *dæg,* DAY.] —**hol′i•day′** *adj.*

ho•li•er-than-thou (hō′lē-ər-*th*ən-*th*ou′) *adj.* Showing an attitude of superior virtue.

ho•li•ness (hō′lē-nĭs) *n.* **1.** The quality of being holy. **2. Holiness.** A title of address used for the pope.

Hol•land (hŏl′ənd). The Netherlands.

hol•lan•daise sauce (hŏl′ən-dāz′, hŏl′ən-dāz′). A creamy sauce of butter, egg yolks, and lemon or vinegar. [< F *Hollandais,* Dutch.]

hol•ler (hŏl′ər) *v.* To yell or shout.

hol•low (hŏl′ō) *adj.* **1.** Having a cavity or space within: *a hollow wall.* **2.** Concave; sunken. **3.** Without substance or validity. **4.** Reverberating: *a hollow sound.* —*n.* **1.** A cavity or space within something. **2.** A concave surface or area. **3.** A valley. —*v.* To make or become hollow. [< OE *holh,* hole, hollow place. See **kel-⁴**.] —**hol′low•ness** *n.*

hol•ly (hŏl′ē) *n., pl.* **-lies.** A tree or shrub characteristically having prickly-edged evergreen leaves and bright-red berries. [< OE *holen.* See **kel-⁵**.]

hol•ly•hock (hŏl′ē-hŏk′) *n.* A tall plant widely cultivated for its showy spike of large, variously colored flowers. [< HOLY + OE *hoc,* a mallow.]

Hol•ly•wood (hŏl′ē-wo͝od′). A district of Los Angeles, California; center of the U.S. motion-picture industry.

hol•mi•um (hōl′mē-əm) *n. Symbol* **Ho** A relatively soft, malleable metallic element. Atomic number 67, atomic weight 164.930. [< Stock*holm,* Sweden.]

holo–. *comb. form.* Whole or entirely. [< Gk *holos,* whole, entire.]

hol•o•caust (hŏl′ə-kôst′, hō′lə-) *n.* Great or total destruction by fire. [< Gk *holokaustos,* burnt whole.]

Hol•o•cene (hŏl′ə-sēn′, hō′lə-) *adj.* Of or belonging to the geologic time or sedimentary deposits of the more recent of the two epochs of the Quaternary period, extending from the end of the Pleistocene to the present. —*n.* The Holocene epoch.

hol•o•crine (hŏl′ə-krĭn, -krēn′, -krīn′, hō′lə-) *adj.* Pertaining to a gland whose secretion is formed by the degeneration of the gland's cells. [HOLO- + Gk *krinein,* to separate.]

hol•o•gram (hŏl′ə-grăm′, hō′lə-) *n.* **1.** The pattern produced on a photosensitive medium by holography. **2.** The photosensitive medium so exposed and developed.

hol•o•graph¹ (hŏl′ə-grăf′, -gräf′, hō′lə-) *n.* **1.** A document written wholly in the handwriting of the person whose signature it bears. **2.** A hologram.

ho•lo•graph² (hŏl′ə-grăf′, -gräf′, hō′lə-) *v.* **1.** To produce an image of (a physical object) by holography. **2.** To form a hologram of (a physical object).

ho•log•raph•y (hō-lŏg′rə-fē, hə-) *n.* The technique of producing images by wave front reconstruction, esp. by using lasers to record on a photographic plate the diffraction pattern from which a three-dimensional image can be projected.

hol•ster (hōl′stər) *n.* A leather case shaped to hold a pistol. [Du.]

ho•ly (hō′lē) *adj.* **-lier, -liest. 1.** Belonging to,

derived from, or associated with a divine power. 2. Living according to a religious system. 3. Specified or set apart for a religious purpose: *a holy hour.* [< OE *hālig.* See **kailo-**.]
Holy Communion. The Eucharist.
Holy Ghost. The third person of the Christian Trinity; Holy Spirit.
Holy Grail. The Grail.
Holy Land. See **Palestine.**
Holy Spirit. The **Holy Ghost.**
holy water. Water blessed by a priest.
hom•age (hŏm'ĭj, ŏm'-) *n.* Honor or respect publicly expressed to a person or idea. [< L *homō,* man.]
Hom•burg (hŏm'bûrg') *n.* A man's felt hat having a dented crown and a shallow brim. [< *Homburg,* West Germany.]
home (hōm) *n.* 1. The place where one resides. 2. A house. 3. A family living in a dwelling. 4. A customary environment; habitat. 5. A place of origin. 6. A headquarters. 7. An objective or place of safety in some games. 8. An institution where people are cared for: *a nursing home.* —*adj.* 1. Of or pertaining to a household or house. 2. Of or pertaining to a headquarters: *a home office.* 3. Taking place in the city where a team is franchised: *a home game.* —*adv.* 1. At or to one's home. 2. On target: *The arrow struck home.* 3. To the center or heart of something; deeply. **—at home.** 1. In one's own house, locale, etc. 2. At ease; comfortable: *feel at home.* 3. Having an easy competence and familiarity: *at home in French.* [< OE *hām.* See **kei-**[1].]
home base. 1. *Baseball.* The plate. 2. A base of operations.
home•bod•y (hōm'bŏd'ē) *n.* One who likes to stay or work at home.
home•com•ing (hōm'kŭm'ĭng) *n.* 1. A coming to or returning home. 2. An annual event for visiting alumni, as in a college.
home economics. The art of home management, including household budgets, clothing, child care, cooking, etc.
home•land (hōm'lănd') *n.* 1. The land of one's allegiance. 2. The place of origin of a people.
home•ly (hōm'lē) *adj.* **-lier, -liest.** 1. Of a nature associated with the home; familiar. 2. Not attractive or good-looking: *a homely girl.* **—home'li•ness** *n.*
home•made (hōm'mād') *adj.* 1. Made or prepared in the home. 2. Crudely or simply made.
home•mak•er (hōm'mā'kər) *n.* One who manages a household, esp. a housewife.
ho•me•o•sta•sis (hō'mē-ō-stā'sĭs, hŏm'ē-) *n.* A state of physiological equilibrium produced by a balance of functions and of chemical composition within an organism.
home plate. *Baseball.* The plate.
hom•er (hō'mər) *n.* *Baseball.* A home run.
Ho•mer (hō'mər). Greek epic poet traditionally believed to have been author of the *Iliad* and the *Odyssey.* **—Ho•mer'ic** (-mĕr'ĭk) *adj.*
home•room (hōm'rōōm', -rōōm') *n.* A classroom to which pupils of the same grade are required to report each day.
home run. *Baseball.* A hit that allows the batter to make a complete circuit of the diamond and score a run.
home•sick (hōm'sĭk') *adj.* Longing for home. **—home'sick'ness** *n.*
home•spun (hōm'spŭn') *adj.* 1. Spun or made at home. 2. Made of a homespun fabric. 3. Simple and homely; unpretentious. —*n.* A plain coarse woolen cloth.
home•stead (hōm'stĕd') *n.* A house, esp. a farmhouse, with adjoining buildings and land.
home•stretch (hōm'strĕch') *n.* 1. The portion of a racetrack from the last turn to the finish line. 2. The final stages of an undertaking.
home•ward (hōm'wərd) *adv.* Also **home•wards** (-wərdz). Toward home. **—home'ward** *adj.*
home•work (hōm'wûrk') *n.* 1. Work, esp. schoolwork, done at home. 2. Any work of a preparatory or preliminary nature.
home•y (hō'mē) *adj.* **-ier, -iest.** Also **hom•y.** *Informal.* Having a feeling of home; homelike. **—hom'ey•ness** *n.*
hom•i•cide (hŏm'ə-sīd', hō'mə-) *n.* 1. The killing of one person by another. 2. A person who kills another person. [< L *homō,* man + -CIDE.] **—hom'i•ci'dal** *adj.*
hom•i•ly (hŏm'ə-lē) *n., pl.* **-lies.** 1. A sermon. 2. A moralizing lecture or admonition. [< Gk *homilia,* discourse.]
hom•ing (hō'mĭng) *adj.* 1. Having the faculty of returning home, esp. from a distance. 2. Assisting in guiding a craft home: *a homing guidance system.*
hom•i•ny grits (hŏm'ə-nē). A coarse white meal of corn kernels. [Perh < Algon.]
homo–. *comb. form.* Same or like. [< Gk *homos,* same.]
ho•mo•ge•ne•ous (hō'mə-jē'nē-əs, -jēn'yəs, hŏm'ə-) *adj.* 1. Like in nature or kind. 2. Uniform in composition throughout. [< HOMO- + Gk *-genēs,* born + -OUS.] **—ho'mo•ge•ne'i•ty** (hō'mō-jĭ-nē'ə-tē) *n.* **—ho'mo•ge'ne•ous•ly** *adv.* **—ho'mo•ge'ne•ous•ness** *n.*
ho•mog•en•ize (hō-mŏj'ə-nīz', hə-) *v.* **-ized, -izing.** 1. To make homogeneous. 2. **a.** To reduce to particles and disperse throughout a fluid. **b.** To make uniform in consistency, esp. to render (milk) uniform in consistency by emulsifying the fat content. **—ho•mog'en•i•za'tion** *n.* **—ho•mog'en•iz'er** *n.*
hom•o•graph (hŏm'ə-grăf', -gräf', hō'mə-) *n.* A word spelled the same as another but differing in meaning and origin.
ho•mol•o•gous (hō-mŏl'ə-gəs, hə-) *adj.* Corresponding or similar in position, structure, etc. [Gk *homologos,* agreeing.]
hom•o•nym (hŏm'ə-nĭm', hō'mə-) *n.* One of two or more words that have the same sound and often the same spelling but differ in meaning. **—hom'o•nym'ic** *adj.*
hom•o•phone (hŏm'ə-fōn', hō'mə-) *n.* A word having the same sound as another but differing from it in spelling, origin, and meaning.
ho•mo•sex•u•al•i•ty (hō'mə-sĕk'shōō-ăl'ə-tē, hŏm'ə-) *n.* 1. Sexual desire for others of one's own sex. 2. Sexual activity with another of the same sex. **—ho'mo•sex'u•al** *adj.* & *n.*
ho•mun•cu•lus (hō-mŭng'kyə-ləs) *n., pl.* **-li** (-lī'). A small man. [< L *homō,* man.]
hon. honorary.
Hon. Honorable (title).
Hon•du•ras (hŏn-d/y/ōōr'əs). A republic of Central America. Pop. 2,315,000. Cap. Tegucigalpa. **—Hon•du'ran** *adj.* & *n.*

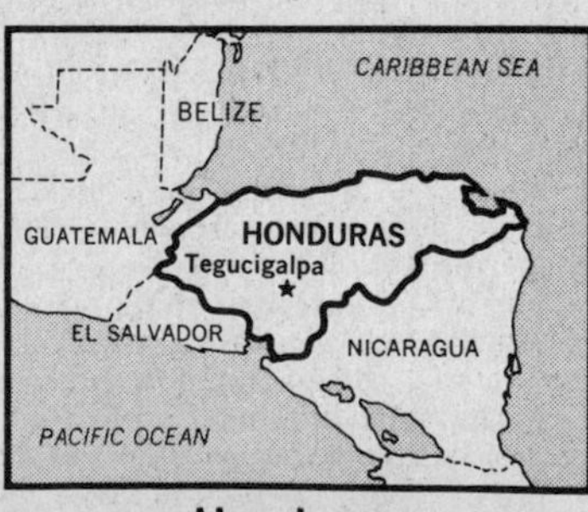

Honduras

hone (hōn) *n.* A fine-grained whetstone. —*v.* **honed, honing.** To sharpen on or as on a hone. [< OE *hān,* stone. See **kē-**.]
hon•est (ŏn'ĭst) *adj.* 1. Not lying, cheating, stealing, or taking unfair advantage; honorable. 2. Not characterized by deception or fraud; genuine. 3. Having or manifesting integrity and truth. 4. Unpretentious; simple. **—honest to goodness.** 1. Absolutely genuine. 2. Expressive of surprise, affirmation, etc. [< L *honōs,* HONOR.] **—hon'est•ly** *adv.* **—hon'es•ty, hon'est•ness** *n.*
hon•ey (hŭn'ē) *n., pl.* **-eys.** 1. A sweet, thick yellowish fluid produced by bees from the nectar of flowers. 2. A sweet substance or quality. 3. *Informal.* Sweet one; dear. [< OE *hunig.* See **kenəko-**.] **—hon'ey** *adj.*
hon•ey•bee (hŭn'ē-bē') *n.* A bee that produces honey.
hon•ey•comb (hŭn'ē-kōm') *n.* 1. A structure of six-sided cells constructed from beeswax by honeybees to hold honey and eggs. 2. Something resembling this. —*v.* To fill with holes; riddle: *His story was honeycombed with lies.*
hon•ey•dew (hŭn'ē-d/y/ōō') *n.* A sweet, sticky substance, as that excreted by aphids.
honeydew melon. A melon with a smooth, whitish rind and green flesh.
hon•eyed (hŭn'ēd) *adj.* Sweet; sugary: *honeyed words.*
hon•ey•moon (hŭn'ē-mōōn') *n.* A holiday or trip taken by a newly married couple. —*v.* To spend a honeymoon.
hon•ey•suck•le (hŭn'ē-sŭk'əl) *n.* A shrub or vine with tubular, often fragrant yellowish, white, or pink flowers.
Hong Kong (hŏng' kŏng', hông' kông'). A British Crown Colony on the S coast of China. Pop. 3,982,000. Cap. Victoria.
honk (hôngk, hŏngk) *n.* A raucous, resonant sound, as that made by a wild goose or an automobile horn. [Imit.] **—honk** *v.*
hon•ky-tonk (hŏng'kē-tôngk', hŏng'kē-tŏngk') *n.* *Slang.* A cheap, noisy bar. [?]
Hon•o•lu•lu (hŏn'ə-lōō'lōō). The capital of Hawaii. Pop. 320,000.
hon•or (ŏn'ər). Also *chiefly Brit.* **hon•our.** *n.* 1. Esteem; respect. 2. **a.** Glory; distinction. **b.** A token or gesture of respect or distinction: *the place of honor.* 3. Great privilege. 4. **Honor.** A title of address often accorded to mayors and judges. 5. Personal integrity maintained without legal or other obligation. 6. **honors. a.** Special recognition for unusual academic achievement. **b.** A program of individual advanced study for exceptional students. —*v.* 1. **a.** To esteem. **b.** To show respect for. 2. To confer distinction upon. 3. To accept or pay as valid (as a check). [< L *honor, honōs.*]
hon•or•a•ble (ŏn'ər-ə-bəl) *adj.* 1. Deserving respect. 2. Bestowing honor or recognition: *honorable mention.* 3. Possessing integrity. 4. **Honorable.** A title of respect for certain high officials: *the Honorable Mayor.* **—hon'or•a•ble•ness** *n.* **—hon'or•a•bly** *adv.*
hon•o•rar•i•um (ŏn'ə-râr'ē-əm) *n., pl.* **-ums** or **-ia** (-ē-ə). A payment given a professional person for services for which fees are not legally or traditionally required.
hon•or•ar•y (ŏn'ə-rĕr'ē) *adj.* Conferred as an honor without the usual duties, privileges, etc.: *an honorary degree.*
hon•or•if•ic (ŏn'ə-rĭf'ĭk) *adj.* Conferring or showing respect or honor. —*n.* A term conveying respect, used esp. when addressing a social superior. **—hon'or•if'i•cal•ly** *adv.*
Hon•shu (hŏn'shōō). The largest island of

Japan.

hood¹ (ho͝od) *n.* **1.** A loose, pliable covering for the head and neck. **2.** Something resembling a hood in shape or function. **3.** The hinged metal lid over an automobile engine. [< OE *hōd.* See **kadh-.**] **—hood'ed** *adj.*

hood² (ho͝od) *n. Slang.* A hoodlum; thug.

–hood. *comb. form.* **1.** The state, condition, or quality of being: **manhood. 2.** All the members of a grouping of a specified nature: **neighborhood.** [< OE *-hād.*]

hood•lum (ho͞od'ləm, ho͝od'-) *n.* A gangster; thug. [?] **—hood'lum•ism'** *n.*

hood•wink (ho͝od'wĭngk') *v.* To deceive; trick; take in.

hoo•ey (ho͞o'ē) *n. Slang.* Nonsense. [?]

hoof (ho͝of, ho͞of) *n., pl.* **hoofs** or **hooves** (ho͝ovz, ho͞ovz). **1.** The horny covering of the foot of horses, cattle, deer, etc. **2.** The foot of such an animal. *—v.* **—hoof it.** *Slang.* To go on foot; walk. [< OE *hōf.* See **kapho-.**] **—hoofed** *adj.*

hook (ho͝ok) *n.* **1.** A curved or sharply bent device, usually of metal, used to catch, drag, suspend, or fasten something. **2.** Something shaped like a hook. **3.** *Boxing.* A short swinging blow delivered with a crooked arm. **—by hook or (by) crook.** By whatever means possible, fair or unfair. **—hook, line, and sinker.** Without reservation; entirely. **—off the hook. 1.** *Slang.* Freed, as from blame or a vexatious obligation. **2.** Off the cradle, as a telephone receiver. *—v.* **1.** To get hold of or catch with or as with a hook. **2.** *Slang.* To become addicted. **3.** *Slang.* To steal; snatch. **4.** To fasten by means of a hook and eye. [< OE *hōc.* See **keg-.**]

hook•ah (ho͝ok'ə) *n.* A smoking pipe with a long tube passing through an urn of water that cools the smoke as it is drawn through. [< Ar *ḥuqqah.*]

hook and eye. A clothes fastener consisting of a small hook with a corresponding loop.

hook up. 1. To connect a mechanism and a source of power. **2.** *Slang.* To form a tie or connection. **3.** To fasten together with a hook or hooks.

hook•up (ho͝ok'ŭp') *n.* **1.** A system of electrical interconnections. **2.** Any configuration of parts or devices acting together.

hook•worm (ho͝ok'wûrm') *n.* A parasitic worm with hooked mouth parts that fasten to the intestinal tract.

hook•y (ho͝ok'ē) *n. Informal.* Truancy: *play hooky.*

hoop (ho͞op, ho͝op) *n.* **1.** A circular band of metal put around a cask or barrel to bind the staves together. **2.** Anything resembling such a band, as: **a.** A large ring used as a plaything. **b.** A ringlike earring. [< OE *hōp* < Gmc **hōpaz.*] **—hoop'less** *adj.*

hoop•la (ho͞op'lä', ho͝op'-) *n. Slang.* **1.** Boisterous commotion or excitement. **2.** Talk intended to mislead or confuse. [F *houp-là.*]

hoo•poe (ho͞o'po͞o, -pō) *n.* An Old World bird with a fanlike crest and a long, slender bill. [< L *upupa* (imit).]

hoo•ray. Variant of **hurrah.**

hoose•gow (ho͞os'gou') *n. Slang.* A jail. [< Span *juzgar,* to judge.]

hoot (ho͞ot) *v.* **1.** To utter the hollow, raucous cry of an owl. **2.** To make a loud derisive or contemptuous cry. **3.** To shout down or drive off with jeering cries. *—n.* **1.** The characteristic cry of an owl. **2.** A cry of contempt or derision. **—not give a hoot.** Not to care at all. [Imit.] **—hoot'er** *n.*

hoot•en•an•ny (ho͞ot'n-ăn'ē) *n., pl.* **-nies.** A gathering of folk singers, typically with audience participation. [?]

hoot owl. Any of various owls having a hooting cry.

Hoo•ver (ho͞o'vər), **Herbert Clark.** 1874–1964. 31st President of the U.S. (1929–33).

Herbert Hoover

hooves. Alternate *pl.* of **hoof.**

hop¹ (hŏp) *v.* **hopped, hopping. 1.** To move with light bounding skips or leaps. **2.** To jump on one foot. **3.** To jump aboard: *hop a freight.* *—n.* **1.** A light springy jump, esp. on one foot. **2.** *Informal.* A dance. **3.** A short airplane trip. [< OE *hoppian.*] **—hop'ping•ly** *adv.*

hop² (hŏp) *n.* **1.** A twining vine with lobed leaves and green, conelike flowers. **2. hops.** The dried flowers of this plant, used as flavoring in brewing beer. *—v.* **hopped, hopping. —hop up.** *Slang.* **1.** To increase the power or energy of. **2.** To stimulate or excite. [< MDu *hoppe.*]

hope (hōp) *v.* **hoped, hoping.** To desire (something) with some confidence of fulfillment. **—hope against hope.** To persist in hoping for something against the odds. *—n.* **1.** A desire supported by some confidence of its fulfillment. **2.** A ground for expectation. **3.** That which is desired. **4.** That in which one places one's confidence. **5.** Expectation; confidence. [< OE *hopian.*] **—hop'er** *n.*

hope•ful (hōp'fəl) *adj.* **1.** Having or manifesting hope. **2.** Inspiring hope. *—n.* A person who aspires to success or shows promise of succeeding. **—hope'ful•ness** *n.*

hope•ful•ly (hōp'fə-lē) *adv.* **1.** In a hopeful manner. **2.** In such a manner as to be hoped; let us hope.

Usage: Hopefully, as used to mean *in such a manner as to be hoped* or *let us hope,* is still unacceptable to a substantial number of authorities on grammar and usage.

hope•less (hōp'lĭs) *adj.* **1.** Having no hope; despairing. **2.** Offering no hope. **3.** Incurable. **4.** Insoluble; discouraging; impossible. **—hope'less•ly** *adv.* **—hope'less•ness** *n.*

Ho•pi (hō'pē) *n., pl.* **-pi** or **-pis. 1.** A member of a tribe of Uto-Aztecan-speaking North American Indians now inhabiting a reservation in NE Arizona. **2.** The language of these people.

hop•per (hŏp'ər) *n.* **1.** One that hops, esp. a hopping insect. **2.** A receptacle in which materials are stored in readiness for dispensation and use.

hop•scotch (hŏp'skŏch') *n.* A children's game in which players toss an object into succeeding sections of a figure on the ground, then hop through the figure and back on one foot as they retrieve the object.

hor. horizontal.

Hor•ace (hôr'ĭs, hŏr'-). 65–8 B.C. Latin poet. **—Ho•ra'tian** (hə-rā'shən) *adj.*

horde (hôrd, hōrd) *n.* A throng or swarm. [< Turk *ordū,* camp.]

hore•hound (hôr'hound', hōr'-) *n.* A downy, aromatic plant yielding a bitter extract used as candy flavoring and as a cough remedy. [< OE *hār,* hoarfrost + *hūne,* horehound.]

ho•ri•zon (hə-rī'zən) *n.* **1.** The apparent intersection of the earth and sky as seen by an observer. **2.** The range of an individual's knowledge, experience, etc. [< Gk *horizein,* to divide, separate.]

hor•i•zon•tal (hôr'ə-zŏnt'l, hŏr'-) *adj.* **1.** Of, relating to, or near the horizon. **2.** Parallel to or in the plane of the horizon. **3.** Occupying or restricted to the same level in a hierarchy. **4.** Flat. *—n.* Anything horizontal. **—hor'i•zon'tal•ly** *adv.*

hor•mone (hôr'mōn') *n.* A substance formed by one organ and conveyed, as by the blood stream, to another, which it stimulates to function by means of its chemical activity. [< Gk *horman,* to urge on.] **—hor'mo'nal** *adj.*

horn (hôrn) *n.* **1.** One of the hard, usually permanent structures projecting from the head of cattle, sheep, goats, etc. **2.** A structure, object, or part suggestive of a horn. **3.** The hard, smooth material forming the outer covering of the horns of cattle or related animals. **4.** A container made from a horn: *a powder horn.* **5.** *Mus.* **a.** A wind instrument made of brass. **b.** A French horn. **6.** A device that produces a sound similar to that of a sounded animal horn. *—v.* **—horn in.** *Slang.* To join without being invited; intrude. [< OE. See **ker-¹.**] **—horned** *adj.* **—horn'y** *adj.*

Horn, Cape. The southernmost point of South America.

horn•blende (hôrn'blĕnd') *n.* A common green or bluish-green to black mineral formed in the late stages of cooling in igneous rock. [G.]

hor•net (hôr'nĭt) *n.* A large, stinging wasp. [< OE *hyrnet.* See **ker-¹.**]

horn of plenty. A cornucopia.

ho•rol•o•gy (hô-rŏl'ə-jē, hō-) *n.* **1.** The science of measuring time. **2.** The art of making timepieces. [< Gk *hōrologos,* "hour-teller."] **—hor'o•log'i•cal** *adj.* **—ho•rol'o•gist** *n.*

hor•o•scope (hôr'ə-skōp', hŏr'-) *n. Astrol.* A forecast of a person's future. [< Gk *hōroskopos,* astrologer, "hour-observer."]

hor•ren•dous (hô-rĕn'dəs, hō-) *adj.* Hideous; dreadful. [< L *horrēre,* to tremble.] **—hor•ren'dous•ly** *adv.*

hor•ri•ble (hôr'ə-bəl, hŏr'-) *adj.* **1.** Causing horror. **2.** Unpleasant; offensive. **—hor'ri•ble•ness** *n.* **—hor'ri•bly** *adv.*

hor•rid (hôr'ĭd, hŏr'-) *adj.* **1.** Causing horror. **2.** Unpleasant; offensive. **—hor'rid•ly** *adv.* **—hor'rid•ness** *n.*

hor•ri•fy (hôr'ə-fī', hŏr'-) *v.* **-fied, -fying. 1.** To cause to feel horror. **2.** To cause unpleasant surprise; shock.

hor•ror (hôr'ər, hŏr'-) *n.* **1.** An intense feeling of repugnance and fear; terror. **2.** Intense dislike; abhorrence. **3.** That which causes horror. [< L *horrēre,* to tremble, be in horror.]

hors d'oeuvre (ôr dûrv') *pl.* **hors d'oeuvres** (ôr dûrvz') or **hors d'oeuvre.** An appetizer or canapé served with cocktails or before a meal. [F, side dish, "outside of work."]

horse (hôrs) *n.* **1.** A large hoofed mammal with

a long mane and tail, domesticated for riding and to pull vehicles or carry loads. **2.** A supportive frame or device, usually having four legs. **3.** Often **horses.** Horsepower. —*v.* **horsed, horsing.** —**horse around.** To engage in horseplay. [< OE *hors* < Gmc **hors-*.]

horse•back (hôrs′băk′) *adv.* On the back of a horse.

horse chestnut. **1.** A tree with erect clusters of white flowers and brown, shiny, inedible nuts. **2.** The nut of such a tree.

horse•flesh (hôrs′flĕsh′) *n.* **1.** Edible horse meat. **2.** Riding or racing horses.

horse•fly (hôrs′flī′) *n.* Also **horse fly.** A large bloodsucking fly.

horse•hair (hôrs′hâr′) *n.* **1.** The hair from a horse's mane or tail. **2.** Cloth made of horsehair.

horse•man (hôrs′mən) *n.* A man who rides a horse or is skilled at horsemanship. —**horse′wom′an** *fem.n.*

horse•man•ship (hôrs′mən-shĭp′) *n.* The art of horseback riding.

horse•play (hôrs′plā′) *n.* Rowdy, prankish play.

horse•pow•er (hôrs′pou′ər) *n.* A U.S. Customary System unit of power, equal to 745.7 watts.

horse•rad•ish (hôrs′răd′ĭsh) *n.* **1.** A coarse plant with a thick, whitish, pungent root. **2.** The grated root of this plant, used as a condiment.

horse•shoe (hôrs′sho͞o′, hôrsh′-) *n.* **1.** A narrow U-shaped iron plate fitted and nailed to a horse's hoof. **2. horseshoes.** A game in which players try to toss horseshoes around a stake.

hors•y (hôr′sē) *adj.* **-ier, -iest.** **1.** Of, pertaining to, or characteristic of a horse. **2.** Devoted to horses and horsemanship: *the horsy crowd.*

hort. horticultural; horticulture.

hor•ta•to•ry (hôr′tə-tôr′ē, -tōr′ē) *adj.* Characterized by or expressing exhortation.

hor•ti•cul•ture (hôr′tə-kŭl′chər) *n.* The science or art of cultivating plants, esp. garden plants. [L *hortus,* garden + (AGRI)CULTURE.] —**hor′ti•cul′tur•al** *adj.* —**hor′ti•cul′tur•ist** *n.*

Hos. Hosea (Old Testament).

ho•san•na (hō-zăn′ə) *interj.* Expressive of praise or adoration to God or the Messiah. [< Heb *hosha′nā,* "save us!"]

hose (hōz) *n.* **1.** *pl.* **hose.** **a.** Stockings. **b.** Socks. **2.** *pl.* **hoses.** A flexible tube for conveying liquids or gases under pressure. —*v.* **hosed, hosing.** To water, drench, or wash with a hose. [< OE *hosa,* leg covering. See **skeu-.**]

ho•sier•y (hō′zhə-rē) *n.* Stockings and socks; hose.

hosp. hospital.

hos•pice (hŏs′pĭs) *n.* A shelter or lodging for travelers, children, or the destitute, often maintained by a monastic order. [<L *hospitium,* hospitality.]

hos•pi•ta•ble (hŏs′pə-tə-bəl, hŏs-pĭt′ə-bəl) *adj.* Welcoming guests or strangers with warmth and generosity. [< L *hospes (hospit-),* HOST.] —**hos′pi•ta•ble•ness** *n.* —**hos′pi•ta•bly** *adv.*

hos•pi•tal (hŏs′pə-təl) *n.* An institution providing medical or surgical care and treatment for the sick and injured. [< L *hospitālis,* of a guest.]

hos•pi•tal•i•ty (hŏs′pə-tăl′ə-tē) *n., pl.* **-ties.** **1.** The act or practice of being hospitable. **2.** An instance of being hospitable.

hos•pi•tal•i•za•tion (hŏs′pə-tə-lə-zā′shən, -lī-zā′shən) *n.* **1.** The state of being hospitalized. **2.** A form of insurance that helps pay a patient's hospital expenses.

hos•pi•tal•ize (hŏs′pə-tə-līz′) *v.* **-ized, -izing.** To put (a person) into a hospital.

host[1] (hōst) *n.* **1.** One who entertains guests. **2.** An organism on or in which a parasite lives. —*v.* *Informal.* To serve as host for (a party, reception, etc.). [< L *hospes (hospit-),* guest, host, stranger.]

host[2] (hōst) *n.* **1.** An army. **2.** A great number. [< L *hostis,* stranger, enemy.]

host[3] (hōst) *n.* Also **Host.** *Eccles.* The consecrated bread or wafer of the Eucharist. [< L *hostia,* sacrifice, victim.]

hos•tage (hŏs′tĭj) *n.* A person held as a security for the fulfillment of certain terms. [< OF *hoste,* guest, host, and < L *obses (obsid-),* a hostage.] —**hos′tage•ship′** *n.*

hos•tel (hŏs′təl) *n.* A supervised, inexpensive lodging house for youthful travelers. [< ML *hospitāle,* inn.]

host•ess (hōs′tĭs) *n.* A woman who acts as a host.

hos•tile (hŏs′təl; *chiefly Brit.* hŏs′tīl′) *adj.* **1.** Of or pertaining to an enemy. **2.** Feeling or showing enmity. [< L *hostis,* HOST.]

hos•til•i•ty (hŏ-stĭl′ə-tē) *n., pl.* **-ties.** **1.** The state of being hostile. **2. hostilities.** Overt warfare.

hot (hŏt) *adj.* **hotter, hottest.** **1. a.** Possessing great heat. **b.** Yielding much heat. **c.** At a high temperature. **2.** Warmer than is normal or desirable. **3.** Pungent; spicy. **4. a.** Charged or as if charged with electricity. **b.** Radioactive. **5.** Angry: *a hot dispute.* **6.** *Slang.* Recently stolen: *hot goods.* **7.** *Informal.* **a.** New; fresh: *hot off the press.* **b.** Currently popular: *a hot sales item.* **8.** *Slang.* **a.** Performing with unusual skill. **b.** Lucky. —**hot under the collar.** Angry. —**in hot water.** In trouble. [< OE *hāt.* See **kai-.**] —**hot′ly** *adv.* —**hot′ness** *n.*

hot air. *Slang.* Boastful nonsense.

hot•bed (hŏt′bĕd′) *n.* **1.** A glass-covered, heated bed of soil used for raising tender plants. **2.** An environment conducive to rapid, vigorous growth, esp. of something bad: *a hotbed of intrigue.*

hot cake. A pancake. —**sell** (or **go**) **like hot cakes.** To be in great demand.

hot dog. A frankfurter, usually served in a long soft roll.

ho•tel (hō-tĕl′) *n.* A public house that provides lodging and usually board. [< OF *hostel,* hostel.]

hot•head•ed (hŏt′hĕd′ĭd) *adj.* **1.** Having a fiery temper. **2.** Impetuous; rash. —**hot′head′ed•ly** *adv.* —**hot′head′ed•ness** *n.*

hot•house (hŏt′hous′) *n.* A heated greenhouse for plants.

hot line. A direct communications link, as a telephone line, especially one between heads of government for use in time of crisis, as to prevent unintentional war.

hot plate. A table-top cooking device having one or two burners.

hot rod. *Slang.* An automobile rebuilt or remodeled for increased speed and acceleration. —**hot rodder.**

hot•shot (hŏt′shŏt′) *n.* *Slang.* An ostentatiously skillful person.

hound (hound) *n.* **1.** Any of various dogs originally bred and used for hunting. **2.** An enthusiast or addict: *a coffee hound.* —*v.* To pursue relentlessly and tenaciously. [< OE *hund.* See **kwon-.**] —**hound′er** *n.*

hour (our) *n.* **1.** The 24th part of a day. **2.** The time of day. **3. a.** A customary time: *dinner hour.* **b. hours.** A specified period: *banking hours.* [< Gk *hōra,* time, season.]

hour•glass (our′glăs′, -gläs′) *n.* An instrument that measures time by the trickling of sand from an upper to a lower glass compartment.

hour•ly (our′lē) *adj.* Every hour. —**hour′ly** *adv.*

house (hous) *n., pl.* **houses** (hou′zĭz). **1.** A structure serving as a dwelling for one or several families. **2.** A building having a specified function. **3.** A household. **4. House.** A noble family: *House of Orange.* **5.** A commercial firm: *banking house.* **6. a.** A theater. **b.** A theater audience. **7.** A legislative assembly. —*v.* (houz) **housed, housing.** **1.** To provide living or working quarters for. **2.** To contain. [< OE *hūs* < Gmc **hūsam.*]

house•boat (hous′bōt′) *n.* A wide, flat-bottomed boat equipped for use as a domicile.

house•break•ing (hous′brā′kĭng) *n.* The unlawful breaking into of another's domicile for the purpose of committing a felony. —**house′break′er** *n.*

house•bro•ken (hous′brō′kən) *adj.* Trained to control excretory functions, as a pet.

house•coat (hous′kōt′) *n.* A woman's garment with a long skirt, worn at home.

house•fly (hous′flī′) *n.* A common fly that frequents human dwellings and is a transmitter of a wide variety of diseases.

house•hold (hous′hōld′) *n.* A domestic establishment including the members of a family and others living under the same roof. —**house′hold′** *adj.*

household word. A commonly used word, phrase, or name.

house•keep•er (hous′kē′pər) *n.* One who has charge of domestic tasks in a household. —**house′keep′ing** *n.*

house•warm•ing (hous′wôr′mĭng) *n.* A party to celebrate the occupancy of a new home.

house•wife (hous′wīf′) *n.* **1.** A woman who manages her own household. **2.** (hŭz′ĭf). *Chiefly Brit.* A pocket container for sewing equipment. —**house′wife′li•ness** *n.* —**house′wife′ly** *adj.* —**house′wif′er•y** *n.*

house•work (hous′wûrk′) *n.* The tasks performed in housekeeping.

hous•ing (hou′zĭng) *n.* **1. a.** Protective shelter; a dwelling. **b.** Dwellings collectively. **2.** A protective covering for something, as a mechanical part.

Hous•ton (hyo͞o′stən). A city of SE Texas. Pop. 1,213,000.

hove (hōv). *Chiefly naut.* Alternate *p.t. & p.p.* of **heave.**

hov•el (hŭv′əl, hŏv′-) *n.* A small, miserable dwelling. [ME.]

hov•er (hŭv′ər, hŏv′-) *v.* **1.** To fly or float as if suspended. **2.** To linger close to a place. **3.** To pause or waver uncertainly. [ME *hoveren.*]

hov•er•craft (hŭv′ər-krăft′, -kräft′, hŏv′-) *n.* A motorized vehicle capable of low-level flight on a cushion of air.

how (hou) *adv.* **1.** In what manner or way; by what means. **2.** In what state or condition. **3.** To what extent, amount, or degree: *How do you like that?* **4.** For what effect or purpose; why. **5.** For what price: *How are these shirts sold on sale?* **6.** With what meaning: *How should I interpret this?* —**how come?** Why? [< OE *hū.* See **kwo-.**]

how•be•it (hou-bē′ĭt) *adv. Archaic.* Be that as it may. —*conj. Obs.* Although.

how•dah (hou′də) *n.* A covered seat, usually enclosed, on the back of an elephant or camel. [< Ar *haudaj,* camel's burden.]

how-do-you-do (hou′də-yə-do͞o′) *n.* Also **how-d'ye-do** (hou′dyə-do͞o′, hou′dē-). *Informal.* A predicament.

how•ev•er (hou-ev′ər) *adv.* **1.** By whatever manner or means. **2.** To whatever degree or extent. *—conj.* Nevertheless; yet.
how•it•zer (hou′ĭt-sər) *n.* A cannon that delivers shells in a high trajectory. [< Czech *houfnice,* catapult.]
howl (houl) *v.* **1.** To utter a long-drawn, mournful cry, as of a wolf. **2.** To utter or produce a similar sound or outcry. *—n.* **1.** A long-drawn wailing sound. **2.** *Slang.* Something uproariously funny. [Perh < MDu *hūlen.*]
howl•er (hou′lər) *n.* **1.** One that howls. **2.** A ridiculous blunder.
howl•ing (hou′lĭng) *adj.* **1.** Characterized by howls. **2.** Very great; vast.
how•so•ev•er (hou′sō-ev′ər) *adv.* **1.** To whatever degree or extent. **2.** By whatever means.
hoy•den (hoid′n) *n.* A boisterous girl. [Prob < MDu *heiden,* "heathen."]
hp horsepower.
HQ, h.q., H.Q. headquarters.
hr hour.
H.R. House of Representatives.
ht height.
hub (hŭb) *n.* **1.** The center portion of a wheel or wheellike part. **2.** A center of activity or interest.
hub•bub (hŭb′ŭb′) *n.* A confused din or uproar. [Ir *hooboobbes.*]
hub•cap (hŭb′kăp′) *n.* A round metal covering clamped over the hub of an automobile wheel.
hu•bris (hyōō′brĭs) *n.* Overbearing pride or presumption. [Gk, insolence, outrage.]
huck•le•ber•ry (hŭk′əl-bĕr′ē) *n.* **1.** A glossy, blackish, edible berry related to the blueberry. **2.** A shrub bearing such berries.
huck•ster (hŭk′stər) *n.* **1.** A peddler. **2.** One who publicizes a commercial product.
hud•dle (hŭd′əl) *v.* **-dled, -dling. 1.** To crowd in a close group. **2.** To hunch up; crouch. **3.** To gather together, as for a conference. *—n.* **1.** A closely crowded group. **2.** A brief gathering together for consultation, as of football players between plays. [?] **—hud′dler** *n.*
Hud•son Bay (hŭd′sən). A part of the Atlantic extending into east-central Canada.
Hudson River. A river of New York State.
hue¹ (hyōō) *n.* **1.** The dimension of color that is referred to a scale of perceptions ranging from red through yellow, green, and blue, and (circularly) back to red. **2.** A particular gradation of color; tint; shade. **3.** Color. [< OE *hēo,* appearance, color, beauty. See **kei-².**]
hue² (hyōō) *n.* **—hue and cry.** A loud outcry, as of pursuit or protest. [< OF *huer,* to cry out (imit).]
huff (hŭf) *n.* A fit of anger or offended annoyance. *—v.* To puff; blow; breathe heavily. [Imit.] **—huf′fi•ness** *n.* **—huf′fy** *adj.*
hug (hŭg) *v.* **hugged, hugging. 1.** To clasp or hold closely; embrace. **2.** To keep or hold close to. **3.** To cling to; cherish. *—n.* A close embrace. [< Scand.] **—hug′ger** *n.*
huge (hyōōj) *adj.* **huger, hugest.** Very large; enormous. [< OF *ahuge.*] **—huge′ly** *adv.* **—huge′ness** *n.*
hug•ger-mug•ger, hug•ger-mug•ger (hŭg′ər-mŭg′ər) *n.* Confused disorder. *—adj.* **1.** Disordered; jumbled. **2.** Secret; clandestine. [?]
Hu•go (hyōō′gō), **Victor.** 1802–1885. French poet.
Hu•gue•not (hyōō′gə-nŏt′) *n.* A French Protestant of the 16th and 17th centuries.
huh (hŭ) *interj.* Expressive of surprise, interrogation, or contempt.
hu•la (hōō′lə) *n.* A Polynesian dance characterized by undulating movements of the hips, arms, and hands.
hulk (hŭlk) *n.* **1.** The hull of a ship, esp. an old or wrecked ship. **2.** A large, clumsy person or object. [< Gk *holkas,* "ship that is towed."]
hulk•ing (hŭl′kĭng) *adj.* Massive and clumsy.
hull (hŭl) *n.* **1.** The dry or leafy outer covering of a fruit, seed, or nut. **2. a.** The main body of a ship. **b.** The outer casing of a rocket, missile, or spacecraft. *—v.* To remove the hulls of (fruit or seeds). [< OE *hulu.* See **kel-⁴.**]
hul•la•ba•loo (hŭl′ə-bə-lōō′) *n.* A loud, confused noise; uproar.
hum (hŭm) *v.* **hummed, humming 1.** To produce a continuous droning sound. **2.** To sing with closed lips. **3.** To be full of activity. *—n.* A continuous droning sound. **—hum′mer** *n.*
hu•man (hyōō′mən) *adj.* **1.** Of, relating to, or characteristic of mankind or of persons. **2.** Having the form or qualities characteristic of man. *—n.* Also **human being.** A person. [< L *hūmānus.*] **—hu′man•ness** *n.*
hu•mane (hyōō-mān′) *adj.* **1.** Having or showing sympathetic concern for others; compassionate; kind. **2.** Of or pertaining to the humanities. [ME *humaine,* human.] **—hu•mane′ly** *adv.* **—hu•mane′ness** *n.*
hu•man•ism (hyōō′mə-nĭz′əm) *n.* **1.** An attitude or system of thought asserting the primacy of man over metaphysical or abstract principles. **2. Humanism.** Study of classical texts as pursued during the Renaissance. **—hu′man•ist** *n.* & *adj.* **—hu′man•is′tic** *adj.*
hu•man•i•tar•i•an (hyōō-măn′ə-târ′ē-ən) *n.* One devoted to the promotion of human welfare. *—adj.* Concerned with human welfare. **—hu•man′i•tar′i•an•ism′** *n.*
hu•man•i•ty (hyōō-măn′ə-tē) *n.* **1.** Human beings collectively; mankind. **2.** The condition or quality of being human. **3.** Humane quality; kindness; mercy. **4. the humanities.** Philosophy, literature, and the fine arts as distinguished from the sciences.
hu•man•ize (hyōō′mə-nīz′) *v.* **-ized, -izing.** To make human or humane. **—hu′man•i•za′tion** *n.*
hu•man•kind (hyōō′mən-kīnd′) *n.* The human race; mankind.
hu•man•ly (hyōō′mən-lē) *adv.* **1.** In a human way. **2.** By human means or powers.
hu•man•oid (hyōō′mə-noid′) *adj.* Resembling a human being in appearance. *—n.* An android.
hum•ble (hŭm′bəl) *adj.* **-bler, -blest. 1.** Showing awareness of one's shortcomings; not proud; meek. **2.** Deeply respectful. **3.** Not high in station; lowly. *—v.* **-bled, -bling. 1.** To make humble in spirit. **2.** To bring low; abase. [< L *humilis,* low, lowly, base.] **—hum′ble•ness** *n.* **—hum′bly** *adv.*
hum•bug (hŭm′bŭg′) *n.* **1.** A hoax; fake. **2.** An impostor; charlatan. **3.** Nonsense; rubbish. *—v.* **-bugged, -bugging.** To trick; cheat. [?] **—hum′bug′ger** *n.*
hum•ding•er (hŭm′dĭng′ər) *n. Informal.* Something extraordinary.
hum•drum (hŭm′drŭm′) *adj.* Monotonous; uneventful. **—hum′drum′ness** *n.*
hu•mer•us (hyōō′mər-əs) *n., pl.* **-meri** (-mə-rī′). The long bone of the upper arm, extending from the shoulder to the elbow. [< L, upper arm, shoulder.] **—hu′mer•al** *adj.*
hu•mid (hyōō′mĭd) *adj.* Having a high concentration of water vapor or moisture. [< L *hūmēre,* to be moist.] **—hu•mid′i•ty** *n.*
hu•mid•i•fy (hyōō-mĭd′ə-fī′) *v.* **-fied, -fying.** To make humid. **—hu•mid′i•fi′er** *n.*
hu•mi•dor (hyōō′mə-dôr′) *n.* A storage case for tobacco products, esp. cigars, equipped with a humidifying device.
hu•mil•i•ate (hyōō-mĭl′ē-āt′) *v.* **-ated, -ating.** To destroy the dignity or pride of; shame; disgrace. [< L *humilis,* HUMBLE.] **—hu•mil′i•at′ing•ly** *adv.* **—hu•mil′i•a′tion** *n.*
hu•mil•i•ty (hyōō-mĭl′ə-tē) *n.* The quality or condition of being humble.
hum•ming•bird (hŭm′ĭng-bûrd′) *n.* A very small, long-billed, often brilliantly colored bird.
hum•mock (hŭm′ək) *n.* A low mound or ridge; knoll. [?]
hu•mor (hyōō′mər). Also *Brit.* **hu•mour.** *n.* **1.** The quality of being laughable or comical. **2.** Ability to perceive or express what is comical, witty, etc. **3.** State of mind; mood; disposition. **4.** Capricious impulse; whim. **5.** Any of various bodily fluids. *—v.* To comply with the whims of; indulge. [ME *humour,* one of the four principal bodily fluids that affected mental disposition.]
hu•mor•ist (hyōō′mər-ĭst) *n.* **1.** One with a sharp sense of humor. **2.** A performer or writer of comedy.
hu•mor•ous (hyōō′mər-əs) *adj.* Comical; funny. **—hu′mor•ous•ly** *adv.* **—hu′mor•ous•ness** *n.*
hump (hŭmp) *n.* **1.** A rounded protuberance, as on the back of a camel. **2.** A hill or hummock. **—over the hump.** Past the worst or most difficult part. *—v.* To make into a hump; to round. [Short for earlier *humpback(ed),* poss < HUNCHBACK(ED).]
hump•back (hŭmp′băk′) *n.* **1.** An abnormally curved or humped back. **2.** One having such a back; a hunchback. **—hump′backed′** *adj.*
humph (hŭmf) *interj.* Expressive of doubt, displeasure, or contempt.
hu•mus (hyōō′məs) *n.* Dark-colored partially or wholly decayed vegetable matter forming a nutrient constituent of soil. [L, earth, ground, soil.]
Hun (hŭn) *n.* One of a nomadic Asiatic people who invaded Europe in the 4th and 5th centuries A.D.
Hun. Hungarian; Hungary.
hunch (hŭnch) *v.* **1.** To arch or draw up into a hump. **2.** To push or thrust forward. *—n.* An intuitive premonitory feeling. [?]
hunch•back (hŭnch′băk′) *n.* **1.** One having an abnormally curved or humped back; a humpback. **2.** An abnormally curved or humped back. **—hunch′backed′** *adj.*
hun•dred (hŭn′drĭd) *n. pl.* **-dreds** or **-dred. 1.** The cardinal number written 100 or in Roman numerals C. **2.** The number in the third position left of the decimal point in an Arabic numeral. **3. hundreds.** The numbers between 100 and 999: *in the hundreds.* [< OE *hundred, hund.*] **—hun′dred** *adj.* & *pron.*
hun•dredth (hŭn′drĭdth) *n.* **1.** The ordinal number 100 in a series. **2.** One of 100 equal parts. **—hun′dredth** *adj.* & *adv.*
hun•dred•weight (hŭn′drĭd-wāt′) *n., pl.* **-weight** or **-weights. 1.** A U.S. Customary System unit of weight equal to 100 pounds. **2.** A British Imperial System unit of weight equal to 112 pounds.
hung (hŭng). Alternate *p.t.* & *p.p.* of **hang.** See Usage note at **hang.**
Hung. Hungarian; Hungary.
Hun•gar•i•an (hŭng-gâr′ē-ən) *n.* **1.** A citizen or native of Hungary. **2.** The Finno-Ugric language spoken in Hungary. **—Hun′gar′i•an** *adj.*
Hun•ga•ry (hŭng′gə-rē). A republic of C Europe. Pop. 10,123,000. Cap. Budapest.
hun•ger (hŭng′gər) *n.* **1.** A strong desire or

need for food. **2.** Weakness or discomfort caused by lack of food. **3.** A strong desire; craving. —*v.* **1.** To be hungry. **2.** To have a strong desire; yearn. [< OE *hungor.* See **kenk-²**.] —**hun'ger•less** *adj.*

hun•gry (hŭng'grē) *adj.* **-grier, -griest. 1. a.** Desiring food. **b.** Weak or uncomfortable from lack of food. **2.** Feeling or showing a strong desire for something. —**hun'gri•ly** *adv.*

Hungary

hunk (hŭngk) *n.* A large piece; chunk.

hun•ker (hŭng'kər) *v.* To squat with one's weight resting on the calves. [Prob < Scand.]

hun•ky-do•ry (hŭng'kē-dôr'ē, -dōr'ē) *adj. Informal.* Quite satisfactory; fine. [< MDu *honc,* hiding place.]

Hun•nish (hŭn'ĭsh) *adj.* **1.** Of or pertaining to the Huns. **2.** Often **hunnish.** Barbarous. —**Hun'nish•ness** *n.*

hunt (hŭnt) *v.* **1.** To pursue (animals) for food, sport, etc. **2.** To make a search (for); seek. **3.** To chase and harass. **4.** To swing back and forth or oscillate, as an indicator on an instrument panel. —*n.* **1.** The act or sport of hunting. **2.** A group or expedition organized for hunting. **3.** A search or pursuit. [< OE *huntian* < Gmc **huntjan.*] —**hunt'er** *n.* —**hunt'ress** *fem.n.*

hunts•man (hŭnts'mən) *n.* One who hunts, esp. one who manages a pack of hunting hounds.

hur•dle (hûrd'l) *n.* **1.** A framelike barrier to be jumped over in obstacle races. **2.** Any obstacle or problem that must be overcome. —*v.* **-dled, -dling. 1.** To jump over (a barrier). **2.** To overcome (an obstacle). [< OE *hyrdel.* See **kert-**.] —**hur'dler** *n.*

hur•dy-gur•dy (hûr'dē-gûr'dē) *n., pl.* **-dies.** A musical instrument, as a barrel organ, played by turning a crank. [Prob imit.]

hurl (hûrl) *v.* **1.** To throw forcefully; fling. **2.** To utter vehemently: *hurl insults.* [ME *hourlen,* to throw, rush on.] —**hurl** *n.* —**hurl'er** *n.*

hur•ly-bur•ly (hûr'lē-bûr'lē) *n., pl.* **-lies.** Commotion; tumult. [< HURL.]

Hu•ron (hyo͝or'ən, -ŏn') *n., pl.* **-ron** or **-rons. 1.** A member of a confederation of four tribes of Iroquoian-speaking North American Indians formerly inhabiting the St. Lawrence Valley region. **2.** The Iroquoian language spoken among these tribes. —**Hu'ron** *adj.*

Huron, Lake. The second largest of the Great Lakes.

hur•rah (ho͝o-rä', -rô') *interj.* Also **hoo•ray** (-rā'), **hur•ray** (-rā'). Expressive of approval, elation, or victory. —**hur•rah'** *n.*

hur•ri•cane (hûr'ə-kān') *n.* A severe tropical cyclone with winds exceeding 75 miles per hour and usually involving heavy rains. [< Carib *huracan, furacan.*]

hur•ry (hûr'ē) *v.* **-ried, -rying. 1.** To move or cause to move with speed or haste. **2.** To proceed or press to proceed with great or undue rapidity; rush. —*n., pl.* **-ries. 1.** The act of hurrying. **2.** Haste; a rush. [Prob imit.] —**hur'ried•ly** *adv.* —**hur'ried•ness** *n.*

hurt (hûrt) *v.* **hurt, hurting. 1.** To feel or cause to feel physical pain. **2.** To offend; distress. **3.** To damage; harm. —*n.* **1.** Physical pain or injury. **2.** Anguish; distress. **3.** Damage; harm. [< OF *hurter.*] —**hurt'ful** *adj.*

hur•tle (hûrt'l) *v.* **-tled, -tling. 1.** To move with forceful, often noisy speed. **2.** To collide violently; crash. [< ME *hurten,* to strike, hurt.]

Hus (ho͞os), **Jan.** 1369?–1415. Bohemian religious reformer.

hus•band (hŭz'bənd) *n.* A married man; male spouse. —*v.* To expend wisely or economically. [< OE *hūsbonda,* master of a household, husband.]

hus•band•man (hŭz'bənd-mən) *n.* A farmer.

hus•band•ry (hŭz'bən-drē) *n.* **1.** Farming; agriculture. **2.** Careful management of resources.

hush (hŭsh) *v.* **1.** To make or become silent. **2.** To quell; calm. **3.** To suppress; conceal. —*n.* A silence; stillness.

hush•pup•py (hŭsh'pŭp'ē) *n. Southern U.S.* A fried cornmeal fritter.

husk (hŭsk) *n.* **1.** A thin or leaflike outer envelope, as of an ear of corn or a nut. **2.** An often worthless or discarded outer shell. —*v.* To remove the husk from. [Prob < MDu *hūs,* house.] —**husk'er** *n.*

husk•y¹ (hŭs'kē) *adj.* **-ier, -iest.** Hoarse; throaty. [Orig "dry as a husk."] —**husk'i•ly** *adv.* —**husk'i•ness** *n.*

husk•y² (hŭs'kē) *adj.* **-ier, -iest.** Large and strong; burly. [< HUSKY¹.] —**husk'i•ness** *n.*

hus•ky³ (hŭs'kē) *n., pl.* **-kies.** An Arctic sled dog with a dense, furry coat. [Prob a shortened var of ESKIMO.]

hus•sar (ho͞o-zär') *n.* A member of a cavalry regiment with a usually much ornamented dress uniform. [Hung *huszár,* "freebooter," hussar.]

hus•sy (hŭz'ē, hŭs'ē) *n., pl.* **-sies. 1.** A saucy girl. **2.** A strumpet; trollop. [Var of HOUSEWIFE.]

hus•tle (hŭs'əl) *v.* **-tled, -tling. 1.** To jostle; shove. **2.** To hurry along. **3.** To work busily. **4.** *Slang.* To make money by questionable means. —*n.* Busy activity. [< MDu *hutsen,* to shake.] —**hus'tler** *n.*

hut (hŭt) *n.* A makeshift or crude dwelling; shack. [OF *hutte.*]

hutch (hŭch) *n.* **1.** A coop for small animals, esp. rabbits. **2.** A cupboard surmounted by usually open shelves. [< OF *huche,* chest.]

huz•za (hə-zä'). Also **huz•zah.** *n.* A shout of encouragement or triumph; a cheer. —**huz•za'** *interj.*

hy•a•cinth (hī'ə-sĭnth) *n.* A bulbous plant with a cluster of variously colored, fragrant flowers. [< Gk *huakinthos,* wild hyacinth.]

hy•ae•na. Variant of **hyena.**

hy•brid (hī'brĭd) *n.* **1.** The offspring of genetically dissimilar parents or stock, as that of plants or animals of different varieties, species, etc. **2.** Something of mixed origin or composition. [L *hybrida,* hybrid, mongrel.] —**hy'brid** *adj.* —**hy'brid•ism'** *n.*

hy•brid•ize (hī'brĭ-dīz') *v.* **-ized, -izing.** To produce or cause to produce a hybrid. —**hy'brid•i•za'tion** *n.*

hy•dran•ge•a (hī-drān'jē-ə, -jə) *n.* A shrub with large, flat-topped or rounded clusters of white, pink, or blue flowers. [< HYDR(O)- + Gk *angos,* vessel.]

hy•drant (hī'drənt) *n.* An upright pipe serving as an outlet from a water main. [HYDR(O)- + -ANT.]

hy•drate (hī'drāt') *n.* A compound containing water combined in a definite ratio, regarded as being retained in its molecular state. —*v.* **-drated, -drating.** To form a hydrate. —**hy•dra'tion** *n.* —**hy'dra'tor** (-drā'tər) *n.*

hy•drau•lic (hī-drô'lĭk) *adj.* **1.** Of, involving, or operated by a fluid, esp. water, under pressure. **2.** Setting and hardening under water: *hydraulic cement.* **3.** Of or pertaining to hydraulics. —*n.* **hydraulics** *(takes sing. v.).* The physical science and technology of the static and dynamic behavior of fluids. [< Gk *hudraulis,* a water organ.] —**hy•drau'li•cal•ly** *adv.*

hydraulic brake. A brake in which the braking force is transmitted to the braking surface by a compressed fluid.

hydro–. *comb. form.* **1.** Water. **2.** Liquid. **3.** Composed of or combined with hydrogen. [< Gk *hudōr,* water.]

hy•dro•car•bon (hī'drə-kär'bən) *n.* An organic compound, such as benzene or methane, that contains only carbon and hydrogen.

hy•dro•ceph•a•ly (hī'drō-sĕf'ə-lē) *n.* A usually congenital condition in which an abnormal accumulation of fluid in the cerebral ventricles causes enlargement of the skull and compression of the brain. —**hy'dro•ce•phal'ic** (-sə-făl'ĭk) *adj.*

hy•dro•chlo•ric acid (hī'drə-klôr'ĭk, -klōr'ĭk). A clear, colorless, highly acidic aqueous solution of hydrogen chloride, HCl, used in petroleum production, ore reduction, food processing, pickling, and metal cleaning.

hy•dro•dy•nam•ics (hī'drō-dī-năm'ĭks) *n. (takes sing. v.).* The dynamics of fluids, esp. incompressible fluids, in motion. —**hy'dro•dy•nam'ic** *adj.*

hy•dro•e•lec•tric (hī'drō-ĭ-lĕk'trĭk) *adj.* Generating electricity by conversion of the energy of running water. —**hy'dro•e•lec'tric'i•ty** (-ĭ-lĕk'trĭs'ə-tē) *n.*

hy•dro•foil (hī'drə-foil') *n.* **1.** One of a set of blades attached to the hull of a boat to lift it out of the water for efficient high-speed operation. **2.** A boat equipped with hydrofoils; hydroplane.

hy•dro•gen (hī'drə-jən) *n. Symbol* **H** A colorless, highly flammable gaseous element used in the production of synthetic ammonia and methanol, in petroleum refining, as a reducing atmosphere, in oxyhydrogen torches, and in rocket fuels. Atomic number 1, atomic weight 1.00797. [F *hydrogène,* "water generating."] —**hy•drog'e•nous** (-drŏj'ə-nəs) *adj.*

hy•dro•gen•ate (hī'drə-jə-nāt', hī-drŏj'ə-) *v.* **-ated, -ating.** To combine with or subject to the action of hydrogen. —**hy'dro•gen•a'tion** *n.*

hydrogen bomb. An explosive weapon of great destructive power derived from the fusion of nuclei of various hydrogen isotopes in the formation of helium nuclei.

hydrogen bond. An essentially ionic chemical bond between a strongly electronegative atom and a hydrogen atom already bonded to another strongly electronegative atom.

hydrogen peroxide. A colorless, heavy, strongly oxidizing liquid, H_2O_2, an essentially unstable compound, used principally in aqueous solution as an antiseptic, bleaching agent, oxidizing agent, and laboratory reagent.

hy•drol•y•sis (hī-drŏl'ə-sĭs) *n.* Decomposition of a chemical compound by reaction with water. —**hy'dro•ly'tic** (hī'drə-lĭt'ĭk) *adj.* —**hy'dro•lyze'** *v.* **(-lyzed, -lyzing.)**

hy•drom•e•ter (hī-drŏm'ə-tər) *n.* A sealed graduated tube, weighted at one end, that sinks in a fluid to a depth used as a measure of the fluid's specific gravity.

hy•dro•pho•bi•a (hī′drə-fō′bē-ə) *n.* Rabies.

hy•dro•plane (hī′drə-plān′) *n.* **1.** A seaplane. **2.** A motorboat designed to skim the water at high speeds. **3.** A hydrofoil.

hy•dro•stat•ic (hī′drə-stăt′ĭk) *adj.* Also **hy•dro•stat•i•cal** (-ĭ-kəl). Pertaining to hydrostatics. —*n.* **hydrostatics** (*takes sing. v.*). The statics of fluids, esp. incompressible fluids.

hy•dro•ther•a•py (hī′drō-thĕr′ə-pē) *n.* The medical use of water in the treatment of certain diseases.

hy•drous (hī′drəs) *adj.* Containing water.

hy•drox•ide (hī-drŏk′sīd′) *n.* A chemical compound containing the univalent group OH. [HYDR(O)- + OXIDE.]

hy•e•na (hī-ē′nə) *n.* Also **hy•ae•na.** A carnivorous African and Asian mammal with powerful jaws. [< Gk *huaina* < *hus,* swine.]

hy•giene (hī′jēn′) *n.* The science or principles of health and the prevention of disease. [< Gk *hugiēs,* healthy.] —**hy′gi•en′ic** *adj.*

hygro–. *comb. form.* Wet. [< Gk *hugros,* wet, moist.]

hy•grom•e•ter (hī-grŏm′ə-tər) *n.* Any of several instruments that measure atmospheric humidity. —**hy•grom′e•try** *n.*

hy•gro•scop•ic (hī′grə-skŏp′ĭk) *adj.* Readily absorbing moisture, as from the atmosphere.

hy•men (hī′mən) *n.* A membranous fold of tissue partly or completely occluding the vaginal external orifice. [< Gk *humēn,* membrane.]

hy•me•ne•al (hī′mə-nē′əl) *adj.* Of or pertaining to a wedding or marriage. [< Gk *Humēn,* god of marriage.]

hymn (hĭm) *n.* A song of praise or thanksgiving, esp. to God. [< Gk *humnos.*]

hym•nal (hĭm′nəl) *n.* A book or collection of hymns.

hy•oid bone (hī′oid′). A U-shaped bone between the mandible and larynx.

hyp. **1.** hypotenuse. **2.** hypothesis.

hyper–. *comb. form.* **1.** Over, above, or in great amount. **2.** In abnormal excess. [< Gk *huper,* over, above, beyond.]

hy•per•bar•ic (hī′pər-băr′ĭk) *adj.* Employing pressures higher than normal atmospheric pressure.

hy•per•bo•la (hī-pûr′bə-lə) *n.* A plane curve having two branches, formed by the locus of points related to two given points such that the difference in the distances of each point from the two given points is a constant. [< Gk *huperbolē,* "a throwing beyond," excess.]

hy•per•bo•le (hī-pûr′bə-lē) *n.* Exaggeration used as a figure of speech. [< Gk *huperbolē,* excess.]

hy•per•bol•ic (hī′pər-bŏl′ĭk) *adj.* **1.** Of or employing hyperbole. **2.** Of or having the form of a hyperbola. —**hy′per•bol′i•cal•ly** *adv.*

hy•per•bo•re•an (hī′pər-bôr′ē-ən, -bōr′ē-ən, -bə-rē′ən) *adj.* Of the far north.

hy•per•crit•i•cal (hī′pər-krĭt′ĭ-kəl) *adj.* Overcritical. —**hy′per•crit′i•cal•ly** *adv.*

hy•per•o•pi•a (hī′pər-ō′pē-ə) *n.* A refractive defect of the eye in which vision is better for distant than for near objects.

hy•per•sen•si•tive (hī′pər-sĕn′sə-tĭv) *adj.* Abnormally sensitive. —**hy′per•sen′si•tiv′i•ty, hy′per•sen′si•tive•ness** *n.*

hy•per•son•ic (hī′pər-sŏn′ĭk) *adj.* Pertaining to speed equal to or exceeding five times the speed of sound.

hy•per•ten•sion (hī′pər-tĕn′shən) *n.* **1.** Abnormally high arterial blood pressure. **2.** A state of high emotional tension.

hy•per•thy•roid•ism (hī′pər-thī′roi-dĭz′əm) *n.* Pathologically excessive production of thyroid hormones. —**hy′per•thy′roid′** *adj.* & *n.*

hy•phen (hī′fən) *n.* A punctuation mark (-) used to connect the parts of a compound word or between syllables of a divided word. [< Gk *huphen,* in the same word.]

hy•phen•ate (hī′fə-nāt′) *v.* **-ated, -ating.** To divide or connect with a hyphen. —**hy′phen•a′tion** *n.*

hyp•no•sis (hĭp-nō′sĭs) *n.* An artificially induced sleeplike condition in which an individual is extremely responsive to suggestion. [< Gk *hupnos,* sleep + -OSIS.] —**hyp′no•tize′** (hĭp′nə-tīz′) *v.* (**-tized, -tizing**).

hyp•not•ic (hĭp-nŏt′ĭk) *adj.* **1.** Of or inducing hypnosis. **2.** Inducing sleep. —*n.* **1.** A hypnotic agent. **2.** A hypnotized person. —**hyp•not′i•cal•ly** *adv.*

hyp•no•tism (hĭp′nə-tĭz′əm) *n.* The theory or practice of inducing hypnosis. —**hyp′no•tist** *n.*

hy•po (hī′pō) *n., pl.* **-pos.** *Informal.* A hypodermic syringe or injection.

hypo–. *comb. form.* **1.** Below or beneath. **2.** At a lower point. **3.** Abnormally low. **4.** Deficient. [< Gk *hupo,* under, beneath.]

hy•po•chon•dri•a (hī′pə-kŏn′drē-ə) *n.* The persistent neurotic conviction that one is or is likely to become ill. [< Gk *hupokhondrion,* belly, abdomen.] —**hy′po•chon′dri•ac′** *n.* & *adj.*

hy•poc•ri•sy (hĭ-pŏk′rə-sē) *n.* The feigning of beliefs, feelings, or virtues that one does not hold or possess. [< Gk *hupokrisis,* playing of a part on the stage.]

hyp•o•crite (hĭp′ə-krĭt′) *n.* A person given to hypocrisy. —**hyp′o•crit′i•cal** *adj.* —**hyp′o•crit′i•cal•ly** *adv.*

hy•po•der•mic (hī′pə-dûr′mĭk) *adj.* **1.** Just beneath the epidermis. **2.** Injected beneath the skin. —*n.* A hypodermic injection.

hy•pot•e•nuse (hī-pŏt′n/y/ōōs′) *n.* The side of a right triangle opposite the right angle. [< Gk *hupoteinousa,* line subtending the right angle.]

hypoth. hypothesis.

hy•po•thal•a•mus (hī′pō-thăl′ə-məs) *n.* The part of the brain that lies below the thalamus and functions to regulate bodily temperature, certain metabolic processes, and other autonomic activities.

hy•poth•e•sis (hī-pŏth′ə-sĭs) *n., pl.* **-ses** (-sēz′). An assumption subject to verification or proof, as a conjecture that accounts for a set of facts and can be used as a basis for further investigation. [< Gk *hupothesis,* proposal.]

hy•poth•e•size (hī-pŏth′ə-sīz′) *v.* **-sized, -sizing.** To assert as or form a hypothesis.

hy•po•thet•i•cal (hī′pə-thĕt′ĭ-kəl) *adj.* Of or based on a hypothesis; conjectural. —**hy′po•thet′i•cal•ly** *adv.*

hy•po•thy•roid•ism (hī′pō-thī′roi-dĭz′əm) *n.* Insufficient production of thyroid hormones.

hys•sop (hĭs′əp) *n.* A bushy, aromatic plant with spikes of small blue flowers. [< Gk *hussōpos.*]

hys•ter•ec•to•my (hĭs′tə-rĕk′tə-mē) *n., pl.* **-mies.** Total or partial surgical removal of the uterus.

hys•ter•e•sis (hĭs′tə-rē′sĭs) *n., pl.* **-ses** (-sēz′). *Phys.* Failure of a property changed by an external agent to return to its original value when the cause of the change is removed. [< Gk *husterēsis,* a shortcoming.]

hys•ter•i•a (hĭ-stĕr′ē-ə) *n.* **1.** A neurosis characterized by symbolic physiological symptoms, hallucination, somnambulism, amnesia, and other mental aberrations. **2.** Uncontrollable fear or other strong emotion. [< Gk *husterikos,* suffering in the womb.] —**hys•ter′ic** *n.* & *adj.* —**hys•ter′ic•al** *adj.* —**hys•ter′ic•al•ly** *adv.*

hys•ter•ics (hĭ-stĕr′ĭks) *n.* (*takes sing. v.*). A fit of uncontrollable laughing and crying.

Hz hertz.

Ii

i, I (ī) *n.* **1.** The 9th letter of the English alphabet. **2.** The 9th in a series.

i **1.** *Math.* imaginary unit. **2.** The Roman numeral for one.

I **1.** iodine. **2.** The Roman numeral for one.

i. **1.** interest. **2.** intransitive.

I. island.

I (ī) *pron.* The 1st person sing. pronoun in the nominative case, used to represent the speaker or writer. [< OE *ic.* See **eg.**]

Ia. Iowa (unofficial).

–ial. *comb. form.* Of, pertaining to, or characterized by: **managerial.** [< L *-iālis.*]

i•amb (ī′ămb′) *n.* A metrical foot consisting of an unstressed syllable followed by a stressed syllable. —**i•am′bic** *adj.* & *n.*

–ian. *comb. form.* Of, belonging to, or resembling: **Bostonian.** [< L *-iānus.*]

–iatrics. *comb. form.* Medical treatment: **pediatrics.** [< Gk *iatros,* healer.]

–iatry. *comb. form.* Medical treatment: **psychiatry.**

I•be•ri•a (ī-bîr′ē-ə). The ancient name for the Spanish-Portuguese peninsula. —**I•be′ri•an** *adj.* & *n.*

i•bex (ī′bĕks′) *n.* An Old World mountain goat with long, curving horns. [L.]

ibid. ibidem.

i•bi•dem (ĭb′ə-dĕm′, ĭ-bī′dəm) *adv.* In the same place, as in a book cited before. [L.]

i•bis (ī′bĭs) *n.* A large wading bird with a long, downward-curving bill. [< Gk < Egypt *hīb.*]

–ible. Variant of **-able.**

Ib•sen (ĭb′sən), **Henrik.** 1828–1906. Norwegian dramatist.
–ic. *comb. form.* **1.** Used to form adjectives meaning of, pertaining to, or characteristic of: **Gaelic. 2.** *Chem.* Having or taking a valence higher than in corresponding *-ous* compounds: **ferric.** [< L *-icus.*]
ICBM intercontinental ballistic missile.
ICC Interstate Commerce Commission.
ice (īs) *n.* **1.** Water frozen solid. **2.** A dessert of sweetened and flavored crushed ice. **—break the ice.** To relax a tense or formal atmosphere. —*v.* **iced, icing. 1.** To form ice. **2.** To coat with ice. **3.** To chill or freeze. **4.** To cover with icing. [< OE *īs.* See **eis-²**.] **—i′ci•ly** *adv.* **—i′cy** *adj.*
ice•berg (īs′bûrg′) *n.* A massive floating body of ice broken away from a glacier.
ice•bound (īs′bound′) *adj.* **1.** Locked in by ice, as a ship. **2.** Obstructed by ice, as a waterway.
ice•box (īs′bŏks′) *n.* A refrigerator.
ice•break•er (īs′brā′kər) *n.* A ship built for breaking a passage through icebound waters.
ice cap. An extensive perennial cover of ice and snow.
ice cream. A food prepared from a frozen mixture of milk products with sweetening.
Icel. Iceland; Icelandic.
Ice•land (īs′lənd). An island republic in the North Atlantic. Pop. 200,000. Cap. Reykjavik. **—Ice′land•er** *n.*

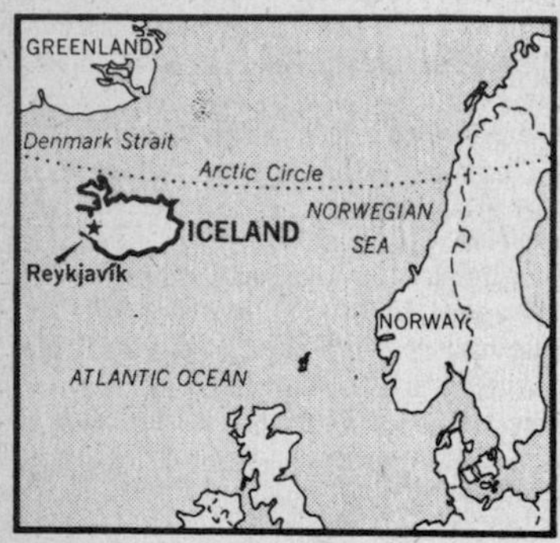

Iceland

Ice•land•ic (īs-lăn′dĭk) *adj.* Of or pertaining to Iceland, its inhabitants, or their language. —*n.* The Germanic language of Iceland as spoken since the 16th century.
ice pick. An awl for chipping ice.
ice point. The temperature at which pure water and ice are in equilibrium in a mixture at one atmosphere of pressure.
ice-skate (īs′skāt′) *v.* **-skated, -skating.** To skate on ice. **—ice skater.**
ice water. Very cold or iced drinking water.
ichthyo–. *comb. form.* Fish. [< Gk *ikhthus,* fish.]
ich•thy•ol•o•gy (ĭk′thē-ŏl′ə-jē) *n.* Zoology specializing in the study of fishes. **—ich′thy•ol′o•gist** *n.*
–ician. *comb. form.* One who practices or is a specialist in a given field: **mortician.**
i•ci•cle (ī′sĭ-kəl) *n.* A tapering spike of ice formed by the freezing of dripping water. [< ICE + OE *gicel,* icicle (see **yeg-**).]
ic•ing (ī′sĭng) *n.* A sweet glaze for cakes and cookies.
ICJ International Court of Justice.
i•con (ī′kŏn′) *n.* Also **i•kon.** A religious image painted on a panel. [< Gk *eikōn,* likeness, image.]
i•con•o•clast (ī-kŏn′ə-klăst′) *n.* Any attacker of established ideas and usages. [< MGk *eikonoklastēs,* "image breaker."] **—i•con′o•clas′tic** (-klăs′tĭk) *adj.*
–ics. *comb. form.* **1.** The science or art of: **acoustics. 2.** The act or practices of: **hysterics.** [< -IC.]
id (ĭd) *n.* The division of the psyche associated with instinctual impulses and primitive needs. [< L, it.]
I'd (īd). **1.** Contraction of *I had.* **2.** Contraction of *I would.* **3.** Contraction of *I should.*
id. idem.
Id. Idaho (unofficial).
I.d. inside diameter.
I.D. identification.
I•da•ho (ī′də-hō). A state of the NW U.S. Pop. 713,000. Cap. Boise.
–ide, –id. *comb. form.* Used to form the names of chemical compounds: **chloride.** [< F *acide,* acid.]
i•de•a (ī-dē′ə) *n.* **1.** A mental representation forming an object of thought. **2.** A product of thought, as: **a.** An opinion. **b.** A plan or method. **c.** A notion; fancy. **3.** The gist or purpose of something. **4.** The Platonic archetype of which a corresponding being in phenomenal reality is assertedly an imperfect replica. [< Gk, form, model, class, notion.]
i•de•al (ī-dē′əl, ī-dēl′) *n.* **1. a.** A standard of absolute perfection, excellence, or beauty. **b.** One regarded as a model of these qualities. **2.** An ultimate object; goal. **3.** An honorable or worthy principle. —*adj.* **1.** Perfect or near-perfect. **2.** Existing only in the mind; visionary. **3.** Existing as a Platonic archetype. [< L *idea,* model, idea.] **—i•de′al•ly** *adv.*
i•de•al•ism (ī-dē′ə-lĭz′əm) *n.* **1.** Pursuit of one's ideals. **2.** Any theory identifying reality with perception or ideation. **—i•de′al•ist** *n.* **—i•de′al•is′tic** *adj.* **—i•de′al•is′ti•cal•ly** *adv.*
i•de•al•ize (ī-dē′ə-līz′) *v.* **-ized, -izing.** To regard or represent as ideal. **—i•de′al•i•za′tion** *n.*
i•de•a•tion (ī′dē-ā′shən) *n.* The process of forming and relating ideas. **—i′de•a′tion•al** *adj.*
i•dem (ī′dĕm′). Used to indicate a reference previously given or mentioned. [L *īdem, idem,* the same.]
i•den•ti•cal (ī-dĕn′tĭ-kəl) *adj.* **1.** Being the same. **2.** Being exactly equal. **3.** Developed from the same ovum. [< LL *identitās,* identity.] **—i•den′ti•cal•ly** *adv.*
i•den•ti•fi•ca•tion (ī-dĕn′tə-fĭ-kā′shən) *n.* **1.** The act of identifying or state of being identified. **2.** Documentary proof of one's identity.
i•den•ti•fy (ī-dĕn′tə-fī′) *v.* **-fied, -fying. 1.** To ascertain or establish the identity of. **2.** To be or cause to be identical; regard as the same. **3.** To associate with, as a political party, business, etc. **—i•den′ti•fi′a•ble** *adj.*
i•den•ti•ty (ī-dĕn′tə-tē) *n., pl.* **-ties. 1.** The collective aspect of the set of characteristics by which a person or thing is recognized or known. **2.** Sameness of character, quality, or condition. **3.** Personal individuality. **4.** An equality satisfied by all values of the variables for which the expressions involved are defined. [LL *identitās* < L *idem,* the same, IDEM.]
ideo–. *comb. form.* Idea.
i•de•ol•o•gy (ī′dē-ŏl′ə-jē, ĭd′ē-) *n., pl.* **-gies.** The body of ideas reflecting the social needs and aspirations of an individual, group, or culture. **—i′de•o•log′i•cal** *adj.*
ides (īdz) *n. (takes sing. v.).* The 15th day of March, May, July, or October or the 13th day of the other months in the ancient Roman calendar. [< L *īdūs.*]
id est (ĭd ĕst′). *Latin.* That is.
id•i•o•cy (ĭd′ē-ə-sē) *n., pl.* **-cies. 1.** Subnormal intellectual development or ability characterized by intelligence in the lowest measurable range. **2.** Extreme folly or stupidity.
id•i•om (ĭd′ē-əm) *n.* **1.** A speech form that is peculiar to itself within the usage of a given language. **2.** A specialized vocabulary; jargon: *legal idiom.* [< Gk *idiōma,* peculiarity, idiom.] **—id′i•o•mat′ic** *adj.*
id•i•o•syn•cra•sy (ĭd′ē-ō-sĭng′krə-sē) *n., pl.* **-sies.** A structural or behavioral peculiarity. [< Gk *idios,* peculiar + *sunkrasis,* mixture.] **—id′i•o•syn•crat′ic** (-sĭn-krăt′ĭk) *adj.*
id•i•ot (ĭd′ē-ət) *n.* **1.** A mentally deficient person having intelligence in the lowest measurable range, being unable to guard against common dangers, and incapable of learning connected speech. **2.** An imbecile; blockhead. [< Gk *idios,* peculiar, private.] **—id′i•ot′ic** *adj.*
i•dle (īd′l) *adj.* **idler, idlest. 1.** Inactive. **2.** Lazy; shiftless. **3.** Useless or groundless: *idle talk.* —*v.* **idled, idling. 1.** To pass time without working. **2.** To move lazily. **3.** To run or cause to run at a slow speed or out of gear: *The motor is idling.* **4.** To cause to be unemployed or inactive. [< OE *īdel* < Gmc **idal.*] **—i′dle•ness** *n.* **—i′dler** *n.* **—i′dly** *adv.*
i•dol (īd′l) *n.* **1.** An image used as an object of worship. **2.** One that is adored. [< Gk *eidōlon,* image, form.]
i•dol•a•try (ī-dŏl′ə-trē) *n.* **1.** The worship of idols. **2.** Blind devotion. **—i•dol′a•ter** *n.* **—i•dol′a•trous** *adj.*
i•dol•ize (īd′l-īz′) *v.* **-ized, -izing. 1.** To regard with blind admiration or devotion. **2.** To worship as an idol.
i•dyll (īd′l) *n.* Also **i•dyl. 1.** A short poem about rustic life. **2.** A scene or event of rural simplicity. **3.** A romantic interlude. [< Gk *eidos,* form, picture.] **—i•dyl′lic** *adj.*
i.e. id est.
if (ĭf) *conj.* **1.** —Used to introduce a subjunctive clause, meaning: **a.** In the event that. **b.** Granting that. **c.** On condition that. **2.** —Used to introduce a negative conditional clause, meaning even though: *a handsome if useless trinket.* **3.** —Used to introduce an indirect question, meaning whether: *Ask if he will come.* —*n.* A condition or stipulation. [< OE *gif.*]
ig•loo (ĭg′lo͞o) *n., pl.* **-loos.** Also **ig•lu.** An Eskimo house, sometimes built of ice blocks. [Esk *iglu,* house.]
ig•ne•ous (ĭg′nē-əs) *adj.* **1.** Characteristic of fire. **2.** Solidified from a molten state. [< L *ignis,* fire.]
ig•nite (ĭg-nīt′) *v.* **-nited, -niting. 1. a.** To cause to burn. **b.** To begin to burn. **2.** To arouse or kindle. [< L *ignis,* fire.]
ig•ni•tion (ĭg-nĭsh′ən) *n.* **1.** An act or instance of igniting. **2.** An electrical system that ignites the fuel mixture in an internal-combustion engine.
ig•no•ble (ĭg-nō′bəl) *adj.* **1.** Dishonorable; base. **2.** Not of the nobility; common. **—ig•no′ble•ness** *n.* **—ig•no′bly** *adv.*
ig•no•min•i•ous (ĭg′nō-mĭn′ē-əs) *adj.* **1.** Characterized by dishonor. **2.** Despicable. **3.** Degrading; debasing. [< L *ignōminia,* dishonor.] **—ig′no•min′i•ous•ly** *adv.* **—ig′no•min′y** *n.*
ig•no•ra•mus (ĭg′nə-rā′məs) *n.* An ignorant person.
ig•no•rance (ĭg′nər-əns) *n.* The condition of being ignorant; lack of knowledge.
ig•no•rant (ĭg′nər-ənt) *adj.* **1.** Without educa-

tion or knowledge. 2. Exhibiting lack of education or knowledge. 3. Unaware or uninformed. [< L *ignōrāre*, to be ignorant, IGNORE.] —**ig'no•rant•ly** *adv.*

ig•nore (ĭg-nôr', -nōr') *v.* **-nored, -noring.** To refuse to pay attention to; disregard. [< L *ignōrāre*, not to know, disregard.]

i•gua•na (ĭ-gwä'nə) *n.* A large tropical American lizard. [< Arawak *iwana*.]

i•kon. Variant of **icon.**

il•e•um (ĭl'ē-əm) *n., pl.* **-ea** (-ē-ə). The portion of the small intestine extending from the jejunum to the cecum. [< L *īleum*, groin, flank.] —**il'e•al** *adj.*

I.L.G.W.U. International Ladies' Garment Workers' Union.

il•i•um (ĭl'ē-əm) *n., pl.* **-ia** (-ē-ə). The uppermost and widest bone of each of the sides of the pelvis.

ilk (ĭlk) *n.* Type or kind: *a remark of that ilk.* [< OE *ilca*, same.]

ill (ĭl) *adj.* **worse, worst. 1.** Not healthy; sick. **2.** Resulting in suffering; distressing. **3.** Hostile. **4.** Unpropitious. **5.** Not up to recognized standards of excellence or conduct. **6.** Harmful; cruel. —*adv.* **worse, worst. 1.** In an ill manner; not well. **2.** Scarcely or with difficulty. —*n.* **1.** Evil. **2.** Disaster or harm. [< ON *illr*, bad.]

I'll (īl). **1.** Contraction of *I will.* **2.** Contraction of *I shall.*

ill. illustrated; illustration.

Ill. Illinois.

ill-ad•vised (ĭl'əd-vīzd') *adj.* Unwise; reckless. —**ill'-ad•vis'ed•ly** *adv.*

ill-bred (ĭl'brĕd') *adj.* Badly brought up; impolite.

il•le•gal (ĭ-lē'gəl) *adj.* Prohibited by law. —**il'le•gal'i•ty** *n.* —**il•le'gal•ly** *adv.*

il•leg•i•ble (ĭ-lĕj'ə-bəl) *adj.* Not legible or decipherable. —**il•leg'i•bil'i•ty** *n.* —**il•leg'i•bly** *adv.*

il•le•git•i•mate (ĭl'ĭ-jĭt'ə-mĭt) *adj.* **1.** Against the law; illegal. **2.** Born out of wedlock; bastard. **3.** Illogical. —**il'le•git'i•ma•cy** *n.* —**il'le•git'i•mate•ly** *adv.*

ill-fat•ed (ĭl'fā'tĭd) *adj.* Doomed or unlucky.

ill-fa•vored (ĭl'fā'vərd) *adj.* **1.** Having an ugly face. **2.** Objectionable; offensive.

ill-got•ten (ĭl'gŏt'n) *adj.* Obtained by dishonest means.

ill-hu•mored (ĭl'hyo͞o'mərd) *adj.* Irritable and surly.

il•lib•er•al (ĭ-lĭb'ər-əl) *adj.* Narrow-minded; bigoted.

il•lic•it (ĭ-lĭs'ĭt) *adj.* Not sanctioned by custom or law; unlawful. [L *illicitus*, not allowed.] —**il•lic'it•ly** *adv.* —**il•lic'it•ness** *n.*

Il•li•nois[1] (ĭl'ə-noi', -noiz') *n., pl.* **-nois. 1.** A member of a confederacy of Algonquian-speaking Indian tribes that inhabited Illinois and parts of Iowa, Wisconsin, and Missouri. **2.** The language of these peoples.

Il•li•nois[2] (ĭl'ə-noi', -noiz'). A Midwestern state of the U.S. Pop. 11,113,976. Cap. Springfield. —**Il'li•nois'an** *adj. & n.*

il•lit•er•a•cy (ĭ-lĭt'ər-ə-sē) *n., pl.* **-cies. 1.** Inability to read and write. **2.** An error characteristic of this condition.

il•lit•er•ate (ĭ-lĭt'ər-ĭt) *adj.* **1.** Unable to read and write. **2. a.** Marked by inferiority to an expected standard of familiarity with language and literature. **b.** Violating prescribed standards of speech or writing. —**il•lit'er•ate** *n.*

ill-man•nered (ĭl'măn'ərd) *adj.* Impolite; rude.

ill-na•tured (ĭl'nā'chərd) *adj.* Disagreeable; surly.

ill•ness (ĭl'nĭs) *n.* Sickness.

il•log•i•cal (ĭ-lŏj'ĭ-kəl) *adj.* Contradicting logic. —**il•log'i•cal'i•ty** *n.* —**il•log'i•cal•ly** *adv.*

ill-starred (ĭl'stärd') *adj.* Ill-fated; unlucky.

ill-tem•pered (ĭl'tĕm'pərd) *adj.* Quarrelsome; irritable.

il•lu•mi•nate (ĭ-lo͞o'mə-nāt') *v.* **-nated, -nating. 1.** To provide or brighten with light. **2.** To decorate (a manuscript) with pictures or designs in brilliant colors. **3.** To clarify. **4.** To enlighten. [L *illūmināre*.] —**il•lu'mi•na'tion** *n.* —**il•lu'mi•na'tor** *n.*

illus. illustrated; illustration.

ill-use (ĭl'yo͞oz') *v.* To maltreat. —*n.* (ĭl'yo͞os'). Also **ill-us•age** (-yo͞o'sĭj). Bad or unjust treatment.

il•lu•sion (ĭ-lo͞o'zhən) *n.* **1.** An erroneous perception of reality. **2.** An erroneous concept; misconception. [< L *illūdere*, to mock.]

il•lu•sive (ĭ-lo͞o'sĭv) *adj.* Illusory. [< ILLUSION.] —**il•lu'sive•ness** *n.*

il•lu•so•ry (ĭ-lo͞o'sə-rē) *adj.* Of the nature of an illusion.

il•lus•trate (ĭl'ə-strāt', ĭ-lŭs'trāt') *v.* **-trated, -trating. 1. a.** To clarify by use of example or comparison. **b.** To exemplify. **2.** To provide (a text) with explanatory or decorative pictures, photographs, or diagrams. [L *illūstrāre*.] —**il'lus•tra'tor** *n.*

il•lus•tra•tion (ĭl'ə-strā'shən) *n.* **1. a.** The act of illustrating. **b.** The state of being illustrated. **2.** An explanatory example. **3.** Visual matter used to elucidate or ornament a text.

il•lus•tra•tive (ĭ-lŭs'trə-tĭv, ĭl'ə-strā'tĭv) *adj.* Serving to elucidate or exemplify. —**il•lus'tra•tive•ly** *adv.*

il•lus•tri•ous (ĭ-lŭs'trē-əs) *adj.* Eminent; celebrated; famous. —**il•lus'tri•ous•ly** *adv.* —**il•lus'tri•ous•ness** *n.*

ill will. Hostility; enmity.

il•ly (ĭl'lē) *adv. Regional.* Badly; ill.

ILO International Labor Organization.

ILS instrument landing system.

I'm (īm). Contraction of *I am.*

im•age (ĭm'ĭj) *n.* **1.** A sculptured likeness. **2.** An optically formed duplicate, counterpart, or other representative reproduction of an object. **3.** One that closely resembles another: *the image of his uncle.* **4.** The concept of someone or something that is held by or projected to the public. **5.** A personification of something specified: *He is the image of health.* **6.** A mental picture. **7.** A representation to the mind by speech or writing. —*v.* **-aged, -aging. 1.** To make a likeness of. **2. a.** To mirror; reflect. **b.** To project. **3.** To symbolize. **4.** To conjure up; imagine. [< L *imāgō*.]

im•age•ry (ĭm'ĭj-rē) *n., pl.* **-ries. 1.** Mental images. **2.** Diction conveying poetic images.

im•ag•i•na•ble (ĭ-măj'ə-nə-bəl) *adj.* Capable of being conceived of by the imagination. —**im•ag'i•na•bly** *adv.*

im•ag•i•nar•y (ĭ-măj'ə-nĕr'ē) *adj.* **1.** Existing only in the imagination. **2.** Of, involving, or being an imaginary number.

imaginary number. A complex number in which the real part is zero and the coefficient of the imaginary unit is not zero.

imaginary unit. The positive square root of −1.

im•ag•i•na•tion (ĭ-măj'ə-nā'shən) *n.* **1.** The process or power of forming a mental image of something that is not or has not been seen or experienced. **2.** Creativity or resourcefulness. **3.** Popular acceptation or belief. —**im•ag'i•na•tive** *adj.* —**im•ag'i•na•tive•ly** *adv.*

im•ag•ine (ĭ-măj'ən) *v.* **-ined, -ining. 1.** To form a mental picture of; fancy. **2.** To think; suppose. [< L *imāginārī*, to picture to oneself < *imāgō*, IMAGE.]

im•be•cile (ĭm'bə-sĭl, -səl) *n.* **1.** A feebleminded person. **2.** A dolt. [< L *imbēcillus*, "without support," feeble.] —**im'be•cile, im'be•cil'ic** (-sĭl'ĭk) *adj.* —**im'be•cil'i•ty** *n.*

im•bed. Variant of **embed.**

im•bibe (ĭm-bīb') *v.* **-bibed, -bibing. 1.** To consume by drinking. **2.** To take in; absorb. **3.** To assimilate in the mind. [< L *imbibere*, to drink in.] —**im•bib'er** *n.*

im•bro•glio (ĭm-brōl'yō) *n., pl.* **-glios. 1. a.** A confused or difficult situation; predicament; mess. **b.** A deeply embarrassing misunderstanding. **2.** A confused heap; a tangle. [It.]

im•brue (ĭm-bro͞o') *v.* **-brued, -bruing.** To stain or drench. [< OF *embruer*, to soak.]

im•bue (ĭm-byo͞o') *v.* **-bued, -buing. 1.** To dye or stain deeply. **2.** To permeate or pervade. [L *imbuere*, to moisten, stain.]

im•i•tate (ĭm'ə-tāt') *v.* **-tated, -tating. 1.** To copy or emulate. **2.** To mimic, ape, or counterfeit. **3.** To reproduce. **4.** To resemble. [L *imitārī*.] —**im'i•ta'tor** (-tā'tər) *n.*

im•i•ta•tion (ĭm'ə-tā'shən) *n.* **1.** An act of imitating. **2.** Something derived or copied from an original. **3.** A counterfeit.

im•i•ta•tive (ĭm'ə-tā'tĭv) *adj.* **1.** Of or involving imitation. **2.** Derivative; copied. **3.** Tending to imitate. **4.** Onomatopoeic. —**im'i•ta'tive•ly** *adv.* —**im'i•ta'tive•ness** *n.*

im•mac•u•late (ĭ-măk'yə-lĭt) *adj.* **1.** Spotless; pure. **2.** Free from sin or error. **3.** Impeccably clean. [< L *immaculātus*, not stained.] —**im•mac'u•late•ly** *adv.* —**im•mac'u•late•ness** *n.*

im•ma•nent (ĭm'ə-nənt) *adj.* **1.** Intrinsic to subjective reality. **2.** Dwelling at the inmost heart of nature and of the human soul. [< L *immanēre*, to remain in.] —**im'ma•nence** *n.*

im•ma•te•ri•al (ĭm'ə-tîr'ē-əl) *adj.* **1.** Having no material body. **2.** Inconsequential; trifling.

im•ma•ture (ĭm'ə-tyo͝or', -cho͝or') *adj.* **1.** Not fully grown or developed. **2.** Exhibiting less than normal maturity. —**im'ma•tur'i•ty** *n.*

im•meas•ur•a•ble (ĭ-mĕzh'ər-ə-bəl) *adj.* Vast; limitless. —**im•meas'ur•a•bly** *adv.*

im•me•di•a•cy (ĭ-mē'dē-ə-sē) *n.* **1.** Directness. **2.** Urgency.

im•me•di•ate (ĭ-mē'dē-ĭt) *adj.* **1.** Being without mediation or interposition; direct. **2.** Intuitive. **3.** Next in line or relation. **4.** Occurring or accomplished without delay; instant. **5.** Near to the present. **6.** Near at hand. [LL *immediātus*.] —**im•me'di•ate•ly** *adv. & conj.* —**im•me'di•ate•ness** *n.*

im•me•mo•ri•al (ĭm'ə-môr'ē-əl, -mōr'ē-əl) *adj.* Reaching beyond memory, tradition, or recorded history. —**im'me•mo'ri•al•ly** *adv.*

im•mense (ĭ-mĕns') *adj.* Vast; huge. [< L *immēnsus*, immeasurable.] —**im•mense'ly** *adv.* —**im•men'si•ty** *n.*

im•merse (ĭ-mûrs') *v.* **-mersed, -mersing. 1.** To plunge into a fluid. **2.** To baptize by submerging in water. **3.** To absorb; engross. [L *immergere*, to dip in.] —**im•mer'sion** *n.*

im•mi•grant (ĭm'ĭ-grənt) *n.* **1.** One who immigrates. **2.** An organism that appears where it was formerly unknown. —**im'mi•grant** *adj.*

im•mi•grate (ĭm'ĭ-grāt') *v.* **-grated, -grating.** To settle permanently in a foreign country. [L *immigrāre*, to remove into, go in.] —**im'mi•gra'tion** *n.*

im•mi•nent (ĭm'ə-nənt) *adj.* About to occur; impending. [< L *imminēre*, to project over or toward, threaten.] —**im'mi•nence** *n.* —**im'mi•nent•ly** *adv.*

im•mo•bile (ĭ-mō'bəl, -bēl') *adj.* **1. a.** Unable to move. **b.** Incapable of being moved. **2.** Not moving. —**im'mo·bil'i·ty** *n.* —**im·mo'bi·lize** *v.* (**-lized, -lizing**). —**im·mo'bi·li·za'tion** *n.*

im·mod·er·ate (ĭ-mŏd'ər-ĭt) *adj.* Extreme or excessive. —**im·mod'er·ate·ly** *adv.* —**im·mod'er·ate·ness, im·mod'er·a'tion** *n.*

im·mod·est (ĭ-mŏd'ĭst) *adj.* **1.** Lacking modesty: *immodest boasting.* **2.** Indecent; brazen. —**im·mod'est·ly** *adv.* —**im·mod'es·ty** *n.*

im·mo·late (ĭm'ə-lāt') *v.* **-lated, -lating.** To kill as a sacrifice. [L *immolāre.*] —**im'mo·la'tion** *n.*

im·mor·al (ĭ-môr'əl, ĭ-mŏr'-) *adj.* **1.** Contrary to established morality. **2.** Licentious or dissolute. —**im'mor·al'i·ty** (ĭm'ô-răl'ə-tē) *n.* —**im·mor'al·ly** *adv.*

im·mor·tal (ĭ-môrt'l) *adj.* **1.** Not subject to death. **2.** Having eternal fame; imperishable. **3.** Of or pertaining to immortality. —*n.* **1.** One exempt from death. **2.** One whose fame is enduring. **3. Immortals.** The gods of the Greek and Roman pantheon. —**im·mor'tal·ly** *adv.*

im·mor·tal·i·ty (ĭm'ôr-tăl'ə-tē) *n.* The quality or condition of being immortal, esp. eternal life.

im·mor·tal·ize (ĭ-môrt'l-īz') *v.* **-ized, -izing.** To make immortal.

im·mov·a·ble (ĭ-mo͞o'və-bəl) *adj.* **1.** Incapable of being moved. **2.** Unyielding; steadfast. **3.** Unimpressionable or impassive. —**im·mov'a·bil'i·ty** *n.* —**im·mov'a·bly** *adv.*

im·mune (ĭ-myo͞on') *adj.* **1. a.** Exempt. **b.** Not affected or responsive. **2.** Resistant to a disease. [L *immūnis.*] —**im·mu'ni·ty** *n.*

im·mu·nize (ĭm'yə-nīz') *v.* **-nized, -nizing.** To render immune. —**im'mu·ni·za'tion** *n.*

im·mure (ĭ-myo͝or') *v.* **-mured, -muring. 1.** To imprison. **2.** To entomb in a wall. [ML *immūrāre.*] —**im·mure'ment** *n.*

im·mu·ta·ble (ĭ-myo͞o'tə-bəl) *adj.* Not susceptible to change. [< L *immūtābilis.*] —**im·mu'ta·bil'i·ty** *n.* —**im·mu'ta·bly** *adv.*

imp (ĭmp) *n.* **1.** A mischievous child. **2.** A small demon. [< OE *impa,* young shoot, sapling < ML *impotus,* graft.]

imp. 1. imperative. **2.** imperfect. **3.** imperial. **4.** import; imported. **5.** important.

im·pact (ĭm'păkt') *n.* **1.** A collision. **2.** The effect of one thing upon another. —*v.* (ĭm-păkt'). **1.** To pack firmly together. **2.** To collide. [< L *impingere,* to strike against, IMPINGE.] —**im·pac'tion** *n.*

im·pact·ed (ĭm-păk'tĭd) *adj.* **1.** Wedged together at the broken ends. **2.** Placed in the alveolus in a manner prohibiting eruption into a normal position: *an impacted tooth.*

im·pair (ĭm-pâr') *v.* To diminish in strength, value, quantity, or quality. [< VL **impējōrāre,* to make worse.] —**im·pair'ment** *n.*

im·pa·la (ĭm-pä'lə) *n.* An African antelope with ridged, curved horns. [Zulu.]

im·pale (ĭm-pāl') *v.* **-paled, -paling. 1.** To pierce or fix by piercing with a sharp point. **2.** To execute by means of a stake driven upward through the body. [ML *impālāre.*] —**im·pale'ment** *n.* —**im·pal'er** *n.*

im·pal·pa·ble (ĭm-păl'pə-bəl) *adj.* **1.** Intangible. **2.** Imperceptible. —**im·pal'pa·bly** *adv.*

im·pan·el (ĭm-păn'əl) *v.* To enroll (a jury).

im·part (ĭm-pärt') *v.* **1.** To transmit. **2.** To disclose.

im·par·tial (ĭm-pär'shəl) *adj.* Unbiased; unprejudiced. —**im'par·ti·al'i·ty** (-shē-ăl'ə-tē) *n.* —**im·par'tial·ly** *adv.*

im·passe (ĭm'păs') *n.* **1.** A dead-end road; cul-de-sac. **2.** A deadlock or dilemma.

im·pas·si·ble (ĭm-păs'ə-bəl) *adj.* **1.** Not subject to pain. **2.** Impassive. [< LL *impassibilis.*] —**im·pas'si·bil'i·ty** *n.* —**im·pas'si·bly** *adv.*

im·pas·sioned (ĭm-păsh'ənd) *adj.* Filled with passion; ardent.

im·pas·sive (ĭm-păs'ĭv) *adj.* Revealing no emotion; expressionless. —**im·pas'sive·ly** *adv.* —**im'pas·siv'i·ty** *n.*

im·pa·tience (ĭm-pā'shəns) *n.* **1.** The inability to wait patiently. **2.** Restive eagerness, desire, or anticipation. —**im·pa'tient** *adj.* —**im·pa'tient·ly** *adv.*

im·peach (ĭm-pēch') *v.* **1.** To charge with malfeasance in office before a proper tribunal. **2.** To challenge or discredit. [< LL *impedicāre,* to entangle, put in fetters.] —**im·peach'a·ble** *adj.* —**im·peach'er** *n.* —**im·peach'ment** *n.*

im·pec·ca·ble (ĭm-pĕk'ə-bəl) *adj.* **1.** Irreproachable; flawless. **2.** Not capable of sin or wrongdoing. [L *impeccābilis,* not liable to sin.] —**im·pec'ca·bly** *adv.* —**im·pec'ca·bil'i·ty** *n.*

im·pe·cu·ni·ous (ĭm'pĭ-kyo͞o'nē-əs) *adj.* Lacking money; penniless. [IN- + L *pecūnia,* money.] —**im'pe·cu'ni·ous·ly** *adv.*

im·pe·dance (ĭm-pē'dəns) *n.* A measure of the total opposition to current flow in an alternating-current circuit. [< IMPEDE.]

im·pede (ĭm-pēd') *v.* **-peded, -peding.** To obstruct the way of; block. [L *impedīre,* to entangle, fetter.] —**im·ped'er** *n.*

im·ped·i·ment (ĭm-pĕd'ə-mənt) *n.* A hindrance; obstruction; block.

im·ped·i·men·ta (ĭm-pĕd'ə-mĕn'tə) *pl.n.* Objects, as provisions or baggage, that impede or encumber.

im·pel (ĭm-pĕl') *v.* **-pelled, -pelling.** To urge; compel. [L *impellere,* to drive on or against.]

im·pend (ĭm-pĕnd') *v.* **1.** To hang or hover menacingly. **2.** To be about to take place. [L *impendēre.*]

im·pend·ing (ĭm-pĕn'dĭng) *adj.* Approaching; imminent.

im·pen·e·tra·ble (ĭm-pĕn'ə-trə-bəl) *adj.* **1.** Not capable of being entered. **2.** Incomprehensible; inscrutable. —**im·pen'e·tra·ble·ness, im·pen'e·tra·bil'i·ty** *n.* —**im·pen'e·tra·bly** *adv.*

im·pen·i·tent (ĭm-pĕn'ə-tənt) *adj.* Not penitent; unrepentant. —**im·pen'i·tence** *n.*

im·per·a·tive (ĭm-pĕr'ə-tĭv) *adj.* **1.** Expressing a command or plea. **2.** Urgent or obligatory. [< L *imperāre,* "to prepare against (an occasion)," to command.] —**im·per'a·tive** *n.* —**im·per'a·tive·ly** *adv.*

im·per·cep·ti·ble (ĭm'pər-sĕp'tə-bəl) *adj.* Not perceptible or barely perceptible. —**im'per·cep'ti·ble·ness** *n.* —**im'per·cep'ti·bly** *adv.*

im·per·fect (ĭm-pûr'fĭkt) *adj.* **1.** Not perfect. **2.** Of or being a verb tense expressing continuous or incomplete action. —*n.* **1.** The imperfect tense. **2.** A verb in this tense. —**im·per'fect·ly** *adv.* —**im·per'fect·ness** *n.*

im·per·fec·tion (ĭm'pər-fĕk'shən) *n.* **1.** The quality or condition of being imperfect. **2.** A defect; flaw.

im·per·fo·rate (ĭm-pûr'fər-ĭt) *adj.* **1.** Not perforated; having no opening. **2.** Not perforated into perforated rows. —*n.* An imperforate stamp.

im·pe·ri·al[1] (ĭm-pîr'ē-əl) *adj.* **1.** Of or pertaining to an empire or emperor. **2.** Designating a nation or government having sovereign rights over colonies or dependencies. [< L *imperium,* command, EMPIRE.]

im·pe·ri·al[2] (ĭm-pîr'ē-əl) *n.* A pointed beard grown from the lower lip.

im·pe·ri·al·ism (ĭm-pîr'ē-ə-lĭz'əm) *n.* The policy of extending economic and political hegemony over other nations. —**im·pe'ri·al·ist** *n.* & *adj.* —**im·pe'ri·al·is'tic** *adj.*

im·per·il (ĭm-pĕr'əl) *v.* **-iled** or **-illed, -iling** or **-illing.** To endanger. —**im·per'il·ment** *n.*

im·pe·ri·ous (ĭm-pîr'ē-əs) *adj.* **1.** Domineering; overbearing. **2.** Urgent; pressing. [< L *imperium,* EMPIRE.] —**im·pe'ri·ous·ly** *adv.* —**im·pe'ri·ous·ness** *n.*

im·per·ish·a·ble (ĭm-pĕr'ĭ-shə-bəl) *adj.* Not perishable. —**im·per'ish·a·bly** *adv.*

im·per·ma·nent (ĭm-pûr'mə-nənt) *adj.* Not permanent; transient. —**im·per'ma·nence** *n.*

im·per·me·a·ble (ĭm-pûr'mē-ə-bəl) *adj.* Not permeable. —**im·per'me·a·bly** *adv.*

im·per·son·al (ĭm-pûr'sə-nəl) *adj.* **1.** Not personal. **2.** Exhibiting no emotion. —**im·per'son·al'i·ty** *n.* —**im·per'son·al·ly** *adv.*

im·per·son·ate (ĭm-pûr'sə-nāt') *v.* **-ated, -ating.** To act the character or part of. —**im·per'son·a'tion** *n.* —**im·per'son·a'tor** *n.*

im·per·ti·nence (ĭm-pûrt'n-əns) *n.* Insolence.

im·per·ti·nent (ĭm-pûrt'n-ənt) *adj.* **1.** Impudent; insolent. **2.** Not pertinent; irrelevant. —**im·per'ti·nent·ly** *adv.*

im·per·turb·a·ble (ĭm'pər-tûr'bə-bəl) *adj.* Not capable of being perturbed. —**im'per·turb'a·bil'i·ty** *n.* —**im'per·turb'a·bly** *adv.*

im·per·vi·ous (ĭm-pûr'vē-əs) *adj.* **1.** Incapable of being penetrated. **2.** Incapable of being affected. —**im·per'vi·ous·ly** *adv.*

im·pe·ti·go (ĭm'pə-tī'gō, -tē'gō) *n.* A contagious skin disease characterized by superficial pustules that burst and form characteristic thick yellow crusts. [L *impetīgō,* "an attack" < *impetere,* to attack.]

im·pet·u·os·i·ty (ĭm-pĕch'o͞o-ŏs'ə-tē) *n.* Also **im·pet·u·ous·ness** (-əs-nĭs). The quality or condition of being impetuous.

im·pet·u·ous (ĭm-pĕch'o͞o-əs) *adj.* **1.** Impulsive; brash. **2.** Having great impetus; rushing with violence. [< L *impetus,* IMPETUS.] —**im·pet'u·ous·ly** *adv.*

im·pe·tus (ĭm'pə-təs) *n., pl.* **-tuses. 1. a.** An impelling force; impulse. **b.** Something that incites; a stimulus. **2.** Force or energy associated with a moving body. [L, attack.]

im·pi·e·ty (ĭm-pī'ə-tē) *n., pl.* **-ties. 1.** The quality or state of being impious. **2.** An impious act. **3.** Undutifulness.

im·pinge (ĭm-pĭnj') *v.* **-pinged, -pinging. 1.** To collide; dash. **2.** To encroach; trespass. [L *impingere,* to push against.]

im·pi·ous (ĭm'pē-əs, ĭm-pī'-) *adj.* Not pious; irreverent. —**im'pi·ous·ly** *adv.*

imp·ish (ĭm'pĭsh) *adj.* Mischievous. —**imp'ish·ly** *adv.* —**imp'ish·ness** *n.*

im·pla·ca·ble (ĭm-plā'kə-bəl, -plăk'ə-bəl) *adj.* Inexorable. —**im·pla'ca·bly** *adv.*

im·plant (ĭm-plănt', -plänt') *v.* **1.** To fix or set firmly. **2.** To inculcate; instill. **3.** To insert or embed in living tissue.

im·plau·si·ble (ĭm-plô'zə-bəl) *adj.* Not plausible. —**im·plau'si·bil'i·ty, im·plau'si·ble·ness** *n.* —**im·plau'si·bly** *adv.*

im·ple·ment (ĭm'plə-mənt) *n.* A tool or utensil. —*v.* To carry into effect. [< L *implēre,* to fill up, fulfill.] —**im'ple·men·ta'tion** *n.*

im·pli·cate (ĭm'plĭ-kāt') *v.* **-cated, -cating. 1.** To involve intimately or incriminatingly. **2.** To imply. [L *implicāre.*] —**im'pli·ca'tion** *n.*

im·plic·it (ĭm-plĭs'ĭt) *adj.* **1.** Implied or understood. **2.** Inherent or contained in the nature of something. **3.** Having no doubts or reservations; unquestioning. [< L *implicāre,* to involve, IMPLICATE.] —**im·plic'it·ly** *adv.* —**im·plic'it·ness** *n.*

im·plode (ĭm-plōd') *v.* **-ploded, -ploding.** To undergo implosion.

im·plore (ĭm-plôr', -plōr') *v.* **-plored, -ploring.** To entreat; beseech. [L *implōrāre,* to invoke with tears.] —**im'plo•ra'tion** *n.*

im•plo•sion (ĭm-plō'zhən) *n.* A more or less violent collapse inward. [IN- (in) + (EX)PLOSION.]

im•ply (ĭm-plī') *v.* **-plied, -plying.** 1. To involve or suggest by logical necessity; entail. 2. To express indirectly. —See Usage note at **infer.** [< L *implicāre,* infold, involve, IMPLICATE.]

im•po•lite (ĭm'pə-līt') *adj.* Discourteous; rude.

im•pol•i•tic (ĭm-pŏl'ə-tĭk) *adj.* Not wise or expedient. —**im•pol'i•tic•ly** *adv.*

im•pon•der•a•ble (ĭm-pŏn'dər-ə-bəl) *adj.* Incapable of being weighed or measured with preciseness.

im•port (ĭm-pôrt', -pōrt', ĭm'pôrt', -pōrt') *v.* 1. To bring in from a foreign country for trade or sale. 2. To mean; signify. —*n.* (ĭm'pôrt', -pōrt'). 1. Meaning; signification. 2. Importance; significance. [< L *importāre,* to carry in.] —**im•port'a•ble** *adj.* —**im•port'er** *n.*

im•por•tance (ĭm-pôr'təns) *n.* The condition or quality of being important; significance; consequence.

im•por•tant (ĭm-pôr'tənt) *adj.* 1. Significant; noteworthy. 2. Having an air of importance. [< L *importāre,* to IMPORT.] —**im•por'tant•ly** *adv.*

im•por•ta•tion (ĭm'pôr-tā'shən, ĭm'pōr-) *n.* 1. The act or occupation of importing. 2. Something imported; import.

im•por•tu•nate (ĭm-pôr'cho͞o-nĭt) *adj.* Stubbornly or unreasonably persistent. —**im•por'tu•nate•ly** *adv.* —**im•por'tu•nate•ness** *n.*

im•por•tune (ĭm'pôr-t/y/o͞on', ĭm-pôr'chən) *v.* **-tuned, -tuning.** To beset with repeated and insistent requests. [< L *importūnus,* "without a port," unsuitable.] —**im'por•tu'ni•ty** *n.*

im•pose (ĭm-pōz') *v.* **-posed, -posing.** 1. To establish or apply as compulsory; levy. 2. To apply or make prevail by or as if by authority. 3. To obtrude. 4. To pass off on others. 5. To take unfair advantage of. [< L *impōnere,* to put on.] —**im•pos'er** *n.*

im•pos•ing (ĭm-pō'zĭng) *adj.* Impressive.

im•po•si•tion (ĭm'pə-zĭsh'ən) *n.* 1. The act of imposing. 2. Something imposed, as a tax, undue burden, etc.

im•pos•si•ble (ĭm-pŏs'ə-bəl) *adj.* 1. Not capable of existing or happening. 2. Unacceptable. 3. Having little likelihood of happening or being accomplished. 4. Not capable of being dealt with or tolerated; objectionable. —**im•pos'si•bil'i•ty** *n.* —**im•pos'si•bly** *adv.*

im•post (ĭm'pōst') *n.* A tax. [< L *impōnere,* IMPOSE.]

im•pos•tor (ĭm-pŏs'tər) *n.* A person who deceives under an assumed identity. [< L *impōnere,* IMPOSE.]

im•pos•ture (ĭm-pŏs'chər) *n.* Deception or fraud, esp. assumption of a false identity.

im•po•tent (ĭm'pə-tənt) *adj.* 1. Lacking physical strength or vigor. 2. Powerless; ineffectual. 3. Incapable of sexual intercourse. —**im'po•tence** *n.* —**im'po•tent•ly** *adv.*

im•pound (ĭm-pound') *v.* 1. To confine in a pound. 2. To seize and retain in legal custody.

im•pov•er•ish (ĭm-pŏv'ər-ĭsh) *v.* 1. To reduce to poverty. 2. To deprive of natural richness or strength. —**im•pov'er•ish•ment** *n.*

im•prac•ti•ca•ble (ĭm-prăk'tĭ-kə-bəl) *adj.* Not capable of being done or carried out.

im•prac•ti•cal (ĭm-prăk'tĭ-kəl) *adj.* 1. Unwise to implement or maintain in practice. 2. Incapable of dealing efficiently with practical matters. 3. Impracticable.

im•pre•cate (ĭm'prə-kāt') *v.* **-cated, -cating.** To invoke (evil or a curse) upon. [L *imprecārī.*] —**im'pre•ca'tion** *n.* —**im'pre•ca'tor** *n.*

im•pre•cise (ĭm'prĭ-sīs') *adj.* Not precise. —**im'pre•cise'ly** *adv.*

im•preg•na•ble (ĭm-prĕg'nə-bəl) *adj.* Able to resist capture or entry by force.

im•preg•nate (ĭm-prĕg'nāt') *v.* **-nated, -nating.** 1. To make pregnant; inseminate. 2. To fertilize (an ovum). 3. To fill throughout or saturate. —**im'preg'na'tion** *n.*

im•pre•sa•ri•o (ĭm'prə-sär'ē-ō', -sâr'ē-ō') *n., pl.* **-rios.** One who sponsors or produces entertainment, esp. the director of an opera company. [< It *imprendere,* to undertake.]

im•press¹ (ĭm-prĕs') *v.* 1. To produce or apply with pressure. 2. To mark or stamp with pressure. 3. To establish firmly in the mind. 4. To affect or influence deeply or forcibly. —*n.* (ĭm'prĕs'). 1. The act of impressing. 2. A mark or pattern produced by impressing. 3. A stamp or seal meant to be impressed.

im•press² (ĭm-prĕs') *v.* 1. To force into military service. 2. To confiscate.

im•pres•sion (ĭm-prĕsh'ən) *n.* 1. An imprint made on a surface by pressure. 2. An effect produced upon the mind. 3. A vague notion, remembrance, or belief.

im•pres•sion•a•ble (ĭm-prĕsh'ən-ə-bəl) *adj.* Readily influenced.

im•pres•sion•ism (ĭm-prĕsh'ə-nĭz'əm) *n.* A theory or style of painting, literature, or music which aims to reflect subjective impressions rather than objective reality. —**im•pres'sion•ist** *n. & adj.* —**im•pres'sion•is'tic** *adj.*

im•pres•sive (ĭm-prĕs'ĭv) *adj.* Commanding attention; making strong impressions. —**im•pres'sive•ly** *adv.* —**im•pres'sive•ness** *n.*

im•pri•ma•tur (ĭm'prə-mā'tər, -mä'tər) *n.* 1. Official approval or license to print or publish. 2. Official sanction; authorization. [< L *imprimere,* to print, impress.]

im•print (ĭm-prĭnt') *v.* To produce or impress (a mark or pattern) on a surface. —*n.* (ĭm'prĭnt'). 1. A mark or pattern produced by imprinting. 2. A distinguishing manifestation: *the imprint of defeat.* 3. The publisher's name, often with other information, printed on a title page. [< L *imprimere,* to impress.]

im•pris•on (ĭm-prĭz'ən) *v.* To put in or as if in prison. —**im•pris'on•ment** *n.*

im•prob•a•ble (ĭm-prŏb'ə-bəl) *adj.* Not probable; doubtful or unlikely. —**im•prob'a•bil'i•ty** *n.* —**im•prob'a•bly** *adv.*

im•promp•tu (ĭm-prŏmp't/y/o͞o) *adj.* Not rehearsed; extempore. [< L *in promptū,* in readiness.] —**im•promp'tu** *adv.*

im•prop•er (ĭm-prŏp'ər) *adj.* 1. Not suited to the given circumstances. 2. Unseemly; indecorous. 3. Not consistent with fact; incorrect. —**im•prop'er•ly** *adv.* —**im•prop'er•ness** *n.*

im•pro•pri•e•ty (ĭm'prə-prī'ə-tē) *n., pl.* **-ties.** 1. The quality of being improper. 2. An improper act or usage.

im•prove (ĭm-pro͞ov') *v.* **-proved, -proving.** 1. To make or become better. 2. To increase the productivity or value of (land). [NF *emprouer,* to turn to profit.]

im•prove•ment (ĭm-pro͞ov'mənt) *n.* 1. The act or procedure of improving. 2. The state of being improved. 3. A change or addition that improves.

im•prov•i•dent (ĭm-prŏv'ə-dənt) *adj.* Not providing for the future; thriftless. —**im•prov'i•dence** *n.* —**im•prov'i•dent•ly** *adv.*

im•pro•vise (ĭm'prə-vīz') *v.* **-vised, -vising.** 1. To invent, compose, or recite without preparation. 2. To make or provide from available materials. [< L *imprōvīsus,* not foreseen.] —**im•pro'vi•sa'tion** *n.* —**im•pro•vis'er** *n.*

im•pru•dent (ĭm-pro͞o'dənt) *adj.* Not prudent; unwise or injudicious. —**im•pru'dence** *n.*

im•pu•dent (ĭm'pyə-dənt) *adj.* Impertinent; rude; disrespectful. [< L *impudēns.*] —**im'pu•dence** *n.*

im•pugn (ĭm-pyo͞on') *v.* To oppose or attack as false; criticize; refute. [< L *impugnāre,* to fight against.] —**im•pugn'er** *n.*

im•pulse (ĭm'pŭls') *n.* 1. An impelling force or the motion it produces. 2. A sudden inclination or urge. 3. A motivating propensity; drive; instinct. 4. A transmission of energy from one neuron to another. [L *impulsus,* pp of *impellere,* IMPEL.]

im•pul•sive (ĭm-pŭl'sĭv) *adj.* 1. Inclined to act on impulse rather than thought. 2. Produced as a result of impulse; precipitate; uncalculated. 3. Having force or power to impel or incite; forceful. 4. *Phys.* Acting within brief time intervals. —**im•pul'sive•ly** *adv.* —**im•pul'sive•ness** *n.*

im•pu•ni•ty (ĭm-pyo͞o'nə-tē) *n.* 1. Exemption from punishment or penalty. 2. Immunity or preservation from recrimination, regret, etc. [< L *impūnis,* not punished.]

im•pure (ĭm-pyo͝or') *adj.* 1. Not pure or clean; contaminated. 2. Immoral or obscene. 3. Mixed with another substance; alloyed; adulterated. —**im•pure'ly** *adv.* —**im•pu'ri•ty** *n.*

im•pute (ĭm-pyo͞ot') *v.* **-puted, -puting.** To ascribe or attribute (a crime or fault) to another. [< L *imputāre,* to bring into the reckoning.] —**im•put'a•ble** *adj.* —**im•pu•ta'tion** *n.*

in (ĭn) *prep.* 1. a. Within the confines of; inside. b. Within the area covered by. 2. On. 3. As a part, aspect, or property of. 4. During. 5. At the position or business of. 6. After the pattern or form of. 7. Into. 8. Out of: *said in anger.* 9. As part of the act or process of: *in hot pursuit.* 10. With the attribute of: *in silence.* 11. a. By means of: *paid in cash.* b. Through the medium of. 12. Within the category of. 13. With reference to. —*adv.* 1. To or toward the inside or center. 2. Into a given place or position. 3. Indoors. 4. Into a given activity together: *joined in and sang.* 5. Inward: *caved in.* —*adj.* 1. Prestigious or appealing to a clique. 2. Available or at home: *He wasn't in.* 3. Incoming or incumbent. —*n.* 1. One in power or having the advantage. 2. *Informal.* Influence. [< OE *in, inn.* See **en.**]

in-.¹ *comb. form.* Not, lacking, or without. [< L.]

in-.² *comb. form.* 1. In, into, within, or inward. 2. Intensive action. 3. Causative function. [< L.]

-in. *comb. form.* 1. Enzyme: **rennin.** 2. Names of drugs and other pharmaceutical products: **aspirin.** 3. Variant of **-ine²**. [< L *-inus,* belonging to.]

in inch.

In indium.

in. inch.

in•a•bil•i•ty (ĭn'ə-bĭl'ə-tē) *n.* Lack of ability or means.

in ab•sen•ti•a (ĭn ăb-sĕn'shē-ə, -shə) *Latin.* In one's absence; while or although not present.

in•ac•ces•si•ble (ĭn'ăk-sĕs'ə-bəl) *adj.* Not accessible; unapproachable.

in•ac•cu•rate (ĭn-ăk'yər-ĭt) *adj.* 1. Not accurate. 2. Mistaken or incorrect. —**in•ac'cu•ra•cy** *n.* —**in•ac'cu•rate•ly** *adv.*

in•ac•tion (ĭn-ăk'shən) *n.* Lack or absence of action.

in•ac•tive (ĭn-ăk'tĭv) *adj.* 1. Not active or not tending to be active. 2. Retired from duty or

service. —**in•ac'tive•ly** *adv.* —**in'ac•tiv'i•ty** *n.*
in•ad•e•quate (ĭn-ăd'ĭ-kwĭt) *adj.* Not adequate; insufficient. —**in•ad'e•qua•cy** *n.*
in•ad•mis•si•ble (ĭn'əd-mĭs'ə-bəl) *adj.* Not admissible. —**in'ad•mis'si•bil'i•ty** *n.*
in•ad•ver•tent (ĭn'əd-vûr'tənt) *adj.* **1.** Not duly attentive. **2.** Accidental; unintentional. —**in'ad•ver'tence** *n.* —**in'ad•ver'tent•ly** *adv.*
in•ad•vis•a•ble (ĭn'əd-vī'zə-bəl) *adj.* Inexpedient; unwise; not recommended. —**in'ad•vis'a•bil'i•ty** *n.* —**in'ad•vis'a•bly** *adv.*
in•al•ien•a•ble (ĭn-āl'yə-nə-bəl) *adj.* Not to be transferred to another; not alienable. —**in•al'ien•a•bly** *adv.*
in•ane (ĭn-ān') *adj.* Lacking sense or substance; empty; silly: *an inane comment.* [L *inānis,* empty, vain.] —**in•an'i•ty** (-ăn'ə-tē) *n.*
in•an•i•mate (ĭn-ăn'ə-mĭt) *adj.* Not having the qualities associated with active, living organisms; not animate. —**in•an'i•mate•ly** *adv.*
in•ap•pli•ca•ble (ĭn-ăp'lĭ-kə-bəl) *adj.* Not applicable. —**in•ap'pli•ca•bil'i•ty** *n.*
in•ap•pre•ci•a•ble (ĭn'ə-prē'shē-ə-bəl) *adj.* Insignificant; negligible. —**in'ap•pre'ci•a•bly** *adv.*
in•ap•pre•ci•a•tive (ĭn'ə-prē'shə-tĭv, -shē-ā'-tĭv) *adj.* Showing no appreciation.
in•ap•pro•pri•ate (ĭn'ə-prō'prē-ĭt) *adj.* Not appropriate. —**in'ap•pro'pri•ate•ly** *adv.*
in•ar•tic•u•late (ĭn'är-tĭk'yə-lĭt) *adj.* **1.** Incomprehensible as speech or language. **2.** Unable to speak; speechless. **3.** Unable to speak with clarity or eloquence. **4.** Unexpressed: *inarticulate sorrow.* —**in'ar•tic'u•late•ly** *adv.* —**in'ar•tic'u•late•ness** *n.*
in•as•much as (ĭn'əz-mŭch'). Because of the fact that; since.
in•at•ten•tion (ĭn'ə-tĕn'shən) *n.* Lack of attention or notice; neglect. —**in'at•ten'tive** *adj.*
in•au•di•ble (ĭn-ô'də-bəl) *adj.* Incapable of being heard; not audible. —**in•au'di•bly** *adv.*
in•au•gu•ral (ĭn-ô'gyər-əl) *adj.* Of, relating to, or characteristic of an inauguration. —*n.* A speech made at an inauguration.
in•au•gu•rate (ĭn-ô'gyə-rāt') *v.* **-rated, -rating.** **1.** To induct into office by a formal ceremony. **2.** To begin or start officially. **3.** To open with a ceremony; dedicate. [L *inaugurāre,* to take omens from the flight of birds, to consecrate, install.] —**in•au'gu•ra'tion** *n.*
in•aus•pi•cious (ĭn'ô-spĭsh'əs) *adj.* Not auspicious; ill-omened. —**in'aus•pi'cious•ly** *adv.*
in•board (ĭn'bôrd', -bōrd') *adj.* **1.** Within the hull of a ship. **2.** Near the fuselage of an aircraft: *inboard engines.* —**in'board'** *adv.*
in•born (ĭn'bôrn') *adj.* Present at birth; inherited; hereditary.
in•bound (ĭn'bound') *adj.* Homeward bound or incoming.
in•bred (ĭn'brĕd') *adj.* **1.** Produced by inbreeding. **2.** Inborn; innate.
in•breed (ĭn'brēd', ĭn-brēd') *v.* To produce by the continued breeding of closely related individuals.
inc. **1.** incorporated. **2.** increase.
Inc. incorporated.
In•ca (ĭng'kə) *n., pl.* **-ca** or **-cas.** A member of a powerful Indian people that ruled Peru before the Spanish conquest.
in•cal•cu•la•ble (ĭn-kăl'kyə-lə-bəl) *adj.* **1.** Not calculable; indeterminate. **2.** Incapable of being foreseen; unpredictable; uncertain. —**in•cal'cu•la•ble•ness** *n.* —**in•cal'cu•la•bly** *adv.*
in•can•des•cent (ĭn'kən-dĕs'ənt) *adj.* **1.** Emitting visible light as a result of being heated. **2.** Shining brilliantly; very bright. —**in'can•des'cence** *n.* —**in'can•des'cent•ly** *adv.*
in•can•ta•tion (ĭn'kăn-tā'shən) *n.* **1.** A recitation of verbal charms or spells to produce a magical effect. **2.** The words, phrases, or sounds used in this manner. [< L *incantāre,* ENCHANT.]
in•ca•pa•ble (ĭn-kā'pə-bəl) *adj.* **1.** Not capable; not able. **2.** Legally unqualified; ineligible. —**in•ca'pa•bil'i•ty** *n.* —**in•ca'pa•bly** *adv.*
in•ca•pac•i•tate (ĭn'kə-păs'ə-tāt') *v.* **-tated, -tating.** **1.** To deprive of strength or ability. **2.** To make legally ineligible; disqualify. —**in'ca•pac'i•ta'tion** *n.*
in•ca•pac•i•ty (ĭn'kə-păs'ə-tē) *n., pl.* **-ties.** **1.** Lack of strength or ability. **2.** That which renders legally ineligible; disqualification.
in•cap•su•late. Variant of **encapsulate.**
in•car•cer•ate (ĭn-kär'sə-rāt') *v.* **-ated, -ating.** To put in jail. [L *incarcerāre.*] —**in•car'cer•a'tion** *n.* —**in•car'cer•a'tor** *n.*
in•car•nate (ĭn-kär'nĭt) *adj.* **1.** Invested with bodily nature and form. **2.** Personified: *wisdom incarnate.* —*v.* (ĭn-kär'nāt') **-nated, -nating.** **1.** To give bodily form to. **2.** To embody or personify. [LL *incarnāre,* to make flesh.] —**in'car•na'tion** *n.*
in•case. Variant of **encase.**
in•cen•di•ar•y (ĭn-sĕn'dē-ĕr'ē) *adj.* **1.** Of or involving arson. **2.** Producing intensely hot fire, as a military weapon. **3.** Tending to inflame; inflammatory. [< L *incendium,* burning.] —**in•cen'di•ar'y** *n.*
in•cense[1] (ĭn-sĕns') *v.* **-censed, -censing.** To infuriate; enrage. [< L *incendere,* to set on fire, enrage.]
in•cense[2] (ĭn'sĕns') *n.* **1.** An aromatic substance burned to produce a pleasant odor. **2.** The smoke or odor thus produced. [< L *incendere,* to set on fire.]
in•cen•tive (ĭn-sĕn'tĭv) *n.* Something inciting to action or effort. [< L *incentīvus,* that sets the tune, inciting.]
in•cep•tion (ĭn-sĕp'shən) *n.* The beginning of something. [< L *incipere,* to take in hand, begin.] —**in•cep'tive** *adj.*
in•cer•ti•tude (ĭn-sûr'tə-t/y/ōōd') *n.* **1.** Uncertainty; doubt. **2.** Insecurity or instability.
in•ces•sant (ĭn-sĕs'ənt) *adj.* Continuing without interruption; unceasing. —**in•ces'sant•ly** *adv.*
in•cest (ĭn'sĕst') *n.* Sexual union between persons so closely related that their marriage is illegal. [< L *incestus,* "unchaste."] —**in•ces'tu•ous** *adj.*
inch (ĭnch) *n.* A unit of length equal to $1/12$ of a foot. —*v.* To move by inches or small degrees. [< L *unica,* twelfth part, inch.]
in•cho•ate (ĭn-kō'ĭt) *adj.* **1.** In an initial or early stage; incipient. **2.** Lacking order or form. [< L *inchoāre,* to begin, orig "to harness."]
inch•worm (ĭnch'wûrm') *n.* A caterpillar that moves by alternately looping and stretching out its body.
in•ci•dence (ĭn'sə-dəns) *n.* The extent or frequency of the occurrence of something.
in•ci•dent (ĭn'sə-dənt) *n.* **1.** A definite, distinct occurrence; an event. **2.** A relatively minor occurrence that precipitates a crisis. —*adj.* **1.** Tending to arise or occur in connection with: *a melancholy incident to his profession.* **2.** Falling upon; striking: *incident radiation.* [< L *incidere,* to fall upon, happen to.]
in•ci•den•tal (ĭn'sə-dĕnt'l) *adj.* Occurring as a fortuitous or minor concomitant. —*n.* Often **incidentals.** A minor concomitant circumstance, expense, etc.
in•ci•den•tal•ly (ĭn'sə-dĕnt'l-ē) *adv.* **1.** Casually; by chance. **2.** Parenthetically.
in•cin•er•ate (ĭn-sĭn'ə-rāt') *v.* **-ated, -ating.** To consume by burning. [ML *incinerāre.*] —**in•cin'er•a'tion** *n.*
in•cin•er•a•tor (ĭn-sĭn'ə-rā'tər) *n.* A furnace or other apparatus for burning waste.
in•cip•i•ent (ĭn-sĭp'ē-ənt) *adj.* In an initial or early stage; just beginning to exist or appear. [L *incipiēns,* beginning.] —**in•cip'i•ence** *n.*
in•cise (ĭn-sīz') *v.* **-cised, -cising.** **1.** To cut into or mark with a sharp instrument. **2.** To cut (designs or writing) into a surface; engrave; carve. [<L *incīdere.*]
in•ci•sion (ĭn-sĭzh'ən) *n.* **1.** A surgical cut into soft tissue. **2.** The scar resulting from such a cut.
in•ci•sive (ĭn-sī'sĭv) *adj.* **1.** Cutting; penetrating. **2.** Trenchant. —**in•ci'sive•ly** *adv.*
in•ci•sor (ĭn-sī'zər) *n.* A tooth adapted for cutting.
in•cite (ĭn-sīt') *v.* **-cited, -citing.** To provoke to action; stir up or urge on. [< L *incitāre,* to urge.] —**in•cite'ment** *n.* —**in•cit'er** *n.*
incl. including; inclusive.
in•clem•ent (ĭn-klĕm'ənt) *adj.* **1.** Stormy. **2.** Severe or unmerciful. [L *inclēmēns.*] —**in•clem'en•cy** *n.*
in•cli•na•tion (ĭn'klə-nā'shən) *n.* **1.** The act of inclining. **2.** A slope; slant. **3.** A tendency; propensity. **4.** A preference or leaning.
in•cline (ĭn-klīn') *v.* **-clined, -clining.** **1.** To lean; slant; slope. **2.** To lower or bend (the head or body) in a nod or bow. **3.** To influence (someone or something) to have a certain preference; dispose. **4.** To tend toward a particular state or condition. —*n.* (ĭn'klīn'). An inclined surface; a slope. [< L *inclīnāre.*]
in•close. Variant of **enclose.**
in•clude (ĭn-klōōd') *v.* **-cluded, -cluding.** **1.** To have as part of a whole; contain. **2.** To consider with or put into a general category. [< L *inclūdere,* to shut in.] —**in•clu'sion** *n.*
in•clu•sive (ĭn-klōō'sĭv) *adj.* **1.** Taking everything into account; comprehensive. **2.** Including the limits specified: *from 11 to 20 inclusive.* —**in•clu'sive•ly** *adv.* —**in•clu'sive•ness** *n.*
in•cog•ni•to (ĭn-kŏg'nə-tō', ĭn'kŏg'nē'tō) *adv.* In a nonofficial capacity or with one's identity concealed. [< L *incognitus,* unknown.] —**in•cog'ni•to'** *adj.*
in•co•her•ent (ĭn'kō-hîr'ənt) *adj.* **1.** Not coherent; disordered; unconnected. **2.** Unable to express one's thoughts in an orderly manner. —**in'co•her'ence** *n.* —**in'co•her'ent•ly** *adv.*
in•com•bus•ti•ble (ĭn'kəm-bŭs'tə-bəl) *adj.* Incapable of burning.
in•come (ĭn'kŭm') *n.* Money received for labor or services, from the sale of property, or from investments. [ME, a coming in, entry.]
income tax. A graduated tax levied on annual income.
in•com•ing (ĭn'kŭm'ĭng) *adj.* **1.** Coming in; entering. **2.** About to take office: *the incoming president.*
in•com•men•su•rate (ĭn'kə-mĕn'shər-ĭt, -sər-ĭt) *adj.* Not commensurate; unequal; disproportionate: *a reward incommensurate with his efforts.* —**in'com•men'su•rate•ly** *adv.*
in•com•mode (ĭn'kə-mōd') *v.* **-moded, -moding.** To inconvenience; disturb. [< L *incommodus,* inconvenient.]
in•com•mo•di•ous (ĭn'kə-mō'dē-əs) *adj.* Inconvenient; uncomfortable.
in•com•mu•ni•ca•do (ĭn'kə-myōō'nĭ-kä'dō) *adj.* Without the means or right to communicate with others, as one held in confinement. —**in'com•mu'ni•ca'do** *adv.*
in•com•pa•ra•ble (ĭn-kŏm'pər-ə-bəl) *adj.* **1.**

Incapable of being compared. **2.** Beyond compare; unsurpassed; matchless.

in•com•pat•i•ble (ĭn′kəm-păt′ə-bəl) *adj.* Not compatible; inharmonious; antagonistic. **—in′com•pat′i•bil′i•ty** *n.* **—in′com•pat′i•bly** *adv.*

in•com•pe•tent (ĭn-kŏm′pə-tənt) *adj.* Not competent. *—n.* An incompetent person. **—in•com′pe•tence** *n.* **—in•com′pe•tent•ly** *adv.*

in•com•plete (ĭn′kəm-plēt′) *adj.* Not complete. **—in′com•plete′ly** *adv.*

in•com•pre•hen•si•ble (ĭn′kŏm-prĭ-hĕn′sə-bəl, ĭn-kŏm′-) *adj.* Not understandable; unintelligible. **—in′com•pre•hen′sion** *n.*

in•com•press•i•ble (ĭn′kəm-prĕs′ə-bəl) *adj.* Incapable of being compressed. **—in′com•press′i•bil′i•ty** *n.*

in•con•ceiv•a•ble (ĭn′kən-sē′və-bəl) *adj.* Incapable of being conceived of; unimaginable.

in•con•clu•sive (ĭn′kən-klo͞o′sĭv) *adj.* Not conclusive. **—in′con•clu′sive•ly** *adv.*

in•con•gru•ous (ĭn-kŏng′gro͞o-əs) *adj.* **1.** Inappropriate; out of place. **2.** Not harmonious; incompatible. **3.** Inconsistent; illogical. **—in′con•gru′i•ty** *n.* **—in•con′gru•ous•ly** *adv.*

in•con•se•quen•tial (ĭn-kŏn′sə-kwĕn′shəl) *adj.* Without consequence; lacking importance.

in•con•sid•er•a•ble (ĭn′kən-sĭd′ər-ə-bəl) *adj.* Small; unimportant.

in•con•sid•er•ate (ĭn′kən-sĭd′ər-ĭt) *adj.* Not considerate. **—in′con•sid′er•ate•ly** *adv.*

in•con•sis•tent (ĭn′kən-sĭs′tənt) *adj.* Not consistent; erratic; contradictory. **—in′con•sis′ten•cy** *n.* **—in′con•sis′tent•ly** *adv.*

in•con•sol•a•ble (ĭn′kən-sō′lə-bəl) *adj.* Incapable of being consoled.

in•con•spic•u•ous (ĭn′kən-spĭk′yo͞o-əs) *adj.* Not readily noticeable. **—in′con•spic′u•ous•ly** *adv.* **—in′con•spic′u•ous•ness** *n.*

in•con•stant (ĭn-kŏn′stənt) *adj.* **1.** Not constant. **2.** Fickle. **—in•con′stan•cy** *n.*

in•con•test•a•ble (ĭn′kən-tĕs′tə-bəl) *adj.* Indisputable; unquestionable. **—in′con•test′a•bil′i•ty** *n.* **—in′con•test′a•bly** *adv.*

in•con•ti•nent (ĭn-kŏn′tə-nənt) *adj.* Not continent; lacking self-restraint. **—in•con′ti•nence** *n.* **—in•con′ti•nent•ly** *adv.*

in•con•tro•vert•i•ble (ĭn′kŏn-trə-vûr′tə-bəl) *adj.* Indisputable; unquestionable.

in•con•ven•ience (ĭn′kən-vēn′yəns) *n.* **1.** The state of being inconvenient; trouble; difficulty. **2.** Something that causes difficulty, trouble, or discomfort. *—v.* **-ienced, -iencing.** To cause inconvenience to; trouble; bother.

in•con•ven•ient (ĭn′kən-vēn′yənt) *adj.* Not convenient; awkward; inopportune.

in•cor•po•rate (ĭn-kôr′pə-rāt′) *v.* **-rated, -rating.** **1.** To form or form into a legal corporation. **2.** To combine together into a united whole. [< LL *incorporāre,* to form into a body.] **—in•cor′po•ra′tion** *n.* **—in•cor′po•ra′tor** *n.*

in•cor•po•re•al (ĭn′kôr-pôr′ē-əl, -pōr′ē-əl) *adj.* Lacking material form or substance.

in•cor•rect (ĭn′kə-rĕkt′) *adj.* **1.** Not correct; erroneous. **2.** Improper; unbecoming. **—in′cor•rect′ly** *adv.* **—in′cor•rect′ness** *n.*

in•cor•ri•gi•ble (ĭn-kôr′ə-jə-bəl, ĭn-kŏr′-) *adj.* Incapable of being corrected or reformed. *—n.* A person that will not be tamed or corrected. **—in•cor′ri•gi•bly** *adv.*

in•cor•rupt•i•ble (ĭn′kə-rŭp′tə-bəl) *adj.* Incapable of being corrupted; not subject to bribery or corruption. **—in′cor•rupt′i•bly** *adv.*

in•crease (ĭn-krēs′) *v.* **-creased, -creasing.** To make or become greater or larger. *—n.* (ĭn′krēs′). **1.** Augmentation; enlargement; multiplication. **2.** The amount of such increase; increment. [< L *incrēscere,* to grow in or on.] **—in•creas′er** *n.* **—in•creas′ing•ly** *adv.*

in•cred•i•ble (ĭn-krĕd′ə-bəl) *adj.* Unbelievable. **—in•cred′i•ble•ness** *n.* **—in•cred′i•bly** *adv.*

in•cred•u•lous (ĭn-krĕj′ə-ləs) *adj.* **1.** Disbelieving; skeptical. **2.** Expressing disbelief. **—in′cre•du′li•ty** (-krə-d/y/o͞o′lə-tē) *n.*

in•cre•ment (ĭn′krə-mənt) *n.* **1.** An increase in number, size, or extent. **2.** Something added or gained. [< L *incrēmentum* < *incrēscere,* to INCREASE.]

in•crim•i•nate (ĭn-krĭm′ə-nāt′) *v.* **-nated, -nating.** To charge with or involve in a crime. **—in•crim′i•na′tion** *n.*

in•crust. Variant of **encrust.**

in•cu•bate (ĭn′kyə-bāt′, ĭng′-) *v.* **-bated, -bating.** **1.** To warm and hatch (eggs), as by bodily heat. **2.** To maintain in favorable environmental conditions for development. [L *incubāre,* to hatch, lie down upon.] **—in′cu•ba′tion** *n.* **—in′cu•ba′tive** *adj.*

in•cu•ba•tor (ĭn′kyə-bā′tər, ĭng′-) *n.* **1.** A cabinet in which a uniform temperature can be maintained, used in growing bacterial cultures. **2.** An apparatus for maintaining a premature infant in an environment of controlled temperature, humidity, and oxygen.

in•cu•bus (ĭn′kyə-bəs, ĭng′-) *n., pl.* **-buses** or **-bi** (-bī′). **1.** An evil spirit believed to descend upon sleeping women. **2.** A nightmare. [< L *incubāre,* to lie down upon, INCUBATE.]

in•cu•des. pl. of **incus.**

in•cul•cate (ĭn-kŭl′kāt′) *v.* **-cated, -cating.** To teach or impress by forceful urging; instill. [L *inculcāre,* to impress upon.] **—in•cul′ca′tion** *n.*

in•cul•pa•ble (ĭn-kŭl′pə-bəl) *adj.* Free from guilt; blameless.

in•cul•pate (ĭn-kŭl′pāt′) *v.* **-pated, -pating.** To incriminate. [LL *inculpāre.*]

in•cum•bent (ĭn-kŭm′bənt) *adj.* **1.** Required; obligatory. **2.** Holding a specified office. *—n.* A person who holds an office. [< L *incumbere,* to lean upon.] **—in•cum′ben•cy** *n.*

in•cu•nab•u•lum (ĭn′kyo͞o-năb′yə-ləm) *n., pl.* **-la** (-lə). A book printed in the earliest stages of movable type (before 1500). [< L *incūnābula,* swaddling clothes, cradle.]

in•cur (ĭn-kûr′) *v.* **-curred, -curring.** To become subject to; bring upon oneself. [L *incurrere,* to run into.]

in•cur•a•ble (ĭn-kyo͝or′ə-bəl) *adj.* Not curable, as a disease. **—in•cur′a•bly** *adv.*

in•cur•sion (ĭn-kûr′zhən, -shən) *n.* **1.** A sudden attack or invasion; a raid. **2.** A running or entering into. [< L *incurrere,* to run into, attack, INCUR.]

in•cus (ĭng′kəs) *n., pl.* **incudes** (ĭn-kyo͞o′dēz). An anvil-shaped bone in the middle ear.

ind. **1.** independence; independent. **2.** index. **3.** industrial; industry.

Ind. **1.** India. **2.** Indian. **3.** Indiana.

in•debt•ed (ĭn-dĕt′ĭd) *adj.* Obligated to another; beholden. **—in•debt′ed•ness** *n.*

in•de•cent (ĭn-dē′sənt) *adj.* Offensive to good taste; unseemly. **—in•de′cen•cy** *n.* **—in•de′cent•ly** *adv.*

in•de•ci•pher•a•ble (ĭn′dĭ-sī′fər-ə-bəl) *adj.* Incapable of being deciphered.

in•de•ci•sion (ĭn′dĭ-sĭzh′ən) *n.* Irresolution.

in•de•ci•sive (ĭn′dĭ-sī′sĭv) *adj.* Not decisive; vacillating; hesitant. **—in′de•ci′sive•ly** *adv.* **—in′de•ci′sive•ness** *n.*

in•dec•o•rous (ĭn-dĕk′ər-əs) *adj.* Lacking propriety or good taste; unseemly. **—in•dec′o•rous•ly** *adv.* **—in•dec′o•rous•ness** *n.*

in•deed (ĭn-dēd′) *adv.* **1.** Truly; certainly. **2.** In fact; in reality. **3.** Admittedly; unquestionably. *—interj.* Expressive of surprise, skepticism, or irony. [ME *in dede,* in reality.]

indef. indefinite.

in•de•fat•i•ga•ble (ĭn′dĭ-făt′ĭ-gə-bəl) *adj.* Untiring; tireless. **—in′de•fat′i•ga•bly** *adv.*

in•de•fen•si•ble (ĭn′dĭ-fĕn′sə-bəl) *adj.* **1.** Not capable of being defended. **2.** Inexcusable. **3.** Untenable. **—in′de•fen′si•bly** *adv.*

in•de•fin•a•ble (ĭn′dĭ-fī′nə-bəl) *adj.* Not capable of being defined, described, or analyzed. *—n.* Something that cannot be defined.

in•def•i•nite (ĭn-dĕf′ə-nĭt) *adj.* Not definite; unclear; uncertain. **—in•def′i•nite•ly** *adv.*

indefinite article. *Gram.* An article, as English *a* or *an,* that does not fix the identity of the noun it modifies.

in•del•i•ble (ĭn-dĕl′ə-bəl) *adj.* **1.** Making a mark not easily erased. **2.** Permanent; lasting. [L *indēlēbilis.*] **—in•del′i•bly** *adv.*

in•del•i•cate (ĭn-dĕl′ĭ-kĭt) *adj.* **1.** Offensive to propriety; coarse. **2.** Tactless. **—in•del′i•ca•cy** *n.* **—in•del′i•cate•ly** *adv.*

in•dem•ni•fy (ĭn-dĕm′nə-fī′) *v.* **-fied, -fying.** **1.** To protect against possible damage; insure. **2.** To make compensation to for incurred damage. **—in•dem′ni•fi•ca′tion** *n.*

in•dem•ni•ty (ĭn-dĕm′nə-tē) *n., pl.* **-ties.** **1.** Insurance against possible damage or loss. **2.** Compensation for damage or loss incurred; indemnification. [< L *indemnis,* unhurt.]

in•dent[1] (ĭn-dĕnt′) *v.* **1.** To notch or serrate the edge of; make jagged. **2.** To set in (the first line of a paragraph) from the margin. [ME *indenten,* to make a toothlike incision into.]

in•dent[2] (ĭn-dĕnt′) *v.* To press down upon so as to form an impression. *—n.* An indentation. [< IN- + DENT.]

in•den•ta•tion (ĭn′dĕn′tā′shən) *n.* **1.** The act of indenting or condition of being indented. **2.** A notch or jagged cut in an edge, as in certain leaves. **3.** A deep recess in a border, coastline, or other boundary. **4.** The blank space between a margin and the beginning of an indented line.

in•den•tion (ĭn-dĕn′shən) *n.* **1.** The act of indenting or the condition of being indented. **2.** The blank space between a margin and the beginning of an indented line.

in•den•ture (ĭn-dĕn′chər) *n.* **1.** A written contract. **2.** Often **indentures.** A contract binding one party into the service of another for a specified term. *—v.* **-tured, -turing.** To bind by indenture.

Independence Day. July 4, a holiday celebrating the adoption of the Declaration of Independence.

in•de•pend•ent (ĭn′dĭ-pĕn′dənt) *adj.* **1.** Politically autonomous; self-governing. **2.** Free from the influence, guidance, or control of others; self-reliant. **3.** Not committed to one political party. **4.** Not dependent on or affiliated with. **5.** Financially self-sufficient. *—n.* One that is independent, esp. a voter not committed to any one political party. **—in′de•pen′dence** *n.* **—in′de•pend′ent•ly** *adv.*

in-depth (ĭn′dĕpth′) *adj.* Detailed; thorough: *an in-depth study.*

in•de•scrib•a•ble (ĭn′dĭ-skrī′bə-bəl) *adj.* Beyond description. **—in′de•scrib′a•bil′i•ty** *n.* **—in′de•scrib′a•bly** *adv.*

in•de•struc•ti•ble (ĭn′dĭ-strŭk′tə-bəl) *adj.* Not capable of being destroyed; unbreakable. **—in′de•struc′ti•bil′i•ty, in′de•struc′ti•ble•ness** *n.* **—in′de•struc′ti•bly** *adv.*

in•de•ter•mi•na•ble (ĭn′dĭ-tûr′mə-nə-bəl) *adj.* Not capable of being ascertained or decided. **—in′de•ter′mi•na•bly** *adv.*

in•de•ter•mi•na•cy (ĭn′dĭ-tûr′mə-nə-sē) *n.*

The state or quality of being indeterminate.

in•de•ter•mi•nate (ĭn'dĭ-tûr'mə-nĭt) *adj.* **1.** Not precisely or quantitatively determined. **2.** Lacking clarity or precision. —**in'de•ter'mi•nate•ly** *adv.* —**in'de•ter'mi•nate•ness, in'de•ter'mi•na'tion** (-nā'shən) *n.*

in•dex (ĭn'dĕks') *n., pl.* **-dexes** or **-dices** (-də-sēz'). **1.** An alphabetized listing of the names, places, and subjects in a printed work, giving the page on which each can be found. **2.** Anything that reveals or indicates; a sign; token. **3.** A number or symbol used to indicate an operation or relationship involving a particular mathematical expression. **4.** A number derived from a formula used to characterize a set of data: *cost-of-living index.* —*v.* **1.** To furnish with an index. **2.** To enter (an item) in an index. [L, forefinger, indicator.]

index finger. The finger next to the thumb.

index of refraction. The ratio of the speed of light in a vacuum to the speed of light in a medium under consideration.

In•di•a (ĭn'dē-ə). **1.** A subcontinent of S Asia. **2.** A republic occupying most of this subcontinent. Pop. 476,278,000. Cap. New Delhi.

India

India ink. A black liquid ink.

In•di•an (ĭn'dē-ən) *n.* **1.** A native or inhabitant of India or the East Indies. **2.** A member of any of the aboriginal peoples of the Americas. —**In'di•an** *adj.*

In•di•an•a (ĭn'dē-ăn'ə). A Midwestern state of the U.S. Pop. 5,194,000. Cap. Indianapolis. —**In'di•an'i•an** *n.* & *adj.*

In•di•an•ap•o•lis (ĭn'dē-ə-năp'ə-lĭs). The capital of Indiana. Pop. 745,000.

Indian Ocean. The ocean between Africa and Australia.

Indian pipe. A waxy white woodland plant with scalelike leaves and a single nodding flower.

Indian summer. A period of mild weather occurring in late autumn or early winter.

In•dic (ĭn'dĭk) *n.* A branch of the Indo-European languages that includes Sanskrit. —**In'dic** *adj.*

indic. indicative.

in•di•cate (ĭn'dĭ-kāt') *v.* **-cated, -cating. 1.** To demonstrate or point out. **2.** To serve as a sign, symptom, or token of; signify. **3.** To suggest the necessity or advisability of. **4.** To state, disclose, or express briefly. [< L *index,* INDEX.] —**in'di•ca'tion** *n.*

in•dic•a•tive (ĭn-dĭk'ə-tĭv) *adj.* **1.** Serving to point out or indicate. **2.** *Gram.* Pertaining to or designating a verbal mood used to indicate that the denoted act or condition is an objective fact. —*n. Gram.* The indicative mood. —**in•dic'a•tive•ly** *adv.*

in•di•ca•tor (ĭn'dĭ-kā'tər) *n.* **1.** One that indicates, esp. a device used to monitor the operation or condition of a system. **2.** A substance such as litmus that indicates the presence, absence, or concentration of a substance, or the degree of reaction between two or more substances, by means of a characteristic change, esp. in color.

in•di•ces. Alternate *pl.* of **index.**

in•dict (ĭn-dīt') *v.* **1.** To accuse of a crime; charge. **2.** To make a formal accusation against by the findings of a grand jury. [< L *indīcere,* to proclaim.] —**in•dict'ment** *n.*

in•dif•fer•ent (ĭn-dĭf'ər-ənt) *adj.* **1.** Having no partiality or bias. **2.** Of no great importance; insignificant. **3.** Having no marked feeling for one way or the other. **4.** Having no particular interest in or concern for; apathetic. **5.** Neither good nor bad; mediocre. —**in•dif'fer•ence** *n.* —**in•dif'fer•ent•ly** *adv.*

in•dig•e•nous (ĭn-dĭj'ə-nəs) *adj.* Living naturally in an area; native. [< L *indigena,* native.]

in•di•gent (ĭn'də-jənt) *adj.* Lacking the means of subsistence; impoverished; needy. —*n.* A destitute or needy person. [< L *indigēre,* to lack.] —**in'di•gence** *n.* —**in'di•gent•ly** *adv.*

in•di•gest•i•ble (ĭn'dĭ-jĕs'tə-bəl, ĭn'dĭ-) *adj.* Difficult or impossible to digest.

in•di•ges•tion (ĭn'dĭ-jĕs'chən, ĭn'dĭ-) *n.* **1.** The inability to digest food. **2.** Discomfort or illness resulting from this.

in•dig•nant (ĭn-dĭg'nənt) *adj.* Feeling or expressing indignation. [< L *indignus,* unworthy.] —**in•dig'nant•ly** *adv.*

in•dig•na•tion (ĭn'dĭg-nā'shən) *n.* Anger aroused by something unjust.

in•dig•ni•ty (ĭn-dĭg'nə-tē) *n., pl.* **-ties.** An offense to one's dignity; affront.

in•di•go (ĭn'dĭ-gō') *n., pl.* **-gos** or **-goes. 1.** A plant that yields a blue dyestuff. **2.** A blue dye obtained from such a plant or produced synthetically. **3.** Dark blue. [< Gk *indikon (pharmakon),* "Indian (dye)."]

in•di•rect (ĭn'dĭ-rĕkt', -dī-rĕkt') *adj.* **1.** Not taking a direct course; roundabout. **2.** Not straight to the point; circumlocutory. **3.** Not immediate; secondary. —**in'di•rec'tion** *n.* —**in•di•rect'ly** *adv.*

indirect object. A grammatical object indirectly affected by the action of a verb.

in•dis•creet (ĭn'dĭs-krēt') *adj.* Lacking discretion; injudicious; imprudent.

in•dis•cre•tion (ĭn'dĭs-krĕsh'ən) *n.* **1.** Lack of discretión. **2.** An indiscreet act or remark.

in•dis•crim•i•nate (ĭn'dĭs-krĭm'ə-nĭt) *adj.* **1.** Not discriminating. **2.** Random; haphazard. **3.** Confused; motley. —**in'dis•crim'i•nate•ly** *adv.* —**in'dis•crim'i•nate•ness** *n.*

in•dis•pen•sa•ble (ĭn'dĭs-pĕn'sə-bəl) *adj.* Absolutely necessary; essential. —**in'dis•pen'sa•bil'i•ty** *n.* —**in'dis•pen'sa•bly** *adv.*

in•dis•posed (ĭn'dĭs-pōzd') *adj.* **1.** Mildly ill. **2.** Disinclined; unwilling. —**in'dis•po•si'tion** *n.*

in•dis•put•a•ble (ĭn'dĭs-pyōō'tə-bəl) *adj.* Beyond doubt; undeniable. —**in'dis•put'a•ble•ness** *n.* —**in'dis•put'a•bly** *adv.*

in•dis•sol•u•ble (ĭn'dĭ-sŏl'yə-bəl) *adj.* **1.** Impossible to break or undo; binding. **2.** Incapable of being dissolved, disintegrated, or decomposed. —**in'dis•sol'u•bly** *adv.*

in•dis•tinct (ĭn'dĭs-tĭngkt') *adj.* **1.** Not clearly delineated. **2.** Faint; dim. —**in'dis•tinct'ly** *adv.*

in•dis•tin•guish•a•ble (ĭn'dĭs-tĭng'gwĭ-shə-bəl) *adj.* **1.** Not readily perceptible. **2.** Without distinctive qualities.

in•di•um (ĭn'dē-əm) *n. Symbol* **In** A soft, malleable, silvery-white metallic element used as a plating over silver in making mirrors and in transistor compounds. Atomic number 49, atomic weight 114.82. [< L *indicum,* indigo.]

in•di•vid•u•al (ĭn'də-vĭj'ōō-əl) *adj.* **1.** Of or relating to a single human being. **2.** By or for one person: *an individual portion.* **3.** Existing as a distinct entity; single; separate. **4.** Distinguished by particular attributes; distinctive. **5.** Indivisible; inseparable. —*n.* **1.** A single person or organism considered separately. **2.** A particular person. [< L *indīviduus,* indivisible.] —**in'di•vid'u•al•ly** *adv.*

in•di•vid•u•al•ism (ĭn'də-vĭj'ōō-ə-lĭz'əm) *n.* **1.** Individuality. **2.** The doctrine that the interests of the individual take precedence over those of the state.

in•di•vid•u•al•ist (ĭn'də-vĭj'ōō-ə-lĭst) *n.* **1.** A person of independent thought and action. **2.** One who advocates individualism. —**in'di•vid'u•al•is'tic** *adj.*

in•di•vid•u•al•i•ty (ĭn'də-vĭj'ōō-ăl'ə-tē) *n.* **1.** The quality of being individual. **2.** The aggregate of distinguishing attributes of a person or thing.

in•di•vid•u•al•ize (ĭn'dĭ-vĭj'ōō-ə-līz') *v.* **-ized, -izing. 1.** To give individuality to. **2.** To consider individually; particularize. **3.** To modify to suit a particular individual.

in•di•vis•i•ble (ĭn'də-vĭz'ə-bəl) *adj.* Incapable of being divided. —**in'di•vis'i•bil'i•ty** *n.*

In•do•chi•na (ĭn'dō-chī'nə). A peninsula in SE Asia. —**In'do•chi'nese'** *adj.* & *n.*

in•doc•tri•nate (ĭn-dŏk'trə-nāt') *v.* **-nated, -nating. 1.** To instruct in a body of doctrine. **2.** To teach to accept a system of thought uncritically. —**in•doc'tri•na'tion** *n.*

In•do-Eu•ro•pe•an (ĭn'dō-yŏŏr'ə-pē'ən) *adj.* Belonging to or constituting a family of languages that includes the Germanic, Celtic, Italic, Baltic, Slavic, Greek, Armenian, Iranian, and Indic groups. —*n.* **1.** The Indo-European family of languages. **2.** Proto-Indo-European. See *Table of Indo-European Languages* on following pages. **3.** A member of the presumed prehistoric people who spoke Proto-Indo-European.

In•do-I•ra•ni•an (ĭn'dō-ĭ-rā'nē-ən, -ī-rā'nē-ən) *n.* The branch of Indo-European including Indic and Iranian. —**In'do-I•ra'ni•an** *adj.*

in•do•lent (ĭn'də-lənt) *adj.* Disinclined to work; habitually lazy. [LL *indolēns,* painless.] —**in'do•lence** *n.* —**in'do•lent•ly** *adv.*

in•dom•i•ta•ble (ĭn-dŏm'ə-tə-bəl) *adj.* Incapable of being overcome or subdued; unconquerable. [LL *indomitābilis,* untamable.]

In•do•ne•sia (ĭn'də-nē'zhə, -shə). A republic in the Malay Archipelago, comprising Java, Sumatra, part of Borneo, and other islands. Pop. 102,200,000. Cap. Djakarta, on Java.

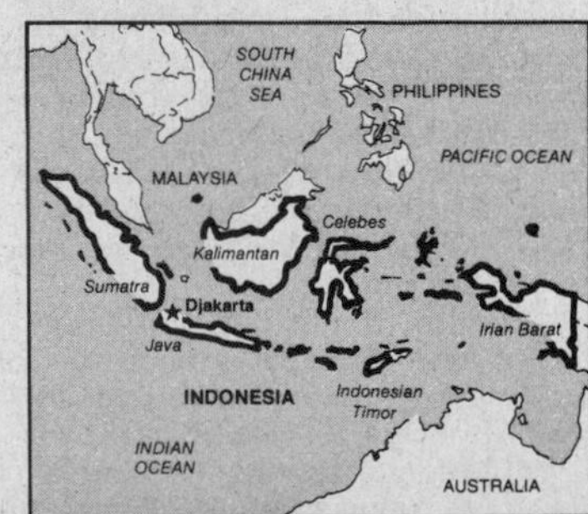

Indonesia

In•do•ne•sian (ĭn'də-nē'zhən, -shən) *n.* **1.** A native or inhabitant of Indonesia. **2.** The national language of Indonesia. —**In'do•ne'sian** *adj.*

in•door (ĭn'dôr', -dōr') *adj.* Pertaining to, situated in, or carried on within the interior of a house.

in•doors (ĭn-dôrz', -dōrz') *adv.* In or into a house or other building.

in•dorse. Variant of **endorse.**

in•du•bi•ta•ble (ĭn-d/y/o͞o'bə-tə-bəl) *adj.* Too apparent to be doubted; unquestionable. —**in•du'bi•ta•bly** *adv.*

in•duce (ĭn-d/y/o͞os') *v.* **-duced, -ducing. 1.** To persuade; prevail upon. **2.** To stimulate the occurrence of; cause. **3.** To infer by inductive reasoning. [< L *indūcere.*]

in•duce•ment (ĭn-d/y/o͞os'mənt) *n.* **1.** The act or process of inducing. **2.** An incentive; motive.

in•duct (ĭn-dŭkt') *v.* **1.** To place formally in office; install. **2.** To admit as a member of; initiate. **3.** To call into military service. [< L *indūcere,* to lead in, INDUCE.] —**in'duc•tee'** *n.*

in•duc•tance (ĭn-dŭk'təns) *n.* A circuit element, typically a conducting coil, in which electromotive force is generated by induction.

in•duc•tion (ĭn-dŭk'shən) *n.* **1.** The act of inducting or being inducted. **2. a.** The generation of electromotive force in a closed circuit by a varying magnetic flux through the circuit. **b.** The charging of an isolated conducting object by momentarily grounding it while a charged body is nearby. **3. a.** Reasoning from the particular to the general. **b.** *Math.* A deductive method of proof in which verification of a proposition consists of proving the first case and the case immediately following an arbitrary case for which the proposition is assumed to be correct.

in•duc•tive (ĭn-dŭk'tĭv) *adj.* **1.** Of or utilizing induction: *inductive method.* **2.** Of or arising from inductance. —**in•duc'tive•ly** *adv.*

in•due. Variant of **endue.**

in•dulge (ĭn-dŭlj') *v.* **-dulged, -dulging. 1.** To yield to the desires and whims of; pamper. **2.** To gratify; satisfy: *indulge a craving for chocolate.* **3.** To allow oneself some special pleasure (with *in*). [L *indulgēre,* to grant as a favor.] —**in•dulg'er** *n.*

in•dul•gence (ĭn-dŭl'jəns) *n.* **1.** The act of indulging or state of being indulgent. **2.** Something indulged in. **3.** Something granted as a favor or privilege. **4.** Liberal or lenient treatment; tolerance. **5.** *R.C.Ch.* The remission of temporal punishment due for a sin after the guilt has been forgiven.

in•dul•gent (ĭn-dŭl'jənt) *adj.* Given to indulgence; lenient. —**in•dul'gent•ly** *adv.*

In•dus (ĭn'dəs). A river of S Asia flowing through West Pakistan.

in•dus•tri•al (ĭn-dŭs'trē-əl) *adj.* **1.** Of or pertaining to industry. **2.** Having highly developed industries: *an industrial nation.*

in•dus•tri•al•ist (ĭn-dŭs'trē-ə-lĭst) *n.* One owning or managing an industrial enterprise.

in•dus•tri•al•ize (ĭn-dŭs'trē-ə-līz') *v.* **-ized, -izing. 1.** To develop industry in. **2.** To become industrial. —**in•dus'tri•al•i•za'tion** *n.*

in•dus•tri•ous (ĭn-dŭs'trē-əs) *adj.* Diligently active; assiduous in work or study. —**in•dus'tri•ous•ly** *adv.* —**in•dus'tri•ous•ness** *n.*

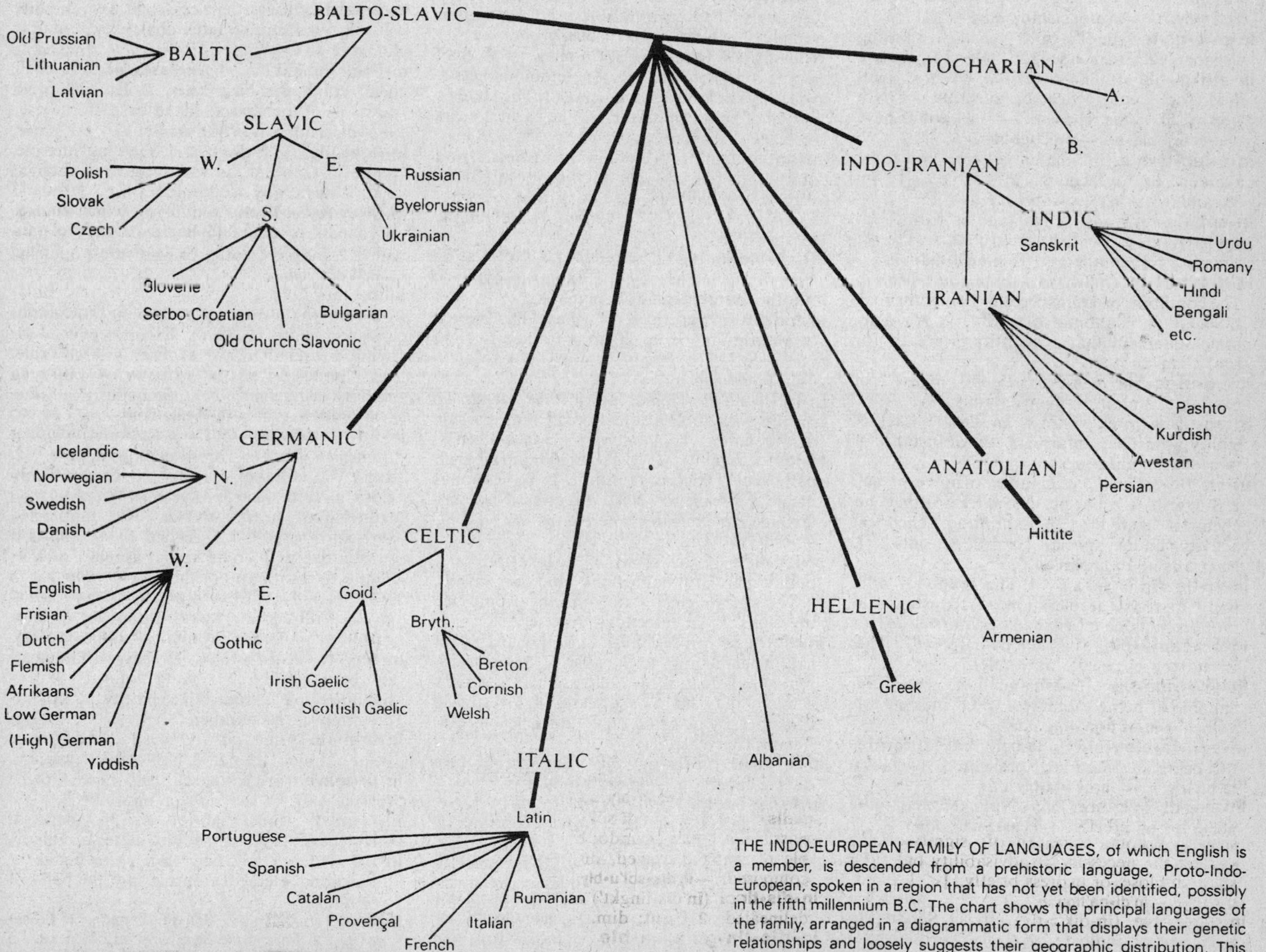

THE INDO-EUROPEAN FAMILY OF LANGUAGES, of which English is a member, is descended from a prehistoric language, Proto-Indo-European, spoken in a region that has not yet been identified, possibly in the fifth millennium B.C. The chart shows the principal languages of the family, arranged in a diagrammatic form that displays their genetic relationships and loosely suggests their geographic distribution. This Dictionary contains an Appendix listing some of the Indo-European roots underlying English words.

in•dus•try (ĭn'də-strē) *n., pl.* **-tries.** 1. The production and sale of goods and services. 2. A specific branch of manufacture and trade. 3. Industrial management as distinguished from labor. 4. Diligence; assiduity. [< L *industria,* skill.]

–ine¹. *comb. form.* Of, pertaining to, belonging to, or resembling: **crystalline.** [< Gk *-inos.*]

–ine², –in. *comb. form.* Halogens: **fluorine.** [< -INE.]

in•e•bri•ate (ĭn-ē'brē-āt') *v.* **-ated, -ating.** To make drunk; intoxicate. —*n.* (ĭn-ē'brē-ĭt). A drunkard. [L *inēbriāre.*] —**in•e'bri•a'tion** *n.*

in•ed•i•ble (ĭn-ĕd'ə-bəl) *adj.* Not suitable for food; not edible.

in•ef•fa•ble (ĭn-ĕf'ə-bəl) *adj.* 1. Beyond expression; indescribable: *ineffable delight.* 2. Not to be uttered; taboo: *the ineffable name of the Deity.* —**in•ef'fa•bly** *adv.*

in•ef•face•a•ble (ĭn'ĭ-fā'sə-bəl) *adj.* Not effaceable; indelible.

in•ef•fec•tive (ĭn'ĭ-fĕk'tĭv) *adj.* 1. Not effective; ineffectual. 2. Incompetent. —**in'ef•fec'tive•ly** *adv.* —**in'ef•fec'tive•ness** *n.*

in•ef•fec•tu•al (ĭn'ĭ-fĕk'cho͞o-əl) *adj.* 1. Unavailing; vain. 2. Powerless; impotent.

in•ef•fi•cient (ĭn'ĭ-fĭsh'ənt) *adj.* Not efficient; wasteful of time, energy, or materials. —**in'ef•fi'cien•cy** *n.* —**in'ef•fi'cient•ly** *adv.*

in•el•e•gant (ĭn-ĕl'ə-gənt) *adj.* 1. Lacking elegance. 2. Coarse; vulgar. —**in•el'e•gance** *n.*

in•el•i•gi•ble (ĭn-ĕl'ə-jə-bəl) *adj.* 1. Not qualified for some office or position. 2. Not worthy of being chosen. —**in•el'i•gi•bil'i•ty** *n.* —**in•el'i•gi•ble** *n.* —**in•el'i•gi•bly** *adv.*

in•e•luc•ta•ble (ĭn'ĭ-lŭk'tə-bəl) *adj.* Not to be avoided or overcome; inevitable. [L *inēluctābilis.*] —**in'e•luc'ta•bly** *adv.*

in•ept (ĭn-ĕpt') *adj.* 1. Not apt or fitting; inappropriate. 2. Foolish; absurd. 3. Awkward; clumsy. 4. Incompetent. —**in•ep'ti•tude'** *n.*

in•e•qual•i•ty (ĭn'ĭ-kwŏl'ə-tē) *n., pl.* **-ties.** 1. The condition or an instance of being unequal. 2. Social or economic disparity. 3. An algebraic statement that a quantity is greater (or less) than another.

in•eq•ui•ta•ble (ĭn-ĕk'wə-tə-bəl) *adj.* Not equitable; unfair. —**in•eq'ui•ta•bly** *adv.*

in•eq•ui•ty (ĭn-ĕk'wə-tē) *n., pl.* **-ties.** 1. Lack of equity; injustice; unfairness. 2. An instance of injustice or unfairness.

in•ert (ĭn-ûrt') *adj.* 1. Unable to move or act. 2. Sluggish; lethargic. 3. a. Exhibiting no chemical activity. b. Exhibiting chemical activity under special conditions only. [L *iners,* inactive, unskilled.]

in•er•tia (ĭn-ûr'shə) *n.* 1. The tendency of a body to resist acceleration. 2. Resistance to motion, action, or change. —**in•er'tial** *adj.*

in•es•cap•a•ble (ĭn'ə-skā'pə-bəl) *adj.* That cannot be escaped; inevitable.

in•es•ti•ma•ble (ĭn-ĕs'tə-mə-bəl) *adj.* 1. Incapable of being estimated. 2. Of incalculable value. —**in•es'ti•ma•bly** *adv.*

in•ev•i•ta•ble (ĭn-ĕv'ə-tə-bəl) *adj.* Incapable of being avoided or prevented. —**in•ev'i•ta•bil'i•ty** *n.* —**in•ev'i•ta•bly** *adv.*

in•ex•act (ĭn'ĭg-zăkt') *adj.* Not exact; not quite accurate or precise. —**in'ex•act'ly** *adv.*

in•ex•cus•a•ble (ĭn'ĭk-skyo͞o'zə-bəl) *adj.* Not excusable; unpardonable. —**in'ex•cus'a•ble•ness** *n.* —**in'ex•cus'a•bly** *adv.*

in•ex•haust•i•ble (ĭn'ĭg-zô'stə-bəl) *adj.* 1. Incapable of being used up. 2. Tireless; indefatigable. —**in'ex•haust'i•bly** *adv.*

in•ex•o•ra•ble (ĭn-ĕk'sər-ə-bəl) *adj.* Not capable of being persuaded by entreaty; relentless. —**in•ex'o•ra•bly** *adv.*

in•ex•pen•sive (ĭn'ĭk-spĕn'sĭv) *adj.* Not expensive; low-priced; cheap. —**in'ex•pen'sive•ly** *adv.* —**in'ex•pen'sive•ness** *n.*

in•ex•pe•ri•ence (ĭn'ĭk-spîr'ē-əns) *n.* Lack of experience. —**in'ex•pe'ri•enced** *adj.*

in•ex•pert (ĭn-ĕk'spûrt') *adj.* Not expert; unskilled. —**in•ex'pert'ly** *adv.*

in•ex•pi•a•ble (ĭn-ĕk'spē-ə-bəl) *adj.* Not capable of being expiated or atoned for.

in•ex•pli•ca•ble (ĭn-ĕk'splĭ-kə-bəl, ĭn'ĭk-splĭk'ə-bəl) *adj.* Not explicable; not possible to explain. —**in•ex'pli•ca•bly** *adv.*

in•ex•press•i•ble (ĭn'ĭk-sprĕs'ə-bəl) *adj.* Not capable of being expressed; indescribable. —**in'ex•press'i•bly** *adv.*

in•ex•tin•guish•a•ble (ĭn'ĭk-stĭng'gwĭ-shə-bəl) *adj.* Not capable of being extinguished.

in•ex•tri•ca•ble (ĭn-ĕk'strĭ-kə-bəl) *adj.* 1. Forming a tangle from which one cannot extricate oneself. 2. Too intricate or complicated to solve. —**in•ex'tri•ca•bly** *adv.*

inf. 1. infantry. 2. inferior. 3. infinitive. 4. information.

in•fal•li•ble (ĭn-făl'ə-bəl) *adj.* Incapable of erring or failing. —**in•fal'li•bil'i•ty, in•fal'li•ble•ness** *n.* —**in•fal'li•bly** *adv.*

in•fa•mous (ĭn'fə-məs) *adj.* 1. Having an exceedingly bad reputation. 2. Loathsome; grossly shocking. —**in'fa•mous•ly** *adv.*

in•fa•my (ĭn'fə-mē) *n., pl.* **-mies.** 1. A bad reputation; notoriety. 2. An infamous act.

in•fan•cy (ĭn'fən-sē) *n., pl.* **-cies.** 1. The state or period of being an infant. 2. The earliest years or stage of something.

in•fant (ĭn'fənt) *n.* A child in the earliest period of its life; a baby. —*adj.* 1. Of or for infants or very young children. 2. Young and growing: *an infant enterprise.* [< L *infāns,* "(one) unable to speak."]

in•fan•tile (ĭn'fən-tīl', -tĭl) *adj.* 1. Of or relating to infants or infancy. 2. Babyish; childish.

infantile paralysis. Poliomyelitis.

in•fan•try (ĭn'fən-trē) *n., pl.* **-tries.** The branch of an army made up of units trained to fight on foot. [< It *infante,* youth, foot soldier.] —**in'fan•try•man** *n.*

in•fat•u•ate (ĭn-făch'o͞o-āt') *v.* **-ated, -ating.** To inspire with foolish and unreasoning passion or attraction. [L *infatuāre.*] —**in•fat'u•a'tion** *n.*

in•fect (ĭn-fĕkt') *v.* 1. To contaminate with pathogenic microorganisms. 2. To communicate a disease to. 3. To affect as if by contagion: *His laughter infected us all.* [< L *inficere,* to work in, dye, taint.]

in•fec•tion (ĭn-fĕk'shən) *n.* 1. Invasion of a bodily part by pathogenic microorganisms. 2. The pathological state resulting from such invasion. 3. An infectious disease.

in•fec•tious (ĭn-fĕk'shəs) *adj.* 1. Capable of causing infection. 2. Capable of being transmitted by infection, as a disease. 3. Caused by a microorganism, as a disease. 4. Tending to spread easily or catch on. —**in•fec'tious•ly** *adv.* —**in•fec'tious•ness** *n.*

in•fec•tive (ĭn-fĕk'tĭv) *adj.* Capable of producing infection. —**in•fec'tive•ness** *n.*

in•fe•lic•i•tous (ĭn'fə-lĭs'ə-təs) *adj.* 1. Not happy; unfortunate; sad. 2. Inappropriate; inopportune. —**in'fe•lic'i•ty** *n.*

in•fer (ĭn-fûr') *v.* **-ferred, -ferring.** 1. To conclude from evidence; deduce. 2. To have as a logical consequence. [< L *inferre,* to bring in, introduce.] —**in•fer'a•ble** *adj.*

Usage: *Infer* and *imply,* in their most frequently used senses, are carefully distinguished in modern usage. To *imply* is to state indirectly, hint, or intimate. To *infer* is to draw a conclusion or make a deduction based on facts or indications. In these senses the words are not interchangeable.

in•fer•ence (ĭn'fər-əns) *n.* 1. The act or process of inferring. 2. Something inferred; a conclusion based on a premise. —**in'fer•en'tial** *adj.* —**in'fer•en'tial•ly** *adv.*

in•fe•ri•or (ĭn-fîr'ē-ər) *adj.* 1. Situated under or beneath. 2. Low or lower in order, degree, or rank. 3. Low or lower in quality. —*n.* A person of lesser rank or status than others. [< L *īnferus,* low.] —**in•fe'ri•or'i•ty** (-ôr'ə-tē, -ŏr'ə-tē) *n.*

in•fer•nal (ĭn-fûr'nəl) *adj.* 1. Of or relating to hell. 2. Abominable; damnable. [< LL *infernus,* hell < L, lower.]

in•fer•no (ĭn-fûr'nō) *n., pl.* **-nos.** 1. Hell. 2. Any place likened to hell.

in•fer•tile (ĭn-fûrt'l) *adj.* Not fertile; unproductive; barren.

in•fest (ĭn-fĕst') *v.* To overrun in large numbers so as to be harmful or unpleasant. [< L *infestus,* hostile.] —**in'fes•ta'tion** *n.*

in•fi•del (ĭn'fə-dəl, -dĕl') *n.* 1. One who has no religious beliefs. 2. One who does not accept a certain religion, esp. Christianity or Islam. [< L *infidēlis,* unfaithful.] —**in'fi•del** *adj.*

in•fi•del•i•ty (ĭn'fə-dĕl'ə-tē) *n., pl.* **-ties.** 1. Lack of religious faith. 2. Lack of fidelity; unfaithfulness.

in•field (ĭn'fēld') *n.* 1. The area of a baseball field within the base lines. 2. The defensive positions of first base, second base, third base, and shortstop. —**in'field'er** *n.*

in•fight•ing (ĭn'fī'tĭng) *n.* 1. Fighting at close range. 2. Conflict, as within an organization, that is generally concealed from outsiders.

in•fil•trate (ĭn-fĭl'trāt', ĭn'fĭl-) *v.* **-trated, -trating.** 1. To pass or cause (a liquid or gas) to pass into. 2. To pass, enter, or join surreptitiously. —**in'fil•tra'tion** *n.*

infin. infinitive.

in•fi•nite (ĭn'fə-nĭt) *adj.* 1. Having no boundaries or limits. 2. *Math.* Existing beyond or being greater than any arbitrarily large value. 3. Unlimited in spatial extent. 4. Continuing endlessly in time. —*n.* Something infinite. —**in'fi•nite•ly** *adv.* —**in'fi•nite•ness** *n.*

in•fin•i•tes•i•mal (ĭn'fə-nə-tĕs'ə-məl) *adj.* 1. Immeasurably or incalculably minute. 2. *Math.* Capable of having values arbitrarily close to zero. —**in'fin•i•tes'i•mal•ly** *adv.*

in•fin•i•tive (ĭn-fĭn'ə-tĭv) *n.* An uninflected verb form used: 1. Preceded by *to:* a. As a substantive with some verbal aspects, such as connection with an object: *To go willingly is to show strength.* b. In verb phrases: *He wished to go.* 2. With certain verbs without *to: He may go.* [< L *infinītus,* infinite.] —**in•fin'i•tive** *adj.*

in•fin•i•ty (ĭn-fĭn'ə-tē) *n., pl.* **-ties.** 1. The quality or condition of being infinite. 2. Unbounded space, time, or quantity. 3. An indefinitely large number.

in•firm (ĭn-fûrm') *adj.* 1. Weak in body, esp. from old age; feeble. 2. Not stable; insecure.

in•fir•ma•ry (ĭn-fûr'mə-rē) *n., pl.* **-ries.** A place for the care of the sick or injured.

in•fir•mi•ty (ĭn-fûr'mə-tē) *n., pl.* **-ties.** 1. Feebleness. 2. An unhealthy state; a malady.

in•fix (ĭn'fĭks') *n.* *Ling.* An inflectional or derivational element inserted into the body of a word.

in•flame (ĭn-flām') *v.* **-flamed, -flaming.** 1. To set on fire. 2. To arouse to strong emotion. 3. To intensify. 4. To produce or be affected by inflammation.

in•flam•ma•ble (ĭn-flăm′ə-bəl) *adj.* **1.** Tending to ignite easily; flammable. **2.** Easily aroused to strong emotion.

in•flam•ma•tion (ĭn′flə-mā′shən) *n.* Localized heat, redness, swelling, and pain as a result of irritation, injury, or infection.

in•flam•ma•to•ry (ĭn-flăm′ə-tôr′ē, -tōr′ē) *adj.* **1.** Arousing strong emotion. **2.** Characterized or caused by inflammation.

in•flate (ĭn-flāt′) *v.* **-flated, -flating. 1.** To fill and swell with a gas. **2.** To cause to increase or puff up. **3.** To raise or expand abnormally, as prices, wages, etc. [L *inflāre,* to blow into.]

in•fla•tion (ĭn-flā′shən) *n.* **1.** The act of inflating or state of being inflated. **2.** An abnormal increase in available currency and credit, resulting in a rise in price levels. **—in•fla′tion•ar′y** (-shə-nĕr′ē) *adj.*

in•flect (ĭn-flĕkt′) *v.* **1.** To alter (the voice) in tone or pitch; modulate. **2.** *Gram.* To subject to or be modified by inflection. [< L *inflectere,* to bend, warp, change.]

in•flec•tion (ĭn-flĕk′shən) *n.* **1.** An alteration in pitch or tone of voice. **2.** *Gram.* **a.** An alteration of the form of a word to indicate different grammatical and syntactic relations. **b.** An element added to a word to denote a grammatical function. **—in•flec′tion•al** *adj.*

in•flexed (ĭn-flĕkst′) *adj.* Bent or curved inward or downward, as petals or sepals.

in•flex•i•ble (ĭn-flĕk′sə-bəl) *adj.* **1.** Not flexible; rigid. **2.** Incapable of being changed; unalterable. **3.** Unyielding. **—in•flex′i•bil′i•ty** *n.* **—in•flex′i•bly** *adv.*

in•flict (ĭn-flĭkt′) *v.* **1.** To cause or carry out by aggressive action. **2.** To impose. **3.** To afflict. [L *inflīgere.*] **—in•flic′tion** *n.*

in•flu•ence (ĭn′flo͞o-əns) *n.* **1.** A power indirectly or intangibly affecting a person or course of events. **2. a.** Power to sway or affect based on prestige, wealth, etc. **b.** A person or thing exercising such power. *—v.* **-enced, -encing. 1.** To have power over; affect. **2.** To modify. [< L *influere,* to flow in.] **—in′flu•enc•er** *n.* **—in′flu•en′tial** (-ĕn′shəl) *adj.*

in•flu•en•za (ĭn′flo͞o-ĕn′zə) *n.* An acute infectious viral disease characterized by inflammation of the respiratory tract, fever, muscular pain, and intestinal irritation. [< ML *influentia,* influence.]

in•flux (ĭn′flŭks′) *n.* A flowing in. [< L *influere,* to flow in.]

in•fold (ĭn-fōld′) *v.* **1.** To fold inward. **2.** Variant of **enfold.** **—in•fold′er** *n.*

in•form (ĭn-fôrm′) *v.* **1.** To impart information to; tell. **2.** To disclose or give often incriminating information. [< L *informāre,* to give form to.] **—in•form′ant, in•form′er** *n.*

in•for•mal (ĭn-fôr′məl) *adj.* **1.** Completed or performed without ceremony or formality. **2.** Of, for, pertaining to, or appropriate to ordinary use; casual. **—in′for•mal′i•ty** (ĭn′fôr-măl′ə-tē) *n.* **—in•for′mal•ly** *adv.*

in•for•ma•tion (ĭn′fər-mā′shən) *n.* **1.** The act of informing or condition of being informed; communication of knowledge. **2.** Knowledge derived from study, experience, or instruction. **3.** Knowledge of a specific event or situation; news. **—in′for•ma′tion•al** *adj.*

in•form•a•tive (ĭn-fôr′mə-tĭv) *adj.* Providing information; instructive.

infra–. *comb. form.* **1.** Below; beneath. **2.** After; later. [L *infrā,* below, beneath.]

in•frac•tion (ĭn-frăk′shən) *n.* The act of breaching; infringement; violation.

in•fra•red (ĭn′frə-rĕd′) *adj.* Pertaining to electromagnetic radiation having wavelengths greater than those of visible light and shorter than those of microwaves.

in•fra•son•ic (ĭn′frə-sŏn′ĭk) *adj.* Generating or using waves or vibrations with frequencies below that of audible sound.

in•fre•quent (ĭn-frē′kwənt) *adj.* **1.** Not frequent; rare. **2.** Not steady; occasional. **—in•fre′quence** *n.* **—in•fre′quent•ly** *adv.*

in•fringe (ĭn-frĭnj′) *v.* **-fringed, -fringing. 1.** To break or ignore the terms or obligations of an agreement, law, etc.; violate. **2.** To trespass; encroach. [L *infringere.*] **—in•fringe′ment** *n.*

in•fu•ri•ate (ĭn-fyo͝or′ē-āt′) *v.* **-ated, -ating.** To make furious; enrage. [ML *infuriāre,* to enrage.]

in•fuse (ĭn-fyo͞oz′) *v.* **-fused, -fusing. 1.** To fill; imbue. **2.** To instill; inculcate. **3.** To steep or soak without boiling. [< L *infundere,* to pour in.] **—in•fus′er** *n.*

in•fus•i•ble (ĭn-fyo͞o′zə-bəl) *adj.* Incapable of being fused or melted; resistant to heat.

in•fu•sion (ĭn-fyo͞o′zhən) *n.* **1.** The act or process of infusing. **2.** An admixture. **3.** The liquid product obtained by infusing.

–ing[1]. *comb. form.* Used to form: **1.** The present participle of verbs: **hoping. 2.** Participial adjectives: **crippling. 3.** Adjectives resembling participial adjectives but not derived from verbs: **swashbuckling.** [< OE *-ende.*]

–ing[2]. *comb. form.* Used to form nouns from verbs, nouns, and other parts of speech. **1.** The act, process, or art of performing an action designated by a root verb: **thinking. 2.** The one that accomplishes such an action: **coating. 3.** Something necessary for the performance of such an action: **mooring. 4.** The result of such an action: **drawing. 5.** Belonging to or connected with the character of the noun root: **boarding. 6.** An action upon or involving the noun root: **sounding.** [< OE.]

in•gen•ious (ĭn-jēn′yəs) *adj.* **1.** Owing to or displaying ingenuity. **2.** Resourceful; clever. [< L *ingenium,* inborn talent, skill.]

in•gé•nue (ăn′zhə-n/y/o͞o′) *n.* **1.** An artless, innocent girl or young woman. **2.** An actress playing an ingénue. [< L *ingenuus,* INGENUOUS.]

in•ge•nu•i•ty (ĭn′jə-n/y/o͞o′ə-tē) *n.* Inventive skill or imagination; cleverness. [< L *ingenuus,* INGENUOUS.]

in•gen•u•ous (ĭn-jĕn′yo͞o-əs) *adj.* **1.** Without sophistication; artless; innocent. **2.** Open or honest; frank; candid. [L *ingenuus,* native, noble, honest.] **—in•gen′u•ous•ly** *adv.*

in•gest (ĭn-jĕst′) *v.* To take in by or as if by swallowing. [L *ingerere,* to carry in.] **—in•ges′tion** *n.*

in•glo•ri•ous (ĭn-glôr′ē-əs, ĭn-glōr′-) *adj.* Ignominious; dishonorable.

in•got (ĭng′gət) *n.* A mass of metal shaped for convenient storage or transportation. [< IN + OE *geotan,* to pour, cast in metal.]

in•grained (ĭn-grānd′) *adj.* **1.** Imbued; deep-seated: *ingrained faults.* **2.** Complete; utter.

in•grate (ĭn′grāt′) *n.* An ungrateful person. [< L *ingrātus,* ungrateful.]

in•gra•ti•ate (ĭn-grā′shē-āt′) *v.* **-ated, -ating.** To bring (oneself) purposely into the favor of another. **—in•gra′ti•a′tion** *n.*

in•grat•i•tude (ĭn-grăt′ə-t/y/o͞od′) *n.* Ungratefulness.

in•gre•di•ent (ĭn-grē′dē-ənt) *n.* **1.** Something added or required to form a mixture or compound. **2.** A component or constituent. [< L *ingredī,* to enter into.]

in•gress (ĭn′grĕs′) *n.* An entrance or entering. [< L *ingredī,* to enter into.]

in•grown (ĭn′grōn′) *adj.* Grown abnormally into the flesh.

in•gui•nal (ĭng′gwə-nəl) *adj.* Of or located in the groin. [< L *inguen,* groin.]

in•hab•it (ĭn-hăb′ĭt) *v.* To live or reside in. [< L *inhabitāre.*] **—in•hab′i•ta•ble** *adj.*

in•hab•i•tant (ĭn-hăb′ə-tənt) *n.* A permanent resident.

in•ha•la•tor (ĭn′hə-lā′tər) *n.* A device that produces a vapor to ease breathing or medicate by inspiration.

in•hale (ĭn-hāl′) *v.* **-haled, -haling.** To draw in by breathing; breathe in. [L *inhālāre.*] **—in•ha′lant** *adj.* & *n.* **—in′ha•la′tion** (ĭn′hə-lā′shən) *n.* **—in•hal′er** *n.*

in•here (ĭn-hîr′) *v.* **-hered, -hering.** To be inherent or innate. [L *inhaerēre.*]

in•her•ent (ĭn-hîr′ənt, -hĕr′ənt) *adj.* Existing as an essential part; intrinsic. **—in•her′ent•ly** *adv.*

in•her•it (ĭn-hĕr′ĭt) *v.* **1.** To receive, esp. by legal succession or will. **2.** To receive (a character or characteristic) genetically from an ancestor. [< L *inhērēditāre.*] **—in•her′it•a•ble** *adj.* **—in•her′i•tor** *n.*

in•her•i•tance (ĭn-hĕr′ə-təns) *n.* **1.** The act of inheriting. **2.** That which is inherited or to be inherited; legacy. **3. a.** The process of genetic transmission of characters or characteristics. **b.** The configuration of characters or characteristics so inherited.

in•hib•it (ĭn-hĭb′ĭt) *v.* **1.** To restrain; repress. **2.** To prohibit; forbid. [< L *inhibēre,* to restrain, hold in.] **—in′hi•bi′tion** *n.*

in•hib•i•tor (ĭn-hĭb′ə-tər) *n.* A substance used to retard or halt an undesirable reaction such as rusting.

in•hos•pi•ta•ble (ĭn-hŏs′pĭ-tə-bəl, ĭn′hŏ-spĭt′ə-bəl) *adj.* **1.** Unfriendly. **2.** Not affording shelter or sustenance; barren.

in•hu•man (ĭn-hyo͞o′mən) *adj.* **1.** Not human. **2.** Lacking kindness or sympathy; cruel. **3.** Not of ordinary human form.

in•hu•mane (ĭn′hyo͞o-mān′) *adj.* Not humane; lacking in pity or compassion.

in•hu•man•i•ty (ĭn′hyo͞o-măn′ə-tē) *n., pl.* **-ties. 1.** Lack of pity or compassion. **2.** An inhuman or cruel act.

in•im•i•cal (ĭn-ĭm′ĭ-kəl) *adj.* **1.** Harmful; adverse. **2.** Unfriendly; hostile. [< L *inimīcus,* enemy.] **—in•im′i•cal•ly** *adv.*

in•im•i•ta•ble (ĭn-ĭm′ĭ-tə-bəl) *adj.* Defying imitation; matchless. **—in•im′i•ta•bly** *adv.*

in•iq•ui•ty (ĭ-nĭk′wə-tē) *n., pl.* **-ties. 1.** Moral turpitude or sin; wickedness. **2.** A grossly immoral act; a sin. [< L *iniquus,* unjust.] **—in•iq′ui•tous** *adj.* **—in•iq′ui•tous•ly** *adv.*

in•i•tial (ĭ-nĭsh′əl) *adj.* Occurring first. *—n.* **1.** Often **initials.** The first letter or letters of a person's name. **2.** The first letter of a word. *—v.* **-tialed, -tialing.** To mark or sign with one's own initials. [< L *initium,* beginning.] **—in•i′tial•ly** *adv.*

in•i•ti•ate (ĭ-nĭsh′ē-āt′) *v.* **-ated, -ating. 1.** To begin or originate. **2.** To introduce (a person) to a new field, interest, skill, etc. **3.** To admit into membership, as with ceremonies. *—n.* (ĭ-nĭsh′ē-ĭt). **1.** One who has been initiated. **2.** A novice; beginner. **—in•i′ti•ate** (-ē-ĭt) *adj.* **—in•i′ti•a′tion** *n.* **—in•i′ti•a′tor** *n.*

in•i•ti•a•tive (ĭ-nĭsh′ē-ə-tĭv, -ē′ā-tĭv, -nĭsh′ə-tĭv) *n.* **1.** The ability to begin or follow through with a plan; enterprise. **2.** The first step or action; opening move. **3.** The procedure by which citizens can propose a law by petition and ensure its submission to the electorate.

in•ject (ĭn-jĕkt′) *v.* **1.** To force or drive (a fluid) into. 2. To introduce (a comment or new element) into conversation or consideration. [L *injicere,* to throw or put in.] —**in•jec'tion** *n.*

in•junc•tion (ĭn-jŭngk'shən) *n.* 1. A command, directive, or order. 2. A court order enjoining or prohibiting a party from a specific course of action. [< L *injungere,* to enjoin.]

in•jure (ĭn'jər) *v.* **-jured, -juring.** 1. To harm; hurt; damage. 2. To commit an offense against; wrong. —**in'jur•er** *n.*

in•ju•ry (ĭn'jə-rē) *n., pl.* **-ries.** 1. Damage of or to a person, property, reputation, or thing. 2. A specific damage or wound. [< L *injūrius,* unjust, wrongful.] —**in•ju'ri•ous** (ĭn-jo͝or'ē-əs) *adj.* —**in•ju'ri•ous•ly** *adv.*

in•jus•tice (ĭn-jŭs'tĭs) *n.* 1. Lack of justice. 2. A specific unjust act; a wrong.

ink (ĭngk) *n.* A pigmented liquid or paste used esp. for writing or printing. [< Gk *enkauston,* purple ink.]

ink•ling (ĭngk'lĭng) *n.* 1. A hint or intimation. 2. A vague idea or notion. [< ME *inkle,* to mutter.]

ink•well (ĭngk'wĕl') *n.* A small reservoir for ink.

ink•y (ĭng'kē) *adj.* **-ier, -iest.** 1. Of or containing ink. 2. Dark or murky. 3. Stained with ink.

in•laid (ĭn'lād', ĭn-lād') *adj.* Decorated with a pattern set into a surface.

in•land (ĭn'lənd) *adj.* 1. Of or located in the interior part of a land mass. 2. Operating or applying within the borders of a country. —*adv.* In, toward, or into the interior of a country. —*n.* The interior of a country.

in-law (ĭn'lô') *n.* Any relative by marriage. [< -IN-LAW.]

-in-law. *comb. form.* Parental, filial, or fraternal relation through marriage: **father-in-law.**

in•lay (ĭn-lā', ĭn'lā') *v.* To set into a surface to form a design. —*n.* (ĭn'lā'). 1. An inlaid object or design. 2. A solid filling, as of gold, fitted to a cavity in a tooth and cemented in place.

in•let (ĭn'lĕt, -lĭt) *n.* 1. A narrow channel or pocket of water. 2. A stream or bay leading inland.

in•mate (ĭn'māt') *n.* 1. A resident in a building. 2. A person confined to an institution, as a prison. [Perh INN + MATE.]

in•most (ĭn'mōst') *adj.* Innermost.

inn (ĭn) *n.* 1. A public lodging house; hotel. 2. A tavern or restaurant. [< OE. See **en.**]

in•nards (ĭn'ərdz) *pl.n. Informal.* 1. Internal bodily organs; viscera. 2. Any inner parts. [Var of INWARDS.]

in•nate (ĭ-nāt', ĭn'āt') *adj.* 1. Possessed at birth; inborn. 2. Possessed as an essential characteristic; inherent. [< L *innāscī,* to be born in.] —**in•nate'ly** *adv.* —**in•nate'ness** *n.*

in•ner (ĭn'ər) *adj.* 1. Located further inside. 2. Occurring within. 3. Pertaining to the soul or mind. 4. More exclusive, private, or important. [< OE *innera, innra.*]

inner city. The older, central part of a city, especially when characterized by crowded, rundown low-income neighborhoods.

in•ner-cit•y (ĭn'ər-sĭt'ē) *adj.* Of or in an inner city.

inner ear. The part of the ear that contains the semicircular canals and cochlea.

in•ner•most (ĭn'ər-mōst') *adj.* 1. Farthest within. 2. Most intimate.

in•ner•vate (ĭ-nûr'vāt', ĭn'ər-) *v.* **-vated, -vating.** To supply (a bodily part) with nerves. —**in'ner•va'tion** *n.*

in•ning (ĭn'ĭng) *n. Baseball.* A division or period of a game in which each team has a turn at bat. [< IN.]

inn•keep•er (ĭn'kē'pər) *n.* One who manages an inn.

in•no•cent (ĭn'ə-sənt) *adj.* 1. Uncorrupted by evil or wrongdoing; pure. 2. Not guilty of a crime. 3. Harmless. 4. Not experienced or worldly; naive. 5. Without deception or guile. [< L *innocēns.*] —**in'no•cence** *n.* —**in'no•cent** *n.* —**in'no•cent•ly** *adv.*

in•noc•u•ous (ĭ-nŏk'yo͞o-əs) *adj.* 1. Having no adverse effect; harmless. 2. Lacking import; insignificant. [< L *innocuus.*]

in•nom•i•nate bone (ĭ-nŏm'ə-nĭt). A large flat bone forming the lateral half of the pelvis; hipbone.

in•no•vate (ĭn'ə-vāt') *v.* **-vated, -vating.** To begin or introduce (something new). [L *innovāre,* to renew.] —**in'no•va'tion** *n.* —**in'no•va'tive** *adj.* —**in'no•va'tor** *n.*

in•nu•en•do (ĭn'yo͞o-ĕn'dō) *n., pl.* **-does.** An indirect, subtle, often derogatory implication. [< L *innuere,* to nod to.]

in•nu•mer•a•ble (ĭ-n/y/o͞o'mər-ə-bəl) *adj.* Too many to be counted.

in•oc•u•late (ĭ-nŏk'yə-lāt') *v.* **-lated, -lating.** To introduce the virus of a disease or other antigenic material into (the body) in order to immunize, cure, or experiment. [< L *inoculāre,* to engraft.] —**in•oc'u•la'tion** *n.*

in•of•fen•sive (ĭn'ə-fĕn'sĭv) *adj.* Giving no offense; unobjectionable.

in•op•er•a•ble (ĭn-ŏp'ər-ə-bəl) *adj.* 1. Not operable. 2. Not susceptible to surgery.

in•op•er•a•tive (ĭn-ŏp'ər-ə-tĭv) *adj.* Not working or functioning.

in•op•por•tune (ĭn-ŏp'ər-t/y/o͞on') *adj.* Inconvenient; ill-timed. —**in•op'por•tune'ly** *adv.*

in•or•di•nate (ĭn-ôrd'n-ĭt) *adj.* 1. Immoderate; unrestrained. 2. Not regulated; disorderly. [< L *inordinātus.*] —**in•or'di•nate•ly** *adv.*

in•or•gan•ic (ĭn'ôr-găn'ĭk) *adj.* 1. Involving neither organic life nor the products of organic life. 2. Relating to the chemistry of compounds not usually classified as organic. —**in'or•gan'i•cal•ly** *adv.*

in•pa•tient (ĭn'pā'shənt) *n.* A patient living in a hospital.

in•put (ĭn'po͝ot') *n.* Anything put into a system or expended in its operation to achieve a result or output.

in•quest (ĭn'kwĕst') *n.* 1. A judicial inquiry, usually before a jury. 2. An investigation.

in•qui•e•tude (ĭn-kwī'ə-t/y/o͞od') *n.* 1. Restlessness. 2. Uneasiness.

in•quire (ĭn-kwīr') *v.* **-quired, -quiring.** 1. To ask or ask about. 2. To examine closely; investigate. [< L *inquīrere.*] —**in•quir'er** *n.* —**in•quir'ing•ly** *adv.*

in•quir•y (ĭn'kwīr'ē, ĭn'kwə-rē) *n., pl.* **-ies.** 1. The act of inquiring. 2. A question; query. 3. A close examination.

in•qui•si•tion (ĭn'kwə-zĭsh'ən) *n.* 1. An official investigation, as an inquest. 2. **Inquisition.** A former Roman Catholic tribunal directed at the suppression of heresy. 3. Any severe scrutiny. —**in'qui•si'tion•al** *adj.* —**in•quis'i•tor** *n.*

in•quis•i•tive (ĭn-kwĭz'ə-tĭv) *adj.* 1. Unduly curious. 2. Eager to learn.

in•road (ĭn'rōd') *n.* 1. An invasion; raid; incursion. 2. An encroachment; intrusion.

in•rush (ĭn'rŭsh') *n.* A sudden rushing in; influx.

ins. insurance.

in•sane (ĭn-sān') *adj.* 1. Of, exhibiting, or afflicted with mental disorder. 2. Used by or for the mentally deranged. 3. Very foolish; wild. —**in•sane'ly** *adv.* —**in•san'i•ty** (-săn'ə-tē) *n.*

in•sa•tia•ble (ĭn-sā'shə-bəl, -shē-ə-bəl) *adj.* Incapable of being satiated.

in•sa•ti•ate (ĭn-sā'shē-ĭt) *adj.* Not satisfied; insatiable. —**in•sa'ti•ate•ly** *adv.*

in•scribe (ĭn-skrīb') *v.* **-scribed, -scribing.** 1. To write, print, or engrave (words or letters) on a surface. 2. To mark or engrave with words or letters. 3. To enter (a name) on a list. 4. To dedicate to another, as a book. 5. To enclose (a polygon or polyhedron) within a closed configuration of lines, curves, or surfaces so that every vertex of the enclosed figure is incident on the enclosing configuration. [L *inscrībere.*] —**in•scrib'er** *n.*

in•scrip•tion (ĭn-skrĭp'shən) *n.* 1. The act or an instance of inscribing. 2. That which is inscribed.

in•scru•ta•ble (ĭn-skro͞o'tə-bəl) *adj.* Impenetrable; enigmatic. —**in•scru'ta•bil'i•ty, in•scru'ta•ble•ness** *n.* —**in•scru'ta•bly** *adv.*

in•sect (ĭn'sĕkt') *n.* Any of numerous usually small, usually winged invertebrate animals having three pairs of legs and a three-segmented body. [< L *insecāre,* to cut into.]

in•sec•ti•cide (ĭn-sĕk'tə-sīd') *n.* A substance used to kill insects.

in•sec•tiv•o•rous (ĭn'sĕk-tĭv'ər-əs) *adj.* Feeding on insects.

in•se•cure (ĭn'sĭ-kyo͝or') *adj.* 1. Not secure or safe. 2. Unstable; shaky. 3. Apprehensive or lacking self-confidence. —**in'se•cure'ly** *adv.* —**in'se•cu'ri•ty, in'se•cure'ness** *n.*

in•sem•i•nate (ĭn-sĕm'ə-nāt') *v.* **-nated, -nating.** To introduce semen into the uterus of. —**in•sem'i•na'tion** *n.* —**in•sem'i•na'tor** *n.*

in•sen•sate (ĭn-sĕn'sāt', -sĭt) *adj.* 1. Inanimate. 2. Inhuman; unfeeling. 3. Lacking sense; foolish. —**in•sen'sate'ly** *adv.*

in•sen•si•ble (ĭn-sĕn'sə-bəl) *adj.* 1. Imperceptible; inappreciable. 2. Unconscious. 3. a. Unsusceptible to or unaffected by. b. Incognizant. c. Indifferent; callous. —**in•sen'si•bil'i•ty** *n.* —**in•sen'si•bly** *adv.*

in•sen•ti•ent (ĭn-sĕn'shənt) *adj.* Without sensation or consciousness. —**in•sen'ti•ence** *n.*

in•sep•a•ra•ble (ĭn-sĕp'ər-ə-bəl) *adj.* Incapable of being separated. —**in•sep'a•ra•bil'i•ty, in•sep'a•ra•ble•ness** *n.* —**in•sep'a•ra•bly** *adv.*

in•sert (ĭn-sûrt') *v.* 1. To put, place, or thrust into. 2. To introduce into; interpolate. —*n.* (ĭn'sûrt'). Something inserted or intended for insertion. [L *inserere.*] —**in•ser'tion** *n.*

in•set (ĭn-sĕt') *v.* To insert; set in. —**in'set'** *n.*

in•side (ĭn-sīd', ĭn'sīd') *n.* 1. The inner or interior part. 2. An inner side or surface. 3. **insides.** *Informal.* a. The inner organs; entrails. b. The inner parts or workings. 4. *Slang.* A position of confidence or influence. —*adj.* 1. Inner; interior. 2. For the interior. —*adv.* (ĭn'sīd'). Into or in the interior; within. —*prep.* (ĭn'sīd'). 1. Within: *inside an hour.* 2. Into: *go inside the house.*

in•sid•er (ĭn-sī'dər) *n.* One having a position of confidence or influence.

in•sid•i•ous (ĭn-sĭd'ē-əs) *adj.* 1. Working or spreading harmfully in a subtle or stealthy manner. 2. Intended to entrap; treacherous. 3. Sly; beguiling. [L *insidiōsus,* "lying in wait for."] —**in•sid'i•ous•ly** *adv.*

in•sight (ĭn'sīt') *n.* 1. The capacity to discern the true nature of a situation. 2. An elucidating glimpse.

in•sig•ni•a (ĭn-sĭg'nē-ə) *n., pl.* **-nia** or **-as.** Also **in•sig•ne** (-nē). 1. A badge of office, rank, etc.; emblem. 2. A distinguishing sign. [< L *insignis,* distinguished, marked.]

in•sig•nif•i•cant (ĭn'sĭg-nĭf'ĭ-kənt) *adj.* 1. Trivial. 2. Small. 3. Meaningless. —**in'sig•nif'i•**

cance *n.* —**in'sig•nif'i•cant•ly** *adv.*

in•sin•cere (ĭn'sĭn-sîr') *adj.* Not sincere; hypocritical. —**in'sin•cere'ly** *adv.* —**in'sin•cer'i•ty** (-sĕr'ə-tē) *n.*

in•sin•u•ate (ĭn-sĭn'yo͞o-āt') *v.* **-ated, -ating. 1. a.** To introduce gradually and insidiously. **b.** To edge or worm (oneself) by subtle and artful means. **2.** To hint covertly. [L *insinuāre,* to wind one's way into.] —**in•sin'u•a'tion** *n.*

in•sip•id (ĭn-sĭp'ĭd) *adj.* **1.** Lacking flavor or zest; tasteless. **2.** Uninteresting; dull; vapid. [LL *insipidus.*] —**in•sip'id•ly** *adv.*

in•sist (ĭn-sĭst') *v.* **1.** To keep resolutely to or emphasize an assertion, demand, or course. **2.** To assert or demand vehemently and persistently. [L *insistere,* to stand on.] —**in•sis'tence, in•sis'ten•cy** *n.* —**in•sis'tent** *adj.*

in•so•far (ĭn'sō-fär') *adv.* —**insofar as.** To such an extent.

in•sole (ĭn'sōl') *n.* **1.** The inner sole of a shoe or boot. **2.** An extra strip put inside a shoe for comfort.

in•so•lent (ĭn'sə-lənt) *adj.* **1.** Insulting in manner or speech; arrogant. **2.** Audaciously impudent. [< L *insolēns.*] —**in'so•lence** *n.*

in•sol•u•ble (ĭn-sŏl'yə-bəl) *adj.* **1.** Incapable of being dissolved. **2.** Incapable of being solved or explained. —**in•sol'u•bil'i•ty** *n.*

in•sol•vent (ĭn-sŏl'vənt) *adj.* Unable to meet debts or discharge liabilities; bankrupt. —**in•sol'ven•cy** *n.*

in•som•ni•a (ĭn-sŏm'nē-ə) *n.* Chronic inability to sleep. [< L *insomnis,* sleepless.] —**in•som'ni•ac'** (-ăk') *n.*

in•so•much (ĭn'sō-mŭch') *adv.* **1.** To such extent or degree. **2. insomuch as.** Since.

in•sou•ci•ant (ĭn-so͞o'sē-ənt) *adj.* Blithely indifferent; carefree. [F.] —**in•sou'ci•ance** *n.*

insp. inspected; inspector.

in•spect (ĭn-spĕkt') *v.* **1.** To examine carefully and critically. **2.** To review or examine officially. [< L *inspicere,* to look into.] —**in•spec'tion** *n.* —**in•spec'tor** *n.*

in•spi•ra•tion (ĭn'spə-rā'shən) *n.* **1.** The act of inspiring. **2.** The condition of being inspired. **3.** An inspiring agency or influence. **4.** Something that is inspired. **5.** Inhalation. —**in'spi•ra'tion•al** *adj.* —**in'spi•ra'tion•al•ly** *adv.*

in•spire (ĭn-spīr') *v.* **-spired, -spiring. 1.** To animate the mind or emotions of. **2.** To stimulate and influence. **3.** To elicit; create. **4.** To inhale. [< L *inspirāre,* to breathe into.]

in•spir•it (ĭn-spĭr'ĭt) *v.* To instill courage or life into; animate.

inst. 1. instant. **2.** institute; institution.

in•sta•bil•i•ty (ĭn'stə-bĭl'ə-tē) *n., pl.* **-ties.** Lack of stability.

in•stall (ĭn-stôl') *v.* Also **in•stal, -stalled, -stalling. 1.** To set in position and adjust for use. **2.** To put in an office, rank, or position. **3.** To establish (oneself or another) in a place or condition indicated. —**in'stal•la'tion** *n.*

in•stall•ment (ĭn-stôl'mənt) *n.* Also **in•stal•ment. 1.** One of several successive payments of a debt. **2.** A portion of anything issued or presented at intervals.

in•stance (ĭn'stəns) *n.* **1.** A case or example. **2.** A step in a series of events; occasion. **3.** A prompting; request. —*v.* **-stanced, -stancing.** To offer as an example; cite.

in•stant (ĭn'stənt) *n.* **1.** A very brief time; a moment. **2.** A particular point in time. —*adj.* **1.** Immediate. **2.** Imperative; urgent. **3.** Prepared for rapid completion with minimal effort. [< L *instāre,* to stand upon, be present.]

in•stan•ta•ne•ous (ĭn'stən-tā'nē-əs) *adj.* Occurring without perceptible delay or at a specific instant. —**in'stan•ta'ne•ous•ly** *adv.*

in•stant•ly (ĭn'stənt-lē) *adv.* At once.

in•stead (ĭn-stĕd') *adv.* As an alternative or substitute. —**instead of.** In lieu of; rather than. [< IN + STEAD.]

in•step (ĭn'stĕp') *n.* The arched medial portion of the human foot. [Prob IN + STEP.]

in•sti•gate (ĭn'stĭ-gāt') *v.* **-gated, -gating. 1.** To urge on; goad. **2.** To incite. [L *instīgāre.*] —**in'sti•ga'tion** *n.* —**in'sti•ga'tor** *n.*

in•still (ĭn-stĭl') *v.* Also **in•stil, -stilled, -stilling. 1.** To introduce gradually; implant. **2.** To pour in drop by drop. [L *instillāre,* to drip in.] —**in•still'er** *n.* —**in•still'ment** *n.*

in•stinct (ĭn'stĭngkt') *n.* **1. a.** The innate aspect of behavior that is unlearned, complex, and normally adaptive. **b.** A powerful motivation or impulse. **2.** An innate aptitude. [< L *instinguere,* to instigate, urge on.] —**in•stinc'tive** *adj.* —**in•stinc'tive•ly** *adv.* —**in•stinc'tu•al** (-cho͞o-əl) *adj.*

in•sti•tute (ĭn'stə-t/y/o͞ot') *v.* **-tuted, -tuting. 1. a.** To establish; organize. **b.** To initiate; begin. **2.** To invest in a position. —*n.* **1.** An authoritative principle. **2.** An organization founded to promote some cause. **3.** An educational institution. **4.** A seminar or workshop. [< L *instituere,* to establish, ordain.]

in•sti•tu•tion (ĭn'stə-t/y/o͞o'shən) *n.* **1.** The act of instituting. **2.** An established custom or practice. **3. a.** An organization, esp. one dedicated to public service. **b.** The building or buildings housing such an organization. **4.** A place of confinement, as a mental asylum. —**in'sti•tu'tion•al** *adj.*

in•sti•tu•tion•al•ize (ĭn'stə-t/y/o͞o'shən-ə-līz') *v.* **-ized, -izing. 1.** To make into an institution. **2.** To confine in an institution.

instr. 1. instructor. **2.** instrument.

in•struct (ĭn-strŭkt') *v.* **1.** To teach; educate. **2.** To direct; give orders to. [< L *instruere,* to build, prepare, instruct.] —**in•struc'tive** *adj.*

in•struc•tion (ĭn-strŭk'shən) *n.* **1.** The act or practice of instructing; education. **2. a.** Imparted knowledge. **b.** A lesson. **3. instructions.** Directions; orders. —**in•struc'tion•al** *adj.*

in•struc•tor (ĭn-strŭk'tər) *n.* One who instructs, esp. a college teacher below the rank of assistant professor. —**in•struc'tor•ship'** *n.*

in•stru•ment (ĭn'strə-mənt) *n.* **1.** A means by which something is done. **2.** A usually small precision tool. **3.** A recording or measuring device functioning as part of a control system. **4.** A device for producing music. **5.** A legal document. —*v.* **1.** To equip with instruments. **2.** To address a legal document to. [< L *instruere,* to prepare, INSTRUCT.]

in•stru•men•tal (ĭn'strə-mĕnt'l) *adj.* **1.** Serving as an instrument. **2.** Pertaining to or accomplished with an instrument. **3.** Performed on or written for a musical instrument. —**in'stru•men'tal•ly** *adv.*

in•stru•men•tal•ist (ĭn-strə-mĕnt'l-ĭst) *n.* One who plays a musical instrument.

in•stru•men•tal•i•ty (ĭn'strə-mĕn-tăl'ə-tē) *n., pl.* **-ties.** Agency; means.

in•stru•men•ta•tion (ĭn'strə-mĕn-tā'shən) *n.* **1.** The application or use of instruments. **2.** The arrangement or composition of music for instruments.

in•sub•or•di•nate (ĭn'sə-bôrd'n-ĭt) *adj.* Not submissive to authority. —**in'sub•or'di•nate•ly** *adv.* —**in'sub•or'di•na'tion** *n.*

in•sub•stan•tial (ĭn'səb-stăn'shəl) *adj.* **1.** Imaginary. **2.** Not firm or solid.

in•suf•fer•a•ble (ĭn-sŭf'ər-ə-bəl) *adj.* Not endurable; intolerable. —**in•suf'fer•a•bly** *adv.*

in•suf•fi•cient (ĭn'sə-fĭsh'ənt) *adj.* Not sufficient; inadequate. —**in'suf•fi'cien•cy** *n.*

in•su•lar (ĭn'sə-lər, ĭns'yə-) *adj.* **1.** Of, constituting, or characteristic of an island or island life. **2.** Circumscribed and detached in outlook and experience. [< L *īnsula,* island.] —**in'su•lar'i•ty** (-lăr'ə-tē) *n.*

in•su•late (ĭn'sə-lāt', ĭns'yə-) *v.* **-lated, -lating. 1.** To detach; isolate. **2.** To prevent the passage of heat, electricity, or sound into or out of (a body or region), esp. by interposition of an appropriate insulator. [< L *īnsula,* island.] —**in'su•la'tion** *n.*

in•su•la•tor (ĭn'sə-lā'tər, ĭns'yə-) *n.* A material or device that insulates.

in•su•lin (ĭn'sə-lən, ĭns'yə-) *n.* A pancreatic hormone that regulates carbohydrate metabolism by controlling blood glucose levels. [< L *insula,* island.]

in•sult (ĭn-sŭlt') *v.* To speak to or treat in a callous or contemptuous way. —*n.* (ĭn'sŭlt'). An offensive remark or act. [< L *insultāre,* to leap on, jump over.]

in•su•per•a•ble (ĭn-so͞o'pər-ə-bəl) *adj.* Incapable of being overcome; insurmountable. —**in•su'per•a•bly** *adv.*

in•sup•port•a•ble (ĭn'sə-pôr'tə-bəl, -pōr'tə-bəl) *adj.* **1.** Unbearable; intolerable. **2.** Unjustifiable.

in•sur•ance (ĭn-sho͝or'əns) *n.* **1. a.** The act, business, or means of insuring persons or property. **b.** The state of being insured. **2.** A contract binding a company to indemnify an insured party against specified loss. **3.** The sum for which something is insured.

in•sure (ĭn-sho͝or') *v.* **-sured, -suring. 1.** To protect against loss, damage, etc., with insurance. **2.** Also **en•sure** (ĕn-). To guarantee. [< NF *enseurer,* to guarantee.] —**in•sur'er** *n.*

in•sur•gent (ĭn-sûr'jənt) *adj.* Rising in revolt against civil authority or a government in power. —*n.* One who revolts against authority. [< L *insurgere,* to rise up.] —**in•sur'gence, in•sur'gen•cy** *n.*

in•sur•mount•a•ble (ĭn'sər-moun'tə-bəl) *adj.* Incapable of being surmounted; insuperable.

in•sur•rec•tion (ĭn'sə-rĕk'shən) *n.* An act of open revolt against civil authority or a constituted government. [< L *insurgere,* to rise up.] —**in'sur•rec'tion•ist** *n.*

int. 1. interest. **2.** interior. **3.** international.

in•tact (ĭn-tăkt') *adj.* **1.** Not impaired in any way. **2.** Having all parts; whole. [< L *intactus,* untouched.] —**in•tact'ness** *n.*

in•ta•glio (ĭn-tăl'yō) *n., pl.* **-glios.** A figure or design incised beneath the surface of a hard material, as stone. [It.]

in•take (ĭn'tāk') *n.* **1.** An opening through which a fluid is admitted into a container or conduit. **2. a.** The act of taking in. **b.** That which is taken in.

in•tan•gi•ble (ĭn-tăn'jə-bəl) *adj.* Not tangible; elusive. —*n.* Something intangible. —**in•tan'gi•bil'i•ty** *n.* —**in•tan'gi•bly** *adv.*

in•te•ger (ĭn'tə-jər) *n.* **1.** Any member of the set of positive whole numbers (1, 2, 3, . . .), negative whole numbers (–1, –2, –3, . . .), and zero (0). **2.** Any intact unit. [L, whole.]

in•te•gral (ĭn'tə-grəl) *adj.* **1.** Essential for completion; constituent. **2.** Whole; entire; intact. **3.** Expressed or expressible as or in terms of integers. —*n.* A complete unit; a whole. [< L *integer,* whole.] —**in'te•gral•ly** *adv.*

in•te•grate (ĭn'tə-grāt') *v.* **-grated, -grating. 1.** To make into a whole; unify. **2.** To join together; unite. **3.** To open to all ethnic groups; desegregate. [L *integrāre,* to make complete.]

—in'te•gra'tion *n.* —in'te•gra'tive *adj.*

in•teg•ri•ty (ĭn-tĕg'rə-tē) *n.* 1. Rigid adherence to a code of values; probity. 2. Soundness; completeness; unity. [< L *integritās,* completeness, purity.]

in•teg•u•ment (ĭn-tĕg'yo͞o-mənt) *n.* An outer covering, as skin or a seed coat. [< L *integere,* to cover.]

in•tel•lect (ĭn'tə-lĕkt') *n.* 1. a. The ability to learn, reason, and think abstractly. b. The capacity for knowledge and understanding. 2. A person of great intellectual ability. [< L *intellegere,* to perceive, choose between.]

in•tel•lec•tu•al (ĭn'tə-lĕk'cho͞o-əl) *adj.* 1. a. Of the intellect. b. Rational. 2. Appealing to or engaging the intellect. 3. Having superior intelligence. —in'tel•lec'tu•al *n.* —in'tel•lec'tu•al•ly *adv.*

in•tel•lec•tu•al•ize (ĭn'tə-lĕk'cho͞o-ə-līz') *v.* -ized, -izing. 1. To make rational. 2. To avoid emotional insight into (an emotional problem) by performing an intellectual analysis. —in'tel•lec'tu•al•i•za'tion *n.*

in•tel•li•gence (ĭn-tĕl'ə-jəns) *n.* 1. a. The capacity to acquire and apply knowledge. b. The faculty of thought and reason. 2. Information; news. 3. a. Secret information, esp. about an enemy. b. An agency engaged in seeking such information.

intelligence quotient. The ratio of tested mental age to chronological age, usually expressed as a quotient multiplied by 100.

in•tel•li•gent (ĭn-tĕl'ə-jənt) *adj.* 1. Having intelligence. 2. Having a high degree of intelligence; mentally acute. 3. Showing intelligence. —in•tel'li•gent•ly *adv.*

in•tel•li•gent•si•a (ĭn-tĕl'ə-jĕnt'sē-ə, -gĕnt'sē-ə) *n.* The intellectual class of a society.

in•tel•li•gi•ble (ĭn-tĕl'ə-jə-bəl) *adj.* Comprehensible. —in•tel'li•gi•bil'i•ty *n.* —in•tel'li•gi•bly *adv.*

in•tem•per•ance (ĭn-tĕm'pər-əns) *n.* Lack of temperance, as in the indulgence of an appetite. —in•tem'per•ate *adj.*

in•tend (ĭn-tĕnd') *v.* 1. To have in mind; plan. 2. To design for a specific purpose. 3. To mean. [< L *intendere,* to stretch toward, direct one's mind to.]

in•tense (ĭn-tĕns') *adj.* 1. Of great intensity. 2. Extreme in degree, strength, or size. 3. Involving or showing strain. 4. Deeply felt; profound. [< L *intensus,* stretched tight.] —in•tense'ly *adv.* —in•tense'ness *n.*

in•ten•si•fy (ĭn-tĕn'sə-fī') *v.* -fied, -fying. To make or become intense or more intense. —in•ten'si•fi•ca'tion *n.*

in•ten•si•ty (ĭn-tĕn'sə-tē) *n., pl.* -ties. 1. Exceptionally great concentration, power, or force. 2. a. The measure of effectiveness of a force field given by the force per unit test element. b. The energy transferred by a wave per unit time across a unit area perpendicular to the direction of propagation.

in•ten•sive (ĭn-tĕn'sĭv) *adj.* 1. Of, pertaining to, or characterized by intensity. 2. Concentrated and exhaustive. —*n. Gram.* A word that serves to emphasize another word or expression. —in•ten'sive•ly *adv.*

in•tent (ĭn-tĕnt') *n.* 1. That which is intended; aim; purpose. 2. The state of mind operative at the time of an action; volition. 3. a. Meaning; purport. b. Connotation. —*adj.* 1. Firmly fixed; concentrated. 2. Engrossed. 3. Determined. [< L *intendere,* to INTEND.]

in•ten•tion (ĭn-tĕn'shən) *n.* 1. A plan of action; design. 2. An aim that guides action; object.

in•ten•tion•al (ĭn-tĕn'shə-nəl) *adj.* Deliberate; intended. —in•ten'tion•al•ly *adv.*

in•ter (ĭn-tûr') *v.* -terred, -terring. To place in a grave; bury. [< L *in,* in + *terra,* earth, ground.]

inter–. *comb. form.* 1. Between or among. 2. Mutually or together. [< L *inter,* among.]

in•ter•act (ĭn'tər-ăkt') *v.* To act on each other. —in'ter•ac'tion *n.* —in'ter•ac'tive *adj.*

in•ter•breed (ĭn'tər-brēd') *v.* 1. To crossbreed; hybridize. 2. To breed within a narrow range; inbreed.

in•ter•ca•lar•y (ĭn-tûr'kə-lĕr'ē) *adj.* 1. Intercalated. 2. Interpolated.

in•ter•ca•late (ĭn-tûr'kə-lāt') *v.* -lated, -lating. 1. To add (a day or month) to a calendar. 2. To insert, interpose, or interpolate. [L *intercalāre,* to proclaim the insertion of a day.] —in•ter'ca•la'tion *n.*

in•ter•cede (ĭn'tər-sēd') *v.* -ceded, -ceding. 1. To plead on another's behalf. 2. To mediate. [L *intercēdere,* to come between.]

in•ter•cel•lu•lar (ĭn'tər-sĕl'yə-lər) *adj.* Among or between cells.

in•ter•cept (ĭn'tər-sĕpt') *v.* 1. To stop or interrupt the progress of. 2. To intersect. 3. *Math.* To cut off or bound a part of (a line, plane, surface, or solid). —*n.* (ĭn'tər-sĕpt'). *Math.* The distance from the origin of coordinates along a coordinate axis to the point at which a line, curve, or surface intersects the axis. [L *intercipere,* to intercept, seize in transit.] —in'ter•cep'tive *adj.*

in•ter•cep•tor (ĭn'tər-sĕp'tər) *n.* A fast-climbing, highly maneuverable fighter plane designed to intercept enemy aircraft.

in•ter•ces•sion (ĭn'tər-sĕsh'ən) *n.* 1. Entreaty in favor of another. 2. Mediation. [< L *intercēdere,* INTERCEDE.] —in'ter•ces'sion•al *adj.* —in'ter•ces'sor *n.* —in'ter•ces'so•ry *adj.*

in•ter•change (ĭn'tər-chānj') *v.* 1. To switch each into the place of the other; change places. 2. To exchange. 3. To alternate. —*n.* (ĭn'tər-chānj'). 1. An exchange. 2. Alternation. 3. A highway intersection designed to permit traffic to move freely from one road to another. —in'ter•change'a•ble *adj.*

in•ter•col•le•giate (ĭn'tər-kə-lē'jĭt, -jē-ĭt) *adj.* Involving two or more colleges.

in•ter•com (ĭn'tər-kŏm') *n.* An intercommunication system, as between two rooms.

in•ter•com•mu•ni•cate (ĭn'tər-kə-myo͞o'nə-kāt') *v.* -cated, -cating. 1. To communicate with each other. 2. To be adjoined, as rooms.

in•ter•con•ti•nen•tal (ĭn'tər-kŏn'tə-nĕnt'l) *adj.* 1. Extending or carried on from one continent to another. 2. Capable of flight from one continent to another.

in•ter•cos•tal (ĭn'tər-kŏst'l) *adj.* Located or occurring between the ribs. [< INTER- + L *costa,* rib.]

in•ter•course (ĭn'tər-kôrs', -kōrs') *n.* 1. Social interchange; communication. 2. Coitus.

in•ter•dict (ĭn'tər-dĭkt') *v.* To prohibit or place under an ecclesiastical or legal sanction. —*n.* An ecclesiastical or legal prohibition. [< L *interdīcere,* to forbid.] —in'ter•dic'tion *n.*

in•ter•est (ĭn'trĭst, -tər-ĭst) *n.* 1. a. A feeling of curiosity, fascination, or absorption. b. The cause of such a feeling. 2. Often **interests.** Advantage; self-interest. 3. A right, claim, or legal share in something. 4. A charge for a financial loan, usually a percentage of the amount loaned. 5. Often **interests.** A group sharing in a financial enterprise. —*v.* 1. To arouse the curiosity or hold the attention of. 2. To cause to become concerned with. [< L *interesse,* "to be in between," be of concern.]

in•ter•face (ĭn'tər-fās') *n.* A surface forming a common boundary between adjacent regions.

in•ter•fere (ĭn'tər-fîr') *v.* -fered, -fering. 1. To hinder; impede. 2. *Football.* To impede illegally the catching of a pass. 3. To intrude in the affairs of others; meddle. 4. To inhibit clear reception of broadcast signals. [OF *(s')entreferir,* to strike each other.] —in'ter•fer'ence *n.* —in'ter•fer'er *n.*

in•ter•fer•on (ĭn'tər-fîr'ŏn) *n.* A cellular protein produced in response to, and acting to prevent reproduction of, an infectious viral form within an infected cell. [INTERFER(E) + -ON.]

in•ter•ga•lac•tic (ĭn'tər-gə-lăk'tĭk) *adj.* Between galaxies.

in•ter•im (ĭn'tər-ĭm) *n.* An intervening period of time. —*adj.* Temporary. [L, in the meantime.]

in•te•ri•or (ĭn-tîr'ē-ər) *adj.* 1. Situated inside; inner. 2. Inland. —*n.* 1. The inner area of something; inside. 2. A representation of the inside of a building. 3. The inland part, as of a country. [L.] —in•te'ri•or•ly *adv.*

interior decorator. One who plans and executes the layout and decoration of an architectural interior.

interj. interjection.

in•ter•ject (ĭn'tər-jĕkt') *v.* To interpose parenthetically; insert. [L *interjicere,* to throw between.] —in'ter•jec'tor *n.*

in•ter•jec•tion (ĭn'tər-jĕk'shən) *n.* 1. An exclamation. 2. A part of speech consisting of exclamatory words capable of standing alone, as *oh!* —in'ter•jec'tion•al *adj.*

in•ter•lace (ĭn'tər-lās') *v.* 1. To interweave; intertwine. 2. To intersperse.

in•ter•lard (ĭn'tər-lärd') *v.* To insert at intervals; intersperse. [OF *entrelarder,* to alternate layers of fat and lean.]

in•ter•leaf (ĭn'tər-lēf') *n.* A blank leaf inserted between the regular pages of a book.

in•ter•leave (ĭn'tər-lēv') *v.* -leaved, -leaving. To provide with an interleaf.

in•ter•lin•e•ar (ĭn'tər-lĭn'ē-ər) *adj.* Inserted between the lines of a text.

in•ter•lock (ĭn'tər-lŏk') *v.* To unite firmly or join closely, as by dovetailing.

in•ter•loc•u•tor (ĭn'tər-lŏk'yə-tər) *n.* One taking part in a conversation. [< L *interloquī,* to speak between.]

in•ter•loc•u•to•ry (ĭn'tər-lŏk'yə-tôr'ē, -tōr'ē) *n.* A temporary decree made during the course of a legal action. —*adj.* Relating to such a decree.

in•ter•lope (ĭn'tər-lōp') *v.* -loped, -loping. To interfere; intrude; meddle. [< INTER- + MDu *loopen,* to run.] —in'ter•lop'er *n.*

in•ter•lude (ĭn'tər-lo͞od') *n.* 1. An intervening period of time; interval. 2. An entertainment between the acts of a play. 3. A short musical piece inserted between parts of a longer composition. [< ML *interlūdium,* performance between acts.]

in•ter•lu•nar (ĭn'tər-lo͞o'nər) *adj.* Of or relating to the period between the old and new moon when the moon is not visible.

in•ter•mar•ry (ĭn'tər-măr'ē) *v.* 1. To marry one of another group. 2. To be bound together by the marriages of members. 3. To marry within one's own group. —in'ter•mar'riage *n.*

in•ter•me•di•ar•y (ĭn'tər-mē'dē-ĕr'ē) *n., pl.* -ies. A mediator or agent. —*adj.* 1. Acting as a mediator. 2. In between; intermediate.

in•ter•me•di•ate (ĭn'tər-mē'dē-ĭt) *adj.* In between; in the middle. —*n.* 1. One that is intermediate. 2. An intermediary.

in•ter•ment (ĭn-tûr′mənt) *n.* The act or ritual of interring.

in•ter•mez•zo (ĭn′tər-mĕt′sō, -mĕd′zō) *n., pl.* **-zos.** **1.** A short movement separating the major sections of a symphonic work. **2.** A short independent instrumental composition.

in•ter•mi•na•ble (ĭn-tûr′mə-nə-bəl) *adj.* Tiresomely protracted; endless. —**in•ter′mi•na•bly** *adv.*

in•ter•min•gle (ĭn′tər-mĭng′gəl) *v.* To mix or mingle.

in•ter•mis•sion (ĭn′tər-mĭsh′ən) *n.* A temporary suspension of activity, as the period between the acts of a theatrical performance.

in•ter•mit (ĭn′tər-mĭt′) *v.* **-mitted, -mitting.** To suspend activity temporarily or repeatedly. [L *intermittere,* to interrupt at intervals.]

in•ter•mit•tent (ĭn′tər-mĭt′ənt) *adj.* Stopping and starting at intervals. —**in′ter•mit′tent•ly** *adv.*

in•ter•mix (ĭn′tər-mĭks′) *v.* To mix together. —**in′ter•mix′ture** *n.*

in•tern (ĭn′tûrn′) *n.* Also **in•terne.** An advanced student or recent graduate, as of a medical school, undergoing supervised practical training. —*v.* **1.** To train or serve as an intern. **2.** (ĭn-tûrn′). To detain or confine, esp. in wartime. [< L *internus,* INTERNAL.] —**in′tern•ship′** *n.*

in•ter•nal (ĭn-tûr′nəl) *adj.* **1.** Inner; interior. **2.** Intrinsic; inherent. **3.** Within the body. **4.** Of or relating to the domestic affairs of a country. [< L *internus* < *inter,* in.] —**in′ter•nal′i•ty** *n.* —**in•ter′nal•ly** *adv.*

in•ter•nal-com•bus•tion engine (ĭn-tûr′nəl-kəm-bŭs′chən). An engine in which fuel is burned within the engine proper rather than in an external furnace as in a steam engine.

internal medicine. The medical study and treatment of nonsurgical constitutional diseases in adults.

in•ter•na•tion•al (ĭn′tər-năsh′ən-əl) *adj.* Of, relating to, or involving two or more nations or nationalities. —*n.* **International.** Any of three successive international associations of Marxist parties. —**in′ter•na′tion•al•ly** *adv.*

in•ter•na•tion•al•ism (ĭn′tər-năsh′ən-ə-lĭz′əm) *n.* A theory or policy of promoting cooperation among nations, esp. in politics and economy. —**in′ter•na′tion•al•ist** *n.*

in•ter•na•tion•al•ize (ĭn′tər-năsh′ən-ə-līz′) *v.* **-ized, -izing.** To put under international control. —**in′ter•na′tion•al•i•za′tion** *n.*

International System. A system of units used for scientific work, based on the metric system with the addition of units of time, electric current, temperature, and luminous intensity.

in•terne. Variant of **intern.**

in•ter•ne•cine (ĭn′tər-nĕs′ēn′, -ən, -nē′sīn′) *adj.* **1.** Mutually destructive. **2.** Relating to struggle within a group. [< L *internecāre,* to slaughter.]

in•tern•ee (ĭn′tûr-nē′) *n.* One who is interned, esp. during a war.

in•ter•nist (ĭn-tûr′nĭst) *n.* A physician who specializes in internal medicine.

in•tern•ment (ĭn-tûrn′mənt) *n.* The act of interning or state of being interned.

in•ter•phase (ĭn′tər-fāz′) *n.* A period or stage between two successive mitotic divisions of a cell nucleus.

in•ter•plan•e•tar•y (ĭn′tər-plăn′ə-tĕr′ē) *adj.* Between planets.

in•ter•play (ĭn′tər-plā′) *n.* Reciprocal action and reaction; interaction. —*v.* To act or react on each other.

in•ter•po•late (ĭn-tûr′pə-lāt′) *v.* **-lated, -lating.** **1.** To insert or introduce between other things or parts. **2.** To change (a text) by introducing new or false material. **3.** *Math.* To determine a value of (a function) between known values by a procedure or algorithm different from that specified by the function itself. [L *interpolāre.*] —**in•ter′po•la′tion** *n.* —**in•ter′po•lat′or** *n.*

in•ter•pose (ĭn′tər-pōz′) *v.* **-posed, -posing.** **1.** To insert or introduce between parts. **2.** To introduce or interject (a remark, question, etc.) during a conversation or speech. **3.** To intrude. **4.** To intervene. [< L *interpōnere,* to place between.] —**in′ter•pos′er** *n.* —**in′ter•po•si′tion** (-pə-zĭsh′ən) *n.*

in•ter•pret (ĭn-tûr′prĭt) *v.* **1.** To clarify; elucidate. **2.** To expound the significance of. **3.** To represent through art. **4.** To translate. **5.** To offer an explanation. [< L *interpretārī.*] —**in•ter′pret•a•ble** *adj.* —**in•ter′pret•er** *n.*

in•ter•pre•ta•tion (ĭn-tûr′prə-tā′shən) *n.* **1.** An explanation. **2.** A concept of a work of art as expressed by its representation or performance. —**in•ter′pre•ta′tion•al** *adj.*

in•ter•pre•ta•tive (ĭn-tûr′prə-tā′tĭv) *adj.* Also **in•ter•pre•tive** (-prə-tĭv). Expository; explanatory. —**in•ter′pre•ta′tive•ly** *adv.*

in•ter•reg•num (ĭn′tər-rĕg′nəm) *n., pl.* **-nums** or **-na** (-nə). **1.** The interval of time between two successive reigns or governments. **2.** A pause in continuity. —**in′ter•reg′nal** *adj.*

in•ter•re•late (ĭn′tər-rĭ-lāt′) *v.* To place in or come into a mutual relationship. —**in′ter•re•la′tion** *n.* —**in′ter•re•la′tion•ship′** *n.*

interrog. interrogative.

in•ter•ro•gate (ĭn-tĕr′ə-gāt′) *v.* **-gated, -gating.** To examine by formal questioning. [L *interrogāre,* to consult, question.] —**in•ter′ro•ga′tion** *n.* —**in•ter′ro•ga′tor** *n.*

in•ter•rog•a•tive (ĭn′tə-rŏg′ə-tĭv) *adj.* **1.** Of the nature of a question. **2.** Designating a word or form used in asking a question. —**in′ter•rog′a•tive** *n.* —**in′ter•rog′a•tive•ly** *adv.*

in•ter•rog•a•to•ry (ĭn′tə-rŏg′ə-tôr′ē, -tōr′ē) *adj.* Interrogative. —**in′ter•rog′a•tor′i•ly** *adv.*

in•ter•rupt (ĭn′tə-rŭpt′) *v.* **1.** To break the continuity or uniformity of. **2.** To hinder or stop by breaking in upon. **3.** To break in upon an action or discourse. [< L *interrumpere,* to break in.] —**in′ter•rup′tion** *n.*

in•ter•scho•las•tic (ĭn′tər-skə-lăs′tĭk) *adj.* Between or among schools.

in•ter•sect (ĭn′tər-sĕkt′) *v.* **1.** To cut across or through. **2.** To form an intersection with.

in•ter•sec•tion (ĭn′tər-sĕk′shən) *n.* **1.** The point or points common to two or more geometric figures. **2. a.** The act or process of intersecting. **b.** A place where things intersect.

in•ter•sperse (ĭn′tər-spûrs′) *v.* **-spersed, -spersing.** To scatter or distribute among other things at irregular intervals. [L *interspergere,* to scatter among.] —**in′ter•sper′sion** (-spûr′zhən, -shən) *n.*

in•ter•state (ĭn′tər-stāt′) *adj.* Pertaining to, existing between, or connecting two or more states.

in•ter•stel•lar (ĭn′tər-stĕl′ər) *adj.* Between the stars.

in•ter•stice (ĭn-tûr′stĭs) *n., pl.* **-stices** (-stĭ-sēz′, -sĭz). A small space between things or parts; crevice. [< L *intersistere,* to stand in the middle of.] —**in′ter•sti′tial** (ĭn′tər-stĭsh′əl) *adj.* —**in′ter•sti′tial•ly** *adv.*

in•ter•tid•al (ĭn′tər-tīd′l) *adj.* Of or being the region between the extremes of high and low tide.

in•ter•twine (ĭn′tər-twīn′) *v.* **1.** To twist or braid together. **2.** To interweave with one another. —**in′ter•twine′ment** *n.*

in•ter•ur•ban (ĭn′tər-ûr′bən) *adj.* Pertaining to or connecting cities.

in•ter•val (ĭn′tər-vəl) *n.* **1.** A space between two objects, points, or units. **2.** The temporal duration between two specified instants, events, or states. **3. a.** A set consisting of all the numbers between, and sometimes including, a pair of given numbers. **b.** A set of numbers greater than or less than, and sometimes including, a given number. **4.** The difference in pitch between two tones. [< L *intervallum,* space between ramparts.]

in•ter•vene (ĭn′tər-vēn′) *v.* **-vened, -vening.** **1.** To enter or occur extraneously. **2.** To occur between two things or two periods of time. **3.** To come between so as to modify. **4.** To interfere in the affairs of another nation. [L *intervenīre,* to come between.] —**in′ter•ven′er** *n.* —**in′ter•ven′tion** (-vĕn′shən) *n.*

in•ter•view (ĭn′tər-vyōō′) *n.* **1. a.** A face-to-face meeting. **b.** Such a meeting arranged for formal discussion. **2.** A conversation between a reporter and one from whom he seeks information. —**in′ter•view′** *v.*

in•ter•weave (ĭn′tər-wēv′) *v.* **1.** To weave together. **2.** To intertwine.

in•tes•tate (ĭn-tĕs′tāt′, -tĭt) *adj.* **1.** Having made no legal will. **2.** Not disposed of by a legal will. —**in•tes′ta•cy** (-tə-sē) *n.*

in•tes•tine (ĭn-tĕs′tən) *n.* The portion of the alimentary canal extending from the stomach to the anus. [< L *intestīnus,* internal.] —**in•tes′ti•nal** *adj.* —**in•tes′ti•nal•ly** *adv.*

in•ti•mate[1] (ĭn′tə-mĭt) *adj.* **1.** Marked by close acquaintance or familiarity. **2.** Essential; innermost. **3.** Characterized by informality and privacy. **4.** Very personal; private. —*n.* A close friend or confidant. [< LL *intimāre,* to put in, INTIMATE[2].] —**in′ti•ma•cy, in′ti•mate•ness** *n.* —**in′ti•mate•ly** *adv.*

in•ti•mate[2] (ĭn′tə-māt′) *v.* **-mated, -mating.** To imply subtly. [LL *intimāre,* to put or bring in.] —**in′ti•mat′er** *n.* —**in′ti•ma′tion** *n.*

in•tim•i•date (ĭn-tĭm′ə-dāt′) *v.* **-dated, -dating.** **1.** To make timid; frighten. **2.** To discourage or inhibit by or as by threats.

intl. international.

in•to (ĭn′tōō) *prep.* **1.** To the inside of. **2.** To the occupation of: *go into banking.* **3.** To the condition or form of. **4.** So as to be in or within. **5.** To a time or place in the course of: *well into the week.* **6.** Against: *ram into a tree.* **7.** Toward.

in•tol•er•a•ble (ĭn-tŏl′ər-ə-bəl) *adj.* Insupportable; unbearable. —**in•tol′er•a•bly** *adv.*

in•tol•er•ant (ĭn-tŏl′ər-ənt) *adj.* Not tolerant, esp.: **a.** Bigoted. **b.** Irritable. **c.** Unable to endure. —**in•tol′er•ance** *n.*

in•to•na•tion (ĭn′tō-nā′shən) *n.* **1. a.** The act of intoning. **b.** An intoned utterance. **2.** A manner of producing or uttering tones, esp. with regard to accuracy of pitch.

in•tone (ĭn-tōn′) *v.* **-toned, -toning.** **1.** To recite in a singing voice. **2.** To utter in a monotone. —**in•ton′er** *n.*

in to•to (ĭn tō′tō). Totally; altogether. [L.]

in•tox•i•cant (ĭn-tŏk′sĭ-kənt) *n.* An agent that intoxicates, esp. an alcoholic beverage.

in•tox•i•cate (ĭn-tŏk′sĭ-kāt′) *v.* **-cated, -cating.** **1.** To induce, esp. with ingested alcohol, effects ranging from exhilaration to stupefaction. **2.** To stimulate or excite. [ML *intoxicāre,* to put poison in.] —**in•tox′i•ca′tion** *n.*

intra–. *comb. form.* In, within, or inside of. [< L *intrā,* on the inside, within.]

in•trac•ta•ble (ĭn-trăk′tə-bəl) *adj.* Difficult to manage or govern; stubborn.

in·tra·cu·ta·ne·ous (ĭn′trə-kyo͞o-tā′nē-əs) *adj.* Within the skin.

in·tra·mu·ral (ĭn′trə-myo͝or′əl) *adj.* Existing within the bounds of an institution, esp. a school. —**in′tra·mu′ral·ly** *adv.*

in·tran·si·gent (ĭn-trăn′sə-jənt) *adj.* Refusing to moderate an extreme position; uncompromising. [< Span *los intransigentes,* "the uncompromising."] —**in·tran′si·gence** *n.* —**in·tran′si·gent·ly** *adv.*

in·tran·si·tive (ĭn-trăn′sə-tĭv) *adj.* Designating a verb or verb construction that does not require a direct object to complete its meaning. —**in·tran′si·tive·ness** *n.*

in·tra·state (ĭn′trə-stāt′) *adj.* Within the boundaries of a state.

in·tra·u·ter·ine (ĭn′trə-yo͞o′tər-ĭn, -tə-rīn′) *adj.* Within the uterus.

in·tra·ve·nous (ĭn′trə-vē′nəs) *adj.* Within a vein or veins. —**in′tra·ve′nous·ly** *adv.*

in·trep·id (ĭn-trĕp′ĭd) *adj.* Resolutely courageous; fearless; bold. [< L *intrepidus.*] —**in′tre·pid′i·ty** (-trə-pĭd′ə-tē) *n.* —**in·trep′id·ly** *adv.*

in·tri·cate (ĭn′trĭ-kĭt) *adj.* **1.** Having many complexly arranged elements. **2.** Difficult to solve or comprehend. [< L *intrīcāre,* to entangle.] —**in′tri·ca·cy** *n.* —**in′tri·cate·ly** *adv.*

in·trigue (ĭn′trēg′, ĭn-trēg′) *n.* **1. a.** A covert or underhand scheme. **b.** The use of such schemes. **2.** A clandestine love affair. **3.** Mystery; suspense. —*v.* (ĭn-trēg′) **-trigued, -triguing.** **1.** To engage in covert schemes. **2.** To arouse the interest or curiosity of. [< L *intrīcāre,* to entangle.] —**in·tri′guer** *n.*

in·trin·sic (ĭn-trĭn′sĭk) *adj.* Pertaining to the essential nature of a thing. [< L *intrinsecus,* inwardly, on the inside.] —**in·trin′si·cal·ly** *adv.*

intro–. *comb. form.* **1.** In or into. **2.** Inward. [< L *intrō,* to the inside, inwardly.]

intro. introduction; introductory.

in·tro·duce (ĭn′trə-d/y/o͞os′) *v.* **-duced, -ducing.** **1.** To identify and present, esp. to make (strangers) acquainted. **2.** To present and recommend, as a plan. **3.** To originate. **4.** To insert or inject. **5.** To inform of something for the first time. **6.** To preface. [L *intrōdūcere,* to lead in.] —**in′tro·duc′er** *n.* —**in′tro·duc′tion** (-dŭk′shən) *n.* —**in′tro·duc′to·ry** *adj.*

in·tro·spec·tion (ĭn′trə-spĕk′shən) *n.* Contemplation of one's own thoughts and sensations; self-examination. —**in′tro·spec′tive** *adj.* —**in′tro·spec′tive·ness** *n.*

in·tro·vert (ĭn′trə-vûrt′) *n.* One whose thoughts and interests are directed inward. [< INTRO- + L *vertere,* to turn.] —**in′tro·ver′sion** *n.*

in·trude (ĭn-tro͞od′) *v.* **-truded, -truding.** To come in rudely or inappropriately; enter as an improper or unwanted element. [L *intrūdere,* to thrust in.] —**in·trud′er** *n.* —**in·tru′sion** *n.* —**in·tru′sive** *adj.* —**in·tru′sive·ly** *adv.*

in·trust. Variant of **entrust.**

in·tu·it (ĭn-t/y/o͞o′ĭt) *v.* To know or sense by intuition.

in·tu·i·tion (ĭn′t/y/o͞o-ĭsh′ən) *n.* **1. a.** The act or faculty of knowing without the use of rational processes. **b.** Knowledge so gained. **2.** Sharp insight. [< L *intuērī,* to look at, contemplate.] —**in·tu′i·tive** *adj.*

in·un·date (ĭn′ŭn-dāt′) *v.* **-dated, -dating.** To overwhelm or cover with or as with a flood. [L *inundāre,* "to flow in."] —**in′un·da′tion** *n.*

in·ure (ĭn-yo͝or′) *v.* **-ured, -uring.** To make used to something undesirable by prolonged subjection. —**in·ure′ment** *n.*

inv. invoice.

in·vade (ĭn-vād′) *v.* **-vaded, -vading.** **1.** To enter by force in order to conquer or overrun. **2.** To encroach or intrude upon. **3.** To infest. **4.** To enter and spread harm through. [< L *invādere,* "to go in."] —**in·vad′er** *n.*

in·va·lid[1] (ĭn′və-lĭd) *n.* A chronically ill or disabled person. —*adj.* Disabled by illness or injury.

in·val·id[2] (ĭn-văl′ĭd) *adj.* **1.** Null; legally ineffective. **2.** Falsely based or reasoned; unjustified. —**in·val′id·ly** *adv.*

in·val·i·date (ĭn-văl′ə-dāt′) *v.* To make void; render invalid. —**in·val′i·da′tion** *n.*

in·val·u·a·ble (ĭn-văl′yo͞o-ə-bəl) *adj.* **1.** Having great value; priceless. **2.** Of inestimable use or help. —**in·val′u·a·bly** *adv.*

in·var·i·a·ble (ĭn-vâr′ē-ə-bəl) *adj.* Not changing or subject to change; constant. —**in·var′i·a·bil′i·ty** *n.* —**in·var′i·a·bly** *adv.*

in·var·i·ant (ĭn-vâr′ē-ənt) *adj.* Unaffected by a designated mathematical operation. —**in·var′i·ance** *n.* —**in·var′i·ant** *n.*

in·va·sion (ĭn-vā′zhən) *n.* **1.** The act of invading, esp. entrance by force. **2.** The onset of something harmful, as a disease.

in·va·sive (ĭn-vā′sĭv) *adj.* Tending to spread, esp. tending to invade healthy tissue.

in·vec·tive (ĭn-vĕk′tĭv) *n.* **1.** An abusive expression. **2.** Vehement denunciation; vituperation. [< L *invehere,* to attack, INVEIGH.]

in·veigh (ĭn-vā′) *v.* To protest vehemently; rail. [< L *invehere,* to carry in, assail.]

in·vei·gle (ĭn-vē′gəl, ĭn-vā′-) *v.* **-gled, -gling.** **1.** To lead astray or win over by deceitful flattery. **2.** To obtain by cajolery. [< OF *aveugler,* to blind.] —**in·vei′gler** *n.*

in·vent (ĭn-vĕnt′) *v.* **1.** To conceive of or devise first; originate. **2.** To fabricate; make up. [< L *invenīre,* to come upon.] —**in·ven′tor** *n.*

in·ven·tion (ĭn-vĕn′shən) *n.* **1.** The act or process of inventing. **2.** A new device or process developed from study and experimentation. **3.** A mental fabrication; falsehood. **4.** Skill at inventing; inventiveness.

in·ven·tive (ĭn-vĕn′tĭv) *adj.* **1.** Of or characterized by invention. **2.** Adept or skillful at inventing. —**in·ven′tive·ness** *n.*

in·ven·to·ry (ĭn′vən-tôr′ē, -tōr′ē) *n., pl.* **-ries.** **1.** A detailed list of things, esp. a periodic survey of goods and materials in stock. **2.** The process of making such a survey. **3.** The items so listed. **4.** The quantity of goods so determined. [< L *invenīre,* to come upon, INVENT.] —**in′ven·to′ry** *v.* **(-ried, -rying).**

in·ver·ness (ĭn′vər-nĕs′) *n.* A loose overcoat with a detachable cape. [< *Inverness,* Scotland.]

in·verse (ĭn-vûrs′, ĭn′vûrs′) *adj.* Reversed in order, nature, or effect. —*n.* That which is opposite, as in sequence or character; the reverse. [< L *invertere,* INVERT.] —**in·verse′ly** *adv.*

in·ver·sion (ĭn-vûr′zhən, -shən) *n.* **1.** The act of inverting or state of being inverted. **2.** An interchange of position, order, etc. **3.** Homosexuality. **4.** *Meteorol.* A state in which the air temperature increases with increasing altitude, holding surface air down along with its pollutants.

in·vert (ĭn-vûrt′) *v.* **1.** To turn inside out or upside down. **2.** To reverse the position, order, or condition of. [L *invertere,* to turn inside out or upside down.] —**in·vert′i·ble** *adj.*

in·ver·te·brate (ĭn-vûr′tə-brĭt, -brāt′) *adj.* Having no backbone or spinal column; not vertebrate. —**in·ver′te·brate** *n.*

in·vest (ĭn-vĕst′) *v.* **1.** To commit (money or capital) in order to gain profit or interest. **2.** To spend or utilize (time or effort) for future benefit. **3.** To endow with rank, authority, or power. **4.** To inaugurate; install in office. **5.** *Rare.* To clothe. **6.** To cover completely; envelop. [< L *investīre,* to clothe in, surround.] —**in·ves′tor** *n.*

in·ves·ti·gate (ĭn-vĕs′tĭ-gāt′) *v.* **-gated, -gating.** To observe or inquire into in detail; examine systematically. [L *investīgāre,* to trace out.] —**in·ves′ti·ga′tion** *n.* —**in·ves′ti·ga′tor** *n.*

in·ves·ti·ture (ĭn-vĕs′tə-cho͝or′) *n.* The act or ceremony of conferring the authority and symbols of a high office.

in·vest·ment (ĭn-vĕst′mənt) *n.* **1.** The act of investing or state of being invested. **2.** An amount invested. **3.** Property acquired for future income. **4.** Investiture. **5.** An outer covering or layer.

in·vet·er·ate (ĭn-vĕt′ər-ĭt) *adj.* **1.** Firmly established by long standing. **2.** Persisting in an ingrained habit: *an inveterate liar.* [< L *inveterāre,* to render old.] —**in·vet′er·a·cy** (-ər-ə-sē) *n.* —**in·vet′er·ate·ly** *adv.*

in·vid·i·ous (ĭn-vĭd′ē-əs) *adj.* **1.** Tending to rouse ill will or animosity. **2.** Containing or implying a slight. [< L *invidia,* envy.] —**in·vid′i·ous·ly** *adv.*

in·vig·or·ate (ĭn-vĭg′ə-rāt′) *v.* **-ated, -ating.** To impart vigor or vitality to. —**in·vig′or·a′tion** *n.*

in·vin·ci·ble (ĭn-vĭn′sə-bəl) *adj.* Unconquerable. —**in·vin′ci·bil′i·ty** *n.* —**in·vin′ci·bly** *adv.*

in·vi·o·la·ble (ĭn-vī′ə-lə-bəl) *adj.* **1.** Safe from violation or profanation. **2.** Impregnable. —**in·vi′o·la·bil′i·ty** *n.* —**in·vi′o·la·bly** *adv.*

in·vi·o·late (ĭn-vī′ə-lĭt) *adj.* Not violated; intact. —**in·vi′o·late·ly** *adv.*

in·vis·i·ble (ĭn-vĭz′ə-bəl) *adj.* **1.** Incapable of being seen; not visible. **2.** Not accessible to view; hidden. **3.** Inconspicuous. —**in·vis′i·bil′i·ty, in·vis′i·ble·ness** *n.* —**in·vis′i·bly** *adv.*

in·vite (ĭn-vīt′) *v.* **-vited, -viting.** **1.** To request the presence or participation of. **2.** To request formally. **3.** To welcome. **4.** To tend to bring on; provoke. **5.** To lure; entice. [< L *invītāre.*] —**in′vi·ta′tion** *n.*

in·vit·ing (ĭn-vī′tĭng) *adj.* Attractive; tempting.

in·vo·ca·tion (ĭn′və-kā′shən) *n.* **1.** The act of invoking, esp. an appeal to a higher power. **2.** A prayer or other formula used in invoking.

in·voice (ĭn′vois′) *n.* A detailed list of goods shipped or services rendered, with an account of all costs; a bill. [< OF *envoy,* a sending.]

in·voke (ĭn-vōk′) *v.* **-voked, -voking.** **1.** To call upon (a higher power) for assistance. **2.** To appeal to; petition. **3.** To call for earnestly; solicit. **4.** To conjure. **5.** To cite in support of one's cause. [< L *invocāre,* "to call upon."]

in·vol·un·tar·y (ĭn-vŏl′ən-tĕr′ē) *adj.* **1.** Not performed willingly. **2.** Not subject to control. —**in·vol′un·tar′i·ly** *adv.* —**in·vol′un·tar′i·ness** *n.*

in·vo·lu·tion (ĭn′və-lo͞o′shən) *n.* **1.** The act of involving or state of being involved. **2.** Anything internally complex or involved. **3.** The multiplying of a quantity by itself a specified number of times; raising to a power.

in·volve (ĭn-vŏlv′) *v.* **-volved, -volving.** **1.** To contain or include. **2.** To have as a necessary feature or consequence. **3.** To draw in; embroil. **4.** To engross completely. **5.** To make complex; complicate. [< L *involvere,* to enwrap, "roll in."] —**in·volve′ment** *n.*

in·vul·ner·a·ble (ĭn-vŭl′nər-ə-bəl) *adj.* **1.** Immune to attack; impregnable. **2.** Incapable of being damaged, injured, or wounded. —**in·vul′ner·a·bil′i·ty** *n.* —**in·vul′ner·a·bly** *adv.*

in·ward (ĭn′wərd) *adj.* **1.** Located inside; inner. **2.** Directed or moving toward the interior. **3.** Existing in the mind. —*adv.* Also **in·wards**

(-wərdz). **1.** Toward the inside or center. **2.** Toward the mind or the self.

In•ward•ly (ĭn'wərd-lē) *adv.* **1.** On or in the inside; within. **2.** Privately; to oneself.

i•o•dide (ī'ə-dīd') *n.* A binary compound of iodine with a more electropositive atom or group.

i•o•dine (ī'ə-dīn', -dĭn, -dēn') *n. Symbol* **I** **1.** A lustrous, grayish-black, corrosive, poisonous element having radioactive isotopes, esp. I 131, used as tracers and in thyroid disease diagnosis and therapy, and compounds used as germicides, antiseptics, and dyes. Atomic number 53, atomic weight 126.9044. **2.** A tincture of iodine and sodium iodide, NaI, or potassium iodide, KI, used as an antiseptic. [< Gk *iōdēs, ioeidēs,* violet-colored.]

i•o•dize (ī'ə-dīz') *v.* **-dized, -dizing.** To treat or combine with iodine or an iodide.

i•on (ī'ən, ī'ŏn') *n.* An atom, group of atoms, or molecule having a net electric charge acquired by gaining or losing electrons from an initially neutral configuration. [< Gk, "going (particle)."] **—i•on'ic** (ī-ŏn'ĭk) *adj.*

ionic bond. A chemical bond formed by the complete transfer of one or more electrons from one kind of atom to another.

Ionic order. One of the three classical orders of architecture, characterized by two opposed volutes in the capital.

i•on•ize (ī'ə-nīz') *v.* **-ized, -izing.** To convert totally or partially into ions. **—i'on•i•za'tion** *n.*

i•on•o•sphere (ī-ŏn'ə-sfîr') *n.* An electrically conducting set of layers of the earth's atmosphere, extending from altitudes of approx. 30 miles to more than 250 miles.

i•o•ta (ī-ō'tə) *n.* **1.** The 9th letter of the Greek alphabet, representing *i.* **2.** A very small amount.

IOU (ī'ō-yōō') *n., pl.* **IOU's, IOUs.** A promise to pay a debt.

I•o•wa¹ (ī'ə-wə). A Midwestern state of the U.S. Pop. 2,825,000. Cap. Des Moines.

I•o•wa² (ī'ə-wə) *n., pl.* **-wa** or **-was.** **1.** A member of a tribe of Siouan-speaking North American Indians formerly inhabiting the region of Minnesota, Iowa, and Missouri. **2.** The language of this tribe. **—I'o•wa** *adj.*

IPA International Phonetic Alphabet.

ip•so fac•to (ĭp'sō făk'tō). By the fact itself; by that very fact. [L.]

IQ intelligence quotient.

Ir **1.** iridium. **2.** Irish.

I•ran (ī-răn', ē-rän'). Formerly **Per•sia** (pûr'zhə, -shə). A kingdom of SW Asia. Pop. 22,860,000. Cap. Teheran.

Iran

I•ra•ni•an (ī-rā'nē-ən) *n.* **1.** A native or inhabitant of Iran. **2.** A group of languages including Persian and Pashto and forming a subbranch of Indo-Iranian. **—I•ra'ni•an** *adj.*

I•raq (ī-răk', ē-räk'). Also **I•rak.** A republic of SW Asia. Pop. 8,262,000. Cap. Baghdad. **—I•ra'qi** *adj. & n.*

Iraq

i•ras•ci•ble (ĭ-răs'ə-bəl, ī-răs'-) *adj.* Prone to outbursts of temper; easily angered. [< L *īrāscī,* to get angry.] **—i•ras'ci•bil'i•ty** *n.*

i•rate (ī'rāt, ī-rāt') *adj.* Angry; enraged. **—i'rate•ly** *adv.*

IRBM Intermediate Range Ballistic Missile.

ire (īr) *n.* Wrath; anger. [< L *īra,* anger.]

Ire. Ireland.

ire•ful (īr'fəl) *adj.* Full of ire; angry; wrathful. **—ire'ful•ly** *adv.*

Ire•land (īr'lənd). **1.** One of the British Isles, divided into the Republic of Ireland and Northern Ireland. **2.** A republic occupying most of Ireland. Pop. 2,849,000. Cap. Dublin.

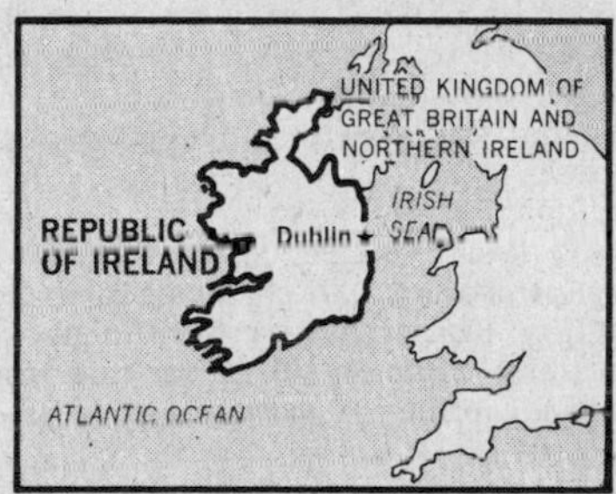

Republic of Ireland

ir•i•des•cent (ĭr'ə-dĕs'ənt) *adj.* Producing a display of lustrous, rainbowlike colors. [L *īris,* rainbow, iris + -ESCENT.] **—ir'i•des'cence** *n.*

i•rid•i•um (ĭ-rĭd'ē-əm, ī-rĭd'-) *n. Symbol* **Ir** A very hard and brittle, exceptionally corrosion-resistant, whitish-yellow metallic element used to harden platinum and in high-temperature materials, electrical contacts, and wear-resistant bearings. Atomic number 77, atomic weight 192.2. [< Gk *iris,* rainbow, IRIS.]

i•ris (ī'rĭs) *n., pl.* **irises** or **irides** (ī'rə-dēz', ĭr'ə-). **1.** The pigmented, round, contractile membrane of the eye, situated between the cornea and lens, and perforated by the pupil. **2.** A plant with narrow, sword-shaped leaves and showy, variously colored flowers. [< Gk, rainbow, iris of the eye.]

I•rish (ī'rĭsh) *adj.* **1. the Irish** *(takes pl. v.).* **a.** The inhabitants of Ireland. **b.** People of immediate Irish descent. **2.** The Celtic language spoken in Ireland. **—I'rish** *adj.*

Irish Gaelic. The Goidelic language of Ireland.

I•rish•man (ī'rĭsh-mən) *n.* A man of Irish birth or descent.

irk (ûrk) *v.* To vex; irritate. [ME *irken.*]

irk•some (ûrk'səm) *adj.* Wearisome; tedious.

i•ron (ī'ərn) *n.* **1.** *Symbol* **Fe** A silvery-white, lustrous, malleable, ductile, magnetic or magnetizable, metallic element used alloyed in many important structural materials. Atomic number 26, atomic weight 55.847. **2.** Great hardness or strength. **3.** An implement made of iron alloy or similar metal. **4.** A golf club with a metal head. **5.** An appliance with a weighted flat bottom, used when heated to press fabric. **6. irons.** Fetters; shackles. *—adj.* Of or like iron. *—v.* To press (fabric) with a heated iron. **—iron out.** To settle through discussion or compromise. [< OE *īren, īsen.*]

Iron Age. A period of human culture succeeding the Bronze Age, characterized by the introduction of iron metallurgy, in Europe beginning around the 8th century B.C.

i•ron•bound (ī'ərn-bound') *adj.* Rigid and unyielding.

i•ron•clad (ī'ərn-klăd') *adj.* **1.** Sheathed with protective iron plates. **2.** Rigid: *an ironclad rule.*

i•ron•ic (ī-rŏn'ĭk) *adj.* Also **i•ron•ic•al** (-ĭ-kəl). **1.** Characterized by or constituting irony. **2.** Given to irony. **—i•ron'i•cal•ly** *adv.*

iron lung. A tank in which the body is enclosed and by means of which pressure is regularly increased and decreased to provide artificial respiration.

i•ron•ware (ī'ərn-wâr') *n.* Iron utensils and other products made of iron.

i•ron•work (ī'ərn-wûrk') *n.* Work in iron, as gratings and rails.

i•ron•works (ī'ərn-wûrks') *n. (takes sing. v.).* An establishment where iron is smelted or where heavy iron products are made.

i•ro•ny (ī'rə-nē) *n., pl.* **-nies.** **1.** The use of words to convey the opposite of their literal meaning. **2.** Incongruity between what might be expected and what actually occurs. [< Gk *eirōneia,* dissembling, feigned ignorance.]

Ir•o•quoi•an (ĭr'ə-kwoi'ən) *n.* **1.** A family of North American Indian languages spoken in Canada and the E U.S. **2.** A member of a tribe using a language of this family. **—Ir'o•quoi'an** *adj.*

Ir•o•quois (ĭr'ə-kwoi', -kwoiz') *n., pl.* **-quois.** **1.** A member of any of several Iroquoian-speaking North American Indian tribes formerly inhabiting New York State. **2.** Any of the languages spoken among these tribes.

ir•ra•di•ate (ĭ-rā'dē-āt') *v.* **-ated, -ating.** **1.** To expose to or treat with radiation. **2.** To emit in a manner analogous to the emission of light. **—ir•ra'di•a'tion** *n.*

ir•ra•tion•al (ĭ-răsh'ən-əl) *adj.* **1. a.** Not endowed with reason. **b.** Incoherent, as from shock. **c.** Illogical. **2.** Incapable of being expressed as an integer or a quotient of integers. **—ir•ra'tion•al•ly** *adv.* **—ir•ra'tion•al•ness** *n.*

Ir•ra•wad•dy (ĭr'ə-wä'dē). A river of Burma.

ir•re•claim•a•ble (ĭr'ĭ-klā'mə-bəl) *adj.* Incapable of being reclaimed.

ir•rec•on•cil•a•ble (ĭ-rĕk'ən-sī'lə-bəl, ĭ-rĕk'ən-sī'-) *adj.* **1.** Incapable of being reconciled; implacably hostile. **2.** Incompatible; incongruous. **—ir•rec'on•cil'a•bly** *adv.*

ir•re•cov•er•a•ble (ĭr'ĭ-kŭv'ər-ə-bəl) *adj.* Incapable of being recovered; irreparable.

ir•re•deem•a•ble (ĭr'ĭ-dē'mə-bəl) *adj.* **1.** Incapable of being bought back or paid off. **2.** Not convertible into coin. **3.** Incapable of being saved or reformed.

ir•re•den•tist (ĭr'ĭ-dĕn'tĭst) *n.* One who advocates the recovery of territory culturally or

historically related to his nation but now subject to a foreign government. [It *irredentista.*]
ir•re•duc•i•ble (ĭr'ĭ-d/y/o͞o'sə-bəl) *adj.* Incapable of being reduced to a desired, simpler, or smaller form or amount.
ir•ref•u•ta•ble (ĭ-rĕf'yə-tə-bəl, ĭr'ĭ-fyo͞o'tə-bəl) *adj.* Incapable of being refuted.
irreg. irregular.
ir•re•gard•less (ĭr'ĭ-gärd'lĭs) *adv. Nonstandard.* Regardless.
Usage: Irregardless, a double negative, is only acceptable when the intent is clearly humorous.
ir•reg•u•lar (ĭ-rĕg'yə-lər) *adj.* **1.** Not according to accepted rules, practice, or order. **2.** Not straight, uniform, or symmetrical. **3.** Of uneven rate, occurrence, or duration. **4.** Asymmetrically arranged or atypical. *—n.* A guerrilla. **—ir•reg'u•lar'i•ty** *n.* **—ir•reg'u•lar•ly** *adv.*
ir•rel•e•vant (ĭ-rĕl'ə-vənt) *adj.* Having no applications or effects in a specified circumstance. **—ir•rel'e•vance** *n.*
ir•re•lig•ious (ĭr'ĭ-lĭj'əs) *adj.* Indifferent or hostile to religion. **—ir're•lig'ious•ness** *n.*
ir•re•me•di•a•ble (ĭr'ĭ-mē'dē-ə-bəl) *adj.* Impossible to remedy; incurable.
ir•re•mov•a•ble (ĭr'ĭ-mo͞o'və-bəl) *adj.* Not removable. **—ir're•mov'a•bly** *adv.*
ir•rep•a•ra•ble (ĭ-rĕp'ər-ə-bəl) *adj.* Incapable of being repaired, rectified, or amended.
ir•re•place•a•ble (ĭr'ĭ-plā'sə-bəl) *adj.* Incapable of being replaced.
ir•re•pres•si•ble (ĭr'ĭ-prĕs'ə-bəl) *adj.* Impossible to control or restrain.
ir•re•proach•a•ble (ĭr'ĭ-prō'chə-bəl) *adj.* Beyond reproach. **—ir're•proach'a•bly** *adv.*
ir•re•sis•ti•ble (ĭr'ĭ-zĭs'tə-bəl) *adj.* **1.** Impossible to resist. **2.** Having an overpowering appeal.
ir•res•o•lute (ĭ-rĕz'ə-lo͞ot') *adj.* **1.** Unresolved as to action or procedure. **2.** Vacillating; indecisive. **—ir•res'o•lute'ly** *adv.*
ir•re•spec•tive (ĭr'ĭ-spĕk'tĭv) *adj.* Regardless of; without consideration of.
ir•re•spon•si•ble (ĭr'ĭ-spŏn'sə-bəl) *adj.* Unreliable. **—ir're•spon'si•bil'i•ty, ir're•spon'si•ble•ness** *n.* **—ir're•spon'si•bly** *adv.*
ir•re•triev•a•ble (ĭr'ĭ-trē'və-bəl) *adj.* Incapable of being retrieved or recovered.
ir•rev•er•ence (ĭ-rĕv'ər-əns) *n.* **1.** Want of reverence or due respect. **2.** A disrespectful act or remark. **—ir•rev'er•ent** *adj.*
ir•re•vers•i•ble (ĭr'ĭ-vûr'sə-bəl) *adj.* Incapable of being reversed. **—ir're•vers'i•bly** *adv.*
ir•rev•o•ca•ble (ĭ-rĕv'ə-kə-bəl) *adj.* Incapable of being retracted or revoked.
ir•ri•gate (ĭr'ĭ-gāt') *v.* **-gated, -gating. 1.** To supply (dry land) with water by artificial means. **2.** To wash out with water or a medicated fluid. [L *irrigāre,* to lead water to.] **—ir'ri•ga'tion** *n.* **—ir'ri•ga'tor** *n.*
ir•ri•ta•ble (ĭr'ə-tə-bəl) *adj.* **1.** Easily annoyed; ill-tempered. **2.** Responsive or abnormally sensitive, as to stimuli. [< L *irritāre,* IRRITATE.] **—ir'ri•ta•bil'i•ty** *n.* **—ir'ri•ta•bly** *adv.*
ir•ri•tate (ĭr'ə-tāt') *v.* **-tated, -tating. 1. a.** To exasperate; vex. **b.** To provoke. **2.** To chafe or inflame. [L *irritāre.*] **—ir'ri•tant** *adj.* & *n.* **—ir'ri•tat'ing•ly** *adv.* **—ir'ri•ta'tion** *n.*
ir•rupt (ĭ-rŭpt') *v.* To break or burst in; make an invasion. [L *irrumpere.*] **—ir•rup'tion** *n.*
Ir•ving (ûr'vĭng), **Washington.** 1783–1859. American author.
is (ĭz). 3rd person sing. present indicative of the verb **be. —as is.** In its present state; as it stands. [< OE. See **es-**.]
Isa. Isaiah (Old Testament).
I•saac (ī'zək). Hebrew patriarch, son of Abraham and father of Jacob. Genesis 21:1–4.
I•sa•iah (ī-zā'ə, ī-zī'ə). Hebrew prophet of the 8th century B.C.
–ise. *Chiefly Brit.* Variant of **-ize.**
–ish. *comb. form.* **1. a.** Of the nationality of: **Finnish. b.** Having the qualities or character of: **sheepish. c.** Tending to or preoccupied with: **selfish. d.** Somewhere near or approximately: *fortyish.* **2.** Somewhat: **greenish.** [< OE *-isc.*]
i•sin•glass (ī'zĭng-glăs', -gläs', ī'zən-) *n.* A transparent, almost pure gelatin prepared from the air bladder of certain fishes. [< MDu *huusblase,* "sturgeon bladder."]
I•sis (ī'sĭs). Egyptian goddess of fertility; sister and wife of Osiris.
isl. island.
Is•lam (ĭs'ləm, ĭz'-, ĭs-läm') *n.* **1.** A religion based upon the teachings of the prophet Mohammed and believing in one God (Allah); the Moslem religion. **2.** Moslems or Moslem nations viewed collectively. **—Is•lam'ic** *adj.*
Is•lam•a•bad (ĭs-lä'mə-bäd', ĭz-). The capital of Pakistan in N West Pakistan. Pop. 50,000.
is•land (ī'lənd) *n.* **1.** A land mass smaller than a continent and surrounded by water. **2.** Anything completely isolated or surrounded. [< OE *iegland, iland.* See **akwā-**.]
is•land•er (ī'lən-dər) *n.* An inhabitant of an island.
islands of Lang•er•hans (läng'ər-häns'). Also **islets of Lang•er•hans.** Irregular masses of small cells that lie in the interstitial tissue of the pancreas and secrete insulin. [< P. *Langerhans* (1847–1888), German physician.]
isle (īl) *n.* An island, esp. a small one. [< L *insula.*]
is•let (ī'lĭt) *n.* A little island.
ism (ĭz'əm) *n. Informal.* A distinctive doctrine or cause.
–ism. *comb. form.* **1.** An action, practice, or process: **favoritism. 2.** A state or condition of being: **parallelism. 3.** A characteristic behavior or quality: **individualism. 4.** A distinctive usage or feature: *Latinism.* **5.** A doctrine, theory, system, or principle: **pacifism, militarism.** [< Gk *-ismos.*]
is•n't (ĭz'ənt). Contraction of *is not.*
iso–. *comb. form.* **1.** Equal, identical, or similar. **2.** *Chem.* Isomeric. [< Gk *isos,* equal.]
i•so•bar (ī'sə-bär') *n.* A line on a map connecting points of equal pressure. **—i'so•bar'ic** *adj.*
i•so•late (ī'sə-lāt', ĭs'ə-) *v.* **-lated, -lating. 1.** To separate from a group or whole and set apart. **2.** To render free of external influence. [< LL *insulātus,* converted into an island.] **—i'so•la'tion** *n.* **—i'so•la'tor** *n.*
i•so•la•tion•ism (ī'sə-lā'shə-nĭz'əm, ĭs'ə-) *n.* A national policy of remaining aloof from political entanglements with other countries. **—i'so•la'tion•ist** *n.* & *adj.*
i•so•mer (ī'sə-mər) *n.* **1.** A compound having the same percentage composition and molecular weight as another compound but differing in chemical or physical properties. **2.** An atom the nucleus of which can exist in any of several bound excited states for a measurable period of time. **—i'so•mer'ic** *adj.* **—i•som'er•ism'** (ī-sŏm'ə-rĭz'əm) *n.*
i•so•met•ric (ī'sə-mĕt'rĭk) *adj.* Also **i•so•met•ri•cal** (-rĭ-kəl). **1.** Exhibiting equality in dimensions or measurements. **2.** Involving muscular contraction occurring when the ends of the muscle are fixed in place so that significant increases in tension occur without appreciable increases in length. [< Gk *isometros,* of equal measure.]
isometric exercise. Exercise involving isometric contraction.
i•so•oc•tane (ī'sō-ŏk'tān') *n.* A highly flammable liquid, C_8H_{18}, used to determine the octane numbers of fuels.
i•so•prene (ī'sə-prēn') *n.* A colorless volatile liquid, C_5H_8, used chiefly to make synthetic rubber.
i•so•pro•pyl alcohol (ī'sə-prō'pəl). A clear, colorless, mobile flammable liquid, C_3H_8O, used in antifreeze compounds, lotions and cosmetics, and as a solvent.
i•sos•ce•les (ī-sŏs'ə-lēz') *adj.* Having two equal sides: *isosceles triangle.* [< Gk *isoskelēs,* "having equal legs."]
i•so•ther•mal (ī'sə-thûr'məl) *adj.* With or at equal temperatures. **—i'so•therm'** *n.*
i•so•tope (ī'sə-tōp') *n.* One of two or more atoms, the nuclei of which have the same number of protons but different numbers of neutrons. **—i'so•top'ic** (-tŏp'ĭk) *adj.* **—i'so•top'i•cal•ly** *adv.*
i•so•trop•ic (ī'sə-trŏp'ĭk) *adj.* Invariant with respect to direction. **—i•sot'ro•py** (ī-sŏt'rə-pē), **i•sot'ro•pism'** *n.*
Is•ra•el[1] (ĭz'rē-əl). **A republic on the E coast of the Mediterranean. Pop. 2,565,000. Cap. Jerusalem. —Is•rae'li** ***adj.*** **&** ***n.***

Israel[1]

Is•ra•el[2] (ĭz'rē-əl) *n.* **1.** The descendants of Jacob. **2.** The whole Hebrew people, past, present, and future, regarded as the chosen people of Jehovah by virtue of the covenant of Jacob. **3.** The Christian church, regarded as the heir to the ancient covenant.
Is•ra•el[3] (ĭz'-rē-əl). A name of the patriarch Jacob.
Is•ra•el•ite (ĭz'rē-ə-līt') *n.* A Hebrew. **—Is'ra•el•ite'** *adj.*
is•su•ance (ĭsh'o͞o-əns) *n.* An act of issuing.
is•sue (ĭsh'o͞o) *n.* **1.** An act or instance of flowing, passing, or giving out. **2.** Something produced, published, or offered, as stamps or coins. **3.** The result of an action. **4.** Proceeds from estates or fines. **5.** Something proceeding from a specified source. **6.** Offspring. **7.** A point of discussion. **8.** An outlet. **9.** A discharge, as of blood. **—at issue.** In dispute. **—take issue.** To disagree. *—v.* **-sued, -suing. 1.** To go or come out. **2.** To come forth or cause to come forth. **3.** To give or distribute, as supplies. **4.** To be descended. **5.** To result

from. **6.** To result in. **7.** To publish or be published. **8.** To circulate or be circulated, as coins. [< VL **exūta,* "exit."] —**is'su•er** *n.*

–ist. *comb. form.* **1.** One who does, makes, produces, etc.: **dramatist. 2.** One who is skilled or trained in a specified field: **industrialist. 3.** An adherent or proponent of a doctrine, system, or school of thought: *Platonist.* **4.** A person characterized by a certain trait: **sadist.** [< Gk *-istēs.*]

Is•tan•bul (ĭs'tăn-bo͞ol', ĭs'tän-). A city of European Turkey. Pop. 1,467,000.

isth•mus (ĭs'məs) *n., pl.* **-muses** or **-mi** (-mī'). **1.** A narrow strip of land connecting two larger masses of land. **2.** *Anat.* **a.** A narrow strip of tissue joining two larger organs or parts of an organ. **b.** A narrow passage connecting two larger cavities. [< Gk *isthmos.*]

it (ĭt) *pron.* The 3rd person sing. pronoun, neuter gender. **1.** —Used to represent the thing last mentioned: *I haven't seen it.* **2.** —Used as the subject of an impersonal verb: *It is raining.* **3.** —Used to represent a word, phrase, or clause that follows: *It is he.* **4.** *Informal.* The best or ultimate in something: *That steak was really it!* —*n.* In the game of tag, the player who must catch the others. [OE *hit.* See **ko-.**]

It., Ital. Italian; Italy.

ital. italic.

I•tal•ian (ĭ-tăl'yən) *adj.* Of Italy, its people, or their language. —*n.* **1.** An inhabitant of Italy, or a person of Italian descent. **2.** The Romance language of Italy.

i•tal•ic (ĭ-tăl'ĭk, ī-tăl'-) *adj.* Being a type with the letters slanting to the right, used to emphasize a word or passage. —**i•tal'ic** *n.*

I•tal•ic (ĭ-tăl'ĭk) *n.* A branch of Indo-European, including Latin and Osco-Umbrian.

i•tal•i•cize (ĭ-tăl'ĭ-sīz') *v.* **-cized, -cizing.** To print in italic type.

It•a•ly (ĭt'ə-lē). A republic of S Europe. Pop. 50,849,000. Cap. Rome.

itch (ĭch) *n.* **1.** A skin sensation causing a desire to scratch. **2.** A contagious skin disease marked by itching. **3.** A restless craving. [< OE *giccan* < Gmc **juk-.*] —**itch** *v.* —**itch'i•ness** *n.* —**itch'y** *adj.*

–ite. *comb. form.* **1.** A native or resident of a specified place: *New Jerseyite.* **2.** An adherent of someone specified: *Trotskyite.* **3.** A mineral or rock: **graphite. 4.** A commercial product: **Lucite.** [< Gk *-itēs.*]

i•tem (ī'təm) *n.* **1.** A single unit in a list, account, or series. **2. a.** A bit of information. **b.** A short piece in a newspaper. [< L *ita,* so.]

i•tem•ize (ī'tə-mīz') *v.* **-ized, -izing.** To set down item by item; list.

it•er•ate (ĭt'ə-rāt') *v.* **-ated, -ating.** To say or perform again; repeat. [< L *iterum,* again.] —**it'er•a'tion** *n.*

i•tin•er•ant (ī-tĭn'ər-ənt, ĭ-tĭn'-) *adj.* Traveling from place to place, esp. to perform some duty or work. —*n.* One who so travels. [< L *iter,* journey.]

i•tin•er•ar•y (ī-tĭn'ə-rĕr'ē, ĭ-tĭn'-) *n., pl.* **-ies. 1.** A route or proposed route of a journey. **2.** An account or record of a journey. **3.** A travelers' guidebook.

–itis. *comb. form.* Inflammation of or inflammatory disease: **bronchitis.** [< Gk.]

its (ĭts). The possessive form of the pronoun *it,* used attributively.

it's (ĭts). 1. Contraction of *it is.* **2.** Contraction of *it has.*

it•self (ĭt-sĕlf') *pron.* A form of the 3rd person sing. neuter pronoun: **1.** —Used reflexively: *This radio turns itself off.* **2.** —Used for emphasis: *The trouble is in the machine itself.* —**by itself. 1.** Alone. **2.** Without help.

–ity. *comb. form.* A state or quality: **authenticity.** [< L *-itās.*]

IUD intrauterine device.

–ium. *comb. form.* The name of an element or chemical group: **ammonium.** [< Gk *-ion,* dim suffix.]

IV intravenous.

I've (īv). Contraction of *I have.*

–ive. *comb. form.* Having a tendency toward or inclination to perform some action: **disruptive.** [< L *-īvus.*]

i•vo•ry (ī'və-rē, īv'rē) *n., pl.* **-ries. 1.** The hard, smooth, yellowish-white substance forming the tusks of certain animals, esp. elephants. **2.** A substance resembling ivory. **3.** Creamy white. [< L *ebur.*] —**i'vo•ry** *adj.*

Ivory Coast. A republic of W Africa. Pop. 3,750,000. Cap. Abidjan.

ivory tower. A place or attitude of intellectual retreat.

i•vy (ī'vē) *n., pl.* **ivies. 1.** A climbing or trailing plant with lobed, evergreen leaves. **2.** Any of various similar plants. [< OE *īfig* < Gmc **ibahs.*] —**i'vied** *adj.*

IWW Industrial Workers of the World.

–ize. Also *chiefly Brit.* **-ise.** *comb. form.* **1. a.** To cause to be or to become; make into: **dramatize. b.** To make conform with: **Anglicize. c.** To treat or regard as: **idolize. 2.** To cause to acquire a specified quality: **sterilize. 3.** To become or become similar to: **materialize. 4. a.** To subject to: **anesthetize. b.** To affect with: **galvanize, magnetize. 5.** To do or follow some practice: **pasteurize.** [< LL *-izāre* < Gk *-izein.*]

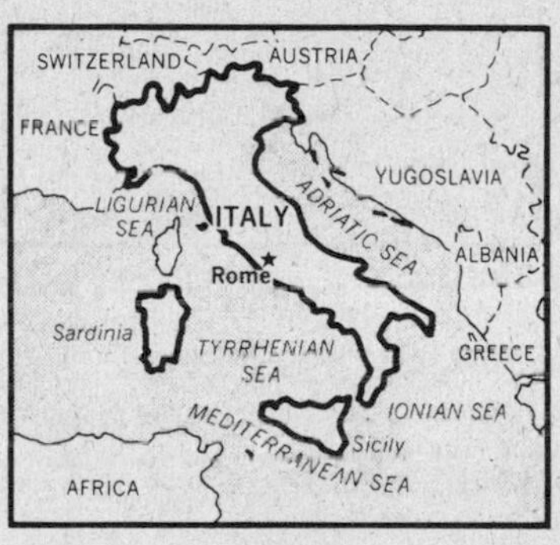

Italy

Ivory Coast

Jj

j, J (jā) *n.* **1.** The 10th letter of the English alphabet. **2.** The 10th in a series.

J joule.

J. 1. journal. **2.** judge.

J.A. judge advocate.

jab (jăb) *v.* **jabbed, jabbing. 1.** To poke abruptly, esp. with something sharp. **2.** To stab or pierce. —*n.* A quick stab or blow. [< ME *jobben.*] —**jab'bing•ly** *adv.*

jab•ber (jăb'ər) *v.* To talk rapidly, unintelligibly, or idly. —**jab'ber** *n.*

jab•ot (zhă-bō', jă-) *n.* A cascade of frills down the front of a shirt or blouse. [F.]

jac•a•ran•da (jăk'ə-răn'də) *n.* **1.** A tropical American tree with feathery leaves and clusters of pale-purple flowers. **2.** Rosewood. [Port *jacarandá.*]

jack (jăk) *n.* **1.** Any of several mechanical devices, esp. one for raising heavy objects a short distance, as by leverage. **2.** A socket that accepts a plug at one end and attaches to circuitry at the other. **3.** A playing card showing the figure of a knave. [Transferred use of the name *Jack.*]

jack•al (jăk'əl, -ôl') *n.* A doglike carnivorous mammal of Africa and Asia. [< Pers *shagāl.*]

jack•ass (jăk'ăs') *n.* **1.** A male ass or donkey. **2.** A foolish or stupid person.

jack•daw (jăk'dô') *n.* A crowlike Eurasian bird.

jack•et (jăk'ĭt) *n.* **1.** A short coat, usually hip-length. **2.** An outer covering or casing, as the dust jacket of a book. [< OF *jaque,* short jacket.] —**jack'et•less** *adj.*

jack-in-the-pul•pit (jăk'ĭn-*th*ə-po͝ol'pĭt, -pŭl'-pĭt) *n.* A plant with a leaflike part enclosing a clublike flower stalk.

jack•knife (jăk'nīf') *n.* **1.** A large pocketknife. **2.** A dive executed by bending at the waist and touching the feet with the hands before straightening out. —*v.* **-knifed, -knifing. 1.** To bend or fold like a jacknife. **2.** To form a 90°angle. [Prob JACK + KNIFE.]

jack-of-all-trades (jăk′əv-ôl′trādz′) *n., pl.* **jacks-of-all-trades.** One who can do many different kinds of work.

jack-o'-lan•tern (jăk′ə-lăn′tərn) *n.* A lantern made from a hollowed pumpkin with a carved face.

jack•pot (jăk′pŏt′) *n.* **1.** The cumulative stakes in various gambling games. **2.** A top prize or reward.

jack rabbit. A large hare of W North America. [JACK(ASS) + RABBIT.]

Jack•son (jăk′sən). The capital of Mississippi. Pop. 154,000.

Andrew Jackson

Jack•son (jăk′sən), **Andrew.** 1767–1845. 7th President of the U.S. (1829–37).

Jack•son•ville (jăk′sən-vĭl). A city of N Florida. Pop. 201,000.

Ja•cob (jā′kəb). Hebrew patriarch, son of Isaac. Genesis 25–50.

jade[1] (jād) *n.* Either of two distinct minerals, nephrite and jadeite, that are generally pale green or white and are used mainly as gemstones. [< Span *(piedra de) ijada,* "(stone of the) flank."]

jade[2] (jād) *n.* **1.** A broken-down horse; nag. **2.** A worthless woman. —*v.* **jaded, jading. 1.** To exhaust or wear out. **2.** To become weary or sated. [ME.] —**jad′ish** *adj.*

jad•ed (jā′dĭd) *adj.* **1.** Wearied; spiritless with fatigue. **2.** Dulled as by surfeit; sated. —**jad′ed•ly** *adv.* —**jad′ed•ness** *n.*

jade•ite (jā′dīt′) *n.* A rare, emerald to light-green, white, red-brown, yellow-brown, or violet jade, $NaAlSi_2O_6$.

jag[1] (jăg) *n.* Also **jagg.** A sharp projection; barb. [ME *jagge.*] —**jag′less** *adj.*

jag[2] (jăg) *n. Slang.* A bout or spree: *a crying jag.* [?]

jag•ged (jăg′ĭd) *adj.* Toothed or serrated; having jags. —**jag′ged•ly** *adv.*

jag•uar (jăg′wär′, -yōō-är′) *n.* A large, leopard-like tropical American wild-cat.

Jah•weh. Variant of **Yahweh.**

jai a•lai (hī′ lī′, hī′ ə-lī′, hī′ ə-lī′). A court game in which players use a long hand-shaped basket strapped to the wrist to propel a ball against a wall. [< Basque.]

jail (jāl). Also *chiefly Brit.* **gaol.** *n.* A prison for the confinement of persons in lawful detention. —*v.* To detain in custody; imprison. [< L *cavea,* a hollow, den, coop.]

jail•bird (jāl′bûrd′) *n. Informal.* A prisoner or ex-convict.

jail•er (jā′lər) *n.* Also **jail•or.** The keeper of a jail.

ja•lop•y (jə-lŏp′ē) *n., pl.* **-ies.** Also **ja•lop•py.** *Informal.* An old, dilapidated automobile. [?]

ja•lou•sie (jăl′ōō-sē) *n.* A blind or shutter having adjustable horizontal slats. [F, "jealousy."]

jam[1] (jăm) *v.* **jammed, jamming. 1.** To drive or wedge forcibly; squeeze into a tight position. **2.** To activate or apply suddenly: *jam the brakes on.* **3.** To become or cause to become locked, stuck, or unworkable. **4.** To pack to excess; cram. **5.** To block or clog. **6.** To interfere with the reception of (broadcast signals) by electronic means. —*n.* **1.** The act of jamming or condition of being jammed. **2.** A crush or congestion. **3.** *Informal.* A predicament.

jam[2] (jăm) *n.* A preserve made by boiling fruit with sugar.

Ja•mai•ca (jə-mā′kə). An island and nation in the Caribbean. Pop. 1,613,000. Cap. Kingston. —**Ja•mai′can** *n.* & *adj.*

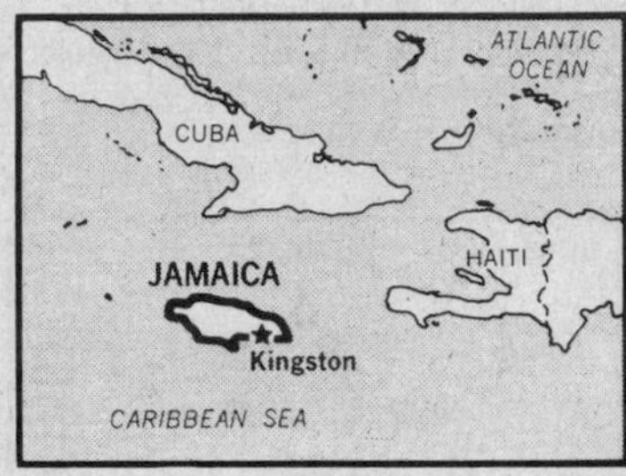

Jamaica

jamb (jăm) *n.* The vertical posts or pieces of a door or window frame. [< Gk *kampē,* joint.]

jam•bo•ree (jăm′bə-rē′) *n.* **1.** A noisy celebration. **2.** A large assembly. [?]

Jan. January.

jan•gle (jăng′gəl) *v.* **-gled, -gling. 1.** To make or cause to make a harsh, metallic sound. **2.** To grate on or jar (the nerves). —*n.* A harsh, metallic sound. [< OF *jangler.*] —**jan′gler** *n.* —**jan′gly** *adj.*

jan•i•tor (jăn′ə-tər) *n.* One who attends to the maintenance or cleaning of a building. [< L *jānus,* arched passage.]

Jan•u•ar•y (jăn′yōō-ĕr′ē) *n., pl.* **-ies.** The 1st month of the year. January has 31 days. [< L *Jānuārius (mensis),* "(month of) Janus."]

Ja•nus (jā′nəs). The Roman god of portals, depicted with two faces looking in opposite directions.

Ja•nus-faced (jā′nəs-fāst′) *adj.* Hypocritical.

Jap. Japan; Japanese.

Ja•pan (jə-păn′). A country of Asia occupying an archipelago off the NE coast of the continent. Pop. 93,419,000. Cap. Tokyo.

Jap•a•nese (jăp′ə-nēz′, -nēs′) *n., pl.* **-nese. 1.** A native or inhabitant of Japan. **2.** The language of Japan. —**Jap′a•nese′** *adj.*

jar[1] (jär) *n.* A cylindrical glass or earthenware vessel with a wide mouth. [< Ar *jarrah,* large earthen vase.]

jar[2] (jär) *v.* **jarred, jarring. 1.** To make or utter a harsh sound. **2.** To disturb. **3.** To shake from impact. **4.** To clash; conflict. **5.** To bump or cause to move or shake. —*n.* **1.** A jolt. **2.** A harsh, grating sound. [Prob imit.]

jar•di•nière (järd′n-îr′) *n.* A large, decorative stand or pot for plants. [< VL **gardīnus,* GARDEN.]

jar•gon (jär′gən) *n.* **1.** Nonsensical or incoherent utterance. **2.** The specialized or technical language of a group or profession. [< OF *jargoun,* "twittering."]

Jas. James (New Testament).

jas•mine (jăz′mən) *n.* Also **jes•sa•mine** (jĕs′ə-mĭn). Any of several vines or shrubs with fragrant, usually yellow or white flowers. [< Pers *yasmīn.*]

jas•per (jăs′pər) *n.* An opaque reddish, brown, or yellow quartz. [< Gk *iaspis.*]

jaun•dice (jôn′dĭs, jän′-) *n.* Yellowish discoloration of tissues and bodily fluids with bile pigment. [< L *galbinus,* greenish yellow.]

jaun•diced (jôn′dĭst, jän′-) *adj.* **1.** Affected with jaundice. **2.** Affected by envy, jealousy, malice, etc.

jaunt (jônt, jänt) *n.* A short trip or outing. [?]

jaun•ty (jôn′tē, jän′-) *adj.* **-tier, -tiest. 1.** Dapper in appearance; natty. **2.** Having a buoyant or self-confident air. [Earlier *jentee,* elegant, "genteel."] —**jaun′ti•ly** *adv.* —**jaun′ti•ness** *n.*

Jav. Javanese.

Ja•va (jä′və, jăv′ə). An island of Indonesia. Pop. 63,000,000.

Jav•a•nese (jăv′ə-nēz′, -nēs′) *n., pl.* **-nese. 1.** A native of Java. **2.** The Indonesian language spoken in Java. —**Jav′a•nese′** *adj.*

jave•lin (jăv′lən, jăv′ə-) *n.* **1.** A light spear thrown as a weapon. **2.** A spear used in contests of distance throwing. [< OF *javelot.*]

jaw (jô) *n.* **1.** Either of two bony or cartilaginous structures in most vertebrates forming the framework of the mouth and holding the teeth. **2.** Either of two opposed hinged parts in a mechanical device. **3. jaws.** A dangerous confrontation: *the jaws of death.* [ME *iawe.*] —**jaw′less** *adj.*

jaw•bone (jô′bōn′) *n.* Any bone of the jaw, esp. the bone of the lower jaw. —*v.* **-boned, -boning.** *Informal.* To urge voluntary compliance or to comply voluntarily, as with governmental guidelines limiting prices and wages. —*adj. Informal.* Urging voluntary compliance: *jawbone controls.*

jaw•break•er (jô′brā′kər) *n.* **1.** A kind of very hard candy. **2.** *Slang.* A word very difficult to pronounce.

jay (jā) *n.* Any of various birds related to the crows, often having a loud, harsh call. [< LL *gāius* and *gāia.*]

jay•walk (jā′wôk′) *v.* To cross a street without regard to traffic rules. —**jay′walk′er** *n.*

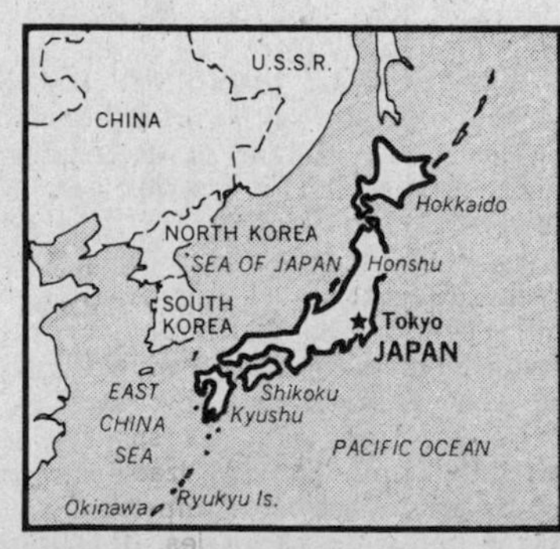

Japan

jazz (jăz) *n.* **1.** A kind of native American music, in most styles having a strong rhythmic understructure with solo and ensemble improvisations. **2.** *Slang.* **a.** Extreme exaggeration. **b.** Nonsense. [?]

jazz•y (jăz'ē) *adj.* **-ier, -iest. 1.** Resembling jazz. **2.** *Slang.* Showy; flashy: *a jazzy red car.* —**jazz'i•ly** *adv.* —**jazz'i•ness** *n.*

J.C.S. Joint Chiefs of Staff.

jct. junction.

jeal•ous (jĕl'əs) *adj.* **1.** Fearful of loss of position or affection. **2.** Resentful in rivalry; envious. **3.** Possessively watchful; vigilant. [< Gk *zēlos,* zeal.] —**jeal'ous•ly** *adv.* —**jeal'ous•y, jeal'ous•ness** *n.*

jeans (jēnz) *pl.n.* Pants made from strong, twilled cotton material. [< Genoa, where it was first made.]

jeep (jēp) *n.* A small, durable motor vehicle used esp. by the armed forces. [Orig *G.P.,* "general purpose."]

jeer (jîr) *v.* To speak or shout derisively; mock; taunt. [?] —**jeer** *n.* —**jeer'ing•ly** *adv.*

Jef•fer•son (jĕf'ər-sən), **Thomas.** 1743–1826. 3rd President of the U.S. (1801–09). —**Jef'fer•so'ni•an** (-sō'nē-ən) *adj.*

Thomas Jefferson

Jef•fer•son City (jĕf'ər-sən). The capital of Missouri. Pop. 32,000.

Je•ho•vah (jĭ-hō'və). God, esp. in Christian translations of the Old Testament.

je•june (jə-jo͞on') *adj.* **1.** Not nourishing; insubstantial. **2.** Not interesting. **3.** Childish. [< L *jējūnus,* hungry, fasting.]

je•ju•num (jə-jo͞o'nəm) *n., pl.* **-na** (-nə). The section of the small intestine between the duodenum and the ileum. [ML *jējūnum (intestīnum),* "the fasting (intestine)."]

jell (jĕl) *v.* **1.** To become or cause to become firm or gelatinous; congeal. **2.** *Informal.* To take shape or fall into place; crystallize.

jel•ly (jĕl'ē) *n., pl.* **-lies. 1.** A soft, resilient food usually made by the setting of a liquid containing pectin or gelatin. **2.** Any substance with the consistency of jelly. —*v.* **-lied, -lying.** To make into or become jelly. [< L *gelāre,* to freeze.]

jel•ly•fish (jĕl'ē-fĭsh') *n.* **1.** A gelatinous, free-swimming, often umbrella-shaped marine organism. **2.** *Informal.* A person who lacks force of character.

jen•ny (jĕn'ē) *n., pl.* **-nies.** A **spinning jenny.**

jeop•ard•ize (jĕp'ər-dīz') *v.* **-ized, -izing.** To invite loss of or injury to; imperil.

jeop•ard•y (jĕp'ər-dē) *n., pl.* **-ies. 1.** Danger or risk of loss or injury. **2.** *Law.* A defendant's risk or danger of conviction. [< OF *jeu parti,* "divided play, even chance."]

Jer. Jeremiah (Old Testament).

jer•e•mi•ad (jĕr'ə-mī'əd) *n.* An elaborate lamentation.

Jer•e•mi•ah (jĕr'ə-mī'ə). Hebrew prophet of the 7th and 6th centuries B.C.

jerk (jûrk) *v.* To move by or with a sharp, suddenly abrupt motion. —*n.* **1.** A sudden, abrupt motion, such as a yank, twist, or lurch. **2.** A sudden spasmodic muscular movement. **3.** *Slang.* A stupid or fatuous person. [?] —**jerk'i•ly** *adv.* —**jerk'i•ness** *n.* —**jerk'y** *adj.*

jer•kin (jûr'kən) *n.* A short, close-fitting coat or jacket, usually sleeveless. [?]

jerk•wa•ter (jûrk'wô'tər, -wŏt'ər) *adj. Informal.* Remote, small, and insignificant: *a jerkwater town.*

jer•ry•build (jĕr'ē-bĭld') *v.* **-built** (-bĭlt'), **-building.** To build flimsily and cheaply. [?]

jer•sey (jûr'zē) *n., pl.* **-seys. 1.** A soft, plain-knitted fabric. **2.** A knitted pullover shirt. **3.** A close-fitting knitted jacket or sweater. [< *Jersey,* one of the Channel Islands.]

Jersey City. A city of NE New Jersey. Pop. 276,000.

Je•ru•sa•lem (jə-ro͞o'sə-ləm, -zə-ləm). The capital of ancient and modern Israel. Pop. 248,000.

jes•sa•mine. Variant of **jasmine.**

jest (jĕst) *n.* **1.** Something said or done to provoke amusement and laughter. **2.** A frivolous attitude: *spoken in jest.* —*v.* To act or speak playfully; joke. [< L *gesta,* exploits.]

jest•er (jĕs'tər) *n.* One given to jesting, esp. a fool or buffoon at medieval courts.

Jes•u•it (jĕzh'o͞o-ĭt, jĕz'yo͞o-) *n.* A member of the Society of Jesus, a Roman Catholic order.

Je•sus (jē'zəs). Also, in various contexts, "Jesus of Nazareth," "Christ," "Jesus Christ," or "Christ Jesus." 4? B.C.–A.D. 29? Son of Mary; founder of the Christian religion; regarded by Christians as the son of God and the Messiah.

jet¹ (jĕt) *n.* **1.** A dense black coal that takes a high polish and is used for jewelry. **2.** A deep black. [< Gk *gagatēs,* "stone of *Gagai*" (town in Asia Minor).] —**jet** *adj.*

jet² (jĕt) *n.* **1. a.** A high-velocity fluid stream forced under pressure out of a small-diameter opening. **b.** Something emitted in or as if in such a stream. **c.** An outlet for emitting such a stream. **2.** A jet-propelled vehicle, esp. a jet-propelled aircraft. —*v.* **jetted, jetting. 1.** To propel outward under pressure. **2.** To travel by jet plane. [< L *jacere,* to throw.]

jet engine. 1. Any engine that develops thrust by ejecting a jet, esp. of gaseous combustion products. **2.** Such an engine equipped to consume atmospheric oxygen as distinguished from rocket engines with self-contained fuel-oxidizer systems.

jet•sam (jĕt'səm) *n.* **1.** Cargo thrown overboard to lighten a ship in distress. **2.** Discarded odds and ends. [< JETTISON.]

jet•ti•son (jĕt'ĭ-sən, -zən) *v.* **1.** To cast off or overboard. **2.** To discard. [< L *jactāre,* to throw.]

jet•ty (jĕt'ē) *n., pl.* **-ties. 1.** A structure projecting into a body of water to influence the current or tide or protect a harbor or shoreline. **2.** A wharf. [< OF *jeter,* to throw, project.]

Jew (jo͞o) *n.* **1.** An adherent of Judaism. **2.** A descendant of the Hebrew people.

jew•el (jo͞o'əl) *n.* **1.** An ornament of precious metal or gems. **2.** A precious stone; a gem. **3.** A small gem or gem substitute used as a bearing in a watch. **4.** A treasured or esteemed person or thing. —*v.* **1.** To adorn with jewels. **2.** To fit with jewels, as a watch. [< NF *juel.*] —**jew'el•ry** *n.*

jew•el•er (jo͞o'ə-lər) *n.* Also *chiefly Brit.* **jew•el•ler.** One who makes, repairs, or deals in jewelry.

Jew•ish (jo͞o'ĭsh) *adj.* **1.** Of, concerning, or characteristic of the Jews, their customs, or their religion. **2.** Yiddish. —*n.* Yiddish.

Jew•ry (jo͞o'rē) *n.* Jews collectively.

jez•e•bel (jĕz'ə-bĕl', -bəl) *n.* Also **Jez•e•bel.** A scheming, wicked woman. [< *Jezebel,* wicked queen of Israel.]

jg junior grade.

jib (jĭb) *n.* A triangular sail attached to the forward mast of a sailing vessel. [?]

jibe¹ (jīb) *v.* **jibed, jibing.** *Informal.* To be in accord; agree. [?]

jibe². Variant of **gibe.**

jif•fy (jĭf'ē) *n., pl.* **-fies.** *Informal.* A moment; no time at all. [?]

jig (jĭg) *n.* **1.** Any of various lively dances in triple time. **2.** A device for guiding a tool or holding machine work in place. —*v.* **jigged, jigging. 1.** To dance a jig. **2.** To move or bob up and down jerkily and rapidly. [?]

jig•ger (jĭg'ər) *n.* **1.** A small measure for liquor, usually holding $1\frac{1}{2}$ ounces. **2.** A short golf club with an iron head. **3.** A short mast set in the stern of a yawl or ketch. **4.** A trivial article whose name eludes one.

jig•gle (jĭg'əl) *v.* **-gled, -gling.** To move lightly and jerkily up and down or to and fro. —*n.* A jiggling motion.

jig•saw (jĭg'sô') *n.* A saw used to cut sharp curves.

jigsaw puzzle. A game consisting of the reassembly of a picture on cardboard or wood that has been cut into numerous interlocking pieces.

jilt (jĭlt) *v.* To discard (a lover) unexpectedly. —*n.* A woman who discards a lover.

Jim Crow. *Slang.* The systematic practice of segregating and suppressing Negroes. —**Jim'-Crow'** *adj.*

jim•my (jĭm'ē) *n., pl.* **-mies.** A short crowbar with curved ends, often regarded as a burglar's tool. —**jim'my** *v.* **(-mied, -mying).**

jim•son•weed (jĭm'sən-wēd') *n.* A coarse, poisonous plant with large, trumpet-shaped white or purplish flowers. [< *Jamestown,* Virginia.]

jin•gle (jĭng'gəl) *v.* **-gled, -gling.** To make or cause to make a tinkling or ringing metallic sound. —*n.* **1.** Such a sound. **2.** Something resembling or suggesting such a sound. **3.** A simple, repetitious, catchy rhyme.

jin•go (jĭng'gō) *n., pl.* **-goes.** An extreme and belligerent nationalist; a blatant patriot. —**jin'go•ish, jin'go•is'tic** *adj.* —**jin'go•ism'** *n.* —**jin'go•ist** *n.*

jink (jĭngk) *v.* To make a quick, evasive turn. —*n.* **1.** A sudden evasive turn. **2. jinks.** Rambunctious play: *high jinks.* [?]

jin•ni (jĭn'ē, jĭ-nē') *n., pl.* **jinn** (jĭn). Also **djin•ni** *pl.* **djinn.** A supernatural being in Moslem folklore.

jin•rik•sha (jĭn-rĭk'shô) *n.* A two-wheeled Oriental carriage drawn by one or two men. [Jap *jinrikisha.*]

jinx (jĭngks). *Informal. n.* Something or someone believed to bring bad luck. —*v.* To bring bad luck to. [Poss < Gk *iunx,* a bird used in magic.]

jit•ney (jĭt'nē) *n., pl.* **-neys.** *Informal.* A small vehicle that transports passengers for a low fare. [?]

jit•ter (jĭt′ər) *v. Informal.* To be nervous or uneasy; fidget. [?] —**jit′ter•y** *adj.*

jit•ter•bug (jĭt′ər-bŭg′) *n.* **1.** A strenuous dance performed to quick-tempo jazz or swing music. **2.** A performer of this dance. —*v.* **-bugged, -bugging.** To dance the jitterbug.

jit•ters (jĭt′ərz) *pl.n. Informal.* A fit of nervousness.

jiu•jit•su, jiu•jut•su. Variants of **jujitsu.**

jive (jīv) *n. Slang.* **1.** Jazz or swing music. **2.** The jargon of jazz musicians and enthusiasts. **3.** Deceptive or glib talk. [?]

jnt. joint.

Joan of Arc (jōn′; ärk′), **Saint.** 1412–1431. French national heroine.

job (jŏb) *n.* **1.** An action requiring some exertion; an undertaking. **2.** An activity performed for payment, esp. one performed regularly as one's occupation. **3. a.** A piece of work to be done for a fee. **b.** The object to be worked on. **c.** Anything resulting from work. **4.** A position in which one is employed. —*v.* **jobbed, jobbing. 1.** To work by the piece. **2.** To act as a middleman or jobber. **3.** To subcontract (work). **4.** To transact (official business) dishonestly for private profit. [?] —**job′less** *adj.* —**job′less•ness** *n.*

Job (jōb). The righteous sufferer of the Old Testament book of Job.

job•ber (jŏb′ər) *n.* **1.** One who buys merchandise from manufacturers and sells it to retailers. **2.** A person who works by the piece. **3.** A public official who exploits his position for personal gain.

job•ber•y (jŏb′ə-rē) *n.* Corruption among public officials.

job•hold•er (jŏb′hōl′dər) *n.* One who has a regular or steady job.

job lot. 1. Miscellaneous merchandise sold in one lot. **2.** Any collection of cheap or almost worthless items.

job printer. A printer who does miscellaneous work, as circulars and cards.

jock•ey (jŏk′ē) *n., pl.* **-eys.** One who rides horses in races, esp. professionally. —*v.* **1.** To ride (a horse) as jockey. **2.** To direct or maneuver by cleverness or skill. **3.** To maneuver for position or a certain advantage.

jo•cose (jō-kōs′) *adj.* Merry; humorous. [< L *jocus,* jest, joke.] —**jo•cose′ly** *adv.*

jo•cos•i•ty (jō-kŏs′ə-tē) *n., pl.* **-ties. 1.** The state or quality of being jocose. **2.** A jocose remark or act.

joc•u•lar (jŏk′yə-lər) *adj.* Humorous; facetious; merry. [< L *jocus,* jest, joke.] —**joc′u•lar•ly** *adv.*

joc•u•lar•i•ty (jŏk′yə-lăr′ə-tē) *n., pl.* **-ties. 1.** The state or quality of being jocular. **2.** Playful humor. **3.** A jocular remark.

joc•und (jŏk′ənd, jō′kənd) *adj.* Cheerful; merry; gay. [< L *jūcundus,* agreeable.] —**joc′und•ly** *adv.*

jo•cun•di•ty (jō-kŭn′də-tē) *n., pl.* **-ties. 1.** The state or quality of being jocund. **2.** A jocund remark or act.

jodh•pur boots (jŏd′pər). Short ankle-height leather boots worn with jodhpurs.

jodh•purs (jŏd′pərz) *pl.n.* Riding breeches that fit tightly at the knees and ankles. [< *Jodhpur,* India.]

jog[1] (jŏg) *v.* **jogged, jogging. 1.** To jolt. **2.** To nudge. **3.** To run or ride at a steady slow trot. **4.** To proceed in a carefree way. —*n.* **1.** A jolt. **2.** A nudge. **3.** A trot. [?]

jog[2] (jŏg) *n.* **1.** A protruding or receding part in a surface or line. **2.** An abrupt change in direction. [Perh var of JAG[1].]

jog•gle (jŏg′əl) *v.* **-gled, -gling.** To shake or jar slightly. —**jog′gle** *n.*

Jo•han•nes•burg (jō-hăn′ĭs-bûrg′, yō-hä′nĭs-). A city of the Republic of South Africa, in the NE. Pop. 1,153,000.

John (jŏn), **Saint.** Called "the Evangelist," "the Divine." Christian apostle; reputed author of the 4th Gospel.

John Doe (jŏn′ dō′). A name used in legal proceedings to designate a fictitious or unidentified person.

john•ny•cake (jŏn′ē-kāk′) *n.* A small bread-like cake made with white cornmeal cooked on a griddle or baked.

John•son (jŏn′sən). **1. Andrew.** 1808–1875. 17th President of the U.S. (1865–69). **2. Lyndon Baines.** 1908–1973. 36th President of the U.S. (1963–69). **3. Samuel.** 1709–1784. English author, critic, and lexicographer.

Andrew Johnson

Lyndon Baines Johnson

John the Baptist, Saint. Baptizer of Jesus.

join (join) *v.* **1.** To put or bring together: *join hands.* **2.** To put or bring into close association: *joined in marriage.* **3.** To connect, as with a straight line. **4.** To form a junction with; combine with. **5.** To come or act together. **6.** To take part; participate. [< L *jungere.*]

join•er (joi′nər) *n.* **1.** One that joins. **2.** *Chiefly Brit.* A carpenter.

joint (joint) *n.* **1.** A point or position at which two or more things are joined. **2.** A point of connection or articulation between more or less movable bodily parts. **3.** A cut of meat for roasting. **4.** *Slang.* Any public establishment or dwelling. **5.** *Slang.* A marijuana cigarette. —*adj.* Shared by or common to two or more.

joist (joist) *n.* A horizontal beam set from wall to wall to support the boards of a floor or ceiling. [< L *jacēre,* to lie down.]

joke (jōk) *n.* **1.** An amusing remark or story. **2.** A mischievous trick. **3.** A ludicrous incident or situation. **4.** A triviality: *His accident was no joke.* **5.** A laughingstock. —*v.* **joked, joking. 1.** To tell or play jokes. **2.** To speak in fun; be facetious. [L *jocus,* jest, joke.] —**joke′less** *adj.* —**jok′ing•ly** *adv.*

jok•er (jō′kər) *n.* **1.** One who tells or plays jokes. **2.** A playing card, usually printed with a picture of a jester, typically used as a wild card. **3.** An element in a situation that acts in an unexpected way.

jol•li•fi•ca•tion (jŏl′ə-fĭ-kā′shən) *n.* Festivity; merrymaking.

jol•li•ty (jŏl′ə-tē) *n.* Merriment.

jol•ly (jŏl′ē) *adj.* **-lier, -liest. 1.** Merry. **2.** Festive. —*adv. Brit. Informal.* Very: *a jolly good cook.* [< OF *jolif, joli,* gay, pleasant.]

jolt (jōlt) *v.* **1.** To bump into; jostle. **2.** To shake or knock about. **3.** To jar with or as if with a sudden, sharp blow. —*n.* **1.** A sudden jarring or jerking. **2.** A sudden shock or reversal. [?] —**jolt′er** *n.* —**jolt′y** *adj.*

Jo•nah (jō′nə) *n.* One thought to bring bad luck. [< *Jonah,* Old Testament prophet whose disobedience to God caused a storm to endanger the ship in which he was traveling. Jonah 1:4.]

Jones (jōnz), **John Paul.** 1747–1792. Scottish-born American naval officer in the Revolutionary War.

jon•quil (jŏng′kwĭl, jŏn′-) *n.* A cultivated plant related to the daffodil, having short-tubed, fragrant yellow flowers. [< Span *junco,* rush, reed.]

Jon•son (jŏn′sən), **Ben(jamin).** 1573–1637. English poet and dramatist.

Jor•dan (jôrd′n). **1.** The principal river of Israel and Jordan. **2.** A kingdom in NW Arabia. Pop. 1,935,000. Cap. Amman. —**Jor•da′ni•an** (jôr-dā′nē-ən) *adj.* & *n.*

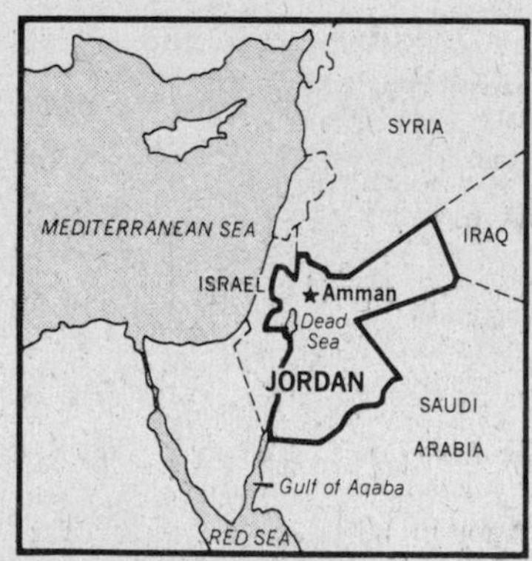

Jordan

Jo•seph (jō′zəf). **1.** Son of Jacob; sold into slavery in Egypt, he became the pharaoh's chief official. Genesis 30–46. **2.** Husband of Mary, mother of Jesus. Matthew 1:16.

josh (jŏsh) *v.* To tease; joke. [?]

Josh. Joshua (Old Testament).

jos•tle (jŏs′əl) *v.* **-tled, -tling. 1.** To come in contact or collide. **2.** To make one's way by pushing or elbowing. —*n.* A rough push or shove. [< OF *juster,* to joust.]

jot (jŏt) *n.* The smallest bit or particle; iota.

—*v.* **jotted, jotting.** To write down briefly and hastily. [< Gk *iōta,* IOTA.]

joule (joul, jo͞ol) *n.* **1.** The International System unit of energy equal to the work done when a current of 1 ampere is passed through a resistance of 1 ohm for 1 second. **2.** A unit of energy equal to the work done when the point of application of a force of 1 newton is displaced 1 meter in the direction of the force. [< J.P. *Joule* (1818–1889), British physicist.]

jounce (jouns) *v.* **jounced, jouncing.** To move with bumps and jolts. [ME *jouncen.*] —**jounce** *n.* —**jounc'y** *adj.*

jour. journal.

jour•nal (jûr'nəl) *n.* **1.** A daily record of occurrences or transactions, as a diary or ship's log. **2.** A newspaper. **3.** A specialized periodical. **4.** The part of a shaft or axle supported by a bearing. [< OF, "daily."]

jour•nal•ese (jûr'nə-lēz', -lēs') *n.* The slick, superficial style of writing often held to be characteristic of newspapers and magazines.

jour•nal•ism (jûr'nə-lĭz'əm) *n.* **1.** The collecting, writing, editing, and publishing of news in periodicals. **2.** Material written for publication in a periodical. —**jour'nal•ist** *n.* —**jour'nal•is'tic** *adj.* —**jour'nal•is'ti•cal•ly** *adv.*

jour•ney (jûr'nē) *n., pl.* **-neys.** Travel from one place to another; a trip. —*v.* To travel. [ME, period of travel, a day's traveling.]

jour•ney•man (jûr'nē-mən) *n.* A workman who has served his apprenticeship.

joust (jŭst, joust, jo͞ost) *n.* **1.** A combat with lances between two mounted knights. **2.** **jousts.** A series of these matches; a tournament. —*v.* To engage in such combat. [< VL **juxtāre,* to come together.]

Jove (jōv) *n.* The god Jupiter.

jo•vi•al (jō'vē-əl) *adj.* Marked by hearty conviviality. [Orig "born under the influence of Jupiter."] —**jo'vi•al'i•ty** (-ăl'ə-tē) *n.*

jowl[1] (joul) *n.* **1.** The jaw, esp. the lower jaw. **2.** The cheek. [< OE *ceafl.* See **geph-.**]

jowl[2] (joul) *n.* The flesh under the lower jaw, esp. when plump or flaccid. [Prob < OE *ceole, ceolu,* throat. See **gwel-**[1].]

joy (joi) *n.* **1.** A feeling of delight; happiness; gladness. **2.** A source of pleasure. [< L *gaudium,* gladness, delight.]

Joyce (jois), **James.** 1882–1941. Irish novelist.

joy•ful (joi'fəl) *adj.* Feeling, causing, or indicating joy. —**joy'ful•ly** *adv.*

joy•ous (joi'əs) *adj.* Feeling or causing joy; joyful. —**joy'ous•ly** *adv.*

J.P. justice of the peace.

Jr., Jr. junior.

ju•bi•lant (jo͞o'bə-lənt) *adj.* **1.** Exultingly joyful. **2.** Expressing joy. [< L *jūbilāre,* to raise a shout of joy.] —**ju'bi•lant•ly** *adv.*

ju•bi•la•tion (jo͞o'bə-lā'shən) *n.* The state of being jubilant; exultation.

ju•bi•lee (jo͞o'bə-lē') *n.* **1. a.** A special anniversary, esp. a 50th anniversary. **b.** The celebration of such an anniversary. **2.** A season or occasion of joyful celebration. **3.** Jubilation; rejoicing. [< LGk *iōbēlos,* jubilee.]

Ju•da•ic (jo͞o-dā'ĭk) *adj.* Also **Ju•da•i•cal** (-ĭ-kəl). Of or pertaining to Jews or Judaism.

Ju•da•ism (jo͞o'dē-ĭz'əm) *n.* The monotheistic religion of the Jewish people.

Ju•das (jo͞o'dəs) *n.* A betrayer in the guise of a friend. [< *Judas* Iscariot, Apostle who betrayed Jesus.]

Judg. Judges (Old Testament).

judge (jŭj) *v.* **judged, judging. 1. a.** To pass judgment upon in a court of law. **b.** To sit in judgment upon; hear. **2.** To determine authoritatively after deliberation; decide. **3.** To form an opinion about. **4.** To criticize; censure. **5.** To think; consider; suppose. —*n.* **1.** A public official who hears and decides cases brought before a court of law; justice; magistrate. **2.** An appointed arbiter in a contest or competition. **3.** One whose critical judgment or opinion is sought; a connoisseur. [< L *jūdex (jūdic-),* judge.] —**judg'er** *n.*

judg•ment (jŭj'mənt) *n.* Also **judge•ment. 1. a.** The ability to perceive and distinguish relationships or alternatives; discernment. **b.** The capacity to make reasonable decisions. **2.** A formal decision, as of an arbiter in a contest. **3.** An estimation. **4.** An idea; opinion; thought. **5.** Criticism; censure. **6.** A judicial decision. —**judg•men'tal** *adj.*

ju•di•ca•ture (jo͞o'dĭ-kə-cho͝or') *n.* **1.** The administering of justice. **2.** A system of law courts and their judges.

ju•di•cial (jo͞o-dĭsh'əl) *adj.* **1.** Of, pertaining to, or proper to courts of law or the administration of justice. **2.** Decreed by or proceeding from a court. **3.** Relative to, characterized by, or expressing judgment.

ju•di•ci•ar•y (jo͞o-dĭsh'ē-ĕr'ē) *adj.* Of or pertaining to courts, judges, or judicial decisions. —*n., pl.* **-ies. 1.** The judicial branch of government. **2.** A system of courts of justice and their judges. —**ju•di'ci•ar'i•ly** *adv.*

ju•di•cious (jo͞o-dĭsh'əs) *adj.* Having or exhibiting sound judgment. —**ju•di'cious•ly** *adv.* —**ju•di'cious•ness** *n.*

ju•do (jo͞o'dō) *n.* A modern form of jujitsu applying principles of balance and leverage. [Jap *jūdō.*] —**ju'do•ist** *n.*

jug (jŭg) *n.* **1.** A small pitcher. **2.** A tall, often rounded vessel with a small mouth, a handle, and usually a stopper, for holding liquids. **3.** *Slang.* A jail. [< *Jug,* pet form of Joan or Judith.]

jug•ger•naut (jŭg'ər-nôt') *n.* Anything that draws blind and destructive devotion, such as a belief.

jug•gle (jŭg'əl) *v.* **-gled, -gling. 1.** To keep (two or more objects) in the air at one time by alternately tossing and catching them. **2.** To manipulate in order to deceive. [< L *joculāri,* to jest.] —**jug'gler** *n.* —**jug'gling•ly** *adv.*

jug•u•lar (jŭg'yə-lər) *adj.* Of or located in the region of the neck or throat. —*n.* A jugular vein. [< L *jugulum,* collarbone.]

juice (jo͞os) *n.* **1. a.** Any fluid naturally contained in plant or animal tissue. **b.** Any bodily secretion. **2.** *Slang.* **a.** Electric current. **b.** Fuel for an engine. —*v.* **juiced, juicing.** To extract the juice from. [< L *jūs,* broth, sauce, juice.] —**juice'less** *adj.*

juic•y (jo͞o'sē) *adj.* **-ier, -iest. 1.** Full of juice; succulent. **2.** Richly interesting; lively; racy.

ju•jit•su (jo͞o-jĭt'so͞o) *n.* Also **ju•jut•su, jiu•jit•su, jiu•jut•su.** A Japanese art of hand-to-hand combat that forces an opponent to use his weight and strength against himself. [Jap *jūjitsu.*]

ju•jube (jo͞o'jo͞ob') *n.* **1.** The fleshy, edible fruit of a spiny tree. **2.** A chewy, fruit-flavored candy or lozenge. [< L *zizyphum.*]

juke box (jo͞ok). A coin-operated phonograph. [< earlier *juke-house,* a brothel.]

ju•lep (jo͞o'lĭp) *n.* A sweetened alcoholic drink made with shaved ice and usually garnished with mint leaves. [< Pers *gulāb,* "rose water."]

Ju•ly (jo͞o-lī', jo͞o-) *n., pl.* **-lys.** The 7th month of the year. July has 31 days. [< L *Jūlius (mēnsis),* (month of) Julius Caesar.]

jum•ble (jŭm'bəl) *v.* **-bled, -bling. 1.** To move, mix, or mingle in a confused, disordered manner. **2.** To confuse. [?] —**jum'ble** *n.*

jum•bo (jŭm'bō) *n., pl.* **-bos.** An unusually large person, animal, or thing. [< *Jumbo,* a large elephant exhibited by P.T. Barnum.] —**jum'bo** *adj.*

jump (jŭmp) *v.* **1.** To spring off the ground or another base by a muscular effort of the legs and feet; leap; leap over. **2.** To throw oneself down, off, out, or into something. **3.** To spring at or upon with the intent to assail or censure. **4.** To arrive at hastily or haphazardly: *jump to conclusions.* **5.** To grab at eagerly: *jump at a bargain.* **6.** To start involuntarily. **7.** To rise suddenly and pronouncedly. **8.** To skip over, leaving a break in continuity. **9.** *Checkers.* To take (an opponent's piece) by moving over it with one's own checker. **10.** To leave (a course or track) through mishap. **11.** *Slang.* To have a lively, pulsating quality. —*n.* **1.** The act of jumping; a leap. **2.** A sudden, pronounced rise. **3.** A level: *a jump ahead of the others.* **4.** An involuntary nervous movement. [Prob imit.] —**jump'a•ble** *adj.*

jump•er[1] (jŭm'pər) *n.* **1.** One that jumps. **2.** A wire used temporarily to complete or by-pass an electric circuit.

jum•per[2] (jŭm'pər) *n.* A sleeveless dress worn over a blouse or sweater. [Prob < Brit dial *jump, jup,* man's loose jacket.]

jump•y (jŭm'pē) *adj.* **-ier, -iest.** Fitful, nervous, or on edge. —**jump'i•ness** *n.*

Jun., Jun. junior.

Junc. junction.

jun•co (jŭng'kō) *n., pl.* **-cos.** A North American bird with predominantly gray plumage. [Span, "rush," junco.]

junc•tion (jŭngk'shən) *n.* **1.** The act or process of joining or condition of being joined. **2.** A place where two things join or meet. [< L *junctus,* pp of *jungere,* to join.]

junc•ture (jŭngk'chər) *n.* **1.** The act of joining or condition of being joined. **2.** The line or point where two things are joined; junction. **3.** A point or interval in time.

June (jo͞on) *n.* The 6th month of the year. June has 30 days. [< L *Jūnius (mēnsis),* (month consecrated to) the goddess JUNO.]

Ju•neau (jo͞o'nō). The capital of Alaska. Pop. 7,000.

jun•gle (jŭng'gəl) *n.* **1.** Land densely overgrown with tropical vegetation and trees. **2.** Any dense thicket or growth. **3.** Any place requiring intense or ruthless struggle for survival. [< Sk *jāṅgala,* "dry," desert.]

jun•ior (jo͞on'yər) *adj.* **1.** Younger. Used to distinguish a son from a father of the same name: *William Jones, Jr.* **2.** Designed for youthful persons: *junior dress sizes.* **3.** Lower in rank or shorter in length of tenure. **4.** Designating the 3rd year of a U.S. high school or college. —*n.* **1.** A younger person. **2.** A subordinate. **3.** One in his junior year of high school or college. [L *jūnior.*]

junior college. A U.S. college offering a two-year course.

junior high school. A U.S. school including the 7th, 8th, and sometimes 9th grades.

ju•ni•per (jo͞o'nə-pər) *n.* An evergreen tree or shrub with scalelike foliage and aromatic, berrylike fruit. [< L *jūniperus.*]

junk[1] (jŭngk) *n.* **1.** Scrapped materials that can be converted into usable stock. **2.** Rubbish; trash. —*v.* To throw away or desert as useless. [< ME *jonke.*]

junk[2] (jŭngk) *n.* A Chinese flat-bottomed sailing ship. [< Malay *jong,* seagoing ship.]

jun•ket (jŭng′kĭt) *n.* **1.** A sweet food made from flavored milk and rennet. **2.** An outing. **3.** A trip taken by an official and underwritten with public funds. [ME *jonket,* a kind of egg custard.]

Ju•no (jo͞o′nō). Chief goddess of the Roman pantheon; sister and wife of Jupiter.

jun•ta (ho͝on′tə, ho͝on′-, jŭn′-) *n.* Those holding state power in a country, esp. after a coup d'état. [< VL **juncta,* "joined."]

Ju•pi•ter (jo͞o′pə-tər) *n.* **1.** The supreme god of the Roman pantheon; Jove. **2.** The 5th planet from the sun, having a diameter of approx. 86,000 miles, a mass approx. 318 times that of Earth, and a sidereal period of revolution about the sun of 11.86 years at a mean distance of 483 million miles.

Ju•ras•sic (jo͞o-răs′ĭk) *adj.* Of or belonging to the geologic time, rock systems, or sedimentary deposits of the second period of the Mesozoic era. —*n.* The Jurassic period. [< the *Jura* Mountains along the French-Swiss border.]

ju•rid•i•cal (jo͞o-rĭd′ĭ-kəl) *adj.* Also **ju•rid•ic** (-ĭk). Of or pertaining to the law. [< L *jūs,* law + *dīcere,* to say.]

ju•ris•dic•tion (jo͝or-əs-dĭk′shən) *n.* **1.** The authority to interpret and apply the law. **2.** The extent or range of such authority. [< L *jūrisdictiō.*] —**ju′ris•dic′tion•al** *adj.*

ju•ris•pru•dence (jo͝or′əs-pro͞o′dəns) *n.* **1.** The science or philosophy of law. **2.** A system of laws. [< LL *jūrisprūdentia,* "skill in law."]

ju•rist (jo͝or′əst) *n.* One skilled in the law. [< L *jūs (jūr-),* law.]

ju•ror (jo͝or′ər, -ôr′) *n.* One who serves on a jury.

ju•ry (jo͝or′ē) *n., pl.* **-ries. 1.** A group of persons forming a body sworn to judge and give a verdict on some matter, esp. one summoned to a court of law. **2.** A committee formed to judge a competition. [< L *jūrāta,* "thing sworn."] —**ju′ry•less** *adj.*

just (jŭst) *adj.* **1.** Honorable and fair in one's dealings and actions; equitable. **2.** Properly due or merited. **3.** Legitimate. **4.** Suitable; fitting. **5.** Sound; well-founded; accurate. **6.** Righteous. —*adv.* (jŭst; *unstressed* jəst, jĭst). **1.** Precisely; exactly. **2.** Only a moment ago. **3.** By a narrow margin; barely. **4.** But a little distance. **5.** Merely; only. **6.** Simply; certainly: *It's just beautiful!* [< L *jūstus.*] —**just′ly** *adv.* —**just′ness** *n.*

jus•tice (jŭs′tĭs) *n.* **1.** Moral rightness; equity. **2.** Honor; fairness. **3.** The administration and procedure of law. **4.** A judge. [< L *jūstus,* JUST.] —**jus′tice•less** *adj.*

justice of the peace. A magistrate of a state court system, having authority chiefly to act on minor offenses, perform marriages, etc.

jus•ti•fy (jŭs′tə-fī′) *v.* **-fied, -fying. 1.** To demonstrate to be just, right, or valid. **2.** To show to be well-founded; warrant. **3.** To declare free of blame; absolve. [< LL *jūstificāre,* to do justice toward, forgive.] —**jus′ti•fi′a•ble** *adj.* —**jus′ti•fi′a•bly** *adv.* —**jus′ti•fi•ca′tion** *n.*

jut (jŭt) *v.* **jutted, jutting.** To project; protrude. [Var of JET^2.] —**jut′ting•ly** *adv.*

jute (jo͞ot) *n.* **1.** The fiber of an Asian plant, used for sacking and cordage. **2.** The plant itself. [< Sk *jūṭa.*]

Jute (jo͞ot) *n.* A member of any of several Germanic tribes, some of whom invaded Britain in the 5th century A.D.

juv. juvenile.

ju•ve•nile (jo͞o′və-nəl, -nīl′) *adj.* **1.** Not yet adult; young. **2.** Immature. —*n.* A young person; child. [< L *juvenis,* young, a youth.]

jux•ta•pose (jŭk′stə-pōz′) *v.* **-posed, -posing.** To situate side by side; place together. —**jux′ta•po•si′tion** (-pə-zĭsh′ən) *n.*

J.V. junior varsity.

Kk

k, K (kā) *n.* The 11th letter of the English alphabet.

K 1. karat. **2.** kilo-.

K 1. Kelvin (temperature scale). **2.** potassium.

ka•bob (kə-bŏb′) *n.* **Shish kebab.**

Ka•bul (kä′bo͝ol). The capital of Afghanistan. Pop. 450,000.

Kaf•ka (käf′kä), **Franz.** 1883–1924. Austrian novelist.

Kai•ser (kī′zər) *n.* The title of the ruler of Germany (1871–1918). [< L *Caesar,* Caesar.]

ka•la-a•zar (kä′lä-ä-zär′) *n.* A chronic, usually fatal disease occurring in Asia, esp. in India, caused by a protozoan parasite and characterized by irregular fever, enlargement of the spleen, hemorrhages, dropsy, and emaciation. [Hindi *kālā-āzār,* "black disease."]

kale (kāl) *n.* A variety of cabbage with crinkled leaves that do not form a tight head. [< L *caulis,* cabbage.]

ka•lei•do•scope (kə-lī′də-skōp′) *n.* **1.** A small tube in which mirrors reflect light transmitted through bits of loose colored glass contained at one end, causing them to appear as symmetrical designs when viewed at the other. **2.** A constantly changing set of colors. **3.** A series of changing phases or events. [Gk *kalos,* beautiful + *eidos,* form + -SCOPE.] —**ka•lei′do•scop′ic** (-skŏp′ĭk) *adj.*

ka•mi•ka•ze (kä′mĭ-kä′zē) *n.* **1.** A Japanese pilot trained to make a suicidal crash attack. **2.** An airplane used in such an attack. [Jap, "divine wind."]

Kam•pa•la (käm-pä′lə). The capital of Uganda. Pop. 45,000.

kan•ga•roo (kăng′gə-ro͞o′) *n.* An Australian marsupial with large hind limbs adapted for leaping and a long, tapered tail. [Prob < a native name in Australia.]

Kan•sas (kăn′zəs). A state of the C U.S. Pop. 2,249,000. Cap. Topeka.

Kansas City. 1. A city of NE Kansas. Pop. 168,000. **2.** A city of NW Missouri. Pop. 507,000.

Kant (kănt, känt), **Immanuel.** 1724–1804. German philosopher. —**Kant′i•an** *adj.*

ka•o•lin (kā′ə-lĭn) *n.* Also **ka•o•line.** A fine whitish clay used in ceramics and refractories. [< Mand Chin *kao^1 ling^3,* "high mountain."]

kaph (käf) *n.* Also **caph.** The 11th letter of the Hebrew alphabet, representing *k(kh).*

ka•pok (kā′pŏk′) *n.* A silky fiber obtained from the fruit of a tropical tree and used as filling for pillows, life preservers, etc. [Malay.]

kap•pa (kăp′ə) *n.* The 10th letter of the Greek alphabet, representing *k.*

Ka•ra•chi (kə-rä′chē). A city of S West Pakistan. Pop. 1,913,000.

Kar•a•kor•am (kăr′ə-kōr′əm). A mountain range of S Asia.

kar•a•kul (kăr′ə-kəl) *n.* Also **car•a•cul. 1.** Fur made from the curled, glossy pelt of the lamb of an Asian sheep. **2.** The sheep itself. [< *Kara Kul,* lake in Tadzhik S.S.R.]

kar•at (kăr′ət) *n.* Also **car•at.** A measure comprising 24 units used to specify the proportion of pure gold in an alloy; for example, 12 karat gold is 50% pure gold. [< CARAT.]

ka•ra•te (kə-rä′tē, kä-rä′tā) *n.* A Japanese system of unarmed self-defense that stresses efficiently struck blows. [Jap, "empty-handed."]

kar•ma (kär′mə) *n.* **1.** *Hinduism & Buddhism.* The sum and consequences of a person's actions during the successive phases of his existence. **2.** Fate; destiny. [Sk *karman,* act, deed.] —**kar′mic** (-mĭk) *adj.*

karyo–. *comb. form.* The nucleus of a living cell. [< Gk *karuon,* kernel, nut.]

kar•y•og•a•my (kăr′ē-ŏg′ə-mē) *n.* The coming together and fusing of gamete nuclei.

Kat•man•du (kät′män-do͞o′). The capital of Nepal. Pop. 123,000.

ka•ty•did (kā′tē-dĭd′) *n.* A green insect related to the grasshoppers, having specialized organs that produce a distinctive sound when rubbed together. [Imit.]

kay•ak (kī′ăk′) *n.* An Eskimo canoe with a deck covering that closes around the waist of the paddler. [Eskimo *qajaq.*]

kay•o (kā′ō, kā′ō′). *Slang. n., pl.* **-os.** A knockout. —*v.* To knock out.

Ka•zakh Soviet Socialist Republic (kə-zăk′). A constituent republic of the Soviet Union, NE of the Caspian Sea. Pop. 12,850,000.

Ka•zan (kə-zăn′). A city of the Soviet Union, on the Volga. Pop. 869,000.

ka•zoo (kə-zo͞o′) *n.* A toy musical instrument in which a paper membrane is vibrated by the performer's voice. [Prob imit.]

kc kilocycle.

K.C. 1. King's Counsel. **2.** Knights of Columbus.

Keats (kēts), **John.** 1795–1821. English poet.

ke•bab (kə-bŏb′) *n.* Also **ke•bob. Shish kebab.**

keel (kēl) *n.* **1.** The principal structural member of a ship, extending from bow to stern and forming the backbone of the vessel, to which the frames are attached. **2.** Any similarly shaped structure. —*v.* —**keel over. 1.** To capsize. **2.** To faint. [< ON *kjölr.*]

keen (kēn) *adj.* **1.** Having a sharp cutting edge.

2. Intellectually acute. 3. Acutely sensitive: *a keen sense of smell.* 4. Sharp; vivid. 5. Intense; piercing. 6. Pungent; acrid. 7. Eager; enthusiastic. 8. *Slang.* Great; splendid. [< OE *cēne,* wise, bold < Gmc **kōnjaz.*] —**keen'ly** *adv.* —**keen'ness** *n.*

keep (kēp) *v.* **kept, keeping.** 1. To retain possession of. 2. To store; put customarily. 3. To take in one's charge temporarily. 4. To provide with the necessities of life; support; raise and feed. 5. To manage; tend; maintain. 6. To remain, continue, or cause to continue in some condition or position. 7. To preserve and protect; save. 8. To detain; confine. 9. To adhere to; fulfill. 10. To refrain from divulging. 11. To celebrate. 12. To remain fresh or unspoiled. —**keep from.** To deter or prevent. —*n.* 1. Care; charge. 2. Means of support. 3. a. The main tower or donjon of a castle. b. A jail. [< OE *cēpan,* to seize, hold, guard.] —**keep'er** *n.*

keep•sake (kēp'sāk') *n.* Something given or kept as a reminder; memento.

keg (kĕg) *n.* A small cask. [< ON *kaggi.*]

Kel•ler (kĕl'ər), **Helen.** 1880–1968. American author; deaf and blind from infancy.

kelp (kĕlp) *n.* Any of various brown, often very large seaweeds. [ME *culpe.*]

Kelt. Variant of **Celt.**

Kelt•ic. Variant of **Celtic.**

Kel•vin (kĕl'vĭn) *adj.* Pertaining to a scale of temperature, the zero point of which is approx. –273.16°C. [< Lord *Kelvin* (1824–1907), British physicist.]

ken (kĕn) *v.* **kenned** or **kent** (kĕnt), **kenning.** *Chiefly Scot.* To know (a person or thing). —*n.* 1. Understanding. 2. View; sight. [< OE *cennan,* to make known.]

Ken•ne•dy (kĕn'ə-dē), **John Fitzgerald.** 1917–1963. 35th President of the U.S. (1961–63).

John F. Kennedy

ken•nel (kĕn'əl) *n.* 1. A shelter for a dog. 2. An establishment where dogs are bred or boarded. [< L *canis,* dog.]

Ken•tuck•y (kən-tŭk'ē). A state of the east-central U.S. Pop. 3,219,000. Cap. Frankfort.

Ken•ya (kĕn'yə, kēn'-). A republic in east-central Africa. Pop. 9,365,000. Cap. Nairobi.

Kep•ler (kĕp'lər), **Johannes.** 1571–1630. German astronomer and mathematician.

kept (kĕpt). *p.t.* & *p.p.* of **keep.**

ker•a•tin (kĕr'ə-tən) *n.* A tough, fibrous protein forming the outer layer of epidermal structures such as hair, nails, horns, and hoofs. [Gk *keras,* horn + -IN.] —**ke•rat'i•nous** (kə-răt'n-əs) *adj.*

kerb. *Brit.* Variant of **curb.**

ker•chief (kûr'chĭf) *n.* 1. A woman's square scarf, often worn as a head covering. 2. A handkerchief. [< OF *couvrechef,* "head covering."]

Ke•ren•sky (kə-rĕn'skē), **Aleksandr Fyodorovich.** 1881–1970. Russian revolutionary leader; prime minister (July–November 1917).

ker•nel (kûr'nəl) *n.* 1. A grain or seed, as of a cereal grass. 2. The inner, often edible part of a nut or fruit stone. 3. A nucleus; essence; core. [< OE *corn,* corn, berry, seed.]

ker•o•sene (kĕr'ə-sēn', kĕr'ə-sēn') *n.* Also **ker•o•sine.** A thin oil distilled from petroleum or shale oil, used as a fuel and alcohol denaturant. [Gk *kēros,* wax + -ENE.]

ketch (kĕch) *n.* A two-masted fore-and-aft-rigged sailing vessel with a smaller mast aft of the mainmast and in front of the tiller. [Earlier *catch.*]

ketch•up (kĕch'əp, kăch'-) *n.* Also **catch•up** (kăch'əp, kĕch'-), **cat•sup** (kăt'səp, kăch'əp, kĕch'-). A condiment consisting of a thick, smooth-textured, spicy tomato sauce. [Malay *kechap.*]

ket•tle (kĕt'l) *n.* A metal pot for boiling. [< L *catillus,* small bowl.]

ket•tle•drum (kĕt'l-drŭm') *n.* A large copper or brass drum with a parchment head.

key¹ (kē) *n.* 1. A notched metallic implement designed to open or close a lock. 2. Any means of control, esp. of entry or possession. 3. a. A small instrument for winding a spring. b. A slotted metal strip used to open cans. 4. a. A crucial fact. b. A set of answers to a test. c. A table, gloss, or cipher for decoding or interpreting. 5. A pin inserted to lock together mechanical or structural parts. 6. a. A control button or lever on a hand-operated machine. b. A button or lever on a musical instrument, used to produce or modulate a sound. 7. *Mus.* A tonal system consisting of seven tones in fixed relationship to a tonic; tonality. 8. The pitch of a voice or other sound. 9. A general tone or level of intensity. —*v.* To bring into harmony; coordinate. —**key up.** To raise to a high pitch; make intense. —*adj.* Of crucial importance; essential; major. [< OE *cǣg(e).*]

key² (kē) *n.* A low offshore island or reef. [Span *cayo.*]

key•board (kē'bôrd', -bōrd') *n.* A set of keys, as on a piano or typewriter.

key•hole (kē'hōl') *n.* The hole in a lock into which a key fits.

key•note (kē'nōt') *n.* 1. The tonic of a musical key. 2. A prime or central element.

keynote address. An opening address, as at a political convention.

key punch. A keyboard machine that is used to punch holes in cards or tapes for data-processing systems.

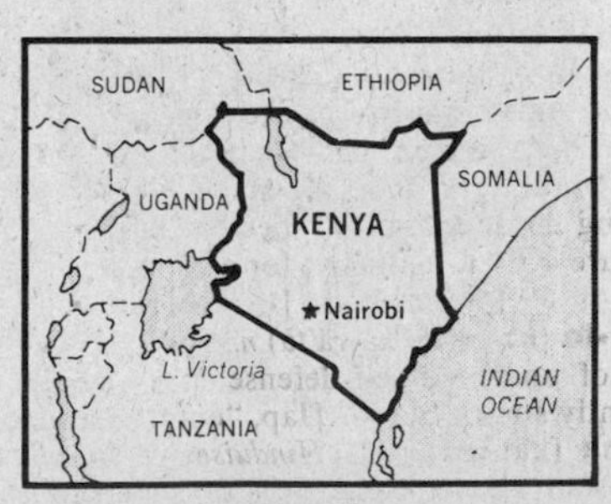

Kenya

key signature. The group of sharps or flats placed to the right of the clef on a musical staff to identify the key.

key•stone (kē'stōn') *n.* The central wedge-shaped stone of an arch that locks the others together.

kg kilogram.

khak•i (kăk'ē, kä'kē) *n., pl.* **-is.** 1. Light olive brown or light yellowish brown. 2. A cloth of this color. 3. **khakis.** A uniform of this cloth. [Urdu *khākī,* dusty.] —**khak'i** *adj.*

khan (kän, kăn) *n.* 1. A title of respect in India and some central Asian countries. 2. **Khan.** The title of the rulers of Mongol, Tartar, or Turkish tribes who succeeded Genghis Khan. [< Turk *khān.*]

Khar•kov (kär'kôf, -kôv). A city of the Soviet Union in the E Ukrainian S.S.R. Pop. 1,223,000.

Khar•toum (kär-to͞om'). The capital of Sudan. Pop. 584,000.

khe•dive (kə-dēv') *n.* The title of the Turkish viceroys of Egypt from 1867 to 1914.

Khmer Republic (kmĕr). A former name for **Cambodia,** a country of SE Asia.

kib•butz (kĭ-bo͝ots') *n., pl.* **-butzim** (-bo͝ot'sēm'). A collective farm or settlement in Israel. [Heb *qibbūtz,* "gathering."]

kib•itz (kĭb'ĭts) *v. Informal.* To act as a kibitzer. [Yid *kibitsen.*]

kib•itz•er (kĭb'ĭt-sər) *n. Informal.* An onlooker who offers unwanted advice, esp. at a card game.

kick (kĭk) *v.* 1. To strike or strike out with the foot or feet. 2. *Sports.* To strike a ball with the foot. 3. To recoil, as a gun when fired. 4. *Informal.* To object vigorously; complain; protest. —*n.* 1. The act of kicking. 2. *Slang.* A stimulating or intoxicating impact. 3. *Slang.* A temporary concentration of interest. [ME *kiken.*]

kick•back (kĭk'băk') *n.* 1. A sharp response or reaction; repercussion. 2. *Slang.* A percentage payment to a person able to influence or control a source of income.

kick off. *Football.* To put the ball in play by kicking it toward the opposing team.

kick•off (kĭk'ôf', -ŏf') *n.* 1. A kick in football or soccer with which play is begun. 2. A beginning.

kid (kĭd) *n.* 1. A young goat. 2. Also **kid•skin** (kĭd'skĭn'). Leather made from the skin of a young goat. 3. *Slang.* A child. —*adj.* 1. Made of kid. 2. *Informal.* Younger: *my kid brother.* —*v.* **kidded, kidding.** *Informal.* 1. To mock playfully. 2. To deceive in fun. [< ON *kidh* < Gmc **kidhja-.*] —**kid'der** *n.*

kid•nap (kĭd'năp') *v.* **-naped** or **-napped, -naping** or **-napping.** To abduct and detain (a person), often for ransom. [< KID + earlier *nap,* to seize.] —**kid'nap'er, kid'nap'per** *n.*

kid•ney (kĭd'nē) *n., pl.* **-neys.** 1. Either of a pair of structures in the dorsal region of the vertebrate abdominal cavity, functioning to maintain proper water balance, regulate acid-base concentration, and excrete metabolic wastes as urine. 2. Disposition; temperament. [ME *kydney.*]

Ki•ev (kē-ĕv', kē'ĕf'). The capital of the Ukrainian S.S.R. Pop. 1,632,000.

Ki•ga•li (kĭ-gä'lē). The capital of Rwanda. Pop. 4,000.

Kil•i•man•ja•ro (kĭl'ə-mən-jär'ō). The highest mountain (19,565 ft.) in Africa, in NE Tanzania.

kill (kĭl) *v.* **1. a.** To put to death; slay. **b.** To deprive of life. **2. a.** To put an end to. **b.** To thwart; veto: *kill a congressional bill.* **3.** To use up: *kill two hours.* **4.** To cause extreme discomfort to. **5.** To mark for deletion; rule out. —*n.* **1.** The act of killing. **2.** That which is killed or destroyed, as an animal in hunting. [< OE **cyllan.* See **gwel-²**.] —**kill'er** *n.*

kill•deer (kĭl'dîr') *n., pl.* **-deers** or **-deer.** A bird with a banded breast and a distinctive cry.

kill•ing (kĭl'ĭng) *n.* **1.** A murder; homicide. **2.** A sudden large profit. —*adj.* **1.** Fatal. **2.** Exhausting. **3.** *Informal.* Hilarious.

kill•joy (kĭl'joi') *n.* One who spoils the fun of others.

kiln (kĭl, kĭln) *n.* An oven for hardening, burning, or drying, esp. one used to bake or fire ceramics. [< L *culīna,* kitchen.]

ki•lo (kē'lō, kĭl'ō) *n., pl.* **-los. 1.** A kilogram. **2.** A kilometer.

kilo–. *comb. form.* 1,000 (10^3). [< Gk *khilioi,* thousand.]

ki•lo•cy•cle (kĭl'ə-sī'kəl) *n.* **1.** A unit equal to 1,000 cycles. **2.** Loosely, 1,000 cycles per second.

kil•o•gram (kĭl'ə-grăm') *n.* The fundamental unit of mass in the International System, about 2.2046 pounds.

kil•o•me•ter (kĭl'ə-mē'tər, kĭ-lŏm'ə-tər) *n.* One thousand meters, approx. 0.62137 mile.

kil•o•ton (kĭl'ə-tŭn') *n.* **1.** One thousand tons. **2.** An explosive force equivalent to that of 1,000 tons of TNT.

kil•o•watt (kĭl'ə-wŏt') *n.* One thousand watts.

kil•o•watt-hour (kĭl'ə-wŏt'our') *n.* The total energy developed by a power of one kilowatt acting for one hour.

kilt (kĭlt) *n.* A skirt with deep pleats, usually of a tartan wool, worn esp. as part of the dress for men in the Scottish Highlands. [< Scand.]

kil•ter (kĭl'tər) *n.* Proper condition: *out of kilter.* [?]

ki•mo•no (kə-mō'nə, -nō) *n., pl.* **-nos. 1.** A wide-sleeved Japanese robe, worn with a broad sash. **2.** A dressing gown resembling this. [Jap, "thing for wearing."]

kin (kĭn) *n.* One's relatives collectively. [< OE *cynn.* See **gene-**.]

–kin. *comb. form.* Small or diminutive: **lambkin.** [< MDu < Gmc **-kin.*]

kin•aes•the•sia. Variant of **kinesthesia.**

kind¹ (kīnd) *adj.* Showing sympathy, concern, or understanding. [< OE *gecynde,* natural, innate. See **gene-**.]

kind² (kīnd) *n.* A class or category of similar or related individuals; sort; type. [< OE *cynd, gecynd,* birth, nature, race. See **gene-**.]
Usage: Kind, denoting a single variety, is used with singular elements in examples such as *This kind of book has little value* (preferable to *these kind of books have*). *Kind* is used acceptably with a plural noun and verb in questions such as *What kind of books are these?* The plural *kinds* is always used, with a plural verb, in examples such as *All kinds of difficulty were involved.*

kin•der•gar•ten (kĭn'dər-gärt'n) *n.* A class for four- to six-year-old children that serves as an introduction to schooling. [G, "children's garden."]

kind•heart•ed (kīnd'här'tĭd) *adj.* Showing a kind nature. —**kind'heart'ed•ly** *adv.* —**kind'heart'ed•ness** *n.*

kin•dle (kĭnd'l) *v.* **-dled, -dling. 1.** To start (a fire); begin to burn. **2.** To glow or cause to glow. **3.** To arouse; inspire. [< ON *kynda.*]

kind•less (kīnd'lĭs) *adj.* **1.** Heartless; cruel. **2.** *Obs.* Inhuman.

kind•li•ness (kīnd'lē-nĭs) *n.* **1.** The quality of being kindly. **2.** A kindly deed.

kin•dling (kĭnd'lĭng) *n.* Material, such as dry sticks of wood, used to start a fire.

kindling point. The minimum temperature at which a substance will continue to burn without additional application of heat.

kind•ly (kīnd'lē) *adj.* **-lier, -liest.** Showing sympathy, considerateness, or helpfulness. —*adv.* **1.** In a kind way or manner. **2.** Please; accommodatingly: *Would you kindly refrain from doing that?*

kind•ness (kīnd'nĭs) *n.* **1.** The quality or state of being kind. **2.** An instance of kind behavior.

kin•dred (kĭn'drĭd) *n.* **1.** A group of related persons. **2.** A person's relatives. —*adj.* Being similar or related. [< KIN + OE *rǣden,* condition.] —**kin'dred•ness** *n.*

kine (kīn) *pl.n.* Cows; cattle.

kin•e•mat•ics (kĭn'ə-măt'ĭks) *n.* *(takes sing. v.).* The study of motion exclusive of the influences of mass and force. [< Gk *kinein,* to move.] —**kin'e•mat'ic, kin'e•mat'i•cal** *adj.* —**kin'e•mat'i•cal•ly** *adv.*

kin•e•scope (kĭn'ə-skōp') *n.* **1.** A cathode-ray tube that translates received TV signals into a visible picture. **2.** A film of a transmitted TV program.

kin•es•the•sia (kĭn'əs-thē'zhə) *n.* Also **kin•aes•the•sia.** The sensation of bodily position, presence, or movement.

ki•net•ic (kĭ-nĕt'ĭk) *adj.* Of or produced by motion. —*n.* **kinetics** *(takes sing. v.).* **1.** The study of all aspects of motion, comprising both kinematics and dynamics. **2.** The study of the relationship between motion and the forces affecting motion. [Gk *kinētikos* < *kinein,* to move.]

kinetic energy. Energy associated with motion.

kin•folk, kin•folks. Variants of **kinsfolk.**

king (kĭng) *n.* **1.** A male monarch. **2.** The most eminent of a group, category, etc. **3.** A playing card bearing a picture of a king. **4.** *Chess.* The principal piece. [< OE *cyning.* See **gene-**.] —**king'li•ness** *n.* —**king'ly** *adj.*

King James Bible (jāmz). A translation of the Bible for use by Protestants.

King (kĭng), **Martin Luther, Jr.** 1929–1968. American Baptist minister and civil-rights leader; assassinated.

Martin Luther King, Jr.

king•dom (kĭng'dəm) *n.* **1.** A country nominally or actually ruled by a king or queen. **2.** An area in which one thing is dominant. **3.** A broad, general category of living or natural forms: *animal kingdom; plant kingdom.*

king•fish•er (kĭng'fĭsh'ər) *n.* A crested, large-billed bird that feeds on fish.

king•let (kĭng'lĭt) *n.* A small bird with a red or yellow head patch.

king•pin (kĭng'pĭn') *n.* **1.** *Bowling.* The foremost or central pin. **2.** A person of central importance. **3.** A vertical bolt used as a pivot.

Kings•ton (kĭngz'tən). The capital of Jamaica. Pop. 123,000.

kink (kĭngk) *n.* **1.** A small, tight curl or twist. **2.** A painful muscle spasm, as in the neck or back. **3.** A slight flaw, as in a plan. —*v.* To form kinks (in). [LG *kinke,* a twist in a rope.] —**kink'i•ness** *n.* —**kink'y** *adj.*

kink•a•jou (kĭng'kə-jōō') *n.* A furry, long-tailed tropical American mammal. [< Algon.]

kins•folk (kĭnz'fōk') *pl.n.* Also *informal* **kin•folk** (kĭn'-), **kin•folks** (-fōks). Members of a family.

Kin•sha•sa (kĭn-shä'sä). The capital of Zaire. Pop. 1,323,000.

kin•ship (kĭn'shĭp') *n.* **1.** The state of being related by blood. **2.** A close connection or relationship.

kins•man (kĭnz'mən) *n.* A male blood relation. —**kins'wo'man** *fem.n.*

ki•osk (kē-ŏsk', kē'ŏsk') *n.* A small structure used as a newsstand, refreshment booth, etc. [< Turk *köshk,* pavilion.]

kip (kĭp) *n., pl.* **kip.** The basic monetary unit of Laos.

Kip•ling (kĭp'lĭng), **Rudyard.** 1865-1936. English author.

kip•per (kĭp'ər) *n.* A herring that has been split, salted, and smoked. [< OE *cypera.*]

Kir•ghiz Soviet Socialist Republic (kîr-gēz'). A constituent republic of the Soviet Union, in C Asia. Pop. 2,933,000.

kis•met (kĭz'mĭt, kĭs'-) *n.* Fate; fortune. [Turk *kismet.*]

kiss (kĭs) *v.* To touch with the lips as a sign of affection, greeting, etc. —*n.* **1.** A touching with the lips. **2.** A small piece of candy. [< OE *cyssan.* See **kus-**.]

kit (kĭt) *n.* **1. a.** A set of instruments or equipment used for a specific purpose. **b.** A container for such a set. **2.** A set of parts or materials to be assembled. [< MDu *kitte,* jug, tankard.]

kitch•en (kĭch'ən) *n.* **1.** An area in which food is cooked or prepared. **2.** A department, as of an institution, that prepares, cooks, and serves food. [< L *coquīnus,* of cooking.]

kitch•en•ette (kĭch'ə-nĕt') *n.* A small kitchen.

kitch•en•ware (kĭch'ən-wâr') *n.* Utensils for kitchen use.

kite (kīt) *n.* **1.** A light framework covered with paper or cloth and designed to hover in the wind at the end of a long string. **2.** A predatory bird with a long, often forked tail. [< OE *cȳta,* kite bird < Gmc **kūtja-.*]

kith (kĭth) *n.* Friends and neighbors: *kith and kin.* [< OE *cȳth,* "knowledge," "acquaintance," friend.]

kit•ten (kĭt'n) *n.* A young cat. [< LL *cattus,* cat.]

kit•ten•ish (kĭt'n-ĭsh) *adj.* Playful; flirtatious; coy. —**kit'ten•ish•ly** *adv.*

kit•ty¹ (kĭt'ē) *n., pl.* **-ties.** A pool or fund of money. [< KIT.]

kit•ty² (kĭt'ē) *n., pl.* **-ties.** *Informal.* A kitten or cat.

K.K.K. Ku Klux Klan.

klep•to•ma•ni•a (klĕp'tə-mā'nē-ə) *n.* An

obsessive impulse to steal, esp. in the absence of economic necessity. [< Gk *kleptein,* to steal + -MANIA.] —**klep'to·ma'ni·ac'** *n.*

klutz (klŭts) *n.* **1.** A clumsy or dim-witted person. **2.** A bungler. [< MHG *kloz,* block, lump. See **gel-**[1].]

km kilometer.

kn. knot.

knack (năk) *n.* **1.** A clever way of doing something. **2.** A specific talent for something. [ME *knak.*]

knap·sack (năp'săk') *n.* A case or bag worn on the back to carry supplies and equipment. [LG.]

knave (nāv) *n.* **1.** An unprincipled, crafty man. **2.** *Card Games.* A jack. [< OE *cnafa,* boy, lad < Gmc **knabōn-.*] —**knav'er·y** *n.* —**knav'ish** *adj.* —**knav'ish·ly** *adv.*

knead (nēd) *v.* **1.** To mix and work (a substance) into a uniform mass. **2.** To massage. [< OE *cnedan.*] —**knead'er** *n.*

knee (nē) *n.* The joint or region between the upper and lower parts of the human leg. [< OE *cnēo.* See **genu-**[1].]

knee·cap (nē'kăp') *n.* The patella.

kneel (nēl) *v.* **knelt** (nĕlt) or **kneeled, kneeling.** To fall or rest on bent knees. [< OE *cnēowlian.* See **genu-**[1].]

knell (nĕl) *v.* **1.** To ring or sound a bell, esp. for a funeral; toll. **2.** To signal, summon, or proclaim by tolling. —*n.* **1.** The slow, solemn sounding of a bell. **2.** An omen of sorrow or death. [< OE *cnyllan.*]

knew (n/y/o͞o). *p.t.* of **know.**

knick·ers (nĭk'ərz) *pl.n.* Also **knick·er·bock·ers** (-ər-bŏk'ərz). Full breeches gathered just below the knee.

knick·knack (nĭk'năk') *n.* A small ornamental article. [Redupl of KNACK.]

knife (nīf) *n., pl.* **knives** (nīvz). **1.** A cutting instrument consisting of a sharp blade with a handle. **2.** Any cutting edge or blade. —*v.* **knifed, knifing. 1.** To use a knife on, esp. to cut, stab, or wound. **2.** *Informal.* To betray by underhand means. [< OE *cnīf.*]

knight (nīt) *n.* **1.** A medieval gentleman-soldier. **2.** The holder of a nonhereditary dignity conferred by a sovereign. **3.** A member of any of several orders or brotherhoods. **4.** A chess piece usually representing a horse's head. —*v.* To raise (a person) to knighthood. [< OE *cniht,* orig "boy," "servant" < Gmc **knihtas.*] —**knight'hood'** *n.* —**knight'ly** *adj.*

knit (nĭt) *v.* **knit** or **knitted, knitting. 1.** To make (a fabric or garment) by intertwining yarn or thread in a series of connected loops. **2.** To join closely. **3.** To draw (the brows) together in wrinkles. —*n.* A fabric or garment made by knitting. [< OE *cnyttan,* to tie in a knot.]

knob (nŏb) *n.* **1.** A rounded protuberance on a surface or extremity. **2.** A rounded handle. [< MLG *knobbe,* tree knot, knob.] —**knobbed** *adj.* —**knob'bi·ness** *n.* —**knob'by** *adj.*

knock (nŏk) *v.* **1.** To strike with a blow or series of blows. **2.** To produce by hitting: *knock a hole in the wall.* **3.** *Slang.* To criticize adversely. **4.** To collide; bump. **5.** To make the pounding noise of a laboring or defective engine. —**knock about** (or **around**). **1.** To be physically brutal with. **2.** To wander aimlessly from place to place. **3.** To discuss. —**knock off. 1.** To rest from or cease work. **2.** To accomplish or consume easily. **3.** To deduct; eliminate. **4.** *Slang.* To kill. [< OE *cnocian.*] —**knock** *n.*

knock·er (nŏk'ər) *n.* A fixture used for knocking on a door.

knock-knee (nŏk'nē') *n.* An abnormal condition in which one or both knees are turned toward the other. —**knock'-kneed'** *adj.*

knock out. 1. To render unconscious. **2.** *Boxing.* To defeat (an opponent) by knocking him to the canvas for a count of ten. **3.** To exhaust (oneself or another).

knock·out (nŏk'out') *n.* **1.** A blow that induces unconsciousness. **2.** *Boxing.* The knocking out of an opponent. **3.** *Slang.* Something very impressive or attractive.

knoll (nōl) *n.* A small rounded hill. [< OE *cnoll.*]

knot (nŏt) *n.* **1.** A compact intersection of interlaced string, rope, etc. **2.** Any tie or bond, esp. a marriage bond. **3.** A cluster of persons or things. **4.** A difficulty; problem. **5.** A hard, dark marking at a point from which a tree branch grows. **6.** A growth on or enlargement of a gland, muscle, etc. **7.** A unit of speed, one nautical mile per hour, about 1.15 statute miles per hour. —**tie the knot.** To get married. —*v.* **knotted, knotting. 1.** To make or become snarled or entangled. **2.** To form a knot or knots (in). [< OE *cnotta.*]

knot·hole (nŏt'hōl') *n.* A hole in a piece of lumber where a knot has dropped out or been removed.

knot·ty (nŏt'ē) *adj.* **-tier, -tiest. 1.** Having knots. **2.** Covered with knots; gnarled. **3.** Difficult to understand or solve; intricate. —**knot'ti·ly** *adv.* —**knot'ti·ness** *n.*

know (nō) *v.* **knew, known, knowing. 1.** To perceive directly with the senses or mind; be aware of as true or factual. **2.** To be capable of: *know how to swim.* **3.** To have a practical understanding of. **4.** To be subjected to. **5.** To have firmly secured in the mind or memory. **6.** To be able to distinguish. **7.** To be acquainted or familiar with. [< OE *(ge)cnāwan.* See **gnō-.**]

Usage: Know, esp. in negative constructions, is often followed by clauses introduced by *that, whether,* or *if,* but not by *as: I don't know that* (not *as*) *I can.*

know-how (nō'hou') *n. Informal.* Skill or ingenuity.

know·ing (nō'ĭng) *adj.* **1.** Possessing or showing knowledge or understanding. **2.** Suggestive of secret or private information: *a knowing glance.* **3.** Clever; shrewd. —**know'ing·ly** *adv.* —**know'ing·ness** *n.*

know-it-all (nō'ĭt-ôl') *n. Informal.* One who talks as if he knew everything.

knowl·edge (nŏl'ĭj) *n.* **1.** The state or fact of knowing. **2.** Familiarity, awareness, or understanding gained through experience or study. **3.** That which is known; the sum or range of what has been perceived, discovered, or inferred. **4.** Learning; erudition.

knowl·edge·a·ble (nŏl'ĭ-jə-bəl) *adj.* Well-informed.

Knox·ville (nŏks'vĭl). A city of E Tennessee. Pop. 172,000.

Knt. knight.

knuck·le (nŭk'əl) *n.* Any joint or region around a joint of a finger, esp. one of the joints connecting the fingers to the hand. —*v.* **-led, -ling.** To press or rub with the knuckles. —**knuckle down.** To apply oneself earnestly. —**knuckle under.** To yield to pressure; give. [< MLG *knōkel.*]

knuck·le·bone (nŭk'əl-bōn') *n.* A knobbed bone, as of a knuckle or joint.

ko·a·la (kō-ä'lə) *n.* Also **koala bear.** A furry, tree-dwelling Australian marsupial. [< native Australian name *kūlla.*]

Ko·be (kō'bē, -bā'). A city of Japan, on Honshu. Pop. 1,181,000.

kohl·ra·bi (kōl-rä'bē, kōl'rä'-) *n.* A plant with a thickened, turniplike stem base that is eaten as a vegetable. [< It *cavolo rapa,* "cabbage turnip."]

ko·la. Variant of **cola.**

ko·lin·sky (kə-lĭn'skē) *n.* The fur of a Eurasian mink. [< *Kola,* district in NW U.S.S.R.]

Ko·ran (kô-răn', -rän', kō-) *n.* The sacred text of Islam, believed to contain the revelations made by Allah to Mohammed. [Ar *qur'ān,* reading, recitation.]

Ko·re·a (kô-rē'ə, kō-). A country of E Asia, divided since 1948 into two states: **a.** the People's Democratic Republic of Korea (North Korea). Pop. 10,930,000. Cap. Pyongyang. **b.** the Republic of Korea (South Korea). Pop. 28,155,000. Cap. Seoul.

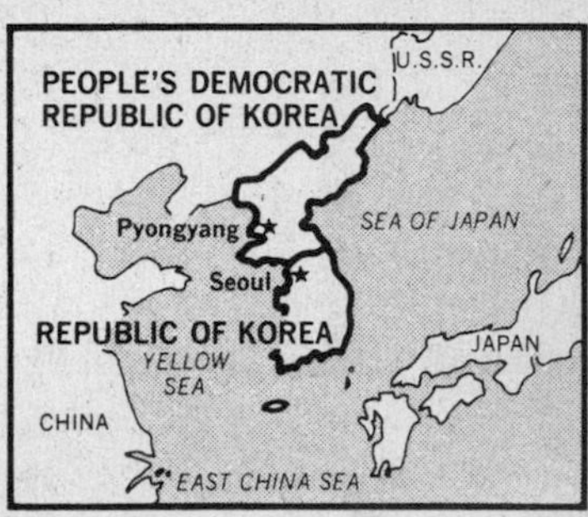

Korea

Ko·re·an (kô-rē'ən, kō-) *adj.* Of or pertaining to Korea, its inhabitants, or their language. —*n.* **1.** A native of Korea. **2.** The language of Korea.

Korean War. A military action between North Korea and United Nations forces (June 1950–July 1953).

ko·ru·na (kôr'o͞o-nä') *n., pl.* **-ny** (-nē) or **-nas.** The basic monetary unit of Czechoslovakia.

ko·sher (kō'shər) *adj.* **1.** Conforming to or prepared in accordance with Jewish dietary laws. **2.** *Slang.* Proper; legitimate. [< Heb *kāshēr,* proper.]

Ko·sy·gin (kə-sē'gĭn), **Aleksei Nikolayevich.** Born 1904. Premier of the Soviet Union (since 1964).

kow·tow (kou'tou', kō'-) *n.* A Chinese salutation in which one touches the forehead to the ground. —*v.* **1.** To perform a kowtow. **2.** To show servile deference. [Mand Chin *k'o*[1] *t'ou*[2].] —**kow'tow'er** *n.*

KP kitchen police.

Kr krypton.

Kra·ków (krä'kou', krăk'ou', krā'kō). A city in S Poland. Pop. 509,000.

Krem·lin (krĕm'lən) *n.* **1.** The citadel of Moscow, housing the offices of the Soviet government. **2.** The executive branch of the Soviet government. [< Russ *kreml',* citadel.]

Krish·na (krĭsh'nə). *Hinduism.* The 8th and principal avatar of Vishnu.

kro·na[1] (krō'nə) *n., pl.* **-nur** (-nər). The basic monetary unit of Iceland.

kro·na[2] (krō'nə) *n., pl.* **-nor** (-nôr'). The basic monetary unit of Sweden.

kro·ne (krō'nə) *n., pl.* **-ner** (-nər). The basic monetary unit of Denmark and Norway.

kryp·ton (krĭp'tŏn') *n. Symbol* **Kr** A whitish, inert gaseous element used chiefly in gas-discharge lamps, fluorescent lamps, and electronic flash tubes. Atomic number 36, atomic weight 83.80. [< Gk *kruptos,* hidden.]

kt. karat.

Kua•la Lum•pur (kwä'lə lo͝om'po͝or). The capital of Malaysia. Pop. 316,000.

Ku•blai Khan (ko͞o'blī kän'). 1216–1294. Founder of Mongol dynasty in China; grandson of Genghis Khan.

ku•dos (kyo͞o'dŏs', -dōs') *n.* Acclaim or prestige in recognition of achievement. [< Gk, glory, fame.]

Kui•by•shev (kwē'bə-shĕf', -shĕv'). A city of the Soviet Union, on the Volga. Pop. 1,047,000.

kum•quat (kŭm'kwŏt') *n.* **1.** A small, thin-skinned, edible orangelike fruit. **2.** A tree bearing such fruit. [Cant *kam kwat.*]

kung fu (ko͝ong' fo͞o', go͝ong'-). A Chinese system of self-defense resembling the Japanese system karate. [<Mand *ch'üan² fa³,* "boxing principles."]

Kurd•ish (kûr'dĭsh, ko͝or'-) *n.* The Iranian language of the Kurds, a nomadic Moslem people of SW Asia. —**Kurd'ish** *adj.*

Ku•wait (ko͞o-wāt', -wīt'). **1.** A republic at the head of the Persian Gulf. Pop. 468,000. **2.** The capital of this republic. Pop. 100,000.

kW kilowatt.

Kwa (kwä) *n.* A branch of the Niger-Congo language family. —**Kwa** *adj.*

kwa•cha (kwä'chä') *n.* The basic monetary unit of Zambia.

kwash•i•or•kor (kwăsh'ē-ôr'kôr, kwä'shē-) *n.* Severe malnutrition, occurring esp. in African children, characterized by anemia, edema, potbelly, depigmentation of the skin, and loss of hair or change in hair color. [Native word in Ghana.]

kWh kilowatt-hour.

Ky. Kentucky.

Kuwait

kyat (kyät, kē-ät') *n.* The basic monetary unit of Burma.

Kyo•to (kyō'tō, kē-ō'-). A city of Japan, in S Honshu. Pop. 1,376,000.

Kyu•shu (kyo͞o'sho͞o). The southernmost island of Japan.

L l

l, L (ĕl) *n.* **1.** The 12th letter of the English alphabet. **2.** **L** Anything shaped like the letter L.

l liter.

L **1.** large. **2.** The Roman numeral for 50.

l. **1.** left. **2.** length. **3.** line.

L. **1.** lake. **2.** Latin.

La lanthanum.

La. Louisiana.

L.A. Los Angeles.

lab (lăb) *n. Informal.* A laboratory.

lab. laboratory.

la•bel (lā'bəl) *n.* Anything functioning as a means of identification, esp. a small piece of paper attached to an article to designate its origin, owner, contents, etc. —*v.* **-beled** or **-belled, -beling** or **-belling. 1.** To attach a label to. **2.** To classify or designate. [< OF, ribbon, strip < Gmc.] —**la'bel•er, la'bel•ler** *n.*

la•bi•al (lā'bē-əl) *adj.* Of or pertaining to the lips or labia. —**la'bi•al•ly** *adv.*

la•bi•um (lā'bē-əm) *n., pl.* **-bia** (-bē-ə). Any of four folds of tissue of the female external genitalia. [< L, lip.]

la•bor (lā'bər). Also *chiefly Brit.* **la•bour.** *n.* **1.** Physical or mental exertion of a practical nature; work. **2.** Work for wages. **3.** Workers collectively. **4.** The physical efforts of childbirth. —*v.* **1.** To work. **2.** To strive painstakingly. **3.** To proceed slowly; plod. **4.** To be hampered: *labor under a misconception.* **5.** To deal with in exhaustive detail. [< L.] —**la'bor•er** *n.* —**la'bor•ing•ly** *adv.*

lab•o•ra•to•ry (lăb'rə-tôr'ē, -tōr'ē) *n., pl.* **-ries. 1.** A place equipped for scientific experimentation, research, or testing. **2.** A place where drugs and chemicals are manufactured. [< L *labor,* LABOR.] —**lab'o•ra•to'ri•al** *adj.*

Labor Day. The first Monday in September, a legal holiday in honor of the workingman.

la•bored (lā'bərd) *adj.* Showing labor; lacking natural ease. —**la'bored•ly** *adv.*

la•bo•ri•ous (lə-bôr'ē-əs, lə-bōr'-) *adj.* Requiring long, hard work. —**la•bo'ri•ous•ly** *adv.*

Lab•ra•dor (lăb'rə-dôr). A peninsula of NE Canada.

la•bur•num (lə-bûr'nəm) *n.* A tree or shrub cultivated for its drooping clusters of yellow flowers. [L.]

lab•y•rinth (lăb'ə-rĭnth') *n.* An intricate structure of interconnecting passages. [< Gk *laburinthos.*] —**lab'y•rin'thine'** (-rĭn'thĭn', -thēn') *adj.*

lac (lăk) *n.* A resinous secretion of an Asian insect used in making shellac. [< Sk *lākshā.*]

lace (lās) *n.* **1.** A cord threaded through eyelets or around hooks on two opposite edges to draw and tie them together. **2.** A delicate fabric woven in a weblike pattern. —*v.* **laced, lacing. 1.** To thread a cord through the eyelets or around the hooks of. **2.** To draw together and tie the laces of. **3.** To add liquor to (a beverage). —**lace into.** To attack; assail. [< L *laqueus,* noose, trap.] —**lac'er** *n.* —**lac'y** *adj.*

lac•er•ate (lăs'ə-rāt') *v.* **-ated, -ating.** To tear; mangle. [< L *lacer,* torn, rent, mangled.] —**lac'er•a'tion** *n.* —**lac'er•a'tive** *adj.*

lach•ry•mal (lăk'rə-məl) *adj.* Also **lac•ri•mal.** Pertaining to tears or tear-producing glands. [< L *lacrima,* tear.]

lach•ry•mose (lăk'rə-mōs') *adj.* Weeping or inclined to weep; tearful.

lack (lăk) *n.* A deficiency or absence. —*v.* **1.** To be entirely without or have very little of. **2.** To be wanting or deficient. [ME *lac, lacke.*]

lack•a•dai•si•cal (lăk'ə-dā'zĭ-kəl) *adj.* Lacking spirit or interest. [< the phrase *alack the day.*] —**lack'a•dai'si•cal•ly** *adv.*

lack•ey (lăk'ē) *n., pl.* **-eys. 1.** A footman. **2.** A servile follower; toady. [< OF *laquais.*]

lack•lus•ter (lăk'lŭs'tər) *adj.* Lacking luster, brightness, or vitality.

la•con•ic (lə-kŏn'ĭk) *adj.* Sparing of words; terse. [< Gk *Lakōnikos,* of the Spartans (known for their brevity of speech).] —**la•con'i•cal•ly** *adv.*

lac•quer (lăk'ər) *n.* Any of various clear or colored synthetic or resinous coatings used to give wood and metal surfaces a high gloss. [< Hindi *lākh,* lac.] —**lac'quer** *v.*

lac•ri•mal. Variant of **lachrymal.**

la•crosse (lə-krôs', -krŏs') *n.* A game played on a field by two teams using long-handled racquets and a hard rubber ball. [< F *la crosse,* a hooked stick.]

lac•ta•ry (lăk'tə-rē) *adj.* Of or pertaining to milk. [< L *lac (lact-),* milk.]

lac•tate (lăk'tāt') *v.* **-tated, -tating.** To secrete or produce milk. —**lac•ta'tion** *n.*

lac•te•al (lăk'tē-əl) *adj.* Of or like milk; milky. —**lac'te•al•ly** *adv.*

lac•tic (lăk'tĭk) *adj.* Of or derived from milk.

lactic acid. A hygroscopic syrupy liquid, $C_3H_6O_3$, present in sour milk, molasses, various fruits, and wines.

lacto–. *comb. form.* Milk. [< L *lac (lact-).*]

lac•to•ba•cil•lus (lăk'tō-bə-sĭl'əs) *n., pl.* **-cilli** (-sĭl'ī'). Any of various bacilli that ferment lactic acid from carbohydrates.

lac•to•pro•te•in (lăk'tō-prō'tē-ən, -prō'tēn') *n.* Any protein normally present in milk.

lac•tose (lăk'tōs') *n.* A white crystalline sugar, $C_{12}H_{22}O_{11}$, made from whey and used in pharmaceuticals, infant foods, and confections.

la•cu•na (lə-kyo͞o'nə) *n., pl.* **-nae** (-nē) or **-nas. 1.** An empty space; gap. **2.** *Anat.* A cavity or depression. [L *lacūna,* pool.]

lad (lăd) *n.* A young man. [ME *ladde.*]

lad•der (lăd'ər) *n.* **1.** A device consisting of two long structural members crossed by parallel rungs, used to climb or descend. **2.** A series of ranked levels: *high on the executive ladder.* [< OE *hlǣdder.* See **klei-.**]

lad•en (lād'n) *adj.* Weighed down; oppressed: *laden with grief.* [< OE *hladan,* to load.]

lad•ing (lā'dĭng) *n.* Cargo; freight: *a bill of lading.*

La•di•no (lə-dē'nō) *n.* A Romance language, derived from Spanish with Hebrew elements and modifications, spoken by Sephardic Jews. [< L Latinus, Latin.]

la•dle (lād'l) *n.* A long-handled spoon with a deep bowl for serving liquids. —*v.* **-dled, -dling.** To lift out with a ladle. [< OE *hladan,* to draw out, load.] —**la'dler** *n.*

la•dy (lā'dē) *n., pl.* **-dies. 1.** A woman of refinement and good manners. **2.** The female head of a household: *the lady of the house.* **3.** A polite term for any adult member of the feminine sex. **4. Lady.** *Brit.* The general feminine title of nobility and other rank. [< OE *hlǣfdige,* "kneader of bread," lady. See **dheigh-**.]

la•dy•bug (lā'dē-bŭg') *n.* Also **la•dy•bird** (lā'dē-bûrd'), **lady beetle.** A small, usually reddish, black-spotted beetle.

la•dy•fin•ger (lā'dē-fĭng'gər) *n.* A small oval sponge cake.

la•dy's-slip•per (lā'dēz-slĭp'ər) *n.* An orchid with an inflated, pouchlike lip.

La•e•trile (lā'ə-trĭl) *n.* The name of a chemical believed by some people to be an antineoplastic agent.

La•fay•ette (lä'fē-ĕt', lăf'ē-), **Marquis de.** 1757–1834. French political leader; commanded American troops in the Revolutionary War.

lag (lăg) *v.* **lagged, lagging. 1.** To fail to keep up a pace; fall behind. **2.** To fail or slacken; flag. —*n.* **1.** A falling behind; retardation. **2.** An interval resulting from this. [?]

la•ger (lä'gər) *n.* Also **lager beer.** Beer aged up to six months to allow sedimentation. [< G *Lager(bier)* (beer) for storing.]

lag•gard (lăg'ərd) *n.* One who lags; a dawdler.

la•gniappe (lăn-yăp', lăn'yăp') *n.* An extra or unexpected gift. [< Amer Span *la ñapa.*]

la•goon (lə-gōōn') *n.* A body of brackish water, esp. one separated from the sea by sandbars or coral reefs. [< L *lacūna,* pool, cavity < *lacus,* LAKE.] —**la•goon'al** *adj.*

La•gos (lä'gŏs', -gəs). The capital of Nigeria. Pop. 450,000.

La•hore (lə-hôr', -hōr'). A city of NE West Pakistan. Pop. 1,296,000.

laid (lād). *p.t. & p.p.* of **lay¹**.

lain (lān). *p.p.* of **lie¹**.

lair (lâr) *n.* The den or dwelling of a wild animal. [< OE *leger.*]

lais•sez faire (lĕs'ā fâr'). Also **lais•ser faire.** Noninterference, esp. the doctrine that government should not interfere with commerce. [F, "allow (them) to do."] —**lais'sez-faire'** *adj.* —**lais'sez-faire'ism** *n.*

la•i•ty (lā'ə-tē) *n.* **1.** Laymen collectively as distinguished from the clergy. **2.** Those outside a given profession, art, etc.; nonprofessionals.

lake (lāk) *n.* **1.** A relatively large inland body of water. **2.** A large pool of other liquid. [< L *lacus,* basin for water.]

lam¹ (lăm) *v.* **lammed, lamming.** *Slang.* To thrash; wallop. [< Scand.]

lam² (lăm) *v.* **lammed, lamming.** *Slang.* To depart swiftly. —*n.* —**on the lam.** In flight, esp. from the law. [?]

Lam. Lamentations (Old Testament).

la•ma (lä'mə) *n.* A Buddhist monk of Tibet or Mongolia.

lamb (lăm) *n.* **1.** A young sheep. **2.** The flesh of a young sheep used as meat. **3.** A mild-mannered or naive person. **4. the Lamb** or **Lamb of God.** Christ. —*v.* To give birth to a lamb. [< OE < Gmc *lambiz-.]

lam•baste (lăm-bāst') *v.* **-basted, -basting. 1.** To thrash; whip. **2.** To scold sharply.

lamb•da (lăm'də) *n.* The 11th letter of the Greek alphabet, representing *l.*

lam•bent (lăm'bənt) *adj.* **1.** Flickering or glowing gently. **2.** Light, effortless, and brilliant: *lambent wit.* [< L *lambere,* to lick, lap.] —**lam'ben•cy** *n.* —**lam'bent•ly** *adv.*

lamb•kin (lăm'kĭn) *n.* **1.** A little lamb. **2.** A small, endearing child.

lame (lām) *adj.* **lamer, lamest. 1.** Crippled, esp. in a leg or foot so as to impair ability to walk. **2.** Ineffectual; unsatisfactory: *a lame excuse.* —*v.* **lamed, laming.** To cause to become lame. [< OE *lama.* See **lem-**.] —**lame'ly** *adv.* —**lame'ness** *n.*

la•mé (lă-mā') *n.* A fabric woven with metallic threads. [F.]

la•med (lä'mĕd', -mĭd) *n.* Also **la•medh.** The 12th letter of the Hebrew alphabet, representing *l.*

lame duck. 1. An elected officeholder continuing in office during the period between the election and inauguration of a successor. **2.** A helpless person; weakling.

la•mel•la (lə-mĕl'ə) *n., pl.* **-lae** (-lē) or **-las.** A thin scale, plate, or layer. [< L *lāmella.*]

la•ment (lə-mĕnt') *v.* **1.** To express sorrow or deep regret (over); mourn. **2.** To wail; complain. —*n.* **1.** An expression of sorrow or mourning. **2.** A dirge or elegy. [< L *lāmentum,* expression of sorrow.] —**lam'en•ta'tion** (lăm'ən-tā'shən) *n.* —**la•ment'er** *n.*

lam•en•ta•ble (lăm'ən-tə-bəl, lə-mĕn'-) *adj.* To be lamented; grievous; deplorable. —**lam'en•ta•bly** *adv.*

lam•i•na (lăm'ə-nə) *n., pl.* **-nae** (-nē') or **-nas.** A thin plate, sheet, or layer. [< L *lāmina,* thin plate.] —**lam'i•nar, lam'i•nal** *adj.*

lam•i•nate (lăm'ə-nāt') *v.* **-nated, -nating. 1.** To form into or bond together in thin layers. **2.** To divide into thin layers. —**lam'i•na'tion** *n.*

lamp (lămp) *n.* **1.** A device, as one equipped with an electric bulb or wick, for providing light. **2.** A similar device, as for therapeutic radiation. [< Gk *lampein,* to shine.]

lamp•black (lămp'blăk') *n.* A gray or black pigment made from soot.

lam•poon (lăm-pōōn') *n.* Broad satire, esp. satire intended as personal ridicule. —*v.* To ridicule in a lampoon. [F.] —**lam•poon'er, lam•poon'ist** *n.* —**lam•poon'er•y** *n.*

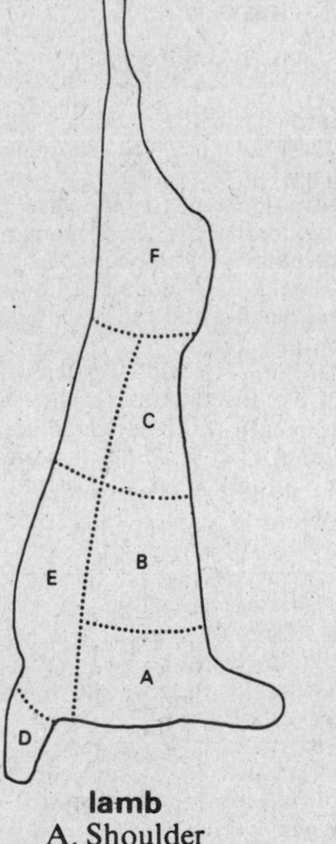

lamb
A. Shoulder
B. Ribs
C. Loin
D. Shank
E. Breast
F. Leg

lam•prey (lăm'prē) *n., pl.* **-preys.** An eellike primitive fish with a jawless sucking mouth. [< ML *lamprēda.*]

la•na•i (lə-nī') *n.* A porch or patio. [Hawaiian.]

lance (lăns, läns) *n.* **1.** A thrusting weapon with a long shaft and a sharp metal head. **2.** A similar implement. —*v.* **lanced, lancing. 1.** To pierce with a lance. **2.** To cut into with a lancet. [< L *lancea.*]

lance corporal. An enlisted man in the U.S. Marine Corps ranking above a private first class and below a corporal. [< OIt *lancia spezzata,* old soldier, "broken lance."]

Lan•ce•lot (lăn'sə-lət, -lŏt', län'-). Knight of Arthurian legend; lover of Guinevere.

lanc•er (lăn'sər, län'-) *n.* A cavalryman armed with a lance.

lan•cet (lăn'sĭt, län'-) *n.* A surgical knife with a short, wide, pointed double-edged blade. [< LANCE.]

land (lănd) *n.* **1. a.** The solid part of the earth's surface. **b.** A portion or region of this. **2.** Earth; soil. **3.** A nation, country, or realm. **4.** A tract owned or sold as property. —*v.* **1.** To put or arrive on land after traveling by water or air. **2.** To arrive or cause to arrive at a certain place. **3.** To come to rest; alight. **4.** To catch by or as by fishing. [< OE. See **lendh-**.]

land•ed (lăn'dĭd) *adj.* **1.** Owning land: *landed gentry.* **2.** Consisting of land: *a landed estate.*

land•fall (lănd'fôl') *n.* **1.** The sighting or reaching of land on a voyage. **2.** The land thus sighted.

land grant. A government grant of public land for a railroad, highway, or state college. —**land'-grant'** *adj.*

land•hold•er (lănd'hōl'dər) *n.* One who owns land. —**land'hold'ing** *n.*

land•ing (lăn'dĭng) *n.* **1.** The act or process of coming to land or rest, as at the end of a voyage or flight. **2.** A site for landing. **3.** A platform at the top, bottom, or between flights of a staircase.

landing field. A tract of land providing a runway for aircraft.

landing gear. The structure that supports an aircraft and its load on the ground.

landing strip. An aircraft runway without airport facilities.

land•locked (lănd'lŏkt') *adj.* **1.** Surrounded or nearly surrounded by land. **2.** Confined to inland waters: *landlocked salmon.*

land•lord (lănd'lôrd') *n.* **1.** One who owns and leases land, buildings, or dwelling units. **2.** A man who runs a rooming house or inn. —**land'la'dy** (-lā'dē) *fem.n.*

land•lub•ber (lănd'lŭb'ər) *n.* One unfamiliar with the sea or seamanship.

land•mark (lănd'märk') *n.* **1.** A fixed marker indicating a boundary line. **2.** A prominent and identifying feature of a landscape. **3.** A historically significant event, building, or site.

land-poor (lănd'pōōr') *adj.* Owning much unprofitable land but lacking the capital to improve or maintain it.

land•scape (lănd'skāp') *n.* **1.** A view or vista of scenery on land. **2.** A pictorial representation of such a scene. —*v.* **-scaped, -scaping.** To improve the appearance of (a piece of ground) by contouring and decorative planting. —**land'scap'er** *n.*

land•slide (lănd'slīd') *n.* **1. a.** The dislodging and fall of a mass of earth and rock. **b.** The dislodged mass. **2.** An overwhelming majority of votes.

land•ward (lănd'wərd) *adv.* Also **land•wards** (-wərdz). Toward the land. —**land'ward** *adj.*

lane (lān) *n.* **1.** A narrow way or road. **2.** A limited passageway or course designated for vehicles, ships, etc. [< OE.]

lang. language.

Lang•er•hans, islands of. See **islands of Langerhans.**

lan•guage (lăng'gwĭj) *n.* **1. a.** The aspect of human behavior that involves the use of vocal sounds in meaningful patterns and, when they exist, corresponding written symbols to form, express, and communicate thoughts and feelings. **b.** A historically established pattern of such behavior that offers substantial communication only within the culture it defines: *the English language.* **2.** Any system of signs, symbols, etc., used for communication. **3.** The special vocabulary, usage, or style of a particular group or individual. **4.** Any particular manner of utterance: *gentle language.* **5.** The manner or means of communication between living creatures other than man. [< L *lingua,* tongue, language.]

lan•guid (lăng'gwĭd) *adj.* **1.** Lacking energy or vitality; weak. **2.** Listless; spiritless; apathetic. **3.** Slow; sluggish. [< L *languēre,* to LANGUISH.] —**lan'guid•ly** *adv.* —**lan'guid•ness** *n.*

lan•guish (lăng'gwĭsh) *v.* **1.** To lose strength or vigor; flag. **2.** To become listless or disconsolate; pine. **3.** To affect a mawkish air of longing or wistfulness. [< L *languēre,* to be faint or weak.] —**lan'guish•er** *n.*

lan•guor (lăng'gər) *n.* Languidness; lassitude; indolence. —**lan'guor•ous** *adj.* —**lan'guor•ous•ly** *adv.* —**lan'guor•ous•ness** *n.*

lank (lăngk) *adj.* **1.** Long and lean; gaunt. **2.** Long, straight, and limp: *lank hair.* [< OE *hlanc,* loose, hollow. See **kleng-.**]

lank•y (lăng'kē) *adj.* **-ier, -iest.** Tall, thin, and ungainly. —**lank'i•ly** *adv.* —**lank'i•ness** *n.*

lan•o•lin (lăn'ə-lən) *n.* A yellowish-white fatty substance obtained from wool and used in soaps, cosmetics, and ointments. [< L *lāna,* wool + -OL + -IN.]

Lan•sing (lăn'sĭng). The capital of Michigan. Pop. 132,000.

lan•tern (lăn'tərn) *n.* A case with transparent or translucent sides for holding and protecting a light. [< Gk *lamptēr,* lantern, torch.]

lan•tha•nide (lăn'thə-nīd') *n.* A **rare-earth element.** [< LANTHANUM.]

lan•tha•num (lăn'thə-nəm) *n. Symbol* **La** A soft, silvery-white metallic element used in glass manufacture and lighting. Atomic number 57, atomic weight 138.91. [< Gk *lanthanein,* to hide.]

lan•yard (lăn'yərd) *n.* A short rope or cord used to secure nautical rigging or worn to carry a knife, whistle, etc. [< OF *lasne,* thong, strap.]

La•os (lä'ōs, lous, lā'ŏs'). A kingdom of SE Asia. Pop. 3,000,000. Caps. Luang Prabang and Vientiane. —**Lao** (lou) *adj.* & *n.* —**La•o'tian** (lā-ō'shən, lou'shən) *adj.* & *n.*

Lao-tse (lou'dzŭ'). 604?–531 B.C. Chinese philosopher.

lap¹ (lăp) *n.* **1.** The front part of a seated person extending from the lower trunk to the knees. **2.** The part of a garment covering this area. **3.** A place of nurture or control: *the lap of luxury; the lap of the gods.* [< OE *læppa,* flap of a garment.]

lap² (lăp) *v.* **lapped, lapping. 1.** To fold or wrap over or around something. **2.** To place or extend so as to overlap. —*n.* **1.** An overlapping part. **2.** A complete turn or circuit, as of a racecourse. [Prob < LAP¹.]

lap³ (lăp) *v.* **lapped, lapping. 1.** To lift and take in (a liquid or food) with the tongue. **2.** To wash or splash with a light slapping sound. —**lap up.** To take in eagerly. —*n.* The act or sound of lapping. [< OE *lapian.* See **lab-.**] —**lap'per** *n.*

La Paz (lə päz', päz'). A capital of Bolivia. Pop. 361,000.

lap dog. A small, easily held pet dog.

la•pel (lə-pĕl') *n.* A part of a coat, jacket, etc., folded back against the chest from the opening at the neckline. [< LAP¹.]

lap•i•dar•y (lăp'ə-dĕr'ē) *n., pl.* **-ies.** One who cuts, polishes, or engraves gems. —*adj.* Of or relating to precious stones or the art of working with them. [L *lapidārius,* stoneworker.]

lap•in (lăp'ən) *n.* Rabbit fur, esp. when sheared. [F.]

lap•is laz•u•li (lăp'ĭs lăz'yo͞o-lē). An opaque, deep-blue gemstone. [< ML.]

Lap•land (lăp'lănd). A region comprising the areas of N Scandinavia and Finland and the NW Soviet Union lying above the Arctic Circle.

Lapp (lăp) *n.* **1.** Also **Lap•land•er** (lăp'lăn'dər). One of a people of nomadic tradition who inhabit Lapland. **2.** Also **Lap•pish** (lăp'ĭsh). The Finno-Ugric language of this people.

lap•pet (lăp'ĭt) *n.* A decorative flap or loose fold on a garment. [< LAP¹.]

lapse (lăps) *v.* **lapsed, lapsing. 1.** To fall away gradually; decline; subside. **2.** To become invalid, as through neglect or the passage of time. **3.** To elapse. —*n.* **1.** A slipping into a lower state; decline. **2.** A minor slip or failure. **3.** A passing or interval of time. **4.** The termination of a right or privilege through disuse or other failure. [< L *lābī* (pp *lapsus*), to slide.] —**laps'er** *n.*

lap•wing (lăp'wĭng') *n.* A crested Old World bird related to the plovers. [< OE *hlēapewince.*]

lar•board (lär'bərd) *n. Naut.* The port side. [ME *ladborde,* prob "the loading side."] —**lar'board** *adj.*

lar•ce•ny (lär'sə-nē) *n., pl.* **-nies.** The crime of stealing; theft. [< L *latrōcinium,* military service for pay.] —**lar'ce•nous** *adj.*

larch (lärch) *n.* A cone-bearing tree with deciduous needles and heavy, durable wood. [< L *larix.*]

lard (lärd) *n.* The white rendered fat of a hog. —*v.* **1.** To insert strips of fat in (lean, uncooked meat). **2.** To enrich or add to (speech or writing). [< L *lārdum.*] —**lard'y** *adj.*

lar•der (lär'dər) *n.* A storage place for food. [< LARD.]

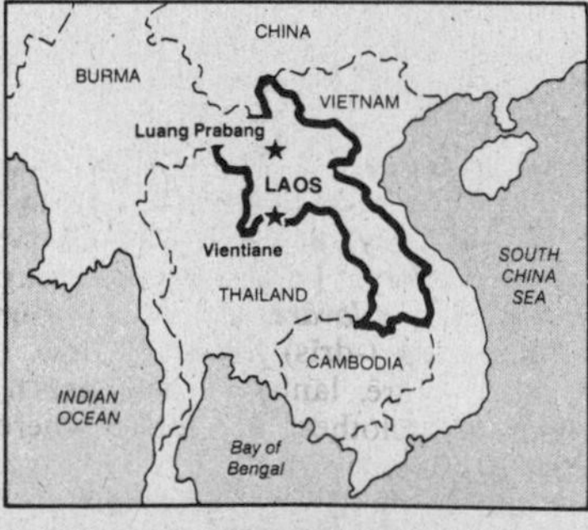

Laos

la•res and pe•na•tes (lâr'ēz; pĕ-nā'tēz, -nä'tēz). **1.** Ancient Roman household gods. **2.** One's household possessions.

large (lärj) *adj.* **larger, largest. 1.** Of considerable size, capacity, etc.; big. **2.** Broad in scope; comprehensive. —**at large. 1.** At liberty; free. **2.** At length; in detail. **3.** Not representing or assigned to a specific country, district, etc. [< L *largus,* generous, bountiful.] —**large'ness** *n.*

large intestine. The lower portion of the intestine, extending to the anus.

large•ly (lärj'lē) *adv.* **1.** For the most part; mainly. **2.** In a large manner.

lar•gess (lär-jĕs', lär'jĭs, -jĕs') *n.* Also **lar•gesse. 1.** Liberality in giving. **2.** Something generously bestowed.

larg•ish (lär'jĭsh) *adj.* Fairly large.

lar•go (lär'gō) *adv. Mus.* Slowly and solemnly. [It, slow, "broad."] —**lar'go** *adj.* & *n.*

lar•i•at (lăr'ē-ət) *n.* A rope with a running noose; a lasso. [Span *la reata.*]

lark¹ (lärk) *n.* **1.** An Old World bird with a sustained, melodious song. **2.** Any of several similar birds. [< OE *lǣwerce* < Gmc **larwarikōn.*]

lark² (lärk) *n.* A carefree romp or prank. —*v.* To romp; frolic. [< ON *leika,* to play.]

lark•spur (lärk'spûr') *n.* A plant with spurred, usually blue or purplish flowers.

lar•rup (lăr'əp) *v. Informal.* To flog; thrash; beat. [?]

lar•va (lär'və) *n., pl.* **-vae** (-vē). **1.** The wingless, often wormlike form of a newly hatched insect. **2.** The newly hatched stage of any of various animals that differ markedly in the adult form, as a tadpole. [L *lārva,* disembodied spirit, mask.] —**lar'val** *adj.*

lar•yn•gi•tis (lăr'ən-jī'tĭs) *n.* Inflammation of the larynx.

lar•ynx (lăr'ĭngks) *n., pl.* **larynges** (lə-rĭn'jēz) or **-ynxes.** The upper part of the respiratory tract between the pharynx and the trachea, containing the vocal cords. [< Gk *larunx.*] —**la•ryn'ge•al** (lə-rĭn'jē-əl) *adj.*

la•sa•gna (lə-zän'yə) *pl.n.* Also **la•sa•gne.** Flat wide noodles, usually baked with tomato sauce and cheese. [It.]

las•civ•i•ous (lə-sĭv'ē-əs) *adj.* Lewd; lecherous. [< L *lascīvus,* wanton, lustful.] —**las•civ'i•ous•ly** *adv.* —**las•civ'i•ous•ness** *n.*

la•ser (lā'zər) *n.* Any of several devices that convert incident electromagnetic radiation of mixed frequencies to one or more discrete frequencies of highly amplified and coherent radiation. [L(ight) a(mplification by) s(timulated) e(mission of) r(adiation).] —**lase** *v.* **(lased, lasing).**

lash¹ (lăsh) *n.* **1.** A whip or thong of a whip. **2.** A stroke or blow with or as with a whip. **3.** An eyelash. —*v.* **1.** To strike with or as with a whip. **2.** To wave or thrash vigorously, as a tail. **3.** To make a violent verbal attack. [ME *lashe.*] —**lash'er** *n.*

lash² (lăsh) *v.* To secure or bind, as with a rope. [< L *laqueus,* snare.] —**lash'er** *n.*

lass (lăs) *n.* A girl or young woman. [ME *lasse.*]

las•sie (lăs'ē) *n.* A girl.

las•si•tude (lăs'ə-t/y/o͞od') *n.* A state of listless weakness or exhaustion. [< L *lassus,* tired, weary.]

las•so (lăs'ō) *n., pl.* **-sos** or **-soes.** A long rope or thong with a running noose at one end, used esp. to catch horses and cattle. [< L *laqueus,* snare.] —**las'so** *v.*

last¹ (lăst, läst) *adj.* **1.** Being, coming, or remaining after all others. **2.** Most recent; latest. **3.** Conclusive and authoritative. **4.** Least likely or expected: *the last man we would have suspected.* —*adv.* **1.** After all others. **2.** Most recently. **3.** In conclusion. —*n.* **1.** One that is last. **2.** The end. —**at last.** Finally. [< OE *latost.* See **lēi-**.] —**last'ly** *adv.*

last[2] (lăst, läst) *v.* **1.** To continue in existence; endure. **2.** To continue to be adequate or sufficient. [< OE *lǣstan.* See **leis-**.]

last[3] (lăst, läst) *n.* A foot-shaped block or form used in making or repairing shoes. [< OE *lāst,* sole, footprint. See **leis-**.]

Las•tex (lăs'tĕks) *n.* A trademark for a yarn of elastic rubber wound with rayon, nylon, silk, or cotton. [(E)las(tic) + tex(tile).]

Last Judgment. The final judgment by God of all mankind.

Last Supper. Christ's supper with his disciples on the night before his Crucifixion.

lat. latitude.

Lat. Latin.

lat•a•ki•a (lăt'ə-kē'ə) *n.* A type of Turkish tobacco.

latch (lăch) *n.* A fastening or lock, as for a door or gate. —*v.* To close with a latch. —**latch on to.** *Informal.* **1.** To get hold or possession of. **2.** To cling to. [< OE *læccan,* to grasp. See **slagw-**.]

late (lāt). **later, latest.** *adj.* **1.** Coming, occurring, or remaining after the usual or expected time. **2.** Being or occurring toward the end. **3.** Recent. **4.** Recently deceased: *the late Mr. Foster.* —*adv.* **1.** After the usual or expected time. **2.** At or into an advanced period or part. **3.** Recently. —**of late.** Recently. [< OE *læt.* See **lēi-**.] —**late'ly** *adv.* —**late'ness** *n.*

Late Greek. Greek from the 4th to the 9th century A.D.

Late Latin. Latin from the 3rd to the 7th century A.D.

la•tent (lā'tənt) *adj.* Present or potential but not manifest. [< L *latēre,* to lie hidden, be concealed.] —**la'ten•cy** *n.* —**la'tent•ly** *adv.*

lat•er•al (lăt'ər-əl) *adj.* Of, at, on, or toward the side. —*n.* Also **lateral pass.** A football pass thrown sideways. [< L *latus (later-),* side.] —**lat'er•al•ly** *adv.*

la•tex (lā'tĕks') *n.* **1.** The milky, viscous sap of certain trees and plants, as the rubber tree. **2.** An emulsion of rubber or plastic globules in water, used in paints, adhesives, etc. [< L, fluid.] —**la'tex'** *adj.*

lath (lăth) *n.* **1.** A narrow, thin strip of wood, used esp. in making a supporting structure for plaster. **2.** A similarly used building material. [< OE *lætt.*]

lathe (lā*th*) *n.* A machine on which a piece is spun and shaped by a fixed cutting or abrading tool. [?] —**lathe** *v.* **(lathed, lathing).**

lath•er (lă*th*'ər) *n.* **1.** Foam or froth, esp. that formed by soap and water. **2.** Frothy sweat. **3.** A dither. —*v.* **1.** To produce lather. **2.** To apply lather to. [< OE *lēathor,* washing soda. See **lou-**.] —**lath'er•y** *adj.*

Lat•in (lăt'n) *adj.* **1.** Of or relating to ancient Rome, its culture, or its language. **2.** Of or relating to peoples using Romance languages. —*n.* **1.** The Italic dialect of ancient Rome. **2.** A member of a Latin people. [< L *Latīnus* < *Latium,* region surrounding Rome.]

Latin America. The Spanish- or Portuguese-speaking countries of the Western Hemisphere. —**Lat'in-A•mer'i•can** *adj.*

lat•i•tude (lăt'ə-t/y/o͞od') *n.* **1.** Extent; range. **2.** Freedom from limitations. **3. a.** The angular distance N or S of the equator, measured in degrees along a meridian. **b.** A region considered in relation to this distance. [< L *lātus,* wide.] —**lat'i•tu'di•al** *adj.*

lat•i•tu•di•nar•i•an (lăt'ə-t/y/o͞od'n-âr'ē-ən) *n.* One favoring freedom of thought and behavior. —**lat'i•tu'di•nar'i•an•ism'** *n.*

la•trine (lə-trēn') *n.* A communal toilet. [< L *latrīna* < *lavāre,* to wash.]

-latry. *comb. form.* Worship: *bibliolatry.* [< Gk *latreia.*]

lat•ter (lăt'ər) *adj.* **1.** Second of two persons or things mentioned. **2.** Further advanced; later. **3.** Closer to the end. [< OE *lætra.* See **lēi-**.] —**lat'ter•ly** *adv.*

Usage: Latter, in contrast with *former,* is acceptable only in contexts limited to two. Otherwise, *last-named* is more appropriate.

lat•ter-day (lăt'ər-dā') *adj.* Of present or recent time.

Latter-day Saint. A Mormon.

lat•tice (lăt'ĭs) *n.* **1.** An open framework made of interwoven strips, as of wood or metal. **2.** Something resembling this, as a window. **3.** *Phys.* A regular periodic configuration throughout an area or space. [< OF *latte,* lath.] —**lat'ticed** *adj.* —**lat'tice•work'** *n.*

Lat•vi•a (lăt'vē-ə). A constituent republic of the Soviet Union, on the Baltic. Pop. 2,365,000. Cap. Riga.

Lat•vi•an (lăt'vē-ən) *n.* **1.** A native of Latvia. **2.** The Baltic language of these people; Lettish. —**Lat'vi•an** *adj.*

laud (lôd) *v.* To praise; extol. —*n.* **1.** Praise. **2. lauds.** A morning church service at which psalms of praise are sung. [L *laudāre,* to praise.] —**laud'er** *n.*

laud•a•ble (lô'də-bəl) *adj.* Praiseworthy; commendable. —**laud'a•bly** *adv.*

lau•da•num (lôd'n-əm) *n.* A tincture of opium. [NL.]

laud•a•to•ry (lô'də-tôr'ē, -tōr'ē) *adj.* Expressing praise. —**laud'a•to'ri•ly** *adv.*

laugh (lăf, läf) *v.* **1.** To produce inarticulate sounds expressive of mirth, joy, or derision. **2.** To drive or influence by or as by laughing: *laughed him off the stage.* —*n.* **1.** The sound or act of laughing: *had a good laugh.* **2.** Something amusing or ridiculous. [< OE *hliehhan.* See **klēg-**.] —**laugh'a•ble** *adj.*

laugh•ing•stock (lăf'ĭng-stŏk', läf'-) *n.* An object of ridicule; butt.

laugh•ter (lăf'tər, läf'-) *n.* The sound or action of laughing.

launch[1] (lônch, länch) *v.* **1.** To set in motion; propel. **2.** To move (a boat) into the water. **3.** To put into action; inaugurate; initiate. —*n.* An act of launching. [< OF *lancier,* to hurl < *lance,* lance.]

launch[2] (lônch, länch) *n.* An open motorboat. [< Malay *lancha.*]

launch•er (lôn'chər, län'-) *n.* A device for launching a grenade or rocket shell.

launching pad. A platform from which a rocket or space vehicle is launched.

launch vehicle. *Aerospace.* A booster.

laun•der (lôn'dər, län'-) *v.* **1.** To wash or wash and iron (clothes or linens). **2.** To conceal the source of (money), as by channeling it through an intermediary. [<L *lavanda,* things that need washing <*lavāre,* to LAVE.] —**laun'der•er** *n.* —**laun'dress** (-drĭs) *fem.n.*

laun•dry (lôn'drē, län'-) *n., pl.* **-dries. 1.** Soiled or laundered clothes. **2.** A place where laundering is done.

lau•re•ate (lôr'ē-ĭt) *n.* One receiving highest honors, as a poet or scientist. [L *laureātus,* crowned with laurel.] —**lau're•ate** *adj.*

lau•rel (lôr'əl, lŏr'-) *n.* **1.** A shrub or tree of the Mediterranean region, having aromatic evergreen leaves. **2.** Any of several similar shrubs or trees. **3.** Often **laurels.** A wreath of laurel leaves. **4. laurels.** Honor; glory. [< L *laurus.*]

la•va (lä'və, lăv'ə) *n.* **1.** Molten rock from a volcano or geologic fissure. **2.** The rock formed by the cooling and solidifying of this substance. [It, lava stream from Vesuvius.]

lav•a•liere (lăv'ə-lîr') *n.* A pendant worn on a chain around the neck. [< Louise de *La Vallière,* a mistress of Louis XIV.]

lav•a•to•ry (lăv'ə-tôr'ē) *n., pl.* **-ries.** A room equipped with washing and toilet facilities. [< L *lavāre,* LAVE.]

lave (lāv) *v.* **laved, laving.** To wash; bathe. [< L *lavāre.*]

lav•en•der (lăv'ən-dər) *n.* **1.** Any of various aromatic plants having small fragrant purplish flowers. **2.** Pale to light purple. [< ML *lavendula.*] —**lav'en•der** *adj.*

lav•ish (lăv'ĭsh) *adj.* Extravagant; profuse. —*v.* To give forth unstintingly. [< OF *lavasse,* torrent of rain.] —**lav'ish•er** *n.* —**lav'ish•ly** *adv.* —**lav'ish•ness** *n.*

La•voi•sier (lȧ-vwȧ-zyā'), **Antoine.** 1743–1794. French chemist.

law (lô) *n.* **1.** A rule established by authority, society, or custom. **2.** A body of such rules. **3.** The science or study of such rules; jurisprudence. **4.** A judicial system or its workings. **5.** A formulation or generalization based on observed phenomena. **6.** A code of ethics or behavior. **7.** Avowed or undisputed authority. [< OE *lagu,* code of rules.]

law•ful (lô'fəl) *adj.* Allowed or established by law. —**law'ful•ly** *adv.*

law•giv•er (lô'gĭv'ər) *n.* **1.** One who gives a code of laws to a people. **2.** A legislator.

law•less (lô'lĭs) *adj.* **1.** Not governed by law. **2.** Heedless of or contrary to law. **3.** Disorderly; unbridled. —**law'less•ly** *adv.* —**law'less•ness** *n.*

law•mak•er (lô'mā'kər) *n.* A legislator.

lawn[1] (lôn) *n.* A closely mown area planted with grass. [< OF *launde,* heath.]

lawn[2] (lôn) *n.* A very fine, thin cotton or linen fabric. [Prob < *Laon,* France, linen-manufacturing town.]

law•ren•ci•um (lô-rĕn'sē-əm, lō-) *n. Symbol* **Lw** A synthetic radioactive element having a single isotope, Lw 257. Atomic number 103. [< E. *Lawrence* (1901–1958), American physicist.]

law•suit (lô'so͞ot') *n.* A case brought before a law court.

law•yer (lô'yər) *n.* One who gives legal advice and assistance to clients and represents them in court.

lax (lăks) *adj.* **1.** Negligent; remiss. **2.** Not strict. **3.** Not tense or taut; slack. **4.** Loose. [< L *laxus,* slack, loose.] —**lax'i•ty, lax'ness** *n.* —**lax'ly** *adv.*

lax•a•tive (lăk'sə-tĭv) *n.* A drug stimulating bowel evacuation. [< L *laxus,* loose, LAX.] —**lax'a•tive** *adj.*

lay[1] (lā) *v.* **laid, laying. 1. a.** To place or rest on a surface. **b.** *Nonstandard.* To recline; lie. **2.** To knock down: *laid him out flat.* **3.** To calm; allay. **4.** To produce and deposit (eggs). **5.** To bet: *laid his life on it.* **6.** To spread: *lay paint on a canvas.* **7.** To apply, assign, or locate. **8.** To bring into a specified condition. **9.** To set or place in a desired position. **10.** To prepare; contrive: *lay plans.* **11.** To sink in the ground: *lay a cable.* **12.** To impose: *laid a heavy fine on him.* **13.** To put forth or submit: *laid the case before us.* —*n.* The relative position or ar-

rangement of something. [< OE *lecgan.* See **legh-**.]
lay² (lā) *adj.* **1.** Of or belonging to the laity. **2.** Nonprofessional. [< Gk *laos,* the people.]
lay³ (lā) *n.* **1.** A ballad. **2.** A song. [< OF *lai.*]
lay⁴ (lā). *p.t.* of **lie¹**.
lay•er (lā'ər) *n.* **1.** A single thickness, coating, or stratum. **2.** One that lays, esp. a hen. [< ME *leyen,* to lay.]
lay•ette (lā-ĕt') *n.* Clothing and other equipment for a newborn child. [< OF *laie,* box.]
lay•man (lā'mən) *n.* **1.** A member of the laity. **2.** A nonprofessional.
lay off. **1.** To suspend from employment, as during a slack period. **2.** To mark off; chart. **3.** *Slang.* **a.** To give up (a habitual indulgence). **b.** To desist.
lay•off (lā'ôf', -ŏf') *n.* **1.** Temporary dismissal of employees. **2.** A period of inactivity.
lay out. **1.** To put or spread out. **2.** To arrange according to plan. **3.** To spend; supply (money). **4.** To prepare for burial. **5.** To knock down; prostrate.
lay•out (lā'out') *n.* **1.** An arrangement or plan. **2.** A set of tools.
lay over. To stop at some place in the course of a journey because of scheduling requirements.
lay•o•ver (lā'ō'vər) *n.* A stop imposed by the scheduling of a carrier.
la•zar (lā'zər) *n.* A leper. [< ML *Lazarus,* LAZARUS.]
Laz•a•rus (lăz'ər-əs). **1.** A man raised from the dead by Jesus. John 11:1–44. **2.** The diseased beggar in the parable of the rich man and the beggar. Luke 16:19–31.
laze (lāz) *v.* **lazed, lazing.** To loaf; idle. [Back-formation < LAZY.]
la•zy (lā'zē) *adj.* **-zier, -ziest.** **1.** Indolent; slothful. **2.** Slow-moving; sluggish. [?] **—la'zi•ly** *adv.* **—la'zi•ness** *n.*
lazy Susan. A revolving tray for condiments or relishes.
lb pound (L *libra*).
l.c. *Ptg.* lower-case.
L.C. Library of Congress.
L/C letter of credit.
l.c.d. lowest common denominator.
l.c.m. least common multiple.
lea (lē, lā) *n.* Grassland; meadow. [< OE *lēah, lēa.*]
leach (lēch) *v.* To remove, or be removed from, by the action of a percolating liquid. [Prob < OE *leccan,* to moisten.] **—leach'er** *n.*
lead¹ (lēd) *v.* **led, leading.** **1.** To guide, conduct, escort, or direct. **2.** To influence; induce. **3.** To be ahead or at the head of: *His name led the list.* **4.** To pursue; live: *lead a hectic life.* **5.** To tend toward a certain goal or result: *led to complications.* **6.** To make the initial play, as in a card game. **—lead astray.** To lead into error or wrongdoing. **—lead on.** To draw along; lure; entice. **—lead up to.** **1.** To result in by a series of steps. **2.** To proceed toward (one's true purpose or subject) with lengthy or evasive preliminary remarks. *—n.* **1.** The first place; foremost position. **2.** The margin by which one is ahead. **3.** A clue. **4.** Command; leadership. **5.** An example; precedent. **6.** The principal role in a play. **7. a.** The prerogative or turn to make the first play in a card game. **b.** The card played. **8.** A leash for leading an animal. [< OE *lǣdan.* See **leith-**.] **—lead'er** *n.* **—lead'er•ship'** *n.*
lead² (lĕd) *n.* **1.** *Symbol* **Pb** A soft, bluish-white, dense metallic element, used in solder and type metal, bullets, radiation shielding, and paints. Atomic number 82, atomic weight 207.19. **2.** A weight used to make soundings. **3.** A thin metal strip used to separate lines of type. **4.** A thin stick of graphitic marking substance in a pencil. *—v.* **1.** To cover, line, or weight with lead. **2.** To secure (window glass) with lead. [< OE *lēad* < Gmc **lauda.*]
lead•en (lĕd'n) *adj.* **1.** Made of lead. **2.** Heavy and inert. **3.** Dull; sluggish. **4.** Weighted down; depressed: *a leaden heart.* **5.** Dull, dark gray. **—lead'en•ly** *adv.*
lead-time (lēd'tīm') *n.* The time needed or available between the decision to start a project and the completion of the work.
leaf (lēf) *n., pl.* **leaves** (lēvz). **1.** A usually green, flattened plant structure attached to a stem and functioning as a principal organ of photosynthesis. **2.** A leaflike part. **3.** Leaves collectively; foliage. **4.** One of the sheets constituting the pages of a book. **5.** A very thin sheet of gold. **6.** A movable section of a table top. **7.** A movable section of a folding door, shutter, or gate. *—v.* **1.** To produce leaves. **2.** To turn pages rapidly: *leaf through a book.* [< OE *lēaf.* See **leup-**.] **—leaf'y** *adj.*
leaf•let (lēf'lĭt) *n.* **1.** A small leaf or leaflike part. **2.** A printed handbill, circular, or flier.
leaf spring. A spring consisting of several metallic strips joined to act as a single unit.
league¹ (lēg) *n.* **1.** An association or alliance, as of states or persons, for common action. **2.** *Informal.* A class of competition: *out of his league.* [< L *ligāre,* to bind.] **—league** *v.* **(leagued, leaguing).**
league² (lēg) *n.* A unit of distance equal to three miles. [< LL *leuga.*]
leak (lēk) *n.* **1. a.** A flaw, crack, or hole permitting accidental admission or escape of fluid or light. **b.** Such admission or escape. **2.** A secret or accidental disclosure of confidential information. *—v.* **1.** To escape or pass through a leak. **2.** To allow something passage through a leak. **3.** To disclose or become known through a breach of secrecy. [ME *leke.*] **—leak'i•ness** *n.* **—leak'y** *adj.*
leak•age (lē'kĭj) *n.* **1.** The process of leaking. **2.** The thing or amount that escapes by leaking.
lean¹ (lēn) *v.* **leaned** or **leant** (lĕnt), **leaning.** **1.** To bend away from the vertical; incline. **2.** To incline one's weight so as to be supported. **3.** To rely on for assistance or support. **4.** To have a tendency or preference. [< OE *hleonian.* See **klei-**.]
lean² (lēn) *adj.* **1.** Not fleshy; thin. **2.** Containing little or no fat: *lean meat.* **3.** Not productive: *lean years.* *—n.* Meat with little or no fat. [< OE *hlǣne* < Gmc **hlainjaz.*] **—lean'ly** *adv.* **—lean'ness** *n.*
lean•ing (lē'nĭng) *n.* A tendency; inclination.
lean-to (lēn'to͞o') *n., pl.* **-tos.** **1.** A shed with a single-pitch roof attached to the side of a building. **2.** A simple shelter resembling this.
leap (lēp) *v.* **leaped** or **leapt** (lĕpt, lēpt), **leaping.** **1.** To jump off the ground; hurdle. **2.** To jump forward; vault; bound. *—n.* A jump or bound. [< OE *hlēapan.*] **—leap'er** *n.*
leap•frog (lēp'frôg', -frŏg') *n.* A game in which one player bends over while the next jumps over him straddle-legged.
leap year. A year having 366 days with February 29 as the extra day.
learn (lûrn) *v.* **learned** or **learnt** (lûrnt), **learning.** **1.** To gain knowledge, comprehension, or mastery through experience or study. **2.** To memorize. **3.** To become informed. [< OE *leornian.* See **leis-**.] **—learn'er** *n.*
learn•ed (lûr'nĭd) *adj.* Erudite; scholarly.
learn•ing (lûr'nĭng) *n.* Erudition.
lease (lēs) *n.* **1.** A contract granting use or occupation of land or holdings during a specified period in exchange for rent. **2.** An extension under improved circumstances: *a new lease on life.* *—v.* **leased, leasing.** **1.** To grant by lease. **2.** To hold under lease. [< L *laxāre,* to let go, loosen < *laxus,* LAX.]
lease•hold (lēs'hōld') *n.* **1.** Possession by lease. **2.** Property held by lease. **—lease'hold'er** *n.*
leash (lēsh) *n.* A restraining chain, strap, etc., attached to the collar or harness of an animal. [< OF *laissier,* to loosen, let (a dog run slack).] **—leash** *v.*
least (lēst). Alternate *superl.* of **little.** *—adj.* **1.** Lowest in importance or rank. **2.** Smallest in magnitude or degree. *—adv.* In the smallest degree. *—n.* The smallest; slightest. [< OE *lǣst* < Gmc **loisiz,* little.]
least common multiple. The least quantity that is exactly divisible by each of two or more designated quantities.
leath•er (lĕth'ər) *n.* The dressed or tanned hide of an animal, usually with the hair removed. [< OE *lether-.* See **letro-**.] **—leath'er** *adj.* **—leath'ern** *adj.*
leath•er•neck (lĕth'ər-nĕk') *n. Slang.* A marine.
leath•er•y (lĕth'ə-rē) *adj.* Resembling leather; tough or weathered.
leave¹ (lēv) *v.* **left, leaving.** **1.** To go out or away from; depart. **2. a.** To let or cause to remain. **b.** To deliver. **3.** To have as a remainder. **4.** To forgo moving or interfering with. **5.** To bequeath. **6.** To abandon; forsake. [< OE *lǣfan.* See **leip-**.]
leave² (lēv) *n.* **1.** Permission. **2.** Official permission to be absent from duty. **3.** Farewell or departure: *take leave.* [< OE *lēaf.*]
leaved (lēvd) *adj.* Having a specified number or kind of leaves: *three-leaved; wide-leaved.*
leav•en (lĕv'ən) *n.* **1.** A substance, such as yeast, used to produce fermentation in batters and doughs. **2.** An element that works to lighten or enliven a whole. *—v.* **1.** To raise dough, as with yeast. **2.** To pervade with a lightening or enlivening influence. [Prob < L *levāre,* to raise.]
leaves. *pl.* of **leaf.**
leave-tak•ing (lēv'tā'kĭng) *n.* Departure.
leav•ings (lē'vĭngz) *pl.n.* Leftovers; residue.
Leb•a•non (lĕb'ə-nən). A republic on the E Mediterranean. Pop. 2,152,000. Cap. Beirut. **—Leb'a•nese'** (-nēz', -nēs') *adj.* & *n.*

Lebanon

lech•er (lĕch'ər) *n.* A man given to inordinate sexual indulgence. [< OF *lechier,* to live in debauchery, lick.] **—lech'er•ous** *adj.* **—lech'er•ous•ly** *adv.* **—lech'er•y** *n.*

lec•tern (lĕk'tərn) *n.* A reading stand for a public speaker. [< L *lectus,* pp of *legere,* to read.]

lec•ture (lĕk'chər) *n.* **1.** An instructional exposition of a given subject delivered before an audience or class. **2.** A solemn scolding. [< L *lectus,* pp of *legere,* to read.] **—lec'ture** *v.* **(-tured, -turing).** **—lec'tur•er** *n.*

led (lĕd). *p.t. & p.p.* of **lead¹.**

ledge (lĕj) *n.* **1.** A shelflike projection on a wall or cliff. **2.** A reef. [ME *legge,* a raised strip or bar.] **—ledge'less** *adj.*

ledg•er (lĕj'ər) *n.* A book in which monetary transactions are posted in the form of debits and credits. [ME *legger,* book remaining in one place.]

lee (lē) *n.* **1.** The side or quarter away from the wind. **2.** Cover; shelter. [< OE *hlēo,* covering, shelter. See **kel-¹.**] **—lee** *adj.*

Lee (lē), **Robert E(dward).** 1807–1870. Commander in chief of the Confederate armies in the Civil War.

leech (lēch) *n.* **1.** Any of various aquatic bloodsucking worms, of which one kind was formerly used by physicians to bleed their patients. **2.** A hanger-on or parasite. [< OE *lǣce.*]

Leeds (lēdz). A city of N England. Pop. 509,000.

leek (lēk) *n.* A vegetable related to the onion, having a white, slender bulb and dark-green leaves. [< OE *lēac.*]

leer (lîr) *n.* A suggestive, cunning, or malicious look. [Prob < *leer,* cheek.] **—leer** *v.*

leer•y (lîr'ē) *adj.* **-ier, -iest.** Distrustful; wary. [< LEER.] **—leer'i•ness** *n.*

lees (lēz) *pl.n.* Dregs. [< ML *lia,* sediment.]

lee•ward (lē'wərd, lo͞o'ərd) *adj.* Located away from the wind. **—lee'ward** *n. & adv.*

lee•way (lē'wā') *n.* **1.** The drift of a ship to leeward of true course. **2.** A margin of freedom or variation; latitude.

left¹ (lĕft) *adj.* **1.** Of, at, or on the side of the body that faces north when the subject is facing east. **2.** Of, at, or on the corresponding side of anything that can be said to have a front. **3.** Often **Left.** Of or belonging to the political Left. *—n.* **1.** The direction or position on the left side of something. **2.** The left side or hand. **3.** A turn in this direction: *take a left.* **4. the Left.** The persons and groups pursuing egalitarian political goals by reformist or revolutionary means. *—adv.* Toward or on the left. [< OE *left, lyft.*]

left² (lĕft). *p.t. & p.p.* of **leave.**

left-hand (lĕft'hănd') *adj.* **1.** Of, at, or on the left. **2.** Intended for the left hand.

left-hand•ed (lĕft'hăn'dĭd) *adj.* **1.** Having more dexterity in the left hand than in the right. **2.** Done with the left hand. **3.** Awkward; maladroit. *—adv.* With the left hand. **—left'-hand'ed•ly** *adv.* **—left'-hand'ed•ness** *n.*

left•ist (lĕf'tĭst) *n.* Also **Left•ist.** One espousing the ideology of the Left. **—left'ist** *adj.*

left•o•vers (lĕft'ō'vərz) *n.* Food left over from one meal and saved for another.

left wing. The leftist faction of a group. **—left'-wing'** *adj.* **—left'-wing'er** *n.*

leg (lĕg) *n.* **1.** A limb of an animal, used for locomotion or support. **2.** Something resembling a leg in shape or function. **3.** The part of a pair of trousers that covers the leg. **4.** A stage of a journey or course. *—v.* **legged, legging.** To use one's legs, esp. to run: *legged it out of there.* [< ON *leggr.*]

leg. **1.** legal. **2.** legislation; legislative; legislature.

leg•a•cy (lĕg'ə-sē) *n., pl.* **-cies.** **1.** A bequest. **2.** Something handed down from an ancestor or predecessor, or from the past. [< L *lēgāre,* to depute, bequeath.]

le•gal (lē'gəl) *adj.* **1.** Of or relating to law or lawyers. **2. a.** Authorized or permitted by law. **b.** Established by law; statutory. **3.** Enforced by law. [< L *lēx (lēg-),* law.] **—le•gal'i•ty** (lē-găl'ə-tē) *n.* **—le'gal•i•za'tion** *n.* **—le'gal•ize'** *v.* **(-ized, -izing).** **—le'gal•ly** *adv.*

le•gal•ism (lē'gə-lĭz'əm) *n.* Strict, literal adherence to law. **—le'gal•is'tic** *adj.*

leg•ate (lĕg'ĭt) *n.* An official emissary, esp. of the pope. [< L *lēgāre,* to depute, send on an embassy.] **—leg'ate•ship'** *n.*

leg•a•tee (lĕg'ə-tē') *n.* The inheritor of a legacy.

le•ga•tion (lə-gā'shən) *n.* **1.** A diplomatic mission headed by a minister. **2.** The premises occupied by the minister and his staff.

le•ga•to (lə-gä'tō) *adv. Mus.* In a connected style. [It, "connected," "bound."] **—le•ga'to** *adj. & n.*

leg•end (lĕj'ənd) *n.* **1.** An unverifiable popular story handed down from the past. **2.** An inscription on an object. **3.** An explanatory caption. [< L *legere,* to collect, gather, read.] **—leg'en•dar'i•ly** *adv.* **—leg'en•dar'y** *adj.*

leg•er•de•main (lĕj'ər-də-mān') *n.* Sleight of hand. [< OF *leger de main,* "light of hand."]

leg•ged (lĕg'ĭd, lĕgd) *adj.* Having a specified number or kind of legs: *six-legged; long-legged.*

leg•gings (lĕg'ĭngz) *pl.n.* Leg coverings, as gaiters or puttees.

leg•horn (lĕg'hôrn', -ərn) *n.* **1. a.** Finely plaited, bleached straw. **b.** A hat made from this. **2.** Often **Leghorn.** One of a breed of domestic fowl noted for egg production. [< *Leghorn,* Italy.]

leg•i•ble (lĕj'ə-bəl) *adj.* Capable of being read. [< L *legere,* to read.] **—leg'i•bil'i•ty, leg'i•ble•ness** *n.* **—leg'i•bly** *adv.*

le•gion (lē'jən) *n.* **1.** The major unit of the Roman army, comprising 3,000 to 6,000 foot soldiers and 100 to 200 mounted soldiers. **2.** A multitude. [< L *legere,* "to gather," levy troops.] **—le'gion•ar'y** *n.*

le•gion•naire (lē'jə-nâr') *n.* A member of the American Legion, an ex-servicemen's organization.

legis. legislation; legislative; legislature.

leg•is•late (lĕj'ĭs-lāt') *v.* **-lated, -lating.** To pass a law or create by legislation. **—leg'is•la'tor** *n.*

leg•is•la•tion (lĕj'ĭs-lā'shən) *n.* **1.** The action of making laws. **2.** Laws made by a legislative body.

leg•is•la•tive (lĕj'ĭs-lā'tĭv) *adj.* **1.** Of or relating to a legislature. **2.** Having the power to make laws. **—leg'is•la'tive•ly** *adv.*

leg•is•la•ture (lĕj'ĭs-lā'chər) *n.* A body of persons vested with the power to legislate.

le•git•i•mate (lə-jĭt'ə-mĭt) *adj.* **1.** In compliance with the law; lawful. **2.** In accordance with accepted standards. **3.** Reasonable: *a legitimate solution.* **4.** Authentic; genuine. **5.** Born in wedlock. *—v.* (lə-jĭt'ə-māt') **-mated, -mating.** To justify as legitimate. [< L *lēgitimus,* lawful, legal.] **—le•git'i•ma•cy** (-mə-sē) *n.* **—le•git'i•mate•ly** *adv.*

leg•ume (lĕg'yo͞om', lə-gyo͞om') *n.* **1.** A bean, pea, or related plant bearing pods that split in two when mature. **2.** The pod or seeds of such a plant, esp. when used as food. [< L *legūmen,* pulse, bean.] **—le•gu'mi•nous** *adj.*

lei¹ (lā, lā'ē) *n.* A garland of flowers. [Hawaiian.]

lei². *pl.* of **leu.**

Leip•zig (līp'sĭg, -sĭk). A city of S East Germany. Pop. 595,000.

lei•sure (lē'zhər, lĕzh'ər) *n.* **1.** Freedom from time-consuming work or duties. **2.** Free time. **—at one's leisure.** At one's convenience. *—adj.* **1.** Not spent in compulsory activity: *leisure hours.* **2.** Having leisure: *the leisure class.* [< L *licēre,* to be lawful, be permitted.] **—lei'sured** *adj.* **—lei'sure•ly** *adj. & adv.*

leit•mo•tif (līt'mō-tēf') *n.* Also **leit•mo•tiv.** A dominant recurrent theme. [G *Leitmotiv,* "leading motif."]

lek (lĕk) *n.* The basic monetary unit of Albania.

lem•ming (lĕm'ĭng) *n.* A rodent of northern regions, noted for its periodic mass migrations. [Norw.]

lem•on (lĕm'ən) *n.* **1.** An egg-shaped yellow citrus fruit with acid, juicy pulp. **2.** A tree bearing such fruit. [< Pers *līmūn.*]

lem•on•ade (lĕm'ə-nād') *n.* A drink of lemon juice, water, and sugar.

lem•pi•ra (lĕm-pîr'ə) *n.* The basic monetary unit of Honduras.

le•mur (lē'mər) *n.* A small African primate with large eyes, soft fur, and a long tail. [< L *lemurēs,* the spirits of the dead in ancient Rome.]

Le•na (lē'nə, lā'-). A river of the E Soviet Union.

lend (lĕnd) *v.* **lent, lending.** **1.** To give out or allow the use of temporarily on condition that the same or its equivalent be returned. **2.** To impart. **3.** To provide: *lend a helping hand.* **4.** To accommodate. [< OE *lǣnan,* to lend, give. See **leikw-.**] **—lend'er** *n.*

length (lĕngkth, lĕngth) *n.* **1. a.** The measure of something along its greatest dimension. **b.** The measure of something from back to front as distinguished from its width or height. **2.** Measured distance or dimension. **3.** Duration or extent. [< OE *lengthu.*] **—length'y** *adj.*

length•en (lĕngk'thən, lĕng'-) *v.* To make or become longer. **—length'en•er** *n.*

length•wise (lĕngkth'wīz', lĕngth'-) *adv.* In or along the direction of the length. **—length'wise'** *adj.*

le•ni•ent (lē'nē-ənt, lēn'yənt) *adj.* Gentle or liberal. [< L *lēnis,* soft.] **—le'ni•en•cy, le'ni•ence** *n.* **—le'ni•ent•ly** *adv.*

Le•nin (lĕn'ĭn, -ēn'), **Vladimir Ilyich.** 1870–1924. Russian revolutionary leader; founder of the modern Soviet state. **—Len'in•ist** *n. & adj.*

Lenin

Len•in•grad (lĕn′ĭn-grăd′). A city of the W Soviet Union. Pop. 3,950,000.

len•i•tive (lĕn′ə-tĭv) *adj.* Easing pain or discomfort. [< L *lēnīre,* to soothe, soften.]

lens (lĕnz) *n.* **1.** A piece of glass or other transparent material made so that either or both of its opposite surfaces are curved, used to make light rays converge or diverge to form an image. **2.** A combination of two or more such lenses used to form an image for viewing or photographing. **3.** A transparent part of the eye that focuses light rays to form an image on the retina. [< L *lēns,* LENTIL.]

lent (lĕnt). *p.t. & p.p.* of **lend.**

Lent (lĕnt) *n.* The 40 weekdays before Easter (beginning on Ash Wednesday), observed as a season of penitence. [< OE *lengten.*]

len•til (lĕn′təl) *n.* **1.** The round, flattened, edible seed of a pealike Old World plant. **2.** The plant itself. [< L *lēns.*]

len•to (lĕn′tō) *adv. Mus.* Slowly. [< L *lentus,* pliant, tenacious, slow.] **—len′to** *adj.*

Le•o (lē′ō) *n.* **1.** A constellation in the N Hemisphere near Cancer and Virgo. **2.** The 5th sign of the zodiac. [< L *leō,* lion.]

Le•o•nar•do da Vin•ci (lē′ə-när′dō də vĭn′chē). 1452–1519. Florentine artist and engineer.

le•one (lē-ōn′) *n.* The basic monetary unit of Sierra Leone.

le•o•nine (lē′ə-nīn′) *adj.* Resembling or characteristic of a lion.

leop•ard (lĕp′ərd) *n.* **1.** A large wild cat of Africa and Asia, usually having a tawny black-spotted coat. **2.** The pelt of a leopard. [< LGk *leopardos,* "lion pard."]

le•o•tard (lē′ə-tärd′) *n.* **1.** A snugly fitting garment worn by dancers or acrobats. **2. leotards.** Tights. [< J. *Léotard,* 19th-century French aerialist.]

lep•er (lĕp′ər) *n.* One afflicted with leprosy.

lep•re•chaun (lĕp′rə-kôn′, -kŏn′) *n.* An elf of Irish folklore. [< OIr *luchorpán,* "small body."]

lep•ro•sy (lĕp′rə-sē) *n.* A chronic infectious disease caused by a bacillus and ranging in severity from noncontagious and spontaneously remitting forms to contagious, malignant forms with progressive tissue degeneration. [< Gk *lepros,* scaly.] **—lep′rous** *adj.*

les•bi•an (lĕz′bē-ən) *n.* A female homosexual. [< *Lesbos,* island in the Aegean.] **—les′bi•an** *adj.* **—les′bi•an•ism′** *n.*

le•sion (lē′zhən) *n.* A wound, injury, or mass of diseased tissue. [< L *laedere,* to injure, damage.]

Le•so•tho (lə-sō′tō). A kingdom of S Africa. Pop. 745,000. Cap. Maseru.

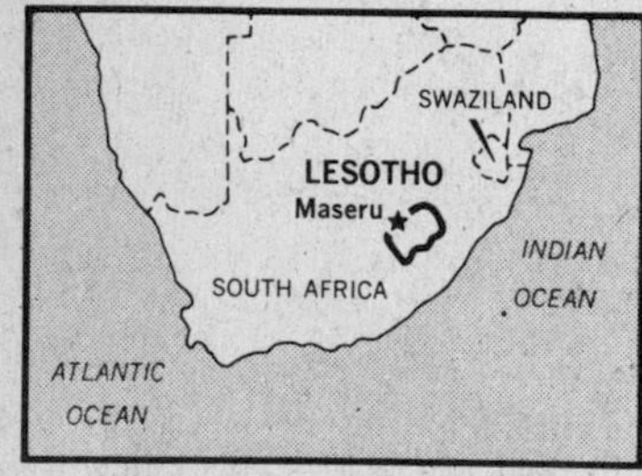

Lesotho

less (lĕs). Alternate comparative of **little.** *—adj.* **1.** Smaller. **2.** Lower in importance, esteem, or rank. *—adv.* To a smaller extent, degree, or frequency. *—n.* A smaller amount. *—prep.* Minus. See Usage note at **few.** [< OE *lǣssa* (adj) and *lǣs* (adv and noun) < Gmc **loisiz,* little.]

–less. *comb. form.* Lack of, free of, or not having: **sleepless.** [< OE *lēas,* lacking, free from.]

les•see (lĕ-sē′) *n.* A tenant holding a lease.

less•en (lĕs′ən) *v.* To make or become less.

less•er (lĕs′ər) *adj.* Smaller in size, amount, value, or importance.

Lesser An•til•les (ăn-tĭl′ēz). An island group in the West Indies.

les•son (lĕs′ən) *n.* **1.** Something learned or to be learned. **2. a.** A period of instruction; a class. **b.** An instructional exercise. **3.** An edifying example or experience. **4.** A reprimand or punishment. **5.** A reading from sacred writings as part of a religious service. [< L *lectiō,* a reading.]

les•sor (lĕs′ôr′, lĕ-sôr′) *n.* One who lets property under a lease.

lest (lĕst) *conj.* For fear that. [< OE *lǣs,* LESS.]

let[1] (lĕt) *v.* **let, letting. 1.** To allow. **2.** To cause to: *He let me know the results.* **3.** —Used in the imperative: **a.** By way of exhortation, command, or warning: *Let's go.* **b.** By way of expressing an assumption or hypothesis: *Let x equal y.* **4.** To rent or lease. [< OE *lǣtan,* to leave behind, leave undone. See **lēi-.**]

let[2] (lĕt) *n.* **1.** Obstacle: *without let or hindrance.* **2.** A stroke in tennis or a similar net game that is invalid. [< OE *lettan,* to hinder. See **lēi-.**]

–let. *comb. form.* **1.** Diminutive size or minor status: **starlet. 2.** An article worn on some part of the body: **bracelet.** [< OF *-elet.*]

let down. 1. To lower. **2.** To disappoint.

let•down (lĕt′doun′) *n.* **1.** A slackening, as of effort. **2.** A disappointment.

le•thal (lē′thəl) *adj.* Fatal or deadly. [< L *lēthum,* death.] **—le•thal′i•ty** (lē-thăl′ə-tē) *n.*

leth•ar•gy (lĕth′ər-jē) *n., pl.* **-gies. 1.** Sluggishness and indifference. **2.** A state of pathological drowsiness. [< Gk *lēthargos,* forgetful.] **—le•thar′gic** (lə-thär′jĭk) *adj.*

let's (lĕts). Contraction of *let us.*

let•ter (lĕt′ər) *n.* **1.** A written symbol representing a speech sound and constituting a unit of an alphabet. **2.** A written or printed communication. **3.** The literal meaning of something. **4. letters.** Literature or learning. *—v.* To write letters on; inscribe. [< L *littera,* letter.] **—let′ter•er** *n.*

let•tered (lĕt′ərd) *adj.* **1. a.** Literate. **b.** Erudite. **2.** Inscribed with letters.

let•ter•head (lĕt′ər-hĕd′) *n.* **1.** Stationery with a printed or engraved heading. **2.** The heading itself.

let•ter-per•fect (lĕt′ər-pûr′fĭkt) *adj.* Correct to the last detail.

let•ter•press (lĕt′ər-prĕs′) *n.* **1. a.** The process of printing from a raised inked surface. **b.** Anything printed in this fashion. **2.** Text as distinct from graphic ornamentation.

Let•tish (lĕt′ĭsh) *n.* Latvian. **—Let′tish** *adj.*

let•tuce (lĕt′əs) *n.* A plant cultivated for its crisp, edible leaves, eaten as salad. [< L *lac (lact-),* milk (< its milky juice).]

let up. 1. To slacken; lessen. **2.** To stop.

let•up (lĕt′ŭp′) *n.* **1.** A slackening or slowdown. **2.** A pause.

le•u (lĕ′ōō) *n., pl.* **lei** (lĕ′ī). The basic monetary unit of Rumania.

leu•ke•mi•a (lōō-kē′mē-ə) *n.* Any of a group of usually fatal diseases involving uncontrolled proliferation of leukocytes. [< LEUK(O)- + -EMIA.]

leuko–. *comb. form.* **1.** White or colorless. **2.** Leukocyte. [< Gk *leukos,* clear, white.]

leu•ko•cyte (lōō′kə-sīt′) *n.* Also **leu•co•cyte.** Any of the white or colorless nucleated cells occurring in blood.

lev (lĕf) *n., pl.* **leva** (lĕv′ə). The basic monetary unit of Bulgaria.

Lev. Leviticus (Old Testament).

Le•vant (lə-vănt′). The countries on the E Mediterranean. **—Le•van′tine** *adj. & n.*

lev•ee (lĕv′ē) *n.* **1.** An embankment raised to prevent a river from overflowing. **2.** A landing place on a river. [< OF *levee,* "raising."]

lev•el (lĕv′əl) *n.* **1.** Relative position or rank on a scale. **2.** A natural or proper position, place, or stage. **3.** Position along a vertical axis; elevation; height. **4. a.** A horizontal line or plane at right angles to the plumb. **b.** The position or height of such a line or plane: *eye level.* **5.** A flat, horizontal surface. **6.** A tract of land of uniform elevation. **7.** An instrument for ascertaining whether a surface is horizontal. *—adj.* **1.** Having a flat, smooth surface. **2.** Horizontal. **3.** At the same height as another; even. **4.** Uniform; consistent. **5.** Steady; cool. *—v.* **-eled** or **-elled, -eling** or **-elling. 1.** To make or become horizontal, flat, or even. **2.** To knock down or raze. **3.** To equalize. **4.** To aim or direct. [< L *lībella,* level, water level, plumb line.] **—lev′el•er** *n.* **—lev′el•ly** *adv.* **—lev′el•ness** *n.*

lev•el•head•ed (lĕv′əl-hĕd′ĭd) *adj.* Cool and steady of judgment. **—lev′el•head′ed•ness** *n.*

le•ver (lĕv′ər, lē′vər) *n.* A simple machine consisting of a rigid body pivoted on a fixed fulcrum. *—v.* To move or lift with a lever. [< OF *lever,* to raise.]

le•ver•age (lĕv′ər-ĭj, lē′vər-) *n.* **1.** The mechanical advantage of a lever. **2.** Positional advantage.

le•vi•a•than (lə-vī′ə-thən) *n.* **1.** A huge sea monster. **2.** Anything unusually large for its kind. [< Heb *libhyāthān.*]

lev•i•tate (lĕv′ə-tāt′) *v.* **-tated, -tating.** To rise or raise in the air in apparent defiance of gravity. [< LEVITY.] **—lev′i•ta′tion** *n.*

lev•i•ty (lĕv′ə-tē) *n., pl.* **-ties.** Lightness of speech or manner; frivolity. [< L *levis,* light.]

lev•y (lĕv′ē) *v.* **-ied, -ying. 1.** To impose or collect (a tax). **2.** To draft into military service. **3.** To wage (a war). **4.** To confiscate property. *—n.* **1.** The act or process of levying. **2.** Money, troops, or property levied. [< OE *levee,* a raising.] **—lev′i•er** *n.*

lewd (lōōd) *adj.* **1.** Licentious; lustful. **2.** Obscene. [< OE *lǣwede,* lay (nonclergy).] **—lewd′ly** *adv.* **—lewd′ness** *n.*

lex. lexicon.

lex•i•cog•ra•phy (lĕk′sĭ-kŏg′rə-fē) *n.* **1.** The writing or compilation of a dictionary. **2.** The principles underlying the making of dictionaries. [LEXICO(N) + -GRAPHY.] **—lex′i•cog′ra•pher** *n.* **—lex′i•co•graph′ic** (-kō-grăf′ĭk), **lex′i•co•graph′i•cal** *adj.* **—lex′i•co•graph′i•cal•ly** *adv.*

lex•i•con (lĕk′sĭ-kŏn′) *n.* **1.** A dictionary. **2.** A vocabulary used in a particular profession, subject, or style. [< Gk *lexikon (biblion),* (book) pertaining to words.] **—lex′i•cal** *adj.*

lf 1. lightface. **2.** low frequency.

LG Low German.

lg., lge. large.

Lha•sa (lä′sə, lăs′ə). The capital of Tibet. Pop. 80,000.

Li lithium.

L.I. Long Island.

li•a•bil•i•ty (lī′ə-bĭl′ə-tē) *n., pl.* **-ties. 1.** The state of being liable. **2. liabilities.** Debts. **3.** A hindrance or drawback.

li•a•ble (lī'ə-bəl) *adj.* **1.** Legally obligated; responsible. **2.** Susceptible; subject. **3.** Likely; apt. [Perh < OF *lier,* to bind.]

li•ai•son (lē'ā-zŏn', lē-ā'zŏn', lē'ə-) *n.* **1.** Communication between groups or units. **2. a.** A close relationship. **b.** An illicit relationship. [F, "binding."]

li•an•a (lē-ăn'ə, -ä'nə) *n.* A high-climbing tropical woody vine. [F *liane.*]

li•ar (lī'ər) *n.* One who tells lies.

li•ba•tion (lī-bā'shən) *n.* **1.** A sacrificial pouring of a liquid or the liquid thus poured. **2.** *Informal.* An alcoholic drink. [< L *lībāre,* to taste, pour out as an offering.]

li•bel (lī'bəl) *n.* **1.** A written, printed, or pictorial statement that unjustly damages a person's reputation. **2.** The action or crime of presenting such a statement to the public. —*v.* **-beled** or **-belled, -beling** or **-belling.** To defame or malign. [< L *libellus,* a little book.] —**li'bel•er** *n.* —**li'bel•ous** *adj.*

lib•er•al (lĭb'ər-əl, lĭb'rəl) *adj.* **1.** Favoring individual freedom and nonrevolutionary reform. **2.** Broad-minded or tolerant. **3.** Generous. **4.** Bountiful: *a liberal serving.* **5.** Not literal. **6.** Of or relating to the cultivation of general knowledge and the humanities: *liberal arts.* —*n.* One holding liberal political or cultural views. [< L *līber,* free.] —**lib'er•al•ism'** *n.* —**lib'er•al'i•ty** (lĭb'ə-răl'ə-tē) *n.* —**lib'er•al•ize'** *v.* (**-ized, -izing**). —**lib'er•al•ly** *adv.*

lib•er•ate (lĭb'ə-rāt') *v.* **-ated, -ating.** To give liberty to; set free. [< L *līber,* free.] —**lib'er•a'tion** *n.* —**lib'er•a'tor** *n.*

Li•be•ri•a (lī-bîr'ē-ə). A republic of W Africa. Pop. 1,066,000. Cap. Monrovia.

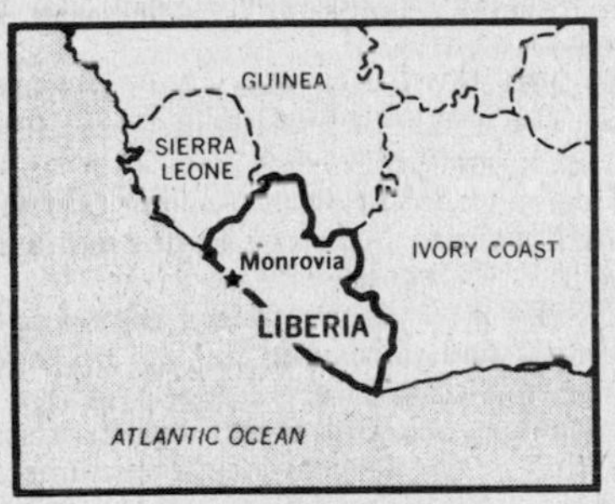

Liberia

lib•er•tine (lĭb'ər-tēn') *n.* A dissolute person. [< L *līber,* free.]

lib•er•ty (lĭb'ər-tē) *n., pl.* **-ties. 1. a.** The condition of being free from restriction or control; freedom. **b.** The right to act as one chooses. **2.** Freedom from confinement or servitude. **3.** Permission to do something; authorization or privilege. **4.** Often **liberties.** Unwarranted familiarity. **5.** Authorized leave from naval duty. [< L *līber,* free.]

li•bi•do (lĭ-bē'dō, -bī'dō) *n., pl.* **-dos. 1.** The psychic and emotional energy associated with instinctual biological drives. **2.** The sexual drive. [L *libīdō,* desire, lust.] —**li•bid'i•nal** (lĭ-bĭd'n-əl) *adj.* —**li•bid'i•nous** *adj.*

Li•bra (lī'brə, lē'-) *n.* **1.** A constellation in the S Hemisphere. **2.** The 7th sign of the zodiac. [< L *lībra,* balance.]

li•brar•i•an (lī-brâr'ē-ən) *n.* A custodian of a library.

li•brar•y (lī'brĕr'ē) *n., pl.* **-ies. 1.** A repository for literary and artistic materials, such as books, records, prints, etc., kept for reading or reference. **2.** A permanent collection of such materials. [< L *liber,* book.]

li•bret•to (lĭ-brĕt'ō) *n., pl.* **-tos** or **-bretti** (-brĕt'ē). The text of an opera or other dramatic musical work as distinct from the musical score. [< It *libro,* book.] —**li•bret'tist** *n.*

Li•bre•ville (lē'brə-vēl'). The capital of Gabon. Pop. 46,000.

Lib•y•a (lĭb'ē-ə). A country of N Africa, on the Mediterranean Sea. Pop. 2,580,000. Cap. Tripoli. —**Lib'yan** *adj. & n.*

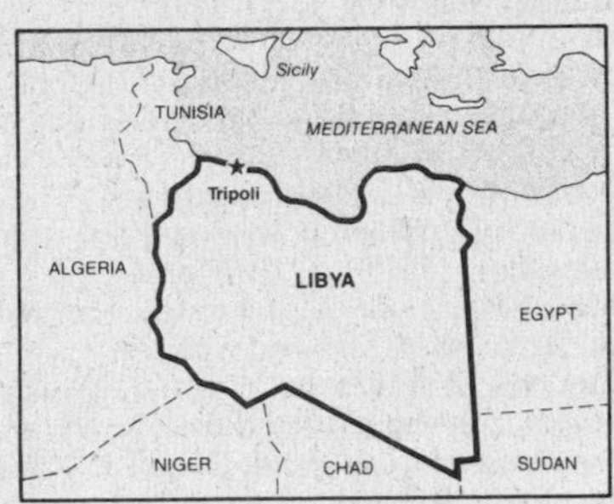

Libya

lice. *pl.* of **louse.**

li•cense (lī'səns). Also *chiefly Brit.* **li•cence.** *n.* **1. a.** Official permission to do or own a specified thing. **b.** Documentary evidence of this. **2.** Unusual freedom justified by extenuating circumstance. **3.** Studied and purposeful irregularity or deviation: *poetic license.* **4.** Excessive or undisciplined freedom. [< L *licēre,* to be lawful, be permitted.] —**li'cens•a•ble** *adj.* —**li'cense** *v.* (**-censed, -censing**).

li•cen•see (lī'sən-sē') *n.* The holder of a license.

li•cen•ti•ate (lī-sĕn'shē-ĭt, -āt') *n.* One who is granted a license, as by a university, to practice a specified profession.

li•cen•tious (lī-sĕn'shəs) *adj.* Lacking moral discipline or sexual restraint; lewd. [< L *licentia,* freedom, license.] —**li•cen'tious•ly** *adv.*

li•chee. Variant of **litchi.**

li•chen (lī'kən) *n.* A plant consisting of a fungus in close combination with certain algae and forming a scaly or branching growth on rocks or tree trunks. [< Gk *leikhēn,* "licker."]

lic•it (lĭs'ĭt) *adj.* Lawful. [< L *licēre,* to be permitted.] —**lic'it•ly** *adv.*

lick (lĭk) *v.* **1.** To pass the tongue over. **2.** To flicker over like a tongue. **3.** To thrash or defeat. —*n.* **1.** The act of licking. **2.** A small quantity. **3.** A place frequented by animals that lick an exposed salt deposit. **4.** A blow. [< OE *liccian.* See **leigh-.**] —**lick'er** *n.*

lick•e•ty-split (lĭk'ə-tē-splĭt') *adv.* With great speed. [< LICK and SPLIT.]

lic•o•rice (lĭk'ər-ĭs, -ĭsh) *n.* Also *chiefly Brit.* **li•quo•rice. 1.** A plant with a sweet, distinctively flavored root. **2.** The root of this plant, used as a flavoring. **3.** A candy made from or flavored with this root. [< Gk *glukurrhiza,* "sweetroot."]

lid (lĭd) *n.* **1.** A cover for any hollow receptacle. **2.** An eyelid. [< OE *hlid,* covering, gate, opening. See **klei-.**] —**lid'ded** *adj.*

lie[1] (lī) *v.* **lay, lain, lying. 1.** To assume or maintain a prostrate or recumbent position; recline. **2.** To be or remain in a specific condition. **3.** To occupy a place. **4.** To extend. —*n.* The position in which something is situated. [< OE *licgan.* See **legh-.**]

lie[2] (lī) *n.* A deliberate falsehood. —*v.* **lied, lying.** To tell a lie or convey a false image or impression; prevaricate. [< OE *lēogan.* See **leugh-.**]

Liech•ten•stein (lĭkн'tən-shtīn). A principality of C Europe. Pop. 19,000. Cap. Vaduz.

lied (lēd) *n., pl.* **lieder** (lē'dər). A German art song.

lie detector. A polygraph used to detect lying.

lief (lēf) *adv.* Readily; willingly. [< OE *lēof,* beloved.]

liege (lēj) *n.* **1.** A feudal lord. **2.** A vassal. —*adj.* **1.** Being in the feudal relationship with another: *liege lord.* **2.** Loyal. [< ML *lētus, litus,* serf.]

lien (lēn, lē'ən) *n.* The right to take and hold or sell the property of a debtor as security or payment for a debt. [< L *ligāre,* to bind.]

lieu (lōō) *n. Archaic.* Place; stead. —**in lieu of.** In place of; instead of. [< L *locus,* place, LOCUS.]

lieu•ten•ant (lōō-tĕn'ənt) *n.* **1.** One of two ranks held by military officers: **a.** A *second lieutenant,* the lowest-ranking commissioned officer; **b.** A *first lieutenant,* an officer ranking next below a captain. **2.** One of two ranks held by naval officers: **a.** A *lieutenant junior grade,* an officer ranking just above an ensign; **b.** A *lieutenant senior grade,* an officer ranking next below a lieutenant commander. **3.** One who acts in place of his superior; a deputy. [< OF, a rank.] —**lieu•ten'an•cy** *n.*

lieutenant colonel. A military officer ranking next below a colonel.

lieutenant commander. A naval officer ranking next below a commander.

lieutenant general. A military officer ranking next below a general.

life (līf) *n., pl.* **lives** (līvz). **1.** The quality manifested in functions such as metabolism, growth, response to stimulation, and reproduction, by which living organisms are distinguished from dead organisms or inanimate matter. **2.** Living organisms collectively: *plant life.* **3.** A living being. **4.** The interval between the birth or inception of an organism and its death. **5.** A biography. **6.** Human activities and relationships: *everyday life.* **7.** A manner of living: *country life.* **8.** Animation; liveliness. [< OE *līf.* See **leip-.**]

life•blood (līf'blŭd') *n.* The indispensable vital part of a thing.

life•boat (līf'bōt') *n.* A boat used for rescue at sea.

life buoy. A buoy.

life•guard (līf'gärd') *n.* An expert swimmer employed to safeguard bathers.

life history. The history of changes undergone by an organism.

life line. 1. A line thrown to a person in danger of drowning. **2.** Any means or route by which necessary supplies are transported.

life•long (līf'lông', -lŏng') *adj.* Continuing for a lifetime.

life preserver. A device designed to keep a person afloat in the water.

life•style (līf'stīl') *n.* Also **life-style, life style.** A way of life or style of living that reflects the attitudes and values of an individual or culture.

life•time (līf'tīm') *n.* **1.** The time during which an individual is alive. **2.** The time during which an object, property, process, or phenomenon persists.

lift (lĭft) *v.* **1. a.** To raise; elevate. **b.** To ascend; rise. **2. a.** To revoke; rescind. **b.** To put an end to. **3.** *Informal.* To steal. **4.** To pay off (a debt). —*n.* **1.** The act or process of raising or rising. 2. Power or force available for raising. 3. A load. 4. The extent or height something is raised. 5. A rise in the level of the ground. 6. A rising of spirits. 7. A machine designed to raise or carry something. 8. *Chiefly Brit.* An elevator. 9. Help or a ride along one's way. 10. The component of the aerodynamic force acting on an aircraft, perpendicular to the relative wind and normally exerted in an upward direction. [< ON *lypta.*]

lift•off (lĭft'ôf', -ŏf') *n.* The initial part of the flight of a rocket or other craft.

lig•a•ment (lĭg'ə-mənt) *n.* A sheet or band of tough, fibrous tissue connecting bones or cartilages, or supporting an organ. [< L *ligāmentum,* bond, bandage.]

lig•a•ture (lĭg'ə-chŏŏr') *n.* 1. A cord, wire, or bandage used for binding or constricting. 2. A character combining two or more letters, such as æ. 3. *Mus.* A slur. [< L *ligāre,* to bind.]

light¹ (līt) *n.* 1. Electromagnetic radiation that may be perceived by the human eye. 2. The sensation of the perception of such radiation; brightness. 3. A source of illumination, such as the sun or an electric lamp. 4. The illumination derived from such a source. 5. Daylight. 6. Dawn; daybreak. 7. A means or agent, as a match or cigarette lighter, for igniting a fire. 8. A way of regarding something; aspect: *see the situation in a different light.* 9. A prominent or distinguished person. —**in (the) light of.** In consideration of. —**shed (or throw) light on.** To provide information about. —*v.* **lighted** or **lit, lighting.** 1. To set on fire; ignite. 2. To cause to give out light: *light a lamp.* 3. To illuminate. 4. To start to burn; be ignited. —**light up.** 1. To become or cause to become light, bright, animated, or cheerful. 2. *Informal.* To start smoking a cigarette, cigar, or pipe. —*adj.* 1. Characterized by or filled with light; radiant; bright. 2. Mixed with white; pale: *light colors.* [< OE *lēoht, līht.* See **leuk-.**]

light² (līt) *adj.* 1. Not heavy. 2. Of relatively low density. 3. Having less force, quantity, intensity, or volume than normal. 4. Moderate; mild. 5. Not serious or profound. 6. Free from worries or troubles; blithe. 7. Frivolous; silly; trivial. 8. Quick to change or be swayed; fickle. 9. Suffering from mild delirium or faintness; dizzy. 10. Moving quickly and easily; graceful. —**make light of.** To regard as insignificant or petty. —*adv.* 1. Lightly. 2. Without additional weight or burdens: *traveling light.* —*v.* **lighted** or **lit, lighting.** 1. To get down, as from a mount or vehicle; dismount. 2. To land. 3. To come upon unexpectedly. [< OE *lēoht, līht.* See **legwh-.**] —**light'ly** *adv.* —**light'ness** *n.*

light•en¹ (līt'n) *v.* To make or become light or lighter; brighten. —**light'en•er** *n.*

light•en² (līt'n) *v.* 1. To make or become less heavy. 2. To make or become less oppressive, burdensome, or severe.

light•er¹ (lī'tər) *n.* 1. One that ignites something. 2. A mechanical device for lighting a cigarette, cigar, or pipe.

light•er² (lī'tər) *n.* A barge used to unload cargo from a larger ship unable to navigate in shallow water. [< MDu *lichten,* to unload.]

light•face (līt'fās') *n. Ptg.* A typeface having relatively thin, light lines. —**light'faced'** *adj.*

light•head•ed (līt'hĕd'ĭd) *adj.* 1. Delirious, giddy, or faint. 2. Frivolous; silly.

light•heart•ed (līt'här'tĭd) *adj.* Blithe; carefree; gay. —**light'heart'ed•ly** *adv.* —**light'heart'ed•ness** *n.*

light•house (līt'hous') *n.* A tall structure topped by a powerful light used for guiding ships.

light•ing (lī'tĭng) *n.* 1. The state of being lighted; illumination. 2. The method or equipment used to provide artificial illumination.

light•ning (līt'nĭng) *n.* A large-scale high-tension natural electric discharge in the atmosphere. —*adj.* Very fast or sudden, like a flash of lightning. [< LIGHT¹.]

lightning rod. A grounded metal rod placed high on a structure to prevent damage by conducting lightning to ground.

light•weight (līt'wāt') *n.* A person weighing relatively little, esp. a fighter weighing between 127 and 135 pounds. —*adj.* Weighing relatively little; not heavy.

light-year (līt'yîr') *n.* Also **light year.** The distance that light travels in one year, approx. 5.878 trillion (5.878 × 10^{12}) miles.

lig•nite (lĭg'nīt') *n.* A low-grade, brownish-black coal. [< L *lignum,* wood.]

lig•num vi•tae (lĭg'nəm vī'tē). 1. A tropical American tree with very hard, heavy wood. 2. The wood of such a tree. [< LL, "tree or wood of life."]

lig•ro•in (lĭg'rō-ən) *n.* A volatile, flammable fraction of petroleum, obtained by distillation, and used as a solvent. [?]

lik•a•ble (lī'kə-bəl) *adj.* Also **like•a•ble.** Pleasing; attractive. —**lik'a•ble•ness** *n.*

like¹ (līk) *v.* **liked, liking.** 1. To find pleasant; enjoy. 2. To want, wish, or prefer. 3. To be fond of. —*n.* —**likes and dislikes.** Preferences, predilections, and aversions. [< OE *līcian,* to please, be sufficient < Gmc **līkjan.*]

like² (līk) *prep.* 1. Similar or similarly to. 2. In the typical manner of: *That's not like you.* 3. Disposed to: *feel like eating.* 4. Indicative of: *It looks like rain.* —*adj.* 1. Similar. 2. Equivalent; equal. —*adv.* As if: *He ran like crazy.* —*n.* Similar or related persons or things: *bills, coins, and the like.* —**the likes of.** *Informal.* An equivalent to a person or thing: *never seen the likes of him.* —*conj. Nonstandard.* 1. In the same way that; as: *Tell it like it is.* 2. As if: *It rained like the skies were falling.* [< OE *līc* < Gmc **līk-.*]

Usage: Like, as a conjunction, is not appropriate to formal usage except when it introduces an elliptical clause in which a verb is not expressed: *He took to politics like a fish to water. The dress looked like new.* If these examples were recast to include full clauses containing verbs, *like* would preferably be replaced, in formal usage, by *as, as if,* or *as though: took to politics as a fish takes to water; dress looked as if it were new.*

like•li•hood (līk'lē-hŏŏd') *n.* 1. The state of being likely or probable; probability. 2. Something that is probable.

like•ly (līk'lē) *adj.* **-lier, -liest.** 1. Apparently destined; apt: *likely to be successful.* 2. Expected to occur. 3. Credible; plausible: *a likely excuse.* 4. Apparently suitable: *a likely place.* 5. Apparently capable of doing well; promising: *a likely lad.* —*adv.* Probably. [< ON *līkr,* like.]

Usage: Likely, as an adverb, is preferably preceded by a qualifying word such as *quite, very,* or *most: He will very likely arrive on Friday.*

lik•en (lī'kən) *v.* To see, mention, or show as like or similar; compare.

like•ness (līk'nĭs) *n.* 1. A resemblance. 2. A semblance; guise. 3. A representation of something; an image.

like•wise (līk'wīz') *adv.* 1. In the same way; similarly. 2. As well; also; too.

lik•ing (lī'kĭng) *n.* 1. A feeling of attraction, tenderness, or love; fondness; affection. 2. Preference; inclination.

li•lac (lī'lək, -lŏk') *n.* 1. A shrub widely cultivated for its clusters of fragrant purplish or white flowers. 2. Pale purple. [< Ar *līlak.*] —**li'lac** *adj.*

Li•long•we (lē-lông'wā). The capital of Malawi. Pop. 20,000.

lilt (lĭlt) *n.* 1. A light, happy tune. 2. A cheerful or lively manner of speaking, in which the pitch of the voice varies pleasantly. 3. A light or resilient manner of walking. [< ME *lulten,* to sound, sing.]

lil•y (lĭl'ē) *n., pl.* **-ies.** 1. Any of various related plants with showy, often trumpet-shaped flowers. 2. Any of various similar plants. [< L *līlium.*]

lily of the valley *pl.* **lilies of the valley.** A plant with a slender cluster of fragrant, bell-shaped white flowers.

lily pad. One of the broad, floating leaves of a water lily.

lim. limit.

Li•ma (lē'mə). The capital of Peru. Pop. 1,716,000.

li•ma bean (lī'mə). 1. A plant having flat pods containing large, light-green, edible seeds. 2. The seed of such a plant. [< LIMA.]

limb (lĭm) *n.* 1. One of the jointed appendages of an animal, used for locomotion or grasping, as an arm, leg, or wing. 2. A large tree branch. [< OE *lim.*]

lim•ber (lĭm'bər) *adj.* 1. Bending or flexing readily; pliable. 2. Capable of moving or bending easily; agile. —*v.* —**limber up.** To make (oneself) limber. [?] —**lim'ber•ly** *adv.* —**lim'ber•ness** *n.*

lim•bo (lĭm'bō) *n., pl.* **-bos.** 1. Often **Limbo.** *Theol.* The abode of souls kept from Heaven through circumstance, such as lack of baptism. 2. A region or condition of oblivion or neglect. [< ML *in limbō,* "(region) on the border (of hell)."]

lime¹ (līm) *n.* 1. A green, egg-shaped citrus fruit with acid juice used as flavoring. 2. A tree bearing such fruit. [< Ar *līmah.*]

lime² (līm) *n.* An Old World linden tree.

lime³ (līm) *n.* 1. **Calcium oxide.** 2. Birdlime. [< OE *līm.*]

lime•light (līm'līt') *n.* 1. A bright light produced by directing a flame at a cylinder of heated lime, formerly used in the theater. 2. **the limelight.** A focus of public attention or notoriety.

lim•er•ick (lĭm'ər-ĭk) *n.* A light humorous or nonsensical verse of five lines with the rhyme scheme *aabba.*

lime•stone (līm'stōn') *n.* A shaly or sandy sedimentary rock composed chiefly of calcium carbonate.

lim•it (lĭm'ĭt) *n.* 1. The point, edge, or line where something ends. 2. **limits.** Bounds: *city limits.* 3. The greatest amount or number allowed. —*v.* To confine or restrict within limits. [< L *līmes,* boundary.] —**lim'it•a•ble** *adj.* —**lim'i•ta'tion** *n.* —**lim'i•ta'tive** *adj.* —**lim'it•less** *adj.* —**lim'it•less•ly** *adv.*

lim•it•ed (lĭm'ə-tĭd) *adj.* 1. Having a limit or limits. 2. *Chiefly Brit.* Limiting the liability of each stockholder to his actual investment: *a limited company.* 3. Designating trains or buses that make few stops. —**lim'i•ted•ly** *adv.* —**lim'i•ted•ness** *n.*

limn (lĭm) *v. Archaic.* 1. To describe. 2. To

depict by painting or drawing. [< L *lūmināre,* to illuminate.] —**lim'ner** (lĭm'nər) *n.*

lim•ou•sine (lĭm'ə-zēn', lĭm'ə-zēn') *n.* A large, luxurious automobile with an enclosed passenger compartment. [Orig a kind of coat < *Limousin,* France.]

limp (lĭmp) *v.* To walk lamely, as if favoring one leg. —*n.* An irregular, jerky, or awkward gait. —*adj.* Lacking rigidity; flabby. [Prob short for obs *limphalt,* lame.] —**limp'ly** *adv.* —**limp'ness** *n.*

lim•pet (lĭm'pĭt) *n.* **1.** A marine mollusk that has a tent-shaped shell and adheres to rocks of tidal areas. **2.** One who clings persistently. [< OE *lempedu* < ML *lamprēda,* LAMPREY.]

lim•pid (lĭm'pĭd) *adj.* Crystal clear; transparent. [< L *limpidus.*] —**lim•pid'i•ty, lim'pid•ness** *n.* —**lim'pid•ly** *adv.*

lin. **1.** lineal. **2.** linear.

lin•age (lī'nĭj) *n.* Also **line•age.** The number of lines of printed or written material.

linch•pin (lĭnch'pĭn') *n.* A locking pin inserted through the end of an axle to prevent a wheel from slipping off. [< OE *lynis,* linchpin + PIN.]

Lin•coln (lĭng'kən). The capital of Nebraska. Pop. 150,000.

Lin•coln (lĭng'kən), **Abraham.** 1809–1865. 16th President of the U.S. (1861–65).

Abraham Lincoln

lin•den (lĭn'dən) *n.* A shade tree with heart-shaped leaves and yellowish, often fragrant flowers. [Perh < OE *linde,* the linden.]

line¹ (līn) *n.* **1. a.** The locus of a point having one degree of freedom; a curve. **b.** A set of points (x, y) that satisfy the equation $ax + by + c = 0$, where a and b are not both zero. **2.** A thin, continuous mark, as that made by a pen, pencil, or brush. **3.** A crease in the skin; wrinkle. **4.** A border or limit. **5.** A contour or outline. **6.** A cable, rope, string, cord, wire, etc. **7.** An electric-power transmission cable. **8.** A telephone connection. **9.** A system of transportation, esp. a company owning such a system. **10.** A course of progress or movement: *line of flight.* **11.** A general manner or course of procedure: *different lines of thought.* **12.** An official or prescribed policy: *the party line.* **13.** Alignment: *bring the wheels into line.* **14. a.** One's trade or occupation. **b.** The range of one's competence: *out of my line.* **15.** Merchandise of a similar nature: *a line of small tools.* **16.** A group of persons or things arranged in a row: *stand in line.* **17.** A row of words printed or written across a page. **18.** A brief letter; a note. **19.** Often **lines.** The dialogue of a play or other theatrical presentation. **20.** A calculated or glib way of speaking. **21.** *Football.* **a.** A line of scrimmage. **b.** The linemen. —**hold the line.** To stand firm. —**in line for.** Next in order for. —**in line with.** In accordance with. —**out of line.** **1.** Not in agreement or conformity. **2.** In an uncalled-for manner. —*v.* **lined, lining. 1.** To mark with lines. **2.** To place in a series or row. **3.** To form a bordering line along: *Small stalls lined the alleys.* [< L *līnea,* thread, line < *līnum,* flax.] —**line'less** *adj.*

line² (līn) *v.* **lined, lining.** To sew or fit a covering to the inside surface of. [< L *līnum,* flax.]

lin•e•age¹ (lĭn'ē-ĭj) *n.* Direct descent from a particular ancestor; ancestry.

line•age². Variant of **linage.**

lin•e•al (lĭn'ē-əl) *adj.* **1.** Being in the direct line of descent from an ancestor. **2.** Linear.

lin•e•a•ment (lĭn'ē-ə-mənt) *n.* A distinctive shape, contour, or line, esp. of the face.

lin•e•ar (lĭn'ē-ər) *adj.* **1.** Of or resembling a line or lines. **2.** Narrow and elongated: *a linear leaf.* —**lin'e•ar•ly** *adv.*

line drive. *Baseball.* A batted ball hit in a roughly straight horizontal line.

line•man (līn'mən) *n.* **1.** One who installs or repairs telephone, telegraph, or other electric power lines. **2.** *Football.* A player positioned on the forward line.

lin•en (lĭn'ən) *n.* **1.** Thread or cloth made of flax. **2.** Garments or articles made from this cloth. [< OE *līnen,* "made of flax" < Gmc **līnin.*] —**lin'en** *adj.*

lin•er (lī'nər) *n.* A commercial ship or airplane, esp. one carrying passengers on a regular route.

lines•man (līnz'mən) *n.* **1.** A football official who marks the downs and the position of the ball. **2.** An official in various court games whose chief duty is to call shots that fall out of bounds.

line up. **1.** To form or take a place in a line. **2.** To put into alignment.

line-up (līn'ŭp') *n.* Also **line•up.** **1.** A line of persons formed for inspection or identification. **2.** The members of a team chosen to start a game.

-ling. *comb. form.* **1.** One who belongs to or is connected with: **hireling. 2.** One who has a specified quality: **underling. 3.** A diminutive: **duckling.** [< OE < Gmc **-linga-.*]

ling. linguistics.

lin•ger (lĭng'gər) *v.* **1.** To remain as though reluctant to leave; tarry. **2.** To persist: *The memory still lingers.* **3.** To be tardy in acting; procrastinate. [< ON *lengja.*]

lin•ge•rie (län'zhə-rā', län'zhə-rē) *n.* Women's underwear. [< L *līnum,* flax.]

lin•go (lĭng'gō) *n., pl.* **-goes.** Language that is unintelligible through being foreign or a special jargon. [Port *lingoa,* "tongue," language.]

lin•gua fran•ca (lĭng'gwə frăng'kə). A language used as a medium of communication between peoples of different languages. [It, "the Frankish tongue."]

lin•guist (lĭng'gwĭst) *n.* **1.** One who speaks several languages. **2.** A specialist in linguistics. [< L *lingua,* language.]

lin•guis•tics (lĭng-gwĭs'tĭks) *n. (takes sing. v.).* The science of language; the study of the nature and structure of human speech. —**lin•guis'tic** *adj.* —**lin•guis'ti•cal•ly** *adv.*

lin•i•ment (lĭn'ə-mənt) *n.* A soothing medicinal fluid applied to the skin, esp. by rubbing. [< L *linere,* to anoint.]

lin•ing (lī'nĭng) *n.* **1.** An interior covering or coating. **2.** A layer of material sewn into the inside of a garment.

link (lĭngk) *n.* **1.** One of the rings or loops forming a chain. **2.** Anything resembling a chain link in its physical arrangement. **3.** Anything that serves to connect; a bond or tie. —*v.* To connect or become connected with or as if with links. [< ON *hlekkr,* link, ring.]

link•age (lĭng'kĭj) *n.* **1.** The act or process of linking. **2.** The state or condition of being linked. **3.** A system of interconnected machine elements used to transmit power or motion.

links (lĭngks) *pl.n.* A golf course. [< OE *hlinc,* ridge. See **kleng-.**]

lin•net (lĭn'ĭt) *n.* A small, brownish Old World songbird. [< OF *lin,* flax (the bird feeds on linseeds).]

li•no•le•um (lĭ-nō'lē-əm) *n.* A durable, washable material made in sheets, used as a floor and counter-top covering. [L *līnum,* flax + *oleum,* OIL.]

Li•no•type (lī'nə-tīp') *n.* A trademark for a keyboard-operated machine that sets an entire line of type on a single metal slug. [LINE + TYPE.]

Lin Pi•ao (lĭn' byou'). Born 1908. Vice-chairman of Chinese Communist Party.

Lin Piao

lin•seed (lĭn'sēd') *n.* The seed of flax, esp. as the source of a yellowish oil, **linseed oil,** used as a drying agent in paints, varnishes, etc. [< L *līnum,* flax + SEED.]

lint (lĭnt) *n.* Clinging bits of fiber and fluff; fuzz. [< L *līnum,* flax.] —**lint'y** *adj.*

lin•tel (lĭnt'l) *n.* The horizontal beam that forms the top of a window or door frame. [< L *līmen,* threshold.]

li•on (lī'ən) *n.* **1.** A very large carnivorous cat of Africa and India, having a short tawny coat and a thick mane in the male. **2. Lion.** Leo. —**the lion's share.** The greatest or best part of a whole. [< Gk *leōn.*] —**li'on•ness** *fem.n.*

li•on•ize (lī'ə-nīz') *v.* **-ized, -izing.** To look upon or treat (a person) as a celebrity.

lip (lĭp) *n.* **1.** Either of two fleshy, muscular folds that together surround the opening of the mouth. **2.** A part that similarly encircles or bounds an opening. **3.** A protruding part or division of a flower. **4.** The tip of a pouring spout. **5.** *Slang.* Insolent talk. [< OE *lippa.* See **leb-.**] —**lip'less** *adj.*

lip reading. The interpretation of inaudible speech by watching lip and facial movements.

lip•stick (lĭp'stĭk') *n.* A stick of waxy lip coloring enclosed in a small cylindrical case.
liq. 1. liquid. 2. liquor.
liq•ue•fy (lĭk'wə-fī') *v.* **-fied, -fying.** Also **liq•ui•fy.** To become or cause to become liquid. —**liq'ue•fac'tion** (-făk'shən) *n.*
li•queur (lĭ-kûr', -kyŏŏr') *n.* A sweet, syrupy alcoholic beverage. [< OF *licour,* liquid, liquor.]
liq•uid (lĭk'wĭd) *n.* A substance capable of flowing or of being poured. —*adj.* 1. Of or being a liquid. 2. Liquefied, esp.: a. Melted by heating: *liquid wax.* b. Condensed by cooling: *liquid oxygen.* 3. Readily converted into cash: *liquid assets.* [< L *liquēre,* to be liquid.]
liq•ui•date (lĭk'wə-dāt') *v.* **-dated, -dating.** 1. To pay off or settle (a debt). 2. To wind up the affairs of (a business firm). 3. To convert (assets) into cash. 4. To do away with; kill. —**liq'ui•da'tion** *n.* —**liq'ui•da'tor** *n.*
liq•uor (lĭk'ər) *n.* 1. An alcoholic beverage made by distillation rather than fermentation. 2. A liquid substance or solution. [< L *liquēre,* to be liquid.] —**liq'uor•y** *adj.*
li•quo•rice. *Chiefly Brit.* Variant of **licorice.**
li•ra (lîr'ə) *n.* 1. *pl.* **-ras** or **-re.** The basic monetary unit of Italy. 2. *pl.* **-re** or **-ras.** The basic monetary unit of Turkey. [< L *lībra,* balance, measure.]
Lis•bon (lĭz'bən). The capital of Portugal. Pop. 802,000.
lisle (līl) *n.* A fine, smooth, tightly twisted thread spun from long-stapled cotton. [< *Lille,* France.]
lisp (lĭsp) *n.* A speech defect characterized by the substitution of the sounds (th) and (*th*) for the sibilants (s) and (z). [< OE *wlisp,* a lisping.] —**lisp** *v.* —**lisp'er** *n.*
lis•some (lĭs'əm) *adj.* 1. Lithe; supple. 2. Agile; nimble. [Var of LITHESOME.] —**lis'some•ly** *adv.* —**lis'some•ness** *n.*
list¹ (lĭst) *n.* A printed or written series of persons or things, often arranged in a particular order. —*v.* 1. To make a list of; itemize. 2. To enter in a list. [OF *liste,* band, strip of paper.]
list² (lĭst) *n.* An inclination to one side, as of a ship; a tilt. —*v.* To lean or tilt to one side. [?]
lis•ten (lĭs'ən) *v.* 1. To apply oneself to hearing something. 2. To pay attention. [< OE *hlysnan.* See **kleu-.**] —**lis'ten•er** *n.*
list•ing (lĭs'tĭng) *n.* 1. An act of making or entering in a list. 2. An entry in a list.
list•less (lĭst'lĭs) *adj.* Marked by lack of energy or enthusiasm; indifferent; languid. [< OE *lystan,* to be pleasing (see **las-**) + -LESS.] —**list'less•ly** *adv.* —**list'less•ness** *n.*
Liszt (lĭst), **Franz.** 1811–1886. Hungarian pianist and composer.
lit (lĭt). 1. Alternate *p.t.* & *p.p.* of **light¹.** 2. Alternate *p.t.* & *p.p.* of **light².**
lit. 1. literal; literally. 2. literary; literature.
lit•a•ny (lĭt'n-ē) *n., pl.* **-nies.** A prayer consisting of phrases recited by a leader alternating with responses by the congregation. [< Gk *litaneia,* entreaty.]
li•tchi (lē'chē) *n.* Also **li•chee.** 1. A Chinese tree bearing edible fruit. 2. Also **litchi nut.** The thin-shelled, fleshy fruit of this tree. [Cant *lai chi.*]
li•ter (lē'tər) *n.* Also *chiefly Brit* **li•tre.** A metric unit of volume, approx. 1.056 liquid quart or 0.908 dry quart. [< Gk *litra,* a unit of weight.]
lit•er•a•cy (lĭt'ər-ə-sē) *n.* The ability to read and write.
lit•er•al (lĭt'ər-əl) *adj.* 1. Upholding the exact meaning of a word or the words of a text. 2. Word for word; verbatim: *a literal translation.* 3. Concerned chiefly with facts; prosaic. [< L *littera,* letter.] —**lit'er•al•ly** *adv.*
lit•er•ar•y (lĭt'ə-rĕr'ē) *adj.* 1. Of or relating to literature. 2. a. Found in or appropriate to literature: *a literary style.* b. Employed chiefly in writing rather than speaking: *literary language.* —**lit'er•ar'i•ness** *n.*
lit•er•ate (lĭt'ər-ĭt) *adj.* 1. Able to read and write. 2. Knowledgeable; educated. [< L *literātus,* acquainted with writings, learned.]
lit•e•ra•ti (lĭt'ə-rä'tē, -rā'tī') *pl.n.* The literary intelligentsia.
lit•er•a•ture (lĭt'ər-ə-chŏŏr') *n.* 1. Imaginative or creative writing; belles-lettres. 2. The body of written work produced in a given field: *medical literature.* 3. Printed material of any kind, as for a political campaign. [< L *literātus,* LITERATE.]
lith. lithograph; lithographic; lithography.
lithe (lī*th*) *adj.* 1. Supple; limber. 2. Marked by effortless grace. [< OE *līthe,* flexible, mild. See **lento-.**] —**lithe'ly** *adv.*
lithe•some (lī*th*'səm) *adj.* Lithe; lissome.
-lithic. *comb. form.* Stone: **Neolithic.**
lith•i•um (lĭth'ē-əm) *n. Symbol* **Li** A soft, silvery, highly reactive metallic element, used as a heat transfer medium, in thermonuclear weapons, and in various alloys. Atomic number 3, atomic weight 6.939.
litho-. *comb. form.* Stone. [< Gk *lithos,* stone.]
litho., lithog. lithograph; lithographic; lithography.
lith•o•graph (lĭth'ə-grăf', -gräf') *n.* A print produced by lithography. —**lith'o•graph'** *v.* —**li•thog'raph•er** (lĭ-thŏg'rə-fər) *n.* —**lith'o•graph'ic** *adj.* —**lith'o•graph'i•cal•ly** *adv.*
li•thog•ra•phy (lĭ-thŏg'rə-fē) *n.* A printing process in which an image is rendered on a surface and treated so that it will retain ink while the other areas will repel ink.
Lith•u•a•ni•a (lĭth'ŏŏ-ā'nē-ə). A Baltic republic of the Soviet Union. Pop. 3,129,000. Cap. Vilnius.
Lith•u•a•ni•an (lĭth'ŏŏ-ā'nē-ən) *n.* 1. An inhabitant or native of Lithuania. 2. The Baltic language of the Lithuanians. —**Lith'u•a'ni•an** *adj.*
lit•i•gant (lĭt'ĭ-gənt) *n.* One engaged in a lawsuit.
lit•i•gate (lĭt'ĭ-gāt') *v.* **-gated, -gating.** To engage in or subject (something) to legal proceedings. [L *lītigāre,* to dispute, quarrel, sue.] —**lit'i•ga'tion** *n.* —**lit'i•ga'tor** *n.*
li•ti•gious (lĭ-tĭj'əs) *adj.* Given to or characterized by litigation. —**li•ti'gious•ness** *n.*
lit•mus (lĭt'məs) *n.* A blue, amorphous powder derived from certain lichens that turns red with increasing acidity and blue with increasing alkalinity. [Perh < ON *litmosi,* "dye moss."]
litmus paper. An unsized white paper impregnated with litmus.
li•tre. *Chiefly Brit.* Variant of **liter.**
lit•ter (lĭt'ər) *n.* 1. A conveyance consisting of a couch mounted between shafts, carried by men or animals. 2. A stretcher for the sick or wounded. 3. Straw or other material used as bedding for animals. 4. The young produced at one birth by certain mammals. 5. Discarded waste materials or scraps. —*v.* 1. To make untidy by discarding rubbish carelessly. 2. To scatter (litter) about. [< L *lectus,* bed.]
lit•ter•bug (lĭt'ər-bŭg') *n. Slang.* One who litters public areas.
lit•tle (lĭt'l) *adj.* **-tler, -tlest.** 1. Small in size, quantity, or degree. 2. Also *compar.* **less,** *superl.* **least.** a. Short in extent or duration; brief: *little time.* b. Unimportant; trivial; insignificant. 3. Without much force; weak. 4. Narrow; petty. 5. Without much power or influence. 6. a. Appealing; endearing: *a little rascal.* b. Contemptible. —*adv.* **less, least.** Not much: *He sleeps little.* —*n.* A small quantity: *Give me a little.* [< OE *lȳtel.* See **leud-.**] —**lit'tle•ness** *n.*
Little Bear. Ursa Minor.
Little Dipper. Ursa Minor.
Little Rock. The capital of Arkansas. Pop. 129,000.
lit•to•ral (lĭt'ər-əl) *adj.* Of or existing on a shore. —*n.* A shore or coastal region. [< L *lītus (lītor-),* shore.]
lit•ur•gy (lĭt'ər-jē) *n., pl.* **-gies.** The system of public worship in the Christian church. [< Gk *leitourgos,* public servant, minister.] —**li•tur'gi•cal** (lĭ-tûr'jĭ-kəl) *adj.*
liv•a•ble (lĭv'ə-bəl) *adj.* Also **live•a•ble** 1. Fit to live in; habitable. 2. Worth living; endurable.
live¹ (lĭv) *v.* **lived, living.** 1. To have life; continue to remain alive. 2. To reside. 3. To pass; spend: *live a full life.* 4. To pass life in a particular manner. 5. To remain in human memory, usage, or general acceptance. —**live down.** To overcome (an adversity) by acceptance over a period of time. —**live up to.** To satisfy (an ideal), justify (an explanation), or fulfill (a bargain). —**live with.** To put up with (a continuing adverse factor). [< OE *libban, lifian.* See **leip-.**]
live² (līv) *adj.* 1. Having life. 2. Of current interest: *a live topic.* 3. Glowing; burning: *a live coal.* 4. Ignitable or explosive: *live ammunition.* 5. Energized. 6. Broadcast at the time of occurrence. [Short for ALIVE.]
live•li•hood (līv'lē-hŏŏd') *n.* Means of support; subsistence. [< OE *līf,* LIFE + *lād,* course (see **leith-**).]
live•ly (līv'lē) *adj.* **-lier, -liest.** 1. Full of life; vigorous. 2. Full of activity, spirit, or excitement. 3. Intense; keen. 4. Cheerful. 5. Bouncing readily upon impact, as a ball. —*adv.* In a vigorous, energetic, or spirited manner. [< OE *līf,* LIFE.] —**live'li•ness** *n.*
li•ven (lī'vən) *v.* To become or cause to become lively or livelier. —**li'ven•er** *n.*
live oak (līv). An evergreen American oak.
liv•er (lĭv'ər) *n.* A large gland that secretes bile and acts in the formation of blood and metabolism of carbohydrates, fats, proteins, minerals, and vitamins. [< OE *lifer.* See **leip-.**]
liv•er•ied (lĭv'ə-rēd) *adj.* Wearing livery, esp. as a servant.
Liv•er•pool (lĭv'ər-pōōl). A city of NW England. Pop. 722,000. —**Liv'er•pud'li•an** (-pŭd'lē-ən) *adj.* & *n.*
liv•er•wort (lĭv'ər-wûrt', -wôrt') *n.* 1. Any of various green nonflowering plants related to the mosses. 2. The hepatica.
liv•er•wurst (lĭv'ər-wûrst') *n.* A type of sausage made with or containing chopped liver.
liv•er•y (lĭv'ə-rē) *n., pl.* **-ies.** 1. The uniform worn by male servants. 2. a. The boarding and care of horses. b. The hiring out of horses and carriages. [< OF *livree,* "something delivered or given," allowance granted to servants.]
liv•er•y•man (lĭv'ə-rē-mən) *n.* A keeper or employee of a livery stable.
lives. *pl.* of **life.**
live•stock (līv'stŏk') *n.* Domestic animals, as cattle, horses, or sheep, raised for home use or profit.
liv•id (lĭv'ĭd) *adj.* 1. Discolored, as from a bruise. 2. Ashen or pallid, as with anger. [< L

līvēre, to be bluish.] **—liv'id•ly** *adv.*

liv•ing (lĭv'ĭng) *adj.* **1.** Possessing life; alive. **2.** In active function or use: *living languages.* **3.** Of or relating to persons who are alive. **4.** Of or characteristic of daily life. *—n.* **1.** The state or condition of being alive. **2.** A means of maintaining life; livelihood. **3.** A manner or style of life: *plain living.* **4. the living.** Those who are alive.

living room. A room for general use and the reception and entertainment of guests in a household.

liz•ard (lĭz'ərd) *n.* **1.** Any of various reptiles having a long, scaly body, four legs, and a tapering tail. **2.** Leather made from the skin of a lizard. [< L *lacertus, lacerta.*]

ll. lines.

lla•ma (lä'mə) *n.* A South American mammal kept as a beast of burden and for its wool. [< Quechua.]

lla•no (lăn'ō, lä'nō) *n., pl.* **-nos.** A large, grassy, almost treeless plain in Latin America and the SW U.S. [< L *plānum,* a plain.]

LL.B. Bachelor of Laws (L *Legum Baccalaureus*).

LL.D. Doctor of Laws (L *Legum Doctor*).

lo (lō) *interj.* Expressive of surprise: *lo and behold.*

load (lōd) *n.* **1. a.** A supported weight or mass. **b.** The overall force to which a structure is subjected. **2.** Material transported by a vehicle or animal. **3.** The share of work allocated to an individual, machine, or group. **4.** A responsibility regarded as an oppressive weight. **5.** Often **loads.** *Informal.* Any large amount or quantity. *—v.* **1.** To place (a load) in or on (a structure, device, or conveyance). **2.** To take on or receive a load. **3.** To weigh down with; burden; oppress. **4.** To charge (a firearm) with ammunition. **5.** To insert (film, tape, etc.) into (a holder or magazine). **6.** To raise the power demand in (a circuit). [< OE *lād,* way, course, conveyance. See **leith-.**]

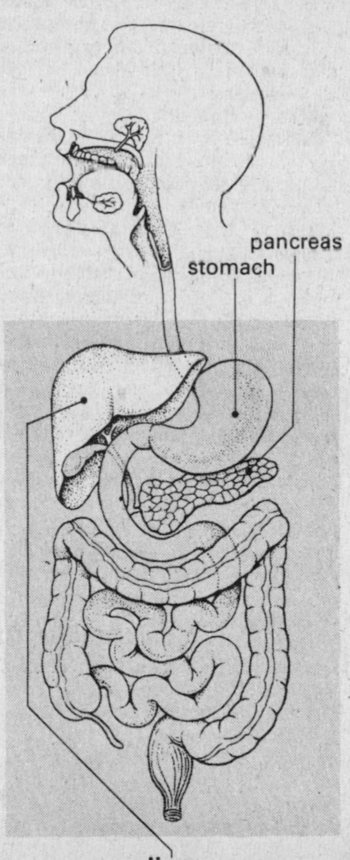

loaf¹ (lōf) *n., pl.* **loaves** (lōvz). A shaped mass of bread or other food baked in one piece. [< OE *hlāf* < Gmc **hlaibaz.*]

loaf² (lōf) *v.* **1.** To spend time lazily or aimlessly. **2.** To waste time on a job. **3.** To spend (time) idly.

loaf•er (lō'fər) *n.* **1.** One who loafs. **2.** A casual moccasinlike shoe.

loam (lōm) *n.* Soil consisting mainly of sand, clay, silt, and organic matter. [< OE *lām.*]

loan (lōn) *n.* **1.** A sum of money lent at interest. **2.** Anything lent for temporary use. *—v.* To lend. [< ON *lān.*] **—loan'er** *n.*

loan-word (lōn'wûrd') *n.* Also **loan word, loan•word.** A word adopted from another language and at least partly naturalized; for example, *encore, kindergarten.*

loath (lōth, lō*th*) *adj.* Unwilling; reluctant; disinclined. [< OE *lāth,* hateful, loathsome. See **leit-.**] **—loath'ness** *n.*

loathe (lō*th*) *v.* **loathed, loathing.** To detest greatly; abhor. [< OE *lāthian.* See **leit-.**] **—loath'er** *n.*

loath•ing (lō'*th*ĭng) *n.* Abhorrence.

loath•some (lō*th*'səm, lōth'-) *adj.* Abhorrent; repulsive; disgusting. **—loath'some•ly** *adv.*

loaves. *pl.* of **loaf¹.**

lob (lŏb) *v.* **lobbed, lobbing.** To hit, toss, or propel (something) slowly in a high arc. *—n.* A ball thus hit or thrown. [Prob < LG.]

lob•by (lŏb'ē) *n., pl.* **-bies. 1.** A hall, foyer, or waiting room in a hotel, apartment house, or theater. **2.** A group of private persons engaged in influencing legislation. *—v.* **-bied, -bying.** To seek to influence legislators in favor of some special interest. [ML *lobium,* a monastic cloister.] **—lob'by•ism'** *n.* **—lob'by•ist** *n.*

lobe (lōb) *n.* **1.** A rounded projection, esp. an anatomical part. **2.** A structurally bounded subdivision of an organ or part. [< Gk *lobos.*] **—lo'bar** *adj.*

lo•bot•o•my (lō-bŏt'ə-mē, lə-) *n., pl.* **-mies.** Surgical incision into a lobe, esp. one in the brain.

lob•ster (lŏb'stər) *n.* **1.** A large, edible marine crustacean with five pairs of legs, of which the first pair is large and clawlike. **2.** Any of several related crustaceans. [< L *locusta,* locust, lobster.]

lo•cal (lō'kəl) *adj.* **1.** Of or relating to a place. **2.** Pertaining to, existing in, or serving a locality: *local government.* **3.** Of or affecting a limited part of the body. **4.** Making many stops: *a local train.* *—n.* **1.** A public conveyance that stops at all stations. **2.** A local branch of an organization, esp. of a labor union. [< L *locus,* place, LOCUS.] **—lo'cal•ly** *adv.*

lo•cale (lō-kăl', -käl') *n.* A locality, with reference to some event.

lo•cal•i•ty (lō-kăl'ə-tē) *n., pl.* **-ties. 1.** A neighborhood, place, or district. **2.** A site, as of an event.

lo•cal•ize (lō'kə-līz') *v.* **-ized, -izing.** To confine or restrict to a particular area or part.

lo•cate (lō'kāt', lō-kāt') *v.* **-cated, -cating. 1.** To determine the position of: *locate Albany on the map.* **2.** To find by searching: *locate the source of error.* **3.** To station, situate, or place. [< L *locus,* place, LOCUS.] **—lo'ca'tor** *n.*

lo•ca•tion (lō-kā'shən) *n.* **1.** A place where something is located. **2.** A site away from the grounds of a motion-picture studio, where a scene is shot: *make a movie on location.*

loc. cit. In the place cited (L *locō citāto*).

loch (lŏKH, lŏk) *n. Scot.* **1.** A lake. **2.** An arm of the sea similar to a fjord. [< Scot Gael.]

lo•ci. *pl.* of **locus.**

lock¹ (lŏk) *n.* **1.** A key- or combination-operated mechanism used to secure a door, lid, etc. **2.** A section of a canal closed off with gates for the purpose of raising or lowering the water level. **3.** A mechanism in a firearm for exploding its charge of ammunition. *—v.* **1.** To fasten or become fastened with a lock. **2. a.** To confine or safeguard by putting behind a lock. **b.** To put in jail (with *up*). **3.** To clasp or embrace tightly. **4.** To entangle in struggle or battle. **5.** To become entangled; interlock. **6.** To jam or force together so as to make unmovable. **7.** To become rigid or unmovable. [< OE *loc.*] **—lock'less** *adj.*

lock² (lŏk) *n.* **1.** A strand or curl of hair. **2. locks.** The hair of the head. [< OE *locc.*]

lock•er (lŏk'ər) *n.* An enclosure that can be locked, esp. one in a gymnasium or public place, for the safekeeping of clothing and valuables.

lock•et (lŏk'ĭt) *n.* A small ornamental case for a picture or keepsake, usually worn as a pendant.

lock•jaw (lŏk'jô') *n. Path.* **1.** Tetanus. **2.** A symptom of tetanus, in which the jaw muscles go into spasm.

lock•out (lŏk'out') *n.* The closing down of a plant by an employer to coerce the workers into meeting his terms.

lock•smith (lŏk'smĭth') *n.* One who makes or repairs locks.

lo•co (lō'kō) *adj. Slang.* Mad; insane. [< Span.]

lo•co•mo•tion (lō'kə-mō'shən) *n.* The act of moving or ability to move from place to place. [< L *locus,* place, LOCUS + MOTION.]

lo•co•mo•tive (lō'kə-mō'tĭv) *n.* A self-propelled engine that moves railroad cars. *—adj.* Of or involved in locomotion.

lo•co•weed (lō'kō-wēd') *n.* Any of several W American plants that are poisonous to livestock.

lo•cus (lō'kəs) *n., pl.* **-ci** (-sī'). **1.** A place. **2.** The set or configuration of all points satisfying geometric conditions. [L *locus,* place.]

lo•cust¹ (lō'kəst) *n.* **1.** A grasshopper that travels in destructive swarms. **2.** A cicada. [< L *lōcusta,* locust, lobster.]

lo•cust² (lō'kəst) *n.* A tree with featherlike compound leaves and clusters of fragrant white flowers.

lo•cu•tion (lō-kyōō'shən) *n.* **1.** A particular word, phrase, or expression. **2.** Style of speaking; phraseology. [< L *loquī* (pp *locūtus*), to speak.]

lode (lōd) *n.* A vein of mineral ore deposited between layers of rock. [< OE *lād,* course, way. See **leith-.**]

lode•star (lōd'stär') *n.* A star that is used as a point of reference, esp. the North Star. [ME *loode sterre,* "guiding star."]

lode•stone (lōd'stōn') *n.* A magnetized piece of magnetite.

lodge (lŏj) *n.* **1.** A cottage or cabin used as a temporary abode by a caretaker, gatekeeper, etc. **2.** An inn. **3. a.** A local chapter of certain fraternal organizations. **b.** The meeting hall of such a society. *—v.* **lodged, lodging. 1.** To provide with or rent quarters temporarily, esp. for sleeping. **2.** To live in a rented room or rooms. **3.** To register (a charge): *lodge a complaint.* **4.** To vest (authority or power). **5.** To

be or become embedded. [< OF *loge,* shed, small house.] —**lodge'a•ble** *adj.*
lodg•er (lŏj'ər) *n.* One who rents and lives in a furnished room or rooms; roomer.
lodg•ing (lŏj'ĭng) *n.* Often **lodgings.** Sleeping accommodations.
Lódź (lo͞oj). A city of C Poland. Pop. 700,000.
loft (lôft, lŏft) *n.* **1.** A large, usually unpartitioned floor over a commercial building. **2.** An open space under a roof; attic. **3.** A gallery or balcony, as in a church: *a choir loft.* —*v.* To send (a ball) in a high arc. [< ON *lopt,* air, attic.]
loft•y (lôf'tē, lŏf'-) *adj.* **-ier, -iest. 1.** Of imposing height; towering. **2.** Elevated in character; noble. **3.** Arrogant; haughty. —**loft'i•ly** *adv.* —**loft'i•ness** *n.*
log (lôg, lŏg) *n.* **1.** A trunk or section of a trunk of a fallen or felled tree. **2.** A device used to determine the speed of a ship through water. **3.** A record of a ship's speed, progress, etc. **4.** Any record of performance, as the flight record of an aircraft. —*v.* **logged, logging. 1.** To cut (trees) into logs. **2. a.** To enter (something) in a ship's or aircraft's log. **b.** To travel (a specified distance, time, or speed). [ME *logge.*] —**log'ger** *n.*
log logarithm.
–log. Variant of **-logue.**
lo•gan•ber•ry (lō'gən-bĕr'ē) *n.* An edible, blackberrylike red fruit. [< J. *Logan* (1841–1928), American horticulturist.]
log•a•rithm (lô'gə-rĭth'əm, lŏg'ə-) *n.* The exponent indicating the power to which a fixed number, the base, must be raised to produce a given number. [< Gk *logos,* reckoning, ratio + *arithmos,* number.] —**log'a•rith'mic** (-rĭth'mĭk), **log'a•rith'mi•cal** *adj.*
loge (lōzh) *n.* **1.** A small compartment, esp. a box in a theater. **2.** The front rows of a theater's mezzanine. [< OF, shed, small house.]
log•ger•head (lô'gər-hĕd', lŏg'ər-) *n.* —**at loggerheads.** In a head-on dispute. [< LOG + HEAD.]
log•ging (lô'gĭng, lŏg'ĭng) *n.* The work of felling and trimming trees and transporting the logs to a mill.
log•ic (lŏj'ĭk) *n.* **1.** The study of the principles of reasoning. **2.** Valid reasoning, esp. as distinguished from invalid or irrational argumentation. [< Gk *logos,* speech, reason.]
log•i•cal (lŏj'ĭ-kəl) *adj.* **1.** Pertaining to or in accordance with logic. **2.** Showing consistency of reasoning. **3.** Reasonable on the basis of earlier statements or events. **4.** Able to reason clearly. —**log'i•cal•ly** *adv.*
lo•gi•cian (lō-jĭsh'ən) *n.* A practitioner of a system of logic.
lo•gis•tics (lō-jĭs'tĭks) *n.* *(takes sing. v.).* The procurement, distribution, maintenance, and replacement of materiel and personnel. —**lo•gis'tic, lo•gis'ti•cal** *adj.*
log•jam (lôg'jăm', lŏg'-) *n.* Also **log-jam, log jam. 1.** A mass of floating logs crowded immovably together. **2.** A deadlock in negotiations, debates, etc.
logo–. *comb. form.* Word or speech. [< Gk *logos,* speech, word, reason.]
log•roll•ing (lôg'rō'lĭng, lŏg'-) *n.* Also **log-roll•ing.** The trading of votes among legislators to achieve passage of projects of interest to one another.
–logue, –log. *comb. form.* Speech, discourse, or recitation: **travelogue.** [< Gk *legein,* to speak.]
lo•gy (lō'gē) *adj.* **-gier, -giest.** Sluggish; lethargic. [Perh < Du *log.*] —**lo'gi•ness** *n.*
–logy. *comb. form.* **1.** Discourse or expression: **phraseology. 2.** The science, theory, or study of: **paleontology.** [< Gk *logos,* word, speech.]
loin (loin) *n.* **1.** The part of the side and back between the ribs and pelvis. **2.** A cut of meat from this part of an animal. **3. loins.** The region of the thighs and groin. [< L *lumbus.*]
loin•cloth (loin'klôth', -klŏth') *n.* A strip of cloth worn around the loins.
Loire (lwär). A river of France.
loi•ter (loi'tər) *v.* **1.** To stand idly about; loaf. **2.** To proceed slowly or with many stops. [ME *loyteren.*] —**loi'ter•er** *n.* —**loi'ter•ing•ly** *adv.*
loll (lŏl) *v.* **1.** To recline in an indolent manner. **2.** To hang or droop laxly. [ME *lollen.*]
lol•li•pop (lŏl'ē-pŏp') *n.* Also **lol•ly•pop.** A piece of hard candy on the end of a stick. [Perh. < LOLL, to hang out (the tongue) + POP.]
Lo•mé (lô'mā'). The capital of Togo. Pop. 80,000.
Lon•don (lŭn'dən). The capital of the United Kingdom, in SE England. Pop. 7,990,000.
lone (lōn) *adj.* **1.** Solitary: *a lone tree.* **2.** Isolated; unfrequented. [Short for ALONE.]
lone•ly (lōn'lē) *adj.* **-lier, -liest. 1.** Without companions or companionship; solitary. **2.** Unfrequented; desolate. **3.** Dejected by the awareness of being alone. [< LONE.] —**lone'li•ly** *adv.* —**lone'li•ness** *n.*
lon•er (lō'nər) *n.* *Informal.* One who avoids other people.
lone•some (lōn'səm) *adj.* **1.** Dejected by being lonely. **2.** Offering solitude; secluded.
long[1] (lông, lŏng) *adj.* **1.** Having great length. **2.** Of relatively great duration: *a long time.* **3.** Of a specified length or duration: *a mile long; an hour long.* **4.** Concerned with distant issues; far-reaching: *a long view.* **5.** Risky; chancy: *long odds.* **6.** Having an abundance or excess of: *long on hope.* —**in the long run.** Ultimately; eventually. —*adv.* **1.** For an extended period of time. **2.** For or throughout a specified period: *all night long.* **3.** At a distant point in time: *long before we were born.* —**as** (or **so**) **long as. 1.** Since; inasmuch as. **2.** During the time that. —**no longer.** Not now as formerly; no more. —**before long.** Soon. —**the long and the short of.** The substance; gist. [< OE *lang.* See **del-**[1].]
long[2] (lông, lŏng) *v.* To yearn; desire greatly. [< OE *langian,* "to seem long (to some)," yearn for. See **del-**[1].]
long. longitude.
long distance. Telephone service between distant points. —**long'-dis'tance** *adj.*
long-drawn (lông'drôn', lŏng'-) *adj.* Prolonged.
lon•gev•i•ty (lŏn-jĕv'ə-tē) *n.* Long duration of life. —**lon•ge'vous** (-jē'vəs) *adj.*
Long•fel•low (lông'fĕl'ō, lŏng'-), **Henry Wadsworth.** 1807–1882. American poet.
long•hair (lông'hâr', lŏng'-) *n.* One dedicated to the arts and esp. to classical music. —**long'-hair', long'haired'** *adj.*
long•hand (lông'hănd', lŏng'-) *n.* Ordinary handwriting.
long•ing (lông'ĭng, lŏng'-) *n.* A persistent yearning or desire that cannot be fulfilled. —*adj.* Showing such a yearning: *longing eyes.* —**long'ing•ly** *adv.*
Long Island. An island of SE New York State.
lon•gi•tude (lŏn'jə-t/y/o͞od') *n.* Angular distance E or W, generally measured with respect to the prime meridian at Greenwich, England. —**lon'gi•tu'di•nal** *adj.* —**lon'gi•tu'di•nal•ly** *adv.*
long-lived (lông'līvd', -lĭvd', lŏng'-) *adj.* Having a long life. —**long'-lived'ness** *n.*
long-play•ing (lông'plā'ĭng, lŏng'-) *adj.* Relating to or being a microgroove phonograph record, esp. one turning at 33⅓ revolutions per minute.
long-range (lông'rānj', lŏng'-) *adj.* **1.** Involving a span of time: *long-range planning.* **2.** Designed to shoot over long distances.
long•shore•man (lông'shôr'mən, -shōr'mən, lŏng'-) *n.* A dock worker who loads and unloads ships.
long shot. An entry, as in a horse race, with only a slight chance of winning.
long-stand•ing (lông'stăn'dĭng, lŏng'-) *adj.* Of long duration.
long-suf•fer•ing (lông'sŭf'ər-ĭng, lŏng'-) *adj.* Patiently enduring wrongs or difficulties.
long-term (lông'tûrm', lŏng'-) *adj.* Involving or maturing after a number of years: *a long-term investment.*
long ton. A unit of weight, a ton.
long-wind•ed (lông'wĭn'dĭd, lŏng'-) *adj.* Wearisomely verbose. —**long'wind'ed•ly** *adv.* —**long'wind'ed•ness** *n.*
look (lo͝ok) *v.* **1.** To employ one's eyes in seeing. **2.** To turn one's eyes on. **3.** To seem or appear to be: *look morose.* **4.** To face in a specified direction. **5.** To have an appearance in conformity with: *look one's age.* —**look after.** To take care of. —**look down on** (or **upon**). To regard with contempt or condescension. —**look for. 1.** To search for. **2.** To expect. —**look forward to.** To anticipate eagerly. —**look into.** To investigate. —**look over.** To inspect, esp. casually. —**look up. 1.** To search for and find, as in a reference book. **2.** To locate and call upon; visit. **3.** *Informal.* To improve. —**look up to.** To admire. —*n.* **1.** The action of looking; a gaze or glance. **2.** Appearance or aspect. **3. looks.** Physical appearance, esp. when pleasing. [< OE *lōcian* < Gmc **lōkōjan.*] —**look'er** *n.*
looking glass. A mirror.
look•out (lo͝ok'out') *n.* **1.** The act of observing or keeping watch. **2.** A high place or structure commanding a wide view for observation. **3.** One who keeps watch.
loom[1] (lo͞om) *v.* **1.** To come into view as a massive, distorted, or indistinct image. **2.** To appear to the mind in a magnified and threatening form. **3.** To seem imminent; impend. [Prob of LG origin.]
loom[2] (lo͞om) *n.* A machine from which cloth is produced by interweaving thread or yarn at right angles. [< OE *gelōma,* utensil, tool.]
loon[1] (lo͞on) *n.* A diving bird with mottled plumage and an eerie, laughlike cry. [Prob < ON *lomr.*]
loon[2] (lo͞on) *n.* A simple-minded or mad person. [ME *loun, lown.*]
loon•y (lo͞o'nē) *adj.* **-ier, -iest.** *Informal.* So odd as to appear demented. —**loon'i•ness** *n.*
loop (lo͞op) *n.* **1.** A length of line, thread, etc., that is folded over and joined at the ends. **2.** Any roughly oval, closed, or nearly closed turn or figure. —*v.* **1.** To form or form into a loop or loops. **2.** To fasten, join, or encircle with a loop or loops. —**loop the loop.** To make a vertical loop or loops in the air, as an aircraft. [ME *loupe.*]
loop•hole (lo͞op'hōl') *n.* **1.** A small hole or slit in a wall. **2.** An omission or ambiguity that provides a means of evasion.
loose (lo͞os) *adj.* **looser, loosest. 1.** Not fastened; unbound. **2.** Not taut or drawn up tightly; slack. **3.** Not tight-fitting or tightly

fitted. **4.** Not compact or dense. **5.** Lacking a sense of restraint or responsibility; idle: *loose talk.* **6.** Licentious; immoral. **7.** Not literal or exact: *a loose translation.* **—at loose ends.** Without plans or direction. *—adv.* In a loose manner. *—v.* **loosed, loosing. 1.** To let loose; set free; release. **2.** To become loose. **3.** To undo, untie, or unwrap. **4.** To release pressure on; make less tight, firm, or compact. **5.** To let fly (a missile). [< ON *lauss, louss.*] **—loose'ly** *adv.* **—loose'ness** *n.*

loos•en (lo͞o'sən) *v.* **1.** To make or become loose or looser. **2.** To free from restraint, pressure, or strictness. **—loos'en•er** *n.*

loot (lo͞ot) *n.* **1.** Valuables pillaged in time of war; spoils. **2.** *Informal.* Goods stolen or illicitly obtained. *—v.* To pillage or engage in pillage. [< Sk *lōptra,* booty.] **—loot'er** *n.*

lop[1] (lŏp) *v.* **lopped, lopping. 1.** To cut off branches or twigs from; trim. **2.** To cut off (a part), esp. with a single swift blow. [?]

lop[2] (lŏp) *v.* **lopped, lopping.** To hang loosely; droop.

lope (lōp) *v.* **loped, loping.** To run or ride with a steady, easy gait. *—n.* A steady, easy gait. [< ON *hlaupa,* to leap.] **—lop'er** *n.*

lop•sid•ed (lŏp'sī'dĭd) *adj.* Heavier, larger, or higher on one side than the other; not symmetrical. **—lop'sid'ed•ness** *n.*

lo•qua•cious (lō-kwā'shəs) *adj.* Very talkative. [< L *loquī,* to speak.] **—lo•qua'cious•ness, lo•quac'i•ty** (-kwăs'ə-tē) *n.*

lord (lôrd) *n.* **1.** A person having dominion over others; a ruler or master. **2. Lord.** *Brit.* The general masculine title of nobility and other rank. **3. Lord.** God. Also used in exclamations, as *Good Lord!* *—v.* To play the lord; domineer: *lording it over the newcomers.* [< OE *hlāfweard,* "keeper of the bread": *hlāf,* LOAF + *weard,* keeper, WARD.]

Lord Chancellor *pl.* **Lords Chancellor.** Also **Lord High Chancellor.** The presiding officer of the House of Lords.

lord•ly (lôrd'lē) *adj.* **-lier, -liest. 1.** Pertaining to a lord. **2.** Dignified; noble. **3.** Arrogant; haughty. **—lord'li•ness** *n.*

Lord's Day, Lord's day. The Sabbath; Sunday.

lord•ship (lôrd'shĭp') *n.* **1. Lordship.** A form of address or a title for a British nobleman, judge, or bishop: *His Lordship.* **2.** The position, authority, or territory of a lord.

Lord's Prayer. The prayer taught by Jesus to his disciples. Matthew 6:9–13.

lore (lôr, lōr) *n.* Accumulated fact, tradition, or belief about a particular subject. [< OE *lār.* See **leis-.**]

lor•gnette (lôrn-yĕt') *n.* Eyeglasses or opera glasses with a short handle. [< OF *lorgne,* squinting.]

lor•ry (lôr'ē, lŏr'ē) *n., pl.* **-ries.** *Chiefly Brit.* A motor truck.

Los An•ge•les (lôs ăn'jə-ləs, -lēz', lŏs). A city of SW California. Pop. 2,782,000.

lose (lo͞oz) *v.* **lost** (lôst, lŏst), **losing. 1.** To be unable to find; mislay. **2.** To be unable to maintain or keep. **3.** To be deprived of: *lose a friend.* **4.** To fail to win; be defeated. **5.** To fail to take advantage of: *lose a chance.* **6.** To rid oneself of. **7.** To allow (oneself) to become engrossed, as in a book. **8.** To result in the loss of: *Failure to reply lost her a job.* **9.** To suffer loss. [< OE *los,* loss, destruction. See **leu-.**]

loss (lôs, lŏs) *n.* **1.** The act or an instance of losing. **2.** Something or someone that is lost. **3. losses.** Casualties. **—at a loss.** Perplexed; puzzled. [< OE *los,* destruction, loss. See **leu-.**]

lost (lôst, lŏst) *adj.* **1.** Strayed or missing. **2.** No longer possessed. **3.** No longer visible. **4.** Not taken advantage of: *a lost opportunity.* **5.** Bewildered; helpless. [< the pp of LOSE.]

lot (lŏt) *n.* **1.** An object used in making a determination by chance. **2.** The use of lots for selection. **3.** One's fortune in life; fate. **4.** A number of people or things. **5.** Often **lots.** A large amount or number. **6.** A piece of land having fixed boundaries. *—adv.* Very much: *Thanks a lot.* [< OE *hlot.*]

Lo•thar•i•o (lō-thâr'ē-ō) *n., pl.* **-os.** A libertine; rake. [< *Lothario,* seducer in *The Fair Penitent* (1703), by Nicholas Rowe.]

lo•tion (lō'shən) *n.* A liquid for external application, esp. one containing a substance in suspension. [< L *lōtiō,* washing.]

lot•ter•y (lŏt'ə-rē) *n., pl.* **-ies.** A contest in which lots are distributed or sold and the winners determined in a chance drawing. [< MDu *lot,* lot.]

lo•tus (lō'təs) *n., pl.* **-tuses. 1.** An Oriental water lily with pinkish flowers and large leaves. **2.** Any of several similar or related plants. **3.** A fruit said in Greek legend to produce a drugged, indolent state in those who eat it. [< Gk *lōtos,* a kind of fruit.]

loud (loud) *adj.* **1.** Characterized by high volume and intensity of sound. **2.** Producing or capable of producing a sound of high volume and intensity. **3.** Having offensively bright colors. [< OE *hlūd.* See **kleu-.**] **—loud, loud'ly** *adv.* **—loud'ness** *n.*

Usage: *Loud* (adverb) and *loudly* are often used interchangeably after certain common verbs, such as *laugh, play, roar, say, scream, shout, sing,* and *talk. Loudly* occurs more frequently in formal usage, esp. in writing. *Loudly* is the idiomatic form after verbs such as *boast, brag, insist,* and *proclaim.*

loud•mouth (loud'mouth') *n.* One whose speech is loud and irritating or indiscreet.

loud-speak•er (loud'spē'kər) *n.* Also **loud•speak•er.** A device that converts electric signals to audible sound.

Lou•is XIV (lo͞o'ē). 1638–1715. King of France (1643–1715).

Lou•is XVI (lo͞o'ē). 1754–1793. King of France (1774–92).

Lou•i•si•an•a (lo͞o-ē'zē-ăn'ə). A state of the S U.S. Pop. 3,643,000. Cap. Baton Rouge.

Louisiana French. French as spoken by descendants of the original settlers of Louisiana.

Lou•is•ville (lo͞o'ē-vĭl). A city of N Kentucky. Pop. 361,000.

lounge (lounj) *v.* **lounged, lounging.** To stand, sit, or lie in a lazy, relaxed way. *—n.* **1.** A comfortably furnished waiting room, as in a hotel or theater. **2.** A long couch. [?]

loupe (lo͞op) *n.* A magnifying glass set in an eyepiece, used by watchmakers and jewelers. [< OF *loupe,* imperfect gem.]

lour. Variant of **lower[1].**

Lou•ren•ço Mar•ques (lō-räɴ'so͞o mər-kăsh'). The capital of Mozambique. Pop. 79,000.

louse (lous) *n.* **1.** *pl.* **lice** (līs). A small, wingless insect that lives as a parasite on various animals, including man. **2.** *pl.* **louses.** *Slang.* A mean or despicable person. *—v.* **loused, lousing.** *Slang.* To bungle (with *up*). [< OE *lūs, lȳs.* See **lus-.**]

lous•y (lou'zē) *adj.* **-ier, -iest. 1.** Infested with lice. **2.** *Slang.* Mean; nasty. **3.** *Slang.* Inferior; worthless. **4.** *Slang.* Having a surfeit of: *lousy with money.* **—lous'i•ly** *adv.* **—lous'i•ness** *n.*

lout (lout) *n.* An awkward, stupid fellow; oaf. [Perh < ON *lūtr,* bent low.] **—lout'ish** *adj.*

lou•ver (lo͞o'vər) *n.* Also **lou•vre. 1.** An opening fitted with fixed or movable slanted slats. **2.** One of the slats used in a louver. [< OF *lovier.*] **—lou'vered** *adj.*

love (lŭv) *n.* **1. a.** An intense affectionate concern for another person. **b.** A passionate attraction to another person. **2.** A beloved person. **3.** A strong liking or enthusiasm for something. **4.** A zero score in tennis. **—in love.** Enamored. *—v.* **loved, loving. 1.** To feel love for. **2.** To like enthusiastically. [< OE *lufu.* See **leubh-.**] **—lov'a•ble, love'a•ble** *adj.*

love•bird (lŭv'bûrd') *n.* A small parrot often kept as a cage bird.

love•lorn (lŭv'lôrn') *adj.* Bereft of love or one's lover. **—love'lorn'ness** *n.*

love•ly (lŭv'lē) *adj.* **-lier, -liest. 1.** Having pleasing or attractive qualities; beautiful. **2.** Enjoyable; delightful. **—love'li•ness** *n.*

lov•er (lŭv'ər) *n.* **1.** A person in love with another. **2. lovers.** A couple in love with each other. **3.** A paramour. **4.** One who is fond of or devoted to something.

love seat. A small sofa or double chair that seats two people.

love•sick (lŭv'sĭk') *adj.* **1.** Stricken, as if with illness, by love. **2.** Showing a lover's yearning. **—love'sick'ness** *n.*

lov•ing (lŭv'ĭng) *adj.* Feeling or exhibiting love; affectionate. **—lov'ing•ly** *adv.*

loving cup. A large, ornamental cup given as an award in sporting events and similar affairs.

low[1] (lō) *adj.* **1.** Having little height. **2.** Situated below normal height. **3.** Situated below surrounding surfaces. **4.** Of less than usual or average depth. **5.** Of inferior quality or character. **6.** Of inferior or relatively simple status. **7.** Morally base. **8.** Emotionally or mentally depressed. **9.** Below average in degree or intensity. **10.** Below an average or standard figure. **11.** Being a sound produced by a relatively small frequency of vibrations. **12.** Not loud. **13.** Depreciatory; disparaging: *a low opinion of his qualities.* *—adv.* **1.** In a low position, level, etc. **2.** In or to a reduced or degraded condition. **3.** At or to a low volume, intensity, etc. **4.** At a small price: *bought low, sold high.* *—n.* **1.** A low level, position, or degree. **2.** A region of depressed barometric pressure. **3.** The gear arrangement that produces the lowest range of output speeds, as in an automotive transmission. [< ON *lāgr.*] **—low'ness** *n.*

low[2] (lō) *v.* To moo. [< OE *hlōwan.* See **kel-[3].**] **—low** *n.*

low•boy (lō'boi') *n.* A low, tablelike chest of drawers.

low•brow (lō'brou') *n.* *Informal.* One having uncultivated tastes. **—low'brow'** *adj.*

Low Countries. Belgium, the Netherlands, and Luxembourg.

low-down (lō'doun') *adj.* Mean; unfair.

low•down (lō'doun') *n.* *Slang.* All the facts; the whole truth.

Low•ell (lō'əl), **James Russell.** 1819–1891. American poet, essayist, and diplomat.

low•er[1] (lou'ər) *v.* Also **lour. 1.** To look angry or sullen; scowl. **2.** To appear dark and threatening, as the weather. [ME *l(o)uren.*]

low•er[2] (lō'ər) *adj.* **1.** Below someone or something, as in rank, position, etc. **2. Lower.** *Geol. & Archaeol.* Being an earlier division of the period named. **3.** Denoting the larger house of a bicameral legislature. *—v.* **1.** To let or move something down to a lower level. **2.** To reduce in value, degree, etc.

Lower Carboniferous. *Geol.* Mississippian.
low•er-case (lō'ər-kās') *adj.* Of or pertaining to small letters as distinguished from capitals.
lower class. Often **lower classes.** The class or classes of lower than middle rank in a society. —**low'er-class'** *adj.*
lowest common denominator. The least common multiple of the denominators of a set of fractions.
low frequency. A radio frequency in the range from 30 to 300 kilocycles per second.
Low German. 1. Any of several German dialects spoken in N Germany. 2. All of the West Germanic languages except High German.
low-keyed (lō'kēd') *adj.* Restrained, as in style or quality.
low•land (lō'lənd) *n.* An area of land that is low in relation to the surrounding country. —**low'land** *adj.*
Low•land (lō'lənd) *n.* The English dialect of the Scottish Lowlands. —*adj.* Of or from the Scottish Lowlands.
Low•lands, The (lō'ləndz). The lowlands of E and S Scotland.
low•ly (lō'lē) *adj.* **-lier, -liest.** 1. Having a low rank or position. 2. Plain; undistinguished. —**low'li•ness** *n.* —**low'ly** *adv.*
low-mind•ed (lō'mīn'dĭd) *adj.* Exhibiting a coarse, vulgar character. —**low'-mind'ed•ly** *adv.* —**low'-mind'ed•ness** *n.*
low profile. Unobtrusive, restrained behavior or stance, esp. an avoidance of militancy or intervention.
low relief. Sculptural relief that projects very little from the background.
low tide. 1. The tide at its lowest ebb. 2. The time of this ebb.
lox[1] (lŏks) *n.* Smoked salmon. [Yid.]
lox[2] (lŏks) *n.* Liquid oxygen.
loy•al (loi'əl) *adj.* 1. Steadfast in allegiance to one's homeland or government. 2. Faithful to a person, ideal, etc. [< L *lēgālis,* legal.] —**loy'al•ly** *adv.* —**loy'al•ty, loy'al•ness** *n.*
loz•enge (lŏz'ĭnj) *n.* 1. A four-sided planar figure with a diamondlike shape. 2. A lozenge-shaped medicated drop for the mouth or throat. [< Gaul **lausa,* flat stone.]
LP (ĕl'pē') *adj.* Long-playing. —*n., pl.* **LP's** or **LPs.** A trademark for a long-playing record.
LSD **Lysergic acid diethylamide;** specifically, this chemical taken as a hallucinogen.
lt. light.
Lt. lieutenant.
Lt. Col. lieutenant colonel.
Lt. Comdr. lieutenant commander.
ltd., Ltd. limited.
Lt. Gen. lieutenant general.
Lu lutetium.
Lu•an•da (lo͞o-ăn'də). The capital of Angola. Pop. 245,000.
Luang Pra•bang (lwăng' prä-băng'). A capital of Laos. Pop. 8,000.
lu•au (lo͞o-ou') *n.* An elaborate Hawaiian feast.
lub. lubricant; lubrication.
Lub•bock (lŭb'ək). A city of NW Texas. Pop. 129,000.
lu•bri•cant (lo͞o'brĭ-kənt) *n.* Any of various materials, such as grease, machine oil, or graphite, that reduce friction when applied as a coating to moving parts.
lu•bri•cate (lo͞o'brĭ-kāt') *v.* **-cated, -cating.** To apply a lubricant to. [< L *lūbricus,* slippery.] —**lu'bri•ca'tion** *n.*
lu•bri•cous (lo͞o'brĭ-kəs) *adj.* Also **lu•bri•cious** (lo͞o-brĭsh'əs). Characterized by lewdness. [< L *lūbricus,* slippery.]
lu•cid (lo͞o'sĭd) *adj.* 1. Easily understood; clear. 2. Rational; clear-minded. [< L *lūcidus* < *lūcēre,* to shine.] —**lu•cid'i•ty, lu'cid•ness** *n.* —**lu'cid•ly** *adv.*
Lu•ci•fer (lo͞o'sə-fər). The archangel cast from Heaven for leading a revolt of the angels; Satan.
Lu•cite (lo͞o'sīt') *n.* A trademark for a transparent, thermoplastic, acrylic resin.
luck (lŭk) *n.* 1. The fortuitous happening of fortunate or adverse events; fortune. 2. Good fortune. [Perh < LG *luk* or MDu *luc.*]
luck•y (lŭk'ē) *adj.* **-ier, -iest.** Having or resulting in good luck; fortunate. —**luck'i•ly** *adv.* —**luck'i•ness** *n.*
lu•cra•tive (lo͞o'krə-tĭv) *adj.* Producing wealth; profitable. [< L *lucrum,* LUCRE.]
lu•cre (lo͞o'kər) *n.* Money; profits. [< L *lucrum,* gain, profit.]
lu•di•crous (lo͞o'dĭ-krəs) *adj.* Laughable because of obvious absurdity or incongruity. [L *lūdicrus,* done playfully.] —**lu'di•crous•ly** *adv.* —**lu'di•crous•ness** *n.*
lug[1] (lŭg) *n.* 1. An earlike handle or projection used as a hold or support. 2. *Mach.* A nut, esp. one closed at one end to serve as a cap. 3. *Slang.* A clumsy fool. [ME *lugge,* flap, ear.]
lug[2] (lŭg) *v.* **lugged, lugging.** To drag or carry (something) laboriously. [Perh < Scand.]
lug•gage (lŭg'ĭj) *n.* Baggage, esp. suitcases. [Prob LUG + (BAG)GAGE.]
lu•gu•bri•ous (lo͝o-g/y/o͞o'brē-əs) *adj.* Mournful, esp. to a ludicrous degree. [L *lūgubris.*] —**lu•gu'bri•ous•ly** *adv.*
Luke (lo͝ok), **Saint.** Christian apostle, reputed author of the 3rd Gospel and Acts.
luke•warm (lo͞ok'wôrm') *adj.* 1. Mildly warm; tepid. 2. Halfhearted; indifferent. [ME.]
lull (lŭl) *v.* 1. To cause to sleep or rest; soothe. 2. To deceive into trustfulness. —*n.* A relatively calm or inactive period. [ME *lullen.*]
lull•a•by (lŭl'ə-bī') *n., pl.* **-bies.** A song with which to lull a child to sleep. [Perh LULL + (GOOD-)BY.]
lum•ba•go (lŭm-bā'gō) *n.* A painful inflammatory rheumatism of the tendons and muscles of the lumbar region.
lum•bar (lŭm'bər, -bär') *adj.* Of or situated in the part of the back and sides between the lowest ribs and pelvis. [< L *lumbus,* loin.]
lum•ber[1] (lŭm'bər) *n.* 1. Timber sawed into boards, planks, etc. 2. Anything useless or cumbersome. —**lum'ber** *adj.*
lum•ber[2] (lŭm'bər) *v.* To walk or move heavily or clumsily. [Perh < Scand.]
lum•ber•jack (lŭm'bər-jăk') *n.* One who fells trees and transports the timber to a mill.
lum•ber•yard (lŭm'bər-yärd') *n.* An establishment that sells lumber and other building materials.
lu•mi•nar•y (lo͞o'mə-nĕr'ē) *n., pl.* **-ies.** 1. An object, as a celestial body, that gives light. 2. A person notable in a specific field. [< L *lūmen,* light.]
lu•mi•nesce (lo͞o'mə-nĕs') *v.* **-nesced, -nescing.** To be or become luminescent.
lu•mi•nes•cence (lo͞o'mə-nĕs'əns) *n.* 1. The emission of light, as in phosphorescence and fluorescence, by means of essentially nonthermal effects. 2. The light so emitted. —**lu'mi•nes'cent** *adj.*
lu•mi•nos•i•ty (lo͞o'mə-nŏs'ə-tē) *n.* 1. The condition or quality of being luminous. 2. Something luminous.
lu•mi•nous (lo͞o'mə-nəs) *adj.* 1. Emitting light, esp. self-generated light. 2. Full of light. [< L *lūmen,* light.] —**lu'mi•nous•ly** *adv.*
lum•mox (lŭm'əks) *n.* An oaf. [?]
lump[1] (lŭmp) *n.* 1. An irregularly shaped mass or piece. 2. *Path.* A swelling or small, palpable mass. 3. An aggregate; collection. —*v.* To put together in a single group or pile. [ME.] —**lump'i•ness** *n.* —**lump'y** *adj.*
lump[2] (lŭmp) *v. Informal.* To tolerate: *like it or lump it.* [?]
lu•na•cy (lo͞o'nə-sē) *n., pl.* **-cies.** 1. Insanity. 2. Foolish conduct.
lu•nar (lo͞o'nər) *adj.* Of or pertaining to the moon. [< L *lūna,* moon.]
lunar excursion module. Also **lunar module.** A spacecraft designed to transport astronauts orbiting the moon to the lunar surface and back.
lu•na•tic (lo͞o'nə-tĭk) *adj.* 1. Of or for the insane. 2. Wildly foolish. [< L *lūnāticus,* "moonstruck," crazy.] —**lu'na•tic** *n.*
lunch (lŭnch) *n.* A meal eaten at midday. [Orig "chunk, thick piece of food."] —**lunch** *v.*
lunch•eon (lŭn'chən) *n.* A lunch, esp. a party at which lunch is served.
lunch•eon•ette (lŭn'chə-nĕt') *n.* A small restaurant that serves simple meals.
lung (lŭng) *n.* Either of two spongy, saclike thoracic organs in most vertebrates, functioning to remove carbon dioxide from the blood and provide it with oxygen. [< OE *lungen.*]
lunge (lŭnj) *n.* Any sudden forward movement or plunge. —*v.* **lunged, lunging.** To move with a lunge. [< OF *allonger,* to lengthen, extend.]
lu•pine (lo͞o'pən) *n.* Also **lu•pin.** A plant with compound leaves and long clusters of variously colored flowers.
lu•pus (lo͞o'pəs) *n.* Any of several diseases of the skin and mucous membranes, many causing disfiguring lesions. [< L, wolf.]
lurch[1] (lûrch) *v.* 1. To stagger. 2. To roll or tip abruptly. —*n.* 1. A staggering movement. 2. An abrupt rolling or tipping. [?]
lurch[2] (lûrch) *n.* A position of difficulty. [< F *lourche,* a game, "defeat."]
lure (lo͝or) *n.* 1. Anything that attracts with the prospect of pleasure or reward. 2. An artificial bait used in catching fish. —*v.* **lured, luring.** To attract by wiles; entice. [< OF *loirre,* bait < Gmc **lōthr.*] —**lur'ing•ly** *adv.*
lu•rid (lo͝or'ĭd) *adj.* Causing shock or horror; sensational. [L *lūridus,* pallid, ghastly.]
lurk (lûrk) *v.* 1. To lie in wait, as in ambush. 2. To move furtively. [ME *lurken.*]
Lu•sa•ka (lo͞o-sä'kə). The capital of Zambia. Pop. 122,000.
lus•cious (lŭsh'əs) *adj.* 1. Pleasant to taste or smell; delicious. 2. Sensually appealing.
lush[1] (lŭsh) *adj.* 1. Characterized by luxuriant growth or vegetation. 2. Luxurious; opulent. [ME *lusch,* lax, soft.] —**lush'ness** *n.*
lush[2] (lŭsh) *n. Slang.* A drunkard. [?]
lust (lŭst) *n.* 1. Sexual craving, esp. when excessive. 2. Any overwhelming craving. —*v.* To have an inordinate desire, esp. a sexual desire. [< OE. See **las-.**] —**lust'ful** *adj.*
lus•ter (lŭs'tər) *n.* Also *chiefly Brit.* **lus•tre.** 1. Soft reflected light; sheen; gloss. 2. Brilliance or radiance. 3. Splendor; glory. [< L *lūstrāre,* to purify, make bright.] —**lus'trous** (-trəs) *adj.*
lust•y (lŭs'tē) *adj.* **-ier, -iest.** Full of vigor; robust. —**lust'i•ly** *adv.* —**lust'i•ness** *n.*
lute (lo͞ot) *n.* A stringed instrument with a fretted fingerboard and a body shaped like half a pear. [< Ar *al-'ud,* "the wood."]
lu•te•ti•um (lo͞o-tē'shē-əm) *n.* Also **lu•te•ci•um.** *Symbol* **Lu** A silvery-white rare-earth element used in nuclear technology. Atomic number 71, atomic weight 174.97. [< *Lūtētia,* Latin

name for Paris.]

Lu•ther (lo͞o'thər), **Martin.** 1483–1546. German theologian and religious reformer.

Martin Luther

Lu•ther•an (lo͞o'thər-ən) *adj.* Of or relating to the branch of the Protestant Church adhering to the views of Martin Luther. —**Lu'ther•an** *n.*

Lux•em•bourg (lŭk'səm-bûrg). Also **Lux•em•burg.** 1. A grand duchy in W Europe. Pop. 331,000. 2. The capital of this grand duchy. Pop. 77,000.

Luxembourg

lux•u•ri•ant (lŭg-zho͝or'ē-ənt, lŭk-sho͝or'-) *adj* 1. Growing abundantly, vigorously, or lushly. 2. Elaborate; ornate; florid. —**lux•u'ri•ance** *n.*

lux•u•ri•ate (lŭg-zho͝or'ē-āt', lŭk-sho͝or'-) *v.* **-ated, -ating.** To take luxurious pleasure; indulge oneself. —**lux•u'ri•a'tion** *n.*

lux•u•ri•ous (lŭg-zho͝or'ē-əs, lŭk-sho͝or'-) *adj.* 1. Fond of or given to luxury. 2. Characterized by luxury. —**lux•u'ri•ous•ly** *adv.*

lux•u•ry (lŭg'zhə-rē, lŭk'shə-) *n., pl.* **-ries.** 1. Something not absolutely necessary that provides comfort or enjoyment. 2. The enjoyment of sumptuous living. [< L *luxus,* excess, extravagance.]

lv. leave.

Lw lawrencium.

–ly¹. *comb. form.* 1. A characteristic or resemblance: **sisterly.** 2. Occurrence at specified intervals: **monthly.** [< OE *-lic,* "having the form of."]

–ly². *comb. form.* 1. In a specified manner: **gradually.** 2. At every specified interval: **daily.** [< OE *-lic,* -LY.]

ly•ce•um (lī-sē'əm) *n.* 1. A hall in which lectures, concerts, etc., are presented. 2. An organization sponsoring such presentations.

lye (lī) *n.* 1. The liquid obtained by leaching wood ashes. 2. **Potassium hydroxide.** 3. **Sodium hydroxide.** [< OE *lēag.* See **lou-.**]

ly•ing (lī'ĭng). 1. *pres.p.* of **lie¹.** 2. *pres.p.* of **lie².**

lymph (lĭmf) *n.* A clear, watery, sometimes faintly yellowish liquid that contains white blood cells and some red blood cells and acts to remove bacteria and certain proteins from the tissues, transport fat from the intestines, and supply lymphocytes to the blood. [L *lympha, limpa,* water.]

lym•phat•ic (lĭm-făt'ĭk) *adj.* Of or relating to lymph or the lymphatic system. —*n.* A vessel that conveys lymph.

lymphatic system. The interconnected system of spaces and vessels between tissues and organs by which lymph is circulated throughout the body.

lymph node. Any of numerous oval or round bodies that supply lymphocytes to the circulatory system and remove bacteria and foreign particles from the lymph.

lym•phoid (lĭm'foid') *adj.* Of or pertaining to lymph, lymphatic tissue, or the lymphatic system.

lynch (lĭnch) *v.* To execute, esp. by hanging, without due process of law. [< C. *Lynch* (1736–1796), Virginia planter and justice of the peace.] —**lynch'er** *n.*

lynx (lĭngks) *n.* A wild cat with thick, soft fur, a short tail, and tufted ears. [< Gk *lunx.*]

lynx-eyed (lĭngks'īd') *adj.* Keen of vision.

Ly•on (lē'ôɴ'). A city of east-central France. Pop. 529,000.

Ly•ra (lī'rə) *n.* A constellation in the N Hemisphere. [L *lyra,* lyre.]

lyre (līr) *n.* A stringed instrument of the harp family used esp. in ancient Greece. [< Gk *lura.*]

lyr•ic (lĭr'ĭk) *adj.* 1. Of or relating to poetry that is a direct, often songlike expression of the poet's thoughts and feelings. 2. Exuberant; unrestrained. —*n.* 1. A lyric poem. 2. **lyrics.** The words of a song. [< Gk *lura,* LYRE.] —**lyr'i•cal** *adj.* —**lyr'i•cal•ly** *adv.*

lyr•i•cist (lĭr'ə-sĭst) *n.* A writer of lyrics.

ly•ser•gic acid (lĭ-sûr'jĭk, lī-). A crystalline alkaloid, $C_{16}H_{16}N_2O_2$, derived from ergot and used in medical research.

lysergic acid di•eth•yl•am•ide (dī'ĕth-əl-ăm'-īd'). A hallucinogenic drug, $C_{20}H_{25}N_3O$, derived from lysergic acid.

ly•sin (lī'sĭn) *n.* A specific antibody that acts to destroy blood cells, tissues, or microorganisms.

–lysis. *comb. form.* Dissolving or decomposition: **hydrolysis.** [< Gk *lusis,* a loosing.]

–lyte. *comb. form.* A substance that can be decomposed by a specific process: **electrolyte.** [< Gk *luein,* to loosen.]

Mm

m, M (ĕm) *n.* The 13th letter of the English alphabet.

m 1. male. 2. *Phys.* mass. 3. medium. 4. meter (measure). 5. milli-.

M 1. male. 2. *Phys.* mass. 3. medium. 4. mega-. 5. The Roman numeral for 1,000 (L *mille*).

m. 1. male. 2. medium. 3. mile.

M. 1. male. 2. master (in titles). 3. medium. 4. minim (liquid measure). 5. Monday.

ma (mä, mô) *n. Informal.* Mother. [Short for MAMA.]

M.A. 1. Master of Arts (L *Magister Artium*). 2. mental age.

Ma'am (măm). A contraction of *Madam.*

ma•ca•bre (mə-kä'brə, -bər) *adj.* Suggesting or concerned unduly with the horror of death; gruesome; ghastly.

mac•ad•am (mə-kăd'əm) *n.* A pavement of layers of compacted small stones bound with tar or asphalt. [< J. *McAdam* (1756–1836), Scottish engineer.] —**mac•ad'am•ize'** *v.* **(-ized, -izing).** —**mac•ad'am•iz'er** *n.*

mac•a•ro•ni (măk'ə-rō'nē) *pl.n.* Also **mac•ca•ro•ni.** Dried, usually tube-shaped pieces of pasta, prepared for eating by boiling. [< obs It *maccaroni.*]

mac•a•roon (măk'ə-ro͞on', măk'ə-ro͞on') *n.* A cooky made with almond paste or coconut. [< It *maccarone,* macaroni.]

Mac•Ar•thur (mək-är'thər), **Douglas.** 1880–1964. American General of the Army.

ma•caw (mə-kô') *n.* A large, often brightly colored tropical American parrot. [Port *macaú.*]

mace¹ (mās) *n.* 1. A heavy medieval war club with a spiked metal head. 2. A ceremonial staff used as a symbol of authority. [< L *mateola,* rod, club.]

mace² (mās) *n.* A spice made from the seed covering of the nutmeg. [< Gk *makir,* an Indian spice.]

Mace (mās) *n.* **Chemical mace.**

Mac•e•do•ni•a (măs'ə-dō'nē-ə). 1. An ancient kingdom, N of Greece. 2. A Balkan region consisting of parts of Greece, Bulgaria, and Yugoslavia.

mac•er•ate (măs'ə-rāt') *v.* **-ated, -ating.** 1. To soften by soaking or steeping in a liquid. 2. To separate into constituents by soaking. 3. To emaciate, usually by starvation. [L *mācerāre,* to soften.] —**mac'er•a'tion** *n.* —**mac'er•a'tor, mac'er•at'er** *n.*

mach. machine; machinery; machinist.

ma•chet•e (mə-shĕt'ē, -chĕt'ē) *n.* A large, broad-bladed knife used esp. for cutting vegetation. [< Span *macho,* ax, club.]

Mach•i•a•vel•li (măk'ē-ə-vĕl'ē), **Niccolò.** 1469–1527. Florentine statesman and political theorist. —**Mach'i•a•vel'li•an** *adj.*

mach•i•na•tion (măk'ĭ-nā'shən, măsh'ĭ-) *n.* 1. The act of plotting. 2. A hostile intrigue.

ma•chine (mə-shēn') *n.* 1. a. Any system formed and connected to alter, transmit, and direct applied forces to accomplish a specific objective. b. A simple device, as a lever, pulley, or inclined plane, that alters an applied

force. 2. Any system or device, as an electronic computer, that assists in the performance of a human task. 3. A powerful political group whose members appear to be under the control of one or more leaders. —*v.* **-chined, -chining.** To cut, shape, or finish by machine. [< Doric Gk *mākhos,* contrivance, means.]
machine gun. A gun that fires rapidly and repeatedly when the trigger is pressed.
ma•chin•er•y (mə-shē'nər-ē, -shēn'rē) *n., pl.* **-ies.** 1. Machines or machine parts collectively. 2. The working parts of a particular machine. 3. Any system of related elements that operates in a definable manner.
ma•chin•ist (mə-shē'nĭst) *n.* One who makes, operates, or repairs machines.
ma•chis•mo (mä-chēz'mō) *n.* An exaggerated sense of masculinity. [< Span *macho,* masculine, virile + -ISM.]
Mach number. Also **mach number.** The ratio of the speed of an object to the speed of sound in the surrounding medium. [< E. *Mach* (1836–1916), Austrian physicist.]
ma•cho (mä'chō') *adj.* Characterized by machismo. —*n.,pl.* **-chos.** 1. A male characterized by machismo. 2. Machismo. [Span]
mac•in•tosh. Variant of **mackintosh.**
Mac•ken•zie (mə-kĕn'zē). A river of NW Canada.
mack•er•el (măk'ər-əl, măk'rəl) *n., pl.* **-el** or **-els.** Any of several widely distributed marine food fishes. [< OF *maquerel.*]
mack•i•naw (măk'ə-nô') *n.* A short coat of heavy woolen material, usually plaid. [< *Mackinac,* island in Michigan.]
mack•in•tosh (măk'ĭn-tŏsh') *n.* Also **mac•in•tosh.** *Chiefly Brit.* A raincoat. [< C. *Macintosh* (1766–1843), Scottish chemist.]
macro–. *comb. form.* 1. Largeness or length in extent or size. 2. Abnormal largeness or overdevelopment. [< Gk *makros,* large, long.]
mac•ro•cosm (măk'rō-kŏz'əm) *n.* 1. The universe itself or the concept of universe. 2. A system regarded as an entity containing subsystems. —**mac'ro•cos'mic** *adj.*
mac•ro•mol•e•cule (măk'rō-mŏl'ə-kyōōl) *n.* A polymer, esp. one composed of more than 100 repeated monomers.
ma•cron (mā'krŏn', -krən) *n.* A mark (¯) placed above a vowel to indicate a long sound, as the (ā) in *make.* [< Gk *makros,* long.]
mac•ro•scop•ic (măk'rə-skŏp'ĭk) *adj.* Also **mac•ro•scop•i•cal** (-ĭ-kəl). 1. Large enough to be perceived or examined without instrumentation, esp. as by the unaided eye. 2. Pertaining to observations made without magnifying instruments, esp. as by the unaided eye. —**mac'ro•scop'i•cal•ly** *adv.*
mac•u•late (măk'yə-lāt') *v.* **-lated, -lating.** To spot, blemish, or pollute.
mad (măd) *adj.* **madder, maddest.** 1. Suffering from a disorder of the mind; insane. 2. Marked by extreme excitement, confusion, or agitation; frantic: *a mad scramble for the bus.* 3. *Informal.* Showing strong liking or enthusiasm: *mad about sports.* 4. Angry; resentful. 5. Lacking restraint or reason; wildly foolish. 6. Affected by rabies. [< OE *gemād.* See **mei-.**] —**mad'ly** *adv.* —**mad'ness** *n.*
Mad•a•gas•car (măd'ə-găs'kər). An island in the Indian Ocean, coextensive with the Malagasy Republic.
Mad•am (măd'əm) *n.* 1. *pl.* **Mesdames** (mā-däm'). A title of courtesy used as a form of address to a woman. 2. **madam.** A woman who manages a brothel. [< MADAME.]
Mad•ame (măd'əm, mə-dăm') *n., pl.* **Mesdames** (mā-däm'). 1. The French title of courtesy for a married woman. 2. A title of courtesy or distinction indicating rank or office: *Madame Ambassador.* [< OF *ma dame,* my lady.]
mad•cap (măd'kăp') *n.* A rash or impulsive person, especially a girl. —*adj.* Rash; impulsive; wild. [MAD + CAP.]
mad•den (măd'n) *v.* 1. To make frantic or insane. 2. To make or become angry.
mad•der (măd'ər) *n.* 1. An Old World plant with small, yellow flowers and a red, fleshy root. 2. A red dye obtained from the root of this plant. [< OE *mædere.*]
made (mād). *p.t.* & *p.p.* of **make.**
made-to-or•der (mād'tōō-ôr'dər) *adj.* Made in accordance with a customer's instructions; custom-made.
made-up (mād'ŭp') *adj.* 1. Fabricated; fictitious; invented: *a made-up story.* 2. Marked by the use of cosmetics or make-up: *a made-up actress.*
mad•house (măd'hous') *n.* 1. An insane asylum. 2. *Informal.* A place of great disorder.
Mad•i•son (măd'ĭ-sən). The capital of Wisconsin. Pop. 173,000.
Mad•i•son (măd'ĭ-sən), **James.** 1751–1836. 4th President of the U.S. (1809–17).

James Madison

mad•man (măd'măn', -mən) *n.* 1. An insane person. 2. A frantic person.
Ma•don•na (mə-dŏn'ə) *n.* 1. The Virgin Mary. 2. An artistic representation of the Virgin Mary.
Ma•dras (mə-drăs', -dräs'). A city of SE India. Pop. 1,729,000.
ma•dras (măd'rəs, mə-drăs', -dräs') *n.* A fine cotton cloth, usually with a plaid or striped pattern. [< MADRAS.]
Ma•drid (mə-drĭd'). The capital of Spain. Pop. 2,559,000.
mad•ri•gal (măd'rĭ-gəl) *n.* 1. An unaccompanied vocal composition for two or three voices in simple harmony. 2. A polyphonic part song, usually unaccompanied. [< It *madriale,* "(piece) without accompaniment."]
mad•ri•lène (măd'rĭ-lĕn) *n.* Also **mad•ri•lene.** A consommé flavored with tomato, generally chilled. [< Span *madrileño,* of Madrid.]
mael•strom (māl'strəm) *n.* 1. A whirlpool of extraordinary size or violence. 2. A situation that resembles such a whirlpool in violence, turbulence, etc. [< Du *maelstrom,* "whirl-stream."]
maes•tro (mīs'trō) *n., pl.* **-tros.** A master in any art, esp. music. [< L *magister,* master.]
mag. 1. magazine. 2. magnetism. 3. magnitude.
mag•a•zine (măg'ə-zēn', măg'ə-zēn') *n.* 1. A place for storage, esp. of ammunition. 2. A periodical containing articles, stories, etc. 3. a. A compartment in some types of firearms for holding cartridges. b. A compartment in a camera for holding film. [< Ar *makhzan,* storehouse.]
Ma•gel•lan (mə-jĕl'ən), **Ferdinand.** 1480?–1521. Portuguese navigator; commander of Spanish expedition that was first to circumnavigate the world.
Ma•gen Da•vid (mä'gən dä'vĭd, mŭ'gən dŭ'-vĭd). A six-pointed star, used as a symbol of Judaism. [Heb *māgen Dāwid,* shield of (King) David.]
ma•gen•ta (mə-jĕn'tə) *n.* Moderate to vivid purplish red. [< the battle of *Magenta* (1859).]
mag•got (măg'ət) *n.* The soft-bodied, wormlike larva of a fly, as the housefly. [ME *magot, maked.*] —**mag'got•y** *adj.*
Ma•gi (mā'jī') *pl.n.* The three wise men from the East who paid homage to the infant Jesus. [< L *magus,* sorcerer.]
mag•ic (măj'ĭk) *n.* 1. The art that purports to produce supernatural effects, as with charms, spells, etc. 2. Any mysterious or overpowering quality that lends enchantment. 3. The exercise of sleight of hand, as for entertainment. [< OPers *maguš,* sorcerer.] —**mag'ic, mag'i•cal** *adj.* —**ma•gi'cian** (mə-jĭsh'ən) *n.*
mag•is•te•ri•al (măj'ĭs-tîr'ē-əl) *adj.* 1. Authoritative; commanding. 2. Of or pertaining to a magistrate or his functions. [< L *magister,* master.] —**mag'is•te'ri•al•ly** *adv.*
mag•is•trate (măj'ĭs-trāt', -trĭt) *n.* A civil officer with power to administer the law. [< L *magister,* master.]
mag•ma (măg'mə, mäg'-) *n., pl.* **-mata** (măg'-mä'tə, mäg'-) or **-mas.** The molten matter under the earth's crust, from which igneous rock is formed by cooling. [< Gk, unguent.]
Mag•na Char•ta, Mag•na Car•ta (măg'nə kär'tə). The charter of English political and civil liberties granted in 1215.
mag•nan•i•mous (măg-năn'ə-məs) *adj.* Generous and noble in forgiving; above revenge or resentment. [L *magnanimus,* "great-souled."] —**mag'na•nim'i•ty** (-nə-nĭm'ĭ-tē) *n.* —**mag•nan'i•mous•ly** *adv.*
mag•nate (măg'nāt') *n.* A powerful or influential man. [< L *magnus,* great.]
mag•ne•sia (măg-nē'zhə, -shə) *n.* **Magnesium oxide.** [< Gk *Magnēsia,* name of an area of Greece.] —**mag•ne'sian** *adj.*
mag•ne•si•um (măg-nē'zē-əm, -shəm) *n.* *Symbol* **Mg** A light, silvery, moderately hard metallic element used in structural alloys, pyrotechnics, flash photography, and incendiary bombs. Atomic number 12, atomic weight 24.312.
magnesium oxide. A white, powdery compound, MgO, having a high melting point and used in high-temperature refractories and electric insulation.
magnesium sulfate. A colorless crystalline compound, $MgSO_4$, used in fireproofing, matches, explosives, and fertilizers.
mag•net (măg'nĭt) *n.* 1. A body that attracts iron and certain other materials by virtue of a surrounding field of force produced by the motion of its atomic electrons and the alignment of its atoms. 2. Anything that attracts. [< Gk *Magnēs lithos,* "the Magnesian stone."]
mag•net•ic (măg-nĕt'ĭk) *adj.* 1. Of or relating to magnetism or magnets. 2. Having the properties of a magnet; exhibiting magnetism. 3. Relating to the magnetic poles of the earth.

4. Capable of being magnetized or of being attracted by a magnet. 5. Exerting attraction.

magnetic compass. An instrument using a magnetic needle to show direction relative to the earth's magnetic field.

magnetic field. A condition in a region of space established by the presence of a magnet or an electric current and characterized by the existence of a detectable magnetic force at every point in the region.

magnetic needle. A needle-shaped bar magnet usually suspended on a low-friction mounting and used in various instruments, esp. in the magnetic compass, to indicate the alignment of a local magnetic field.

magnetic north. The direction of the earth's magnetic pole, to which the north-seeking pole of a magnetic needle points when free from local magnetic influence.

magnetic pickup. A type of phonograph pickup that utilizes a coil in a magnetic field to convert motions of the stylus into electric impulses.

magnetic pole. 1. Either of two limited regions in a magnet at which the magnet's field is most intense. 2. Either of two variable points on the earth, close to but not coinciding with the geographic poles, where the earth's magnetic field is most intense.

magnetic recording. The recording of a signal, such as sound or computer instructions, in the form of a magnetic pattern.

magnetic storm. A severe but transitory fluctuation in the earth's magnetic field.

magnetic tape. A plastic tape coated with magnetic material for use in magnetic recording.

mag•net•ism (măg'nə-tĭz'əm) *n.* 1. The class of phenomena exhibited by the field of force produced by a magnet or electric current. 2. The study of magnets and their effects. 3. The force exerted by a magnetic field. 4. Power to attract.

mag•net•ite (măg'nə-tīt') *n.* A magnetic black iron oxide, Fe_3O_4, an important ore of iron.

mag•net•ize (măg'nə-tīz') *v.* **-ized, -izing.** 1. To make magnetic. 2. To attract. **—mag'net•i•za'tion** *n.* **—mag'net•iz'er** *n.*

mag•ne•to (măg-nē'tō) *n., pl.* **-tos.** A small generator of alternating current using permanent magnets, used in the ignition systems of some internal-combustion engines.

mag•ni•fi•ca•tion (măg'nĭ-fĭ-kā'shən) *n.* 1. a. The act of magnifying or state of being magnified. b. The process of enlarging the size of something, as an optical image. c. Something magnified; an enlarged representation, image, or model. 2. *Opt.* The ratio of image size to object size.

mag•nif•i•cent (măg-nĭf'ĭ-sənt) *adj.* 1. Splendid; lavish; sumptuous. 2. Noble in thought or deed; exalted. 3. Impressive. [< L *magnificus,* "great in deeds."] **—mag•nif'i•cence** *n.* **—mag•nif'i•cent•ly** *adv.*

mag•ni•fi•er (măg'nĭ-fī'ər) *n.* A magnifying glass or other system of components that magnifies.

mag•ni•fy (măg'nĭ-fī') *v.* **-fied, -fying.** 1. To make greater in size; enlarge. 2. To exaggerate. 3. To increase the apparent size of, esp. by means of a lens. 4. To glorify. [< L *magnificāre,* to make great.]

magnifying glass. A converging lens that enlarges the image of an object.

mag•ni•tude (măg'nĭ-t/y/ōōd') *n.* 1. Greatness in size, extent, or significance. 2. Size; quantity. 3. The relative brightness of a celestial body designated on a numerical scale, where 6 denotes faint visibility and decreases of 1 unit represent an increase in apparent brightness by a factor of 2.512. [< L *magnus,* great.]

mag•no•lia (măg-nōl'yə) *n.* A tree or shrub with large, showy, usually white or pinkish flowers. [< P. *Magnol* (1638–1715), French botanist.]

mag•pie (măg'pī) *n.* A long-tailed, loud-voiced, chiefly black and white bird related to the crows and jays.

Mag•yar (măg'yär', mäg'-) *n.* Hungarian. **—Mag'yar** *adj.*

ma•ha•ra•jah, ma•ha•ra•ja (mä'hə-rä'jä, -zhä) *n.* A king or prince in India. [< Sk *mahārājā,* "great king."]

ma•ha•ra•ni, ma•ha•ra•nee (mä'hə-rä'nē) *n.* A queen or princess in India. [< Sk *mahārājnī,* "great queen."]

ma•hat•ma (mä-hät'mä, mə-hăt'mə) *n.* 1. One venerated for great knowledge and love of humanity. 2. **Mahatma.** A Hindu title of respect for a man renowned for spirituality. [Sk *mahātman,* "great soul."]

Mah•di (mä'dē). The Islamic messiah.

Ma•hi•can (mə-hē'kən) *n., pl.* **-can** or **-cans.** Also **Mo•hi•can** (mō-hē'kən, mə-). A member of a tribe or confederacy of Algonquian-speaking Indians that formerly lived in N New York State.

mah-jong (mä'zhŏng', -zhông') *n.* Also **mah-jongg.** A game of Chinese origin played with tiles resembling dominoes.

ma•hog•a•ny (mə-hŏg'ə-nē) *n., pl.* **-nies.** 1. A tropical American tree with hard, reddish-brown wood. 2. The wood of such a tree. 3. Any of several similar trees or their wood.

ma•hout (mə-hout') *n.* The keeper and driver of an elephant. [< Sk *mahāmātra,* "of great measure."]

maid (mād) *n.* 1. A girl or an unmarried woman. 2. A female servant. [< MAIDEN.]

maid•en (mād'n) *n.* An unmarried girl or woman. *—adj.* 1. Of, pertaining to, or befitting a maiden. 2. First or earliest: *a maiden voyage.* [< OE *mægden.* See **maghu-.**] **—maid'en•hood'** *n.* **—maid'en•ly** *adj.*

maid•en•hair (mād'n-hâr') *n.* A fern having feathery fronds with fan-shaped leaflets.

maid of honor *pl.* **maids of honor.** The chief unmarried female attendant of a bride.

Mai•du (mī'dōō) *n., pl.* **-du** or **-dus.** 1. A member of a Penutian-speaking Indian tribe, formerly living in the Sacramento Valley area of California. 2. The language of this tribe. [Maidu, "man."] **—Mai'du** *adj.*

mail¹ (māl) *n.* 1. a. Letters, packages, etc., handled by a postal system. b. Postal material for a specific person or organization. 2. A postal system. *—v.* To send by mail. [< OF *male,* pouch, bag.] **—mail'er** *n.*

mail² (māl) *n.* Armor made of small overlapping metal rings, loops of chain, or scales. [< L *macula,* spot, mesh.]

mail•box (māl'bŏks') *n.* 1. A public box for deposit of outgoing mail. 2. A private box for incoming mail.

mail•man (māl'măn', -mən) *n.* One who delivers mail.

maim (mām) *v.* 1. To mutilate; disable; cripple. 2. To impair. [< OF *mahaignier,* to wound.]

main (mān) *adj.* 1. Most important; principal; major. 2. Exerted to the utmost; sheer; utter. *—n.* 1. The principal part or point. 2. The principal pipe or conduit in a utility system. 3. Physical strength: *might and main.* [< OE *mægen,* strength. See **magh-.**] **—main'ly** *adv.*

Maine (mān). A state of the NE U.S. Pop. 994,000. Cap. Augusta.

main•land (mān'lănd', -lənd) *n.* The principal land mass of a country or continent.

main•mast (mān'məst) *n.* The principal mast of a vessel.

main•sail (mān'səl) *n.* The principal sail of a vessel, as one set from the mainmast.

main•spring (mān'sprĭng') *n.* 1. The principal spring in a mechanical device, esp. in a watch or clock. 2. A chief motivating force.

main•stay (mān'stā') *n.* 1. A rope that supports a mainmast. 2. A principal support.

main•stream (mān'strēm') *n.* The prevailing direction of a movement or influence.

main•tain (mān-tān') *v.* 1. To continue; carry on. 2. To preserve or retain. 3. To keep in repair. 4. To provide for; support. 5. To defend or sustain. 6. To assert or declare. [< L *manū tenēre,* "to hold in the hand."] **—main'te•nance** (mān'tə-nəns) *n.*

main top•sail (tŏp'səl). The sail that is set above the mainsail.

maî•tre d'hô•tel (mĕ'tr' dō-tĕl') *pl.* **maîtres d'hôtel** (mĕ'tr' dō-tĕl'). 1. A head steward. 2. A headwaiter. [F, "master of hotel."]

maize (māz) *n.* Corn. [< Taino *mahiz.*]

Maj. major.

maj•es•ty (măj'ĭs-tē) *n., pl.* **-ties.** 1. Sovereign greatness, power, and authority. 2. **Majesty.** A title used in speaking of or to a monarch: *at His Majesty's request.* 3. Regal dignity, splendor, and grandeur. [< L *mājestās,* authority, grandeur.] **—ma•jes'tic** (mə-jĕs'tĭk) *adj.*

Maj. Gen. major general.

ma•jor (mā'jər) *adj.* 1. Greater in importance, rank, or extent. 2. Serious or dangerous: *a major illness.* 3. *Mus.* Of or based on a major scale. *—n.* 1. A military officer ranking next above a captain. 2. a. The principal field of specialization of a college student. b. A student specializing in such a field. *—v.* To pursue academic studies in a major field. [< L *mājor,* greater.]

ma•jor-do•mo (mā'jər-dō'mō) *n., pl.* **-mos.** A head steward or butler. [< ML *mājor domūs,* "head of the house."]

major general. A military officer who ranks next above a brigadier general.

ma•jor•i•ty (mə-jôr'ĭ-tē, mə-jŏr'-) *n., pl.* **-ties.** 1. The greater number or part of something. 2. a. A number more than half of a total. b. The number of votes cast in any election above the total of all other votes cast. 3. The status of legal age.

major scale. *Mus.* A diatonic scale having half steps between the 3rd and 4th and the 7th and 8th tones.

make (māk) *v.* **made, making.** 1. To create; construct; form; shape. 2. To cause to be, become, or seem. 3. To compel. 4. To appoint. 5. To perform. 6. To do; execute. 7. To arrive at. 8. To acquire. 9. To achieve; attain. 10. To prepare. 11. To provide. 12. To develop into. 13. To admit of being transformed into. 14. To constitute. 15. To behave or act in a specified manner. 16. To set out; proceed. **—make away with.** To carry off, esp. to steal. **—make out.** 1. To discern or see, esp. with difficulty. 2. To comprehend. 3. To write out or draw up. 4. To attempt to prove or imply. 5. *Slang.* To get along; succeed. 6. *Slang.* To neck; pet. *—n.* 1. The style or manner in which a thing is made. 2. A specific line of manufactured goods. 3. The physical or moral nature of a person. 4. The yield or output, as of a factory. [< OE *macian.* See **mag-**.] —**mak'er** *n.*

make believe. To feign; pretend.

make-be•lieve (māk'bĭ-lēv') *n.* 1. Playful pretense. 2. *Psychol.* A tendency to live in a world of fantasy. —**make'-be•lieve'** *adj.*

make•shift (māk'shĭft') *n.* A temporary or expedient substitute. —**make'shift'** *adj.*

make up. 1. To construct. 2. To arrange or organize. 3. To apply cosmetics. 4. To decide. 5. To constitute; amount to. 6. To invent or improvise. 7. To compensate for; fill a deficiency. 8. To resolve a personal difference.

make-up (māk'ŭp') *n.* Also **make•up.** 1. The way in which something is arranged or constructed. 2. One's constitution, temperament, or disposition. 3. Cosmetics.

mal–. *comb. form.* Bad, badly, or wrongly. [< L *malus,* bad.]

Mal. 1. Malachi (Old Testament). 2. Malay; Malayan.

Ma•la•bo (mə-lä'bō). **The capital of Equatorial Guinea. Pop. 38,000.**

mal•ad•just•ment (măl'ə-jŭst'mənt) *n.* 1. Faulty adjustment, as in a machine. 2. Inability to adjust personality needs to environmental demands. —**mal'ad•just'ed** *adj.*

mal•a•droit (măl'ə-droit') *adj.* 1. Awkward; clumsy. 2. Tactless. —**mal'a•droit'ly** *adv.*

mal•a•dy (măl'ə-dē) *n., pl.* **-dies.** A disease, disorder, or ailment. [< L *male habitus,* "ill-kept."]

Mal•a•gas•y (măl'ə-găs'ē) *n.* 1. A native of the Malagasy Republic. 2. The language spoken in the Malagasy Republic. —**Mal'a•gas'y** *adj.*

Malagasy Republic. A country occupying the island of Madagascar. Pop. 5,862,000. Cap. Tananarive.

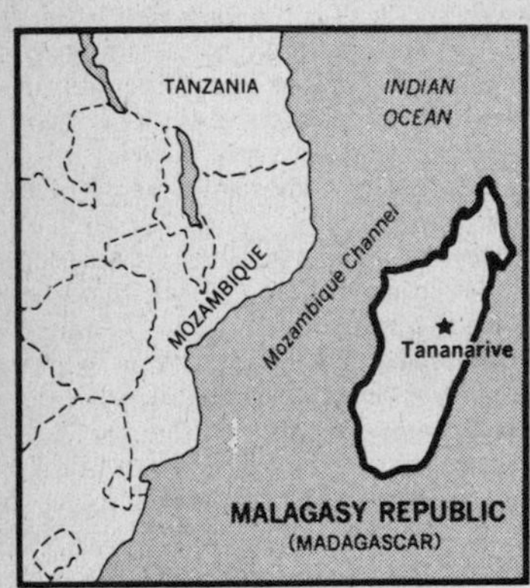

Malagasy Republic

mal•aise (măl-āz') *n.* A feeling of illness or depression. [F.]

mal•a•prop•ism (măl'ə-prŏp-ĭz'əm) *n.* A humorous misuse of a word. [< Mrs. *Malaprop* in Sheridan's play *The Rivals* < MALAPROPOS.]

ma•lar•i•a (mə-lâr'ē-ə) *n.* A disease characterized by cycles of chills, fever, and sweating, transmitted by the bite of an infected mosquito. [It *mal'aria,* foul air.] —**ma•lar'i•al, ma•lar'i•an, ma•lar'i•ous** *adj.*

ma•lar•key (mə-lär'kē) *n.* Also **ma•lar•ky.** *Slang.* Nonsense. [?]

Ma•la•wi (mə-lä'wē). **A republic of SE Africa. Pop. 4,530,000. Cap. Lilongwe.**

Ma•lay (mā'lā', mə-lā') *n.* 1. One of a people inhabiting the Malay Peninsula, other parts of Malaysia, Indonesia, and some adjacent areas. 2. The language of the Malays. —*adj.* 1. Of or pertaining to the Malays or their language. 2. Of or pertaining to Malaysia. —**Ma•lay'an** *adj. & n.*

Mal•a•ya•lam (măl'ə-yä'ləm) *n.* A Dravidian language spoken in SW India.

Malay Archipelago. A group of islands in the Indian and Pacific Oceans, including Sumatra, Java, Borneo, and other islands.

Malay Peninsula. A peninsula of SE Asia.

Ma•lay•sia (mə-lā'zhə, -shə). A country of SE Asia. Pop. 9,137,000. Cap. Kuala Lumpur. —**Ma•lay'sian** *adj. & n.*

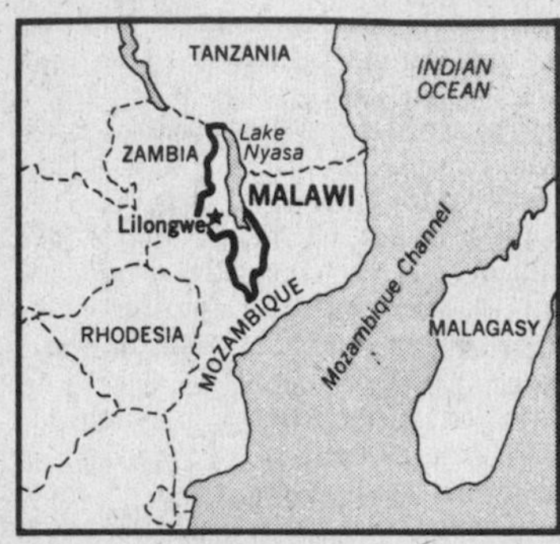

Malawi

mal•con•tent (măl'kən-tĕnt') *adj.* Discontented. —*n.* A discontented person.

Mal•dive Islands (măl'dīv'). A sultanate in the Indian Ocean. Pop. 96,000. Cap. Malé.

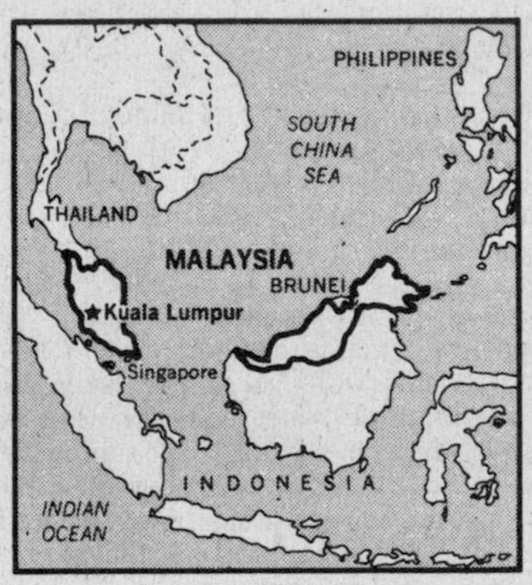

Malaysia

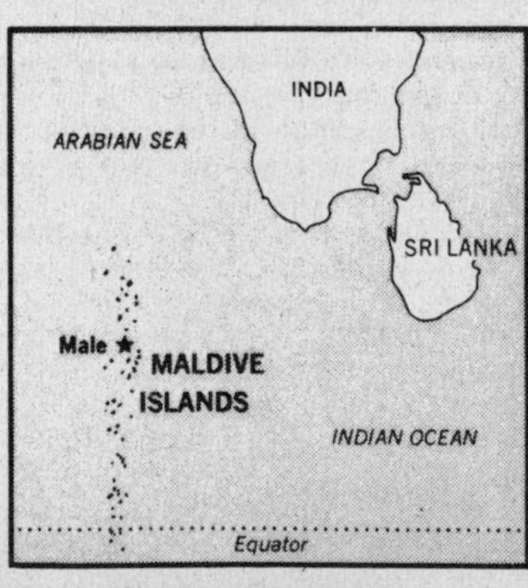

Maldive Islands

male (māl) *adj.* 1. Of, pertaining to, or designating the sex capable of fertilizing ova or begetting young. 2. Characteristic of the male sex; masculine. 3. Designating an object, such as an electric plug, designed for insertion into a fitted bore or socket. —*n.* One that is male. [< L *masculus,* dim of *mas,* male.]

Ma•lé (mä'lā). The capital of the Maldive Islands. Pop. 11,000.

mal•e•dic•tion (măl'ə-dĭk'shən) *n.* 1. A curse. 2. Slander; calumny.

mal•e•fac•tor (măl'ə-făk'tər) *n.* 1. A criminal. 2. One who does evil. [< L *malefacere,* to do wrong.] —**mal'e•fac'tion** *n.*

ma•lef•ic (mə-lĕf'ĭk) *adj.* 1. Baleful. 2. Malicious. [L *maleficus,* wrongdoing.]

ma•lev•o•lent (mə-lĕv'ə-lənt) *adj.* 1. Having or exhibiting ill will or malice. 2. Having an evil influence. [L *malevolēns.*] —**ma•lev'o•lence** *n.* —**ma•lev'o•lent•ly** *adv.*

mal•fea•sance (măl-fē'zəns) *n.* Wrongdoing, esp. if contrary to official obligations. [MAL- + OF *faisance,* doing.] —**mal•fea'sant** *adj. & n.*

mal•for•ma•tion (măl'fôr-mā'shən) *n.* An abnormal or irregular structure or form. —**mal•formed'** *adj.*

mal•func•tion (măl-fŭngk'shən) *v.* To fail to function normally. —**mal•func'tion** *n.*

Ma•li (mä'lē). A republic of W Africa. Pop. 4,485,000. Cap. Bamako. —**Ma'li** *adj.*

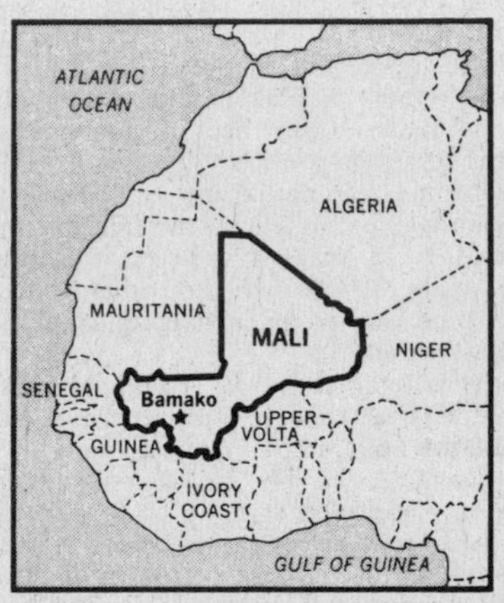

Mali

mal•ice (măl'ĭs) *n.* Ill will with a desire to harm; spite. [< L *malus,* bad.] —**ma•li'cious** (mə-lĭsh'əs) *adj.* —**ma•li'cious•ly** *adv.*

ma•lign (mə-līn') *v.* To speak evil of; slander; defame. —*adj.* 1. Evil in nature, intent, or influence. 2. Malevolent. [< L *malus,* bad.]

ma•lig•nant (mə-lĭg'nənt) *adj.* 1. Showing great malevolence. 2. Highly injurious. 3. Designating a pathological growth that tends to spread. —**ma•lig'nan•cy** *n.*

ma•lig•ni•ty (mə-lĭg'nə-tē) *n., pl.* **-ties.** 1. a. Intense ill will; great malice. b. An instance of great malice. 2. The quality of being highly evil or injurious.

ma•lin•ger (mə-lĭng'gər) *v.* To feign illness to avoid duty or work. [< OF *malingre.*] —**ma•lin'ger•er** *n.*

mall (môl, măl) *n.* 1. A shady public walk or promenade. 2. A street lined with shops and closed to vehicles. 3. A median strip dividing a road or highway. [< The *Mall,* a tree-lined street in London.]

mal•lard (măl'ərd) *n.* A wild duck of which the male has a green head and neck. [< OF *mallart.*]

mal•le•a•ble (măl'ē-ə-bəl) *adj.* **1.** Capable of being shaped or formed, as by hammering or pressure. **2.** Tractable; pliable. [< ML *malleāre,* to hammer.] —**mal'le•a•bil'i•ty** *n.* —**mal'le•a•bly** *adv.*

mal•let (măl'ĭt) *n.* **1.** A short-handled hammer, usually with a cylindrical wooden head, used chiefly to drive a chisel or wedge. **2.** A longer-handled hammer, as for use in croquet and polo. [< L *malleus,* hammer.]

mal•le•us (măl'ē-əs) *n., pl.* **mallei** (măl'ē-ī', -ē-ē'). The largest of three small bones in the middle ear.

mal•low (măl'ō) *n.* Any of various related plants usually having pink or white, often showy flowers. [< L *malva.*]

mal•nour•ished (măl-nûr'ĭsht) *adj.* Suffering from improper nutrition or insufficient food.

mal•nu•tri•tion (măl'n/y/o͞o-trĭsh'ən) *n.* Poor nutrition, esp. because of insufficient or poorly balanced diet.

mal•oc•clu•sion (măl'ə-klo͞o'zhən) *n.* Faulty closure of teeth.

mal•o•dor•ous (măl-ō'dər-əs) *adj.* Having a bad odor; ill-smelling. —**mal•o'dor•ous•ly** *adv.* —**mal•o'dor•ous•ness** *n.*

mal•prac•tice (măl-prăk'tĭs) *n.* Improper or negligent conduct or treatment, esp. by a physician. —**mal'prac•ti'tion•er** *n.*

malt (môlt) *n.* **1.** Soaked, sprouted, and dried grain, usually barley, used chiefly in brewing and distilling. **2.** Any alcoholic beverage brewed from malt. [< OE *mealt.* See **mel-.**]

Mal•ta (môl'tə). An island nation in the Mediterranean. Pop. 324,000. Cap. Valletta.

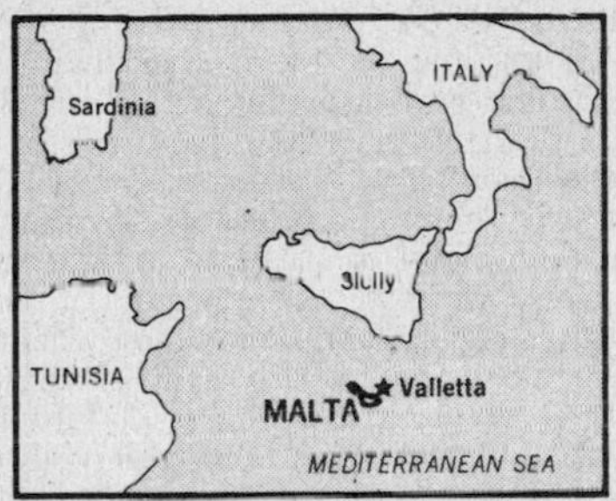

Malta

Mal•tese (môl-tēz', -tēs') *adj.* Pertaining to Malta, its inhabitants, or the language spoken in Malta. —*n., pl.* **-tese. 1.** A native of Malta. **2.** The language of Malta, a dialect of North Arabic with elements of Italian.

mal•tose (môl'tōs', -tōz') *n.* A sugar, $C_{12}H_{22}O_{11} \cdot H_2O$. [< MALT + -OSE.]

mal•treat (măl-trēt') *v.* To treat cruelly; handle roughly. —**mal•treat'ment** *n.*

ma•ma (mä'mə, mə-mä') *n.* Also **mam•ma.** *Informal.* Mother. [Baby talk.]

mam•ba (mäm'bə) *n.* A venomous tropical African snake.

mam•mal (măm'əl) *n.* Any of a group of warm-blooded vertebrate animals, including man, characterized by the presence of hair and by milk-producing glands in the females. [< L *mamma,* breast.] —**mam•mal'i•an** (mă-mā'lē-ən) *adj.* & *n.*

mam•ma•ry (măm'ər-ē) *adj.* Of or pertaining to a breast or milk-producing organ.

mam•mo•gram (măm'ə-grăm') *n.* An x-ray photograph or radiograph of the breast. [L *mamma,* breast + -GRAM.]

mam•mog•ra•phy (mə-mŏg'rə-fē) *n.* Examination of the breast by x-rays in order to detect tumors before they can be felt by hand. [L *mamma,* breast + -GRAPHY.]

mam•mon (măm'ən) *n.* Also **Mam•mon.** Money personified as a false god. [< Aram *māmōnā,* riches.]

mam•moth (măm'əth) *n.* An extinct elephant that formerly existed throughout the N Hemisphere. —*adj.* Huge; gigantic. [Obs Russ *mammot'.*]

man (măn) *n., pl.* **men** (mĕn). **1.** An adult male human being. **2.** A human being; a person. **3.** Mankind. **4.** A male human being having qualities considered characteristic of manhood. **5.** A husband, lover, or sweetheart. **6.** Any workman, servant, or subordinate. **7.** Any of the pieces used in board games, as chess. —*v.* **manned, manning. 1.** To supply or furnish with men for defense, service, etc. **2.** To strengthen; fortify. [< OE *mann.* See **man-.**]

Man, Isle of (măn). A British island between Britain and Ireland. —**Manx** *adj.* & *n.*

Man. Manitoba.

man•a•cle (măn'ə-kəl) *n.* **1.** Often **manacles.** A restraining device, as handcuffs, for the hands. **2.** Anything that confines or restrains. —*v.* **-cled, -cling.** To restrain with manacles. [< L *manicula,* little hand, handle.]

man•age (măn'ĭj) *v.* **-aged, -aging. 1.** To direct, control, or handle. **2.** To administer or regulate. **3.** To make submissive. **4.** To contrive or arrange. **5.** To get along. [Prob < VL **manidiāre,* to handle.] —**man'age•a•ble** *adj.* —**man'age•a•bil'i•ty** *n.* —**man'age•a•bly** *adv.*

man•age•ment (măn'ĭj-mənt) *n.* **1.** The act or practice of managing. **2.** The person or persons who manage a business. **3.** Skill in managing.

man•ag•er (măn'ĭj-ər) *n.* **1.** One who manages. **2.** One in charge of the business affairs or training of a person or group. —**man'a•ger'i•al** (măn'ə-jîr'ē-əl) *adj.*

Ma•na•gua (mä-nä'gwä). The capital of Nicaragua. Pop. 275,000.

ma•ña•na (mä-nyä'nä) *n.* Some indefinite time in the future. [Span, tomorrow.]

man•a•tee (măn'ə-tē') *n.* A large aquatic mammal of warm Atlantic coastal waters. [Span *manatí.*]

Man•ches•ter (măn'chĕs'tər, -chĭs-tər). A city of NW England. Pop. 638,000.

Man•chu (măn'cho͞o, măn-cho͞o') *n., pl.* **-chu** or **-chus. 1.** One of a nomadic Mongoloid people, native to Manchuria, who ruled China from 1644 to 1911. **2.** The Tungusic language of the Manchu. —**Man'chu** *adj.*

Man•chu•ri•a (măn-cho͝or'ē-ə). The northernmost region and administrative division of China. —**Man•chu'ri•an** *adj.* & *n.*

Manchuria

man•da•rin (măn'də-rĭn) *n.* **1.** In imperial China, a high-ranking public official. **2. Mandarin. a. Mandarin Chinese. b.** In imperial China, the dialect used by mandarins and other officials of the empire. [< Sk *mantrin,* counselor.]

Mandarin Chinese. The national language of China, based on the principal dialect spoken in the area around Peking.

man•date (măn'dāt') *n.* **1.** An authoritative command or instruction. **2.** The wishes of a political electorate, expressed to its representatives. **3. a.** A commission from the League of Nations authorizing a nation to administer a territory. **b.** Any region under such administration. [< L *mandāre,* to command.]

man•da•to•ry (măn'də-tôr'ē, -tōr'ē) *adj.* **1.** Of or pertaining to a mandate. **2.** Required; obligatory.

Man•de (män'dā) *n., pl.* **-de** or **-des. 1.** A people of W Africa in the upper Niger valley. **2.** A branch of the Niger-Congo language family.

man•di•ble (măn'də-bəl) *n.* A jaw or jawlike part, esp. the lower jaw in vertebrates. [< L *mandere,* to chew.] —**man•dib'u•lar** (măn-dĭb'yə-lər) *adj.*

Man•din•go (măn-dĭng'gō) *n., pl.* **-gos** or **-goes. 1.** A member of any of various Negroid peoples inhabiting the region of the upper Niger River valley of W Africa. **2.** Any language or dialect of the Mandingos.

man•do•lin (măn'də-lĭn', măn'də-lĭn') *n.* A stringed musical instrument with a usually pear-shaped wooden body and a fretted neck. [< It *mandola, mandora,* lute.]

man•drag•o•ra (măn-drăg'ə-rə) *n. Chiefly Poetic.* The mandrake or a narcotic prepared from it.

man•drake (măn'drāk') *n.* **1.** A Eurasian plant with a branched root thought to resemble the human body and believed to have magical powers. **2.** The **May apple.** [< Gk *mandragoras.*]

man•drel, man•dril (măn'drəl) *n.* **1.** A spindle or axle used to secure or support material being machined or milled. **2.** A shaft on which a working tool is mounted. [Prob < F *mandrin,* a lathe.]

man•drill (măn'drĭl) *n.* A large African monkey with brilliantly colored markings on the face and buttocks. [MAN + DRILL.]

mane (mān) *n.* The long hair growing from the neck of a horse, male lion, etc. [< OE *manu.* See **mon-.**]

ma•nège (mă-nĕzh') *n.* Also **ma•nege.** The art of training or managing horses. [< It *maneggiare,* to manage.]

ma•nes, Ma•nes (mā'nēz, mä'nās) *pl.n.* **1.** The deified spirits of the dead. **2.** *(takes sing. v.).* Any revered spirit of one who has died. [L *mānēs,* prob "the good ones."]

Ma•net (mă-nā'), **Edouard.** 1832–1883. French painter.

ma•neu•ver (mə-n/y/o͞o'vər). Also *chiefly Brit.* **ma•noeu•vre.** *n.* **1. a.** A strategic or tactical military movement. **b.** Often **maneuvers.** A large-scale military training exercise simulating combat. **2. a.** A procedure requiring skill. **b.** A controlled change in the path of a vehicle. **3.** A stratagem. —*v.* **1.** To perform a military maneuver. **2.** To change tactics. **3.** To scheme. **4.** To manipulate into a desired position. [< L *manū operārī,* to work by hand.] —**ma•neu'ver•a•bil'i•ty** *n.*

man•ful (măn'fəl) *adj.* Displaying manly qualities; brave and resolute. —**man'ful•ly** *adv.* —**man'ful•ness** *n.*

man•ga•nese (măng'gə-nēz', -nēs') *n. Symbol* **Mn** A gray-white, brittle metallic element, alloyed with steel to increase strength, hardness, wear resistance, and other properties. Atomic number 25, atomic weight 54.9380. [< It.]

mange (mānj) *n.* A skin disease, esp. of animals, caused by parasitic mites and characterized by itching and loss of hair. [< OF *mangier,* to eat.] —**man'gy** *adj.*

man•ger (mān'jər) *n.* A trough or open box in which feed for horses or cattle is placed. [< VL **mandūcātōria,* feeding place.]

man•gle¹ (măng'gəl) *v.* **-gled, -gling. 1.** To mutilate or disfigure by battering, hacking, etc. **2.** To ruin or spoil through ineptitude. [< NF *mangler, mahangler.*] —**man'gler** *n.*

man•gle² (măng'gəl) *n.* A laundry machine for pressing fabrics. [Du *mangel.*]

man•go (măng'gō) *n., pl.* **-goes** or **-gos. 1.** A tropical fruit with sweet, juicy, yellow-orange flesh. **2.** A tree bearing such fruit. [< Tamil *mānkāy.*]

man•grove (măn'grōv', măng'grōv') *n.* A tropical evergreen tree that has stiltlike roots and forms dense thickets along tidal shores. [< Port *mangue.*]

man•han•dle (măn'hăn'dəl) *v.* To handle roughly. —**man'han'dler** *n.*

Man•hat•tan¹ (măn-hăt'n, mən-) *n., pl.* **-tan** or **-tans.** A member of a tribe of Algonquian-speaking Indians, formerly inhabiting the area that is now roughly New York City.

Man•hat•tan² (măn-hăt'n, mən-). A borough of New York City. Pop. 1,698,000.

man•hole (măn'hōl') *n.* A hole through which one enters a sewer, boiler, etc.

man•hood (măn'hŏŏd) *n.* **1.** The state or condition of being an adult male. **2.** The composite of manly qualities, as courage and determination. **3.** Men collectively.

man-hour (măn'our') *n., pl.* **man-hours.** A unit equal to the work a man can produce in one hour.

man•hunt (măn'hŭnt') *n., pl.* **manhunts.** An organized search for someone, esp. a fugitive criminal.

ma•ni•a (mā'nē-ə, mān'yə) *n.* **1.** An inordinately intense enthusiasm; craze. **2.** A manifestation of manic-depressive psychosis. [< Gk.] —**man'ic** (măn'ĭk) *adj.*

-mania. *comb. form.* An exaggerated desire for, pleasure in, or excitement induced by (something): **monomania.**
In the following list, the English meaning is indicated for the form with which **-mania** is combined:

- **acromania** (heights)
- **ailuromania** (cats)
- **cynomania** (dogs)
- **gymnomania** (nudity)
- **hedonomania** (pleasure)
- **heliomania** (sunbathing)
- **hippomania** (horses)
- **hypnomania** (sleep)
- **necromania** (death)
- **noctimania** (night)
- **ochlomania** (crowds)
- **ophidiomania** (reptiles)
- **ornithomania** (birds)
- **pharmacomania** (medicines)
- **sitomania** (food)
- **xenomania** (foreigners)
- **zoomania** (animals)

ma•ni•ac (mā'nē-ăk') *n.* **1.** An insane person; lunatic. **2.** One who has an excessive enthusiasm for something. —**ma'ni•ac', ma•ni'a•cal** (mə-nī'ə-kəl) *adj.*

man•ic-de•pres•sive (măn'ĭk-dĭ-prĕs'ĭv) *adj.* Of or afflicted with a psychosis in which periods of manic excitation alternate with melancholic depression. —*n.* A person so afflicted.

man•i•cure (măn'ĭ-kyŏŏr') *n.* Treatment of the hands and fingernails. —*v.* **-cured, -curing. 1.** To care for (the fingernails). **2.** To trim closely. [F, "hand care."] —**man'i•cur'ist** *n.*

man•i•fest (măn'ə-fĕst') *adj.* Clearly apparent, esp. to the sight; obvious. —*v.* **1.** To show plainly; reveal. **2.** To be evidence of; prove. —*n.* A list of cargo or passengers. [< L *manifestus,* palpable, "grasped by hand."]

man•i•fes•ta•tion (măn'ə-fĕs-tā'shən) *n.* **1.** A demonstration or display. **2.** One of the forms in which someone or something, such as a divine being or an idea, is revealed.

man•i•fes•to (măn'ə-fĕs'tō) *n., pl.* **-toes** or **-tos.** A public declaration of principles or intentions.

man•i•fold (măn'ə-fōld) *adj.* **1.** Of many kinds; varied. **2.** Having many forms. **3.** Consisting of or operating several of one kind. —*n.* **1.** One of many copies. **2.** A pipe having apertures for multiple connections. —*v.* **1.** To make several copies of. **2.** To multiply.

man•i•kin, man•ni•kin (măn'ĭ-kĭn) *n.* **1.** A little man; dwarf. **2.** An anatomical model of the human body, as used in medical study. **3.** A mannequin. [MDu *mannekīn.*]

Ma•nil•a (mə-nĭl'ə). The largest city of the Philippines. Pop. 1,139,000.

ma•nip•u•late (mə-nĭp'yə-lāt') *v.* **-lated, -lating. 1.** To handle or control skillfully. **2.** To influence or manage shrewdly or deviously. [< L *manipulus,* handful.] —**ma•nip'u•la'tion** *n.* —**ma•nip'u•la'tor** *n.*

Man•i•to•ba (măn'ĭ-tō'bə). A province of C Canada. Pop. 958,000. Cap. Winnipeg.

man•kind. *n.* **1.** (măn'kīnd', -kīnd'). The human race. **2.** (măn'kīnd'). Men as distinguished from women.

man•ly (măn'lē) *adj.* **-lier, -liest.** Having the admirable qualities attributed to a man. —**man'li•ness** *n.*

man•made (măn'mād') *adj.* Made by man; not of natural origin.

Mann (män), **Thomas.** 1875–1955. German author.

man•na (măn'ə) *n.* **1.** The food miraculously provided for the Israelites in the wilderness. Exodus 16:14–36. **2.** Something of value received unexpectedly. [Aram *mannā.*]

man•ne•quin (măn'ĭ-kĭn) *n.* **1.** A representation of the human body, used for displaying clothes. **2.** A woman who models clothes. [< MDu *mannekin,* MANIKIN.]

man•ner (măn'ər) *n.* **1.** A way of doing something. **2.** One's natural bearing or behavior. **3. manners. a.** Social behavior. **b.** Polite social behavior. **4.** A style or method in the arts. **5.** Kind or sort. [< VL **manuāria,* "way of handling."]

man•nered (măn'ərd) *adj.* **1.** Having manners of a specific kind: *ill-mannered.* **2.** Artificial or affected.

man•ner•ism (măn'ər-ĭz'əm) *n.* **1.** A distinctive behavioral trait; idiosyncrasy. **2.** Exaggerated or affected style or habit.

man•ner•ly (măn'ər-lē) *adj.* Polite; well-behaved.

man•ni•kin. Variant of **manikin.**

man•nish (măn'ĭsh) *adj.* Of, befitting, or resembling a man. —**man'nish•ly** *adv.* —**man'nish•ness** *n.*

ma•noeu•vre. *Chiefly Brit.* Variant of **maneuver.**

man-of-war (măn'ə-wôr') *n., pl.* **men-of-war. 1.** A warship. **2.** See **Portuguese man-of-war.**

man•or (măn'ər) *n.* **1.** The estate of a feudal lord. **2.** Any landed estate. **3.** The main house on any estate; mansion. [< L *manēre,* to dwell, remain.] —**ma•no'ri•al** (mă-nôr'ē-əl, mă-nōr'-) *adj.*

man•pow•er (măn'pou'ər) *n.* **1.** The power of human strength. **2.** The men available to a particular group or required for a particular task.

man•qué (mäɴ-kā') *adj.* Unfulfilled; frustrated: *an artist manqué.* [F < It *manco,* lacking, defective.]

man•sard (măn'särd) *n.* A roof having two slopes on all four sides, with the lower slope steeper than the upper. [< F. *Mansart* (1598–1666), French architect.]

manse (măns) *n.* A clergyman's residence. [< L *manēre,* to dwell, remain.]

man•sion (măn'shən) *n.* A large, stately house. [< L *mānsiō,* dwelling.]

man•slaugh•ter (măn'slô'tər) *n.* The unlawful killing of someone without premeditation.

man•tel (măn'təl) *n.* Also **man•tle. 1.** A facing around a fireplace. **2.** A mantelpiece. [< L *mantellum,* MANTLE.]

man•tel•piece (măn'təl-pēs') *n.* Also **man•tle•piece.** The shelf over a fireplace.

man•til•la (măn-tē'yə, -tĭl'ə) *n.* A scarf, usually of lace, worn over the head and shoulders by women in Spain and Latin America. [< Span *manta,* cape.]

man•tis (măn'tĭs) *n.* A predatory grasshopper-like insect that holds its forelimbs in a praying position. [< Gk, prophet, diviner.]

man•tis•sa (măn-tĭs'ə) *n.* The decimal part of a logarithm written as the sum of an integer and a decimal. [L, a gain.]

man•tle (măn'təl) *n.* **1.** A loose, sleeveless coat worn over outer garments. **2.** Anything that covers, envelops, or conceals. **3.** A device in gas lamps consisting of a sheath of threads that gives off brilliant illumination when heated by the flame. **4.** The layer of the earth between the crust and core. **5.** Variant of **mantel.** —*v.* **-tled, -tling.** To cover with or as with a mantle; cloak. [< L *mantellum,* cloak.]

man•u•al (măn'yōō-əl) *adj.* **1.** Of or operated by the hands. **2.** Employing human rather than mechanical energy: *manual labor.* —*n.* **1.** Any small reference book, esp. one giving instructions. **2.** A keyboard of an organ played with the hands. **3.** Prescribed movements in the handling of a rifle. [< L *manus,* hand.] —**man'u•al•ly** *adv.*

manual alphabet. An alphabet of hand signals used for communication by deaf-mutes.

man•u•fac•ture (măn'yə-făk'chər) *v.* **-tured, -turing. 1.** To make or process into a finished product, esp. through a large-scale industrial operation. **2.** To concoct or invent. —*n.* **1.** The act or process of manufacturing. **2.** A manufactured product. [< LL *manūfactus,* handmade.] —**man'u•fac'tur•er** *n.*

man•u•mit (măn'yōō-mĭt') *v.* **-mitted, -mitting.** To free from slavery. [< L *manū ēmittere,* to liberate, release from one's hand.] —**man'u•mis'sion** (-mĭsh'ən) *n.*

ma•nure (mə-n/y/ŏŏr') *n.* Animal dung or other material used to fertilize soil. —*v.* **-nured, -nuring.** To apply manure to. [< OF *manoeuvrer,* to till, "work by hand."]

man•u•script (măn'yə-skrĭpt') *n.* **1.** A book or other composition written by hand. **2.** A typewritten or handwritten version of a book,

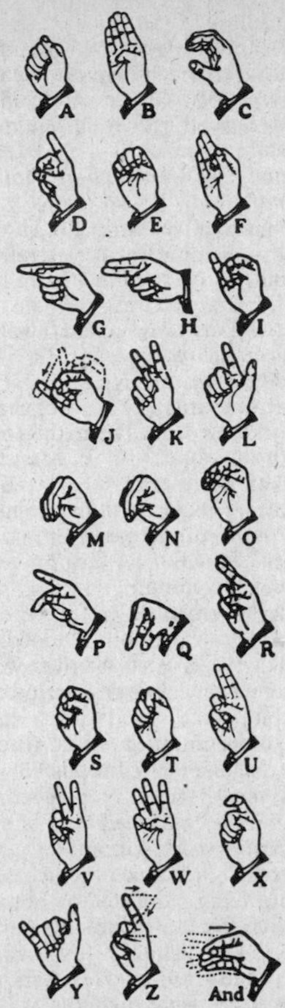

manual alphabet

article, etc., esp. the author's own copy, submitted for publication. **3.** Handwriting as opposed to printing. [ML *manūscriptus*, handwritten.]

man•y (mĕn'ē) *adj.* **more, most.** Amounting to or consisting of a large, indefinite number: *many friends.* —*n.* *(takes pl. v.).* A large, indefinite number. —*pron.* *(takes pl. v.).* A large number of persons or things. [< OE *manig, mænig.* See **menegh-**.]

Ma•o•ri (mou'rē) *n., pl.* **-ri** or **-ris.** **1.** A member of the aboriginal people of New Zealand. **2.** The language of the Maori. —**Ma'o•ri** *adj.*

Mao Tse-tung (mou'tsĭ-to͝ong', mou'dzŭ'-do͝ong'). 1893–1976. Political theorist; leader of the Chinese revolution; head of state (1949–59); party chairman (from 1943). —**Mao'ism'** *n.* —**Mao'ist** *n.* & *adj.*

Mao Tse-tung

map (măp) *n.* A representation, usually on a plane surface, of a region of the earth or heavens. —*v.* **mapped, mapping.** **1.** To make a map of. **2.** To plan, esp. in detail; arrange: *mapping out their vacation.* [< ML *mappa,* napkin, sheet, cloth.] —**map'per** *n.*

ma•ple (mā'pəl) *n.* **1.** Any of various trees with lobed leaves and close-grained, usually hard wood and, in a North American species, sap that is boiled to produce a sweet syrup (**maple syrup**) or sugar (**maple sugar**). **2.** The wood of such a tree. [< OE *mapel(treow),* maple (tree).]

mar (mär) *v.* **marred, marring.** To damage, deface, or spoil. [< OE *merran, mierran.* See **mer-[2]**.]

mar. **1.** maritime. **2.** married.

Mar. March.

mar•a•bou (măr'ə-bo͞o') *n.* **1.** A large, Old World stork having soft down used to trim women's garments. **2.** The down of this bird. [< Ar *murābit,* stork.]

ma•ra•ca (mə-rä'kə) *n.* A percussion instrument consisting of a hollow-gourd rattle. [< Tupi.]

mar•a•schi•no (măr'ə-skē'nō, -shē'nō) *n.* A cordial made from the juice and pits of an Old World cherry. [It.]

maraschino cherry. A maraschino-flavored preserved cherry.

mar•a•thon (măr'ə-thŏn') *n.* **1.** A long-distance race, esp. one on foot. **2.** A contest of endurance. —**mar'a•thon'** *adj.*

ma•raud (mə-rôd') *v.* To rove in search of booty; raid for plunder. [F *marauder.*] —**ma•raud'er** *n.*

mar•ble (mär'bəl) *n.* **1.** A metamorphic rock, chiefly calcium carbonate, often irregularly colored by impurities. **2. a.** A small ball used in children's games. **b. marbles** *(takes sing. v.).* A game played with such balls. —*adj.* Consisting of or resembling marble. [< Gk *marmaros,* marble, any hard stone.]

mar•bling (mär'blĭng) *n.* A mottling or streaking that resembles marble.

march[1] (märch) *v.* **1.** To walk or cause to walk in a military manner with measured steps at a steady rate. **2.** To advance or proceed with steady movement. **3.** To traverse by marching. —*n.* **1.** The act of marching. **2.** Forward movement. **3.** A regulated pace. **4.** The distance covered by marching. **5.** A musical composition in regularly accented meter, to accompany marching. [OF *marcher, marchier,* to walk, trample.]

march[2] (märch) *n.* A border region or frontier. [< OF *marche, marc,* borderland.]

March (märch) *n.* The 3rd month of the year. March has 31 days. [< L *Mārtius (mēnsis),* (month) of Mars.]

mar•chion•ess (mär'shən-ĭs, mär'shə-nĕs') *n.* **1.** The wife or widow of a marquis. **2.** A peeress of the rank of marquis in her own right. [< ML *marchiō,* marquis.]

Mar•di gras (mär'dē grä'). The last day before Lent. [F, "fat Tuesday."]

mare[1] (mâr) *n.* A female horse, zebra, etc. [< OE *mere, miere.* See **marko-**.]

ma•re[2] (mä'rā) *n., pl.* **-ria** (-rē-ə). *Astron.* Any of the large dark areas on the moon or Mars. [< L, sea.]

mar•ga•rine (mär'jə-rĭn) *n.* A butter substitute made with vegetable oils. [F.]

mar•gin (mär'jən) *n.* **1.** An edge and the area immediately adjacent to it; border. **2.** The blank space bordering the printed area on a page. **3.** A limit of a state or process: *the margin of reality.* **4.** A surplus measure or amount: *a margin of safety.* **5.** A measure or degree of difference: *a margin of 500 votes.* [< L *margō (margin-).*] —**mar'gin•al** *adj.*

mar•gi•na•li•a (mär'jə-nā'lē-ə) *pl.n.* Notes in a book margin.

Ma•rie An•toi•nette (mə-rē' ăn'twə-nĕt'). 1755–1793. Queen of France; wife (1770) of Louis XVI; guillotined.

mar•i•gold (măr'ə-gōld', mâr'-) *n.* A widely cultivated plant with showy yellow, orange, or reddish flowers. [ME *marygould.*]

mar•i•jua•na, mar•i•hua•na (măr'ə-wä'nə) *n.* **1.** The hemp plant. **2.** The dried flowers and leaves of this plant, esp. when smoked to induce euphoria. [Mex Span *mariguana, marihuana.*]

ma•rim•ba (mə-rĭm'bə) *n.* A large xylophone with resonators.

ma•ri•na (mə-rē'nə) *n.* A boat basin for small pleasure boats. [< L *marīnus,* MARINE.]

mar•i•nade (măr'ə-nād') *n.* A liquid, as vinegar or wine, in which food is soaked before cooking. [< Span *marino,* "briny," marine.]

mar•i•nate (măr'ə-nāt') *v.* **-nated, -nating.** To soak (meat or fish) in a marinade. [Var of MARINADE.]

ma•rine (mə-rēn') *adj.* **1. a.** Of or pertaining to the sea: *marine exploration.* **b.** Native to the sea: *marine life.* **2.** Pertaining to shipping or maritime affairs. **3.** Pertaining to sea navigation: *marine chart.* —*n.* **1.** Shipping in general; maritime interests as represented by ships: *merchant marine.* **2. a.** A soldier serving on a ship. **b. Marine.** A member of the U.S. Marine Corps. [< L *marīnus* < *mare,* sea.]

Marine Corps. A branch of the U.S. Armed Forces composed chiefly of amphibious troops.

mar•i•ner (măr'ə-nər) *n.* A sailor or seaman.

mar•i•o•nette (măr'ē-ə-nĕt') *n.* A jointed puppet manipulated by strings.

mar•i•tal (măr'ə-təl) *adj.* Of or pertaining to marriage. [< L *maritus,* married, husband.]

mar•i•time (măr'ə-tīm') *adj.* **1.** Located on or near the sea. **2.** Of or concerned with shipping or navigation. [< L *mare,* sea.]

mar•jo•ram (mär'jər-əm) *n.* An aromatic plant with leaves used as seasoning. [< ML *majorāna.*]

mark[1] (märk) *n.* **1.** A visible trace or impression on something, as a spot, dent, or line. **2.** A written or printed symbol: *a punctuation mark.* **3.** A grade, as in school. **4.** A name, stamp, etc., placed on an article to signify ownership, quality, etc. **5.** A visible indication of some quality, property, etc. **6.** A standard or criterion of quality. **7.** Quality; note; importance. **8.** A target. **9.** That which one wishes to achieve; a goal. **10.** An object or point that serves as a guide. —*v.* **1.** To make a visible impression (on). **2.** To form, distinguish, or separate by making a visible impression on. **3.** To pay attention to. **4.** To characterize; set off. **5.** To grade (school papers). [< OE *mearc,* boundary, landmark, sign. See **merg-**.] —**mark'er** *n.*

mark[2] (märk) *n.* See **Deutsche mark, ostmark.**

Mark (märk), **Saint.** Christian apostle; reputed author of the 2nd Gospel of the New Testament.

marked (märkt) *adj.* **1.** Having a mark or marks. **2.** Having a noticeable trait. —**mark'ed•ly** (mär'kĭd-lē) *adv.*

mar•ket (mär'kĭt) *n.* **1.** An open place or building where merchandise is offered for sale. **2.** A store that sells a particular type of merchandise: *a meat market.* **3. a.** A region in which goods can be bought and sold: *the*

European market. **b.** A type of buyer or demand: *the college market.* **4.** Demand for goods. —*v.* **1.** To offer for sale. **2.** To sell. **3.** To buy household supplies. [< L *mercārī,* to trade.] —**mar'ket·er, mar'ke·teer'** *n.*

mar·ket·place (mär'kĭt-plās') *n.* **1.** A public square in which a market is set up. **2.** The world of trade.

mark·ka (mär'kä') *n., pl.* **-kaa** (-kä'). The basic monetary unit of Finland.

marks·man (märks'mən) *n.* One skilled at shooting a gun or other weapon. —**marks'man·ship'** *n.*

mark·up (märk'ŭp') *n.* **1.** A raise in price. **2.** The amount added to the cost of an item when figuring the selling price.

marl (märl) *n.* A loam used as fertilizer. [< LL *marga.*]

mar·lin (mär'lən) *n.* A large marine game fish resembling the swordfish.

mar·line·spike (mär'lən-spīk') *n.* A metal spike used to separate strands of rope and wire cable in splicing.

Mar·lowe (mär'lō), **Christopher.** 1564–1593. English poet and dramatist.

mar·ma·lade (mär'mə-lād') *n.* A jellylike preserve made of the pulp and rind of fruits, esp. citrus fruits. [< Gk *melimēlon,* "honey-apple."]

mar·mo·re·al (mär-môr'ē-əl, -mōr'ē-əl) *adj.* Pertaining to or resembling marble. [< L *marmor,* marble.]

mar·mo·set (mär'mə-sĕt', -zĕt') *n.* Any of various small, furry, long-tailed tropical American monkeys. [< OF, grotesque figure.]

mar·mot (mär'mət) *n.* A stocky, short-legged burrowing rodent such as the woodchuck. [< ML *mormotāna,* "mountain mouse."]

ma·roon[1] (mə-ro͞on') *v.* **1.** To put (a person) ashore on a deserted island or coast. **2.** To abandon (a person) with little hope of rescue or escape. [F *marron.*]

ma·roon[2] (mə-ro͞on') *n.* Dark red. [< F *marron,* chestnut.]

mar·quee (mär-kē') *n.* **1.** A large tent, used chiefly for outdoor entertainment. **2.** A rooflike structure projecting over an entrance, as to a theater. [F *marquise,* a linen tent pitched atop an officer's tent.]

mar·quis (mär'kwĭs) *n., pl.* **-quis** or **-quises.** Also *chiefly Brit.* **mar·quess.** The title of a nobleman ranking below a duke. [< OF, "count of the march (frontier)."]

mar·riage (măr'ĭj) *n.* **1.** The state of being married; wedlock. **2.** A wedding. **3.** Any close union. —**mar'riage·a·ble** *adj.*

mar·row (măr'ō) *n.* **1.** The soft material that fills bone cavities, consisting of fat cells and maturing blood cells, with supporting connective tissue and blood vessels. **2.** Spinal marrow; the spinal cord. [< OE *mærg, mærh.* See **mozgo-.**]

mar·ry (măr'ē) *v.* **-ried, -rying. 1.** To join as husband and wife. **2.** To take as husband or wife. **3.** To enter into a close relationship. [< L *marītus,* husband.]

Mars (märz) *n.* **1.** The Roman god of war. **2.** The 4th planet from the sun, having a sidereal period of revolution about the sun of 687 days at a mean distance of 141.6 million miles, a mean radius of approx. 2,090 miles, and a mass approx. 0.15 that of Earth.

Mar·seille (mär-sā'). A city of SE France. Pop. 778,000.

marsh (märsh) *n.* An area of low-lying, wet land; a swamp. [< OE *mersc, merisc.* See **mori-.**] —**marsh'y** *adj.*

mar·shal (mär'shəl) *n.* **1.** In some countries, a military officer of the highest rank. **2.** In the U.S.: **a.** A Federal or city officer who carries out court orders. **b.** The head of a police or fire department. **3.** One in charge of a ceremony. —*v.* **1.** To arrange or place in order. **2.** To guide (a person) ceremoniously; usher. [< OHG *marahscalc,* "keeper of the horses," marshal.]

Mar·shall (mär'shəl). **1. George Catlett.** 1880–1959. American General of the Army, statesman, and diplomat. **2. John.** 1755–1835. American jurist, Chief Justice of the U.S. (1801–35).

marsh·mal·low (märsh'mĕl'ō, -măl'ō) *n.* **1.** A confection of sweetened paste, formerly made from the root of a mallow. **2.** A confection made of corn syrup, gelatin, etc., and dusted with powdered sugar.

marsh marigold. A North American swamp plant with yellow, buttercuplike flowers.

mar·su·pi·al (mär-so͞o'pē-əl) *n.* Any of a group of mammals including the kangaroo and the opossum, of which the females have an external pouch in which the newly born young are fed and sheltered. [< Gk *marsupion,* pouch.] —**mar·su'pi·al** *adj.*

mart (märt) *n.* A market. [< MARKET.]

mar·ten (märt'n) *n.* **1.** A thick-furred, weasellike mammal of N regions. **2.** The fur of a marten. [< OF *martre.*]

mar·tial (mär'shəl) *adj.* **1.** Of, pertaining to, or suggestive of war or warriors. **2.** Pertaining to the army or the military profession. [< L *Mārs,* Mars.] —**mar'tial·ism'** *n.* —**mar'tial·ist** *n.* —**mar'tial·ly** *adv.*

martial law. Temporary military rule imposed upon a civilian population, as in time of war.

Mar·tian (mär'shən) *adj.* Of or pertaining to the planet Mars. —*n.* A fictitious inhabitant of the planet Mars.

mar·tin (märt'n) *n.* Any of several birds resembling and closely related to the swallows. [ME.]

mar·ti·net (mär'tə-nĕt') *n.* A rigid disciplinarian. [< J. *Martinet,* 17th-century French general.]

mar·tin·gale (mär'tən-gāl') *n.* A part of a harness designed to prevent a horse from throwing back its head. [< *Martigue,* small village in Provence.]

mar·ti·ni (mär-tē'nē) *n., pl.* **-nis.** A cocktail usually made of three parts of gin to one part of dry vermouth.

mar·tyr (mär'tər) *n.* **1.** One who chooses to suffer death rather than renounce religious principles. **2.** One who makes a great sacrifice for his principles. **3.** One who endures great suffering. [< Gk *martus,* witness, witness (of Christ).] —**mar'tyr** *v.* —**mar'tyr·dom** *n.*

mar·vel (mär'vəl) *n.* **1.** Something that evokes surprise, admiration, or wonder. **2.** A sense of profound wonder or astonishment. —*v.* To feel wonder or astonishment. [< L *mīrābilis,* wonderful.]

mar·vel·ous (mär'vəl-əs) *adj.* Also **mar·vel·lous. 1.** Causing wonder or astonishment. **2.** Miraculous. **3.** Of the highest kind or quality. —**mar'vel·ous·ly** *adv.*

Marx (märks), **Karl.** 1818–1883. German philosopher and political economist; founder of Communism. —**Marx'ism'** *n.* —**Marx'ist** *n.* & *adj.*

Mar·y (mâr'ē). The mother of Jesus. Matthew 1:18–25.

Mar·y·land (mâr'ə-lənd). A state of the E U.S. Pop. 3,922,000. Cap. Annapolis.

masc. masculine.

mas·car·a (măs-kăr'ə) *n.* A cosmetic used to darken the eyelashes. [Span *máscara,* "mask."]

mas·cot (măs'kŏt, -kət) *n.* A person, animal, or object believed to bring good luck. [F *mascotte.*]

mas·cu·line (măs'kyə-lĭn) *adj.* **1.** Of or pertaining to men or boys; male. **2.** Mannish. **3.** Of, designating, or constituting the gender of words or grammatical forms referring normally to males. —*n.* **1.** The masculine gender. **2.** A word or word form of the masculine gender. [< L *masculus,* male.] —**mas'cu·line·ly** *adv.* —**mas'cu·lin'i·ty** (măs'kyə-lĭn'ə-tē) *n.*

ma·ser (mā'zər) *n.* A device similar to a laser that operates at microwave frequencies.

Mas·er·u (măz'ə-ro͞o'). The capital of Lesotho. Pop. 9,000.

mash (măsh) *n.* **1.** Any fermentable starchy mixture from which alcohol can be distilled. **2.** A mixture of ground grain and nutrients fed to livestock. **3.** Any soft, pulpy mass. —*v.* **1.** To convert (something) into a soft, pulpy mixture. **2.** To crush or grind. [< OE *māsc.*] —**mash'er** *n.*

mask (măsk, mäsk) *n.* **1.** A cover worn on the face to protect or conceal identity. **2.** A mold of a person's face, as a death mask. **3.** A grotesque representation of a face. **4.** Anything that disguises or conceals. **5.** A masque. —*v.* To cover, disguise, or protect with or as with a mask. [F *masque.*]

mas·o·chism (măs'ə-kĭz'əm) *n.* **1.** An abnormal sexual condition in which satisfaction depends on being subjected to abuse or pain. **2.** The deriving of pleasure from being mistreated in some way. [< L. von Sacher-*Masoch* (1836–1895), Austrian novelist.] —**mas'o·chist** *n.* —**mas'o·chis'tic** (măs'ə-kĭs'tĭk) *adj.* —**mas'o·chis'ti·cal·ly** *adv.*

ma·son (mā'sən) *n.* **1.** One who builds or works with stone or brick. **2. Mason.** A Freemason. [< Frank *_makōn,_ to make.]

Ma·son·ic (mə-sŏn'ĭk) *adj.* Of or pertaining to Freemasons or Freemasonry.

ma·son·ry (mā'sən-rē) *n., pl.* **-ries. 1.** The trade of a mason. **2.** Stonework or brickwork. **3. Masonry.** Freemasonry.

Ma·so·ra (mə-sôr'ə, -sōr'ə) *n.* The tradition relating to correct textual reading of the Hebrew Scriptures, as embodied in critical notes made by Jewish scholars before the 10th century A.D. —**Mas'o·ret'ic** (măs'ə-rĕt'ĭk) *adj.*

masque (măsk, mäsk) *n.* A dramatic entertainment, usually mythological or allegorical in theme, popular in England in the 16th and

Karl Marx

early 17th centuries; a mask. [Var of MASK.]

mas•quer•ade (măs'kə-rād') *n.* **1. a.** A costume ball at which masks are worn. **b.** The costume for such a ball. **2.** Any disguise or false outward show. —*v.* **-aded, -ading. 1.** To wear a disguise, as at a masquerade. **2.** To go about as if in disguise; put on a deceptive appearance. [< It *maschera,* mask.] —**mas'-quer•ad'er** *n.*

mass (măs) *n.* **1.** A unified body of matter with no specific shape. **2.** Any large but nonspecific amount or number. **3.** The major part of something; majority. **4.** The physical volume or bulk of a solid body. **5.** The measure of a body's resistance to acceleration, different from but proportional to its weight. —**the masses.** The body of common people. —*v.* To gather, form, or assemble into a mass. [< Gk *maza,* barley cake, lump, mass.]

Mass (măs) *n.* In Roman Catholic and some Protestant churches, the celebration of the Eucharist. [< LL *missa,* eucharist.]

Mass. Massachusetts.

Mas•sa•chu•set (măs'ə-cho͞o'sĭt, -zĭt) *n.* Also **Mas•sa•chu•sett. 1.** A member of a large tribe of Algonquian-speaking Indians who lived on or near the coast in Massachusetts. **2.** The language of these Indians.

Mas•sa•chu•setts (măs'ə-cho͞o'sĭts, -zĭts). A state of the NE U.S. Pop. 5,689,000. Cap. Boston.

mas•sa•cre (măs'ə-kər) *n.* **1.** Savage and indiscriminate killing; slaughter. **2.** *Informal.* A severe defeat, as in sports. [< L *mateola,* a kind of mallet.] —**mas'sa•cre** *v.* **(-cred, -cring).**

mas•sage (mə-säzh') *n.* The rubbing or kneading of the body to aid circulation or relax the muscles. [< F *masser,* to massage.] —**mas•sage'** *v.* **(-saged, -saging).**

mass communication. Communication directed at or reaching many people.

mas•seur (mă-sûr') *n.* A man who gives massages professionally. [< F *masser,* to MASSAGE.] —**mas•seuse'** (-sœz') *fem.n.*

mas•sive (măs'ĭv) *adj.* **1.** Consisting of or making up a large mass; bulky. **2.** Imposing in quantity, scope, degree, intensity, or scale.

mass number. The total number of neutrons and protons in an atomic nucleus.

mass production. The manufacture of goods in large quantities, often using assembly-line techniques.

mast (măst, mäst) *n.* **1.** A tall vertical spar that rises from the keel of a ship to support the sails and rigging. **2.** Any vertical pole. [< OE *mæst.*]

mas•ter (măs'tər, mäs'-) *n.* **1.** A man having control over others; an employer; owner. **2.** The captain of a merchant ship. **3.** A teacher or tutor. **4.** One highly skilled, as in a trade. **5. Master.** A title preceding the name of a boy too young to be addressed as Mister. **6. a.** A college or university degree granted to a person who has completed at least one year of study beyond the bachelor's degree. **b.** One holding such a degree. —*v.* **1.** To make oneself a master of (an art, craft, or science). **2.** To overcome or subdue. [< L *magister.*]

mas•ter•ful (măs'tər-fəl, mäs'-) *adj.* **1.** Given to playing the master; domineering. **2.** Expert; skillful. —**mas'ter•ful•ly** *adv.*

mas•ter•ly (măs'tər-lē, mäs'-) *adj.* Indicating the knowledge or skill of a master.

mas•ter•mind (măs'tər-mīnd', mäs'-) *n.* A person who plans and directs a project. —**mas'-ter•mind'** *v.*

master of ceremonies. One who acts as host at a formal event or program of varied entertainment.

mas•ter•piece (măs'tər-pēs', mäs'-) *n.* **1.** An outstanding work of art. **2.** Anything superlative.

master sergeant. A U.S. noncommissioned officer of the next to highest rating.

mas•ter•work (măs'tər-wûrk', mäs'-) *n.* A masterpiece.

mas•ter•y (măs'tər-ē, mäs'-) *n., pl.* **-ies. 1.** Possession of consummate skill. **2.** The status of master; dominion. **3.** Full command of some subject of study.

mast•head (măst'hĕd', mäst'-) *n.* **1:** The top of a ship's mast. **2.** The listing in a publication of information about its staff and operation.

mas•tic (măs'tĭk) *n.* A pastelike cement. [< Gk *mastikhē,* mastic, "chewing gum."]

mas•ti•cate (măs'tə-kāt') *v.* **-cated, -cating.** To chew. [< Gk *mastikhān,* to grind the teeth.] —**mas'ti•ca'tion** *n.* —**mas'ti•ca•to'ry** (-tĭ-kə-tôr'ē, -tōr'ē) *adj.*

mas•tiff (măs'tĭf) *n.* A large dog with a short brownish coat. [< L *mānsuētus,* tamed, "accustomed to the hand."]

masto–. *comb. form.* The breast or protuberances resembling a breast or nipple. [< Gk *mastos,* breast.]

mas•to•don (măs'tə-dŏn') *n.* An extinct elephantlike mammal. [NL, "breast-tooth."]

mas•toid (măs'toid') *n.* The **mastoid process.**

mas•toid•ec•to•my (măs'toid-ĕk'tə-mē) *n., pl.* **-mies.** Removal of part or all of the mastoid process.

mas•toid•i•tis (măs'toid-ī'tĭs) *n.* Inflammation of part or all of the mastoid process.

mastoid process. The rear portion of the temporal bone.

mas•tur•ba•tion (măs'tər-bā'shən) *n.* Excitation of the genital organs, usually to orgasm, by means other than sexual intercourse. [< L *masturbāri,* to masturbate.] —**mas'tur•bate'** *v.* **(-bated, bating).**

mat¹ (măt) *n.* **1.** A flat piece of fabric or other material used as a floor covering, table pad, etc. **2.** A floor pad to protect athletes, as in wrestling. **3.** A dense or tangled mass. —*v.* **matted, matting. 1.** To cover, protect, or decorate with a mat. **2.** To form into a mat. [< LL *matta.*]

mat² (măt) *n.* **1.** A border placed around a picture to serve as a frame or provide contrast between the picture and frame. **2.** A dull finish, as on paper. **3.** *Ptg.* A matrix. —*adj.* Having a dull finish. [< L *mattus,* dull, vague.]

mat•a•dor (măt'ə-dôr') *n.* The bullfighter with the role of killing the bull. [Span, "killer."]

match¹ (măch) *n.* **1.** One equal or similar to another. **2.** Two persons or things that harmonize. **3.** A game or contest. **4.** A marriage or arrangement of marriage. —*v.* **1.** To be or make similar or equal to. **2.** To harmonize with. **3.** To place in competition with. **4.** To join in marriage. [< OE *gemæcca,* mate. See **mag-.**] —**match'er** *n.*

match² (măch) *n.* A narrow strip of wood, cardboard, or wax coated on one end with a compound that ignites easily by friction. [< ML *myxa,* lamp wick.]

match•book (măch'bo͝ok') *n.* A small folder containing safety matches.

match•less (măch'lĭs) *adj.* Having no equal; peerless. —**match'less•ly** *adv.*

match•lock (măch'lŏk') *n.* A musket in which powder is ignited by a match.

match•mak•er (măch'mā'kər) *n.* **1.** One who arranges marriages. **2.** One who arranges athletic competitions.

mate (māt) *n.* **1.** One of a matched pair. **2.** A spouse. **3.** One of a pair of breeding animals. **4.** An associate. **5.** A deck officer on a merchant ship ranking below the master. —*v.* **mated, mating. 1.** To join closely; couple. **2.** To unite in marriage or for breeding. [< MLG *mate, gemate,* companion.]

ma•té (mä'tā') *n.* A tealike beverage made from the dried leaves of a South American tree.

ma•te•ri•al (mə-tîr'ē-əl) *n.* **1.** The substance out of which a thing is or can be constructed. **2. materials.** Tools or apparatus for the performance of a given task. —*adj.* **1.** Composed of or pertaining to physical substances. **2.** Of or affecting the enjoyment of physical well-being. **3.** Of or concerned with the physical as distinct from the spiritual. **4.** Of importance to an argument; relevant. [< L *māteria,* matter.] —**ma•te'ri•al•ly** *adv.*

ma•te•ri•al•ism (mə-tîr'ē-əl-ĭz'əm) *n.* **1.** The view that matter and material process are the sole constituents of reality. **2.** Preoccupation with money and possessions to the exclusion of spiritual or intellectual things. —**ma•te'ri•al•ist** *adj.* & *n.* —**ma•te'ri•al•is'tic** *adj.*

ma•te•ri•al•ize (mə-tîr'ē-əl-īz') *v.* **-ized, -izing. 1.** To assume or cause to assume material or effective form. **2.** To take form or shape. —**ma•te'ri•al•i•za'tion** *n.*

ma•te•ri•el, ma•té•ri•el (mə-tîr'ē-ĕl') *n.* The equipment, apparatus, and supplies of an organization, esp. of an army.

ma•ter•nal (mə-tûr'nəl) *adj.* **1.** Relating to or characteristic of a mother or motherhood; motherly. **2.** Inherited from or related to through one's mother. [< L *māter,* mother.] —**ma•ter'nal•ly** *adv.*

ma•ter•ni•ty (mə-tûr'nə-tē) *n.* The state of being a mother; motherhood.

math (măth) *n.* Mathematics.

math. mathematical; mathematician; mathematics.

math•e•mat•ics (măth'ə-măt'ĭks) *n.* *(takes sing. v.)* The study of number, form, arrangement, and associated relationships, using rigorously defined literal, numerical, and operational symbols. [< Gk *mathēma,* science.] —**math'e•mat'i•cal** *adj.* —**math'e•mat'i•cal•ly** *adv.* —**math'e•ma•ti'cian** (-mə-tĭsh'ən) *n.*

mat•i•nee, mat•i•née (măt'n-ā') *n.* A dramatic or musical performance given usually in the afternoon. [< L *(tempus) mātūtīnum,* morning (time).]

matri–. *comb. form.* Motherhood. [< L *māter,* mother.]

ma•tri•arch (mā'trē-ärk') *n.* A woman who rules a family, clan, or tribe. —**ma'tri•ar'chal** *adj.*

ma•tri•ar•chy (mā'trē-är'kē) *n., pl.* **-chies.** A social system in which descent is traced through the mother's side of the family.

ma•tric•u•late (mə-trĭk'yə-lāt') *v.* **-lated, -lating.** To enroll in a group, esp. in a college or university. [< L *mātrīx,* list, womb, source.] —**ma•tric'u•la'tion** *n.*

mat•ri•mo•ny (măt'rə-mō'nē) *n.* The act or state of being married; the sacrament or rite of marriage. [< L *mātrimōnium,* marriage, "motherhood."] —**mat'ri•mo'ni•al** *adj.*

ma•trix (mā'trĭks) *n., pl.* **-trices** (-trə-sēz', măt'rə-) or **-trixes. 1.** A medium within which something originates, develops, or is contained. **2.** *Ptg.* A mold from which metal plates can be cast. [L *mātrix,* womb, pregnant animal.]

ma•tron (mā'trən) *n.* **1.** A married woman, esp. a mature woman with dignity and social position. **2.** A woman who supervises a public institution, such as a prison. [< L *māter,* mother.] **—ma'tron•li•ness** *n.* **—ma'tron•ly** *adj.* & *adv.*

matron of honor *pl.* **matrons of honor.** A married woman serving as chief attendant of the bride at a wedding.

Matt. Matthew (New Testament).

mat•ter (măt'ər) *n.* **1. a.** That which occupies space, can be perceived by the senses, and constitutes any physical body or the universe as a whole. **b.** Any entity displaying gravitation and inertia when at rest as well as when in motion. **2.** A specific type of substance: *inorganic matter.* **3.** The substance of thought or expression. **4.** Any subject of concern or action. **5.** A difficulty: *What's the matter?* **6.** An indefinite quantity: *a matter of a few cents.* **7.** Something written or printed. *—v.* To be of importance. [< L *māteria,* matter.]

mat•ter-of-fact (măt'ər-əv-făkt') *adj.* Pertaining or adhering to facts; literal.

Mat•thew (măth'yo͞o), **Saint.** Christian apostle; reputed author of 1st Gospel.

mat•ting (măt'ĭng) *n.* A coarsely woven fabric used for covering floors and similar purposes.

mat•tock (măt'ək) *n.* A digging tool with a blade set at right angles to the handle. [< OE *mattuc.*]

mat•tress (măt'rĭs) *n.* A rectangular pad of heavy cloth filled with soft material, used as or on a bed. [< Ar *maṭraḥ,* place where something is thrown.]

mat•u•rate (măch'o͞o-rāt') *v.* **-rated, -rating.** To mature or ripen. **—mat'u•ra'tion** *n.*

ma•ture (mə-t/y/o͞or', -cho͞or') *adj.* **-turer, -turest.** **1.** Fully grown or developed. **2.** Fully aged or ripened. **3.** Worked out fully by the mind; perfected. **4.** Payable; due: *a mature bond.* *—v.* **-tured, -turing.** To bring or come to full development. [< L *mātūrus.*] **—ma•ture'ly** *adv.* **—ma•tur'i•ty** *n.*

mat•zo (mät'sə) *n., pl.* **-zoth** (-sōṯh', -sōt', -sōs') or **-zos** (-səz, -səs, -sōz') or **-zot** (-sōt'). A brittle, flat piece of unleavened bread, eaten esp. during the Passover. [Yid *matse.*]

maud•lin (môd'lĭn) *adj.* Effusively sentimental. **—maud'lin•ly** *adv.*

maul (môl) *n.* A heavy hammer used to drive stakes, piles, or wedges. *—v.* To handle roughly; bruise or tear. [< L *malleus,* hammer.] **—maul'er** *n.*

maun•der (môn'dər, män'-) *v.* **1.** To talk incoherently or aimlessly. **2.** To move or act aimlessly or vaguely.

Mau•pas•sant (mō-pȧ-säN'), **Guy de.** 1850–1893. French novelist and short-story writer.

Mau•ri•ta•ni•a (môr'ə-tā'nē-ə). A republic of NW Africa. Pop. 900,000. Cap. Nouakchott. **—Mau'ri•ta'ni•an** *adj.* & *n.*

Mau•ri•ti•us (mô-rĭsh'ē-əs, -rĭsh'əs). An island nation in the Indian Ocean, formerly a British crown colony. Pop. 734,000. Cap. Port Louis. **—Mau•ri'ti•an** (-rĭsh'ən) *adj.* & *n.*

mau•so•le•um (mô'sə-lē'əm, mô'zə-) *n., pl.* **-leums** or **-lea** (-lē'ə). A large and stately tomb. [L *mausōlēum.*]

mauve (mōv) *n.* Moderate purple or pale violet. [F *mauve,* "mallow(-colored)."]

mav•er•ick (măv'ər-ĭk, măv'rĭk) *n.* **1.** An unbranded or orphaned range animal, esp. a calf. **2. a.** A nonconformist. **b.** An independent, as in politics. [< S.A. *Maverick* (1803–1870), Texas cattleman.]

maw (mô) *n.* **1.** The stomach, mouth, or gullet of a voracious animal. **2.** An opening that gapes. [< OE *maga.*]

mawk•ish (mô'kĭsh) *adj.* Excessively and objectionably sentimental. **—mawk'ish•ly** *adv.*

max. maximum.

max•il•la (măk-sĭl'ə) *n., pl.* **-lae** (-sĭl'ē) or **-las.** One of a pair of bones forming the upper jaw. [L, "lower jaw."] **—max'il•lar** (măk'sə-lər, măk-sĭl'ər), **max'il•lar'y** (-sə-lĕr'ē) *adj.*

max•im (măk'sĭm) *n.* A succinct formulation of some fundamental principle or rule of conduct. [< ML *(prōpositiō) maxima,* "greatest proposition."]

max•i•mal (măk'sə-məl) *adj.* Of or designating a maximum. **—max'i•mal•ly** *adv.*

max•i•mum (măk'sə-məm) *n., pl.* **-mums** or **-ma** (-mə). **1. a.** The greatest possible quantity, degree, or number. **b.** The period during which the highest point or degree is attained. **2.** An upper limit stipulated by law or other authority. *—adj.* Having or being the greatest quantity or highest degree that has been or can be attained. [L, "greatest (quantity)."]

may¹ (mā) *v. p.t.* **might.** —Used as an auxiliary to indicate: **1.** A requesting or granting of permission: *May I take a swim? You may.* **2.** Possibility: *It may rain.* **3.** Ability or capacity, with the force of *can: If I may be of service.* **4.** Obligation or function, with the force of *must* or *shall: "Congress may determine the time of choosing the electors."* (Constitution). **5.** Desire or fervent wish: *Long may he live!* **6.** Contingency, purpose, or result: *so that the average man may understand.* [< OE *magan,* to be able. See **magh-.**]

may² (mā) *n. Brit.* The blossoms of the hawthorn. [< MAY.]

May (mā) *n.* The 5th month of the year. May has 31 days. [< L *Maius (mēnsis),* (the month) of *Maia,* Italic goddess.]

Ma•ya (mä'yə) *n., pl.* **-ya** or **-yas.** **1.** A member of a race of Indians in S Mexico and Central America. **2.** Their language. **—Ma'ya** *adj.*

Ma•yan (mä'yən) *adj.* Of or pertaining to the Maya. *—n.* **1.** A Maya. **2.** A family of Central American languages, including the language of the Maya.

May apple. A North American plant with poisonous seeds and foliage, a single white flower, and yellowish fruit.

may•be (mā'bē) *adv.* Perhaps; possibly.

May Day. **1.** May 1, marked by the celebration of spring. **2.** May 1, regarded in a number of places as an international holiday to celebrate labor organizations.

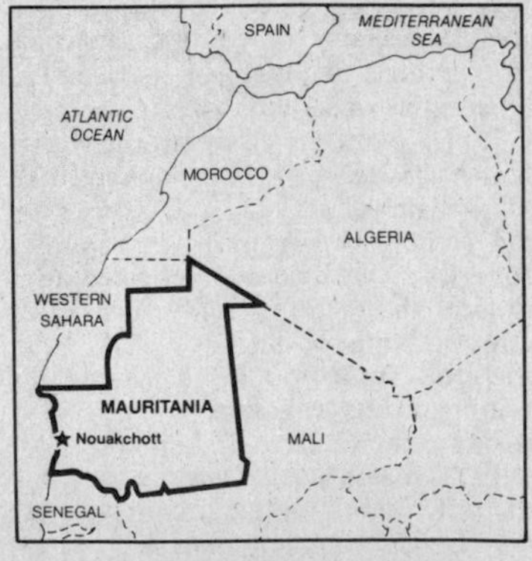

Mauritania

may•flow•er (mā'flou'ər) *n.* A spring-blooming flower, esp. the arbutus.

may•hem (mā'hĕm', mā'əm) *n. Law.* The offense of willfully maiming or crippling a person. [< OF *mahaignier,* maim.]

may•n't (mā'ənt, mānt). Contraction of *may not.*

may•on•naise (mā'ə-nāz') *n.* A dressing of beaten raw egg yolk, oil, and lemon juice or vinegar. [F.]

may•or (mā'ər, mâr) *n.* The chief magistrate of a city or borough. [< L *mājor,* "greater."] **—may'or•al** *adj.* **—may'or•al•ty** *n.*

May•pole (mā'pōl') *n.* Also **may•pole.** A pole decorated with streamers that May Day celebrators hold while dancing.

maze (māz) *n.* **1.** An intricate, usually confusing, network of walled or hedged pathways; a labyrinth. **2.** Anything resembling or likened to such a network, as a puzzle. [< OE *ā-masian.*] **—maz'y** *adj.*

ma•zur•ka (mə-zûr'kə, -zo͞or'kə) *n.* **1.** A lively Polish dance. **2.** Music for such a dance. [F.]

Mba•bane (əm-bä-bän'). The capital of Swaziland. Pop. 8,400.

MC **1.** Marine Corps. **2.** Medical Corps. **3.** Member of Congress.

m.c. master of ceremonies.

M.C. **1.** Master of Ceremonies. **2.** Member of Congress.

Mc•Kin•ley (mə-kĭn'lē), **William.** 1843–1901. 25th President of the U.S. (1897–1901).

William McKinley

Md mendelevium.

Md. Maryland.

M.D. Doctor of Medicine (L *Medicinae Doctor*).

mdse. merchandise.

me (mē) *pron.* The objective case of the 1st person pronoun *I,* used as the direct or indirect object of a verb or as the object of a preposition. [< OE *mē, me.* See **me-.**]

Usage: I, rather than *me,* is the grammatically prescribed 1st person pronoun for use after the verb *be: It is I.* But *it is me* (or *it's me*) is acceptable in informal writing and in speech on all levels as a more natural variant.

ME Middle English.

Me. Maine (unofficial).

M.E. **1.** mechanical engineer. **2.** Middle English. **3.** mining engineer.

mead¹ (mēd) *n.* An alcoholic beverage made from fermented honey and water. [< OE *medu, meodu.* See **medhu-.**]

mead² (mēd) *n. Archaic.* A meadow. [< OE *mæd.*]

mead•ow (mĕd'ō) *n.* A tract of grassland, as one used for pasture or growing hay. [< OE *mæd,* MEAD².]

mea•ger (mē'gər) *adj.* Also **mea•gre. 1.** Having little flesh; thin; lean. **2.** Conspicuously deficient in quantity. **3.** Deficient in richness or fertility. [< L *macer,* thin.] **—mea'ger•ly** *adv.* **—mea'ger•ness** *n.*

meal¹ (mēl) *n.* **1.** Coarsely ground edible grain. **2.** A similar granular substance. [< OE *melu,* flour. See **melə-**.] **—meal'y** *adj.*

meal² (mēl) *n.* The food served and eaten in one sitting. [< OE *mǣl,* fixed time, mealtime. See **mē-²**.]

meal•time (mēl'tīm') *n.* The usual time for eating a meal.

meal•y-mouthed (mē'lē-mou*th*d', -moutht') *adj.* Unwilling to speak simply and directly.

mean¹ (mēn) *v.* **meant, meaning. 1. a.** To be defined as; denote. **b.** To act as a symbol of; represent. **2.** To intend to convey or indicate: *What do you mean by that look?* **3.** To have as a purpose or intention. **4.** To have as a consequence: *Friction means heat.* **5.** To be of a specified importance; matter: *Advice meant little to him.* [< OE *mǣnan,* to intend, tell, signify. See **mei-no-**.]

mean² (mēn) *adj.* **1.** Low in quality or grade. **2.** Low in social status. **3.** Ignoble; base; petty. **4.** Low in value or amount. **5.** Miserly. **6.** Lacking elevating human qualities, as kindness and good will. **7.** *Informal.* Ill-tempered. **8.** *Slang.* Hard to cope with. [< OE *gemǣne,* "common."] **—mean'ly** *adv.* **—mean'ness** *n.*

mean³ (mēn) *n.* **1.** The middle point or state between two extremes. **2.** Moderation. **3.** *Math.* **a.** A number that represents a set of numbers in a way determined by a rule involving all members of the set; average. **b.** The **arithmetic mean. 4. means.** A course of action or instrument by which some act can be accomplished or some end achieved. **5. means.** Money, property, or other wealth. **—by all means.** Without fail; certainly. *—adj.* Occupying a middle or intermediate position, esp. one between two extremes. [< L *mediānus,* median.]

me•an•der (mē-ăn'dər) *v.* **1.** To follow a winding course. **2.** To wander aimlessly and idly. [< Gk *Maiandros,* a river in Phrygia noted for its windings.] **—me•an'der•er** *n.*

mean•ing (mē'nĭng) *n.* **1.** That which is signified by something; sense; import. **2.** That which one wishes to convey. **3.** Functional value; efficacy; significance. **—mean'ing•ful** *adj.* **—mean'ing•less** *adj.*

meant (mĕnt). *p.t.* & *p.p.* of **mean.**

mean•time (mēn'tīm') *n.* The time between one occurrence and another. *—adv.* Meanwhile.

mean•while (mēn'hwīl') *n.* The intervening time. *—adv.* In the intervening time.

meas. measurable; measure.

mea•sles (mē'zəlz) *n.* *(takes sing. v.).* **1.** An acute, contagious viral disease, usually involving the eruption of red spots. **2. German measles.** [< MDu *māsel,* blemish.]

mea•sly (mēz'lē) *adj.* **-slier, -sliest.** *Slang.* Contemptibly small.

meas•ure (mĕzh'ər) *n.* **1.** The dimensions, quantity, or capacity of anything as ascertained by measuring. See tables of measurement on following pages. **2.** A reference standard or sample used for the quantitative comparison of properties. **3.** A unit specified by a scale, as an inch, or by variable conditions, as a day's march. **4.** A device, such as

Measurement Units

Length

U.S. Customary Unit	U.S. Equivalents	Metric Equivalents
inch	0.083 foot	2.54 centimeters
foot	⅓ yard, 12 inches	0.3048 meter
yard	3 feet, 36 inches	0.9144 meter
rod	5½ yards, 16½ feet	5.0292 meters
mile (statute, land)	1,760 yards, 5,280 feet	1.609 kilometers
mile (nautical, international)	1.151 statute miles	1.852 kilometers

Area

U.S. Customary Unit	U.S. Equivalents	Metric Equivalents
square inch	0.007 square foot	6.4516 square centimeters
square foot	144 square inches	929.030 square centimeters
square yard	1,296 square inches, 9 square feet	0.836 square meter
acre	43,560 square feet, 4,840 square yards	4,047 square meters
square mile	640 acres	2.590 square kilometers

Volume or Capacity

U.S. Customary Unit	U.S. Equivalents	Metric Equivalents
cubic inch	0.00058 cubic foot	16.387 cubic centimeters
cubic foot	1,728 cubic inches	0.028 cubic meter
cubic yard	27 cubic feet	0.765 cubic meter

U.S. Customary Liquid Measure	U.S. Equivalents	Metric Equivalents
fluid ounce	8 fluid drams, 1.804 cubic inches	29.573 milliliters
pint	16 fluid ounces, 28.875 cubic inches	0.473 liter
quart	2 pints, 57.75 cubic inches	0.946 liter
gallon	4 quarts, 231 cubic inches	3.785 liters
barrel	varies from 31 to 42 gallons, established by law or usage	

U.S. Customary Dry Measure	U.S. Equivalents	Metric Equivalents
pint	½ quart, 33.6 cubic inches	0.551 liter
quart	2 pints, 67.2 cubic inches	1.101 liters
peck	8 quarts, 537.605 cubic inches	8.810 liters
bushel	4 pecks, 2,150.42 cubic inches	35.238 liters

British Imperial Liquid and Dry Measure	U.S. Customary Equivalents	Metric Equivalents
fluid ounce	0.961 U.S. fluid ounce, 1.734 cubic inches	28.412 milliliters
pint	1.032 U.S. dry pints, 1.201 U.S. liquid pints, 34.678 cubic inches	568.26 milliliters
quart	1.032 U.S. dry quarts, 1.201 U.S. liquid quarts, 69.354 cubic inches	1.136 liters
gallon	1.201 U.S. gallons, 277.420 cubic inches	4.546 liters
peck	554.84 cubic inches	0.009 cubic meter
bushel	1.032 U.S. bushels, 2,219.36 cubic inches	0.036 cubic meter

Weight

U.S. Customary Unit (Avoirdupois)	U.S. Equivalents	Metric Equivalents
grain	0.036 dram, 0.002285 ounce	64.79891 milligrams
dram	27.344 grains, 0.0625 ounce	1.772 grams
ounce	16 drams, 437.5 grains	28.350 grams
pound	16 ounces, 7,000 grains	453.59237 grams
ton (short)	2,000 pounds	0.907 metric ton (1,000 kilograms)
ton (long)	1.12 short tons, 2,240 pounds	1.016 metric tons

Apothecary Weight Unit	U.S. Customary Equivalents	Metric Equivalents
scruple	20 grains	1.296 grams
dram	60 grains	3.888 grams
ounce	480 grains, 1.097 avoirdupois ounces	31.103 grams
pound	5,760 grains, 0.823 avoirdupois pound	373.242 grams

a marked tape, used for measuring. **5.** An act of measuring. **6.** A criterion. **7.** Extent or degree. **8.** A limited amount or degree. **9.** An action taken as a means to an end. **10.** A legislative bill or enactment. **11.** Poetic meter. **12.** *Mus.* The metrical unit between two bars on the staff; a bar. **—for good measure.** In addition to the required amount. *—v.* **-ured, -uring. 1.** To ascertain or mark off the dimensions, quantity, or capacity of. **2.** To have a specified measure. **3.** To bring into opposition: *measured her power with that of her rival.* **4.** To choose with care; weigh: *measured his words.* [< L *mēnsūra.*] **—meas'ur•a•ble** *adj.* **—meas'ure•ment** *n.* **—meas'ur•er** *n.*

meat (mēt) *n.* **1.** The edible flesh of animals, esp. mammals, as distinguished from fish or poultry. **2.** The edible portion of fruits, nuts, etc. **3.** The essence or principal part of something. **4.** *Slang.* Something one enjoys or excels in. [< OE *mete,* food. See **mad-**.] **—meat'i•ness** *n.* **—meat'y** *adj.*

Mec•ca (mĕk'ə). A capital of Saudi Arabia and holy city of Islam. Pop. 200,000.

mec•ca (mĕk'ə) *n.* Often **Mecca.** A place regarded as the center of an activity or interest; a goal to which adherents of a faith or practice aspire.

mech. mechanical; mechanics.

me•chan•ic (mĭ-kăn'ĭk) *n.* A worker skilled in making, using, or repairing machines and tools.

me•chan•i•cal (mĭ-kăn'ĭ-kəl) *adj.* **1.** Of or pertaining to machines or tools. **2.** Operated or produced by a machine. **3.** Acting or performing like a machine. **4.** Of or dominated by physical forces. [< Gk *mēkhanē,* contrivance, machine.] **—me•chan'i•cal•ly** *adv.*

mechanical advantage. The ratio of the output force of a machine to the input force.

mechanical engineering. The branch of engineering that encompasses the production of mechanical power and the design, production, and use of machines and tools. **—mechanical engineer.**

me•chan•ics (mĭ-kăn'ĭks) *n.* *(takes sing. v.).* **1.** The analysis of the action of forces on matter or material systems. **2.** The design, construction, operation, and application of machinery or mechanical structures.

mech•a•nism (mĕk'ə-nĭz'əm) *n.* **1. a.** A machine. **b.** The arrangement of connected parts in a machine. **2.** Any system of parts that interact like those of a machine. **3.** An instrument or process by which something is done or comes into being.

mech•a•nis•tic (měk'ə-nĭs'tĭk) *adj.* Pertaining to mechanics as a branch of physics. —**mech'-a•nis'ti•cal•ly** *adv.*

mech•a•nize (měk'ə-nīz') *v.* **-nized, -nizing. 1.** To equip with machinery or mechanical devices. **2.** To make automatic or mechanical. —**mech'a•ni•za'tion** *n.*

med. 1. medical; medicine. **2.** medieval. **3.** medium.

med•al (měd'l) *n.* **1.** A piece of metal stamped with a design or inscription commemorating an event or person, often given as an award. **2.** A piece of metal stamped with a religious device. [< L *metallum,* metal.]

me•dal•lion (mə-dăl'yən) *n.* **1.** A large medal. **2.** Something resembling a large medal, such as a decorative design.

med•dle (měd'l) *v.* **-dled, -dling.** To intrude in other people's affairs; interfere. [< L *miscēre,* to mix.] —**med'dler** *n.*

me•di•a. Alternate *pl.* of **medium.**

me•di•al (mē'dē-əl) *adj.* Situated in or extending toward the middle; median. [< L *medius,* middle.]

me•di•an (mē'dē-ən) *adj.* **1.** Of, at, or toward the middle; medial. **2.** Of or lying in the plane that divides a symmetrical organism into right and left halves. **3.** *Stat.* Relating to the middle value in a distribution. —*n.* **1.** A median point, plane, line, or part. **2.** *Stat.* The middle value in a distribution, above and below which lie an equal number of values. **3.** A line that joins a vertex of a triangle to the midpoint of the opposite side. [< L *medius,* middle.]

me•di•ate (mē'dē-āt') *v.* **-ated, -ating.** To act as an intermediary, esp. to seek to resolve (differences) between two or more conflicting parties. [L *mediāre,* to be in the middle.] —**me'di•a'tion** *n.* —**me'di•a'tor** *n.*

med•ic (měd'ĭk) *n. Informal.* **1.** A physician or surgeon. **2.** A military medical corpsman. [L *medicus,* doctor.]

Med•i•caid (měd'ĭ-kād') *n.* Also **med•i•caid.** A program, jointly funded by the states and the federal government, that provides medical aid for people who fall below a certain income level. [MEDIC(AL) + AID.]

med•i•cal (měd'ĭ-kəl) *adj.* **1.** Of or pertaining to the study or practice of medicine. **2.** Requiring medical as distinct from surgical treatment. [< L *medicus,* doctor.]

me•dic•a•ment (mĭ-dĭk'ə-mənt, měd'ĭ-kə-mənt) *n.* An agent that promotes recovery from injury or ailment; medicine.

Med•i•care (měd'ə-kâr') *n.* Also **med•i•care.** A government program that provides medical care for the aged.

med•i•cate (měd'ə-kāt') *v.* **-cated, -cating. 1.** To treat medicinally. **2.** To tincture or permeate with a medicinal substance. —**med'i•ca'tive** *adj.*

med•i•ca•tion (měd'ə-kā'shən) *n.* **1.** A medicine. **2.** The act or process of being medicated. **3.** The administration of medicine.

me•dic•i•nal (mə-dĭs'ə-nəl) *adj.* Pertaining to or having the properties of medicine; healing; curative. —**me•dic'i•nal•ly** *adv.*

med•i•cine (měd'ə-sən) *n.* **1. a.** The science of diagnosing, treating, or preventing disease. **b.** The branch of this science encompassing treatment by drugs, diet, exercise, and other nonsurgical means. **2.** Any drug or other agent used to treat disease or injury. [< L *medicīna,* the art of a physician.]

medicine man. One believed among preliterate peoples to possess supernatural powers for healing and invoking spirits.

med•i•co (měd'ĭ-kō') *n., pl.* **-cos.** *Informal.* A doctor or medical student. [< L *medicus,* doctor.]

me•di•e•val (mē'dē-ē'vəl, měd'ē'vəl) *adj.* Also **me•di•ae•val.** Pertaining or belonging to the Middle Ages. [< NL *Medium Aevum,* the Middle Age.] —**me'di•e'val•ly** *adv.*

Medieval Greek. Greek from about A.D. 700 to 1500.

Medieval Latin. Latin as used throughout Europe from about A.D. 700 to 1500.

Me•di•na (mə-dē'nə). A city of NW Saudi Arabia; a sacred center of Islam. Pop. 30,000.

me•di•o•cre (mē'dē-ō'kər) *adj.* Of medium and unimpressive quality. [< L *mediocris,* "halfway up the mountain," in a middle state.] —**me'di•oc'ri•ty** (-ŏk'rə-tē) *n.*

med•i•tate (měd'ə-tāt') *v.* **-tated, -tating. 1.** To reflect upon; contemplate. **2.** To intend. **3.** To engage in contemplation. [L *meditārī.*] —**med'i•ta'tion** *n.* —**med'i•ta'tive** *adj.*

Med•i•ter•ra•ne•an (měd'ə-tə-rā'nē-ən, -rān'-yən) *adj.* **1.** Of, pertaining to, or characteristic of the Mediterranean Sea or the areas that border on it. **2.** Designating languages spoken in the Mediterranean region before the coming of the Indo-Europeans. —*n.* **1.** The Mediterranean Sea. **2.** The Mediterranean languages.

Mediterranean Sea. The world's largest inland sea, bounded by Africa in the S, Asia in the E, and Europe in the N and W.

me•di•um (mē'dē-əm) *n., pl.* **-dia** (-dē-ə) or **-ums. 1.** Something occupying a position or having a condition midway between extremes. **2.** An intervening substance through which something is transmitted or carried on. **3.** An agency by means of which something is accomplished, conveyed, or transferred. **4.** A means of mass communication. **5.** *pl.* **-ums** *only.* One thought to have powers of communicating with the spirits of the dead. **6.** An environment in which something functions and thrives. **7.** A means of expression as determined by the materials or creative methods involved. —*adj.* Intermediate in degree, amount, quantity, or quality. [< L *medius,* middle.]

med•ley (měd'lē) *n., pl.* **-leys. 1.** A jumbled assortment; mixture. **2.** A musical arrangement made from various melodies. [< OF *meslee.*]

me•dul•la (mə-dŭl'ə) *n., pl.* **-las** or **-lae** (-ē). **1.** *Anat.* The inner core of certain vertebrate body structures, such as the marrow of bone. **2.** The **medulla oblongata.** [L, marrow.] —**me•dul'lar** (mə-dŭl'ər), **med'ul•lar'y** (měd'ə-lĕr'ē, mə-dŭl'ə-rē) *adj.*

medulla ob•lon•ga•ta (ŏb'lông-gä'tə) *pl.* **medulla oblongatas** or **medullae oblongatae** (-gä'tē). The nervous tissue at the bottom of the brain that controls respiration, circulation, and certain other bodily functions.

meed (mēd) *n. Archaic.* A merited gift or reward. [< OE *mēd.*]

meek (mēk) *adj.* **1.** Humble and patient. **2.** Submissive. [< ON *mjūkr,* soft.] —**meek'ly** *adv.* —**meek'ness** *n.*

meer•schaum (mîr'shəm, -shôm) *n.* A tough, compact, usually white mineral, $H_4Mg_2Si_3O_{10}$, used in fashioning tobacco pipes and as a building stone. [G, "sea-foam."]

meet[1] (mēt) *v.* **met, meeting. 1.** To come upon. **2.** To be present at the arrival of: *meet a train.* **3.** To be introduced (to). **4.** To come into conjunction (with); join: *where sea meets sky.* **5.** To come into the company of, as for a conference. **6.** To come to the notice of (the senses): *more than meets the eye.* **7.** To cope or contend effectively with. **8.** To satisfy (a demand, need, etc.). **9.** To come together: *Let's meet tonight.* —*n.* A meeting or contest. [< OE *mētan.* See **mōd-.**]

meet[2] (mēt) *adj. Archaic.* Fitting; proper. [< OE *gemǣte.*] —**meet'ly** *adv.*

meet•ing (mēt'ĭng) *n.* **1.** A coming together; assembly. **2.** A joining. **3.** A hostile encounter, as a duel.

mega-. *comb. form.* **1.** One million (10^6). **2.** Large. [< Gk *megas,* great.]

meg•a•cy•cle (mĕg'ə-sī'kəl) *n.* **1.** One million cycles. **2.** One million cycles per second.

megalo-. *comb. form.* Largeness or exaggerated size. [< Gk *megas,* great.]

meg•a•lo•ma•ni•a (mĕg'ə-lō-mā'nē-ə, -mān'-yə) *n.* A psychopathological condition marked by fantasies of self-grandeur and omnipotence. —**meg'a•lo•ma'ni•ac** *adj.* & *n.*

meg•a•lop•o•lis (mĕg'ə-lŏp'ə-lĭs) *n.* A region made up of several large cities and their surrounding areas.

meg•a•phone (mĕg'ə-fōn') *n.* A horn-shaped device used to project the voice.

meg•a•ton (mĕg'ə-tŭn') *n.* A unit of explosive force equal to one million tons of TNT.

me•gil•lah (mə-gĭl'ə) *n. Slang.* A prolix, tediously detailed or embroidered account. [Heb *məgillāh,* "scroll."]

me•grim (mē'grĭm) *n.* **1.** A migraine. **2.** Often **megrims.** A caprice. **3. megrims.** Depression. **4. megrims.** A disease of cattle and horses. [< OF *migraine,* migraine.]

mei•o•sis (mī-ō'sĭs) *n., pl.* **-ses** (-sēz'). The cell division in sexually reproducing organisms that reduces the number of chromosomes in reproductive cells. [< Gk *meiōsis,* diminution.]

Me•kong (mā'kŏng'). A river of SE Asia.

mel•an•cho•li•a (mĕl'ən-kō'lē-ə) *n.* A mental disorder characterized by feelings of dejection and usually by withdrawal.

mel•an•chol•ic (mĕl'ən-kŏl'ĭk) *adj.* **1.** Subject to melancholy. **2.** Of or afflicted with melancholia. —**mel'an•chol'i•cal•ly** *adv.*

mel•an•chol•y (mĕl'ən-kŏl'ē) *n.* **1.** Sadness; gloom. **2.** Pensive reflection. —*adj.* **1.** Sad; gloomy. **2.** Pensive; thoughtful. [< Gk *melankholia,* sadness, "(an excess of) black bile."] —**mel'an•chol'i•ness** *n.*

Mel•a•ne•sia (mĕl'ə-nē'zhə, -shə). An island group in the SW Pacific Ocean. —**Mel'a•ne'sian** *adj.*

mé•lange (mā-läNzh') *n.* Also **me•lange.** A mixture. [F.]

mel•a•nin (mĕl'ə-nĭn) *n.* A dark pigment found in the skin, retina, and hair. [< Gk *melas,* black.]

mel•a•no•ma (mĕl'ə-nō'mə) *n., pl.* **-mas** or **-mata** (-mə-tə). A dark-pigmented malignant tumor.

Mel•ba toast (mĕl'bə). Very thinly sliced crisp toast. [< Dame Nellie *Melba* (1861–1931), Australian soprano.]

Mel•bourne (mĕl'bərn). A city of SE Australia. Pop. 2,122,000.

meld[1] (mĕld) *v.* To declare or display (a card or combination of cards in a hand) for inclusion in one's score in a game such as pinochle. —*n.* A combination of cards to be declared for a score. [G *melden,* to declare.]

meld[2] (mĕld) *v.* To be or cause to become blended. [Blend of MELT + WELD.]

me•lee (mā'lā', mā-lā') *n.* Also **mê•lée** (mĕ-lā'). **1.** Hand-to-hand fighting. **2.** A brawl. **3.** A crowded tumult. [< OF *meslee,* MEDLEY.]

mel•io•rate (mēl'yə-rāt', mē'lē-ə-) *v.* **-rated, -rating.** To make or become better; improve. [< L *melior,* better.] —**mel'io•ra'tion** *n.*

mel•lif•lu•ous (mə-lĭf'lo͞o-əs) *adj.* **1.** Flowing with honey. **2.** Euphoniously smooth and sweet. [< L *mellifluus.*]

mel•low (mĕl'ō) *adj.* **1. a.** Soft, sweet, juicy, and full-flavored because of ripeness. **b.** Suggesting these qualities. **2.** Rich and soft in quality. **3.** Gently and maturely dignified. **4.** Relaxed and at ease. **5.** Slightly and pleasantly intoxicated. —*v.* To make or become mellow. [Perh < OE *melu,* meal, "soft and rich."] —**mel'low•ly** *adv.* —**mel'low•ness** *n.*

me•lo•de•on (mə-lō'dē-ən) *n.* A small reed organ.

me•lo•di•ous (mə-lō'dē-əs) *adj.* **1.** Tuneful. **2.** Agreeable to hear.

mel•o•dra•ma (mĕl'ə-drä'mə, -drăm'ə) *n.* **1.** A sentimental dramatic presentation characterized by heavy use of suspense and sensational episodes. **2.** Melodramatic behavior or occurrences. [F *mélodrame,* "musical drama."]

mel•o•dra•mat•ic (mĕl'ə-drə-măt'ĭk) *adj.* **1.** Having the excitement and emotional appeal of melodrama. **2.** Exaggeratedly emotional or sentimental; histrionic.

mel•o•dy (mĕl'ə-dē) *n., pl.* **-dies. 1.** A pleasing succession or arrangement of sounds. **2.** Musical quality. **3.** *Mus.* **a.** A sequence of single tones. **b.** The structure of music with respect to the succession of single tones. **c.** The leading part in a composition. [< Gk *melōidia,* choral song.] —**me•lod'ic** (mə-lŏd'ĭk) *adj.*

mel•on (mĕl'ən) *n.* Any of several fruits, as a cantaloupe or watermelon, having a hard rind and juicy flesh. [< Gk *mēlo(pepōn),* melon, "apple(-gourd)."]

melt (mĕlt) *v.* **1.** To change or be changed from a solid to a liquid state by the application of heat, pressure, or both. **2.** To dissolve. **3.** To disappear or cause to disappear gradually. **4.** To pass or merge imperceptibly into something else; blend or cause to blend gradually. **5.** To become softened in feeling; be made gentle. [< OE *meltan.* See **mel-**.]

melting point. The temperature at which a solid and its liquid are in equilibrium, at any fixed pressure.

Mel•ville (mĕl'vĭl), **Herman.** 1819–1891. American novelist.

mem (mĕm) *n.* The 13th letter of the Hebrew alphabet, representing *m.*

mem. 1. member. **2.** memoir. **3.** memorial.

mem•ber (mĕm'bər) *n.* **1.** A distinct part of a whole. **2.** A part or organ, as of the human body. **3.** One who belongs to a group or organization. **4.** One elected to a political body such as Congress. [< L *membrum.*]

mem•ber•ship (mĕm'bər-shĭp') *n.* **1.** The state of being a member. **2.** The total number of members in a group.

mem•brane (mĕm'brān') *n.* **1.** A thin, pliable layer of animal or plant tissue covering or separating structures or organs. **2.** A thin sheet of natural or synthetic material that is permeable to substances in solution. [L *membrāna,* "skin covering a member of the body."] —**mem'bra•nous** (-brə-nəs) *adj.*

me•men•to (mə-mĕn'tō) *n., pl.* **-tos** or **-toes.** Any reminder of the past; a souvenir. [< L *meminisse,* to remember.]

mem•o (mĕm'ō) *n., pl.* **-os.** A memorandum.

mem•oir (mĕm'wär', -wôr') *n.* **1. memoirs.** An autobiography; biography. **2.** A written reminder; memorandum. **3.** The report of the proceedings of a learned society. [< L *memoria,* MEMORY.]

mem•o•ra•bil•i•a (mĕm'ər-ə-bĭl'ē-ə, -bĭl'yə) *pl.n.* Things worthy of remembrance.

mem•o•ra•ble (mĕm'ər-ə-bəl) *adj.* Worth being remembered or noted; remarkable. [< L *memor,* mindful.] —**mem'o•ra•bly** *adv.*

mem•o•ran•dum (mĕm'ə-răn'dəm) *n., pl.* **-dums** or **-da** (-də). **1.** A short note written as a reminder. **2.** A written record or communication, as in a business office.

me•mo•ri•al (mə-môr'ē-əl, mə-mōr'-) *n.* **1.** An established remembrance of a person or event; monument. **2.** A written statement of facts or a petition. —*adj.* Commemorative. —**me•mo'ri•al•ize'** *v.* **(-ized, -izing).**

mem•o•rize (mĕm'ə-rīz') *v.* **-rized, -rizing.** To commit to memory; learn by heart. —**mem'o•ri•za'tion** (-rī-zā'shən) *n.* —**mem'o•riz'er** *n.*

mem•o•ry (mĕm'ər-ē) *n., pl.* **-ries. 1.** The faculty of retaining and recalling past experience; the ability to remember. **2.** A remembrance; recollection. **3.** All that a person can remember. **4.** Something remembered of a person, thing, or event. **5.** The period of time covered by remembrance or recollection. [< L *memoria.*]

Mem•phis (mĕm'fĭs). A city of SW Tennessee. Pop. 624,000.

men. *pl.* of **man.**

men•ace (mĕn'ĭs) *n.* **1.** A threat. **2.** A troublesome or annoying person. —*v.* **-aced, -acing.** To threaten. [< L *minacia,* menace, orig "threatening things."] —**men'ac•ing•ly** *adv.*

mé•nage (mā-näzh') *n.* Also **me•nage.** A household. [< VL **mansiōnāticum,* household.]

me•nag•er•ie (mə-năj'ə-rē, mə-năzh'-) *n.* A collection of live wild animals on exhibition. [F *ménagerie,* orig "the management of domestic animals."]

mend (mĕnd) *v.* **1.** To make right or correct; repair. **2.** To reform or improve. **3.** To improve in health or heal. **4.** To correct errors. —*n.* **1.** The act of mending. **2.** A mended place. [< ME *amenden,* to amend.]

men•da•cious (mĕn-dā'shəs) *adj.* **1.** Lying; untruthful. **2.** False; untrue. [< L *mendāx.*] —**men•dac'i•ty** (-dăs'ə-tē) *n.*

men•de•le•vi•um (mĕn'də-lē'vē-əm) *n. Symbol* **Md** A radioactive element with two isotopes, Md^{255} and Md^{256}. [< D. *Mendeleev* (1834–1907), Russian chemist.]

Men•dels•sohn (mĕn'dəl-sən), **Felix.** 1809–1847. German composer.

men•di•cant (mĕn'dĭ-kənt) *adj.* Depending upon alms for a living; practicing begging. —*n.* **1.** A beggar. **2.** A mendicant friar. [< L *mendīcāre,* to beg.]

me•ni•al (mē'nē-əl, mēn'yəl) *adj.* **1.** Pertaining to or appropriate for a servant. **2.** Of or pertaining to work regarded as servile. —*n.* A servant, esp. a domestic servant. [< VL **mansiōnāta,* household.] —**me'ni•al•ly** *adv.*

men•in•gi•tis (mĕn'ĭn-jī'tĭs) *n.* Inflammation of any or all of the meninges of the brain and spinal cord, usually caused by a bacterial infection. [< MENING(ES) + -ITIS.]

me•ninx (mē'nĭngks) *n., pl.* **meninges** (mə-nĭn'jēz). Any of the membranes enclosing the brain and spinal cord in vertebrates. [< Gk *mēninx,* membrane.] —**me•nin'ge•al** *adj.*

me•nis•cus (mə-nĭs'kəs) *n., pl.* **menisci** (-nĭs'ī') or **-cuses. 1.** A crescent-shaped body. **2.** The curved upper surface of a nonturbulent liquid in a container. [< Gk *mēniskos,* crescent.] —**me•nis'cal** (-kəl), **me•nis'coid'** (-koid'), **men'is•col'dal** (mĕn'ĭs-koid'l) *adj.*

Men•non•ite (mĕn'ən-īt') *n.* A member of an Evangelical Protestant Christian sect opposed to taking oaths, performing military service, etc. [< *Menno* Simons (1492–1559), religious reformer.]

men•o•pause (mĕn'ə-pôz') *n.* The period of cessation of menstruation, occurring usually between the ages of 45 and 50. [< Gk *mēn,* moon + PAUSE.] —**men'o•paus'al** *adj.*

men•ses (mĕn'sēz) *pl.n.* Blood and dead cell debris discharged from the uterus through the vagina by adult women at approximately monthly intervals between puberty and menopause. [L *mēnsēs,* months.]

men•stru•al (mĕn'stro͞o-əl) *adj.* Relating to menstruation. [< L *mēnstruus,* menstrual, monthly.]

men•stru•ate (mĕn'stro͞o-āt') *v.* **-ated, -ating.** To undergo menstruation.

men•stru•a•tion (mĕn'stro͞o-ā'shən) *n.* The process or an instance of discharging the menses.

men•su•ra•ble (mĕn'sər-ə-bəl, mĕn'shər-ə-) *adj.* Capable of being measured. [< L *mēnsūra,* measure.] —**men'su•ra•bil'i•ty** *n.*

men•su•ra•tion (mĕn'sə-rā'shən, mĕn'shə-) *n.* The process, act, or art of measuring. —**men'su•ral** *adj.* —**men'su•ra'tive** *adj.*

-ment. *comb. form.* Product, means, action, or state: **measurement.** [< L *-mentum.*]

men•tal (mĕn'təl) *adj.* **1.** Pertaining to the mind; intellectual. **2.** Done or performed by the mind. [< L *mēns (ment-),* mind.] —**men'tal•ly** *adv.*

mental deficiency. Subnormal intellectual development.

men•tal•i•ty (mĕn-tăl'ə-tē) *n., pl.* **-ties. 1.** Intellectual capability or endowment; intelligence. **2.** Mental status or inclination.

mental retardation. Mental deficiency.

men•thol (mĕn'thôl') *n.* A white, crystalline organic compound, $C_{10}H_{19}OH$, used in perfumes, as a mild anesthetic, and as a flavoring. [< L *mentha,* MINT² + -OL.] —**men'tho•lat'ed** *adj.*

men•tion (mĕn'shən) *v.* To cite or refer to incidentally. —*n.* An act of mentioning. [< L *mentiō,* remembrance, mention.]

men•tor (mĕn'tôr', -tər) *n.* A wise and trusted counselor or teacher. [< *Mentor,* a character in Fénelon's *Télémaque* (1699).]

men•u (mĕn'yo͞o, mān'yo͞o) *n.* A list of dishes to be served or available for a meal; bill of fare. [F, menu, list.]

me•ow (mē-ou'). Also **mi•aow, mi•aou.** *n.* The cry of a cat. [Imit.] —**me•ow'** *v.*

mep, m.e.p. mean effective pressure.

me•phi•tis (mə-fī'tĭs) *n.* **1.** An offensive smell; stench. **2.** A poisonous or foul-smelling gas emitted from the earth. [L *mefitis,* stench.] —**me•phit'ic** (-fĭt'ĭk), **me•phit'i•cal** *adj.*

meq. milliequivalent.

mer•can•tile (mûr'kən-tēl', -tīl', -tĭl) *adj.* Of or pertaining to merchants or trade. [< VL **mercātāns,* merchant.]

Mer•ca•tor projection (mər-kā'tər). Also **Mer•ca•tor's projection.** A map projection in which the meridians and parallels appear as straight lines crossing at right angles and areas appear greater farther from the equator. [< G. *Mercator* (1512–1594), Flemish cartographer.]

mer•ce•nar•y (mûr'sə-nĕr'ē) *adj.* **1.** Motivated solely by a desire for monetary or material gain. **2.** Hired for service in a foreign army. [< L *mercēs,* pay.] —**mer'ce•nar'i•ly** *adv.* —**mer'ce•nar'i•ness** *n.* —**mer'ce•nar'y** *n.*

mer•cer (mûr'sər) *n. Brit.* A dealer in textiles, esp. silks. [< L *merx (merc-),* merchandise.]
mer•cer•ize (mûr'sə-rīz') *v.* **-ized, -izing.** To treat (cotton thread) with sodium hydroxide, so as to shrink the fiber and increase its color absorption and luster. [< J. *Mercer* (1791–1866), English textile maker.]
mer•chan•dise (mûr'chən-dīz', -dīs'). Also **mer•chan•dize.** *n.* The commodities of commerce; goods that can be bought or sold. —*v.* (mûr'chən-dīz') **-dised, -dising.** To buy and sell (commodities). —**mer'chan•dis'er** *n.*
mer•chant (mûr'chənt) *n.* **1.** One whose occupation is the wholesale purchase and retail sale of goods for profit. **2.** A shopkeeper. [< L *mercārī,* to trade.]
mer•chant•man (mûr'chənt-mən) *n.* A ship used in commerce.
merchant marine. 1. A nation's ships that are engaged in commerce. **2.** The personnel of such ships.
mer•cu•ri•al (mər-kyŏŏr'ē-əl) *n.* A medical or chemical preparation containing mercury. —*adj.* **1.** Containing or caused by the action of the element mercury. **2.** Quick and changeable in character. [< L *Mercurius,* the god Mercury.] —**mer•cu'ri•al•ly** *adv.*
mer•cu•ri•al•ism (mər-kyŏŏr'ē-əl-ĭz'əm) *n.* Poisoning caused by mercury or any of its compounds.
mer•cu•ric (mər-kyŏŏr'ĭk) *adj.* Of or containing bivalent mercury.
Mer•cu•ro•chrome (mər-kyŏŏr'ə-krōm') *n.* A trademark for an organic mercury compound used as an antiseptic.
mer•cu•ry (mûr'kyə-rē) *n.* **1.** *Symbol* **Hg** A silvery-white, poisonous metallic element, liquid at room temperature, used in thermometers, barometers, vapor lamps, and batteries and in the preparation of chemical pesticides. Atomic number 80, atomic weight 200.59. **2. Mercury.** The planet nearest the sun, having a sidereal period of revolution about the sun of 88.0 days at a mean distance of 36.2 million miles, a mean radius of approx. 1,500 miles, and a mass approx. 0.05 that of Earth. **3. Mercury.** Roman god of commerce and science, serving as messenger to the other gods. [ME *Mercurie,* god, planet, and metal.]
mer•cy (mûr'sē) *n., pl.* **-cies. 1.** Compassionate treatment of an offender, enemy, etc.; clemency. **2.** A disposition to be kind and forgiving. **3.** A fortunate occurrence. **4.** Alleviation of distress; relief. [< LL *mercēs,* reward, God's gratuitous compassion.] —**mer'ci•ful** *adj.* —**mer'ci•less** *adj.*
mercy killing. Euthanasia.
mere (mîr) *adj. superl.* **merest.** Being nothing more than what is specified. [L *merus,* clear, pure, unmixed.] —**mere'ly** *adv.*
mer•e•tri•cious (mĕr'ə-trĭsh'əs) *adj.* Attracting attention in a vulgar manner. [< L *meretrix,* a prostitute.] —**mer'e•tri'cious•ly** *adv.* —**mer'e•tri'cious•ness** *n.*
merge (mûrj) *v.* **merged, merging.** To blend together or cause to be absorbed so as to lose identity. [< L *mergere,* to dive, plunge.] —**mer'gence** *n.*
merg•er (mûr'jər) *n.* The union of two or more commercial interests or corporations.
me•rid•i•an (mə-rĭd'ē-ən) *n.* **1. a.** A great circle on the earth's surface passing through both geophysical poles. **b.** Either half of such a great circle lying between the poles. **2.** A great circle passing through the two poles of the celestial sphere and the observer's zenith. **3.** The highest point or stage of development; zenith. [< L *merīdiēs,* midday.] —**me•rid'i•an** *adj.*
me•ringue (mə-răng') *n.* A dessert topping made of beaten egg whites, sweetened and baked. [F *méringue.*]
me•ri•no (mə-rē'nō) *n., pl.* **-nos. 1.** A sheep of a breed having fine, soft wool. **2.** The wool of such a sheep or fabric made from it. [Span.] —**me•ri'no** *adj.*
mer•it (mĕr'ĭt) *n.* **1.** Value, excellence, or superior quality. **2.** Often **merits.** An aspect of a person's character deserving approval or disapproval. **3. a.** The intrinsic right or wrong of any matter. **b.** The actual facts of a legal matter. —*v.* To earn; deserve; warrant. [< L *merēre* (pp *meritus*), to earn, deserve.] —**mer'it•ed•ly** *adv.*
mer•i•to•ri•ous (mĕr'ə-tôr'ē-əs, -tōr'ē-əs) *adj.* Deserving reward or praise; having merit. —**mer'i•to'ri•ous•ly** *adv.*
Mer•lin (mûr'lən). Magician and prophet of Arthurian legend.
mer•maid (mûr'mād') *n.* A fabled creature of the sea with the head and upper body of a woman and the tail of a fish. [ME *meremaide,* "sea creature."]
mer•ri•ment (mĕr'ĭ-mənt) *n.* Gay conviviality; hilarity.
mer•ry (mĕr'ē) *adj.* **-rier, -riest. 1.** Full of high-spirited gaiety; jolly. **2.** Marked by fun and gaiety; festive. **3.** Pleasurable; entertaining. [< OE *mirige,* pleasant. See **mreghu-.**] —**mer'ri•ly** *adv.* —**mer'ri•ness** *n.*
mer•ry-go-round (mĕr'ē-gō-round') *n.* **1.** A circular revolving platform fitted with seats, often animal-shaped, ridden for amusement. **2.** Any whirl or swift round.
mer•ry•mak•ing (mĕr'ē-mā'kĭng) *n.* **1.** Participation in a revel. **2.** A festivity; revelry. —**mer'ry•mak'er** *n.*
Mer•thi•o•late (mər-thī'ə-lāt') *n.* A trademark for an organic mercury compound used as an antiseptic.
me•sa (mā'sə) *n.* A flat-topped elevation with clifflike sides, common in the SW U.S. [< L *mēnsa,* table.]
mes•ca•line (mĕs'kə-lēn') *n.* A psychedelic drug, $C_{11}H_{17}NO_3$. [< Nah *mexcalli.*]
Mes•dames. *pl.* of **Madame** and **Madam.**
mes•en•ter•y (mĕs'ən-tĕr'ē) *n., pl.* **-ies.** Also **mes•en•ter•i•um** (mĕs'ən-tîr'ē-əm) *pl.* **-ia** (-ē-ə). Any of several peritoneal folds that connect the intestines to the dorsal abdominal wall. [< Gk *mesenterion,* "middle intestine."] —**mes'en•ter'ic** *adj.*
mesh (mĕsh) *n.* **1.** Any of the open spaces in a cord, thread, or wire network. **2.** A net or network. **3.** The engagement of gear teeth. —*v.* **1.** To entangle or ensnare. **2.** To engage or become engaged, as gear teeth. **3.** To coordinate; harmonize. [< MDu *masche, maesche.*] —**mesh'y** *adj.*
mesh•work (mĕsh'wûrk') *n.* Meshes; network.
mes•mer•ize (mĕz'mə-rīz', mĕs'-) *v.* **-ized, -izing.** To hypnotize. —**mes'mer•ism'** *n.* —**mes'mer•iz'er** *n.*
meso–. *comb. form.* Middle, center, or intermediate. [< Gk *mesos,* middle.]
Mes•o•lith•ic (mĕz'ə-lĭth'ĭk, mĕs'-) *adj.* Pertaining to a period of human culture between the Paleolithic and Neolithic ages, marked by the appearance of the bow and of cutting tools. —*n.* The Mesolithic Age.
Mes•o•po•ta•mi•a (mĕs'ə-pə-tā'mē-ə). The ancient country between the Tigris and Euphrates rivers. —**Mes'o•po•ta'mi•an** *adj.* & *n.*

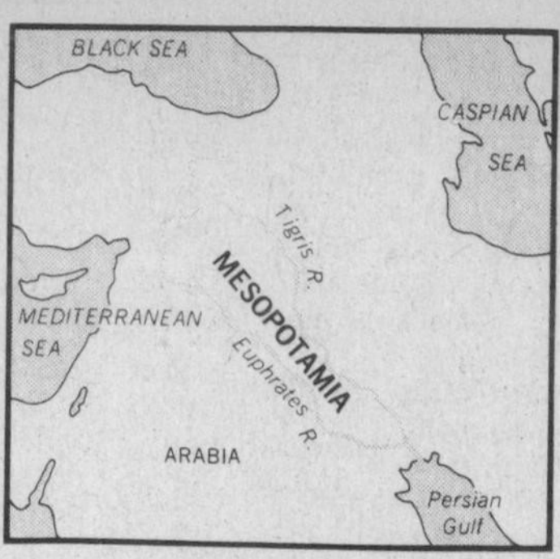

Mesopotamia

Mes•o•zo•ic (mĕz'ə-zō'ĭk, mĕs'-) *adj.* Of or belonging to the geologic time, rock systems, or deposits of the era between the Paleozoic and Cenozoic, and including the Cretaceous, Jurassic, and Triassic periods. —*n.* The Mesozoic era.
mes•quite (mĕs-kēt', mə-skēt') *n.* A thorny, pod-bearing shrub of SW North America. [< Nah *mizquitl.*]
mess (mĕs) *n.* **1.** A disorderly accumulation of items; jumble. **2.** A confusing state of affairs; muddle; chaos. **3.** A quantity of food: *a mess of fish.* **4. a.** A group of persons who regularly eat meals together. **b.** The meal eaten by such a group. —*v.* **1.** To make disorderly and soiled; clutter. **2.** To bungle or mismanage. **3.** To interfere; meddle. [< L *missus,* "placement," course of a meal.]
mes•sage (mĕs'ĭj) *n.* **1.** A communication transmitted from one person or group to another. **2.** The basic theme or significance of something. [< VL **missāticum,* "something sent."]
mes•sen•ger (mĕs'ən-jər) *n.* One who transmits messages or performs errands.
Mes•si•ah (mə-sī'ə) *n.* **1.** The anticipated deliverer and king of the Jews. **2.** Jesus Christ. **3. messiah.** Any expected deliverer or liberator. [Aram *məshīḥa* or Heb *māshiaḥ.*]
Messrs. *pl.* of **Mr.**
mess•y (mĕs'ē) *adj.* **-ier, -iest.** Untidy; dirty; disordered. —**mess'i•ly** *adv.* —**mess'i•ness** *n.*
mes•ti•zo (mĕs-tē'zō) *n., pl.* **-zos** or **-zoes.** A person of mixed European and Indian ancestry. [Span, "mixed."]
met (mĕt). *p.t.* & *p.p.* of **meet¹.**
met. 1. meteorology. **2.** metropolitan.
meta–. *comb. form.* **1.** *Anat.* Situated behind. **2.** Occurring later. **3.** Beyond; transcending. **4.** Changed or involving change. **5.** Alternating. **6.** *Geol.* Having undergone metamorphic change. [< Gk *meta,* between, with, beside, after.]
me•tab•o•lism (mə-tăb'ə-lĭz'əm) *n.* **1.** The complex of physical and chemical processes involved in the maintenance of life. **2.** The functioning of any specific substance within the living body: *water metabolism; iodine metabolism.* —**met'a•bol'ic** (mĕt'ə-bŏl'ĭk) *adj.* —**me•tab'o•lize'** *v.* (**-lized, -lizing**).
met•a•car•pus (mĕt'ə-kär'pəs) *n.* The part of the hand or forefoot that includes the five bones between the phalanges and carpus.
met•al (mĕt'l) *n.* **1.** Any of a category of electropositive elements that are usually whitish, lustrous, and often ductile and malleable with high tensile strength. **2.** An alloy of two or more metallic elements. **3.** An object made of metal. **4.** Basic character; mettle. [< Gk *met-*

allon, a mine, mineral, metal.] **—me•tal'lic** (mə-tăl'ĭk) *adj.* **—me•tal'li•cal•ly** *adv.*

metall. metallurgical; metallurgy.

met•al•lur•gy (mĕt'l-ûr'jē) *n.* The science or technology of extracting metals from their ores, of purifying metals, and of creating useful objects from metals. [< Gk *metallourgos,* a miner.] **—met'al•lur'gic, met'al•lur'gi•cal** *adj.* **—met'al•lur'gist** *n.*

met•a•mor•phic (mĕt'ə-môr'fĭk) *adj.* Also **met•a•mor•phous** (-môr'fəs). **1.** Of or relating to metamorphosis. **2.** Characteristic of, pertaining to, or changed by metamorphism.

met•a•mor•phism (mĕt'ə-môr'fĭz'əm) *n.* Any alteration in composition, texture, or structure of rock masses, caused by great heat or pressure.

met•a•mor•phose (mĕt'ə-môr'fōz', -fōs') *v.* **-phosed, -phosing.** To change or be changed by metamorphosis.

met•a•mor•pho•sis (mĕt'ə-môr'fə-sĭs) *n., pl.* **-ses** (-sēz'). **1.** A transformation, as by magic. **2.** A marked change in appearance, character, etc. **3.** Marked changes in form and mode of life during development to maturity, as in insects. [< Gk *metamorphōsis.*]

met•a•phase (mĕt'ə-fāz') *n.* The stage of mitosis during which the chromosomes are aligned along the equator of the mitotic spindle.

met•a•phor (mĕt'ə-fôr', -fər) *n.* A figure of speech in which a term is transferred from the object it ordinarily designates to one it can designate only by implicit comparison or analogy, as in the phrase *evening of life.* [< Gk *metaphora,* transference.] **—met'a•phor'ic** (-fôr'ĭk, -fŏr'ĭk), **met'a•phor'i•cal** *adj.*

met•a•phys•i•cal (mĕt'ə-fĭz'ĭ-kəl) *adj.* **1.** Of or pertaining to metaphysics. **2.** Based on speculative or abstract reasoning. **3.** Abstruse. **4.** Immaterial or imaginary.

met•a•phys•ics (mĕt'ə-fĭz'ĭks) *n. (takes sing. v.).* The systematic investigation of the nature of first principles and problems of ultimate reality. [ML *metaphysica.*] **met'a•phy•si'cian** (-fə-zish'ən) *n.*

me•tas•ta•sis (mə-tăs'tə-sĭs) *n., pl.* **-ses** (-sēz'). Transmission of disease from an original site to one or more sites elsewhere in the body, as in tuberculosis or cancer. [< LL, transition.] **—me•tas'ta•size'** *v.* **(-sized, -sizing).**

met•a•tar•sus (mĕt'ə-tăr'səs) *n., pl.* **-si** (-sī'). The middle part of the foot, composed of the five bones between the toes and tarsus, that forms the instep. **—met'a•tar'sal** *adj.* & *n.*

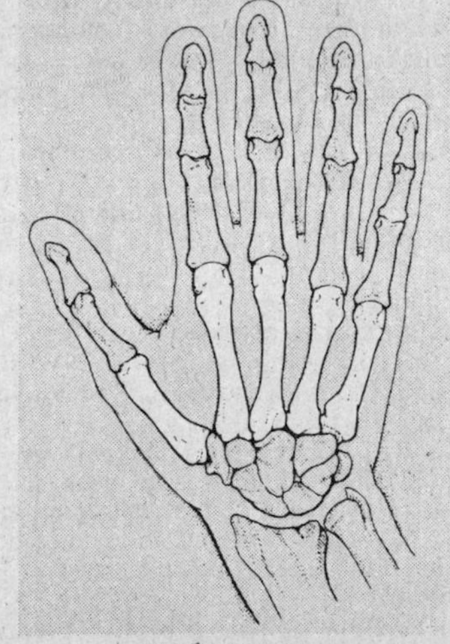

metacarpus

mete (mēt) *v.* **meted, meting.** To deal out; allot. [< OE *metan.* See **med-.**]

me•tem•psy•cho•sis (mə-tĕm'sĭ-kō'sĭs, mĕt'-əm-sī-kō'sĭs) *n., pl.* **-ses** (-sēz'). The transmigration of souls. [Gk *metempsukhōsis.*]

me•te•or (mē'tē-ər, -ôr') *n.* **1.** The luminous trail or streak that appears in the sky when a meteoroid is made incandescent by the earth's atmosphere. **2.** A meteoroid. [< Gk *meteōros,* high in the air.]

me•te•or•ic (mē'tē-ôr'ĭk, -ŏr'ĭk) *adj.* **1.** Of or formed by a meteor or meteors. **2.** Resembling a meteor in speed and brilliance.

me•te•or•ite (mē'tē-ə-rīt') *n.* The stony or metallic material of a meteoroid that survives passage through the atmosphere and reaches the earth's surface.

me•te•or•oid (mē'tē-ə-roid') *n.* Any of numerous celestial bodies, ranging in size from specks of dust to asteroids weighing thousands of tons, that appear as meteors when entering the earth's atmosphere.

meteorol. meteorology.

me•te•or•ol•o•gy (mē'tē-ə-rŏl'ə-jē) *n.* The science of the earth's atmosphere, esp. weather conditions. **—me'te•or'o•log'i•cal** (-ôr'ə-lŏj'ĭ-kəl, -ŏr'ə-lŏj'ĭ-kəl) *adj.* **—me'te•or•ol'o•gist** *n.*

me•ter[1] (mē'tər) *n.* Also *chiefly Brit.* **me•tre. 1.** The measured rhythm characteristic of verse. **2. a.** The division of music into measures or bars. **b.** A specific division of this kind. [< Gk *metron,* measure.]

me•ter[2] (mē'tər) *n.* Also *chiefly Brit.* **me•tre.** The fundamental metric unit of length, approx. 39.37 inches. [< Gk *metron,* meter, measure.]

me•ter[3] (mē'tər) *n.* Any of various devices designed to measure or indicate and record. —*v.* **1.** To measure with a meter. **2.** To imprint with postage by means of a postage meter or other similar device.

-meter. *comb. form.* A measuring device: **barometer.**

meth-. *comb. form.* Chemical compounds containing methyl.

meth•a•done hydrochloride (mĕth'ə-dōn'). An organic compound, $C_{21}H_{27}NO{\cdot}HCL$, used as an analgesic and in treating heroin addiction.

meth•ane (mĕth'ān') *n.* An odorless, colorless, flammable gas, CH_4, that is the major constituent of natural gas, used as a fuel and as a source of hydrogen and a wide variety of organic compounds.

meth•a•nol (mĕth'ə-nôl', -nōl') *n.* A colorless, flammable liquid, CH_3OH, used as an antifreeze, solvent, fuel, and denaturant for ethanol.

me•thinks (mĭ-thĭngks') *v. Archaic.* It seems to me.

meth•od (mĕth'əd) *n.* **1.** A systematic means or manner of procedure. **2.** Orderliness; regularity. [< Gk *methodos,* "a going after."] **—me•thod'i•cal** (mə-thŏd'ĭ-kəl) *adj.*

Meth•od•ist (mĕth'ə-dĭst) *n.* A Protestant Christian denomination developed from the doctrines of John Wesley concerning free grace and individual responsibility. **—Meth'od•ism'** *n.* **—Meth'od•ist** *adj.*

meth•od•ol•o•gy (mĕth'ə-dŏl'ə-jē) *n., pl.* **-gies. 1.** The system of principles and procedures applied in a science or discipline. **2.** The theoretical foundations of a given practical activity. **—meth'od•o•log'i•cal** (mĕth'ə-də-lŏj'ĭ-kəl) *adj.* **—meth'od•o•log'i•cal•ly** *adv.*

me•thu•se•lah (mə-thōō'zə-lə) *n.* An extremely old man. [< *Methuselah,* Biblical patriarch said to have lived 969 years. Genesis 5:27.]

meth•yl (mĕth'əl) *n.* The univalent organic radical CH_3. [< Gk *methu,* wine, mead.]

methyl alcohol. Methanol.

meth•yl•at•ed spirit (mĕth'ə-lā'tĭd). Often **methylated spirits.** A denatured alcohol consisting of a mixture of ethanol and methanol.

me•tic•u•lous (mə-tĭk'yə-ləs) *adj.* Extremely or excessively careful and precise; scrupulous. [L *meticulōsus,* overly concerned, fearful.] **—me•tic'u•los'i•ty** (mə-tĭk'yə-lŏs'ə-tē) *n.*

mé•tier (mā-tyā') *n.* **1.** An occupation, trade, or profession. **2.** One's specialty. [< VL **misterium.*]

me•tre. *Chiefly Brit.* Variant of **meter.**

met•ric (mĕt'rĭk) *adj.* Of or using the metric system.

met•ri•cal (mĕt'rĭ-kəl) *adj.* **1.** Pertaining to versification or measure in music or poetry. **2.** Composed in poetic meter. **3.** Pertaining to measurement. [< Gk *metron,* measure, meter.] **—met'ri•cal•ly** *adv.*

metric system. A decimal system of weights and measures based on the meter as a unit length and the kilogram as a unit mass. Derived units include the liter for liquid volume, the stere for solid volume, and the are for area.

metric ton. A unit of mass equal to 1,000 kilograms.

met•ri•fy (mĕt'rə-fī') *v.* **-fied, -fying.** To convert to or adopt the metric system. **—met'ri•ca'tion, met'ri•fi•ca'tion** *n.*

met•ro•nome (mĕt'rə-nōm') *n.* A device that marks time at a steady beat in adjustable intervals. [Gk *metron,* measure + *nomos,* rule, law.] **—met'ro•nom'ic** (mĕt'rə-nŏm'ĭk) *adj.*

me•trop•o•lis (mə-trŏp'ə-lĭs) *n., pl.* **-lises. 1.** A major city, esp. the capital of a country, state, or region. **2.** A large urban center of culture, trade, etc. [< Gk *mētropolis.*] **—met'ro•pol'i•tan** (mĕt'rə-pŏl'ə tən) *adj.*

-metry. *comb. form.* The science or process of measuring: **optometry.** [< Gk *metron,* meter, measure.]

met•tle (mĕt'l) *n.* **1.** Inherent quality of character and temperament. **2.** Courage and fortitude; spirit. [ME *metel,* fortitude, metal.]

met•tle•some (mĕt'l-səm) *adj.* Plucky.

mew[1] (myōō) *v.* To confine in or as if in a cage. [ME *mewe,* cage for molting hawks.]

mew[2] (myōō) *v.* To utter the high-pitched, crying sound of a cat. [ME *mewen* (imit).] **—mew** *n.*

mews (myōōz) *n. (takes sing. v.).* A small street containing private stables, now mostly converted into apartments. [< the *Mews* at Charing Cross, London.]

Mex. Mexican; Mexico.

Mex•i•co (mĕk'sĭ-kō'). A republic of SW North America. Pop. 39,643,000. Cap. Mexico City. **—Mex'i•can** (-kən) *adj.*

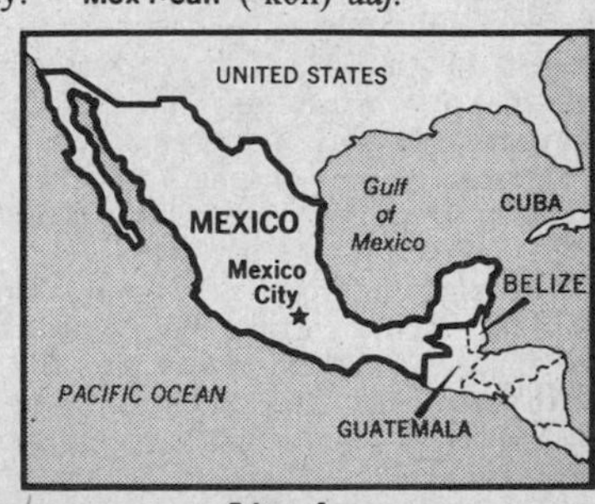

Mexico

Mexico, Gulf of. An inlet of the Atlantic Ocean, surrounded by the U.S., Mexico, and Cuba.

Mexico City. The capital of Mexico. Pop. 3,193,000.

mez•za•nine (mĕz'ə-nēn', mĕz'ə-nēn') *n.* **1.** A partial story between two main stories of a building. **2.** The lowest balcony in a theater or its first few rows. [< It *mezzano,* middle.]

mez•zo-so•pran•o (mĕt'sō-sə-prăn'ō, -prä'nō, mĕd'zō-, mĕz'ō-) *n., pl.* **-os.** Also **mez•zo.** **1.** The range between soprano and contralto. **2.** A woman having such a range.

mfg. manufacturing.

mfr. manufacture; manufacturer.

mg milligram.

Mg magnesium.

M.G. Major General.

mgr. manager.

MH Medal of Honor.

mi. mile.

Mi•am•i (mī-ăm'ē, -ăm'ə). A city of SE Florida. Pop. 335,000.

mi•aou, mi•aow. Variants of **meow.**

mi•as•ma (mī-ăz'mə, mē-) *n., pl.* **-mas** or **-mata** (-mə-tə). **1.** A poisonous atmosphere formerly thought to rise from swamps and cause disease. **2.** Any noxious atmosphere or influence. [< Gk *miainein,* to pollute.] **—mi•as'mal** (-məl), **mi'as•mat'ic** (mī'əz-măt'ĭk), **mi•as'mic** *adj.*

Mic. Micah (Old Testament).

mi•ca (mī'kə) *n.* Any of a group of chemically and physically related mineral silicates, common in igneous and metamorphic rocks. [< L *mica,* grain.]

mice. *pl.* of **mouse.**

Mich. Michigan.

Mi•chel•an•ge•lo (mī'kəl-ăn'jə-lō', mĭk'əl-). 1475–1564. Italian sculptor, painter, and architect.

Mich•i•gan (mĭsh'ĭ-gən). A state of the north-central U.S. Pop. 8,875,000. Cap. Lansing.

Michigan, Lake. The third largest of the Great Lakes.

mi•cra. Alternate *pl.* of **micron.**

micro–. *comb. form.* **1.** Small or smaller than. **2.** Invisible to the naked eye. **3.** *Symbol* μ One-millionth (10^{-6}). [< Gk *mikros,* small.]

mi•crobe (mī'krōb') *n.* A minute life form; a microorganism, esp. one that causes disease. **—mi•cro'bi•al** (mī-krō'bē-əl), **mi•cro'bic** *adj.*

mi•cro•cosm (mī'krə-kŏz'əm) *n.* A diminutive, representative world; a system analogous to a much larger system in constitution, configuration, or development. [< Gk *mikros kosmos,* small world.] **—mi'cro•cos'mic, mi'cro•cos'mi•cal** *adj.*

mi•cro•film (mī'krə-fĭlm') *n.* **1.** A film upon which documents are photographed greatly reduced in size. **2.** A reproduction on microfilm. **—mi'cro•film'** *v.*

Mi•cro•groove (mī'krō-gr o͞o v') *n.* A trademark for a long-playing phonograph record.

mi•crom•e•ter (mī-krŏm'ə-tər) *n.* Any of various devices for measuring minute distances.

mi•cron (mī'krŏn') *n., pl.* **-crons** or **-cra** (-krə). Also **mi•kron.** A unit of length equal to one-millionth (10^{-6}) of a meter. [< Gk *mikros,* small.]

Mi•cro•ne•sia (mī'krō-nē'zhə, -shə). The islands in the Pacific E of the Philippines and N of the equator. **—Mi'cro•ne'sian** *adj. & n.*

mi•cro•or•gan•ism (mī'krō-ôr'gən-ĭz'əm) *n.* An organism, as a bacterium or protozoan, of microscopic size.

mi•cro•phone (mī'krə-fōn') *n.* An instrument that converts acoustical waves into an electric current, usually fed into an amplifier, recorder, or broadcast transmitter.

mi•cro•scope (mī'krə-skōp') *n.* An instrument that uses a combination of lenses to produce magnified images of small objects, esp. of objects too small to be seen by the unaided eye.

mi•cro•scop•ic (mī'krə-skŏp'ĭk) *adj.* Also **mi•cro•scop•i•cal** (-ĭ-kəl). **1.** Invisible to the naked eye but large enough to be studied under a microscope. **2.** Exceedingly small; minute. **3.** Extremely detailed. **4.** Of or pertaining to a microscope. **—mi'cro•scop'i•cal•ly** *adv.*

mi•cro•wave (mī'krə-wāv') *n.* Any electromagnetic radiation having a wavelength in the approximate range from one millimeter to one meter, the region between infrared and shortwave radio wavelengths.

mid (mĭd) *adj.* Middle; central.

mid•air (mĭd'âr') *n.* A point or region in the middle of the air.

mid•day (mĭd'dā') *n.* The middle of the day; noon. **—mid'day'** *adj.*

mid•dle (mĭd'l) *adj.* **1.** Equally distant from extremes or limits; central; mean. **2.** Intermediate; in-between. **3.** Medium; moderate. *—n.* **1.** A middle area or point. **2.** The waist. [< OE *middel.* See **medhyo-.**]

middle age. The time of life between 40 and 60. **—mid'dle-aged'** *adj.*

Middle Ages. The period in European history between antiquity and the Renaissance, regarded as dating from A.D. 476 to 1453.

Middle America. **1.** Mexico and Central America. **2. a.** That part of the U.S. middle class thought of as being conservative in values and attitudes. **b.** The American heartland, thought of as being made up of small towns, small cities, and suburbs.

mid•dle•brow (mĭd'l-brou') *n. Informal.* A person of mediocre culture.

middle class. The members of society occupying an intermediate social and economic position. **—mid'dle-class'** *adj.*

Middle Dutch. Dutch from about 1150 to 1500.

middle ear. The tympanic membrane together with the malleus, incus, and stapes and the structure that encloses them.

Middle East. The area in Asia and Africa from Libya in the W to Pakistan in the E.

Middle English. English from about 1100 to 1500.

Middle High German. High German from about 1000 to 1500.

Middle Low German. Low German from about 1250 to 1500.

mid•dle•man (mĭd'l-măn') *n.* An intermediary or go-between, esp. one who buys from producers and sells to retailers or consumers.

mid•dle•weight (mĭd'l-wāt') *n.* A boxer or wrestler weighing between 147 and 160 pounds.

Middle West. A region of the U.S. from Ohio through Iowa and from the Ohio and Missouri rivers through the Great Lakes. **—Middle Western. —Middle Westerner.**

mid•dling (mĭd'lĭng, -lĭn) *adj.* Of medium size, quality, etc.; fair. *—adv.* Fairly; moderately.

mid•dy (mĭd'ē) *n., pl.* **-dies.** **1.** *Informal.* A midshipman. **2.** Also **middy blouse.** A woman's or child's loose blouse with a sailor collar.

midge (mĭj) *n.* A small, gnatlike fly. [< OE *mycg.*]

midg•et (mĭj'ĭt) *n.* **1.** An extremely small person. **2.** Something very small of its kind. [Dim of MIDGE.] **—midg'et** *adj.*

mid•night (mĭd'nīt') *n.* The middle of the night; specifically, twelve o'clock at night.

mid•point (mĭd'point') *n.* A point or position midway between two extremes.

mid•riff (mĭd'rĭf') *n.* **1.** The diaphragm. **2.** The outer part of the human body, extending from the chest to the waistline. [< MID + OE *hrif,* belly (see **krep-**).] **—mid'riff'** *adj.*

mid•ship•man (mĭd'shĭp'mən, mĭd-shĭp'mən) *n.* A student training to be commissioned as an officer in the U.S. Navy or Coast Guard.

mid•ships (mĭd'shĭps') *adv.* Amidships.

midst (mĭdst, mĭtst) *n.* **1.** The middle portion or part; center. •**2.** The condition of being surrounded by or enveloped in something. *—prep.* Among.

mid•sum•mer (mĭd'sŭm'ər) *n.* **1.** The middle of the summer. **2.** The summer solstice, about June 21.

mid•way (mĭd'wā') *n.* The area of a fair, carnival, etc., where side shows and other amusements are located. *—adv. & adj.* In the middle; halfway.

Mid•west (mĭd'wĕst') *n.* The **Middle West.** **—Mid'west', Mid'west'ern** (-wĕs'tərn) *adj.* **—Mid'west'ern•er** *n.*

mid•wife (mĭd'wīf') *n.* A woman who assists women in childbirth. [< OE *mid,* with + *wīf,* WIFE.] **—mid'wife'ry** (-wīf'rē, -wĭ'fə-rē) *n.*

mid•win•ter (mĭd'wĭn'tər) *n.* **1.** The middle of the winter. **2.** The winter solstice, about December 22.

mien (mēn) *n.* Manner; appearance; aspect.

miff (mĭf) *v.* To offend; upset.

might[1] (mīt) *n.* **1.** Great or supreme power. **2.** Great physical strength. [< OE *miht.* See **magh-.**]

might[2] (mīt). *p.t.* of **may**[1].

might•y (mī'tē) *adj.* **-ier, -iest.** **1.** Powerful. **2.** Great; pre-eminent. *—adv. Informal.* Very. **—might'i•ly** *adv.* **—might'i•ness** *n.*

mi•gnon•ette (mĭn'yən-ĕt') *n.* A plant cultivated for its small, fragrant greenish flowers. [< F *mignon,* dainty, small.]

mi•graine (mī'grān') *n.* Severe, recurrent headache, usually affecting only one side of the head. [< LL *hēmicrānia,* pain in half of the head.]

mi•grant (mī'grənt) *n.* **1.** One that migrates. **2.** One who travels from place to place in search of work. **—mi'grant** *adj.*

mi•grate (mī'grāt') *v.* **-grated, -grating.** **1.** To move from one country or region and settle in another. **2.** To move seasonally from one region to another. [L *migrāre.*] **—mi•gra'tion** *n.* **—mi'gra•to'ry** (-grə-tôr'ē, -tōr'ē) *adj.*

mi•ka•do (mĭ-kä'dō) *n., pl.* **-dos.** The emperor of Japan. [Jap, "exalted gate."]

mike (mīk) *n. Informal.* A microphone.

mi•kron. Variant of **micron.**

mil (mĭl) *n.* A unit of length equal to one-thousandth (10^{-3}) of an inch. [< L *mille,* thousand.]

mil. military.

mil•age. Variant of **mileage.**

Mi•lan (mĭ-lăn', -län'). A city of NW Italy. Pop. 1,666,000. **—Mil'an•ese'** (mĭl'ə-nēz', -nēs') *adj. & n.*

milch (mĭlch) *adj.* Giving milk: *a milch cow.*

mild (mīld) *adj.* **1.** Gentle or meek in disposition or behavior. **2.** Not extreme; moderate. **3.** Not sharp or strong in taste or odor. [< OE *milde.* See **mel-.**] **—mild'ly** *adv.* **—mild'ness** *n.*

mil•dew (mĭl'd/y/o͞o') *n.* A white or grayish coating formed by fungi on plant leaves, cloth, paper, etc. [< OE *mildēaw.*] —**mil'dew'** *v.*

mile (mīl) *n.* **1.** A unit of length, equal to 5,280 feet, 1,760 yards, or 1,609.34 meters, used in the U.S. and other English-speaking countries; statute mile. **2.** A **nautical mile.** **3.** An **air mile.** [< L *mīle, mīlle,* thousand.]

mile•age (mī'lĭj) *n.* Also **mil•age.** **1.** Distance measured or expressed in miles. **2.** Service or wear estimated by or as by miles used or traveled. **3.** An allowance for travel expenses established at a specified rate per mile.

mile•stone (mīl'stōn') *n.* **1.** A stone marker indicating the distance in miles from a given point. **2.** An important event or turning point.

mi•lieu (mē-lyœ') *n.* Environment or surroundings. [< OF, midst, center.]

mil•i•tant (mĭl'ə-tənt) *adj.* **1.** Fighting or warring. **2.** Aggressive, esp. in the service of some cause. —*n.* One who is militant. [< L *mīlitāre,* to MILITATE.] —**mil'i•tan•cy** (mĭl'ə-tən-sē) *n.* —**mil'i•tant•ly** *adv.*

mil•i•ta•rism (mĭl'ə-tə-rĭz'əm) *n.* The glorification of a professional military class or policies arising from its predominance in state affairs. —**mil'i•ta•rist** *n.* —**mil'i•ta•ris'tic** *adj.*

mil•i•ta•rize (mĭl'ə-tə-rīz') *v.* **-rized, -rizing.** **1.** To equip or train for war. **2.** To imbue with militarism.

mil•i•tar•y (mĭl'ə-tĕr'ē) *adj.* Of, pertaining to, or associated with soldiers, the armed forces, or warfare. —*n.* —**the military.** The armed forces; soldiers collectively. [< L *mīles (mīlit-),* soldier.] —**mil'i•tar'i•ly** *adv.*

mil•i•tate (mĭl'ə-tāt') *v.* **-tated, -tating.** To have force as evidence. [L *mīlitāre,* to serve as a soldier.]

mi•li•tia (mə-lĭsh'ə) *n.* Those who are not members of the regular armed forces, but who are called to military service in an emergency. —**mi•li'tia•man** *n.*

milk (mĭlk) *n.* **1. a.** A whitish liquid produced by the mammary glands of female mammals for feeding their young. **b.** Cows' milk used as human food. **2.** A milklike liquid, as a plant juice. —*v.* **1.** To draw milk from (a female mammal) **2.** To press or extract something from as by milking. [< OE *milc, meolc.* See **melg-.**] —**milk'er** *n.* —**milk'y** *adj.*

milk fever. A disease affecting dairy cows and occasionally sheep or goats, esp. soon after giving birth.

milk•maid (mĭlk'mād') *n.* A girl or woman who milks cows.

milk•man (mĭlk'măn') *n.* A man who sells or delivers milk.

milk of magnesia. A liquid suspension of magnesium hydroxide, $Mg(OH)_2$, used as an antacid and laxative.

milk shake. A whipped beverage made of milk, flavoring, and usually ice cream.

milk•sop (mĭlk'sŏp') *n.* A man lacking manly qualities; a mollycoddle.

milk•weed (mĭlk'wēd') *n.* A plant with milky juice and large pods that split open to release downy seeds.

Milky Way. The galaxy in which the solar system is located, visible as a luminous band in the night sky.

mill¹ (mĭl) *n.* **1.** A building or establishment equipped with machinery for grinding grain. **2.** A machine or device for grinding, crushing, cutting, rolling, etc. **3.** A place where materials are processed; a factory. **4.** A place, institution, etc., that turns out something routinely and in large quantities. —*v.* **1.** To grind or process in or as in a mill. **2.** To move with a circular or whirling motion. [< OE *mylen* < Gmc **mulīna* < LL *molīna.*]

mill² (mĭl) *n.* A monetary unit equal to 1/1000 of a U.S. dollar. [< L *millēsimus,* thousandth.]

Mill (mĭl), **John Stuart.** 1806–1873. English economist, philosopher, and political theorist.

mil•len•ni•um (mə-lĕn'ē-əm) *n., pl.* **-ums** or **-lennia** (-lĕn'ē-ə). **1.** A span of one thousand years. **2.** A thousand-year period of holiness during which Christ is to rule on earth. Revelation 20:1–5. **3.** A hoped-for period of prosperity and justice. [< L *mīlle,* thousand + *annus,* year.] —**mil•len'ni•al** *adj.*

mill•er (mĭl'ər) *n.* One who operates or owns a mill for grinding grain.

mil•let (mĭl'ĭt) *n.* **1.** A grass cultivated for its edible seed and for hay. **2.** The white seeds of this plant. [< L *milium.*]

milli–. *comb. form.* One-thousandth (10^{-3}). [< L *mīlle,* thousand.]

mil•liard (mĭl'yərd, -yärd', mĭl'ē-ärd') *n. Brit.* A billion.

mil•li•me•ter (mĭl'ĭ-mē'tər) *n.* One-thousandth of a meter.

mil•li•ner (mĭl'ə-nər) *n.* One who makes, trims, designs, or sells women's hats. [< *Milaner,* native of Milan.]

mil•li•ner•y (mĭl'ə-nĕr'ē) *n.* **1.** Merchandise sold by a milliner. **2.** The business of a milliner.

mil•lion (mĭl'yən) *n., pl.* **-lion** or **-lions.** **1.** The cardinal number written 1,000,000. **2.** A million monetary units, as of dollars. **3.** Often **millions.** An indefinitely large number. [< L *mīlle,* thousand.] —**mil'lion** *adj.*

Usage: *Million,* preceded by a number or numeral, is used to signify a specific amount: *two million. Millions* is rarely used with a specific number: *many millions; millions of victims of war.*

mil•lion•aire (mĭl'yə-nâr') *n.* A person whose wealth amounts to a million or more in dollars or other currency.

mil•lionth (mĭl'yənth) *n.* **1.** The ordinal number one million in a series. **2.** One of a million equal parts. —**mil'lionth** *adj.*

mill•pond (mĭl'pŏnd') *n.* A pond formed by a dam to supply power for operating a mill.

mill•stone (mĭl'stōn') *n.* **1.** One of a pair of cylindrical stones used in a mill for grinding grain. **2.** A heavy burden.

mill•stream (mĭl'strēm') *n.* A stream whose flow is used to run a mill.

milque•toast (mĭlk'tōst') *n.* A meek, timid man. [< Caspar *Milquetoast,* a character in the newspaper cartoon *The Timid Soul.*]

milt (mĭlt) *n.* The sperm of fishes. [Prob < MDu *milte,* milt, spleen.]

Mil•ton (mĭl'tən), **John.** 1608–1674. English poet.

Mil•wau•kee (mĭl-wô'kē). A city of SE Wisconsin. Pop. 717,000.

mime (mīm) *n.* **1.** The art of pantomime. **2.** A performer in pantomime. **3.** A mimic. —*v.* **mimed, miming.** **1.** To mimic; ape. **2.** To act or portray in pantomime. [< Gk *mimos,* imitator.] —**mim'er** *n.*

mim•e•o•graph (mĭm'ē-ə-grăf', -gräf') *n.* A duplicator that makes copies of written or typed material from a stencil fitted around an inked drum. [< Gk *mimeisthai,* to imitate.] —**mim'e•o•graph'** *v.*

mi•me•sis (mĭ-mē'sĭs, mī-) *n. Med.* The appearance, often due to hysteria, of symptoms of a disease not actually present. [< Gk *mimeisthai,* to imitate.]

mi•met•ic (mĭ-mĕt'ĭk, mī-) *adj.* Of, pertaining to, or using mimicry; imitative. —**mi•met'i•cal•ly** *adv.*

mim•ic (mĭm'ĭk) *v.* **-icked, -icking.** **1.** To imitate another's speech, gestures, etc., as in mockery; ape. **2.** To resemble closely; simulate. —*n.* One who mimics others, as for amusement. —*adj.* Of or pertaining to mimicry; imitative. [L *mīmicus,* imitative.] —**mim'ick•er** *n.*

mim•ic•ry (mĭm'ĭk-rē) *n.* The act or practice of mimicking; imitation.

mi•mo•sa (mĭ-mō'sə, -zə) *n.* Any of various plants, shrubs, and trees with compound leaves and ball-like clusters of small flowers. [< MIME.]

min minute (unit of time).

min. **1.** minimum. **2.** mining.

min•a•ret (mĭn'ə-rĕt') *n.* A tall, slender tower on a mosque. [< Ar *manārat,* lamp.]

min•a•to•ry (mĭn'ə-tôr'ē, -tōr'ē) *adj.* Menacing; threatening. [< L *minārī,* to menace.]

mince (mĭns) *v.* **minced, mincing.** **1.** To cut into very small pieces. **2.** To pronounce with forced refinement or restraint. **3.** To walk primly or affectedly. [< L *minuere,* to diminish.] —**minc'er** *n.*

mince•meat (mĭns'mēt') *n.* A mixture of finely chopped apples, raisins, spices, suet, and sometimes meat, used esp. as pie filling.

mince pie. A pie filled with mincemeat.

mind (mīnd) *n.* **1.** The consciousness that originates in the brain and directs mental and physical behavior. **2.** Memory; recollection. **3.** Conscious thoughts; attention. **4.** Opinion or intentions. **5.** Intellect; intelligence. **6.** One considered with regard to intellectual ability. **7.** Mental or emotional health; sanity. —*v.* **1.** To attend to; heed. **2.** To obey. **3.** To take care of; tend. **4.** To be careful about. **5.** To be concerned or troubled (about); object (to). [< OE *gemynd,* memory, mind. See **men-.**]

mind•ful (mīnd'fəl) *adj.* Attentive; heedful. —**mind'ful•ly** *adv.* —**mind'ful•ness** *n.*

mind•less (mīnd'lĭs) *adj.* **1.** Lacking intelligence or sensible intention. **2.** Careless; heedless. —**mind'less•ly** *adv.* —**mind'less•ness** *n.*

mine¹ (mīn) *n.* **1.** An excavation made in the earth to extract metals, coal, salt, or other minerals. **2.** A natural deposit of ore or minerals. **3.** An abundant supply or source. **4.** A tunnel dug under an enemy emplacement. **5.** An explosive device usually placed in a concealed position and detonated by contact or a time fuse. —*v.* **mined, mining.** **1.** To dig from or as from a mine. **2.** To dig a mine (in). **3.** To lay explosive mines in or under. **4.** To undermine. [< VL **mina* < Celt **meini-,* ore.] —**min'er** *n.*

mine² (mīn). The possessive form of the pronoun *I,* used as a predicate adjective or as a substantive: *This nearly was mine. If you can't find your hat, take mine.* —**of mine.** Belonging to me: *a friend of mine.* [< OE *mīn.* See **me-.**]

min•er•al (mĭn'ər-əl) *n.* **1.** Any naturally occurring, homogeneous inorganic substance having a definite chemical composition and characteristic crystalline structure, color, and hardness. **2. a.** An element, such as gold or silver. **b.** A mixture of inorganic compounds, such as hornblende or granite. **c.** An organic derivative, such as coal or petroleum. **3.** Any substance that is neither animal nor vegetable; inorganic matter. **4.** An ore. —*adj.* **1.** Of or pertaining to minerals: *a mineral deposit.* **2.** Impregnated with minerals: *mineral water.* [< MINE¹.]

min•er•al•o•gy (mĭn'ə-rŏl'ə-jē, -răl'ə-jē) *n.* The scientific study of minerals. [MINERA(L) + -LOGY.] —**min'er•al'o•gist** *n.*

mineral oil. Any of various light hydrocarbon oils, esp. a refined distillate of petroleum used medicinally as a laxative.
mineral water. Water containing dissolved minerals or gases.
Mi•ner•va (mĭ-nûr'və). Roman goddess of wisdom, invention, and the arts.
min•e•stro•ne (mĭn'ə-strō'nē) *n.* An Italian soup containing a variety of vegetables in a broth base. [< It *minestrare,* to serve, dish out.]
min•gle (mĭng'gəl) *v.* **-gled, -gling.** To mix together in close association. [< OE *mengan,* to mix. See **mag-.**] **—min'gler** *n.*
mini-. *comb. form.* Something distinctively smaller or shorter than other members of its class: *miniskirt.*
min•i•a•ture (mĭn'ē-ə-cho͝or', mĭn'ə-cho͝or', -chər) *n.* **1.** A very small or greatly reduced copy or model. **2.** A small painting executed with great detail. *—adj.* On a small or greatly reduced scale. [It *miniatura,* painting.]
min•im (mĭn'əm) *n.* **1.** A unit of fluid measure: **a.** In the U.S., 1/60 of a fluid dram or 0.00376 cubic inches. **b.** In Great Britain, 1/20 of a scruple or 0.00361 cubic inches. **2.** A very small amount. [< L *minimus,* least.]
min•i•mal (mĭn'ə-məl) *adj.* Least in amount or degree. **—min'i•mal•ly** *adv.*
min•i•mize (mĭn'ə-mīz') *v.* **-mized, -mizing.** To reduce to or represent as having minimum importance, value, etc. **—min'i•miz'er** *n.*
min•i•mum (mĭn'ə-məm) *n., pl.* **-mums** or **-ma** (-mə). **1.** The least possible quantity or degree. **2.** The lowest amount or degree reached or permitted. **3.** A number not greater than any other in a finite set of numbers. [< L *minimus,* least.] **—min'i•mum** *adj.*
min•ion (mĭn'yən) *n.* **1.** An obsequious follower or subordinate agent. **2.** *Archaic.* A favorite. [F *mignon,* darling.]
min•is•ter (mĭn'ĭ-stər) *n.* **1.** A person serving as an agent for another by carrying out specified orders. **2.** A clergyman; pastor. **3.** A high officer of state appointed to head an executive or administrative department of government. **4.** A diplomat, usually ranking next below an ambassador. *—v.* **1.** To attend to the wants and needs of others. **2.** *Eccles.* To administer or dispense. [< L, attendant, servant.] **—min'is•te'ri•al** (-stîr'ē-əl) *adj.* **—min'is•trant** (-strənt) *adj. & n.* **—min'is•tra'tion** *n.*
min•is•try (mĭn'ĭ-strē) *n., pl.* **-tries.** **1.** The act of ministering or serving. **2. a.** The profession of a minister of religion. **b.** The clergy. **c.** The period of service of a minister of religion. **3. a.** A governmental department presided over by a minister. **b.** The building in which it is housed. **c.** The duties or term of a governmental minister.
mink (mĭngk) *n.* **1.** A semiaquatic weasellike mammal with soft, lustrous, brownish fur. **2.** The fur of this animal. [< Scand.]
Minn. Minnesota.
Min•ne•ap•o•lis (mĭn'ē-ăp'ə-lĭs). A city of SE Minnesota. Pop. 434,000.
Min•ne•so•ta (mĭn'ə-sō'tə). A state in the north-central U.S. Pop. 3,805,000. Cap. St. Paul. **—Min'ne•so'tan** (mĭn'ə-sō'tən) *n. & adj.*
min•now (mĭn'ō) *n.* Any of numerous small freshwater fishes often used as bait. [< OE *mynwe.*]
mi•nor (mī'nər) *adj.* **1.** Lesser or smaller in amount, size, or importance. **2.** Lesser in seriousness or danger: *minor difficulties; a minor injury.* **3.** Designating a field of academic specialization requiring fewer credits than a major field. **4.** *Mus.* Of or based on a minor scale. *—n.* **1.** One who has not reached full legal age. **2.** An area of minor study. *—v.* To pursue academic studies in a minor field. [< L, less.]
mi•nor•i•ty (mə-nôr'ə-tē, -nŏr'ə-tē, mī-) *n., pl.* **-ties.** **1.** A group of persons or things numbering less than half of a total. **2.** A racial, religious, political, national, or other group regarded as being different from the larger group of which it is part. **3.** The state or period of being under legal age.
minor scale. *Mus.* A diatonic scale having a minor third between the 1st and 3rd tones.
Mi•nos (mī'nəs, -nŏs'). Mythical king of Crete.
Min•o•taur (mĭn'ə-tôr', mīn'ə-tôr'). *Gk.Myth.* A monster having the body of a man and the head of a bull.
Minsk (mĭnsk). Capital of the Byelorussian S.S.R. Pop. 916,000.
min•ster (mĭn'stər) *n. Brit.* A monastery church. [< LL *monastērium,* monastery.]
min•strel (mĭn'strəl) *n.* **1.** A medieval singer who traveled from place to place. **2.** A performer in a minstrel show. [< LL *ministeriālis,* household officer.] **—min'strel•sy** *n.*
minstrel show. A variety show, formerly popular in the U.S., in which performers, some in black facial make-up, sing, dance, and tell jokes.
mint[1] (mĭnt) *n.* **1.** A place where coins are manufactured by a government. **2.** An abundant amount, esp. of money. *—v.* To produce (money) by stamping metal. *—adj.* In original condition; unused. [< OE *mynet,* money < Gmc ***munita** < L *monēta.*] **—mint'age** (mĭn'tĭj) *n.*
mint[2] (mĭnt) *n.* **1.** Any of various related plants, many of which yield an aromatic oil used as flavoring. **2.** A candy flavored with mint. [< OE *minte* < Gmc ***minta** < L *mentha.*] **—mint'y** *adj.*
min•u•end (mĭn'yo͞o-ĕnd') *n.* The quantity from which another quantity is to be subtracted. [< L *minuere,* to lessen.]
min•u•et (mĭn'yo͞o-ĕt') *n.* **1.** A stately dance originated in 17th-century France. **2.** The music for this dance. [< obs F *menuet,* dainty, small.]
mi•nus (mī'nəs) *prep.* **1.** *Math.* Reduced by the subtraction of; less: *Seven minus four equals three.* **2.** *Informal.* Lacking; without. *—adj.* **1.** *Math.* Negative or on the negative part of a scale: *a minus value; minus five degrees.* **2.** Designating one subdivision of a grade less than; slightly less than: *a grade of B minus.* *—n.* **1.** The minus sign (–). **2.** A negative quantity. **3.** A loss, deficiency, or disadvantage. [< L *minus,* less.]
min•us•cule (mĭn'ə-skyo͞ol', mĭ-nŭs'kyo͞ol) *adj.* Very small; tiny; minute. [< L *minusculus,* less.] **—mi•nus'cu•lar** (-kyə-lər) *adj.*
minus sign. The symbol –, used to indicate subtraction or a negative quantity.
min•ute[1] (mĭn'ĭt) *n.* **1. a.** A unit of time equal to 1/60 of an hour, or 60 seconds. **b.** A unit of angular measurement equal to 1/60 of a degree, or 60 seconds. **2.** Any short interval of time; a moment. **3.** A specific point in time. **4. minutes.** An official record of proceedings at a meeting of an organization. [< L *minūtus,* small, MINUTE.]
mi•nute[2] (mī-n/y/o͞ot', mĭ-) *adj.* **1.** Exceptionally small; tiny. **2.** Insignificant; trifling. **3.** Characterized by close examination. [L *minūtus,* small.] **—mi•nute'ly** *adv.* **—mi•nute'ness** *n.*
min•ute•man (mĭn'ĭt-măn') *n.* Also **Min•ute•man.** A Revolutionary War militiaman or any armed civilian pledged to be ready to fight on a minute's notice.
mi•nu•ti•a (mĭ-n/y/o͞o'shē-ə, -shə) *n., pl.* **-tiae** (-shē-ē'). A small or trivial detail.
minx (mĭngks) *n., pl.* **minxes.** A pert, impudent, or flirtatious young girl. [LG *minsk,* hussy.]
Mi•o•cene (mī'ə-sēn') *adj.* Of or belonging to the geologic time, rock series, or sedimentary deposits of the fourth epoch of the Tertiary period. *—n.* The Miocene epoch. [G *meiōn,* less + -CENE.]
mir•a•cle (mĭr'ə-kəl) *n.* **1.** An event that appears unexplainable by the laws of nature and so is held to be supernatural or an act of God. **2.** A person, thing, or event that excites admiring awe. [< L *mīrārī,* to wonder at.] **—mi•rac'u•lous** (mĭ-răk'yə-ləs) *adj.* **—mi•rac'u•lous•ly** *adv.* **—mi•rac'u•lous•ness** *n.*
mi•rage (mĭ-räzh') *n.* **1.** An optical phenomenon that creates the illusion of water, often with inverted reflections of distant objects. **2.** Something that is illusory like a mirage. [< L *mīrus,* wonder.]
mire (mīr) *n.* **1.** A bog. **2.** Deep, slimy soil or mud. *—v.* **mired, miring.** **1.** To cause to sink or become stuck in or as in mire. **2.** To soil with mud. [< ON *mȳrr,* a bog.] **—mir'y** *adj.*
mir•ror (mĭr'ər) *n.* **1.** Any surface capable of reflecting sufficient undiffused light to form a virtual image of an object placed in front of it. **2.** Anything that gives a true picture of something else. *—v.* To reflect in or as in a mirror. [< L *mīrārī,* to wonder at.]
mirth (mûrth) *n.* Rejoicing or enjoyment, esp. when expressed by laughter. [< OE *myrgth.* See **mreghu-.**] **—mirth'ful** *adj.* **—mirth'ful•ly** *adv.* **—mirth'ful•ness** *n.*
mis-. *comb. form.* **1.** Error or wrongness. **2.** Badness or impropriety. **3.** Unsuitableness. **4.** Opposite or lack of. **5.** Failure. [< OE (see **mei-**) and < L *minus,* MINUS.]
mis•ad•ven•ture (mĭs'əd-vĕn'chər) *n.* A mishap; misfortune.
mis•al•li•ance (mĭs'ə-lī'əns) *n.* An unsuitable marriage.
mis•an•thrope (mĭs'ən-thrōp', mĭz'-) *n.* A hater of mankind. [Gk *misanthrōpos,* hating mankind.] **—mis'an•throp'ic** (-thrŏp'ĭk) *adj.* **—mis•an'thro•py** (mĭs-ăn'thrə-pē, mĭz-) *n.*
mis•ap•ply (mĭs'ə-plī') *v.* To apply wrongly. **—mis'ap•pli•ca'tion** (-ăp-lĭ-kā'shən) *n.*
mis•ap•pre•hend (mĭs'ăp-rĭ-hĕnd') *v.* To fail to interpret correctly; misunderstand. **—mis'ap•pre•hen'sion** (-hĕn'shən) *n.*
mis•ap•pro•pri•ate (mĭs'ə-prō'prē-āt') *v.* To appropriate dishonestly for one's own use. **—mis'ap•pro'pri•a'tion** *n.*
mis•be•got•ten (mĭs'bĭ-gŏt'n) *adj.* Illegally begotten, esp. illegitimate.
mis•be•have (mĭs'bĭ-hāv') *v.* To behave badly. **—mis'be•hav'ior** *n.*
misc. miscellaneous.
mis•cal•cu•late (mĭs-kăl'kyə-lāt') *v.* To calculate wrongly; make a wrong estimate of. **—mis'cal•cu•la'tion** *n.*
mis•call (mĭs-kôl') *v.* To call by a wrong name.
mis•car•riage (mĭs-kăr'ĭj) *n.* **1. a.** Mismanagement. **b.** Failure. **2.** Premature expulsion of a nonviable fetus from the uterus.
mis•car•ry (mĭs-kăr'ē) *v.* **1.** To go wrong. **2.** To abort.
mis•cast (mĭs-kăst', -käst') *v.* To cast in an unsuitable role.
mis•ce•ge•na•tion (mĭs'ĭ-jə-nā'shən, mĭ-sĕj'ə-nā'shən) *n.* The interbreeding of what are

presumed to be distinct human races, esp. marriage between white and nonwhite persons. [< L *miscēre,* to mix + *genus,* race.]

mis•cel•la•ne•ous (mĭs'ə-lā'nē-əs) *adj.* Made up of a variety of parts, members, or characteristics. [< L *miscellus,* mixed.] **—mis'cel•la'ne•ous•ly** *adv.*

mis•cel•la•ny (mĭs'ə-lā'nē) *n., pl.* **-nies. 1.** A collection of various items or ingredients. **2.** A collection of diverse literary works.

mis•chance (mĭs-chăns', -chäns') *n.* **1.** An unfortunate occurrence; mishap. **2.** Bad luck.

mis•chief (mĭs'chĭf) *n.* **1.** A cause of discomfiture or annoyance. **2.** An inclination to play pranks. **3.** Injury caused by a specified human agency. [< OF *meschever,* to meet with misfortune.]

mis•chie•vous (mĭs'chə-vəs) *adj.* **1.** Playful, teasing, or troublesome. **2.** Causing harm or injury. **—mis'chie•vous•ly** *adv.* **—mis'chie•vous•ness** *n.*

mis•ci•ble (mĭs'ə-bəl) *adj.* Capable of being mixed in all proportions. [< L *miscēre,* to mix.] **—mis'ci•bil'i•ty** *n.*

mis•con•ceive (mĭs'kən-sēv') *v.* To interpret incorrectly; misunderstand. **—mis'con•cep'tion** (-sĕp'shən) *n.*

mis•con•duct (mĭs-kŏn'dŭkt) *n.* **1.** Improper behavior; impropriety. **2.** Dishonest or bad management. **3.** Malfeasance.

mis•con•strue (mĭs'kən-stro͞o') *v.* To misinterpret. **—mis'con•struc'tion** (-strŭk'shən) *n.*

mis•count (mĭs-kount') *v.* To count incorrectly; miscalculate.

mis•cre•ant (mĭs'krē-ənt) *n.* An evildoer. [< OF *mescroire,* to disbelieve.] **—mis'cre•ant** *adj.*

mis•cue (mĭs-kyo͞o') *n.* A blunder or mistake. **—mis•cue'** *v.*

mis•deed (mĭs-dēd') *n.* A wicked deed.

mis•de•mean•or (mĭs'dĭ-mē'nər) *n.* **1.** A misdeed. **2.** *Law.* An offense of lesser gravity than a felony.

mis•di•rect (mĭs'dĭ-rĕkt', -dī-rĕkt') *v.* To direct incorrectly. **—mis'di•rec'tion** *n.*

mise en scène (mēz äɴ sĕn'). **1.** The setting and staging of a play. **2.** Any setting or environment. [F, "placing on stage."]

mis•em•ploy (mĭs'ĕm-ploi') *v.* To put to a wrong use. **—mis'em•ploy'ment** *n.*

mi•ser (mī'zər) *n.* **1.** One who hoards money. **2.** A greedy or avaricious person. [< L, wretched, unfortunate.] **—mi'ser•li•ness** *n.* **—mi'ser•ly** *adj.*

mis•er•a•ble (mĭz'ər-ə-bəl, mĭz'rə-bəl) *adj.* **1.** Very uncomfortable or unhappy; wretched. **2.** Causing wretchedness. **3.** Wretchedly inadequate or inferior. [< L *miser,* wretched, unfortunate.] **—mis'er•a•bly** *adv.*

mis•er•y (mĭz'ər-ē) *n., pl.* **-ies. 1.** Prolonged or extreme suffering; wretchedness. **2.** An affliction or deprivation.

mis•fea•sance (mĭs-fē'zəns) *n.* The improper and unlawful execution of an act that in itself is lawful and proper. [< OF *mesfaire,* to misdo.] **—mis•fea'sor** *n.*

mis•fire (mĭs-fīr') *v.* **1.** To fail to explode or ignite, as a gun or engine. **2.** To fail to achieve an anticipated result. **—mis'fire** *n.*

mis•fit (mĭs'fĭt', mĭs-fĭt') *n.* **1.** A poor fit. **2.** A maladjusted person.

mis•for•tune (mĭs-fôr'chən) *n.* **1.** Bad fortune. **2.** A mishap.

mis•giv•ing (mĭs-gĭv'ĭng) *n.* Often **misgivings.** A feeling of uncertainty or apprehension.

mis•gov•ern (mĭs-gŭv'ərn) *v.* To govern badly. **—mis•gov'ern•ment** *n.*

mis•guide (mĭs-gīd') *v.* To give misleading direction to; lead astray. **—mis•guid'ance** *n.* **—mis•guid'ed•ly** *adv.* **—mis•guid'er** *n.*

mis•han•dle (mĭs-hăn'dəl) *v.* To deal with clumsily or inefficiently.

mis•hap (mĭs'hăp', mĭs-hăp') *n.* An unfortunate accident.

mis•hear (mĭs-hîr') *v.* To hear wrongly.

mish•mash (mĭsh'măsh', -mŏsh') *n.* A hodgepodge. [Redupl of MASH.]

mis•in•form (mĭs'ĭn-fôrm') *v.* To give wrong or inaccurate information to. **—mis'in•form'ant** (-fôr'mənt) *n.* **—mis'in•for•ma'tion** *n.*

mis•in•ter•pret (mĭs'ĭn-tûr'prĭt) *v.* **1.** To explain inaccurately. **2.** To err in understanding. **—mis'in•ter'pre•ta'tion** *n.*

mis•judge (mĭs-jŭj') *v.* To judge or estimate wrongly. **—mis•judg'ment** *n.*

mis•lay (mĭs-lā') *v.* **1.** To lose. **2.** To put in a place that is afterward forgotten.

mis•lead (mĭs-lēd') *v.* **1.** To lead in the wrong direction. **2.** To lead into error of action or belief.

mis•lead•ing (mĭs-lē'dĭng) *adj.* Deceptive.

mis•man•age (mĭs-măn'ĭj) *v.* To manage badly or carelessly. **—mis•man'age•ment** *n.*

mis•match (mĭs-măch') *v.* To match unsuitably, esp. in marriage. **—mis'match** *n.*

mis•name (mĭs-nām') *v.* To call by a wrong name.

mis•no•mer (mĭs-nō'mər) *n.* A name or designation wrongly applied. [< OF *mesnommer,* to misname.]

miso–. *comb. form.* Hating or hatred. [< Gk *misein,* to hate, and *misos,* hatred.]

mi•sog•y•ny (mĭ-sŏj'ə-nē) *n.* Hatred of women. **—mi•sog'y•nist** *n.* **—mi•sog'y•nous** *adj.*

mis•place (mĭs-plās') *v.* **1. a.** To put in a wrong place. **b.** To lose. **2.** To bestow on a wrong object: *misplacing her trust.*

mis•play (mĭs'plā) *n.* A mistaken action in a game. **—mis•play'** *v.*

mis•print (mĭs-prĭnt') *v.* To print incorrectly. **—mis'print'** *n.*

mis•pri•sion (mĭs-prĭzh'ən) *n.* Maladministration of public office. [< NF *mesprendre,* to take wrongly.]

mis•pro•nounce (mĭs'prə-nouns') *v.* To pronounce incorrectly. **—mis'pro•nun'ci•a'tion** (-nŭn'sē-ā'shən) *n.*

mis•quote (mĭs-kwōt') *v.* To quote incorrectly. **—mis'quo•ta'tion** (-kwō-tā'shən) *n.*

mis•read (mĭs-rēd') *v.* **1.** To read incorrectly. **2.** To misinterpret.

mis•rep•re•sent (mĭs'rĕp-rĭ-zĕnt') *v.* To give an incorrect or dishonest representation of. **—mis'rep•re•sen•ta'tion** *n.*

mis•rule (mĭs-ro͞ol') *v.* To misgovern. **—mis•rule'** *n.*

miss[1] (mĭs) *v.* **1.** To fail to hit, reach, or otherwise make contact with. **2.** To fail to perceive or understand. **3.** To fail to achieve or obtain. **4.** To fail to attend or perform. **5.** To omit. **6.** To avoid. **7.** To discover or feel the absence of. **8.** To misfire. **—*n.* 1.** A failure to hit or succeed. **2.** A misfire. [< OE *missan.* See **mei-.**]

miss[2] (mĭs) *n., pl.* **misses. 1. Miss.** A title preceding the name of an unmarried woman or girl. **2.** *Informal.* An unmarried woman or girl. [Short for MISTRESS.]

Miss. Mississippi.

mis•sal (mĭs'əl) *n.* A book containing all the prayers and responses necessary for celebrating the Roman Catholic Mass. [< LL *missa,* Mass.]

mis•shape (mĭs-shāp') *v.* To shape badly; deform. **—mis•shap'en** *adj.*

mis•sile (mĭs'əl) *n.* Any object or weapon fired, thrown, dropped, or otherwise projected at a target. [< L *mittere* (pp *missus*), to let go, send.]

mis•sile•ry (mĭs'əl-rē) *n.* Also **mis•sil•ry.** The science of making and using guided missiles.

miss•ing (mĭs'ĭng) *adj.* Absent; lost; lacking.

mis•sion (mĭsh'ən) *n.* **1.** A body of envoys to a foreign country. **2.** A body of missionaries, their ministry, or the place of its exercise. **3.** A permanent diplomatic office in a foreign country. **4.** A combat assignment. **5.** A function or task. [< L *mittere* (pp *missus*), to let go, send.] **—mis'sion•al** *adj.*

mis•sion•ar•y (mĭsh'ə-nĕr'ē) *n., pl.* **-ies.** One sent to do religious or charitable work in some territory or foreign country. *—adj.* Of or pertaining to church missions or missionaries.

Mis•sis•sip•pi (mĭs'ə-sĭp'ē). **1.** A state of the SE U.S. Pop. 2,217,000. Cap. Jackson. **2.** A river of the C U.S.

Mis•sis•sip•pi•an (mĭs'ə-sĭp'ē-ən) *adj.* Of or belonging to the geologic time, rock system, or sedimentary deposits of the fifth period of the Paleozoic era. **—*n.* 1.** The Mississippian period. **2.** A native or inhabitant of Mississippi.

mis•sive (mĭs'ĭv) *n.* A letter or message. [< L *mittere* (pp *missus*), to send.]

Mis•sou•ri (mĭ-zo͝or'ē, -zo͝or'ə). **1.** A state of the C U.S. Pop. 4,677,000. Cap. Jefferson City. **2.** A river flowing from Montana to the Mississippi.

mis•spell (mĭs-spĕl') *v.* To spell incorrectly. **—mis•spell'ing** *n.*

mis•state (mĭs-stāt') *v.* To state wrongly or falsely. **—mis•state'ment** *n.*

mis•step (mĭs-stĕp') *n.* **1.** A wrong step. **2.** An instance of wrong or improper conduct.

mist (mĭst) *n.* **1.** A mass of fine droplets of water in the atmosphere. **2.** Water vapor condensed on and clouding the appearance of a surface. **3.** Fine drops of any liquid, as perfume, sprayed into the air. **4.** Something that dims or obscures; a haze. *—v.* To make or become misty or obscured. [< OE. See **meigh-.**]

mis•take (mĭ-stāk') *n.* **1.** An error or blunder. **2.** A misconception or misunderstanding. [< ON *mistaka,* to take in error.] **—mis•take'** *v.* **(-took, -taken).**

mis•tak•en (mĭ-stā'kən) *adj.* **1.** Wrong or incorrect, as in opinion, understanding, etc. **2.** Misunderstood. **—mis•tak'en•ly** *adv.*

Mis•ter (mĭs'tər) *n.* A courtesy title preceding a man's surname or title of office: *Mr. Secretary.* [< MASTER.]

mis•tle•toe (mĭs'əl-tō') *n.* A plant growing as a parasite on trees and having leathery evergreen leaves and waxy white berries. [< OE *mistel,* mistletoe + *tān,* twig < Gmc **tainaz.*]

mis•treat (mĭs-trēt') *v.* To treat roughly or wrongly; abuse. **—mis•treat'ment** *n.*

mis•tress (mĭs'trĭs) *n.* **1.** A woman in a position of authority, control, or ownership. **2.** A country enjoying hegemony: *mistress of the seas.* **3.** A man's female lover. **4. Mistress.** *Archaic.* Mrs.

mis•tri•al (mĭs-trī'əl, -trīl') *n. Law.* **1.** A trial that becomes invalid because of basic error in procedure. **2.** An inconclusive trial, as one in which the jurors fail to reach a verdict.

mis•trust (mĭs-trŭst') *n.* Lack of trust; suspicion. *—v.* To regard without confidence. **—mis•trust'ful** *adj.* **—mis•trust'ing•ly** *adv.*

mist•y (mĭs'tē) *adj.* **-ier, -iest. 1.** Consisting of or resembling mist. **2.** Obscured by or as by mist;

vague. —**mist'i•ly** *adv.* —**mist'i•ness** *n.*

mis•un•der•stand (mĭs'ŭn-dər-stănd') *v.* **1.** To fail to understand. **2.** To understand incorrectly.

mis•un•der•stand•ing (mĭs'ŭn-dər-stăn'dĭng) *n.* **1.** A failure to understand correctly. **2.** A disagreement or quarrel.

mis•use (mĭs-yo͞os') *n.* Improper use; misapplication. —*v.* (mĭs-yo͞oz'). **1.** To misapply. **2.** To abuse.

mite[1] (mīt) *n.* Any of various small, spiderlike, often parasitic organisms. [< OE *mīte.* See **mai-**[1].]

mite[2] (mīt) *n.* **1.** A very small contribution or amount of money. **2.** A tiny thing or amount. [< MDu *mīte.*]

mi•ter (mī'tər) *n.* Also *chiefly Brit.* **mi•tre. 1.** A hat with peaks in front and back, worn by bishops. **2.** A joint made by beveling each of two surfaces at an angle and fitting them to form a 90° corner. [< Gk *mitra,* headband.]

mit•i•gate (mĭt'ə-gāt') *v.* **-gated, -gating.** To make or become less harsh or severe; alleviate. [< L *mītis,* gentle, mild.] —**mit'i•ga'tion** *n.* —**mit'i•ga'tor** *n.*

mi•to•sis (mī-tō'sĭs) *n.* **1.** The sequential differentiation and segregation of replicated chromosomes in a cell nucleus that precedes complete cell division. **2.** The sequence of processes by which a cell divides to form two daughter cells having the normal number of chromosomes. [< Gk *mitos,* a thread + -OSIS.] —**mi•tot'ic** (-tŏt'ĭk) *adj.*

mitt (mĭt) *n.* **1.** A large glove worn by baseball catchers and first basemen. **2. mitts.** *Slang.* Hands. [Short for MITTEN.]

mit•ten (mĭt'n) *n.* A covering for the hand that encases the thumb separately and the four fingers together. [< OF *mitaine.*]

mix (mĭks) *v.* **1.** To combine or blend so that the constituent parts are indistinguishable. **2.** To form by blending. **3.** To combine or join: *mix joy with sorrow.* **4.** To crossbreed. **5.** To associate socially. —*n.* A packaged mixture, as of baking ingredients. [< L *miscēre* (pp *mixtus*), to mix.] —**mix'a•ble** *adj.* —**mix'er** *n.*

mix•ture (mĭks'chər) *n.* **1.** Something produced by mixing. **2.** Anything consisting of diverse elements. **3.** The act or process of mixing or being mixed. **4.** Any blend of substances not chemically bound to each other.

mix-up (mĭks'ŭp') *n.* A state or instance of confusion.

miz•zen, miz•en (mĭz'ən) *n.* A fore-and-aft sail set on the mizzenmast. [< L *medietās,* half.] —**miz'zen** *adj.*

miz•zen•mast, miz•en•mast (mĭz'ən-məst, -măst', -mäst') *n.* The third mast aft on sailing ships carrying three or more masts.

mk. mark.

mkt. market.

ml milliliter.

ML Medieval Latin.

Mlle. Mademoiselle.

mm millimeter.

MM. Messieurs.

Mme. Madame.

Mmes. Mesdames.

Mn manganese.

mne•mon•ic (nĭ-mŏn'ĭk) *adj.* Assisting or designed to aid the memory. [< Gk *mnēmōn,* mindful.] —**mne•mon'i•cal•ly** *adv.*

Mo molybdenum.

mo. month.

Mo. Missouri.

m.o. 1. mail order. **2.** medical officer. **3.** money order.

moan (mōn) *n.* A low, sustained, mournful sound, as of sorrow or pain. [< OE **mān,* complaint. See **mei-no-.**] —**moan** *v.*

moat (mōt) *n.* A wide, deep ditch, usually filled with water, surrounding a medieval town or fortress. [ME *mote,* orig "mound," "embankment" < OF *mote, motte,* clod, hill, mound, prob < Gaul **mutt(a).*]

mob (mŏb) *n.* **1.** A large, disorderly crowd. **2.** The rabble. **3.** An organized gang of hoodlums. —*v.* **mobbed, mobbing. 1.** To crowd around and jostle or attack. **2.** To crowd into (a place). [< L *mōbile (vulgus),* "the fickle (crowd)."]

mo•bile (mō'bəl, -bēl', -bīl') *adj.* **1.** Capable of moving or being moved. **2.** Moving quickly from one condition to another. —*n.* (mō'bēl'). A type of sculpture consisting of parts that move, esp. in response to air currents. [< L *mōbilis.*] —**mo•bil'i•ty** (-bĭl'ə-tē) *n.*

Mo•bile (mō'bēl'). A city of SW Alabama. Pop. 203,000.

-mobile. *comb. form.* A specialized kind of vehicle: **bookmobile.** [< AUTOMOBILE.]

mo•bi•lize (mō'bə-līz') *v.* **-lized, -lizing. 1.** To make mobile or capable of movement. **2.** To assemble and prepare for war or a similar emergency. —**mo'bi•li•za'tion** *n.*

mob•ster (mŏb'stər) *n.* A member of a criminal gang.

moc•ca•sin (mŏk'ə-sĭn) *n.* **1.** A soft leather slipper or shoe. **2.** A snake, the **water moccasin.** [< Algon.]

mo•cha (mō'kə) *n.* **1.** A type of coffee originally produced in Arabia. **2.** Coffee flavoring, often mixed with chocolate. [< *Mocha,* a port of Yemen.] —**mo'cha** *adj.*

mock (mŏk) *v.* **1.** To treat with scorn or contempt; deride. **2. a.** To mimic in sport or derision. **b.** To imitate. —*adj.* Simulated; sham. [< OF *mocquer,* to deride.] —**mock'er** *n.* —**mock'er•y** *n.* —**mock'ing•ly** *adv.*

mock•ing•bird (mŏk'ĭng-bûrd') *n.* A gray and white songbird common in the S U.S.

mock•up (mŏk'ŭp') *n.* Also **mock-up. 1.** A full-sized scale model for study, testing, etc. **2.** A layout of printed matter.

mod. 1. moderate. **2.** modern.

mode (mōd) *n.* **1. a.** A manner, way, or method of doing or acting. **b.** A particular form, variety, or manner. **2.** The current fashion or style. **3.** *Mus.* Any of certain arrangements of the diatonic tones of an octave. [< L *modus,* measure, manner, melody.] —**mo'dal** *adj.*

mod•el (mŏd'l) *n.* **1.** A miniature representation of some existing object. **2.** A preliminary pattern. **3.** A tentative ideational structure used as a testing device. **4.** A type or design. **5.** An example to be emulated. **6.** One who poses for an artist or photographer. **7.** A mannequin. —*v.* **1.** To plan or construct. **2.** To display (clothes) by wearing. **3.** To work as a model. [< L *modulus,* little measure.] —**mod'el** *adj.* —**mod'el•er** *n.*

mod•er•ate (mŏd'ər-ĭt) *adj.* **1.** Not excessive or extreme. **2.** Temperate. **3.** Average; mediocre. **4.** Opposed to radical views or measures. —*n.* One who holds moderate views. —*v.* (mŏd'ə-rāt') **-ated, -ating. 1.** To make or become less violent, severe, or extreme. **2.** To preside over as a moderator. [< L *moderārī, moderāre,* to reduce, control.] —**mod'er•ate•ly** *adv.* —**mod'er•a'tion** *n.*

mod•er•a•tor (mŏd'ə-rā'tər) *n.* **1.** One that moderates. **2.** A presiding officer, as of a general assembly.

mod•ern (mŏd'ərn) *adj.* Of, pertaining to, or characteristic of recent times or the present. [< LL *modernus.*] —**mod'ern** *n.* —**mod•ern'i•ty** (mō-dûr'nə-tē) *n.* —**mod'ern•ly** *adv.*

Modern English. English since the early 16th century.

Modern Greek. Greek since the early 16th century.

mod•ern•ism (mŏd'ər-nĭz'əm) *n.* A theory, practice, or belief that is peculiar to modern times. —**mod'ern•ist** *n.* —**mod'ern•ist'ic** *adj.*

mod•ern•ize (mŏd'ər-nīz') *v.* **-ized, -izing.** To make or become modern in appearance, style, etc. —**mod'ern•i•za'tion** *n.*

mod•est (mŏd'ĭst) *adj.* **1.** Having or showing a moderate estimation of oneself. **2.** Shy; reserved. **3.** Decent. **4.** Unpretentious. **5.** Moderate; not extreme: *a modest charge.* [< L *modestus,* "keeping due measure."] —**mod'est•ly** *adv.* —**mod'es•ty** *n.*

mod•i•cum (mŏd'ĭ-kəm) *n.* A small or moderate amount. [< L *modicus,* moderate.]

mod•i•fy (mŏd'ə-fī') *v.* **-fied, -fying. 1.** To change; alter. **2.** To make or become less extreme, severe, or strong. **3.** *Gram.* To qualify or limit the meaning of. [< L *modus,* a measure + *facere,* to do, make.] —**mod'i•fi•ca'tion** *n.* —**mod'i•fi'er** *n.*

mod•ish (mō'dĭsh) *adj.* Stylish; fashionable. [< MODE.] —**mod'ish•ly** *adv.*

mo•diste (mō-dēst') *n.* One who produces or designs ladies' fashions.

mod•u•late (mŏj'o͝o-lāt', mŏd'yə-) *v.* **-lated, -lating. 1.** To regulate; temper. **2.** To change or vary the pitch, intensity, or tone of. **3.** *Mus.* To pass from one tonality to another by means of harmonic progression. **4.** To vary the frequency, amplitude, phase, or other characteristic of (any carrier wave). [< L *modus,* measure, rhythm.] —**mod'u•la'tion** *n.* —**mod'u•la'tive, mod'u•la•to'ry** *adj.* —**mod'u•la'tor** *n.*

mod•ule (mŏj'o͞ol, mŏd'yo͞ol) *n.* A standardized unit or component, generally having a defined function in a system. [L *modulus,* a small measure.] —**mod'u•lar** *adj.*

Mog•a•dish•u (mŏg'ə-dĭsh'o͞o). The capital of Somalia. Pop. 100,000.

mo•gul (mō'gəl) *n.* A very rich or powerful person.

mo•hair (mō'hâr') *n.* **1.** The soft, silky hair of the Angora goat. **2.** A fabric made from this hair. [< Ar *mukhayyar,* "select," cloth of goat's hair.]

Mo•ham•med (mō-hăm'ĭd, -hä'mĭd). A.D. 570?–632. Prophet and founder of Islam.

Mo•hawk (mō'hôk') *n., pl.* **-hawk** or **-hawks. 1.** A member of an Iroquoian-speaking tribe of North American Indians formerly living in N New York State and SE Canada. **2.** The language of this tribe. —**Mo'hawk'** *adj.*

Mo•he•gan (mō-hē'gən) *n., pl.* **-gan** or **-gans.** A member of a tribe of Algonquian-speaking Indians formerly living in E Connecticut. —**Mo•he'gan** *adj.*

Mo•hi•can. Variant of **Mahican.**

moi•e•ty (moi'ə-tē) *n., pl.* **-ties. 1.** A half. **2.** A part or share of indefinite size. [< L *medietās,* half.]

moil (moil) *v.* To toil or slave. [< OF *moillier,* to moisten, paddle in mud.] —**moil** *n.*

moi•ré (mwä-rā'). Also **moire** (mwär). *n.* **1.** Cloth, esp. silk, that has a watered or wavy pattern. **2.** A watered pattern produced on cloth by engraved rollers. [< MOHAIR.] —**moi•ré'** *adj.*

moist (moist) *adj.* Slightly wet or damp; humid. [< VL **muscidus,* moldy, wet.] —**moist'ly** *adv.* —**moist'ness** *n.*

mois•ten (mois'ən) *v.* To make or become moist. —**mois'ten•er** *n.*

mois•ture (mois'chər) *n.* Diffuse wetness; dampness.

mo•lar (mō'lər) *n.* A tooth with a broad crown for grinding food, located behind the bicuspids. [< L *mola,* millstone.] —**mo'lar** *adj.*

mo•las•ses (mə-lăs'ĭz) *n.* Any of various thick syrups produced in refining sugar. [< LL *mellāceum,* must.]

mold[1] (mōld). Also *chiefly Brit.* **mould.** *n.* **1.** A form or matrix for shaping a fluid or plastic substance. **2.** A frame or model for shaping or forming something. **3.** Something made in or shaped on a mold. **4.** General shape or form: *the oval mold of her face.* **5.** Distinctive shape, character, or type. —*v.* To shape in or on a mold. [< L *modulus,* a small measure.] —**mold'a•ble** *adj.*

mold[2] (mōld). Also *chiefly Brit.* **mould.** *n.* **1.** Any of various fungous growths formed on the surface of organic matter. **2.** A fungus that causes mold. —*v.* To become moldy. [< ON *mugla, mygla,* mold.]

mold[3] (mōld) *n.* Also *chiefly Brit.* **mould.** Loose soil rich in humus. [< OE *molde.*]

Mol•da•vi•a (mŏl-dā'vē-ə, -vyə). **1.** A historic region of E Rumania. **2.** The Moldavian Soviet Socialist Republic.

Mol•da•vi•an Soviet Socialist Republic (mŏl-dā'vē-ən, -vyən). A republic of the SW Soviet Union. Pop. 3,572,000. Cap. Kishinev. —**Mol•da'vi•an** *n.* & *adj.*

mold•er (mōl'dər) *v.* Also *chiefly Brit.* **mould•er.** To decay or crumble into dust. [Prob < Scand.]

mold•ing (mōl'dĭng) *n.* Also *chiefly Brit.* **mould•ing. 1. a.** Anything that is molded. **b.** The process of shaping in a mold. **2.** An embellishment in strip form used to decorate a surface.

mold•y (mōl'dē) *adj.* **-ier, -iest.** Also *chiefly Brit.* **mould•y. 1.** Covered with or containing mold. **2.** Musty or stale. —**mold'i•ness** *n.*

mole[1] (mōl) *n.* A small congenital growth on the human skin, usually slightly raised and dark and sometimes hairy. [< OE *māl.* See **mai-**[2].]

mole[2] (mōl) *n.* A small, burrowing mammal with minute eyes, a narrow snout, and silky fur. [< MDu *mol* and ML *mulus.*]

mole[3] (mōl) *n.* The amount of a substance that has a weight in grams numerically equal to the molecular weight of the substance. [< G *Molekulargewicht,* molecular weight.]

mol•e•cule (mŏl'ə-kyōōl') *n.* **1.** A stable configuration of atomic nuclei and electrons bound together by electrostatic and electromagnetic forces, the simplest structural unit that displays the characteristic physical and chemical properties of a compound. **2.** A small particle; tiny bit. [< L *mōlēs,* mass, bulk, burden.] —**mo•lec'u•lar** (mə-lĕk'yə-lər) *adj.*

mole•hill (mōl'hĭl') *n.* A small mound of loose earth thrown up by a burrowing mole.

mole•skin (mōl'skĭn') *n.* **1.** The fur of a mole. **2.** A napped cotton fabric.

mo•lest (mə-lĕst') *v.* **1.** To interfere with or annoy. **2.** To accost and harass sexually. [< L *molestus,* troublesome.] —**mo'les•ta'tion** *n.* —**mo•lest'er** *n.*

Mo•lière (mōl-yâr'). Pen name of Jean-Baptiste Poquelin. 1622–1673. French dramatist.

moll (mŏl) *n. Slang.* A female companion of a gangster.

mol•li•fy (mŏl'ə-fī') *v.* **-fied, -fying. 1.** To placate; calm. **2.** To soften or ease. [< L *mollificāre,* to make soft.] —**mol'li•fi•ca'tion** (mŏl'ə-fĭ-kā'shən) *n.*

mol•lusk (mŏl'əsk) *n.* Also **mol•lusc.** Any of a large group of soft-bodied, usually shell-bearing invertebrates, including the snails, oysters, clams, etc. [< L *mollis,* soft.]

mol•ly•cod•dle (mŏl'ē-kŏd'l) *n.* A pampered boy or man. —*v.* **-dled, -dling.** To spoil by pampering. —**mol'ly•cod'dler** *n.*

molt (mōlt). Also *chiefly Brit.* **moult.** *v.* To shed an outer covering, as feathers or skin, that is replaced periodically by a new growth. —*n.* The process of molting. [< L *mūtāre,* to change.]

mol•ten (mōlt'n) *adj.* Made liquid and glowing by heat; melted.

mo•lyb•de•num (mə-lĭb'də-nəm) *n. Symbol* **Mo** A hard, gray metallic element used to toughen alloy steels. Atomic number 42, atomic weight 95.94. [< Gk *molubdos,* lead.]

mom (mŏm) *n. Informal.* Mother.

mo•ment (mō'mənt) *n.* **1.** A brief interval of time. **2.** A specific point in time: *He is reading at the moment.* **3.** A particular period of importance or excellence. **4.** Importance. [< L *mōmentum,* MOMENTUM.]

mo•men•tar•y (mō'mən-tĕr'ē) *adj.* **1.** Lasting only a brief time. **2.** Occurring or present at every moment. **3.** Short-lived; ephemeral. —**mo'men•tar'i•ly** *adv.* —**mo'men•tar'i•ness** *n.*

mo•ment•ly (mō'mənt-lē) *adv.* From moment to moment.

mo•men•tous (mō-mĕn'təs) *adj.* Of utmost importance or outstanding significance. —**mo•men'tous•ly** *adv.* —**mo•men'tous•ness** *n.*

mo•men•tum (mō-mĕn'təm) *n., pl.* **-ta** (-tə) or **-tums. 1.** The product of a body's mass and linear velocity. **2.** Impetus. [L *mōmentum,* motion, movement < *movēre,* to move.]

mon (mŏn) *n. Scot.* Man.

Mon. Monday.

Mon•a•co (mŏn'ə-kō', mə-nä'kō). A principality on the Mediterranean coast of France. Pop. 22,000. Cap. Monaco-Ville.

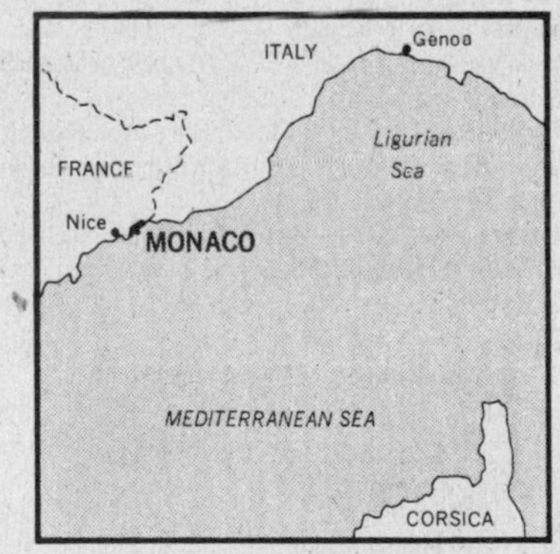

Monaco

mon•arch (mŏn'ərk) *n.* **1.** A sovereign, such as a king or emperor. **2.** One that presides over or rules. **3.** A large orange and black butterfly. [< Gk *monarkhēs.*] —**mon•ar'chic, mon•ar'chi•cal** *adj.*

mon•ar•chism (mŏn'ər-kĭz'əm) *n.* Belief in or advocacy of monarchy. —**mon'ar•chist** (-kĭst) *n.* & *adj.* —**mon'ar•chis'tic** *adj.*

mon•ar•chy (mŏn'ər-kē) *n., pl.* **-chies. 1.** Government by a monarch. **2.** A state ruled by a monarch.

mon•as•ter•y (mŏn'ə-stĕr'ē) *n., pl.* **-ies.** The dwelling place of a community of monks. [< Gk *monazein,* to live alone.] —**mon'as•te'ri•al** (-stîr'ē-əl, -stĕr'ē-əl) *adj.*

mo•nas•tic (mə-năs'tĭk) *adj.* Of or pertaining to monasteries or persons living in religious or contemplative seclusion.

mo•nas•ti•cism (mə-năs'tə-sĭz'əm) *n.* The monastic life or system.

mon•au•ral (mŏn-ôr'əl, mō-nôr'əl) *adj.* **1.** Designating sound reception by one ear. **2.** Monophonic.

Mon•day (mŭn'dē, -dā') *n.* The 2nd day of the week. [< OE *mōnan dæg,* moon's day.]

Mo•net (mō-nā'), **Claude.** 1840–1926. French painter.

mon•e•tar•y (mŏn'ə-tĕr'ē, mŭn'-) *adj.* **1.** Of or pertaining to money. **2.** Of or pertaining to a nation's currency or coinage.

mon•ey (mŭn'ē) *n., pl.* **-eys** or **-ies. 1.** A commodity that is legally established as an exchangeable equivalent of all other commodities and used as a measure of their comparative market value. **2.** The official currency issued by a government. **3.** Assets and property that can be converted into actual currency. **4.** Pecuniary profit or loss. [< L *monēta,* money, mint.]

mon•eyed (mŭn'ēd) *adj.* Also **mon•ied. 1.** Having a great deal of money. **2.** Representing or arising from the possession of money.

mon•ger (mŭng'gər, mŏng'-) *n.* A dealer: *ironmonger.* [< L *mangō,* (fraudulent) dealer.]

Mon•gol (mŏng'gəl, -gōl') *n.* **1.** A member of one of the nomadic tribes of Mongolia or a native of Mongolia. **2.** Any of the languages of Mongolia. **3.** A member of the Mongoloid ethnic group. —**Mon'gol** *adj.*

Mon•go•li•a (mŏng-gō'lē-ə, -gōl'yə, mŏn-). A region of east-central Asia, now consisting of the Mongolian People's Republic (Outer Mongolia) and the Inner Mongolian Autonomous Region of China (Inner Mongolia).

Mon•go•li•an (mŏng-gō'lē-ən, -gōl'yən, mŏn-) *n.* **1.** A native of Mongolia. **2.** A member of the Mongoloid ethnic division. **3. a.** The Mongolic subfamily of the Altaic languages. **b.** Any of the Mongolic languages of Mongolia. —**Mon•go'li•an** *adj.*

Mongolian People's Republic. A republic of east-central Asia. Pop. 1,050,000. Cap. Ulan Bator.

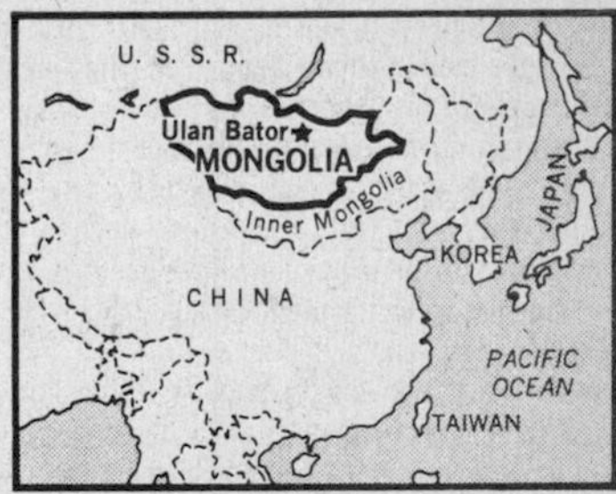

Mongolian People's Republic

Mon•gol•ic (mŏng-gŏl'ĭk, mŏn-) *n.* The Altaic subfamily that includes the various languages of Mongolia. —*adj.* Of or pertaining to the Mongoloid ethnic division or to the subfamily of Altaic languages spoken in Mongolia.

mon•gol•ism (mŏng'gə-lĭz'əm, mŏn'-) *n.* A congenital idiocy in which a child is born with a short, flattened skull, slanting eyes, and other anomalies. —**mon'gol•oid'** (-loid') *adj.*

Mon•gol•oid (mŏng'gə-loid', mŏn'-) *adj.* **1.** Pertaining to a major ethnic division of the human species having yellowish-brown to white skin color. **2.** Characteristic of or like a Mongol. —**Mon'gol•oid'** *n.*

mon•goose (mŏng'go͞os', mŏn'-) *n., pl.* **-gooses.** Any of various weasellike, chiefly African or Asian mammals noted for their ability to kill venomous snakes. [< Dravid.]

mon•grel (mŭng'grəl, mŏng'-) *n.* A plant or animal, esp. a dog, of mixed breed. [Prob < OE *gemang,* mixture. See **mag-**.]

mon•ied. Variant of **moneyed.**

mo•nism (mō'nĭz'əm, mŏn'ĭz'əm) *n.* A metaphysical system in which reality is conceived as a unified whole. —**mo'nist** *n.* & *adj.* —**mo•nis'tic** (mō-nĭs'tĭk, mŏ-) *adj.*

mo•ni•tion (mō-nĭsh'ən, mə-) *n.* A warning or admonition. [< L *monēre,* to warn.]

mon•i•tor (mŏn'ə-tər) *n.* **1.** A student who assists a teacher. **2.** Any device used to record or control a process. —*v.* To check, watch, or keep track of, often by means of an electronic device. [L, one who warns.]

mon•i•to•ry (mŏn'ə-tôr'ē, -tōr'ē) *adj.* Conveying an admonition.

monk (mŭngk) *n.* A member of a religious brotherhood living in a monastery. [< LGk *monakhos,* solitary, monk.]

mon•key (mŭng'kē) *n., pl.* **-keys.** Any member of the primates except man, esp. one of the long-tailed small- to medium-sized species as distinguished from the larger apes and the smaller lemurs. —*v. Informal.* To play or tamper with something.

mon•key•shine (mŭng'kē-shīn') *n.* Often **monkeyshines.** *Slang.* A prank.

monkey wrench. A hand tool with adjustable jaws for turning nuts.

monks•hood (mŭngks'ho͝od') *n.* Any of several poisonous plants with hood-shaped, usually purplish flowers.

mono–. *comb. form.* **1.** One; single; alone. **2.** The presence of a single atom, radical, or group in a compound. [< Gk *monos,* single, sole, alone.]

mon•o•chro•mat•ic (mŏn'ə-krō-măt'ĭk) *adj.* Also **mon•o•chro•ic** (-krō'ĭk). Of only one color. —**mon'o•chro•mat'i•cal•ly** *adv.*

mon•o•cle (mŏn'ə-kəl) *n.* An eyeglass for one eye. [< LL *monoculus,* one-eyed.]

mon•o•cot•y•le•don (mŏn'ə-kŏt'l-ēd'n) *n.* Also **mon•o•cot** (mŏn'ə-kŏt'). A plant, as a grass, with a single embryonic seed leaf that appears at germination. —**mon'o•cot'y•le'don•ous** *adj.*

mo•noc•u•lar (mŏ-nŏk'yə-lər, mə-) *adj.* **1.** Of or having one eye. **2.** Adapted for the use of only one eye.

mon•o•dy (mŏn'ə-dē) *n., pl.* **-dies.** An ode or elegy. —**mo•nod'ic** (mə-nŏd'ĭk) *adj.* —**mon'o•dist** (mŏn'ə-dĭst) *n.*

mo•nog•a•my (mə-nŏg'ə-mē) *n.* The custom or condition of being married to only one person at a time. —**mo•nog'a•mist** *n.* —**mo•nog'a•mous** *adj.* —**mo•nog'a•mous•ly** *adv.*

mon•o•gram (mŏn'ə-grăm') *n.* A design composed of one or more initials of a name. —**mon'o•gram'** *v.* **(-grammed** or **-gramed, -gramming** or **-graming).**

mon•o•graph (mŏn'ə-grăf', -gräf') *n.* A scholarly paper or treatise. —**mo•nog'ra•pher** (mə-nŏg'rə-fər) *n.* —**mon'o•graph'ic** *adj.*

mon•o•lith (mŏn'ə-lĭth') *n.* A large block of stone used in architecture or sculpture.

mon•o•lith•ic (mŏn'ə-lĭth'ĭk) *adj.* **1.** Consisting of a monolith. **2.** Like a monolith; massive and uniform.

mon•o•logue (mŏn'ə-lôg', -lŏg') *n.* **1.** A long speech. **2.** A soliloquy. [< MONO- + (DIA)-LOGUE.]

mon•o•ma•ni•a (mŏn'ō-mā'nē-ə, -măn'yə) *n.* **1.** Obsession with one idea. **2.** Obsessive concentration on a single subject. —**mon'o•ma'ni•ac'** (-ăk') *n.*

mon•o•mer (mŏn'ə-mər) *n.* Any molecule that can be chemically bound as a unit of a polymer.

mo•no•mi•al (mŏ-nō'mē-əl, mō-, mə-) *n.* An algebraic expression consisting of only one term. [MON(O)- + (BIN)OMIAL.] —**mo•no'mi•al** *adj.*

mon•o•nu•cle•o•sis (mŏn'ō-n/y/o͞o'klē-ō'sĭs) *n.* An infectious disease characterized by an abnormally large number of leukocytes with single nuclei in the bloodstream. [< MONO- + NUCLE(US) + -OSIS.]

mon•o•phon•ic (mŏn'ə-fŏn'ĭk) *adj. Electronics.* Using one channel to carry or reproduce sounds through audio devices; monaural.

mon•o•plane (mŏn'ə-plān') *n.* An airplane with only one pair of wings.

mo•nop•o•ly (mə-nŏp'ə-lē) *n., pl.* **-lies. 1.** Exclusive ownership or control, as of a given commodity or business activity. **2. a.** A company or group having such control. **b.** A commodity or service thus controlled. [< Gk *monopōlion,* sole selling rights.] —**mo•nop'o•list** *n.* & *adj.* —**mo•nop'o•lis'tic** *adj.* —**mo•nop'o•li•za'tion** *n.* —**mo•nop'o•lize'** *v.* **(-lized, -lizing).**

mon•o•rail (mŏn'ə-rāl') *n.* A single-rail railway track or system.

mon•o•so•di•um glu•ta•mate (mŏn'ə-sō'dē-əm glo͞o'tə-māt'). **Sodium glutamate.**

mon•o•syl•la•ble (mŏn'ə-sĭl'ə-bəl) *n.* A word of one syllable. —**mon'o•syl•lab'ic** (-sĭ-lăb'ĭk) *adj.* —**mon'o•syl•lab'i•cal•ly** *adv.*

mon•o•the•ism (mŏn'ə-thē-ĭz'əm) *n.* The doctrine or belief that there is only one God. —**mon'o•the'ist** *n.* & *adj.* —**mon'o•the•is'tic** *adj.*

mon•o•tone (mŏn'ə-tōn') *n.* A succession of sounds or words uttered in a single tone of voice or sung at a single pitch.

mo•not•o•nous (mə-nŏt'n-əs) *adj.* **1.** Unvarying in inflection or pitch. **2.** Repetitiously dull. —**mo•not'o•nous•ly** *adv.* —**mo•not'o•ny** *n.*

mon•o•va•lent (mŏn'ə-vā'lənt) *adj.* Possessing a valence of 1; univalent.

mon•ox•ide (mŏ-nŏk'sīd', mə-) *n.* An oxide with each molecule containing one oxygen atom.

Mon•roe (mən-rō'), **James.** 1758–1831. 5th President of the U.S. (1817–25).

James Monroe

Mon•ro•vi•a (mən-rō'vē-ə). The capital of Liberia. Pop. 80,000.

Mon•si•gnor (mŏn-sēn'yər) *n.* Also **mon•si•gnor.** A title of certain officials of the Roman Catholic Church.

mon•soon (mŏn-so͞on') *n.* A wind system that influences large climatic regions and reverses direction seasonally, esp. the Asiatic monsoon that produces dry and wet seasons in India and S Asia. [< Ar *mausim,* season, monsoon season.]

mon•ster (mŏn'stər) *n.* **1.** An animal or plant that is structurally abnormal or grotesquely deformed. **2.** Any very large animal, plant, or object. **3.** One who inspires horror or disgust. —*adj.* Gigantic; huge. [< L *mōnstrum,* prodigy, portent.] —**mon•stros'i•ty** (-strŏs'ə-tē) *n.* —**mon'strous** *adj.* —**mon'strous•ly** *adv.* —**mon'strous•ness** *n.*

mon•strance (mŏn'strəns) *n. R.C.Ch.* A receptacle in which the Host is held. [< L *mōnstrum,* portent, MONSTER.]

Mont. Montana.

mon•tage (mŏn-täzh') *n.* A composite photograph or other artistic composition consisting of several superimposed components.

Mon•tan•a (mŏn-tăn'ə). A state of the W U.S. Pop. 694,000. Cap. Helena. —**Mon•tan'an** *adj.* & *n.*

Mont Blanc (môɴ bläɴ'). The highest mountain in the Alps (15,781 ft.).

Mon•te•vi•de•o (mŏn'tə-vĭ-dā'ō). The capital of Uruguay. Pop. 1,204,000.

Mont•gom•er•y (mŏnt-gŭm'ər-ē, -gŭm'rē, mənt-). The capital of Alabama. Pop. 134,000.

month (mŭnth) *n.* **1.** One of the 12 divisions of a year as determined by the Gregorian calendar. **2.** Any period extending from a date in one calendar month to the corresponding date in the following month. **3. a.** A period of four weeks. **b.** A period of 30 days. **4.** One twelfth of a tropical year. [< OE *mōnath.* See **mē-²**.]

Usage: The singular *month,* preceded by a numeral (or number) and a hyphen, is used as a compound attributive: *a three-month vacation.* The plural possessive form without a hyphen is also possible: *a three months' vacation.*

month•ly (mŭnth'lē) *adj.* **1.** Of, occurring, coming due, or published every month. **2.** Lasting for a month. —*n., pl.* **-lies.** A monthly publication. —**month'ly** *adv.*

Mont•pe•lier (mŏnt-pēl'yər). The capital of Vermont. Pop. 9,000.

Mon•tre•al (mŏn'trē-ôl', mŭn'-). Canada's largest city. Pop. 1,191,000.

mon•u•ment (mŏn'yə-mənt) *n.* **1.** A structure erected as a memorial. **2.** A tombstone. **3.** Any place or region officially designated and preserved as having special interest or significance. **4.** Something that commemorates by association. **5.** An exceptional example of something. [< L *monumentum* < *monēre,* to remind, warn.] —**mon'u•men'tal** (-mĕn'tl) *adj.* —**mon'u•men'tal•ly** *adv.*

moo (mo͞o) *v.* To emit the deep, bellowing sound made by a cow. [Imit.] —**moo** *n.*

mooch (mo͞och) *v. Slang.* **1.** To obtain free of charge, as by begging. **2.** To steal or filch.

mood¹ (mo͞od) *n.* **1.** A state of mind or feeling. **2.** Inclination or disposition. [< OE *mōd.* See **mē-¹**.]

mood² (mo͞od) *n.* A set of verb forms used to indicate the speaker's attitude toward the factuality, likelihood, or desirability of the action or condition expressed. [Var of MODE.]

mood•y (mo͞o'dē) *adj.* **-ier, -iest. 1.** Given to

changeable emotional states. **2.** Gloomy; uneasy. **—mood'i•ly** *adv.* **—mood'i•ness** *n.*

moon (mo͞on) *n.* **1.** The natural satellite of the earth, varying in distance from the earth between 221,600 and 252,950 miles, having a mean diameter of 2,160 miles, a mass approx. 1/80 that of the earth, and an average period of revolution around the earth of 29 days 12 hours 44 minutes. **2.** Any natural satellite revolving around a planet. **3.** The moon as it appears at a particular time in its cycle of phases: *the full moon.* **4.** A month. **5.** Any disk, globe, or crescent resembling the moon. **6.** Moonlight. *—v.*. **1.** To dream or wander about aimlessly. **2.** To exhibit infatuation. [< OE *mōna.* See **mē-**[2].]

moon•light (mo͞on'līt') *n.* The light of the moon. **—moon'lit'** (-lĭt') *adj.*

moon•shine (mo͞on'shīn') *n.* **1.** Moonlight. **2.** *Informal.* Foolish talk. **3.** *Slang.* Illegally distilled whiskey. **—moon'shine'** *adj.* **—moon'-shin'er** *n.*

moon•stone (mo͞on'stōn') *n.* A form of feldspar valued as a gem for its pearly translucence.

moon•struck (mo͞on'strŭk') *adj.* Also **moon•strick•en** (mo͞on'strĭk'ən). **1.** Afflicted with insanity; crazed. **2.** Distracted with romantic sentiment.

moor[1] (mo͝or) *v.* To secure or make fast, as with cables or anchors. [< MLG *mōren.*]

moor[2] (mo͝or) *n.* A broad tract of open, often boggy land. [< OE *mōr.* See **mā-.**]

Moor (mo͝or) *n.* **1.** One of a Moslem people now living chiefly in N Africa. **2.** One of a Moslem people who invaded Spain in the 8th century A.D. **—Moor'ish** *adj.*

moor•ing (mo͝or'ĭng) *n.* **1.** A place at which a vessel or aircraft can be moored. **2.** Often **moorings.** Elements providing stability or security.

moose (mo͞os) *n., pl.* **moose.** A very large deer of N North America, having broad, flattened antlers. [< Algon.]

moot (mo͞ot) *adj.* **1.** Subject to debate; arguable: *a moot question.* **2.** Without legal significance. [< OE *mōt,* moot, assembly.]

mop (mŏp) *n.* A household implement made of absorbent material attached to a handle and used for cleaning floors. [Perh < *mappa,* cloth.] **—mop** *v.* **(mopped, mopping).**

mope (mōp) *v.* **moped, moping. 1.** To be gloomy or dejected. **2.** To dawdle. [Orig, to move as in a daze.] **—mop'er** *n.*

mo•ped (mō'pĕd') *n.* A low, two-wheeled, motor-driven vehicle having two pedals and resembling a bicycle. [MO(TOR) PED(AL).]

mo•raine (mə-rān') *n.* An accumulation of boulders, stones, or other debris carried and deposited by a glacier. [F.]

mor•al (môr'əl, mŏr'-) *adj.* 1. Of or concerned with the discernment or instruction of what is good and evil. 2. Being or acting in accordance with established standards of good behavior. 3. Arising from conscience. 4. Having psychological rather than tangible effects. 5. Based on likelihood rather than evidence. —*n.* 1. The principle taught by a story or event. 2. morals. Rules or habits of conduct, esp. sexual conduct. [< L *mōs* (*mōr-*), custom.] —mor'al•ly *adv.*

mo•rale (mə-răl') *n.* The state of mind of an individual or group with respect to confidence, cheerfulness, discipline, etc. [< F *moral,* moral.]

mor•al•ist (môr'ə-lĭst, mŏr'-) *n.* **1.** A teacher or student of ethics. **2.** One who follows a system of moral principles rather than an established religion. **—mor'a•lis'tic** *adj.*

mo•ral•i•ty (mə-răl'ə-tē, mô-) *n.* **1.** The quality of being moral. **2.** A set of ideas or customs of a given religion, society, or social class. **3.** Virtuous conduct.

mor•al•ize (môr'ə-līz', mŏr'-) *v.* **-ized, -izing.** To think about or discuss moral or ethical issues. **—mor'al•i•za'tion** *n.* **—mor'al•iz'er** *n.*

mo•rass (mə-răs', mô-) *n.* **1.** An area of low-lying, soggy ground; a bog or marsh. **2.** Any difficult or perplexing situation. [< OF *marasc.*]

mor•a•to•ri•um (môr'ə-tôr'ē-əm, -tōr'ē-əm, mŏr'-) *n., pl.* **-ums** or **-toria** (-tôr'ē-ə, -tōr'ē-ə). **1.** An authorization to a debtor permitting temporary suspension of payments. **2.** A deferment or delay of any action. [< L *morārī,* to delay.]

mo•ray (môr'ā, mōr'ā, mə-rā') *n.* Any of various often voracious tropical marine eels. [< Gk *muraina.*]

mor•bid (môr'bĭd) *adj.* **1.** Of, relating to, or caused by disease. **2.** Characterized by preoccupation with unwholesome matters. **3.** Gruesome; grisly. [L *morbidus,* diseased.] **—mor•bid'i•ty** *n.* **—mor'bid•ly** *adv.*

mor•dant (môr'dənt) *adj.* **1.** Bitingly sarcastic. **2.** Incisive and trenchant. [< OF *mordre,* to bite.] **—mor'dan•cy** *n.* **—mor'dant•ly** *adv.*

more (môr, mōr) *adj. superl.* **most. 1. a.** *compar. of* **many.** Greater in number. **b.** *compar. of* **much.** Greater in size, amount, extent, or degree. **2.** Additional; extra: *They need more food.* *—n.* A greater or additional quantity, number, degree, or amount. *—adv.* **1.** —Used to form the comparative of many adjectives and adverbs: *more difficult; more intelligently.* **2.** In addition; further; again; longer. **—more or less. 1.** About; approximately. **2.** To an undetermined degree. [< OE *māra* (adj), *māre* (adv and n). See **mē-**[3].]

More (môr, mōr), **Saint** (Sir) **Thomas.** 1478–1535. English statesman and author.

mo•rel (mə-rĕl', mô-) *n.* An edible mushroom with a brownish, spongelike cap. [< L *Maurus,* Moor.]

more•o•ver (môr-ō'vər, mōr-, môr'ō'vər, mōr'-) *adv.* Beyond what has been stated; further; besides.

mo•res (môr'āz, mōr'-, -ēz) *pl.n.* The traditional customs of a social group that come through general observance to have the force of law. [< L *mōs,* custom.]

Mor•gan (môr'gən), **J(ohn) P(ierpont).** 1837–1913. American capitalist and financier.

morgue (môrg) *n.* A place in which the bodies of persons found dead are temporarily kept. [< *le Morgue,* the mortuary building in Paris.]

mor•i•bund (môr'ə-bŭnd', mŏr'-) *adj.* At the point of death; about to die. [< L *morī,* to die.] **—mor'i•bund'ly** *adv.*

Mor•mon (môr'mən) *n.* A member of the Church of Jesus Christ of Latter-day Saints. **—Mor'mon** *adj.* **—Mor'mon•ism'** *n.*

morn (môrn) *n. Poetic.* The morning. [< OE *morgen.* See **mer-**[1].]

morn•ing (môr'nĭng) *n.* The first or early part of the day, esp. from sunrise to noon. [< MORN.] **—morn'ing** *adj.*

morn•ing-glo•ry (môr'nĭng-glôr'ē, -glōr'ē) *n.* Any of various twining vines with funnel-shaped, variously colored flowers that close late in the day.

mo•roc•co (mə-rŏk'ō) *n., pl.* **-cos.** A soft, grainy-textured goatskin leather.

Mo•roc•co (mə-rŏk'ō). A kingdom of NW Africa. Pop. 11,598,000. Cap. Rabat. **—Mo•roc'can** (mə-rŏk'ən) *adj.* & *n.*

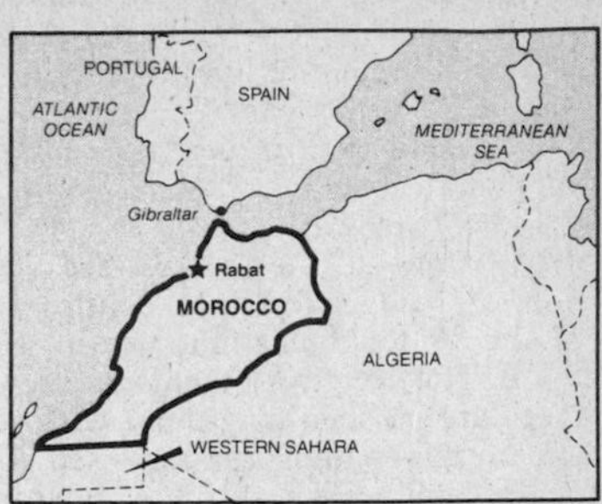

Morocco

mo•ron (môr'ŏn', mōr'-) *n.* A mentally retarded person, esp. one having mental age between 7 and 12 years. [< Gk *mōros,* foolish.] **—mo•ron'ic** (mə-rŏn'ĭk, mô-) *adj.*

mo•rose (mə-rōs', mô-) *adj.* Sullenly melancholy; gloomy. [L *mōrōsus,* captious, fretful.]

mor•pheme (môr'fēm') *n.* A linguistic unit that cannot be divided into smaller meaningful parts. [< Gk *morphē,* form.]

Mor•phe•us (môr'fē-əs, -fyo͞os') *n.* Something that causes sleep. [< *Morpheus,* Ovid's name for the god of dreams.]

-morphic, -morphous. *comb. form.* Possession of (some specified) shape or form: *polymorphic,* **amorphous.** [< Gk *morphē,* form.]

mor•phine (môr'fēn') *n.* An organic compound, $C_{17}H_{19}NO_3$, extracted from opium, the soluble salts of which are used in medicine as an anesthetic or sedative. [< MORPHEUS.]

mor•phol•o•gy (môr-fŏl'ə-jē) *n.* **1.** The biological study of the form and structure of organisms. **2.** *Ling.* The study of word formation, including the origin and function of inflections and derivations. [< Gk *morphē,* form + -LOGY.] **—mor'pho•log'i•cal** (-fə-lŏj'ĭ-kəl) *adj.* **—mor'pho•log'i•cal•ly** *adv.*

mor•row (môr'ō, mŏr'ō) *n.* **1.** The day following some specified day. **2.** *Archaic.* The morning. [< OE *morgen,* MORN.]

Morse code (môrs). A system of communication used in telegraphy in which letters and numbers are represented by short and long patterns of sounds, flashes of light, written dots and dashes, etc. [< S. *Morse* (1791–1872), American artist and inventor.]

A	•–	O	–––	É	••–••
B	–•••	P	•––•	Ñ	––•––
C	–•–•	Q	––•–	Ö	–––•
D	–••	R	•–•	Ü	••––
E	•	S	•••	1	•––––
F	••–•	T	–	2	••–––
G	––•	U	••–	3	•••––
H	••••	V	•••–	4	••••–
I	••	W	•––	5	•••••
J	•–––	X	–••–	6	–••••
K	–•–	Y	–•––	7	––•••
L	•–••	Z	––••	8	–––••
M	––	Á	•––•–	9	––––•
N	–•	Ä	•–•–	0	–––––

, (comma)	––••––	/	–••–•
. (period)	•–•–•–	- (hyphen)	–••••–
?	••––••	apostrophe	•––––•
;	–•–•–•	parenthesis	–•––•–
:	–––•••	underline	••––•–

Morse code

mor•sel (môr'səl) *n.* **1.** A small piece or bite of food. **2.** A tasty tidbit. [< L *mordēre,* to bite.]
mor•tal (môrt'l) *adj.* **1.** Liable or subject to death. **2.** Causing death; fatal. **3.** Fought to the death. **4.** Unrelenting; implacable: *a mortal enemy.* **5.** Like the fear of death: *in mortal terror.* **6.** Causing spiritual death: *a mortal sin.* —*n.* A human being. [< L *mors (mort-),* death.] —**mor'tal•ly** *adv.*
mor•tal•i•ty (môr-tăl'ə-tē) *n., pl.* **-ties. 1.** The condition of being subject to death. **2.** The ratio of deaths to population; death rate.
mor•tar (môr'tər) *n.* **1.** A receptacle in which substances are crushed or ground with a pestle. **2.** A muzzle-loading cannon used to fire shells in a high trajectory. **3.** A mixture of cement or lime with sand and water, used in building. [< L *mortārium,* a mortar and the substance made in it.]
mort•gage (môr'gĭj) *n.* **1.** A pledge of property to a creditor as security against a debt. **2.** A contract or deed specifying the terms of such a pledge. —*v.* **-gaged, -gaging.** To pledge (property) by mortgage. [< OF, "dead pledge."]
mort•ga•gee (môr'gĭ-jē') *n.* The holder of a mortgage.
mort•ga•gor (môr'gĭ-jôr', môr'gĭ-jər) *n.* One who mortgages his property.
mor•ti•cian (môr-tĭsh'ən) *n.* A funeral director; undertaker.
mor•ti•fy (môr'tə-fī') *v.* **-fied, -fying. 1.** To shame; humiliate. **2.** To discipline (one's body and appetites) by self-denial. **3.** To cause gangrene or become gangrenous. [< LL *mortificāre,* to cause to die.] —**mor'ti•fi•ca'tion** (-fĭ-kā'shən) *n.* —**mor'ti•fy'ing•ly** *adv.*
mor•tise (môr'tĭs) *n.* Also **mor•tice.** A cavity, usually rectangular, in a piece of wood or other material, prepared to receive a tenon of another piece, to join the two. [< OF *mortoise.*]
mor•tu•ar•y (môr'chōō-ĕr'ē) *n., pl.* **-ies.** A place where dead bodies are prepared or kept prior to burial or cremation. [< LL *mortuārius,* of burial.]
mos. months.
mo•sa•ic (mō-zā'ĭk) *n.* A picture or decorative design made by setting small colored pieces, such as tile, in mortar. [< Gk *mouseios,* belonging to the Muses.] —**mo•sa'ic** *adj.*
Mos•cow (mŏs'kou', -kō). The capital of the Soviet Union. Pop. 7,061,000.
Mo•ses (mō'zĭz, -zĭs). Hebrew prophet and lawgiver. —**Mo•sa'ic** (-zā'ĭk) *adj.*
mo•sey (mō'zē) *v. Informal.* To amble along. [?]
Mos•lem (mŏz'ləm, mŏs'-) *n.* Also **Mus•lim** (mŭz'ləm, mōōz'-, mŭs'-, mōōs'-), *archaic* **Mus•sul•man** (mŭs'əl-mən, mōōs'-). A believer in or adherent of Islam. —**Mos'lem** *adj.*
mosque (mŏsk) *n.* A Moslem house of worship.
mos•qui•to (mə-skē'tō) *n., pl.* **-toes** or **-tos.** Any of various winged insects of which the females suck blood and in some species transmit diseases. [< L *musca,* fly.]
moss (môs, mŏs) *n.* Any of various small, green, nonflowering plants often forming a dense, matlike growth. [< OE *mos.* See **meu-.**] —**moss'i•ness** *n.* —**moss'y** *adj.*
most (mōst) *adj.* **1. a.** *superl.* of **many.** Greatest in number. **b.** *superl.* of **much.** Greatest in amount, size, or degree. **2.** In the greatest number of instances: *Most fish have fins.* —*n.* **1.** The greatest amount, quantity, or degree; the largest part. **2.** *(takes pl. v.).* The greatest number (of a group or classification); the majority. —**at (the) most.** Not over; at the absolute limit: *four miles at most.* —**make the most of.** To use as advantageously as possible. —*adv.* **1.** In the highest degree, quantity, or extent: *most honest; what I need most.* **2.** Very: *a most impressive book.* **3.** *Informal.* Almost: *Most everyone agrees.* [< OE *mǣst.* See **mē-³.**]
-most. *comb. form.* Forms the superlative degree of adverbs and adjectives: **innermost.** [< OE *-mǣst, -mest.*]
most•ly (mōst'lē) *adv.* For the most part; almost entirely.
mote (mōt) *n.* A speck, esp. of dust. [< OE *mot.*]
mo•tel (mō-tĕl') *n.* A hotel for motorists, usually opening directly on a parking area. [Blend of MOTOR and HOTEL.]
mo•tet (mō-tĕt') *n.* A polyphonic musical composition based on a sacred text. [< OF *mot,* phrase, word.]
moth (môth, mŏth) *n., pl.* **moths** (mô*thz,* mŏ*thz,* môths, mŏths). **1.** Any of various insects related to and resembling the butterflies but generally night-flying and with featherlike antennae. **2.** Also **clothes moth.** A small whitish moth with larvae that feed on wool, fur, etc. [< OE *moththe.*]
moth ball. 1. A marble-sized ball of naphthalene, stored with clothes to repel moths. **2. moth balls.** Protective storage: *warships put into moth balls.*
moth•er (mŭ*th*'ər) *n.* **1.** A female parent. **2.** A creative or environmental source: *Necessity is the mother of invention.* —*adj.* **1.** Being a mother: *a mother hen.* **2.** Characteristic of a mother: *mother love.* **3.** Native: *one's mother tongue.* —*v.* **1.** To give birth to; be the mother of. **2.** To care for; nourish and protect. [< OE *mōdor.* See **māter-.**] —**moth'er•hood'** *n.*
moth•er-in-law (mŭ*th*'ər-ĭn-lô') *n., pl.* **mothers-in-law.** The mother of one's wife or husband.
moth•er•land (mŭ*th*'ər-lănd') *n.* One's native land.
moth•er•ly (mŭ*th*'ər-lē) *adj.* Of or characteristic of a mother; maternal.
moth•er-of-pearl (mŭ*th*'ər-əv-pûrl') *n.* The pearly internal layer of certain mollusk shells, used to make decorative objects.
mo•tif (mō-tēf') *n.* Also **mo•tive** (mō'tĭv, mō-tēv'). A recurrent thematic element used in the development of a musical, artistic, or literary work. [< OF, motive.]
mo•tile (mōt'l, mō'tĭl') *adj.* Moving or having the power to move spontaneously. [< MOTION.] —**mo•til'i•ty** (mō-tĭl'ə-tē) *n.*
mo•tion (mō'shən) *n.* **1.** The action or process of change of position. **2.** A significant movement of a part of the body; a gesture. **3.** A formal proposal put to vote under parliamentary procedures. —*v.* **1.** To signal to or direct by making a gesture. **2.** To make a gesture signifying something. [< L *movēre* (pp *mōtus*), to move.]
mo•tion•less (mō'shən-lĭs) *adj.* Not moving. —**mo'tion•less•ly** *adv.*
motion picture. A series of filmed images viewed in sufficiently rapid succession to create the illusion of motion and continuity. —**mo'tion-pic'ture** *adj.*
mo•ti•vate (mō'tə-vāt') *v.* **-vated, -vating.** To stimulate to action; provide with an incentive or motive. —**mo'ti•va'tion** *n.*
mo•tive (mō'tĭv) *n.* **1.** An impulse acting as an incitement to action. **2.** Variant of **motif.** —*adj.* Causing or able to cause motion. [< OF *motif,* "causing to move."]
mot•ley (mŏt'lē) *adj.* **1.** Having components of great variety; heterogeneous; varied. **2.** Having or exhibiting many colors; multicolored. [ME *motteley.*]
mo•tor (mō'tər) *n.* **1.** Anything that imparts or produces motion. **2.** A device that converts any form of energy into mechanical energy, esp. a device that converts electric current into mechanical power. —*adj.* **1.** Causing or producing motion. **2.** Driven by or having a motor. **3.** Of or for motor vehicles: *motor oil.* **4.** Relating to movements of the muscles. —*v.* To drive or travel in a motor vehicle. [< L *movēre* (pp *mōtus*), to move.]
mo•tor•boat (mō'tər-bōt') *n.* A boat propelled by an internal-combustion engine.
mo•tor•cade (mō'tər-kād') *n.* A procession of automobiles or other motor vehicles. [MOTOR + (CAVAL)CADE.]
mo•tor•car (mō'tər-kär') *n.* An automobile.
motor court. A motel.
mo•tor•cy•cle (mō'tər-sī'kəl) *n.* A vehicle with two wheels in tandem, propelled by an internal-combustion engine. —**mo'tor•cy'clist** (-sī'klĭst) *n.*
mo•tor•ist (mō'tər-ĭst) *n.* One who travels in an automobile.
mo•tor•ize (mō'tə-rīz') *v.* **-ized, -izing.** To equip with a motor or motors.
mo•tor•man (mō'tər-mən) *n.* One who drives an electrically powered streetcar, locomotive, or subway train.
motor scooter. A small two-wheeled vehicle powered by a gasoline engine.
mo•tor•ship (mō'tər-shĭp') *n.* A ship powered by an internal-combustion engine.
motor vehicle. Any self-propelled land vehicle that does not run on rails.
mot•tle (mŏt'l) *v.* **-tled, -tling.** To cover (a surface) with spots or streaks of different shades or colors.
mot•to (mŏt'ō) *n., pl.* **-toes** or **-tos.** A brief sentence, phrase, or single word used to express a principle, goal, or ideal; maxim. [It, "a word."]
mould. *Chiefly Brit.* Variant of **mold.**
mould•er. *Chiefly Brit.* Variant of **molder.**
moult. *Chiefly Brit.* Variant of **molt.**
mound (mound) *n.* **1.** A pile or bank of earth, sand, or rocks. **2.** A natural elevation, as a small hill. **3.** The slightly elevated pitcher's area in the center of a baseball diamond. [Perh < Du *mond,* protection.]
mount¹ (mount) *v.* **1.** To climb or ascend. **2.** To get up on: *mount a horse.* **3.** To increase in amount, degree, extent, intensity, or number. **4.** To place in an appropriate setting, as for display, study, etc. **5. a.** To set (guns) in position. **b.** To launch and carry out: *mount an attack.* —*n.* **1.** A horse or other animal on which to ride. **2.** An object to which another is affixed for accessibility, display, or use. [< VL **montāre,* "to climb a mountain."] —**mount'a•ble** *adj.*
mount² (mount) *n.* A mountain or hill. [< L *mōns,* mountain.]
moun•tain (moun'tən) *n.* A natural elevation of the earth's surface having a height greater than that of a hill. [< L *mōns,* mountain.] —**moun'tain** *adj.*
moun•tain•eer (moun'tən-îr') *n.* **1.** An inhabitant of a mountainous area. **2.** One who climbs mountains for sport. —*v.* To climb mountains for sport.
mountain lion. A large, tawny wild cat of mountainous regions of the W Hemisphere.
moun•tain•ous (moun'tən-əs) *adj.* Having

many mountains.

moun•te•bank (moun'tə-băngk') *n.* **1.** A hawker of quack medicines. **2.** Any charlatan or trickster. [It *montambanco,* "one who climbs on a bench."]

mount•ing (moun'tĭng) *n.* Something that provides a setting: *a mounting for a gem.*

mourn (môrn, mōrn) *v.* To feel or express sorrow (for or over). [< OE *murnan.* See **smer-¹.**] —**mourn'er** *n.*

mourn•ful (môrn'fəl, mōrn'-) *adj.* **1.** Feeling or expressing grief. **2.** Arousing or suggesting grief. —**mourn'ful•ly** *adv.*

mourn•ing (môr'nĭng, mōr'-) *n.* **1.** The actions or expressions of one who has suffered a bereavement. **2.** Clothes worn as a sign of grief for the dead. **3.** The period during which a death is mourned.

mouse (mous) *n., pl.* **mice** (mīs). Any of various small, usually long-tailed rodents, some of which live in or near human dwellings. —*v.* (mouz) **moused, mousing.** To hunt or catch mice. [< OE *mūs.* See **mū-.**]

mousse (mo͞os) *n.* Any of various chilled desserts made with whipped cream, gelatin, and flavoring. [F, "froth."]

mous•tache. *Chiefly Brit.* Variant of **mustache.**

mous•y (mou'sē, -zē) *adj.* **-ier, -iest.** Mouselike in color, features, or shyness: *mousy hair; a mousy person.* —**mous'i•ness** *n.*

mouth (mouth) *n., pl.* **mouths** (mou*thz*). **1.** The body opening and related organs with which food is taken in, chewed, and swallowed and sounds and speech are articulated. **2.** A natural opening, such as the part of a river that empties into a larger body of water or the entrance to a harbor, canyon, etc. **3.** The opening through which any container is filled or emptied. —*v.* (mou*th*). **1.** To utter in a meaninglessly declamatory manner. **2.** To put, take, or move around in the mouth. [< OE *mūth.* See **menth-.**]

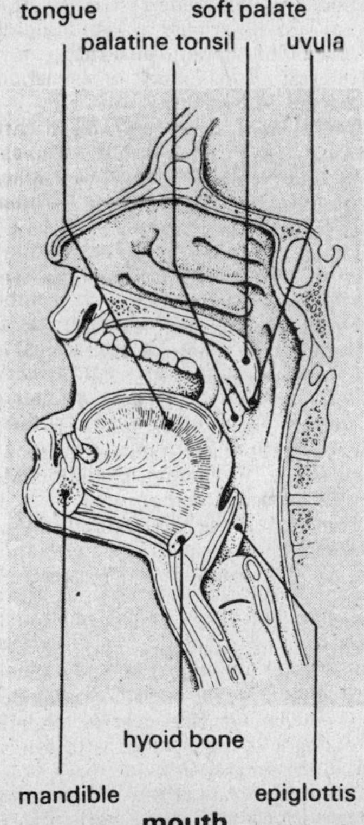

mouth

mouth organ. A harmonica.

mouth•piece (mouth'pēs') *n.* **1.** A part of an instrument that functions in or near the mouth. **2.** *Informal.* A spokesman.

mou•ton (mo͞o'tŏn') *n.* Sheepskin sheared and processed to resemble beaver or seal. [F, "sheep."]

move (mo͞ov) *v.* **moved, moving.** **1.** To change in position from one point to another. **2.** To transfer (a piece) in a board game. **3.** To settle in a new place. **4.** To change hands commercially: *Furs move slowly in summer.* **5.** To affect deeply. **6.** To take some action. **7.** To make a formal motion in parliamentary procedure. **8.** To cause (the bowels) to evacuate. —*n.* **1.** An act of moving. **2.** A change of residence or place of business. **3. a.** The transferring of a piece from one position to another in a board game. **b.** A player's turn to maneuver one of his pieces. **4.** One of a series of actions undertaken to achieve some end. [< L *movēre,* to move.]

move•ment (mo͞ov'mənt) *n.* **1. a.** An act of moving; a change in position. **b.** A maneuver in which military or naval units are moved toward some tactical or strategic objective. **2.** The activities of a group toward the achievement of a specific goal: *the labor movement.* **3.** Activity, esp. in business or commerce. **4.** An evacuation of the bowels. **5.** *Mus.* A primary section of a composition. **6.** A mechanism that produces or transmits motion, as the works of a watch.

mov•er (mo͞o'vər) *n.* **1.** One that moves. **2.** One whose occupation is transporting furnishings.

mov•ie (mo͞o'vē) *n. Informal.* **1.** A **motion picture.** **2.** A theater that shows motion pictures. **3. the movies.** A showing of a motion picture. [Short for moving picture.]

mow¹ (mō) *v.* **mowed, mowed** or **mown** (mōn), **mowing.** **1.** To cut down (grain, grass, etc.) with a scythe or mechanical device. **2.** To cut (such growth) from. —**mow down.** To fell in great numbers, as in battle. [< OE *māwan.* See **mē-⁴.**] —**mow'er** (mō'ər) *n.*

mow² (mou) *n.* A place for storing hay or grain. [< OE *mūwa.*]

Mo•zam•bique (mō'zăm-bēk'). A country in SE Africa, formerly an overseas province of Portugal. Pop. 7,376,000. Cap. Lourenço Marques.

Mo•zart (mōt'särt'), **Wolfgang Amadeus.** 1756–1791. Austrian composer.

MP military police; military policeman.

M.P. **1.** Member of Parliament. **2.** military police; military policeman.

mph, m.p.h. miles per hour.

Mr. (mĭs'tər) *n., pl.* **Messrs.** The abbreviated form of the title **Mister** when used with a name.

Mrs. (mĭs'ĭz) *n., pl.* **Mmes.** A title of courtesy used in speaking to or of a married woman, preceding her surname.

ms manuscript.

Ms., Ms (mĭz, ĕm'ĕs') *n., pl.* **Mses** or **Mss.** A title of courtesy used before a woman's surname or before her given name and surname without regard to her marital status. [Abbr. of **mistress,** formed by combining and shortening Miss and Mrs.]

mss, MSS, mss., MSS. manuscripts.

MST, M.S.T. Mountain Standard Time.

mt., Mt. mount; mountain.

m.t., M.T. Mountain Time.

mtn. mountain.

mu (m/y/o͞o) *n.* The 12th letter of the Greek alphabet, representing *m.*

much (mŭch) *adj.* **more, most.** Great in quantity, degree, or extent: *much rain.* —*n.* **1.** A large quantity or amount. **2.** Anything impressive or important: *not much of a swimmer.* —*adv.* **more, most.** **1.** To a great degree; to a large extent: *much better.* **2.** Just about; almost: *much the same.* [< OE *mycel, micel,* great, large, greatly. See **meg-.**]

mu•ci•lage (myo͞o'sə-lĭj) *n.* A sticky substance used as an adhesive. [< L *mūcus,* MUCUS.] —**mu'ci•lag'i•nous** (-lăj'ə-nəs) *adj.*

muck (mŭk) *n.* **1.** A moist, sticky mixture, esp. of mud and filth. **2.** Moist animal dung. **3.** Dark, fertile soil containing putrid vegetable matter. [< ON *mykr.*] —**muck'y** *adj.*

muck•rake (mŭk'rāk') *v.* **-raked, -raking.** To search for and expose political or commercial corruption. —**muck'rak'er** *n.*

mu•cous (myo͞o'kəs) *adj.* Also **mu•cose** (-kōs'). Producing or secreting mucus.

mucous membrane. The membrane lining all bodily channels that communicate with the air, the glands of which secrete mucus.

mu•cus (myo͞o'kəs) *n.* The viscous material secreted as a protective lubricant coating by glands in the mucous membrane. [L *mūcus.*]

mud (mŭd) *n.* **1.** Wet, sticky, soft earth. **2.** Slanderous charges; calumny. [ME *mudde.*]

mud•dle (mŭd'l) *v.* **-dled, -dling.** **1.** To make turbid; muddy. **2.** To mix confusedly; jumble. **3.** To mix up (the mind), as with alcohol; confuse. **4.** To mismanage or bungle. —*n.* A confusion, jumble, or mess. [Perh < MDu *moddelen,* to make muddy.]

mud•dy (mŭd'ē) *adj.* **-dier, -diest.** **1.** Covered, full of, or spattered with mud. **2.** Not clear or pure, as a color or liquid. —*v.* **-died, -dying.** **1.** To make muddy or dirty. **2.** To make dull or cloudy. —**mud'di•ness** *n.*

mud•guard (mŭd'gärd') *n.* A shield over a vehicle's wheel.

mud•sling•er (mŭd'slĭng'ər) *n.* One who makes malicious charges against an opponent. —**mud'sling'ing** *n.*

mu•ez•zin (m/y/o͞o-ĕz'ĭn) *n.* A Moslem crier who calls the faithful to prayer, usually from a minaret.

muff¹ (mŭf) *v.* To perform (an act) clumsily; bungle. [?] —**muff** *n.*

muff² (mŭf) *n.* A small cylindrical cover, open at both ends, for keeping the hands warm. [< MDu *moffel.*]

muf•fin (mŭf'ĭn) *n.* A small, cup-shaped bread, usually served hot. [Prob < LG *muffen.*]

muf•fle (mŭf'əl) *v.* **-fled, -fling.** **1.** To wrap up snugly for warmth or protection. **2.** To wrap or cover in order to deaden a sound. **3.** To deaden (a sound). [< OF *moufle,* mitten.]

muf•fler (mŭf'lər) *n.* **1.** A heavy scarf worn around the neck. **2.** Any device that absorbs noise, esp. that of an internal-combustion engine.

muf•ti (mŭf'tē) *n.* Civilian dress as distinguished from a uniform.

mug¹ (mŭg) *n.* A cylindrical drinking vessel, often having a handle. [?]

mug² (mŭg). *Slang. n.* **1.** The face of a person. **2.** A grimace. **3.** A hoodlum. —*v.* **mugged, mugging.** To waylay and beat severely, usually with intent to rob. —**mug'ger** *n.*

mug•gy (mŭg'ē) *adj.* **-gier, -giest.** Warm and extremely humid. [< ON *mugga,* to drizzle.] —**mug'gi•ly** *adv.* —**mug'gi•ness** *n.*

mu•lat•to (m/y/o͞o-lăt'ō, -lä'tō) *n., pl.* **-tos** or **-toes.** A person having one white and one Negro parent. [Span *mulato,* young mule, mulatto.] —**mu•lat'to** *adj.*

mul•ber•ry (mŭl'bĕr'ē, -bə-rē) *n.* **1.** A tree bearing sweet reddish or purplish berrylike fruit. 2. The fruit of such a tree. [< OE *mōrberie.*] —**mul'ber•ry** *adj.*

mulch (mŭlch) *n.* A protective covering, as of leaves, manure, or hay, placed around plants to prevent evaporation of moisture and freezing of roots. —*v.* To cover with a mulch. [Prob < OE *melisc,* mild, mellow.]

mulct (mŭlkt) *n.* A fine or similar penalty. —*v.* 1. To penalize by fining. 2. To acquire or take away from by trickery or deception. [L *mulcta,* a fine.]

mule¹ (myo͞ol) *n.* 1. The sterile hybrid offspring of a male ass and a female horse. 2. *Informal.* A stubborn person. [< L *mūlus,* mule.]

mule² (myo͞ol) *n.* A slipper that has no strap to fit around the heel. [< L *mulleus (calceus),* "red (shoe)."]

mu•le•teer (myo͞o'lə-tîr') *n.* A mule driver.

mul•ish (myo͞o'lĭsh) *adj.* Like a mule; stubborn. —**mul'ish•ness** *n.*

mull¹ (mŭl) *v.* To heat and spice (a beverage, such as wine). [Perh < ME *mul,* dust, meal, powdered spice.]

mull² (mŭl) *v.* To ponder or ruminate on (with *over*). [< ME *mullen,* to pulverize.]

mul•let (mŭl'ĭt) *n.* Any of various widely distributed, chiefly marine food fishes. [< L *mullus,* red mullet.]

mul•li•ga•taw•ny (mŭl'ĭ-gə-tô'nē) *n.* An East Indian meat soup strongly flavored with curry.

multi–. *comb. form.* 1. Many or much. 2. More than one. [< L *multus,* much.]

mul•ti•col•ored (mŭl'tĭ-kŭl'ərd) *adj.* Having many colors.

mul•ti•far•i•ous (mŭl'tə-fâr'ē-əs) *adj.* Having great variety; made up of many parts or kinds. [L *multifārius.*] —**mul'ti•far'i•ous•ness** *n.*

mul•ti•form (mŭl'tə-fôrm') *adj.* Having many forms, shapes, or appearances.

mul•ti•mil•lion•aire (mŭl'tə-mĭl'yə-nâr') *n.* One whose financial assets equal many millions of dollars.

mul•ti•na•tion•al (mŭl'tē-năsh'ə-nəl, -năsh'nəl) *adj.* 1. Having operations, subsidiaries, or investments in more than one country: *a multinational corporation.* 2. Of or in several or many countries: *a multinational research project.* —*n.* A multinational company or corporation.

mul•ti•ple (mŭl'tə-pəl) *adj.* Of or having more than one element, component, etc. —*n.* A quantity into which another can be divided with zero remainder. [< LL *multiplus.*]

mul•ti•ple-choice (mŭl'tə-pəl-chois') *adj.* Offering a number of answers from which the correct one is to be chosen.

multiple sclerosis. A degenerative disease of the central nervous system, in which hardening of tissue occurs.

mul•ti•pli•cand (mŭl'tə-plĭ-kănd') *n.* The number that is or is to be multiplied by another.

mul•ti•pli•ca•tion (mŭl'tə-plĭ-kā'shən) *n.* 1. The act of multiplying or process of being multiplied. 2. The propagation of plants and animals. 3. a. An operation on two real numbers in which the number of times either is taken in summation is determined by the value of the other. b. An extension of this operation to quantities other than real numbers.

multiplication sign. The sign ×, placed between multiplicand and multiplier.

mul•ti•plic•i•ty (mŭl'tə-plĭs'ə-tē) *n.* 1. The state of being various or manifold. 2. A large number.

mul•ti•pli•er (mŭl'tə-plī'ər) *n.* The number by which the multiplicand is multiplied. If 3 is multiplied by 2, 3 is the multiplicand and 2 is the multiplier.

mul•ti•ply (mŭl'tə-plī') *v.* **-plied, -plying.** 1. To increase in number, amount, or degree. 2. To breed; propagate. 3. To perform multiplication (on). [< L *multiplicāre.*]

mul•ti•stage (mŭl'tə-stāj') *adj.* Functioning by stages.

mul•ti•tude (mŭl'tə-t/y/o͞od') *n.* A great, indefinite number. [< L *multus,* many.]

mul•ti•tu•di•nous (mŭl'tə-t/y/o͞od'n-əs) *adj.* Very numerous; existing in great numbers.

mum¹ (mŭm) *adj.* Not talking. [Prob < LG.]

mum² (mŭm) *n. Informal.* A chrysanthemum.

mum•ble (mŭm'bəl) *v.* **-bled, -bling.** To speak or utter indistinctly by lowering the voice or partially closing the mouth. [< MUM¹.] —**mum'ble** *n.* —**mum'bler** *n.*

mum•bo jum•bo (mŭm'bō jŭm'bō). 1. An object believed to have supernatural powers; a fetish. 2. Confusing or meaningless activity; obscure ritual. [Mandingo *mā-mā-gyo-mbō,* "magician who makes the troubled spirits of ancestors go away."]

mum•mer (mŭm'ər) *n.* One who acts or plays in a mask or costume. [< MDu *mommer.*] —**mum'mer•y** *n.*

mum•mi•fy (mŭm'ə-fī') *v.* **-fied, -fying.** 1. To make into a mummy. 2. To shrivel up like a mummy. —**mum'mi•fi•ca'tion** *n.*

mum•my (mŭm'ē) *n., pl.* **-ies.** A body embalmed after death, as by the ancient Egyptians. [< Ar *mūmiyā.*]

mumps (mŭmps) *n. (takes sing. v.).* An inflammatory, contagious viral disease of the salivary glands and, sometimes, of the ovaries or testes. [Prob < Scand.]

munch (mŭnch) *v.* To chew steadily with a crunching sound. [ME *monchen.*]

mun•dane (mŭn'dān', mŭn'dān') *adj.* 1. Bound to earth; worldly. 2. Typical of or concerned with the ordinary. [< L *mundus,* the world.] —**mun•dane'ly** *adv.*

Mu•nich (myo͞o'nĭk). A city of SE West Germany. Pop. 1,193,000.

mu•nic•i•pal (myo͞o-nĭs'ə-pəl) *adj.* 1. Of or pertaining to a city or its government. 2. Having local self-government: *a municipal borough.* [< L *mūnicipium,* a franchised city.]

mu•nic•i•pal•i•ty (myo͞o-nĭs'ə-păl'ə-tē) *n., pl.* **-ties.** A city, town, or other district incorporated for local self-government.

mu•nif•i•cent (myo͞o-nĭf'ə-sənt) *adj.* Extremely liberal in giving; very generous. [< L *mūnificus,* "present-making," generous.] —**mu•nif'i•cence** *n.* —**mu•nif'i•cent•ly** *adv.*

mu•ni•tions (myo͞o-nĭsh'ənz) *pl.n.* War materiel. [< L *mūnīre,* to defend, fortify.]

mu•ral (myo͞or'əl) *n.* A picture or decoration, usually very large, applied directly to a wall or ceiling. —*adj.* 1. Of or like a wall. 2. Painted on a wall. [< L *mūrus,* a wall.] —**mu'ral•ist** *n.*

mur•der (mûr'dər) *n.* The unlawful killing of one human being by another, esp. with malice aforethought. —*v.* 1. To kill (a human being) unlawfully. 2. To mar or spoil by ineptness: *murder the English language.* [< OE *morthor.*] —**mur'der•er** *n.* —**mur'der•ess** *fem.n.*

mur•der•ous (mûr'dər-əs) *adj.* 1. Capable of, guilty of, or intending murder. 2. Characteristic of murder; brutal. 3. *Informal.* Very difficult or dangerous: *a murderous exam.*

murk (mûrk) *n.* Darkness; gloom. [< OE *mirce,* darkness.]

murk•y (mûr'kē) *adj.* **-ier, -iest.** 1. Dark or gloomy. 2. a. Heavy and thick with smoke, mist, etc. b. Turbid with sediment: *murky waters.* —**murk'i•ly** *adv.* —**murk'i•ness** *n.*

mur•mur (mûr'mər) *n.* 1. A low, indistinct, and continuous sound. 2. An indistinct complaint. 3. An abnormal sound, as from the heart or lungs. —*v.* To make or utter in a low, continuous, and indistinct sound. [< L.]

Mur•ray River (mûr'ē). A river of SE Australia.

mus. 1. museum. 2. music.

mus•cat (mŭs'kăt', -kət) *n.* A sweet white grape used for making wine or raisins. [< LL *muscus,* musk.]

Mus•cat (mŭs'kăt'). The capital of Oman. Pop. 6,000.

Mus•cat and O•man. See **Oman.**

mus•ca•tel (mŭs'kə-tĕl') *n.* A rich, sweet wine made from muscat grapes.

mus•cle (mŭs'əl) *n.* 1. A tissue composed of fibers capable of contracting and relaxing to effect bodily movement. 2. A contractile organ consisting of muscle tissue. 3. Muscular strength. —*v.* **-cled, -cling.** To force one's way. [< L *mūsculus,* "little mouse," muscle.]

mus•cle-bound (mŭs'əl-bound') *adj.* Having stiff, overdeveloped muscles, as from excessive exercise.

mus•cu•lar (mŭs'kyə-lər) *adj.* 1. Pertaining to or consisting of muscle or muscles. 2. Having strong muscles. —**mus'cu•lar'i•ty** (-lăr'ə-tē) *n.*

muscular dystrophy. A chronic, noncontagious disease of unknown cause, in which there is gradual but irreversible muscular deterioration.

mus•cu•la•ture (mŭs'kyə-lə-cho͝or') *n.* The system of muscles of an animal or a body part.

muse (myo͞oz) *v.* **mused, musing.** To ponder or meditate (on); consider reflectively or at length. [< OF *muser,* to muse, "sniff around."] —**mus'er** *n.*

Muse (myo͞oz) *n.* 1. *Gk.Myth.* Any of the nine daughters of Zeus, each of whom presided over a different art or science. 2. **muse.** The spirit regarded as inspiring a poet; a source of inspiration. [< Gk *Mousa.*]

mu•se•um (myo͞o-zē'əm) *n.* A building in which works of artistic, historical, and scientific interest are exhibited. [< Gk *mouseion,* "place of the Muses."]

mush (mŭsh) *n.* 1. Boiled cornmeal. 2. Anything thick, soft, and pulpy. 3. *Informal.* Maudlin sentimentality. [Prob var of MASH.]

mush•room (mŭsh'ro͞om', -ro͝om') *n.* Any of various fleshy fungi having an umbrella-shaped cap borne on a stalk, esp. one that is edible. —*v.* To multiply, grow, or expand rapidly. [< OF *mousseron.*]

mush•y (mŭsh'ē) *adj.* **-ier, -iest.** 1. Like mush; soft and pulpy. 2. *Informal.* Excessively sentimental. —**mush'i•ness** *n.*

mu•sic (myo͞o'zĭk) *n.* 1. The art of organizing sound so as to elicit an aesthetic response in a listener. 2. Vocal or instrumental sounds having some degree of rhythm, melody, and harmony. 3. A musical composition or body of such compositions. 4. Any aesthetically pleasing or harmonious sound or combination of sounds. [< Gk *mousikē (tekhnē),* (art) of the Muses.]

mu•si•cal (myo͞o'zĭ-kəl) *adj.* 1. Of, pertaining to, or capable of producing music. 2. Resembling music; melodious. 3. Set to or accompanied by music. 4. Devoted to or skilled in music. —*n.* Also **musical comedy.** A play in which dialogue is interspersed with songs and dances. —**mu'si•cal•ly** *adv.*

mu•si•cale (myo͞o'zĭ-kăl') *n.* A program of music performed at a social gathering.

mu•si•cian (myo͞o-zĭsh'ən) *n.* One skilled in composing or performing music.

mu•si•col•o•gy (myo͞o'zĭ-kŏl'ə-jē) *n.* The historic and scientific study of music. **—mu'si•col'o•gist** *n.*

musk (mŭsk) *n.* An odorous substance secreted by an Asian deer or produced synthetically, used in perfumery. [< Pers *mushk.*] **—musk'i•ness** *n.* **—musk'y** *adj.*

mus•kel•lunge (mŭs'kə-lŭnj') *n.* A large North American freshwater game fish similar to the pike. [< Algon.]

mus•ket (mŭs'kĭt) *n.* A smoothbore shoulder gun used in the 17th and 18th centuries. [< It *moschetto.*] **—mus'ket•eer'** (mŭs'kĭ-tîr') *n.*

mus•ket•ry (mŭs'kĭ-trē) *n.* **1.** Muskets collectively. **2.** The fire of muskets. **3.** The technique of using small arms.

Mus•kho•ge•an (mŭs-kō'gē-ən) *n.* Also **Mus•ko•ge•an.** A North American Indian language family, including Creek and Seminole. **—Mus•kho'ge•an** *adj.*

musk•mel•on (mŭsk'mĕl'ən) *n.* A melon, as the cantaloupe, having flesh with a musky aroma.

musk ox. A large, shaggy, horned mammal of N Canada and Greenland.

musk•rat (mŭs'krăt') *n.* **1.** An aquatic North American rodent with dense brown fur. **2.** The fur of this rodent.

Mus•lim (mŭz'ləm, mo͝os'-, mo͝oz'-) *n.* **1.** See **Moslem. 2.** A member of the **Nation of Islam. —Mus'lim** *adj.*

mus•lin (mŭz'lĭn) *n.* Any of various sturdy, plain-weave cotton fabrics, used esp. for sheets. [< It *mussolina,* "cloth of Mosul," city in Iraq.]

mus•quash (mŭs'kwăsh', -kwôsh') *n. Chiefly Brit.* The muskrat or its fur. [< Algon.]

muss (mŭs) *v.* To make messy or untidy; rumple. *—n.* A state of disorder; mess. [Perh var of MESS.] **—muss'y** *adj.*

mus•sel (mŭs'əl) *n.* Any of various narrow-shelled bivalve mollusks, esp. an edible marine species. [< L *mūsculus,* "little mouse," muscle, mussel.]

Mus•so•li•ni (mo͞os'sō-lē'nē), **Benito.** 1883–1945. Fascist dictator of Italy (1922–43).

Benito Mussolini

Mus•sul•man (mŭs'əl-mən) *n., pl.* **-men** or **-mans.** *Archaic.* A Moslem.

must (mŭst) *v.* —Used as an auxiliary to indicate: **1.** Necessity or obligation: *You must register in order to vote.* **2.** Probability: *It must be midnight.* **3.** Inevitability or certainty: *To each of us, death must come.* *—n.* An absolute requirement; something that should be done without fail. [< OE *mōtan,* to be allowed.]

mus•tache (mŭs'tăsh', mə-stăsh') *n.* Also *chiefly Brit.* **mous•tache.** The hair growing on the upper lip, esp. when cultivated and groomed. [< Gk *mustax,* the upper lip, mustache.]

mus•tang (mŭs'tăng') *n.* A wild horse of the W North American plains. [< Span *mestengo,* stray (animal).]

mus•tard (mŭs'tərd) *n.* **1.** Any of various plants with yellow flowers and often pungent seeds. **2.** A condiment made from powdered mustard seeds. **3.** Dark brownish yellow. [< OF *moustarde.*]

mustard gas. An oily, volatile liquid, $(ClCH_2CH_2)_2S$, used in warfare as a gaseous blistering agent.

mus•ter (mŭs'tər) *v.* **1.** To summon or assemble (troops). **2.** To gather up: *muster up courage.* **—muster in** (or **out**). To enlist (someone) in, or discharge (someone) from, military service. *—n.* A gathering, esp. of troops, as for inspection. **—pass muster.** To be acceptable. [< L *monstrāre,* to show, indicate.]

must•y (mŭs'tē) *adj.* **-ier, -iest.** Having a stale or moldy odor. [Var of obs *moisty* < MOIST.]

mu•ta•ble (myo͞o'tə-bəl) *adj.* **1.** Subject to change. **2.** Prone to frequent change; fickle. [< L *mūtāre,* to change.] **—mu'ta•bil'i•ty** *n.*

mu•tant (myo͞o'tənt) *n.* An organism differing from the parental strain or strains as a result of mutation. [< L *mūtāre,* to MUTATE.] **—mu'tant** *adj.*

mu•tate (myoo'tāt', myo͞o-tāt') *v.* **-tated, -tating.** To undergo or cause to undergo alteration, esp. by mutation. [L *mūtāre.*] **—mu'ta'tive** (myo͞o'tā'tĭv, myo͞o'tə-) *adj.*

mu•ta•tion (myo͞o-tā'shən) *n.* **1.** An alteration or change, as in nature, form, or quality. **2.** *Biol.* Any heritable alteration of an organism.

mute (myo͞ot) *adj.* **1.** Incapable of producing speech or vocal sound. **2.** Not speaking or spoken; silent. *—n.* **1.** A person incapable of speech, esp. one both deaf and mute. **2.** A device used to muffle or soften the tone of a musical instrument. *—v.* **muted, muting.** To soften the sound, color, or shade of. [< L *mūtus,* silent, dumb.] **—mute'ness** *n.*

mu•ti•late (myo͞ot'l-āt') *v.* **-lated, -lating. 1.** To deprive of a limb or other essential part. **2.** To disfigure by seriously damaging a part. [< L *mutilus,* maimed.] **—mu'ti•la'tion** *n.*

mu•ti•neer (myo͞ot'n-îr') *n.* One who takes part in a mutiny.

mu•ti•nous (myo͞ot'n-əs) *adj.* Engaged in or disposed toward mutiny.

mu•ti•ny (myo͞ot'n-ē) *n., pl.* **-nies.** Open rebellion against constituted authority, esp. by sailors or soldiers against their officers. [< OF *muete,* revolt, "movement."] **—mu'ti•ny** *v.* **(-nied, -nying).**

mutt (mŭt) *n. Slang.* A mongrel dog. [Short for *muttonhead.*]

mut•ter (mŭt'ər) *v.* **1.** To speak or utter in low, indistinct tones. **2.** To complain or grumble morosely. *—n.* A low, indistinct uttering or utterance. [ME *muteren.*]

mut•ton (mŭt'n) *n.* The flesh of fully grown sheep. [< ML *multō,* sheep.]

mu•tu•al (myo͞o'cho͞o-əl) *adj.* **1.** Having the same feelings each for the other: *mutual enemies.* **2.** Felt or directed for or toward each other: *mutual respect; mutual recriminations.* **3.** Possessed in common: *mutual interests.* [< L *mūtuus,* exchanged, mutual.] **—mu'tu•al'i•ty** (-ăl'ə-tē) *n.* **—mu'tu•al•ly** *adv.*

muz•zle (mŭz'əl) *n.* **1.** The usually projecting jaws and nose of certain animals. **2.** A device fitted over an animal's snout to prevent biting or eating. **3.** The front end of the barrel of a firearm. *—v.* **-zled, -zling. 1.** To put a muzzle on (an animal). **2.** To restrain (someone) from expressing opinions. [< LL *mūsum,* snout.]

muz•zle•load•er (mŭz'əl-lō'dər) *n.* A firearm loaded through the muzzle. **—muz'zle•load'ing** *adj.*

mV millivolt.

MV motor vessel.

my (mī). The possessive form of the pronoun *I,* used attributively: *my book.* *—interj.* Expressive of surprise, pleasure, or dismay. [< OE *mīn.* See **me-.**]

-mycin. *comb. form.* Derivation of a specified substance from bacteria or fungi: **streptomycin.** [< Gk *mukēs,* fungus.]

my•col•o•gy (mī-kŏl'ə-jē) *n.* The botanical study of fungi. [< Gk *mukēs,* fungus + -LOGY.] **—my'co•log'i•cal** (mī'kə-lŏj'ĭ-kəl) *adj.* **—my•col'o•gist** *n.*

my•e•lin (mī'ə-lĭn) *n.* Also **my•e•line** (mī'ə-lĭn, -lēn'). A white, fatty material that encloses some nerve fibers.

my•e•li•tis (mī'ə-lī'tĭs) *n.* Inflammation of the spinal column or bone marrow. [< Gk *muelos,* marrow + -ITIS.]

my•na (mī'nə) *n.* Also **my•nah.** Any of various Asian birds related to the starlings. [< Sk *madana.*]

my•o•pi•a (mī-ō'pē-ə) *n.* **1.** A visual defect in which distant objects appear blurred because their images are focused in front of the retina rather than on it; nearsightedness. **2.** Shortsightedness in thinking or planning. [< Gk *muōps,* myopic, "closing the eyes."] **—my•op'ic** (mī-ŏp'ĭk, -ō'pĭk) *adj.*

my•o•sin (mī'ə-sĭn) *n.* The commonest protein in muscle.

myr•i•ad (mîr'ē-əd) *adj.* Amounting to a very large, indefinite number. *—n.* A vast number. [< Gk *murios,* countless.]

myr•mi•don (mûr'mə-dŏn', -dən) *n.* A faithful follower who carries out orders without question.

myrrh (mûr) *n.* An aromatic gum resin obtained from several Asian or African trees and shrubs and used in perfume and incense. [< Gk *murrha.*]

myr•tle (mûrt'l) *n.* **1.** An Old World shrub with pink or white flowers and blackish berries. **2.** A trailing vine with evergreen leaves and usually blue flowers. [< Gk *murtos.*]

my•self (mī-sĕlf') *pron.* A form of the 1st person sing. pronoun: **1.** —Used reflexively: *I hurt myself.* **2.** —Used for emphasis: *I told him so myself.* **3.** —Used to indicate one's normal or proper state: *I am not myself today.* **—by myself. 1.** Alone. **2.** Without help.

mys•te•ri•ous (mĭ-stîr'ē-əs) *adj.* **1.** Full of mystery; difficult to explain or account for. **2.** Implying a mystery. **3.** Enigmatic. **—mys•te'ri•ous•ly** *adv.* **—mys•te'ri•ous•ness** *n.*

mys•ter•y (mĭs'tər-ē) *n., pl.* **-ies. 1.** Anything that arouses curiosity because it is unexplained, inexplicable, or secret. **2.** The quality of being inexplicable or secret. **3.** A piece of fiction dealing with a puzzling crime. **4.** A religious truth revealed through Christ to the elect. **5. mysteries.** Any of certain ancient Mediterranean cults and secret rites to which only initiates were admitted. [< Gk *mustērion,* "secret rites."]

mystery play. A medieval drama based on episodes in the life of Christ.

mys•tic (mĭs′tĭk) *adj.* **1.** Of or pertaining to mystics or mysticism. **2.** Mysterious. —*n.* One who practices a specified form of mysticism. [< Gk *mustikos.*]

mys•ti•cal (mĭs′tĭ-kəl) *adj.* **1.** Of or pertaining to the experience described by mystics. **2.** Spiritually symbolic. —**mys′ti•cal•ly** *adv.*

mys•ti•cism (mĭs′tə-sĭz′əm) *n.* A spiritual discipline aiming at union with the divine through deep meditation or contemplation.

mys•ti•fy (mĭs′tə-fī′) *v.* **-fied, -fying. 1.** To awe or perplex; bewilder. **2.** To make obscure or difficult to comprehend. [< F *mystère,* mystery.] —**mys′ti•fi•ca′tion** *n.* —**mys′ti•fi′er** *n.* —**mys′ti•fy′ing•ly** *adv.*

mys•tique (mĭ-stēk′) *n.* **1.** An attitude of mystical veneration conferring upon a person or thing an awesome and mythical status. **2.** The object of such veneration. [< L *mysticus,* mystic.]

myth (mĭth) *n.* **1.** A traditional story presenting supernatural beings, ancestors, or heroes that serve as primordial types in a primitive view of the world. **2.** Any fictitious or imaginary story, person, or thing. **3.** A notion based more on tradition or convenience than on fact. [< Gk *muthos.*] —**myth′i•cal** *adj.*

myth. mythological; mythology.

my•thol•o•gy (mĭ-thŏl′ə-jē) *n., pl.* **-gies.** A body of myths about the origin and history of a people. —**myth′o•log′i•cal** (mĭth′ə-lŏj′ĭ-kəl) *adj.* —**my•thol′o•gist** *n.*

Nn

n, N (ĕn) *n.* The 14th letter of the English alphabet.

n **1.** nano-. **2.** north; northern.

N **1.** nitrogen. **2.** north; northern.

n. **1.** net. **2.** north; northern. **3.** noun. **4.** number.

N. **1.** Norse. **2.** north; northern. **3.** November.

Na sodium (L *natrium*).

NAACP, N.A.A.C.P. National Association for the Advancement of Colored People.

nab (năb) *v.* **nabbed, nabbing.** *Slang.* **1.** To arrest. **2.** To grab. [Prob < Scand.]

na•bob (nā′bŏb′) *n.* A man of wealth or prominence.

na•cre (nā′kər) *n.* Mother-of-pearl. [< Ar *naqqārah,* shell.] —**na′cre•ous** (-krē-əs) *adj.*

Na-De•ne (nä-dā′nē) *n.* Also **Na-Dé•né.** A phylum of North American Indian languages including Athapascan.

na•dir (nā′dər, nā′dîr′) *n.* **1.** A point on the celestial sphere diametrically opposite the zenith. **2.** The lowest point. [< Ar *nazīr (as-samt),* opposite (the zenith).]

nae•vus. Variant of **nevus.**

nag¹ (năg) *v.* **nagged, nagging. 1.** To annoy by constant scolding, complaining, or urging. **2.** To torment with anxiety or discomfort: *nagged by worries.* **3.** To complain or find fault constantly. —*n.* One who nags. [< ON *gnaga,* to bite.] —**nag′ging•ly** *adv.*

nag² (năg) *n.* A horse, esp. an old or worn-out horse. [< MDu *negghe,* horse.]

Na•hua•tl (nä′wät′l) *n., pl.* **-tl** or **-tls. 1.** A member of a group of Mexican and Central American Indian tribes, including the Aztecs. **2.** The language of the Nahuatl.

nai•ad (nā′əd, nā′ăd′, nī′-) *n., pl.* **-ades** (-ə-dēz′) or **-ads.** *Gk. Myth.* One of the nymphs living in brooks, springs, and fountains.

na•if, na•ïf. Variants of **naive.**

nail (nāl) *n.* **1.** A slim, pointed piece of metal hammered into wood or other material as a fastener. **2.** A fingernail or toenail. —**hit the nail on the head.** To express the sense of something exactly and concisely. —*v.* **1.** To fasten with or as with nails. **2.** To secure or make sure of: *nail down the facts.* **3.** *Informal.* To stop and seize; catch. **4.** *Informal.* To strike; hit. [< OE *nægl.* See **nogh-.**]

Nai•ro•bi (nī-rō′bē). The capital of Kenya. Pop. 267,000.

na•ive, na•ïve (nä-ēv′) *adj.* Also **na•if, na•ïf** (nä-ēf′). Lacking worldliness and sophistication; artless; ingenuous. [< OF, ingenuous, natural < L *nātivus,* native.]

na•ive•té, na•ïve•té (nä′ēv-tā′) *n.* **1.** The quality of being naive. **2.** A naive statement or action.

na•ked (nā′kĭd) *adj.* **1.** Without clothing on the body; nude. **2.** Without covering, esp. without usual or natural covering. **3.** Without addition, concealment, etc.: *the naked facts.* [< OE *nacod.* See **nogw-.**] —**na′ked•ness** *n.*

N.A.M. National Association of Manufacturers.

Na•mib•i•a (nə-mĭb′ē-ə). A country of SW Africa. Pop. 900,000. Cap. Windhoek.

nam•by-pam•by (năm′bē-păm′bē) *adj.* **1.** Insipidly affected. **2.** Lacking vigor or decisiveness. [< *Namby-Pamby,* a satire on sentimental pastorals, by Henry Carey (died 1743).]

name (nām) *n.* **1.** A word or words by which any entity is designated. **2.** A disparaging designation: *called him names.* **3.** Verbal representation as opposed to reality: *a democracy in name only.* **4.** Reputation; renown. **5.** *Informal.* A famous or outstanding person. —*v.* **named, naming. 1.** To give a name to. **2.** To mention, specify, or identify by name. **3.** To nominate or appoint. —*adj. Informal.* Well-known by a name: *name brands.* [< OE *nama.* See **nomen-.**] —**nam′er** *n.*

name•less (nām′lĭs) *adj.* **1.** Having no name. **2.** Unknown by name. **3.** Inexpressible; indescribable: *nameless horror.*

name•ly (nām′lē) *adv.* That is to say; specifically.

nan•keen (năn-kēn′) *n.* Also **nan•kin** (năn-kēn′, -kĭn′). A sturdy yellow or buff cotton cloth. [< NANKING.]

Nan•king (năn′kĭng′). A city of E China. Pop. 1,419,000.

nan•ny (năn′ē) *n., pl.* **-nies.** *Chiefly Brit.* A children's nurse. [< baby-talk *nana.*]

nanny goat. A female goat. [< *Nanny,* pet form for Ann.]

nano–. *comb. form.* One-billionth of (a specified unit). [L *nānus,* dwarf.]

na•no•sec•ond (năn′ə-sĕk′ənd, nā′nə-) *n.* One-billionth of a second.

nap¹ (năp) *n.* A brief sleep, often during a period other than one's regular sleeping hours. —*v.* **napped, napping. 1.** To doze or sleep lightly for a brief period. **2.** To be unaware of imminent danger or trouble. [< OE *hnappian.*] —**nap′per** *n.*

nap² (năp) *n.* A soft, fuzzy surface on certain textiles, usually formed by raising fibers from the underlying material. —*v.* **napped, napping.** To form or raise a nap on (fabric or leather). [< MDu *noppe.*] —**nap′less** *adj.*

na•palm (nā′päm′) *n.* An incendiary mixture composed of gasoline, thickening agents, and other hydrocarbons.

nape (nāp) *n.* The back of the neck.

naph•tha (năf′thə, năp′-) *n.* A colorless flammable liquid obtained from crude petroleum, used as a solvent and as a raw material for gasoline. [Gk.]

naph•tha•lene (năf′thə-lēn′, năp′-) *n.* A white crystalline compound, $C_{10}H_8$, used to manufacture dyes, moth repellents, explosives, and solvents.

nap•kin (năp′kĭn) *n.* **1.** A soft piece of fabric or paper used at table to protect the clothes or wipe the lips. **2.** Any similar cloth or towel. [< L *mappa,* napkin, towel.]

Na•ples (nā′pəlz). A city of SW Italy. Pop. 1,221,000.

Na•po•le•on I (nə-pō′lē-ən, -pōl′yən). Surname, Bonaparte. 1769–1821. Emperor of the French (1804–15). —**Na•po′le•on′ic** (nə-pō′lē-ŏn′ĭk) *adj.*

Napoleon I

nar•cis•sism (när′sə-sĭz′əm) *n.* Excessive admiration of oneself. [< NARCISSUS.] —**nar′cis•**

sist (när'sə-sĭst) *n.* —**nar'cis•sis'tic** (när'sə-sĭs'-tĭk) *adj.*

nar•cis•sus (när-sĭs'əs) *n., pl.* **-suses** or **-cissi** (-sĭs'ī', -sĭs'ē). A widely cultivated plant having grasslike leaves and white or yellow flowers with a cup-shaped or trumpet-shaped central part. [< Gk *narkissos.*]

Nar•cis•sus (när-sĭs'əs). *Gk.Myth.* A youth who pined away for love of his own image reflected in a pool and was transformed into a flower.

nar•co•sis (när-kō'sĭs) *n.* Deep unconsciousness produced by a drug. [Gk *narkōsis,* a numbing.]

nar•cot•ic (när-kŏt'ĭk) *n.* Any drug that dulls the senses, induces sleep, and with prolonged use becomes addictive. [< Gk *narkōtikos,* numbing, narcotic.] —**nar•cot'ic** *adj.*

nar•co•tism (när'kə-tĭz'əm) *n.* Addiction to narcotics such as opium, heroin, or morphine.

nar•co•tize (när'kə-tīz') *v.* **-tized, -tizing. 1.** To place under the influence of a narcotic. **2.** To lull or induce to sleep.

nard (närd) *n.* A plant, spikenard, or a fragrant ointment obtained from it. [< Gk *nardos.*]

nar•es (nâr'ēz) *pl.n. Sing.* **-is** (-ĭs). The nostrils. [< L *nāris,* nostril.]

nar•rate (năr'āt', nă-rāt') *v.* **-rated, -rating. 1.** To tell (a story). **2.** To give an account or commentary. [L *narrāre.*] —**nar•ra'tion** *n.* —**nar'ra'tor, nar'ra'ter** *n.*

nar•ra•tive (năr'ə-tĭv) *n.* **1.** A story or description of actual or fictional events. **2.** The technique or process of narrating.

nar•row (năr'ō) *adj.* **1.** Of small or limited width, esp. in comparison with length. **2.** Limited in area or scope. **3.** Barely sufficient or successful: *a narrow margin of victory.* —*v.* To make or become narrow or narrower; lessen in width or extent. —*n.* **narrows.** A narrow body of water connecting two larger ones. [< OE *nearu.*] —**nar'row•ly** *adv.* —**nar'row•ness** *n.*

nar•row-mind•ed (năr'ō-mīn'dĭd) *adj.* Lacking breadth of view, tolerance, etc.; bigoted. —**nar'row-mind'ed•ness** *n.*

nar•whal (när'wəl) *n.* A whalelike mammal of arctic seas, having a long spiral tusk. [< ON *nāhvalr,* "corpse-whale."]

NASA (năs'ə) National Aeronautics and Space Administration.

na•sal (nā'zəl) *adj.* **1.** Of or pertaining to the nose. **2.** Uttered so that the air passes through the nose: *a nasal twang.* [< L *nāsus,* nose.] —**na•sal'i•ty** (nā-zăl'ə-tē) *n.*

nas•cent (năs'ənt, nā'sənt) *adj.* Coming into existence; in the process of emerging. [< L *nāscī,* to be born.] —**nas'cence** *n.*

Nash•ville (năsh'vĭl'). The capital of Tennessee. Pop. 448,000.

Nas•sau (năs'ô'). The capital of the Bahama Islands. Pop. 82,000.

na•stur•tium (nə-stûr'shəm, nă-) *n.* A plant with showy orange or yellow flowers and pungent leaves and seeds. [L *nāsturtium,* a kind of cress.]

nas•ty (năs'tē) *adj.* **-tier, -tiest. 1.** Disgusting to see, smell, or touch; filthy. **2.** Malicious; spiteful. **3.** Unpleasant: *nasty weather.* **4.** Painful and dangerous: *a nasty accident.* [ME.] —**nas'ti•ly** *adv.* —**nas'ti•ness** *n.*

nat. 1. national. **2.** native. **3.** natural.

na•tal (nāt'l) *adj.* **1.** Of, relating to, or accompanying birth. **2.** Of or pertaining to the time or place of one's birth. [< L *nāscī* (pp *nātus*), to be born.]

na•tion (nā'shən) *n.* **1.** An aggregation of people organized under a single government. **2.** A federation or tribe, esp. one composed of North American Indians. [< L *nātiō,* "race," "breed."]

na•tion•al (năsh'ən-əl, năsh'nəl) *adj.* **1.** Of, pertaining to, or characteristic of a nation. **2.** Of or relating to nationality. —*n.* A citizen of a particular nation. —**na'tion•al•ly** *adv.*

National Guard. The military reserve units controlled by each state of the U.S.

na•tion•al•ism (năsh'ən-əl-ĭz'əm, năsh'nəl-) *n.* **1.** Devotion to the interests of a particular nation. **2.** Aspirations for national independence. —**na'tion•al•ist** *adj.* & *n.* —**na'tion•al•is'tic** *adj.* —**na'tion•al•is'ti•cal•ly** *adv.*

na•tion•al•i•ty (năsh'ə-năl'ə-tē) *n., pl.* **-ties. 1.** The status of belonging to a particular nation by origin, birth, or naturalization. **2.** A people having common origins or traditions and constituting or considered to constitute a nation. **3.** Existence as a politically autonomous entity; the status of a nation. **4.** National character.

na•tion•al•ize (năsh'ən-əl-īz', năsh'nəl-) *v.* **-ized, -izing. 1.** To convert from private to governmental ownership and control. **2.** To make national. —**na'tion•al•i•za'tion** *n.*

Nation of Islam. An organization of American Negroes who follow the religious practices of Islam.

na•tion•wide (nā'shən-wīd') *adj.* Throughout a whole nation.

na•tive (nā'tĭv) *adj.* **1.** Inborn; innate. **2.** Being such by birth or origin. **3.** One's own because of the place or circumstances of one's birth: *his native land.* **4.** Originating or produced in a certain place; indigenous. —*n.* **1.** One born in or connected with a place by birth. **2.** An original inhabitant of a place. **3.** One belonging to a people of primitive culture originally occupying a country. [< L *nātīvus,* born, native.] —**na'tive•ly** *adv.*

na•tiv•i•ty (nə-tĭv'ə-tē, nā-) *n., pl.* **-ties. 1.** Birth, esp. the conditions or circumstances of one's birth. **2. Nativity.** The birth of Jesus. [< L *nātīvus,* born, NATIVE.]

natl. national.

NATO (nā'tō) North Atlantic Treaty Organization.

nat•ty (năt'ē) *adj.* **-tier, -tiest.** Neat, trim, and smart. [Perh < OF *net,* neat.]

nat•u•ral (năch'ər-əl, năch'rəl) *adj.* **1.** Present in or produced by nature; not artificial. **2.** Pertaining to or concerning nature. **3.** Produced solely by nature: *a natural death.* **4. a.** Inherent; innate. **b.** Distinguished by innate qualities or aptitudes. **5.** Free from affectation. **6.** Consonant with particular circumstances; expected and accepted. **7.** *Mus.* Not sharped or flatted. —*n.* **1.** *Informal.* One with talent for a particular endeavor. **2.** *Mus.* The sign (♮) placed before a note to cancel a preceding sharp or flat. —**nat'u•ral•ness** *n.*

natural history. The study of natural objects and organisms and their origins and interrelationships.

nat•u•ral•ism (năch'ər-ə-lĭz'əm, năch'rə-) *n.* Conformity to nature; factual or realistic representation, esp. in art and literature. —**nat'u•ral•is'tic** *adj.*

nat•u•ral•ist (năch'ər-ə-lĭst, năch'rə-) *n.* One who studies plants and animals in their natural environment.

nat•u•ral•ize (năch'ər-ə-līz', năch'rə-) *v.* **-ized, -izing. 1.** To grant full citizenship to. **2.** To adapt or acclimate (a plant or animal) to life in a new environment. —**nat'u•ral•i•za'tion** *n.*

nat•u•ral•ly (năch'ər-ə-lē, năch'rə-) *adv.* **1.** In a natural manner. **2.** By nature; inherently. **3.** Without a doubt; of course.

natural science. A science, such as biology, chemistry, or physics, based chiefly on objective quantitative hypotheses.

natural selection. 1. The principle that individuals possessing characteristics advantageous for survival in a specific environment constitute an increasing proportion of their species in that environment with each succeeding generation. **2.** The natural phenomenon of such a selective increase leading to new species.

na•ture (nā'chər) *n.* **1.** The intrinsic character of a person or thing. **2.** The order, disposition, and essence of all entities composing the physical universe. **3.** The physical world, including living things, natural phenomena, etc. **4.** The primitive state of existence. **5.** Kind; type: *something of that nature.* **6.** Disposition; temperament: *a sweet nature.* [< L *nātūra,* nature, "birth."] —**na'tured** *adj.*

naught (nôt) *n.* Also **nought. 1.** Nothing. **2.** A cipher; zero. [< OE *nā,* NO[1] + *wiht,* creature, thing.]

naugh•ty (nô'tē) *adj.* **-tier, -tiest.** Disobedient; mischievous: *a naughty child.* [< ME *nauht,* "worthless," naught.] —**naugh'ti•ly** *adv.* —**naugh'ti•ness** *n.*

nau•se•a (nô'zē-ə, -zhə, -sē-ə, -shə) *n.* **1.** A stomach disturbance characterized by a feeling of the need to vomit. **2.** Strong disgust. [< Gk *nausia,* seasickness.]

nau•se•ate (nô'zē-āt', -zhē-āt', -sē-āt', -shē-āt') *v.* **-ated, -ating.** To feel or cause to feel nausea. —**nau'se•a'tion** *n.*

nau•seous (nô'shəs, nô'zē-əs) *adj.* **1.** Causing nausea; sickening. **2.** Nauseated.

naut. nautical.

nau•ti•cal (nô'tĭ-kəl) *adj.* Of or pertaining to ships, seamen, or navigation. [< Gk *naus,* ship.] —**nau'ti•cal•ly** *adv.*

nautical mile. A unit of length used in sea and air navigation, esp. an international and U.S. unit equal to 1,852 meters, or about 6,076 feet.

nau•ti•lus (nô'tə-ləs) *n., pl.* **-luses** or **-li** (-lī'). A tropical marine mollusk with a partitioned spiral shell. [< Gk *nautilos,* sailor.]

nav. 1. naval. **2.** navigation.

Nav•a•ho (năv'ə-hō', nä'və-) *n., pl.* **-ho, -hos,** or **-hoes. 1.** A member of a group of Athapascan-speaking Indians occupying an extensive reservation in parts of New Mexico, Arizona, and Utah. **2.** The language of this group. —**Nav'a•ho'** *adj.*

na•val (nā'vəl) *adj.* Of, pertaining to, or possessing a navy.

nave (nāv) *n.* The central part of a church. [ML *nāvis,* "ship."]

na•vel (nā'vəl) *n.* The mark on the abdomen where the umbilical cord was attached during gestation. [< OE *nafela.* See **nobh-.**]

nav•i•ga•ble (năv'ə-gə-bəl) *adj.* **1.** Sufficiently deep or wide to provide passage for vessels. **2.** Capable of being steered, as a vessel or aircraft. —**nav'i•ga•bil'i•ty** *n.*

nav•i•gate (năv'ə-gāt') *v.* **-gated, -gating. 1.** To control the course of a ship or aircraft. **2.** To voyage over water in a boat or ship; sail. [L *nāvigāre,* to manage a ship.] —**nav'i•ga'tion** *n.* —**nav'i•ga'tor** *n.*

na•vy (nā'vē) *n., pl.* **-vies. 1.** All of a nation's warships. **2.** Often **Navy.** A nation's entire military organization for sea warfare and defense. [< L *nāvis,* ship.]

nay (nā) *adv.* **1.** No. **2.** And moreover: *He was ill-favored, nay, hideous.* —*n.* A negative vote.

[< ON *nei.*]

Naz•a•reth (năz'ə-rĭth). A town in N Israel, site of Jesus' childhood.

Na•zi (nät'sē, năt'-) *n., pl.* **-zis.** A member or supporter of the fascist National Socialist German Workers' Party, brought to power in 1933 under Adolf Hitler. —**Na'zi** *adj.* —**Na'zism',** **Na'zi•ism'** *n.*

Nb niobium.

N.B. 1. New Brunswick. 2. nota bene.

N.C. North Carolina.

NCO, N.C.O. noncommissioned officer.

Nd neodymium.

N.D. North Dakota (unofficial).

N. Dak. North Dakota.

N'Dja•me•na (ĕn-jä'mə-nə). The capital of Chad. Pop. 135,000.

Ne neon.

NE northeast.

N.E. New England.

NEA, N.E.A. National Education Association.

Ne•an•der•thal (nē-ăn'dər-thôl', -tôl', nā-än'-dər-täl') *adj.* 1. Of, pertaining to, or designating an extinct primitive man of the Stone Age. 2. Crude, primitive, or boorish.

neap tide (nēp). A tide of lowest range. [< OE *nēp(flōd),* neap (tide).]

near (nîr) *adv.* To, at, or within a short distance or interval in space or time. —*adj.* 1. Close in time, space, position, or degree. 2. Closely related; intimate. 3. Accomplished or missed by a small margin: *a near accident.* 4. Closer of two or more. —*prep.* Close to; within a short distance or time of. —*v.* To come close or closer to; draw near. [< OE *nēah,* near < Gmc **nēwh-iz.*] —**near'ness** *n.*

near•by (nîr'bī') *adj. & adv.* Not far away; adjacent.

Near East. The countries of the E Mediterranean and the Arabian Peninsula.

near•ly (nîr'lē) *adv.* Almost but not quite.

near•sight•ed (nîr'sī'tĭd) *adj.* 1. Afflicted with myopia. 2. Shortsighted. —**near'sight'ed•ly** *adv.* —**near'sight'ed•ness** *n.*

neat (nēt) *adj.* 1. In good order or clean condition; tidy. 2. Orderly in appearance or procedure. 3. Skillfully executed; adroit. 4. Simple and smoothly consistent. 5. Not diluted with other substances: *neat whiskey.* 6. *Slang.* Stylish; appealing. [< L *nitidus,* elegant, shiny.] —**neat'ly** *adv.* —**neat'ness** *n.*

Nebr. Nebraska.

Ne•bras•ka (nə-brăs'kə). A Midwestern state of the U.S. Pop. 1,484,000. Cap. Lincoln. —**Ne•bras'kan** *adj. & n.*

Neb•u•chad•nez•zar II (nĕb'ə-kəd-nĕz'ər, nĕb'yŏŏ-). King of Babylon (605–562 B.C.).

neb•u•la (nĕb'yə-lə) *n., pl.* **-lae** (-lē', -lī') or **-las.** Any diffuse mass of interstellar dust or gas or both. [< L, cloud.] —**neb'u•lar** *adj.*

neb•u•los•i•ty (nĕb'yə-lŏs'ə-tē) *n., pl.* **-ties.** The quality or condition of being nebulous.

neb•u•lous (nĕb'yə-ləs) *adj.* Lacking definite form or limits; unclearly established. [< L *nebula,* cloud.] —**neb'u•lous•ly** *adv.*

nec•es•sar•i•ly (nĕs'ə-sĕr'ə-lē) *adv.* 1. By necessity. 2. Inevitably.

nec•es•sar•y (nĕs'ə-sĕr'ē) *adj.* 1. Needed for the continuing existence or functioning of something; essential. 2. Needed to achieve a certain result; requisite. 3. Required by obligation, compulsion, etc. —*n.* Often **necessaries.** That which is needed. [< L *necesse,* necessary.]

ne•ces•si•tate (nə-sĕs'ə-tāt') *v.* **-tated, -tating.** To make necessary or unavoidable. —**ne•ces'si•ta'tion** *n.*

ne•ces•si•tous (nə-sĕs'ə-təs) *adj.* Needy; indigent. —**ne•ces'si•tous•ly** *adv.*

ne•ces•si•ty (nə-sĕs'ə-tē) *n., pl.* **-ties.** 1. Something necessary. 2. The state or fact of being necessary or unavoidable. 3. Pressing or urgent need.

neck (nĕk) *n.* 1. The part of the body joining the head to the trunk. 2. The part of a garment around or near the neck of the wearer. 3. Any relatively narrow elongation or connecting part: *a neck of land.* 4. a. The length of the head and neck of a horse: *won the race by a neck.* b. *Slang.* Any narrow margin by which a competition is won. —*v. Slang.* To kiss and caress. [< OE *hnecca.*]

neck•er•chief (nĕk'ər-chĭf) *n.* A kerchief worn around the neck.

neck•lace (nĕk'lĭs) *n.* An ornament, such as a string of beads, worn around the neck.

neck•line (nĕk'līn') *n.* The line formed by the edge of a garment at the neck.

neck•tie (nĕk'tī') *n.* A narrow band of fabric worn around the neck and tied in a knot or bow.

nec•ro•man•cy (nĕk'rə-măn'sē) *n.* The art that professes to conjure up and commune with the spirits of the dead in order to predict the future. [< Gk *nekromanteia,* divination by corpses, and < ML *nigromantia,* black magic.] —**nec'ro•man'cer** *n.*

nec•tar (nĕk'tər) *n.* 1. *Gk.&Rom.Myth.* The drink of the gods. 2. The undiluted juice of a fruit. 3. A sweet liquid secreted by flowers. [< Gk *nektar.*]

nec•tar•ine (nĕk'tə-rēn') *n.* A smooth-skinned variety of peach. [< obs *nectarine,* "sweet as nectar."]

née (nā) *adj.* Also **nee.** Born: *Mrs. Mary Parks, née Case.* [< F *naître,* to be born.]

need (nēd) *n.* 1. A state in which something necessary or desirable is required or wanted. 2. A wish for something lacking or desired. 3. Necessity; obligation. 4. Poverty. —*v.* 1. —Used with an infinitive to express necessity or obligation: *He needs to study.* 2. To want urgently; require. 3. To be in want. [< OE *nēd,* necessity, distress. See **nāu-.**]

Usage: Need, as an auxiliary verb, is not inflected in the third person singular present tense in negative statements and questions: *He need not come. Need it have happened?*

need•ful (nēd'fəl) *adj.* Necessary; required.

nee•dle (nēd'l) *n.* 1. A small, slender sewing implement, made of steel, pointed at one end and having an eye at the other to hold thread. 2. Any of various implements similar in shape and use, as a knitting needle. 3. A small, pointed stylus used to transmit vibrations from the grooves of a phonograph record. 4. Any slender pointer or indicator, as on a magnet. 5. A stiff, narrow leaf, as of a pine. 6. Any fine, sharp projection. —*v.* **-dled, -dling.** To goad, provoke, or tease. [< OE *nǣdl.* See **snē-¹.**]

nee•dle•point (nēd'l-point') *n.* 1. Decorative needlework on canvas. 2. A type of lace worked on paper patterns with a needle.

need•less (nēd'lĭs) *adj.* Not needed; unnecessary. —**need'less•ly** *adv.*

nee•dle•work (nēd'l-wûrk') *n.* Work done with a needle, esp. embroidery.

need•n't (nēd'ənt). Contraction of *need not.*

needs (nēdz) *adv.* Necessarily: *He must needs go.*

need•y (nē'dē) *adj.* **-ier, -iest.** Being in need; impoverished. —**need'i•ness** *n.*

ne'er (nâr). *Poetic.* Contraction of *never.*

ne'er-do-well (nâr'dŏŏ-wĕl') *n.* An irresponsible person.

ne•far•i•ous (nĭ-fâr'ē-əs) *adj.* Evil; wicked. [< L *nefās,* sin.] —**ne•far'i•ous•ness** *n.*

neg. negative.

ne•gate (nĭ-gāt') *v.* **-gated, -gating.** 1. To render ineffective or invalid; nullify. 2. To rule out; deny. [L *negāre,* to deny.]

ne•ga•tion (nĭ-gā'shən) *n.* 1. The act of negating. 2. A denial, contradiction, or negative statement.

neg•a•tive (nĕg'ə-tĭv) *adj.* 1. Expressing negation, refusal, or denial. 2. Lacking the quality of being positive or affirmative. 3. Pertaining to or denoting a quantity less than zero or a quantity, number, angle, velocity, or direction in a sense opposite to another indicated or understood to be positive. 4. Pertaining to or denoting electric charge of the same sign as that of an electron, designated by the symbol (-). —*n.* 1. A negative word, statement, or concept. 2. The side opposing the opinion upheld by the affirmative side in a debate. 3. a. An image in which the light areas of the object rendered appear dark and the dark areas appear light. b. A film, plate, or other photographic material containing such an image. —*adv.* No. —*v.* **-tived, -tiving.** 1. To refuse to approve; veto. 2. To deny; contradict. [< L *negāre,* to NEGATE.] —**neg'a•tive•ly** *adv.* —**neg'a•tive•ness, neg'a•tiv'i•ty** *n.*

ne•glect (nĭ-glĕkt') *v.* 1. To disregard; ignore. 2. To fail to care for or give proper attention to. 3. To fail to do through oversight. —*n.* 1. The act or an instance of neglecting something. 2. The state of being neglected. [< L *neglegere,* "not to choose," not to heed.] —**ne•glect'er, ne•glec'tor** *n.*

ne•glect•ful (nĭ-glĕkt'fəl) *adj.* Careless; heedless. —**ne•glect'ful•ly** *adv.*

neg•li•gee (nĕg'lĭ-zhā') *n.* A woman's dressing gown, often of delicate fabric. [F, "casual," "neglected."]

neg•li•gence (nĕg'lĭ-jəns) *n.* 1. The state or quality of being negligent. 2. Any negligent act or failure to act.

neg•li•gent (nĕg'lĭ-jənt) *adj.* 1. Habitually guilty of neglect. 2. Extremely careless.

neg•li•gi•ble (nĕg'lĭ-jə-bəl) *adj.* Not worth considering; trifling: *a negligible amount.* [< L *negligere,* to neglect.] —**neg'li•gi•bly** *adv.*

ne•go•tia•ble (nĭ-gō'shə-bəl, -shē-ə-bəl) *adj.* 1. Capable of being negotiated. 2. Capable of being legally transferred from one person to another. —**ne•go'tia•bil'i•ty** *n.*

ne•go•ti•ate (nĭ-gō'shē-āt') *v.* **-ated, -ating.** 1. To confer with another or others in order to come to terms. 2. To arrange by conferring: *negotiate a contract.* 3. To transfer ownership of (financial documents) to another party in return for value received. 4. To succeed in getting across, through, or around: *negotiate a curve.* [< L *negōtium,* business, "lack of leisure."] —**ne•go'ti•a'tion** *n.* —**ne•go'ti•a'tor** *n.*

Ne•gril•lo (nĭ-grĭl'ō, -grē'yō) *n., pl.* **-los** or **-loes.** One of a group of Negroid peoples of Africa who are short in stature.

Ne•gri•to (nĭ-grē'tō) *n., pl.* **-tos** or **-toes.** 1. A Negrillo. 2. One of various groups of Negroid people of short stature inhabiting parts of Malaysia, the Philippines, and SE Asia.

Ne•gro (nē'grō) *n., pl.* **-groes.** 1. A member of the Negroid ethnic division of the human species, esp. one of various peoples of C and S Africa. 2. A descendant of these or other Negroid peoples. —*adj.* 1. Pertaining to or characteristic of a Negro or Negroes. 2. Negroid.

Ne•groid (nē'groid') *adj.* **1.** Pertaining to a major ethnic division of the human species having brown to black skin color. **2.** Of or characteristic of Negroes. —**Ne'groid'** *n.*

Neh. Nehemiah.

Neh•ru (nā'rōō), **Jawaharlal.** 1889–1964. Indian nationalist leader; first prime minister (1947–64).

neigh (nā) *v.* To utter the breathy, prolonged cry of a horse. [< OE *hnǣgan.*] —**neigh** *n.*

neigh•bor (nā'bər). Also *chiefly Brit.* **neigh•bour.** *n.* One living or located near or next to another. —*v.* To lie close to; live or be situated nearby. [< OE *nēah,* near + *gebūr,* dweller (see **bheu-**).]

neigh•bor•hood (nā'bər-hŏŏd') *n.* **1.** A district considered in regard to its inhabitants or characteristics. **2.** The people who live in a particular vicinity. **3.** *Informal.* Approximate amount: *in the neighborhood of ten dollars.*

neigh•bor•ing (nā'bər-ĭng) *adj.* Living or situated close by.

neigh•bor•ly (nā'bər-lē) *adj.* Of or characteristic of a neighbor; friendly; helpful. —**neigh'bor•li•ness** *n.*

nei•ther (nē'*th*ər, nī'-) *adj.* Not one or the other: *Neither shoe fits.* —*pron.* Not the one nor the other: *Neither of them fits.* —*conj.* Not either; not in either case (with *nor*): *Neither we nor they want it.* [< OE *nā,* no, not + *hwæther,* which of two (see **kwo-**).]

Usage: When all the elements within a *neither . . . nor* construction are singular, the verb is always singular: *Neither he nor she was told.* When the elements are all plural, the verb is plural. When the elements differ in number, the verb agrees in number with the element to which it is nearer: *Neither my father nor my uncles were included.* When the nearer element is a personal pronoun, the verb agrees with it: *Neither Tom nor I know.* The same rule applies to *either. . . or* constructions.

nem•e•sis (nĕm'ə-sĭs) *n., pl.* **-ses** (-sēz'). **1.** An inflicter of retribution; avenger. **2.** An unbeatable rival, as in sports. **3.** Retributive justice. [< Gk, retribution.]

neo–, Neo–. *comb. form.* **1.** A new or recent form, development, or type. **2.** A recent formation, modification, or abnormal change. **3.** The most recent subdivision of a series of periods. [< Gk *neos,* new.]

ne•o•clas•si•cism (nē'ō-klăs'ə-sĭz'əm) *n.* A revival of classical aesthetics and forms in art, music, and literature. —**ne'o•clas'sic, ne'o•clas'si•cal** *adj.*

ne•o•dym•i•um (nē'ō-dĭm'ē-əm) *n. Symbol* **Nd** A bright, silvery rare-earth metallic element, used for coloring glass and in some lasers. Atomic number 60, atomic weight 144.24

Ne•o•lith•ic (nē'ə-lĭth'ĭk) *adj.* Of or denoting a period of human culture beginning around 10,000 B.C. in the Middle East and later elsewhere and characterized by the invention of farming and the making of technically advanced stone implements. —*n.* The Neolithic Age.

ne•ol•o•gism (nē-ŏl'ə-jĭz'əm) *n.* A newly coined word or expression.

ne•on (nē'ŏn') *n. Symbol* **Ne** An inert gaseous element occurring in the atmosphere to the extent of 18 parts per million, used in display and television tubes. Atomic number 10, atomic weight 20.183. [< Gk *neos,* new.]

ne•o•phyte (nē'ə-fīt') *n.* **1.** A recent convert. **2.** A beginner; novice. [< Gk *neophutos,* "newly planted."]

ne•o•plasm (nē'ə-plăz'əm) *n.* An abnormal new growth of tissue; tumor.

ne•o•prene (nē'ə-prēn') *n.* A synthetic rubber used in weather-resistant products, adhesives, and shoe soles.

Ne•pal (nə-pôl', -päl'). A kingdom in the Himalayas. Pop. 9,500,000. Cap. Katmandu.

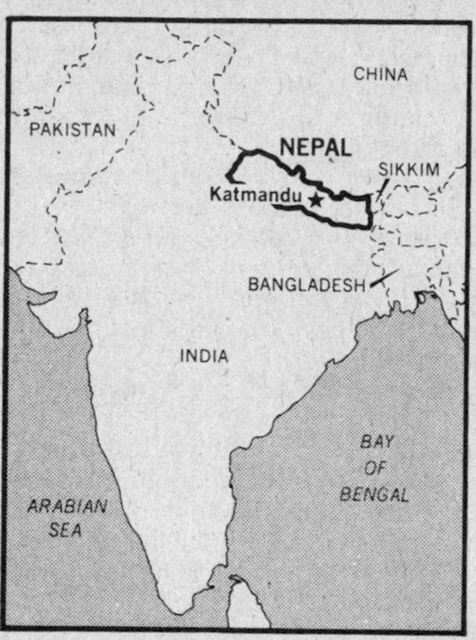

Nepal

Nep•al•ese (nĕp'əl-ēz') *n., pl.* **-ese. 1.** A native or resident of Nepal. **2.** The central Indic language of Nepal. —**Nep'al•ese'** *adj.*

ne•pen•the (nĭ-pĕn'thē) *n.* **1.** A drug of ancient times used to remedy grief and pain. **2.** Anything that eases suffering. [Gk *nēpenthes (pharmakon),* "grief-banishing (drug)."]

neph•ew (nĕf'yōō) *n.* The son of one's brother, sister, brother-in-law, or sister-in-law. [< L *nepōs,* nephew, grandson.]

neph•rite (nĕf'rīt') *n.* A white to dark green variety of jade. [G *Nephrit,* "kidney mineral."]

ne•phri•tis (nə-frī'tĭs) *n.* Any of various acute or chronic inflammations of the kidneys.

nephro–. *comb. form.* The kidney. [< Gk *nephros,* kidney.]

nep•o•tism (nĕp'ə-tĭz'əm) *n.* Favoritism shown to relatives, esp. in filling political positions. [< It *nepotismo,* "favoring of nephews."] —**nep'o•tis'tic, nep'o•tis'ti•cal** *adj.*

Nep•tune (nĕp't/y/ōōn') *n.* **1.** Roman god of the sea. **2.** The 8th planet from the sun, having a sidereal period of revolution around the sun of 164.8 years at a mean distance of 2.8 billion miles, a mean radius of 14,000 miles, and a density 17.2 times that of Earth. —**Nep•tu'ni•an** *adj.*

nep•tu•ni•um (nĕp-t/y/ōō'nē-əm) *n. Symbol* **Np** A silvery, metallic, naturally radioactive element. Atomic number 93, longest-lived isotope Np 237.

Ne•ro (nîr'ō). Roman emperor (A.D. 54–68).

nerve (nûrv) *n.* **1.** Any of the bundles of fibers interconnecting the central nervous system and the organs or parts of the body, capable of transmitting both sensory stimuli and motor impulses from one part of the body to another. **2. a.** Forcefulness; stamina. **b.** Strong will; courage. **c.** *Informal.* Brazenness; effrontery. **3. nerves.** Neurological manifestations, such as involuntary trembling, agitation, or hysteria. [L *nervus,* sinew, nerve.]

nerve cell. Any of the cells of nerve tissue consisting of a nucleated portion, and cytoplasmic extensions, the cell body, the dendrites, and axons.

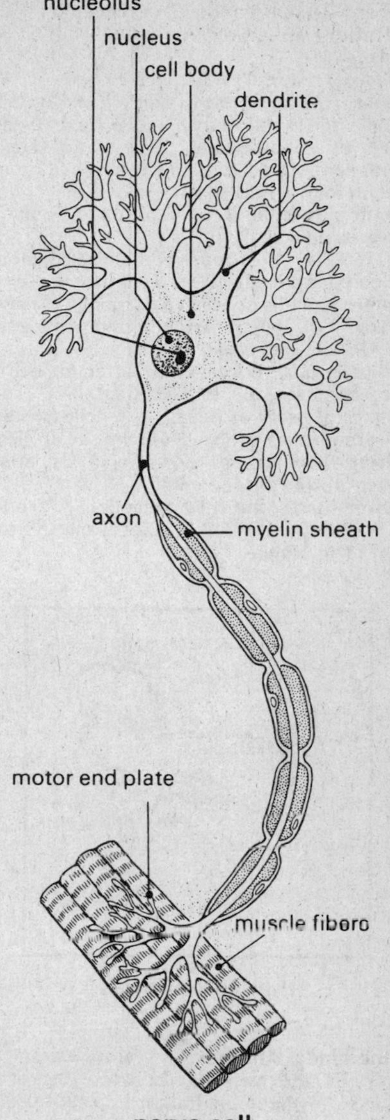

nerve cell

nerve•less (nûrv'lĭs) *adj.* **1.** Listless; inert. **2.** Self-controlled. —**nerve'less•ly** *adv.*

nerve-rack•ing (nûrv'răk'ĭng) *adj.* Also **nerve-wrack•ing.** Intensely distressing.

nerv•ous (nûr'vəs) *adj.* **1.** High-strung; excitable. **2.** Spirited. **3. a.** Of or relating to the nerves or nervous system. **b.** Stemming from or affecting the nerves or nervous system: *a nervous disorder.* **4.** Uneasy; anxious. —**ner'vous•ly** *adv.* —**ner'vous•ness** *n.*

nervous system. A coordinating mechanism in all multicellular animals, except sponges, that regulates internal body functions and responses to external stimuli.

nerv•y (nûr'vē) *adj.* **-ier, -iest. 1.** Brazen; rude. **2.** Showing fortitude or endurance. **3.** Nervous. —**nerv'i•ly** *adv.* —**nerv'i•ness** *n.*

–ness. *comb. form.* **1.** State, quality, or condition of being: **quietness. 2.** An instance or example of a state, quality, or condition: **kindness.** [< OE.]

nest (nĕst) *n.* **1. a.** The structure made by a bird for holding its eggs and young. **b.** A similar structure, as for fish or insect eggs. **2.** A snug, secluded place. **3.** A den; haunt.

4. A set of objects that can be stacked together. —*v.* **1.** To build or occupy a nest. **2.** To fit or place snugly together. [< OE. See **nizdo-.**]

nest egg. A reserve fund of money.

nes•tle (nĕs'əl) *v.* **-tled, -tling. 1. a.** To settle snugly and comfortably. **b.** To lie half-sheltered, as a house near trees. **2.** To snuggle contentedly. [< OE *nestlian,* to make a nest. See **nizdo-.**] —**nes'tler** *n.*

nest•ling (nĕst'lĭng) *n.* A bird too young to leave its nest.

net[1] (nĕt) *n.* **1.** An openwork meshed fabric. **2.** Something made of net, as a device used to capture animals or act as a barrier. —*v.* **netted, netting.** To catch or surround in or as in a net. [< OE *net.* See **ned-.**]

net[2] (nĕt) *adj.* **1.** Remaining after all deductions or losses. **2.** Ultimate; final. —*n.* Total gain, as of profit or weight. —*v.* **netted, netting.** To bring in as profit. [ME *net,* neat, clear.]

neth•er (nĕ*th*'ər) *adj.* Lower. [< OE *nither,* down, downward. See **ni.**]

Neth•er•lands, the (nĕ*th*'ər-ləndz). A country of W Europe. Pop. 12,212,000. Caps. Amsterdam, The Hague.

the Netherlands

Netherlands Antilles. An autonomous territory of the Netherlands, consisting of six islands, in the West Indies. Pop. 204,000.

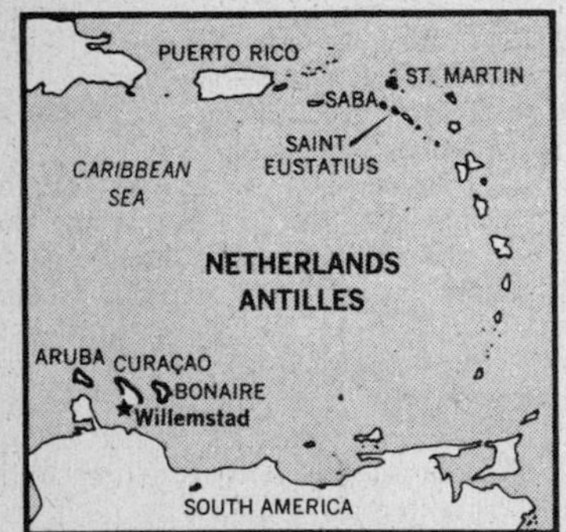

Netherlands Antilles

neth•er•most (nĕ*th*'ər-mōst') *adj.* Lowest.

net•ting (nĕt'ĭng) *n.* A net or network.

net•tle (nĕt'l) *n.* A plant covered with stinging hairs. —*v.* **-tled, -tling.** To irritate; vex. [< OE *netle.* See **ned-.**] —**net'tler** *n.*

net ton. See **ton.**

net•work (nĕt'wûrk') *n.* **1.** Something, as a net, having ropes, threads, etc., that cross at regular intervals. **2.** Any pattern or system that interconnects.

neu•ral (n/y/ŏŏr'əl) *adj.* Of or pertaining to the nerves.

neu•ral•gia (n/y/ŏŏ-răl'jə) *n.* Paroxysmal pain along a nerve. —**neu•ral'gic** *adj.*

neu•ras•the•ni•a (n/y/ŏŏr'əs-thē'nē-ə) *n.* A condition marked by fatigue, loss of energy and memory, and feelings of inadequacy.

neu•ri•tis (n/y/ŏŏ-rī'tĭs) *n.* Inflammation of a nerve, causing pain, loss of reflexes, and muscular atrophy.

neuro–. *comb. form.* Nerve or nervous system. [< Gk *neuron,* tendon, nerve.]

neu•rol•o•gy (n/y/ŏŏ-rŏl'ə-jē) *n.* The medical science of the nervous system and its disorders. [L *neurologia* : NEURO- + -LOGY.] —**neu'ro•log'i•cal** (n/y/ŏŏr'ə-lŏj'ĭ-kəl) *adj.* —**neu•rol'o•gist** *n.*

neu•ron (n/y/ŏŏr'ŏn') *n.* A **nerve cell.** [Gk, sinew, nerve.]

neu•ro•sis (n/y/ŏŏ-rō'sĭs) *n., pl.* **-ses** (-sēz'). Any of various functional disorders of the mind or emotions, without obvious organic lesion or change, and involving anxiety, phobia, or other abnormal behavior symptoms. —**neu•rot'ic** (-rŏt'ĭk) *adj.* & *n.*

neut. neuter.

neu•ter (n/y/ōō'tər) *adj.* **1.** *Gram.* Neither masculine nor feminine in gender. **2. a.** *Biol.* Having no functional sexual organs. **b.** *Bot.* Having no pistils or stamens; asexual. —*n.* **1.** *Gram.* **a.** The neuter gender. **b.** A neuter word. **2. a.** A castrated animal. **b.** A sexually undeveloped or imperfectly developed female insect; worker. **c.** A plant without stamens or pistils. [< L, neither.]

neu•tral (n/y/ōō'trəl) *adj.* **1.** Not favoring either side in a dispute. **2.** Belonging to neither side nor party. **3.** Indifferent. **4.** *Chem.* Neither acidic nor basic. **5.** Having a net electric charge of zero. **6.** Designating a color with no hue. —*n.* **1.** One that is neutral. **2.** A neutral color. **3.** The position of gears that are not engaged. —**neu'tral•ly** *adv.*

neu•tral•ism (n/y/ōō'trə-lĭz'əm) *n.* A neutral policy in foreign affairs.

neu•tral•i•ty (n/y/ōō-trăl'ə-tē) *n.* The quality or state of being neutral, esp. nonparticipation in war.

neu•tral•ize (n/y/ōō'trə-līz') *v.* **-ized, -izing.** To make neutral or ineffective. —**neu'tral•i•za'tion** *n.* —**neu'tral•iz'er** *n.*

neu•tron (n/y/ōō'trŏn') *n. Symbol* **n** *Phys.* An electrically neutral subatomic particle, having a mass 1,839 times that of the electron, stable when bound in an atomic nucleus, and having a mean lifetime of approx. 16.6 minutes as a free particle. [NEUTR(AL) + -ON.]

Nev. Nevada.

Ne•vad•a (nə-văd'ə, -vä'də). A state of the W U.S. Pop. 489,000. Cap. Carson City.

nev•er (nĕv'ər) *adv.* **1.** Not ever; on no occasion. **2.** Not at all; in no way. [< OE *nǣfre,* "not ever."]

nev•er•more (nĕv'ər-môr', -mōr') *adv.* Never again.

nev•er•the•less (nĕv'ər-*th*ə-lĕs') *adv.* None the less; however.

ne•vus (nē'vəs) *n., pl.* **-vi** (-vī'). Also **nae•vus.** Any congenital growth or mark on the skin, such as a birthmark. [L *naevus.*] —**ne'void'** (nē'void') *adj.*

new (n/y/ōō) *adj.* **1. a.** Not old; recent. **b.** Used for the first time. **2.** Recently become known. **3.** Unfamiliar. **4.** Unaccustomed. **5.** Begun afresh. **6.** Refreshed; rejuvenated. **7.** Different and distinct from what was before. **8. a.** Modern; current. **b.** In the most recent form, period, or development of something: *New Latin.* —*n.* That which is new. —*adv.* Freshly; recently. [< OE *nēowe, nīwe.* See **newo-.**] —**new'ness** *n.*

New•ark (n/y/ōō'ərk). A city of NE New Jersey. Pop. 382,000.

New Bed•ford (bĕd'fərd). A port of SE Massachusetts. Pop. 102,000.

new•born (n/y/ōō'bôrn') *adj.* **1.** Very recently born. **2.** Reborn.

New Bruns•wick (brŭnz'wĭk). A province of SE Canada. Pop. 623,000. Cap. Fredericton.

new•com•er (n/y/ōō'kŭm'ər) *n.* One who has lately come to a place or situation.

New Deal. The programs and policies for economic recovery and reform introduced during the 1930's by President Franklin D. Roosevelt. —**New Dealer.**

New Del•hi (dĕl'ē). The capital of the Republic of India. Pop. 295,000.

new•el (n/y/ōō'əl) *n.* **1.** The vertical post at the center of a winding staircase. **2.** A post at the bottom or landing of a staircase. [< OF *nouel,* "kernel," newel.]

New England. The NE U.S., comprising Maine, New Hampshire, Vermont, Massachusetts, Connecticut, and Rhode Island. —**New Englander.**

Newf. Newfoundland.

new•fan•gled (n/y/ōō'făng'gəld) *adj.* **1.** Novel. **2.** Fond of novelty. [< ME *newefangel,* fond of new things.]

New•found•land (n/y/ōō'fən-lənd, -lănd'). **1.** An island off the SE coast of Canada. **2.** A province of Canada, comprising this island and Labrador. Pop. 498,000. Cap. St. John's.

New Greek. Modern Greek.

New Guinea. A large island in the Pacific N of Australia.

New Hamp•shire (hămp'shər, hăm'shər, -shîr'). A state of the NE U.S. Pop. 738,000. Cap. Concord.

New Ha•ven (hā'vən). A city of S Connecticut. Pop. 152,000.

New High German. German.

New Jer•sey (jûr'zē). A state of the E U.S. Pop. 7,168,000. Cap. Trenton.

New Latin. The form of Latin in use, esp. in scientific nomenclature, since the beginning of the Renaissance.

new•ly (n/y/ōō'lē) *adv.* **1.** Lately; recently. **2.** Once more; anew. **3.** In a different way.

new•ly•wed (n/y/ōō'lē-wĕd') *n.* Also **new•ly•wed.** One recently married.

New Mexico. A state of the SW U.S. Pop. 1,016,000. Cap. Santa Fe.

new moon. 1. The phase of the moon occurring when it passes between the earth and sun and is invisible or visible only as a narrow crescent at sunset. **2.** The crescent moon.

New Or•le•ans (ôr'lē-ənz, ôr'lənz, ôr-lēnz'). A city of SE Louisiana. Pop. 593,000.

New•port News (n/y/ōō'pôrt' n/y/ōōz, -pōrt'). A city in SE Virginia. Pop. 114,000.

news (n/y/ōōz) *n. (takes sing. v.).* **1.** Recent events and happenings. **2.** A report about recent events. **3.** New information.

news•boy (n/y/ōōz'boi') *n.* A boy who sells newspapers.

news•cast (n/y/ōōz'kăst', -käst') *n.* A broadcast of news events.

news•let•ter (n/y/ōōz'lĕt'ər) *n.* A news periodical for a special-interest group.

news•pa•per (n/y/ōōz'pā'pər) *n.* A typically

daily or weekly publication containing news, feature articles, advertising, etc.
news•pa•per•man (n/y/o͞oz'pā'pər-măn') *n.* One who owns or is employed on a newspaper.
news•print (n/y/o͞oz'prĭnt') *n.* Inexpensive paper used chiefly for printing newspapers.
news•reel (n/y/o͞oz'rēl') *n.* A short film of current events.
news•stand (n/y/o͞oz'stănd') *n.* An open booth or shop at which newspapers are sold.
news•y (n/y/o͞o'zē) *adj.* **-ier, -iest.** Full of news. **—news'i•ness** *n.*
newt (n/y/o͞ot) *n.* Any of several small, semiaquatic salamanders. [< ME *an ewt,* an eft.]
New Test. New Testament.
New Testament. The Gospels, Acts, Pauline and other Epistles, and the Book of Revelation, which together have been viewed by Christians as forming the record of the new dispensation belonging to the Church, as distinct from the Old Testament dispensation shared with Judaism.
new•ton (n/y/o͞ot'n) *n.* A unit equal to the force required to accelerate a mass of one kilogram one meter per second per second. [< Sir Isaac NEWTON.]
New•ton (n/y/o͞ot'n), Sir **Isaac.** 1642–1727. English philosopher and scientist.
New•to•ni•an (n/y/o͞o-tō'nē-ən) *adj.* Pertaining to or in accordance with the work of Newton, esp. that in mechanics and gravitation.
New World. The W Hemisphere.
new year. The year about to begin or just begun.
New Year's Day. The 1st day of the year, as reckoned according to the Gregorian calendar; January 1.
New York (yôrk). **1.** A state of the NE U.S. Pop. 18,191,000. Cap. Albany. **2.** Also **New York City.** The largest city of the U.S., in SE New York State. Pop. 7,782,000. **—New Yorker.**
New Zea•land (zē'lənd). An insular nation in the S Pacific. Pop. 2,640,000. Cap. Wellington. **—New Zealander.**

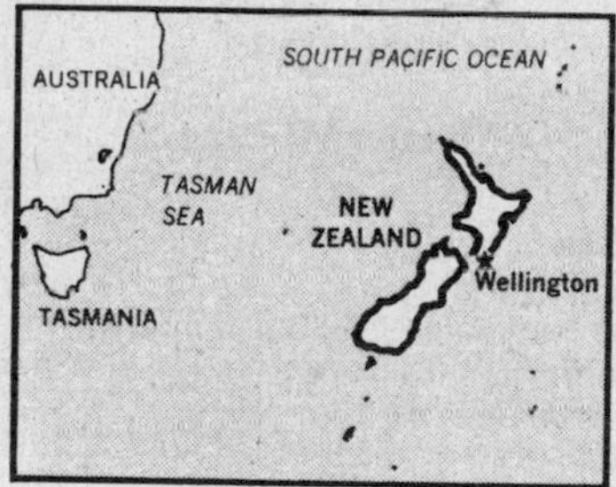

New Zealand

next (nĕkst) *adj.* **1.** Nearest in space; adjacent. **2.** Immediately succeeding. *—adv.* **1.** In the time, order, or place immediately following. **2.** On the first subsequent occasion. *—prep.* Close to; nearest. [< OE *nēahst,* superl of *nēah,* near.]
nex•us (nĕk'səs) *n., pl.* **-us** or **-uses. 1.** A means of connection; link. **2.** A connected series or group. [< L *nectere,* to bind, connect.]
N.F. Norman French.
Nfld. Newfoundland.
NG, N.G. National Guard.
NGk New Greek.
N.H. New Hampshire.
NHG New High German.
Ni nickel.
ni•a•cin (nī'ə-sĭn) *n.* **Nicotinic acid.**
Nia•mey (nyä-mā'). The capital of Niger. Pop. 30,000.
nib (nĭb) *n.* The point of a pen. [?]
nib•ble (nĭb'əl) *v.* **-bled, -bling. 1.** To bite gently and repeatedly. **2.** To take small or hesitant bites. *—n.* A small bite. [Prob < LG *nibbeln.*]
Nic•a•ra•gua (nĭk'ə-rä'gwə). A republic of Central America. Pop. 1,593,000. Cap. Managua. **—Nic'a•ra'guan** *adj.* & *n.*

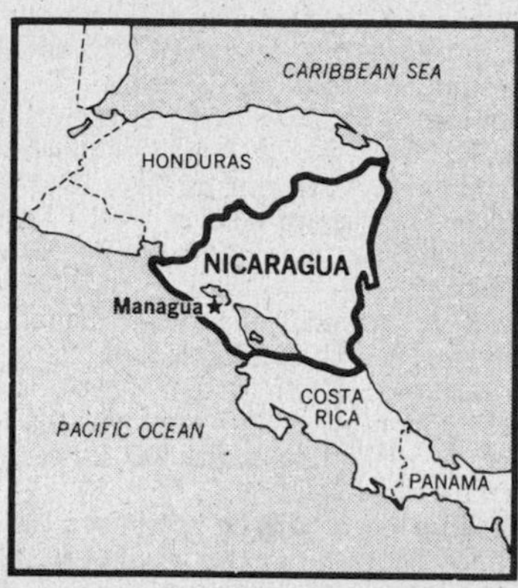

Nicaragua

nice (nīs) *adj.* **nicer, nicest. 1.** Pleasing; appealing. **2.** Considerate; well-mannered. **3.** Respectable; virtuous. **4.** Proper; seemly. **5.** Fastidious; exacting. **6. a.** Showing or requiring sensitive discernment. **b.** Done with skill. [< L *nescire,* to be ignorant.] **—nice'ly** *adv.*
ni•ce•ty (nī'sə-tē) *n., pl.* **-ties. 1.** Precision or accuracy. **2.** Fastidiousness. **3.** A subtle point, detail, or distinction. **4.** Often **niceties.** An elegant or dainty thing.
niche (nĭch) *n.* **1.** A recess in a wall, as for holding a statue. **2.** A suitable situation or activity. [< OF *niche,* "nest."]
nick (nĭk) *n.* A shallow notch or indentation on a surface. **—in the nick of time.** Just at the critical moment. *—v.* **1.** To cut a nick in. **2.** To cut short. [ME *nyke.*] **—nick'er** *n.*
nick•el (nĭk'əl) *n.* **1.** *Symbol* **Ni** A silvery, hard, ductile metallic element. It is used in alloys, in corrosion-resistant surfaces and batteries, and for electroplating. Atomic number 28, atomic weight 58.71. **2.** A U.S. coin worth five cents. [< G *Kupfernickel,* "copper-demon."]
nick•el•o•de•on (nĭk'ə-lō'dē-ən) *n.* **1.** An early movie house charging an admission price of five cents. **2.** A juke box.
nickel silver. A silvery, hard, corrosion-resistant, malleable alloy of copper, zinc, and nickel, used in tableware and as a structural material for hospital and restaurant equipment.
nick•name (nĭk'nām') *n.* **1.** A descriptive appellation added to or replacing one's actual name. **2.** A familiar form of a proper name. *—v.* **-named, -naming.** To call by a nickname. [< ME *an ekename,* an additional name.]
Nic•o•si•a (nĭk'ə-sē'ə). The capital of Cyprus. Pop. 103,000.
nic•o•tine (nĭk'ə-tēn') *n.* A poisonous alkaloid, $C_5H_4NC_4H_7NCH_3$, derived from the tobacco plant, used in medicine and as an insecticide. [F.]
nic•o•tin•ic acid (nĭk'ə-tĭn'ĭk). A member of the vitamin B complex, C_5H_4NCOOH, occurring in living cells and synthesized for use in treating pellagra.
niece (nēs) *n.* A daughter of one's brother, sister, brother-in-law, or sister-in-law. [< L *neptis.*]
Nie•tzsche (nē'chə, -chē), **Friedrich.** 1844–1900. German philosopher, poet, and critic.
nif•ty (nĭf'tē) *adj.* **-tier, -tiest.** *Slang.* Stylish; pleasing. [Poss < MAGNIFICENT.]
Ni•ger (nī'jər). **1.** A republic in west-central Africa. Pop. 3,100,000. Cap. Niamey. **2.** A river in W Africa.

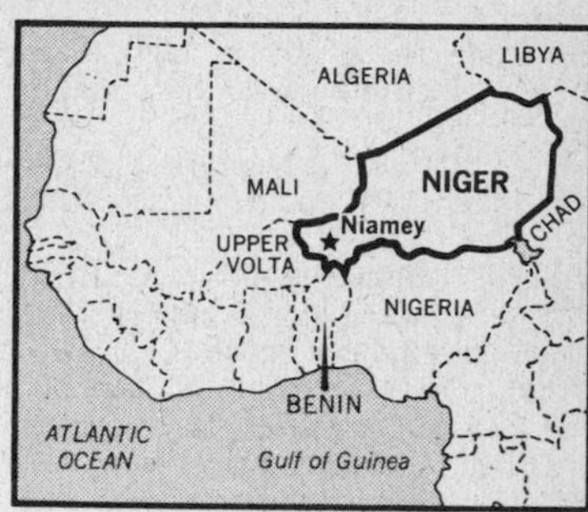

Niger

Ni•ger-Con•go (nī'jər-kŏng'gō) *n.* A large language family of Africa that includes the Mande, Kwa, and Bantu languages.
Ni•ge•ri•a (nī-jîr'ē-ə). A nation of W Africa. Pop. 55,654,000. Cap. Lagos. **—Ni•ge'ri•an** *adj.* & *n.*

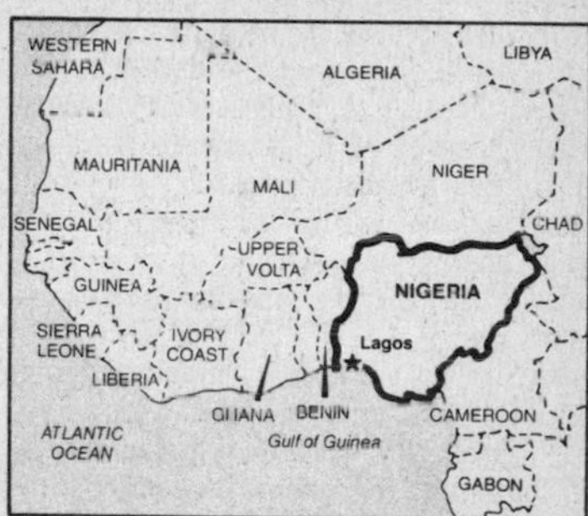

Nigeria

nig•gard (nĭg'ərd) *n.* A stingy, grasping person. *—adj.* Parsimonious. [< Scand.]
nig•gard•ly (nĭg'ərd-lē) *adj.* **-lier, -liest. 1.** Unwilling to part with anything; stingy. **2.** Meager. **—nig'gard•li•ness** *n.* **—nig'gard•ly** *adv.*
nig•gling (nĭg'lĭng) *adj.* **1.** Fussy. **2.** Petty. **3.** Showing or requiring close attention to details. [Prob < Scand.] **—nig'gling•ly** *adv.*
nigh (nī) *adj.* **nigher, nighest** or **next.** Close; near. *—adv.* **1.** Near in time or location. **2.** Nearly; almost *—prep.* Not far from; near to. [< OE *nēah,* NEAR.]
night (nīt) *n.* **1.** The period of darkness between sunset and sunrise. **2.** Darkness. [< OE *niht, neaht.* See **nekwt-.**] **—night** *adj.*
night blindness. Poor vision in the dark. **—night'-blind'** *adj.*
night•cap (nīt'kăp') *n.* **1.** A cloth cap worn in bed. **2.** A drink taken just before bedtime.
night•clothes (nīt'klōz', -klō*thz'*) *pl.n.* Clothes worn in bed.
night•club (nīt'klŭb') *n.* An establishment that stays open late at night and provides food, drink, and entertainment.

night crawler. An earthworm that emerges from the ground at night.
night•dress (nīt'drĕs') *n.* A nightgown.
night•fall (nīt'fôl') *n.* The approach of darkness.
night•gown (nīt'goun') *n.* A loose gown worn to bed.
night•hawk (nīt'hôk') *n.* **1.** A night-flying bird related to and resembling the whippoorwill. **2.** *Informal.* One who stays up late at night.
night•in•gale (nīt'n-gāl', nī'tĭng-) *n.* A brownish Old World songbird that sings at night. [< OE *nihtegale,* "night-singer."]
Night•in•gale (nīt'n-gāl', nī'tĭng-), **Florence.** 1820–1910. British nurse and hospital reformer.
night•ly (nīt'lē) *adj.* **1.** Nocturnal. **2.** Happening or done every night. *—adv.* On every night.
night•mare (nīt'mâr') *n.* **1.** A frightening dream. **2.** A horrifying event or condition. [ME *nihtmare,* female incubus.]
night owl. One who stays up late at night.
night•shade (nīt'shād') *n.* Any of several related, often poisonous plants with variously colored flowers and berries.
night•shirt (nīt'shûrt') *n.* A long shirt worn as nightclothes.
night•stick (nīt'stĭk') *n.* A club carried by a policeman.
night•time (nīt'tīm') *n.* The time between sunset and sunrise.
night watchman. One who acts as a guard at night.
ni•hil•ism (nī'əl-ĭz'əm, nī'hĭl-, nē'-) *n.* Systematic denial of the reality of experience and rejection of all value or meaning attributed to it. [< L *nihil,* nothing.] **—ni'hil•ist** *n.*
nil (nĭl) *n.* Nothing; naught. [< L *nihil.*]
Nile (nīl). A river of E Africa, flowing through Egypt to the Mediterranean.
Ni•lo-Sa•har•an (nī'lō-sə-hâr'ən) *n.* A large language family of Africa, including Chari-Nile and a number of smaller groups. **—Ni'lo-Sa•har'an** *adj.*
nim•ble (nĭm'bəl) *adj.* **-bler, -blest. 1.** Quick and agile; deft. **2.** Cleverly alert; acute. [< OE *nǣmel,* quick to seize or understand, and *numol,* seizing. See **nem-.**] **—nim'ble•ness** *n.* **—nim'bly** *adv.*
nim•bo•stra•tus (nĭm'bō-strā'təs, -străt'əs) *n.* A low, gray cloud, often dark, that precipitates rain, snow, or sleet.
nim•bus (nĭm'bəs) *n., pl.* **-bi** (-bī') or **-buses.** A surrounding radiance or circle of light, as in a representation of a holy person. [L, heavy rain, rain cloud.]
Nim•rod (nĭm'rŏd') *n.* A hunter. [< *Nimrod,* son of Cush, described as a mighty man and hunter. Genesis 10:8.]
nin•com•poop (nĭn'kəm-po͞op', nĭng'-) *n.* A fool; simpleton. [?]
nine (nīn) *n.* The cardinal number written 9 or in Roman numerals IX. [< OE *nigon.* See **newn.**] **—nine** *adj. & pron.*
nine•teen (nīn'tēn') *n.* The cardinal number written 19 or in Roman numerals XIX. **—nine'teen'** *adj. & pron.*
nine•teenth (nīn'tēnth') *n.* **1.** The ordinal number 19 in a series. **2.** One of 19 equal parts. **—nine'teenth'** *adj. & adv.*
nine•ti•eth (nīn'tē-ĭth) *n.* **1.** The ordinal number 90 in a series. **2.** One of 90 equal parts. **—nine'ti•eth** *adj. & adv.*
nine•ty (nīn'tē) *n.* The cardinal number written 90 or in Roman numerals XC or LXXXX. **—nine'ty** *adj. & pron.*
nin•ny (nĭn'ē) *n., pl.* **-nies.** A fool; simpleton. [< INNOCENT.]
ni•non (nē'nŏn') *n.* A sheer lightweight fabric.
ninth (nīnth) *n.* **1.** The ordinal number 9 in a series. **2.** One of 9 equal parts. **—ninth** *adj. & adv.*
ni•o•bi•um (nī-ō'bē-əm) *n. Symbol* **Nb** A silvery, soft, ductile metallic element, used in steel alloys, arc welding, and superconductivity research. Atomic number 41, atomic weight 92.906.
nip[1] (nĭp) *v.* **nipped, nipping. 1. a.** To squeeze, pinch, or press between two points. **b.** To give a small, sharp bite to. **2.** To clip or sever. **3.** To sting, as cold. **4.** To check growth or development. **5.** *Slang.* **a.** To snatch up hastily. **b.** To steal. *—n.* **1.** A bite or pinch. **2.** A small bit. **3. a.** A stinging quality, as of frosty air. **b.** Severely sharp cold or frost. **—nip and tuck.** Very close; closely contested. [Prob < ON *hnippa.*]
nip[2] (nĭp) *n.* A small quantity of liquor. *—v.* **nipped, nipping.** To drink (alcoholic liquor) in small portions. [Prob < Du *nippen,* to sip.]
nip•per (nĭp'ər) *n.* **1.** One that nips. **2.** Often **nippers.** A pincerlike device or structure, as pliers or a lobster claw.
nip•ple (nĭp'əl) *n.* **1.** The small conical protuberance near the center of the mammary gland, containing the outlets of the milk ducts. **2.** The rubber cap on a nursing bottle. **3.** Anything resembling or functioning like a nipple, as: **a.** A regulated opening for discharging a liquid, as in a small stopcock. **b.** A pipe threaded on both ends. [< OE *nebb,* a beak < Gmc **nabja-.*]
nip•py (nĭp'ē) *adj.* **-pier, -piest.** Sharp or biting.
nir•va•na (nîr-vä'nə, nər-) *n.* **1. Nirvana.** The Buddhist state of absolute blessedness, characterized by release from the cycle of reincarnations and attained through the extinction of the self. **2.** Oblivion; bliss. [Sk *nirvāna,* "extinction (of individual existence)."]
Ni•sei (nē-sā', nē'sā') *n., pl.* **-sei** or **-seis.** One born in America of immigrant Japanese parents. [Jap, "second generation."]
nit (nĭt) *n.* The egg or young of a parasitic insect, as a louse. [< OE *hnitu,* louse egg.] **—nit'ty** *adj.*
ni•ter (nī'tər) *n.* Also *chiefly Brit.* **ni•tre.** A white, gray, or colorless mineral of potassium nitrate, KNO_3, used in making gunpowder. [< Gk *nitron.*]
ni•trate (nī'trāt', -trĭt) *n.* A salt or ester of nitric acid. *—v.* **-trated, -trating.** To treat with nitric acid or with a nitrate, usually to change an organic compound into a nitrate. **—ni•tra'tion** *n.*
ni•tric acid (nī'trĭk). A corrosive liquid, HNO_3, used in the production of fertilizers, explosives, and rocket fuels, and in a wide variety of industrial metallurgical processes.
nitric oxide. A colorless, poisonous gas, NO, produced as an intermediate during the manufacture of nitric acid from ammonia or atmospheric nitrogen.
ni•tride (nī'trīd') *n.* A compound containing nitrogen with another, more electropositive element.
ni•trid•ing (nī'trī'dĭng) *n. Metall.* The casehardening of a ferrous alloy, such as steel, by heating it in ammonia.
ni•tri•fy (nī'trə-fī') *v.* **-fied, -fying. 1.** To oxidize into nitric acid, a nitrate, or a related nitrogen compound, as by the action of bacteria. **2.** To treat or combine with nitrogen or compounds containing nitrogen. **—ni'tri•fi•ca'tion** *n.*
nitro–. *comb. form.* A compound containing the univalent group NO_2. [< Gk *nitron.*]
ni•tro•cel•lu•lose (nī'trō-sĕl'yə-lōs') *n.* A pulpy or cottonlike material derived from cellulose treated with sulfuric and nitric acids and used in the manufacture of explosives and plastics.
ni•tro•gen (nī'trə-jən) *n. Symbol* **N** A nonmetallic element constituting nearly four-fifths of the air by volume, occurring as a colorless, odorless, almost inert gas in various minerals and all proteins. Atomic number 7, atomic weight 14.0067. **—ni•trog'e•nous** (nī-trŏj'ə-nəs) *adj.*
ni•tro•glyc•er•in (nī'trō-glĭs'ər-ĭn) *n.* Also **ni•tro•glyc•er•ine.** A thick, pale-yellow liquid, $C_3N_3H_5O_9$, explosive on concussion or exposure to sudden heat.
ni•trous oxide (nī'trəs). A colorless, sweet inorganic gas, N_2O, used as a mild anesthetic.
nit•ty-grit•ty (nĭt'ē-grĭt'ē) *n. Slang.* The essence of a matter.
nit•wit (nĭt'wĭt') *n. Informal.* A stupid or silly person.
nix (nĭks). *Slang. n.* Nothing. *—adv.* No. *—v.* To forbid; veto. [< G *nichts,* nothing.]
Nix•on (nĭk'sən), **Richard Milhous.** Born 1913. 37th President of the United States (1969–74); resigned.

Richard M. Nixon

N.J. New Jersey.
NL New Latin.
NLRB National Labor Relations Board.
nm, n.m. nautical mile.
N.M. New Mexico (unofficial).
N. Mex. New Mexico.
NNE north-northeast.
NNW north-northwest.
no[1] (nō) *adv.* **1.** Not so; opposed to "yes." Used in expressing refusal, denial, or disagreement. **2.** Not by any degree: *no better.* **3.** Not: *whether or no.* *—n., pl.* **noes.** A negative response. [< OE *nā* : *ne,* no (see **ne**) + *ā,* ever (see **aiw-**).]
no[2] (nō) *adj.* **1.** Not any. **2.** Not at all. [< OE *nān,* NONE.]
No nobelium.
no., No. 1. north; northern. **2.** number.
No•ah (nō'ə). Biblical patriarch commanded by God to build the ark.
no•bel•i•um (nō-bĕl'ē-əm) *n. Symbol* **No** A synthetic radioactive element produced in trace amounts. Atomic number 102, longest-lived isotope No 254. [< the *Nobel* Institute at Stockholm.]

No•bel Prize (nō-bĕl′). Any of the annual prizes awarded for distinction in literature, medicine, chemistry, physics, and economics, and for the promotion of world peace. [< A. *Nobel* (1833–1896), Swedish chemist whose will set up the Nobel Prize.]

no•ble (nō′bəl) *adj.* **-bler, -blest. 1.** Of high hereditary rank. **2.** Showing greatness and magnanimity of character; illustrious. **3.** Grand; stately; magnificent. —*n.* A person of noble rank. [< L *nōbilis,* knowable, famous, noble.] —**no•bil′i•ty** (nō-bĭl′ə-tē) *n.* —**no′ble•ness** *n.* —**no′bly** *adv.*

no•ble•man (nō′bəl-mən) *n.* A man of noble rank.

no•bod•y (nō′bŏd′ē, -bə-dē) *pron.* No person; no one. —*n., pl.* **-bodies.** One without fame or influence.

noc•tur•nal (nŏk-tûr′nəl) *adj.* **1.** Of, suitable to, or occurring at night. **2.** Active or functioning by night: *nocturnal animals.* [< L *nox (noct-),* night.] —**noc•tur′nal•ly** *adv.*

noc•turne (nŏk′tûrn′) *n.* A romantic musical composition intended to embody sentiments appropriate to the evening or night.

nod (nŏd) *v.* **nodded, nodding. 1.** To bow the head briefly, as in a gesture of agreement or in dozing. **2.** To express (greeting, approval, or acknowledgement) by bowing the head. **3.** To be briefly inattentive, as if sleepy. **4.** To sway or bend, as plants in the wind. —*n.* A nodding motion. [ME *nodden.*] —**nod′der** *n.*

node (nōd) *n.* **1.** A knob, knot, protuberance, or swelling: *a lymph node.* **2.** The often enlarged point on a plant stem where a leaf or other organ is attached. [L *nōdus,* a knob, knot.] —**nod′al** *adj.*

nod•ule (nŏj′o͞ol) *n.* A small, knotlike protuberance; a small node. —**nod′u•lar** (nŏj′o͞o-lər) *adj.*

No•ël (nō-ĕl′) *n.* **1.** Christmas. **2. noël.** A Christmas carol. [< L *nātālis (dies),* "birth(day) of Christ."]

no-fault (nō′fôlt′) *adj.* Of a system of automobile insurance in which accident victims are compensated by their insurance companies without any assignment of blame.

nog•gin (nŏg′ĭn) *n.* **1.** A small mug or cup. **2.** A unit of liquid measure equal to one-quarter of a pint. **3.** The head. [?]

noise (noiz) *n.* **1.** A sound or sounds, esp. when loud, unexpected, or disagreeable. **2.** An outcry, clamor, or din. **3.** *Phys.* Any disturbance, esp. a random and persistent disturbance, that obscures or reduces the clarity or quality of a signal. —*v.* **noised, noising.** To spread the rumor or report of. [< L *nausea,* seasickness.] —**nois′y** *adj.*

noi•some (noi′səm) *adj.* **1.** Offensive; disgusting. **2.** Harmful or dangerous. [< ME *anoien,* ANNOY + -SOME.] —**noi′some•ly** *adv.*

Noah

no•mad (nō′măd′) *n.* **1.** One of a people having no fixed abode and moving from place to place. **2.** A wanderer. [< Gk *nomas,* one that wanders about for pasture.] —**no•mad′ic** *adj.*

nom de plume (nŏm′ də plo͞om′). A pseudonym; pen name. [F, "pen name."]

no•men•cla•ture (nō′mən-klā′chər, nō-mĕn′klə-chər) *n.* A system of names; systematic naming in an art or science. [L *nōmenclātūra.*]

nom•i•nal (nŏm′ə-nəl) *adj.* **1.** Of or like a name. **2.** In name only. **3.** Insignificant. [< L *nōmen,* name.] —**nom′i•nal•ly** *adv.*

nom•i•nate (nŏm′ə-nāt′) *v.* **-nated, -nating. 1.** To propose as a candidate. **2.** To designate or appoint to an office, honor, etc. —**nom′i•na′tion** *n.* —**nom′i•nee′** (-nē′) *n.*

nom•i•na•tive (nŏm′ə-nə-tĭv, nŏm′nə-tĭv). *Gram. adj.* Of or designating the case of the subject of a finite verb and of words identified with the subject. —*n.* The nominative case or a word in that case.

-nomy. *comb. form.* The systematization of knowledge about a specified field: **astronomy.** [< Gk *nomos,* law.]

non-. *comb. form.* Not. [< L *nōn,* not.]

non•age (nŏn′ĭj, nō′nĭj) *n.* **1.** Legal minority. **2.** Immaturity.

non•a•ligned (nŏn′ə-līnd′) *adj.* Not in alliance with any power bloc; neutral: *a nonaligned nation.*

nonce (nŏns) *n.* The present or a particular time or occasion: *for the nonce.* [< ME *for then anes,* "for the one (purpose or occasion)."]

non•cha•lant (nŏn′shə-länt′) *adj.* Appearing casually unconcerned or indifferent. [< OF *nonchaloir,* to be unconcerned.] —**non′cha•lance′** *n.* —**non′cha•lant′ly** *adv.*

non•com•bat•ant (nŏn′kəm-băt′ənt, -kŏm′bə-tənt) *n.* **1.** One in the armed forces whose duties exclude fighting. **2.** A civilian in wartime.

non•com•mis•sioned officer (nŏn′kə-mĭsh′-ənd). An enlisted member of the armed forces appointed to a rank conferring leadership.

non•com•mit•tal (nŏn′kə-mĭt′l) *adj.* Revealing no preference or purpose.

non com•pos men•tis (nŏn kŏm′pəs mĕn′tĭs). Not of sound mind. [L, "not having control of the mind."]

non•con•duc•tor (nŏn′kən-dŭk′tər) *n.* A substance that conducts little or no electricity or heat. —**non′con•duct′ing** *adj.*

non•con•form•ist (nŏn′kən-fôr′mĭst) *n.* One who does not conform to accepted rules, beliefs, or practices. —**non′con•form′i•ty** *n.*

non•co•op•er•a•tion (nŏn′kō-ŏp′ə-rā′shən) *n.* Failure or refusal to cooperate, esp. refusal to perform civil duties.

non•de•nom•i•na•tion•al (nŏn′dĭ-nŏm′ə-nā′shən-əl) *adj.* Not restricted to or associated with a religious denomination.

non•de•script (nŏn′dĭ-skrĭpt′) *adj.* Lacking in distinctive qualities. [< NON- + L *dēscrībere,* DESCRIBE.]

none (nŭn) *pron.* **1.** No one; nobody. **2.** Not any of a specified group. **3.** No part; not any. —*adj.* Not one; no. —*adv.* In no way; not at all. [< OE *nān* : *ne,* no + *ān,* one.]

Usage: None (pronoun) can take either a singular or a plural verb. A singular verb is used when *none* can logically be construed as singular (when *not one* or *no one* can be substituted for *none*) or when *none* precedes a singular noun. A plural verb is used when *none*

Note: Many compounds are formed with *non-*. Normally, *non-* combines with a second element without an intervening hyphen. However, if the second element begins with a capital letter, it is separated with a hyphen: *non-French.*

non′a•ban′don•ment *n.*
non′ab•di•ca′tion *n.*
non′ab•o•li′tion *n.*
non′a•bra′sive *adj.*
non′a•bridg′ment *n.*
non•ab′so•lute *adj.* & *n.*
non′ab•sorb′ent *adj.* & *n.*
non′ab•sorp′tion *n.*
non′ab•stain′er *n.*
non•ab′stract *adj.* & *n.*
non′a•bu′sive *adj.*
non′ac•a•dem′ic *adj.*
non′ac•cel′er•a′tion *n.*
non•ac′cent *n.*
non′ac•cept′ance *n.*
non′ac•ces′so•ry *adj.* & *n.*
non′ac•ci•den′tal *adj.* & *n.*
non′ac•com′mo•dat′ing *adj.*
non′ac•cord′ *n.*
non′ac•cu•mu•la′tion *n.*
non•ac′id *n.* & *adj.*
non′ac•qui•es′cent *adj.*
non′ac•quit′tal *n.*
non•ac′tion *n.*
non•ac′tive *adj.*
non•ac′tu•al *adj.*
non′a•cute′ *adj.*
non′a•dapt′a•ble *adj.*
non′ad•dic′tive *adj.*
non′a•dept′ *adj.*
non′ad•her′ence *n.*
non′ad•he′sive *adj.*
non′ad•ja′cent *adj.*
non′ad•jec•ti′val *adj.*
non′ad•join′ing *adj.*
non′ad•just′a•ble *adj.*
non′ad•min′is•tra′tive *adj.*
non′ad•mis′sion *n.*
non′a•dult′ *adj.* & *n.*
non′ad•vance′ment *n*
non′ad•van•ta′geous *adj.*
non′ad•ven′tur•ous *adj.*
non′ad•ver′bi•al *adj.*
non′aes•thet′ic *adj.*
non′af•fec•ta′tion *n.*
non′af•fil′i•a′tion *n.*
non-Af′ri•can *adj.* & *n.*
non′al•co•hol′ic *adj.*
non′a•pol′o•get′ic *adj.*
non′ap•par′ent *adj.*
non′ap•pear′ance *n.*
non′ap•pre′ci•a′tion *n.*
non′ap•proach′a•ble *adj.*
non•a′que•ous *adj.*
non•ar′bi•trar′y *adj.*
non′ar•o•mat′ic *adj.*
non-Ar′y•an *n.* & *adj.*
non-A′sian *n.* & *adj.*
non′as•ser′tive *adj.*
non′as•sim′i•la′tion *n.*
non•ath′lete *n.*
non′a•tom′ic *adj.*
non′at•tach′ment *n.*
non′at•tain′a•ble *adj.*

applies to more than one (when *not any of a group of persons or things* can be substituted for *none*). When *none* can logically be construed as either singular or plural, either a singular or a plural verb is possible.

non•en•ti•ty (nŏn-ĕn'tə-tē) *n., pl.* **-ties.** An insignificant person or thing.

none•such (nŭn'sŭch') *n.* A person or thing without equal.

none•the•less (nŭn'*th*ə-lĕs') *adv.* Nevertheless.

non•ex•ist•ence (nŏn'ĭg-zĭs'təns) *n.* The condition of not existing. **—non'ex•ist'ent** *adj.*

non•fic•tion (nŏn-fĭk'shən) *n.* Prose works other than fiction. **—non•fic'tion•al** *adj.*

no•nil•lion (nō-nĭl'yən) *n.* **1.** The cardinal number represented by the figure 1 followed by 30 zeros. **2.** In Great Britain, the cardinal number represented by the figure 1 followed by 54 zeros. [< OF, "the ninth power of a million."] **—no•nil'lion** *adj.*

no•nil•lionth (nō-nĭl'yənth) *n.* The ordinal number nonillion in a series. **—no•nil'lionth** *adj.*

non•in•ter•ven•tion (nŏn'ĭn-tər-vĕn'shən) *n.* Failure or refusal to intervene in the affairs of another, esp. in international affairs. **—non'in•ter•ven'tion•ist** *n.* & *adj.*

non•met•al (nŏn-mĕt'l) *n.* Any of a number of elements, such as oxygen or sulfur, that generally occur as negatively charged ions or radicals, form oxides that produce acids, and are poor conductors of heat and of electricity when solid. **—non'me•tal'lic** (nŏn'-mə-tăl'ĭk) *adj.*

non•ob•jec•tive (nŏn'əb-jĕk'tĭv) *adj.* Designating a style of graphic art that does not represent objects.

non•pa•reil (nŏn'pə-rĕl') *adj.* Without rival; matchless; peerless. *—n.* One without equal; a paragon.

non•par•ti•san (nŏn-pär'tə-zən) *adj.* **1.** Not partisan. **2.** Not influenced by the policies of any one political party.

non•plus (nŏn-plŭs') *v.* **-plused** or **-plussed, -plusing** or **-plussing.** To perplex; baffle. [L *nōn plūs,* "no more (can be said)."]

non•prof•it (nŏn-prŏf'ĭt) *adj.* Not seeking profit.

non•sec•tar•i•an (nŏn'sĕk-târ'ē-ən) *adj.* Not limited to or associated with any particular religious denomination.

non•sense (nŏn'sĕns', -səns) *n.* **1.** Something that does not make or have sense, esp. meaningless or absurd behavior or language. **2.** Extravagant foolishness or frivolity. **—non•sen'si•cal** (nŏn-sĕn'sĭ-kəl) *adj.*

non se•qui•tur (nŏn sĕk'wĭ-to͝or'). An inference that does not follow from established premises. [L, "it does not follow."]

non•skid (nŏn'skĭd') *adj.* Designed to prevent or inhibit skidding.

non•stan•dard (nŏn-stăn'dərd) *adj.* **1.** Not adhering to a standard. **2.** *Ling.* Of or pertaining to usages or varieties of a language that do not conform to those approved by educated native users of the language.

non•stop (nŏn'stŏp') *adj.* Making or having made no stops. **—non'stop'** *adv.*

non•sup•port (nŏn'sə-pôrt', -pōrt') *n.* Failure to provide for the maintenance of one's legal dependents.

non•un•ion (nŏn-yo͞on'yən) *adj.* **1. a.** Not belonging to a labor union. **b.** Not unionized: *a nonunion shop.* **2.** Not produced by union labor.

non•vi•o•lence (nŏn-vī'ə-ləns) *n.* A social philosophy based on the rejection of violent means to gain objectives. **—non•vi'o•lent** *adj.*

noo•dle (no͞od'l) *n.* A thin strip of food paste, usually made of flour and eggs. [G *Nudel.*]

nook (no͝ok) *n.* **1.** A corner, esp. in a room. **2.** A quiet or secluded spot. [Perh < Scand.]

noon (no͞on) *n.* Twelve o'clock in the daytime; midday. [< OE *nōn,* "the ninth hour (after sunrise)."]

noon•day (no͞on'dā') *n.* Noon.

no one (nō'wŭn'). No person; nobody.

noon•tide (no͞on'tīd') *n.* Noon.

noon•time (no͞on'tīm') *n.* Noon.

noose (no͞os) *n.* A loop formed by a running knot in a rope or cord, as in a lasso. [< L *nōdus,* a knot.]

nor (nôr; *unstressed* nər) *conj.* And not; or not; likewise not; not either. —Used: **a.** As a correlative to give continuing negative force: *He never worked nor offered to help.* **b.** For rhetorical effect: *The day was bright, nor were there clouds above.* [< ME *nother,* neither.]

Nor•dic (nôr'dĭk) *adj.* Of, pertaining to, or relating to the Caucasoid ethnic group most predominant in Scandinavia. [< OE *north,* NORTH.] **—Nor'dic** *n.*

Nor•folk (nôr'fək). A port of SE Virginia. Pop. 306,000.

norm (nôrm) *n.* A standard, model, or pattern regarded as typical. [L *norma,* carpenter's square, pattern.]

nor•mal (nôr'məl) *adj.* **1.** Conforming to a usu-

---

non'at·ten'dance *n.*
non'at·trib'u·tive *adj.* & *n.*
non'au·to·mat'ic *adj.*
non'bac·te'ri·al *adj.*
non-Bap'tist *n.*
non·ba'sic *adj.*
non·beau'ty *n.*
non·be'ing *n.*
non'be·liev'er *n.*
non'be·nev'o·lent *adj.*
non-Bib'li·cal *adj.*
non-Brit'ish *adj.*
non·bus'y *adj.*
non·caf·feine' *n.*
non·cak'ing *adj.* & *n.*
non·can'cer·ous *adj.*
non'ca·non'i·cal *adj.*
non'cap·i·tal·is'tic *adj.*
non'car·niv'o·rous *adj.*
non'cat·e·gor'i·cal *adj.*
non-Cath'o·lic *adj.* & *n.*
non'-Cau·ca'sian *adj.* & *n.*
non'ce·les'tial *adj.*
non·cel'lu·lar *adj.*
non-Celt'ic *adj.*
non'cer·e·mo'ni·al *adj.*
non·cer'ti·fied' *adj.*
non·chem'i·cal *adj.* & *n.*
non'-Chi·nese' *adj.* & *n.*
non-Chris'tian *adj.* & *n.*
non·cit'i·zen *n.*
non·civ'i·lized' *adj.*
non'clas·si·fi·ca'tion *n.*
non·cler'i·cal *adj.*
non·clin'i·cal *adj.*
non'co·er'cive *adj.*
non'co·he'sive *adj.*
non'col·laps'i·ble *adj.*
non'col·le'giate *adj.*
non'com'bat·ant *n.*
non'com·bus'ti·ble *adj.* & *n.*
non'com·mer'cial *adj.* & *n.*
non'com·mu'ni·ca·ble *adj.*
non·com'mu·nist *n.* & *adj.*
non'com·pen·sa'tion *n.*
non·com'pe·tent *adj.*
non·com'pe·tent·ly *adv.*
non'com·pet'i·tive *adj.*
non'com·pet'i·tive·ness *n.*
non'com·ple'tion *n.*
non'com·pres'sion *n.*
non'com·pul'sion *n.*
non'con·cur'rence *n.*
non'con·cur'rent *adj.*
non'con·den·sa'tion *n.*
non'con·duc'tive *adj.*
non'con·fi·den'tial *adj.*
non'con·fine'ment *n.*
non'con·flic'tive *adj.*
non'con·form'i·ty *n.*
non'con·ges'tion *n.*
non'-Con·gres'sion·al *adj.*
non'con·nec'tive *adj.* & *n.*
non·con'no·ta'tive *adj.*
non·con'scious *adj.*
non'con·sec'u·tive *adj.*
non'con·sent' *n.*
non'con·ser'va·tive *adj.* & *n.*
non'con·sid'er·a'tion *n.*
non'con·spir'a·tor *n.*
non'con·sult'a·tive *adj.*
non'con·ta'gious *adj.*
non'con·tem'po·rar'y *adj.* & *n.*
non'con·tin'u·ous *adj.*
non·con'tra·band' *n.* & *adj.*
non'con·tra·dic'tion *n.*
non'con·tri·bu'tion *n.*
non'con·trib'u·tor *n.*
non'con·tro·ver'sial *adj.*
non'con·ver'gence *n.*
non'con·ver'sion *n.*
non'con·vic'tion *n.*
non'co·or'di·na'tion *n.*
non·cor'po·rate *adj.*
non'cor·rec'tive *adj.* & *n.*
non·cor're·lat'ing *adj.*
non'cor·re·la'tion *n.*
non·cos'mic *adj.*
non'cre·a'tive *adj.*
non·cred'i·ble *adj.*
non·crim'i·nal *adj.* & *n.*
non·cul'pa·ble *adj.*
non·cul'ture *n.*
non·cu'mu·la'tive *adj*
non·cur'rent *adj.*
non'cur·tail'ment *n.*
non·cus'tom·ar'y *adj.*
non'de·cay'ing *adj.*
non'de·cep'tive *adj.*
non'de·liv'er·y *n.*
non'dem·o·crat'ic *adj.*
non'de·part·men'tal *adj.*
non'de·par'ture *n.*
non'de·pen'dence *n.*
non'de·pos'i·tor *n.*
non'de·pre'ci·a'tion *n.*
non'de·riv'a·tive *adj.* & *n.*
non'de·rog'a·to'ry *adj.*
non'de·struc'tive *adj.*
non'de·tach'a·ble *adj.*
non'det·ri·men'tal *adj.*
non'de·vel'op·ment *n.*
non'de·vi·a'tion *n.*
non'de·vo'tion·al *adj.*
non'di·a·lec'tal *adj.*
non'di·dac'tic *adj.*
non'dif·fer·en'ti·a'tion *n.*
non'di·gest'i·ble *adj.*
non'di·rec'tion·al *adj.*
non'dis·cern'ment *n.*
non·dis'ci·pli·nar'y *adj.*

---

al or typical pattern. 2. *Math.* Perpendicular. —*n.* 1. Anything normal; the standard. 2. The usual state, amount, etc. 3. A perpendicular. [< L *normālis,* made according to the carpenter's square.] —**nor·mal'i·ty** (-măl'ə-tē), **nor'mal·cy** *n.* —**nor'mal·ly** *adv.*

normal school. A school that trains teachers, chiefly for the elementary grades.

Nor·man (nôr'mən) *n.* 1. One of a Scandinavian people who conquered Normandy in the 10th century. 2. One of the people of Normandy who conquered England in 1066. 3. A native of Normandy. —**Nor'man** *adj.*

Nor·man·dy (nôr'mən-dē). A region of NW France on the English Channel.

Norman French. 1. The dialect of Old French used in medieval Normandy and England. 2. The form of this dialect used in English court and legal circles from the Norman conquest until the 15th century.

Norse (nôrs) *adj.* Of or pertaining to ancient Scandinavia, its people, or their language. —**Norse** *n.*

Norse·man (nôrs'mən) *n.* Any of the ancient Scandinavians.

north (nôrth) *n.* 1. a. The direction along a meridian to the left of an observer facing in the direction of the earth's rotation. b. The point on a mariner's compass located at 0°. 2. Often **North.** a. The N or arctic part of the earth. b. The N part of any country or region. —**the North:** In the U.S., the states N of Maryland, the Ohio River, and Missouri. —*adj.* 1. To or from the north. 2. **North.** Designating the N part of a country, continent, or other geographical area: *North Korea.* —*adv.* In, from, or toward the north. [< OE. See ner-.]

North America. The northern continent of the W Hemisphere.

North Car·o·li·na (kăr'ə-lī'nə). A state of the S U.S. Pop. 5,082,000. Cap. Raleigh.

North Da·ko·ta (də-kō'tə). A state of the Midwestern U.S. Pop. 618,000. Cap. Bismarck.

north·east (nôrth-ēst') *n.* 1. The direction halfway between north and east. 2. Any area or region lying in this direction. —**the Northeast.** In the U.S., New England, New York, and sometimes Pennsylvania and New Jersey. —*adj.* To, from, or in the northeast. —*adv.* In, from, or toward the northeast. —**north·east'ern** *adj.*

north·east·er (nôrth-ē'stər) *n.* A storm or gale from the northeast.

north·east·er·ly (nôrth-ē'stər-lē) *adj.* 1. Toward the northeast. 2. From the northeast. —**north·east'er·ly** *adv.*

north·er (nôr'*th*ər) *n.* A sudden cold gale from the north.

north·er·ly (nôr'*th*ər-lē) *adj.* 1. Toward the north. 2. From the north. —**north'er·ly** *adv.*

north·ern (nôr'*th*ərn) *adj.* 1. Toward, in, or facing the north. 2. Coming from the north. 3. Often **Northern.** Of or characteristic of northern regions or the North.

north·ern·er (nôr'*th*ər-nər) *n.* 1. A native or inhabitant of the north. 2. Often **Northerner.** A native or inhabitant of the NE U.S.

Northern Hemisphere. The half of the earth north of the equator.

Northern Ireland. A component of the United Kingdom in NE Ireland. Pop. 1,458,000. Cap. Belfast.

northern lights. The **aurora borealis.**

North Germanic. A branch of Germanic including Danish, Norwegian, and Swedish.

North Korea. The unofficial name for the People's Democratic Republic of Korea. See **Korea.**

North Pole. 1. The northern end of the earth's axis of rotation. 2. The celestial zenith of this terrestrial point. 3. **north pole.** The north-seeking magnetic pole of a magnet.

North Sea. A part of the Atlantic between Great Britain and Denmark.

North Star. The polar star; Polaris.

North Vietnam. The former unofficial name for the Democratic Republic of Vietnam. See **Vietnam.**

north·ward (nôrth'wərd) *adv.* Also **north·wards** (-wərdz). Toward the north. —*adj.* Toward, facing, or in the north. —*n.* 1. A direction toward the north. 2. A region in or toward the north. —**north'ward·ly** *adj.* & *adv.*

north·west (nôrth-wĕst') *n.* 1. The direction halfway between north and west. 2. Any area or region lying in this direction. —**the Northwest.** In the U.S.: 1. Formerly, the area W of the Mississippi and N of the Missouri. 2. The present states of Washington, Oregon, and Idaho. —*adj.* To, from, or in the northwest. —*adv.* In, from, or toward the northwest. —**north·west'ern** *adj.*

north·west·er·ly (nôrth-wĕs'tər-lē) *adj.* 1. Toward the northwest. 2. From the northwest. —**north·west'er·ly** *adv.*

Norw. Norway; Norwegian.

Nor·way (nôr'wā'). A kingdom of NW

---

non'dis·crim'i·na'tion *n.*
non'dis·pos'al *n.*
non'dis·rup'tive *adj.*
non·dis'si·dence *n.*
non'dis·tinc'tive *adj.*
non'dis·tri·bu'tion *n.*
non'di·ver'gence *n.*
non'di·ver'si·fi·ca'tion *n.*
non'di·vis'i·ble *adj.*
non·doc'tri·nal *adj.*
non'doc·u·men'ta·ry *adj.* & *n.*
non'dog·mat'ic *adj.*
non'do·mes'tic *adj.* & *n.*
non'dra·mat'ic *adj.*
non·dry'ing *adj.*
non'ec·cle'si·as'ti·cal *adj.*
non'ec·lec'tic *adj.*
non'ec·o·nom'ic *adj.*
non·ed'i·ble *adj.* & *n.*
non'ed·i·to'ri·al *adj.*
non·ed'u·ca·ble *adj.*
non'ed·u·ca'tion·al *adj.*
non'ef·fec'tive *adj.*
non'ef·fer·ves'cent *adj.*
non'ef·fi'cien·cy *n.*
non'e·las'tic *adj.*
non'e·lect' *n.*
non'e·lec'tion *n.*
non'e·lec'tive *adj*
non'e·lec'tric *adj.*
non'el·e·men'ta·ry *adj.*
non'e·lim'i·na'tion *n.*
non'e·mo'tion·al *adj.*
non'em·pir'i·cal *adj.*
non'en·cy'clo·pe'dic *adj.*
non'en·force'a·ble *adj.*
non-Eng'lish *adj.* & *n.*
non·en'ter·pris'ing *adj.*
non'-E·pis'co·pa'lian *adj.* & *n.*
non·e'qual *adj.* & *n.*
non'e·quiv'a·lent *adj.* & *n.*
non'e·ra'sure *n.*
non'e·rot'ic *adj.*
non·er'u·dite' *adj.*
non'es·sen'tial *adj.* & *n.*
non'es·thet'ic *adj.*
non'e·ter'nal *adj.*
non·eth'i·cal *adj.*
non'eth·no·log'i·cal *adj.*
non'-Eu·clid'e·an *adj.*
non'-Eu·ro·pe'an *adj.* & *n.*
non'e·vac'u·a'tion *n.*
non'e·va'sion *n.*
non'e·va'sive *adj.*
non'e·vic'tion *n.*
non'ev·o·lu'tion·ar'y *adj.*
non'ex·pan'sive *adj.*
non'ex·pend'a·ble *adj.*
non'ex·per'i·men'tal *adj.*
non'ex·plo'sive *adj.* & *n.*
non·ex'tant *adj.*
non'ex·ter'nal *adj.*
non'ex·tinct' *adj.*
non'ex·tra·di'tion *n.*
non'ex·tra'ne·ous *adj.*
non·fa·ce'tious *adj.*
non·fac'tu·al *adj.*
non·fan'ta·sy *n.*
non·fas'cist *n.* & *adj.*
non'fas·tid'i·ous *adj.*
non·fa'tal *adj.*
non·fed'er·al *adj.*
non·fer'tile *adj.*
non·fes'tive *adj.*
non·feu'dal *adj.*
non·fig'ur·a·tive *adj.*
non'fi·nan'cial *adj.*
non·fi'nite *adj.* & *n.*
non·fire'proof' *adj.*
non·for'mal *adj.*
non'for·tu'i·tous *adj.*
non'fra·ter'nal *adj.*
non·fraud'u·lent *adj.*
non·free'dom *n.*
non-French' *adj.* & *n.*
non·fre'quent *adj.*
non'ful·fill'ment *n.*
non·func'tion·al *adj.*
non'fun·da·men'tal *adj.* & *n.*
non·gas'e·ous *adj.*
non'ge·lat'i·nous *adj.*
non'ge·net'ic *adj.*
non'gov·ern·ment'al *adj.*
non'gre·gar'i·ous *adj.*
non·hab'it·a·ble *adj.*
non'ha·bit'u·al *adj.*
non·haz'ard·ous *adj.*
non·hea'then *n.* & *adj.*
non'he·red'i·tar'y *adj.*
non'he·ret'i·cal *adj.*
non'he·ro'ic *adj.*
non'his·tor'ic *adj.*
non'ho·mo·ge'ne·ous *adj.*
non·hos'tile *adj.*
non·hu'man *adj.*
non·hu'man·ness *n.*
non·hu'mor·ous *adj.*
non'i·den'ti·cal *adj.*
non'i·den'ti·ty *n.*
non'id·i·o·mat'ic *adj.*
non'i·dol'a·trous *adj.*
non'im·ag'i·nar'y *adj.*
non·im'i·ta'tive *adj.*
non'im·mune' *adj.*
non'im·pair'ment *n.*
non'im·pe'ri·al *adj.*
non'im·prove'ment *n.*
non'im·pul'sive *adj.*
non'in·can·des'cent *adj.*
non'in·clu'sive *adj.*
non·in'crease *n.*
non'in·de·pend'ent *adj.*
non·in'dexed *adj.*
non'in·dict'ment *n.*
non'in·di·vid'u·al *adj.*
non'in·duc'tive *adj.*
non'in·dus'tri·al *adj.*
non'in·fal'li·ble *adj.*
non'in·flam'ma·ble *adj.*
non'in·flec'tion·al *adj.*
non'in·form'a·tive *adj.*
non·in'ju·ry *n.*
non'in·quir'ing *adj.*
non'in·struc'tion·al *adj.*
non'in·stru·men'tal *adj.*
non'in·tel·lec'tu·al *adj.* & *n.*

Europe. Pop. 3,708,000. Cap. Oslo.
Nor•we•gian (nôr-wē′jən) *n.* **1.** A native or inhabitant of Norway. **2.** The North Germanic language of the Norwegians. —**Nor•we′gian** *adj.*

Norway

nose (nōz) *n.* **1.** The facial part or structure bearing the nostrils and containing the organ of smell and the beginning of the respiratory tract. **2. a.** The sense of smell. **b.** The ability to discover, as if by smell: *a nose for news.* **3.** Anything resembling a nose in shape or position. —*v.* **nosed, nosing. 1.** To find out by or as by smell. **2.** To touch with the nose; nuzzle. **3.** To steer or move forward with care. **4.** To pry curiously. [< OE *nosu.* See **nas-**.]
nose•bleed (nōz′blēd′) *n.* A nasal hemorrhage.
nose cone. The forwardmost section of a rocket or guided missile.
nose dive. 1. A sudden plunge of an aircraft, nose toward the earth. **2.** Any sudden plunge. —**nose′-dive′** (nōz′dīv′) *v.*
nose•gay (nōz′gā′) *n.* A small bunch of flowers.
nose•piece (nōz′pēs′) *n.* A piece of armor serving as a guard for the nose.
nos•tal•gi•a (nŏ-stăl′jə, nə-) *n.* **1.** A longing for things, persons, or situations that are not present. **2.** Homesickness. [< Gk *nostos,* a return + -ALGIA.] —**nos•tal′gic** *adj.*
Nos•tra•da•mus (nŏs′trə-dā′məs, nŏs′trə-dā′məs). 1503–1566. French astrologer; author of prophecies (1555).
nos•tril (nŏs′trəl) *n.* An external opening of the nose. [< OE *nosthyrl,* "nose hole."]
nos•trum (nŏs′trəm) *n.* A quack medicine or remedy. [NL, "our own."]
nos•y, nos•ey (nō′zē) *adj.* **-ier, -iest.** *Informal.* Prying; inquisitive. —**nos′i•ness** *n.*
not (nŏt) *adv.* In no way; to no degree: *I will not go. You may not have any.* [< OE *nāwiht* : *nā,* no + *wiht,* a man, thing (see **wekti-**).]
no•ta be•ne (nō′tə bĕn′ē, nō′tä bā′nā). Note well. [L.]
no•ta•ble (nō′tə-bəl) *adj.* Worthy of notice; remarkable; striking. —*n.* A person of note or distinction. [< L *notāre,* to note.] —**no′ta•bil′i•ty** *n.* —**no′ta•bly** *adv.*
no•ta•rize (nō′tə-rīz′) *v.* **-rized, -rizing.** To authenticate or attest to as a notary. —**no′ta•ri•za′tion** *n.*
no•ta•ry (nō′tə-rē) *n., pl.* **-ries.** A notary public. [< L *notārius,* "stenographer."]

frontal sinuses
sphenoid sinus
Eustachian tube
pharyngeal tonsil

nose

notary public *pl.* **notaries public.** A public officer authorized to certify documents, take

non′in·tel′li·gent *adj.*
non′in·ter·change′a·ble *adj.*
non′in·tox′i·cant *adj.*
non·ir′ri·tant *adj.* & *n.*
non-Jew′ *n.*
non′ju·di′cial *adj.*
non·ju′ror *n.*
non·ko′sher *adj.*
non-Lat′in *adj.* & *n.*
non·le′gal *adj.*
non·le′thal *adj.*
non′lib·er·a′tion *n.*
non·life′ *n.*
non′lim·i·ta′tion *n.*
non′liq·ui·da′tion *n.*
non·list′ing *adj.*
non·lit′er·a·cy *n.*
non·lit′er·ar′y *adj.*
non′li·tur′gi·cal *adj.*
non·liv′ing *adj.* & *n.*
non·lo′cal *adj.* & *n.*
non·lov′ing *adj.*
non·lu′cid *adj.*
non′lu·mi·nes′cent *adj.*
non′mag·net′ic *adj.*
non·main′te·nance *n.*
non′ma·lig′nant *adj.*
non·mal′le·a·ble *adj.*
non·mar′i·tal *adj.*
non·mar′i·time′ *adj.*
non·mar′ry·ing *adj.*
non·mar′tial *adj.*
non′ma·te′ri·al *adj.*
non′ma·ter′nal *adj.*
non′me·chan′i·cal *adj.*
non·med′i·cal *adj.*
non′me·lo′di·ous *adj.*
non·mem′ber *n.*
non′-Meth′od·ist *adj.* & *n.*
non′met·ro·pol′i·tan *adj.* & *n.*
non·mi′gra·to′ry *adj.*
non·mil′i·tant *adj.* & *n.*
non·min′er·al *n.* & *adj.*
non′min·is·te′ri·al *adj.*
non·mo′bile *adj.*
non·mor′tal *adj.* & *n.*
non-Mos′lem *adj.* & *n.*
non·mo′tile *adj.*
non′mu·nic′i·pal *adj.*
non·mus′cu·lar *adj.*
non·mys′ti·cal *adj.*
non·myth′i·cal *adj.*
non·na′tion·al *adj.* & *n.*
non·nau′ti·cal *adj.*
non·na′val *adj.*
non′ne·go′tia·ble *adj.*
non-Ne′gro *n.* & *adj.*
non·neu′tral *adj.* & *n.*
non·nu′cle·ar *adj.*
non·nu′tri·ent *n.* & *adj.*
non′o·be′di·ence *n.*
non′o·blig′a·to′ry *adj.*
non′ob·ser′vance *n.*
non′ob·struc′tive *adj.*
non′oc·cu·pa′tion *n.*
non′oc·cur′rence *n.*
non·o′dor·ous *adj.*
non′of·fen′sive *adj.*
non′of·fi′cial *adj.*
non·op′er·a′tive *adj.*
non·op′tion·al *adj.*
non′or·gan′ic *adj.*
non·own′er *n.*
non′pa·cif′ic *adj.*
non·pa′gan *n.* & *adj.*
non·pa′pal *adj.*
non·par′ *adj.*
non·par′al·lel′ *adj.* & *n.*
non′par·a·sit′ic *adj.*
non′pa·ren′tal *adj.*
non′pa·rish′ion·er *n.*
non′par·lia·men′ta·ry *adj.*
non′pa·ro′chi·al *adj.*
non·par′tial *adj.*
non′par·tic′i·pant *n.*
non′par·tic′i·pat′ing *adj.*
non′par·tic′i·pa′tion *n.*
non′pa·ter′nal *adj.*
non′path·o·gen′ic *adj.*
non·pay′ment *n.*
non′per·cep′tu·al *adj.*
non′per·form′ance *n.*
non′pe·ri·od′i·cal *adj.* & *n.*
non·per′ish·a·ble *adj.* & *n.*
non·per′ma·nent *adj.*
non·per′me·a·ble *adj.*
non′per·pet′u·al *adj.*
non′per·sist′ence *n.*
non′per·sist′ent *adj.*
non′phil·an·throp′ic *adj.*
non·phys′i·cal *adj.*
non′phys·i·o·log′i·cal *adj.*
non·plan′e·tar′y *adj.*
non′po·et′ic *adj.*
non·poi′son·ous *adj.*
non′po·lit′i·cal *adj.*
non·po′rous *adj.*
non·pred′a·to′ry *adj.*
non′pre·dict′a·ble *adj.*
non′pref·er·en′tial *adj.*
non′pres·i·den′tial *adj.*
non·prev′a·lent *adj.*
non·priest′ly *adj.*
non′pro·duc′er *n.*
non′pro·duc′tive *adj.*
non′pro·fes′sion·al *adj.* & *n.*
non′pro·fi′cien·cy *n.*
non′pro·gres′sive *adj.* & *n.*
non′pro·lif′ic *adj.*
non′pro·por′tion·al *adj.*
non′pro·pri′e·ty *n.*
non′pro·tec′tion *n.*
non-Prot′es·tant *n.* & *adj.*
non·psy′chic *adj.* & *n.*
non·pub′lic *adj.*
non·ra′cial *adj.*
non·rad′i·cal *adj.* & *n.*
non·ra′tion·al *adj.*
non′re·ac′tive *adj.*
non′re·ceiv′a·ble *adj.* & *n.*
non′re·cip′ro·cal *adj.* & *n.*
non′rec·og·ni′tion *n.*
non′rec·tan′gu·lar *adj.*

affidavits, and administer oaths.

no•ta•tion (nō-tā'shən) *n.* **1.** A system of figures or symbols used to represent numbers, quantities, etc. **2.** The act or process of using such a system. [< L.]

notch (nŏch) *n.* **1.** A V-shaped cut, esp. one used for keeping count. **2.** A narrow pass between mountains. *—v.* **1.** To cut notches in. **2.** To record by or as by making notches. [< OF *ochier,* to notch.] **—notch'y** *adj.*

note (nōt) *n.* **1.** A brief written record or communication. **2.** A formal diplomatic or official communication. **3.** A commentary to a passage in a text. **4. a.** A piece of paper currency. **b.** A certificate issued by a government or bank, often negotiable. **c.** A **promissory note. 5.** *Mus.* **a.** A tone of definite pitch. **b.** The symbol of such a tone in musical notation. **6.** A musical call or cry, as of a bird. **7.** An indication of some quality or aspect: *a note of suspicion.* **8.** Importance; consequence. **9.** Notice; observation. *—v.* **noted, noting. 1.** To observe carefully; notice; perceive. **2.** To write down; make a note of. **3.** To make particular mention of; remark. [< L *nota,* mark, sign, cipher.]

note•book (nōt'bo͝ok') *n.* A book of blank pages for notes.

not•ed (nō'tĭd) *adj.* Distinguished by reputation; eminent. **—not'ed•ly** *adv.*

note•wor•thy (nōt'wûr'*th*ē) *adj.* Worthy of notice; remarkable. **—note'wor'thi•ness** *n.*

noth•ing (nŭth'ĭng) *n.* **1.** No thing; not anything. **2.** No significant thing. **3.** No portion. **4.** Insignificance; obscurity. **5.** A person or thing of no consequence. **6.** Absence of anything perceptible; nonexistence. **7.** Zero. *—adv.* In no way or degree; not at all. [< OE nān, NONE + *thing,* THING.]

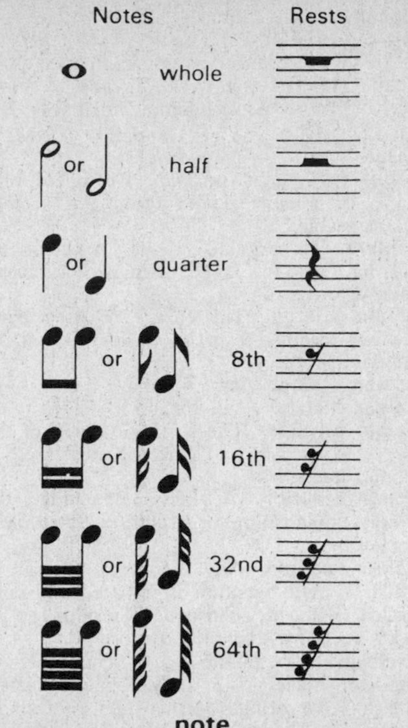

note

noth•ing•ness (nŭth'ĭng-nĭs) *n.* **1.** The condition or quality of being nothing; nonexistence. **2.** Insignificance.

no•tice (nō'tĭs) *n.* **1.** The act of observing; attention. **2.** An announcement or indication of some event. **3.** A formal announcement of intent to leave a job. **4.** A critical review, as of a play. *—v.* **-ticed, -ticing. 1.** To observe; perceive; be aware of. **2.** To take note of; remark on. [< L *nōtus,* pp of *nōscere,* to get acquainted with.]

no•tice•a•ble (nō'tĭs-ə-bəl) *adj.* **1.** Readily observed; evident. **2.** Worth noticing; significant. **—no'tice•a•bly** *adv.*

no•ti•fy (nō'tə-fī') *v.* **-fied, -fying. 1.** To give notice to; inform. **2.** To give notice of; proclaim. **—no'ti•fi•ca'tion** (-fĭ-kā'shən) *n.* **—no'ti•fi'er** *n.*

no•tion (nō'shən) *n.* **1.** A general impression or feeling. **2.** A view; conception; theory. **3.** Intention or inclination. **4. notions.** Small items for household and clothing use. [L *nōtiō,* "a becoming acquainted."]

no•to•ri•ous (nō-tôr'ē-əs, -tōr'ē-əs) *adj.* **1.** Known widely and regarded unfavorably; infamous. **2.** Generally known and discussed. [< L *nōtus,* known.] **—no'to•ri'e•ty** (nō'tə-rī'ə-tē) *n.* **—no•to'ri•ous•ly** *adv.*

no-trump (nō'trŭmp') *n.* **1.** A declaration to play a hand without a trump suit, as in bridge. **2.** A hand so played. **—no'-trump'** *adj.*

not•with•stand•ing (nŏt'wĭth-stăn'dĭng, nŏt'wĭ*th*-) *prep.* In spite of. *—adv.* All the same; nevertheless. *—conj.* Although.

Nouak•chott (nwäk'shŏt'). The capital of Mauritania. Pop. 13,000.

nou•gat (no͞o'gət) *n.* A confection made from a sweet paste into which nuts are mixed. [< OProv *nogat,* confection of nuts.]

nought. Variant of **naught.**

noun (noun) *n.* A word used to denote or

non're·cur'rent *adj.*
non're·deem'a·ble *adj.*
non're·gen'er·a'tive *adj.*
non'reg·i·men'tal *adj.*
non'reg·is·tra'tion *n.*
non're·li'ance *n.*
non're·lig'ious *adj.*
non're·mu'ner·a'tive *adj.*
non're·new'a·ble *adj.*
non're·pay'a·ble *adj.*
non're·pen'tant *adj.*
non're·pet'i·tive *adj.*
non'rep·re·hen'si·bly *adv.*
non'rep·re·sen·ta'tion *n.*
non'rep·re·sen'ta·tive *n.* & *adj.*
non're·pro·duc'tive *adj.*
non're·sem'blance *n.*
non'res·i·den'tial *adj.*
non're·sid'u·al *adj.*
non're·solv'a·ble *adj.*
non're·stric'tive *adj.*
non're·ten'tion *n.*
non're·ten'tive *adj.*
non're·tir'ing *adj.*
non're·turn'a·ble *adj.*
non're·vers'i·ble *adj.*
non're·volt'ing *adj.*
non'rhe·tor'i·cal *adj.*
non·rig'id *adj.*
non·ri'val *n.* & *adj.*
non-Ro'man *adj.* & *n.*
non·ru'ral *adj.*
non'sac·ra·men'tal *adj.*
non·sa'cred *adj.*
non·sal'a·ble *adj.*
non·sal'a·ried *adj.*
non·sched'uled *adj.*
non'scho·las'tic *adj.*
non'sci·en·tif'ic *adj.*
non·scor'ing *adj.*
non·sea'son·al *adj.*
non'sec·re·tar'i·al *adj.*
non·sec'u·lar *adj.*
non'seg·men'tal *adj.*
non'se·lec'tive *adj.*
non-Sem'ite *n.*
non'sen·a·to'ri·al *adj.*
non·sen'si·tive *adj.*
non·sen'su·al *adj.*
non·ser'vile *adj.*
non·sex'u·al *adj.*
non'sig·nif'i·cant *adj.*
non·slip'per·y *adj.*
non·smok'er *n.*
non·so'cial *adj.*
non·so'cial·ist *n.* & *adj.*
non·sol'vent *n.*
non·spar'ing *adj.*
non·spar'kling *adj.*
non'spe·cif'ic *adj.*
non'spec·tac'u·lar *adj.*
non·spec'u·la'tive *adj.*
non·spher'i·cal *adj.*
non·spir'i·tu·al *adj.* & *n.*
non'spon·ta'ne·ous *adj.*
non·sport'ing *adj.*
non·stand'ard·ized' *adj.*
non·sta'tion·ar'y *adj.*
non·stat'u·to'ry *adj.*
non'stim·u·la'tion *n.*
non'stra·te'gic *adj.*
non·stretch'a·ble *adj.*
non·stri'at·ed *adj.*
non·strik'er *n.*
non·struc'tur·al *adj.*
non'sub·mis'sive *adj.*
non'sub·scrib'er *n.*
non'suc·cess' *n.*
non'sup·port'er *n.*
non·sur'gi·cal *adj.*
non'sus·tain'ing *adj.*
non'sym·pa·thet'ic *adj.*
non·sym'pa·thy *n.*
non'sym·phon'ic *adj.*
non'symp·to·mat'ic *adj.*
non·syn'chro·nous *adj.*
non'syn·tac'tic *adj.*
non'sys·tem·at'ic *adj.*
non·talk'a·tive *adj.*
non·tech'ni·cal *adj.*
non·tem'po·ral *adj.*
non'ter·ri·to'ri·al *adj.*
non·tex'tu·al *adj.*
non'the·at'ri·cal *adj.*
non'ther·a·peu'tic *adj.*
non·ther'mal *adj.*
non·think'er *n.*
non·tox'ic *adj.*
non'tra·di'tion·al *adj.*
non·trag'ic *adj.*
non·trans·fer'a·ble *adj.*
non'tran·si'tion·al *adj.*
non'trans·par'ent *adj.*
non·triv'i·al *adj.*
non·truth' *n.*
non'tu·ber'cu·lar *adj.*
non·typ'i·cal *adj.*
non'ty·po·graph'ic *adj.*
non'ty·po·graph'i·cal *adj.*
non'un·der·stand'a·ble *adj.*
non'un·der·stand'ing *adj.* & *n.*
non·u'ni·form' *adj.*
non'u·ni·ver'sal *adj.* & *n.*
non·ur'ban *adj.*
non·us'er *n.*
non'u·til'i·tar'i·an *adj.*
non'va·lid'i·ty *n.*
non·val'ue *n.*
non·vas'cu·lar *adj.*
non·ven'om·ous *adj.*
non·ver'bal *adj.*
non·ver'ti·cal *adj.*
non·vet'er·an *n.*
non'vi·o·la'tion *n.*
non·vi'o·lence *n.*
non·vis'u·al *adj.*
non·vi'tal *adj.*
non·vo'cal *adj.*
non'vo·ca'tion·al *adj.*
non·vol'a·tile *adj.*
non·vol'un·tar'y *adj.*
non·vot'er *n.*
non·white' *n.* & *adj.*
non·work'er *n.*
non·yield'ing *adj.*

name a person, place, thing, quality, or act. [< L *nōmen,* name.]
nour•ish (nûr'ĭsh) *v.* **1.** To provide with food or other substances necessary for life and growth. **2.** To foster the development of; promote and sustain. [< L *nūtrīre,* to feed.] —**nour'ish•er** *n.* —**nour'ish•ment** *n.*
nou•veau riche (no͞o-vō rēsh') *pl.* **nouveaux riches** (no͞o-vō rēsh'). One who has lately become rich. [F, "new rich."]
Nov. November.
no•va (nō'və) *n., pl.* **-vae** (-vē) or **-vas.** A star that suddenly increases in brightness to several times its normal magnitude and then returns to its original appearance. [< L *novus,* new.]
No•va Sco•tia (nō'və skō'shə). A province of SE Canada. Pop. 763,000. Cap. Halifax. —**Nova Scotian.**
nov•el[1] (nŏv'əl) *n.* A fictional prose narrative of considerable length, typically having a plot unfolded by the actions, speech, and thoughts of the characters. [< L *novellus,* new.] —**nov'el•ist** *n.* —**nov'el•is'tic** *adj.*
nov•el[2] (nŏv'əl) *adj.* Strikingly new, unusual, or different. [< L *novus,* new.]
nov•el•ette (nŏv'ə-lĕt') *n.* A short novel.
no•vel•la (nō-vĕl'ə) *n., pl.* **-las** or **-le** (-vĕl'ē). A short novel.
nov•el•ty (nŏv'əl-tē) *n., pl.* **-ties. 1.** Newness; originality. **2.** Something that is novel; a new or unusual thing; an innovation. **3. novelties.** Small mass-produced articles, as trinkets. [< NOVEL[2].]
No•vem•ber (nō-vĕm'bər) *n.* The 11th month of the year. November has 30 days. [< L *Novembris (mēnsis),* the ninth (month) (of the Roman calendar).]
no•ve•na (nō-vē'nə) *n., pl.* **-nas** or **-nae** (-nē). *R.C.Ch.* A nine-days' devotion. [< L *novem,* nine.]
nov•ice (nŏv'ĭs) *n.* **1.** One new to any activity; a beginner. **2.** One who has entered a religious order but is on probation before taking final vows. [< L *novus,* new.]
no•vi•ti•ate (nō-vĭsh'ē-ĭt, -āt') *n.* **1.** The period or state of being a novice. **2.** A novice.
No•vo•cain (nō'və-kān') *n.* A trademark for **procaine hydrochloride.**
No•vo•si•birsk (nō'vō-sĭ-bîrsk'). A city in south-central Siberia. Pop. 1,161,000.
now (nou) *adv.* **1.** At the present time. **2.** At once; immediately. **3.** Very recently. **4.** Very soon. **5.** At this point in a narrative or series of events; then. **6.** Nowadays. **7.** In these circumstances. —*conj.* Since; seeing that. —*n.* The present time or moment: *Now is the time to act.* [< OE *nū.* See **nu-**.]
NOW (nou). **National Organization for Women.**
now•a•days (nou'ə-dāz') *adv.* In these days.
no•way (nō'wā') *adv.* Also **no•ways** (-wāz'). Nowise.
no•where (nō'hwâr') *adv.* In, to, or at no place; not anywhere. —*n.* A nonexistent or insignificant place.
no•wise (nō'wīz') *adv.* In no way, manner, or degree.
nox•ious (nŏk'shəs) *adj.* **Injurious to health or morals.** [< L *noxa,* **injury, damage.]**
noz•zle (nŏz'əl) *n.* A spout, as the end of a hose, through which gas or liquid is discharged. [< NOSE.]
Np neptunium.
N.P. notary public.
N.S. 1. Nova Scotia. **2.** not specified.
NT, N.T. New Testament.
nu (n/y/o͞o) *n.* The 13th letter of the Greek alphabet, representing *n.*
nu•ance (n/y/o͞o-äns', n/y/o͞o'äns') *n.* A subtle or slight variation, as in meaning, color, or quality. [< OF *nuer,* to show shades of color.]
nub (nŭb) *n.* **1.** A protuberance or knob. **2.** A small lump. **3.** The gist or point. [< MLG *knobbe,* knob.] —**nub'by** *adj.*
nu•bile (n/y/o͞o'bĭl,-bīl') *adj.* Ready for marriage; of a marriageable age. [< L *nūbilis,* marriageable.]
nu•cle•ar (n/y/o͞o'klē-ər) *adj.* **1.** Of or involving a nucleus. **2.** Of or involving nuclear energy.
nuclear energy. The energy released by a nuclear reaction, esp. by fission, fusion, or radioactive decay.
nuclear fission. *Phys.* Fission.
nuclear fusion. *Phys.* Fusion.
nuclear physics. The scientific study of the forces, reactions, and internal structures of atomic nuclei.
nuclear reaction. A reaction that alters the energy, composition, or structure of an atomic nucleus.
nuclear reactor. Any of several devices in which a chain reaction is initiated and controlled, with the consequent production of heat, neutrons, and fission products.
nu•cle•ate (n/y/o͞o'klē-ĭt) *adj.* Having a nucleus or nuclei. —*v.* (n/y/o͞o'klē-āt') **-ated, -ating. 1.** To bring together into or form a nucleus. **2.** To act as a nucleus for. —**nu'cle•a'tion** *n.* —**nu'cle•a'tor** *n.*
nu•cle•ic acid (n/y/o͞o-klē'ĭk). Any member of either of two groups of complex compounds found in all living cells.
nucleo–. *comb. form.* Nucleus.
nu•cle•o•lus (n/y/o͞o-klē'ə-ləs, -klē-ō'ləs) *n., pl.* **-li** (-lī'). A small particle of protein and ribonucleic acid in the nucleus of a cell. —**nu•cle'o•lar** (-lər) *adj.*
nu•cle•on (n/y/o͞o'klē-ŏn') *n.* A proton or neutron, esp. as part of an atomic nucleus. —**nu'cle•on'ic** *adj.*
nu•cle•us (n/y/o͞o'klē-əs) *n., pl.* **-clei** (-klē-ī') or *rare* **-uses. 1.** A central thing or part around which other things are grouped; core. **2.** Anything regarded as a basis for development and growth. **3.** A complex, usually spherical, protoplasmic body within a living cell that contains the cell's hereditary material and controls its metabolism, growth, and reproduction. **4.** The positively charged central region of an atom, composed of protons and neutrons and containing almost all of the mass of the atom. [L, "nut," "kernel."]
nude (n/y/o͞od) *adj.* Without clothing; naked. —*n.* **1.** The nude human figure or a representation of it. **2.** Nude state: *in the nude.* [L *nūdus.*] —**nu'di•ty** *n.*
nudge (nuj) *v.* **nudged, nudging.** To push against gently, esp. to gain attention or give a signal. [Prob < Scand.] —**nudge** *n.*
nud•ism (n/y/o͞o'dĭz'əm) *n.* The doctrine or practice of living in the nude for reasons of health. —**nud'ist** *adj. & n.*
nug•get (nŭg'ĭt) *n.* A small lump, esp. of natural gold.
nui•sance (n/y/o͞o'səns) *n.* A source of inconvenience, annoyance, or vexation; a bother. [< OF.]
null (nŭl) *adj.* **1.** Having no legal force; invalid. **2.** Of no consequence, effect, or value; insignificant. **3.** Amounting to nothing. **4.** Of zero magnitude. [< L *nūllus.*] —**nul'li•ty** *n.*
nul•li•fy (nŭl'ə-fī') *v.* **-fied, -fying. 1.** To deprive of legal force; annul. **2.** To make ineffective or useless. —**nul'li•fi•ca'tion** (-fĭ-kā'shən) *n.* —**nul'li•fi'er** *n.*
Num. Numbers.
numb (nŭm) *adj.* **1.** Insensible, as from excessive chill. **2.** Stunned, as from shock. [< OE *niman,* take, seize. See **nem-**.] —**numb** *v.* —**numb'ly** *adv.* —**numb'ness** *n.*
num•ber (nŭm'bər) *n.* **1. a.** A member of the set of positive integers. **b.** A member of any of the further sets of mathematical objects that can be derived from the positive integers. **2. numbers.** Arithmetic: **3.** A numeral or series of numerals designating a specific object. **4.** A specific quantity composed of equal units. **5.** Quantity of units: *The crowd was small in number.* **6.** A multitude. **7.** One item in a sequence or series. —*v.* **1.** To add up to. **2.** To count or enumerate. **3.** To include in or be one of a group. **4.** To assign a number to. **5.** To limit in number. [< L *numerus.*]
num•ber•less (nŭm'bər-lĭs) *adj.* Countless; innumerable.
nu•mer•a•ble (n/y/o͞o'mər-ə-bəl) *adj.* Capable of being counted.
nu•mer•al (n/y/o͞o'mər-əl) *n.* A symbol used to denote a number. [< L *numerus,* NUMBER.] —**nu'mer•al** *adj.*
nu•mer•ate (n/y/o͞o'mə-rāt') *v.* **-ated, -ating.** To enumerate; number; reckon.
nu•mer•a•tor (n/y/o͞o'mə-rā'tər) *n.* The expression written above the line in a common fraction.
nu•mer•i•cal (n/y/o͞o-mĕr'ĭ-kəl) *adj.* Also **nu•mer•ic** (n/y/o͞o-mĕr'ĭk). **1.** Pertaining to a number or series of numbers. **2.** Expressed in or counted by numbers. —**nu•mer'i•cal•ly** *adv.*
nu•mer•ol•o•gy (n/y/o͞o'mə-rŏl'ə-jē) *n.* The study of the occult meanings of numbers.
nu•mer•ous (n/y/o͞o'mər-əs) *adj.* **1.** Consisting of many persons or things: *a numerous collection.* **2.** Many: *numerous books.* —**nu'mer•ous•ly** *adv.* —**nu'mer•ous•ness** *n.*
nu•mis•mat•ics (n/y/o͞o'mĭz-măt'ĭks, n/y/o͞o'mĭs-) *n. (takes sing. v.).* The study and collection of money and medals. [< Gk *nomisma,* usage, current coin.] —**nu•mis'ma•tist** *n.*
num•skull (nŭm'skŭl') *n.* A stupid person; blockhead.
nun[1] (nŭn) *n.* A woman who belongs to a religious order, usually under vows of poverty, chastity, and obedience. [< ML *nonna.*]
nun[2] (no͞on, no͝on) *n.* The 14th letter of the Hebrew alphabet, representing *n.*
nun•ci•o (nŭn'sē-ō', no͝on'-) *n., pl.* **-os.** An ambassador from the pope. [< L *nūntius,* messenger.]
nun•ner•y (nŭn'ə-rē) *n., pl.* **-ies.** A community of nuns or the buildings in which they live.
nup•tial (nŭp'shəl, -chəl) *adj.* Pertaining to marriage or the wedding ceremony. —*n.* Often **nuptials.** A wedding ceremony. [L *nuptiālis.*] —**nup'tial•ly** *adv.*
nurse (nûrs) *n.* **1.** A person trained to care for the sick. **2.** A woman employed to take care of another's children. —*v.* **nursed, nursing. 1.** To suckle. **2.** To care for or tend (a child or invalid). **3.** To take special care of; foster. **4.** To bear privately in the mind: *nurse a grudge.* **5.** To hold or clasp carefully. [< L *nutrix,* a nurse.] —**nurs'er** *n.*
nurse•maid (nûrs'mād') *n.* A woman employed to take care of children.
nurs•er•y (nûr'sə-rē, nûrs'rē) *n.,pl.* **-ies. 1.** A room set apart for the use of children. **2.** A place where plants are grown, esp. for sale.
nurs•er•y•man (nûr'sə-rē-mən, nûrs'rē-) *n.* One who owns or works in a nursery for

plants.

nursery school. A school for children not old enough to attend kindergarten.

nurs•ling (nûrs'lĭng) *n.* **1.** A nursing infant or young animal. **2.** A carefully nurtured person or thing.

nur•ture (nûr'chər) *n.* **1.** Anything that nourishes; sustenance; food. **2.** The promotion or influencing of development or growth; upbringing; rearing. —*v.* **-tured, -turing. 1.** To nourish. **2.** To train. [< L *nūtrīre,* to feed, suckle.] **—nur'tur•er** *n.*

nut (nŭt) *n.* **1. a.** A fruit or seed with a hard shell and usually a single kernel. **b.** The kernel itself. **2.** *Slang.* An eccentric or deranged person. **3.** A small block of metal or wood having a central, threaded hole, designed to fit around and secure a bolt or screw. [< OE *hnutu.*]

nut•crack•er (nŭt'krăk'ər) *n.* An implement used to crack nuts.

nut•hatch (nŭt'hăch') *n.* A small, grayish, sharp-billed bird that climbs up and down tree trunks.

nut•meat (nŭt'mēt') *n.* The edible kernel of a nut.

nut•meg (nŭt'mĕg') *n.* The hard, aromatic seed of a tropical tree, grated or ground for use as a spice. [< VL **nuce muscāta,* "musky nut."]

nu•tri•a (n/y/o͞o'trē-ə) *n.* The thick, brownish fur of a beaverlike South American rodent. [Span.]

nu•tri•ent (n/y/o͞o'trē-ənt) *n.* A nourishing ingredient or substance. —*adj.* Having nutritive value. [< L *nūtrīre,* to feed, nourish.]

nu•tri•ment (n/y/o͞o'trə-mənt) *n.* Anything that nourishes; food. [< L *nūtrīre,* to feed, nourish.] **—nu'tri•men'tal** (-mĕn'təl) *adj.*

nu•tri•tion (n/y/o͞o-trĭsh'ən) *n.* The process of nourishing, esp. the interrelated steps by which a living organism assimilates and uses food. [< L *nūtrīre,* to feed, nourish.] **—nu•tri'tion•al** *adj.* **—nu•tri'tion•al•ly** *adv.*

nu•tri•tion•ist (n/y/o͞o-trĭsh'ən-ĭst) *n.* One who specializes in the study of nutrition.

nu•tri•tious (n/y/o͞o-trĭsh'əs) *adj.* Aiding growth and development; nourishing.

nu•tri•tive (n/y/o͞o'trə-tĭv) *adj.* Promoting nutrition; nourishing.

nuts (nŭts) *adj. Slang.* **1.** Crazy; insane. **2.** Extremely enthusiastic.

nut•shell (nŭt'shĕl') *n.* The shell enclosing the kernel of a nut. **—in a nutshell.** In concise or brief form.

nut•ty (nŭt'ē) *adj.* **-tier, -tiest. 1.** Having a flavor like that of nuts. **2.** *Informal.* Eccentric.

nuz•zle (nŭz'əl) *v.* **-zled, -zling. 1.** To rub or push against gently with the nose or snout. **2.** To nestle or cuddle together. [< NOSE.]

NW northwest.

n.wt. net weight.

N.Y. New York.

N.Y.C. New York City.

nyc•ta•lo•pi•a (nĭk'tə-lō'pē-ə) *n.* Vision that is normal in daylight but abnormally weak when the light is dim.

ny•lon (nī'lŏn') *n.* **1.** Any of a family of high-strength, resilient synthetic materials. **2.** Cloth or yarn made from nylon. **3. nylons.** Stockings made of nylon.

nymph (nĭmf) *n.* **1.** *Gk.&Rom.Myth.* Any of numerous female spirits, inhabiting and animistically representing features of nature. **2.** A young stage of an insect that undergoes incomplete metamorphosis. [< Gk *numphē,* nymph, bride.]

nym•pho•ma•ni•a (nĭm'fə-mā'nē-ə, -măn'yə) *n.* Abnormally strong and uncontrollable sexual desire in women. **—nym'pho•ma'ni•ac'** *adj.* & *n.*

N.Z. New Zealand.

Oo

o, O (ō) *n.* **1.** The 15th letter of the English alphabet. **2.** A zero. **3.** Anything shaped like the letter **O**; a circle.

O 1. ocean. **2.** order. **3.** oxygen.

O. 1. ocean. **2.** Ohio (unofficial). **3.** order.

O (ō). Used before the substantive in prayer or invocation.

o' (ə, ō) *prep.* A reduced form of the preposition *of* used esp. in the phrase *o'clock* but also found in such terms as *will-o'-the-wisp.*

O'. *comb. form.* A descendant of: *O'Connor.*

oaf (ōf) *n.* A stupid or clumsy person. [< ON *alfr,* elf.] **—oaf'ish** *adj.* **—oaf'ish•ly** *adv.* **—oaf'ish•ness** *n.*

oak (ōk) *n.* **1.** Any of various trees having usually lobed leaves and bearing acorns. **2.** The hard, durable wood of such a tree. [< OE *āc* < Gmc **aik-.*] **—oak'en** *adj.*

Oak•land (ōk'lənd). A city of W California. Pop. 368,000.

oa•kum (ō'kəm) *n.* Loose hemp or jute fiber, sometimes treated with tar, used for caulking ships. [< OE *ācumba,* "off-combings."]

oar (ôr, ōr) *n.* **1.** A long, thin pole with a blade at one end, used to row and, occasionally, steer a boat. **2.** One who rows; rower. [< OE *ār* < Gmc **airo.*] **—oared** *adj.*

oar•lock (ôr'lŏk', ōr'-) *n.* A U-shaped device used to hold an oar in place.

oars•man (ôrz'mən, ōrz'-) *n.* One who rows, esp. an expert in rowing.

OAS Organization of American States.

o•a•sis (ō-ā'sĭs) *n., pl.* **-ses** (-sēz'). A fertile or green spot in a desert or waste. [< Gk.]

oat (ōt) *n.* Often **oats. 1.** A cereal grass widely cultivated for its edible seeds. **2.** The seeds of this plant. [< OE *āte.*] **—oat'en** *adj.*

oath (ōth) *n., pl.* **oaths** (ōthz, ōths). **1.** A formal promise to fulfill a pledge, often calling upon God as witness. **2.** A blasphemous use of a sacred name. [< OE *āth.* See **oito-**.]

oat•meal (ōt'mēl') *n.* **1.** Meal made by rolling or grinding oats. **2.** Porridge made from this.

Ob (ŏb, ôb). A river of W Siberia.

ob–. *comb. form.* Inverse shape or attachment. [< L, to, toward, in front of, on account of, against.]

ob. 1. incidentally (L *obiter*). **2.** obstetric; obstetrics.

Obad. Obadiah (Old Testament).

ob•bli•ga•to (ŏb'lə-gä'tō) *n., pl.* **-tos.** *Mus.* An accompaniment that is an integral, indispensable part of a piece. [< It *obbligare,* to obligate.]

ob•du•rate (ŏb'd/y/o͞o-rĭt) *adj.* Hardened against influence or feeling; unyielding. [< L *obdūrāre,* to harden.] **—ob'du•ra•cy** *n.*

o•be•di•ent (ō-bē'dē-ənt) *adj.* Obeying a request, command, etc.; submissive to control; dutiful. [< L *oboedīre,* OBEY.] **—o•be'di•ence** *n.* **—o•be'di•ent•ly** *adv.*

o•bei•sance (ō-bā'səns, ō-bē'-) *n.* **1.** A gesture, as a bow, expressing respect. **2.** An attitude, as deference, associated with this gesture. [< OF *obeir,* to obey.] **—o•bei'sant** *adj.*

ob•e•lisk (ŏb'ə-lĭsk) *n.* A tall, four-sided shaft of stone, usually tapering to a pyramidal point. [< Gk *obeliskos.*]

o•bese (ō-bēs') *adj.* Extremely fat. [L *obēsus,* "grown fat by eating."] **—o•be'si•ty** *n.*

o•bey (ō-bā') *v.* **1.** To carry out the commands of; behave obediently. **2.** To comply with (a command, order, or request). [< L *oboedīre,* "to listen to."] **—o•bey'er** *n.*

ob•fus•cate (ŏb'fə-skāt', ŏb-fŭs'kāt') *v.* **-cated, -cating. 1.** To render indistinct or dim; darken. **2.** To confuse or becloud. [LL *obfuscāre,* to darken.] **—ob'fus•ca'tion** *n.*

o•bit (ō'bĭt, ō-bĭt') *n. Informal.* An obituary.

o•bit•u•ar•y (ō-bĭch'o͞o-ĕr'ē) *n., pl.* **-ies.** A notice of a death, usually with a brief biography. [< L *obīre,* to fall, die.]

obj. *Gram.* object; objective.

ob•ject¹ (əb-jĕkt') *v.* **1.** To present a dissenting or opposing argument. **2.** To feel or express disapproval of something. [< L *objicere,* to throw against, oppose.] **—ob•jec'tion** *n.*

ob•ject² (ŏb'jĭkt, -jĕkt') *n.* **1.** Anything perceptible by the senses; a material thing. **2.** *Phil.* Anything intelligible or perceptible by the mind. **3.** Anything serving as a focus of attention or action. **4.** The purpose of a specific action. **5.** *Gram.* A noun that receives or is affected by the action of a verb or that follows and is governed by a preposition. [< L *objectus,* "something thrown before or presented to (the mind)."]

ob•jec•tion•a•ble (əb-jĕk'shən-ə-bəl) *adj.* Arousing disapproval; offensive; unpleasant.

ob•jec•tive (əb-jĕk'tĭv) *adj.* **1.** Of or having to do with a material object as distinguished from a mental concept, idea, or belief. **2.** Having actual existence. **3. a.** Uninfluenced by emotion or personal prejudice. **b.** Based on observable phenomena. **4.** *Gram.* Denoting the case of a noun or pronoun serving as the object of a verb or preposition. **5.** Serving as the goal of a course of action. —*n.* **1.** Something worked toward or striven for; a goal. **2.** *Gram.* The objective case or a noun or pronoun in the objective case. **3.** The lens in an optical system that is closest to the object. **—ob•jec'tive•ly** *adv.* **—ob•jec'tive•ness** *n.* **—ob'jec•tiv'i•ty** (ŏb'jĕk-tĭv'ə-tē) *n.*

ob•jet d'art (ôb-zhĕ där') *pl.* **objets d'art** (ôb-zhĕ där'). An object valued for its artistry.

obl. 1. oblique. 2. oblong.

ob•late (ŏb'lāt', ŏb-lāt') *adj.* Having an equatorial diameter greater than the distance between poles; compressed along or flattened at the poles. [NL *oblatus,* "carried toward," stretched.]

ob•la•tion (ŏb-lā'shən) *n.* The ritual of offering something to a deity. [< L *oblātus,* "one offered."] **—ob•la'tion•al** *adj.*

ob•li•gate (ŏb'lə-gāt') *v.* **-gated, -gating.** To bind, compel, or constrain by a legal or moral tie. [L *obligāre,* to OBLIGE.]

ob•li•ga•tion (ŏb'lə-gā'shən) *n.* 1. The act of binding oneself by a social, legal, or moral tie. 2. The contract, promise, etc., that compels one to follow a certain course of action. 3. The constraining power of a law, promise, contract, or sense of duty. 4. The state, fact, or condition of being indebted for a favor received.

o•blig•a•to•ry (ə-blĭg'ə-tôr'ē, -tōr'ē, ŏb'lĭ-gə-) *adj.* 1. Legally or morally constraining. 2. Compulsory. **—o•blig'a•to'ri•ly** *adv.*

o•blige (ə-blīj') *v.* **obliged, obliging.** 1. To constrain by physical, legal, or moral means. 2. To make indebted for a favor. 3. To do a service or favor for. [< L *obligāre,* to tie to.] **—o•blig'er** *n.* **—o•blig'ing•ly** *adv.*

o•blique (ō-blēk', ə-) *adj.* 1. a. Slanting or sloping. b. Neither parallel nor perpendicular. 2. Indirect or evasive in action or expression; not straightforward. [< L *oblīquus.*] **—o•blique'ly** *adv.* **—o•bliq'ui•ty** (-blĭk'wə-tē), **o•blique'ness** *n.*

o•blit•er•ate (ə-blĭt'ə-rāt') *v.* **-ated, -ating.** 1. To destroy so as to leave no trace. 2. To wipe out; erase. [L *obliterāre,* "to strike out words."] **—o•blit'er•a'tion** *n.* **—o•blit'er•a'tor** *n.*

o•bliv•i•on (ə-blĭv'ē-ən) *n.* 1. The state or condition of being completely forgotten. 2. Forgetfulness. [< L *oblīvīscī,* to forget.]

o•bliv•i•ous (ə-blĭv'ē-əs) *adj.* 1. Lacking all memory of something; forgetful. 2. Unaware or unmindful. **—o•bliv'i•ous•ly** *adv.* **—o•bliv'i•ous•ness** *n.*

ob•long (ŏb'lông', -lŏng') *adj.* 1. Having one of two perpendicular dimensions, as length or width, greater than the other; rectangular. 2. Elongated. **—ob'long'** *n.*

ob•lo•quy (ŏb'lə-kwē) *n., pl.* **-quies.** 1. Abusively detractive language or utterance. 2. Ill repute or discredit. [< L *obloquī,* to speak against.]

ob•nox•ious (ŏb-nŏk'shəs, əb-) *adj.* Highly disagreeable or offensive; odious. [L *obnoxiōsus,* injurious.] **—ob•nox'ious•ly** *adv.* **—ob•nox'ious•ness** *n.*

o•boe (ō'bō) *n.* A woodwind instrument with a conical bore and a double-reed mouthpiece. [< F *hautbois,* "high wood."] **—o'bo•ist** *n.*

obs. obsolete.

ob•scene (ŏb-sēn', əb-) *adj.* 1. Offensive to accepted standards of decency. 2. Inciting lustful feelings. 3. Offensive to the senses. [< L *obscēnus,* ill-boding, repulsive.] **—ob•scene'ly** *adv.* **—ob•scen'i•ty** (-sĕn'ə-tē) *n.*

ob•scur•ant•ism (ŏb-skyŏŏr'ən-tĭz'əm, əb-, ŏb'skyŏŏ-răn'tĭz'əm) *n.* 1. Deliberate abstruseness. 2. Opposition to the diffusion of enlightenment. **—ob•scur'ant•ist** *n.* & *adj.*

ob•scure (ŏb-skyŏŏr', əb-) *adj.* **-scurer, -scurest.** 1. Dark; gloomy. 2. Indistinctly heard or perceived. 3. Out of sight; hidden. 4. Inconspicuous. 5. Difficult to understand. **—***v.* **-scured, -scuring.** 1. To make indistinct or unclear. 2. To conceal from view; hide. [< L *obscūrus.*] **—ob•scure'ly** *adv.* **—ob•scu'ri•ty** *n.*

ob•se•qui•ous (ŏb-sē'kwē-əs, əb-) *adj.* Full of servile compliance; fawning. [< L *obsequī,* to comply with.] **—ob•se'qui•ous•ly** *adv.* **—ob•se'qui•ous•ness** *n.*

ob•se•quy (ŏb'sə-kwē) *n., pl.* **-quies.** Often **obsequies.** A funeral rite or ceremony. [< L *obsequium,* compliance, service.]

ob•ser•vance (əb-zûr'vəns) *n.* 1. The act of observing or complying with something prescribed, as a law or custom. 2. The keeping or celebrating of a holiday or other ritual occasion. 3. Observation.

ob•ser•vant (əb-zûr'vənt) *adj.* 1. Quick to perceive or apprehend; alert. 2. Diligent in observing a law, custom, duty, etc.

ob•ser•va•tion (ŏb'zər-vā'shən) *n.* 1. The act or faculty of paying attention or noticing; the fact of being observed. 2. a. The noting and recording of a phenomenon. b. The record of such notation. 3. A comment or remark.

ob•ser•va•to•ry (əb-zûr'və-tôr'ē, -tōr'ē) *n., pl.* **-ries.** A building equipped for making observations of astronomical, meteorological, or other natural phenomena.

ob•serve (əb-zûrv') *v.* **-served, -serving.** 1. To perceive; take notice. 2. To watch attentively. 3. To make a systematic observation of. 4. To say; make a comment. 5. To adhere to or abide by. 6. To keep or pay tribute to (a holiday, rite, etc.). 7. To watch or be present without participating actively. [< L *observāre,* to pay attention to, look to.] **—ob•serv'a•ble** *adj.* **—ob•serv'er** *n.*

ob•sess (əb-sĕs', ŏb-) *v.* To haunt as a fixed idea. [L *obsidēre* (pp *obsessus*), to sit down before, besiege.] **—ob•ses'sive** *adj.*

ob•ses•sion (əb-sĕsh'ən, ŏb-) *n.* 1. Compulsive preoccupation with a fixed idea or unwanted feeling. 2. An idea or emotion causing such preoccupation. **—ob•ses'sion•al** *adj.*

ob•sid•i•an (ŏb-sĭd'ē-ən) *n.* An acid-resistant, lustrous volcanic glass, usually black or banded. [L *obsidiānus.*]

ob•so•les•cent (ŏb'sə-lĕs'ənt) *adj.* Becoming obsolete. [< L *obsolēscere,* to grow old.] **—ob'so•les'cence** *n.* **—ob'so•les'cent•ly** *adv.*

ob•so•lete (ŏb'sə-lēt', ŏb'sə-lēt') *adj.* 1. No longer in use or fashion. 2. No longer useful or functioning. [< L *obsolēre, to be old or in disuse.] **—ob'so•lete'ly** *adv.*

ob•sta•cle (ŏb'stə-kəl) *n.* One that opposes, stands in the way of, or holds up progress toward some goal. [< L *obstāre,* to hinder.]

ob•ste•tri•cian (ŏb'stə-trĭsh'ən) *n.* A physician specializing in obstetrics.

ob•stet•rics (ŏb-stĕt'rĭks, əb-) *n. (takes sing. or pl. v.).* The branch of medicine concerned with the care of women during pregnancy, childbirth, and the period following delivery. [< L *obstetrīx,* midwife.] **—ob•stet'ric** *adj.*

ob•sti•nate (ŏb'stə-nĭt) *adj.* 1. Stubbornly adhering to an idea or course; inflexible. 2. Difficult to control or subdue. [< L *obstināre,* to persist.] **—ob'sti•na•cy** (-nə-sē), **ob'sti•nate•ness** *n.* **—ob'sti•nate•ly** *adv.*

ob•strep•er•ous (ŏb-strĕp'ər-əs, əb-) *adj.* Noisily defiant; unruly. [< L *obstrepere,* to make noise against.] **—ob•strep'er•ous•ness** *n.*

ob•struct (əb-strŭkt', ŏb-) *v.* 1. To block (a passage) with obstacles. 2. To impede or retard. 3. To get in the way of; hide, as a view. [< L *obstruere* (pp *obstructus*).] **—ob•struct'er, ob•struc'tor** *n.* **—ob•struc'tive** *adj.*

ob•struc•tion (əb-strŭk'shən, ŏb-) *n.* 1. An obstacle. 2. An act or instance of obstructing. 3. The causing of delay.

ob•struc•tion•ist (əb-strŭk'shən-ĭst, ŏb-) *n.* One who systematically obstructs or interrupts progress. **—ob•struc'tion•ism'** *n.*

ob•tain (əb-tān', ŏb-) *v.* 1. To succeed in gaining; get or acquire. 2. To be established or accepted: *Certain customs still obtain.* [< L *obtinēre,* attain.] **—ob•tain'a•ble** *adj.*

ob•trude (ŏb-trōōd', əb-) *v.* **-truded, -truding.** 1. To force (oneself or one's ideas) upon others. 2. To thrust out; push forward. [L *obtrūdere.*] **—ob•tru'sion** (-trōō'zhən) *n.* **—ob•tru'sive** (-trōō'sĭv) *adj.*

ob•tuse (ŏb-t/y/ōōs', əb-) *adj.* 1. Not sharp, pointed, or acute; blunt. 2. Slow to apprehend or perceive. [L *obtūsus,* pp of *obtundere,* to blunt.] **—ob•tuse'ly** *adv.* **—ob•tuse'ness** *n.*

obtuse angle. An angle greater than 90° and less than 180°.

ob•verse (ŏb-vûrs', ŏb'vûrs') *adj.* 1. Facing the observer. 2. Serving as a counterpart or complement. **—***n.* (ŏb'vûrs', ŏb-vûrs'). 1. The side of a coin or medal that bears the principal stamp or design and, on U.S. coins, the date. 2. A counterpart or complement. [< L *obvertere,* to turn toward.]

ob•vi•ate (ŏb'vē-āt') *v.* **-ated, -ating.** To prevent or dispose of effectively; anticipate so as to render unnecessary. [LL *obviāre,* "to meet in the way," prevent.] **—ob'vi•a'tion** *n.*

ob•vi•ous (ŏb'vē-əs) *adj.* 1. Easily perceived or understood. 2. Easily seen through; lacking subtlety. [< L *obviam,* in the way.] **—ob'vi•ous•ly** *adv.* **—ob'vi•ous•ness** *n.*

oc•a•ri•na (ŏk'ə-rē'nə) *n.* A small terra-cotta or plastic wind instrument with a mouthpiece, finger holes, and a bulbous shape. [It, "little goose."]

OCAS Organization of Central American States.

occ. occupation.

oc•ca•sion (ə-kā'zhən) *n.* 1. An event or happening, esp. a significant event. 2. The time of an occurrence. 3. A favorable time; opportunity. 4. That which brings on an action. 5. Ground; reason. 6. Need; necessity. **—***v.* To provide occasion for. [< L *occāsiō,* "a falling down, happening."]

oc•ca•sion•al (ə-kā'zhən-əl) *adj.* 1. Occurring from time to time. 2. Occurring, used on, or created for a special occasion. **—oc•ca'sion•al•ly** *adv.*

Oc•ci•dent (ŏk'sə-dənt, -dĕnt') *n.* Europe and the W Hemisphere. [< L *occidēns,* "quarter of the setting sun," west.]

Oc•ci•den•tal (ŏk'sə-dĕn'təl) *adj.* Pertaining to the Occident. **—***n.* An inhabitant of the Occident.

oc•clude (ə-klōōd') *v.* **-cluded, -cluding.** 1. To close or shut off; obstruct. 2. To make contact at opposing surfaces. 3. *Chem.* To absorb or adsorb. [L *occlūdere.*] **—oc•clu'sion** *n.*

oc•cult (ə-kŭlt', ō-kŭlt', ŏk'ŭlt') *adj.* 1. Of or relating to supernatural influences, agencies, or phenomena. 2. Beyond human comprehension. 3. Available only to the initiate; secret. [< L *occulere,* to conceal.]

oc•cu•pan•cy (ŏk'yə-pən-sē) *n., pl.* **-cies.** 1. The act of occupying or condition of being occupied; occupation. 2. The period during which one owns, rents, or uses premises or land.

oc•cu•pant (ŏk'yə-pənt) *n.* 1. One who occupies a position or place. 2. A tenant or an owner of premises.

oc•cu•pa•tion (ŏk'yə-pā'shən) *n.* 1. An activity that serves as one's regular source of livelihood. 2. The act of occupying or state of being occupied. 3. The invasion, conquest, and control of a nation or territory by a foreign military force. —**oc'cu•pa'tion•al** *adj.*

occupational therapy. Therapy in which the principal element is some form of productive or creative activity.

oc•cu•py (ŏk'yə-pī') *v.* **-pied, -pying. 1.** To seize possession of and maintain control over (a place or region). **2.** To fill or take (time or space). **3.** To dwell or reside in. **4.** To hold or fill (an office). **5.** To engage or busy (oneself). [< L *occupāre,* to seize.]

oc•cur (ə-kûr') *v.* **-curred, -curring. 1.** To take place. **2.** To be found to exist or appear. **3.** To come to mind. [L *occurrere,* to run to meet.]

oc•cur•rence (ə-kûr'əns) *n.* **1.** An act or instance of occurring. **2.** Something that takes place. —**oc•cur'rent** *adj.*

OCD Office of Civil Defense.

o•cean (ō'shən) *n.* **1.** The entire body of salt water that covers about 72% of the earth's surface. **2.** Often **Ocean.** Any of the principal divisions of this body of water, including the Atlantic, Pacific, and Indian oceans, their southern extensions in Antarctica, and the Arctic Ocean. **3.** A great expanse or amount. [< Gk *Ōkeanos,* god of the outer sea encircling the earth.] —**o'ce•an'ic** (ō'shē-ăn'ĭk) *adj.*

o•cean•og•ra•phy (ō'shə-nŏg'rə-fē) *n.* The exploration and scientific study of the ocean. —**o'cean•og'ra•pher** *n.*

oc•e•lot (ŏs'ə-lŏt', ō'sə-) *n.* A spotted wild cat of the SW U.S. and Central and South America. [< Nah *ocelotl.*]

o•cher (ō'kər) *n.* Also **o•chre. 1.** Any of several earthy mineral oxides of iron mingled with varying amounts of clay and sand, occurring in yellow, brown, or red, and used as pigments. **2.** Moderate orange yellow. [< Gk *ōkhros,* yellow.]

o'clock (ə-klŏk') *adv.* Of or according to the clock: *three o'clock.* [< *of the clock.*]

OCS Officer Candidate School.

oct. octavo.

Oct. October.

oc•ta•gon (ŏk'tə-gŏn') *n.* A polygon with eight sides. [< Gk *oktagōnos,* having eight angles.] —**oc•tag'o•nal** (ŏk-tăg'ə-nəl) *adj.*

oc•ta•he•dron (ŏk'tə-hē'drən) *n., pl.* **-drons** or **-dra** (-drə). A polyhedron with eight surfaces. —**oc'ta•he'dral** (-drəl) *adj.*

oc•tane (ŏk'tān') *n.* **1.** Any of various hydrocarbons with the formula C_8H_{18}. **2.** Also **octane number.** A numerical measure of the antiknock properties of motor fuel, based on the percentage by volume of one particular octane in a standard reference fuel.

oc•tant (ŏk'tənt) *n.* One-eighth of a circle or of an arc of a circle. [< L *octō,* eight.]

oc•tave (ŏk'tĭv, -tāv') *n.* **1.** The interval of eight diatonic degrees between two musical tones. **2.** Any group or series of eight. [< L *octō,* eight.]

oc•ta•vo (ŏk-tā'vō, -tä'vō) *n., pl.* **-vos. 1.** The page size (from 5 × 8 to 6 × 9 1/2 inches) of a book composed of printer's sheets folded into eight leaves. **2.** A book composed of pages of this size. [L *(in) octāvō,* "in eighth."]

oc•tet (ŏk-tĕt') *n.* Also **oc•tette. 1.** A musical composition written for eight voices or instruments. **2.** Any group of eight. [< It *otto,* eight.]

octo–. *comb. form.* Eight. [< L *octō,* eight, and < Gk *oktō,* eight.]

Oc•to•ber (ŏk-tō'bər) *n.* The 10th month of the year. October has 31 days. [< L *Octōber,* "eighth month."]

oc•to•ge•nar•i•an (ŏk'tə-jə-nâr'ē-ən) *n.* Someone between eighty and ninety years of age. [< L *octōgintā,* eighty.]

oc•to•pus (ŏk'tə-pəs) *n., pl.* **-puses** or **-pi** (-pī'). A marine mollusk with a rounded, saclike body and eight sucker-bearing tentacles. [< Gk *oktōpous,* eight-footed.]

oc•to•roon (ŏk'tə-rōōn') *n.* A person who is one-eighth Negro.

oc•u•lar (ŏk'yə-lər) *adj.* **1.** Pertaining to the eye. **2.** Visual. —*n.* The eyepiece of an optical instrument. [< L *oculus,* eye.]

oc•u•list (ŏk'yə-lĭst) *n.* **1.** A physician who treats diseases of the eyes; an ophthalmologist. **2.** An optometrist.

O.D. 1. Doctor of Optometry. **2.** officer of the day. **3.** overdraft. **4.** overdrawn.

odd (ŏd) *adj.* **1. a.** Strange; unusual. **b.** Queer or eccentric in conduct. **2.** In addition to or in excess of what is usual, regular, or approximated: *odd jobs; 40-odd persons.* **3.** Being one of an incomplete pair or set; extra. **4.** Not divisible by two. [< ON *oddi,* triangle, third, odd number.] —**odd'ly** *adv.*

odd•i•ty (ŏd'ə-tē) *n., pl.* **-ties. 1.** One that is odd. **2.** The state or quality of being odd.

odd•ment (ŏd'mənt) *n.* Something left over.

odds (ŏdz) *pl.n.* **1.** An advantage given to a weaker side in a contest to equalize the chances of the participants. **2.** A ratio expressing the probability of an event or outcome. —**at odds.** In disagreement.

odds and ends. Miscellaneous items.

ode (ōd) *n.* A lyric poem often addressed to some praised object or person and characterized by exalted style. [< Gk *ōidē, aoidē,* song.]

–ode. *comb. form.* A way or path: **cathode.** [< Gk *hodos,* a way.]

O•des•sa (ō-dĕs'ə). A city of the SW Soviet Union. Pop. 735,000.

O•din (ō'dĭn). Supreme god of the Norse pantheon.

o•di•ous (ō'dē-əs) *adj.* Offensive; hateful; repugnant. [< L *odium,* ODIUM.] —**o'di•ous•ly** *adv.* —**o'di•ous•ness** *n.*

o•di•um (ō'dē-əm) *n.* **1.** The state or quality of being odious. **2.** Disgrace resulting from hateful conduct. [L, hatred.]

o•dom•e•ter (ō-dŏm'ə-tər) *n.* An instrument that indicates distance traveled by a vehicle. [< Gk *hodos,* road, journey + *metron,* METER.]

o•dor (ō'dər) *n.* Also *chiefly Brit.* **o•dour. 1.** The property or quality of a thing that stimulates or is perceived by the sense of smell. **2.** Esteem; repute. [< L.] —**o'dor•less** *adj.* —**o'dor•ous** *adj.*

o•dor•if•er•ous (ō'də-rĭf'ər-əs) *adj.* Having or giving off an odor.

O•dys•seus (ō-dĭs'yōōs', ō-dĭs'ē-əs). The hero of Homer's *Odyssey.*

od•ys•sey (ŏd'ə-sē) *n.* An extended adventurous wandering. [< Homer's *Odyssey,* which recounted the wanderings of Odysseus.]

OE Old English

OED, O.E.D. Oxford English Dictionary.

Oed•i•pus complex (ĕd'ə-pəs, ē'də-). Libidinal feelings in a male child for the mother, often accompanied by hostility to the father. [< *Oedipus,* mythical Greek king who unwittingly killed his father and married his mother.]

OEO Office of Economic Opportunity.

o'er. *Poetic.* Contraction of **over.**

of (ŭv; *unstressed* əv) *prep.* **1.** From. **2.** Owing to. **3.** Away from. **4.** So as to be separated or relieved from: *robbed of his dignity.* **5.** From the total or group comprising. **6.** Composed or made from. **7.** Associated with or adhering to. **8.** Belonging or connected to. **9.** Possessing; having: *a man of honor.* **10.** Containing or carrying. **11.** Specified as; named or called: *a depth of ten feet; the Garden of Eden.* **12.** Centering on or directed toward. **13.** Produced by; issuing from. **14.** Characterized or identified by. **15.** With reference to; about. **16.** Set aside for; taken up by: *a day of rest.* **17.** Before; until: *five minutes of two.* **18.** During or on (a specified time): *of recent years.* [< OE. See **apo-.**]

off (ôf, ŏf) *adv.* **1.** At or to a distance from a nearer place. **2.** Distant in time. **3.** So as to be unattached, disconnected, or removed. **4.** So as to be smaller, fewer, or less. **5.** So as to be away from work or duty. —*adj.* **1.** More distant or removed. **2.** Not on, attached, or connected. **3.** Not continuing, operating, or functioning. **4.** No longer existing or effective; canceled. **5.** Fewer, smaller, or less. **6.** Inferior. **7.** In a specified condition: *well off.* **8.** In error. **9.** Absent or away from work or duty: *He's off Tuesday.* —*prep.* **1.** So as to be removed or distant from. **2.** Away or relieved from: *off duty.* **3. a.** By consuming: *living off honey.* **b.** With the means provided by: *living off his pension.* **4.** Extending or branching out from: *an artery off the heart.* **5.** Below the usual level of: *off his game.* **6.** Abstaining from. **7.** Seaward of: *a mile off Sandy Hook.* [< OE *of.* See **apo-.**]

off. office; officer; official.

of•fal (ô'fəl, ŏf'əl) *n.* **1.** Waste parts, esp. of a butchered animal. **2.** Refuse; rubbish. [< MDu *afval,* "that which falls off," refuse.]

off•beat (ôf'bēt', ŏf'-) *n.* An unaccented beat in a musical measure. —*adj.* (ôf'bĕt', ŏf'-). *Slang.* Unconventional.

off-col•or (ôf'kŭl'ər, ŏf'-) *adj.* **1.** Varying from the expected or required color. **2.** In bad taste: *an off-color joke.* **3.** *Chiefly Brit.* Not in good health.

of•fend (ə-fĕnd') *v.* **1.** To create anger, resentment, or annoyance in; affront. **2.** To be displeasing or disagreeable (to). **3.** To sin. [< L *offendere,* to strike against.] —**of•fend'er** *n.*

of•fense (ə-fĕns') *n.* Also *chiefly Brit.* **of•fence. 1.** The act of offending. **2. a.** Any violation of a moral or social code. **b.** A crime. **3.** (ŏf'ĕns'). The act of attacking or assaulting. —**take offense.** To become displeased or resentful. —**of•fen'sive** *adj.* —**of•fen'sive•ly** *adv.* —**of•fen'sive•ness** *n.*

of•fer (ô'fər, ŏf'ər) *v.* **1.** To present for acceptance or rejection. **2.** To present for sale. **3.** To propose as payment; bid. **4.** To present as an act of worship. **5.** To volunteer. **6.** To provide; furnish; afford. **7.** To produce or introduce on the stage. [< L *offerre.*] —**of'fer** *n.* —**of'fer•er, of'fer•or** *n.*

of•fer•ing (ô'fər-ĭng, ŏf'ər-) *n.* **1.** The act of making an offer. **2.** Something offered. **3.** A presentation made to a deity as an act of worship or sacrifice. **4.** A contribution, esp. at a religious service.

of•fer•to•ry (ô'fər-tôr'ē, -tōr'ē, ŏf'ər-) *n., pl.* **-ries. 1.** Often **Offertory.** The part of the Eucharistic liturgy at which bread and wine are offered by the celebrant. **2.** The collection of offerings at a church service.

off•hand (ôf'hănd', ŏf'-) *adv. & adj.* Without preparation or forethought; impromptu.

of•fice (ô'fĭs, ŏf'ĭs) *n.* **1. a.** A place in which services, clerical work, professional duties, etc., are carried out. **b.** The staff working in such a place. **2.** A duty or function assigned to or assumed by someone. **3.** A position of authority given to a person, as in a government or other organization. **4.** A branch of the Federal government of the U.S. ranking just below a department. **5.** A public position: *seek office.* **6.** Often **offices.** A favor. **7.** *Eccles.* A ceremony, usually prescribed by liturgy, esp. a rite for the dead. [< L *officium,* performance of duty.]

of•fice•hold•er (ô'fĭs-hōl'dər, ŏf'ĭs-) *n.* One who holds a public office.

of•fi•cer (ô'fĭ-sər, ŏf'ĭ-) *n.* **1.** One who holds an office of authority or trust in a corporation, government, or other institution. **2.** One holding a commission in the armed forces. **3.** A man licensed in the merchant marine as master, mate, chief engineer, or assistant engineer. **4.** A policeman.

of•fi•cial (ə-fĭsh'əl) *adj.* **1.** Of, pertaining to, or authorized by a proper authority; authoritative. **2.** Formal or ceremonious: *an official banquet.* —*n.* One who holds an office or position. —**of•fi'cial•dom** *n.* —**of•fi'cial•ly** *adv.*

of•fi•cial•ism (ə-fĭsh'ə-lĭz'əm) *n.* Rigid adherence to official regulations, forms, and procedures.

of•fi•ci•ant (ə-fĭsh'ē-ənt) *n. Eccles.* The celebrant at a religious service.

of•fi•ci•ate (ə-fĭsh'ē-āt') *v.* **-ated, -ating.** To perform the duties and functions of an office or position of authority, esp. as a priest or minister at a religious service.

of•fi•cious (ə-fĭsh'əs) *adj.* Excessively forward in offering one's services or advice to others. [< L *officium,* duty, service, OFFICE.] —**of•fi'cious•ly** *adv.* —**of•fi'cious•ness** *n.*

off•ing (ô'fĭng, ŏf'ĭng) *n.* The part of the sea that is visible from the shore. —**in the offing.** In the near or immediate future. [< OFF.]

off•ish (ô'fĭsh, ŏf'ĭsh) *adj.* Inclined to be reserved in manner; aloof. —**off'ish•ness** *n.*

off•set (ôf'sĕt', ŏf'-) *n.* **1.** Something that balances, counteracts, or compensates. **2.** A ledge or recess in a wall. **3.** A bend in a pipe or bar to allow it to pass around an obstruction. **4.** Printing by indirect image transfer. —*v.* (ôf'sĕt', ŏf'-) **-set, -setting. 1.** To counterbalance, counteract, or compensate for. **2.** To print by offset. **3.** To make or form an offset in (a wall, bar, or pipe). —**off'set'** *adj.*

off•shoot (ôf'sho͞ot', ŏf'-) *n.* Something that branches out or originates from a particular source, as a shoot from a plant stem.

off•shore (ôf'shôr', -shōr', ŏf'-) *adj.* **1.** Moving or directed away from the shore. **2.** Located or occurring at a distance from the shore. —**off'shore'** *adv.*

off•spring (ôf'sprĭng', ŏf'-) *n., pl.* **-spring.** Progeny; young.

off-stage (ôf'stāj', ŏf'-) *adj. & adv.* Away from the area of a stage visible to the audience.

off-the-rec•ord (ôf'*th*ə-rĕk'ərd, ŏf'-) *adj.* Not intended for publication, not to be repeated. —**off'-the-rec'ord** *adv.*

oft (ôft, ŏft) *adv. Poetic.* Often. [< OE *oft.* See **op-.**]

of•ten (ô'fən, ŏf'ən) *adv.* Frequently; repeatedly. [< OFT.]

of•ten•times (ô'fən-tīmz', ŏf'ən-) *adv.* Often.

o•gle (ō'gəl, ô'-) *v.* **ogled, ogling. 1.** To stare at. **2.** To stare in an impertinent or amorous manner. [Prob < LG *oegeln.*] —**o'gle** *n.*

o•gre (ō'gər) *n.* **1.** A fabled man-eating giant or monster. **2.** Anyone who is esp. cruel or hideous. [F.] —**o'gress** (ō'grĭs) *fem.n.*

oh (ō) *interj.* Expressive of strong emotion, as surprise, fear, etc. —*n., pl.* **oh's** or **ohs.** The exclamation *oh.*

O•hi•o (ō-hī'ō). A state of the C U.S. Pop. 10,652,000. Cap. Columbus. —**O•hi'o•an** *n.*

Ohio River. A river of the C U.S.

ohm (ōm) *n.* A unit of electrical resistance equal to that of a conductor in which a current of one ampere is produced by a potential of one volt across its terminals. [< G. *Ohm* (1787–1854), German physicist.]

o•ho (ō-hō') *interj.* Expressive of surprise or mock astonishment.

-oid. *comb. form.* Likeness, resemblance, or similarity to: **planetoid.** [< Gk *eidos,* form, shape.]

oil (oil) *n.* **1.** Any of numerous mineral, vegetable, and synthetic substances and animal and vegetable fats, that are generally slippery, combustible, viscous, liquid or liquefiable at room temperatures, soluble in various organic solvents, such as ether, but not in water, and used in a great variety of products, esp. lubricants and fuels. **2.** Petroleum. **3.** Any substance with an oily consistency. **4.** An **oil color. 5.** An **oil painting. 6.** *Informal.* Insincere flattery. —*v.* **1.** To lubricate, supply, cover, or polish with oil. **2.** To load up with or take on fuel oil. **3.** To become oil by melting. [< L *oleum.*] —**oil** *adj.*

oil•cloth (oil'klôth', -klŏth') *n.* A fabric treated with clay, oil, and pigments to make it waterproof.

oil color. A color consisting of pigment ground in oil, usually linseed, used in oil painting.

oil paint. Any paint in which the vehicle is a drying oil.

oil painting. 1. A painting in oil colors. **2.** The art of painting with oil colors.

oil•skin (oil'skĭn') *n.* **1.** Cloth treated with oil so that it is waterproof. **2.** A garment made of this material.

oil well. A hole dug or drilled in the earth to obtain petroleum.

oil•y (oi'lē) *adj.* **-ier, -iest. 1.** Of, pertaining to, or smeared with oil; greasy. **2.** Unctuous.

oint•ment (oint'mənt) *n.* Any of numerous highly viscous or semisolid substances used on the skin for cosmetic or medical purposes. [< L *unguere,* to anoint.]

O•jib•wa (ō-jĭb'wā', -wə) *n., pl.* **-wa** or **-was.** Also **O•jib•way** (ō-jĭb'wā') *pl.* **-way** or **-ways. 1.** A member of a tribe of Algonquian-speaking North American Indians inhabiting regions of the U.S. and Canada around Lake Superior. **2.** The language of this tribe.

O.K., OK, o•kay (ō-kā') *n., pl.* **O.K.'s** or **OK's** or **okays.** *Informal.* Approval; endorsement; agreement. —*v.* **O.K.'d** or **OK'd** or **okayed, O.K.'ing** or **OK'ing** or **okaying.** To approve or endorse by signing with an O.K.; agree to. —*interj.* Expressive of approval or agreement. —**O.K.** *adj. & adv.*

Usage: O.K. (or *OK*) is especially appropriate to business correspondence and informal speech and writing and is usually inappropriate to expressly formal usage. In written usage, it is generally most acceptable when used as a noun or verb, not as an adjective or adverb.

O•ki•na•wa (ō'kĭ-nä'wə). The largest of the Ryukyu Islands, off the S tip of Japan. Pop. 759,000.

O•kla•ho•ma (ō'klə-hō'mə). A state of the SW U.S. Pop. 2,559,000. Cap. Oklahoma City. —**O'kla•ho'man** *adj. & n.*

Oklahoma City. The capital of Oklahoma. Pop. 366,000.

o•kra (ō'krə) *n.* **1.** A tall plant with edible, mucilaginous green pods. **2.** The pods of this plant, used esp. in soups. [West African native name *nkruma.*]

-ol. *comb. form. Chem.* Alcohol or phenol: **menthol.** [< ALCOHOL.]

old (ōld) *adj.* **older** or **elder, oldest** or **eldest. 1.** Having lived or existed for a relatively long time; far advanced in years or life. **2.** Made long ago; ancient. **3.** Characteristic of an aged person. **4.** Mature; sensible. **5.** Having a specified age: *She was two years old.* **6.** Of an earlier time: *his old classmates.* **7.** Worn-out. **8.** Dear or cherished through long acquaintance: *good old Harry.* —*n.* Former times; yore: *in days of old.* [< OE *eald, ald.* See **al-²**.] —**old'ness** *n.*

Old Church Sla•von•ic (slə-vŏn'ĭk). The literary language of the oldest Slavic manuscripts (10th or early 11th century).

old•en (ōl'dən) *adj. Archaic & Poetic.* Old.

Old English. English from about 700 to 1150; Anglo-Saxon.

old fashioned. A cocktail made of whiskey, bitters, sugar, and fruit.

old-fash•ioned (ōld'făsh'ənd) *adj.* Outdated.

old fogy. Also **old fogey.** One who is tiresomely conservative or old-fashioned.

Old French. French from about 800 to 1500.

Old High German. High German from about 850 to 1100.

Old Iranian. Iranian before the Christian era.

Old Irish. Irish from 725 to 950.

Old Italian. Italian before 1550.

old-line (ōld'līn') *adj.* **1.** Conservative or reactionary. **2.** Traditional.

old maid. 1. An unmarried older woman; a spinster. **2.** A primly fastidious person.

Old Norse. The North Germanic language from which the modern Scandinavian languages are descended.

Old North French. The northern dialect of Old French.

Old Persian. An ancient form of Persian, recorded in inscriptions from the sixth to the fifth century B.C.

Old Provençal. Provençal before 1550.

Old Prussian. The Baltic language of the Prussians, which became extinct in the 18th century.

Old Saxon. Low German from about 850 to 1250.

old school. Any group committed to traditional ideas or practices. —**old'-school'** *adj.*

Old Spanish. Spanish before 1550.

old•ster (ōld'stər) *n.* An old or elderly person.

Old Testament. 1. The first of the two main divisions of the Christian Bible, containing the Hebrew Scriptures. **2.** The covenant of God with Israel as distinguished in Christianity from the dispensation of Christ constituting the New Testament.

old-tim•er (ōld'tī'mər) *n. Informal.* **1.** One who has been a resident, member, employee, etc., for a long time. **2.** Something very old or antiquated.

Old World. The E Hemisphere, esp. Europe.

old-world (ōld'wûrld') *adj.* **1.** Antique; old-fashioned; quaint. **2.** Often **Old-World.** Native or pertaining to the E Hemisphere, or Old World.

o•le•an•der (ō'lē-ăn'dər, ō'lē-ăn'dər) *n.* A poisonous, chiefly tropical shrub with clusters of white or reddish flowers. [ML.]

o•le•ic acid (ō-lē'ĭk). An oily liquid, $CH_3(CH_2)_7CH{:}CH(CH_2)_7COOH$, occurring in animal and vegetable oils.

oleo–. *comb. form.* Oil or pertaining to oil. [< L *oleum,* (olive) oil.]

o•le•o•mar•ga•rine (ō'lē-ō-mär'jə-rĭn, -gə-rĭn, -rēn') *n.* Margarine.

ol•fac•to•ry (ŏl-făk'tər-ē, -trē, ōl-) *adj.* Of or contributing to the sense of smell. [< L *olfacere,* to smell.]

ol•i•gar•chy (ŏl'ə-gär'kē) *n., pl.* **-chies. 1. a.** Government by the few, esp. by a small faction. **b.** Those making up such a faction. **2.** A state so governed. **—ol'i•garch'** *n.* **—ol'i•gar'-chic, ol'i•gar'chi•cal** *adj.*

oligo–. *comb. form.* Few. [< Gk *oligos,* few, little.]

Ol•i•go•cene (ŏl'ĭ-gō-sēn') *adj.* Of or belonging to the geologic time, rock series, or sedimentary deposits of the third epoch of the Tertiary period. *—n.* The Oligocene epoch.

ol•ive (ŏl'ĭv) *n.* **1.** The small, edible ovoid fruit of an Old World tree, pressed to extract a yellowish oil, **olive oil,** used in cooking. **2.** A tree bearing such fruit. **3.** Dull yellowish green. [< L *olīva* < Gk *elaia.*] **—ol'ive** *adj.*

O•lym•pi•a (ō-lĭm'pē-ə). The capital of the state of Washington. Pop. 23,000.

O•lym•pic games (ō-lĭm'pĭk). **1.** An ancient Greek festival of athletic games and other contests. **2.** An international athletic contest held every four years.

O•lym•pus (ō-lĭm'pəs). A mountain of Greece, the abode of the gods in ancient mythology.

–oma. *comb. form.* Tumor: **melanoma.** [< Gk *-ōma,* abstract nominal ending.]

O•ma•ha (ō'mə-hô', -hä'). A city in E Nebraska. Pop. 347,000.

O•man (ō-män'). A sultanate of the E Arabian peninsula. Pop. 750,000. Cap. Muscat.

om•buds•man (ŏm'bŭdz-mən) *n.* A government official who investigates citizens' complaints. [Norw.]

o•me•ga (ō-mĕg'ə, ō-mē'gə, ō-mā'-) *n.* The 24th and final letter of the Greek alphabet, representing long *o.* [Gk *ō mega,* "large o."]

om•e•let (ŏm'lĭt, ŏm'ə-lĭt) *n.* Also **om•e•lette.** A dish consisting of beaten eggs cooked and folded, often around a filling. [< L *lāmella,* thin metal plate.]

o•men (ō'mən) *n.* **1.** A prophetic sign. **2.** Portent: *birds of ill omen.* [L *ōmen.*]

om•i•cron (ŏm'ə-krŏn', ō'mə-) *n.* The 15th letter of the Greek alphabet, representing *o.* [Gk *o mikron,* "small o."]

om•i•nous (ŏm'ə-nəs) *adj.* **1.** Being or pertaining to an evil omen; foreboding; portentous. **2.** Menacing; threatening. **—om'i•nous•ly** *adv.* **—om'i•nous•ness** *n.*

o•mit (ō-mĭt') *v.* **omitted, omitting. 1.** To leave out; fail to include. **2.** To neglect; fail (to do). [< L *omittere.*] **—o•mis'sion** (-mĭsh'ən) *n.*

omni–. *comb. form.* All. [< L *omnis,* all.]

om•ni•bus (ŏm'nĭ-bŭs') *n., pl.* **-buses.** A bus. *—adj.* Including many things or classes; covering many situations at once. [< L, "for all."]

om•nip•o•tent (ŏm-nĭp'ə-tənt) *adj.* Having unlimited power, authority, or force; all-powerful. *—n.* **the Omnipotent.** God. **—om•nip'o•tence** *n.* **—om•nip'o•tent•ly** *adv.*

om•ni•pres•ence (ŏm'nĭ-prĕz'əns) *n.* The fact of being present everywhere. **—om'ni•pres'ent** *adj.*

om•nis•cient (ŏm-nĭsh'ənt) *adj.* Having total knowledge; knowing everything. [ML *omnisciēns.*] **—om•nis'cience** *n.*

om•niv•o•rous (ŏm-nĭv'ər-əs) *adj.* **1.** Eating all kinds of food, including animal and vegetable substances. **2.** Taking in everything available, as with the mind. **—om•niv'o•rous•ly** *adv.* **—om•niv'o•rous•ness** *n.*

on (ŏn, ôn) *prep.* **1.** —Used to indicate: **a.** Position upon. **b.** Contact with. **c.** Location at or along. **d.** Proximity. **e.** Attachment to or suspension from. **2.** —Used to indicate motion or direction toward or against. **3.** —Used to indicate: **a.** Occurrence during: *on July 3rd.* **b.** The occasion of what is stated: *On entering the room, she saw him.* **c.** The exact moment or point of: *every hour on the hour.* **4.** —Used to indicate: **a.** The object affected by an action: *The spotlight fell on the actress.* **b.** The agent or agency performing a specified action: *He cut his foot on the broken glass.* **c.** Something used to perform a stated action: *talk on the telephone.* **5.** —Used to indicate an originating or sustaining source or agency: *live on bread and water.* **6.** —Used to indicate: **a.** The state, condition, or process of: *on leave; on fire.* **b.** The purpose of: *travel on business.* **c.** A means of conveyance: *ride on a train.* **d.** Availability by means of: *beer on tap.* **e.** Association with: *a doctor on the staff.* **f.** The ground or basis for: *on principle.* **g.** Addition or repetition: *error on error.* **7.** Concerning; about: *a book on astronomy.* **8.** In one's possession; with: *I haven't a cent on me.* **9.** At the expense of: *drinks on the house.* *—adv.* **1.** In or into a position of being attached to or covering something. **2.** In the direction of: *He looked on while the ship docked.* **3.** Toward or at a point lying ahead in space or time; forward. **4.** In a continuous course. **5.** In or into action or operation. **6.** In or at the present position: *stay on; hang on.* [< OE *on, an.* See **an¹**.]

ON Old Norse.

–on. *comb. form.* Subatomic particle, unit, or quantum: **photon.** [< (I)ON.]

once (wŭns) *adv.* **1.** One time only: *once a day.* **2.** At one time in the past; formerly. **3.** At any time; ever. **—at once. 1.** Simultaneously. **2.** Immediately. *—conj.* As soon as; when. [< OE *ān,* ONE.]

once-o•ver (wŭns'ō'vər) *n.* A quick but comprehensive survey or performance.

on•com•ing (ŏn'kŭm'ĭng, ôn'-) *adj.* Approaching.

one (wŭn) *adj.* **1.** Being a single entity or being; single; individual. **2.** Of a single kind or nature; undivided. **3.** Designating an unspecified person or thing. **4.** Single in kind; alike or the same. *—n.* **1.** The cardinal number written 1 or in Roman numerals I. **2.** A single person or thing; unit. *—pron.* **1.** A certain person or thing. **2.** Any person or thing. **3.** A single person or thing among persons or things already mentioned. [< OE *ān.* See **oino-.**]

–one. *comb. form.* An oxygen-containing compound: **acetone.** [< Gk *-ōnē.*]

O'Neill (ō-nēl'), **Eugene.** 1888–1953. American dramatist.

one•ness (wŭn'nĭs) *n.* **1.** The quality or state of being one. **2.** Identity of character, as of several things. **3.** Unison; agreement.

on•er•ous (ŏn'ər-əs, ō'nər-) *adj.* Troublesome or oppressive; burdensome. [< L *onus (oner-),* burden.] **—on'er•ous•ness** *n.*

one•self (wŭn-sĕlf') *pron.* A form of the 3rd person sing. pronoun *one:* **1.** —Used reflexively: *to hurt oneself.* **2.** —Used for emphasis: *to take the initiative oneself.* **—by oneself. 1.** Alone. **2.** Without help.

one-sid•ed (wŭn'sī'dĭd) *adj.* **1.** Partial; biased. **2.** More developed on one side.

one-time (wŭn'tīm') *adj.* Also **one•time.** At or in some past time; former.

one-track (wŭn'trăk') *adj.* Obsessively limited to a single idea: *a one-track mind.*

one-way (wŭn'wā') *adj.* Moving or permitting movement in one direction only.

on•go•ing (ŏn'gō-ĭng, ôn'-) *adj.* Progressing or evolving.

on•ion (ŭn'yən) *n.* **1.** A plant widely cultivated for its pungent edible bulb. **2.** The bulb of this plant. [< OF *oignon.*]

on•ion•skin (ŭn'yən-skĭn') *n.* A thin, strong, translucent paper.

on•look•er (ŏn'lo͝ok'ər, ôn'-) *n.* A spectator.

on•ly (ōn'lē) *adj.* Alone in kind or class; sole. *—adv.* **1.** Without anyone or anything else; alone. **2. a.** No more than; at least; just. **b.** Merely. **3.** Exclusively; solely. *—conj.* But; except (that). [< OE *ānlīc* : *ān,* ONE + *-līc,* -LY.]

on•o•mat•o•poe•ia (ŏn'ə-măt'ə-pē'ə) *n.* The formation or use of a word that sounds like its referent, as *buzz* or *cuckoo.* [< Gk *onomatopoiein,* to coin names.] **—on'o•mat'o•poe'ic** (-pē'ĭk) *adj.*

on•rush (ŏn'rŭsh', ôn'-) *n.* **1.** A forward rush. **2.** An assault.

on•set (ŏn'sĕt', ôn'-) *n.* **1.** An onslaught. **2.** A beginning; start.

on•slaught (ŏn'slôt', ôn'-) *n.* A violent attack.

On•tar•i•o (ŏn-târ'ē-ō'). A province of C Canada. Pop. 6,731,000. Cap. Toronto.

Ontario, Lake. The smallest and easternmost of the Great Lakes.

on•to (ŏn'to͞o', ôn'-, ŏn'tə, ôn'-) *prep.* **1.** On top of; upon. **2.** *Informal.* Aware of: *I'm onto your schemes.* [ON + TO.]

on•tol•o•gy (ŏn-tŏl'ə-jē) *n.* The systematic study of being. [< Gk *ōn,* being + -LOGY.] **—on'to•log'i•cal** (ŏn'tə-lŏj'ĭ-kəl) *adj.*

o•nus (ō'nəs) *n.* **1.** A burden, esp. a disagreeable responsibility. **2.** A stigma or blame. [< L, burden.]

on•ward (ŏn'wərd, ôn'-) *adv.* Also **on•wards** (-wərdz). In a direction or toward a position that is ahead; forward. *—adj.* Moving or tending forward.

–onym. *comb. form.* Word or name: **acronym.** [< Gk *onuma, onoma,* name.]

on•yx (ŏn'ĭks) *n.* A kind of translucent quartz that occurs in bands of different colors and is used as a gemstone. [< Gk *onux,* claw, fingernail, onyx.]

oo•dles (o͞od'ləlz) *pl.n. Informal.* A great amount. [Perh < HUDDLE.]

oo•mi•ak. Variant of **umiak.**

oomph (o͝omf) *n. Slang.* **1.** Spirited vigor. **2.** Sex appeal.

ooze¹ (o͞oz) *v.* **oozed, oozing. 1.** To flow or leak out slowly; exude. **2.** To disappear or ebb slowly. [< OE *wōs,* juice. See **wes-²**.] **—ooze** *n.* **—ooz'i•ness** *n.* **—ooz'y** *adj.*

ooze² (o͞oz) *n.* Soft, thin mud or mudlike sediment, as on the floor of oceans and lakes. [< OE *wāse.* See **wels-.**] **—ooz'y** *adj.*

op., OP. opus.

o•pal (ō'pəl) *n.* A translucent mineral of hydrated silicon dioxide, often used as a gem. [< Sk *úpala,* (precious) stone.] **—o'pal•ine'** (ō'pə-līn', -lēn') *adj.*

o•pal•es•cence (ō'pə-lĕs'əns) *n.* A milky iridescence like that of an opal. **—o'pal•es'cent** *adj.*

o•paque (ō-pāk') *adj.* **1. a.** Impenetrable by light. **b.** Not reflecting light; dull. **2.** Obtuse; dense. [< L *opācus,* dark.] **—o•pac'i•ty** (-păs'ə-tē), **o•paque'ness** *n.*

op. cit. In the work cited (L *opere citato*).

OPEC (ō′pĕk′) Organization of Petroleum Exporting Countries.

o•pen (ō′pən) *adj.* **1.** Affording unobstructed passage or entrance and exit; not shut or closed; spacious. **2.** Having no cover; exposed. **3.** Not sealed, tied, or folded. **4.** Having interspersed gaps, spaces, or intervals. **5.** Accessible to all; unrestricted. **6.** Susceptible; vulnerable. **7.** Available; obtainable. **8.** Ready to transact business. **9.** Unoccupied. **10.** Characterized by lack of pretense; candid; receptive. —*v.* **1.** To become or cause to become open; release from a closed position. **2.** To remove obstructions from; clear. **3.** To spread out or apart. **4.** To remove the cover or wrapping from; expose; undo. **5.** To begin; initiate; commence. **6.** To make available. **7.** To make or become more responsive or understanding. **8.** To reveal the secrets of. **9.** To come into view; become revealed. —*n.* **1. the open.** The outdoors. **2.** A contest with both professional and amateur participants. [< OE. See **upo.**] —**o′pen•er** *n.* —**o′pen•ly** *adv.* —**o′pen•ness** *n.*

o•pen-air (ō′pən-âr′) *adj.* Occurring, done, or existing outdoors.

o•pen•hand•ed (ō′pən-hăn′dĭd) *adj.* Giving freely; generous. —**o′pen•hand′ed•ly** *adv.* —**o′pen•hand′ed•ness** *n.*

o•pen-heart (ō′pən-härt′) *adj.* Involving surgery in which the heart is open while its normal functions are assumed by external apparatus.

o•pen-hearth (ō′pən-härth′) *adj.* Designating a reverberatory furnace used in the production of high-quality steel.

o•pen•ing (ō′pən-ĭng) *n.* **1.** The act of becoming open or being made to open. **2.** An open space; a hole. **3.** The first stage of or occasion for something. **4.** A series of beginning moves in chess. **5.** An unfilled job.

o•pen-mind•ed (ō′pən-mīn′dĭd) *adj.* Receptive to new ideas; free from prejudice.

open shop. A business establishment or factory having nonunion employees.

o•pen•work (ō′pən-wûrk′) *n.* Ornamental or structural work containing numerous openings.

op•er•a[1] (ŏp′rə, ŏp′ər-ə) *n.* **1.** A form of theatrical presentation in which a dramatic performance is set to music. **2.** A work of this kind. [< L, work.] —**op′er•at′ic** (ŏp′ə-răt′ĭk) *adj.* —**op′er•at′i•cal•ly** *adv.*

o•pe•ra[2]. Alternate *pl.* of **opus.**

op•er•a•ble (ŏp′ər-ə-bəl, ŏp′rə-) *adj.* **1.** Capable of being used or operated. **2.** Capable of being treated by surgery. —**op′er•a•bil′i•ty** *n.*

opera glasses. Small binoculars for use at a theatrical performance.

op•er•ate (ŏp′ə-rāt′) *v.* **-ated, -ating. 1.** To function effectively; work. **2.** To bring about a desired effect. **3.** To perform surgery. **4.** To run; control the functioning of. [L *operārī*, to work, labor.]

op•er•a•tion (ŏp′ə-rā′shən) *n.* **1.** The act, process, or way of operating. **2.** The state of being operative. **3.** A method of productive activity. **4.** *Med.* Any procedure for remedying an injury or ailment in a living body, esp. one performed with instruments. **5.** *Math.* A process or action, such as addition, substitution, or transposition, performed in accordance with specific rules of procedure.

op•er•a•tion•al (ŏp′ə-rā′shən-əl) *adj.* **1.** Pertaining to an operation or series of operations. **2.** Fit for proper functioning.

op•er•a•tive (ŏp′ər-ə-tĭv, ŏp′rə-, ŏp′ə-rā′tĭv) *adj.* **1.** Exerting influence or force. **2.** Functioning effectively; efficient. **3.** In operation. **4.** Engaged in or related to physical or mechanical activity. **5.** Of, pertaining to, or resulting from a surgical operation. —*n.* **1.** A skilled worker. **2.** A secret agent.

op•er•a•tor (ŏp′ə-rā′tər) *n.* **1.** One who operates a mechanical device: *a telephone operator.* **2.** A symbol that represents a mathematical operation. **3.** *Informal.* A shrewd and sometimes unscrupulous person.

op•e•ret•ta (ŏp′ə-rĕt′ə) *n.* A theatrical production that has many of the elements of opera but is lighter and more popular in subject and style.

Oph•i•u•chus (ŏf′ē-yōō′kəs, ō′fē-) *n.* A constellation in the equatorial region. [< Gk *ophioukhos*, "serpent-holder."]

oph•thal•mic (ŏf-thăl′mĭk, ŏp-thăl′-) *adj.* Of or pertaining to the eye or eyes; ocular.

ophthalmo–. *comb. form.* The eye or eyeball. [< Gk *ophthalmos*, eye.]

oph•thal•mol•o•gy (ŏf′thăl-mŏl′ə-jē, ŏf′thəl-, ŏp′-) *n.* The medical specialty encompassing the anatomy, functions, pathology, and treatment of the eye. —**oph′thal•mol′o•gist** *n.*

–opia. *comb. form.* A specific visual condition or defect: **myopia.** [< Gk *ōps*, eye.]

o•pi•ate (ō′pē-ĭt, -āt′) *n.* **1.** A narcotic containing opium or its derivatives. **2.** Any sedative or narcotic drug. **3.** Anything that relaxes or induces sleep or torpor. —*adj.* (ō′pē-ĭt, -āt′). **1.** Consisting of or containing opium. **2.** Causing or producing sleep or sedation. —*v.* (ō′pē-āt′) **-ated, -ating. 1.** To subject to the action of an opiate. **2.** To dull or deaden as if with a narcotic drug.

o•pine (ō-pīn′) *v.* **opined, opining.** To hold or state as an opinion.

o•pin•ion (ə-pĭn′yən) *n.* **1.** A belief, conclusion, or judgment not substantiated by positive knowledge or proof. **2.** An evaluation based on special knowledge. **3.** Prevailing feeling or sentiment: *public opinion.* [< L *opīnārī*, to think.]

o•pin•ion•at•ed (ə-pĭn′yə-nā′tĭd) *adj.* Holding stubbornly to one's own opinions.

o•pi•um (ō′pē-əm) *n.* **1.** A bitter, yellowish-brown, strongly addictive narcotic prepared from the dried juice of unripe pods of an Old World poppy, containing morphine and other alkaloids. **2.** Something that numbs or stupefies. [< Gk *opion*, poppy juice, opium, dim of *opos*, juice.]

o•pos•sum (ə-pŏs′əm, pŏs′əm) *n.* Also **pos•sum** (pŏs′əm). Any of various furry, mostly tree-dwelling marsupials of the New World and Australia. [< Algon.]

opp. opposite.

op•po•nent (ə-pō′nənt) *n.* One that opposes, as in a battle, controversy, etc.; an adversary.

op•por•tune (ŏp′ər-t/y/ōōn′) *adj.* **1.** Suited for a particular purpose. **2.** Occurring at a fitting or advantageous time. [< L *opportūnus*, seasonable.] —**op′por•tune′ly** *adv.*

op•por•tun•ist (ŏp′ər-t/y/ōō′nĭst) *n.* One who takes advantage of any opportunity, usually with little regard for moral principles. —**op′por•tun′ism′** *n.* —**op′por•tun•is′tic** *adj.*

op•por•tu•ni•ty (ŏp′ər-t/y/ōō′nə-tē) *n.*, *pl.* **-ties.** A favorable or advantageous combination of circumstances.

op•pose (ə-pōz′) *v.* **-posed, -posing. 1.** To be in contention or conflict with; resist. **2.** To be against. **3.** To place in opposition; contrast. [< L *oppōnere*, to set against.] —**op•pos′a•ble** *adj.* —**op′po•si′tion** (ŏp′ə-zĭsh′ən) *n.*

op•po•site (ŏp′ə-zĭt) *adj.* **1.** Placed or located directly across from; lying in a corresponding position to: *opposite sides of a building.* **2.** Facing the other way. **3.** Diametrically opposed; altogether different. —*n.* One that is opposite or contrary to another. —*prep.* Across from or facing. —**op′po•site** *adv.*

op•press (ə-prĕs′) *v.* **1.** To subjugate or persecute by unjust use of force. **2.** To weigh heavily upon, esp. so as to depress. [< L *opprimere* (pp *oppressus*), to press against.] —**op•pres′sion** *n.* —**op•pres′sor** (ə-prĕs′ər) *n.*

op•pres•sive (ə-prĕs′ĭv) *adj.* **1.** Difficult to bear; harsh. **2.** Physically or mentally distressing. —**op•pres′sive•ness** *n.*

op•pro•bri•ous (ə-prō′brē-əs) *adj.* **1.** Contemptuously scornful. **2.** Shameful; infamous.

op•pro•bri•um (ə-prō′brē-əm) *n.* **1.** Disgrace arising from shameful conduct; ignominy. **2.** Scornful reproach or contempt. **3.** A cause of shame. [L, "a reproach against."]

–opsy. *comb. form.* An examination: **biopsy.** [< Gk *opsis*, sight, appearance.]

opt (ŏpt) *v.* To make a choice. [< L *optāre.*]

opt. **1.** optical; optician; optics. **2.** optional.

op•tic (ŏp′tĭk) *adj.* Pertaining to the eye or vision. [< Gk *optos*, visible.]

op•ti•cal (ŏp′tĭ-kəl) *adj.* **1.** Of or pertaining to sight. **2.** Of or pertaining to optics. —**op′ti•cal•ly** *adv.*

op•ti•cian (ŏp-tĭsh′ən) *n.* One who makes or sells lenses and eyeglasses.

op•tics (ŏp′tĭks) *n. (takes sing. v.).* The scientific study of light and vision.

op•ti•mism (ŏp′tə-mĭz′əm) *n.* **1.** A tendency to expect the best possible outcome or to dwell upon the most hopeful aspects of a situation. **2.** *Phil.* The doctrine that this world is the best of all possible worlds. [< L *optimum*, best.] —**op′ti•mist** *n.* —**op′ti•mis′tic** *adj.*

op•ti•mum (ŏp′tə-məm) *n.*, *pl.* **-ma** (-mə) or **-mums.** The best or most favorable condition for a particular situation. [< L *optimus*, best.] —**op′ti•mal** *adj.* —**op′ti•mal•ly** *adv.*

op•tion (ŏp′shən) *n.* **1.** The act of choosing; choice. **2.** The freedom to choose. **3.** The right to buy or sell something within a specified time and at a specified price. [< L *optiō*, choice.] —**op′tion•al** *adj.* —**op′tion•al•ly** *adv.*

op•tom•e•try (ŏp-tŏm′ə-trē) *n.* The profession of examining, measuring, and treating certain visual defects by means of corrective lenses or other methods that do not require license as a physician. [Gk *optos*, visible + -METRY.] —**op•tom′e•trist** *n.*

op•u•lent (ŏp′yə-lənt) *adj.* **1.** Extremely wealthy; rich; affluent. **2.** Abundant; luxuriant. [L *opulentus.*] —**op′u•lence** *n.*

o•pus (ō′pəs) *n.*, *pl.* **opera** (ō′pər-ə, ŏp′ər-ə) or **opuses.** A creative work, esp. a musical composition. [L, work.]

or (ôr; *unstressed* ər) *conj.* —Used to indicate: **1. a.** An alternative. **b.** The second of two alternatives: *either right or wrong.* **2.** A synonymous or equivalent expression: *acrophobia, or fear of great heights.* **3.** Uncertainty or indefiniteness: *two or three.* [< OE *oththe.*]

Usage: When all of the elements connected by *or* are singular, the verb they govern must be singular: *Tom or Jack is coming. Beer or ale or wine is included in the charge.* When the elements are all plural, the verb is plural. When the elements do not agree in number, or when one or more of the elements is a personal pronoun, the verb is governed by the element to which it is nearer: *Tom or his brothers are going.*

–or¹. *comb. form.* One that performs the action expressed by the root verb: **percolator.** [< L.]

–or². *comb. form.* Also *Brit.* **-our.** A state, quality, or activity: **behavior.** [< L, abstract suffix.]

or•a•cle (ôr'ə-kəl, ŏr'-) *n.* **1. a.** A shrine consecrated to a prophetic god. **b.** The priest at such a shrine. **c.** A prophecy made known at such a shrine. **2.** A wise person. [< L *ōrāre,* to speak.] —**o•rac'u•lar** (ô-răk'yə-lər, ō-răk'-) *adj.* —**o•rac'u•lar•ly** *adv.*

o•ral (ôr'əl, ŏr'-) *adj.* **1.** Spoken rather than written. **2.** Of or pertaining to speech. **3.** Of, used in, or taken through the mouth. [< L *ōs (ōr-),* the mouth.] —**o'ral•ly** *adv.*

oral contraceptive. Any of various hormone compounds in pill form, used in specific sequence to prevent ovulation and conception.

or•ange (ôr'ĭnj, ŏr'-) *n.* **1.** A round citrus fruit with a reddish-yellow rind and juicy, sectioned pulp. **2.** An evergreen, white-flowered tree bearing such fruit. **3.** A color between yellow and red. [< Sk *nāranga,* orange, orange tree.] —**or'ange** *adj.*

or•ange•ade (ôr'ĭn-jād', ŏr'-) *n.* A beverage of orange juice, sugar, and water.

o•rang-u•tan (ō-răng'ə-tăn', ə-răng'-) *n.* Also **o•rang•u•tan, o•rang•ou•tan, o•rang•u•tang** (ō-răng'ə-tăng', ə-răng'-). A large, shaggy-haired, long-armed ape of Borneo and Sumatra. [Malay *orang hutan.*]

o•rate (ô-rāt', ō-rāt', ôr'āt', ŏr'āt') *v.* **orated, orating.** To speak publicly in a grandiloquent manner.

o•ra•tion (ô-rā'shən, ō-rā'-) *n.* A formal address or speech, esp. one at an academic celebration, funeral, etc. [< L *ōrāre,* to speak.]

or•a•tor (ôr'ə-tər, ŏr'-) *n.* **1.** One who delivers an oration. **2.** One skilled in the art of public address. —**or'a•tor'i•cal** (ôr'ə-tôr'ĭ-kəl, ŏr'ə-tŏr'-) *adj.* —**or'a•tor'i•cal•ly** *adv.*

or•a•to•ri•o (ôr'ə-tôr'ē-ō', -tōr'ē-ō', ŏr'-) *n., pl.* **-os.** A musical composition for voices and orchestra, telling a sacred story. [< the *Oratory* of St. Philip Neri at Rome.]

or•a•to•ry¹ (ôr'ə-tôr'ē, -tōr'ē, ŏr'-) *n.* **1.** The art of public speaking; rhetoric. **2.** Rhetorical style or skill.

or•a•to•ry² (ôr'ə-tôr'ē, -tōr'ē, ŏr'-) *n., pl.* **-ries.** A small private chapel. [< LL *ōrātōrium (templum),* (place) of prayer.]

orb (ôrb) *n.* **1.** A sphere. **2.** A heavenly body. **3.** One of a series of concentric transparent spheres revolving about the earth, postulated by medieval astronomers as support for the stars and planets. [< L *orbis,* orb, disk.]

or•bit (ôr'bĭt) *n.* **1.** The path of a celestial body or man-made satellite as it revolves around another body. **2.** The path of any body in a field of force surrounding another body, as the movement of an atomic electron in relation to a nucleus. **3.** A range of activity, experience, or influence. **4.** Either of two bony cavities in the skull containing an eye and its external structures; eye socket. —*v.* **1.** To put into or cause to move in an orbit. **2.** To revolve or move in orbit. [< L *orbis,* ORB.] —**or'bit•al** *adj.*

or•chard (ôr'chərd) *n.* **1.** A tract of land where fruit or nut trees are cultivated. **2.** The trees cultivated in such an area. [< L *hortus,* a garden + OE *geard,* yard.]

or•ches•tra (ôr'kĭ-strə, ôr'kĕs'trə) *n.* **1.** A large group of musicians who play together on various instruments. **2. a.** The section of seats nearest the orchestra pit in a theater. **b.** The entire main floor of a theater. [< Gk *orkheisthai,* to dance.] —**or•ches'tral** (ôr-kĕs'trəl) *adj.* —**or•ches'tral•ly** *adv.*

or•ches•trate (ôr'kĭ-strāt') *v.* **-trated, -trating.** To compose or arrange (music) for an orchestra. —**or ches•tra'tion** *n.*

or•chid (ôr'kĭd) *n.* **1.** Any of numerous chiefly tropical plants with irregularly shaped flowers. **2.** The flower of such a plant. **3.** Light reddish purple. [< Gk *orkhis,* testicle, orchid.]

ord. order.

or•dain (ôr-dān') *v.* **1.** To invest with ministerial or priestly authority; confer holy orders upon. **2.** To order or decree. **3.** To predestine: *by fate ordained.* [< L *ōrdināre,* to arrange in order.] —**or•dain'ment** *n.*

or•deal (ôr-dēl') *n.* A severely difficult or painful experience. [< OE *ordāl.*]

or•der (ôr'dər) *n.* **1.** A condition of logical or comprehensible arrangement among the separate elements of a group. **2.** The state, condition, or disposition of a thing. **3. a.** The existing structures of a given society. **b.** The condition in which these structures are maintained and preserved by the rule of law. **4.** A sequence, arrangement, or category of successive things. **5.** The established sequence; customary procedure. **6.** A command or direction. **7.** A commission or instruction to buy, sell, or supply something. **8.** A portion of food requested by a customer at a restaurant. **9. a.** Any of several grades of the Christian ministry. **b. orders.** Ordination. **10.** A monastic institution. **11.** An organization of people bound by some common fraternal bond or social aim. **12.** A group of persons upon whom a government or sovereign has formally conferred honor: *the Order of the Garter.* **13.** Degree of quality; distinction; rank. **14.** Approximate size or magnitude. —*v.* **1.** To issue a command or instruction (to). **2.** To request to be supplied with (something). **3.** To put in a systematic arrangement. [< L *ōrdō.*]

or•der•ly (ôr'dər-lē) *adj.* **1.** Tidy; neat. **2.** Peaceful; well-behaved. —*n., pl.* **-lies. 1.** A male hospital attendant. **2.** A soldier assigned to attend upon a superior officer.

or•di•nal (ôrd'n-əl) *adj.* **1.** Of a specified position in a numbered series. **2.** Pertaining to a biological order.

ordinal number. A number indicating position in a series or order. The ordinal numbers are first (1st), second (2nd), third (3rd), etc.

or•di•nance (ôrd'n-əns) *n.* **1.** An authoritative command or order. **2.** A municipal statute or regulation. **3.** A long-established custom. [< L *ōrdināre,* to put in order.]

or•di•nar•i•ly (ôrd'n-ĕr'ə-lē, ôrd'n-ĕr'-) *adv.* Usually; as a general rule.

or•di•nar•y (ôrd'n-ĕr'ē) *adj.* **1.** Commonly encountered; usual; regular; normal. **2.** Average in rank or merit; commonplace. [< L *ōrdō,* order.] —**or'di•nar'i•ness** *n.*

or•di•nate (ôrd'n-ĭt, -āt') *adj.* The plane Cartesian coordinate representing the distance from a specified point to the *x*-axis, measured parallel to the *y*-axis.

or•di•na•tion (ôrd'n-ā'shən) *n. Eccles.* The ceremony during which a person is ordained.

ord•nance (ôrd'nəns) *n.* **1.** Military supplies, esp. weapons, ammunition, etc. **2.** Heavy guns; artillery. [< ORDINANCE.]

Or•do•vi•cian (ôr'də-vĭsh'ən) *adj.* Of or belonging to the geologic time, system of rocks, or sedimentary deposits of the second period of the Paleozoic era. —*n.* The Ordovician period. [< the *Ordovices,* an ancient Celtic tribe of N Wales.]

or•dure (ôr'jər, ôr'dyo͝or) *n.* Excrement; dung. [< L *horridus,* horrid.]

ore (ôr, ōr) *n.* A mineral or aggregate of minerals from which a valuable constituent, esp. a metal, can profitably be mined or extracted. [< OE *ār,* brass. See **ayos-.**]

Ore. Oregon (unofficial).

Oreg. Oregon.

o•reg•a•no (ə-rĕg'ə-nō', ô-rĕg'-) *n.* The dried leaves of a type of marjoram, used as seasoning. [< Gk *origanon,* oregano, marjoram.]

Or•e•gon (ôr'ə-gən, -gŏn', ŏr'-). A state of the NW U.S. Pop. 2,091,000. Cap. Salem. —**Or'e•go'ni•an** (ôr'ə-gō'nē-ən, ŏr'-) *adj.* & *n.*

org. 1. organic. **2.** organization; organized.

or•gan (ôr'gən) *n.* **1.** A musical instrument consisting of a keyboard and pipes supplied with wind by means of bellows. **2.** A differentiated part of an organism, adapted for a specific function. **3.** A medium by means of which some action is performed. **4.** An instrument of communication, esp. a periodical publication. [< L *organum,* implement, instrument.]

or•gan•dy (ôr'gən-dē) *n., pl.* **-dies.** Also **or•gan•die.** A transparent crisp fabric of cotton or silk. [F *organdi.*]

or•gan•elle (ôr'gə-nĕl') *n. Biol.* A specialized part of a cell that resembles and functions as an organ.

organ grinder. A street musician who plays a hurdy-gurdy.

or•gan•ic (ôr-găn'ĭk) *adj.* **1.** Of or affecting an organ of the body. **2.** Of or derived from living organisms. **3.** Likened to an organism in organization or development. **4.** Of or constituting the essential part of something; constitutional; substantive. **5.** *Chem.* Of or designating carbon compounds. —**or•gan'i•cal•ly** *adv.*

organic chemistry. The chemistry of carbon compounds.

or•gan•ism (ôr'gə-nĭz'əm) *n.* Any living being; a plant or animal. —**or'gan•is'mal** (ôr'gə-nĭz'məl), **or'gan•is'mic** *adj.*

or•gan•ist (ôr'gə-nĭst) *n.* One who plays the organ.

or•gan•i•za•tion (ôr'gə-nə-zā'shən) *n.* **1.** The act of organizing or the process or state of being organized. **2.** Something that has been organized. **3.** A number of persons united for some purpose or work. —**or'gan•i•za'tion•al** *adj.* —**or'gan•i•za'tion•al•ly** *adv.*

or•gan•ize (ôr'gə-nīz') *v.* **-ized, -izing. 1.** To form an orderly, functional, structured whole. **2.** To arrange; systematize. **3.** To establish as an organization. **4.** To induce employees to form or join a union. [< L *organum,* instrument, ORGAN.] —**or'gan•iz'er** *n.*

organo–. *comb. form.* Organ or organic.

or•gan•za (ôr-găn'zə) *n.* A sheer, stiff fabric of silk or synthetic fibers.

or•gasm (ôr'găz'əm) *n.* The climax of sexual excitement. [< Gk *organ,* to swell (with lust), be excited.] —**or•gas'mic, or•gas'tic** *adj.*

or•gy (ôr'jē) *n., pl.* **-gies. 1.** A revel involving unrestrained indulgence, as in drinking or sexual activity. **2.** Excessive indulgence in any activity: *an orgy of reading.* [< Gk *orgia.*] —**or'gi•as'tic** (-ăs'tĭk) *adj.*

o•ri•el (ôr'ē-əl, ōr'-) *n.* A projecting bay window supported from below. [< ML *oriolum,* upper chamber.]

o•ri•ent (ôr'ē-ənt, -ĕnt', ōr'-) *n.* **1.** The east; eastern regions. **2. Orient.** The countries of

Asia, esp. of E Asia. **3.** In ancient times, the regions east of the Mediterranean. —*v.* (ôr'ē-ĕnt', ōr'-). **1.** To align or position with respect to a specific direction or reference system. **2.** To familiarize with or adjust to a situation. [< L *oriēns,* rising, rising sun, east.] **—o'ri•en•ta'tion** *n.*

O•ri•en•tal (ôr'ē-ĕn'təl, ōr'-) *adj.* Of or pertaining to the Orient. —*n.* An inhabitant of the Orient.

or•i•fice (ôr'ə-fĭs, ŏr'-) *n.* An opening; mouth; vent. [< LL *ōrificium.*]

orig. original; originally.

o•ri•ga•mi (ôr'ĭ-gä'mē) *n.* The Japanese art of folding paper into decorative shapes. [Jap.]

or•i•gin (ôr'ə-jĭn, ŏr'-) *n.* **1.** A source or cause of existence. **2.** Ancestry; derivation. **3.** A coming into being. **4.** *Math.* The point of intersection of coordinate axes. [< L *orīrī,* to rise.]

o•rig•i•nal (ə-rĭj'ən-əl) *adj.* **1.** Primary; first. **2.** Fresh and novel. **3.** Creative; inventive. —*n.* **1.** The primary form from which copies are made or varieties arise. **2.** An authentic work of art as distinguished from a copy. [< L *origō,* origin.] **—o•rig'i•nal'i•ty** (ə-rĭj'ə-năl'ə-tē) *n.* **—o•rig'i•nal•ly** *adv.*

o•rig•i•nate (ə-rĭj'ə-nāt') *v.* **-nated, -nating.** To come or bring into being; begin. **—o•rig'i•na'tion** *n.* **—o•rig'i•na'tor** *n.*

O•ri•no•co (ôr'ə-nō'kō, ōr'-). A river of NW South America.

o•ri•ole (ôr'ē-ōl', ōr'-) *n.* A songbird with bright orange or yellow and black plumage. [< ML *oriolus,* "golden (bird)."]

O•ri•on (ō-rī'ən) *n.* A constellation on the celestial equator.

Or•lon (ôr'lŏn') *n.* A trademark for a synthetic fiber used in a variety of fabrics.

or•mo•lu (ôr'mə-lo͞o') *n.* A copper and tin or zinc alloy resembling gold, used for decorative work. [F *or moulu,* "ground gold."]

or•na•ment (ôr'nə-mənt) *n.* **1.** Something used for decoration or adornment. **2.** One who does honor or credit: *an ornament to his profession.* —*v.* (ôr'nə-mĕnt'). To decorate; adorn. [< L *ōrnāre,* to adorn.] **—or'na•men'tal** (-mĕn'təl) *adj.* **—or'na•men•ta'tion** *n.*

or•nate (ôr-nāt') *adj.* **1.** Elaborately ornamented. **2.** Showy in style; florid. [< L *ōrnāre,* to adorn.] **—or•nate'ly** *adv.* **—or•nate'ness** *n.*

or•ner•y (ôr'nə-rē) *adj.* **-ier, -iest.** Ill-tempered; perversely stubborn. [Var of ORDINARY.]

ornitho–. *comb. form.* Bird or birds. [< Gk *ornis (ornith-),* bird.]

or•ni•thol•o•gy (ôr'nə-thŏl'ə-jē) *n.* The scientific study of birds. **—or'ni•tho•log'i•cal** (ôr'nĭ-thə-lŏj'ĭ-kəl) *adj.* **—or'ni•thol'o•gist** *n.*

o•ro•tund (ôr'ə-tŭnd', ōr'-) *adj.* **1.** Full in sound; sonorous. **2.** Pompous; bombastic. [L *ōre rotundō,* "with round mouth."]

or•phan (ôr'fən) *n.* A child whose parents are dead. —*v.* To cause to become an orphan. [< Gk *orphanos,* orphaned.]

or•phan•age (ôr'fə-nĭj) *n.* An institution for the care of orphans.

Or•phe•us (ôr'fē-əs, -fyo͞os'). Legendary Thracian poet and musician; reputed founder of a mystery religion. **—Or'phic** (-fĭk) *adj.*

or•ris•root (ôr'ĭs-ro͞ot', -ro͝ot', ōr'-) *n.* The fragrant root of an Old World iris, used in perfumes and cosmetics.

orth. orthopedic; orthopedics.

ortho–. *comb. form.* **1.** Straight or upright. **2.** *Math.* Perpendicular to or at right angles. **3.** Correct or standard. **4.** *Med.* Correction of maladjustments or deformities. [< Gk *orthos,* straight, correct.]

or•tho•don•tia (ôr'thə-dŏn'shə) *n.* The dental specialty and practice of correcting abnormally aligned or positioned teeth. [ORTHO- + Gk *odous (odont-),* tooth.] **—or'tho•don'tic** *adj.* **—or'tho•don'tist** *n.*

or•tho•dox (ôr'thə-dŏks') *adj.* **1.** Adhering to traditional and established beliefs and practices, esp. in religion. **2. Orthodox. a.** Of or belonging to Christian churches derived from the church of the Byzantine Empire. **b.** Of or belonging to a branch of Judaism adhering strictly to the ancient Hebrew law. [< Gk *orthodoxos,* having the right opinion.] **—or'tho•dox'y** *n.*

or•thog•o•nal (ôr-thŏg'ə-nəl) *adj.* Pertaining to or composed of right angles. [Gk *orthogōnios.*]

or•thog•ra•phy (ôr-thŏg'rə-fē) *n.* **1.** Correct spelling. **2.** The study and formulation of systems of spelling. **—or'tho•graph'ic** (-thə-grăf'ĭk) *adj.* **—or'tho•graph'i•cal•ly** *adv.*

or•tho•pe•dics (ôr'thə-pē'dĭks) *n. (takes sing. v.).* The surgical or manipulative treatment of disorders of the skeletal system and associated motor organs. [< ORTHO- + Gk *paideia,* education.] **—or'tho•pe'dic** *adj.* **—or'tho•pe'dist** *n.*

–ory[1]. *comb. form.* A place for or something used as: **observatory.** [< L *-ōrius,* adj suffix.]

–ory[2]. *comb. form.* Characterization by, possession of the nature of, or tendency toward: **compensatory.** [< L *-ōrius,* adj suffix.]

Os osmium.

O•sage (ō'sāj', ō-sāj') *n., pl.* **Osage** or **Osages. 1.** A member of a tribe of Siouan-speaking North American Indians, formerly inhabiting the region between the Missouri and Arkansas rivers. **2.** The language of this tribe. **—O'sage'** *adj.*

O•sa•ka (ō-sä'kə). A city of Japan, on Honshu Island. Pop. 3,119,000.

Os•can (ŏs'kən) *n.* **1.** One of an ancient people of S Italy. **2.** The Italic language of this people. **—Os'can** *adj.*

os•cil•late (ŏs'ə-lāt') *v.* **-lated, -lating. 1.** To swing back and forth steadily. **2.** To waver; vacillate. **3.** *Phys.* To vary between alternate extremes. [L *ōscillāre.*] **—os'cil•la'tion** *n.* **—os'cil•la'tor** *n.* **—os'cil•la•to'ry** (ŏs'ə-lə-tôr'ē, -tōr'ē) *adj.*

os•cil•lo•scope (ŏ-sĭl'ə-skōp', ə-sĭl'-) *n.* An electronic instrument that produces a visual display on the screen of a cathode-ray tube corresponding to some external signal. **—os•cil'lo•scop'ic** (-skŏp'ĭk) *adj.*

Os•co-Um•bri•an (ŏs'kō-ŭm'brē-ən) *n.* A subdivision of Italic, consisting of Oscan and Umbrian.

os•cu•late (ŏs'kyə-lāt') *v.* **-lated, -lating.** To kiss. [L *ōsculārī.*] **—os'cu•la'tion** *n.*

–ose[1]. *comb. form.* Possession of or similarity to: **grandiose.** [< L *-ōsus.*]

–ose[2]. *comb. form.* A carbohydrate: **fructose.** [< GLUCOSE.]

o•sier (ō'zhər) *n.* **1.** A willow with long, flexible twigs used in basketry. **2.** A twig of such a willow. [< ML *ausēria,* willow bed.]

O•si•ris (ō-sī'rĭs). Egyptian fertility god.

–osis. *comb. form.* **1.** A condition or process: **osmosis. 2.** A diseased or abnormal condition: **neurosis. 3.** An increase or formation of: **sclerosis.** [< Gk *-ōsis,* abstract noun suffix.]

Os•lo (ŏz'lō, ŏs'lō). The capital of Norway. Pop. 483,000.

os•mi•um (ŏz'mē-əm) *n. Symbol* **Os** A bluish-white, hard metallic element, used as a platinum hardener and in making pen points, phonograph needles, and instrument pivots. Atomic number 76, atomic weight 190.2. [< Gk *osmē,* odor.]

os•mo•sis (ŏz-mō'sĭs, ŏs-) *n.* **1.** The diffusion of fluid through a semipermeable membrane until there is an equal concentration of fluid on either side of the membrane. **2.** A gradual process resembling this. [< Gk *ōsmos,* action of pushing.] **—os•mot'ic** (-mŏt'ĭk) *adj.*

os•prey (ŏs'prē, -prā') *n., pl.* **-preys.** A large fish-eating hawk with blackish and white plumage. [< L *avis praedae,* "bird of prey."]

os•si•fi•ca•tion (ŏs'ə-fĭ-kā'shən) *n.* **1.** The natural process of bone formation. **2. a.** The abnormal hardening or calcification of soft tissue into a bonelike material. **b.** A mass or deposit of such material. **3.** A being or becoming set in a rigidly conventional pattern, as of habits or beliefs.

os•si•fy (ŏs'ə-fī') *v.* **-fied, -fying. 1.** To change into bone. **2.** To set into a rigidly conventional pattern. [L *os,* bone + -FY.]

os•ten•si•ble (ŏ-stĕn'sə-bəl) *adj.* Outwardly apparent; seeming; professed. [< L *ostendere,* to show.] **—os•ten'si•bly** *adv.*

os•ten•ta•tion (ŏs'tĕn-tā'shən, ŏs'tən-) *n.* Pretentious display or showiness. [< L *ostendere,* to show.] **—os'ten•ta'tious** *adj.* **—os'ten•ta'tious•ly** *adv.*

osteo–. *comb. form.* Bone or bones. [< Gk *osteon,* bone.]

os•te•op•a•thy (ŏs'tē-ŏp'ə-thē) *n.* A medical therapy that emphasizes manipulative techniques for correcting somatic abnormalities thought to cause disease and inhibit recovery. **—os'te•o•path'** (ŏs'tē-ə-păth') *n.* **—os'te•o•path'ic** (-ə-păth'ĭk) *adj.*

ost•mark (ôst'märk', ōst'-) *n.* The basic monetary unit of East Germany.

os•tra•cize (ŏs'trə-sīz') *v.* **-cized, -cizing.** To banish or exclude from a group. [< Gk *ostrakon,* shell, shard (with which the Athenian citizen voted for ostracism).] **—os'tra•cism'** (-sĭz'əm) *n.*

os•trich (ŏs'trĭch, ôs'-) *n.* A very large, long-necked, long-legged, flightless African bird. [< VL **avistrūthius.*]

OT Old Testament.

oth•er (ŭth'ər) *adj.* **1.** Being or designating the remaining or alternate one or ones: *the other ear.* **2.** Different or apart from that or those under consideration: *any other man.* **3.** Additional; extra: *I have no other shoes.* **4.** Alternating: *every other day.* **5.** Recently past: *the other day.* —*pron.* **1.** The remaining or alternate one. **2.** A different or additional person or thing. —*adv.* Differently. [< OE *ōther.* See **an[2].**]

oth•er•wise (ŭth'ər-wīz') *adv.* **1.** In another way; differently. **2.** Under other circumstances. **3.** In other respects: *an otherwise logical mind.* —*adj.* Other than supposed; different.

oth•er•world•ly (ŭth'ər-wûrld'lē) *adj.* Transcending concrete or mundane matters or considerations. **—oth'er•world'li•ness** *n.*

–otic. *comb. form.* **1.** Affected with or by: **sclerotic. 2.** Having a specific disease: **neurotic.** [< Gk *-ōtikos,* adj suffix.]

OTS Officer's Training School.

Ot•ta•wa[1] (ŏt'ə-wə, -wä', -wô') *n., pl.* **-wa** or **-was. 1.** A group of Algonquian-speaking Indians, originally inhabiting the region of the Ottawa River in Ontario, Canada. **2.** A member of this group. **3.** The Ojibwa dialect of this group.

Ot•ta•wa[2] (ŏt'ə-wə, -wä', -wô'). The capital of

Canada. Pop. 281,000.

ot•ter (ŏt'ər) *n.* **1.** A weasellike aquatic mammal with webbed feet and dense, dark-brown fur. **2.** The fur of such an animal. [< OE *otor.* See **wed-**.]

ot•to•man (ŏt'ə-mən) *n., pl.* **-mans.** **1.** A low, backless, armless seat or cushioned footstool. **2.** A heavy ribbed fabric. [< OTTOMAN.]

Ot•to•man (ŏt'ə-mən) *n., pl.* **-mans.** A Turk. *—adj.* Turkish.

Oua•ga•dou•gou (wä'gə-dōō'gōō). The capital of Upper Volta. Pop. 51,000.

ou•bli•ette (ōō'blē-ĕt') *n.* A dungeon entered through a trap door in the ceiling. [< F *oublier,* to forget.]

ouch (ouch) *interj.* Expressive of sudden pain.

ought[1] (ôt) *v.* —Used as an auxiliary verb followed by an infinitive with *to.* Indicates: **1.** Obligation: *You ought to work harder than that.* **2.** Expediency or prudence: *You ought to wear a raincoat.* **3.** Desirability: *You ought to have been there; it was great fun.* **4.** Probability: *She ought to finish by next week.* [< OE *āhte,* 1st & 3rd sing past indicative of *āgan,* to possess. See **ēik-**.]

ought[2]. Variant of **aught.**

ounce (ouns) *n.* **1. a.** A U.S. Customary System unit of weight equal to 16 drams or 437.5 grains. **b.** A unit of apothecary weight equal to 480 grains or 1.097 avoirdupois ounces. **2. a.** A U.S. Customary System unit of volume or capacity used in liquid measure, equal to 8 fluid drams or 1.804 cubic inches. **b.** A British Imperial System unit of volume or capacity used in dry and liquid measure, equal to 1.734 cubic inches. **3.** A tiny bit. [< L *uncia,* a twelfth, ounce.]

our (our) *adj.* The possessive form of the pronoun *we,* used attributively. [< OE *ūre.* See **nes-**.]

-our. *Brit.* Variant of **-or**[2].

ours (ourz). The possessive form of the pronoun *we,* used as a predicate adjective or as a substantive: *This house is ours. Ours is the best.* **—of ours.** Belonging to us: *a friend of ours.*

our•selves (our-sĕlvz', är-) *pron.* A form of the 1st person pl. pronoun: **1.** —Used reflexively: *We are only deceiving ourselves.* **2.** —Used for emphasis: *We did it ourselves.* **—by ourselves.** **1.** Alone. **2.** Without help.

-ous. *comb. form.* **1.** Possessing or full of: **joyous.** **2.** *Chem.* Occurring with a valence that is lower than that in a comparable *-ic* system: **ferrous.** [< L *-ōsus, -us,* adj suffixes.]

oust (oust) *v.* To evict; force out. [< L *obstāre,* to hinder.]

oust•er (ous'tər) *n.* Eviction; expulsion.

out (out) *adv.* **1.** Away or forth from inside. **2.** Away from the center or middle. **3.** Away from a usual place. **4.** To depletion or extinction: *Supplies have run out.* **5.** Into being or view: *The moon came out.* **6.** Without inhibition; boldly: *Speak out.* **7.** Into disuse or an unfashionable status. **8.** *Baseball.* So as to be retired. *—adj.* **1.** Exterior; external. **2.** Unable to be used. **3.** *Informal.* Not available for use or consideration. **4.** Bare or threadbare. *—prep.* **1.** Through; forth from: *fall out the window.* **2.** Beyond or outside of. *—n.* **1.** A person or thing that is out. **2.** A means of escape. **3.** *Baseball.* Any play in which a batter or base runner is retired. [< OE *ūt.* See **ud-**.]

out-. *comb. form.* **1.** To a surpassing or superior degree. **2.** Located outside.

out-and-out (out'n-out') *adj.* Complete; thoroughgoing.

out•bid (out-bĭd') *v.* To bid higher than (another).

out•board (out'bôrd', -bōrd') *adj.* **1.** Situated or attached on the outside of the hull of a vessel: *an outboard motor.* **2.** Situated toward or nearer the end of an aircraft wing. **—out'board'** *adv.*

out•bound (out'bound') *adj.* Outward bound; headed outward.

out•break (out'brāk') *n.* A sudden eruptive occurrence.

out•build•ing (out'bĭl'dĭng) *n.* A building separate from but associated with a main building.

out•burst (out'bûrst') *n.* A sudden, violent manifestation, as of activity or emotion: *an outburst of hatred.*

out•cast (out'kăst', -käst') *n.* One that has been rejected or excluded, as from society. **—out'cast'** *adj.*

out•class (out-klăs', -kläs') *v.* To surpass decisively.

out•come (out'kŭm') *n.* A natural result; consequence.

out•crop (out'krŏp') *n. Geol.* A portion of bedrock or other stratum protruding through the soil level.

out•cry (out'krī') *n.* **1.** A loud cry or clamor. **2.** A strong protest.

out•dat•ed (out-dā'tĭd) *adj.* Old-fashioned; obsolete.

out•dis•tance (out-dĭs'təns) *v.* **-tanced, -tancing.** To go far beyond or surpass, as in a race or competition.

out•do (out-dōō') *v.* To exceed in performance.

out•door (out'dôr', -dōr') *adj.* Located in, done in, or suited to the open air.

out•doors (out-dôrz', -dōrz') *adv.* In or into the open; outside of a house or shelter. *—n.* The open air; the area away from human habitation.

out•er (out'ər) *adj.* **1.** Located on the outside; external. **2.** Farther from the center or middle.

Outer Mongolia. The Mongolian People's Republic. See **Mongolia.**

out•er•most (out'ər-mōst') *adj.* Farthest out.

out•face (out-fās') *v.* To overcome or defy with bold self-assurance.

out•field (out'fēld') *n.* **1.** The area of a baseball field extending beyond the base lines. **2.** The members of a baseball team playing in the outfield. **—out'field'er** *n.*

out•fit (out'fĭt') *n.* **1.** A set of equipment or clothing, esp. for a special purpose. **2.** *Informal.* An association of persons, as a military unit or business organization. *—v.* To provide with an outfit. **—out'fit'ter** *n.*

out•flank (out-flăngk') *v.* To maneuver around the flank of (an opposing force).

out•fox (out-fŏks') *v.* To get the better of by cunning.

out•go (out'gō') *n., pl.* **-goes.** An expenditure or cost.

out•go•ing (out'gō'ĭng) *adj.* **1.** Departing; going out. **2.** Friendly and unreserved.

out•grow (out-grō') *v.* **1.** To grow too large for. **2.** To lose or discard in the course of maturing. **3.** To surpass in growth.

out•growth (out'grōth') *n.* **1.** A part growing out; an offshoot. **2.** A result or consequence.

out•guess (out-gĕs') *v.* **1.** To anticipate correctly the actions of. **2.** To outwit.

out•house (out'hous') *n.* An enclosed outdoor toilet; a privy.

out•ing (ou'tĭng) *n.* **1.** An excursion or pleasure trip. **2.** A walk outdoors; an airing.

out•land•ish (out-lăn'dĭsh) *adj.* **1.** Foreign and unusual. **2.** Conspicuously odd or unconventional; bizarre. [< OE *ūtlandisc.*] **—out•land'ish•ly** *adv.* **—out•land'ish•ness** *n.*

out•last (out-lăst', -läst') *v.* To endure or live longer than.

out•law (out'lô') *n.* **1.** A person excluded from normal legal protection and rights. **2.** One who lives lawlessly. *—v.* **1.** To declare illegal; ban. **2.** To deprive of the protection of the law.

out•lay (out'lā') *n.* **1.** The spending or disbursing of money. **2.** An amount spent.

out•let (out'lĕt', -lĭt) *n.* **1.** A passage for escape or exit; vent. **2.** A means of releasing emotions, energies, etc. **3.** A market for commercial goods. **4.** *Elec.* A receptacle that is connected to a power supply and equipped with a socket for a plug.

out•line (out'līn') *n.* **1.** A line forming the boundary of an object or figure. **2.** Drawing in which objects are depicted in lines without shading. **3.** A general description, plan, or summary. *—v.* **1.** To draw or show the outline of. **2.** To give the main points of; summarize.

out•live (out-lĭv') *v.* To live longer than; outlast; survive.

out•look (out'lŏŏk') *n.* **1.** The prospect seen from a viewing place. **2.** A point of view; attitude. **3.** A probable result; expectation.

out•ly•ing (out'lī'ĭng) *adj.* Distant or remote from a point or center.

out•mod•ed (out-mō'dĭd) *adj.* No longer in use or fashion; obsolete.

out•num•ber (out-nŭm'bər) *v.* To be more numerous than.

out-of-date (out'əv-dāt') *adj.* Outmoded; old-fashioned.

out-of-the-way (out'əv-*th*ə-wā') *adj.* **1.** Remote; secluded. **2.** Out of the ordinary.

out•pa•tient (out'pā'shənt) *n.* A patient who receives treatment at a hospital or clinic without being hospitalized.

out•play (out-plā') *v.* To play better than (an opponent).

out•post (out'pōst') *n.* **1.** A detachment of troops stationed at a distance from a main unit. **2.** The station occupied by such troops. **3.** An outlying settlement.

out•put (out'pŏŏt') *n.* **1.** Production, esp. the amount produced or manufactured during a given span of time. **2.** *Technology.* **a.** The energy, power, or work produced by a system. **b.** The information produced by a computer from a specific input.

out•rage (out'rāj') *n.* **1.** A viciously violent or grossly offensive act. **2.** A severe insult or offense. **3.** Resentful anger. *—v.* **-raged, -raging.** **1.** To commit an outrage upon. **2.** To rape. **3.** To fill with angry resentment. [< OF, "excess," atrocity.]

out•ra•geous (out-rā'jəs) *adj.* **1.** Grossly offensive; heinous. **2.** Disgraceful; shocking. **—out•ra'geous•ly** *adv.* **—out•ra'geous•ness** *n.*

ou•tré (ōō-trā') *adj.* Outlandishly improper or unconventional. [< F *outrer,* to pass beyond.]

out•reach (out-rēch') *v.* **1.** To surpass in reach. **2.** To reach out. **3.** To outdo by trickery.

out•rig•ger (out'rĭg'ər) *n.* **1.** A float attached to the laterally projecting spars of a seagoing canoe, riding parallel on either side to prevent capsizing. **2.** A vessel fitted with such a float.

out•right (out'rīt', -rīt') *adv.* **1.** Entirely; wholly. **2.** Without delay; at once. *—adj.* (out'rīt'). **1.** Unqualified: *an outright gift.* **2.** Complete or thoroughgoing; out-and-out. **3.** *Archaic.* Proceeding straight onward: *"an even,* *outright, but imperceptible speed*" (R.L. Stevenson).

out•run (out-rŭn′) *v.* **1.** To run faster than. **2.** To escape from. **3.** To exceed.

out•sell (out-sĕl′) *v.* To surpass in sales or selling.

out•set (out′sĕt′) *n.* Beginning; start.

out•shine (out-shīn′) *v.* **1.** To shine brighter than. **2.** To surpass.

out•side (out-sīd′, out′sīd′) *n.* **1.** The outer surface; exterior. **2.** The external or surface aspect. **3.** The space beyond a boundary or limit. **4.** The utmost limit or extent. *—adj.* **1.** Coming from without: *outside agitators.* **2.** External: *an outside door.* **3.** Apart from one's regular occupation. **4.** Maximum: *an outside estimate.* **5.** Slight; remote: *an outside possibility.* *—adv.* On or to the outside. *—prep.* **1.** On or to the outer side of. **2.** Beyond the limits of. **3.** Except. **—outside of.** Outside.

out•sid•er (out-sī′dər) *n.* **1.** A nonmember of a given group. **2.** A contestant given little chance of winning.

out•size (out′sīz′) *n.* A very large size. **—out′size′, out′sized′** *adj.*

out•skirts (out′skûrts′) *pl.n.* The peripheral parts, as of a town.

out•smart (out-smärt′) *v.* To outwit.

out•spo•ken (out-spō′kən) *adj.* Frank and direct. **—out•spo′ken•ly** *adv.*

out•spread (out-sprĕd′) *adj.* Spread out; extended.

out•stand•ing (out′stăn′dĭng, out-stăn′dĭng) *adj.* **1.** Projecting upward or outward. **2.** Prominent; salient. **3.** Distinguished; excellent. **4.** Not paid, settled, or resolved.

out•sta•tion (out′stā′shən) *n.* A remote station or post.

out•stay (out-stā′) *v.* **1.** To stay longer than. **2.** To outdo in staying power.

out•stretch (out-strĕch′) *v.* To extend.

out•strip (out-strĭp′) *v.* To leave behind; outrun.

out•ward (out′wərd) *adj.* **1.** Heading toward the outside. **2.** Outer; exterior. **3.** Manifest or external. *—adv.* Also **out•wards** (-wərdz). Toward the outside. **—out′ward•ly** *adv.*

out•wear (out-wâr′) *v.* **1.** To wear out; exhaust. **2.** To outlast.

out•weigh (out-wā′) *v.* **1.** To weigh more than. **2.** To be more significant than.

out•wit (out-wĭt′) *v.* To best by cleverness or cunning.

out•work[1] (out-wûrk′) *v.* To work better or faster than.

out•work[2] (out′wûrk′) *n.* A minor fortification outside the main defenses.

o•va. *pl.* of **ovum.**

o•val (ō′vəl) *adj.* Egg-shaped; ellipsoidal or elliptical. [< L *ōvum,* egg.] **—o′val** *n.*

o•va•ry (ō′və-rē) *n., pl.* **-ries.** **1.** One of a pair of female reproductive glands that produce ova. **2.** The plant structure at the base of the pistil, in which seeds are produced. **—o•var′i•an** (ō-vâr′ē-ən), **o•var′i•al** *adj.*

o•vate (ō′vāt′) *adj.* Oval; egg-shaped.

o•va•tion (ō-vā′shən) *n.* An enthusiastic show of public homage; applause. [< L *ovāre,* to rejoice.]

ov•en (ŭv′ən) *n.* A compartment, as in a stove, for baking or heating. [< OE *ofen.* See **aukwh-.**]

o•ver (ō′vər) *prep.* **1.** Above. **2.** On or above and across. **3.** On the other side of. **4.** Upon. **5.** Throughout or during. **6.** Along the length of. **7.** In excess of; more than. **8.** While engaged in or partaking of: *a chat over coffee.* **9.** On account of or with reference to: *an argument over methods.* *—adv.* **1.** Above. **2. a.** Across to another or opposite side. **b.** Across the edge or brim. **3.** Across an intervening distance. **4.** To a different opinion or allegiance: *win him over.* **5.** To a different person, condition, or title: *sign over land.* **6.** So as to be completely covered: *The river froze over.* **7.** Through or thoroughly: *think it over.* **8. a.** From an upright position. **b.** From an upward to an inverted or reversed position. **9. a.** Again. **b.** In repetition: *ten times over.* **10.** In addition or excess. *—adj.* **1.** Finished: *The war is over.* **2. a.** Upper; higher. **b.** Covering; outer. **3.** In excess: *His estimate was fifty dollars over.* *—interj.* Used in radio conversations to mark the end of a transmission by one speaker. [< OE *ofer.* See **uper.**]

over–. *comb. form.* **1.** Superiority of rank or power. **2.** Location above or across a specified position. **3.** Passage beyond or above a limit. **4.** Movement or transferal to a lower or inferior position. **5.** Quantity in excess of what is normal or desirable.

o•ver•act (ō′vər-ăkt′) *v.* To act with unnecessary exaggeration.

o•ver•age (ō′vər-ăj′) *adj.* Beyond the proper or normal age.

o•ver•all (ō′vər-ôl′) *adj.* Comprehensive.

o•ver•alls (ō′vər-ôlz′) *pl.n.* Coarse, loose-fitting trousers with a bib front and shoulder straps.

o•ver•arm (ō′vər-ärm′) *adj.* Executed with the arm raised above the shoulder: *an overarm throw of the ball.*

o•ver•awe (ō′vər-ô′) *v.* To subdue by inspiring awe.

o•ver•bal•ance (ō′vər-băl′əns) *v.* **1.** To outweigh. **2.** To throw off balance.

o•ver•bear (ō′vər-bâr′) *v.* **1.** To crush or press down upon. **2.** To prevail over; dominate.

o•ver•bear•ing (ō′vər-bâr′ĭng) *adj.* Domineering; arrogant. **—o′ver•bear′ing•ly** *adv.*

o•ver•blown[1] (ō′vər-blōn′) *adj.* **1.** Blown down or over. **2.** Blown up with conceit.

o•ver•blown[2] (ō′vər-blōn′) *adj.* Past the stage of full bloom.

o•ver•board (ō′vər-bôrd′, -bōrd′) *adv.* Over the side of a boat or ship.

o•ver•cast (ō′vər-kăst′, -käst′, ō′vər-kăst′, -käst′) *adj.* Clouded; gloomy; dark.

o•ver•charge (ō′vər-chärj′) *v.* **1.** To charge (a person) too high a price for something. **2.** To fill too full. **—o′ver•charge′** *n.*

o•ver•cloud (ō′vər-kloud′) *v.* To cover or become covered with clouds or gloom.

o•ver•coat (ō′vər-kōt′) *n.* A heavy outdoor coat.

o•ver•come (ō′vər-kŭm′) *v.* **1.** To conquer; defeat. **2.** To surmount; prevail over. **3.** To overpower or exhaust.

---

o′ver·a·bound′ *v.*
o′ver·a·bun′dance *n.*
o′ver·a·bun′dant *adj.*
o′ver·ac′tive *adj.*
o′ver·anx′ious *adj.*
o′ver·at·tached′ *adj.*
o′ver·care′ful *adj.*
o′ver·cau′tious *adj.*
o′ver·cau′tious·ly *adv.*
o′ver·cau′tious·ness *n.*
o′ver·chill′ *v.*
o′ver·con′fi·dence *n.*
o′ver·con′fi·dent *adj.*
o′ver·con′fi·dent·ly *adv.*
o′ver·cook′ *v.*
o′ver·cool′ *adj.*
o′ver·cour′te·ous *adj.*
o′ver·crit′i·cal *adj.*
o′ver·crowd′ *v.*
o′ver·dar′ing *adj.*
o′ver·dec′o·rate′ *v.*
o′ver·de·mand′ *v.*
o′ver·de·vot′ed *adj.*
o′ver·de·vo′tion *n.*
o′ver·dil′i·gence *n.*
o′ver·dil′i·gent *adj.*
o′ver·dis′ci·pline *v.*
o′ver·dose′ *n.*
o′ver·dra·mat′ic *adj.*
o′ver·drink′ *v.*
o′ver·ea′ger *adj.*
o′ver·ear′nest *adj.*
o′ver·ear′nest·ly *adv.*
o′ver·eas′y *adj.*
o′ver·eat′ *v.*
o′ver·ed′u·cate′ *v.*
o′ver·e·lab′o·rate *adj.*
o′ver·el′e·gant *adj.*
o′ver·em·bel′lish *v.*
o′ver·e·mo′tion·al *adj.*
o′ver·em′pha·sis *n.*
o′ver·em′pha·size′ *v.*
o′ver·em·phat′ic *adj.*
o′ver·en·thu′si·as′tic *adj.*
o′ver·es′ti·mate′ *v.*
o′ver·ex·cit′a·ble *adj.*
o′ver·ex·cite′ *v.*
o′ver·ex·cite′ment *n.*
o′ver·ex·ert′ *v.*
o′ver·ex·er′tion *n.*
o′ver·ex·pand′ *v.*
o′ver·ex·pan′sion *n.*
o′ver·ex·pect′ant *adj.*
o′ver·ex·u′ber·ant *adj.*
o′ver·faith′ful *adj.*
o′ver·fa·mil′iar *adj.*
o′ver·fan′ci·ful *adj.*
o′ver·fas·tid′i·ous *adj.*
o′ver·fat′ten *v.*
o′ver·fed′ *adj.*
o′ver·feed′ *v.*
o′ver·fem′i·nine *adj.*
o′ver·fierce′ *adj.*
o′ver·fill′ *v.*
o′ver·fond′ness *n.*
o′ver·frank′ *adj.*
o′ver·free′ly *adv.*
o′ver·fre′quent *adj.*
o′ver·full′ *adj.*
o′ver·full′ness *n.*
o′ver·fur′nish *v.*
o′ver·gen′er·al·ize′ *v.*
o′ver·gen′er·ous *adj.*
o′ver·gift′ed *adj.*
o′ver·glad′ *adj.*
o′ver·gra′cious *adj.*
o′ver·grate′ful *adj.*
o′ver·greas′y *adj.*
o′ver·hard′ *adj.*
o′ver·hard′en *v.*
o′ver·harsh′ *adj.*
o′ver·hast′y *adj.*
o′ver·help′ful *adj.*
o′ver·hon′est *adj.*
o′ver·i·de′al·ism′ *n.*
o′ver·im·ag′i·na′tive *adj.*
o′ver·im·press′ *v.*
o′ver·in·clined′ *adj.*
o′ver·in·dulge′ *v.*
o′ver·in·dul′gence *n.*
o′ver·in·dul′gent *adj.*
o′ver·in·flate′ *v.*
o′ver·in·fla′tion *n.*
o′ver·in′flu·en′tial *adj.*
o′ver·in·sist′ence *n.*
o′ver·in·sist′ent *adj.*
o′ver·in·sure′ *v.*
o′ver·in′tel·lec′tu·al *adj.*
o′ver·in·tense′ *adj.*
o′ver·in′ter·est *n.*
o′ver·in·vest′ *v.*
o′ver·jeal′ous *adj.*
o′ver·keen′ *adj.*
o′ver·kind′ *adj.*
o′ver·large′ *adj.*
o′ver·late′ *adj.*
o′ver·lav′ish *adj.*
o′ver·lax′ *adj.*
o′ver·lib′er·al *adj.*
o′ver·live′ly *adj.*
o′ver·load′ *v.*
o′ver·long′ *adj.* & *adv.*
o′ver·loud′ *adj.*
o′ver·loy′al *adj.*
o′ver·mag′ni·fy′ *v.*

---

o•ver•do (ō′vər-dōō′) *v.* **1.** To exaggerate. **2.** To do too much. **3.** To wear oneself out. **4.** To cook too much or too long.

o•ver•draft (ō′vər-drăft′, -dräft′) *n.* An amount overdrawn on a bank account.

o•ver•draw (ō′vər-drô′) *v.* **1.** To draw against (an account) in excess of credit. **2.** To exaggerate or overstate.

o•ver•drive (ō′vər-drīv′) *n.* A gearing mechanism of an automobile that increases the ratio of drive shaft to engine speed in a given speed range.

o•ver•flow (ō′vər-flō′) *v.* **1.** To flow over the top, brim, or banks (of). **2.** To inundate; flood. **3.** To be filled beyond capacity. **4.** To be superabundant. *—n.* (ō′vər-flō′). **1.** A flood. **2.** An excess; surplus. **3.** An outlet through which excess liquid can escape.

o•ver•glaze (ō′vər-glāz′) *n.* An outer glaze in ceramics.

o•ver•grown (ō′vər-grōn′) *adj.* **1.** Covered with growth. **2.** Grown beyond normal size. **—o′ver•growth′** *n.*

o•ver•hand (ō′vər-hănd′) *adj.* Thrown, struck, or executed with the hand brought down from above. **—o′ver•hand′** *adv.*

o•ver•hang (ō′vər-hăng′) *v.* **1.** To project or extend over, out, or beyond. **2.** To threaten or menace; loom over. *—n.* (ō′vər-hăng′). **1.** A projecting part, as of a roof or rock face. **2.** The amount of projection.

o•ver•haul (ō′vər-hôl′, ō′vər-hôl′) *v.* **1.** To examine or dismantle for needed repairs. **2.** To fix; renovate. *—n.* (ō′vər-hôl′). A repair job; renovation.

o•ver•head (ō′vər-hĕd′) *adj.* **1.** Located or functioning above the level of the head. **2.** Of or pertaining to operating expenses. *—n.* (ō′vər-hĕd′). **1.** The operating expenses of a business. **2.** The top surface in an enclosed space of a ship. *—adv.* (ō′vər-hĕd′). Over or above the level of the head.

o•ver•hear (ō′vər-hîr′) *v.* To hear without being noticed or addressed by the speaker.

o•ver•joyed (ō′vər-joid′) *adj.* Filled with joy; delighted.

o•ver•kill (ō′vər-kĭl′) *n.* Nuclear destructive capacity exceeding the amount needed to destroy an enemy.

o•ver•land (ō′vər-lănd′, -lənd) *adj.* Traversing land: *an overland trip.* **—o′ver•land′** *adv.*

o•ver•lap (ō′vər-lăp′) *v.* **-lapped, -lapping. 1.** To extend over and cover part of. **2.** To coincide partly. **—o′ver•lap′** *n.*

o•ver•lay (ō′vər-lā′) *v.* **1.** To lay or spread over or upon. **2.** To cover or embellish the surface of: *overlay wood with silver.* **—o′ver•lay′** *n.*

o•ver•leap (ō′vər-lēp′) *v.* **1.** To leap across or over. **2.** To pass over; omit.

o•ver•lie (ō′vər-lī′) *v.* To lie over or upon.

o•ver•look (ō′vər-lŏŏk′) *v.* **1.** To look over from a higher place. **2.** To afford a view over. **3.** To miss, ignore, or disregard. **4.** To inspect or examine. **5.** To supervise.

o•ver•lord (ō′vər-lôrd′) *n.* A lord having supremacy over other lords.

o•ver•ly (ō′vər-lē) *adv.* Excessively; too.

o•ver•mas•ter (ō′vər-măs′tər, -mäs′tər) *v.* To overpower; overcome.

o•ver•match (ō′vər-măch′) *v.* **1.** To be more than the match of; defeat. **2.** To match with a superior opponent.

o•ver•night (ō′vər-nīt′) *adj.* **1.** Lasting or remaining for a night. **2.** For use on a short journey. *—adv.* (ō′vər-nīt′). **1.** On or during the night. **2.** Suddenly: *The political situation changed overnight.*

o•ver•pass (ō′vər-păs′, -päs′) *n.* A roadway or bridge that crosses above another thoroughfare.

o•ver•play (ō′vər-plā′) *v.* **1.** To play (a role) in an exaggerated manner; overact. **2.** To overestimate the strength of (one's position): *overplay one's hand.*

o•ver•pow•er (ō′vər-pou′ər) *v.* **1.** To vanquish by superior force; subdue. **2.** To overwhelm.

o•ver•reach (ō′vər-rēch′) *v.* **1.** To reach or extend over or beyond. **2.** To miss by reaching too far or attempting too much: *overreach a goal.* **3.** To defeat (oneself) by going too far. **—o′ver•reach′er** *n.*

o•ver•ride (ō′vər-rīd′) *v.* **1.** To ride across. **2.** To trample upon. **3.** To prevail over. **4.** To declare null and void; set aside.

o•ver•rule (ō′vər-rōōl′) *v.* **1.** To disallow or rule against. **2.** To invalidate; reverse. **3.** To prevail over.

o•ver•run (ō′vər-rŭn′) *v.* **1.** To attack and defeat conclusively. **2. a.** To spread or swarm over destructively. **b.** To infest. **3.** To spread swiftly throughout. **4.** To overflow. **5.** To go beyond.

o•ver•seas (ō′vər-sēz′, ō′vər-sēz′) *adv.* Beyond the sea; abroad. **—o′ver•seas′** *adj.*

o•ver•see (ō′vər-sē′) *v.* **1.** To supervise. **2.** To inspect.

o•ver•se•er (ō′vər-sē′ər) *n.* A supervisor or foreman.

o•ver•sexed (ō′vər-sĕkst′) *adj.* Obsessed with sex.

o•ver•shad•ow (ō′vər-shăd′ō) *v.* **1.** To cast a shadow over. **2.** To make insignificant by comparison.

o•ver•shoe (ō′vər-shōō′) *n.* An article of footwear worn over shoes as protection from water or snow.

o•ver•shoot (ō′vər-shōōt′) *v.* **1.** To shoot over or beyond. **2.** To miss by shooting or flying over and beyond. **3.** To exceed.

o•ver•shot (ō′vər-shŏt′) *adj.* **1.** Having an upper part projecting beyond the lower: *an overshot jaw.* **2.** Designating a water wheel turned by a stream at the top of its circumference.

o•ver•sight (ō′vər-sīt′) *n.* **1.** An unintentional omission or mistake. **2.** Watchful care or management; supervision.

o•ver•sleep (ō′vər-slēp′) *v.* To sleep beyond one's usual time for waking.

o•ver•state (ō′vər-stāt′) *v.* To exaggerate. **—o′ver•state′ment** *n.*

o•ver•stay (ō′vər-stā′) *v.* To stay beyond the set limits or expected duration of.

o•ver•step (ō′vər-stĕp′) *v.* To go beyond; transgress.

o•ver•stuffed (ō′vər-stŭft′) *adj.* **1.** Excessively stuffed. **2.** Thickly upholstered.

o•ver•sub•scribe (ō′vər-səb-skrīb′) *v.* To sub-

---

o′ver•man′y *adj.*
o′ver•ma•ture′ *adj.*
o′ver•meek′ *adj.*
o′ver•mer′ci•ful *adj.*
o′ver•might′y *adj.*
o′ver•mix′ *v.*
o′ver•mod′est *adj.*
o′ver•moist′ *adj.*
o′ver•mois′ten *v.*
o′ver•mort′gage *v.*
o′ver•near′ *adj.*
o′ver•neat′ *adj.*
o′ver•neg•lect′ *v.*
o′ver•ner′vous *adj.*
o′ver•nour′ish *v.*
o′ver•o•bese′ *adj.*
o′ver•o•blige′ *v.*
o′ver•ob•se′qui•ous *adj.*
o′ver•of•fi′cious *adj.*
o′ver•op′ti•mis′tic *adj.*
o′ver•or•nate′ *adj.*
o′ver•par•tic′u•lar *adj.*
o′ver•pas′sion•ate *adj.*
o′ver•pas′sion•ate•ly *adv.*
o′ver•pa′tri•ot′ic *adj.*
o′ver•pes′si•mis′tic *adj.*
o′ver•plain′ *adj.*
o′ver•pol′ish *v.*
o′ver•pop′u•lar *adj.*
o′ver•pop′u•la′tion *n.*
o′ver•pop′u•lous *adj.*
o′ver•pre•cise′ *adj.*
o′ver•press′ *v.*
o′ver•print′ed *adj.*
o′ver•pro•cras′ti•na′tion *n.*
o′ver•pro•duc′tive *adj.*
o′ver•pro•lif′ic *adj.*
o′ver•prom′i•nent *adj.*
o′ver•prompt′ *adj.*
o′ver•proud′ *adj.*
o′ver•pro•vide′ *v.*
o′ver•pro•voke′ *v.*
o′ver•pub′lic *adj.*
o′ver•pun′ish *v.*
o′ver•pun′ish•ment *n.*
o′ver•quan′ti•ty *n.*
o′ver•quick′ *adj.*
o′ver•qui′et *adj.*
o′ver•ra′tion•al *adj.*
o′ver•re•act′ *v.*
o′ver•re•ac′tion *n.*
o′ver•read′y *adj.*
o′ver•re′al•is′tic *adj.*
o′ver•re•fined′ *adj.*
o′ver•re•fine′ment *n.*
o′ver•re•flec′tive *adj.*
o′ver•re•li′ant *adj.*
o′ver•re•lig′ious *adj.*
o′ver•re•served′ *adj.*
o′ver•re•strain′ *v.*
o′ver•rich′ *adj.*
o′ver•rife′ *adj.*
o′ver•right′eous *adj.*
o′ver•right′eous•ness *n.*
o′ver•rig′id *adj.*
o′ver•rig′or•ous *adj.*
o′ver•ripe′ *adj.*
o′ver•rip′en *v.*
o′ver•rough′ *adj.*
o′ver•rude′ *adj.*
o′ver•sad′ *adj.*
o′ver•sale′ *n.*
o′ver•salt′ *v.*
o′ver•salt′y *adj.*
o′ver•sat′u•rate′ *v.*
o′ver•sat′u•ra′tion *n.*
o′ver•scent′ed *adj.*
o′ver•scru′pu•lous *adj.*
o′ver•scru′pu•lous•ness *n.*
o′ver•sea′son *v.*
o′ver•sea′soned *adj.*
o′ver•se•cure′ *adj.*
o′ver•sell′ *v.*
o′ver•sen′si•tive *adj.*
o′ver•sen′ti•men′tal *adj.*
o′ver•se′ri•ous *adj.*
o′ver•se•vere′ *adj.*
o′ver•sharp′ *adj.*
o′ver•short′ *adj.*
o′ver•short′en *v.*
o′ver•shrink′ *v.*
o′ver•si′lent *adj.*
o′ver•sim′ple *adj.*
o′ver•sim•plic′i•ty *n.*
o′ver•sim′pli•fi•ca′tion *n.*
o′ver•sim′pli•fy′ *v.*
o′ver•skep′ti•cal *adj.*
o′ver•slow′ *adj.*
o′ver•small′ *adj.*
o′ver•smooth′ *adj.*
o′ver•soak′ *v.*
o′ver•soft′ *adj.*
o′ver•sol′emn *adj.*
o′ver•so•lic′i•tous *adj.*
o′ver•so•phis′ti•cat′ed *adj.*
o′ver•so•phis′ti•ca′tion *n.*
o′ver•spar′ing *adj.*
o′ver•spar′ing•ly *adv.*
o′ver•spe′cial•i•za′tion *n.*
o′ver•spe′cial•ize′ *v.*

---

scribe for in excess of available supply or accommodation.
o•vert (ō-vûrt′, ō′vûrt′) *adj.* Not concealed or hidden; open. [< OF, pp of *ovrir,* to open.] —**o•vert′ly** *adv.*
o•ver•take (ō′vər-tāk′) *v.* To catch up with.
o•ver•throw (ō′vər-thrō′) *v.* **1.** To overturn. **2.** To bring about the downfall of, esp. by force or concerted action. **3.** To throw something over and beyond. —**o′ver•throw′** *n.*
o•ver•time (ō′vər-tīm′) *n.* Time beyond an established limit, esp. working hours in addition to those of the regular schedule. —**o′ver•time′** *adv.* & *adj.*
o•ver•tone (ō′vər-tōn′) *n.* **1.** One of the series of higher tones produced by a fundamental tone. **2.** An implication or suggestion.
o•ver•top (ō′vər-tŏp′) *v.* **1.** To tower above. **2.** To surpass in importance.
o•ver•ture (ō′vər-cho͝or′) *n.* **1.** An instrumental introduction to an extended musical work, as an opera. **2.** Any introductory section or part. **3.** An offer or proposal. [< L *apertūra,* an opening.]
o•ver•turn (ō′vər-tûrn′) *v.* **1.** To capsize; upset. **2.** To overthrow; defeat.
o•ver•view (ō′vər-vyo͞o′) *n.* A comprehensive view; survey.
o•ver•ween•ing (ō′vər-wē′nĭng) *adj.* **1.** Arrogant; overbearing. **2.** Excessive; immoderate.
o•ver•weigh (ō′vər-wā′) *v.* **1.** To outweigh. **2.** To oppress.
o•ver•whelm (ō′vər-hwĕlm′) *v.* **1.** To submerge; engulf. **2.** To overcome; overpower. **3.** To upset; overthrow. —**o′ver•whelm′ing** *adj.*
o•ver•wrought (ō′vər-rôt′) *adj.* **1.** Excessively nervous. **2.** Extremely elaborate.
ovi–. *comb. form.* Egg or ovum. [< L *ōvum,* egg.]
Ov•id (ŏv′ĭd). 43 B.C.–A.D. 17? Roman poet.
o•vip•a•rous (ō-vĭp′ər-əs) *adj.* Producing eggs that hatch outside the body. —**o′vi•par′i•ty** (ō′və-păr′ə-tē) *n.* —**o•vip′a•rous•ly** *adv.*
o•void (ō′void′) *adj.* Egg-shaped. [< OV(I)- + -OID.] —**o′void′** *n.*
o•vu•late (ō′vyə-lāt′) *v.* **-lated, -lating.** To produce or discharge ova. —**o′vu•la′tion** *n.*
o•vule (ō′vyo͞ol) *n.* A minute plant structure that after fertilization becomes a seed. [< L *ōvum,* egg.]
o•vum (ō′vəm) *n., pl.* **ova** (ō′və). A female reproductive cell; an egg. [< L *ōvum,* egg.]
owe (ō) *v.* **owed, owing. 1.** To have to pay or repay. **2.** To be morally obligated to: *I owe him an apology.* **3.** To be in debt to. **4.** To be obliged for. **5.** To bear (a feeling) toward a person: *He owes them a grudge.* **6.** *Obs.* To own; have. —**owing to.** Because of. [< OE *āgan,* to possess. See **ēik-.**]
owl (oul) *n.* A usually night-flying bird of prey with a large head, a short, hooked bill, and a disklike face. [< OE *ūle.*] —**owl′ish** *adj.*
owl•et (ou′lĭt) *n.* A young or small owl.
own (ōn) *adj.* Of or belonging to oneself. —Used as an intensive adjective: *my own book.* —*n.* That which belongs to one: *It is my own.* —*v.* **1.** To have or possess. **2.** To acknowledge, admit, or confess. [< OE *āgen.* See **ēik-.**] —**own′er** *n.* —**own′er•ship′** *n.*
ox (ŏks) *n., pl.* **oxen** (ŏk′sən). **1.** An adult castrated bull. **2.** Any of various bovine mammals. [< OE *oxa.*]
ox•al•ic acid (ŏk-săl′ĭk). A poisonous, crystalline organic acid, $C_2H_2O_4 \cdot 2H_2O$, used as a cleansing agent and bleach.
ox•bow (ŏks′bō′) *n.* **1.** A U-shaped collar for a draft ox. **2.** A U-shaped bend in a river.
ox•ford (ŏks′fərd) *n.* A low shoe that laces over the instep. [< OXFORD, England.]
Ox•ford (ŏks′fərd). A city of S England; site of Oxford University. Pop. 109,000. —**Ox•o′ni•an** (ŏk-sō′nē-ən) *adj.*
ox•i•dant (ŏk′sə-dənt) *n.* A chemical reagent that oxidizes.

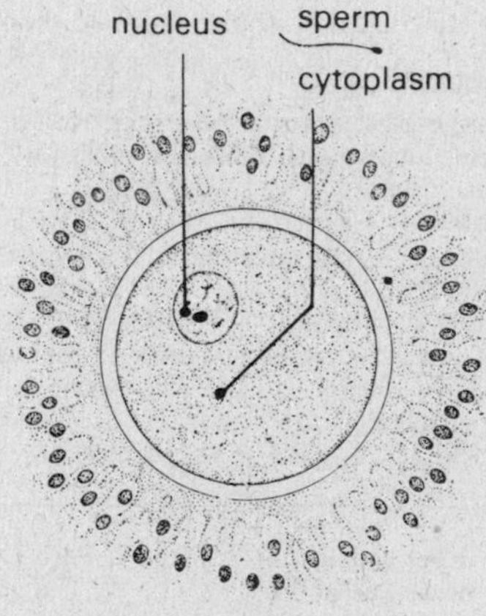

ovum
Human ovum, enlarged 126 diameters

ox•i•da•tion (ŏk′sə-dā′shən) *n.* **1.** The combination of a substance with oxygen. **2.** A reaction in which the atoms in an element lose electrons and its valence is correspondingly increased. —**ox′i•da′tive** (ŏk′sə-dā′tĭv) *adj.* —**ox′i•da′tive•ly** *adv.*
ox•ide (ŏk′sīd′) *n.* A binary compound of an element or radical with oxygen. [< OXYGEN.] —**ox•id′ic** (ŏk-sĭd′ĭk) *adj.*
ox•i•dize (ŏk′sə-dīz′) *v.* **-dized, -dizing. 1.** To combine with oxygen. **2.** To increase the positive charge or valence of (an element) by removing electrons. **3.** To coat with oxide. [< OXIDE.] —**ox′i•di•za′tion** *n.*
ox•i•diz•er (ŏk′sə-dī′zər) *n.* Any substance that oxidizes or induces another substance to oxidize.
oxy–. *comb. form. Chem.* Containing oxygen.
ox•y•a•cet•y•lene (ŏk′sē-ə-sĕt′l-ĭn, -ə-sĕt′l-ēn′) *adj.* Containing a mixture of acetylene and oxygen, as commonly used in metal welding and cutting torches.
ox•y•gen (ŏk′sĭ-jən) *n. Symbol* **O** A colorless, odorless, tasteless gaseous element constituting 21% of the atmosphere by volume, required for nearly all combustion and combustive processes. Atomic number 8, atomic weight 15.9994. [F *oxygène,* "acid-former" : Gk *oxus,* sharp + -GEN.] —**ox′y•gen′ic** (ŏk′sĭ-jĕn′ĭk), **ox•yg′e•nous** (ŏk-sĭj′ə-nəs) *adj.*
ox•y•gen•ate (ŏk′sĭ-jə-nāt′) *v.* **-ated, -ating.** To treat, combine, or infuse with oxygen. —**ox′y•gen•a′tion** *n.*
oxygen mask. A masklike device covering the mouth and nose through which oxygen is supplied from a tank or other source.
oxygen tent. A canopy placed over the head and shoulders to provide oxygen therapy.
ox•y•mo•ron (ŏk′sē-môr′ŏn′, -mōr′ŏn′) *n., pl.* **-mora** (-môr′ə, -mōr′ə). A rhetorical figure in which an epigrammatic effect is created by a paradoxical conjunction of terms. [< Gk *oxumōros,* "sharp-foolish."]
oys•ter (oi′stər) *n.* Any of several often edible bivalve mollusks with an irregularly shaped shell. [< Gk *ostreon.*]
oz ounce.
oz ap apothecaries' ounce.
O•zark Mountains (ō′zärk). A range of low mountains in the south-central U.S.
o•zone (ō′zōn′) *n.* **1.** A blue, gaseous, powerfully oxidizing form of oxygen, O_3, derived from O_2 by electric discharge or exposure to ultraviolet radiation. **2.** *Informal.* Fresh, pure air. [< Gk *ozein,* to smell, reek.]

---

o′ver·spec′u·late′ *v.*
o′ver·spec′u·la′tion *n.*
o′ver·spec′u·la′tive *adj.*
o′ver·spent′ *adj.*
o′ver·stim′u·late′ *v.*
o′ver·stim′u·la′tion *n.*
o′ver·stock′ *v.*
o′ver·strain′ *v.*
o′ver·stress′ *v.*
o′ver·stretch′ *v.*
o′ver·striv′ing *adj.* & *n.*
o′ver·sub·scrip′tion *n.*
o′ver·sub′tle *adj.*
o′ver·sub′tle·ty *n.*
o′ver·suf·fi′cient *adj.*
o′ver·su′per·sti′tious *adj.*
o′ver·sure′ *adj.*
o′ver·sus·pi′cious *adj.*
o′ver·sus·pi′cious·ly *adv.*
o′ver·sweet′ *adj.*
o′ver·sys′tem·at′ic *adj.*
o′ver·talk′a·tive *adj.*
o′ver·talk′a·tive·ness *n.*
o′ver·tax′ *v.*
o′ver·tax·a′tion *n.*
o′ver·teach′ *v.*
o′ver·tech′ni·cal *adj.*
o′ver·te·na′cious *adj.*
o′ver·ten′der *adj.*
o′ver·ten′der·ness *n.*
o′ver·tense′ *adj.*
o′ver·ten′sion *n.*
o′ver·thick′ *adj.*
o′ver·thin′ *adj.*
o′ver·thought′ful *adj.*
o′ver·thrift′y *adj.*
o′ver·tight′ *adj.*
o′ver·tire′ *v.*
o′ver·train′ *v.*
o′ver·truth′ful *adj.*
o′ver·use′ *v.*
o′ver·val′u·a·ble *adj.*
o′ver·va·ri′e·ty *n.*
o′ver·ve′he·ment *adj.*
o′ver·ven′ti·late′ *v.*
o′ver·ven′tur·ous *adj.*
o′ver·vig′or·ous *adj.*
o′ver·vi′o·lent *adj.*
o′ver·warm′ *v.*
o′ver·warmed′ *adj.*
o′ver·weak′ *adj.*
o′ver·wet′ *adj.*
o′ver·will′ing *adj.*
o′ver·wise′ *adj.*
o′ver·wor′ry *v.*
o′ver·write′ *v.*
o′ver·writ′ten *adj.*
o′ver·young′ *adj.*
o′ver·youth′ful *adj.*
o′ver·zeal′ *n.*
o′ver·zeal′ous *adj.*
o′ver·zeal′ous·ly *adv.*
o′ver·zeal′ous·ness *n.*

Pp

p, P (pē) *n.* The 16th letter of the English alphabet.
p **1.** pico-. **2.** proton.
P phosphorous.
p. **1.** page. **2.** participle. **3.** past. **4.** per. **5.** pint. **6.** population. **7.** president.
P. president.
pa (pä) *n. Informal.* Father.
Pa protactinium.
PA public-address system.
Pa. Pennsylvania.
p.a. per annum.
P.A. power of attorney.
pab•u•lum (păb'yə-ləm) *n.* Food; nourishment. [L *pābulum,* food, fodder.]
Pac. Pacific.
pace (pās) *n.* **1.** A step made in walking. **2.** The distance spanned by a step taken as a unit of measurement. **3.** Rate of movement or progress. **4.** A manner of walking or running. **5.** A horse's gait in which both feet on one side move together. —*v.* **paced, pacing. 1.** To walk or cover at a slow pace. **2.** To measure by paces. **3.** To set or regulate the rate of speed for. **4.** To train (a horse) in a particular gait, esp. the pace. [< L *passus,* a step, "stretch of the leg."] —**pac'er** *n.*
pace•mak•er (pās'mā'kər) *n.* **1.** One who sets the pace in a race. **2.** A leader in any field. **3. a.** A mass of specialized muscle fibers of the heart that regulate the heartbeat. **b.** Any of several usually miniaturized and surgically implanted electronic devices used to regulate the heartbeat.
pace•set•ter (pās'sĕt'ər) *n.* A pacemaker. —**pace'set'ting** *adj.*
pach•y•derm (păk'ĭ-dûrm') *n.* A large, thick-skinned mammal, as the elephant or rhinoceros. [< Gk *pakhudermos,* thick-skinned.]
pach•y•san•dra (păk'ĭ-săn'drə) *n.* A low-growing plant with evergreen leaves, cultivated as a ground cover. [NL, "with thick stamens."]
pa•cif•ic (pə-sĭf'ĭk) *adj.* **1.** Tending to diminish conflict. **2.** Peaceful; tranquil. [< L *pāx,* peace + -FIC.] —**pa•cif'i•cal•ly** *adv.*
pac•i•fi•ca•tion (păs'ə-fĭ-kā'shən) *n.* **1.** Placation; appeasement. **2.** Reduction to peaceful submission.
Pacific Ocean. The earth's largest body of water, between Asia and the Americas.
pac•i•fi•er (păs'ə-fī'ər) *n.* **1.** One that pacifies. **2.** A rubber or plastic nipple for a baby to suck on.
pac•i•fism (păs'ə-fĭz'əm) *n.* Opposition to war or violence as a means of resolving disputes. —**pac'i•fist** *n.* & *adj.*
pac•i•fy (păs'ə-fī') *v.* **-fied, -fying. 1.** To calm; appease. **2.** To subdue. [< L *pācificāre.*]
pack (păk) *n.* **1.** A collection of items tied up or wrapped; bundle. **2.** A container carried on the back of a person or animal. **3.** A small package containing a standard number of identical or similar items. **4.** A deck of playing cards. **5.** A large amount; heap. **6. a.** A group of animals, as wolves, that run together. **b.** A gang or band of people. **7.** A compacted mass of ice floes. **8.** *Med.* **a.** The swathing of a patient in hot, cold, wet, or dry sheets or blankets. **b.** The sheets or blankets so used. **c.** A material, as gauze, therapeutically inserted into a cavity or wound. **9.** A folded cloth filled with crushed ice and applied to sore or swollen parts of the body. —*v.* **1.** To combine into a bundle. **2. a.** To put into a protective receptacle. **b.** To stow luggage or belongings. **3.** To crowd together. **4.** To fill up tight; cram. **5.** *Med.* To apply a pack. **6.** To compact firmly. **7.** *Informal.* To carry: *pack a pistol.* **8.** To send or be sent off peremptorily. **9.** To rig (a voting panel) to be fraudulently favorable: *pack the jury.* [ME.]
pack•age (păk'ĭj) *n.* **1.** A parcel or bundle. **2.** A configuration of several related items offered for sale. —*v.* **-aged, -aging.** To put or make into a package.
pack•er (păk'ər) *n.* One that packs, esp. a wholesaler of meat products.
pack•et (păk'ĭt) *n.* **1.** A small package or bundle. **2.** A regularly scheduled passenger and cargo boat.
pack•ing (păk'ĭng) *n.* **1.** The processing and packaging of food products. **2.** Material used to prevent leakage or seepage.
pact (păkt) *n.* A treaty or compact. [< L *pactum.*]
pad¹ (păd) *n.* **1.** A cushion or something functioning as a cushion. **2.** A number of sheets of paper, stacked and glued together at one end. **3.** A broad, floating leaf, as of a water lily. **4.** The cushionlike flesh on the underpart of the foot of an animal. —*v.* **padded, padding.** To line or stuff with padding. [Akin to Flem *pad.*]
pad² (păd) *v.* **padded, padding.** To move or walk about quietly on foot. [Prob < MDu *paden,* to walk along a path.]
pad•ding (păd'ĭng) *n.* **1.** Material used as stuffing, filling, or lining. **2.** Unnecessary matter added to a text to make it longer.
pad•dle¹ (păd'l) *n.* **1.** An oar for a canoe. **2.** An implement or part resembling this. **3.** A ping-pong racket. **4.** A board of a paddle wheel. —*v.* **-dled, -dling. 1.** To row or swim with or as with a paddle. **2.** To stir or beat with a paddle. **3.** To spank. [ME *padell.*] —**pad'dler** *n.*
pad•dle² (păd'l) *v.* **-dled, -dling. 1.** To dabble or wade about in shallow water. **2.** To toddle. [?]
paddle wheel. A wheel with paddles on its rim, used to propel a ship.
pad•dock (păd'ək) *n.* A fenced area in which horses are kept, as for grazing or for preparation and display before a race. [< OE *pearroc* < Gmc **parruk.*]
pad•dy (păd'ē) *n., pl.* **-dies.** An irrigated or flooded field where rice is grown. [Malay *padi.*]
paddy wagon. A police van for taking suspects into custody.
pad•lock (păd'lŏk') *n.* A lock with a U-shaped bar that can be passed through the staple of a hasp and then snapped shut. [ME *padlok.*] —**pad'lock'** *v.*
pae•an (pē'ən) *n.* A song of joyful praise or exultation. [L *paeān.*]
pa•gan (pā'gən) *n.* One who is not a Christian, Moslem, or Jew. [< L *pāgānus,* country-dweller.] —**pa'gan** *adj.* —**pa'gan•ism'** *n.*
page¹ (pāj) *n.* **1.** An errand boy or messenger. **2.** A youth in knightly or ceremonial attendance at court. —*v.* **paged, paging.** To summon by calling the name of. [Prob < Gk *paidion,* child.]
page² (pāj) *n.* A leaf of a book or manuscript or one side of it. —*v.* **paged, paging. 1.** To number the pages of; paginate. **2.** To thumb through. [< L *pāgina.*]
pag•eant (păj'ənt) *n.* An elaborate and colorful public spectacle. [< ML *pāgina,* scene of a play < L, PAGE².] —**pag'eant•ry** (-ən-trē) *n.*
pag•i•na•tion (păj'ə-nā'shən) *n.* **1.** The numbering of pages. **2.** The arrangement and number of pages in a book.
pa•go•da (pə-gō'də) *n.* A many-storied Buddhist tower. [< Dravid.]
paid (pād) *p.t.* & *p.p.* of **pay.**
pail (pāl) *n.* A cylindrical vessel with a handle; bucket. [< ML *pagella,* a measure.]
pain (pān) *n.* **1.** An unpleasant sensation arising from injury, disease, or emotional disorder. **2.** Suffering or distress. **3. pains.** Trouble; effort. **4.** Penalty: *pain of death.* —*v.* To cause or suffer pain. [< Gk *poinē,* penalty.] —**pain'ful** *adj.* —**pain'ful•ly** *adv.*
Paine (pān), **Thomas.** 1737–1809. Political leader in the American Revolution.
pain•kill•er (pān'kĭl'ər) *n.* Something that relieves pain. —**pain'kill'ing** *adj.*
pain•less (pān'lĭs) *adj.* Free from pain. —**pain'less•ly** *adv.* —**pain'less•ness** *n.*
pains•tak•ing (pānz'tā'kĭng) *adj.* Taking pains; careful. —**pains'tak'ing•ly** *adv.*
paint (pānt) *n.* **1. a.** A mixture of a pigment in a liquid, used as a decorative or protective coating. **b.** The dry film formed by such a mixture applied to a surface. **2.** A cosmetic. —*v.* **1.** To represent with or as with paints. **2.** To coat with paint. **3.** To apply cosmetics. **4.** To practice the art of painting pictures. [< L *pingere.*] —**paint'er** *n.*
paint•ing (pān'tĭng) *n.* **1.** The art or occupation of working with paint. **2.** A painted picture.
pair (pâr) *n., pl.* **pairs** or *informal* **pair. 1.** Two corresponding persons or items, similar in form or function. **2.** Something composed of two corresponding parts. **3.** Two associated persons or animals considered together. —*v.* **1.** To arrange in sets of two. **2.** To form a pair or pairs. [< L *paria,* equal things.]
pais•ley (pāz'lē) *adj.* Having a colorful, swirled pattern of curved shapes. [< *Paisley,* Scotland.]
pa•ja•mas (pə-jä'məz, -jăm'əz) *pl.n.* A loose-fitting garment consisting of trousers and a

jacket, for sleeping or lounging. [Hindi *pāe-jāma.*]
Pak•i•stan (păk′ĭ-stăn′, pä′kĭ-stän′). A republic in southern Asia. Pop. 112,600,000. Cap. Islamabad. —**Pak′i•stan′i** *adj.* & *n.*

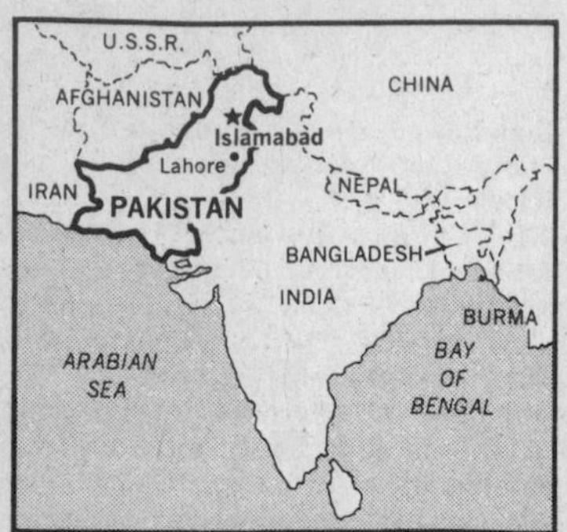

Pakistan

pal (păl) *n. Informal.* A friend; chum. [< Sk *bhrātar-,* brother.]
pal•ace (păl′ĭs) *n.* **1.** The official residence of a royal person. **2.** Any splendid residence; mansion. [< L *palātium.*]
pal•a•din (păl′ə-dĭn) *n.* **1.** Any of the 12 peers of Charlemagne's court. **2.** A paragon of chivalry; knightly champion. [< L *palātium,* PALACE.]
pal•an•quin (păl′ən-kēn′) *n.* A covered litter, carried on poles on the shoulders of two or four men.
pal•at•a•ble (păl′ĭt-ə-bəl) *adj.* **1.** Acceptable to the taste. **2.** Acceptable to the mind or sensibilities: *a palatable solution to the problem.* [< PALATE.]
pal•ate (păl′ĭt) *n.* **1.** The roof of the mouth, consisting of the **hard palate** and the **soft palate.** **2.** The sense of taste. [< L *palātum.*] —**pal′a•tal** *adj.*
pa•la•tial (pə-lā′shəl) *adj.* **1.** Of or suitable for a palace. **2.** Spacious and ornate.
pa•lat•i•nate (pə-lăt′n-āt′, -ĭt) *n.* The territory of a palatine.
pal•a•tine¹ (păl′ə-tīn′) *n.* **1.** A title of various administrative officials of the late Roman and Byzantine empires. **2.** A feudal lord delegated with royal powers. —*adj.* **1.** Belonging to or fit for a palace. **2.** Of or designating a palatine or palatinate. [< L *palātium,* a PALACE.]
pal•a•tine² (păl′ə-tīn′) *adj.* **1.** Pertaining to the palate. **2.** Designating either of the two bones that make up the hard palate. —*n.* Either of these bones.
pa•lav•er (pə-lăv′ər, -lä′vər) *n.* Long and idle chatter or cajolery. [< LL *parabola,* speech, parable.] —**pa•lav′er** *v.*
pale¹ (pāl) *n.* **1.** A stake or picket. **2.** The area enclosed by a fence or boundary. [< L *pālus.*]
pale² (pāl) *adj.* **paler, palest.** **1.** Pallid; wan. **2.** Of a low intensity of color; light. **3.** Of a low intensity of light; dim. **4.** Feeble; weak. —*v.* **paled, paling.** To make or become pale. [< L *pallēre,* to be pale.] —**pale′ness** *n.*
paleo–. *comb. form.* Ancient or prehistoric. [< Gk *palaios,* ancient.]
Pa•le•o•cene (pā′lē-ə-sēn′) *adj.* Of or belonging to the geologic time, rock series, or sedimentary deposits of the first epoch of the Tertiary period. —*n.* The Paleocene epoch.
pa•le•og•ra•phy (pā′lē-ŏg′rə-fē) *n.* The study and interpretation of ancient documents. —**pa′le•og′ra•pher** *n.* —**pa′le•o•graph′ic** (-ə-grăf′ĭk), **pa′le•o•graph′i•cal** *adj.*
Pa•le•o•lith•ic (pā′lē-ə-lĭth′ĭk) *adj.* Of or belonging to the period of human culture beginning with the earliest chipped stone tools, about 750,000 years ago, until the beginning of the Mesolithic, about 15,000 years ago. —*n.* The Paleolithic Age.
pa•le•on•tol•o•gy (pā′lē-ŏn-tŏl′ə-jē) *n.* The study of fossils and ancient life forms. —**pa′le•on•tol′o•gist** *n.*
Pa•le•o•zo•ic (pā′lē-ə-zō′ĭk) *adj.* Of or belonging to the geologic time, rock series, or sedimentary deposits of the era preceding the Mesozoic, divided into seven periods from the Cambrian to the Permian. —*n.* The Paleozoic era.
Pa•ler•mo (pä-lĕr′mō). The capital of Sicily. Pop. 623,000.
Pal•es•tine (păl′ĭ-stīn′). **1.** The land between the Mediterranean Sea and the Jordan River that was occupied by the Hebrews in Biblical times. **2.** This territory, occupied today by Israel. —**Pal′es•tin′i•an** (păl′ĭ-stĭn′ē-ən) *n.*
pal•ette (păl′ĭt) *n.* **1.** A board, typically with a hole for the thumb, upon which an artist mixes colors. **2.** The range of colors on a palette. [< L *pāla,* spade, shovel.]
Pa•li (pä′lē) *n.* An ancient Indic language.
pal•imp•sest (păl′ĭmp-sĕst′) *n.* Vellum or parchment that has been written upon several times, often with remnants of earlier, imperfectly erased writing still visible. [< Gk *palimpsēstos,* rubbed again.]
pal•in•drome (păl′ĭn-drōm′) *n.* A word, verse, or sentence that reads the same backward and forward, as *A man, a plan, a canal, Panama!* [Gk *palindromos,* running back again.]
pal•ing (pā′lĭng) *n.* **1.** A pale; picket. **2.** Pointed sticks used in making fences. **3.** A fence of pales.
pal•i•node (păl′ə-nōd′) *n.* A poem of retraction or recantation. [< Gk *palinōidia.*]
pal•i•sade (păl′ə-sād′) *n.* **1.** A fence of pales forming a fortification. **2.** A line of steep cliffs, usually along a river.
pall¹ (pôl) *n.* **1.** A cloth covering for a coffin or bier. **2.** A coffin. **3.** Something that covers with darkness or gloom. [< L *pallium,* a cover, cloak.]
pall² (pôl) *v.* **1.** To make or become insipid, boring, or wearisome. **2.** To cloy; satiate. [< ME *appallen,* appall.]
pal•la•di•um (pə-lā′dē-əm) *n. Symbol* **Pd** A soft, ductile, steel-white, tarnish-resistant metallic element alloyed for use in electric contacts, jewelry, nonmagnetic watch parts, and surgical instruments. Atomic number 46, atomic weight 106.4.
Pal•las (păl′əs) *n.* The second-largest asteroid of the solar system, approx. 300 miles in diameter. [< P. *Pallas* (died 1811), German naturalist.]
pall•bear•er (pôl′bâr′ər) *n.* One of the persons carrying or attending the coffin at a funeral.
pal•let (păl′ĭt) *n.* A narrow, hard bed or straw-filled mattress. [< L *palea,* chaff.]
pal•li•ate (păl′ē-āt′) *v.* **-ated, -ating.** **1.** To extenuate; excuse. **2.** To alleviate without curing. [< L *pallium,* cloak.] —**pal′li•a′tion** *n.* —**pal′li•a′tive** (-ā′tĭv, -ə-tĭv) *adj.* & *n.*
pal•lid (păl′ĭd) *adj.* Pale in color or complexion; wan. [< L *pallēre,* to be pale.]
pal•lor (păl′ər) *n.* Extreme or unnatural paleness.
palm¹ (päm) *n.* The inner surface of the hand, extending from the wrist to the base of the fingers. —*v.* **1.** To conceal in the palm of the hand. **2.** To pick up furtively. —**palm off.** To dispose of fraudulently. [< L *palma,* palm of the hand, palm tree.]
palm² (päm) *n.* **1.** Any of various chiefly tropical trees usually having an unbranched trunk with a crown of large featherlike or fanlike leaves. **2. a.** An emblem of victory. **b.** Triumph; victory. [< OE < L *palma,* PALM.]
pal•mate (păl′māt′, päl′-, pä′māt′) *adj.* Also **pal•mat•ed** (păl′mā′tĭd, päl′-, pä′mā′-). Resembling a hand with the fingers extended.
palm•er (pä′mər) *n.* Formerly, a person who wore two crossed palm leaves as a token of having visited the Holy Land.
pal•met•to (păl-mĕt′ō) *n., pl.* **-tos** or **-toes.** Any of several small palms with fan-shaped leaves.
palm•is•try (pä′mĭ-strē) *n.* The practice or art of telling fortunes from the lines, marks, and patterns on the palms of the hands. —**palm′ist, palm′is•ter** (pä′mĭ-stər) *n.*
Palm Sunday. The Sunday before Easter, commemorating Christ's triumphal entry into Jerusalem.
palm•y (pä′mē) *adj.* **-ier, -iest.** **1.** Of or covered with palm trees. **2.** Prosperous; flourishing.
pal•o•mi•no (păl′ə-mē′nō) *n., pl.* **-nos.** A horse with a light tan coat and a whitish mane and tail. [< Span, dove-colored.]
pal•pa•ble (păl′pə-bəl) *adj.* **1.** Capable of being felt; tangible. **2.** Easily perceived; obvious. [< L *palpāre,* to touch.] —**pal′pa•bil′i•ty** *n.* —**pal′pa•bly** *adv.*
pal•pate (păl′pāt′) *v.* **-pated, -pating.** *Med.* To examine by touching. [L *palpāre,* to touch.]
pal•pi•tate (păl′pə-tāt′) *v.* **-tated, -tating.** To shake, quiver, or throb. [< L *palpāre,* to touch.] —**pal′pi•ta′tion** *n.*
pal•sy (pôl′zē) *n., pl.* **-sies.** **1.** Paralysis. **2.** A condition marked by loss of power to feel or to control movement in any part of the body. **3. a.** A weakening or debilitating influence. **b.** An enfeebled condition or debilitated state thought to result from such an influence. [< L *paralysis,* paralysis.] —**pal′sied** *adj.*
pal•ter (pôl′tər) *v.* **1.** To talk or act insincerely; equivocate. **2.** To quibble. [?]
pal•try (pôl′trē) *adj.* **-trier, -triest.** **1.** Petty; trifling. **2.** Worthless; trashy. **3.** Contemptible; vile. [?] —**pal′tri•ly** *adv.*
pam•pas (păm′pəz) *pl.n. Sing.* **-pa** (-pə). A nearly treeless grassland area of South America, chiefly in C Argentina and Uruguay. [< Amer Span *pampa.*]
pam•per (păm′pər) *v.* To treat with excessive indulgence; coddle; cater to. [ME *pamperen.*] —**pam′per•er** *n.*
pam•phlet (păm′flĭt) *n.* A short essay or treatise, usually on a current topic, published without a binding. [< *Pamphilus,* a popular short Latin poem of the 12th century.] —**pam′phle•teer′** (-flə-tîr′) *n.*
pan (păn) *n.* **1.** A shallow, wide, open container for holding liquids, cooking, etc. **2.** A similar container or object. —*v.* **panned, panning.** **1.** To wash (gravel, sand, etc.) in a pan to separate precious metal. **2.** *Informal.* To criticize harshly. —**pan out.** *Informal.* To turn out well; be successful. [< OE *panne* < Gmc **panna.*]
pan–. *comb. form.* All. [< Gk *pas (pant-),* all.]
pan•a•ce•a (păn′ə-sē′ə) *n.* A remedy for all diseases, evils, or difficulties; cure-all. [< Gk *panakēs,* all-healing.]
pa•nache (pə-năsh′, -näsh′) *n.* **1.** A bunch of feathers or a plume, esp. on a helmet. **2.** Dash; swagger; verve. [< L *pinna,* feather.]
Pan•a•ma (păn′ə-mä′). **1.** A republic of Cen-

tral America. Pop. 1,076,000. 2. Also **Panama City.** Its capital. Pop. 273,000. —**Pan'a•ma'ni•an** (păn'ə-mā'nē-ən) *adj.* & *n.*

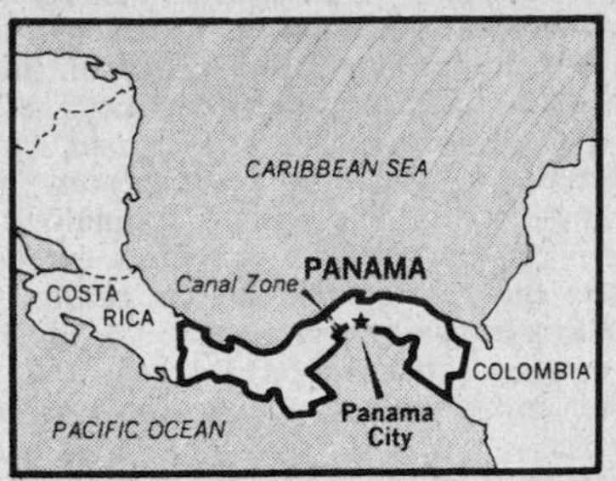

Panama

Panama, Isthmus of. An isthmus connecting North and South America and separating the Pacific from the Caribbean.

Panama Canal. A ship canal across the Isthmus of Panama, connecting the Caribbean with the Pacific.

Pan-A•mer•i•can (păn'ə-mĕr'ə-kən) *adj.* Of or pertaining to North, South, and Central America collectively.

pan•a•tel•a (păn'ə-tĕl'ə) *n.* A long, slender cigar. [< Amer Span, a long thin biscuit.]

pan•cake (păn'kāk') *n.* A thin cake made of batter, cooked on a hot, greased skillet.

pan•chro•mat•ic (păn'krō-măt'ĭk) *adj.* Sensitive to all colors, as film.

pan•cre•as (păng'krē-əs, păn'-) *n.* A long, soft, irregularly shaped gland that secretes pancreatic juice into the duodenum and, in the islands of Langerhans, produces insulin. [Gk *pankreas,* "all-flesh."] —**pan'cre•at'ic** (-ăt'ĭk) *adj.*

pancreatic juice. A clear, alkaline secretion of the pancreas containing enzymes that aid in the digestion of proteins, carbohydrates, and fats.

pan•da (păn'də) *n.* 1. Also **giant panda.** A bearlike black and white mammal of the mountains of China and Tibet. 2. Also **lesser panda.** A related raccoonlike mammal. [F.]

pan•dem•ic (păn-dĕm'ĭk) *adj.* Prevalent over a wide geographic area, as a disease. [< Gk *pandēmos,* of all the people.]

pan•de•mo•ni•um (păn'də-mō'nē-əm) *n.* Wild uproar or noise. [< *Pandæmonium,* capital of Hell in Milton's *Paradise Lost.*]

pan•der (păn'dər) *n.* Also **pan•der•er** (păn'dər-ər). A go-between in sexual intrigues; pimp; procurer. —*v.* 1. To act as a pander. 2. To cater to the vices or weaknesses of others. [< *Pandare,* character in Chaucer's *Troilus and Criseyde.*]

Pan•do•ra (păn-dôr'ə, -dōr'ə). *Gk.Myth.* The first woman; opened a box containing all the ills that could plague mankind.

pane (pān) *n.* A sheet of glass in a window or door. [ME, piece of cloth, section.]

pan•e•gyr•ic (păn'ə-jĭr'ĭk, -jī'rĭk) *n.* Elaborate praise expressed formally; an encomium. [< Gk *(logos) panēgurikos,* "(speech) for a public festival."] —**pan'e•gyr'i•cal** *adj.*

pan•el (păn'əl) *n.* 1. A flat, usually rectangular, raised, recessed or framed piece forming a part of a surface in which it is set. 2. A board containing instruments or controls. 3. A group of people gathered or selected to discuss an issue, make a judgment, etc. —*v.* **-eled** or **-elled, -eling** or **-elling.** To cover, furnish, or decorate with panels. [< OF, piece of parchment on which names of a jury were written.]

pan•el•ing (păn'əl-ĭng) *n.* Panels, esp. decorative panels.

pan•el•ist (păn'əl-ĭst) *n.* A member of a panel.

panel truck. A small delivery truck with a fully enclosed body.

pang (păng) *n.* A sudden, sharp feeling of pain or distress.

pan•han•dle¹ (păn'hănd'l) *n.* A narrow strip of territory projecting from a larger, broader area to which it belongs.

pan•han•dle² (păn'hănd'l) *v.* **-dled, -dling.** *Informal.* To beg, esp. on the streets. —**pan'han'dler** *n.*

pan•ic (păn'ĭk) *n.* A sudden, overpowering, often contagious terror. —*v.* **-icked, -icking.** To affect or be affected with panic. [< Gk *panikos,* of Pan (god who aroused terror in lonely places).] —**pan'ick•y** *adv.*

pan•i•cle (păn'ĭ-kəl) *n.* A loosely and irregularly branched flower cluster. [< L *pānus,* tuft.] —**pan'i•cled** *adj.*

pan•nier (păn'yər, păn'ē-ər) *n.* 1. A large wicker basket, esp. one carried on the back. 2. A part of a skirt or overskirt puffed out at the hips. [< L *pānārium,* breadbasket.]

pan•o•ply (păn'ə-plē) *n., pl.* **-plies.** 1. The complete arms and armor of a warrior. 2. Any magnificent, shining array. [< PAN- + Gk *hoplon,* weapon.]

pan•o•ram•a (păn'ə-răm'ə, -rä'mə) *n.* 1. An unlimited view over a wide area. 2. A picture or representation of a continuous scene or series of events. [PAN- + Gk *horāma,* sight.] —**pan'o•ram'ic** *adj.* —**pan'o•ram'i•cal•ly** *adv.*

pan•sy (păn'zē) *n., pl.* **-sies.** A garden plant having variously colored flowers with rounded, velvety petals. [< F *pensée,* "thought."]

pant (pănt) *v.* 1. To breathe rapidly in short gasps, as after exertion. 2. To utter hurriedly or breathlessly. —*n.* A short, labored breath, gasp. [< VL **phantasiāre,* to gasp with horror.] —**pant'ing•ly** *adv.*

pan•ta•loons (păn'tə-lōōnz') *pl.n.* Trousers. [< OIt *Pantalone,* orig a nickname for a Venetian.]

pan•the•ism (păn'thē-ĭz'əm) *n.* The doctrine identifying the Deity with the various forces and workings of nature. —**pan'the•ist** *n.* —**pan'the•is'tic, pan'the•is'ti•cal** *adj.*

pan•the•on (păn'thē-ŏn', -ən) *n.* 1. A temple dedicated to all gods. 2. A public building commemorating and dedicated to the great persons of a nation. 3. All the gods of a people. [< PAN- + Gk *theos,* god.]

pan•ther (păn'thər) *n.* A large wild cat, esp. a leopard or a mountain lion. [< Gk *panthēr.*]

pant•ies (păn'tēz) *pl.n. Informal.* A pair of women's or children's underpants.

pan•to•mime (păn'tə-mīm') *n.* 1. A type of theatrical performance in which the actors use motions and gestures rather than speech. 2. Such motions or gestures used for expressive communication. —*v.* **-mimed, -miming.** To express or act in pantomime. [L *pantomimus,* "the complete mime."]

pan•try (păn'trē) *n., pl.* **-tries.** A small room or closet, usually off a kitchen, where food, china, silver, linens, etc., are stored. [< OF *panetier,* servant in charge of the bread.]

pants (pănts) *pl.n.* 1. A pair of trousers. 2. A pair of underpants. [Short for PANTALOONS.]

pant•suit (pănt'sōōt') *n.* Also **pants suit.** A woman's suit having trousers instead of a skirt.

pant•y•hose (păn'tē-hōz') *n., pl.* **pantyhose.** A garment consisting of stretchable stockings and underpants in one piece.

pap (păp) *n.* Soft or semiliquid food, as for infants. [Prob < L *pappa,* baby talk for food.]

pa•pa (pä'pə, pə-pä') *n. Informal.* Father. [< OF.]

pa•pa•cy (pā'pə-sē) *n., pl.* **-cies.** 1. The office and jurisdiction of a pope. 2. The period of time during which a pope is in office. 3. **Papacy.** The system of church government headed by the pope.

pa•pal (pā'pəl) *adj.* Of or pertaining to the pope or the papacy. —**pa'pal•ly** *adv.*

pa•paw (pô'pô') *n.* Also **paw•paw.** 1. A North American tree, with fleshy, edible fruit. 2. The fruit of this tree. [Prob < Span *papaya,* papaya.]

pa•pa•ya (pə-pä'yə) *n.* The large, yellow, edible fruit of a tropical American tree. [< Cariban.]

pa•per (pā'pər) *n.* 1. A thin sheet material made of cellulose pulp, derived mainly from wood and rags, and used chiefly for writing, printing, drawing, wrapping, and covering walls. 2. A single sheet or leaf of this material. 3. An official document. 4. An essay, report, or scholarly dissertation. 5. A newspaper. 6. **papers.** Documents establishing the identity of the bearer. —*v.* To cover with wallpaper. —*adj.* Made of paper. [< Gk *papuros,* PAPYRUS.] —**pa'per•er** *n.* —**pa'per•y** *adj.*

pa•per•back (pā'pər-băk') *n.* A book having a flexible paper binding.

pa•per•weight (pā'pər-wāt') *n.* A small heavy object placed on top of loose papers to keep them in place.

pa•per•work (pā'pər-wûrk') *n.* Also **paper work.** Work involving the handling of reports, letters, forms, etc.

pa•pier-mâ•ché (pā'pər-mə-shā') *n.* A material made from paper pulp mixed with glue or paste, that can be molded into various shapes when wet. [F, "chewed paper."]

pa•pil•la (pə-pĭl'ə) *n., pl.* **-pillae** (-pĭl'ē). A small, nipplelike projection, as on the tongue. [< L, nipple.] —**pap'il•lar'y**

pa•poose (pă-pōōs', pə-) *n.* A North American Indian infant or young child. [Algon *papoos.*]

pa•pri•ka (pă-prē'kə, pə-, păp'rĭ-kə) *n.* A mild, powdered seasoning made from sweet red peppers. [Hung.]

Pap test (păp). A test in which a smear of a bodily secretion, esp. from the cervix or vagina, is immediately fixed and examined to detect cancer in an early stage or to evaluate hormonal condition. [< G. *Papanicolaou* (1883–1962), American scientist.]

pa•py•rus (pə-pī'rəs) *n., pl.* **-ruses** or **-ri** (-rī'). 1. A tall, grasslike water plant of N Africa. 2. Paper made from the pith or stems of this plant. [< Gk *papuros.*]

par (pär) *n.* 1. An accepted average; normal standard: *up to par.* 2. An equal status, level, or footing: *on a par.* 3. a. The established face value of the monetary unit of a country. b. The face value of a stock, bond, etc. 4. *Golf.* The number of strokes considered necessary to complete a hole or course in expert play. [L, equal.] —**par** *adj.*

par. 1. paragraph. 2. parallel. 3. parish.

para–. *comb. form.* 1. Alongside; beside. 2. Beyond. 3. Resembling or similar to. 4. Subsidiary to. 5. Isomeric to or polymeric to. [< Gk *para,* beside, for.]

par•a•ble (păr'ə-bəl) *n.* A simple story illustrating a moral or religious lesson. [< Gk *parabolē,* comparison.]

pa•rab•o•la (pə-răb'ə-lə) *n.* A plane curve formed by the locus of points equidistant from a fixed line and a fixed point not on the line. [< Gk *parabolē,* juxtaposition, parallelism.] —**par'a•bol'ic** (păr'ə-bŏl'ĭk) *adj.*

par•a•chute (păr'ə-sho͞ot') *n.* An umbrella-shaped apparatus used to retard free fall from an aircraft. —*v.* **-chuted, -chuting.** To drop or descend by means of a parachute. —**par'a•chut'ist** *n.*

Par•a•clete (păr'ə-klēt') *n.* The Holy Ghost. [< Gk *Paraklētos,* "the Comforter."]

pa•rade (pə-rād') *n.* **1.** A public procession held on a festive or ceremonial occasion. **2.** A ceremonial review of troops. —*v.* **-raded, -rading.** **1.** To march in or as in a parade. **2.** To exhibit ostentatiously; flaunt. [< VL **parāta,* "a making ready."] —**pa•rad'er** *n.*

par•a•digm (păr'ə-dĭm', -dīm') *n.* **1.** A list of all the inflectional forms of a word taken as an illustrative example. **2.** An example or model. [< Gk *paradeiknunai,* to compare, exhibit.]

par•a•dise (păr'ə-dīs', -dīz') *n.* **1. Paradise. a.** Heaven, the abode of righteous souls after death. **b.** Eden. **2.** Any place of ideal beauty or loveliness. [< Gk *paradeisos,* garden, park, paradise.]

par•a•dox (păr'ə-dŏks') *n.* **1.** A seemingly contradictory statement that may nonetheless be true. **2.** A person or situation having contradictory aspects. [< Gk *paradoxos,* incredible, conflicting with expectation.] —**par'a•dox'i•cal** *adj.* —**par'a•dox'i•cal•ly** *adv.*

par•af•fin (păr'ə-fĭn) *n.* **1.** A waxy, white or colorless, solid hydrocarbon mixture used to make candles, wax paper, lubricants, and sealing materials. **2.** *Brit.* Kerosene. [< L *parum,* too little + *affinis,* neighboring.]

par•a•gon (păr'ə-gŏn', -gən) *n.* A model or pattern of excellence; peerless example: *the paragon of virtue.* [< Gk *parakonan,* to sharpen against, compare.]

par•a•graph (păr'ə-grăf', -gräf') *n.* **1.** A distinct division of a written work or composition, begun on a new line and indented. **2.** A mark (¶) used to indicate a new paragraph. —*v.* To divide or arrange in paragraphs. [< Gk *paragraphein,* to write beside.]

Par•a•guay (păr'ə-gwī', -gwā'). A republic of C South America. Pop. 1,817,000. Cap. Asunción. —**Par'a•guay'an** (păr'ə-gwī'ən, -gwā'ən) *adj.* & *n.*

Paraguay

par•a•keet (păr'ə-kēt') *n.* A small parrot with a long, pointed tail. [OF *paroquet.*]

par•al•lax (păr'ə-lăks') *n.* An apparent change in the direction of an object, caused by a change in the viewer's position. [< Gk *parallassein,* to change.]

par•al•lel (păr'ə-lĕl') *adj.* **1.** Being an equal distance at every point so as never to intersect. **2.** Having comparable parts, analogous aspects, or readily recognized similarities. —*adv.* In a parallel relationship or manner. —*n.* **1.** A surface or line that is equidistant from another. **2.** One of a set of parallel geometric figures, usually lines. **3. a.** Anything that closely resembles or is analogous to something else. **b.** A comparison indicating likeness or analogy. **4.** Any of the imaginary lines of the earth's surface parallel to the equator, representing a given latitude. —*v.* **-leled** or **-lelled, -leling** or **-lelling.** **1.** To extend parallel to. **2.** To be similar or analogous to. [< Gk *parallēlos.*] —**par'al•lel•ism'** *n.*

par•al•lel•o•gram (păr'ə-lĕl'ə-grăm') *n.* A four-sided plane figure with opposite sides parallel.

pa•ral•y•sis (pə-răl'ə-sĭs) *n., pl.* **-ses** (-sēz'). **1.** Loss or impairment of the ability to move or have sensation in a bodily part. **2.** A stoppage or crippling of activity. [< Gk *paraluein,* to loosen, disable.] —**par'a•lyt'ic** (păr'ə-lĭt'ĭk) *adj.* & *n.*

par•a•lyze (păr'ə-līz') *v.* **-lyzed, -lyzing.** **1.** To affect with paralysis. **2.** To make inoperative or powerless. —**par'a•lyz'er** *n.*

par•a•me•ci•um (păr'ə-mē'shē-əm, -sē-əm) *n., pl.* **-cia** (-shē-ə, -sē-ə) or **-ums.** A usually oval, aquatic protozoan that moves by means of cilia. [< Gk *paramēkēs,* oblong.]

par•a•med•ic (păr'ə-mĕd'ĭk) *n.* **A person who assists a medical professional, as a nurse or corpsman. [PARA- + MEDIC]**

par•a•mil•i•tar•y (păr'ə-mĭl'ə-tĕr'e) *adj.* **Designating forces organized after a military pattern, as an auxiliar military force.**

pa•ram•e•ter (pə-răm'ə-tər) *n.* A variable or an arbitrary constant appearing in a mathematical expression, each value of which restricts or determines the specific form of the expression. —**par'a•met'ric** (păr'ə-mĕt'rĭk) *adj.*

par•a•mount (păr'ə-mount') *adj.* Of chief rank or importance; primary; foremost. [NF *paramont,* "superior."] —**par'a•mount'ly** *adv.*

par•a•mour (păr'ə-mo͝or') *n.* A lover, esp. in an adulterous relationship. [< OF *par amour,* "by love."]

Pa•ra•ná (păr'ə-nä'). A river of E South America.

par•a•noi•a (păr'ə-noi'ə) *n.* A chronic psychosis characterized by well-rationalized delusions of persecution or of grandeur. [< Gk, madness.] —**par'a•noi'ac** (-noi'ăk, -noi'ĭk) *n.* —**par'a•noid'** (păr'ə-noid') *adj.*

par•a•pet (păr'ə-pĭt, -pĕt') *n.* **1.** A low wall or railing along the edge of a roof, balcony, etc. **2.** An embankment protecting soldiers from enemy fire. [< It *parapetto,* chest-high wall.]

par•a•pher•na•lia (păr'ə-fər-nāl'yə, -fə-nāl'yə) *n. (takes sing. or pl. v.).* **1.** Personal belongings. **2.** The articles used in some activity; equipment; gear. [< Gk *parapherna,* a woman's property beyond her dowry.]

par•a•phrase (păr'ə-frāz') *n.* A restatement of a passage in other words, often to clarify the meaning. [< Gk *paraphrazein,* to paraphrase.] —**par'a•phrase'** *v.* —**par'a•phras'er** *n.*

par•a•ple•gi•a (păr'ə-plē'jē-ə, -jə) *n.* Complete paralysis of the lower half of the body. [< Gk *paraplēssein,* to strike on one side.] —**par'a•ple'gic** (-plē'jĭk) *adj.* & *n.*

par•a•pro•fes•sion•al (păr'ə-prə-fĕsh'ə-nəl) *n.* **A worker who is not a member of a given profession but who assists a professional. [PARA- (alongside) + PROFESSIONAL.]**

par•a•site (păr'ə-sīt') *n.* **1.** An often harmful organism that lives on or in a different organism. **2.** A person who habitually takes advantage of the generosity of others without making any useful return. [< Gk *parasitos,* "fellow guest."] —**par'a•sit'ic** (-sĭt'ĭk) *adj.* —**par'a•sit•ism'** (-sĭt-ĭz'əm) *n.*

par•a•sol (păr'ə-sôl', -sŏl') *n.* A light, usually small umbrella carried as protection from the sun. [< OIt *parasole.*]

par•a•sym•pa•thet•ic nervous system (păr'ə-sĭm'pə-thĕt'ĭk). The part of the autonomic nervous system that, in general, inhibits or opposes the physiological effects of the sympathetic nervous system.

par•a•troops (păr'ə-tro͞ops') *pl.n.* Infantry trained and equipped to parachute. —**par'a•troop'er** *n.*

par•boil (pär'boil') *v.* To cook partially by boiling for a brief period. [ME *parboilen,* "to boil thoroughly."]

par•cel (pär'səl) *n.* **1.** Something wrapped up or packaged; bundle; package. **2.** A portion or plot of land, usually a division of a larger area. —*v.* **-celed** or **-celled, -celing** or **-celling.** To divide into portions and distribute. [< *particula,* portion, particle.]

parcel post. The branch of the postal service that handles and delivers parcels.

parch (pärch) *v.* **1.** To make very dry, esp. by the action of heat. **2.** To make thirsty. [ME *parchen.*]

parch•ment (pärch'mənt) *n.* **1.** The skin of a sheep or goat, prepared for writing upon. **2.** A written text on this material. [< VL **particaminum.*]

par•don (pärd'n) *v.* **1.** To release (a person) from punishment. **2.** To pass over (an offense) without punishment. **3.** To make courteous allowance for; excuse. —*n.* **1.** The act of forgiving. **2.** *Law.* **a.** An exemption from the penalties of an offense or crime. **b.** The official document declaring such an exemption. [< LL *perdōnāre,* to give wholeheartedly.] —**par'don•a•ble** *adj.* —**par'don•a•bly** *adv.*

pare (pâr) *v.* **pared, paring.** **1.** To remove the outer skin of; peel. **2.** To reduce little by little. [< L *parāre,* to prepare.]

par•e•gor•ic (păr'ə-gôr'ĭk, -gŏr'ĭk) *n.* Camphorated tincture of opium, taken chiefly for the relief of diarrhea. [< Gk *parēgoros,* encouraging, soothing.]

paren. parenthesis.

par•ent (pâr'ənt) *n.* **1.** A father or mother. **2.** A forefather; ancestor; progenitor. **3.** The source or cause of something; origin. [< L *parere,* to give birth.] —**pa•ren'tal** (pə-rĕnt'l) *adj.* —**par'ent•hood'** *n.*

par•ent•age (pâr'ən-tĭj) *n.* Descent from parents or ancestors; lineage; origin.

pa•ren•the•sis (pə-rĕn'thə-sĭs) *n., pl.* **-ses (-sēz'). Either of the upright curved lines, ( ), used to mark off explanatory or qualifying remarks. [< Gk, "a putting in beside."]**

par•en•thet•i•cal (păr'ən-thĕt'ĭ-kəl) *adj.* Also **par•en•thet•ic** (-thĕt'ĭk). Contained, or as if contained, in parentheses; qualifying or explanatory. —**par'en•thet'i•cal•ly** *adv.*

pa•re•sis (pə-rē'sĭs, păr'ə-sĭs) *n.* Slight or partial paralysis. [< Gk, act of letting go.] —**pa•ret'ic** (-rĕt'ĭk) *n.* & *adj.*

par ex•cel•lence (pär ĕk-sə-läNs'). The highest degree or epitome of something; preeminently.

par•fait (pär-fā') *n.* A dessert made of cream, eggs, and sugar, or different flavors of ice cream, served in a tall glass. [< L *perfectus,* perfect.]

ă pat/ā ate/âr care/ä bar/b **bib**/ch **chew**/d **deed**/ĕ pet/ē be/f fit/g **gag**/h hat/hw **what**/
ĭ pit/ī pie/îr pier/j **judge**/k **kick**/l lid, fatal/m **mum**/n no, sudden/ng sing/ŏ pot/ō go/

pa•ri•ah (pə-rī'ə) *n.* **1.** A member of a low caste in S India. **2.** A social outcast. [Tamil *paraiyan,* drummer.]

pa•ri•e•tal bone (pə-rī'ə-təl). Either of the two large bones that make up the top and sides of the skull.

par•i-mu•tu•el (păr'ĭ-myōō'chōō-əl) *n., pl.* **-els.** A system of betting on races whereby the winners divide the net amount bet in proportion to the sums they have wagered. [F *pari mutuel,* mutual stake.]

Par•is[1] (păr'ĭs). *Gk.Myth.* The prince of Troy whose abduction of Helen provoked the Trojan War.

Par•is[2] (păr'ĭs). The capital of France, in the NW. Pop. 2,790,000. **—Pa•ri'sian** (pə-rĭzh'ən, -rē'zhən) *adj.* & *n.*

par•ish (păr'ĭsh) *n.* **1.** An administrative part of a diocese that has its own church. **2.** A civil district in Louisiana, corresponding to a county in other states. **3.** Members of a parish; the community of parishioners. [< LGk *paroikos,* Christian.]

pa•rish•ion•er (pə-rĭsh'ən-ər) *n.* A member of a parish.

par•i•ty (păr'ə-tē) *n., pl.* **-ties. 1.** Equality, as in amount, status, or value. **2.** The equivalent in value of a sum of money expressed in terms of a different currency. **3.** A level for farm-product prices, maintained by governmental support. [< L *pār,* equal.]

park (pärk) *n.* **1.** An expanse of enclosed grounds for recreational use. **2.** A stadium or enclosed playing field: *ball park.* —*v.* **1.** To put or leave (a vehicle) for a time in a certain location. **2.** To place, put, set, or leave (something) somewhere. [< OF *parc,* enclosure.]

par•ka (pär'kə) *n.* A hooded fur jacket. [< Russ, pelt of a reindeer.]

parking lot. An area for parking motor vehicles.

Par•kin•son's disease (pär'kĭn-sənz). A progressive nervous disease of the later years, characterized by muscular tremor, slowing of movement, partial facial paralysis, and impaired motor control. [< J. *Parkinson* (1755–1824), English surgeon.]

park•way (pärk'wā') *n.* A broad landscaped highway.

Parl. Parliament.

par•lance (pär'ləns) *n.* Manner of speaking; language, style, or idiom: *legal parlance.* [< ML *parabolāre,* to parley.]

par•lay (pär'lā, -lē) *v.* To bet (an original wager and its winnings) on a subsequent event. —*n.* A bet comprising the sum of an original wager plus its winnings. [< It *parolo,* a set of dice.]

par•ley (pär'lē) *n., pl.* **-leys.** A discussion or conference, esp. between enemies. [< LL *parabola,* discourse, parable.] **—par'ley** *v.*

par•lia•ment (pär'lə-mənt) *n.* **1.** A legislative body. **2. Parliament.** The legislative body of various countries, esp. that of the United Kingdom. [< OF *parler,* to talk.] **—par•lia•men'ta•ry** (-mĕn'tə-rē) *adj.*

par•lia•men•tar•i•an (pär'lə-mĕn-târ'ē-ən) *n.* An expert in parliamentary procedures, rules, or debate.

par•lor (pär'lər) *n.* Also *chiefly Brit.* **par•lour. 1.** A room for the entertainment of visitors. **2.** A room designed for some special function or business: *beauty parlor.* [< OF *parleur,* room used for conversation.]

par•lous (pär'ləs) *adj. Archaic.* Perilous; dangerous. [< PERIL.] **—par'lous•ly** *adv.*

Par•me•san (pär'mə-zän', -zăn', -zən) *n.* A hard, dry Italian cheese usually served grated as a garnish. [< *Parma,* Italy.]

pa•ro•chi•al (pə-rō'kē-əl) *adj.* **1.** Of, pertaining to, supported by, or located in a parish. **2.** Narrow; provincial: *parochial attitudes.* [< LL *parochia,* parish.] **—pa•ro'chi•al•ly** *adv.*

parochial school. A school supported by a church parish.

par•o•dy (păr'ə-dē) *n., pl.* **-dies. 1.** A satirical imitation of a work of literature or music. **2.** A travesty: *a parody of justice.* [< Gk *parōidia,* "mock-song."] **—par'o•dy** *v.* **(-died, -dying).**

pa•role (pə-rōl') *n.* The release of a prisoner before his term has expired on condition of good behavior. —*v.* **-roled, -roling.** To release (a prisoner) on parole. [F, word of honor.] **—pa•rol'ee'** *n.*

pa•rot•id gland (pə-rŏt'ĭd). Either of the salivary glands located ahead of and below each ear.

-parous. *comb. form.* Giving birth to or bearing: **viviparous.** [< L *parere,* to give birth to.]

par•ox•ysm (păr'ək-sĭz'əm) *n.* **1.** A sudden outburst: *a paroxysm of laughter.* **2. a.** A crisis in or recurrent intensification of a disease. **b.** A spasm or fit; convulsion. [< Gk *paroxusmos,* irritation, paroxysm.] **—par'ox•ys'mal** (păr'ək-sĭz'məl) *adj.*

par•quet (pär-kā') *n.* **1.** The main floor of a theater; the orchestra. **2.** A floor of parquetry. —*v.* **-queted** (-kād'), **-queting** (-kā'ĭng). To make (a floor) of parquetry. [< OF *parc,* enclosure, PARK.]

par•quet•ry (pär'kĭ-trē) *n., pl.* **-ries.** Wood worked into an inlaid mosaic, used esp. for floors.

par•rot (păr'ət) *n.* **1.** Any of various chiefly tropical birds having a short, hooked bill, brightly colored plumage, and sometimes the ability to mimic human speech. **2.** One who mindlessly imitates words or actions of another. —*v.* To repeat or imitate without meaning or understanding. [< OF *paroquet,* PARAKEET.] **—par'rot•er** *n.*

par•ry (păr'ē) *v.* **-ried, -rying. 1.** To deflect or ward off. **2.** To avoid or evade: *He skillfully parried her questions.* [< F *parer,* to defend, parry.]

parse (pärs) *v.* **parsed, parsing.** To describe the form, function, and syntactical relationship of each part of a sentence. [< L *pars,* part.]

par•si•mo•ny (pär'sə-mō'nē) *n.* Unusual or excessive frugality; extreme economy; stinginess. [< L *parcere.*] **—par'si•mo'ni•ous** *adj.*

pars•ley (pär'slē) *n.* A plant with much-divided, curled leaves used as a seasoning and garnish. [< Gk *petroselinon,* rock parsley.]

pars•nip (pär'snĭp') *n.* **1.** A plant cultivated for its long edible root. **2.** The root of this plant. [< L *pastināca,* parsnip, carrot.]

par•son (pär'sən) *n.* A clergyman in charge of a parish. [< L *persōna (ecclēsiae),* "person (of the church)."]

par•son•age (pär'sən-ĭj) *n.* The official residence of a parson, as provided by his church.

part (pärt) *n.* **1.** A portion, division, or segment of a whole. **2.** An essential component: *a machine part.* **3.** A role. **4.** One's share in responsibility or obligation; duty. **5.** Often **parts.** A region, land, or territory: *foreign parts.* **6.** The line where the hair on the head is parted. **7.** One of the melodic lines in concerted music or in harmony. **—for one's part.** So far as one is concerned. **—for the most part.** Generally; mostly. **—in part.** To some extent; partly. **—take part in.** To join in; participate. —*v.* **1.** To divide into separate parts. **2.** To separate by coming between; keep apart. **3.** To comb (the hair) away from a dividing line on the scalp. **4.** To go away from one another; separate. **5.** To leave; depart. **—part with.** To give up; relinquish. —*adv.* Partially; in part: *part yellow.* —*adj.* Not full or complete; partial: *a part owner.* [< L *pars (part-).*]

part. participle.

par•take (pär-tāk') *v.* **-took, -taken, -taking. 1.** To take part; participate. **2.** To take or be given part or portion. [Back-formation < partaker < *part taker.*] **—par•tak'er** *n.*

par•the•no•gen•e•sis (pär'thə-nō-jĕn'ə-sĭs) *n.* Reproduction of organisms without conjunction of gametes of opposite sexes. [< Gk *parthenos,* virgin, girl + -GENESIS.]

par•tial (pär'shəl) *adj.* **1.** Not total; incomplete. **2.** Biased; prejudiced. **3.** Especially fond. [< L *pars (part-),* PART.] **—par'ti•al'i•ty** (pär'shē-ăl'ə-tē) *n.* **—par'tial•ly** *adv.*

par•tic•i•pant (pär-tĭs'ə-pənt) *n.* One who participates or takes part in something.

par•tic•i•pate (pär-tĭs'ə-pāt') *v.* **-pated, -pating.** To take part; join or share with others. [< L *particeps,* a partaker.] **—par•tic'i•pa'tion** *n.*

par•ti•ci•ple (pär'tə-sĭp'əl) *n.* A form of a verb that is used with an auxiliary verb to indicate certain tenses and that can also function independently as an adjective. [< L *particeps,* partaker.] **—par'ti•cip'i•al** *adj.*

par•ti•cle (pär'tĭ-kəl) *n.* **1.** A very small piece or part; speck. **2.** A very small amount: *not a particle of difference.* **3.** One of a class of words, such as prepositions or conjunctions. [< L *pars,* PART.]

par•ti-col•ored (pär'tē-kŭl'ərd) *adj.* Having different parts or sections colored differently. [< OF *parti,* striped.]

par•tic•u•lar (pər-tĭk'yə-lər) *adj.* **1.** Pertaining to a single person, group, or thing; not general or universal. **2.** Separate and distinct from others; specific. **3.** Worthy of note; exceptional; special. **4.** Especially concerned with details or niceties; fussy. —*n.* An individual item, fact, or detail. **—in particular.** Particularly; especially. [< L *particula,* detail, particle.] **—par•tic'u•lar'i•ty** (-lăr'ə-tē) *n.* **—par•tic'u•lar•ly** *adv.*

par•tic•u•lar•ize (pər-tĭk'yə-lə-rīz') *v.* **-ized, -izing. 1.** To state or enumerate in detail; itemize. **2.** To give particulars.

par•tic•u•late (pər-tĭk'yə-lĭt, -lāt') *adj.* Of, pertaining to, or formed of separate particles.

part•ing (pär'tĭng) *n.* **1.** The act of separating or dividing. **2.** A departure or leave-taking. —*adj.* Done, given, or said on departing or separating.

par•ti•san (pär'tə-zən) *n.* **1.** A militant supporter of a party, cause, faction, person, or idea. **2.** A guerrilla. [< L *pars,* PART.] **—par'ti•san** *adj.* **—par'ti•san•ship'** *n.*

par•ti•ta (pär-tē'tə) *n. Mus.* A composition similar to a suite. [< L *partīre,* to divide.]

par•ti•tion (pär-tĭsh'ən) *n.* **1.** The act or process of dividing something into parts. **2.** Something that separates, such as a partial wall dividing a larger area. —*v.* **1.** To divide into parts or sections. **2.** To divide or separate by means of a partition.

par•ti•tive (pär'tə-tĭv) *Gram. adj.* Indicating a part as distinct from a whole. —*n.* A partitive word or construction.

part•ly (pärt'lē) *adv.* In part; in some degree; not completely.

part•ner (pärt'nər) *n.* A person associated with another in some common activity, esp.: **a.** A member of a business partnership. **b.** Either of two persons dancing together. **c.** One of two players on the same side in a game or sport. [< L *partitiō*, partition.] **—part'ner•ship'** *n.*

part of speech. One of the traditional classifications of words according to their functions in context, such as noun, verb, etc.

par•took (pär-to͝ok'). *p.t.* of **partake.**

par•tridge (pär'trij) *n.* Any of several plump-bodied game birds. [< Gk *perdix.*]

part-time (pärt'tīm') *adj.* For or during less than the customary time: *a part-time job.* **—part'-time'** *adv.*

par•tu•ri•tion (pär't/y/o͞o-rĭsh'ən, pär'cho͞o-) *n.* The act of giving birth; childbirth. [< L *parturīre,* to be in labor.]

par•ty (pär'tē) *n., pl.* **-ties. 1.** A social gathering for pleasure or entertainment. **2.** A group of persons participating in some common activity. **3.** A political group organized to promote its principles and candidates for public office. **4.** A person or group involved in a legal proceeding. **5.** A participant or accessory. [< OF *partir,* to divide.] **—par'ty** *adj.*

party line. 1. A telephone circuit used by two or more subscribers. **2.** The official policies of a political party to which loyal members are expected to adhere.

par•ve•nu (pär'və-n/y/o͞o') *n.* One who has suddenly risen above his social and economic class; an upstart. [< F *parvenir,* to arrive.]

Pas•a•de•na (păs'ə-dē'nə). A city in SW California. Pop. 116,000.

pas•chal (păs'kəl) *adj.* Of or pertaining to the Passover or to Easter. [< LL *pascha,* Passover, Easter.]

pa•sha (pä'shə, păsh'ə) *n.* A former Turkish title of honor placed after the name.

Pash•to (pŭsh'tō) *n.* An Iranian language that is a major language of Afghanistan.

pas•qui•nade (păs'kwə-nād') *n.* A lampoon posted in a public place. [< It *pasquinata.*]

pass (păs, päs) *v.* **1.** To go by without stopping. **2.** To move on or ahead; proceed. **3.** To run; extend: *The river passes through our land.* **4.** To cause to move: *pass one's hand over the fabric.* **5.** To hand over to someone else: *pass the bread.* **6.** To move past in time; elapse. **7.** To be communicated, exchanged, transferred, or conveyed. **8.** To allow to go by or elapse; spend. **9.** To come to an end; be terminated. **10.** To happen; take place. **11.** To be allowed to happen without challenge: *Let a remark pass.* **12.** To undergo (an examination or trial) with favorable results. **13. a.** To approve; adopt: *The legislature passed the bill.* **b.** To be sanctioned, ratified, or approved (by). **14.** To pronounce; utter: *pass judgment.* **15.** To be accepted as something different. **16.** To transfer (a ball or puck) to a teammate. **17.** To decline to bid in a card game. **18.** To discharge; void (bodily waste). **—come to pass.** To happen. **—pass away.** To die. **—pass for.** To be accepted as being something one is not. **—pass out. 1.** To distribute. **2.** To faint. **—pass up.** To reject; let go by. *—n.* **1.** The act of passing; passage. **2.** A narrow passage between mountains. **3. a.** A permit, ticket, or authorization to come and go at will or without charge. **b.** Written leave of absence from military duty. **4.** A sweep or run by an aircraft over an area or target. **5.** A critical condition or situation; predicament. **6.** A sexual invitation or overture. **7.** A motion of the hand or the waving of a wand for magic. [< L *passus,* step, pace, pp of *pandere,* to stretch out.] **—pass'less** *adj.*

pass. 1. passenger. **2.** passive.

pass•a•ble (păs'ə-bəl, päs'-) *adj.* **1.** Capable of being passed, traversed, or crossed. **2.** Satisfactory but not outstanding. **—pass'a•bly** *adv.*

pas•sage (păs'ĭj) *n.* **1.** The act or process of passing: **a.** Movement; transit. **b.** The process of elapsing. **c.** Transition. **d.** The enactment of a legislative measure. **2.** A journey. **3. a.** The right to travel, esp. on a ship: *to book passage.* **b.** The price paid for this. **4.** A path, channel, or duct through, over, or along which something may pass. **5.** A segment of a literary work or musical composition.

pas•sage•way (păs'ĭj-wā') *n.* A corridor.

pass•book (păs'bo͝ok', päs'-) *n.* A bankbook.

pas•sé (pă-sā') *adj.* **1.** Out-of-date; old-fashioned. **2.** Past one's prime. [< F *passer,* to pass.]

pas•sen•ger (păs'ən-jər) *n.* A person traveling in a train, airplane, ship, bus, or other conveyance. [< OF *passager,* passing.]

pas•ser-by (păs'ər-bī', päs'-) *n., pl.* **passers-by.** One who passes by, often by chance.

pas•sim (păs'ĭm) *adv.* Throughout; here and there, as occurrence of a word or passage in a text. [L, here and there.]

pass•ing (păs'ĭng, päs'-) *adj.* **1.** Of brief duration; transitory. **2.** Cursory; superficial; casual. **3.** Satisfactory: *a passing mark.* *—n.* **1.** The act of one that passes. **2.** Death.

pas•sion (păsh'ən) *n.* **1.** Any powerful emotion or appetite, such as love, joy, hatred, anger, or greed. **2. a.** Ardent adoring love. **b.** Strong sexual desire; lust. **c.** The object of such love or desire. **3. a.** Boundless enthusiasm. **b.** The object of such enthusiasm. **4.** An outburst of emotion, esp. of anger. **5. Passion.** The sufferings of Christ in the period following the Last Supper and including the Crucifixion. [< L *patī* (pp *passus*), to suffer.]

pas•sion•ate (păsh'ən-ĭt) *adj.* **1.** Capable of or having intense feelings. **2.** Ardent; fervent. **—pas'sion•ate•ly** *adv.*

pas•sive (păs'ĭv) *adj.* **1.** Not active but acted upon. **2.** Accepting without resistance; submissive. **3.** Not participating, acting, or operating; inert. **4.** Denoting a verb form or voice used to indicate that the subject is the object of the action. *—n.* **1.** The passive voice. **2.** A verb or construction in this voice. [< L *passīvus,* capable of suffering.] **—pas'sive•ly** *adv.* **—pas•siv'i•ty, pas'sive•ness** *n.*

Pass•o•ver (păs'ō'vər, päs'-) *n.* A Jewish festival commemorating the exodus from Egypt. [< the phrase *pass over.*]

pass•port (păs'pôrt', -pōrt', päs'-) *n.* An official governmental document that certifies the identity and citizenship of a person traveling abroad. [F *passeport,* permission to pass through a port.]

pass•word (păs'wûrd', päs'-) *n.* A secret word or phrase which indicates that the speaker is to be admitted.

past (păst, päst) *adj.* **1.** No longer current; gone by; over. **2.** Having existed or occurred in an earlier time; bygone. **3.** Just gone by or elapsed. **4.** Having served formerly in some official capacity. **5.** Denoting a verb tense or form used to express an action or condition prior to the time it is expressed. *—n.* **1.** The time before the present. **2.** Former background, career, experiences, and activities. **3. a.** The past tense. **b.** A verb form in the past tense. *—adv.* So as to pass by or go beyond: *He waved as he walked past.* *—prep.* **1.** By and beyond: *walk past the theater.* **2.** Beyond in position, time, extent, or amount. [ME, pp of *passen,* to pass.]

pas•ta (päs'tə) *n.* **1.** Paste or dough made of flour and water, as in macaroni and ravioli. **2.** A prepared dish of pasta. [< LL, paste.]

paste[1] (pāst) *n.* **1.** A smooth viscous adhesive, made of flour and water or starch and water. **2.** Any similar soft, moist, smooth substance: *toothpaste.* **3.** A smooth dough used in making pastry. **4.** A hard, brilliant glass used in making artificial gems. *—v.* **pasted, pasting.** To cause to adhere by applying paste. [< Gk *pastē,* barley porridge.]

paste[2] (pāst). *Slang. v.* **pasted, pasting.** To hit with a hard blow; punch. *—n.* A hard blow. [Var of BASTE[3].]

paste•board (pāst'bôrd', -bōrd') *n.* A thin, firm material made of sheets of paper pasted together.

pas•tel (pă-stĕl') *n.* **1.** A crayon made of a paste of ground and mixed pigment, chalk, water, and gum. **2.** A picture drawn with this type of crayon. **3.** The art or process of drawing with such crayons. **4.** A soft, delicate hue. [< LL *pastellus,* woad dye, crayon.] **—pas•tel'** *adj.* **—pas•tel'ist, pas•tel'list** *n.*

pas•tern (păs'tərn) *n.* The part of a horse's foot between the fetlock and hoof. [< LL *pāstōria,* a sheep's hobble.]

Pas•teur (pă-stûr'), **Louis.** 1822–1895. French chemist.

pas•teur•i•za•tion (păs'chər-ə-zā'shən, păs'-tər-) *n.* The process of destroying most disease-producing microorganisms and limiting fermentation in milk, beer, and other liquids by partial or complete sterilization. [< L. PASTEUR.] **—pas'teur•ize'** (păs'chə-rīz', păs'tə-) *v.* **(-ized, -izing).**

pas•tille (pă-stēl') *n.* A small tablet or lozenge. [< L *pāstillus,* little loaf, roll.]

pas•time (păs'tīm', päs'-) *n.* An activity that occupies one's time pleasantly.

pas•tor (păs'tər, päs'-) *n.* A Christian minister in charge of a congregation. [< L *pāstor,* shepherd.]

pas•tor•al (păs'tər-əl, päs'-) *adj.* **1.** Of or pertaining to shepherds. **2. a.** Of or pertaining to the country or country life; rural. **b.** Having the qualities of idealized country life, as simplicity and a leisurely pace. **3.** Of or pertaining to a pastor or his duties. *—n.* A literary or other artistic work that portrays rural life, usually in an idealized manner. [< L *pāstor,* shepherd, PASTOR.]

pas•tor•ate (păs'tər-ĭt, päs'-) *n.* The office, rank, or jurisdiction of a pastor.

past participle. A verb form indicating past or completed action or time.

pas•tra•mi (pə-strä'mē) *n.* A highly seasoned smoked cut of beef, usually from the breast or shoulder. [Yidd.]

pas•try (pās'trē) *n., pl.* **-tries. 1.** A baked paste of flour, water, and shortening, used for the crusts of pies, tarts, etc. **2.** Baked foods, such as pies or tarts, made with this paste. [< PASTE.]

past tense. A verb tense used to express an action or condition that occurred in or during the past.

pas•ture (păs'chər, päs'-) *n.* Also **pas•tur•age** (păs'chər-ĭj, päs'-). **1.** Grass or other plants eaten by grazing animals. **2.** Land used for grazing. *—v.* **-tured, -turing. 1.** To put in a pasture. **2.** To graze. [< L *pāscere* (pp *pāstus*), to pasture, feed.] **—pas'tur•er** *n.*

past•y (pā'stē) *adj.* **-ier, -iest. 1.** Resembling paste in color or consistency. **2.** Pale and lifeless-looking.

pat[1] (păt) *v.* **patted, patting.** To tap gently with the open hand or with something flat. *—n.* **1.** A light stroke or tap. **2.** The sound made by such a stroke or tap. **3.** A small mass: *a pat of butter.* [ME *patte* (prob imit).]

pat² (păt) *adj.* **1.** Timely; opportune; fitting: *a pat answer.* **2.** Facile; glib. **3.** Needing no change; exactly right. *—adv.* **1.** Without changing position; steadfastly. **2.** Perfectly; precisely; aptly. [Prob < PAT.]

pat. patent.

patch (păch) *n.* **1.** A small piece of material affixed to another to conceal or reinforce a weakened or worn area. **2.** *Mil.* A small cloth badge affixed to a sleeve to indicate the unit to which one belongs. **3. a.** A dressing for a wound. **b.** A small shield of cloth worn over an injured eye. **4.** A small piece of land. **5.** A small piece or part of anything: *a patch of blue sky.* *—v.* To put a patch or patches on. **—patch up.** To settle; make up: *patched up a quarrel.* [< OF *pece, pieche,* piece.]

patch test. A test for allergic sensitivity made by applying a suspected allergen to the skin by a small surgical pad.

patch•work (păch'wûrk') *n.* **1.** Needlework consisting of varicolored patches of material sewed together, as in a quilt. **2.** A collection of miscellaneous parts; jumble.

pate (pāt) *n.* The head, esp. the top of the head. [ME.]

pâ•té (pä-tā') *n.* A seasoned meat paste. [< OF *paste,* paste.]

pa•tel•la (pə-tĕl'ə) *n., pl.* **-tellae** (-tĕl'ē). A flat, triangular bone located at the front of the knee joint. [L, dim of *patina,* plate.] **—pa•tel'lar, pa•tel'late** (pə-tĕl'ĭt, -āt') *adj.*

pat•ent (păt'ənt) *n.* A grant made by a government to an inventor, assuring him the sole right to make, use, and sell his invention over a certain period of time. *—adj.* **1.** Open to general inspection; unsealed: *letters patent.* **2.** (pāt'ənt). Obvious; plain. **3.** Protected by a patent. **4.** Of or pertaining to patents: *patent law.* *—v.* To obtain a patent on. [< ML *(litterae) patentes,* "open (letters)."]

pat•ent•ee (păt'n-tē') *n.* One who has been granted a patent.

patent leather. Black leather finished to a hard, glossy surface. [Made by a once-patented process.]

pa•ter•nal (pə-tûr'nəl) *adj.* **1.** Of, pertaining to, or characteristic of a father; fatherly. **2.** Inherited from a father. **3.** On the father's side of a family. [< L *pater,* father.]

pa•ter•nal•ism (pə-tûr'nəl-ĭz'əm) *n.* A practice of treating or governing people in a fatherly manner, esp. by providing for their needs without giving them responsibility. **—pa•ter'nal•is'tic** (-ĭs'tĭk) *adj.*

pa•ter•ni•ty (pə-tûr'nə-tē) *n.* The fact or condition of being a father; fatherhood.

Pat•er•son (păt'ər-sən). A city in NE New Jersey. Pop. 144,000.

path (păth, päth) *n., pl.* **paths** (păthz, päthz, păths, päths). **1.** A trodden track or way. **2.** Any road, way, or track. **3.** The route or course along which something moves. **4.** A course of action or conduct. [< OE *pæth.*]

path. pathological; pathology.

pa•thet•ic (pə-thĕt'ĭk) *adj.* Arousing pity, sympathy, or tenderness. [< Gk *pathos,* passion, suffering.] **—pa•thet'i•cal•ly** *adv.*

path•find•er (păth'fīn'dər, päth'-) *n.* One who discovers a way through or into unexplored regions.

patho–. *comb. form.* Disease or suffering. [< Gk *pathos,* emotion, suffering.]

path•o•gen (păth'ə-jən) *n.* Any agent that causes disease, esp. a microorganism such as a bacterium or fungus.

path•o•gen•ic (păth'ə-jĕn'ĭk) *adj.* Capable of causing disease.

pathol. pathological; pathology.

pa•thol•o•gy (pă-thŏl'ə-jē) *n., pl.* **-gies.** **1.** The scientific study of disease. **2.** The anatomic or functional manifestations of disease. **—path'o•log'i•cal** *adj.* **—path'o•log'i•cal•ly** *adv.* **—pa•thol'o•gist** *n.*

pa•thos (pā'thŏs', -thôs') *n.* A quality in something or someone that arouses feelings of pity, sympathy, tenderness, or sorrow in another. [Gk, passion, suffering.]

path•way (păth'wā', päth'-) *n.* A path.

–pathy. *comb. form.* Feeling; perception: **telepathy.** [< Gk *pathos,* suffering.]

pa•tience (pā'shəns) *n.* The capacity of calm endurance.

pa•tient (pā'shənt) *adj.* **1.** Capable of bearing affliction with calmness. **2.** Capable of bearing delay and waiting for the right moment. **3.** Persevering; constant. *—n.* One under medical treatment. [< L *patiēns,* pres part of *pati,* to suffer.] **—pa'tient•ly** *adv.*

pat•i•na (păt'ə-nə) *n.* A thin layer of corrosion, usually brown or green, that appears on copper or bronze as a result of oxidation. [It.]

pat•i•o (păt'ē-ō', pä'tē-ō') *n., pl.* **-os.** **1.** An inner, roofless courtyard. **2.** A space for dining or recreation, adjacent to a house. [Span.]

pat•ois (păt'wä') *n., pl.* **patois** (păt'wäz'). **1.** A nonstandard regional dialect. **2.** The special jargon of a group. [< OF.]

patri–. *comb. form.* Father. [< L *pater,* father, and Gk *patēr,* father.]

pa•tri•arch (pā'trē-ärk') *n.* **1.** The paternal leader of a family or tribe. **2.** One of the founders of the Israelites. **3.** An ecclesiastical dignitary, esp. in Eastern churches. **4.** A venerable old man. **—pa'tri•ar'chal** *adj.*

pa•tri•cian (pə-trĭsh'ən) *n.* A person of high rank, an aristocrat. [< L *patres,* "fathers," senators.] **—pa•tri'cian** *adj.*

Pat•rick (păt'rĭk), **Saint.** A.D. 389?–461? Patron saint and apostle of Ireland.

pat•ri•mo•ny (păt'rə-mō'nē) *n., pl.* **-nies.** An inheritance, esp. from one's father. **—pat'ri•mo'ni•al** (-mō'nē-əl) *adj.*

pa•tri•ot (pā'trē-ət, -ŏt') *n.* One who loves and defends his country. [< Gk *patris,* fatherland.] **—pa'tri•ot'ic** (-ŏt'ĭk) *adj.* **—pa'tri•ot'i•cal•ly** *adv.* **—pa'tri•ot•ism'** (-ə-tĭz'əm) *n.*

pa•trol (pə-trōl') *n.* **1.** The action of moving about an area for observation or security. **2.** A person or group performing such an action. **3.** A military unit sent out to reconnoiter. *—v.* **-trolled, -trolling.** To engage in a patrol. [< OF *patouiller,* to paw or paddle around in mud.] **—pa•trol'ler** *n.*

pa•trol•man (pə-trōl'mən) *n.* A policeman or guard who patrols an assigned area.

patrol wagon. A police truck used to convey prisoners.

pa•tron (pā'trən) *n.* **1.** One who supports or protects; benefactor. **2.** A regular customer. [< L *patrōnus,* defender, advocate < *pater,* father.] **—pa'tron•ness** *fem.n.*

pa•tron•age (pā'trə-nĭj, păt'rə-) *n.* **1.** Support from a patron. **2.** The trade of customers. **3.** Customers; clientele. **4.** The action of distributing governmental positions.

pa•tron•ize (pā'trə-nīz', păt'rə-) *v.* **-ized, -izing.** **1.** To act as a patron to. **2.** To treat condescendingly. **—pa'tron•iz'er** *n.*

pat•ro•nym•ic (păt'rə-nĭm'ĭk) *n.* A name received from a paternal ancestor, esp. one formed by a prefix or suffix. [< LL *patrōnymicus,* "derived from the name of a father."] **—pat'ro•nym'ic** *adj.*

pat•sy (păt'sē) *n., pl.* **-sies.** *Slang.* One who is cheated or victimized. [?]

pat•ter¹ (păt'ər) *v.* To make a quick succession of light taps. *—n.* A succession of quick, light taps. [Freq of PAT¹.]

pat•ter² (păt'ər) *v.* To chatter glibly or mumble mechanically. *—n.* **1.** The jargon of a particular group; cant. **2.** Glib, rapid speech. [ME *patren.*] **—pat'ter•er** *n.*

pat•tern (păt'ərn) *n.* **1.** An ideal worthy of imitation. **2.** A model to be followed in making things. **3.** A sample. **4.** Any artistic or decorative design. **5.** A composite of traits or characteristics. *—v.* To make by following a pattern. [< ML *patrōnus,* patron, "something to be imitated," pattern.]

pat•ty (păt'ē) *n., pl.* **-ties.** **1.** A small, flattened cake of chopped food. **2.** A small pie. [< OF *paste,* paste.]

pau•ci•ty (pô'sə-tē) *n.* Smallness of number or quantity. [< L *paucus,* little, few.]

Paul (pôl), **Saint.** A.D. 5?–67? Christian apostle. **—Paul'ine** (pô'līn') *adj.*

paunch (pônch, pänch) *n.* The belly, esp. a potbelly. [< L *pantex.*] **—paunch'y** *adj.*

pau•per (pô'pər) *n.* A very poor person, esp. one living on charity. [L, poor.] **—pau'per•ism'** (-pə-rĭz'əm) *n.* **—pau'per•i•za'tion** *n.* **—pau'per•ize'** *v.* **(-ized, -izing).**

pause (pôz) *v.* **paused, pausing.** To cease action for a time; linger or hesitate. *—n.* **1.** A temporary stop. **2.** A hesitation. **3.** A reason for hesitation: *give one pause.* [< Gk *pausis,* a stopping.]

pave (pāv) *v.* **paved, paving.** To cover with a hard, smooth surface that will bear travel. **—pave the way.** To make progress or development easier. [< L *pavīre,* to strike, stamp.] **—pav'er** *n.*

pave•ment (pāv'mənt) *n.* **1.** A hard, paved surface. **2.** The material used for such a surface.

pa•vil•ion (pə-vĭl'yən) *n.* **1.** An ornate tent. **2.** A temporary, often open structure, used at parks or fairs for amusement or shelter. **3.** An annex of a building. [< L *pāpiliō,* butterfly, tent.]

pav•ing (pā'vĭng) *n.* Pavement.

Pav•lov (păv'lôf', păv'lŏv'), **Ivan Petrovich.** 1849–1936. Russian physiologist.

paw (pô) *n.* **1.** The clawed foot of an animal, as a dog or cat. **2.** *Informal.* A human hand. *—v.* **1.** To strike, touch, or scrape with a paw or forefoot. **2.** To handle clumsily or rudely. [< OF *poue* < Gmc **pauta.*]

pawl (pôl) *n.* A hinged or pivoted device fit into a notch of a ratchet wheel to impart forward or prevent backward motion. [Du *pal.*]

pawn¹ (pôn) *n.* **1. Something given as security for a loan. 2. The condition of being held as security.** *—v.* **1. To give as security for money borrowed. 2. To risk; hazard; stake:** ***pawn one's honor.*** **[< OF** ***pan.*****]**

pawn² (pôn) *n.* **1.** A chessman of lowest value. **2.** One used to further the purposes of another. [< ML *pedō,* a foot soldier.]

pawn•bro•ker (pôn'brō'kər) *n.* One who lends money for personal property left as security.

Paw•nee (pô-nē') *n., pl.* **-nee** or **-nees.** **1.** A confederation of four Caddoan-speaking North American Plains Indian tribes in the region of Kansas and Nebraska. **2.** The lan-

guage or a member of this confederation.
pawn•shop (pôn'shŏp') *n.* The shop of a pawnbroker.
paw•paw. Variant of **papaw.**
pay (pā) *v.* **paid, paying 1.** To recompense for goods or services. **2.** To discharge (a debt or obligation). **3.** To requite. **4.** To yield as recompense. **5.** To be profitable or worthwhile. **6.** To give or bestow. **7.** To make (a visit or call). **—pay out. 1.** To expend or hand out (money). **2.** *p.t.* **payed out.** *Naut.* To let out (a line or cable) by slackening. **—pay up.** To pay in full. *—adj.* **1.** Requiring payment to operate. **2.** Yielding valuable metal in mining: *pay streak.* *—n.* **1.** Salary; wages. **2.** Recompense or reward. **3.** Paid employment. [< ML *pācāre,* to satisfy, pay.] **—pay'a•ble** *adj.* **—pay•ee'** (pā-ē') *n.* **—pay'er** *n.*
pay•check (pā'chĕk') *n.* A check to an employee in payment of his salary or wages.
pay dirt. Earth, ore, or gravel with a rich enough metal content to make mining profitable.
pay•load (pā'lōd') *n.* The significant part of a transported burden or cargo.
pay•mas•ter (pā'măs'tər, -mäs'tər) *n.* One in charge of paying wages.
pay•ment (pā'mənt) *n.* **1.** The act of paying. **2.** That which is paid.
pay off. 1. a. To pay the full amount owed. **b.** To requite. **2.** To pay the due wages and discharge. **3.** To bribe. **4.** To be profitable.
pay•off (pā'ôf', -ŏf') *n.* **1.** Full payment of a salary or wages. **2.** The climax of a sequence of events. **3.** A bribe.
pay•roll (pā'rōl') *n.* Also **pay roll. 1.** A list of employees and the wages due to each. **2.** The total sum of all these wages.
pay station. A coin-operated telephone.
Pb lead (L *plumbum*).
p.c. 1. after meals (L *post cibum*). **2.** per cent. **3.** petty cash. **4.** post card.
pct. per cent.
Pd palladium.
pd. paid.
p.d. per diem.
P.D. Police Department.
pe (pā) *n.* The 17th letter of the Hebrew alphabet, representing *p(ph).*
pea (pē) *n.* **1.** A vine cultivated for its round, edible green seeds enclosed in green pods. **2.** A seed of this plant. **3.** Any of several similar or related plants. [< Gk *pison,* a pea.]
peace (pēs) *n.* **1.** The absence of war or other hostilities. **2.** An agreement to end hostilities. **3.** Freedom from quarrels and disagreement. **4.** Public security. **5.** Calm; serenity: *peace of mind.* [< L *pāx.*] **—peace'a•ble** (pē'sə-bəl) *adj.* **—peace'ful** *adj.* **—peace'ful•ly** *adv.*
peace•mak•er (pēs'mā'kər) *n.* One who makes peace, esp. by settling disputes.
peace officer. A law officer, such as a sheriff, responsible for maintaining civil peace.
Peace River. A river of W Canada.
peace•time (pēs'tīm') *n.* A time of absence of war. **—peace'time'** *adj.*
peach (pēch) *n.* **1.** A sweet, juicy fruit with downy reddish or yellowish skin. **2.** A tree bearing such fruit. **3.** Light yellowish pink. [< L *persicum (mālum),* "Persian (apple)."]
pea•cock (pē'kŏk') *n.* The male of a large Asian bird, the **peafowl,** having brilliant blue or green plumage and long tail feathers with eyelike spots. [< L *pāvō,* peacock + COCK.]
pea green. Strong yellow green to moderate yellowish green. **—pea'-green'** *adj.*
peak (pēk) *n.* **1.** A pointed extremity. **2. a.** The pointed summit of a mountain. **b.** A mountain. **3.** The point of greatest development, value, or intensity. **4.** The highest value attained by a varying quantity. *—v.* **1.** To be formed into a peak or peaks. **2.** To achieve a maximum. [Prob < ME *pike,* summit.]
peak•ed (pē'kĭd) *adj.* Sickly, pale, or emaciated. **—peak'ed•ness** *n.*
peal (pēl) *n.* **1.** A ringing of bells. **2.** A set of tuned bells. **3.** A loud sound or series of sounds. *—v.* To ring or resound. [< ME *appel,* an appeal.]
pea•nut (pē'nŭt') *n.* **1.** A pealike vine bearing brittle-shelled pods that ripen underground. **2.** The pod or edible, nutlike seed of this vine.
pear (pâr) *n.* **1.** An edible fruit with a rounded base and a tapering stem end. **2.** A tree bearing such fruit. [< L *pirus,* pear tree, and *pirum,* pear.]
pearl (pûrl) *n.* **1.** A smooth, often rounded, lustrous deposit formed in the shells of certain oysters and other mollusks and valued as a gem. **2.** Mother-of-pearl. **3.** Something likened to a pearl in value. [< L *perna,* ham, sea-mussel.] **—pearl, pearl'y** *adj.*
peas•ant (pĕz'ənt) *n.* **1.** A member of the agricultural class, including farmers, laborers, etc. **2.** A countryman; rustic. **3.** An ill-bred person. [< ML *pāgēnsis,* "inhabitant of a district," peasant.] **—peas'ant•ry** *n.*
peat (pēt) *n.* Partially carbonized moss or other matter, found in bogs and used as fuel. [< ML *peta.*] **—peat'y** *adj.*
peb•ble (pĕb'əl) *n.* **1.** A small stone eroded smooth. **2. a.** Clear, colorless quartz; rock crystal. **b.** A lens made of such quartz. **3.** A crinkled surface, as on leather or paper. *—v.* **-bled, -bling. 1.** To pave or pelt with pebbles. **2.** To impart a rough, grainy surface to (leather or paper). [< OE *papol-,* pebble.] **—peb'bly** *adj.*
pe•can (pĭ-kän', -kăn') *n.* **1.** A smooth-shelled, oval, edible nut. **2.** A tree bearing such nuts. [< Algon.]
pec•ca•dil•lo (pĕk'ə-dĭl'ō) *n., pl.* **-loes** or **-los.** A minor offense. [< L *peccāre,* to sin.]
pec•ca•ry (pĕk'ə-rē) *n., pl.* **-ries.** A piglike tropical American mammal with long, dark bristles. [< Cariban *pakira.*]
pec•ca•vi (pĕ-kā'vī, -kä'vē) *n., pl.* **-vis.** A confession of sin. [L, "I have sinned."]
peck[1] (pĕk) *v.* **1.** To strike or form by striking with or as with the beak. **2.** To pick up with the beak. **3.** To kiss briefly and casually. *—n.* **1.** A stroke or mark made with the beak. **2.** A light, quick kiss. [ME *pecken.*]
peck[2] (pĕk) *n.* **1.** A U.S. Customary System unit of volume or capacity, used in dry measure, equal to 8 quarts or 537.605 cubic inches. **2.** A corresponding British Imperial System unit, used in dry and liquid measure, equal to 554.84 cubic inches. [< NF *pek.*]
pec•tin (pĕk'tĭn) *n.* Any of a group of complex colloidal substances of high molecular weight found in ripe fruits, such as apples, and used to jell various foods, drugs, and cosmetics. [< Gk *pēktikos,* coagulating.] **—pec'tic, pec'tin•ous** *adj.*
pec•to•ral (pĕk'tər-əl) *adj.* Of or pertaining to the breast or chest: *a pectoral muscle.* [< L *pectus (pector-),* breast.]
pec•u•late (pĕk'yə-lāt') *v.* **-lated, -lating.** To embezzle. [< L *pecūlium,* "wealth in cattle."] **—pec'u•la'tion** *n.* **—pec'u•la'tor** *n.*
pe•cu•liar (pĭ-kyōōl'yər) *adj.* **1.** Unusual or eccentric; odd. **2.** Distinct and particular. **3. a.** Exclusive. **b.** Belonging distinctively to one person or group. [< L *pecūliāris,* individual, peculiar, of private property.] **—pe•cu'li•ar'i•ty** (pĭ-kyōō'lē-ăr'ə-tē) *n.* **—pe•cu'liar•ly** *adv.*
pe•cu•ni•ar•y (pĭ-kyōō'nē-ĕr'ē) *adj.* Of or pertaining to money. [< L *pecūnia,* "wealth in cattle," money.]
-ped, -pede. *comb. form.* Foot or feet: **biped, centipede.** [L *pēs (ped-),* foot.]
ped•a•gogue (pĕd'ə-gŏg', -gôg') *n.* A schoolteacher. [< Gk *paidagōgos,* teacher, trainer (of boys).]
ped•a•go•gy (pĕd'ə-gō'jē, -gŏj'ē) *n.* The art, profession, or study of teaching. **—ped'a•gog'ic** (pĕd'ə-gŏj'ĭk, -gō'jĭk), **ped'a•gog'i•cal** (-ĭ-kəl) *adj.* **—ped'a•gog'i•cal•ly** *adv.*
ped•al (pĕd'l) *n.* **1.** A lever operated by the foot on various musical instruments, such as the piano, organ, or harp. **2.** A lever worked by the foot. *—adj.* Of or pertaining to a foot or footlike part: *the pedal extremities.* *—v.* **-aled** or **-alled, -aling** or **-alling. 1.** To use or operate a pedal or pedals. **2.** To ride a bicycle. [< L *pedālis,* of the foot.]
ped•ant (pĕd'ənt) *n.* **1.** One who stresses trivial details of learning. **2.** One who parades learning. **3.** *Archaic.* A schoolmaster. [< It *pedante.*] **—pe•dan'tic** (pə-dăn'tĭk) *adj.* **—ped'ant•ry** (pĕd'n-trē) *n.*
ped•dle (pĕd'l) *v.* **-dled, -dling.** To travel about selling (wares). [< ME *pedlere,* a peddler.] **—ped'dler** *n.*
-pede. Variant of **-ped.**
ped•er•as•ty (pĕd'ə-răs'tē) *n.* Sexual relations between a man and a boy. [< Gk *paiderastēs,* "a lover of boys."] **—ped'er•ast'** *n.*
ped•es•tal (pĕd'ə-stəl) *n.* **1.** A support or base, as for a column or statue. **2.** A position of esteem. [< OIt *pie di stallo,* "foot of a stall."]
pe•des•tri•an (pə-dĕs'trē-ən) *n.* One traveling on foot. *—adj.* **1.** Going or performed on foot. **2.** Commonplace; undistinguished. [< L *pedester,* going on foot, prosaic.]
pedi-. *comb. form.* Foot. [< L *pēs (ped-),* foot.]
pe•di•at•rics (pē'dē-ăt'rĭks) *n. (takes sing. v.).* The branch of medicine that deals with the care of infants and children and the treatment of their diseases. **—pe'di•at'ric** *adj.*
ped•i•cure (pĕd'ĭ-kyŏŏr') *n.* Cosmetic care or treatment of the feet and toenails. *—v.* **-cured, -curing.** To give a pedicure to.
ped•i•form (pĕd'ə-fôrm') *adj.* Shaped like a foot.
ped•i•gree (pĕd'ə-grē') *n.* **1.** Ancestry; lineage. **2.** A list or record of ancestors or descent, as of a purebred animal. [< OF *pie de grue,* "crane's foot" < the claw-shaped marks used in pedigrees.] **—ped'i•greed'** *adj.*
ped•i•ment (pĕd'ə-mənt) *n.* A wide, low-pitched gable surmounting the façade of a building in the Classical style. [Prob < a var of PYRAMID.]
pe•dom•e•ter (pĭ-dŏm'ə-tər) *n.* An instrument that gauges the approximate distance traveled on foot by registering the number of steps taken. [< PEDI- + -METER.]
peek (pēk) *v.* **1.** To glance quickly. **2.** To peer furtively. *—n.* A furtive or brief look.
peek•a•boo (pēk'ə-bōō') *n.* A child's game in which one suddenly exposes the face, exclaiming "peekaboo!"
peel (pēl) *n.* Skin or rind, esp. of a fruit. *—v.* **1.** To strip or cut away the skin, rind, or bark from; pare. **2.** To strip away; pull off (an outer covering). **3.** To come off in thin strips or pieces. [< OF *peler.*] **—peel'er** *n.*
peel•ing (pē'lĭng) *n.* A peeled-off piece or strip of skin or rind.

peen (pēn) *n.* The end of a hammerhead opposite the flat striking surface, often wedge-shaped or ball-shaped. [?]

peep¹ (pēp) *v.* To utter a short, high-pitched sound, as of a baby bird. —*n.* **1.** A weak, shrill sound. **2.** Any slight utterance.

peep² (pēp) *v.* **1.** To peek furtively, as through a small aperture. **2.** To become visible gradually. —*n.* **1.** A quick or furtive look. **2.** A first glimpse or appearance.

peep•hole (pēp'hōl') *n.* A small hole through which one may peep.

peer¹ (pîr) *v.* **1.** To look intently. **2.** To be partially visible. [Perh contraction of APPEAR.]

peer² (pîr) *n.* **1.** One who has equal standing with another. **2.** A member of the British peerage; a duke, marquis, earl, viscount, or baron. [< OF *per,* equal.] —**peer'age** *n.* —**peer'ess** *fem.n.*

peer•less (pîr'lĭs) *adj.* Without peer; unmatched. —**peer'less•ly** *adv.*

peeve (pēv) *v.* **peeved, peeving.** To annoy or vex. —*n.* **1.** A vexation; grievance. **2.** A resentful mood. [Back-formation < PEEVISH.]

pee•vish (pē'vĭsh) *adj.* Querulous; irritable. [Perh < F *pervers,* perverse.] —**pee'vish•ly** *adv.* —**pee'vish•ness** *n.*

pee•wee (pē'wē) *n.* One that is noticeably small. —**pee'wee** *adj.*

peg (pĕg) *n.* **1.** A small cylindrical pin, as of wood, used to fasten things. **2.** A projection used as a support or as a boundary marker. **3.** A degree or notch. **4.** A pretext or occasion for. —*v.* **pegged, pegging. 1.** To put or insert a peg into. **2.** To mark with pegs. **3.** To stabilize prices. **4.** To throw. **5.** To work steadily. [ME *pegge.*]

peg leg. *Informal.* An artificial leg.

pei•gnoir (pān-wär', pĕn-) *n.* A woman's loose-fitting dressing gown. [F, "garment worn while combing the hair."]

pe•jor•a•tive (pĭ-jôr'ə-tĭv, -jŏr'ə-tĭv, pĕj'ə-rā'-tĭv, pē'jə-) *adj.* Tending to make or become worse; disparaging; downgrading. —*n.* A pejorative word. [< L *pējor,* worse.] —**pe•jor'a•tive•ly** *adv.*

Pe•king (pē'kĭng'). The capital of the People's Republic of China. Pop. 5,420,000.

Pe•king•ese (pē'kĭng-ēz', -ēs') *n., pl.* **-ese.** Also **Pe•kin•ese** (pē'kə-nēz', -nēs'). **1.** A resident or native of Peking, China. **2.** (pē'kə-nēz', -nēs'). A small, short-legged, long-haired dog with a flat nose. —**Pe'king•ese'** *adj.*

pe•koe (pē'kō, pĕk'ō) *n.* Black tea made from relatively small leaves. [Chin (Amoy) *peh ho.*]

pel•age (pĕl'ĭj) *n.* The hairy, furry, or woolly coat of an animal. [< L *pilus,* hair.]

pe•lag•ic (pə-lăj'ĭk) *adj.* Of open oceans or seas. [< Gk *pelagos,* sea.]

pelf (pĕlf) *n.* Wealth or riches. [< OF *pelfre,* booty.]

pel•i•can (pĕl'ĭ-kən) *n.* A large, web-footed bird with a large pouch under the lower bill, used for catching fish. [< Gk *pelekan, pelekinos.*]

pel•lag•ra (pə-lăg'rə, -lā'grə, -lä'grə) *n.* A chronic niacin deficiency disease, marked by skin eruptions and digestive and nervous disturbances. [< L *pellis,* skin + Gk *agra,* seizure.] —**pel•lag'rous** *adj.*

pel•let (pĕl'ĭt) *n.* **1.** A small, solid or densely packed ball or mass, as of medicine. **2.** A bullet or piece of small shot. —*v.* To strike with pellets. [< L *pila,* ball, pill.]

pell-mell (pĕl'mĕl') *adv.* Also **pell•mell. 1.** In a confused manner. **2.** In disorderly haste; headlong. [F *pêle-mêle.*]

pel•lu•cid (pə-lo͞o'sĭd) *adj.* **1.** Admitting the maximum passage of light; transparent; translucent. **2.** Clear. [< L *pellūcēre,* to shine through.] —**pel•lu'cid•ly** *adv.*

pelt¹ (pĕlt) *n.* An animal skin, esp. with the fur or hair still on it. [ME.]

pelt² (pĕlt) *v.* To strike repeatedly with or as with blows or missiles. [ME *pelten.*]

pel•vis (pĕl'vĭs) *n., pl.* **-vises** or **-ves** (-vēz'). A basin-shaped skeletal structure that rests on the lower limbs and supports the spinal column. [< L *pēlvis,* basin.] —**pel'vic** *adj.*

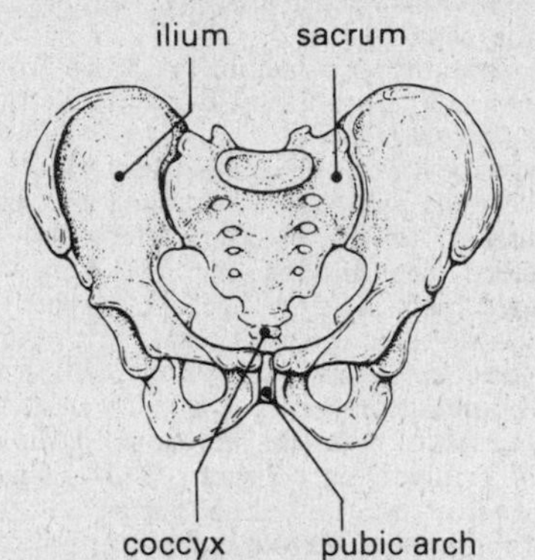

pelvis
Male pelvis

pem•mi•can (pĕm'ĭ-kən) *n.* A food prepared from dried meat pounded into paste and mixed with fat. [< Algon.]

pen¹ (pĕn) *n.* An instrument for writing or drawing with ink. —*v.* **penned, penning.** To write. [< L *penna,* feather.]

pen² (pĕn) *n.* A small fenced enclosure, as for animals. —*v.* **penned** or **pent, penning.** To confine in or as in a pen. [< OE *penn.* See **bend-.**]

pen. peninsula.

pe•nal (pē'nəl) *adj.* Of or pertaining to punishment, esp. for breaking the law. [< L *poena,* penalty.] —**pe'nal•ly** *adv.*

pe•nal•ize (pē'nəl-īz', pĕn'əl-) *v.* **-ized, -izing.** To subject to a penalty.

pen•al•ty (pĕn'əl-tē) *n., pl.* **-ties. 1.** A punishment for a crime or offense. **2.** Something required as a forfeit for an offense. **3.** A punishment, handicap, or disadvantage imposed for some action.

pen•ance (pĕn'əns) *n.* **1.** An act of contrition. **2.** *Eccles.* A sacrament that includes contrition, confession to a priest, acceptance of punishment, and absolution. [< L *paenitēns,* penitent.]

pe•na•tes (pə-nā'tēz, -nä'tēz) *pl.n.* See **lares and penates.**

pence. *Brit.* Alternate *pl.* of **penny:** *twopence.*

pen•chant (pĕn'chənt) *n.* A strong inclination or liking. [< F *pencher,* to incline.]

pen•cil (pĕn'səl) *n.* A writing implement consisting of a thin rod of graphite or similar substance encased in wood or held in a plastic or metal mechanical device. —*v.* **-ciled** or **-cilled, -ciling** or **-cilling.** To write, draw, or mark with a pencil. [< L *pēnicillus,* a brush, pencil.] —**pen'cil•er** *n.*

pen•dant (pĕn'dənt) *n.* Something suspended from something else, esp. an ornament. [< L *pendēre,* to hang.]

pen•dent (pĕn'dənt) *adj.* Also **pen•dant.** Hanging down; dangling; suspended. [< L *pendēre,* to hang.] —**pen'dent•ly** *adv.*

pend•ing (pĕn'dĭng) *adj.* **1.** Not yet decided or settled. **2.** Impending. —*prep.* **1.** During. **2.** While awaiting; until. [< OF *pendant,* "hanging."]

pen•du•lar (pĕn'jo͝o-lər, pĕn'dyə-) *adj.* Of or resembling the motion of a pendulum; swinging back and forth.

pen•du•lous (pĕn'jo͝o-ləs, pĕn'dyə-) *adj.* Hanging loosely. [< L *pendēre,* to hang.]

pen•du•lum (pĕn'jo͝o-ləm, pĕn'dyə-, pĕn'də-) *n.* A mass suspended so that it is free to swing in a vertical plane under the influence of gravitational force only. [< L *pendēre,* to hang.]

Pe•nel•o•pe (pə-nĕl'ə-pē). The faithful wife of Odysseus in Homer's *Odyssey.*

pe•nes. Alternate *pl.* of **penis.**

pen•e•tra•ble (pĕn'ə-trə-bəl) *adj.* Capable of being penetrated. —**pen'e•tra•bil'i•ty** *n.*

pen•e•trate (pĕn'ə-trāt') *v.* **-trated, -trating. 1.** To enter into; pierce. **2.** To permeate. **3.** To grasp the meaning of; understand. **4.** To see through. **5.** To affect deeply. [< L *penus,* the interior of a house.] —**pen'e•tra'tion** (pĕn'ə-trā'shən) *n.*

pen•e•trat•ing (pĕn'ə-trā'tĭng) *adj.* **1.** Piercing. **2.** Keenly perceptive; discerning: *penetrating insight.* —**pen'e•trat'ing•ly** *adv.*

pen•e•tra•tive (pĕn'ə-trā'tĭv) *adj.* Capable of penetrating; piercing.

pen•guin (pĕn'gwĭn, pĕng'gwĭn) *n.* A flightless sea bird of cool regions of the S Hemisphere, having flipperlike wings and webbed feet. [Perh < W *pen gwyn.*]

pen•i•cil•lin (pĕn'ə-sĭl'ĭn) *n.* Any of several antibiotic compounds obtained from certain molds or produced synthetically, and used to treat a wide variety of diseases and infections.

pen•in•su•la (pə-nĭn's/y/ə-lə) *n.* A long projection of land into water. [L *pēninsula.*] —**pen•in'su•lar** *adj.*

pe•nis (pē'nĭs) *n., pl.* **-nises** or **-nes** (-nēz'). The male organ of copulation, esp. in higher vertebrates. [L *pēnis,* tail, penis.]

pen•i•tent (pĕn'ə-tənt) *adj.* Repentant of misdeeds or sins. [< L *paenitēre,* to repent.] —**pen'i•tence** *n.* —**pen'i•ten'tial** (pĕn'ə-tĕn'shəl) *adj.* —**pen'i•tent•ly** *adv.*

pen•i•ten•tia•ry (pĕn'ə-tĕn'shə-rē) *n., pl.* **-ries.** A prison for those convicted of major crimes. —*adj.* Of, pertaining to, or incurring imprisonment in a penitentiary. [< L *paenitēns,* penitent.]

pen•knife (pĕn'nīf') *n.* A small pocketknife.

pen•man (pĕn'mən) *n.* **1.** A copyist. **2.** An expert in penmanship. **3.** An author.

pen•man•ship (pĕn'mən-shĭp') *n.* The skill or style of handwriting.

Penn (pĕn), **William.** 1644–1718. English Quaker leader; founder of Pennsylvania (1681).

Penn., Penna. Pennsylvania (unofficial).

pen name. A literary pseudonym.

pen•nant (pĕn'ənt) *n.* **1.** A long narrow flag, as one used for signaling. **2.** Such a flag as a symbol of championship. [Blend of PENDANT and PENNON.]

pen•ni•less (pĕn'ē-lĭs, -ə-lĭs) *adj.* Without money. —**pen'ni•less•ness** *n.*

pen•non (pĕn'ən) *n.* A long, narrow banner borne on a lance. [< OF *penne,* feather, wing.]

Penn•syl•va•nia (pĕn'səl-vān'yə, -vā'nē-ə). A state of the E U.S. Pop. 11,794,000. Cap. Harrisburg.

Penn•syl•va•nian (pĕn'səl-vān'yən, -vā'nē-ən) *adj.* **1.** Of or pertaining to the state of Pennsylvania. **2.** Of or belonging to the geologic time, system of rocks, or sedimentary deposits of the sixth period of the Paleozoic era. —*n.* **1.** A native of Pennsylvania. **2.** The Pennsylvanian period.

pen•ny (pĕn'ē) *n., pl.* **-nies. 1.** A coin of the U.S. and Canada, the cent. **2.** *pl.* **-nies** or **pence** (pĕns). **a.** A subdivision of the pound of the United Kingdom. After 1971, it will equal 1/100 of the pound. **b.** A subdivision of the pound of Gambia, the Republic of Ireland, Jamaica, Malawi, Malta, Nigeria, Rhodesia, and various dependent territories of the United Kingdom. [< OE *penig, penning* < Gmc **panninga.*]

pen•ny•roy•al (pĕn'ē-roi'əl) *n.* An aromatic plant with hairy leaves and small bluish flowers.

pen•ny•weight (pĕn'ē-wāt') *n.* A unit of troy weight equal to 1/20 of a troy ounce or approx. 1.555 grams.

pe•nol•o•gy (pē-nŏl'ə-jē) *n.* The theory and practice of prison management and criminal rehabilitation. [L *poena,* penalty + -LOGY.]

pen•sion (pĕn'shən) *n.* A sum of money paid regularly, esp. as a retirement benefit. —*v.* To give a pension to. [< L *pēnsiō,* payment.] **—pen'sion•er** *n.*

pen•sive (pĕn'sĭv) *adj.* Wistfully or sadly thoughtful. [< OF *penser,* to think.] **—pen'sive•ly** *adv.* **—pen'sive•ness** *n.*

pent (pĕnt). Alternate *p.t.* & *p.p.* of **pen²**. —*adj.* Penned or shut up; closely confined.

penta–. *comb. form.* Five. [< Gk *pente,* five.]

pen•ta•cle (pĕn'tə-kəl) *n.* A five-pointed star formed by five straight lines connecting the vertices of a pentagon.

pen•ta•gon (pĕn'tə-gŏn') *n.* A polygon having five sides. **—pen•tag'o•nal** (pĕn-tăg'ə-nəl) *adj.*

pen•tam•e•ter (pĕn-tăm'ə-tər) *n.* A line of verse composed of five metrical feet.

Pen•ta•teuch (pĕn'tə-t/y/o͞ok') *n.* The first five books of the Bible: Genesis, Exodus, Leviticus, Numbers, and Deuteronomy. See **Bible. —Pen'ta•teuch'al** *adj.*

Pen•te•cost (pĕn'tĭ-kôst', -kŏst') *n.* A church festival occurring on the 7th Sunday after Easter, to celebrate the descent of the Holy Ghost upon the disciples; Whitsunday. [< Gk *pentēkostē (hēmera),* the 50th day (after the Resurrection).] **—Pen'te•cos'tal** *adj.*

pent•house (pĕnt'hous') *n.* An apartment situated on the roof of a building. [< ML *appenticium,* appendage.]

pe•nul•ti•mate (pĭ-nŭl'tə-mĭt) *adj.* Next to last. [< L *paenultimus,* last but one.]

pe•nu•ri•ous (pə-n/y/o͝or'ē-əs) *adj.* Miserly; stingy. **—pe•nu'ri•ous•ness** *n.*

pen•u•ry (pĕn'yə-rē) *n.* Extreme poverty. [< L *paenūria,* scarcity.]

Pe•nu•ti•an (pə-no͞o'tē-ən, -shən) *n.* A family or phylum of North American Indian languages of Pacific coastal areas.

pe•on (pē'ŏn', pē'ən) *n.* **1.** A laborer of Latin America or the SW U.S. **2.** One bound in servitude to a creditor. [< ML *pedo,* a foot soldier.] **—pe'on•age** (-ə-nĭj) *n.*

pe•o•ny (pē'ə-nē) *n., pl.* **-nies.** A garden plant with large pink, red, or white flowers. [< Gk *paiōnia.*]

peo•ple (pē'pəl) *n., pl.* **-ple. 1.** *pl.* **-ples** (only form for sense 1). A body of persons of the same country, culture, etc. **2. a.** The mass of ordinary persons; populace. **b.** The electorate. **3.** Persons loyal to a superior. **4.** One's relatives. **5.** Human beings. —*v.* **-pled, -pling.** To populate. [< L *populus.*]

pep (pĕp) *Informal. n.* Energy; vim. —*v.* **pepped, pepping. —pep up.** To invigorate. [Short for PEPPER.] **—pep'py** *adj.*

pep•per (pĕp'ər) *n.* **1. a.** The small, pungent berry of a tropical Asian vine, used ground or whole as a condiment. **b.** The vine itself. **2. a.** The podlike or bell-shaped fruit of several related bushy plants, having a mild to pungent flavor and used as a vegetable or condiment. **b.** A plant bearing such fruit. —*v.* **1.** To season or sprinkle with or as with pepper. **2.** To pelt with numerous small missiles. [< Gk *peperi* < Sk *pippalī,* berry.]

pep•per•corn (pĕp'ər-kôrn') *n.* A dried berry of the pepper vine.

pep•per•mint (pĕp'ər-mĭnt') *n.* **1.** An aromatic plant yielding a pungent oil. **2.** A candy with this flavoring.

pep•per•y (pĕp'ə-rē) *adj.* **-ier, -iest. 1.** Of, like, or containing pepper; pungent. **2.** Sharp-tempered; touchy. **3.** Vivid; fiery: *a peppery speech.* **—pep'per•i•ness** *n.*

pep•sin (pĕp'sĭn) *n.* A digestive enzyme found in gastric juice. [< Gk *pepsis,* digestion.]

pep•tic (pĕp'tĭk) *adj.* **1. a.** Of or assisting digestion: *peptic secretion.* **b.** Of or associated with the action of digestive secretions: *peptic ulcer.* **2.** Of or involving pepsin. [< Gk *peptein,* to digest.]

per (pûr) *prep.* **1.** Through; by means of. **2.** To, for, or by each. **3.** According to. [L.]

per–. *comb. form. Chem.* A compound that includes an element in its highest oxidation state. [< L *per,* through, by, away.]

per. period.

per•ad•ven•ture (pûr'əd-vĕn'chər, pĕr'-) *adv. Archaic.* Perhaps.

per•am•bu•late (pə-răm'byə-lāt') *v.* **-lated, -lating.** To walk about; stroll. [L *perambulāre.*] **—per•am'bu•la'tion** *n.*

per•am•bu•la•tor (pə-răm'byə-lā'tər) *n. Chiefly Brit.* A baby carriage.

per an•num (ăn'əm). By the year; annually. [L.]

per•cale (pər-kāl') *n.* A close-woven cotton fabric used esp. to make sheets. [< Pers *pargālah.*]

per cap•i•ta (kăp'ə-tə). Per person. [L, "by heads."]

per•ceive (pər-sēv') *v.* **-ceived, -ceiving. 1.** To become aware of through the senses. **2.** To observe; detect. **3.** To achieve understanding of. [< L *percipere,* "to seize wholly."]

per cent. Also **per•cent** (pər-sĕnt'). Per hundred; for or out of each hundred. [< L *per centum,* by the hundred.]

per•cent•age (pər-sĕn'tĭj) *n.* **1.** A fraction or ratio with 100 fixed and understood as the denominator. **2.** A proportion or share in relation to a whole.

per•cen•tile (pər-sĕn'tīl') *n. Stat.* A number that divides the range of a set of data so that a given percentage lies below this number.

per•cept (pûr'sĕpt') *n.* An impression in the mind of something perceived by the senses. [Back-formation < PERCEPTION.]

per•cep•ti•ble (pər-sĕp'tə-bəl) *adj.* Capable of being perceived. **—per•cep'ti•bly** *adv.*

per•cep•tion (pər-sĕp'shən) *n.* **1.** The act or result of perceiving. **2.** Awareness; discernment; insight. [< L *percipere,* PERCEIVE.]

per•cep•tive (pər-sĕp'tĭv) *adj.* **1.** Of or pertaining to perception. **2.** Having the ability to perceive; discerning.

per•cep•tu•al (pər-sĕp'cho͞o-əl) *adj.* Of, based on, or involving perception. **—per•cep'tu•al•ly** *adv.*

perch¹ (pûrch) *n.* **1.** A rod or branch serving as a roost for a bird. **2.** A place for resting or sitting. —*v.* To alight or rest on a perch. [< L *pertica,* stick.]

perch² (pûrch) *n., pl.* **perch** or **perches. 1.** A freshwater food fish. **2.** Any of various related or similar fishes. [< Gk *perkē.*]

per•chance (pər-chăns', -chäns') *adv.* Perhaps.

per•co•late (pûr'kə-lāt') *v.* **-lated, -lating. 1.** To cause (fluid) to pass through a porous substance; filter. **2.** To pass or ooze through. **3.** To make (coffee) in a percolator. [L *percōlāre.*] **—per'co•la'tion** *n.*

per•co•la•tor (pûr'kə-lā'tər) *n.* A coffeepot in which boiling water is forced up through a center tube to filter through ground coffee.

per•cus•sion (pər-kŭsh'ən) *n.* **1.** The striking together of two bodies, esp. when noise is produced. **2.** The act of detonating a cap in a firearm. **3.** Musical percussion instruments collectively. [< L *percutere* (pp *percussus*), to strike hard.]

percussion instrument. A musical instrument in which sound is produced by striking.

per di•em (dē'əm, dī'əm). Per day. [L.]

per•di•tion (pər-dĭsh'ən) *n.* **1.** Eternal damnation. **2.** Hell. [< L *perdere,* to destroy, lose.]

per•e•gri•nate (pĕr'ə-grə-nāt') *v.* **-nated, -nating.** To travel from place to place. [L *peregrīnārī,* to travel in foreign lands.] **—per'e•gri•na'tion** *n.*

per•emp•to•ry (pə-rĕmp'tə-rē) *adj.* **1.** *Law.* Precluding further debate or action. **2.** Not admitting denial; imperative. **3.** Expressing a command; urgent. **4.** Dictatorial; imperious. [LL *peremptōrius,* "precluding debate," decisive.] **—per•emp'to•ri•ly** *adv.*

per•en•ni•al (pə-rĕn'ē-əl) *adj.* **1.** Lasting through a year or many years. **2. a.** Everlasting; perpetual. **b.** Continually recurring. **3.** *Bot.* Having a life span of more than two years. —*n.* A perennial plant. [< L *perennis.*] **—per•en'ni•al•ly** *adv.*

perf. **1.** perfect. **2.** perforated.

per•fect (pûr'fĭkt) *adj.* **1.** Without defect; flawless. **2.** Accurate; exact. **3.** Complete; utter. **4.** Excellent in all respects. **5.** *Gram.* Of, pertaining to, or constituting a verb tense expressing completed past action. —*n. Gram.* **1.** The perfect tense. **2.** A verb or verb form in this tense. —*v.* (pər-fĕkt'). To bring to perfection. [< L *perficere,* to complete.] **—per•fect'er** *n.* **—per'fect•ly** *adv.*

per•fec•tion (pər-fĕk'shən) *n.* **1.** The state or quality of being perfect. **2.** The act of perfecting. **3.** A person or thing that perfectly embodies something.

per•fec•tion•ism (pər-fĕk'shə-nĭz'əm) *n.* A propensity for setting extremely high standards and being displeased with anything less. **—per•fec'tion•ist** *n.*

per•fi•dy (pûr'fə-dē) *n., pl.* **-dies.** Deliberate breach of faith; treachery. [< L *perfidus,* treacherous.] **—per•fid'i•ous** (pər-fĭd'ē-əs) *adj.*

per•fo•rate (pûr'fə-rāt') *v.* **-rated, -rating. 1.** To pierce, punch, or bore a hole or holes in. **2.** To pierce or stamp with rows of holes to allow easy separation. [L *perforāre.*] **—per'fo•ra'tion** *n.* **—per'fo•ra'tor** *n.*

per•force (pər-fôrs', -fōrs') *adv.* By necessity.

per•form (pər-fôrm') *v.* **1.** To carry out (an action); function. **2.** To fulfill, as a duty or obligation. **3.** To give a public presentation, as of a dramatic work or musical composition. [< OF *parfornir.*] **—per•form'er** *n.*

per•form•ance (pər-fôr'məns) *n.* **1.** The act or manner of performing. **2.** A presentation before an audience. **3.** A deed; feat.

per•fume (pûr'fyo͞om', pər-fyo͞om') *n.* **1.** A fragrant volatile liquid, as one distilled from flowers. **2.** Any pleasing odor. *—v.* (pər-fyo͞om') **-fumed, -fuming.** To impart a pleasant odor to. [< OIt *parfumare,* to smoke through.]

per•fum•er•y (pər-fyo͞o'mə-rē) *n., pl.* **-ies. 1.** Perfumes in general. **2.** An establishment that makes or sells perfume.

per•func•to•ry (pər-fŭngk'tə-rē) *adj.* Done or acting routinely and with little interest or care. [< L *perfungī,* "to get through with."] **—per•func'to•ri•ly** *adv.* **—per•func'to•ri•ness** *n.*

per•go•la (pûr'gə-lə) *n.* An arbor or passageway with a roof of latticework. [< L *pergula.*]

per•haps (pər-hăps') *adv.* Maybe; possibly. [PER + HAP (chance).]

peri–. *comb. form.* **1.** About, around, encircling, or enclosing. **2.** Close at hand; adjacent. [< Gk *peri,* about, near, around.]

Per•i•cles (pĕr'ə-klēz'). 495?–429 B.C. Athenian statesman, orator, and general.

Pericles

per•i•gee (pĕr'ə-jē) *n.* The point nearest the earth in the orbit of the moon or a satellite. [< Gk *perigeios,* near the earth.]

per•i•he•li•on (pĕr'ə-hē'lē-ən, -hēl'yən) *n., pl.* **-helia** (-hē'lē-ə, -hēl'yə). The point nearest the sun in the orbit of a planet or other body.

per•il (pĕr'əl) *n.* **1.** A condition of imminent danger. **2.** Something that endangers. [< L *periculum,* trial, danger.] **—per'il•ous** *adj.* **—per'il•ous•ly** *adv.*

pe•rim•e•ter (pə-rĭm'ə-tər) *n.* **1.** A closed curve bounding a plane area. **2.** The length of such a boundary.

pe•ri•od (pîr'ē-əd) *n.* **1.** An interval of time characterized by the occurrence or prevalence of certain conditions or events. **2.** A unit of geologic time longer than an epoch and shorter than an era. **3.** An interval regarded as a developmental phase; stage. **4.** Any of various arbitrary temporal units, as of an academic day. **5.** An instance of menstruation. **6.** A point or portion of time at which something is ended; completion. **7.** A punctuation mark (.) indicating a full stop and placed esp. at the end of sentences. *—adj.* Of a certain historical age or time: *a period piece.* [< Gk *periodos,* circuit, rhetorical period.]

pe•ri•od•ic (pîr'ē-ŏd'ĭk) *adj.* **1.** Having periods or repeated cycles. **2.** Happening or appearing at regular intervals. **3.** Taking place now and then; intermittent. **—pe'ri•od'i•cal•ly** *adv.* **—pe'ri•o•dic'i•ty** (-ə-dĭs'ə-tē) *n.*

pe•ri•od•i•cal (pîr'ē-ŏd'ĭ-kəl) *adj.* **1.** Periodic. **2. a.** Published at regular intervals of more than one day. **b.** Of or pertaining to a publication issued at such intervals. *—n.* A periodical publication.

per•i•o•don•tal (pĕr'ē-ō-dŏnt'l) *adj.* Of or designating tissue and structures that surround and support the teeth.

per•i•pa•tet•ic (pĕr'ə-pə-tĕt'ĭk) *adj.* **1.** Walking about from place to place. **2.** Carried on while walking about. [< Gk *peripatein,* to walk about while teaching.]

pe•riph•er•al (pə-rĭf'ər-əl) *adj.* **1.** Of or on the periphery. **2.** Relatively unimportant. **—pe•riph'er•al•ly** *adv.*

pe•riph•er•y (pə-rĭf'ə-rē) *n., pl.* **-ies. 1.** The outermost region within a precise boundary. **2.** The region immediately beyond a precise boundary. **3.** A zone constituting an imprecise boundary. **4.** Perimeter. [< Gk *peripherein,* to carry around.]

per•i•scope (pĕr'ə-skōp') *n.* Any of various optical instruments that permit observation from a position displaced from a direct line of sight.

per•ish (pĕr'ĭsh) *v.* **1.** To die, esp. in a violent or untimely manner. **2.** To disappear gradually. [< L *perīre,* to pass away.]

per•ish•a•ble (pĕr'ĭsh-ə-bəl) *adj.* Easily destroyed or spoiled. **—per'ish•a•bly** *adv.*

per•i•stal•sis (pĕr'ə-stôl'sĭs, -stăl'sĭs) *n., pl.* **-ses** (-sēz'). Wavelike muscular contractions that propel contained matter along the tubular organs, as in the alimentary canal. [< Gk *peristellein,* to wrap around.] **—per'i•stal'tic** (-stôl'tĭk, -stăl'tĭk) *adj.*

per•i•to•ne•um (pĕr'ə-tə-nē'əm) *n., pl.* **-nea** (-nē'ə). Also **per•i•to•nae•um.** The membrane lining the walls of the abdominal cavity. [< Gk *peritonaios,* stretched across.] **—per'i•to•ne'al** *adj.*

per•i•to•ni•tis (pĕr'ə-tə-nī'tĭs) *n.* Inflammation of the peritoneum.

per•i•wig (pĕr'ĭ-wĭg') *n.* A wig. [< OF *perruque.*]

per•i•win•kle¹ (pĕr'ĭ-wĭng'kəl) *n.* A small, edible marine snail with a cone-shaped shell. [Prob < L *pina,* a mussel + OE *-wincel,* snail shell (see **weng-**).]

per•i•win•kle² (pĕr'ĭ-wĭng'kəl) *n.* A trailing blue-flowered myrtle. [< L *pervinca.*]

per•jure (pûr'jər) *v.* **-jured, -juring.** To testify falsely and deliberately under oath. [< L *perjūrāre.*] **—per'jur•er** *n.* **—per'ju•ry** *n.*

perk (pûrk) *v.* **1.** To raise, as the head, smartly and quickly. **2.** To make or become vigorous and lively again (with *up*). [< NF *perquer,* to perch.] **—perk'i•ness** *n.* **—perk'y** *adj.*

perm. permanent.

per•ma•frost (pûr'mə-frôst', -frŏst') *n.* Permanently frozen subsoil in frigid areas.

per•ma•nent (pûr'mə-nənt) *adj.* Fixed and lasting. *—n.* A long-lasting hair setting. [< L *permanēre,* to remain throughout.] **—per'ma•nence** *n.* **—per'ma•nen•cy** *n.* **—per'ma•nent•ly** *adv.*

per•me•a•ble (pûr'mē-ə-bəl) *adj.* Capable of being permeated. **—per'me•a•bly** *adv.*

per•me•ate (pûr'mē-āt') *v.* **-ated, -ating. 1.** To pervade. **2.** To pass through the openings or interstices of. [L *permeāre.*] **—per'me•a'tion** *n.*

Per•mi•an (pûr'mē-ən, pĕr'-) *adj.* Of or belonging to the geologic time, system of rocks, or sedimentary deposits of the seventh and last period of the Paleozoic era. *—n.* The Permian period. [< *Perm,* former Russian province.]

per•mis•si•ble (pər-mĭs'ə-bəl) *adj.* That can be permitted; allowable.

per•mis•sion (pər-mĭsh'ən) *n.* Consent, esp. formal consent.

per•mis•sive (pər-mĭs'ĭv) *adj.* **1.** Granting permission. **2.** Lenient; tolerant.

per•mit (pər-mĭt') *v.* **-mitted, -mitting. 1.** To allow; consent to. **2.** To afford opportunity to. *—n.* (pûr'mĭt, pər-mĭt'). A document granting permission. [L *permittere.*]

per•mu•ta•tion (pûr'myo͞o-tā'shən) *n.* **1.** A transformation. **2.** The act of altering a given set of objects in a group. **3.** *Math.* An ordered arrangement of all or some of the elements of a set.

per•ni•cious (pər-nĭsh'əs) *adj.* Destructive or deadly. [< L *perniciēs,* destruction.]

per•o•ra•tion (pĕr'ə-rā'shən) *n.* The formal recapitulation at the end of a speech. [< L *perōrāre,* to harangue at length.]

per•ox•ide (pə-rŏk'sīd') *n.* **1. Hydrogen peroxide. 2.** Any compound containing oxygen that yields hydrogen peroxide with an acid, such as sodium peroxide, Na_2O_2.

per•pen•dic•u•lar (pûr'pən-dĭk'yə-lər) *adj.* **1.** Intersecting at or forming right angles. **2.** At right angles to the horizontal; vertical. [< L *perpendiculum,* plumb line.] **—per'pen•dic'u•lar** *n.* **—per'pen•dic'u•lar•ly** *adv.*

per•pe•trate (pûr'pə-trāt') *v.* **-trated, -trating. 1.** To be guilty of; commit. **2.** To carry out; perform. [L *perpetrāre,* to accomplish.] **—per'pe•tra'tion** *n.* **—per'pe•tra'tor** (-trā'tər) *n.*

per•pet•u•al (pər-pĕch'o͞o-əl) *adj.* **1.** Lasting for eternity. **2.** Lasting for an indefinitely long duration. **3.** Ceaselessly repeated. [< L *perpetuus,* continuous, permanent.] **—per•pet'u•al•ly** *adv.* **—per•pet'u•al•ness** *n.*

per•pet•u•ate (pər-pĕch'o͞o-āt') *v.* **-ated, -ating. 1.** To make perpetual. **2.** To prolong the existence of. **—per•pet'u•a'tion** *n.*

per•pe•tu•i•ty (pûr'pə-t/y/o͞o'ə-tē) *n., pl.* **-ties.** The quality or condition of being perpetual.

per•plex (pər-plĕks') *v.* To confuse or puzzle; bewilder. [< L *perplexus,* intricate.] **—per•plex'i•ty** *n.*

per•qui•site (pûr'kwə-zĭt) *n.* **1.** A payment or profit received in addition to a regular wage or salary. **2.** Something claimed as an exclusive right. [< L *perquīrere,* to search for.]

Pers. Persia; Persian.

per se (sā', sē'). In or by itself; intrinsically. [L *per sē.*]

per•se•cute (pûr'sə-kyo͞ot') *v.* **-cuted, -cuting. 1.** To oppress or harass with ill-treatment. **2.** To annoy persistently. [< L *persequī,* to pursue.] **—per'se•cu'tion** *n.* **—per'se•cu'tor** (-kyo͞o'tər) *n.*

per•se•vere (pûr'sə-vîr') *v.* **-vered, -vering.** To persist in or remain constant to a purpose, idea, or task in the face of obstacles. [< L *persevērus,* very serious.] **—per'se•ver'ance** *n.*

Per•sia (pûr'zhə). The former name for Iran.

Per•sian (pûr'zhən) *n.* **1.** A native or inhabitant of ancient Persia or modern Iran. **2.** The Iranian language of the Persians. **—Per'sian** *adj.*

Persian Gulf. An inlet of the Arabian Sea between the Arabian Peninsula and Iran.

Persian lamb. The glossy, tightly curled fur of a young lamb of the karakul sheep.

per•sim•mon (pər-sĭm'ən) *n.* **1.** A tree with hard wood and orange-red, edible fruit. **2.** The fruit of such a tree. [< Algon.]

per•sist (pər-sĭst', -zĭst') *v.* **1.** To hold firmly and steadfastly to some purpose or undertaking, despite obstacles. **2.** To continue in existence. [L *persistere.*] **—per•sist'ence** *n.* **—per•sist'ent** *adj.* **—per•sist'ent•ly** *adv.*

per•snick•e•ty (pər-snĭk'ə-tē) *adj.* Fastidious.

per•son (pûr'sən) *n.* **1.** A human being. **2.** The

living body of a human being. **3.** The personality of a human being; self. **4.** Any of three groups of pronouns with corresponding verb inflections that distinguish between the speaker (first person), the individual addressed (second person), and the individual or thing spoken of (third person). [< L *persōna,* mask.]

per•son•a•ble (pûr'sən-ə-bəl) *adj.* Pleasing in appearance or personality.

per•son•age (pûr'sən-ĭj) *n.* A person of distinction.

per•son•al (pûr'sən-əl) *adj.* **1.** Of or pertaining to a particular person; private. **2.** Done in person: *a personal appearance.* **3.** Of or pertaining to the body of a human being. **4.** Pertaining to an individual, esp. in an offensive way: *a highly personal remark.* **5.** *Law.* Pertaining to a person's movable property. **6.** Indicating grammatical person. *—n.* A personal item or notice in a newspaper. **—per'son•al•ly** *adv.*

per•son•al•i•ty (pûr'sən-ăl'ə-tē) *n., pl.* **-ties. 1.** The state or quality of being a person. **2.** The totality of distinctive traits of an individual. **3.** The personal traits that make one socially appealing. **4.** A person of renown.

per•son•al•ize (pûr'sən-əl-īz') *v.* **-ized, -izing. 1.** To make personal. **2.** To mark with one's name or initials.

per•so•na non gra•ta (pər-sō'nə nōn grä'tə, grăt'ə). A person who is not acceptable or welcome. [L, "unacceptable person."]

per•son•i•fy (pər-sŏn'ə-fī') *v.* **-fied, -fying. 1.** To think of or represent (an inanimate object or abstraction) as a person. **2.** To be the embodiment or perfect example of. **—per•son'i•fi•ca'tion** (-fĭ-kā'shən) *n.*

per•son•nel (pûr'sən-ĕl') *n.* **1.** The body of persons employed by or active in an organization. **2.** An administrative division concerned with this body of persons.

per•spec•tive (pər-spĕk'tĭv) *n.* **1.** Any of various techniques for representing three-dimensional objects and depth relationships on a two-dimensional surface. **2.** The relationship of aspects of a subject to each other and to a whole: *a perspective of history.* **3.** Point of view. [< L *perspicere,* to see through or into.]

per•spi•cac•i•ty (pûr'spĭ-kăs'ə-tē) *n.* Acuteness of perception or understanding. [< L *perspicere,* to see through.] **—per'spi•ca'cious** (-kā'shəs) *adj.* **—per'spi•ca'cious•ly** *adv.*

per•spic•u•ous (pər-spĭk'yōō-əs) *adj.* Clearly expressed or presented; lucid. [< L *perspicere,* to see through.] **—per'spi•cu'i•ty** (pûr'spĭ-kyōō'ə-tē), **per•spic'u•ous•ness** *n.*

per•spi•ra•tion (pûr'spə-rā'shən) *n.* **1.** The saline moisture excreted through the pores of the skin by the sweat glands; sweat. **2.** The act or process of perspiring.

per•spire (pər-spīr') *v.* **-spired, -spiring.** To excrete perspiration through the pores of the skin. [< L *perspīrāre,* breathe through.]

per•suade (pər-swād') *v.* **-suaded, -suading. 1.** To cause (someone) to do something by means of argument, reasoning, or entreaty. **2.** To make (someone) believe something. [L *persuādēre.*] **—per•suad'a•ble** *adj.* **—per•suad'er** *n.* **—per•sua'sive** *adj.*

per•sua•sion (pər-swā'zhən) *n.* **1.** The act of persuading or the state of being persuaded. **2.** The ability to persuade. **3.** A body of religious beliefs: *worshipers of various persuasions.*

pert (pûrt) *adj.* **1.** Impudently bold. **2.** High-spirited. **3.** Jaunty: *a pert little hat.* [< OF *apert,* straightforward, open.]

pert. pertaining.

per•tain (pər-tān') *v.* **1.** To have reference; relate. **2.** To belong as an adjunct or accessory. **3.** To be suitable. [< L *pertinēre,* to relate to, to reach to.]

Perth (pûrth). A city of W Australia. Pop. 465,000.

per•ti•na•cious (pûr'tə-nā'shəs) *adj.* **1.** Holding firmly to some purpose or opinion. **2.** Stubbornly persistent. [< L *pertināx.*] **—per'ti•nac'i•ty** (-năs'ə-tē) *n.*

per•ti•nent (pûr'tə-nənt) *adj.* Relating to a specific matter; apposite: *a pertinent fact.* [< L *pertinēre,* to reach, concern.] **—per'ti•nence, per'ti•nen•cy** *n.* **—per'ti•nent•ly** *adv.*

per•turb (pər-tûrb') *v.* To disturb greatly; make uneasy or anxious. [< L *perturbāre.*] **—per'tur•ba'tion** (pûr'tər-bā'shən) *n.*

Pe•ru (pə-rōō'). A republic in W South America. Pop. 10,365,000. Cap. Lima. **—Pe•ru'vi•an** *adj.* & *n.*

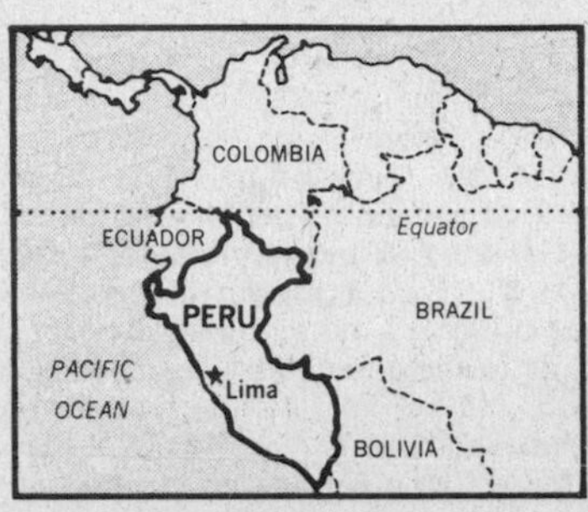

Peru

pe•ruse (pə-rōōz') *v.* **-rused, -rusing.** To read or examine, esp. with great care. [ME *perusen,* to use up.] **—pe•rus'al** *n.* **—pe•rus'er** *n.*

per•vade (pər-vād') *v.* **-vaded, -vading.** To spread throughout; permeate. [L *pervādere.*] **—per•va'sive** (-vā'sĭv, -zĭv) *adj.*

per•verse (pər-vûrs') *adj.* **1.** Directed away from what is right or good. **2.** Obstinately persisting in an error or fault. **3.** Cranky; peevish. [< L *pervertere,* to PERVERT.] **—per•verse'ly** *adv.* **—per•ver'si•ty** *n.*

per•ver•sion (pər-vûr'zhən, -shən) *n.* **1.** The act of perverting or the state of being perverted. **2.** A deviant sexual practice.

per•vert (pər-vûrt') *v.* **1.** To corrupt or debase. **2.** To misuse. **3.** To interpret incorrectly. *—n.* (pûr'vûrt'). One who practices sexual perversion. [< L *pervertere,* to turn the wrong way, turn around.] **—per•vert'ed** *adj.*

pe•se•ta (pə-sā'tə) *n.* The basic monetary unit of Spain.

pes•ky (pĕs'kē) *adj.* **-kier, -kiest.** Annoying. [Prob < PEST.] **—pes'ki•ness** *n.*

pe•so (pā'sō) *n., pl.* **-sos.** The basic monetary unit of Argentina, Bolivia, Colombia, Cuba, the Dominican Republic, Mexico, the Philippines, and Uruguay. [Span, "weight."]

pes•si•mism (pĕs'ə-mĭz'əm) *n.* **1.** A tendency to take the gloomiest possible view of a situation. **2.** The belief that the evil in the world outweighs the good. [< L *pessimus,* worst.] **—pes'si•mist** *n.* **—pes'si•mis'tic** *adj.*

pest (pĕst) *n.* **1.** An annoying person or thing; nuisance. **2.** An injurious plant or animal. [< L *pestis.*]

pes•ter (pĕs'tər) *v.* To harass with petty annoyances; bother. [Prob < OF *espestrer,* to tie up (an animal), impede.] **—pes'ter•er** *n.*

pes•ti•cide (pĕs'tə-sīd') *n.* A chemical used to kill pests, esp. insects and rodents.

pes•tif•er•ous (pĕs-tĭf'ər-əs) *adj.* **1.** Producing or breeding infectious disease. **2.** Bothersome.

pes•ti•lence (pĕs'tə-ləns) *n.* A fatal epidemic disease, esp. bubonic plague.

pes•ti•lent (pĕs'tə-lənt) *adj.* Also **pes•ti•len•tial** (pĕs'tə-lĕn'shəl). **1.** Tending to cause death. **2.** Likely to cause an epidemic disease. [< L *pestis,* plague, PEST.]

pes•tle (pĕs'əl, pĕs'təl) *n.* A club-shaped hand tool for grinding or mashing substances in a mortar. [< L *pistillum.*]

pet (pĕt) *n.* **1.** An animal kept for amusement or companionship. **2.** Any object of the affections. **3.** A favorite: *teacher's pet.* *—adj.* **1.** Kept as a pet. **2.** Especially cherished or indulged. *—v.* **petted, petting. 1.** To stroke or caress gently. **2.** To fondle and caress. [?]

pet•al (pĕt'l) *n.* A separate segment of a flower corolla. [< Gk *petalon,* leaf.] **—pet'aled, pet'alled** *adj.*

pe•tard (pĭ-tärd') *n.* A small bell-shaped bomb used to breach a gate or wall. **—hoist with one's own petard.** Injured by one's own cleverness.

pe•ter (pē'tər) *v.* **—peter out. 1.** To diminish gradually. **2.** To become exhausted.

Pe•ter I (pē'tər). Called "Peter the Great." 1672–1725. Czar of Russia (1682–1725).

Pe•ter (pē'tər), **Saint.** Died A.D. 67? The chief of the Apostles; traditionally regarded as first bishop of Rome.

Saint Peter

pe•tite (pə-tēt') *adj.* Small, slender, and trim, as a girl or woman. [F.]

pe•ti•tion (pə-tĭsh'ən) *n.* **1.** A solemn request; an entreaty. **2.** A formal document containing such a request. *—v.* **1.** To address a petition to. **2.** To request formally. **3.** To make an entreaty: *petition for retrial.* [< L *petere,* to seek, demand.] **—pe•ti'tion•er** *n.*

Pe•trarch (pē'trärk'). 1304–1374. Italian poet.

pet•rel (pĕt'rəl) *n.* Any of various small, blackish sea birds.

pet•ri•fy (pĕt'rə-fī') *v.* **-fied, -fying. 1.** To convert (wood or other organic matter) into a stony replica by structural impregnation with dissolved minerals. **2.** To cause to become stonelike; deaden. **3.** To stun or paralyze with terror. [< L *petra,* stone + *facere,* to make.]

pet•ro•chem•i•cal (pĕt'rō-kĕm'ĭ-kəl) *n.* Any chemical derived from petroleum or natural gas. **—pet'ro•chem'i•cal** *adj.*

pet•ro•dol•lar (pĕt'rō-dŏl'ər) *n.* A unit of hard currency, as a dollar, held by oil-exporting countries.

pet•rol (pĕt'rəl) *n. Chiefly Brit.* Gasoline. [< PETROLEUM.]

pet•ro•la•tum (pĕt'rə-lā'təm, -lä'təm) *n.* A colorless-to-amber gelatinous semisolid, obtained from petroleum and used in lubricants and medicinal ointments.

pe•tro•le•um (pə-trō'lē-əm) *n.* A natural, yellow-to-black, thick, flammable liquid hydrocarbon mixture found principally beneath the earth's surface and processed for fractions including natural gas, gasoline, naphtha, kerosene, fuel and lubricating oils, paraffin wax, and asphalt. [< Gk *petros,* stone + L *oleum,* oil.]

pet•ti•coat (pĕt'ē-kōt') *n.* A skirt, esp. a woman's slip or underskirt. [< ME *pety,* small, petty + *cote,* coat.]

pet•ti•fog•ger (pĕt'ē-fŏg'ər, -fôg'ər) *n.* A petty, quibbling, unscrupulous lawyer.

pet•tish (pĕt'ĭsh) *adj.* Ill-tempered; petulant.

pet•ty (pĕt'ē) *adj.* **-tier, -tiest. 1.** Small, trivial, or insignificant in quantity or quality. **2.** Of contemptibly narrow mind or views. **3.** Spiteful; mean. [< OF *petit,* small.] **—pet'ti•ly** *adv.* **—pet'ti•ness** *n.*

petty officer. A naval noncommissioned officer.

pet•u•lant (pĕch'o͝o-lənt) *adj.* Unreasonably irritable; peevish. [< L **petulāre,* to jab at.] **—pet'u•lance** *n.* **—pet'u•lant•ly** *adv.*

pe•tu•nia (pə-t/y/o͞on'yə) *n.* A cultivated plant with funnel-shaped variously colored flowers. [< Tupi *petyn, petyma.*]

pew (pyo͞o) *n.* A bench for the congregation in a church. [< L *podium,* podium, balcony.]

pe•wee (pē'wē) *n.* A small, brownish North American bird. [Imit.]

pew•ter (pyo͞o'tər) *n.* An alloy of tin with various amounts of antimony, copper, and lead, used for kitchen utensils and tableware. [< OF *peltre,* tin.] **—pew'ter** *adj.*

pe•yo•te (pā-ō'tē) *n.* A hallucinatory drug derived from a species of cactus. [< Nah.]

Pfc, Pfc. private first class.

P.G. postgraduate.

pH A measure of the acidity or alkalinity of a solution, numerically equal to 7 for neutral solutions, increasing with increasing alkalinity and decreasing with increasing acidity. [P(otential of) h(ydrogen).]

pha•lanx (fā'lăngks') *n., pl.* **-lanxes** or **phalanges** (fə-lăn'jēz, fā-). **1.** A formation of foot soldiers carrying overlapping shields and long spears, used by Alexander the Great. **2.** Any close-knit or compact group. **3.** *pl.* **phalanges.** Any bone of a finger or toe. [< Gk, wooden beam, line of battle.]

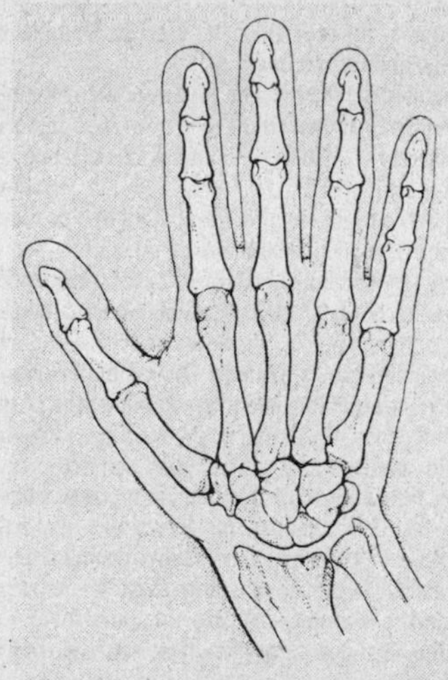

phalanx
Phalanges of the hand

phal•a•rope (făl'ə-rōp') *n.* Any of several small wading birds with lobed toes that enable them to swim. [< Gk *phalaros,* having a white spot + *pous,* foot.]

phal•lus (făl'əs) *n., pl.* **phalli** (făl'ī') or **-luses. 1.** The penis. **2.** A representation of the penis and testes as a symbol of generative power. [< Gk *phallos.*] **—phal'lic** *adj.*

phan•tasm (făn'tăz'əm) *n.* A phantom. [< Gk *phantasma,* apparition, specter.]

phan•tas•ma•go•ri•a (făn-tăz'mə-gôr'ē-ə, -gōr'ē-ə) *n.* A fantastic sequence of haphazardly associative imagery, as in dreams.

phan•tom (făn'təm) *n.* **1.** Something apparently seen, heard, or sensed, but having no physical reality; ghost; specter. **2.** An illusory mental image. [< Gk *phantasma,* PHANTASM.] **—phan'tom** *adj.*

Phar•aoh (fâr'ō, fā'rō) *n.* A king of ancient Egypt.

phar•i•see (făr'ə-sē) *n.* **1. Pharisee.** A member of an ancient Jewish sect that emphasized strict interpretation and observance of the Mosaic law. **2.** A hypocritically self-righteous person. [< Aram *perīshayyā.*] **—phar'i•sa'ic** (-sā'ĭk) *adj.*

pharm. pharmaceutical; pharmacist; pharmacy.

phar•ma•ceu•ti•cal (fär'mə-so͞o'tĭ-kəl) *adj.* Pertaining to pharmacy or pharmacists. *—n.* A pharmaceutical product or preparation.

phar•ma•cist (fär'mə-sĭst) *n.* A person trained in pharmacy; druggist.

pharmaco–. *comb. form.* Drugs. [< Gk *pharmakon,* drug, poison, potion.]

phar•ma•col•o•gy (fär'mə-kŏl'ə-jē) *n.* The science of drugs, including their composition, uses, and effects.

phar•ma•co•poe•ia (fär'mə-kə-pē'ə) *n., pl.* **-ias. 1.** A book listing medicinal drugs together with articles on their preparation and use. **2.** A collection or stock of drugs.

phar•ma•cy (fär'mə-sē) *n., pl.* **-cies. 1.** The art of preparing and dispensing drugs. **2.** A drugstore. [< Gk *pharmakon,* drug.]

phar•ynx (făr'ĭngks) *n., pl.* **pharynges** (fə-rĭn'jēz) or **-ynxes.** The section of the digestive tract that extends from the nasal cavities to the larynx, there becoming continuous with the esophagus. [< Gk *pharunx,* throat, pharynx.] **—pha•ryn'ge•al** (fə-rĭn'jē-əl, făr'ĭn-jē'əl) *adj.*

phase (fāz) *n.* **1.** One of a sequence of apparent forms. **2.** A distinct stage of development. **3.** A temporary pattern of behavior: *a passing phase.* **4.** One of the cyclically recurring apparent forms of the moon or a planet. *—v.* **phased, phasing. —phase out.** To eliminate by one stage at a time. [< Gk *phasis,* appearance, phase of the moon.]

Ph.D. Doctor of Philosophy (L *Philosophiae Doctor*).

pheas•ant (fĕz'ənt) *n.* Any of various long-tailed, often brightly colored chickenlike birds. [< Gk *phasianos,* "the Phasian (bird)," of the Phasis River in the Caucasus.]

pheno–. *comb. form. Chem.* **1.** Showing or displaying. **2.** A compound derived from, containing, or related to benzene. [< Gk *phainein,* to show.]

phe•no•bar•bi•tal (fē'nō-bär'bə-tôl') *n.* A white, shiny, crystalline compound, $C_{12}H_{12}N_2O_3$, used in medicine as a sedative and hypnotic.

phe•nol (fē'nōl', -nôl') *n.* A caustic, poisonous, white, crystalline compound, C_6H_5OH, derived from benzene and used in various resins, plastics, disinfectants, and pharmaceuticals.

phe•nom•e•nal (fĭ-nŏm'ə-nəl) *adj.* **1.** Pertaining to a phenomenon or phenomena. **2.** Extraordinary; outstanding.

phe•nom•e•non (fĭ-nŏm'ə-nŏn') *n., pl.* **-na** (-nə). **1.** Any occurrence or fact that is directly perceptible. **2.** Also *pl.* **-nons. a.** An unusual fact or occurrence. **b.** A person outstanding for some extreme quality or achievement. [< Gk *phainesthai,* to appear.]

phe•no•type (fē'nə-tīp') *n.* **1.** The environmentally and genetically determined observable appearance of an organism. **2.** An individual or group of organisms exhibiting a particular phenotype. **—phe'no•typ'ic** (-tĭp'ĭk) *adj.*

phi (fī) *n.* The 21st letter of the Greek alphabet, representing *ph.*

phi•al (fī'əl) *n.* A small bottle; a vial. [< Gk *phialē,* broad vessel.]

Phi Be•ta Kap•pa (fī' bā'tə kăp'ə). An honorary fraternity whose members are chosen on the basis of high academic standing. [< Gk *philosophia biou kubernētēs,* "philosophy, the guide of life."]

phil. philosophy.

Phil. Philippians (New Testament).

Phil•a•del•phi•a (fĭl'ə-dĕl'fē-ə). A city in SE Pennsylvania. Pop. 1,928,000. [Gk, "brotherly love."] **—Phil'a•del'phi•an** *adj. & n.*

phi•lan•der (fĭ-lăn'dər) *v.* To engage in love affairs frivolously; flirt. [< Gk *philandros,* "loving men," "loving one's husband."] **—phi•lan'der•er** *n.*

phi•lan•thro•py (fĭ-lăn'thrə-pē) *n., pl.* **-pies. 1.** The effort to increase the well-being of mankind, as by charitable donations. **2.** Love of mankind in general. **3.** A charitable action or institution. [< Gk *philanthrōpos,* "lover of mankind."] **—phil'an•throp'ic** (fĭl'ən-thrŏp'ĭk) *adj.* **—phi•lan'thro•pist** *n.*

phi•lat•e•ly (fĭ-lăt'l-ē) *n.* The collection and study of postage stamps and related materials. [< F *philatélie.*] **—phil'a•tel'ic** (fĭl'ə-tĕl'ĭk) *adj.* **—phi•lat'e•list** *n.*

–phile, –phil. *comb. form.* One having love, strong affinity, or preference for: **Anglophile.** [< Gk *philos,* beloved, dear, loving.]

Philem. Philemon (New Testament).

phil•har•mon•ic (fĭl'här-mŏn'ĭk, fĭl'ər-) *adj.* Pertaining to a symphony orchestra. *—n.* Also **Phil•har•mon•ic.** A symphony orchestra or the group that supports it. [< It *filarmonico.*]

–philia. *comb. form.* Tendency toward or attraction to: **hemophilia.** [< Gk *philos,* loving.]

Phil•ip•pines, Republic of the (fĭl'ə-pēnz',

Republic of the Philippines

ô paw, for/oi boy/ou out/o͝o took/o͞o coo/p pop/r run/s sauce/sh shy/t to/th thin/*th* the/
ŭ cut/ûr fur/v van/w wag/y yes/z size/zh vision/ə ago, item, edible, gallop, circus/

fĭl'ə-pēnz'). A republic consisting of the Philippine Islands, a group of islands in the W Pacific. Pop. 27,088,000. Cap. Quezon City.

Phi•lis•tine (fĭ-lĭs'tĭn, -tēn', fĭl'ĭ-stēn') *n.* **1.** One of an ancient people of SW Palestine. **2.** One who is annoyingly indifferent to artistic and cultural values. *—adj.* **1.** Of or pertaining to the ancient Philistines. **2.** Often **philistine.** Boorish; barbarous: "*Interpretation amounts to the philistine refusal to leave the work of art alone.*" (Susan Sontag). [< Heb *pelesheth,* "land of the Philistines."]

philo–. *comb. form.* Love. [< Gk *philos,* loving.]

phil•o•den•dron (fĭl'ə-dĕn'drən) *n., pl.* **-drons** or **-dra** (-drə). Any of various climbing tropical American plants often cultivated as house plants. [< Gk *philodendros,* "tree-loving."]

phi•lol•o•gy (fĭ-lŏl'ə-jē) *n.* **1.** Historical linguistics. **2.** Literary study or classical scholarship. [< Gk *philologos,* loving reason or learning.] **—phi•lol'o•gist** *n.*

philos. philosopher; philosophy.

phi•los•o•pher (fĭ-lŏs'ə-fər) *n.* **1.** A specialist in philosophy. **2.** One who lives by a particular philosophy. **3.** One who is calm and rational under any circumstances. [< Gk *philosophos,* "loving wisdom."]

phi•los•o•phize (fĭ-lŏs'ə-fīz') *v.* **-phized, -phizing.** To speculate in a philosophical manner.

phi•los•o•phy (fĭ-lŏs'ə-fē) *n., pl.* **-phies. 1. a.** Speculative inquiry concerning the source and nature of human knowledge. **b.** Any system of ideas based on such thinking. **2.** *Archaic.* The investigation of natural phenomena: *natural philosophy.* **3.** The sciences and liberal arts, excluding medicine, law, and theology: *Doctor of Philosophy.* **4.** A basic theory concerning a particular subject: *philosophy of education.* **5.** The set of values of an individual, culture, etc. **—phil'o•soph'i•cal** (fĭl'ə-sŏf'ĭ-kəl) *adj.* **—phil'o•soph'i•cal•ly** *adv.*

–philous. *comb. form.* A love of or fondness for: **photophilous.** [< Gk *philos,* beloved, loving.]

phil•ter (fĭl'tər) *n.* Also **phil•tre. 1.** A love potion. **2.** Any magic potion or charm. [< Gk *philtron,* "love charm."]

phle•bi•tis (flĭ-bī'tĭs) *n.* Inflammation of a vein.

phlebo–. *comb. form.* A vein. [< Gk *phleps (phleb-),* blood vessel, vein.]

phle•bot•o•my (flĭ-bŏt'ə-mē) *n., pl.* **-mies.** The therapeutic practice of opening a vein to draw blood.

phlegm (flĕm) *n.* Stringy, thick mucus produced in the respiratory tract. [< Gk *phlegma,* flame, inflammation, phlegm.]

phleg•mat•ic (flĕg-măt'ĭk) *adj.* Having or suggesting a calm, sluggish temperament; unemotional. [< Gk *phlegma,* PHLEGM.]

phlox (flŏks) *n., pl.* **phlox** or **phloxes.** A plant with clusters of white, red, or purple flowers. [< Gk, wallflower, flame.]

Phnom Penh (pə-nôm' pĕn'). The capital of Cambodia. Pop. 403,000.

–phobe. *comb. form.* One who fears or is averse to something: **xenophobe.** [< Gk *phobos,* fear.]

pho•bi•a (fō'bē-ə) *n.* **1.** A persistent, illogical fear of a specific thing or situation. **2.** Any strong fear or aversion. **—pho'bic** (-bĭk) *adj.*

–phobia. *comb. form.* Persistent, abnormal, or intense fear: **claustrophobia.** [< Gk *phobos,* fear, flight.]

phoe•be (fē'bē) *n.* A small, grayish North American bird.

Phoe•ni•cia (fĭ-nĭsh'ə, -nē'shə). An ancient kingdom of the E Mediterranean.

Phoe•ni•cian (fĭ-nĭsh'ən, -nē'shən) *n.* **1.** A native, inhabitant, or subject of ancient Phoenicia. **2.** The Semitic language of ancient Phoenicia. **—Phoe•ni'cian** *adj.*

phoe•nix (fē'nĭks) *n.* *Egyptian Myth.* A bird that consumed itself by fire after 500 years, and rose renewed from its ashes. [< Gk *phoinix.*]

Phoe•nix (fē'nĭks). The capital of Arizona. Pop. 580,000.

phon. phonetics.

phone (fōn). *Informal. n.* A telephone. *—v.* **phoned, phoning.** To telephone.

–phone. *comb. form.* A sound or sound-emitting device: **telephone.** [< Gk *phōnē,* sound, voice.]

pho•neme (fō'nēm') *n. Ling.* One of the smallest units of speech that distinguish one utterance or word from another. [< Gk *phōnēma,* an utterance.] **—pho•ne'mic** (fə-nē'mĭk, fō-) *adj.* **—pho•ne'mi•cal•ly** *adv.*

pho•net•ic (fə-nĕt'ĭk) *adj.* **1.** Pertaining to phonetics. **2.** Representing the sounds of speech with a set of distinct symbols, each denoting a single sound: *phonetic alphabet.* [< Gk *phōnein,* to sound, speak.]

pho•net•ics (fə-nĕt'ĭks) *n. (takes sing. v.).* The branch of linguistics dealing with the study of the sounds of speech.

phono–. *comb. form.* Sound or voice. [Gk *phōnē,* sound, voice.]

pho•no•graph (fō'nə-grăf', -gräf') *n.* A machine that reproduces sound from a disc. **—pho'no•graph'ic** *adj.*

pho•ny (fō'nē) *adj.* **-nier, -niest.** Not genuine; spurious; fake. [?] **—pho'ni•ly** *adv.* **—pho'ni•ness** *n.* **—pho'ny** *n.*

–phony. *comb. form.* Sound of a specified kind: **telephony.** [< Gk *phōnē,* sound.]

–phore. *comb. form.* A bearer or producer of: **semaphore.** [< Gk *pherein,* to bear.]

phos•phate (fŏs'fāt') *n.* **1.** A salt or ester of phosphoric acid. **2.** A fertilizer containing phosphorus compounds. [< PHOSPHORUS.] **—phos'phat'ic** (fŏs'făt'ĭk) *adj.*

phos•phor (fŏs'fər, -fôr') *n.* **1.** Any substance that can be stimulated to emit light by incident radiation. **2.** Something exhibiting phosphorescence. [< PHOSPHORUS.]

phos•pho•res•cence (fŏs'fə-rĕs'əns) *n.* **1.** Persistent emission of light following exposure to and removal of incident radiation. **2.** Organically generated light emission. **—phos'pho•resce'** *v.* **(-resced, -rescing). —phos'pho•res'cent** *adj.*

phos•phor•ic acid (fŏs-fôr'ĭk, -fŏr'ĭk). A clear colorless liquid, H_3PO_4, used in fertilizers, soaps, and detergents.

phos•pho•rus (fŏs'fər-əs) *n.* **1.** *Symbol* **P** A highly reactive, poisonous, nonmetallic element used in safety matches, pyrotechnics, incendiary shells, fertilizers, glass, and steel. Atomic number 15, atomic weight 30.9738. **2.** Any phosphorescent substance. [< Gk *phōsphoros,* "light-bearing."]

pho•to (fō'tō) *n., pl.* **-tos.** A photograph.

photo–. *comb. form.* **1.** Light. **2.** Photographic. [Gk *phōs (phōt-),* light.]

pho•to•cell (fō'tō-sĕl') *n.* A **photoelectric cell.**

pho•to•cop•y (fō'tō-kŏp'ē) *v.* **-ied, -ying.** To make a photographic reproduction of. *—n., pl.* **-ies.** A photographic reproduction. **—pho'to•cop'i•er** *n.*

pho•to•e•lec•tric (fō'tō-ĭ-lĕk'trĭk) *adj.* Pertaining to electric effects, esp. increased electrical conduction, caused by illumination.

photoelectric cell. An electronic device having an electrical output that varies in response to incident radiation, esp. to visible light.

pho•to•en•grave (fō'tō-ĕn-grāv') *v.* **-graved, -graving.** To reproduce by photoengraving. **—pho'to•en•grav'er** *n.*

pho•to•en•grav•ing (fō'tō-ĕn-grā'vĭng) *n.* **1.** The process of reproducing graphic material by transferring the image photographically to a plate or other surface in etched relief for printing. **2.** A reproduction made by this method.

photo finish. A race so closely contested that the winner must be determined by a photograph taken of the finish.

pho•to•flash (fō'tō-flăsh') *n.* A **flash bulb.**

pho•to•flood (fō'tō-flŭd') *n.* An electric lamp that produces a bright continuous light for photographic illumination.

pho•to•gen•ic (fō'tə-jĕn'ĭk) *adj.* Attractive as a subject for photography. **—pho'to•gen'i•cal•ly** *adv.*

pho•to•graph (fō'tə-grăf', -gräf') *n.* An image, esp. a positive print, recorded by a camera and reproduced on a photosensitive surface. *—v.* **1.** To take a photograph of. **2.** To be the subject for photographs.

pho•to•graph•ic (fō'tə-grăf'ĭk) *adj.* **1.** Pertaining to photography or a photograph. **2.** Used in photography. **3.** Like a photograph in accuracy or detail. **—pho'to•graph'i•cal•ly** *adv.*

pho•tog•ra•phy (fə-tŏg'rə-fē) *n.* **1.** The process of rendering optical images on photosensitive surfaces. **2.** The art, practice, or occupation of taking and printing photographs. **3.** A body of photographs. **—pho•tog'ra•pher** *n.*

pho•to•me•chan•i•cal (fō'tō-mĭ-kăn'ĭ-kəl) *adj.* Of or designating any of various methods by which plates are prepared for printing by means of photography.

pho•to•mi•cro•graph (fō'tō-mī'krə-grăf', -gräf') *n.* A photograph made through a microscope.

pho•ton (fō'tŏn') *n.* The quantum of electromagnetic energy, generally regarded as a discrete particle having zero mass, no electric charge, and an indefinitely long lifetime. [PHOT(O)- + -ON.] **—pho'ton'ic** *adj.*

pho•to•play (fō'tō-plā') *n.* A play filmed or arranged for filming as a motion picture.

pho•to•re•cep•tion (fō'tō-rĭ-sĕp'shən) *n.* The detection or perception of visible light; vision. **—pho'to•re•cep'tive** *adj.*

pho•to•re•cep•tor (fō'tō-rĭ-sĕp'tər) *n.* A photoreceptive nerve.

pho•to•sen•si•tive (fō'tō-sĕn'sə-tĭv) *adj.* Sensitive to light.

pho•to•sen•si•tize (fō'tō-sĕn'sə-tīz') *v.* **-tized, -tizing.** To make sensitive to light.

Pho•to•stat (fō'tə-stăt') *n.* **1.** A trademark for a device used to make photographic copies of written, printed, or graphic material. **2.** Often **photostat.** A copy made by Photostat. *—v.* **-stated** or **-statted, -stating** or **-statting.** Often **photostat.** To make a copy of by Photostat.

pho•to•syn•the•sis (fō'tō-sĭn'thə-sĭs) *v.* The process by which chlorophyll-containing cells in green plants use the energy of light to synthesize carbohydrates from carbon dioxide and water. **—pho'to•syn'the•size'** (-sĭn'thə-sīz') *v.* **(-sized, -sizing). —pho'to•syn•thet'ic** (-sĭn-thĕt'ĭk) *adj.* **—pho'to•syn•thet'i•cal•ly** *adv.*

phr. phrase.

phrase (frāz) *n.* **1.** Any sequence of words intended to have meaning. **2.** A brief, cogent expression. **3.** *Gram.* Two or more words in sequence that form a syntactic unit or group of syntactic units, less completely predicated than a sentence. **4.** A segment of a musical composition, usually consisting of several measures. —*v.* **phrased, phrasing. 1.** To express orally or in writing. **2.** *Mus.* To render in phrases. [< Gk *phrasis,* speech, style of speech.] —**phras'al** *adj.*

phra•se•ol•o•gy (frā'zē-ŏl'ə-jē) *n., pl.* **-gies.** The way in which words and phrases are used; style.

phre•net•ic, phre•net•i•cal. Variants of **frenetic.**

-phrenia. *comb. form.* Mental disorder: **schizophrenia.** [< Gk *phrēn,* mind.]

phren•ic (frĕn'ĭk, frē'nĭk) *adj.* Pertaining to the mind.

phreno-. *comb. form.* **1.** The mind. **2.** The diaphragm. [< Gk *phrēn,* diaphragm, mind.]

phre•nol•o•gy (frĭ-nŏl'ə-jē) *n.* The practice of studying character and mental capacity from the conformation of the human skull. —**phre•nol'o•gist** *n.*

phy•lac•ter•y (fĭ-lăk'tə-rē) *n., pl.* **-ies.** *Judaism.* Either of two small leather boxes containing quotations from the Hebrew Scriptures. One is strapped to the forehead and the other to the left arm by observant Jewish men during morning worship, except on the Sabbath and holidays. [< Gk *phulaktērion,* safeguard.]

-phyll. *comb. form.* Leaf: **chlorophyll.** [< Gk *phullon,* leaf.]

phy•lum (fī'ləm) *n., pl.* **-la** (-lə). **1.** One of the broad categories, esp. of the animal kingdom, used in the classification of organisms. **2.** A large division of genetically related families of languages or linguistic stocks. [< Gk *phulon,* tribe, class, race.]

phys. 1. physical. **2.** physician. **3.** physicist; physics.

phys•ic (fĭz'ĭk) *n.* **1.** Any medicine or drug. **2.** A cathartic. —*v.* **-icked, -icking.** To act upon as a cathartic. [< L *physica,* natural medicine or science, physics.]

phys•i•cal (fĭz'ĭ-kəl) *adj.* **1.** Of or pertaining to the body, as distinguished from the mind or spirit. **2.** Of or pertaining to material things. **3.** Of or pertaining to matter and energy or the sciences dealing with them, esp. physics. —*n.* A medical examination. [< L *physica,* natural medicine.] —**phys'i•cal•ly** *adv.*

physical education. Education in the care and development of the human body, stressing athletics.

physical geography. The study of the structure and phenomena of the earth's surface.

physical science. Any of the sciences, such as physics, chemistry, astronomy, and geology, that analyzes the nature and properties of energy and nonliving matter.

physical therapy. The treatment of disease and injury by mechanical means such as exercise, heat, light, and massage.

phy•si•cian (fĭ-zĭsh'ən) *n.* A medical doctor. [< OF *fisique,* medicine, physic.]

phy•si•cian•ly (fĭ-zĭsh'ən-lē) *adj.* Characteristic of a physician.

phys•i•cist (fĭz'ə-sĭst) *n.* A scientist who specializes in physics.

phys•ics (fĭz'ĭks) *n. (takes sing. v.).* The science of matter and energy and of interactions between the two. [Pl of PHYSIC.]

physio-. *comb. form.* **1.** Natural or nature. **2.** Physical. [< Gk *phusis,* nature.]

phys•i•og•no•my (fĭz'ē-ŏg'nə-mē, -ŏn'ə-mē) *n., pl.* **-mies.** Facial features, esp. when regarded as revealing character. [< PHYSIO- + Gk *gnōmōn,* "judge."]

physiol. physiological; physiology.

phys•i•ol•o•gy (fĭz'ē-ŏl'ə-jē) *n.* **1.** The biological science of life processes, activities, and functions. **2.** The vital processes of an organism. —**phys'i•o•log'i•cal** (-ə-lŏj'ĭ-kəl) *adj.* —**phys'i•ol'o•gist** *n.*

phys•i•o•ther•a•py (fĭz'ē-ō-thĕr'ə-pē) *n.* **Physical therapy.**

phy•sique (fĭ-zēk') *n.* The body, considered with reference to its proportions, muscular development, and appearance. [< F, "physical."]

pi (pī) *n., pl.* **pis. 1.** The 16th letter of the Greek alphabet, representing *p.* **2.** *Symbol* ρ *Math.* A transcendental number, approx. 3.14159, representing the ratio of the circumference to the diameter of a circle.

pi•a•nis•si•mo (pē'ə-nĭs'ə-mō') *adv. Mus.* Very softly or quietly. [It, superl of PIANO².] —**pi'a•nis'si•mo'** *adj.*

pi•an•ist (pē-ăn'ĭst, pē'ə-nĭst) *n.* One who plays the piano.

pi•an•o¹ (pē-ăn'ō) *n., pl.* **-os.** A musical keyboard instrument with hammers that strike wire strings. [It, short for PIANOFORTE.]

pi•a•no² (pē-ä'nō) *adv. Mus.* Softly; quietly. [It.] —**pi•a'no** *adj.*

pi•an•o•for•te (pē-ăn'ō-fôr'tā, -fôr'tē, -fôrt') *n.* A piano. [< It *piano e forte,* soft and loud.]

pi•as•ter (pē-ăs'tər, -ä'stər) *n.* Also **pi•as•tre.** The basic monetary unit of South Vietnam.

pi•az•za (pē-ăz'ə, -ä'zə) *n., pl.* **-zas.** A veranda; porch.

pi•ca (pī'kə) *n.* A printer's unit of type size, equal to 12 points or about 1/6 inch. [Prob < ML *pica,* almanac.]

pic•a•resque (pĭk'ə-rĕsk', pē'kə-) *adj.* Of or involving clever rogues or adventurers. [< Span *picaro,* rogue.]

Pi•cas•so (pĭ-kä'sō, pē-), **Pablo.** Born 1881. Spanish painter and sculptor, resident in France.

pic•a•yune (pĭk'ē-yo͞on') *adj.* **1.** Of little value or importance. **2.** Petty; mean. [< F *picaillon,* small copper coin.]

pic•ca•lil•li (pĭk'ə-lĭl'ē) *n., pl.* **-lis.** A pickled relish made of chopped vegetables. [Perh blend of PICKLE and CHILI.]

pic•co•lo (pĭk'ə-lō') *n., pl.* **-los.** A small flute pitched an octave above a regular flute. [< It *piccolo,* small.]

pick¹ (pĭk) *v.* **1.** To select from a group. **2.** To gather in; harvest. **3. a.** To remove the outer covering of; pluck. **b.** To tear off bit by bit. **4.** To poke at with the fingers. **5.** To break up or detach with a pointed instrument. **6.** To pierce with a sharp instrument. **7.** To steal the contents of. **8.** To open (a lock) without the use of a key. **9.** To make (one's way) carefully. **10.** To provoke: *pick a fight.* —**pick off.** To shoot after singling out. —**pick on.** To tease or bully. —*n.* **1.** The act of selecting; choice. **2.** The best or choicest part. [Prob < VL **piccāre,* to prick, pierce.] —**pick'er** *n.*

pick² (pĭk) *n.* **1.** A tool for breaking hard surfaces, consisting of a curved bar sharpened at both ends and fitted to a long handle. **2.** *Mus.* A plectrum. [ME *pik.*]

pick•ax, pick•axe (pĭk'ăks') *n.* A pick, esp. with one end of the head pointed and the other end with a chisel edge. [< OF *picois.*]

pick•er•el (pĭk'ər-əl, pĭk'rəl) *n., pl.* **-el** or **-els.** A North American freshwater fish related to the pike. [< PIKE².]

pick•et (pĭk'ĭt) *n.* **1.** A pointed stake driven into the ground to support a fence, secure a tent, tether an animal, etc. **2.** A soldier or group of soldiers on guard against enemy approach. **3. a.** A worker on strike, stationed outside a place of employment to express grievance or protest. **b.** Any protester. —*v.* **1.** To enclose, secure, tether, etc., with pickets. **2.** To guard with pickets. **3.** To post a picket or pickets. **4.** To act as a picket. [< OF *piquer,* to prick, pierce.] —**pick'et•er** *n.*

pick•ing (pĭk'ĭng) *n.* **1.** The act of one that picks. **2. pickings.** Something that is or may be picked. **3.** Often **pickings. a.** Leftovers. **b.** A share of spoils.

pick•le (pĭk'əl) *n.* **1.** A food, esp. a cucumber, preserved in a solution of brine or vinegar. **2.** A solution of brine or vinegar for preserving and flavoring food. **3.** *Informal.* An embarrassing or difficult situation. —*v.* **-led, -ling.** To preserve or flavor in a solution of brine or vinegar. [ME *pekille.*]

pick•pock•et (pĭk'pŏk'ĭt) *n.* One who steals from pockets.

pick up. 1. To take or lift up. **2.** To take on (passengers, freight, etc.). **3.** To fetch or acquire. **4.** To accelerate.

pick•up (pĭk'ŭp') *n.* **1.** The action or process of picking up. **2.** Capacity for acceleration. **3.** One that is picked up. **4.** A light truck with an open body and low sides. **5.** A device that converts the oscillations of a phonograph needle into electrical impulses.

pick•y (pĭk'ē) *adj.* **-ier, -iest.** Excessively meticulous.

pic•nic (pĭk'nĭk) *n.* **1.** A meal eaten outdoors on an excursion. **2.** *Slang.* An easy task. —*v.* **-nicked, -nicking.** To go on a picnic. [F *piquenique.*] —**pic'nick•er** *n.*

pico-. *comb. form.* One trillionth, 10^{-12}: *picosecond,* one-trillionth of a second. [Span *pico,* small quantity, peak.]

pi•cot (pē'kō, pē-kō') *n.* A small loop forming an ornamental edging, as on ribbon. [F, "small point."]

pic•to•ri•al (pĭk-tôr'ē-əl, -tōr'ē-əl) *adj.* **1.** Of, characterized by, or composed of pictures. **2.** Illustrated by pictures.

pic•ture (pĭk'chər) *n.* **1.** A visual representation or image painted, drawn, photographed, or otherwise rendered on a flat surface. **2.** A vivid verbal description. **3.** One that bears a striking resemblance to another. **4.** One that typifies or embodies an emotion, state of mind, or mood. **5.** The chief circumstances of; a situation. **6.** A motion picture. —*v.* **-tured, -turing. 1.** To make a visible representation or picture of. **2.** To visualize. **3.** To describe vividly in words. [< L *pingere* (pp *pictus*), to paint.] —**pic'tur•er** *n.*

pic•tur•esque (pĭk'chə-rĕsk') *adj.* **1.** Of, suggesting, or suitable for a picture. **2.** Unusually or quaintly attractive; charming. **3.** Strikingly expressive or vivid. —**pic'tur•esque'ly** *adv.*

pid•dling (pĭd'lĭng) *adj.* Trifling; trivial.

pidg•in (pĭj'ən) *n.* A simplified mixture of two or more languages, used for communication between groups speaking different languages.

Pidgin English. A pidgin based on English and used as a trade language in Far Eastern ports. [A pidgin corruption of *business English.*]

pie (pī) *n.* A baked pastry shell filled with fruit, meat, etc., and often covered with a pastry crust. [ME.]

pie•bald (pī'bôld') *adj.* Having spotted or patchy markings: *a piebald horse.*

piece (pēs) *n.* **1.** A unit or element of a larger

quantity or class; portion. **2.** An artistic, musical, or literary work. **3.** An instance; specimen. **4.** One's mind: *speak one's piece.* **5.** A coin or counter. **6.** A figure used in a game. **7.** A firearm, esp. a rifle. **8.** A short or manageable distance: *down the road a piece.* —*v.* **pieced, piecing. 1.** To mend by adding a piece to. **2.** To join the pieces of. [< Gaul **pettia.*]

pièce de ré•sis•tance (pyĕs də rā-zē-stäNs'). **1.** The principal dish of a meal. **2.** An outstanding accomplishment. [F.]

piece•meal (pēs'mēl') *adv.* Piece by piece. —*adj.* Made piece by piece.

piece•work (pēs'wûrk') *n.* Work paid for by the piece.

pied (pīd) *adj.* Having spots or patches of different colors.

pier (pîr) *n.* **1.** A platform extending from a shore over water, used to secure, protect, and provide access to ships or boats. **2.** A support for the spans of a bridge. **3.** *Archit.* Any of various vertical supporting structures. [< L *podium,* raised platform, podium.]

pierce (pîrs) *v.* **pierced, piercing. 1.** To cut or pass through with or as with a sharp instrument; stab. **2.** To perforate. **3.** To penetrate through. [< L *pertundere* (pp *pertūsus*), to pierce through.] —**pierc'ing•ly** *adv.*

Pierce (pîrs), **Franklin.** 1804–1869. 14th President of the U.S. (1853–57).

Franklin Pierce

Pierre (pîr). The capital of South Dakota. Pop. 10,000.

pi•e•ty (pī'ə-tē) *n., pl.* **-ties. 1.** Devotion and reverence, esp. to God and family. **2.** A pious act or thought. [< L *pius,* PIOUS.]

pif•fle (pĭf'əl) *n.* Foolish or futile talk or ideas; nonsense. [?]

pig (pĭg) *n.* **1.** A hoofed mammal with short legs, bristly hair, and a blunt snout used for digging, esp. one of a kind raised for meat. **2.** A person regarded as being piglike, greedy, or gross. **3.** An oblong block of metal, chiefly iron or lead, poured from a smelting furnace. [Prob < OE **picga.*]

pi•geon (pĭj'ən) *n.* **1.** Any of various related birds with a deep-chested body, a small head, and short legs, esp. a common, often domesticated species. **2.** *Slang.* One easily swindled; a dupe. [< L *pīpiō,* squab, young chirping bird.]

pi•geon•hole (pĭj'ən-hōl') *n.* A small compartment, as in a desk. —*v.* **-holed, -holing. 1.** To place or file in a pigeonhole. **2.** To categorize. **3.** To put aside and ignore.

pi•geon-toed (pĭj'ən-tōd') *adj.* Having the toes turned inward.

pig•gish (pĭg'ĭsh) *adj.* Like a pig; greedy.

pig•gy•back (pĭg'ē-băk') *adv.* **1.** On the shoulders or back. **2.** By a method of transportation in which truck trailers are carried on trains. —**pig'gy•back'** *adj.*

pig•head•ed (pĭg'hĕd'ĭd) *adj.* Stubborn.

pig iron. Crude iron cast in blocks or pigs.

pig•ment (pĭg'mənt) *n.* **1.** A coloring substance or matter. **2.** A substance, such as chlorophyll or hemoglobin, that produces a characteristic color in plant or animal tissue. [L *pigmentum* < *pingere,* to paint.]

pig•men•ta•tion (pĭg'mən-tā'shən) *n. Biol.* **1.** Coloration of tissues by pigment. **2.** Deposition of pigment by cells.

pig•my. Variant of **pygmy.**

Pig•my. Variant of **Pygmy.**

pig•pen (pĭg'pĕn') *n.* **1.** A pen for pigs. **2.** A dirty place.

pig•skin (pĭg'skĭn') *n.* **1.** The skin of a pig or leather made from it. **2.** A football.

pig•sty (pĭg'stī') *n., pl.* **-sties.** A shelter where pigs are kept.

pig•tail (pĭg'tāl') *n.* A braid of hair.

pike[1] (pīk) *n.* A long spear formerly used by infantry. [< VL **piccāre,* to pierce.]

pike[2] (pīk) *n., pl.* **pike** or **pikes.** A narrow-bodied freshwater game and food fish with a long snout. [ME.]

pike[3] (pīk) *n.* A turnpike.

pike[4] (pīk) *n.* A spike or sharp point. [< OE *pīc.*]

pik•er (pī'kər) *n. Slang.* A stingy, petty person. [?]

pi•las•ter (pĭ-lăs'tər) *n.* A rectangular column set into a wall, often as an ornament. [< ML *pilastrum.*]

Pi•late (pī'lĭt), **Pontius.** Roman procurator of Judea (A.D. 26?–36?); assumed to have authorized the execution of Jesus.

pil•chard (pĭl'chərd) *n.* Any of various small marine fishes related to the herrings. [?]

pile[1] (pīl) *n.* **1.** A quantity of objects in a heap. **2.** A large accumulation or quantity. **3.** A funeral pyre. **4.** A large building or complex of buildings. **5.** A **nuclear reactor.** —*v.* **piled, piling. 1.** To stack in or form a pile. **2.** To load with a pile. [< L *pīla,* PILLAR.]

pile[2] (pīl) *n.* A heavy beam driven into the earth as a support for a structure. [< L *pīlum,* heavy javelin, pestle.]

pile[3] (pīl) *n.* Cut or uncut loops of yarn forming the surface of certain fabrics, as velvet, plush, etc. [< L *pilus,* hair.] —**piled** *adj.*

piles (pīlz) *pl.n.* Hemorrhoids. [< L *pila,* ball.]

pil•fer (pĭl'fər) *v.* To steal; filch. [< OF *pelfre,* booty.] —**pil'fer•age** (-ĭj) *n.* —**pil'fer•er** *n.*

pil•grim (pĭl'grĭm, -grəm) *n.* **1.** One who goes on a pilgrimage. **2.** Any traveler. **3. Pilgrim.** One of the English Puritans who migrated to New England (1620). [< L *peregrīnus,* a foreigner.]

pil•grim•age (pĭl'grə-mĭj) *n.* **1.** A journey to a sacred place or shrine. **2.** A long journey or search.

pill (pĭl) *n.* **1.** A small pellet or tablet of medicine. **2. the Pill.** An oral contraceptive. **3.** Anything distasteful but necessary. **4.** *Slang.* An ill-natured person. [< L *pila,* ball.]

pil•lage (pĭl'ĭj) *v.* **-laged, -laging. 1.** To plunder. **2.** To take as spoils. —*n.* **1.** The act of pillaging. **2.** Spoils. [< OF *piller,* to tear up, plunder.] —**pil'lag•er** *n.*

pil•lar (pĭl'ər) *n.* **1.** A slender, freestanding vertical support; a column. **2.** One occupying a central or responsible position. [< L *pīla,* pillar.]

pill•box (pĭl'bŏks') *n.* **1.** A small box for pills. **2.** A roofed concrete emplacement for a weapon.

pil•lion (pĭl'yən) *n.* A seat for an extra rider behind the saddle on a horse or motorcycle. [< L *pellis,* skin, hide.]

pil•lo•ry (pĭl'ə-rē) *n., pl.* **-ries.** A wooden framework with holes for the head and hands, in which offenders were formerly locked to be exposed to public scorn as punishment. —*v.* **-ried, -rying. 1.** To put in a pillory. **2.** To expose to ridicule and abuse. [Prob < L *pīla,* PILLAR.]

pil•low (pĭl'ō) *n.* **1.** A cloth case stuffed with something soft and used to cushion the head during sleep. **2.** A decorative cushion. —*v.* **1.** To rest (one's head) on or as on a pillow. **2.** To act as a pillow for. [< L *pulvīnus,* pillow.] —**pil'low•y** *adj.*

pil•low•case (pĭl'ō-kās') *n.* A removable pillow covering.

pi•lot (pī'lət) *n.* **1.** One who operates or is licensed to operate an aircraft. **2. a.** One who is licensed to conduct ships into and out of port. **b.** The helmsman of a ship. **3.** One who guides or directs. —*v.* **1.** To serve as the pilot of. **2.** To steer or control the course of. —*adj.* Serving as a tentative model for future development. [< It *pilota.*]

pi•lot•house (pī'lət-hous') *n.* An enclosed area on the deck or bridge of a vessel from which the vessel is controlled.

pilot light. A small flame kept burning in order to ignite a burner, as in a stove.

pi•men•to (pĭ-mĕn'tō) *n., pl.* **-tos.** Also **pi•mien•to** (pĭ-mĕn'tō, -myĕn'-). A mild-flavored red pepper. [< LL *pigmentum,* plant juice, pigment.]

pimp (pĭmp) *n.* A procurer; pander. —*v.* To serve as a pimp. [?]

pim•per•nel (pĭm'pər-nĕl', -nəl) *n.* A plant with red, purple, or white flowers that close in bad weather. [< VL **piperīnella.*]

pim•ple (pĭm'pəl) *n.* A small swelling of the skin, sometimes containing pus. [ME *pinple.*] —**pim'pled, pim'ply** *adj.*

pin (pĭn) *n.* **1.** A short, straight, stiff piece of wire with a blunt head and a sharp point, used for fastening. **2.** Anything resembling a pin in shape or use, as a hairpin. **3.** An ornament fastened to the clothing with a clasp. **4.** A slender, cylindrical piece of wood or metal for holding, fastening, or supporting. **5.** One of the wooden clubs at which the ball is aimed in bowling. **6.** *Golf.* The pole bearing a pennant to mark a hole. **7. pins.** The legs. —*v.* **pinned, pinning. 1.** To fasten or secure with or as with a pin or pins. **2.** To place in a position of trusting dependence: *pinned his hopes on his victory.* **3.** To hold fast; immobilize. **4.** To oblige (someone) to make a definite response. —**pin on.** To attribute (a wrongdoing or crime). [< OE *pinn.*] —**pin'ner** *n.*

pin•a•fore (pĭn'ə-fôr', -fōr') *n.* A sleeveless garment similar to an apron.

pince-nez (păns'nā', pĭns'-) *n., pl.* **-nez** (-nāz', -nā'). Eyeglasses clipped to the nose. [F, "pinch-nose."]

pin•cers (pĭn'sərz) *n.* Also **pin•chers** (pĭn'chərz). *(often takes sing. v.).* **1.** A grasping tool having a pair of jaws and handles pivoted together to work in opposition. **2.** A jointed, clawlike grasping part, as of a lobster. [< OF *pincier,* to PINCH.]

pinch (pĭnch) *v.* **1.** To squeeze between the thumb and a finger, the jaws of a tool, etc. **2.** To squeeze or bind (a part of the body) painfully. **3.** To wither or shrivel. **4.** To be miserly. **5.** *Slang.* To steal. **6.** *Slang.* To arrest. —*n.* **1.** The act of pinching. **2.** An amount that can be held between thumb and forefinger. **3.** A difficult or straitened circumstance. **4.** Any emergency. [< OF *pincier.*]

pinch-hit (pĭnch'hĭt') *v.* To substitute for another, esp. to bat in place of another in a baseball game. —**pinch hitter.**

pin•cush•ion (pĭn'ko͝osh'ən) *n.* A cushion in which pins are stuck when not in use.

pine[1] (pīn) *n.* **1.** Any of various cone-bearing evergreen trees with clustered, needle-shaped leaves. **2.** The wood of such a tree. [< L *pīnus.*]

pine[2] (pīn) *v.* **pined, pining. 1.** To suffer intense longing or yearning. **2.** To wither away from longing or grief. [< Gk *poinē,* payment, punishment.]

pin•e•al body (pĭn'ē-əl, pīn'-). A small glandlike body of uncertain function located in the brain.

pine•ap•ple (pīn'ăp-əl) *n.* **1.** A tropical American plant with swordlike leaves and a large, fleshy, edible fruit. **2.** The fruit of this plant. **3.** *Slang.* A small hand grenade. [< PINE + APPLE.]

pin•feath•er (pĭn'fĕth'ər) *n.* A feather still enclosed in its horny sheath and just emerging through the skin.

ping (pĭng) *n.* A brief, high-pitched sound, as that made by a bullet striking metal. [Imit.] —**ping** *v.*

pin•hole (pĭn'hōl') *n.* A tiny puncture made by or as if by a pin.

pin•ion[1] (pĭn'yən) *n.* A bird's wing. —*v.* **1.** To restrain or immobilize by binding the wings or arms. **2.** To fix in one place. [< L *pinna, penna,* a feather, wing.]

pin•ion[2] (pĭn'yən) *n.* A small cogwheel that engages or is engaged by a larger cogwheel or a rack. [< L *pecten,* a comb.]

pink[1] (pĭngk) *n.* **1.** Any of various plants related to the carnation, often cultivated for their fragrant flowers. **2.** Light red. **3.** The highest degree of excellence: *in the pink of health.* **4.** *Slang.* A pinko. [Poss short for *pink eye,* "small eye."] —**pink, pink'ish** *adj.*

pink[2] (pĭngk) *v.* **1.** To stab lightly. **2.** To decorate with a perforated pattern. [ME *pynken.*]

pink•eye (pĭngk'ī') *n.* Also **pink eye.** Acute contagious conjunctivitis. [Part trans of obs Du *pinck oog(en),* "small eye(s)."]

pink•ie (pĭng'kē) *n.* Also **pink•y** *pl.* **-ies.** The little finger. [< Du *pink,* little finger.]

pink•o (pĭng'kō) *n., pl.* **-os.** *Slang.* One in sympathy with Communist doctrine.

pin•nace (pĭn'ĭs) *n.* **1.** A small sailing boat. **2.** A ship's boat. [< VL **pīnācea (nāvis),* "(ship) of pine-wood."]

pin•na•cle (pĭn'ə-kəl) *n.* **1.** A small turret or spire on a roof or buttress. **2.** Any tall, pointed formation. **3.** The highest point; summit. [< LL *pinnāculum,* "little wing."]

pin•nate (pĭn'āt') *adj.* Featherlike, as compound leaves with leaflets along each side of a stalk. [L *pinnātus,* feathered.]

pi•noch•le (pē'nŭk'əl, -nŏk'əl) *n.* A card game for two to four persons, played with a deck of 48 cards. [Earlier *binuochle.*]

pi•ñon (pĭn'yōn', -yən) *n.* Also **pin•yon.** Any pine tree bearing edible, nutlike seeds. [< Span, pine nut, pine cone.]

pin•point (pĭn'point') *n.* An extremely small thing or spot; particle. —*v.* **1.** To pierce. **2.** To locate and identify precisely.

pin•prick (pĭn'prĭk') *n.* **1.** A slight puncture made by or as if by a pin. **2.** A minor annoyance.

pins and needles. A tingling felt in a part of the body that has been numbed from lack of circulation.

pin•stripe (pĭn'strīp') *n.* **1.** A thin stripe on a fabric. **2.** A thinly striped fabric.

pint (pīnt) *n.* **1.** A U.S. Customary System unit of volume or capacity, used in liquid measure, equal to 16 fluid ounces or 28.875 cubic inches. **2.** A U.S. Customary System unit of volume or capacity, used in dry measure, equal to 1/2 quart or 33.6 cubic inches. **3.** A British Imperial System unit of volume or capacity, used in dry and liquid measure, equal to 34.678 cubic inches. **4.** A container with such a capacity or the amount it will hold. [< OF *pinte.*]

pin•to (pĭn'tō) *n., pl.* **-tos** or **-toes.** A horse with irregular spots or markings. [< obs Span, "painted."]

pin•up (pĭn'ŭp') *n.* A picture to be pinned up on a wall, esp. a photograph of a sexually attractive girl. —*adj.* Pertaining to or suitable for a pinup.

pin•wale (pĭn'wāl') *n.* A corduroy having narrow ribs or wales. —**pin'wale'** *adj.*

pin•wheel (pĭn'hwēl') *n.* **1.** A toy consisting of colored vanes pinned to the end of a stick in such a way that they turn when blown upon. **2.** A firework that forms a rotating wheel of colored flames.

pin•yon. Variant of **piñon.**

pi•o•neer (pī'ə-nîr') *n.* **1.** One who ventures into unknown or unclaimed territory to settle. **2.** An innovator in any field. [OF *pionier,* orig "a foot soldier sent out to clear the way."] —**pi'o•neer'** *v.*

pi•ous (pī'əs) *adj.* **1.** Reverently observant of religion; devout. **2.** Solemnly hypocritical. **3.** Devotional. **4.** High-minded. **5.** Commendable; worthy. [L *pius.*] —**pi'ous•ly** *adv.* —**pi'ous•ness** *n.*

pip[1] (pĭp) *n.* A small fruit seed, as of an orange. [Short for PIPPIN.]

pip[2] (pĭp) *n.* A dot indicating a unit of numerical value on dice or dominoes. [Earlier *peepe.*]

pip[3] (pĭp) *n.* A short, high-pitched radio signal. [Var of PEEP.]

pip[4] (pĭp) *n.* **1.** A disease of birds. **2.** *Slang.* Any minor or imaginary human ailment. [Prob < L *pituita,* phlegm.]

pipe (pīp) *n.* **1.** Any hollow cylinder or tubular conveyance for a fluid or gas. **2.** A tube of wood or clay with a mouthpiece at one end and a small bowl at the other, used for smoking. **3. a.** A tubular part or organ. **b. pipes.** *Informal.* The human respiratory system. **4. a.** A tubular wind instrument, such as a flute. **b.** Any of the tubes in an organ. **5. pipes. a.** A small wind instrument, consisting of tubes of different lengths bound together: *pipes of Pan.* **b.** A bagpipe. —*v.* **piped, piping. 1.** To convey (liquid or gas) by means of pipes. **2.** To play (a tune) on pipes. **3.** To make a shrill or whistling noise. [< Gmc **pīpa* < L *pīpāre,* to chirp.]

pipe•line (pīp'līn') *n.* **1.** A conduit of pipe for the conveyance of water or petroleum products. **2.** A channel by which secret information is transmitted. **3.** A line of supply.

pipe organ. An organ whose sound is made by pipes.

pip•er (pī'pər) *n.* One who plays pipes.

pip•ing (pī'pĭng) *n.* **1.** The act of playing pipes. **2.** A rounded strip of cloth used for trimming seams of fabric.

pip•pin (pĭp'ĭn) *n.* Any of several varieties of apple. [< OF *pepin,* seed, seedling apple.]

pip-squeak (pĭp'skwēk') *n.* A small or insignificant person.

pi•quant (pē'kənt, -känt', pē-känt') *adj.* **1.** Pleasantly pungent. **2.** Appealingly provocative. [< OF *piquer,* to pierce.] —**pi'quan•cy** *n.*

pique (pēk) *n.* Resentment or vexation arising from wounded pride or vanity. —*v.* **piqued, piquing. 1.** To cause such resentment. **2.** To provoke; arouse. [< OF *piquer,* to pierce.]

pi•qué (pĭ-kā', pē-) *n.* A fabric with various patterns of wales. [F, "quilting."]

pi•ra•nha (pĭ-rän'/y/ə, -răn'/y/ə) *n.* Also **pi•ra•ña.** A sharp-toothed tropical American freshwater fish that often attacks and destroys living animals. [< Tupi, "toothed fish."]

pi•rate (pī'rĭt) *n.* **1.** One who robs at sea or plunders the land from the sea. **2.** One who makes use of the copyrighted or patented work of another without permission or illicitly. [< Gk *peiratēs,* "attacker."] —**pi'ra•cy** *n.* —**pi'rate** *v.* **(-rated, -rating).**

pir•ou•ette (pĭr'o͞o-ĕt') *n. Ballet.* A full turn on the tip of the toe or on the ball of the foot. [< OF *pirouet,* a spinning top.] —**pir'ou•ette'** *v.* **(-etted, -etting).**

pis•ca•to•ri•al (pĭs'kə-tôr'ē-əl, -tōr'ē-əl) *adj.* Of or pertaining to fishing. [< L *piscis,* fish.]

Pi•sces (pī'sēz) *n.* **1.** A constellation in the equatorial region of the N Hemisphere. **2.** The 12th sign of the zodiac. [< L *piscis,* fish.]

pis•mire (pĭs'mīr', pĭz'-) *n.* An ant. [ME *pissemyre.*]

pis•ta•chi•o (pĭ-stăsh'ē-ō', -stä'shē-ō') *n., pl.* **-os. 1.** A tree bearing hard-shelled, edible nuts with a green kernel. **2.** Also **pistachio nut.** The nut of this tree. [< Pers *pistah.*]

pis•til (pĭs'tĭl) *n.* The seed-bearing reproductive organ of a flower. [< L *pistillum,* pestle.]

pis•tol (pĭs'təl) *n.* A firearm designed to be held and fired with one hand. [< Czech *pištala,* "pipe."]

pis•ton (pĭs'tən) *n.* A solid cylinder or disk that fits snugly into a larger cylinder and moves back and forth under fluid pressure. [< OIt *pistone,* a large pestle.]

pit[1] (pĭt) *n.* **1.** A relatively deep hole in the ground. **2.** A trap; pitfall. **3.** Hell. **4.** An enclosed space in which animals are placed for fighting. **5. a.** A natural depression in the surface of the body. **b.** A small indentation in the skin left by disease or injury; pockmark. **6.** The musician's section directly in front of the stage of a theater. **7.** *Bot.* A thin-walled spot or depression in the wall of some plant cells. —*v.* **pitted, pitting. 1.** To make cavities, depressions, or scars in. **2.** To place in contest against another. [< Gmc **putti* < L *puteus,* a pit, well.]

pit[2] (pĭt) *n.* The single, hard-shelled seed of certain fruits, as a peach or cherry; stone. —*v.* **pitted, pitting.** To extract pits from (fruit). [< Gmc **pithan,* pit, pith.]

pit•a•pat (pĭt'ə-păt') *v.* **-patted, -patting.** To make a repeated tapping sound. —*n.* A series of quick steps, taps, or beats. [Imit.]

pitch[1] (pĭch) *n.* Any of various thick, dark, sticky substances, as those obtained from the distillation residue of coal tar, wood tar, or petroleum, used for waterproofing, roofing, caulking, and paving. [< L *pix.*]

pitch[2] (pĭch) *v.* **1.** To throw in a specific, intended direction; hurl. **2.** *Baseball.* To throw (the ball) from the mound to the batter. **3.** To put up or in position; establish. **4.** To set firmly; implant. **5.** To fix the level of. **6.** To plunge; fall, esp. forward. **7.** To dip bow and stern alternately, as a ship in rough seas. **pitch in.** *Informal.* **1.** To set to work vigorously. **2.** To help; cooperate. —*n.* **1.** An act or instance of pitching. **2. a.** Any downward slant. **b.** The degree of such a slant. **3.** A point or stage of development. **4.** The subjective quality of a complex sound, as a musical tone, that is dependent mostly on frequency. **5. a.** The distance traveled by a screw in a single revolution. **b.** The distance between two corresponding points on adjacent screw threads or gear teeth. **6.** *Slang.* A set talk designed to persuade. [< OE **pician,* to PICK.]

pitch-black (pĭch'blăk') *adj.* Extremely black.

pitch•blende (pĭch'blĕnd') *n.* A brownish-black mineral, the principal ore of uranium.

pitch-dark (pĭch'därk') *adj.* Extremely dark.

pitch•er[1] (pĭch'ər) *n.* One that pitches in a baseball game.

pitch•er[2] (pĭch'ər) *n.* **1.** A vessel for liquids, with a handle and a lip or spout for pouring. **2.** *Bot.* A pitcherlike part such as the leaf of a pitcher plant. [< ML *bicārius,* goblet.]

pitch•fork (pĭch'fôrk') *n.* A large fork with widely spaced prongs for pitching hay and breaking ground. [< PICK + FORK.]

pitch•man (pĭch'mən) *n.* A peddler or vender.

pit•e•ous (pĭt'ē-əs) *adj.* Exciting pity; pathetic.

pit•fall (pĭt'fôl') *n.* **1.** A trap made by digging a hole in the ground and concealing its opening. **2.** A danger or difficulty.

pith (pĭth) *n.* **1.** The soft, spongelike central substance in the stems of many plants. **2.** The essential or central part of anything. **3.** Force; strength. [< OE *pitha* < Gmc **pithan.*]

pith•y (pĭth'ē) *adj.* **-ier, -iest. 1.** Of or resembling pith. **2.** Precisely meaningful.

pit•i•a•ble (pĭt'ē-ə-bəl) *adj.* Arousing or deserving of pity. —**pit'i•a•bly** *adv.*

pit•i•ful (pĭt'ĭ-fəl) *adj.* **1.** Arousing pity; pathetic. **2.** So inferior or insignificant as to be contemptible. —**pit'i•ful•ly** *adv.*

pit•i•less (pĭt'ĭ-lĭs) *adj.* Having no pity; without mercy. —**pit'i•less•ness** *n.*

pi•ton (pē'tŏn') *n.* A metal spike having a ring through which to pass a rope, used in mountain climbing as a hold. [< OF, "nail."]

pit•tance (pĭt'əns) *n.* **1.** A meager amount, esp. of money. **2.** A very small salary. [< VL **pietantia,* pious donation, portion.]

pit•ter-pat•ter (pĭt'ər-păt'ər) *n.* A rapid series of light, tapping sounds. [Imit.] —**pit'ter-pat'ter** *adv.*

Pitts•burgh (pĭts'bûrg'). A city in SW Pennsylvania. Pop. 513,000.

pi•tu•i•tar•y (pĭ-t/y/ōō'ə-tĕr'ē) *n., pl.* **-ies.** The **pituitary gland.** [< L *pituita,* phlegm.] —**pi•tu'i•tar'y** *adj.*

pituitary gland. A small, oval endocrine gland attached to the base of the vertebrate brain, the secretions of which control the other endocrine glands and influence growth, metabolism, and maturation.

pit•y (pĭt'ē) *n., pl.* **-ies. 1. a.** Sorrow or grief aroused by the misfortune of another. **b.** Condescending sympathy. **2.** A regrettable or disagreeable fact or necessity. —*v.* **-ied, -ying.** To feel pity (for). [< L *pius,* pious.] —**pit'y•ing•ly** *adv.*

piv•ot (pĭv'ət) *n.* **1.** A short rod or shaft about which a related part rotates or swings. **2.** One that determines the direction or effect of something. **3.** The act of turning on or as if on a pivot. —*v.* To turn or cause to turn on or as if on a pivot. [< OF.] —**piv'ot•al** *adj.*

pix. Variant of **pyx.**

pix•y (pĭk'sē) *n., pl.* **-ies.** Also **pix•ie.** A fairylike or elfin creature. [?]

Pi•zar•ro (pĭ-zär'ō), **Francisco.** 1470?–1541. Spanish explorer; conqueror of Peru.

piz•za (pēt'sə) *n.* An Italian baked dish having a pielike crust covered usually with a spiced mixture of tomatoes and cheese.

piz•zazz (pĭ-zăz') *n. Slang.* Flamboyance; zest; flair. [Expr.]

piz•ze•ri•a (pēt'sə-rē'ə) *n.* A place where pizzas are made and sold.

piz•zi•ca•to (pĭt'sĭ-kä'tō) *adj.* Played by plucking the strings of an instrument. [It.] —**piz'zi•ca'to** *adv.* & *n.*

pk. 1. pack. **2.** park. **3.** peak. **4.** peck.

pkg. package.

pkt. packet.

pl. plural.

Pl. Place.

plac•ard (plăk'ärd', -ərd) *n.* **1.** A poster for public display. **2.** A nameplate, as on the door of a house. —*v.* **1.** To announce on a placard. **2.** To post placards on or in. [< OF *plaquart,* plate.] —**plac'ard'er** *n.*

pla•cate (plā'kāt', plăk'āt') *v.* **-cated, -cating.** To allay the anger of; appease. [L *plācāre.*] —**pla•ca'tion** (plā-kā'shən) *n.*

place (plās) *n.* **1.** A portion of space; an area with or without definite boundaries. **2.** An area occupied by or set aside for someone or something. **3.** A definite location. **4. Place.** A public square or thoroughfare in a town. **5.** A table setting. **6.** A position regarded as possessed by someone or something else; stead: *I was chosen in his place.* **7.** A relative position in a series; standing: *fourth place.* —*v.* **placed, placing. 1.** To put in some particular position; set. **2.** To appoint to a post. **3.** To rank (someone or something) in an order or sequence. **4.** To make: *place a telephone call.* **5.** To request formally: *place an order.* **6.** To finish in second place or among the first three finishers in a race. [< L *platea,* "broad street," space.]

pla•ce•bo (plə-sē'bō) *n., pl.* **-bos** or **-boes. 1.** A substance containing no medication and given merely to humor a patient. **2.** An inactive substance used as a control in an experiment. [< L *placēre,* to please.]

place•ment (plās'mənt) *n.* **1.** The act of placing or arranging. **2.** The act or business of finding jobs, lodgings, or other positions for applicants.

pla•cen•ta (plə-sĕn'tə) *n., pl.* **-tas** or **-tae** (-tē). A vascular, membranous organ that develops in female mammals during pregnancy, lining the uterine wall and partially enveloping the fetus, to which it is attached by the umbilical cord. [< L, flat cake.] —**pla•cen'tal** *adj.*

plac•er (plăs'ər) *n.* **1.** A glacial or alluvial deposit of sand or gravel containing eroded particles of valuable minerals. **2.** A place where such a deposit is washed to extract its mineral content. [< L *platea,* "broad road," PLACE.]

plac•id (plăs'ĭd) *adj.* **1.** Outwardly calm or composed. **2.** Self-satisfied. [< L *placēre,* to please.] —**plac'id•ly** *adv.*

plack•et (plăk'ĭt) *n.* A slit in a garment. [< PLACARD.]

pla•gia•rize (plā'jə-rīz') *v.* **-rized, -rizing.** To steal and use (the ideas or writings of another) as one's own. [< L *plagium,* kidnaping.] —**pla'gia•rism'** *n.* —**pla'gia•riz'er** *n.*

plague (plāg) *n.* **1.** A pestilence, affliction, or calamity. **2.** Any cause for annoyance; a nuisance. **3.** A highly infectious, usually fatal, epidemic disease, esp. the bubonic plague. —*v.* **plagued, plaguing.** To harass, pester, or annoy. [< L *plāga,* a stroke, wound.]

plaid (plăd) *n.* **1.** A rectangular woolen scarf of a checked or tartan pattern worn over one shoulder by Scottish Highlanders. **2.** Cloth with a tartan or checked pattern. —*adj.* Having a tartan or checked pattern. [Scot Gael *plaide.*] —**plaid'ed** *adj.*

plain (plān) *adj.* **1.** Free from obstructions; open to view; clear. **2.** Easily understood; clearly evident. **3.** Uncomplicated; simple. **4.** Straightforward. **5.** Not mixed with other substances; pure. **6.** Common in rank or station; ordinary. **7.** Not pretentious; unsophisticated; simple. **8.** Unattractive. **9.** Sheer; unqualified: *plain terror.* —*n.* An extensive, level, treeless land region, such as a valley floor or a plateau summit. —*adv.* In a clear or intelligible manner. [< L *plānus,* flat, clear.] —**plain'ly** *adv.* —**plain'ness** *n.*

plain•clothes man (plān'klōz'). Also **plain•clothes•man** (plān'klōz'mən). A member of a police force who wears civilian clothes on duty.

Plains Indian. A member of any of the tribes of North American Indians that once inhabited the plains of the C U.S. and Canada.

plaint (plānt) *n.* **1.** A complaint. **2.** Lamentation. [< L *plangere,* to strike (one's breast), lament.]

plain•tiff (plān'tĭf) *n. Law.* The party that institutes a suit in a court.

plain•tive (plān'tĭv) *adj.* Expressing sorrow; mournful. —**plain'tive•ly** *adv.*

plait (plāt, plăt) *n.* A braid, esp. of hair. —*v.* To braid. [< L *plicāre,* to fold.]

plan (plăn) *n.* **1.** A detailed scheme or method for the accomplishment of an object. **2.** A proposed or tentative project or goal. **3.** An outline or sketch, esp. a drawing or diagram made to scale. —*v.* **planned, planning. 1.** To formulate, draw up, or make a plan or plans. **2.** To intend. [< L *plānus,* flat, and *planta,* sole of the foot.] —**plan'ner** *n.*

pla•nar (plā'nər) *adj.* **1.** Of or in a plane. **2.** Flat. —**pla•nar'i•ty** (plə-nâr'ə-tē) *n.*

plane[1] (plān) *n.* **1.** A surface containing all the straight lines connecting any two points on it. **2.** Any flat or level surface. **3.** A level of development. **4.** An airplane. **5.** A supporting surface of an airplane. [< L *plānus,* flat.] —**plane'ness** *n.*

plane[2] (plān) *n.* A carpenter's tool for smoothing and leveling wood. —*v.* **planed, planing.** To smooth or finish with or as with a plane. [< L *plānus,* level.] —**plan'er** *n.*

plane[3] (plān) *n.* Also **plane tree.** A sycamore or related tree with maplelike leaves and ball-like fruit clusters.

plan•et (plăn'ət) *n.* A nonluminous celestial body illuminated by light from a star around which it revolves. [< Gk *planētos,* wandering planet.] —**plan'e•tar'y** *adj.*

plan•e•tar•i•um (plăn'ə-târ'ē-əm) *n., pl.* **-iums** or **-ia** (-ē-ə). **1.** An apparatus or model representing the solar system. **2.** A device for projecting images of celestial bodies in their courses, on the inner surface of a hemispherical dome. **3.** A building or room containing such a device. [PLANET + -ARIUM.]

plan•e•toid (plăn'ə-toid') *n.* An asteroid.

plank (plăngk) *n.* **1.** A thick piece of lumber. **2.** One of the articles of a political platform. —*v.* **1.** To cover with planks. **2.** To bake or broil and serve (fish or meat) on a board. **3.** To put or set down with force. [< L *planca.*] —**plank'less** *adj.*

plank•ing (plăng'kĭng) *n.* **1.** Planks collectively. **2.** A covering of planks.

plank•ton (plăngk'tən) *n.* Usually minute plants and animals floating in bodies of water. [< Gk, "wanderer."] —**plank•ton'ic** (plăngk-tŏn'ĭk) *adj.*

plant (plănt, plänt) *n.* **1.** An organism characteristically having cellulose cell walls, growing by synthesis of inorganic substances, and lacking the power of locomotion. **2.** A plant without a permanent woody stem, as distinguished from a tree or shrub. **3.** A factory. **4.** The buildings, equipment, and fixtures of any institution. —*v.* **1.** To place in the ground to grow. **2.** To sow or supply with or as if with seeds or plants. **3.** To fix or set firmly in position. **4.** To establish. **5.** To implant in the mind. **6.** To place for the purpose of spying or deception. [< L *plantāre,* to plant.]

plan•tain¹ (plăn'tən) *n.* A weedy plant with a dense spike of small, greenish or whitish flowers. [< L *plantāgō.*]

plan•tain² (plăn'tən) *n.* A bananalike tropical plant or its fruit. [< L *platanus,* plane tree.]

plan•ta•tion (plăn-tā'shən) *n.* **1.** A group of cultivated trees or plants. **2.** A large estate or farm on which crops are worked by resident workers.

plant•er (plăn'tər) *n.* **1.** One that plants. **2.** A decorative plant container.

plaque (plăk) *n.* **1.** An ornamented or engraved plate, slab, or disk used for decoration or on a monument for information. **2.** A small ornament or a badge of membership. [< OF, metal plate, coin.]

plash (plăsh) *v.* To splash. [< MDu *plasschen* (imit).]

-plasm. *comb. form. Biol.* Cell-forming material: **protoplasm.** [< PLASMA.]

plas•ma (plăz'mə) *n.* Also **plasm** (plăz'əm). **1.** The clear, yellowish fluid portion of blood, lymph, or intramuscular fluid in which cells are suspended. **2.** The fluid portion of milk from which the curd has been separated; whey. **3.** A highly ionized gas composed of ions, electrons, and neutral particles. [< LL, a form, mold.] —**plas•mat'ic** (plăz-măt'ĭk), **plas'mic** *adj.*

plas•ter (plăs'tər, plas'-) *n.* A paste that hardens to a smooth solid and is used for coating walls and ceilings. **2. plaster of Paris. 3.** A pastelike mixture applied to a part of the body for healing or cosmetic purposes. —*v.* **1.** To cover with or as if with plaster. **2.** To cover conspicuously or to excess. [< Gk *emplassein,* to daub on, plaster.] —**plas'ter•er** *n.*

plaster of Paris. Any of a group of gypsum cements, essentially partially hydrated calcium sulfate, $CaSO_4 \cdot 1/2 H_2O$, a powder that hardens into a solid when mixed with water.

plas•tic (plăs'tĭk) *adj.* **1.** Capable of being shaped or formed; pliable. **2.** Pertaining to or dealing with shaping or modeling. **3.** Made of a plastic or plastics. —*n.* Any of various complex organic compounds produced by polymerization. They can be molded, extruded, or cast into various shapes and films, or drawn into filaments used as textile fibers. [< Gk *plassein,* to mold.] —**plas•tic'i•ty** *n.*

plastic surgery. Surgery to remodel, repair, or restore injured or defective tissue or body parts. —**plastic surgeon.**

plate (plāt) *n.* **1.** A smooth, flat, relatively thin, rigid body of uniform thickness. **2. a.** A sheet of hammered, rolled, or cast metal. **b.** A flat piece of metal on which something is engraved. **3. a.** A sheet of material converted into a printing surface, such as an electrotype. **b.** An impression taken from such a surface. **c.** A full-page book illustration, often in color. **4.** A sheet of glass or metal upon which a photographic image can be recorded. **5.** A thin metallic or plastic support fitted to the gums to anchor artificial teeth. **6.** *Baseball.* Home base or plate, usually a flat piece of heavy rubber. **7.** A shallow dish from which food is served or eaten. **8.** Food and service for one person at a meal. **9.** Household articles covered with a thin layer of metal. —*v.* **1.** To cover with a thin layer of metal. **2.** To armor. [< Gk *platus,* broad, flat.] —**plat'ed** *adj.*

pla•teau (plă-tō') *n., pl.* **-teaus** or **-teaux** (-tōz'). **1.** An elevated, level expanse of land. **2.** A leveling off. [< Gk *platus,* broad, flat.]

plat•en (plăt'n) *n.* **1.** One of the two flat members in a printing press that holds the paper against the inked type. **2.** The roller on a typewriter. [Earlier *plattin* < OF *plate,* plate.]

plat•form (plăt'fôrm') *n.* **1.** Any horizontal surface raised above the level of the adjacent area. **2.** A formal declaration of the policy of a group, such as a political party. [OF *plate-forme,* "flat form."]

plat•ing (plā'tĭng) *n.* **1.** A thin layer or coating of metal, such as gold or silver. **2.** A covering or layer of metal plates.

plat•i•num (plăt'ə-nəm) *n. Symbol* **Pt** A silver-white, corrosive-resistant, metallic element used in electrical components, jewelry, dentistry, electroplating, and as a catalyst. Atomic number 78, atomic weight 195.09. [< Span *plata,* silver, plate.]

plat•i•tude (plăt'ə-t/y/o͞od') *n.* A trite remark, statement, or idea. [F, "flatness."] —**plat'i•tu'di•nous** *adj.* —**plat'i•tu'di•nous•ly** *adv.*

Pla•to (plā'tō). 427?–347 B.C. Greek philosopher.

Pla•ton•ic (plə-tŏn'ĭk, plā-) *adj.* **1.** Of or characteristic of Plato or his philosophy. **2.** Often **platonic.** Transcending physical desire; spiritual. **Pla•ton'i•cal•ly** *adv.*

pla•toon (plə-to͞on') *n.* **1.** A subdivision of a military company usually consisting of two or more squads. **2.** A body of persons working together. [F *peloton,* "little ball," group of soldiers.]

plat•ter (plăt'ər) *n.* **1.** A large, shallow dish or plate. **2.** A meal served on such a dish. [< OF *plate,* plate.]

plat•y•pus (plăt'ĭ-pəs) *n., pl.* **-puses.** A semi-aquatic, egg-laying, Australian mammal with webbed feet and a snout resembling a duck's bill. [< Gk *platupous,* "flat-footed."]

plau•dit (plô'dĭt) *n.* An expression of praise. [< L *plaudere,* to applaud.]

plau•si•ble (plô'zə-bəl) *adj.* Apparently valid or likely. [Orig "deserving applause" < L *plaudere,* to applaud.] —**plau'si•bil'i•ty, plau'si•ble•ness** *n.* —**plau'si•bly** *adv.*

play (plā) *v.* **1.** To occupy oneself in amusement, sport, etc. **2.** To take part in (a game or sport). **3.** To act or perform in jest. **4.** To toy; trifle. **5.** To act in a specified way: *play fair.* **6.** To act or perform (a role). **7.** To perform (on a musical instrument). **8.** To be performed: Othello *is playing next week.* **9.** To move lightly or irregularly: *The breeze played on the water.* **10.** To pretend to be. **11.** To compete against in a game. **12. a.** To occupy (a position) in a game: *He plays first base.* **b.** To employ (a player) in a game or position. **c.** To use (a card, piece, etc.) in a game. **13.** To manipulate: *He played his two opponents against each other.* **14.** To bet or wager. **15.** To cause (a record, radio, etc.) to emit sounds. —**play down.** To minimize the importance of. —**play on** (or **upon**). To take advantage of (another's feelings). —**play up.** *Informal.* To emphasize or publicize. —**play up to.** *Informal.* To curry favor with. —*n.* **1. a.** A literary work written for the stage. **b.** The performance of such a work. **2.** Activity engaged in for enjoyment or recreation. **3.** Fun: *It was done in play.* **4.** The act or manner of playing a game or sport. **5.** A method of dealing with people generally: *fair play.* **6.** A move in a game: *It's your play.* **7.** *Sports.* Legitimate use: *The ball was in play.* **8.** Action or use: *the play of the imagination.* **9.** Free movement, as of mechanical parts. —**make a play for.** To attempt to attract or obtain. [< OE *plegan* < Gmc **plegan,* to exercise oneself.] —**play'a•ble** *adj.* —**play'ing•ly** *adv.*

play-act (plā'ăkt') *v.* **1.** To play a pretended role. **2.** To behave in an artificial manner.

play•bill (plā'bĭl') *n.* A program for a theatrical performance.

play•boy (plā'boi') *n.* A wealthy man devoted to the pleasures of nightclubs, sports, and female company.

play•er (plā'ər) *n.* **1.** One who participates in a game or sport. **2.** An actor. **3.** One who plays a musical instrument.

play•ful (plā'fəl) *adj.* **1.** Full of fun; sportive. **2.** Humorous; jesting. —**play'ful•ly** *adv.* —**play'ful•ness** *n.*

play•go•er (plā'gō'ər) *n.* One who attends the theater.

play•ground (plā'ground') *n.* An outdoor area set aside for recreation and play.

playing card. A card marked with its rank and suit belonging to any of several decks used in playing various games.

play•mate (plā'māt') *n.* A companion in play.

play-off (plā'ôf', -ŏf') *n. Sports.* A final game or series of games played to determine a championship.

play•pen (plā'pĕn') *n.* A portable enclosure in which a baby can be left to play.

play•thing (plā'thĭng') *n.* A toy.

play•wright (plā'rīt') *n.* One who writes plays.

pla•za (plä'zə, plăz'ə) *n.* A public square or similar open area in a town or city. [< L *platea,* broad street, courtyard.]

plea (plē) *n.* **1.** An appeal or entreaty. **2.** An excuse; pretext. **3.** *Law.* The answer of the accused to a charge or indictment. [< OF *plaid,* legal action, agreement.]

plead (plēd) *v.* **pleaded** or **pled, pleading. 1.** To appeal earnestly; implore. **2.** To argue for or against something. **3.** To submit as an excuse or defense: *plead illness.* **4.** To put forward a plea of a specific nature in a court of law. **5.** To argue or present (a case) in a court. [< OF *plaidier.*] —**plead'er** *n.*

pleas•ant (plĕz'ənt) *adj.* **1.** Giving or affording mild pleasure; agreeable. **2.** Pleasing in manner, appearance, etc. [< L *placēre,* to please.] —**pleas'ant•ly** *adv.* —**pleas'ant•ness** *n.*

pleas•ant•ry (plĕz'ən-trē) *n., pl.* **-ries.** A jesting or friendly remark.

please (plēz) *v.* **pleased, pleasing. 1.** To make glad; give enjoyment or satisfaction to. **2.** To be the will or desire of: *may it please the court.* **3.** To be willing to. Used to introduce or indicate a politely intended request: *Please read it now.* **4.** To like; wish: *Do whatever you please.* [< L *placēre.*] —**pleas'er** *n.*

pleas•ing (plē'zĭng) *adj.* Agreeable; gratifying.

pleas•ur•a•ble (plĕzh'ər-ə-bəl) *adj.* Giving pleasure; gratifying. —**pleas'ur•a•bly** *adv.*

pleas•ure (plĕzh'ər) *n.* **1.** Enjoyment; satisfaction. 2. A source of enjoyment. 3. One's preference, wish, or choice: *What is your pleasure?* [< OF *plaisir,* to please.]

pleat (plēt) *n.* A fold in cloth made by doubling the material upon itself. [< PLAIT.] —**pleat** *v.*

ple•be•ian (plĭ-bē'ən) *adj.* Common; vulgar. —*n.* Someone who is common or crude. [< L *plēbs,* common people.]

pleb•i•scite (plĕb'ə-sīt', -sĭt) *n.* A vote in which the entire people is called to accept or refuse a political proposal. [< L *plēbiscītum,* people's decree.]

plec•trum (plĕk'trəm) *n., pl.* **-trums** or **-tra** (-trə). Also **plec•tron** (plĕk'trŏn'). A small, thin piece of metal, plastic, etc., used to play a stringed instrument. [< Gk *plēktron.*]

pled (plĕd). Alternate *p.t.* & *p.p.* of **plead.**

pledge (plĕj) *n.* 1. A formal promise. 2. Something given or held as security in a loan, contract, etc. 3. One who has promised to join a fraternity, club, etc. —*v.* **pledged, pledging.** 1. To promise solemnly. 2. To bind by or as by a pledge. 3. To deposit as security. 4. To promise to join (a fraternity, club, etc.). [< LL *plebium.*] —**pledg'er** *n.*

-plegia. *comb. form.* A form of paralysis: **paraplegia.** [< Gk *plēgē,* a stroke, blow.]

Plei•a•des (plē'ə-dēz') *pl.n.* An open star cluster in the constellation Taurus, consisting of several hundred stars, of which six are visible to the naked eye.

Pleis•to•cene (plī'stə-sēn') *adj.* Of or belonging to the geologic time, rock series, or sedimentary deposits of the earlier of the two epochs of the Quaternary period. —*n.* The Pleistocene epoch. [Gk *pleistos,* most + -CENE.]

ple•na•ry (plē'nə-rē, plĕn'ə-) *adj.* 1. Full; absolute: *a diplomat with plenary powers.* 2. Fully attended by qualified members. [< L *plēnus,* full.] —**ple'na•ri•ly** *adv.*

plen•i•po•ten•ti•ar•y (plĕn'ē-pə-tĕn'shē-ĕr'ē, -shə-rē) *adj.* Invested with full powers. —*n., pl.* **-ies.** A diplomatic agent, as an ambassador, fully authorized to represent his government. [< LL *plēnipotens.*]

plen•i•tude (plĕn'ə-t/y/o͞od') *n.* 1. Abundance; copiousness. 2. The condition of being full or complete. [< L *plēnus,* full.]

plen•te•ous (plĕn'tē-əs) *adj.* 1. Abundant; copious. 2. Producing or yielding in abundance. —**plen'te•ous•ness** *n.*

plen•ti•ful (plĕn'tĭ-fəl) *adj.* 1. Existing in great quantity; abundant. 2. Providing an abundance. —**plen'ti•ful•ly** *adv.*

plen•ty (plĕn'tē) *n.* 1. A large quantity or amount; abundance: *goods in plenty.* 2. A condition of general abundance or prosperity. [< L *plēnus,* full.]

pleth•o•ra (plĕth'ər-ə) *n.* Superabundance; excess. [< Gk *plēthōra,* fullness.]

pleu•ri•sy (plo͝or'ə-sē) *n.* Inflammation of the membranous sacs that enclose the lungs. [< Gk *pleura,* side, rib.]

plex•us (plĕk'səs) *n., pl.* **-us** or **-uses.** A structure in the form of a network, esp. of nerves, blood vessels, or lymphatics. [< L, pp of *plectere,* to plait.]

pli•a•ble (plī'ə-bəl) *adj.* 1. Easily bent or shaped; flexible. 2. Easily influenced or persuaded; tractable. —**pli'a•bil'i•ty** *n.*

pli•ant (plī'ənt) *adj.* 1. Easily bent or flexed; supple. 2. Receptive to change; adaptable. [< L *plicāre,* to fold.] —**pli'an•cy** (-ən-sē) *n.*

pli•ers (plī'ərz) *pl.n.* Any of variously shaped tools having a pair of pivoted jaws, used for holding, bending, etc.

plight[1] (plīt) *n.* A condition or situation of difficulty or adversity. [< OF *pleit, ploit,* "a fold."]

plight[2] (plīt) *v.* To promise or bind by a solemn pledge, esp. to betroth. [< OE *pliht,* peril < Gmc **plegan,* to risk, pledge.]

plinth (plĭnth) *n.* A block or slab upon which a pedestal, column, or statue is placed. [< Gk *plinthos,* brick, square stone block.]

Pli•o•cene (plī'ə-sēn') *adj.* Of or belonging to the geologic time, rock series, or sedimentary deposits of the last of the five epochs of the Tertiary period. —*n.* The Pliocene epoch. [< Gk *pleiōn,* more + -CENE.]

plod (plŏd) *v.* **plodded, plodding.** 1. To walk heavily or laboriously; trudge. 2. To work perseveringly or monotonously. [Imit.] —**plod'der** *n.* —**plod'ding•ly** *adv.*

-ploid. *comb. form.* A specific multiple of a set of chromosomes: **haploid.** [< Gk *-ploos,* -fold.]

plop (plŏp) *v.* **plopped, plopping.** 1. To fall with a sound like that of an object falling into water. 2. To drop or sink heavily. [Imit.] —**plop** *n.*

plot (plŏt) *n.* 1. A small piece of ground. 2. The series of events constituting an outline of the action of a narrative or drama. 3. A secret plan; scheme. —*v.* **plotted, plotting.** 1. To represent graphically, as on a chart. 2. To plan secretly; scheme; conspire. [< OE *plot,* piece of ground, and OF *complote,* secret plan.] —**plot'ter** *n.*

plov•er (plŭv'ər, plō'vər) *n.* Any of various relatively small, short-billed wading birds. [< VL **pluviārius,* "rain-bird."]

plow (plou) Also *chiefly Brit.* **plough.** *n.* 1. A farm implement used for breaking up soil and cutting furrows. 2. Any implement of similar function, as a snowplow. —*v.* 1. To break and turn up (earth) with a plow. 2. To make (one's way) forcefully: *plowed through the crowd.* [< OE *plōg, plōh,* plowland.]

plow•share (plou'shâr') *n.* The cutting blade of a plow.

ploy (ploi) *n.* A stratagem to obtain an advantage over one's opponent. [< EMPLOY.]

pluck (plŭk) *v.* 1. To pull off or out; pick. 2. To pull the hair or feathers from. 3. To sound (the strings of an instrument) by pulling and releasing them. —*n.* 1. The act of plucking. 2. Resourceful courage; spirit. [< VL **piluccāre,* to remove the hair.]

pluck•y (plŭk'ē) *adj.* **-ier, -iest.** Courageous in trying circumstances. —**pluck'i•ly** *adv.*

plug (plŭg) *n.* 1. An object used to stop a hole. 2. a. A fitting, commonly with metal prongs for insertion in a fixed socket, used to make electric connections. b. A **spark plug.** 3. A fireplug. 4. A portion of chewing tobacco. 5. *Informal.* A favorable public mention of a product, business, etc. —*v.* **plugged, plugging.** 1. To fill (a hole) tightly with or as with a plug. 2. To connect to a socket by means of a plug. 3. *Slang.* To hit with a bullet. 4. *Informal.* To make favorable public mention of (a product, business, etc.). 5. *Informal.* To work doggedly at some activity. [MDu *plugge.*]

plum (plŭm) *n.* 1. A smooth-skinned, fleshy fruit with a hard-shelled pit. 2. A tree bearing such fruit. 3. Something especially desirable, as a good position. [< OE *plūme* < Gmc < L *prūnum.*]

plum•age (plo͞o'mĭj) *n.* The feathers of a bird. [< OE *plume,* plume.]

plumb (plŭm) *n.* 1. A weight suspended from the end of a line, used to determine water depth. 2. Such a device used to establish a true vertical. —*adj.* 1. Exactly vertical. 2. *Informal.* Utter; sheer: *a plumb fool.* —*v.* 1. To test the alignment or angle of with a plumb. 2. To determine the depth of; sound. [< L *plumbum,* lead.] —**plumb** *adv.* —**plumb'a•ble** *adj.*

plumb bob. A usually conical weight attached to a plumb line.

plumb•er (plŭm'ər) *n.* One who installs and repairs pipes and plumbing. [< LL *plumbārius,* lead worker.]

plumb•ing (plŭm'ĭng) *n.* 1. The pipes and fixtures of a water or sewage system. 2. The trade of a plumber.

plumb line. A line from which a weight is suspended to determine verticality or depth.

plume (plo͞om) *n.* 1. A feather, esp. a large or showy one. 2. A featherlike form: *a plume of smoke.* —*v.* **plumed, pluming.** 1. To decorate with or as with plumes. 2. To pride or congratulate (oneself). [< L *plūma.*]

plum•met (plŭm'ĭt) *v.* To drop straight down; plunge. [< L *plumbum,* lead.]

plump[1] (plŭmp) *adj.* Well-rounded and full in form; chubby. —*v.* To make well-rounded: *plump up a pillow.* [MLG, thick, blunt, dull.] —**plump'ly** *adv.* —**plump'ness** *n.*

plump[2] (plŭmp) *v.* 1. To drop abruptly or heavily. 2. To give full support or praise. —*n.* 1. A heavy or abrupt fall. 2. The sound of this. —*adv.* 1. With a heavy impact. 2. Straight down or ahead. [MLG *plumpen,* to plunge into water.]

plun•der (plŭn'dər) *v.* To rob of goods, esp. by force; pillage. —*n.* Property stolen by fraud or force; booty. [MDu *plunderen* or Fris *plunderje,* "to rob (of household goods)."] —**plun'der•a•ble** *adj.* —**plun'der•er** *n.*

plunge (plŭnj) *v.* **plunged, plunging.** 1. To thrust or throw oneself forcefully into a substance or place. 2. To enter or cast suddenly into a given state, situation, or activity. 3. To descend steeply or suddenly. [< VL **plumbicāre,* to sound with a plumb.] —**plunge** *n.*

plung•er (plŭn'jər) *n.* 1. A machine part that operates with a repeated thrusting or plunging movement. 2. A device consisting of a rubber suction cup at the end of a stick, used to unclog drains and pipes.

plunk (plŭngk) *v.* 1. To pluck (the strings of a musical instrument). 2. To drop heavily or abruptly. 3. To emit a hollow, twanging sound. —*n.* A hollow, twanging sound. [Imit.] —**plunk'er** *n.*

plu•per•fect (plo͞o-pûr'fĭkt) *Gram. adj.* Of or designating a verb tense used to express action completed prior to a specified or implied past time. —*n.* 1. The pluperfect tense. 2. A verb or form in this tense. [< L *(tempus praeteritum) plūs quam perfectum,* "(past tense) more than perfect."]

plu•ral (plo͝or'əl) *Gram. adj.* Of or relating to a form that designates more than one of the things specified. —*n.* 1. The plural number or form. 2. A word or term in this form. [< L *plūs (plūr-),* more.] —**plu'ral•ly** *adv.*

Usage: Terms made up of single letters or numbers, or groups of letters or numbers, are made plural by the addition of *'s* or *s,* as *two R's* (or *Rs*), *two 6's* (or *6s*), *GI's* (or *GIs*), *the 1930's* (or *1930s*). The *'s* form is usually used for lower-case letters: *two t's.* Plurals of surnames of one syllable ending in *s* are formed by adding *es: Joneses.* Plurals of given names ending in *y* preceded by a consonant are formed by adding *s: the three Marys.*

plu•ral•i•ty (plōō-răl'ə-tē) *n., pl.* **-ties.** **1.** In a contest of more than two alternatives, the number of votes cast for the winning alternative, if this number is not more than one half of the total votes cast. **2.** The number by which the vote of a winning candidate exceeds that of his closest opponent.

plus (plŭs) *prep.* **1.** Added to. **2.** Increased by; along with: *earnings plus dividends.* —*adj.* **1.** Positive, as on a scale or in polarity. **2.** Being in addition to what is expected or specified. —*n.* **1.** The symbol +, used to indicate addition or a positive quantity. **2.** A favorable factor. [L *plūs,* more.]

plush (plŭsh) *n.* A fabric with a thick, deep pile. —*adj.* Luxurious. [< OF *peluchier,* to pluck.] —**plush'ly** *adv.*

Plu•to (plōō'tō) *n.* **1.** The 9th and farthest planet from the sun, having a sidereal period of revolution about the sun of 248.4 years, 2.8 billion miles distant at perihelion and 4.6 billion miles at aphelion, and a diameter approx. half that of the earth. **2.** Roman god of the dead.

plu•toc•ra•cy (plōō-tŏk'rə-sē) *n., pl.* **-cies.** **1.** Government by the wealthy. **2.** A wealthy class that controls a government. [< Gk *ploutos,* wealth + -CRACY.] —**plu'to•crat'** (-tə-krăt') *n.* —**plu'to•crat'ic** *adj.*

plu•ton•ic (plōō-tŏn'ĭk) *adj. Geol.* Of deep igneous or magmatic origin: *plutonic water.*

plu•to•ni•um (plōō-tō'nē-əm) *n. Symbol* **Pu** A naturally radioactive, silvery metallic element, used as a reactor fuel and in nuclear weapons. Atomic number 94, longest-lived isotope Pu 244. [< PLUTO.]

ply[1] (plī) *n., pl.* **plies.** **1.** A layer, as of doubled-over cloth. **2.** One of the layers or strands of which something, as plywood, rope, or yarn, is composed. [< L *plicāre,* to fold.]

ply[2] (plī) *v.* **plied, plying.** **1.** To use diligently, as a tool or weapon. **2.** To engage in, as a trade; work diligently. **3.** To traverse or sail over regularly. **4.** To continue supplying: *ply guests with food.* [< APPLY.]

ply•wood (plī'wŏŏd') *n.* A material made of layers of wood glued tightly together. [PLY[1] + WOOD.]

Pm promethium.

PM postmaster.

P.M. **1.** postmaster. **2.** post meridiem. **3.** postmortem examination. **4.** prime minister.

p.n. promissory note.

pneu•mat•ic (n/y/ōō-măt'ĭk) *adj.* Of, operated by, or filled with air or another gas. [< Gk *pneuma,* wind, spirit.]

pneu•mo•nia (n/y/ōō-mōn'yə) *n.* An acute or chronic disease marked by inflammation of the lungs and caused by viruses, bacteria, and physical and chemical agents. [< Gk *pneumonia,* var of *pleumonia,* disease of the lungs.]

Po polonium.

Po (pō). A river of N Italy.

P.O. **1.** petty officer. **2.** postal (money) order. **3.** post office.

poach[1] (pōch) *v.* To cook in boiling or simmering liquid. [< OF *pochier (des œufs),* "to put (egg yolks) in pockets."]

poach[2] (pōch) *v.* **1.** To trespass on another's property in order to take fish or game. **2.** To take (fish or game) in a forbidden area. [OF *pochier,* to trample, poach into.] —**poach'er** *n.*

pock (pŏk) *n.* **1.** A pustule caused by smallpox or a similar eruptive disease. **2.** A mark or scar left in the skin by such a pustule; pockmark. [< OE *pocc.* See **beu-**.]

pock•et (pŏk'ĭt) *n.* **1.** A pouch or piece of material sewn onto a garment with one edge open. **2.** Any receptacle or cavity. **3.** Financial means. **4.** A small isolated or protected area or group. —*adj.* **1.** Suitable for or capable of being carried in a pocket. **2.** Tiny; miniature. —*v.* **1.** To place in or as in a pocket. **2.** To take possession of for oneself, esp. dishonestly. [< OF *poche,* pocket.]

pock•et•book (pŏk'ĭt-bŏŏk') *n.* **1.** A wallet; billfold. **2.** A handbag; purse. **3.** Financial resources. **4.** A pocket-sized, usually paper-bound book.

pock•et•knife (pŏk'ĭt-nīf') *n.* A small knife with a blade or blades folding into the handle.

pock•mark (pŏk'märk') *n.* A pitlike scar left on the skin by smallpox or another eruptive disease. —**pock'marked'** *adj.*

pod (pŏd) *n.* **1.** A seed vessel, as of a pea or bean, that splits open. **2.** A housing that encloses an externally mounted part of an aircraft. [Prob var of COD.]

po•di•a•try (pə-dī'ə-trē) *n.* The study and treatment of foot ailments. [Gk *pous (pod-),* foot + -IATRY.] —**po•di'a•trist** *n.*

po•di•um (pō'dē-əm) *n., pl.* **-dia** (-dē-ə) or **-ums.** An elevated platform for an orchestra conductor, lecturer, etc. [< Gk *podion,* "small foot," base.]

P.O.E. port of entry.

Poe (pō), **Edgar Allan.** 1809–1849. American poet and critic.

po•em (pō'əm, -ĭm) *n.* A verbal composition having the suggestive power to engage the feelings and imagination, typically through the highly structured patterning and movement of sound, rhythm, and meaning characteristic of verse. [< Gk *poiēma,* "created thing," work, poem.]

po•e•sy (pō'ə-zē, -sē) *n. Archaic.* Poetry.

po•et (pō'ĭt) *n.* A writer of poems. [< Gk *poiētēs,* "maker," poet.]

po•et•as•ter (pō'ĭt-ăs'tər) *n.* An inferior poet.

po•et•ic (pō-ĕt'ĭk) *adj.* Also **po•et•i•cal** (-ĭ-kəl). Of, pertaining to, or characteristic of poetry or poets. —**po•et'i•cal•ly** *adv.*

po•et•ry (pō'ĭ-trē) *n.* **1.** The art or work of a poet. **2.** Verse as distinguished from prose. **3.** The quality characteristic of the poetic experience.

po•grom (pō'grəm, pō-grŏm') *n.* An organized massacre of a minority group, esp. Jews. [Russ, "like thunder," devastation.]

poign•ant (poin'yənt, poi'nənt) *adj.* **1.** Keenly distressing to the mind or feelings: *poignant anxiety.* **2.** Affecting; touching: *poignant sentiment.* [< L *pungere,* to prick, pierce.] —**poign'an•cy** *n.* —**poign'ant•ly** *adv.*

poin•set•ti•a (poin-sĕt'ē-ə) *n.* A tropical American shrub with showy, usually scarlet petallike leaves beneath the small yellow flowers. [< J.R. *Poinsett* (1799–1851), U.S. minister to Mexico.]

point (point) *n.* **1.** The sharp or tapered end of something. **2.** A tapering extension of land projecting into water. **3.** A dimensionless geometric object having no property but location. **4.** A position or place. **5.** A specified or distinct degree or condition. **6.** A specific moment in time. **7.** An important, essential, or primary factor or idea. **8.** A purpose; reason. **9.** An individual item or element. **10.** A distinctive characteristic or quality. **11.** A single unit, as in counting, rating, or measuring. **12.** An electrical contact, esp. one in the distributor of an automobile engine. **13.** A unit equal to one dollar, used to quote or state the current prices of stocks, commodities, etc. —*v.* **1.** To direct or aim. **2.** To bring to notice: *pointed out the landmarks.* **3.** To indicate the position or direction of with or as with the finger. **4.** To give emphasis to; stress: *pointed up the difference.* [< L *punctus,* pp of *pungere,* to pierce, prick.]

point•blank (point'blăngk') *adj.* **1. a.** So close to a target that a weapon can be aimed directly at it: *pointblank range.* **b.** Close enough so that missing the target is unlikely. **2.** Straightforward; blunt. —*adv.* **1.** With a straight aim: *fired pointblank.* **2.** Without hesitation or equivocation: *answer pointblank.*

point•ed (poin'tĭd) *adj.* **1.** Having a point. **2.** Pertinent; incisive. **3.** Obviously making reference to something or someone. **4.** Conspicuous; marked: *a pointed lack of interest.* —**point'ed•ly** *adv.* —**point'ed•ness** *n.*

point•er (poin'tər) *n.* **1.** An indicator on a watch, balance, etc. **2.** A long stick for indicating objects on a chart, blackboard, etc. **3.** A hunting dog with a short, smooth coat. **4.** A suggestion; piece of advice.

point•less (point'lĭs) *adj.* Meaningless; irrelevant. —**point'less•ly** *adv.*

point of view. **1.** The position from which something is observed or considered. **2.** One's manner of viewing things; attitude.

poise (poiz) *v.* **poised, poising.** To balance or be balanced. —*n.* **1.** Balance; stability. **2. a.** Composure. **b.** Dignity of manner. [< OF *poiser,* to weigh.]

poi•son (poi'zən) *n.* Any substance that causes injury or death, esp. by chemical means. —*v.* **1.** To give poison to; kill or harm with poison. **2.** To make poisonous. **3.** To have a harmful influence on; corrupt or ruin. [< L *pōtiō,* potion.] —**poi'son•ous** *adj.*

poison ivy. A North American plant having leaflets in groups of three and causing a rash on contact.

poke (pōk) *v.* **poked, poking.** **1.** To push or jab, as with a finger or stick. **2.** To make (a hole or pathway) by or as by prodding or thrusting. **3.** To thrust forward; appear. **4.** To pry or meddle. **5.** To search curiously; rummage. —*n.* A push, thrust, or jab. [< MDu and MLG *poken,* to strike, thrust.]

pok•er[1] (pō'kər) *n.* A metal rod used to stir a fire.

pok•er[2] (pō'kər) *n.* Any of various card games played by two or more players who bet on the value of their hands. [?]

po•key (pō'kē) *n., pl.* **-keys.** *Slang.* Jail. [< POKY.]

pok•y (pō'kē) *adj.* **-ier, -iest.** Dawdling; slow. [< POKE.] —**pok'i•ness** *n.*

Pol. Poland; Polish.

Po•land (pō'lənd). A republic of C Europe. Pop. 31,340,000. Cap. Warsaw.

Poland

po•lar (pō'lər) *adj.* **1.** Of, measured from, or referred to a pole or poles. **2.** Of or near the North or South Pole. **3.** Occupying or characterized by opposite extremes.

polar bear. A large white bear of Arctic regions.

polar cap. 1. A high-altitude icecap. **2.** The polar regions of ice.

Po•lar•is (pō-lăr'ĭs, -lâr'ĭs) *n.* A star at the end of the handle of the Little Dipper and almost at the N celestial pole. [NL *(Stella) Polāris,* polar (star).]

po•lar•i•ty (pō-lăr'ə-tē, pō-lâr'-) *n., pl.* **-ties. 1.** Intrinsic polar separation, alignment, or orientation, esp. of a physical property. **2.** The manifestation of two opposing tendencies. **3.** An indicated polar extreme.

po•lar•ize (pō'lə-rīz') *v.* **-ized, -izing. 1.** To impart polarity to. **2.** To cause to concentrate about two opposing positions. **3.** To acquire polarity. **—po'lar•i•za'tion** *n.*

pole[1] (pōl) *n.* **1.** Either axial extremity of any axis through a sphere. **2.** The **North Pole** or the **South Pole. 3.** A magnetic pole. **4.** Either of two oppositely charged terminals, as in an electric cell or battery. **5.** Either of two opposing forces. [< Gk *polos,* axis of the sphere.]

pole[2] (pōl) *n.* A long, slender piece of wood or other material. [< L *pālus,* stake.]

Pole (pōl) *n.* A native of Poland.

pole•cat (pōl'kăt') *n.* **1.** A weasellike Old World mammal. **2.** A skunk.

po•lem•ic (pə-lĕm'ĭk) *n.* **1.** A controversy, argument, or refutation. **2. polemics.** The art or practice of argumentation or controversy. [< Gk *polemos,* war.] **—po•lem'ic, po•lem'i•cal** *adj.*

pole•star (pōl'stär') *n.* **1.** Polaris. **2.** A guiding principle.

pole vault. *Sports.* A field event in which the contestant vaults over a high crossbar with the aid of a long pole. **—pole'-vault'er** (pōl'vôlt'ər) *n.*

po•lice (pə-lēs') *n., pl.* **-lice. 1. a.** A governmental department established to maintain order, enforce the law, and prevent and detect crime. **b.** *(takes pl. v.).* The members of such a department. **2.** Any group of persons resembling the police force of a community in function: *campus police.* **3.** Soldiers assigned to a specified maintenance duty: *kitchen police.* **—***v.* **-liced, -licing. 1.** To control or keep in order with or as with police. **2.** To make (a military area) neat and orderly. [< Gk *polis,* city.]

po•lice•man (pə-lēs'mən) *n.* A member of a police department.

pol•i•cy[1] (pŏl'ə-sē) *n., pl.* **-cies. 1.** A method or course of action adopted by a government, business organization, etc., designed to influence and determine decisions. **2.** A guiding principle or procedure. **3.** Shrewdness; sagacity. [< Gk *politeia,* citizenship.]

pol•i•cy[2] (pŏl'ə-sē) *n., pl.* **-cies.** A written contract or certificate of insurance. [< Gk *apodeixis,* "a showing or making known."]

po•li•o (pō'lē-ō') *n.* Poliomyelitis.

po•li•o•my•e•li•tis (pō'lē-ō-mī'ə-lī'tĭs) *n.* An infectious viral disease occurring mainly in children and in its acute forms attacking the central nervous system and producing paralysis, muscular atrophy, and often death. [Gk *polios,* gray + MYELITIS.]

pol•ish (pŏl'ĭsh) *v.* **1.** To make smooth or shiny, as by abrasion or rubbing. **2.** To remove flaws from; perfect; refine. **—***n.* **1.** Smoothness or shininess of surface. **2.** A substance used to shine a surface. **3.** Elegance of style or manners. [< L *polīre.*] **—pol'ish•er** *n.*

Po•lish (pō'lĭsh) *adj.* Of or pertaining to Poland, its inhabitants, or their language. **—***n.* The Slavic language of Poland.

polit. political; politics.

po•lite (pə-līt') *adj.* **-liter, -litest. 1.** Marked by consideration and correct manners; courteous. **2.** Refined; cultivated. [< L *polītus,* "polished."] **—po•lite'ly** *adv.* **—po•lite'ness** *n.*

pol•i•tic (pŏl'ə-tĭk) *adj.* **1.** Shrewd and tactful. **2.** Prudent; judicious.

po•lit•i•cal (pə-lĭt'ĭ-kəl) *adj.* **1.** Of or pertaining to government or politics. **2.** Characteristic of political parties or politicians. [< Gk *politikos,* of a citizen.] **—po•lit'i•cal•ly** *adv.*

pol•i•ti•cian (pŏl'ə-tĭsh'ən) *n.* **1.** One actively involved in politics, esp. party politics. **2.** One who holds or seeks a political office.

pol•i•tick (pŏl'ə-tĭk) *v.* To engage in or talk politics.

pol•i•tics (pŏl'ə-tĭks) *n. (takes sing. v.).* **1.** The art or science of political government. **2.** The policies or affairs of a government. **3. a.** The conducting of or engaging in political affairs, often professionally. **b.** The profession of a person so involved. **4.** *(takes pl. v.).* Political opinions or principles.

pol•i•ty (pŏl'ə-tē) *n., pl.* **-ties.** Any organized society, as a nation, having one specific form of government. [< Gk *politēs,* citizen.]

Polk (pōk), **James Knox.** 1795–1849. 11th President of the U.S. (1845–49).

James K. Polk

pol•ka (pōl'kə, pō'kə) *n.* **1.** A lively round dance performed by couples. **2.** Music for this dance. [< Pol *polka,* Polish woman.]

polka dot. A pattern or fabric with uniform dots. [Perh < *poke a dot.*]

poll (pōl) *n.* **1. a.** The casting and registering of votes in an election. **b.** The number of votes cast or recorded. **c.** Often **polls.** The place where votes are cast and registered. **2.** A canvassing of persons to analyze public opinion on a particular question. **—***v.* **1. a.** To receive (a given number of votes). **b.** To receive or record the votes of. **2.** To canvass (persons) to survey public opinion. **3.** To cut off; trim; clip. [ME *pol, polle,* head.] **—poll'er** *n.*

pol•len (pŏl'ən) *n.* The powderlike material produced by the anthers of flowering plants and functioning as the male element in fertilization. [< L, flour, dust.]

pollen count. The average number of pollen grains, usually of ragweed, in a cubic yard or other standard volume of air over a 24-hour period at a specified time and place, used to estimate the possible severity of hay-fever attacks.

pol•li•nate (pŏl'ə-nāt') *v.* **-nated, -nating.** To fertilize by transferring pollen to a stigma of (a plant or flower). **—pol'li•na'tion** *n.*

pol•li•wog (pŏl'ē-wŏg', -wôg') *n.* Also **pol•ly•wog.** A tadpole. [< POLL + WIGGLE.]

pol•lut•ant (pə-lo͞ot'nt) *n.* Anything that pollutes, esp. any gaseous, chemical, or organic waste that contaminates air, soil, or water.

pol•lute (pə-lo͞ot') *v.* **-luted, -luting.** To make impure or unclean; contaminate. [< L *polluere.*] **—pol•lu'tion** *n.*

Pol•lux (pŏl'əks) *n.* A bright star in the constellation Gemini.

po•lo (pō'lō) *n.* A game played by two teams on horseback, equipped with long-handled mallets for driving a wooden ball. [Akin to Tibetan *bo-lo.*]

Po•lo (pō'lō), **Marco.** 1254?–1324? Venetian traveler to the court of Kublai Khan.

po•lo•ni•um (pə-lō'nē-əm) *n. Symbol* **Po** A naturally radioactive metallic element, occurring in minute quantities as a product of radium disintegration and produced by bombarding bismuth or lead with neutrons. Atomic number 84, longest-lived isotope Po 210. [< L *Polōnia,* Poland.]

pol•ter•geist (pōl'tər-gīst') *n.* A ghost that manifests itself by noises and rappings. [G.]

pol•troon (pŏl-tro͞on') *n. Archaic.* A coward. [< OIt *poltrone,* "foal."]

poly–. *comb. form.* **1.** More than one; many. **2.** More than usual. [< Gk *polus,* much, many.]

pol•y•clin•ic (pŏl'ē-klĭn'ĭk) *n.* A clinic that treats all types of diseases and injuries.

pol•y•es•ter (pŏl'ē-ĕs'tər) *n.* Any of numerous synthetic resins. [POLY(MER) + ESTER.]

pol•y•eth•yl•ene (pŏl'ē-ĕth'ə-lēn') *n.* A synthetic resin, used esp. in the form of films and sheets. [POLY(MER) + ETHYLENE.]

po•lyg•a•my (pə-lĭg'ə-mē) *n.* The practice of having more than one wife or husband at one time. **—po•lyg'a•mist** (-mĭst) *n.* **—po•lyg'a•mous** (-məs) *adj.*

pol•y•glot (pŏl'ē-glŏt') *n.* One with a reading, writing, or speaking knowledge of several languages. [< Gk *poluglōttos.*]

pol•y•gon (pŏl'ē-gŏn') *n.* A closed plane figure bounded by three or more line segments. [< Gk *polugōnos,* "having many angles."] **—po•lyg'o•nal** (pə-lĭg'ə-nəl) *adj.*

pol•y•graph (pŏl'ē-grăf', -gräf') *n.* An instrument that records changes in such physiological processes as heartbeat, blood pressure, and respiration, and is sometimes used in lie detection. [Gk *polugraphos,* "writing a lot."]

pol•y•he•dron (pŏl'ē-hē'drən) *n., pl.* **-drons** or **-dra** (-drə). A solid bounded by polygons. **—pol'y•he'dral** *adj.*

pol•y•mer (pŏl'ə-mər) *n.* Any of numerous natural and synthetic compounds of usually high molecular weight consisting of repeated linked units, each a relatively light and simple molecule. **—pol'y•mer'ic** (-mĕr'ĭk) *adj.*

pol•y•mer•ize (pŏl'ə-mə-rīz', pə-lĭm'ə-) *v.* **-ized, -izing.** To unite two or more monomers to form a polymer. **—po•lym'er•i•za'tion** (pə-lĭm'ər-ə-zā'shən, pŏl'ə-mər-) *n.*

Pol•y•ne•sia (pŏl'ə-nē'zhə, -shə). A scattered group of islands of the E and SE Pacific. **—Pol'y•ne'sian** *adj. & n.*

pol•y•no•mi•al (pŏl'ē-nō'mē-əl) *adj.* Of, pertaining to, or consisting of more than two names or terms. **—***n.* An algebraic function of two or more summed terms, each term consisting of a constant multiplier and one or more variables raised, in general, to integral powers. [POLY- + (BI)NOMIAL.]

pol•yp (pŏl'ĭp) *n.* **1.** An organism, as a coral, with a cylindrical body and a mouth opening surrounded by tentacles. **2.** A pathological growth protruding from the mucous lining of an organ. [< Gk *polupous,* "many-footed."]

po•lyph•o•ny (pə-lĭf'ə-nē) *n.* The simultaneous combination of two or more independent melodic parts. [Gk *poluphōnia,* variety of tones.] **—pol'y•phon'ic** (pŏl'ē-fŏn'ĭk) *adj.*

pol•y•sty•rene (pŏl'ē-stī'rēn') *n.* A hard, rigid, dimensionally stable, clear thermoplastic polymer.

pol•y•syl•la•ble (pŏl'ē-sĭl'ə-bəl) *n.* A word of more than three syllables. **—pol'y•syl•lab'ic** (-sĭ-lăb'ĭk) *adj.*

pol•y•tech•nic (pŏl'ē-tĕk'nĭk) *adj.* Of or involving many arts or sciences.

pol•y•the•ism (pŏl'ē-thē-ĭz'əm) *n.* The worship of or belief in more than one god. **—pol'y•the'ist** *n.* **—pol'y•the•is'tic** *adj.*

pol•y•un•sat•u•rat•ed (pŏl'ē-ŭn-săch'ə-rā'tĭd) *adj.* Pertaining to long-chain carbon compounds, esp. fats, having many unsaturated bonds.

pol•y•vi•nyl chloride (pŏl'ē-vī'nəl). A common thermoplastic resin, used in a wide variety of manufactured products.

po•made (pə-măd', -mäd', pō-) *n.* A perfumed hair ointment. [< It *pomata,* hair ointment orig apple-scented.]

pome•gran•ate (pŏm'grăn'ĭt, pŭm'-) *n.* **1.** A fruit with a tough, reddish rind and many seeds enclosed in juicy, red pulp. **2.** A tree bearing such fruit. [< OF *pome grenate,* "many-seeded apple."]

pom•mel (pŭm'əl, pŏm'-) *n.* **1.** A knob on the hilt of a sword. **2.** The upper front part of a saddle. —*v.* To beat; pummel. [< VL **pōmellum,* rounded knob.]

pomp (pŏmp) *n.* **1.** Magnificent display; splendor. **2.** Ostentatious display. [< Gk *pompē,* "a sending," solemn procession.]

pom•pa•no (pŏm'pə-nō', pŭm'-) *n., pl.* **-no** or **-nos.** A food fish of tropical and temperate Atlantic waters. [Span *pámpano,* name of a fish.]

pom•pon (pŏm'pŏn') *n.* Also **pom•pom** (-pŏm'). **1.** A tuft or ball of material worn as decoration. **2.** A small, buttonlike chrysanthemum. [F.]

pom•pous (pŏm'pəs) *adj.* **1.** Self-important; pretentious. **2.** Characterized by pomp or stately display. **—pom'pos'i•ty** (pŏm'pŏs'ə-tē), **pom'pous•ness** *n.* **—pom'pous•ly** *adv.*

pon•cho (pŏn'chō) *n., pl.* **-chos.** **1.** A blanketlike cloak with a center hole for the head. **2.** A similar garment used as a raincoat. [Amer Span.]

pond (pŏnd) *n.* A still body of water, smaller than a lake. [< OE *pund-,* enclosure.]

pon•der (pŏn'dər) *v.* **1.** To consider carefully. **2.** To meditate; reflect. [< L *ponderāre,* to weigh, ponder.] **—pon'der•er** *n.*

pon•der•ous (pŏn'dər-əs) *adj.* **1.** Having great weight; massive; unwieldy. **2.** Lacking fluency; dull. [< L *pondus (ponder-),* weight.]

pone (pōn) *n.* A cornmeal patty usually made without milk or eggs. [< Algon.]

pon•gee (pŏn-jē', pŏn'jē) *n.* A soft, thin silk cloth. [Mand Chin *pen*[3] *chi*[1], "(made by) one's own loom."]

pon•iard (pŏn'yərd) *n.* A dagger. [F *poignard.*]

pons (pŏnz) *n., pl.* **pontes** (pŏn'tēz). Any slender tissue joining two parts of an organ. [L *pōns,* bridge.]

pon•tiff (pŏn'tĭf) *n.* **1.** The pope. **2.** A bishop. [< L *pontifex,* Roman high priest.]

pon•tif•i•cal (pŏn-tĭf'ĭ-kəl) *adj.* Of or pertaining to a pope or bishop. —*n.* **pontificals.** The vestments and insignia of a pontiff.

pon•toon (pŏn-to͞on') *n.* **1.** A flat-bottomed boat or other structure used to support a floating bridge. **2.** A float on a seaplane. [< L *pontō,* boat bridge.]

po•ny (pō'nē) *n., pl.* **-nies.** A small horse. [< L *pullus,* foal.]

pooch (po͞och) *n. Slang.* A dog. [?]

poo•dle (po͞od'l) *n.* A dog with thick, curly hair. [G *Pudel(hund),* "poodle (dog)."]

pooh (po͞o) *interj.* Expressive of disdain.

pooh-pooh (po͞o'po͞o') *v. Informal.* To express contempt or disdain for.

pool[1] (po͞ol) *n.* **1.** A small pond. **2.** A puddle of any liquid. **3.** A deep place in a river or stream. [< OE *pōl* < Gmc **pōla-.*]

pool[2] (po͞ol) *n.* **1.** In certain gambling games, the total amount staked by all players. **2.** Any grouping of resources for the common advantage of the participants. **3.** An agreement between competing business concerns to establish certain controls for common profit. **4.** Any of several games played on a six-pocket billiard table. —*v.* To combine (money, funds, or interests) for mutual benefit. [F *poule,* stakes, target.]

poop[1] (po͞op) *n.* **1.** The stern superstructure of a ship. **2.** A **poop deck.** [< L *puppis.*]

poop[2] (po͞op) *v. Slang.* To become or cause to become fatigued; tire. [?]

poop deck. The aftermost deck of a ship.

poor (po͝or) *adj.* **1. a.** Having little or no wealth. **b.** Destitute. **2.** Inferior; inadequate; inefficient. **3. a.** Lacking desirable elements or constituents. **b.** Undernourished; lean. **4.** Lacking in value. **5. a.** Humble. **b.** Pitiable. [< L *pauper.*] **poor'ly** *adv.*

poor•house (po͝or'hous') *n.* A publicly supported establishment for paupers.

pop[1] (pŏp) *v.* **popped, popping.** **1.** To make or cause to make a short, sharp, explosive sound. **2.** To burst open with such a sound. **3.** To appear abruptly. **4.** To open the eyes wide suddenly. **5.** To put or thrust suddenly: *popped the cooky into her mouth.* **6.** To fire (a pistol or other firearm). —*n.* **1.** A sudden sharp, explosive sound. **2.** A shot with a firearm. **3.** A nonalcoholic carbonated beverage. [ME *poppen.*]

pop[2] (pŏp) *n. Informal.* Father.

pop[3] (pŏp) *adj. Informal.* **1.** Pertaining to or specializing in popular music. **2.** Suggestive of pop art.

pop. **1.** popular. **2.** population.

pop art. A form of art that depicts objects of everyday life and adapts techniques of commercial art.

pop•corn (pŏp'kôrn') *n.* **1.** A variety of corn with hard kernels that burst to form white puffs when heated. **2.** The edible popped kernels of popcorn. [< *popped corn.*]

pope (pōp) *n.* **1.** Often **Pope.** The bishop of Rome and head of the Roman Catholic Church. **2.** *E.O.Ch.* A priest. [< Gk *pappas,* title of bishops.]

Pope (pōp), **Alexander.** 1688–1744. English poet and satirist.

pop•eyed (pŏp'īd') *adj.* Having bulging eyes.

pop•gun (pŏp'gŭn') *n.* A toy gun operating by compressed air to fire corks or pellets.

pop•in•jay (pŏp'ĭn-jā') *n.* A vain, supercilious person. [< OF *papegai,* a parrot.]

pop•lar (pŏp'lər) *n.* Any of several trees with triangular leaves and soft wood. [< L *pōpulus.*]

pop•lin (pŏp'lĭn) *n.* A ribbed fabric used in making clothing and upholstery. [< It *papalino,* papal.]

pop•o•ver (pŏp'ō'vər) *n.* A light, puffy, hollow muffin made with eggs, milk, and flour.

pop•py (pŏp'ē) *n., pl.* **-pies.** Any of various plants with showy red, orange, or white flowers and milky juice. [< L *papāver.*]

pop•py•cock (pŏp'ē-kŏk') *n.* Senseless talk. [Du dial *pappekak,* "soft dung."]

pop•u•lace (pŏp'yə-lĭs) *n.* **1.** The common people; masses. **2.** A population. [< L *populus,* people.]

pop•u•lar (pŏp'yə-lər) *adj.* **1.** Widely liked or appreciated. **2.** Of, representing, or carried on by the people at large. **3.** Accepted by or suited to the people in general. [L *populāris,* of the people.] **—pop'u•lar'i•ty** (-lăr'ə-tē) *n.* **—pop'u•lar•ly** *adv.*

pop•u•lar•ize (pŏp'yə-lə-rīz') *v.* **-ized, -izing.** To make popular.

pop•u•late (pŏp'yə-lāt') *v.* **-lated, -lating.** **1.** To supply with inhabitants. **2.** To inhabit. [< L *populus,* people.]

pop•u•la•tion (pŏp'yə-lā'shən) *n.* **1.** The people or total number of people inhabiting a specified area. **2.** *Stat.* The entire set of individuals, items, or scores from which a sample is drawn.

pop•u•lous (pŏp'yə-ləs) *adj.* Thickly settled or populated. **—pop'u•lous•ness** *n.*

p.o.r. pay on return.

por•ce•lain (pôrs'lĭn, pōrs'-, pôr'sə-lĭn, pōr'sə-) *n.* **1.** A hard, white, translucent ceramic. **2.** An object made of this material. [< OF *pourcelaine.*]

porch (pôrch, pōrch) *n.* **1.** A platform, usually with a separate roof, at an entrance to a house. **2.** A gallery or room attached to the outside of a building. [< L *porticus,* PORTICO.]

por•cine (pôr'sīn') *adj.* Of or like swine or a pig. [< L *porcus,* pig.]

por•cu•pine (pôr'kyə-pīn') *n.* A rodent having the back covered with long, sharp spines. [< OF *porc espin,* "spiny pig."]

pore[1] (pôr, pōr) *v.* **pored, poring.** **1.** To read or study attentively. **2.** To ponder. [ME *pouren.*]

pore[2] (pôr, pōr) *n.* A minute opening, as in an animal's skin or a plant leaf, esp. for the passage of fluid. [< Gk *poros,* passage.]

por•gy (pôr'gē) *n., pl.* **-gies.** A deep-bodied marine food fish. [< Gk *phagros.*]

pork (pôrk, pōrk) *n.* The flesh of a pig, used as food. [< L *porcus,* pig.]

pork•er (pôr'kər, pōr'-) *n.* A fattened young pig.

por•no (pôr'nō) *n.,pl.* **-nos.** *Slang.* **1.** Pornography. **2.** A pornographic motion picture, book, etc. **—por'no** *adj.*

por•nog•ra•phy (pôr-nŏg'rə-fē) *n.* Written or graphic material intended to excite lascivious feeling. [< Gk *pornographos,* writing about prostitutes.] **—por'no•graph'ic** (pôr'nə-grăf'ĭk) *adj.* **—por'no•graph'i•cal•ly** *adv.*

po•ros•i•ty (pə-rŏs'ə-tē, pō-) *n., pl.* **-ties.** **1.** The state or property of being porous. **2.** A porous structure or part.

po•rous (pôr'əs, pōr'-) *adj.* **1.** Having or full of pores. **2.** Admitting the passage of gas or liquid through pores or interstices. **—po'rous•ly** *adv.* **—po'rous•ness** *n.*

por•phy•ry (pôr'fə-rē) *n., pl.* **-ries.** Rock containing relatively large, conspicuous crystals, esp. feldspar, in a fine-grained igneous matrix. [< L *porphyrītes,* purple-colored stone.]

por•poise (pôr'pəs) *n.* A marine mammal related to the whales but smaller, usually having a blunt snout. [< VL **porcopiscis,* "pig fish."]

por•ridge (pôr'ĭj, pŏr'-) *n.* Boiled oatmeal, usually eaten with milk. [Var of POTTAGE.]

por•rin•ger (pôr'ĭn-jər, pŏr'-) *n.* A shallow cup or bowl with a handle. [< OF *potage,* pottage.]

port[1] (pôrt, pōrt) *n.* **1.** A town having a harbor. **2.** A harbor or waterfront district. [< L *portus,* house door, port.]

port[2] (pôrt, pōrt) *n.* The left-hand side of a ship or aircraft facing forward. *—adj.* Of, pertaining to, or on the port. *—v.* To turn or shift (the helm of a vessel) to the left. [?]

port[3] (pôrt, pōrt) *n.* **1.** A porthole. **2.** An opening for the passage of steam or fluid. [< L *porta,* gate.]

port[4] (pôrt, pōrt) *n.* A rich, sweet fortified wine. [< Port *o porto,* "the port."]

port[5] (pôrt, pōrt) *v.* To carry (a rifle, sword, etc.) diagonally across the body, with the muzzle or blade near the left shoulder. [< OF *porter,* to bear.]

Port. Portugal; Portuguese.

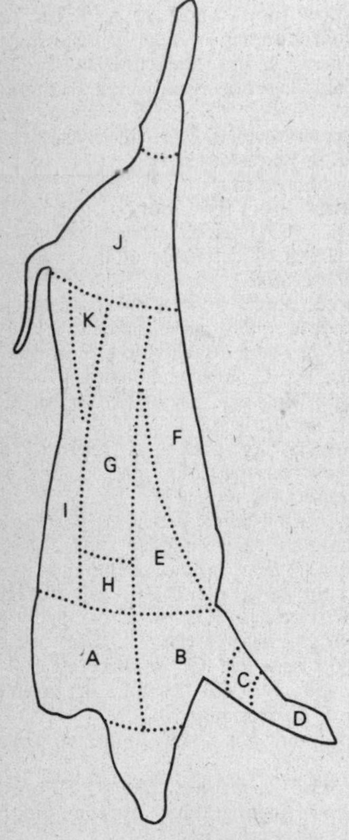

pork

A. Boston butt
B. Picnic ham
C. Hock
D. Foot
E. Spareribs
F. Bacon
G. Center loin
H. Rib chops
I. Fatback for salt pork
J. Ham
K. Tenderloin

port•a•ble (pôr'tə-bəl, pōr'-) *adj.* **1.** Capable of being carried. **2.** Easily moved. [< L *portāre,* to carry.] **—port'a•bil'i•ty** *n.*

port•age (pôr'tĭj, pōr'-, pôr-täzh') *n.* **1.** The carrying of boats and supplies overland between two waterways. **2.** A route by which this is done. *—v.* **-aged, -aging.** To transport by portage. [< L *portāre,* to carry.]

por•tal (pôrt'l, pōrt'l) *n.* A doorway or entrance. [<L *porta,* a gate.]

Port-au-Prince (pôrt'ō-prĭns', pōrt'-). The capital of Haiti. Pop. 250,000.

port•cul•lis (pôrt-kŭl'ĭs, pōrt-) *n.* A grating suspended in the gateway of a fortified place. [<OF *porte coleīce.*]

porte-co•chère, porte-co•chere (pôrt'kō-shâr', pōrt'-) *n.* A projecting roof at a building entrance, providing shelter for those getting in and out of vehicles. [F *porte cochère,* "coach-door."]

por•tend (pôr-tĕnd', pōr-) *v.* To serve as an omen of. [<L *portendere.*]

por•tent (pôr'tĕnt', pōr'-) *n.* **1.** An indication of something about to occur; an omen. **2.** Something amazing; a prodigy. [< L *portendere,* to PORTEND.]

por•ten•tous (pôr-tĕn'təs, pōr-) *adj.* **1.** Of the nature of or constituting a portent. **2.** Exciting wonder and awe; prodigious. **—por•ten'tous•ly** *adv.* **—por•ten'tous•ness** *n.*

por•ter[1] (pôr'tər, pōr'-) *n.* **1.** One employed to carry luggage. **2.** A railroad employee who waits on passengers. [< L *portāre,* to carry.]

por•ter[2] (pôr'tər, pōr'-) *n. Chiefly Brit.* A gatekeeper; doorman. [< L *porta,* a gate.]

por•ter[3] (pôr'tər, pōr'-) *n.* A dark beer. [Short for *porter's beer.*]

por•ter•house (pôr'tər-hous', pōr'-) *n.* A cut of beef having a T-bone and a sizable piece of tenderloin.

port•fo•li•o (pôrt-fō'lē-ō', pōrt-) *n., pl.* **-os. 1.** A portable case for holding papers, drawings, etc. **2.** The office or post of a minister of state. **3.** An itemized list of investments or securities. [It *portafoglio.*]

port•hole (pôrt'hōl', pōrt'-) *n.* A small, usually circular window in a ship's side.

por•ti•co (pôr'tĭ-kō', pōr'-) *n., pl.* **-coes** or **-cos.** A porch or walkway with a roof supported by columns. [< L *porticus,* porch.]

por•tière, por•tiere (pôr-tyâr', pōr-) *n.* A heavy curtain hung across a doorway. [< F *porte,* door.]

por•tion (pôr'shən, pōr'-) *n.* **1.** A section or quantity within a larger thing; a part of a whole. **2.** A part that is allotted to a person or group. **3.** One's lot or fate. *—v.* **1.** To divide into parts or shares (with *out*). **2.** To provide with a share or inheritance. [< L *portiō.*]

Port•land (pôrt'lənd, pōrt'-). A city of NW Oregon. Pop. 375,000.

Portland cement. A hydraulic cement made from a mixture of limestone and clay. [< *Portland,* England.]

Port Lou•is (lōō'ĭs, lōō'ē, lōō-ē'). The capital of Mauritius. Pop. 128,000.

port•ly (pôrt'lē, pōrt'-) *adj.* **-lier, -liest.** Comfortably stout. [< OF *porter,* to bear.]

port•man•teau (pôrt-măn'tō, pōrt-, pôrt'măn-tō', pōrt'-) *n., pl.* **-teaus** or **-teaux** (-tōz). *Chiefly Brit.* A large leather suitcase with two hinged compartments. [< OF *portemanteau,* "coat-carrier."]

port of call. A port where ships dock in the course of voyages to load or unload cargo, obtain supplies, etc.

port of entry. A place where travelers or goods can enter or leave a country under official supervision.

Port-of-Spain (pôrt'əv-spān', pōrt'-). The capital of Trinidad and Tobago. Pop. 94,000.

Por•to-No•vo (pôr'tō-nō'vō). The capital of Benin. Pop. 80,000.

por•trait (pôr'trĭt, -trāt', pōr'-) *n.* A painting, photograph, etc., esp. one showing the face. [< OF *portraire,* portray.]

por•trait•ist (pôr'trə-tĭst, pōr-) *n.* One who makes portraits.

por•trai•ture (pôr'trĭ-chŏŏr', pōr'-) *n.* The practice or art of making portraits.

por•tray (pôr-trā', pōr-) *v.* **1.** To depict pictorially. **2.** To describe in words. **3.** To represent dramatically. [< L *prōtrahere,* to draw forth, reveal.] **—por•tray'al** *n.*

Por•tu•gal (pôr'chə-gəl, pōr'-). A republic of SW Europe. Pop. 8,889,000. Cap. Lisbon.

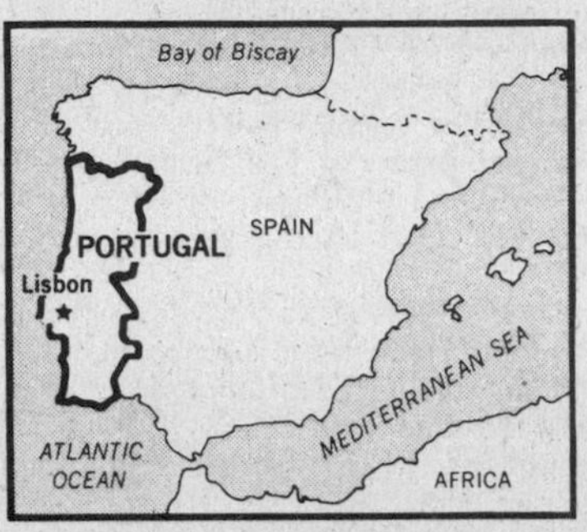

Portugal

Por•tu•guese (pôr'chə-gēz', -gēs', pōr'-; pôr'chə-gēz', -gēs', pōr'-) *n., pl.* **-guese. 1.** A native or inhabitant of Portugal. **2.** The Romance language of Portugal and Brazil. **—Por'tu•guese'** *adj.*

Portuguese man-of-war. A chiefly tropical marine organism having a bluish, bladderlike float and numerous long stinging tentacles.

pos. **1.** position. **2.** positive.

pose[1] (pōz) *v.* **posed, posing. 1.** To assume or hold a particular position or posture, as in sitting for a portrait. **2.** To place in a specific position. **3.** To affect a particular attitude. **4.** To propound or assert. *—n.* **1.** A bodily attitude or position, esp. one assumed in modeling. **2.** An affected attitude of mind or body. [< LL *pausāre,* to cease.]

pose[2] (pōz) *v.* **posed, posing.** To puzzle with a difficult question. [< OF *opposer,* to oppose.]

Po•sei•don (pō-sī'dən). Greek god of the sea.

pos•er[1] (pō'zər) *n.* One who poses.

pos•er[2] (pō'zər) *n.* A baffling question.

po•seur (pō-zœr') *n.* One who affects a particular attitude to impress others. [< OF *poser,* POSE[1].]

posh (pŏsh) *adj. Informal.* Fashionable.

pos•it (pŏz'ĭt) *v.* To put forward as a truth; postulate. [L *pōnere* (pp *positus*), to place.]

po•si•tion (pə-zĭsh'ən) *n.* **1.** A place or location. **2.** The appropriate place. **3. a.** The way in which something is placed. **b.** The arrangement of bodily parts; posture. **4.** A point of view. **5.** A situation relative to circumstances. **6.** Status; rank. **7.** A post of employment. *—v.* To place. [< L *pōnere* (pp *positus*), to place.] **—po•si'tion•al** *adj.*

pos•i•tive (pŏz'ə-tĭv) *adj.* **1.** Characterized by or displaying affirmation. **2.** Explicitly expressed. **3.** Admitting of no doubt; irrefutable. **4.** Confident. **5.** Overconfident; dogmatic. **6.**

Concerned with practical matters. **7.** Real, not fictitious. **8. a.** Of or being a quantity greater than zero. **b.** Of or being the opposite of something negative. **c.** Of or having electric charge of a sign opposite to that of an electron. **9.** *Photog.* Having the areas of light and dark in their original and normal relationship, as in a print made from a negative. **10.** *Gram.* Of, pertaining to, or denoting the simple uncompared degree of an adjective or adverb. —*n.* **1.** That which is positive. **2.** *Photog.* An image in which the lights and darks appear as they do in nature. **3.** *Gram.* The uncompared degree of an adjective or adverb. [< L *pōnere* (pp *positus*), to place.] —**pos'i•tive•ly** *adv.* —**pos'i•tive•ness** *n.*

pos•i•tron (pŏz'ə-trŏn') *n.* The antiparticle of the electron.

poss. possessive.

pos•se (pŏs'ē) *n.* A body of men summoned to aid a peace officer. [< ML *posse,* power.]

pos•sess (pə-zĕs') *v.* **1.** To have as property; own. **2.** To have as an attribute. **3.** To have knowledge of. **4.** To exert influence or control over; dominate. [< L *possidere,* "to sit as master," and L *possidēre,* to own, possess.] —**pos•ses'sor** *n.*

pos•sessed (pə-zĕst') *adj.* **1.** Owning or having. **2.** Controlled by or as by a spirit or other force. **3.** Calm; collected.

pos•ses•sion (pə-zĕsh'ən) *n.* **1.** The act or fact of possessing. **2.** The state of being possessed. **3.** That which is owned or possessed. **4.** Self-control. **5.** The state of being dominated.

pos•ses•sive (pə-zĕs'ĭv) *adj.* **1.** Of or pertaining to ownership or possession. **2.** Having a desire to control or dominate. **3.** *Gram.* Of, pertaining to, or designating a noun or pronoun case that expresses belonging or other similar relation. —*n. Gram.* **1.** The possessive case. **2.** A possessive form or construction. —**po•ses'sive•ly** *adv.* —**pos•ses'sive•ness** *n.*

Usage: Possessive forms are made in English in the following ways: **1.** By adding an apostrophe *s ('s)*: **a.** To the singular of most nouns, proper names, and irregular plurals: *the boy's chair, Bill's car, the men's hats.* **b.** To monosyllabic singular nouns and proper names ending in a sibilant: *the boss's car, Marx's philosophy.* **2.** By adding an apostrophe (') alone: **a.** To regular plurals: *the girls' dresses, the ladies' furs.* **b.** To certain expressions with *sake: for appearance' sake, for goodness' sake.* **c.** To plurals of proper nouns: *the Joneses' house.* **d.** To proper nouns when a sibilant occurs before the last syllable: *Moses' law, Xerxes' palace.* **e.** To ancient or classical names: *Achilles' heel.* When a singular noun or a proper name ending in a sibilant has two or more syllables, the possessive may be formed by the apostrophe alone or by *'s: Dickens'* or *Dickens's* and *witness'* or *witness's.*

pos•si•ble (pŏs'ə-bəl) *adj.* **1.** Capable of happening, existing, or being true. **2.** Capable of occurring or being done. **3.** Potential. **4.** That may or may not occur. [< L *posse,* to be able.] —**pos'si•bil'i•ty** *n.* —**pos'si•bly** *adv.*

pos•sum (pŏs'əm) *n.* An opossum. —**play possum.** To pretend to be dead, asleep, or unaware.

post¹ (pōst) *n.* **1.** A stake set upright in the ground to serve as a marker or support. **2.** Anything resembling this. —*v.* **1.** To fasten up (an announcement) in a place of public view. **2.** To announce by or as by posters. **3.** To publish (a name) on a list. [< L *postis.*]

post² (pōst) *n.* **1.** A military base where troops are stationed. **2.** An assigned position or station, as of a sentry. **3.** A position of employment, esp. an appointive public office. **4.** A trading post. —*v.* **1.** To assign to a position or station. **2.** To put forward; present: *post bail.* [< L *positum,* neut pp of *pōnere,* to place.]

post³ (pōst) *n.* **1.** A rider on a mail route; courier. **2.** *Brit.* **a.** The mail. **b.** A post office. —*v.* **1.** To travel quickly; hasten. **2.** To mail (a letter). **3.** To inform of the latest news. [< L *posita,* fem pp of *pōnere,* to place.]

post–. *comb. form.* **1.** After in time; later; subsequent to. **2.** After in position; behind; posterior to. [< L *post,* behind, after.]

post•age (pō'stĭj) *n.* The charge for mailing an item.

postage stamp. A small engraved adhesive label affixed to items of mail as evidence of the payment of postage.

post•al (pōst'l) *adj.* Of or pertaining to the post office or mail service. —**post'al•ly** *adv.*

postal card. A card printed with a postage stamp for sending messages at low rates; post card.

post card. Also **post•card.** **1.** An unofficial card, usually bearing a picture on one side, with space for an address, postage stamp, and short message. **2.** A **postal card.**

post•date (pōst-dāt') *v.* **1.** To put a date on (a check, letter, or document) that is later than the actual date. **2.** To occur later than; follow in time.

post•er (pō'stər) *n.* A large placard, bill, or announcement posted to advertise or publicize something.

pos•te•ri•or (pō-stîr'ē-ər, pō-) *adj.* **1.** Located behind a part or toward the rear of a structure. **2.** Following in time; later. —*n.* The buttocks. [< L *posterus,* coming after, next.]

pos•ter•i•ty (pō-stĕr'ə-tē) *n.* **1.** Future generations. **2.** All of a person's descendants. [< L *posterus,* next.]

pos•tern (pō'stərn, pŏs'tərn) *n.* A small rear gate, esp. in a fort or castle. [< LL *postera,* back door.]

poster paint. Opaque water-color paint in bright colors.

Post Exchange, post exchange. A store on a military base that sells to military personnel and their families.

post•grad•u•ate (pōst-grăj'o͞o-ĭt, -āt') *adj.* Of, pertaining to, or pursuing studies beyond the bachelor's degree. —*n.* A person engaged in such study.

post•haste (pōst'hāst') *adv.* With great speed; hastily; rapidly.

post•hu•mous (pŏs'cho͞o-məs) *adj.* **1.** Occurring or continuing after one's death. **2.** Born after the death of the father. [L *posthumus.*] —**post'hu•mous•ly** *adv.*

post•hyp•not•ic suggestion (pōst'hĭp-nŏt'ĭk). A suggestion made to a hypnotized person specifying an action to be performed in a subsequent waking state.

pos•til•ion (pō-stĭl'yən, pŏ-) *n.* Also **pos•til•lion.** One who rides and guides the near horse of a pair or of one of the pairs drawing a coach. [< It *posta,* post (mail).]

post•man (pōst'mən) *n.* A mailman.

post•mark (pōst'märk') *n.* An official mark stamped on mail that cancels the postage stamp and records the date and place of mailing. —**post'mark'** *v.*

post•mas•ter (pōst'măs'tər, -mäs'tər) *n.* A government official in charge of the operations of a local post office.

postmaster general *pl.* **postmasters general.** The executive head of a national postal service.

post•me•rid•i•an (pōst'mə-rĭd'ē-ən) *adj.* Of or taking place in the afternoon.

post me•rid•i•em (pōst' mə-rĭd'ē-əm). After noon. [L *post meridiem,* after midday.]

post-mor•tem (pōst-môr'təm) *adj.* After death. —*n.* **1.** A post-mortem examination, esp. an autopsy. **2.** *Informal.* An analysis or review of some completed event. [L *post mortem,* after death.]

post•na•tal (pōst-nāt'l) *adj.* After birth.

post office. **1.** The public department responsible for the transportation and delivery of the mails. **2.** Any local office where mail is sorted, stamps sold, etc.

post•op•er•a•tive (pōst-ŏp'ər-ə-tĭv, -ŏp'rə-tĭv, -ŏp'ə-rā'tĭv) *adj.* After surgery. —**post•op'er•a•tive•ly** *adv.*

post•or•bi•tal (pōst-ôr'bĭ-təl) *adj.* Located behind the eye socket: *a postorbital bone.*

post•paid (pōst'pād') *adj.* With the postage paid in advance.

post•pone (pōst-pōn', pōs-pōn') *v.* **-poned, -poning.** To delay until a future time; put off. [L *postpōnere,* to place after.] —**post•pone'ment** *n.* —**post•pon'er** *n.*

post•script (pōst'skrĭpt', pōs'skrĭpt') *n.* A message appended at the end of a letter after the writer's signature. [< L *postscrībere,* to write after.]

pos•tu•late (pŏs'cho͞o-lāt') *v.* **-lated, -lating.** **1.** To assume the truth or reality of with no proof, esp. as a basis of an argument. **2.** To assume as a premise or axiom; take for granted. —*n.* (pŏs'cho͞o-lĭt, -lāt'). Something assumed without proof as being self-evident or generally accepted. [L *postulāre,* to request, demand.] —**pos'tu•la'tion** *n.*

pos•ture (pŏs'chər) *n.* **1.** A position or attitude of the body. **2.** A characteristic way of bearing one's body; carriage. **3.** The present condition of something: *a nation's military posture.* —*v.* **-tured, -turing.** To assume an exaggerated or unnatural pose. [< L *positūra,* position.] —**pos'tur•al** *adj.*

post•war (pōst'wôr') *adj.* Occurring after a war.

po•sy (pō'zē) *n., pl.* **-sies.** A flower or bunch of flowers. [Var of POESY.]

pot (pŏt) *n.* **1.** A round, fairly deep vessel or container, as for cooking. **2.** The amount such a vessel will hold; potful. **3.** A container in which plants are grown. **4.** *Card Games.* The total amount staked by all the players in one hand. **5.** *Slang.* Marijuana. —**go to pot.** *Informal.* To deteriorate. —*v.* **potted, potting.** **1.** To place or plant in a pot. **2.** To cook in a pot. [< OE *pott* < VL **pottus.*]

pot. potential.

po•ta•ble (pō'tə-bəl) *adj.* Fit to drink. [< L *pōtāre,* to drink.]

pot•ash (pŏt'ăsh') *n.* **1. Potassium carbonate.** **2. Potassium hydroxide.** **3.** Any of several compounds containing potassium, esp. soluble basic compounds.

po•tas•si•um (pə-tăs'ē-əm) *n.* *Symbol* **K** A soft, silver-white, light, highly reactive metallic element found in, or converted to, a wide variety of salts used in fertilizers and soaps. Atomic number 19, atomic weight 39.102. [< POTASH.]

potassium bromide. A white crystalline solid or powder, KBr, used as a sedative and in photographic emulsions.

potassium carbonate. A transparent, white, granular powder, K_2CO_3, used in making glass, pigments, ceramics, and soaps.

potassium hydroxide. A caustic solid, KOH, used as a bleach and in the manufacture of liquid detergents and soaps.

potassium nitrate. A transparent white crystalline compound, KNO_3, used to pickle meat and in the manufacture of explosives, matches, and fertilizers.

po•ta•to (pə-tā'tō) *n., pl.* **-toes.** **1.** The starchy, edible tuber of a widely cultivated plant. **2.** The plant itself. [< Arawakan *batata.*]

potato chip. A thin slice of potato fried in deep fat until crisp and then salted.

pot•bel•ly (pŏt'bĕl'ē) *n., pl.* **-lies.** A protruding abdominal region. **—pot'bel'lied** *adj.*

pot•boil•er (pŏt'boi'lər) *n.* A literary or artistic work of poor quality, produced as quickly as possible for profit.

pot cheese. **Cottage cheese.**

po•tent (pōt'nt) *adj.* **1.** Possessing great strength; powerful. **2.** Cogent; convincing. **3.** Producing strong effects, as medicines or alcoholic beverages. **4.** Able to perform sexually, as a male. [< L *potēns.*] **—po'ten•cy** *n.*

po•ten•tate (pōt'n-tāt') *n.* One who has the power and position to rule over others; monarch. [< L *potēns,* POTENT.]

po•ten•tial (pə-tĕn'shəl) *adj.* Possible but not yet realized; latent. *—n.* **1.** The inherent ability or capacity for growth, development, or coming into being. **2.** The potential energy possessed by a unit charge by virtue of its location in an electric field; voltage. [< L *potēns,* POTENT.] **—po•ten'ti•al'i•ty** *n.* **—po•ten'tial•ly** *adv.*

potential energy. The energy derived from position, rather than motion, with respect to a field of force.

poth•er (pŏ*th*'ər) *n.* **1.** A commotion; disturbance. **2.** A fuss. [?]

pot•hold•er (pŏt'hōl'dər) *n.* A cloth pad for holding hot cooking utensils.

pot•hole (pŏt'hōl') *n.* A deep hole or pit, esp. in a road.

pot•hook (pŏt'ho͝ok') *n.* A bent or hooked piece of iron for hanging a pot or kettle over a fire or for lifting hot pots or stove lids.

po•tion (pō'shən) *n.* A liquid dose, esp. of medicinal, magic, or poisonous content. [< L *pōtāre,* to drink.]

pot•luck (pŏt'lŭk') *n.* Whatever food happens to be available to a guest.

Po•to•mac (pə-tō'mək). A river of the E U.S.

pot•pie (pŏt'pī') *n.* **1.** A mixture of meat or poultry and vegetables covered with a pastry crust and baked in a deep dish. **2.** A meat or poultry stew with dumplings.

pot•pour•ri (pō'po͞o-rē') *n.* **1.** A combination of various incongruous elements. **2.** A fragrant mixture of dried flower petals and spices. [F *pot pourri,* "rotten pot."]

pot roast. A cut of beef that is browned and then cooked in a covered pot.

pot•sherd (pŏt'shûrd') *n.* A fragment of broken pottery, esp. one found in an archaeological excavation.

pot shot. **1.** A shot aimed to kill, without regard for sporting rules. **2.** A shot fired at an animal or person within easy range.

pot•tage (pŏt'ĭj) *n.* A thick soup or stew of vegetables and sometimes meat. [< OF *potage.*]

pot•ted (pŏt'ĭd) *adj.* **1.** Grown in a pot, as a plant. **2.** *Slang.* Intoxicated.

pot•ter¹ (pŏt'ər) *n.* One who makes earthenware pots, dishes, or other vessels.

pot•ter². *Chiefly Brit.* Variant of **putter.**

pot•ter•y (pŏt'ə-rē) *n., pl.* **-ies.** **1.** Ware, such as vases, pots, etc., shaped from moist clay and hardened by heat. **2.** The craft or occupation of a potter. **3.** The establishment in which this craft is pursued.

pouch (pouch) *n.* **1.** A small flexible receptacle, esp. for carrying loose pipe tobacco. **2.** A mailbag, esp. one for diplomatic dispatches. **3.** A saclike structure, as the external abdominal pocket in which marsupials carry their young. [< OF *pouche.*]

poul•tice (pōl'tĭs) *n.* A moist, soft mass of bread, meal, clay, or other adhesive substance spread on cloth, and applied to warm, moisten, or stimulate an aching or inflamed part of the body. [< ML *pultēs,* pulp, thick paste.]

poul•try (pōl'trē) *n.* Domestic fowls, as chickens, turkeys, or ducks, raised for flesh or eggs. [< OF *poule,* hen, chicken.]

pounce (pouns) *v.* **pounced, pouncing.** To spring or swoop with intent to seize someone or something. *—n.* The act of pouncing. [Prob < OF *poinçon,* pointed tool.]

pound¹ (pound) *n., pl.* **pound** or **pounds.** **1.** The fundamental unit of weight in the U.S. Customary and British Imperial Systems, equal to 16 ounces or 7,000 grains; avoirdupois pound. **2.** An apothecary unit of weight, equal to 0.823 of the avoirdupois pound. **3.** Also **pound sterling.** **a.** The basic monetary unit of the United Kingdom, originally equal to 20 shillings or 240 pence, but after 1971 equal to 100 new pence. **b.** The basic monetary unit of Gambia, Ireland, Malawi, Malta, Nigeria, Rhodesia, and of various dependent territories of the United Kingdom. **4. a.** The basic monetary unit of Lebanon, Libya, Sudan, Syria, and the United Arab Republic. **b.** The basic monetary unit of Cyprus. **c.** The basic monetary unit of Israel. [< OE *pund* < L *pondō.*]

pound² (pound) *v.* **1.** To strike heavily; hammer or thump. **2.** To beat to a powder or pulp; pulverize or crush. [< OE *pūnian.*]

pound³ (pound) *n.* A public enclosure for confining stray animals. [< OE *pund-.*]

pound cake. A rich cake containing eggs and originally made with a pound each of flour, butter, and sugar.

pour (pôr, pōr) *v.* **1.** To flow or cause to flow in a stream or flood. **2.** To rain hard or heavily. **3.** To go forth in large numbers. [ME *pouren.*]

pout (pout) *v.* **1.** To protrude the lips in displeasure. **2.** To show displeasure or disappointment; sulk. [ME *pouten.*] **—pout** *n.*

pov•er•ty (pŏv'ər-tē) *n.* **1.** The state or condition of being poor. **2.** Deficiency in amount; scantiness. [< L *pauper,* poor.]

pov•er•ty-strick•en (pŏv'ər-tē-strĭk'ən) *adj.* Poor; destitute.

POW, P.O.W. prisoner of war.

pow•der (pou'dər) *n.* **1.** A substance consisting of ground, pulverized particles. **2.** Any of various preparations in this form, as certain cosmetics and medicines. **3.** Gunpowder or a similar explosive substance. *—v.* **1.** To reduce to powder; pulverize. **2.** To apply powder to. [< L *pulvis (pulver-).*] **—pow'der•er** *n.*

powder puff. A soft pad for applying powder to the skin.

powder room. A lavatory for women.

pow•der•y (pou'də-rē) *adj.* Composed of or similar to powder.

pow•er (pou'ər) *n.* **1.** The ability or capacity to act or perform effectively. **2.** Often **powers.** A specific capacity, faculty, or aptitude: *powers of concentration.* **3.** Strength or force capable of being exerted; might. **4.** The ability or capacity to exercise control; authority. **5.** A nation having influence over other nations. **6.** *Math.* An exponent. **7.** A measure of the magnification of an optical instrument. *—v.* To supply with power, esp. mechanical power. [< OF *povoir.*]

pow•er•boat (pou'ər-bōt') *n.* A motorboat.

pow•er•ful (pou'ər-fəl) *adj.* **1.** Having or capable of exerting power. **2.** Effective or potent, as medicine. **—pow'er•ful•ly** *adv.*

pow•er•house (pou'ər-hous') *n.* **1.** A station for the generating of electricity. **2.** One who possesses great force or energy.

pow•er•less (pou'ər-lĭs) *adj.* **1.** Lacking strength or power; helpless; ineffectual. **2.** Lacking legal or other authority.

power of attorney. A legal instrument authorizing one to act as another's attorney or agent.

pow•wow (pou'wou') *n. Informal.* A conference or gathering. [< Algon.]

pox (pŏks) *n.* **1.** Any disease characterized by purulent skin eruptions, such as chicken pox or smallpox. **2.** Syphilis. **3.** *Archaic.* Misfortune and calamity. [< POCK.]

pp. **1.** pages. **2.** past participle. **3.** *Mus.* pianissimo.

P.P. parcel post.

ppd. **1.** postpaid. **2.** prepaid.

P.P.S. additional postscript (L *post postscriptum).*

p.q. previous question.

P.Q. Province of Quebec.

Pr praseodymium.

PR public relations.

pr. **1.** pair. **2.** present. **3.** price. **4.** pronoun.

P.R. **1.** proportional representation. **2.** public relations. **3.** Puerto Rico.

prac•ti•ca•ble (prăk'tĭ-kə-bəl) *adj.* **1.** Capable of being effected, done, or executed; feasible. **2.** Capable of being used for a specified purpose. **—prac'ti•ca•bil'i•ty** *n.*

prac•ti•cal (prăk'tĭ-kəl) *adj.* **1.** Acquired through practice or action, rather than theory or speculation. **2.** Capable of being used or put into effect. **3.** Designed to serve a purpose; useful. **4.** Level-headed, efficient, and unspeculative. **5.** Being actually so in almost every respect; virtual. [< Gk *prattein, prassein,* to practice.] **—prac'ti•cal'i•ty** (prăk'tĭ-kăl'ə-tē) *n.*

practical joke. A mischievous trick played on a person.

prac•ti•cal•ly (prăk'tĭk-lē) *adj.* **1.** In a way that is practical. **2.** In every important respect; virtually. **3.** Almost.

prac•tice (prăk'tĭs) *v.* **-ticed, -ticing.** Also *chiefly Brit.* **prac•tise.** **1.** To do or perform (something) habitually or customarily. **2.** To exercise or perform (something) repeatedly in order to acquire a skill. **3.** To work at (a profession). *—n.* Also *chiefly Brit.* **prac•tise.** **1.** A habitual or customary action or way of doing something. **2. a.** Repeated performance of an activity in order to learn or perfect a skill. **b.** Proficiency gained through repeated exercise: *out of practice.* **3.** The act of doing something; performance. **4.** The exercise of an occupation or profession. **5.** The business of a professional person. **6. practices.** Questionable or unacceptable actions. [< LL *practicus,* practical.]

prac•ticed (prăk'tĭst) *adj.* Proficient; skilled.

prac•ti•tion•er (prăk-tĭsh'ən-ər) *n.* One who practices an occupation, profession, or technique.

prae•tor (prē'tər) *n.* A high elected Roman

magistrate ranking below a consul. [L, "leader," "chief."]

prag•mat•ic (prăg-măt'ĭk) *adj.* **1.** Dealing with facts or actual occurrences; practical. **2.** Emphasizing the practical outcome of events and historical phenomena. [L *pragmaticus,* skilled in affairs.] —**prag•mat'i•cal•ly** *adv.*

prag•ma•tism (prăg'mə-tĭz'əm) *n.* A method used in the conduct of affairs based on practical means and expedients. —**prag'ma•tist** *n.*

Prague (präg). The capital of Czechoslovakia. Pop. 1,021,000.

prai•rie (prâr'ē) *n.* An extensive area of flat or rolling grassland, esp. the plains of C North America. [< L *prātum,* meadow.]

prairie dog. A burrowing rodent of C North America.

prairie schooner. A canvas-covered wagon used by pioneers crossing the North American prairies.

prairie state. Any of the states in the Midwestern and W U.S. prairie regions.

praise (prāz) *n.* **1.** An expression of warm approval or admiration. **2.** The extolling of a deity, ruler, or hero. —*v.* **praised, praising.** **1.** To express warm approval of or admiration for; commend; applaud. **2.** To extol or exalt; worship. [< LL *pretiāre,* to prize, praise.]

praise•wor•thy (prāz'wûr'*th*ē) *adj.* Meriting praise; highly commendable.

pram (prăm) *n. Chiefly Brit.* A perambulator.

prance (prăns, präns) *v.* **pranced, prancing.** **1.** To spring forward on the hind legs, as a horse. **2.** To walk or move about in a lively manner; caper; strut. —*n.* An act of prancing; caper. [ME *prauncen.*] —**pranc'er** *n.*

prank (prăngk) *n.* A mischievous trick; practical joke. [?]

prank•ster (prăngk'stər) *n.* One who plays tricks or pranks.

pra•se•o•dym•i•um (prā'zē-ō-dĭm'ē-əm, prā'sē-) *n. Symbol* **Pr** A soft, silvery, malleable, ductile rare-earth element, used to color glass yellow and in metallic alloys. Atomic number 59, atomic weight 140.907. [< Gk *prasios,* "leek-green" + DIDYMIUM.]

prate (prāt) *v.* **prated, prating.** To talk idly and at great length; chatter. [ME *praten.*]

prat•tle (prăt'l) *v.* **-tled, -tling.** To talk idly or meaninglessly; babble. —*n.* Childish or meaningless sounds; babble. [Freq of PRATE.]

prawn (prôn) *n.* An edible crustacean related to and resembling the shrimps. [ME *prayne.*]

pray (prā) *v.* **1.** To utter or address a prayer to a deity or other object of worship. **2.** To ask (someone) imploringly; beseech: *Pray, be careful.* [< L *precārī,* to entreat.]

prayer (prâr) *n.* **1.** A reverent petition made to a deity or other object of worship. **2.** The act of making such a petition. **3.** A specially worded or spontaneously expressed appeal to God. **4.** Often **prayers.** A religious service in which praying predominates. [< L *precārī,* to entreat, PRAY.]

prayer•ful (prâr'fəl) *adj.* Inclined to pray frequently; devout. —**prayer'ful•ly** *adv.*

pre–. *comb. form.* **1.** An earlier or prior time. **2.** Preliminary or preparatory work or activity. **3.** A location in front of or anterior to. [< L *prae,* before, in front.]

preach (prēch) *v.* **1.** To deliver (a sermon). **2.** To advocate earnestly. **3.** To give moral advice, esp. in a tiresome manner. [< L *praedīcāre,* to proclaim.] —**preach'er** *n.*

pre•am•ble (prē'ăm'bəl) *n.* An introduction to a formal document, explaining its purpose. [< LL *praeambulus,* walking in front.]

pre•ar•range (prē'ə-rānj') *v.* To arrange in advance. —**pre'ar•range'ment** *n.*

Pre•cam•bri•an (prē-kăm'brē-ən) *adj.* Of or belonging to the oldest and largest division of geologic time, preceding the Cambrian and characterized by the appearance of primitive forms of life. —*n.* The Precambrian era.

pre•car•i•ous (prĭ-kâr'ē-əs) *adj.* **1.** Dangerously lacking in stability. **2.** Subject to chance or unknown conditions. [< L *precārius,* dependent on prayer.] —**pre•car'i•ous•ly** *adv.*

pre•cau•tion (prĭ-kô'shən) *n.* An action taken in advance to protect against possible failure or danger. —**pre•cau'tion•ar'y** (-shə-nĕr'ē) *adj.*

pre•cede (prĭ-sēd') *v.* **-ceded, -ceding.** To come before in time, place, or rank. [< L *praecēdere.*] —**pre•ced'a•ble** *adj.*

pre•ced•ence (prĭ-sēd'əns, prĕs'ə-dəns) *n.* The act, state, or right of preceding; priority.

prec•e•dent (prĕs'ə-dənt) *n.* **1.** An act or instance that can be used as an example in dealing with subsequent similar cases. **2.** Convention or custom. —*adj.* (prĭ-sēd'ənt). Preceding; prior. [< L *praecēdere,* PRECEDE.]

pre•ced•ing (prĭ-sē'dĭng) *adj.* Existing or coming before; previous.

pre•cept (prē'sĕpt') *n.* A rule or principle imposing a standard of action or conduct. [< L *praecipere* (pp *praeceptus*), to take beforehand, warn, teach.]

pre•cep•tor (prĭ-sĕp'tər, prē'sĕp'tər) *n.* A teacher; instructor.

pre•cinct (prē'sĭngkt) *n.* **1.** A subdivision of a city patrolled by a unit of the police force. **2.** An election district. **3.** Often **precincts.** A place or enclosure marked off by definite limits. **4. precincts.** Neighborhood; environs. [< ML *praecinctum,* "enclosure."]

pre•cious (prĕsh'əs) *adj.* **1.** Of high cost or worth; valuable. **2.** Dear; beloved. **3.** Affectedly dainty or overrefined. [< L *pretium,* price.] —**pre'cious•ly** *adv.*

prec•i•pice (prĕs'ə-pĭs) *n.* An extremely steep or overhanging mass of rock, as the face of a cliff. [< L *praecipitāre,* to throw headlong.]

pre•cip•i•tate (prĭ-sĭp'ə-tāt') *v.* **-tated, -tating.** **1.** To hurl downward. **2.** To cause to happen before anticipated or required. **3.** *Meteorol.* To condense and fall. **4.** To separate from a solution as a precipitate. —*adj.* (prĭ-sĭp'ə-tĭt, -tāt'). **1.** Speeding headlong; moving rapidly and heedlessly. **2.** Acting with excessive haste or impulse. —*n.* (prĭ-sĭp'ə-tāt', -tĭt). A solid separated from a solution. [L *praecipitāre,* to throw headlong.] —**pre•cip'i•tate•ly** *adv.*

pre•cip•i•ta•tion (prĭ-sĭp'ə-tā'shən) *n.* **1.** Abrupt or impulsive haste. **2.** Any form of rain or snow. **3.** The production of a precipitate.

pre•cip•i•tous (prĭ-sĭp'ə-təs) *adj.* **1.** Like a precipice; extremely steep. **2.** Precipitate. —**pre•cip'i•tous•ly** *adv.* —**pre•cip'i•tous•ness** *n.*

pré•cis (prā'sē, prā-sē') *n., pl.* **-cis** (-sēz, -sēz'). A concise summary; an abstract. [F, "precise."]

pre•cise (prĭ-sīs') *adj.* **1.** Clearly expressed or delineated; definite. **2.** Exactly corresponding to what is indicated; correct. **3.** Strictly distinguished from others; very: *at that precise moment.* **4.** Conforming strictly to rule. [< L *praecīsus,* shortened.] —**pre•cise'ly** *adv.* —**pre•cise'ness** *n.*

pre•ci•sion (prĭ-sĭzh'ən) *n.* The state or quality of being precise. —*adj.* Used or intended for precise measurement: *a precision tool.*

pre•clude (prĭ-klōōd') *v.* **-cluded, -cluding.** **1.** To make impossible; prevent. **2.** To exclude; debar. [L *praeclūdere.*]

pre•co•cious (prĭ-kō'shəs) *adj.* Early in development or maturity, esp. in mental aptitude. [< L *praecox,* "ripening before its time."] —**pre•co'cious•ness, pre•coc'i•ty** (-kŏs'ə-tē) *n.*

pre•cog•ni•tion (prē'kŏg-nĭsh'ən) *n.* Knowledge of something in advance of its occurrence. [< L *praecognōscere,* to know before.]

pre•con•ceive (prē'kən-sēv') *v.* To form an opinion of (something) beforehand. —**pre'con•cep'tion** (-sĕp'shən) *n.*

pre•con•di•tion (prē'kən-dĭsh'ən) *n.* A prerequisite. —*v.* To condition, train, or accustom in advance.

pre•cur•sor (prĭ-kûr'sər, prē'kûr'sər) *n.* **1.** A forerunner; harbinger. **2.** One that precedes another; predecessor. [< L *praecurrere,* to run before.]

pred. predicate.

pre•da•cious, pre•da•ceous (prĭ-dā'shəs) *adj.* Living by seizing prey; predatory. [< L *praedārī,* to plunder.]

pre•date (prē-dāt') *v.* **1.** To mark with an earlier date than the actual one. **2.** To precede in time; antedate.

pred•a•tor (prĕd'ə-tər, -tôr') *n.* **1.** An animal that preys upon others. **2.** One that preys, destroys, or devours.

pred•a•to•ry (prĕd'ə-tôr'ē, -tōr'ē) *adj.* **1.** Characterized by plundering or pillaging. **2.** Preying on other animals. [< L *praedārī,* to plunder.] —**pred'a•to'ri•ness** *n.*

pre•de•cease (prē'dĭ-sēs') *v.* To die before (some other person).

pred•e•ces•sor (prĕd'ə-sĕs'ər, prē'də-) *n.* One who precedes another in time, esp. in an office or position. [< LL *praedecessor.*]

pre•des•ti•na•tion (prē-dĕs'tə-nā'shən) *n.* **1.** The act whereby God is believed to have foreordained all things. **2.** The doctrine asserting this.

pre•des•tine (prē-dĕs'tĭn) *v.* To decide or decree in advance; foreordain.

pre•de•ter•mine (prē'dĭ-tûr'mĭn) *v.* To determine or decide in advance. —**pre'de•ter'mi•na'tion** *n.*

pre•dic•a•ment (prĭ-dĭk'ə-mənt) *n.* A troublesome, embarrassing, or ludicrous situation. [< LL *praedicāmentum,* something predicated, condition.]

pred•i•cate (prĕd'ə-kāt') *v.* **-cated, -cating.** **1.** To base or establish (a concept, statement, or action): *predicate an argument on the facts.* **2.** To affirm as an attribute or quality of something. —*n.* (prĕd'-ĭ-kĭt). The part of a sentence or clause that expresses something about the subject. —*adj.* (prĕd'ĭ-kĭt). Of or belonging to the predicate of a sentence or clause. [LL *praedicāre,* to proclaim.] —**pred'i•ca'tion** (-ĭ-kā'shən) *n.* —**pred'i•ca'tive** *adj.*

predicate adjective. *Gram.* An adjective that follows certain verbs and describes the subject of the verb. In the sentence *The man is good,* the predicate adjective is *good.*

predicate nominative. *Gram.* A noun, or a pronoun in the subject form, that follows certain verbs, and is identified with the subject of the verb. In the sentence *It is I,* the predicate nominative is *I.*

pre•dict (prĭ-dĭkt') *v.* To foretell; prophesy. [L *praedīcere.*] —**pre•dict'a•ble** *adj.* —**pre•dic'tion** (-dĭk'shən) *n.* —**pre•dic'tor** *n.*

pre•di•lec•tion (prĕd'ə-lĕk'shən, prē'də-) *n.* A preference or partiality. [< ML *praedīligere,* to prefer.]

pre•dis•pose (prē'dĭs-pōz') *v.* To make (someone) inclined to something in advance; put into a certain mood. —**pre'dis•po•si'tion** *n.*

pre•dom•i•nant (prĭ-dŏm'ə-nənt) *adj.* **1.** Having greatest importance or authority. **2.** Most common or conspicuous; prevalent. —**pre•dom'i•nance** *n.* —**pre•dom'i•nant•ly** *adv.*

pre•dom•i•nate (prĭ-dŏm'ə-nāt') *v.* **1.** To be most numerous, important, or outstanding. **2.** To have authority, power, or controlling influence; prevail. —**pre•dom'i•nate•ly** (-nĭt-lē) *adv.* —**pre•dom'i•na'tion** *n.*

pre-em•i•nent (prē-ĕm'ə-nənt) *adj.* Also **pre•em•i•nent.** Superior to all others; outstanding. —**pre-em'i•nence** *n.* —**pre-em'i•nent•ly** *adv.*

pre-empt (prē-ĕmpt') *v.* Also **pre•empt.** **1.** To gain possession of by prior right, esp. to settle on (public land) so as to obtain the right to buy before others. **2.** To appropriate, seize, or act for oneself before others. [< ML *praeemere,* to buy beforehand.] —**pre-emp'tion** *n.* —**pre-emp'tive** *adj.* —**pre-emp'tive•ly** *adv.*

preen (prēn) *v.* **1.** To smooth or clean (feathers) with the beak. **2.** To adorn (oneself) carefully; primp. [Poss < OF *poroindre,* to anoint before.] —**preen'er** *n.*

pref. **1.** preface. **2.** preference; preferred. **3.** prefix.

pre•fab•ri•cate (prē-făb'rĭ-kāt') *v.* To construct in standard sections that can be easily shipped and assembled.

pref•ace (prĕf'ĭs) *n.* An introduction to a book, speech, etc. —*v.* **-aced, -acing.** To introduce by or provide with a preface. [< L *praefāri,* to say beforehand.] —**pref'ac•er** *n.* —**pref'a•to'ry** (-ə-tôr'ē, -tōr'ē) *adj.*

pre•fect (prē'fĕkt') *n.* Also **prae•fect.** A high administrative official. [< L *praefectus,* overseer, chief.] —**pre'fec'ture** (-fĕk'chər) *n.*

pre•fer (prĭ-fûr') *v.* **-ferred, -ferring.** **1.** To value more highly; like better. **2.** To file before a court: *prefer charges.* [< L *praeferre,* to hold or set before.] —**pre•fer'rer** *n.*

pref•er•a•ble (prĕf'ər-ə-bəl) *adj.* More desirable; preferred. —**pref'er•a•bly** *adv.*

pref•er•ence (prĕf'ər-əns) *n.* **1.** The selecting of or right to select someone or something over another or others. **2.** That which is preferred. **3.** An advantage given to one over others. —**pref'er•en'tial** (-ə-rĕn'shəl) *adj.*

pre•fix (prē-fĭks') *n. Gram.* An affix put before a word, changing or modifying the meaning. —*v.* (prē-fĭks'). **1.** (*also* prē'fĭks'). To put or fix before. **2.** To add as a prefix. —**pre'fix•al** *adj.* —**pre'fix'al•ly** *adv.*

preg•nant (prĕg'nənt) *adj.* **1.** Carrying a developing fetus within the uterus. **2.** Creative; inventive. **3.** Fraught with significance or implication. **4.** Filled; charged; fraught. [< L *praegnāns, praegnās.*] —**preg'nan•cy** *n.*

pre•hen•sile (prĭ-hĕn'sĭl) *adj.* Adapted for seizing or holding, esp. by wrapping around: *a prehensile tail.* [< L *prehendere,* to seize.]

pre•his•tor•ic (prē'hĭs-tôr'ĭk, -tŏr'ĭk) *adj.* Of the era before recorded history.

pre•judge (prē-jŭj') *v.* To judge beforehand without possessing adequate evidence.

prej•u•dice (prĕj'ə-dĭs) *n.* **1.** A preconceived preference; bias. **2.** Irrational hatred of a particular group, race, or religion. **3.** Detriment or injury. —*v.* **-diced, -dicing.** **1.** To cause to judge prematurely; bias. **2.** To affect injuriously or detrimentally. [< L *praejūdicium.*] —**prej'u•di'cial** (-dĭsh'əl) *adj.*

prel•ate (prĕl'ĭt) *n.* A high-ranking clergyman, as a bishop. [< ML *praelātus.*] —**prel'a•cy** (-ə-sē) *n.*

pre•lim•i•nar•y (prĭ-lĭm'ə-nĕr'ē) *adj.* Prior to the main action or business; introductory; prefatory. —*n., pl.* **-ies.** Something antecedent or preparatory. [< ML *praelīmināris.*]

pre•lit•er•ate (prē-lĭt'ər-ĭt) *adj.* Of or pertaining to any culture not having a written language.

prel•ude (prĕl'yo͞od', prē'lo͞od') *n.* **1.** A preliminary part; preface. **2.** A piece or movement serving as an introduction to a musical composition. [< L *praelūdere,* to play beforehand.]

prem. premium.

pre•ma•ture (prē'mə-cho͝or', -t/y/o͝or') *adj.* Occurring, born, or done prior to the customary or correct time; too early. —**pre'ma•ture'ly** *adv.* —**pre'ma•ture'ness** *n.*

pre•med•i•cal (prē'mĕd'ĭ-kəl) *adj.* Of or involving preparation for the study of medicine.

pre•med•i•tate (prē-mĕd'ə-tāt') *v.* To plan, arrange, or plot in advance. —**pre•med'i•ta'tion** *n.* —**pre•med'i•ta'tor** *n.*

pre•mier (prē'mē-ər, prĭ-mîr') *adj.* First in status or importance; chief. —*n.* (prĭ-mîr'). A **prime minister.** [< L *prīmus,* first.]

pre•mière (prĭ-mîr') *n.* The first public presentation of a movie, play, etc. [< F *premier,* first, chief, premier.]

prem•ise (prĕm'ĭs) *n.* **1.** A proposition upon which an argument is based or from which a conclusion is drawn. **2. premises.** Land and the buildings on it. [< ML *praemissa (prōpositiō),* "(proposition) put before."]

pre•mi•um (prē'mē-əm) *n.* **1.** A prize awarded, esp. as an inducement to buy. **2.** A sum of money paid in addition to a regular amount. **3.** The amount paid, often in installments, for an insurance policy. **4.** An unusual or high value: *put a premium on hard work.* [L *praemium,* "that which is obtained before others."]

pre•mo•lar (prē-mō'lər) *n.* Any of eight bicuspid teeth located in pairs between the canines and molars.

pre•mo•ni•tion (prē'mə-nĭsh'ən, prĕm'ə-) *n.* **1.** A warning in advance; forewarning. **2.** A presentiment of the future; foreboding. [< L *praemonēre,* to warn beforehand.] —**pre•mon'i•to'ry** (-mŏn'ə-tôr'ē, -tōr'ē) *adj.*

pre•na•tal (prē-nāt'l) *adj.* Existing or taking place prior to birth.

pre•oc•cu•py (prē-ŏk'yə-pī') *v.* **1.** To occupy the mind of completely; engross. **2.** To occupy in advance or before another. —**pre•oc'cu•pa'tion** (-pā'shən) *n.*

pre•or•dain (prē'ôr-dān') *v.* To decree or ordain in advance; foreordain.

prep•a•ra•tion (prĕp'ə-rā'shən) *n.* **1.** The act or process of preparing. **2.** Readiness. **3.** Often **preparations.** Preliminary measures. **4.** A substance, as a medicine, prepared for a particular purpose.

pre•par•a•to•ry (prĭ-păr'ə-tôr'ē, -tōr'ē, prĭ-pâr'-) *adj.* Serving to make ready or prepare; introductory.

pre•pare (prĭ-pâr') *v.* **-pared, -paring.** **1.** To make or get ready. **2.** To put together or make by combining various elements or ingredients. **3.** To fit out; equip. [< L *praeparāre,* to prepare in advance.] —**pre•par'er** *n.*

pre•par•ed•ness (prĭ-pâr'ĭd-nĭs) *n.* The state of being prepared, esp. military readiness for war.

pre•pay (prē-pā') *v.* To pay or pay for beforehand. —**pre•pay'ment** *n.*

pre•pon•der•ate (prĭ-pŏn'də-rāt') *v.* **-ated, -ating.** To be greater in power, force, quantity, importance, etc.; predominate. [L *praeponderāre,* to exceed in weight.] —**pre•pon'der•ance** (-dər-əns) *n.* —**pre•pon'der•ant** *adj.*

prep•o•si•tion (prĕp'ə-zĭsh'ən) *n.* A word that indicates the relation of a substantive to a verb, an adjective, or another substantive. [< L *praepōnere* (pp *praepositus*), to place in front.] —**prep'o•si'tion•al** *adj.*

pre•pos•sess (prē'pə-zĕs') *v.* **1.** To influence beforehand; prejudice; bias. **2.** To impress favorably in advance.

pre•pos•sess•ing (prē'pə-zĕs'ĭng) *adj.* Impressing favorably; pleasing.

pre•pos•ter•ous (prĭ-pŏs'tər-əs) *adj.* Contrary to nature, reason, or common sense; absurd. [L *praeposterus,* "inverted," perverted, absurd.]

pre•puce (prē'pyo͞os') *n.* **1.** The loose fold of skin that covers the glans of the penis. **2.** A similar structure covering the glans of the clitoris. [< L *praepūtium.*]

pre•req•ui•site (prē-rĕk'wə-zĭt) *adj.* Required as a prior condition to something. —*n.* That which is prerequisite.

pre•rog•a•tive (prĭ-rŏg'ə-tĭv) *n.* An exclusive right or privilege. [< L *praerogātīvus,* asked to vote first.]

pres. **1.** present (time). **2.** president.

Pres. President.

pres•age (prĕs'ĭj) *n.* **1.** An omen; portent. **2.** A presentiment; foreboding. —*v.* **pre•sage** (prĭ-sāj') **-saged, -saging.** **1.** To indicate or warn of in advance; portend. **2.** To foretell or predict. [< L *praesāgīre,* to perceive beforehand.]

pres•by•ter (prĕz'bə-tər, prĕs'-) *n. Eccles.* **1.** In various hierarchical churches, a priest. **2.** In the Presbyterian Church, an elder. [< Gk *presbuteros,* a priest, "elder."]

Pres•by•te•ri•an (prĕz'bə-tîr'ē-ən, prĕs'-) *adj.* Of or pertaining to a Protestant church governed by presbyters and traditionally Calvinist in doctrine. —*n.* A member or adherent of a Presbyterian Church. —**Pres'by•te'ri•an•ism'** *n.*

pre•sci•ence (prē'shē-əns, prĕsh'ē-) *n.* Knowledge of actions or events before they occur. —**pre'sci•ent** *adj.*

pre•scribe (prĭ-skrīb') *v.* **-scribed, -scribing.** **1.** To set down as a rule or guide. **2.** To order or recommend a remedy or treatment. [< L *praescrībere,* to write at the beginning, prescribe.] —**pre•scrip'tive** (-skrĭp'tĭv) *adj.*

pre•scrip•tion (prĭ-skrĭp'shən) *n.* **1.** The act of prescribing. **2. a.** A written instruction by a physician for the preparation and administration of a medicine. **b.** A prescribed medicine.

pres•ence (prĕz'əns) *n.* **1.** The state or fact of being present. **2.** Immediate proximity: *in the presence of ladies.* **3.** A manner of carrying oneself; bearing.

pres•ent[1] (prĕz'ənt) *n.* **1.** A moment or period in time intermediate between past and future; now. **2.** The present tense. —*adj.* **1.** Being or occurring at the present time. **2.** Being at hand. **3.** Denoting a verb tense or form that expresses current time. [< L *praeesse,* to be before one, be present.]

pre•sent[2] (prĭ-zĕnt') *v.* **1.** To introduce. **2.** To bring before the public: *present a play.* **3. a.** To make a gift or award of. **b.** To make a gift to; bestow formally. **4.** To offer formally: *present one's credentials.* **5.** To offer for consideration. **6.** To salute with or aim (a weapon). —*n.* **pres•ent** (prĕz'ənt). Something presented; a gift. [< L *praesēns,* present, being at hand.]

pre•sent•a•ble (prĭ-zĕn'tə-bəl) *adj.* **1.** Capable of being given, displayed, or offered. **2.** Fit for introduction to others. —**pre•sent'a•bly** *adv.*

pres•en•ta•tion (prĕz'ən-tā'shən, prē'zən-) *n.* **1.** The act of presenting. **2.** A performance, as of a drama.

pres•ent-day (prĕz'ənt-dā') *adj.* Current.

ă pat/ā ate/âr care/ä bar/b **b**i**b**/ch **ch**ew/d **d**ee**d**/ĕ pet/ē be/f **f**it/g **g**a**g**/h **h**at/hw **wh**at/
ĭ pit/ī pie/îr pier/j **j**u**dg**e/k **k**ic**k**/l **l**id, fata**l**/m **m**u**m**/n **n**o, sudde**n**/ng si**ng**/ŏ pot/ō go/

pre•sen•ti•ment (prĭ-zĕn'tə-mənt) *n.* A sense of something about to occur; premonition. [< L *praesentire*, to perceive beforehand.]

pres•ent•ly (prĕz'ənt-lē) *adv.* **1.** In a short time; soon; directly. **2.** At this time or period; now.

pre•serv•a•tive (prĭ-zûr'və-tĭv) *adj.* Tending to preserve. *—n.* Something used to preserve, esp. a chemical used in foods to inhibit spoilage.

pre•serve (prĭ-zûrv') *v.* **-served, -serving. 1.** To protect from injury, peril, or other adversity. **2.** To keep or maintain intact. **3.** To treat or prepare so as to prevent decay. *—n.* **1.** Often **preserves.** Fruit cooked with sugar to protect against decay. **2.** An area maintained for the protection of wildlife or natural resources. [< ML *praeservāre*, "to guard beforehand."] **—pres'er•va'tion** (prĕz'ər-vā'shən) *n.*

pre•side (prĭ-zīd') *v.* **-sided, -siding. 1.** To act as chairman or president. **2.** To possess or exercise authority or control. [< L *praesidēre*, "to sit in front of," superintend.]

pres•i•dent (prĕz'ə-dənt, -dĕnt') *n.* **1.** One chosen to preside over an assembly or meeting. **2.** Often **President.** The chief executive of a republic, esp. of the U.S. **3.** The chief officer of a branch of government, a corporation, a university, etc. [< L *praesidēre*, PRESIDE.] **—pres'i•den•cy** *n.* **—pres'i•den'tial** *adj.*

press (prĕs) *v.* **1.** To exert steady weight or force (against). **2.** To squeeze the juice from. **3.** To iron (clothing). **4.** To clasp or embrace closely. **5.** To entreat insistently; urge on; spur. **6.** To distress by constraining circumstances: *pressed for time.* **7.** To put forward importunately or insistently. **8.** To advance eagerly; push forward; crowd. *—n.* **1.** Any of various machines or devices that apply pressure. **2.** A **printing press. 3.** A printing or publishing establishment. **4.** Printed matter as a whole, esp. newspapers and periodicals. **5.** A crowding or pushing forward; crush. **6.** The pressure or urgency of business or affairs. **7.** The set of proper creases in a garment. [< L *premere* (pp *pressus*), to press.]

press conference. An interview held for newsmen by a political figure or celebrity.

press•ing (prĕs'ĭng) *adj.* Demanding immediate attention; urgent. **—press'ing•ly** *adv.*

press•man (prĕs'mən, -măn') *n.* **1.** A printing press operator. **2.** *Brit.* A newspaperman.

pres•sure (prĕsh'ər) *n.* **1. a.** The act of pressing. **b.** The condition of being pressed. **2.** The application of continuous force. **3.** Force applied over a surface measured as force per unit of area. **4.** A compelling influence. **5.** Urgent claim or demand: *the pressure of business.* *—v.* **-sured, -suring.** To force, as by overpowering influence or persuasion.

pres•sur•ize (prĕsh'ə-rīz') *v.* **-ized, -izing. 1.** To maintain normal air pressure in (an aircraft, submarine, etc.). **2.** To put under a greater than normal pressure. **—pres'sur•i•za'tion** *n.*

pres•ti•dig•i•ta•tion (prĕs'tə-dĭj'ĭ-tā'shən) *n.* Sleight of hand. [< F *prestidigitateur*, juggler.] **—pres'ti•dig'i•ta•tor** *n.*

pres•tige (prĕ-stēzh', -stēj') *n.* Prominence or influential status achieved through success, renown, or wealth. [< L *praestigiae*, "juggler's tricks," illusions.] **—pres•tig'ious** (prĕ-stĭj'əs, -stē'jəs) *adj.* **—pres•tig'ious•ly** *adv.*

pres•to (prĕs'tō) *adv.* **1.** *Mus.* In rapid tempo. **2.** Suddenly; at once. [< L *praestus*, ready.] **—pres'to** *adj.*

pre•sume (prĭ-zōōm') *v.* **-sumed, -suming. 1.** To assume; take for granted. **2.** To venture; dare. **3.** To take unwarranted advantage of something. [< L *praesūmere*, "to take in advance," presuppose.] **—pre•sum'a•ble** *adj.* **—pre•sum'ab•ly** *adv.*

pre•sump•tion (prĭ-zŭmp'shən) *n.* **1.** Behavior or language that is boldly arrogant or offensive; effrontery. **2.** Acceptance or belief based on reasonable evidence; an assumption or supposition. [< L *praesūmere*, PRESUME.] **—pre•sump'tive** *adj.*

pre•sump•tu•ous (prĭ-zŭmp'chōō-əs) *adj.* Excessively forward or confident; arrogant. **—pre•sump'tu•ous•ly** *adv.* **—pre•sump'tu•ous•ness** *n.*

pre•sup•pose (prē'sə-pōz') *v.* **1.** To assume or suppose in advance. **2.** To require or involve necessarily as an antecedent condition. **—pre'sup•po•si'tion** (-sŭp-ə-zĭsh'ən) *n.*

pre•tend (prĭ-tĕnd') *v.* **1.** To make believe. **2.** To claim or allege insincerely or falsely; profess. **3.** To take upon oneself; venture. **4.** To put forward a claim. [< L *praetendere*, "to stretch forth," hold out as a pretext.] **—pre•tend'ed•ly** *adv.*

pre•tend•er (prĭ-tĕn'dər) *n.* **1.** One who pretends; a hypocrite or dissembler. **2.** A claimant to a throne.

pre•tense (prē'tĕns', prĭ-tĕns') *n.* Also *chiefly Brit.* **pre•tence. 1.** A false appearance or action intended to deceive. **2.** A false reason or excuse; pretext. **3.** A claim asserted without foundation.

pre•ten•sion (prĭ-tĕn'shən) *n.* **1.** A claim to something. **2.** Pretentiousness.

pre•ten•tious (prĭ-tĕn'shəs) *adj.* **1.** Claiming or demanding a position of distinction or merit. **2.** Making an extravagant outer show; ostentatious. **—pre•ten'tious•ness** *n.*

pret•er•it, pret•er•ite (prĕt'ər-ĭt) *adj.* Denoting the verb tense that expresses a past or completed action. *—n.* **1.** The past tense. **2.** A verb in this tense. [< L *praeteritus*, gone by, past.]

pre•ter•nat•u•ral (prē'tər-năch'ər-əl) *adj.* **1.** Transcending the normal course of nature; abnormal; exceptional. **2.** Supernatural. [< L *praeter nātūram*, beyond nature.]

pre•test (prē'tĕst') *n.* **1.** A test given in advance of an action, use, or experiment. **2.** The condition existing before an experiment. *—v.* (prē-tĕst'). To subject to a pretest.

pre•text (prē'tĕkst') *n.* An ostensible or professed purpose; pretense; excuse. [L *praetextus*, outward show, pretense.]

Pre•to•ri•a (prĭ-tôr'ē-ə, -tōr'ē-ə). The administrative capital of the Republic of South Africa. Pop. 423,000.

pret•ti•fy (prĭt'ĭ-fī') *v.* **-fied, -fying.** To make pretty. **—pret'ti•fi'er** *n.*

pret•ty (prĭt'ē) *adj.* **-tier, -tiest. 1.** Pleasing or attractive. **2.** Excellent; fine; good. Often used ironically: *a pretty mess.* **3.** *Informal.* Considerable in size or extent: *a pretty penny.* *—adv.* To a fair degree; somewhat; moderately: *a pretty good student.* *—v.* **-tied, -tying.** *Informal.* To make pretty. [< OE *prætt*, trick, wile < Gmc **pratt-*.] **—pret'ti•ly** *adv.*

pret•zel (prĕt'səl) *n.* A glazed biscuit, salted on the outside, usually baked in the form of a loose knot or stick. [< OHG *brezitella*.]

pre•vail (prĭ-vāl') *v.* **1.** To triumph; be victorious. **2.** To prove superior in strength or influence. **3.** To be most common or frequent; be predominant. **4.** To be in force, use, or effect; be current. **5.** To persuade. [< L *praevalēre*, to be more powerful.]

pre•vail•ing (prĭ-vā'lĭng) *adj.* **1.** Most frequent or common; predominant. **2.** Generally current; widespread; prevalent.

prev•a•lent (prĕv'ə-lənt) *adj.* Widely or commonly occurring or existing; generally accepted or practiced. [< L *praevalēre*, to PREVAIL.] **—prev'a•lence** *n.* **—prev'a•lent•ly** *adv.*

pre•var•i•cate (prĭ-văr'ə-kāt') *v.* **-cated, -cating.** To stray from or evade the truth; equivocate. [L *praevāricārī*, to walk crookedly, deviate.] **—pre•var'i•ca'tion** *n.* **—pre•var'i•ca'tor** *n.*

pre•vent (prĭ-vĕnt') *v.* **1.** To keep from happening; avert; thwart. **2.** To keep (someone) from doing something; hinder; impede: *He kept him from his work.* [< L *praevenīre*, to come before, anticipate.] **—pre•vent'a•ble, pre•vent'i•ble** *adj.* **—pre•ven'tion** *n.*

pre•ven•tive (prĭ-vĕn'tĭv) *adj.* Also **pre•ven•ta•tive** (-tə-tĭv). **1.** Designed or used to prevent or ward off; precautionary. **2.** Preventing illness or disease; prophylactic. **—pre•ven'tive** *n.*

pre•view (prē'vyōō') *n.* Also **pre•vue. 1.** An advance showing of a motion picture or play. **2.** An advance showing of several scenes advertising a forthcoming motion picture.

pre•vi•ous (prē'vē-əs) *adj.* Existing or occurring prior to something else in time or order; antecedent. **—previous to.** Prior to; before. [L *praevius*, going before, leading the way.] **—pre'vi•ous•ly** *adv.*

pre•war (prē'wôr') *adj.* Existing or occurring before a war.

prey (prā) *n.* **1.** An animal hunted or caught for food. **2.** A victim. **3.** The act of seizing animals to devour: *bird of prey.* *—v.* **1.** To feed by seizing as prey. **2.** To victimize. **3.** To plunder or pillage. **4.** To exert a wearing effect: *prey upon one's mind.* [L < *praeda* "booty," prey.]

price (prīs) *n.* **1.** The sum of money or goods asked or given for something. **2.** The cost at which something is obtained. **3.** Value or worth. *—v.* **priced, pricing. 1.** To fix or establish a price for. **2.** To find out the price of. [< L *pretium*, price, value, reward.]

price•less (prīs'lĭs) *adj.* Of inestimable worth; invaluable. **—price'less•ly** *adv.*

prick (prĭk) *n.* **1. a.** An instance of pricking. **b.** The sensation of being pricked. **2.** A small mark or puncture made by a pointed object. **3.** Something that pricks, as a thorn or bee sting. *—v.* **1.** To puncture lightly. **2.** To sting. **3.** To incite; impel. **4.** To outline by means of small punctures. **5.** *Archaic.* To ride at a gallop: *"A gentle knight was pricking on the plain"* (Spenser). **—prick up one's ears.** To listen with attentive interest. [< OE *prica*, pricked mark, puncture < Gmc **prikk-*.]

prick•le (prĭk'əl) *n.* **1.** A small, sharp spine or thorn. **2.** A slight stinging sensation. *—v.* **-led, -ling. 1.** To prick as with a thorn. **2.** To tingle. **—prick'li•ness** *n.* **—prick'ly** *adj.*

prickly heat. A skin disease caused by inflammation of the sweat glands.

prickly pear. 1. A cactus bearing egg-shaped, often edible fruit. **2.** The fruit of such a cactus.

pride (prīd) *n.* **1.** Self-respect. **2.** Elation or satisfaction over one's achievements or possessions. **3. a.** A cause or source of pride. **b.** The prime; flower: *the flush and pride of youth.* **4.** Conceit, arrogance, or disdain. **5.** A group of lions. *—v.* **prided, priding.** To esteem (oneself) for: *I pride myself on my garden.* [< OE *prūt, prūd*, PROUD.] **—pride'ful** *adj.*

prie•dieu (prē-dyœ') *n., pl.* **-dieus.** A low desk with space for a book above and with a foot piece below for kneeling in prayer. [F *prie-Dieu*, "pray God."]

pri•er (prī'ər) *n.* Also **pry•er.** One who pries.
priest (prēst) *n.* In the Roman Catholic, Eastern Orthodox, Anglican, Armenian, and separated Catholic hierarchies, a member of the second grade of clergy ranking below a bishop but above a deacon and having authority to pronounce absolution and administer all sacraments save that of ordination. [< Gk *presbuteros,* "elder."] —**priest'ess** *fem.n.* —**priest'hood'** *n.* —**priest'li•ness** *n.* —**priest'ly** *adj.*
prig (prĭg) *n.* A person regarded as overprecise and smugly narrow-minded. [?] —**prig'gish** *adj.* —**prig'gish•ly** *adv.*
prim (prĭm) *adj.* **primmer, primmest.** Precise, neat, or proper to the point of affectation. [?]
prim. 1. primary. **2.** primitive.
pri•ma•cy (prī'mə-sē) *n., pl.* **-cies. 1.** The state of being first or foremost. **2.** The office or rank of an ecclesiastical primate.
pri•ma don•na (prē'mə dŏn'ə, prĭm'ə). **1.** The leading female soloist in an opera company. **2.** A temperamental or conceited performer. [It, "first lady."]
pri•ma fa•cie (prī'mə fā'shē, fā'shə). At first sight. [L *prīmā faciē,* "on first appearance."] —**pri'ma-fa'cie** *adj.*
pri•mal (prī'məl) *adj.* **1.** Original; archetypal. **2.** Fundamental; primary. [< L *prīmus,* first.]
pri•ma•ri•ly (prī-mĕr'ə-lē, prī'mĕr'ə-lē) *adv.* **1.** At first; originally. **2.** Chiefly; principally.
pri•ma•ry (prī'mĕr'ē, -mə-rē) *adj.* **1.** Occurring first in time, sequence, or importance. **2.** Primal. **3.** Fundamental. **4.** Immediate; direct. **5.** Of or being a fundamental or generative part. —*n., pl.* **-ries. 1.** Something that is first in time, order, or importance. **2.** A preliminary election in which the registered voters of a political party nominate candidates for office. [< L *prīmus,* first.]
primary school. A school usually comprising the first three or four grades of elementary school and sometimes kindergarten.
pri•mate (prī'māt) *n.* **1.** One of the group of mammals that includes the monkeys, apes, and man. **2.** A bishop of highest rank in a province or country. [< L *prīmus,* first.] —**pri•ma'tial** (prī-mā'shəl) *adj.*
prime (prīm) *adj.* **1.** First in quality, degree, or sequence. **2.** Designating a **prime number.** —*n.* **1.** The earliest stage of something. **2.** Springtime. **3.** The period of ideal or peak condition. **4.** A mark (′) written above and to the right of a letter in order to distinguish it from the same letter already in use or to designate a related quantity or thing, as feet, minutes of angle, or minutes of time. **5.** *Math.* A **prime number.** —*v.* **primed, priming. 1.** To make ready; prepare. **2.** To load for firing. **3.** To prepare for operation, as by pouring water into a pump. [< L *prīmus,* first.]
prime meridian. The zero meridian from which longitude E and W is measured and which passes through Greenwich, England.
prime minister. 1. A chief minister appointed by a ruler. **2.** The chief executive in various kinds of parliamentary democracy.
prime number. A number that has itself and unity as its only factors.
prim•er¹ (prĭm'ər) *n.* **1.** An elementary textbook. **2.** A basic handbook of any subject. [< L *prīmārius,* basic, primary.]
prim•er² (prī'mər) *n.* **1.** A device for detonating an explosive charge. **2.** Someone or something that primes. **3.** An undercoat of paint or size used to prime a surface.
pri•me•val (prī-mē'vəl) *adj.* Belonging to the earliest ages. [< L *prīmaevus,* in the first period of life.] —**pri•me'val•ly** *adv.*
prim•i•tive (prĭm'ə-tĭv) *adj.* **1.** Of or pertaining to an early or original stage or state of development, evolution, etc. **2.** Crude or unsophisticated. **3.** Of or pertaining to early stages in the evolution of human culture. [< L *prīmitīvus,* first of its kind.] —**prim'i•tive** *n.* —**prim'i•tive•ly** *adv.*
pri•mo•gen•i•tor (prī'mō-jĕn'ə-tər) *n.* The earliest ancestor. [ML.]
pri•mo•gen•i•ture (prī'mō-jĕn'ə-cho͝or') *n.* **1.** The state of being the eldest child of the same parents. **2.** The right of the eldest son to inherit his parents' entire estate. [ML *prīmōgenitūra.*]
pri•mor•di•al (prī-môr'dē-əl) *adj.* Primary, primeval, original, or fundamental. —*n.* A basic principle. [< L *prīmōrdius.*] —**pri•mor'di•al•ly** *adv.*
primp (prĭmp) *v.* To dress or groom oneself with finicky attention to detail. [Akin to PRIM.]
prim•rose (prĭm'rōz') *n.* A plant with clustered, variously colored flowers. [< ML *prīma rosa,* "first (or earliest) rose."]
primrose path. A way of life of worldly ease or pleasure.
prin. principal.
prince (prĭns) *n.* **1. a.** A male member of a royal family. **b.** *Archaic.* A hereditary ruler. **2.** An outstanding man: *a merchant prince.* [< L *princeps,* first in rank, sovereign, ruler.] —**prince'li•ness** *n.* —**prince'ly** *adj.*
Prince Edward Island. A province of SE Canada. Pop. 108,000. Cap. Charlottetown.
prince•ling (prĭns'lĭng) *n.* A petty prince.
prin•cess (prĭn'sĭs, -sĕs', prĭn-sĕs') *n.* **1.** A female member of a royal family other than the monarch. **2.** The consort of a prince.
prin•ci•pal (prĭn'sə-pəl) *adj.* First or foremost in importance; chief. —*n.* **1.** The head of a school. **2.** A main participant. **3.** A leading person, as in a play. **4. a.** Capital, as distinguished from the revenue from it. **b.** A sum of money owed as a debt, upon which interest is calculated. **5. a.** A person who empowers another to act as his representative. **b.** The person having prime responsibility for an obligation, as distinguished from one who acts as his agent. [< L *princeps,* first one in rank, PRINCE.] —**prin'ci•pal•ly** *adv.*
prin•ci•pal•i•ty (prĭn'sə-păl'ə-tē) *n., pl.* **-ties.** A territory ruled by a prince or from which a prince derives his title.
principal parts. In traditional grammars of inflected languages, the primary forms of a verb from which all other forms can be derived. In English, the principal parts are generally considered to be the present infinitive *(play, eat),* the past tense *(played, ate),* the past participle *(played, eaten),* and the present participle *(playing, eating).*
prin•ci•ple (prĭn'sə-pəl) *n.* **1.** A basic truth, law, or assumption. **2.** An ethical code or standard. **3.** A fixed policy or mode of action. **4.** A basic quality determining intrinsic nature or characteristic behavior. **5.** A basic source. [< L *principium* < *princeps,* first.]
prin•ci•pled (prĭn'sə-pəld) *adj.* Motivated by or based on ethical principles.
print (prĭnt) *n.* **1.** A mark or impression made by pressure. **2.** Something marked with an impression. **3. a.** Lettering or other impressions produced in ink. **b.** The state or form of matter so produced. **4.** A design or picture reproduced by printing. **5.** A photographic copy. **6.** A fabric with a stamped dyed pattern. —*v.* **1.** To press as a mark onto a surface. **2.** To produce by means of pressed type on a paper surface. **3.** To publish. **4.** To write in characters similar to those commonly used in print. **5.** To produce (a positive photograph) by passing light through a negative onto sensitized paper. [< OF *preindre,* to press.] —**print'er** *n.*
print. printing.
print•a•ble (prĭn'tə-bəl) *adj.* **1.** Capable of being printed or of producing a print. **2.** Fit for publication.
print•ing (prĭn'tĭng) *n.* **1.** The process, art, or business of producing printed material. **2.** All the copies of a publication that are printed at one time. **3.** Written characters resembling those appearing in print.
printing press. A machine that transfers lettering or images by contact with various forms of inked surface onto paper or similar material.
pri•or¹ (prī'ər) *adj.* **1.** Preceding in time or order. **2.** Preceding in importance. [L.] —**pri•or'i•ty** (-ôr'ə-tē, -ŏr'ə-tē) *n.*
pri•or² (prī'ər) *n.* A monastic officer in charge of a priory. [< L, former, superior.] —**pri'or•ess** *fem.n.*
pri•or•y (prī'ə-rē) *n., pl.* **-ies.** A religious house governed by a prior or prioress.
prism (prĭz'əm) *n.* **1.** *Geom.* A polyhedron having parallel, congruent polygons as bases and parallelograms as sides. **2.** A homogeneous transparent solid, usually with triangular bases and rectangular sides, used to produce or analyze a continuous spectrum. **3.** A cut-glass object, such as a pendant of a chandelier. [< Gk *prisma,* "a thing sawed," prism.] —**pris•mat'ic** (-măt'ĭk) *adj.*
pris•on (prĭz'ən) *n.* A place of confinement for persons convicted or accused of crimes. [< L *prehendere,* to seize.]
pris•on•er (prĭz'ə-nər, prĭz'nər) *n.* A person held in custody, captivity, or a condition of forcible restraint.
pris•sy (prĭs'ē) *adj.* **-sier, -siest.** Finicky, fussy, and prudish. [Blend of PRIM and SISSY.] —**pris'si•ly** *adv.* —**pris'si•ness** *n.*
pris•tine (prĭs'tēn', prĭ-stēn') *adj.* **1.** Primitive or original. **2.** Remaining in a pure and uncorrupted state. [L *prīstīnus,* original.]
prith•ee (prĭth'ē, prĭth'ē) *interj. Archaic.* Please. [< (I) *pray thee.*]
pri•va•cy (prī'və-sē) *n., pl.* **-cies. 1.** The condition of being secluded. **2.** Secrecy.
pri•vate (prī'vĭt) *adj.* **1.** Secluded from the sight, presence, or intrusion of others. **2.** Of or confined to one person; personal. **3.** Not available for public use or participation. **4.** Belonging to a particular person or persons. **5.** Not holding an official or public position. **6.** Intimate; secret. —*n.* An enlisted man ranking below private first class in the Army or Marine Corps. —**in private.** Secretly; confidentially. [< L *prīvātus,* not in public life.] —**pri'vate•ly** *adv.* —**pri'vate•ness** *n.*
pri•va•teer (prī'və-tîr') *n.* **1.** A ship privately owned and manned but authorized to attack and capture enemy vessels. **2.** The commander or one of the crew of such a ship.
private first class. An enlisted man ranking below corporal and above private in the Army or Marine Corps.
pri•va•tion (prī-vā'shən) *n.* **1.** Lack of the basic necessities or comforts of life. **2.** The condition resulting from such lack. [< L *prīvāre,* to deprive.]
priv•et (prĭv'ĭt) *n.* A shrub with small, dark-

green leaves, widely used for hedges. [?]

priv•i•lege (prĭv'ə-lĭj) *n.* A special immunity, right, or benefit enjoyed by an individual or class. —*v.* **-leged, -leging.** To grant a privilege to. [< L *prīvilēgium,* law affecting an individual, prerogative.]

priv•i•leged (prĭv'ə-lĭjd) *adj.* Enjoying a privilege or having privileges.

privileged communication. A confidential communication that one cannot be made to divulge.

priv•y (prĭv'ē) *adj.* **1.** Made a participant in a secret: *privy to the plan.* **2.** Belonging to a person, as the British sovereign, in his private rather than his official capacity: *Privy Council.* —*n. pl.* **-ies.** A latrine or outhouse. [< L *prīvātus,* PRIVATE.] —**priv'i•ly** *adv.*

prize¹ (prīz) *n.* **1.** Something offered or won as an award in a competition or game of chance. **2.** Anything worth striving for. —*adj.* **1.** Offered or given as a prize. **2.** Given a prize. **3.** Outstanding; first-class. —*v.* **prized, prizing.** To value highly; esteem. [ME *pris,* value, price.]

prize² (prīz) *n.* Something, as an enemy ship, seized during wartime. [< VL **prensa,* "something seized."]

prize³ (prīz) *v.* **prized, prizing.** To pry. [< PRIZE².]

prize fight. Also **prize•fight** (prīz'fīt'). A professional boxing match. —**prize'fight'er** *n.* —**prize'fight'ing.** *n.*

pro¹ (prō) *n., pl.* **pros. 1.** An argument in favor of something. **2.** One who takes the affirmative side in debate. —*adv.* In favor of. —*adj.* Favoring; supporting. [< L *prō,* for.]

pro² (prō) *n., pl.* **pros.** *Informal.* A professional or expert.

pro–. *comb. form.* **1.** Favor or support. **2.** Acting as. [< L *prō,* before, in front of, according to, for.]

prob. **1.** probable; probably. **2.** problem.

prob•a•bil•i•ty (prŏb'ə-bĭl'ə-tē) *n., pl.* **-ties. 1.** The quality or condition of being probable; likelihood. **2.** A probable situation, condition, or event. **3.** A number expressing the likelihood of occurrence of a specific event. —**in all probability.** Most probably; very likely.

prob•a•ble (prŏb'ə-bəl) *adj.* **1.** Likely to happen or to be true. **2.** Apparently true; plausible. [< L *probābilis,* provable, laudable.] —**prob'a•bly** *adv.*

pro•bate (prō'bāt') *n.* Legal establishment of the validity of a will. [< L *probāre,* to examine, demonstrate as good, PROVE.] —**pro'bate'** *v.* **(-bated, -bating).**

pro•ba•tion (prō-bā'shən) *n.* **1.** A trial period. **2.** The action of granting a convicted offender provisional freedom on the promise of good behavior. [< L *probāre,* to try, PROVE.] —**pro•ba'tion•al, pro•ba'tion•ar'y** *adj.*

pro•ba•tion•er (prō-bā'shən-ər) *n.* A person on probation.

pro•ba•tive (prō'bə-tĭv) *adj.* Serving to test, try, or prove.

probe (prōb) *n.* **1.** A slender instrument used to explore a wound or body cavity. **2.** A penetrating investigation. [< L *probāre,* to test, PROVE.] —**probe** *v.* **(probed, probing).**

pro•bi•ty (prō'bə-tē) *n.* Integrity; uprightness. [< L *probus,* good, virtuous.]

prob•lem (prŏb'ləm) *n.* **1.** A question or situation that presents uncertainty or difficulty. **2.** A source of trouble or annoyance. **3.** A question put forward for consideration or solution. [< Gk *problēma,* "thing thrown forward," projection, problem.]

prob•lem•at•i•cal (prŏb'lə-măt'ĭ-kəl) *adj.* Also **prob•lem•at•ic** (-ĭk). **1.** Difficult to solve. **2.** Open to doubt; debatable.

pro•bos•cis (prō-bŏs'ĭs) *n., pl.* **-cises** or **-boscides** (-bŏs'ə-dēz'). A long, flexible snout, as an elephant's trunk. [< Gk *pro-,* in front + *boskein,* to feed.]

pro•caine hydrochloride (prō'kān'). A white crystalline powder, $C_{13}H_{20}O_2N_2 \cdot HCl$, used as a local anesthetic in medicine and dentistry.

pro•ce•dure (prə-sē'jər) *n.* **1.** A manner of proceeding. **2.** A series of steps or course of action. **3.** A set of established forms for conducting business or public affairs. —**pro•ce'dur•al** *adj.*

pro•ceed (prō-sēd', prə-) *v.* **1.** To advance or continue. **2.** To undertake and carry on some action. **3.** To move on in an orderly manner. **4.** To issue forth; originate. **5.** To take legal action. [< L *prōcēdere.*] —**pro•ceed'er** *n.*

pro•ceed•ing (prō-sē'dĭng, prə-) *n.* **1.** A procedure. **2.** A transaction. **3. a. proceedings.** Events or doings. **b.** Minutes, as of a meeting. **c.** Legal action.

pro•ceeds (prō'sēdz') *pl.n.* The amount of money derived from a commercial venture; profits.

proc•ess (prŏs'ĕs', prō'sĕs') *n.* **1.** A system of operations in the production of something. **2.** A series of actions, changes, or functions that bring about a particular result. **3.** Ongoing movement; progession. **4. a.** A court summons or writ. **b.** The entire course of a judicial proceeding. **5.** *Biol.* A part extending or projecting from an organ or organism; an appendage. **6.** Any of various photomechanical or photoengraving methods. —*v* **1.** To put through the steps of a prescribed procedure. **2.** To prepare or convert by subjecting to some special process. [< L *prōcessus,* pp of *prōcēdere,* to PROCEED.] —**proc'es'sor, proc'es'ser** *n*

pro•ces•sion (prə-sĕsh'ən) *n.* **1.** A group of persons moving along in an orderly and formal manner. **2.** Any continuous and orderly course.

pro•ces•sion•al (prə-sĕsh'ən-əl) *n.* A hymn sung when the clergy enter a church at the beginning of the service.

pro•claim (prō-klām', prə-) *v.* To announce officially and publicly; declare. [< L *prōclāmāre.*] —**pro•claim'er** *n.* —**proc'la•ma'tion** (prŏk'lə-mā'shən) *n.*

pro•cliv•i•ty (prō-klĭv'ə-tē) *n., pl.* **-ties.** A natural propensity. [< L *prōclīvus,* sloping forward.]

pro•cras•ti•nate (prō-krăs'tə-nāt', prə-) *v.* **-nated, -nating.** To put off doing something until a future time. [L *prōcrāstināre,* "to put forward until tomorrow."] —**pro•cras'ti•na'tion** *n.* —**pro•cras'ti•na'tor** *n.*

pro•cre•ate (prō'krē-āt') *v.* **-ated, -ating.** To beget or reproduce. —**pro'cre•ant** *adj.* —**pro'cre•a'tion** *n.* —**pro'cre•a'tive** *adj.* —**pro'cre•a'tor** (-ā'tər) *n.*

pro•crus•te•an (prō-krŭs'tē-ən) *adj.* Forcing conformity by ruthless or arbitrary means. [< *Procrustes,* a Greek giant who stretched or shortened captives to fit one of his iron beds.]

proc•tol•o•gy (prŏk-tŏl'ə-jē) *n.* The physiology and pathology of the rectum and anus. [Gk *prōktos,* anus + -LOGY.] —**proc•tol'o•gist** *n.*

proc•tor (prŏk'tər) *n.* An examination supervisor. [< PROCURATOR.] —**proc'tor** *v.* —**proc•to'ri•al** (-tôr'ē-əl, -tōr'ē-əl) *adj.*

proc•u•ra•tor (prŏk'yə-rā'tər) *n.* An administrator of a minor Roman province. [< L *prōcūrāre,* to take care of, PROCURE.]

pro•cure (prō-kyŏŏr', prə-) *v.* **-cured, -curing. 1.** To obtain; acquire. **2.** To bring about; effect. **3.** To obtain (a woman) to serve as a prostitute. [< L *prōcūrāre,* to take care of, manage for someone else.] —**pro•cur'er** *n.* —**pro•cur'ess** *fem.n.* —**pro•cure'ment** *n.*

Pro•cy•on (prō'sē-ŏn') *n.* **A double star in the constellation Canis Minor; Dog Star. [< Gk *Prokuōn,* "before the dog star."]**

prod (prŏd) *v.* **prodded, prodding. 1.** To jab or poke. **2.** To urge; goad. [Perh blend of POKE and *brod,* var of BRAD.] —**prod** *n.*

prod. **1.** produce. **2.** produced. **3.** product.

prod•i•gal (prŏd'ĭ-gəl) *adj.* **1.** Recklessly wasteful; extravagant. **2.** Profuse in giving. **3.** Profuse; lavish. [< L *prōdigere,* to drive away, squander.] —**prod'i•gal** *n.* —**prod'i•gal'i•ty** (-găl'ə-tē) *n.*

pro•di•gious (prə-dĭj'əs) *adj.* **1.** Enormous. **2.** Extraordinary; marvelous. [< L *prōdigium,* omen, PRODIGY.] —**pro•di'gious•ly** *adv.* —**pro•di'gious•ness** *n.*

prod•i•gy (prŏd'ə-jē) *n., pl.* **-gies. 1.** A person with exceptional talents or powers. **2.** A marvel. [L *prōdigium,* prophetic sign, marvel.]

pro•duce (prə-d/y/ōōs', prō-) *v.* **-duced, -ducing. 1.** To bring forth; yield. **2.** To manufacture. **3.** To cause or give rise to. **4.** To bring forward; exhibit. —*n.* (prŏd'yōōs, prō'dyōōs). Something produced; a product, esp. farm products, as fruits and vegetables. [L *prōdūcere,* to lead or bring forth.] —**pro•duc'er** *n.* —**pro•duc'i•ble** *adj.*

prod•uct (prŏd'əkt) *n.* **1.** Anything produced by labor. **2.** The result obtained by performing multiplication.

pro•duc•tion (prə-dŭk'shən, prō-) *n.* **1.** The act or process of producing. **2.** The creation of value by producing goods and services. **3.** A product. **4.** The total number of products; output. **5.** A public performance. **pro•duc'tive** *adj.* —**pro•duc'tive•ly** *adv.* —**pro'duc•tiv'i•ty** *n.*

pro•em (prō'ĕm') *n.* A short introduction; preface. [< Gk *prooimion.*]

prof (prŏf) *n.* *Informal.* A professor.

Prof. professor.

pro•fane (prō-fān', prə-) *adj.* **1.** Blasphemous. **2.** Nonreligious; secular. **3.** Impure. [< L *profānus,* "before (i.e., outside) the temple," not sacred.] —**prof'a•na'tion** (prŏf'ə-nā'shən) *n.* —**pro•fane'** *v.* **(-faned, -faning).** —**pro•fan'i•ty** (-făn'ə-tē) *n.*

pro•fess (prə-fĕs', prō-) *v.* **1.** To affirm. **2.** To make a pretense of. **3.** To claim skill in or knowledge of. **4.** To affirm belief in. [L *prōfitēri* (pp *prōfessus*), to declare publicly.] —**pro•fessed'** *adj.* —**pro•fess'ed•ly** *adv.*

pro•fes•sion (prə-fĕsh'ən) *n.* **1.** An occupation or vocation requiring advanced study in a specialized field. **2.** The body of qualified persons of one specific field. **3.** The act or an instance of professing; declaration. **4.** An avowal of faith. [< L *prōfessiō,* declaration, confession < *prōfitēri,* PROFESS.]

pro•fes•sion•al (prə-fĕsh'ən-əl) *adj.* **1.** Of, related to, or suitable for a profession. **2.** Engaged in one of the learned professions, as law. **3.** Participating for pay in a sport. —*n.* **1.** A person following a profession. **2.** One who earns his livelihood as an athlete. **3.** One who has an assured competence in a particular field or occupation. —**pro•fes'sion•al•ly** *adv.*

pro•fes•sion•al•ism (prə-fĕsh'ən-ə-lĭz'əm) *n.* **1.** Professional status, methods, character, or standards. **2.** The use of professional players in organized athletics.

pro•fes•sor (prə-fĕs'ər) *n.* 1. A teacher of the highest rank in an institution of higher learning. 2. A teacher or instructor. —**pro'fes•so'ri•al** *adj.* —**pro•fes'sor•ship'** *n.*

prof•fer (prŏf'ər) *v.* To offer or tender. [< OF *proffrir.*] —**prof'fer** *n.*

pro•fi•cien•cy (prə-fĭsh'ən-sē) *n., pl.* **-cies.** The state or quality of being proficient; skill; competence.

pro•fi•cient (prə-fĭsh'ənt) *adj.* Performing in a given art, skill, or branch of learning with expert correctness and facility; adept. —*n.* An expert. [< L *prōficere,* to make progress.] —**pro•fi'cien•cy** *n.* —**pro•fi'cient•ly** *adv.*

pro•file (prō'fīl') *n.* 1. A side view of the human head. 2. An outline of any object. 3. A biographical sketch. [< It *profilare,* to draw in outline.]

prof•it (prŏf'ĭt) *n.* 1. A gain or return; benefit. 2. The return received on a business undertaking after costs have been met. —*v.* 1. To make a gain or profit. 2. To be advantageous; benefit. [< L *prōficere,* to go forward, make progress.] —**prof'it•a•bil'i•ty** *n.* —**prof'it•a•ble** *adj.* —**prof'it•a•bly** *adv.*

prof•i•teer (prŏf'ə-tîr') *n.* One who makes excessive profits on commodities in short supply. —**prof'i•teer'** *v.*

prof•li•gate (prŏf'lĭ-gĭt, -gāt') *adj.* 1. Dissolute. 2. Recklessly extravagant. —*n.* A wastrel. [< L *prōflīgāre,* to strike down, destroy.] —**prof'li•ga•cy** (-lĭ-gə-sē) *n.*

pro for•ma (prō fôr'mə). As a matter of form. [L.]

pro•found (prə-found', prō-) *adj.* 1. Extended to or coming from a great depth; deep. 2. Coming as if from the depths of one's being: *profound contempt.* 3. Thoroughgoing. 4. Penetrating beyond what is superficial or obvious. 5. Absolute; complete: *a profound silence.* [< L *profundus.*] —**pro•found'ly** *adv.* —**pro•fun'di•ty** (-fŭn'də-tē) *n.*

pro•fuse (prə-fyōōs', prō-) *adj.* Copious or abundant. [< L *prōfundere,* to pour forth.] —**pro•fuse'ly** *adv.* —**pro•fu'sion** (-fyōō'zhən), **pro•fuse'ness** *n.*

pro•gen•i•tor (prō-jĕn'ə-tər) *n.* 1. A direct ancestor. 2. An originator of a line of descent. [< L *prōgignere,* to beget.]

prog•e•ny (prŏj'ə-nē) *n.* Children or descendants; offspring. [< L *prōgignere,* to beget.]

prog•no•sis (prŏg-nō'sĭs) *n., pl.* **-ses** (-sēz'). 1. A prediction of the probable course and outcome of a disease. 2. The likelihood of recovery from a disease. [< Gk *progignōskein,* to foreknow, predict.]

prog•nos•tic (prŏg-nŏs'tĭk) *n.* 1. A portent; omen. 2. A prophecy. [< Gk *progignōskein,* to predict.] —**prog•nos'tic** *adj.*

prog•nos•ti•cate (prŏg-nŏs'tĭ-kāt') *v.* **-cated, -cating.** To predict on the basis of present indications. —**prog•nos'ti•ca'tion** *n.* —**prog•nos'ti•ca'tor** *n.*

pro•gram (prō'grăm', -grəm) *n.* Also *chiefly Brit.* **pro•gramme.** 1. A listing of the order of events for some public presentation. 2. Any organized list of procedures; schedule. 3. Instructions coded for a computer. —*v.* **-grammed** or **-gramed, -gramming** or **-graming.** 1. To include in a program. 2. To provide (a computer) with a set of instructions. [< Gk *programma,* public notice.] —**pro'gram•mat'ic** (-grə-măt'ĭk) *adj.* —**pro'gram'mer** *n.*

prog•ress (prŏg'rĕs', -rəs) *n.* 1. Movement toward a goal. 2. Development; unfolding. 3. Steady improvement. —*v.* **pro•gress** (prə-grĕs'). 1. To advance; proceed. 2. To improve. [< L *prōgredī,* to go forward.]

pro•gres•sion (prə-grĕsh'ən) *n.* 1. Progress. 2. Advance. 3. A sequence. 4. A series of numbers or quantities, each derived from the one preceding by some consistent operation. —**pro•gres'sion•al** *adj.*

pro•gres•sive (prə-grĕs'ĭv) *adj.* 1. Moving forward; ongoing. 2. Proceeding in steps or by stages. 3. Promoting or favoring political reform. 4. *Gram.* Designating a verb form that expresses an action or condition in progress. —*n.* A partisan of reform in politics, education, or other fields.

pro•hib•it (prō-hĭb'ĭt) *v.* 1. To forbid by authority. 2. To prevent or debar. [< L *prōhibēre,* to hold in front, hinder.]

pro•hi•bi•tion (prō'ə-bĭsh'ən) *n.* 1. The act of prohibiting. 2. A ban on the manufacture and sale of alcoholic beverages.

pro•hib•i•tive (prō-hĭb'ə-tĭv) *adj.* 1. Prohibiting. 2. Discouraging purchase or use.

proj•ect (prŏj'ĕkt', -ĭkt) *n.* 1. A plan; scheme. 2. An undertaking requiring concerted effort. —*v.* **pro•ject** (prə-jĕkt'). 1. To protrude. 2. To throw forward. 3. To direct one's voice so as to be heard clearly at a distance. 4. To form a plan or intention for. 5. To cause (an image) to appear upon a surface. [< L *prōjicere,* to throw forth.] —**pro•jec'tion** (prə-jĕk'shən) *n.*

pro•jec•tile (prə-jĕk'təl, -tīl') *n.* 1. A fired, thrown, or otherwise projected object, as a bullet. 2. A self-propelling missile, as a rocket. [< L *prōjicere,* to throw forth, PROJECT.]

pro•jec•tor (prə-jĕk'tər) *n.* A device for projecting an image onto a screen.

pro•le•tar•i•an (prō'lə-târ'ē-ən) *n.* A member of the proletariat. [< L *prōlētārius,* Roman citizen of the lowest class.]

pro•le•tar•i•at (prō'lə-târ'ē-ĭt) *n.* The class of industrial wage earners.

pro•lif•er•ate (prō-lĭf'ə-rāt') *v.* **-ated, -ating.** To reproduce or increase rapidly and repeatedly. [< ML *prōlifer,* producing offspring.] —**pro•lif'er•a'tion** *n.*

pro•lif•ic (prō-lĭf'ĭk) *adj.* 1. Producing offspring in abundance. 2. Producing abundant works or results. [< ML *prōlificus.*] —**pro•lif'i•cal•ly** *adv.*

pro•lix (prō-lĭks', prō'lĭks) *adj.* Wordy; verbose. [< L *prōlixus,* "poured forth," extended.] —**pro•lix'i•ty** *n.* —**pro•lix'ly** *adv.*

pro•logue (prō'lôg', -lŏg') *n.* An introduction, as to a play. [< Gk *prologos,* (speaker of) a prologue.]

pro•long (prə-lông', -lŏng') *v.* 1. To lengthen in duration; protract. 2. To lengthen in extent; elongate. —**pro'lon•ga'tion** (-gā'shən) *n.*

prom (prŏm) *n.* A formal dance held for a high-school or college class. [Short for PROMENADE.]

prom•e•nade (prŏm'ə-nād', -näd') *n.* 1. A leisurely walk; stroll. 2. A public place for such walking. 3. A formal march by the guests at the opening of a ball. —*v.* **-naded, -nading.** To go on a leisurely walk. [< LL *prōmināre,* to drive forward.]

pro•me•thi•um (prə-mē'thē-əm) *n. Symbol* **Pm** A radioactive rare-earth element. Atomic number 61, longest-lived isotope Pm 145. [NL.]

prom•i•nence (prŏm'ə-nəns) *n.* 1. The condition or quality of being prominent. 2. Something prominent; a projection.

prom•i•nent (prŏm'ə-nənt) *adj.* 1. Projecting outward. 2. Immediately noticeable; conspicuous. 3. Widely known; eminent. [< L *prōminēre,* to jut out.] —**prom'i•nent•ly** *adv.*

pro•mis•cu•ous (prə-mĭs'kyōō-əs) *adj.* 1. Consisting of diverse and unrelated parts or individuals; confused. 2. Indiscriminate, esp. in sexual relations. 3. Casual; random. [L *prōmiscuus,* mixed.] —**prom'is•cu'i•ty** (prŏm'ĭ-skyōō'ə-tē, prō'mĭ-), —**pro•mis'cu•ous•ness** *n.* —**pro•mis'cu•ous•ly** *adv.*

prom•ise (prŏm'ĭs) *n.* 1. A declaration assuring that one will or will not do something. 2. Something promised. 3. Indication of future excellence or success. —*v.* **-ised, -ising.** 1. To pledge or offer assurance. 2. To make a promise of. 3. To afford a basis for expecting. [< L *prōmittere,* "to send forth," promise.]

Promised Land. 1. The land of Canaan. Genesis 12:7. 2. **promised land.** Any place of anticipated happiness.

prom•is•ing (prŏm'ĭ-sĭng) *adj.* Likely to develop in a desirable manner. —**prom'is•ing•ly** *adv.*

prom•is•so•ry note (prŏm'ĭ-sôr'ē, -sōr'ē). A written promise to pay a specified sum of money at a stated time or on demand.

prom•on•to•ry (prŏm'ən-tôr'ē, -tōr'ē) *n., pl.* **-ries.** A high ridge of land or rock jutting out into a sea or other expanse of water. [< L *prōmunturium.*]

pro•mote (prə-mōt') *v.* **-moted, -moting.** 1. To raise in position or rank. 2. To contribute to the progress or growth of; further. 3. To urge the adoption of; advocate. 4. To attempt to sell or popularize. [< L *prōmovēre* (pp *prōmōtus*), to move forward, advance.] —**pro•mo'tion** *n.* —**pro•mo'tion•al** *adj.*

pro•mot•er (prə-mō'tər) *n.* 1. An active supporter; advocate. 2. A finance and publicity organizer.

prompt (prŏmpt) *adj.* 1. On time; punctual. 2. Done without delay. —*v.* 1. To press into action; incite. 2. To give rise to; inspire. 3. To assist with a reminder; remind. 4. To give a cue to, as in the theater. [< L *promptus,* "brought to light," "visible," at hand, prompt.] —**prompt'er** *n.* —**promp'ti•tude', prompt'ness** *n.* —**prompt'ly** *adv.*

prom•ul•gate (prŏm'əl-gāt', prō-mŭl'gāt') *v.* **-gated, -gating.** To make known or put into effect by public declaration. [L *prōmulgāre.*] —**prom'ul•ga'tion** (prŏm'əl-gā'shən, prō'-məl-) *n.* —**prom'ul•ga'tor** *n.*

pron. 1. pronoun. 2. pronunciation.

pro•na•tal•ism (prō-nāt'l-ĭz'əm) *n.* Any policy that encourages childbearing. [PRO- + NATAL + -ISM.] — **pro•na'tal•ist** *adj.* & *n.*

prone (prōn) *adj.* 1. Lying with the front or face downward. 2. Tending: *prone to mischief.* [< L *prōnus,* "bending."] —**prone'ness** *n.*

prong (prông, prŏng) *n.* 1. A sharply pointed part, as a tine of a fork. 2. Any slender projection. [ME *pronge,* forked instrument.]

pro•noun (prō'noun') *n.* One of a class of words that function as substitutes for nouns. [< L *prōnōmen.*]

pro•nounce (prə-nouns') *v.* **-nounced, -nouncing.** 1. To articulate (a word or speech sound). 2. To state officially and formally; declare. [< L *prōnuntiāre,* to speak in public, declare.] —**pro•nounce'a•ble** *adj.* —**pro•nun'ci•a'tion** (-nŭn'sē-ā'shən) *n.*

pro•nounced (prə-nounst') *adj.* Distinct; strongly marked.

pro•nounce•ment (prə-nouns'mənt) *n.* A formal declaration or statement.

pron•to (prŏn'tō) *adv. Informal.* Without delay; quickly. [< L *promptus,* PROMPT.]

proof (prōōf) *n.* 1. The evidence establishing

PROOFREADERS' MARKS

Instruction	Mark in Margin	Mark in Type	Corrected Type
Delete	℘	the ~~good~~ word	the word
Insert indicated material	good	the ‸ word	the good word
Let it stand	(stet)	the ~~good~~ word	the good word
Make capital	(cap)	the word	the Word
Make lower case	(lc)	The Word	the Word
Set in small capitals	(SC)	See word.	See WORD.
Set in italic type	(ital)	The word is word.	The word is *word.*
Set in roman type	(rom)	the (word)	the word
Set in boldface type	(bf)	the entry word	the entry **word**
Set in lightface type	(lf)	the entry (word)	the entry word
Transpose	(tr)	the word good	the good word
Close up space	⁀	the wo rd	the word
Delete and close up space	℘	the woord	the word
Spell out	(sp)	(2) words	two words
Insert: space	#	theword	the word
period	⊙	This is the word‸	This is the word.
comma	‸	words‸ words, words	words, words, words
hyphen	=/=	word‸ for‸ word test	word-for-word test
colon	(:)	The following words‸	The following words:
semicolon	;	Scan the words‸ skim the words.	Scan the words; skim the words.
apostrophe	’	Johns words	John's words
quotation marks	“/”	the word word	the word “word”
parentheses	(/)/	The word‸ word‸ is in parentheses.	The word (word) is in parentheses.
brackets	[/]/	He read from the Word ‸ the Bible‸	He read from the Word [the Bible].

Instruction	Mark in Margin	Mark in Type	Corrected Type
en dash	1/N	1964‸ 1972	1964–1972
em dash	1/M	The dictionary‸ how often it is needed‸ belongs in every home.	The dictionary—how often it is needed—belongs in every home.
superior type	∨ 2	2‸ = 4	$2^2 = 4$
inferior type	∧ 2	H‸ O	H_2O
asterisk	*	word‸	word*
dagger	†	a word‸	a word†
double dagger	‡	words and words‸	words and words‡
section symbol	§	‸ Book Reviews	§Book Reviews
virgule	/	either‸ or	either/or
Start paragraph	¶	“Where is it?” ‸ “It's on the shelf.”	“Where is it?” “It's on the shelf.”
Run in	(run in)	The entry word is printed in boldface. The pronunciation follows.	The entry word is printed in boldface. The pronunciation follows.
Turn right side up	◌	the word	the word
Move left	⊏	⊏ the word	the word
Move right	⊐	the word	the word
Move up	⊓	the word	the word
Move down	⊔	the word	the word
Align	‖	the word / the word / the word	the word / the word / the word
Straighten line	=	the word	the word
Wrong font	(wf)	the word	the word
Broken type	×	the word	the word

the validity of a given assertion. **2.** Conclusive demonstration of something. **3.** The proving of something. **4.** The alcoholic strength of a liquor. **5.** A trial sheet of printed material on which corrections are made before publication. **6.** A photographer's trial print. *—adj.* **1.** Fully resistant: *proof against fire.* **2.** Of standard alcoholic strength. [< L *probāre,* to test, prove.]

-proof. *comb. form.* Impervious to or able to resist: *shockproof.*

proof•read (pro͞of′rēd′) *v.* To read (copy or a printer's proof) against the original manuscript for corrections. **—proof′read′er** *n.*

prop¹ (prŏp) *n.* A support or stay. [ME *proppe.*] **—prop** *v.* **(propped, propping).**

prop² (prŏp) *n.* A stage property.

prop³ (prŏp) *n. Informal.* A propeller.

prop. **1.** property. **2.** proposition. **3.** proprietary; proprietor.

prop•a•gan•da (prŏp′ə-găn′də) *n.* **1.** The systematic propagation of a given doctrine. **2.** Material disseminated by the proselytizers of a doctrine. [< L *prōpāgāre,* to PROPAGATE.] **—prop′a•gan′dist** *n.* **—prop′a•gan′dize′** *v.* **(-dized, -dizing).**

prop•a•gate (prŏp′ə-gāt′) *v.* **-gated, -gating.** **1.** To produce or cause to produce offspring; reproduce; breed. **2.** To move through a medium. [L *prōpāgāre.*] **—prop′a•ga′tion** *n.*

pro•pane (prō′pān′) *n.* A colorless gas, C_3H_8, found in natural gas and petroleum, used as a fuel.

pro•pel (prə-pĕl′) *v.* **-pelled, -pelling.** To cause to move or sustain in motion. [< L *prōpellere.*]

pro•pel•lant (prə-pĕl′ənt) *n.* Also **pro•pel•lent.** Something that propels, as an explosive charge or a rocket fuel.

pro•pel•ler (prə-pĕl′ər) *n.* Also **pro•pel•lor.** A device for propelling aircraft or boats, esp. one having radiating blades mounted on a revolving power-driven shaft.

pro•pen•si•ty (prə-pĕn′sə-tē) *n., pl.* **-ties.** An innate inclination; tendency; bent. [< L *prōpendēre,* to be inclined or favorable.]

prop•er (prŏp′ər) *adj.* **1.** Suitable; fitting. **2.** Out-and-out; thorough: *a proper whipping.* **3.** Worthy of the name. **4.** Meeting a requisite standard. **5. a.** Within the strict limitation of a term: *France proper.* **b.** Rigorously correct; exact. **6.** Seemly; decorous. [< L *proprius,* one's own, personal, particular.] **—prop′er•ly** *adv.* **—prop′er•ness** *n.*

proper fraction. A numerical fraction in which the numerator is less than the denominator.

proper noun. Also **proper name.** A noun designating by name a being or thing without a limiting modifier.

prop•er•ty (prŏp′ər-tē) *n., pl.* **-ties.** **1.** Ownership. **2.** A possession or possessions. **3.** Any article, except costumes and scenery, used as part of a play. **4.** A characteristic trait or quality. [< L *proprius,* own, PROPER.]

pro•phase (prō′fāz′) *n.* The first stage of cell division by mitosis.

proph•e•cy (prŏf′ə-sē) *n., pl.* **-cies.** **1.** A prediction. **2.** The inspired utterance of a prophet.

proph•e•sy (prŏf′ə-sī′) *v.* **-sied, -sying.** **1.** To reveal by divine inspiration. **2.** To predict. **—proph′e•si′er** *n.*

proph•et (prŏf′ĭt) *n.* **1.** One who speaks by divine inspiration. **2.** A predictor. **3. The Prophets.** The prophetic writings of the Hebrew Scriptures. [< Gk *prophētēs,* "one who speaks beforehand," proclaimer.] **—proph′et•ess** *fem.n.*

pro•phet•ic (prə-fĕt′ĭk) *adj.* Of or belonging to a prophet or prophecy.

pro•phy•lac•tic (prō′fə-lăk′tĭk, prŏf′ə-) *adj.* Acting against or to prevent something, esp. disease. *—n.* A prophylactic medicine, device, or measure, esp. a condom. [< Gk *prophulassein,* to stand on guard before (a place), take precautions against.]

pro•pin•qui•ty (prō-pĭng′kwə-tē) *n.* **1.** Nearness; proximity. **2.** Kinship. [< L *propinquus,* near.]

pro•pi•ti•ate (prō-pĭsh′ē-āt′) *v.* **-ated, -ating.** To conciliate; appease. [< L *propitius,* PROPITIOUS.] **—pro•pi′ti•a′tion** *n.* **—pro•pi′ti•a•to′ry** (-ə-tôr′ē, -tōr′ē) *adj.*

pro•pi•tious (prə-pĭsh′əs) *adj.* Presenting favorable circumstances; auspicious. [< L *propitius,* favorable, kind.]

pro•po•nent (prə-pō′nənt) *n.* One who argues in support of something; an advocate. [< L *prōpōnere,* to PROPOSE.]

pro•por•tion (prə-pôr′shən, -pōr′shən) *n.* **1.** A part considered in relation to the whole. **2.** A relationship between things or variable quantities. **3.** A relation between quantities such that if one varies, another varies as a multiple of the first; ratio. **4.** Harmonious relation; balance. **5.** Often **proportions.** Dimensions; size. —*v.* **1.** To adjust so that proper relations between parts are attained. **2.** To form with symmetry. [< L *prō portiōne,* "for (its or his) share," proportionally.] —**pro•por′tion•al** *adj.* —**pro•por′tion•al′i•ty** (-shə-năl′ə-tē) *n.* —**pro•por′tion•al•ly** *adv.* —**pro•por′tion•ate** *adj.*

pro•pose (prə-pōz′) *v.* **-posed, -posing. 1.** To put forward for consideration; suggest. **2.** To present or nominate (a person) for a position, office, etc. **3.** To purpose; intend. **4.** To make an offer, esp. of marriage. [< L *prōpōnere* (pp *prōpositus*), to put or set forth, declare.] —**pro•pos′al** *n.* —**pro•pos′er** *n.*

prop•o•si•tion (prŏp′ə-zĭsh′ən) *n.* **1.** A plan or scheme suggested for acceptance. **2.** *Informal.* A matter requiring special handling. **3.** A subject for discussion or analysis. [<L *prōpōnere,* PROPOSE.]

pro•pound (prə-pound′) *v.* To put forward for consideration or debate. [< L *prōpōnere,* to PROPOSE.] —**pro•pound′er** *n.*

pro•pri•e•tar•y (prə-prī′ə-tĕr′ē) *adj.* **1.** Of or characteristic of a proprietor or proprietors. **2.** Exclusively owned; private. [< L *proprietās,* property, propriety.]

pro•pri•e•tor (prə-prī′ə-tər) *n.* An owner. [Var of PROPRIETARY.] —**pro•pri′e•tor•ship′** *n.* —**pro•pri′e•tress** *fem.n.*

pro•pri•e•ty (prə-prī′ə-tē) *n., pl.* **-ties. 1.** The quality of being proper; appropriateness. **2.** Conformity to prevailing customs and usages. [< L *proprius,* PROPER.]

pro•pul•sion (prə-pŭl′shən) *n.* **1.** The process of propelling. **2.** A driving force. [< L *prōpellere* (pp *prōpulsus*), to drive forward, PROPEL.] —**pro•pul′sive** *adj.*

pro ra•ta (prō rā′tə, răt′ə, rä′tə). In proportion. [L *pro rata (parte),* according to the calculated (share).]

pro•rate (prō-rāt′, prō′rāt′) *v.* **-rated, -rating.** To divide, distribute, or assess proportionately. [< PRO RATA.] —**pro•ra′tion** *n.*

pro•rogue (prō-rōg′) *v.* **-rogued, -roguing.** To discontinue a session of (a legislative body). [< L *prōrogāre,* "to ask publicly," defer.] —**pro′ro•ga′tion** *n.*

pros. prosody.

pro•sa•ic (prō-zā′ĭk) *adj.* **1.** Matter-of-fact; straightforward. **2.** Dull; ordinary. [< L *prōsa,* PROSE.] —**pro•sa′i•cal•ly** *adv.*

pro•sce•ni•um (prō-sē′nē-əm) *n., pl.* **-nia** (-nē-ə). The area located between the curtain and orchestra in a theater. [< Gk *proskēnion.*]

pro•scribe (prō-skrīb′) *v.* **-scribed, -scribing. 1.** To outlaw. **2.** To prohibit; forbid. [L *prōscrībere,* to publish in writing, proscribe.] —**pro•scrip′tion** (-skrĭp′shən) *n.*

prose (prōz) *n.* Ordinary speech or writing as distinguished from verse. [< L *prōsa (ōrātiō),* "straightforward discourse."]

pros•e•cute (prŏs′ə-kyōōt′) *v.* **-cuted, -cuting. 1.** To pursue or persist in so as to complete. **2.** To initiate and conduct court action against. [< L *prōsequī,* to follow up or forward.] —**pros′e•cu′tion** *n.* —**pros′e•cu′tor** *n.*

pros•e•lyte (prŏs′ə-līt′) *n.* A new convert to a religion or doctrine. [< Gk *prosēlutos,* "one who comes to a place," stranger, religious convert.]

pros•e•lyt•ize (prŏs′ə-lə-tīz′) *v.* **-ized, -izing.** To convert from one doctrine to another. —**pros′e•lyt•iz′er** *n.*

pros•o•dy (prŏs′ə-dē) *n.* The study of the metrical structures of verse. [< Gk *prosōidia,* accompanied song, modulation of voice.] —**pro•sod′ic** (prō-sŏd′ĭk) *adj.*

pros•pect (prŏs′pĕkt′) *n.* **1.** Something expected; a possibility. **2. prospects.** Chances for success. **3.** A potential customer or candidate. **4.** The direction in which something faces; an outlook. **5.** A scene; view. —*v.* To explore for mineral deposits. [< L *prōspectus,* pp of *prōspicere,* to look forward, foresee.] —**pros′pec′tor** *n.*

pro•spec•tive (prə-spĕk′tĭv) *adj.* Expected. —**pro•spec′tive•ly** *adv.*

pro•spec•tus (prə-spĕk′təs) *n., pl.* **-tuses.** A formal summary of a proposed commercial venture. [L, PROSPECT.]

pros•per (prŏs′pər) *v.* To be successful; thrive. [< L *prosperus,* fortunate.]

pros•per•i•ty (prŏs-pĕr′ə-tē) *n.* Financial success or well-being.

pros•per•ous (prŏs′pər-əs) *adj.* **1.** Flourishing or wealthy. **2.** Propitious; favorable.

pros•tate (prŏs′tāt′) *n.* A gland in male mammals composed of muscular and glandular tissue that surrounds the urethra at the bladder. [< Gk *prostatēs,* "one that stands before (the bladder)."]

pros•the•sis (prŏs-thē′sĭs) *n., pl.* **-ses** (-sēz′). An artificial replacement for a limb, tooth, or other part of the body. [< Gk, attachment, addition.] —**pros•thet′ic** (-thĕt′ĭk) *adj.* —**pros•thet′i•cal•ly** *adv.*

pros•thet•ics (prŏs-thĕt′ĭks) *n. (takes sing. v.).* Prosthetic surgery or dentistry.

pros•ti•tute (prŏs′tə-t/y/ōōt′) *n.* A whore. —*v.* **-tuted, -tuting. 1.** To offer (oneself or another) for sexual hire. **2.** To sell (one's talents) to an unworthy cause. [< L *prōstituere,* to expose publicly, prostitute.] —**pros′ti•tu′tion** *n.*

pros•trate (prŏs′trāt′) *v.* **-trated, -trating. 1.** To put or throw down in a posture of adoration or submission. **2.** To lay low; overcome. —*adj.* **1.** Lying face down. **2.** Exhausted; incapacitated. [< L *prōsternere,* to throw down, prostrate.] —**pros•tra′tion** *n.*

Prot. Protestant.

pro•tac•tin•i•um (prō′tăk-tĭn′ē-əm) *n. Symbol* **Pa** A rare radioactive element chemically similar to uranium. Atomic number 91, longest-lived isotope Pa 231. [< PROT(O)- + ACTINIUM.]

pro•tag•o•nist (prō-tăg′ə-nĭst) *n.* **1.** A leading character in a drama or story. **2.** Any leading figure. [< PROT(O)- + Gk *agōnistēs,* actor.]

pro•tect (prə-tĕkt′) *v.* To keep from harm or injury; guard. [L *prōtegere* (pp *prōtectus*), to cover in front, protect.] —**pro•tec′tion** *n.* —**pro•tec′tive** *adj.* —**pro•tec′tor** *n.*

pro•tec•tor•ate (prə-tĕk′tər-ĭt) *n.* **1.** A relationship of partial control assumed by a superior power over a dependent country or region. **2.** The dependent country.

pro•té•gé (prō′tə-zhā′) *n.* One whose welfare or career is promoted by an influential person. [< L *prōtegere,* PROTECT.]

pro•tein (prō′tēn, -tē-ĭn) *n.* Any of a group of complex organic compounds that contain amino acids as their basic structural units, occur in all living matter, and are essential for the growth and repair of animal tissue. [F *protéine,* "primary substance."]

pro•test (prə-tĕst′, prō-tĕst′, prō′tĕst′) *v.* **1.** To object (to). **2.** To promise or affirm solemnly. —*n.* (prō′tĕst′). **1.** The act of protesting. **2.** A strong or solemn objection. [< L *prōtestārī,* to declare in public, testify.] —**prot′es•ta′tion** (prŏt′ĭs-tā′shən, prō′tĭs-) *n.* —**pro•test′er** *n.*

Prot•es•tant (prŏt′ĭs-tənt) *n.* Any Christian belonging to a sect descending from those that seceded from the Church of Rome at the time of the Reformation. [< L *prōtestārī,* to PROTEST.] —**Prot′es•tant•ism′** *n.*

Protestant Episcopal Church. A church body in the U.S. originally associated with the Church of England, but a separate entity since 1789.

proto–. *comb. form.* **1.** The earliest form or the first in rank or time. **2. Proto-.** The earliest reconstructed form of a language: *Proto-Indo-European.* [< Gk *prōtos,* first.]

pro•to•col (prō′tə-kôl′, -kōl′, -kŏl′) *n.* **1.** The forms of ceremony and etiquette observed by diplomats and heads of state. **2.** The first copy of a treaty prior to ratification. **3.** Any preliminary draft or record. [< Gk *prōtokollon,* first sheet glued to a papyrus roll, bearing a table of contents.]

pro•ton (prō′tŏn′) *n. Symbol* **p** A stable, positively charged subatomic particle having a mass 1,836 times that of the electron. [< Gk *prōtos,* first.]

pro•to•plasm (prō′tə-plăz′əm) *n.* A complex, jellylike colloidal substance constituting the living matter of plant and animal cells. —**pro′to•plas′mic, pro′to•plas′mal, pro′to•plas•mat′ic** (-plăz-măt′ĭk) *adj.*

pro•to•type (prō′tə-tīp′) *n.* An original form or model.

pro•to•zo•an (prō′tə-zō′ən) *n., pl.* **-ans** or **-zoa** (-zō′ə). Any of numerous single-celled, usually microscopic organisms belonging to a group that includes the most primitive forms of animal life. [< PROTO- + Gk *zōion,* animal.] —**pro′to•zo′an, pro′to•zo′ic** (-zō′ĭk) *adj.*

pro•tract (prō-trăkt′) *v.* To draw out; prolong. [L *prōtrahere,* to drag out, lengthen.] —**pro•trac′tion** *n.*

pro•trac•tor (prō-trăk′tər) *n.* A semicircular instrument for measuring and constructing angles.

pro•trude (prō-trōōd′) *v.* **-truded, -truding.** To push or jut outward; project. [L *prōtrūdere.*] —**pro•tru′sion** *n.*

pro•tu•ber•ance (prō-t/y/ōō′bər-əns) *n.* A bulge or swelling. [< LL *prōtūberāre,* to bulge out.] —**pro•tu′ber•ant** *adj.*

proud (proud) *adj.* **1.** Feeling pleasurable satisfaction. **2.** Occasioning pride; gratifying. **3.** Marked by exacting self-respect. **4.** Having excessive self-esteem; haughty; arrogant. **5.** Of great dignity; honored. **6.** Majestic; magnificent. **7.** Spirited. [< LL *prōde,* advantageous.] —**proud′ly** *adv.*

prov. 1. province; provincial. **2.** provisional. **3.** provost.

Prov. 1. Provençal. **2.** Proverbs (Old Testament).

prove (prōōv) *v.* **proved, proved** or **proven** (prōō′vən), **proving. 1.** To establish the truth or validity of by presentation of argument or evidence. **2.** To determine the quality of by testing; try out. **3.** To be shown to be; turn out. [< L *probāre,* to test, demonstrate as good.] —**prov′a•ble** *adj.* —**prov′er** *n.*

prov•e•nance (prŏv′ə-nəns, -näns′) *n.* Place of origin; derivation. [< L *prōvenīre,* to come forth.]

Pro•ven•çal (prō′vən-säl′, prŏv′ən-) *n.* **1.** A native or inhabitant of Provence, France. **2.** The Romance language of Provence, esp. the literary language of the troubadours. —**Pro′-**

ven•çal′ *adj.*

Pro•vence (prô-väNs′). A region of SE France.

prov•en•der (prŏv′ən-dər) *n.* **1.** Dry food for livestock. **2.** Food or provisions. [< LL *praebenda,* support, subsistence.]

pro•ve•nience (prə-vēn′yəns, -vē′nē-əns) *n.* Origin; source. [< L *prōvenire,* to come forth.]

prov•erb (prŏv′ûrb′) *n.* A short, popular saying expressing a well-known truth or fact. [< L *prōverbium,* "set of words put forth."] **—pro•ver′bi•al** (prə-vûr′bē-əl) *adj.*

pro•vide (prə-vīd′) *v.* **-vided, -viding. 1.** To furnish; supply. **2.** To make ready; prepare. **3.** To make available; afford. **4.** To set down as a stipulation. [< L *prōvidēre,* to foresee.] **—pro•vid′er** *n.*

prov•i•dence (prŏv′ə-dəns, -dĕns′) *n.* **1.** Foresight. **2.** Economy. **3.** Divine direction. **4. Providence.** God.

Prov•i•dence (prŏv′ə-dəns, -dĕns′). The capital of Rhode Island. Pop. 177,000.

prov•i•dent (prŏv′ə-dənt, -dĕnt′) *adj.* **1.** Providing for future needs. **2.** Frugal; economical. **—prov′i•dent•ly** *adv.*

prov•i•den•tial (prŏv′ə-dĕn′shəl) *adj.* **1.** Of or resulting from divine providence. **2.** Fortunate; opportune. **—prov′i•den′tial•ly** *adv.*

prov•ince (prŏv′ĭns) *n.* **1.** A territory governed as an administrative or political unit of a country or empire. **2.** A comprehensive area of interest; sphere. [< L *prōvincia.*]

pro•vin•cial (prə-vĭn′shəl) *adj.* **1.** Of or pertaining to a province. **2.** Limited in perspective; narrow. **—pro•vin′cial•ism′** *n.*

pro•vi•sion (prə-vĭzh′ən) *n.* **1.** The act of supplying or fitting out. **2.** That which is provided. **3.** A preparatory measure. **4. provisions.** A stock of necessary supplies, esp. food. **5.** A stipulation or qualification. *—v.* To supply with provisions. [< L *provisus,* pp of *prōvidēre,* to PROVIDE.]

pro•vi•sion•al (prə-vĭzh′ən-əl) *adj.* Provided for the time being, pending permanent arrangements. **—pro•vi′sion•al•ly** *adv.*

pro•vi•so (prə-vī′zō) *n., pl.* **-sos** or **-soes.** A qualifying clause or stipulation. [< L *prōvidēre,* to PROVIDE.]

prov•o•ca•tion (prŏv′ə-kā′shən) *n.* **1.** The act of provoking or inciting. **2.** A cause of irritation.

pro•voc•a•tive (prə-vŏk′ə-tĭv) *adj.* Exciting; stimulating. **—pro•voc′a•tive•ly** *adv.*

pro•voke (prə-vōk′) *v.* **-voked, -voking. 1.** To incite to anger or resentment. **2.** To incite to action; arouse. **3.** To bring on by inciting: *provoke a fight.* [< L *prōvocāre,* to call forth, challenge.] **—pro•vok′ing•ly** *adv.*

pro•vost (prō′vōst′, prŏv′əst, prō′vəst) *n.* A chief officer, as in some colleges. [< L *praepositus,* "(one) placed before (others)," president.]

prow (prou) *n.* The forward part of a ship's hull. [F *proue.*]

prow•ess (prou′ĭs) *n.* Superior skill, strength, or courage. [< OF *prod, prud,* gallant, proud.]

prowl (proul) *v.* To roam about furtively, as in search of prey. [ME *prollen.*] **—prowl** *n.* **—prowl′er** *n.*

prowl car. A **squad car.**

prox•im•i•ty (prŏk-sĭm′ə-tē) *n.* Nearness; closeness. [< L *proximus,* nearest.]

prox•y (prŏk′sē) *n., pl.* **-ies. 1.** A person authorized to act for another; agent. **2.** The written authorization for such action. [< L *prōcūrātiō,* a caring for.]

prude (prōōd) *n.* One who is overconcerned with being or seeming to be modest or proper. [< OF *preudefemme,* virtuous woman.] **—prud′ish** *adj.* **—prud′ish•ness** *n.*

pru•dence (prōōd′əns) *n.* **1.** The state, quality, or fact of being prudent; discretion. **2.** Careful management; economy. **—pru•den′tial** *adj.* **—pru•den′tial•ly** *adv.*

pru•dent (prōōd′ənt) *adj.* **1.** Wise in handling practical matters. **2.** Provident. **3.** Careful about one's conduct. [< L *prūdēns,* foreseeing, wise < *prōvidens,* provident.] **—pru′dent•ly** *adv.*

prud•er•y (prōō′də-rē) *n., pl.* **-ies. 1.** Excessive regard for propriety, modesty, or morality. **2.** An instance of prudish behavior. [< PRUDE.]

prune[1] (prōōn) *n.* A partially dried plum. [< L *prūnum,* plum.]

prune[2] (prōōn) *v.* **pruned, pruning. 1** To cut branches, stems, etc., from (a plant) to improve shape or growth. **2.** To remove as superfluous. **3.** To reduce; retrench. [< VL **prōrotundiāre,* to cut round in front.] **—prun′er** *n.*

pru•ri•ent (prōōr′ē-ənt) *adj.* Obsessively interested in matters of a sexual nature. [< L *prūrīre,* to itch, be lascivious.] **—pru′ri•ence** *n.*

Prus•sia (prŭsh′ə). A former German kingdom and state in N and C Germany. **—Prus′sian** *adj.* & *n.*

pry[1] (prī) *v.* **pried, prying.** To look closely, curiously, or inquisitively; snoop. [ME *prien.*] **—pry** *n.* **—pry′ing•ly** *adv.*

pry[2] (prī) *v.* **pried, prying. 1.** To raise, move, or force open with a lever. **2.** To obtain with difficulty. *—n., pl.* **pries. 1.** Something used to apply leverage, such as a crowbar. **2.** Leverage. [Var of PRIZE[3].]

pry•er. Variant of **prier.**

Ps. Psalm; Psalms (Old Testament).

p.s. postscript.

P.S. 1. postscript. **2.** public school.

Psa. Psalm; Psalms (Old Testament).

psalm (säm) *n.* **1.** A sacred song; hymn. **2.** Often **Psalm.** Any of the sacred songs or hymns collected in the Old Testament Book of Psalms. [< Gk *psalmos,* song sung to the harp, psalm.] **—psalm′ist** *n.*

pseud. pseudonym.

pseu•do (sōō′dō) *adj.* Counterfeit; fake.

pseudo–. *comb. form.* **1.** Lack of authenticity; sham. **2.** Deceptive similarity. [< Gk *pseudēs,* false.]

pseu•do•nym (sōō′də-nĭm′) *n.* A fictitious name assumed by an author; pen name.

psf, p.s.f. pounds per square foot.

pshaw (shô) *interj.* Expressive of impatience, irritation, or disbelief.

psi (psī, sī) *n.* The 23rd letter of the Greek alphabet, representing *ps.*

psi, p.s.i. pounds per square inch.

pso•ri•a•sis (sə-rī′ə-sĭs) *n.* A chronic, noncontagious skin disease characterized by inflammation and white, scaly patches. [< Gk *psōrian,* to have the itch.]

PST, P.S.T. Pacific Standard Time.

psych (sīk) *n. Informal.* Psychology.

psych. psychologist; psychology.

psy•che (sī′kē) *n.* **1.** The soul or spirit as distinguished from the body. **2.** The mind functioning as the center of thought, feeling, and behavior. [Gk *psukhē,* breath, life, soul.]

psych•e•del•ic (sī′kə-dĕl′ĭk) *adj.* Of or generating hallucinations, distortions of perception, and, occasionally, states resembling psychosis. [< PSYCHE + Gk *dēlos,* clear, visible.]

psy•chi•a•try (sĭ-kī′ə-trē, sī-) *n.* The medical study, diagnosis, treatment, and prevention of mental illness. [PSYCH(O)- + -IATRY.] **—psy′chi•at′ric** (sī′kē-ăt′rĭk) *adj.* **—psy•chi′a•trist** *n.*

psy•chic (sī′kĭk) *adj.* Also **psy•chi•cal** (-kĭ-kəl). **1.** Pertaining to the human mind or psyche. **2.** Pertaining to extraordinary, esp. extrasensory and nonphysical, mental processes, such as extrasensory perception and mental telepathy. *—n.* **1.** An individual apparently responsive to psychic forces. **2.** A medium. [< Gk *psukhē,* soul, life, PSYCHE.] **—psy′chi•cal•ly** *adv.*

psy•cho (sī′kō) *n., pl.* **-chos.** *Slang.* A psychopath.

psycho–. *comb. form.* The mind or mental processes. [< Gk *psukhē,* breath, life, PSYCHE.]

psy•cho•a•nal•y•sis (sī′kō-ə-năl′ə-sĭs) *n.* **1.** The analytic technique originated by Sigmund Freud to investigate mental processes. **2.** The theory of human psychology founded by Freud. **3.** Any psychiatric therapy incorporating such an analytic technique in such a theoretical framework. **—psy′cho•an′a•lyst** (-ăn′ə-lĭst) *n.* **—psy′cho•an′a•lyt′ic** (-ăn′ə-lĭt′ĭk), **psy′cho•an′a•lyt′i•cal** *adj.* **—psy′cho•an′a•lyt′i•cal•ly** *adv.* **—psy′cho•an′a•lyze** *v.* **(-lyzed, -lyzing).**

psychol. psychologist; psychology.

psy•cho•log•i•cal (sī′kə-lŏj′ĭ-kəl) *adj.* **1.** Pertaining to psychology. **2.** Of or involving the mind or emotions. **—psy′cho•log′i•cal•ly** *adv.*

psy•chol•o•gy (sī-kŏl′ə-jē) *n., pl.* **-gies. 1.** The science of mental processes and behavior. **2.** The emotional and behavioral characteristics of an individual, group, or activity: *the psychology of war.* **3.** Subtle tactical action or argument. **—psy•chol′o•gist** *n.*

psy•cho•path (sī′kə-păth′) *n.* A person with a personality disorder, esp. one manifested in aggressively antisocial behavior. **—psy′cho•path′ic** *adj.*

psy•cho•sis (sī-kō′sĭs) *n., pl.* **-ses** (-sēz′). Any severe mental disorder, with or without organic damage, characterized by deterioration of normal intellectual and social functioning and by partial or complete withdrawal from reality.

psy•cho•so•mat•ic (sī′kō-sō-măt′ĭk) *adj.* Both physiological and psychological.

psy•cho•ther•a•py (sī′kō-thĕr′ə-pē) *n.* The psychological treatment of mental, emotional, and nervous disorders. **—psy′cho•ther′a•pist** *n.*

psy•chot•ic (sī-kŏt′ĭk) *n.* One afflicted with a psychosis. *—adj.* Of or caused by psychosis. **—psy•chot′i•cal•ly** *adv.*

Pt platinum.

pt. 1. part. **2.** payment. **3.** pint. **4.** point. **5.** port.

p.t. pro tempore.

P.T. 1. Pacific Time. **2.** physical therapy. **3.** physical training.

PTA, P.T.A. Parent-Teachers Association.

ptar•mi•gan (tär′mĭ-gən) *n., pl.* **-gan** or **-gans.** A grouselike bird of northern regions. [Var of Scot Gael *tarmachan.*]

PT boat. A fast, lightly armed vessel used to torpedo enemy shipping. [< patrol torpedo boat.]

ptero–. *comb. form.* Feather, wing, or winglike part. [< Gk *pteron,* feather, wing.]

pter•o•dac•tyl (tĕr′ə-dăk′tĭl) *n.* An extinct flying reptile.

ptg. printing.

Ptol•e•my (tŏl′ə-mē). Greek astronomer of the 2nd century A.D. **—Ptol′e•ma′ic** (tŏl′ə-mā′ĭk) *adj.*

pto•maine (tō′mān′, tō-mān′) *n.* Also **pto•main.** Any of various basic nitrogenous materials, some poisonous, produced by the putrefaction and decomposition of protein. [Gk *ptōma,* "fall, fallen body," corpse.]

pty. proprietary.

Pu plutonium.

pub (pŭb) *n.* A tavern; bar. [Short for PUBLIC HOUSE.]

pub. 1. public. 2. publication. 3. published; publisher.

pu•ber•ty (pyo͞o'bər-tē) *n.* The stage of maturation in which the individual becomes physiologically capable of sexual reproduction. [< L *pūber,* adult.]

pu•bic (pyo͞o'bĭk) *adj.* Of or in the region of the lower part of the abdomen.

publ. 1. public. 2. publication. 3. published; publisher.

pub•lic (pŭb'lĭk) *adj.* 1. Of, concerning, or affecting the community or the people. 2. Maintained for, used by, or open to the people or community: *a public park.* 3. Serving or acting on behalf of the people or community: *public office.* 4. Open to general knowledge; widely known. —*n.* 1. The community or the people as a whole. 2. A group of people sharing a common interest. [< L *populus,* people.] —**pub'lic•ly** *adv.*

pub•li•can (pŭb'lĭ-kən) *n.* 1. *Chiefly Brit.* The keeper of a public house. 2. A tax collector in the ancient Roman Empire.

pub•li•ca•tion (pŭb'lĭ-kā'shən) *n.* 1. The act or process of publishing. 2. Published material. [< L *pūblicāre,* to make public.]

public domain. The status of being unprotected by patent or copyright.

public house. *Chiefly Brit.* A licensed tavern or bar.

pub•li•cist (pŭb'lə-sĭst) *n.* One who publicizes, esp. a press or publicity agent.

pub•lic•i•ty (pŭ-blĭs'ə-tē) *n.* 1. Information that attracts public notice. 2. Public interest or notice.

pub•li•cize (pŭb'lə-sīz') *v.* **-cized, -cizing.** To give publicity to.

public relations. The activities undertaken by an organization to promote a favorable relationship with the public.

public school. 1. In the U.S., a tax-supported school. 2. In Great Britain, a private secondary boarding school.

pub•lic-spir•i•ted (pŭb'lĭk-spĭr'ĭ-tĭd) *adj.* Motivated by devotion to public welfare.

pub•lish (pŭb'lĭsh) *v.* 1. To prepare and issue (printed material) for public distribution or sale. 2. To announce to the public. [< L *pūblicāre,* to make public.] —**pub'lish•a•ble** *adj.* —**pub'lish•er** *n.*

Puc•ci•ni (po͞ot-chē'nē), **Giacomo.** 1858–1924. Italian composer of operas.

puce (pyo͞os) *n.* Deep red to dark grayish purple. [F *(couleur) puce,* "flea (color)."] —**puce** *adj.*

puck (pŭk) *n.* A hard rubber disk used in ice hockey. [< POKE.]

Puck (pŭk) *n.* A mischievous sprite. [< OE *pūca.*] —**puck'ish** *adj.*

puck•a. Variant of **pukka.**

puck•er (pŭk'ər) *v.* To gather into wrinkles or folds. —*n.* A wrinkle or wrinkled part. [Perh < POCKET.]

pud•ding (po͝od'ĭng) *n.* A soft dessert usually containing flour or a cereal product. [< OF *boudin.*]

pud•dle (pŭd'l) *n.* A small pool of liquid, as of muddy water. [< OE *pudd,* ditch.]

pud•dling (pŭd'lĭng) *n.* The purification of impure metal, esp. pig iron, by agitation of a molten bath of the metal in an oxidizing atmosphere.

pudg•y (pŭj'ē) *adj.* **-ier, -iest.** Short and fat; chubby. [Prob < Scot *pud,* belly.]

pueb•lo (pwĕb'lō) *n., pl.* **-los.** 1. A flat-roofed community dwelling, up to five stories high, of Indian tribes of the SW U.S. 2. **Pueblo.** A member of a tribe, as the Hopi, inhabiting such dwellings. [Span, "people."]

pu•er•ile (pyo͞o'ər-ĭl, pyo͝or'ĭl, -īl', pwĕr'ĭl, -īl') *adj.* Immature; childish. [< L *puer,* child, boy.] —**pu'er•il'i•ty** *n.*

Puer•to Ri•co (pwĕr'tō rē'kō, pōr'-). An island in the Caribbean; a self-governing U.S. Commonwealth. Pop. 2,584,000. Cap. San Juan. —**Puerto Rican.**

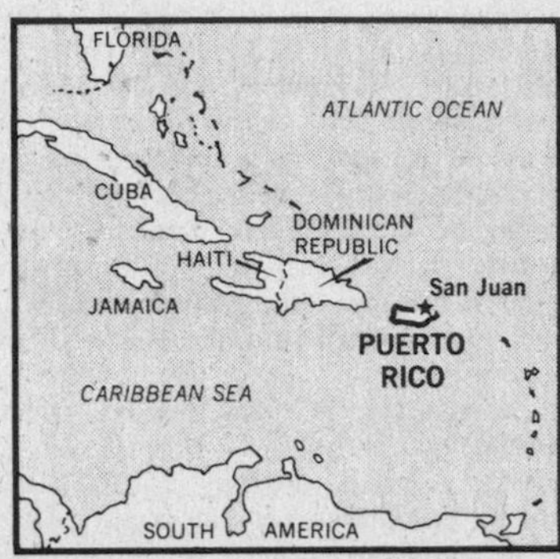

Puerto Rico

puff (pŭf) *n.* 1. a. A short, forceful discharge, as of smoke or air. b. A short, sibilant sound produced by a puff. 2. A swelling or rounded protuberance. 3. A light, inflated pastry. 4. A soft pad for applying cosmetic powder. 5. An approving or flattering recommendation. —*v.* 1. To blow in puffs. 2. To breathe forcefully and rapidly. 3. To emit clouds of smoke, vapor, etc. 4. To swell or seem to swell. 5. To fill with pride or conceit. 6. To praise exaggeratedly. [< OE *pyffan.*] —**puff'er** *n.* —**puff'i•ness** *n.* —**puff'y** *adj.*

puff•ball (pŭf'bôl') *n.* A ball-shaped fungus that releases dustlike spores when broken open.

puf•fin (pŭf'ĭn) *n.* A black and white northern sea bird with a flattened, brightly colored bill. [ME *poffoun.*]

pug (pŭg) *n.* 1. A small, short-haired dog with a square, flat muzzle. 2. A short, turned-up nose. [?]

pu•gi•lism (pyo͞o'jə-lĭz'əm) *n.* Boxing. [< L *pugil,* fighter.] —**pu'gi•list** *n.* —**pu'gi•lis'tic** *adj.*

pug•na•cious (pŭg-nā'shəs) *adj.* Eager to fight; aggressive by nature. [< L *pugnus,* fist.] —**pug•nac'i•ty** (pŭg-năs'ə-tē) *n.*

puis•sance (pwĭs'əns, pyo͞o'ə-səns, pyo͞o-ĭs'-əns) *n.* Power; might. [< L *posse,* to be powerful.] —**puis'sant** *adj.* —**puis'sant•ly** *adv.*

puke (pyo͞ok) *v.* **puked, puking.** To vomit.

puk•ka (pŭk'ə) *adj.* Also **puck•a.** 1. Genuine; authentic. 2. Superior; first-class. [Hindi *pakkā,* cooked, ripe, firm.]

pul•chri•tude (pŭl'krĭ-t/y/o͞od') *n.* Physical beauty. [< L *pulcher,* beautiful.]

pule (pyo͞ol) *v.* **puled, puling.** To whine; whimper. —**pul'er** *n.*

pull (po͝ol) *v.* 1. To apply force so as to draw something toward the force. 2. To move. 3. To extract. 4. To tug; jerk. 5. To rip or tear. 6. To stretch. 7. To strain. 8. *Informal.* To attract. 9. *Informal.* To perform, esp. with skill. 10. To draw (a knife or gun). 11. To produce (an impression) from type. —*n.* 1. The action or process of pulling. 2. Force exerted in pulling. 3. Something used for pulling. 4. *Slang.* Special influence. 5. *Informal.* Ability to attract; appeal. [< OE *pullian.*]

pul•let (po͝ol'ĭt) *n.* A young hen. [< L *pullus,* young of an animal, chicken.]

pul•ley (po͝ol'ē) *n., pl.* **-leys.** 1. A simple machine used esp. for lifting weight, consisting essentially of a wheel with a grooved rim in which a pulled rope or chain is run. 2. A wheel turned by or driving a belt. [Prob < Gk *polos,* pole, pivot.]

Pull•man (po͝ol'mən) *n.* Also **Pullman car.** A railroad parlor car or sleeping car. [< G.M. *Pullman* (1831–1897), American industrialist.]

pull•o•ver (po͝ol'ō'vər) *n.* A garment, as a sweater, put on by being drawn over the head.

pul•mo•nar•y (po͝ol'mə-nĕr'ē, pŭl'-) *adj.* Of or involving the lungs. [< L *pulmō,* lung.]

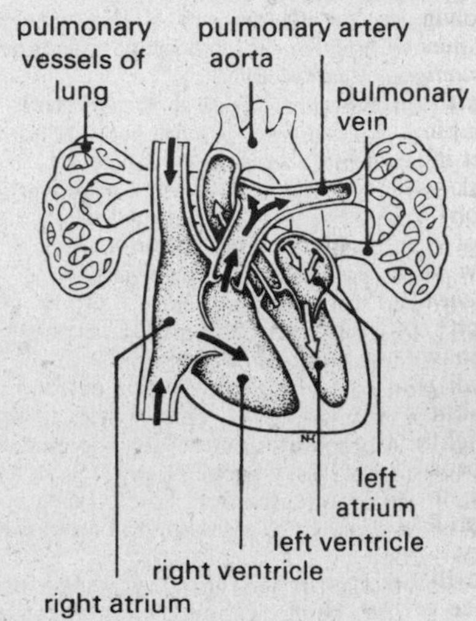

pulmonary
Pulmonary circulation

pulp (pŭlp) *n.* 1. A soft, moist mass. 2. The soft, moist part of fruit. 3. A moist mixture of ground wood, rags, etc., used to make paper. 4. The soft inner structure of a tooth, consisting of nerve and blood vessels. 5. A magazine with lurid subject matter, usually printed on rough paper. [L *pulpa,* solid flesh, pulp.] —**pulp'y** *adj.*

pul•pit (po͝ol'pĭt, pŭl'-) *n.* An elevated platform or lectern, as one used in conducting a religious service. [< L *pulpitum,* scaffold, platform.]

pul•sar (pŭl'sär') *n.* *Astron.* Any of several very short-period variable Galactic radio sources.

pul•sate (pŭl'sāt') *v.* **-sated, -sating.** To expand and contract rhythmically. —**pul•sa'tion** *n.*

pulse (pŭls) *n.* 1. The rhythmical throbbing of arteries produced by the regular contractions of the heart. 2. *Electronics.* A transient amplification or intensification of a characteristic of a system. —*v.* **pulsed, pulsing.** To pulsate. [< L *pulsus,* pp of *pellere,* to push, beat.]

pul•ver•ize (pŭl'və-rīz') *v.* **-ized, -izing.** To crush or grind to a powder or dust. [< L *pulvis (pulver-),* dust.]

pu•ma (pyo͞o'mə) *n.* The **mountain lion.** [< Quechua.]

pum•ice (pŭm'ĭs) *n.* A porous, lightweight volcanic rock used as an abrasive and polish.

[< L *pūmex.*]

pum•mel (pŭm′əl) *v.* **-meled** or **-melled, -meling** or **-melling.** To beat; pommel.

pump¹ (pŭmp) *n.* A machine or device for transferring a liquid or gas from a source or container through tubes or pipes to another container or receiver. —*v.* **1.** To propel, eject, or insert with or as with a pump. **2.** To question closely or persistently: *pump a witness.* **3.** To move up and down in the manner of a pump handle. [< MLG *pumpe* or MDu *pompe.*] —**pump′er** *n.*

pump² (pŭmp) *n.* A low-cut shoe without fastenings. [?]

pum•per•nick•el (pŭm′pər-nĭk′əl) *n.* A dark, coarse rye bread. [G.]

pump•kin (pŭmp′kĭn, pŭm′-, pŭng′-) *n.* **1.** A large, round fruit with a thick, orange rind. **2.** A vine bearing such fruit. [< Gk *pepōn,* a large melon.]

pun (pŭn) *n.* A humorous use of a word involving two interpretations of the meaning. —*v.* **punned, punning.** To make a pun. [Perh < It *puntiglio,* fine point, quibble.]

punch¹ (pŭnch) *n.* **1.** A tool for piercing or stamping. **2.** A tool for forcing a pin, bolt, or rivet in or out of a hole. —*v.* To perforate or mark with a punch. [Short for PUNCHEON.]

punch² (pŭnch) *v.* **1.** To hit with a sharp blow, as of the fist. **2.** To herd (cattle). —*n.* **1.** A blow with the fist. **2.** Vigor or drive. [ME *punchen.*]

punch³ (pŭnch) *n.* A beverage of fruit juices, often with a wine or liquor base. [Perh < Hindi *pānch.*]

pun•cheon (pŭn′chən) *n.* **1.** A short, wooden upright used in structural framing. **2.** A piece of broad, roughly dressed timber. [< L *pungere,* to prick.]

punch line. The climax of a joke or humorous story.

punc•til•i•o (pŭngk-tĭl′ē-ō′) *n.* Precise observance of formalities. [It *punctiglio,* PUN.]

punc•til•i•ous (pŭngk-tĭl′ē-əs) *adj.* **1.** Attentive to details of formal conduct. **2.** Precise; scrupulous. —**punc•til′i•ous•ly** *adv.*

punc•tu•al (pŭngk′cho͞o-əl) *adj.* Acting or arriving at the time appointed; prompt. [ML *punctuālis,* "to the point."] —**punc•tu•al′i•ty** *n.* —**punc′tu•al•ly** *adv.*

punc•tu•ate (pŭngk′cho͞o-āt′) *v.* **-ated, -ating.** **1.** To provide (a text) with punctuation. **2.** To interrupt periodically. **3.** To emphasize. [< L *punctum,* pricked mark, point.]

punc•tu•a•tion (pŭngk′cho͞o-ā′shən) *n.* **1.** The use of standard marks in writing and printing to separate units and clarify meaning. **2.** The marks so used.

punc•ture (pŭngk′chər) *v.* **-tured, -turing.** **1.** To pierce with or as with a sharp or pointed object. **2.** To deflate by or as by piercing. —*n.* **1.** An act or instance of puncturing. **2.** A hole made by a sharp or pointed object. [L *punctūra,* a pricking, puncture.]

pun•dit (pŭn′dĭt) *n.* A learned person. [< Sk *paṇḍita.*]

pun•gent (pŭn′jənt) *adj.* **1.** Sharp and acrid to taste or smell. **2.** Penetrating; biting; caustic. [< L *pungere,* to prick, sting.] —**pun′gen•cy** *n.* —**pun′gent•ly** *adv.*

Pu•nic (pyo͞o′nĭk) *adj.* Of or pertaining to ancient Carthage. [< L *Poenus,* a Carthaginian.]

pun•ish (pŭn′ĭsh) *v.* **1.** To subject to penalty for a crime or offense. **2.** To inflict a penalty for (an offense). **3.** To injure; hurt. [< L *pūnīre, poenīre.*] —**pun′ish•a•ble** *adj.*

pun•ish•ment (pŭn′ĭsh-mənt) *n.* **1. a.** An act of punishing. **b.** The condition of being punished. **2.** A penalty imposed for wrongdoing. **3.** Rough handling.

pu•ni•tive (pyo͞o′nə-tĭv) *adj.* Inflicting or aiming to inflict punishment. —**pu′ni•tive•ly** *adv.*

punk¹ (pŭngk) *n.* Dry, decayed wood or fungi, used as tinder. [?]

punk² (pŭngk) *n. Slang.* **1.** An inexperienced youth. **2.** A young ruffian. —*adj.* Of poor quality. [Earlier *punck.*]

punt¹ (pŭnt) *n.* An open, flat-bottomed boat propelled by a pole. —*v.* To propel (a boat) with a pole. [< L *pontō,* floating bridge, pontoon.] —**punt′er** *n.*

punt² (pŭnt) *n.* A kick in which a football is dropped and kicked before touching the ground. —*v.* To kick by means of a punt. [Prob dial *bunt, punt,* to push, kick.]

pu•ny (pyo͞o′nē) *adj.* **-nier, -niest.** Of inferior size, strength, or significance; weak. [OF *puisne,* "born afterward."] —**pu′ni•ly** *adv.* —**pu′ni•ness** *n.*

pup (pŭp) *n.* **1.** A young dog; puppy. **2.** A young seal or similar animal. [Back-formation < PUPPY.]

pu•pa (pyo͞o′pə) *n., pl.* **-pae** (-pē′) or **-pas.** An inactive stage in the life cycle of an insect, between the larval and adult forms. [< L *pūpa,* girl, doll.] —**pu′pal** *adj.*

pu•pil¹ (pyo͞o′pəl) *n.* A student supervised by a teacher. [< L *pūpus,* boy.]

pu•pil² (pyo͞o′pəl) *n.* The apparently black circular aperture in the center of the iris of the eye. [< L *pūpilla,* "little orphan girl," pupil.]

pup•pet (pŭp′ĭt) *n.* **1.** A small figure of a person or animal, moved by strings or by the hand. **2.** One whose behavior is controlled by others. [< L *pūpa,* girl, doll.]

pup•py (pŭp′ē) *n., pl.* **-pies.** A young dog. [< L *pūpa,* doll.]

pur•blind (pûr′blīnd′) *adj.* **1.** Nearly or partly blind. **2.** Slow in understanding or discerning. [ME *pureblind,* orig "totally blind" : PURE + BLIND.] —**pur′blind′ness** *n.*

pur•chase (pûr′chĭs) *v.* **-chased, -chasing.** To obtain in exchange for money or its equivalent; buy. —*n.* **1.** That which is bought. **2.** The act or an instance of buying. **3.** A secure hold. [< OF *purchacier,* to pursue, seek to obtain.] —**pur′chas•er** *n.*

pure (pyo͝or) *adj.* **purer, purest.** **1.** Having a uniform composition; not mixed. **2.** Free from adulterants or impurities. **3.** Free from contaminants; clean. **4.** Complete; utter. **5.** Without faults; perfect; sinless. **6.** Chaste; virgin. **7.** Theoretical rather than applied: *pure science.* [< L *pūrus,* clean.] —**pure′ly** *adv.*

pure•bred (pyo͝or′brĕd′) *adj.* Of a strain established through constant breeding of unmixed stock.

pu•rée (pyo͝o-rā′, pyo͝or′ā) *v.* **-réed, -réeing.** To rub (food) through a strainer. —*n.* Food so prepared. [< OF *purer,* to purify, strain.]

pur•ga•tion (pûr-gā′shən) *n.* The act of purging or purifying.

pur•ga•tive (pûr′gə-tĭv) *adj.* Tending to cleanse or purge, esp. tending to cause evacuation of the bowels. —*n.* A purgative agent or medicine.

pur•ga•to•ry (pûr′gə-tôr′ē, -tōr′ē) *n., pl.* **-ries.** **1.** *R.C.Ch.* A state in which the souls of those who have died in grace must expiate their sins. **2.** Any place of expiation or remorse. [< L *purgāre,* to PURGE.] —**pur′ga•to′ri•al** (-tôr′ē-əl, -tōr′ē-əl) *adj.*

purge (pûrj) *v.* **purged, purging.** **1.** To purify. **2.** To rid of sin or guilt. **3.** To rid (a nation, political party, etc.) of persons considered undesirable. **4.** To cause evacuation of the bowels. —*n.* **1.** The act or process of purging. **2.** That which purges. [< L *purgāre,* to cleanse.] —**purg′er** *n.*

pu•ri•fy (pyo͝or′ə-fī′) *v.* **-fied, -fying.** To make or become clean or pure. —**pu′ri•fi•ca′tion** *n.* —**pu•rif′i•ca•to′ry** (pyo͝o-rĭf′ĭ-kə-tôr′ē, -tōr′ē) *adj.* —**pu′ri•fi′er** *n.*

pur•ism (pyo͝or′ĭz′əm) *n.* Strict observance of traditional correctness, esp. of language. —**pur′ist** *n.*

pu•ri•tan (pyo͝or′ə-tən) *n.* **1. Puritan.** A member of the 16th- and 17th-century English Protestant group advocating simplification of the ceremonies of the Church of England. **2.** One who advocates strict religious and moral discipline. [< LL *pūritās,* purity.] —**pu′ri•tan′i•cal** *adj.* —**pu′ri•tan′i•cal•ly** *adv.*

pu•ri•ty (pyo͝or′ə-tē) *n.* The quality or condition of being pure.

purl¹ (pûrl) *v.* To flow or ripple with a murmuring sound. —*n.* The sound made by rippling water. [Norw *purla.*]

purl² (pûrl) *v.* To knit with an inverted stitch. —*n.* An inverted knitting stitch. [Earlier *pyrle.*]

pur•lieu (pûrl′yo͞o, pûr′lo͞o) *n.* **1.** Any outlying area. **2. purlieus.** Outskirts; environs. [< NF *puralée,* perambulation.]

pur•loin (pər-loin′, pûr′loin′) *v.* To steal; filch. [< NF *purloigner,* "to put far away."]

pur•ple (pûr′pəl) *n.* **1.** A bluish red color. **2.** Cloth of this color, worn as a symbol of royalty or high office. —*adj.* **1.** Of the color purple. **2.** Elaborate: *purple prose.* [< Gk *porphura,* shellfish yielding a purple dye, purple dye.] —**pur′plish** *adj.*

pur•port (pər-pôrt′, -pōrt′, pûr′pôrt′, -pōrt′) *v.* **1.** To claim or profess as the meaning. **2.** To have or give the impression, often falsely, of being. —*n.* (pûr′pôrt′, -pōrt′). An apparent meaning or significance. [< ML *prōportāre,* to carry forth.] —**pur•port′ed•ly** (pər-pôr′tĭd-lē, pər-pōr′-) *adv.*

pur•pose (pûr′pəs) *n.* **1.** A result or effect that is intended or desired; intention. **2.** Determination; resolution. —**on purpose.** Intentionally. —*v.* **-posed, -posing.** To resolve to perform or accomplish. [< L *prōpōnere* (pp *prōpositus*), to PROPOSE.] —**pur′pose•ful** *adj.* —**pur′pose•ly** *adv.*

purr (pûr) *n.* **1.** The low, vibrant sound made by a cat to express contentment. **2.** A similar sound. —**purr** *v.*

purse (pûrs) *n.* **1.** A small bag or pouch for carrying money. **2.** A woman's handbag. **3.** Available wealth or resources. **4.** A sum of money offered as a present or prize. —*v.* **pursed, pursing.** To pucker. [< Gk *bursa,* leather, hide.]

purs•er (pûr′sər) *n.* The officer in charge of money matters on board a ship. [< PURSE.]

pur•su•ance (pər-so͞o′əns) *n.* A carrying out or putting into effect.

pur•su•ant (pər-so͞o′ənt) *adj.* —**pursuant to.** In accordance with.

pur•sue (pər-so͞o′) *v.* **-sued, -suing.** **1.** To follow in an effort to overtake; chase. **2.** To strive to accomplish. **3.** To follow. **4.** To engage in (a vocation, hobby, etc.). [< L *prōsequī.*] —**pur•su′a•ble** *adj.* —**pur•su′er** *n.*

pur•suit (pər-so͞ot′) *n.* **1.** The act or an instance of pursuing. **2.** Any vocation, hobby, etc.

pu•ru•lence (pyo͝or′ə-ləns, pyo͝or′yə-) *n.* **1.** The condition of secreting or containing pus.

2. Pus.

pu•ru•lent (pyŏŏr'ə-lənt, pyŏŏr'yə-) *adj.* Containing or secreting pus. [L *pūrulentus.*] —**pu'ru•lent•ly** *adv.*

pur•vey (pər-vā', pûr'vā') *v.* To supply (food, information, etc.); furnish. [< L *prōvidēre,* to foresee, PROVIDE.] —**pur•vey'or** *n.*

pur•vey•ance (pər-vā'əns) *n.* Procurement of supplies.

pur•view (pûr'vyōō) *n.* **1.** The range of function, power, or competence. **2.** Range of vision or comprehension. [< OF *porveeir,* to provide.]

pus (pŭs) *n.* A viscous, yellowish-white fluid formed in infected tissue, consisting chiefly of leukocytes, cellular debris, and liquefied tissue elements. [L *pūs.*]

Pu•san (pōō'sän'). A port of SE South Korea. Pop. 1,391,000.

push (pŏŏsh) *v.* **1.** To exert force against (an object) to move it. **2.** To thrust; shove. **3.** To press or urge forward. **4.** *Slang.* To promote or sell (a product). —*n.* **1.** The act of pushing; a thrust. **2.** A vigorous effort; drive. **3.** A provocation to action. [< L *pellere* (pp *pulsus*), to push, beat.] —**push'er** *n.*

push•cart (pŏŏsh'kärt') *n.* A light cart pushed by hand.

Push•kin (pŏŏsh'kĭn), **Aleksandr Sergeyevich.** 1799–1837. Russian poet.

push•o•ver (pŏŏsh'ō'vər) *n.* **1.** Anything easily accomplished. **2.** A person or group easily defeated or taken advantage of.

Push•tu (pŭsh'tōō) *n.* Pashto.

push•y (pŏŏsh'ē) *adj.* **-ier, -iest.** *Informal.* Disagreeably forward or aggressive. —**push'i•ly** *adv.* —**push'i•ness** *n.*

pu•sil•lan•i•mous (pyōō'sə-lăn'ə-məs) *adj.* Cowardly; faint-hearted. [< L *pūsillus,* weak + *animus,* mind.] —**pu'sil•la•nim'i•ty** (-lə-nĭm'ə-tē) *n.* —**pu'sil•lan'i•mous•ly** *adv.*

puss[1] (pŏŏs) *n. Informal.* A cat.

puss[2] (pŏŏs) *n. Slang.* The face. [Ir *bus,* lip, mouth.]

puss•y[1] (pŏŏs'ē) *n., pl.* **-ies.** *Informal.* A cat.

pus•sy[2] (pŭs'ē) *adj.* **-sier, -siest.** Resembling or containing pus.

puss•y•foot (pŏŏs'ē-fŏŏt') *v.* **1.** To move stealthily or cautiously. **2.** *Slang.* To avoid committing oneself.

pussy willow. A shrub with silky catkins.

pus•tule (pŭs'chōōl, pŭs'tyōōl) *n.* A slight, inflamed elevation of the skin filled with pus. [< L *pustula,* a blister.]

put (pŏŏt) *v.* **put, putting. 1.** To place in a specified location; set. **2.** To cause to be in a specified condition. **3.** To subject. **4.** To assign; attribute. **5.** To estimate. **6.** To impose or levy. **7.** To hurl with an overhand pushing motion: *put the shot.* **8.** To bring up for consideration. **9.** To express; state. **10.** To adapt. **11.** To apply. **12.** To proceed. —**put across.** To state so as to be understood or accepted. —**put down. 1.** To record. **2.** To repress. **3.** *Slang.* To reject. —**put forth.** To grow: *The plant put forth leaves.* —**put off. 1.** To postpone. **2.** To discard. —**put on. 1.** To clothe oneself with. **2.** To apply. **3.** To pretend. —**put out. 1.** To extinguish. **2.** *Baseball.* To retire (a runner). **3.** To inconvenience. —**put up. 1.** To erect. **2.** To preserve. **3.** To provide (funds). **4.** To provide lodgings for. **5.** To incite to some action. —**put upon.** To impose on. —**put up with.** To endure. [< OE *pūtian,* to push, thrust.]

pu•ta•tive (pyōō'tə-tĭv) *adj.* Generally regarded as such; reputed. [< L *putāre,* to compute, consider.] —**pu'ta•tive•ly** *adv.*

pu•tre•fy (pyōō'trə-fī') *v.* **-fied, -fying. 1.** To decompose; decay. **2.** To become gangrenous. [< L *putrefacere.*] —**pu'tre•fac'tion** *n.* —**pu'tre•fac'tive** *adj.*

pu•trid (pyōō'trĭd) *adj.* **1.** Decayed; rotten. **2.** Proceeding from, pertaining to, or displaying putrefaction. **3.** Corrupt. **4.** Vile. [L *putridus.*] —**pu•trid'i•ty, pu'trid•ness** *n.*

putsch (pŏŏch) *n.* A suddenly effected attempt by a group to overthrow a government. [G.]

putt (pŭt) *n.* A golf stroke made in an effort to place the ball into the hole. [Var of PUT.] —**putt** *v.* **(putted, putting).**

put•tee (pŭ-tē', pŭt'ē) *n.* **1.** A strip of cloth wound around the lower leg. **2.** A gaiter covering the lower leg. [Hindi *paṭṭī.*]

put•ter[1] (pŭt'ər) *n. Golf.* **1.** A short, stiff-shafted club used for putting. **2.** A golfer who is putting.

put•ter[2] (pŭt'ər) *v.* Also *chiefly Brit.* **pot•ter** (pŏt'ər). To move about or act aimlessly. [< OE *potian,* to push, kick.]

putting green. *Golf.* The area at the end of a fairway in which the hole is placed.

put•ty (pŭt'ē) *n., pl.* **-ties. 1.** A doughlike cement made by mixing whiting and linseed oil, used to fill holes in woodwork and secure panes of glass. **2.** A fine lime cement used as a finishing on plaster. [< OF *potee,* contents of a pot, a potful.]

puz•zle (pŭz'əl) *v.* **-zled, -zling. 1.** To bewilder; perplex. **2.** To clarify or solve by reasoning or study (with *out*). **3.** To ponder over a problem. —*n.* **1.** Something that puzzles. **2.** A toy, game, or device that tests ingenuity. **3.** Perplexity; bewilderment. [?] —**puz'zler** *n.* —**puz'zle•ment** *n.*

pvt., Pvt. private.

pwt. pennyweight.

PX post exchange; Post Exchange.

Pyg•ma•lion (pĭg-māl'yən, -mā'lē-ən). *Gk.Myth.* A sculptor who fell in love with his statue of a woman.

pyg•my (pĭg'mē) *n., pl.* **-mies.** Also **pig•my. 1.** One of unusually small size or significance. **2. Pygmy.** A member of any of several African and Asian peoples with a hereditary stature of from four to five feet. —*adj.* **1.** Unusually or atypically small. **2. Pygmy.** Of or pertaining to the Pygmies. [< Gk *pugmē,* fist, the length from the elbow to the knuckles.]

py•lon (pī'lŏn') *n.* **1.** A monumental gateway in the form of a pair of truncated pyramids, as the entrance to an Egyptian temple. **2.** A tower marking a turning point in an air race. **3.** A steel tower supporting high-tension wires. [< Gk *pulē,* a gate.]

py•lo•rus (pī-lôr'əs, -lōr'əs, pĭ-) *n.* The passage connecting the stomach and duodenum. [< Gk *pulōros,* "a gatekeeper."]

pyo–. *comb. form.* Pus. [< Gk *puon,* pus.]

Pyong•yang (pyŭng'yăng'). The capital of North Korea. Pop. 940,000.

py•or•rhe•a, py•or•rhoe•a (pī'ə-rē'ə) *n.* **1.** A discharge of pus. **2.** Inflammation of the gum and tooth sockets leading to loosening of the teeth. [< PYO- + -RRHEA.]

pyr•a•mid (pĭr'ə-mĭd) *n.* **1.** A polyhedron with a polygonal base and triangular faces meeting in a common vertex. **2.** A pyramidal monument. —*v.* **1.** To place or build in the shape of a pyramid. **2.** To increase rapidly and on a widening base. [< Gk *puramis.*] —**py•ram'i•dal** (pĭ-răm'ə-dəl) *adj.*

pyre (pīr) *n.* A combustible heap, esp. for burning a corpse. [< Gk *pur,* fire.]

Pyr•e•nees (pĭr'ə-nēz'). A mountain range between France and Spain.

py•rite (pī'rīt') *n.* A yellow to brown, widely occurring mineral, FeS_2, used as a source of iron and sulfur. [L *pyrītes,* pyrites.]

py•ri•tes (pī-rī'tēz, pə-) *n., pl.* **-tes.** Any of various natural metallic sulfides, esp. of iron. [< Gk *puritēs (lithos),* "fire (stone)."]

pyro–. *comb. form.* Fire. [< Gk *pur,* fire.]

py•ro•ma•ni•a (pī'rō-mā'nē-ə, -măn'yə) *n.* The uncontrollable impulse to start fires. —**py'ro•ma'ni•ac'** (-mā'nē-ăk') *adj.* & *n.*

py•ro•tech•nics (pī'rə-tĕk'nĭks, pĭr'ə-) *n.* **1.** A display of fireworks. **2.** A brilliant display, as of rhetoric or wit.

Py•thag•o•ras (pĭ-thăg'ər-əs). Greek philosopher of the 6th century B.C. —**Py•thag'o•re'an** (-ə-rē'ən) *adj.*

Pythagorean theorem. The theorem that the sum of the squares of the lengths of the sides of a right triangle is equal to the square of the length of the hypotenuse.

py•thon (pī'thŏn', -thən) *n.* A large, nonvenomous Old World snake that coils around and crushes its prey. [< *Python,* Greek mythological serpent or dragon.]

pyx (pĭks) *n.* Also **pix.** A container in which the Eucharist is carried to the sick.

Qq

q, Q (kyo͞o) *n.* The 17th letter of the English alphabet.
q. **1.** quart. **2.** question.
qb quarterback.
Q.E.D. which was to be demonstrated or proved (L *quod erat demonstrandum*).
QM quartermaster.
qoph (kôf) *n.* The 19th letter of the Hebrew alphabet, representing *q*.
qq.v. which (things) see (NL *quae vide*).
qr. quarter.
qt quart.
q.t. *Slang.* Quiet; in secret.
qto. quarto.
qty. quantity.
qua (kwā, kwä) *adv.* In the function or character of. [L *quā*, abl of *quī*, who.]
quack[1] (kwăk) *n.* The hoarse sound uttered by a duck. —**quack** *v.*
quack[2] (kwăk) *n.* **1.** One who pretends to have medical knowledge. **2.** A charlatan. [Short for QUACKSALVER.] —**quack** *adj.* —**quack′er•y** *n.*
quack•sal•ver (kwăk′săl′vər) *n. Archaic.* A charlatan; quack. [< MDu *quacsalven*, to cure with home remedies.]
quad[1] (kwŏd) *n. Informal.* A quadrangle.
quad[2] (kwŏd) *n.* Shortened form of **quadruplet.**
quad•ran•gle (kwŏd′răng′gəl) *n.* **1.** A plane figure consisting of four points, no three of which are collinear, connected by straight lines. **2.** A rectangular area bordered by buildings. [< L *quadriangulus*, having four angles.]
quad•rant (kwŏd′rənt) *n.* **1. a.** A circular arc subtending a central angle of 90°. **b.** The plane area bounded by two perpendicular radii and the arc they subtend. **2.** An early instrument for measuring altitudes, consisting of a 90° graduated arc with a movable radius for measuring angles. [< L *quadrāns*, fourth part, quarter.]
quad•ra•phon•ic (kwŏd′rə-fŏn′ĭk) *adj.* Of or for an extension of stereophonic sound reproduction in which two additional channels are used at the rear of the listening space, reproducing signals that are independent of or derived from the front channels. [Prob < QUADR(I)- + PHONIC.]
quad•rat•ic (kwŏ-drăt′ĭk) *adj.* Of or containing mathematical quantities of the second degree and no higher. —**quad•rat′ic** *n.*
quad•ren•ni•al (kwŏ-drĕn′ē-əl) *adj.* **1.** Happening once in four years. **2.** Lasting for four years.
quad•ren•ni•um (kwŏ-drĕn′ē-əm) *n., pl.* **-ums** or **quadrennia** (-drĕn′ē-ə). A period of four years. [L *quadriennium.*]
quadri–. *comb. form.* Four. [L.]
quad•ri•cen•ten•ni•al (kwŏd′rĭ-sĕn-tĕn′ē-əl) *n.* A 400th anniversary. —**quad′ri•cen•ten′ni•al** *adj.*
quad•ri•lat•er•al (kwŏd′rə-lăt′ər-əl) *n.* A four-sided polygon. —*adj.* Having four sides.
qua•drille (kwŏ-drĭl′, kwə-, kə-) *n.* A square dance composed of five figures and performed by four couples. [F, orig "one of the four divisions of an army."]
quad•ril•lion (kwŏ-drĭl′yən) *n.* **1.** The cardinal number represented by 1 followed by 15 zeros. **2.** In British usage, the cardinal number represented by 1 followed by 24 zeros. [< QUADR(I)- + (M)ILLION.] —**quad•ril′lion** *adj.*
quad•ril•lionth (kwŏ-drĭl′yənth) *n.* The ordinal number quadrillion in a series. —**quad•ril′lionth** *adj. & adv.*
quad•ri•par•tite (kwŏd′rə-pär′tīt′) *adj.* **1.** Consisting of four parts. **2.** Involving four participants.
quadru–. *comb. form.* Four. [L.]
quad•ru•ped (kwŏd′ro͞o-pĕd′) *n.* A four-footed animal.
quad•ru•ple (kwŏ-dro͞o′pəl, -drŭp′əl, kwŏd′-ro͞o-pəl) *adj.* **1.** Having four parts. **2.** Multiplied by four. —*n.* A number or amount four times as many or as much as another. —*v.* **-pled, -pling.** To multiply or increase by four. [< L *quadruplus.*]
quad•ru•plet (kwŏ-drŭp′lĭt, -dro͞o′plĭt, kwŏd′-ro͞o-plĭt) *n.* **1.** A group or combination of four. **2.** One of four offspring born in a single birth.
quad•ru•pli•cate (kwŏ-dro͞o′plĭ-kĭt) *adj.* **1.** Multiplied by four; quadruple. **2.** Fourth in a group or set. —*n.* One of a set or group of four. —*v.* (kwŏ-dro͞o′plĭ-kāt′) **-cated, -cating.** To multiply four times. —**quad•ru′pli•ca′tion** *n.*
quaff (kwŏf, kwăf, kwôf) *v.* To drink heartily. [Perh imit.] —**quaff** *n.* —**quaff′er** *n.*
quag•mire (kwăg′mīr′, kwŏg′-) *n.* A bog having a surface that yields when stepped on.
qua•hog (kwô′hôg′, -hŏg′, kwō′-, kō′-) *n.* A hard-shelled, edible clam of the North American Atlantic coast. [< Algon.]
quail[1] (kwāl) *n., pl.* **quail** or **quails.** Any of various small, short-tailed chickenlike birds. [< ML *quaccula.*]
quail[2] (kwāl) *v.* To lose courage; cower. [Perh < L *coāgulāre*, to curdle, COAGULATE.]
quaint (kwānt) *adj.* **1.** Agreeably curious and old-fashioned. **2.** Unfamiliar or unusual; strange. [< OF *cointe*, expert, elegant.] —**quaint′ly** *adv.* —**quaint′ness** *n.*
quake (kwāk) *v.* **quaked, quaking. 1.** To shake or tremble. **2.** To shiver, as with cold or emotion. —*n.* **1.** An instance of quaking. **2.** An earthquake. [< OE *cwacian* < Gmc **kwei-*, to shake.] —**quak′y** *adj.*
Quak•er (kwā′kər) *n.* A member of the Society of Friends.
qual•i•fi•ca•tion (kwŏl′ə-fĭ-kā′shən) *n.* **1.** The act of qualifying or condition of being qualified. **2.** A quality or ability that suits a person to a specific position or task.
qual•i•fy (kwŏl′ə-fī′) *v.* **-fied, -fying. 1.** To describe; characterize. **2.** To make competent or suitable for an office, position, etc. **3.** To give legal power to. **4.** To limit or restrict. **5.** To make less harsh. **6.** To modify the meaning of (a word or phrase). [< ML *quālificāre*, to attribute a quality to.]
qual•i•ta•tive (kwŏl′ə-tā′tĭv) *adj.* Of or pertaining to quality or qualities. —**qual′i•ta′tive•ly** *adv.*
qual•i•ty (kwŏl′ə-tē) *n., pl.* **-ties. 1.** A characteristic or attribute; a property. **2.** The natural or essential character of something. **3.** Degree of excellence. **4.** High social position. [< L *quālis*, of what kind.]
qualm (kwäm, kwôm) *n.* **1.** A sudden feeling of sickness, nausea, etc. **2.** Doubt or misgiving; uneasiness. **3.** A pang of conscience. [?]
quan•da•ry (kwŏn′drē, -də-rē) *n., pl.* **-ries.** A state of uncertainty or perplexity. [?]
quan•ti•ta•tive (kwŏn′tə-tā′tĭv) *adj.* Of or pertaining to number or quantity. —**quan′ti•ta′tive•ly** *adv.*
quan•ti•ty (kwŏn′tə-tē) *n., pl.* **-ties. 1.** A number or amount of anything, either specified or indefinite. **2.** A sufficient or considerable amount or number: *sell books in quantity.* [< L *quantus*, how great.]
quan•tum (kwŏn′təm) *n., pl.* **-ta** (-tə). **1.** Quantity or amount. **2.** An indivisible unit of energy. [< L *quantus*, how great.]
quar•an•tine (kwôr′ən-tēn′, kwŏr′-) *n.* **1. a.** A period of time during which one suspected of carrying a contagious disease is detained. **b.** A place for such detention. **2.** Enforced isolation or restriction of free movement imposed to prevent the spread of a contagious disease. —*v.* **-tined, -tining.** To place in quarantine. [It *quarantina (giorni)*, forty days.]
quark (kwôrk) *n.* Any of three hypothetical subatomic particles with fractional electric charges, proposed as the fundamental units of matter.
quar•rel (kwôr′əl, kwŏr′-) *n.* **1.** An angry dispute or argument. **2.** A cause for a dispute. —*v.* **-reled** or **-relled, -reling** or **-relling. 1.** To engage in a quarrel. **2.** To find fault. [< L *querī*, to complain.] —**quar′rel•some** *adj.*
quar•ry[1] (kwôr′ē, kwŏr′ē) *n., pl.* **-ries. 1.** A hunted animal. **2.** Any object of pursuit. [ME *querre*, entrails of a beast given to the hounds.]
quar•ry[2] (kwôr′ē, kwŏr′ē) *n., pl.* **-ries.** An open excavation from which stone is obtained. —*v.* **-ried, -rying.** To obtain (stone) from a quarry. [< OF *quarre*, "square stone."]
quart (kwôrt) *n.* **1.** A U.S. Customary System unit of volume or capacity, used in liquid measure, equal to two pints or 57.75 cubic inches. **2.** A corresponding U.S. Customary System unit, used in dry measure, equal to two pints or 67.2 cubic inches. **3.** A corresponding British Imperial System unit, used in liquid and dry measure, equal to 1.201 U.S. liquid quarts, 1.032 U.S. dry quarts, or 69.354 cubic inches. [< L *quārtus*, fourth (part of a gallon).]
quar•ter (kwôr′tər) *n.* **1.** One of four equal parts of something. **2.** A coin equal to one-fourth of the dollar of the U.S. and Canada. **3.** Mercy; clemency. **4.** Either side of a horse's hoof. **5. quarters.** A place of residence; lodgings. **6.** A district of a city. —*v.* **1.** To divide into four equal or equivalent parts. **2.** To dismember (a human body). **3.** To furnish with lodgings. —*adj.* **1.** Being one of four equal or equivalent parts. **2.** Being one-fourth of a standard or usual value. [< L *quārtus*, fourth.]
quar•ter•back (kwôr′tər-băk′) *n.* The backfield football player who usually calls the signals.

ô paw, for/oi boy/ou out/o͝o took/o͞o coo/p pop/r run/s sauce/sh shy/t to/th thin/*th* the/
ŭ cut/ûr fur/v van/w wag/y yes/z size/zh vision/ə ago, item, edible, gallop, circus/

quar•ter-deck (kwôr'tər-dĕk') *n.* The after part of a ship's upper deck.

quar•ter•ly (kwôr'tər-lē) *adj.* **1.** Made up of four parts. **2.** Being one of four parts. **3.** Occurring at regular intervals of three months. *—n., pl.* **-lies.** A quarterly publication. *—adv.* In or by quarters.

quar•ter•mas•ter (kwôr'tər-măs'tər, -mäs'tər) *n.* **1.** A military officer responsible for the food, clothing, and equipment of troops. **2.** A naval petty officer responsible for the navigation of a ship. [< QUARTER (residence).]

quarter note. *Mus.* A note having one-fourth the time value of a whole note.

quar•ter•staff (kwôr'tər-stăf', -stäf') *n.* A long wooden staff formerly used as a weapon.

quar•tet (kwôr-tĕt') *n.* Also **quar•tette.** **1. a.** A musical composition for four instruments. **b.** A group of four performing musicians. **2.** Any set of four persons or things. [L *quārtus,* fourth.]

quar•to (kwôr'tō) *n., pl.* **-tos.** **1.** The page size obtained by folding a whole sheet into four leaves. **2.** A book composed of such pages. [L *(in) quārto,* in quarter.]

quartz (kwôrts) *n.* A hard, crystalline, vitreous mineral silicon dioxide, SiO_2, found worldwide as a component of sandstone and granite or as pure crystals. [G.]

qua•sar (kwā'zär', -sär', -zər, -sər) *n.* A **quasi-stellar object.**

quash[1] (kwŏsh) *v. Law.* To set aside or annul. [< LL *cassāre.*]

quash[2] (kwŏsh) *v.* To put down or suppress completely. [< L *quatere* (pp *quassus*), to shake, shatter.]

qua•si (kwā'zī', -sī', kwä'zē, -sē) *adv.* To some degree; almost or somewhat. *—adj.* Resembling but not being: *a quasi-victory.* [L < **quānsei,* as if.]

qua•si-stel•lar object (kwā'zī'stĕl'ər, kwā'sī'-, kwä'zē-, kwä'sē-). *Astron.* A member of any of several classes of starlike objects having exceptionally large red shifts and apparently immense speeds, energies, and distances from earth.

Qua•ter•nar•y (kwŏt'ər-nĕr'ē, kwə-tûr'nə-rē) *adj.* Of or belonging to the geologic time, system of rocks, or sedimentary deposits of the second period of the Cenozoic era, including the Pleistocene and Holocene epochs. *—n.* The Quaternary period. [< L *quaternārius,* consisting of four.]

quat•rain (kwŏt'rān', kwŏ-trān') *n.* A typically rhyming four-line stanza. [< L *quattuor,* four.]

qua•ver (kwā'vər) *v.* **1.** To quiver; tremble. **2.** To speak in a quivering voice. [< ME *quaven,* to tremble.] **—qua'ver** *n.*

quay (kē) *n.* A wharf. [< Gaul *caio,* rampart, retaining wall.]

Que. Quebec.

quea•sy (kwē'zē) *adj.* **-sier, -siest.** **1.** Nauseated. **2.** Uneasy. [ME *coysy,* perh orig "wounded."] **—quea'si•ness** *n.*

Que•bec (kwĭ-bĕk'). **1.** A province of E Canada. Pop. 5,657,000. **2.** The capital of this province. Pop. 331,000.

Quech•ua (kĕch'wə, -wä') *n., pl.* **-ua** or **-uas.** **1.** A member of a tribe of South American Indians formerly living chiefly in Peru, Bolivia, and Ecuador. **2.** The language of this tribe.

queen (kwēn) *n.* **1.** The wife or widow of a king. **2.** A female monarch. **3.** A woman who is eminent or supreme in a given domain. **4.** The most powerful chessman. **5.** A playing card bearing the figure of a queen. **6.** The fertile female in a colony of bees, ants, etc. [< OE *cwēn,* woman, wife, queen. See **gwen-.**] **—queen'li•ness** *n.* **—queen'ly** *adj.*

Queens (kwēnz). A borough of New York City. Pop. 1,810,000.

queer (kwîr) *adj.* **1.** Deviating from the expected or normal; strange; peculiar. **2.** Eccentric. *—v. Slang.* To ruin or thwart. [Perh < G *quer,* perverse, cross.] **—queer'ly** *adv.*

quell (kwĕl) *v.* **1.** To put down forcibly. **2.** To pacify. [< OE *cwellan,* to destroy. See **gwel-**[2]**.**]

quench (kwĕnch) *v.* **1.** To put out; extinguish. **2.** To suppress; squelch. **3.** To slake; satisfy. **4.** To cool (hot metal) by thrusting in water or other liquid. [< OE *ācwencan.*]

quer•u•lous (kwĕr'ə-ləs, kwĕr'yə-) *adj.* **1.** Given to complaining or fretting. **2.** Expressing a complaint. [< L *queri,* to complain.]

que•ry (kwîr'ē) *n., pl.* **-ries.** **1.** A question. **2.** A notation calling attention to an item to question its accuracy. *—v.* **-ried, -rying.** To question. [< L *quaerere,* to seek, ask.]

quest (kwĕst) *n.* **1.** An act or instance of seeking; a search. **2.** An expedition undertaken by a medieval knight: *the quest for the Holy Grail.* [< L *quaerere,* to seek.]

ques•tion (kwĕs'chən) *n.* **1.** An expression of inquiry that invites or calls for a reply; an interrogative sentence or phrase. **2.** A controversial subject or point. **3.** A difficult matter; problem: *a question of ethics.* **4.** A proposal or subject under discussion. **5.** Uncertainty; doubt: *no question about it.* **6.** Possibility: *out of the question.* *—v.* **1.** To put a question to; ask questions. **2.** To interrogate, as a witness. **3.** To express doubt about; dispute. [< L *quaerere* (pp *quaestus*), to seek, ask.]

ques•tion•a•ble (kwĕs'chən-ə-bəl) *adj.* **1.** Open to doubt; uncertain. **2.** Of dubious morality or respectability.

question mark. A punctuation symbol (?) written at the end of a sentence or phrase to indicate a direct question.

ques•tion•naire (kwĕs'chə-nâr') *n.* A printed form containing a set of questions, esp. one used in a survey.

quet•zal (kĕt-säl') *n.* **1.** A long-tailed Central American bird with brilliant green and red plumage. **2.** *pl.* **-zales** (-sä'lās). The basic monetary unit of Guatemala. [< Nah *quetzall,* large brilliant tail feather.]

Quet•zal•co•a•tl (kĕt-säl'kō-ät'l). The plumed serpent god of the Toltecs and Aztecs.

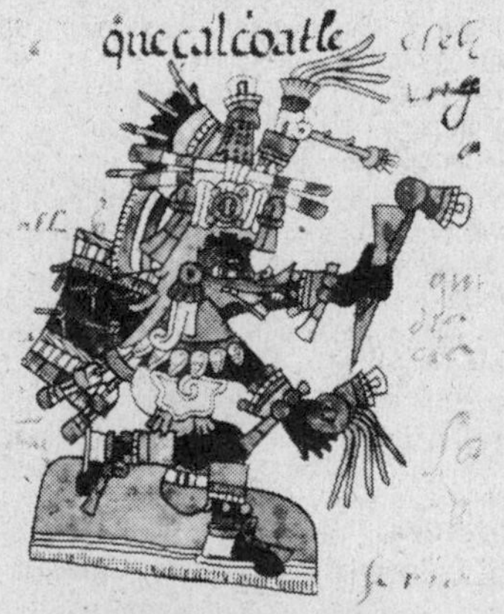

Quetzalcoatl
Aztec pictorial manuscript

queue (kyōō) *n.* **1.** A line of people or vehicles awaiting a turn, as at a ticket window. **2.** A braid of hair worn hanging down the back of the neck. *—v.* **queued, queuing.** To wait in a queue. [F, tail, pigtail, line.]

Que•zon City (kā'sôn'). The capital of the Philippines. Pop. 398,000.

quib•ble (kwĭb'əl) *v.* **-bled, -bling.** To make petty distinctions or raise objections to unimportant details. [Perh < obs *quib,* pun.] **—quib'ble** *n.* **—quib'bler** *n.*

quick (kwĭk) *adj.* **1.** Moving or functioning rapidly; speedy. **2.** Occurring or achieved in a brief space of time. **3.** Understanding, perceiving, or learning with speed; alert; keen. **4.** Hasty or sharp in reacting. *—n.* **1.** Sensitive exposed flesh, as under the fingernails. **2.** The most sensitive aspect of the emotions: *cut to the quick.* **3.** The living: *the quick and the dead.* [< OE *cwic,* living, alive. See **gwei-.**] **—quick** *adv.* **—quick'ly** *adv.* **—quick'ness** *n.*

Usage: Quick (adverb) is used frequently in speech and written dialogue: *Come quick!* In other written contexts, *quickly* is much more common.

quick•en (kwĭk'ən) *v.* **1.** To make or become more rapid; accelerate. **2.** To revive; come to life. **3.** To excite and stimulate.

quick•ie (kwĭk'ē) *n. Informal.* Something made or done hastily.

quick•sand (kwĭk'sănd') *n.* A bed of loose sand mixed with water forming a soft, shifting mass that yields easily to pressure and tends to suck down any object resting on its surface.

quick•sil•ver (kwĭk'sĭl'vər) *n.* The element mercury.

quick•step (kwĭk'stĕp') *n.* A march for accompanying military quick time.

quick-tem•pered (kwĭk'tĕm'pərd) *adj.* Easily aroused to anger.

quick time. A military marching pace of 120 steps per minute.

quick-wit•ted (kwĭk'wĭt'ĭd) *adj.* Mentally alert and sharp.

quid[1] (kwĭd) *n.* A cut of something to be chewed, such as tobacco. [< OE *cwidu.*]

quid[2] (kwĭd) *n., pl.* **quid** or **quids.** *Brit. Slang.* A **pound sterling.** [?]

quid pro quo (kwĭd' prō kwō'). An equal exchange or substitution. [L, "something for something."]

qui•es•cent (kwī-ĕs'ənt, kwē-) *adj.* Inactive or still; dormant. [< L *quiēscere,* to be quiet.] **—qui•es'cence** *n.* **—qui•es'cent•ly** *adv.*

qui•et (kwī'ĭt) *adj.* **1.** Silent; hushed. **2.** Still. **3.** Untroubled; peaceful. **4.** Unobtrusive; restrained. *—n.* Tranquillity; repose. *—v.* To become or cause to become quiet or calm. [< L *quiēs,* quiet.] **—qui'et•ly** *adv.* **—qui'et•ness** *n.*

qui•e•tude (kwī'ə-t/y/ōōd') *n.* A condition of tranquillity.

qui•e•tus (kwī-ē'təs) *n., pl.* **-tuses.** **1.** Death. **2.** A final discharge, as of a debt. [< L *quiētus,* at rest, quiet.]

quill (kwĭl) *n.* **1.** The hollow main shaft of a feather. **2.** A large, stiff feather. **3.** A writing pen made from such a feather. **4.** A sharp, hollow spine, as of a porcupine. [ME *quille.*]

quilt (kwĭlt) *n.* A padded coverlet for a bed. [< L *culcita,* sack filled with feathers.]

quince (kwĭns) *n.* **1.** An applelike, aromatic fruit used chiefly for preserves. **2.** A tree bearing such fruit. [< L *cotōneum, cydōneum.*]

qui•nine (kwī'nīn') *n.* A bitter alkaloid, $C_{20}H_{24}N_2O_2{\cdot}3H_2O$, used to treat malaria. [< Span *quina,* cinchona bark + -INE.]

quin•sy (kwĭn'zē) *n.* Acute inflammation of

the tonsils and the surrounding tissue, often leading to the formation of an abscess. [< Gk *kunanchē,* dog quinsy, sore throat.]
quint (kwĭnt) *n.* Shortened form of **quintuplet.**
quin•tes•sence (kwĭn-tĕs'əns) *n.* **1.** The pure, highly concentrated essence of something. **2.** The purest or most typical instance. [< ML *quinta essentia,* fifth essence.]
quin•tet (kwĭn-tĕt') *n.* **1.** A group of five, esp. of musicians. **2.** A musical composition for five voices or instruments. [< L *quintus,* fifth.]
quin•til•lion (kwĭn-tĭl'yən) *n.* **1.** The cardinal number represented by 1 followed by 18 zeros. **2.** In British usage, the cardinal number represented by 1 followed by 30 zeros. [L *quintus,* fifth + (M)ILLION.] **—quin•til'lion** *adj.*
quin•til•lionth (kwĭn-tĭl'yənth) *n.* The ordinal number quintillion in a series. **—quin•til'lionth** *adj.*
quin•tu•ple (kwĭn-t/y/ōō'pəl, -tŭp'əl, kwĭn'-tŏŏ-pəl) *adj.* **1.** Having five parts. **2.** Multiplied by five. *—n.* A number or amount five times as many or as much as another. *—v.* **-pled, -pling.** To multiply or increase by five. [< LL *quintuplex.*]
quin•tu•plet (kwĭn-tŭp'lĭt, -t/y/ōō'plĭt, kwĭn'-tŏŏ-plĭt) *n.* **1.** A group of five. **2.** One of five offspring born in a single birth.
quip (kwĭp) *n.* A witty or sarcastic remark. *—v.* **quipped, quipping.** To make quips. [Perh < L *quippe,* indeed, certainly.]
quire (kwīr) *n.* A set of 24 or sometimes 25 sheets of paper of the same size and stock. [< OF *quaer,* set of four sheets.]
quirk (kwûrk) *n.* **1.** A sudden sharp turn or twist. **2.** A peculiarity of behavior or action. [?] **—quirk'i•ness** *n.*
quirt (kwûrt) *n.* A riding whip with a short handle and a lash of rawhide. [Perh < Span *cuerda,* whip, chord.]
quis•ling (kwĭz'lĭng) *n.* A traitor who serves as the puppet of the enemy occupying his country. [< V. *Quisling* (1887–1945), head of the State Council of Norway during the German occupation (1940–45).]
quit (kwĭt) *v.* **quit** or **quitted, quitting. 1.** To end one's involvement in; leave abruptly. **2.** To give up; relinquish. **3.** To stop. **4.** To conduct (oneself) in a specified way. *—n.* **—call it quits.** To stop. [< ML *quiētāre,* to set free, quit, discharge.] **—quit'ter** *n.*
quite (kwīt) *adv.* **1.** Entirely; completely. **2.** Actually; really. **3.** Somewhat; rather. **—quite a** (or **an**). **1.** Considerable; notable. **2.** Extraordinary; impressive. [< L *quiētus,* freed, quiet.]
Qui•to (kē'tō). The capital of Ecuador. Pop. 348,000.
quits (kwĭts) *adj.* Even (with someone) by payment or requital. [< ML *quittus,* discharged, var of *quiētus,* freed.]
quit•tance (kwĭt'ns) *n.* **1.** Release from a debt. **2.** Something given as recompense. [< OF *quiter,* to discharge a debt, quit.]
quit•ter (kwĭt'ər) *n.* One who gives up easily.
quiv•er¹ (kwĭv'ər) *v.* To shake or cause to shake with a rapid slight agitating motion; tremble; vibrate. *—n.* The act of quivering. [ME *quiveren.*]
quiv•er² (kwĭv'ər) *n.* A portable case for arrows. [Prob < ML *cucurum.*]
quix•ot•ic (kwĭk-sŏt'ĭk) *adj.* Idealistic without regard to practicality. [< DON QUIXOTE.]
quiz (kwĭz) *v.* **quizzed, quizzing. 1.** To question closely; interrogate. **2.** To test the knowledge of by posing questions. *—n., pl.* **quizzes. 1.** A questioning or inquiry. **2.** A short oral or written test. [?] **—quiz'zer** *n.*
quiz•zi•cal (kwĭz'ĭ-kəl) *adj.* **1.** Suggesting puzzlement. **2.** Teasing; mocking.
quoin (koin, kwoin) *n.* **1. a.** An exterior angle of a wall or other masonry. **b.** A stone serving to form such an angle; cornerstone. **2.** A keystone. [Var of COIN.]
quoit (kwoit, koit) *n.* **1. quoits.** A game in which flat rings are pitched at a stake. **2.** One of the rings used in this game. [ME *coite.*]
quon•dam (kwŏn'dəm, -dăm') *adj.* That once was; former. [L, formerly.]
quo•rum (kwôr'əm, kwōr'-) *n.* The minimum number of members of an organization who must be present for the valid transaction of business. [< L, gen pl of *quī,* who.]
quot. quotation.
quo•ta (kwō'tə) *n.* **1. a.** An allotment. **b.** A production assignment. **2.** The maximum number of persons who may be admitted, as to a nation, group, or institution. [< L *quotus,* of what number.]
quo•ta•tion (kwō-tā'shən) *n.* **1.** The act of quoting. **2.** A passage that is quoted. **3.** The quoting of current prices and bids for securities and goods. **—quo•ta'tion•al** *adj.* **—quo•ta'tion•al•ly** *adv.*
quotation mark. Either of a pair of punctuation marks used to mark the beginning and end of a passage attributed to another and repeated word for word. They usually appear in the form (" "). Single quotation marks (' ') are usually reserved to set off a quotation within a quotation.
quote (kwōt) *v.* **quoted, quoting. 1.** To repeat or copy the words of (another), usually with acknowledgment. **2.** To cite or refer to for illustration or proof. **3.** To state (a price) for securities, goods, or services. *—n.* A quotation. [ME *coten,* to mark with numbers < L *quot,* how many.] **—quot'er** *n.*
quoth (kwōth) *v. Archaic.* Uttered; said: *"Quoth the raven 'Nevermore!'"* (Poe). [< OE *cwethan,* to say. See **gwet-.**]
quo•tid•i•an (kwō-tĭd'ē-ən) *adj.* **1.** Recurring daily. **2.** Commonplace. [< L *quotīdiē,* each day.]
quo•tient (kwō'shənt) *n.* The quantity resulting from division of one quantity by another. [< L *quotiēns,* how many times.]
q.v. which see (L *quod vide*).
qy. query.

Rr

r, R (är) *n.* The 18th letter of the English alphabet.
r 1. radius. **2.** *Elec.* resistance.
R 1. radius. **2.** Republican. **3.** *Elec.* resistance.
r. 1. right. **2.** rod (unit of length).
R. 1. railroad; railway. **2.** Republican. **3.** right. **4.** river. **5.** road.
Ra (rä). Egyptian sun god and supreme deity.
Ra radium.
Ra•bat (rä-bät'). The capital of Morocco. Pop. 227,000.
rab•bet (răb'ĭt) *n.* A groove along or near the edge of a piece of wood that allows another piece to fit into it to form a joint. *—v.* **1.** To cut a rabbet in. **2.** To join by a rabbet. [< OF *rabat,* a beating down.]
rab•bi (răb'ī) *n.* **1.** The ordained spiritual leader of a Jewish congregation. **2.** Formerly, a person authorized to interpret Jewish law. [Heb *rabbī,* my master.] **—rab•bin'i•cal** (rə-bĭn'ĭk-əl) *adj.*
rab•bin•ate (răb'ĭn-āt') *n.* The office or function of a rabbi.
rab•bit (răb'ĭt) *n.* **1.** A long-eared, short-tailed, burrowing mammal with soft fur. **2.** The fur of a rabbit. [ME *rabet.*]
rabbit fever. A disease, tularemia.
rab•ble (răb'əl) *n.* **1.** A mob. **2.** Any group regarded contemptuously. [?]
rab•ble-rous•er (răb'əl-rou'zər) *n.* A demagogue.
Rab•e•lais (răb'ə-lā), **François.** 1494?–1553. French humanist and satirist. **—Rab'e•lai'si•an** (-lā'zē-ən) *adj.*
rab•id (răb'ĭd) *adj.* **1.** Of or afflicted with rabies. **2.** Fanatical. **3.** Raging: *rabid thirst.* [L *rabidus,* raving.] **—ra•bid'i•ty** (rə-bĭd'ə-tē, ră-), **rab'id•ness** *n.* **—rab'id•ly** *adv.*
ra•bies (rā'bēz) *n.* An acute, infectious, often fatal, viral disease of most warm-blooded animals, esp. wolves, cats, and dogs, that attacks the central nervous system and is transmitted by the bite of infected animals. [< L *rabiēs,* rage.]
rac•coon (ră-kōōn') *n.* **1.** A North American mammal with a bushy, black-ringed tail. **2.** The fur of this animal. [< Algon.]
race¹ (rās) *n.* **1.** A local geographic or global human population distinguished by genetically transmitted physical characteristics. **2.** Any group of people more or less distinct, as on the basis of nationality. **3.** A subspecies, breed, or strain of plants or animals. [F, group of people, generation.]
race² (rās) *n.* **1.** A competition of speed. **2.** Any contest for supremacy: *the Presidential race.* **3.** Steady or rapid onward movement. **4. a.** A strong current of water. **b.** The channel of such a current. *—v.* **raced, racing. 1.** To compete in a race. **2.** To rush. **3.** To cause an engine to run swiftly or too swiftly. [< ON *rās.*] **—rac'er** *n.*
race•course (rās'kôrs') *n.* A racetrack.

race•horse (rās'hôrs') *n.* A horse bred and trained to race.

ra•ceme (rā-sēm', rə-) *n.* A flower cluster with stalked flowers arranged singly along a stem. [L *racēmus,* stalk of a cluster of grapes, bunch of berries.]

race•track (rās'trăk') *n.* A course laid out for racing.

Rach•ma•ni•noff (räkH-mä'nĭ-nôf), **Sergei.** 1873–1943. Russian composer and pianist.

ra•cial (rā'shəl) *adj.* **1.** Pertaining to or typical of an ethnic group or groups. **2.** Arising from or based upon differences between ethnic groups. **—ra'cial•ly** *adv.*

Ra•cine (rȧ-sēn'), **Jean.** 1639–1699. French playwright.

ra•cism (rā'sĭz'əm) *n.* The notion that one's own ethnic stock is superior. **—rac'ist, ra'cial•ist** *n. & adj.*

rack (răk) *n.* **1.** A framework or stand in which to hold or display various articles. **2.** A toothed bar that meshes with another toothed structure, such as a pinion or gearwheel. **3.** A framelike instrument of torture. **4.** A state or cause of torment. *—v.* **1.** To torture by means of the rack. **2.** To torment. **3.** To strain with great effort: *rack one's brain.* [Prob < MDu *rec,* framework.] **—rack'er** *n.*

rack•et[1] (răk'ĭt) *n.* Also **rac•quet.** A light bat with a nearly elliptical hoop strung with a network of catgut, nylon, or silk, used in various ball games. [< dial Ar *râhet,* palm of the hand.]

rack•et[2] (răk'ĭt) *n.* **1.** A clamor; uproar. **2. a.** A business that obtains money through fraud or extortion. **b.** An illegal or dishonest practice. [?]

rack•et•eer (răk'ə-tîr') *n.* One engaged in an illegal business.

rack•et•y (răk'ĭt-ē) *adj.* Noisy.

rac•on•teur (răk'ŏn-tûr') *n.* One who recounts stories and anecdotes with skill and wit. [< OF *raconter,* to tell.]

rac•y (rā'sē) *adj.* **-ier, -iest. 1.** Piquant or pungent. **2.** Risqué; ribald. [< RACE (lineage, hence kind, type).] **—rac'i•ness** *n.*

rad. 1. radical. **2.** radius.

ra•dar (rā'där) *n.* **1.** A method of detecting distant objects and determining their position, velocity, or other characteristics by analysis of very high frequency radio waves reflected from their surfaces. **2.** The equipment used in such detection. [Ra(dio) d(etecting) a(nd) r(anging).]

ra•di•al (rā'dē-əl) *adj.* **1.** Of or arranged like rays or radii. **2.** Radiating from or converging to a common center. [< L *radius,* rod, ray.]

ra•di•ant (rā'dē-ənt) *adj.* **1.** Emitting heat or light. **2.** Consisting of or emitted as radiation: *radiant heat.* **3. a.** Bright. **b.** Glowing. [< L *radiāre,* to RADIATE.] **—ra'di•ance** *n.* **—ra'di•ant•ly** *adv.*

radiant energy. Energy transferred by radiation, esp. by an electromagnetic wave.

ra•di•ate (rā'dē-āt') *v.* **-ated, -ating. 1.** To emit radiation. **2.** To issue or emerge in rays. **3.** To spread out or converge radially, as the spokes of a wheel. **4.** To manifest in a glowing manner: *He radiated confidence.* [< L *radiāre,* to emit beams.] **—ra'di•a'tive** *adj.*

ra•di•a•tion (rā'dē-ā'shən) *n.* **1.** The act or process of radiating. **2.** The emission and propagation of waves or particles, such as light, sound, radiant heat, or particles emitted by radioactivity.

radiation sickness. Illness induced by ionizing radiation, ranging in severity of effects from nausea to death.

ra•di•a•tor (rā'dē-ā'tər) *n.* **1.** A heating device for the circulation of steam or hot water. **2.** A cooling device, as in automotive engines. **3.** Something that emits radiation.

rad•i•cal (răd'ĭ-kəl) *adj.* **1.** Fundamental; basic. **2.** Carried to the farthest limit; extreme; sweeping: *radical social change.* **3.** Favoring revolutionary changes, as in politics. *—n.* **1.** One who advocates political and social revolution. **2.** *Math.* The root of a quantity as indicated by the **radical sign. 3.** An atom or group of atoms with at least one unpaired electron. [< LL *rādīcālis,* having roots.] **—rad'i•cal•ly** *adv.* **—rad'i•cal•ness** *n.*

rad•i•cal•ism (răd'ĭ-kəl-ĭz'əm) *n.* **1.** The quality of being radical. **2.** The doctrines or practices of political radicals.

rad•i•cal•ize (răd'ĭ-kə-līz') *v.* **-ized, -izing.** To make radical or more radical. **—rad'i•cal•i•za'tion** *n.*

radical sign. The sign $\surd$ placed before a quantity, indicating extraction of the root designated by a raised integral index.

ra•di•i. *pl.* of **radius.**

ra•di•o (rā'dē-ō) *n., pl.* **-os. 1.** The use of electromagnetic waves in the approximate frequency range from 10 kilocycles/second to 300,000 megacycles/second to transmit or receive electric signals without wires connecting the points of transmission and reception. **2.** Communication of audible signals, such as music, encoded in electromagnetic waves so transmitted and received. **3.** Transmission of programs for the public by this means; radio broadcast. **4.** The equipment used for transmitting or receiving radio signals. *—adj.* **1.** Of or sent by radio. **2.** Of or using oscillations of radio frequency. *—v.* To transmit a message to, or communicate with, by radio. [Short for RADIOTELEGRAPHY.]

radio–. *comb. form.* Emission and propagation of radiation.

radioactive decay. A progressive decrease in the number of radioactive atoms in a substance by spontaneous nuclear disintegration or transformation.

ra•di•o•ac•tiv•i•ty (rā'dē-ō-ăk'tĭv'ə-tē) *n.* **1.** The spontaneous emission of radiation, either directly from unstable atomic nuclei or as a consequence of a nuclear reaction. **2.** Broadly, the radiation so emitted, including alpha particles, nucleons, electrons, and gamma rays. **—ra'di•o•ac'tive** (rā'dē-ō-ăk'tĭv) *adj.* **—ra'di•o•ac'tive•ly** *adv.*

radio astronomy. The study of celestial objects and phenomena by observation and analysis of emitted or reflected radio-frequency waves.

ra•di•o•broad•cast (rā'dē-ō-brôd'kăst', -käst') *v.* To broadcast by radio. **—ra'di•o•broad'cast'er** *n.*

ra•di•o•chem•is•try (rā'dē-ō-kĕm'ĭs-trē) *n.* The chemistry of radioactive materials. **—ra'di•o•chem'i•cal** *adj.*

radio frequency. Any frequency in the range within which radio waves may be transmitted, from about 10 kilocycles/second to about 300,000 megacycles/second.

ra•di•o•gram (rā'dē-ō-grăm') *n.* A message transmitted by wireless telegraphy.

ra•di•o•graph (rā'dē-ō-grăf', -gräf') *n.* An image produced on a radiosensitive surface, such as a photographic film, by radiation other than visible light, esp. by x rays. *—v.* To make a radiograph of. **—ra'di•o•graph'ic** *adj.* **—ra'di•og'ra•phy** (-ŏg'rə-fē) *n.*

ra•di•o•i•so•tope (rā'dē-ō-ī'sə-tōp') *n.* A radioactive isotope.

ra•di•ol•o•gy (rā'dē-ŏl'ə-jē) *n.* The use of ionizing radiation for medical diagnosis, esp. of x rays in medical radiography and for radiotherapy. **—ra'di•o•log'i•cal** (-ə-lŏj'ĭ-kəl) *adj.* **—ra'di•ol'o•gist** *n.*

ra•di•o•man (rā'dē-ō-măn') *n.* A radio technician or operator.

ra•di•os•co•py (rā'dē-ŏs'kə-pē) *n.* The examination of the inner structure of optically opaque objects by x rays or other penetrating radiation. **—ra'di•o•scop'ic** (-ō-skŏp'ĭk), **ra'di•o•scop'i•cal** *adj.*

ra•di•o•sen•si•tive (rā'dē-ō-sĕn'sə-tĭv) *adj.* Sensitive to radiation.

ra•di•o•te•leg•ra•phy (rā'dē-ō-tə-lĕg'rə-fē) *n.* Wireless telegraphy, in which messages are sent by radio. [RADI(ATE) + TELEGRAPHY.] **—ra'di•o•tel'e•graph'ic** *adj.*

ra•di•o•tel•e•phone (rā'dē-ō-tĕl'ə-fōn') *n.* A telephone in which communication is established by radio. **—ra'di•o•tel'e•phon'ic** (-ə-fŏn'ĭk) *adj.*

radio telescope. A sensitive, directional radio-antenna system used to detect and analyze radio waves of extraterrestrial origin.

ra•di•o•ther•a•py (rā'dē-ō-thĕr'ə-pē) *n.* The treatment of disease with radiation.

radio wave. A radio-frequency electromagnetic wave.

rad•ish (răd'ĭsh) *n.* **1.** A plant cultivated for its pungent, edible root. **2.** The root of this plant, eaten raw as an appetizer and in salads. [< L *rādix (rādīc-),* root.]

ra•di•um (rā'dē-əm) *n. Symbol* **Ra** A rare brilliant-white, luminescent, highly radioactive metallic element, used in radiotherapy, as a neutron source, and as a constituent of luminescent paints. Atomic number 88, longest-lived isotope Ra 226. [< L *radius,* ray.]

radium therapy. The use of radium in radiotherapy, esp. in treating cancer.

ra•di•us (rā'dē-əs) *n., pl.* **-dii** (-dē-ī') or **-uses. 1. a.** A line segment that joins the center of a circle with any point on its circumference. **b.** A line segment that joins the center of a sphere with any point on its surface. **c.** A line segment that joins the center of a regular polygon to any of its vertices. **2.** A measure of range of activity or influence. **3.** The shorter and thicker of the two forearm bones, located on the lateral side of the ulna. [L *radius,* spoke of a wheel, ray.]

ra•don (rā'dŏn) *n. Symbol* **Rn** A colorless, radioactive, inert gaseous element formed by disintegration of radium and used in radiotherapy. Atomic number 86, atomic weight 222. [< RADIUM.]

RAF Royal Air Force.

raf•fi•a (răf'ē-ə) *n.* A fiber from the leaves of an African palm, used for mats, baskets, etc. [Malagasy *rafia, rofia.*]

raff•ish (răf'ĭsh) *adj.* **1.** Vulgar; showy. **2.** Rakish. [Prob < dial *raff,* trash.] **—raff'ish•ly** *adv.* **—raff'ish•ness** *n.*

raf•fle (răf'əl) *n.* A lottery in which a number of persons buy chances on a prize. *—v.* **-fled, -fling.** To dispose of in a raffle. [< OF, act of snatching.] **—raf'fler** *n.*

raft[1] (răft, räft) *n.* A flat structure, typically made of planks, logs, or barrels, that floats on water and is used for transport or as a platform for swimmers. [< ON *raptr,* beam, rafter.]

raft[2] (răft, räft) *n. Informal.* A great number or amount. [Perh < Scand.]

raft•er (răf'tər, räf'-) *n.* One of the sloping beams that support a pitched roof. [< OE *ræfter.* See **rĕp-.**]

rag¹ (răg) *n.* A scrap of cloth. [< ON *rögg,* tuft.]

rag² (răg) *v.* **ragged, ragging.** *Slang.* **1.** To taunt. **2.** To scold. [?]

rag•a•muf•fin (răg'ə-mŭf'ĭn) *n.* A dirty or unkempt child. [< *Ragamoffyn,* demon in *Piers Plowman* (1393).]

rage (rāj) *n.* **1.** Violent anger. **2.** A fad; craze. —*v.* **raged, raging. 1.** To speak or act furiously. **2.** To move with great violence or intensity. **3.** To spread or prevail unchecked. [< L *rabere,* to rave.]

rag•ged (răg'ĭd) *adj.* **1.** Tattered. **2.** Dressed in tattered clothes. **3.** Having a rough surface or edges. **4.** Imperfect; sloppy: *a ragged performance.* [< RAG.] —**rag'ged•ly** *adv.* —**rag'ged•ness** *n.*

rag•lan (răg'lən) *n.* A loose coat, jacket, or sweater with slanted shoulder seams and with the sleeves extending in one piece to the neckline. [< Field Marshal Lord *Raglan* (1788–1855), British soldier.] —**rag'lan** *adj.*

ra•gout (ră-go͞o') *n.* A meat and vegetable stew. [< F *ragoûter,* to renew the taste.]

rag•tag (răg'tăg') *n.* Rabble; riffraff. [RAG + TAG.]

rag•time (răg'tīm') *n.* A style of jazz characterized by elaborately syncopated rhythm in the melody. [Perh < *ragged time.*]

rag•weed (răg'wēd') *n.* A weedy plant whose pollen is one of the chief causes of hay fever.

raid (rād) *n.* A small-scale surprise attack. —*v.* To make a raid on. [< OE *rād,* ride, road. See **reidh-.**] —**raid'er** *n.*

rail¹ (rāl) *n.* **1.** A horizontal bar supported by vertical posts, as in a fence. **2.** A railing or balustrade. **3.** A bar used as a track for railroad cars and similar vehicles. **4.** The railroad: *It was transported by rail.* —*v.* To supply or enclose with a rail or rails. [< OF *reille,* bar.]

rail² (rāl) *n.* A brownish, short-winged marsh bird. [< OProv *rasclar,* to scrape, make a scraping noise.]

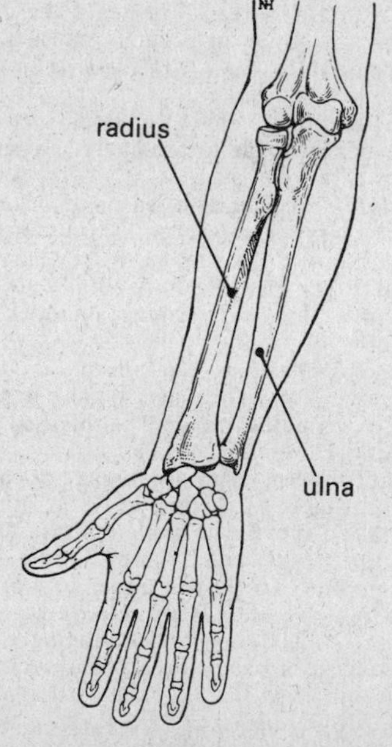

radius

rail³ (rāl) *v.* To use bitter or abusive language. [< LL *ragere,* to neigh, roar.]

rail•ing (rā'lĭng) *n.* A banister, fence, etc., made of rails.

rail•ler•y (rā'lər-ē) *n., pl.* **-ies.** Good-natured teasing or ridicule. [< RAIL³.]

rail•road (rāl'rōd') *n.* **1.** A road composed of parallel steel rails supported by ties and providing a track for trains. **2.** An entire system of such track, together with the land, stations, and rolling stock belonging to it. —*v.* **1.** To transport by railroad. **2.** To rush through quickly in order to prevent careful consideration: *railroad a law through Congress.*

rail•way (rāl'wā') *n.* **1.** A railroad. **2.** A track providing a runway for wheeled equipment.

rai•ment (rā'mənt) *n.* Clothing. [< OF *araie,* an array.]

rain (rān) *n.* **1. a.** Water condensed from atmospheric vapor, falling to earth in drops. **b.** Rainy weather. **2.** The rapid falling of anything in this manner. —*v.* To fall or release as or like rain. [< OF *regn, rēn.* See **reg-².**] —**rain'i•ness** *n.* —**rain'y** *adj.*

rain•bow (rān'bō') *n.* **1.** An arc of spectral colors appearing in the sky opposite the sun as a result of the refractive dispersion of sunlight in drops of rain or mist. **2.** Any similar arc or graded display of colors.

rain•coat (rān'kōt') *n.* A waterproof or water-resistant coat.

rain•fall (rān'fôl') *n.* **1.** A shower of rain. **2.** The quantity of water, expressed in inches, precipitated as rain, snow, hail, or sleet in a specified area and time interval.

rain•storm (rān'stôrm) *n.* A storm accompanied by rain.

rain•wat•er (rān'wô'tər, -wŏt'ər) *n.* Water precipitated as rain.

raise (rāz) *v.* **raised, raising. 1.** To elevate; lift. **2.** To make erect. **3.** To build. **4.** To cause to arise or appear: *raise from the dead.* **5.** To increase in size, worth, degree, etc. **6.** To improve in rank or status. **7.** To breed or rear. **8.** To utter (a cry, shout, etc.). **9.** To arouse or stir up. **10.** To collect: *raise money.* **11.** To cause (dough) to puff up. **12.** To end (a siege). —*n.* **1.** An act of raising or increasing. **2.** An increase in salary. [< ON *reisa.*]

rai•sin (rā'zən) *n.* A sweet dried grape. [< OF, grape.]

rai•son d'ê•tre (rĕ-zôN' dĕ'tr). Reason for being. [F.]

ra•jah, ra•ja (rä'jə) *n.* A prince in India. [Hindi *rājā.*]

rake¹ (rāk) *n.* A long-handled implement with a row of projecting teeth at its head, used to gather leaves and grass. —*v.* **raked, raking. 1.** To gather, move, or loosen with or as with a rake. **2.** To aim heavy gunfire along the length of. [< OE *raca, racu.* See **reg-¹.**]

rake² (rāk) *n.* A profligate man; roué.

rake³ (rāk) *n.* Inclination from the vertical or from the horizontal. [?]

rake-off (rāk'ŏf') *n.* A share of the profits of an enterprise, esp. one accepted as a bribe.

rak•ish¹ (rā'kĭsh) *adj.* **1.** *Naut.* Having a trim, streamlined appearance. **2.** Gay and showy; jaunty. —**rak'ish•ly** *adv.*

rak•ish² (rā'kĭsh) *adj.* Debauched; libertine.

Ra•leigh (rô'lē). The capital of North Carolina. Pop. 94,000.

Ra•leigh (rô'lē), Sir **Walter.** 1552?–1618. English courtier, navigator, colonizer, and writer.

ral•ly¹ (răl'ē) *v.* **-lied, -lying. 1.** To call or join together for a common purpose. **2.** To reassemble. **3.** To recover (one's strength). —*n., pl.* **-lies. 1.** A mass assembly, esp. to inspire enthusiasm for a cause. **2.** A reassembling. **3.** A notable rise in market prices and active trading after a decline. [< OF *ralier,* to ally again.] —**ral'li•er** *n.*

ral•ly² (răl'ē) *v.* **-lied, -lying.** To banter; tease. [< OF *railler,* to RAIL³.] —**ral'li•er** *n.*

ram (răm) *n.* **1.** A male sheep. **2. Ram.** A constellation and sign of the zodiac, Aries. **3.** Any of several devices used to drive, batter, or crush by forceful impact. —*v.* **rammed, ramming. 1.** To strike or drive against with a heavy impact. **2.** To force into place. **3.** To cram; stuff. [< OE *ramm* < Gmc **ramma-.*]

ram•ble (răm'bəl) *v.* **-bled, -bling. 1.** To walk or wander aimlessly. **2.** To follow an irregularly winding course. **3.** To speak or write with many digressions. —*n.* A leisurely stroll. [< ME *romen,* to roam.]

ram•bler (răm'blər) *n.* **1.** One who rambles. **2.** A climbing rose with numerous small flowers.

ram•bunc•tious (răm-bŭngk'shəs) *adj.* Boisterous. [< L *robustus,* oaken, strong.]

ram•ie (răm'ē) *n.* A textile fiber obtained from the stems of an Asian plant. [Malay *rami.*]

ram•i•fy (răm'ə-fī') *v.* **-fied, -fying.** To divide into branchlike parts; branch out. [< L *rāmus,* branch.] —**ram'i•fi•ca'tion** *n.*

ram•jet (răm'jĕt') *n.* A jet engine that propels aircraft by igniting fuel with air taken and compressed by the engine in a fashion that produces greater exhaust than intake velocity.

ramp (rămp) *n.* An inclined passage connecting different levels, as of a building or road. [< F *ramper,* to slope, creep.]

ram•page (răm'pāj) *n.* A course of violent, frenzied behavior. —*v.* (răm-pāj') **-paged, -paging.** To move about wildly or violently. [Scot.] —**ram•pag'er** *n.*

ram•pant (răm'pənt) *adj.* **1.** Extending unchecked; unrestrained. **2.** *Heraldry.* Rearing on the left hind leg with the forelegs elevated, the right above the left, and usually with the head in profile. [< OF *ramper,* to climb.]

ram•part (răm'pärt) *n.* **1.** A fortification consisting of an embankment, often with a parapet. **2.** Anything that serves to protect. [< OF *ramparer,* to fortify.]

ram•rod (răm'rŏd') *n.* **1.** A metal rod used to force the charge into a muzzleloading firearm. **2.** A rod used to clean the barrel of a firearm. —*adj.* Like a rod in stiffness.

ram•shack•le (răm'shăk'əl) *adj.* Shoddily constructed; rickety. [< ME *ransaken,* to ransack.]

ran (răn). *p.t.* of **run.**

ranch (rănch) *n.* A large farm, as in the W U.S., esp. for raising cattle, sheep, or horses. —*v.* To work on or manage a ranch. [< OF *ranger,* to put in a line.] —**ranch'er** *n.*

ran•cid (răn'sĭd) *adj.* Having the disagreeable odor or taste of decomposed oils or fats; rank. [< L *rancēre,* to stink.] —**ran'cid•ness** *n.*

ran•cor (răng'kər) *n.* Deep-seated ill will. [< L *rancēre,* to stink.] —**ran'cor•ous** *adj.*

rand (rănd, ränd) *n.* The basic monetary unit of the Republic of South Africa.

ran•dom (răn'dəm) *adj.* Having no specific pattern or objective; haphazard. —**at random.** Without definite method or purpose. [< OF *randon,* haphazard.] —**ran'dom•ly** *adv.*

rang (răng). *p.t.* of **ring.**

range (rānj) *n.* **1. a.** The extent of perception, knowledge, experience, or ability. **b.** The area, sphere, or scope of activity or occurrence. **2.** The extent of variation: *price range.* **3.** The maximum distance that a ship or other vehicle can travel before exhausting its fuel supply. **4.** A place for shooting at targets. **5.** Open land on which livestock wander and graze. **6.** The act of roaming. **7.** An extended series of mountains. **8.** A type of cooking stove. —*v.* **ranged, ranging. 1.** To arrange in order, esp. in rows or lines. **2.** To classify. **3.** To roam through; explore. **4.** To roam freely. **5.** To extend in a particular direction. **6.** To vary within limits. [< OF, range, rank.]

rang•er (rān'jər) *n.* **1.** A wanderer or rover. **2.** One of an armed troop who patrols a specific region. **3.** A warden employed to patrol a forest.

Ran•goon (răng-gōōn'). The capital of Burma. Pop. 1,530,000.

rang•y (rān'jē) *adj.* **-ier, -iest.** Slender and long-limbed. —**rang'i•ness** *n.*

rank¹ (răngk) *n.* **1.** Relative position or status in a group. **2.** Official position. **3.** Eminent position. **4.** A row, line, or series. **5.** A line of soldiers or military vehicles standing side by side in close order. **6. ranks. a.** The armed forces. **b.** Enlisted men. —*v.* **1.** To place in or form a row or rows. **2.** To classify. **3.** To hold a particular rank. **4.** To take precedence over. [OF *ranc, renc,* rank, range.]

rank² (răngk) *adj.* **1.** Growing profusely or with excessive vigor. **2.** Strong and offensive in odor or flavor. [< OE *ranc,* haughty, full-grown.] —**rank'ly** *adv.* —**rank'ness** *n.*

rank•ing (răngk'ĭng) *adj.* Of the highest rank.

ran•kle (răng'kəl) *v.* **-kled, -kling. 1.** To cause irritation or resentment. **2.** To become sore or inflamed. [< OF *rancle, draoncle,* ulcer, festering sore.]

ran•sack (răn'săk') *v.* **1.** To search thoroughly. **2.** To pillage. [< ON *rannsaka,* search a house.] —**ran'sack'er** *n.*

ran•som (răn'səm) *n.* **1.** The release of a person in return for payment. **2.** The price demanded or paid. [< L *redemptiō,* redemption.] —**ran'som** *v.* —**ran'som•er** *n.*

rant (rănt) *v.* To speak or declaim in a vehement manner; rave. [Prob < Du *ranten.*] —**rant'er** *n.*

rap (răp) *v.* **rapped, rapping. 1.** To strike quickly and lightly. **2.** To utter sharply. **3.** *Slang.* To talk. —*n.* **1.** A knock. **2.** A reprimand. **3.** *Slang.* A talk. —**beat the rap.** *Slang.* To escape legal punishment. [ME *rappen.*]

ra•pa•cious (rə-pā'shəs) *adj.* **1.** Taking by force; plundering. **2.** Greedy; ravenous. **3.** Subsisting on prey. [< L *rapere,* to seize.] —**ra•pa'cious•ly** *adv.* —**ra•pa'cious•ness, ra•pac'i•ty** (rə-păs'ə-tē) *n.*

rape¹ (rāp) *n.* **1.** The crime of forcing a female to submit to sexual intercourse. **2.** The act of carrying off by force. **3.** Profanation. [< L *rapere,* to seize.] —**rape** *v.* **(raped, raping).** —**rap'ist** *n.*

rape² (rāp) *n.* A plant with oil-rich seeds used as animal feed. [< L *rāpa, rāpum,* turnip.]

Raph•a•el (răf'ē-əl, rā'fē-). 1483–1520. Italian painter.

rap•id (răp'ĭd) *adj.* Very fast; swift. —*n.* Often **rapids.** An extremely fast-moving part of a river. [L *rapidus,* hurrying, seizing.] —**ra•pid'i•ty** (rə-pĭd'ə-tē), **rap'id•ness** *n.* —**rap'id•ly** *adv.*

ra•pi•er (rā'pē-ər, rāp'yər) *n.* **1.** A long, slender, two-edged sword used in the 16th and 17th centuries. **2.** An 18th-century, lighter, sharp-pointed sword, used only for thrusting. [F *rapière.*]

rap•ine (răp'ĭn) *n.* Pillage. [< L *rapere,* to RAPE.]

rap•pel (rā-pĕl') *n.* The method of descending from a steep height by means of a double rope passed under one thigh and over the opposite shoulder. [F, "recall."] —**rap•pel'** *v.* **(-pelled, -pelling).**

rap•port (rə-pôr', -pōr') *n.* Relationship, esp. one of mutual trust or understanding. [< F *rapporter,* to bring back, yield.]

rap•proche•ment (rà-prôsh-mäN') *n.* **1.** A reestablishing of cordial relations. **2.** The state of cordial relations. [< F *rapprocher,* to bring together.]

rap•scal•lion (răp-skăl'yən) *n.* A rascal; scamp. [< RASCAL.]

rapt (răpt) *adj.* Deeply absorbed; engrossed. [< L *raptus,* "seized."]

rap•ture (răp'chər) *n.* A state of ecstasy. [< L *raptus,* RAPT.] —**rap'tur•ous** *adj.*

ra•ra a•vis (râr'ə ā'vĭs) *pl.* **rara avises** or **rarae aves** (râr'ē ā'vēz). A rare or unique person or thing. [L, "rare bird."]

rare¹ (râr) *adj.* **rarer, rarest. 1.** Unusual. **2.** Special. **3.** Thin in density; rarefied: *the rare air of the high altitudes.* [< L *rārus,* loose, thin, scarce.] —**rare'ly** *adv.* —**rare'ness, rar'i•ty** *n.*

rare² (râr) *adj.* **rarer, rarest.** Cooked a short time to retain juice and redness: *rare meat.* [< OE *hrēr,* soft-boiled.] —**rare'ness** *n.*

rare•bit (râr'bĭt) *n.* **Welsh rabbit.** [Var of (WELSH) RABBIT.]

rare-earth element (râr'ûrth'). Any of the related series of metallic elements of atomic number 57 through 71.

rar•e•fied (râr'ə-fīd') *adj.* Elevated in character or style; esoteric.

rar•e•fy (râr'ə-fī') *v.* **-fied, -fying. 1.** To make or become thin or less dense. **2.** To purify or refine. —**rar'e•fac'tion** *n.*

rar•ing (râr'ĭng) *adj. Informal.* Full of eagerness. [< REAR².]

ras•cal (răs'kəl) *n.* **1.** An unscrupulous or dishonest person. **2.** One who is playfully mischievous. [Perh < OF *rasque, rasche,* mud, filth.] —**ras'cal•ly** *adj.*

rash¹ (răsh) *adj.* Acting without forethought or due caution; hasty. [ME *rasch,* nimble, quick.] —**rash'ly** *adv.* —**rash'ness** *n.*

rash² (răsh) *n.* **1.** A skin eruption. **2.** A wide recurrence of something within a given period. [Poss < VL **rasciāre,* to scrape.]

rash•er (răsh'ər) *n.* A thin slice of bacon to be fried or broiled. [?]

rasp (răsp, räsp) *v.* **1.** To file or scrape with a rasp. **2.** To speak in a grating voice. **3.** To grate upon (nerves or feelings). —*n.* A file having abrasive, pointed projections. [< OHG *raspōn.*] —**rasp'er** *n.* —**rasp'ing•ly** *adv.* —**rasp'y** *adj.*

rasp•ber•ry (răz'bĕr'ē, -bə-rē, räz'-) *n.* **1.** The sweet, usually red berry of a prickly woody plant. **2.** A plant bearing such berries. [< earlier *raspis.*]

Ras•pu•tin (răs-pyōō'tĭn), **Grigori.** 1871?–1916. Russian mystic monk; favorite of the imperial family.

rat (răt) *n.* **1.** Any of various long-tailed, often destructive rodents resembling but larger than a mouse. **2.** A sneaky person, esp. one who betrays his associates. —*v.* **ratted, ratting. 1.** To hunt for or catch rats. **2.** *Slang.* To desert or betray one's comrades: *rat on a friend.* [< OE *ræt* < Gmc **ratt-.*] —**rat'ter** *n.*

ratch•et (răch'ĭt) *n.* A mechanism consisting of a pawl, or hinged catch, that engages the sloping teeth of a wheel or bar, permitting motion in one direction only. [< OF *rocquet,* head of a lance.]

rate¹ (rāt) *n.* **1.** A measured quantity within the limits of a fixed quantity of something else. **2.** A quantitative measure of a part to a whole; proportion. **3. a.** A charge or payment. **b.** A cost per unit. **4.** Level of quality. —**at any rate. 1.** Whatever the case may be. **2.** At least. —*v.* **rated, rating. 1.** To calculate the value of. **2.** To classify or be classified. **3.** To regard. **4.** To deserve. **5.** To have importance or status. [< ML *rata,* calculated, fixed.]

rate² (rāt) *v.* **rated, rating.** To scold. [Perh < ON *hrata.*]

rath•er (răth'ər, rä'thər) *adv.* **1.** Preferably. **2.** With more reason. **3.** With more accuracy. **4.** Somewhat. **5.** On the contrary. **6.** *Chiefly Brit.* Most certainly. Used as an emphatic reply. [< OE *hræth,* early.]

rat•i•fy (răt'ə-fī') *v.* **-fied, -fying.** To give formal sanction to; approve and so make valid. [< ML *ratificāre.*] —**rat'i•fi•ca'tion** *n.*

rat•ing (rā'tĭng) *n.* **1.** A place assigned on a scale; a standing or rank. **2.** A classification according to specialty or proficiency.

ra•tio (rā'shō, rā'shē-ō') *n., pl.* **-tios. 1.** Relation in degree or number between two similar things; rate. **2.** *Math.* The relative size of two quantities expressed as the quotient of one divided by the other. [L *ratiō,* computation.]

ra•ti•oc•i•nate (răsh'ē-ŏs'ə-nāt') *v.* **-nated, -nating.** To reason methodically and logically. [< L *ratiō,* RATIO.] —**ra'ti•oc'i•na'tion** *n.* —**ra'ti•oc'i•na'tive** *adj.* —**ra'ti•oc'i•na'tor** *n.*

ra•tion (răsh'ən, rā'shən) *n.* **1.** A fixed portion, esp. an amount of food allotted to persons in military service or to civilians in times of scarcity. **2. rations.** *Mil.* Food. —*v.* **1.** To supply with rations. **2.** To restrict to limited allotments. [< L *ratiō (ratiōn-),* RATIO.]

ra•tion•al (răsh'ən-əl) *adj.* **1.** Having or exercising the ability to reason. **2.** Of sound mind. **3.** Manifesting or based upon reason; logical. **4.** *Math.* Expressible as a ratio of two integers. [< L *ratiō,* reason, RATIO.] —**ra'tion•al'i•ty** *n.* —**ra'tion•al•ly** *adv.*

ra•tion•ale (răsh'ə-năl') *n.* **1.** The fundamental reasons for something. **2.** An exposition of principles or reasons.

ra•tion•al•ism (răsh'ən-əl-ĭz'əm) *n.* The theory that the exercise of reason provides the only valid basis for action or belief. —**ra'tion•al•ist** *n.* —**ra'tion•al•is'tic** *adj.* —**ra'tion•al•is'ti•cal•ly** *adv.*

ra•tion•al•ize (răsh'ən-əl-īz') *v.* **-ized, -izing. 1.** To make conformable to reason. **2.** To interpret from a rational standpoint. **3.** To devise self-satisfying but incorrect reasons for (one's behavior). —**ra'tion•al•i•za'tion** (-ə-zā'shən) *n.*

rat•line (răt'lĭn) *n.* Also **rat•lin.** *Naut.* Any of the small ropes fastened horizontally to the shrouds of a ship and forming a ladder for going aloft. [?]

rats•bane (răts'bān') *n.* Rat poison.

rat•tan (ră-tăn') *n.* The long, tough, slender stems of a climbing tropical palm, used for wickerwork, canes, etc. [Malay *rotan.*]

rat•tle (răt'l) *v.* **-tled, -tling. 1.** To make or cause to emit a quick succession of short, sharp sounds. **2.** To move with such sounds. **3.** To talk or utter rapidly and at length: *rattle off a list.* **4.** *Informal.* To fluster; unnerve. —*n.* **1.** Short, percussive sounds produced in rapid succession. **2.** A device for producing these sounds, such as a baby's toy. **3.** The series of horny structures at the end of a rattlesnake's tail. [< MLG *rattelen.*]

rat•tler (răt'lər) *n.* A rattlesnake.

rat•tle•snake (răt'l-snāk') *n.* A venomous

New World snake with a series of loose, horny segments at the end of the tail.
rat•tle•trap (răt'l-trăp') *n.* A rickety, worn-out vehicle.
rat•ty (răt'ē) *adj.* **-tier, -tiest.** 1. Of or characteristic of rats. 2. *Slang.* Disreputable; dilapidated.
rau•cous (rô'kəs) *adj.* Rough-sounding; harsh. [< L *raucus,* hoarse, harsh.] —**rau'cous•ly** *adv.* —**rau'cous•ness** *n.*
rav•age (răv'ĭj) *v.* **-aged, -aging.** To destroy or despoil. —*n.* 1. The act of ravaging. 2. Grievous damage. [< OF *ravir,* to ravish.] —**rav'ag•er** *n.*
rave (rāv) *v.* **raved, raving.** 1. To speak or utter wildly, irrationally, or incoherently. 2. To roar; rage. 3. To speak with wild enthusiasm. —*n.* 1. The state or act of raving. 2. *Informal.* An extravagantly enthusiastic opinion or review. [< ONF *raver.*]
rav•el (răv'əl) *v.* **-eled** or **-elled, -eling** or **-elling.** 1. To separate the fibers or threads of (cloth); unravel; fray. 2. To tangle or become confused. —*n.* 1. A raveling. 2. A loose thread. 3. A tangle. [< Du *rafelen,* to unravel.]
Ra•vel (rə-vĕl', ră-), **Maurice.** 1875–1937. French composer and pianist.
ra•ven (rā'vən) *n.* A large crowlike bird with a croaking cry. —*adj.* Black and shiny. [< OE *hræfn.* See **ker-**[2].]
rav•en•ing (răv'ən-ĭng) *adj.* Predatory; voracious. [< OF *raviner,* to ravage.]
rav•en•ous (răv'ən-əs) *adj.* 1. Extremely hungry. 2. Predatory. 3. Greedy for gratification. [< OF *raviner,* to ravage.] —**rav'en•ous•ly** *adv.*
ra•vine (rə-vēn') *n.* A deep, narrow cleft or gorge in the earth's surface, esp. one worn by water. [F, mountain torrent.]
ra•vi•o•li (ră'vē-ō'lē) *pl.n. (takes sing.* or *pl. v.).* Small casings of pasta with various fillings, as chopped meat or cheese. [< It *rava,* turnip.]
rav•ish (răv'ĭsh) *v.* 1. To seize and carry away by force. 2. To rape. 3. To enrapture. [< L *rapere,* seize.] —**rav'ish•er** *n.* —**rav'ish•ment** *n.*
rav•ish•ing (răv'ĭsh-ĭng) *adj.* Entrancing.
raw (rô) *adj.* 1. Uncooked. 2. In a natural condition; not subjected to manufacturing or refining. 3. Untrained. 4. Having subcutaneous tissue exposed: *a raw wound.* 5. Penetratingly damp. 6. Cruel and unfair. 7. Outspoken; crude. [< OE *hrēaw.* See **kreu-**[1].] —**raw'ly** *adv.* —**raw'ness** *n.*
raw•boned (rô'bōnd') *adj.* Having a lean, gaunt frame with prominent bones.
raw•hide (rô'hīd') *n.* 1. The untanned hide of cattle. 2. A whip or rope made of such hide.
ray[1] (rā) *n.* 1. A thin line or narrow beam of radiation, esp. of visible light. 2. A trace; hint: *a ray of hope.* 3. A straight line extending from a point. 4. A part or structure having this form. [< L *radius.*]
ray[2] (rā) *n.* A marine fish with a broad, flattened body and a long, narrow tail. [< L *raia.*]
ray•on (rā'ŏn) *n.* 1. A synthetic fiber produced by forcing a cellulose solution through a plate with fine holes and solidifying the resulting filaments. 2. Fabric made from such fibers. [< RAY[1].]
raze (rāz) *v.* **razed, razing.** 1. To tear down or demolish. 2. To scrape or shave off. [< L *rādere* (pp *rāsus*), to scrape.]
ra•zor (rā'zər) *n.* A sharp-edged cutting instrument used esp. for shaving. [< OF *raser,* to scrape, raze.]
razz (răz) *v. Slang.* To deride or tease.
Rb rubidium.
r.b.i. *Baseball.* run or runs batted in.
R.C. 1. Red Cross. 2. Roman Catholic.
R.C.Ch. Roman Catholic Church.
rcpt. receipt.
rd rod (unit of length).
rd. 1. road. 2. round.
R.D. rural delivery.
re (rē) *prep.* Concerning; in reference to; in the case of. [< L *rēs,* thing.]
Re rhenium.
re–. *comb. form.* 1. Restoration to a previous condition. 2. Repetition of a previous action. [< L.]
reach (rēch) *v.* 1. To stretch out or extend (a bodily part). 2. To touch, take hold of, or try to grasp (something) by extending a bodily part, esp. the hand. 3. To get to or arrive at. 4. To succeed in communicating with. 5. To extend or carry as far as. 6. To aggregate or amount to. —*n.* 1. The act or power of stretching or thrusting out. 2. The extent or distance something can reach. 3. An unbroken expanse. [< OE *rǣcan.* See **reig-.**]
re•act (rē-ăkt') *v.* 1. To act in response or opposition to some former act or state. 2. To be affected or influenced by circumstances or events. 3. To undergo chemical change.
re•ac•tant (rē-ăk'tənt) *n.* A substance participating in a chemical reaction.
re•ac•tion (rē-ăk'shən) *n.* 1. A response to a stimulus or the state resulting from such a response. 2. A reverse or opposing action. 3. Opposition to progress or liberalism. 4. A chemical change or transformation. 5. A nu-

Note: Many compounds may be formed with *re-*. In forming compounds *re-* is normally joined with the following element without space or hyphen: *reopen.* If the second element begins with *e,* it is preferable to separate it with a hyphen. However, such compounds may often be found written solid: *reenter; reexamine.*

re'a•ban'don *v.*
re'ab•sorb' *v.*
re'ab•sorp'tion *n.*
re'ac•cept' *v.*
re'ac•com'mo•date' *v.*
re'ac•com'pa•ny *v.*
re'ac•cuse' *v.*
re'ac•quire' *v.*
re•ac'ti•vate' *v.*
re'a•dapt' *v.*
re'ad•dress' *v.*
re'ad•journ' *v.*
re'ad•journ'ment *n.*
re'ad•just' *v.*
re'ad•just'ment *n.*
re'ad•mis'sion *n.*
re'ad•mit' *v.*
re'a•dopt' *v.*
re'a•dorn' *v.*
re'ad•vance' *v.*
re'af•firm' *v.*
re'a•lign' *v.*
re'a•lign'ment *n.*
re•an'i•mate' *v.*
re'an•nex' *v.*
re'a•noint' *v.*
re'ap•pear' *v.*
re'ap•pear'ance *n.*
re'ap•ply' *v.*
re'ap•point' *v.*
re'ap•point'ment *n.*
re'ap•por'tion *v.*
re'ap•por'tion•ment *n.*
re•ar'gue *v.*
re•ar'gu•ment *n.*
re•arm' *v.*
re•ar'ma•ment *n.*
re'ar•range' *v.*
re'ar•range'ment *n.*
re'as•cend' *v.*
re'as•cent' *n.*
re'as•sem'ble *v.*
re'as•sem'bly *n.*
re'as•sert' *v.*
re'as•ser'tion *n.*
re'as•sign' *v.*
re'as•sim'i•late' *v.*
re'as•sim'i•la'tion *n.*
re'as•so'ci•ate' *v.*
re'as•sume' *v.*
re'as•sump'tion *n.*
re'at•tach' *v.*
re'at•tack' *v.*
re'at•tain' *v.*
re'at•tempt' *v.*
re'a•vow' *v.*
re'a•wake' *v.*
re'a•wak'en *v.*
re•bill' *v.*
re•bind' *v.*
re•bloom' *v.*
re•blos'som *v.*
re•boil' *v.*
re•broad'cast' *v.* & *n.*
re•build' *v.*
re•bur'y *v.*
re•car'ry *v.*
re•cast' *v.* & *n.*
re•cel'e•brate' *v.*
re•chal'lenge *v.*
re•charge' *v.*
re•char'ter *v.*
re•check' *v.*
re•choose' *v.*
re•chris'ten *v.*
re•cir'cle *v.*
re•cir'cu•late' *v.*
re•clasp' *v.*
re•clean' *v.*
re•clothe' *v.*
re•coin' *v.*
re•coin'age *n.*
re'-col•lect' *v.*
re•col'o•nize' *v.*
re•col'or *v.*
re'com•bine' *v.*
re'com•mence' *v.*
re'com•mis'sion *n.*
re'com•pose' *v.*
re'con•dense' *v.*
re'con•duct' *v.*
re'con•firm' *v.*
re•con'quer *v.*
re•con'quest *n.*
re•con'se•crate' *v.*
re'con•sol'i•date' *v.*
re•con'sti•tute *v.*
re•con'sti•tu'tion *n.*
re'con•vene' *v.*
re'con•vert' *v.*
re'con•vey' *v.*
re•cop'y *v.*
re'cor•o•na'tion *n.*
re•cross' *v.*
re•crown' *v.*
re'crys•tal•li•za'tion *n.*
re•crys'tal•lize' *v.*
re•cul'ti•vate' *v.*
re'cy'cle *v.*
re'ded•i•ca'tion *n.*
re'de•feat' *v.* & *n.*
re'de•fine' *v.*
re'de•liv'er *v.*
re'de•mand' *v.*
re•dem'on•strate' *v.*
re'de•ny' *v.*
re'de•pos'it *v.* & *n.*
re'de•scend' *v.*
re'de•scent' *n.*
re'de•scribe' *v.*
re'de•ter'mine *v.*
re'de•vel'op *v.*
re'di•gest' *v.*
re'dis•cov'er *v.*
re'dis•cov'er•y *n.*
re'dis•solve' *v.*
re'dis•till' *v.*
re'dis•trib'ute *v.*
re'di•vide' *v.*
re'di•vi'sion *n.*
re'do' *v.*
re•dou'ble *v.*
re'draft' *n.*
re•draw' *v.*
re•drive' *v.*
re•dry' *v.*
re•dye' *v.*
re•ech'o *n.* & *v.*
re•ed'it *v.*
re•ed'u•cate' *v.*
re'-e•lect' *v.*
re'-e•lec'tion *n.*
re•el'e•vate' *v.*
re'-em•bark' *v.*
re'-em•bod'y *v.*
re'-em•brace' *v.*
re'-e•merge' *v.*
re'-e•mer'gence *n.*
re•em'i•grate' *v.*
re'-en•act' *v.*
re'-en•act'ment *n.*
re'-en•cour'age *v.*
re'-en•cour'age•ment *n.*
re'-en•dow' *v.*

ô paw, for/oi boy/ou out/ŏŏ took/ōō coo/p pop/r run/s sauce/sh shy/t to/th thin/*th* the/ ŭ cut/ûr fur/v van/w wag/y yes/z size/zh vision/ə ago, item, edible, gallop, circus/

clear reaction.
re•ac•tion•ar•y (rē-ăk′shə-nĕr′ē) *adj.* Characterized by reaction, esp. opposing progress or liberalism. *—n., pl.* **-ies.** An opponent of progress or liberalism.
re•ac•tive (rē-ăk′tĭv) *adj.* **1.** Tending to be responsive or to react to a stimulus. **2.** Characterized by reaction.
re•ac•tor (rē-ăk′tər) *n.* **1.** One that reacts. **2.** A nuclear reactor.
read (rēd) *v.* **read** (rĕd), **reading. 1.** To comprehend the meaning of (something written or printed). **2.** To utter or render aloud (something written or printed). **3.** To ascertain the intent or mood of: *He read her mind.* **4.** To derive a special meaning from or ascribe a special significance to: *read improper motives into his actions.* **5.** To foretell or predict. **6.** To comprehend (a signal, message, etc.). **7.** To study. **8.** To learn by reading. **9.** To indicate or register: *The dial reads 0°.* **10.** To have a particular wording. **11.** To contain a specific meaning. [< OE *rǣdan,* advise, explain, read.] **—read′a•bil′i•ty, read′a•ble•ness** *n.* **—read′a•ble** *adj.* **—read′er** *n.*
read•i•ly (rĕd′ə-lē) *adv.* **1.** Promptly. **2.** Willingly. **3.** Easily.
read•ing (rē′dĭng) *n.* **1.** The act or practice of a reader. **2.** Written or printed material. **3.** A public recitation of literary or other written material. **4.** A personal interpretation or appraisal. **5.** The specific form of a particular passage in a text. **6.** Information indicated, as by a gauge.
read•y (rĕd′ē) *adj.* **-ier, -iest. 1.** Prepared or available for service or action. **2.** Mentally disposed; willing. **3.** Prompt in apprehending or reacting. [< OE *rǣde.* See **reidh-.**] **—read′i•ness** *n.*
read•y-made (rĕd′ē-mād′) *adj.* Made to a set pattern; not custom-made.
read•y•wit•ted (rĕd′ē-wĭt′ĭd) *adj.* Quick-witted. **—read′y•wit′ted•ly** *adv.*
re•a•gent (rē-ā′jənt) *n.* Any substance used in a chemical reaction to detect, measure, examine, or produce other substances. [RE- + AGENT.]
re•al (rē′əl, rēl) *adj.* **1.** Being or occurring in fact or actuality. **2.** Genuine; authentic. **3.** *Opt.* Pertaining to an image formed by light rays that converge in space. **4.** *Law.* Of or pertaining to stationary or fixed property, as buildings or land. *—adv. Informal.* Very: *I'm real sorry.* [< LL *reālis,* actual, real < L *rēs,* thing.]
real estate. Landed property including all inherent natural resources and any man-made improvements established thereon; realty. **—re′al-es•tate′** *adj.*
re•al•ism (rē′ə-lĭz′əm) *n.* **1.** Inclination toward

re′-en·gage′ *v.*
re′-en·gage′ment *n.*
re′-en·grave′ *v.*
re′-en·list′ *v.*
re′-en·list′ment *n.*
re′-en·slave′ *v.*
re-en′ter *v.*
re′-e·rect′ *v.*
re′-es·tab′lish *v.*
re′-es·tab′lish·ment *n.*
re′-e·val′u·ate′ *v.*
re′-e·val′u·a′tion *n.*
re′-ex·am′i·na′tion *n.*
re′-ex·am′ine *v.*
re′-ex·change′ *v.*
re′-ex·hib′it *v.*
re′-ex·pel′ *v.*
re′-ex·pe′ri·ence *v.*
re′ex·port′ *v.*
re·face′ *v.*
re·fash′ion *v.*
re·fas′ten *v.*
re·fer′ti·lize′ *v.*
re·fire′ *v.*
re′flow′ *v.*
re·flow′er *v.*
re·fold′ *v.*
re·forge′ *v.*
re·for′mu·late′ *v.*
re′for·ti·fi·ca′tion *n.*
re·for′ti·fy′ *v.*
re·frame′ *v.*
re·freeze′ *v.*
re·fu′el *v.*
re·fur′nish *v.*
re·gath′er *v.*
re·gear′ *v.*
re·ger′mi·nate′ *v.*
re′ger·mi·na′tion *n.*
re·gild′ *v.*
re·glaze′ *v.*
re·glue′ *v.*
re·grade′ *v.*
re·graft′ *v.*
re·grant′ *v.*
re·group′ *v.*
re·han′dle *v.*
re·hear′ing *n.*
re·heat′ *v.*
re·heel′ *v.*
re′hire′ *v.*
re′ig·nite′ *v.*
re′im·plant′ *v.*
re′im·port′ *v.*
re′im·pose′ *v.*
re′im·po·si′tion *n.*
re′im·preg′nate *v.*
re′im·press′ *v.*
re′im·print′ *v.*
re′im·pris′on *v.*
re′im·pris′on·ment *n.*
re′in·au′gu·rate′ *v.*
re′in·cite′ *v.*
re′in·cor′po·rate′ *v.*
re′in·cur′ *v.*
re′in·duce′ *v.*
re′in·fect′ *v.*
re′in·fec′tion *n.*
re′in·flame′ *v.*
re′in·form′ *v.*
re′in·fuse′ *v.*
re′in·hab′it *v.*
re′in·oc′u·late′ *v.*
re′in·oc′u·la′tion *n.*
re′in·scribe′ *v.*
re′in·sert′ *v.*
re′in·ser′tion *n.*
re′in·spect′ *v.*
re′in·spec′tion *n.*
re′in·spire′ *v.*
re′in·stall′ *v.*
re′in·stal·la′tion *n.*
re′in·struct′ *v.*
re′in·sure′ *v.*
re′in′te·grate′ *v.*
re′in·te·gra′tion *n.*
re′in·ter′ *v.*
re′in·ter′ro·gate′ *v.*
re′in·tro·duce′ *v.*
re′in·tro·duc′tion *n.*
re′in·vent′ *v.*
re′in·vest′ *v.*
re′in·ves′ti·gate′ *v.*
re′in·ves·ti·ga′tion *n.*
re′in·vest′ment *n.*
re′in·vig′or·ate′ *v.*
re′in·vig′or·a′tion *n.*
re′in·vite′ *v.*
re′in·volve′ *v.*
re·is′sue *n.* & *v.*
re·judge′ *v.*
re·kin′dle *v.*
re·la′bel *v.*
re·lace′ *v.*
re·launch′ *v.*
re·learn′ *v.*
re·light′ *v.*
re·line′ *v.*
re·liq′ui·date′ *v.*
re′liq·ui·da′tion *n.*
re·load′ *n.* & *v.*
re·loan′ *n.* & *v.*
re·lo′cate *v.*
re′lo·ca′tion *n.*
re·make′ *v.* & *n.*
re′man·u·fac′ture *v.*
re·mar′ry *v.*
re′match′ *n.*
re·meas′ure *v.*
re·melt′ *v.*
re·merge′ *v.*
re·mi′grate *v.*
re′mi·gra′tion *n.*
re·mil′i·ta·rize′ *v.*
re·mix′ *v.*
re′mod·i·fi·ca′tion *n.*
re·mod′i·fy′ *v.*
re·mold′ *v.*
re·mount′ *v.* & *n.*
re·name′ *v.*
re·nav′i·gate′ *v.*
re·nom′i·nate′ *v.*
re′nom·i·na′tion *n.*
re·no′ti·fy′ *v.*
re·num′ber *v.*
re′ob·tain′ *v.*
re′ob·tain′a·ble *adj.*
re′oc·cu·pa′tion *n.*
re·oc′cu·py′ *v.*
re′oc·cur′ *v.*
re′oc·cur′rence *n.*
re·o′pen *v.*
re′op·pose′ *v.*
re′or·dain′ *v.*
re′or·di·na′tion *n.*
re·o′ri·ent′ *v.*
re·pac′i·fy′ *v.*
re·pack′ *v.*
re·pack′age *v.*
re·paint′ *v.* & *n.*
re·pa′per *v.*
re·pass′ *v.*
re·pave′ *v.*
re·pe′nal·ize′ *v.*
re·plant′ *v.*
re·play′ *v.*
re′play *n.*
re·pledge′ *v.*
re·plunge′ *v.*
re·pol′ish *v.* & *n.*
re·pop′u·late′ *v.*
re′pop·u·la′tion *n.*
re·pour′ *v.*
re′-press′ *v.*
re′print′ *n.*
re·proc′ess *v.*
re′pro·claim′ *v.*
re′pub·li·ca′tion *n.*
re·pub′lish *v.*
re·pur′chase *v.*
re·pu′ri·fy′ *v.*
re′pur·sue′ *v.*
re·ra′di·ate′ *v.*
re·read′ *v.*
re′re·cord′ *v.*
re·rise′ *v.*
re·roll′ *v.*
re·route′ *v.*
re·sad′dle *v.*
re·sail′ *v.*
re′sale *n.*
re·sa·lute′ *v.*
re·seal′ *v.*
re·seat′ *v.*
re·seed′ *v.*
re·seek′ *v.*
re·seg′re·gate′ *v.*
re·seize′ *v.*
re·sei′zure *n.*
re·sell′ *v.*
re·set′ *v.* & *n.*
re·set′tle *v.*
re·set′tle·ment *n.*
re·shape′ *v.*
re·sharp′en *v.*
re·ship′ *v.*
re·ship′ment *n.*
re·shuf′fle *v.*
re·sift′ *v.*
re·sol′der *v.*
re·sole′ *v.*
re′so·lid′i·fy′ *v.*
re·sow′ *v.*
re·spell′ *v.*
re·spread′ *v.*
re·stack′ *v.*
re·state′ *v.*
re·state′ment *n.*
re·stip′u·late′ *v.*
re′stip·u·la′tion *n.*
re·stock′ *v.*
re·strength′en *v.*
re·string′ *v.*
re·strive′ *v.*
re·stud′y *n.* & *v.*
re′sub·ject′ *v.*
re′sub·jec′tion *n.*
re·sum′mon *v.*
re·sum′mons *n.*
re′sup·ply′ *v.*
re′sur·vey′ *v.* & *n.*
re·teach′ *v.*
re·tell′ *v.*
re·test′ *v.*
re·tie′ *v.*
re′trans·late′ *v.*
re·trav′erse *v.*
re·type′ *v.*
re·u′ni·fy′ *v.*
re′u·ni·fi·ca′tion *n.*
re·use′ *v.*
re·u′til·ize′ *v.*
re·ut′ter *v.*
re·val′ue *v.*
re·var′nish *v.*
re′ver·i·fi·ca′tion *n.*
re·ver′i·fy′ *v.*
re·vin′di·cate′ *v.*
re·vin′di·ca′tion *n.*
re·vis′it *v.*
re·voice′ *v.*
re·warm′ *v.*
re·wash′ *v.*
re·weigh′ *v.*
re·wind′ *v.*
re·wire′ *v.*
re·work′ *v.*

literal truth and pragmatism. 2. Artistic representation felt to be accurate. —**re'al•ist** *n.* —**re'al•is'tic** *adj.* —**re'al•is'ti•cal•ly** *adv.*

re•al•i•ty (rē-ăl'ə-tē) *n., pl.* **-ties.** 1. The quality or state of being actual or true. 2. The totality of all things possessing actuality, existence, or essence.

re•al•ize (rē'ə-līz') *v.* **-ized, -izing.** 1. To comprehend completely or correctly. 2. To make real or actualize (a plan, ambition, etc.). 3. To obtain or achieve, esp. from a commercial transaction. —**re'al•iz'a•ble** *adj.* —**re'al•i•za'tion** (-lə-zā'shən) *n.* —**re'al•iz'er** *n.*

re•al•ly (rē'ə-lē', rē'lē) *adv.* 1. In reality. 2. Truly.

realm (rĕlm) *n.* 1. A kingdom. 2. Any field, sphere, or province. [< L *regimen,* system of government.]

Re•al•tor (rē'əl-tər, -tôr') *n.* Also **re•al•tor.** A real-estate agent affiliated with the National Association of Real Estate Boards. [< REALTY.]

re•al•ty (rē'əl-tē) *n., pl.* **-ties. Real estate.** [REAL + -TY.]

ream¹ (rēm) *n.* 1. A quantity of paper, 500 sheets or, in a printer's ream, 516. 2. Often **reams.** Very much: *reams of verse.* [< Ar *rizmah,* bundle.]

ream² (rēm) *v.* 1. To form, taper, or enlarge (a hole) with or as with a reamer. 2. To remove (material) by reaming. [Perh < OE *rȳman,* to widen.]

ream•er (rē'mər) *n.* Any of various tools used to shape or enlarge holes.

reap (rēp) *v.* 1. To harvest by cutting with or as with a scythe, sickle, etc. 2. To obtain as a result of effort; receive as reward or punishment. [< OE *rīpan.* See **rei-¹**.]

reap•er (rē'pər) *n.* 1. One who reaps. 2. A machine for harvesting.

rear¹ (rîr) *n.* The back or hind part. —**bring up the rear.** To be last in a line. —*adj.* Of or located in the rear. [Short for ARREAR.]

rear² (rîr) *v.* 1. To care for during the early stages of life; bring up. 2. To lift upright. 3. To build. 4. To rise on the hind legs, as a horse. [< OE *rǣran,* to raise < Gmc **raizjan.*] —**rear'er** *n.*

rear admiral. A naval officer ranking next below a vice admiral.

rear guard. A detachment of troops that protects the rear of a military force. —**rear'guard'** (rîr'gärd') *adj.*

rear•most (rîr'mōst') *adj.* Farthest in the rear; in the last position.

rear•ward (rîr'wərd) *adj.* Directed toward or situated at the rear. —*adv.* Also **rear•wards** (-wərdz). Toward, to, or at the rear.

rea•son (rē'zən) *n.* 1. The basis or motive for an action, decision, or conviction. 2. An underlying fact or cause that provides logical sense for a premise or occurrence. 3. The capacity for rational thought, inference, or discrimination. —**stand to reason.** To be logical or likely. —*v.* 1. To use the faculty of reason; think logically. 2. To talk or argue logically and persuasively. 3. To determine or conclude by logical thinking. [< L *ratiō,* calculation, judgment.] —**rea'son•er** *n.* —**rea'son•ing** *n.*

rea•son•a•ble (rē'zən-ə-bəl) *adj.* 1. Capable of reasoning; rational. 2. In accordance with reason or sound thinking. 3. Not excessive or extreme. —**rea'son•a•bil'i•ty, rea'son•a•ble•ness** *n.* —**rea'son•a•bly** *adv.*

re•as•sure (rē'ə-sho͝or') *v.* 1. To restore confidence to. 2. To assure again. —**re'as•sur'ance** *n.* —**re'as•sur'ing•ly** *adv.*

re•bate (rē'bāt') *n.* A deduction from an amount to be paid or a return of part of an amount paid. —*v.* (rē'bāt', rĭ-bāt') **-bated, -bating.** To deduct or return (an amount) from a payment or bill. [< OF *rabattre,* to beat down again, reduce.] —**re'bat'er** (rē'bā'tər, rĭ-bā'tər) *n.*

re•bel (rĭ-bĕl') *v.* **-belled, -belling.** 1. To refuse allegiance to and oppose by force an established government or ruling authority. 2. To resist or defy any authority or generally accepted convention. —*n.* **reb•el** (rĕb'əl). 1. One who rebels or is in rebellion. 2. **Rebel.** A Confederate soldier in the Civil War. —*adj.* Of or pertaining to rebels. [< L *rebellāre,* to make war again.]

re•bel•lion (rĭ-bĕl'yən) *n.* 1. An uprising intended to change or overthrow an existing government or ruling authority. 2. An act or show of defiance of any authority or established convention.

re•bel•lious (rĭ-bĕl'yəs) *adj.* 1. Participating in or tending toward rebellion. 2. Resisting control; unruly. —**re•bel'lious•ly** *adv.* —**re•bel'lious•ness** *n.*

re•birth (rē-bûrth', rē'bûrth') *n.* 1. A second or new birth. 2. A renaissance; revival.

re•born (rē-bôrn') *adj.* Born again; spiritually revived or regenerated.

re•bound (rē'bound', rĭ-) *v.* 1. To spring or bounce back after hitting or colliding with something. 2. To recover, as from depression or disappointment. —**re'bound'** (rē'bound', rĭ-bound') *n.*

re•buff (rĭ-bŭf') *n.* 1. A blunt or abrupt repulse or refusal. 2. Any abrupt setback to progress or action. —*v.* 1. To refuse bluntly or contemptuously; snub. 2. To repel or drive back. [< It *ribuffo,* reprimand.]

re•buke (rĭ-byo͞ok') *v.* **-buked, -buking.** To criticize sharply; reprimand. —*n.* A sharp reproof. [< ONF *rebuker.*]

re•bus (rē'bəs) *n., pl.* **-buses.** A riddle composed of pictures that suggest the sound of the words or syllables they represent. [L *rēbus,* by things.]

re•but (rĭ-bŭt') *v.* **-butted, -butting.** To refute, esp. by offering opposing evidence or arguments, as in a legal case. [< OF *rebuter.*] —**re•but'tal** *n.*

rec. 1. receipt. 2. recipe. 3. record; recording. 4. recreation.

re•cal•ci•trant (rĭ-kăl'sə-trənt) *adj.* Stubbornly resistant to authority or guidance. [< L *recalcitrāre,* to kick back.] —**re•cal'ci•trance, re•cal'ci•tran•cy** *n.*

re•call (rĭ-kôl') *v.* 1. To call back; ask or order to return. 2. To remember or recollect. 3. To cancel; take back. 4. To bring back; restore. —*n.* (rĭ-kôl', rē'kôl'). 1. The act of recalling. 2. The ability to remember information or experiences. 3. a. The procedure by which a public official can be removed from office by popular vote. b. The right to employ this procedure. —**re•call'a•ble** *adj.*

re•call•ment (rĭ-kôl'mənt) *n.* Recall.

re•cant (rĭ-kănt') *v.* To make a formal retraction or disavowal of (a previously held statement, position, or belief). [L *recantāre.*] —**re'can•ta'tion** (rē'kăn-tā'shən) *n.* —**re•cant'er** *n.* —**re•cant'ing•ly** *adv.*

re•cap¹ (rē-kăp') *v.* To restore (a used automobile tire) to usable condition by bonding new rubber onto the worn tread and lateral surface. —*n.* (rē'kăp'). A tire thus reconditioned.

re•cap² (rē'kăp') *v.* **-capped, -capping.** To summarize. —*n.* A summary. [Short for RECAPITULATE.]

re•ca•pit•u•late (rē'kə-pĭch'o͞o-lāt') *v.* **-lated, -lating.** To repeat in concise form; summarize. [LL *recapitulāre.*] —**re'ca•pit'u•la'tion** *n.* —**re•ca•pit'u•la'tive** *adj.*

re•cap•ture (rē-kăp'chər) *v.* 1. To capture again; retake or recover. 2. To recall: *an attempt to recapture the past.*

recd. received.

re•cede (rĭ-sēd') *v.* **-ceded, -ceding.** 1. To move back or away; retreat. 2. To slope backward. 3. To become or seem to become more distant. [L *recēdere,* to go back.]

re•ceipt (rĭ-sēt') *n.* 1. The act of receiving or fact of being received. 2. Often **receipts.** The amount of something received: *cash receipts.* 3. A written acknowledgment that something specified has been received. 4. *Regional.* A recipe. —*v.* 1. To mark (a bill) as paid. 2. To give a receipt for. [< L *recipere* (pp *receptus*), to take, RECEIVE.]

re•ceiv•a•ble (rĭ-sē'və-bəl) *adj.* 1. Suitable for being received; acceptable as payment. 2. Awaiting or requiring payment; due or collectable: *accounts receivable.*

re•ceive (rĭ-sēv') *v.* **-ceived, -ceiving.** 1. To take or acquire (something given, offered, or transmitted); get. 2. To meet with; experience. 3. To take in, hold, or contain. 4. To admit or welcome (members, guests, etc.). 5. To regard in a specified manner: *theories well received.* [< L *recipere,* to take back, regain.]

re•ceiv•er (rĭ-sē'vər) *n.* 1. One that receives something; a recipient; receptacle. 2. A person appointed by a court to take into custody the property or funds of others pending litigation. 3. A device, as a radio, television set, or telephone, that receives incoming signals and converts them to perceptible forms.

re•ceiv•er•ship (rĭ-sē'vər-shĭp') *n. Law.* 1. The office or functions of a receiver. 2. The state of being held by a receiver.

re•cent (rē'sənt) *adj.* 1. Of, belonging to, or occurring at a time immediately prior to the present. 2. Modern; new. [L *recēns,* fresh, new.] —**re'cent•ly** *adv.*

re•cep•ta•cle (rĭ-sĕp'tə-kəl) *n.* 1. A container. 2. *Elec.* A fitting connected to a power supply and equipped to receive a plug. [< L *receptāre,* to take again.]

re•cep•tion (rĭ-sĕp'shən) *n.* 1. The act or process of receiving or being received. 2. A welcome, greeting, or acceptance. 3. A formal social function. 4. a. The receiving of electromagnetic signals. b. The condition or quality of received signals.

re•cep•tion•ist (rĭ-sĕp'shə-nĭst) *n.* One employed to receive callers and answer the telephone.

re•cep•tive (rĭ-sĕp'tĭv) *adj.* 1. Able or willing to receive favorably. 2. Capable of or qualified for receiving. —**re•cep'tive•ly** *adv.* —**re'cep•tiv'i•ty, re•cep'tive•ness** *n.*

re•cep•tor (rĭ-sĕp'tər) *n.* A nerve ending specialized to sense or receive stimuli.

re•cess (rē'sĕs', rĭ-sĕs') *n.* 1. a. A cessation of customary activities. b. The period of such cessation. 2. A remote or secret place. 3. An indentation or small hollow. —*v.* 1. To place in a recess. 2. To make a recess in. 3. To suspend for a recess. [< L *recēdere,* to RECEDE.]

re•ces•sion (rĭ-sĕsh'ən) *n.* 1. The act of withdrawing. 2. The filing out of clergy and choir members after a church service. 3. A moderate and temporary decline in economic activity.

re•ces•sion•al (rĭ-sĕsh'ən-əl) *n.* A hymn that accompanies the exit of the clergy and choir after a church service.

re•ces•sive (rĭ-sĕs'ĭv) *adj.* **1.** Tending to go backward or recede. **2.** *Genetics.* Incapable of being manifested when occurring with a dominant form of a gene.

recip. reciprocal; reciprocity.

rec•i•pe (rĕs'ə-pē') *n.* A formula for preparing something, esp. in cooking or pharmacology. [< L *recipere,* to RECEIVE.]

re•cip•i•ent (rĭ-sĭp'ē-ənt) *n.* One that receives.

re•cip•ro•cal (rĭ-sĭp'rə-kəl) *adj.* **1.** Concerning each of two or more persons or things. **2.** Mutual. **3.** Interchangeable. *—n.* **1.** One that is reciprocal to another; a converse or complement. **2.** *Math.* Either of a pair of quantities whose product is unity. [L *reciprocus,* alternating, returning.] **—re•cip'ro•cal•ly** *adv.*

re•cip•ro•cate (rĭ-sĭp'rə-kāt') *v.* **-cated, -cating. 1.** To give or take mutually; interchange. **2.** To show or feel in response or return. **3.** To make a return for something given or done. **4.** To be equivalent. **—re•cip'ro•ca'tion** *n.* **—re•cip'ro•ca'tive** *adj.*

rec•i•proc•i•ty (rĕs'ə-prŏs'ə-tē) *n.* **1.** A reciprocal condition or relationship. **2.** A commercial policy or trade agreement between two or more parties.

re•cit•al (rĭ-sīt'l) *n.* **1.** A public reading of memorized materials. **2.** A narration. **3.** A performance of music or dance, esp. by one performer.

rec•i•ta•tion (rĕs'ə-tā'shən) *n.* **1. a.** The act of reciting. **b.** The material recited. **2. a.** The oral delivery of prepared lessons by a pupil. **b.** The class period within which this occurs.

rec•i•ta•tive (rĕs'ə-tə-tēv') *n.* **1.** A musical style used in opera or oratorio, in which the text is declaimed in the rhythm of natural speech. **2.** A passage rendered in this form.

re•cite (rĭ-sīt') *v.* **-cited, -citing. 1.** To repeat or utter aloud something rehearsed or memorized, esp. publicly. **2.** To relate in detail. **3.** To enumerate or list. [< L *recitāre,* to cite again.] **—re•cit'er** *n.*

reck•less (rĕk'lĭs) *adj.* **1. a.** Careless. **b.** Headstrong; rash. **2.** Uncontrolled; wild. [< OE *rēceléas.* See **reg-¹**.] **—reck'less•ly** *adv.* **—reck'less•ness** *n.*

reck•on (rĕk'ən) *v.* **1.** To count or compute. **2.** To regard as. **3.** *Informal.* To think or assume. [< OE *gerecenian,* to enumerate. See **reg-¹**.] **—reck'on•er** *n.*

reck•on•ing (rĕk'ən-ĭng) *n.* **1.** The act of counting. **2.** The settlement of an account. **3.** The calculated position of a ship, aircraft, etc.

re•claim (rĭ-klām') *v.* **1.** To make (marsh land or desert) suitable for cultivation or habitation. **2.** To procure (usable substances) from refuse or waste products. **3.** To reform. **—re•claim'a•ble** *adj.* **—rec'la•ma'tion** (rĕk'lə-mā'shən) *n.*

re•cline (rĭ-klīn') *v.* **-clined, -clining.** To assume or cause to assume a leaning or prone position. [< L *reclīnāre,* to bend back.] **—re•clin'er** *n.*

re•cluse (rĕk'lo͞os', rĭ-klo͞os') *n.* One who lives in solitude and seclusion; a hermit. [< L *reclūdere,* to close off.]

rec•og•ni•tion (rĕk'əg-nĭsh'ən) *n.* **1.** The act of recognizing or state of being recognized. **2.** An awareness that something perceived has been perceived before. **3.** An acknowledgment.

re•cog•ni•zance (rĭ-kŏg'nə-zəns, -kŏn'ə-zəns) *n.* An obligation of record entered into before a court with the condition to perform a particular act, as to appear in court. **—re•cog'ni•zant** *adj.*

rec•og•nize (rĕk'əg-nīz') *v.* **-nized, -nizing. 1.** To know or be aware that something perceived has been perceived before. **2.** To identify from past experience or knowledge. **3.** To acknowledge the validity of. **4.** To acknowledge as a speaker. **5.** To acknowledge or accept the national status of as a new government. **6.** To admit the acquaintance of. [< L *recognōscere,* to know again.] **—rec'og•niz'a•ble** *adj.* **—rec'og•niz'a•bly** *adv.*

re•coil (rĭ-koil') *v.* **1.** To spring back, as a gun upon firing. **2.** To shrink back in fear or repugnance. **—re'coil'** (rē'koil', rĭ-koil') *n.*

rec•ol•lect (rĕk'ə-lĕkt') *v.* To recall to mind; remember. [< L *recolligere,* to gather again.] **—rec'ol•lec'tion** *n.*

rec•om•mend (rĕk'ə-mĕnd') *v.* **1.** To commend to the attention of another as reputable, worthy, or desirable. **2.** To make attractive or acceptable. **3.** To entrust. **4.** To counsel or advise. **—rec'om•mend'a•ble** *adj.* **—rec'om•men•da'tion** *n.*

rec•om•pense (rĕk'əm-pĕns') *v.* **-pensed, -pensing.** To award compensation to or for. *—n.* **1.** Amends made for damage or loss. **2.** Payment in return for services. [< LL *recompensāre.*]

rec•on•cile (rĕk'ən-sīl') *v.* **-ciled, -ciling. 1.** To re-establish friendship between. **2.** To settle, as a dispute. **3.** To bring to acquiescence: *reconcile oneself to defeat.* **4.** To make compatible or consistent. [< L *reconciliāre.*] **—rec'on•cil'a•ble** *adj.* **—rec'on•cil'i•a'tion** (-sĭl'ē-ā'shən) *n.*

rec•on•dite (rĕk'ən-dīt', rĭ-kŏn'dīt') *adj.* **1.** Not easily understood; abstruse. **2.** Concealed; hidden. [< L *recondere,* to hide, put up again.]

re•con•nais•sance (rĭ-kŏn'ə-səns, -zəns) *n.* A preliminary survey of a region to examine its terrain or to determine the disposition of military forces.

re•con•noi•ter (rē'kə-noi'tər, rĕk'ə-) *v.* To make a preliminary inspection (of).

re•con•sid•er (rē'kən-sĭd'ər) *v.* To consider again, esp. with intent to modify a previous decision. **—re'con•sid'er•a'tion** *n.*

re•con•struct (rē'kən-strŭkt') *v.* To construct again.

re•con•struc•tion (rē'kən-strŭk'shən) *n.* **1.** The act or result of reconstructing. **2. Reconstruction.** The period (1865–77) during which the Confederate states were forced to change politically and socially as prerequisite to full readmission to the Union.

rec•ord (rĕk'ərd) *n.* **1.** A written account of events or facts. **2.** Something on which such an account is made. **3.** Information on a particular subject collected and preserved: *the coldest day on record.* **4.** The known history of performance. **5.** The best performance known, as in a sport. **6.** A disk structurally coded to reproduce sound; phonograph record. *—v.* **re•cord** (rĭ-kôrd'). **1.** To set down for preservation in a record. **2.** To register or indicate. **3.** To register (sound) in permanent form on a record or a tape. *—adj.* **rec•ord** (rĕk'ərd). Establishing a record: *a record crowd.* [< L *recordārī,* to remember.]

re•cord•er (rĭ-kôr'dər) *n.* **1.** One that records. **2.** A horizontal flute usually of wood.

re•cord•ing (rĭ-kôr'dĭng) *n.* Sound recorded on a phonograph record or magnetic tape or wire.

re-count (rē-kount') *v.* To count again. *—n.* (rē'kount', rē-kount'). An additional count, esp. of votes in an election.

re•count (rĭ-kount') *v.* **1.** To narrate the facts or particulars of. **2.** To enumerate.

re•coup (rĭ-ko͞op') *v.* **1.** To receive an equivalent for. **2.** To reimburse. **3.** To regain. [< OF *recouper,* to cut back.]

re•course (rē'kôrs', -kōrs', rĭ-kôrs', -kōrs') *n.* **1.** A turning or applying to a person or thing for aid or security. **2.** One that is turned to for such aid or security.

re•cov•er (rĭ-kŭv'ər) *v.* **1.** To get back; regain. **2.** To regain a normal or usual condition or state. **3.** To receive a favorable judgment in a lawsuit. [< L *recuperāre,* to RECUPERATE.] **—re•cov'er•a•ble** *adj.* **—re•cov'er•y** *n.*

rec•re•ant (rĕk'rē-ənt) *adj.* **1.** Unfaithful. **2.** Craven or cowardly. *—n.* **1.** A disloyal person. **2.** A coward. [< OF *recroire,* to yield, surrender.] **—rec're•ant•ly** *adv.*

re-cre•ate (rē'krē-āt') *v.* To create anew.

rec•re•a•tion (rĕk'rē-ā'shən) *n.* Refreshment of one's mind or body after labor through diverting activity; play. **—rec're•a'tion•al** *adj.*

re•crim•i•nate (rĭ-krĭm'ə-nāt') *v.* **-nated, -nating.** To counter one accusation with another. **—re•crim'i•na'tion** *n.*

re•cruit (rĭ-kro͞ot') *v.* **1.** To engage for military service. **2.** To enroll as a supporter. **3.** To replenish. **4.** To renew or restore (health or vitality). *—n.* A newly engaged member of a military force or an organization. [< L *recrēscere,* to grow again.] **—re•cruit'er** *n.* **—re•cruit'ment** *n.*

rect. **1.** receipt. **2.** rectangle. **3.** rector; rectory.

rec•tan•gle (rĕk'tăng'gəl) *n.* A parallelogram with a right angle. [< L *rēctus,* right + *angulus,* ANGLE.] **—rec•tan'gu•lar** *adj.*

rec•ti•fy (rĕk'tə-fī') *v.* **-fied, -fying.** To set right; correct. [< L *rēctus,* straight + *facere,* to make.] **—rec'ti•fi•ca'tion** *n.* **—rec'ti•fi'er** *n.*

rec•ti•lin•e•ar (rĕk'tə-lĭn'ē-ər) *adj.* Of, moving in, or bounded by a straight line or lines.

rec•ti•tude (rĕk'tə-t/y/o͞od') *n.* **1.** Moral uprightness. **2.** Sound intellectual judgment. [< L *rēctus,* straight.]

rec•to (rĕk'tō) *n., pl.* **-tos.** A right-hand page. [< L *rēctus,* right, straight.]

rec•tor (rĕk'tər) *n.* **1.** A clergyman in charge of a parish. **2.** The principal of certain schools, colleges, and universities. **3.** A priest serving as head of a seminary or university. [L *rēctor,* governor.] **—rec'tor•ate** (-ĭt) *n.* **—rec•to'ri•al** (-tôr'ē-əl, -tōr'-) *adj.*

rec•to•ry (rĕk'tə-rē) *n., pl.* **-ries.** A rector's dwelling.

rec•tum (rĕk'təm) *n., pl.* **-tums** or **-ta** (-tə). The portion of the large intestine extending from the sigmoid flexure to the anal canal. [NL *rectum (intestinum),* straight (intestine).] **—rec'tal** *adj.*

re•cum•bent (rĭ-kŭm'bənt) *adj.* Lying down; reclining. [< L *recumbere,* to lie down.]

re•cu•per•ate (rĭ-k/y/o͞o'pə-rāt') *v.* **-ated, -ating. 1.** To return to health or strength; recover. **2.** To recover or regain. [L *recuperāre.*] **—re•cu'per•a'tion** *n.*

re•cur (rĭ-kûr') *v.* **-curred, -curring.** To happen, come up, or show up again or repeatedly; return. [L *recurrere,* run back.] **—re•cur'rence** *n.* **—re•cur'rent** *adj.* **—re•cur'rent•ly** *adv.*

re•cy•cle (rē-sī'kəl) *v.* **-cled, -cling. 1.** To start a different cycle in. **2. a.** To extract useful materials from (garbage, waste, etc.). **b.** To extract and reuse (useful substances found in garbage, waste, etc.).

red (rĕd) *n.* **1.** Any of a group of colors whose hue resembles that of blood. **2.** A pigment or dye having or giving this hue. **3.** Something that has this hue. **4.** Often **Red.** A communist or revolutionary activist. —*adj.* **redder, reddest. 1.** Having a color resembling that of blood. **2.** Having a coppery skin tone. **3.** Having a ruddy or flushed complexion. **4.** Often **Red. a.** Revolutionary. **b.** Of, pertaining to, or aroused by revolution or revolutionaries. **c.** Composed of or directed by Communists. [< OE *rēad.* See **reudh-.**] —**red'ness** *n.*

red•blood•ed (rĕd'blŭd'ĭd) *adj.* Strong or virile. —**red'-blood'ed•ness** *n.*

red•coat (rĕd'kōt') *n.* A British soldier during the American Revolution and the War of 1812.

Red Cross. Officially, Red Cross Society. An international organization, formed for the care of the wounded, sick, and homeless.

red•den (rĕd'n) *v.* To make or become red.

red•dish (rĕd'ĭsh) *adj.* Mixed or tinged with red. —**red'dish•ness** *n.*

re•deem (rĭ-dēm') *v.* **1.** To recover ownership of by paying a specified sum. **2.** To pay off, as a promissory note. **3.** To turn in (coupons, certificates, etc.) and receive something in exchange. **4.** To fulfill (an oath or promise). **5.** To cash. **6.** To rescue or ransom. **7.** To save from sin. [< L *redimere,* to buy back.] —**re•deem'a•ble** *adj.* —**re•deem'er** *n.*

re•demp•tion (rĭ-dĕmp'shən) *n.* The act of redeeming or the condition of being redeemed.

red-hand•ed (rĕd'hăn'dĭd) *adj.* & *adv.* In the act of committing, or having just committed, a crime. —**red'-hand'ed•ly** *adv.*

red•head (rĕd'hĕd') *n.* A person with red hair.

red herring. Something that draws attention away from the matter at hand. [< the use of red herring to distract hunting dogs from the scent.]

red hot (rĕd'hŏt') *adj.* **1.** Glowing hot; very hot. **2.** New; very recent.

re•dis•trict (rē-dĭs'trĭkt) *v.* To divide again, as into administrative or election districts.

red-let•ter (rĕd'lĕt'ər) *adj.* Memorably happy: *a red-letter day.*

red•o•lent (rĕd'ə-lənt) *adj.* **1.** Emitting fragrance; pleasantly odorous. **2.** Smelling: *boatyards redolent of tar.* [< L *redolēre,* to emit an odor.] —**red'o•lence, red'o•len•cy** *n.* —**red'o•lent•ly** *adv.*

re•doubt (rĭ-dout') *n.* A defensive fortification. [< ML *reductus,* concealed place.]

re•doubt•a•ble (rĭ-dou'tə-bəl) *adj.* **1.** Awesome; formidable. **2.** Worthy of respect or honor. [< OF *redouter,* to dread.]

re•dound (rĭ-dound') *v.* **1.** To have an effect or consequence. **2.** To contribute; accrue. [< L *redundāre,* to overflow.]

re•dress (rĭ-drĕs') *v.* **1.** To set right; remedy or rectify. **2.** To make amends to or for. —*n.* (rĭ-drĕs', rē'drĕs). **1.** Satisfaction for wrong done. **2.** Correction.

Red River. A river of the SW U.S.

Red Sea. A body of water separating the Arabian Peninsula from Africa and connected with the Mediterranean by the Suez Canal.

red shift. 1. An apparent increase in the wavelength of radiation emitted by a receding celestial body. **2.** A similar increase in wavelength resulting from loss of energy by radiation moving against a gravitational field.

red•skin (rĕd'skĭn') *n. Informal.* A North American Indian.

red tape. Impedimental use of official forms and procedures.

re•duce (rĭ-d/y/ōōs') *v.* **-duced, -ducing. 1.** To lessen in extent, amount, etc.; diminish or become diminished. **2.** To gain control of; conquer. **3.** To put in order systematically. **4.** To separate into orderly components by analysis. **5.** To bring to a certain state. **6.** To pulverize. **7.** *Chem.* **a.** To decrease the valence of (an atom) by adding electrons. **b.** To deoxidize. **c.** To add hydrogen to. **8.** To lose weight, as by dieting. [< L *redūcere,* bring back.] —**re•duc'i•ble** *adj.* —**re•duc'i•bly** *adv.* —**re•duc'tion** (-dŭk'shən) *n.* —**re•duc'tive** *adj.*

re•dun•dant (rĭ-dŭn'dənt) *adj.* **1.** Exceeding what is necessary or natural. **2.** Needlessly repetitive. [< L *redundāre,* to overflow.] —**re•dun'dan•cy** *n.* —**re•dun'dant•ly** *adv.*

redupl. reduplicate; reduplication; reduplicative.

re•du•pli•ca•tion (rĭ-d/y/ōō'plə-kā'shən) *n.* A doubling of an initial syllable or a whole word to form a new word. —**re•du'pli•cate'** *v.*

red•wood (rĕd'wŏŏd') *n.* **1.** A very tall evergreen tree of coastal California. **2.** The soft, reddish wood of this tree.

reed (rēd) *n.* **1. a.** Any of various tall hollow-stemmed swamp or marsh grasses. **b.** The stalk of such a grass. **2. a.** A strip of cane or metal set into certain musical instruments to produce tone by vibration. **b.** An instrument fitted with a reed. [< OE *hrēod.* See **kreut-.**] —**reed'i•ness** *n.* —**reed'y** *adj.*

reef[1] (rēf) *n.* A strip or ridge of rocks, sand, or coral that rises to or near the surface of a body of water. [< MDu *rif,* ridge.]

reef[2] (rēf) *n. Naut.* A portion of a sail rolled and tied down to lessen the area exposed to the wind. —*v.* To reduce the size of (a sail) by tucking in a part. [< ON *rif,* ridge, rib.]

reef•er (rē'fər) *n. Slang.* A marijuana cigarette.

reek (rēk) *v.* **1.** To smoke, steam, or fume. **2.** To emit or be pervaded by something unpleasant. **3.** To give off or become permeated with a strong and unpleasant odor. —*n.* **1.** A stench. **2.** Vapor; steam. [< OE *rēocan.* See **reug-.**] —**reek'er** *n.* —**reek'y** *adj.*

reel[1] (rēl) *n.* **1.** A cylinder, spool, or frame that turns on an axis and is used for winding rope, tape, etc. **2.** Such a device on a fishing rod to let out or wind up the line. **3.** The quantity of something wound on one reel. —*v.* **1.** To wind on a reel. **2.** To recover by winding on a reel: *reel in the marlin.* **3.** To recite fluently: *reel off the names.* [< OE *hrēol.*]

reel[2] (rēl) *v.* **1.** To throw or be thrown off balance; fall back. **2.** To stagger, lurch, or sway. **3.** To go round and round in a whirling motion. **4.** To feel dizzy.

reel[3] (rēl) *n.* A fast dance of Scottish origin.

re-en•try (rē-ĕn'trē) *n., pl.* **-tries.** Also **re•en•try. 1.** A second or subsequent entry. **2.** The return of a missile or spacecraft into the earth's atmosphere.

reeve (rēv) *v.* **reeved** or **rove, reeving.** *Naut.* To pass (a rope) through a hole. [?]

ref. 1. reference; referred. **2.** refining. **3.** reformation; reformed.

re•fec•tion (rĭ-fĕk'shən) *n.* **1.** Refreshment with food and drink. **2.** A light meal or repast. [< L *reficere,* to refresh.]

re•fec•to•ry (rĭ-fĕk'tə-rē) *n., pl.* **-ries.** A room where meals are served.

re•fer (rĭ-fûr') *v.* **-ferred, -ferring. 1.** To turn or direct to a source for help or information. **2.** To assign or attribute to. **3.** To submit (a matter in dispute) to an authority for decision or examination. **4.** To direct the attention of. **5.** To pertain. **6.** To allude or make reference. [< L *referre,* refer to, carry back.] —**ref'er•a•ble** (rĕf'ər-ə-bəl, rĭ-fûr'-) *adj.* —**re•fer'ral** *n.* —**re•fer'rer** *n.*

ref•e•ree (rĕf'ə-rē') *n.* **1.** One to whom something is referred, esp. in a court of law; an arbitrator. **2.** An official supervising a game; an umpire. —*v.* **-reed, -reeing.** To act as referee.

ref•er•ence (rĕf'ər-əns, rĕf'rəns) *n.* **1.** An act of referring. **2.** One that is referred to. **3.** The state of being related or referred: *with reference to; in reference to.* **4.** An allusion. **5.** A note in a publication referring the reader to another passage or source. **6.** A statement attesting to personal qualifications of one seeking employment.

ref•er•en•dum (rĕf'ə-rĕn'dəm) *n., pl.* **-dums** or **-da** (-də). **1.** The submission of a proposed public measure or actual statute to a direct popular vote. **2.** Such a vote.

ref•er•ent (rĕf'ər-ənt, rĭ-fûr'ənt) *n.* **1.** Something that refers, esp. a linguistic item in its capacity of referring to a meaning. **2.** Something referred to.

re•fill (rē-fĭl') *v.* To fill again. —*n.* (rē'fĭl'). **1.** A replacement for the used contents of a container. **2.** A second or subsequent filling.

re•fine (rĭ-fīn') *v.* **-fined, -fining. 1.** To reduce to a pure state; become pure; purify. **2.** To free from coarse characteristics. **3.** To improve. —**re•fin'er** *n.*

re•fined (rĭ-fīnd') *adj.* **1.** Free from coarseness or vulgarity. **2.** Free of impurities. **3.** Precise to a fine degree; subtle; exact.

re•fine•ment (rĭ-fīn'mənt) *n.* **1. a.** An act of refining. **b.** The state of being refined. **2.** An improvement. **3.** Fineness of thought or expression. **4.** A keen or precise phrasing.

re•fin•er•y (rĭ-fī'nə-rē) *n., pl.* **-ies.** An industrial plant for purifying a crude substance, such as petroleum or ore.

refl. 1. reflection. **2.** reflexive.

re•flect (rĭ-flĕkt') *v.* **1.** To throw or bend back (heat, light, or sound) from a surface. **2.** To mirror or become mirrored. **3.** To manifest as a result of one's actions. **4.** To think or consider seriously. **5.** To bring blame or reproach. [< L *reflectere,* to bend back.] —**re•flec'tion** *n.* —**re•flec'tive** *adj.* —**re•flec'tive•ly** *adv.*

re•flec•tor (rĭ-flĕk'tər) *n.* **1.** That which reflects. **2.** A surface that reflects radiation.

re•flex (rē'flĕks') *adj.* **1.** Turned, thrown, or bent backward. **2.** *Physiol.* Designating an involuntary action or response, as a sneeze, blink, or hiccup. —*n.* (rē'flĕks'). **1.** Reflection or an image produced by reflection. **2.** An unlearned, involuntary, or instinctive response to a stimulus.

re•flex•ive (rĭ-flĕk'sĭv) *adj. Gram.* **1.** Designating a verb having an identical subject and direct object, as *dressed* in *She dressed herself.* **2.** Designating the pronoun used as the direct object in the preceding example. —**re•flex'ive** *n.* —**re•flex'ive•ly** *adv.* —**re•flex'ive•ness** *n.*

re•for•est (rē-fôr'ĭst, -fŏr'ĭst) *v.* To replant with forest trees. —**re'for•es•ta'tion** *n.*

re-form (rē-fôrm') *v.* To form again.

re•form (rĭ-fôrm') *v.* **1.** To improve, as by alteration. **2.** To abolish malpractice in. **3.** To give up or cause to abandon immoral practices. —*n.* **1.** A change for the better. **2.** A movement that attempts to improve social and political conditions without revolutionary change. **3.** Moral improvement. —**re•for'ma•tive** *adj.* —**re•formed'** *adj.* —**re•form'er** *n.*

ref•or•ma•tion (rĕf'ər-mā'shən) *n.* **1.** The act of reforming or state of being reformed. **2.**

Reformation. A 16th-century movement resulting in the separation of the Protestant churches from the Roman Catholic Church.
re•for•ma•to•ry (rĭ-fôr'mə-tôr'ē, -tōr'ē) *n., pl.* **-ries.** A penal institution for juvenile and first offenders.
re•fract (rĭ-frăkt') *v.* To deflect by refraction. [L *refringere* (pp *refractus*), to break off.]
re•frac•tion (rĭ-frăk'shən) *n.* The deflection of a propagating wave, as of light or sound, at the boundary between two mediums with different characteristics. **—re•frac'tive** *adj.* **—re•frac'tive•ness, re'frac•tiv'i•ty** *n.*
re•frac•to•ry (rĭ-frăk'tə-rē) *adj.* **1.** Obstinate; unmanageable. **2.** Difficult to melt or work; resistant to heat. *—n., pl.* **-ries.** A material that does not significantly deform or change chemically at high temperatures.
re•frain¹ (rĭ-frān') *v.* To hold oneself back; forbear: *Kindly refrain from singing.* [< L *refrēnāre*, hold back, bridle.]
re•frain² (rĭ-frān') *n.* A phrase or verse repeated at intervals throughout a song or poem. [< OF *refraindre*, echo, to break off.]
re•fresh (rĭ-frĕsh') *v.* **1.** To revive or become revived, as with rest, food, or drink. **2.** To make cool, clean, or damp; freshen. **3.** To renew by stimulation: *refresh one's memory.* **—re•fresh'er** *n.* & *adj.* **—re•fresh'ing** *adj.*
re•fresh•ment (rĭ-frĕsh'mənt) *n.* **1.** The act of refreshing or state of being refreshed. **2.** Something that refreshes. **3. refreshments.** A light meal or snack.
re•frig•er•ant (rĭ-frĭj'ər-ənt) *adj.* Cooling or freezing; refrigerating. *—n.* A substance used to produce refrigeration, either as the working substance of a refrigerator or by direct absorption of heat.
re•frig•er•ate (rĭ-frĭj'ə-rāt') *v.* **-ated, -ating. 1.** To cool or chill (a substance). **2.** To preserve (food) by chilling. **—re•frig'er•a'tion** *n.*
re•frig•er•a•tor (rĭ-frĭj'ə-rā'tər) *n.* An apparatus for refrigerating and freezing food.
ref•uge (rĕf'yōōj) *n.* **1.** Protection or shelter, as from danger or hardship. **2.** A haven or sanctuary. **3.** Anything to which one may turn for help, relief, or escape. [< L *refugere*, flee back.]
ref•u•gee (rĕf'yŏŏ-jē') *n.* One who flees to find refuge, esp. one who escapes from political persecution.
re•ful•gent (rĭ-fŭl'jənt) *adj.* Shining radiantly; brilliant. [< L *refulgēre*, to flash back.] **—re•ful'gence** *n.* **—re•ful'gent•ly** *adv.*
re•fund (rĭ-fŭnd', rē'fŭnd') *v.* To return or repay; give back; reimburse. *—n.* (rē'fŭnd'). **1.** A repayment of funds. **2.** The amount repaid. **—re•fund'er** *n.*
re•fur•bish (rē-fûr'bĭsh) *v.* To make clean, bright, or fresh again; renovate.
re•fuse¹ (rĭ-fyōōz') *v.* **-fused, -fusing.** To decline to do, accept, give, or allow. [< L *refundere*, to pour back.] **—re•fus'al** *n.*
ref•use² (rĕf'yōōs) *n.* Anything discarded or rejected as useless or worthless; trash; rubbish.
re•fute (rĭ-fyōōt') *v.* **-futed, -futing.** To prove to be false or erroneous; disprove. [L *refutāre*, rebut, drive back.] **—re•fut'a•ble** *adj.* **—ref'u•ta'tion** (ref'yŏŏ-tā'shən) *n.* **—re•fut'er** *n.*
reg. 1. regent. **2.** regiment. **3.** region. **4.** register; registered. **5.** registrar. **6.** registry. **7.** regular. **8.** regulation.
re•gain (rē-gān') *v.* **1.** To get back again. **2.** To reach again. **—re•gain'er** *n.*
re•gal (rē'gəl) *adj.* Of or pertaining to a king; royal. [< L *rēx*, king.] **—re'gal•ly** *adv.*
re•gale (rĭ-gāl') *v.* **-galed, -galing. 1.** To delight or entertain; give pleasure to. **2.** To entertain sumptuously. **—re•gale'ment** *n.*
re•ga•lia (rĭ-gāl'yə, -gā'lē-ə) *pl.n. (often takes sing. v.).* **1.** The emblems and symbols of royalty. **2.** The rights and privileges of royalty. **3.** The distinguishing symbols of any rank, office, etc.
re•gard (rĭ-gärd') *v.* **1.** To observe closely. **2.** To look upon or consider in a particular way. **3.** To have great affection or admiration for. **4.** To relate, concern, or refer to. **5.** To take into account. **6.** To pay attention. *—n.* **1.** A look or gaze. **2.** Careful thought or attention; concern. **3.** Respect, affection, or esteem. **4. regards.** Good wishes: *send one's regards.* **5.** Reference or relation: *in regard to this case.* **6.** A particular point: *I agree in this regard.* [< OF *reguarder*, to look at, regard.]
re•gard•ing (rĭ-gär'dĭng) *prep.* In reference to; with respect to; concerning.
re•gard•less (rĭ-gärd'lĭs) *adj.* In spite of everything; anyway.
re•gat•ta (rĭ-gä'tə, -găt'ə) *n.* A boat race or an organized series of boat races. [It *regata*, gondola race.]
regd. registered.
re•gen•cy (rē'jən-sē) *n., pl.* **-cies. 1.** The office, area of jurisdiction, or government of a regent or regents. **2.** The period during which a regent governs.
re•gen•er•ate (rĭ-jĕn'ə-rāt') *v.* **-ated, -ating. 1.** To reform spiritually or morally. **2.** To form, construct, or create anew. *—adj.* (rĭ-jĕn'ər-ĭt). **1.** Spiritually or morally revitalized. **2.** Restored; refreshed; renewed. **—re•gen'er•a'tion** *n.* **—re•gen'er•a'tive** *adj.* **—re•gen'er•a'tor** *n.*
re•gent (rē'jənt) *n.* **1.** One who rules during the absence or disability of a sovereign. **2.** One acting as a ruler or governor. **3.** One serving on a board that governs an educational institution in the U.S. [< L *regere*, to rule.] **—re'gent** *adj.*
reg•i•cide (rĕj'ə-sīd') *n.* **1.** The killing of a king. **2.** One who kills a king. [L *rēx*, king.] **—reg'i•ci'dal** (-sīd'l) *adj.*
re•gime (rā-zhēm', rĭ-) *n.* **1.** A system of management of government; an administration. **2.** A regimen. [< L *regere*, to rule.]
reg•i•men (rĕj'ə-mən, -mĕn') *n.* **1.** Governmental rule or control. **2.** A systematic procedure of therapy.
reg•i•ment (rĕj'ə-mənt) *n.* A military unit of ground troops, consisting of several battalions. *—v.* (rĕj'ə-mĕnt'). **1.** To organize; systematize. **2.** To force uniformity and discipline upon. [< L *regere*, to rule.] **—reg'i•men'tal** *adj.* **—reg'i•men•ta'tion** *n.*
Re•gi•na (rĭ-jī'nə). The capital of Saskatchewan, Canada. Pop. 112,000.
re•gion (rē'jən) *n.* **1.** Any large, usually continuous segment of a surface or space; an area. **2.** An area of the body: *the abdominal region.* [< L *regiō*, direction, boundary.]
re•gion•al (rē'jən-əl) *adj.* **1.** Of, pertaining to, or characteristic of a large geographic region. **2.** Of, pertaining to, or characteristic of a particular region. **—re'gion•al•ly** *adv.*
reg•is•ter (rĕj'ĭ-stər) *n.* **1. a.** A formal or official recording of items, names, or actions. **b.** A book for such entries. **2.** A device that automatically registers a quantity or number. **3.** An adjustable device through which heated or cooled air is released into a room. **4.** A part of the range of a voice or instrument that is similar in timbre. *—v.* **1.** To enter in a register; enroll. **2.** To indicate, as on a scale. **3.** To show (emotion). **4.** To cause (mail) to be officially recorded by payment of a fee. **5.** To have one's name officially placed on a list of eligible voters. [< LL *regesta*, list.]
registered nurse. A graduate trained nurse who has passed a state registration examination.
reg•is•trar (rĕj'ĭ-strär', rĕj'ĭ-strär') *n.* One who keeps records, esp. in a college or university.
reg•is•tra•tion (rĕj'ĭ-strā'shən) *n.* **1.** A registering, as of voters or students. **2.** The number of persons registered; enrollment.
reg•is•try (rĕj'ĭ-strē) *n., pl.* **-tries. 1.** Registration. **2.** A place where registers are kept.
re•gress (rĭ-grĕs') *v.* To go back; return to a previous condition or state. *—n.* (rē'grĕs'). Return or withdrawal. [< L *regredī*, to go back.] **—re•gres'sive** *adj.*
re•gres•sion (rĭ-grĕsh'ən) *n.* **1.** Reversion; retrogression. **2.** Relapse to a less perfect or developed state.
re•gret (rĭ-grĕt') *v.* **-gretted, -gretting. 1.** To feel sorry, disappointed, or distressed about. **2.** To mourn. *—n.* **1.** Distress over a desire unfulfilled or an action performed or not performed. **2.** An expression of grief or disappointment. **3. regrets.** A courteous declining to accept an invitation. [< OF *regreter*, to lament.] **—re•gret'ful** *adj.* **—re•gret'ful•ly** *adv.* **—re•gret'ta•ble** *adj.*
regt. regiment.
reg•u•lar (rĕg'yə-lər) *adj.* **1.** Customary, usual, or normal. **2.** Orderly or symmetrical. **3.** Conforming to set procedure, principle, or discipline. **4.** Methodical; well-ordered. **5.** Occurring at fixed intervals; periodic. **6.** Constant; not varying. **7.** Proper. **8.** Complete; thorough: *a regular villain.* **9.** *Gram.* Belonging to a standard mode of inflection or conjugation. **10.** Belonging to a religious order and bound by its rules. **11.** *Geom.* **a.** Having equal sides and equal angles. **b.** Having faces that are congruent regular polygons and congruent polyhedral angles. **12.** Belonging to or constituting the permanent army of a nation. *—n.* A soldier belonging to a regular army. [< L *rēgulāris*, containing rules.] **—reg'u•lar'i•ty** (-lăr'ə-tē) *n.* **—reg'u•lar•ize'** (-lə-rīz') *v.* **(-ized, -izing). —reg'u•lar•ly** *adv.*
reg•u•late (rĕg'yə-lāt') *v.* **-lated, -lating. 1.** To control or direct according to a rule. **2.** To adjust in conformity to a specification or requirement. **3.** To adjust for accurate and proper functioning. **—reg'u•la'tive, reg'u•la•to'ry** (-lə-tôr'ē, -tōr'ē) *adj.* **—reg'u•la'tor** *n.*
reg•u•la•tion (rĕg'yə-lā'shən) *n.* **1.** A principle, rule, or law designed to govern behavior. **2.** A governmental order having the force of law. *—adj.* Prescribed in accordance with a rule.
re•gur•gi•tate (rē-gûr'jə-tāt') *v.* **-tated, -tating.** To pour back, esp. to cast up (partially digested food); vomit. [ML *regurgitāre*.] **—re•gur'gi•ta'tion** *n.*
re•ha•bil•i•tate (rē'hə-bĭl'ə-tāt') *v.* **-tated, -tating. 1.** To restore to good condition, as through education and therapy. **2.** To reinstate the good name of. **3.** To restore the former rank, privileges, or rights of. **—re'ha•bil'i•ta'tion** *n.* **—re'ha•bil'i•ta'tive** *adj.*
re•hash (rē-hăsh') *v.* To repeat or rework (old material). **—re'hash'** (rē'hăsh') *n.*
re•hear•ing (rē-hîr'ĭng) *n.* *Law.* A second or new consideration of a case.
re•hears•al (rĭ-hûr'səl) *n.* **1.** The act or process of rehearsing. **2.** A verbal repetition or recital.
re•hearse (rĭ-hûrs') *v.* **-hearsed, -hearsing. 1.** To practice in preparation for a public performance. **2.** To perfect or cause to perfect (an

action) by repetition. **3.** To retell. [< OF *rehercer,* to repeat.] —**re•hears'er** *n.*

Reich (rīk) *n.* Formerly, the territory or government of a German empire or republic. [< OHG *rīhhi,* realm.]

reign (rān) *n.* **1.** The exercise of sovereign power. **2.** The term during which sovereignty is held. **3.** Dominance or widespread influence. —*v.* **1.** To rule with sovereign power. **2.** To be prevalent. [< L *rēx,* a king.]

re•im•burse (rē'ĭm-bûrs') *v.* **-bursed, -bursing.** **1.** To repay. **2.** To compensate for money spent or losses incurred. —**re'im•burse'ment** *n.*

rein (rān) *n.* **1.** Often **reins.** Two narrow leather straps attached to the bit of a bridle and used by a rider to control a horse. **2.** Any means of restraint, check, or guidance. —**give (free) rein to.** To release from restraints. —*v.* **1.** To check or hold back. **2.** To guide or control. [< L *retinēre,* to RETAIN.]

re•in•car•nate (rē'ĭn-kär'nāt') *v.* **-nated, -nating.** To be reborn in another body. —**re'in•car•na'tion** *n.*

rein•deer (rān'dîr') *n.* A large deer of arctic regions, domesticated in the Old World. [< ON *hreindȳri.*]

re•in•force (rē'ĭn-fôrs', -fōrs') *v.* **-forced,-forcing.** **1.** To strengthen; support. **2.** To strengthen with additional troops or equipment. —**re'in•force'ment** *n.*

re•in•state (rē'ĭn-stāt') *v.* **-stated, -stating.** To restore to a previous condition or position. —**re'in•state'ment** *n.*

re•it•er•ate (rē-ĭt'ə-rāt') *v.* **-ated, -ating.** To say over again. [L *reiterāre.*] —**re•it'er•a'tion** *n.*

re•ject (rĭ-jĕkt') *v.* **1.** To refuse to accept, recognize, or make use of; repudiate. **2.** To refuse to grant; deny. **3.** To discard as defective or useless; throw away. —*n.* (rē'jĕkt). One that has been rejected. [< L *rejicere,* to throw back.] —**re•jec'tion** *n.*

re•joice (rĭ-jois') *v.* **-joiced, -joicing.** **1.** To feel or be joyful. **2.** To fill with joy. —**re•joic'er** *n.*

re•join¹ (rē'join') *v.* To come or join together again.

re•join² (rĭ-join') *v.* To respond; answer. [< OF *rejoindre.*]

re•join•der (rĭ-join'dər) *n.* An answer, esp. in response to a reply.

re•ju•ve•nate (rĭ-jōō'və-nāt') *v.* **-nated, -nating.** To restore the youthful vigor or appearance of. —**re•ju've•na'tion** *n.*

rel. **1.** relating. **2.** relative. **3.** released. **4.** religion; religious.

re•lapse (rĭ-lăps') *v.* **-lapsed, -lapsing.** To fall back or revert to a former state, esp. to regress after partial recovery from illness. —*n.* (rē'-lăps, rĭ-lăps'). The act or result of relapsing. [< L *relābī,* to slide back.]

re•late (rĭ-lāt') *v.* **-lated, -lating.** **1.** To narrate or tell. **2.** To bring into logical or natural association. **3.** To have relation or reference to. **4.** To interact with others meaningfully. [L *relātus.*] —**re•lat'er** *n.*

re•lat•ed (rĭ-lā'tĭd) *adj.* Connected, as by kinship, marriage, or common origin.

re•la•tion (rĭ-lā'shən) *n.* **1.** A logical or natural association between two or more things; relevance of one to another; connection. **2.** Connection by blood or marriage; kinship. **3.** A relative. **4.** The mode in which a person or thing is connected with another. **5. relations.** Business or diplomatic connections or associations. **6.** Reference; regard. **7.** A narration; account. —**re•la'tion•al** *adj.*

re•la•tion•ship (rĭ-lā'shən-shĭp') *n.* **1.** The condition or fact of being related. **2.** Kinship.

rel•a•tive (rĕl'ə-tĭv) *adj.* **1.** Relevant; connected; related. **2.** Considered in comparison to or relationship with something else. **3.** Dependent upon something else for significance; not absolute. **4.** *Gram.* Referring to or qualifying an antecedent. —*n.* **1.** One related by kinship. **2.** One that is relative. **3.** A relative term. [< L *relātus.*] —**rel'a•tive•ly** *adv.*

relative clause. A dependent clause introduced by a relative pronoun. In *He who hesitates is lost,* the relative clause is *who hesitates.*

relative pronoun. A pronoun that introduces a relative clause and has reference to an antecedent.

rel•a•tiv•i•ty (rĕl'ə-tĭv'ə-tē) *n.* **1.** The quality or state of being relative. **2.** *Phys.* **a. Special relativity. b. General relativity.**

re•lax (rĭ-lăks') *v.* **1.** To make or become lax or loose. **2.** To make or become less severe. **3.** To slacken. **4.** To relieve from strain. **5.** To take one's ease; rest. **6.** To become less formal or tense. —**re•lax'er** *n.*

re•lax•a•tion (rē'lăk'sā'shən) *n.* **1.** The act of relaxing or state of being relaxed. **2.** Recreation. **3.** The lengthening of inactive muscle or muscle fibers. —**re•lax'ant** *adj.* & *n.*

re•lay (rē'lā, rĭ-lā') *n.* **1.** A fresh team or crew to relieve others in work, a journey, etc. **2.** The act of relaying. **3.** A race between two teams, in which each team member runs a set part of the total race. **4.** A device that responds to a small current or voltage change by activating switches or other devices in an electric circuit. —*v.* **1.** To pass or send along from one group or station to another: *relay a message.* **2.** To supply with fresh relays. [< OF *relaier,* to relay, leave behind.]

re•lease (rĭ-lēs') *v.* **-leased, -leasing.** **1.** To set free, as from confinement or bondage; liberate. **2.** To free; unfasten. **3.** To allow performance, sale, publication, or circulation of. **4.** To relinquish, as a right or claim. —*n.* **1.** The act of releasing or state of being released. **2.** A device or catch for locking or releasing a mechanism. [< L *relaxāre,* to relax.] —**re•leas'er** *n.*

rel•e•gate (rĕl'ə-gāt') *v.* **-gated, -gating.** **1.** To consign, esp. to an obscure place, position, or condition. **2.** To assign to a particular category. **3.** To refer for decision or performance. **4.** To banish; exile. [L *relēgāre,* to send away.] —**rel'e•ga'tion** *n.*

re•lent (rĭ-lĕnt') *v.* To become softened or gentler in attitude or determination; abate. [< ML **relentāre.*]

re•lent•less (rĭ-lĕnt'lĭs) *adj.* **1.** Unyielding; pitiless. **2.** Steady and persistent. —**re•lent'less•ly** *adv.* —**re•lent'less•ness** *n.*

rel•e•vant (rĕl'ə-vənt) *adj.* Related to the matter at hand; pertinent. [< L *relevāre,* to lift up, RELIEVE.] —**rel'e•vance, rel'e•van•cy** *n.* —**rel'e•vant•ly** *adv.*

re•li•a•ble (rĭ-lī'ə-bəl) *adj.* Able to be relied upon; dependable. —**re•li'a•bil'i•ty, re•li'a•ble•ness** *n.* —**re•li'a•bly** *adv.*

re•li•ance (rĭ-lī'əns) *n.* **1.** The act of relying. **2.** Confidence; dependence; trust. **3.** One depended on. —**re•li'ant** *adj.*

rel•ic (rĕl'ĭk) *n.* **1.** Something that has survived the passage of time, esp., an object or custom whose original cultural environment has disappeared. **2.** A keepsake. **3.** An object of religious veneration. **4. relics.** Remains. [< L *relinquere,* to RELINQUISH.]

re•lief (rĭ-lēf') *n.* **1.** Ease from or lessening of pain or discomfort. **2.** Anything that lessens pain, anxiety, etc. **3.** Assistance given to the needy or aged. **4.** The projection of figures or forms from a flat background, as in sculpture. **5.** The variations in elevation of any area of the earth's surface.

re•lieve (rĭ-lēv') *v.* **-lieved, -lieving.** **1.** To lessen or alleviate; ease. **2.** To free from pain, anxiety, etc. **3.** To aid. **4.** To free from a specified duty by providing a substitute. **5.** To make less unpleasant or monotonous. **6.** To make distinct through contrast. [< L *relevāre,* to raise again.] —**re•liev'er** *n.*

re•lig•ion (rĭ-lĭj'ən) *n.* **1. a.** An organized system of beliefs and rituals centering on a supernatural being or beings. **b.** Adherence to such a system. **2.** A belief upheld or pursued with zeal and devotion. [< L *religiō,* bond between man and the gods.] —**re•lig'ious** *adj.*

re•lin•quish (rĭ-lĭng'kwĭsh) *v.* **1.** To retire from; leave; abandon. **2.** To put aside or desist from. **3.** To surrender; renounce. **4.** To release. [< L *relinquere,* to leave behind.] —**re•lin'quish•er** *n.* —**re•lin'quish•ment** *n.*

rel•ish (rĕl'ĭsh) *n.* **1.** An appetite for something; appreciation. **2.** Pleasure; zest. **3.** A spicy or savory condiment served with other food. **4.** The flavor of a food, esp. when appetizing. —*v.* **1.** To take pleasure in. **2.** To like the flavor of. [< L *relaxāre,* to loosen, relax.] —**rel'ish•a•ble** *adj.*

re•live (rē-lĭv') *v.* To undergo again, as an experience.

re•luc•tant (rĭ-lŭk'tənt) *adj.* Unwilling; averse. [< L *reluctārī,* to struggle against.] —**re•luc'tance, re•luc'tan•cy** (-tən-sē) *n.* —**re•luc'tant•ly** *adv.*

re•ly (rĭ-lī') *v.* **-lied, -lying.** —**rely on** (or **upon**). **1.** To depend. **2.** To trust confidently. [< L *religāre,* to bind back.]

re•main (rĭ-mān') *v.* **1.** To continue without change of condition, quality, or place. **2.** To stay or be left over after the removal, departure, or destruction of others. **3.** To be left as still to be dealt with: *A cure remains to be found.* **4.** To endure or persist. [< L *remanēre,* to stay behind.]

re•main•der (rĭ-mān'dər) *n.* **1.** Something left over after other parts have been taken away. **2. a.** In division, the dividend minus the product of the divisor and quotient. **b.** In subtraction, the difference between the minuend and subtrahend.

re•mains (rĭ-mānz') *pl.n.* **1.** All that is left after other parts have been taken away. **2.** A corpse.

re•mand (rĭ-mănd') *v.* To send or order back, as someone in custody to prison, to another court, etc. [< LL *remandāre,* to send back word.] —**re•mand'ment** *n.*

re•mark (rĭ-märk') *v.* **1.** To say or write briefly and casually as a comment. **2.** To take notice of; observe. —*n.* **1.** The act of noticing or observing; mention. **2.** A casual comment.

re•mark•a•ble (rĭ-mär'kə-bəl) *adj.* **1.** Worthy of notice. **2.** Extraordinary; uncommon. —**re•mark'a•bly** *adv.*

Rem•brandt (rĕm'brănt). 1606–1669. Dutch painter and graphic artist.

re•me•di•al (rĭ-mē'dē-əl) *adj.* **1.** Supplying a remedy. **2.** Intended to correct something, esp. study or reading habits. —**re•me'di•al•ly** *adv.*

rem•e•dy (rĕm'ə-dē) *n., pl.* **-dies.** **1.** Something, as medicine or therapy, that relieves pain, cures disease, or corrects a disorder. **2.** Something that corrects any evil, fault, or error. —*v.* **-died, -dying.** **1.** To relieve or cure. **2.** To counteract or rectify. [< L *remedium,* medicine.]

re•mem•ber (rĭ-mĕm′bər) *v.* **1.** To recall to the mind; think of again. **2.** To retain in the mind. **3.** To keep (someone) in mind. **4.** To mention (someone) to another as sending greetings. [< LL *rememorārī,* to remember again.] **—re•mem′ber•a•ble** *adj.* **—re•mem′ber•er** *n.*

re•mem•brance (rĭ-mĕm′brəns) *n.* **1.** The act of remembering or state of being remembered. **2.** A memorial. **3.** The length of time over which one's memory extends. **4.** Something remembered. **5.** A memento or souvenir. **6.** **remembrances.** Greetings.

re•mind (rĭ-mīnd′) *v.* To cause (someone) to remember. [RE- + MIND.] **—re•mind′er** *n.*

rem•i•nisce (rĕm′ə-nĭs′) *v.* **-nisced, -niscing.** To recollect and tell of past experiences or events.

rem•i•nis•cence (rĕm′ə-nĭs′əns) *n.* **1.** The act or process of recalling the past. **2.** A memory. **3.** Often **reminiscences.** A narration of past experiences.

rem•i•nis•cent (rĕm′ə-nĭs′ənt) *adj.* **1.** Having the quality of or containing reminiscence. **2.** Tending to recall or talk of the past. [< L *reminiscī,* to recollect.]

re•miss (rĭ-mĭs′) *adj.* Lax in attending to duty; negligent. [< L *remissus,* slack.] **—re•miss′ness** *n.*

re•mis•sion (rĭ-mĭsh′ən) *n.* The act of remitting or condition of being remitted.

re•mit (rĭ-mĭt′) *v.* **-mitted, -mitting.** **1.** To send (money). **2. a.** To cancel (a penalty or punishment). **b.** To pardon; forgive. **3.** To relax; slacken. **4.** To diminish; abate. [< L *remittere,* to send back, release.]

re•mit•tance (rĭ-mĭt′əns) *n.* Money or credit sent to someone.

rem•nant (rĕm′nənt) *n.* **1.** Something left over; a remainder. **2.** A surviving trace or vestige. [< OF *remanoir, remaindre,* to remain.]

re•mod•el (rē-mŏd′l) *v.* To remake with a new structure; renovate. **—re•mod′el•er** *n.*

re•mon•strance (rĭ-mŏn′strəns) *n.* The act or an instance of remonstrating.

re•mon•strate (rĭ-mŏn′strāt′) *v.* **-strated, -strating.** To say or plead in protest, objection, or reproof. [ML *remōnstrāre,* to demonstrate.] **—re′mon•stra′tion** (rē′mŏn-strā′shən, rĕm′ən-) *n.* **—re•mon′stra•tive** (-strə-tĭv) *adj.*

re•morse (rĭ-môrs′) *n.* Moral anguish arising from repentance for past misdeeds; bitter regret. [< L *remorsus,* a biting back.] **—re•morse′ful** *adj.* **—re•morse′ful•ly** *adv.*

re•morse•less (rĭ-môrs′lĭs) *adj.* Having no pity or compassion; merciless.

re•mote (rĭ-mōt′) *adj.* **-moter, -motest.** **1.** Located far away. **2.** Distant in time. **3.** Barely discernible; slight. **4.** Distantly related: *a remote descendant.* **5.** Distant in manner; aloof. [L *remōtus,* pp of *removēre,* to move back.] **—re•mote′ly** *adv.* **—re•mote′ness** *n.*

re•move (rĭ-mo͞ov′) *v.* **-moved, -moving.** **1.** To move from a position occupied; convey from one place to another. **2.** To take away; extract; do away with. **3.** To dismiss from office. **4.** To change one's residence; move. **—***n.* **1.** The act of removing. **2.** Distance or degree away or apart. [< L *removēre,* to move back.] **—re•mov′a•ble** *adj.* **—re•mov′al** *n.*

re•mu•ner•ate (rĭ-myo͞o′nə-rāt′) *v.* **-ated, -ating.** To pay (a person) for goods provided, services rendered, or losses incurred. [L *remūnerāre.*] **—re•mu′ner•a′tion** *n.* **—re•mu′ner•a′tive** *adj.*

ren•ais•sance (rĕn′ə-säns′, -zäns′) *n.* **1.** A rebirth; revival. **2. Renaissance. a.** The humanistic revival of art, literature, and learning in Europe. **b.** The period of this revival, roughly from the 14th through the 16th century. **3.** Often **Renaissance.** Any similar period of revived intellectual or artistic achievement. [< L *renascī,* to be born again.]

re•nal (rē′nəl) *adj.* Of, pertaining to, or in the region of the kidneys. [< L *rēnēs,* kidneys.]

re•nas•cence (rĭ-năs′əns, -nā′səns) *n.* A rebirth; renaissance.

rend (rĕnd) *v.* **rent** or **rended, rending.** **1.** To tear apart or into pieces violently; split. **2.** To remove forcibly. **3.** To penetrate and disturb as if by tearing. [< OE *rendan.* See **rendh-.**] **—rend′er** *n.*

ren•der (rĕn′dər) *v.* **1.** To submit: *render a bill.* **2.** To give or make available: *render assistance.* **3.** To give what is due. **4.** To represent in a verbal or artistic form. **5.** To translate. **6.** To cause to become; make: *renders me helpless.* **7.** To liquefy (fat) by heating. [< OF *rendre,* to give back.] **—ren′der•er** *n.*

ren•dez•vous (rän′dā-vo͞o′, rän′də-) *n., pl.* **-vous** (-vo͞oz′). **1.** A prearranged meeting place. **2.** The meeting itself. **3.** A popular gathering place. **—***v.* To meet together at a specified time and place. [< OF *rendez vous,* "present yourselves."]

ren•di•tion (rĕn-dĭsh′ən) *n.* The act or result of rendering, as: **a.** An interpretation or performance of a musical score or dramatic piece. **b.** A translation.

ren•e•gade (rĕn′ə-găd′) *n.* **1.** One who rejects his religion or allegiance for another. **2.** An outlaw. [< ML *renegāre,* to deny.]

re•nege (rĭ-nĭg′, -nĕg′, -nēg′) *v.* **-neged, -neging.** To fail to carry out a promise or commitment. [ML *renegāre,* to deny.] **—re•neg′er** *n.*

re•new (rĭ-n/y/o͞o′) *v.* **1.** To make new or as if new again; restore. **2.** To take up again; resume. **3.** To grant or obtain for the extension of: *renew a contract.* **4.** To replenish. [RE- + NEW.] **—re•new′a•ble** *adj.* **—re•new′al** *n.*

ren•net (rĕn′ĭt) *n.* An extract from the lining of a calf's stomach, used to curdle milk in making cheese or junket. [< OE **rynet.*]

ren•nin (rĕn′ĭn) *n.* A milk-coagulating enzyme produced from rennet. [RENN(ET) + -IN.]

Re•noir (rĕn′wär′), **Pierre Auguste.** 1841–1919. French painter.

re•nounce (rĭ-nouns′) *v.* **-nounced, -nouncing.** **1.** To give up (a title or activity), esp. by formal announcement. **2.** To reject; disown. [< L *renūntiāre,* to bring back word, protest against.] **—re•nounce′ment** *n.*

ren•o•vate (rĕn′ə-vāt′) *v.* **-vated, -vating.** To restore to an earlier condition. [L *renovāre.*] **—ren′o•va′tion** *n.* **—ren′o•va′tor** *n.*

re•nown (rĭ-noun′) *n.* The quality of being widely honored and acclaimed. [< OF *renomer,* to name again, make famous.] **—re•nowned′** *adj.*

rent¹ (rĕnt) *n.* Periodic payment made by one in return for the right to use the property of another. **—***v.* **1.** To pay for and obtain use of (another's property). **2.** To be for rent. [< VL **rendere,* to render.]

rent² (rĕnt). Alternate *p.t. & p.p.* of **rend.** **—***n.* An opening made by rending; rip.

rent•al (rĕnt′l) *n.* **1.** An amount paid out or taken in as rent. **2.** An act of renting. **3.** Property rented.

re•nun•ci•a•tion (rĭ-nŭn′sē-ā′shən) *n.* The act or practice of renouncing.

re•or•der (rē-ôr′dər) *v.* **1.** To rearrange. **2.** To order (the same goods) again.

re•or•gan•ize (rē-ôr′gə-nīz′) *v.* **-ized, -izing.** To organize again or anew. **—re•or′gan•i•za′tion** *n.*

rep (rĕp) *n.* A ribbed or corded fabric. [F *reps.*]

rep. **1.** repair. **2.** report. **3.** reporter. **4.** representative. **5.** republic.

Rep. **1.** representative. **2.** republic. **3.** Republican (Party).

re•pair¹ (rĭ-pâr′) *v.* To restore to sound condition after damage or injury. **—***n.* **1.** The work or act of repairing. **2.** General condition after use or repairing: *in good repair.* **3.** Often **repairs.** An instance of repairing. [< L *reparāre.*] **—re•pair′a•ble** *adj.* **—re•pair′er** *n.*

re•pair² (rĭ-pâr′) *v.* To betake oneself. [< OF *repairer,* to return.]

rep•a•ra•tion (rĕp′ə-rā′shən) *n.* **1.** The act or process of making amends. **2.** Something done or paid to make up for. **3. reparations.** Compensation required from a defeated nation for damage or injury during a war. [< L *reparāre,* REPAIR.] **—re•par′a•tive** (rĭ-păr′ə-tĭv), **re•par′a•to′ry** (-tôr′ē, -tōr′ē) *adj.*

rep•ar•tee (rĕp′ər-tē′, -ər-tā′, -är-tē′, -är-tā′) *n.* **1.** A swift, witty reply. **2.** Conversation characterized by such replies. [< F *repartir,* to reply readily.]

re•past (rĭ-păst′, -päst′) *n.* A meal, or the food eaten or provided at a meal. [< LL *repascere,* to feed again.]

re•pay (rĭ-pā′) *v.* **1.** To pay back (money). **2.** To pay (someone) back, either in return or in requital. **3.** To make or do in return: *repay a call.* **—re•pay′a•ble** *adj.* **—re•pay′ment** *n.*

re•peal (rĭ-pēl′) *v.* To withdraw or annul officially or formally. [< OF *rapeler.*] **—re•peal′** *n.* **—re•peal′er** *n.*

re•peat (rĭ-pēt′) *v.* **1.** To say or do (something) again. **2.** To manifest or express in the same way or words: *History repeats itself.* **—***n.* **1.** The act of repeating. **2.** Something repeated. [< L *repetere,* to go back to, seek again.] **—re•peat′er** *n.*

re•peat•ed (rĭ-pē′tĭd) *adj.* Said, done, or occurring again and again. **—re•peat′ed•ly** *adv.*

re•pel (rĭ-pĕl′) *v.* **-pelled, -pelling.** **1.** To drive back; ward off or keep away. **2.** To cause aversion or distaste in. **3.** To be incapable of absorbing or mixing with. **4.** To present an opposing force to: *Electric charges of the same sign repel one another.* [< L *repellere.*]

re•pel•lent (rĭ-pĕl′ənt) *adj.* **1.** Serving or tending to repel. **2.** Resistant to some substance. **—***n.* **1.** A substance used to repel insects. **2.** A substance for making a surface resistant to something.

re•pent (rĭ-pĕnt′) *v.* **1.** To feel regret for (what one has done or failed to do). **2.** To feel contrition for one's sins and to abjure sinful ways. [< OF *repentir.*] **—re•pen′tance** *n.* **—re•pen′tant** *adj.* **—re•pent′er** *n.*

re•per•cus•sion (rē′pər-kŭsh′ən) *n.* **1.** An indirect effect produced by an event or action. **2.** A reciprocal action. [< L *repercutere,* to cause to rebound.] **—re′per•cus′sive** *adj.*

rep•er•toire (rĕp′ər-twär, -twôr) *n.* Also **rep•er•to•ry** (-tôr′ē, -tōr′ē). **1.** The stock of songs, plays, etc., that a person or group is prepared to perform. **2.** The skills or accomplishments of a person or group. [< LL *repertōrium,* repertory.]

rep•er•to•ry (rĕp′ər-tôr′ē, -tōr′ē) *n., pl.* **-ries.** **1.** A repertoire. **2.** A theatrical company that presents plays from a specified repertoire. [< L *reperīre,* to find out, find again.]

rep•e•ti•tion (rĕp′ə-tĭsh′ən) *n.* **1.** The act of repeating. **2.** Something repeated.

rep•e•ti•tious (rĕp′ə-tĭsh′əs) *adj.* Characterized by repetition, esp. needless repetition. **—rep′e•ti′tious•ly** *adv.* **—rep′e•ti′tious•ness** *n.*

re•pet•i•tive (rĭ-pĕt′ə-tĭv) *adj.* Characterized

by repetition. —**re•pet'i•tive•ly** *adv.* —**re•pet'i•tive•ness** *n.*

re•phrase (rē-frāz') *v.* To state in a new or different way.

repl. replacement.

re•place (rĭ-plās') *v.* **1.** To put back in place. **2.** To take or fill the place of. —**re•place'a•ble** *adj.* —**re•place'ment** *n.* —**re•plac'er** *n.*

re•play (rē-plā') *v.* To play (a record, video tape, etc.) again. —**re'play'** *n.*

re•plen•ish (rĭ-plĕn'ĭsh) *v.* To fill or make complete again. [< OF *replenir.*] —**re•plen'ish•er** *n.* —**re•plen'ish•ment** *n.*

re•plete (rĭ-plēt') *adj.* Plentifully supplied; abounding. [< L *replēre,* to refill.]

rep•li•ca (rĕp'lə-kə) *n.* A copy or close reproduction. [< It *replicare,* to repeat.]

re•ply (rĭ-plī') *v.* **-plied, -plying.** To say or give as an answer. —*n., pl.* **-plies.** An answer; response. [< OF *replier,* to fold back, reply.] —**re•pli'er** *n.*

re•port (rĭ-pôrt') *n.* **1.** An account that is prepared or presented, usually in formal or organized form. **2.** Rumor. **3.** Reputation. **4.** An explosive noise. —*v.* **1.** To make or present an account of (something). **2.** To relate or tell about; present. **3.** To complain about or make known to the proper authorities. **4.** To serve as a reporter. **5.** To present oneself: *report for duty.* [< L *reportāre,* "to carry back."] —**re•port'a•ble** *adj.*

re•port•ed•ly (rĭ-pôr'tĭd-lē, rĭ-pōr'-) *adv.* By report; supposedly.

re•port•er (rĭ-pôr'tər, rĭ-pōr'-) *n.* A person who reports, esp. a writer of news stories.

re•pose[1] (rĭ-pōz') *n.* **1. a.** The act of resting; a rest. **b.** The state of being at rest; relaxation. **2.** Calmness; tranquillity. —*v.* **-posed, -posing.** **1.** To lie at rest; relax. **2.** To lie supported by something. [< LL *repausāre.*]

re•pose[2] (rĭ-pōz') *v.* **-posed, -posing.** To place, as faith or trust in. [< RE- + POSE.]

re•pos•i•to•ry (rĭ-pŏz'ə-tôr'ē, -tōr'ē) *n., pl.* **-ries.** A place where things can be put for safekeeping. [< L *repōnere* (pp *repositus*), to put back.]

re•pos•sess (rē'pə-zĕs') *v.* To regain possession of (property). —**re'pos•ses'sion** *n.*

rep•re•hend (rĕp'rĭ-hĕnd') *v.* To reprove; censure. [< L *reprehendere,* to rebuke, hold back.]

rep•re•hen•si•ble (rĕp'rĭ-hĕn'sə-bəl) *adj.* Deserving of rebuke or censure; blameworthy. [< L *reprehendere,* to REPREHEND.] —**rep're•hen'si•bly** *adv.*

rep•re•sent (rĕp'rĭ-zĕnt') *v.* **1.** To stand for; symbolize. **2.** To depict; portray. **3.** To serve as the authorized delegate or agent for. **4.** To serve as an example of. [< L *repraesentāre,* show, bring back.]

rep•re•sen•ta•tion (rĕp'rĭ-zĕn-tā'shən, rĕp'rĭ-zən-) *n.* **1.** The act of representing or state of being represented. **2.** That which represents. **3.** The right of being represented by delegates in a legislative body.

rep•re•sen•ta•tive (rĕp'rĭ-zĕn'tə-tĭv) *n.* **1.** A person or thing serving as an example or type. **2.** One who serves as a delegate, esp. a member of a governmental body, usually legislative. —*adj.* **1.** Of or pertaining to government by representation. **2.** Exemplary of others in the same class; typical.

re•press (rĭ-prĕs') *v.* **1.** To hold back; restrain. **2.** To suppress; quell. **3.** To force (memories, ideas, or fears) into the subconscious mind. [< L *reprimere,* to press back.] —**re•pres'sion** *n.* —**re•pres'sive** *adj.*

re•prieve (rĭ-prēv') *v.* **-prieved, -prieving.** To postpone the punishment of. —*n.* The postponement of a punishment. [< L *reprehendere,* to hold back, REPREHEND.]

rep•ri•mand (rĕp'rə-mănd', -mänd') *v.* To rebuke or censure severely. —*n.* A severe or formal rebuke. [< L *reprimere,* to REPRESS.]

re•pri•sal (rĭ-prī'zəl) *n.* Retaliation for an injury with the intent of inflicting at least as much injury in return. [< L *reprehensus,* pp of *reprehendere,* to REPREHEND.]

re•proach (rĭ-prōch') *v.* To blame for something; rebuke. —*n.* **1.** Rebuke; blame. **2.** Disgrace; shame. [< VL **repropiāre,* bring back near.] —**re•proach'a•ble** *adj.*

re•proach•ful (rĭ-prōch'fəl) *adj.* Expressing reproach or blame. —**re•proach'ful•ly** *adv.*

rep•ro•bate (rĕp'rə-bāt') *n.* A morally unprincipled person. [< LL *reprobāre,* to reprove.]

re•pro•duce (rē'prə-d/y/o͞os') *v.* **-duced, -ducing.** **1.** To produce a counterpart, image, or copy of. **2.** To produce offspring. **3.** To produce again or anew; re-create. **4.** To undergo copying. —**re'pro•duc'tion** (-dŭk'shən) *n.* —**re'pro•duc'tive** (-dŭk'tĭv) *adj.*

re•proof (rĭ-pro͞of') *n.* An act or expression of reproving.

re•prove (rĭ-pro͞ov') *v.* **-proved, -proving.** **1.** To rebuke; scold. **2.** To find fault with. [< LL *reprobāre.*] —**re•prov'ing•ly** *adv.*

rept. **1.** receipt. **2.** report.

rep•tile (rĕp'tĭl, -tīl') *n.* Any of various cold-blooded vertebrates covered with scales or horny plates, as a lizard, snake, or turtle. [< L *repere,* to creep.] —**rep•til'i•an** (-tĭl'ē-ən, -tĭl'yən) *adj.* & *n.*

re•pub•lic (rĭ-pŭb'lĭk) *n.* **1.** Any political order that is not a monarchy. **2.** A constitutional form of government, esp. a democratic one. [< L *rēspublica,* "public matter."]

re•pub•li•can (rĭ-pŭb'lĭ-kən) *adj.* **1.** Of, pertaining to, or characteristic of a republic. **2.** **Republican.** Of, pertaining to, characteristic of, or belonging to the Republican Party of the U.S. —*n.* **1.** One who favors a republican form of government. **2.** **Republican.** A member of the Republican Party of the U.S.

Republican Party. One of the two major political parties of the U.S.

re•pu•di•ate (rĭ-pyo͞o'dē-āt') *v.* **-ated, -ating.** **1.** To reject the validity of. **2.** To refuse to recognize, acknowledge, or pay. [L *repudiāre,* to reject, cast off.] —**re•pu'di•a'tion** *n.*

re•pug•nant (rĭ-pŭg'nənt) *adj.* Offensive; distasteful; repulsive. [< L *repugnāre,* to fight against.] —**re•pug'nance** *n.*

re•pulse (rĭ-pŭls') *v.* **-pulsed, -pulsing.** **1.** To drive back; repel. **2.** To repel with rudeness, coldness, or denial. —*n.* **1.** The act of repulsing or state of being repulsed. **2.** Rejection; refusal. [L *repulsus,* pp of *repellere,* to REPEL.]

re•pul•sion (rĭ-pŭl'shən) *n.* **1.** The act of repulsing or condition of being repulsed. **2.** Extreme aversion or dislike.

re•pul•sive (rĭ-pŭl'sĭv) *adj.* **1.** Causing extreme dislike or aversion; disgusting. **2.** Tending to repel or drive off. —**re•pul'sive•ly** *adv.* —**re•pul'sive•ness** *n.*

rep•u•ta•ble (rĕp'yə-tə-bəl) *adj.* Having a good reputation; honorable. —**rep'u•ta•bly** *adv.*

rep•u•ta•tion (rĕp'yə-tā'shən) *n.* **1.** The general estimation in which one is held by the public. **2.** The state of being held in high repute. **3.** A specific character or trait ascribed to one: *a reputation for courtesy.* [< L *reputāre,* to consider, REPUTE.]

re•pute (rĭ-pyo͞ot') *v.* **-puted, -puting.** To assign a reputation to: *He was reputed to be honest.* —*n.* **1.** Reputation. **2.** A good reputation. [< L *reputāre,* to count over, consider.]

re•put•ed (rĭ-pyo͞o'tĭd) *adj.* Generally considered or supposed. —**re•put'ed•ly** *adv.*

req. **1.** require; required. **2.** requisition.

re•quest (rĭ-kwĕst') *v.* **1.** To ask for. **2.** To ask (a person) to do something. —*n.* **1.** An expressed desire; the act of asking. **2.** That which is asked for. [< L *requīrere,* to seek again, REQUIRE.]

re•qui•em (rĕk'wē-əm, rē'kwē-) *n.* **1.** **Requiem.** *R.C.Ch.* A mass for a deceased person. **2.** A hymn, composition, or service for the dead. [< L *requiēs,* rest, "after-rest."]

re•quire (rĭ-kwīr') *v.* **-quired, -quiring.** **1.** To have use for as a necessity; need. **2.** To demand; insist upon. [< L *requīrere,* to seek again, inquire.] —**re•quire'ment** *n.*

req•ui•site (rĕk'wə-zĭt) *adj.* Required; absolutely needed. —*n.* A necessity; something absolutely essential. —**req'ui•site•ly** *adv.*

req•ui•si•tion (rĕk'wə-zĭsh'ən) *n.* A formal written request for something needed. —*v.* To demand, as for military needs.

re•quite (rĭ-kwīt') *v.* **-quited, -quiting.** **1.** To make repayment or return for. **2.** To avenge. [RE- + obs *quite,* to repay, var of QUIT.] —**re•qui'tal** *n.* —**re•quit'er** *n.*

re•run (rē'rŭn') *n.* A repetition of a recorded performance, as a television program.

res. **1.** research. **2.** reserve. **3.** residence. **4.** resolution.

re•scind (rĭ-sĭnd') *v.* To void; repeal. [L *rēscindere,* to cut off, abolish.] —**re•scind'a•ble** *adj.* —**re•scis'sion** (-sĭzh'ən) *n.*

res•cue (rĕs'kyo͞o) *v.* **-cued, -cuing.** To save, as from danger. —*n.* An act of saving; deliverance. [< VL **reexcutere,* to drive away, shake off.] —**res'cu•er** *n.*

re•search (rĭ-sûrch', rē'sûrch) *n.* Scholarly or scientific investigation or inquiry. [< OF *recercher,* to seek out, search again.] —**re•search'** *v.* —**re•search'er** *n.*

re•sec•tion (rĭ-sĕk'shən) *n.* The surgical removal of part of an organ or structure.

re•sem•blance (rĭ-zĕm'bləns) *n.* The condition or quality of resembling something.

re•sem•ble (rĭ-zĕm'bəl) *v.* **-bled, -bling.** To have a similarity to. [< OF *resembler.*]

re•sent (rĭ-zĕnt') *v.* To feel indignantly aggrieved at (an act, situation, or person). [Obs *resentir,* to feel strongly.] —**re•sent'ful** *adj.* —**re•sent'ful•ly** *adv.* —**re•sent'ment** *n.*

res•er•va•tion (rĕz'ər-vā'shən) *n.* **1.** The act of reserving. **2.** A limiting qualification, condition, or exception. **3.** A tract of land set apart by the Federal government for a special purpose. **4.** An arrangement by which accommodations are secured in advance.

re•serve (rĭ-zûrv') *v.* **-served, -serving.** **1.** To save for future use. **2.** To set apart for a particular person or use. **3.** To retain: *I reserve the right to disagree.* —*n.* **1.** Something saved for future use. **2.** The state of being set aside or saved: *funds held in reserve.* **3.** Reticence; discretion. **4.** A reservation of public land. **5.** Often **reserves.** The part of a country's armed forces subject to call in an emergency. [< L *reservāre,* to keep back.]

re•served (rĭ-zûrvd') *adj.* **1.** Held in reserve. **2.** Characterized by self-restraint or reticence.

re•serv•ist (rĭ-zûr'vĭst) *n.* A member of a military reserve.

res•er•voir (rĕz'ər-vwär', -vwôr', -vôr') *n.* **1.** A body of water stored in a natural or artificial lake. **2.** A chamber for storing a fluid.

resh (rĕsh) *n.* The 20th letter of the Hebrew alphabet, representing *r.*

re•side (rĭ-zīd′) *v.* **-sided, -siding.** 1. To live in a place. 2. To be inherently present; exist (with *in*). [< L *residēre,* "to sit back," "remain sitting."] —**re•sid′er** *n.*

res•i•dence (rĕz′ə-dəns, -dĕns′) *n.* 1. The place in which one lives; a dwelling. 2. The act or a period of residing somewhere.

res•i•den•cy (rĕz′ə-dən-sē, -dĕn′sē) *n., pl.* **-cies.** The period during which a physician receives specialized clinical training.

res•i•dent (rĕz′ə-dənt, -dĕnt′) *n.* 1. One who makes his home in a particular place. 2. A physician serving his period of residency.

res•i•den•tial (rĕz′ə-dĕn′shəl) *adj.* Of, characterized by, suitable for, or limited to dwellings.

re•sid•u•al (rĭ-zĭj′o͞o-əl) *adj.* Remaining as a residue.

res•i•due (rĕz′ə-d/y/o͞o′) *n.* Matter remaining after completion of a process such as evaporation, combustion, distillation, or filtration. [< L *residēre,* RESIDE.]

re•sign (rĭ-zīn′) *v.* 1. To give over or submit (oneself). 2. To give up (a position); quit. 3. To relinquish (a privilege, right, or claim). [< L *resignāre,* to unseal, resign.]

res•ig•na•tion (rĕz′ĭg-nā′shən) *n.* 1. The act of resigning. 2. A written or oral statement that one is resigning a position or office. 3. Acceptance; submission.

re•signed (rĭ-zīnd′) *adj.* Feeling or marked by resignation; acquiescent. —**re•sign′ed•ly** (rĭ-zī′nĭd-lē) *adv.*

re•sil•ience (rĭ-zĭl′yəns) *n.* Also **re•sil•ien•cy** (-yən-sē). 1. The ability to recover quickly, as from illness; buoyancy. 2. The property of a material that enables it to resume an original shape after being bent, stretched, etc. [< L *resilīre,* to leap back.] —**re•sil′ient** *adj.*

res•in (rĕz′ĭn) *n.* 1. A plant substance, as rosin or amber, used in lacquers, varnishes, adhesives, etc. 2. Any of numerous physically similar polymerized synthetics or chemically modified natural resins used in making plastics. [< Gk *rhētinē.*] —**res′in•ous** (rĕz′ə-nəs) *adj.*

re•sist (rĭ-zĭst′) *v.* 1. To strive or work against; fight off. 2. To withstand. [< L *resistere,* to stand back, resist.] —**re•sist′er** *n.*

re•sis•tance (rĭ-zĭs′təns) *n.* 1. The act of resisting or capacity to resist. 2. Any force that tends to oppose or retard motion. 3. The opposition to electric current characteristic of a medium, substance, or circuit element.

re•sis•tor (rĭ-zĭs′tər) *n.* An electric circuit element used to provide resistance.

res•o•lute (rĕz′ə-lo͞ot′) *adj.* Characterized by firmness or determination. [< L *resolvere,* to RESOLVE.] —**res′o•lute′ly** *adv.*

res•o•lu•tion (rĕz′ə-lo͞o′shən) *n.* 1. The state or quality of being resolute. 2. A course of action determined or decided upon. 3. A formal statement of a decision put before or adopted by an assembly. 4. The action of separating something into its constituent parts.

re•solve (rĭ-zŏlv′) *v.* **-solved, -solving.** 1. To make a firm decision about. 2. To cause (a person) to reach a decision. 3. To decide or express by formal vote. 4. To separate (something) into constituent parts. 5. To find a solution to. —*n.* 1. Firmness of purpose; resolution. 2. A determination or decision. [< L *resolvere,* to release, resolve.] —**re•solv′a•ble** *adj.* —**re•solv′er** *n.*

re•solved (rĭ-zŏlvd′) *adj.* Firmly determined; resolute.

res•o•nance (rĕz′ə-nəns) *n.* 1. The enhancement of the response of an electric or mechanical system to a periodic driving force when the driving frequency is equal to the natural undamped frequency of the system. 2. The intensification and prolongation of a tone by sympathetic vibration. [< L *resonāre,* to RESOUND.] —**res′o•nant** *adj.*

res•o•nate (rĕz′ə-nāt′) *v.* **-nated, -nating.** 1. To exhibit resonance or resonant effects. 2. To resound. —**res′o•na′tor** *n.*

re•sort (rĭ-zôrt′) *v.* To seek assistance or relief; have recourse: *resorted to censorship.* —*n.* 1. A place frequented by people for relaxation or recreation. 2. A person or thing turned to for aid or relief: *a last resort.* [< OF *resortir,* to come out again, to resort.]

re•sound (rĭ-zound′) *v.* 1. To be filled with sound; reverberate. 2. To sound loudly; ring. [< L *resonāre,* to sound again, echo.] —**re•sound′ing** *adj.* —**re•sound′ing•ly** *adv.*

re•source (rē′sôrs′, rĭ-sôrs′) *n.* 1. An available supply that can be drawn upon when needed. 2. An ability to deal with a situation effectively. 3. Often **resources.** Available capital; assets. [< L *resurgere,* to rise or surge again.]

re•source•ful (rĭ-sôrs′fəl) *adj.* Readily able to act effectively. —**re•source′ful•ness** *n.*

resp. respective; respectively.

re•spect (rĭ-spĕkt′) *v.* 1. To feel or show esteem for. 2. To show consideration for. 3. To relate or refer to; concern. —*n.* 1. A feeling of deferential regard. 2. The state of being regarded with esteem. 3. A particular aspect, feature, or detail. 4. Relation; reference. 5. **respects.** Polite expressions of deference: *pay one's respects.* [L *respectus,* pp of *respicere,* to regard, look back.] —**re•spect′ful** *adj.* —**re•spect′ful•ly** *adv.* —**re•spect′ful•ness** *n.*

re•spect•a•ble (rĭ-spĕk′tə-bəl) *adj.* 1. Meriting respect; worthy. 2. Proper or conventional in conduct. 3. Of moderately good quality. —**re•spect′a•bil′i•ty** *n.* —**re•spect′a•bly** *adv.*

re•spect•ing (rĭ-spĕk′tĭng) *prep.* In relation to; concerning.

re•spec•tive (rĭ-spĕk′tĭv) *adj.* Pertaining to two or more persons or things regarded individually: *They took their respective seats.*

re•spec•tive•ly (rĭ-spĕk′tĭv-lē) *adv.* Singly in the order designated or mentioned.

res•pi•ra•ble (rĕs′pər-ə-bəl, rĭ-spīr′-) *adj.* 1. Fit for breathing. 2. Capable of breathing. —**res′pi•ra•bil′i•ty** *n.*

res•pi•ra•tion (rĕs′pə-rā′shən) *n.* 1. The act or process of inhaling and exhaling. 2. The metabolic process by which an organism assimilates oxygen and releases carbon dioxide and other products. —**res′pi•ra•to′ry** (rĕs′pər-ə-tôr′ē, -tōr′ē, rĭ-spīr′ə-) *adj.*

res•pi•ra•tor (rĕs′pə-rā′tər) *n.* 1. An apparatus used in administering artificial respiration. 2. A screenlike device worn over the mouth or nose, or both, to protect the respiratory tract.

re•spire (rĭ-spīr′) *v.* **-spired, -spiring.** 1. To inhale and exhale. 2. To undergo the metabolic process of respiration. [< L *respīrāre,* to breathe again.]

res•pite (rĕs′pĭt) *n.* A temporary cessation or postponement, usually of something disagreeable. [< L *respectus,* a looking back, a refuge.]

re•splend•ent (rĭ-splĕn′dənt) *adj.* Having splendor; brilliant. [< L *resplendēre,* to shine brightly.] —**re•splen′dence** *n.*

re•spond (rĭ-spŏnd′) *v.* 1. To reply; answer. 2. To act in return or in answer. 3. To react positively or cooperatively. [L *respondēre,* "to promise in return."]

re•sponse (rĭ-spŏns′) *n.* 1. A reply or answer. 2. A reaction to a stimulus.

re•spon•si•bil•i•ty (rĭ-spŏn′sə-bĭl′ə-tē) *n., pl.* **-ties.** 1. The state or fact of being responsible. 2. A person or thing that one is answerable for; a duty or obligation.

re•spon•si•ble (rĭ-spŏn′sə-bəl) *adj.* 1. Involving personal ability to act without superior authority: *a responsible position.* 2. Being the source or cause of something (with *for*). 3. Able to be trusted or depended upon; reliable. 4. Accountable; answerable (with *to*). [< L *respondēre,* to RESPOND.] —**re•spon′si•bly** *adv.*

re•spon•sive (rĭ-spŏn′sĭv) *adj.* Readily reacting to suggestions, appeals, etc. —**re•spon′sive•ly** *adv.* —**re•spon′sive•ness** *n.*

rest[1] (rĕst) *n.* 1. The act or state of ceasing from work, activity, or motion. 2. Ease or refreshment resulting from sleep or the cessation of an activity. 3. Sleep. 4. *Mus.* An interval of silence. —*v.* 1. To refresh (oneself) by rest. 2. To sleep. 3. To be, become, or remain temporarily still, quiet, or inactive. 4. a. To be supported: *rests against the wall.* b. To place or lay: *rest it against the wall.* 5. To be imposed as a responsibility or burden. 6. To depend or rely. [< OE *reste* < Gmc **rast-.*] —**rest′er** *n.*

rest[2] (rĕst) *n.* 1. That which is left over; remainder. 2. Those remaining: *The rest are coming later.* —*v.* To be or continue to be: *rest easy.* [< OF *rester,* to remain.]

res•tau•rant (rĕs′tər-ənt, -tə-ränt′) *n.* A place where meals are served to the public. [F, "restorative."]

res•tau•ra•teur (rĕs′tər-ə-tûr′) *n.* The manager of a restaurant.

rest•ful (rĕst′fəl) *adj.* Affording tranquillity.

res•ti•tu•tion (rĕs′tə-t/y/o͞o′shən) *n.* 1. The act of restoring to the rightful owner something taken away, lost, or surrendered. 2. The act of compensating for loss, damage, or injury; indemnification.

res•tive (rĕs′tĭv) *adj.* 1. Impatient or nervous under restriction or delay; restless. 2. Difficult to control; unruly. [< L *restāre,* to keep back.] —**res′tive•ly** *adv.* —**res′tive•ness** *n.*

rest•less (rĕst′lĭs) *adj.* 1. Without quiet or rest: *a restless night.* 2. Incapable of or opposed to resting or relaxing: *a restless child.* —**rest′less•ly** *adv.* —**rest′less•ness** *n.*

res•to•ra•tion (rĕs′tə-rā′shən) *n.* 1. The act of restoring or state of being restored. 2. That which has been restored, such as a renovated building.

re•stor•a•tive (rĭ-stôr′ə-tĭv, rĭ-stōr′-) *adj.* Tending to restore something, such as health. —*n.* Something that restores.

re•store (rĭ-stôr′, -stōr′) *v.* **-stored, -storing.** 1. To bring back into existence or use. 2. To bring back to a previous, normal condition. 3. To put (someone) back in a prior position. 4. To give or bring back; make restitution of. [< L *restaurāre.*] —**re•stor′er** *n.*

re•strain (rĭ-strān′) *v.* 1. To control; check. 2. To limit or restrict. [< L *restringere,* to bind back, RESTRICT.]

re•straint (rĭ-strānt′) *n.* 1. The act of restraining. 2. Any influence that restrains. 3. An instrument or means of restraining. 4. Control of feelings; constraint.

re•strict (rĭ-strĭkt′) *v.* To hold down or keep within limits. [L *restringere* (pp *restrictus*), to bind back.] —**re•stric′tive** *adj.*

re•stric•tion (rĭ-strĭk′shən) *n.* 1. The act of limiting or restricting or state of being limited or restricted. **2.** That which restrains or restricts; a limitation.

re•sult (rĭ-zŭlt′) *v.* **1.** To occur or exist as a consequence of a particular cause. **2.** To end in a particular way. *—n.* The consequence of a particular action, operation, or course; outcome. [< L *resultāre,* to leap back, rebound.]

re•sul•tant (rĭ-zŭl′tənt) *adj.* Issuing or following as a consequence or result.

re•sume (rĭ-zo͞om′) *v.* **-sumed, -suming. 1.** To begin again; continue after interruption. **2.** To occupy or take again. [< L *resūmere,* to take up again.] **—re•sump′tion** (-zŭmp′shən) *n.*

rés•u•mé (rĕz′o͞o-mā′, rĕz′o͞o-mā′) *n.* A summary, esp. a summary of experience submitted with a job application. [< OF *resumer,* resume.]

re•sur•gent (rĭ-sûr′jənt) *adj.* Rising or tending to rise again. **—re•sur′gence** *n.*

res•ur•rect (rĕz′ə-rĕkt′) *v.* **1.** To bring back to life. **2.** To bring back into practice, notice, or use.

res•ur•rec•tion (rĕz′ə-rĕk′shən) *n.* **1.** A returning to life. **2.** A returning to practice, notice, or use. **3. the Resurrection.** The rising again of Christ on the third day after the Crucifixion. [< L *resurgere,* to rise again.]

re•sus•ci•tate (rĭ-sŭs′ə-tāt′) *v.* **-tated, -tating.** To return to life or consciousness; revive. [L *resuscitāre.*] **—re•sus′ci•ta′tion** *n.*

re•tail (rē′tāl′) *n.* The sale of commodities in small quantities to the consumer. *—v.* To sell at retail. [< OF *retailler,* to cut up.] **—re′tail′** *adj.* **—re′tail′er** *n.*

re•tain (rĭ-tān′) *v.* **1.** To keep in one's possession. **2.** To continue to practice, employ, etc. **3.** To keep in a particular place, condition, or position. **4.** To hire (a lawyer) by the payment of a fee. **5.** To keep in one's service or pay. **6.** To keep in mind; remember. [< L *retinēre.*] **—re•tain′ment** *n.*

re•tain•er (rĭ-tā′nər) *n.* **1.** A person or thing that retains. **2.** One who served in a noble household as an attendant. **3.** The fee paid to engage the services of a lawyer, consultant, etc.

re•tal•i•ate (rĭ-tăl′ē-āt′) *v.* **-ated, -ating.** To return like for like, esp. to return evil for evil. [L *retaliāre,* repay in kind.] **—re•tal′i•a′tion** *n.* **—re•tal′i•a•to′ry** (-ē-ə-tôr′ē, -tōr′ē) *adj.*

re•tard (rĭ-tärd′) *v.* To impede or delay. [< L *retardāre.*]

re•tar•date (rĭ-tär′dāt′, -dĭt) *n.* A mentally retarded person.

re•tar•da•tion (rē′tär-dā′shən) *n.* **1.** The act of retarding or condition of being retarded. **2. a.** That which retards; a delay or hindrance. **b.** The amount or time of delay or hindrance. **3. Mental deficiency.**

re•tard•ed (rĭ-tär′dĭd) *adj.* Slow or deficient in mental or emotional development.

retch (rĕch) *v.* To vomit or attempt to vomit. [< OE *hrǣcan,* to cough up phlegm. See **ker-**[2].]

re•ten•tion (rĭ-tĕn′shən) *n.* **1.** The act of retaining or condition of being retained. **2.** The capacity to remember. **—re•ten′tive** *adj.*

ret•i•cent (rĕt′ə-sənt) *adj.* Not inclined to speak; uncommunicative. [< L *reticēre,* to keep silent.] **—ret′i•cence** *n.*

ret•i•na (rĕt′n-ə) *n., pl.* **-nas** or **-nae** (-n-ē′). A delicate multilayer light-sensitive membrane lining the inner eyeball and connected by the optic nerve to the brain. [< ML *retina.*] **—ret′i•nal** *adj.*

ret•i•nue (rĕt′n-/y/o͞o′) *n.* The attendants accompanying a person of rank. [< OF *retenir,* to retain.]

re•tire (rĭ-tīr′) *v.* **-tired, -tiring. 1.** To go away; depart, as for rest or seclusion. **2.** To go to bed. **3.** To withdraw from business or public life. **4.** To remove from active service: *retire an old career officer.* **5.** To withdraw troops. **6.** To take out of circulation: *retire bonds.* **7.** *Baseball.* To put out (a batter). [< OF *retirer,* to draw back.] **—re•tire′ment** *n.*

re•tired (rĭ-tīrd′) *adj.* Withdrawn from business or public life.

re•tir•ing (rĭ-tī′rĭng) *adj.* Shy and modest; reticent. **—re•tir′ing•ly** *adv.*

re•tort[1] (rĭ-tôrt′) *v.* **1.** To reply, esp. to answer in a quick, direct manner. **2.** To present a counterargument. **3.** To return in kind; pay back. *—n.* A quick, incisive reply. [L *retorquēre* (pp *retortus*), to bend back.]

re•tort[2] (rĭ-tôrt′, rē′tôrt′) *n.* A closed laboratory vessel with an outlet tube, used for distillation, sublimation, or decomposition by heat. [< L *retortus,* "bent back."]

re•touch (rē-tŭch′) *v.* To add new details or touches to (a photograph, painting, etc.) for correction or improvement.

re•trace (rē-trās′) *v.* To go back over: *retraced his steps.* **—re•trace′a•ble** *adj.*

re•tract (rĭ-trăkt′) *v.* **1.** To take back or disavow (a statement, offer, etc.). **2.** To draw back or in: *The turtle retracted its head.* [< L *retrahere* (pp *retractus*), to draw back.] **—re•tract′a•ble** *adj.* **—re•trac′tion** *n.*

re•trac•tile (rĭ-trăk′tĭl) *adj.* Capable of being drawn back or in: *retractile claws.*

re•tread (rē′trĕd′) *n.* A worn automobile tire fitted with a new tread.

re•treat (rĭ-trēt′) *n.* **1.** The act of going backward or withdrawing. **2.** A quiet, private, or secure place; refuge. **3.** A period of seclusion or solitude. **4.** The withdrawal of a military force from a dangerous position or from an enemy attack. *—v.* To withdraw; go back. [< L *retrahere,* to RETRACT.]

re•trench (rĭ-trĕnch′) *v.* **1.** To cut down; reduce. **2.** To curtail expenses; economize. [< OF *retrenchier.*] **—re•trench′ment** *n.*

ret•ri•bu•tion (rĕt′rə-byo͞o′shən) *n.* Something given or demanded in repayment, esp. punishment. [< L *retribuere,* to pay back.] **—re•trib′u•tive** (rĭ-trĭb′yə-tĭv), **re•trib′u•to′ry** (-tôr′ē, -tōr′ē) *adj.*

re•trieve (rĭ-trēv′) *v.* **-trieved, -trieving. 1.** To get back; regain. **2.** To find and carry back; fetch. **3.** To find and bring back game. [< OF *retrover,* to find again.] **—re•triev′a•ble** *adj.* **—re•triev′al** *n.*

re•triev•er (rĭ-trē′vər) *n.* A dog bred or trained to retrieve game.

retro–. *comb. form.* **1.** Backward or back. **2.** Situated behind. [< L *retrō,* backward, behind.]

ret•ro•ac•tive (rĕt′rō-ăk′tĭv) *adj.* Influencing or applying to a period prior to enactment. [< L *retroagere,* to drive back.]

ret•ro•grade (rĕt′rə-grād′) *adj.* **1.** Moving or tending backward. **2.** Reverting to an earlier or inferior condition. [< L *retrōgradus.*]

ret•ro•gress (rĕt′rə-grĕs′, rĕt′rə-grĕs′) *v.* To return to an earlier, inferior, or less complex condition. [L *retrōgradī* (pp *retrōgressus*), to go backward.] **—ret′ro•gres′sion** *n.* **—ret′ro•gres′sive** *adj.*

ret•ro•rock•et (rĕt′rō-rŏk′ĭt) *n.* A rocket engine used to retard, arrest, or reverse motion.

ret•ro•spect (rĕt′rə-spĕkt′) *n.* A review or contemplation of things in the past. [< L *retrōspicere,* to look back at.] **—ret′ro•spec′tive** *adj.* **—ret′ro•spec′tive•ly** *adv.*

re•turn (rĭ-tûrn′) *v.* **1.** To go or come back, as to an earlier condition or place. **2.** To answer; respond. **3.** To send, put, or carry back. **4.** To give in reciprocation: *She returned his praise.* **5.** To yield (profit or interest). **6.** To deliver (a verdict). **7.** To re-elect, as to a legislative body. *—n.* **1.** The act of going, coming, bringing, or sending back. **2. a.** Something brought or sent back. **b.** Something that goes or comes back. **3.** Often **returns.** A profit or yield, as from investments. **4.** Often **returns.** A report on the vote in an election. *—adj.* **1.** Of or for coming back: *the return voyage.* **2.** Given, sent, or done in reciprocation or exchange: *a return visit.* [< VL **retornāre,* to turn back.] **—re•turn′a•ble** *adj.*

re•un•ion (rē-yo͞on′yən) *n.* **1.** The act of reuniting or state of being reunited. **2.** A gathering of the members of a group who have been separated.

re•u•nite (rē′yo͞o-nīt′) *v.* To bring or come together again.

rev (rĕv). *Informal. n.* A revolution, as of a motor. *—v.* **revved, revving.** To increase the speed of a motor.

rev. 1. revenue. **2.** reverse; reversed. **3.** review; reviewed. **4.** revise; revision. **5.** revolution. **6.** revolving.

Rev. 1. Revelation (New Testament). **2.** reverend (title).

re•vamp (rē-vămp′) *v.* **1.** To reconstruct or restore. **2.** To vamp (a shoe or boot) anew.

re•veal (rĭ-vēl′) *v.* **1.** To divulge or disclose; make known. **2.** To bring to view; expose. [< L *revēlāre,* to unveil, reveal.]

rev•eil•le (rĕv′ə-lē) *n.* The sounding of a bugle in the morning to awaken soldiers. [< OF *reveiller,* to rouse.]

rev•el (rĕv′əl) *v.* **-eled** or **-elled, -eling** or **-elling. 1.** To take great pleasure or delight (with *in*). **2.** To engage in uproarious festivities. *—n.* Often **revels.** A noisy festivity. [< OF *reveler,* to make noise, "rebel."] **—rev′el•er** *n.*

rev•e•la•tion (rĕv′ə-lā′shən) *n.* **1.** Something revealed. **2.** An act of revealing. **3.** A manifestation of divine will or truth. **4. Revelation.** The last book in the New Testament, attributed to Saint John.

rev•el•ry (rĕv′əl-rē) *n., pl.* **-ries.** Boisterous merrymaking.

re•venge (rĭ-vĕnj′) *v.* **-venged, -venging.** To inflict punishment in return for (injury or insult); avenge. *—n.* **1.** Vengeance; retaliation. **2.** The act of taking vengeance. **3.** A desire for revenge. [< LL *revindicāre,* to avenge.] **—re•venge′ful** *adj.*

rev•e•nue (rĕv′ə-n/y/o͞o) *n.* **1.** The income of a government. **2.** Yield from property or investment. [< OF *revenir,* to return.]

re•ver•ber•ate (rĭ-vûr′bə-rāt′) *v.* **-ated, -ating.** To re-echo; resound. [L *reverberāre,* to cause to rebound.] **—re•ver′ber•a′tion** *n.*

re•vere (rĭ-vîr′) *v.* **-vered, -vering.** To regard with awe, great respect, or devotion. [L *reverērī.*] **—re•ver′er** *n.*

Re•vere (rĭ-vîr′), **Paul.** 1735–1818. American silversmith and Revolutionary patriot.

rev•er•ence (rĕv′ər-əns) *n.* **1.** A feeling of profound awe and respect. **2.** An act of showing respect. **3.** The state of being revered. **4. Reverence.** A title of respect for a clergyman: *Your Reverence.*

rev•er•end (rĕv′ər-ənd) *adj.* **1.** Deserving of reverence. **2.** Often **Reverend.** Designating a member of the clergy. [< L *reverērī,* REVERE.]

rev•er•ent (rĕv′ər-ənt) *adj.* Feeling or expressing reverence. **—rev′er•ent•ly** *adv.*

rev•er•en•tial (rĕv'ə-rĕn'shəl) *adj.* Expressing reverence; reverent.

rev•er•ie (rĕv'ər-ē) *n.* **1.** Abstracted musing; daydreaming. **2.** A daydream. [< OF *rever,* to dream.]

re•ver•sal (rĭ-vûr'səl) *n.* **1.** An act or instance of reversing. **2.** The state of being reversed.

re•verse (rĭ-vûrs') *adj.* **1.** Turned backward in position, direction, or order. **2.** Causing backward movement: *a reverse gear.* —*n.* **1.** The opposite or contrary of something. **2.** The back or rear of something, as of a coin. **3.** A change in fortune from better to worse. **4.** A mechanism for reversing movement, as a gear in an automobile. —*v.* **-versed, -versing. 1.** To turn to the opposite direction or tendency. **2.** To exchange the positions of; transpose. **3.** *Law.* To revoke or annul (a decision or decree). **4.** To turn or move in the opposite direction. [< L *reversus,* pp of *revertere,* REVERT.] —**re•vers'er** *n.*

re•vers•i•ble (rĭ-vûr'sə-bəl) *adj.* Capable of being reversed. —**re•vers'i•bil'i•ty, re•vers'i•ble•ness** *n.* —**re•vers'i•bly** *adv.*

re•vert (rĭ-vûrt') *v.* To return to a former condition, practice, or belief. [< L *revertere,* to turn back.] —**re•ver'sion** (-vûr'zhən) *n.*

re•view (rĭ-vyōō') *v.* **1.** To look over or study (material) again. **2.** To look back on. **3.** To examine with an eye to criticism or correction. **4.** To write or give a critical report on (a new work or performance). **5.** To subject to a military inspection. —*n.* **1.** A re-examination or reconsideration. **2.** A retrospective survey. **3.** A restudying of subject matter. **4.** An inspection or examination for the purpose of evaluating. **5.** A report or essay giving a critical estimate of a work or performance. [OF *revoir,* to see again, look over.] —**re•view'er** *n.*

re•vile (rĭ-vīl') *v.* **-viled, -viling.** To denounce with abusive language. [< OF *reviler.*]

re•vise (rĭ-vīz') *v.* **-vised, -vising. 1.** To prepare a newly edited version of (a text). **2.** To change or modify. [L *revīsere,* to look back.] —**re•vi'sion** (-vĭzh'ən) *n.*

Revised Standard Version. A modern translation of the Bible existing in both Protestant and Catholic editions.

re•vi•tal•ize (rē-vīt'l-īz') *v.* **-ized, -izing.** To impart new life or vigor to; restore the vitality of. —**re•vi'tal•i•za'tion** *n.*

re•viv•al (rĭ-vī'vəl) *n.* **1.** The act of reviving or condition of being revived. **2.** A restoration to use, acceptance, or vigor. **3.** A new presentation of an old play or motion picture. **4.** A meeting or series of meetings for the purpose of reawakening religious faith.

re•vive (rĭ-vīv') *v.* **-vived, -viving. 1.** To bring or come back to life or consciousness. **2.** To impart or regain vigor or spirit. **3.** To restore to use. [< LL *revīvere.*]

re•viv•i•fy (rē-vĭv'ə-fī') *v.* **-fied, -fying.** To impart new life to. —**re•viv'i•fi•ca'tion** *n.*

re•voke (rĭ-vōk') *v.* **-voked, -voking.** To annul by recalling or withdrawing; cancel; rescind: *revoke a license.* [< L *revocāre,* to call back.] —**re•vok'er** *n.*

re•volt (rĭ-vōlt') *v.* **1.** To institute or take part in a rebellion against authority. **2.** To fill or be filled with disgust or abhorrence. —*n.* An uprising against authority; rebellion. [< L *revolvere,* to roll back, REVOLVE.]

re•volt•ing (rĭ-vōl'tĭng) *adj.* Causing disgust; repulsive. —**re•volt'ing•ly** *adv.*

rev•o•lu•tion (rĕv'ə-lōō'shən) *n.* **1. a.** Orbital motion about a point, esp. as distinguished from axial rotation. **b.** A turning or rotational motion about an axis. **c.** A single complete cycle of such orbital or axial motion. **2.** A momentous change in any situation. **3.** A sudden political overthrow brought about from within a given system. [< L *revolvere,* REVOLVE.]

rev•o•lu•tion•ar•y (rĕv'ə-lōō'shə-nĕr'ē) *adj.* Of, pertaining to, or bringing about a revolution. —*n., pl.* **-ies.** A militant in the struggle for revolution.

Revolutionary War. The **American Revolution.**

rev•o•lu•tion•ize (rĕv'ə-lōō'shə-nīz') *v.* **-ized, -izing.** To bring about a radical change in; alter drastically.

re•volve (rĭ-vŏlv') *v.* **-volved, -volving. 1.** To orbit a central point. **2.** To turn on an axis; rotate. **3.** To recur in cycles or at periodic intervals. [< L *revolvere,* to roll back.] —**re•volv'a•ble** *adj.*

re•volv•er (rĭ-vŏl'vər) *n.* A pistol having a revolving cylinder with several cartridge chambers.

re•vue (rĭ-vyōō') *n.* A show consisting of skits, songs, and dances, often of a satirical nature. [< OF *revoir,* to REVIEW.]

re•vul•sion (rĭ-vŭl'shən) *n.* A sudden and strong change or reaction in feeling, esp. a feeling of violent disgust or loathing. [< L *revellere* (pp *revulsus*), to pull back or away.]

re•ward (rĭ-wôrd') *n.* **1.** Something given or received in recompense. **2.** Money offered for some special service, as for the return of something lost. —*v.* **1.** To bestow a reward on. **2.** To give a reward in return for. [< NF *rewarder,* "to look at."]

re•word (rē-wûrd') *v.* To state or express again in different words.

re•write (rē-rīt') *v.* To write again, esp. in a different form. —**re•writ'er** *n.*

Rey•kja•vík (rā'kyə-vēk'). The capital of Iceland. Pop. 75,000.

RF radio frequency.

RFD. rural free delivery.

Rh rhodium.

r.h. right hand.

rhap•so•dize (răp'sə-dīz') *v.* **-dized, -dizing.** To express oneself in a rhapsodic manner.

rhap•so•dy (răp'sə-dē) *n., pl.* **-dies. 1.** Exalted or excessively enthusiastic expression of feeling in speech or writing. **2.** *Mus.* A composition that is free or irregular in form. [< Gk *rhapsōidos,* "weaver of songs," rhapsodist.] —**rhap•sod'ic** (-sŏd'ĭk) *adj.* —**rhap'so•dist** *n.*

rhe•a (rē'ə) *n.* A large South American bird resembling the ostrich.

rhe•ni•um (rē'nē-əm) *n. Symbol* **Re** A rare dense, silvery-white metallic element with a very high melting point, used for electrical contacts and with tungsten for high-temperature thermocouples. Atomic number 75, atomic weight 186.2. [< L *Rhēnus,* the Rhine.]

rhe•o•stat (rē'ə-stăt') *n.* A variable electrical resistor used to regulate current. [Gk *rheos,* current + -STAT.]

rhet•o•ric (rĕt'ər-ĭk) *n.* The art of effective expression in speech or writing. [< Gk *rhētorikē,* rhetorical.]

rhe•tor•i•cal (rĭ-tôr'ĭ-kəl, rĭ-tŏr'-) *adj.* Concerned primarily with style or effect.

rhetorical question. A question to which no answer is expected or to which only one answer can be made.

rheum (rōōm) *n.* A watery or thin mucous discharge from the eyes or nose. [< Gk *rheuma,* stream, humor of the body, rheum.] —**rheum'y** *adj.*

rheu•mat•ic (rōō-măt'ĭk) *adj.* Of, pertaining to, or afflicted with rheumatism. —*n.* A person afflicted with rheumatism.

rheumatic fever. A severe infectious disease occurring chiefly in children and frequently resulting in permanent damage to the valves of the heart.

rheu•ma•tism (rōō'mə-tĭz'əm) *n.* **1.** Any of several pathological conditions of the muscles, tendons, joints, bones, or nerves, characterized by discomfort and disability. **2. Rheumatoid arthritis.** [< Gk *rheuma,* stream, flux, RHEUM.]

rheu•ma•toid arthritis (rōō'mə-toid'). A chronic disease marked by stiffness and inflammation of the joints.

Rh factor. Any of several substances on the surface of red blood cells that induce antigenic reactions with Rh negative blood cells. [First discovered in the blood of the *rhesus monkey,* a brownish monkey of India.]

Rhine (rīn). A river of W Europe.

rhine•stone (rīn'stōn') *n.* A colorless artificial gem of paste or glass. [Trans of F *caillou du Rhin.*]

rhi•noc•er•os (rī-nŏs'ər-əs) *n.* A large, thick-skinned African or Asian mammal with one or two upright horns on the snout. [< Gk *rhinokerōs,* "nose-horned."]

rhi•zome (rī'zōm') *n.* A rootlike plant stem sending out roots from its lower surface and leaves or shoots from its upper surface. [< Gk *rhizōma,* mass of roots of a tree.]

Rh negative. Lacking an **Rh factor.**

rho (rō) *n.* The 17th letter of the Greek alphabet, representing *r(rh).*

Rhode Island (rōd). A state of the NE U.S. Pop. 950,000. Cap. Providence.

Rho•de•sia (rō-dē'zhə). A self-governing British protectorate in central-south Africa. In 1965 it unilaterally declared its independence. Pop. 3,849,000. Cap. Salisbury. —**Rho•de'sian** *adj.* & *n.*

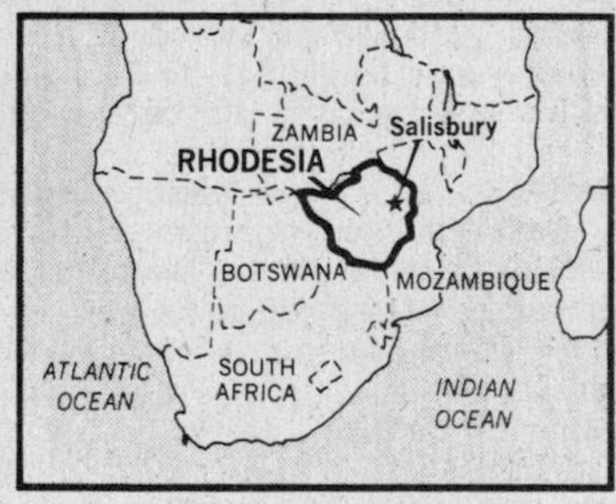

Rhodesia

rho•di•um (rō'dē-əm) *n. Symbol* **Rh** A hard, durable, silvery-white metallic element that is used to form high-temperature alloys with platinum and is plated on other metals to produce a durable corrosion-resistant coating. Atomic number 45, atomic weight 102.905. [< Gk *rhodon,* rose (color).]

rho•do•den•dron (rō'də-dĕn'drən) *n.* A shrub with evergreen leaves and clusters of variously colored flowers. [< Gk, "rose tree."]

rhom•bus (rŏm'bəs) *n., pl.* **-buses** or **-bi** (-bī'). An equilateral parallelogram. [< Gk *rhombos,* magic wheel, rhombus.] —**rhom'bic** (-bĭk) *adj.*

Rhône (rōn). A river of W Europe.

Rh positive. Containing an **Rh factor.**

rhu•barb (rōō'bärb') *n.* **1.** A plant with large leaves and long, fleshy, edible leafstalks. **2.** *Slang.* A quarrel. [Prob < ML *rha barbarum,* barbarian rhubarb.]

rhyme (rīm). Also **rime.** *n.* **1.** Correspondence

of terminal sounds of words or lines of verse. **2.** A rhyming poem or verse: *nursery rhyme.* **3.** A word that corresponds with another in terminal sound. —*v.* **rhymed, rhyming. 1.** To form a rhyme; correspond in sound. **2.** To make use of rhymes in composing verse. **3.** To use (a word or words) as a rhyme or rhymes. [< L *rhythmus,* rhythm.]

rhythm (rĭth'əm) *n.* **1. a.** Any kind of movement characterized by the regular recurrence of strong and weak elements: *the rhythm of the tides.* **b.** The pattern of this, as in verse. **2.** The element of music that derives mainly from the relative duration and intensity of sounds. [< Gk *rhuthmos,* recurring motion, measure, rhythm.] —**rhyth'mi•cal** (-mĭ-kəl), **rhyth'mic** *adj.* —**rhyth'mi•cal•ly** *adv.*

rhythm method. A birth-control method dependent on continence during ovulation.

R.I. Rhode Island.

ri•al (rē-ôl', -äl') *n.* **1.** The basic monetary unit of Iran. **2.** Variant of **riyal.**

rib (rĭb) *n.* **1.** One of a series of long, curved, paired bones extending from the spine to or toward the breastbone. **2.** A part or piece similar to a rib and serving to shape or support. **3.** A raised ridge, as in fabric. —*v.* **ribbed, ribbing. 1.** To shape or support with a rib or ribs. **2.** To make with ridges. **3.** *Slang.* To tease. [< OE. See **rebh-.**]

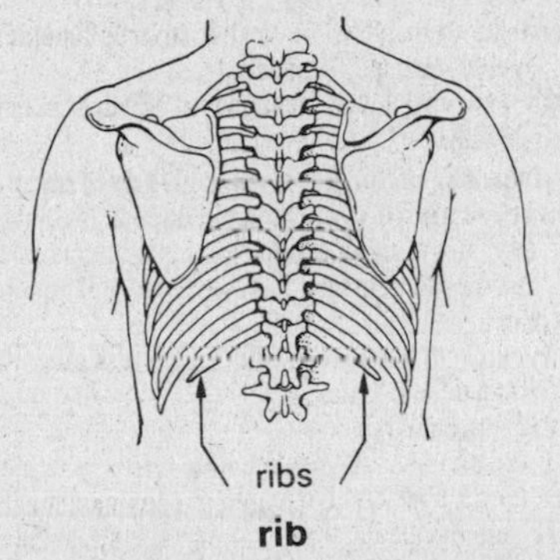

rib

rib•ald (rĭb'əld) *adj.* Pertaining to or indulging in vulgar, lewd humor. —*n.* A ribald person. [< OF *riber,* to be wanton.] —**rib'ald•ry** (-əl-drē) *n.*

rib•bon (rĭb'ən) *n.* **1.** A narrow strip or band of fine fabric, such as satin or velvet, finished at the edges and used for trimming or tying. **2. ribbons.** Tattered or ragged strips: *torn to ribbons.* **3.** An inked strip of cloth, as for a typewriter. [< MDu *ringhband,* necklace.]

ri•bo•fla•vin (rī'bō-flā'vĭn) *n.* A crystalline orange-yellow pigment, $C_{17}H_{20}O_6N_4$, the principal growth-promoting factor in the vitamin B_2 complex, found in milk, leafy vegetables, fresh meat, and egg yolks.

ri•bo•nu•cle•ic acid (rī'bō-n/y/o͞o-klē'ĭk). A universal polymeric constituent of all living cells, consisting of a single-stranded chain of alternating units, the structure and sequence of which are determinants of protein synthesis. [RIBO(SE) + NUCLEIC ACID.]

ri•bose (rī'bōs') *n.* A sugar, $C_5H_{10}O_5$, occurring as a component of nucleic acids. [< G *Ribon(säure),* acid from which ribose is obtained.]

ri•bo•some (rī'bə-sōm) *n.* A cytoplasmic particle that contains RNA and acts in protein synthesis.

rice (rīs) *n.* **1.** A cereal grass cultivated extensively in warm climates. **2.** The starchy edible seed of this grass. —*v.* **riced, ricing.** To sieve (food) to the consistency of rice. [< Gk *oruzon, oruza.*] —**ric'er** *n.*

rich (rĭch) *adj.* **1.** Possessing great wealth. **2.** Of great worth; valuable. **3.** Elaborate or sumptuous. **4.** Plentiful; abundant. **5.** Abounding in natural resources. **6.** Producing or yielding much. **7.** Containing a large proportion of tasty ingredients. **8.** Pleasing and satisfying to the senses. —*n.* **the rich.** Wealthy people collectively. [< OF *riche,* powerful, and OE *rīce.*] —**rich'ly** *adv.* —**rich'ness** *n.*

Ri•che•lieu (rē-shə-lyœ'), **Duc de.** 1585–1642. French cardinal and statesman.

rich•es (rĭch'ĭz) *pl.n.* Abundant wealth.

Rich•mond (rĭch'mənd). **1.** The capital of Virginia. Pop. 250,000. **2.** A borough of New York City, coextensive with Staten Island.

rick•ets (rĭk'ĭts) *n.* A deficiency disease resulting from a lack of vitamin D and from insufficient exposure to sunlight, characterized by defective bone growth. [< Gk *rakhitis,* a disease of the spine.]

rick•et•y (rĭk'ĭt-ē) *adj.* **-ier, -iest. 1.** Likely to break or fall apart; shaky. **2.** Of or having rickets. —**rick'et•i•ness** *n.*

ric•o•chet (rĭk'ə-shā', -shĕt') *v.* **-cheted** (-shād') or **-chetted** (-shĕt'ĭd), **-cheting** (-shā'ĭng) or **-chetting** (-shĕt'ĭng). To rebound at least once from a surface. [F.] —**ric'o•chet'** *n.*

rid (rĭd) *v.* **rid** or **ridded, ridding.** To free from something objectionable or undesirable. [< ON *rythja* < Gmc **rudjan.*]

rid•dance (rĭd'əns) *n.* —**good riddance.** A welcome removal of or deliverance from something. [RID + -ANCE.]

rid•den (rĭd'n). *p.p.* of **ride.** —*adj.* Dominated by: *grief-ridden.*

rid•dle¹ (rĭd'l) *v.* **-dled, -dling.** To pierce with numerous holes; perforate: *riddle with bullets.* [< OE *hriddel, hridder,* sieve.]

rid•dle² (rĭd'l) *n.* A question or problem requiring a clever answer or solution. [< OE *rǣdelse.*]

ride (rīd) *v.* **rode, ridden, riding. 1.** To sit on and be conveyed by an animal. **2.** To be conveyed in a vehicle. **3.** To travel over a surface: *This car rides well.* **4.** To float or move on or as on water. **5.** To sit on and drive. **6.** To be supported or carried upon. **7.** To take part in or do by riding: *rode his last race.* **8.** To cause to be carried: *rode him out of town.* **9.** To tease or ridicule. —*n.* **1.** An excursion or journey by any means of conveyance. **2.** In amusement parks, any of various structures in which persons ride for excitement. [< OE *rīdan.* See **reidh-.**]

rid•er (rī'dər) *n.* **1.** One who rides. **2.** A clause, usually having little relevance to the main issue, added to a legislative bill. **3.** An amendment or addition to a document or record.

ridge (rĭj) *n.* **1.** The long, narrow crest of something. **2.** A long, narrow land elevation. **3.** The horizontal line formed by the juncture of two sloping planes. **4.** Any narrow raised strip. —*v.* **ridged, ridging.** To mark with, form into, or provide with ridges. [< OE *hrycg.* See **sker-².**]

rid•i•cule (rĭd'ə-kyo͞ol') *n.* Words or actions intended to evoke contemptuous laughter at a person or thing. —*v.* **-culed, -culing.** To engage in ridicule. [< L *rīdiculus,* RIDICULOUS.]

ri•dic•u•lous (rĭ-dĭk'yə-ləs) *adj.* Deserving or inspiring ridicule; absurd or preposterous. [L *rīdiculōsus, rīdiculus,* laughable.] —**ri•dic'u•lous•ly** *adv.* —**ri•dic'u•lous•ness** *n.*

ri•el (rē-ĕl') *n.* The basic monetary unit of Cambodia.

rife (rīf) *adj.* **rifer, rifest. 1.** Widespread; prevalent. **2.** Abundant. **3.** Abounding: *a department rife with incompetents.* [< OE *rȳfe.*]

riff•raff (rĭf'răf') *n.* Worthless or disreputable persons. [< OF *rif et raf.*]

ri•fle¹ (rī'fəl) *n.* A firearm with a rifled bore, designed to be fired from the shoulder. —*v.* **-fled, -fling.** To cut spiral grooves within (a gun barrel). [< OF *rifler,* to file.]

ri•fle² (rī'fəl) *v.* **-fled, -fling. 1.** To search with intent to steal. **2.** To rob: *rifle a safe.* [< OF *rifler,* to scratch, file, plunder.] —**ri'fler** *n.*

rift (rĭft) *n.* **1. a.** *Geol.* A fault. **b.** A narrow fissure in rock. **2.** A break in friendly relations. [< Scand.]

rig (rĭg) *v.* **rigged, rigging. 1.** To fit out; equip. **2.** To equip (a ship) with rigging. **3.** To make in a makeshift manner. **4.** To manipulate dishonestly for personal gain. —*n.* **1.** The arrangement of masts, spars, and sails on a sailing vessel: *a square rig.* **2.** A vehicle with one or more horses harnessed to it. **3.** The special apparatus used for drilling oil wells. [Prob < Scand.]

Ri•ga (rē'gə). The capital of Latvia. Pop. 733,000.

rig•a•ma•role. Variant of **rigmarole.**

rig•ging (rĭg'ĭng) *n.* The system of ropes, chains, and tackle used to support and control the masts, sails, and yards of a sailing vessel.

right (rīt) *adj.* **1.** In accordance with justice, law, or morality; fitting; proper. **2.** In accordance with fact or truth. **3.** Most appropriate, desirable, or convenient: *the right time to act.* **4.** Sound or normal: *in one's right mind.* **5.** Intended to be worn facing outward: *the right side of cloth.* **6. a.** Of, pertaining to, or toward that side of the human body in which the liver is normally located. **b.** Of, pertaining to, or toward the corresponding side of something relative to the observer's point of view. **7.** Often **Right.** Of or tending toward conservative or reactionary political policies or views. —*n.* **1.** That which is just, morally good, legal, proper, or fitting. **2.** The right-hand side. **3. the Right.** A political group whose policies are conservative or reactionary. **4.** That which is due to anyone by law, tradition, or nature. **5.** A just or legal claim or title. —*adv.* **1.** Directly; straight: *right to the heart of the matter.* **2.** Properly; correctly: *The suit doesn't fit right.* **3.** Exactly; just: *happened right there.* **4.** Immediately: *She will be right down.* **5.** Completely: *The bullet went right through him.* **6.** According to law, morality, or justice. **7.** On or toward the right side or direction. **8.** Extremely: *answered right well.* **9.** —Used in certain titles: *the Right Reverend.* —*v.* **1.** To restore to or regain an upright or proper position or order. **2.** To redress: *right a wrong.* [< OE *riht.* See **reg-¹.**] —**right'ness** *n.*

right angle. A 90° angle.

right•eous (rī'chəs) *adj.* Meeting the standards of what is right and just. [< OE *rihtwīs.*] —**right'eous•ly** *adv.* —**right'eous•ness** *n.*

right•ful (rīt'fəl) *adj.* **1.** Right or proper; just. **2.** Having or held by a just or proper claim. —**right'ful•ly** *adv.* —**right'ful•ness** *n.*

right-hand (rīt'hănd') *adj.* **1.** Located on or directed toward the right side. **2.** Of, for, or done by the right hand. **3.** Helpful; reliable: *my right-hand man.*

right-hand•ed (rīt'hăn'dĭd) *adj.* **1.** Using the

right hand more easily than the left. **2.** Made to be used by the right hand.

right•ly (rīt′lē) *adv.* **1.** With correctness. **2.** Properly; suitably.

right of way. **1.** *Law.* **a.** The right to pass over property owned by another. **b.** The path or thoroughfare on which such passage is made. **2.** The strip of land over which highways, railroads, etc., are built. **3.** The customary or legal right of a person, vessel, or vehicle to pass in front of another.

right on *Slang.* Expressive of encouragement, approval, support, etc.

right triangle. A triangle containing a 90° angle.

rig•id (rĭ′jĭd) *adj.* **1.** Not bending; stiff; inflexible. **2.** Not moving; fixed. **3.** Harsh; severe. [< L *rigēre,* to be stiff.] **—ri•gid′i•ty** *n.*

rig•ma•role (rĭg′mə-rōl) *n.* Also **rig•a•ma•role** (-ə-mə-rōl). **1.** Confused or incoherent discourse; nonsense. **2.** A complicated and petty set of procedures. [< ME *Ragmane rolle,* scroll used in a medieval game.]

rig•or (rĭg′ər) *n.* **1.** Strictness or severity, as in temperament, action, or judgment. **2.** A harsh or trying circumstance; hardship. **3.** Strict precision; accuracy. [< L *rigēre,* to be stiff.] **—rig′or•ous** *adj.* **—rig′or•ous•ly** *adv.*

rig•or mor•tis (rĭg′ər môr′tĭs). Muscular stiffening following death. [L, "the stiffness of death."]

rile (rīl) *v.* **riled, riling.** **1.** To vex; anger. **2.** To stir up (liquid); roil. [Var of ROIL.]

rill (rĭl) *n.* A small brook; rivulet. [Du *ril* or LG *rille.*]

rim (rĭm) *n.* **1.** The border or edge of an object. **2.** The circular outer part of a wheel, furthest from the axle, around which a tire is fitted. *—v.* **rimmed, rimming.** To furnish with a rim. [< OE *rima* < Gmc **rimō.*]

rime. Variant of **rhyme.**

rind (rīnd) *n.* A tough outer covering, as the skin of some fruits or the coating on cheese. [< OE *rinde.* See **rendh-.**]

ring[1] (rĭng) *n.* **1.** A circular object, form, or arrangement with a vacant circular center. **2.** A small circular band, generally of precious metal, worn on a finger. **3.** Any circular band used for carrying, holding, or containing something. **4. a.** An area in which prize fights, exhibitions, etc., are held. **b. the ring.** The sport of prize fighting. **5.** An exclusive group of persons acting privately or illegally. *—v.* **1.** To surround with a ring; encircle. **2.** To move in a spiral or circular course. [< OE *hring.* See **sker-[2].**]

ring[2] (rĭng) *v.* **rang, rung, ringing.** **1.** To give forth a clear, resonant sound when caused to vibrate. **2.** To cause (a bell, chimes, etc.) to sound. **3.** To sound a bell in order to summon someone. **4.** To have a character suggestive of a particular quality: *a perception that rings true.* **5.** To resound. **6.** To hear a persistent humming or buzzing: *ears ringing from the blast.* **7.** To call (someone) on the telephone. *—n.* **1.** The sound created by a bell or other sonorous, vibrating object. **2.** A telephone call. **3.** A particular quality: *a suspicious ring.* [< OE *hringan.* See **ker-[2].**]

ring•let (rĭng′lĭt) *n.* A long, spirally curled lock of hair.

ring•side (rĭng′sīd′) *n.* The seats immediately outside an arena or ring, as at a prize fight.

ring•worm (rĭng′wûrm′) *n.* A contagious skin disease caused by a fungus and characterized by ring-shaped itching patches.

rink (rĭngk) *n.* **1.** An area surfaced with smooth ice for skating. **2.** A smooth floor suited for roller-skating. [< OF *renc,* row, range.]

rinse (rĭns) *v.* **rinsed, rinsing.** **1.** To wash lightly. **2.** To remove (soap, dirt, etc.) with water. *—n.* **1. a.** The act of washing lightly. **b.** The water or solution used in this process. **2.** A cosmetic solution used in conditioning or tinting the hair. [Prob < L *recēns,* fresh, recent.]

Ri•o de Ja•nei•ro (rē′ō dĭ jə-nâr′ō, zhə-nâr′ō). A city of SE Brazil. Pop. 3,223,000.

Ri•o Grande (rē′ō grănd). A river forming much of the U.S.-Mexican border.

ri•ot (rī′ət) *n.* **1.** A wild or turbulent disturbance created by a large number of people. **2.** A profusion, as of colors. **—run riot.** **1.** To move or act with wild abandon. **2.** To grow abundantly. *—v.* **1.** To take part in a riot. **2.** To engage in uncontrolled revelry. [< OF *ruihoter,* to quarrel.] **—ri′ot•er** *n.* **—ri′ot•ous** *adj.* **—ri′ot•ous•ly** *adv.* **—ri′ot•ous•ness** *n.*

rip (rĭp) *v.* **ripped, ripping.** **1.** To tear or become torn apart. **2.** To remove by pulling or tearing roughly. **3.** To move quickly or violently. **4.** To attack or censure: *ripped into his opponent's record.* *—n.* A torn or split place. [Prob < Flem *rippen.*] **—rip′per** *n.*

rip•cord (rĭp′kôrd′) *n.* A cord pulled to release the pack of a parachute.

ripe (rīp) *adj.* **1.** Fully developed; mature: *ripe fruit.* **2.** Sufficiently advanced; opportune: *The time is ripe.* [< OE *rīpe.* See **rei-[1].**]

rip•en (rī′pən) *v.* To become or make ripe.

rip off. *Slang.* **1.** To steal from; rob: *rip off a store.* **2.** To steal: *rip off merchandise.* **3.** To exploit or swindle.

rip-off (rĭp′ôf′, -ŏf′) *n. Slang.* **1.** A theft. **2.** One who steals; a thief. **3.** An act of exploitation; a swindle.

rip•ple (rĭp′əl) *v.* **-pled, -pling.** **1.** To form small waves on the surface. **2.** To rise and fall gently in tone or volume. *—n.* **1.** A slight wave or undulation. **2.** An indistinct vibrating sound. [Perh freq of RIP.]

rip•saw (rĭp′sô′) *n.* A coarse-toothed saw for cutting wood along the grain.

rise (rīz) *v.* **rose, risen** (rĭz′ən), **rising.** **1.** To assume a standing position. **2.** To get out of bed. **3.** To move from a lower to a higher position. **4.** To increase in amount, value, etc. **5.** To appear above the horizon. **6.** To extend upward. **7.** To originate. **8.** To puff up or swell up, as dough. **9.** To increase in intensity, force, or pitch. **10.** To meet a demand or challenge. **11.** To return to life. **12.** To rebel. *—n.* **1.** The act of rising; an ascent. **2.** The degree of elevation; upward slope. **3.** An increase in height, as of the level of water. **4.** An origin or beginning. **5.** Occasion or opportunity: *give rise to doubt.* **6.** An increase in price, worth, quantity, or degree. **7.** An increase in intensity, volume, or pitch. **8.** Elevation in social status, prosperity, or importance. [< OE *rīsan* < Gmc.]

ris•er (rī′zər) *n.* A person who rises, esp. from sleep: *a late riser.*

ris•i•ble (rĭz′ə-bəl) *adj.* **1.** Inclined to laugh. **2.** Causing laughter; ludicrous; laughable. [< L *rīdēre* (pp *rīsus*), to laugh.]

risk (rĭsk) *n.* **1.** The possibility of suffering harm or loss; danger. **2.** A person considered with respect to the possibility of loss to an insurer: *a poor risk.* *—v.* **1.** To expose to a chance of loss or damage. **2.** To incur the risk of. [< VL *resecum,* risk at sea, danger, "that which cuts."] **—risk′y** *adj.*

ris•qué (rĭs-kā′) *adj.* Suggestive of or bordering on indelicacy or impropriety. [< F *risquer,* to risk.]

rite (rīt) *n.* **1.** The prescribed form for conducting a religious or other solemn ceremony. **2.** A ceremonial act or series of acts: *fertility rites.* [< L *rītus.*]

rit•u•al (rĭch′o͞o-əl) *n.* **1.** The prescribed form for conducting a solemn ceremony. **2.** A body of ceremonies or rites. [< L *rītus,* RITE.] **—rit′u•al** *adj.* **—rit′u•al•ly** *adv.*

ri•val (rī′vəl) *n.* **1.** A person who pursues the same object as another; competitor. **2.** One that equals or almost equals another in some respect. *—adj.* Acting as or being a rival; competing. *—v.* **1.** To attempt to equal or surpass. **2.** To be the equal of; be a match for. [< L *rīvālis,* "one using the same brook as another," rival.] **—ri′val•ry** *n.*

rive (rīv) *v.* **rived, rived** or **riven** (rĭv′ən), **riving.** **1.** To rend or tear apart. **2.** To cleave or split asunder. [< ON *rīfa.*]

riv•er (rĭv′ər) *n.* A large natural stream of water emptying into an ocean, lake, or other body of water. [< L *rīpārius,* on a bank.]

riv•er•side (rĭv′ər-sīd′) *n.* The bank of a river. *—adj.* On or near the bank of a river.

riv•et (rĭv′ĭt) *n.* A metal bolt or pin, having a head on one end, used to fasten metal plates or other objects together by inserting the shank through a hole in each piece and forming the plain end into a new head. *—v.* **1.** To fasten or secure with a rivet. **2.** To engross or hold (the attention). [< OF *river,* to fix.]

riv•u•let (rĭv′yə-lĭt) *n.* A small brook or stream. [< L *rīvus,* brook, stream.]

Ri•yadh (rē-yäd′). A capital of Saudi Arabia. Pop. 300,000.

ri•yal (rē-ôl′, -äl′) *n.* **1.** Also **ri•al.** The basic monetary unit of Saudi Arabia. **2.** The basic monetary unit of Yemen.

rm. **1.** ream. **2.** room.

Rn radon.

R.N. **1.** registered nurse. **2.** Royal Navy.

RNA ribonucleic acid.

ro. rood (measure).

roach[1] (rōch) *n.* A cockroach.

roach[2] (rōch) *n.* A European freshwater fish. [< OF *roche.*]

road (rōd) *n.* **1.** An open way for the passage of vehicles, persons, and animals. **2.** A way or course toward the achievement of something. [< OE *rād,* riding, journey. See **reidh-.**]

road•bed (rōd′bĕd′) *n.* The foundation laid for railroad tracks or a road.

road•run•ner (rōd′rŭn′ər) *n.* A swift-running, long-tailed, crested bird of SW North America.

road•side (rōd′sīd′) *n.* The area on the side of a road. **—road′side′** *adj.*

road•ster (rōd′stər) *n.* An open automobile having a single seat for two or three people.

road•way (rōd′wā′) *n.* A road, esp. the part over which vehicles travel.

roam (rōm) *v.* To move or travel (through) without purpose or plan. [ME *romen.*]

roan (rōn) *adj.* Having a brownish coat sprinkled with white or gray, as a horse. *—n.* A roan horse or other animal. [< OSpan *roano.*]

roar (rôr) *v.* **1.** To utter a loud, deep, prolonged sound. **2.** To utter or express with a roar. **3.** To laugh loudly or excitedly. *—n.* **1.** A loud, deep sound, cry, or noise. **2.** A loud burst of laughter. [< OE *rārian.*]

roast (rōst) *v.* **1.** To cook with dry heat. **2.** To expose to great or excessive heat. **3.** To heat (ores) in a furnace in order to dehydrate, purify, or oxidize. **4.** *Informal.* To criticize or ridicule harshly. *—n.* **1.** Something roasted.

2. A cut of meat suitable or prepared for roasting. —*adj.* Roasted. [< OF *rostir.*] —**roast'er** *n.*

rob (rŏb) *v.* **robbed, robbing.** 1. To steal (from). 2. To deprive of something. [< OF *rober.*] —**rob'ber** *n.*

rob•ber•y (rŏb'ər-ē) *n., pl.* **-ies.** 1. The act of robbing. 2. An instance of this.

robe (rōb) *n.* 1. A long, loose, flowing outer garment, esp. one worn on formal occasions. 2. A dressing gown or bathrobe. 3. A blanket or covering: *a lap robe.* —*v.* **robed, robing.** To dress in a robe or robes. [< VL **rauba,* "clothes taken away as booty," robe.]

Robes•pierre (rōbz'pē-âr), **Maximilien de.** 1758–1794. French revolutionary leader.

rob•in (rŏb'ĭn) *n.* 1. A North American songbird with a rust-red breast and a dark back. 2. A small Old World bird with an orange breast and a brown back. [< *Robin,* given name.]

Rob•in Hood (rŏb'ĭn ho͝od). One who takes from the rich to give to the poor. [< *Robin Hood,* legendary 12th-century English outlaw.]

ro•bot (rō'bət, rŏb'ət) *n.* 1. A manlike mechanical device capable of performing human tasks. 2. A person who works mechanically without original thought. 3. Any machine or device that works automatically. [Czech.]

ro•bust (rō-bŭst', rō'bŭst) *adj.* Full of health and strength; vigorous; hardy. [L *rōbustus,* oaken.] —**ro•bust'ly** *adv.* —**ro•bust'ness** *n.*

Roch•es•ter (rŏch'ĕs-tər). A city in W New York State. Pop. 319,000.

rock¹ (rŏk) *n.* 1. Any relatively hard naturally formed mass of mineral or petrified matter; stone. 2. A support, foundation, or source of strength. —**on the rocks.** 1. In a state of ruin. 2. Served over ice cubes without water or mix. [< VL **rocca.*]

rock² (rŏk) *v.* 1. To move or sway back and forth or from side to side, esp. gently or rhythmically. 2. To shake violently, as from a blow or shock. —*n.* 1. A rocking motion. 2. **Rock 'n' roll.** [< OE *roccian.*]

rock-and-roll. Variant of **rock 'n' roll.**

rock-bound (rŏk'bound') *adj.* Hemmed in by or bordered with rocks.

Rock•e•fel•ler (rŏk'ə-fĕl'ər), **John D(avison).** 1839–1937. American capitalist.

rock•er (rŏk'ər) *n.* 1. A rocking chair. 2. One of the two curved pieces upon which a cradle or rocking chair rocks. —**off one's rocker.** *Slang.* Out of one's mind; crazy.

rock•et (rŏk'ĭt) *n.* 1. a. Any device propelled by ejection of matter, esp. by the high-velocity ejection of gaseous combustion products. b. An engine that propels in this manner; a rocket engine. 2. A rocket-propelled explosive weapon. —*v.* To move swiftly, as a rocket. [It *rocchetta,* rocket, small distaff.]

rock•et•ry (rŏk'ĭt-rē) *n.* The science and technology of rocket design, construction, and flight.

Rock•ies (rŏk'ēz). *Informal.* The Rocky Mountains.

rocking chair. A chair mounted on rockers or springs.

rocking horse. A toy horse large enough for a child to ride, mounted upon rockers or springs.

rock 'n' roll (rŏk' ən rōl'). Also **rock-and-roll** (rŏk'ən-rōl'). Popular music combining elements of rhythm and blues with country and western music and having a heavily accented beat. —**rock 'n' roll** *adj.*

rock-ribbed (rŏk'rĭbd') *adj.* 1. Having rocks or rock outcroppings. 2. Stern and unyielding.

rock salt. Common salt, essentially sodium chloride, occurring in large solid masses.

rock•y¹ (rŏk'ē) *adj.* **-ier, -iest.** 1. Consisting of or abounding in rocks. 2. Marked by hazards or difficulties.

rock•y² (rŏk'ē) *adj.* **-ier, -iest.** 1. Unsteady; shaky. 2. Weak, dizzy, or nauseated.

Rock•y Mountains (rŏk'ē). The major mountain system of North America, extending from Mexico to Alaska.

ro•co•co (rə-kō'kō, rō'kə-kō') *n.* A style of architecture and decoration characterized by elaborate, profuse designs intended to produce a delicate effect. [< F *rocaille,* rockwork.] —**ro•co'co** *adj.*

rod (rŏd) *n.* 1. A straight, thin piece or bar of metal, wood, or other material. 2. A stick or bundle of sticks used for chastisement. 3. A scepter or staff symbolizing power or authority; wand. 4. A metal bar in a machine: *a piston rod.* 5. A linear measure equal to 5.5 yards, 16.5 feet, or 5.03 meters. 6. *Slang.* A pistol or revolver. [< OE *rodd.* See **rēt-.**]

rode (rōd). *p.t.* of **ride.**

ro•dent (rōd'ənt) *n.* Any of various related mammals, as a mouse, rat, squirrel, or beaver, having teeth adapted for gnawing. [< L *rōdere,* to gnaw.]

ro•de•o (rō'dē-ō', rō-dā'ō) *n., pl.* **-os.** 1. A cattle roundup. 2. A public exhibition of cowboy skills, including riding broncos, lassoing, etc. [< Span *rodear,* to surround.]

Ro•din (rō-dăN'), **Auguste.** 1840–1917. French sculptor.

roe¹ (rō) *n.* The eggs or egg-laden ovary of a fish. [< MLG or MDu *roge.*]

roe² (rō) *n.* Also **roe deer.** A small Old World deer with short antlers. [< OE *rā.* See **rei-².**]

roe•buck (rō'bŭk') *n.* A male roe deer.

roent•gen (rĕnt'gən, rŭnt'-) *n.* An obsolete unit of radiation dosage, equal to the quantity of ionizing radiation that will produce a standard amount of electricity in one cubic centimeter of dry air at 0°C and standard atmospheric pressure. [< W. *Roentgen* (1845–1923), German physicist.]

Roentgen ray. **X ray.**

Rog•er (rŏj'ər) *interj.* Also **rog•er.** Used in radio communications to indicate message received.

rogue (rōg) *n.* 1. An unprincipled person; a scoundrel or rascal. 2. A playfully mischievous person; scamp. [Orig "beggar," prob < L *rogāre,* to ask, beg.] —**ro'guer•y** *n.*

roil (roil) *v.* 1. To make (a liquid) muddy or cloudy by stirring up sediment. 2. To displease; irritate; vex. [?]

roist•er (rois'tər) *v.* 1. To engage in boisterous merrymaking. 2. To behave in a blustering manner; swagger. [Prob < OF *rustre,* churl, boor.] —**roist'er•er** *n.*

Ro•land (rō'lənd). Legendary paladin and nephew of Charlemagne.

role (rōl) *n.* Also **rôle.** 1. A character or part played by an actor. 2. A function or position. [< OF *rolle,* roll (on which a part is written).]

roll (rōl) *v.* 1. To move by turning over and over. 2. To move on wheels. 3. To gain momentum. 4. To go by; elapse. 5. To turn over and over: *roll in the mud.* 6. To advance with a rising and falling motion, as waves. 7. To move or rock from side to side, as a ship. 8. To make a deep, prolonged, surging sound, as thunder. 9. To rotate: *roll one's eyes.* 10. To pronounce or utter with a trill: *roll one's "r's".* 11. To wrap (something) round and round upon itself or around something else. 12. To envelop or enfold in a covering. 13. To spread, compress, or flatten by applying pressure with a roller. 14. To throw (dice) in craps or other games. —**roll in.** To arrive in large numbers; pour in. —**roll out.** To unroll and spread out. —**roll up.** *Informal.* To arrive in a vehicle. —*n.* 1. An instance of rolling. 2. A quantity of something rolled up in the form of a cylinder. 3. A piece of parchment or paper that can be or is rolled up; scroll. 4. A list of names of persons belonging to a given group. 5. a. A small rounded portion of bread. b. Any food that is prepared by rolling up: *an egg roll.* 6. A rolling, swaying, or rocking motion. 7. A deep reverberation or rumble. 8. A rapid succession of short sounds: *the roll of a drum.* [< L *rota,* wheel.]

roll call. The reading aloud of a list of names to determine who is absent.

roll•er (rō'lər) *n.* 1. A small, spokeless wheel, as that of a roller skate or caster. 2. An elongated cylinder upon which something is wound. 3. Any of various cylindrical devices used for leveling, crushing, or curling. 4. A heavy wave that breaks on the coast.

roller coaster. A sharply banked railway with small open cars, operated in amusement parks.

roller skate. A skate having four small wheels instead of a runner. —**roll'er-skate'** *v.* **(-skated, -skating).**

rol•lick (rŏl'ĭk) *v.* To behave or move in a carefree manner; romp. [Prob a blend of ROMP or ROLL and FROLIC.] —**rol'lick•ing** *adj.*

rolling pin. A smooth cylinder, usually of wood, used for rolling out dough.

rolling stock. A railroad's wheeled vehicles.

ro•ly-po•ly (rō'lē-pō'lē) *adj.* Short and plump; pudgy. [Perh < ROLL + POLL.]

rom. roman (type).

Rom. 1. Roman. 2. Romance (language). 3. Romans (New Testament).

ro•maine (rō-mān') *n.* A type of lettuce with long leaves forming a head. [< F *Romain,* Roman.]

Ro•man (rō'mən) *adj.* 1. Of or characteristic of Rome and its people, esp. ancient Rome. 2. Of or pertaining to the Roman Catholic Church. 3. **roman.** Designating the most common style of type, with letters having serifs and vertical lines thicker than horizontal lines. —*n.* A native, resident, or citizen of Rome, esp. ancient Rome.

Roman Catholic. 1. Of or pertaining to the Roman Catholic Church. 2. A member of the Roman Catholic Church.

Roman Catholic Church. The Christian church that is characterized by a hierarchic structure of bishops and priests, with the pope as head of the episcopal college. —**Roman Catholicism.**

ro•mance (rō-măns', rō'măns) *n.* 1. A long medieval narrative in prose or verse, telling of the adventures of chivalric heroes. 2. Any long, fictitious tale of heroes and extraordinary or mysterious events. 3. The quality of adventure and idealized exploits found in such tales. 4. A novel or story dealing with a love affair. 5. A love affair. [< VL **Rōmānicē,* in the Roman manner.]

Ro•mance (rō-măns', rō'măns) *n.* The languages that developed from Vulgar Latin, the principal ones being French, Italian, Portuguese, Rumanian, and Spanish. —**Ro•mance'** *adj.*

Roman Empire. The empire of the ancient Romans from 27 B.C. to A.D. 395.

Ro•man•esque (rō'mən-ĕsk') *adj.* Designating

a transitional style of European architecture prevalent from the 9th to the 12th century. [< ROMAN.] —**Ro'man•esque'** *n.*

Ro•ma•ni•a. Variant of **Rumania.**

Ro•ma•ni•an. Variant of **Rumanian.**

Roman numeral. One of the letters employed in the ancient Roman system of numeration, still used in certain formal contexts.

I	1
II	2
III	3
IV	4
V	5
VI	6
VII	7
VIII	8
IX	9
X	10
XI	11
XII	12
XIII	13
XIV	14
XV	15
XVI	16
XVII	17
XVIII	18
XIX	19
XX	20
XXI	21
XXIX	29
XXX	30
XL	40
XLVIII	48
IL	49
L	50
LX	60
XC	90
XCVIII	98
IC	99
C	100
CI	101
CC	200
D	500
DC	600
CM	900
M	1000
MDCLXVI	1666
MCMLXX	1970

Roman numeral

ro•man•tic (rō-măn'tĭk) *adj.* **1.** Of, pertaining to, or characteristic of romance. **2.** Given to thoughts or feelings of romance. **3.** Conducive to romance. **4.** Imaginative but impractical: *romantic notions.* **5.** Not based on fact; imaginary. **6.** Of or characteristic of romanticism in the arts. —*n.* A romantic person. —**ro•man'ti•cal•ly** *adv.*

ro•man•ti•cism (rō-măn'tə-sĭz'əm) *n.* A literary movement originating toward the end of the 18th century that sought to assert the validity of subjective experience and escape from the prevailing subordination to classical forms. —**ro•man'ti•cist** *n.*

ro•man•ti•cize (rō-măn'tə-sīz') *v.* **-cized, -cizing. 1.** To interpret romantically. **2.** To think in a romantic way.

Rom•a•ny (rŏm'ə-nē, rō'mə-) *n., pl.* **-ny** or **-nies. 1.** A Gypsy. **2.** The Indic language spoken by the Gypsies; Gypsy. —**Rom'a•ny** *adj.*

Rome (rōm). **1.** The capital of Italy and site of Vatican City; formerly the capital of the Roman Empire. Pop. 2,445,000. **2.** The ancient Roman kingdom, republic, and empire.

Ro•me•o (rō'mē-ō) *n., pl.* **-os.** One given over to courtship or lovemaking. [< *Romeo,* lover in Shakespeare's *Romeo and Juliet.*]

romp (rŏmp) *v.* **1.** To play or frolic boisterously. **2.** *Slang.* To win a race easily. —*n.* **1.** Lively, merry play; frolic. **2.** *Slang.* An easy win.

romp•er (rŏm'pər) *n.* **1.** One who romps, esp. a small child. **2. rompers.** A loose-fitting sports or play outfit with short bloomers.

roof (ro͞of, ro͝of) *n.* **1.** The exterior top covering of a building. **2.** The top covering of anything: *the roof of a car.* **3.** The upper part of the mouth. —*v.* To cover with a roof. [< OE *hrōf.* See **krapo-.**]

roof garden. 1. A garden on the roof of a building. **2.** A restaurant on the roof of a building.

roof•ing (ro͞o'fĭng, ro͝of'ĭng) *n.* Materials used in building a roof.

rook[1] (ro͝ok) *n.* A crowlike Old World bird. —*v. Slang.* To swindle. [< OE *hrōc.*]

rook[2] (ro͝ok) *n.* A chess piece that may move in a straight line over any number of empty squares; castle. [< Pers *rukh.*]

rook•er•y (ro͝ok'ər-ē) *n., pl.* **-ies.** A breeding place of rooks or certain animals, as seals.

rook•ie (ro͝ok'ē) *n. Slang.* **1.** An untrained recruit. **2.** A novice player in baseball or football. [Var of RECRUIT.]

room (ro͞om, ro͝om) *n.* **1.** Space: *This desk takes up too much room.* **2. a.** An area of a building set off by walls or partitions. **b.** The people present in such an area: *The whole room laughed.* **3. rooms.** Living quarters. **4.** Suitable opportunity: *room for error.* —*v.* To occupy a room; live or lodge. [< OE *rūm.* See **rewə-.**]

room•er (ro͞o'mər, ro͝om'ər) *n.* A lodger.

room•ette (ro͞o-mĕt', ro͝om-ĕt') *n.* A small private compartment in a railroad sleeping car.

room•ful (ro͞om'fo͝ol', ro͝om'-) *n., pl.* **-fuls. 1.** As much or as many as a room will hold. **2.** The number of people in a room.

rooming house. A house where lodgers can rent rooms.

room•mate (ro͞om'māt', ro͝om'-) *n.* A person with whom one shares a room or apartment.

room•y (ro͞o'mē, ro͝om'ē) *adj.* **-ier, -iest.** Having plenty of room; spacious; large. —**room'i•ly** *adv.* —**room'i•ness** *n.*

Roo•se•velt (rō'zə-vĕlt, rōz'vĕlt, -vəlt). **1. Franklin Delano.** 1882–1945. 32nd President of the U.S. (1933–45). **2. Theodore.** 1858–1919. 26th President of the U.S. (1901–09).

roost (ro͞ost) *n.* **1.** A perch on which domestic fowls or other birds rest. **2.** A place with such perches. —**rule the roost.** To be in charge. —*v.* To rest or sleep on a perch or roost. [< OE *hrōst.*]

roost•er (ro͞os'tər) *n.* The adult male of the common domestic fowl.

root[1] (ro͞ot, ro͝ot) *n.* **1.** The usually underground portion of a plant that serves as support and absorbs and stores food. **2.** The embedded part of an organ or structure such as a hair, tooth, or nerve. **3.** An essential element; core. **4.** A primary source; origin. **5.** *Ling.* **a.** In etymology, a word or word element from which other words are formed. **b.** In morphology, a base to which prefixes and suffixes may be added. **6.** A number that when multiplied by itself an indicated number of times equals a specified number. —**take root. 1.** To put forth roots and begin to grow. **2.** To become firmly fixed or established. —*v.* **1.** To put forth roots. **2.** To implant or become fixed by or as by roots. **3.** To pull up by or as by the roots. [< OE *rōt* < ON.]

root[2] (ro͞ot, ro͝ot) *v.* To dig with or as with the snout or nose. [< OE *wrōtan.* See **wrōd-.**]

root[3] (ro͞ot, ro͝ot) *v.* To support a contestant or team; cheer (with *for).* [Perh < ROOT[2].] —**root'er** *n.*

Franklin Delano Roosevelt

root beer. A carbonated soft drink made from extracts of the roots of several plants.

root•stock (ro͞ot'stŏk', ro͝ot'-) *n.* A rootlike stem; a rhizome.

rope (rōp) *n.* A flexible, heavy cord of twisted hemp or other fiber. —**know the ropes.** To be experienced with the details of an operation. —*v.* **roped, roping. 1.** To tie or fasten with rope. **2.** To enclose with a rope. **3.** To lasso. **4.** *Informal.* To entice or deceive. [< OE *rāp.* See **rei-**[1].]

Theodore Roosevelt

Roque•fort cheese (rōk′fərt). A French cheese made from goat's and ewe's milk and containing a blue mold. [< *Roquefort,* village in S France.]

Ror•schach test (rôr′shäk, -shäkh, rōr′-). A psychological test of personality in which a subject's interpretations of ten standard abstract designs are analyzed as a measure of emotional and intellectual functioning and integration. [< H. *Rorschach* (1884–1922), Swiss psychiatrist.]

ro•sa•ry (rō′zə-rē) *n., pl.* **-ries.** A string of beads on which prayers are counted. [< ML *rosārium.*]

rose[1] (rōz) *n.* **1.** Any of various usually prickly shrubs or vines with compound leaves and showy, often fragrant flowers. **2.** The flower of such a plant. **3.** Dark pink. **4.** Something resembling a rose in form. [< L *rosa.*]

rose[2] (rōz). *p.t.* of **rise.**

ro•sé (rō-zā′) *n.* A light, pink table wine. [F, "pink."]

ro•se•ate (rō′zē-ĭt, -āt′) *adj.* **1.** Rose-colored. **2.** Cheerful; optimistic; rosy.

rose-col•ored (rōz′kŭl′ərd) *adj.* **1.** Having the color rose. **2.** Seeing or seen overoptimistically.

rose fever. A spring or early summer hay fever.

rose•mar•y (rōz′mâr′ē) *n., pl.* **-ies.** An aromatic shrub with grayish-green leaves used as seasoning. [< L *rōs marīnus,* "sea dew."]

ro•sette (rō-zĕt′) *n.* An ornament or badge made of ribbon or silk gathered and tufted to resemble a rose. [F, "small rose."]

rose water. A fragrant preparation made by steeping or distilling rose petals in water, used in cosmetics and cookery.

rose•wood (rōz′wo͝od′) *n.* The hard, dark or reddish wood of a tropical tree.

Rosh Ha•sha•nah (rōsh hə-shä′nə, rōsh). Also **Rosh Ha•sha•na, Rosh Ha•sho•na** (hə-shō′nə), **Rosh Ha•sho•nah.** The Jewish New Year, celebrated in September or early October. [Heb *rōsh hashānāh,* beginning of the year.]

ros•in (rŏz′ĭn) *n.* A brown or yellowish resin derived from the sap of pine trees and used to increase friction on the bows of certain stringed instruments and in varnishes and other products. [< RESIN.]

ros•ter (rŏs′tər) *n.* A list of names, esp. of officers and men enrolled for military duty. [Du *rooster,* gridiron, list.]

Ros•tov (rŏs′tŏv). A Soviet city on the Don. Pop. 789,000.

ros•trum (rŏs′trəm) *n., pl.* **-trums** or **-tra.** (-trə). A dais or platform for public speaking. [L, beak, ship's prow.]

ros•y (rō′zē) *adj.* **-ier, -iest. 1.** Having the characteristic pink or red color of a rose. **2.** Bright; cheery; optimistic. **3.** Flushed with a healthy glow. **—ros′i•ly** *adv.* **—ros′i•ness** *n.*

rot (rŏt) *v.* **rotted, rotting. 1.** To decompose; decay. **2.** To disappear or fall by decaying. *—n.* **1.** The process of rotting. **2.** Anything rotting or rotten. **3.** Pointless talk. [< OE *rotian* < Gmc **rutjan.*]

ro•ta•ry (rō′tə-rē) *adj.* Of or involving rotation, esp. axial rotation.

ro•tate (rō′tāt′) *v.* **-tated, -tating. 1.** To turn or spin on an axis. **2.** To alternate in sequence. [L *rotāre,* to revolve.] **—ro′ta′tor** *n.* **—ro′ta•to′ry** (rō′tə-tôr′ē, -tōr′ē) *adj.*

ro•ta•tion (rō-tā′shən) *n.* **1.** Motion in which the path of every point in the moving object is a circle or circular arc centered on a specified axis, esp. on an internal axis. **2.** A single complete cycle of such motion; revolution. **3.** Uniform sequential variation; alternation. **—ro•ta′tion•al** *adj.*

ROTC Reserve Officers' Training Corps.

rote (rōt) *n.* A memorizing process using routine or repetition without full comprehension: *learn by rote.* [ME.]

ro•tis•se•rie (rō-tĭs′ə-rē) *n.* A cooking device equipped with a rotating spit for roasting. [< OF *rostir,* to roast.]

ro•to•gra•vure (rō′tə-grə-vyo͝or′, -grā′vyər) *n.* **1.** A process in which letters and pictures are printed from an etched copper cylinder in a rotary press. **2.** Material thus printed. [L *rota,* wheel + GRAVURE.]

ro•tor (rō′tər) *n.* A rotating part of an electrical or mechanical device. [Short for ROTATOR.]

rot•ten (rŏt′n) *adj.* **1.** Decayed; decomposed. **2.** Putrid; stinking. **3.** Made unsound by or as by rot. **4.** Very bad; wretched. [< ON *rotinn* < Gmc **ruteno-,* akin to **rutjan,* to ROT.] **—rot′ten•ly** *adv.* **—rot′ten•ness** *n.*

Rot•ter•dam (rŏt′ər-dăm). A city of the Netherlands. Pop. 732,000.

ro•tund (rō-tŭnd′) *adj.* Rounded; plump. [L *rotundus,* round.] **—ro•tun′di•ty** *n.*

ro•tun•da (rō-tŭn′də) *n.* **1.** A circular building or hall, esp. one with a dome. **2.** A large room with a high ceiling. [< L *rotundus,* round.]

rou•ble, ru•ble (ro͞o′bəl) *n.* The basic monetary unit of the Soviet Union.

rou•é (ro͞o-ā′) *n.* A lecherous and dissipated man. [F, "broken on the wheel," completely tired.]

rouge (ro͞ozh) *n.* **1.** A red or pink cosmetic for coloring the cheeks or lips. **2.** A reddish powder used to polish metals or glass. *—v.* **rouged, rouging.** To color with rouge. [< L *rubeus,* red.]

rough (rŭf) *adj.* **1.** Having an uneven surface; not smooth. **2.** Coarse; shaggy. **3.** Turbulent; agitated: *rough waters.* **4.** Not gentle or careful; violent: *rough handling.* **5.** Rude; unmannerly; uncouth. **6.** *Informal.* Difficult or unpleasant: *a rough time.* **7.** In a crude or unpolished state. **8.** Not perfected, elaborated, or completed: *a rough drawing.* *—n.* **1.** The part of a golf course left unmowed and uncultivated. **2.** Something in an unfinished or hastily worked-out state. **—in the rough.** In a crude or unfinished state. *—v.* **1.** To make rough; roughen. **2.** To treat roughly or with physical violence. **3.** To prepare or indicate in a rough or unfinished form: *rough in the illustrations.* **—rough it.** To get along without the usual comforts. [< OE *rūh.* See **ruk-.**] **—rough′ly** *adv.* **—rough′ness** *n.*

rough•age (rŭf′ĭj) *n.* The relatively coarse, indigestible parts of certain foods.

rough•en (rŭf′ən) *v.* To make or become rough.

rough•hew (rŭf′hyo͞o′) *v.* **1.** To hew or shape roughly, without finishing. **2.** To make in rough form.

rough•house (rŭf′hous′) *n.* Rowdy, uproarious play or behavior. *—v.* **-housed, -housing.** To engage in roughhouse.

rough•neck (rŭf′nĕk′) *n.* A pugnacious fellow; a rowdy.

rough•shod (rŭf′shŏd′) *adj.* **—ride roughshod over.** To treat inconsiderately or arrogantly.

rou•lette (ro͞o-lĕt′) *n.* A gambling game played with a rotating disk having numbered slots in which a small ball will come to rest. [< L *rota,* a wheel.]

Rou•ma•ni•a. See **Rumania.**

Rou•ma•ni•an. Variant of **Rumanian.**

round (round) *adj.* **1.** Spherical; globular; ball-shaped. **2.** Circular. **3.** Curved. **4.** Complete; full: *a round dozen.* **5.** Expressed or designated as a whole number or integer; not fractional. **6.** Approximate; not exact: *a round estimate.* *—n.* **1.** Something round, as a circle, disk, globe, or ring. **2.** A cut of beef between the rump and shank. **3.** A complete course, succession, or series: *a round of parties.* **4.** Often **rounds.** A course of customary or prescribed actions, duties, or places. **5.** A single distribution, as of drinks. **6.** A single outburst of applause. **7. a.** A single shot or volley. **b.** Ammunition for a single shot; a cartridge. **8.** A period of play or action in various sports. **9.** *Mus.* A musical form in which the same melody is repeated by successive overlapping voices. *—v.* **1.** To make or become round. **2.** To make or become plump. **3.** To bring to completion or perfection. **4.** To go or pass around. **5.** To make a turn about or to the other side of. **6.** To encompass; surround. *—adv.* **1.** Around. **2.** Throughout: *the year round.* *—prep.* Around. [< L *rotundus.*] **—round′ness** *n.*

round•a•bout (round′ə-bout′) *adj.* Indirect; circuitous.

roun•de•lay (roun′də-lā′) *n.* A poem or song with a regularly recurring refrain. [< OF *rondel,* "small circle."]

round•house (round′hous′) *n.* **1.** A circular building for housing and switching locomotives. **2.** *Slang.* A punch or swing delivered with a sweeping sidearm movement.

round•ly (round′lē) *adv.* **1.** In the form of a circle or sphere. **2.** Vigorously; bluntly. **3.** Fully; thoroughly.

round robin. A tournament in which each contestant is matched against every other contestant.

round-shoul•dered (round′shōl′dərd) *adj.* Having the shoulders and upper back rounded: *a round-shouldered man.*

round-the-clock (round′*th*ə-klŏk′) *adj.* Throughout the entire day; continuous.

round trip. A trip from one place to another and back; two-way trip. **—round′-trip′** *adj.*

round up. 1. To seek out and bring together; gather. **2.** To herd (cattle) together.

round•up (round′ŭp′) *n.* **1.** The herding together of cattle. **2.** A gathering up of persons under suspicion by the police. **3.** A summing up; summation; résumé.

rouse (rouz) *v.* **roused, rousing. 1.** To bring out of a state of slumber or apathy. **2.** To excite, as to anger or action; spur. [< ME *rowsen,* to shake feathers or body.] **—rous′er** *n.*

Rous•seau (ro͞o-sō′), **Jean Jacques.** 1712–1778. French philosopher and social reformer.

roust•a•bout (rous′tə-bout′) *n.* A laborer employed for transient or unskilled jobs, as on a wharf or in a circus or oil field. [< ROUSE + ABOUT.]

rout (rout) *n.* **1.** A disorderly retreat or flight following defeat. **2.** An overwhelming defeat. *—v.* **1.** To put to disorderly flight or retreat. **2.** To defeat overwhelmingly. [< L *rumpere* (pp *ruptus*), to break.]

route (ro͞ot, rout) *n.* **1.** A road, course, or way for travel from one place to another. **2.** A fixed course or territory assigned to a salesman or deliveryman. *—v.* **1.** To send along; forward. **2.** To schedule or dispatch on a certain route. [< VL **rupta (via),* "broken or beaten (way)."]

rou•tine (ro͞o-tēn′) *n.* **1.** A prescribed and detailed method of procedure. **2.** A set of customary and often mechanically performed activities. —*adj.* 1. Habitual; regular. 2. Lacking in interest or originality. [< ROUTE.] —**rou·tine'ly** *adv.*

rove[1] (rōv) *v.* **roved, roving.** To wander about at random, esp. over a wide area; roam. [Prob < Scand.]

rove[2] (rov). Alternate *p.t.* & *p.p.* of **reeve.**

rov·er (rō'vər) *n.* 1. One who roves; wanderer; nomad. 2. A pirate or pirate vessel. [Sense 2 < MDu *rōven,* to rob.]

row[1] (rō) *n.* 1. A horizontal linear arrangement or array. 2. A line of adjacent seats, as in a theater. [< OE *rāw, rǣw.* See **rei-**[1].]

row[2] (rō) *v.* **rowed, rowing.** 1. To propel (a boat) with or as with oars. 2. To travel or carry in a rowboat. —*n.* A trip or excursion in a rowboat. [< OE *rōwan.* See **erə-.**] —**row'er** *n.*

row[3] (rou) *n.* A boisterous disturbance or quarrel; brawl. —*v.* To take part in a row. [?]

row·an (rou'ən) *n.* A small tree with white flowers and orange-red berries. [< Scand.]

row·boat (rō'bōt') *n.* A small boat propelled by oars.

row·dy (rou'dē) *n., pl.* **-dies.** A rough, disorderly person. —*adj.* **-dier, -diest.** Disorderly; rough. [Prob < ROW[3].]

row·el (rou'əl) *n.* A sharp-toothed wheel inserted into the end of a spur. [< L *rota,* a wheel.]

roy·al (roi'əl) *adj.* 1. Of or pertaining to a king, queen, or other monarch. 2. Befitting a king; stately. [< L *rēgālis,* regal.] —**roy'al·ly** *adv.*

royal blue. Deep to strong blue.

roy·al·ist (roi'əl-ĭst) *n.* A supporter of a king or monarchy.

roy·al·ty (roi'əl-tē) *n., pl.* **-ties.** 1. Monarchs and their families collectively. 2. The power, status, or authority of monarchs. 3. Royal quality or bearing. 4. a. A share paid to an author or composer out of the proceeds resulting from the sale or performance of his work. b. A share paid to an inventor for the right to use his invention.

r.p.m. revolutions per minute.

r.p.s. revolutions per second.

rpt. report.

RR railroad.

-rrhea. *comb. form.* A flow or discharge: **pyorrhea.** [< Gk *rhein,* to flow.]

R.S. 1. recording secretary. 2. right side. 3. Royal Society.

R.S.V. Revised Standard Version (of the Bible).

r.s.v.p. répondez s'il vous plaît (English *please reply).*

rt. right.

rte. route.

Ru ruthenium.

rub (rŭb) *v.* **rubbed, rubbing.** 1. To apply pressure and friction to (a surface). 2. To apply firmly and with friction upon a surface. 3. To contact or cause to contact repeatedly and with friction; scrape. 4. To become or cause to become chafed or irritated. 5. To remove or erase (with *out* or *off*). —*n.* 1. The act of rubbing. 2. An obstacle or difficulty. [ME *rubben.*]

rub·ber[1] (rŭb'ər) *n.* 1. Any of numerous elastic materials of varying chemical composition, some natural and others synthetic. 2. Often **rubbers.** A low overshoe made of rubber.

rub·ber[2] (rŭb'ər) *n.* A series of games of which two out of three must be won to terminate the play. [?]

rub·ber·ize (rŭb'ər-īz') *v.* **-ized, -izing.** To coat, treat, or impregnate with rubber.

rub·ber·y (rŭb'ər-ē) *adj.* Of or like rubber; elastic; resilient.

rub·bish (rŭb'ĭsh) *n.* 1. Refuse; garbage; litter. 2. Worthless material. 3. Nonsense. [< NF **robel,* RUBBLE.]

rub·ble (rŭb'əl) *n.* 1. Fragments of stone or brick used in masonry. 2. The debris remaining after severe destruction: *reduce to rubble.* [< NF **robel,* "rubbings."]

rub·down (rŭb'doun') *n.* A vigorous massage of the body.

rube (ro͞ob) *n. Slang.* An unsophisticated country fellow.

ru·bel·la (ro͞o-bĕl'ə) *n.* **German measles.** [< L *rubellus,* reddish.]

Ru·bens (ro͞o'bənz), **Peter Paul.** 1577–1640. Flemish painter.

ru·bi·cund (ro͞o'bə-kənd) *adj.* Inclined to a healthy rosiness; ruddy. [L *rubicundus.*]

ru·bid·i·um (ro͞o-bĭd'ē-əm) *n. Symbol* **Rb** A soft silvery-white, highly reactive alkali element used in photoelectric cells and in the manufacture of vacuum tubes. Atomic number 37, atomic weight 85.47. [< L *rubidus,* red.]

ru·ble. Variant of **rouble.**

ru·bric (ro͞o'brĭk) *n.* 1. A title, heading, or initial letter, usually written in red. 2. A title or heading of a statute or chapter in a code of law. 3. A direction in a missal, hymnal, or other liturgical book. [< L *rubrīca (terra),* "red earth."]

ru·by (ro͞o'bē) *n., pl.* **-bies.** 1. A deep-red, translucent corundum, highly valued as a precious stone. 2. A dark red. [< L *rubeus,* red.]

ruck·us (rŭk'əs) *n. Informal.* A noisy disturbance; commotion.

rud·der (rŭd'ər) *n.* A vertically hinged plate mounted at the rear of a vessel or aircraft, used for directing or altering its course. [< OE *rōther,* steering oar. See **erə-.**]

rud·dy (rŭd'ē) *adj.* **-dier, -diest.** 1. Having a healthy, reddish color. 2. Reddish; rosy. [< OE *rudu,* red color. See **reudh-.**] —**rud'di·ly** *adv.* —**rud'di·ness** *n.*

rude (ro͞od) *adj.* **ruder, rudest.** 1. Impolite; uncivil; discourteous. 2. Formed without skill or precision; makeshift; crude. [< L *rudis,* rough, raw.] —**rude'ly** *adv.* —**rude'ness** *n.*

ru·di·ment (ro͞o'də-mənt) *n.* Often **rudiments.** 1. A fundamental element, principle, or skill. 2. Something in an incipient or incompletely developed form. [< L *rudis,* RUDE.] —**ru'di·men'ta·ry** (-mĕn'tər-ē) *adj.*

rue[1] (ro͞o) *v.* **rued, ruing.** To feel remorse or sorrow for; regret; repent. [< OE *hrēowan,* to make penitent, distress. See **kreu-**[2].]

rue[2] (ro͞o) *n.* A strong-smelling Old World plant formerly used in medicine. [< Gk *rhutē.*]

rue·ful (ro͞o'fəl) *adj.* 1. Inspiring pity or compassion. 2. Expressive of a bitter, faintly sardonic compassion; wry. —**rue'ful·ly** *adv.*

ruff (rŭf) *n.* 1. A stiffly starched frilled collar worn in the 16th and 17th centuries. 2. A collarlike projecting growth, as of feathers or fur. [Short for RUFFLE.]

ruf·fi·an (rŭf'ē-ən, rŭf'yən) *n.* A tough or rowdy fellow. [< It *ruffiano,* pander, "filthy or scabby person."]

ruf·fle (rŭf'əl) *n.* 1. A strip of frilled or closely pleated fabric used for trimming or decoration. 2. A slight disturbance. —*v.* **-fled, -fling.** 1. To disturb the smoothness of; ripple. 2. To pleat or gather (fabric) into a ruffle. 3. To erect (the feathers). 4. To discompose; fluster. 5. To flip through (the pages of a book). [ME *ruffelen,* to roughen, disarrange.]

rug (rŭg) *n.* A piece of heavy fabric or animal skin used as a floor covering. [Prob < Swed *rugg,* ruffled hair.]

Rug·by football (rŭg'bē). A British form of football. [< *Rugby* School, Warwickshire, England.]

rug·ged (rŭg'ĭd) *adj.* 1. Having a rough, irregular surface. 2. Marked with furrows or wrinkles. 3. Hard; trying; severe. 4. Vigorously healthy; hardy. [< Scand.] —**rug'ged·ness** *n.*

Ruhr (ro͝or). A river of West Germany.

ru·in (ro͞o'ĭn) *n.* 1. a. Total destruction or disintegration. b. The cause of such destruction. 2. Often **ruins.** The remains of something destroyed. —*v.* 1. To reduce to ruin. 2. To harm irreparably. 3. To reduce to poverty or bankruptcy. [< L *ruīna,* "fall."] —**ru'in·a'tion** *n.* —**ru'in·ous** *adj.* —**ru'in·ous·ly** *adv.*

rule (ro͞ol) *n.* 1. Governing power. 2. An authoritative direction for conduct or procedure. 3. Something that generally prevails or obtains. 4. A standard method or procedure. 5. A straight-edge; ruler. —*v.* **ruled, ruling.** 1. To exercise control (over); govern. 2. To dominate; hold sway over. 3. To decide judicially; decree. 4. To mark with straight parallel lines. —**rule out.** To exclude. [< L *rēgula,* straight stick, ruler, rule, pattern.]

rul·er (ro͞o'lər) *n.* 1. One who rules or governs, as a sovereign. 2. A straight-edged strip for drawing straight lines and measuring lengths.

rul·ing (ro͞o'lĭng) *adj.* Exercising control; governing. —*n.* 1. The act of governing or controlling. 2. An authoritative or official decision.

rum (rŭm) *n.* An alcoholic liquor distilled from fermented molasses or sugar cane.

Ru·ma·ni·a (ro͞o-mā'nē-ə, -nyə). Also **Ro·ma·ni·a** (rō-), **Rou·ma·ni·a** (ro͞o-). A country of SE Europe. Pop. 18,927,000. Cap. Bucharest.

Ru·ma·ni·an (ro͞o-mā'nē-ən, -mān'yən) *n.* Also **Ro·ma·ni·an** (rō-mā'nē-ən, -nyən), **Rou·ma·ni·an** (ro͞o-mā'nē-ən, -nyən). 1. An inhabitant or native of Rumania. 2. The Romance language of the Rumanian people. —**Ru·ma'ni·an** *adj.*

Rumania

rum·ba (rŭm'bə) *n.* A rhythmical dance that originated among Cuban Negroes. [< Amer Span *rumbo,* carousel.]

rum·ble (rŭm'bəl) *v.* **-bled, -bling.** 1. To make a continuous deep, heavy, reverberating sound. 2. To move or proceed with such a sound. —*n.* A continuous deep, heavy, rolling sound. [ME *romblen.*] —**rum'bly** *adj.*

ru·mi·nant (ro͞o'mə-nənt) *n.* Any of a group of hoofed, cud-chewing mammals, including cattle, sheep, goats, and deer. —*adj.* 1. Chewing cud. 2. Meditative; contemplative. [< L *rūmināre,* to RUMINATE.]

ru•mi•nate (ro͞o'mə-nāt') *v.* **-nated, -nating. 1.** To chew cud. **2.** To meditate at length; muse. [L *rūmināre.*] **—ru'mi•na'tion** *n.*

rum•mage (rŭm'ĭj) *v.* **-maged, -maging. 1.** To discover by searching thoroughly. **2.** To make an energetic, hasty search. [Orig "arrangement of cargo in a ship's hold," odds and ends.] **—rum'mag•er** *n.*

rummage sale. A sale of secondhand miscellaneous objects.

rum•my (rŭm'ē) *n.* A card game in which the object is to obtain sets of three or more cards of the same denomination or suit. [?]

ru•mor (ro͞o'mər). Also *chiefly Brit.* **ru•mour.** *n.* Unverified information of uncertain origin. *—v.* To spread rumor. [< L *rūmor.*]

rump (rŭmp) *n.* **1. a.** The often fleshy hind part of an animal. **b.** A cut of beef or veal from this part. **2.** The last or inferior part of something. [< Scand.]

rum•ple (rŭm'pəl) *v.* **-pled, -pling.** To wrinkle or form into folds or creases. [< MDu *rumpelen.*] **—rum'ple** *n.* **—rum'ply** *adj.*

rum•pus (rŭm'pəs) *n.* A noisy clamor. [?]

rum•run•ner (rŭm'rŭn'ər) *n.* One who illegally transports liquor across a border.

run (rŭn) *v.* **ran, run, running. I.** To move or cause to move rapidly. **1.** To move on foot at a pace faster than the walk. **2.** To retreat rapidly; flee. **3.** To move without hindrance or restraint. **4.** To make a short, quick trip. **5.** To swim in large numbers, as in migrating. **6. a.** To hurry; hasten. **b.** To have frequent recourse to someone or something. **II.** To compete or cause to compete. **7.** To take part in a race. **8.** To compete for elected office. **9.** To finish a race in a specified position. **III.** To move or cause to move in a specified way. **10.** To move freely, as by rolling or sliding. **11.** To be in operation. **12.** To go regularly. **13.** To sail or steer before the wind or on an indicated course. **IV.** To flow or cause to flow. **14.** To flow in a steady stream. **15.** To melt and flow. **16.** To flow and spread. **17.** To be wet with: *streets running with blood.* **18.** To overflow. **19.** To discharge; drain. **20.** To surge, as waves. **V.** To extend in space. **21.** To extend, stretch, or reach. **22.** To spread or climb, as vines. **23.** To spread rapidly. **24.** To be valid in a given area: *The writ runs only to the county line.* **25.** To unravel along a line. **VI.** To extend in time. **26.** To continue. **27.** To pass. **28.** To persist or recur. **29.** *Law.* **a.** To be effective. **b.** To be concurrent with: *Fishing tickets run with the ownership of land.* **30. a.** To accumulate or accrue. **b.** To become payable. **31.** To be expressed in a given way. **32.** To tend or incline. **33.** To be channeled. **34.** To vary or range in quality, price, size, proportion, etc. **35.** To come into or out of a specified condition. *—n.* **I. 1. a.** A pace faster than the walk. **b.** A gait faster than the canter. **2.** An act of running. **3. a.** A distance covered by or as by running. **b.** The time taken to cover it. **4.** A quick trip or visit. **5.** *Baseball.* **a.** The process of scoring a point by running from home plate around the bases and back to home plate. **b.** The point so scored. **6.** A shoaling or migrating of fish prior to spawning. **7.** Unrestricted freedom or use of: *the run of the library.* **II. 8. a.** A journey between points on a scheduled route. **b.** The time taken to cover this distance. **9.** A continuous period of operation by a machine, factory, etc. **III. 10.** A movement or flow, as of fluid or sand. **11.** A pipe or channel through which something flows: *a mill run.* **IV. 12.** A continuous length or extent of something. **13.** The direction, configuration, or lie of something: *the run of the grain in leather.* **14.** An outdoor enclosure for domestic animals or poultry. **15.** A length of torn or unraveled stitches in a knitted fabric. **V. 16.** An unbroken series or sequence. **17.** An unbroken sequence of theatrical performances. **18.** A series of unexpected and urgent demands by customers: *a run on a bank.* **19. a.** In certain games, a continuous set or sequence, as of playing cards in one suit. **b.** A successful sequence of shots or points. **20.** A sustained state or condition: *a run of good luck.* **21.** A trend or tendency. **22.** An average type, group, or category; majority: *the broad run of voters.* **—in the long run.** In the final analysis or outcome. **—on the run. 1.** In hiding. **2.** Hurrying busily from place to place. [< OE *rinnan.* See **er-¹**.]

run•a•bout (rŭn'ə-bout') *n.* A small open automobile, wagon, or motorboat.

run-a•round (rŭn'ə-round') *n.* Deception in the form of evasive excuses.

run•a•way (rŭn'ə-wā') *n.* **1.** One that runs away. **2.** An act of running away. **3.** *Informal.* An easy victory. *—adj.* **1.** Escaping or having escaped from captivity or control. **2.** Of or done by running away. **3.** Easily won, as a race.

run down. 1. a. To slow down and stop because of a failure of motive power. **b.** To exhaust or wear out. **2.** To pursue and capture. **3.** To hit with a moving vehicle. **4.** To disparage; decry. **5.** To give a brief or summary account of.

run-down (rŭn'doun') *n.* A summary or résumé. *—adj.* **1.** In poor condition. **2.** Unwound and not running.

rune (ro͞on) *n.* **1.** One of the letters of an alphabet used by ancient Germanic peoples. **2.** A poem written in runic characters. **3.** Magic. [< ON *rūn,* secret writing, rune.] **—run'ic** *adj.*

basic Germanic runic alphabet

two later runes used in English

rune

rung¹ (rŭng) *n.* **1.** A bar forming a step of a ladder. **2.** A crosspiece supporting the legs or back of a chair. **3.** A spoke in a wheel. [< OE *hrung.*]

rung² (rŭng). *p.p.* of **ring.**

run in. 1. To insert or include as something extra. **2.** *Slang.* To take into legal custody.

run-in (rŭn'ĭn') *n.* A quarrel or fight.

run•let (rŭn'lĭt) *n.* A rivulet. [Dim of RUN (stream).]

run•nel (rŭn'əl) *n.* A narrow channel or rivulet. [< OE *rinnan,* to RUN.]

run•ner (rŭn'ər) *n.* **1.** One who or that which runs, as a messenger or errand boy. **2.** A device in or on which something slides or moves, as the blade of a skate. **3.** A long narrow carpet or tablecloth. **4.** A creeping stem that roots at intervals along its length.

run•ner-up (rŭn'ər-ŭp') *n.* One that takes second place.

running gear. 1. The working parts of an automobile or other vehicle. **2.** The part of a ship's rigging that comprises the ropes with which sails are raised or lowered, booms are operated, etc.

run•ny (rŭn'ē) *adj.* **-nier, -niest.** Inclined to run.

run-off (rŭn'ôf', -ŏf') *n.* An extra competition held to break a tie.

runt (rŭnt) *n.* **1.** An undersized animal, esp. the smallest of a litter. **2.** An undersized person. [Poss < Du *rund,* small ox.] **—runt'i•ness** *n.* **—runt'y** *adj.*

run through. 1. To pierce. **2.** To use up (money) quickly. **3.** To examine or rehearse quickly.

run-through (rŭn'thro͞o') *n.* A complete but rapid review or rehearsal of something.

run•way (rŭn'wā') *n.* **1.** A path, channel, or track over which something runs. **2.** A narrow walkway extending from a stage into an auditorium. **3.** A strip on which aircraft take off and land.

ru•pee (ro͞o-pē', ro͞o'pē) *n.* **1.** The basic monetary unit of Ceylon and Mauritius. **2.** The basic monetary unit of India. **3.** The basic monetary unit of Nepal. **4.** The basic monetary unit of Pakistan.

ru•pi•ah (ro͞o-pē'ä) *n., pl.* **-ah** or **-ahs.** The basic monetary unit of Indonesia.

rup•ture (rŭp'chər) *n.* **1.** A breaking open or bursting. **2.** A tear in bodily tissue. [< L *rumpere* (pp *ruptus*), to break.] **—rup'ture** *v.* **(-tured, -turing).**

ru•ral (ro͝or'əl) *adj.* Of or pertaining to the country as opposed to the city; rustic. [< L *rūs (rūr-),* country.] **—ru'ral•ly** *adv.*

ruse (ro͞oz) *n.* A trick; artifice; strategem. [< OF *ruser,* to repulse, detour.]

rush¹ (rŭsh) *v.* **1.** To move or act swiftly. **2.** To attack; charge. **3.** To perform with great haste. *—n.* **1.** A sudden forward motion. **2.** General haste or busyness. **3.** A sudden onslaught. **4.** A great flurry of activity or press of business. [< L *recusāre,* to object to.] **—rush'er** *n.*

rush² (rŭsh) *n.* A grasslike marsh plant with hollow or pithy stems. [< OE *rysc.* See **rezg-.**]

Russ. Russia; Russian.

rus•set (rŭs'ĭt) *n.* **1.** Moderate to strong brown. **2.** A reddish-brown homespun cloth. **3.** A winter apple with a reddish-brown skin. [< L *russus,* red.] **—rus'set** *adj.*

Rus•sia (rŭsh'ə). **1.** The name commonly applied to the **Union of Soviet Socialist Republics. 2.** The **Russian Soviet Federated Socialist Republic.**

Rus•sian (rŭsh'ən) *n.* **1.** A native or inhabitant

of Russia. 2. One of Russian descent. 3. The Slavic language of the Russian people. —**Rus'sian** *adj.*
Russian dressing. Mayonnaise with chili sauce, chopped pickles, and pimientos.
Russian Orthodox Church. 1. An independent branch of the Eastern Orthodox Church in the Soviet Union headed by the Patriarch of Moscow. 2. A branch of this church outside the Soviet Union.
Russian Soviet Federated Socialist Republic. The largest republic of the Soviet Union, in Europe and Asia. Pop. 130,090,000. Cap. Moscow.
rust (rŭst) *n.* 1. Any of various reddish oxides formed on iron by low-temperature oxidation in the presence of water. 2. A stain or coating resembling iron dust. 3. A plant disease caused by parasitic fungi, characterized by brownish spots on leaves and stems. 4. Reddish brown. —*v.* 1. To corrode. 2. To deteriorate through inactivity. 3. To become the color of rust. [< OE *rūst.* See **reudh-**.] —**rust'i•ness** *n.* —**rust'y** *adj.*
rus•tic (rŭs'tĭk) *adj.* 1. Typical of country life. 2. Unsophisticated; bucolic. 3. Made of rough tree branches: *rustic furniture.* —*n.* 1. A country person. 2. A simpleton. [< L *rūs,* country.] —**rus'ti•cal•ly** *adv.* —**rus•tic'i•ty** (-tĭs'ə-tē) *n.*
rus•ti•cate (rŭs'tĭ-kāt') *v.* **-cated, -cating.** To go to or live in the country. —**rus'ti•ca'tion** *n.* —**rus'ti•ca'tor** *n.*
rus•tle[1] (rŭs'əl) *v.* **-tled, -tling.** 1. To move with soft whispering sounds. 2. To cause to make such sounds. [ME *rustelen.*] —**rus'tle** *n.* —**rus'tler** *n.* —**rus'tling•ly** *adv.*
rus•tle[2] (rŭs'əl) *v.* **-tled, -tling.** 1. To steal cattle. 2. *Informal.* To forage. [Prob < RUSTLE.] —**rus'tler** *n.*
rut[1] (rŭt) *n.* 1. A sunken track or groove made by the passage of wheels. 2. A fixed routine of thought or action. [OF *route,* way, route.]
rut[2] (rŭt) *n.* A condition of sexual excitement and reproductive activity in male mammals, as deer. —*v.* **rutted, rutting.** To be in rut. [< L *rūgire,* to roar.]
ru•ta•ba•ga (ro͞o'tə-bā'gə) *n.* A turniplike plant with a thick, bulbous, edible root. [Swed (dial) *rotabagge,* "baggy root."]
ru•the•ni•um (ro͞o-thē'nē-əm) *n.* *Symbol* **Ru** A hard white acid-resistant metallic element used to harden platinum and palladium and in nonmagnetic wear-resistant alloys. Atomic number 44, atomic weight 101.07. [< ML *Ruthenia,* Russia.]
ruth•less (ro͞oth'lĭs) *adj.* Having no compassion or pity; merciless. [< OE *hrēowan,* to rue + -LESS.] —**ruth'less•ly** *adv.* —**ruth'less•ness** *n.*
Rwan•da (rwän'dä, ro͞o-än'-). A republic of east-central Africa. Pop. 3,000,000. Cap. Kigali.

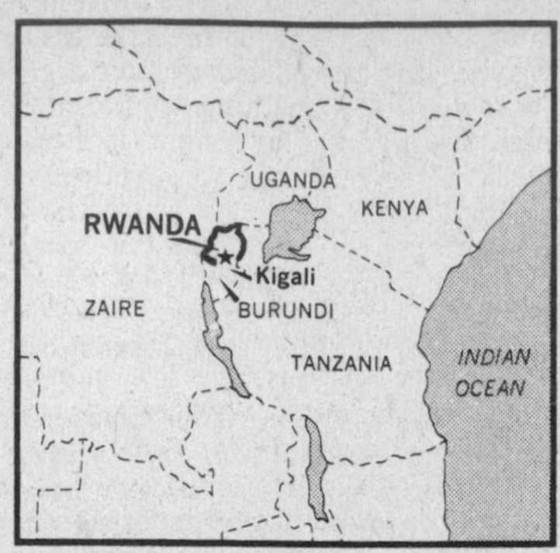

Rwanda

Rwy., Ry. railway.
-ry. Variant of **-ery.**
rye (rī) *n.* 1. A widely cultivated cereal grass. 2. The grain of this plant, used in making flour and whiskey. 3. Whiskey made from rye. [< OE *ryge.* See **wrughyo-**.]
Ryu•kyu Islands (ryo͞o'kyo͞o'). A group of islands in the Pacific between Kyushu, Japan, and Taiwan.

Ss

s, S (ĕs) *n.* 1. The 19th letter of the English alphabet. 2. **S** Anything shaped like the letter **S.**
s 1. second. 2. south; southern. 3. stere.
S 1. small. 2. south; southern. 3. sulfur.
s. 1. small. 2. son. 3. south; southern. 4. substantive.
S. 1. Saturday. 2. school. 3. sea. 4. September. 5. south; southern. 6. Sunday.
-s[1]. *comb. form.* Indicates the plural form: *toys.* [< OE *-as.*]
-s[2]. *comb. form.* Indicates the 3rd person sing. form of the present indicative: *She sleeps.* [< OE *-es, -as.*]
-s[3]. *comb. form.* Used in the formation of certain adverbs from nouns and adjectives: *unawares.*
-'s[1]. *comb. form.* Indicates the possessive case: *men's.* [< OE *-es.*]
-'s[2]. 1. Contraction of **is:** *She's here.* 2. Contraction of **has:** *He's been eating.* 3. Contraction of **us:** *Let's go.*
Sab•bath (săb'əth) *n.* 1. The 7th day of the week, Saturday, observed as the day of rest and worship by Jews and some Christian sects. 2. The 1st day of the week, Sunday, observed as the day of rest by most Christian churches. [< Heb *shābhath,* to rest.]
sa•ber (sā'bər) *n.* Also *chiefly Brit.* **sa•bre.** 1. A heavy cavalry sword with a one-edged, slightly curved blade. 2. A two-edged sword used in fencing. [< MHG *sabel, sebel.*]
Sa•bin vaccine (sā'bĭn). A live attenuated virus taken orally to immunize against poliomyelitis. [< A. *Sabin* (born 1906), American physician.]
sa•ble (sā'bəl) *n.* 1. A weasellike mammal of N Eurasia, having soft, dark fur. 2. The valuable fur of this animal. 3. a. The color black. b. **sables.** Black garments worn in mourning. [< ML *sabelum.*] —**sa'ble** *adj.*
sab•o•tage (săb'ə-täzh') *n.* 1. The damaging of property or procedure so as to obstruct productivity or normal functioning. 2. Any underhanded effort to defeat or do harm to an endeavor; deliberate subversion. [< F *saboter,* "to clatter shoes," work clumsily.] —**sab'o•tage'** *v.* **(-taged, -taging).**
sab•o•teur (săb'ə-tûr') *n.* One who commits sabotage.
sa•bra (sä'brə, -brä) *n.* A native-born Israeli. [Heb *Ṣabēr.*]
sa•bre. *Chiefly Brit.* Variant of **saber.**
sac (săk) *n.* A pouchlike plant or animal structure. [< L *saccus,* a sack.]
SAC Strategic Air Command.
sac•cha•rin (săk'ə-rĭn) *n.* An extremely sweet crystalline powder, $C_7H_5NO_3S$, used as a calorie-free sweetener. [< Gk *sakkharon,* sugar.]
sac•cha•rine (săk'ə-rĭn, -rīn') *adj.* 1. Of, relating to, or of the nature of sugar or saccharin; sweet. 2. Having a cloyingly sweet attitude, tone, or character.
sac•er•do•tal (săs'ər-dōt'l, săk'-) *adj.* Of or pertaining to priests or the priesthood; priestly. [< L *sacerdōs,* a priest.]
sa•chem (sā'chəm) *n.* The chief of a tribe or confederation among some North American Indians. [< Algon.]
sa•chet (să-shā') *n.* A small bag containing perfumed powder, used to scent clothes. [< OF, a small bag.]
sack[1] (săk) *n.* 1. A large bag of strong, coarse material. 2. A similar but smaller container, often of paper or plastic. 3. A short, loose-fitting coat or dress. 4. *Slang.* Dismissal from employment: *get the sack.* 5. *Slang.* A bed. —*v.* 1. To place in a sack. 2. *Slang.* To discharge from employment. [< Gk *sakkos.*]
sack[2] (săk) *v.* To loot or pillage. [< OF *(mettre a) sac,* (to put in) a sack, plunder.] —**sack** *n.*
sack•cloth (săk'klôth') *n.* 1. A rough cloth. 2. Garments made of this cloth, worn as a symbol of mourning or penitence.
sack•ing (săk'ĭng) *n.* Stout woven cloth used for making sacks.
sac•ra•ment (săk'rə-mənt) *n.* 1. Any of the rites of the Christian church considered to have been instituted by Christ, as the Eucharist, baptism, etc. 2. **Sacrament.** The consecrated elements of the Eucharist. [< L *sacrāre,* to consecrate.] —**sac'ra•men'tal** (-mĕn'təl) *adj.* —**sac'ra•men'tal•ly** *adv.*
Sac•ra•men•to (săk'rə-mĕn'tō). The capital of California. Pop. 258,000.
sa•cred (sā'krĭd) *adj.* 1. Dedicated to or set apart for worship. 2. Made or declared holy. 3. Dedicated or devoted exclusively to a single use or person. 4. Worthy of reverence or respect. 5. Of or pertaining to religious as opposed to secular things; not secular or profane.

[< L *sacer,* dedicated, holy, sacred.] **—sa'cred•ly** *adv.* **—sa'cred•ness** *n.*

sac•ri•fice (săk'rə-fīs') *n.* **1.** The offering of something to a deity. **2. a.** The forfeiture of something highly valued for the sake of someone or something considered to have a greater value or claim. **b.** Something so forfeited. **3. a.** A relinquishing of something at less than its presumed value. **b.** A loss so sustained. *—v.* **-ficed, -ficing. 1.** To offer as a sacrifice. **2.** To forfeit something for something considered to have a greater value or claim. **3.** To sell or give away at a loss. [< L *sacrificium.*] **—sac'ri•fic'er** *n.* **—sac'ri•fi'cial** (-fĭsh'əl) *adj.* **—sac'ri•fi'cial•ly** *adv.*

sac•ri•lege (săk'rə-lĭj) *n.* The misuse, theft, desecration, or profanation of anything regarded as sacred. [< L *sacrilegus,* one who steals sacred things.] **—sac'ri•le'gious** (-lē'jəs) *adj.* **—sac'ri•le'gious•ness** *n.*

sac•ris•tan (săk'rĭs-tən) *n.* **1.** A person in charge of a sacristy. **2.** A sexton. [< ML *sacrista,* "one in charge of sacred vessels."]

sac•ris•ty (săk'rĭs-tē) *n., pl.* **-ties.** A room in a church housing the sacred vessels and vestments; vestry.

sac•ro•sanct (săk'rō-săngkt') *adj.* Regarded as inviolably sacred. [L *sacrōsanctus,* consecrated with religious ceremonies.]

sa•crum (sā'krəm) *n., pl.* **-cra** (-krə). A triangular bone that forms the posterior section of the pelvis. [< LL *(os) sacrum,* "sacred bone."]

sad (săd) *adj.* **sadder, saddest. 1.** Sorrowful; unhappy. **2.** Causing or expressing sorrow. **3.** Deplorable; sorry. [< OE *sæd,* sated, weary. See **sā-.**] **—sad'ly** *adv.* **—sad'ness** *n.*

sad•den (săd'n) *v.* To make or become sad.

sad•dle (săd'l) *n.* **1.** A leather seat for a rider, secured on an animal's back by a girth. **2.** A cut of meat, as lamb, including the backbone. **—in the saddle.** In a position of control. *—v.* **-dled, -dling. 1.** To put a saddle on (a horse). **2.** To load or burden; encumber. [< OE *sadol.* See **sed-.**]

sad•dle•bow (săd'l-bō') *n.* The arched upper front part of a saddle; pommel.

saddle horse. A horse bred or schooled for riding.

saddle shoe. A flat casual shoe, usually white, having a band of leather in a contrasting color across the instep.

Sad•du•cee (săj'o͝o-sē, săd'yo͝o-) *n.* An ancient Jewish priestly sect that opposed the Pharisees. **—Sad'du•ce'an** (-sē'ən) *adj.*

sa•de, sa•dhe (sä'də, -dē) *n.* Also **tsa•de** (tsä'də, -dē). The 18th letter of the Hebrew alphabet, representing *s.*

sad•i•ron (săd'ī'ərn) *n.* A heavy flatiron with a removable handle. [SAD (in the dial sense of "heavy") + IRON.]

sa•dism (sā'dĭz'əm, săd'ĭz'əm) *n.* **1.** The association of sexual satisfaction with the infliction of pain on others. **2.** Broadly, delight in cruelty. [< D.A.F. de *Sade* (1740–1814), who expounded principles of anarchic sexual violence.] **—sa'dist** *n.* **—sa•dis'tic** (sə-dĭs'tĭk) *adj.* **—sa•dis'ti•cal•ly** *adv.*

sa•fa•ri (sə-fä'rē) *n.* An overland expedition, esp. for hunting or exploration in Africa. [Ar *safarīy,* a journey.]

safe (sāf) *adj.* **safer, safest. 1.** Not apt to cause or incur danger or harm. **2.** Unhurt: *safe and sound.* **3.** Free from hazard; sure: *a safe bet.* **4.** Affording protection: *a safe place.* **5.** *Baseball.* Having reached a base without being put out. *—n.* A metal container or enclosure for storing valuables; strongbox. [< L *salvus,* healthy, uninjured, safe.] **—safe'ly** *adv.*

safe-con•duct (sāf'kŏn'dŭkt) *n.* A document assuring unmolested passage, as through enemy lines.

safe•guard (sāf'gärd') *n.* A precautionary measure or device. *—v.* To insure the safety of; protect.

safe•keep•ing (sāf'kē'pĭng) *n.* Protection; care.

safe•ty (sāf'tē) *n., pl.* **-ties. 1.** Freedom from danger or injury. **2.** Any of various protective devices. **3.** *Football.* **a.** A play in which the offensive team downs the ball behind its own goal line. **b.** A defensive back closest to his own goal line.

safety match. A match that can be lighted only by being struck against a chemically prepared friction surface.

safety pin. A pin in the form of a clasp, having a sheath to cover and hold the point.

saf•fron (săf'rən) *n.* **1.** The dried orange-yellow stigmas of a kind of crocus, used to color and flavor food and as a dye. **2.** Orange-yellow. [< Ar *za'farān.*] **—saf'fron** *adj.*

sag (săg) *v.* **sagged, sagging. 1.** To sink or bend downward, as from pressure or slackness. **2.** To droop. [Perh < Scand.] **—sag** *n.*

sa•ga (sä'gə) *n.* **1.** An Icelandic prose narrative of the 12th and 13th centuries. **2.** A long heroic narrative. [ON, a story, legend.]

sa•ga•cious (sə-gā'shəs) *adj.* Shrewd and wise. [< L *sagāx.*] **—sa•gac'i•ty** (-găs'ə-tē) *n.*

sage[1] (sāj) *n.* A venerable wise man. *—adj.* **sager, sagest.** Judicious; wise. [< L *sapere,* to be sensible, be wise.] **—sage'ly** *adv.*

sage[2] (sāj) *n.* **1.** An aromatic plant with grayish-green leaves used as seasoning. **2.** Sagebrush. [< L *salvia,* "the healing plant."]

sage•brush (sāj'brŭsh') *n.* An aromatic shrub of arid regions of W North America.

sag•it•tal (săj'ə-təl) *adj.* **1.** Of or like an arrow or arrowhead. **2.** Relating to the suture uniting the two parietal bones of the skull. [< L *sagitta,* arrow.] **—sag'it•tal•ly** *adv.*

Sag•it•ta•ri•us (săj'ə-târ'ē-əs) *n.* **1.** A constellation in the S Hemisphere. **2.** The 9th sign of the zodiac. [< L *sagittārius,* an archer, Sagittarius.]

sa•go (sā'gō) *n.* A powdery starch obtained from the trunks of an Asian palm. [Malay *sagu.*]

sa•gua•ro (sə-gwär'ō, sə-wär'ō) *n., pl.* **-ros.** Also **sa•hua•ro** (sə-wär'ō). A very large branching cactus of SW North America. [Mex Span.]

Sa•har•a (sə-hâr'ə, -hä'rə). A desert of N Africa.

sa•hib (sä'ĭb) *n.* A title of respect for Europeans in colonial India, equivalent to *master* or *sir.* [Hindi *ṣāḥib,* master, lord.]

said (sĕd). *p.t. & p.p.* of **say.** *—adj.* Aforementioned.

Sai•gon (sī-gŏn'). Officially, Ho Chi Minh City. A port of Vietnam. Pop. 1,707,000.

sail (sāl) *n.* **1.** A length of shaped fabric that catches the wind and propels or aids in maneuvering a vessel. **2.** A sailing ship. **3.** A trip in a sailing craft. **4.** Something resembling a sail. *—v.* **1.** To move across the surface of water by means of a sail. **2.** To travel by water in a vessel. **3.** To start out on a voyage. **4.** To operate a sailing craft; navigate or manage (a vessel). **5.** To glide through the air; soar. [< OE *segl* < Gmc **seglam.*]

sail•boat (sāl'bōt') *n.* A small boat propelled by a sail or sails.

sail•fish (sāl'fĭsh') *n.* A large marine fish with a large dorsal fin and a spearlike projection from the upper jaw.

sail•or (sā'lər) *n.* **1.** One who serves in a navy or earns his living working on a ship. **2.** A straw hat with a flat top and brim.

saint (sānt) *n.* **1.** *Theol.* **a.** A person officially entitled to public veneration for extreme holiness. **b.** A human soul inhabiting heaven. **2.** A very holy or unselfish person. [< L *sanctus,* sacred.] **—saint'dom** *n.* **—saint'hood'** *n.*

saint•ly (sānt'lē) *adj.* **-lier, -liest.** Of or befitting a saint. **—saint'li•ness** *n.*

Saint-Saëns (săN-säNs'), **Camille.** 1835–1921. French composer.

saith (sĕth, sā'əth). *Archaic.* 3rd person sing. present indicative of **say.**

sake[1] (sāk) *n.* **1.** Purpose; motive: *for the sake of argument.* **2.** Advantage, benefit, or welfare. [< OE *sacu,* lawsuit. See **sāg-.**]

sa•ke[2] (sä'kē) *n.* Also **sa•ki.** A Japanese liquor made from fermented rice.

sa•laam (sə-läm') *n.* An Oriental obeisance performed by bowing low while placing the right palm on the forehead. [Ar *salām,* "peace."] **—sa•laam'** *v.*

sa•la•cious (sə-lā'shəs) *adj.* Lewd; bawdy. [< L *salāx,* fond of leaping, lustful.] **—sa•la'cious•ly** *adv.* **—sa•la'cious•ness, sa•lac'i•ty** (sə-lăs'ə-tē) *n.*

sal•ad (săl'əd) *n.* A dish usually consisting of raw green vegetables tossed with a dressing. [< VL **salāre,* to salt.]

sal•a•man•der (săl'ə-măn'dər) *n.* **1.** A small, lizardlike amphibian. **2.** A portable stove used to heat or dry buildings under construction. [< Gk *salamandra.*]

sa•la•mi (sə-lä'mē) *n.* A highly spiced and salted sausage. [< It *salame,* "salted pork."]

sal•a•ried (săl'ə-rēd) *adj.* Earning or yielding a regular salary.

sal•a•ry (săl'ə-rē, săl'rē) *n., pl.* **-ries.** A fixed compensation for services, paid on a regular basis. [< L *salārium,* orig "money given to Roman soldiers to buy salt."]

sale (sāl) *n.* **1.** The exchange of property or ownership for money. **2.** Demand; ready market. **3.** Availability for purchase: *on sale.* **4.** An auction. **5.** A special disposal of goods at lowered prices. [< OE *sala* < ON.] **—sal'a•ble, sale'a•ble** *adj.*

Sa•lem (sā'ləm). The capital of Oregon. Pop. 68,000.

sales•man (sālz'mən) *n.* A man employed to sell merchandise, insurance, etc. **—sales'man•ship'** *n.* **—sales'wom'an** *fem.n.*

sal•i•cyl•ic acid (săl'ə-sĭl'ĭk). A white crystalline acid, $C_7H_6O_3$, used in making aspirin. [< L *salix,* willow.]

sa•li•ent (sā'lē-ənt) *adj.* **1.** Projecting or jutting beyond a line. **2.** Striking; conspicuous. [< L *salīre,* to leap, jump.] **—sa'li•ence, sa'li•en•cy** *n.*

sa•line (sā'lēn', -līn') *adj.* Of or containing salt. [< L *sāl,* salt.] **—sa•lin'i•ty** (sə-lĭn'ə-tē) *n.*

Salis•bur•y (sôlz'bĕr-ē, -brē). The capital of Rhodesia. Pop. 314,000.

Sa•lish (sā'lĭsh) *n.* Also **Sa•lish•an** (sā'lĭsh-ən, săl'ĭsh-). **1.** A family of languages spoken by North American Indian tribes in the NW U.S. and British Columbia. **2.** The Indians speaking languages of this family. **—Sa'lish•an** *adj.*

sa•li•va (sə-lī'və) *n.* The watery, tasteless liquid mixture of salivary and oral mucous gland secretions that lubricates chewed food, moistens the oral walls, and functions in the digestion of starches. [L *salīva.*] **—sal'i•var'y** (săl'ə-vĕr'ē) *adj.*

salivary gland. A gland that secretes saliva, esp. any of three pairs of large glands the secretions of which enter the mouth and mingle in saliva.

sal•i•vate (săl'ə-vāt') *v.* **-vated, -vating.** To secrete or produce saliva. **—sal'i•va'tion** *n.*

Salk vaccine (sôlk). A killed-virus vaccine used to immunize actively against poliomyelitis. [< J. *Salk* (born 1914), American microbiologist.]

sal•low (săl'ō) *adj.* Of a sickly yellowish hue or complexion. [< OE *salo.* See **sal-²**.] **—sal'low•ly** *adv.* **—sal'low•ness** *n.*

sal•ly (săl'ē) *n., pl.* **-lies. 1.** A sudden assault from a defensive position. **2.** A quick witticism; quip. **3.** A short excursion; jaunt. [< L *salīre,* to leap.] **—sal'ly** *v.* **(-lied, -lying).**

salm•on (săm'ən) *n., pl.* **-on** or **-ons. 1.** Any of various food and game fishes of northern waters, usually having pinkish flesh. **2.** Yellowish pink to reddish orange. [< L *salmō.*] **—salm'on** *adj.*

sa•lon (sə-lŏn') *n.* **1.** An elegant drawing room. **2.** An assemblage of persons, usually of social or intellectual distinction, who frequent such a room. **3.** A shop offering something related to fashion: *beauty salon.* [< It *sala,* a hall, room.]

sa•loon (sə-lo͞on') *n.* **1.** A barroom. **2.** A large lounge or ballroom on a ship. [F *salon,* salon.]

sal soda. A hydrated sodium carbonate used as a general cleanser.

salt (sôlt) *n.* **1.** A colorless or white crystalline solid, chiefly sodium chloride, extensively used as a food seasoning and preservative. **2.** A chemical compound formed by replacing all or part of the hydrogen ions of an acid with one or more metallic ions. **3. salts.** Any of various mineral salts used as a laxative or cathartic. **4.** An element that gives flavor or zest. **5.** Wit or pungency of expression. **6.** *Informal.* A veteran sailor. *—adj.* **1.** Tasting of salt. **2.** Preserved in salt. *—v.* To season, cure, or feed with salt. [< OE *sealt.* See **sal-¹**.] **—salt'i•ness** *n.* **—salt'y** *adj.*

salt•cel•lar (sôlt'sĕl'ər) *n.* A small dish or shaker for salt. [Var of ME *salt saler.*]

sal•tine (sôl-tēn') *n.* A thin salted cracker.

Salt Lake City. The capital of Utah. Pop. 177,000.

salt lick. A deposit or block of exposed salt that animals lick.

salt marsh. Low coastal grassland frequently overflowed by the tide.

salt•pe•ter (sôlt'pē'tər) *n.* Also *chiefly Brit.* **salt•pe•tre. 1. Potassium nitrate. 2. Sodium nitrate.** [< ML *salpetra,* prob "salt rock."]

salt•shak•er (sôlt'shā'kər) *n.* A container for sprinkling table salt.

salt•wat•er (sôlt'wô'tər, -wŏt'ər) *adj.* Consisting of or inhabiting salt water.

sa•lu•bri•ous (sə-lo͞o'brē-əs) *adj.* Conducive to health or well-being. [< L *salūs,* health.] **—sa•lu'bri•ous•ly** *adv.*

sal•u•tar•y (săl'yə-tĕr'ē) *adj.* **1.** Beneficially corrective; remedial. **2.** Wholesome. [< L *salūs,* health.]

sal•u•ta•tion (săl'yə-tā'shən) *n.* An expression of greeting, good will, or courtesy. [< L *salūtāre,* to SALUTE.]

sa•lute (sə-lo͞ot') *v.* **-luted, -luting. 1.** To greet. **2.** To recognize (a military superior) with a prescribed gesture. **3.** To honor formally. *—n.* **1.** A greeting. **2.** A prescribed military display of honor or greeting. [< L *salūtāre,* to preserve, salute, wish health to.]

sal•vage (săl'vĭj) *v.* **1.** The rescue of a ship. **2.** Compensation given to those who voluntarily aid in such a rescue. **3. a.** The saving of any imperiled property from loss. **b.** The property so saved. *—v.* **-vaging, -vages.** To save from loss or destruction. [< F, the act of saving.] **—sal'vage•a•ble** *adj.*

sal•va•tion (săl-vā'shən) *n.* **1.** Preservation or deliverance from evil or difficulty. **2.** A means or cause of such deliverance. **3.** Deliverance from the power or penalty of sin; redemption. [< LL *salvāre,* to save.]

salve (săv, säv) *n.* An analgesic or medicinal ointment. *—v.* **salved, salving. 1.** To dress (a wound or sore) with salve. **2.** To soothe; ease. [< OE *salf, sealf.* See **selp-**.]

sal•ver (săl'vər) *n.* A serving platter or tray. [< F *salve,* a tray for presenting food (to the king).]

sal•vo (săl'vō) *n., pl.* **-vos** or **-voes.** A simultaneous firing of guns. [< It *salva,* salute, volley.]

sa•mar•i•um (sə-mâr'ē-əm) *n. Symbol* **Sm** A silvery or pale-gray metallic rare-earth element used in laser materials, in infrared absorbing glass, and as a neutron absorber. Atomic number 62, atomic weight 150.35.

same (sām) *adj.* **1.** Being the very one; not different; identical. **2.** Similar or corresponding. *—pron.* **1.** A person, thing, or event identical with or similar to another. **2.** An aforesaid person or thing. *—adv.* In like or identical manner. [< ON *samr.*] **—same'ness** *n.*

sa•mekh (sä'mĕk) *n.* Also **sa•mech, sa•mek.** The 15th letter of the Hebrew alphabet, representing *s.*

Sa•mo•a (sə-mō'ə). An island group in the South Pacific. **—Sa•mo'an** *adj.*

sam•o•var (săm'ə-vär') *n.* A metal urn with a spigot, used to boil water for tea. [Russ, "self-boiler."]

Sam•o•yed (săm'ə-yĕd') *n.* Also **Sam•o•yede. 1.** A member of a Ural-Altaic people inhabiting the tundra lands of the NE European Soviet Union and NW Siberia. **2.** A branch of the Uralic family of languages including four languages spoken by the Samoyed tribes inhabiting this region. **—Sam'o•yed'ic** *adj.*

sam•pan (săm'păn') *n.* Any of various flat-bottomed skiffs used in the Orient. [Chin *san¹ pan³* (obs).]

sam•ple (săm'pəl) *n.* A portion, piece, or segment regarded as representative of a whole. *—v.* **-pled, -pling.** To take a sample of, esp. to test or examine by a sample. [< OF *essample,* example.]

sam•pler (săm'plər) *n.* **1.** One employed to appraise samples. **2.** A piece of cloth embroidered with various designs.

sam•u•rai (săm'o͞o-rī') *n., pl.* **-rai** or **-rais.** The military aristocracy of feudal Japan, or one of its members.

San•a (sä-nä'). Also **Sa•n'a.** The capital of Yemen. Pop. 135,000.

San An•to•ni•o (săn' ăn-tō'nē-ō). A city of Texas. Pop. 588,000.

san•a•to•ri•um (săn'ə-tôr'ē-əm, -tōr'ē-əm) *n.* **1.** An institution for the treatment of chronic diseases. **2.** A sanitarium. [< L *sānus,* healthy, sane.]

sanc•ti•fy (săngk'tə-fī') *v.* **-fied, -fying. 1.** To reserve for sacred use; consecrate. **2.** To make holy; purify. [< LL *sanctificāre.*] **—sanc'ti•fi•ca'tion** *n.* **—sanc'ti•fi'er** *n.*

sanc•ti•mo•ni•ous (săngk'tə-mō'nē-əs) *adj.* Making a pretense of piety. [< L *sanctus,* sacred.] **—sanc'ti•mo'ni•ous•ly** *adv.* **—sanc'ti•mo'ni•ous•ness** *n.*

sanc•tion (săngk'shən) *n.* **1.** Authoritative permission or approval. **2.** A penalty intended to enforce compliance or conformity. **3.** A coercive measure adopted usually by several nations against a nation violating international law. *—v.* To authorize, approve, or encourage. [< L *sanctus,* sacred.]

sanc•ti•ty (săngk'tə-tē) *n., pl.* **-ties. 1.** Saintliness or godliness. **2.** Sacredness or inviolability: *the sanctity of a church.* [< L *sanctus,* sacred.]

sanc•tu•ar•y (săngk'cho͞o-ĕr'ē) *n., pl.* **-ies. 1.** A consecrated place, as of a house of worship. **2.** A place of refuge, asylum, or protection. [< L *sanctus,* sacred.]

sanc•tum (săngk'təm) *n., pl.* **-tums** or **-ta** (-tə). A private room or study. [< L *sanctus,* sacred.]

sand (sănd) *n.* Loose, granular, gritty particles of worn or disintegrated rock, finer than gravel and coarser than dust. *—v.* **1.** To polish or scour with sand or sandpaper. **2.** To fill up (a harbor) with sand. [< OE.] **—sand'er** *n.* **—sand'i•ness** *n.* **—sand'y** *adj.*

san•dal (săn'dəl) *n.* **1.** A shoe consisting of a sole fastened to the foot by thongs or straps. **2.** A light slipper or low-cut shoe. [< Gk *sandalon.*]

san•dal•wood (săn'dəl-wo͝od') *n.* **1.** An Asian tree with aromatic wood used for carving and in perfumery. **2.** The wood of this tree. [< Gk *sandanon.*]

sand•bar (sănd'bär') *n.* A ridge or shoal of sand in a river, off a shore, etc.

sand•blast (sănd'blăst', -bläst') *n.* A blast of air carrying sand at high velocity, as for cleaning stone or metal surfaces. **—sand'blast'** *v.* **—sand'blast'er** *n.*

sand•box (sănd'bŏks') *n.* A low, sand-filled box in which children play.

sand•cast (sănd'kăst', -käst') *v.* To make (a casting of something) by pouring molten metal into a sand mold.

sand•hog (sănd'hôg', -hŏg') *n.* A laborer who works under compressed air, as in underwater tunnel-building.

San Di•e•go (săn' dē-ā'gō). A city in S California. Pop. 676,000.

sand-lot (sănd'lŏt') *adj.* Designating a game played by amateurs, esp. children, usually in a vacant lot: *sand-lot baseball.*

sand•man (sănd'măn') *n.* A mysterious character of folklore who causes children to sleep by sprinkling sand in their eyes.

sand•pa•per (sănd'pā'pər) *n.* Heavy paper coated on one side with a particulate abrasive, used for smoothing. **—sand'pa'per** *v.*

sand•pi•per (sănd'pī'pər) *n.* Any of various small, slender-billed shore birds.

sand•stone (sănd'stōn') *n.* Variously colored sedimentary rock composed predominantly of sandlike quartz.

sand•storm (sănd'stôrm') *n.* A strong wind carrying clouds of sand.

sand•wich (sănd'wĭch, săn'-) *n.* Two or more slices of bread with meat, cheese, or other filling placed between them. [< the Fourth Earl of *Sandwich* (1718–92).]

sane (sān) *adj.* **saner, sanest. 1.** Of sound mind. **2.** Having sound judgment; reasonable; rational. [L *sānus,* sound, whole, healthy.] **—sane'ly** *adv.* **—sane'ness** *n.*

San Fran•cis•co (săn' frən-sĭs'kō). A city of N California. Pop. 704,000.

sang (săng). *p.t.* of **sing.**

sang-froid (säN-frwä') *n.* Composure; imperturbability. [F, "cold blood."]

san•gui•nar•y (săng'gwə-nĕr'ē) *adj.* **1.** Bloody.

2. Bloodthirsty. [L *sanguinārius,* of blood.] **—san'gui•nar'i•ly** *adv.*

san•guine (săng'gwĭn) *adj.* 1. Ruddy, as the complexion. 2. Eagerly optimistic; cheerful. [< L *sanguis,* blood.] **—san'guine•ly** *adv.* **—san'guine•ness** *n.*

san•i•tar•i•um (săn'ə-târ'ē-əm) *n.* 1. A health resort. 2. A sanatorium. [< L *sānitās,* health, sanity.]

san•i•tar•y (săn'ə-tĕr'ē) *adj.* 1. Of or used to preserve health. 2. Clean; hygienic. [< L *sānitās,* health, sanity.]

san•i•ta•tion (săn'ə-tā'shən) *n.* 1. The formulation and application of public health measures. 2. The disposal of sewage and garbage.

san•i•tize (săn'ə-tīz') *v.* **-tized, -tizing.** To make sanitary.

san•i•ty (săn'ə-tē) *n.* Soundness of mind or reason. [< L *sānus,* healthy, SANE.]

San Jo•se (săn' hō-zā'). A city of W California. Pop. 204,000.

San Jo•sé (sän' hō-zā'). The capital of Costa Rica. Pop. 114,000.

San Juan (sän' hwän'). The capital of Puerto Rico. Pop. 452,000.

sank (săngk). *p.t.* of **sink.**

San Ma•ri•no (săn' mə-rē'nō). 1. A republic in the Apennines of Italy. Pop. 17,000. 2. The capital of this republic.

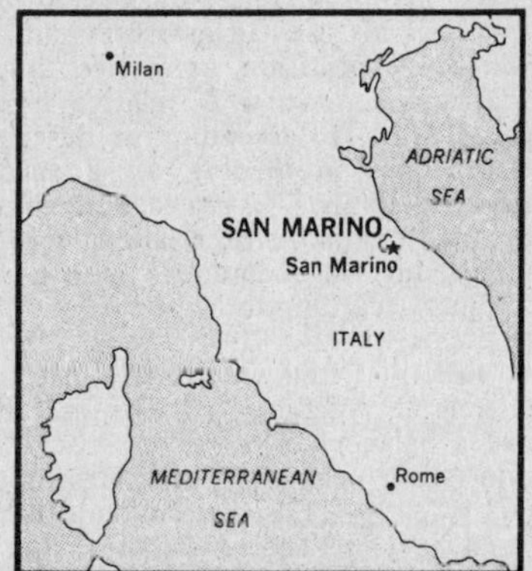

San Marino

sans (sănz) *prep.* Without. [< L *sine.*]

San Sal•va•dor (săn' săl'və-dôr). The capital of El Salvador. Pop. 281,000.

San•skrit (săn'skrĭt') *n.* An ancient Indic language of India, now used only for sacred or scholarly writings.

San•ta Claus (săn'tə klôz'). The personification of the spirit of Christmas as a fat old man with a white beard and a red suit. [< MDu *Sint Nicolaes,* Saint Nicholas, the patron saint of children.]

San•ta Fe (săn'tə fā'). The capital of New Mexico. Pop. 39,000.

San•ta Is•a•bel (săn'tə ĭz'ə-bĕl'). The capital of Equatorial Guinea. Pop. 20,000.

San•ti•a•go (săn-tyä'gō). The capital of Chile. Pop. 1,907,000.

San•to Do•min•go (săn'tō dō-mēng'gō). The capital of the Dominican Republic. Pop. 478,000.

São Pau•lo (souN pou'lo͞o). A city of SE Brazil. Pop. 3,825,000.

sap[1] (săp) *n.* 1. The watery fluid that circulates through plant tissue. 2. A similar juice or fluid. 3. Health and energy; vitality. 4. *Slang.* A dupe; fool. [< OE *sæp.* See **sab-.**]

sap[2] (săp) *v.* **sapped, sapping.** 1. To undermine the foundations of. 2. To deplete or weaken gradually. [< OF *sappe,* "an undermining."]

sa•pi•ent (sā'pē-ənt) *adj.* Having wisdom; discerning. [< L *sapere,* to taste, to have good taste.] **—sa'pi•ence** *n.* **—sa'pi•ent•ly** *adv.*

sap•ling (săp'lĭng) *n.* A young tree.

sap•phire (săf'īr) *n.* 1. Any of several relatively pure forms of corundum, esp. a blue form used as a gemstone. 2. A corundum gem. 3. The blue color of a gem sapphire. [< Gk *sappheiros.*]

sap•py (săp'ē) *adj.* **-pier, -piest.** 1. Full of sap; juicy. 2. Vital; vigorous. 3. *Slang.* Silly or foolish. **—sap'pi•ness** *n.*

sap•suck•er (săp'sŭk'ər) *n.* A small North American woodpecker that drills into trees to drink the sap.

sar•a•band (săr'ə-bănd') *n.* 1. A stately dance of the 17th and 18th centuries. 2. Music for this dance. [< Span *zarabanda.*]

Sar•a•cen (săr'ə-sən) *n.* 1. Any Moslem, esp. of the time of the Crusades. 2. An Arab.

sa•ra•pe. Variant of **serape.**

sar•casm (sär'kăz'əm) *n.* 1. A mocking remark utilizing statements opposite or irrelevant to the underlying meaning. 2. The use of such remarks. [< Gk *sarkazein,* "to tear flesh," bite the lips in rage.] **—sar•cas'tic** (-kăs'tĭk) *adj.*

sar•coph•a•gus (sär-kŏf'ə-gəs) *n., pl.* **-gi** (-jī'). A stone coffin. [L *sarcophagus (lapis),* "flesh-eating (stone)."]

sar•dine (sär-dēn') *n.* A small herring or similar fish, often canned in oil. [< Gk *sardinos.*]

Sar•din•i•a (sär-dĭn'ē-ə). An Italian island in the W Mediterranean. **—Sar•din'i•an** *adj.* & *n.*

sar•don•ic (sär-dŏn'ĭk) *adj.* Scornful; cynical. [< L *Sardonius (rīsus),* bitter (laugh).] **—sar•don'i•cal•ly** *adv.*

sarge (särj) *n. Informal.* Sergeant.

sa•ri (sär'ē) *n., pl.* **-ris.** A lightweight garment worn chiefly by women of India and Pakistan. [Hindi *sārī.*]

sa•rong (sə-rông', -rŏng') *n.* A brightly colored cloth garment worn by both men and women of the Malay Archipelago and the Pacific islands. [Malay, sarong, sheath.]

sar•sa•pa•ril•la (săs'pə-rĭl'ə, sär'sə-pə-rĭl'ə) *n.* 1. The dried roots of a tropical American plant, used as a flavoring. 2. A soft drink flavored with sarsaparilla. [Span *zarzaparrilla.*]

sar•to•ri•al (sär-tôr'ē-əl, -tōr'ē-əl) *adj.* 1. Pertaining to tailors or tailoring. 2. Pertaining to clothing, esp. men's. [< L *sartor,* a tailor.]

sash[1] (săsh) *n.* A band or ribbon worn about the waist or over the shoulder. [< Ar *shāsh,* muslin.]

sash[2] (săsh) *n.* A frame in which the panes of a window or door are set. [< F *châssis,* a frame, chassis.]

sa•shay (să-shā') *v. Informal.* To strut or flounce. [< F *chasser,* to chase.]

Sas•katch•e•wan (săs-kăch'ə-wän', -wən). A province of W Canada. Pop. 953,000. Cap. Regina.

sass (săs). *Informal. n.* Impertinence; back talk. *—v.* To talk back to. [Back-formation < SASSY.]

sas•sa•fras (săs'ə-frăs') *n.* 1. A North American tree with irregularly lobed leaves and aromatic bark. 2. The dried root bark of this tree, used as flavoring. [< Span *sasafrás.*]

sas•sy (săs'ē) *adj.* **-sier, -siest.** *Informal.* Impudent; saucy. [Var of SAUCY.]

sat (săt). *p.t.* & *p.p.* of **sit.**

SAT Scholastic Aptitude Test.

Sat. Saturday.

Sa•tan (sāt'n) *n.* The Devil. [< Heb *śāṭān,* devil, adversary.]

sa•tan•ic (sə-tăn'ĭk) *adj.* Also **sa•tan•i•cal** (-ĭ-kəl). 1. Pertaining to or suggestive of Satan. 2. Profoundly cruel or evil.

satch•el (săch'əl) *n.* A small valise or bag. [< L *saccus,* a bag, SACK.]

sate[1] (sāt) *v.* **sated, sating.** 1. To indulge (an appetite) fully. 2. To indulge to excess; glut. [Prob < OE *sadian.* See **sā-.**]

sate[2] (săt, sāt). *Archaic. p.t.* of **sit.**

sa•teen (să-tēn') *n.* A cotton fabric with a satin finish. [Var of SATIN.]

sat•el•lite (săt'l-īt') *n.* 1. A relatively small body, natural or artificial, orbiting a planet. 2. One who attends a dignitary. 3. A nation dominated politically by another. [< L *satelles,* an attendant, escort.]

sa•ti•ate (sā'shē-āt') *v.* **-ated, -ating.** 1. To satisfy fully. 2. To gratify to excess. [< L *satis,* sufficient, enough.] **—sa'ti•a'tion** *n.*

sa•ti•e•ty (sə-tī'ə-tē) *n.* The condition of being satiated.

sat•in (săt'n) *n.* A smooth, close-woven fabric with a glossy face. [Prob < Ar *Zaytūn,* Ar form of Chin *Tseutung,* former name of *Tsinkiang,* city in S China.] **—sat'in•y** *adj.*

sat•ire (săt'īr) *n.* 1. A literary work in which irony, derision, or wit is used to expose folly or wickedness. 2. The use of derisive wit to attack folly or wickedness. [< L *satira,* satire, medley, mixture.] **—sa•tir'i•cal** (sə-tĭr'ĭ-kəl), **sa•tir'ic** *adj.* **—sat'i•rist** (săt'ə-rĭst) *n.*

sat•i•rize (săt'ə-rīz') *v.* **-rized, -rizing.** To ridicule by means of satire.

sat•is•fac•tion (săt'ĭs-făk'shən) *n.* 1. Fulfillment or gratification of a desire, need, etc. 2. Pleasure derived from gratification. 3. Reparation in the form of penance. 4. Compensation for injury or loss.

sat•is•fac•to•ry (săt'ĭs-făk'tə-rē) *adj.* Giving satisfaction; adequate. **—sat'is•fac'to•ri•ly** *adv.*

sat•is•fy (săt'ĭs-fī') *v.* **-fied, -fying.** 1. To gratify or fulfill a need, desire, etc. 2. To relieve of doubt or question; assure. 3. To fulfill or discharge an obligation. 4. To conform to the requirements of. 5. To give satisfaction. [< L *satisfacere.*] **—sat'is•fi'er** *n.*

sa•trap (sā'trăp, săt'răp) *n.* A subordinate ruler. [< OPers *khshathrapāvan,* "protector of the country."]

sat•u•rate (săch'ə-rāt') *v.* **-rated, -rating.** 1. To soak thoroughly. 2. To fill to capacity. [L *saturāre,* to fill, satiate.] **—sat'u•ra•ble** (săch'ər-ə-bəl) *adj.* **—sat'u•ra'tion** *n.*

Sat•ur•day (săt'ər-dē, -dā') *n.* The 7th day of the week. [< OE *sæternesdæg,* "Saturn's day."]

Sat•urn (săt'ərn) *n.* The 6th planet from the sun, having a diameter of 74,000 miles, a mass 95 times that of Earth, and an orbital period of 29.5 years at a mean distance of about 886,000,000 miles. [< L *Sāturnus,* Roman deity.]

sat•ur•nine (săt'ər-nīn') *adj.* 1. Morose and sardonic. 2. Pertaining to or resembling lead or produced by the absorption of lead.

sat•yr (săt'ər, sā'tər) *n.* 1. *Gk.Myth.* A woodland god often with the ears, legs, and horns of a goat. 2. A lecher. [< Gk *saturos.*]

sat•y•ri•a•sis (săt'ə-rī'ə-sĭs) *n.* Excessive, often uncontrollable sexual desire in men.

sauce (sôs) *n.* 1. A soft or liquid dressing served as an accompaniment to food. 2. Stewed or puréed fruit. 3. *Informal.* Impudence. *—v.* **sauced, saucing.** 1. To add zest to.

2. *Informal.* To be impudent to. [< L *salsus*, salted.]

sauce•pan (sôs'păn') *n.* A long-handled cooking pan.

sau•cer (sô'sər) *n.* A small, shallow dish for holding a cup. [ME, sauce dish.]

sau•cy (sô'sē) *adj.* **-cier, -ciest.** 1. Impudent. 2. Piquant; pert. —**sau'ci•ly** *adv.*

Sa•u•di A•ra•bi•a (sä-ōō'dē ə-rā'bē-ə). A kingdom of the Arabian peninsula. Pop. 6,000,000. Caps. Riyadh and Mecca.

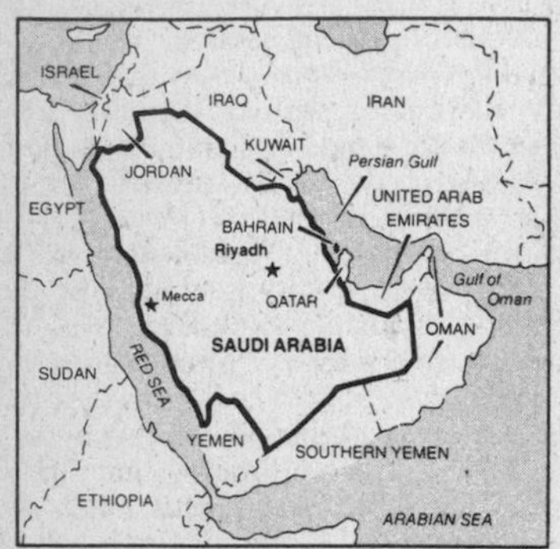

Saudi Arabia

sauer•kraut (sour'krout') *n.* Shredded cabbage that is salted and fermented in its own juice. [G.]

Saul (sôl). 1st king of Israel.

sau•na (sou'nə) *n.* A heat and bath treatment in which one is subjected to heat produced usually by running water over heated rocks. [Finn.]

saun•ter (sôn'tər) *v.* To stroll. —*n.* A leisurely pace; stroll. [Prob ME *santeren*, to muse.]

-saur, -saurus. *comb. form.* Lizard: **brontosaur.** [< Gk *sauros*, lizard.]

sau•sage (sô'sĭj) *n.* Finely chopped and seasoned meat, stuffed into a prepared casing. [< LL *salsīcius*, prepared by salting.]

sau•té (sō-tā', sô-) *v.* **-téed, -téing.** To fry lightly in fat. [F, "tossed (in a pan)."]

sau•terne, sau•ternes (sō-tûrn', sô-) *n.* A delicate, sweet white dessert wine. [< *Sauternes*, commune in SW France.]

sav•age (săv'ĭj) *adj.* 1. Not domesticated or cultivated; wild. 2. Not civilized; primitive. 3. Ferocious; fierce. —*n.* 1. A primitive or uncivilized person. 2. A brutal person. 3. A rude person. [< L *silvāticus*, of the woods, wild.] —**sav'age•ly** *adv.* —**sav'age•ry** *n.*

Sa•van•nah (sə-văn'ə). A city of Georgia. Pop. 149,000.

sa•vant (sə-vänt', săv'ənt) *n.* A learned man. [< L *sapere*, to be sensible, be wise.]

save¹ (sāv) *v.* **saved, saving.** 1. To rescue from danger. 2. To preserve or safeguard. 3. To keep for future use; store. 4. To prevent waste. 5. To avoid fatigue, wear, or damage; spare. 6. To redeem from sin. [< L *salvus*, safe.] —**sav'er** *n.*

save² (sāv) *prep.* With the exception of; except. —*conj.* Except; but. [< L *salvō*, without injury or prejudice to.]

sav•ing (sā'vĭng) *adj.* 1. Serving to save. 2. Redeeming. 3. Economical. —*n.* 1. The act or condition of being saved. 2. A reduction, as in expenditure. 3. That which is saved. 4. **savings.** Sums of money saved. —*prep.* With the exception of. —*conj.* Except; save.

sav•ior (săv'yər) *n.* Also **sav•iour.** One who saves or preserves. —**the Saviour.** Christ.

sa•voir-faire (să-vwär-fâr') *n.* Experienced social skill or tact. [F, "to know how to do."]

sa•vor (sā'vər). Also *chiefly Brit.* **sa•vour.** *n.* 1. Taste or aroma. 2. A specific taste, smell, or quality. —*v.* 1. To have a particular savor. 2. To taste with zest; relish. [< L *sapor*, taste, savor.] —**sa'vor•i•ness** *n.* —**sa'vor•y** *adj.*

sav•vy (săv'ē) *v.* **-vied, -vying.** *Slang.* To understand. [< Span *sabe (usted)*, (you) know.]

saw¹ (sô) *n.* A cutting tool having a thin metal blade or disk with a sharp-toothed edge. —*v.* **sawed, sawed** or **sawn, sawing.** To cut with or as if with a saw. [< OE *sagu, sage.* See **sek-.**]

saw² (sô) *n.* A saying discredited through long repetition. [< OE *sagu*, speech, talk. See **sekw-¹.**]

saw³ (sô). *p.t.* of **see.**

saw•buck (sô'bŭk') *n.* 1. A sawhorse, esp. one with X-shaped legs projecting above the crossbar. 2. *Slang.* A ten-dollar bill.

saw•dust (sô'dŭst') *n.* The small waste particles resulting from sawing.

saw•horse (sô'hôrs') *n.* A rack or trestle used to support wood being sawed.

saw•mill (sô'mĭl') *n.* A mill where logs are cut into lumber.

sawn (sôn). Alternate *p.p.* of **saw.**

saw•yer (sô'yər) *n.* One employed to saw wood, as in a sawmill.

sax (săks) *n.* *Informal.* A saxophone.

Sax•on (săk'sən) *n.* 1. A member of a Germanic tribal group that invaded England in the 5th century and with the Angles and Jutes formed the Anglo-Saxon peoples. 2. The Germanic language or dialect spoken by any Saxon people. —**Sax'on** *adj.*

sax•o•phone (săk'sə-fōn') *n.* A wind instrument having a single-reed mouthpiece, a usually curved conical metal bore, and finger keys, and made in a variety of sizes. [Invented (1846) by Adolphe *Sax.*] —**sax'o•phon'ist** (-fō'-nĭst) *n.*

say (sā) *v.* **said, saying.** 1. To utter aloud; pronounce; speak. 2. To express in words. 3. To state with assurance. 4. To recite. 5. To allege. 6. To estimate or suppose. —**that is to say.** In other words. —*n.* 1. A positive assurance. 2. One's chance to speak. 3. Authority. —*adv.* 1. Approximately. 2. For instance. [< OE *secgan.* See **sekw-¹.**]

say•ing (sā'ĭng) *n.* An often repeated expression.

Sb antimony (L *stibium*).

sb. substantive.

Sc scandium.

sc. 1. scene. 2. sculpsit.

s.c. *Ptg.* small capitals.

S.C. South Carolina.

scab (skăb) *n.* 1. The crustlike exudate that covers a healing wound. 2. *Informal.* A worker who refuses membership in a labor union or who works while others are on strike. —*v.* **scabbed, scabbing.** 1. a. To form a scab. b. To become covered with a scab. 2. *Informal.* To work as a scab. [< ON *skabb.*]

scab•bard (skăb'ərd) *n.* A sheath for a dagger, sword, etc. [< NF *escaubers* (pl).]

scab•by (skăb'ē) *adj.* **-bier, -biest.** 1. Having, consisting of, or covered with scabs or something resembling scabs. 2. Afflicted with scabies. —**scab'bi•ly** *adv.* —**scab'bi•ness** *n.*

sca•bies (skā'bēz') *n. (takes sing. v.).* A contagious skin disease caused by a mite and characterized by intense itching. [L *scabiēs*, roughness, scurf.]

scab•rous (skăb'rəs, skā'brəs) *adj.* Rough or harsh. [< L *scaber*, rough, scurfy.]

scads (skădz) *pl.n.* *Informal.* A large number. [?]

scaf•fold (skăf'əld, -ōld') *n.* 1. A temporary platform for supporting workers. 2. A platform for the execution of condemned prisoners. [< OF *chafaud.*]

scaf•fold•ing (skăf'əl-dĭng, skăf'ōl'-) *n.* 1. A system of scaffolds. 2. The materials for scaffolds.

scal•a•wag (skăl'ə-wăg') *n.* *Informal.* A rascal.

scald¹ (skôld) *v.* 1. To burn with or as if with hot liquid or steam. 2. To subject to or treat with boiling water. 3. To heat (a liquid) almost to the boiling point. —*n.* An injury caused by scalding. [< LL *excaldāre*, to wash in hot water.]

scald². Variant of **scall.**

scale¹ (skāl) *n.* 1. One of the small, platelike structures forming the external covering of fishes, reptiles, etc. 2. A similar structure or part. 3. A dry, thin flake of epidermis shed from the skin. 4. A small, thin piece of anything. 5. Also **scale insect.** A destructive insect that forms and remains under waxy scales on plants. 6. A flaky oxide film formed on a metal. —*v.* **scaled, scaling.** 1. To clear or strip of scale or scales. 2. To remove or come off in layers or scales. 3. To cover with scales or become covered with encrustation. [< OF *escale*, "shell," "husk" < Gmc.] —**scal'y** *adj.*

scale² (skāl) *n.* 1. A system of ordered marks at fixed intervals used in measurement. 2. A progressive classification, as of size, amount, importance, or rank. 3. A relative level or degree. 4. *Mus.* An ascending or descending series of tones proceeding by a specified scheme of intervals. —*v.* **scaled, scaling.** 1. To climb up with or as if with a ladder, rope, etc. 2. To reproduce in accordance with a scale. 3. To adjust according to a proportion. [< L *scālae*, stairs.]

scale³ (skāl) *n.* Often **scales.** Any instrument or machine for weighing. [< ON *skāl*, bowl, scale of a balance.]

sca•lene (skā'lēn', skā-lēn') *adj.* Having three unequal sides. [< Gk *skalēnos*, uneven.]

Scales (skālz) *pl.n.* The constellation and sign of the zodiac Libra.

scall (skôl) *n.* Also **scald** (skôld). A scaly eruption of the skin or scalp. [< ON *skalli*, baldhead.]

scal•lion (skăl'yən) *n.* A young onion before the bulb enlarges. [< L *Ascalōnia (caepa)*, (onion) of Ascalon, port in S Palestine.]

scal•lop (skŏl'əp, skăl'-) *n.* 1. A bivalve marine mollusk with a fan-shaped, ridged shell. 2. The edible muscle of a scallop. 3. One of a series of curved projections forming an ornamental border. —*v.* 1. To border with scallops. 2. Also **es•cal•lop** (ĕ-skŏl'əp, ĕ-skăl'-). To bake in a casserole with milk or a sauce and often with bread crumbs. [< OF *escalope*, shell.] —**scal'lop•er** *n.*

scalp (skălp) *n.* The skin covering the top of the head. —*v.* 1. To cut or tear the scalp from; deprive of the scalp. 2. *Informal.* To sell at a price higher than the established value. [Prob < Scand.] —**scalp'er** *n.*

scal•pel (skăl'pəl, skăl-pĕl') *n.* A small straight surgical knife with a very thin, sharp blade. [< L *scalpere*, to cut, scratch.]

scamp (skămp) *n.* A rogue; rascal. [< obs *scamp*, to slip away, bolt.]

scam•per (skăm'pər) *v.* To run nimbly. —*n.* A hasty run or departure. [Flem *scamperen*, to decamp.] —**scam'per•er** *n.*

scam•pi (skăm'pē) *pl.n.* Large shrimps used in

Italian cooking. [It.]

scan (skăn) *v.* **scanned, scanning.** **1.** To examine closely. **2.** To inspect or look over quickly. **3.** To analyze (verse) into metrical patterns. —*n.* An act or instance of scanning. [< LL *scandere,* "to analyze the rising and falling rhythm in verses."] —**scan'ner** *n.*

Scand. Scandinavia; Scandinavian.

scan•dal (skăn'dəl) *n.* **1.** Public disgrace. **2.** Outrage; shame. **3.** Malicious gossip. [< Gk *skandalon,* trap, snare, stumbling block.] —**scan'dal•ous** *adj.* —**scan'dal•ous•ly** *adv.*

scan•dal•ize (skăn'də-līz') *v.* **-ized, -izing.** To shock or outrage the propriety of.

Scan•di•na•vi•a (skăn'də-nā'vē-ə, -nāv'yə). **1.** The NW European countries of Norway, Sweden, and Denmark. **2.** These countries and Iceland considered as a linguistic and cultural unit. **3.** These countries, Iceland, and Finland.

Scan•di•na•vi•an (skăn'də-nā'vē-ən, -nāv'yən) *n.* **1.** A native or inhabitant of Scandinavia. **2.** A branch of Germanic including Norwegian, Swedish, Danish, and Icelandic. —**Scan'di•na'vi•an** *adj.*

scan•di•um (skăn'dē-əm) *n.* *Symbol* **Sc** A silvery-white, very lightweight metallic element found in various rare minerals. Atomic number 21, atomic weight 44.956. [< L *Scandia,* ancient name for Scandinavia.]

scan•sion (skăn'shən) *n.* The analysis of verse into metrical patterns. [LL *scansiō.*]

scant (skănt) *adj.* **1.** Barely enough; meager; inadequate. **2.** Being just short of a specific measure. —*v.* **1.** To skimp. **2.** To limit, as in amount; stint. [< ON *skammr,* short.]

scant•ling (skănt'lĭng, -lĭn) *n.* A small piece of timber, esp. one used as an upright in a building frame. [Prob < VL **scandilia,* measure, scale.]

scant•y (skăn'tē) *adj.* **-ier, -iest.** Deficient in extent or degree; skimpy. —**scant'i•ly** *adv.* —**scant'i•ness** *n.*

scape•goat (skāp'gōt') *n.* One bearing blame for others. [(E)SCAPE + GOAT.]

scape•grace (skāp'grās') *n.* An incorrigible rascal. [(E)SCAPE + GRACE.]

scap•u•la (skăp'yə-lə) *n., pl.* **-las** or **-lae** (-lē'). Either of two large, flat, triangular bones forming the back part of the shoulder. [L, shoulder blade, shoulder.] —**scap'u•lar** *adj.*

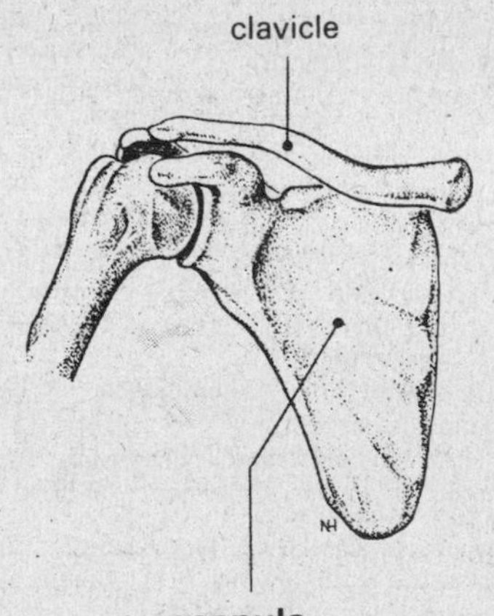

scapula

scar (skär) *n.* **1.** A mark left on the skin following the healing of a surface injury or wound. **2.** Any sign remaining as evidence of injury, damage, or an injurious mental or physical condition. —*v.* **scarred, scarring.** To mark or become marked with a scar. [< Gk *eskhara,* hearth, scab caused by burning.] —**scar'less** *adj.*

scar•ab (skăr'əb) *n.* Also **scar•a•bae•us** (skăr'ə-bē'əs) *pl.* **-uses** or **-baei** (-bē'ī'). **1.** Any of numerous often large beetles, esp. one regarded as sacred by the ancient Egyptians. **2.** A representation of a scarab beetle. [< L *scarabaeus.*]

scarce (skârs) *adj.* **scarcer, scarcest. 1.** Infrequently seen or found. **2.** Not plentiful or abundant. [< VL **excarpsus,* "picked," "choice."] —**scar'ci•ty** *n.*

scarce•ly (skârs'lē) *adv.* **1.** By a small margin; just; barely. **2.** Almost not; hardly. **3.** Assuredly not.

Usage: *Scarcely* has a negative sense, and is therefore not preceded by another negative in standard usage: *He could scarcely hear* (not *couldn't scarcely*). *Scarcely* is preferably followed by *when* or (less often) *before,* rather than by *than,* in constructions such as: *Scarcely had he entered when the telephone rang.*

scare (skâr) *v.* **scared, scaring.** To startle; frighten. —*n.* **1.** A fright. **2.** Panic. [< ON *skjarr,* shy, timid.]

scare•crow (skâr'krō') *n.* A crude figure set up in a cultivated area to scare birds away.

scarf (skärf) *n., pl.* **scarfs** or **scarves** (skärvz). **1.** A rectangular or triangular piece of cloth, worn about the neck or head. **2.** A runner, as for a bureau. [< OF *escherpe,* orig "pilgrim's wallet suspended from the neck."]

Scar•lat•ti (skär-lät'ē), **Domenico.** 1683–1757. Italian harpsichordist and composer.

scar•let (skär'lĭt) *n.* Strong to vivid red or reddish orange. [< Pers *säqirlat,* silk material dyed red.]

scarlet fever. An acute contagious disease caused by a bacterium, occurring predominantly among children and characterized by a scarlet skin eruption and high fever.

scar•y (skâr'ē) *adj.* **-ier, -iest.** *Informal.* **1.** Frightening. **2.** Easily scared.

scat (skăt) *v.* **scatted, scatting.** *Informal.* To leave hastily. [Poss short for SCATTER.]

scath•ing (skā'*th*ĭng) *adj.* Extremely severe or harsh. [< ON *skadha,* to harm.]

scat•ter (skăt'ər) *v.* **1.** To disperse. **2.** To distribute loosely by or as if by sprinkling or strewing. [Poss < SHATTER.] —**scat'ter•er** *n.*

scat•ter•brain (skăt'ər-brān') *n.* A flighty or disorganized person. —**scat'ter•brained'** *adj.*

scat•ter•ing (skăt'ər-ĭng) *n.* **1. a.** The act or process of scattering. **b.** The state of being scattered. **2.** A sparse distribution. —*adj.* Placed at intervals or occurring irregularly.

scav•enge (skăv'ĭnj) *v.* **-enged, -enging. 1.** To act as a scavenger. **2.** To search through for salvageable material.

scav•en•ger (skăv'ĭn-jər) *n.* **1.** An animal that feeds on dead flesh or other decaying matter. **2.** One who scavenges. [< ME *skawager,* collector of tolls.]

sce•nar•i•o (sĭ-nâr'ē-ō', sĭ-när'-) *n., pl.* **-os.** A script or an outline of the plot of a motion picture. [It, "scenery."] —**sce•nar'ist** *n.*

scene (sēn) *n.* **1.** A prospect; view. **2.** The setting of some action. **3.** A subdivision of an act of a play. **4.** A unit of continuous related action in a film. **5.** The scenery for a dramatic presentation. **6.** A display of temper. [< Gk *skēnē,* "tent."]

scen•er•y (sē'nə-rē) *n.* **1.** The landscape. **2.** The painted backdrops on a theatrical stage. [It *scenario,* SCENARIO.] —**sce'nic** *adj.*

scent (sĕnt) *n.* **1.** A distinctive odor. **2.** A perfume. **3.** The trail of a hunted animal or fugitive. —*v.* **1.** To smell; hunt by smell. **2.** To fill with an odor. [< L *sentīre,* to feel.]

scep•ter (sĕp'tər) *n.* Also *chiefly Brit.* **scep•tre.** A staff held by a sovereign as an emblem of authority. [< Gk *skēptron,* "staff," "stick."]

scep•tic. Variant of **skeptic.**

sch. school.

sched•ule (skĕj'ōōl, -ōō-əl, skĕj'əl) *n.* **1.** A list of items. **2.** A program. **3.** A timetable. **4.** A production plan. —*v.* **-uled, -uling. 1.** To enter on a schedule. **2.** To make up a schedule for. **3.** To plan for a certain time. [< L *scheda,* papyrus leaf.]

sche•mat•ic (skē-măt'ĭk) *adj.* Pertaining to or in the form of a scheme; diagrammatic. —*n.* A structural or procedural diagram, esp. of an electrical or mechanical system.

scheme (skēm) *n.* **1.** A systematic plan or design. **2.** A secret plan; plot; intrigue. —*v.* **schemed, scheming. 1.** To contrive a scheme for. **2.** To plot. [< Gk *skhēma,* form, figure.]

scher•zo (skĕr'tsō) *n., pl.* **-zos.** *Mus.* A lively movement commonly in 3/4 time. [It, joke.]

Schick test (shĭk). An intracutaneous skin test of susceptibility to diphtheria. [< B. *Schick* (1877–1967), American pediatrician.]

Schil•ler (shĭl'ər), **Friedrich von.** 1759–1805. German poet.

schil•ling (shĭl'ĭng) *n.* The basic monetary unit of Austria. [G.]

schism (sĭz'əm, skĭz'-) *n.* A separation or division into factions, esp. within a Christian church. [< Gk *skhisma,* a split, division.] —**schis•mat'ic** (sĭz-măt'ĭk, skĭz-) *adj.* —**schis•mat'i•cal•ly** *adv.*

schist (shĭst) *n.* Also **shist.** A metamorphic rock consisting of laminated, often flaky, parallel layers. [< L *(lapis) schistos,* "fissile (stone)."] —**schis'tose'** (shĭs'tōs'), **schis'tous** (shĭs'təs) *adj.*

schizo–. *comb. form.* Division, split, or cleavage. [< Gk *skhizein,* to split.]

schiz•oid (skĭt'soid') *adj.* Of or resembling schizophrenia. —*n.* A schizophrenic. [SCHIZ(O)- + -OID.]

schiz•o•phre•ni•a (skĭt'sə-frē'nē-ə, -frĕn'ē-ə) *n.* Any of a group of psychotic reactions characterized by withdrawal from reality with highly variable accompanying affective, behavioral, and intellectual disturbances. —**schiz'o•phren'ic** (-frĕn'ĭk) *adj.* & *n.*

schnapps (shnäps, shnăps) *n.* Any of various strong liquors. [G *Schnaps.*]

schnit•zel (shnĭt'səl) *n.* A thin cutlet of veal fried lightly in butter. [< G *Schnitz,* slice.]

schol•ar (skŏl'ər) *n.* **1.** A learned person. **2.** A pupil or student. [< LL *scholāris,* of a school.] —**schol'ar•li•ness** *n.* —**schol'ar•ly** *adj.*

schol•ar•ship (skŏl'ər-shĭp') *n.* **1.** The knowledge or discipline of a scholar. **2.** A grant-in-aid awarded to a student.

scho•las•tic (skə-lăs'tĭk) *adj.* Of or pertaining to schools or scholarship. [< Gk *skholē,* school.] —**scho•las'ti•cal•ly** *adv.*

school¹ (skōōl) *n.* **1.** An institution for instruction and learning. **2.** The student body of an educational institution. **3.** The process of being educated. **4.** A group of persons under some common influence or sharing a unifying belief. —*v.* **1.** To instruct. **2.** To train; discipline. [< Gk *skholē,* leisure (devoted to learning), lecture, school.]

school² (skōōl) *n.* A group of fish or other aquatic animals swimming together. [< MDu *schōle,* troop, group.]

school•boy (sko͞ol'boi') *n.* A boy attending school.
school•child (sko͞ol'chīld') *n.* A child attending school.
school•girl (sko͞ol'gûrl') *n.* A girl attending school.
school•house (sko͞ol'hous') *n.* A building used as a school.
school•marm (sko͞ol'märm') *n. Informal.* A woman schoolteacher, esp. an old-fashioned disciplinarian.
school•mas•ter (sko͞ol'măs'tər, -mäs'tər) *n.* A male teacher.
school•mate (sko͞ol'māt') *n.* A school companion.
school•mis•tress (sko͞ol'mĭs'trĭs) *n.* A woman teacher.
school•room (sko͞ol'ro͞om', -ro͝om') *n.* A classroom.
school•teach•er (sko͞ol'tē'chər) *n.* One who teaches in a school below the college level.
schoo•ner (sko͞o'nər) *n.* **1.** A fore-and-aft-rigged ship with two or more masts, the mainmast being taller than the foremast. **2.** A large beer glass, generally holding a pint or more. [Earlier *scooner.*]
Scho•pen•hau•er (shō'pən-hou'ər), **Arthur.** 1788–1860. German philosopher.
Schu•bert (sho͞o'bərt), **Franz.** 1797–1828. Austrian composer.
Schu•mann (sho͞o'män), **Robert.** 1810–1856. German composer.
schwa (shwä, shvä) *n.* A symbol (ə) for an indeterminate vowel sound, in English occurring in many unstressed syllables. [< Heb *shəwā'.*]
Schwei•tzer (shwīt'sər, shvīt'sər), **Albert.** 1875–1965. French missionary doctor in Africa.
sci. science.
sci•at•i•ca (sī-ăt'ĭ-kə) *n.* Chronic neuralgic pain in the area of the hip or thigh. [< ML *sciatica (passiō),* "(suffering) in the hip."]
sci•ence (sī'əns) *n.* **1.** The observation, identification, description, experimental investigation, and theoretical explanation of natural phenomena. **2.** Any methodological activity, discipline, or study. **3.** Any activity that appears to require study and method. **4.** Knowledge, esp. knowledge gained through experience. [< L *sciēns,* pres part of *scīre,* to know.] **—sci'en•tif'ic** (sī'ən-tĭf'ĭc) *adj.* **—sci'en•tif'i•cal•ly** *adv.*
science fiction. Fiction based on elements of scientific discovery and prediction.
sci•en•tist (sī'ən-tĭst) *n.* A person having expert knowledge of one or more sciences.
scim•i•tar (sĭm'ə-tər, -tär') *n.* A curved Oriental sword. [< Pers *šimšīr.*]
scin•til•la (sĭn-tĭl'ə) *n.* A minute amount; trace. [L, spark.]
scin•til•late (sĭn'tə-lāt') *v.* **-lated, -lating.** To throw off sparks; flash and sparkle. [< L *scintilla,* spark.] **—scin'til•la'tion** *n.*
sci•on (sī'ən) *n.* **1.** A descendant or heir. **2.** A detached plant shoot used in grafting. [< OF *ciun, cion.*]
sci•roc•co. Variant of **sirocco.**
scis•sors (sĭz'ərz) *n. (takes sing.* or *pl. v.).* A cutting implement of two blades, joined by a swivel pin that allows the cutting edges to be opened and closed. [< LL *cisōrium,* cutting instrument.]
scissors kick. A swimming kick in which one leg is swung forward, the other bent back at the knee, and then both straightened and snapped together.
scle•ra (sklîr'ə) *n.* The tough, fibrous tissue that covers all of the eyeball except the cornea.
scle•ro•sis (sklə-rō'sĭs) *n., pl.* **-ses** (-sēz'). A thickening or hardening of a body part, esp. from tissue overgrowth or disease. [< Gk *sklēros,* hard.] **—scle•rot'ic** (-rŏt'ĭk) *adj.*
scoff (skôf, skŏf) *v.* To mock at or scorn. *—n.* An expression of scorn; a jeer. [Prob < Scand.] **—scoff'er** *n.*
scold (skōld) *v.* To reprimand harshly. *—n.* One who persistently rails against others. [< ME, ribald or abusive person.]
scold•ing (skōl'dĭng) *n.* A sharp reprimand.
sconce¹ (skŏns) *n.* A small fort. [< It *scanso,* defense.]
sconce² (skŏns) *n.* A decorative wall bracket for candles or lights. [< OF *esconse,* lantern, hiding place.]
scone (skōn, skŏn) *n.* A round, soft, doughy pastry. [Short for Du *schoonbrood,* fine white bread.]
scoop (sko͞op) *n.* **1.** A small, shovellike utensil. **2.** The bucket or shovel of a steam shovel or dredge. **3.** The amount taken with one scoop. **4.** *Slang.* An exclusive news story acquired by luck or initiative. *—v.* **1.** To take up with or as with a scoop. **2.** To hollow out. **3.** *Slang.* To outmaneuver in acquiring a news story. [< MLG and MDu *schōpe.*]
scoot (sko͞ot) *v.* To go speedily. *—n.* A darting or scurrying off. [Prob < Scand.]
scoot•er (sko͞o'tər) *n.* A child's vehicle consisting of a long footboard between two small end wheels.
scope (skōp) *n.* **1.** The range of one's perceptions, thoughts, or actions. **2.** Breadth or opportunity to function. **3.** The area covered by a given activity or subject. [< Gk *skopos,* watcher, goal, aim.]
-scope. *comb. form.* An instrument for observing or detecting: **microscope.** [< Gk *skopein,* to see.]
sco•pol•a•mine (skō-pŏl'ə-mēn', -mĭn) *n.* A thick, syrupy, colorless alkaloid, $C_{17}H_{21}NO_4$, used as a sedative and truth serum.
scor•bu•tic (skôr-byo͞o'tĭk) *adj.* Also **scor•bu•ti•cal** (-tĭ-kəl). Related to, resembling, or afflicted with scurvy. [< LL *scorbūtus,* scurvy.]
scorch (skôrch) *v.* **1.** To burn the surface of. **2.** To wither or parch. *—n.* **1.** A slight or surface burn. **2.** A discoloration caused by heat. [ME *scorchen.*] **—scorch'ing•ly** *adv.*
score (skôr, skōr) *n.* **1.** A notch or incision. **2.** A record of points made in a competitive event. **3.** A result of a test or examination. **4.** A debt. **5.** A reason; account. **6.** A group of 20 items. **7.** The written form of a musical composition. **8.** The music composed for a stage show or film. *—v.* **scored, scoring. 1.** To mark with lines or notches. **2.** To gain (a point) in a game or contest. **3.** To record the score in a contest. **4.** To achieve; win. **5.** To evaluate and assign a grade to. **6.** *Mus.* **a.** To orchestrate. **b.** To arrange for a specific instrument. [< ON *skor,* notch, twenty.]
scorn (skôrn) *n.* **1.** Contempt or disdain. **2.** Derision. *—v.* To consider or treat as contemptible; disdain. [< OF *escharnir.*] **—scorn'ful** *adj.* **—scorn'ful•ly** *adv.*
scor•pi•on (skôr'pē-ən) *n.* **1.** An arachnid with a segmented body and a tail tipped with a venomous sting. **2. Scorpion.** The constellation and sign of the zodiac Scorpius. [< Gk *skorpios.*]
Scor•pi•us (skôr'pē-əs) *n.* Also **Scor•pi•o** (skôr'pē-ō'). **1.** A constellation in the S Hemisphere. **2.** The 8th sign of the zodiac. [< L *scorpiō,* scorpion.]
Scot (skŏt) *n.* **1.** A native or inhabitant of Scotland. **2.** A member of the ancient Gaelic tribe that migrated to N Great Britain from Ireland in about the 6th century A.D.
Scot. Scotch; Scotland; Scottish.
scotch (skŏch) *v.* **1.** To cut or scratch. **2.** To cripple. **3.** To put an end to; stifle. [< NF *escocher,* to cut a notch.]
Scotch (skŏch) *n.* **1.** The people of Scotland. **2.** Any of the English dialects spoken in Scotland. **3. Scotch whisky.** [Contraction of SCOTTISH.] **—Scotch** *adj.*
Scotch•man (skŏch'mən) *n.* A Scot.
Scotch whisky. A smoky-flavored whiskey distilled in Scotland from malted barley, the malt having been dried over a peat fire.
scot-free (skŏt'frē') *adj.* Free from obligation or penalty. [< ME *scot,* tax.]
Scot•land (skŏt'lənd). A constituent country of the United Kingdom, located in N Great Britain. Pop. 5,178,000. Cap. Edinburgh.
Scotland Yard. The headquarters of the London Metropolitan Police.
Scots•man (skŏts'mən) *n.* A Scot.
Scott (skŏt), Sir **Walter.** 1771–1832. Scottish poet and historical novelist.
Scot•tie (skŏt'ē) *n.* A Scotsman.
Scot•tish (skŏt'ĭsh) *n.* **1.** A dialect of English spoken by the Lowlanders of Scotland. **2.** The people of Scotland. **—Scot'tish** *adj.*
Scottish Gaelic. The Gaelic language of the Scottish Highlanders.
scoun•drel (skoun'drəl) *n.* A villain. [?]
scour¹ (skour) *v.* **1.** To clean by scrubbing vigorously, as with an abrasive. **2.** To scrub something in order to clean it. [< LL *excūrāre,* to clean out.]
scour² (skour) *v.* **1.** To search through or over thoroughly. **2.** To move swiftly. [Prob < ON *skȳra,* to rush in.]
scourge (skûrj) *n.* **1.** A whip used to inflict punishment. **2.** Any means of inflicting punishment. **3.** A cause of affliction, as pestilence or war. *—v.* **scourged, scourging. 1.** To flog. **2.** To chastise severely; excoriate. **3.** To devastate; ravage. [< OF *escorgier,* to whip.] **—scourg'er** *n.*
scout¹ (skout) *n.* **1.** One dispatched to gather information. **2.** A watchman or sentinel. *—v.* **1.** To reconnoiter. **2.** To observe and evaluate. [< OF *escoute,* "listener;" spy.]
scout² (skout) *v.* **1.** To reject contemptuously. **2.** To scoff. [< Scand.]
scow (skou) *n.* A flat-bottomed boat with square ends. [Du *schouw.*]
scowl (skoul) *n.* An angry frown. *—v.* To form a scowl. [Prob < Scand.]
scrab•ble (skrăb'əl) *v.* **-bled, -bling. 1.** To grope about frenetically with the hands. **2.** To struggle. **3.** To scribble. **4.** To make or obtain by scraping together. [< MDu *schrabben,* to scrape.] **—scrab'ble** *n.*
scrag•gly (skrăg'lē) *adj.* **-glier, -gliest.** Ragged or irregular; unkempt.
scram (skrăm) *v.* **scrammed, scramming.** *Slang.* To leave a scene at once. [Short for SCRAMBLE.]
scram•ble (skrăm'bəl) *v.* **-bled, -bling. 1.** To move or climb hurriedly. **2.** To compete frantically. **3.** To mix confusedly. **4.** To fry (eggs) with the yolks and whites mixed together. **5.** *Electronics.* To distort (a signal) so as to render it unintelligible without a special receiver. [Blend of obs *scamble,* to struggle for, and *cramble,* to crawl.] **—scram'ble** *n.* **—scram'bler** *n.*

scrap[1] (skrăp) *n.* 1. A fragment or shred. 2. **scraps.** Leftover food. 3. Construction material left over or discarded as refuse. —*v.* **scrapped, scrapping.** 1. To break down into parts for disposal or salvage. 2. To discard as worthless. [< ON *skrap,* trifles, remains.]

scrap[2] (skrăp) *v.* **scrapped, scrapping.** To fight or quarrel. —*n.* A quarrel. [Perh var of SCRAPE.] —**scrap'per** *n.* —**scrap'py** *adj.*

scrap•book (skrăp'bo͝ok') *n.* A book with blank pages for mounting pictures or other mementos.

scrape (skrāp) *v.* **scraped, scraping.** 1. To rub (a surface) with considerable pressure. 2. To draw (a hard or abrasive object) forcefully over a surface. 3. To abrade, smooth, injure, or remove by this procedure. 4. To come into abrasive contact. 5. To rub or move with a grating noise. 6. To amass or produce with difficulty: *He scraped together the money.* —*n.* 1. The act or result of scraping. 2. a. A predicament. b. A scuffle. [< ON *skrapa.*] —**scrap'er** *n.*

scratch (skrăch) *v.* 1. To make a shallow cut or mark with something sharp. 2. To use the nails or claws to dig, scrape, or wound. 3. To rub (the skin) to relieve itching. 4. To strike out or cancel (a word, name, or passage) by or as if by drawing lines through. —*n.* A mark or wound produced by scratching. —**from scratch.** From the beginning. —*adj.* 1. Done by chance. 2. Assembled at random. 3. Used for hasty jottings: *scratch paper.* [Blend of obs *scrat* and *cratch.*] —**scratch'y** *adj.*

scrawl (skrôl) *v.* To write hastily or illegibly. —*n.* Irregular or illegible handwriting. [Blend of SPRAWL and CRAWL.] —**scrawl'y** *adj.*

scraw•ny (skrô'nē) *adj.* **-nier, -niest.** Gaunt and bony; skinny. [?] —**scraw'ni•ness** *n.*

scream (skrēm) *v.* 1. To cry out loudly and shrilly, as from pain or fear. 2. To have a blatantly arresting effect. —*n.* A loud piercing sound. [< ON *skræma.*]

screech (skrēch) *n.* 1. A shriek. 2. A sound resembling this. [< ON *skrækja.*] —**screech** *v.*

screen (skrēn) *n.* 1. Something that serves to divide, conceal, or protect, as a movable room partition. 2. A coarse sieve. 3. A window insertion of framed mesh used to keep out insects. 4. a. The white or silver surface upon which a picture is projected for viewing. b. The motion-picture industry. —*v.* 1. To provide with a screen. 2. To conceal or protect. 3. To separate with or as if with a sieve. 4. To show on a screen, as a motion picture. [< MDu *scherm,* "shield," "protection."]

screen•play (skrēn'plā') *n.* The script for a motion picture.

screw (skro͞o) *n.* 1. A metal pin with incised thread or threads, having a broad slotted head so that it can be driven as a fastener by turning it with a screwdriver. 2. A propeller. —*v.* 1. To fasten, tighten, adjust, or attach by or as if by means of a screw. 2. To turn or twist. 3. To become attached by means of screw threads. [< L *scrōfa,* sow (prob because screw threads coil like a sow's tail).]

screw•ball (skro͞o'bôl') *n.* 1. *Baseball.* A pitched ball curving in the direction opposite to a normal curve. 2. *Slang.* An eccentric or irrational person.

screw•driv•er (skro͞o'drī'vər) *n.* 1. A tool used for turning screws. 2. A cocktail of vodka and orange juice.

scrib•ble (skrĭb'əl) *v.* **-bled, -bling.** To write hurriedly and carelessly. [< L *scrībere,* to write.] —**scrib'ble** *n.* —**scrib'bler** *n.*

scribe (skrīb) *n.* 1. A public clerk. 2. A professional copyist of manuscripts. 3. A writer. [< L *scrībere,* to write.]

scrim•mage (skrĭm'ĭj) *n. Football.* 1. The contest between two teams from the time the ball is snapped back until it becomes out of play. 2. A team's practice session. —**line of scrimmage.** *Football.* An imaginary line across the field on which the ball rests and at which the teams line up for a new play. [< var of SKIRMISH.]

scrimp (skrĭmp) *v.* To economize severely. [Perh < Scand.] —**scrimp'y** *adj.*

scrip[1] (skrĭp) *n.* Paper money issued for temporary and often emergency use. [Var of SCRIPT.]

scrip[2] (skrĭp) *n.* A certificate entitling the holder to a fractional share of stock or of other property. [Short for *subscription (receipt).*]

script (skrĭpt) *n.* 1. Handwriting as distinguished from print. 2. Cursive writing. 3. The text of a play, broadcast, or motion picture. [< L *scrīptus,* pp of *scrībere,* to write.]

Script. Scriptural; Scriptures.

Scrip•ture (skrĭp'chər) *n.* Often **Scriptures.** 1. A sacred writing or book, esp. the Bible. 2. A passage from such a writing. [< L *scrīptūra,* act of writing.] —**Scrip'tur•al** *adj.*

scriv•en•er (skrĭv'nər) *n. Archaic.* 1. A professional copyist; scribe. 2. A notary. [< L *scrība,* scribe.]

scrod (skrŏd) *n.* A young cod or haddock. [Obs Du *schrood,* slice, shred.]

scroll (skrōl) *n.* 1. A roll of parchment, papyrus, etc., used esp. for writing a document. 2. Ornamentation resembling a partially rolled scroll of paper. [< OF *escroue,* strip of parchment.]

Scrooge (skro͞oj) *n.* A mean, miserly person. [< the character in Dickens' *Christmas Carol.*]

scro•tum (skrō'təm) *n., pl.* **-ta** (-tə) or **-tums.** The external sac of skin enclosing the testes. [L *scrōtum.*] —**scro'tal** (skrōt'l) *adj.*

scrounge (skrounj) *v.* **scrounged, scrounging.** 1. To forage about in an effort to acquire (something) at no cost. 2. To wheedle. [Var of dial *scrunge,* to steal.] —**scroung'er** *n.*

scrub[1] (skrŭb) *v.* **scrubbed, scrubbing.** 1. To rub hard, as with a brush, soap, and water, in order to clean. 2. To clean by hard rubbing. [< MLG or MDu *schrobben, schrubben.*] —**scrub** *n.* —**scrub'ber** *n.*

scrub[2] (skrŭb) *n.* 1. A growth of stunted trees or shrubs. 2. A stunted or inferior domestic animal, tree, etc. [< SHRUB.] —**scrub** *adj.* —**scrub'by** *adj.*

scruff (skrŭf) *n.* The back of the neck; nape. [Var of obs *scuff.*]

scrump•tious (skrŭmp'shəs) *adj. Slang.* Splendid; delectable. [Perh var of SUMPTUOUS.]

scru•ple (skro͞o'pəl) *n.* 1. Ethical objection to certain actions; principle; dictate of conscience. 2. A unit of apothecary weight equal to 20 grains. [< L *scrūpulus,* small sharp stone, scruple.]

scru•pu•lous (skro͞o'pyə-ləs) *adj.* 1. Having scruples; principled. 2. Very conscientious and exacting. —**scru'pu•lous•ly** *adv.* —**scru'pu•lous•ness** *n.*

scru•ti•nize (skro͞ot'n-īz') *v.* **-nized, -nizing.** To examine or observe with great care.

scru•ti•ny (skro͞ot'n-ē) *n., pl.* **-nies.** A close, careful examination or study. [< L *scrūtārī,* to search, examine.]

scu•ba (sko͞o'bə) *n.* An apparatus containing compressed air and used for free-swimming underwater breathing. [S(elf)-c(ontained) u(nderwater) b(reathing) a(pparatus).]

scud (skŭd) *v.* **scudded, scudding.** To run or skim along swiftly and easily. —*n.* Wind-driven clouds or mist.

scuff (skŭf) *v.* 1. To scrape the feet while walking. 2. To scrape and roughen the surface of (shoes). —*n.* 1. The sound or act of scuffing. 2. A spot left as a result of scuffing. [Prob < Scand.]

scuf•fle (skŭf'əl) *v.* **-fled, -fling.** 1. To fight confusedly at close quarters. 2. To shuffle. —*n.* A disorderly struggle at close quarters. [Prob < Scand.] —**scuf'fler** *n.*

scull (skŭl) *n.* 1. A long oar twisted from side to side over the stern of a boat to propel it. 2. One of a pair of short-handled oars used by a single rower. —*v.* To propel (a boat) with a scull or sculls. [ME *sculle.*]

scul•ler•y (skŭl'ə-rē) *n., pl.* **-ies.** A room adjoining the kitchen where dishwashing and other chores are done. [< OF *escuelier,* keeper of dishes.]

sculp•sit (skŭlp'sĭt). He (or she) sculptured (it). [L.]

sculpt (skŭlpt) *v.* To sculpture.

sculp•tor (skŭlp'tər) *n.* One who sculptures, esp. an artist who works in stone or metal. —**sculp'tress** *fem.n.*

sculp•ture (skŭlp'chər) *n.* 1. The art or practice of shaping figures or designs in the round or in relief, as by carving wood, chiseling marble, modeling clay, or casting in metal. 2. A work or formation created in this manner. —*v.* **-tured, -turing.** 1. To fashion into a three-dimensional figure. 2. To represent in sculpture. [< L *sculpere* (pp *sculptus*), to carve.]

scum (skŭm) *n.* 1. A filmy layer of impure matter on the surface of a liquid or body of water. 2. Any refuse or worthless matter. 3. An element of society regarded as being vile or worthless. [< MDu *schūm.*]

scup•per (skŭp'ər) *n.* An opening in the side of a ship at deck level to allow water to run off. [ME *skopper.*]

scurf (skûrf) *n.* Scaly or shredded dry skin, such as dandruff. —**scurf'i•ness** *n.* —**scurf'y** *adj.*

scur•ri•lous (skûr'ə-ləs) *adj.* Vulgar; abusive; obscene. [< L *scurrīlis,* buffoonlike, jeering.]

scur•ry (skûr'ē) *v.* **-ried, -rying.** 1. To scamper. 2. To flurry or swirl about.

scur•vy (skûr'vē) *n.* A disease caused by deficiency of vitamin C, characterized by spongy and bleeding gums, bleeding under the skin, and extreme weakness. —*adj.* **-vier, -viest.** Mean; worthless. [< SCURF.]

scut•tle[1] (skŭt'l) *n.* A small hatch, esp. in the deck or side of a ship. —*v.* **-tled, -tling.** To sink (a ship) by cutting or opening a hole in the hull. [< OF *escoutille.*]

scut•tle[2] (skŭt'l) *n.* A pail for carrying coal. [< L *scutella,* salver.]

scut•tle[3] (skŭt'l) *v.* **-tled, -tling.** To run hastily; scurry. [< SCUD.]

scut•tle•butt (skŭt'l-bŭt') *n. Slang.* Gossip; rumor.

scythe (sīth) *n.* An implement with a long, curved single-edged blade, used for mowing or reaping. [< OE *sīthe.* See **sek-.**] —**scythe** *v.* **(scythed, scything).**

s.d. Indefinitely (L *sine die*).

S.D. 1. special delivery. 2. South Dakota (unofficial).

S.Dak. South Dakota.

Se selenium.

SE southeast; southeastern.

sea (sē) *n.* **1. a.** The continuous body of salt water covering most of the earth's surface, esp. this body regarded as a geophysical entity distinct from the earth and sky. **b.** A tract of water within an ocean. **c.** A relatively large body of salt water completely or partly landlocked. **d.** A body of fresh water. **2.** The condition of the ocean's surface: *a high sea.* **3.** Something that suggests the sea in its overwhelming sweep or vastness. [< OE *sǣ* < Gmc **saiwa-.*]

sea anemone. A marine organism with a flexible, cylindrical body and numerous tentacles.

sea•board (sē'bôrd', -bōrd') *n.* **1.** The seacoast. **2.** The land near the sea.

sea•coast (sē'kōst') *n.* Land bordering the sea.

sea•far•er (sē'fâr'ər) *n.* A sailor.

sea•far•ing (sē'fâr'ĭng) *n.* The occupation of a sailor. *—adj.* Following a life at sea.

sea•food (sē'fo͞od') *n.* Edible fish or shellfish from the sea.

sea•go•ing (sē'gō'ĭng) *adj.* **1.** Made or used for ocean voyages. **2.** Seafaring.

sea horse. A small marine fish with a horselike head and a body covered with bony plates.

seal[1] (sēl) *n.* **1. a.** A die or signet having a raised or incised emblem, used to stamp an impression upon a substance such as wax or lead. **b.** The impression made. **c.** The design or emblem itself. **d.** A small disk or wafer bearing such an imprint and affixed to a document to prove authenticity or seal it shut. **2.** Something (as a commercial hallmark) that serves similarly to authenticate, confirm, or attest. *—v.* **1.** To affix a seal to so as to prove authenticity or attest to accuracy, quality, etc. **2.** To close with or as with a seal; make fast. **3.** To establish or determine irrevocably. [< L *signum,* sign.] **—seal'er** *n.*

seal[2] (sēl) *n.* **1.** An aquatic mammal with a torpedo-shaped body and limbs in the form of flippers. **2.** Also **seal•skin** (sēl'skĭn'). The pelt or fur of a seal. *—v.* To hunt seals. [< OE *seolh.*] **—seal'er** *n.*

sea level. The level of the ocean's surface, esp. the mean level halfway between high and low tide.

sea lion. A brown seal of Pacific waters.

seam (sēm) *n.* **1. a.** A line formed by sewing together two pieces of material. **b.** A similar line, ridge, or groove. **2.** Any line across a surface, as a fissure or wrinkle. **3.** A thin layer or stratum, as of coal. *—v.* **1.** To join with or as with a seam. **2.** To mark with a wrinkle, scar, or other seamlike line. [< OE *sēam.* See **syū-.**] **—seam'er** *n.* **—seam'less** *adj.*

sea•man (sē'mən) *n.* **1.** A sailor. **2.** *U.S. Navy.* An enlisted man ranking below petty officer.

sea•man•ship (sē'mən-shĭp') *n.* Skill in managing or navigating a boat or ship.

seam•stress (sēm'strĭs) *n.* A woman who makes her living by sewing.

seam•y (sē'mē) *adj.* **-ier, -iest. 1.** Having or showing a seam. **2.** Rough and raw; sordid.

sé•ance (sā'äns') *n.* A meeting of persons to receive spiritualistic messages. [F, "a sitting."]

sea•plane (sē'plān') *n.* An aircraft equipped to land on or take off from a body of water.

sea•port (sē'pôrt', -pōrt') *n.* A port with facilities for seagoing ships.

sear (sîr) *v.* **1.** To make or become withered; dry up. **2.** To char, scorch, or burn the surface of. [< OE *sēar,* withered. See **saus-.**]

search (sûrch) *v.* **1.** To make a thorough examination of in order to find something; explore. **2.** To make a careful investigation of; probe. **3.** To make a thorough check of; scrutinize. [< OF *cerchier,* "to go around."] **—search** *n.* **—search'er** *n.*

search•light (sûrch'līt') *n.* **1.** An apparatus for projecting a bright beam of light. **2.** The beam so projected.

sea•shell (sē'shĕl') *n.* The shell of a marine mollusk.

sea•shore (sē'shôr', -shōr') *n.* Land by the sea.

sea•sick•ness (sē'sĭk'nĭs) *n.* Nausea and other malaise provoked by the motion of a vessel at sea. **—sea'sick'** *adj.*

sea•side (sē'sīd') *n.* The seashore.

sea•son (sē'zən) *n.* **1. a.** One of the four equal divisions of the year, spring, summer, autumn, and winter. **b.** The two divisions of the year, rainy and dry, in tropical climates. **2.** A recurrent period characterized by certain occupations, festivities, or crops. *—v.* **1.** To improve or enhance the flavor of (food) by adding spices, herbs, etc. **2.** To add zest or interest to. **3.** To accustom; inure. **4.** To make or become usable, as by aging or drying. [< L *satiō,* act of sowing.] **—sea'son•al** *adj.*

sea•son•a•ble (sē'zə-nə-bəl) *adj.* **1.** In keeping with the season. **2.** Occurring at the proper time; timely. **—sea'son•a•bly** *adv.*

sea•son•ing (sē'zə-nĭng) *n.* Anything used to flavor food.

seat (sēt) *n.* **1.** Something that may be sat upon, as a chair. **2.** A place in which one may sit. **3.** The part of something on which one rests in sitting. **4.** The buttocks. **5. a.** The place where anything is located or based. **b.** A center of authority; capital. **6.** Membership, as in a legislative body. *—v.* **1.** To place in or on a seat. **2.** To have or provide seats for. **3.** To install in a position of authority or eminence. [< ON *sæti.*]

seat belt. A safety strap attached to the seat of a passenger vehicle.

SEATO (sē'tō) Southeast Asia Treaty Organization.

Se•at•tle (sē-ăt'l). A city in W Washington. Pop. 524,000.

sea urchin. A marine organism with a spiny globular shell.

sea•ward (sē'wərd) *adv.* Also **sea•wards** (-wərdz). Toward the sea. **—sea'ward** *adj.*

sea•way (sē'wā') *n.* An inland waterway for ocean shipping.

sea•weed (sē'wēd') *n.* Any of various large or branching marine algae.

sea•wor•thy (sē'wûr'thē) *adj.* Designating a vessel that is fit to sail.

se•ba•ceous (sĭ-bā'shəs) *adj.* Of or secreting fat. [< L *sēbum,* tallow + -ACEOUS.]

sec, sec. 1. second[1]. **2.** secretary. **3.** sector.

se•cant (sē'kənt, -kănt') *n.* A straight line intersecting a curve at two or more points. [F *(ligne) secante,* "cutting (line)."]

se•cede (sĭ-sēd', sē'-) *v.* **-ceded, -ceding.** To withdraw formally from membership in an organization or alliance. [L *sēcēdere,* to go away.]

se•ces•sion (sĭ-sĕsh'ən) *n.* The act of seceding.

se•clude (sĭ-klo͞od') *v.* **-cluded, -cluding. 1.** To set apart from others; isolate. **2.** To screen from view. [< L *sēclūdere.*] **—se•clu'sion** (-klo͞o'zhən) *n.*

sec•ond[1] (sĕk'ənd) *n.* **1.** A unit of time equal to $^1/_{60}$ of a minute. **2.** A moment. **3.** *Geom.* A unit of angular measure equal to $^1/_{60}$ of a minute of arc. [< ML *(pars minūta) secunda,* "second (small part)."]

sec•ond[2] (sĕk'ənd) *adj.* **1.** Next after the first. **2.** Inferior to another; subordinate. *—n.* **1.** The ordinal number two in a series. **2.** One that is next after the first. **3.** The forward gears in an automobile transmission having the second highest ratio. **4.** Often **seconds.** Merchandise of inferior quality. **5.** The official attendant of a contestant in a duel or boxing match. *—v.* **1.** To attend as an aide or assistant. **2.** To promote or encourage. **3.** To endorse (a motion or nomination). [< L *secundus,* following, coming next.] **—sec'ond, sec'ond•ly** *adv.*

sec•on•dar•y (sĕk'ən-dĕr'ē) *adj.* **1. a.** One step removed from the first; not primary. **b.** Inferior; minor. **2.** Derived from what is original: *a secondary source.* **3.** Of or relating to education between elementary school and college. *—n., pl.* **-ies.** One that acts in an auxiliary or subordinate capacity.

sec•ond-class (sĕk'ənd-klăs', -kläs') *adj.* **1.** In the rank or class next below the first or best. **2.** Inferior. **—sec'ond-class'** *adv.*

sec•ond-guess (sĕk'ənd-gĕs') *v.* **1.** To criticize (a decision) after the outcome is known; reconsider from hindsight. **2.** To outguess.

sec•ond•hand (sĕk'ənd-hănd') *adj.* **1.** Previously used; not new. **2.** Dealing in used merchandise. **3.** Not original; borrowed. *—adv.* Indirectly.

second person. A set of grammatical forms used in referring to the person addressed.

se•cre•cy (sē'krə-sē) *n.* **1.** The quality or condition of being secret. **2.** The ability to keep or habit of keeping secrets.

se•cret (sē'krĭt) *adj.* **1.** Concealed from general knowledge or view; kept hidden. **2.** Operating covertly: *a secret agent.* **3.** Beyond ordinary understanding; mysterious. *—n.* **1.** Something kept hidden from others. **2.** Something beyond understanding or explanation; a mystery. [< L *sēcrētus,* separate, out of the way, secret.] **—se'cret•ly** *adv.*

sec•re•tar•i•at (sĕk'rə-târ'ē-ĭt) *n.* **1.** The department administered by a governmental secretary. **2.** The position of a governmental secretary.

sec•re•tar•y (sĕk'rə-tĕr'ē) *n., pl.* **-ies. 1.** One employed to handle correspondence and do clerical work. **2.** An officer, as of a corporation, in charge of correspondence or records. **3.** An official in charge of a governmental department. **4.** A writing desk. [< ML *sēcrētārius,* confidential officer, secretary < L *sēcrētus,* SECRET.] **—sec're•tar'i•al** (-târ'ē-əl) *adj.*

se•crete[1] (sĭ-krēt') *v.* **-creted, -creting.** To generate and separate out (a substance) from cells or bodily fluids. [< L *sēcernere,* to separate.] **—se•cre'tion** *n.* **—se•cre'to•ry** (-krē'tə-rē) *adj.*

se•crete[2] (sĭ-krēt') *v.* **-creted, -creting.** To conceal; cache. [< SECRET.]

se•cre•tive (sē'krə-tĭv, sĭ-krē'tĭv) *adj.* Close-mouthed. **—se'cre•tive•ness** *n.*

sect (sĕkt) *n.* **1.** A group of people forming a distinct unit within a larger group and united by common beliefs, interests, etc. **2.** A schismatic religious body. **3.** A religious denomination. [< L *secta,* "following."]

-sect. *comb. form.* Cut or divide: **bisect.** [< L *secāre,* to cut.]

sec•tar•i•an (sĕk-târ'ē-ən) *adj.* **1.** Of or pertaining to a sect or sects. **2.** Adhering to a sect. **3.** Narrow-minded. *—n.* **1.** A member of a sect. **2.** One characterized by a narrow or factional viewpoint.

sec•tion (sĕk'shən) *n.* **1.** A component part or subdivision of something; a portion. **2.** The representation of a solid object as it would appear if cut by an intersecting plane, so that the internal structure is displayed. —*v.* To separate or divide into parts. [< L *secāre,* to cut.]

–section. *comb. form.* The act or process of dividing or cutting: **vivisection.**

sec•tion•al (sĕk'shən-əl) *adj.* **1.** Of or pertaining to a particular district. **2.** Composed of or divided into component sections.

sec•tor (sĕk'tər, -tôr') *n.* **1.** The portion of a circle bounded by two radii and one of the intercepted arcs. **2.** A division of a military position for which one unit is responsible. [< L *secāre,* to cut.]

sec•u•lar (sĕk'yə-lər) *adj.* **1.** Temporal rather than spiritual. **2.** Not pertaining to religion or a religious body. **3.** Not under monastic vows: *secular clergy.* [< L *saeculum,* generation, age.] —**sec'u•lar•ly** *adv.*

se•cure (sĭ-kyŏŏr') *adj.* **-curer, -curest. 1.** Free from danger; safe. **2.** Free from fear or doubt. **3.** Not likely to fail or give way; stable. **4.** Assured; certain. —*v.* **-cured, -curing. 1.** To guard from danger or risk of loss. **2.** To make firm; fasten. **3.** To make certain; guarantee. **4.** To acquire. [L *sēcūrus,* "without care."] —**se•cure'ly** *adv.* —**se•cure'ness** *n.*

se•cu•ri•ty (sĭ-kyŏŏr'ə-tē) *n., pl.* **-ties. 1.** Safety. **2.** Confidence. **3.** Anything that gives or assures safety. **4.** Something deposited as assurance of the fulfillment of an obligation. **5. securities.** Written evidence of ownership, as stocks, bonds, notes, etc.

secy. secretary.

se•dan (sĭ-dăn') *n.* **1.** A closed automobile having a front and rear seat. **2.** An enclosed chair carried on poles by two men.

se•date[1] (sĭ-dāt') *adj.* Serenely deliberate in character or manner. [< L *sēdāre,* to settle, calm, compose.] —**se•date'ly** *adv.* —**se•date'ness** *n.*

se•date[2] (sĭ-dāt') *v.* **-dated, -dating.** To administer a sedative to. —**se•da'tion** *n.*

sed•a•tive (sĕd'ə-tĭv) *adj.* Having a soothing, calming, or tranquilizing effect. —*n.* A sedative agent or drug.

sed•en•tar•y (sĕd'n-tĕr'ē) *adj.* Characterized by much sitting: *a sedentary job.*

Se•der (sā'dər) *n., pl.* **Seders** or **Sedarim** (sĭ-där'ĭm). *Judaism.* The feast commemorating the departure of the Israelites from Egypt, celebrated on the eves of the first and second days of Passover or only on the eve of the first day. [Heb *sēdher,* "order."]

sedge (sĕj) *n.* Any of various grasslike plants growing chiefly in wet places. [< OE *secg.*]

sed•i•ment (sĕd'ə-mənt) *n.* Material that settles to the bottom of a liquid. [< L *sedēre,* to sit, settle.] —**sed'i•men•ta'tion** *n.*

sed•i•men•ta•ry (sĕd'ə-mĕn'tə-rē, -mĕn'trē) *adj.* **1.** Of or resembling sediment. **2.** Pertaining to rocks formed from sediment.

se•di•tion (sĭ-dĭsh'ən) *n.* Conduct or language inciting to rebellion against the authority of the state. [< L *sēditiō,* "a going apart," separation.] —**se•di'tious** *adj.*

se•duce (sĭ-d/y/ōōs') *v.* **-duced, -ducing. 1.** To entice into wrongful behavior; corrupt. **2.** To induce to have sexual intercourse. [< L *sēdūcere,* to lead away.] —**se•duc'er** *n.* —**se•duc'tion** (-dŭk'shən) *n.* —**se•duc'tive** *adj.*

sed•u•lous (sĕj'ŏŏ-ləs) *adj.* Diligent; industrious. [< L *sē doliō,* "without guile."]

see[1] (sē) *v.* **saw, seen, seeing. 1.** To perceive with the eye; have the power of sight. **2.** To understand; comprehend. **3.** To regard; view; imagine. **4.** To foresee. **5.** To know through experience; undergo. **6.** To find out; ascertain. **7.** To take note of. **8.** To meet; visit socially or for consultation. **9.** To escort: *see someone to the door.* **10.** To make sure: *See that it gets done.* [< OE *sēon.* See **sekw-[2]**.]

see[2] (sē) *n.* The official seat, center of authority, jurisdiction, or office of a bishop. [< L *sēdes,* "seat," "residence."]

seed (sēd) *n.,pl.* **seeds** or **seed. 1.** A fertilized plant ovule containing an embryo capable of developing a new plant. **2.** Seeds collectively. **3.** A source or germ. **4.** Offspring. **5.** Ancestry. —*v.* **1.** To plant seeds in. **2.** To remove seeds from. [<OE *sǣd* See **sē-**.]

seed•ling (sēd'lĭng) *n.* A young, newly developing plant.

seed money. Money needed or provided to start a new project.

seed•y (sē'dē) *adj.* **-ier, -iest. 1.** Having many seeds. **2.** Worn and shabby. **3.** Somewhat disreputable; squalid. —**seed'i•ness** *n.*

see•ing (sē'ĭng) *conj.* Inasmuch as.

seek (sēk) *v.* **sought, seeking. 1.** To search for. **2.** To endeavor to obtain or reach. **3.** To try; attempt. [< OE *sēcan.* See **sāg-**.] —**seek'er** *n.*

seem (sēm) *v.* **1.** To give the impression of being; appear. **2.** To appear to one's own mind. **3.** To be evident. **4.** To appear to exist. [< ON *sœma,* to conform to, honor.]

seem•ing (sē'mĭng) *adj.* Apparent; ostensible. —**seem'ing•ly** *adv.* —**seem'ing•ness** *n.*

seem•ly (sēm'lē) *adj.* **-lier, -liest. 1.** Proper; suitable. **2.** Of pleasing appearance. [< ON *sœmr,* fitting.] —**seem'li•ness** *n.*

seen (sēn). *p.p.* of **see.**

seep (sēp) *v.* **1.** To pass slowly through small openings. **2.** To enter, depart, or become diffused gradually. —**seep'age** *n.*

seer (sē'ər) *n.* **1.** A prophet. **2.** A clairvoyant.

see•saw (sē'sô') *n.* **1.** A long plank balanced on a central fulcrum so that with a person riding on either end, one end goes up as the other goes down. **2.** A back-and-forth or up-and-down movement. [Redupl of SAW[1].] —**see'saw'** *v.*

seethe (sē*th*) *v.* **seethed, seething. 1.** To churn and foam as if boiling. **2.** To be violently agitated. [< OE *sēothan.* See **seu-[1]**.]

seg•ment (sĕg'mənt) *n.* A part into which something can be divided; a subdivision or section. —*v.* (sĕg-mĕnt'). To divide or become divided into segments. [< L *secāre,* to cut.] —**seg'men'tal** *adj.* —**seg'men•ta'tion** *n.*

seg•re•gate (sĕg'rə-gāt') *v.* **-gated, -gating. 1.** To separate or isolate from others or from a main body or group. **2.** To impose the separation of (a race or class) from the rest of society. [L *sēgregāre,* "to separate from the flock."] —**seg're•ga'tion** *n.*

seg•re•ga•tion•ist (sĕg'rə-gā'shən-ĭst) *n.* One who advocates or practices a policy of racial segregation.

seign•ior (sān'yôr) *n.* A feudal landlord. [< L *senior,* older.] —**sei•gnio'ri•al** *adj.*

seine (sān) *n.* A large fishing net with weights at the lower edge and floats at the top. —*v.* **seined, seining.** To fish or catch with a seine. [< Gk *sagēnē.*]

Seine (sĕn). A river of N France.

seis•mic (sīz'mĭk) *adj.* Of or caused by an earthquake. [SEISM(O)- + -IC.] —**seis'mi•cal•ly** *adv.*

seismo–. *comb. form.* Earthquake. [< Gk *seismos,* earthquake.]

seis•mo•graph (sīz'mə-grăf', -gräf') *n.* An instrument for automatically detecting and recording the intensity, direction, and duration of any movement of the ground. —**seis•mog'ra•pher** (sīz-mŏg'rə-fər) *n.* —**seis'mo•graph'ic** *adj.* —**seis•mog'ra•phy** *n.*

seize (sēz) *v.* **seized, seizing. 1.** To grasp suddenly and forcibly. **2.** To have a sudden effect upon; overwhelm. **3.** To take into legal custody; confiscate. [< OF *seisir.*]

sei•zure (sē'zhər) *n.* **1.** The act of seizing or state of being seized. **2.** A sudden paroxysm, as an epileptic convulsion.

sel. select; selected.

sel•dom (sĕl'dəm) *adv.* Not often; infrequently. [< OE *seldan* < Gmc **seldo-*.] —**sel'dom•ness** *n.*

se•lect (sĭ-lĕkt') *v.* To choose from among several; make a choice. —*adj.* Also **se•lect•ed** (sĭ-lĕk'tĭd). **1.** Chosen; picked out. **2.** Of special value or quality. [L *sēligere* (pp *sēlectus*), to choose out.] —**se•lec'tive** *adj.* —**se•lec'tiv'i•ty** *n.* —**se•lec'tor** *n.*

se•lec•tion (sĭ-lĕk'shən) *n.* **1. a.** The act of selecting or fact of being selected; choice. **b.** That which is selected. **2.** A literary or musical text chosen for reading or performance. **3.** A process that promotes the continued existence of certain organisms in competition with others.

selective service. Compulsory military service according to stipulated requirements for induction.

se•lect•man (sĭ-lĕkt'mən) *n.* One of a board of town officers of New England communities.

se•le•ni•um (sĭ-lē'nē-əm) *n. Symbol* **Se** A nonmetallic element resembling sulfur, used as a semiconductor and in xerography. Atomic number 34, atomic weight 78.96. [< Gk *selēnē,* moon.]

self (sĕlf) *n., pl.* **selves** (sĕlvz). **1.** The total being of one person; the individual. **2.** Individuality. **3.** One's own interests, welfare, or advantage. —*pron.* Myself, yourself, himself, or herself. [< OE *self, silf.* See **seu-[2]**.]

self–. *comb. form.* Forms hyphenated compounds indicating: **1.** Oneself or itself. **2.** Of, to, toward, in, on, with, by, for, or from the self, oneself, or itself. **3.** Autonomous, automatic, or automatically.

self-ad•dressed (sĕlf'ə-drĕst') *adj.* Addressed to oneself.

self-cen•tered (sĕlf'sĕn'tərd) *adj.* Engrossed in oneself and one's affairs. —**self'-cen'tered•ly** *adv.* —**self'-cen'tered•ness** *n.*

self-con•fi•dence (sĕlf'kŏn'fə-dəns) *n.* Confidence in oneself or one's abilities. —**self'-con'fi•dent** *adj.* —**self'-con'fi•dent•ly** *adv.*

self-con•scious (sĕlf'kŏn'shəs) *adj.* **1.** Excessively conscious of one's appearance or manner. **2.** Not natural; stilted. —**self'-con'scious•ly** *adv.* —**self'-con'scious•ness** *n.*

self-con•tained (sĕlf'kən-tānd') *adj.* **1.** Self-sufficient. **2.** Keeping to oneself; reserved.

self-con•trol (sĕlf'kən-trōl') *n.* Control of one's emotions, desires, or actions by one's own will. —**self'-con•trolled'** *adj.*

self-de•fense (sĕlf'dĭ-fĕns') *n.* **1.** Defense against attack on oneself, one's property, or one's reputation. **2.** *Law.* The right to protect oneself against violence or threatened violence with whatever means are reasonably necessary.

self-de•ni•al (sĕlf'dĭ-nī'əl) *n.* Sacrifice of one's own comfort or gratification. —**self'-de•ny'ing** *adj.* —**self'-de•ny'ing•ly** *adv.*

self-de•ter•mi•na•tion (sĕlf'dĭ-tûr'mə-nā'shən) *n.* **1.** Determination of one's own fate or course of action without compulsion. **2.** Freedom of a people or area to determine its own political status.

self-ef•fac•ing (sĕlf'ĭ-fā'sĭng) *adj.* Not drawing attention to oneself; modest. —**self'-ef•face'ment** *n.*

self-ev•i•dent (sĕlf'ĕv'ə-dənt) *adj.* Requiring no proof or explanation.

self-ex•plan•a•to•ry (sĕlf'ĭk-splăn'ə-tôr'ē, -tōr'ē) *adj.* Needing no explanation.

self-ex•pres•sion (sĕlf'ĭk-sprĕsh'ən) *n.* Expression of one's own personality, as through speech or art.

self-gov•ern•ment (sĕlf'gŭv'ərn-mənt) *n.* **1.** Political independence; autonomy. **2.** Democracy. —**self'-gov'ern•ing** *adj.*

self-im•por•tance (sĕlf'ĭm-pôr'təns) *n.* Excessively high opinion of one's own importance; conceit. —**self'-im•por'tant** *adj.*

self-in•ter•est (sĕlf'ĭn'trĭst, -ĭn'tər-ĭst) *n.* Personal advantage or interest; selfish motive or gain. —**self'-in'ter•est•ed** *adj.*

self•ish (sĕl'fĭsh) *adj.* Concerned chiefly or only with oneself, without regard for the well-being of others; egotistic. —**self'ish•ly** *adv.* —**self'ish•ness** *n.*

self-knowl•edge (sĕlf'nŏl'ĭj) *n.* Knowledge of one's own nature; insight into oneself.

self•less (sĕlf'lĭs) *adj.* Without concern for oneself; unselfish. —**self'less•ly** *adv.* —**self'-less•ness** *n.*

self-made (sĕlf'mād') *adj.* **1.** Having achieved success unaided. **2.** Made by oneself or itself.

self-pos•ses•sion (sĕlf'pə-zĕsh'ən) *n.* Full command of one's faculties, feelings, and behavior; poise. —**self'-pos•sessed'** *adj.*

self-re•li•ance (sĕlf'rĭ-lī'əns) *n.* Reliance upon one's own capabilities or resources. —**self'-re•li'ant** *adj.* —**self'-re•li'ant•ly** *adv.*

self-re•spect (sĕlf'rĭ-spĕkt') *n.* Due respect for oneself, one's character, and one's conduct. —**self'-re•spect'ing** *adj.*

self-right•eous (sĕlf'rī'chəs) *adj.* Piously sure of one's righteousness. —**self'-right'eous•ly** *adv.* —**self'-right'eous•ness** *n.*

self•same (sĕlf'sām') *adj.* The very same; identical.

self-seek•ing (sĕlf'sē'kĭng) *adj.* Pursuing or seeking only for oneself. —**self'-seek'er** *n.*

self-styled (sĕlf'stīld') *adj.* As characterized by oneself.

self-suf•fi•cient (sĕlf'sə-fĭsh'ənt) *adj.* Also **self-suf•fic•ing** (-fī'sĭng). Able to provide for oneself without help; not dependent. —**self'-suf•fi'cien•cy** *n.*

self-will (sĕlf'wĭl') *n.* Willfulness, esp. in satisfying one's own desires. —**self'-willed'** *adj.*

self-wind•ing (sĕlf'wīn'dĭng) *adj.* Winding automatically.

sell (sĕl) *v.* **sold, selling. 1.** To exchange for money or its equivalent. **2.** To offer for sale, as for one's livelihood: *He sells textiles.* **3.** To be sold or be on sale. **4.** To attract prospective buyers: *an item that sells well.* **5.** To convince: *They sold him on the idea.* [< OE *sellan,* to give, betray, sell. See **sel-**[1].] —**sell'er** *n.*

sell out. 1. To sell all one's goods or possessions. **2.** *Slang.* To betray one's cause or colleagues. —**sell'out'** *n.*

selt•zer (sĕlt'sər) *n.* **1.** A natural effervescent spring water of high mineral content. **2.** Such water artificially prepared and containing carbon dioxide. [G *Selterser (Wasser),* "(water) of Nieder Selters," a district near Wiesbaden, West Germany.]

sel•vage (sĕl'vĭj) *n.* Also **sel•vedge.** The edge of a fabric woven so that it will not ravel. [< SELF + EDGE.]

selves. *pl.* of **self.**

se•man•tic (sə-măn'tĭk) *adj.* Pertaining to meaning, esp. in language. [Gk *sēmantikos,* significant.]

se•man•tics (sə-măn'tĭks) *n.* *(takes sing. v.).* The study or science of meaning in language forms, esp. with regard to its historical change.

sem•a•phore (sĕm'ə-fôr', -fōr') *n.* Any visual signaling apparatus with flags, lights, or mechanically moving arms. [Gk *sēma,* sign + -PHORE.]

sem•blance (sĕm'bləns) *n.* **1.** An outward or token appearance. **2.** A representation; resemblance. **3.** The barest trace. [< OF *sembler,* to resemble, seem.]

se•men (sē'mən) *n.* A viscous whitish secretion of the male reproductive organs, the transporting medium for spermatozoa; sperm. [< L *sēmen,* "seed."]

se•mes•ter (sə-mĕs'tər) *n.* One of two divisions of 15 to 18 weeks each of an academic year. [< L *(cursus) sēmēstris,* "(period) of six months."]

semi–. *comb. form.* **1.** Partly or partially. **2.** Half of. **3.** Occurring twice within a particular period of time. [L *sēmi-.*]

sem•i•an•nu•al (sĕm'ē-ăn'yo͞o-əl, sĕm'ī-) *adj.* Happening or issued twice a year.

sem•i•cir•cle (sĕm'ĭ-sûr'kəl) *n.* A half of a circle as divided by a diameter. —**sem'i•cir'cu•lar** (-sûr'kyə-lər) *adj.*

semicircular canal. Any of the three looped, fluid-containing tubes in the inner ear that function in maintaining the sense of balance and orientation.

sem•i•co•lon (sĕm'ĭ-kō'lən) *n.* A mark of punctuation (;) indicating a degree of separation intermediate between the comma and the period.

sem•i•con•duc•tor (sĕm'ē-kən-dŭk'tər, sĕm'ī-) *n.* Any of various solid crystalline substances, such as germanium or silicon, having electrical conductivity greater than insulators but less than good conductors.

sem•i•fi•nal (sĕm'ē-fī'nəl, sĕm'ī-) *adj.* Immediately preceding the final, as in a series of competitions.

sem•i•month•ly (sĕm'ē-mŭnth'lē, sĕm'ī-) *adj.* Occurring or issued twice a month. See Usage note at **bimonthly.** —*adv.* Twice monthly.

sem•i•nal (sĕm'ə-nəl) *adj.* Of, relating to, or containing semen.

sem•i•nar (sĕm'ə-när') *n.* **1.** A small group of advanced college students engaged in original research under the guidance of a professor. **2.** A course of study so pursued. [< L *sēminārium,* seed plot, nursery.]

sem•i•nar•y (sĕm'ə-nĕr'ē) *n., pl.* **-ies.** A school, esp. a theological school for the training of priests, ministers, or rabbis. [< L *sēminārium,* garden, seed plot, nursery.] —**sem'i•nar'i•an** (sĕm'ə-nâr'ē-ən) *n.*

Sem•i•nole (sĕm'ə-nōl') *n., pl.* **-nole** or **-noles. 1.** A member of a tribe of Muskhogean-speaking North American Indians, now living chiefly in Oklahoma and Florida. **2.** The language of this tribe.

sem•i•per•me•a•ble (sĕm'ē-pûr'mē-ə-bəl, sĕm'ī-) *adj.* **1.** Partially permeable. **2.** Pertaining to a membrane that is permeable to some molecules in a solution but not to all.

sem•i•pre•cious (sĕm'ē-prĕsh'əs, sĕm'ī-) *adj.* Of less value than precious stones, as a topaz.

sem•i•pri•vate (sĕm'ē-prī'vĭt, sĕm'ī-) *adj.* Shared with other occupants.

sem•i•skilled (sĕm'ē-skĭld', sĕm'ī-) *adj.* Possessing minimal skills.

sem•i•sol•id (sĕm'ē-sŏl'ĭd, sĕm'ī-) *adj.* Intermediate in properties, esp. in rigidity, between solids and liquids. —*n.* A semisolid substance.

Sem•ite (sĕm'īt') *n.* Also **Shem•ite** (shĕm'īt'). A member of any of a group of Caucasoid peoples, chiefly Jews and Arabs, of the E Mediterranean area.

Se•mit•ic (sə-mĭt'ĭk) *adj.* **1.** Of or pertaining to the Semites, esp. Jewish or Arabic. **2.** Pertaining to a subfamily of Afro-Asiatic, including Arabic, Hebrew, and Aramaic. —*n.* **1.** The Semitic subfamily of languages. **2.** Any one of these languages.

Sem•i•to-Ha•mit•ic (sĕm'ə-tō'hă-mĭt'ĭk) *n.* Afro-Asiatic. —**Sem'i•to'-Ha•mit'ic** *adj.*

sem•i•vow•el (sĕm'ĭ-vou'əl) *n.* A letter or vocal sound having the sound of a vowel but used as a consonant, as *y* and *w.*

sem•i•week•ly (sĕm'ē-wēk'lē, sĕm'ī-) *adj.* Issued or happening twice a week. See Usage note at **bimonthly.** —*adv.* Twice weekly.

sem•i•year•ly (sĕm'ē-yîr'lē, sĕm'ī-) *adj.* Happening or issued twice a year or once every half year. See Usage note at **bimonthly.** —*adv.* Every half year.

sen., Sen. 1. senate; senator. **2.** senior.

Sen•ate (sĕn'ĭt) *n.* **1. senate.** A legislative and deliberative assembly. **2.** The upper house of Congress in the U.S. **3.** The upper house in the bicameral legislature of many U.S. states. **4.** The upper legislative house in Canada, France, and other countries. [< L *senātus.*]

sen•a•tor (sĕn'ə-tər) *n.* Also **Sen•a•tor.** A member of a senate. —**sen'a•to'ri•al** (-tôr'ē-əl, -tōr'ē-əl) *adj.*

send (sĕnd) *v.* **sent, sending. 1.** To cause to be conveyed by an intermediary to a destination. **2. a.** To direct to go on a mission. **b.** To enable to go. **3.** To command or request to go. **4.** To cause to depart. **5.** To emit. **6.** To direct or propel with force. **7.** To cause to take place or befall. **8.** To put into some state or condition. —**send for. 1.** To order. **2.** To summon. [< OE *sendan.* See **sent-.**] —**send'er** *n.*

send•off (sĕnd'ôf', -ŏf') *n.* **1.** A demonstration of good wishes for one about to leave on a journey or begin a new undertaking. **2.** A start given to someone or something.

Sen•e•gal (sĕn'ə-gôl'). A republic in W Africa. Pop. 3,100,000. Cap. Dakar.

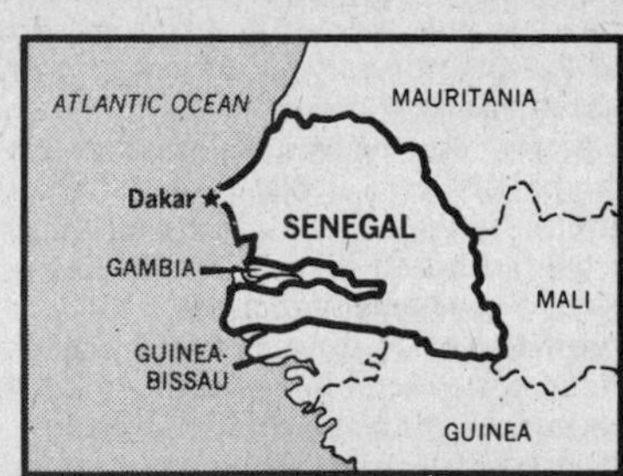

Senegal

Senegal River. A river of W Africa.

se•nile (sē'nīl', sĕn'īl') *adj.* **1.** Characteristic of or proceeding from old age. **2.** Mentally and physically deteriorating with old age. [< L *senex,* old.] —**se•nil'i•ty** (sĭ-nĭl'ə-tē) *n.*

sen•ior (sēn'yər) *adj.* **1.** Of or designating the older of two, esp. the older of two persons having the same name. **2.** Above others in rank or length of service. **3.** Pertaining to the fourth and last year of high school or college.

—*n.* **1.** A senior person. **2.** A student in his fourth year of high school or college. [< L *senex*, old.]

senior high school. A high school usually including grades 10, 11, and 12.

sen•ior•i•ty (sēn-yôr'ə-tē, -yŏr'ə-tē) *n., pl.* **-ties.** **1.** The state of being older or higher in rank. **2.** Precedence of position, esp. by reason of longer service.

sen•na (sĕn'ə) *n.* **1.** A plant with compound leaves and yellow flowers. **2.** The dried leaves of such a plant, used as a cathartic. [< Ar *sanā'*.]

sen•sa•tion (sĕn'sā'shən, sən-) *n.* **1. a.** A perception associated with stimulation of a sense organ or with a specific bodily condition. **b.** The faculty to feel or perceive. **2.** A state of heightened interest or emotion. **3. a.** A condition of intense public interest and excitement. **b.** An event or object causing such public excitement. —**sen'sa'tion•al** *adj.*

sen•sa•tion•al•ism (sĕn'sā'shən-əl-ĭz'əm, sən-) *n.* The use of sensational matter or methods in writing, art, politics, etc. —**sen'sa'tion•al•ist** *n.*

sense (sĕns) *n.* **1.** Any of the functions of hearing, sight, smell, touch, and taste. **2.** The faculty of external or self-perception exemplified by these functions. **3. senses.** The faculties of sensation as means of providing physical gratification and pleasure. **4.** A feeling or perception either through the senses or the intellect. **5.** Correct judgment. **6. a.** Import; point. **b.** Lexical meaning. —*v.* **sensed, sensing. 1.** To become aware of; perceive. **2.** To understand. **3.** To detect something automatically: *sense radioactivity.* [< L *sentīre*, to perceive by the senses, to feel.]

sense•less (sĕns'lĭs) *adj.* **1.** Without sense or meaning; meaningless. **2.** Foolish; lacking sense. **3.** Unconscious.

sen•si•bil•i•ty (sĕn'sə-bĭl'ə-tē) *n., pl.* **-ties. 1.** The ability to feel or perceive. **2.** Keen perception. **3.** Delicate sensitivity to. **4.** The aptness of plant organisms and instruments to be affected by environment.

sen•si•ble (sĕn'sə-bəl) *adj.* **1.** Perceptible by the senses or mind. **2.** Readily perceived; appreciable. **3.** Able to feel or perceive. **4.** Cognizant; aware. **5.** Acting with or showing good sense: *a sensible choice.* —**sen'si•bly** *adv.*

sen•si•tive (sĕn'sə-tĭv) *adj.* **1.** Capable of perceiving with a sense or senses. **2.** Responsive to external conditions or stimulation. **3.** Susceptible to the feelings of others. **4.** Quick to take offense; touchy. **5. a.** Easily irritated. **b.** Easily altered. **6.** Registering very slight differences or changes of condition. —**sen'si•tive•ly** *adv.* —**sen'si•tiv'i•ty, sen'si•tive•ness** *n.*

sen•si•tize (sĕn'sə-tīz') *v.* **-tized, -tizing.** To make or become sensitive. —**sen'si•ti•za'tion** *n.*

sen•sor (sĕn'sər, -sôr') *n.* A device, such as a photoelectric cell, that receives and responds to a signal or stimulus.

sen•so•ry (sĕn'sər-ē) *adj.* Pertaining to the senses.

sen•su•al (sĕn'sho͞o-əl) *adj.* **1.** Of or affecting the senses. **2. a.** Pertaining to the gratification of the physical appetites. **b.** Suggesting sexuality. **c.** Carnal rather than intellectual. **3.** Sensory. —**sen'su•al•ist** *n.* —**sen'su•al'i•ty, sen'su•al•ness** *n.* —**sen'su•al•ly** *adv.*

sen•su•ous (sĕn'sho͞o-əs) *adj.* **1.** Pertaining to, derived from, or appealing to the senses. **2.** Highly appreciative of the pleasures of sensation. —**sen'su•ous•ly** *adv.* —**sen'su•ous•ness** *n.*

sent (sĕnt). *p.t.* & *p.p.* of **send.**

sen•tence (sĕn'təns) *n.* **1.** A grammatical unit comprising a word or group of words that usually consists of at least one subject and a finite verb or verb phrase. **2. a.** A court judgment, esp. a decision of the penalty to be given a convicted person. **b.** The penalty meted out. —*v.* **-tenced, -tencing.** To pass sentence upon (a convicted person). [< L *sententia*, a way of thinking < *sentīre*, to feel.] —**sen•ten'tial** (sĕn-tĕn'shəl) *adj.* —**sen'ten'tial•ly** *adv.*

sen•ten•tious (sĕn-tĕn'shəs) *adj.* **1.** Terse and energetic in expression. **2. a.** Fond of aphoristic utterances. **b.** Given to pompous moralizing. [< L *sententia*, opinion, SENTENCE.] —**sen•ten'tious•ly** *adv.*

sen•ti•ent (sĕn'chĭ-ənt) *adj.* **1.** Having sense perception. **2.** Experiencing sensation. [< L *sentīre*, to feel.] —**sen'ti•ent•ly** *adv.*

sen•ti•ment (sĕn'tə-mənt) *n.* **1. a.** A cast of mind regarding something. **b.** An opinion; view. **2.** A thought or attitude based on emotion instead of reason. **3.** The emotional import of something. [< L *sentīre*, to feel.]

sen•ti•men•tal (sĕn'tə-mĕnt'l) *adj.* **1. a.** Characterized by or swayed by sentiment. **b.** Extravagantly emotional. **2.** Appealing to the sentiments, esp. to romantic feelings. —**sen'ti•men'tal•ism', sen'ti•men•tal'i•ty** *n.* —**sen'ti•men'tal•ize** *v.* **(-ized, -izing).** —**sen'ti•men'tal•ly** *adv.*

sen•ti•nel (sĕnt'n-əl) *n.* One that keeps guard; a sentry. [< It *sentinella.*]

sen•try (sĕn'trē) *n., pl.* **-tries. 1.** A guard, esp. a soldier posted to prevent the passage of unauthorized persons. **2.** The duty of a sentry. [Perh short for obs *centrinell*, var of SENTINEL.]

Seoul (sōl). The capital of South Korea. Pop. 3,376,000.

se•pal (sē'pəl) *n.* One of the leaflike segments of a flower calyx. [< Gk *skepē*, covering + (PET)AL.]

sep•a•ra•ble (sĕp'ər-ə-bəl, sĕp'rə-) *adj.* Capable of being separated.

sep•a•rate (sĕp'ə-rāt') *v.* **-rated, -rating. 1. a.** To set, keep, or come apart; divide or become divided; disunite. **b.** To sort. **2.** To differentiate between; distinguish. **3.** To remove from a mixture or combination; isolate. **4.** To part, as a married couple, by decree. **5.** To part company; disperse. —*adj.* (sĕp'ər-ĭt, sĕp'rĭt). **1.** Set apart from the rest; not connected. **2.** Existing as an entity; independent. **3.** Dissimilar; distinct. **4.** Not shared; individual. [< L *sēparāre.*] —**sep'a•rate•ly** *adv.* —**sep'a•rate•ness** *n.*

sep•a•ra•tion (sĕp'ə-rā'shən) *n.* **1. a.** The act or process of separating. **b.** The state of being separated. **2.** The place where a division occurs.

sep•a•ra•tist (sĕp'ər-ə-tĭst, sĕp'rə-, sĕp'ə-rā'tĭst) *n.* Also **sep•a•ra•tion•ist** (sĕp'ə-rā'shən-ĭst). One who advocates separation, esp. from an established church. —**sep'a•ra•tism'** *n.*

sep•a•ra•tor (sĕp'ə-rā'tər) *n.* **1.** One that separates. **2.** A device for separating cream from milk.

se•pi•a (sē'pē-ə) *n.* **1.** A dark-brown pigment or color. **2.** Dark yellowish brown. [< L *sēpia*, cuttlefish (pigment).]

sep•sis (sĕp'sĭs) *n.* The presence of pathogenic organisms, or their toxins, in the blood or tissues. [< Gk *sēpein*, to make rotten.]

Sept. September.

Sep•tem•ber (sĕp-tĕm'bər) *n.* The 9th month of the year. September has 30 days. [< L *September*, the 7th month (of the Roman calendar).]

septi–. *comb. form.* Seven. [< L *septem*, seven.]

sep•tic (sĕp'tĭk) *adj.* **1.** Pertaining to sepsis. **2.** Causing sepsis; putrefactive.

sep•ti•ce•mi•a (sĕp'tĭ-sē'mē-ə) *n.* A systemic disease caused by pathogenic organisms or their toxins in the bloodstream. [< L *sēpticus*, septic + -EMIA.]

septic tank. A sewage-disposal tank in which waste material is decomposed by certain bacteria.

sep•til•lion (sĕp-tĭl'yən) *n.* **1.** The cardinal number represented by 1 followed by 24 zeros. **2.** In British usage, the cardinal number represented by 1 followed by 42 zeros. —**sep•til'lion** *adj.*

sep•til•lionth (sĕp-tĭl'yənth) *n.* **1.** The ordinal number septillion in a series. **2.** One of a septillion equal parts. —**sep•til'lionth** *adj.* & *adv.*

Sep•tu•a•gint (sĕp'cho͞o-ə-jĭnt', sĕp'to͞o-) *n.* A Greek translation of the Old Testament dating from the 3rd century B.C. [L *septuāgintā*, seventy, "the Seventy" < the 70 or 72 Jewish scholars who are traditionally recognized as having done the translation.]

sep•tu•ple (sĕp't/y/o͞o-pəl, sĕp-t/y/o͞o'pəl) *adj.* **1.** Consisting of or containing seven. **2.** Multiplied by seven. —*v.* **-pled, -pling.** To multiply by seven.

sep•ul•cher (sĕp'əl-kər). Also *chiefly Brit.* **sep•ul•chre.** *n.* A burial vault. —*v.* To inter. [< L *sepulchrum* < *sepelīre*, to bury.] —**se•pul'chral** (sə-pŭl'krəl) *adj.*

seq. the following (L *sequēns*).

se•quel (sē'kwĕl) *n.* **1.** Something that follows; a continuation. **2.** A literary work continuing the narrative of an earlier work. **3.** A consequence. [< L *sĕquī*, to follow.]

se•quence (sē'kwəns) *n.* **1.** A following of one thing after another; succession. **2.** An order of succession; arrangement. **3.** A related or continuous series. [< L *sequī*, to follow.] —**se•quen'tial** (sĭ-kwĕn'shəl) *adj.* —**se•quen'ti•al'i•ty** *n.* —**se•quen'tial•ly** *adv.*

se•ques•ter (sĭ-kwĕs'tər) *v.* **1.** To remove or set apart; segregate. **2.** To withdraw into seclusion. [< L, depository.]

se•ques•trate (sĭ-kwĕs'trāt') *v.* **-trated, -trating.** To sequester. —**se'ques•tra'tion** *n.*

se•quin (sē'kwĭn) *n.* A small, shiny ornamental disk, often sewn on cloth. [< Ar *sikkah*, coin die.]

se•quoi•a (sĭ-kwoi'ə) *n.* A very tall, massive evergreen tree of the mountains of California. [< *Sequoya* (died 1843), American Indian scholar.]

ser. **1.** serial. **2.** series. **3.** sermon.

se•ra. Alternate *pl.* of **serum.**

se•ra•glio (sĭ-răl'yō, -räl'yō) *n., pl.* **-glios. 1.** A large harem. **2.** A sultan's palace. [Prob < Turk *serai*, a palace.]

se•ra•pe (sə-rä'pē) *n.* Also **sa•ra•pe.** A woolen poncho worn by Latin-American men.

ser•aph (sĕr'əf) *n., pl.* **-aphs** or **-aphim** (-ə-fĭm) or **-aphin** (-ə-fĭn). A celestial being or angel. [< Heb *sārāph.*] —**se•raph'ic** (sĭ-răf'ĭk) *adj.*

Serb (sûrb) *n.* A Serbian.

Ser•bi•a (sûr'bē-ə). A constituent republic of Yugoslavia, in the E part of the country.

Ser•bi•an (sûr'bē-ən) *n.* **1.** A member of a southern Slavic people that is the dominant ethnic group of Serbia and adjacent republics of Yugoslavia. **2.** A Serbo-Croatian. —*adj.* **1.** Of Serbia or the Serbians. **2.** Serbo-Croatian.

Ser•bo-Cro•a•tian (sûr'bō-krō-ā'shən) *n.* **1.**

The Slavic language of the Serbs and Croats of Yugoslavia. **2.** A speaker of this language. **—Ser'bo-Cro•a'tian** *adj.*

sere (sîr) *adj.* Withered; dry. [< OE *sēar.* See **saus-.**]

ser•e•nade (sĕr'ə-nād', sĕr'ə-nād') *n.* An honorific musical performance, esp. one given by a lover for his sweetheart. *—v.* (sĕr'ə-nād') **-naded, -nading.** To perform a serenade (for). [< L *serēnus,* SERENE.] **—ser'e•nad'er** *n.*

ser•en•dip•i•ty (sĕr'ən-dĭp'ə-tē) *n.* The faculty of making fortunate and unexpected discoveries by accident. [< the fairy tale *The Three Princes of Serendip.*] **—ser'en•dip'i•tous** *adj.*

se•rene (sĭ-rēn') *adj.* **1.** Unruffled; tranquil; dignified. **2.** Unclouded; bright. [L *serēnus.*] **—se•rene'ly** *adv.* **—se•ren'i•ty** (sĭ-rĕn'ə-tē) *n.*

serf (sûrf) *n.* **1.** A member of the lowest feudal class, bound to the land and owned by a lord. **2.** A slave. [< L *servus,* slave.] **—serf'dom** *n.*

serge (sûrj) *n.* A cloth of worsted or worsted and wool, often used for suits. [< L *sēricus,* of Seres (a people).]

ser•geant (sär'jənt) *n.* **1. a.** Any of several ranks of noncommissioned officers in the U.S. Army, Air Force, or Marine Corps. **b.** One holding any of these ranks. **2.** Also *chiefly Brit.* **ser•jeant. a.** The rank of police officer next below a captain, lieutenant, or inspector. **b.** One holding this rank. [< L *servus,* slave.] **—ser'gean•cy, ser'geant•ship'** *n.*

sergeant at arms. An officer appointed to keep order within an organization, as in a legislative body.

sergeant first class. A noncommissioned officer next below master sergeant in the U.S. Army.

sergeant major. 1. A noncommissioned officer serving as chief administrative assistant of a headquarters unit of the U.S. Army, Air Force, or Marine Corps. **2.** *Brit.* A noncommissioned officer of the highest rank.

se•ri•al (sîr'ē-əl) *adj.* **1.** Of, forming, or arranged in a series. **2.** Published or produced in installments. *—n.* A work published or produced in installments. [< SERIES.] **—se'ri•al•ize'** *v.* **(-ized, -izing). —se'ri•al•ly** *adv.*

se•ries (sîr'ēz) *n., pl.* **-ries. 1. a.** A group of events related by order of occurrence. **b.** A group of thematically connected works or performances. **2.** A group of related objects. [L *seriēs* < *serere,* to join.]

ser•if (sĕr'ĭf) *n.* Also *chiefly Brit.* **cer•iph.** *Ptg.* A fine line finishing off the main strokes of a letter. [Perh < L *scribere,* to write.]

se•ri•ous (sîr'ē-əs) *adj.* **1.** Grave in character, quality, or mien; sober. **2.** Sincere; earnest. **3.** Concerned with important rather than trivial matters. **4.** Difficult. **5.** Causing anxiety; critical. [< L *sērius.*] **—se'ri•ous•ly** *adv.* **—se'ri•ous•ness** *n.*

ser•jeant. *Chiefly Brit.* Variant of **sergeant.**

ser•mon (sûr'mən) *n.* **1.** A religious discourse delivered as part of a church service. **2.** A lengthy and tedious reproof or exhortation. [< L *sermō,* a discourse.]

se•rous (sîr'əs) *adj.* Containing, secreting, or resembling serum.

ser•pent (sûr'pənt) *n.* A snake. [< L *serpēns,* "crawling thing."]

ser•pen•tine (sûr'pən-tēn', -tīn') *adj.* Snakelike, as in form, movement, or insinuating slyness.

ser•rate (sĕr'āt', -ĭt) *adj.* Also **ser•rat•ed** (-rā'-tĭd). Edged with notched, toothlike projections. [< L *serra,* saw.] **—ser•ra'tion** *n.*

ser•ried (sĕr'ēd) *adj.* Pressed together in rows; in close order. [< OF *serrer,* to crowd.]

se•rum (sîr'əm) *n., pl.* **-rums** or **sera** (sîr'ə). **1.** The clear yellowish fluid obtained upon separating whole blood into its solid and liquid components. **2.** The fluid from the tissues of immunized animals, used esp. as an antitoxin. [L, whey, serum.]

serv. service.

ser•vant (sûr'vənt) *n.* One employed to perform domestic or other services.

serve (sûrv) *v.* **served, serving. 1.** To work for; be a servant to. **2.** To act in a particular capacity. **3.** To place food before; wait on. **4.** To provide goods and services for. **5.** To be of assistance to. **6.** To spend or complete (time), as in prison or in elective office. **7.** To undergo military service for. **8.** To requite: *Punish her; it will serve her right.* **9.** To meet a need; satisfy. **10.** To be used by or of use to. **11.** To give homage to. **12.** To present (a legal writ or summons). **13.** To put (a ball) in play, as in tennis. *—n.* The right, manner, or act of serving in many games played on a court. [< L *servīre* < *servus,* slave.] **—serv'er** *n.*

serv•ice (sûr'vĭs) *n.* **1.** The occupation or duties of a servant. **2.** The act or means of serving. **3.** A government department and its employees: *civil service.* **4.** The armed forces of a nation, or any branch thereof. **5.** Duties performed as an occupation. **6.** Installation, maintenance, or repairs provided or guaranteed by a dealer or manufacturer. **7.** A set of dishes or utensils: *a tea service.* **8.** A serve in a game. *—adj.* **1.** Useful. **2.** Reserved for employees, deliveries, etc.: *a service elevator.* *—v.* **-iced, -icing. 1.** To adjust; repair; maintain. **2.** To provide services to. [< L *servus,* slave.]

serv•ice•a•ble (sûr'vĭs-ə-bəl) *adj.* **1.** Ready for service; usable. **2.** Able to give good service; durable. **—serv'ice•a•bil'i•ty, serv'ice•a•ble•ness** *n.* **—serv'ice•a•bly** *adv.*

serv•ice•man (sûr'vĭs-măn', -mən) *n.* **1.** A member of the armed forces. **2.** Also **service man.** One whose work is the maintenance and repair of equipment.

ser•vile (sûr'vəl, -vīl') *adj.* Slavish in character or attitude; submissive. [< L *servus,* slave.] **—ser•vil'i•ty** (sər-vĭl'ə-tē) *n.*

ser•vi•tor (sûr'və-tər, -tôr') *n.* An attendant; servant. [< L *servire,* to SERVE.]

ser•vi•tude (sûr'və-t/y/ōōd') *n.* Submission to a master; slavery. [< L *servus,* slave.]

ses•a•me (sĕs'ə-mē) *n.* **1.** An Asian plant bearing small, edible, oil-rich seeds. **2.** The seeds of this plant. [< Gk *sēsamē* < Sem.]

ses•sion (sĕsh'ən) *n.* **1. a.** A meeting of a legislative or judicial body. **b.** A series of such meetings. **c.** The duration of such a series of meetings. **2.** The part of a year or of a day during which a school holds classes. [< L *sessus,* pp of *sedēre,* to sit.] **—ses'sion•al** *adj.* **—ses'sion•al•ly** *adv.*

set¹ (sĕt) *v.* **set, setting. 1.** To put in a specified position or state. **2.** To put into a stable position; fix. **3.** To restore to a proper and normal state. **4.** To adjust, as for proper functioning. **5.** To arrange tableware upon (a table) preparatory to eating. **6.** To apply curlers and clips to (one's hair) in order to style. **7.** To arrange (type) into words and sentences preparatory to printing; compose. **8.** To prescribe, establish, or assign. **9.** To put forth as a model to be emulated. **10.** To put in a mounting; mount. **11.** To cause to sit. **12.** To sit on eggs, as a hen. **13.** To affix (a price or value). **14.** To disappear below the horizon, as the sun. **15.** To diminish or decline; wane. **16.** To become fixed; harden or congeal. **—set about.** To start or begin doing. **—set aside. 1.** To separate and reserve for a special purpose. **2.** To annul. **—set forth. 1.** To utter or express. **2.** To embark on a journey. **—set out.** To begin any procedure or progress; start. *—adj.* **1.** Fixed or established. **2.** Stereotyped. **3.** Fixed and rigid; unflinching. **4.** Unyielding; firm. **5.** Ready: *get set.* *—n.* **1.** The act or process of setting. **2.** The condition resulting from setting. [< OE *settan,* to cause to sit, place. See **sed-.**]

set² (sĕt) *n.* **1.** A group of persons or things connected by or collected for their similar appearance, interest, importance, etc.: *a chess set.* **2.** A group of circumstances, situations, etc., joined to be treated as a whole. **3.** A group of books published as a unit. **4. a.** The scenery constructed for a theatrical performance. **b.** The enclosure in which a motion picture is being filmed; studio. **5.** The receiving apparatus assembled to operate a radio or television. **6.** *Math.* Any collection of distinct elements. **7.** In tennis and other games, a group of games constituting one division or unit of a match. [< L *secta,* SECT.]

set•back (sĕt'băk') *n.* An unanticipated or sudden check in progress; a reverse.

set•tee (sĕt-tē') *n.* **1.** A wooden bench with a high back. **2.** A small sofa.

set•ter (sĕt'ər) *n.* A long-haired dog of a breed originally trained to hunt game.

set•ting (sĕt'ĭng) *n.* **1.** The act of a person or thing that sets. **2.** The context in which a situation is set. **3.** A jewelry mounting. **4.** The scenery for a theatrical performance. **5.** The descent of the sun or other celestial body below the horizon.

set•tle (sĕt'l) *v.* **-tled, -tling. 1.** To put into order; place; arrange or fix definitely as desired. **2.** To establish residence in. **3.** To restore calmness or comfort to. **4. a.** To come or cause to come to rest, sink, or become compact. **b.** To cause (a liquid) to become clear by forming a sediment. **5.** To stabilize; assure. **6. a.** To make compensation for (a claim). **b.** To pay (a debt). **7.** To decide by mutual agreement. [< OE *setl,* seat. See **sed-.**] **—set'tler** *n.*

set•tle•ment (sĕt'l-mənt) *n.* **1.** The act or process of settling. **2. a.** Establishment in a new business or region. **b.** A newly colonized region. **3.** A small community. **4.** An understanding reached, as in financial matters. **5.** A welfare center providing community services in an underprivileged area.

sev•en (sĕv'ən) *n.* The cardinal number written 7 or in Roman numerals VII. [< OE *seofon.* See **septṃ.**] **—sev'en** *adj. & pron.*

sev•en•teen (sĕv'ən-tēn', sĕv'ən-tēn') *n.* The cardinal number written 17 or in Roman numerals XVII. **—sev'en•teen'** *adj. & pron.*

sev•en•teenth (sĕv'ən-tĕnth', sĕv'ən-tĕnth') *n.* **1.** The ordinal number 17 in a series. **2.** One of 17 equal parts. **—sev'en•teenth'** *adj. & adv.*

sev•enth (sĕv'ənth) *n.* **1.** The ordinal number 7 in a series. **2.** One of 7 equal parts. **—sev'enth** *adj. & adv.*

sev•en•ti•eth (sĕv'ən-tē-ĭth) *n.* **1.** The ordinal number 70 in a series. **2.** One of 70 equal parts. **—sev'en•ti•eth** *adj. & adv.*

sev•en•ty (sĕv'ən-tē) *n.* The cardinal number written 70 or in Roman numerals LXX. **—sev'en•ty** *adj. & pron.*

sev•er (sĕv'ər) *v.* **1.** To divide or separate into parts; keep apart. **2.** To cut or become cut into two or more parts. **3.** To break off (a relationship); dissolve. [< L *sēparāre,* to SEPARATE.]

sev•er•al (sĕv′ər-əl) *adj.* **1.** Being of a number more than two or three, but not many; of an indefinitely small number. **2.** Single; distinct. —*n.* Several ones; a few. [< L *sēparāre,* to SEPARATE.] —**sev′er•al•ly** *adv.*

sev•er•ance (sĕv′ər-əns) *n.* **1. a.** The act or process of severing. **b.** The condition of being severed. **2.** Extra pay given an employee upon leaving a job.

se•vere (sə-vîr′) *adj.* **-verer, -verest. 1.** Unsparing and harsh in treating others; stern; strict. **2.** Maintained rigidly; accurate. **3.** Austere in appearance or temperament; grave; forbidding. **4.** Extremely plain; conservatively presented. **5.** Causing intense pain or distress; violent; sharp. **6.** Extremely difficult to perform or accomplish; rigorous; trying. [< L *sevērus.*] —**se•vere′ly** *adv.* —**se•ver′i•ty** (-vĕr′ə-tē), **se•vere′ness** *n.*

Se•ville (sə-vĭl′). A city of SW Spain. Pop. 532,000.

sew (sō) *v.* **sewed, sewn** or **sewed, sewing. 1.** To make, repair, or fasten with a needle and thread or a sewing machine. **2.** To furnish with stitches for the purpose of closing, fastening, etc. [< OE *seowian.* See **syū-.**]

sew•age (so͞o′ĭj) *n.* Waste carried off with ground water in sewers or drains.

sew•er (so͞o′ər) *n.* An artificial, usually underground conduit for carrying off sewage or rainwater. [< VL **exaquāria.*]

sew•er•age (so͞o′ər-ĭj) *n.* **1.** A system of sewers. **2.** The removal of waste materials by means of sewers. **3.** Sewage.

sew•ing (sō′ĭng) *n.* **1.** The act of one who sews. **2.** The article upon which one sews; needlework.

sewing machine. A machine for sewing.

sewn (sōn). *p.p.* of **sew.**

sex (sĕks) *n.* **1. a.** The property or quality by which organisms are classified according to their reproductive functions. **b.** Either of two divisions, designated *male* and *female,* of this classification. **2.** Males or females collectively. **3.** The sexual urge or instinct as it manifests itself in behavior. **4.** Sexual intercourse. [< L *sexus.*]

sex–. *comb. form.* Six. [< L *sex,* six.]

sex•ism (sĕk′sĭz′əm) *n.* Discrimination by members of one sex against the other, esp. by males against females, based on the assumption that one sex is superior. —**sex′ist** *adj.* & *n.*

sex•less (sĕks′lĭs) *adj.* **1.** Lacking sexual characteristics; asexual; neuter. **2.** Arousing or exhibiting no sexual interest or desire. —**sex′less•ly** *adv.* —**sex′less•ness** *n.*

sex reversal. The natural, artificial, or pathological functional transformation from one sex to another.

sex•tant (sĕks′tənt) *n.* A navigational instrument used for measuring the altitudes of celestial bodies.

sex•tet (sĕks-tĕt′) *n.* **1. a.** A group of six musicians. **b.** A musical composition for six performers. **2.** A group of six.

sex•tile (sĕks′tĭl′) *adj.* Designating the position of two celestial bodies when they are 60° apart. [L *sextīlis,* one sixth (of a circle).]

sex•til•lion (sĕks-tĭl′yən) *n.* **1.** The cardinal number represented by 1 followed by 21 zeros. **2.** In British usage, the cardinal number represented by 1 followed by 36 zeros. [< SEX- + (M)ILLION.] —**sex•til′lion** *adj.*

sex•til•lionth (sĕks-tĭl′yənth) *n.* **1.** The ordinal number sextillion in a series. **2.** One of sextillion equal parts. —**sex•til′lionth** *adj.* & *adv.*

sex•ton (sĕks′tən) *n.* One responsible for the care and upkeep of church property. [< ML *sacristānus.*]

sex•tu•ple (sĕks-t/y/o͞o′pəl, -tŭp′əl, sĕks′to͞o-pəl) *adj.* **1.** Having six parts. **2.** Multiplied by six. —*n.* A number or amount six times as many or as much as another. —*v.* **-pled, -pling.** To multiply or increase by six. [Prob SEX- + (QUIN)TUPLE.]

sex•tu•plet (sĕks-tŭp′lĭt, -t/y/o͞o′plĭt, sĕks′to͞o-plĭt) *n.* One of six offspring delivered at one birth.

sex•u•al (sĕk′sho͞o-əl) *adj.* **1.** Of or involving sex, the sexes, or the sex organs and their functions. **2.** Having a sex or sexual organs. **3.** Implying or symbolizing erotic desires or activity. **4.** Pertaining to or designating reproduction involving the union of male and female gametes. —**sex′u•al•ly** *adv.*

sexual intercourse. Coitus, esp. between humans.

sex•u•al•i•ty (sĕk′sho͞o-ăl′ə-tē) *n.* **1.** The condition of being characterized and distinguished by sex. **2.** Concern or preoccupation with sex. **3.** The quality of possessing a sexual character or potency.

sex•y (sĕk′sē) *adj.* **-ier, -iest.** *Slang.* Arousing or intending to arouse sexual desire or interest. —**sex′i•ness** *n.*

Sfc. sergeant first class.

S.G. solicitor general.

sgd. signed.

Sgt. sergeant.

sh (sh) *interj.* Used to urge silence.

sh. **1.** share (capital stock). **2.** sheet. **3.** shilling.

shab•by (shăb′ē) *adj.* **-bier, -biest. 1.** Threadbare; worn-out. **2.** Wearing worn garments; seedy. **3.** Dilapidated; deteriorated. **4.** Despicable; mean. **5.** Unfair. [< OE *sceabb,* a scab. See **skep-.**] —**shab′bi•ly** *adv.* —**shab′bi•ness** *n.*

shack (shăk) *n.* A small, crudely built cabin. [< Aztec *xacalli,* thatched cabin.]

shack•le (shăk′əl) *n.* **1.** A metal fastening, usually one of a pair, for encircling the ankle or wrist of a prisoner or captive; fetter; manacle. **2.** Anything that confines or restrains. —*v.* **-led, -ling.** To put shackles on; fetter. [< OE *sceacel,* fetter < Gmc **skakulo-.*] —**shack′ler** *n.*

shad (shăd) *n., pl.* **shad** or **shads.** A food fish that swims up streams from marine waters to spawn. [< OE *sceadd.*]

shade (shād) *n.* **1. a.** Diminished or partial light; comparative darkness or obscurity. **b.** An area or space of such partial darkness or obscurity. **2.** Cover or shelter from the sun or its rays. **3. shades.** *Slang.* Sunglasses. **4.** The degree to which a color is mixed with black or otherwise darkened. **5.** A slight variation; nuance. **6.** A small amount; trace. —*v.* **shaded, shading. 1.** To screen from light or heat. **2.** To obscure or darken. **3.** To represent or produce degrees of darkness in (a picture). **4.** To change or vary by slight degrees. [< OE *sceadu, scead.* See **skot-.**]

shad•ing (shā′dĭng) *n.* The lines or other marks used to fill in outlines of a sketch, engraving, etc., to represent gradations of colors or darkness.

shad•ow (shăd′ō) *n.* **1.** A partially or totally unilluminated area, caused by an object blocking rays of light. **2.** The outline of an object that casts a shadow. **3.** Gloom or an influence that causes such feeling. **4.** A shaded area in a picture. **5.** A phantom; ghost. **6.** A faint indication. **7.** A remnant. **8.** A slight trace. —*v.* **1.** To cast a shadow upon; shade. **2.** To make gloomy or dark. **3.** To represent vaguely or mysteriously. **4.** To darken in a painting; shade in. **5.** To follow after, esp. in secret. [< OE *sceaduwe* < *sceadu,* SHADE.] —**shad′ow•er** *n.* —**shad′ow•i•ness** *n.* —**shad′ow•y** *adj.*

shad•y (shā′dē) *adj.* **-ier, -iest. 1.** Full of shade; shaded. **2.** Hidden. **3.** Of dubious character or honesty; questionable.

shaft¹ (shăft, shäft) *n.* **1.** The long, narrow stem or body of a spear or arrow. **2.** A spear or arrow. **3.** Something suggestive of a missile in appearance. **4.** The handle of any of various tools or implements. **5.** A long, generally cylindrical bar, esp. one that rotates and transmits power. [< OE *sceaft.* See **skep-.**]

shaft² (shăft, shäft) *n.* A long, narrow passage, duct, or conduit. [Prob < MLG *schacht.*]

shag (shăg) *n.* **1.** A tangle or mass, esp. of rough, matted hair. **2.** A coarse, long nap, as on some woolen cloth. [< OE *sceacga* < Gmc **skag-.*]

shag•gy (shăg′ē) *adj.* **-gier, -giest. 1.** Having long, rough hair or wool. **2.** Bushy and matted. **3.** Poorly groomed. —**shag′gi•ness** *n.*

shah (shä) *n.* The monarch of certain lands of the Middle East, esp. Iran. [Pers *shāh.*]

shake (shāk) *v.* **shook, shaken** (shā′kən), **shaking. 1.** To move or cause to move to and fro with short jerky movements. **2.** To vibrate or rock; tremble. **3.** To cause to stagger; waver; unsettle. **4.** To remove or dislodge by or as by jerky movements. **5.** To brandish or wave: *shake one's fist.* **6.** To clasp (hands or another's hand) in greeting or leave-taking or as a sign of agreement. —**shake up.** To unnerve; disturb or agitate. —*n.* **1.** An act of shaking. **2.** A beverage mixed by shaking: *a milk shake.* —**get a fair** (or **good**) **shake.** *Slang.* To be treated with fairness. [< OE *sceacan* < Gmc **skakan.*] —**shak′a•ble, shake′a•ble** *adj.* —**shak′er** *n.*

shake•down (shāk′doun′) *n. Informal.* An extortion of money by blackmail or other means.

Shak•er (shā′kər) *n.* A member of a sect practicing communal living and observing celibacy.

Shake•speare (shāk′spîr), **William.** Also **Shak•spere.** 1564–1616. English dramatist and poet. —**Shake•spear′e•an** *adj.*

shake•up (shāk′ŭp′) *n.* A thorough or drastic reorganization, as in a business or government.

shak•y (shā′kē) *adj.* **-ier, -iest. 1.** Trembling or quivering. **2.** Unsteady; weak. **3.** Wavering; insecure. —**shak′i•ly** *adv.* —**shak′i•ness** *n.*

shale (shāl) *n.* A rock composed of layers of claylike, fine-grained sediments. [Prob < OE *sc(e)alu,* shell.]

shall (shăl) *v.* past **should.** —Used as an auxiliary followed by a simple infinitive to indicate (often with future reference) willingness, intention, obligation, compulsion, permission, or necessity. *Shall* is rarely used in speech outside of questions with subject *I* or *we.* See Usage note at **will².** [< OE *sceal.* See **skel-².**]

shal•lot (shə-lŏt′) *n.* **1.** An onionlike plant with an edible bulb divided into sections. **2.** The bulb of this plant. [< L *Ascalōnia (caepa).* See **scallion.**]

shal•low (shăl′ō) *adj.* **1.** Measuring little from bottom to top or surface; not deep. **2.** Lacking depth, as in intellect or significance. —*n.* A shallow part of a body of water. [ME *schalowe.*] —**shal′low•ness** *n.*

shalt (shălt). *Archaic.* 2nd person sing. present tense of **shall.**

sham (shăm) *n.* **1.** Something false or empty

purporting to be genuine. **2.** A person who assumes a false character. *—adj.* Not genuine; counterfeit. *—v.* **shammed, shamming.** To assume a false appearance or character; feign. [Poss var of SHAME.]

sham•ble (shăm'bəl) *v.* **-bled, -bling.** To walk in an awkward, lazy, or unsteady manner, shuffling the feet. [< earlier *shamble,* ungainly.] **—sham'ble** *n.*

sham•bles (shăm'bəlz) *n. (takes sing. v.).* A scene or condition of complete disorder or ruin. [< earlier *shamble,* table for display or sale of meat.]

shame (shām) *n.* **1.** A painful emotion caused by a strong sense of guilt, unworthiness, or disgrace. **2.** Capacity for such a feeling: *Have you no shame?* **3.** A person or thing that brings dishonor or disgrace. **4.** A condition of dishonor or disgrace. **5.** A great disappointment. *—v.* **shamed, shaming.** **1.** To cause to feel shame. **2.** To bring dishonor or disgrace upon. **3.** To force by making ashamed: *shamed into an apology.* [< OE *sceamu* < Gmc **skamō.*]

shame•faced (shām'fāst') *adj.* **1.** Indicative of shame: *a shamefaced explanation.* **2.** Modest; shy. [< OE *sceamu,* SHAME + *fæst,* FAST (firm).] **—shame'fac'ed•ly** (-fā'sĭd-lē) *adv.* **—shame'fac'ed•ness** *n.*

shame•ful (shām'fəl) *adj.* Bringing or deserving shame; disgraceful. **—shame'ful•ly** *adv.* **—shame'ful•ness** *n.*

shame•less (shām'lĭs) *adj.* Without shame; impudent; brazen. **—shame'less•ly** *adv.* **—shame'less•ness** *n.*

sham•poo (shăm-pōō') *n.* **1.** Any of various preparations used to wash the hair and scalp. **2.** Any of various cleaning agents for rugs or upholstery. **3.** The act or process of washing or cleaning with shampoo. [Hindi *chāmpo.*] **—sham•poo'** *v.*

sham•rock (shăm'rŏk') *n.* A plant, as a clover, having leaves with three leaflets, considered the national emblem of Ireland. [Ir *seamrog.*]

shang•hai (shăng-hī') *v.* To kidnap (a man) for compulsory service aboard a ship, esp. after rendering him insensible. [< SHANGHAI.]

Shang•hai (shăng-hī'). A city of E China. Pop. 7,000,000.

shank (shăngk) *n.* **1.** The part of the leg between the knee and the ankle or a corresponding part. **2.** A cut of meat from the leg of a steer or lamb. **3.** The section of a tool or instrument connecting the functioning part and handle. [< OE *sceanca.* See **skeng-.**]

shan't, sha'nt (shănt, shänt). Contractions of *shall not.*

shan•tung (shăn'tŭng') *n.* A plain-woven fabric with an irregular texture, originally of silk. [< *Shantung,* province of E China.]

shan•ty (shăn'tē) *n., pl.* **-ties.** A roughly built or ramshackle cabin; shack. [Perh < Ir *sean tig,* "old house."]

shape (shāp) *n.* **1.** The outline or characteristic surface configuration of a thing; contour; form. **2.** The contour of a person's body; figure. **3.** Developed or definite form. **4.** Any form or condition in which something may exist or appear. *—v.* **shaped, shaping.** **1.** To give a particular form to. **2.** To take a definite form; develop. [< OE *(ge)sceap.* See **skep-.**]

shape•less (shāp'lĭs) *adj.* **1.** Having no distinct shape. **2.** Lacking symmetrical or attractive form. **—shape'less•ness** *n.*

shape•ly (shāp'lē) *adj.* **-lier, -liest.** Having a pleasing shape; well-proportioned. **—shape'li•ness** *n.*

shard (shärd) *n.* A fragment of a brittle substance, as of glass or metal. [< OE *sceard.* See **sker-[1].**]

share[1] (shâr) *n.* **1.** A part or portion belonging to a person or group. **2.** An equitable or full portion. **3.** Any of the equal parts into which the capital stock of a corporation or company is divided. *—v.* **shared, sharing.** **1.** To divide and parcel out in shares; apportion. **2.** To have, use, or experience in common. **3.** To participate; join: *share in an effort.* [< OE *scearu,* division or fork of the body, tonsure. See **sker-[1].**] **—shar'er** *n.*

share[2] (shâr) *n.* A plowshare. [< OE *scēar.* See **sker-[1].**]

share•crop•per (shâr'krŏp'ər) *n.* A tenant farmer who gives a share of his crop to the landlord in lieu of rent.

share•hold•er (shâr'hōl'dər) *n.* A person who owns a share or shares of stock.

shark (shärk) *n.* **1.** Any of various often large and voracious marine fishes with tough skin and small, toothlike scales. **2.** A ruthless, greedy, or dishonest person. [?]

shark•skin (shärk'skĭn') *n.* **1.** A shark's skin or leather made from it. **2.** A plain-woven, smooth-textured fabric.

sharp (shärp) *adj.* **1.** Having a thin, keen edge or a fine, acute point. **2.** Not rounded or blunt; pointed: *a sharp nose.* **3.** Abrupt; sudden. **4.** Clear or marked; distinct. **5.** Shrewd; astute. **6.** Artful; underhand. **7.** Alert. **8.** Harsh; biting. **9.** Sudden and shrill. **10.** Angular; not rounded. **11.** *Mus.* **a.** Being one half step higher than the corresponding natural key. **b.** Being below the intended pitch. **12.** *Slang.* Attractive or stylish. *—adv.* **1.** In a sharp manner. **2.** Punctually; exactly. **3.** *Mus.* Above the proper pitch. *—n. Mus.* **1.** A sign (#) affixed to a note to indicate that it is to be raised by a half step. **2.** A note that is raised by a half step. *—v. Mus.* **1.** To raise (a note) a half step. **2.** To sing or play above the proper pitch. [< OE *scearp.* See **sker-[1].**] **—sharp'ly** *adv.* **—sharp'ness** *n.*

sharp•en (shär'pən) *v.* To make or grow sharp or sharper. **—sharp'en•er** *n.*

sharp•shoot•er (shärp'shōō'tər) *n.* An expert marksman.

shat•ter (shăt'ər) *v.* To break or burst suddenly into pieces, as with a violent blow. [< OE *sceaterian.* See **skhed-.**]

shave (shāv) *v.* **shaved, shaved** or **shaven** (shā'vən), **shaving.** **1.** To remove (the beard or other body hair) from with a razor. **2.** To remove thin slices from. **3.** To cut or scrape into thin slices. **4.** To come close to or graze in passing. *—n.* The act, process, or result of shaving. **—close shave.** A narrow escape. [< OE *sceafan.* See **skep-.**]

shav•er (shā'vər) *n.* **1.** An electric or mechanical device used to shave. **2.** *Informal.* A small boy.

shav•ing (shā'vĭng) *n.* **1.** A thin slice; sliver. **2.** The action of one that shaves.

Shaw (shô), **George Bernard.** 1856–1950. Irish-born English dramatist, critic, and essayist.

shawl (shôl) *n.* A piece of cloth worn by women as a covering for the head, neck, and shoulders. [< Pers *shāl.*]

she (shē) *pron.* The 3rd person sing. pronoun in the nominative case, feminine gender. **1.** —Used to represent the female person last mentioned. **2.** —Used traditionally of certain objects and institutions, such as ships and nations. *—n.* A female animal or person: *Is the cat a she?* [< OE *sēo.* See **so-.**]

sheaf (shēf) *n., pl.* **sheaves** (shēvz). **1.** A bundle of cut stalks, esp. of grain. **2.** Any collection of articles held or bound together. [< OE *scēaf.* See **skeup-.**]

shear (shîr) *v.* **sheared, sheared** or **shorn, shearing.** **1.** To remove (fleece, hair, etc.) by cutting or clipping with a sharp instrument. **2.** To remove the hair or fleece from. **3.** To cut with or as with shears. **4.** To strip or deprive of. [< OE *sceran.* See **sker-[1].**]

shears (shîrz) *pl.n.* **1.** Large-sized scissors. **2.** Any of various other implements or machines that cut with scissorlike action. [< OE *scēara,* scissors. See **sker-[1].**]

sheath (shēth) *n., pl.* **sheaths** (shē*thz,* shēths). **1.** A case for the blade of a knife, sword, etc. **2.** A part or covering resembling this. **3.** A close-fitting dress. [< OE *scēath.*]

sheathe (shē*th*) *v.* **sheathed, sheathing.** To insert into or provide with a sheath.

sheaves. *pl.* of **sheaf.**

shed[1] (shĕd) *v.* **shed, shedding.** **1.** To pour forth or cause to pour forth: *shed tears.* **2.** To diffuse or radiate: *shed light.* **3.** To repel without allowing penetration: *A duck's feathers shed water.* **4.** To lose, drop, or cast off, as a covering, by a natural process. **—shed blood.** To take life; kill. [< OE *scēadan,* to divide. See **skei-.**]

shed[2] (shĕd) *n.* A small structure for storage or shelter. [Perh < SHADE.]

she'd (shēd). **1.** Contraction of *she had.* **2.** Contraction of *she would.*

sheen (shēn) *n.* Glistening brightness; shininess. [< OE *sciene,* beautiful, bright. See **keu-.**]

sheep (shēp) *n., pl.* **sheep.** **1.** A hoofed, thick-fleeced mammal widely domesticated for wool and meat. **2.** One who is meek and submissive. [< OE *scēap* < Gmc **skǣpa.*]

sheep•ish (shēp'ĭsh) *adj.* Embarrassed, as by consciousness of a fault: *a sheepish grin.* **—sheep'ish•ly** *adv.* **—sheep'ish•ness** *n.*

sheep•skin (shēp'skĭn') *n.* **1.** The skin of a sheep. **2.** A diploma.

sheer[1] (shîr) *v.* To swerve or deviate from a course. [Perh var of SHEAR.]

sheer[2] (shîr) *adj.* **1.** Thin, fine, and transparent, as a fabric. **2.** Undiluted; pure: *sheer happiness.* **3.** Perpendicular or nearly perpendicular; steep. [Perh < ME *schir,* bright, shining.] **—sheer'ly** *adv.* **—sheer'ness** *n.*

sheet[1] (shēt) *n.* **1.** A rectangular piece of linen or similar material serving as a basic article of bedding. **2.** A broad, thin, usually rectangular mass or piece of any material, as paper, metal, glass, etc. [< OE *scēte.*]

sheet[2] (shēt) *n. Naut.* A rope attached to one or both of the lower corners of a sail. [< OE *scēata,* corner of a sail.]

sheik (shēk, shāk) *n.* The leader of an Arab family, village, or tribe.

shelf (shĕlf) *n., pl.* **shelves** (shĕlvz). **1.** A flat, usually rectangular structure of a rigid material fixed at right angles to a wall or other surface and used to hold objects. **2.** Anything resembling such an object, as a balcony or a ledge of rock. [ME *shelfe.*]

shell (shĕl) *n.* **1.** A hard or brittle outer covering, as of a mollusk, egg, or nut. **2.** Anything resembling or having the form of such a covering, as: **a.** A framework or exterior, as of a building. **b.** A thin layer of pastry. **c.** A long, narrow racing boat propelled by oarsmen. **3.** A projectile or piece of ammunition. *—v.* **1.** To remove from a shell, pod, etc. **2.** To fire shells at; bombard. **3.** *Informal.* To pay: *shell* *out five dollars.* [< OE *scell, scill.* See **skel-**[1].]

shel•lac (shə-lăk') *n.* **1.** A purified lac formed into thin yellow or orange flakes, often bleached white, and widely used in varnishes, paints, stains, inks, and sealing wax. **2.** A thin varnish made by dissolving flake shellac in denatured alcohol. —*v.* **-lacked, -lacking. 1.** To apply shellac. **2.** *Slang.* To defeat decisively. [SHEL(L) + LAC (lacquer).]

Shel•ley (shĕl'ē), **Percy Bysshe.** 1792–1822. English poet.

shell•fish (shĕl'fĭsh') *n., pl.* **-fish** or **-fishes.** An aquatic animal, as a mollusk or crustacean, with a shell or shell-like covering.

shell shock. **Combat fatigue.** —**shell'-shocked'** *adj.*

shel•ter (shĕl'tər) *n.* **1.** Something that provides cover or protection, as from the weather. **2.** The state of being covered or protected. —*v.* To provide cover or protection for. [?]

shelve (shĕlv) *v.* **shelved, shelving. 1.** To place on a shelf or shelves. **2.** To put aside; postpone.

shelves. *pl.* of **shelf.**

Shem•ite. Variant of **Semite.**

Shen•yang (shŭn'yäng'). A city of NE China. Pop. 2,411,000.

shep•herd (shĕp'ərd) *n.* One that herds or tends sheep. —*v.* To herd, guard, or care for as or in the manner of a shepherd. [< OE *scēap,* SHEEP + *hirde,* HERD (herdsman).] —**shep'herd•ess** *fem.n.*

sher•bet (shûr'bĭt) *n.* A sweet-flavored water ice to which milk, egg white, or gelatin has been added. [< Ar *sharbah,* drink.]

sher•iff (shĕr'ĭf) *n.* The chief law-enforcement officer in a county. [< OE *scīr,* SHIRE + *gerēfa,* officer.]

Sher•pa (shûr'pə) *n., pl.* **-pa** or **-pas.** A member of a Tibetan people living in N Nepal.

sher•ry (shĕr'ē) *n., pl.* **-ries. 1.** An amber-colored fortified Spanish wine ranging from very dry to sweet. **2.** Any similar wine. [Earlier *sherris,* "wine of Jerez," city in Spain.]

shib•bo•leth (shĭb'ə-lĭth, -lĕth') *n.* A slogan or saying, esp. one distinctive of a particular group. [Heb *shibbōleth,* an ear of corn, stream.]

shield (shēld) *n.* **1.** An article of protective armor made of leather, metal, or wood, carried on the forearm. **2.** A similar protective plate or covering. **3.** Something resembling a shield in shape. —*v.* **1.** To protect or defend with or as if with a shield. **2.** To cover up; conceal. [< OE *scild, sceld.* See **skel-**[1].]

shift (shĭft) *v.* **1.** To move or transfer (something) from one place or position to another. **2.** To change gears. **3.** To change position, direction, etc. **4.** To provide for one's needs. —*n.* **1.** A change, transference, or displacement. **2.** A change of direction or form. **3. a.** A change of workers. **b.** The working period of such a group: *the night shift.* **4.** A dodge, evasion, or trick. **5.** A chemise. [< OE *sciftan,* to arrange < Gmc **skip-.*]

shift•less (shĭft'lĭs) *adj.* Showing a lack of ambition, purpose, or resourcefulness. —**shift'less•ly** *adv.* —**shift'less•ness** *n.*

shift•y (shĭf'tē) *adj.* **-ier, -iest. 1.** Tricky; crafty. **2.** Suggesting craft or guile. —**shift'i•ness** *n.*

Shi•ko•ku (shĭ-kō'kōō). The smallest of the major islands of Japan, between SW Honshu and E Kyushu.

shil•le•lagh (shə-lā'lē, -lə) *n.* A club or cudgel. [< *Shillelagh,* town in Ireland.]

shil•ling (shĭl'ĭng) *n.* **1.** The basic monetary unit of Kenya, the Somali Republic, Tanzania, and Uganda. **2.** A subdivision of the pound of the United Kingdom, Gambia, Republic of Ireland, Malawi, Malta, Nigeria, Rhodesia, and various dependent territories of the United Kingdom, such as Bermuda. [< OE *scilling* < Gmc **skillingaz.*]

shil•ly-shal•ly (shĭl'ē-shăl'ē) *v.* **-lied, -lying.** To put off acting; hesitate or waver. [Short for *to stand* (or *go*), *shill I? shall I?* redupl of *shall I?*] —**shil'ly-shal'li•er** *n.*

shim (shĭm) *n.* A thin, often tapered piece of material used to fill a space between parts or to level a structure. [?]

shim•mer (shĭm'ər) *v.* To shine with a soft, tremulous light. —*n.* A glimmering or tremulous light. [< OE *scimerian, scimrian.* See **skī-.**] —**shim'mer•y** *adj.*

shim•my (shĭm'ē) *n., pl.* **-mies. 1.** Abnormal vibration or wobbling, as in an automobile chassis. **2.** *Regional.* A chemise. —*v.* **-mied, -mying.** To vibrate or wobble. [Short for *shimmy-shake,* "to shake one's chemise."]

shin[1] (shĭn) *n.* The front part of the leg below the knee and above the ankle. —*v.* **shinned, shinning.** To climb (a rope, pole, etc.) by gripping and pulling alternately with the hands and legs. [< OE *scinu.* See **skei-.**]

shin[2] (shēn) *n.* The 22nd letter of the Hebrew alphabet, representing *sh.*

shin•dig (shĭn'dĭg') *n. Slang.* A festive party or celebration.

shine (shīn) *v.* **shone** or **shined, shining. 1.** To emit light; be radiant. **2.** To reflect light; glint or glisten. **3.** To distinguish oneself in some sphere; excel. **4.** To aim the beam or glow of. **5.** To make glossy or bright by polishing. —*n.* **1.** Brightness; radiance. **2.** The act or an instance of polishing shoes. **3.** Fair weather: *rain or shine.* —**take a shine to.** To like spontaneously. [< OE *scīnan.* See **skī-.**]

shin•er (shī'nər) *n.* **1.** A black eye. **2.** A small, silvery fish.

shin•gle[1] (shĭng'gəl) *n.* **1.** A thin oblong piece of wood, asbestos, etc., laid in overlapping rows to cover the roofs or sides of houses. **2.** A small signboard, as one indicating a doctor's office. —*v.* **-gled, -gling.** To cover (a roof or building) with shingles. [< L *scindula.*] —**shin'gler** *n.*

shin•gle[2] (shĭng'gəl) *n.* **1.** Beach gravel consisting of large smooth pebbles. **2.** A beach covered with such gravel. [Prob < MLG *singele,* outermost wall.]

shin•ny (shĭn'ē) *v.* **-nied, -nying.** To climb by shinning.

Shin•to (shĭn'tō) *n.* Also **Shin•to•ism** (-ĭz'əm). The aboriginal religion of Japan, marked by the veneration of nature spirits and ancestors. —**Shin'to•ist** *n.*

shin•y (shī'nē) *adj.* **-ier, -iest.** Bright; glistening. —**shin'i•ness** *n.*

ship (shĭp) *n.* **1.** Any large vessel adapted for deep-water navigation. **2.** A ship's company. **3.** An airplane. —*v.* **shipped, shipping. 1.** To place or take on board a ship. **2.** To send or cause to be transported. **3.** To take in (water) over the side. [< OE *scip* < Gmc **skipam.*]

-ship. *comb. form.* **1.** The quality or condition of: **friendship. 2.** The status, rank, or office of: **professorship. 3.** The art or functioning of: **penmanship.** [< OE *-scipe.* See **skep-.**]

ship•board (shĭp'bôrd', -bōrd') *n.* A ship. —**on shipboard.** On board a ship.

ship•build•ing (shĭp'bĭl'dĭng) *n.* The business of constructing ships. —**ship'build'er** *n.*

ship•mate (shĭp'māt') *n.* A fellow sailor.

ship•ment (shĭp'mənt) *n.* **1.** The act of sending or transporting goods. **2.** The goods or cargo transported.

ship•ping (shĭp'ĭng) *n.* **1.** The act or business of transporting goods. **2.** The body of ships belonging to one port or country.

ship•shape (shĭp'shāp') *adj.* Neatly arranged; orderly; tidy.

ship•wreck (shĭp'rĕk') *n.* **1.** The remains of a wrecked ship. **2.** The destruction of a ship, as by storm or collision. —*v.* To cause to suffer shipwreck. [SHIP + OE *wræc,* thing driven by the sea.]

ship•yard (shĭp'yärd') *n.* An area where ships are built or repaired.

shire (shīr) *n.* One of the counties of Great Britain. [< OE *scīr,* official charge, province, shire.]

shirk (shûrk) *v.* To put off or avoid (work or duty). [Prob < G *Schurke,* scoundrel.] —**shirk'er** *n.*

shirr (shûr) *v.* **1.** To gather (cloth) into parallel rows. **2.** To bake (eggs) in molds. —*n.* A decorative gathering of cloth into parallel rows. [?]

shirt (shûrt) *n.* **1.** A garment for the upper part of the body, typically having a collar, sleeves, and a front opening. **2.** An undershirt. [< OE *scyrte.* See **sker-**[1].]

shish ke•bab (shĭsh' kə-bŏb'). Pieces of seasoned meat roasted and served with condiments on skewers. [Turk *sıs kebabı.*]

shist. Variant of **schist.**

Shi•va (shē'və). Hindu god of destruction and reproduction.

shiv•er[1] (shĭv'ər) *v.* To shudder or shake, as from cold. [ME *shiveren.*] —**shiv'er** *n.*

shiv•er[2] (shĭv'ər) *v.* To break suddenly into fragments or splinters; shatter. [< ME *scivre,* fragment.]

shoal[1] (shōl) *n.* **1.** A shallow. **2.** A sandy elevation of the bottom of a body of water, constituting a hazard to navigation. [< OE *sceald,* shallow < Gmc **skaldaz.*]

shoal[2] (shōl) *n.* **1.** A large group. **2.** A school of fish. —*v.* To form a shoal; school. [Prob < MDu or MLG *schōle,* school of fish.]

shoat (shōt) *n.* Also **shote.** A young pig. [ME *shote.*]

shock[1] (shŏk) *n.* **1.** A violent collision or impact. **2. a.** Something that jars the mind or emotions as if with a violent, unexpected blow. **b.** The disturbance of function or equilibrium caused by such a blow. **3.** A severe offense to one's sense of propriety or decency. **4.** A massive physiological reaction to bodily trauma, usually characterized by loss of blood pressure and depression of vital processes. **5.** The sensation and muscular spasm caused by an electric current passing through a bodily part. —*v.* **1.** To strike with great surprise and agitation. **2.** To strike with disgust; offend. **3.** To induce shock in (a person). **4.** To subject to an electric shock. [< OF *choquer,* to strike (with fear).]

shock[2] (shŏk) *n.* A number of sheaves of grain stacked upright in a field for drying. [ME *shokke.*]

shock[3] (shŏk) *n.* A thick, heavy mass: *a shock of hair.* [Perh < SHOCK[2].]

shock•ing (shŏk'ĭng) *adj.* **1.** Highly disturbing emotionally. **2.** Highly offensive; distasteful. —**shock'ing•ly** *adv.*

shock wave. A large-amplitude compression wave, such as that produced by an explosion, caused by supersonic motion of a body in a medium.

shod•dy (shŏd'ē) *adj.* **-dier, -diest.** **1.** Made of or containing inferior material. **2.** Imitative; ersatz. **3.** Shabby. [?] **—shod'di•ly** *adv.* **—shod'di•ness** *n.*

shoe (sho͞o) *n.* **1.** A durable covering for the human foot. **2.** A horseshoe. **3.** The outer covering, casing, or tread of a pneumatic rubber tire. **4.** The part of a brake that presses against the wheel or drum to retard its motion. *—v.* **shod** (shŏd), **shod** or **shodden** (shŏd'n), **shoeing.** To furnish or fit with shoes. [< OE *scōh* < Gmc **skōhaz.*]

shoe•horn (sho͞o'hôrn') *n.* A curved implement used to help slip a shoe on the foot.

shoe•lace (sho͞o'lās') *n.* A string or cord used for lacing and fastening shoes.

shoe•mak•er (sho͞o'mā'kər) *n.* One who makes or repairs shoes.

shoe•tree (sho͞o'trē') *n.* A foot-shaped form inserted into a shoe to preserve its shape.

shone (shōn). *p.t.* & *p.p.* of **shine.**

shoo (sho͞o) *interj.* Used to scare away something. *—v.* To drive or scare away, as by crying "shoo." [ME *schowe* (imit).]

shook (sho͝ok). *p.t.* of **shake.**

shoot (sho͞ot) *v.* **shot, shooting.** **1.** To hit, wound, or kill with a missile. **2.** To fire or let fly (a missile) from a weapon. **3.** To discharge (a weapon); go off. **4.** To move or send forth swiftly. **5.** To pass over or through swiftly: *shoot the rapids.* **6.** To record on film. **7.** To project or cause to project or protrude. **8.** To put forth; begin to grow; sprout. **9.** To move or propel (a marble or ball) toward a goal. *—n.* **1.** A newly sprouting plant growth or part. **2.** A skeet tournament, hunt, etc. [< OE *scēotan.* See **skeud-.**] **—shoot'er** *n.*

shooting star. A briefly visible meteor.

shop (shŏp) *n.* **1.** A small retail store. **2.** A business or industrial establishment. **3.** A workshop. *—v.* **shopped, shopping.** To visit stores for the purpose of inspecting and buying merchandise. [< OE *sceoppa,* booth, stall < Gmc **skupp-.*] **—shop'per** *n.*

shop•keep•er (shŏp'kē'pər) *n.* An owner or manager of a shop.

shop•lift•er (shŏp'lĭf'tər) *n.* One who steals goods on display in a store. **—shop'lift'ing** *n.*

shop•worn (shŏp'wôrn', -wōrn') *adj.* **1.** Soiled, faded, etc., from being on display in a store. **2.** Trite; hackneyed.

shore¹ (shôr, shōr) *n.* The land along the edge of an ocean, sea, lake, or river. [< MDu and MLG *schore.*]

shore² (shôr, shōr) *v.* **shored, shoring.** To prop up, as with an inclined timber. [< MDu *schōren.*]

shore•line (shôr'līn', shōr'-) *n.* The line marking the edge of a body of water.

shorn (shôrn, shōrn). Alternate *p.p.* of **shear.**

short (shôrt) *adj.* **1.** Having little length. **2.** Having little height. **3.** Having a small extent in time. **4.** Not attaining that which is required. **5.** Lacking in length or amount. **6.** Rudely brief; curt. **7.** Containing shortening; crisp, as pastry. **8.** Designating a particular pronunciation of the letters for vowel sounds, as the sound of (ă) in *pan.* *—adv.* **1.** Abruptly; quickly. **2.** Concisely. **3.** Without getting to. **4.** Without owning what one is selling: *sell short.* *—n.* **1.** Anything that is short. **2. shorts.** Short drawers or trousers. **3.** A **short circuit.** *—v.* To cause a short circuit in. [< OE *scort.* See **sker-¹.**] **—short'ness** *n.*

short•age (shôr'tĭj) *n.* A deficiency in amount.

short•cake (shôrt'kāk') *n.* A cake made of biscuit dough, split and filled with fruit.

short•change (shôrt'chānj') *v.* To give (someone) less than what is due.

short circuit. A low-resistance connection, often unintended, between two points in an electric circuit.

short-cir•cuit (shôrt'sûr'kĭt) *v.* To cause or have a short circuit.

short•com•ing (shôrt'kŭm'ĭng) *n.* A deficiency or flaw.

short cut. **1.** A more direct route than the customary one. **2.** Any means of saving time or effort.

short•en (shôrt'n) *v.* To make or become short or shorter. **—short'en•er** *n.*

short•en•ing (shôrt'n-ĭng, shôrt'nĭng) *n.* A fat, as butter or lard, used to make pastry light or flaky.

short•fall (shôrt'fôl) *n.* **1.** A shortage. **2.** The amount by which a supply falls short. **3.** A monetary deficit. [SHORT + FALL.]

short•hand (shôrt'hănd') *n.* A system of rapid handwriting employing symbols to represent words, phrases, and letters; stenography.

short-lived (shôrt'līvd', -lĭvd') *adj.* Living or lasting only a short time.

short•ly (shôrt'lē) *adv.* **1.** In a short time; soon. **2.** In a few words; concisely.

short•sight•ed (shôrt'sī'tĭd) *adj.* **1.** Nearsighted; myopic. **2.** Lacking foresight. **—short'sight'ed•ness** *n.*

short•stop (shôrt'stŏp') *n.* *Baseball.* The field position or player between second and third bases.

short story. A short prose fiction aiming at unity of characterization, theme, and effect.

short-tem•pered (shôrt'tĕm'pərd) *adj.* Easily angered.

short ton. A unit of weight, the ton.

short wave. An electromagnetic wave with a wavelength of 80 meters or less. **—short'-wave'** (shôrt'wāv') *adj.*

Sho•sho•ne (shō-shō'nē) *n., pl.* **-ne** or **-nes.** Also **Sho•sho•ni.** **1.** A member of a tribe of Uto-Aztecan-speaking North American Indians, formerly occupying parts of the W U.S. **2.** The language of this tribe.

Sho•sho•ne•an (shō-shō'nē-ən) *n.* An Indian linguistic group in W North America, comprising most of the Uto-Aztecan languages found in the U.S. **—Sho•sho'ne•an** *adj.*

shot¹ (shŏt) *n.* **1.** The firing or discharge of a weapon. **2.** *pl.* **shots** or **shot.** A pellet, bullet, etc., fired from various firearms. **3.** A throw, hit, or drive in any of several games. **4.** One who shoots: *a good shot.* **5.** Scope; range. **6.** An attempt, guess, or opportunity. **7.** The heavy metal ball put for distance in the shot-put. **8.** A photograph or single cinematic view. **9.** A hypodermic injection. **10.** A drink of liquor, esp. a jigger. [< OE *scot.* See **skeud-.**]

shot² (shŏt). *p.t.* & *p.p.* of **shoot.**

shote. Variant of **shoat.**

shot•gun (shŏt'gŭn') *n.* A firearm that fires a charge of pellets through a smooth bore.

shot-put (shŏt'po͝ot') *n.* An athletic event in which the contestants attempt to throw or put a shot as far as possible. **—shot'-put'ter** *n.*

should (sho͝od). *p.t.* of **shall,** used as an auxiliary expressing obligation, necessity, anticipation, contingency, or uncertainty. [< OE *sceolde.* See **skel-².**]

Usage: In sentences expressing simple conditions (contingency of one clause on another clause or phrase), both *would* and *should* are employed, but *would* is much more frequent in American usage: *If I had known that, I would* (or *should*) *have made a different reply. We would* (or *should*) *not have succeeded without your assistance.* Either *would* or *should* (indicating condition, not obligation) is acceptable on all levels of usage in the preceding examples. *Would* is employed in such constructions in all three grammatical persons, whereas *should* is limited to the first person. Either *would* or *should* is possible in the first person, as an auxiliary, with *like, be inclined, be glad, prefer,* and related verbs: *I would* (or *should*) *like to call your attention to an oversight.*

shoul•der (shōl'dər) *n.* **1. a.** The part of the body between the neck and the upper arm or forelimb. **b.** The joint connecting the arm with the trunk. **2. shoulders.** The two shoulders and the area of the back between them. **3.** The edge or ridge on either side of a roadway. *—v.* **1.** To carry on or as on the shoulders. **2.** To push with or as with the shoulder. [< OE *sculdor* < Gmc **skuldra-.*]

shoulder blade. Either of two flat bones forming the back of the shoulders.

should•n't (sho͝od'ənt). Contraction of *should not.*

shouldst (sho͝odst). Also **should•est** (sho͝od'ĭst). *Archaic.* 2nd person sing. past tense of **shall.**

shout (shout) *n.* A loud cry, often expressing strong emotion or a command. [ME *shouten.*] **—shout** *v.* **—shout'er** *n.*

shove (shŭv) *v.* **shoved, shoving.** To prod or give thrust to; push roughly or rudely. *—n.* The act of shoving, esp. a rude push. [< OE *scūfan.* See **skeubh-.**] **—shov'er** *n.*

shov•el (shŭv'əl) *n.* **1.** A tool with a handle and a scoop for picking up dirt, snow, etc. **2.** A large mechanical device for heavy digging or excavation. *—v.* **-eled** or **-elled, -eling** or **-elling.** **1.** To dig or move with a shovel. **2.** To convey in a rough way, as with a shovel. [< OE *scofl.* See **skeubh-.**]

show (shō) *v.* **showed, shown** or **showed, showing.** **1.** To cause or allow to be seen; display. **2.** To conduct; guide. **3.** To point out; demonstrate. **4.** To manifest; reveal. **5.** To grant; confer. **6.** To instruct. **7.** To be visible or evident. **8.** To finish third in a horse race. *—n.* **1.** A display; demonstration. **2.** An appearance; semblance. **3.** A spectacle. **4.** A public exhibition or entertainment. **5.** Third place in a horse race. [< OE *scēawian,* to look at, see. See **keu-.**]

show bill. An advertising poster.

show•case (shō'kās') *n.* A display case or cabinet, as in a store or museum.

show•down (shō'doun') *n.* An event or circumstance that forces an issue to a conclusion.

show•er (shou'ər) *n.* **1.** A brief fall of rain. **2.** An outpouring: *a shower of abuse.* **3.** A party held to honor and present gifts to someone. **4.** A bath in which water is sprayed on the bather. *—v.* **1.** To sprinkle; spray. **2.** To bestow abundantly. **3.** To fall or pour down in a shower. **4.** To bathe by taking a shower. [< OE *scūr.* See **kēwero-.**]

show•ing (shō'ĭng) *n.* **1.** The presenting or displaying of something. **2.** A show. **3.** Performance: *a poor showing.*

show•man (shō'mən) *n.* **1.** A theatrical producer. **2.** A person having a flair for doing things dramatically. **—show'man•ship'** *n.*

shown (shōn). Alternate *p.p.* of **show.**

show off. To behave in an impudent and exhibitionistic manner.

show•off (shō'ôf', -ŏf') *n.* An exhibitionist.

show place. A place that is exhibited for its beauty, historical interest, etc.

show room. A room in which merchandise is

on display.

show•y (shō'ē) *adj.* **-ier, -iest.** Making a conspicuous display; ostentatious; gaudy. —**show'i•ly** *adv.* —**show'i•ness** *n.*

shpt. shipment.

shr. share (capital stock).

shrank (shrăngk). Alternate *p.t.* of **shrink.**

shrap•nel (shrăp'nəl) *n., pl.* **-nel.** **1. a.** A projectile containing metal balls, fused to explode in the air above enemy troops. **b.** The metal balls in such a weapon. **2.** Shell fragments from any high-explosive shell. [< Gen. Henry *Shrapnel* (1761–1842), British artillery officer.]

shred (shrĕd) *n.* **1.** A long, irregular strip cut or torn off. **2.** A small amount; particle. —*v.* **shredded** or **shred, shredding.** To cut or tear into shreds. [< OE *scrēade.* See **skeru-.**] —**shred'der** *n.*

Shreve•port (shrēv'pôrt', -pōrt'). A city of NW Louisiana. Pop. 178,000.

shrew (shro͞o) *n.* **1.** A very small mouselike mammal with a pointed nose. **2.** A woman who constantly nags or scolds. [< OE *scrēawa.* See **skeru-.**] —**shrew'ish** *adj.*

shrewd (shro͞od) *adj.* **1.** Having keen insight; discerning; astute. **2.** Artful; cunning. [< SHREW.] —**shrewd'ly** *adv.* —**shrewd'ness** *n.*

shriek (shrēk) *n.* A shrill outcry; screech. —*v.* To utter such a cry. [Prob < ON *skrækja.*]

shrike (shrīk) *n.* A predatory bird with a hooked bill, often impaling its prey on thorns. [Prob < OE *scrīc,* thrush.]

shrill (shrĭl) *adj.* High-pitched and piercing: *a shrill whistle.* [Prob < Scand.] —**shrill'ness** *n.* —**shril'ly** *adv.*

shrimp (shrĭmp) *n.* **1.** A small, often edible marine crustacean. **2.** *Slang.* A diminutive or unimportant person. [ME *shrimpe,* pigmy, shrimp.]

shrine (shrīn) *n.* **1.** A container for sacred relics. **2.** The tomb of a saint. **3.** A site hallowed by a venerated object or its associations. [< L *scrīnium,* box, bookcase.]

shrink (shrĭngk) *v.* **shrank** or **shrunk, shrunk** or **shrunken, shrinking.** **1.** To draw together or contract from heat, moisture, or cold. **2.** To diminish in amount or value; dwindle. **3.** To draw back; recoil. **4.** To be reluctant to do or say something. [< OE *scrincan.* See **sker-[2].**] —**shrink'age** *n.*

shrive (shrīv) *v.* **shrove** (shrōv) or **shrived, shriven** (shrĭv'ən) or **shrived, shriving.** To confess and give absolution to (a penitent). [< OE *scrīfan* < Gmc **skrīban,* to write, "prescribe (penance)."]

shriv•el (shrĭv'əl) *v.* **-eled** or **-elled, -eling** or **-elling.** **1.** To shrink and wrinkle, often in drying. **2.** To cause to become shriveled. [Poss < ON **skrifla,* to wrinkle.]

shroud (shroud) *n.* **1.** A cloth used to wrap a body for burial. **2.** Something that conceals, protects, or screens. —*v.* To envelop; screen; hide. [< OE *scrūd.* See **skeru-.**]

Shrove•tide (shrōv'tīd') *n.* The three days preceding Ash Wednesday. [< ME *schrof-,* "shriving" + TIDE (time).]

shrub (shrŭb) *n.* A many-stemmed woody plant of relatively low height. [< OE *scrybb.* See **sker-[1].**] —**shrub'by** *adj.*

shrub•ber•y (shrŭb'ə-rē) *n., pl.* **-ies.** A group or planting of shrubs.

shrug (shrŭg) *v.* **shrugged, shrugging.** To raise (the shoulders) as a gesture of doubt, disdain, or indifference. —**shrug off.** To minimize the importance of. —*n.* The expressive gesture so made. [Perh < Scand.]

shrunk (shrŭngk). Alternate *p.t. & p.p.* of **shrink.**

shrunken (shrŭng'kən). Alternate *p.p.* of **shrink.**

shtg. shortage.

shuck (shŭk) *n.* A husk, shell, etc. —**not worth shucks.** Of little value; worthless. —*v.* To remove the husk or shell from. [?]

shucks (shŭks) *interj.* Expressive of disappointment, disgust, or annoyance. [< SHUCK.]

shud•der (shŭd'ər) *v.* To tremble or shiver convulsively, as from fear or aversion. —*n.* A convulsive shiver, as from fear, aversion, or cold; a tremor. [< MLG *schōderen.*] —**shud'der•ing•ly** *adv.*

shuf•fle (shŭf'əl) *v.* **-fled, -fling.** **1.** To move with a shambling, idle gait. **2.** To mix together (playing cards, dominoes, etc.) to change their order. **3.** To mix together in a disordered, haphazard fashion. —*n.* **1.** A shuffling gait or movement. **2.** The mixing of cards, dominoes, etc. [Prob < LG *schüffeln,* to walk clumsily, shuffle cards.] —**shuf'fler** *n.*

shuf•fle•board (shŭf'əl-bôrd', -bōrd') *n.* A game in which disks are pushed along a smooth, level surface toward numbered squares with a pronged cue. [Var of earlier *shove-board.*]

shun (shŭn) *v.* **shunned, shunning.** To avoid (a person, group, or thing) deliberately and consistently; keep away from. [< OE *scunian,* to avoid, be afraid, abhor.] —**shun'ner** *n.*

shunt (shŭnt) *v.* **1.** To turn or move (something) aside or onto another course. **2.** To shift or switch (a train or car) from one track to another. **3.** To divert by means of a shunt. —*n.* **1.** The act of shunting. **2.** A railroad switch. **3.** A low resistance alternative path for a portion of an electric current. [Perh < ME *shunnen,* shun.]

shush (shŭsh) *interj.* Used to express a demand for silence. —*v.* To demand silence from by saying "shush."

shut (shŭt) *v.* **shut, shutting.** **1.** To move (a door, lid, valve, etc.) into closed position. **2.** To block passage or access to; close. **3.** To move or become moved to a closed position. —**shut off.** **1.** To turn off. **2.** To isolate. **3.** To cease operating automatically. —**shut up.** **1.** To silence (a person). **2.** To be or become silenced. [< OE *scyttan.*]

shut•down (shŭt'doun') *n.* A temporary closing of an industrial plant.

shut•eye (shŭt'ī') *n.* *Slang.* Sleep.

shut-in (shŭt'ĭn') *n.* An invalid.

shut out. **1.** To keep out. **2.** *Sports.* To prevent (the opposing team) from scoring.

shut•out (shŭt'out') *n.* A game in which one side does not score.

shut•ter (shŭt'ər) *n.* **1.** A hinged cover or screen for a window. **2.** A device that opens and shuts the lens aperture of a camera. —*v.* To furnish or close with a shutter.

shut•tle (shŭt'l) *n.* **1.** A device used in weaving to carry the thread back and forth. **2.** A device for holding the thread in tatting, in a sewing machine, etc. **3.** A train, bus, or plane making short, frequent trips between two points. —*v.* **-tled, -tling.** To move back and forth by shuttle: *shuttle between New York and Boston.* [< OE *scytel,* dart, missile. See **skeud-.**]

shut•tle•cock (shŭt'l-kŏk') *n.* A small rounded piece of cork, plastic, etc., with a crown of feathers, used in badminton. [SHUTTLE + COCK (bird).]

shy[1] (shī) *adj.* **shier** or **shyer, shiest** or **shyest.** **1.** Easily startled; timid. **2.** Bashful; reserved. **3.** Distrustful; wary; cautious. **4.** *Informal.* Short; lacking. —*v.* **shied, shying.** **1.** To move suddenly, as if startled. **2.** To draw back, as from fear or caution. [< OE *scēoh* < Gmc **skiuhwaz.*] —**shi'er, shy'er** *n.* —**shy'ly, shi'ly** *adv.* —**shy'ness** *n.*

shy[2] (shī) *v.* **shied, shying.** To throw (something) with a swift sideways motion. [Prob < SHY.]

shy•ster (shī'stər) *n.* *Slang.* An unethical or unscrupulous lawyer. [Poss < *Scheuster,* an unscrupulous 19th-century New York lawyer.]

Si silicon.

Si•am. The former name for **Thailand.**

Si•a•mese (sī'ə-mēz', -mēs') *adj.* Thai. —*n., pl.* **-mese.** Thai.

Siamese twins. Twins born with their bodies joined together.

Si•be•li•us (sĭ-bā'lē-əs, -bāl'yəs), **Jean.** 1865–1957. Finnish composer.

Si•be•ri•a (sī-bîr'ē-ə). A large region of the Soviet Union in Asia. —**Si•be'ri•an** *adj. & n.*

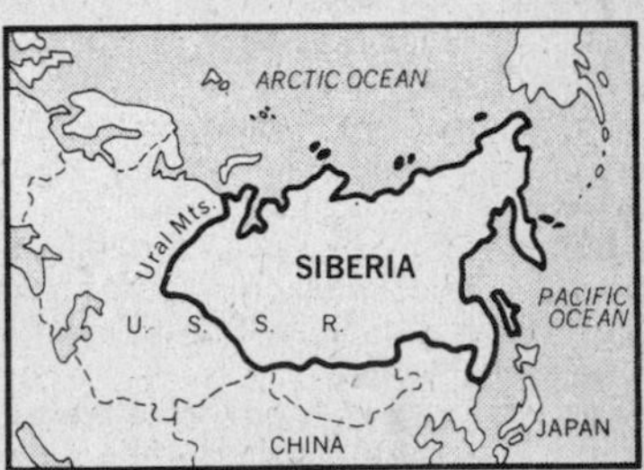

Siberia

sib•i•lant (sĭb'ə-lənt) *adj.* Producing a hissing sound. —*n.* A speech sound that suggests hissing, as (s), (sh), (z), or (zh). [< L *sibilāre,* to hiss, whistle.]

sib•ling (sĭb'lĭng) *n.* An offspring of the same parents; a brother or sister. [< OE *sibb,* kin + -LING.]

sic[1] (sĭk, sēk) *adv.* Thus; so. Used in written texts to indicate that a surprising quotation is not a mistake and is to be read as it stands. [L *sic.*]

sic[2] (sĭk) *v.* **sicced, siccing.** Also **sick.** **1.** To urge to attack or chase. **2.** To set upon or chase. [Dial var of SEEK.]

Sic•i•ly (sĭs'ə-lē). An Italian island in the Mediterranean. Pop. 4,712,000. Cap. Palermo. —**Si•cil'ian** *adj. & n.*

sick[1] (sĭk) *adj.* **1. a.** Ailing; ill; unwell. **b.** Violently nauseated. **2.** Of or for sick persons. **3. a.** Mentally ill or disturbed. **b.** Morbid or unwholesome: *a sick joke.* **4. a.** Deeply distressed; chagrined; upset. **b.** Disgusted; revolted. **c.** Weary; tired: *sick of it all.* [< OE *sēoc* < Gmc **siukaz.*] —**sick'ish** *adj.* —**sick'ness** *n.*

sick[2]. Variant of **sic[2].**

sick•bay (sĭk'bā') *n.* The hospital and dispensary of a ship.

sick•bed (sĭk'bĕd') *n.* A sick person's bed.

sick•en (sĭk'ən) *v.* To make or become sick.

sick•en•ing (sĭk'ə-nĭng) *adj.* **1.** Causing sickness or nausea. **2.** Revolting or disgusting; loathsome. —**sick'en•ing•ly** *adv.*

sick•le (sĭk'əl) *n.* An implement having a semicircular blade attached to a short handle, for cutting grain or tall grass. [< L *sēcula.*]

sick leave. Time off from work with pay allowed an employee because of sickness.

sick•ly (sĭk'lē) *adj.* **-lier, -liest.** **1.** Prone to sickness; ailing. **2.** Of, caused by, or associated with sickness: *a sickly pallor.* 3. Nauseating; sickening

side (sīd) *n.* 1. A surface of an object, esp. a surface joining a top and a bottom. 2. Either of the two surfaces of a flat object, such as a piece of paper. 3. The left or right half in reference to a vertical axis, as of the body. 4. The space immediately next to someone or something: *stood at her side.* 5. An area separated from another by some intervening line, barrier, or other feature: *on this side of the Atlantic.* 6. One of two or more opposing groups, teams, or sets of opinions. 7. A distinct aspect of something: *the cruel side of her nature.* 8. Line of descent: *my aunt on my mother's side.* —**on the side.** In addition to the main portion, occupation, or arrangement. —**side by side.** Next to each other. —**take sides.** To associate oneself with a faction, contested opinion, or cause. —*adj.* 1. Located on a side: *a side door.* 2. From or to one side; oblique: *a side view.* 3. Minor; incidental; secondary: *a side interest.* —*v.* **sided, siding.** —**side with** (or **against**). To align oneself with (or against). [< OE *sīde.*]

side•board (sīd'bôrd', -bōrd') *n.* A piece of dining-room furniture for holding linens and tableware.

side•burns (sīd'bûrnz') *pl.n.* Growths of hair down the sides of the face in front of the ears. [Var of *burnsides* < A. Burnside (1824–81), U.S. military leader.]

side•car (sīd'kär) *n.* A one-wheeled car for a single passenger, attached to the side of a motorcycle.

side•kick (sīd'kĭk') *n. Slang.* A close friend or associate.

side•line (sīd'līn') *n.* Also **side line.** 1. a. A line along either side of a playing field, marking its limits. b. **sidelines.** The space outside such limits, occupied by spectators and inactive players. 2. A subsidiary line of merchandise. 3. An activity pursued in addition to one's regular occupation. —*v.* **-lined, -lining.** To keep from active participation, as in athletic contests.

side•long (sīd'lông', -lŏng') *adj.* Directed to one side; sideways: *a sidelong glance.*

si•de•re•al (sī-dîr'ē-əl) *adj.* Relative to the stars. [< L *sīdus,* constellation.]

side•sad•dle (sīd'săd'l) *n.* A woman's saddle enabling her to sit with both legs on one side of the horse. —*adv.* On a sidesaddle.

side•step (sīd'stĕp') *v.* **-stepped, -stepping.** 1. To step out of the way of. 2. To evade; skirt. —**side'step'per** *n.*

side stroke. A stroke in which a person swims on one side and thrusts his arms forward alternately while performing a scissors kick.

side•swipe (sīd'swīp') *v.* **-swiped, -swiping.** To strike along the side in passing.

side•track (sīd'trăk') *v.* 1. To switch from a main track to a siding. 2. To divert from a main issue or course. —*n.* A railroad siding.

side•walk (sīd'wôk') *n.* A walk or raised path along the side of a road for pedestrians.

side•ways (sīd'wāz') *adv.* 1. Toward or from one side. 2. With one side forward. —*adj.* Toward or from one side.

sid•ing (sī'dĭng) *n.* 1. A short section of railroad track connected by switches with a main track. 2. Material used for surfacing a frame building.

si•dle (sīd'l) *v.* **-dled, -dling.** To move sideways; edge along furtively or indirectly. [Back-formation < SIDELONG.]

siege (sēj) *n.* 1. The surrounding and blockading of a town or fortress by an army bent on capturing it. 2. A prolonged period, as of illness. [< OF, "seat."]

si•er•ra (sē-ĕr'ə) *n.* A rugged range of mountains having an irregular or serrated profile. [Span, "a saw."]

Si•er•ra Le•one (sē-ĕr'ə lē-ōn'). A country of W Africa. Pop. 2,183,000. Cap. Freetown.

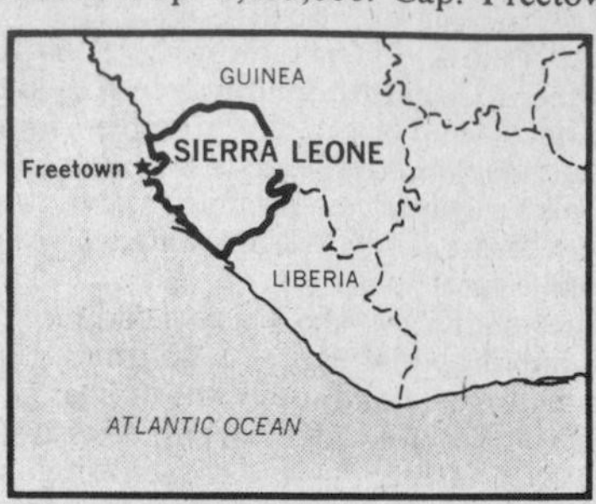

Sierra Leone

Si•er•ra Ne•vad•a (sē-ĕr'ə nə-vä'də, -văd'ə). A mountain range in E California.

si•es•ta (sē-ĕs'tə) *n.* A rest, usually taken after the midday meal. [< L *sexta (hora),* 6th (hour after sunrise), noon.]

sieve (sĭv) *n.* A utensil of wire mesh or closely perforated metal, used for straining or sifting. [< OE *sife* < Gmc **sib-*.]

sift (sĭft) *v.* 1. To put through a sieve to separate fine particles from coarse ones. 2. To examine closely and carefully: *sift the evidence.* [< OE *siftan* < Gmc **sib-*.] —**sift'er** *n.*

sig. 1. signal. 2. signature.

sigh (sī) *v.* To exhale audibly in a long, deep breath, as in sorrow, weariness, or relief. —*n.* The act or sound of sighing. [Prob < OE *sīcan* < Gmc **sīk-*.]

sight (sīt) *n.* 1. The ability to see. 2. The act or fact of seeing. 3. The field of one's vision. 4. Something that is seen. 5. Something worth seeing: *the sights of London.* 6. *Informal.* Something unsightly: *Her hair was a sight.* 7. A device used to assist in aiming, as on a gun. —*v.* 1. To see or observe within one's field of vision: *sight land.* 2. To take aim with (a firearm). [< OE *sihth,* eyesight, thing seen. See **sekw-²**.]

sight•ed (sī'tĭd) *adj.* Having sight; not blind.

sight•less (sīt'lĭs) *adj.* 1. Blind. 2. Invisible.

sight•ly (sīt'lē) *adj.* **-lier, -liest.** Pleasing to the eye; handsome. —**sight'li•ness** *n.*

sight-read (sīt'rēd') *v.* To read or perform, as music, without preparation or prior acquaintance. —**sight'-read'er** *n.*

sight•see•ing (sīt'sē'ĭng) *n.* The act or pastime of touring places of interest. —*adj.* Used or engaged in seeing sights. —**sight'se'er** *n.*

sig•ma (sĭg'mə) *n.* The 18th letter of the Greek alphabet, representing *s.*

sig•moid flex•ure (sĭg'moid'; flĕk'shər). *Anat.* An S-shaped bend in the colon between the descending section and the rectum.

sign (sīn) *n.* 1. Something that suggests a fact, condition, or quality not immediately evident; an indication. 2. An action or gesture used to convey an idea, desire, information, or a command. 3. A board, poster, or placard displayed to advertise or convey information. 4. A conventional figure or device that stands for a word, phrase, or operation. 5. A trace or vestige: *no sign of life.* —*v.* 1. To affix one's signature to. 2. To write (one's name). 3. To approve (a document) by affixing one's signature. 4. To hire by written contract. 5. To relinquish or transfer title to by signature. —**sign off.** *Broadcasting.* To cease transmission. —**sign up.** To volunteer one's services; enlist. [< L *signum,* distinctive mark or figure, seal, signal.] —**sign'er** *n.*

sig•nal (sĭg'nəl) *n.* 1. A sign or other indicator serving as a means of communication. 2. a. A fluctuating quantity, such as voltage or current strength, the variations of which represent information. b. Information so represented. —*adj.* 1. Out of the ordinary; remarkable; conspicuous: *a signal feat.* 2. Used or acting as a signal: *a signal flare.* —*v.* **-naled** or **-nalled, -naling** or **-nalling.** 1. To make a signal or signals (to). 2. To relate or make known by signals. [< L *signum,* SIGN.]

sig•nal•ize (sĭg'nə-līz') *v.* **-ized, -izing.** 1. To make remarkable or conspicuous. 2. To point out particularly.

sig•na•to•ry (sĭg'nə-tôr'ē, -tōr'ē) *adj.* Bound by signed agreement. —*n., pl.* **-ries.** A person or nation that has signed a treaty or other document.

sig•na•ture (sĭg'nə-cho͝or') *n.* 1. The name of a person as written by himself. 2. *Mus.* A sign used to indicate key or tempo. [< L *signāre,* to mark with a sign.]

sign•board (sīn'bôrd', -bōrd') *n.* A board bearing a sign.

sig•net (sĭg'nĭt) *n.* A small seal used to authenticate a document. [< OF *signe,* sign.]

sig•nif•i•cance (sĭg-nĭf'ĭ-kəns) *n.* 1. Importance; consequence. 2. Meaning; import.

sig•nif•i•cant (sĭg-nĭf'ĭ-kənt) *adj.* 1. Having a meaning; meaningful. 2. Full of meaning: *a significant glance.* 3. Important; notable.

sig•ni•fy (sĭg'nə-fī') *v.* **-fied, -fying.** 1. To serve as a sign of; betoken; denote. 2. To make known; communicate.

sign language. A system of communication by means of hand gestures.

sign•post (sīn'pōst') *n.* A post supporting a sign.

Sikh (sēk) *n.* An adherent of Sikhism. —*adj.* Of or pertaining to the Sikhs. [Hindi.]

Sikh•ism (sē'kĭz'əm) *n.* The doctrines and practices of a monotheistic Hindu religious sect founded in the 16th century.

Sik•kim (sĭk'ĭm). A kingdom between India and China. Pop. 162,000. Cap. Gangtok.

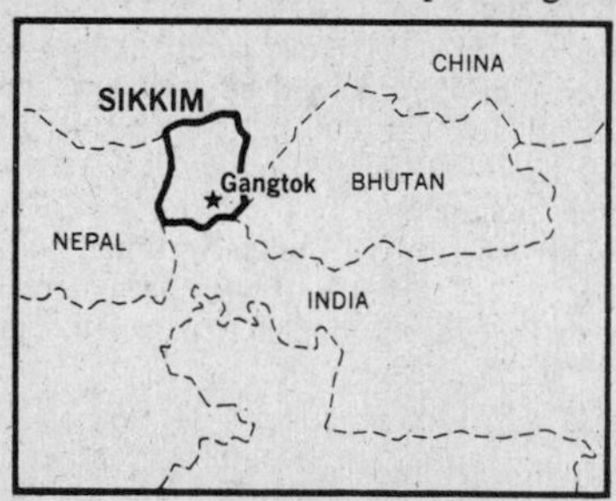

Sikkim

si•lage (sī'lĭj) *n.* Fodder made from green plants stored and fermented in a silo.

si•lence (sī'ləns) *n.* 1. The condition or quality of being silent. 2. The absence of sound; stillness. 3. Refusal or failure to speak out. —*v.* **-lenced, -lencing.** 1. To make silent or bring to silence. 2. To suppress: *silence all criticism.*

si•lenc•er (sī'lən-sər) *n.* A device for muffling the sound of a firearm.

si•lent (sī'lənt) *adj.* 1. Making no sound or noise; quiet. 2. Not disposed to speak; taciturn. 3. Unable to speak; mute. 4. Not voiced or expressed; tacit. 5. Having no phonetic value; unpronounced, as the *b* in *subtle.* **6.** Having no soundtrack: *silent motion pictures.* [< L *silēre,* to be silent.] —**si'lent•ly** *adv.*

sil•hou•ette (sĭl'o͞o-ĕt') *n.* A representation of the outline of something, usually filled in with black or another solid color. —*v.* **-etted, -etting.** To cause to be seen as a silhouette; outline. [< Étienne de *Silhouette* (1709–67), French official.]

sil•i•ca (sĭl'ĭ-kə) *n.* A white or colorless crystalline compound, SiO_2, occurring abundantly as quartz, sand, flint, agate, and many other minerals. [< L *silex (silic-),* flint.]

sil•i•cate (sĭl'ĭ-kāt', -kĭt) *n.* Any of numerous compounds containing silicon, oxygen, and a metallic or organic radical.

si•li•ceous (sĭ-lĭsh'əs) *adj.* Containing, resembling, or consisting of silica.

sil•i•con (sĭl'ĭ-kən, -kŏn') *n. Symbol* **Si** A nonmetallic element occurring extensively in the earth's crust in silica and silicates, and used in glass, semiconducting devices, concrete, brick, refractories, pottery, and silicones. Atomic number 14, atomic weight 28.086. [< SILICA.]

silicon carbide. A bluish-black crystalline compound, SiC, one of the hardest known substances, used as an abrasive and heat-refractory material.

silicon dioxide. Silica.

sil•i•cone (sĭl'ĭ-kōn') *n.* Any of a group of materials based on the structural unit R_2SiO, where R is an organic group, used in adhesives, lubricants, protective coatings, paints, and electrical insulation. [< SILICA.]

sil•i•co•sis (sĭl'ĭ-kō'sĭs) *n.* A disease of the lungs caused by long-term inhalation of silica dust and resulting in a chronic shortness of breath.

silk (sĭlk) *n.* **1.** The fine, lustrous fiber produced by a silkworm to form its cocoon. **2.** Thread or fabric made from this fiber. **3.** Fibers or material resembling silk. [< OE *sioloc, seoluc.*] —**silk'en** *adj.* —**silk'y** *adj.*

silk•worm (sĭlk'wûrm') *n.* The larva of an Asian moth whose cocoons are the source of commercial silk.

sill (sĭl) *n.* The horizontal member that bears the upright portion of a frame, esp. the base of a window. [< OE *sylle,* threshold, sill. See **swel-³**.]

sil•ly (sĭl'ē) *adj.* **-lier, -liest.** Showing a lack of good sense; foolish; stupid. [< OE *gesǣlig,* happy. See **sel-²**.] —**sil'li•ness** *n.*

si•lo (sī'lō) *n., pl.* **-los. 1.** A tall, cylindrical structure or a pit in which fodder is stored. **2.** A sunken shelter for storing and launching missiles. [< Gk *siros,* pit for keeping grain in.]

silt (sĭlt) *n.* Fine mineral particles deposited as sediment in rivers and lakes. —*v.* To fill or become filled with silt. [Prob < Scand.]

Si•lu•ri•an (sĭ-lo͝or'ē-ən, sī-) *adj.* Of or belonging to the geologic time, system of rocks, or sedimentary deposits of the third period of the Paleozoic era. —*n.* The Silurian period.

sil•van. Variant of **sylvan.**

sil•ver (sĭl'vər) *n.* **1.** *Symbol* **Ag** A lustrous white, ductile, malleable metallic element, highly valued for jewelry and tableware and widely used in coinage, photography, dental and soldering alloys, and electrical contacts. Atomic number 47, atomic weight 107.87. **2.** Coins made of this metal. **3.** Tableware made of this metal. **4.** A lustrous medium-gray color. —*adj.* **1.** Made of, containing, or pertaining to silver. **2.** Having a lustrous medium-gray color. **3.** Of or designating a 25th anniversary. —*v.* To cover, plate, or adorn with silver. [< OE *siolfor, seolfor* < Gmc **silubhra-*.]

sil•ver•fish (sĭl'vər-fĭsh') *n.* A silvery, wingless insect found in human dwellings.

silver iodide. A pale-yellow, odorless powder, AgI, that darkens on exposure to light and is used in artificial rainmaking and in photography.

silver nitrate. A poisonous, colorless crystalline compound, $AgNO_3$, that becomes grayish black when exposed to light in the presence of organic matter and is used in photography, manufacturing, and medicine.

sil•ver•smith (sĭl'vər-smĭth') *n.* One who makes, repairs, or replates articles of silver.

sil•ver•ware (sĭl'vər-wâr') *n.* Articles made of or plated with silver, esp. tableware.

sil•ver•y (sĭl'və-rē) *adj.* **1.** Containing or coated with silver. **2.** Like silver in luster; shining; glittering. —**sil'ver•i•ness** *n.*

sim•i•an (sĭm'ē-ən) *adj.* Pertaining to or characteristic of apes or monkeys. —*n.* An ape or monkey. [< L *sīmia,* ape.]

sim•i•lar (sĭm'ə-lər) *adj.* **1.** Showing some resemblance; related in appearance or nature; alike though not identical. **2.** *Geom.* Having corresponding angles equal and corresponding line segments proportional. [< L *similis,* like.] —**sim'i•lar'i•ty** *n.* —**sim'i•lar•ly** *adv.*

Usage: Similar is an adjective only, and is not employed adverbially in standard usage: *The heating mechanism is similar to that of a drier* or *works like that* (or *similarly to that*) *of a drier,* but not *works similar to that of a drier.*

sim•i•le (sĭm'ə-lē) *n.* A figure of speech in which two essentially unlike things are compared. [< L *similis,* SIMILAR.]

si•mil•i•tude (sĭ-mĭl'ə-t/y/o͞od') *n.* Similarity.

sim•mer (sĭm'ər) *v.* **1.** To cook below or just at the boiling point. **2.** To be filled with barely controlled anger or resentment; seethe. —**simmer down.** To become calm after excitement or anger. —*n.* The state of simmering. [< ME *simperen* (imit).]

si•mon•ize (sī'mə-nīz') *v.* **-ized, -izing.** To clean and polish (an automobile) with wax.

si•mon-pure (sī'mən-pyo͝or') *adj.* Genuine; real.

sim•o•ny (sĭm'ə-nē, sī'mə-) *n.* The buying or selling of ecclesiastical pardons, offices, or emoluments.

sim•per (sĭm'pər) *v.* To smile in a silly or self-conscious manner. [< Scand.] —**sim'per** *n.* —**sim'per•er** *n.*

sim•ple (sĭm'pəl) *adj.* **-pler, -plest. 1.** Consisting of one thing or part only; not compound. **2.** Not involved or complicated; easy. **3.** Without additions or modifications; bare; mere. **4.** Without embellishment; not ornate or luxurious. **5.** Not affected; unassuming or unpretentious. **6.** Not guileful or deceitful; sincere. **7.** Humble or lowly in condition or rank. **8.** Ordinary or common. **9.** Having little sense or intellect; silly. [< L *simplus.*]

sim•ple-mind•ed (sĭm'pəl-mīn'dĭd) *adj.* **1.** Not sophisticated; artless. **2.** Stupid or silly. **3.** Mentally defective.

sim•ple•ton (sĭm'pəl-tən) *n.* A silly or stupid person; a fool.

sim•plic•i•ty (sĭm-plĭs'ə-tē) *n., pl.* **-ties.** The state or quality of being simple; absence of complexity, intricacy, or artificiality.

sim•pli•fy (sĭm'plə-fī') *v.* **-fied, -fying.** To make simple or simpler; render less complex or intricate. —**sim'pli•fi•ca'tion** *n.*

sim•ply (sĭm'plē) *adv.* **1.** In a simple manner; plainly. **2.** Merely; only. **3.** Absolutely; altogether.

sim•u•late (sĭm'yə-lāt') *v.* **-lated, -lating. 1.** To have or take on the appearance of; imitate. **2.** To make a pretense of; feign. [< L *similis,* SIMILAR.] —**sim'u•la'tion** *n.* —**sim'u•la'tive** *adj.* —**sim'u•la'tor** *n.*

si•mul•ta•ne•ous (sī'məl-tā'nē-əs, sĭm'əl-) *adj.* Happening, existing, or done at the same time. [< L *simul,* at the same time.] —**si'mul•ta'ne•ous•ness, si'mul•ta•ne'i•ty** (-tə-nē'ə-tē) *n.* —**si'mul•ta'ne•ous•ly** *adv.*

Usage: Simultaneous is an adjective only. Its use as an adverb, for *simultaneously,* is not standard: *The referendum was conducted simultaneously* (not *simultaneous*) *with the general election.*

sin¹ (sĭn) *n.* **1.** A transgression of a religious or moral law, esp. when deliberate. **2.** Any offense, violation, fault, or error. —*v.* **sinned, sinning.** To commit a sinful act; do wrong. [< OE *synn.* See **es-**.]

sin² (sēn) *n.* The 21st letter of the Hebrew alphabet, representing *s.*

since (sĭns) *adv.* **1.** From then until now. **2.** Between then and now. **3.** At some past time; before now; ago: *long since forgotten.* —*prep.* **1.** During the time after. **2.** Continuously throughout the time following. —*conj.* **1.** During the time after which. **2.** Continuously from the time when. **3.** As a result of the fact that; inasmuch as. [< OE *siththan,* "after that."]

sin•cere (sĭn-sîr') *adj.* **-cerer, -cerest. 1.** Not feigned or affected; true. **2.** Presenting no false appearance; not hypocritical; honest. [L *sincērus,* clean, pure, genuine, honest.] —**sin•cere'ly** *adv.* —**sin•cer'i•ty** (-sĕr'ə-tē, -sîr'-) *n.*

si•ne•cure (sī'nə-kyo͝or', sĭn'ə-) *n.* An office, commission, or charge that requires no work yet provides compensation. [ML *(beneficium) sine cūrā,* (benefice) without cure (of souls).] —**si'ne•cur•ist** *n.*

sin•ew (sĭn'yo͞o) *n.* **1.** A tendon. **2.** Vigorous strength; muscular power. [< OE *sinu, seonu.* See **snēu-**.] —**sin'ew•y** *adj.*

sin•ful (sĭn'fəl) *adj.* Marked by or full of sin; wicked. —**sin'ful•ly** *adv.* —**sin'ful•ness** *n.*

sing (sĭng) *v.* **sang** or **sung, sung, singing. 1.** To utter a series of words or sounds in musical tones. **2.** To render in tones with musical inflections of the voice. **3.** To proclaim or extol, esp. in verse. **4.** To bring to a specified state by singing: *She sang him to sleep.* **5.** *Slang.* To give information or evidence against someone. —*n.* A gathering of people for group singing. [< OE *singan.* See **sengwh-**.] —**sing'er** *n.*

sing. singular.

Sin•ga•pore (sĭng'gə-pôr', -pōr', sĭng'ə-). **1.** A

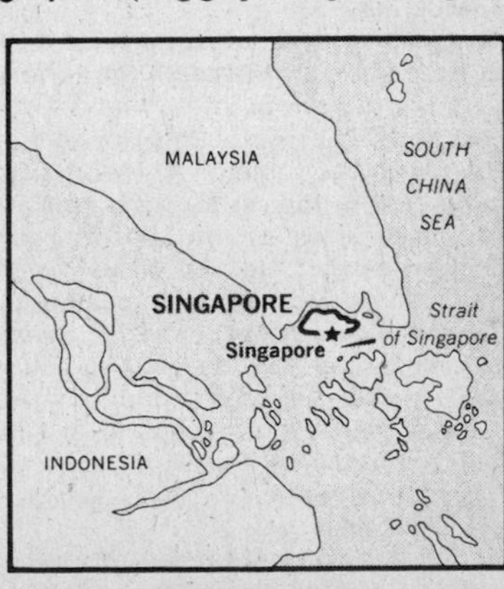

Singapore

country on an island off the S tip of the Malay Peninsula. 2. The capital of this country. Pop. 1,775,000.

singe (sĭnj) *v.* **singed, singeing.** 1. To burn superficially. 2. To burn off the feathers or bristles of by subjecting briefly to flame. [< OE *sengan.* See **senk-.**]

Sin•gha•lese (sĭng'gə-lēz', -lēs') *n., pl.* **-lese.** Also **Sin•ha•lese** (sĭn'hə-). 1. A people constituting the major portion of the population of Ceylon. 2. The Indic language of these people. —**Sin'gha•lese'** *adj.*

sin•gle (sĭng'gəl) *adj.* 1. One only; lone; sole; solitary. 2. Consisting of one form, part, or element. 3. Separate; individual: *every single one.* 4. Intended or designed to accommodate one person: *a single bed.* 5. Unmarried. 6. One-against-one; man-to-man: *single combat.* —*n.* 1. A separate unit; individual. 2. An accommodation for one person. 3. A one-dollar bill. 4. **singles.** A tennis match between two players. —*v.* **-gled, -gling.** To separate or distinguish from among others (with *out*). [< L *singulus.*] —**sin'gle•ness** *n.*

sin•gle-breast•ed (sĭng'gəl-brĕs'tĭd) *adj.* Closing with a narrow overlap and a single row of fasteners: *a single-breasted coat.*

single file. A line of people, animals, or things standing or moving one behind the other.

sin•gle-hand•ed (sĭng'gəl-hăn'dĭd) *adj.* 1. Working or done without help; unassisted. 2. Having or using only one hand. —**sin'gle-hand'ed•ly** *adv.*

sin•gle-mind•ed (sĭng'gəl-mīn'dĭd) *adj.* Having one overriding aim or purpose. —**sin'gle-mind'ed•ness** *n.*

sin•gle-space (sĭng'gəl-spās') *v.* To type (copy) without leaving a blank line between lines.

sin•gle•ton (sĭng'gəl-tən) *n.* A playing card that is the only one of its suit in a player's hand.

sin•gly (sĭng'glē) *adv.* 1. Without company or help; alone. 2. One by one; individually.

sing•song (sĭng'sông', -sŏng') *n.* Monotonous regularity of rhythm and rhyme. —**sing'song'** *adj.*

sin•gu•lar (sĭng'gyə-lər) *adj.* 1. Being only one; separate; individual. 2. Exceptional; extraordinary. 3. *Gram.* Denoting a single person or thing. —*n. Gram.* The singular number or the form denoting it. —**sin'gu•lar'i•ty** *n.* —**sin'gu•lar•ly** *adv.*

Sin•ha•lese. Variant of **Singhalese.**

sin•is•ter (sĭn'ĭ-stər) *adj.* 1. Suggesting an evil force or motive. 2. Presaging trouble; ominous. [< L, left, on the left, evil, unlucky.] —**sin'is•ter•ly** *adv.*

sink (sĭngk) *v.* **sank** or **sunk, sunk** or **sunken, sinking.** 1. To submerge beneath the surface or descend to the bottom of a liquid or soft substance. 2. To descend slowly or in stages. 3. To force into the ground. 4. To dig or drill (a mine or well) in the earth. 5. To pass into a worsened physical condition; approach death. 6. To become weaker, quieter, or less forceful. 7. To diminish or decline. 8. To penetrate the mind; become understood: *The facts sank in finally.* 9. To invest. 10. To get the ball into the hole or basket, as in golf, pool, or basketball. —*n.* A water basin fixed to a wall or floor and having a drainpipe and generally a piped supply of water. [< OE *sincan.* See **sengw-.**] —**sink'a•ble** *adj.*

Usage: As the past tense, *sank* is now preferable to the alternative form *sunk,* esp. in formal usage: *The bow sank beneath the water. Sunk* (not *sank*) is the past participle: *They have sunk both destroyers. The skiff may have sunk.*

sink•er (sĭng'kər) *n.* 1. One that sinks. 2. A weight used for sinking fishing lines, nets, etc.

sinking fund. A fund accumulated to pay off a public or corporate debt.

sin•ner (sĭn'ər) *n.* One who sins.

Sino–. *comb. form.* Chinese.

Sin•o-Ti•bet•an (sī'nō-tĭ-bĕt'n, sĭn'ō-) *n.* A linguistic group that includes Tibeto-Burman. —**Sin'o-Ti•bet'an** *adj.*

sin•u•ous (sĭn'yōō-əs) *adj.* Having many curves or turns; winding. [< L *sinus,* a bend, curve, fold.] —**sin'u•os'i•ty** (-ŏs'ə-tē) *n.*

si•nus (sī'nəs) *n.* 1. A depression or cavity formed by a bending or curving. 2. Any of various air-filled cavities in the skull, esp. one communicating with the nostrils. [L *sinus,* a bend, curve, fold, hollow.]

Si•on. Variant of **Zion.**

Siou•an (sōō'ən) *n.* A large North American Indian language family spoken from Lake Michigan to the Rocky Mountains and southward to Arkansas. —**Siou'an** *adj.*

Sioux (sōō) *n., pl.* **Sioux.** 1. A member of or any of the various groups of Siouan-speaking North American Indian peoples formerly occupying parts of C North America. 2. The language of one of the Sioux groups. —**Sioux** *adj.*

sip (sĭp) *v.* **sipped, sipping.** To drink delicately and in small quantities. —*n.* 1. The act of sipping. 2. A small quantity of liquid sipped. [ME *sippen.*]

si•phon (sī'fən). Also **sy•phon.** *n.* A pipe or tube having an inverted U shape and filled until atmospheric pressure is sufficient to force a liquid from a reservoir into one end of the tube over a barrier higher than the reservoir and out the other end. —*v.* To draw off with or as if with a siphon. [< Gk *siphōn,* pipe, tube.] —**si'phon•al, si•phon'ic** (sī-fŏn'ĭk) *adj.*

sir (sûr) *n.* 1. Often **Sir.** A respectful form of address used instead of a man's name. 2. **Sir.** A title of honor used before the name of baronets and knights. [< SIRE.]

sire (sīr) *n.* 1. A father or forefather. 2. The male parent of an animal, as a horse. 3. *Archaic.* A title and form of address used esp. in addressing a king. —*v.* **sired, siring.** To beget. [< L *senior,* older.]

si•ren (sī'rən) *n.* 1. Often **Siren.** *Gk.Myth.* One of a group of sea nymphs whose singing lured mariners to destruction on the rocks surrounding their island. 2. A device producing a loud, penetrating whistle, wailing, or other sound as a signal or warning.

Sir•i•us (sĭr'ē-əs) *n.* A star in the constellation Canis Major, the brightest star in the sky.

sir•loin (sûr'loin') *n.* A cut of beef from the upper part of the loin. [< OF *surlonge.*]

si•roc•co (sə-rŏk'ō) *n., pl.* **-cos.** Also **sci•roc•co** (shə-). A hot, humid wind originating in the Sahara Desert and blowing into S Europe. [< Ar *sharq, sharuq,* "east (wind)."]

sir•up. Variant of **syrup.**

sis (sĭs) *n. Informal.* Sister.

si•sal (sī'zəl, -səl) *n.* A cordage fiber obtained from the leaves of a Mexican plant. [< *Sisal,* town in Yucatán, Mexico.]

sis•sy (sĭs'ē) *n., pl.* **-sies.** An effeminate boy or man. [< SIS.]

sis•ter (sĭs'tər) *n.* 1. A female having the same mother and father as another. 2. A female who shares a common ancestry, allegiance, character, or purpose with another. 3. **Sister.** A member of a religious order of women; a nun. —*adj.* Related by or as by sisterhood. [< OE *sweostor.* See **swesor-.**] —**sis'ter•ly** *adj.*

sis•ter•hood (sĭs'tər-hŏŏd') *n.* 1. The state or relationship of being a sister or sisters. 2. A women's auxiliary organization, esp. in a church or synagogue.

sis•ter-in-law (sĭs'tər-ĭn-lô') *n., pl.* **sisters-in-law.** 1. The sister of one's spouse. 2. The wife of one's brother. 3. The wife of the brother of one's spouse.

Sis•y•phus (sĭs'ĭ-fəs). *Gk.Myth.* A king of Corinth condemned forever to roll a stone up a hill in Hades only to have it roll down again on nearing the top.

sit (sĭt) *v.* **sat, sitting.** 1. To rest with the body supported upon the buttocks or hindquarters. 2. To perch, as a bird. 3. To rest on and cover eggs for hatching. 4. To maintain a seated position on (a horse). 5. To be situated; lie. 6. To pose for an artist or photographer. 7. To be in session. 8. To remain inactive or unused. 9. To baby-sit. 10. To cause to sit; seat. [<OE *sittan.* See **sed-.**] —**sit'ter** *n.*

si•tar (sĭ-tär') *n.* A Hindu stringed instrument.

sit•com (sĭt'kŏm) *n.* Also **sit-com.** *Informal.* A situation comedy. —**sit'com'** *adj.*

site (sīt) *n.* The place or plot of land where something was, is, or is to be located. [< L *situs,* place.]

sit•ting (sĭt'ĭng) *n.* 1. The act or position of one that sits. 2. A period during which one is seated, as when posing for a portrait. 3. A term or session, as of a legislature.

Sit•ting Bull (sĭt'ĭng bŏŏl). 1834?–1890. American Indian leader; chief of the Dakota; leader in Sioux war (1876–77).

Sitting Bull

sitting room. A small living room.

sit•u•ate (sĭch'ōō-āt') *v.* **-ated, -ating.** To place in a certain spot or position; locate. [< L *situs,* place, SITE.]

sit•u•a•tion (sĭch'ōō-ā'shən) *n.* 1. A location; position. 2. A state of affairs. 3. A position of employment. —**sit'u•a'tion•al** *adj.*

situation comedy. A humorous television series with a continuing cast of characters.

six (sĭks) *n.* The cardinal number written 6 or in Roman numerals VI. [< OE *sex, six.* See **sweks.**] —**six** *adj.* & *pron.*

six•teen (sĭk'stēn') *n.* The cardinal number written 16 or in Roman numerals XVI. —**six'-**

teen' *adj.* & *pron.*

six•teenth (sĭk'stēnth') *n.* **1.** The ordinal number 16 in a series. **2.** One of 16 equal parts. —**six'teenth'** *adj.* & *adv.*

sixth (sĭksth) *n.* **1.** The ordinal number 6 in a series. **2.** One of 6 equal parts. —**sixth** *adj.* & *adv.*

six•ti•eth (sĭk'stē-ĭth) *n.* **1.** The ordinal number 60 in a series. **2.** One of 60 equal parts. —**six'ti•eth** *adj.* & *adv.*

six•ty (sĭk'stē) *n.* The cardinal number written 60 or in Roman numerals LX. —**six'ty** *adj.* & *pron.*

siz•a•ble (sī'zə-bəl) *adj.* Also **size•a•ble.** Of considerable size; fairly large. —**siz'a•bly** *adv.*

size[1] (sīz) *n.* **1.** The physical dimensions, magnitude, or extent of something. **2.** Any of a series of graduated categories of dimension whereby manufactured articles are classified. **3.** Actual state of affairs: *That's about the size of it.* —*v.* **sized, sizing.** To arrange according to size. [ME *syse,* fixed amount, assize.]

size[2] (sīz) *n.* A gelatinous or glutinous substance used as a glaze or filler for porous materials such as paper, cloth, or wall surfaces. —*v.* **sized, sizing.** To treat or coat with size. [Prob < SIZE[1].]

siz•ing (sī'zĭng) *n.* **1.** A glaze or filler, size. **2.** The treatment of a surface with size.

siz•zle (sĭz'əl) *v.* **-zled, -zling.** To make the hissing sound characteristic of frying fat. [Imit.] —**siz'zle** *n.*

S.J. Society of Jesus.

skate[1] (skāt) *n.* **1. a.** A bladelike metal runner fixed to a shoe, enabling the wearer to glide easily over ice. **b.** A shoe having such a runner or runners. **2.** A **roller skate.** [< ONF *escace,* stilt.] —**skate** *v.* **(skated, skating).** —**skat'er** *n.*

skate[2] (skāt) *n.* A marine fish having a flattened body with fins forming winglike extensions. [< ON *skata.*]

skeet (skēt) *n.* A kind of trapshooting in which clay targets are used to simulate birds in flight.

skein (skān) *n.* A length of thread or yarn wound in a loose, elongated coil. [< OF *escaigne.*]

skel•e•ton (skĕl'ə-tən) *n.* **1. a.** The internal vertebrate structure composed of bone and cartilage that protects and supports the soft organs, tissues, and parts. **b.** The hard external supporting and protecting structure in many invertebrates and certain vertebrates, such as turtles. **2.** Any supporting structure or framework. **3.** An outline or sketch. [< Gk *skeletos,* dried up, withered.] —**skel'e•tal** *adj.* —**skel'e•tal•ly** *adv.*

skeleton key. A key with a slender bit that can open different locks.

skep•tic (skĕp'tĭk) *n.* Also **scep•tic. 1.** One who habitually questions assertions or generally accepted conclusions. **2.** One inclined to skepticism in religious matters. **3.** An adherent of any philosophical school of skepticism. [< Gk *skeptesthai,* to examine, consider.]

skep•ti•cal (skĕp'tĭ-kəl) *adj.* Doubting; questioning; disbelieving. —**skep'ti•cal•ly** *adv.*

skep•ti•cism (skĕp'tə-sĭz'əm) *n.* **1.** A doubting or questioning attitude or state of mind. **2.** The philosophical doctrine that absolute knowledge is impossible. **3.** Doubt or disbelief of religious tenets.

sketch (skĕch) *n.* **1.** A rough preliminary drawing or painting. **2.** A brief outline. **3.** A brief, light, or informal short story, play, etc. —*v.* To make a sketch (of). [< It *schizzare,* to sketch.] —**sketch'er** *n.*

sketch•y (skĕch'ē) *adj.* **-ier, -iest. 1.** Resembling a sketch. **2.** Incomplete; slight; superficial. —**sketch'i•ness** *n.*

skew (skyōō) *v.* To turn or place at an angle; slant. —*adj.* Placed or turned to one side; slanting; oblique. [< ONF *eskuer.*]

skew•er (skyōō'ər) *n.* A long pin used to secure or suspend meat during cooking; a spit. [Var of dial *skiver.*]

ski (skē, shē) *n., pl.* **skis** or **ski.** One of a pair of long, flat runners attached to a boot for gliding or traveling over snow. —*v.* To travel on skis, esp. as a sport. [< ON *skīth,* ski, snowshoe.] —**ski'er** *n.*

skid (skĭd) *n.* **1.** The act of sliding or slipping over a surface. **2.** A plank or log, usually one of a pair, used for sliding or rolling heavy objects. **3.** A runner in the landing gear of certain aircraft. —*v.* **skidded, skidding. 1.** To slip or slide sideways because of loss of traction, as a vehicle. **2.** To slide without revolving, as a wheel. [?]

skiff (skĭf) *n.* A small, flat-bottomed open boat. [< It *schifo.*]

skill (skĭl) *n.* **1.** Proficiency; expertness. **2.** An art, trade, or technique, esp. one requiring use of the hands or body. [< ON *skil.*] —**skilled** *adj.*

skil•let (skĭl'ĭt) *n.* A frying pan. [Prob < Scand.]

skill•ful (skĭl'fəl) *adj.* **1.** Possessing or exercising skill. **2.** Characterized by or requiring skill. —**skill'ful•ly** *adv.* —**skill'ful•ness** *n.*

skim (skĭm) *v.* **skimmed, skimming. 1.** To remove (floating matter) from (a liquid). **2.** To glide quickly and lightly over. **3.** To read or glance through quickly or superficially. [< OF *escume,* foam.]

skim milk. Milk from which the cream has been removed.

skimp (skĭmp) *v.* **1.** To do hastily, carelessly, or with poor material. **2.** To be extremely sparing with; scrimp. [Poss a var of SCRIMP.]

skimp•y (skĭm'pē) *adj.* **-ier, -iest. 1.** Inadequate in size, fullness, or amount; scanty. **2.** Unduly thrifty; stingy; niggardly.

skin (skĭn) *n.* **1.** The membranous tissue forming the external covering of the animal body. **2.** An animal pelt. **3.** An outer layer or covering, as the rind of fruit. **4.** A liquid container made of animal skin. —*v.* **skinned, skinning. 1.** To remove skin from; flay or peel. **2.** To bruise, cut, or injure the skin or surface of. [< ON *skinn.*]

skin diving. Underwater swimming in which the diver is equipped with a snorkel or other breathing device. —**skin'-dive'** (skĭn'dīv') *v.* —**skin diver.**

skin•flint (skĭn'flĭnt') *n.* A miser.

skin•ny (skĭn'ē) *adj.* **-nier, -niest.** Very thin.

skin•ny-dip (skĭn'ē-dĭp') *v.* **-dipped, -dipping.** *Informal.* To swim in the nude. —**skin'ny-dip'per** *n.*

skip (skĭp) *v.* **skipped, skipping. 1.** To leap or spring lightly (over). **2.** To ricochet. **3.** To pass from point to point omitting what intervenes. **4.** To pass over, omit, or disregard. **5.** To be promoted beyond (the next grade or level). **6.** *Informal.* To leave hastily: *skip town.* —*n.* **1.** A gait in which hops and steps alternate. **2.** A passing over or omission. [ME *skippen.*] —**skip'per** *n.*

skip•per (skĭp'ər) *n.* The master of a ship. [< MDu *schip,* ship.]

skir•mish (skûr'mĭsh) *n.* **1.** A minor encounter between small bodies of troops. **2.** Any minor or preliminary conflict. [< OF *eskermir,* to fight with the sword.] —**skir'mish** *v.*

skirt (skûrt) *n.* **1.** That part of a garment, such as a dress, that hangs from the waist down. **2.** A separate garment hanging from the waist. —*v.* **1.** To lie along; bound. **2.** To pass around rather than across or through. **3.** To avoid (a subject) by circumlocution. [< ON *skyrta,* shirt.]

skit (skĭt) *n.* A short, usually comic theatrical sketch. [?]

skit•ter (skĭt'ər) *v.* To skip, glide, or move lightly or rapidly along a surface. [Prob < dial *skite,* to run rapidly, shoot about.]

skit•tish (skĭt'ĭsh) *adj.* **1.** Excitable or nervous. **2.** Shy, coy, or timid. **3.** Undependable or fickle. [ME.] —**skit'tish•ness** *n.*

skiv•vy (skĭv'ē) *n., pl.* **-vies.** *Slang.* **1.** Also **skivvy shirt.** A man's cotton knit undershirt. **2. skivvies.** A man's underwear consisting of shirt and shorts. [?]

Skr., Skt. Sanskrit.

skulk (skŭlk) *v.* To move about stealthily. [< Scand.] —**skulk'er** *n.*

skull (skŭl) *n.* The bony framework of the head. [ME *skulle.*]

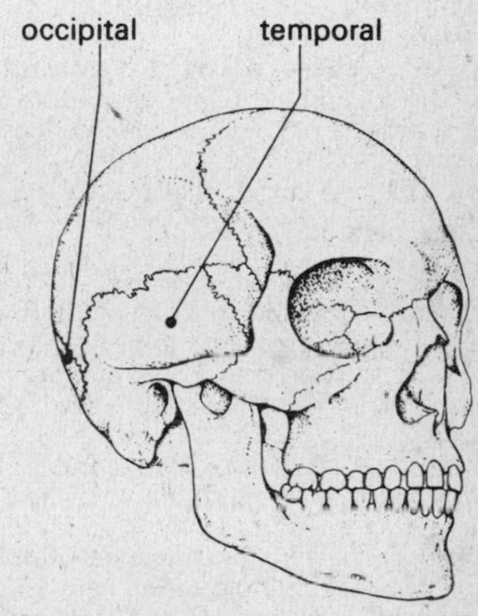

skull

skull and crossbones. A representation of the human skull above two long crossed bones, a symbol of death once used by pirates and now used as a warning label on poisons.

skull•cap (skŭl'kăp') *n.* A close-fitting, brimless cap.

skull•dug•ger•y (skŭl-dŭg'ə-rē) *n.* Also **skul•dug•ger•y.** Crafty deception or trickery. [?]

skunk (skŭngk) *n.* **1.** A New World mammal having black and white fur and ejecting a malodorous secretion. **2.** *Slang.* A despicable person. [< Algon.]

sky (skī) *n., pl.* **skies. 1.** The upper atmosphere, appearing as a hemisphere above the earth. **2.** The celestial or heavenly regions. [< ON *skȳ,* cloud < Gmc **skewja-*.]

sky•jack (skī'jăk') *v.* **-jacked, -jacking.** *Informal.* To hijack (an airplane), as through the use or threat of force. —**sky'jack'er** *n.*

sky•lark (skī'lärk') *n.* An Old World bird that sings while in flight. —*v.* To indulge in frolic.

sky•light (skī'līt') *n.* An overhead window admitting daylight.

sky•line (skī'līn') *n.* **1.** The horizon. **2.** The outline of a group of buildings seen against the sky.

sky•rock•et (skī'rŏk'ĭt) *n.* A firework that ascends high into the air, where it explodes in a cascade of flares and sparks. —*v.* To rise rapidly or suddenly, as in amount, position, reputation, etc.

sky•scrap•er (skī'skrā'pər) *n.* A very tall building.

sky•ward (skī'wərd) *adv.* Also **sky•wards** (-wərdz). Toward the sky. —**sky'ward** *adj.*

slab (slăb) *n.* A broad, flat, somewhat thick piece, as of cake, stone, or cheese. [ME *slabbe.*]

slack (slăk) *adj.* **1.** Slow; dull; sluggish. **2.** Not busy: *a slack business season.* **3.** Not tense or taut; loose. **4.** Careless; negligent. —*v.* To slacken. —*n.* **1.** A loose or slack part or portion of something. **2.** A lack of tension; looseness. **3.** A period of little activity; a lull. **4.** **slacks.** Trousers for casual wear. [< OE *slæc.* See **slēg-.**] —**slack'ness** *n.*

slack•en (slăk'ən) *v.* **1.** To slow down. **2.** To loosen. **3.** To make or become less vigorous or intense.

slack•er (slăk'ər) *n.* One who shirks work or responsibility.

slag (slăg) *n.* **1.** The vitreous mass left as a residue by the smelting of metallic ore. **2.** Volcanic refuse. [MLG *slagge.*]

slain (slān). *p.p.* of **slay.**

slake (slāk) *v.* **slaked, slaking. 1.** To quench, as thirst. **2.** To combine (lime) chemically with water or moist air. [< OE *slacian,* to loose < *slæc,* SLACK.]

sla•lom (slä'ləm) *n.* A skiing race along a downhill zigzag course. [Norw, "sloping path."]

slam¹ (slăm) *v.* **slammed, slamming. 1.** To shut with force and loud noise. **2.** To put, throw, or strike with great force so as to produce a loud noise. —*n.* **1.** A forceful closing that produces a loud noise. **2.** The noise so produced. [Perh < Scand.]

slam² (slăm) *n.* In bridge, the winning of all the tricks, **grand slam,** or all but one, **little slam.** [?]

slan•der (slăn'dər) *n.* The utterance of defamatory statements injurious to the reputation or well-being of a person. —*v.* To utter damaging reports about. [< L *scandalum,* scandal.] —**slan'der•er** *n.* —**slan'der•ous** *adj.* —**slan'der•ous•ly** *adv.*

slang (slăng) *n.* Nonstandard vocabulary consisting typically of arbitrary and often ephemeral coinages and figures of speech. [?] —**slang'i•ness** *n.* —**slang'y** *adj.*

slant (slănt, slänt) *v.* **1.** To incline; slope. **2.** To present so as to conform with a particular bias. —*n.* **1.** A sloping direction, plane, or course; incline. **2.** A bias or point of view. [< ME *slenten.*] —**slant'ing•ly** *adv.*

slap (slăp) *n.* **1.** A smacking blow made with the open hand. **2.** An insult; rebuff. —*v.* **slapped, slapping.** To strike with a flat object, as the palm of the hand. [LG *slapp.*]

slap•dash (slăp'dăsh') *adj.* Hasty; careless. —*adv.* Recklessly; haphazardly.

slap•stick (slăp'stĭk') *n.* Comedy characterized by loud and boisterous farce.

slash (slăsh) *v.* **1.** To cut or lash with violent sweeping strokes. **2.** To make a gash or gashes in. **3.** To reduce or curtail drastically. —*n.* **1.** A sweeping stroke made with a sharp instrument. **2.** A cut or other injury made by such a stroke; a gash. **3.** *Ptg.* A virgule. [ME *slaschen.*] —**slash'er** *n.*

slat (slăt) *n.* A narrow strip of metal or wood. [< OF *esclater,* to splinter.]

slate (slāt) *n.* **1.** A fine-grained rock that splits into thin, smooth-surfaced layers. **2.** A piece of this material cut for use as roofing material or a writing surface. **3.** A list of the candidates of a political party running for various offices. —*v.* **slated, slating. 1.** To cover with slate. **2.** To designate; schedule: *slated to arrive at noon.* [< OF *esclat,* fragment, splinter.]

slat•tern (slăt'ərn) *n.* A woman untidy or slovenly in person or habits. [Perh < dial *slatter,* to spill awkwardly.]

slaugh•ter (slô'tər) *n.* **1.** The killing of animals for food. **2.** The killing of a large number of persons; carnage; massacre. —*v.* **1.** To kill (animals) for food; butcher. **2.** To kill (persons) in large numbers; massacre. [ME.]

slaugh•ter•house (slô'tər-hous') *n.* A place where animals are butchered.

Slav (släv) *n.* A member of one of the Slavic-speaking peoples of eastern Europe.

Slav. Slavic.

slave (slāv) *n.* **1.** One bound in servitude as an instrument of labor. **2.** One completely under the domination of a specified person or influence. —*v.* **slaved, slaving.** To work like a slave; drudge. [< ML *Sclavus,* Slav.]

slave driver. 1. A severely exacting employer or supervisor. **2.** An overseer of slaves at work.

slav•er (slăv'ər) *v.* To slobber. —*n.* Saliva drooling from the mouth. [Prob < ON *slafra.*]

slav•er•y (slā'və-rē, slāv'rē) *n.* Bondage to a master or household.

Slav•ic (slä'vĭk) *adj.* Of or pertaining to the Slavs or their languages. —*n.* A branch of Indo-European including Czech, Bulgarian, Polish, Russian, and Serbo-Croatian.

slav•ish (slā'vĭsh) *adj.* **1.** Of or like a slave; servile. **2.** Of or like the institution of slavery; oppressive. **3.** Blindly dependent on or imitative. —**slav'ish•ly** *adv.* —**slav'ish•ness** *n.*

slaw (slô) *n.* Coleslaw.

slay (slā) *v.* **slew, slain, slaying.** To kill by violent means. [< OE *slēan.* See **slak-.**] —**slay'er** *n.*

sld. 1. sailed. **2.** sealed.

slea•zy (slē'zē) *adj.* **-zier, -ziest. 1.** Flimsy or thin, as fabric. **2.** Cheap; shoddy. [?] —**slea'zi•ly** *adv.* —**slea'zi•ness** *n.*

sled (slĕd) *n.* A vehicle mounted on runners, used for moving over ice and snow. —*v.* **sledded, sledding.** To ride or use a sled. [ME *sledde.*] —**sled'der** *n.*

sledge (slĕdj) *n.* A vehicle on low runners used for transporting loads across ice and snow. [< MDu *sleedse.*]

sledge•ham•mer (slĕdj'hăm'ər) *n.* A long, heavy hammer, often wielded with both hands. [< OE *slecg.* See **slak-.**]

sleek (slēk) *adj.* **1.** Smooth and lustrous as if polished; glossy. **2.** Well-groomed and neatly tailored in appearance. —*v.* **1.** To make lustrous or smooth; polish. **2.** To gloss over; conceal. [Var of SLICK.] —**sleek'ness** *n.*

sleep (slēp) *n.* **1.** A natural, periodically recurring state of rest, characterized by relative physical and nervous inactivity, unconsciousness, and lessened responsiveness to external stimuli. **2.** Any similar condition of inactivity, as unconsciousness or hibernation. —*v.* **slept, sleeping. 1.** To be in the state of sleep or fall asleep. **2.** To pass or get rid of by sleeping: *He went home to sleep it off.* [< OE *slǣp.*]

sleep•er (slē'pər) *n.* **1.** A person or animal that sleeps. **2.** A sleeping car on a railroad train. **3.** *Brit.* A heavy beam used as a support for rails in a railroad track.

sleeping bag. A warmly lined zippered bag in which one may sleep outdoors.

sleeping car. A railroad car having accommodations for sleeping.

sleeping pill. A sedative, esp. a barbiturate, in the form of a pill or capsule.

sleeping sickness. Any of various often fatal diseases of man and animals in tropical Africa, characterized by fever and lethargy.

sleep•less (slēp'lĭs) *adj.* Without sleep; wakeful; restless. —**sleep'less•ness** *n.*

sleep•walk•ing (slēp'wô'kĭng) *n.* The act of walking in one's sleep. —**sleep'walk'er** *n.*

sleep•y (slē'pē) *adj.* **-ier, -iest. 1.** Ready for or needing sleep; drowsy. **2.** Quiet: *a sleepy town.* —**sleep'i•ly** *adv.* —**sleep'i•ness** *n.*

sleep•y•head (slē'pē-hĕd') *n. Informal.* A sleepy person.

sleet (slēt) *n.* **1.** Partially frozen rain. **2.** A mixture of rain and snow. —*v.* To shower sleet. [< OE *slēte.] —**sleet'y** *adj.*

sleeve (slēv) *n.* **1.** The part of a garment that covers the arm. **2.** Any encasement or shell into which a piece of equipment fits. [< OE *slīf, slēf.* See **sleubh-.**] —**sleeve'less** *adj.*

sleigh (slā) *n.* A light vehicle mounted on runners for use on snow or ice, and usually drawn by a horse. [< MDu *slēde.*]

sleight of hand. 1. Tricks or feats performed by jugglers or magicians so quickly that their manner of execution cannot be observed. **2.** Skill in performing such feats.

slen•der (slĕn'dər) *adj.* **1.** Gracefully slim. **2.** Meager; inadequate. **3.** Slight; feeble: *a slender chance.* [ME *slendre.*] —**slen'der•ly** *adv.*

slen•der•ize (slĕn'də-rīz') *v.* **-ized, -izing.** To make or become slender.

slept (slĕpt). *p.t.* & *p.p.* of **sleep.**

sleuth (slo͞oth) *n. Informal.* A detective. [< ME, track of an animal.]

slew¹ (slo͞o) *n.* Also **slue.** *Informal.* A large amount or number; a lot. [Ir Gael *sluagh.*]

slew² (slo͞o). *p.t.* of **slay.**

slice (slīs) *n.* **1.** A thin, broad piece cut from a larger object. **2.** A portion or share. **3.** A stroke that causes a ball to curve off course. —*v.* **sliced, slicing. 1.** To cut or divide into slices. **2.** To cut or remove from a larger piece. **3.** To hit (a ball) with a slice. [< OF *esclicer,* to reduce to splinters < Gmc *slītjan.] —**slice'a•ble** *adj.* —**slic'er** *n.*

slick (slĭk) *adj.* **1.** Smooth, glossy, and slippery, as if covered with oil or ice. **2.** Deftly executed; adroit; facile. **3.** Shrewd; wily. **4.** Superficially attractive but without depth. —*n.* A smooth or slippery surface or area. —*v.* **1.** To make smooth, glossy, or oily. **2.** *Informal.* To make neat, trim, or tidy; spruce. [ME *slike.*]

slick•er (slĭk'ər) *n.* **1.** A glossy raincoat, esp. one made of oilskin. **2.** *Informal.* A stylish city dweller; a dude.

slide (slīd) *v.* **slid** (slĭd), **slid** or **slidden** (slĭd'n), **sliding. 1.** To move or cause to move in smooth, continuous contact with a surface. **2.** *Baseball.* To drop down and skid into a base to avoid being tagged out. —*n.* **1.** A sliding movement or action. **2.** A playground apparatus for children to slide upon. **3.** An image on a transparent plate for projection on a screen. **4.** A small glass plate for mounting specimens to be examined under a microscope. **5.** An avalanche. [< OE *slīdan.* See **sleidh-.**] —**slid'er** *n.*

slide rule. A device consisting essentially of two scaled rules mounted to slide along each other so that computations can be performed mechanically.

slight (slīt) *adj.* **1.** Small in size, degree, or

amount; meager. **2.** Of small importance or consideration. **3.** Slender or frail; delicate. —*v.* **1.** To treat with disrespect. **2.** To do negligently; shirk. **3.** To treat as unimportant. —*n.* An act of pointed disrespect or discourtesy. [ME.] —**slight'ness** *n.*

slight•ly (slīt'lē) *adv.* To a small degree or extent; somewhat.

slim (slĭm) *adj.* **slimmer, slimmest. 1.** Small in girth or thickness; slender. **2.** Small in quality or amount; scant; meager. —*v.* **slimmed, slimming.** To make or become slim. [Du, small, inferior.] —**slim'ly** *adv.* —**slim'ness** *n.*

slime (slīm) *n.* A moist, sticky substance or coating. [< OE *slīm.* See **lei-**.] —**slim'y** *adj.*

sling (slĭng) *n.* **1.** A weapon consisting of a looped strap in which a stone is whirled and then let fly. **2.** A looped rope, strap, or chain for supporting, cradling, or hoisting something, esp. a band suspended from the neck to support an injured arm or hand. —*v.* **slung, slinging.** To hurl from or as if from a sling; fling. [ME.] —**sling'er** *n.*

sling•shot (slĭng'shŏt') *n.* A Y-shaped stick with an elastic strap attached to the prongs, used for flinging small stones.

slink (slĭngk) *v.* **slunk, slinking.** To move in a quiet, furtive manner. [< OE *slincan.* See **slenk-**.]

slip[1] (slĭp) *v.* **slipped, slipping. 1.** To move quietly and stealthily. **2.** To slide accidentally; lose one's balance. **3.** To slide out of place or from one's grasp. **4.** To get away (from); escape unnoticed. **5.** *Informal.* To decline in ability, strength, or keenness. **6.** *Informal.* To decline; fall off. **7.** To place or insert smoothly and quietly. **8.** To put on or remove (clothing) easily or quickly. —**let slip.** To say inadvertently. —**slip up.** *Informal.* To make a mistake; err. —*n.* **1.** The act of slipping. **2.** A slight error or oversight. **3.** A docking place for a ship between two piers. **4.** A woman's undergarment of various lengths. **5.** A pillowcase. [ME *slippen,* to slip, slip away.]

slip[2] (slĭp) *n.* **1.** A plant part removed for grafting or planting. **2.** A youthful, slender person: *a slip of a girl.* **3.** A small piece of paper. [ME *slippe,* a strip.]

slip•cov•er (slĭp'kŭv'ər) *n.* A fitted, removable cover for a piece of upholstered furniture.

slip•knot (slĭp'nŏt') *n.* A knot made with a loop so that it slips along the rope around which it is tied.

slip•o•ver (slĭp'ō'vər) *adj.* Designed to be put on or taken off over the head. —*n.* A slipover garment, such as a sweater.

slip•page (slĭp'ĭj) *n.* **1.** A slipping. **2.** Loss of motion or power due to slipping.

slip•per (slĭp'ər) *n.* A light, low shoe, worn mainly indoors, that may be slipped on and off easily.

slip•per•y (slĭp'ə-rē) *adj.* **-ier, -iest. 1.** Causing or tending to cause sliding or slipping. **2.** Elusive; evasive. [< OE *slipor.* See **lei-**.]

slip•shod (slĭp'shŏd') *adj.* Poorly made or done; careless.

slip-up (slĭp'ŭp') *n. Informal.* An error or oversight.

slit (slĭt) *n.* A long, narrow cut or opening. —*v.* **slit, slitting. 1.** To make a long, narrow incision in. **2.** To cut lengthwise into strips; split. [ME *slitte.*]

slith•er (slĭth'ər) *v.* To slip and slide, as on a loose or uneven surface. [< OE *slīdan,* to SLIDE.] —**slith'er•y** *adj.*

sliv•er (slĭv'ər) *n.* A slender piece cut, split, or broken off; a splinter. [< ME *slyven,* to cleave, split.]

slob (slŏb) *n. Informal.* A crude, slovenly person. [Ir *slab,* mud.]

slob•ber (slŏb'ər) *v.* **1.** To drool; slaver. **2.** To spill (liquid or food) from the mouth while eating or drinking. —*n.* Saliva running from the mouth; drivel. [ME *sloberen.*]

sloe (slō) *n.* The blackish, plumlike fruit of the blackthorn. [< OE *slāh.*]

slog (slŏg) *v.* **slogged, slogging.** To walk with a slow, plodding gait. [?]

slo•gan (slō'gən) *n.* **1.** The motto of a political party, school, or other group. **2.** An often repeated word or phrase used in advertising or promotion. [< Gael *sluagh-ghairm.*]

sloop (slo͞op) *n.* A single-masted, fore-and-aft-rigged sailing boat. [Du *sloep.*]

slop (slŏp) *n.* **1.** Liquid spilled or splashed. **2.** Soft mud or slush. **3.** Unappetizing, watery food or soup. **4.** Refuse used as animal feed. —*v.* **slopped, slopping.** To spill or splash. [ME *sloppe,* a muddy place.]

slope (slōp) *v.* **sloped, sloping.** To incline upward or downward. —*n.* **1.** Any inclined line, surface, plane, position, or direction. **2.** A stretch of ground forming a natural or artificial incline: *ski slope.* [< ME, sloping.]

slop•py (slŏp'ē) *adj.* **-pier, -piest. 1.** Of, like, or covered with slop; splashy; muddy. **2.** *Informal.* Untidy; messy. **3.** *Informal.* Careless; slipshod. —**slop'pi•ly** *adv.* —**slop'pi•ness** *n.*

slosh (slŏsh) *v.* To splash or flounder, as in water or another liquid. —*n.* Slush. [Var of SLUSH.] —**slosh'y** *adj.*

slot (slŏt) *n.* A long narrow groove or opening. [ME, hollow between the breasts.]

sloth (slōth, slôth, slŏth) *n.* **1.** Laziness; indolence; sluggishness. **2.** A slow-moving, tree-dwelling, tropical American mammal. [ME *slowthe* < *slow,* slow.] —**sloth'ful** *adj.*

slot machine. A coin-operated vending or gambling machine.

slouch (slouch) *n.* **1.** A drooping posture or gait. **2.** A lazy or inept person. [?] —**slouch** *v.*

slough[1] (slo͞o, slou) *n.* **1.** A mud hollow. **2.** A swamp. **3.** A state of dejection or despondency. [< OE *slōh.*]

slough[2] (slŭf) *n.* **1.** *Med.* Dead tissue separated from a living structure. **2.** Any outer layer or covering that is shed. —*v.* To cast off or shed, as dead skin. [ME *slouh.*] —**slough'y** *adj.*

Slo•vak (slō'väk', -văk') *n.* **1.** Any of a Slavic people living in Slovakia. **2.** The Slavic language of these people, closely related to Czech. —*adj.* Of or pertaining to Slovakia, the Slovaks, or their language.

Slo•vak•i•a (slō-vä'kē-ə). The E region and a former province of Czechoslovakia.

slov•en (slŭv'ən) *n.* A habitually unwashed and untidy person. [ME *sloveyn.*]

Slo•vene (slō'vēn') *n.* The Slavic language of NW Yugoslavia. —**Slo'vene'** *adj.*

slov•en•ly (slŭv'ən-lē) *adj.* **-lier, -liest. 1.** Untidy; messy. **2.** Careless; slipshod. —**slov'en•li•ness** *n.*

slow (slō) *adj.* **1.** Moving or proceeding at a low speed. **2. a.** Taking a long or inordinate time. **b.** Gradual. **3. a.** Registering behind the correct time. **b.** Tardy. **4.** Not precipitate. **5.** Sluggish; inactive. **6.** Boring. **7.** Dull; stupid. —*v.* **1.** To make or become slow or slower. **2.** To delay; retard. [< OE *slāw* < Gmc **slǣwaz.*] —**slow, slow'ly** *adv.* —**slow'ness** *n.*

sludge (slŭj) *n.* **1.** Mire or ooze, as on a river bed. **2.** Material precipitated by the treatment of sewage. —**sludg'y** *adj.*

slue. Variant of **slew**[1].

slug[1] (slŭg) *n.* **1. a.** A lump of metal. **b.** A bullet. **2.** A shot of liquor. **3.** A metal disk for use in a slot machine. [Prob < SLUG[2].]

slug[2] (slŭg) *n.* **1.** A land mollusk related to the snails but having no shell. **2.** A sluggard. [Prob < Scand.]

slug[3] (slŭg) *v.* **slugged, slugging.** To strike hard and heavily. [Perh < SLUG[1].] —**slug'ger** *n.*

slug•gard (slŭg'ərd) *n.* A slothful person. [Prob < Scand.]

slug•gish (slŭg'ĭsh) *adj.* **1.** Slow; inactive. **2.** Lazy or dull. [ME.] —**slug'gish•ly** *adv.* —**slug'gish•ness** *n.*

sluice (slo͞os) *n.* **1.** A man-made channel for water with a gate to regulate the flow. **2.** The gate used in this way. **3.** Any artificial channel for carrying off excess water. **4.** An inclined trough, as for floating logs or separating gold ore. —*v.* **sluiced, sluicing. 1.** To wash with a sudden flow of water; flush. **2.** To draw off or let out by a sluice. **3.** To send (logs) down a sluice. [< L *exclūdere,* to shut out, EXCLUDE.]

slum (slŭm) *n.* A squalid and overcrowded district inhabited by the poor. —*v.* **slummed, slumming.** To visit a slum. [?]

slum•ber (slŭm'bər) *v.* **1.** To sleep or doze. **2.** To be dormant or sluggish. —*n.* Sleep. [ME *slumberen.*] —**slum'ber•er** *n.*

slum•ber•ous (slŭm'bər-əs) *adj.* **1.** Sleepy; drowsy. **2.** Quiet; inactive.

slump (slŭmp) *v.* **1.** To decline or sink suddenly; collapse. **2.** To droop or slouch. [Prob < Scand.] —**slump** *n.*

slung (slŭng). *p.t.* & *p.p.* of **sling.**

slunk (slŭngk). *p.t.* & *p.p.* of **slink.**

slur (slûr) *v.* **slurred, slurring. 1.** To pass over lightly or carelessly. **2.** To pronounce indistinctly. **3.** To disparage; calumniate. **4.** To glide over (a series of musical notes) smoothly without a break. —*n.* **1.** A disparaging remark; aspersion. **2.** *Mus.* A curved line connecting notes on a score to indicate that they are to be played or sung legato. [< ME *sloor.*]

slurp (slûrp) *v.* To eat or drink noisily. [< MDu *slorpen.*]

slush (slŭsh) *n.* **1.** Partially melted snow or ice. **2.** Soft mud; mire. [Perh < Scand.] —**slush'i•ness** *n.* —**slush'y** *adj.*

slut (slŭt) *n.* **1.** A slovenly woman. **2.** A whorish woman. [ME *slutte.*] —**slut'tish** *adj.*

sly (slī) *adj.* **slier** or **slyer, sliest** or **slyest. 1.** Stealthily clever; cunning. **2.** Secretive or underhand. **3.** Roguish; arch. [< ON *slœgr,* cunning, clever.] —**sly'ly** *adv.* —**sly'ness** *n.*

Sm samarium.

sm. small.

smack[1] (smăk) *v.* **1.** To compress and open (the lips) with a sharp sound expressive of relish. **2.** To kiss or slap noisily. —*n.* **1.** The sound produced by smacking the lips. **2.** A noisy kiss. **3.** A sharp blow or loud slap. —*adv.* **1.** With a smack: *fell smack on her head.* **2.** Directly; completely: *smack against the rules.* [< MLG or MDu *smacken.*]

smack[2] (smăk) *n.* **1.** A savor or hint. **2.** A smattering. —*v.* **1.** To taste of: *cheese that smacks of mold.* **2.** To be distinctly suggestive of. [< OE *smæc.* See **smeg-**.]

smack[3] (smăk) *n.* A sloop-rigged fishing vessel with a well for live fish. [< MDu *smacke.*]

small (smôl) *adj.* **1.** Little. **2.** Trifling or trivial. **3.** Limited in operation or scope. **4.** Of low or minor status. **5.** Unpretentious; modest. **6.** Petty or mean. **7.** Diluted; weak: *small beer.* **8.** Soft; low: *a small voice.* —*adv.* **1.** In small pieces: *Cut it up small.* **2.** Softly and timidly: *sing small.* —*n.* Something smaller than the

ô paw, for/oi boy/ou out/o͝o took/o͞o coo/p pop/r run/s sauce/sh shy/t to/th thin/*th* the/
ŭ cut/ûr fur/v van/w wag/y yes/z size/zh vision/ə ago, item, edible, gallop, circus/

rest: *the small of the back.* [< OE *smæl.* See **mēlo-**.] —**small'ness** *n.*

small capital. A smaller letter having the form of a capital letter: SMALL CAPITALS.

small intestine. The part of the intestine between the outlet of the stomach and the large intestine.

small•pox (smôl'pŏks') *n.* An acute, highly infectious viral disease, characterized by chills, high fever, headache, and backache, with subsequent eruption of pimples that form pockmarks.

small talk. Casual or trivial conversation.

smar•my (smär'mē) *adj.* **-mier, -miest.** Marked by an exaggerated or insincere earnestness; smug and self-righteous. [?]

smart (smärt) *v.* **1.** To cause or feel a stinging pain. **2.** To feel or suffer distress. —*n.* A stinging pain. —*adj.* **1. a.** Mentally alert; bright. **b.** Clever or skillful. **2.** Impertinently witty: *a smart reply.* **3.** Sharp and quick: *a smart pace.* **4.** Shrewd: *a smart lawyer.* **5.** Stylish or fashionable. [< OE *smeortan.* See **smerd-**.] —**smart'ly** *adv.* —**smart'ness** *n.*

smart al•eck (ăl'ĭk). *Informal.* A pretentiously clever person.

smart•en (smärt'n) *v.* To make or become smart.

smash (smăsh) *v.* **1.** To break or be broken into pieces. **2.** To throw or move violently so as to shatter or crush. **3.** To destroy completely; wreck. —*n.* **1.** The act or sound of smashing. **2. a.** Collapse; ruin. **b.** Bankruptcy. **3.** A collision or crash. **4.** A violent overhand stroke in tennis. [Perh blend of SMACK and CRASH.] —**smash'er** *n.*

smat•ter•ing (smăt'ər-ĭng) *n.* Fragmented or superficial knowledge.

smear (smîr) *v.* **1.** To daub with a sticky or greasy substance. **2.** To smudge or soil. **3.** To sully; vilify. —*n.* **1.** A smudge or blot. **2.** Vilification; slander. [< OE *smierwan, smerian.* See **smer-**[2].]

smell (smĕl) *v.* **smelled** or **smelt, smelling. 1.** To perceive by means of the olfactory nerves. **2.** To sense the presence of by or as if by the olfactory nerves. **3.** To have or emit an odor. **4.** To stink. —*n.* **1.** The olfactory sense. **2.** Odor; scent. **3.** The act or an instance of smelling. [ME *smellen.*]

smell•y (smĕl'ē) *adj.* **-ier, -iest.** *Informal.* Having an unpleasant odor.

smelt[1] (smĕlt) *v.* To melt or fuse (ores), separating the metallic constituents. [Du or LG *smelten.*]

smelt[2] (smĕlt) *n.* A small silvery, narrow-bodied food fish. [< OE.]

smelt[3] (smĕlt). Alternate *p.t.* & *p.p.* of **smell.**

smelt•er (smĕl'tər) *n.* **1.** A worker who smelts ore. **2.** Also **smelt•er•y** (-tə-rē). A smelting works.

smi•lax (smī'lăks') *n.* A climbing vine with glossy leaves, used for decoration. [< Gk.]

smile (smīl) *n.* A facial expression indicative of pleasure, affection, or amusement and formed by an upward curving of the corners of the mouth. —*v.* **smiled, smiling. 1.** To have or form a smile. **2.** To express favor or approval. **3.** To express with a smile. [Perh < Scand.]

smirch (smûrch) *v.* **1.** To soil, stain, or dirty. **2.** To dishonor or disgrace. [ME *smorchen.*] —**smirch** *n.*

smirk (smûrk) *v.* To smile in an obnoxiously arch or simpering manner. [< OE *smearcian,* to smile. See **smei-**.] —**smirk** *n.*

smite (smīt) *v.* **smote, smitten** (smĭt'n) or **smit** (smĭt) or **smote, smiting. 1. a.** To inflict a heavy blow on. **b.** To kill by striking. **2.** To afflict: *smitten with cholera.* [< OE *smītan.* See **smē-**.] —**smit'er** *n.*

smith (smĭth) *n.* One who works in metals, esp. a blacksmith. [< OE. See **smi-**.]

Smith, Adam. 1723–1790. Scottish political economist and philosopher.

smith•er•eens (smĭth'ə-rēnz') *pl.n.* Splintered pieces; bits. [< Ir *smiodar,* small fragment.]

smith•y (smĭth'ē, smĭth'ē) *n., pl.* **-ies.** A blacksmith's shop. [< ON *smidhja.*]

smock (smŏk) *n.* A loose outer garment worn to protect the clothes while working. —*v.* To decorate (fabric) with small, regularly spaced stitches forming a gathered pattern. [< OE *smoc.*]

smog (smŏg, smôg) *n.* Fog that has become mixed and polluted with smoke. [Blend of SMOKE and FOG.] —**smog'gy** *adj.*

smoke (smōk) *n.* **1.** The vapor made up of small particles of matter in the air, resulting from the incomplete combustion of material such as wood or coal. **2.** Any cloud of fine particles. **3.** The act of smoking tobacco. **4.** *Informal.* A cigarette. —*v.* **smoked, smoking. 1.** To emit smoke. **2.** To emit smoke excessively. **3.** To draw in and exhale the smoke of tobacco or the like. **4.** To preserve (meat or fish) by exposure to smoke. **5.** To fumigate or discolor with smoke. [< OE *smoca.* See **smeug-**.] —**smok'i•ness** *n.* —**smok'y** *adj.*

smoke•house (smōk'hous') *n.* A structure in which meat or fish is cured with smoke.

smok•er (smō'kər) *n.* **1.** One that smokes. **2.** A railroad car in which smoking is permitted.

smoke•stack (smōk'stăk') *n.* A large vertical pipe through which smoke, gases, etc., are discharged, as from a factory.

smol•der (smōl'dər). Also **smoul•der.** *v.* **1.** To burn with little smoke and no flame. **2.** To burn or exist inwardly. —*n.* Thick smoke resulting from a slow fire. [ME *smolderen.*]

smooth (smo͞oth) *adj.* **1.** Not irregular or rough; even. **2.** Having a fine consistency or texture. **3.** Having an even or gentle motion. **4.** Agreeable; mild. —*v.* **1.** To make or become smooth. **2.** To rid of hindrances, difficulties, etc. **3.** To soothe or tranquilize. [< OE *smōth.*] —**smooth'er** *n.* —**smooth'ly** *adv.* —**smooth'ness** *n.*

smooth•bore (smo͞oth'bôr', -bōr') *adj.* Having no rifling within the barrel, as a firearm. —*n.* Also **smooth bore.** A firearm having no rifling.

smor•gas•bord (smôr'gəs-bôrd', -bōrd') *n.* A meal consisting of a number of dishes served buffet-style. [Swed *smörgåsbord.*]

smote (smōt). *p.t.* & alternate *p.p.* of **smite.**

smoth•er (smŭth'ər) *v.* **1.** To suffocate. **2.** To suppress. **3.** To cook or cover (a foodstuff) under a thick mass of another foodstuff. —*n.* A dense cloud of smoke or dust or a welter of spume. [< OE *smorian,* to suffocate, smother.] —**smoth'er•y** *adj.*

smoul•der. Variant of **smolder.**

smudge (smŭj) *v.* **smudged, smudging.** To smear or blur. —*n.* **1.** A blotch or smear. **2.** A smoky fire used against insects or frost. [ME *smogen.*] —**smudg'y** *adj.*

smug (smŭg) *adj.* **smugger, smuggest.** Complacent or self-satisfied. [Prob < LG *smuck,* neat, smooth.] —**smug'ly** *adv.* —**smug'ness** *n.*

smug•gle (smŭg'əl) *v.* **-gled, -gling. 1.** To import or export without paying lawful customs charges or duties. **2.** To convey illicitly or by stealth. [< LG *smuggeln* and Du *smokkelen.*] —**smug'gler** *n.*

smut (smŭt) *n.* **1.** A smudge or something that smudges. **2.** Obscenity. **3.** A plant disease caused by fungi and characterized by black, powdery masses. [Perh < LG *smutt.*] —**smut'ti•ness** *n.* —**smut'ty** *adj.*

smutch (smŭch) *n.* A stain or smudge. [Perh related to SMUDGE.]

Sn tin (L *stannum*).

snack (snăk) *n.* A light meal. [ME *snake,* a snatch with the teeth, bite.]

snaf•fle (snăf'əl) *n.* A jointed bit for a horse. [?]

snag (snăg) **1.** A sharp or jagged projection. **2.** An unforeseen or hidden obstacle. —*v.* **snagged, snagging. 1.** To get caught by or as by a snag. **2.** To snatch. [Prob < Scand.] —**snag'gy** *adj.*

snail (snāl) *n.* A mollusk with a spirally coiled shell into which the head and body can be withdrawn. [< OE *snægel.* See **sneg-**.]

snake (snāk) *n.* Any of various legless, long-bodied, sometimes venomous reptiles. —*v.* **snaked, snaking.** To move, crawl, or drag with a snakelike motion. [< OE *snaca.* See **sneg-**.] —**snak'i•ly** *adv.* —**snak'y** *adj.*

Snake River. A river of the NW U.S.

snap (snăp) *v.* **snapped, snapping. 1.** To make or cause to make a sharp cracking sound. **2.** To break suddenly with a sharp sound. **3.** To give way abruptly. **4.** To bite or seize with a snatching motion. **5.** To speak abruptly or sharply. **6.** To move smartly. **7.** To flash or sparkle. **8.** *Football.* To pass the ball so as to initiate a play. **9.** To open or close with a click. —*n.* **1.** A sharp cracking sound. **2.** A sudden breaking or release of something under pressure. **3.** A clasp, catch, or other fastening device. **4.** A thin, crisp cooky. **5.** Briskness; energy. **6.** A spell of cold weather. **7.** The passing of the ball that initiates each play in football. [Prob < MLG or MDu *snappen,* to seize, speak hastily.] —**snap'pish** *adj.* —**snap'py** *adj.*

snap•drag•on (snăp'drăg'ən) *n.* A cultivated plant with showy clusters of two-lipped flowers.

snap•per (snăp'ər) *n.* **1.** One that snaps. **2.** Any of various marine food fishes.

snap•shot (snăp'shŏt') *n.* A casual photograph taken with a small camera.

snare[1] (snâr) *n.* **1.** A trap consisting of a noose for capturing birds and other small animals. **2.** Anything that entangles the unwary. **3.** A surgical instrument with a wire loop controlled by a mechanism in the handle, used to remove growths, such as tumors and polyps. [< ON *snara.*] —**snare** *v.* **(snared, snaring).**

snare[2] (snâr) *n.* Any of the wires or cords stretched across the lower skin of a drum to increase reverberation. [Prob Du *snaar,* string.]

snarl[1] (snärl) *v.* **1.** To growl with bared teeth. **2.** To speak angrily or threateningly. [< MLG *snarren.*] —**snarl** *n.* —**snarl'y** *adj.*

snarl[2] (snärl) *n.* A tangle. [Prob < SNARE[1].] —**snarl** *v.* —**snarl'y** *adj.*

snatch (snăch) *v.* **1.** To try to grasp or seize. **2.** To seize or grab. —*n.* **1.** The act of snatching. **2.** A brief period. **3.** A small part: *a snatch of song.* [ME *snacchen,* make a sudden gesture.] —**snatch'er** *n.*

sneak (snēk) *v.* **sneaked** or *nonstandard* **snuck, sneaking.** To move, give, or take in a stealthy way. —*n.* **1.** A cowardly or underhand person. **2.** A stealthy move. [Of dial origin.] —**sneak'i•ness** *n.* —**sneak'y** *adj.*

sneak•er (snē'kər) *n.* A canvas shoe with a soft rubber sole.

sneer (snîr) *n.* A slight raising of one corner of the upper lip, expressive of contempt. —**sneer** *v.* —**sneer'er** *n.* —**sneer'ful** *adj.*

sneeze (snēz) *v.* **sneezed, sneezing.** To expel air forcibly from the mouth and nose in an explosive, spasmodic, involuntary action. [< OE *fnēosan.* See **pneu-.**] —**sneeze** *n.*

snick•er (snĭk'ər) *n.* Also **snig•ger** (snĭg'ər). A snide, partly stifled laugh. [Imit.] —**snick'er** *v.* —**snick'er•ing•ly** *adv.*

snide (snīd) *adj.* **1.** Slyly derogatory or sarcastic. **2.** Mean. [?]

sniff (snĭf) *v.* **sniffed, sniffing. 1.** To inhale a short, audible breath through the nose. **2.** To indicate contempt or disdain. **3.** To detect by or as if by sniffing. [ME *sniffen.*] —**sniff** *n.* —**sniff'er** *n.* —**sniff'ing•ly** *adv.*

snif•fle (snĭf'əl) *v.* **-fled, -fling.** To snuffle or whimper. [Freq of SNIFF.] —**snif'fle** *n.*

snif•ter (snĭf'tər) *n.* A pear-shaped brandy glass. [< dial *snifter,* to sniff.]

snip (snĭp) *v.* **snipped, snipping.** To cut or clip with short, quick strokes. —*n.* **1.** A stroke of the scissors. **2.** A small piece clipped off. [LG or Du *snippen,* to snap.]

snipe (snīp) *n., pl.* **snipe** or **snipes.** A long-billed, brownish wading bird. —*v.* **sniped, sniping.** To shoot at an enemy from a concealed place. [ME.]

snip•er (snī'pər) *n.* A rifleman detailed to pick off enemy soldiers from a concealed position.

snip•pet (snĭp'ĭt) *n.* A tidbit or morsel. [< SNIP.]

snitch (snĭch) *v. Slang.* **1.** To steal. **2.** To turn informer. [?] —**snitch'er** *n.*

sniv•el (snĭv'əl) *v.* **-eled** or **-elled, -eling** or **-elling. 1.** To whine tearfully. **2.** To run at the nose. [< OE **snyflan.* See **snē-²**.] —**sniv'el** *n.*

snob (snŏb) *n.* One who is convinced of and flaunts his social or other superiority. [?] —**snob'ber•y** *n.* —**snob'bish** *adj.* —**snob'bish•ly** *adv.* —**snob'bish•ness** *n.*

snoop (snōōp) *v.* To pry furtively. —*n. Informal.* One who pries or meddles. [Du *snoepen,* to eat on the sly.] —**snoop'er** *n.* —**snoop'y** *adj.*

snooze (snōōz) *v.* **snoozed, snoozing.** To doze. [?] —**snooze** *n.*

snore (snôr, snōr) *v.* **snored, snoring.** To make snorting sounds while sleeping. [ME *snoren,* to snort.] —**snore** *n.* —**snor'er** *n.*

snor•kel (snôr'kəl) *n.* **1.** A retractable vertical tube in a submarine, containing air-intake and exhaust pipes that permit extended periods of submergence. **2.** A breathing apparatus used by skin divers, consisting of a long tube held in the mouth. [G *Schnorchel.*]

snort (snôrt) *v.* **1.** To exhale or inhale forcibly and noisily through the nostrils in the manner of a horse. **2.** To laugh or express contempt with or as if with a snort. [ME *snorten.*] —**snort** *n.* —**snort'er** *n.*

snout (snout) *n.* An animal's projecting nose or facial part. [ME *snoute.*]

snow (snō) *n.* **1.** Solid precipitation in the form of white or translucent ice crystals. **2.** A falling of snow; snowstorm. —*v.* **1.** To fall as snow. **2.** To cover or close off with snow. [< OE *snāw.* See **sneigwh-.**] —**snow'y** *adj.*

snow•ball (snō'bôl') *n.* **1.** A mass of soft, wet snow packed into a ball. **2.** A shrub with rounded clusters of white flowers. —*v.* **1.** To throw snowballs. **2.** To grow rapidly in significance, importance, or size.

snow•bound (snō'bound') *adj.* Confined in one place by heavy snow.

snow•drift (snō'drĭft') *n.* Snow banked up by the wind.

snow•fall (snō'fôl') *n.* **1.** The amount of snow that falls during a given period or in a specified area. **2.** A fall of snow.

snow•mo•bile (snō'mō-bēl') *n.* A small motor vehicle with skilike runners, used for driving in or traveling on snow.

snow•plow (snō'plou') *n.* Any plowlike device for snow removal.

snow•shoe (snō'shōō') *n.* A racket-shaped frame worn under the shoe to facilitate walking on deep snow. —**snow'shoe'** *v.*

snow•storm (snō'stôrm') *n.* A storm marked by heavy snowfall.

snub (snŭb) *v.* **snubbed, snubbing.** To treat with scorn. [< ON *snubba.*] —**snub** *n.*

snub-nosed (snŭb'nōzd') *adj.* Having a short, turned-up nose.

snuck (snŭk). *Nonstandard. p.t. & p.p.* of **sneak.**

snuff¹ (snŭf) *v.* **1.** To inhale through the nose; sniff. **2.** To smell. **3.** To use snuff. —*n.* **1.** Finely pulverized tobacco for snorting up the nostrils. **2.** A sniff. [Prob < MDu *snuffen.*]

snuff² (snŭf) *v.* **1.** To cut off the charred end of (a candle). **2.** To extinguish (a candle). [ME *snoffe.*]

snuf•fle (snŭf'əl) *v.* **-fled, -fling. 1.** To breathe or sniff noisily. **2.** To sniffle. [Prob < LG or Du *snuffelen.*] —**snuf'fle** *n.*

snug (snŭg) *adj.* **snugger, snuggest. 1.** Cozy. **2.** Close-fitting, compact, or tight. [Perh < Scand.] —**snug, snug'ly** *adv.* —**snug'ness** *n.*

snug•gle (snŭg'əl) *v.* **-gled, -gling.** To nestle or cuddle.

so (sō) *adv.* **1.** In the manner expressed or indicated. **2.** To the degree expressed. **3.** To an evident degree. **4.** Therefore; consequently. **5.** Thereabouts: *ten dollars or so.* **6.** Likewise; also. **7.** Then. **8.** Indeed. —*adj.* True; factual. —*conj.* For that reason or with the consequence that: *He agreed, so they went ahead with plans.* —**so that.** With the purpose or result that. [< OE *swā.* See **swo-.**]

So. south; southern.

s.o. 1. seller's option. **2.** strikeout.

soak (sōk) *v.* **1.** To wet or saturate, as by immersing for a period of time. **2.** To absorb. **3.** To be immersed. **4.** To permeate; seep. **5.** *Slang.* To overcharge. —*n.* **1.** The act or process of soaking. **2.** Liquid in which something is soaked. **3.** *Slang.* A drunkard. [< OE *socian.* See **seu-⁴**.] —**soak'er** *n.*

soap (sōp) *n.* A cleansing agent made from an alkali acting on natural oils and fats. —*v.* To treat or cover with soap. [< OE *sāpe* < Gmc **saip-,* "dripping thing."] —**soap'i•ly** *adv.* —**soap'i•ness** *n.* —**soap'y** *adj.*

soap opera. A daytime radio or television serial drama.

soap•stone (sōp'stōn') *n.* Steatite.

soar (sôr, sōr) *v.* To rise, fly upward, or glide high in the air. [< VL **exaurāre.*]

sob (sŏb) *v.* **sobbed, sobbing.** To weep convulsively. [ME *sobben,* to catch breath.] —**sob** *n.* —**sob'bing•ly** *adv.*

so•ber (sō'bər) *adj.* **1.** Abstemious or temperate. **2.** Not drunk. **3.** Serious or grave. **4.** Plain or subdued. **5.** Without frivolity, excess, or exaggeration. **6.** Rational and impartial. —*v.* To make or become sober. [< L *sōbrius.*] —**so'ber•ly** *adv.* —**so'ber•ness** *n.*

so•bri•e•ty (sō-brī'ə-tē) *n.* **1.** Seriousness, gravity, or solemnity. **2.** Absence of alcoholic intoxication.

so•bri•quet (sō'brĭ-kā', -kĕt', sō'brĭ-kā', -kĕt') *n.* A nickname. [F.]

soc. 1. socialist. **2.** society.

so-called (sō'kôld') *adj.* Thus (but often wrongly thus) designated: *our so-called allies.*

soc•cer (sŏk'ər) *n.* A kind of football in which two teams maneuver a round ball mainly by kicking in attempts to score points. [Short var of ASSOCIATION (football).]

so•cia•ble (sō'shə-bəl) *adj.* Friendly; companionable; convivial. [< L *socius,* partner, sharer.] —**so'cia•bil'i•ty** (sō'shə-bĭl'ə-tē) *n.* —**so'cia•ble•ness** *n.* —**so'cia•bly** *adv.*

so•cial (sō'shəl) *adj.* **1.** Living together in communities or organized groups. **2.** Of or pertaining to human society or its class and individual interrelationships. **3.** Of or pertaining to fashionable society. **4.** Sociable or convivial. —*n.* A social gathering: *church social.* [< L *socius,* companion, partner.] —**so'cial•ly** *adv.*

so•cial•ism (sō'shə-lĭz'əm) *n.* A system or theory of social organization in which the producers possess both political power and production and distribution means. —**so'cial•ist** *n.* & *adj.* —**so'cial•is'tic** *adj.*

so•cial•ize (sō'shə-līz') *v.* **-ized, -izing. 1.** To place under public ownership or control. **2.** To convert or adapt to social needs. **3.** To take part in social activities. —**so'cial•i•za'tion** *n.* —**so'cial•iz'er** *n.*

social security. A U.S. governmental system providing people with economic assistance for unemployment, disability, or old age.

so•ci•e•ty (sə-sī'ə-tē) *n., pl.* **-ties. 1. a.** The totality of human interrelationships. **b.** A given human group distinguished by participation in characteristic economic and political relationships and a common culture. **2.** The fashionable social class. **3.** Companionship; company. [< L *societās,* fellowship, union, society.] —**so•ci'e•tal** (-təl) *adj.*

Society of Friends. A Christian sect founded in about 1650 in England. It rejects ritual, formal sacraments, a priesthood, and violence.

socio-. *comb. form.* **1.** Society. **2.** Social. [< L *socius,* a sharing.]

so•ci•ol•o•gy (sō'sē-ŏl'ə-jē, sō'shē-) *n.* The study of human social structures and relationships. —**so'ci•o•log'ic** (-ə-lŏj'ĭk), **so'ci•o•log'i•cal** *adj.* —**so'ci•ol'o•gist** *n.*

sock¹ (sŏk) *n.* **1.** *pl.* **socks** or **sox.** A short stocking. **2.** *pl.* **socks. a.** A light shoe worn in the comedy of antiquity. **b.** Comic drama; comedy. [< OE *socc,* a kind of light shoe < L *soccus.*]

sock² (sŏk) *v. Slang.* To hit forcefully; punch. [?] —**sock** *n.*

sock•et (sŏk'ĭt) *n.* **1.** A cavity that acts as the receptacle for an inserted part. **2. a.** The hollow part of a joint that receives the end of a bone. **b.** A hollow into which a part, such as the eye, fits. [ME *soket.*]

Soc•ra•tes (sŏk'rə-tēz'). 470?–399 B.C. Greek philosopher and teacher. —**So•crat'ic** (sō-krăt'ĭk) *adj.*

sod (sŏd) *n.* Grass-covered surface soil held together by matted roots. —*v.* **sodded, sodding.** To cover with sod. [ME.]

so•da (sō'də) *n.* **1.** Any of various carbonates or bicarbonates of sodium. **2.** Carbonated water or a soft drink containing it. [ML.]

soda pop. *Informal.* A soft drink; soda.

sod•den (sŏd'n) *adj.* **1.** Thoroughly soaked; saturated. **2.** Bloated and dull, as from drink. [ME *soden,* pp of *sethen,* to seethe.] —**sod'den•ly** *adv.* —**sod'den•ness** *n.*

so•di•um (sō'dē-əm) *n. Symbol* **Na** A soft, light, extremely malleable silver-white metallic element, used esp. in the production of many industrially important compounds. Atomic number 11, atomic weight 22.99. [< SOD(A) + -IUM.]

sodium bicarbonate. A white crystalline compound, $NaHCO_3$, used in making effervescent salts and beverages, artificial mineral water, baking soda, and pharmaceuticals, and in fire extinguishers; bicarbonate of soda.

sodium borate. A crystalline compound, $Na_2B_4O_7 \cdot 10H_2O_2$, used in the manufacture of glass, detergents, and pharmaceuticals.

sodium carbonate. A white powdery compound, Na_2CO_3, used to manufacture various sodium compounds, ceramics, detergents, and soap.

sodium chloride. A colorless crystalline compound, NaCl, used to manufacture chemicals and as a food preservative and seasoning.

sodium glutamate. A white crystalline compound, $C_5H_8O_4NaM$, having a meatlike taste, used in cooking.

sodium hydroxide. A strongly alkaline compound, NaOH, used to manufacture chemicals and soaps and in petroleum refining.

sodium peroxide. A yellowish-white powder, Na_2O_2, employed as an oxidizing and bleaching agent.

sod•om•y (sŏd'ə-mē) *n.* Anal copulation of one male with another.

so•fa (sō'fə) *n.* A long upholstered couch with a back and arms. [< Ar *suffah,* a cushioned dais.]

So•fi•a (sō'fē-ə, sō-fē'ə). The capital of Bulgaria. Pop. 747,000.

soft (sôft, sŏft) *adj.* **1. a.** Offering little resistance; not hard. **b.** Yielding readily; not firm. **2.** Flabby. **3. a.** Smooth or fine. **b.** Bland. **4.** Not loud. **5.** Subdued. **6.** Not sharp. **7.** Gentle; mild. **8. a.** Compassionate. **b.** Affectionate; tender. **9.** Easy: *a soft job.* **10.** Having low dissolved mineral content. *—adv.* Softly; gently. [< OE *sôfte, sēfte* < Gmc **samfti-*.] **—soft'ly** *adv.* **—soft'ness** *n.*

soft•ball (sôft'bôl', sŏft'-) *n.* **1.** A variation of baseball played with a larger, softer ball. **2.** The ball used.

soft drink. A nonalcoholic, usually carbonated beverage.

soft drug. A drug, such as marijuana, that is considered to be less damaging to the health than a hard drug.

sof•ten (sôf'ən, sŏf'-) *v.* To make or become soft or softer. **—sof'ten•er** *n.*

soft palate. The movable fold of muscular fibers suspended from the rear of the hard palate that closes off the nasal cavity from the oral cavity during swallowing.

soft•ware (sôft'wâr', sŏft'-) *n.* **1. Written or printed data, as programs, essential to the operation of computers. 2. Documents, as manuals, containing information on the operation and maintenance of computers.**

sog•gy (sŏg'ē) *adj.* **-gier, -giest. 1.** Sodden; soaked. **2.** Humid; sultry. **—sog'gi•ly** *adv.* **—sog'gi•ness** *n.*

soil¹ (soil) *n.* **1.** The loose top layer of the earth's surface. **2.** Country; region: *native soil.* [< L *solium,* seat.]

soil² (soil) *v.* **1.** To make or become dirty; begrime. **2.** To disgrace; tarnish. **3.** To pollute; defile. *—n.* **1.** A stain or defilement. **2.** Human excrement used as fertilizer. [< VL **suculāre.*]

soi•ree (swä-rā') *n.* Also **soi•rée.** An evening party. [< F *soir,* evening.]

so•journ (sō'jûrn, sō-jûrn') *v.* To stay for a time; reside temporarily. [< OF *sojorner.*] **—so'journ** *n.* **—so'journ•er** *n.*

sol (sōl) *n.* The basic monetary unit of Peru.

sol•ace (sŏl'ĭs) *n.* **1.** Comfort in distress; consolation. **2.** That which furnishes comfort or consolation. [< L *sōlārī,* to comfort, console.] **—sol'ace** *v.* **(-aced, -acing).**

so•lar (sō'lər) *adj.* **1.** Of or proceeding from the sun. **2.** Utilizing or operated by energy derived from the sun: *solar battery.* **3.** Determined or measured with respect to the sun. [< L *sōl,* sun.]

so•lar•i•um (sō-lâr'ē-əm) *n., pl.* **-laria** (-lâr'ē-ə) or **-iums.** A room, gallery, etc., exposed to the sun, as in a sanitarium. [L *sōlārium,* sundial, terrace, balcony.]

solar plexus. 1. The large network of nerves located behind the stomach. **2.** *Informal.* The pit of the stomach.

solar system. The sun together with the nine planets and all other celestial bodies that orbit the sun.

sold (sōld). *p.t. & p.p.* of **sell.**

sol•der (sŏd'ər, sôd'-) *n.* **1.** Any of various fusible alloys, usually tin and lead, used to join metallic parts. **2.** Anything that joins or cements. *—v.* To join or repair with or as with solder. [< L *solidāre,* to make solid.]

sol•dier (sōl'jər) *n.* **1.** One who serves in an army. **2.** An enlisted man as distinguished from a commissioned officer. **3.** A sexually undeveloped form of certain ants and termites, having the jaws specialized to serve as fighting weapons. *—v.* To be or serve as a soldier. [< OF *soulde,* pay.] **—sol'dier•ly** *adj.*

sol•dier•y (sōl'jə-rē) *n., pl.* **-ies. 1.** A body of soldiers. **2.** The military profession.

sole¹ (sōl) *n.* **1.** The undersurface of the foot. **2.** The undersurface of a shoe or boot. *—v.* **soled, soling.** To furnish (a shoe or boot) with a sole. [< L *solum,* bottom, ground, sole of the foot.]

sole² (sōl) *adj.* Single; only. [< L *sōlus,* alone, single.] **—sole'ly** *adv.*

sole³ (sōl) *n., pl.* **sole** or **soles.** A marine flatfish valued as food. [< OF, sole (fish), SOLE¹, from the shape of the fish.]

sol•e•cism (sŏl'ə-sĭz'əm, sō'lə-) *n.* **1.** A nonstandard usage or grammatical construction. **2.** A violation of etiquette. [< Gk *soloikos,* speaking incorrectly.]

sol•emn (sŏl'əm) *adj.* **1.** Deeply earnest; grave. **2.** Performed with full ceremony: *a Solemn High Mass.* **3.** Gloomy; somber. [< L *sollemnis,* stated, established, appointed.] **—so•lem'ni•ty** (sə-lĕm'nə-tē), **sol'emn•ness** *n.* **—sol'emn•ly** *adv.*

sol•em•nize (sŏl'əm-nīz') *v.* **-nized, -nizing. 1.** To observe with formal ceremonies or rites. **2.** To perform with formal ceremony: *solemnize a marriage.* **—sol'em•ni•za'tion** *n.*

so•lic•it (sə-lĭs'ĭt) *v.* **1.** To seek to obtain: *solicit votes.* **2.** To entreat; importune. **3.** To entice; tempt. [< L *sollicitāre,* to disturb, agitate.] **—so•lic'i•ta'tion** *n.*

so•lic•i•tor (sə-lĭs'ə-tər) *n.* **1.** One who solicits contributions, subscriptions, etc. **2.** The chief law officer of a city or government department. **3.** *Brit.* A lawyer who is not a member of the bar and who may be heard only in the lower courts.

so•lic•i•tous (sə-lĭs'ə-təs) *adj.* **1.** Concerned; attentive. **2.** Eager. [L *sollicitus,* thoroughly moved, agitated.] **—so•lic'i•tous•ly** *adv.* **—so•lic'i•tous•ness** *n.*

so•lic•i•tude (sə-lĭs'ə-t/y/o͞od') *n.* The state of being solicitous; concern.

sol•id (sŏl'ĭd) *adj.* **1.** Not liquid or gaseous. **2.** Not hollowed out. **3.** Being the same substance throughout. **4.** Of or pertaining to three-dimensional geometric figures or bodies. **5.** Without breaks; continuous. **6.** Well-made. **7.** Forceful; hearty. **8.** Substantial. **9.** Sound; concrete. **10.** Upstanding and dependable. *—n.* **1.** A solid substance. **2.** A geometric figure having three dimensions. [< L *solidus.*] **—so•lid'i•ty** (sə-lĭd'ə-tē), **sol'id•ness** *n.* **—sol'id•ly** *adv.*

sol•i•dar•i•ty (sŏl'ə-dăr'ə-tē) *n.* Unity of purpose, interest, or sympathy.

so•lid•i•fy (sə-lĭd'ə-fī') *v.* **-fied, -fying.** To make or become solid. **—so•lid'i•fi•ca'tion** *n.*

sol•id-state (sŏl'ĭd-stāt') *adj.* **1.** Of or involving the physical properties of solid materials, esp. the electromagnetic, thermodynamic, and structural properties of crystalline solids. **2.** Based on or using semiconducting materials.

so•lil•o•quize (sə-lĭl'ə-kwīz') *v.* **-quized, -quizing.** To utter a soliloquy.

so•lil•o•quy (sə-lĭl'ə-kwē) *n., pl.* **-quies. 1.** A dramatic discourse in which a character expresses his thoughts verbally without addressing a listener. **2.** The act of talking to oneself. [LL *sōliloquium.*]

sol•ip•sism (sŏl'əp-sĭz'əm, sō'ləp-) *n.* The theory that the self is the only reality. [L *sōlus,* alone + *ipse,* self + -ISM.] **—sol'ip•sist** *n.* **—sol'ip•sis'tic** *adj.*

sol•i•taire (sŏl'ə-târ') *n.* **1.** A gemstone set alone, as in a ring. **2.** A card game played by one person. [< L *sōlitārius,* solitary.]

sol•i•tar•y (sŏl'ə-tĕr'ē) *adj.* **1.** Existing or living alone. **2.** Happening or done alone. **3.** Secluded. **4.** Lonely. **5.** Single; sole. [L *sōlus,* alone.] **—sol'i•tar'i•ness** *n.*

sol•i•tude (sŏl'ə-t/y/o͞od') *n.* **1.** The state of being alone. **2.** A lonely or secluded place. [< L *sōlus,* alone.]

soln solution.

so•lo (sō'lō) *n., pl.* **-los. 1.** A musical composition for an individual voice or instrument, with or without accompaniment. **2.** Any performance accomplished by a single individual. *—v.* To perform alone, esp. to fly an airplane without an instructor. [< L *sōlus,* alone.] **—so'lo** *adj.* & *adv.* **—so'lo•ist** *n.*

Sol•o•mon (sŏl'ə-mən). King of Israel in the 10th century B.C.; noted for his wisdom.

so long. *Informal.* Good-by.

sol•stice (sŏl'stəs, sōl'-) *n.* Either of two times of the year when the sun has no apparent northward or southward motion. [< L *sōlstitium.*] **—sol•sti'tial** (-stĭsh'əl) *adj.*

sol•u•ble (sŏl'yə-bəl) *adj.* **1.** Capable of being dissolved, esp. easily dissolved. **2.** Capable of being solved. [< L *solvere,* to loosen.] **—sol'u•bil'i•ty** *n.* **—sol'u•bly** *adv.*

sol•ute (sŏl'yo͞ot', sō'lo͞ot') *n.* A substance dissolved in another substance, usually the component of a solution present in the lesser amount. *—adj.* In solution; dissolved. [L *solūtus,* pp of *solvere,* to loosen.]

so•lu•tion (sə-lo͞o'shən) *n.* **1.** A spontaneously forming homogeneous mixture of two or more substances, retaining its constitution in subdivision to molecular volumes and having various possible proportions of the constituents. **2.** The process of forming such a mixture. **3.** The state of being dissolved. **4.** The method or process of solving a problem. **5.** The answer to or disposition of a problem. [< L *solūtus.* See **solute.**]

solv•a•ble (sŏl'və-bəl) *adj.* Capable of being solved. **—solv'a•bil'i•ty** *n.*

solve (sŏlv) *v.* **solved, solving.** To find a solution to (a problem). [< L *solvere,* to loosen.]

sol•vent (sŏl'vənt) *adj.* **1.** Able to meet financial obligations. **2.** Capable of dissolving another substance. —*n. Chem.* **1.** The component of a solution that is present in excess or that undergoes no change of state. **2.** A liquid capable of dissolving another substance. [< L *solvere,* to loosen.] —**sol'ven•cy** *n.*

So•ma•li•a (sō-mä'lē-ə). A republic of E Africa. Pop. about 2,000,000. Cap. Mogadishu.

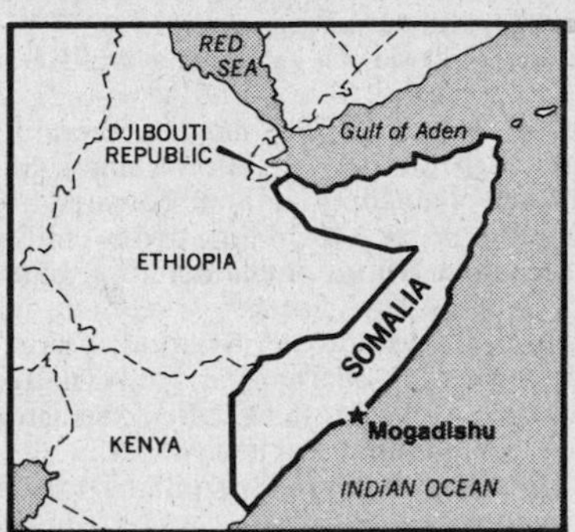

Somalia

so•mat•ic (sə-măt'ĭk) *adj.* Of or pertaining to the body, esp. as distinguished from a bodily part, the mind, or the environment. [< Gk *sōma,* body.]

som•ber (sŏm'bər) *adj.* Also **som•bre. 1.** Dark; gloomy. **2.** Melancholy; dismal. [< VL **subombrāre,* to shade.] —**som'ber•ly** *adv.*

som•bre•ro (sŏm-brâr'ō) *n., pl.* **-ros.** A broad-brimmed Spanish or Mexican hat. [< VL **subombrāre,* to shade.]

some (sŭm) *adj.* **1.** Being an unspecified number or part: *Some laws are bad.* **2.** Being unknown or unspecified by name: *Some fool laughed.* **3.** *Informal.* Remarkable: *He is some skier.* —*pron.* **1.** An unspecified number or portion. **2.** An indefinite additional quantity: *three and some.* —*adv.* **1.** Approximately: *some 40 people.* **2.** *Informal.* Somewhat. [< OE *sum,* one, a certain one. See **sem-¹.**]

-some¹. *comb. form.* Being or tending to be: **burdensome.** [< OE *-sum.*]

-some². *comb. form.* Body: **chromosome.** [< Gk *sōma,* body.]

-some³. *comb. form.* A group of. Used with numerals: **threesome.** [< SOME.]

some•bod•y (sŭm'bŏd'ē, -bŭd'ē, -bə-dē) *pron.* An unspecified person; someone. —*n. Informal.* A person of importance.

some•day (sŭm'dā') *adv.* At a future time.

some•how (sŭm'hou') *adv.* In a way not specified or known.

some•one (sŭm'wŭn', -wən) *pron.* Some person; somebody.

some•place (sŭm'plās') *adv. Informal.* Somewhere.

som•er•sault (sŭm'ər-sôlt') *n.* An acrobatic stunt in which the body rolls in a complete circle, heels over head. [< OProv **sobresaut.*] —**som'er•sault'** *v.*

some•thing (sŭm'thĭng) *pron.* An unspecified thing. —*n.* An important person or thing.

some•time (sŭm'tīm') *adv.* At an indefinite time. —*adj.* **1.** Having been at some prior time; former. **2.** *Nonstandard.* Occasional.

some•times (sŭm'tīmz') *adv.* Upon occasion; now and then.

some•way (sŭm'wā') *adv.* Also **some•ways** (-wāz'). *Informal.* Somehow.

some•what (sŭm'hwăt, sŭm-hwăt') *adv.* To some extent; rather. —*n.* Some amount, part, or degree: *He is somewhat of a fool.*

some•where (sŭm'hwĕr') *adv.* **1.** At, in, or to a place not specified or known; someplace. **2.** At or to some unspecified point in time, amount, or degree. —*n.* An unknown or unspecified place.

som•nam•bu•lism (sŏm-năm'byə-lĭz'əm) *n.* Walking while asleep or in a sleeplike condition. —**som•nam'bu•list** *n.*

somni-. *comb. form.* Sleep. [< L *somnus,* sleep.]

som•no•lent (sŏm'nə-lənt) *adj.* **1.** Drowsy; sleepy. **2.** Inducing or tending to induce sleep; soporific. [< L *somnus,* sleep.] —**som'no•lence** *n.* —**som'no•lent•ly** *adv.*

son (sŭn) *n.* **1.** A male offspring. **2.** Any male descendant. **3. the Son.** The second person of the Trinity, Christ. [< OE *sunu.* See **seu-³.**]

so•nar (sō'när') *n.* A system using transmitted and reflected acoustic waves to detect and locate submerged objects. [So(und) na(vigation) r(anging).]

so•na•ta (sō-nä'tä) *n. Mus.* An instrumental composition consisting of three or four movements. [It.]

song (sông, sŏng) *n.* **1.** Sound produced by singing. **2.** A brief musical composition for singing. **3.** The act of singing. **4.** A lyric poem or ballad. [< OE *sang.* See **sengwh-.**] —**song'ful** *adj.* —**song'ful•ly** *adv.*

song•bird (sông'bûrd', sŏng'-) *n.* A bird with a melodious song or call.

song•ster (sông'stər, sŏng'-) *n.* One that sings.

son•ic (sŏn'ĭk) *adj.* Of or relating to sound or its speed of propagation. [< L *sonus,* sound.]

sonic boom. A loud, transient explosive sound caused by the shock wave preceding an aircraft traveling at supersonic speeds.

son-in-law (sŭn'ĭn-lô') *n., pl.* **sons-in-law** (sŭnz'-). The husband of one's daughter.

son•net (sŏn'ĭt) *n.* A 14-line poetic form embodying the statement and resolution of a single theme. [< OProv *sonet.*]

so•no•rous (sə-nôr'əs, sə-nōr'-, sŏn'ər-) *adj.* **1.** Producing sound. **2.** Producing a full, rich sound when struck, as a gong. **3.** Impressive. [< It *sonāre,* to sound.] —**so•nor'i•ty** *n.*

soon (so͞on) *adv.* **1.** In the near future. **2.** Promptly. **3.** Early. **4.** Readily. [< OE *sōna* < Gmc **sǣnō.*]

Usage: *No sooner* is preferably followed by *than,* rather than by *when,* as in the following typical example: *No sooner had she come than the maid knocked.*

soot (so͝ot, sŭt, so͞ot) *n.* A fine dispersion of black particles, chiefly carbon, produced by the incomplete combustion of fuels. [< OE *sōt.* See **sed-.**] —**soot'y** *adj.*

sooth (so͞oth) *n. Archaic.* Truth. [< OE *sōth.* See **es-.**]

soothe (so͞o*th*) *v.* **soothed, soothing. 1.** To calm; mollify; placate. **2.** To ease or relieve the pain of. [< OE *sōth,* truth, SOOTH.] —**sooth'er** *n.*

sooth•say•er (so͞oth'sā'ər) *n.* One who foretells events.

sop (sŏp) *v.* **sopped, sopping. 1.** To dip, soak, or steep in a liquid; saturate. **2.** To take up by absorption. —*n.* **1.** A bit of food soaked in a liquid. **2.** Something yielded to placate; a bribe. [< OE *sopp,* dipped bread.]

soph. sophomore.

soph•ism (sŏf'ĭz'əm) *n.* **1.** A plausible but fallacious argument. **2.** Any deceptive or fallacious argumentation. [< Gk *sophisma,* acquired skill, clever device.]

soph•ist (sŏf'ĭst) *n.* One skillful in devious argumentation. [< Gk *sophistēs,* expert, deviser.]

so•phis•tic (sə-fĭs'tĭk) *adj.* Also **so•phis•ti•cal** (-tĭ-kəl). **1.** Of or characteristic of sophists. **2.** Specious; fallacious.

so•phis•ti•cat•ed (sə-fĭs'tĭ-kā'tĭd) *adj.* **1.** Lacking natural simplicity or naiveté. **2.** Complex or complicated. **3.** Suitable for the tastes of sophisticates. [< Gk *sophistēs,* SOPHIST.] —**so•phis'ti•cate** (-kĭt) *n.* —**so•phis'ti•ca'tion** *n.*

soph•is•try (sŏf'əs-trē) *n., pl.* **-tries.** Plausible but misleading or fallacious argumentation.

Soph•o•cles (sŏf'ə-klēz'). 496?–406 B.C. Athenian tragic poet. —**Soph'o•cle'an** *adj.*

soph•o•more (sŏf'ə-môr') *n.* A second-year student in a four-year American college or high school. [Prob < earlier *sophumer,* arguments.]

so•po•rif•ic (sŏp'ə-rĭf'ĭk) *adj.* **1.** Inducing sleep. **2.** Drowsy. [< L *sopor,* sleep.] —**so'po•rif'ic** *n.*

so•pran•o (sə-prăn'ō, -prä'nō) *n., pl.* **-os. 1.** The highest natural human voice, found in some women and boys. **2.** A singer having such a voice. **3.** A part for such a voice. [< It *sopra,* above.] —**so•pran'o** *adj.*

sor•cer•y (sôr'sər-ē) *n.* Black magic; witchcraft. [< VL **sortiārius,* caster of lots.] —**sor'cer•er** *n.* —**sor'cer•ess** *fem.n.*

sor•did (sôr'dĭd) *adj.* **1.** Filthy; foul. **2.** Squalid; wretched. **3.** Vile; base. **4.** Grasping; selfish. [< L *sordidus.*] —**sor'did•ly** *adv.* —**sor'did•ness** *n.*

sore (sôr, sōr) *adj.* **sorer, sorest. 1.** Painful; tender. **2.** Feeling physical pain; hurting. **3.** Causing sorrow or distress; grievous. —*n.* An open skin lesion, wound, or ulcer. [< OE *sār.* See **sai-.**] —**sore'ly** *adv.* —**sore'ness** *n.*

sor•ghum (sôr'gəm, sōr'-) *n.* A cereal grass cultivated for grain, forage, or as a source of syrup. [< VL **syricum (grānum),* "Syrian (grain)."]

so•ror•i•ty (sə-rôr'ə-tē, sə-rōr'-) *n., pl.* **-ties.** A social club for female students, as at a college. [< L *soror,* sister.]

sor•rel¹ (sôr'əl) *n.* Any of several plants with acid-tasting leaves. [< OF *sur,* sour.]

sor•rel² (sôr'əl) *n.* **1.** Yellowish or reddish brown. **2.** A horse of this color. [< OF *sor,* red-brown.] —**sor'rel** *adj.*

sor•row (sŏr'ō, sôr'ō) *n.* **1.** Mental suffering because of injury or loss. **2.** A misfortune. **3.** Grief. —*v.* To feel or display sorrow; grieve. [< OE *sorh, sorg,* anxiety, sorrow. See **swergh-.**] —**sor'row•ful** *adj.* —**sor'row•ful•ly** *adv.* —**sor'row•ful•ness** *n.*

sor•ry (sŏr'ē, sôr'ē) *adj.* **-rier, -riest. 1.** Feeling or expressing sympathy or regret. **2.** Poor; paltry. **3.** Grievous; sad. [< OE *sārig,* painful, sad. See **sai-.**] —**sor'ri•ness** *n.*

sort (sôrt) *n.* **1.** A group or collection of similar persons or things; class; kind. **2.** Type; quality. **3.** Manner; style. —*v.* To arrange according to class, kind, or size; classify. [Prob < L *sors (sort-),* lot, fortune.]

Usage: *Sort* (noun), in written usage, usually takes a singular modifier and verb: *This sort of problem is not new.* In the plural: *These sorts of problems are not new.* An alternative form, *these sort of problems are,* is more common to speech. *All sort of problems* (for *all sorts*) has less standing.

sor•tie (sôr'tē) *n.* **1.** A sally by besieged forces upon the besiegers. **2.** A single flight of an airplane on a combat mission. [F, "a going out."]

so-so (sō'sō') *adv.* Indifferently; passably.

sot (sŏt) *n.* A chronic drunkard. [< ML *sottus.*] **—sot'tish** *adj.* **—sot'tish•ly** *adv.*

So•tho (sō'thō) *n.* A group of Bantu languages spoken in Lesotho, Botswana, and South Africa.

sou•brette (so͞o-brĕt') *n.* A lady's maid in comedies or comic opera. [< Prov *soubret,* conceited.]

souf•flé (so͞o-flā') *n.* A light, fluffy baked dish made with egg yolks and beaten egg whites. [< F *souffler,* to puff up.]

sough (sŭf, sou) *v.* To make a soft murmuring or rustling sound. [< OE *swōgan.*] **—sough** *n.*

sought (sôt). *p.t.* & *p.p.* of **seek.**

soul (sōl) *n.* **1.** An immaterial entity said to be the animating and vital principle in man. **2.** A person: *a trusting soul.* **3.** The vital core of something. **4.** An inspiring leader: *the soul of our enterprise.* [< OE *sāwol* < Gmc *saiwalō.] **—soul'less** *adj.* **—soul'less•ness** *n.*

soul•ful (sōl'fəl) *adj.* Full of or expressing deep feeling. **—soul'ful•ly** *adv.* **—soul'ful•ness** *n.*

sound¹ (sound) *n.* **1.** A vibratory disturbance, with frequency in the approximate range between 20 and 20,000 cycles per second, capable of being heard. **2. a.** The sensation stimulated in the organs of hearing by such a disturbance. **b.** Such sensations collectively. **3.** An articulation made by the vocal apparatus. **4.** Audible material recorded, as for a motion picture. *—v.* **1.** To make or cause to make a sound. **2.** To seem to be. **3.** To summon, announce, or signal by a sound: *sound a warning.* [< L *sonus.*]

sound² (sound) *adj.* **1.** In good condition. **2.** Healthy. **3.** Solid; unshakable. **4.** Reliable. **5.** Sensible and correct. **6.** Thorough; complete. **7.** Unbroken; undisturbed: *a sound sleep.* **8.** Upright; honorable. [< OE *gesund.* See **swento-.**] **—sound'ly** *adv.* **—sound'ness** *n.*

sound³ (sound) *n.* **1.** A body of water larger than a strait or channel, connecting larger bodies of water. **2.** A long, wide ocean inlet. [< OE *sund,* swimming.]

sound⁴ (sound) *v.* **1.** To measure the depth of (water). **2.** To try to learn the opinions of a person. **3.** To dive swiftly downward, as a whale. [< OF *sonde,* a sounding line.] **—sound'er** *n.*

sound effects. Imitative sounds produced artificially for theatrical purposes.

sound•ing (soun'dĭng) *n.* **1.** The act of one that sounds. **2.** A measured depth of water.

sounding board. **1.** A thin board that acts to reinforce the sound in a musical instrument, as a violin or piano. **2.** One whose reactions serve as a test of the effectiveness or acceptability of one's ideas.

sound•proof (sound'pro͞of') *adj.* Not penetrable by audible sound. *—v.* To make soundproof.

sound•track (sound'trăk') *n.* The narrow strip at one side of a motion-picture film that carries the sound recording.

soup (so͞op) *n.* A liquid food prepared from meat, fish, or vegetable stock, often with various other ingredients added. *—v.* **—soup up.** *Slang.* To add greater speed potential to (an engine). [< OF *soupe.*]

sour (sour) *adj.* **1.** Having a sharp or acid taste. **2.** Spoiled; rank. **3.** Bad-tempered; disagreeable. *—v.* To make or become sour. [< OE *sūr.* See **sūro-.**] **—sour'ly** *adv.* **—sour'ness** *n.*

source (sôrs, sōrs) *n.* **1.** A point of origin. **2.** The beginning of a stream of water. **3.** One that supplies information. [< OF *sourdre,* to rise.]

sour•puss (sour'po͝os') *n. Slang.* A gloomy or sullen person.

sour salt. Crystals of citric acid used in cooking.

souse (sous) *v.* **soused, sousing. 1.** To plunge into a liquid. **2.** To drench. **3.** To steep in a mixture, as in pickling. **4.** *Slang.* To make intoxicated. *—n.* **1.** The act or process of sousing. **2.** Food steeped in pickle, as pigs' feet. **3.** *Slang.* A drunkard. [ME *sousen,* to souse, to pickle.]

south (south) *n.* **1. a.** The direction along a meridian to the right of an observer facing in the direction of the earth's rotation. **b.** The point on the mariner's compass 180° clockwise from north. **2.** Often **South. a.** The S part of the earth. **b.** The S part of any country or region. **—the South.** In the U.S., the states S of Pennsylvania and the Ohio River and E of the Mississippi. *—adj.* **1.** To or from the south. **2. South.** Designating the S part of a country, continent, or other geographical area: *South America.* *—adv.* In, from, or toward the south. [< OE *sūth.* See **sāwel-.**]

South Africa, Republic of. A country in the extreme S of Africa. Pop. 17,474,000. Caps. Pretoria and Cape Town.

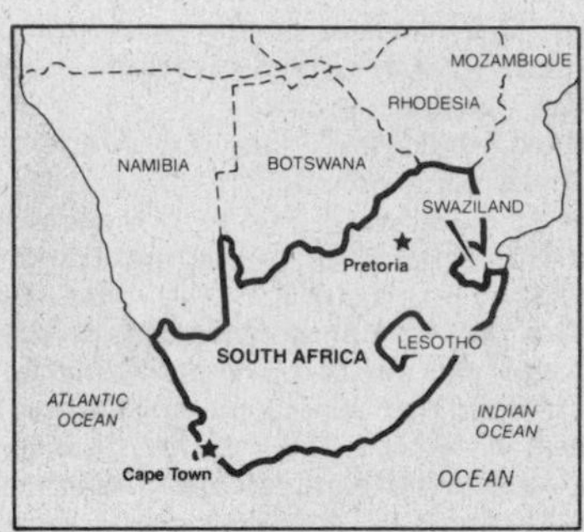

South Africa

South African. **1.** A native of the Republic of South Africa, esp. one of European descent; an Afrikaner. **2.** Of or pertaining to South Africa or its inhabitants.

South African Dutch. **1.** See **Boer.** **2.** Afrikaans.

South America. The southern of the two continents of the W Hemisphere. **—South American.**

South•amp•ton (south-hămp'tən, sou-thămp'-). A city and major seaport in England. Pop. 210,000.

South Bend. A city of N Indiana. Pop. 132,000.

south•bound (south'bound') *adj.* Going toward the south.

South Carolina. A state of the SE U.S. Pop. 2,591,000. Cap. Columbia. **—South Car'o•lin'i•an** (-lĭn'ē-ən).

South China Sea. A section of the Pacific SE of China.

South Dakota. A Middle Western state of the U.S. Pop. 666,000. Cap. Pierre. **—South Dakotan.**

South•down (south'doun') *n.* Any of a breed of small, hornless sheep of English origin, having dense, short, fine-textured wool. [< SOUTH DOWNS.]

South Downs. A range of hills extending W to E in SE England.

south•east (south-ēst') *n.* **1.** The direction halfway between south and east. **2.** Any area or region lying in this direction. *—adj.* To, from, or in the southeast. *—adv.* From or toward the southeast. **—south•east'ern** *adj.*

Southeast Asia. A region generally considered to include Indochina, Malaysia, Indonesia, and the Philippines.

south•east•er (south-ē'stər) *n.* A storm or gale blowing from the southeast.

south•east•er•ly (south-ē'stər-lē) *adj.* **1.** Toward the southeast. **2.** From the southeast. **—south•east'er•ly** *adv.*

south•er (sou'*th*ər) *n.* A strong wind coming from the south.

south•er•ly (sŭ*th*'ər-lē) *adj.* **1.** Toward the south. **2.** From the south. **—south'er•ly** *adv.*

south•ern (sŭ*th*'ərn) *adj.* **1.** Toward, in, or facing the south. **2.** Coming from the south. **3.** Often **Southern.** Of or characteristic of southern regions or the South.

Southern Cross. A constellation, Crux.

south•ern•er (sŭ*th*'ər-nər) *n.* **1.** A native or inhabitant of the South. **2.** Often **Southerner.** A native or inhabitant of the S U.S.

Southern Hemisphere. The half of the earth south of the equator.

southern lights. The **aurora australis.**

south•ern•most (sŭ*th*'ərn-mōst') *adj.* Farthest south.

south•ern•wood (sŭ*th*'ərn-wo͝od') *n.* An aromatic woody plant native to Europe, having finely divided grayish foliage.

Southern Yemen. A former name for the People's Democratic Republic of Yemen.

South Korea. The unofficial name for the Republic of Korea. See **Korea.**

south•paw (south'pô') *n. Informal.* A left-handed player, especially a left-handed baseball pitcher. *—adj. Informal.* Left-handed.

South Pole. **1.** The southern end of the earth's axis of rotation. **2.** The celestial zenith of the heavens as viewed from the south terrestrial pole. **3. south pole.** The south-seeking magnetic pole of a magnet.

South Sea Islands. The islands of the South Pacific.

South Seas. The South Pacific.

South Vietnam. The unofficial name for the former Republic of Vietnam. See **Vietnam.**

south•ward (south'wərd) *adv.* Also **south•wards** (south'wərdz). Toward the south. *—adj.* Toward, facing, or in the south. **—south'ward•ly** *adj.* & *adv.*

south•west (south-wĕst') *n.* **1.** The direction halfway between south and west. **2.** Any area or region lying in this direction. **—the Southwest.** A region of the SW U.S. including New Mexico, Texas, Arizona, California, Nevada, Utah, and Colorado. *—adj.* To, from, or in the southwest. *—adv.* In, from, or toward the southwest. **—south•west'ern** *adj.*

south•west•er (south-wĕs'tər) *n.* Also **sou•west•er** (sou-wĕs'tər). **1.** A storm or strong wind from the southwest. **2.** A sailor's waterproof hat with a broad brim to protect the neck.

south•west•er•ly (south-wĕs'tər-lē) *adj.* **1.** Toward the southwest. **2.** From the southwest. **—south•west'er•ly** *adv.*

Sou•tine (so͞o-tēn'), **Chaim.** 1894–1943. Lithuanian painter.

sou•ve•nir (so͞o'və-nîr') *n.* Something serving as a remembrance; a memento. [< L *subvenīre,* to come to aid, come to mind.]

sov. sovereign.

sov•er•eign (sŏv'ər-ən) *n.* **1.** The chief of state in a monarchy. **2.** A British gold coin worth one pound. *—adj.* **1.** Paramount; supreme.

2. Having supreme rank or power. 3. Independent: *a sovereign state.* 4. Unsurpassed; excellent. [< VL **superānus.*]

sov•er•eign•ty (sŏv'ər-ən-tē) *n.* 1. Supremacy of authority or rule. 2. Royal rank, authority, or power. 3. Complete independence and self-government.

so•vi•et (sō'vē-ĕt', sō-vyĕt', sŏv'ē-ĕt) *n.* In the Soviet Union, one of the popularly elected legislative assemblies. *—adj.* 1. Of or pertaining to a soviet. 2. **Soviet.** Of or pertaining to the U.S.S.R. [Russ *sovet,* "council."]

Soviet Union. See **Union of Soviet Socialist Republics.**

sow[1] (sō) *v.* **sowed, sown** (sōn) or **sowed, sowing.** 1. To scatter (seed) over the ground for growing. 2. To strew with seed. 3. To propagate. [< OE *sāwan.* See **sē-**.] **—sow'er** *n.*

sow[2] (sou) *n.* An adult female pig. [< OE *sugu.* See **su-**.]

sox. Alternate *pl.* of **sock**[1].

soy (soi) *n.* 1. The soybean. 2. Also **soy sauce.** A brown, salty liquid condiment made from fermented soybeans. [Jap *shō-yu.*]

soy•bean (soi'bēn') *n.* An Asian bean cultivated for its nutritious seeds.

SP shore patrol; shore police.

sp. 1. special. 2. species. 3. spelling.

Sp. Spain; Spanish.

spa (spä) *n.* 1. A mineral spring. 2. A resort area with such a spring. [< *Spa,* town in Belgium.]

space (spās) *n.* 1. a. A set of elements or points satisfying specified geometric conditions. b. The three-dimensional field of everyday experience or its infinite extension. 2. The expanse in which the solar system, stars, and galaxies exist; the universe. 3. Broadly, the distance between two points or the area or volume between specified boundaries. 4. A particular area. 5. a. A period or interval of time. b. A little while: *for a space.* *—v.* **spaced, spacing.** To organize or arrange with spaces between. [< L *spatium,* space, distance.]

space•craft (spās'krăft, -kräft) *n.,pl.* **-craft.** A vehicle designed to be launched into space.

space•ship (spās'shĭp) *n.* A spacecraft.

space shuttle. A space vehicle designed to transport astronauts to and from between Earth and an orbiting space station.

space station. A large manned satellite designed for permanent orbit around Earth.

space suit. A protective pressure suit having an independent air supply and other devices designed to permit the wearer relatively free movement in space.

space-time (spās'tīm') *n.* The four-dimensional continuum of one temporal and three spatial coordinates, in which any event or physical object is located.

spa•cial. Variant of **spatial.**

spa•cious (spā'shəs) *adj.* 1. Having much space; extensive. 2. Vast in range or scope. **—spa'cious•ly** *adv.* **—spa'cious•ness** *n.*

spade[1] (spād) *n.* A digging tool having a thick handle and a flat blade. *—v.* **spaded, spading.** To dig with a spade. [< OE *spadu.* See **sphē-**.]

spade[2] (spād) *n.* Any of a suit of playing cards marked with a symbol in the shape of an inverted heart with a short stalk. [It *spada,* "broad sword."]

spa•ghet•ti (spə-gĕt'ē) *n.* An Italian pasta consisting of long strings of flour paste. [< It *spago,* string.]

Spain (spān). A country of W Europe. Pop. 30,903,000. Cap. Madrid.

spait. Variant of **spate.**

spake (spāk). *Archaic. p.t.* of **speak.**

span[1] (spăn) *n.* 1. The extent or measure of space between two points or extremities. 2. Something that extends over or across. 3. *Archaic.* A unit of measure equal to the length of the fully extended hand from the tip of the thumb to the tip of the little finger, generally considered as nine inches. 4. A period of time: *a life span.* *—v.* **spanned, spanning.** 1. To measure by or as by the fully extended hand. 2. To reach or extend over or from one side to the other. [< OE. See **spen-**.]

span[2] (spăn) *n.* A pair of animals, such as oxen, matched in size, strength, or color. [MDu *spannen.*]

span[3] (spăn). *Archaic. p.t. & p.p.* of **spin.**

Span. Spanish.

span•gle (spăng'gəl) *n.* A small piece of bright, shiny metal used on a garment for decoration. *—v.* **-gled, -gling.** To adorn with or as with spangles. [< MDu *spange,* ornament, clasp.] **—span'gly** *adv.*

Span•iard (spăn'yərd) *n.* A native or inhabitant of Spain.

span•iel (spăn'yəl) *n.* A dog with drooping ears, short legs, and a silky, wavy coat. [< OF *espaignol,* "Spanish."]

Span•ish (spăn'ĭsh) *n.* 1. The Romance language of Spain and Spanish America. 2. **the Spanish.** The inhabitants of Spain. **—Span'ish** *adj.*

Spanish America. The parts of the W Hemisphere inhabited mostly by Spanish-speaking people.

Span•ish-A•mer•i•can (spăn'ĭsh-ə-mĕr'ĭ-kən) *n.* 1. A native or inhabitant of a country of Spanish America. 2. A person of Spanish descent who lives in the U.S. **—Span'ish-A•mer'i•can** *adj.*

Spanish moss. A plant of the SE U.S. and tropical America that grows on trees in long, threadlike tangled masses.

spank (spăngk) *v.* To slap on the buttocks with the open hand. *—n.* A slap on the buttocks.

spank•ing (spăng'kĭng) *adj.* 1. *Informal.* Exceptional of its kind in size, quality, or, esp., smartness. 2. Bright; fast: *a spanking pace.* [?]

spar[1] (spär) *n.* A wooden or metal pole used to support sail rigging. [< ON *sperra,* beam.]

spar[2] (spär) *v.* **sparred, sparring.** 1. To go through the motions of boxing. 2. To bandy words about in argument. [< OE *sperran,* to strike.]

spare (spâr) *v.* **spared, sparing.** 1. a. To treat mercifully. b. To refrain from harming or destroying. 2. To save or relieve (one) from pain, trouble, etc. 3. To use frugally. 4. To do without. *—adj.* **sparer, sparest.** 1. a. Ready when needed. b. Extra: *spare cash.* c. Unoccupied: *spare time.* 2. a. Without excess; meager. b. Thin or lean. *—n.* 1. A replacement, as a tire, reserved for future use. 2. The knocking down of all ten bowling pins with two successive rolls of the ball. [< OE *sparian* < Gmc **sparōjan.*] **—spare'ness** *n.*

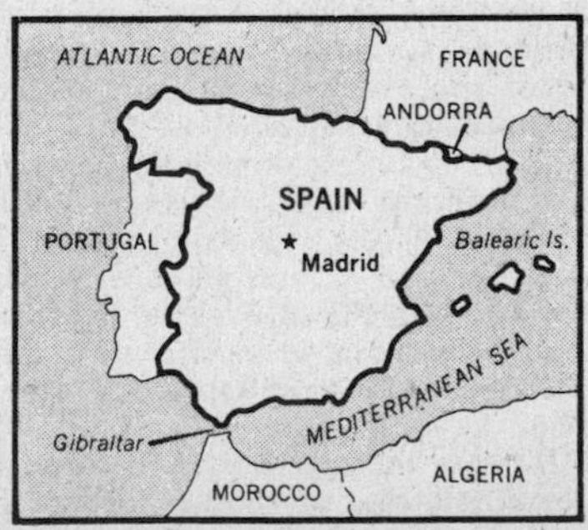

Spain

spare•ribs (spâr'rĭbz') *pl.n.* A cut of pork consisting usually of the lower ribs with the meat closely trimmed. [Inverted var of LG *ribbespēr.*]

spar•ing (spâr'ĭng) *adj.* Thrifty; frugal.

spark[1] (spärk) *n.* 1. An incandescent particle, as one thrown off from a burning substance or resulting from friction; ember. 2. a. A flash of light, esp. a flash produced by electric discharge. b. A short pulse or flow of electric current. 3. Something, as a quality or factor, with latent potential; seed: *the spark of genius.* *—v.* 1. To give off sparks. 2. To set in motion; activate; ignite. [< OE *spearca, spærca.*]

spark[2] (spärk) *n.* 1. A young dandy. 2. A suitor. *—v.* To court or woo.

spar•kle (spär'kəl) *v.* **-kled, -kling.** 1. To give off or reflect flashes of light; glitter. 2. To effervesce. *—n.* 1. A small spark or gleaming particle. 2. Animation; vivacity. 3. Effervescence. [< SPARK.] **—spar'kler** *n.*

spark plug. A device in an internal-combustion-engine cylinder that ignites the fuel mixture by means of an electric spark.

spar•row (spăr'ō) *n.* Any of various small birds with grayish or brownish plumage. [< OE *spearwa.* See **sper-**[3].]

sparse (spärs) *adj.* **sparser, sparsest.** Growing or settled at widely spaced intervals; not dense or crowded. [L *sparsus,* pp of *spargere,* to strew, scatter.] **—spar'si•ty** (spär'sə-tē) *n.*

Spar•ta (spär'tə). A city state of ancient Greece, renowned for military prowess and austerity.

Spar•tan (spärt'n) *adj.* 1. Of or pertaining to Sparta or its people. 2. Resembling the Spartans; austere. *—n.* 1. A citizen of Sparta. 2. Someone of Spartan character.

spasm (spăz'əm) *n.* 1. A sudden, involuntary muscular contraction. 2. Any sudden burst of activity, emotion, etc. [< Gk *spasmos* < *span,* to draw, pull.]

spas•mod•ic (spăz-mŏd'ĭk) *adj.* 1. Pertaining to, affected by, or having the character of a spasm; convulsive. 2. Happening intermittently; fitful. **—spas•mod'i•cal•ly** *adv.*

spas•tic (spăs'tĭk) *adj.* Continuously convulsing or contracting. *—n.* A person suffering from chronic spasms. [< Gk *spastikos* < *span,* to draw, pull.] **—spas'ti•cal•ly** *adv.*

spat[1] (spăt). *p.t. & p.p.* of **spit**[1].

spat[2] (spăt) *n.* A gaiter covering the upper shoe and ankle. [Short for earlier *spatterdash.*]

spat[3] (spăt) *n.* A brief, petty quarrel. [?] **—spat** *v.* **(spatted, spatting).**

spate, spait (spāt) *n.* A sudden flood, rush, or outpouring. [ME *spate.*]

spa•tial (spā'shəl) *adj.* Also **spa•cial.** Of or involving space.

spat•ter (spăt'ər) *v.* 1. To scatter in drops or small splashes. 2. To splash. 3. To fall with a splash or a splashing sound. *—n.* 1. The act of spattering. 2. A spot or stain of something spattered. 3. A spattering sound.

spat•u•la (spăch'ə-lə) *n.* A small flat-bladed implement used to spread or mix plaster, paint, etc. [< Gk *spathē,* blade, broad sword.]

spav•in (spăv'ən) *n.* A disease affecting the hock joint of horses. [< OF *espavin.*] **—spav'ined** *adj.*

spawn (spôn) *n.* 1. The eggs of aquatic animals such as oysters, fish, or frogs. 2. Offspring produced in large numbers. —*v.* 1. To produce spawn. 2. To produce offspring in large numbers. 3. To bring forth. [< NF *espaundre,* to shed roe.]

spay (spā) *v.* To remove the ovaries of (a female animal). [< OF *espeer,* to cut with a sword.]

S.P.C.A. Society for the Prevention of Cruelty to Animals.

speak (spēk) *v.* **spoke, spoken, speaking.** 1. To utter words; talk. 2. To express oneself. 3. To deliver an address or lecture; make a speech. 4. To converse in or be able to converse in (a language). [< OE *specan.* See **spreg-**.]

speak•eas•y (spēk'ē'zē) *n., pl.* **-ies.** *Slang.* A place for the illegal sale of alcoholic drinks.

speak•er (spē'kər) *n.* 1. a. One who speaks. b. A spokesman. 2. One who delivers a public speech. 3. The presiding officer of a legislative assembly.

spear (spîr) *n.* 1. A sharply pointed weapon with a long shaft. 2. A sharp, barbed shaft for spearing fish. 3. A slender stalk, as of asparagus. —*v.* To pierce or stab with or as with a spear. [< OE *spere.* See **sper-¹**.]

spear•mint (spîr'mĭnt') *n.* A common mint widely used as flavoring.

spec. 1. special. 2. specification.

spe•cial (spĕsh'əl) *adj.* 1. Surpassing what is common or usual; exceptional. 2. Distinct among others of a kind. 3. Peculiar to a specific person or thing. 4. Having a specific function, application, etc. 5. Esteemed: *special friends.* 6. Additional; extra. —*n.* 1. Something arranged or designed for a particular service or occasion. 2. A featured attraction such as a reduced price: *a special on lamb chops.* 3. A single television production of unusual importance. [< L *speciālis,* special, of a particular kind.] —**spe'cial•ly** *adv.*

spe•cial•ist (spĕsh'ə-lĭst) *n.* One who has devoted himself to a particular branch of study or research.

spe•cial•ize (spĕsh'ə-līz') *v.* **-ized, -izing.** 1. To train or employ oneself in a special study or activity. 2. To adapt to a specific environment or function. —**spe'cial•i•za'tion** *n.*

special relativity. The physical theory of space and time developed by Albert Einstein.

spe•cial•ty (spĕsh'əl-tē) *n., pl.* **-ties.** 1. A special pursuit, occupation, service, etc. 2. An aspect of medicine to which physicians confine their practice after certification of special knowledge by examination. 3. A special feature or characteristic.

spe•cie (spē'shē, -sē) *n.* Coined money; coin. [L *(in) specie,* (in) kind.]

spe•cies (spē'shēz, -sēz) *n., pl.* **species.** 1. Kind; type; sort. 2. a. A category of similar, closely related organisms capable of interbreeding. b. A member of such a category. [L *speciēs,* a seeing, likeness, kind, species.]

specif. specifically.

spe•cif•ic (spə-sĭf'ĭk) *adj.* 1. Explicitly set forth; definite. 2. Pertaining to, characterizing, or distinguishing a species. 3. Special, distinctive, or unique, as a quality or attribute. —*n.* 1. A distinct quality, statement, attribute, etc. 2. A remedy intended for a particular disorder. [< L *speciēs,* kind, SPECIES.] —**spe•cif'i•cal•ly** *adv.*

spec•i•fi•ca•tion (spĕs'ə-fĭ-kā'shən) *n.* 1. Often **specifications.** A detailed description of materials, dimensions, and workmanship for something to be built, installed, or manufactured. 2. A specified item.

specific gravity. The ratio of the mass of a solid or liquid to the mass of an equal volume of distilled water at 4°C, or of a gas to an equal volume of air or hydrogen under prescribed conditions of temperature and pressure.

spec•i•fy (spĕs'ə-fī') *v.* **-fied, -fying.** 1. To state explicitly. 2. To include in a specification.

spec•i•men (spĕs'ə-mən) *n.* An individual, item, or part representative of a class or whole; example. [L, mark, token.]

spe•cious (spē'shəs) *adj.* Seemingly fair, attractive, sound, or true, but actually not so; deceptive. [< L *speciōsus,* good-looking.] —**spe'cious•ly** *adv.* —**spe'cious•ness** *n.*

speck (spĕk) *n.* 1. A small spot, mark, or discoloration. 2. A small bit or particle. —*v.* To mark with specks. [< OE *specca.*]

speck•le (spĕk'əl) *n.* A speck or small spot, esp. a natural marking. —*v.* **-led, -ling.** To mark or cover with or as with speckles. [MDu *spekkel.*]

spec•ta•cle (spĕk'tə-kəl) *n.* 1. A public performance or display. 2. A marvel or curiosity. 3. **spectacles.** A pair of eyeglasses. [< L *spectāre,* to look at.]

spec•tac•u•lar (spĕk-tăk'yə-lər) *adj.* Of the nature of a spectacle; unusual or sensational.

spec•ta•tor (spĕk'tā-tər) *n.* One who views an event; an observer or onlooker. [< L *spectāre,* look at.]

spec•ter (spĕk'tər) *n.* Also *chiefly Brit.* **spec•tre.** A phantom; apparition. [< L *spectrum,* appearance, image.]

spec•tral (spĕk'trəl) *adj.* 1. Of or resembling a specter. 2. Of, pertaining to, or produced by a spectrum.

spectro–. *comb. form.* Spectrum.

spec•tro•scope (spĕk'trə-skōp') *n. Phys.* Any of various instruments for resolving and observing or recording spectra. —**spec'tro•scop'ic** (-skŏp'ĭk), **spec'tro•scop'i•cal** *adj.* —**spec'tro•scop'i•cal•ly** *adv.*

spec•trum (spĕk'trəm) *n., pl.* **-tra** (-trə) or **-trums.** 1. The distribution of a characteristic of a physical system or phenomenon, esp. the distribution of energy emitted by a radiant source, as by an incandescent body, arranged in order of wavelengths. 2. A broad sequence or range of related qualities, ideas, etc. [L, appearance, image, form.]

spec•u•late (spĕk'yə-lāt') *v.* **-lated, -lating.** 1. To meditate on a given subject; reflect. 2. To engage in risky business transactions on the chance of great profit. [L *speculārī,* to spy out, watch, observe.] —**spec'u•la'tion** *n.* —**spec'u•la•tive** (-lə-tĭv, -lā'tĭv) *adj.*

speech (spēch) *n.* 1. The faculty or act of speaking. 2. Conversation; vocal communication. 3. A talk or public address. 4. A person's habitual manner of speaking. 5. The language or dialect of a nation or region. [< OE *spēc, sprǣc.* See **spreg-**.]

speech•less (spēch'lĭs) *adj.* 1. Lacking the faculty of speech. 2. Temporarily unable to speak. —**speech'less•ly** *adv.*

speed (spēd) *n.* 1. Rate of motion. 2. A rate of performance; swiftness of action. 3. Rapid movement. 4. A gear in a motor vehicle. 5. a. The sensitivity of a film, plate, or paper to light. b. The capacity of a lens to accumulate light. c. The time in which a camera shutter exposes film. —*v.* **sped** (spĕd) or **speeded, speeding.** 1. To move rapidly. 2. To accelerate; increase the speed of. 3. To drive at a high or illegal rate of speed. 4. To help to succeed; aid. [< OE *spēd,* success, prosperity. See **spēi-**.] —**speed'y** *adj.*

speed•ing (spē'dĭng) *adj.* Moving with speed. —*n.* The act of driving faster than is allowed by law.

speed•om•e•ter (spē-dŏm'ə-tər, spĭ-) *n.* An instrument for indicating speed or distance traveled.

speed•way (spēd'wā') *n.* 1. A course for automobile racing. 2. A road designed for fast-moving traffic.

speed•well (spēd'wĕl') *n.* A low-growing plant with small blue flowers.

spell¹ (spĕl) *v.* **spelled** or **spelt, spelling.** 1. To name or write in order the letters constituting (a word or part of a word). 2. To mean; signify. [< OF *espeller,* to read out.]

spell² (spĕl) *n.* 1. An incantational word or formula. 2. Compelling attraction; fascination. 3. A bewitched state. [< OE, story, fable. See **spel-²**.]

spell³ (spĕl) *n.* 1. A short, indefinite period of time. 2. *Informal.* A period of weather of a particular kind. 3. A short turn of work. 4. *Informal.* A period of illness or indisposition. —*v.* To relieve (someone) from work temporarily. [< OE *spelian,* to substitute.]

spell•bind (spĕl'bīnd') *v.* To hold under or as if under a spell; enchant.

spell•bind•er (spĕl'bīn'dər) *n.* One who holds others spellbound.

spell•bound (spĕl'bound') *adj.* Entranced; fascinated.

spell•er (spĕl'ər) *n.* 1. One who spells words. 2. A textbook to teach spelling.

spell•ing (spĕl'ĭng) *n.* 1. The forming of words with letters. 2. The way in which a word is spelled.

spelt (spĕlt). Alternate *p.t.* & *p.p.* of **spell¹**.

spe•lun•ker (spĭ-lŭng'kər, spē'lŭng-kər) *n.* One who explores and studies caves. [< Gk *spēlunx,* cave.]

spend (spĕnd) *v.* **spent, spending.** 1. To pay out (money). 2. To exhaust; wear out. 3. To pass (time). 4. To waste; squander. [< L *expendere,* to EXPEND, and < OF *despendre,* to dispend.] —**spend'er** *n.*

spending money. Cash for small personal needs.

spend•thrift (spĕnd'thrĭft') *n.* One who spends money wastefully. —*adj.* Wasteful or extravagant.

spent (spĕnt). *p.t.* & *p.p.* of **spend.** —*adj.* 1. Consumed; used up; expended. 2. Passed; over with. 3. Depleted of energy or strength; exhausted.

sperm (spûrm) *n.* 1. A male gamete or reproductive cell; spermatozoon. 2. The male fluid of fertilization; semen. [< Gk *sperma.*] —**sper•mat'ic** (spûr-măt'ĭk) *adj.*

spermato–. *comb. form.* 1. Sperm. 2. Seed.

sper•ma•to•gen•e•sis (spûr-măt'ə-jĕn'ə-sĭs, spûr'mə-tə-) *n.* The generation of sperm.

sper•ma•to•zo•on (spûr-măt'ə-zō'ən, spûr'mə-tə-zō'ən) *n., pl.* **-zoa** (-zō'ə). The fertilizing gamete of a male animal, usually a long nucleated cell with a thin, motile tail.

spew (spyōō) *v.* 1. To vomit. 2. To force out in a stream; eject. [< OE *spīwan* and *spīowan.* See **spyeu-**.]

sphe•noid (sfē'noid') *n.* The **sphenoid bone.** —*adj.* Also **sphe•noid•al** (sfē-noid'l). 1. Wedge-shaped. 2. Of or pertaining to the sphenoid bone.

sphenoid bone. A compound bone situated at the base of the skull.

sphere (sfîr) *n.* 1. A three-dimensional surface, all points of which are equidistant from a fixed point. 2. A spherical object or figure. 3. A planet, star, or other heavenly body. **4.** The sky, appearing as a hemisphere to an observer. **5.** The environment in which one exists or acts; range. [< Gk *sphaira.*] **—spher'i•cal** (sfîr'ĭ-kəl, sfĕr'-) *adj.* **—spher'i•cal•ly** *adv.* **—sphe•ric'i•ty** (sfîr-ĭs'ə-tē) *n.*

-sphere. *comb. form.* The shape of a sphere: **bathysphere.**

sphinc•ter (sfĭngk'tər) *n.* A ringlike muscle that normally maintains constriction of a bodily passage or orifice and relaxes as required by normal physiological functioning. [< Gk *sphinktēr,* that which binds tight.]

sphinx (sfĭnks) *n., pl.* **sphinxes** or **sphinges** (sfĭn'jēz'). **1.** An ancient Egyptian figure with the body of a lion and the head of a man, ram, or hawk. **2.** *Gk.Myth.* A winged monster that destroyed all who could not answer its riddle. **3.** Any mysterious or enigmatic person. [< Gk *Sphinx.*]

spice (spīs) *n.* **1.** An aromatic or pungent plant substance, as cinnamon or pepper, used as flavoring. **2.** Something that adds zest or flavor. [< LL *speciēs,* goods, spices.] **—spice** *v.* **(spiced, spicing). —spic'i•ly** *adv.* **—spic'i•ness** *n.* **—spic'y** *adj.*

spick-and-span (spĭk'ən-spăn') *adj.* **1.** Neat and clean. **2.** Brand-new. [Short for obs *spick and spannew.*]

spic•ule (spĭk'yo͞ol) *n.* A small needlelike structure or part. [L *spīculum.*] **—spic'u•lar, spic'u•late** (-yə-lĭt, -lāt') *adj.*

spi•der (spī'dər) *n.* **1.** Any of various eight-legged arachnids that have a body divided into two parts and that spin webs to trap insects. **2.** A long-handled frying pan, often with short legs. [< OE *spīthra.*] **—spi'der•y** *adj.*

spig•ot (spĭg'ət) *n.* **1.** A faucet. **2.** The vent plug of a cask. [ME.]

spike¹ (spīk) *n.* **1.** A heavy nail. **2.** A sharp-pointed projection. *—v.* **spiked, spiking. 1.** To secure or provide with a spike. **2.** To impale, pierce, or injure with a spike. **3.** To put an end to; thwart; block. **4.** *Slang.* To add alcoholic liquor to. [ME *spyk.*]

spike² (spīk) *n.* **1.** An ear of grain. **2.** A long cluster of stalkless or nearly stalkless flowers. [< L *spīca,* point, ear of grain.]

spike•nard (spīk'närd') *n.* An aromatic plant from which a fragrant ointment was obtained in ancient times.

spill (spĭl) *v.* **spilled** or **spilt** (spĭlt), **spilling. 1.** To cause or allow to run or fall out of a container. **2.** To shed (blood). **3.** To cause to fall. *—n.* **1.** An act of spilling. **2.** The amount spilled. **3.** A fall, as from a horse. [< OE *spillan,* to destroy, spill (blood). See **spel-¹.**]

spill•way (spĭl'wā') *n.* A channel for reservoir overflow.

spin (spĭn) *v.* **spun, spinning. 1.** To draw out and twist fibers into thread. **2.** To form thread or yarn in this manner. **3.** To form (a thread, web, etc.) by extruding a viscous substance. **4.** To relate, esp. imaginatively: *spin a story.* **5.** To twirl. **6.** To rotate rapidly; whirl. *—n.* **1.** A swift whirling motion. **2.** A state of mental confusion. **3.** A short excursion in a vehicle. **4.** The flight condition of an aircraft in a nose-down, spiraling, stalled descent. [< OE *spinnan.* See **spen-.**] **—spin'ner** *n.*

spin•ach (spĭn'ĭch) *n.* A plant cultivated for its dark-green edible leaves. [< Ar *isfānākh.*]

spi•nal (spī'nəl) *adj.* **1.** Of, pertaining to, or situated near the spine or spinal cord. **2.** Resembling a spine or spiny part. *—n.* A spinal anesthetic. **—spi'nal•ly** *adv.*

spinal canal. The canal formed by the successive openings in the vertebrae through which the spinal cord and its membranes pass.

spinal column. The columnar assemblage of vertebrae extending from the cranium to the coccyx or the end of the tail, encasing the spinal cord and forming the supporting axis of the body; the backbone.

spinal cord. The part of the central nervous system contained within the spinal canal.

spin•dle (spĭnd'l) *n.* **1.** A stick or rod used in spinning for twisting or winding thread. **2.** Any of various slender mechanical parts that revolve or serve as axes for larger revolving parts, as in a lock or axle. *—v.* **-dled, -dling. 1.** To perforate on or as on the spike of a spindle. **2.** To grow into a thin, elongated, or weakly form. [< OE *spinel,* rod of a spinning wheel. See **spen-.**]

spin•dly (spĭnd'lē) *adj.* **-dlier, -dliest.** Also **spind•ling** (-lĭng). Long, thin, and often weak.

spine (spīn) *n.* **1.** The spinal column of a vertebrate. **2.** A sharp-pointed projecting plant or animal part; a thorn, prickle, or quill. [< L *spīna,* thorn, prickle, spine.] **—spin'y** *adj.*

spine•less (spīn'lĭs) *adj.* **1.** Lacking a spine or spines. **2.** Lacking in courage or will power. **—spine'less•ness** *n.*

spin•et (spĭn'ĭt) *n.* A small piano or harpsichord. [< It *spinetta.*]

spin•ning (spĭn'ĭng) *n.* The process of making fibrous material into yarn or thread. *—adj.* Of, for, or used in spinning.

spinning jenny. An early form of spinning machine having several spindles.

spinning wheel. An apparatus for making yarn or thread, consisting of a foot- or hand-driven wheel and a single spindle.

spin-off (spĭn'ôf', -ŏf') *n.* An object, product, etc., derived from a larger, more or less unrelated enterprise.

spin•ster (spĭn'stər) *n.* A woman who has remained single beyond the conventional age for marrying. [ME *spinnester,* "one who spins."] **—spin'ster•hood'** *n.*

spi•ral (spī'rəl) *n.* **1.** The path in a plane of a point moving around a fixed center at an increasing or decreasing distance. **2.** The path of a point moving parallel to and about a central axis; helix. **3.** Something having the form of such a curve. **4.** A continuously accelerating increase or decrease. *—adj.* **1.** Of or resembling a spiral. **2.** Coiling in a constantly changing plane; helical. **3.** Circling around to form a series of constantly changing planes, as a spring. *—v.* **-raled** or **-ralled, -raling** or **-ralling. 1.** To take a spiral form or course. **2.** To rise or fall with steady acceleration. [< L *spīra,* coil.] **—spi'ral•ly** *adv.*

spire¹ (spīr) *n.* **1.** The top part or point of something that tapers upward. **2.** A pointed formation or structure, as a steeple. [< OE *spīr,* slender stalk. See **spei-.**]

spire² (spīr) *n.* A spiral, esp. a single turn of a spiral; whorl. [< Gk *speira.*]

spir•it (spĭr'ĭt) *n.* **1.** The vital principle or animating force within living beings; the soul. **2. Spirit.** The Holy Ghost. **3.** A supernatural being. **4.** An individual. **5.** Mood or emotional state. **6.** Vivacity and courage. **7.** Loyalty or dedication. **8.** The real sense or significance of something. **9.** Often **spirits.** An alcohol solution of an essential or volatile substance. **10. spirits.** An alcoholic beverage. *—v.* To carry off mysteriously or secretly. [< L *spīritus,* breath, breath of a god, inspiration.]

spir•it•ed (spĭr'ĭ-tĭd) *adj.* Energetic; vigorous.

spir•it•less (spĭr'ĭt-lĭs) *adj.* Lacking energy or enthusiasm. **—spir'it•less•ly** *adv.*

spir•i•tu•al (spĭr'ĭ-cho͞o-əl) *adj.* **1.** Of, relating to, or consisting of spirit; not tangible or material. **2.** Sacred. **3.** Ecclesiastical. *—n.* A religious folk song of American Negro origin. **—spir'i•tu•al'i•ty** *n.* **—spir'i•tu•al•ly** *adv.*

spir•i•tu•al•ism (spĭr'ĭ-cho͞o-ə-lĭz'əm, -chə-lĭz'-əm) *n.* The belief that the dead communicate with the living. **—spir'i•tu•al•ist** *n.* **—spir'i•tu•al•is'tic** *adj.*

spir•i•tu•ous (spĭr'ĭ-cho͞o-əs) *adj.* Having the nature of or containing alcohol.

spi•ro•chete (spī'rə-kēt') *n.* Any of various slender, twisted microorganisms, including those causing syphilis and other diseases. [< L *spīra,* coil + Gk *khaitē,* long hair.] **—spi'ro•che'tal** *adj.*

spi•roid (spī'roid) *adj.* Having resemblance to a spiral.

spit¹ (spĭt) *n.* **1.** Saliva, esp. when expectorated; spittle. **2.** The act of spitting. *—v.* **spat** or **spit, spitting. 1.** To eject from the mouth. **2.** To eject as if by spitting. [< OE *spittan.* See **spyeu-.**]

spit² (spĭt) *n.* **1.** A pointed rod on which meat is impaled for broiling. **2.** A narrow point of land extending into a body of water. [< OE *spitu.* See **spei-.**]

spite (spīt) *n.* Malicious ill will prompting an urge to hurt or humiliate. **—in spite of.** Regardless of; despite. *—v.* **spited, spiting.** To treat with malice. [ME, insult, ill will.]

spite•ful (spīt'fəl) *adj.* Filled with spite; vindictive. **—spite'ful•ly** *adv.*

spit•tle (spĭt'l) *n.* Spit; saliva. [< OE *spātl.* See **spyeu-.**]

spit•toon (spĭ-to͞on') *n.* A bowl-shaped vessel for spit. [< SPIT¹.]

splash (splăsh) *v.* **1.** To dash or scatter (a liquid) about in masses. **2.** To dash liquid upon. **3.** To fall into or move through liquid with the sound of splashing. *—n.* **1.** The act or sound of splashing. **2.** A flying mass of liquid. **3.** A marking produced by or as if by scattered liquid. [Var of PLASH.] **—splash'er** *n.*

splash•down (splăsh'doun') *n.* The landing of a missile or spacecraft on water.

splat¹ (splăt) *n.* A slat of wood, as one in the middle of a chair back. [?]

splat² (splăt) *n.* A slapping noise. [?]

splat•ter (splăt'ər) *v.* To spatter with splashes of liquid. *—n.* A splash of liquid. [Perh a blend of SPLASH and SPATTER.]

splay (splā) *adj.* **1.** Spread or turned out. **2.** Clumsy or clumsily formed; awkward. *—v.* **1.** To spread out or apart. **2.** To slant or slope. [< ME *displayen,* to display.]

splay•foot (splā'fo͝ot') *n.* A deformity characterized by abnormally flat and turned-out feet. **—splay'foot'ed** *adj.*

spleen (splēn) *n.* **1.** A visceral organ composed of a white pulp of lymphatic nodules and tissue and a red pulp of venous tissue, functioning as a blood filter and to store blood. **2.** Ill temper. [< Gk *splēn.*]

splen•did (splĕn'dĭd) *adj.* **1.** Brilliant; radiant. **2.** Magnificent; grand. **3.** Very satisfying; praiseworthy. [< L *splendēre,* to shine.] **—splen'did•ly** *adv.*

splen•dor (splĕn'dər) *n.* Also *Brit.* **splen•dour. 1.** Great light or luster; brilliance. **2.** Magnificence; grandeur.

splice (splīs) *v.* **spliced, splicing. 1.** To join (pieces of material) at the ends. **2.** To join (pieces of wood) by overlapping and binding at the ends. *—n.* A joint made by splicing. [Prob < MDu *splissen.*] **—splic'er** *n.*

splint (splĭnt) *n.* 1. A rigid device used to prevent motion of a joint or the ends of a fractured bone. 2. A thin, flexible wooden strip, as used in making baskets. [ME, small strip of metal, splint.]

splin•ter (splĭn'tər) *n.* A sharp, slender piece, as of wood, bone, glass, etc., split or broken off from a main body. —*v.* To split or break into splinters. [< MDu.] —**splin'ter•y** *adj.*

split (splĭt) *v.* **split, splitting.** 1. To divide, esp. into lengthwise sections. 2. To break, burst, or rip apart with force. 3. To disunite. 4. To divide and share. 5. To separate into layers or sections. —*n.* 1. The act or result of splitting. 2. A breach or rupture in a group. —*adj.* 1. Divided or separated. 2. Fissured longitudinally; cleft. [Du *splitten.*]

split•ting (splĭt'ĭng) *adj.* 1. Acute; piercing. 2. Very severe, as a headache.

splotch (splŏch) *n.* An irregularly shaped stain, spot, or blotch. [Perh a blend of SPOT and BLOTCH.] —**splotch** *v.* —**splotch'y** *adj.*

splurge (splûrj) *n.* An extravagant expense or luxury. [?] —**splurge** *v.* **(splurged, splurging).**

splut•ter (splŭt'ər) *v.* 1. To make a spitting sound. 2. To speak hastily and incoherently. —*n.* A spluttering noise. [Perh var of SPUTTER.] —**splut'ter•er** *n.*

spoil (spoil) *v.* **spoiled** or **spoilt** (spoilt), **spoiling.** 1. To damage. 2. To impair the completeness, perfection, or unity of. 3. To disrupt; disturb. 4. To overindulge so as to harm the character. 5. *Obs.* To plunder; pillage. 6. To become tainted or rotten; decay, as food. —*n.* **spoils.** 1. Goods or property seized by force; plunder. 2. Political patronage enjoyed by a successful party or candidate. [< L *spolium,* hide torn from an animal, booty.] —**spoil'age** *n.* —**spoil'er** *n.*

Spo•kane (spō-kăn'). A city of E Washington. Pop. 182,000.

spoke¹ (spōk) *n.* 1. One of the rods that connect the hub and rim of a wheel. 2. A rung of a ladder. [< OE *spāca.* See **spei-.**]

spoke² (spōk). *p.t. & archaic p.p.* of **speak.**

spo•ken (spō'kən). *p.p.* of **speak.**

spokes•man (spōks'mən) *n.* One who speaks on behalf of others. [< obs *spoke,* "speaking" + MAN.]

spo•li•a•tion (spō'lē-ā'shən) *n.* The act of despoiling or plundering. [< L *spoliāre,* to despoil.] —**spo'li•a'tor** *n.*

sponge (spŭnj) *n.* 1. A primitive marine animal with a porous skeleton. 2. The absorbent, fibrous skeletal part of such an animal, used for bathing, cleaning, etc. 3. A substance having spongelike qualities. 4. A gauze pad used to absorb blood and other fluids, as in surgery. —*v.* **sponged, sponging.** 1. To wipe or clean with a sponge. 2. *Informal.* To live by relying on another's generosity. [< Gk *sphongos,* sponge.] —**spong'er** *n.* —**spon'gy** *adj.*

spon•sor (spŏn'sər) *n.* 1. One who vouches or assumes responsibility for a person or thing. 2. A godparent. 3. A business enterprise that pays for a radio or television program, usually in return for advertising time. [< L *spondēre,* to make a solemn pledge.] —**spon'sor** *v.* —**spon'sor•ship'** *n.*

spon•ta•ne•ous (spŏn-tā'nē-əs) *adj.* 1. Happening or arising without external cause. 2. Voluntary; unpremeditated. 3. Natural and unstudied in manner or behavior. [< L *sponte,* of one's own accord, out of free will.] —**spon'ta•ne'i•ty** (-tə-nē'ə-tē), **spon•ta'ne•ous•ness** *n.* —**spon•ta'ne•ous•ly** *adv.*

spontaneous combustion. Ignition in a thermally isolated substance, as oily rags or hay, caused by a localized heat-increasing reaction between the oxidant and fuel.

spoof (spo͞of) *n.* 1. A hoax. 2. A light parody. [< *spoof,* a card game characterized by nonsense and hoaxing.] —**spoof** *v.*

spook (spo͝ok). *Informal. n.* A ghost; specter. —*v.* 1. To haunt. 2. To frighten; startle. [< MDu *spoocke.*] —**spook'y** *adj.*

spool (spo͞ol) *n.* A small cylinder upon which wire, thread, or string is wound. [< MDu *spoele.*]

spoon (spo͞on) *n.* 1. A utensil consisting of a shallow bowl on a handle, used in preparing or eating food. 2. A shiny, curved metallic fishing lure. —*v.* To lift, scoop up, or carry with or as with a spoon. [< OE *spōn,* chip of wood. See **sphē-.**]

spoon•er•ism (spo͞o'nə-rĭz'əm) *n.* An unintentional transposition of sounds in spoken language, as *Let me sew you to your sheet* for *Let me show you to your seat.* [< W.A. *Spooner* (1844–1930), English clergyman noted for such slips.]

spoor (spo͝or) *n.* The track or trail of an animal. [< MDu.]

spo•rad•ic (spô-răd'ĭk, spō-) *adj.* Occurring at irregular intervals. [< Gk *sporas,* scattered, dispersed.] —**spo•rad'i•cal•ly** *adv.*

spore (spôr, spōr) *n.* A usually single-celled reproductive structure or resting stage, as of a fern, fungus, or bacterium. [< Gk *spora,* a sowing, seed.]

sport (spôrt, spōrt) *n.* 1. An active pastime or diversion. 2. A specific diversion, as athletics or hunting. 3. Light mockery. 4. One known for the manner of his acceptance of rules or a difficult situation: *a poor sport.* 5. *Informal.* One who lives a gay, extravagant life. 6. *Archaic.* Amorous dalliance; lovemaking. —*v.* 1. To play; frolic. 2. To joke or trifle. 3. To display or show off. —*adj.* Of, relating to, or appropriate for sports. [ME *sporten,* to amuse, divert.]

spor•tive (spôr'tĭv, spōr'-) *adj.* 1. Full of fun; frisky. 2. Of or interested in sports.

sports•man (spôrts'mən, spōrts'-) *n.* 1. A participant in sports. 2. One who abides by rules and accepts victory or defeat graciously. —**sports'wom'an** *fem.n.*

sports•man•ship (spôrts'mən-shĭp', spōrts'-) *n.* The qualities and conduct befitting a sportsman.

sports•wear (spôrts'wâr', spōrts'-) *n.* Clothes for casual wear.

sport•y (spôr'tē, spōr'-) *adj.* **-ier, -iest.** *Informal.* 1. Appropriate to sport. 2. Casual in style, as clothes. 3. Gay; carefree.

spot (spŏt) *n.* 1. A particular place of relatively small and definite limits. 2. A mark on a surface differing sharply in color from the surroundings, esp. a stain or blot. 3. A position; location. 4. *Informal.* A situation, esp. a difficult one. 5. A blot on one's reputation. —*v.* **spotted, spotting.** 1. To mark or become marked with a spot or spots. 2. To detect; locate; discern. [ME.] —**spot'less** *adj.*

spot•light (spŏt'līt') *n.* 1. A strong beam of light that illuminates only a small area, as on a stage. 2. A lamp that produces such a light. 3. Public notoriety.

spot•ter (spŏt'ər) *n.* One that looks for and reports something, as a military lookout.

spot•ty (spŏt'ē) *adj.* **-tier, -tiest.** 1. Having or marked with spots. 2. Lacking consistency; uneven. —**spot'ti•ness** *n.*

spouse (spous, spouz) *n.* One's husband or wife. [< L *spōnsus,* betrothed (person), betrothal.]

spout (spout) *v.* 1. To gush forth or discharge in a rapid stream or in spurts. 2. To speak volubly and pompously. —*n.* 1. A pipe through which liquid is released. 2. A continuous stream of liquid. [ME *spouten.*]

spp. species (plural).

sprain (sprān) *n.* 1. A painful wrenching or laceration of the ligaments of a joint. 2. The resulting condition. —*v.* To cause a sprain in (a muscle or joint). [Perh < OF *espraindre,* to squeeze out, strain.]

sprang (sprăng). *p.t.* of **spring.**

sprat (sprăt) *n.* A small herring or similar fish. [< OE *sprott.*]

sprawl (sprôl) *v.* 1. To sit or lie with the limbs spread out awkwardly. 2. To spread out awkwardly, as handwriting. [< OE *sprēawlian.* See **sper-².**] —**sprawl** *n.* —**sprawl'er** *n.*

spray¹ (sprā) *n.* 1. Liquid moving in a mass of dispersed droplets, as from a wave. 2. a. A fine jet of liquid discharged from a pressurized container. b. Such a pressurized container; an atomizer. —*v.* 1. To disperse (a liquid) in a spray. 2. To apply a spray to (a surface). [< MDu *spraeyen,* to sprinkle.] —**spray'er** *n.*

spray² (sprā) *n.* A small leafy or flowery branch. [< OE **sprǣg.*]

spread (sprĕd) *v.* 1. To open or be extended more fully; stretch. 2. To separate or become separated more widely; move farther apart. 3. To distribute over a surface in a layer; apply. 4. To extend or cause to extend over a considerable area; distribute widely. 5. To become or cause to become widely known; disseminate. —*n.* 1. The act of spreading. 2. An open area of land; expanse. 3. The extent or limit to which something is or can be spread; a range. 4. A cloth covering for a bed, table, or other piece of furniture. 5. *Informal.* An abundant meal laid out on a table. 6. A food to be spread on bread or crackers. 7. Printed matter running across two or more columns in a magazine, newspaper, etc. [< OE *sprǣdan.* See **sper-².**] —**spread'er** *n.*

spree (sprē) *n.* 1. A gay, lively outing. 2. A drinking bout. 3. An overindulgence in some activity. [Perh Scot *spreath,* cattle taken as booty, raid, plunder.]

sprig (sprĭg) *n.* A small twig or shoot. [ME *sprigg.*]

spright•ly (sprīt'lē) *adj.* **-lier, -liest.** Animated; full of life. [< SPRITE.] —**spright'li•ness** *n.*

spring (sprĭng) *v.* **sprang** or **sprung, sprung, springing.** 1. To move upward or forward suddenly; leap. 2. To emerge suddenly. 3. To shift position suddenly. 4. To arise from a source; develop. 5. To be or become warped or bent, as wood. 6. To actuate: *spring a trap.* 7. To present suddenly: *spring a surprise.* —*n.* 1. An elastic device, as a coil of wire, that regains its original shape after being compressed or extended. 2. Elasticity; resilience. 3. The act of springing. 4. A natural fountain or flow of water. 5. A source or origin. 6. The season between winter and summer. [< OE *springan.* See **spergh-.**] —**spring'y** *adj.*

spring•board (sprĭng'bôrd', -bōrd') *n.* A flexible board used by gymnasts, divers, etc.

Spring•field (sprĭng'fēld). 1. The capital of Illinois. Pop. 90,000. 2. A city in SW Massachusetts. Pop. 162,000.

spring•time (sprĭng'tīm') *n.* The season of spring.

sprin•kle (sprĭng'kəl) *v.* **-kled, -kling.** To scatter or release in drops or small particles, as water.

—*n.* A light rainfall. [ME *sprenklen.*] —**sprin'kler** *n.*
sprint (sprĭnt) *n.* A short race run at top speed. —*v.* To run at top speed. [< Scand.] —**sprint'er** *n.*
sprite (sprīt) *n.* A small or elusive supernatural being; an elf or pixie. [< L *spiritus,* SPIRIT.]
sprock•et (sprŏk'ĭt) *n.* Any of various toothlike projections arranged on a wheel rim to engage the links of a chain. [?]
sprout (sprout) *v.* To begin to grow; produce or appear as a bud, shoot, or new growth. —*n.* A young plant growth, as a bud or shoot. [< OE *sprūtan.* See **sper-²**.]
spruce¹ (sprōōs) *n.* **1.** A cone-bearing evergreen tree with short, pointed needles and soft wood. **2.** The wood of such a tree. [Short for earlier *Spruce fir,* "Prussian fir."]
spruce² (sprōōs) *adj.* **sprucer, sprucest.** Having a neat or dapper appearance. —*v.* **spruced, sprucing.** To make or become spruce: *He spruced himself up for the evening.*
sprue (sprōō) *n.* A chronic, chiefly tropical disease characterized by diarrhea, emaciation, and anemia. [Du *spruw.*]
sprung (sprŭng). *p.p.* & alternate *p.t.* of **spring.**
spry (sprī) *adj.* **sprier** or **spryer, spriest** or **spryest.** Active; nimble; lively. [Perh < Scand.]
spud (spŭd) *n. Slang.* A potato. [ME *spudde,* short knife.]
spume (spyōōm) *n.* Foam or froth on a liquid. [< L *spūma.*]
spun (spŭn). *p.t.* & *p.p.* of **spin.**
spunk (spŭngk) *n. Informal.* Spirit; mettle. [Scot Gael *spong,* tinder, sponge.] —**spunk'i•ness** *n.* —**spunk'y** *adj.*
spur (spûr) *n.* **1.** One of a pair of spiked devices attached to a rider's heels and used to urge the horse forward. **2.** An incentive or goad. **3.** A narrow pointed projection, as on the back of a bird's leg or on certain flowers. **4.** A lateral ridge projecting from a mountain or mountain range. —*v.* **spurred, spurring. 1.** To urge (a horse) on by the use of spurs. **2.** To incite; stimulate. [< OE *spora, spura.* See **spher-.**] —**spurred** *adj.*
spurge (spûrj) *n.* Any of various plants with milky juice and small flowers. [< OF *espurge,* "purge."]
spu•ri•ous (spyōōr'ē-əs) *adj.* Lacking authenticity; counterfeit; false. [< L *spurius,* illegitimate.] —**spu'ri•ous•ly** *adv.*
spurn (spûrn) *v.* To reject or refuse disdainfully; scorn. [< OE *spurnan, spornan.* See **spher-.**] —**spurn'er** *n.*
spurt (spûrt) *n.* **1.** A sudden and forcible gush, as of water. **2.** Any sudden burst of activity. —*v.* **1.** To burst forth. **2.** To force out in a burst; squirt. [< OE *spryttan,* to sprout. See **sper-².**]
sput•nik (spŭt'nĭk, spōōt'-) *n.* Any of the artificial Earth satellites launched by the U.S.S.R. [Russ *sputnik (zemlyi),* "fellow traveler (of Earth)."]
sput•ter (spŭt'ər) *v.* **1. a.** To spit out small particles in short bursts. **b.** To make the sporadic coughing noise characteristic of such activity. **2.** To stammer. [< Du *sputteren.*] —**sput'ter** *n.* —**sput'ter•er** *n.*
spu•tum (spyōō'təm) *n., pl.* **-ta** (-tə). Expectorated matter, including saliva, substances from the respiratory tract, and foreign material. [< L *spuere,* to spit.]
spy (spī) *n., pl.* **spies. 1.** A clandestine agent employed to obtain intelligence. **2.** One who secretly watches another or others. —*v.* **spied, spying. 1.** To keep under surveillance with hostile intent. **2.** To catch sight of; see. **3.** To investigate; pry: *spying into their activities.* [< OF *espier,* to spy, watch.]
spy•glass (spī'glăs', -gläs') *n.* A small telescope.
sq. 1. squadron. **2.** square.
squab (skwŏb) *n.* A young pigeon. [Prob < Scand.]
squab•ble (skwŏb'əl) *n.* A trivial quarrel. [Prob < Scand.] —**squab'ble** *v.* **(-bled, -bling).**
squad (skwŏd) *n.* **1.** A small group of persons organized for a specific purpose. **2.** *Mil.* The smallest unit of personnel. [< OSpan *escuadra,* "square," "square formation (of troops)."]
squad car. A police patrol car connected by radiotelephone with headquarters.
squad•ron (skwŏd'rən) *n.* **1.** A group of naval vessels constituting two or more divisions of a fleet. **2.** An armored cavalry unit. **3.** The basic air force tactical unit, consisting of two or more flights. [It *squadrone,* "square formation (of troops)."]
squal•id (skwŏl'ĭd) *adj.* **1.** Having a dirty or wretched appearance. **2.** Morally repulsive; sordid. [< L *squālus,* scabby, filthy.] —**squal'id•ly** *adv.* —**squal'id•ness** *n.*
squall¹ (skwôl) *n.* A loud, harsh outcry. [Prob < Scand.] —**squall** *v.*
squall² (skwôl) *n.* A brief, sudden, and violent windstorm, often with rain or snow. [Prob < Scand.] —**squall'y** *adj.*
squal•or (skwŏl'ər) *n.* The state or quality of being squalid.
squan•der (skwŏn'dər) *v.* To spend wastefully or extravagantly. [?]
square (skwâr) *n.* **1.** A rectangle having four equal sides. **2.** Anything with this form. **3.** An instrument for drawing or testing right angles. **4.** The product of a number or quantity multiplied by itself. **5.** Any of the quadrilateral spaces on a checkerboard. **6. a.** An open area at the intersection of two or more streets. **b.** A rectangular space enclosed by streets; a block. **7.** *Slang.* One characterized by rigid conventionality. —*adj.* **squarer, squarest. 1.** Having four equal sides and four right angles. **2.** Forming a right angle. **3. a.** Expressed in units measuring area: *square feet.* **b.** Having a specified length in each of two equal dimensions. **4.** Of more or less quadrate dimensions. **5.** Honest; direct. **6.** Just; equitable. **7.** Paid-up; settled. **8.** *Slang.* Rigidly conventional. —*v.* **squared, squaring. 1.** To cut to a square or rectangular shape. **2.** To bring into balance; settle: *square a debt.* **3.** To raise (a number or quantity) to the second power. **4.** To agree or conform. [< VL **exquadrāre,* to square.] —**square'ly** *adv.*
square dance. A dance in which sets of four couples form squares.
square rig. A sailing-ship rig with rectangular sails set approx. at right angles to the keel line from horizontal yards. —**square'-rigged'** *adj.*
square root. A divisor of a quantity that when squared gives the quantity.
squash¹ (skwŏsh, skwôsh) *n.* **1.** A fleshy fruit related to the pumpkins and gourds, eaten as a vegetable. **2.** A plant bearing such fruit. [< Algon.]
squash² (skwŏsh, skwôsh) *v.* **1.** To beat or flatten to a pulp; crush. **2.** To be crushed or flattened. **3.** To suppress; quash. —*n.* **1.** The impact or sound of a soft body dropping against a surface. **2.** A crush of people; a crowd. **3.** A game played in a walled court with a racket and a hard rubber ball. [< VL **exquassāre,* "to break to pieces."]
squat (skwŏt) *v.* **squatted** or **squat, squatting. 1.** To sit on one's heels. **2.** To settle on unoccupied land without legal claim. **3.** To occupy a given piece of public land in order to acquire title to it. —*adj.* **squatter, squattest.** Short and thick; low and broad. —*n.* The act or posture of squatting. [< OF *esquatir,* to flatten.] —**squat'ter** *n.*
squaw (skwô) *n.* A North American Indian woman. [< Algon.]
squawk (skwôk) *n.* **1.** A loud screech. **2.** A loud or insistent protest. [Perh blend of SQUALL and SQUEAK.] —**squawk** *v.*
squeak (skwēk) *v.* To utter, speak in, or make a brief thin, shrill cry or sound. [Prob < Scand.] —**squeak** *n.* —**squeak'y** *adj.*
squeal (skwēl) *v.* **1.** To make a loud, shrill cry or sound. **2.** *Slang.* To turn informer. —*n.* A loud, shrill cry or sound. [Prob < Scand.] —**squeal'er** *n.*
squeam•ish (skwē'mĭsh) *adj.* **1. a.** Easily nauseated or sickened. **b.** Nauseated. **2.** Easily disgusted. **3.** Excessively fastidious. [< OE *swima,* dizziness. See **swei-.**] —**squeam'ish•ly** *adv.* —**squeam'ish•ness** *n.*
squeeze (skwēz) *v.* **squeezed, squeezing. 1.** To press hard upon or together; compress. **2.** To exert pressure. **3.** To extract from by applying pressure: *squeeze juice from a lemon.* **4.** To force by pressure; cram. —*n.* **1.** An act or instance of squeezing. **2.** An amount squeezed. [< OE *cwȳsan,* to press.]
squelch (skwĕlch) *v.* **1.** To suppress completely. **2.** To silence, as with a crushing remark. —*n.* A crushing reply. [Imit.]
squid (skwĭd) *n., pl.* **squids** or **squid.** A marine mollusk with a long body and ten arms surrounding the mouth. [?]
squint (skwĭnt) *v.* **1. a.** To look with the eyes partly open. **b.** To close (the eyes) partly. **2.** To glance to the side. [< ME *asquint,* with a sidelong glance.] —**squint** *n.*
squire (skwīr) *n.* **1.** A young nobleman attendant upon a knight. **2.** An English country gentleman. **3.** A judge or other local dignitary. **4.** A man who attends or escorts a woman. —*v.* **squired, squiring.** To attend as a squire or escort. [< OF *esquier,* "shield-bearer."]
squirm (skwûrm) *v.* **1.** To twist about in a wriggling motion; writhe. **2.** To feel or show signs of humiliation or embarrassment.
squir•rel (skwûr'əl, skwĭr'əl) *n.* **1.** Any of various tree-climbing rodents with gray or reddish-brown fur and a long bushy tail. **2.** The fur of a squirrel. [< Gk *skiouros,* "shadow-tail."]
squirt (skwûrt) *v.* To eject liquid in a thin swift stream. —*n.* **1. a.** A device used to squirt. **b.** The stream squirted. **2.** *Informal.* An insignificant but arrogant person. [ME *squirten.*]
Sr strontium.
sr. senior.
Sri Lan•ka (srē lăng'kə). An insular nation off the SE coast of India. Pop. 12,510,000. Cap. Colombo.
SSE south-southeast.
S.S.R. Soviet Socialist Republic.
SSW south-southwest.
-st. Variant of **-est².**
St. 1. saint. **2.** strait. **3.** street.
sta. station.
stab (stăb) *v.* **stabbed, stabbing. 1.** To pierce or wound with or as with a pointed weapon. **2.** To lunge with or as with a pointed weapon. —*n.* **1.** A thrust made with a pointed weapon. **2.** A wound inflicted by stabbing. **3.** An at-

tempt. [< ME *stabbe,* wound by stabbing.]

sta•bi•lize (stā'bə-līz') *v.* **-lized, -lizing. 1.** To make, hold, or become stable. **2.** To maintain the stability of. **—sta'bi•li•za'tion** *n.* **—sta'bi•liz'er** *n.*

sta•ble¹ (stā'bəl) *adj.* **-bler, -blest. 1.** Resistant to sudden change. **2.** Maintaining equilibrium. **3.** Enduring. [< L *stabilis,* standing firm.] **—sta•bil'i•ty** (stə-bĭl'ə-tē) *n.*

sta•ble² (stā'bəl) *n.* **1.** A building for the shelter and feeding of domestic animals, esp. horses. **2.** All of the racehorses belonging to a single owner. [< L *stabulum,* "standing place," enclosure, stable.]

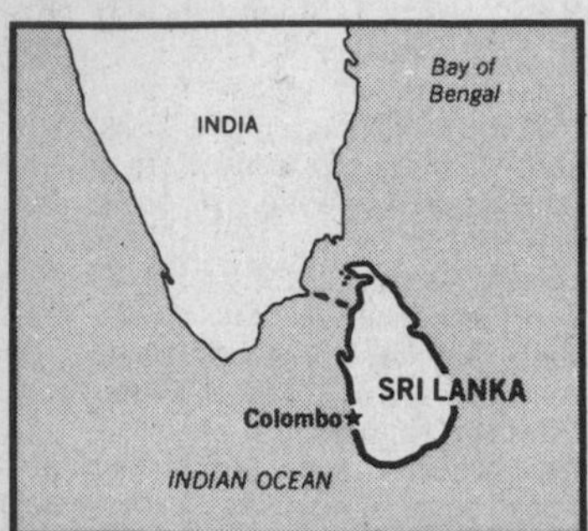

Sri Lanka

stack (stăk) *n.* **1.** A large conical pile of straw. **2.** A pile arranged in layers. **3.** A large quantity. **4.** A chimney or vertical exhaust pipe. **5. stacks.** The area of a library in which books are shelved. *—v.* **1.** To arrange in a stack; to pile. **2.** To prearrange the order of (playing cards) so as to cheat. [< ON *stakkr.*]

sta•di•um (stā'dē-əm) *n.* A large, often unroofed structure in which athletic events are held. [< Gk *spadion,* racetrack.]

staff (stăf) *n.* **1.** *pl.* **staffs** or **staves** (stāvz). A rod or stick carried as a weapon, an aid in walking, etc. **2.** *pl.* **staffs. a.** A group of assistants to an executive or military commander. **b.** The personnel of an enterprise. **3.** *pl.* **staves.** The set of lines on which music is written. *—v.* To provide with a staff of employees. [< OE *stæf,* stick, rod. See **stebh-**.]

staff sergeant. 1. A noncommissioned army officer ranking next below a sergeant first class. **2.** A noncommissioned air force officer ranking next below a technical sergeant. **3.** A noncommissioned marine officer ranking next below a gunnery sergeant.

stag (stăg) *n.* **1.** An adult male deer. **2.** A man who attends a social affair without escorting a woman. *—adj.* For or attended by men only. [< OE *stagga.* See **stegh-**.]

stage (stāj) *n.* **1.** Any raised platform, as a workmen's scaffold. **2. a.** The raised platform upon which theatrical performances are presented. **b.** Any area in which actors perform. **c.** The acting profession. **3.** The scene or setting of an event. **4.** A leg of a journey. **5.** A step in development. *—v.* **staged, staging. 1.** To present or perform on or as if on a stage. **2.** To arrange and carry out: *stage an invasion.* [< VL **staticum,* "standing place," position.]

stage•coach (stāj'kōch') *n.* A horse-drawn vehicle formerly used to transport mail and passengers.

stage-struck (stāj'strŭk') *adj.* Enthralled with hopes of becoming an actor.

stag•ger (stăg'ər) *v.* **1.** To move or cause to move unsteadily; totter. **2.** To overwhelm with emotion or surprise. **3.** To arrange in alternating or overlapping time periods. *—n.* **1.** The act of staggering; a tottering or reeling motion. **2. staggers** *(takes sing. v.).* A disease of animals, esp. horses, characterized by staggering and falling. [< ON *staka,* to push, cause to stumble.] **—stag'ger•er** *n.*

stag•ing (stā'jĭng) *n.* The process of producing and directing a stage play.

stag•nant (stăg'nənt) *adj.* **1.** Not moving or flowing. **2.** Foul from standing still. **3.** Inactive; sluggish. [< L *stagnum,* pond, swamp.]

stag•nate (stăg'nāt') *v.* **-nated, -nating.** To lie inactive; fail to progress or develop. **—stag'na'tion** *n.*

staid (stād) *adj.* Reserved and colorless; grave; sober. [< *staid,* obs pp of STAY.]

stain (stān) *v.* **1.** To discolor or spot. **2.** To corrupt or disgrace. **3.** To color, as wood, with a penetrating dye. *—n.* **1.** A spot or smudge of foreign matter. **2.** A blemish upon one's name; stigma. **3.** A dye. [< VL **distingere,* to deprive of color.] **—stain'er** *n.*

stain•less (stān'lĭs) *adj.* **1.** Without stain or blemish. **2.** Resistant to corrosion.

stainless steel. Any of various steels alloyed with sufficient chromium to resist corrosion, oxidation, or rusting.

stair (stâr) *n.* **1.** Often **stairs.** A flight of steps; a staircase. **2.** One of a flight of steps. [< OE *stǣger.* See **steigh-**.]

stair•case (stâr'kās') *n.* A flight of steps and its supporting structure.

stair•way (stâr'wā') *n.* A flight of stairs.

stake¹ (stāk) *n.* **1.** A pointed piece of wood or metal for driving into the ground, as a marker, a fence pole, or a tent peg. **2.** A vertical post to which an offender is bound for execution by burning. *—v.* **staked, staking. 1.** To indicate the limits of with or as if with stakes: *stake out a claim.* **2.** To attach or support with stakes. **3.** To tie to a stake. [< OE *staca.* See **steg-²**.]

stake² (stāk) *n.* **1.** Often **stakes. a.** Money or property risked in a wager or gambling game. **b.** The prize in a contest or race. **2.** A share or interest in any enterprise. *—v.* **staked, staking. 1.** To gamble or risk. **2.** To finance.

sta•lac•tite (stə-lăk'tīt', stăl'ək-) *n.* A cylindrical or conical deposit projecting downward from the roof of a cavern. [< Gk *stalaktos,* dripping.]

sta•lag•mite (stə-lăg'mīt', stăl'əg-) *n.* A cylindrical or conical deposit projecting upward from the floor of a cavern. [< Gk *stalagmos,* dripping.]

stale (stāl) *adj.* **staler, stalest. 1.** Having lost freshness or palatability. **2.** Lacking in originality. **3.** Impaired in strength. *—v.* **staled, staling.** To make or become stale. [Prob < OF *estale,* not moving, slack.]

stale•mate (stāl'māt') *n.* **1.** *Chess.* A drawing position in which only the king can move and although not in check can move only into check. **2.** A deadlock. **—stale'mate'** *v.* **(-mated, -mating).**

Sta•lin (stä'lĭn), **Joseph.** 1879–1953. General secretary of the Communist Party of the Soviet Union (1922–53); premier (1941–53). **—Sta'lin•ism'** *n.* **—Sta'lin•ist** *adj.* & *n.*

stalk¹ (stôk) *n.* **1.** A stem of a plant or plant part. **2.** A similar supporting structure. [Prob < Scand.]

stalk² (stôk) *v.* **1.** To walk with a stiff, haughty gait. **2.** To move menacingly. **3.** To track (game). [< OE *stealcian,* to walk cautiously. See **ster-⁴**.] **—stalk'er** *n.*

stall (stôl) *n.* **1.** A compartment for one domestic animal in a barn or shed. **2.** Any small compartment or booth. *—v.* **1.** To bring or come to a standstill accidentally: *stall an engine.* **2.** To employ delaying tactics: *stall for time.* [< OE *steall,* standing place, stable.]

stal•lion (stăl'yən) *n.* An uncastrated adult male horse. [< Frank **stal,* stable.]

stal•wart (stôl'wərt) *adj.* **1.** Having physical strength; sturdy. **2.** Resolute; uncompromising. [< OE *stælwierthe,* serviceable.]

sta•men (stā'mən) *n.* The pollen-producing reproductive organ of a flower. [L *stāmen,* thread of the warp, stamen.]

stam•i•na (stăm'ə-nə) *n.* Physical or moral power of endurance. [< L *stāmen,* thread of the warp, thread of human life.]

stam•mer (stăm'ər) *v.* To intrude involuntary pauses and sometimes syllabic repetitions into one's speaking; falter. [< OE *stamerian* < Gmc **stam-*.] **—stam'mer** *n.* **—stam'mer•er** *n.*

stamp (stămp) *v.* **1.** To bring the foot down upon (a surface or object) forcibly. **2.** To thrust the foot forcibly downward. **3.** To imprint or impress with a mark. **4.** To affix an adhesive stamp to. **5.** To form or cut out with a mold, form, or die. **6.** To characterize or identify. *—n.* **1.** The act of stamping. **2.** A mark or seal indicating ownership, approval, etc. **3.** A small piece of gummed paper, as used for postage. **4.** Any identifying mark. **5. a.** An implement used to impress, cut out, or shape. **b.** The impression or shape thus formed. [< OE **stampian,* to pound, stamp. See **stebh-**.]

stam•pede (stăm'pēd') *n.* A sudden headlong rush, as of startled animals. *—v.* **-peded, -peding.** To participate in or cause a stampede. [< Span *estampar,* to pound, stamp.]

stance (stăns) *n.* The posture of a standing person. [< VL **stantia,* a standing.]

stanch (stänch, stănch) *v.* To check the flow of blood, as from a wound. [< L *stāre,* to stand.]

stan•chion (stăn'chən, -shən) *n.* An upright pole or post. [< OF *estanche,* a stay, prop.]

stand (stănd) *v.* **stood, standing. 1.** To take, cause to take, or maintain an upright position on the feet. **2.** To assume an erect position in a specified manner: *stand straight.* **3.** To measure or equal a specified height. **4.** To remain stable or intact. **5.** To remain unchanged; stagnate. **6.** To withstand. **7.** To tolerate; endure. **8.** To rank. **9.** To undergo: *stand trial.* *—n.* **1.** The act of standing. **2.** A halt; standstill. **3.** A stop on a performance tour. **4.** The place where a person stands, as a witness box in a courtroom. **5.** A counter for the display of

Joseph Stalin

goods. **6.** A small rack or prop for holding various articles. **7. stands.** Bleachers, as at a stadium. **8.** A parking space reserved for taxis. **9.** A group or growth of tall plants or trees. [< OE *standan.* See **stā-**.]

stan•dard (stăn'dərd) *n.* **1.** A flag, banner, or ensign. **2.** An acknowledged measure of comparison for quantitative or qualitative value; criterion; norm. **3.** The commodity or commodities, such as gold, used to back a monetary system. **4.** A degree or level or excellence. **5.** A pedestal or stand. [Prob < Frank **standhard,* "standing firmly."] **—stan'dard** *adj.*

stan•dard•ize (stăn'dər-dīz') *v.* **-ized, -izing.** To make, cause, or adapt to fit a standard. **—stan'dard•i•za'tion** *n.*

standard time. The time in any of 24 time zones, usually the mean solar time at the central meridian of each zone.

stand•by (stănd'bī') *n., pl.* **-bys. 1.** One that can be depended upon. **2.** One ready to serve as a substitute.

stand-in (stănd'ĭn') *n.* A substitute, as for an actor.

stand•ing (stăn'dĭng) *n.* **1.** Status with respect to credit, rank, etc. **2.** Length of time. *—adj.* **1.** Remaining upright. **2.** Performed from an upright position: *standing jumps.* **3.** Permanent. **4.** Stationary. **5.** Stagnant.

stand•off•ish (stănd-ôf'ĭsh, -ŏf'ĭsh) *adj.* Unsociable; aloof.

stand•pipe (stănd'pīp') *n.* A large vertical pipe into which water is pumped in order to produce a desired pressure.

stand•point (stănd'point') *n.* A position from which things are considered; point of view.

stand•still (stănd'stĭl') *n.* A halt: *came to a standstill.*

stank (stăngk). *p.t.* of **stink.**

stan•za (stăn'zə) *n.* One of the divisions of a poem having two or more lines. [It, "a stopping or standing."]

sta•pes (stā'pēz') *n., pl.* **-pes** or **stapedes** (stə-pē'dēz'). One of three small bones located in the middle ear. [< ML *stapēs.*]

staph•y•lo•coc•cus (stăf'ə-lō-kŏk'əs) *n., pl.* **-cocci** (-kŏk'sī'). Any of various spherical parasitic bacteria occurring in grapelike clusters and causing boils, septicemia, and other infections. [< Gk *staphulē,* bunch of grapes + *kokkos,* a berry.]

sta•ple¹ (stā'pəl) *n.* **1.** A major commodity or product. **2.** A major part or element. **3.** Raw material. **4.** The fiber of cotton, wool, etc. [ME, market town, trade center.]

sta•ple² (stā'pəl) *n.* **1.** A U-shaped metal loop with pointed ends, driven into a surface to hold a bolt, hook, etc., or to hold wiring in place. **2.** A thin piece of wire having the shape of a square bracket, used as a fastening for papers. [< OE *stapol,* post, pillar.] **—sta'ple** *v.* **(-pled, -pling). —sta'pler** *n.*

star (stär) *n.* **1.** *Astron.* A celestial object consisting of a self-luminous, self-containing mass of gas. **2.** Any of the celestial bodies visible at night from Earth as relatively stationary, usually twinkling points of light. **3.** Anything regarded as resembling such a body. **4.** A graphic design with radiating points, esp. one with five points. **5. a.** A superior performer. **b.** A leading actor or actress. **6.** An asterisk. **7. stars.** *Astrol.* **a.** The constellations of the zodiac believed to influence personal destiny. **b.** Loosely, the planets in relation to them. *—v.* **starred, starring. 1.** To ornament with stars. **2.** To mark with an asterisk. **3.** To play the leading role in a theatrical production. [< OE *steorra.* See **ster-³**.] **—star'ry** *adj.*

star•board (stär'bərd) *n.* The right-hand side of a ship or aircraft as one faces forward. [< OE *stēorbord,* "rudder side."] **—star'board** *adj.* & *adv.*

starch (stärch) *n.* **1.** A carbohydrate, $(C_6H_{10}O_5)_n$, found chiefly in the seeds, fruits, tubers, and roots of plants, as corn, potatoes, or wheat, and commonly prepared as a white, tasteless powder. **2.** Any of various substances, including natural starch, used to stiffen fabrics. **3.** A food having a high starch content. *—v.* To stiffen with starch. [< OE *stercan,* to stiffen. See **ster-¹**.] **—starch'y** *adj.*

stare (stâr) *v.* **stared, staring.** To fix with a steady, often wide-eyed gaze. [< OE *starian.* See **ster-¹**.] **—stare** *n.*

star•fish (stär'fĭsh') *n.* A marine animal having a star-shaped form with five radiating arms.

stark (stärk) *adj.* **1.** Bare; blunt. **2.** Utter; extreme. **3.** Harsh in appearance; grim. *—adv.* Utterly; absolutely: *stark raving mad.* [< OE *stearc,* hard, stern, severe, cruel. See **ster-¹**.]

stark naked. Completely naked. [< ME *stert naked,* "naked to the tail."]

star•let (stär'lĭt) *n.* A young actress publicized as a future star.

star•light (stär'līt') *n.* The light given by the stars.

star•ling (stär'lĭng) *n.* An Old World bird with dark plumage, widely naturalized in North America. [< OE *stær,* starling (see **storos**) + -LING.]

Stars and Stripes, The. The flag of the U.S.

Star-Span•gled Banner, The (stär'spăng'-gəld). **1.** The flag of the U.S. **2.** The national anthem of the U.S.

start (stärt) *v.* **1.** To commence; begin. **2.** To set in motion, operation, or activity. **3.** To establish: *start a business.* **4.** To move suddenly and involuntarily. *—n.* **1. a.** A beginning. **b.** A place or time of beginning. **2.** A position of advantage, as in a race. **3.** A sudden, involuntary movement. [< OE *styrtan,* to leap up. See **ster-¹**.] **—start'er** *n.*

star•tle (stär'təl) *v.* **-tled, -tling. 1.** To cause to make a quick, involuntary movement, as in fright. **2.** To become startled. [< OE *steartlian,* to kick, struggle. See **ster-¹**.]

starve (stärv) *v.* **starved, starving. 1.** To die or cause to die from hunger. **2.** To suffer or cause to suffer from or as from hunger. [< OE *steorfan,* to die. See **ster-¹**.] **—star•va'tion** *n.*

stash (stăsh) *v.* To store away in a secret place. [?]

-stasis. *comb. form.* A stable state or a balance: **homeostasis.** [< Gk *stasis,* a standing, standstill.]

-stat. *comb. form.* Stationary or making stationary: **thermostat.** [< Gk *-statēs,* one that causes to stand.]

stat. statute.

state (stāt) *n.* **1.** A condition of being with regard to a set of circumstances. **2.** A condition of being in a stage or form, as of structure, growth, or development. **3.** A mental or emotional condition. **4. a.** The supreme public power within a sovereign political entity. **b.** The sphere of supreme civil power within a given polity: *matters of state.* **5.** A specific mode of government: *a welfare state.* **6.** A body politic, esp. one constituting a nation: *the states of eastern Europe.* **7.** One of the internally autonomous political units composing a federation under a sovereign government: *New York State.* *—v.* **stated, stating.** To set forth in words; declare. [< L *status,* manner of standing, condition, position, attitude.] **—state'hood'** *n.*

state•ly (stāt'lē) *adj.* **-lier, -liest. 1.** Dignified; formal. **2.** Majestic; lofty. **—state'li•ness** *n.*

state•ment (stāt'mənt) *n.* **1.** The act of stating. **2.** Something stated; an account. **3.** An abstract of a financial account.

Stat•en Island (stăt'n). An island in the bay of New York.

state•room (stāt'ro͞om') *n.* A private room on a ship or train.

state•side (stāt'sīd') *adj.* Of or in the continental U.S. **—state'side'** *adv.*

states•man (stāts'mən) *n.* **1.** One who is a leader in public affairs. **2.** A political leader regarded as a promoter of the public good. **—states'man•like'** *adj.* **—states'man•ship'** *n.*

stat•ic (stăt'ĭk) *adj.* **1.** Having no motion; quiescent. **2.** Of or produced by random radio noise. *—n.* Random noise produced in a radio or television receiver. [< Gk *statikos,* causing to stand.] **—stat'i•cal•ly** *adv.*

static electricity. **1.** An accumulation of electric charge on an insulated body. **2.** Electric discharge resulting from such accumulation.

sta•tion (stā'shən) *n.* **1.** The position where a person or thing stands or is placed. **2.** The place from which a service is provided or operations directed: *a police station.* **3.** A transportation depot. **4.** Social position; status. **5.** An establishmen for radio or television transmission. *—v.* To assign to a position; to post. [< L *statiō,* a standing.]

sta•tion•ar•y (stā'shə-nĕr'ē) *adj.* **1.** Fixed in a position; not moving. **2.** Remaining in a fixed condition. [< L *statiō,* a standstill, STATION.]

sta•tion•er (stā'shən-ər) *n.* One who sells stationery.

sta•tion•er•y (stā'shə-nĕr'ē) *n.* **1.** Writing materials and office supplies. **2.** A store that sells stationery and related items.

station wagon. An automobile having an extended interior with a luggage platform and a hinged rear wall that can be let down.

sta•tis•tic (stə-tĭs'tĭk) *n.* Any numerical datum. **—sta•tis'ti•cal** *adj.*

sta•tis•tics (stə-tĭs'tĭks) *n.* **1.** *(takes sing. v.)* The mathematics of the collection, organization, and interpretation of numerical data, esp. the analysis of population characteristics by inference from sampling. **2.** *(takes pl. v.)* A collection of numerical data. [G *Statistik,* orig "political science dealing with state affairs."] **—stat'is•ti'cian** (stat'ə-stĭsh'ən) *n.*

stat•u•ar•y (stăch'o͞o-ĕr'ē) *n.* Statues collectively.

stat•ue (stăch'o͞o) *n.* A form or likeness sculpted, modeled, carved, or cast in a material such as stone, clay, wood, or bronze. [< L *statuere,* to set up, erect.]

stat•u•esque (stăch'o͞o-ĕsk') *adj.* Suggestive of a statue, as in proportion, grace, or dignity.

stat•u•ette (stăch'o͞o-ĕt') *n.* A small statue.

stat•ure (stăch'ər) *n.* **1.** Natural height in an upright position, esp. of a person. **2.** A level achieved; status; caliber. [< L *statūra.*]

stat•us (stā'təs, stăt'əs) *n.* **1.** The legal condition of a person or thing. **2.** A relative position, esp. social standing. **3.** High standing. **4.** A state of affairs. [L, manner of standing, posture, condition.]

sta•tus quo (stā'təs kwō', stăt'əs). The existing state of affairs. [L, "state in which."]

stat•ute (stăch'o͞ot) *n.* **1.** A law enacted by a legislative body. **2.** A decree or edict. **3.** An established rule, as of a corporation. [< L *statuere,* to set up, decree.]

ô **paw**, **for**/oi **boy**/ou **out**/o͝o **took**/o͞o **coo**/p **pop**/r **run**/s **sauce**/sh **shy**/t **to**/th **thin**/*th* **the**/
ŭ **cut**/ûr **fur**/v **van**/w **wag**/y **yes**/z **size**/zh **vision**/ə **ago**, **item**, **edible**, **gallop**, **circus**/

statute mile. The standard mile, 5,280 feet.
stat•u•to•ry (stăch'ə-tôr'ē, -tōr'ē) *adj.* Enacted, regulated, or defined by statute.
staunch (stônch, stänch) *adj.* **1.** Firm and steadfast; true. **2.** Having a strong construction or constitution. [< OF *estanchier*, stanch.] **—staunch'ly** *adv.* **—staunch'ness** *n.*
stave (stāv) *n.* **1.** A narrow strip of wood forming part of the sides of a barrel, tub, etc. **2.** A staff or cudgel. **3.** A stanza. *—v.* **staved** or **stove, staving. 1.** To break in the staves of. **2.** To break or smash a hole in. **3.** To ward or keep off: *He staved off hunger.* [Back-formation < STAVES.]
staves. Alternate *pl.* of **staff.**
stay¹ (stā) *v.* **1.** To remain or cause to remain. **2.** To stop; halt. **3.** To pause; wait. **4.** To hold on; endure. **5.** To postpone. **6.** To keep up, as in a race. *—n.* **1.** The action of halting. **2.** A sojourn or visit. **3.** A postponement. [< L *stāre*, to stand.]
stay² (stā) *v.* To support or prop up. *—n.* **1.** A support or brace. **2.** A strip of bone, plastic, or metal, used to stiffen a garment or part, as a shirt collar. **3. stays.** A corset. [< OF *estaie*, support.]
stay³ (stā) *n.* A heavy rope or cable used as a support, as for a ship's mast. *—v.* To brace or support with a stay or stays. [< OE *stæg*. See **stāk-.**]
St. Ber•nard (sānt bər-närd'). A large dog of a breed used by monks of the hospice of St. Bernard in the Swiss Alps to help travelers.
St. Croix (sānt' kroi'). The largest island of the Virgin Islands of the U.S.
std. standard.
stead (stĕd) *n.* **1.** The place or function properly occupied by another. **2.** Advantage; avail: *stand one in good stead.* [< OE *stede*. See **stā-.**]
stead•fast (stĕd'făst') *adj.* **1.** Fixed or unchanging. **2.** Firmly loyal or constant. [< OE *stedefæst*, fixed in one place.] **—stead'fast'ly** *adv.* **—stead'fast'ness** *n.*
stead•y (stĕd'ē) *adj.* **-ier, -iest. 1.** Firm in position or place. **2.** Unfaltering; sure. **3.** Having a continuous movement or quality. **4.** Calm; controlled. **5.** Reliable. *—v.* **-ied, -ying.** To make or become steady. [< STEAD, place.] **—stead'i•ly** *adv.* **—stead'i•ness** *n.*
steak (stāk) *n.* A slice of meat, usually beef, cooked by broiling or frying. [< ON *steikja*, to roast on a spit.]
steal (stēl) *v.* **stole, stolen, stealing. 1.** To take without right or permission, generally in a surreptitious way. **2.** To get or effect secretly or artfully. **3.** To move or happen stealthily or unobtrusively. **4.** *Baseball.* To gain (a base) without a hit, error, or wild pitch. *—n.* **1.** The act of stealing; theft. **2.** *Slang.* A bargain. [< OE *stelan*. See **ster-⁴.**]
stealth (stĕlth) *n.* The quality or state of being secret, sly, or surreptitious. **—stealth'i•ly** *adv.* **—stealth'i•ness** *n.* **—stealth'y** *adj.*
steam (stēm) *n.* **1. a.** The vapor phase of water. **b.** The mist of cooling water vapor. **2.** Power; energy. *—v.* **1.** To produce or emit steam. **2.** To move or be powered by steam. **3.** To expose to steam, as in cooking. [< OE *stēam* < Gmc **stauma*.] **—steam'y** *adj.*
steam•boat (stēm'bōt') *n.* A steamship.
steam engine. An engine that converts the heat energy of pressurized steam into mechanical energy.
steam•er (stē'mər) *n.* **1.** A steamship. **2.** A container in which something is steamed.
steam•rol•ler (stēm'rō'lər) *n.* A steam-driven machine used chiefly for rolling road surfaces flat. *—v.* To overwhelm or crush.
steam•ship (stēm'shĭp') *n.* A large vessel propelled by steam-driven screws or propellers.
steam shovel. A steam-driven machine for digging.
ste•a•tite (stē'ə-tīt') *n.* A massive, white-to-green talc used in paints, ceramics, and insulation. [< Gk *steatitis*, "tallow stone."]
steed (stēd) *n.* A horse, esp. a spirited mount. [< OE *stēda*, stallion.]
steel (stēl) *n.* **1.** Any of various generally hard, strong, durable, malleable alloys of iron and carbon, often with other constituents. **2.** A quality suggestive of steel, esp. a hard, unflinching character. *—adj.* **1.** Made of or with steel. **2.** Resembling the properties of steel. *—v.* To make hard, strong, or obdurate. [< OE *stēli*. See **stāk-.**] **—steel'y** *adj.*
steel wool. Fine fibers of woven or matted steel used esp. for scouring.
steep¹ (stēp) *adj.* **1.** Having a sharp inclination; nearly perpendicular; precipitous. **2.** Excessive; exorbitant: *a steep price.* [< OE *stēap*, lofty, deep, projecting. See **steu-.**] **—steep'ly** *adv.* **—steep'ness** *n.*
steep² (stēp) *v.* **1.** To soak or be soaked in liquid in order to cleanse, soften, or extract some property from. **2.** To saturate. [ME *stepen*.] **—steep'er** *n.*
steep•en (stē'pən) *v.* To make or become steeper.
stee•ple (stē'pəl) *n.* **1.** A tall tower forming the superstructure of a building, such as a church, and usually surmounted by a spire. **2.** A spire. [< OE *stȳpel*. See **steu-.**]
stee•ple•chase (stē'pəl-chās') *n.* A horse race across open country or over a course provided artificially with obstacles.
stee•ple•jack (stē'pəl-jăk') *n.* A worker on steeples or other very high structures.
steer¹ (stîr) *v.* **1.** To guide (a vessel or vehicle) by means of a rudder, wheel, paddle, etc. **2.** To direct the course of. **3.** To move in a set course. **4.** To allow of being steered or guided: *The boat steers easily.* [< OE *stīeran*. See **stā-.**]
steer² (stîr) *n.* A young ox, esp. one raised for beef. [< OE *stēor*.]
steer•age (stîr'ĭj) *n.* **1.** The action of steering. **2.** The section of a passenger ship providing the cheapest accommodations for passengers.
steg•o•saur (stĕg'ə-sôr') *n.* Also **steg•o•sau•rus** (stĕg'ə-sôr'əs). A dinosaur with a double row of upright bony plates along the back. [< Gk *stegos*, roof, "ridge of plates" + -SAUR.]
stein (stīn) *n.* An earthenware mug, esp. one for beer. [G.]
Stein•beck (stīn'bĕk), **John.** 1902–1968. American novelist.
stel•lar (stĕl'ər) *adj.* Of or relating to stars or a star performer. [< L *stella*, star.]
stem¹ (stĕm) *n.* **1.** The main axis of a plant or a slender supporting or connecting plant part; a stalk. **2. a.** Something similar to a plant stem. **b.** A stemlike part, as of a pipe, wine glass, etc. **3.** The main part of a word to which affixes are added. **4.** The prow of a vessel. *—v.* **stemmed, stemming. 1.** To derive or develop (from). **2.** To make headway against (a tide, current, or comparable force). [< OE *stemn, stefn*, stem, tree trunk. See **stā-.**] **—stem'less** *adj.*
stem² (stĕm) *v.* **stemmed, stemming.** To stop or hold back, by or as if by damming. [< ON *stemma*.]
stemmed (stĕmd) *adj.* **1.** Having the stems removed. **2.** Provided with a stem.
stem•ware (stĕm'wâr') *n.* Glassware mounted on a stem.
stench (stĕnch) *n.* A strong and foul odor. [< OE *stenc* < Gmc **stenkw-*.]
sten•cil (stĕn'səl) *n.* A sheet of material in which a desired lettering or design has been cut so that when ink or paint is passed over the sheet the pattern will be reproduced on the surface placed below. *—v.* **-ciled** or **-cilled, -ciling** or **-cilling.** To mark or produce with a stencil. [< OF *estenceler*, "to cause to sparkle."]
sten•o (stĕn'ō) *n., pl.* **-os. 1.** A stenographer. **2.** Stenography.
steno, stenog. stenographer; stenography.
ste•nog•ra•pher (stə-nŏg'rə-fər) *n.* A person employed to take and transcribe dictation.
ste•nog•ra•phy (stə-nŏg'rə-fē) *n.* The art or process of writing in shorthand. [< Gk *stenos*, narrow + -GRAPHY.] **—sten'o•graph'ic** (stĕn'ə-grăf'ĭk) *adj.*
sten•to•ri•an (stĕn-tôr'ē-ən, stĕn-tōr'-) *adj.* Extremely loud. [Gk *Stentōr*, name of a loud-voiced herald in the *Iliad*.]
step (stĕp) *n.* **1. a.** The single complete movement of raising one foot and putting it down in another spot in the act of walking. **b.** A manner of walking. **c.** The rhythm or pace of another or others, as in a march. **d.** The sound of a tread. **2. a.** The distance traversed by moving one foot ahead of the other. **b.** A very short distance. **c. steps.** Course: *followed in his father's steps.* **3. a.** A rest for the foot in ascending or descending. **b. steps.** Stairs. **4. a.** One of a series of actions taken toward some end. **b.** A stage in a process. **5.** A degree in progress or a grade or rank in a scale. **—in step. 1.** Moving in rhythm. **2.** *Informal.* In conformity with one's environment. *—v.* **stepped, stepping. 1.** To put or press the foot down (on). **2.** To shift or move slightly: *step back.* **3.** To walk a short distance to a specified place: *step over.* **4.** To move with the feet in a particular manner: *step lively.* **5.** To measure by pacing: *step off ten yards.* **—step up. 1.** To increase. **2.** To advance; put oneself forward. [< OE *stæpe, stepe*. See **stebh-.**]
step–. *comb. form.* Relationship through the previous marriage of a spouse or through the remarriage of a parent, rather than by blood. [< OE *stēop-*.]
step•broth•er (stĕp'brŭth'ər) *n.* The son of one's stepparent by a previous marriage.
step•child (stĕp'chīld') *n.* The child of one's spouse by a former marriage.
step•daugh•ter (stĕp'dô'tər) *n.* The daughter of one's spouse by a former marriage.
step•fa•ther (stĕp'fä'thər) *n.* The husband of one's mother by a later marriage.
step•lad•der (stĕp'lăd'ər) *n.* A portable ladder with a hinged supporting frame and usually topped with a small platform.
step•moth•er (stĕp'mŭth'ər) *n.* The wife of one's father by a later marriage.
step•par•ent (stĕp'pâr'ənt) *n.* A stepfather or a stepmother.
steppe (stĕp) *n.* A vast semiarid plain, as found in SE Europe and Siberia. [Russ *step'*.]
step•ping•stone (stĕp'ĭng-stōn') *n.* **1.** A stone that provides a place to step. **2.** An advantageous position for advancement toward some goal.
step•sis•ter (stĕp'sĭs'tər) *n.* The daughter of one's stepparent by a previous marriage.
step•son (stĕp'sŭn') *n.* The son of one's spouse by a former marriage.
–ster. *comb. form.* **1.** One who does: **teamster. 2.** One who is associated with: **gangster. 3.** One

who is given to making: **prankster.** **4.** One who is: **youngster.** [< OE *-estre* < Gmc **-strjōn,* agent-noun suffix.]

ster. sterling.

stere (stîr) *n.* A unit of volume equal to one cubic meter. [< Gk *stereos,* solid, hard.]

ste•re•o (stĕr'ē-ō', stîr'-) *n., pl.* **-os.** **1. a.** A stereophonic sound-reproduction system. **b.** Stereophonic sound. **2.** A stereoscopic system or photograph. **—ste're•o'** *adj.*

stereo–. *comb. form.* Solid, firm, or three-dimensional. [< Gk *stereos,* solid, hard.]

ster•e•o•phon•ic (stĕr'ē-ō-fŏn'ĭk, -fō'nĭk, stîr'-) *adj.* Having or rendering the illusion of having a natural distribution of sources of sound. **—ster'e•o•phon'i•cal•ly** *adv.*

ster•e•o•scope (stĕr'ē-ə-skōp', stîr'-) *n.* An optical instrument used to impart a three-dimensional effect to two photographs of the same scene taken at slightly different angles and viewed through two eyepieces. **—ster'e•o•scop'ic** (-skŏp'ĭk) *adj.*

ster•e•o•type (stĕr'ē-ə-tīp', stîr'-) *n.* **1.** A metal printing plate cast from a matrix that is molded from a raised printing surface, such as type. **2.** A conventional and usually oversimplified conception or belief. **3.** One considered typical of an unvarying pattern or manner. **—ster'e•o•typ'er** *n.*

ster•e•o•typed (stĕr'ē-ə-tīpt', stîr'-) *adj.* **1.** Printed or reproduced from stereotype plates. **2.** Not individualized; unoriginal; conventional.

ster•ile (stĕr'əl) *adj.* **1.** Incapable of reproducing sexually. **2.** Incapable of producing fruit, vegetation, etc. **3.** Free from bacteria or other microorganisms. **4.** Not productive or effective. [< L *sterilis,* unfruitful.] **—ste•ril'i•ty** (stə-rĭl'ə-tē) *n.*

ster•il•ize (stĕr'ə-līz') *v.* **-ized, -izing.** To render sterile. **—ster'il•i•za'tion** (-lə-zā'shən, -lī-zā'shən) *n.* **—ster'il•iz'er** *n.*

ster•ling (stûr'lĭng) *n.* **1.** British money, esp. the pound as the basic monetary unit. **2.** Sterling silver. *—adj.* **1.** Consisting of or relating to British money. **2.** Made of sterling silver. **3.** Of the highest quality. [ME, "small star" (stamped on silver pennies).]

sterling silver. An alloy of 92.5% silver with copper or another metal.

stern[1] (stûrn) *adj.* **1.** Firm or unyielding. **2.** Grave or severe in manner or appearance. **3.** Inexorable; relentless. [< OE *stierne.* See **ster-**[1].] **—stern'ly** *adv.*

stern[2] (stûrn) *n.* The rear part of a ship or boat. [ME *sterne.*]

ster•num (stûr'nəm) *n., pl.* **-na** (-nə) or **-nums.** A long flat bone forming the midventral support of most of the ribs. [< Gk *sternon,* breast, breastbone.]

steth•o•scope (stĕth'ə-skōp') *n.* An instrument used for listening to sounds produced within the body. [< Gk *stēthos,* chest, breast + -SCOPE.] **—steth'o•scop'ic** (-skŏp'ĭk) *adj.*

ste•ve•dore (stē'və-dôr', -dōr') *n.* A person employed in loading or unloading ships. [< Span *estivar,* to stow, pack.]

Ste•ven•son (stē'vən-sən). **1. Adlai Ewing.** 1900–1965. American statesman; twice Democratic candidate for President (1952 and 1956). **2. Robert Louis.** 1850–1894. Scottish poet and novelist.

stew (st/y/ōō) *v.* **1.** To cook (food) by simmering or boiling slowly. **2.** *Informal.* To worry; fret. *—n.* **1.** A dish cooked by stewing, esp. a mixture of meat or fish and vegetables. **2.** *Informal.* Mental agitation. [ME *stewen,* orig "to bathe in hot water."]

stew•ard (st/y/ōō'ərd) *n.* **1.** One who manages another's property, finances, or other affairs. **2.** One in charge of the household affairs of a hotel, resort, etc. **3.** An officer on a ship in charge of provisions and dining arrangements. **4.** A male member of the staff of a ship or airplane who waits on the passengers. [< OE *stigweard,* "keeper of the hall."] **—stew'ard•ess** *fem.n.*

stg. sterling.

stick (stĭk) *n.* **1.** A long, slender piece of wood, esp. a branch or stem from a tree or shrub. **2.** Any of various sticklike implements, as a cane or baton. **3.** Something having the shape of a stick. **4. sticks.** *Informal.* An area far from a city or town. **5.** *Informal.* A stiff, spiritless, or boring person. *—v.* **stuck, sticking.** **1.** To pierce, puncture, or penetrate with a pointed instrument. **2.** To fasten or attach. **3.** To fix or impale on a pointed object. **4.** To adhere (to); cling. **5.** To be or become fixed or embedded in place. **6.** To be at or come to a standstill; become fixed or obstructed. **7.** To put, thrust, or poke into a specified place or position. **8.** To put responsibility on; burden: *stuck with paying the bill.* **9.** To persist, endure, or persevere. **10.** To remain in a vicinity; linger: *Stick around a while.* **11.** To extend, project, or protrude. [< OE *sticca,* a stick, and < OE *stician,* to pierce, stab. See **steig-.**]

stick•er (stĭk'ər) *n.* **1.** A person or thing that sticks. **2.** A gummed or adhesive label or patch.

stick•ler (stĭk'lər) *n.* **1.** A person who insists on something unyieldingly. **2.** Anything puzzling or difficult. [< OE *stihtan,* to order, arrange.]

stick•y (stĭk'ē) *adj.* **-ier, -iest.** **1.** Adhering or sticking to a surface; adhesive. **2.** Warm and humid; muggy. **3.** *Informal.* Painful or difficult. **—stick'i•ly** *adv.* **—stick'i•ness** *n.*

stiff (stĭf) *adj.* **1.** Difficult to bend or stretch; not flexible. **2.** Not moving or operating easily; not limber. **3.** Excessively formal, awkward, or constrained. **4.** Not liquid, loose, or fluid. **5.** Having a strong, swift, steady force or movement. **6.** Potent or strong: *a stiff drink.* **7.** Difficult; arduous. **8.** Harsh or severe. *—adv.* **1.** In a stiff manner. **2.** Completely: *bored stiff.* [< OE *stīf.* See **steip-.**] **—stiff'ly** *adv.* **—stiff'ness** *n.*

stiff•en (stĭf'ən) *v.* To make or become stiff or stiffer. **—stiff'en•er** *n.*

stiff-necked (stĭf'nĕkt') *adj.* Stubborn; unyielding.

sti•fle (stī'fəl) *v.* **-fled, -fling.** **1.** To kill by preventing respiration; smother or suffocate. **2.** To interrupt or cut off (the voice or breath). **3.** To keep or hold back; suppress. [< OF *estouffer,* to choke, smother.] **—sti'fler** *n.*

stig•ma (stĭg'mə) *n., pl.* **stigmata** (stĭg-mä'tə, stĭg'mə-tə). **1.** A mark or token of disgrace or reproach. **2.** Usually *pl.* **stigmas.** The tip of a flower pistil, upon which pollen is deposited. **3. stigmata.** Marks or sores corresponding to and resembling the crucifixion wounds of Jesus. [< Gk, tattoo mark.] **—stig•mat'ic** (stĭg-măt'ĭk) *adj.*

stig•ma•tize (stĭg'mə-tīz') *v.* **-tized, -tizing.** **1.** To characterize as disgraceful or ignominious. **2.** To brand or mark with a stigma or stigmata.

stile (stīl) *n.* A set or series of steps for getting over a fence or wall. [< OE *stigel.*]

sti•let•to (stĭ-lĕt'ō) *n., pl.* **-tos** or **-toes.** A small dagger with a slender, tapering blade. [< It *stilo,* dagger.]

still[1] (stĭl) *adj.* **1.** Free from sound; silent. **2.** Low in sound; subdued. **3.** Without movement. **4.** Free from disturbance. **5.** Pertaining to a single or static photograph as opposed to a motion picture. *—n.* **1.** Silence; calm. **2.** A still photograph, esp. one from a motion picture. *—adv.* **1.** Without movement. **2.** Now as before: *He is still sick.* **3.** In increasing amount or degree: *still further complaints.* **4.** Nevertheless; all the same. *—conj.* Nevertheless: *It was difficult, still he tried.* *—v.* **1.** To make or become still. **2.** To allay; calm. [< OE *stille.* See **stel-.**] **—still'ness** *n.*

still[2] (stĭl) *n.* An apparatus for distilling liquids, particularly alcohols. [< ME *distillen,* distill.]

still•birth (stĭl'bûrth') *n.* The birth of a dead child or fetus. **—still'born'** (stĭl'bôrn', -bōrn') *adj.*

still life *pl.* **still lifes.** A painting or picture of inanimate objects. **—still'-life'** *adj.*

stilt (stĭlt) *n.* **1.** Either of a pair of long, slender poles, each equipped with a raised footrest to permit walking elevated above the ground. **2.** Any of various tall posts or pillars used as support, as for a building. [ME *stilte,* stilt, crutch.]

stilt•ed (stĭl'tĭd) *adj.* Stiffly or artificially formal; pompous. **—stilt'ed•ly** *adv.*

stim•u•late (stĭm'yə-lāt') *v.* **-lated, -lating.** To rouse to activity or heightened action; excite. [L *stimulāre,* to goad on.] **—stim'u•lant** (-lənt) *adj.* & *n.* **—stim'u•la'tion** *n.*

stim•u•lus (stĭm'yə-ləs) *n., pl.* **-li** (-lī', -lē'). **1.** Anything causing or regarded as causing a response. **2.** Something that rouses to action; an incentive. [L *stimulus,* a goad.] **—stim'u•la'tive** (-lā'tĭv) *adj.* & *n.*

sting (stĭng) *v.* **stung, stinging.** **1.** To pierce with or as with a sharp-pointed structure or organ. **2.** To cause pain by or as by pricking with a sharp point. **3.** To cause to suffer keenly. *—n.* **1.** The act of stinging. **2.** The wound or pain caused by or as by stinging. **3.** A sharp, piercing organ or part, as of certain insects. [< OE *stingan.* See **stegh-.**] **—sting'er** *n.*

stin•gy (stĭn'jē) *adj.* **-gier, -giest.** **1.** Giving or spending reluctantly. **2.** Scanty or meager. [Perh < OE *stingan,* to STING.] **—stin'gi•ly** *adv.* **—stin'gi•ness** *n.*

stink (stĭngk) *v.* **stank** or **stunk, stunk, stinking.** **1.** To emit or cause to emit a strong foul odor. **2.** To be highly offensive. *—n.* A strong offensive odor. [< OE *stincan* < Gmc **stinkwan.*] **—stink'er** *n.*

stint (stĭnt) *v.* **1.** To restrict or limit; be sparing with. **2.** To subsist on a meager allowance; be frugal. *—n.* **1.** A duty to be performed within a given period of time. **2.** A limitation or restriction. [< OE *styntan,* to blunt, dull. See **steu-.**] **—stint'er** *n.*

sti•pend (stī'pĕnd', -pənd) *n.* A fixed or regular payment, as a salary or allowance. [< L *stīpendium,* tax, tribute.]

stip•ple (stĭp'əl) *v.* **-pled, -pling.** To draw, engrave, or paint in dots or short touches. *—n.* **1.** The method of painting, drawing, or engraving by stippling. **2.** The effect produced by stippling. [< MDu *stip,* dot, point.]

stip•u•late (stĭp'yə-lāt') *v.* **-lated, -lating.** **1.** To specify as a condition of an agreement; require by contract. **2.** To guarantee in an agreement. [L *stipulārī,* to bargain, demand.] **—stip'u•la'tion** *n.* **—stip'u•la'tor** *n.*

stir (stûr) *v.* **stirred, stirring.** **1.** To mix a liquid by passing an implement through it in circular motions. **2.** To change or alter the placement of slightly; disarrange. **3.** To move briskly or vigorously. **4.** To rouse (someone) from sleep or indifference. 5. To incite or instigate: *stir up trouble.* 6. To move or affect strongly. —*n.* 1. An act of stirring; a mixing or poking movement. 2. A disturbance or commotion. 3. An excited reaction; a ferment. [< OE *styrian,* to move, excite. See **twer-.**] —**stir'rer** *n.*

stir•ring (stûr'ĭng) *adj.* 1. Rousing; exciting. 2. Active; lively. —**stir'ring•ly** *adv.*

stir•rup (stûr'əp, stĭr'-) *n.* 1. A flat-based loop or ring hung from either side of a horse's saddle to support the rider's foot. 2. Any similar device in which something is supported. [< OE *stigrāp.*]

stitch (stĭch) *n.* 1. A single complete movement of a threaded needle in sewing or surgical suturing. 2. A single loop of yarn around a knitting needle or similar implement. 3. A sudden sharp pain in the side. 4. *Informal.* An article of clothing: *not a stitch on.* 5. *Informal.* The least part; a bit: *He didn't do a stitch of work.* —*v.* 1. To fasten, join, or ornament with stitches. 2. To sew. [< OE *stice,* a sting, prick. See **steig-.**] —**stitch'er** *n.*

St. John (sānt jŏn'). An island of the Virgin Islands of the U.S.

St. Johns (sānt jŏnz'). The capital of Antigua.

stk. stock.

St. Law•rence River (sānt lôr'əns). A river of SE Canada.

St. Lou•is (sānt lo͞o'ĭs). A city of E Missouri. Pop. 608,000.

stoat (stōt) *n. Chiefly Brit.* The ermine, esp. in its brown color phase.

stock (stŏk) *n.* 1. A supply accumulated for future use. 2. The total merchandise kept on hand by a commercial establishment. 3. Domestic animals; livestock. 4. a. The capital that a corporation raises through the sale of shares entitling the holder to dividends and other rights of ownership. b. A certificate that shows such ownership. 5. a. The original progenitor of a family line or group of descendants. b. Ancestry or lineage. c. A group, as of organisms or languages, descended from a common ancestor. 6. The raw material out of which something is made. 7. Broth used as a base for soup, gravy, or sauces. 8. A supporting structure, block, or frame. 9. **stocks.** A pillory. 10. A theatrical activity, esp. one outside a main theatrical center. —*v.* 1. To provide with stock or a stock. 2. To keep for future sale or use. 3. To put forth or sprout new shoots. —*adj.* 1. Kept regularly available for sale or use. 2. Commonplace: *a stock answer.* [< OE *stocc,* tree trunk. See **steu-.**]

stock•ade (stŏk'ād') *n.* A barrier or enclosure made of strong posts driven upright side by side in the ground, used for protection or imprisonment. [< Span *estaca,* stake < Gmc.]

stock•bro•ker (stŏk'brō'kər) *n.* One who acts as an agent in the buying and selling of securities.

stock car. 1. An automobile of a standard make, modified for racing. 2. A railroad car carrying livestock.

stock exchange. 1. A place where stocks, bonds, or other securities are bought and sold. 2. An association of stockbrokers.

stock•hold•er (stŏk'hōl'dər) *n.* One who owns stock in a company.

Stock•holm (stŏk'hōlm). The capital of Sweden. Pop. 794,000.

stock•ing (stŏk'ĭng) *n.* A close-fitting covering for the foot and leg. [< dial *stock,* stocking.]

stock market. 1. A stock exchange. 2. The business transacted at a stock exchange.

stock•pile (stŏk'pīl') *n.* Also **stock pile.** A supply of material stored for future use. —*v.* **-piled, -piling.** To accumulate a stockpile of.

stock•y (stŏk'ē) *adj.* **-ier, -iest.** Solidly built; thickset. —**stock'i•ness** *n.*

stock•yard (stŏk'yärd') *n.* A large enclosed yard in which livestock is kept until being slaughtered or shipped elsewhere.

stodg•y (stŏj'ē) *adj.* **-ier, -iest.** 1. a. Dull, narrow, and commonplace. b. Prim or pompous; stuffy. 2. Heavy. [< earlier *stodge,* to cram, gorge.] —**stodg'i•ly** *adv.* —**stodg'i•ness** *n.*

sto•ic (stō'ĭk) *n.* One seemingly indifferent to or unaffected by joy, grief, pleasure, or pain. —*adj.* Also **sto•i•cal** (-ĭ-kəl). Indifferent to or unaffected by pleasure or pain; impassive. [< Gk *Stōikos,* a member of a school of philosophy that held that all occurrences were the unavoidable result of divine will.] —**sto'i•cal•ly** *adv.* —**sto'i•cism'** (stō'ĭ-sĭz'əm) *n.*

stoke (stōk) *v.* **stoked, stoking.** 1. To stir up (a fire or furnace). 2. To tend a fire or furnace. [< MDu *stoken,* to poke.] —**stok'er** *n.*

stole¹ (stōl) *n.* 1. A long scarf worn by some clergymen while officiating. 2. A women's long scarf worn about the shoulders. [< OE *stol,* a long robe < L *stola.*]

stole² (stōl). *p.t.* of **steal.**

sto•len (stō'lən). *p.p.* of **steal.**

stol•id (stŏl'ĭd) *adj.* Having or showing little emotion; impassive. [L *stolidus.*] —**sto•lid'i•ty** (stə-lĭd'ə-tē) *n.* —**stol'id•ly** *adv.*

stom•ach (stŭm'ək) *n.* 1. A large, saclike digestive organ of the alimentary canal, located in vertebrates between the esophagus and small intestine. 2. *Informal.* The abdomen or belly. 3. An appetite for food. 4. Any desire or inclination. —*v.* 1. To bear; tolerate; endure. 2. To digest. [< Gk *stomakhos,* throat, mouth, gullet.]

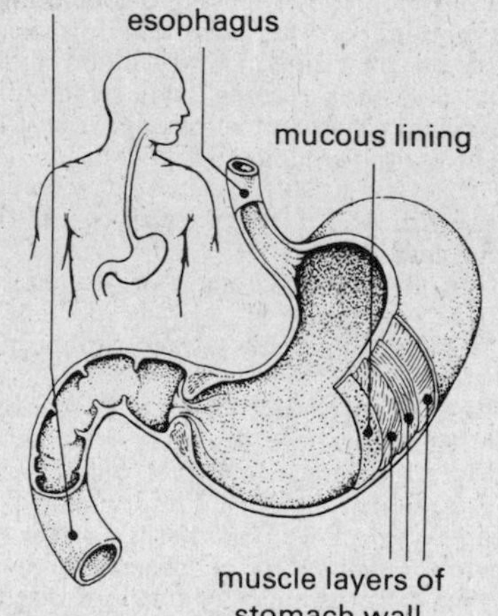

stomach

stom•ach•er (stŭm'ə-kər) *n.* An embroidered or jeweled garment formerly worn over the chest and stomach, esp. by women.

stomp (stômp, stŏmp) *v.* To tread or trample heavily (on). [Var of STAMP.]

stone (stōn) *n.* 1. Concreted earthy or mineral matter; rock. 2. Such material used for construction. 3. A small piece of rock. 4. A piece of rock shaped for a particular purpose, as a gravestone or millstone. 5. A gem or precious stone. 6. A seed with a hard covering, as of a cherry or plum. 7. *Path.* A mineral concretion in a hollow organ, as in the kidney. 8. *pl.* **stone.** A unit of weight in Britain, 14 pounds avoirdupois. —*adv.* Utterly; completely: *stone-blind.* —*v.* **stoned, stoning.** 1. To hurl or throw stones at; pelt or kill with stones. 2. To remove the stones or pits from. [< OE *stān.* See **stei-.**] —**stone** *adj.*

Stone Age. The early period of human culture characterized by the use of stone tools.

stoned (stōnd) *adj. Slang.* Intoxicated; drunk.

stone•wall (stōn'wôl') *v.* **-walled, -walling.** 1. *Cricket.* To play defensively. 2. *Informal.* To refuse to answer or cooperate (with).

ston•y (stō'nē) *adj.* **-ier, -iest.** Also **ston•ey.** 1. Covered with or full of stones. 2. Hard as a stone. 3. Hard-hearted; unemotional. 4. Emotionally numbing: *stony fear.*

stood (sto͝od). *p.t.* & *p.p.* of **stand.**

stooge (sto͞oj) *n.* 1. One who allows himself to be used for another's profit. 2. One placed to spy or inform on others.

stool (sto͞ol) *n.* 1. A backless and armless single seat supported on legs or a pedestal. 2. A low bench or support for the feet. 3. A bowel movement. [< OE *stōl.*]

stool pigeon. 1. A pigeon used as a decoy. 2. An informer, esp. for the police.

stoop¹ (sto͞op) *v.* 1. To bend from the waist or middle of the back. 2. To lower or debase oneself. —*n.* The act of stooping. [< OE *stūpian.* See **steu-.**]

stoop² (sto͞op) *n.* A small porch, platform, or staircase leading to the entrance of a house or building. [Du *stoep,* front verandah.]

stop (stŏp) *v.* **stopped, stopping.** 1. To close (an opening) by covering, filling in, or plugging up. 2. To adjust a vibrating medium to produce a desired musical pitch. 3. To obstruct or block passage on. 4. To prevent the flow or passage of. 5. To cause to halt, cease, or desist. 6. To desist from; cease; come to a halt. 7. To visit briefly; stay. —*n.* 1. The act of stopping or condition of being stopped. 2. A finish; an end. 3. A stay or visit. 4. A place stopped at. 5. A device or means that obstructs, blocks, etc. 6. An order given to a bank to withhold payment on a check. 7. A mark of punctuation, esp. a period. 8. *Mus.* A tuned set of pipes, as in an organ. [< Gmc **stoppōn,* to plug up < LL *stuppāre,* to stop up with a tow.]

stop•gap (stŏp'găp') *n.* A temporary expedient.

stop•page (stŏp'ĭj) *n.* The act of stopping or condition of being stopped; a halt.

stop•per (stŏp'ər) *n.* Any device inserted to close an opening. —**stop'per** *v.*

stop•watch (stŏp'wŏch') *n.* A timepiece with a sweep hand operated by an external trigger to measure duration of time.

stor•age (stôr'ĭj, stōr'-) *n.* 1. The act of storing goods. 2. A space for storing goods. 3. The price charged for storing goods.

storage battery. *Elec.* A group of rechargeable cells acting as a unit.

store (stôr, stōr) *n.* 1. A place where merchandise is offered for sale; a shop. 2. A stock or supply reserved for future use. 3. A warehouse or storehouse. 4. An abundance. —*v.* **stored, storing.** 1. To put away for future use. 2. To stock with something. 3. To deposit or receive in a warehouse for safekeeping. [< L *instaurāre,* to restore.]

store•house (stôr'hous', stōr'-) *n.* 1. A warehouse. 2. An abundant source or supply.

store•room (stôr'ro͞om', -ro͝om', stōr'-) *n.* A

room in which things are stored.

sto•rey. *Chiefly Brit.* Variant of **story²**.

sto•ried (stôr'ēd, stōr'-) *adj.* Celebrated in history or story.

stork (stôrk) *n.* A large wading bird with long legs and a long bill. [< OE *storc.* See **ster-¹**.]

storm (stôrm) *n.* **1.** An atmospheric disturbance manifested in strong winds accompanied by rain, snow, or other precipitation, and often by thunder and lightning. **2.** A violent, sudden attack. —*v.* **1.** To rain, snow, hail, or otherwise precipitate violently: *It stormed last night.* **2.** To rant and rage. **3.** To try to capture by a violent, sudden attack. [< OE. See **twer-**.] —**storm'y** *adj.*

sto•ry¹ (stôr'ē, stōr'ē) *n., pl.* **-ries.** **1.** The narrating or relating of an event or series of events, either true or fictitious. **2.** A tale. **3.** A short fictional literary composition: *short story.* **4.** The plot of a novel, play, etc. **5.** A statement or allegation of facts. **6.** An anecdote. **7.** A lie. [< Gk *historia.*]

sto•ry² (stôr'ē, stōr'ē) *n., pl.* **-ries.** Also *chiefly Brit.* **sto•rey.** A complete horizontal division of a building, comprising the area between two adjacent levels. [< ML *historia,* orig a row of windows with pictures on them < STORY.]

stoup (sto͞op) *n.* A basin for holy water in a church. [< ON *staup,* vessel.]

stout (stout) *adj.* **1.** Determined, bold, or brave. **2.** Strong; sturdy; solid. **3.** Bulky in figure; corpulent. —*n.* Strong, very dark beer or ale. [< OF *estout* < Gmc.] —**stout'ly** *adv.* —**stout'ness** *n.*

stout•heart•ed (stout'här'tĭd) *adj.* Brave; courageous. —**stout'heart'ed•ness** *n.*

stove¹ (stōv) *n.* An apparatus in which electricity or a fuel is used to furnish heat, as for cooking or comfort. [< MLG or MDu.]

stove² (stōv). Alternate *p.t.* & *p.p.* of **stave.**

stove•pipe (stōv'pīp') *n.* **1.** A pipe used to conduct smoke from a stove into a chimney flue. **2.** A man's tall silk hat.

stow (stō) *v.* **1.** To place, arrange, or store away. **2.** To fill by packing tightly. [< OE *stōw,* a place.]

stow•a•way (stō'ə-wā') *n.* One who hides aboard a ship or other conveyance in order to obtain free passage.

St. Paul (sānt pôl'). The capital of Minnesota. Pop. 309,000.

St. Pe•ters•burg (sānt pē'tərz-bûrg'). **1.** A former name for Leningrad. **2.** A city of W Florida. Pop. 181,000.

stra•bis•mus (strə-bĭz'məs) *n.* A visual defect in which one eye cannot focus with the other on an objective because of imbalance of the eye muscles. [< Gk *strabizein,* to squint.]

strad•dle (străd'l) *v.* **-dled, -dling.** **1.** To sit astride (of). **2.** To appear to favor both sides of (an issue). [< STRIDE.] —**strad'dle** *n.*

strafe (strāf, sträf) *v.* **strafed, strafing.** To attack with machine-gun fire from low-flying aircraft. [< G *strafen,* to punish.]

strag•gle (străg'əl) *v.* **-gled, -gling.** **1.** To stray or fall behind. **2.** To spread out in a scattered or irregular group. [ME *straglen.*] —**strag'gler** *n.* —**strag'gly** *adj.*

straight (strāt) *adj.* **1.** Extending continously in the same direction without curving. **2.** Having no irregularities. **3.** Upright. **4.** Direct and candid. **5.** Uninterrupted. **6.** Accurate; true. **7.** Unmodified or unaltered. **8.** Undiluted. **9.** *Slang.* **a.** Conventional and law-abiding. **b.** Not being a criminal, drug user, homosexual, etc. —*adv.* In a straight course or manner. —*n.* **1.** The straight part of a racecourse between the winning post and the last turn. **2.** A straight line, piece or position. **3.** In poker, a sequence of five consecutive cards. [ME *streight,* pp of *strecchen* to stretch.] —**straight'ly** *adv.* —**straight'ness** *n.*

straight•edge (strāt'ĕj') *n.* A rigid flat rectangular bar with a straight edge for testing or drawing straight lines.

straight•en (strāt'n) *v.* To make or become straight. —**straight'en•er** *n.*

straight•for•ward (strāt-fôr'wərd) *adj.* **1.** Proceeding in a straight course. **2.** Honest; candid. —*adv.* Also **straight•for•wards** (-wərdz). In a straightforward course or manner. —**straight•for'ward•ness** *n.*

straight jacket. Variant of **strait jacket.**

strain¹ (strān) *v.* **1.** To pull, draw, or stretch tight. **2.** To exert, tax, or be taxed to the utmost. **3.** To injure or become injured by overexertion. **4.** To stretch beyond the proper point or limit. **5.** To strive hard. **6.** To filter; pass through a strainer. —*n.* **1. a.** The act of straining. **b.** The state of being strained. **2.** A great effort, exertion, or tension. **3.** *Phys.* A deformation produced by stress. [< L *stringere,* to draw tight, tie.]

strain² (strān) *n.* **1.** A group of the same ancestry or species having shared distinctive characteristics. **2.** Ancestry; lineage. **3.** A kind; sort. **4.** A streak; trace. **5.** The tone or tenor of something. [< OE *strēon,* generation, offspring. See **ster-²**.]

strain•er (strā'nər) *n.* **1.** A filter, sieve, colander, etc., used to separate liquids from solids. **2.** One that strains.

strait (strāt) *n.* **1.** A narrow passage of water joining two larger bodies of water. **2.** Often **straits.** A position of difficulty or need. —*adj. Archaic.* **1.** Narrow or constricted. **2.** Strict, rigid, or righteous. [< L *strictus,* pp of *stringere,* to draw tight.]

strait•en (strāt'n) *v.* **1.** To make narrow; restrict. **2.** To bring into difficulty or distress: *in straitened circumstances.*

strait jacket. Also **straight jacket.** A jacketlike garment used to bind the arms tightly as a means of restraining a violent patient or prisoner.

strait-laced (strāt'lāst') *adj.* Prudish.

strand¹ (strănd) *n.* A shore; beach. —*v.* **1.** To drive or be driven aground, as a ship. **2.** To leave or be left in a difficult or helpless position. [< OE.]

strand² (strănd) *n.* **1.** Each of the fibers or filaments that are twisted together to form a rope, cable, etc. **2.** A string of beads, pearls, etc. [ME *strond.*]

strange (strānj) *adj.* **stranger, strangest.** **1.** Previously unknown; unfamiliar. **2.** Unusual; extraordinary. **3.** Peculiar; queer. **4.** Not of one's own or a particular locality or kind; exotic. **5.** Lacking experience. [< L *extrāneus,* foreign, strange.] —**strange'ly** *adv.* —**strange'ness** *n.*

stran•ger (strān'jər) *n.* **1.** One who is neither friend nor acquaintance. **2.** A foreigner, newcomer, or outsider.

stran•gle (străng'gəl) *v.* **-gled, -gling.** **1. a.** To kill by choking or suffocating. **b.** To smother. **2.** To suppress or stifle. **3.** To restrict. [< L *strangulāre,* STRANGULATE.] —**stran'gler** *n.*

stran•gu•late (străng'gyə-lāt') *v.* **-lated, -lating.** **1.** To strangle. **2.** *Path.* To constrict so as to cut off the flow of blood or other fluid. [L *strangulāre.*] —**stran'gu•la'tion** *n.*

strap (străp) *n.* A long, narrow strip of leather or other similar material, esp. one with a buckle for binding or securing objects. —*v.* **strapped, strapping.** To fasten or secure with a strap. [Var of STROP.]

strap•less (străp'lĭs) *adj.* Without a strap or straps. —*n.* A strapless garment.

strap•ping (străp'ĭng) *adj.* Tall and sturdy.

stra•ta. *pl.* of **stratum.** See Usage note at **stratum.**

strat•a•gem (străt'ə-jəm) *n.* **1.** A trick or artifice designed to deceive or surprise an enemy. **2.** A deception. [< Gk *stratēgēma,* "act of a general."]

strat•e•gy (străt'ə-jē) *n., pl.* **-gies.** **1.** The science or art of military command as applied to the overall planning and conduct of combat operations. **2.** A plan of action resulting from the practice of this science. [< Gk *stratēgos,* general.] —**stra•te'gic** (strə-tē'jĭk) *adj.* —**strat'e•gist** *n.*

strat•i•fy (străt'ə-fī') *v.* **-fied, -fying.** To form strata. —**strat'i•fi•ca'tion** *n.*

stra•to•cu•mu•lus (străt'ō-kyo͞om'yə-ləs) *n., pl.* **-li** (-lī'). A low-lying cloud occurring in extensive horizontal layers with massive rounded summits.

strat•o•sphere (străt'ə-sfîr') *n.* The part of the atmosphere above the troposphere. —**strat'o•spher'ic** (-sfîr'ĭk, -sfĕr'ĭk) *adj.*

stra•tum (strā'təm, stră'-, străt'əm) *n., pl.* **-ta** (-tə) or *rare* **-tums.** **1.** A horizontal layer of any material, esp. one of several parallel layers arranged one on top of another. **2.** A level in a hierarchy. [< L *strātus,* stretched out, pp of *sternere,* to stretch out.] —**stra'tal** *adj.*

Usage: Strata is standard as a plural form but not as a singular: *All strata of society are represented. Each stratum is accounted for. Stratas* (plural) is not a standard form.

stra•tus (strā'təs, străt'əs) *n., pl.* **-ti** (-tī'). A low-altitude cloud typically resembling a horizontal layer of fog.

Strauss (strous), **Johann.** 1825–1899. Austrian composer.

Stra•vin•sky (strə-vĭn'skē), **Igor.** Born 1882. Russian-born American composer.

straw (strô) *n.* **1.** A stalk or stalks of threshed grain. **2.** A slender tube used for sucking up a liquid. **3.** Something of minimal value. —*adj.* **1.** Pertaining to, used for, or like straw. **2.** Made of straw. [< OE *strēaw.* See **ster-²**.]

straw•ber•ry (strô'bĕr'ē, -bə-rē) *n.* **1.** The red, fleshy, edible fruit of a low-growing plant with white flowers. **2.** The plant itself. [< STRAW + BERRY.]

straw vote. An unofficial vote or poll.

stray (strā) *v.* **1. a.** To wander beyond established limits; roam. **b.** To become lost. **2.** To wander about or meander. **3.** To go astray; err. **4.** To digress. —*n.* One that has strayed, esp. a lost domestic animal. —*adj.* **1. a.** Straying or having strayed; out of place. **b.** Lost. **2.** Scattered or separate. [< VL **estragāre.*] —**stray'er** *n.*

streak (strēk) *n.* **1.** A line, mark, or smear differentiated by color or texture from its surroundings. **2.** A trait. **3.** A brief stretch of time: *a streak of good luck.* —*v.* **1.** To mark with or form a streak or streaks. **2.** To move at high speed; rush. [< OE *strica.* See **streig-**.] —**streak'i•ness** *n.* —**streak'y** *adj.*

stream (strēm) *n.* **1. a.** A body of running water. **b.** A steady current in such a body. **2.** A course or drift, as of opinion or history. —*v.* **1.** To flow in or as in a stream. **2.** To pour forth or emit. **3.** To move in large numbers. **4.** To extend, wave, or float outward. **5.** To give forth a continuous stream of light rays or

beams; shine. [< OE *strēam.* See **sreu-.**] —**stream'y** *adj.*
stream•er (strē'mər) *n.* **1.** A long narrow flag or banner. **2.** A long narrow strip of material. **3.** A ray of light extending upward. **4.** A newspaper headline that runs across a full page.
stream•lined (strēm'līnd') *adj.* Also **stream•line** (-līn'). **1.** Designed or arranged to offer the least resistance to fluid flow. **2.** Improved in efficiency; modernized. —**stream'line'** *v.* (**-lined, -lining**).
street (strēt) *n.* **1.** A public way or thoroughfare, as in a city or town. **2.** The people living along such a roadway. [< OE *strǣt* < Gmc **strāta* < L *strātus,* pp of *sternere,* to extend.]
street•car (strēt'kär') *n.* A public passenger car operated on rails along the streets of a city.
street•walk•er (strēt'wô'kər) *n.* A prostitute.
strength (strĕngkth, strĕngth) *n.* **1.** The state, quality, or property of being strong; physical power; muscularity. **2.** The power of resisting force or stress; durability; impregnability. **3.** Power or capability. **4.** A source of power or force. **5.** Moral courage or power. **6.** Effective or binding force: *the strength of an argument.* **7.** Degree of concentration, distillation, or saturation; potency. **8.** Intensity. **9.** A concentration of available force or personnel. [< OE *strengthu.*]
strength•en (strĕngk'thən, strĕng'-) *v.* To make or become strong or stronger. —**strength'en•er** *n.*
stren•u•ous (strĕn'yōō-əs) *adj.* **1.** Requiring great effort, energy, or exertion. **2.** Vigorously active; energetic. [L *strēnuus,* brisk, nimble.] —**stren'u•ous•ly** *adv.* —**stren'u•ous•ness** *n.*
strepto–. *comb. form.* A twisted chain. [< Gk *streptos,* twisted.]
strep•to•coc•cus (strĕp'tə-kŏk'əs) *n., pl.* **-ci** (-sī'). Any of various rounded bacteria occurring in pairs or chains and often causing disease.
strep•to•my•cin (strĕp'tə-mī'sən) *n.* An antibiotic, $C_{21}H_{39}N_7O_{12}$, produced from mold cultures and used medicinally to combat various bacteria.
stress (strĕs) *n.* **1.** Importance, significance, or emphasis placed upon something. **2. a.** The emphasis placed upon the sound or syllable spoken loudest in a given word or phrase. **b.** A syllable receiving such emphasis. **3.** *Mus.* An accent. **4.** *Phys.* A force that tends to deform a body. **5.** A mentally or emotionally disruptive influence; distress. —*v.* **1.** To place emphasis on; accent. **2.** To subject to pressure or strain. **3.** To subject to mechanical pressure or force. [< L *strictus,* strict.]
–stress. *comb. form.* A feminine agent: **seamstress.** [-ST(ER) + -ESS.]
stretch (strĕch) *v.* **1. a.** To lengthen, widen, or distend by pulling. **b.** To become lengthened, widened, or distended. **2.** To cause to extend across a given space. **3.** To make taut; tighten. **4.** To reach or put forth; extend: *He stretched out his hand.* **5.** To extend (oneself) at full length in a prone position. **6.** To flex one's muscles. **7.** To strain. **8.** To cause to suffice; make do with. **9.** To extend the limits of credulity, conscience, etc. **10.** To prolong. —*n.* **1.** The act of stretching or state of being stretched. **2.** The extent to which something can be stretched; elasticity. **3.** A continuous or unbroken length, area, or expanse. **4.** A straight section of a racecourse or track leading to the finish line. **5.** A continuous period of time. —*adj.* Capable of being stretched; elastic: *a stretch sock.* [< OE *streccan,* to spread out < Gmc **strakkjan.*] —**stretch'a•ble** *adj.* —**stretch'y** *adj.*
stretch•er (strĕch'ər) *n.* **1.** One that stretches. **2.** A canvas-covered frame used to transport the sick, wounded, or dead.
strew (strōō) *v.* **strewn** (strōōn) or **strewed, strewing. 1.** To spread here and there; scatter; sprinkle. **2.** To cover (a surface) with things scattered or sprinkled. **3.** To be or become dispersed over (a surface). [< OE *strēowian.* See **ster-2**.]
stri•a (strī'ə) *n., pl.* **striae** (strī'ē'). **1.** A thin, narrow groove or channel. **2.** A thin line or band. [L, furrow, channel.] —**stri'at'ed** (-ā'tĭd) *adj.* —**stri•a'tion** *n.*
strick•en (strĭk'ən). Alternate *p.p.* of **strike.** —*adj.* **1.** Struck or wounded, as by a projectile. **2.** Afflicted with something overwhelming, such as a disease, emotion, etc.
strict (strĭkt) *adj.* **1.** Precise; accurate; exact. **2.** Complete; absolute. **3.** Kept within narrow and specific limits; stringent. **4.** Imposing an exacting discipline. **5.** Rigidly conforming; devout: *a strict Catholic.* [L *strictus,* tight, narrow < *stringere,* to draw tight, tighten.] —**strict'ly** *adv.* —**strict'ness** *n.*
stric•ture (strĭk'chər) *n.* **1.** Something that restrains, limits, or restricts. **2.** An adverse criticism; censure. **3.** *Path.* An abnormal narrowing of a duct or passage. [< L *strictus,* STRICT.]
stride (strīd) *v.* **strode, stridden** (strĭd'n), **striding.** To walk vigorously with long steps. —*n.* **1.** The act of striding. **2.** A long step. **3.** A characteristic motion or manner of striding or running. **4.** A step forward; an advance. [< OE *strīdan* < Gmc.] —**strid'er** *n.*
stri•dent (strīd'ənt) *adj.* Loud and harsh; shrill. [< L *strīdēre,* to make a harsh sound.]
strife (strīf) *n.* **1.** Violent dissension; bitter conflict. **2.** A struggle between rivals. [< OF *estrif.*]
strike (strīk) *v.* **struck, struck** or **stricken, striking. 1. a.** To hit sharply, as with the hand, fist, or a weapon. **b.** To inflict (a blow). **2.** To collide (with) or crash into. **3.** To attack or begin an attack. **4.** To afflict suddenly with a disease. **5.** To impress by stamping or printing. **6.** To produce by hitting some agent, as a key on a musical instrument. **7.** To indicate by a percussive sound: *The clock struck nine.* **8.** To produce (a flame or spark) by friction. **9.** To eliminate: *struck out the error.* **10.** To come upon; discover. **11.** To reach; fall upon. **12.** To impress abruptly or freshly: *strikes me as a good idea.* **13.** To cause (an emotion) to penetrate deeply. **14. a.** To make or conclude (a bargain). **b.** To achieve (a balance). **15.** To fall into or assume (a pose). **16.** To proceed, esp. in a new direction; set out; head. **17.** To engage in a strike against an employer. —*n.* **1.** An act of striking. **2.** An attack. **3.** A cessation of work by employees in support of demands made upon their employer, as for higher pay. **4.** *Baseball.* A pitched ball that is counted against the batter, typically one swung at and missed or one taken and judged to have been in the strike zone. **5.** *Bowling.* The knocking down of all the pins with one ball. [< OE *strīcan,* to stroke, rub. See **streig-.**] —**strik'er** *n.*
strike out. *Baseball.* To retire (a batter) or be retired by the recording of three strikes.
strike•out (strīk'out') *n.* The act or an instance of striking out.
strike zone. *Baseball.* The area over the plate between the batter's armpits and knees.
strik•ing (strī'kĭng) *adj.* Impressing the mind or senses with immediacy; prominent.
string (strĭng) *n.* **1.** A cord usually made of fiber, thicker than thread, used for fastening or lacing. **2.** Anything shaped into a long, thin line. **3.** A set of objects threaded together: *a string of beads.* **4.** *Mus.* **a.** A stretched cord that is struck, plucked, or bowed to produce tones. **b. strings.** Instruments having such strings, esp. the instruments of the violin family. —*v.* **strung, stringing. 1.** To furnish with a string or strings. **2.** To thread on a string. **3.** To arrange in a series. **4.** To fasten, tie, or hang with a string. **5.** To stretch out. [< OE *streng.*] —**string'i•ness** *n.* —**string'y** *adj.*
string bean. 1. A narrow, green, edible bean pod. **2.** A plant bearing such pods.
strin•gent (strĭn'jənt) *adj.* **1.** Imposing rigorous standards of performance; severe. **2.** Constricted; tight. [< L *stringere,* to tighten.] —**strin'gen•cy** *n.* —**strin'gent•ly** *adv.*
strip1 (strĭp) *v.* **stripped, stripping. 1.** To undress. **2.** To deprive of honors, rank, etc. **3.** To remove all excess detail from. **4.** To dismantle piece by piece. **5.** To denude; bare. [< OE *(be)strīepan,* to plunder < Gmc **straupjan.*]
strip2 (strĭp) *n.* **1.** A long, narrow piece, usually of uniform width: *a strip of paper.* **2.** An airstrip. [Perh var of STRIPE.]
stripe (strīp) *n.* **1.** A long, narrow band distinguished, as by color or texture, from the surrounding material or surface. **2.** A strip of cloth worn on a uniform to indicate rank, awards, etc.; a chevron. **3.** Sort; kind. —*v.* **striped, striping.** To mark with a stripe or stripes. [< MDu *stripe.*] —**striped** (strīpt, strī'pĭd) *adj.*
strip•ling (strĭp'lĭng) *n.* A youth. [ME, prob "slender as a strip."]
strive (strīv) *v.* **strove, striven** (strĭv'ən) or **strived, striving. 1.** To exert much effort or energy. **2.** To struggle; contend. [< OF *estriver.*] —**striv'er** *n.*
strob•o•scope (strō'bə-skōp') *n.* Any of various instruments used to make moving objects appear stationary by intermittent illumination or observation. [Gk *strobos,* a whirling round + -SCOPE.] —**strob'o•scop'ic** (-skŏp'ĭk) *adj.* —**strob'o•scop'i•cal•ly** *adv.*
strode (strōd). *p.t.* of **stride.**
stroke (strōk) *n.* **1.** An impact; blow; strike. **2.** An act of striking. **3.** An event having a powerful immediate effect: *a stroke of luck.* **4.** Apoplexy. **5.** An inspired idea or act: *a stroke of genius.* **6.** A single completed movement, as in swimming or rowing. **7.** The member of a rowing crew who sets the tempo of the oarsmen. **8.** Any of a series of movements of a piston from one end of the limit of its motion to the other. **9.** A single mark made by a pen or other marking implement. **10.** A light caressing movement. —*v.* **stroked, stroking. 1.** To rub lightly, as with the hand; caress. **2.** To set the pace for (a rowing crew). [< OE **strāc.* See **streig-.**]
stroll (strōl) *v.* To walk at a leisurely pace. [Perh < G dial *strollen.*] —**stroll** *n.*
stroll•er (strō'lər) *n.* **1.** One who strolls. **2.** A light four-wheeled chair for transporting small children.
strong (strông) *adj.* **1. a.** Having great physical strength; muscular. **b.** Powerful; forceful. **2.** In sound health; thriving. **3.** Capable of enduring; solid. **4.** Having a specified number of units or members. **5. a.** Persuasive and effective. **b.** Emphatic. **6.** Extreme; drastic. **7.** Intense in degree or quality. [< OE *strang.*]

—**strong'ly** *adv.*

strong•box (strông'bŏks') *n.* A stoutly made box or safe in which valuables are deposited.

strong•hold (strông'hōld') *n.* **1.** A fortress. **2.** An area of predominance.

stron•ti•um (strŏn'chē-əm, -tē-əm) *n. Symbol* **Sr** A soft, silvery, easily oxidized metallic element used in pyrotechnic compounds and various alloys. Atomic number 38, atomic weight 87.62. [< *Strontian,* mining village in Scotland.]

strop (strŏp) *n.* A flexible strip of leather or canvas used for sharpening a razor. —*v.* **stropped, stropping.** To sharpen on a strop. [< Gk *strophos,* twisted cord.]

stro•phe (strō'fē, strō'fē') *n.* A stanza of a poem. [Gk *strophē,* a turning.] —**stroph'ic** *adj.*

strove (strōv). *p.t.* of **strive.**

struck (strŭk). *p.t.* & *p.p.* of **strike.**

struc•ture (strŭk'chər) *n.* **1.** A complex entity. **2. a.** Organization; arrangement. **b.** Constitution; make-up. **3.** Something constructed, esp. a building or part. —*v.* **-tured, -turing.** To construct or give structure to. [< L *struere* (pp *structus*), to construct.] —**struc'tur•al** *adj.* —**struc'tur•al•ly** *adv.*

stru•del (strōōd'l) *n.* A rolled sheet of dough filled with fruit or cheese and baked. [G.]

strug•gle (strŭg'əl) *v.* **-gled, -gling. 1.** To exert muscular energy, as against a material force or mass; wrestle. **2.** To be strenuously engaged with a problem, task, etc. **3. a.** To contend against. **b.** To compete with. —*n.* **1.** An act of struggling. **2.** Strenuous effort. **3.** Combat; strife. [ME *struglen.*] —**strug'gler** *n.*

strum (strŭm) *v.* **strummed, strumming.** To play idly on (a stringed musical instrument) by plucking the strings with the fingers. [Perh blend of STRING and THRUM.]

strum•pet (strŭm'pĭt) *n.* A whore.

strung (strŭng). *p.t.* & *p.p.* of **string.**

strut (strŭt) *v.* **strutted, strutting.** To walk with pompous bearing; swagger. —*n.* **1.** A stiff, self-important gait. **2.** A bar or rod used to strengthen a framework by resisting longitudinal thrust. [< OE *strūtian,* to stand out stiffly. See **ster-**[1].] —**strut'ter** *n.* —**strut'ting•ly** *adv.*

strych•nine (strĭk'nīn', -nən, -nēn') *n.* An extremely poisonous white crystalline alkaloid, $C_{21}H_{22}N_2O_2$. [< Gk *strukhnos,* a kind of plant.]

St. Thom•as (sānt' tŏm'əs). The second-largest of the Virgin Islands of the U.S.

stub (stŭb) *n.* **1.** The short blunt end remaining after something has been cut, broken off, or worn down. **2. a.** The part of a check or receipt retained as a record. **b.** The part of a ticket returned as a voucher of payment. —*v.* **stubbed, stubbing.** To strike (one's toe or foot) against something. [< OE *stybb.* See **steu-.**]

stub•ble (stŭb'əl) *n.* **1.** Short, stiff stalks, as of grain, left on a field after harvesting. **2.** Anything resembling stubble. [< L *stipula,* straw.] —**stub'bly** *adj.*

stub•born (stŭb'ərn) *adj.* **1.** Unduly determined to exert one's will; obstinate. **2.** Persistent. **3.** Difficult to handle or work. [ME *stoborne.*] —**stub'born•ness** *n.*

stub•by (stŭb'ē) *adj.* **-bier, -biest.** Short and stocky. —**stub'bi•ness** *n.*

stuc•co (stŭk'ō) *n., pl.* **-coes** or **-cos.** A plaster or cement finish for walls. —*v.* To finish or decorate with stucco. [< OHG *stukki,* fragment, covering.]

stuck (stŭk). *p.t.* & *p.p.* of **stick.**

stuck-up (stŭk'ŭp') *adj. Informal.* Snobbish; conceited.

stud[1] (stŭd) *n.* **1.** An upright post in the framework of a wall for supporting sheets of lath, wallboard, etc. **2.** A small knob, nail head, etc., fixed in and slightly projecting from a surface. **3.** A small ornamental button, as on a dress shirt. —*v.* **studded, studding.** To provide with or construct with a stud or studs. [< OE *studu,* post, prop.]

stud[2] (stŭd) *n.* **1.** A stallion or other male animal kept for breeding. **2.** A group of such animals. [< OE *stōd,* stable for breeding.]

stud. student.

stu•dent (st/y/ōō'dənt) *n.* One who studies, esp. at a school.

stud•ied (stŭd'ēd) *adj.* Carefully contrived; deliberate; lacking spontaneity.

stu•di•o (st/y/ōō'dē-ō) *n., pl.* **-os. 1.** An artist's workroom. **2.** An establishment where an art is taught or studied. **3.** A room or building for motion-picture, television, or radio productions. [< L *studium,* study.]

stu•di•ous (st/y/ōō'dē-əs) *adj.* **1.** Devoted to study. **2.** Earnest; diligent. —**stu'di•ous•ly** *adv.*

stud•y (stŭd'ē) *n., pl.* **-ies. 1.** The act or process of studying; the pursuit of knowledge. **2.** A branch of knowledge. **3.** A work on a particular subject. **4.** A room intended or equipped for studying. —*v.* **-ied, -ying. 1.** To apply one's mind purposefully to the acquisition of knowledge or understanding of (any subject). **2.** To take (a course) at a school. **3.** To inquire into; investigate. **4.** To examine closely; contemplate. [< L *studium* < *studēre,* to be eager, study.] —**stud'i•er** *n.*

stuff (stŭf) *n.* **1.** The material out of which something is made or formed; substance. **2.** The basic elements of; essence. **3.** Material not specifically identified. **4.** Woven material, esp. woolens. —*v.* **1. a.** To pack tightly; fill up; cram. **b.** To block or obstruct. **2.** To fill with an appropriate stuffing. **3.** To eat to excess. [< LL *stuppāre,* to plug up.]

stuff•ing (stŭf'ĭng) *n.* Material used to stuff or fill, esp. padding put in cushions or food put in a cavity of meat or vegetables.

stuff•y (stŭf'ē) *adj.* **-ier, -iest. 1.** Lacking sufficient ventilation. **2.** Blocked: *a stuffy nose.* **3.** Formal; straitlaced. —**stuff'i•ness** *n.*

stul•ti•fy (stŭl'tə-fī') *v.* **-fied, -fying. 1.** To render useless or ineffectual. **2.** To cause to appear stupid, ridiculous, etc. [< L *stultus,* foolish + *facere,* to make.] —**stul'ti•fi•ca'tion** *n.*

stum•ble (stŭm'bəl) *v.* **-bled, -bling. 1. a.** To trip and almost fall. **b.** To proceed unsteadily or falteringly. **2.** To make a mistake; blunder. **3.** To come upon accidentally or unexpectedly. [ME *stumblen.*] —**stum'ble** *n.* —**stum'bler** *n.* —**stum'bling•ly** *adv.*

stumbling block. An obstacle or impediment.

stump (stŭmp) *n.* **1.** The part of a tree trunk remaining rooted after the tree has been felled. **2.** A part, as of a limb, remaining after the main part has been cut away. —*v.* **1.** To traverse (a district) making political speeches. **2.** To bring to a halt; perplex. [< MLG.] —**stump'er** *n.* —**stump'y** *adj.*

stun (stŭn) *v.* **stunned, stunning. 1.** To daze or render senseless, as by a blow. **2.** To stupefy, as with the emotional impact of an experience. [< VL **extonāre.*]

stung (stŭng). *p.t.* & *p.p.* of **sting.**

stunk (stŭngk). *p.p.* & alternate *p.t.* of **stink.**

stun•ning (stŭn'ĭng) *adj.* **1.** Causing loss of consciousness or emotional shock. **2.** *Informal.* Of a strikingly attractive appearance.

stunt[1] (stŭnt) *v.* To check the growth or development of; dwarf. [Perh < ME *stont,* short in duration.] —**stunt'ed•ness** *n.*

stunt[2] (stŭnt) *n.* **1.** A feat displaying unusual skill or daring. **2.** Something of an unusual nature: *publicity stunt.* [?]

stu•pe•fy (st/y/ōō'pə-fī') *v.* **-fied, -fying. 1.** To dull the senses of. **2.** To amaze; astonish. [< L *stupefacere.*] —**stu'pe•fa'cient** (-fā'shənt) *adj.* & *n.* —**stu'pe•fac'tion** *n.*

stu•pen•dous (st/y/ōō-pĕn'dəs) *adj.* **1.** Of astounding force, volume, degree, or excellence. **2.** Of tremendous size; huge. [< L *stupēre,* to be stunned.] —**stu•pen'dous•ly** *adv.*

stu•pid (st/y/ōō'pĭd) *adj.* **1.** Slow to apprehend; dull; obtuse. **2.** Showing a lack of sense or intelligence. **3.** Uninteresting; trite: *a stupid job.* [< L *stupēre,* to be stunned.] —**stu•pid'i•ty** *n.* —**stu'pid•ly** *adv.*

stu•por (st/y/ōō'pər) *n.* **1.** A state of reduced sensibility; lethargy. **2.** Mental confusion; daze. [< L *stupēre,* to be stunned.] —**stu'por•ous** *adj.*

stur•dy (stûr'dē) *adj.* **-dier, -diest.** Substantially built; durable; strong. [< OF *estourir,* to stun, daze.] —**stur'di•ly** *adv.* —**stur'di•ness** *n.*

stur•geon (stûr'jən) *n.* A large food fish whose roe is valued as caviar. [< VL **sturiō* < Gmc **strujōn.*]

stut•ter (stŭt'ər) *v.* To speak with a spasmodic hesitation, prolongation, or repetition of sounds. —*n.* The act or habit of stuttering. [< ME *stutten.*] —**stut'ter•er** *n.* —**stut'ter•ing•ly** *adv.*

Stutt•gart (stŭt'gärt). A city of SW West Germany. Pop. 632,000.

St. Vi•tus' dance (sānt' vī'təs-ĭz). Also **St. Vi•tus's dance.** *Path.* Chorea. [< St. *Vitus,* 3rd-century Christian martyr, venerated by sufferers of the disease.]

sty[1] (stī) *n., pl.* **sties.** An enclosure for pigs. [< OE *stī, stig* < Gmc **stijam.*]

sty[2] (stī) *n., pl.* **sties** or **styes.** Inflammation of a sebaceous gland of an eyelid. [< OE *stīgan,* to rise. See **steigh-.**]

style (stīl) *n.* **1.** The way in which something is said or done. **2.** The combination of distinctive features of literary or artistic expression characterizing a particular person, school, etc. **3.** Sort; kind; type: *a style of furniture.* **4.** Individuality expressed in one's actions and tastes. **5.** An elegant mode of existence: *live in style.* **6.** The fashion of the moment. **7.** A customary manner of presenting printed material, including usage, punctuation, spelling, typography, and arrangement. **8.** The slender stalk of a flower pistil. —*v.* **styled, styling. 1.** To call or name; designate. **2.** To design: *style hair.* [< L *stilus,* writing instrument, style.] —**styl'er** *n.*

styl•ish (stī'lĭsh) *adj.* In step with current fashion; modish; smart; elegant. —**styl'ish•ly** *adv.* —**styl'ish•ness** *n.*

styl•ist (stī'lĭst) *n.* One who cultivates an artful style, esp. a writer.

sty•lis•tic (stī-lĭs'tĭk) *adj.* Of or relating to style, esp. literary style. —**sty•lis'ti•cal•ly** *adv.*

styl•ize (stī'līz') *v.* **-ized, -izing.** To subordinate verisimilitude to principles of design in the representation of.

sty•lus (stī'ləs) *n., pl.* **-luses** or **-li** (-lī'). **1.** A sharp, pointed instrument used for writing, marking, or engraving. **2.** A phonograph needle. [L *stilus,* STYLE.]

sty•mie (stī'mē) *v.* **-mied, -mieing** or **-mying.** To block; thwart. [?]

styp•tic (stĭp'tĭk) *adj.* **1.** Contracting the tissues or blood vessels; astringent. **2.** Tending to check bleeding. —*n.* A styptic drug or substance. [< Gk *stuphein,* to contract.]

sty•rene (stī'rēn') *n.* A colorless oily liquid, C_8H_8, the monomer for polystyrene.

suave (swäv, swāv) *adj.* Smoothly gracious in social manner; urbane. [< L *suāvis,* delightful.] —**suave'ly** *adv.* —**suav'i•ty, suave'ness** *n.*

sub (sŭb) *n. Informal.* **1.** A submarine. **2.** A substitute. —*v.* **subbed, subbing.** To act as a substitute.

sub–. *comb. form.* **1.** Under or beneath. **2.** Inferior in rank. **3.** Somewhat short of or less than. **4.** Forming a subordinate or constituent part of a whole. [< L *sub,* under, from below.]

sub. subscription.

sub•al•tern (sŭb'ôl'tərn) *n.* A subordinate. [LL *subalternus.*]

sub•a•tom•ic (sŭb'ə-tŏm'ĭk) *adj.* **1.** Pertaining to the constituents of the atom. **2.** Participating in reactions characteristic of these constituents.

sub•com•mit•tee (sŭb'kə-mĭt'ē) *n.* A subordinate committee composed of members appointed from the main committee.

sub•con•scious (sŭb'kŏn'shəs) *adj.* Not wholly conscious but capable of being made conscious. —**sub'con'scious•ly** *adv.*

sub•con•ti•nent (sŭb'kŏn'tə-nənt) *n.* A large land mass on a continent, but in some geographic respect independent of it, as India or S Africa.

sub•con•tract (sŭb'kŏn'trăkt') *n.* A contract that assigns some of the obligations of a prior contract to another party. —**sub'con'tract'** *v.*

sub•cu•ta•ne•ous (sŭb'kyōō-tā'nē-əs) *adj.* Just beneath the skin. —**sub'cu•ta'ne•ous•ly** *adv.*

sub•di•vide (sŭb'də-vīd') *v.* **-vided, -viding.** To divide into smaller parts. —**sub'di•vi'sion** (-vĭzh'ən) *n.*

sub•due (səb-d/y/ōō') *v.* **-dued, -duing. 1.** To conquer and subjugate. **2.** To quiet or bring under control. **3.** To make less intense. [< L *subdūcere,* to lead away, withdraw.]

sub•e•qua•to•ri•al (sŭb'ē-kwə-tôr'ē-əl, -tōr'ē-əl, sŭb'ĕk-wə-) *adj.* Belonging to a region adjacent to the equatorial area.

sub•group (sŭb'grōōp') *n.* A subordinate group.

subj. **1.** subject. **2.** subjunctive.

sub•ja•cent (sŭb'jā'sənt) *adj.* **1.** Located beneath or below. **2.** Lying at a lower level but not directly beneath. [< L *subjacēre,* to lie under.]

sub•ject (sŭb'jĭkt) *adj.* **1.** Under the power or authority of another. **2.** Prone; disposed: *subject to colds.* **3.** Liable to incur or receive: *subject to misinterpretation.* **4.** Contingent or dependent: *subject to rules.* —*n.* **1.** One who owes allegiance to a government or ruler. **2.** A person or thing concerning which something is said or done. **3.** A course or area of study. **4.** One that experiences or is subjected to something. **5.** *Gram.* A word or phrase in a sentence that denotes the doer of the action or the receiver of the action in passive constructions. —*v.* (sŭb-jĕkt'). **1.** To subjugate; subdue. **2.** To submit to the authority of. **3.** To cause to experience or undergo. [< L *subicere,* to bring under.] —**sub•jec'tion** (-jĕk'shən) *n.*

sub•jec•tive (səb-jĕk'tĭv) *adj.* **1.** Proceeding from or taking place within an individual's mind. **2.** Particular to a given individual; personal. —**sub•jec'tive•ly** *adv.* —**sub•jec'tive•ness, sub'jec•tiv'i•ty** *n.*

subject matter. Matter under consideration in a written work or speech.

sub•join (sŭb-join') *v.* To add at the end; append.

sub•ju•gate (sŭb'jə-gāt') *v.* **-gated, -gating.** To bring under dominion; conquer. [< L *subjugāre,* to place under a yoke.] —**sub'ju•ga'tion** *n.* —**sub'ju•ga'tor** *n.*

sub•junc•tive (sŭb-jŭngk'tĭv) *adj.* Designating a verb form or set of forms used in English to express a contingent or hypothetical action. [< L *subjungere,* subjoin.] —**sub•junc'tive** *n.*

sub•let (sŭb'lĕt') *v.* **-let, -letting.** To rent (property one holds by lease) to another.

sub•li•mate (sŭb'lə-māt') *v.* **-mated, -mating. 1.** To modify the natural expression of (an instinctual impulse) in a socially acceptable manner. **2.** To transform directly from the solid to the gaseous or from the gaseous to the solid state. [L *sublīmāre,* to raise.] —**sub'li•ma'tion** *n.*

sub•lime (sə-blīm') *adj.* **1.** Exalted; lofty. **2.** Inspiring awe; impressive; moving. [L *sublīmis.*] —**sub•lime'ly** *adv.* —**sub•lim'i•ty** (sə-blĭm'ə-tē), **sub•lime'ness** *n.*

sub•lim•i•nal (sŭb-lĭm'ə-nəl) *adj.* Below the threshold of conscious perception. [SUB- + L *līmen,* threshold.] —**sub•lim'i•nal•ly** *adv.*

sub•ma•chine gun (sŭb'mə-shēn'). A lightweight automatic or semiautomatic gun fired from the shoulder or hip.

sub•ma•rine (sŭb'mə-rēn', sŭb'mə-rēn') *adj.* Beneath the surface of the water; undersea. —*n.* A ship capable of operating submerged.

sub•merge (səb-mûrj') *v.* **-merged, -merging. 1.** To place or go under or as if under water or other liquid. **2.** To cover with water. [L *submergere.*] —**sub•mer'gence** *n.* —**sub•mer'gi•ble** *adj.* —**sub•mer'gi•bil'i•ty** *n.*

sub•merse (səb-mûrs') *v.* **-mersed, -mersing.** To submerge. —**sub•mers'i•bil'i•ty** *n.* —**sub•mers'i•ble** *adj.* —**sub•mer'sion** *n.*

sub•mi•cro•scop•ic (sŭb'mī'krə-skŏp'ĭk) *adj.* Too small to be resolved by an optical microscope.

sub•min•i•a•ture (sŭb'mĭn'ē-ə-chŏŏr', -chər) *adj.* Smaller than miniature; exceedingly small. —**sub'min'i•a•tur•ize'** (-chə-rīz') *v.* **(-ized, -izing).**

sub•mit (səb-mĭt') *v.* **-mitted, -mitting. 1.** To yield or surrender (oneself) to the will or authority of another; give in. **2.** To commit (something) to the consideration of another. **3.** To offer as a proposition or contention: *I submit that the terms are unreasonable.* **4.** To allow oneself to be subjected to; acquiesce. [< L *submittere,* to place under.] —**sub•mis'sion** *n.* —**sub•mis'sive** *adj.*

sub•nor•mal (sŭb'nôr'məl) *adj.* Less than normal; below the average.

sub•or•di•nate (sə-bôr'də-nĭt) *adj.* **1.** Belonging to a lower or inferior class or rank. **2.** Subject to the authority or control of another. **3.** *Gram.* Dependent on another clause. —*n.* One that is subordinate. —*v.* (sə-bôr'də-nāt') **-nated, -nating. 1.** To put in a lower or inferior rank or class. **2.** To make subservient. [< ML *subōrdināre,* to put in a lower rank.] —**sub•or'di•na'tion** *n.*

sub•orn (sə-bôrn') *v.* To induce (a person) to commit a wrong or unlawful act, as perjury. [L *subōrnāre.*] —**sub'or•na'tion** *n.*

sub•poe•na (sə-pē'nə). Also **sub•pe•na.** *n.* A legal writ requiring appearance in court to give testimony. —*v.* To serve or summon with such a writ. [< L *sub poenā,* under penalty (first words in the writ).]

sub ro•sa (sŭb rō'zə). In secret; privately.

sub•scribe (səb-scrīb') *v.* **-scribed, -scribing. 1.** To sign (one's name). **2.** To sign one's name to in testimony or consent: *subscribe a will.* **3.** To pledge or contribute (a sum of money). **4.** To express concurrence or approval (with *to*). **5.** To receive and pay for a certain number of issues of a periodical (with *to*). [< L *subscrībere.*] —**sub•scrib'er** *n.*

sub•script (sŭb'skrĭpt') *adj.* Written beneath. —*n.* A character or symbol written next to and slightly below a letter or number. [L *subscriptus,* pp of *subscrībere,* SUBSCRIBE.]

sub•scrip•tion (səb-skrĭp'shən) *n.* **1.** The signing of one's name, as to a document. **2.** A purchase made by signed order, as for the issues of a periodical or a series of theatrical performances.

sub•se•quent (sŭb'sə-kwənt) *adj.* Following in time or order; succeeding. [< L *subsequī,* to follow close after.] —**sub'se•quent•ly** *adv.*

sub•ser•vi•ent (səb-sûr'vē-ənt) *adj.* **1.** Subordinate in capacity or function. **2.** Servile. —**sub•ser'vi•ent•ly** *adv.* —**sub•ser'vi•ence** *n.*

sub•set (sŭb'sĕt') *n.* A mathematical set contained within a set.

sub•side (səb-sīd') *v.* **-sided, -siding. 1.** To sink to a lower or normal level. **2.** To become less agitated or active; abate. [L *subsīdere,* to sink down.] —**sub•si'dence** *n.*

sub•sid•i•ar•y (səb-sĭd'ē-ăr'ē) *adj.* **1.** Serving to assist or supplement. **2.** Secondary in importance. —*n., pl.* **-ies. 1.** One that is subsidiary. **2.** A company having more than half of its stock owned by another company. [< L *subsidium,* support, SUBSIDY.]

sub•si•dize (sŭb'sə-dīz') *v.* **-dized, -dizing.** To assist or support with a subsidy.

sub•si•dy (sŭb'sə-dē) *n., pl.* **-dies.** Monetary assistance, as that granted by a government to a private commercial enterprise. [< L *subsidium,* reserve troops, support, help.]

sub•sist (səb-sĭst') *v.* **1.** To exist. **2.** To be sustained, nourished, etc.; live. [L *subsistere,* to stand still, stand up.]

sub•sis•tence (səb-sĭs'təns) *n.* The act, state, or a means of subsisting.

sub•soil (sŭb'soil') *n.* The layer of earth beneath the surface soil.

sub•son•ic (sŭb'sŏn'ĭk) *adj.* **1.** Of less than audible frequency. **2.** Having a speed less than that of sound in a designated medium.

sub•stance (sŭb'stəns) *n.* **1. a.** Matter. **b.** Material of a specified, esp. complex, constitution. **2.** The essence of what is said or written; gist. **3.** That which is solid or real; reality as opposed to appearance. **4.** Density; body. **5.** Material possessions; wealth. [< L *substāre,* to be present, stand up.]

sub•stan•dard (sŭb'stăn'dərd) *adj.* Failing to meet a standard; below standard.

sub•stan•tial (səb-stăn'shəl) *adj.* **1.** Of or having substance; material. **2.** Not imaginary; real. **3.** Solidly built; strong. **4.** Ample; sustaining. **5.** Considerable in amount, extent, etc. [< L *substantia,* substance.] —**sub•stan'tial•ly** *adv.*

sub•stan•ti•ate (səb-stăn'shē-āt') *v.* **-ated, -ating.** To support with proof or evidence; verify. —**sub•stan'ti•a'tion** *n.*

sub•stan•tive (sŭb'stən-tĭv) *adj.* Of substantial amount; considerable. —*n.* A word or group of words functioning as a noun. —**sub'stan•ti'val** (-tī'vəl) *adj.*

sub•sta•tion (sŭb'stā'shən) *n.* A branch station, as of a post office.

sub•sti•tute (sŭb'stə-t/y/ōōt') *n.* One that takes the place of another; a replacement. —*v.*

-tuted, -tuting. 1. To put or use (a person or thing) in place of another. 2. To take the place of another. [< L *substituere.*] —**sub'sti•tut'a•bil'i•ty** *n.* —**sub'sti•tu'tion** *n.*

sub•stra•tum (sŭb'strā'təm, -străt'əm) *n., pl.* **-ta** (-tə) or **-tums.** An underlying layer. —**sub'stra'tive** *adj.*

sub•sume (sŭb-s/y/o͞om') *v.* **-sumed, -suming.** To place in a more comprehensive category. —**sub•sum'a•ble** *adj.*

sub•tend (səb-tĕnd') *v. Geom.* To be opposite to and delimit. [L *subtendere,* to extend beneath.]

sub•ter•fuge (sŭb'tər-fyo͞oj') *n.* An evasive tactic or a trick. [< L *subterfugere,* to flee secretly.]

sub•ter•ra•ne•an (sŭb'tə-rā'nē-ən) *adj.* 1. Situated beneath the earth's surface; underground. 2. Hidden; secret. [< L *subterrāneus.*] —**sub'ter•ra'ne•an•ly** *adv.*

sub•ti•tle (sŭb'tīt'l) *n.* 1. A secondary and usually explanatory title, as of a literary work. 2. A printed narration or portion of dialogue shown on the screen during or between the scenes of a motion picture.

sub•tle (sŭt'l) *adj.* **-tler, -tlest.** 1. So slight as to be difficult to detect or analyze; elusive. 2. Not immediately obvious; abstruse. 3. Able to make fine distinctions; keen. 4. Characterized by skill or ingenuity. 5. Characterized by craft or slyness. [< L *subtīlis,* thin, fine.] —**sub'tle•ty, sub'tle•ness** *n.* —**sub'tly** *adv.*

sub•tract (səb-trăkt') *v.* 1. To take away; deduct. 2. To find the arithmetic difference between two quantities. [L *substrahere,* to draw away.] —**sub•trac'tion** *n.*

sub•tra•hend (sŭb'trə-hĕnd') *n.* A quantity to be subtracted from another.

sub•trop•i•cal (sŭb'trŏp'ĭ-kəl) *adj.* Of or being the geographical areas adjacent to the tropics.

sub•trop•ics (sŭb'trŏp'ĭks) *pl.n.* Subtropical regions.

sub•urb (sŭb'ûrb') *n.* 1. A usually residential community outlying a city. 2. **the suburbs.** The perimeter of country around a major city; environs. [< L *sub-,* near + *urbs,* city.] —**sub•ur'ban** (sə-bûr'bən) *adj.*

sub•ur•ban•ite (sə-bûr'bə-nīt') *n.* One who lives in a suburb.

sub•ur•bi•a (sə-bûr'bē-ə) *n.* Suburbs or suburbanites collectively.

sub•ver•sive (səb-vûr'sĭv, -zĭv) *adj.* Intended or serving to subvert. —*n.* One who advocates subversive means or policies.

sub•vert (səb-vûrt') *v.* 1. To destroy completely; ruin. 2. To undermine the character, morals, or allegiance of; corrupt. 3. To overthrow completely. [< L *subvertere,* to turn upside down.] —**sub•ver'sion** (-vûr'zhən, -shən) *n.* —**sub•vert'er** *n.*

sub•way (sŭb'wā') *n.* An underground urban railroad, usually operated by electricity.

suc•ceed (sək-sēd') *v.* 1. To follow or come next in time or order; replace, esp. in an office or position. 2. To accomplish something desired or attempted. [< L *succēdere,* to follow closely, go after.] —**suc•ceed'er** *n.*

suc•cess (sək-sĕs') *n.* 1. The achievement of something desired or attempted. 2. The gaining of fame or prosperity. 3. One that succeeds. [L *successus,* pp of *succēdere,* SUCCEED.] —**suc•cess'ful** *adj.* —**suc•cess'ful•ly** *adv.*

suc•ces•sion (sək-sĕsh'ən) *n.* 1. The act or process of following in order or sequence. 2. A group of persons or things following in order; sequence. 3. The sequence, right, or act of succeeding to a title, throne, dignity, or estate. —**suc•ces'sion•al** *adj.*

suc•ces•sive (sək-sĕs'ĭv) *adj.* Following in uninterrupted order or sequence. —**suc•ces'sive•ly** *adv.*

suc•ces•sor (sək-sĕs'ər) *n.* One that succeeds another.

suc•cinct (sək-sĭngkt') *adj.* Clearly expressed in few words; concise; terse. [L *succinctus,* girdled, concise.] —**suc•cinct'ly** *adv.* —**suc•cinct'ness** *n.*

suc•cor (sŭk'ər) *n.* Also *Brit.* **suc•cour.** Assistance or help in time of distress; relief. [< L *succurrere,* to run to the aid of, run under.] —**suc'cor** *v.*

suc•co•tash (sŭk'ə-tăsh') *n.* Corn kernels and lima beans cooked together. [< Algon.]

Suc•coth (so͝ok'ōt, -əs) *n.* Also **Suk•koth.** A Jewish harvest festival. [Heb *sukkōth,* "(feast of) booths."]

suc•cu•lent (sŭk'yə-lənt) *adj.* 1. Full of juice; juicy. 2. Having thick, fleshy leaves or stems. —*n.* A succulent plant, as a cactus. [< L *succus,* juice.] —**suc'cu•lence, suc'cu•len•cy** *n.* —**suc'cu•lent•ly** *adv.*

suc•cumb (sə-kŭm') *v.* 1. To yield or submit to an overpowering force. 2. To die. [< L *succumbere,* to lie down under.]

such (sŭch) *adj.* 1. Of this or that kind. 2. Being the same as that which has been mentioned or implied. 3. Being the same in quality or kind: *pins, needles, and other such trivia.* 4. Of so great a degree or quality. —**such as.** 1. For example. 2. Of the stated or implied kind or degree. —*pron.* Such a one or ones. —*adv.* 1. To such an extent or degree. 2. Very. [< OE *swylc, swelc.* See **swo-.**]

suck (sŭk) *v.* 1. To draw (liquid) into the mouth by inhalation. 2. a. To draw in by establishing a partial vacuum. b. To draw in by or as by suction. 3. To draw nourishment through or from with the mouth. —*n.* The act of sucking. [< OE *sūcan.* See **seu-**[4].]

suck•er (sŭk'ər) *n.* 1. One that sucks. 2. *Slang.* One who is easily deceived; a dupe. 3. A lollipop. 4. A structure or part adapted for clinging by suction. 5. A shoot arising from the base of a tree trunk or shrub.

suck•le (sŭk'əl) *v.* **-led, -ling.** 1. To feed at the breast or udder. 2. To rear; nourish.

suck•ling (sŭk'lĭng) *n.* A young unweaned mammal.

su•cre (so͞o'krā) *n.* The basic monetary unit of Ecuador.

Su•cre (so͞o'krā). A capital of Bolivia. Pop. 541,000.

su•crose (so͞o'krōs') *n.* A sugar, $C_{12}H_{22}O_{11}$, found in sugar cane, sugar beets, etc., and used widely as a sweetener. [F *sucre,* sugar + -OSE.]

suc•tion (sŭk'shən) *n.* 1. The act or process of sucking. 2. A force that causes a fluid or solid to be drawn into an interior space or to adhere to a surface. —*adj.* 1. Creating suction. 2. Operating by suction. [< L *sūgere* (pp *sūctus*), to suck.]

Su•dan (so͞o-dăn'). A region lying across Africa, S of the Sahara and N of the equator. —**Su•da•nese'** (-də-nēz', -nēs') *adj. & n.*

Su•dan, Republic of the (so͞o-dăn'). A country in NE Africa. Pop. 13,011,000. Cap. Khartoum. —**Su•dan'ic** *adj. & n.*

sud•den (sŭd'n) *adj.* 1. Happening without warning; unforeseen. 2. Characterized by hastiness; rash. 3. Characterized by rapidity; quick; swift. [< L *subitus.*] —**sud'den•ly** *adv.* —**sud'den•ness** *n.*

suds (sŭdz) *pl.n.* 1. Soapy water. 2. Foam; lather. [Orig, dregs, muddy water.] —**suds'y** *adj.*

sue (so͞o) *v.* **sued, suing.** 1. To institute legal proceedings; bring suit against (a person) for redress of grievances. 2. To make an appeal or entreaty. [ME *sewen,* to pursue, prosecute.]

suede (swād) *n.* Also **suède.** 1. Leather with a soft napped surface. 2. Fabric resembling this. [< F *(gants) de suède,* "(gloves) of Sweden."]

su•et (so͞o'ĭt) *n.* Hard fat of cattle and sheep, used in cooking and making tallow. [< L *sēbum,* tallow, suet.]

Su•ez Canal (so͞o-ĕz', so͞o'ĕz). A waterway in NE Egypt, connecting the Mediterranean and Gulf of Suez.

suf. suffix.

suff. 1. sufficient. 2. suffix.

suf•fer (sŭf'ər) *v.* 1. To feel pain or distress. 2. To experience or sustain (an injury, loss, disadvantage, etc.). 3. To endure or bear; stand. 4. To permit; allow. [< L *sufferre,* to sustain, "to bear up."] —**suf'fer•a•ble** *adj.* —**suf'fer•er** *n.* —**suf'fer•ing•ly** *adv.*

suf•fer•ance (sŭf'ər-əns, sŭf'rəns) *n.* Sanction or permission implied or given by failure to prohibit; tacit assent.

suf•fer•ing (sŭf'ər-ĭng, sŭf'rĭng) *n.* The act or condition of one who suffers.

suf•fice (sə-fīs') *v.* **-ficed, -ficing.** 1. To meet present needs or requirements; be sufficient or adequate for. 2. To be capable or competent. [< L *sufficere,* to put under, substitute, suffice.] —**suf•fic'er** *n.*

suf•fi•cient (sə-fĭsh'ənt) *adj.* As much as is needed; enough. [< L *sufficere,* SUFFICE.] —**suf•fi'cien•cy** *n.* —**suf•fi'cient•ly** *adv.*

suf•fix (sŭf'ĭks') *n. Gram.* An affix added to the end of a word or stem, serving to form a new word or an inflectional ending. [< L *suffigere,* to affix, fasten beneath.]

suf•fo•cate (sŭf'ə-kāt') *v.* **-cated, -cating.** 1. To kill or destroy by cutting off from oxygen. 2. To impair the respiration of. 3. To cause discomfort by or as by cutting off the supply of air. 4. To die from suffocation. [L *suffocāre.*] —**suf'fo•ca'tion** *n.*

suf•frage (sŭf'rĭj) *n.* 1. The right or privilege of voting; franchise. 2. The exercise of such a right. [< ML *suffrāgium,* vote, support, prayer.]

suf•fra•gette (sŭf'rə-jĕt') *n.* A female advocate of suffrage for women.

suf•fuse (sə-fyo͞oz') *v.* **-fused, -fusing.** To spread through or over, as with color or light. [L *suffundere* (pp *suffūsus*), to pour underneath or into.] —**suf•fu'sion** *n.*

sug•ar (sho͝og'ər) *n.* Any of a class of water-soluble crystalline carbohydrates having a

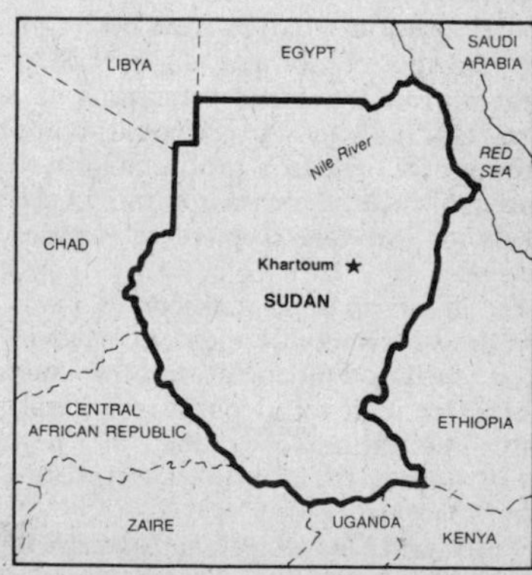

Republic of the Sudan

characteristically sweet taste. —*v.* To coat or sweeten with sugar. [< Ar *sukkar.*]
sugar beet. A beet with white roots from which sugar is obtained.
sugar cane. A tall grass of warm regions, having thick stems that are a major commercial source of sugar.
sug•ar•plum (shŏŏg'ər-plŭm') *n.* A small piece of candy.
sug•ar•y (shŏŏg'ə-rē) *adj.* **-ier, -iest. 1.** Containing or tasting like sugar. **2.** Deceitfully or cloyingly sweet.
sug•gest (səg-jĕst', sə-jĕst') *v.* **1.** To offer for consideration or action; propose. **2.** To bring or call to mind by association; evoke. **3.** To make evident indirectly; imply. [L *suggerere,* to carry or put underneath, furnish, suggest.]
sug•ges•tion (səg-jĕs'chən, sə-jĕs'-) *n.* **1.** The act of suggesting. **2.** Something suggested. **3.** A trace; touch.
sug•ges•tive (səg-jĕs'tĭv, sə-jĕs'-) *adj.* **1.** Tending to suggest thoughts or ideas. **2.** Tending to suggest something improper or indecent. —**sug•ges'tive•ly** *adv.* —**sug•ges'tive•ness** *n.*
su•i•cide (s/y/ōō'ə-sīd') *n.* **1.** The act or an instance of intentionally killing oneself. **2.** One who commits suicide. [< L *suī,* of oneself + -CIDE.] —**su'i•ci'dal** *adj.*
su•i gen•e•ris (s/y/ōō'ī jĕn'ər-ĭs). Unique. [L, "of one's own kind."]
suit (sōōt) *n.* **1.** A set of outer garments consisting of a coat and trousers or skirt. **2.** Any of the four sets of playing cards that constitute a deck. **3.** Any proceeding in a court of law to recover a right or claim. —*v.* **1.** To meet the requirements of. **2.** To be or make appropriate; adapt. **3.** To please; satisfy. [< VL **sequita,* pursuit.]
suit•a•ble (s/y/ōō'tə-bəl) *adj.* Appropriate to a given purpose or occasion. —**suit'a•bil'i•ty** (-bĭl'ə-tē) *n.* —**suit'a•bly** *adv.*
suit•case (s/y/ōōt'kās') *n.* A rectangular, flat piece of luggage.
suite (swēt) *n.* **1.** A staff of attendants; retinue. **2.** A series of connected rooms used as a living unit. **3.** (*also* sōōt). A set of matched furniture pieces. **4.** An instrumental composition consisting of a succession of short pieces. [< OF *sieute,* following, retinue.]
suit•ing (sōō'tĭng) *n.* Fabric from which suits are made.
suit•or (sōō'tər) *n.* A man in the process of courting a woman. [< L *sequī,* to follow.]
Suk•koth. Variant of **Succoth.**
sulf–. *comb. form.* Sulfur. [< SULFUR.]
sul•fa drug (sŭl'fə). Any of a group of synthetic organic compounds, such as sulfanilamide, capable of inhibiting bacterial growth and activity.
sul•fa•nil•a•mide (sŭl'fə-nĭl'ə-mīd') *n.* A white, odorless compound, $C_6H_8N_2SO_2$, used to treat various bacterial infections.
sul•fate (sŭl'fāt') *n.* A chemical compound containing the bivalent group SO_4.
sul•fide (sŭl'fīd') *n.* A compound of bivalent sulfur with an electropositive element or group.
sul•fur (sŭl'fər) *n.* Also **sul•phur.** *Symbol* **S** A pale-yellow nonmetallic element used in gunpowder, rubber vulcanization, the manufacture of insecticides and pharmaceuticals, and in the preparation of industrial chemicals. Atomic number 16, atomic weight 32.064. [< L *sulfur, sulphur.*]
sulfur dioxide. A colorless, extremely irritating gas or liquid, SO_2, used to manufacture sulfuric acid.
sul•fu•ric (sŭl'fyŏŏr'ĭk) *adj.* Of or containing sulfur.
sulfuric acid. A highly corrosive, dense oily liquid, H_2SO_4, used to manufacture fertilizers, paints, detergents, and explosives.
sul•fur•ous (sŭl'fə-rəs, sŭl'fyŏŏr'əs) *adj.* Of, relating to, derived from, or containing sulfur.
sulk (sŭlk) *v.* To be sullenly aloof or withdrawn. —*n.* A mood or display of sulking. [Back-formation < SULKY[1].]
sulk•y[1] (sŭl'kē) *adj.* **-ier, -iest.** Sullenly aloof or withdrawn. [Perh < obs *sulke,* sluggish.] —**sulk'i•ly** *adv.* —**sulk'i•ness** *n.*
sulk•y[2] (sŭl'kē) *n., pl.* **-ies.** A light two-wheeled vehicle accommodating one person and drawn by one horse. [< SULKY.]
sul•len (sŭl'ən) *adj.* **1.** Showing a brooding ill humor or resentment; morose; sulky. **2.** Gloomy or somber in tone, color, etc. [< NF **solein,* alone, sullen.] —**sul'len•ly** *adv.* —**sul'len•ness** *n.*
sul•ly (sŭl'ē) *v.* **-lied, -lying. 1.** To mar the cleanness or luster of. **2.** To defile; taint. [Prob < OF *souiller,* to soil.]
sul•phur. Variant of **sulfur.**
sul•tan (sŭl'tən) *n.* A Moslem ruler. [< Ar *sulṭān,* ruler.] —**sul'tan•ate'** (-āt') *n.*
sul•tan•a (sŭl-tăn'ə, -tä'nə) *n.* The wife, mother, sister, or daughter of a sultan.
sul•try (sŭl'trē) *adj.* **-trier, -triest. 1.** Very hot and humid. **2.** Extremely hot; torrid. [< SWELTER.] —**sul'tri•ness** *n.*
sum (sŭm) *n.* **1.** The amount obtained as a result of adding. **2.** The whole amount or number; aggregate: *the sum of our knowledge.* **3.** An amount of money. **4.** An arithmetic problem. **5.** A summary: *in sum.* —*v.* **summed, summing.** To give a brief review; summarize. [< L *(res) summa,* the highest thing, sum, total.]
su•mac (sōō'măk', shōō'-) *n.* Also **su•mach.** Any of various shrubs or small trees with compound leaves and pointed clusters of small, usually red, hairy fruits. [< Ar *summaq,* sumac tree.]
Su•ma•tra (sōō-mä'trə). The second-largest island of Indonesia.
sum•ma•rize (sŭm'ə-rīz') *v.* **-rized, -rizing.** To make a summary of; restate briefly. —**sum'ma•ri•za'tion** *n.*
sum•ma•ry (sŭm'ə-rē) *adj.* **1.** Presenting the substance in a condensed form; concise. **2.** Performed speedily and without ceremony: *summary justice.* —*n., pl.* **-ries.** A condensation of the substance of a work. [< L *summa,* SUM.] —**sum•ma'ri•ly** (sə-măr'ə-lē, sŭm'ər-ə-lē) *adv.*
sum•ma•tion (sə-mā'shən) *n.* A summing up, esp. a concluding statement containing a summary of the principal points of a case before a court of law.
sum•mer (sŭm'ər) *n.* The usually warmest season of the year, occurring between spring and autumn. [< OE *sumor.* See **sem-**[2].] —**sum'mer, sum'mer•y** *adj.*
sum•mer•time (sŭm'ər-tīm') *n.* The summer season.
sum•mit (sŭm'ĭt) *n.* The highest point or part; the top, esp. of a mountain. [< L *summus,* highest, topmost.]
sum•mon (sŭm'ən) *v.* **1.** To call together; convene. **2.** To send for; request to appear. **3.** To order (a person) to appear in court. **4.** To call forth; muster: *summoned up a smile.* [< L *summonēre,* to remind secretly.]
sum•mons (sŭm'ənz) *n., pl.* **-monses. 1.** A call or order to appear or come. **2.** A notice summoning a defendant to report to a court.
sump•tu•ous (sŭmp'chōō-əs) *adj.* Of a size or splendor suggesting great expense; lavish. [< L *sumptus,* expense.] —**sump'tu•ous•ly** *adv.* —**sump'tu•ous•ness** *n.*
sun (sŭn) *n.* **1.** The central star of the solar system, having a mean distance from Earth of about 93 million miles, a diameter of approx. 864,000 miles, and a mass about 330,000 times that of Earth. **2.** Any star that is the center of a planetary system. **3.** The radiant energy, esp. heat and visible light, emitted by the sun; sunshine. —*v.* **sunned, sunning.** To expose to or bask in the sun's rays. [< OE *sunne.* See **sāwel-.**]
Sun. Sunday.
sun-bathe (sŭn'bāth') *v.* To expose the body to the sun. —**sun'-bath'er** *n.*
sun•burn (sŭn'bûrn') *n.* An inflammation or blistering of the skin caused by overexposure to sunlight. —*v.* To afflict with or be subjected to a sunburn.
sun•dae (sŭn'dē, -dā') *n.* A dish of ice cream topped with syrup, fruits, nuts, and whipped cream. [?]
Sun•day (sŭn'dē, -dā') *n.* The first day of the week and the Christian Sabbath. [< OE *sunnandæg,* "day of the sun."]
sun•der (sŭn'dər) *v.* To break apart; divide. [< OE *syndrian, sundrian.* See **sen-.**]
sun•di•al (sŭn'dī'əl) *n.* An instrument that indicates local apparent solar time by measuring the hour angle of the sun with a pointer that casts a shadow on a calibrated dial.
sun•down (sŭn'doun') *n.* The time of sunset.
sun•dries (sŭn'drēz) *pl.n.* Miscellaneous articles. [< SUNDRY.]
sun•dry (sŭn'drē) *adj.* Various; miscellaneous. [< OE *syndrig,* apart, separate. See **sen-.**]
sun•fish (sŭn'fĭsh') *n.* **1.** Any of various flat-bodied North American freshwater fishes. **2.** A large marine fish with a rounded body.
sun•flow•er (sŭn'flou'ər) *n.* A tall plant bearing large, yellow-rayed flowers and oil-rich, edible seeds.
sung (sŭng). *p.p.* & alternate *p.t.* of **sing.**
sun•glass•es (sŭn'glăs'ĭz, -glä'sĭz) *pl.n.* Eyeglasses with tinted lenses to protect the eyes from the sun's glare.
sunk (sŭngk). *p.p.* & alternate *p.t.* of **sink.** See Usage note at **sink.**
sunk•en (sŭng'kən). Alternate *p.p.* of **sink.** —*adj.* **1.** Depressed, fallen in, or hollowed. **2.** Submerged. **3.** Below the surrounding level.
sun•light (sŭn'līt') *n.* The light of the sun; sunshine.
sun•lit (sŭn'lĭt') *adj.* Illuminated by the sun.
sun•ny (sŭn'ē) *adj.* **-nier, -niest. 1.** Exposed to or abounding in sunshine. **2.** Cheerful; genial.
sun•rise (sŭn'rīz') *n.* The first appearance of the sun above the E horizon.
sun•set (sŭn'sĕt') *n.* The disappearance of the sun below the W horizon.
sun•shine (sŭn'shīn') *n.* The light of the sun; the direct rays from the sun.
sun•spot (sŭn'spŏt') *n.* Any of the relatively dark spots that appear in groups on the surface of the sun.
sun•stroke (sŭn'strōk') *n.* Heat stroke caused by exposure to the sun and characterized by a rise in temperature, convulsions, and coma. —**sun'struck'** (-strŭk') *adj.*
sun tan. Also **sun•tan** (sŭn'tăn'). A tan color on the skin from exposure to the sun. —**sun'-tanned'** *adj.*
sun•up (sŭn'ŭp') *n.* The time of sunrise.
Sun Yat-sen (sōōn' yät'sĕn'). 1866–1925.

Founder of the Republic of China (1911).

sup (sŭp) *v.* **supped, supping.** To eat the evening meal; dine. [< OF *soup,* piece of bread dipped in broth, soup.]

sup. 1. above (L *supra*). 2. superior. 3. *Gram.* superlative. 4. supplement. 5. supply.

su•per (sōō'pər) *n. Informal.* A superintendent in an apartment or office building. —*adj. Slang.* Ideal; first-rate.

super–. *comb. form.* 1. Placement above, over, or outside. 2. Superiority in size, quality, number, or degree. 3. A degree exceeding a norm. 4. *Chem.* Presence of an ingredient in a high proportion. [< L *super,* above, over.]

super. 1. superintendent. 2. superior.

su•per•a•bun•dant (sōō'pər-ə-bŭn'dənt) *adj.* Abundant to excess; more than ample. —**su'per•a•bun'dance** *n.*

su•per•an•nu•at•ed (sōō'pər-ăn'yōō-ā'tĭd) *adj.* 1. Retired or discharged because of age or infirmity. 2. Obsolete; antiquated. [< ML *superannuārī,* to be too old.]

su•perb (sōō-pûrb', sə-) *adj.* 1. Of unusually high quality. 2. Majestic; imposing. [< L *superbus,* superior, proud, arrogant.]

su•per•charge (sōō'pər-chärj') *v.* To increase the power of (an engine). —**su'per•charg'er** *n.*

su•per•cil•i•ar•y (sōō'pər-sĭl'ē-ĕr'ē) *adj.* 1. Pertaining to the eyebrow. 2. Located over the eyebrow. [< L *supercilium,* eyebrow.]

su•per•cil•i•ous (sōō'pər-sĭl'ē-əs) *adj.* Characterized by haughty scorn; disdainful; arrogant. [< L *supercilium,* "upper eyelid," eyebrow, pride.] —**su'per•cil'i•ous•ly** *adv.* —**su'per•cil'i•ous•ness** *n.*

su•per•con•duc•tiv•i•ty (sōō'pər-kŏn'dŭk'-tĭv'ə-tē) *n.* The flow of electric current without resistance in certain metals and alloys at temperatures near absolute zero. —**su'per•con•duc'tor** *n.*

su•per•e•go (sōō'pər-ē'gō, -ĕg'ō) *n.* The division of the psyche that develops by the incorporation of the perceived moral standards of the community, is mainly unconscious, and includes the conscience.

su•per•e•rog•a•to•ry (sōō'pər-ə-rŏg'ə-tôr'ē, -tōr'ē) *adj.* Superfluous; unnecessary.

su•per•fi•cial (sōō'pər-fĭsh'əl) *adj.* 1. Of or being on or near the surface. 2. Concerned with or comprehending only what is apparent or obvious. 3. a. Apparent rather than actual or substantial. b. Trivial. [< L *superficiēs,* surface.] —**su'per•fi'ci•al'i•ty, su'per•fi'cial•ness** *n.* —**su'per•fi'cial•ly** *adv.*

su•per•flu•id (sōō'pər-flōō'ĭd) *n.* A fluid exhibiting frictionless flow at temperatures close to absolute zero. —**su'per•flu•id'i•ty** *n.*

su•per•flu•i•ty (sōō'pər-flōō'ə-tē) *n., pl.* **-ties.** 1. The quality or condition of being superfluous. 2. Something that is superfluous.

su•per•flu•ous (sōō-pûr'flōō-əs) *adj.* Beyond what is required or sufficient; extra. [< L *superfluere,* to overflow.] —**su•per'flu•ous•ly** *adv.* —**su•per'flu•ous•ness** *n.*

su•per•high•way (sōō'pər-hī'wā') *n.* A broad highway for high-speed traffic.

su•per•hu•man (sōō'pər-hyōō'mən) *adj.* 1. Divine; supernatural. 2. Beyond ordinary or normal human ability, power, or experience.

su•per•im•pose (sōō'pər-ĭm-pōz') *v.* To lay or place upon or over something else. —**su'per•im'po•si'tion** *n.*

su•per•in•tend (sōō'pər-ĭn-tĕnd') *v.* To have charge of; exercise supervision over; manage. [LL *superintendere,* to oversee.] —**su'per•in•ten'dence** *n.*

su•per•in•ten•dent (sōō'pər-ĭn-tĕn'dənt) *n.* One who supervises or is in charge of some undertaking, building, etc.

su•pe•ri•or (sə-pîr'ē-ər) *adj.* 1. Higher in rank, station, or authority. 2. Of a higher nature or kind. 3. Of great value or excellence. 4. Greater in number or amount. 5. Haughty. 6. *Ptg.* Set above the main line of type. —*n.* 1. One who surpasses another in rank or quality. 2. The head of a monastery, convent, etc. 3. *Ptg.* A superior character. [< L *superus,* situated above, upper.] —**su•pe'ri•or'i•ty** (-pîr'ē-ôr'ə-tē, -ŏr'ə-tē) *n.*

Superior, Lake. The largest of the Great Lakes.

su•per•la•tive (sōō-pûr'lə-tĭv) *adj.* 1. Of the highest order, quality, or degree. 2. *Gram.* Expressing the extreme degree of comparison of an adjective or adverb. —*n.* 1. The highest degree; acme. 2. *Gram.* a. The superlative degree. b. An adjective or adverb expressing the superlative degree. [< LL *superlātīvus.*] —**su•per'la•tive•ly** *adv.* —**su•per'la•tive•ness** *n.*

su•per•man (sōō'pər-măn') *n.* A man with more than human powers.

su•per•mar•ket (sōō'pər-mär'kĭt) *n.* A large self-service retail food and household-goods store.

su•per•nal (sōō-pûr'nəl) *adj.* 1. Celestial; heavenly. 2. Exalted. [< L *supernus.*]

su•per•nat•u•ral (sōō'pər-năch'ər-əl) *adj.* 1. Not attributable to natural forces. 2. Attributable to divine power. —*n.* That which is supernatural. —**su'per•nat'u•ral•ly** *adj.* —**su'per•nat'u•ral•ness** *n.*

su•per•no•va (sōō'pər-nō'və) *n., pl.* **-vae** (-vē'). The explosion of most of the material in a star, resulting in an extremely bright, short-lived object that emits vast amounts of energy.

su•per•nu•mer•ar•y (sōō'pər-n/y/ōō'mər-ĕr'ē) *n., pl.* **-ries.** 1. Someone or something in excess of the regular, necessary, or usual number. 2. *Theater.* A performer without a speaking part. —**su'per•nu'mer•ar•y** *adj.*

su•per•pow•er (sōō'pər-pou'ər) *n.* A powerful and influential nation, esp. a nuclear power that dominates its satellites and allies in an international power bloc.

su•per•sat•u•rate (sōō'pər-săch'ər-āt') *v.* **-rated, -rating.** To cause (a chemical solution) to be more highly concentrated than is normally possible under given conditions of temperature and pressure.

su•per•scribe (sōō'pər-skrīb') *v.* **-scribed, -scribing.** To write (something) on the outside or upper part of, as on a letter, envelope, etc. [L *superscrībere,* to write over.]

su•per•script (sōō'pər-skrĭpt') *adj.* Written above, as a diacritical mark. —*n.* A character printed or written above and immediately to one side of another; *2* is the superscript in x^2. [L *superscriptus,* pp of *superscrībere,* SUPERSCRIBE.]

su•per•sede (sōō'pər-sēd') *v.* **-seded, -seding.** 1. To take the place of; replace or succeed. 2. To cause to be set aside or displaced. [< L *supersedēre,* to sit above, desist from.]

su•per•son•ic (sōō'pər-sŏn'ĭk) *adj.* Of, at, or caused by a speed greater than the speed of sound in a specified medium.

su•per•sti•tion (sōō'pər-stĭsh'ən) *n.* 1. A belief that some action not logically related to a course of events influences its outcome. 2. Any belief, practice, or rite unreasoningly upheld by faith in magic, chance, or dogma. [< L *superstitiō,* excessive fear, superstition.] —**su'per•sti'tious** *adj.*

su•per•struc•ture (sōō'pər-strŭk'chər) *n.* 1. Any structure built on top of something else. 2. That part of a building above the foundation.

su•per•vise (sōō'pər-vīz') *v.* **-vised, -vising.** To direct and inspect the performance of (workers or work); oversee. [ML *supervidēre,* to look over.] —**su'per•vi'sion** (-vĭzh'ən) *n.* —**su'per•vi'sor** *n.* —**su'per•vi'so•ry** (-vī'zə-rē) *adj.*

su•pine (sōō'pīn', sōō'pīn') *adj.* 1. Lying on the back or having the face upward. 2. Indisposed to act; lethargic; passive. [L *supinus.*]

sup•per (sŭp'ər) *n.* An evening meal, esp. a light one. [< SUP.]

suppl. supplement; supplementary.

sup•plant (sə-plănt') *v.* To take the place of; supersede or displace. [< L *supplantāre,* to trip up one's heel.] —**sup•plant'er** *n.*

sup•ple (sŭp'əl) *adj.* **-pler, -plest.** 1. Readily bent; pliant. 2. Moving and bending with agility; limber. 3. Compliant or adaptable. [< L *supplex,* beseeching, submissive.] —**sup'ple•ness** *n.*

sup•ple•ment (sŭp'lə-mənt) *n.* 1. Something added to complete a thing or make up for a deficiency. 2. A section added to a newspaper, book, or document to give further information. —*v.* (sŭp'lə-mĕnt'). To provide or form a supplement to. [< L *supplēre,* to complete, SUPPLY.] —**sup'ple•men'ta•ry** (-tə-rē, -trē), **sup'ple•men'tal** *adj.*

sup•pli•ant (sŭp'lĭ-ənt) *adj.* Asking humbly and earnestly; beseeching. —*n.* One who supplicates. [< L *supplicāre,* SUPPLICATE.]

sup•pli•cant (sŭp'lĭ-kənt) *n.* A suppliant.

sup•pli•cate (sŭp'lĭ-kāt') *v.* **-cated, -cating.** 1. To ask for humbly or earnestly, as by praying. 2. To make a humble entreaty to; beseech. [< L *supplicāre,* to kneel down, beg humbly.] —**sup'pli•ca'tion** *n.*

sup•ply (sə-plī') *v.* **-plied, -plying.** 1. To make available for use; provide. 2. To furnish or equip with what is needed or lacking. 3. To fill sufficiently; satisfy: *supply a need.* —*n., pl.* **-plies.** 1. The act of supplying. 2. An amount available for a given use; stock. 3. Often **supplies.** Materials or provisions stored and dispensed when needed. 4. *Econ.* The amount of a commodity available for meeting a demand or for purchase at a given price. [< L *supplēre,* to fill up, complete.] —**sup•pli'er** *n.*

sup•port (sə-pôrt', -pōrt') *v.* 1. To bear the weight of, esp. from below. 2. To hold in position; prevent from falling. 3. To be capable of bearing; withstand. 4. To provide for or maintain by supplying with money or other necessities. 5. To corroborate or substantiate. 6. To aid the cause of by approving, favoring, or advocating. 7. To endure; tolerate. 8. To act in a subordinate role to (a leading actor). —*n.* 1. The act of supporting. 2. Someone or something that supports. 3. Maintenance or subsistence. [< L *supportāre,* to carry, convey.] —**sup•port'er** *n.* —**sup•por'tive** *adj.*

sup•pose (sə-pōz') *v.* **-posed, -posing.** 1. To assume to be true for argument's sake. 2. To believe probable; be inclined to think. 3. To consider as a suggestion: *Suppose we dine together.* 4. To expect or require: *He is supposed to come at 8:00.* [< L *suppōnere* (pp *suppositus*), to put under, substitute.]

sup•po•si•tion (sŭp'ə-zĭsh'ən) *n.* 1. The act of supposing. 2. An unproven statement or assumption.

sup•pos•i•to•ry (sə-pŏz'ə-tôr'ē, -tōr'ē) *n., pl.* **-ries.** A solid medication designed to melt within a bodily cavity other than the mouth. [< L *suppositōrius,* "placed under."]

sup•press (sə-prĕs') *v.* **1.** To put an end to forcibly; subdue; crush. **2.** To curtail or prohibit the activities of. **3.** To keep from being revealed, published, or circulated. **4.** To hold back, as an impulse; check. [< L *supprimere,* to press down.] **—sup•pres'sion** *n.* **—sup•pres'sive** *adj.*

sup•pu•rate (sŭp'yə-rāt') *v.* **-rated, -rating.** To form pus, as a wound. [L *suppūrāre.*] **—sup'pu•ra'tion** *n.*

su•prem•a•cy (sə-prĕm'ə-sē) *n., pl.* **-cies. 1.** The condition or quality of being supreme. **2.** Supreme power or authority.

su•preme (sə-prēm') *adj.* **1.** Greatest in power, authority, or rank. **2.** Greatest in importance or degree. **3.** Ultimate; final. [L *suprēmus,* superl of *superus,* situated above, upper.] **—su•preme'ly** *adv.*

Supreme Court. 1. The highest Federal court in the U.S. **2.** The highest court in a state within the U.S.

Supreme Soviet. The legislature of the Soviet Union.

supt., Supt. superintendent.

sur–. *comb. form.* **1.** Over, beyond, or above. **2.** Excessively; extremely. [< L *super,* above, over.]

Su•ra•ba•ya (sŏŏr'ə-bī'ə). A city of NE Java. Pop. 1,008,000.

su•rah (sŏŏr'ə) *n.* A soft twilled fabric of silk, rayon, etc. [< *Surat,* republic of India.]

sur•cease (sûr'sēs', sər-sēs') *n.* A ceasing; end.

sur•charge (sûr'chärj') *n.* **1.** An additional sum added to the usual amount or cost. **2.** A new value or denomination printed over a postage stamp. *—v.* **1.** To overcharge (a person). **2.** To print a surcharge on (a postage stamp).

sur•cin•gle (sûr'sĭng'gəl) *n.* A girth that binds a saddle, pack, or blanket to the body of a horse. [< OF *sur-,* over + *cengle,* belt.]

sur•coat (sûr'kōt') *n.* **1.** A loose outer coat or gown. **2.** A tunic worn in the Middle Ages by a knight over his armor.

sure (shŏŏr) *adj.* **surer, surest. 1.** Incapable of being doubted. **2.** Having no doubt; certain; confident. **3.** Not liable to fail; thoroughly dependable. **4. a.** Bound to happen; inevitable. **b.** Destined: *sure to succeed.* **—make sure.** To establish without doubt; make certain. **—to be sure.** Indeed; certainly. *—adv. Informal.* Surely; indeed; undoubtedly. **—for sure.** Certainly; unquestionably: *We'll win for sure.* [< L *sēcūrus,* "free from care," safe.]

sure-fire (shŏŏr'fīr') *adj. Informal.* Bound to be successful or perform as expected: *a sure-fire plan.*

sure-foot•ed (shŏŏr'fŏŏt'ĭd) *adj.* Not liable to stumble or fall.

sure•ly (shŏŏr'lē) *adv.* **1.** Firmly and with confidence. **2.** Undoubtedly; certainly.

sure•ty (shŏŏr'ə-tē) *n., pl.* **-ties. 1.** Confidence in one's abilities; poise. **2.** A certainty. **3.** A guarantee against loss, damage, or default. **4.** A guarantor.

surf (sûrf) *n.* The mass of foamy water caused by the breaking of the sea against the shore. *—v.* To engage in surfing. [?]

sur•face (sûr'fəs) *n.* **1. a.** The outer or the topmost boundary of an object. **b.** A material layer constituting such a boundary. **2.** The superficial or outward appearance of anything. *—v.* **-faced, -facing. 1.** To give a surface to by smoothing or leveling. **2.** To rise to the surface. **3.** To emerge after concealment. [< F *sur,* above + FACE.] **—sur'face** *adj.*

surf•board (sûrf'bôrd', -bōrd') *n.* The narrow, somewhat rounded board used by surfers for riding waves into shore.

sur•feit (sûr'fĭt) *v.* To feed or supply to fullness or excess; satiate. *—n.* **1.** Overindulgence in food or drink. **2.** The result of such overindulgence; satiety. **3.** An excessive amount. [< VL **superficere,* to overdo.]

surf•er (sûr'fər) *n.* One who engages in surfing.

surf•ing (sûr'fĭng) *n.* A sport in which one attempts to ride a surfboard toward the shore.

surg. surgeon; surgery; surgical.

surge (sûrj) *v.* **surged, surging. 1.** To move in a billowing or swelling manner. **2.** To move forward in great numbers. **3.** To increase suddenly. *—n.* **1.** A heavy, billowing, or swelling motion like that of great waves. **2.** A sudden increase or onrush: *a surge of joy.* [< L *surgere,* "to lead straight up," rise.]

sur•geon (sûr'jən) *n.* A physician specializing in surgery.

sur•ger•y (sûr'jə-rē) *n., pl.* **-ies. 1.** The medical diagnosis and treatment of injury, deformity, and disease by manual and instrumental operations. **2.** A surgical operating room or laboratory. [< Gk *kheirurgos,* working by hand.] **—sur'gi•cal** *adj.*

Su•ri•nam (sŏŏr'ə-năm). A territory of the Netherlands, in N South America. Pop. 362,000. Cap. Paramaribo.

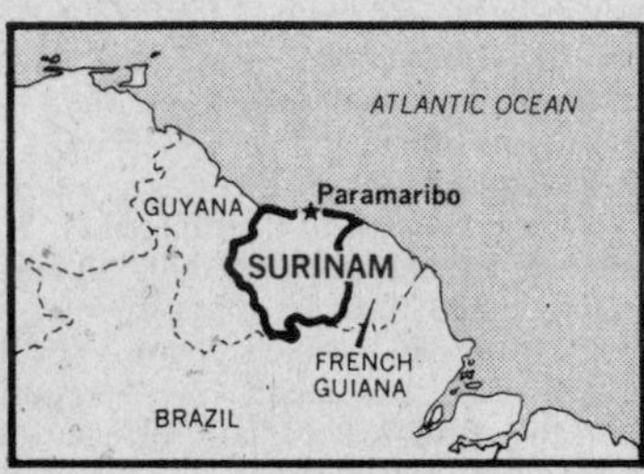

Surinam

sur•ly (sûr'lē) *adj.* **-lier, -liest.** Sullenly rude and ill-humored; brazenly uncivil; gruff. [Earlier *sirly,* orig "lordly" < SIR.] **—sur'li•ness** *n.*

sur•mise (sər-mīz') *v.* **-mised, -mising.** To infer (something) without sufficiently conclusive evidence. *—n.* A guess; conjecture. [< LL *supermittere,* to throw upon.]

sur•mount (sər-mount') *v.* **1.** To overcome (an obstacle). **2.** To ascend to the top of and cross over. **3.** To place something above; to top. **4.** To be above or on top of.

sur•name (sûr'nām') *n.* One's family name as distinguished from his given name.

sur•pass (sər-păs', -päs') *v.* **1.** To go beyond the limit, powers, or extent of; transcend. **2.** To be or go beyond in quantity, degree, amount, etc.

sur•plice (sûr'plĭs) *n.* A loose-fitting white gown worn over a cassock by some clergymen. [< ML *superpellicium.*]

sur•plus (sûr'pləs) *adj.* Being in excess of what is needed or required. *—n.* A quantity in excess of what is needed. [< ML *superplūs.*]

sur•prise (sər-prīz') *v.* **-prised, -prising. 1.** To encounter suddenly or unexpectedly; take or catch (a person) unawares. **2.** To attack or capture suddenly and without warning. **3.** To cause to feel astonishment or amazement. *—n.* **1.** The act of surprising. **2.** A feeling of amazement or wonder. **3.** An unexpected encounter, event, or gift. [< OF *surprendre,* "to overtake."] **—sur•pris'er** *n.*

sur•re•al•ism (sə-rē'əl-ĭz'əm) *n.* A literary and artistic movement that attempts to express the workings of the subconscious mind. **—sur•re'al•ist** *adj.* & *n.* **—sur•re'al•is'tic** *adj.*

sur•ren•der (sə-rĕn'dər) *v.* **1.** To relinquish possession or control of to another because of demand or compulsion. **2.** To give oneself up, as to an enemy. [< OF *surrendre.*] **—sur•ren'der** *n.*

sur•rep•ti•tious (sûr'əp-tĭsh'əs) *adj.* Performed, made, or acquired by secret, clandestine, or stealthy means. [< L *surripere,* to seize secretly.] **—sur'rep•ti'tious•ly** *adv.*

sur•rey (sûr'ē) *n., pl.* **-reys.** A horse-drawn four-wheeled vehicle with two seats. [< *Surrey,* county in England.]

sur•ro•gate (sûr'ə-gĭt, -gāt') *n.* **1.** One that is substituted for another; a substitute. **2.** A judge having jurisdiction over the probate of wills and settlement of estates. [L *subrogāre,* to substitute.]

sur•round (sə-round') *v.* **1.** To enclose on all sides; encircle; ring. **2.** To confine on all sides so as to bar escape. [< LL *superundāre.*]

sur•round•ings (sə-roun'dĭngz) *pl.n.* External circumstances, conditions, and objects; environment.

sur•tax (sûr'tăks') *n.* An additional tax.

sur•veil•lance (sər-vā'ləns) *n.* Close observation of a person or group, esp. of one under suspicion. [< F *surveiller,* to watch over.]

sur•vey (sər-vā', sûr'vā') *v.* **1.** To examine or look at in a comprehensive way. **2.** To determine the boundaries, area, or elevations of by measuring angles and distances. *—n.* (sûr'vā'). **1.** A detailed inspection or investigation. **2.** A general or comprehensive view. **3. a.** The process of surveying. **b.** A report on or map of that which is surveyed. [< ML *supervidēre,* to look over.] **—sur•vey'al** *n.* **—sur•vey'or** *n.*

sur•vey•ing (sər-vā'ĭng) *n.* The measurement of dimensional relationships, as of horizontal distances, elevations, directions, and angles, on the earth's surface.

sur•vive (sər-vīv') *v.* **-vived, -viving. 1.** To remain alive or in existence; continue life or activity. **2.** To live longer than; outlive. [< LL *supervīvere.*] **—sur•viv'al** *n.* **—sur•vi'vor** *n.*

sus•cep•ti•ble (sə-sĕp'tə-bəl) *adj.* **1.** Readily subject to an influence or agency. **2.** Liable to be stricken with or by: *susceptible to colds.* **3.** Especially sensitive or impressionable. [< L *suscipere,* to take up, receive.] **—sus•cep'ti•bil'i•ty** *n.* **—sus•cep'ti•bly** *adv.*

sus•pect (sə-spĕkt') *v.* **1.** To have suspicion; mistrust. **2.** To surmise to be probable; imagine. **3.** To think (a person) guilty without proof. *—n.* (sŭs'pĕkt'). One who is suspected, esp. of committing a crime. *—adj.* (sŭs'pĕkt'). Open to or viewed with suspicion. [< L *suspicere,* to look up at, watch.]

sus•pend (sə-spĕnd') *v.* **1.** To bar for a period from a privilege, office, or position. **2.** To interrupt or stop temporarily. **3. a.** To hold in abeyance: *suspend judgment.* **b.** To render ineffective temporarily: *suspend a sentence.* **4.** To hang so as to allow free movement. **5.** To support or keep from falling without apparent attachment. **6.** To fail to make payments or meet obligations. [< L *suspendēre,* to hang up.]

sus•pend•er (sə-spĕn'dər) *n.* **1.** One of a pair of straps worn over the shoulders to support trousers. **2.** *Brit.* A garter.

sus•pense (sə-spĕns') *n.* **1.** The condition of being suspended; suspension. **2.** A state of uncertainty. **3.** Anxiety or apprehension.

—**sus•pense'ful** *adj.*

sus•pen•sion (sə-spĕn'shən) *n.* **1.** The act of suspending or condition of being suspended, as temporary abrogation or postponement. **2.** A device from which something is suspended. **3.** A relatively coarse, noncolloidal dispersion of solid particles in a liquid.

sus•pi•cion (sə-spĭsh'ən) *n.* **1.** The act or an instance of suspecting something without proof. **2.** A minute amount; hint; trace. [< L *suspicere,* to look at secretly, SUSPECT.]

sus•pi•cious (sə-spĭsh'əs) *adj.* **1.** Arousing or open to suspicion; questionable. **2.** Tending to suspect; distrustful. —**sus•pi'cious•ly** *adv.*

sus•tain (sə-stān') *v.* **1.** To maintain; prolong. **2.** To supply with necessities or nourishment; provide for. **3.** To keep from falling or sinking. **4.** To support or encourage. **5.** To endure or withstand. **6.** To suffer (loss or injury). **7.** To affirm the validity or justice of. **8.** To prove or confirm. [< L *sustinēre,* to hold up.] —**sus•tain'a•ble** *adj.*

sus•te•nance (sŭs'tə-nəns) *n.* **1.** The act of sustaining or condition of being sustained. **2.** The supporting of life or health; maintenance. **3.** Nourishment; food. **4.** Means of support. [< OF *sustenir,* sustain.]

su•tra (sōō'trə) *n.* Also **sut•ta** (sōō'tə). Any of various aphoristic discourses or narratives traditional in Buddhism and Hinduism. [Sk *sūtra,* thread, string, collection of rules.]

sut•tee (sŭ'tē', sŭt'ē') *n.* The act or practice of a Hindu widow cremating herself on her husband's funeral pyre.

su•ture (sōō'chər) *n.* **1. a.** The process of joining by or as if by sewing. **b.** The material used in this procedure, as thread, gut, etc. **c.** The line so formed. **2.** The line of junction or an immovable joint between two bones of the skull. —*v.* **-tured, -turing.** To join surgically by means of sutures; sew up. [< L *sūtūra,* a sewing together, seam.]

su•ze•rain (sōō'zə-rən, -rān') *n.* **1.** A feudal lord to whom fealty was due. **2.** A nation that controls another nation politically. [F.] —**su'ze•rain** *adj.* —**su'ze•rain•ty** *n.*

svelte (svĕlt) *adj.* **svelter, sveltest.** Slender; willowy; lithe. [< It *svelto,* "stretched," slender.]

Sverd•lovsk (sfĕrd'lôfsk'). A city of the Soviet Union, in the W Russian S.F.S.R. Pop. 1,026,000.

sw short wave; short-wave.

SW southwest.

Sw. Swedish.

swab (swŏb). Also **swob.** *n.* **1.** Absorbent material attached to the end of a stick or wire and used for cleansing or applying medicine. **2.** A mop for cleaning decks. **3.** A sailor. —*v.* **swabbed, swabbing.** To clean or treat with a swab. [Prob < MDu *swabbe,* mop.]

swad•dle (swŏd'l) *v.* **-dled, -dling. 1.** To wrap in bandages; swathe. **2.** To wrap (a baby) in strips of linen or other cloth. [< OE *swæthel,* swaddling clothes.]

swag (swăg) *n.* Goods or property obtained forcibly or illicitly. [Prob < Scand.]

swage (swāj) *n.* A tool used in bending or shaping cold metal. [< OF *souaige.*] —**swage** *v.* **(swaged, swaging).**

swag•ger (swăg'ər) *v.* **1.** To walk with an insolent air; strut. **2.** To brag; bluster. [Prob < SWAG.] —**swag'ger** *n.* —**swag'ger•er** *n.*

swagger stick. A short cane carried by military officers.

Swa•hi•li (swä-hē'lē) *n.* A Bantu language of E and C Africa, widely used as a lingua franca. —**Swa•hi'li•an** *adj.*

swain (swān) *n.* **1.** A country youth, esp. a young shepherd. **2.** A lover. [< ON *sveinn,* a boy, herdsman.]

swal•low[1] (swä'lō) *v.* **1.** To cause to pass from the mouth into the stomach; ingest. **2.** To consume or devour. **3.** To ingest reluctantly. **4. a.** To bear humbly; tolerate: *swallow an insult.* **b.** To believe without question. **5. a.** To suppress: *swallow one's feelings.* **b.** To take back; retract: *swallow one's words.* —*n.* **1.** The act of swallowing. **2.** The amount or matter that can be swallowed at one time. [< OE *swelgan.* See **swel-[1]**.]

swal•low[2] (swä'lō) *n.* Any of various birds with narrow, pointed wings and a usually notched or forked tail. [< OE *swealwe* < Gmc **swalwi.*]

swal•low•tail (swä'lō-tāl') *n.* **1.** Something resembling or suggestive of the deeply forked tail of a swallow. **2.** A man's fitted formal coat with a long, divided back part. **3.** Any of various butterflies with a taillike extension at the end of each hind wing.

swam (swăm). *p.t.* of **swim.**

swa•mi (swä'mē) *n.* **1.** A Hindu religious teacher. **2.** A spiritualist seer.

swamp (swämp, swômp) *n.* Land saturated with water; marsh. —*v.* **1.** To drench in or deluge with water. **2.** To overwhelm. **3.** To sink by filling with water. —**swamp'i•ness** *n.* —**swamp'y** *adj.*

swan (swän) *n.* A large, usually white aquatic bird with webbed feet and a long slender neck. [< OE *swan, suan.* See **swen-.**]

swang (swăng). *Rare. p.t.* of **swing.**

swank (swăngk) *adj.* Also **swank•y** (swăng'kē), **-ier, -iest. 1.** Imposingly fashionable or elegant. **2.** Ostentatious; pretentious. —*n.* **1.** Smartness; elegance. **2.** Swagger; pretentiousness. [< MHG *swanken,* to swing, swag.] —**swank'i•ly** *adv.* —**swank'i•ness** *n.*

swan's-down (swänz'doun') *n.* Also **swans•down. 1.** The down of a swan. **2.** A soft woolen or cotton fabric.

swap (swäp). Also **swop.** *v.* **swapped, swapping.** *Informal.* To trade one thing for another; exchange. [ME *swappen,* to strike, hit.] —**swap** *n.* —**swap'per** *n.*

sward (swôrd) *n.* Land covered with grassy turf. [< OE *sweard,* skin of the body, rind of bacon.]

sware (swâr). *Archaic. p.t.* of **swear.**

swarm (swôrm) *n.* **1.** A large number of insects or other small organisms, esp. when in motion. **2.** A throng of persons or animals. —*v.* **1.** To move in a swarm. **2.** To leave a beehive to form a new colony. **3.** To move or congregate in great numbers; throng. **4.** To be overrun or filled. [< OE *swearm.* See **swer-[2]**.]

swarth•y (swôr'*th*ē) *adj.* **-ier, -iest.** Having a dark or sunburned complexion. [< OE *sweart.* See **swordo-.**] —**swarth'i•ness** *n.*

swash (swäsh, swôsh) *n.* A splash or splashing sound. [Prob imit.] —**swash** *v.*

swash•buck•ler (swäsh'bŭk'lər) *n.* A flamboyant swordsman or daredevil. —**swash'buck'ling** *adj.*

swas•ti•ka (swäs'tĭ-kə, swä-stē'kə) *n.* **1.** An ancient symbol formed by a cross with the ends of the arms bent at right angles. **2.** The emblem of Nazi Germany. [Sk *svastika,* a sign of good luck.]

swat (swät) *v.* **swatted, swatting.** To deal a sharp blow to; slap. [Var of SQUAT.] —**swat** *n.* —**swat'ter** *n.*

swath (swäth, swôth) *n.* Also **swathe** (swä*th,* swô*th*). **1.** The width of the stroke of a scythe or mowing machine. **2. a.** A path made in mowing. **b.** A row of mown grass or grain. [< OE *swæth,* track, trace < Gmc **swath-.*]

swathe (swä*th*) *v.* **swathed, swathing.** To wrap or bind with or as with bandages. [< OE *swathian,* to wrap up.]

sway (swā) *v.* **1.** To swing or cause to swing from side to side. **2.** To bend; swerve. **3.** To vacillate. **4.** To persuade; exert influence on. **5.** *Archaic.* To rule or govern. —*n.* **1.** A gentle swinging from side to side. **2.** Power; influence. **3.** Dominion; sovereign power. [Prob < ON *sveigja,* to bend, yield.]

Swa•zi•land (swä'zĭ-lănd'). A kingdom in SE Africa. Pop. 400,000. Cap. Mbabane.

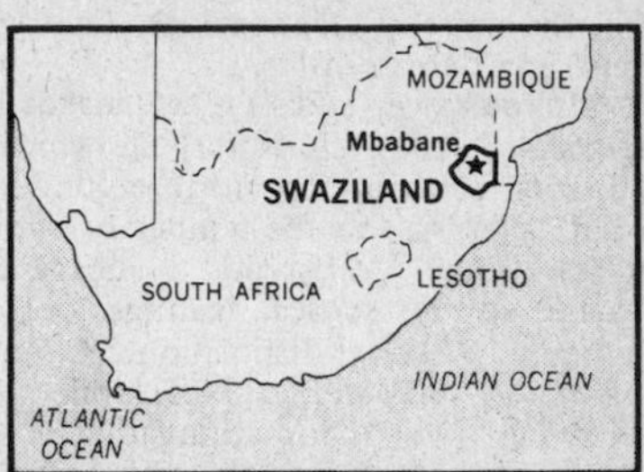

Swaziland

swear (swâr) *v.* **swore, sworn, swearing. 1.** To make a solemn declaration or promise. **2.** To curse or blaspheme. **3.** To assert under oath. **4.** To pledge with a solemn oath; vow. **5.** To administer a legal oath to. **6.** To affirm earnestly and with great conviction. [< OE *swerian.* See **swer-[1]**.] —**swear'er** *n.*

sweat (swĕt) *v.* **sweated** or **sweat, sweating. 1.** To excrete perspiration through the pores in the skin; perspire. **2.** To exude in or become moist with surface droplets. **3.** To condense atmospheric moisture. **4.** *Informal.* To work or cause to work long and hard. **5.** *Informal.* To worry or suffer. —*n.* **1.** Perspiration. **2.** Any condensation of moisture on a surface. **3.** Strenuous exercise or labor. [< OE *swǣtan.* See **sweid-.**] —**sweat'y** *adj.*

sweat•er (swĕt'ər) *n.* A knitted or crocheted garment worn on the upper part of the body.

sweat gland. Any of the numerous small, tubular glands that in man are found everywhere in the skin and that secrete perspiration externally through pores.

Swed. Swedish.

Swede (swēd) *n.* **1.** A native or inhabitant of Sweden. **2.** A person of Swedish descent.

Swe•den (swēd'n). A kingdom in NW Europe. Pop. 7,495,000. Cap. Stockholm.

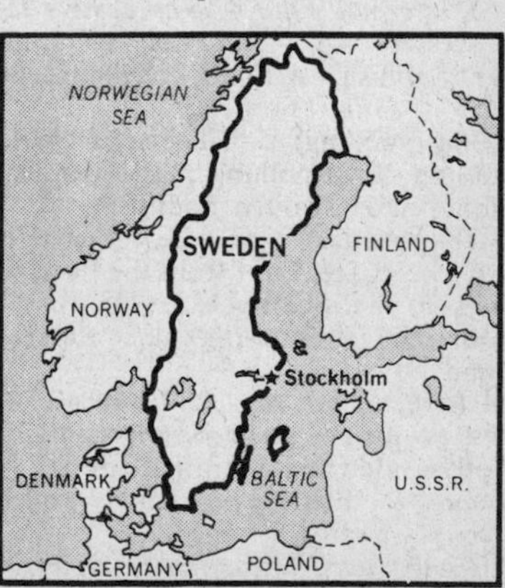

Sweden

ô paw, for/oi boy/ou out/ŏŏ took/ōō coo/p pop/r run/s sauce/sh shy/t to/th thin/*th* the/
ŭ cut/ûr fur/v van/w wag/y yes/z size/zh vision/ə ago, item, edible, gallop, circus/

Swed•ish (swē′dĭsh) *adj.* Of or pertaining to Sweden, the Swedes, or their language. *—n.* The Germanic language of Sweden.

sweep (swēp) *v.* **swept, sweeping.** **1.** To clean or clear with or as with a broom. **2.** To brush. **3.** To move, remove, or clear, as by wind or rain. **4.** To move or unbalance emotionally. **5.** To traverse with speed or intensity. **6.** To encompass in a wide curve. *—n.* **1.** A clearing or removal with or as with a broom. **2.** The motion of sweeping: *a sweep of the arm.* **3.** An encompassed range or scope. **4.** A reach or extent. **5.** Any curve or contour. [< OE *swāpan,* to sweep. See **swei-.**] **—sweep′er** *n.*

sweep•ing (swē′pĭng) *adj.* Extending over a great area; wide-ranging. *—n.* **1.** The action of one who sweeps. **2. sweepings.** That which is swept up; debris; litter.

sweep•stakes (swēp′stāks′) *n., pl.* **-stakes.** Also **sweep•stake** (-stāk′). A lottery in which the participants' contributions form a fund to be awarded as a prize to the winner or winners.

sweet (swēt) *adj.* **1.** Having a sugary taste. **2.** Pleasing to the senses, feelings, or mind. **3.** Having a pleasing disposition. **4.** Not saline; fresh: *sweet water.* **5.** Not spoiled, sour, or decaying. *—n.* **1.** Something that is sweet or contains sugar. **2.** A dear or beloved person. [< OE *swēte.* See **swād-.**] **—sweet′ly** *adv.* **—sweet′ness** *n.*

sweet•bread (swēt′brĕd′) *n.* The thymus gland of an animal, used for food.

sweet•bri•er (swēt′brī′ər) *n.* Also **sweet•bri•ar.** A rose with prickly stems and fragrant pink flowers.

sweet•en (swēt′n) *v.* **1.** To make sweet or sweeter by the addition of sugar. **2.** To make pleasurable or gratifying. **3.** To make bearable; alleviate. **—sweet′en•er** *n.*

sweet•en•ing (swēt′n-ĭng) *n.* **1.** The act or process of making sweet. **2.** Something used to sweeten.

sweet•heart (swēt′härt′) *n.* One who is loved by another.

sweet•meat (swēt′mēt′) *n.* A candy.

sweet pea. A climbing plant cultivated for its variously colored, fragrant flowers.

sweet potato. **1.** The thick, sweetish, orange-colored, edible root of a tropical vine. **2.** The vine itself.

swell (swĕl) *v.* **swelled, swelled** or **swollen, swelling.** **1.** To increase in size or volume as a result of internal pressure; expand; protrude. **2.** To increase in force, number, or intensity. **3.** To fill or become filled with an emotion, as pride. *—n.* **1.** A bulge or protuberance. **2.** A long wave that moves continuously without breaking. **3.** *Informal.* One who is always fashionably dressed. *—adj. Informal.* **1.** Fashionably elegant; stylish. **2.** Fine; excellent. [< OE *swellan* < Gmc **swaljan.*]

swell•ing (swĕl′ĭng) *n.* **1.** The act of swelling or expanding. **2.** Something that is swollen, esp. an abnormally swollen bodily part.

swel•ter (swĕl′tər) *v.* To be affected by oppressive heat; feel faint from the heat. [< OE *sweltan,* to die. See **swel-[2].**]

swel•ter•ing (swĕl′tər-ĭng) *adj.* Oppressively hot and humid.

swept (swĕpt). *p.t. & p.p.* of **sweep.**

swerve (swûrv) *v.* **swerved, swerving.** To turn abruptly aside from a straight course. [< OE *sweorfan,* to file away, scour, polish. See **swerbh-.**] **—swerve** *n.*

swift (swĭft) *adj.* **1.** Moving or able to move with speed; fast; fleet. **2.** Coming, occurring, or accomplished quickly. *—n.* A dark-colored, narrow-winged, swallowlike bird. [< OE. See **swei-.**] **—swift′ly** *adv.* **—swift′ness** *n.*

Swift (swĭft), **Jonathan.** 1667–1745. English satirist.

swig (swĭg) *n. Informal.* A large swallow or draft, as of a liquid; a gulp. [?] **—swig** *v.* **(swigged, swigging).**

swill (swĭl) *v.* **swilled, swilling.** To drink eagerly, greedily, or to excess. *—n.* **1.** A mixture of liquid and solid food fed to animals. **2.** Garbage; refuse. [< OE *swilian,* to wash out.] **—swill′er** *n.*

swim[1] (swĭm) *v.* **swam, swum, swimming.** **1.** To propel oneself through water by bodily movements. **2.** To swim across (a body of water). *—n.* **1.** The act of one that swims. **2.** A period or instance of swimming. [< OE *swimman.*] **—swim′mer** *n.*

swim[2] (swĭm) *v.* **swam, swum, swimming.** To be dizzy; feel faint or giddy: *my head is swimming.* [< OE *swīma,* dizziness. See **swei-.**]

swin•dle (swĭnd′l) *v.* **-dled, -dling.** To cheat or defraud (someone) of money or property. *—n.* The act or an instance of swindling; a fraud. [< G *schwindeln,* to be dizzy, swindle, cheat.] **—swin′dler** *n.*

swine (swīn) *n., pl.* **swine.** **1.** Often *pl.* A pig or related animal. **2.** A contemptible, vicious, or greedy person. [< OE *swīn.* See **su-.**] **—swin′ish** *adj.*

swing (swĭng) *v.* **swung, swinging.** **1.** To move rhythmically back and forth. **2.** To ride on a swing. **3.** To move, walk, or run with a free-swaying motion. **4.** To turn in place, as on a hinge or other pivot. **5.** To move with a swinging motion; brandish. **6.** *Slang.* To be executed by hanging. **7.** *Slang.* To manipulate or manage successfully. *—n.* **1.** A rhythmic back-and-forth movement. **2.** A sweeping blow or stroke. **3.** The manner in which a person or thing swings something, as a baseball bat or golf club. **4.** A seat suspended from above for the enjoyment of those who sit and swing thereon. **5.** A type of dance music based on jazz but employing a larger band and simpler harmonic and rhythmic patterns. **—in full swing.** In action to the maximum speed, capacity, or ability. [< OE *swingan,* to whip, strike, fling oneself. See **sweng-.**]

swing•er (swĭng′ər) *n. Slang.* One who participates actively in youthful fads.

swipe (swīp) *n.* A heavy, sweeping blow. *—v.* **swiped, swiping.** **1.** To hit with a sweeping blow. **2.** *Slang.* To steal; filch.

swirl (swûrl) *v.* To rotate or spin in or as in a whirlpool or eddy. *—n.* **1.** The motion of whirling or spinning. **2.** Something that swirls; a whirlpool or eddy. [ME *swyrl,* eddy, whirlpool.] **—swirl′y** *adj.*

swish (swĭsh) *v.* **1.** To move with a whistle or hiss. **2.** To rustle, as certain fabrics. *—n.* **1.** A sharp sibilant or rustling sound. **2.** A movement making such a sound. [Prob imit.]

swiss (swĭs) *n.* Also **Swiss.** A crisp, sheer cotton cloth used for curtains, light garments, etc. [< SWISS.]

Swiss (swĭs) *adj.* Of or pertaining to Switzerland, its inhabitants, or its culture. *—n., pl.* **Swiss.** A native or inhabitant of Switzerland.

Swiss cheese. A firm white or pale-yellow cheese with many large holes.

switch (swĭch) *n.* **1.** A slender flexible rod, stick, twig, etc., used for whipping. **2.** A flailing or lashing, as with a slender rod. **3.** A device used to break or open an electrical circuit. **4.** A device used to transfer rolling stock from one track to another. **5.** A shift, as of opinion. *—v.* **1.** To whip with or as with a switch. **2.** To shift, transfer, or change: *switch the conversation.* **3.** To cause (an electric current or appliance) to begin or cease operation: *switch off the radio.* [Perh < MDu *swijch,* bough, twig.] **—switch′er** *n.*

switch•board (swĭch′bôrd′, -bōrd′) *n.* A panel containing control switches and other apparatus for operating electric circuits.

switch•man (swĭch′mən) *n.* One who operates railroad switches.

Swit•zer•land (swĭt′sər-lənd). A federal republic in C Europe. Pop. 5,429,000. Cap. Bern.

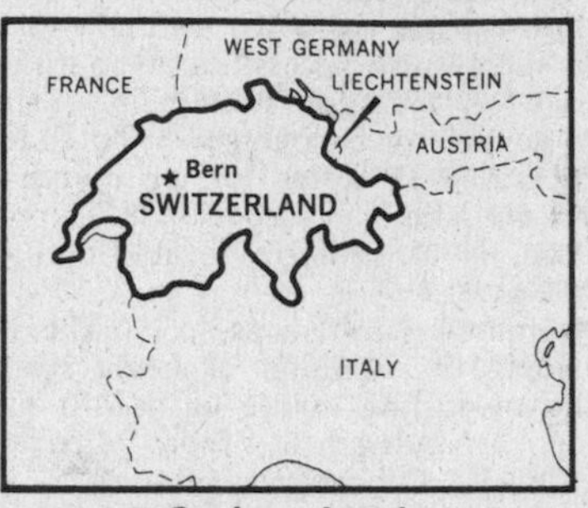

Switzerland

swiv•el (swĭv′əl) *n.* A link, pivot, or other fastening that permits free turning of attached parts. *—v.* **-eled** or **-elled, -eling** or **-elling.** To turn or rotate on or as on a swivel. [Perh < OE *swīfan,* to revolve. See **swei-.**]

swob. Variant of **swab.**

swol•len (swōl′ən). Alternate *p.p.* of **swell.**

swoon (swo͞on) *v.* To faint. *—n.* A fainting spell. [< OE *swōgan,* to suffocate, choke.]

swoop (swo͞op) *v.* To make a sudden sweeping movement, as a bird descending upon its prey. *—n.* A swift, sudden descent. [< OE *swāpan,* to swing, sweep, drive. See **swei-.**]

swop. Variant of **swap.**

sword (sôrd) *n.* A weapon having a long blade for cutting or thrusting, often worn ceremonially as a symbol of power or authority. **—at swords' points.** Ready for combat; antagonistic. [< OE. See **swer-[3].**]

sword•fish (sôrd′fĭsh′) *n.* A large marine game and food fish with a long, swordlike extension of the upper jaw.

sword•play (sôrd′plā′) *n.* The action or art of using a sword; fencing.

swords•man (sôrdz′mən) *n.* **1.** A person skilled in the use of the sword. **2.** A person armed with a sword, as a fencer or soldier. **—swords′man•ship′** *n.*

swore (swôr). *p.t.* of **swear.**

sworn (swôrn). *p.p.* of **swear.**

swum (swŭm). *p.p. & archaic p.t.* of **swim.**

swung (swŭng). *p.t. & p.p.* of **swing.**

syb•a•rite (sĭb′ər-īt) *n.* Also **Syb•a•rite.** A person devoted to pleasure and luxury. [L *Sybarita,* native of Sybaris, ancient Greek city.] **—syb′a•rit′ic** (-ə-rĭt′ĭk) *adj.*

syc•a•more (sĭk′ə-môr′, -mōr′) *n.* **1.** A large North American tree with maplelike leaves, ball-like seed clusters, and patchy bark. **2.** An Old World tree related to the maples. [< Gk *sukamoros.*]

syc•o•phant (sĭk′ə-fənt) *n.* One who attempts to win favor or advance himself by flattering persons of influence; a servile self-seeker. [< Gk *sukophantēs,* "fig-shower," "accuser."] **—syc′o•phan•cy** *n.*

Syd•ney (sĭd′nē). A city of SE Australia. Pop. 2,300,000.

syl., syll. **1.** syllable. **2.** syllabus.

syl•lab•i•cate (sĭ-lăb′ə-kāt′) *v.* **-cated, -cating.** Also **syl•lab•i•fy** (-fī′), **-fied, -fying.** To divide into syllables. **—syl•lab′i•ca′tion** *n.*

syl•la•ble (sĭl′ə-bəl) *n.* A single uninterrupted sound forming part of a word or, in some cases, an entire word. [< Gk *sullabē,* "a gathering (of letters)."] **—syl•lab′ic** (sĭ-lăb′ĭk) *adj.*

syl•la•bus (sĭl′ə-bəs) *n., pl.* **-buses** or **-bi** (-bī′). An outline of the main subjects covered in a course of study. [< Gk *sittuba,* book title, label, table of contents.]

syl•lo•gism (sĭl′ə-jĭz′əm) *n.* A form of deductive reasoning consisting of a major premise and a minor premise that, taken together, lead to a conclusion. [< Gk *sullogismos,* "a reckoning together."] **—syl′lo•gis′tic** (-jĭs′tĭk) *adj.* **—syl′lo•gis′ti•cal•ly** *adv.*

sylph (sĭlf) *n.* **1.** Any of a class of elemental beings believed to inhabit the air. **2.** A slim, graceful woman or girl. [NL *sylphus.*]

syl•van (sĭl′vən) *adj.* **1.** Of, pertaining to, or characteristic of woods or forest regions. **2.** Abounding in trees; wooded. [< L *silva, sylva,* forest.]

sym–. Variant of **syn–.**

sym. **1.** symbol. **2.** symphony.

sym•bol (sĭm′bəl) *n.* **1.** Something that represents something else by association, resemblance, or convention. **2.** A sign used to represent an operation, element, quantity, quality, or relation, as in mathematics or music. [L *symbolum,* sign, token.] **—sym•bol′ic** (-bŏl′ĭk) *adj.* **—sym•bol′i•cal•ly** *adv.*

sym•bol•ism (sĭm′bə-lĭz′əm) *n.* The representation of things by means of symbols.

sym•bol•ize (sĭm′bə-līz′) *v.* **-ized, -izing.** **1.** To be or serve as a symbol of. **2.** To represent by a symbol or symbols.

sym•me•try (sĭm′ə-trē) *n.* **1.** A relationship of characteristic correspondence, equivalence, or identity among constituents of a system or between different systems. **2.** Exact correspondence of form and constituent configuration on opposite sides of a dividing line or plane or about a center or axis. [< Gk *summetros,* "of like measure," symmetrical.] **—sym•met′ri•cal** (sĭ-mĕt′rĭ-kəl) *adj.*

sym•pa•thet•ic (sĭm′pə-thĕt′ĭk) *adj.* **1.** Of, expressing, feeling, or resulting from sympathy. **2.** In agreement; favorable; inclined. **—sym′pa•thet′i•cal•ly** *adv.*

sympathetic nervous system. The part of the autonomic nervous system whose stimulation increases the blood pressure, heart rate, and respiration rate, and, in general, prepares an organism for vigorous activity, as in response to danger.

sym•pa•thize (sĭm′pə-thīz′) *v.* **-thized, -thizing.** **1.** To feel or express compassion; commiserate (with *with*). **2.** To share or understand another's feelings or ideas (with *with*). **—sym′pa•thiz′er** *n.*

sym•pa•thy (sĭm′pə-thē) *n., pl.* **-thies.** **1.** Mutual understanding between persons. **2.** A feeling or expression of pity or sorrow for the distress of another; compassion. **3.** Favor; agreement; approval: *in sympathy with one's ideas.* [< Gk *sumpathēs,* affected by like feelings.]

sym•pho•ny (sĭm′fə-nē) *n., pl.* **-nies.** **1.** *Mus.* A

SYMBOLS AND SIGNS

+ plus
− minus
± plus or minus
∓ minus or plus
× multiplied by
÷ divided by
= equal to
≠ or ≢ not equal to
≈ or ≒ nearly equal to
≡ identical with
≢ not identical with
≎ equivalent
∼ difference
≅ congruent to
> greater than
≯ not greater than
< less than
≮ not less than
≧ or ≥ greater than or equal to
≦ or ≤ less than or equal to
absolute value
∪ logical sum or union
∩ logical product or intersection
⊂ is contained in
ε is a member of; permittivity; mean error
: is to; ratio

∷ as; proportion
≐ approaches
⟶ approaches limit of
∝ varies as
∥ parallel
⊥ perpendicular
∠ angle
∟ right angle
△ triangle
□ square
▭ rectangle
▱ parallelogram
○ circle
⌒ arc of circle
≟ equilateral
≙ equiangular
√ radical; root; square root
∛ cube root
∜ fourth root
Σ sum
! or ∟ factorial product
∞ infinity
∫ integral
f function
∂ or δ differential; variation
π pi
∴ therefore
∵ because
— vinculum (above letter)

( ) parentheses
[ ] brackets
{ } braces
° degree
′ minute
″ second
Δ increment
ω angular frequency; solid angle
Ω ohm
μΩ microhm
MΩ megohm
Φ magnetic flux
Ψ dielectric flux; electrostatic flux
ρ resistivity
Λ equivalent conductivity
ℛ reluctance
→ direction of flow
⇄ electric current
⬭ benzene ring
→ yields
⇌ reversible reaction
↓ precipitate
↑ gas
‰ salinity
☉ or ☼ sun
● or ◍ new moon
☽ first quarter

long orchestral composition, usually consisting of three or four related movements. **2.** A **symphony orchestra.** [< Gk *sumphōnos,* harmonious.] —**sym•phon'ic** (-fŏn'ĭk) *adj.*

symphony orchestra. A large orchestra composed of string, wind, and percussion sections.

sym•po•si•um (sĭm-pō'zē-əm) *n., pl.* **-ums** or **-sia** (-zē-ə). **1.** A conference for discussion of some topic. **2.** A collection of writings on a particular topic. [< Gk *sumposion,* drinking party.]

symp•tom (sĭm'təm, sĭmp'-) *n.* **1.** A circumstance or phenomenon regarded as an indication of a certain condition. **2.** A phenomenon experienced by an individual as a departure from normal function, sensation, or appearance, generally indicating disorder or disease. [< Gk *sumptōma,* occurrence, phenomenon.] —**symp'to•mat'ic** *adj.*

syn–, sym–. *comb. form.* **1.** Together or with. **2.** Same, alike, similar, or at the same time. **3.** Union or fusion. [< Gk *sun, xun,* together, with.]

syn. synonym; synonymous; synonymy.

syn•a•gogue (sĭn'ə-gŏg') *n.* A building or place of meeting for Jewish worship and religious instruction. [< Gk *sunagōgē,* assembly.]

syn•apse (sĭn'ăps) *n.* The point at which a nerve impulse passes between neurons. [< Gk *sunapsis,* point of contact.]

syn•chro•nize (sĭn'krə-nīz', sĭng'-) *v.* **-nized, -nizing. 1.** To occur at the same time; be simultaneous. **2.** To cause to operate with exact coincidence in time or rate. —**syn'chro•ni•za'tion** *n.* —**syn'chro•niz'er** *n.*

syn•chro•nous (sĭn'krə-nəs, sĭng'-) *adj.* Occurring at the same time; simultaneous. [< Gk *sunkhronos.*] —**syn'chro•nous•ly** *adv.*

syn•cline (sĭn'klīn') *n.* A low, troughlike area in bedrock, in which rocks incline together from opposite sides.

syn•co•pate (sĭn'kə-pāt', sĭng'-) *v.* **-pated, -pating.** To modify (musical rhythm) by syncopation. [< Gk *sunkopē,* a cutting off.]

syn•co•pa•tion (sĭn'kə-pā'shən, sĭng'-) *n. Mus.* A shift in which a normally weak beat is stressed.

syn•cre•tism (sĭn'krə-tĭz'əm, sĭng'-) *n.* The attempt or tendency to combine or reconcile differing beliefs, as in philosophy or religion. [< Gk *sunkrētismos,* union.] —**syn'cre•tis'tic, syn•cret'ic** (-krĕt'ĭk) *adj.*

synd. syndicate.

syn•di•cate (sĭn'dĭ-kĭt) *n.* **1.** An association of people formed to carry out a large business undertaking. **2.** An agency that sells articles for simultaneous publication in a number of newspapers or periodicals. [< Gk *sundikos,* public advocate.] —**syn'di•cate'** (sĭn'dĭ-kāt') *v.* **(-cated, -cating).**

syn•drome (sĭn'drōm') *n.* A group of signs and symptoms that collectively indicate a disease or disorder. [< Gk *sundromē,* a running together, concurrence (of symptoms).]

syn•er•gism (sĭn'ər-jĭz'əm) *n.* Also **syn•er•gy** (-ər-jē). The action of two or more substances, organs, or organisms to achieve an effect of which each is individually incapable. [< Gk *sunergos,* working together.]

○ or ☻ full moon
☾ last quarter
☿ Mercury
♀ Venus
⊖ or ⊕ Earth
♂ Mars
♃ Jupiter
♄ Saturn
♅ Uranus
♆ Neptune
♇ Pluto
♈ Aries
♉ Taurus
♊ Gemini
♋ Cancer
♌ Leo
♍ Virgo
♎ Libra
♏ Scorpius
♐ Sagittarius
♑ Capricornus
♒ Aquarius
♓ Pisces
☌ conjunction
☍ opposition
△ trine
□ quadrature
✶ sextile
☊ dragon's head, ascending node
☋ dragon's tail, descending node
◍ rain
✶ snow
⊠ snow on ground
⟵ floating ice crystals
▲ hail
△ sleet
V frostwork
⊔ hoarfrost
≡ fog
∞ haze; dust haze
T thunder
< sheet lightning
⦶ solar corona
⊕ solar halo
⌈< thunderstorm
╲ direction
○ or ⊙ or ① annual
⊙⊙ or ② biennial
♃ perennial
♂ or ♂ male
♀ female
□ male (in charts)
○ female (in charts)
℞ take (from Latin *Recipe*)
ĀĀ or Ā or āā of each (doctor's prescription)
℔ pound
℥ ounce
ʒ dram
℈ scruple
ƒ℥ fluid ounce
ƒʒ fluid dram
♏ minim
& or & and; ampersand
℘ per
number
/ virgule; slash; solidus; shilling
© copyright
% per cent
℅ care of
℀ account of
@ at
* asterisk
† dagger
‡ double dagger
§ section
☞ index
´ acute
` grave
~ tilde
ˆ circumflex
¯ macron
˘ breve
¨ dieresis
¸ cedilla
∧ caret

---

syn•od (sĭn'əd) *n.* **1.** A council or assembly of churches. **2.** Any council or assembly. [< Gk *sunodos,* meeting.]

syn•o•nym (sĭn'ə-nĭm') *n.* A word having a meaning similar to that of another. [< Gk *sunōnumon.*]

syn•op•sis (sĭ-nŏp'sĭs) *n., pl.* **-ses** (-sēz'). A brief statement or outline of a subject. [< Gk *sunopsis,* a viewing all together, general view.]

syn•tax (sĭn'tăks') *n.* The way in which words are put together to form phrases and sentences. [< Gk *suntassein,* to put together, arrange in order.] **—syn•tac'tic** (-tăk'tĭk), **syn•tac'ti•cal** *adj.*

syn•the•sis (sĭn'thə-sĭs) *n., pl.* **-ses** (-sēz'). The combining of separate elements or substances to form a coherent whole. [< Gk, a putting together.] **—syn'the•size'** (-sīz') *v.* **(-sized, -sizing).**

syn•thet•ic (sĭn-thĕt'ĭk) *adj.* Also **syn•thet•i•cal** (-ĭ-kəl). **1.** Of, pertaining to, involving, or produced by synthesis. **2.** Not genuine; artificial. [< Gk *suntithenai,* to put together.] **—syn•thet'i•cal•ly** *adv.*

syph•i•lis (sĭf'ə-lĭs) *n.* A chronic infectious venereal disease transmitted by direct contact, usually in sexual intercourse, and sometimes progressing from its local phase through three stages to systemic infection. **—syph'i•lit'ic** (-lĭt'ĭk) *adj.* & *n.*

sy•phon. Variant of **siphon.**

Syr•a•cuse (sĭr'ə-kyōōz', -kyōōs'). A city of C New York State. Pop. 216,000.

Syr•i•a (sĭr'ē-ə). A country on the E Mediterranean coast. Pop. 5,067,000. Cap. Damascus. **—Syr'i•an** *adj.* & *n.*

Syria

syr•inge (sə-rĭnj', sĭr'ĭnj) *n.* A medical instrument used to inject fluids into the body or draw them from it. [< Gk *surinx,* shepherd's pipe.]

syr•up (sûr'əp, sĭr'-) *n.* Also **sir•up.** A thick, sweet, sticky liquid, as a sugar solution or boiled plant sap. [< Ar *sharāb,* beverage, syrup.] **—syr'up•y** *adj.*

sys•tem (sĭs'təm) *n.* **1.** A group of interrelated elements forming a collective entity. **2.** The human body regarded as a functional physiological unit. **3.** A network, as for communications, travel, or distribution. **4.** A set of interrelated ideas, principles, rules, procedures, laws, etc. **5.** A social, economic, or political organizational form. **6.** The state or condition of harmonious, orderly interaction. [< Gk *sustēma,* a composite whole.] **—sys'tem•at'ic** *adj.* **—sys'tem•at'i•cal•ly** *adv.*

sys•tem•a•tize (sĭs'tə-mə-tīz') *v.* **-tized, -tizing.** To formulate into or reduce to a system. **—sys'tem•a•ti•za'tion** *n.*

sys•tem•ic (sĭ-stĕm'ĭk) *adj.* **1.** Pertaining to a system or systems. **2.** Of or affecting the entire body. **—sys•tem'i•cal•ly** *adv.*

sys•to•le (sĭs'tə-lē) *n.* The rhythmic contraction of the heart, esp. of the ventricles. [Gk *sustolē,* contraction.] **—sys•tol'ic** (-tŏl'ĭk) *adj.*

Tt

t, T (tē) *n.* **1.** The 20th letter of the English alphabet. **2.** T Anything shaped like the letter T. **—to a T.** Perfectly; precisely.

t **1.** ton. **2.** troy.

T temperature.

t. **1.** teaspoon. **2.** *Gram.* tense. **3.** time. **4.** *Gram.* transitive.

T. **1.** tablespoon. **2.** territory. **3.** Testament. **4.** time. **5.** transit.

Ta tantalum.

tab (tăb) *n.* **1.** A projection, flap, or short strip attached to an object to facilitate opening, handling, or identification. **2.** A bill or check, as in a restaurant. [?]

tab•by (tăb'ē) *n., pl.* **-bies.** **1.** A black and grayish striped or mottled domestic cat. **2.** A female domestic cat. [F *tabis.*]

tab•er•na•cle (tăb'ər-năk'əl) *n.* Often **Tabernacle.** **1.** The portable sanctuary in which the Jews carried the ark of the covenant through the desert. **2.** A receptacle on a church altar containing the consecrated elements of the Eucharist. [< L *taberna,* hut.]

ta•ble (tā'bəl) *n.* **1.** An article of furniture having a flat horizontal surface supported by vertical legs. **2.** An orderly display of data, usually arranged in rows and columns. **3.** An abbreviated list, as of contents; a synopsis. **4.** A slab or tablet, as of stone, bearing an inscription or device. *—v.* **-bled, -bling.** **1.** To put or place on a table. **2.** To postpone consideration of; shelve. [< L *tabula,* board, list.]

tab•leau (tăb'lō', tă-blō') *n., pl.* **-leaux** (tăb'lōz', tă-blōz') or **-leaus.** **1.** A vivid or graphic description. **2.** A scene presented on stage by costumed actors who remain silent and motionless as if in a picture. [F.]

ta•ble•cloth (tā'bəl-klôth', -klŏth') *n.* A cloth to cover a table.

ta•ble d'hote (ta'bəl dōt') *pl.* **tables d'hôte** (tä'bəl dōt'). A full meal served in a restaurant at a fixed price. [F, "table of (the) host."]

ta•ble•land (tā'bəl-lănd') *n.* A plateau.

ta•ble•spoon (tā'bəl-spōōn') *n.* **1.** A large spoon used for serving food. **2.** A household cooking measure, three teaspoons or four liquid drams.

tab•let (tăb'lĭt) *n.* **1.** A slab or plaque, as of stone or ivory, bearing an inscription. **2.** A pad of writing paper glued together along one edge. **3.** A small flat pellet of oral medication. [< OF *table,* table.]

table tennis. A game similar to tennis, played on a table with wooden paddles and a small Celluloid ball.

ta•ble•ware (tā'bəl-wâr') *n.* Dishes, glassware, etc., used in setting a table for a meal.

tab•loid (tăb'loid') *n.* A newspaper of small format giving the news in condensed form, usually with illustrated, often sensational material. [< TABL(ET) + -OID.]

ta•boo, ta•bu (tə-bōō', tă-) *n., pl.* **-boos.** **1.** A prohibition excluding something from use, approach, or mention because of its sacred and inviolable nature. **2.** A ban attached to something by social custom. *—adj.* Excluded or forbidden from use, approach, or mention. *—v.* To place under taboo.

ta•bor (tā'bər) *n.* A small drum used to accompany a fife. [< OF *tabour.*]

tab•u•lar (tăb'yə-lər) *adj.* Organized as a table or list. **—tab'u•lar•ly** *adv.*

tab•u•late (tăb'yə-lāt') *v.* **-lated, -lating.** To arrange in tabular form; condense and list. **—tab'u•la'tion** *n.* **—tab'u•la'tor** *n.*

ta•chom•e•ter (tə-kŏm'ə-tər) *n.* An instrument used to determine speed, esp. rotational speed. [Gk *takhos,* speed + -METER.]

tac•it (tăs'ĭt) *adj.* **1.** Not spoken: *tacit consent.* **2.** Implied by or inferred from actions or statements. [< L *tacēre,* to be silent.]

tac•i•turn (tăs'ə-tərn) *adj.* Habitually untalkative; laconic; uncommunicative. [< L *tacitus,* silent, tacit.] **—tac'i•tur'ni•ty** (-tûr'nə-tē) *n.*

tack (tăk) *n.* **1.** A short, light nail with a sharp point and a flat head. **2.** The position of a vessel relative to the trim of its sails. **3.** A course of action. *—v.* **1.** To fasten or attach with a tack. **2.** To append; add (with *on*). **3.** To change the course of a vessel. [< OF *tache,* nail, fastening.]

tack•le (tăk'əl) *n.* **1.** The equipment used in a sport or occupation, esp. in fishing; gear. **2.** (*also* tā'kəl). A system of ropes and blocks for raising and lowering weights. **3.** *Football.* **a.** A lineman stationed between guard and end. **b.** The seizing and throwing to the ground of an opposing player. *—v.* **-led, -ling.** **1.** To take on; come to grips with: *tackle a problem.* **2.** *Football.* To seize and throw (an opposing player) to the ground. [Prob < MLG *taken,* to seize.] **—tack'ler** *n.*

tack•y¹ (tăk'ē) *adj.* **-ier, -iest.** Slightly adhesive or gummy to the touch; sticky. [< TACK.] **—tack'i•ness** *n.*

tack•y² (tăk'ē) *adj.* **-ier, -iest.** *Informal.* **1.** Rundown; shabby. **2.** Lacking style; dowdy. [< dial *tacky,* an inferior horse.] **—tack'i•ness** *n.*

Ta•co•ma (tə-kō'mə). A city of W Washington. Pop. 152,000.

tact (tăkt) *n.* The ability to appreciate the

delicacy of a situation and do or say the most fitting thing. [< L *tactus,* sense of touch.] —**tact'ful** *adj.* —**tact'less** *adj.*

tac•tics (tăk'tĭks) *n. (takes sing. v.).* The technique or science of securing strategic objectives, esp. the art of deploying and directing one's forces against an enemy. [< Gk *(ta) taktika,* "(the) matters of arrangement."] —**tac'ti•cal** *adj.* —**tac'ti'cian** *n.*

tac•tile (tăk'təl, -tīl') *adj.* Of, pertaining to, or perceptible to the sense of touch. [< L *tactus,* sense of touch.]

tad•pole (tăd'pōl') *n.* The aquatic larval stage of a frog or toad, having a tail and external gills. [ME *taddepol,* "toad head."]

Ta•dzhik Soviet Socialist Republic (tä'jĭk, -jēk'). A republic of the south-central Soviet Union. Pop. 2,900,000. Cap. Dushanbe.

taf•fe•ta (tăf'ə-tə) *n.* A glossy, plain-woven fabric of silk, rayon, or nylon. [< Pers *tāftah,* "woven."]

taf•fy (tăf'ē) *n.* A sweet, chewy candy made of molasses or brown sugar.

Taft (tăft), **William Howard.** 1857–1930. 27th President of the U.S. (1909–13).

William Howard Taft
Photographed during a 1908 speech in Wisconsin

tag¹ (tăg) *n.* **1.** A strip of paper, metal, etc., attached to something for purposes of identification, classification, or labeling. **2.** A plastic or metal tip on shoelaces. **3.** A designation or epithet. —*v.* **tagged, tagging. 1.** To label or identify with a tag. **2.** To follow closely. [Prob < Scand.] —**tag'ger** *n.*

tag² (tăg) *n.* **1.** A children's game in which one player pursues the others until he can touch one of them. **2.** *Baseball.* The act of touching a runner to retire him. —*v.* **tagged, tagging. 1.** To touch (another player) in the game of tag. **2.** *Baseball.* To touch (a runner) with the ball in order to retire him. —**tag'ger** *n.*

Ta•ga•log (tə-gä'lôg') *n., pl.* **-log** or **-logs. 1.** A member of a people native to the Philippines. **2.** The language of the Austronesian family spoken by this people.

Ta•gus (tā'gəs). A river of Spain and Portugal.

Ta•hi•ti (tə-hē'tē). An island of Polynesia, in the SE Pacific.

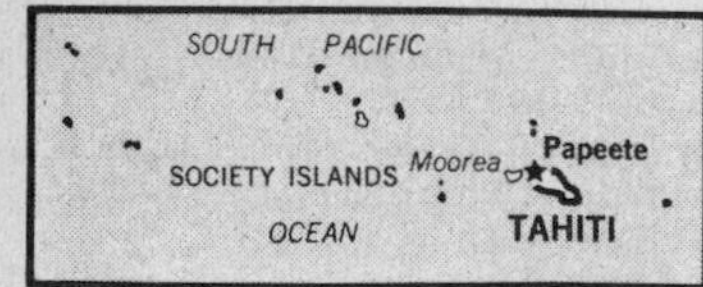

Tahiti

Ta•hi•tian (tə-hē'shən, -hē'tē-ən) *n.* **1.** A native or inhabitant of Tahiti. **2.** The Polynesian language of Tahiti. —**Ta•hi'tian** *adj.*

Tai (tī) *n.* A family of languages spoken in SE Asia and S China, including Thai and other languages.

tai•ga (tī-gä') *n.* The evergreen forest of Siberia and of similar regions elsewhere in Eurasia and North America. [Russ *taiga.*]

tail (tāl) *n.* **1.** The hind part of an animal, esp. when elongated and extending beyond the main part of the body. **2.** Anything resembling an animal's tail. **3.** The bottom, rear, or hindmost part of anything. **4. a.** The rear of an aircraft. **b.** An assembly of stabilizing planes and control surfaces in this region. **5. tails.** The reverse of a coin: *heads or tails.* **6. tails.** A formal evening costume worn by men. —*v. Informal.* To follow and keep under surveillance. —*adj.* **1.** Posterior; hindmost. **2.** Coming from behind: *a tail wind.* [< OE *tægel.* See **dek-.**]

tail•light (tāl'līt') *n.* A light mounted on the rear end of a vehicle.

tai•lor (tā'lər) *n.* One who makes, repairs, and alters garments. —*v.* **1.** To make (a garment). **2.** To make, alter, or adapt for a particular purpose. [< VL **tāliātor,* "cutter."]

tai•lor-made (tā'lər-mād') *adj.* Made or as if made to order.

tail•spin (tāl'spĭn') *n.* **1.** The descent of an aircraft in a nose-down spiraling motion. **2.** A sudden precipitous decline or slump.

taint (tānt) *v.* **1.** To affect slightly with something undesirable. **2.** To make poisonous or rotten; infect or spoil. —*n.* **1.** A moral defect considered as a stain or spot. **2.** An infecting touch, influence, or tinge. [< L *tingere,* to dip in liquid, dye.]

Tai•pei (tī'pā'). The capital of the Republic of China, on Taiwan. Pop. 1,028,000.

Tai•wan (tī'wän'). An island off the SE coast of China, constituting along with smaller islands the Republic of China.

Ta•iz (tă-ĭz'). A former capital of the Yemen Arab Republic. Pop. 80,000.

take (tāk) *v.* **took, taken** (tā'kən), **taking. 1.** To get possession of; capture; seize. **2.** To grasp with the hands. **3.** To carry with one to another place. **4.** To lead or convey to another place. **5.** To remove from a place. **6.** To charm; captivate. **7.** To eat, drink, consume, or inhale. **8.** To assume upon oneself; commit oneself to. **9.** *Gram.* To govern: *Intransitive verbs take no direct object.* **10.** To select; pick out; choose. **11.** To use as a means of conveyance or transportation. **12.** To occupy: *take a seat.* **13.** To require: *It takes money to do that.* **14.** To determine through measurement or observation. **15.** To write down: *take notes.* **16.** To make by photography: *take a picture.* **17.** To accept (something owed, offered, or given). **18.** To endure: *take criticism.* **19.** To follow (advice, a suggestion, etc.). **20.** To indulge in; do; perform: *take a step.* **21.** To allow to come in; admit. **22.** To interpret or react to in a certain manner: *take literally.* **23.** To subtract. **24.** To commit oneself to the study of: *take a course.* **25.** To have the intended effect; work. **26.** To become: *take sick.* **27.** To set out for; make one's way; go. —**take aback.** To bewilder; astonish; nonplus. —**take after. 1.** To pursue; chase. **2.** To resemble. —**take down. 1.** To bring to a lower position from a higher. **2.** To dismantle; take apart. **3.** To put down in writing. —**take for.** To consider or suppose to be. —**take in. 1.** To grant admittance to. **2.** To make smaller or shorter. **3.** To include or comprise. **4.** To deceive; swindle. **5.** To look at thoroughly; view. —**take it. 1.** To understand; assume: *as I take it.* **2.** *Informal.* To endure abuse, criticism, etc. —**take on. 1.** To hire. **2.** To undertake. **3.** To oppose in competition. —**take out. 1.** To extract; remove. **2.** *Informal.* To escort, as on a date. —**take over.** To assume the control or management of. —**take place.** To happen. —**take to. 1.** To go to, as for safety. **2.** To develop as a habit or steady practice. **3.** To become fond of. —**take up. 1.** To raise up; lift. **2.** To reduce in size; shorten or tighten. **3.** To accept, as an option, bet, or challenge. **4.** To begin again; resume. **5.** To use up, consume, or occupy (space, time, etc.). **6.** To develop an interest in. —**take up with.** *Informal.* To develop a friendship or association with. —*n.* **1. a.** The act or process of taking. **b.** That which is taken. **2.** The amount of money collected as admission to a sporting event. [< OE *tacan* < ON *taka.*]

take off. 1. To remove, as clothing. **2.** To deduct. **3.** *Slang.* To leave; depart. **4.** To leave the ground, as an airplane.

take•off (tāk'ôf', -ŏf') *n.* **1.** The act of leaving the ground. **2.** *Informal.* An amusing imitative caricature or burlesque.

tak•er (tā'kər) *n.* A person who takes or takes up something, as a wager.

tak•ing (tā'kĭng) *adj.* Fetching; winning. —*n.* **1.** The act of a person or thing that takes. **2. takings.** Receipts, esp. of money.

talc (tălk) *n.* A fine-grained mineral used in making talcum powder. [< Ar *talq.*]

tal•cum powder (tăl'kəm). A fine powder made from purified talc, for use on the skin.

tale (tāl) *n.* **1.** A recital of events or happenings. **2.** A malicious story; piece of gossip. **3.** A deliberate lie; falsehood. [< OE *talu,* discourse, narrative. See **del-².**]

tale•bear•er (tāl'bâr'ər) *n.* One who spreads malicious stories or gossip.

tal•ent (tăl'ənt) *n.* **1.** A natural or acquired ability; aptitude. **2.** Natural endowment or ability of a superior quality. **3.** A variable unit of weight and money used in ancient times. [< L *talentum,* unit of weight or money.]

ta•ler (tä'lər) *n.* Also **tha•ler.** Any of numerous silver coins formerly used in certain Germanic countries. [G.]

tal•is•man (tăl'ĭs-mən, tăl'ĭz-) *n.* An object marked with magical signs and believed to confer on its bearer supernatural powers or protection. [< LGk *telesma,* completion, consecrated object.]

talk (tôk) *v.* **1.** To articulate words. **2.** To converse by means of spoken language. **3.** To speak (an idiom). **4.** To gossip. **5.** To parley or negotiate. **6.** To consult or confer. —**talk back.** To make an impertinent reply. —**talk down to.** To address someone with insulting condescension. —**talk (someone) into.** To persuade. —**talk (someone) out of.** To dissuade. —**talk over.** To discuss. —*n.* **1.** The act of talking; conversation. **2.** An informal speech. **3.** Any hearsay, rumor, or speculation concerning something: *talk of war.* **4.** Any subject of conversation. **5.** A conference. [< OE *talian,* to reckon, tell, relate. See **del-².**] —**talk'er** *n.*

talk•a•tive (tô'kə-tĭv) *adj.* Having an inclination to talk; loquacious.

talk•ing-to (tô'kĭng-tōō') *n., pl.* **-tos.** *Informal.* A scolding.

tall (tôl) *adj.* **1.** Having greater than ordinary height. **2.** Having a stated height: *six feet tall.* **3.** *Informal.* Fanciful; boastful: *tall tales.* [ME, seemly, handsome, valiant.]

Tal•la•has•see (tăl'ə-hăs'ē). The capital of Florida. Pop. 72,000.

tal•low (tăl'ō) *n.* Whitish, tasteless solid or hard fat obtained from cattle, sheep, etc., and used in edibles or to make candles, leather dressing, soap, and lubricants. [< MLG *talg, talch.*] —**tal'low•y** *adj.*

tal•ly (tăl'ē) *n., pl.* **-lies.** **1.** A stick on which notches are made to keep a count or score. **2.** A reckoning or score. —*v.* **-lied, -lying.** **1.** To reckon or count. **2.** To correspond; agree. [< L *tālea,* twig, cutting, stick.]

tal•ly•ho (tăl'ē-hō') *interj.* Used to urge hounds in fox hunting. [Prob < OF *thialau,* cry used to urge hounds.]

Tal•mud (täl'mo͝od', tăl'məd) *n.* The collection of ancient Rabbinic writings constituting the basis of religious authority for traditional Judaism. [Heb *talmūd,* learning, instruction.]

tal•on (tăl'ən) *n.* The claw of a bird of prey or other predatory animal. [< L *tālus,* ankle.]

ta•ma•le (tə-mä'lē) *n.* A Mexican dish of fried chopped meat and crushed peppers, wrapped in corn husks and steamed. [< Nah *tamalli.*]

tam•a•rack (tăm'ə-răk') *n.* An American larch tree. [< Algon.]

tam•a•rind (tăm'ə-rĭnd') *n.* **1.** A tropical tree with pulpy, acid-flavored pods. **2.** The fruit of this tree. [< Ar *tamr hindī,* "date of India."]

tam•a•risk (tăm'ə-rĭsk') *n.* A shrub or small tree with small, scalelike leaves and clusters of pink flowers. [< L *tamarīx.*]

tam•bou•rine (tăm'bə-rēn') *n.* A musical instrument consisting of a small drumhead with jingling disks fitted into the rim. [F *tambourin.*]

tame (tām) *adj.* **tamer, tamest.** **1.** Brought from wildness into a domesticated state. **2.** Gentle; docile. **3.** Insipid; flat. —*v.* **tamed, taming.** **1.** To domesticate. **2.** To subdue or curb. [< OE *tam.* See **demə-²**.]

Tam•er•lane (tăm'ər-lān'). 1336?–1405. Islamic conqueror of much of C Asia and E Europe.

Tam•il (tăm'əl, tŭm'-) *n.* **1.** A member of a Dravidian people of S India and Ceylon. **2.** The language spoken by this people. —**Tam'il** *adj.*

tam-o'-shan•ter (tăm'ə-shăn'tər) *n.* A tight-fitting Scottish cap, sometimes having a pompon, tassel, or feather in the center. [< the hero of Burns's poem *Tam o'Shanter.*]

tamp (tămp) *v.* To pack down tightly by a succession of blows or taps.

Tam•pa (tăm'pə). A city of W Florida. Pop. 302,000.

tam•per (tăm'pər) *v.* —**tamper with.** **1.** To interfere in a harmful manner. **2.** To meddle rashly or foolishly. **3.** To engage in underhand dealings. [Orig "to prepare (clay) by mixing," var of TEMPER.] —**tam'per•er** *n.*

tan (tăn) *v.* **tanned, tanning.** **1.** To convert (hide) into leather, as by treating with tannin. **2.** To make or become brown by exposure to the sun. **3.** *Informal.* To thrash; beat. —*n.* **1.** A light brown. **2.** The brown color sun rays impart to the skin. —*adj.* **tanner, tannest.** **1.** Of the color tan. **2.** Having a sun tan. [< ML *tannāre.*]

tan•a•ger (tăn'ĭ-jər) *n.* Any of various New World birds often having brightly colored plumage. [< Port *tangará.*]

Ta•nan•a•rive (tə-năn'ə-rēv'). The capital of the Malagasy Republic. Pop. 299,000.

tan•bark (tăn'bärk') *n.* **1.** Tree bark used as a source of tannin. **2.** Shredded bark used to cover circus arenas, racetracks, etc.

tan•dem (tăn'dəm) *n.* **1.** A two-wheeled carriage drawn by horses harnessed one behind the other. **2.** A bicycle built for two. —*adv.* One behind the other. [L, "exactly then," at length.] —**tan'dem** *adj.*

tang (tăng) *n.* **1.** A sharp, often acrid taste, flavor, or odor. **2.** A projection by which a tool is attached to its handle. [Prob < ON *tangi,* a sting, point.] —**tang'y** *adj.*

tan•ge•lo (tăn'jə-lō') *n., pl.* **-los.** A citrus fruit that is a cross between a grapefruit and a tangerine. [Blend of TANGE(RINE) and *pomelo,* a grapefruit.]

tan•gent (tăn'jənt) *adj.* Making contact at a single point or along a line; touching but not intersecting. —*n.* **1.** A line, curve, or surface touching but not intersecting another line, curve, or surface. **2.** A sudden digression or change of course. [< L *tangere,* to touch.] —**tan•gen'tial** (-jĕn'shəl) *adj.* —**tan•gen'ti•al'i•ty** (-shē-ăl'ə-tē) *n.* —**tan•gen'tial•ly** *adv.*

tan•ger•ine (tăn'jə-rēn') *n.* A citrus fruit with easily peeled deep-orange skin. [Short for *tangerine orange,* "orange of Tangier."]

tan•gi•ble (tăn'jə-bəl) *adj.* **1.** Discernible by the touch; palpable. **2.** Real; concrete: *tangible evidence.* —*n.* **1.** Something palpable or concrete. **2. tangibles.** Material assets. [< L *tangere,* to touch.] —**tan'gi•bil'i•ty, tan'gi•ble•ness** *n.* —**tan'gi•bly** *adv.*

Tan•gier (tăn-jîr'). A city and port in N Morocco. Pop. 142,000.

tan•gle (tăng'gəl) *v.* **-gled, -gling.** **1.** To intertwine in a confused mass; snarl. **2.** To be or become entangled. —*n.* **1.** A confused, intertwined mass. **2.** A jumbled or confused state or condition. [Prob < Scand.]

tan•go (tăng'gō) *n., pl.* **-gos.** A Latin-American ballroom dance. [Amer Span.] —**tan'go** *v.*

tank (tăngk) *n.* **1.** A large container for fluids. **2.** An enclosed, heavily armored combat vehicle mounted with cannon and guns and moving on caterpillar treads. [Perh < Sk *taḍāga,* pond.]

tank•ard (tăng'kərd) *n.* A large drinking cup having a single handle and often a hinged cover. [ME.]

tank•er (tăng'kər) *n.* A ship, plane, or truck constructed to transport oil or other liquids in bulk.

tan•ner (tăn'ər) *n.* One who tans hides.

tan•ner•y (tăn'ər-ē) *n., pl.* **-ies.** A place where hides are tanned.

tan•nic acid (tăn'ĭk). A lustrous yellowish to light-brown powdered, flaked, or spongy mass having the approximate composition $C_{76}H_{52}O_{46}$, used in tanning and as an astringent and styptic. [< TANNIN.]

tan•nin (tăn'ən) *n.* Tannic acid or some compound having similar uses. [< F *tanner,* to tan.]

Ta•no•an (tä'nō-ən) *n.* A language family of several Indian peoples of New Mexico and NE Arizona. —**Ta'no•an** *adj.*

tan•sy (tăn'zē) *n., pl.* **-sies.** A pungently aromatic plant with buttonlike yellow flowers. [Perh < ML *athanasia,* an elixir of life.]

tan•ta•lize (tăn'tə-līz') *v.* **-lized, -lizing.** To tease or torment by exposing to view but keeping out of reach something much desired. [< *Tantalus,* Greek mythological king who was punished thus.] —**tan'ta•li•za'tion** *n.* —**tan'ta•liz'er** *n.*

tan•ta•lum (tăn'tə-ləm) *n.* *Symbol* **Ta** A very hard, heavy, gray metallic element used to make electric-light-bulb filaments, lightning arresters, nuclear reactor parts, and some surgical instruments. Atomic number 73, atomic weight 180.948. [< *Tantalus.*]

tan•ta•mount (tăn'tə-mount') *adj.* Equivalent in effect or value. [< NF *tant amunter,* to amount to so much.]

tan•trum (tăn'trəm) *n.* A fit of bad temper. [?]

Tan•za•ni•a (tăn'zə-nē'ə, tăn-zä'nē-ə). A republic of E Africa. Pop. 10,514,000. Cap. Dar es Salaam.

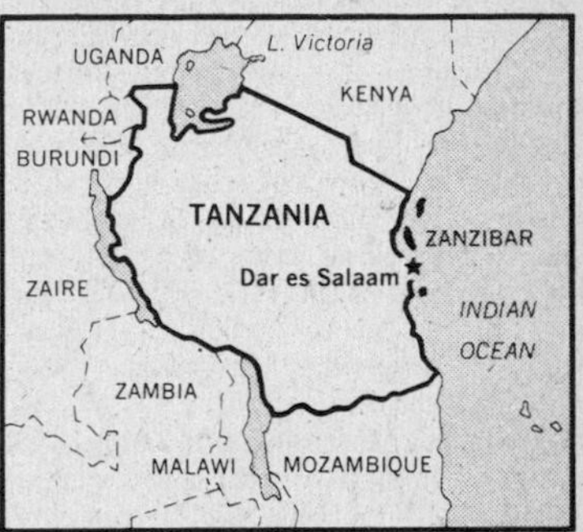

Tanzania

Tao•ism (tou'ĭz'əm, dou'-) *n.* A principal philosophy and religious system of China based upon the teachings of Lao-tse in the 6th century B.C. [< Mand Chin *tao⁴,* "the Way."]

tap¹ (tăp) *v.* **tapped, tapping.** **1.** To strike gently; rap. **2.** To repair (shoe heels or toes) by applying a tap. —*n.* **1.** A gentle but audible blow. **2.** A metal plate attached to the toe or heel of a shoe. [< OF *taper.*]

tap² (tăp) *n.* **1.** A faucet; spigot. **2.** Liquor drawn from a tap. **3.** A tool for cutting an internal screw thread. **4.** A makeshift terminal in an electric circuit. —*v.* **tapped, tapping.** **1.** To furnish with a spigot or tap. **2.** To pierce in order to draw off liquid. **3.** To draw (liquid) from a vessel or container. **4.** To open outlets from: *tap a water main.* **5. a.** To wiretap. **b.** To establish an electric connection in (a power line). **6.** To cut screw threads in. [< OE *tæppa* < Gmc **tap-.*]

tape (tāp) *n.* **1.** A narrow strip of woven fabric. **2.** Any continuous narrow, flexible strip, as adhesive tape. **3.** A string stretched across a finish line. **4.** A **tape recording.** —*v.* **taped, taping.** **1.** To bind or wrap with tape. **2.** To measure with a tape measure. **3.** To tape-record. [< OE *tæppa, tæppe.*]

tape measure. A tape marked off in a linear scale, as inches, and used for taking measurements.

ta•per (tā'pər) *n.* **1.** A slender candle or waxed wick. **2.** A gradual decrease in thickness or width of an elongated object. —*v.* **1.** To make or become gradually narrower toward one end. **2.** To become gradually smaller; slacken off. [< OE *tapor, tapur.*] —**ta'per•ing•ly** *adv.*

tape recorder. A device for recording and playing back sound on magnetic tape.

tape recording. **1.** Magnetized recording tape. **2.** The sound recorded on a magnetic tape. —**tape'-re•cord'** *v.*

tap•es•try (tăp'ĭ-strē) *n., pl.* **-tries.** A heavy textile with a varicolored design woven across the warp, used esp. for a wall hanging. [< Gk *tapēs,* carpet.]

tape•worm (tāp'wûrm') *n.* A long, ribbonlike worm that lives as a parasite in the intestines of vertebrates, including man.

tap•i•o•ca (tăp'ē-ō'kə) *n.* A beady starch obtained from cassava root and used for thickening puddings, soups, etc. [< Tupi *tipioca,* "residue."]

ta•pir (tā'pər, tə-pîr') *n.* A tropical American or Asian mammal with a heavy body, short legs, and a fleshy proboscis.

tap•room (tăp'ro͞om', -ro͝om') *n.* A barroom.

tap•root (tăp'ro͞ot', -ro͝ot') *n.* The often stout main root of a plant, growing straight downward from the stem.

taps (tăps) *n. (takes sing. v.).* A military bugle call blown as an order to put out lights and at military funerals and memorial services. [< TAP[1].]

tar[1] (tär) *n.* A dark, oily, viscid mixture, consisting mainly of hydrocarbons, produced by the destructive distillation of organic substances such as wood, coal, or peat. —*v.* **tarred, tarring.** To coat with tar. [< OE *teru.* See **deru-.**]

tar[2] (tär) *n. Informal.* A sailor. [Short for TARPAULIN.]

ta•ran•tu•la (tə-răn'cho͞o-lə) *n.* Any of various large, hairy, chiefly tropical spiders capable of inflicting a painful bite. [< It *tarantola.*]

tar•dy (tär'dē) *adj.* **-dier, -diest. 1. a.** Late. **b.** Dilatory. **2.** Slow; sluggish. [< L *tardus,* slow.] —**tar'di•ly** *adv.* —**tar'di•ness** *n.*

tare[1] (târ) *n.* Any of several weeds that grow in grain fields. [ME, seed of the vetch.]

tare[2] (târ) *n.* The weight of a container or wrapper that is deducted from the gross weight to obtain net weight. [< Ar *ṭarḥah,* thing thrown away.]

tar•get (tär'gĭt) *n.* **1.** An object with a marked surface that is shot at to test accuracy. **2.** Anything aimed or fired at. **3.** An object of criticism or attack. **4.** A desired goal. [< OF *targe,* light shield.]

tar•iff (tăr'ĭf) *n.* **1. a.** A list or system of duties imposed on imported or exported goods. **b.** A duty of this kind. **2.** Any schedule of rates or fees. [< Turk *ta'rifa.*]

tar•nish (tär'nĭsh) *v.* **1.** To make or become dull or discolored. **2.** To sully or taint. [OF *ternir.*] —**tar'nish** *n.* —**tar'nish•a•ble** *adj.*

ta•ro (tär'ō, tăr'ō) *n., pl.* **-ros.** A tropical plant with broad leaves and a large, starchy, edible root. [Tahitian and Maori.]

tar•ot (tăr'ō) *n.* Any of a set of playing cards used in fortunetelling. [< It *tarocco.*]

tar•pau•lin (tär-pô'lĭn, tär'pə-lĭn) *n.* Waterproof canvas used for covering and protecting. [Earlier *tarpawling.*]

tar•pon (tär'pən) *n., pl.* **-pon** or **-pons.** A large, silvery game fish of Atlantic coastal waters. [?]

tar•ra•gon (tăr'ə-gŏn', -gən) *n.* An aromatic herb with leaves used as seasoning. [< Ar *tarkhūn.*]

tar•ry (tăr'ē) *v.* **-ried, -rying. 1.** To delay or be late; linger. **2.** To stay temporarily; sojourn. [ME *tarien.*] —**tar'ri•er** *n.*

tart[1] (tärt) *adj.* **1.** Agreeably pungent or sour. **2.** Caustic; cutting. [< OE *teart,* sharp, severe.] —**tart'ly** *adv.* —**tart'ness** *n.*

tart[2] (tärt) *n.* **1.** A small open pie with a sweet filling. **2.** A whore. [< L *torta,* round bread, "twisted."]

tar•tan (tärt'n) *n.* Any of numerous textile patterns of Scottish origin consisting of stripes of varying widths and colors crossed at right angles against a solid background. [Prob < OF *tertaine,* a kind of fabric.] —**tar'tan** *adj.*

tar•tar[1] (tär'tər) *n.* **1.** A reddish acid material found in the juice of grapes and deposited on the sides of casks during wine-making. **2.** A hard, yellowish deposit on the teeth. [< MGk *tartaron.*] —**tar•tar'ic** (-tăr'ĭc) *adj.*

tar•tar[2] (tär'tər) *n.* Also **Tar•tar.** A ferocious or violent-tempered person. [< TATAR.]

Tar•tar. Variant of **Tatar.**

Tash•kent (tăsh-kĕnt'). The capital of the Uzbek S.S.R. Pop. 1,385,000.

task (tăsk, täsk) *n.* **1.** A piece of assigned work. **2.** A difficult or tedious undertaking. [ME *taske,* tax, work imposed, task.]

task•mas•ter (tăsk'măs'tər, täsk'mäs'tər) *n.* One who imposes heavy work on another.

tas•sel (tăs'əl) *n.* **1.** A pendent ornament consisting of a bunch of loose threads or cords bound at one end. **2.** Something resembling a tassel, as the pollen-bearing flower cluster of a corn plant. —*v.* **-seled** or **-selled, -seling** or **-selling. 1.** To fringe or decorate with tassels. **2.** To put forth a tassellike inflorescence. [< OF.]

taste (tāst) *v.* **tasted, tasting. 1.** To distinguish the flavor of by taking into the mouth. **2.** To eat or drink a small quantity of. **3.** To experience, esp. for the first time. **4.** To have a distinct flavor. —*n.* **1. a.** The sense that distinguishes the sweet, sour, salty, and bitter qualities of dissolved substances in contact with the taste buds on the tongue. **b.** A sensation of such a quality, or a combination of such qualities, perceived with this sense. **2.** The act of tasting. **3.** A small quantity eaten or tasted. **4.** A limited or first experience. **5.** A personal preference or inclination. **6.** Discernment of what is aesthetically excellent or appropriate. **7.** The sense of what is proper in a given social situation. [< L *taxāre,* to touch.] —**tast'er** *n.*

taste bud. Any of numerous nests of cells distributed over the tongue that are primarily responsible for the sense of taste.

taste•ful (tāst'fəl) *adj.* Having or exhibiting good taste. —**taste'ful•ly** *adv.*

taste•less (tāst'lĭs) *adj.* **1.** Lacking flavor; insipid. **2.** Having or exhibiting poor taste.

tast•y (tā'stē) *adj.* **-ier, -iest.** Having a pleasing flavor; savory. —**tast'i•ness** *n.*

tat (tăt) *v.* **tatted, tatting.** To make tatting or produce by tatting. —**tat'ter** *n.*

Ta•tar (tä'tər) *n.* Also **Tar•tar** (tär'tər). **1.** A member of one of the Mongolian peoples who invaded much of C and W Asia and E Europe in the 13th century. **2.** Any of the Turkic languages of the Tatars. —**Ta'tar** *adj.*

tat•ter (tăt'ər) *n.* **1.** A torn and hanging piece of cloth; shred. **2. tatters.** Torn and ragged clothing; rags. —*v.* To make or become ragged. [< ON *tōturr.*]

tat•ter•de•mal•ion (tăt'ər-də-mā'lē-ən, -măl'ē-ən) *n.* A person wearing tattered clothing; ragamuffin. [< TATTER.]

tat•ting (tăt'ĭng) *n.* **1.** Handmade lace fashioned by looping and knotting a single strand of heavy-duty thread on a small hand shuttle. **2.** The art of making tatting.

tat•tle (tăt'l) *v.* **-tled, -tling. 1.** To reveal the secrets of another. **2.** To chatter; prate. —**tat'tler** *n.*

tat•tle•tale (tăt'l-tāl') *n.* A talebearer.

tat•too[1] (tă-to͞o') *n.* **1.** A call sounded to summon soldiers or sailors to quarters at night. **2.** A rhythmic tapping. [< Du *taptoe,* "the shutting off of the taps (at taverns at the end of the day)."]

tat•too[2] (tă-to͞o') *n.* A permanent mark or design made on the skin by a process of pricking and ingraining an indelible pigment or by raising scars. —*v.* To mark (the skin) with a tattoo or tattoos. [Of Polynesian origin.] —**tat•too'er** *n.*

tau (tou, tô) *n.* The 19th letter of the Greek alphabet, representing *t.*

taught (tôt). *p.t.* & *p.p.* of **teach.**

taunt (tônt) *v.* To jeer or challenge mockingly. —*n.* A scornful jeer or challenge. [Perh < L *temptāre,* TEMPT.] —**taunt'er** *n.*

taupe (tōp) *n.* Brownish gray. [< L *talpa,* mole.] —**taupe** *adj.*

Tau•rus (tôr'əs) *n.* **1.** A constellation in the N Hemisphere. **2.** The 2nd sign of the zodiac. [< L, bull.]

taut (tôt) *adj.* **1.** Tight; not slack. **2.** Strained; tense. **3.** Trim; tidy. [< OE *togian,* to pull. See **deuk-.**] —**taut'ly** *adv.* —**taut'ness** *n.*

tau•tol•o•gy (tô-tŏl'ə-jē) *n., pl.* **-gies. 1. a.** Needless repetition of the same sense in different words; redundancy. **b.** An instance of such repetition. **2.** A statement composed of simpler statements in a fashion that makes it true whether the simpler statements are true or false, as *Either it will rain tomorrow or it will not rain tomorrow.* [< Gk *tautologos,* repeating the same ideas.] —**tau'to•log'i•cal** (tô'tə-lŏj'ĭ-kəl) *adj.* —**tau'to•log'i•cal•ly** *adv.*

tav (täf, tôf) *n.* Also **taw.** The 23rd letter of the Hebrew alphabet, representing *t(th).*

tav•ern (tăv'ərn) *n.* **1.** A saloon; bar. **2.** A public house or inn. [< L *taberna,* hut, inn.]

taw•dry (tô'drē) *adj.* **-drier, -driest.** Gaudy and cheap; vulgarly ornamental.

taw•ny (tô'nē) *n.* Light brown to brownish orange. [< OF *tane,* tanned.] —**taw'ny** *adj.*

tax (tăks) *n.* **1.** A contribution for the support of a government required of persons, groups, or businesses within the domain of that government. **2.** A burdensome or excessive demand; a strain. —*v.* **1.** To place a tax on. **2.** To make difficult or excessive demands upon. **3.** To make a charge against; accuse. [< L *taxāre* < *tangere,* to touch.] —**tax'a•ble** *adj.* —**tax•a'tion** *n.* —**tax'er** *n.*

tax•i (tăk'sē) *n., pl.* **-is** or **-ies.** A taxicab. —*v.* **-ied, -iing** or **-ying. 1.** To be transported by taxi. **2.** To move slowly on the ground or water before takeoff or after landing. [Short for TAXICAB.]

tax•i•cab (tăk'sē-kăb') *n.* An automobile that carries passengers for a fare. [< F *taxe,* charge + CAB.]

tax•i•der•my (tăk'sə-dûr'mē) *n.* The art or process of stuffing and mounting animal skins in lifelike form. [< TAXO- + -DERM + -Y.] —**tax'i•der'mist** *n.*

tax•ing (tăk'sĭng) *adj.* Burdensome.

taxo–. *comb. form.* Arrangement or order. [< Gk *taxis,* arrangement, order.]

tax•on•o•my (tăk-sŏn'ə-mē) *n.* The science, laws, or principles of classification, esp. the classification of organisms in categories based on common characteristics. —**tax'o•nom'ic** (-sə-nŏm'ĭk) *adj.* —**tax'o•nom'i•cal•ly** *adv.* —**tax•on'o•mist** *n.*

tax shelter. Any financial operation, such as the acquisition of expenses, that reduces taxes on current earnings.

Tay•lor (tā'lər), **Zachary.** 1784–1850. 12th President of the U.S. (1849–50).

Tb terbium.

TB tuberculosis.

Tbi•li•si (tə-bē-lē'sē). The capital of the Georgian S.S.R. Pop. 889,000.

tbs., tbsp. tablespoon.

Tc technetium.

Tchai•kov•sky (chī-kôf'skē, -kŏf'skē), **Peter Ilyich.** 1840–1893. Russian composer.

TD touchdown.

Te tellurium.

tea (tē) *n.* **1.** An Asian shrub with evergreen leaves. **2.** The dried, processed leaves of this shrub, steeped in boiling water to make a beverage. **3.** The beverage thus prepared. **4.** A similar beverage. **5.** An afternoon refreshment or social gathering at which tea is taken. [< Ancient Chin *d'a.*]

tea bag. A small porous sac holding tea leaves to make an individual serving of tea.

teach (tēch) *v.* **taught, teaching. 1.** To impart knowledge or skill to; give instruction. **2.** To instruct in. **3.** To cause to learn by example or experience. **4.** To advocate or expound. [< OE *tǣcan.* See **deik-.**]

teach•er (tē'chər) *n.* One who teaches, esp. a person hired by a school to teach.

teach•ing (tē'ching) *n.* **1.** The occupation of teachers. **2.** A precept or doctrine.

teak (tēk) *n.* **1.** An Asian tree with hard, durable, yellowish-brown wood. **2.** The wood of this tree. [Port *teca.*]

teal (tēl) *n.* Any of several small wild ducks. [ME *tele.*]

team (tēm) *n.* **1.** Two or more harnessed draft animals. **2.** A group of players in a game. **3.** Any group organized to work together. —*v.* **1.** To harness together to form a team. **2.** To form a team. [< OE *tēam,* offspring, brood, team of animals. See **deuk-.**]

team•mate (tēm'māt') *n.* A fellow member of a team.

team•ster (tēm'stər) *n.* **1.** One who drives a team. **2.** A truck driver.

tear[1] (târ) *v.* **tore, torn, tearing. 1.** To pull apart or into pieces; rend. **2.** To make (an opening) by ripping. **3.** To lacerate. **4.** To extract or separate forcefully; wrench. **5.** To divide; disunite. **6.** To rush headlong. —*n.* A rip or rent. [< OE *teran.* See **der-**[2]**.**]

tear[2] (tîr) *n.* **1.** A drop of the clear saline liquid that lubricates the surface between the eyeball and eyelid. **2.** A drop of any liquid or hardened fluid. **3. tears.** The act of weeping: *left in tears.* [< OE *tēar, tehher.* See **dakru-.**] —**tear'ful** *adj.* —**tear'ful•ly** *adv.*

tear•drop (tîr'drŏp') *n.* **1.** A single tear. **2.** An object having the shape of a tear.

tear gas (tîr). Any of various agents that on dispersal irritate the eyes and cause blinding tears.

tease (tēz) *v.* **teased, teasing. 1.** To annoy; vex. **2.** To make fun of. **3.** To coax. **4.** To disentangle and dress the fibers of (wool). **5.** To raise the nap of (cloth). —*n.* **1.** One given to playful mocking. **2.** A coquettish woman. [< OE *tǣsan,* to pull, tear < Gmc **taisan.*] —**teas'er** *n.* —**teas'ing•ly** *adv.*

Zachary Taylor

tea•sel (tē'zəl) *n.* Also **tea•zel, tea•zle. 1.** A plant with thistlelike flowers surrounded by stiff bristles. **2.** The flower head of such a plant, used to raise a nap on fabrics. [< OE *tǣsel* < Gmc **taisilā.*]

tea•spoon (tē'spōōn') *n.* **1.** The common small spoon used esp. with tea, coffee, and desserts. **2.** A household cooking measure, 1/3 tablespoon or 1 1/3 drams.

teat (tēt, tĭt) *n.* A mammary gland or nipple. [< Gmc **titta,* TIT.]

tech. technical.

tech•ne•ti•um (tĕk'nē'shē-əm) *n. Symbol* **Tc** A silvery-gray, radioactive metallic element, used as a tracer and to eliminate corrosion in steel. Atomic number 43, longest-lived isotope Tc 97. [< Gk *tekhnētos,* artificial.]

tech•ni•cal (tĕk'nĭ-kəl) *adj.* **1.** Of, pertaining to, or derived from technique. **2.** Specialized. **3. a.** Abstract or theoretical. **b.** Scientific. **4.** Formal rather than practical. **5.** Technological. [< Gk *tekhnikos,* of art or skill.] —**tech'ni•cal•ly** *adv.* —**tech'ni•cal•ness** *n.*

tech•ni•cal•i•ty (tĕk'nĭ-kăl'ə-tē) *n., pl.* **-ties. 1.** The condition or quality of being technical. **2.** Something meaningful or relevant in principle only.

tech•ni•cian (tĕk-nĭsh'ən) *n.* An expert in a technique or technology.

tech•nique (tĕk-nēk') *n.* **1.** The systematic procedure by which a task is accomplished. **2.** Also **tech•nic** (tĕk'nĭk). The degree of skill shown in any performance. [F, "technical."]

tech•nol•o•gy (tĕk-nŏl'ə-jē) *n., pl.* **-gies. 1.** The application of science, esp. in industry or commerce. **2.** The methods and materials thus used. [Gk *tekhnē,* skill, art + -LOGY.] —**tech'no•log'i•cal** (-nə-lŏj'ĭ-kəl) *adj.* —**tech'no•log'i•cal•ly** *adv.* —**tech•nol'o•gist** *n.*

ted•dy bear (tĕd'ē). A child's toy bear.

te•di•ous (tē'dē-əs) *adj.* Tiresome by reason of length or slowness; boring. [L *taedium,* TEDIUM.] —**te'di•ous•ly** *adv.* —**te'di•ous•ness** *n.*

te•di•um (tē'dē-əm) *n.* Boredom; tediousness. [L *taedium* < *taedēre,* to bore, weary.]

tee (tē) *n.* **1.** A small peg with a concave top for holding a golf ball for an initial drive. **2.** The place from which a player makes his first stroke in golf. —*v.* **teed, teeing.** To place (a golf ball) on a tee. —**tee off. 1.** To drive a golf ball from the tee. **2.** *Slang.* To start. [Earlier *teaz.*]

teem (tēm) *v.* To abound or swarm. [< OE *tīeman,* to breed. See **deuk-.**]

teem•ing (tē'mĭng) *adj.* Abounding in or swarming with.

-teen. *comb. form.* Used in the names of the cardinal numbers **thirteen** through **nineteen.** [< OE *-tēne, -tȳne.*]

tee•ter (tē'tər) *v.* **1.** To totter. **2.** To seesaw; vacillate. [Prob < ON *titra,* to tremble.]

teeth. *pl.* of **tooth.**

teethe (tē*th*) *v.* **teethed, teething.** To grow teeth; cut one's teeth in infancy.

tee•to•tal•er (tē'tōt'l-ər) *n.* One who abstains completely from alcoholic liquors. [*Tee,* first letter in TOTAL + total (abstinence).]

Te•gu•ci•gal•pa (tā-gōō'sē-gäl'pä). The capital of Honduras. Pop. 168,000.

Te•he•ran (tĕ'ə-răn', -rän'). The capital of Iran. Pop. 2,317,000.

tel. **1.** telegram; telegraph. **2.** telephone.

Tel A•viv (tĕl' ə-vēv'). A city of W Israel. Pop. 394,000.

tele-. *comb. form.* **1.** Distance. **2.** Television. [< Gk *tēle,* at a distance, far off.]

tel•e•cast (tĕl'ə-kăst', -käst') *v.* **-cast** or **-casted, -casting.** To broadcast by television. —*n.* A television broadcast.

tel•e•com•mu•ni•ca•tion (tĕl'ə-kə-myōō'nĭ-kā'shən) *n.* Often **telecommunications.** The science and technology of communication by electrical or electronic means.

tel•e•gram (tĕl'ə-grăm') *n.* A communication transmitted by telegraph.

tel•e•graph (tĕl'ə-grăf', -gräf') *n.* **1.** Any communications system that transmits and receives unmodulated electric impulses, esp. one in which the transmission and reception stations are connected by wires. **2.** A telegram. —*v.* To transmit (a message) by telegraph. —**tel'e•graph'ic** *adj.* —**tel'e•graph'i•cal•ly** *adv.* —**te•leg'ra•phy** (tə-lĕg'rə-fē) *n.*

Tel•e•gu (tĕl'ə-gōō') *n.* A Dravidian language spoken in SE India.

tel•e•ki•ne•sis (tĕl'ə-kĭ-nē'sĭs, -kī-nē'sĭs) *n.* The movement of, or ability to move, objects by scientifically unknown or inexplicable means, as by the exercise of mystical powers.

te•lem•e•try (tə-lĕm'ə-trē) *n.* The science and technology of automatic acquisition and transmission of data from remote sources.

te•lep•a•thy (tə-lĕp'ə-thē) *n.* Communication by scientifically unknown means. —**tel'e•path'ic** (tĕl'ə-păth'ĭk) *adj.*

tel•e•phone (tĕl'ə-fōn') *n.* **1.** An electrical or electronic device that transmits voice or other acoustic signals to remote locations. **2.** A system of such devices together with connecting and supporting equipment. —*v.* **-phoned, -phoning.** To communicate, or communicate with, by telephone. —**tel'e•phon'er** *n.* —**tel'e•phon'ic** (-fŏn'ĭk) *adj.*

te•leph•o•ny (tə-lĕf'ə-nē) *n.* The electrical transmission of sound between distant stations.

tel•e•pho•to (tĕl'ə-fō'tō) *adj.* Of or pertaining to a photographic lens or lens system used to produce a large image of a distant object.

tel•e•scope (tĕl'ə-skōp') *n.* **1.** An arrangement of lenses or mirrors or both that gathers light, permitting direct observation or photographic recording of distant objects. **2.** Any of various devices used to detect and observe distant objects by their emission or reflection of radiant energy. —*v.* **-scoped, -scoping. 1.** To slide inward or outward in overlapping sections, as the cylindrical sections of a small hand telescope. **2.** To crush or compress inward. **3.** To make shorter or more precise; condense. [< Gk *teleskopos,* farseeing.] —**tel'e•scop'ic** (-skŏp'ĭk) *adj.*

tel•e•type•writ•er (tĕl'ə-tīp'rī'tər) *n.* An electromechanical typewriter that either transmits or receives messages coded in electrical signals.

tel•e•vise (tĕl'ə-vīz') *v.* **-vised, -vising.** To broadcast (a program) by television.

tel•e•vi•sion (tĕl'ə-vĭzh'ən) *n.* **1.** The transmission and reception of images of moving and stationary objects, generally with accompanying sound, by electronic means. **2.** The receiving apparatus used in this process. **3.** The industry of broadcasting television programs.

tell (tĕl) *v.* **told, telling. 1.** To narrate; recount. **2.** To express with words. **3.** To notify; inform. **4.** To command; order. **5.** To discern; identify. **6.** To have an effect or impact: *In this game every move tells.* [< OE *tellan.* See **del-**[2]**.**] —**tell'a•ble** *adj.*

tell•er (tĕl'ər) *n.* A bank employee who receives and pays out money.

tell•ing (tĕl'ĭng) *adj.* **1.** Having force or effect. **2.** Revealing. —**tell'ing•ly** *adv.*

tell•tale (tĕl'tāl') *n.* **1.** A talebearer. **2.** A sign; token. **3.** Any of various devices that indicate or register information. *—adj.* Serving to indicate, reveal, or betray.

tel•lu•ri•um (tĕ-lo͝or'ē-əm) *n. Symbol* **Te** A brittle, silvery-white metallic element used to alloy stainless steel and lead, in ceramics, and in thermoelectric devices. Atomic number 52, atomic weight 127.60. [< L *tellūs,* earth.]

Tell (tĕl), **William.** Legendary Swiss independence hero.

te•mer•i•ty (tə-mĕr'ə-tē) *n.* Rashness; foolish boldness. [< L *temere,* blindly, rashly.]

temp. 1. in the time of (L *tempore*). **2.** temperature. **3.** temporary.

tem•per (tĕm'pər) *v.* **1.** To modify; moderate. **2.** To bring to a specified consistency, as by blending, kneading, etc. **3.** To harden or toughen (a metal), as by alternate heating and cooling. *—n.* **1.** A state of mind or emotions; mood; disposition. **2.** Equanimity; composure. **3. a.** Irascibility. **b.** An outburst of rage: *a fit of temper.* **4.** The condition or degree of being tempered. [< L *temperāre,* "to mingle in due proportion."]

tem•per•a (tĕm'pər-ə) *n.* **1.** A painting medium in which pigment is mixed with water-soluble glutinous materials such as size or egg yolk. **2.** Painting done with this medium. [< It *temperare,* to mingle, temper.]

tem•per•a•ment (tĕm'prə-mənt, tĕm'pər-ə-) *n.* **1.** The manner of thinking, behaving, and reacting characteristic of a specific individual. **2.** Excessive irritability or sensitiveness. [< L *temperāmentum,* "a mixing (of the humors)."] **—tem'per•a•men'tal** *adj.* **—tem'per•a•men'tal•ly** *adv.*

tem•per•ance (tĕm'pər-əns, tĕm'prəns) *n.* **1.** Moderation or self-restraint. **2.** Total abstinence from alcoholic liquors.

tem•per•ate (tĕm'pər-ĭt, tĕm'prĭt) *adj.* **1.** Exercising moderation and self-restraint. **2.** Moderate; mild. **3.** Neither hot nor cold in climate. [< L *temperāre,* to moderate, TEMPER.] **—tem'per•ate•ly** *adv.*

Temperate Zone. Either of two middle latitude zones of the earth lying between 23½° and 66½° N and S.

tem•per•a•ture (tĕm'pər-ə-cho͝or', tĕm'prə-) *n.* **1.** The degree of hotness or coldness of a body or environment. **2.** A bodily temperature above normal, caused by illness; fever. [< L *temperāre,* to mix, TEMPER.]

tem•pered (tĕm'pərd) *adj.* **1.** Having a specified temper or disposition. **2.** Moderated: *justice tempered with clemency.*

tem•pest (tĕm'pĭst) *n.* A violent storm. [< L *tempestās,* storm, weather, season.] **—tem•pes'tu•ous** (-pĕs'cho͞o-əs) *adj.*

tem•plate (tĕm'plĭt) *n.* Also **tem•plet.** A pattern or gauge used as a guide in making something accurately. [< F *templet.*]

tem•ple¹ (tĕm'pəl) *n.* A building or place dedicated to the worship or the presence of a deity. [< L *templum,* sanctuary.]

tem•ple² (tĕm'pəl) *n.* The flat region on either side of the forehead. [< L *tempus,* temple of the head.]

tem•po (tĕm'pō) *n., pl.* **-pos. 1.** The relative speed at which music is to be played. **2.** A characteristic rate of activity; pace. [It, "time."]

tem•po•ral¹ (tĕm'pər-əl, tĕm'prəl) *adj.* **1.** Pertaining to or limited by time. **2.** Secular as distinguished from ecclesiastical. [< L *tempus,* time.] **—tem'po•ral•ly** *adv.*

tem•po•ral² (tĕm'pər-əl, tĕm'prəl) *adj.* Of, pertaining to, or near the temples of the skull. [< L *tempus,* TEMPLE².]

tem•po•rar•y (tĕm'pə-rĕr'ē) *adj.* Lasting, used, or enjoyed for a limited time; not permanent. [< L *tempus,* time.] **—tem'po•rar'i•ly** *adv.*

tem•po•rize (tĕm'pə-rīz') *v.* **-rized, -rizing.** To compromise or act evasively in order to gain time or postpone a decision. [< L *tempus,* time.] **—tem'po•ri•za'tion** *n.*

tempt (tĕmpt) *v.* **1.** To entice (someone) to commit an unwise or immoral act. **2.** To be attractive to. **3.** To provoke or risk provoking. **4.** To incline or dispose strongly. [< L *temptāre,* to try, touch, tempt.] **—temp•ta'tion** *n.* **—tempt'er** *n.* **—tempt'ress** (tĕmp'trĭs) *fem.n.*

ten (tĕn) *n.* The cardinal number written 10 or in Roman numerals X. [< OE *tien, tȳn.* See **dekm̥-.**] **—ten** *adj.* & *pron.*

ten. tenor.

ten•a•ble (tĕn'ə-bəl) *adj.* Defensible or logical. [< L *tenēre,* to hold.] **—ten'a•bil'i•ty, ten'a•ble•ness** *n.* **—ten'a•bly** *adv.*

te•na•cious (tə-nā'shəs) *adj.* **1.** Persistent; stubborn. **2.** Cohesive or adhesive. **3.** Tending to retain; retentive. [< L *tenēre,* to hold.] **—te•nac'i•ty** (-năs'ə-tē) *n.*

ten•an•cy (tĕn'ən-sē) *n., pl.* **-cies. 1.** The possession or occupancy of lands or tenements by lease or rent. **2.** The period of a tenant's occupancy or possession.

ten•ant (tĕn'ənt) *n.* **1.** One who temporarily holds or occupies property owned by another. **2.** An occupant or inhabitant. [< L *tenēre,* to hold.]

Ten Commandments. The ten injunctions received by Moses.

tend¹ (tĕnd) *v.* **1.** To move or extend in a certain direction. **2.** To be likely. **3.** To be disposed or inclined. [< L *tendere,* to stretch, direct one's course, be inclined.]

tend² (tĕnd) *v.* **1.** To look after. **2.** To serve at: *tend bar.* [< ME *attenden,* attend.]

ten•den•cy (tĕn'dən-sē) *n., pl.* **-cies. 1.** A demonstrated inclination to think, act, or behave in a certain way; propensity. **2.** The drift or purport of a literary work. [< L *tendere,* to stretch, TEND.]

ten•der¹ (tĕn'dər) *adj.* **1.** Delicate; soft; fragile. **2.** Young and vulnerable. **3.** Frail; weakly delicate. **4.** Sensitive or sore. **5.** Gentle and loving. [< L *tener,* tender, delicate.] **—ten'der•ly** *adv.* **—ten'der•ness** *n.*

ten•der² (tĕn'dər) *n.* **1.** A formal offer or bid. **2.** Money: *legal tender.* *—v.* To offer formally. [< L *tendere,* to stretch.]

tend•er³ (tĕn'dər) *n.* **1.** One who tends something. **2.** *Naut.* A vessel attendant on another vessel or vessels. **3.** A railroad car attached to the locomotive, carrying fuel and water.

ten•der•foot (tĕn'dər-fo͝ot') *n., pl.* **-foots** or **-feet.** A greenhorn; novice.

ten•der•heart•ed (tĕn'dər-här'tĭd) *adj.* Compassionate.

ten•der•iz•er (tĕn'də-rī'zər) *n.* A substance applied to meat to make it tender.

ten•der•loin (tĕn'dər-loin') *n.* The tenderest part of a loin of beef, pork, etc.

ten•don (tĕn'dən) *n.* A band of tough, inelastic fibrous tissue that connects a muscle with its bony attachment. [< L *tendere,* to stretch.]

ten•dril (tĕn'drəl) *n.* **1.** A slender, coiling extension by which a climbing plant clings to a support. **2.** Something resembling this. [< OF *tendron,* cartilage, young shoot.]

ten•e•ment (tĕn'ə-mənt) *n.* **1.** A building to live in, esp. one intended for rent. **2.** A cheap apartment house whose facilities and maintenance barely meet minimum standards. [< ML *tenementum,* feudal holding, house.]

ten•et (tĕn'ĭt) *n.* A fundamental principle or dogma. [< L *tenēre,* to hold.]

Tenn. Tennessee.

Ten•nes•see (tĕn'ə-sē'). A state of the SE U.S. Pop. 3,924,000. Cap. Nashville.

ten•nis (tĕn'ĭs) *n.* A game played with rackets and a light ball by two players *(singles)* or two pairs of players *(doubles)* on a court divided by a net. [ME *tennys.*]

Ten•ny•son (tĕn'ə-sən), **Alfred Lord.** 1809–1892. English poet.

ten•on (tĕn'ən) *n.* A projection on the end of a piece of wood shaped for insertion into a mortise. [< L *tenēre,* to hold.]

ten•or (tĕn'ər) *n.* **1.** Flow of meaning; gist; purport. **2. a.** *Law.* The exact meaning or actual wording of a document as distinct from its effect. **b.** An exact copy or transcript of a document. **3. a.** The highest natural adult male voice. **b.** A part for this voice. **c.** One who sings this part. [< L, uninterrupted course, a holding on.]

ten•pin (tĕn'pĭn') *n.* **1.** A bowling pin used in playing tenpins. **2. tenpins.** A game, bowling.

tense¹ (tĕns) *adj.* **tenser, tensest. 1.** Taut; strained. **2.** Nerveracking; suspenseful: *a tense situation.* *—v.* **tensed, tensing.** To make or become tense. [L *tensus,* pp of *tendere,* to stretch out.] **—tense'ness** *n.*

tense² (tĕns) *n.* Any of the inflected forms of a verb that indicate the time and continuance or completion of the action or state. [< L *tempus,* time.]

ten•sile (tĕn'səl, -sīl') *adj.* Of or involving a force that produces stretching. [< L *tensus,* "stretched," TENSE.]

ten•sion (tĕn'shən) *n.* **1.** The act of stretching or the condition of being stretched. **2.** A force tending to produce elongation or extension. **3. a.** Mental strain. **b.** A strained relation between persons or groups. **c.** Uneasy suspense. [< L *tensus,* TENSE.] **—ten'sion•al** *adj.*

tent (tĕnt) *n.* A portable shelter, as of canvas stretched over a supporting framework of poles, ropes, and pegs. [< L *tendere,* to stretch.]

ten•ta•cle (tĕn'tə-kəl) *n.* A flexible, unjointed, projecting appendage, as of an octopus or sea anemone. [< L *temptāre,* to touch, feel, TEMPT.] **—ten•tac'u•lar** (-tăk'yə-lər) *adj.*

ten•ta•tive (tĕn'tə-tĭv) *adj.* **1.** Of an experimental nature. **2.** Uncertain. [< L *temptāre,* to feel, try, TEMPT.] **—ten'ta•tive•ly** *adv.*

ten•ter•hook (tĕn'tər-ho͝ok') *n.* A hooked nail for securing cloth on a drying framework. **—on tenterhooks.** In a state of suspense or anxiety.

tenth (tĕnth) *n.* **1.** The ordinal number 10 in a series. **2.** One of 10 equal parts. **—tenth** *adj.* & *adv.*

ten•u•ous (tĕn'yo͞o-əs) *adj.* **1.** Slender or thin; rarefied. **2.** Unsubstantial; flimsy. [< L *tenuis,* thin, rare, fine.] **—ten'u•ous•ly** *adv.* **—ten'u•ous•ness** *n.*

ten•ure (tĕn'yər, -yo͝or') *n.* **1.** The holding of something, as an office; occupation. **2.** The terms under which something is held. **3. a.** The period of holding. **b.** Permanence of position. [< L *tenēre,* to hold.]

te•pee (tē'pē) *n.* A cone-shaped tent of skins or bark used by North American Indians.

tep•id (tĕp'ĭd) *adj.* Moderately warm; lukewarm. [< L *tepēre,* to be lukewarm.]

te•qui•la (tə-kē'lə) *n.* An alcoholic liquor distilled from a fleshy-leaved Central American plant. [< *Tequila,* district in Mexico.]

ter. territorial; territory.

tera–. Indicates a trillion (10^{12}): *terahertz.* [< Gk *teras,* monster.]

ter•bi•um (tûr'bē-əm) *n. Symbol* **Tb** A soft, silvery-gray metallic rare-earth element, used in electronics and as a laser material. Atomic number 65, atomic weight 158.924. [< *Ytterby,* a village in Sweden.]

ter•cen•te•nar•y (tûr'sĕn-tĕn'ə-rē, tûr-sĕn'-tə-nĕr'ē) *n., pl.* **-ies.** Also **ter•cen•ten•ni•al** (tûr'-sĕn-tĕn'ē-əl). A 300th anniversary or its celebration. **—ter'cen•te'nar•y** *adj.*

term (tûrm) *n.* **1. a.** A limited period of time. **b.** An assigned period for a person to serve. **2. a.** A point of time beginning or ending a period. **b.** A deadline, as for making a payment. **c.** The end of a normal gestation period. **3. a.** A word having a precise meaning. **b. terms.** Language or manner of expression employed: *no uncertain terms.* **4. terms. a.** Conditions or stipulations: *peace terms.* **b.** The relation between two persons or groups: *on speaking terms.* **5.** *Math.* Each of the quantities connected by addition or subtraction signs in an equation or series. *—v.* To designate; call. [< L *terminus,* boundary line, boundary, limit.] **—term'ly** *adv.*

ter•ma•gant (tûr'mə-gənt) *n.* A shrew. [ME *Termagaunt,* imaginary Moslem deity who appeared as such a character in mystery plays.]

ter•mi•nal (tûr'mə-nəl) *adj.* **1.** Pertaining to, situated at, or forming the end or boundary of something. **2.** Concluding; final. **3.** Pertaining to or occurring in a term or each term. *—n.* **1.** A terminating point, limit, or part. **2.** A point at which a connection to an electrical component is normally made. **3.** A railroad or bus station, esp. a terminus. [< L *terminus,* boundary, TERMINUS.] **—ter'mi•nal•ly** *adv.*

ter•mi•nate (tûr'mə-nāt') *v.* **-nated, -nating.** To end or conclude. [< L *terminus,* TERMINUS.] **—ter'mi•na'tion** *n.* **—ter'mi•na'tive** *adj.*

ter•mi•nol•o•gy (tûr'mə-nŏl'ə-jē) *n., pl.* **-gies.** The technical terms of a particular trade, science, or art; nomenclature. [< L *terminus,* limit + -LOGY.] **—ter'mi•no•log'i•cal** (-nə-lŏj'ĭ-kəl) *adj.* **—ter'mi•no•log'i•cal•ly** *adv.* **—ter'mi•nol'o•gist** *n.*

ter•mi•nus (tûr'mə-nəs) *n., pl.* **-nuses** or **-ni** (-nī'). **1.** The end of something. **2. a.** A terminal on a transportation line. **b.** The last stop on such a line. [L, boundary line, boundary, limit.]

ter•mite (tûr'mīt') *n.* Any of various superficially antlike social insects that feed on and destroy wood. [< L *tarmes,* wood-eating worm.]

tern (tûrn) *n.* Any of various sea birds related to and resembling the gulls but usually smaller and with a forked tail. [< Scand.]

ter•na•ry (tûr'nə-rē) *adj.* **1.** Composed of three or arranged in threes. **2.** *Math.* **a.** Having the base three. **b.** Involving three variables. [< L *ternī,* three each.]

terp•si•cho•re•an (tûrp'sĭk-ə-rē'ən, tûrp'sə-kôr'ē-ən, -kōr'ē-ən) *adj.* Pertaining to dancing. [< *Terpsichore,* Greek muse of dancing.]

terr. territorial; territory.

ter•race (tĕr'ĭs) *n.* **1.** A porch or balcony. **2.** An open area adjacent to a house; patio. **3.** A raised bank of earth having vertical or sloping sides and a flat top. **4.** A row of buildings erected on raised ground or on a sloping site. [< L *terra,* earth.]

ter•ra cot•ta (tĕr'ə kŏt'ə). A hard ceramic clay used in pottery and construction. [It, "cooked earth."] **—ter'ra-cot'ta** *adj.*

ter•ra fir•ma (tĕr'ə fûr'mə). Dry land. [L, "firm land."]

ter•rain (tə-rān', tĕ-) *n.* **1.** A tract of land; ground. **2.** The character of land. [< L *terra,* earth.]

ter•ra•pin (tĕr'ə-pən) *n.* Any of various aquatic North American turtles. [< Algon.]

ter•rar•i•um (tə-rār'ē-əm) *n., pl.* **-ums** or **-ia** (-ē-ə). A closed container in which small plants are grown or small animals, as turtles or lizards, are kept. [< L *terra,* earth + -ARIUM.]

ter•res•tri•al (tə-rĕs'trē-əl) *adj.* **1.** Pertaining to the earth or its inhabitants. **2.** Of, pertaining to, or composed of land as distinct from water or air. **3.** Living or growing on land. [< L *terra,* earth.]

terre-verte (tĕr'vĕrt') *n.* An olive-green pigment. [F, "green earth."]

ter•ri•ble (tĕr'ə-bəl) *adj.* **1.** Causing terror or fear; dreadful. **2.** Eliciting awe. **3.** Intense; severe. **4.** Unpleasant; disagreeable. [< L *terrēre,* to frighten.] **—ter'ri•ble•ness** *n.* **—ter'ri•bly** *adv.*

ter•ri•er (tĕr'ē-ər) *n.* Any of various usually small, active dogs originally bred for hunting burrowing animals. [< F *terrier,* burrow.]

ter•rif•ic (tə-rĭf'ĭk) *adj.* **1.** Terrifying or frightful. **2.** Splendid; magnificent. **3.** Awesome; astounding: *a terrific speed.* [< L *terrēre,* to frighten + -FIC.] **—ter•rif'i•cal•ly** *adv.*

ter•ri•fy (tĕr'ə-fī') *v.* **-fied, -fying.** To fill with terror. **—ter'ri•fy'ing•ly** *adv.*

ter•ri•to•ri•al (tĕr'ə-tôr'ē-əl, -tōr'ē-əl) *adj.* **1.** Of or pertaining to a territory or to its powers of jurisdiction. **2.** Pertaining or restricted to a particular territory; regional; local.

territorial waters. Inland and coastal waters under the jurisdiction of a state.

ter•ri•to•ry (tĕr'ə-tôr'ē, -tōr'ē) *n., pl.* **-ries. 1.** A region. **2.** The land and waters under the jurisdiction of a state. **3. Territory. a.** A part of the U.S. not admitted as a state. **b.** A part of Canada or Australia not accorded statehood or provincial status. **4.** The area for which a person is responsible. **5.** A sphere of action or interest; province. [< L *terra,* land.]

ter•ror (tĕr'ər) *n.* **1.** Intense, overpowering fear. **2.** A terrifying object or occurrence. **3.** A policy of violence aiming to achieve or maintain supremacy. [< L *terrēre,* to frighten.]

ter•ror•ism (tĕr'ər-ĭz'əm) *n.* The political use of terror and intimidation. **—ter'ror•ist** *n.* & *adj.*

ter•ror•ize (tĕr'ər-īz') *v.* **-ized, -izing. 1.** To fill with terror. **2.** To coerce by intimidation.

ter•ry (tĕr'ē) *n., pl.* **-ries. 1.** Any of the uncut loops that form the pile of a fabric. **2.** A looped pile fabric used for bath towels and robes. [?]

terse (tûrs) *adj.* **terser, tersest.** Effectively concise. [< L *tersus,* pp of *tergēre,* to wipe off, polish.] **—terse'ly** *adv.* **—terse'ness** *n.*

ter•ti•ar•y (tûr'shē-ĕr'ē) *adj.* **1.** Third in place, order, degree, or rank. **2. Tertiary.** Of or belonging to the geologic time, system of rocks, and sedimentary deposits of the first period of the Cenozoic era. *—n.* The Tertiary period. [< L *tertius,* third.]

tes•sel•late (tĕs'ə-lāt') *v.* **-lated, -lating.** To form into a mosaic pattern, as by using small squares of stone or glass. [< L *tessella,* a small cube.] **—tes'sel•la'tion** *n.*

test (tĕst) *n.* **1.** A means of examination, trial, or proof. **2.** A series of questions or problems designed to determine knowledge or intelligence. **3.** A criterion; standard. [< L *testum,* earthen vessel.] **—test** *v.* **—test'er** *n.*

test. 1. testator. **2.** testimony.

Test. Testament.

tes•ta•ment (tĕs'tə-mənt) *n.* **1. a.** A document providing for the disposition of personal property after death. **b.** A will. **2. a.** Any proof that serves as evidence of something. **b.** A statement of belief. **3. Testament. a.** Either of the two main divisions of the Bible, the Old Testament and the New Testament. **b.** The New Testament. [< L *testis,* witness.]

tes•tate (tĕs'tāt') *adj.* Having made a legally valid will before death. [< L *testārī,* to make a will.]

tes•ta•tor (tĕs'tā'tər, tĕs-tā'tər) *n.* One who has made a legally valid will before death.

tes•ti•cle (tĕs'tĭ-kəl) *n.* A testis.

tes•ti•fy (tĕs'tə-fī') *v.* **-fied, -fying. 1.** To make a declaration of fact under oath. **2.** To make a serious or solemn statement in support of an argument or asserted fact. **3.** To declare publicly; make known. [< L *testificārī.*]

tes•ti•mo•ni•al (tĕs'tə-mō'nē-əl) *n.* **1.** A formal statement testifying to a particular fact. **2.** A written affirmation of another's character or worth. **3.** Something given as a tribute for a person's achievement. **—tes'ti•mo'ni•al** *adj.*

tes•ti•mo•ny (tĕs'tə-mō'nē) *n., pl.* **-nies. 1.** A declaration or affirmation of fact or truth. **2.** Any evidence in support of a fact or assertion; proof. **3.** The collective testimony in a legal case. **4.** A public declaration regarding a religious experience. [< L *testis,* witness.]

tes•tis (tĕs'tĭs) *n., pl.* **-tes** (-tēz'). The male reproductive gland. [L, "witness" (to virility).]

test tube. A cylindrical clear glass tube usually open at one end and rounded at the other, used in laboratory experimentation.

tes•ty (tĕs'tē) *adj.* **-tier, -tiest. 1.** Irritable; touchy; peevish. **2.** Characterized by irritability, impatience, or exasperation: *a testy remark.* [ME *testif,* headstrong.] **—tes'ti•ly** *adv.* **—tes'ti•ness** *n.*

tet•a•nus (tĕt'n-əs) *n.* An acute, often fatal infectious disease caused by a bacillus and characterized by rigidity and spasmodic contraction of the voluntary muscles. [< Gk *tetanos,* "stretched."]

tête-à-tête (tāt'ə-tāt') *adv.* Together without a third person; in privacy. *—n.* A private conversation between two people. *—adj.* For or between two only; private. [F, "head to head."]

teth (tĕt, tĕs) *n.* The 9th letter of the Hebrew alphabet, representing *ṭ.*

teth•er (tĕ*th*'ər) *n.* **1.** A rope or chain for an animal, allowing it a short radius to move about. **2.** The range or scope of one's resources or abilities. *—v.* To restrict with a tether. [< ON *tjōthr.*]

tetra–. *comb. form.* Four. [Gk.]

tet•ra•he•dron (tĕt'rə-hē'drən) *n., pl.* **-drons** or **-dra** (-drə). A polyhedron with four faces. [< Gk *tetraedros,* four-faced.] **—tet'ra•he'dral** (-drəl) *adj.*

te•tram•e•ter (tĕ-trăm'ə-tər) *n.* A line of verse consisting of four metrical feet.

Teu•ton (t/y/ōōt'n) *n.* **1. Teutons.** An ancient people, probably of Germanic or Celtic origin, who lived in N Europe until about 100 B.C. **2.** One of the peoples speaking a Germanic language, esp. a German.

Teu•ton•ic (t/y/ōō-tŏn'ĭk) *adj.* **1.** Of or relating to the Teutons. **2.** Of or relating to the Germanic languages. *—n.* The Germanic languages.

Tex. Texas.

Tex•as (tĕk'səs). A state of the south-central U.S. Pop. 11,197,000. Cap. Austin. —**Tex'an** *adj.* & *n.*

text (tĕkst) *n.* **1.** The wording or words of something written or printed. **2.** The body of a printed work as distinct from a preface, footnote, or appendix. **3.** A Scriptural passage to be read and expounded upon in a sermon. **4.** The subject matter of a discourse. **5.** A textbook. [< L *textus,* literary composition, "woven thing."] —**tex'tu•al** (tĕks'cho͞o-əl) *adj.*

text•book (tĕkst'bo͝ok') *n.* A book used for the study of a particular subject.

tex•tile (tĕks'tīl', -tĭl) *n.* **1.** Cloth; fabric, esp. a woven or knitted one. **2.** Fiber or yarn used for making fabric. *—adj.* Pertaining to textiles or their manufacture. [< L *textus,* "woven thing."]

tex•ture (tĕks'chər) *n.* **1.** The appearance of a fabric resulting from the woven arrangement of its yarns or fibers. **2.** The composition or structure of a substance; grain. [< L *textus,* woven thing.] —**tex'tur•al** *adj.*

–th[1]. *comb. form.* **1.** The act or result of the act expressed in the verb root: *spilth.* **2.** The quality suggested by the adjective root: **width.** [< OE *-thu, -tho.*]

–th[2], **–eth.** *comb. form.* Ordinal numbers: **millionth.** [< OE *-tha, -the.*]

–th[3]. Variant of **-eth**[1].

Th thorium.

Thack•er•ay (thăk'ə-rē, 'thăk'rē), **William Makepeace.** 1811–1863. English novelist.

Thai (tī) *n., pl.* **Thai. 1.** A native or citizen of Thailand. **2.** The official language of Thailand, a member of the Tai family; Siamese. —**Thai** *adj.*

Thai•land (tī'lănd'). A kingdom of SE Asia. Pop. 26,258,000. Cap. Bangkok.

Thailand

thal•a•mus (thăl'ə-məs) *n., pl.* **-mi** (-mī'). A large mass of gray matter that relays sensory stimuli to the cerebral cortex. [< Gk *thalamos,* inner chamber.] —**tha•lam'ic** (thə-lăm'ĭk) *adj.*

tha•ler. Variant of **taler.**

thal•li•um (thăl'ē-əm) *n. Symbol* **Tl** A soft, malleable, highly toxic metallic element, used in rodent and ant poisons, photocells, and low-melting glass. Atomic number 81, atomic weight 204.37. [< L *thallus,* green shoot + -IUM.]

Thames (tĕmz). A river of S England.

than (*th*ăn) *conj.* **1.** —Used in comparative statements to introduce the second element of a comparison or inequality. **2.** —Used in statements of preference to introduce the rejected alternative: *I would rather dance than eat.* **3.** —Used with the sense of "beyond" with adverbs of degree or quantity: *Read more than the first page.* [< OE *thanne, thǣnne.* See **to-.**]

Usage: In sentences involving comparison, the case of the word following *than* is governed by its function in the clause introduced by *than: He speaks better than I do.* This is true also of elliptical clauses in which the unexpressed words are clearly indicated: *He is a better speaker than I* (that is, *than I am*). *The students disliked no one more than her* (that is, *than they disliked her*). In the first example, *I* is construed as the subject of an unexpressed verb; in the second, *her* is construed as an object. See Usage note at **different.**

thane (thān) *n.* Also **thegn. 1.** In Anglo-Saxon England, a freeman granted land by the king in return for military service. **2.** A feudal lord in Scotland. [< OE *thegen.*]

thank (thăngk) *v.* To express gratitude to. [< OE *thancian.* See **tong-.**]

thank•ful (thăngk'fəl) *adj.* Grateful. —**thank'ful•ly** *adv.* —**thank'ful•ness** *n.*

thank•less (thăngk'lĭs) *adj.* **1.** Not feeling or showing gratitude; ungrateful. **2.** Not apt to be appreciated: *a thankless task.*

thanks (thăngks) *pl.n.* An acknowledgment of a favor, gift, etc. —**thanks to.** On account of; because of. *—interj.* Expressive of gratitude.

thanks•giv•ing (thăngks'gĭv'ĭng) *n.* An act of giving thanks; an expression of gratitude, esp. to God.

Thanksgiving Day. A U.S. national holiday set apart for giving thanks to God, celebrated on the fourth Thursday of November.

that (*th*ăt; *unstressed th*ət) *adj., pl.* **those** (*th*ōz). **1.** Being the one singled out, implied, or understood. **2.** Being the one further removed or less obvious. *—pron., pl.* **those. 1. a.** The one designated, implied, mentioned, or understood. **b.** The further or less immediate one. **2.** —Used as a relative pronoun to introduce a clause. **3.** Something: *There is that about him which mystifies me.* *—adv.* To such an extent: *Is it that complicated?* *—conj.* **1.** —Used chiefly to introduce a subordinate clause stating a fact, wish, consequence, or reason: *We supposed that you were lost.* **2.** —Used to introduce an elliptical exclamation of desire: *Oh, that I were rich!* [< OE *thæt.* See **to-.**]

thatch (thăch) *n.* Plant stalks or foliage, as reeds or palm fronds, used for roofing. *—v.* To cover with or as if with thatch. [< OE *theccan,* to thatch, cover. See **steg-**[1].]

thaw (thô) *v.* **1.** To change from a frozen solid to a liquid by gradual warming. **2.** To become warm enough to melt snow and ice. **3.** To become less reserved. *—n.* **1.** The process of thawing. **2.** A period during which ice and snow melt. [< OE *thāwian.* See **tā-.**]

the[1] (*thē before a vowel; thə before a consonant*). The definite article, functioning as an adjective before singular or plural nouns and noun phrases that denote particular specified persons or things and before certain nouns and adjectives with generic force. [< OE *thĕ.* See **to-.**]

the[2] (*thē before a vowel; thə before a consonant*) *adv.* To that extent; by that much: *the sooner the better.* [< OE *thĕ,* THE and *thæt,* THAT.]

the•a•ter (thē'ə-tər) *n.* Also **the•a•tre. 1.** A building for the presentation of motion pictures and dramatic performances. **2.** Any similar place with tiers of seats. **3.** Dramatic literature or performance. **4.** A place that is the setting for dramatic events. [< Gk *theatron.*]

the•at•ri•cal (thē-ăt'rĭ-kəl) *adj.* **1.** Of, relating to, or suitable for the theater. **2.** Affectedly dramatic. —**the•at'ri•cal'i•ty** *n.*

thee (*th*ē) *pron. Archaic & Poetic.* The objective case of the 2nd person pronoun *thou.*

theft (thĕft) *n.* The act or an instance of stealing; larceny. [< OE *thēofth* < Gmc **thiufith.*]

thegn. Variant of **thane.**

their (*th*âr). The possessive form of the pronoun *they,* used attributively: *their books.* [< ON *theirra.*]

theirs (*th*ârz). The possessive form of the pronoun *they,* used as a predicate adjective or as a substantive: *The choice ought to be theirs. Theirs is better than ours.* —**of theirs.** Belonging to them: *a friend of theirs.*

the•ism (thē'ĭz'əm) *n.* Belief in the existence of a god or gods. [THE(O)- + -ISM.] —**the'ist** *n.* —**the•is'tic** *adj.* —**the•is'ti•cal•ly** *adv.*

them (*th*ĕm) *pron.* The objective case of the 3rd person pl. pronoun *they,* used as the direct or indirect object of a verb or as the object of a preposition. [< ON *theim* and OE *thǣm.* See **to-.**]

the•mat•ic (thĭ-măt'ĭk) *adj.* Of, constituting, or relating to a theme or themes. —**the•mat'i•cal•ly** *adv.*

theme (thēm) *n.* **1.** A topic of discourse or discussion. **2.** The subject of an artistic work. **3.** A short written composition. **4.** *Mus.* A melody forming the basis of variations or other development in a composition. [< Gk *thema,* "thing placed," proposition.]

them•selves (*th*ĕm'sĕlvz', *th*əm'-) *pron.* A form of the 3rd person pl. pronoun: **1.** —Used reflexively: *They have only themselves to blame.* **2.** —Used for emphasis: *They did it themselves.* —**by themselves. 1.** Alone. **2.** Without help.

then (*th*ĕn) *adv.* **1.** At that time in the past. **2.** Next in time, space, or order. **3.** At another time in the future. **4.** In that case; accordingly. **5.** In addition; besides. **6.** Yet; on the other hand. *—n.* A particular time or moment. *—adj.* Being so at that time. [< OE *thanne, thænne.* See **to-.**]

thence (*th*ĕns, thĕns) *adv.* **1.** From that place. **2.** From that time; thenceforth. **3.** From that circumstance or source. [< OE *thanon,* from there. See **to-.**]

thence•forth (*th*ĕns-fôrth', thĕns-) *adv.* From that time forward; thereafter.

thence•for•ward (*th*ĕns-fôr'wərd, thĕns-) *adv.* Also **thence•for•wards** (-wərdz). **1.** Thenceforth. **2.** From that time or place onward.

theo–. *comb. form.* A god or gods. [< Gk *theos,* god.]

the•oc•ra•cy (thē-ŏk'rə-sē) *n., pl.* **-cies. 1.** Government by a god regarded as the ruling power or by officials claiming divine sanction. **2.** A state so governed. —**the'o•crat'ic** *adj.* —**the'o•crat'i•cal•ly** *adv.*

theol. theological; theology.

the•ol•o•gy (thē-ŏl'ə-jē) *n., pl.* **-gies. 1.** The study of the nature of God and religious truth. **2.** An organized body of opinions concerning God and man's relationship to God. —**the'o•lo'gi•an** (thē'ə-lō'jən) *n.* —**the'o•log'i•cal** (-lŏg'ĭ-kəl) *adj.* —**the'o•log'i•cal•ly** *adv.*

the•o•rem (thē'ə-rəm, thîr'əm) *n.* **1.** An idea that is demonstrably true or is assumed to be so. **2.** *Math.* A proposition that is proven or to be proved. [< Gk *theōrein,* to observe.]

the•o•rize (thē'ə-rīz') *v.* **-rized, -rizing. 1.** To formulate or analyze theories. **2.** To speculate.

—**the'o•rist** *n.* —**the'o•riz'er** *n.*

the•o•ry (thē'ə-rē, thîr'ē) *n., pl.* **-ries. 1. a.** Systematically organized knowledge applicable in a relatively wide variety of circumstances, esp. a system of assumptions, accepted principles, and rules of procedure devised to analyze, predict, or otherwise explain a specified set of phenomena. **b.** Such knowledge or such a system distinguished from experiment or practice. **2.** Abstract reasoning; speculation. **3.** Broadly, hypothesis or supposition. [< Gk *theōria,* contemplation, theory.] —**the'o•ret'i•cal** (-rĕt'ĭ-kəl) *adj.* —**the'o•ret'i•cal•ly** *adv.*

the•os•o•phy (thē-ŏs'ə-fē) *n.* Religious speculation dealing with the mystical apprehension of God. —**the'o•soph'i•cal** (-ə-sŏf'ĭ-kəl) *adj.* —**the•os'o•phist** *n.*

ther•a•peu•tic (thĕr'ə-pyōō'tĭk) *adj.* Having healing or curative powers. [< Gk *therapeuein,* to administer to (medically).] —**ther'a•peu'ti•cal•ly** *adv.*

ther•a•peu•tics (thĕr'ə-pyōō'tĭks) *n. (takes sing. v.).* The medical treatment of disease.

ther•a•py (thĕr'ə-pē) *n., pl.* **-pies.** The treatment of illness or disability. [< Gk *theraps,* attendant.] —**ther'a•pist** *n.*

there (*th*âr) *adv.* **1.** At or in that place. **2.** To, into, or toward that place; thither. **3.** At a point of action or time. —*n.* That place. —*interj.* Expressive of an emotion, as relief or satisfaction. [< OE *thǣr, thēr.* See **to-**.]

Usage: *There* frequently precedes a linking verb such as *be, seem,* or *appear* in beginning a sentence or clause: *There has been much trouble.* The number of the verb is governed by the subject, which in such constructions follows the verb: *There is a garage across the street. There seem to be many good candidates.* But a singular verb is also possible before a compound subject whose parts are joined by a conjunction or conjunctions, especially when the parts are singular: *There is much pain and toil involved.* When the first element of such a subject is singular, a singular verb is also possible even though the other elements are plural: *There was* (or *were*) *a man and two children in the car.*

there•a•bout (*th*âr'ə-bout') *adv.* Also **there•a•bouts** (-bouts'). Approximately.

there•af•ter (*th*âr'ăf'tər, -äf'tər) *adv.* From a specified time onward; from then on.

there•at (*th*âr'ăt') *adv.* **1.** At a specified place. **2.** At such time. **3.** By reason of that.

there•by (*th*âr'bī') *adv.* **1.** By that means; as a result. **2.** In a specified connection or relation wherein.

there•for (*th*âr'fôr') *adv.* For that, this, or it.

there•fore (*th*âr'fôr', -fōr') *adv. & conj.* For that reason; consequently; hence.

there•from (*th*âr'frŏm', -frŭm') *adv.* From that, this, or it.

there•in (*th*âr'ĭn', *th*âr'ĭn') *adv.* In that place or context.

there•in•af•ter (*th*âr'ĭn-ăf'tər, -äf'tər) *adv.* In a later or subsequent portion.

there•of (*th*âr'ŏv', -ŭv') *adv.* **1.** Of or concerning this, that, or it. **2.** From a stated cause or origin.

there•on (*th*âr'ŏn', -ôn') *adv.* **1.** On or upon this, that, or it. **2.** Following that immediately.

there•to (*th*âr'tōō') *adv.* **1.** To that, this, or it. **2.** *Archaic.* Furthermore.

there•to•fore (*th*âr'tə-fôr', -fōr') *adv.* Until or prior to a specified time.

there•un•to (*th*âr'ŭn-tōō') *adv.* To that, this, or it.

there•up•on (*th*âr'ə-pŏn', -ə-pôn') *adv.* **1.** Upon this, that, or it. **2.** Directly following that.

there•with (*th*âr'wĭth', -wĭ*th*') *adv.* **1.** With that, this, or it. **2.** Immediately thereafter.

there•with•al (*th*âr'wĭ*th*-ôl') *adv.* **1.** With all that, this, or it; besides. **2.** *Obs.* Therewith; with that, this, or it.

ther•mal (thûr'məl) *adj.* Also **ther•mic** (-mĭk). Of, pertaining to, using, producing, or caused by heat. [< Gk *thermē,* heat.] —**ther'mal•ly** *adv.*

thermo–. *comb. form.* Pertaining to or caused by heat. [< Gk *thermē,* heat < *thermos,* hot.]

ther•mo•cou•ple (thûr'mə-kŭp'əl) *n.* A device consisting of two dissimilar metals joined at two points, the potential difference between the two junctions being a measure of their difference in temperature.

ther•mo•dy•nam•ics (thûr'mō-dī-năm'ĭks) *n. (takes sing. v.).* The physics of the relationships between heat and other forms of energy. —**ther'mo•dy•nam'ic** *adj.*

ther•mom•e•ter (thər-mŏm'ə-tər) *n.* An instrument for measuring temperature. —**ther'mo•met'ric** (thûr'mō-mĕt'rĭk), **ther'mo•met'ri•cal** *adj.* —**ther•mom'e•try** *n.*

ther•mo•nu•cle•ar (thûr'mō-n/y/ōō'klē-ər) *adj.* **1.** Of or derived from the fusion of atomic nuclei at high temperatures. **2.** Pertaining to atomic weapons based on fusion.

ther•mo•plas•tic (thûr'mə-plăs'tĭk) *adj.* Becoming soft when heated and hardening when cooled. —*n.* A thermoplastic material.

ther•mos bottle (thûr'məs). A commercially produced heat-insulated flask.

ther•mo•set•ting (thûr'mō-sĕt'ĭng) *adj.* Permanently hardening or solidifying on being heated, as certain synthetic resins.

ther•mo•stat (thûr'mə-stăt') *n.* A device that automatically responds to temperature changes and activates switches controlling equipment such as furnaces, refrigerators, and air conditioners.

the•sau•rus (thĭ-sôr'əs) *n., pl.* **-sauri** (-sôr'ī') or **-ruses.** A book of selected words, esp. a book of synonyms and antonyms. [L *thēsaurus,* treasure.]

these. *pl.* of **this.**

the•sis (thē'sĭs) *n., pl.* **-ses** (-sēz'). **1.** A proposition maintained by argument. **2.** A dissertation resulting from original research, esp. as a requirement for an academic degree. [< Gk, a placing, a laying down, position.]

Thes•pi•an (thĕs'pē-ən) *adj.* Also **thes•pi•an.** Of or pertaining to drama; dramatic. —*n.* An actor or actress. [< *Thespis,* Greek poet of the 6th cent. B.C.]

Thess. Thessalonians (New Testament).

the•ta (thā'tə, thē'-) *n.* The 8th letter in the Greek alphabet, representing *th.*

thew (thyōō) *n.* **1.** A well-developed sinew or muscle. **2. thews.** Muscular power or strength. [< OE *thēaw,* usage, custom, characteristic.]

they (*th*ā) *pron.* The 3rd person pl. pronoun in the nominative case, used to represent the persons or things last mentioned. [< ON *their* and OE *thā.* See **to-**.]

they'd (*th*ād). Contraction of *they had* or *they would.*

they'll (*th*āl). Contraction of *they will.*

they're (*th*âr). Contraction of *they are.*

they've (*th*āv). Contraction of *they have.*

thi•a•mine (thī'ə-mĭn, -mēn') *n.* A B-complex vitamin, $C_{12}H_{17}ClN_4OS$, occurring in the bran coat of grains, in yeast, and in meat, that is necessary for carbohydrate metabolism, maintenance of normal nerve function, and the prevention of beriberi. [< Gk *theion,* sulfur + (VIT)AMIN.]

thick (thĭk) *adj.* **1.** Relatively great in depth or in extent from one surface to the opposite; not thin. **2.** Measuring in this dimension. **3.** Thickset. **4.** Dense; concentrated. **5.** Having a viscous consistency; not transparent or fluid. **6.** Having a great number of; abounding. **7.** Indistinctly articulated. **8.** Pronounced; heavy. **9.** Lacking mental agility; stupid. **10.** *Informal.* Very friendly; intimate. **11.** *Informal.* Excessive. —*n.* **1.** The thickset part of something. **2.** The most active or intense part. [< OE *thicce.* See **tegu-**.] —**thick'ly** *adv.* —**thick'ness** *n.*

thick•en (thĭk'ən) *v.* To make or become thick or thicker. —**thick'en•er** *n.*

thick•en•ing (thĭk'ən-ĭng) *n.* **1.** The act or process of making or becoming thick. **2.** Any material used to thicken liquid.

thick•et (thĭk'ĭt) *n.* A dense growth of shrubs or underbrush. [< OE *thiccet* < *thicce,* THICK.]

thick•set (thĭk'sĕt') *adj.* **1.** Having a short, stocky body; stout. **2.** Positioned or placed closely together.

thief (thēf) *n., pl.* **thieves** (thēvz). One who steals. [< OE *thīof, thēof* < Gmc **thiuf.*]

thieve (thēv) *v.* **thieved, thieving.** To take by theft; steal. —**thiev'er•y** *n.*

thigh (thī) *n.* The portion of the leg between the hip and the knee. [< OE *thēoh.* See **teuə-**.]

thigh•bone (thī'bōn') *n.* The femur.

thim•ble (thĭm'bəl) *n.* A small cuplike guard worn to protect the finger that pushes the needle in sewing. [< OE *thȳmel* < *thūma,* THUMB.]

thim•ble•ful (thĭm'bəl-fəl) *n.* A very small quantity.

Thim•phu (thĭm'pōō'). The capital of Bhutan.

thin (thĭn) *adj.* **thinner, thinnest. 1.** Having a relatively small distance between opposite sides or surfaces. **2.** Not great in diameter or cross section; fine. **3.** Lean or slender. **4.** Not dense or concentrated; sparse. **5.** Not rich or heavy in consistency. **6.** Lacking force or substance; flimsy. —*v.* **thinned, thinning.** To become or make thin or thinner. [< OE *thynne.* See **ten-**.] —**thin'ly** *adv.* —**thin'ness** *n.*

thine (*th*īn). **1.** The possessive form of the pronoun *thee,* used as a predicate adjective or as a substantive. **2.** —Used instead of *thy* before an initial vowel or *h: thine enemy.* [OE *thīn.* See **tu-**.]

thing (thĭng) *n.* **1.** Something that exists; an entity. **2.** A tangible object. **3.** An inanimate object. **4.** A creature. **5. things.** Possessions; belongings. **6.** An article of clothing. **7.** An act, deed, or work. **8.** A thought or notion. **9.** A piece of information. **10.** A matter to be dealt with. **11.** A turn of events. **12. things.** The general state of affairs; conditions. [< OE, creature, thing, deed, assembly.]

think (thĭngk) *v.* **thought, thinking. 1.** To have as a thought; formulate in the mind. **2.** To ponder. **3.** To reason. **4.** To believe; suppose. **5.** To remember; call to mind. **6.** To visualize; imagine. **7.** To devise or invent. **8.** To consider. [< OE *thencan.* See **tong-**.] —**think'er** *n.*

think•a•ble (thĭng'kə-bəl) *adj.* Fit to be considered; possible. —**think'a•bly** *adv.*

thin•ner (thĭn'ər) *n.* A liquid, such as turpentine, mixed with paint to reduce viscosity.

thin-skinned (thĭn'skĭnd') *adj.* **1.** Having a thin rind or skin. **2.** Excessively sensitive.

thi•on•ic (thī-ŏn'ĭk) *adj.* Of, containing, or derived from sulfur. [< Gk *theion,* sulfur.]

third (thûrd) *n.* **1.** The ordinal number 3 in a series. **2.** One of 3 equal parts. **3.** The gear next higher after second in an automobile transmission. —*adj.* **1.** Being number 3 in a series; next after second. **2.** Being one of 3 equal parts. —*adv.* Also **third•ly** (thûrd'lē). In the 3rd place, rank, or order. [< OE *thridda.* See **trei-.**]

third person. A set of grammatical forms used in referring to a person or thing other than the speaker or the one spoken to.

Third World. Also **third world.** The underdeveloped or developing countries of Africa, Asia, and Latin America, esp. those not allied with any superpower.

thirst (thûrst) *n.* **1. a.** A sensation of dryness in the mouth related to a desire to drink. **b.** The desire to drink. **2.** An insistent desire; craving. —*v.* **1.** To feel a need to drink. **2.** To have a strong craving. [< OE *thurst.* See **ters-.**] —**thirst'i•ly** *adv.* —**thirst'y** *adj.*

thir•teen (thûr'tēn') *n.* The cardinal number written 13 or in Roman numerals XIII. [< OE *thrēotīne.* See **trei-.**] —**thir'teen'** *adj.* & *pron.*

thir•teenth (thûr'tēnth') *n.* **1.** The ordinal number 13 in a series. **2.** One of 13 equal parts. —**thir'teenth'** *adj.* & *adv.*

thir•ti•eth (thûr'tē-ĭth) *n.* **1.** The ordinal number 30 in a series. **2.** One of 30 equal parts. —**thir'ti•eth** *adj.* & *adv.*

thir•ty (thûr'tē) *n.* The cardinal number written 30 or in Roman numerals XXX. [< OE *thrītig.* See **trei-.**] —**thir'ty** *adj.* & *pron.*

this (*th*ĭs) *pron., pl.* **these** (thēz). **1.** The person or thing present, nearby, or just mentioned. **2.** What is about to be said. **3.** The one that is nearer than another or the one compared with the other. **4.** The present occasion or time. —*adj., pl.* **these.** **1.** Being just mentioned or present. **2.** Being nearer than another or compared with another. **3.** Being about to be stated or described. —*adv.* To this extent. [< OE *thes* or *thēs.* See **to-.**]

this•tle (thĭs'əl) *n.* Any of various prickly plants with usually purplish flowers. [< OE *thistel* < Gmc **thistilaz.*]

this•tle•down (thĭs'əl-doun') *n.* The silky down attached to the seeds of a thistle.

thith•er (thĭ*th*'ər, *th*ĭ*th*'-) *adv.* To or toward that place; there. —*adj.* Being on the more distant side. [< OE *thider.* See **to-.**]

thith•er•ward (thĭ*th*'ər-wərd, *th*ĭ*th*'-) *adv.* In that direction; thither.

thole pin (thōl). A peg set in pairs in the gunwale of a boat to serve as an oarlock. [< OE *tholl.*]

thong (thông, thŏng) *n.* A strip of leather used for binding or lashing. [< OE *thwong, thwang.* See **twengh-.**]

tho•rax (thôr'ăks', thōr'-) *n., pl.* **-raxes** or **thoraces** (thôr'ə-sēz', thōr'-, thô-rā'-). The part of the body between the neck and the diaphragm, partially encased by the ribs; the chest. [< Gk *thōrax,* breastplate, chest covering.] —**tho•rac'ic** (thə-răs'ĭk) *adj.*

tho•ri•um (thôr'ē-əm, thōr'-) *n. Symbol* **Th** A silvery-white metallic element used in magnesium alloys. Atomic number 90, atomic weight 232.038. [< *Thor,* Norse god of thunder.]

thorn (thôrn) *n.* **1.** A sharp, woody spine protruding from a plant stem. **2.** Any of various shrubs, trees, or plants bearing such spines. **3.** One that causes pain or discomfort. [< OE, thorn, thornbush. See **stern-.**] —**thorn'y** *adj.*

thor•ough (thûr'ō) *adj.* **1.** Fully done; finished. **2.** Completely as described; absolute. **3.** Painstakingly careful. [< OE *thurh,* THROUGH.] —**thor'ough•ly** *adv.* —**thor'ough•ness** *n.*

thor•ough•bred (thûr'ō-brĕd', thûr'ə-) *adj.* Bred of pure or pedigreed stock. —*n.* **1.** A purebred or pedigreed animal. **2. Thoroughbred.** Any of a breed of horse originating from a cross of Arabian stallions with English mares.

thor•ough•fare (thûr'ō-fâr', thûr'ə-) *n.* A main road or public highway.

thor•ough•go•ing (thûr'ō-gō'ĭng, thûr'ə-) *adj.* **1.** Very thorough. **2.** Absolute.

those. *pl.* of **that.**

thou (*th*ou) *pron. Archaic & Poetic.* The 2nd person sing. in the nominative case, equivalent to *you.* [< OE *thū.* See **tu-.**]

though (*th*ō) *conj.* **1.** Despite the fact that; although. **2.** Conceding or supposing that. **3.** However; yet. —*adv.* However; nevertheless. [< ON *thō.*]

thought (thôt). *p.t.* & *p.p.* of **think.** —*n.* **1.** The act or process of thinking. **2.** An idea. **3.** The power to reason or imagine. **4.** Consideration; concern. **5.** Expectation. **6.** A trifle; a bit. [< OE *thōht.* See **tong-.**]

thought•ful (thôt'fəl) *adj.* **1.** Contemplative; meditative. **2.** Well thought-out. **3.** Considerate. —**thought'ful•ly** *adv.* —**thought'ful•ness** *n.*

thought•less (thôt'lĭs) *adj.* **1.** Careless; unthinking. **2.** Reckless. **3.** Inconsiderate. —**thought'less•ly** *adv.* —**thought'less•ness** *n.*

thou•sand (thou'zənd) *n.* The cardinal number written 1,000 or in Roman numerals M. [< OE *thūsend.* See **teuə-.**] —**thou'sand** *adj.* & *pron.*

thou•sandth (thou'zəndth, -zənth) *n.* **1.** The ordinal number 1,000 in a series. **2.** One of 1,000 equal parts. —**thou'sandth** *adj.* & *adv.*

thrall (thrôl) *n.* **1.** A slave, serf, or bondman. **2.** Servitude; bondage. [< OE *thrǣl* < ON *thrǣll.*] —**thrall'dom** (-dəm), **thral'dom** *n.*

thrash (thrăsh) *v.* **1.** To beat or flog with or as with a flail. **2.** To defeat utterly. **3.** To move wildly or violently. [Orig a var of THRESH.] —**thrash'er** *n.*

thrash•er (thrăsh'ər) *n.* A long-tailed New World songbird often having a spotted breast.

thrash•ing (thrăsh'ĭng) *n.* A whipping.

thread (thrĕd) *n.* **1.** A fine cord of a fibrous material made of filaments twisted together. **2.** Anything suggestive of the fineness of thread. **3.** Anything suggestive of the continuousness and sequence of thread. **4.** A helical or spiral ridge on a screw, nut, or bolt. —*v.* **1.** To pass one end of a thread through the eye of (a needle or the various hooks and holes on a sewing machine). **2.** To pass cautiously through. **3.** To machine a thread on (a screw, nut, or bolt). [< OE *thrǣd.* See **ter-2.**] —**thread'er** *n.*

thread•bare (thrĕd'bâr') *adj.* **1.** Having the nap worn down so threads show through; frayed or shabby. **2.** Hackneyed; trite.

thread•y (thrĕd'ē) *adj.* **-ier, -iest.** **1.** Consisting of or resembling thread; fibrous; filamentous. **2.** *Med.* Weak and shallow, as a pulse.

threat (thrĕt) *n.* **1.** An expression of an intention to inflict pain, injury, evil, etc. **2.** One regarded as a possible danger. [< OE *thrēat,* oppression, use of force, threat. See **treud-.**]

threat•en (thrĕt'n) *v.* **1.** To express a threat against. **2.** To serve as a threat to. **3.** To portend. —**threat'en•ing•ly** *adv.*

three (thrē) *n.* The cardinal number written 3 or in Roman numerals III. [< OE *thrēo.* See **trei-.**] —**three** *adj.* & *pron.*

three-di•men•sion•al (thrē'dĭ-mĕn'shən-əl) *adj.* **1.** Of, having, or existing in three dimensions. **2.** Having or appearing to have extension in depth.

three•score (thrē'skôr', -skōr') *adj.* Sixty; three times twenty. —**three'score'** *n.*

three•some (thrē'səm) *n.* A group of three.

thren•o•dy (thrĕn'ə-dē) *n., pl.* **-dies.** A song of lamentation. [< Gk *thrēnos,* dirge, lament + *ōidē,* song, ODE.]

thresh (thrĕsh) *v.* **1.** To beat (cereal plants), as with a flail, to remove the grain or seeds. **2.** *Rare.* To thrash. [< OE *therscan.* See **ter-2.**] —**thresh'er** *n.*

thresh•old (thrĕsh'ōld', thrĕsh'hōld') *n.* **1.** The piece of wood or stone placed beneath a door. **2.** An entrance. **3.** The intensity below which a stimulus produces no response. [< OE *therscold, threscold.* See **ter-2.**]

threw (thrōō). *p.t.* of **throw.**

thrice (thrīs) *adv.* Three times. [< OE *thriga, thriwa.* See **trei-.**]

thrift (thrĭft) *n.* Wise economy in the management of money; frugality. [< ON, prosperity.] —**thrift'i•ly** *adv.* —**thrift'y** *adj.*

thrill (thrĭl) *v.* **1.** To feel or cause to feel a sudden intense sensation. **2.** To quiver or vibrate or cause to quiver or vibrate. —*n.* **1.** A quivering or trembling. **2.** That which produces great excitement. [< OE *thyrlian,* to pierce < *thyrl,* hole.] —**thrill'er** *n.*

thrive (thrīv) *v.* **throve** or **thrived, thrived** or **thriven, thriving.** **1.** To prosper. **2.** To grow vigorously; flourish. [< ON *thrīfask,* "to grasp for oneself."] —**thriv'er** *n.*

throat (thrōt) *n.* **1.** The portion of the digestive tract lying between the rear of the mouth and the esophagus. **2.** The anterior portion of the neck. [< OE *throte, throtu* < Gmc **thrut-.*]

throat•y (thrō'tē) *adj.* **-ier, -iest.** Uttered or sounding as if uttered deep in the throat. —**throat'i•ly** *adv.* —**throat'i•ness** *n.*

throb (thrŏb) *v.* **throbbed, throbbing.** **1.** To beat rapidly or violently; pound. **2.** To vibrate, pulsate, or sound with a steady, pronounced rhythm. —*n.* The act of throbbing.

throe (thrō) *n.* **1.** Often **throes.** A violent pang or spasm of pain. **2. throes.** A condition of agonizing struggle or effort. [< OE *thrawe,* paroxysm.]

throm•bo•sis (thrŏm-bō'sĭs) *n., pl.* **-ses** (-sēz'). The formation, presence, or development of a thrombus.

throm•bus (thrŏm'bəs) *n., pl.* **-bi** (-bī'). A blood clot blocking a blood vessel or formed in a heart cavity. [< Gk *thrombos,* lump, clot.]

throne (thrōn) *n.* **1.** The chair occupied by a sovereign, bishop, or other exalted personage on ceremonial occasions. **2.** Sovereign power or rank. [< Gk *thronos.*]

throng (thrŏng) *n.* A large group of people or things crowded together; a multitude. —*v.* **1.** To crowd into. **2.** To move in a throng. [< OE *thrang,* prob < Gmc **thring-,* to press, crowd.]

throt•tle (thrŏt'l) *n.* **1. a.** A valve in an internal-combustion engine that regulates the amount of vaporized fuel entering the cylinders. **b.** A similar valve in a steam engine regulating the amount of steam. **2.** A lever or pedal controlling this valve. —*v.* **-tled, -tling.** **1.** To regulate the speed of (an engine) with a throttle. **2.** To strangle; choke. **3.** To suppress. [Perh < THROAT.] —**throt'tler** *n.*

through (thrōō) *prep.* **1.** In one side and out another side of. **2.** In the midst of. **3.** By way of. **4.** By the means or agency of. **5.** Here and there in; around. **6.** From the beginning to the end of. **7.** Done or finished with. *—adv.* **1.** From one end or side to another end or side. **2.** From beginning to end. **3.** To a conclusion. **4.** Out into the open. *—adj.* **1.** Passing or extending from one end, side, or surface to another. **2.** Allowing continuous passage; unobstructed. **3.** Finished; done. [< OE *thurh, thuruh.* See **ter-**[1].]

through•out (thro͞o-out′) *prep.* In, to, through, or during every part of. *—adv.* **1.** Everywhere. **2.** During the entire duration or extent.

through•way. Variant of **thruway.**

throve (thrōv). *p.t.* of **thrive.**

throw (thrō) *v.* **threw, thrown** (thrōn), **throwing. 1.** To propel through the air with a swift motion of the arm; cast. **2.** To hurl. **3.** To perplex. **4.** To put on or off casually. **5.** To put quickly into use or place. **6.** To put into a specified condition. **7.** To move (a controlling lever or switch). **—throw away.** To discard. **—throw off. 1.** To cast out; to reject; spurn. **2.** To rid oneself of; evade. **—throw out.** To reject or discard. **—throw up. 1.** To abandon. **2.** To vomit. *—n.* **1.** The act of throwing; a cast. **2.** The distance, height, or direction of something thrown. **3.** A light coverlet. [< OE *thrāwan,* to turn, twist. See **ter-**[2].] **—throw′er** *n.*

throw back. To revert to a type or stage in one's ancestral past.

throw•back (thrō′băk′) *n.* A reversion to a former type or ancestral characteristic.

thrum (thrŭm) *v.* **thrummed, thrumming.** To play (a stringed instrument) idly or monotonously; strum. [Imit.]

thrush (thrŭsh) *n.* Any of various songbirds usually having brownish upper plumage and a spotted breast. [< OE *thrysce.* See **trozdos-.**]

thrust (thrŭst) *v.* **1.** To push or drive forcibly. **2.** To stab; pierce. **3.** To force into a specified condition or situation. **4.** To interject. *—n.* **1.** A forceful shove or push. **2. a.** A driving force or pressure. **b.** The forward-directed force developed in a jet or rocket engine as a reaction to the rearward ejection of fuel gases. **3.** A stab. **4.** Outward or lateral stress in a structure. [< ON *thrȳsta,* to thrust, compress.]

thru•way (thro͞o′wā′) *n.* Also **through•way.** An expressway.

thud (thŭd) *n.* **1.** A dull sound. **2.** A blow or fall causing such a sound. *—v.* **thudded, thudding.** To make such a sound. [< OE *thyddan* (imit).] **—thud′ding•ly** *adv.*

thug (thŭg) *n.* A ruffian; hoodlum. [Hindi *thag,* cheat, thief.]

thu•li•um (tho͞o′lē-əm) *n.* *Symbol* **Tm** A bright silvery rare-earth element, one isotope of which is used in small portable medical x-ray units. Atomic number 69, atomic weight 168.934.

thumb (thŭm) *n.* **1.** The short first digit of the hand, opposable to each of the other four digits. **2.** The part of a glove or mitten that covers the thumb. **—all thumbs.** Clumsy. **—thumbs down.** Expressive of refusal or disapproval. **—under the thumb of.** Under the influence or power of. *—v.* **1.** To disarrange, soil, or wear by handling. **2.** *Informal.* To hitchhike. [< OE *thūma.* See **teuə-.**]

thumb index. A series of indentations in the front edge of a reference book, each labeled to indicate a section of the book.

thumb•nail (thŭm′nāl′) *n.* The nail of the thumb. *—adj.* **1.** Of the size of a thumbnail. **2.** Brief.

thumb•screw (thŭm′skro͞o′) *n.* **1.** A screw so designed that it can be turned with the thumb and fingers. **2.** An instrument of torture used to compress the thumb.

thumb•tack (thŭm′tăk′) *n.* A tack with a smooth head that can be pressed into place with the thumb. *—v.* To affix with a thumbtack.

thump (thŭmp) *n.* **1.** A blow with a blunt instrument. **2.** The muffled sound produced by such a blow. *—v.* **1.** To strike with a blunt or dull instrument so as to produce a muffled sound. **2.** To pound. [Imit.]

thun•der (thŭn′dər) *n.* **1.** The explosive sound emitted as a result of the electrical discharge of lightning. **2.** Any similar sound. *—v.* **1.** To produce thunder. **2.** To produce sounds like thunder. **3.** To utter loudly. [< OE *thunor.* See **stenə-.**] **—thun′der•er** *n.*

thun•der•bolt (thŭn′dər-bōlt′) *n.* The discharge of lightning that accompanies thunder.

thun•der•clap (thŭn′dər-klăp′) *n.* A single sharp crash of thunder.

thun•der•cloud (thŭn′dər-kloud′) *n.* A large, dark cloud charged with electricity and producing thunder and lightning.

thun•der•head (thŭn′dər-hĕd′) *n.* The upper portion of a thundercloud.

thun•der•ous (thŭn′dər-əs) *adj.* **1.** Producing thunder or a similar sound. **2.** Loud and unrestrained. **—thun′der•ous•ly** *adv.*

thun•der•show•er (thŭn′dər-shou′ər) *n.* A brief rainstorm accompanied by thunder and lightning.

thun•der•stone (thŭn′dər-stōn′) *n.* Any of various mineral concretions formerly supposed to be thunderbolts.

thun•der•storm (thŭn′dər-stôrm′) *n.* An electrical storm accompanied by heavy rain.

thun•der•struck (thŭn′dər-strŭk′) *adj.* Astonished; amazed.

Thurs•day (thûrz′dē, -dā′) *n.* The 5th day of the week. [< OE *thunresdæg,* "day of Thor" (Old Norse god of thunder).]

thus (*th*ŭs) *adv.* **1.** In a manner previously stated or to be stated. **2.** To a stated degree or extent; so. **3.** Therefore; consequently. [< OE. See **to-.**]

Usage: Except when it is used to provide intentional humor, *thusly* is not an acceptable variant of *thus,* which is itself an adverb.

thwack (thwăk) *v.* To strike or hit with something flat; whack. [Imit.] **—thwack** *n.*

thwart (thwôrt) *v.* **1.** To prevent from taking place; frustrate. **2.** To oppose directly. *—n.* A seat across a boat, on which the oarsman sits. *—adj.* Extending across something. *—adv.* Athwart. [< ON *thverr,* transverse.]

thy (*th*ī). *Archaic & Poetic.* The possessive form of the pronoun *thee,* used attributively. [< OE *thīn.* See **tu-.**]

thyme (tīm) *n.* An aromatic plant with leaves used as seasoning. [< Gk *thumon.*]

thy•mus (thī′məs) *n.* A ductless glandlike structure, situated near the throat, that plays some part in building resistance to disease but is usually vestigial in adults. [< Gk *thumos.*] **—thy′mic** *adj.*

thy•roid (thī′roid′) *adj.* Of or relating to the thyroid gland. *—n.* **1.** The **thyroid gland. 2.** A dried and powdered preparation of the thyroid gland of certain domestic animals, used in medicine. [< Gk *thuroeidēs,* shaped like a door or oblong shield.]

thyroid gland. A two-lobed endocrine gland found in all vertebrates, located in front of and on either side of the trachea in humans, and producing a hormone that regulates metabolism.

thy•self (*th*ī-sĕlf′) *pron.* *Archaic & Poetic.* Yourself. —Used as the reflexive or emphatic form of *thee* or *thou.*

Ti titanium.

ti•ar•a (tē-ăr′ə, -âr′ə, -är′ə) *n.* **1.** The triple crown worn by the pope. **2.** A woman's ornamental headpiece worn on formal occasions. [< Gk, a kind of Persian headdress.]

Ti•ber (tī′bər). A river of C Italy.

Ti•bet (tĭ-bĕt′). A former state in S Asia, now a region of S China. Pop. 1,270,000. Cap. Lhasa.

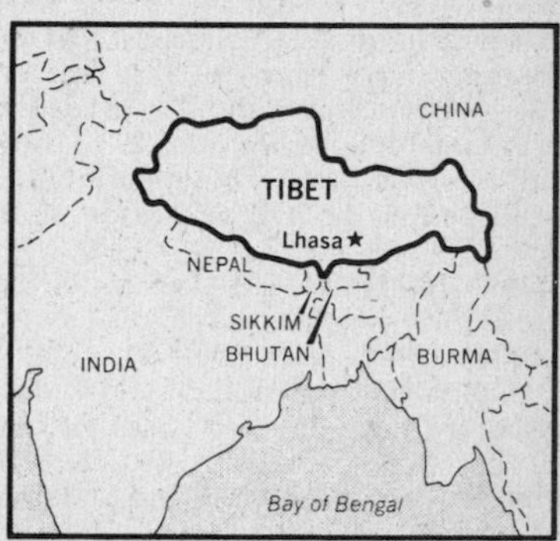

Tibet

Ti•bet•an (tĭ-bĕt′n) *adj.* Of or pertaining to Tibet, its people, or their language or culture. *—n.* **1.** One of the Mongoloid people of Tibet. **2.** The Tibeto-Burman language of Tibet.

Ti•bet•o-Bur•man (tĭ-bĕt′ō-bûr′mən) *n.* A language family including Tibetan and Burmese, usually classed as a subgroup of Sino-Tibetan. **—Ti•bet′o-Bur′man** *adj.*

tib•i•a (tĭb′ē-ə) *n., pl.* **-iae** (-ē-ē′) or **-ias.** The inner and larger of the two bones of the lower leg from the knee to the ankle. [L *tibia,* shinbone, pipe.] **—tib′i•al** *adj.*

tic (tĭk) *n.* A spasmodic muscular contraction, usually in the face or extremities. [F.]

tick[1] (tĭk) *n.* **1.** The recurring clicking sound made by a machine, esp. by a clock. **2.** A light mark used to check off or call attention to an item. [ME *tek.*] **—tick** *v.*

tick[2] (tĭk) *n.* Any of various bloodsucking parasitic arachnids or louselike insects, many of which transmit diseases. [< OE *ticia.* See **deigh-.**]

tick[3] (tĭk) *n.* **1.** The cloth case of a mattress or pillow. **2.** Ticking. [< Gk *thēkē,* cover, case.]

tick•er (tĭk′ər) *n.* A telegraphic printing or display device that receives and records stock-market quotations.

ticker tape. The paper strip on which a ticker prints.

tick•et (tĭk′ĭt) *n.* **1.** A paper slip or card indicating that its holder has paid for admission. **2.** A certificate or license. **3.** An identifying tag; a label. **4.** A list of candidates endorsed by a political party. **5.** A summons, esp. for a traffic violation. *—v.* **1.** To provide with a ticket. **2.** To attach a tag to; label. [Obs F *etiquet,* ticket, label.]

tick•ing (tĭk′ĭng) *n.* A strong, tightly woven fabric used to make ticks.

tick•le (tĭk′əl) *v.* **-led, -ling. 1.** To feel a tingling sensation. **2.** To touch (the body) lightly causing laughter or twitching movements. **3.** To tease or excite pleasurably. *—n.* The act or sensation of tickling. [< ME *ticken,* to touch lightly.] **—tick′ler** *n.*

tick•lish (tĭk'lĭsh) *adj.* **1.** Sensitive to tickling. **2.** Easily offended or upset. **3.** Requiring skillful handling. —**tick'lish•ly** *adv.*

tid•al (tīd'l) *adj.* **1.** Having tides: *a tidal river.* **2.** Scheduled by the time of high tide: *a tidal ship.* —**tid'al•ly** *adv.*

tidal wave. **1.** An unusual rise or incursion of water along the seashore. **2.** Loosely, a tsunami.

tid•bit (tĭd'bĭt') *n.* A choice morsel.

tide (tīd) *n.* **1. a.** The periodic variation in the surface level of the oceans and of bays, gulfs, inlets, etc., caused by the gravitational attraction of the moon and sun. **b.** A specific occurrence of such a variation. **c.** The waters in such a variation. **2.** A tendency regarded as alternating and inexorable. **3.** A time or season: *eventide; Christmastide.* —*v.* **tided, tiding.** **1.** To rise and fall like the tide. **2.** To drift with the tide. —**tide over.** To support through a difficult period. [< OE *tīd,* season, time. See **dā-**.]

tide•land (tīd'lănd') *n.* Coastal land submerged during high tide.

tide•wa•ter (tīd'wô'tər, -wŏt'ər) *n.* **1.** Water that inundates land at flood tide. **2.** Water affected by the tides, esp. tidal streams. **3.** Low coastal land drained by tidal streams.

ti•dings (tī'dĭngz) *pl.n.* Information; news. [Perh < ON *tidhendi,* events.]

ti•dy (tī'dē) *adj.* **-dier, -diest.** **1.** Orderly and neat. **2.** *Informal.* Considerable. —*v.* **-died, -dying.** To put in order. —*n., pl.* **-dies.** A fancy protective covering for the arms or headrest of a chair. [ME, timely, seasonable < TIDE.] —**ti'di•ly** *adv.* —**ti'di•ness** *n.*

tie (tī) *v.* **tied, tying.** **1.** To fasten or secure with a cord, rope, etc. **2.** To draw together and knot with strings or laces. **3.** To make (a knot or bow). **4.** To bring together; unite. **5.** To equal (an opponent or his score) in a contest. —*n.* **1.** A cord, string, etc., by which something is tied. **2.** That which unites; a bond. **3.** A necktie. **4.** A beam or rod that joins and supports parts. **5.** One of the timbers laid across a railroad bed to support the tracks. **6.** An equality of scores, votes, or performance in a contest. [< OE *tīgan.* See **deuk-**.]

Tien•tsin (tĭn'tsĭn'). A city of NE China. Pop. 3,320,000.

tier (tîr) *n.* One of a series of rows placed one above another. [< OF *tire,* sequence, rank.]

Ti•er•ra del Fu•e•go (tĭ-ĕr'ə dĕl f/y/o͞o-ā'gō). **1.** A group of islands at the extreme S tip of South America. **2.** The main island of this group.

tiff (tĭf) *n.* **1.** A fit of irritation. **2.** A petty quarrel. [?] —**tiff** *v.*

Tif•lis (tĭf'lĭs). The former Russian name for Tbilisi.

ti•ger (tī'gər) *n.* A large carnivorous Asian cat having a tawny coat with black stripes. [< Gk *tigris.*] —**ti'gress** *fem.n.*

tight (tīt) *adj.* **1.** Of such a close construction, texture, or organization as to be impermeable, esp. by water or air. **2.** Fastened, held, or closed securely. **3.** Compact. **4.** Drawn out; taut. **5.** Snug, often uncomfortably so. **6.** Constricted. **7.** Stingy. **8.** Difficult to deal with or get out of: *a tight spot.* **9.** Closely contested. **10.** *Slang.* Drunk. —*adv.* **1.** Firmly; securely. **2.** Soundly: *sleep tight.* [< ON *thēttr,* watertight, dense.] —**tight'ly** *adv.* —**tight'ness** *n.*

tight•en (tīt'n) *v.* To make or become tight or tighter. —**tight'en•er** *n.*

tight•fist•ed (tīt'fĭs'tĭd) *adj.* Stingy.

tight•lipped (tīt'lĭpt') *adj.* **1.** Having the lips pressed together. **2.** Reticent.

tight•rope (tīt'rōp') *n.* A tightly stretched rope or wire on which acrobats perform.

tights (tīts) *pl.n.* A snug stretchable garment covering the body from the waist down.

tight•wad (tīt'wŏd') *n. Slang.* A stingy person.

Ti•gris (tī'grĭs). A river of SW Asia.

til•de (tĭl'də) *n.* A diacritical mark (˜) used in Spanish and Portuguese to indicate certain nasal sounds, as in *cañon.*

tile (tīl) *n.* **1.** A slab of baked clay, plastic, etc., laid to cover walls, floors, and roofs. **2.** A length of clay or concrete pipe used in sewers and drains. **3.** A marked playing piece, as in mahjong. —*v.* **tiled, tiling.** To cover or provide with tiles. [< L *tegere,* to cover.]

till¹ (tĭl) *v.* To prepare (land) for the raising of crops by plowing, harrowing, and fertilizing. [< OE *tilian,* to work at, cultivate < Gmc **tilōjan.*] —**till'a•ble** *adj.*

till² (tĭl) *prep.* Until. —*conj.* Until. [< OE *til,* prob < Gmc **tilam,* fixed point.]

Usage: *Till* and *until* are generally interchangeable, and each is appropriate to the highest level of usage. *'Til* is a rare variant form of *until; 'till* is nonstandard.

till³ (tĭl) *n.* A drawer or compartment for money, esp. in a store. [ME *tylle.*]

till•age (tĭl'ĭj) *n.* **1.** The cultivation of land. **2.** Tilled land.

till•er¹ (tĭl'ər) *n.* One that tills land.

till•er² (tĭl'ər) *n.* A lever used to turn a boat's rudder. [< L *tēla,* web, warp of a fabric, weaver's beam.]

tilt (tĭlt) *v.* **1.** To slope or cause to slope, as by raising one end; incline; tip. **2.** To thrust (a lance) in a joust. —*n.* **1.** A slant; slope. **2.** A joust. **3.** A verbal duel. [Perh < Scand.]

tilth (tĭlth) *n.* Tillage.

Tim. Timothy (New Testament).

tim•ber (tĭm'bər) *n.* **1.** Trees or wooded land considered as a source of wood. **2. a.** Wood as a building material. **b.** A dressed piece of wood, esp. a beam in a structure. **c.** A rib in a ship's frame. —*interj.* Used to warn of a falling tree. [< OE, building. See **demə-¹**.]

tim•ber•line (tĭm'bər-līn') *n.* Also **timber line.** The limit of altitude in mountainous regions beyond which trees do not grow.

tim•bre (tĭm'bər, tăm'-) *n.* The quality of a sound that distinguishes it from others of the same pitch and volume. [< Gk *tumpanon.*]

time (tīm) *n.* **1.** A nonspatial continuum in which events occur in apparently irreversible succession. **2.** An interval separating two points on this continuum, measured essentially in terms of occurrences or a regularly recurring event. **3.** A number, as of years, days, or minutes, representing such an interval. **4.** A similar number representing a specific point, as the present, as reckoned from an arbitrary past point on the continuum. **5.** A system by which such intervals are measured or such numbers reckoned. **6.** Often **times.** A span of years; era. **7.** One's heyday. **8.** A suitable or opportune moment. **9.** A designated moment or period: *harvest time.* **10.** One of several instances. **11.** An occasion. **12.** *Informal.* A prison sentence. **13.** The rate of speed of a measured activity. **14.** The characteristic beat of musical rhythm. —*adj.* **1.** Of or relating to time. **2.** Constructed to operate at a particular moment: *time bomb.* **3.** Of or relating to installment buying. —*v.* **timed, timing.** **1.** To set the time for (an event or occasion). **2.** To adjust to keep accurate time. **3.** To regulate for orderly sequence of movements or events. **4.** To record, set, or maintain the speed, duration, or tempo of. [< OE *tīma.* See **dā-**.] —**tim'er** *n.*

time clock. A device that records the arrival and departure times of employees.

time-hon•ored (tīm'ŏn'ərd) *adj.* Honored because of age or age-old observance.

time•keep•er (tīm'kē'pər) *n.* One who keeps track of time, as in a sports event.

time•less (tīm'lĭs) *adj.* **1.** Unending. **2.** Unaffected by time. —**time'less•ly** *adv.*

time•ly (tīm'lē) *adj.* **-lier, -liest.** Occurring at a suitable or opportune time; well-timed.

time•piece (tīm'pēs') *n.* An instrument that measures, registers, or records time.

times (tīmz) *prep.* Multiplied by: *Five times two is ten.*

time•ta•ble (tīm'tā'bəl) *n.* A table listing the scheduled arrival and departure times of trains, buses, etc.

time•worn (tīm'wôrn', -wōrn') *adj.* **1.** Showing the effects of long use or wear. **2.** Used too often; trite.

tim•id (tĭm'ĭd) *adj.* **1.** Hesitant or fearful. **2.** Shy. [< L *timēre,* to fear.] —**ti•mid'i•ty, tim'id•ness** *n.* —**tim'id•ly** *adv.*

tim•ing (tī'mĭng) *n.* The regulating of occurrence, pace, or coordination to achieve the most desirable effects.

tim•or•ous (tĭm'ər-əs) *adj.* Apprehensive; timid. [< L *timēre,* to fear.] —**tim'or•ous•ly** *adv.* —**tim'or•ous•ness** *n.*

tim•o•thy (tĭm'ə-thē) *n.* A grass with narrow, cylindrical flower spikes, widely cultivated for hay. [< *Timothy* Hanson, 18th-century American farmer.]

tim•pa•ni (tĭm'pə-nē) *pl.n.* Also **tym•pa•ni.** A set of kettle-drums. [< L *tympanum,* tympanum.] —**tim'pa•nist** *n.*

tim•pa•num. Variant of **tympanum.**

tin (tĭn) *n.* **1.** *Symbol* **Sn** A malleable, silvery metallic element used to coat other metals to prevent corrosion and in numerous alloys, such as soft solder, pewter, type metal, and bronze. Atomic number 50, atomic weight 118.69. **2.** A tin container or box. —*v.* **tinned, tinning.** **1.** To plate or coat with tin. **2.** To preserve or pack in tins; can. [< OE < Gmc **tinam.*]

tinc•ture (tĭngk'chər) *n.* **1.** A dyeing substance; pigment. **2.** A trace; vestige. **3.** An alcohol solution of a nonvolatile medicine: *tincture of iodine.* [< L *tinctūra,* a dyeing.]

tin•der (tĭn'dər) *n.* Readily combustible material used to kindle fires. [< OE *tynder* < Gmc **tund-.*]

tin•der•box (tĭn'dər-bŏks') *n.* A metal box for holding tinder.

tine (tīn) *n.* A pointed part or prong, as of a fork or an antler. [< OE *tind* < Gmc **tind-,* point.]

tin•foil (tĭn'foil') *n.* Also **tin foil.** A thin, pliable sheet of tin or tin-lead alloy.

tinge (tĭnj) *v.* **tinged** (tĭnjd), **tingeing** or **tinging.** **1.** To color slightly; tint. **2.** To affect slightly, as with a contrasting quality. —*n.* A faint trace of color, flavor, etc. [< L *tingere,* to moisten, plunge, dye.]

tin•gle (tĭng'gəl) *v.* **-gled, -gling.** To have a prickling, stinging sensation as from cold or excitement. [ME *tinglen,* orig, to be affected with a ringing sound in the ears.] —**tin'gle** *n.* —**tin'gler** *n.* —**tin'gly** *adj.*

tink•er (tĭng'kər) *n.* **1.** A traveling mender of metal household utensils. **2.** One who is clumsy at his work; a bungler. —*v.* **1.** To work as a tinker. **2.** To play with machine parts experimentally. [ME *tynkere.*]

tin•kle (tĭng'kəl) *v.* **-kled, -kling.** To make or cause to make light metallic sounds, as of a small bell. —*n.* A light metallic sound.

tin•ny (tĭn'ē) *adj.* **-nier, -niest. 1.** Of, containing, or yielding tin. **2.** Having a thin metallic sound. **3.** Tasting or smelling of tin.

tin•sel (tĭn'səl) *n.* **1.** Very thin sheets, strips, or threads of a glittering material used as decoration. **2.** Anything superficially showy but basically valueless. [< OF *estincelle,* a spark.]

tin•smith (tĭn'smĭth') *n.* One who works with light metal, as tin.

tint (tĭnt) *n.* **1.** A shade of a color, esp. a pale or delicate variation. **2.** A slight coloration. —*v.* To imbue with a tint; color. [< L *tinctus,* a dipping or dyeing.] —**tint'er** *n.*

tin•tin•nab•u•la•tion (tĭn'tĭ-năb'yə-lā'shən) *n.* The ringing or sounding of bells. [< L *tinnīre,* to ring.]

tin•type (tĭn'tĭp') *n.* A ferrotype.

ti•ny (tī'nē) *adj.* **-nier, -niest.** Extremely small. [< ME *tine.*] —**ti'ni•ness** *n.*

-tion. *comb. form.* Action or process involved with: **adsorption.** [< L *-tiō (-tiōn).*]

tip[1] (tĭp) *n.* **1.** The end or extremity of something. **2.** A piece meant to be fitted to the end of something. —*v.* **tipped, tipping. 1.** To furnish with a tip. **2.** To cover, decorate, or remove the tip of. [Prob < ON *typpi.*]

tip[2] (tĭp) *v.* **tipped, tipping. 1.** To knock over or upset; topple over. **2.** To slant; tilt. —*n.* A slant or tilt. [ME *tipen.*]

tip[3] (tĭp) *v.* **tipped, tipping.** To strike gently; tap. [ME *tippen.*] —**tip** *n.*

tip[4] (tĭp) *n.* **1.** A sum of money given for services rendered; gratuity. **2.** Useful information; a helpful hint. [Orig "to pass to" < TIP[3].] —**tip** *v.* **(tipped, tipping).** —**tip'per** *n.*

ti•pi. Variant of **tepee.**

tip•pet (tĭp'ĭt) *n.* A covering for the shoulders, as a cape or scarf. [ME *tipet.*]

tip•ple (tĭp'əl) *v.* **-pled, -pling.** To drink alcoholic liquor, esp. habitually or intemperately. [Back-formation < *tippler,* a bartender.] —**tip'-pler** *n.*

tip•ster (tĭp'stər) *n. Informal.* One who sells tips to bettors or speculators.

tip•sy (tĭp'sē) *adj.* **-sier, -siest.** Slightly drunk. [< TIP[2].] —**tip'si•ness** *n.*

tip•toe (tĭp'tō') *v.* To walk or move on or as on the tips of one's toes. —*n.* The tip of a toe. —*adv.* On tiptoe.

tip•top (tĭp'tŏp') *n.* The highest point; summit. —*adj.* Excellent; first-rate.

ti•rade (tī'răd', tĭ-răd') *n.* A long violent or harshly censorious speech; a diatribe. [F, "a stretching."]

Ti•ra•na (tĭ-rä'nə). The capital of Albania. Pop. 153,000.

tire[1] (tīr) *v.* **tired, tiring. 1.** To make or become weary or fatigued. **2.** To make or become bored; lose interest. [< OE *tēorian.*]

tire[2] (tīr) *n.* Also *Brit.* **tyre. 1.** A solid or air-filled covering for a wheel, typically of rubber, fitted around the wheel's rim to absorb shock and provide traction. **2.** A hoop of iron or heavy rubber fitted about the rim of a wheel. [Prob < TIRE.]

tired (tīrd) *adj.* **1. a.** Fatigued. **b.** Impatient; bored. **2.** Hackneyed.

tire•less (tīr'lĭs) *adj.* Untiring; indefatigable. —**tire'less•ly** *adv.* —**tire'less•ness** *n.*

tire•some (tīr'səm) *adj.* Causing fatigue or boredom; tedious. —**tire'some•ly** *adv.*

'tis (tĭz). *Archaic & Poetic.* Contraction of *it is.*

ti•sane (tĭ-zăn', -zän') *n.* A herbal infusion or similar preparation, drunk as a beverage or for its mildly medicinal effect. [< L *ptisana,* barley.]

tis•sue (tĭsh'o͞o) *n.* **1.** *Biol.* **a.** A group of cells that are similar in form or function. **b.** Cellular matter in general. **2.** A soft, absorbent piece of paper used as a handkerchief. **3.** A thin, translucent paper used for packing, wrapping, etc. **4.** A fine sheer cloth, as gauze. **5.** A web; network. [< L *texere,* to weave.]

tit[1] (tĭt) *n.* Any of various small Old World birds related to and resembling the New World chickadees. [Short for TITMOUSE.]

tit[2] (tĭt) *n.* A teat. [< OE *titt* < Gmc **titta.*]

Tit. Titus (New Testament).

ti•tan (tĭt'n) *n.* A person of colossal size or strength. [< *Titan,* one of a family of Greek gods.]

ti•tan•ic (tī-tăn'ĭk) *adj.* Having great stature, strength, or power.

ti•ta•ni•um (tī-tā'nē-əm, tĭ-) *n. Symbol* **Ti** A strong, low-density, highly corrosion-resistant, lustrous white metallic element used in alloys requiring low weight, strength, and high-temperature stability. Atomic number 22, atomic weight 47.90.

tithe (tī*th*) *n.* **1.** A tenth part of one's annual income, paid for the support of a church. **2.** A tenth part. [< OE *tēotha, teogetha,* tenth.] —**tithe** *v.* **(tithed, tithing).** —**tith'er** (tī'*th*ər) *n.*

tit•il•late (tĭt'ə-lāt') *v.* **-lated, -lating. 1.** To tickle. **2.** To excite agreeably. [L *tītillāre.*] —**tit'il•la'tion** *n.* —**tit'il•la'tive** *adj.*

ti•tle (tīt'l) *n.* **1.** An identifying name given to a book, painting, etc. **2.** A claim or right, esp. a legal right to ownership. **3. a.** A formal appellation, as of rank or office. **b.** Such an appellation used to indicate nobility. **4.** *Law.* **a.** Just cause of possession or control. **b.** The evidence of such means. **c.** The instrument constituting this evidence, such as a deed. **5.** *Sports.* A championship. —*v.* **-tled, -tling.** To give a title to. [< L *titulus,* superscription, label, title.]

ti•tled (tīt'əld) *adj.* Having a title, esp. of nobility.

tit•mouse (tĭt'mous') *n., pl.* **-mice** (-mīs'). A small grayish, crested North American bird. [Perh dial *tit,* small object + MOUSE.]

tit•ter (tĭt'ər) *v.* To utter a restrained, nervous giggle. [Imit.] —**tit'ter** *n.*

tit•tle (tĭt'l) *n.* The tiniest bit; an iota. [< L *titulus,* TITLE.]

tit•u•lar (tĭch'o͞o-lər) *adj.* **1.** Of, relating to, or constituting a title. **2.** Existing as such in name only; nominal.

tiz•zy (tĭz'ē) *n., pl.* **-zies.** *Slang.* A state of nervous confusion; a dither. [?]

tk. truck.

TKO technical knockout.

tkt. ticket.

Tl thallium.

Tm thulium.

tn. 1. town. **2.** train.

tnpk. turnpike.

TNT (tē'ĕn-tē') *n.* Trinitrotoluene.

to (to͞o; *unstressed* tə) *prep.* **1.** In a direction toward. **2.** In the direction of. **3.** Reaching as far as. **4.** Toward or reaching the state of. **5.** To the extent of. **6.** In contact with: *cheek to cheek.* **7.** In front of: *face to face.* **8.** Through and including; until: *from three to five.* **9.** For the attention, benefit, or possession of. **10.** For the purpose of; for: *to that end.* **11.** For or of: *the belt to this dress.* **12.** Concerning or regarding: *deaf to her pleas.* **13.** In relation to: *parallel to the road.* **14.** With the resulting condition of: *torn to shreds.* **15.** As an accompaniment for. **16.** With regard to. **17.** Composing or constituting; in: *two pints to the quart.* **18.** In accord with: *not to my liking.* **19.** As compared with: *a score of four to three.* **20.** Before: *ten to five.* **21.** In honor of: *a toast to his success.* —*adv.* **1.** Into a shut or closed position: *slammed the door to.* **2.** Into consciousness: *He came to.* **3.** Into a state of application to the action or work at hand: *to fall to.* **4.** *Naut.* Turned into the wind. [< OE *tō, te.* See **de-.**]

t.o. turnover.

toad (tōd) *n.* A froglike, mostly land-dwelling amphibian with rough, warty skin. [< OE *tādige.*]

toad•stool (tōd'sto͞ol') *n.* An inedible or poisonous mushroom.

toad•y (tō'dē) *n., pl.* **-ies.** A servile flatterer; a sycophant. —**toad'y** *v.* **(-ied, -ying).**

toast[1] (tōst) *v.* **1.** To heat and brown (bread, rolls, etc.). **2.** To warm thoroughly: *toast one's feet.* —*n.* Sliced bread heated and browned. [< L *torrēre* (pp *tostus*), to dry, parch.]

toast[2] (tōst) *n.* **1.** A person or thing in whose honor persons drink. **2.** The act of proposing the honor of a person or thing as a toast. —*v.* To drink to or propose as a toast.

toast•er (tō'stər) *n.* An electrical appliance used to toast bread.

to•bac•co (tə-băk'ō) *n., pl.* **-cos** or **-coes. 1.** A plant native to tropical America, having broad leaves used chiefly for smoking. **2.** The leaves of this plant processed for use in cigarettes, cigars, pipes, etc. **3.** Such products collectively. [Prob < Ar *tabāq,* euphoria-causing herb.]

to•bac•co•nist (tə-băk'ə-nĭst) *n.* A dealer in tobacco.

To•ba•go (tə-bā'gō). See **Trinidad and Tobago.**

to•bog•gan (tə-bŏg'ən) *n.* A long, runnerless sled constructed of thin boards curled upward at the front. —*v.* **1.** To ride on a toboggan. **2.** To decline or fall rapidly. [< Algon.] —**to•bog'gan•ist** *n.*

To•char•i•an (tō-kâr'ē-ən, -kär'ē-ən) *n.* Also **To•khar•i•an. 1.** A people of possible European origin living in Asia until about the 10th century A.D. **2.** An Indo-European language with eastern and western dialects, *Tocharian A* and *B* respectively, known from documents of the 7th century A.D.

toc•sin (tŏk'sĭn) *n.* **1.** An alarm sounded on a bell. **2.** A warning; omen. [< OProv *tocar,* to strike (a bell), touch + *senh,* bell.]

to•day (tə-dā'). Also **to-day.** *adv.* **1.** During or on the present day. **2.** During or at the present time. —*n.* The present day, time, or age. [< OE *tōdæge,* on this day : TO + *dæge,* dat of *dæg,* DAY.]

tod•dle (tŏd'l) *v.* **-dled, -dling.** To walk with short, unsteady steps, as a small child. [?] —**tod'dle** *n.* —**tod'dler** *n.*

tod•dy (tŏd'ē) *n., pl.* **-dies.** A drink consisting of liquor with hot water, sugar, and spices. [< Hindi *tāṛī,* sap of a palm.]

to-do (tə-do͞o') *n. Informal.* Commotion or bustle; a stir.

toe (tō) *n.* **1.** One of the digits of the foot. **2.** The forward part of something worn on the foot. **3.** Anything suggestive of a toe in form, function, or location. —*v.* **toed, toeing.** To touch, kick, follow, or trace with the toe. [< OE *tā* < Gmc **taihwō.*]

tof•fee (tŏf'ē, tô'fē) *n.* Also **tof•fy** *pl.* **-fies.** A candy of brown sugar and butter. [Var of TAFFY.]

to•ga (tō'gə) *n.* A draped one-piece outer garment worn in public by citizens of ancient Rome. [L < *tegere,* to cover.]

to•geth•er (tə-gĕth'ər) *adv.* **1.** In or into a single group or place. **2.** Against or in relationship to one another. **3.** Regarded collectively; in total. **4.** Simultaneously. **5.** In harmony, accord, or cooperation. [< OE *tōgædere.* See **ghedh-.**]

To•go (tō'gō). A republic of W Africa. Pop. 1,500,000. Cap. Lomé.

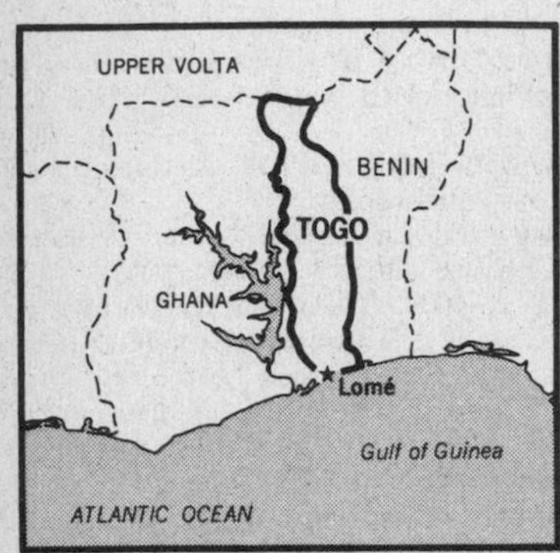

Togo

togs (tŏgz) *pl.n.* Clothes: *gardening togs.* [Short for cant *togman.*]

toil¹ (toil) *v.* **1.** To labor continuously and untiringly; work strenuously. **2.** To proceed with difficulty. *—n.* Exhausting labor or effort. [< L *tudiculāre,* to stir about.]

toil² (toil) *n.* Often **toils.** An entrapment: *in the toils of despair.* [< L *tēla,* a net.]

toi•let (toi'lĭt) *n.* **1.** A disposal apparatus used for urination and defecation. **2.** A room or booth containing such an apparatus. **3.** The act or process of grooming and dressing oneself. [F *toilette,* lavatory.]

toi•let•ry (toi'lĭ-trē) *n., pl.* **-ries.** Any article or cosmetic used in dressing or grooming oneself.

toi•lette (twä-lĕt') *n.* **1.** The act or process of dressing or grooming oneself. **2.** A person's dress or style of dress. [F, TOILET.]

to•ken (tō'kən) *n.* **1.** Something that serves as an indication or representation; a sign; symbol. **2.** Something that tangibly signifies authority, validity, etc. **3.** A keepsake. **4.** A piece of stamped metal used as a substitute for currency. *—adj.* Done as an indication or pledge: *a token payment.* [< OE *tācen.* See **deik-.**]

to•ken•ism (tō'kə-nĭz'əm) *n.* The policy of making only a superficial effort or symbolic gesture toward the accomplishment of a goal, such as racial integration.

To•khar•i•an. Variant of **Tocharian.**

To•ky•o (tō'kē-ō). The capital of Japan. Pop. 8,527,000.

told (tōld). *p.t.* & *p.p.* of **tell.**

To•le•do (tə-lē'dō). A city of NW Ohio. Pop. 363,000.

tol•er•a•ble (tŏl'ər-ə-bəl) *adj.* **1.** Able to be tolerated; endurable. **2.** Adequate; passable. **—tol'er•a•bly** *adv.*

tol•er•ance (tŏl'ər-əns) *n.* **1.** The capacity for or practice of recognizing and respecting the opinions, practices, or behavior of others. **2.** Leeway for variation, as from a standard. **3.** The capacity to endure hardship, pain, etc. **—tol'er•ant** *adj.* **—tol'er•ant•ly** *adv.*

tol•er•ate (tŏl'ə-rāt') *v.* **-ated, -ating. 1.** To allow without prohibiting or opposing; permit. **2.** To recognize and respect, as the opinions, practices, or behavior of others, whether agreeing with them or not. **3.** To put up with; endure. [L *tolerāre,* to bear, tolerate.] **—tol'er•a'tion** *n.* **—tol'er•a'tive** *adj.* **—tol'er•a'tor** *n.*

toll¹ (tōl) *n.* **1.** A fixed tax for a privilege, as passage across a bridge. **2.** A charge for a service, as a long-distance telephone call. **3.** A quantity of people or things destroyed or adversely affected, as in a disaster. [< Gk *telōnēs,* a tax collector.]

toll² (tōl) *v.* **1.** To sound (a bell) slowly at regular intervals. **2.** To announce or summon by tolling. **3.** To sound in slowly repeated single tones. *—n.* The sound of a tolling bell. [ME *tollen.*]

toll•gate (tōl'gāt') *n.* A gate barring passage of vehicles until a toll is paid.

Tol•stoi (tōl'stoi', tŏl'-), Count **Lev Nikolayevich.** English name, Leo Tolstoy. 1828–1910. Russian novelist.

Tol•tec (tōl'tĕk', tŏl'-) *n.* One of an ancient Nahuatl people of C and S Mexico. **—Tol'tec'** *adj.*

tom (tŏm) *n.* A male animal, as a cat or turkey.

tom•a•hawk (tŏm'ə-hôk') *n.* A light ax used as a tool or weapon by North American Indians. *—v.* To strike with a tomahawk. [< Algon.]

to•ma•to (tə-mā'tō, -mä'tō) *n., pl.* **-toes. 1.** A fleshy, smooth-skinned reddish fruit eaten in salads or as a vegetable. **2.** A plant bearing such fruit. [< Nah *tomatl.*]

tomb (to͞om) *n.* **1.** A vault or chamber for the dead. **2.** Any place of burial. [< Gk *tombos,* sepulchral mound.]

tom•boy (tŏm'boi') *n.* A girl who behaves like a spirited boy. **—tom'boy'ish** *adj.*

tomb•stone (to͞om'stōn') *n.* A stone marking a grave.

tom•cat (tŏm'kăt') *n.* A male cat.

tome (tōm) *n.* A book, esp. a large or scholarly one. [< L *tomus,* cut, tome, roll of paper.]

tom•fool•er•y (tŏm'fo͞o'lə-rē) *n.* **1.** Foolish behavior. **2.** Nonsense.

to•mor•row (tə-môr'ō, -mŏr'ō). Also **to-morrow.** *n.* **1.** The day following today. **2.** The near future. *—adv.* On or for the day following today. [< TO (at, on) + OE *morgenne,* dat of *morgen,* MORROW.]

tom•tit (tŏm'tĭt') *n. Brit.* A tit or other small bird.

tom-tom (tŏm'tŏm') *n.* Any of various small-headed drums that are beaten with the hands. [Hindi *ṭamṭam.*]

-tomy. *comb. form.* A cutting of (a specified part or tissue): **lobotomy.** [< Gk *tomos,* a cutting.]

ton (tŭn) *n.* **1. a.** A U.S. Customary System unit of weight equal to 2,240 pounds; long ton. **b.** A U.S. Customary System unit of weight equal to 2,000 pounds; short ton; net ton. **2.** Loosely, a very large quantity of anything. [ME *tonne,* a measure of wine, tun.]

to•nal•i•ty (tō-năl'ə-tē) *n., pl.* **-ties.** *Mus.* The arrangement of the tones of a composition in relation to a tonic.

tone (tōn) *n.* **1. a.** A sound of distinct pitch, quality, and duration. **b.** Quality of sound. **2.** *Mus.* The largest interval between adjacent notes of a diatonic scale. **3.** The pitch of a word or phrase. **4.** Manner of expression: *an angry tone of voice.* **5.** A general quality or atmosphere: *the tone of the debate.* **6. a.** A color or shade of color. **b.** Quality of color. **7. a.** The tension in resting muscles. **b.** Normal tissue firmness. *—v.* **toned, toning. 1.** To give a particular tone or inflection to. **2.** To soften or change the color of. **3.** To harmonize in color. [< L *tonus,* a stretching, tone, sound.] **—to'nal** *adj.* **—to'nal•ly** *adv.*

tongs (tôngz, tŏngz) *n.* (*often takes sing. v.*). A grasping device consisting of two arms joined at one end by a pivot or hinge. [< OE *tange* (sing). See **denk-.**]

tongue (tŭng) *n.* **1.** The fleshy, movable, muscular organ in the mouth that functions in tasting, speech, and as an aid in chewing and swallowing. **2.** The tongue of an animal, as a cow, used as food. **3.** Anything resembling a tongue in form or function. **4.** A spoken language. **5.** Quality of utterance: *her sharp tongue.* [< OE *tunge.* See **dṇghū.**]

tongue-tied (tŭng'tīd') *adj.* Speechless or confused in expression, as from shyness, embarrassment, or astonishment.

ton•ic (tŏn'ĭk) *n.* **1.** Anything that invigorates, refreshes, or restores. **2.** *Mus.* The primary tone of a diatonic scale. *—adj.* **1.** Producing or stimulating physical or mental vigor. **2.** *Mus.* Pertaining to or based on the tonic. [< Gk *tonos,* a stretching, tone.]

to•night (tə-nīt'). Also **to-night.** *adv.* On or during the present or coming night. *—n.* This night or the night of this day.

ton•nage (tŭn'ĭj) *n.* **1.** The number of tons of water a ship displaces afloat. **2.** The capacity of a merchant ship in units of 100 cubic feet. **3.** A charge per ton on cargo. **4.** The total shipping of a country or port, figured in tons. **5.** Weight, measured in tons.

ton•neau (tŭn-ō') *n.* The rear seating compartment of an early type of automobile. [F, "barrel," "cask."]

ton•sil (tŏn'səl) *n.* A mass of lymphoid tissue, esp. either of two such masses, embedded in the lateral walls of the aperture between the mouth and pharynx. [L *tonsillae.*] **—ton'sil•ar** *adj.*

ton•sil•lec•to•my (tŏn'sə-lĕk'tə-mē) *n., pl.* **-mies.** The surgical removal of a tonsil.

ton•sil•li•tis (tŏn'sə-lī'tĭs) *n.* Tonsil inflammation.

ton•so•ri•al (tŏn-sôr'ē-əl, -sōr'ē-əl) *adj.* Of or pertaining to a barber or barbering. [< L *tonsor,* a barber.]

ton•sure (tŏn'shər) *n.* **1.** The act of shaving the head, esp. as a preliminary to becoming a member of a monastic order. **2.** The part of a monk's head so shaven. [< L *tonsūra,* a shearing.]

too (to͞o) *adv.* **1.** In addition; also; as well. **2.** More than sufficient; excessively. **3.** Very; extremely; immensely. **4.** *Informal.* Indeed; so. [ME *to,* in addition to, to.]

Usage: The phrase *not too* is employed, principally informally, in the approximate sense of *not very: Ratification of the treaty is not considered too likely.*

took (to͝ok). *p.t.* of **take.**

tool (to͞ol) *n.* **1.** An instrument, as a hammer, used or worked by hand. **2. a.** A machine, as a lathe, used to cut and shape machinery parts. **b.** The cutting part of such a machine. **3.** Anything used in the performance of an operation; an instrument. **4.** Anything necessary to the carrying out of one's occupation: *tools of the trade.* **5.** A dupe. *—v.* **1.** To form or work with a tool or tools. **2.** To furnish tools or machinery for (a factory). [< OE *tōl* < Gmc **tōwlam.*]

toot (to͞ot) *v.* **1.** To sound (a horn or whistle) in short blasts. **2.** To sound (a blast or series of blasts) on a horn or whistle. *—n.* The act or sound of tooting. [Prob < MDu *tūten* (imit).]

tooth (to͞oth) *n., pl.* **teeth** (tēth). **1.** One of a set of hard, bonelike structures rooted in sockets in the jaws, typically composed of a core of soft pulp surrounded by a layer of hard dentine that is coated with cement or enamel at the crown, and used to seize, hold, or masticate. **2.** A structure or projection resembling a tooth in shape or function, as on a comb, gear, or saw. [< OE *tōth.* See **dent-**.] **—toothed** *adj.*

tooth•paste (to͞oth'pāst') *n.* A paste dentifrice.

tooth•pick (to͞oth'pĭk') *n.* A small piece of wood or other material, for removing food particles from between the teeth.

tooth•some (to͞oth'səm) *adj.* Delicious; savory. **—tooth'some•ness** *n.*

top¹ (tŏp) *n.* **1.** The uppermost part, point, surface, or end of something. **2.** A lid or cap. **3. a.** The highest rank or position. **b.** The highest degree or pitch; acme; zenith. *—adj.* Of, pertaining to, at, or forming the top. *—v.* **topped, topping. 1.** To remove the top from. **2.** To furnish with, form, or serve as a top. **3.** To reach the top of. **4.** To go over the top of. **5.** To exceed or surpass. [< OE *topp.*]

top² (tŏp) *n.* A toy consisting of a symmetrical rigid body spun on a pointed end about the axis of symmetry.

to•paz (tō'păz') *n.* **1.** A colorless, blue, yellow, brown, or pink mineral, often found in association with granitic rocks and valued as a gemstone. **2.** Any of various yellow gemstones, esp. a yellow variety of sapphire. **3.** A light-yellow variety of quartz. [< Gk *topazos.*]

top•coat (tŏp'kōt') *n.* A lightweight overcoat.

tope (tōp) *v.* **toped, toping.** To drink (alcoholic liquors) habitually and excessively. **—top'er** *n.*

To•pe•ka (tə-pē'kə). The capital of Kansas. Pop. 119,000.

top•flight (tŏp'flīt') *adj.* First-rate; superior: *a topflight athlete.*

top-heav•y (tŏp'hĕv'ē) *adj.* Likely to topple because overloaded at the top.

top•ic (tŏp'ĭk) *n.* **1.** A subject treated in a speech, essay, or portion of a discourse; theme. **2.** A subject of discussion or conversation. **3.** A subdivision of a theme, thesis, or outline. [< Aristotle's *Topics.*]

top•i•cal (tŏp'ĭ-kəl) *adj.* **1.** Pertaining or belonging to a particular location or place; local. **2.** Contemporary. **3.** Of or pertaining to a particular topic. **4.** *Med.* Applied or pertaining to a local part of the body.

top•knot (tŏp'nŏt') *n.* **1.** A crest of hair or feathers on the crown of the head. **2.** Any decorative ribbon, bow, etc., worn as a headdress.

top•most (tŏp'mōst') *adj.* Highest; uppermost.

top•notch (tŏp'nŏch') *adj. Informal.* First-rate; excellent.

topo–. *comb. form.* Place or region. [< Gk *topos,* a place.]

topog. topography.

to•pog•ra•phy (tə-pŏg'rə-fē) *n., pl.* **-phies. 1.** The art of graphically representing on a map the exact physical configuration of a place or region. **2.** The features of a place or region. **—to•pog'ra•pher** *n.* **—top'o•graph'ic** (tŏp'ə-grăf'ĭk), **top'o•graph'i•cal** *adj.*

top•ping (tŏp'ĭng) *n.* A sauce, frosting, or garnish for food.

top•ple (tŏp'əl) *v.* **-pled, -pling. 1.** To push over; overturn. **2.** To totter and fall. [Freq of TOP.]

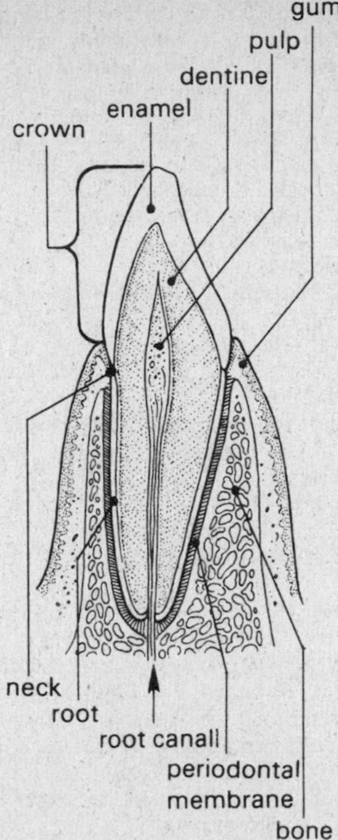

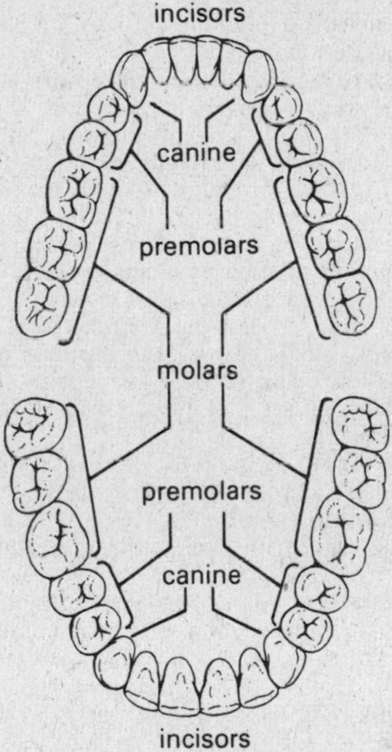

tooth
Above: Cross section of a human incisor
Below: The upper and lower teeth of an adult human

tops (tŏps) *adj. Slang.* First-rate; excellent.

top•sail (tŏp'səl, -sāl') *n.* A square sail set above the lowest sail on the mast of a square-rigged ship.

top-se•cret (tŏp'sē'krĭt) *adj.* Designating information of the highest level of security classification.

top•soil (tŏp'soil') *n.* The surface layer of soil.

top•sy-tur•vy (tŏp'sē-tûr'vē) *adv.* **1.** Upside-down. **2.** In a state of utter disorder or confusion. *—adj.* In a disordered condition.

toque (tōk) *n.* A small brimless, close-fitting woman's hat. [< Span *toca.*]

to•rah (tôr'ə, tōr'ə) *n.* **1.** The body of Jewish literature and oral tradition as a whole. **2. Torah. a.** The Pentateuch. **b.** A scroll on which the Pentateuch is written, used in a synagogue during services. [Heb *tōrāh,* a law, instruction.]

torch (tôrch) *n.* **1.** A portable light produced by the flame of an inflammable material wound about the end of a stick of wood. **2.** A portable apparatus that produces a very hot flame by the combustion of gases, as used in welding. **3.** Anything that serves to illuminate or guide. **4.** *Brit.* A flashlight. [< L *torquēs,* a twisted necklace, wreath.]

tore (tôr, tōr). *p.t.* of **tear¹**.

tor•e•a•dor (tôr'ē-ə-dôr') *n.* A bullfighter. [< Span *torear,* to fight bulls.]

tor•ment (tôr'mĕnt') *n.* **1.** Great pain or anguish. **2.** A source of harassment or pain. *—v.* (tôr-mĕnt', tôr'mĕnt'). **1.** To cause to undergo great pain or anguish. **2.** To agitate or upset greatly. **3.** To annoy or harass. [< L *tormentum,* **torquementum,* a twisted rope.] **—tor•ment'ing•ly** *adv.* **—tor•men'tor** *n.*

torn (tôrn, tōrn). *p.p.* of **tear¹**.

tor•na•do (tôr-nā'dō) *n., pl.* **-does** or **-dos.** A rotating column of air usually accompanied by a funnel-shaped downward extension of a cloud and having a vortex several hundred yards in diameter whirling at speeds of up to 300 miles per hour. [Var of Span *tronada,* thunderstorm.]

To•ron•to (tə-rŏn'tō). The capital of Ontario. Pop. 665,000.

tor•pe•do (tôr-pē'dō) *n., pl.* **-does. 1.** A cigar-shaped, self-propelled underwater projectile launched from a plane, ship, or submarine and designed to detonate on contact with or in the vicinity of a target. **2.** Any of various submarine explosive devices, esp. a submarine mine. **3.** Any of various devices that contain explosives. *—v.* To attack or destroy with or as with a torpedo or torpedoes. [< L *torpēdō,* stiffness, numbness.]

tor•pid (tôr'pĭd) *adj.* In a sluggish, benumbed, or lethargic state of inactivity. [< L *torpēre,* to be stiff.] **—tor'pid•ly** *adv.*

tor•por (tôr'pər) *n.* **1.** A condition of inactivity or insensibility. **2.** Lethargy; apathy. [< L *torpēre,* to be stiff.]

torque (tôrk) *n.* The tendency of a force to produce rotation about an axis. [< L *torquēre,* to twist.]

tor•rent (tôr'ənt, tŏr'-) *n.* **1.** A turbulent, swift-flowing stream. **2.** A raging flood; deluge. **3.** Any turbulent or overwhelming flow. [< L *torrēns,* a burning, a torrent.] **—tor•ren'tial** (tô-rĕn'shəl, tə-) *adj.*

tor•rid (tôr'ĭd, tŏr'-) *adj.* **1.** Parched with the heat of the sun. **2.** Scorching. **3.** Passionate. [< L *torrēre,* to dry, parch.]

Torrid Zone. The region of the earth's surface between the tropics of Cancer and Capricorn.

tor•sion (tôr'shən) *n.* **1.** A twisting or turning. **2.** The stress caused when one end of an object is twisted in one direction and the other end is held motionless. [< LL *torsus,* "twisted."]

tor•so (tôr'sō) *n., pl.* **-sos** or **-si** (-sē'). The trunk of the human body. [It, a stalk, trunk of a statue.]

tort (tôrt) *n. Law.* Any wrongful act, not involving breach of contract, for which a civil suit can be brought. [< L *tortum,* twisted, distorted.]

tor•til•la (tôr-tē'yə) *n.* A thin unleavened pancake characteristic of Mexican cookery. [< Span *torta,* a round cake.]

tor•toise (tôr'təs) *n.* A turtle, esp. a land turtle. [< OF *tortue.*]

tor•toise•shell (tôr'təs-shĕl') *n.* **1.** The translucent brownish outer covering of certain sea turtles, used to make combs, jewelry, etc. **2.** A domestic cat with brown, black, and yellowish fur.

tor•tu•ous (tôr'cho͞o-əs) *adj.* **1.** Winding; twisting. **2.** Devious; deceitful. **3.** Complex. [< L *tortus,* a twist, pp of *torquēre,* to twist.]

tor•ture (tôr'chər) *n.* **1.** The infliction of severe pain as a means of punishment or coercion. **2.** Pain or mental anguish. —*v.* **-tured, -turing. 1.** To subject (a person or animal) to torture. **2.** To afflict with great pain or anguish. [< LL *tortūra,* a twisting, torment.] —**tor'tur•er** *n.*

To•ry (tôr'ē, tōr'ē) *n., pl.* **-ries. 1.** A member of the Conservative Party in Great Britain. **2.** An American who during the American Revolution favored the British side. —**To'ry** *adj.*

toss (tôs, tŏs) *v.* **1.** To throw or be thrown to and fro. **2.** To throw lightly. **3.** To move or lift (the head) with rapidity. **4.** To flip a coin to decide something. **5.** To move oneself about vigorously. —*n.* **1.** An act of tossing. **2.** A rapid lift, as of the head. [?]

toss•up (tôs'ŭp', tŏs'-) *n. Informal.* An even chance or choice.

tot (tŏt) *n.* **1.** A small child. **2.** A small amount of something, as of liquor. [?]

to•tal (tōt'l) *n.* **1.** The amount or quantity obtained by addition. **2.** A whole quantity; an entirety. —*adj.* **1.** Constituting or pertaining to the whole. **2.** Complete; utter; absolute. —*v.* **-taled** or **-talled, -taling** or **-talling. 1.** To determine the sum or total of. **2.** To amount to. [< L *tōtus,* whole.] —**to'tal•ly** *adv.*

to•tal•i•tar•i•an (tō-tăl'ə-târ'ē-ən) *adj.* Of, pertaining to, or designating a polity based on monolithic unity and authoritarianism. —**to•tal'i•tar'i•an•ism'** *n.*

to•tal•i•ty (tō-tăl'ə-tē) *n., pl.* **-ties. 1.** The state or condition of being total. **2.** The aggregate amount; a sum.

tote (tōt) *v.* **toted, toting.** To haul; carry.

to•tem (tō'təm) *n.* **1.** An animal, plant, or natural object serving among certain primitive peoples as the emblem of a clan or family. **2.** A representation of this. —**to•tem'ic** (tō-tĕm'ĭk) *adj.*

totem pole. A post carved and painted with a series of totemic symbols, as among certain Indian peoples of the NW coast of North America.

tot•ter (tŏt'ər) *v.* **1.** To sway as if about to fall. **2.** To walk unsteadily. [< MDu *touteren,* to stagger.] —**tot'ter•er** *n.*

tou•can (to͞o'kăn', -kän') *n.* A tropical American bird with brightly colored plumage and a very large bill. [< Tupi *tucana.*]

touch (tŭch) *v.* **1.** To cause or permit a part of the body to come in contact with so as to feel. **2.** To be or come into contact. **3.** To tap or nudge lightly. **4.** To partake of: *didn't touch her food.* **5.** To move by handling. **6.** To adjoin; border. **7.** To come up to; equal. **8.** To treat of a subject, as in a lecture. **9.** To be pertinent to. **10.** To have an effect upon; act on; change. **11.** To move to tender response. —*n.* **1.** The act or an instance of touching. **2.** The physiological sense by which bodily contact is registered. **3.** The sensation from a specific contact. **4.** A mark or effect left by a specific contact. **5.** A small amount; tinge; trace. **6.** A mild tap or stroke. **7.** A facility; knack. **8.** A characteristic manner of doing something. **9.** The state of being in contact with a specified or unspecified reality: *getting out of touch.* [< VL **toccāre,* to strike, ring a bell, touch.] —**touch'a•ble** *adj.*

touch and go. A precarious state of affairs. —**touch'-and-go'** *adj.*

touch•down (tŭch'doun') *n.* **1.** *Football.* A play worth six points, accomplished by carrying or passing the ball across the opponent's goal line. **2.** The contact, or moment of contact, of a landing aircraft or spacecraft with the landing surface.

tou•ché (to͞o-shā') *interj.* Expressive of concession to an opponent for a point well made, as in an argument. [F, "touched."]

touch•ing (tŭch'ĭng) *adj.* Eliciting a tender reaction. —**touch'ing•ly** *adv.*

touch•stone (tŭch'stōn') *n.* A criterion; standard.

touch•y (tŭch'ē) *adj.* **-ier, -iest. 1.** Oversensitive; irritable. **2.** Precarious; risky.

tough (tŭf) *adj.* **1.** Strong and resilient. **2.** Hard to cut or chew. **3.** Physically rugged. **4.** Severe; harsh. **5.** Aggressive; pugnacious. **6.** Difficult; demanding. **7.** Having a determined will. **8.** *Informal.* Unfortunate; too bad. —*n.* A hoodlum. [< OE *tōh.* See **denk-.**] —**tough'ly** *adv.* —**tough'ness** *n.*

tough•en (tŭf'ən) *v.* To make or become tough. —**tough'en•er** *n.*

tough-mind•ed (tŭf'mīn'dĭd) *adj.* Not sentimental or timorous.

tou•pee (to͞o-pā') *n.* A hair piece worn to cover a bald spot. [< OF *top, toup,* top, summit.]

tour (to͝or) *n.* **1.** A comprehensive trip with visits to places of established interest. **2.** A brief trip to or through a place for the purpose of seeing it. **3.** A journey to fulfill a round of engagements in several places: *a concert tour.* **4.** A period of duty at a single place or job. —*v.* To go on a tour; make a tour of. [< L *tornus,* tool for drawing a circle, lathe.]

tour•ism (to͝or'ĭz'əm) *n.* The business of providing tours and services for tourists.

tour•ist (to͝or'ĭst) *n.* A person who is traveling for pleasure.

tourist class. A grade of travel accommodations less luxurious than first class.

tour•ma•line (to͝or'mə-lĭn, -lēn') *n.* A mineral valued, esp. in its green, clear, and blue varieties, as a gemstone. [F.]

tour•na•ment (to͝or'nə-mənt, tûr'-) *n.* **1.** A contest composed of a series of elimination games or trials. **2.** A medieval jousting match. [< OF *torneier,* "to turn around."]

tour•ney (to͝or'nē, tûr'-) *n., pl.* **-neys.** A tournament. [< OF *torneier,* "to turn around."]

tour•ni•quet (to͝or'nĭ-kĭt, -kā', tûr'-) *n.* Any device used to stop temporarily the flow of blood through a large artery in a limb, esp. a cloth band tightened around a limb. [F, "a turning instrument."]

tou•sle (tou'zəl) *v.* **-sled, -sling.** To disarrange or rumple; dishevel. [ME *touselen.*]

tout (tout) *v.* **1.** To obtain and deal in information regarding horse races. **2.** To publicize as being of great worth. [< OE *tūtian* < Gmc **tūt-,* to stick out, protrude.] —**tout** *n.*

tow¹ (tō) *v.* To draw or pull along behind by a chain or line. —*n.* **1.** An act of towing or the condition of being towed. **2.** Something being towed, as a barge. [< OE *togian.* See **deuk-.**]

tow² (tō) *n.* Coarse broken flax or hemp fiber prepared for spinning. [ME *towe.*]

to•ward (tôrd, tōrd, tə-wôrd') *prep.* Also **to•wards** (tôrdz, tōrdz, tə-wôrdz'). **1.** In the direction of. **2.** In a position facing. **3.** Somewhat before in time. **4.** With regard to. **5.** In furtherance of. **6.** By way of achieving. [< OE *tōweard,* coming, favorable, future : TO + -WARD.]

tow•el (tou'əl) *n.* An absorbent cloth or paper used for wiping or drying. [< OF *toaille.*]

tow•el•ing (tou'əl-ĭng) *n.* Any of various fabrics used for making towels.

tow•er (tou'ər) *n.* **1.** A tall building or part of a building. **2.** A tall framework or structure used for observation, signaling, etc. —*v.* To rise to a conspicuous height. [< Gk *turris.*]

tow•er•ing (tou'ər-ĭng) *adj.* **1.** Of imposing height. **2.** Outstanding. **3.** Awesomely intense. —**tow'er•ing•ly** *adv.*

tow•head (tō'hĕd') *n.* One having white-blond hair. [< TOW².] —**tow'head'ed** *adj.*

tow•hee (tō'hē, tō-hē') *n.* A North American bird with black, white, and rust-colored plumage. [Imit.]

town (toun) *n.* **1.** A population center, often incorporated, larger than a village and smaller than a city. **2.** *Informal.* A city. [< OE *tūn,* enclosed place, homestead, village.]

town•ship (toun'shĭp') *n.* **1.** A subdivision of a county in most Northeastern and Midwestern states. **2.** A public land surveying unit of 36 square miles.

towns•man (tounz'mən) *n.* **1.** A resident of a town. **2.** A fellow resident of one's town.

towns•peo•ple (tounz'pē'pəl) *pl.n.* The inhabitants or citizens of a town or city.

tow•path (tō'păth', -päth') *n.* A path along a canal or river used by animals towing boats.

tox–. *comb. form.* Poison. [< L *toxicum,* poison.]

tox•e•mi•a (tŏk-sē'mē-ə) *n.* A condition in which toxins produced locally by body cells are contained in the blood. [< TOX- + -EMIA.]

tox•ic (tŏk'sĭk) *adj.* **1.** Of or pertaining to a toxin. **2.** Harmful; deadly; poisonous. [< L *toxicum,* poisons for arrows.] —**tox'i•cal•ly** *adv.* —**tox•ic'i•ty** (-sĭs'ə-tē) *n.*

tox•i•col•o•gy (tŏk'sĭ-kŏl'ə-jē) *n.* The study of poisons and the treatment of poisoning. —**tox'i•co•log'i•cal** (-kə-lŏj'ĭ-kəl) *adj.* —**tox'i•co•log'i•cal•ly** *adv.* —**tox'i•col'o•gist** *n.*

tox•in (tŏk'sĭn) *n.* A substance, having a protein structure, secreted by certain organisms and capable of causing poisoning when introduced into the body tissues but also capable of inducing a counteragent or antitoxin. [TOX- + -IN.]

toy (toi) *n.* **1.** An object for children to play with. **2.** Something of little importance; a trinket. **3.** A small ornament. —*v.* To amuse oneself idly; trifle (with *with*). —*adj.* **1.** Designed as a toy. **2.** Miniature. [ME *toye,* dallying, amorous sport.]

tp. township.

tpk. turnpike

tr. **1.** transitive. **2.** translated; translation; translator. **3.** transpose; transposition. **4.** treasurer.

trace¹ (trās) *n.* **1.** A visible mark or sign of the former presence or passage of some person, thing, or event. **2.** A barely perceivable indication of something; a touch. **3.** A minute quantity. —*v.* **traced, tracing. 1.** To follow the trail of. **2.** To ascertain the successive stages in the development of. **3.** To locate or discover, as a cause. **4.** To delineate or sketch (a figure). **5.** To form (letters) with special care. **6.** To copy by following lines seen through transparent paper. [< VL **tractiāre,* to drag.] —**trace'a•ble** *adj.* —**trac'er** *n.*

trace² (trās) *n.* One of two side straps or chains connecting a harnessed draft animal to a vehicle. [< L *tractus,* a dragging.]

trac•er•y (trā'sə-rē) *n., pl.* **-ies.** Ornamental work of interlaced and ramified lines.

tra•che•a (trā'kē-ə) *n., pl.* **-cheae** (-kē-ē') or **-as.** A thin-walled tube of cartilaginous and membranous tissue descending from the larynx to the bronchi and carrying air to the lungs. [< Gk *(artēria) trakheia,* "rough (artery)."] —**tra'che•al** *adj.*

tra•che•ot•o•my (trā'kē-ŏt'ə-mē) *n., pl.* **-mies.** The act or procedure of cutting into the trachea through the neck.

track (trăk) *n.* **1.** A mark, as a footprint, left by the passage of something; a trace. **2.** A path, route, or course; trail. **3. a.** A road or course, as of cinder, laid out for racing. **b.** Athletic competition on such a course. **4.** A set of parallel rails upon which a train or trolley runs. —*v.* **1.** To follow the footprints or traces of; trail. **2.** To carry on the shoes and deposit as tracks. **3.** To observe or monitor, as by radar. [ME *trak,* trace, trail, footprints.] —**track'a•ble** *adj.* —**track'er** *n.*

tract¹ (trăkt) *n.* **1.** An expanse of land. **2.** A system of organs and tissues that together perform one specialized function: *the alimentary tract.* [L *tractus,* "a drawing," course, tract.]

tract² (trăkt) *n.* A propaganda pamphlet, esp. one put out by a religious or political group. [< L *tractātus,* a discussion, treatise.]

tract•a•ble (trăk'tə-bəl) *adj.* **1.** Easily controlled; governable. **2.** Easily worked; malleable. [< L *tractāre,* to pull violently, take in hand, manage.] —**tract'a•bly** *adv.*

trac•tion (trăk'shən) *n.* **1.** The act of drawing or pulling or condition of being drawn or pulled. **2.** Adhesive friction, as of a wheel on a track. **3.** The pulling power of a railroad engine. [< L *trahere,* to draw, pull.]

trac•tor (trăk'tər) *n.* **1.** An automotive vehicle designed for pulling machinery. **2.** A truck having a cab and no body, used for pulling large vehicles. [< L *trahere,* to pull.]

trade (trād) *n.* **1.** An occupation, esp. one requiring skill; a craft. **2.** The business of buying and selling commodities; commerce. **3.** The persons associated with a specified business or industry. **4.** An exchange of one thing for another. —*v.* **traded, trading. 1.** To engage in buying and selling. **2.** To exchange one thing for another. **3.** To shop regularly at a given store. [< MLG, a track, path.]

trade•mark (trād'märk') *n.* A name, symbol, or other device identifying a product, legally restricted to the use of the owner or manufacturer. —*v.* **1.** To label (a product) with a trademark. **2.** To register as a trademark.

trade name. 1. The name by which a commodity, service, process, etc., is known to the trade. **2.** The name under which a business firm operates.

trad•er (trā'dər) *n.* **1.** One who trades; a dealer. **2.** A ship employed in foreign trade.

trades•man (trādz'mən) *n.* **1.** One engaged in retail trade, esp. a shopkeeper. **2.** A skilled worker; craftsman.

trade wind. A system of winds occupying most of the tropics, blowing northeasterly in the N Hemisphere and southeasterly in the S Hemisphere.

trading post. A station or store in a sparsely settled area established by traders to barter supplies for local products.

tra•di•tion (trə-dĭsh'ən) *n.* **1.** The passing down of elements of a culture from generation to generation, esp. orally. **2. a.** A cultural custom or usage. **b.** A set of such customs and usages viewed as a coherent body of precedents. **3.** Any time-honored set of practices. [< L *trādere,* to hand over.] —**tra•di'tion•al** *adj.* —**tra•di'tion•al•ly** *adv.*

tra•duce (trə-d/y/o͞os') *v.* **-duced, -ducing.** To speak falsely or maliciously of; slander. [L *trādūcere,* to lead across, make public.] —**tra•duce'ment** *n.* —**tra•duc'er** *n.*

traf•fic (trăf'ĭk) *n.* **1. a.** The commercial exchange of goods; trade. **b.** The quantity of goods traded. **2. a.** The passage of persons, vehicles, or messages through routes of transportation or communication. **b.** The amount, as of vehicles, in transit. **3.** Connections; dealings. —*v.* **-ficked, -ficking.** To carry on trade in. [< It *trafficare,* to trade.] —**traf'fick•er** *n.*

tra•ge•di•an (trə-jē'dē-ən) *n.* An actor of tragic roles. —**tra•ge'di•enne'** (-dē-ĕn') *fem.n.*

trag•e•dy (trăj'ə-dē) *n., pl.* **-dies. 1.** A dramatic or literary work depicting a protagonist engaged in a morally significant struggle ending in ruin or profound unhappiness. **2.** Any dramatic, disastrous event. [< Gk *tragōidia,* "goat-song."]

trag•ic (trăj'ĭk) *adj.* Also **trag•i•cal** (trăj'ĭ-kəl). **1.** Pertaining to, in the style of, or having the character of tragedy. **2.** Calamitous; disastrous. —**trag'i•cal•ly** *adv.*

trag•i•com•e•dy (trăj'ĭ-kŏm'ə-dē) *n., pl.* **-dies.** A drama that combines elements of both tragedy and comedy. —**trag'i•com'ic** *adj.*

trail (trāl) *v.* **1.** To drag or allow to drag or stream behind, as along the ground. **2.** To follow the traces or scent of; track. **3.** To lag behind (an opponent). **4.** To extend or grow along the ground or over a surface. **5.** To drift in a tenuous stream, as smoke. **6.** To become gradually fainter: *Her voice trailed off.* —*n.* **1.** Something that trails, esp. something that hangs loose and long. **2. a.** A mark, trace, or path left by a moving body. **b.** The scent of a person or animal. **c.** A path or beaten track. [Prob < VL **trāgulāre,* to drag.]

trail•er (trā'lər) *n.* **1.** One that trails. **2.** A large transport vehicle hauled by a truck or tractor. **3.** A van drawn by a truck or automobile and used as a home.

train (trān) *n.* **1.** Something that follows or is drawn along behind, as the part of a gown that trails. **2.** A staff of followers; retinue. **3.** A long line of moving persons, animals, or vehicles. **4.** A string of connected railroad cars. **5.** An orderly succession of related events or thoughts. —*v.* **1.** To coach in or accustom to some mode of behavior or performance. **2.** To make or become proficient with specialized instruction and practice. **3.** To prepare physically, as with a regimen. **4.** To cause (a plant or one's hair) to take a desired course or shape. **5.** To focus (on); aim. [< OF *trahiner,* to drag.] —**train'a•ble** *adj.* —**train•ee'** *n.* —**train'er** *n.* —**train'ing** *n.*

train•man (trān'mən) *n.* A member of the operating crew on a railroad train.

traipse (trāps) *v.* **traipsed, traipsing.** *Informal.* To walk about idly. [?]

trait (trāt) *n.* A distinguishing feature, as of character. [< L *tractus,* a pulling, a drawing.]

trai•tor (trā'tər) *n.* One who betrays his country, a cause, or a trust, esp. one who has committed treason. [< L *trādere,* to hand over, betray.] —**trai'tor•ous** *adj.*

tra•jec•to•ry (trə-jĕk'tə-rē) *n., pl.* **-ries.** The path of a moving particle or body, esp. such a path in three dimensions. [< L *trājicere,* to throw across.]

tram (trăm) *n.* **1.** *Chiefly Brit.* A streetcar. **2.** An open wagon or car run on tracks in a coal mine. [Perh < Scand.]

tram•mel (trăm'əl) *n.* Often **trammels.** Something that restricts activity or free movement; a hindrance. —*v.* **-meled** or **-melled, -meling** or **-melling. 1.** To confine or hinder. **2.** To entrap. [< LL *tremaculum.*]

tramp (trămp) *v.* **1.** To walk with a firm, heavy step. **2.** To traverse on foot. **3.** To tread down; trample. —*n.* **1.** The sound of heavy walking or marching. **2.** A walking trip. **3.** One who travels aimlessly about as a vagrant. **4.** An immoral woman. **5.** A cargo vessel that has no regular schedule but takes on freight wherever it can be found and discharges it wherever required. [ME *trampen.*] —**tramp'er** *n.*

tram•ple (trăm'pəl) *v.* **-pled, -pling. 1.** To tread heavily so as to injure or destroy. **2.** To treat harshly, as if tramping upon. —*n.* The action or sound of treading underfoot. [< ME *trampen,* to TRAMP.] —**tram'pler** *n.*

trance (trăns) *n.* **1.** A hypnotic, cataleptic, or ecstatic state. **2.** A state of detachment from one's physical surroundings, as in contemplation. **3.** A dazed state. [< OF *transir,* "to pass (from life to death)," depart.]

tran•quil (trăn'kwəl) *adj.* **-quiler** or **-quiller, -quilest** or **-quillest.** Free from agitation; calm. [L *tranquillus.*] —**tran'quil•ly** *adv.* —**tran•quil'li•ty, tran•quil'i•ty** *n.*

tran•quil•ize (trăn'kwə-līz') *v.* **-ized, -izing.** Also **tran•quil•lize.** To make or become tranquil.

tran•quil•iz•er (trăn'kwə-līz'ər) *n.* A tranquilizing drug.

trans–. *comb. form.* **1.** Across or over. **2.** Beyond or above. **3.** From one place to another. **4.** Transferring or transporting. **5.** Changing. **6.** Having a greater atomic number. [< L *trāns,* across, over, beyond, through, through and through.]

trans. 1. transaction. **2.** transitive. **3.** translated; translation; translator. **4.** transportation.

trans•act (trăn-săkt', -zăkt') *v.* To carry out or conduct (business or affairs).

trans•ac•tion (trăn-săk'shən, -zăk'shən) *n.* **1.** The act of transacting or fact of being transacted. **2.** Something transacted. **3. transactions.** The proceedings, as of a convention.

trans•at•lan•tic (trăns'ət-lăn'tĭk, trănz'ət-) *adj.* **1.** On the other side of the Atlantic. **2.** Spanning or crossing the Atlantic.

tran•scend (trăn-sĕnd') *v.* **1.** To exist above and independent of. **2.** To rise above; surpass; exceed. [< L *transcendere,* "to climb over."] —**tran•scen'dent** *adj.*

tran•scen•den•tal (trăn'sĕn-dĕnt'l) *adj.* **1.** Of or pertaining to transcendentalism. **2.** Rising above common thought or ideas; mystical.

tran•scen•den•tal•ism (trăn'sən-dĕnt'l-ĭz'əm) *n. Phil.* The belief or doctrine that knowledge of reality is derived from intuitive sources rather than objective experience. —**tran'scen•den'tal•ist** *n.*

trans•con•ti•nen•tal (trăns'kŏn'tə-nĕn'təl, trănz'-) *adj.* Spanning or crossing a continent.

tran•scribe (trăn-skrīb') *v.* **-scribed, -scribing. 1.** To write or type a copy of; write out fully, as from shorthand notes. **2.** To adapt or arrange (a musical composition). **3.** To record for broadcasting at a later date. [L *transcrībere,* to copy, "write over."]

tran•script (trăn'skrĭpt') *n.* Something transcribed; a written or printed copy.

tran•scrip•tion (trăn-skrĭp'shən) *n.* **1.** The act or process of transcribing. **2.** Something transcribed, esp.: **a.** An adaptation of a musical composition. **b.** A recorded radio or television program.

tran•sept (trăn'sĕpt') *n.* Either of the two lateral arms of a cruciform church. [< TRANS- + L *sēptum,* partition.]

trans•fer (trăns-fûr', trăns'fər) *v.* **-ferred, -ferring. 1.** To convey, shift, or change from one person or place to another. **2.** To make over the possession or title of to another. **3.** To convey (a drawing or design) from one surface to another. **4.** To change from one train, airplane, or bus to another. —*n.* **1.** Also **trans•fer•al** (trăns-fûr'əl), **trans•fer•ral.** The conveyance of something from one person or place to another. **2.** Also **trans•fer•al, trans•fer•ral.** Any person or thing that has or has been transferred. **3.** A ticket entitling a passenger to change from one carrier to another. **4.** *Law.* The conveyance of title or property from one person to another. [< L *trānsferre,* to bear across.] —**trans•fer'a•bil'i•ty** *n.* —**trans•fer'a•ble** *adj.* —**trans•fer'ence** *n.*

trans•fig•ure (trăns-fĭg'yər) *v.* **-ured, -uring. 1.** To change radically the figure or appearance of. **2.** To exalt; glorify. —**trans'fig•u•ra'tion** *n.*

trans•fix (trăns-fĭks') *v.* **1.** To pierce through with or as with a pointed weapon; impale. **2.** To render motionless, as with terror.

trans•form (trăns-fôrm') *v.* **1.** To change markedly in form or appearance. **2.** To change the nature, function, or condition of; convert or be converted. —**trans'for•ma'tion** *n.*

trans•form•er (trăns-fôr'mər) *n.* **1.** One that transforms. **2.** A device used to transfer electric energy, usually that of an alternating current, from one circuit to another, often with a change in voltage, current, or other electric characteristic.

trans•fuse (trăns-fyo͞oz') *v.* **-fused, -fusing. 1.** To transfer (liquid) from one vessel to another. **2.** To permeate; instill. **3.** To administer a transfusion of or to. [< L *trānsfundere,* "to pour over."] —**trans•fus'er** *n.*

trans•fu•sion (trăns-fyo͞o'zhən) *n.* **1.** The act or process of transfusing. **2.** The direct injection of whole blood, plasma, or another solution into the blood stream.

trans•gress (trăns-grĕs', trănz-) *v.* **1.** To go beyond or over (a limit or boundary). **2.** To act in violation of (a law, commandment, etc.); sin. [L *trānsgredī,* to step across.] —**trans•gres'sion** *n.* —**trans•gres'sor** *n.*

tran•ship. Variant of **transship.**

tran•sient (trăn'shənt, -zhənt, -zē-ənt) *adj.* **1.** Passing away with time; transitory. **2.** Passing through from one place to another; stopping only briefly. —*n.* One that is transient, esp. a person making a brief stay at a hotel. [< L *transīre,* to go over.] —**tran'sience, tran'sien•cy** *n.* —**tran'sient•ly** *adv.*

tran•sis•tor (trăn-zĭs'tər, trăn-sĭs'-) *n.* **1.** A three-terminal semiconductor device used for amplification, switching, etc. **2.** A radio equipped with transistors. [TRAN(SFER) + (RE)SISTOR.]

tran•sit (trăn'sĭt, -zĭt) *n.* **1. a.** The act of passing over, across, or through. **b.** The conveyance of persons or goods from one place to another, esp. on a local public transportation system. **2.** A surveying instrument that measures horizontal and vertical angles. [< L *transīre,* to go across.]

tran•si•tion (trăn-zĭsh'ən, -sĭsh'ən) *n.* The process or an instance of changing or passing from one form, state, subject, or place to another. —**tran•si'tion•al** *adj.*

tran•si•tive (trăn'sə-tĭv, trăn'zə-) *adj. Gram.* Designating a verb or verb construction that requires a direct object to complete its meaning. [LL *transitīvus,* passing over (as from the subject to the object).]

tran•si•to•ry (trăn'sə-tôr'ē, -tōr'ē, trăn'zə-) *adj.* Existing or occurring only briefly; short-lived. [< L *transitus,* TRANSIT.]

transl. translated; translation.

trans•late (trăns-lāt', trănz-, trăns'lāt', trănz'-) *v.* **-lated, -lating. 1.** To express or admit of being expressed in another language. **2.** To put in simpler terms; explain. **3.** To convey from one form or style to another. **4.** *Phys.* To move from one place to another without rotation. [< L *translātus,* "carried across."] —**trans•lat'a•ble** *adj.* —**trans•la'tion** *n.* —**trans•la'tor** *n.*

trans•lit•er•ate (trăns-lĭt'ə-rāt', trănz-) *v.* **-ated, -ating.** To represent (letters or words) in the characters of another alphabet. [TRANS- + L *littera,* LETTER + -ATE.] —**trans•lit'er•a'tion** *n.*

trans•lu•cent (trăns-lo͞o'sənt, trănz-) *adj.* Transmitting light but causing sufficient diffusion to eliminate perception of distinct images. [< L *translūcēre,* to shine through.] —**trans•lu'cence, trans•lu'cen•cy** *n.*

trans•mi•grate (trăns-mī'grāt', trănz-) *v.* **-grated, -grating.** *Theol.* To pass into another body after death. —**trans'mi•gra'tion** *n.*

trans•mis•sion (trăns-mĭsh'ən, trănz-) *n.* **1.** The act or process of transmitting. **2.** Something transmitted. **3. a.** An assembly of gears that links an engine to a driving axle. **b.** A system of gears. **4.** The sending of a signal, as by radio.

trans•mit (trăns-mĭt', trănz-) *v.* **-mitted, -mitting. 1.** To send from one person, thing, or place to another. **2.** To cause to spread, as an infection. **3.** To impart by heredity. **4.** To send (a signal), as by radio. **5.** To convey (force or energy) from one part of a mechanism to another. [< L *transmittere,* to send across.] —**trans•mis'si•ble, trans•mit'ta•ble** *adj.* —**trans•mit'tal** *n.*

trans•mit•ter (trăns-mĭt'ər, trănz-) *n.* **1.** One that transmits. **2.** Any of various electrical or electronic devices used to originate signals, as in radio or telegraphy.

trans•mute (trăns-myo͞ot', trănz-) *v.* **-muted, -muting.** To change from one form, nature, substance, or state into another; transform. [< L *transmūtāre.*] —**trans•mut'a•ble** *adj.* —**trans'mu•ta'tion** *n.*

trans•o•ce•an•ic (trăns'ō-shē-ăn'ĭk, trănz'-) *adj.* **1.** Situated beyond the ocean. **2.** Spanning or crossing the ocean.

tran•som (trăn'səm) *n.* **1.** A small hinged window above a door or another window. **2.** A horizontal dividing piece in a window. [ME *traunson,* crossbeam, lintel.]

transp. transportation.

trans•pa•cif•ic (trăns'pə-sĭf'ĭk) *adj.* **1.** Crossing the Pacific Ocean. **2.** Situated beyond the Pacific Ocean.

trans•par•ent (trăns-pâr'ənt, -păr'ənt) *adj.* **1.** Capable of transmitting light so that objects or images can be seen as if there were no intervening material. **2.** Of such texture that objects can be seen on the other side; sheer. **3.** Easily detected; flimsy: *transparent lies.* **4.** Guileless; candid; open. [< ML *trānspārēre,* to be seen through.] —**trans•par'en•cy** *n.* —**trans•par'ent•ly** *adv.*

tran•spire (trăn-spīr') *v.* **-spired, -spiring. 1.** To give off vapor containing waste products through pores. **2.** To become known; come to light. **3.** To happen; occur. [< L *trāns-,* out + *spīrāre,* to breathe.] —**tran'spi•ra'tion** *n.*

Usage: *Transpire,* in the sense of happen or occur, is widely employed but still disputed.

trans•plant (trăns-plănt', -plänt') *v.* **1.** To uproot and replant (a growing plant). **2.** To transfer from one place or residence to another. **3.** To transfer (tissue or an organ) from one body, or body part, to another. —**trans'plant'** *n.* —**trans'plan•ta'tion** *n.*

trans•port (trăns-pôrt', -pōrt') *v.* **1.** To carry from one place to another. **2.** To move to strong emotion; enrapture. **3.** To send abroad to a penal colony. —*n.* (trăns'pôrt', -pōrt'). **1.** The act of transporting; conveyance. **2.** Rapture. **3.** A ship used to transport troops or military equipment. **4.** A vehicle, as an aircraft, used to transport passengers or freight. [< L *trānsportāre.*] —**trans'por•ta'tion** *n.*

trans•pose (trăns-pōz') *v.* **-posed, -posing. 1.** To reverse or transfer the order or place of; interchange. **2.** *Mus.* To write or perform (a composition) in a key other than the original. —**trans'po•si'tion** *n.*

trans•ship (trăns-shĭp') *v.* **-shipped, -shipping.** Also **tran•ship.** To transfer (cargo) from one vessel or vehicle to another for reshipment. —**trans•ship'ment** *n.*

tran•sub•stan•ti•a•tion (trăn'səb-stăn'shē-ā'shən) *n.* The doctrine that the bread and wine of the Eucharist are transformed into the true presence of Christ, although their appearance remains the same.

trans•verse (trăns-vûrs', trănz-, trăns'vûrs', trănz'-) *adj.* Situated or lying across; crosswise. [< L *trānsvertere,* to turn or direct across.] —**trans•verse'** *n.* —**trans•verse'ly** *adv.*

trap (trăp) *n.* **1.** A device for catching and holding animals. **2.** A stratagem for betraying, tricking, or exposing an unsuspecting person. **3. a.** A receptacle for collecting waste or other materials. **b.** A device for sealing a passage against the escape of gases, as in a drainpipe. **4.** *Golf.* A land hazard or bunker. **5.** A light two-wheeled carriage. **6.** Often **traps.** Percussion instruments. —*v.* **trapped, trapping. 1.** To catch in or as in a trap. **2.** To trap fur-bearing animals, esp. as a business. [< OE *træppe.* See **der-**[1].] —**trap'per** *n.*

trap door. A hinged or sliding door in a floor or roof.

tra•peze (tră-pēz') *n.* A short horizontal bar suspended from two parallel ropes, used for acrobatics. [< Gk *trapeza,* "four-footed," table.]

trap•e•zoid (trăp'ə-zoid') *n.* A quadrilateral having two parallel sides. [< Gk *trapeza,* table + -OID.] —**trap'e•zoi'dal** *adj.*

trap•pings (trăp'ĭngz) *pl.n.* Ornamental coverings or dress, esp. for a horse.

trap•shoot•ing (trăp'sho͞o'tĭng) *n.* The sport of shooting at clay disks hurled into the air from traps.

trash (trăsh) *n.* **1.** Worthless or discarded material or objects; refuse. **2.** Cheap or empty expressions or ideas. **3.** An ignorant or contemptible person. [?] —**trash'y** *adj.*

trau•ma (trou'mə, trô'-) *n., pl.* **-mas** or **-mata** (-mə-tə). **1.** *Path.* A wound, esp. one produced by sudden physical injury. **2.** An emotional shock that creates substantial and lasting psychological damage. [Gk, wound, hurt.] —**trau•mat'ic** (-măt'ĭk) *adj.* —**trau•mat'i•cal•ly** *adv.* —**trau'ma•tize'** *v.* **(-tized, -tizing).**

tra•vail (trə-vāl', trăv'āl') *n.* **1.** Strenuous exertion; toil. **2.** Tribulation or agony; anguish. **3.** The labor of childbirth. —*v.* **1.** To toil. **2.** To be in the labor of childbirth. [< VL **tripālium,* torture instrument (made of three stakes).]

trav•el (trăv'əl) *v.* **-eled** or **-elled, -eling** or **-elling.** **1.** To go from one place to another; journey (through). **2.** To journey from one place to another as a salesman. **3.** To be transmitted; move, as light. **4.** To associate: *travel in wealthy circles.* **5.** To move swiftly. **6.** *Basketball.* To walk or run illegally while holding the ball. —*n.* **1.** The act or process of traveling. **2. travels.** A series of journeys. [ME *travailen,* to toil, make a (toilsome) journey.] —**trav'el•er, trav'el•ler** *n.*

trav•e•logue (trăv'ə-lôg', -lŏg') *n.* Also **trav•e•log.** A lecture on travel, illustrated by slides or films.

trav•erse (trăv'ərs, trə-vûrs') *v.* **-ersed, -ersing.** **1.** To travel across, over, or through. **2.** To move forward and backward over. **3.** To turn laterally; swivel. **4.** To extend across; cross. —*n.* One lying across something else, esp. a structural crosspiece. —*adj.* Lying or extending across. [< L *trānsversus,* transverse.] —**tra•vers'al** (trə-vûr'səl) *n.*

trav•er•tine (trăv'ər-tēn', -tĭn) *n.* A light-colored, porous calcium carbonate deposited from solution in ground or surface waters. [< L *(lapis) Tīburtīnus,* "(stone) of Tibur."]

trav•es•ty (trăv'ĭ-stē) *n., pl.* **-ties.** A grotesque imitation with intent to ridicule. —*v.* **-tied, -tying.** To make a travesty on or of. [< It *travestire,* "to disguise."]

trawl (trôl) *n.* **1.** A large, tapered fishing net towed along the sea bottom. **2.** A multiple fishing line. —*v.* To fish or catch (fish) with a trawl. [Perh < Du *tragel,* dragnet.]

trawl•er (trô'lər) *n.* A boat used for trawling.

tray (trā) *n.* A flat, shallow receptacle of wood, metal, etc., with a raised edge or rim, used for carrying, holding, or displaying articles. [< OE *trig, trēg.* See **deru-.**]

treach•er•ous (trĕch'ər-əs) *adj.* **1.** Betraying a trust; disloyal. **2. a.** Not dependable. **b.** Not to be trusted; deceptive; dangerous.

treach•er•y (trĕch'ə-rē) *n., pl.* **-ies.** Willful betrayal of trust; perfidy; treason. [< OF *trichier,* to trick.]

trea•cle (trē'kəl) *n. Brit.* Molasses. [ME *triacle,* antidote for poison.]

tread (trĕd) *v.* **trod, trodden** or **trod, treading.** **1.** To walk on, over, or along. **2.** To press beneath the foot; trample. **3.** To walk; dance. —*n.* **1.** The act, manner, or sound of treading. **2.** The horizontal part of a step in a staircase. **3.** The grooved face of an automobile tire. **4.** The part of the sole of a shoe that touches the ground. [< OE *tredan.* See **der-**[1].]

tread•le (trĕd'l) *n.* A pedal or lever operated by the foot, as in a sewing machine.

tread•mill (trĕd'mĭl') *n.* **1.** A mechanism operated by walking on the moving steps of a wheel or treading an endless sloping belt. **2.** A monotonous routine.

treas. treasurer; treasury.

trea•son (trē'zən) *n.* Violation of allegiance toward one's sovereign or country. [< L *trāditiō,* a handing over.] —**trea'son•a•ble** *adj.* —**trea'son•ous** *adj.*

treas•ure (trĕzh'ər) *n.* **1.** Accumulated, stored, or cached wealth in the form of valuables, as jewels. **2.** One considered especially precious or valuable. —*v.* **-ured, -uring.** **1.** To accumulate; hoard. **2.** To value highly. [< Gk *thēsauros.*] —**treas'ure•a•ble** *adj.*

treas•ur•er (trĕzh'ər-ər) *n.* One in charge of funds or revenues, esp. a financial officer for a government or society.

treas•ure-trove (trĕzh'ər-trōv') *n.* **1.** Any treasure found hidden and not claimed by its owner. **2.** A discovery of great value. [NF *tresor trove,* "discovered treasure."]

treas•ur•y (trĕzh'ə-rē) *n., pl.* **-ies.** **1.** A place where treasure is kept or stored. **2.** A place where private or public funds are received, kept, managed, and disbursed. **3. Treasury.** A governmental department in charge of public revenue.

treat (trēt) *v.* **1.** To act or behave in a specified manner toward. **2.** To regard or consider in a certain way. **3.** To deal with in a specified manner or style, esp. in art or literature. **4.** To entertain at one's own expense. **5.** To subject to a process. **6.** To give medical aid to. —*n.* **1.** Something generously paid for by someone else. **2.** The act of providing a treat. **3.** A special delight or pleasure. [< L *tractāre,* to drag, handle, treat.] —**treat'er** *n.*

trea•tise (trē'tĭs) *n.* A formal, systematic account in writing of some subject.

treat•ment (trēt'mənt) *n.* **1.** The act or manner of treating something. **2.** The application of remedies with the aim of effecting a cure; therapy.

trea•ty (trē'tē) *n., pl.* **-ties.** **1. a.** A formal agreement between two or more states containing terms of trade, peace, etc.; a pact. **b.** A document embodying this. **2.** Any contract or agreement. [< L *tractāre,* TREAT.]

treb•le (trĕb'əl) *adj.* **1.** Triple. **2.** *Mus.* Of, having, or performing the highest part, voice, or range. **3.** High-pitched; shrill. —*n.* **1.** *Mus.* The highest part, voice, instrument, performer, or range; soprano. **2.** A high, shrill sound or voice. —*v.* **-led, -ling.** To triple. [< L *triplus,* TRIPLE.] —**treb'ly** *adv.*

treble clef. *Mus.* A symbol centered on the second line of the staff to indicate the position of G above middle C.

tree (trē) *n.* **1.** A usually tall woody plant with a single main stem or trunk. **2.** Something suggestive of a tree: *a clothes tree.* **3.** A diagram showing a family lineage; family tree. —*v.* **treed, treeing.** To force to climb a tree in evasion of pursuit. [< OE *trēow.* See **deru-.**]

tre•foil (trē'foil', trĕf'oil') *n.* **1.** A plant, as a clover, having compound leaves with three leaflets. **2.** Any ornament resembling the leaves of such a plant. [< L *trifolium,* three-leaved grass.]

trek (trĕk) *v.* **trekked, trekking.** To make a slow or arduous journey. —*n.* **1.** An arduous journey. **2.** A migration. [< MDu *trekken,* to pull, draw, travel.] —**trek'ker** *n.*

trel•lis (trĕl'ĭs) *n.* An open latticework used for training creeping plants. [< L *trilīx,* triple-twilled.]

trem•ble (trĕm'bəl) *v.* **-bled, -bling.** **1.** To shake involuntarily, as from fear, cold, etc.; quake; shiver; quiver. **2.** To feel or express fear or anxiety. —*n.* The act or state of trembling. [< L *tremulus,* TREMULOUS.] —**trem'bler** *n.* —**trem'bling•ly** *adv.*

tre•men•dous (trĭ-mĕn'dəs) *adj.* **1.** Capable of making one tremble; terrible. **2. a.** Extremely large; enormous. **b.** Marvelous; wonderful. [< L *tremere,* to tremble.] —**tre•men'dous•ly** *adv.* —**tre•men'dous•ness** *n.*

trem•o•lo (trĕm'ə-lō') *n., pl.* **-los.** *Mus.* A tremulous effect produced by the rapid repetition of a single tone or the rapid alternation of two tones. [It, "tremulous."]

trem•or (trĕm'ər) *n.* **1.** A quick shaking or vibrating movement. **2.** An involuntary trembling motion of the body; a nervous quiver or shiver. [< L *tremere,* to tremble.]

trem•u•lous (trĕm'yə-ləs) *adj.* **1.** Vibrating or quivering; trembling. **2.** Timid; fearful. [L *tremulus* < *tremere,* to tremble.]

trench (trĕnch) *n.* **1.** A deep furrow. **2.** A ditch, esp. one embanked with its own soil and used for concealment and protection in warfare. —*v.* **1.** To cut trenches in. **2.** To fortify with trenches. **3.** To verge or encroach. [< OF *trenchier,* to cut, dig.]

trench•ant (trĕn'chənt) *adj.* **1.** Keen; incisive. **2.** Forceful; effective. **3.** Distinct; sharply defined. [< OF *trenchier,* to cut.] —**trench'an•cy** *n.* —**trench'ant•ly** *adv.*

trench coat. A loose-fitting, belted raincoat having many pockets and flaps.

trench•er (trĕn'chər) *n.* A wooden board or plate on which food is cut or served. [< OF *trenchier,* to cut.]

trench fever. An acute infectious relapsing fever caused by a microorganism transmitted by lice.

trench foot. Frostbite of the feet, often afflicting soldiers obliged to stand in cold water over long periods of time.

trench mouth. An oral disease characterized by pain, foul odor, and the formation of a gray film over the diseased area.

trend (trĕnd) *n.* **1.** A direction of movement; a flow. **2.** A general tendency. —*v.* **1.** To move in a specified direction. **2.** To tend. [< OE *trendan,* to turn < Gmc **trand-.*]

tren•dy (trĕn'dē) *adj.* **-ier, -iest.** *Informal.* According to the latest fad or fashion; modish and unconventional. —**trend'i•ness** *n.*

Tren•ton (trĕn'tən). The capital of New Jersey. Pop. 105,000.

tre•pan (trĭ-păn') *n.* A trephine. —*v.* **-panned, -panning.** To trephine. [< Gk *trupanon,* auger, borer.] —**trep'a•na'tion** (trĕp'ə-nā'shən, trĭ-păn'ā'shən) *n.* —**tre•pan'ner** *n.*

tre•phine (trĭ-fīn', -fēn') *n.* A surgical instrument having circular, sawlike edges, used to cut out disks of bone, usually from the skull. —*v.* **-phined, -phining.** To operate on with or extract by means of a trephine. [< L *trēs fīnes,* three ends.] —**treph'i•na'tion** (trĕf'ə-nā'shən, trĭ-fī'-, trĭ-fē'-) *n.*

trep•i•da•tion (trĕp'ə-dā'shən) *n.* **1.** A state of alarm or dread; apprehension. **2.** A trembling. [< L *trepidus,* alarmed.]

tres•pass (trĕs'pəs, -păs') *v.* **1.** To commit an offense or sin; err; transgress. **2.** To infringe upon the privacy or attention of another. **3.** To invade the property or rights of another without his consent. —*n.* **1.** A transgression. **2.** The act of trespassing. [< ML *transpassāre,* to pass across.] —**tres'pass•er** *n.*

tress (trĕs) *n.* A lock of hair. [< OF *tresse.*]

tres•tle (trĕs'əl) *n.* **1.** A horizontal bar held up by two pairs of divergent legs and used as a support. **2.** A framework consisting of vertical, slanted supports and horizontal crosspieces supporting a bridge. [< L *transtrum,* cross-beam.]

trey (trā) *n.* A card, die, or domino with three pips; a three. [< L *trēs,* three.]

tri–. *comb. form.* **1.** Three. **2.** Every three or every third. [L and Gk, three.]

tri•ad (trī'ăd', -əd) *n.* A group of three persons or things; trinity. [< Gk *trias.*] —**tri•ad'ic** *adj.*

tri•al (trī'əl, trīl) *n.* **1.** The examination of evidence and applicable law to determine the issue of specified charges or claims. **2.** The act or process of testing and trying by use and experience. **3.** An effort or attempt. **4.** A state of pain or anguish. **5.** A test of patience or endurance. *—adj.* **1.** Of or pertaining to a trial or trials. **2.** Made, done, or used during the course of a test or tests. [< OF *trier,* try.]

tri•an•gle (trī'ăng'gəl) *n.* **1.** The plane figure formed by connecting three points not in a straight line by straight line segments. **2.** Something having the shape of this figure. [< L *triangulus,* three-angled.] **—tri•an'gu•lar** *adj.*

tri•an•gu•late (trī-ăng'gyə-lāt') *v.* **-lated, -lating.** To measure by using trigonometry. **—tri•an'gu•la'tion** *n.*

Tri•as•sic (trī-ăs'ĭk) *adj.* Of or belonging to the geologic time, rock systems, and sedimentary deposits of the first period of the Mesozoic era. *—n.* The Triassic period. [< LL *trias,* triad.]

tribe (trīb) *n.* **1.** A social organization or division comprising several local villages, bands, lineages, or other groups and sharing a common ancestry, language, culture, and name. **2.** A group having a common distinguishing characteristic. [< L *tribus,* division of the Roman people.] **—trib'al** *adj.*

tribes•man (trībz'mən) *n.* A member of a tribe.

trib•u•la•tion (trĭb'yə-lā'shən) *n.* **1.** Great affliction or distress. **2.** That which causes such distress. [< LL *trībulāre,* to oppress.]

tri•bu•nal (trī-byōō'nəl, trĭ-) *n.* **1.** A seat or court of justice. **2.** One having the power of determining. [< L *tribūnus,* TRIBUNE.]

trib•une (trĭb'yōōn', trĭ-byōōn') *n.* **1.** An official of ancient Rome chosen by the common people to protect their rights. **2.** A protector or champion of the people. [< L *tribūnus,* "head of the tribe."] **—trib'u•nar'y** (trĭb'yə-nĕr'ē) *adj.*

trib•u•tar•y (trĭb'yə-tĕr'ē) *adj.* **1.** Contributory; subsidiary. **2.** Having the nature of or paying tribute. *—n., pl.* **-ries. 1.** One that pays tribute. **2.** A stream or river flowing into a larger stream or river.

trib•ute (trĭb'yōōt) *n.* **1.** A gift or other acknowledgment of gratitude, respect, or admiration. **2. a.** A sum of money paid by one ruler or nation to another as acknowledgment of submission or as the price for protection by that nation. **b.** A forced levy. [< L *tribuere,* to distribute (as among the Roman tribes) < *tribus,* TRIBE.]

trice (trīs) *n.* A very short period of time; a moment; an instant: *in a trice.* [< ME *at a tryse,* immediately.]

tri•ceps (trī'sĕps') *n.* A large muscle running along the back of the upper arm and serving to extend the forearm. [L, three-headed.]

tri•cer•a•tops (trī-sĕr'ə-tŏps') *n.* A horned plant-eating dinosaur with a bony plate covering the neck. [< TRI- + Gk *keras,* horn + *ōps,* eye, face.]

trich•i•no•sis (trĭk'ə-nō'sĭs) *n.* A disease characterized by intestinal disorders, fever, muscular swelling, pain, and insomnia, and caused by eating inadequately cooked pork infested with parasitic worms. [< NL *trichina,* a parasitic worm + -OSIS.]

trick (trĭk) *n.* **1.** A device or action designed to achieve an end by deceptive or fraudulent means; stratagem. **2.** A practical joke; prank. **3.** A childish act or performance. **4.** A peculiar trait; mannerism. **5.** The quality necessary to accomplish something easily. **6.** A feat of magic. **7.** A clever act. **8.** *Card Games.* All the cards played in a single round. *—v.* **1.** To swindle or cheat; deceive. **2.** To ornament or adorn. [Perh < L *trīcae,* trifles, tricks.] **—trick** *adj.* **—trick'er** *n.*

trick•er•y (trĭk'ə-rē) *n., pl.* **-ies. 1.** The practice or use of tricks; artifice; deception by stratagem. **2.** A trick used to deceive.

trick•ish (trĭk'ĭsh) *adj.* Characterized by or tending to use tricks or trickery. **—trick'ish•ly** *adv.* **—trick'ish•ness** *n.*

trick•le (trĭk'əl) *v.* **-led, -ling. 1.** To flow or fall in drops or in a thin, intermittent stream; drip steadily. **2.** To proceed slowly or bit by bit. *—n.* **1.** The act or condition of trickling. **2.** Any slow, small, or irregular quantity of trickling. [ME *triklen.*]

trick•ster (trĭk'stər) *n.* One who tricks; a cheater; deceiver.

trick•y (trĭk'ē) *adj.* **-ier, -iest. 1.** Crafty; sly; wily. **2.** Requiring caution or skill. **—trick'i•ly** *adv.* **—trick'i•ness** *n.*

tri•col•or (trī'kŭl'ər) *n.* A flag with three stripes of different colors, esp. the French flag. *—adj.* Having three colors.

tri•cot (trē'kō) *n.* A knitted fabric. [< F *tricoter,* to knit.]

tri•cy•cle (trī'sĭk'əl, -sĭ-kəl) *n.* A vehicle with three wheels usually propelled by pedals.

tri•dent (trīd'ənt) *n.* A long, three-pronged weapon. [L *tridēns,* three-toothed.]

tried (trīd) *adj.* Thoroughly tested and proved to be good or trustworthy.

tri•en•ni•al (trī-ĕn'ē-əl) *adj.* **1.** Occurring every third year. **2.** Lasting three years. *—n.* A third anniversary.

tri•fle (trī'fəl) *n.* **1.** Something of slight importance or very little value. **2.** A small amount; a little. **—a trifle.** Very little; somewhat: *"A couple of the very youngest children dragged the tempo a trifle . . . "* (J.D. Salinger). *—v.* **-fled, -fling. 1.** To deal with something as if it were of little significance or value. **2.** To jest. **3.** To play or toy with something; handle things idly. **4.** To waste. [< OF *truffle,* trickery.] **—tri'fler** (trī'flər) *n.*

tri•fling (trī'flĭng) *adj.* **1.** Of slight importance; insignificant. **2.** Frivolous.

tri•fo•cal (trī-fō'kəl) *adj.* Having three focal lengths. *—pl.n.* **trifocals.** Eyeglasses having trifocal lenses.

trig (trĭg) *adj.* **1.** Trim; neat; tidy. **2.** Firm; strong. [< ON *tryggr,* active.]

trig. trigonometry.

trig•ger (trĭg'ər) *n.* **1.** The lever pressed by the finger to discharge a firearm. **2.** A device used to release or activate a mechanism. **3.** A stimulus. *—v.* To initiate; activate; set off. [< MDu *trecken,* to pull, travel.]

trig•o•nom•e•try (trĭg'ə-nŏm'ə-trē) *n.* The study of the relations between the sides and angles of triangles. [< Gk *trigōnon,* triangle + -METRY.] **—trig'o•no•met'ric** (-nə-mĕt'rĭk) *adj.*

trill (trĭl) *n.* **1.** A fluttering or tremulous sound, as that made by certain birds; warble. **2.** *Mus.* The rapid alternation of two tones either a whole or a half tone apart. **3.** *Phon.* **a.** A rapid vibration of one speech organ against another. **b.** A speech sound pronounced with such a vibration. *—v.* **1.** To sound, sing, play with, or give forth a trill. **2.** *Phon.* To articulate with a trill. [It *trillo.*]

tril•lion (trĭl'yən) *n.* **1.** The cardinal number represented by 1 followed by 12 zeros. **2.** In Great Britain, the cardinal number represented by 1 followed by 18 zeros. [< TRI- + (M)ILLION.] **—tril'lion** *adj.*

tril•lionth (trĭl'yənth) *n.* **1.** The ordinal number one trillion in a series. **2.** One of a trillion equal parts. **—tril'lionth** *adj. & adv.*

tril•o•gy (trĭl'ə-jē) *n., pl.* **-gies.** A group of three dramatic or literary works related in subject or theme. [< TRI- + -LOGY.]

trim (trĭm) *v.* **trimmed, trimming. 1.** To make neat or tidy by clipping, smoothing, or pruning. **2.** To rid of excess or remove by cutting. **3.** To ornament; decorate. **4. a.** To adjust (the sails and yards) so that they receive the wind properly. **b.** To balance (a ship) by shifting its cargo or contents. **5.** To balance (an airplane) in flight. *—n.* **1.** State of order or appearance; condition. **2.** Ornamentation. **3.** Excised or rejected material. **4. a.** The readiness of a vessel for sailing. **b.** The balance of a ship. *—adj.* **trimmer, trimmest. 1.** In good or neat order. **2.** Having lines of neat and pleasing simplicity. [Perh < OE *trymian,* to strengthen, arrange.] **—trim'ly** *adv.* **—trim'mer** *n.* **—trim'ness** *n.*

trim•ming (trĭm'ĭng) *n.* **1.** That which is added as decoration; an ornament. **2. trimmings.** Accessories; extras. **3.** That which is trimmed.

trine (trīn) *adj.* Threefold; triple. [< L *trīnī,* three each.]

Trin•i•dad and To•ba•go (trĭn'ə-dăd'; tə-bā'-gō). A state comprising the islands of Trinidad and Tobago, off the coast of Venezuela. Pop. 932,000. Cap. Port-of-Spain.

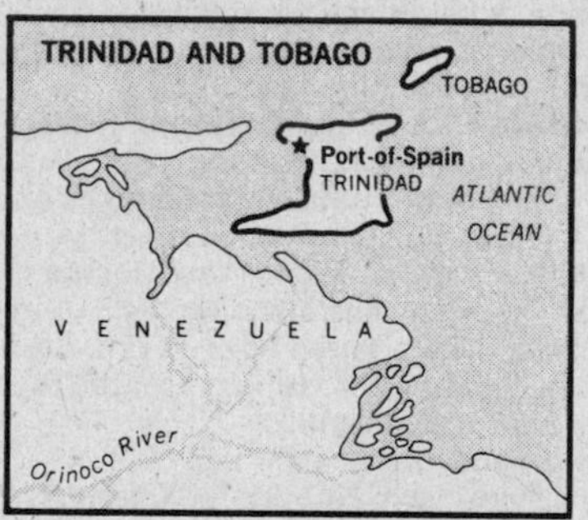

Trinidad and Tobago

tri•ni•tro•tol•u•ene (trī'nī'trō-tŏl'yōō-ēn') *n.* A yellow crystalline compound, $C_7H_5N_3O_6$, used mainly as a high explosive.

trin•i•ty (trĭn'ə-tē) *n., pl.* **-ties. 1.** Any three parts in union; a triad. **2. Trinity.** The Godhead of orthodox Christian belief, constituted by the persons of the Father, Son, and Holy Ghost.

trin•ket (trĭng'kĭt) *n.* **1.** Any small ornament, as a piece of jewelry. **2.** A trivial thing. [?]

tri•o (trē'ō) *n., pl.* **-os. 1.** A group of three. **2.** *Mus.* **a.** A composition for three performers. **b.** The people who perform this composition. [It.]

trip (trĭp) *n.* **1.** A going from one place to another; journey. **2.** *Slang.* An extended hallucination induced by a hallucinogen, as LSD. **3.** A stumble or fall caused by an obstacle or loss of balance. **4. a.** A device for tripping a mechanism. **b.** The action of such a device. *—v.* **tripped, tripping. 1.** To stumble or cause to stumble; make a false step. **2.** To move quickly or nimbly with light, rapid steps; skip. **3.** To make or catch in a mistake; err. **4.** To release or be released, as a catch, trigger, etc. [< MDu *trippen,* to hop.]

tri•par•tite (trī-pär'tīt') *adj.* 1. Composed of or divided into three parts. 2. Relating to or executed by three parties.

tripe (trīp) *n.* 1. The light-colored, rubbery lining of the stomach of cattle or other ruminants, used as food. 2. *Informal.* Anything with no value; rubbish. [< OF.]

trip•le (trĭp'əl) *adj.* 1. Consisting of three parts. 2. Thrice multiplied. —*n.* 1. A quantity three times as great as another. 2. A group or set of three; triad. —*v.* **-led, -ling.** 1. To make or become three times as great in number or amount. 2. *Baseball.* To make a three-base hit. [< L *triplus.*] —**trip'ly** *adv.*

trip•let (trĭp'lĭt) *n.* 1. A group or set of three of one kind. 2. One of three children born at one birth.

trip•lex (trĭp'lĕks', trī'plĕks') *adj.* Triple.

trip•li•cate (trĭp'lĭ-kĭt) *adj.* Made with three identical copies. —*n.* One of a set of three identical objects. —*v.* (trĭp'lĭ-kāt') **-cated, -cating.** 1. To triple. 2. To make three identical copies of. —**trip'li•ca'tion** *n.*

tri•pod (trī'pŏd') *n.* A three-legged utensil, stool, or stand used for support. [< Gk *tripous,* three-footed.]

Trip•o•li (trĭp'ə-lē). The capital of Libya. Pop. 162,000.

trip•tych (trĭp'tĭk) *n.* A three-paneled picture. [Gk *triptukhos,* threefold.]

tri•sect (trī'sĕkt', trī-sĕkt') *v.* To divide into three equal parts.

trit. triturate.

trite (trīt) *adj.* **triter, tritest.** Overused and commonplace; lacking interest or originality. [L *trītus,* pp of *terere,* to rub (away).] —**trite'ly** *adv.* —**trite'ness** *n.*

trit•i•um (trĭt'ē-əm, trĭsh'ē-) *n.* A rare radioactive hydrogen isotope with atomic mass 3 and half-life 12.5 years. [< Gk *tritos,* third.]

tri•umph (trī'əmf) *v.* 1. To be victorious; win; prevail. 2. To rejoice over a victory. —*n.* 1. The instance or fact of being victorious; success. 2. Exultation derived from victory. [< L *triumphus.*] —**tri•um'phal** *adj.* —**tri•um'phant** *adj.* —**tri•um'phant•ly** *adv.*

tri•um•vir (trī-ŭm'vər) *n., pl.* **-virs** or **-viri** (-və-rī'). One of three men sharing civil authority, as in ancient Rome. [L.] —**tri•um'vi•ral** *adj.* —**tri•um'vi•rate** *n.*

tri•une (trī'yo͞on') *adj.* Being three in one. —*n.* A trinity.

triv•et (trĭv'ĭt) *n.* 1. A three-legged stand. 2. A metal stand with short feet, used under a hot dish. [< L *tripēs,* "three-footed."]

triv•i•a (trĭv'ē-ə) *pl.n. (takes sing. or pl. v.).* Insignificant or inessential matters; trivialities; trifles. [NL, "that which comes from the street."]

triv•i•al (trĭv'ē-əl) *adj.* 1. Of little importance or significance; trifling. 2. Ordinary; commonplace. —**triv'i•al'i•ty** *n.* —**triv'i•al•ly** *adv.*

tro•che (trō'kē) *n.* A small circular medicinal lozenge; pastille. [< Gk *trokhos,* wheel.]

trod (trŏd). *p.t.* & alternate *p.p.* of **tread.**

trod•den (trŏd'n). *p.p.* of **tread.**

Tro•jan (trō'jən) *n.* A native or inhabitant of ancient Troy. —*adj.* Of or pertaining to ancient Troy or its residents.

Trojan War. The prehistoric ten-year war waged against Troy by the confederated Greeks, ending in the burning of Troy.

troll¹ (trōl) *v.* 1. To fish by trailing a baited line from behind a slowly moving boat. 2. To sing in succession the parts of (a round). 3. To sing heartily. —*n.* 1. The act of trolling for fish. 2. A lure used for trolling. [ME *trollen,* to ramble, roll.] —**troll'er** *n.*

troll² (trōl) *n.* A supernatural creature of Scandinavian folklore. [< ON, monster, demon.]

trol•ley (trŏl'ē) *n., pl.* **-leys.** Also **trol•ly** *pl.* **-lies.** 1. An electric car; a streetcar. 2. A wheeled carriage or basket suspended from an overhead track. 3. A device that collects electric current and transmits it to the motor of an electric vehicle. [Prob < TROLL¹.]

trolley bus. An electric bus that is powered by electricity from an overhead wire.

trol•lop (trŏl'əp) *n.* 1. A slovenly, untidy woman. 2. A loose woman; strumpet.

trom•bone (trŏm-bōn', trəm-, trŏm'bōn') *n.* A low-pitched brass musical instrument related to the trumpet. [< It.] —**trom•bon'ist** *n.*

-tron. *comb. form.* 1. Vacuum tube: *dynatron.* 2. Device for manipulating subatomic particles: **cyclotron.** [Gk, suffix denoting instrument.]

troop (tro͞op) *n.* 1. A group or company of people, animals, or things. 2. A group of soldiers. 3. **troops.** Military units; soldiers. —*v.* To move or go as a throng. [< F *troupeau,* herd.]

troop•er (tro͞o'pər) *n.* 1. a. A cavalryman. b. A cavalry horse. 2. A mounted policeman. 3. A state policeman.

troop•ship (tro͞op'shĭp') *n.* A transport ship designed for carrying troops.

trop. tropic; tropical.

trope (trōp) *n.* The figurative use of a word or expression. [< Gk *tropos,* a turn, way, manner.]

tro•phy (trō'fē) *n., pl.* **-phies.** A prize or memento received as a symbol of victory. [< Gk *tropaios,* of turning, of defeat.]

trop•ic (trŏp'ĭk) *n.* 1. Two parallels of latitude 23 degrees 27 minutes N and S of the equator that are the boundaries of the Torrid Zone. 2. **tropics.** The region of the earth's surface lying between these latitudes; the Torrid Zone. —*adj.* Of or relating to the tropics; tropical. [ME *tropik,* solstice point at which the sun "turns."]

trop•i•cal (trŏp'ĭ-kəl) *adj.* 1. Of, indigenous to, or characteristic of the tropics. 2. Hot and humid; sultry; torrid. —**trop'i•cal•ly** *adv.*

tropical year. The time interval between two successive passages of the sun through the vernal equinox; the calendar year.

tropic of Cancer. The parallel of latitude 23 degrees 27 minutes N of the equator, the northern boundary of the Torrid Zone.

tropic of Capricorn. The parallel of latitude 23 degrees 27 minutes S of the equator, the southern boundary of the Torrid Zone.

tro•pism (trō'pĭz'əm) *n.* Responsive growth or movement of an organism toward or away from an external stimulus. [< Gk *tropos,* turn.]

tro•po•sphere (trō'pə-sfîr', trŏp'ə-) *n.* The lowest region of the earth's atmosphere, characterized by decreasing temperature with increasing altitude. [< Gk *tropos,* a turn, change + SPHERE.]

trot (trŏt) *n.* 1. A gait of a four-footed animal in which diagonal pairs of legs move forward together. 2. A gait faster than a walk; a jog. —*v.* **trotted, trotting.** 1. To go or move at a trot. 2. To proceed rapidly; hurry. [< OF *troter.*] —**trot'ter** *n.*

troth (trôth, trŏth, trōth) *n.* 1. Good faith; fidelity. 2. One's pledged fidelity; betrothal. [< OE *trēowth,* TRUTH.]

Trots•ky (trŏt'skē), **Leon.** 1879–1940. Russian revolutionary leader.

trou•ba•dour (tro͞o'bə-dôr', -dōr', -do͝or') *n.* One of a class of lyric poets of the 12th and 13th centuries, attached to the courts of Provence and N Italy, who composed songs. [< OProv *trobador.*]

troub•le (trŭb'əl) *n.* 1. A state of distress, affliction, danger, or need. 2. Something that contributes to such a state. 3. Exertion; effort; pains. 4. A condition of pain, disease, or malfunction: *heart trouble.* —*v.* **-led, -ling.** 1. To agitate; stir up. 2. To afflict with pain or discomfort. 3. To perturb. 4. To inconvenience; bother. 5. To take pains. [< L *turbidus,* TURBID.] —**troub'le•some** *adj.*

troub•le•mak•er (trŭb'əl-mā'kər) *n.* One who habitually stirs up trouble.

troub•le-shoot•er (trŭb'əl-sho͞o'tər) *n.* One who locates and eliminates sources of trouble.

trough (trôf, trŏf) *n.* 1. A long, narrow, generally shallow receptacle, esp. one for holding water or feed for animals. 2. A gutter under the eaves of a roof. 3. A long, narrow depression, as between waves or ridges. [< OE *trog.* See **deru-.**]

trounce (trouns) *v.* **trounced, trouncing.** 1. To thrash; beat. 2. To defeat decisively. [?]

troupe (tro͞op) *n.* A company or group, esp. of touring actors, singers, or dancers. [F, troop.] —**troup'er** *n.*

trou•sers (trou'zərz) *pl.n.* Also **trow•sers.** A garment covering the body from the waist to the ankles, divided into sections to fit each leg separately, worn esp. by men and boys. [< Scot Gael *triubhas.*]

trous•seau (tro͞o'sō, tro͞o-sō') *n., pl.* **-seaux** (-sōz, -sōz') or **-seaus.** The special wardrobe a bride assembles for her marriage. [< OF *trusse,* a bundle.]

trout (trout) *n., pl.* **trout** or **trouts.** Any of various chiefly freshwater food and game fishes related to the salmon. [< LL *tructa.*]

trow (trō) *v. Archaic.* To think; suppose. [< OE *trēowian* and *trūwian.*]

trow•el (trou'əl) *n.* 1. A flat-bladed hand tool used for shaping substances such as cement or mortar. 2. A small gardening implement with a scoop-shaped blade. [< L *trua,* stirring spoon, ladle.]

troy (troi) *adj.* Of or expressed in troy weight. [Prob < *Troyes,* France.]

Troy (troi). An ancient city in NW Asia Minor.

troy weight. A system of units of weight in which the grain is the same as in the avoirdupois system and the pound contains 12 ounces.

tru•ant (tro͞o'ənt) *n.* 1. One who is absent without permission, esp. from school. 2. One who shirks his work or duty. —*adj.* 1. Absent without permission. 2. Idle, lazy, or neglectful. [< OF, idle rogue.] —**tru'an•cy** *n.*

truce (tro͞os) *n.* A temporary cessation of hostilities by agreement of the contending forces; an armistice. [< OE *trēow,* faith, pledge. See **deru-.**]

truck¹ (trŭk) *n.* 1. Any of various heavy automotive vehicles designed for transporting loads. 2. A two-wheeled barrow for moving heavy objects by hand. 3. One of the swiveling frames of wheels under each end of a railroad car, trolley car, etc. —*v.* 1. To transport by truck. 2. To drive a truck. [Perh < L *trochus,* a wheel.]

truck² (trŭk) *v.* 1. To exchange; barter. 2. To have dealings; traffic. —*n.* 1. Trade goods. 2. Garden produce raised for the market. 3. Barter; exchange. 4. Dealings; business. [< OF *troquer.*]

truck•age (trŭk'ĭj) *n.* 1. Transportation of goods by truck. 2. A charge for this.

truck•le (trŭk'əl) *n.* 1. A small wheel or roller; caster. 2. A trundle bed. —*v.* **-led, -ling.** To be servile; yield weakly. [< L *trochlea,* system of pulleys.] —**truck'ler** *n.*

truck•load (trŭk'lōd') *n.* The quantity or weight that a truck carries.

truc•u•lent (trŭk'yə-lənt) *adj.* 1. Savage and cruel; fierce. 2. Pugnacious; defiant. [L *truculentus.*] —**truc'u•lence** *n.* —**truc'u•lent•ly** *adv.*

trudge (trŭj) *v.* **trudged, trudging.** To walk in a heavy-footed way; plod. —*n.* A long, tedious walk. [?] —**trudg'er** *n.*

true (trōō) *adj.* **truer, truest.** 1. Consistent with fact or reality; not false or erroneous. 2. Exactly conforming to a rule, standard, or pattern. 3. Reliable; accurate. 4. Real; genuine. 5. Faithful; loyal. 6. Fundamental; essential: *his true motive.* 7. Rightful; legitimate. 8. Determined with reference to the earth's axis, not the magnetic poles: *true north.* —*adv.* 1. Rightly; truthfully. 2. Unswervingly; exactly. 3. So as to conform to an ancestral type or stock: *breed true.* —*v.* **trued, truing** or **trueing.** To adjust so as to conform with a standard. —*n.* 1. Truth. 2. Proper alignment or adjustment. [< OE *trēowe,* loyal, trustworthy. See **deru-.**] —**true'ness** *n.*

true•blue (trōō'blōō') *n.* Also **true blue.** One of unswerving loyalty. —**true'-blue'** *adj.*

true•love (trōō'lŭv') *n.* One's beloved; a sweetheart.

truf•fle (trŭf'əl) *n.* An underground fungus esteemed as a food delicacy. [< L *tūber,* tuber, truffle.]

tru•ism (trōō'ĭz'əm) *n.* A statement of an obvious truth.

tru•ly (trōō'lē) *adv.* 1. Sincerely; genuinely. 2. Truthfully; accurately. 3. Indeed: *truly ugly.*

Tru•man (trōō'mən), **Harry S** Born 1884–1972. 33rd President of the U.S. (1945–53).

trump (trŭmp) *n.* 1. A suit the cards of which are declared as outranking all other cards for the duration of a hand. 2. A card of such a suit. —*v.* To play a trump card. —**trump up.** To devise fraudulently. [Var of TRIUMPH.]

Harry S Truman

trump•er•y (trŭm'pə-rē) *n., pl.* **-ies.** 1. Showy but worthless finery. 2. Nonsense. 3. Deception. [< OF *tromper,* to cheat.]

trum•pet (trŭm'pĭt) *n.* 1. A soprano brass wind instrument consisting of a long metal tube ending in a flared bell. 2. Something shaped or sounding like a trumpet. —*v.* 1. To play a trumpet. 2. To give forth a resounding call. [< OF *trompe.*]

trum•pet•er (trŭm'pĭt-ər) *n.* 1. A trumpet player. 2. One who announces something, as on a trumpet; herald.

trun•cate (trŭng'kāt') *v.* **-cated, -cating.** To shorten by or as by cutting; lop. [< L *truncus,* torso, TRUNK.] —**trun'ca'tion** *n.*

trun•cheon (trŭn'chən) *n.* A short stick carried by policemen; billy. [< L *truncus,* torso, TRUNK.]

trun•dle (trŭnd'l) *v.* **-dled, -dling.** To push or propel on wheels or rollers. [< OE *trendel,* circle.] —**trun'dler** *n.*

trundle bed. A low bed on casters that can be rolled under another bed when not in use.

trunk (trŭngk) *n.* 1. The main woody stem of a tree. 2. The human body excluding the head and limbs; torso. 3. A main body, apart from tributaries or appendages. 4. A large packing case or box that clasps shut, used as luggage or for storage. 5. A covered compartment of an automobile, used for luggage and storage. 6. A proboscis, esp. the long, prehensile proboscis of an elephant. 7. **trunks.** Men's shorts worn for swimming or athletics. —*adj.* Of or designating the main body or line of a system. [< L *truncus.*]

trunk line. 1. A direct line between two telephone switchboards. 2. The main line of a communication or transportation system.

truss (trŭs) *n.* 1. A supportive device worn to prevent enlargement of a hernia or the return of a reduced hernia. 2. A wooden or metal framework used to support a roof, bridge, or similar structure. —*v.* 1. To tie up or bind. 2. To bind or skewer the wings or legs of (a fowl) before cooking. 3. To support or brace with a truss. [< OF *trousser,* to tie in a bundle.] —**truss'er** *n.*

trust (trŭst) *n.* 1. Firm reliance; confident belief; faith. 2. The person or thing in which confidence is placed. 3. Custody; care. 4. One committed into the care of another; charge. 5. The condition and resulting obligation of having confidence placed in one. 6. Reliance on something in the future; hope. 7. A legal title to property held by one party for the benefit of another. 8. A combination of firms for the purpose of reducing competition. —*v.* 1. To rely; depend; have confidence in. 2. To be confident; hope. 3. To expect with assurance; assume. 4. To believe. 5. To entrust. 6. To grant discretion to confidently. 7. To extend credit to. —*adj.* Maintained in trust. [Prob < ON *traust,* confidence, firmness.] —**trust'er** *n.*

trus•tee (trŭs'tē') *n.* 1. A person or agent holding legal title to property in order to administer it for a beneficiary. 2. A member of a board that directs the funds and policy of an institution. —**trus'tee'ship'** *n.*

trust•ful (trŭst'fəl) *adj.* Full of trust. —**trust'ful•ly** *adv.* —**trust'ful•ness** *n.*

trust•wor•thy (trŭst'wûr'*thē*) *adj.* Dependable; reliable. —**trust'wor'thi•ness** *n.*

trust•y (trŭs'tē) *adj.* **-ier, -iest.** Dependable; faithful. —*n., pl.* **-ies.** A trusted person, esp. a convict granted special privileges.

truth (trōōth) *n., pl.* **truths** (trōō*thz,* trōōths). 1. Conformity to knowledge, fact, actuality, or logic. 2. Fidelity to an original or standard. 3. Reality; actuality. 4. A statement proven to be or accepted as true. 5. Sincerity; integrity. [< OE *trēowth, trīewth.*]

truth•ful (trōōth'fəl) *adj.* 1. Honest. 2. Corresponding to reality. —**truth'ful•ly** *adv.* —**truth'ful•ness** *n.*

try (trī) *v.* **tried, trying.** 1. To test in order to determine strength, effect, etc. 2. a. To examine or hear (evidence or a case) by judicial process. b. To put (an accused person) on trial. 3. To subject to great strain or hardship; tax. 4. To melt (fat) to separate out impurities; render. 5. To make an effort (to do something); attempt. 6. To smooth, fit, or align accurately. —*n., pl.* **tries.** An attempt; effort. [ME *trien,* to separate, pick out, sift.]

Usage: Try and is common in speech for *try to,* esp. in such established combinations as *try and stop me* (defiance) and *try and get some rest* (exhortation). In most contexts, however, it is usually not interchangeable with *try to* unless the level is expressly informal.

try•ing (trī'ĭng) *adj.* Causing severe strain or distress. —**try'ing•ly** *adv.*

try•out (trī'out') *n.* A test to ascertain the qualifications of applicants, as for a theatrical role.

tryst (trĭst) *n.* 1. An agreement between lovers to meet. 2. The meeting or meeting place so arranged. [Perh < Scand.]

tsa•de. Variant of **sade.**

tsar. Variant of **czar.**

tset•se fly (tsĕt'sē, tsēt'sē). A bloodsucking African fly that transmits microorganisms causing diseases such as sleeping sickness.

Tshi. Variant of **Twi.**

T-shirt (tē'shûrt') *n.* A short-sleeved, collarless shirt worn by men.

tsp. teaspoon; teaspoonful.

tsu•na•mi (tsōō-nä'mē) *n.* A very large ocean wave caused by an underwater earthquake or volcanic eruption. [Jap.]

tub (tŭb) *n.* 1. A round, open, flat-bottomed vessel used for packing, storing, or washing. 2. A bathtub. [< MDu and MLG *tubbe.*]

tu•ba (t/y/ōō'bə) *n.* A large brass musical wind instrument with a bass pitch and several valves. [< L, a trumpet.]

tub•by (tŭb'ē) *adj.* **-bier, -biest.** Short and fat.

tube (t/y/ōōb) *n.* 1. A hollow cylinder that conveys a fluid or functions as a passage. 2. A flexible cylindrical container sealed at one end and having a screw cap at the other, for pigments, toothpaste, etc. 3. An electron tube or vacuum tube. 4. A subway. [< L *tubus.*]

tu•ber (t/y/ōō'bər) *n.* 1. A swollen, usually underground stem, as a potato, bearing buds from which new plants sprout. 2. A swelling; tubercle. [L *tūber,* a lump, swelling, tumor.] —**tu'ber•ous** *adj.*

tu•ber•cle (t/y/ōō'bər-kəl) *n.* 1. A small, rounded prominence or process, such as a wartlike excrescence on the roots of some leguminous plants or a knoblike process in the skin or on a bone. 2. The characteristic lesion of tuberculosis. [< L *tūber,* a lump, TUBER.]

tubercle bacillus. A rod-shaped bacterium that causes tuberculosis.

tu•ber•cu•lar (t/y/ōō-bûr'kyə-lər) *adj.* 1. Of or covered with tubercles. 2. Of or afflicted with tuberculosis.

tu•ber•cu•late (t/y/ōō-bûr'kyə-lĭt) *adj.* 1. Having tubercles. 2. Tubercular.

tu•ber•cu•lin (t/y/ōō-bûr'kyə-lĭn) *n.* A substance derived from tubercle bacilli, used in the diagnosis and treatment of tuberculosis.

tu•ber•cu•loid (t/y/ōō-bûr'kyə-loid') *adj.* 1. Resembling tuberculosis. 2. Resembling a tubercle.

tu•ber•cu•lo•sis (t/y/ōō-bûr'kyə-lō'sĭs) *n.* 1. A communicable disease of man and animals, caused by a microorganism and manifesting itself in bodily lesions, esp. of the lung. **2.** Tuberculosis of the lungs. **—tu•ber'cu•lous** *adj.*

tube•rose (t/y/o͞ob'rōz', t/y/o͞o'bə-rōz', -rōs') *n.* A tuber-bearing plant native to Mexico, cultivated for its fragrant white flowers. [< L *tūberōsus,* full of lumps.]

tu•bu•lar (t/y/o͞o'byə-lər) *adj.* Having the form of a tube. **—tu'bu•lar•ly** *adv.*

tuck (tŭk) *v.* **1.** To make one or more folds in. **2.** To thrust or turn in the end or edge of (a shirt, blanket, etc.) in order to secure. **3.** To put in an out-of-the-way and snug place. **4.** To draw in; contract. *—n.* A flattened pleat or fold, esp. a very narrow one stitched in place. [< OE *tūcian,* to punish, torment.]

tuck•er (tŭk'ər) *v.* To weary; exhaust. [Freq of TUCK.]

Tuc•son (to͞o'sŏn'). A city of S Arizona. Pop. 213,000.

-tude. *comb. form.* A condition or state of being: **exactitude.** [< L *-tūdō.*]

Tues•day (t/y/o͞oz'dē, -dā') *n.* The 3rd day of the week. [< OE *tīwesdæg,* "day of Tiu," Germanic god of war.]

tu•fa (t/y/o͞o'fə) *n.* The calcareous and siliceous rock deposits of springs, lakes, or ground water. [< L *tōphus, tōfus.*] **—tu•fa'ceous** (-fā'shəs) *adj.*

tuft (tŭft) *n.* A cluster of yarn, hair, grass, etc., held or growing close together. [< OF *toffe.*]

tug (tŭg) *v.* **tugged, tugging. 1.** To pull at vigorously. **2.** To move by pulling with great effort or exertion. *—n.* **1.** A strong pull or pulling force. **2.** A tugboat. [< OE *tēon.* See **deuk-.**] **—tug'ger** *n.*

tug•boat (tŭg'bōt') *n.* A powerful small boat designed for towing larger vessels.

tug of war. A contest in which two teams tug on opposite ends of a rope, each trying to pull the other across a dividing line.

tu•i•tion (t/y/o͞o-ĭsh'ən) *n.* **1.** A fee for instruction, esp. at a formal institution of learning. **2.** Instruction; teaching. [< L *tuitiō,* protection, a watching.]

tu•la•re•mi•a (t/y/o͞o'lə-rē'mē-ə) *n.* An infectious disease transmitted from infected rodents to man and characterized by fever and swelling of the lymph nodes. [< *Tulare,* a county in California + -EMIA.]

tu•lip (t/y/o͞o'lĭp) *n.* A bulb-bearing plant widely cultivated for its showy, variously colored flowers. [NL *Tulipa.*]

tulip tree. A tall tree with tuliplike green and orange flowers and soft yellowish, easily worked wood.

tulle (to͞ol) *n.* A fine starched net of silk, rayon, or nylon, used for veils, gowns, etc. [< *Tulle,* city in central France.]

Tul•sa (tŭl'sə). A city of NE Oklahoma. Pop. 262,000.

tum•ble (tŭm'bəl) *v.* **-bled, -bling. 1.** To perform acrobatic feats, such as somersaults. **2.** To fall or roll end over end. **3.** To spill or roll out in confusion or disorder. **4.** To pitch headlong; fall. **5.** To drop: *Prices tumbled.* **6.** To cause to fall; bring down. *—n.* **1.** An act of tumbling; a fall. **2.** A condition of confusion or disorder. [< OE *tumbian.*]

tum•ble-down (tŭm'bəl-doun') *adj.* Dilapidated; rickety.

tum•bler (tŭm'blər) *n.* **1.** An acrobat or gymnast. **2.** A drinking glass having no handle or stem. **3.** The part in a lock that releases the bolt when moved by a key.

tum•ble•weed (tŭm'bəl-wēd') *n.* A densely branched plant that when withered breaks off and is rolled about by the wind.

tum•bling (tŭm'blĭng) *n.* The skill or practice of gymnastic falling, rolling, or somersaulting.

tum•brel, tum•bril (tŭm'brəl) *n.* A two-wheeled cart, esp. one that can be tilted to dump a load. [< OF *tomberel,* a dumpcart.]

tu•mid (t/y/o͞o'mĭd) *adj.* **1.** Swollen; distended. **2.** Overblown; bombastic. [< L *tumēre,* to swell.] **—tu•mid'i•ty** *n.*

tum•my (tŭm'ē) *n., pl.* **-mies.** *Informal.* The stomach. [Baby-talk var of STOMACH.]

tu•mor (t/y/o͞o'mər) *n.* A circumscribed, noninflammatory growth arising from existing tissue but growing independently and serving no physiological function. [< L *tumēre,* to swell.]

tu•mult (t/y/o͞o'məlt) *n.* **1.** The din and commotion of a great crowd. **2.** Agitation of the mind or emotions. [< L *tumultus.*] **—tu•mul'tu•ous** (tə-mŭl'cho͞o-əs) *adj.*

tun (tŭn) *n.* A large cask. [< OE *tunne,* cask, vat < ML *tunna.*]

tu•na (t/y/o͞o'nə) *n., pl.* **-na** or **-nas. 1.** Any of various often large marine food fishes. **2.** Also **tuna fish.** The canned or commercially processed flesh of such a fish. [< L *thunnus,* tunny.]

tun•dra (tŭn'drə) *n.* A treeless area of arctic regions, having a permanently frozen subsoil and low-growing vegetation such as lichens, mosses, and stunted shrubs. [< Lapp *tundar.*]

tune (t/y/o͞on) *n.* **1.** A melody, esp. an easily remembered one. **2. a.** Correct musical pitch. **b.** The state of being properly in agreement or adjustment with respect to pitch. **3.** Concord or agreement; harmony: *in tune with the times.* **4.** *Electronics.* Adjustment of a receiver or circuit for maximum response to a given signal or frequency. *—v.* **tuned, tuning. 1.** To put into tune. **2.** To adjust for maximum performance. **3.** To adjust a radio or television receiver to receive signals at a particular frequency. [< TONE.] **—tun'a•ble** *adj.*

tune•ful (t/y/o͞on'fəl) *adj.* Melodious; musical. **—tune'ful•ly** *adv.* **—tune'ful•ness** *n.*

tune•less (t/y/o͞on'lĭs) *adj.* Deficient in melody; unmusical. **—tune'less•ly** *adv.*

tun•er (t/y/o͞o'nər) *n.* **1.** One that tunes: *a piano tuner.* **2.** An electronic device used to select signals at a specific radio frequency for amplification and conversion to sound.

tune-up (t/y/o͞on'ŭp') *n.* An adjustment of a motor or engine to put it in efficient working order.

tung•sten (tŭng'stən) *n.* *Symbol* **W** A hard, brittle, corrosion-resistant gray to white metallic element used in high-temperature structural materials and electrical elements, notably lamp filaments requiring thermally compatible glass-to-metal seals. Atomic number 74, atomic weight 183.85. [Swed, "heavy stone."]

Tun•gus (to͝ong-go͞oz') *n., pl.* **-guses** or **-gus. 1.** A Mongoloid people inhabiting E Siberia. **2.** The Tungusic language of this people.

Tun•gus•ic (to͝ong-go͞o'zĭk) *n.* A subgroup of Altaic, including Tungus and Manchu, spoken in E Siberia and N Manchuria. *—adj.* Of or pertaining to the Tungus peoples or to Tungusic.

tu•nic (t/y/o͞o'nĭk) *n.* **1.** A loose-fitting garment extending to the knees, worn by men and women esp. in ancient Greece and Rome. **2.** A long plain sleeved or sleeveless blouse worn over a skirt by women. [L *tunica,* a sheath, tunic.]

tuning fork. A small two-pronged instrument that when struck produces a sound of fixed pitch.

Tu•nis (t/y/o͞o'nĭs). **1.** The capital of Tunisia. Pop. 714,000. **2.** A former kingdom on the N coast of Africa.

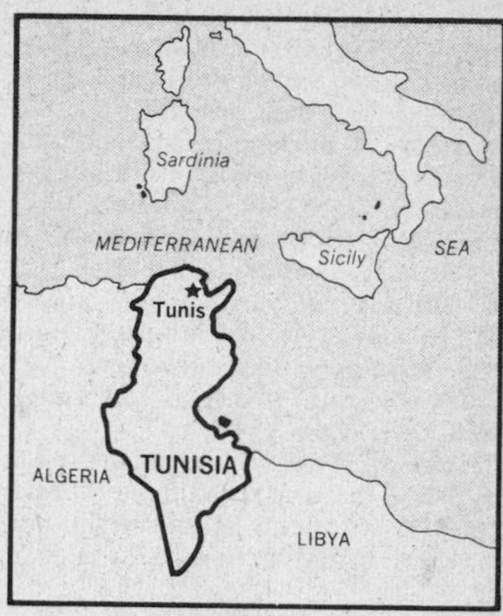

Tunisia

Tu•ni•sia (t/y/o͞o-nē'zhə, -nĭzh'ə, -nĭsh'ə). A republic in N Africa. Pop. 4,030,000. Cap. Tunis. **—Tu•ni'sian** *adj.* & *n.*

tun•nel (tŭn'əl) *n.* An underground or underwater passage. *—v.* **-neled** or **-nelled, -neling** or **-nelling. 1.** To make a tunnel under or through. **2.** To dig in the form of a tunnel. [< ML *tunna, tonna,* TUN.]

tun•ny (tŭn'ē) *n., pl.* **-nies.** *Chiefly Brit.* The tuna. [< Gk *thunnos.*]

Tu•pi (to͞o'pē, to͞o-pē') *n., pl.* **-pi** or **-pis. 1.** A member of any of a group of peoples formerly living along the coast of Brazil and in the Amazon River valley. **2.** The language of these peoples.

Tu•pi•an (to͞o'pē-ən, to͞o-pē'ən) *adj.* Of or pertaining to the Tupi. *—n.* A major division of Tupi-Guarani that includes Tupi.

Tu•pi-Gua•ra•ni (to͞o-pē'gwär'ən-ē', to͞o'pē'-) *n.* A family of languages, of which the chief divisions are Tupian and Guarani, spread throughout large areas of coastal Brazil and NE South America. **—Tu•pi'-Gua'ra•ni', Tu•pi'-Gua'ra•ni'an** *adj.*

tur•ban (tûr'bən) *n.* A headdress of Moslem origin, consisting of a long scarf of linen, cotton, or silk wound around the head or a cap. [< Pers *dulband.*]

tur•bid (tûr'bĭd) *adj.* **1.** Having sediment or foreign particles stirred up or suspended: *turbid water.* **2.** Heavy, dark, or dense, as smoke. **3.** In turmoil; muddled: *turbid feelings.* [< L *turba,* turmoil, uproar.]

tur•bine (tûr'bĭn, -bīn') *n.* Any of various machines in which the kinetic energy of a moving fluid is converted to useful rotational power by the interaction of the fluid with a series of vanes arrayed about the circumference of a wheel or cylinder. [< L *turbō (turbin-),* a spinning thing, top, whirlwind.]

turbo-. *comb. form.* Turbine.

tur•bo•jet (tûr'bō-jĕt') *n.* A jet engine having a turbine-driven compressor.

tur•bo•prop (tûr'bō-prŏp') *n.* A turbojet engine used to drive an external propeller.

tur•bo•ram•jet (tûr'bō-răm'jĕt') *n.* A turbojet engine that at high speeds compresses air taken in as a ramjet and increases exhaust velocities with an afterburner.

tur•bot (tûr'bət) *n., pl.* **-bot** or **-bots.** A European flatfish esteemed as food. [< OF.]

tur•bu•lent (tûr'byə-lənt) *adj.* **1.** Violently agitated or disturbed; stormy: *turbulent waters.* **2.** Causing unrest or disturbance; unruly: *turbulent troops.* [< L *turba,* confusion.] **—tur'bu•lence** *n.* **—tur'bu•lent•ly** *adv.*

tu•reen (t/y/ōō-rēn') *n.* A broad, deep dish with a cover, used for serving soups, stews, etc. [< F *terrine,* "earthen vessel."]

turf (tûrf) *n.* **1.** Surface earth containing a dense growth of grass and its matted roots. **2.** A piece cut from this. **—the turf. 1.** A racetrack. **2.** The sport or business of racing horses. [< OE.] **—turf'y** *adj.*

tur•gid (tûr'jĭd) *adj.* **1.** Swollen; bloated. **2.** Overornate in style or language; grandiloquent. [L *turgēre,* to be swollen, to swell.]

Tu•rin (t/y/ōō'-rĭn). A city of NW Italy. Pop. 1,117,000.

Turk (tûrk) *n.* **1.** A native or inhabitant of Turkey. **2.** A person speaking a Turkic language. **3.** A Moslem. **4.** Formerly, an Ottoman. **5.** A brutal or tyrannical person. **6.** Turkic.

Turk. Turkey; Turkish.

tur•key (tûr'kē) *n., pl.* **-keys. 1.** A large, widely domesticated North American bird with a bare wattled head and neck. **2.** The edible flesh of such a bird. **—talk turkey.** To discuss in a straightforward and direct manner.

Tur•key (tûr'kē). A republic mainly in Asia Minor and partly in SE Europe. Pop. 31,391,000. Cap. Ankara.

Turkey

Tur•kic (tûr'kĭk) *n.* A subdivision of Altaic including Turkish. *—adj.* **1.** Of or pertaining to the Turks. **2.** Of or pertaining to Turkic.

Turk•ish (tûr'kĭsh) *adj.* **1.** Of or relating to Turkey or the Turks. **2.** Of or relating to the Turkic language of Turkey. *—n.* The Turkic language of Turkey.

Turk•men Soviet Socialist Republic (tûrk'mĕn, -mən). A republic of the Soviet Union in C Asia. Pop. 2,158,000. Cap. Ashkhabad.

tur•moil (tûr'moil) *n.* Utter confusion; extreme agitation. [?]

turn (tûrn) *v.* **1.** To move around an axis or center; rotate; revolve. **2.** To shape (something) on a lathe. **3.** To give distinctive form to: *turn a phrase.* **4.** To change the position of so as to show another side of. **5.** To injure by twisting: *turn an ankle.* **6.** To upset; be or become nauseated. **7. a.** To change the direction or course of: *turn the car left.* **b.** To direct or change one's way or course. **8.** To make a course around or about: *turn the corner.* **9.** To set in a specified way or direction. **10.** To direct (the attention, interest, etc.) toward or away from something: *turn to music.* **11.** To antagonize or become antagonistic. **12.** To send, drive, or let go: *turn the dog loose.* **13.** To change; transform or become transformed. **14.** To become: *She turns twelve today.* **15.** To have recourse to a person or thing for help. **16.** To depend upon for success or failure; rely. **17.** To change color. **18.** To make or become sour; ferment. **—turn down. 1.** To diminish, as the volume of. **2.** To reject or refuse. **—turn in. 1.** To turn or go into. **2.** To hand in; give over. **3.** To go to bed. **—turn off. 1.** To stop the operation of. **2.** To leave a path or road at a point and enter another. **3.** *Slang.* To affect with dislike or displeasure. **—turn on. 1.** To cause to begin the operation of: *turn on the light.* **2.** *Slang.* **a.** To affect with great pleasure. **b.** To smoke or ingest a drug. **—turn tail.** To run away; flee. **—turn up. 1.** To increase, as the volume of. **2.** To find or be found. **3.** To arrive; appear. *—n.* **1.** The act of turning or condition of being turned; a rotation; revolution. **2.** A change of direction: *a right turn.* **3.** A departure or deviation, as in a trend: *a turn of events.* **4.** A chance or opportunity to do something accorded individuals in scheduled order. **5.** Natural inclination: *a speculative turn of mind.* **6.** A deed or action: *did her a good turn.* **7.** A short excursion: *a turn in the park.* **8.** A single wind or convolution, as of wire upon a spool. **9.** A rendering or fashioning: *an interesting turn of phrase.* **10.** A momentary shock or scare. **—at every turn.** In every place; at every moment. **—in turn.** In the proper order or sequence. **—take turns.** To take part or do in order, one after another. **—to a turn.** Perfectly: *The roast was done to a turn.* [< L *tornāre,* to turn in a lathe, round off.]

turn•a•bout (tûrn'ə-bout') *n.* A shift or change in opinion or allegiance.

turn•coat (tûrn'kōt') *n.* One who traitorously switches allegiance.

turning point. A point at which a crucial decision must be made; decisive moment.

tur•nip (tûr'nĭp) *n.* **1.** A cultivated plant with a large, edible yellow or white root. **2.** The root of this plant. [Earlier *turnepe.*]

turn out. 1. To shut off, as a light. **2.** To arrive or assemble. **3.** To produce; make. **4.** To result; end up.

turn•out (tûrn'out') *n.* **1.** The act of turning out. **2.** The number of people at a gathering; attendance. **3.** An outfit.

turn over. 1. To bring the bottom to the top or vice versa. **2.** To think about; consider. **3.** To transfer to another.

turn•o•ver (tûrn'ō'vər) *n.* **1.** The act of turning over; an upset. **2.** An abrupt change; reversal. **3.** A small filled pastry with half the crust turned back over the other half. **4.** The number of times a particular stock of goods is sold and restocked during a given period. **5.** The amount of business transacted during a given period. **6.** The number of workers hired by an establishment to replace those who have left. *—adj.* Capable of being folded over.

turn•pike (tûrn'pīk') *n.* A road, esp. a wide highway with tollgates. [ME *turnepike,* a revolving barrier used to block a road.]

turn•stile (tûrn'stīl') *n.* A device used to control passage from one area to another, typically consisting of revolving horizontal arms projecting from a central post.

turn•ta•ble (tûrn'tā'bəl) *n.* A circular rotating platform, used for turning locomotives, phonograph records, etc.

tur•pen•tine (tûr'pən-tīn') *n.* A thin, volatile oil, $C_{10}H_{16}$, obtained from the wood or exudate of certain pine trees and used as a paint thinner, solvent, and medicinally as a liniment. [< L *terebinthus.*]

tur•pi•tude (tûr'pə-t/y/ōōd') *n.* Baseness; depravity. [< L *turpis,* ugly, vile.]

tur•quoise (tûr'kwoiz', -koiz') *n.* **1.** A blue to blue-green mineral of aluminum and copper, esteemed as a gemstone. **2.** Light to brilliant bluish green. [< OF *(pierre) turqueise,* "Turkish (stone)."]

tur•ret (tûr'ĭt) *n.* **1.** A small tower-shaped projection on a building. **2.** A projecting armored structure, usually rotating horizontally, containing mounted guns and their gunners, as on a warship or tank. **3.** An attachment for a lathe, consisting of a rotating cylindrical block holding various cutting tools. [< OF *tour,* a TOWER.] **—tur'ret•ed** *adj.*

tur•tle[1] (tûrt'l) *n.* Any of various reptiles having beaklike jaws and the body enclosed in a bony or leathery shell. [Perh var of F *tortue,* tortoise.]

tur•tle[2] (tûrt'l) *n. Archaic.* A turtledove. [< L *turtur.*]

tur•tle•dove (tûrt'l-dŭv') *n.* An Old World dove with a soft, purring voice.

tusk (tŭsk) *n.* A long pointed tooth, as of an elephant or walrus, extending outside of the mouth. [< OE *tūx, tūsc.*]

tus•sle (tŭs'əl) *v.* **-sled, -sling.** To struggle; scuffle. [ME *tussillen.*] **—tus'sle** *n.*

tus•sock (tŭs'ək) *n.* A clump or tuft, as of grass.

tu•te•lage (t/y/ōō'tə-lĭj) *n.* **1.** The function or capacity of a guardian; guardianship. **2.** The act or capacity of a tutor; instruction. **3.** The state of being under a guardian or tutor. [< L *tūtor,* TUTOR.] **—tu'te•lar'y** (-lĕr'ē) *adj.*

tu•tor (t/y/ōō'tər) *n.* **1.** A private instructor. **2.** *Law.* The guardian of a minor and his property. *—v.* To act as a tutor to. [< L *tūtor,* a guardian, tutor.] **—tu•to'ri•al** (-tôr'ē-əl, -tōr'ē-əl) *adj.*

tut•ti-frut•ti (tōō'tē-frōō'tē) *n.* A confection, esp. ice cream, containing a variety of chopped candied fruits. [It, "all fruits."]

tux•e•do (tŭk-sē'dō) *n., pl.* **-dos.** A man's suit, usually black, designed to be worn for semiformal occasions. [< *Tuxedo* Park, New York.]

TV television.

TVA Tennessee Valley Authority.

twad•dle (twŏd'l) *n.* Foolish, trivial, or idle talk. [Prob < Scand.] **—twad'dle** *v.* **(-dled, -dling). —twad'dler** *n.*

twain (twān) *n. Poetic.* A set of two. [< OE *twēgen,* two. See **dwō.**]

twang (twăng) *v.* **1.** To emit or cause to emit a sharp, vibrating sound, as the string of a musical instrument when plucked. **2.** To utter with a twang. *—n.* **1.** A sharp, vibrating sound, as that of a plucked string. **2.** An excessively nasal tone of voice. [Imit.] **—twang'y** *adj.*

tweak (twēk) *v.* To pinch or twist sharply. [Prob < OE *twiccian* < Gmc **twik-.*] **—tweak** *n.* **—tweak'y** *adj.*

tweed (twēd) *n.* **1.** A rough-textured woolen fabric made in any of various twill weaves. **2. tweeds.** Clothing made of this fabric. [< TWILL.] **—tweed'y** *adj.*

tweet (twēt) *n.* A chirping sound, as of a small bird. [Imit.] **—tweet** *v.*

tweet•er (twē'tər) *n.* A loud-speaker designed to reproduce high-pitched sounds in a high-fidelity audio system.

tweez•ers (twē'zərz) *pl.n.* Any small, usually metal, pincerlike tool used for plucking or handling small objects. [Orig "a set or case of small instruments."]

twelfth (twĕlfth) *n.* **1.** The ordinal number 12

in a series. **2.** One of 12 equal parts. **—twelfth** *adj. & adv.*

twelve (twĕlv) *n.* The cardinal number written 12 or in Roman numerals XII. [< OE *twelf.* See **dwō.**] **—twelve** *adj. & pron.*

twelve•month (twĕlv′mŭnth′) *n.* A year.

twen•ti•eth (twĕn′tē-ĭth) *n.* **1.** The ordinal number 20 in a series. **2.** One of 20 equal parts. **—twen′ti•eth** *adj. & adv.*

twen•ty (twĕn′tē) *n.* The cardinal number written 20 or in Roman numerals XX. [< OE *twēntig.* See **dwō.**] **—twen′ty** *adj. & pron.*

Twi (chwē, chē). Also **Tshi.** A language spoken in W Africa.

twice (twīs) *adv.* **1.** In two cases or on two occasions; two times. **2.** In doubled degree or amount. [< OE *twige, twiga,* twice. See **dwō.**]

twid•dle (twĭd′l) *v.* **-dled, -dling. 1.** To turn over or around idly or lightly. **2.** To trifle with something. [Prob a blend of TWIRL and FIDDLE.] **—twid′dler** *n.*

twig (twĭg) *n.* A small slender branch. [< OE *twigge.* See **dwō.**] **—twig′gy** *adj.*

twi•light (twī′līt′) *n.* **1.** The time interval during which the sun is at a small angle below the horizon. **2.** The illumination of the atmosphere during this interval, esp. after a sunset. **3.** A period or condition of decline. [ME, "light between (night and day)," half-light.]

twill (twĭl) *n.* A fabric with parallel diagonal ribs. [< OE *twilic,* "two-threaded."] **—twilled** *adj.*

twin (twĭn) *n.* **1.** One of two offspring born at the same birth. **2.** One of two identical or similar things. **3. Twins.** The constellation and sign of the zodiac Gemini. *—adj.* **1.** Born at the same birth. **2.** Being one of two identical or similar things. **3.** Consisting of two identical or similar parts. [< OE *getwinn.* See **dwō.**]

twine (twīn) *v.* **twined, twining. 1.** To twist together; intertwine. **2.** To form by twisting. **3.** To encircle or coil about. **4.** To go in a winding course; twist about. *—n.* A strong string or cord formed of two or more threads twisted together. [< OE *twīn,* a rope of two strands. See **dwō.**] **—twin′er** *n.*

twinge (twĭnj) *n.* A sharp and sudden physical, mental, or emotional pain. [< OE *twengan.* See **twengh-.**]

twin•kle (twĭng′kəl) *v.* **-kled, -kling. 1.** To shine with slight, intermittent gleams; sparkle. **2.** To be bright or sparkling: *Her eyes twinkle.* *—n.* **1.** A slight, intermittent gleam of light. **2.** A sparkle of delight in the eye. **3.** A brief interval; a twinkling. [< OE **twincan,* to wink < Gmc **twink-.*] **—twin′kler** *n.*

twin•kling (twĭng′klĭng) *n.* A brief interval; an instant.

twirl (twûrl) *v.* To rotate or revolve briskly; spin. [Poss a blend of TRILL or TWIST and WHIRL.] **—twirl** *n.*

twist (twĭst) *v.* **1.** To entwine (two or more threads) so as to produce a single strand. **2.** To coil (vines, rope, etc.) about something. **3. a.** To impart a coiling or spiral shape to. **b.** To assume a spiral shape. **4. a.** To turn or open by turning. **b.** To break by turning: *twist off a dead branch.* **5.** To wrench or sprain: *twist one's wrist.* **6.** To distort the intended meaning of. **7.** To move in a winding course. **8.** To rotate or revolve. *—n.* **1.** Something twisted or formed by winding. **2.** The act of twisting or condition of being twisted; a spin or twirl. **3.** A spiral curve or turn. **4.** A sprain or wrench, as of a muscle. **5.** An unexpected change in a process or a departure from a pattern. [< OE *-twist,* a rope.] **—twist′a•ble** *adj.* **—twist′er** *n.*

twit (twĭt) *v.* **twitted, twitting.** To taunt or tease, esp. for embarrassing mistakes or faults. [< OE *æt,* AT + *witan,* to reproach, ascribe to (see **weid-**).]

twitch (twĭch) *v.* To move or cause to move jerkily or spasmodically. *—n.* **1.** A sudden involuntary muscular movement: *a twitch in the eye.* **2.** A sudden pulling; a jerk. [ME *twicchen.*]

twit•ter (twĭt′ər) *v.* To make tremulous chirping sounds. *—n.* A tremulous chirping sound. [ME *twiteren.*] **—twit′ter•y** *adj.*

two (to͞o) *n.* The cardinal number written 2 or in Roman numerals II. **—in two.** So as to be in two separate units. [< OE *twā, tū.* See **dwō.**] **—two** *adj. & pron.*

two-faced (to͞o′fāst′) *adj.* **1.** Having two faces or surfaces. **2.** Hypocritical or double-dealing; deceitful.

two-ply (to͞o′plī′) *adj.* **1.** Made of two interwoven layers. **2.** Consisting of two thicknesses or strands: *two-ply yarn.*

two•some (to͞o′səm) *n.* Two people together; a pair or couple; a duo.

two-way (to͞o′wā′) *adj.* **1.** Affording passage in two directions. **2.** Permitting communication in two directions, as a radio. **3.** Involving mutual action or responsibility.

-ty¹. *comb. form.* A condition or quality: **reality.** [< L *-tās.*]

-ty². *comb. form.* A multiple of ten: **sixty.** [< OE *-tig.*]

ty•coon (tī-ko͞on′) *n.* A wealthy and powerful businessman or industrialist; magnate. [Jap *taikun,* a military title.]

tyke (tīk) *n.* A small child, esp. a mischievous one. [< ON *tīk,* a bitch.]

Ty•ler (tī′lər), **John.** 1790–1862. 10th President of the U.S. (1841–45).

John Tyler

tym•pa•ni. Variant of **timpani.**

tym•pan•ic membrane (tĭm-păn′ĭk). The thin, semitransparent, oval-shaped membrane separating the middle ear from the external ear.

tym•pa•num (tĭm′pə-nəm) *n., pl.* **-na** (-nə) or **-nums.** Also **tim•pa•num.** The eardrum or the middle part of the ear that the eardrum separates from the outer part. [< Gk *tumpanon,* a drum.]

tym•pa•ny (tĭm′pə-nē) *n.* Variant of **timpani.**

typ. typographer; typographical.

type (tīp) *n.* **1.** A group or category of persons or things sharing common traits or characteristics that distinguish them as an identifiable class. **2.** One belonging to such a group or category. **3.** An example or model; embodiment. **4. a.** A small block of metal bearing a raised character that when inked and pressed upon paper leaves a printed impression. **b.** Such pieces collectively. **5.** Printed or typewritten characters; print. *—v.* **typed, typing. 1.** To typewrite. **2.** To classify according to a particular type. **3.** To represent or typify. [< Gk *tupos,* a blow, impression.]

Usage: Type (noun) is followed by *of* in constructions such as *that type of leather.* The variant form omitting *of, that type leather,* is not standard usage.

-type. *comb. form.* **1.** Type or representative form: **prototype. 2.** Stamping or printing type or photographic process: **Linotype.**

type•face (tīp′fās′) *n. Ptg.* The size and style of the characters on type.

type foundry. A factory where type metal is cast. **—type founder.**

type•set•ter (tīp′sĕt′ər) *n.* **1.** One who sets type; compositor. **2.** A machine used for setting type. **—type′set′ting** *n.*

type•write (tīp′rīt′) *v.* To write (something) with a typewriter; type.

type•writ•er (tīp′rī′tər) *n.* A manually operated keyboard machine that prints characters by means of a set of metal hammers bearing raised, inked type that strike the paper.

ty•phoid (tī′foid′) *n.* An acute, highly infectious disease caused by a bacillus transmitted by contaminated food or water and characterized by red rashes, high fever, bronchitis, and intestinal hemorrhaging.

ty•phoon (tī-fo͞on′) *n.* A severe tropical hurricane occurring in the western Pacific or the China Sea. [Cant *tai fung,* "great wind."]

ty•phus (tī′fəs) *n.* Any of several forms of an infectious disease caused by microorganisms and characterized generally by severe headache, sustained high fever, depression, delirium, and red rashes. [< Gk *tuphos,* (fever-causing) delusion.] **—ty′phous** (-fəs) *adj.*

typ•i•cal (tĭp′ĭ-kəl) *adj.* **1.** Exhibiting the traits or characteristics peculiar to a kind, group, or category. **2.** Pertaining to a representative specimen; characteristic. **3.** Constituting or serving as a type. [< Gk *tupikos,* impressionable < *tupos,* impression, TYPE.] **—typ′i•cal•ly** *adv.* **—typ′i•cal•ness** *n.*

typ•i•fy (tĭp′ə-fī′) *v.* **-fied, -fying. 1.** To serve as a typical example of. **2.** To represent by an image, form, or model; symbolize. **—typ′i•fi•ca′tion** *n.* **—typ′i•fi′er** *n.*

typ•ist (tī′pĭst) *n.* One who operates a typewriter.

typo., typog. typographer; typographical; typography.

ty•pog•ra•pher (tī-pŏg′rə-fər) *n.* A printer or compositor.

typographical error. A mistake in printing, typing, or writing.

ty•pog•ra•phy (tī-pŏg′rə-fē) *n.* **1.** The composition of printed material from movable type. **2.** The arrangement and appearance of such matter. **—ty′po•graph′i•cal** (tī′pə-grăf′ĭ-kəl), **ty′po•graph′ic** *adj.*

ty•ran•ni•cal (tĭ-răn′ĭ-kəl, tī-) *adj.* Also **ty•ran•nic** (-răn′ĭk). Of, pertaining to, or characteristic of a tyrant; despotic. **—ty•ran′ni•cal•ly** *adv.* **—ty•ran′ni•cal•ness** *n.*

tyr•an•nize (tĭr′ə-nīz′) *v.* **-nized, -nizing. 1.** To rule as a tyrant. **2.** To treat tyrannically. **—tyr′an•niz′er** *n.*

ty•ran•no•saur (tĭ-răn′ə-sôr′, tī-) *n.* Also **ty•ran•no•saur•us** (tĭ-răn′ə-sôr′əs, tī-). A carnivorous dinosaur with small forelimbs and a large head. [< Gk *turannos,* TYRANT + -SAUR.]

tyr•an•nous (tĭr′ə-nəs) *adj.* Characterized by tyranny; despotic; cruel; tyrannical. —**tyr′an•nous•ly** *adv.*

tyr•an•ny (tĭr′ə-nē) *n., pl.* **-nies. 1.** A government in which a single ruler is vested with absolute power. **2.** Absolute power, esp. when exercised unjustly or cruelly. **3.** A tyrannical act.

ty•rant (tī′rənt) *n.* **1.** A ruler who exercises power in a harsh, cruel manner; an oppressor. **2.** Any tyrannical or despotic person. [< Gk *turannos.*]

tyre. *Brit.* Variant of **tire²**.

Tyre (tīr). The capital of ancient Phoenicia.

ty•ro (tī′rō) *n., pl.* **-ros.** An inexperienced person; a beginner. [< L *tīrō,* a young soldier, recruit.]

tzar. Variant of **czar.**

Uu

u, U (yo͞o) *n.* **1.** The 21st letter of the English alphabet. **2. U** Anything shaped like the letter **U.**

U uranium.

U. 1. university. **2.** upper.

UAR United Arab Republic.

UAW United Automobile Workers.

u•biq•ui•tous (yo͞o-bĭk′wə-təs) *adj.* Being or seeming to be everywhere at the same time. [< L *ubīque,* everywhere.] —**u•biq′ui•tous•ly** *adv.* —**u•biq′ui•ty** *n.*

ud•der (ŭd′ər) *n.* The baglike mammary organ of cows, sheep, and goats. [< OE *ūder.* See **eudh-.**]

UFO unidentified flying object.

U•gan•da (yo͞o-găn′də, o͞o-gän′dä). A country in east-central Africa. Pop. 7,190,000. Cap. Kampala.

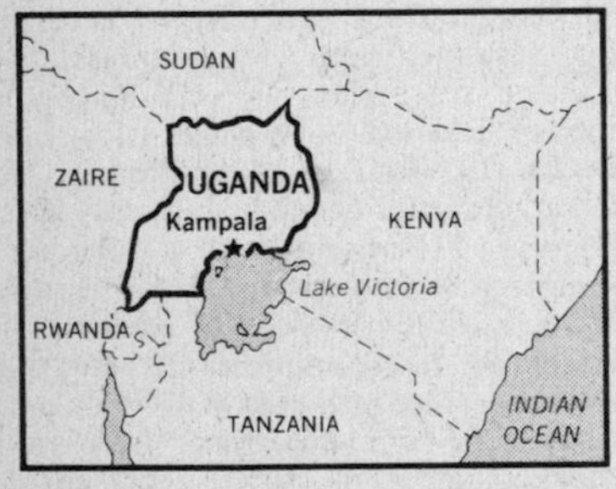

Uganda

ug•ly (ŭg′lē) *adj.* **-lier, -liest. 1.** Displeasing to the eye; unsightly. **2.** Repulsive or offensive in any way; objectionable. [< ON *uggr,* fear.] —**ug′li•ness** *n.*

U•gric (/y/o͞o′grĭk) *n.* A branch of Finno-Ugric, including Hungarian. —**U′gric** *adj.*

uhf ultrahigh frequency.

U.K. United Kingdom.

u•kase (yo͞o-kās′, -kāz′, yo͞o′kās′, -kāz′) *n.* **1.** A decree of the czar in imperial Russia. **2.** Any authoritative decree; an edict. [< Russ *ukaz,* decree.]

U•krain•i•an (yo͞o-krā′nē-ən) *n.* **1.** An inhabitant or native of the Ukraine. **2.** A Slavic language of the Ukraine, similar to but distinct from Russian. —**U•krain′i•an** *adj.*

Ukrainian Soviet Socialist Republic. Also **U•kraine** (yo͞o-krān′, yo͞o-krīn′, yo͞o′krān). A republic of the SW Soviet Union. Pop. 47,136,000. Cap. Kiev.

u•ku•le•le (/y/o͞o′kə-lā′lē) *n.* A small four-stringed guitar popularized in Hawaii. [Hawaiian *'ukulele,* "jumping little flea."]

U•lan Ba•tor (o͞o′län bä′tôr). The capital of the Mongolian People's Republic. Pop. 250,000.

–ular. *comb. form.* A relationship or resemblance: **tubular.** [< L *-ulus.*]

ul•cer (ŭl′sər) *n.* An inflammatory lesion on the skin or an internal mucous surface of the body. [< L *ulcus (ulcer-),* a sore, ulcer.]

ul•cer•ate (ŭl′sə-rāt′) *v.* **-ated, -ating.** To affect or become affected with or as with an ulcer. —**ul′cer•a′tive** (ŭl′sə-rā′tĭv, ŭl′sər-ə-tĭv), **ul′cer•ous** *adj.*

ul•na (ŭl′nə) *n., pl.* **-nae** (-nē′) or **-nas.** The bone extending from the elbow to the wrist on the side opposite the thumb. [< L, elbow, arm.] —**ul′nar** *adj.*

ul•ster (ŭl′stər) *n.* A loose, long overcoat. [< *Ulster,* province of the Republic of Ireland.]

ult. 1. ultimate; ultimately. **2.** ultimo.

ul•te•ri•or (ŭl′tîr′ē-ər) *adj.* **1.** Lying beyond or outside the area of immediate interest. **2.** Lying beyond what is evident or avowed: *an ulterior motive.* **3.** Occurring later; subsequent. [L, farther.] —**ul′te′ri•or•ly** *adv.*

ul•ti•mate (ŭl′tə-mĭt) *adj.* **1.** Final; conclusive. **2.** Representing the furthest possible extent of analysis or division into parts: *ultimate particle.* **3.** Fundamental; elemental. **4.** Maximum. **5.** Farthest; most remote. —*n.* **1.** The basic or fundamental fact. **2.** A conclusive result; conclusion. **3.** The maximum. [< L *ultimus,* farthest, last.] —**ul′ti•mate•ly** *adv.*

ul•ti•ma•tum (ŭl′tə-mā′təm, -mä′təm) *n., pl.* **-tums** or **-ta** (-tə). A statement of terms that expresses or implies the threat of serious penalties if the terms are not accepted. [< L *ultimātus,* last.]

ul•ti•mo (ŭl′tə-mō′) *adv.* In or of the month before the present one. [L *ultimo (mense),* in last (month).]

ul•tra (ŭl′trə) *adj.* Extreme. —*n.* An extremist.

ultra–. *comb. form.* **1.** A surpassing of a specified limit or range. **2.** An exceeding of what is common, moderate, or proper. [< L *ultrā,* beyond.]

ul•tra•con•ser•va•tive (ŭl′trə-kən-sûr′və-tĭv) *adj.* Extremely conservative; reactionary. —**ul′tra•con•ser′va•tive** *n.*

ul•tra•high frequency (ŭl′trə-hī′). A band of radio frequencies from 300 to 3,000 megacycles per second.

ul•tra•ma•rine (ŭl′trə-mə-rēn′) *n.* **1.** A blue pigment. **2.** Vivid or strong blue to purplish blue. [ML *ultrāmarīnus,* "(coming from) beyond the sea."]

ul•tra•mod•ern (ŭl′trə-mŏd′ərn) *adj.* Extremely modern in style.

ul•tra•son•ic (ŭl′trə-sŏn′ĭk) *adj.* Pertaining to acoustic frequencies above the range audible to the human ear, approx. above 20,000 cycles per second.

ul•tra•vi•o•let (ŭl′trə-vī′ə-lĭt) *adj.* Pertaining to the range of radiation wavelengths from just beyond the violet in the visible spectrum to the border of the x-ray region. —**ul′tra•vi′o•let** *n.*

ul•u•late (ŭl′yə-lāt′, yo͞ol′-) *v.* **-lated, -lating.** To howl, hoot, wail, or lament loudly. [L *ululāre,* to howl.] —**ul′u•la′tion** *n.*

U•lys•ses. Latin name for **Odysseus.**

um•bel (ŭm′bəl) *n.* A flat-topped or rounded flower cluster in which the individual flower stalks arise from about the same point. [< L *umbella,* an umbrella.]

um•ber (ŭm′bər) *n.* **1.** A natural brown earth composed of iron oxide, silica, alumina, lime, and manganese oxides and used as pigment. **2.** Any of the shades of brown produced by umber in its various states. —*adj.* Having a brownish hue. [< OF *terre d'Umbre,* "earth of Umbria."]

um•bil•i•cal (ŭm′bĭl′ĭ-kəl) *adj.* **1.** Of or resembling an umbilicus. **2.** Pertaining to or located near the central area of the abdomen.

umbilical cord. The flexible, cordlike structure connecting the fetus at the navel with the placenta and containing two arteries and one vein that nourish the fetus and remove its wastes.

um•bil•i•cus (ŭm′bĭl′ĭ-kəs, ŭm′bə-lī′kəs) *n.* The navel. [L *umbilīcus.*]

um•bra (ŭm′brə) *n., pl.* **-brae** (-brē). **1.** A dark area; specifically, the blackest part of a shadow from which all light is cut off. **2.** The shadow region over an area of the earth where a solar eclipse is total. [L *umbra,* shadow.]

um•brage (ŭm′brĭj) *n.* **1.** Offense: *take umbrage.* **2.** *Archaic.* Shade or foliage. [< L *umbrāticus,* of a shadow.]

um•brel•la (ŭm′brĕl′ə) *n.* A device for protection from the weather consisting of a collapsible canopy mounted on a central rod. [< L *umbra,* shade.]

Um•bri•a (ŭm′brē-ə). A region of C Italy.

Um•bri•an (ŭm′brē-ən) *n.* **1.** An inhabitant or native of ancient or modern Umbria. **2.** The extinct Italic language of ancient Umbria. —**Um′bri•an** *adj.*

u•mi•ak (o͞o′mē-ăk′) *n.* Also **oo•mi•ak.** An open Eskimo boat made of skins stretched on a wooden frame.

um•laut (o͝om′lout′) *n. Ling.* **1.** A change in a vowel sound caused by partial assimilation to a vowel or semivowel originally occurring in the following syllable. **2.** A vowel sound changed in this manner, such as the German *ä, ö,* or *ü.* **3.** The diacritical mark (¨) placed over a vowel to indicate an umlaut. [G.]

um•pire (ŭm'pīr') *n.* **1.** A person appointed to rule on plays in various sports. **2.** A person empowered to settle a dispute. **3.** A judge. [< ME *(a) noumpere,* (an) umpire.] **—um'pire'** *v.* **(-pired, -piring).**

ump•teen (ŭmp-tēn', ŭm-) *adj. Informal.* Large but indefinite in number. **—ump•teenth'** *adj.*

UMW United Mine Workers.

un-¹. *comb. form.* Not or contrary to. [< OE *un-.* See **ne.**]

un-². *comb. form.* **1.** Reversal of an action. **2.** Deprivation. **3.** Release or removal from. **4.** Intensified action. [< OE *ond-, and-,* against. See **anti.**]

UN United Nations.

un•a•ble (ŭn-ā'bəl) *adj.* **1.** Not able; incapable. **2.** Incompetent.

un•a•bridged (ŭn'ə-brĭjd') *adj.* Not condensed: *an unabridged edition.*

un•ac•com•pa•nied (ŭn'ə-kŭm'pə-nēd) *adj.* Not accompanied, esp. without instrumental accompaniment.

un•ac•count•a•ble (ŭn'ə-koun'tə-bəl) *adj.* **1.** Inexplicable; mysterious. **2.** Not responsible. **—un'ac•count'a•bly** *adv.*

un•ac•cus•tomed (ŭn'ə-kŭs'təmd) *adj.* **1.** Not used to. **2.** Unfamiliar or unusual.

un•a•dorned (ŭn'ə-dôrnd') *adj.* Without embellishment or artificiality; simple.

un•a•dul•ter•at•ed (ŭn'ə-dŭl'tə-rā'tĭd) *adj.* Not mixed or diluted; pure.

un•ad•vised (ŭn'əd-vīzd') *adj.* **1.** Having received no advice. **2.** Ill-advised; rash; imprudent. **—un'ad•vis'ed•ly** (-vī'zĭd-lē) *adv.*

un•af•fect•ed (ŭn'ə-fĕk'tĭd) *adj.* **1.** Not changed or affected. **2.** Natural; sincere; genuine. **—un'af•fect'ed•ly** *adv.*

un•al•ien•a•ble (ŭn-āl'yə-nə-bəl) *adj. Archaic.* Inalienable.

un-A•mer•i•can (ŭn'ə-mĕr'ĭ-kən) *adj.* Considered subversive to the institutions or interests of the U.S.

u•nan•i•mous (yo͞o-năn'ə-məs) *adj.* **1.** Sharing the same opinions or views. **2.** Based on complete assent or agreement. [L *ūnanimus,* "of one mind."] **—u'na•nim'i•ty** (-nə-nĭm'ə-tē) *n.* **—u•nan'i•mous•ly** *adv.*

un•armed (ŭn'ärmd') *adj.* Lacking weapons or armor.

un•as•sail•a•ble (ŭn'ə-sā'lə-bəl) *adj.* **1.** Undeniable; unquestionable. **2.** Impregnable. **—un'as•sail'a•bly** *adv.*

un•as•sum•ing (ŭn'ə-so͞o'mĭng) *adj.* Not pretentious; modest. **—un'as•sum'ing•ly** *adv.*

un•at•tached (ŭn'ə-tăcht') *adj.* **1.** Not attached. **2.** Not engaged or married.

un•at•test•ed (ŭn'ə-tĕs'tĭd) *adj.* Not attested.

un•a•void•a•ble (ŭn'ə-voi'də-bəl) *adj.* Not able to be avoided; inevitable. **—un'a•void'a•bil'i•ty** *n.* **—un'a•void'a•bly** *adv.*

un•a•ware (ŭn'ə-wâr') *adj.* Not aware or cognizant.

un•a•wares (ŭn'ə-wârz') *adv.* **1.** By surprise; unexpectedly. **2.** Without forethought or plan.

un•bal•anced (ŭn'băl'ənst) *adj.* **1.** Not in proper balance. **2. a.** Mentally deranged. **b.** Not of sound judgment; irrational. **3.** Not adjusted so that debit and credit correspond.

un•bar (ŭn'bär') *v.* **-barred, -barring.** To open.

un•bear•a•ble (ŭn'bâr'ə-bəl) *adj.* Unendurable; intolerable. **—un'bear'a•bly** *adv.*

un•beat•a•ble (ŭn'bē'tə-bəl) *adj.* Impossible to surpass or defeat. **—un'beat'a•bly** *adv.*

un•beat•en (ŭn'bēt'n) *adj.* **1.** Undefeated. **2.** Not traversed; untrod. **3.** Not beaten or pounded.

un•be•com•ing (ŭn'bĭ-kŭm'ĭng) *adj.* **1.** Not appropriate or attractive. **2.** Not seemly; indecorous. **—un'be•com'ing•ly** *adv.*

un•be•known (ŭn'bĭ-nōn') *adj.* Occurring or existing without the knowledge of; unknown.

un•be•lief (ŭn'bĭ-lēf') *n.* Lack of religious belief. **—un'be•liev'er** *n.*

un•be•liev•a•ble (ŭn'bĭ-lē'və-bəl) *adj.* Not to be believed; incredible. **—un'be•liev'a•bly** *adv.*

un•bend (ŭn'bĕnd') *v.* **1.** To release from tension. **2.** *Naut.* To untie or loosen. **3.** To make or become less tense.

un•bend•ing (ŭn'bĕn'dĭng) *adj.* Resolute; uncompromising.

un•bi•ased (ŭn'bī'əst) *adj.* Without bias; impartial. **—un'bi'ased•ly** *adv.*

un•bid•den (ŭn'bĭd'n) *adj.* Not invited.

un•bind (ŭn'bīnd') *v.* **1.** To untie or unfasten. **2.** To release.

un•blessed (ŭn'blĕst') *adj.* **1.** Not blessed. **2.** Unholy; evil.

un•blush•ing (ŭn'blŭsh'ĭng) *adj.* **1.** Without shame or remorse. **2.** Not blushing.

un•bolt (ŭn'bōlt') *v.* To release the bolts of (a door or gate); unlock.

un•born (ŭn'bôrn') *adj.* Not yet born.

un•bos•om (ŭn'bo͝oz'əm, -bo͞o'zəm) *v.* **1.** To confide or disclose. **2.** To reveal one's thoughts or feelings.

un•bound•ed (ŭn'boun'dĭd) *adj.* Having no limits. **—un'bound'ed•ly** *adv.*

un•bowed (ŭn'boud') *adj.* **1.** Not bowed. **2.** Not subdued.

un•bri•dled (ŭn'brī'dəld) *adj.* **1.** Not fitted with a bridle. **2.** Unrestrained; uncontrolled. **—un'bri'dled•ly** *adv.*

un•bro•ken (ŭn'brō'kən) *adj.* **1.** Not broken; intact. **2.** Not violated or breached. **3.** Uninterrupted; continuous. **4.** Not tamed or broken to harness.

un•buck•le (ŭn'bŭk'əl) *v.* To loosen or undo the buckle of.

un•bur•den (ŭn'bûrd'n) *v.* To free or relieve, as from a burden: *unburden one's mind.*

un•but•ton (ŭn'bŭt'n) *v.* To unfasten the buttons of.

un•can•ny (ŭn'kăn'ē) *adj.* **-nier, -niest. 1.** Inexplicable; strange. **2.** So keen as to seem preternatural: *uncanny insight.* **—un'can'ni•ly** *adv.*

un•cap (ŭn'kăp') *v.* To remove the cap or covering of.

un•ceas•ing (ŭn'sē'sĭng) *adj.* Continuous. **—un'ceas'ing•ly** *adv.*

un•cer•e•mo•ni•ous (ŭn'sĕr'ə-mō'nē-əs) *adj.* Without the due formalities; abrupt. **—un'cer'e•mo'ni•ous•ly** *adv.*

un•cer•tain (ŭn'sûrt'n) *adj.* **1.** Not known or established. **2.** Vague; undecided. **3.** Subject to change; variable. **4.** Unsteady; fitful. **5.** Not sure. **—un'cer'tain•ly** *adv.*

un•cer•tain•ty (ŭn'sûrt'n-tē) *n., pl.* **-ties. 1.** Lack of certainty. **2.** Something that is uncertain.

un•chain (ŭn'chān') *v.* To set free.

un•char•i•ta•ble (ŭn'chăr'ə-tə-bəl) *adj.* Not

Note: Many compounds are formed with *un-*. Normally *un-* combines with a second element without an intervening hyphen. However, if the second element begins with a capital letter, it is separated with a hyphen: *un-American.*

un'ac•cept'a•ble *adj.*
un'ac•quaint'ed *adj.*
un'a•fraid' *adj.*
un'aid'ed *adj.*
un'an•nounced' *adj.*
un'a•shamed' *adj.*
un'au'thor•ized' *adj.*
un'bap'tized *adj.*
un'bleached' *adj.*
un'break'a•ble *adj.*
un'called'-for *adj.*
un'cared'-for *adj.*
un'chal'lenged *adj.*
un'checked' *adj.*
un'claimed' *adj.*
un'clear' *adj.*
un'clut'tered *adj.*
un'con•test'ed *adj.*
un'con•vinced' *adj.*
un'cov'ered *adj.*
un'dam'aged *adj.*
un'damped' *adj.*
un'de•fined' *adj.*
un'de•vel'oped *adj.*
un'dig'ni•fied' *adj.*
un'ed'u•cat'ed *adj.*
un'e•mo'tion•al *adj.*
un'end'ing *adj.*
un'fal'ter•ing *adj.*
un'fath'omed *adj.*
un'fin'ished *adj.*
un'flag'ging *adj.*
un'fore•seen' *adj.*
un'for•giv'a•ble *adj.*
un'grace'ful *adj.*
un'ham'pered *adj.*
un'harmed' *adj.*
un'heat'ed *adj.*
un'i•den'ti•fied' *adj.*
un'im•por'tant *adj.*
un'in•sured' *adj.*
un'in•vit'ed *adj.*
un'la'beled *adj.*
un'leav'ened *adj.*
un'li'censed *adj.*
un'list'ed *adj.*
un'loved' *adj.*
un'marked' *adj.*
un'mar'ried *adj.*
un'mer'it•ed *adj.*
un'named' *adj.*
un'no'ticed *adj.*
un'num'bered *adj.*
un'ob•struct'ed *adj.*
un'o'pened *adj.*
un'par'don•a•ble *adj.*
un'pa'tri•ot'ic *adj.*
un'pol'ished *adj.*
un'polled' *adj.*
un'pol•lut'ed *adj.*
un'prej'u•diced *adj.*
un'pressed' *adj.*
un'proc'essed *adj.*
un'pro•tect'ed *adj.*
un'prov'en *adj.*
un'pro•voked' *adj.*
un'pub'lished *adj.*
un'ques'tion•ing *adj.*
un'rea'son•ing *adj.*
un're•cord'ed *adj.*
un'reg'is•tered *adj.*
un're•port'ed *adj.*
un're•quit'ed *adj.*
un'ro•man'tic *adj.*
un'salt'ed *adj.*
un'san'i•tar'y *adj.*
un'sat'u•rat'ed *adj.*
un'sched'uled *adj.*
un'sea'soned *adj.*
un'shaved' *adj.*
un'signed' *adj.*
un'sink'a•ble *adj.*
un'so•lic'it•ed *adj.*
un'spoiled' *adj.*
un'suit'ed *adj.*
un'sure' *adj.*
un'sus•pect'ing *adj.*
un'tal'ent•ed *adj.*
un'trained' *adj.*
un'tried' *adj.*
un'var'y•ing *adj.*
un'want'ed *adj.*
un'wed' *adj.*
un'wel'come *adj.*
un'yield'ing *adj.*

ô paw, for/oi boy/ou out/o͝o took/o͞o coo/p pop/r run/s sauce/sh shy/t to/th thin/*th* the/
ŭ cut/ûr fur/v van/w wag/y yes/z size/zh vision/ə ago, item, edible, gallop, circus/

generous; unkind. —un'char'i•ta•ble•ness *n.* —un'char'i•ta•bly *adv.*

un•chaste (ŭn'chāst') *adj.* Not chaste or modest. —un'chaste'ly *adv.*

un•chris•tian (ŭn'krĭs'chən) *adj.* 1. Not Christian. 2. Not in accordance with the Christian spirit.

un•cial (ŭn'shəl, -shē-əl) *adj.* Of or pertaining to a script with rounded capital letters found in Greek and Latin manuscripts of the 4th to the 8th centuries A.D. [LL *unciāles (litterae),* "(letters) of an inch long."] —un'cial *n.*

un•cir•cum•cised (ŭn'sûr'kəm-sīzd') *adj.* 1. Not circumcised. 2. Not Jewish; Gentile.

un•civ•il (ŭn'sĭv'əl) *adj.* 1. Impolite; rude. 2. Uncivilized; barbarous. —un'civ'il•ly *adv.*

un•civ•i•lized (ŭn'sĭv'ə-līzd') *adj.* Not civilized.

un•clad (ŭn'klăd') *adj.* Naked.

un•clasp (ŭn'klăsp', -kläsp') *v.* 1. To release or loosen the clasp of. 2. To release from a clasp or embrace.

un•cle (ŭng'kəl) *n.* 1. The brother of one's mother or father. 2. The husband of one's aunt. —*interj. Slang.* Expressive of surrender: *They beat him until he cried uncle.* [< L *avunculus,* maternal uncle.]

un•clean (ŭn'klēn') *adj.* 1. Foul or dirty. 2. Morally defiled. 3. Ceremonially impure. —un'clean'ly (ŭn'klēn'lē) *adv.*

un•clean•ly (ŭn'klĕn'lē) *adj.* -lier, -liest. Unclean. —un'clean'li•ness (ŭn'klĕn'lē-nĭs) *n.*

un•clench (ŭn'klĕnch') *v.* To loosen from a clenched position; relax.

Uncle Sam. A personification of the U.S. Government, represented as a tall, thin man with a white beard, dressed in red, white, and blue. [< *U.S.* (for *U*nited *S*tates).]

un•close (ŭn'klōz') *v.* To open.

un•clothe (ŭn'klōth') *v.* To remove the clothing or cover from.

un•coil (ŭn'koil') *v.* To unwind.

un•com•fort•a•ble (ŭn'kŭmf'tə-bəl, -kŭm'fər-tə-bəl) *adj.* 1. Experiencing discomfort; uneasy. 2. Causing discomfort. —un'com'fort•a•ble•ness *n.* —un'com'fort•a•bly *adv.*

un•com•mit•ted (ŭn'kə-mĭt'ĭd) *adj.* Not pledged to a specific cause or course of action.

un•com•mon (ŭn'kŏm'ən) *adj.* 1. Not common; unusual; rare. 2. Wonderful; remarkable. —un'com'mon•ly *adv.*

un•com•mu•ni•ca•tive (ŭn'kə-myōō'nĭ-kā'tĭv, -nĭ-kə-tĭv) *adj.* Not disposed to be communicative; reserved.

un•com•pro•mis•ing (ŭn'kŏm'prə-mī'zĭng) *adj.* Not granting concessions; inflexible.

un•con•cern (ŭn'kən-sûrn') *n.* 1. Lack of interest; indifference. 2. Lack of worry or apprehensiveness.

un•con•cerned (ŭn'kən-sûrnd') *adj.* 1. Not interested; indifferent. 2. Not anxious or apprehensive; unworried. —un'con•cern'ed•ly (-kən-sûr'nĭd-lē) *adv.*

un•con•di•tion•al (ŭn'kən-dĭsh'ən-əl) *adj.* Without conditions or limitations; absolute. —un'con•di'tion•al•ly *adv.*

un•con•di•tioned (ŭn'kən-dĭsh'ənd) *adj.* 1. Unconditional; unrestricted. 2. Not the result of conditioning.

un•con•quer•a•ble (ŭn'kŏng'kər-ə-bəl) *adj.* Incapable of being overcome or defeated.

un•con•scion•a•ble (ŭn'kŏn'shən-ə-bəl) *adj.* 1. Not governed or restrained by conscience. 2. Unreasonable; immoderate; excessive. —un'con'scion•a•bly *adv.*

un•con•scious (ŭn'kŏn'shəs) *adj.* 1. Without conscious awareness, esp. psychological rather than physiological, and unavailable for direct conscious scrutiny. 2. Temporarily lacking consciousness. 3. Without conscious control; involuntary. —*n.* The division of the psyche not subject to direct conscious observation but inferred from its effects on conscious processes and behavior. —un'con'scious•ly *adv.* —un'con'scious•ness *n.*

un•con•sti•tu•tion•al (ŭn'kŏn-stə-t/y/ōō'-shən-əl) *adj.* Not in accord with the principles set forth in the constitution of a country. —un'con•sti•tu'tion•al'i•ty *n.* —un'con•sti•tu'tion•al•ly *adv.*

un•con•trol•la•ble (ŭn'kən-trō'lə-bəl) *adj.* Not able to be controlled or governed. —un'con•trol'la•bly *adv.*

un•con•ven•tion•al (ŭn'kən-vĕn'shən-əl) *adj.* Not adhering to convention. —un'con•ven'tion•al'i•ty *n.* —un'con•ven'tion•al•ly *adv.*

un•cork (ŭn'kôrk') *v.* 1. To draw the cork from. 2. To free from a constrained state.

un•count•ed (ŭn'koun'tĭd) *adj.* Unable to be counted; innumerable.

un•coup•le (ŭn'kŭp'əl) *v.* To disconnect: *uncouple railroad cars.*

un•couth (ŭn'kōōth') *adj.* 1. Crude or unrefined. 2. Awkward or ungraceful. [< OE *un-,* not + *cūth,* known (see **gnō-**).]

un•cov•er (ŭn'kŭv'ər) *v.* 1. To remove the cover from. 2. To disclose; reveal. 3. To bare (the head) in respect or reverence.

un•cross (ŭn'krôs', -krŏs') *v.* To move (one's legs) from a crossed position.

unc•tion (ŭngk'shən) *n.* 1. The act of anointing as part of a ceremonial or healing ritual. 2. An ointment or oil; salve. 3. Something that serves to soothe or restore; balm. 4. Affected or exaggerated earnestness. [< L *unguere,* to anoint.]

unc•tu•ous (ŭngk'chōō-əs) *adj.* 1. Greasy. 2. Containing or composed of oil or fat. 3. Characterized by affected or insincere earnestness: *unctuous flattery.* [< L *unctum,* ointment.] —unc'tu•ous•ly *adv.* —unc'tu•ous•ness, unc'tu•os'i•ty (-ŏs'ə-tē) *n.*

un•cut (ŭn'kŭt') *adj.* 1. Not cut. 2. *Bookbinding.* Having the page edge not slit or trimmed. 3. Not ground to a specific shape: *uncut diamonds.* 4. Unabridged.

un•daunt•ed (ŭn'dôn'tĭd, -dän'tĭd) *adj.* Not discouraged or disheartened; resolute; fearless. —un'daunt'ed•ly *adv.*

un•de•cid•ed (ŭn'dĭ-sī'dĭd) *adj.* 1. Not yet determined or settled; open. 2. Not having reached a decision; uncommitted.

un•de•mon•stra•tive (ŭn'dĭ-mŏn'strə-tĭv) *adj.* Not disposed to expressions of feeling; reserved. —un'de•mon'stra•tive•ness *n.*

un•de•ni•a•ble (ŭn'dĭ-nī'ə-bəl) *adj.* 1. Not able to be denied; irrefutable. 2. Unquestionably good; excellent. —un'de•ni'a•bly *adv.*

un•der (ŭn'dər) *prep.* 1. In a lower position or place than. 2. Beneath the surface of. 3. Beneath the guise of: *under a false name.* 4. Less than; smaller than. 5. Less than the required amount or degree of: *under voting age.* 6. Inferior to. 7. Subject to the authority of. 8. Undergoing or receiving the effects of: *under intensive care.* 9. Subject to the obligation of: *under contract.* 10. Within the group or classification of: *listed under biology.* 11. In the process of: *under discussion.* 12. Because of: *under these conditions.* —*adv.* 1. In or into a place below or beneath. 2. In or into a subordinate or inferior condition or position. 3. So as to be covered or enveloped by. 4. So as to be less than the required amount or degree. —*adj.* 1. Located or moving on a lower level. 2. Lower in rank. 3. Substandard. 4. Lower in strength or intensity; held in restraint or check. [< OE. See **ṇdher-**.]

under–. *comb. form.* 1. Location below or under. 2. Inferiority in rank or importance. 3. Degree, rate, or quantity that is lower or less than normal or proper. 4. Secrecy or treachery.

un•der•a•chieve (ŭn'dər-ə-chēv') *v.* To perform below the expected level, as indicated by tests of intelligence, aptitude, or ability, esp. in school. —un'der•a•chiev'er *n.*

un•der•act (ŭn'dər-ăkt') *v.* To perform (a role) weakly or in an understated way.

un•der•age (ŭn'dər-āj') *adj.* Below the customary, required, or legal age.

un•der•arm¹ (ŭn'dər-ärm') *adj.* Located, placed, or used under the arm. —*n.* The armpit.

un•der•arm² (ŭn'dər-ärm') *adj.* Executed with the hand kept below the level of the shoulder; underhand: *an underarm pitch.*

un•der•bid (ŭn'dər-bĭd') *v.* 1. To bid lower than (a competitor). 2. *Bridge.* To bid less than the full value of (one's hand).

un•der•brush (ŭn'dər-brŭsh') *n.* Small trees, shrubs, etc., growing beneath taller trees.

un•der•car•riage (ŭn'dər-kăr'ĭj) *n.* 1. A supporting framework, as for the body of an automobile. 2. The landing gear of an aircraft.

un•der•charge (ŭn'dər-chärj') *v.* 1. To charge less than is customary or required. 2. To load (a firearm) with an insufficient charge. —*n.* (ŭn'dər-chärj'). An insufficient or improper charge.

un•der•class•man (ŭn'dər-klăs'mən, -kläs'-mən) *n.* A student in the freshman or sophomore class at a secondary school or college.

un•der•clothes (ŭn'dər-klōz', -klōthz') *pl.n.* Also **un•der•cloth•ing** (-klō'thĭng). Underwear.

un•der•coat (ŭn'dər-kōt') *n.* 1. A coat worn beneath another. 2. Short hairs or fur concealed by the longer outer hairs of an animal's coat. 3. A coat of sealing material applied to a surface before the top coat is applied.

un•der•cov•er (ŭn'dər-kŭv'ər) *adj.* Performed or occurring in secret.

un•der•cur•rent (ŭn'dər-kûr'ənt) *n.* 1. A current, as of air or water, below another current or surface. 2. An underlying tendency or force, often contrary to what is superficially evident.

un•der•cut (ŭn'dər-kŭt') *v.* 1. To make a cut under or below. 2. To sell at a lower price or work for lower wages than (a competitor). 3. *Sports.* a. To impart backspin to (a ball) by striking downward as well as forward, as in golf. b. To cut or slice (a ball) with an underarm stroke, as in tennis. —un'der•cut' *n.*

un•der•de•vel•oped (ŭn'dər-dĭ-vĕl'əpt) *adj.* 1. Not adequately or normally developed; immature. 2. Economically backward; having potential but not yet self-sufficient.

un•der•dog (ŭn'dər-dôg', -dŏg') *n.* 1. One who is expected to lose a contest or struggle. 2. One who is at a disadvantage.

un•der•done (ŭn'dər-dŭn') *adj.* Insufficiently cooked.

un•der•draw•ers (ŭn'dər-drôrz') *pl.n.* Shorts worn as undergarments; underpants.

un•der•es•ti•mate (ŭn'dər-ĕs'tə-māt') *v.* To estimate too low the quantity, degree, or worth of. —un'der•es'ti•ma'tion *n.*

un•der•ex•pose (ŭn'dər-ĭk-spōz') *v.* To expose (film) to light for too short a time. —un'der•ex•po'sure (-spō'zhər) *n.*

un•der•feed (ŭn'dər-fēd') *v.* To feed insufficiently.

un•der•foot (ŭn'dər-fo͝ot') *adv.* **1.** Below or under the foot or feet; directly below. **2.** In the way.

un•der•gar•ment (ŭn'dər-gär'mənt) *n.* A garment worn under outer garments.

un•der•gird (ŭn'dər-gûrd') *v.* To gird or support from beneath.

un•der•go (ŭn'dər-gō') *v.* **1.** To experience; be subjected to. **2.** To endure; suffer.

un•der•grad•u•ate (ŭn'dər-grăj'o͞o-ĭt) *n.* A college or university student who has not yet received a degree.

un•der•ground (ŭn'dər-ground') *adj.* **1.** Below the surface of the earth. **2.** Hidden; clandestine. *—n.* (ŭn'dər-ground'). **1.** A clandestine subversive organization. **2.** *Brit.* A subway system. *—adv.* (ŭn'dər-ground'). **1.** Below the surface of the earth. **2.** In secret; stealthily; furtively.

un•der•growth (ŭn'dər-grōth') *n.* Low-growing plants, shrubs, etc., beneath trees in a forest.

un•der•hand (ŭn'dər-hănd') *adj.* **1.** Deceitful; sneaky; base. **2.** Underarm. *—adv.* **1.** With an underhand movement. **2.** Slyly; secretly.

un•der•hand•ed (ŭn'dər-hăn'dĭd) *adj.* Underhand. **—un'der•hand'ed•ly** *adv.* **—un'der•hand'ed•ness** *n.*

un•der•lie (ŭn'dər-lī') *v.* **1.** To be located under or below. **2.** To be the support or basis of; account for.

un•der•line (ŭn'dər-līn', ŭn'dər-līn') *v.* **1.** To draw a line under; underscore. **2.** To emphasize. **—un'der•line'** *n.*

un•der•ling (ŭn'dər-lĭng) *n.* A subordinate; lackey.

un•der•ly•ing (ŭn'dər-lī'ĭng) *adj.* **1.** Lying under or beneath something. **2.** Basic; fundamental. **3.** Implicit; hidden.

un•der•mine (ŭn'dər-mīn') *v.* **1.** To dig a mine or tunnel beneath. **2.** To weaken by wearing away; subvert.

un•der•most (ŭn'dər-mōst') *adj.* Lowest in position, rank, or place. *—adv.* Lowest.

un•der•neath (ŭn'dər-nēth') *adv.* **1.** In a place beneath; below. **2.** On the lower face or underside. *—prep.* **1.** Under; below; beneath. **2.** Under the power or control of. *—adj.* Lower; under. *—n.* The part or side below or under. [< UNDER + OE *neothan,* below (see **ni**).]

un•der•nour•ish (ŭn'dər-nûr'ĭsh) *v.* To provide with insufficient nourishment. **—un'der•nour'ish•ment** *n.*

un•der•pants (ŭn'dər-pănts') *pl.n.* An undergarment worn over the loins; drawers; shorts.

un•der•pass (ŭn'dər-păs', -päs') *n.* A section of road that passes under another road or a railroad.

un•der•pay (ŭn'dər-pā') *v.* To pay insufficiently.

un•der•play (ŭn'dər-plā', ŭn'dər-plā') *v.* To act (a role) subtly or with restraint.

un•der•priv•i•leged (ŭn'dər-prĭv'ə-lĭjd) *adj.* Socially or economically deprived.

un•der•pro•duc•tion (ŭn'dər-prə-dŭk'shən) *n.* **1.** Production below full capacity. **2.** Production below demand.

un•der•rate (ŭn'dər-rāt') *v.* To rate too low; underestimate.

un•der•score (ŭn'dər-skôr', -skōr') *v.* **1.** To underline. **2.** To emphasize or stress. **—un'der•score'** *n.*

un•der•sea (ŭn'dər-sē') *adj.* Pertaining to, existing, or created for use beneath the surface of the sea.

un•der•sec•re•tar•y (ŭn'dər-sĕk'rə-tĕr'ē) *n.* An official directly subordinate to a Cabinet member.

un•der•sell (ŭn'dər-sĕl') *v.* To sell for a lower price than.

un•der•shirt (ŭn'dər-shûrt') *n.* An undergarment worn next to the skin under a shirt.

un•der•shot (ŭn'dər-shŏt') *adj.* **1.** Driven by water passing from below, as a water wheel. **2.** Projecting from below.

un•der•side (ŭn'dər-sīd') *n.* The side or surface that is underneath; bottom side.

un•der•signed (ŭn'dər-sīnd') *n.* The person or persons who have signed at the bottom of a document.

un•der•sized (ŭn'dər-sīzd') *adj.* Also **un•der•size** (-sīz'). Being of subnormal or insufficient size.

un•der•slung (ŭn'dər-slŭng') *adj.* Having springs attached to the axles from below, as a vehicle.

un•der•staffed (ŭn'dər-stăft') *adj.* Having too small a staff.

un•der•stand (ŭn'dər-stănd') *v.* **-stood, -stand•ing.** **1.** To perceive and comprehend the nature and significance of; know. **2.** To know thoroughly. **3.** To grasp or comprehend. **4.** To be tolerant or sympathetic toward. **5.** To learn indirectly, as by hearsay; gather. **6.** To conclude; infer. **7.** To accept as an agreed fact: *It is understood that the fee is five dollars.* [< OE *understandan.* See **stā-**.] **—un'der•stand'a•ble** *adj.* **—un'der•stand'a•bly** *adv.*

un•der•stand•ing (ŭn'dər-stăn'dĭng) *n.* **1.** The quality of comprehension; discernment. **2.** The faculty by which one understands; intelligence. **3.** Individual or specified judgment or opinion; interpretation. **4. a.** A compact implicit between two or more persons or groups. **b.** The matter implicit in such a compact. **5.** A reconciliation of differences. *—adj.* **1.** Characterized by comprehension or good sense. **2.** Compassionate and sympathetic.

un•der•state (ŭn'dər-stāt') *v.* **1.** To state with less completeness or truth than seems warranted by the facts. **2.** To express with restraint or lack of emphasis. **3.** To state (a number, quantity, etc.) that is too low. **—un'der•state'ment** *n.*

un•der•stood (ŭn'dər-sto͝od') *adj.* **1.** Agreed upon. **2.** Not expressed in writing; implied.

un•der•stud•y (ŭn'dər-stŭd'ē) *v.* **1.** To study or know (a role) so as to be able to replace the regular actor. **2.** To act as an understudy to. *—n., pl.* **-ies.** An actor trained to do the work of another.

un•der•take (ŭn'dər-tāk') *v.* **1.** To take upon oneself; decide or agree to do. **2.** To pledge or commit oneself.

un•der•tak•er (ŭn'dər-tā'kər) *n.* One whose business it is to arrange for the burial or cremation of the dead.

un•der•tak•ing (ŭn'dər-tā'kĭng) *n.* **1.** An enterprise or venture. **2.** A guaranty, engagement, or promise. **3.** The occupation of an undertaker.

un•der-the-count•er (ŭn'dər-*th*ə-koun'tər) *adj.* Transacted or sold illicitly.

un•der•tone (ŭn'dər-tōn') *n.* **1.** A speech tone of low pitch or volume. **2.** A pale or subdued color. **3.** An implied tendency or meaning; undercurrent.

un•der•tow (ŭn'dər-tō') *n.* The seaward pull of receding waves breaking on a shore.

un•der•val•ue (ŭn'dər-văl'yo͞o) *v.* **1.** To assign too low a value to; underestimate. **2.** To have too little regard or esteem for.

un•der•wa•ter (ŭn'dər-wô'tər, -wŏt'ər) *adj.* Occurring, used, or performed beneath the surface of water. **—un'der•wa'ter** *adv.*

under way. 1. In motion or operation; started. **2.** Already in progress; afoot. **3.** Not anchored and not moored to a fixed object.

un•der•wear (ŭn'dər-wâr') *n.* Clothing worn under the outer clothes and next to the skin; underclothes.

un•der•weight (ŭn'dər-wāt') *adj.* Weighing less than is normal.

un•der•world (ŭn'dər-wûrld') *n.* **1.** The world of the dead, conceived to be below the surface of the earth. **2.** The part of society engaged in and organized for the purpose of crime and vice.

un•der•write (ŭn'dər-rīt') *v.* **1.** To subscribe, esp. to endorse (a document). **2.** To assume financial responsibility for (an enterprise). **3. a.** To sign an insurance policy, thus assuming liability in case of specified losses. **b.** To insure. **c.** To insure against losses totaling (a given amount). **4.** To agree to buy (the stock in a new enterprise not yet sold publicly) at a fixed time and price. **—un'der•writ'er** *n.*

un•de•sir•a•ble (ŭn'dĭ-zīr'ə-bəl) *adj.* Not desirable; objectionable.

un•dies (ŭn'dēz) *pl.n. Informal.* Underwear.

un•do (ŭn'do͞o') *v.* **1.** To reverse; cancel; annul. **2.** To untie or loosen. **3.** To open; unwrap. **4.** To ruin or destroy.

un•do•ing (ŭn'do͞o'ĭng) *n.* **1.** The act of reversing or annulling; cancellation. **2.** The act of unfastening or loosening. **3. a.** The act of bringing to ruin. **b.** The cause of ruin.

un•doubt•ed (ŭn'dou'tĭd) *adj.* Accepted as beyond question; undisputed. **—un•doubt'ed•ly** *adv.*

un•dress (ŭn'drĕs') *v.* To remove the clothing of; disrobe; strip. *—n.* **1.** Informal attire. **2.** Nakedness.

un•due (ŭn'd/y/o͞o') *adj.* **1.** Exceeding what is appropriate or normal; excessive. **2.** Not just, proper, or legal. **3.** Not yet payable or due.

un•du•lant (ŭn'jo͞o-lənt, ŭn'd/y/ə-) *adj.* Undulating.

un•du•late (ŭn'jo͞o-lāt', ŭn'd/y/ə-) *v.* **-lated, -lating.** **1.** To move or cause to move in a wavelike motion. **2.** To have a wavelike appearance or form. [< L *undu,* wave.]

un•du•la•tion (ŭn'jo͞o-lā'shən, ŭn'd/y/ə-) *n.* **1.** A wavelike movement, outline, appearance, or form. **2.** One of a series of waves or wavelike segments; a pulsation.

un•du•ly (ŭn'd/y/o͞o'lē) *adv.* **1.** Excessively; immoderately. **2.** In disregard of a legal or moral precept.

un•dy•ing (ŭn'dī'ĭng) *adj.* Endless; everlasting; immortal.

un•earned (ŭn'ûrnd') *adj.* **1.** Not gained by work or service. **2.** Not deserved.

un•earth (ŭn'ûrth') *v.* **1.** To dig up; uproot. **2.** To bring to public notice; uncover.

un•earth•ly (ŭn'ûrth'lē) *adj.* **1.** Not of the earth; supernatural. **2.** Frighteningly weird and unaccountable. **3.** Outlandish.

un•eas•y (ŭn'ē'zē) *adj.* **1.** Lacking ease, comfort, or a sense of security. **2.** Affording no ease; difficult. **3.** Awkward or unsure in manner; constrained. **—un'eas'i•ly** *adv.* **—un'eas'i•ness** *n.*

un•em•ployed (ŭn'ĭm-ploid') *adj.* Out of work; without a job. **—un'em•ploy'ment** *n.*

un•e•qual (ŭn'ē'kwəl) *adj.* **1.** Not equal. **2.** Asymmetric. **3.** Irregular. **4.** Inadequate. **—un'e'qual•ly** *adv.*

un•e•qualed (ŭn'ē'kwəld) *adj.* Also **un•e•qualled.** Not equaled; unrivaled.

un•e•quiv•o•cal (ŭn'ĭ-kwĭv'ə-kəl) *adj.* Admitting of no doubt or misunderstanding; clear. —**un'e•quiv'o•cal•ly** *adv.*

un•err•ing (ŭn'ûr'ĭng, -ĕr'ĭng) *adj.* Consistently accurate; without error. —**un'err'ing•ly** *adv.*

un•e•ven (ŭn'ē'vən) *adj.* **1.** Not equal, as in size, length, or quality. **2.** Not consistent or uniform. **3.** Not smooth or level. **4.** Not straight or parallel. —**un'e'ven•ly** *adv.* —**un'e'ven•ness** *n.*

un•e•vent•ful (ŭn'ĭ-vĕnt'fəl) *adj.* Lacking in significant events; without incident.

un•ex•am•pled (ŭn'ĭg-zăm'pəld, -zäm'pəld) *adj.* Without precedent; unparalleled.

un•ex•cep•tion•a•ble (ŭn'ĭk-sĕp'shən-ə-bəl) *adj.* Beyond the least reasonable objection; irreproachable. —**un'ex•cep'tion•a•bly** *adv.*

un•ex•cep•tion•al (ŭn'ĭk-sĕp'shən-əl) *adj.* **1.** Not varying from a norm; usual. **2.** Not subject to exceptions; absolute.
Usage: Unexceptional is often confused with *unexceptionable,* for which it can only be substituted loosely. When the desired meaning is "not open to objection," the term is *unexceptionable.*

un•ex•pect•ed (ŭn'ĭk-spĕk'tĭd) *adj.* Coming without warning; unforeseen. —**un'ex•pect'ed•ly** *adv.* —**un'ex•pect'ed•ness** *n.*

un•fail•ing (ŭn'fā'lĭng) *adj.* **1.** Inexhaustible. **2.** Constant; unflagging. **3.** Infallible. —**un'fail'ing•ly** *adv.* —**un'fail'ing•ness** *n.*

un•fair (ŭn'fâr') *adj.* **1.** Not just; biased. **2.** Unethical: *unfair practices.* —**un'fair'ly** *adv.* —**un'fair'ness** *n.*

un•faith•ful (ŭn'fāth'fəl) *adj.* **1.** Not adhering to a pledge or contract; disloyal. **2.** Not justly representing or reflecting an original; inaccurate. —**un'faith'ful•ly** *adv.* —**un'faith'ful•ness** *n.*

un•fa•mil•iar (ŭn'fə-mĭl'yər) *adj.* **1.** Not within one's knowledge; strange. **2.** Not acquainted; not conversant. —**un'fa•mil'i•ar'i•ty** (-mĭl'yăr'ə-tē, -mĭl'ē-ăr'ə-tē) *n.*

un•fas•ten (ŭn'făs'ən, -fä'sən) *v.* To separate the connected parts of; become loosened or separated.

un•fa•vor•a•ble (ŭn'fā'vər-ə-bəl, -fā'vrə-bəl) *adj.* **1.** Not propitious. **2.** Adverse; opposed. —**un'fa'vor•a•bly** *adv.*

un•feel•ing (ŭn'fē'lĭng) *adj.* **1.** Having no sensation; insentient. **2.** Not sympathetic; callous. —**un'feel'ing•ly** *adv.*

un•feigned (ŭn'fānd') *adj.* Not simulated; genuine.

un•fit (ŭn'fĭt') *adj.* **1.** Inappropriate. **2.** Unqualified. **3.** Not in good health. —**un'fit'ly** *adv.* —**un'fit'ness** *n.*

un•fix (ŭn'fĭks') *v.* **1.** To detach or unfasten. **2.** To unsettle; disturb.

un•fledged (ŭn'flĕjd') *adj.* **1.** Immature with plumage insufficiently developed for flight. **2.** Inexperienced, immature, or untried.

un•flinch•ing (ŭn'flĭn'chĭng) *adj.* Not betraying fear or indecision; resolute. —**un'flinch'ing•ly** *adv.*

un•fold (ŭn'fōld') *v.* **1.** To open and spread out; extend. **2.** To disclose to view. **3.** To reveal or be revealed gradually.

un•for•get•ta•ble (ŭn'fər-gĕt'ə-bəl) *adj.* Earning a permanent place in the memory; memorable. —**un'for•get'ta•bly** *adv.*

un•formed (ŭn'fôrmd') *adj.* **1.** Having no definite shape or structure; unorganized. **2.** Not yet developed to maturity.

un•for•tu•nate (ŭn'fôr'chə-nĭt) *adj.* **1.** Unlucky. **2.** Causing misfortune; disastrous. **3.** Regrettable; deplorable. —*n.* A victim of bad luck, disaster, poverty, etc. —**un'for'tu•nate•ly** *adv.* —**un'for'tu•nate•ness** *n.*

un•found•ed (ŭn'foun'dĭd) *adj.* Not based on fact or sound observation; groundless.

un•fre•quent•ed (ŭn'frĭ-kwĕn'tĭd, ŭn'frē'-kwən-tĭd) *adj.* Receiving few or no visitors.

un•friend•ly (ŭn'frĕnd'lē) *adj.* **1.** Not disposed to friendship; hostile. **2.** Indicating a bad prospect; unfavorable. —**un'friend'li•ness** *n.*

un•frock (ŭn'frŏk') *v.* To strip of priestly privileges and functions.

un•furl (ŭn'fûrl') *v.* To spread or open out; unroll.

un•fur•nished (ŭn'fûr'nĭsht) *adj.* Not containing or provided with furniture.

un•gain•ly (ŭn'gān'lē) *adj.* **-lier, -liest.** Awkward; clumsy. —**un'gain'li•ness** *n.*

un•glued (ŭn-glo͞od') *adj.* Loosened or separated. —**come unglued.** *Slang.* To become upset and lose one's composure, as in a crisis.

un•god•ly (ŭn'gŏd'lē) *adj.* **-lier, -liest. 1.** Not revering God. **2.** Sinful; wicked. **3.** *Informal.* Outrageous. —**un'god'li•ness** *n.*

un•gov•ern•a•ble (ŭn'gŭv'ər-nə-bəl) *adj.* Not able to be governed; uncontrollable; unruly.

un•gra•cious (ŭn'grā'shəs) *adj.* **1.** Discourteous; rude. **2.** Unacceptable; unattractive. —**un'gra'cious•ly** *adv.*

un•grate•ful (ŭn'grāt'fəl) *adj.* **1.** Without a feeling of gratitude or appreciation. **2.** Disagreeable; repellent.

un•guard•ed (ŭn'gär'dĭd) *adj.* **1.** Unprotected. **2.** Without discretion; imprudent.

un•guent (ŭng'gwənt) *n.* A salve; ointment. [< L *unguere,* to anoint.]

un•gu•late (ŭng'gyə-lĭt, -lāt') *adj.* Having hoofs. —*n.* A hoofed mammal. [< L *ungula,* hoof.]

un•hand (ŭn'hănd') *v.* To remove one's hands from; let go.

un•hap•py (ŭn'hăp'ē) *adj.* **1.** Not happy; sad. **2.** Unlucky. **3.** Not suitable or tactful; inappropriate. —**un'hap'pi•ly** (-hăp'ə-lē) *adv.* —**un'hap'pi•ness** *n.*

un•har•ness (ŭn'här'nĭs) *v.* **1.** To remove the harness from. **2.** To release, as energy.

un•health•y (ŭn'hĕl'thē) *adj.* **1.** In ill health; sick. **2.** Symptomatic of ill health. **3.** Likely to cause illness. **4.** Harmful to morals; corruptive. —**un'health'i•ness** *n.*

un•heard (ŭn'hûrd') *adj.* **1.** Not heard. **2.** Not given a hearing.

un•heard-of (ŭn'hûrd'ŭv', -ŏv') *adj.* **1.** Not previously known. **2.** Without precedent.

un•hinge (ŭn'hĭnj') *v.* **1.** To remove from hinges. **2.** To unbalance (the mind).

un•hitch (ŭn'hĭch') *v.* To unfasten.

un•ho•ly (ŭn'hō'lē) *adj.* **1.** Not hallowed or consecrated. **2.** Wicked; immoral. **3.** *Informal.* Outrageous.

un•hook (ŭn'ho͝ok') *v.* **1.** To remove from a hook. **2.** To unfasten the hooks of.

un•horse (ŭn'hôrs') *v.* **-horsed, -horsing.** To cause to fall from a horse.

uni–. *comb. form.* Single. [< L *ūnus,* one.]

u•ni•cam•er•al (yo͞o'nĭ-kăm'ər-əl) *adj.* Consisting of a single legislative chamber.

u•ni•cel•lu•lar (yo͞o'nĭ-sĕl'yə-lər) *adj.* Consisting of a single cell; one-celled: *unicellular organisms.*

u•ni•corn (yo͞o'nə-kôrn') *n.* A fabled creature usually represented as a horse with a single spiraled horn on its forehead. [< UNI- + L *cornū,* horn.]

u•ni•di•rec•tion•al (yo͞o'nĭ-dĭ-rĕk'shən-əl, -dī-rĕk'shən-əl) *adj.* Having, operating, or moving in one direction only.

u•ni•form (yo͞o'nə-fôrm') *adj.* **1.** Unchanging; consistent. **2.** Being the same everywhere; identical. —*n.* A distinctive outfit intended to identify those who wear it as members of a specific group. [< L *ūniformis,* of one form.] —**u'ni•for'mi•ty, u'ni•form'ness** *n.* —**u'ni•form'ly** *adv.*

u•ni•fy (yo͞o'nə-fī') *v.* **-fied, -fying.** To make into a unit; unite; consolidate. [< UNI- + L *facere,* to make.] —**u'ni•fi•ca'tion** *n.* —**u'ni•fi'er** *n.*

u•ni•lat•er•al (yo͞o'nĭ-lăt'ər-əl) *adj.* **1.** Of, on, pertaining to, involving, or affecting only one side. **2.** Having only one side. —**u'ni•lat'er•al•ly** *adv.*

un•im•peach•a•ble (ŭn'ĭm-pē'chə-bəl) *adj.* Beyond doubt or reproach; unquestionable. —**un'im•peach'a•bly** *adv.*

un•in•hib•i•ted (ŭn'ĭn-hĭb'ə-tĭd) *adj.* Free from inhibition. —**un'in•hib'i•ted•ly** *adv.*

un•in•tel•li•gent (ŭn'ĭn-tĕl'ə-jənt) *adj.* **1.** Lacking intelligence; stupid. **2.** Uneducated; ignorant. —**un'in•tel'li•gent•ly** *adv.*

un•in•ten•tion•al (ŭn'ĭn-tĕn'shən-əl) *adj.* Not intentional; not done or said on purpose. —**un'in•ten'tion•al•ly** *adv.*

un•in•ter•est•ed (ŭn-ĭn'trĭs-tĭd, -ĭn'tə-rĕs'tĭd) *adj.* Not paying attention; indifferent.

un•ion (yo͞on'yən) *n.* **1.** The act of uniting or state of being united. **2.** A combination so formed; an alliance or confederation. **3.** The state of matrimony; marriage. **4.** An organization of wage earners formed for the purpose of serving their class interests with respect to wages and working conditions. **5.** A coupling device for connecting parts, as pipes or rods. **6.** A device on a flag signifying the union of two or more sovereignties. —**the Union.** The United States of America, esp. during the Civil War. —*adj.* **1.** Of or pertaining to a union, esp. a labor union. **2. Union.** Supporting the Federal government during the Civil War. [< L *ūnus,* one.]

un•ion•ize (yo͞on'yə-nīz') *v.* **-ized, -izing.** To organize (into) a labor union.

union jack. 1. Any flag consisting entirely of a union. **2.** Often **Union Jack.** The flag of the United Kingdom.

Union of Soviet Socialist Republics. A country of 15 constituent republics in N Eurasia; Soviet Union; Russia. Pop. 241,748,000. Cap. Moscow.

Union of Soviet Socialist Republics

union shop A business or industrial establishment whose employees are required to be union members or agree to join the union within a specified time after being hired.

u•nique (yo͞o-nēk') *adj.* **1.** Being the only one of its kind; solitary; sole; single. **2.** Being without an equal or equivalent; unparalleled. [< L *ūnicus,* only, sole.] —**u•nique'ly** *adv.* —**u•nique'ness** *n.*

Usage: *Unique,* in careful usage, is not preceded by adverbs that qualify it with respect to degree. By definition, *unique* cannot strictly be said to vary in degree or intensity. Therefore, constructions such as *rather* (or *somewhat* or *very*) *unique* and *more* (or *most*) *unique* are rendered more appropriately by substituting for *unique* less special terms, such as *unusual, rare,* or *remarkable.*

u•ni•sex (yo͞o'nĭ-sĕks') *n.* The elimination of gender distinctions, as in dress. —*adj.* Not distinguished or distinguishable on the basis of gender: *unisex hair styles.*

u•ni•son (yo͞o'nə-sən, -zən) *n.* **1. a.** Identity of musical pitch. **b.** The combination of musical parts at the same pitch or in octaves. **2.** Any speaking of the same words simultaneously by two or more speakers. **3.** Agreement; concord. [< ML *ūnisonus,* of the same sound.]

u•nit (yo͞o'nĭt) *n.* **1.** Anything regarded as an elementary structural or functional constituent of a whole. **2. a.** A mechanical part or module. **b.** An entire apparatus. **3.** A precisely specified quantity in terms of which the magnitudes of other quantities of the same kind can be stated. [Back-formation < UNITY.]

U•ni•tar•i•an (yo͞o'nə-târ'ē-ən) *n.* A member of a Christian denomination that rejects the doctrine of the Trinity and emphasizes freedom and tolerance in religious belief. [< L *ūnitās,* unity.] —**U'ni•tar'i•an•ism'** *n.*

u•nite (yo͞o-nīt') *v.* **united, uniting.** **1.** To bring together so as to form a whole. **2.** To combine (people) in interest, attitude, or action. **3.** To become joined, formed, or combined into a unit. [< L *ūnus,* one.]

United Arab Emirates. A federation in E Arabia. Pop. 179,000. Cap. Abu Dhabi.

United Kingdom. In full, United Kingdom of Great Britain and Northern Ireland. A kingdom of W Europe, consisting of England, Scotland, Wales, and Northern Ireland. Pop. 54,068,000. Cap. London.

United Kingdom

United Nations. An international organization of 144 independent countries, with headquarters in New York City.

United States of America. A North American republic composed of 50 states. Pop. 200,000,000. Cap. Washington. See map on following page.

u•ni•ty (yo͞o'nə-tē) *n., pl.* **-ties.** **1.** The state of being one; singleness. **2.** Oneness of mind; agreement; concord. **3.** An ordering of all elements in a work of art so that each contributes to a unified aesthetic effect. **4.** Singleness of purpose or action; continuity. **5.** The number 1. [< L *ūnus,* one.]

univ. **1.** universal. **2.** university.

Univ. university.

u•ni•va•lent (yo͞o'nĭ-vā'lənt) *adj.* **1.** Having valence 1. **2.** Having only one valence.

u•ni•valve (yo͞o'nĭ-vălv') *n.* A mollusk, as a snail, having a single shell. —**u'ni•valve'** *adj.*

u•ni•ver•sal (yo͞o'nə-vûr'səl) *adj.* **1.** Extending to or affecting the entire world; worldwide. **2.** Including or affecting all members of a class or group. **3.** Applicable to all purposes, conditions, or situations. **4.** Of or pertaining to the universe or cosmos; cosmic. **5.** Comprising all or many subjects: *a universal genius.* —**u'ni•ver•sal'i•ty** *n.* —**u'ni•ver'sal•ly** *adv.*

universal joint. A joint that allows parts of a machine limited movement in any direction while transmitting rotary motion.

u•ni•verse (yo͞o'nə-vûrs') *n.* All existing things regarded as a collective entity. [< L *ūniversus,* whole, entire, "turned into one."]

u•ni•ver•si•ty (yo͞o'nə-vûr'sə-tē) *n., pl.* **-ties.** An institution for higher learning comprising a graduate school, professional schools, and an undergraduate division. [< LL *ūniversitās,* a society, guild.]

un•just (ŭn'jŭst') *adj.* Violating principles of justice or fairness; unfair. —**un'just'ly** *adv.*

un•kempt (ŭn'kĕmpt') *adj.* **1.** Not combed: *unkempt hair.* **2.** Untidy; messy. [< UN-[1] + OE *cemban,* to comb.]

un•kind (ŭn'kīnd') *adj.* Lacking kindness; unsympathetic. —**un'kind'ly** *adv.*

un•know•ing (ŭn'nō'ĭng) *adj.* Not knowing; unaware. —**un'know'ing•ly** *adv.*

un•known (ŭn'nōn') *adj.* **1.** Not known; unfamiliar; strange. **2.** Not identified or ascertained. —*n.* **1.** One that is unknown. **2.** A quantity of unknown numerical value.

un•lace (ŭn'lās') *v.* To loosen or undo the lace or laces of.

un•latch (ŭn'lăch') *v.* To unfasten or open by releasing a latch.

un•law•ful (ŭn'lô'fəl) *adj.* Not lawful; in violation of law; illegal. —**un'law'ful•ly** *adv.* —**un'law'ful•ness** *n.*

un•learn (ŭn'lûrn') *v.* To put (something learned) out of the mind; forget.

un•learn•ed. *adj.* **1.** (ŭn'lûr'nĭd). Not educated; ignorant or illiterate. **2.** (ŭn'lûrnd'). Not acquired by training or studying.

un•leash (ŭn'lēsh') *v.* To release or loose from or as from a leash.

un•less (ŭn-lĕs') *conj.* Except on the condition that; except under the circumstances that. [< ME *(up)on less than,* "on a less condition than."]

un•let•tered (ŭn'lĕt'ərd) *adj.* Not educated; illiterate.

un•like (ŭn'līk') *adj.* Not alike; different; dissimilar. —*prep.* **1.** Different from; not like. **2.** Not typical of.

un•like•ly (ŭn'līk'lē) *adj.* **1.** Not likely; improbable. **2.** Likely to fail. —**un'like'li•hood',** **un'like'li•ness** *n.*

un•lim•ber (ŭn'lĭm'bər) *v.* To prepare for action.

un•lim•it•ed (ŭn'lĭm'ĭ-tĭd) *adj.* Having no limits, bounds, or qualifications.

un•load (ŭn'lōd') *v.* **1. a.** To remove the load or cargo from. **b.** To discharge (a cargo or load). **2.** To remove the charge from (a firearm). **3.** To dispose of, esp. by selling in great quantity; dump.

un•lock (ŭn'lŏk') *v.* **1.** To undo (a lock). **2.** To undo the lock of.

un•looked-for (ŭn'lo͝okt'fôr') *adj.* Not looked for or expected.

un•loose (ŭn'lo͞os') *v.* **1.** To let loose or unfasten; release; set free. **2.** To relax; ease, as a hold.

un•loos•en (ŭn'lo͞o'sən) *v.* To unloose.

un•luck•y (ŭn'lŭk'ē) *adj.* Marked by or bringing bad luck; unfortunate.

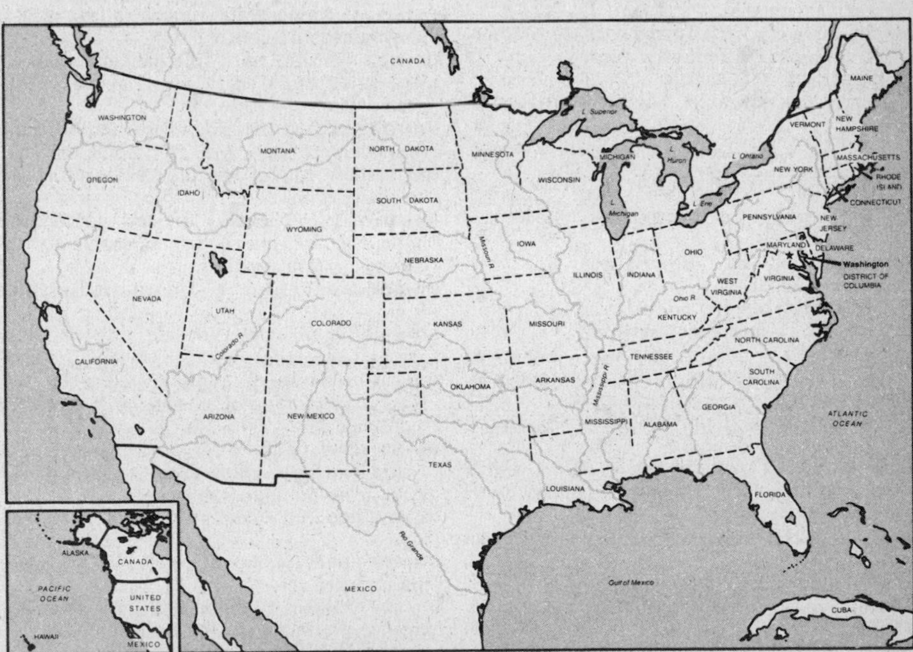

United States of America

un•man•ly (ŭn'măn'lē) *adj.* 1. Weak; cowardly. 2. Effeminate. —**un'man'li•ness** *n.*
un•manned (ŭn'mănd') *adj.* Operated without a crew on board.
un•man•ner•ly (ŭn'măn'ər-lē) *adj.* Rude; ill-mannered. —**un'man'ner•li•ness** *n.*
un•mar•ried (ŭn'măr'ēd) *adj.* Not married.
un•mask (ŭn'măsk', -mäsk') *v.* 1. To remove a mask from. 2. To disclose the true character of; expose.
un•men•tion•a•ble (ŭn'mĕn'shən-ə-bəl) *adj.* Not fit for polite conversation.
un•mer•ci•ful (ŭn'mûr'sĭ-fəl) *adj.* Having no mercy; merciless.
un•mind•ful (ŭn'mīnd'fəl) *adj.* Careless; forgetful; oblivious: *unmindful of the time.*
un•mis•tak•a•ble (ŭn'mĭ-stā'kə-bəl) *adj.* Obvious; evident. —**un'mis•tak'a•bly** *adv.*
un•mit•i•gat•ed (ŭn'mĭt'ə-gā'tĭd) *adj.* 1. Not diminished in intensity or severity; unrelieved. 2. Absolute; out-and-out.
un•nat•u•ral (ŭn'năch'ər-əl) *adj.* 1. Violating natural law. 2. Deviating from a behavioral, ethical, or social norm. 3. Contrived or constrained; artificial.
un•nec•es•sar•y (ŭn'nĕs'ə-sĕr'ē) *adj.* Not necessary; needless. —**un'nec'es•sar'i•ly** (-sâr'ə-lē) *adv.* —**un'nec'es•sar'i•ness** *n.*
un•nerve (ŭn'nûrv') *v.* **-nerved, -nerving.** To deprive of composure, energy, or firmness.
un•ob•tru•sive (ŭn'əb-trōō'sĭv) *adj.* Not readily noticeable; inconspicuous.
un•oc•cu•pied (ŭn'ŏk'yə-pīd') *adj.* Not occupied; vacant.
un•of•fi•cial (ŭn'ə-fĭsh'əl) *adj.* 1. Not official. 2. Not acting officially. —**un'of•fi'cial•ly** *adv.*
un•or•gan•ized (ŭn'ôr'gə-nīzd') *adj.* 1. Lacking order, system, or unity. 2. Not unionized.
un•or•tho•dox (ŭn'ôr'thə-dŏks') *adj.* Not orthodox; unconventional.
un•pack (ŭn'păk') *v.* 1. To remove the contents of (a suitcase). 2. To remove from a container or from packaging.
un•paid (ŭn'pād') *adj.* 1. Not yet paid. 2. Serving without pay.
un•par•al•leled (ŭn'păr'ə-lĕld') *adj.* Without parallel; unequaled.
un•pin (ŭn'pĭn') *v.* 1. To remove a pin from. 2. To unfasten by removing pins.
un•pleas•ant (ŭn'plĕz'ənt) *adj.* Not pleasing; offensive; disagreeable. —**un'pleas'ant•ness** *n.*
un•plug (ŭn'plŭg') *v.* 1. To remove a plug or stopper from. 2. To disconnect from a source of electric power.
un•pop•u•lar (ŭn'pŏp'yə-lər) *adj.* Lacking general approval or acceptance. —**un'pop'u•lar'i•ty** (-lăr'ə-tē) *n.*
un•prec•e•dent•ed (ŭn'prĕs'ə-dĕn'tĭd) *adj.* Without precedent.
un•pre•dict•a•ble (ŭn'prĭ-dĭk'tə-bəl) *adj.* Not predictable. —**un'pre•dict'a•bly** *adv.*
un•pre•pared (ŭn'prĭ-pârd') *adj.* 1. Having made no preparations. 2. Not equipped to meet a contingency. 3. Impromptu.
un•pre•ten•tious (ŭn'prĭ-tĕn'shəs) *adj.* Lacking pretention; modest.
un•prin•ci•pled (ŭn'prĭn'sə-pəld) *adj.* Lacking principles or moral scruples; unscrupulous: *unprincipled behavior.*
un•print•a•ble (ŭn'prĭn'tə-bəl) *adj.* Not suitable for publication.
un•pro•duc•tive (ŭn'prə-dŭk'tĭv) *adj.* Producing or yielding little or nothing.
un•pro•fes•sion•al (ŭn'prə-fĕsh'ən-əl) *adj.* 1. Not a qualified member of a professional group. 2. Not conforming to the standards of a profession. —**un'pro•fes'sion•al•ly** *adv.*
un•prof•it•a•ble (ŭn'prŏf'ĭ-tə-bəl) *adj.* 1. Yielding no profit. 2. Serving no purpose; useless. —**un'prof'it•a•bly** *adv.*
un•qual•i•fied (ŭn'kwŏl'ə-fīd') *adj.* 1. Lacking the proper or required qualifications. 2. Without reservations.
un•ques•tion•a•ble (ŭn'kwĕs'chən-ə-bəl) *adj.* Beyond question or doubt; indisputable. —**un'ques'tion•a•bly** *adv.*
un•ques•tioned (ŭn'kwĕs'chənd) *adj.* Not questioned or doubted; unquestionable.
un•quote (ŭn'kwōt') *v.* To close (a quotation). Used by a speaker to indicate the termination of a quotation.
un•rav•el (ŭn'răv'əl) *v.* 1. To separate (entangled threads). 2. To solve; clear up (something mysterious or baffling).
un•read (ŭn'rĕd') *adj.* 1. Not read, studied, or perused. 2. Having read little; ignorant.
un•read•a•ble (ŭn'rē'də-bəl) *adj.* 1. Illegible. 2. Incomprehensible; obscure.
un•read•y (ŭn'rĕd'ē) *adj.* 1. Not ready or prepared. 2. Slow to see or respond. —**un'read'i•ly** *adv.* —**un'read'i•ness** *n.*
un•re•al (ŭn'rē'əl, -rēl') *adj.* Not real or substantial; imaginary; artificial; illusory.
un•rea•son•a•ble (ŭn'rē'zə-nə-bəl) *adj.* 1. Not governed by or predicated upon reason. 2. Exorbitant; immoderate.
un•re•hearsed (ŭn'rĭ-hûrst') *adj.* Not rehearsed; extemporaneous.
un•re•lent•ing (ŭn'rĭ-lĕn'tĭng) *adj.* 1. Not relenting; inexorable. 2. Not diminishing in intensity, speed, or effort.
un•re•li•a•ble (ŭn'rĭ-lī'ə-bəl) *adj.* Not reliable. —**un're•li'a•bil'i•ty** *n.* —**un're•li'a•bly** *adv.*
un•re•mit•ting (ŭn'rĭ-mĭt'ĭng) *adj.* Never slackening; incessant; persistent.
un•re•served (ŭn'rĭ-zûrvd') *adj.* 1. Not reserved for a particular person: *an unreserved seat.* 2. Given without reservation; unqualified. 3. Not reserved in manner; open; candid. —**un're•serv'ed•ly** (-zûr'vĭd-lē) *adv.*
un•rest (ŭn'rĕst') *n.* Uneasiness; disquiet: *social unrest.*
un•re•strained (ŭn'rĭ-strānd') *adj.* 1. Not restrained; immoderate; uncontrolled. 2. Not constrained; natural.
un•ripe (ŭn'rīp') *adj.* Not ripe; immature.
un•ri•valed (ŭn'rī'vəld) *adj.* Unequaled; supreme.
un•roll (ŭn'rōl') *v.* 1. To unwind and open out (something rolled up). 2. To become unrolled.
un•ruf•fled (ŭn'rŭf'əld) *adj.* Not ruffled or agitated; calm.
un•ru•ly (ŭn'rōō'lē) *adj.* **-lier, -liest.** Difficult or impossible to govern; not amenable to discipline. —**un'ru'li•ness** *n.*
un•sad•dle (ŭn'săd'l) *v.* To remove the saddle from.
un•safe (ŭn'sāf') *adj.* Not safe; involving danger or risk; dangerous.
un•sat•is•fac•to•ry (ŭn'săt'ĭs-făk'tə-rē) *adj.* Not satisfactory; not meeting the necessary requirements.
un•sa•vor•y (ŭn'sā'və-rē) *adj.* 1. Tasteless. 2. Having an unpleasant taste. 3. Socially objectionable or undesirable.
un•scathed (ŭn'skā*th*d') *adj.* Unharmed; uninjured.
un•schooled (ŭn'skōōld') *adj.* Not schooled; uninstructed.
un•sci•en•tif•ic (ŭn'sī-ən-tĭf'ĭk) *adj.* Not scientific, esp. lacking in method or objectivity. —**un'sci•en•tif'i•cal•ly** *adv.*
un•scram•ble (ŭn'skrăm'bəl) *v.* To disentangle; straighten out; resolve.
un•screw (ŭn'skrōō') *v.* 1. To take out the screws from. 2. To loosen, adjust, or detach by rotating.
un•scru•pu•lous (ŭn'skrōō'pyə-ləs) *adj.* Without scruples; contemptuous of what is right or honorable. —**un'scru'pu•lous•ly** *adv.*
un•seal (ŭn'sēl') *v.* To break or remove the seal of.
un•sea•son•a•ble (ŭn'sē'zə-nə-bəl) *adj.* 1. Not characteristic of the time of year. 2. Poorly timed. —**un'sea'son•a•bly** *adv.*
un•seat (ŭn'sēt') *v.* 1. To remove from a seat, esp. from a saddle. 2. To dislodge from a position or office.
un•seem•ly (ŭn'sēm'lē) *adj.* Not in good taste; indecorous; unbecoming.
un•seen (ŭn'sēn') *adj.* Not directly evident; invisible.
un•sel•fish (ŭn'sĕl'fĭsh) *adj.* Not selfish; generous. —**un'sel'fish•ly** *adv.* —**un'sel'fish•ness** *n.*
un•set•tle (ŭn'sĕt'l) *v.* To disrupt; disturb.
un•set•tled (ŭn'sĕt'əld) *adj.* 1. Disordered; disturbed. 2. Not determined or resolved. 3. Not paid or adjusted. 4. Unpopulated. 5. Not fixed or established, as in a residence.
un•shack•le (ŭn'shăk'əl) *v.* To release from or as from confinement or shackles; set free.
un•sheathe (ŭn'shē*th*') *v.* To draw from a sheath or scabbard.
un•sight•ly (ŭn'sīt'lē) *adj.* Unpleasant or offensive to look at; unattractive. —**un'sight'li•ness** *n.*
un•skilled (ŭn'skĭld') *adj.* 1. Lacking skill or technical training. 2. Requiring no training or skill.
un•skill•ful (ŭn'skĭl'fəl) *adj.* Lacking skill or proficiency; inexpert. —**un'skill'ful•ly** *adv.*
un•snap (ŭn'snăp') *v.* To undo the snaps of; unfasten.
un•snarl (ŭn'snärl') *v.* To free of snarls; disentangle.
un•so•cia•ble (ŭn'sō'shə-bəl) *adj.* Not disposed to seek the company of others; not companionable. —**un'so'cia•bil'i•ty** *n.*
un•so•phis•ti•cat•ed (ŭn'sə-fĭs'tĭ-kā'tĭd) *adj.* Not sophisticated.
un•sound (ŭn'sound') *adj.* 1. Not dependably strong or solid. 2. Not physically healthy; diseased. 3. Not logically founded; fallacious; invalid. —**un'sound'ly** *adv.*
un•spar•ing (ŭn'spâr'ĭng) *adj.* 1. Not frugal; lavish. 2. Unmerciful; severe. —**un'spar'ing•ly** *adv.* —**un'spar'ing•ness** *n.*
un•speak•a•ble (ŭn'spē'kə-bəl) *adj.* 1. Beyond description; inexpressible. 2. Inexpressibly bad or objectionable. —**un'speak'a•bly** *adv.*
un•sta•ble (ŭn'stā'bəl) *adj.* 1. Lacking stability or firmness. 2. a. Of fickle temperament; irresponsible; flighty. b. Psychologically maladjusted. 3. Decomposing or decaying readily. —**un'sta'ble•ness** *n.*
un•stead•y (ŭn'stĕd'ē) *adj.* 1. Not securely in place; unstable. 2. Fluctuating; inconstant. 3. Wavering; uneven; erratic.
un•stop (ŭn'stŏp') *v.* To remove a stopper or obstruction from; open.
un•stressed (ŭn'strĕst') *adj.* 1. Not stressed or having the weakest stress, as a speech segment. 2. Not emphasized.
un•strung (ŭn'strŭng') *adj.* 1. Having the strings loosened or removed. 2. Emotionally upset; unnerved.
un•suc•cess•ful (ŭn'sək-sĕs'fəl) *adj.* Not succeeding; without success. —**un'suc•cess'ful•ly** *adv.* —**un'suc•cess'ful•ness** *n.*
un•suit•a•ble (ŭn'sōō'tə-bəl) *adj.* Not suitable; inappropriate. —**un'suit'a•bil'i•ty** *n.*

un•sung (ŭn'sŭng') *adj.* **1.** Not sung. **2.** Not honored or praised in song; uncelebrated: *unsung heroes.*

un•sure (ŭn'sho͝or') *adj.* Lacking confidence or assurance; uncertain.

un•tan•gle (ŭn'tăng'gəl) *v.* **1.** To disentangle. **2.** To clarify; resolve.

un•ten•a•ble (ŭn'tĕn'ə-bəl) *adj.* **1.** Indefensible. **2.** Not suitable for occupation.

un•think•a•ble (ŭn'thĭng'kə-bəl) *adj.* Not thinkable; inconceivable; out of the question.

un•think•ing (ŭn'thĭng'kĭng) *adj.* Not thinking or mindful; inattentive.

un•ti•dy (ŭn'tī'dē) *adj.* Not neat and tidy; slovenly. **—un'ti'di•ly** *adv.* **—un'ti'di•ness** *n.*

un•tie (ŭn'tī') *v.* **1.** To undo or loosen (a knot). **2.** To free from something that binds or restrains.

un•til (ŭn-tĭl') *prep.* **1.** Up to the time of. **2.** Before a specified time: *not until Friday.* *—conj.* **1.** Up to the time that. **2.** Before. **3.** To the point or extent that. —See Usage note at **till.** [ME, to, toward, up to, till.]

un•time•ly (ŭn'tīm'lē) *adj.* **1.** Occurring or done at an inappropriate time; inopportune. **2.** Occurring too soon; premature. **—un'time'ly** *adv.* **—un'time'li•ness** *n.*

un•tir•ing (ŭn'tīr'ĭng) *adj.* **1.** Not tiring. **2.** Not ceasing despite fatigue; indefatigable. **—un'tir'ing•ly** *adv.*

un•to (ŭn'to͞o) *prep. Poetic & Archaic.* To.

un•told (ŭn'tōld') *adj.* **1.** Not told or revealed. **2.** Beyond description or enumeration.

un•touch•a•ble (ŭn'tŭch'ə-bəl) *adj.* **1.** Not to be touched. **2.** Out of reach; unobtainable. *—n.* A Hindu of the lowest caste, whose touch is considered to defile those of higher castes.

un•to•ward (ŭn'tôrd', -tōrd') *adj.* **1.** Unfavorable; unpropitious. **2.** Hard to control; refractory.

un•true (ŭn'tro͞o') *adj.* **1.** Contrary to fact; false. **2.** Disloyal; unfaithful.

un•truth (ŭn'tro͞oth') *n.* **1.** A lie. **2.** Falsity. **—un'truth'ful** *adj.* **—un'truth'ful•ness** *n.*

un•tu•tored (ŭn't/y/o͞o'tərd) *adj.* Having had no formal education.

un•twist (ŭn'twĭst') *v.* To loosen or separate (that which is twisted together) by turning in the opposite direction.

un•used (ŭn'yo͞ozd') *adj.* **1.** Not in use. **2.** Never having been used. **3.** (ŭn'yo͞ost'). Not accustomed: *unused to city traffic.*

un•u•su•al (ŭn'yo͞o'zho͞o-əl) *adj.* Not usual, common, or ordinary.

un•ut•ter•a•ble (ŭn'ŭt'ər-ə-bəl) *adj.* Not capable of being expressed; too profound for oral expression. **—un'ut'ter•a•bly** *adv.*

un•var•nished (ŭn'vär'nĭsht) *adj.* **1.** Not varnished. **2.** Stated without any effort to soften or disguise: *the unvarnished truth.*

un•veil (ŭn'vāl') *v.* **1.** To remove a veil from. **2.** To disclose; reveal.

un•voiced (ŭn'voist') *adj.* **1.** Not expressed or uttered. **2.** *Phon.* Voiceless.

un•war•rant•ed (ŭn'wôr'ən-tĭd, ŭn'wŏr'-) *adj.* Having no justification; groundless.

un•war•y (ŭn'wâr'ē) *adj.* Not alert to danger or deception; not cautious.

un•well (ŭn'wĕl') *adj.* Not well; ailing; ill.

un•whole•some (ŭn'hōl'səm) *adj.* Injurious to physical, mental, or moral health. **—un'whole'some•ly** *adv.* **—un'whole'some•ness** *n.*

un•wield•y (ŭn'wēl'dē) *adj.* **-ier, -iest.** Difficult to carry or manage because of bulk or shape.

un•will•ing (ŭn'wĭl'ĭng) *adj.* **1.** Hesitant; loath. **2.** Done, given, or said reluctantly. **—un'will'ing•ly** *adv.* **—un'will'ing•ness** *n.*

un•wind (ŭn'wīnd') *v.* **1.** To unroll; uncoil. **2.** To become unrolled or uncoiled.

un•wise (ŭn'wīz') *adj.* Lacking wisdom; foolish or imprudent. **—un'wise'ly** *adv.*

un•wit•ting (ŭn'wĭt'ĭng) *adj.* **1.** Not knowing; unaware. **2.** Not intended; unintentional. [< UN-[1] + OE *witan,* to know (see **weid-**).] **—un'wit'ting•ly** *adv.*

un•wont•ed (ŭn'wôn'tĭd, -wōn'tĭd, -wŭn'tĭd) *adj.* Not habitual or ordinary; unusual.

un•wor•thy (ŭn'wûr'*th*ē) *adj.* **1.** Insufficient in worth; undeserving: *unworthy of the award.* **2.** Not suiting or befitting. **—un'wor'thi•ness** *n.*

un•wrap (ŭn'răp') *v.* To remove the wrappings from; open.

un•writ•ten (ŭn'rĭt'n) *adj.* **1.** Not written or recorded. **2.** Not formulated; operating through custom; traditional.

un•zip (ŭn'zĭp') *v.* To open or unfasten (a zipper).

up (ŭp) *adv.* **1.** From a lower to a higher position. **2.** In or toward a higher position. **3.** From a reclining to an upright position. **4. a.** Above a surface. **b.** Above the horizon. **5.** Into view or consideration. **6.** In or toward a position conventionally regarded as higher. **7.** To or at a higher price. **8.** So as to advance, increase, or improve. **9.** With or to a greater pitch or volume. **10.** Into a state of excitement or turbulence. **11.** So as to detach or unearth: *pulling up weeds.* **12.** To a stop. **13.** Apart; into pieces: *tore it up.* **14.** To windward. **15.** Each; apiece: *The score was eight up.* **16.** Completely; entirely. **17.** —Used as an intensifier: *cleaning up.* *—adj.* **1.** High or relatively high. **2. a.** Standing; erect. **b.** Out of bed. **3.** Moving or directed upward: *an up elevator.* **4.** Actively functioning: *up and around.* **5.** Rising toward the flood level. **6.** Marked by agitation or acceleration: *The winds are up.* **7.** *Informal.* Going on: *What's up?* **8.** Being considered; under study: *a contract up for renewal.* **9.** Running as a candidate. **10.** Charged; on trial. **11.** Finished; over: *His time was up.* **12.** *Informal.* Well-informed: *not up on sports.* **13.** Being ahead of the opponent: *up two holes in a golf match.* **14.** *Baseball.* At bat. **15.** As a bet; at stake. *—prep.* **1.** From a lower to or toward a higher point on. **2.** Toward or at a point farther along: *up the road.* **3.** In a direction toward the source of: *up the Hudson.* **4.** Against: *up the wind.* *—n.* **1.** A rise or ascent. **2.** An upward movement or trend. *—v.* **upped, upping. 1.** To increase or improve. **2.** To raise. **3.** *Informal.* To act suddenly or unexpectedly: *upped and went home.* [< OE *ūp* and *uppe.* See **upo.**]

up–. *comb. form.* **1.** Up. **2.** Upper.

up-and-com•ing (ŭp'ən-kŭm'ĭng) *adj.* Marked for future success; promising.

up•beat (ŭp'bēt') *n. Mus.* An unaccented beat, esp. the last beat of a measure.

up•braid (ŭp'brād') *v.* To reprove sharply; scold or chide vehemently; censure. [< OE *ūpbrēdan,* "to throw up against," reproach.] **—up'braid'er** *n.*

up•bring•ing (ŭp'brĭng'ĭng) *n.* The rearing and training received during childhood.

up•com•ing (ŭp'kŭm'ĭng) *adj.* About to take place; approaching.

up•coun•try (ŭp'kŭn'trē) *n.* The interior of a country. *—adj.* (ŭp'kŭn'trē). Located, originating from, or characteristic of the upcountry. **—up'coun'try** *adv.*

up•date (ŭp'dāt') *v.* To bring up to date.

up•draft (ŭp'drăft', -dräft') *n.* An upward current of air.

up•end (ŭp'ĕnd') *v.* **1.** To stand, set, or turn on one end. **2.** To overturn or overthrow.

up•grade (ŭp'grād') *v.* To raise to a higher grade or standard. *—n.* An incline leading uphill.

up•heav•al (ŭp'hē'vəl) *n.* **1.** The process or an instance of being heaved upward. **2.** A sudden and violent disruption. **3.** A lifting of the earth's crust.

up•hill (ŭp'hĭl') *adj.* **1.** Going up a hill or slope. **2.** Prolonged and laborious. *—n.* (ŭp'hĭl'). An upward incline. *—adv.* (ŭp'hĭl'). Toward higher ground; upward.

up•hold (ŭp-hōld') *v.* **1.** To hold aloft. **2.** To prevent from falling; support. **3.** To maintain or affirm in the face of a challenge.

up•hol•ster (ŭp-hōl'stər) *v.* To furnish (chairs, sofas, etc.) with stuffing, springs, cushions, and covering fabric. [< ME *upholdester,* one who upholds or repairs.] **—up•hol'ster•er** *n.*

up•hol•ster•y (ŭp-hōl'stər-ē, -strē) *n., pl.* **-ies. 1.** The materials used in upholstering. **2.** The business of upholstering.

UPI, U.P.I. United Press International.

up•keep (ŭp'kēp') *n.* **1.** Maintenance in proper condition. **2.** The cost of such maintenance.

up•land (ŭp'lənd, -lănd') *n.* The higher parts of a region or tract of land. **—up'land** *adj.*

up•lift (ŭp-lĭft') *v.* **1.** To raise up or aloft; elevate. **2.** To raise to a higher social, intellectual, or moral level. *—n.* (ŭp'lĭft'). **1.** The act, process, or result of lifting up. **2.** A movement to improve social, moral, or intellectual standards.

up•on (ə-pŏn', ə-pôn') *prep.* On.

up•per (ŭp'ər) *adj.* **1.** Higher in place, position, or rank. **2. Upper.** *Geol. & Archaeol.* Being a later division of the period named. *—n.* That part of a shoe above the sole.

up•per-case (ŭp'ər-kās') *adj.* Pertaining to or printed in capital letters.

up•per-class (ŭp'ər-klăs', -kläs') *adj.* **1.** Pertaining to an upper social class. **2.** Of or characteristic of the junior and senior classes in a school or college.

upper crust. *Informal.* The highest social class or group.

up•per•cut (ŭp'ər-kŭt') *n. Boxing.* A short swinging blow directed upward, as to the opponent's chin. **—up'per•cut'** *v.*

upper hand. A position of control or advantage.

up•per•most (ŭp'ər-mōst') *adj.* Highest in position, place, rank, or influence; foremost. *—adv.* In the first or highest rank, position, or place; first.

Upper Vol•ta (vŏl'tə). A republic of W Africa. Pop. 4,600,000. Cap. Ouagadougou.

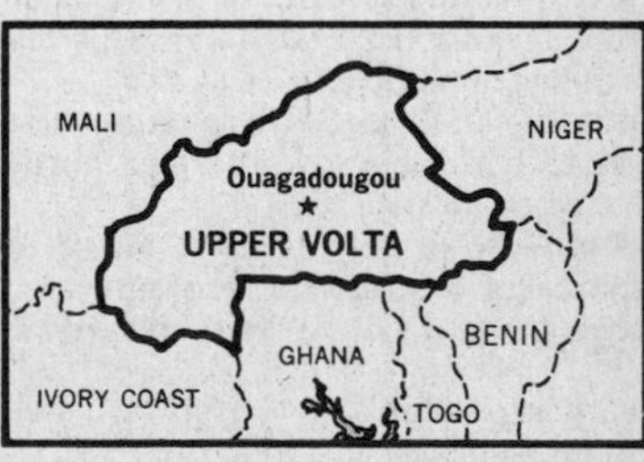

Upper Volta

up•pi•ty (ŭp'ə-tē) *adj. Informal.* Tending to be snobbish or arrogant. [< UP.]

up•raise (ŭp-rāz') *v.* To raise or lift up; elevate.

up•right (ŭp'rīt') *adj.* 1. a. In a vertical position, direction, or stance. b. Erect in posture or carriage. 2. Morally respectable; honorable. —*n.* Something standing upright, as a beam. —**up'right'ness** *n.*

upright piano. A piano having vertically mounted strings.

up•ris•ing (ŭp'rī'zĭng) *n.* 1. The act of rising or rising up. 2. A revolt; insurrection.

up•roar (ŭp'rôr', -rōr') *n.* A condition of noisy excitement and confusion; a tumult. [< MDu *op,* up + *roer,* motion.]

up•roar•i•ous (ŭp'rôr'ē-əs, ŭp'rōr'-) *adj.* 1. Causing or accompanied by an uproar. 2. Boisterous. —**up'roar'i•ous•ly** *adv.*

up•root (ŭp-ro͞ot', -ro͝ot') *v.* 1. To tear or remove (a plant and its roots) from the ground. 2. To destroy completely; eradicate. 3. To force to leave an accustomed or native location. —**up•root'er** *n.*

up•set (ŭp-sĕt') *v.* **-set, -setting.** 1. To overturn or capsize; tip over. 2. To disturb the usual or normal functioning of. 3. To distress or perturb mentally or emotionally. 4. To defeat unexpectedly. —*n.* (ŭp'sĕt'). 1. a. An act of upsetting. b. The condition of being upset. 2. A disturbance, disorder, or agitation. 3. A game or contest in which the favorite is defeated. —*adj.* (ŭp-sĕt'). 1. Overturned; capsized. 2. Disordered; disturbed. 3. Distressed; distraught; agitated. [Orig "to set up," "erect."] —**up•set'ter** *n.*

up•shot (ŭp'shŏt') *n.* The final result; outcome. [Orig the last shot in an archery contest.]

up•side-down (ŭp'sīd'doun') *adj.* 1. Overturned completely so that the upper side is down. 2. In great disorder or confusion; topsy-turvy. —*adv.* Also **upside down.** 1. With the upper and lower parts reversed in position. 2. In or into great disorder. [< ME *up so doun,* "up as if down."]

up•si•lon (ŭp'sə-lŏn') *n.* The 20th letter of the Greek alphabet, representing *u* (sometimes *y*).

up•stage (ŭp'stāj') *adj.* Pertaining to the rear of a stage. —*adv.* Toward, to, on, or at the back part of a stage. —*v.* (ŭp'stāj'). 1. To distract audience attention from (another actor). 2. To steal the show from.

up•stairs (ŭp'stârz') *adv.* In, on, or to an upper floor; up the stairs. —*adj.* (ŭp'stârz'). Of or pertaining to an upper floor or floors. —*n.* (ŭp'stârz'). (*takes sing. or pl. v.*). A floor above the ground level.

up•stand•ing (ŭp'stăn'dĭng, ŭp'-) *adj.* 1. Standing erect or upright. 2. Morally upright; honest.

up•start (ŭp'stärt') *n.* One of humble origin who attains sudden wealth or prominence, esp. one having an exaggerated sense of his own importance or ability.

up•state (ŭp'stāt') *adj.* Designating that part of a state lying inland or farther north of a large city. —**up'state'** *adv.*

up•stream (ŭp'strēm') *adv.* In, at, or toward the source of a stream or current.

up•surge (ŭp'sûrj') *n.* A rapid upward swell or rise.

up•swing (ŭp'swĭng') *n.* An upward swing or trend; an increase.

up•take (ŭp'tāk') *n.* 1. A passage for drawing up smoke or air. 2. Understanding; comprehension: *quick on the uptake.*

up tight. Also **up•tight** (ŭp'tīt'). *Slang.* Tense; nervous.

up-to-date (ŭp'tə-dāt') *adj.* Informed of or reflecting the latest improvement, facts, or style; modern.

up•town (ŭp'toun') *adv.* In or toward the upper part of a city. —*n.* The upper part of a city. —**up'town'** *adj.*

up•turn (ŭp'tûrn') *n.* An upward movement, curve, or trend.

up•ward (ŭp'wərd) *adv.* Also **up•wards** (-wərdz). In, to, or toward a higher place, level, or position. —**upward** (or **upwards**) **of.** More than; in excess of. —*adj.* Ascending.

U•ral-Al•ta•ic (yo͝or'əl-ăl-tā'ĭk) *n.* A hypothetical group of languages including Uralic and Altaic. —**U'ral-Al•ta'ic** *adj.*

U•ral•ic (yo͞o-răl'ĭk) *n.* A family of languages including Finno-Ugric and Samoyed. —**U•ral'ic** *adj.*

U•ral Mountains (yo͝or'əl). A mountain system of the Soviet Union, constituting the traditional boundary between Europe and Asia.

u•ra•ni•um (yo͞o-rā'nē-əm) *n.* *Symbol* **U** A heavy, silvery-white radioactive metallic element used in research, nuclear fuels, and nuclear weapons. Atomic number 92, atomic weight 238.03. [< URANUS.]

U•ra•nus (yo͝or'ə-nəs, yo͞o-rā'nəs) *n.* The 7th planet from the sun, revolving about it every 84.02 years at a distance of approx. 1,790,000,000 miles. It has an equatorial diameter of 30,000 miles, a mass 14.6 times that of Earth, and five satellites. [< Gk *Ouranos,* "heaven," god of the sky.] —**U•ra'ni•an** (yo͞o-rā'nē-ən, -rān'yən) *adj.*

u•ra•ri. Variant of **curare.**

ur•ban (ûr'bən) *adj.* 1. Pertaining to, located in, or constituting a city. 2. Characteristic of the city or city life. [< L *urbs,* city.]

ur•bane (ûr'bān') *adj.* Having the refined manners of polite society; suave. [< L *urbānus,* characteristic of city life.] —**ur'bane'ly** *adv.* —**ur'ban'i•ty** (-băn'ə-tē) *n.*

ur•ban•ize (ûr'bə-nīz') *v.* **-ized, -izing.** To cause to become urban in nature or character. —**ur'ban•i•za'tion** *n.*

ur•chin (ûr'chĭn) *n.* 1. A small, mischievous boy; a scamp. 2. See **sea urchin.** [< L *hēr,* hedgehog.]

Ur•du (o͝or'do͞o, ûr'-) *n.* 1. A Hindustani language spoken in West Pakistan. 2. Hindustani.

-ure. *comb. form.* 1. An act or process: **erasure.** 2. A function or office or a body performing a function: **legislature.** [< L *-ūra.*]

u•re•a (yo͞o-rē'ə) *n.* A white crystalline or powdery compound, CON_2H_4, found in mammalian urine and other body fluids. [< URINE.]

u•re•mi•a (yo͞o-rē'mē-ə) *n.* An excess of urea in the blood, characterized by headache, nausea, vomiting, and coma.

u•re•ter (yo͞o-rē'tər) *n.* The long, narrow duct that conveys urine from the kidney to the urinary bladder. [< Gk *ouron,* urine.]

u•re•thra (yo͞o-rē'thrə) *n., pl.* **-thras** or **-thrae** (-thrē). The canal through which urine is discharged and which serves as the male genital duct. [< Gk *ouron,* urine.] —**u•re'thral** *adj.*

urge (ûrj) *v.* **urged, urging.** 1. To drive onward forcefully; impel; spur. 2. To entreat earnestly and repeatedly; plead with; exhort. 3. To advocate persistently; press emphatically. —*n.* An irresistible or impelling force, influence, or instinct. [L *urgēre,* to push, press.]

ur•gent (ûr'jənt) *adj.* 1. Compelling immediate action; pressing: *a crisis of an urgent nature.* 2. Conveying a sense of pressing importance or necessity. [< L *urgēre,* to push, press, URGE.] —**ur'gen•cy** *n.* —**ur'gent•ly** *adv.*

-urgy. *comb. form.* A technology: **metallurgy.** [< Gk *ergon,* work.]

u•ric (yo͝or'ĭk) *adj.* Of, in, or obtained from urine.

u•ri•nal (yo͝or'ə-nəl) *n.* 1. An upright wall fixture used by men for urinating. 2. A place containing such a fixture or fixtures.

u•ri•nal•y•sis (yo͝or'ə-năl'ə-sĭs) *n.* The chemical analysis of urine.

u•ri•nar•y (yo͝or'ə-nĕr'ē) *adj.* Pertaining to urine, its production, function, or excretion.

urinary bladder. A muscular membrane-lined sac situated in the anterior part of the pelvic cavity and used as a urine reservoir prior to excretion.

u•ri•nate (yo͝or'ə-nāt') *v.* **-nated, -nating.** To excrete urine.

u•rine (yo͝or'ĭn) *n.* The fluid and dissolved substances secreted by the kidneys, stored in the bladder, and excreted from the body through the urethra. [< L *ūrina.*]

urn (ûrn) *n.* 1. A vase with a pedestal, used esp. as a receptacle for the ashes of the cremated dead. 2. A closed metal vessel with a spigot, used for warming or serving tea or coffee; a samovar. [< L *urna.*]

Ur•sa Major (ûr'sə). A constellation in the region of the N celestial pole, containing the Big Dipper. [< L *ursus,* bear.]

Ursa Minor. A constellation having the shape of a ladle with Polaris at the tip of its handle.

ur•sine (ûr'sīn') *adj.* Of or characteristic of a bear. [< L *ursus,* bear.]

ur•ti•car•i•a (ûr'tĭ-kâr'ē-ə) *n.* A skin condition having various causes, characterized by intensely itching welts. [< L *urtīca,* nettle.]

U•ru•guay (yo͝or'ə-gwā', -gwī'). A republic of SE South America. Pop. 2,590,000. Cap. Montevideo.

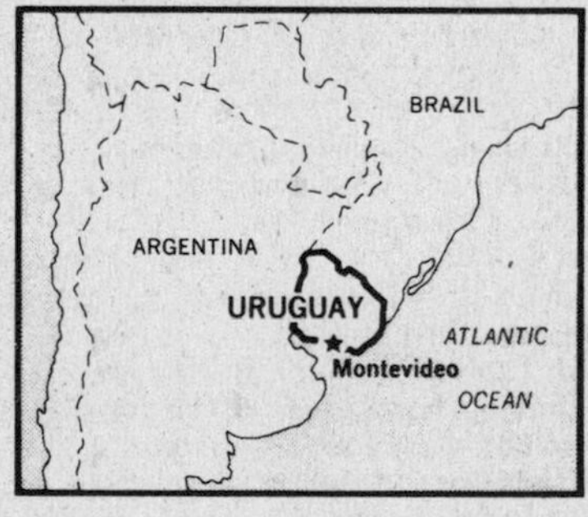

Uruguay

us (ŭs) *pron.* The objective case of the 1st person pl. pronoun *we,* used as the direct or indirect object of a verb or as the object of a preposition. [< OE *ūs.* See **nes-.**]

US, U.S. United States.

USA, U.S.A. 1. United States Army. 2. United States of America.

us•a•ble (yo͞o'zə-bəl) *adj.* Also **use•a•ble.** 1. Capable of being used. 2. In a fit condition for use. —**us'a•ble•ness** *n.*

USAF, U.S.A.F. United States Air Force.

us•age (yo͞o'sĭj, -zĭj) *n.* 1. The act or manner of using; use or employment. 2. Customary practice; habitual use. 3. The actual way in which a language or its elements are used, interrelated, or pronounced.

USCG, U.S.C.G. United States Coast Guard.

USDA, U.S.D.A. United States Department of Agriculture.

use (yo͞oz) *v.* **used, using.** 1. To bring or put into service; employ for some purpose. 2. To consume or expend. **3.** *Informal.* To exploit for one's own advantage. —Used as an auxiliary in the past tense to express former practice, fact, or state: *I used to go; he didn't use to.* —**used to.** Accustomed to. —*n.* (yo͞os). **1. a.** The act of using. **b.** The condition or fact of being used. **2.** The manner of using; usage. **3. a.** The permission to use or privilege of using something: *have use of the car.* **b.** The power or ability to use something: *lose the use of one arm.* **4.** The need or occasion to use: *Do you have any use for this book?* **5.** The quality of being suitable or adaptable to an end; usefulness. **6.** The goal, object, or purpose for which something is used. —**have no use for. 1.** To have no need of. **2.** To have no tolerance for; dislike. —**in use.** Being used; occupied. [< L *ūtī* (pp *ūsus*).] —**us'er** *n.*

used (yo͞ozd) *adj.* Not new; secondhand.

use•ful (yo͞os'fəl) *adj.* Capable of being used advantageously or beneficially. —**use'ful•ly** *adv.* —**use'ful•ness** *n.*

use•less (yo͞os'lĭs) *adj.* Having no beneficial purpose or use; of little or no worth. —**use'less•ly** *adv.* —**use'less•ness** *n.*

ush•er (ŭsh'ər) *n.* **1.** An official doorkeeper, as in a courtroom or legislative chamber. **2.** One who escorts people to their seats in a theater, church, stadium, etc. **3.** A male attendant at a wedding. —*v.* **1.** To escort; lead or conduct. **2.** To precede and introduce; be a forerunner of. [< L *ōstiārius,* doorkeeper.]

USIA United States Information Agency.

U.S.M. United States Mail.

USMC, U.S.M.C. United States Marine Corps.

USN, U.S.N. United States Navy.

USO, U.S.O. United Service Organizations.

U.S.S. United States Ship.

U.S.S.R. Union of Soviet Socialist Republics.

u•su•al (yo͞o'zho͞o-əl) *adj.* **1.** Such as is commonly or frequently encountered or used; ordinary; normal. **2.** Habitual or customary. [< L *ūsus,* use, custom.] —**u'su•al•ly** *adv.* —**u'su•al•ness** *n.*

u•surp (yo͞o-sûrp', -zûrp') *v.* To seize and hold by force and without legal right or authority. [< L *ūsūrpāre,* to take into use.] —**u'sur•pa'tion** *n.* —**u•surp'er** *n.*

u•su•ry (yo͞o'zhə-rē) *n., pl.* **-ries. 1.** The lending of money at an exorbitant rate of interest. **2.** Such an excessive rate of interest. [< L *ūsūra,* use of money lent, interest.] —**u'su•rer** *n.* —**u•su'ri•ous** (yo͞o-zho͝or'ē-əs) *adj.*

U•tah (yo͞o'tô, -tä). A state of the W U.S. Pop. 1,059,000. Cap. Salt Lake City.

u•ten•sil (yo͞o-tĕn'səl) *n.* Any instrument or container, esp. one used domestically, as in a kitchen or on a farm. [< L *ūtēnsilia,* "things for use."]

u•ter•us (yo͞o'tər-əs) *n.* A pear-shaped muscular organ located in the pelvic cavity of female mammals that holds the fertilized ovum during the development of the fetus and is the principal agent in its expulsion at birth. [L.] —**u'ter•ine** (-ĭn, -tə-rīn') *adj.*

u•til•i•tar•i•an (yo͞o-tĭl'ə-târ'ē-ən) *adj.* **1.** Pertaining to or associated with utility. **2.** Stressing utility over aesthetic qualities.

u•til•i•ty (yo͞o-tĭl'ə-tē) *n., pl.* **-ties. 1.** Usefulness. **2.** A public service, such as gas, electricity, water, or transportation. [< L *ūtī,* to USE.]

u•til•ize (yo͞o'tə-līz') *v.* **-ized, -izing.** To put to use for a certain purpose. —**u'til•i•za'tion** *n.*

ut•most (ŭt'mōst') *adj.* **1.** Being or situated at the farthest limit or point. **2.** Of the highest or greatest degree, amount, or intensity. —*n.* The greatest possible amount, degree, or extent; maximum. [< OE *ūtemest,* outermost.]

U•to-Az•tec•an (yo͞o'tō-ăz'tĕk'ən) *n.* **1.** A large language family of North and Central American Indians, including Nahuatl. **2.** A tribe speaking a Uto-Aztecan language. **3.** A member of such a tribe. —**U'to-Az'tec'an** *adj.*

u•to•pi•a (yo͞o-tō'pē-ə) *n.* **1.** Any condition, place, or situation of social or political perfection. **2.** Any idealistic goal or concept for social and political reform. [NL, "no-place."] —**u•to'pi•an** *adj.*

ut•ter[1] (ŭt'ər) *v.* **1.** To express audibly; pronounce; say. **2.** To give forth as a sound: *utter a sigh.* [< MDu *ūteren,* to drive away, announce, speak.] —**ut'ter•er** *n.*

ut•ter[2] (ŭt'ər) *adj.* Complete; absolute; entire. [< OE *ūtera, ūttra,* outer, external. See **ud-.**] —**ut'ter•ly** *adv.*

ut•ter•ance (ŭt'ər-əns) *n.* **1.** The act of uttering. **2.** Something that is uttered or expressed.

ut•ter•most (ŭt'ər-mōst') *adj.* **1.** Utmost. **2.** Outermost. —*n.* Utmost.

U-turn (yo͞o'tûrn') *n.* A turn, as by a vehicle, completely reversing the direction of travel.

u•vu•la (yo͞o'vyə-lə) *n.* The small, conical, fleshy mass of tissue suspended from the center of the soft palate above the back of the tongue. [< LL, "small grape."] —**u'vu•lar** *adj.*

ux•o•ri•ous (ŭk'sôr'ē-əs, ŭk'sōr'-, ŭg'zôr'-, ŭg'zōr'-) *adj.* Excessively submissive or devoted to one's wife. [< L *uxor,* wife.]

Uz•bek Soviet Socialist Republic (o͞oz'bĕk, ŭz'-). A republic of the Soviet Union, in C Asia. Pop. 11,963,000. Cap. Tashkent.

Vv

v, V (vē) *n.* **1.** The 22nd letter of the English alphabet. **2.** Anything shaped like the letter **V.**

v The Roman numeral for five.

V 1. vanadium. **2.** velocity. **3.** volt. **4.** volume. **5.** The Roman numeral for five.

v. 1. verb. **2.** verse. **3.** version. **4.** versus. **5.** vide. **6.** voice. **7.** volume (book).

V. 1. vice (in titles). **2.** village.

VA Veterans' Administration.

Va. Virginia.

va•can•cy (vā'kən-sē) *n., pl.* **-cies. 1.** The state or condition of being vacant. **2.** A position, office, or accommodation that is unfilled or unoccupied.

va•cant (vā'kənt) *adj.* **1.** Containing nothing; empty. **2.** Not occupied. **3.** Expressionless; blank: *a vacant stare.* [< L *vacāre,* to be empty.] —**va'cant•ly** *adv.*

va•cate (vā'kāt') *v.* **-cated, -cating.** To cease to occupy or hold; give up; leave. [L *vacāre,* to be empty.] —**va'cat'a•ble** *adj.*

va•ca•tion (vā-kā'shən) *n.* An interval of time devoted to rest or relaxation from work, study, etc. —*v.* To take or spend a vacation. [< L *vacātiō,* freedom, release from occupation.] —**va•ca'tion•er** *n.*

vac•ci•nate (văk'sə-nāt') *v.* **-nated, -nating.** To inoculate with a vaccine to produce immunity against one of various diseases. —**vac'ci•na'tion** *n.* —**vac'ci•na'tor** *n.*

vac•cine (văk-sēn') *n.* A suspension of attenuated or killed microorganisms, as of viruses or bacteria, incapable of inducing severe infection but capable, when inoculated, of counteracting the unmodified species. [F *(virus) vaccine,* (virus) of cowpox.]

vac•il•late (văs'ə-lāt') *v.* **-lated, -lating. 1.** To sway to and fro; oscillate. **2.** To swing indecisively from one course of action or opinion to another; waver. [L *vacillāre,* to waver.] —**vac'il•la'tion** *n.* —**vac'il•la'tor** *n.*

va•cu•i•ty (vă-kyo͞o'ə-tē) *n., pl.* **-ties. 1.** Emptiness. **2.** An empty space; vacuum. **3.** Emptiness of mind. [< L *vacuus,* empty.]

vac•u•ous (văk'yo͞o-əs) *adj.* **1.** Devoid of matter; empty. **2.** Stupid; dull; inane. [L *vacuus,* empty.] —**vac'u•ous•ness** *n.*

vac•u•um (văk'yo͞o-əm, -yo͞om) *n., pl.* **-ums** or **vacua** (vak'yo͞o-ə). **1.** A space empty or relatively empty of matter. **2.** A state of emptiness; a void. —*v.* To clean with a vacuum cleaner. [< L *vacuus,* empty.] —**vac'u•um** *adj.*

vacuum cleaner. An electrical appliance that draws light dirt from surfaces by suction.

vacuum tube. An electron tube having an internal vacuum sufficiently high to permit electrons to move with low interaction with any remaining gas molecules.

Va•duz (fä-do͞ots'). The capital of Liechtenstein. Pop. 4,000.

vag•a•bond (văg'ə-bŏnd') *n.* A person who wanders from place to place with no apparent means of support. [< L *vagus,* wandering, undecided, VAGUE.] —**vag'a•bond'** *adj.*

va•gar•y (vā'gə-rē, və-gâr'ē) *n., pl.* **-ies. 1.** A whimsical notion or action. **2.** Often **vagaries.** An unpredictable change or fluctuation: *vagaries of weather.* [< L *vagārī,* to wander.]

va•gi•na (və-jī'nə) *n., pl.* **-nas** or **-nae** (-nē). The passage leading from the external genital orifice to the uterus in female mammals. [L *vāgīna,* sheath.] —**vag'i•nal** (văj'ə-nəl) *adj.*

va•grant (vā'grənt) *n.* A person who wanders from place to place and ekes out a living by begging or stealing; a tramp; vagabond. —*adj.* **1.** Wandering from place to place; roving. **2.** Moving in a random fashion; not fixed in place. [Prob < L *vagus,* wandering, undecided, VAGUE.] —**va'gran•cy** *n.*

vague (vāg) *adj.* **vaguer, vaguest. 1.** Not clearly expressed or outlined; inexplicit. **2.** Lacking definite shape, form, or character. **3.** Indistinctly felt, perceived, understood, or recalled. [< L *vagus,* wandering, undecided, vague.] **—vague'ly** *adv.* **—vague'ness** *n.*

vain (vān) *adj.* **1.** Unsuccessful; futile; fruitless. **2.** Lacking substance or worth; hollow. **3.** Showing undue preoccupation with one's appearance or accomplishments; conceited. **—in vain. 1.** To no avail. **2.** Irreverently. [< L *vānus,* empty.] **—vain'ly** *adv.*

vain•glo•ry (vān'glôr'ē, -glōr'ē) *n., pl.* **-ries. 1.** Excessive vanity. **2.** Vain and ostentatious display. **—vain•glo'ri•ous** *adj.*

val. value.

val•ance (văl'əns) *n.* A short ornamental drapery hung across the top of a window or along a bed, shelf, etc. [ME *valaunce.*]

vale (vāl) *n.* A valley; dale. [< L *vallis.*]

val•e•dic•to•ri•an (văl'ə-dĭk-tôr'ē-ən, -tōr'ē-ən) *n.* A student, usually of the highest scholastic standing, who delivers the valedictory at commencement.

val•e•dic•to•ry (văl'ə-dĭk'tə-rē) *n., pl.* **-ries.** A farewell address, esp. one delivered by a valedictorian. [< L *valedīcere,* to say farewell.]

va•lence (vā'ləns) *n.* Also **va•len•cy** (vā'lən-sē) *pl.* **-cies. 1.** *Chem.* The capacity of an atom or group of atoms to combine in specific proportions with other atoms or groups of atoms. **2.** An integer used to represent this capacity. [< L *valēre,* to be strong.]

Va•len•ci•a (və-lĕn'shē-ə, -shə). A city of E Spain. Pop. 583,000.

val•en•tine (văl'ən-tīn') *n.* **1.** A greeting card sent on Saint Valentine's Day, February 14. **2.** A person singled out as one's sweetheart on Saint Valentine's Day.

val•et (văl'ĭt, vă-lā') *n.* **1.** A man's personal attendant. **2.** A hotel employee who performs personal services for patrons. [< OF *vaslet,* orig "young nobleman," "squire."]

val•e•tu•di•nar•i•an (văl'ə-t/y/ōōd'n-âr'e-ən) *n.* A person constantly and morbidly concerned with his health. [L *valētūdinārius,* in poor health.] **—val'e•tu'di•nar'i•an•ism'** *n.*

Val•hal•la (văl-hăl'ə) *n.* Also **Wal•hal•la** (văl-, wŏl-). *Norse Myth.* The hall in which the souls of slain warriors were received by Odin.

val•iant (văl'yənt) *adj.* Possessing, showing, or acting with valor; brave; courageous; stouthearted. [< L *valēre,* to be strong.] **—val'ian•cy** *n.* **—val'iant•ly** *adv.*

val•id (văl'ĭd) *adj.* **1.** Well-grounded; sound; supportable: *a valid objection.* **2.** Having legal force: *a valid passport.* [< L *validus,* strong, effective.] **—va•lid'i•ty** (və-lĭd'ə-tē) *n.*

val•i•date (văl'ə-dāt') *v.* **-dated, -dating. 1.** To declare or make legally valid. **2.** To substantiate; verify. **—val'i•da'tion** *n.*

va•lise (və-lēs') *n.* A small piece of hand luggage. [< ML *valisia.*]

Val•let•ta (və-lĕt'ə). The capital of Malta. Pop. 18,000.

val•ley (văl'ē) *n., pl.* **-leys. 1.** An elongated lowland between ranges of mountains or hills. **2.** The land area drained by a river system. [< L *vallis.*]

val•or (văl'ər) *n.* Also *chiefly Brit.* **val•our.** Courage and boldness; bravery. [< L *valēre,* to be strong, be of value.] **—val'or•ous** *adj.*

val•u•a•ble (văl'yōō-ə-bəl, văl'yə-) *adj.* **1.** Having high monetary or material value. **2.** Having useful or admirable qualities or characteristics. *—n.* Often **valuables.** A valuable personal possession, as a piece of jewelry.

val•u•a•tion (văl'yōō-ā'shən) *n.* **1.** The act of assessing the value or price of something; an appraisal. **2.** The assessed value or price of something.

val•ue (văl'yōō) *n.* **1.** An amount considered a suitable equivalent for something else; a fair return for goods or services. **2.** Monetary or material worth. **3.** Worth in usefulness or importance to the possessor; merit. **4.** A principle, standard, or quality considered worthwhile or desirable. **5.** Precise meaning. **6.** An assigned or calculated numerical quantity. **7.** *Mus.* The relative duration of a tone or rest. **8.** The relative darkness or lightness of a color in a picture. *—v.* **-ued, -uing. 1.** To determine or estimate the value of; appraise. **2.** To prize; esteem. **3.** To rate according to relative estimate of worth or desirability; evaluate. [< L *valēre,* to be strong, be of value.]

valve (vălv) *n.* **1.** A membranous bodily structure that retards or prevents the return flow of a bodily fluid. **2. a.** Any of various devices that regulate gas or liquid flow by opening, closing, or obstructing its passage, as through piping. **b.** The control element of such a device. **c.** A device in a brass wind instrument that permits rapid variation of tube length to produce changes in pitch. **3.** A paired or separable structure or part, as of a seed pod or mollusk shell. [< L *valva,* the leaf of a door.]

va•moose (vă-mōōs', və-) *v.* **-moosed, -moosing.** *Slang.* To leave or go away hastily. [Span *vamos,* "let's go."]

vamp[1] (vămp) *n.* The part of a boot or shoe covering the instep and sometimes the toe. *—v.* **1.** To provide with a new vamp. **2.** To refurbish. **3.** To improvise. [< OF *avantpie.*]

vamp[2] (vămp). *Informal. n.* An unscrupulously seductive woman. *—v.* To play the vamp; seduce and exploit. [Short for VAMPIRE.]

vam•pire (văm'pīr') *n.* **1.** In folklore, one that rises from the grave by night to suck the blood of sleeping persons. **2.** One who preys upon others, esp. an extortionist or exploiter. **3.** Also **vampire bat.** Any of various tropical bats thought to feed on the blood of living mammals. [< Hung *vampir.*]

vam•pir•ism (văm'pī-rĭz'əm) *n.* **1.** Belief in the vampires of folklore. **2.** The practice of a vampire; bloodsucking.

van[1] (văn) *n.* **1.** A covered truck or wagon for transporting goods or livestock. **2.** *Brit.* A closed railroad car for baggage or freight. [Short for CARAVAN.]

van[2] (văn) *n.* The vanguard. [Short for VANGUARD.]

va•na•di•um (və-nā'dē-əm) *n.* *Symbol* **V** A bright, white, soft, ductile metallic element, used in rust-resistant high-speed tools, as a carbon stabilizer in some steels, and as a catalyst. Atomic number 23, atomic weight 50.942. [< ON *Vanadīs,* name of Freya, goddess of love and beauty.]

Van Al•len belt (văn ăl'ən). Either of two zones of high-intensity radiation trapped in the earth's magnetic field, beginning at an altitude of approx. 800 kilometers and extending thousands of kilometers into space. [< J. *Van Allen* (born 1914), American physicist.]

Van Bu•ren (văn byŏŏr'ən), **Martin.** 1782–1862. 8th President of the U.S. (1837–41).

Van•cou•ver (văn-kōō'vər). A city of SW British Columbia, Canada. Pop. 385,000.

van•dal (vănd'l) *n.* One who willfully or maliciously defaces or destroys public or private property. [< VANDAL.] **—van'dal•ism'** *n.*

Van•dal (vănd'l) *n.* A member of a Germanic people that sacked Rome in A.D. 455. [L *Vandalus,* "wanderer" < Gmc.]

Van de Graaff generator (văn' də grăf'). An electrostatic generator in which electric charge is either removed from or transferred to a large, hollow spherical electrode by a rapidly moving belt. [< R. *Van de Graaff* (1901–67), American physicist.]

Van•dyke beard (văn-dīk'). A short pointed beard. [< Sir Anthony *Vandyke* (1599–1641), Flemish painter.]

vane (vān) *n.* **1.** A device that pivots on an elevated vertical spindle to indicate wind direction. **2.** One of several surfaces radially mounted along an axis that is turned by or used to turn a fluid. [< OE *fana,* banner. See **pan-.**]

van Gogh (văn gō', gôKH'), **Vincent.** 1853–1890. Dutch painter.

van•guard (văn'gärd') *n.* **1.** The foremost position in an army or fleet; van. **2.** The leading position in a trend or movement. [< OF *avant-garde.*]

va•nil•la (və-nĭl'ə) *n.* **1.** A flavoring obtained from the narrow, beanlike pods of a tropical American orchid. **2.** An orchid bearing such pods. [Span *vainilla,* "little sheath."]

van•ish (văn'ĭsh) *v.* **1.** To disappear or become invisible, esp. quickly. **2.** To pass out of existence. [< L *ēvānēscere.*]

van•i•ty (văn'ə-tē) *n., pl.* **-ties. 1.** Excessive pride; conceit. **2.** Futility; worthlessness. **3.** Something vain, futile, or worthless. **4.** A case for cosmetics. [< L *vānus,* empty, vain.]

van•quish (văng'kwĭsh, văn'-) *v.* **1.** To defeat; subjugate. **2.** To overcome; suppress. [< L *vincere.*] **—van'quish•er** *n.*

van•tage (văn'tĭj) *n.* **1. a.** An advantage in a competition. **b.** Something providing superiority or advantage. **2.** A commanding view or outlook. [< OF *avantage,* advantage.]

vap•id (văp'ĭd) *adj.* Insipid; flat; stale. [< L *vapidus.*] **—vap'id•ly** *adv.* **—vap'id•ness** *n.*

va•por (vā'pər) *n.* Also *chiefly Brit.* **va•pour. 1.** Any barely visible or cloudy diffused matter, as mist, fumes, or smoke, suspended in the air. **2.** The gaseous state of any substance that is liquid or solid under ordinary conditions. **3. vapors.** *Archaic.* Depression or hysteria. [< L, steam.]

va•por•ize (vā'pə-rīz') *v.* **-ized, -izing.** To convert or be converted into vapor, esp. by heating. **—va'por•i•za'tion** *n.* **—va'por•iz'er** *n.*

va•por•ous (vā'pər-əs) *adj.* **1.** Pertaining to or resembling vapor. **2. a.** Volatile. **b.** Giving off vapors. **3.** Insubstantial, vague, or ethereal.

Martin Van Buren

4. Extravagantly fanciful. —**va'por•ous•ly** *adv.* —**va'por•ous•ness** *n.*

var. 1. variable. 2. variant. 3. variation. 4. variety. 5. various.

var•i•a•ble (vâr'ē-ə-bəl) *adj.* 1. a. Subject to variation; changeable. b. Inconstant; fickle. 2. *Math.* Having no fixed quantitative value. —*n.* 1. Anything that varies or is prone to variation. 2. *Math.* A quantity capable of assuming any of a set of values. —**var'i•a•bil'i•ty, var'i•a•ble•ness** *n.* —**var'i•a•bly** *adv.*

var•i•ance (vâr'ē-əns) *n.* 1. a. The act of varying. b. Variation; difference. 2. A difference of opinion; dispute. 3. A license to engage in an act contrary to a usual rule.

var•i•ant (vâr'ē-ənt) *adj.* 1. Exhibiting variation; differing. 2. Tending to vary; variable. 3. Deviant. —*n.* Something exhibiting slight variation in form from another, as a different spelling of the same word.

var•i•a•tion (vâr'ē-ā'shən) *n.* 1. The act, process, or result of varying; change or deviation. 2. The extent or degree of such change. 3. Something that is slightly different from another of the same type. 4. A musical form that is an altered version of a given theme, diverging from it by melodic ornamentation and changes in harmony, rhythm, or key.

var•i•col•ored (vâr'ĭ-kŭl'ərd) *adj.* Having a variety of colors; variegated.

var•i•cose (văr'ə-kōs') *adj.* Designating blood or lymph vessels that are abnormally dilated, knotted, and tortuous. [< L *varix,* swollen vein.]

var•ied (vâr'ēd) *adj.* 1. Marked by variety. 2. Modified or altered. 3. Varicolored. —**var'ied•ly** *adv.*

var•i•e•gate (vâr'ē-ə-gāt') *v.* **-gated, -gating.** 1. To impart a variety of colors to. 2. To give variety to; diversify. —**var'i•e•ga'tion** *n.*

va•ri•e•ty (və-rī'ə-tē) *n., pl.* **-ties.** 1. The condition or quality of being various or varied; diversity. 2. A number of varied things, esp. of a particular group; an assortment. 3. A different kind, sort, or form of something of the same general classification. 4. An organism, esp. a plant, belonging to a naturally occurring or selectively bred subdivision of a species. [< L *varius,* VARIOUS.]

var•i•ous (vâr'ē-əs) *adj.* 1. a. Of diverse kinds. b. Unlike; different. 2. More than one; several. 3. Many-sided; versatile. 4. Having a variegated nature or appearance. 5. Individual and separate: *The various reports all agreed.* [L *varius,* speckled, changeable.] —**var'i•ous•ly** *adv.* —**var'i•ous•ness** *n.*

Usage: *Various* sometimes appears as a plural collective pronoun followed by *of* rather than by a noun, but the usage is not standard: *He spoke to various of the members. Various* has its proper function as an adjective in *He spoke to various members.*

var•let (vär'lĭt) *n. Archaic.* 1. An attendant. 2. A rascal; knave. [OF *vaslet, valet,* VALET.]

var•mint (vär'mənt) *n. Regional.* An animal or person considered objectionable or troublesome. [Var of VERMIN.]

var•nish (vär'nĭsh) *n.* 1. An oil-based liquid covering used to coat a surface with a hard, glossy, thin film. 2. a. The smooth coating or gloss resulting from the application of varnish. b. Something resembling varnish. 3. Outward show; gloss. [< OF *vernis.*] —**var'nish** *v.*

var•si•ty (vär'sə-tē) *n., pl.* **-ties.** 1. The principal team representing a university, college, or school, as in sports. 2. *Brit. Slang.* A university. [Short for UNIVERSITY.] —**var'si•ty** *adj.*

var•y (vâr'ē) *v.* **-ied, -ying.** 1. To cause or undergo change; modify or alter. 2. To give variety to; diversify. 3. To deviate; diverge; differ. [< L *varius,* speckled, changeable.]

vas•cu•lar (văs'kyə-lər) *adj.* Of or containing vessels for the circulation of fluids such as blood, lymph, or sap. [< L *vās,* vessel.]

vase (vās, vāz, väz) *n.* A tall open vessel used chiefly for holding and displaying flowers. [< L *vās,* vessel.]

Vas•e•line (văs'ə-lēn', -lĭn) *n.* A trademark for a petroleum jelly used primarily as a vehicle for ointments and as a protective coating for metals. [< G *Wasser,* water.]

vas•o•mo•tor (văs'ō-mō'tər, vā'sō-) *adj.* Causing or regulating constriction or dilation of blood vessels.

vas•sal (văs'əl) *n.* 1. One who holds land from a feudal lord and receives protection in return for homage and allegiance. 2. One subservient to another; a subordinate or dependent. [< ML *vassus,* servant, valet.]

vas•sal•age (văs'ə-lĭj) *n.* 1. The condition of being a vassal. 2. The service, homage, and fealty required of a vassal. 3. Subordination or subjection: *"Am I the man to reproach Coleridge with this vassalage to opium?"* (De Quincey). 4. A fief.

vast (văst, väst) *adj.* 1. Very great in size, amount, or quantity. 2. Very great in area or extent; immense. [L *vastus,* immense, vast.] —**vast'ly** *adv.* —**vast'ness** *n.*

vat (văt) *n.* A large tub or barrel used to store or hold liquids. [< OE *fæt.* See **ped-**[2].]

vat•ic (văt'ĭk) *adj.* Prophetic; oracular. [< L *vātēs,* prophet.]

Vat•i•can (văt'ĭ-kən) *n.* 1. **the Vatican.** The official residence of the pope in Vatican City. 2. The papal government.

Vatican City. A sovereign papal state in Rome, Italy. Pop. 900.

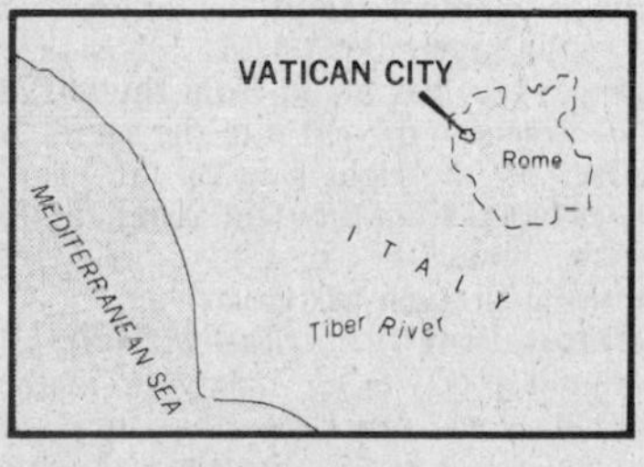

Vatican City

vau. Variant of **vav.**

vaude•ville (vôd'vĭl, vōd'-, vô'də-vĭl') *n.* Stage entertainment offering a variety of short acts. [< OF *vaudevire.*]

vault[1] (vôlt) *n.* 1. An arched structure forming a ceiling or roof. 2. A room with arched walls and ceiling, esp. when underground, as a storeroom. 3. A compartment for the safekeeping of valuables. 4. A burial chamber. —*v.* To construct or cover with a vault. [< VL **volvita,* a turn, vault.]

vault[2] (vôlt) *v.* To jump or leap over, esp. with the aid of a support, as the hands or a pole. —*n.* The act of vaulting; a leap. [< L *volvere,* to turn.] —**vault'er** *n.*

vaunt (vônt, vänt) *v.* To boast; brag. [< L *vānus,* empty, vain.] —**vaunt** *n.*

vav (väv, vôv) *n.* Also **vau, waw.** The 6th letter of the Hebrew alphabet, representing *w.*

vb. verb.

V.C. Vietcong.

VD venereal disease.

veal (vēl) *n.* The meat of a calf. [< L *vitulus,* calf, "yearling."]

vec•tor (vĕk'tər) *n.* 1. *Math.* A quantity completely specified by a magnitude and a direction. 2. An organism that transmits microorganisms that cause disease. [L, carrier.] —**vec•to'ri•al** (vĕk-tôr'ē-əl, -tōr'ē-əl) *adj.*

Ve•da (vā'də, vē'-) *n.* Any of the oldest sacred writings of Hinduism. [Sk *veda,* "knowledge."] —**Ve'dic** *adj.*

Ve•dan•ta (vĭ-dän'tə, -dăn'tə) *n.* The Hindu doctrine that all reality is a single principle, Brahman, and that the believer's goal is to transcend the limitations of self-identity and realize his unity with Brahman. [Sk *vedanta,* "complete knowledge of the Veda."] —**Ve•dan'tic** *adj.*

veer (vîr) *v.* To turn aside from a course or direction; swerve; shift. [< VL **vīrāre.*] —**veer** *n.* —**veer'ing•ly** *adv.*

Ve•ga (vē'gə, vā'-) *n.* The brightest star in the constellation Lyra. [ML.]

veg•e•ta•ble (vĕj'tə-bəl, vĕj'ə-tə-) *n.* 1. a. A plant cultivated for an edible part, as roots, stems, leaves, or flowers. b. The edible part of such a plant. 2. A plant as distinguished from an animal or mineral. 3. A person who leads a passive or inert existence. —*adj.* 1. Of, pertaining to, or derived from plants. 2. Suggestive of inactivity. [< L *vegetus,* lively.]

veg•e•tar•i•an (vĕj'ə-târ'ē-ən) *n.* One who practices or advocates vegetarianism. —**veg'e•tar'i•an** *adj.*

veg•e•tar•i•an•ism (vĕj'ə-târ'ē-ə-nĭz'əm) *n.* 1. The practice of eating only vegetables and plant products. 2. The practice of not eating meat.

veg•e•tate (vĕj'ə-tāt') *v.* **-tated, -tating.** 1. To grow or sprout as a plant does. 2. To lead a passive or inert existence. [LL *vegetāre,* to grow.]

veg•e•ta•tion (vĕj'ə-tā'shən) *n.* 1. The act or process of vegetating. 2. Plant life collectively.

veg•e•ta•tive (vĕj'ə-tā'tĭv) *adj.* 1. Of, pertaining to, or characteristic of plants or plant growth. 2. *Biol.* a. Of, pertaining to, or capable of growth. b. Of, pertaining to, or functioning in processes such as growth or nutrition rather than sexual reproduction.

ve•he•ment (vē'ə-mənt) *adj.* 1. Forceful; intense; ardent. 2. Strong; violent. [< L *vehemēns.*] —**ve'he•mence** *n.* —**ve'he•ment•ly** *adv.*

ve•hi•cle (vē'ĭ-kəl) *n.* 1. Any device for carrying passengers, goods, or equipment; a conveyance. 2. A medium through which something is expressed or conveyed. 3. A substance used as the medium in which active ingredients are applied or administered. [< L *vehere,* to carry.] —**ve•hic'u•lar** (vē-hĭk'yə-lər) *adj.*

veil (vāl) *n.* 1. A piece of cloth, often transparent, worn by women over the head or face. 2. The life or vows of a nun: *take the veil.* 3. Anything that conceals, separates, or screens: *a veil of secrecy.* —*v.* To cover with or as with a veil. [< L *vēlum,* covering, veil.]

veil•ing (vā'lĭng) *n.* 1. A veil. 2. Gauzy material used for veils.

vein (vān) *n.* 1. A vessel that transports blood toward the heart. 2. Loosely, any blood vessel. 3. One of the branching structures forming the framework of a leaf or an insect's wing. 4. A regularly shaped and lengthy occurrence of an ore; a lode. 5. A long, wavy strip of color, as in marble. 6. Any fissure, crack, or cleft. 7. Inherent character or quality; a strain or streak. **8.** Style or mode of expression: *talk in a serious vein.* —*v.* To form or mark with veins. [< L *vēna,* vein.]

Ve•láz•quez (və-läs′kĭs, -kās, və-lăs′-), **Diego.** 1599–1660. Spanish painter.

veldt (fĕlt, vĕlt) *n.* Also **veld.** Any of the open grasslands of S Africa. [Afrik *veld.*]

vel•le•i•ty (vĕ-lē′ə-tē) *n., pl.* **-ties. 1.** The lowest level of volition. **2.** A mere wish. [< L *velle,* to wish.]

vel•lum (vĕl′əm) *n.* **1.** A fine parchment made from the skins of calf, lamb, or kid and used for the pages and binding of fine books. **2.** A paper resembling vellum. [< OF *veel,* calf, veal.]

ve•loc•i•pede (və-lŏs′ə-pēd′) *n.* A tricycle. [F *vélocipède,* "swift-footed."]

ve•loc•i•ty (və-lŏs′ə-tē) *n., pl.* **-ties. 1.** Rapidity or speed. **2.** *Phys.* A vector quantity, the magnitude of which is a body's speed and the direction of which is the body's direction of motion. [< L *vēlōx,* fast.]

ve•lours, ve•lour (və-lo͝or′) *n., pl.* **-lours** (-lo͝or′). A closely napped, velvetlike fabric. [< L *villus,* shaggy hair, wool.]

ve•lum (vē′ləm) *n., pl.* **-la** (-lə). A covering or partition of thin membranous tissue. [< L *vēlum,* veil, covering, sail.]

vel•vet (vĕl′vĭt) *n.* **1. a.** A fabric of silk or a synthetic fiber such as rayon, having a smooth, dense pile and a plain back. **b.** Anything resembling this fabric. **2.** Smoothness; softness. **3.** The soft covering on the newly developing antlers of deer. —*adj.* Made of, covered with, or resembling velvet. [< L *villus,* shaggy hair, wool.] —**vel′vet•y** *adj.*

vel•vet•een (vĕl′və-tēn′) *n.* A velvetlike fabric made of cotton.

ve•nal (vē′nəl) *adj.* Open or susceptible to bribery; corrupt or corruptible. [< L *vēnum,* sale.] —**ve•nal′i•ty** (-năl′ə-tē) *n.* —**ve′nal•ly** *adv.*

vend (vĕnd) *v.* To sell, esp. as a vender. [< L *vēndere.*]

vend•ee (vĕn-dē′) *n.* A buyer.

ven•der (vĕn′dər) *n.* Also **ven•dor. 1.** One who vends; a peddler. **2.** A vending machine.

ven•det•ta (vĕn-dĕt′ə) *n.* A hereditary blood feud between two families. [< L *vindicāre,* to revenge, VINDICATE.]

vending machine. A coin-operated machine that dispenses small articles.

ve•neer (və-nîr′) *n.* **1.** A thin finishing or surface layer bonded to an inferior substratum. **2.** Surface show; gloss. —*v.* To overlay with a veneer. [< G *furniren,* to furnish, veneer.]

ven•er•a•ble (vĕn′ər-ə-bəl) *adj.* **1.** Worthy of reverence or respect by virtue of dignity, position, or age. **2.** Commanding reverence by association: *venerable relics.* [< L *venerārī,* VENERATE.] —**ven′er•a•bil′i•ty** *n.*

ven•er•ate (vĕn′ə-rāt′) *v.* **-ated, -ating.** To regard with respect and reverence. [L *venerārī.*] —**ven′er•a′tion** *n.* —**ven′er•a′tor** *n.*

ve•ne•re•al (və-nîr′ē-əl) *adj.* **1.** Pertaining to sexual intercourse. **2.** Transmitted by sexual intercourse. **3.** Pertaining to the genitals. [< L *venus,* love, lust.]

Venetian blind. A window blind consisting of adjustable horizontal or sometimes vertical slats that can be set at a desired angle to regulate the amount of light admitted.

Ven•e•zue•la (vĕn′ə-zwā′lə, -zwē′lə). A republic in N South America. Pop. 8,722,000. Cap. Caracas.

venge•ance (vĕn′jəns) *n.* Retaliation for a wrong or injury; retribution. [< L *vindicāre,* to revenge, VINDICATE.]

venge•ful (vĕnj′fəl) *adj.* Desiring vengeance; vindictive. —**venge′ful•ness** *n.*

ve•ni•al (vē′nē-əl, vēn′yəl) *adj.* Easily excused or forgiven; pardonable: *a venial offense.* [< L *venia,* forgiveness.]

Ven•ice (vĕn′ĭs). A city of NE Italy. Pop. 360,000. —**Ve•ne′tian** (və-nē′shən) *adj.* & *n.*

ven•i•son (vĕn′ə-sən, -zən) *n.* The flesh of a deer used for food. [< L *vēnātiō,* hunting, game.]

ven•om (vĕn′əm) *n.* **1.** A poisonous secretion of some animals, as certain snakes or spiders, usually transmitted by a bite or sting. **2.** Malice; evil; spite. [< L *venēnum.*]

ven•om•ous (vĕn′ə-məs) *adj.* **1.** Secreting venom: *a venomous snake.* **2.** Full of or containing venom. **3.** Malicious; malignant.

ve•nous (vē′nəs) *adj.* **1.** Of or pertaining to a vein or veins. **2.** Returning to the heart through the great veins.

vent¹ (vĕnt) *n.* **1.** A means of escaping; an outlet or exit. **2.** An opening for the passage or escape of liquids or gases. —*v.* **1.** To give expression to. **2.** To discharge through a vent. **3.** To provide with a vent. [< OF *esventer,* to let out air.] —**vent′er** *n.*

vent² (vĕnt) *n.* A slit at the bottom of a seam in a skirt or jacket: *side vents.* [< OF *fente,* slit.]

ven•ti•late (vĕnt′l-āt′) *v.* **-lated, -lating. 1.** To admit fresh air into in order to replace stale air. **2.** To provide with a vent or a similar means of airing. **3.** To vent: *ventilate one's grievances.* **4.** To expose to public discussion. [< L *ventilāre,* to fan.] —**ven′ti•la′tion** *n.* —**ven′ti•la′tor** *n.* —**ven′ti•la•to′ry** (vĕnt′l-ə-tôr′ē, -tōr′ē) *adj.*

ven•tral (vĕn′trəl) *adj.* **1.** Of, on, or near the belly; abdominal. **2.** Pertaining to the anterior aspect of the human body or the lower surface of the body of an animal. [< L *venter,* the belly.]

ven•tri•cle (vĕn′trĭ-kəl) *n.* A small anatomical cavity or chamber, as of the brain or heart, esp.: **a.** The chamber on the left side of the heart that receives blood from the left atrium and contracts to drive it into the aorta. **b.** The chamber on the right side of the heart that receives blood from the right atrium and sends it to the lungs. [< L *venter,* belly, womb.] —**ven•tric′u•lar** (vĕn-trĭk′yə-lər) *adj.*

ven•tril•o•quism (vĕn-trĭl′ə-kwĭz′əm) *n.* Also **ven•tril•o•quy** (-kwē) *pl.* **-quies.** A method of producing vocal sounds so that they seem to originate in a source other than the speaker. [< LL *ventriloquus,* "speaking from the belly."] —**ven•tril′o•quist** (-ə-kwĭst) *n.*

ven•ture (vĕn′chər) *n.* **1.** A speculative or risky undertaking. **2.** Something at hazard in such an undertaking; stake. —*v.* **-tured, -turing. 1.** To hazard; stake. **2.** To brave the dangers of. **3.** To express at the risk of denial, criticism, or censure. [< ME *aventure,* adventure.] —**ven′tur•er** *n.*

Venezuela

ven•ture•some (vĕn′chər-səm) *adj.* **1.** Daring; bold. **2.** Hazardous.

ven•tur•ous (vĕn′chər-əs) *adj.* Venturesome. —**ven′tur•ous•ly** *adv.*

ven•ue (vĕn′yo͞o) *n.* **1.** The locality where a crime is committed or a cause of action occurs. **2.** The locality from which a jury must be called and in which a trial must be held. [ME, arrival, assault.]

Ve•nus (vē′nəs) *n.* **1.** The second planet from the sun, having an average radius of 3,800 miles, a mass 0.816 times that of the earth, and a period of revolution about the sun of 224.7 days at a mean distance of approx. 67.2 million miles. **2.** Roman goddess of love.

ver. version.

ve•ra•cious (və-rā′shəs) *adj.* **1.** Honest; truthful. **2.** Accurate; precise. [< L *vērāx,* truth.] —**ve•ra′cious•ly** *adv.* —**ve•ra′cious•ness** *n.*

ve•rac•i•ty (və-răs′ə-tē) *n., pl.* **-ties. 1.** Habitual adherence to the truth. **2.** Conformity to fact; accuracy. **3.** Something true.

ve•ran•dah, ve•ran•da (və-răn′də) *n.* A roofed porch or balcony. [Hindi.]

verb (vûrb) *n.* Any of a class of words functioning to express existence, action, or occurrence. [< L *verbum,* word.]

ver•bal (vûr′bəl) *adj.* **1.** Of, pertaining to, or associated with words. **2.** Concerned with words rather than the ideas they represent. **3.** Expressed in speech; unwritten: *a verbal contract.* **4.** Literal; word for word: *a verbal translation.* **5.** Having the nature or function of a verb. —*n.* A verb or verb phrase functioning as a noun, adjective, or adverb. [< L *verbum,* word, VERB.] —**ver′bal•ly** *adv.*

ver•bal•ize (vûr′bə-līz′) *v.* **-ized, -izing.** To express (oneself) in words. —**ver′bal•i•za′tion** *n.*

ver•ba•tim (vûr-bā′tĭm) *adj.* Literal; word for word. [< L *verbum,* word, VERB.] —**ver•ba′tim** *adv.*

ver•be•na (vər-bē′nə) *n.* Any of various plants cultivated for their clusters of variously colored, sometimes fragrant flowers. [< L *verbēnae,* sacred boughs of olive or myrtle.]

ver•bi•age (vûr′bē-ĭj) *n.* **1.** Excess of words; wordiness. **2.** Wording; diction. [< L *verbum,* word, VERB.]

ver•bose (vər-bōs′) *adj.* Characterized by dull and windy speech; wordy; prolix. [< L *verbum,* word, VERB.] —**ver•bose′ly** *adv.* —**ver•bose′ness, ver•bos′i•ty** (-bŏs′ə-tē) *n.*

ver•bo•ten (fĕr-bōt′n) *adj.* Forbidden, as by arbitrary or dictatorial authority. [G.]

ver•dant (vûr′dənt) *adj.* **1.** Green with plant growth. **2.** Inexperienced or unsophisticated; green. [< OF *verd,* green.] —**ver′dant•ly** *adv.*

Ver•di (vâr′dē), **Giuseppe.** 1813–1901. Italian composer of operas.

ver•dict (vûr′dĭkt) *n.* **1.** The decision reached by a jury at the conclusion of a legal proceeding. **2.** A conclusion or judgment. [< OF *voirdit,* "true saying."]

ver•di•gris (vûr′də-grēs, -grĭs) *n.* A green patina or crust of copper sulfate or copper chloride formed on copper, brass, and bronze exposed to air or sea water for long periods of time. [< OF *vert-de-Grice,* "green of Greece."]

ver•dure (vûr′jər) *n.* The fresh greenness of flourishing vegetation. [< OF *verd,* green.]

verge¹ (vûrj) *n.* **1.** The extreme edge, rim, or margin of something. **2.** A brink or threshold. **3.** A staff carried as an emblem of authority or office. —*v.* **verged, verging.** To approach, come near, or border upon. [< L *virga,* rod, strip.]

verge[2] (vûrj) *v.* **verged, verging. 1.** To slope or incline. **2.** To be in the process of becoming something else. [L *vergere,* to tend toward.]

verg•er (vûr'jər) *n. Chiefly Brit.* **1.** One who carries the verge before a dignitary in a procession. **2.** A person who has charge of the interior of a church.

ver•i•fy (vĕr'ə-fī') *v.* **-fied, -fying. 1.** To prove the truth of; substantiate. **2.** To test the truth or accuracy of, as by comparison. [< L *vērus,* true + *facere,* to make.] **—ver'i•fi'a•ble** *adj.* **—ver'i•fi•ca'tion** (-fə-kā'shən) *n.*

ver•i•ly (vĕr'ə-lē) *adv. Archaic.* **1.** In truth; of a certainty. **2.** Assuredly. [< ME *verray,* true, very.]

ver•i•si•mil•i•tude (vĕr'ə-sĭm-ĭl'ə-t/y/ōōd') *n.* **1.** The quality of appearing to be true or real; likelihood. **2.** Something that has the appearance of being true or real. [L *vērisimilitūdō.*]

ver•i•ta•ble (vĕr'ə-tə-bəl) *adj.* Unquestionable; actual; true. [< OF.] **—ver'i•ta•bly** *adv.*

ver•i•ty (vĕr'ə-tē) *n., pl.* **-ties. 1.** The condition or quality of being true. **2.** A true statement or principle. [< L *vērus,* true.]

ver•meil (vûr'mĭl) *n.* **1.** Vermilion. **2.** Gilded metal, such as silver, bronze, or copper. [< LL *vermiculus.*]

vermi–. *comb. form.* Worm. [< L *vermis,* worm.]

ver•mi•cel•li (vûr'mə-chĕl'ē, -sĕl'ē) *n.* A very thin spaghettilike pasta. [It, "little worms."]

ver•mi•form (vûr'mə-fôrm') *adj.* Resembling or having the shape of a worm.

vermiform appendix. A wormlike vestigial organ of the cecum found in man and some other mammals.

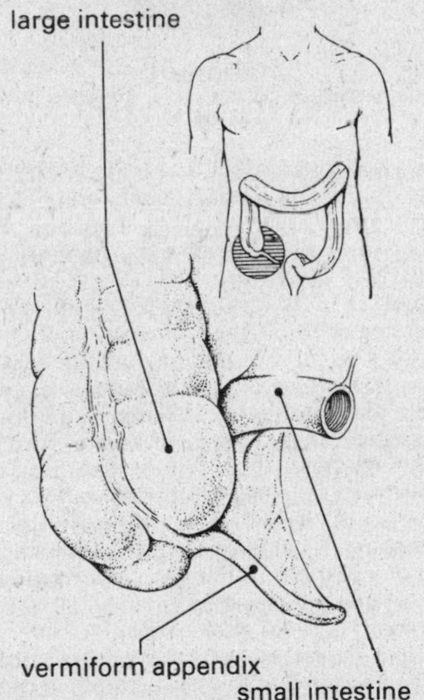

vermiform appendix

ver•mi•fuge (vûr'mə-fyōōj') *n.* Any agent that expels or destroys intestinal worms.

ver•mil•ion (vər-mĭl'yən) *n.* Also **ver•mil•lion.** Vivid red to reddish orange. [< OF *vermeillon.*]

ver•min (vûr'mĭn) *n., pl.* **vermin.** Any of various small destructive or obnoxious animals, as cockroaches or rats. [< L *vermis,* worm.] **—ver'min•ous** *adj.*

Ver•mont (vər-mŏnt'). A state of the NE U.S. Pop. 445,000. Cap. Montpelier.

ver•mouth (vər-mōōth') *n.* A fortified wine flavored with aromatic herbs. [< G *Wermut,* wormwood.]

ver•nac•u•lar (vər-năk'yə-lər) *n.* **1.** The normal spoken language of a country or region as distinct from literary or learned language. **2.** The idiom of a particular trade or profession: *legal vernacular.* [< L *vernāculus,* domestic.] **—ver•nac'u•lar** *adj.*

ver•nal (vûr'nəl) *adj.* Of, pertaining to, or occurring in the spring. [< L *vernus,* of spring.] **—ver'nal•ly** *adv.*

vernal equinox. 1. The point at which the ecliptic intersects the celestial equator, the sun having a northerly motion. **2.** The moment at which the sun passes through this point, about March 21, marking the beginning of spring.

ver•ni•er (vûr'nē-ər) *n.* A small scale attached to a main scale to indicate fractional parts of the subdivisions of the larger scale. [< P. *Vernier* (1580–1637), French mathematician.]

ver•sa•tile (vûr'sə-təl) *adj.* **1.** Skillfully adaptable; having a generalized aptitude. **2.** Having varied uses or functions. [< L *vertere,* to turn.] **—ver'sa•til'i•ty** *n.*

verse (vûrs) *n.* **1. a.** A line of poetry. **b.** A stanza. **2.** Poetry. **3.** A specific type of metrical composition: *blank verse.* **4.** One of the numbered subdivisions of a chapter in the Bible. [< L *versus,* "a turning of the plow," furrow, line.]

versed (vûrst) *adj.* Knowledgeable, practiced, or skilled.

ver•si•cle (vûr'sĭ-kəl) *n.* A short verse or sentence spoken or chanted by a priest and followed by a response from the congregation.

ver•si•fy (vûr'sə-fī') *v.* **-fied, -fying.** To write verses or put into verse. **—ver'si•fi•ca'tion** *n.* **—ver'si•fi'er** *n.*

ver•sion (vûr'zhən, -shən) *n.* **1.** A description, narration, or account related from a specific or subjective viewpoint. **2.** A translation. Often used to designate one of the various Christian revisions of the Bible as translated into the vernacular. **3.** A variation of any prototype; variant. **4.** An adaptation into another medium or style. [< L *vertere,* to turn, change.] **—ver'sion•al** *adj.*

vers li•bre (vĕr lē'br'). Free verse. [F.]

ver•so (vûr'sō) *n., pl.* **-sos. 1.** *Ptg.* A left-hand page of a book or the reverse side of a leaf. **2.** The back of a coin or medal. [L *versō (folio),* "(the page) being turned."]

ver•sus (vûr'səs) *prep.* **1.** Against: *the plaintiff versus the defendant.* **2.** As an alternative to; in contrast with: *death versus dishonor.* [< L *vertere,* to turn.]

vert. vertical.

ver•te•bra (vûr'tə-brə) *n., pl.* **-brae** (-brē) or **-bras.** Any of the bones or cartilaginous segments forming the spinal column. [L, joint, vertebra, "something to turn on."] **—ver'te•bral** *adj.*

ver•te•brate (vûr'tə-brāt', -brĭt) *adj.* **1.** Having a backbone or spinal column. **2.** Of or characteristic of vertebrates. *—n.* Any of a group of animals having a backbone, including the fishes, amphibians, reptiles, birds, and mammals.

ver•tex (vûr'tĕks') *n., pl.* **-texes** or **-tices** (-tə-sēz'). **1.** The highest point of anything; apex; summit. **2. a.** The point at which the sides of an angle intersect. **b.** The point on a triangle opposite to and farthest away from its base. **c.** A point on a polyhedron common to three or more sides. [L, whirl, crown of the head.]

ver•ti•cal (vûr'tĭ-kəl) *adj.* **1. a.** At right angles to the horizon. **b.** Extending perpendicularly from a plane. **2.** Of or at the vertex or highest point; directly overhead. *—n.* **1.** A vertical line, plane, circle, etc. **2.** A vertical position. [< L *vertex,* VERTEX.] **—ver'ti•cal'i•ty, ver'ti•cal•ness** *n.* **—ver'ti•cal•ly** *adv.*

ver•tig•i•nous (vər-tĭj'ə-nəs) *adj.* **1.** Revolving; whirling; rotary. **2.** Affected by vertigo; dizzy. **3.** Tending to produce vertigo. [< L *vertīgō,* VERTIGO.] **—ver•tig'i•nous•ly** *adv.*

ver•ti•go (vûr'tĭ-gō') *n., pl.* **-goes** or **vertigines** (vər-tĭj'ə-nēz'). Severe dizziness. [L *vertīgō,* "a whirling."]

verve (vûrv) *n.* Vitality; liveliness; vivacity. [< OF, fancy, fanciful expression.]

ver•y (vĕr'ē) *adv.* **1.** Extremely; exceedingly: *very happy.* **2.** Truly: *the very best way.* **3.** Precisely: *the very same one.* *—adj.* **1.** Absolute; utter: *the very end.* **2.** Identical; selfsame. **3.** —Used as an intensive to emphasize the importance of the thing described: *The very mountains crumbled.* **4.** Particular; precise. **5.** Mere: *The very mention of the name was frightening.* **6.** Actual: *caught in the very act.* [< L *vērus,* true.]

Usage: *Very* (adverb) is sometimes employed to qualify directly a past participle used predicatively in passive constructions: *He was very tired* (or *very discouraged*). This usage is generally acceptable when the participle is felt to have the nature of a true adjective, as in the foregoing. When the participle remains essentially a verb form, it is preferable to replace *very* with *very much, much, greatly,* or a like term: *much disliked; greatly inconvenienced.*

very high frequency. A band of radio frequencies between 30 and 300 megacycles per second.

very low frequency. A band of radio frequencies between 3 and 30 kilocycles per second.

ves•i•cant (vĕs'ĭ-kənt) *n.* A blistering agent, as mustard gas, used in chemical warfare. *—adj.* Causing blisters.

ves•i•cle (vĕs'ĭ-kəl) *n.* **1.** A small bladderlike cell or cavity. **2.** A blister. [< L *vēsīca,* bladder.] **—ve•sic'u•lar** (və-sĭk'yə-lər) *adj.*

ves•per (vĕs'pər) *n.* **1.** A bell used to summon persons to vespers. **2.** *Archaic.* Evening. **3. Vesper.** The **evening star.** *—adj.* Of or pertaining to the evening or vespers.

ves•pers (vĕs'pərz) *pl.n.* Also **Ves•pers.** A worship service held in the late afternoon or evening. [< L *vesper,* evening, evening star.]

Ves•puc•ci (vĕs-pōōt'chē), **Amerigo.** 1451–1512. Italian navigator for whom America was named.

ves•sel (vĕs'əl) *n.* **1.** A container or receptacle. **2.** A craft larger than a rowboat, designed to navigate on water. **3.** A bodily duct, canal, etc., for containing or circulating a bodily fluid. [< L *vās,* vessel.]

vest (vĕst) *n.* **1.** A sleeveless garment, buttoning in front, worn typically under a suit coat. **2.** *Chiefly Brit.* An undershirt. *—v.* **1.** To clothe, as with ecclesiastical vestments. **2.** To place (authority or ownership) in the control of. **3.** To place (authority or power). [< L *vestis,* garment.]

Ves•ta (vĕs'tə). Roman goddess of the hearth.

ves•tal (vĕs'təl) *adj.* **1.** Pertaining to or sacred to Vesta. **2.** Pertaining to or characteristic of the priestesses of Vesta; chaste. *—n.* Also **vestal virgin.** One of the six virgin priestesses who tended the sacred fire in the temple of Vesta.

ves•ti•bule (vĕs'tə-byo͞ol') *n.* **1.** A small entrance hall or lobby. **2.** An enclosed area at the end of a railroad passenger car. **3.** Any body cavity, chamber, or channel that serves as an approach or entrance to another cavity. [< L *vestibulum.*] **—ves•tib'u•lar** (vĕ-stĭb'yə-lər) *adj.*

ves•tige (vĕs'tĭj) *n.* A visible trace or sign of something that exists or appears no more. [< L *vestigium,* footprint, trace.]

ves•tig•i•al (vĕ-stĭj'ē-əl) *adj.* **1.** Of, pertaining to, or constituting a vestige. **2.** Occurring or persisting as a rudimentary or degenerate bodily structure. **—ves•tig'i•al•ly** *adv.*

vest•ment (vĕst'mənt) *n.* **1.** An official or ceremonial gown. **2.** Any of the robes worn by clergymen or other assistants at ecclesiastical ceremonies. [< L *vestis,* garment.]

ves•try (vĕs'trē) *n., pl.* **-tries. 1.** A room in a church where vestments and sacred objects are stored. **2.** A meeting room in a church. **3.** A committee that administers the temporal affairs of an Episcopal parish. [ME *vestrie.*]

ves•try•man (vĕs'trē-mən) *n.* A member of a vestry.

ves•ture (vĕs'chər) *n.* **1.** Clothing; apparel. **2.** Something that covers or cloaks. [< L *vestire,* to clothe.]

Ve•su•vi•us (və-so͞o'vē-əs). An active volcano in SW Italy near Naples.

vet (vĕt) *n. Informal.* **1.** A veterinarian. **2.** A veteran.

vet. 1. veteran. **2.** veterinarian; veterinary.

vetch (vĕch) *n.* A climbing or twining plant with featherlike leaves and usually purplish flowers. [< L *vicia.*]

vet•er•an (vĕt'ər-ən, vĕt'rən) *n.* **1.** One of long experience in a given activity. **2.** A former member of the armed forces. **3.** An old soldier. [< L *vetus (veter-),* old.] **—vet'er•an** *adj.*

vet•er•i•nar•i•an (vĕt'ər-ə-nâr'ē-ən, vĕt'rə-) *n.* One trained and authorized to treat animals medically.

vet•er•i•nar•y (vĕt'ər-ə-nĕr'ē, vĕt'rə-) *adj.* Of or pertaining to the diagnosis and treatment of diseases and injuries of animals. *—n., pl.* **-ies.** A veterinarian. [< L *veterīnus,* of cattle.]

ve•to (vē'tō) *n., pl.* **-toes. 1.** The vested power or constitutional right of a branch of government, esp. of a chief executive, to reject a bill passed by a legislative body and thus prevent or delay its enactment into law. **2.** The exercise of this right. **3.** The official document communicating the rejection and the reasons for it. **4.** Any authoritative prohibition or rejection of a proposed or intended act. [L *vetō,* I forbid.] **—ve'to** *v.* **—ve'to'er** *n.*

vex (vĕks) *v.* **1.** To irritate or annoy; bother. **2.** To perplex. **3.** To debate at length. **4.** To agitate. [< L *vexāre.*] **—vex•a'tion** *n.* **—vex•a'tious** *adj.* **—vex•a'tious•ly** *adv.*

vhf, VHF very high frequency.

VI, V.I. Virgin Islands.

vi•a (vī'ə, vē'ə) *prep.* By way of. [< L, road, way.]

vi•a•ble (vī'ə-bəl) *adj.* **1.** Capable of living or developing under normal or favorable conditions. **2.** Capable of actualization; practicable. [< OF *vie,* life.] **—vi'a•bil'i•ty** *n.*

vi•a•duct (vī'ə-dŭkt') *n.* A series of spans or arches used to carry a road or railroad over a wide valley or other roads. [L *via,* road, way + (AQUE)DUCT.]

vi•al (vī'əl) *n.* A small container for liquids. [ME *viole.*]

vi•ands (vī'əndz) *pl.n.* Food; victuals. [< L *vivere,* to live.]

vi•at•i•cum (vī-ăt'ĭ-kəm, vē-) *n., pl.* **-ca** (-kə) or **-cums.** The Eucharist as given to a dying person or one in danger of death. [< L *viāticus,* of a road or journey.]

vi•brant (vī'brənt) *adj.* **1.** Exhibiting, characterized by, or resulting from vibration; vibrating. **2.** Pulsing with energy or activity. **—vi'bran•cy** *n.* **—vi'brant•ly** *adv.*

vi•brate (vī'brāt') *v.* **-brated, -brating. 1.** To move or cause to move back and forth rapidly. **2.** To produce a sound; resonate. [L *vibrāre.*] **—vi•bra'tion** (vī-brā'shən) *n.* **—vi•bra'tion•al** *adj.* **—vi'bra'tor** *n.* **—vi'bra•to'ry** *adj.*

vi•bra•to (vĭ-brä'tō, vē-) *n.* A tremulous or pulsating effect produced in a musical tone by minute and rapid variations in pitch. [< L *vibrāre,* VIBRATE.]

vic. 1. vicar. **2.** vicinity.

vic•ar (vĭk'ər) *n.* **1.** An Anglican priest of a parish. **2.** A substitute; deputy. [< L *vicārius,* a substitute.] **—vi•car'i•al** (vī-kâr'ē-əl) *adj.*

vic•ar•age (vĭk'ər-ĭj) *n.* The residence or benefice of a vicar.

vicar general *pl.* **vicars general.** An administrative deputy to a Roman Catholic bishop.

vi•car•i•ous (vī-kâr'ē-əs, vĭ-) *adj.* **1.** Performed or endured by one person substituting for another. **2.** Experienced through sympathetic participation in the experience of another. [< L *vicis,* change, turn, office.] **—vi•car'i•ous•ly** *adv.* **—vi•car'i•ous•ness** *n.*

vice¹ (vīs) *n.* **1.** An immoral practice or habit. **2.** Depravity; corruption. **3.** A flaw or blemish. [< L *vitium,* blemish, offense, vice.]

vice². Variant of **vise.**

vice³ (vīs) *adj.* Substituting for; deputy: *vice chairman.* *—prep.* Replacing or succeeding. [< L *vicis,* change.]

vice–. *comb. form.* One substituting for another. [< L *vice,* in place of, vice.]

vice admiral. A naval officer ranking next below an admiral.

vice president. 1. An officer ranking next below a president, usually empowered to assume the president's duties under such conditions as absence, illness, or death. **2.** A deputy of a president, as in a corporation. **—vice'-pres'i•den•cy** *n.* **—vice'-pres•i•den'tial** *adj.*

vice•re•gal (vīs-rē'gəl) *adj.* Of or pertaining to a viceroy. **—vice•re'gal•ly** *adv.*

vice•roy (vīs'roi') *n.* A governor of a country, province, or colony, ruling as the representative of a sovereign. **—vice'roy'al•ty** *n.*

vi•ce ver•sa (vī'sē vûr'sə, vīs', vī'sə). Conversely. [L, "the position being changed."]

vi•chy•ssoise (vĭsh'ē-swäz', vē'shē-) *n.* A creamy potato soup flavored with leeks or onions and usually served cold. [F, "(cream) of *Vichy,*" city in C France.]

vic•i•nage (vĭs'ə-nĭj) *n.* Neighborhood or vicinity. [< L *vicīnus,* neighbor.]

vic•i•nal (vĭs'ə-nəl) *adj.* Restricted to a limited area; local. [< L *vicīnus,* neighbor.]

vi•cin•i•ty (vĭ-sĭn'ə-tē) *n., pl.* **-ties. 1.** The state of being near in space or relationship; proximity. **2.** A neighborhood; locality. [< L *vicīnus,* neighbor.]

vi•cious (vĭsh'əs) *adj.* **1.** Depraved; debased. **2.** Malicious; reprobate; evil. **3.** Failing to meet a standard or criterion; defective. **4.** Impure; foul. **5.** Characterized by a tendency to worsen. [< L *vitium,* VICE¹.] **—vi'cious•ly** *adv.* **—vi'cious•ness** *n.*

vi•cis•si•tude (vĭ-sĭs'ə-t/y/o͞od') *n.* **1.** The quality of being changeable; mutability. **2. vicissitudes.** Sudden changes or alterations. [< L *vicissim,* in turn.]

vic•tim (vĭk'tĭm) *n.* **1.** A living being slain and offered as a sacrifice to a deity. **2.** One who is harmed or killed, as by accident. **3.** A person who is tricked, swindled, or injured. [L *victima.*]

vic•tim•ize (vĭk'tə-mīz') *v.* **-ized, -izing.** To make a victim of. **—vic'tim•i•za'tion** *n.*

vic•tor (vĭk'tər) *n.* **1.** One who defeats or vanquishes an adversary. **2.** A winner. [< L *vincere* (pp *victus*), to conquer.]

vic•to•ri•a (vĭk-tôr'ē-ə, -tōr'ē-ə) *n.* A low four-wheeled carriage for two with a folding top and an elevated driver's seat in front. [< Queen VICTORIA.]

Vic•to•ri•a¹ (vĭk-tôr'ē-ə, -tōr'ē-ə). 1819–1901. Queen of the United Kingdom of Great Britain and Ireland (1837–1901); Empress of India (1876–1901).

Victoria¹
Photographed in 1876

Vic•to•ri•a² (vĭk-tôr'ē-ə, -tōr'ē-ə). **1.** The capital of British Columbia, Canada. Pop. 55,000. **2.** The capital of Hong Kong. Pop. 1,005,000.

Vic•to•ri•a, Lake (vĭk-tôr'ē-ə, -tōr'ē-ə). The largest lake in Africa.

Vic•to•ri•an (vĭk-tôr'ē-ən, -tōr'ē-ən) *adj.* **1.** Pertaining or belonging to the period of Queen Victoria's reign. **2.** Exhibiting qualities associated with the time of Queen Victoria, as prudishness and stuffiness. **3.** Being in the highly ornamented, massive style of architecture and furnishings popular in 19th-century England. **—Vic•to'ri•an** *n.* **—Vic•to'ri•an•ism'** *n.*

vic•to•ri•ous (vĭk-tôr'ē-əs, -tōr'ē-əs) *adj.* **1.** Triumphant; conquering. **2.** Expressing a sense of victory or fulfillment. **—vic•to'ri•ous•ly** *adv.* **—vic•to'ri•ous•ness** *n.*

vic•to•ry (vĭk'tə-rē) *n., pl.* **-ries. 1.** Final and complete defeat of the enemy in a military engagement. **2.** Any successful struggle against an opponent or obstacle.

vict•ual (vĭt'l) *n.* **1.** Food fit for human consumption. **2. victuals.** Food; provisions. *—v.* **1.** To provide with food. **2.** To lay in food supplies. [< L *victus,* sustenance.]

vict•ual•er (vĭt'l-ər) *n.* **1.** A supplier of victuals, as to an army or ship. **2.** An innkeeper.

vi•cu•ña (və-ko͞on'yə, -k/y/o͞o'nə, vī-) *n.* Also **vi•cu•na. 1.** A South American mammal, related to the llama, having fine, silky fleece. **2. a.** The fleece of this animal. **b.** Fabric made from this fleece. [< Quechua *wikuña.*]

vi•de (vī'dē) *v.* See. Used to direct a reader's attention: *vide page 64.* [< L *vidēre,* to see.]

vi•de•li•cet (vĭ-dĕl'ə-sĭt) *adv.* That is; namely. [L *vidēlicet,* it is easy (permissible) to see.]

vid•e•o (vĭd'ē-ō') *adj.* Pertaining to television, esp. to televised images. *—n.* **1.** The visual portion of a televised broadcast. **2.** Television. [< L *vidēre,* to see.]

vie (vī) *v.* **vied, vying.** To strive; contend; compete. [< OF *envier,* to challenge, bid.]

Vi•en•na (vē-ĕn'ə). The capital of Austria. Pop. 1,628,000. **—Vi'en•nese'** (vē'ə-nēz', -nēs') *adj.*

Vien•tiane (vyăN-tyän'). The administrative capital of Laos. Pop. 100,000.

Vi•et•cong (vē-ĕt'kŏng', vyĕt'-) *n., pl.* **Vietcong.** Also **Vi•et Cong. 1.** A Vietnamese supporting the National Liberation Front of South Vietnam. **2.** The Front itself, esp. its armed forces. **—Vi•et'cong'** *adj.*

Vi•et•minh (vē-ĕt'mĭn', vyĕt'-) *n., pl.* **Vietminh.** Also **Vi•et Minh. 1.** The Vietnamese national independence front (1941–54) led by Ho Chi Minh. **2.** A member or members of this front, esp. of its armed forces. **—Vi•et'minh'** *adj.*

Viet•nam (vē-ĕt'näm', -năm', vyĕt'-). **A country of SE Asia, divided from 1954 to 1975 into the Democratic Republic of Vietnam (North Vietnam), pop. 21,340,000, cap. Hanoi, and the Republic of Vietnam (South Vietnam), pop. 16,543,000, cap. Saigon. In 1975 the country was reunified under the government of the Democratic Republic of Vietnam.**

Vietnam

Vi•et•nam•ese (vē-ĕt'nə-mēz', -mēs', vyĕt'-) *n.* **1.** A native of Vietnam. **2.** The language of Vietnam. **—Vi•et'nam•ese'** *adj.*

view (vyōō) *n.* **1.** An examination or inspection. **2.** A systematic survey; coverage. **3. views.** Thoughts or opinions. **4.** The field of vision. **5.** A prospect or vista. **6.** An aspect, as from a given vantage point. **7.** An aim; intention. **8.** Expectation; chance: *no view of success.* *—v.* **1.** To see; behold. **2. a.** To examine; inspect. **b.** To survey or consider. [< L *vidēre,* to see.] **—view'er** *n.*

view•point (vyōō'point') *n.* A point of view.

vig•il (vĭj'əl) *n.* **1.** A watch kept during normal sleeping hours. **2.** The eve of a religious festival as observed by devotional watching. **3. vigils.** Ritual devotions observed on the eve of a holy day. [< L, alert.]

vig•i•lance (vĭj'ə-ləns) *n.* Watchfulness.

vig•i•lant (vĭj'ə-lənt) *adj.* On the alert; watchful. [< L *vigilāre,* to be alert.] **—vig'i•lant•ly** *adv.* **—vig'i•lant•ness** *n.*

vig•i•lan•te (vĭj'ə-lăn'tē) *n.* A member of an unauthorized group exercising police power, esp. in the 19th-century South.

vi•gnette (vĭn-yĕt') *n.* **1.** An unenclosed decorative design placed at the beginning or end of a book or chapter. **2.** An unbordered portrait that shades off into the surrounding ground. **3.** A brief literary sketch. *—v.* **-gnetted, -gnetting.** To soften the edges of (a picture) in vignette style. [< OF, "young vine."]

vig•or (vĭg'ər) *n.* Also *chiefly Brit.* **vig•our. 1.** Active physical or mental strength. **2.** Effectiveness or force. [< L *vigēre,* to be lively or vigorous.]

vig•or•ous (vĭg'ər-əs) *adj.* **1.** Robust; hardy. **2.** Energetic; forceful. **—vig'or•ous•ly** *adv.* **—vig'or•ous•ness** *n.*

vi•king (vī'kĭng) *n.* Also **Vi•king.** One of the Scandinavian mariners and marauders of the 8th through the 10th century. [ON *víkingr.*]

vil. village.

vile (vīl) *adj.* **viler, vilest. 1.** Wretched; base. **2.** Depraved; ignoble. **3.** Loathsome; disgusting. **4.** Unpleasant or objectionable. [< L *vīlis.*] **—vile'ly** *adv.* **—vile'ness** *n.*

vil•i•fy (vĭl'ə-fī') *v.* **-fied, -fying.** To defame; denigrate. [< L *vīlis,* VILE + *facere,* to make.] **—vil'i•fi•ca'tion** *n.* **—vil'i•fi'er** *n.*

vil•la (vĭl'ə) *n.* **1.** A resort or country estate. **2.** *Brit.* A middle-class house in the suburbs. [< L *villa,* country home.]

vil•lage (vĭl'ĭj) *n.* **1.** A rural settlement ranking in size between a hamlet and a town. **2.** An incorporated municipality smaller than a town. **3.** The inhabitants of a village. [< L *villa,* VILLA.] **—vil'lage** *adj.*

vil•lag•er (vĭl'ĭ-jər) *n.* An inhabitant of a village.

vil•lain (vĭl'ən) *n.* **1.** One of wicked deeds; scoundrel. **2.** Variant of **villein.** [< OF *vilain,* "feudal serf."]

vil•lain•ous (vĭl'ə-nəs) *adj.* **1.** Viciously wicked or criminal. **2.** Obnoxious. **—vil'lain•ous•ly** *adv.* **—vil'lain•ous•ness** *n.*

vil•lain•y (vĭl'ə-nē) *n., pl.* **-ies. 1.** Viciousness of conduct or action. **2.** Baseness of mind or character. **3.** A treacherous or vicious act.

vil•lein (vĭl'ən) *n.* Also **vil•lain.** One of a class of feudal serfs who held the legal status of freemen in their dealings with all persons except their lord. [< VILLAIN.]

Vil•lon (vē-yôN'), **François.** 1431–1463? French poet.

Vil•ni•us (vĭl'nē-əs, vēl'-). The capital of Lithuania. Pop. 372,000.

vim (vĭm) *n.* Ebullient vitality and energy. [< L *vis,* power.]

Vin•ci, Leonardo da. See **Leonardo da Vinci.**

vin•di•ca•ble (vĭn'dĭ-kə-bəl) *adj.* Capable of being vindicated; justifiable.

vin•di•cate (vĭn'dĭ-kāt') *v.* **-cated, -cating. 1.** To clear of accusation, blame, etc., with supporting proof. **2.** To justify: *vindicate one's claim.* [L *vindicāre,* to claim, defend, revenge.] **—vin'di•ca'tion** *n.*

vin•dic•tive (vĭn-dĭk'tĭv) *adj.* **1.** Disposed to seek revenge; revengeful. **2.** Unforgiving; bitter; spiteful. **—vin•dic'tive•ly** *adv.* **—vin•dic'tive•ness** *n.*

vine (vīn) *n.* **1.** A plant having a stem supported by climbing, twining, or creeping along a surface. **2.** A grapevine or grapevines collectively. [< L *vinum,* wine.]

vin•e•gar (vĭn'ĭ-gər) *n.* An impure dilute solution of acetic acid obtained by fermentation beyond the alcohol stage and used as a condiment and preservative. [< OF *vin,* wine + *aigre,* sour.]

vin•e•gar•y (vĭn'ĭ-gə-rē) *adj.* **1.** Having the nature of vinegar; sour; acid. **2.** Sour in disposition or speech.

vine•yard (vĭn'yərd) *n.* Ground planted with cultivated grapevines.

vin•tage (vĭn'tĭj) *n.* **1.** The yield of wine or grapes from a particular vineyard or district during one season. **2.** Wine, usually of high quality, identified as to year and vineyard or district of origin. **3.** The year in which or place where a particular wine was bottled. **4.** The harvesting of a grape crop or the initial stages of wine-making. **5.** A year or period of origin: *a car of 1942 vintage.* *—adj.* **1.** Venerable; classic. **2.** Old or outmoded. [< L *vindēmia,* grape gathering.]

vint•ner (vĭnt'nər) *n.* A wine merchant. [< L *vīnētum,* vineyard.]

vi•nyl (vī'nəl) *n.* Any of various plastics, typically tough, flexible, and shiny, often used for coverings and clothing. **—vi'nyl** *adj.*

vi•o•la (vē-ō'lə, vī-) *n.* A stringed musical instrument of the violin family, slightly larger than a violin, tuned a fifth lower, and having a deeper, more sonorous tone. [It.]

vi•o•late (vī'ə-lāt') *v.* **-lated, -lating. 1.** To break (a law or regulation) intentionally or unintentionally. **2.** To injure the person or property of, esp. to rape. **3.** To profane; desecrate. [< L *violāre* < *vis,* force.] **—vi'o•la•ble** *adj.* **—vi'o•la•bly** *adv.* **—vi'o•la'tion** *n.* **—vi'o•la'tive** *adj.* **—vi'o•la'tor** *n.*

vi•o•lence (vī'ə-ləns) *n.* **1.** Physical force exerted, as for violating, damaging, or abusing. **2.** An act of violent action or behavior. **3.** Intensity or severity: *the violence of a hurricane.* **4.** Fanaticism.

vi•o•lent (vī'ə-lənt) *adj.* **1.** Displaying extreme physical or emotional force. **2.** Extreme; severe: *violent contrast.* **3.** Severe; harsh. **4.** Caused by unexpected force or injury rather than by natural causes: *a violent death.* [< L *violentus.*] **—vi'o•lent•ly** *adv.*

vi•o•let (vī'ə-lĭt) *n.* **1.** Any of various low-growing plants with spurred, irregular flowers that are usually purplish-blue but sometimes yellow or white. **2.** Any of several similar plants. **3.** Any of a group of colors, reddish blue in hue. [< L *viola.*] **—vi'o•let** *adj.*

vi•o•lin (vī'ə-lĭn') *n.* A stringed instrument played with a bow, having four strings tuned at intervals of a fifth and an unfretted fingerboard. [< VIOLA.]

vi•o•lin•ist (vī'ə-lĭn'ĭst) *n.* One who plays the violin.

vi•o•list (vē-ō'lĭst) *n.* A person who plays the viola.

vi•o•lon•cel•list (vē'ə-lən-chĕl'ĭst) *n.* A cellist.

vi•o•lon•cel•lo (vē'ə-lən-chĕl'ō) *n., pl.* **-los.** A cello. [< VIOLONE.]

vio•lo•ne (vyō-lō'nā) *n.* A **double bass.** [< VIOLA.]

VIP *Informal.* very important person.

vi•per (vī'pər) *n.* **1.** Any of various venomous Old World snakes. **2.** Any of various other venomous or supposedly venomous snakes. **3.** A malicious person. [< L *vīpera,* snake.]

vi•ra•go (vĭ-rä'gō, -rā'gō, vī-) *n., pl.* **-goes** or **-gos.** A noisy, domineering woman; a scold. [L *virāgō.*]

vi•ral (vī'rəl) *adj.* Of, pertaining to, or caused by a virus.

vir•e•o (vĭr'ē-ō') *n., pl.* **-os.** Any of several small grayish or greenish New World birds. [L.]

Vir•gil (vûr'jəl). 70–19 B.C. Latin poet.

vir•gin (vûr'jĭn) *n.* **1.** One who has not experienced sexual intercourse. **2.** A chaste or unmarried woman. **3. the Virgin.** Mary, the mother of Jesus. —*adj.* 1. Chaste. 2. In a pure or natural state: *virgin snow.* [< L *virgō.*] —**vir•gin'i•ty** *n.*

vir•gin•al (vûr'jə-nəl) *adj.* 1. Chaste; pure. 2. Remaining in a state of virginity. 3. Untouched or unsullied.

Vir•gin•ia (vər-jĭn'yə). A state of the SE U.S. Pop. 4,648,000. Cap. Richmond. —**Vir•gin'ian** *adj. & n.*

Virginia creeper. A North American climbing vine with compound leaves and bluish-black berries.

Virginia reel. A country dance in which couples perform various figures to the instructions called out by a leader.

Virgin Islands. An island group E of Puerto Rico in the Caribbean, divided into: a. The British Virgin Islands, a British colony. Pop. 9,000. b. The Virgin Islands of the U.S., including the islands of St. Thomas, St. John, and St. Croix. Pop. 32,000. Cap. Charlotte Amalie on St. Thomas.

Virgin Mary. The mother of Jesus.

Vir•go (vûr'gō) *n.* 1. A constellation in the region of the celestial equator. 2. The sixth sign of the zodiac. [L *virgō,* VIRGIN.]

vir•gu•late (vûr'gyə-lĭt, -lāt') *adj.* Shaped like a small rod. [< L *virgula,* small rod.]

vir•gule (vûr'gyo͞ol) *n.* A diagonal mark (/) used esp. to separate alternatives, as in *and/or,* or to represent the word *per,* as in *miles/hour.* [< L *virgula,* small rod.]

vir•ile (vĭr'əl) *adj.* 1. Having masculine strength, vigor, force, etc. 2. Pertaining to male sexual functions. [< L *vir,* man.] —**vi•ril'i•ty** (və-rĭl'ə-tē) *n.*

vi•rol•o•gy (vī-rŏl'ə-jē) *n.* The study of viruses and viral diseases. —**vi•rol'o•gist** *n.*

vir•tu•al (vûr'cho͞o-əl) *adj.* Existing in essence or effect though not in actual fact or form. [< L *virtūs,* capacity, VIRTUE.]

virtual image. An image from which rays of reflected or refracted light appear to diverge, as from an image seen in a plane mirror.

vir•tu•al•ly (vûr'cho͞o-ə-lē) *adv.* Essentially; practically.

vir•tue (vûr'cho͞o) *n.* 1. Moral excellence, righteousness, and responsibility; goodness. 2. Conformity to standard morality or mores; rectitude. 3. Chastity. 4. A particular beneficial or efficacious quality; an advantage. —**by** (or **in**) **virtue of.** On the grounds or basis of; by reason of. [< L *virtūs,* manliness, strength, capacity.] —**vir'tu•ous** *adj.* —**vir'tu•ous•ly** *adv.* —**vir'tu•ous•ness** *n.*

vir•tu•os•i•ty (vûr'cho͞o-ŏs'ə-tē) *n., pl.* **-ties.** The technical skill, fluency, or style exhibited by a virtuoso.

vir•tu•o•so (vûr'cho͞o-ō'sō) *n., pl.* **-sos** or **-si** (-sē). 1. A musician with masterly ability, technique, or personal style. 2. One with masterly skill or technique in any field, esp. in the arts. [< L *virtūs,* VIRTUE.]

vir•u•lent (vĭr'/y/ə-lənt) *adj.* 1. Extremely poisonous or harmful, as a disease or microorganism. 2. Bitterly hostile or antagonistic; venomously spiteful; full of hate. 3. Intensely irritating, obnoxious, or harsh: *virulent antirationalism.* [< L *vīrus,* VIRUS.] —**vir'u•lence** (-ləns) *n.* —**vir'u•lent•ly** *adv.*

vi•rus (vī'rəs) *n., pl.* **-ruses.** 1. Any of various submicroscopic disease-causing agents consisting essentially of a core of a nucleic acid surrounded by a protein coat, having the ability to reproduce only inside a living cell. 2. Any specific disease-causing agent. [L *vīrus,* poison, slime.]

vis. 1. visibility. 2. visual.

vi•sa (vē'zə) *n.* An official authorization appended to a passport, permitting entry into and travel within a particular country or region. [< L *vīsa,* "things seen."]

vis•age (vĭz'ĭj) *n.* The face or facial expression of a person. [< OF *vis,* face.]

vis-à-vis (vē'zə-vē') *adv.* Face to face. —*prep.* Compared with; in relation to. [F, "face to face."] —**vis'-à-vis'** *adj.*

vis•cer•a (vĭs'ər-ə) *pl.n. Sing.* **viscus** (vĭs'kəs). 1. The internal organs of the body, esp. those contained within the abdominal and thoracic cavities. 2. Broadly, the intestines. [< L *viscus,* body organ.]

vis•cer•al (vĭs'ər-əl) *adj.* 1. Of, in, or affecting the viscera. 2. Intensely emotional.

vis•cid (vĭs'ĭd) *adj.* 1. Thick and adhesive: *a viscid fluid.* 2. Covered with a sticky coating. [< L *viscum,* mistletoe, birdlime.] —**vis•cid'i•ty** *n.* —**vis'cid•ly** *adv.*

vis•cose (vĭs'kōs') *n.* A thick, golden-brown viscous solution derived from cellulose, used in the manufacture of rayon and cellophane. [< LL *viscōsus,* VISCOUS.]

vis•cos•i•ty (vĭs-kŏs'ə-tē) *n., pl.* **-ties.** The condition, property, or degree of being viscous.

vis•count (vī'kount') *n.* A peer ranking below an earl and above a baron. [< VICE[3] + ML *comes,* count.]

vis•cous (vĭs'kəs) *adj.* 1. Having relatively high resistance to flow. 2. Viscid. [< LL *viscōsus.*] —**vis'cous•ly** *adv.* —**vis'cous•ness** *n.*

vis•cus. *Sing.* of **viscera.**

vise (vīs) *n.* Also **vice.** A clamping device, usually consisting of two jaws closed by a screw or lever, used, as in carpentry, to hold work in position. [< L *vītis,* (winding) vine.]

Vish•nu (vĭsh'no͞o) *n. Hinduism.* Second member of the trinity including also Brahma and Shiva.

vis•i•bil•i•ty (vĭz'ə-bĭl'ə-tē) *n., pl.* **-ties.** 1. The fact, state, or degree of being visible. 2. The greatest distance under given weather conditions to which it is possible to see without instrumental assistance.

vis•i•ble (vĭz'ə-bəl) *adj.* 1. Capable of being seen; perceptible to the eye. 2. Manifest; apparent. [< L *vīsus,* sight, VISION.] —**vis'i•ble•ness** *n.* —**vis'i•bly** *adv.*

vi•sion (vĭzh'ən) *n.* 1. The faculty of sight. 2. Intelligent foresight. 3. A mental image produced by the imagination. 4. Something perceived through unusual means, as a supernatural sight. 5. Something of extraordinary beauty. [< L *vīsus,* pp of *vidēre,* to see.]

vi•sion•ar•y (vĭzh'ən-ĕr'ē) *adj.* 1. Characterized by vision or foresight. 2. Having the nature of a vision. 3. Not practicable; utopian. —*n., pl.* **-ies.** 1. One who has visions. 2. One given to impractical ideas.

vis•it (vĭz'ĭt) *v.* 1. To go or come to see for reasons of business, duty, or pleasure. 2. To stay with as a guest. 3. To afflict; assail. 4. To inflict punishment; avenge. 5. To pay a call. 6. To converse or chat. —*n.* 1. An act or instance of visiting. 2. A stay or sojourn as a guest. [< L *vīsāre,* to view < *vīsus,* sight, VISION.] —**vis'it•a•ble** *adj.*

vis•i•ta•tion (vĭz'ə-tā'shən) *n.* 1. An official visit. 2. A visit of affliction or blessing, regarded as being ordained by God. —**vis'i•ta'tion•al** *adj.*

vis•i•tor (vĭz'ə-tər) *n.* One who pays a visit; a guest.

vi•sor (vī'zər, vĭz'ər) *n.* Also **vi•zor.** 1. A piece projecting from the front of a cap or the windshield of a vehicle to shade the eyes. 2. The front piece of a helmet, capable of being raised and lowered. [< L *vīsus,* sight, VISION.]

vis•ta (vĭs'tə) *n.* 1. A distant view seen through a passage or opening. 2. A comprehensive awareness of a series of events. [< L *vidēre,* to see.]

Vis•tu•la (vĭs'cho͞o-lə). A river of Poland.

vis•u•al (vĭzh'o͞o-əl) *adj.* 1. Of or involving the sense of sight. 2. Capable of being seen by the eye; visible. 3. Done, maintained, or executed by the sight only. 4. Designating instruction involving sight: *visual aids.* [< L *vīsus,* VISION.] —**vis'u•al•ly** *adv.*

vis•u•al•ize (vĭzh'o͞o-ə-līz') *v.* **-ized, -izing.** To form a mental image or vision of. —**vis'u•al•i•za'tion** *n.* —**vis'u•al•iz'er** *n.*

vi•ta (vī'tə, vē'-) *n.* **An outline of one's personal history and experience, as one submitted when applying for a job.**

vi•tal (vī'təl, vīt'l) *adj.* 1. Of or characteristic of life. 2. Necessary to the continuation of life. 3. Full of life; vigorous; animated. 4. Essential. 5. Concerned with data pertinent to lives. [< L *vīta,* life.] —**vi'tal•ly** *adv.*

vi•tal•i•ty (vī-tăl'ə-tē) *n., pl.* **-ties.** 1. That which distinguishes the living from the nonliving. 2. The capacity to live, grow, develop, or survive. 3. Vigor; energy.

vi•tal•ize (vīt'l-īz') *v.* **-ized, -izing.** To endow with life or vigor. —**vi'tal•i•za'tion** *n.* —**vi'tal•iz'er** *n.*

vi•tals (vī'təlz) *pl.n.* 1. Any bodily parts or organs regarded as vital. 2. Essential elements.

vi•ta•min (vī'tə-mən) *n.* Also *rare* **vi•ta•mine** (-mēn, -mĭn). Any of various relatively complex organic substances occurring naturally in plant and animal tissue and essential in small amounts for metabolic processes. [< L *vīta,* life + AMINE.]

vitamin A. A vitamin or mixture of vitamins occurring principally in fish-liver oils and some yellow and dark-green vegetables, functioning in normal cell growth and development and responsible in deficiency for night blindness and degeneration of mucous membranes.

vitamin B. 1. **Vitamin B complex.** 2. A member of the vitamin B complex.

vitamin B_{12}. A complex, cobalt-containing compound found in liver and widely used to treat some forms of anemia.

vitamin B complex. A group of vitamins important for growth, occurring chiefly in yeast, liver, eggs, and some vegetables.

vitamin C. **Ascorbic acid.**

vitamin D. Any of several chemically similar compounds obtained from milk, fish, and eggs, required for normal bone growth and used to treat rickets in children.

vitamin K. Any of several natural and synthetic substances essential for the promotion of blood clotting and prevention of hemorrhage.

vi•ti•ate (vĭsh'ē-āt') *v.* **-ated, -ating.** 1. To impair the value or quality of; spoil. 2. To debase; pervert. 3. To invalidate or render legally ineffective. [< L *vitium,* defect, fault.] —**vi'ti•a'tion** *n.* —**vi'ti•a'tor** *n.*

vit•re•ous (vĭt'rē-əs) *adj.* 1. Of or resembling glass; glassy. 2. Obtained or made from glass. [< L *vitrum,* glass.]

vit•ri•fy (vĭt'rə-fī') *v.* **-fied, -fying.** To change into glass or a similar substance. [< L *vitrum,* glass + -FY.] —**vit'ri•fi'a•ble** *adj.*

vit•ri•ol (vĭt'rē-ōl') *n.* 1. a. **Sulfuric acid.** b. Any of various salts of sulfuric acid. 2. Vituperative feeling or utterance. [< L *vitrum,* glass.]

vit•ri•ol•ic (vĭt'rē-ŏl'ĭk) *adj.* 1. Of or derived from vitriol. 2. Bitterly scathing; caustic.

vit•tles (vĭt'lz) *pl.n. Nonstandard.* Victuals.

vi•tu•per•ate (vī-t/y/o͞o'pə-rāt', vĭ-) *v.* **-ated, -ating.** To rail against abusively; revile; berate. [L *vituperāre.*] **—vi•tu'per•a'tion** *n.* **—vi•tu'per•a•tive** (-pər-ə-tĭv) *adj.*

vi•va•ce (ve-vä'chā) *adv. Mus.* Lively; vivaciously; briskly. [It.] **—vi•va'ce** *adj.*

vi•va•cious (vĭ-vā'shəs, vī-) *adj.* Animated; lively; spirited. [L *vīvāx,* lively.] **—vi•va'cious•ly** *adv.* **—vi•vac'i•ty** (-văs'ə-tē) *n.*

viv•id (vĭv'ĭd) *adj.* 1. Perceived as bright and distinct; brilliant; intense. 2. Full of the vigor and freshness of immediate experience. 3. Evoking lifelike images within the mind. [L *vīvidus,* full of life, lifelike.] **—viv'id•ly** *adv.* **—viv'id•ness** *n.*

viv•i•fy (vĭv'ə-fī') *v.* **-fied, -fying.** 1. To impart life to; animate. 2. To make more lively or intense. [< L *vīvus,* alive + *facere,* to do.] **—viv'i•fi•ca'tion** *n.* **—viv'i•fi'er** *n.*

vi•vip•a•rous (vī-vĭp'ər-əs) *adj.* Giving birth to offspring that develop within the mother's body rather than hatching from eggs. [< L *vīvus,* alive + -PAROUS.]

viv•i•sec•tion (vĭv'ə-sĕk'shən) *n.* The act of cutting into or dissecting the body of a living animal, esp. for scientific research. **—viv'i•sect'** (-sĕkt') *v.*

vix•en (vĭk'sən) *n.* 1. A female fox. 2. A quarrelsome, shrewish woman. [< OE *fyxe,* she-fox. See **puk-**.]

viz. videlicet.

viz•ard (vĭz'ərd) *n.* 1. A visor. 2. A mask.

vi•zier (vĭ-zîr', vĭz'yər) *n.* Also **vi•zir** (vĭ-zîr'). A high officer in a Moslem government, esp. in the old Turkish Empire.

vi•zor. Variant of **visor.**

V.M.D. Doctor of Veterinary Medicine (L *Veterinariae Medicinae Doctor*).

voc. vocative.

vocab. vocabulary.

vo•cab•u•lar•y (vō-kăb'yə-lĕr'ē) *n., pl.* **-ies.** 1. A list of words and phrases, usually arranged alphabetically and defined or translated; a lexicon. 2. All the words of a language. 3. The sum of words used by a particular person, profession, etc. [< L *vocābulum,* an appellation, name.]

vo•cal (vō'kəl) *adj.* 1. Of or pertaining to the voice. 2. Uttered by the voice. 3. Capable of emitting sound or speech. 4. Full of voices; resounding with speech. 5. Outspoken. *—n.* 1. A vocal sound. 2. A popular piece of music for a singer. [< L *vōx,* voice.] **—vo'cal•ly** *adv.*

vocal cords. The lower of two pairs of bands or folds in the larynx that vibrate when pulled together and when air is passed up from the lungs, thereby producing vocal sounds.

vo•cal•ic (vō-kăl'ĭk) *adj.* Pertaining to or having the nature of a vowel.

vo•cal•ist (vō'kə-lĭst) *n.* A singer.

vo•cal•ize (vō'kə-līz') *v.* **-ized, -izing.** To make vocal; articulate or sing.

vo•ca•tion (vō-kā'shən) *n.* 1. A profession, esp. one for which one is specially suited or trained. 2. An urge to undertake a certain kind of work. [< L *vōcātiō,* a calling, summoning.] **—vo•ca'tion•al** *adj.*

voc•a•tive (vŏk'ə-tĭv) *adj. Gram.* Pertaining to or designating a case used to indicate the one being addressed. *—n.* 1. The vocative case. 2. A word in this case. [< L *vōcāre,* to call.]

vo•cif•er•ate (vō-sĭf'ə-rāt') *v.* **-ated, -ating.** To cry out vehemently; clamor. [< L *vōx,* voice + *ferre,* to bear.] **—vo•cif'er•a'tion** *n.*

vo•cif•er•ous (vō-sĭf'ər-əs) *adj.* Making an outcry; clamorous. **—vo•cif'er•ous•ly** *adv.*

vod•ka (vŏd'kə) *n.* A colorless alcoholic liquor distilled from wheat, potatoes, etc. [< Russ *voda,* water.]

vogue (vōg) *n.* 1. The prevailing fashion, practice, or style. 2. Popular acceptance; popularity. [F, fashion, "rowing."]

voice (vois) *n.* 1. The sound or sounds produced by the vocal organs of a vertebrate. 2. The specified quality, condition, or timbre of vocal sound. 3. A medium or agency of expression. 4. *Gram.* A verb form indicating the relation between the subject and the action expressed by the verb. 5. The expiration of air through vibrating vocal cords, used in the production of vowels and voiced consonants. 6. Musical tone produced by the vibration of vocal cords. 7. Any of the melodic parts for a musical composition. *—v.* **voiced, voicing.** To express or utter; give voice to. [< L *vōx.*]

voiced (voist) *adj.* 1. Having a voice or a specified kind of voice. 2. Expressed by voice. 3. *Phon.* Uttered with vibration of the vocal cords, as the consonant *d.*

voice•less (vois'lĭs) *adj.* 1. Having no voice. 2. *Phon.* Uttered without vibration of the vocal cords, as the consonant *t.*

voice-o•ver (vois'ō'vər) *n.* In motion pictures and television, the voice of a narrator who does not appear on camera.

void (void) *adj.* 1. Containing no matter; empty. 2. Unoccupied. 3. Devoid; lacking: *void of understanding.* 4. Ineffective; useless. 5. Having no legal force or validity; null. *—n.* 1. Something void; empty space. 2. A feeling of emptiness, loneliness, or loss. *—v.* 1. To invalidate; annul. 2. a. To empty. b. To evacuate (body wastes). 3. To leave; vacate. [< L *vocāre,* to be empty.] **—void'er** *n.*

voile (voil) *n.* A sheer fabric used for making dresses, curtains, etc. [< L *vēlum,* cloth, veil.]

vol. 1. volume. 2. volunteer.

vol•a•tile (vŏl'ə-tĭl) *adj.* 1. Evaporating readily at normal temperatures and pressures. 2. Capable of being readily vaporized. 3. Changeable. 4. Lighthearted. [< L *volāre,* to fly.] **—vol'a•til'i•ty** *n.*

vol•a•til•ize (vŏl'ə-tə-līz') *v.* **-ized, -izing.** 1. To make or become volatile. 2. To evaporate or cause to evaporate.

vol•ca•no (vŏl-kā'nō) *n., pl.* **-noes** or **-nos.** 1. A vent in the earth's crust through which molten lava and gases are ejected. 2. A mountain formed by the materials so ejected. [< L *Volcānus,* VULCAN.] **—vol•can'ic** (-kăn'ĭk) *adj.* **—vol•can'i•cal•ly** *adv.*

vole (vōl) *n.* Any of various rodents resembling rats or mice but having a shorter tail. [Earlier *volemouse,* "field mouse."]

Vol•ga (vŏl'gə). A river of the W Soviet Union.

Vol•go•grad (vŏl'gə-grăd'). A city of the SW Russian S.F.S.R. Pop. 818,000.

vo•li•tion (və-lĭsh'ən) *n.* 1. A conscious choice; decision. 2. The power of choosing; the will. [< L *velle,* to wish.] **—vo•li'tion•al** *adj.* **—vo•li'tion•al•ly** *adv.*

vol•ley (vŏl'ē) *n., pl.* **-leys.** 1. a. The simultaneous discharge of a number of missiles. b. The missiles thus discharged. 2. A bursting forth of a number of things simultaneously. *—v.* To discharge in or as in a volley. [< L *volāre,* to fly.] **—vol'ley•er** *n.*

vol•ley•ball (vŏl'ē-bôl') *n.* 1. A court game in which a score is made by grounding a ball on the opposing team's side of a high net. 2. The large ball used in this game.

volt (vōlt) *n.* A unit of electric potential and electromotive force, equal to the difference of electric potential between two points on a conducting wire carrying a constant current of one ampere when the power dissipated between the points is one watt. [< Count A. *Volta* (1745–1827), Italian physicist.]

volt•age (vōl'tĭj) *n.* Electromotive force or potential difference.

vol•ta•ic (vŏl-tā'ĭk) *adj.* Of or involving electricity produced by chemical action.

Vol•taire (vŏl-târ', vōl-). Pen name of François Marie Arouet. 1694–1778. French poet, dramatist, satirist, and historian.

volt•me•ter (vōlt'mē'tər) *n.* An instrument for measuring potential differences in volts.

vol•u•ble (vŏl'yə-bəl) *adj.* Characterized by ready, fluent speech; garrulous. [< L *volūbilis.*] **—vol'u•bil'i•ty** *n.* **—vol'u•bly** *adv.*

vol•ume (vŏl'yo͞om, -yəm) *n.* 1. A collection of written or printed sheets bound together; a book. 2. One book of a set. 3. The measure of a three-dimensional object or region of space. 4. A large amount. 5. a. The loudness of a sound. b. A control for adjusting loudness. [< L *volvere,* to roll, turn.]

vol•u•met•ric (vŏl'yə-mĕt'rĭk) *adj.* Pertaining to measurement of volume.

vo•lu•mi•nous (və-lo͞o'mə-nəs) *adj.* 1. Having great volume, fullness, size, or number. 2. Filling or capable of filling volumes. 3. Having many coils; winding.

vol•un•tar•y (vŏl'ən-tĕr'ē) *adj.* 1. Arising from one's own free will. 2. Acting by choice and without constraint or guarantee of reward. 3. Normally controlled by individual volition. 4. Not accidental; intentional. [< L *voluntās,* will, free will.] **—vol'un•tar'i•ly** *adv.*

vol•un•teer (vŏl'ən-tîr') *n.* One who performs or gives services of his own free will. *—v.* 1. To give or offer to give on one's own initiative. 2. To enter into or offer to enter into an undertaking of one's own free will. **—vol'un•teer'** *adj.*

vo•lup•tu•ar•y (və-lŭp'cho͞o-ĕr'ē) *n., pl.* **-ies.** One given to luxury and sensual pleasures. [< L *voluptās,* pleasure.]

vo•lup•tu•ous (və-lŭp'cho͞o-əs) *adj.* 1. Consisting of, devoted to, or characterized by sensual pleasures. 2. Full and appealing in form. [< L *voluptās,* pleasure.] **—vo•lup'tu•ous•ness** *n.*

vo•lute (və-lo͞ot') *n.* A spiral, scroll-like formation or decoration. [< L *volūta,* scroll.]

vom•it (vŏm'ĭt) *v.* 1. To eject part or all of the contents of the stomach through the mouth. 2. To eject or discharge in a gush. *—n.* Matter ejected from the stomach. [< L *vomere.*]

voo•doo (vo͞o'do͞o) *n.* A religious cult of African origin characterized by a belief in sorcery and fetishes and rituals in which participants communicate by trance with ancestors, saints, or animistic deities. **—voo'doo** *adj.* **—voo'doo•ism'** *n.*

vo•ra•cious (vô-rā'shəs, vō-, və-) *adj.* 1. Greedy for food; ravenous. 2. Too eager; insatiable. [< L *vorāre,* to devour.] **—vo•ra'ci•ty** (vô-răs'ə-tē, vō-, və-), **vo•ra'cious•ness** *n.*

Vo•ro•nezh (vŏ-rô'nĭsh). A city of the W Russian S.F.S.R. Pop. 576,000.

-vorous. *comb. form.* Eating or feeding on: **herbivorous.** [< L *vorāre,* to devour.]

vor•tex (vôr'tĕks) *n., pl.* **-texes** or **-tices** (-tə-sēz'). 1. Fluid flow involving rotation about an axis. 2. A situation that draws into its center all surrounding it. [L *vortex, vertex.*]

vo•ta•ry (vō'tə-rē) *n., pl.* **-ries. 1.** One bound by religious vows. **2.** A devotee. [< L *vovēre,* to vow.]
vote (vōt) *n.* **1.** A formal expression of preference for a candidate or a proposed resolution. **2.** That by which such a preference is made known. **3.** A group of voters: *the labor vote.* **4.** The result of an election, referendum, etc. **5.** Suffrage. *—v.* **voted, voting. 1.** To express preference by a vote. **2.** To bring into existence or make available by vote. **3.** To declare or pronounce by general consent. [L *vōtum,* vow.] **—vot'er** *n.*
vo•tive (vō'tĭv) *adj.* Given or dedicated in fulfillment of a vow or pledge. [< L *vōtum,* vow.]
vouch (vouch) *v.* **1.** To substantiate by supplying evidence; verify. **2.** To function or serve as a guarantee; furnish supporting evidence: *He vouched for her courage.* [< L *vocāre,* to call.]
vouch•er (vou'chər) *n.* **1.** One who vouches. **2.** A document serving as proof that the terms of a transaction have been met.
vouch•safe (vouch'sāf') *v.* **-safed, -safing.** To condescend to grant or bestow; deign. [ME *vouchen sauf,* "to warrant as safe."]
vow (vou) *n.* **1.** An earnest promise or pledge that binds one to a specified act or mode of behavior. **2.** A formal declaration. *—v.* **1.** To promise or pledge solemnly; make a vow. **2.** To declare formally. [< L *vōtum,* pp of *vovēre,* to pledge, promise.] **—vow'er** *n.*
vow•el (vou'əl) *n.* **1.** A speech sound created by the relatively free passage of breath through the larynx and oral cavity. **2.** A letter that represents such a sound. [< L *(littera) vōcālis,* "sounding (letter)."]
voy•age (voi'ĭj) *n.* A long journey, esp. one across a sea or ocean. *—v.* **-aged, -aging.** To make a voyage; travel. [< L *via,* road, way.] **—voy'ag•er** *n.*
vo•yeur (vwä-yûr') *n.* One who derives sexual gratification by secretly observing the sex organs or sexual acts of others. [< OF, "one who sees."] **—vo•yeur'ism'** *n.* **—vo'yeur•is'tic** (vwä'yə-rĭs'tĭk) *adj.*
V.P. vice president.
vs. versus.
v.s. vide supra.
Vt. Vermont.
VTOL vertical takeoff and landing.
Vul. Vulgate.
Vul•can (vŭl'kən). Roman god of fire and craftsmanship. [L *Vulcānus, Volcānus.*]
vul•can•ize (vŭl'kə-nīz') *v.* **-ized, -izing. 1.** To modify the properties of rubber by treatment with sulfur or other additives in the presence of heat and pressure. **2.** To treat (other substances) similarly. [< VULCAN.] **—vul'can•i•za'tion** *n.* **—vul'can•iz'er** *n.*
Vulg. Vulgate.
vul•gar (vŭl'gər) *adj.* **1.** Of or associated with the common people. **2.** Vernacular. **3.** Ill-bred; boorish. **4.** Obscene; offensive; coarse. [< L *vulgus,* the common people.] **—vul'gar•ly** *adv.* **—vul'gar•ness** *n.*
vul•gar•i•an (vŭl'gâr'ē-ən) *n.* A vulgar person, esp. one who makes a display of his money.
vul•gar•ism (vŭl'gə-rĭz'əm) *n.* **1.** Vulgarity. **2.** A word or expression used mainly by uncultivated people.
vul•gar•i•ty (vŭl'găr'ə-tē) *n., pl.* **-ties. 1.** The condition or quality of being vulgar. **2.** Something that offends good taste or propriety.
vul•gar•ize (vŭl'gə-rīz') *v.* **-ized, -izing. 1.** To render vulgar; debase; cheapen. **2.** To popularize. **—vul'gar•i•za'tion** *n.*
Vulgar Latin. The common speech of ancient Rome, differing from literary or standard Latin and forming the basis for the development of the Romance languages.
vul•ner•a•ble (vŭl'nər-ə-bəl) *adj.* **1.** Susceptible to injury; unprotected from danger. **2.** Susceptible to attack; insufficiently defended. **3.** *Bridge.* In a position to receive greater penalties. [< L *vulnerāre,* to wound.] **—vul'ner•a•bil'i•ty** *n.* **—vul'ner•a•bly** *adv.*
vul•pine (vŭl'pīn, -pĭn') *adj.* **1.** Resembling or characteristic of a fox. **2.** Clever; devious; cunning. [< L *vulpēs,* fox.]
vul•ture (vŭl'chər) *n.* Any of various large birds characteristically having dark plumage, a naked head and neck, and feeding on carrion. [< L *vultur.*]
vul•va (vŭl'və) *n., pl.* **-vae** (-vē). The external female genitalia. [L *vulva, volva,* womb, covering.]
vv. verses.
v.v. vice versa.
vy•ing (vī'ĭng) *adj.* Competing; contending.

w, W (dŭb'əl-yōō, -yōō) *n.* **1.** The 23rd letter of the English alphabet. **2.** Anything shaped like the letter **W.**
w 1. west; western. **2.** width.
W 1. tungsten. **2.** watt. **3.** west; western. **4.** *Broadcasting.* A letter prefixed to the call letters of some U.S. radio and TV stations.
w. west; western.
W. 1. Wednesday. **2.** Welsh. **3.** west; western.
Wac (wăk) *n.* A member of the Women's Army Corps of the U.S. Army.
wack•y (wăk'ē) *adj.* **-ier, -iest.** Also **whack•y.** *Slang.* Highly irrational or erratic. [Prob < WHACK.] **—wack'i•ness** *n.*
wad (wŏd) *n.* **1.** A small mass of soft material. **2.** A compressed ball, roll, or lump, as of tobacco. **3.** A disk, as of felt, to keep the powder and shot in place in a shotgun cartridge. **4.** *Informal.* **a.** A large amount. **b.** A sizable roll of paper money. *—v.* **wadded, wadding. 1.** To compress into a wad. **2.** To pad or plug with wadding. **3.** To hold (shot or powder) in place with a wad. [?]
wad•ding (wŏd'ĭng) *n.* **1.** A wad or wads collectively. **2.** A soft layer of fibrous cotton or wool used for padding or stuffing.
wad•dle (wŏd'l) *v.* **-dled, -dling.** To walk with short steps that tilt the body from side to side, as a duck does. *—n.* A waddling gait. [Prob freq of WADE.] **—wad'dler** *n.*
wade (wād) *v.* **waded, wading. 1.** To walk in or through water or something that similarly impedes movement. **2.** To make one's way arduously. *—n.* The act of wading. [< OE *wadan,* to go, wade. See **wādh-.**]
wad•er (wā'dər) *n.* **1.** One that wades. **2.** A long-legged bird that frequents shallow water. **3. waders.** Waterproof hip boots or trousers worn esp. by fishermen or hunters.
wa•di (wä'dē) *n.* In N Africa and SW Asia, a valley or gully that remains dry except during the rainy season. [Ar *wādī.*]
wa•fer (wā'fər) *n.* **1.** A small, thin, crisp cake, biscuit, or candy. **2.** A small disk. [< MLG *wāfel.*]
waf•fle[1] (wŏf'əl) *n.* A crisp batter cake baked in a waffle iron. [Du *wafel.*]
waf•fle[2] (wŏf'əl) *v.* **-fled, -fling.** *Informal.* To speak or write evasively. *—n. Informal.* Vague or misleading language. [Prob imit.]
waffle iron. An appliance with hinged metal plates that impress a grid pattern into waffle batter.
waft (wăft, wäft) *v.* To carry or cause to go gently and smoothly through the air or over water. *—n.* **1.** Something, as an odor, carried through the air. **2.** A light breeze. **3.** A waving. [< MDu *wachten,* to watch, guard.]
wag[1] (wăg) *v.* **wagged, wagging.** To move briskly and repeatedly from side to side, to and fro, or up and down. *—n.* The act or motion of wagging. [< OE *wagian,* to totter.]
wag[2] (wăg) *n.* One who jests. [?]
wage (wāj) *n.* **1.** Often **wages.** Payment for services. **2. wages** *(takes sing. or pl. v.).* Recompense; requital. *—v.* **waged, waging.** To engage in (a war or campaign). [ME, a pledge, wage, soldier's pay.]
wa•ger (wā'jər) *n.* A bet. *—v.* To bet. [< ONF *wage,* a pledge, wage.]
wag•gish (wăg'ĭsh) *adj.* Playfully humorous.
wag•gle (wăg'əl) *v.* **-gled, -gling.** To move with short, quick motions. *—n.* A waggling motion. [Freq of **WAG.**] **—wag'gly** *adj.*
Wag•ner (väg'nər), **Richard.** 1813–1883. German poet and composer. **—Wag•ne'ri•an** *adj.*
wag•on (wăg'ən) *n.* **1.** A 4-wheeled, usually horse-drawn vehicle having a large rectangular body. **2. a.** A **station wagon. b.** A police patrol wagon. **3.** A child's low four-wheeled cart. **—on the wagon.** *Slang.* Abstaining from liquor. [< MDu *wagen, waghen.*]
wag•on•er (wăg'ə-nər) *n.* A wagon driver.
wag•on•ette (wăg'ə-nĕt') *n.* A light wagon with two facing seats behind the driver's seat.
wa•gon-lit (vá-gôɴ-lē') *n., pl.* **wagons-lits** or **wagon-lits** (vá-gôɴ-lē'). A railroad sleeping car. [F.]
waif (wāf) *n.* **1. a.** A forsaken or orphaned child. **b.** A stray young animal. **2.** Something found and unclaimed. [ME *waife,* property without owner.]
wail (wāl) *v.* **1.** To grieve or protest audibly; to

lament. 2. To make a high-pitched mournful sound. —*n.* 1. A high-pitched mournful cry. 2. Any similar sound. [Prob < ON **veila,* to moan, lament.] —**wail'er** *n.*

wail•ful (wāl'fəl) *adj.* Mournful.

wain (wān) *n.* A large open farm wagon. [< OE *wægen.*]

wain•scot (wān'skət, -skŏt', -skōt') *n.* Wall paneling, esp. on the lower part of an interior wall. —*v.* **-scoted** or **-scotted, -scoting** or **-scotting.** To line or panel (a room or wall) with wainscot. [< MDu *wagenschot,* perh "timber for wagons."]

wain•scot•ing (wān'skə-tĭng, -skŏt'ĭng, -skō'-tĭng) *n.* Also **wain•scot•ting.** 1. A wainscoted wall or walls. 2. Material for a wainscot.

wain•wright (wān'rīt') *n.* A builder and repairer of wagons.

waist (wāst) *n.* 1. The part of the human trunk between the bottom of the rib cage and the pelvis. 2. a. The part of a garment from the shoulders to the waistline. b. A blouse. c. A child's undershirt. 3. The middle section or part of something. [< OE **wæst,* growth, size of body. See **aug-.**]

waist•coat (wĕs'kĭt, wāst'kōt') *n. Chiefly Brit.* A vest.

waist•line (wāst'līn') *n.* 1. a. The place at which the circumference of the waist is smallest. b. The measurement of this circumference. 2. The line at which the skirt and bodice of a dress join.

wait (wāt) *v.* 1. To remain inactive in anticipation. 2. To delay; postpone. 3. To serve as a waiter or waitress. 4. To attend, as a clerk or servant: *He waited on her.* —*n.* The act of waiting or the time spent waiting. [ME *waiten,* to watch, lie in wait, wait.]

wait•er (wā'tər) *n.* 1. A man who waits on table. 2. A tray.

wait•ress (wā'trĭs) *n.* A woman or girl who waits on table.

waive (wāv) *v.* **waived, waiving.** 1. To relinquish or give up (a claim or right) voluntarily. 2. To put aside or off for the time. [ME *weiven,* to outlaw, abandon, relinquish.]

waiv•er (wā'vər) *n.* 1. The intentional relinquishment of a right, claim, or privilege. 2. A document that evidences such an act.

Wa•kash•an (wô'kə-shăn', wä-kăsh'ən) *n.* A family of North American Indian languages spoken by certain tribes of Washington and British Columbia. —**Wa'kash•an** *adj.*

wake[1] (wāk) *v.* **woke, waked** or *chiefly Brit. & regional* **woke** or **woken, waking.** 1. To awaken: *He woke up with a start.* 2. To keep watch or guard, esp. over a corpse. 3. To remain awake. 4. To make aware of; alert. —*n.* 1. A watch, esp. over the body of a deceased person before burial. 2. The condition of being awake. [< OE *wacian,* to be awake, and **wacan,* to rouse. See **weg-.**]

Usage: The verbs *wake, waken, awake,* and *awaken* are alike in meaning but differentiated in usage. Each has transitive and intransitive senses, but *awake* is used largely intransitively and *waken* transitively. In the passive voice, *awaken* and *waken* are the more frequent. In figurative usage, *awake* and *awaken* are the more prevalent: *He awoke to the danger. His suspicions were awakened. Wake* is frequently used with *up;* the others do not take a preposition. The preferred past participle of *wake* is *waked,* not *woke* or *woken.* The preferred past participle of *awake* is *awaked,* not *awoke.*

wake[2] (wāk) *n.* 1. The track of turbulence left by something moving through water. 2. The track or course left behind anything. [Prob < ON *vök,* a hole or crack in ice.]

wake•ful (wāk'fəl) *adj.* 1. a. Not sleeping. b. Sleepless. 2. Alert. —**wake'ful•ness** *n.*

wak•en (wā'kən) *v.* 1. To rouse from sleep; awake. 2. To rouse from an inactive state. —See Usage note at **wake.** [< OE *wæcnian.*]

wale (wāl) *n.* 1. A welt on the skin. 2. a. One of the ribs or ridges in the surface of a fabric. b. The texture of such a fabric. —*v.* **waled, waling.** To mark (the skin) with wales. [< OE *walu,* a ridge of earth or stone, weal.]

Wales (wālz). A principality comprising part of the United Kingdom located in W Great Britain. Pop. 2,676,000.

Wal•hal•la. Variant of **Valhalla.**

walk (wôk) *v.* 1. To go, cause to go, or lead around on foot. 2. To pass over, on, or through on foot. 3. To conduct oneself in a particular manner. 4. *Baseball.* To go to first base after the pitcher has thrown four balls. —*n.* 1. a. The act or an instance of walking. b. A relatively slow gait in which the feet are lifted alternately. 2. a. Walking pace. b. The characteristic way in which one walks. 3. The distance to be covered in walking. 4. A place on which one may walk. [< OE *wealcan,* to roll, toss, and *wealcian,* to roll up, muffle up.] —**walk'er** *n.*

walk•ie-talk•ie (wô'kē-tô'kē) *n.* A portable sending and receiving radio set.

walk-in (wôk'ĭn') *adj.* Large enough to admit entrance, as a closet. —**walk'-in'** *n.*

walking stick. A cane used as an aid in walking.

walk-on (wôk'ŏn', -ôn') *n.* A minor role in a theatrical production.

walk•out (wôk'out') *n.* A strike of workmen.

walk•up (wôk'ŭp') *n.* 1. A building with no elevator. 2. An apartment in such a building.

wall (wôl) *n.* 1. A vertical construction forming an inner partition or exterior siding of a building. 2. A continuous structure forming a rampart and built for defensive purposes. 3. Something resembling a wall in appearance, function, or construction. —*v.* 1. To enclose, surround, or fortify with or as if with a wall. 2. To separate with or as if with a wall. [< OE *weall* < L *vallum,* palisade, wall.]

wal•la•by (wŏl'ə-bē) *n., pl.* **-bies.** Any of various Australian marsupials related to and resembling the kangaroos but generally smaller.

wall•board (wôl'bôrd', -bōrd') *n.* A structural material used as a substitute for plaster or wood panels.

wal•let (wŏl'ĭt) *n.* A small, flat folding case for holding paper money, cards, photographs, etc. [ME *walet,* a pilgrim's knapsack or provisions bag.]

wall•eye (wôl'ī') *n.* 1. An eye in which the cornea is white or opaque. 2. An eye abnormally turned away from the center of the face. 3. Also **walleyed pike.** A North American freshwater food and game fish with large, conspicuous eyes. [Back-formation < WALL-EYED.]

wall•eyed (wôl'īd') *adj.* Having a walleye. [< ON *vagleygr.*]

wall•flow•er (wôl'flou'ər) *n.* 1. A cultivated plant with fragrant yellowish or brownish flowers. 2. *Informal.* One who does not participate in social activity because of shyness or unpopularity.

Wal•loon (wŏ-lo͞on') *n.* 1. One of a French-speaking people of Celtic descent inhabiting SE Belgium and adjacent regions of France. 2. The French dialect of this people. —**Wal•loon'** *adj.*

wal•lop (wŏl'əp) *v.* 1. To beat soundly; thrash. 2. To strike with a hard blow. —*n.* 1. A severe blow. 2. The ability to strike such a blow. [< ME *walopen,* to gallop.]

wal•lop•ing (wŏl'ə-pĭng) *adj. Informal.* Very large; huge.

wal•low (wŏl'ō) *v.* 1. To roll the body about in or as in water, snow, or mud. 2. To luxuriate; revel. —*n.* A place where animals go to wallow. [< OE *wealwian.* See **wel-**[3].]

wall•pa•per (wôl'pā'pər) *n.* Paper printed with designs used as a wall covering. —*v.* To cover with wallpaper.

wal•nut (wôl'nŭt', -nət) *n.* 1. An edible nut with a hard, corrugated shell. 2. A tree bearing such nuts. 3. The hard, dark wood of such a tree. [< OE *wealhhnutu,* "Gaulish nut."]

wal•rus (wôl'rəs, wŏl'-) *n., pl.* **-ruses** or **-rus.** A large Arctic marine mammal with tough, wrinkled skin and large tusks. [< Scand.]

waltz (wôlts) *n.* A dance in triple time with a strong accent on the first beat. —*v.* 1. To dance the waltz (with). 2. To move briskly and with ease. [< MHG *walzen,* to roll, turn, dance.] —**waltz'er** *n.*

wam•pum (wŏm'pəm, wôm'-) *n.* Small beads made from polished shells, formerly used by North American Indians as currency and as jewelry. [< Algon.]

wan (wŏn) *adj.* 1. Unnaturally pale. 2. Languid; melancholy. [< OE *wann,* dusky, dark, livid.] —**wan'ly** *adv.* —**wan'ness** *n.*

wand (wŏnd) *n.* 1. A slender rod carried as a symbol of office in a procession. 2. A musician's baton. 3. A rod used by a magician, diviner, or conjurer. [< ON *vöndr.*]

wan•der (wŏn'dər) *v.* 1. To roam aimlessly. 2. To go by an indirect route or at no set pace. 3. To go astray. 4. To think or express oneself incoherently. [< OE *wandrian.* See **wendh-.**] —**wan'der•er** *n.*

wandering Jew. A trailing plant often with variegated foliage, popular as a house plant.

wan•der•lust (wŏn'dər-lŭst') *n.* A strong impulse to travel. [G.]

wane (wān) *v.* **waned, waning.** 1. To decrease gradually; dwindle; decline. 2. To show decreasing illuminated area from full moon to new moon. 3. To approach an end. —*n.* 1. The act or process of waning. 2. A period of waning, esp. the period of the decrease of the moon's illuminated visible surface. [< OE *wanian,* to lessen. See **eu-.**]

wan•gle (wăng'gəl) *v.* **-gled, -gling.** 1. To make, achieve, or get by contrivance. 2. To manipulate or juggle. 3. To use tricky or fraudulent methods. [Orig "to manipulate or devise a substitute for."] —**wan'gler** *n.*

Wan•kel engine (väng'kəl, wäng'-). A rotary internal-combustion engine in which a triangular rotor turning in a specially shaped housing performs the functions alloted to the pistons of a conventional engine. [< Felix *Wankel* (born 1902), German engineer.]

want (wŏnt, wônt) *v.* 1. To fail to have; lack. 2. To desire; wish for: *He wants to leave.* 3. To need or require. 4. a. To request the presence of. b. To seek with intent to capture. —*n.* 1. The condition or quality of lacking a usual or necessary amount. 2. Pressing need. 3. Something needed. 4. A fault. [< ON *vanta,* to be lacking.]

want•ing (wŏn'tĭng, wôn'-) *adj.* 1. Absent; lacking. 2. Not up to standards or expectations. —*prep.* 1. Without. 2. Minus; less.

wan•ton (wŏn'tən) *adj.* 1. Immoral or unchaste; lewd. **2.** Maliciously cruel. **3.** Freely extravagant. **4.** Luxuriant. —*n.* A wanton person, esp. an immoral woman. [ME *wantowen,* lacking discipline, lewd.] —**wan'ton•ly** *adv.* —**wan'ton•ness** *n.*

wap•i•ti (wŏp'ə-tē) *n.* A large North American deer with many-branched antlers; an elk. [< Algon.]

war (wôr) *n.* **1. a.** A state of open, armed conflict between nations, states, or parties. **b.** The period of such conflict. **2.** Any condition of active antagonism. **3.** Military science; strategy. —*v.* **warred, warring. 1.** To wage war. **2.** To be in a state of hostility. [< OHG *werra,* confusion, strife.]

War Between the States. The **Civil War.**

war•ble (wôr'bəl) *v.* **-bled, -bling.** To sing with trills, runs, or other melodic embellishments. —*n.* The act of warbling. [< ONF *werble,* a warbling, melody.]

war•bler (wôr'blər) *n.* **1.** Any of various small, often yellowish New World birds. **2.** Any of various small brownish or grayish Old World birds.

war bonnet. A feathered ceremonial headdress used by some North American Plains Indians, consisting of a cap or band and a trailing extension decorated with erect feathers.

war cry. 1. A cry uttered by combatants as they attack. **2.** A slogan used to rally people to a cause.

ward (wôrd) *n.* **1.** A division of a city for administrative and representative purposes. **2.** A division in a hospital. **3.** A division of a prison. **4.** *Law.* A child or incompetent person placed under the care or protection of a guardian or court. **5.** The state of being under guard. **6.** The act of guarding. **7.** A means of protection. —*v.* To turn aside; parry; avert; repel: *ward off a blow.* [< OE *weard,* a watching over. See **wer-[4]**.]

-ward, -wards. *comb. form.* Direction toward: **skyward, westwards.** [< OE *-weard.* See **wer-[3]**.]

war•den (wôrd'n) *n.* **1.** The chief administrative official of a prison. **2.** An official charged with the enforcement of certain laws and regulations, as an air-raid warden. [< ONF *warder,* to guard.]

ward•er (wôr'dər) *n.* A guard, porter, or watchman of a gate or tower. [< ONF *warder,* to guard, keep.]

ward•robe (wôrd'rōb') *n.* **1.** A tall cabinet, closet, or small room designed to hold clothes. **2.** Garments collectively, esp. all the articles of clothing belonging to one person. [< ONF *warderobe.*]

ward•ship (wôrd'shĭp') *n.* **1.** The state of being in the charge of a guardian. **2.** Guardianship.

-ware. *comb. form.* **1.** Articles of the same general kind: *glassware.* **2.** Pottery or ceramics: *earthenware.*

ware•house (wâr'hous') *n.* A place in which goods or merchandise is stored.

wares (wârz) *pl.n.* Articles of commerce; goods. [< OE *waru* (sing).]

war•fare (wôr'fâr') *n.* **1.** The waging of war. **2.** Conflict of any kind. [ME *werrefare,* a going to war.]

war•head (wôr'hĕd') *n.* A part of the system in the forward part of a projectile, as a guided missile, that contains the explosive charge.

war-horse (wôr'hôrs') *n.* **1.** A horse used in combat. **2.** One who has been through many struggles.

war•like (wôr'līk') *adj.* **1.** Belligerent; hostile. **2.** Of or pertaining to war.

war•lock (wôr'lŏk') *n.* A male witch, sorcerer, or wizard. [< OE *wǣrloga,* "oath-breaker."]

war•lord (wôr'lôrd') *n.* A military commander exercising civil power in a given region, often in defiance of the national government.

warm (wôrm) *adj.* **1.** Moderately hot. **2.** Having the natural heat of living beings. **3.** Preserving or imparting heat. **4.** Having a sensation of unusually high bodily heat, as from exercise. **5.** Marked by enthusiasm. **6.** Sympathetic; cordial. **7.** Loving; passionate. **8.** Quick to be aroused; fiery. **9.** Recently made: *a warm trail.* **10.** Close to discovering something. —*v.* To increase slightly in temperature; make or become warm. —**warm up.** To make or become ready for operation, as an engine. [< OE *wearm.*] —**warm'ly** *adv.*

warm-blood•ed (wôrm'blŭd'ĭd) *adj.* Maintaining a relatively constant, warm body temperature independent of environmental temperature, as a mammal.

warm-heart•ed (wôrm'här'tĭd) *adj.* Friendly; sympathetic. —**warm'-heart'ed•ly** *adv.*

war•mon•ger (wôr'mŭng'gər, -mŏng'ər) *n.* One who advocates or attempts to stir up war.

warmth (wôrmth) *n.* **1.** The state, sensation, or quality of moderate heat. **2.** Excitement or intensity, as of love or passion; ardor; zeal. [< OE **wiermthu.*]

warn (wôrn) *v.* **1.** To make aware of potential danger; caution. **2.** To admonish as to action or manners. **3.** To notify (a person) to go or stay away. **4.** To notify in advance. [< OE *wearnian,* to take heed, warn. See **wer-[5]**.]

warn•ing (wôr'nĭng) *n.* **1.** An intimation or sign of impending danger. **2. a.** Advice to beware. **b.** Counsel to desist from a given course of action. —*adj.* Acting or serving as a warning. —**warn'ing•ly** *adv.*

warp (wôrp) *v.* **1.** To twist or become twisted out of shape. **2.** To pervert; corrupt. **3.** *Naut.* To move (a vessel) by hauling on a line fastened to a piling, anchor, or pier. —*n.* **1.** The state of being twisted or bent out of shape. **2.** A distortion or twist. **3.** The threads that run lengthwise in a fabric, crossed at right angles by the woof. [< OE *weorpan,* to throw (away). See **wer-[3]**.] —**warp'er** *n.*

war paint. Pigments applied to the face or body by certain tribes preparatory to going to war.

war•path (wôr'păth', -päth') *n.* **1.** The route taken by a party of North American Indians on the attack. **2.** A hostile course or mood: *on the warpath.*

war•rant (wôr'ənt, wŏr'-) *n.* **1.** Authorization or certification. **2.** Justification for some action; grounds. **3.** Evidence; proof. **4.** A writ or other order that serves as authorization for something, esp. a judicial writ authorizing a search, seizure, or arrest. —*v.* **1.** To guarantee or attest to the quality or accuracy of. **2.** To vouch for. **3. a.** To guarantee (a product). **b.** To guarantee (a purchaser) indemnification against damage or loss. **4.** To guarantee the security of. **5.** To call for; deserve. **6.** To authorize or empower. [Prob < OHG *werenti,* "the one protecting."]

war•ran•ty (wôr'ən-tē, wŏr'-) *n., pl.* **-ties. 1.** Official authorization, sanction, or warrant. **2.** Justification for an act or course of action. **3.** A legally binding guarantee.

war•ren (wôr'ən, wŏr'-) *n.* **1.** An area where rabbits live in burrows. **2.** Any overcrowded place of habitation. [< ONF *warenne.*]

war•ri•or (wôr'ē-ər, -yər, wŏr'-) *n.* One engaged or experienced in battle.

War•saw (wôr'sô). The capital of Poland. Pop. 1,241,000.

war•ship (wôr'shĭp') *n.* A ship equipped for use in battle.

wart (wôrt) *n.* **1.** A small, hard growth on the outer skin, caused by a virus and occurring typically on the hands or feet. **2.** Any similar protuberance, as on a plant. [< OE *wearte.* See **wer-[1]**.] —**wart'y** *adj.*

wart hog. An African hog with curved tusks and wartlike protuberances on the face.

war•time (wôr'tīm') *n.* A time of war.

war•y (wâr'ē) *adj.* **-ier, -iest. 1.** On one's guard; cautious; watchful. **2.** Characterized by caution. [< OE *wær.* See **wer-[4]**.] —**war'i•ness** *n.*

was (wŏz, wŭz; *unstressed* wəz). 1st and 3rd person sing. past indicative of **be.** See Usage note at **were.** [< OE *wæs.* See **wes-[3]**.]

wash (wŏsh, wôsh) *v.* **1.** To cleanse, using water or other liquid, usually with soap, detergent, etc., by immersing, dipping, rubbing, or scrubbing. **2.** To cleanse oneself. **3.** To rid of corruption; purify. **4.** To make moist or wet. **5.** To flow over, against, or past: *shores washed by ocean tides.* **6.** To sweep or carry away: *The rain had washed them away.* **7.** To erode or destroy by moving water: *The roads were washed out.* **8.** To coat with a watery layer of paint or other coloring substance. **9.** To remove particulate constituents from (an ore) by immersion in or agitation with water. **10.** *Brit. Informal.* To hold up under examination: *Your excuse won't wash!* —*n.* **1.** The act or process of washing or cleansing. **2.** A quantity of articles washed or intended for washing. **3.** Waste liquid; swill. **4.** Any preparation or product used in washing or coating. **5.** A light tint or hue: *a wash of red sunset.* **6. a.** The rush or surge of water or waves. **b.** The sound of this. **7.** The removal or erosion of soil, subsoil, etc., by the action of moving water. **8.** *Western U.S.* The dry bed of a stream. [< OE *wæscan, wacsan.* See **wed-.**]

Wash. Washington.

wash•a•ble (wŏsh'ə-bəl, wôsh'-) *adj.* Capable of being washed without injury.

wash-and-wear (wŏsh'ən-wâr', wôsh'-) *adj.* Treated so as to require little or no ironing.

wash•board (wŏsh'bôrd', -bōrd', wôsh'-) *n.* A board with a corrugated surface upon which clothes can be rubbed in the process of laundering.

wash•cloth (wŏsh'klôth', -klŏth', wôsh'-) *n.* A small, usually square cloth used for washing the face or body.

washed-out (wŏsht'out', wôsht'-) *adj.* **1.** Pale; faded. **2.** *Informal.* Exhausted.

wash•er (wŏsh'ər, wôsh'-) *n.* **1.** One that washes. **2.** A small perforated disk, as of metal, rubber, or plastic, placed beneath a nut or at an axle bearing to relieve friction, prevent leakage, or distribute pressure. **3.** A machine or apparatus for washing.

wash•er•wom•an (wŏsh'ər-wo͝om'ən, wô'-shər-) *n.* A laundress.

wash•ing (wŏsh'ĭng, wôsh'-) *n.* **1.** A quantity of articles washed at one time: *the week's washing.* **2.** The residue after an ore or other material has been washed.

washing soda. A hydrated sodium carbonate, used as a general cleanser.

Wash•ing•ton (wŏsh'ĭng-tən, wôsh'-). **1.** A state of the NW U.S. Pop. 3,409,000. Cap. Olympia. **2.** The capital of the U.S., a city coextensive with the District of Columbia. Pop. 757,000.

Wash•ing•ton (wŏsh'ĭng-tən, wôsh'-). **1. Booker T(aliaferro).** 1856–1915. American Negro educator. **2. George.** 1732–1799. 1st President of the U.S. (1789–97).

Booker T. Washington

George Washington

wash•out (wŏsh'out', wôsh'-) *n.* **1. a.** The erosion, as of a roadbed, by a transient stream of water. **b.** A channel produced by washout. **2.** A total failure.

wash•room (wŏsh'ro͞om', -ro͝om', wôsh'-) *n.* A bathroom or lavatory, esp. in a public place.

wash•stand (wŏsh'stănd', wôsh'-) *n.* **1.** A stand designed to hold a basin and pitcher of water for washing. **2.** A bathroom sink.

wash•tub (wŏsh'tŭb', wôsh'-) *n.* A tub used for washing clothes.

wash•y (wŏsh'ē, wôsh'ē) *adj.* **-ier, -iest. 1.** Watery; diluted. **2.** Lacking intensity or strength. **—wash'i•ness** *n.*

was•n't (wŏz'ənt, wŭz'-). Contraction of *was not.*

wasp (wŏsp, wôsp) *n.* Any of various insects having a slender body with a narrow mid-section and often inflicting a painful sting. [< OE *wæsp, wæps.* See **wopsā.**] **—wasp'y** *adj.*

wasp•ish (wŏs'pĭsh, wôs'-) *adj.* **1.** Suggestive of a wasp. **2.** Easily irritated or annoyed. **—wasp'ish•ly** *adv.* **—wasp'ish•ness** *n.*

wasp waist. A very slender or tightly corseted woman's waist. **—wasp'-waist'ed** (wŏsp'wās'tĭd, wôsp'-) *adj.*

was•sail (wŏs'əl, wăs'-, wŏ-sāl') *n.* **1. a.** A toast formerly given in drinking someone's health. **b.** The drink used in such toasting. **2.** A festivity characterized by much drinking. *—v.* To drink to the health of. [< ON *ves heill,* be in good health.]

Was•ser•mann test (wä'sər-mən). A diagnostic blood test for syphilis. [< A. von *Wassermann* (1866–1925), German bacteriologist.]

wast (wŏst). *Archaic.* 2nd person sing. *p.t.* of **be.**

wast•age (wā'stĭj) *n.* Loss by deterioration, wear, destruction, etc.

waste (wāst) *v.* **wasted, wasting. 1.** To consume thoughtlessly or carelessly. **2.** To weaken or become weak. **3.** To fail to take advantage of: *waste an opportunity.* *—n.* **1.** The act of wasting or condition of being wasted. **2.** A desert or wilderness. **3.** A useless or worthless by-product of a process. **4.** The undigested residue of food eliminated from the body. *—adj.* **1.** Discarded as worthless or useless: *waste paper.* **2.** Used as a container for refuse: *a waste can.* **3.** Not cultivated or inhabited. **4.** Excreted from the body as useless. [< L *vāstāre,* to make empty.]

waste•ful (wāst'fəl) *adj.* Characterized by heedless wasting; extravagant. **—waste'ful•ly** *adv.* **—waste'ful•ness** *n.*

waste•land (wāst'lănd') *n.* Uncultivated or desolate land.

wast•rel (wā'strəl) *n.* **1.** One who wastes. **2.** An idler or loafer.

watch (wŏch) *v.* **1.** To look or observe carefully and continuously. **2.** To look and wait expectantly or in anticipation: *watch for an opportunity.* **3.** To be on the lookout or alert; guard. **4.** To stay alert as a devotional or religious exercise; keep vigil. **5.** To observe the course of mentally. **6.** To tend, as flocks. **—watch out.** To be careful or on the alert. *—n.* **1.** The act of watching. **2.** Formerly, any of the periods into which the night was divided. **3.** A period of close observation. **4.** A person or group of persons serving, esp. at night, to guard or protect. **5.** The post or period of duty of a guard, sentinel, or watchman. **6.** A small, portable timepiece, esp. one worn on the wrist or carried in the pocket. **7.** A vigil. **8.** A period of assignment to duty on a ship. [< OE *wæccan,* to be or stay awake, keep vigil. See **weg-.**]

watch•dog (wŏch'dôg', -dŏg') *n.* A dog trained to guard property.

watch•ful (wŏch'fəl) *adj.* Alert; vigilant. **—watch'ful•ly** *adv.* **—watch'ful•ness** *n.*

watch•man (wŏch'mən) *n.* A man employed to stand guard or keep watch.

watch•tow•er (wŏch'tou'ər) *n.* An observation tower for a guard.

watch•word (wŏch'wûrd') *n.* **1.** A password. **2.** A rallying cry; slogan.

wa•ter (wô'tər, wŏt'ər) *n.* **1.** A clear, colorless, nearly odorless and tasteless liquid, H_2O, essential for most plant and animal life and the most widely used of all solvents. **2.** Any of various forms of water, as rain. **3.** Any body of water, as a sea, lake, river, or stream. **4.** An aqueous solution of a substance. *—v.* **-tered, -tering. 1.** To pour water upon; make wet. **2.** To supply with drinking water. **3.** To dilute by or as by adding water. **4.** To produce or discharge fluid, as from the eyes. **5.** To treat so as to produce a wavy surface effect, as on silk. [< OE *wæter.* See **wed-.**]

Water Bearer. The constellation and sign of the zodiac Aquarius.

water buffalo. An African or Asian buffalo with large, spreading horns, often domesticated as a draft animal.

Wa•ter•bur•y (wô'tər-bĕr'ē, wŏt'ər-). A city of west-central Connecticut. Pop. 142,000.

water closet. A room or booth containing a toilet and often a sink.

water color. 1. A paint composed of a water-soluble pigment. **2.** A work done in water colors. **3.** The art of using water colors.

water cooler. A device for cooling, storing, and dispensing drinking water.

wa•ter•course (wô'tər-kôrs', -kōrs', wŏt'ər-) *n.* **1.** A waterway. **2.** The bed or channel of a waterway.

wa•ter•cress (wô'tər-krĕs', wŏt'ər-) *n.* A plant growing in freshwater ponds and streams and having pungent edible leaves.

wa•ter•fall (wô'tər-fôl', wŏt'ər-) *n.* A steep descent of water from a height.

wa•ter•fowl (wô'tər-foul', wŏt'ər-) *n.* **1.** A swimming bird, as a duck or goose. **2.** Such birds collectively.

wa•ter•front (wô'tər-frŭnt', wŏt'ər-) *n.* Improved or unimproved land abutting on a body of water.

Wa•ter•gate (wô'tər-gāt', wŏt'ər-) *n. Informal.* A scandal that involves officials violating public or corporate trust through acts of abuse of power. [< *Watergate,* a building complex in Washington, D.C.]

watering place. A health resort featuring water activities or mineral springs.

water lily. Any of various aquatic plants with broad floating leaves and showy, variously colored flowers.

water line. Any of several lines marked on the hull of a ship, indicating the depth to which the ship sinks under various loads.

wa•ter-logged (wô'tər-lôgd', -lŏgd', wŏt'ər-) *adj.* Soaked or saturated with water.

water main. A principal pipe in a system of pipes for conveying water.

wa•ter•mark (wô'tər-märk', wŏt'ər-) *n.* **1.** A mark showing the height to which water has risen. **2.** A translucent design impressed on paper during manufacture and visible when the paper is held to the light.

wa•ter•mel•on (wô'tər-mĕl'ən, wŏt'ər-) *n.* A large melon with a hard green rind and watery, reddish flesh.

water moccasin. A venomous snake of swampy regions of the S U.S.

wa•ter•pow•er (wô'tər-pou'ər, wŏt'ər-) *n.* **1.** The energy of running or falling water as used for driving machinery, esp. for generating electricity. **2.** A source of such power.

wa•ter•proof (wô'tər-pro͞of', wŏt'ər-) *adj.* Impenetrable to or unaffected by water. *—n. Chiefly Brit.* A raincoat or other waterproof garment. *—v.* To make waterproof.

wa•ter-re•pel•lent (wô'tər-rĭ-pĕl'ənt, wŏt'ər-) *adj.* Repelling water but not waterproof.

wa•ter-re•sis•tant (wô'tər-rĭ-zĭs'tənt, wŏt'ər-) *adj.* Resistant to wetting but not waterproof.

wa•ter•shed (wô'tər-shĕd', wŏt'ər-) *n.* **1.** A ridge of high land dividing two areas that are drained by different river systems. **2.** The region draining into a body of water.

wa•ter-ski (wô'tər-skē', wŏt'ər-) *v.* To ski on water while being towed by a power boat. *—n.* A broad ski used in water-skiing.

wa•ter•spout (wô'tər-spout', wŏt'ər-) *n.* **1.** A tornado or lesser whirlwind occurring over water and resulting in a whirling column of spray and mist. **2.** A pipe from which water is discharged.

water system. 1. A river and all its tributaries. **2. a.** The water available for a community or region. **b.** The sources and delivery system of such water.

water table. The surface in a permeable body of rock of a zone saturated with water.

wa•ter•tight (wô′tər-tīt′, wŏt′ər-) *adj.* **1.** Permitting neither entry nor escape of water. **2.** Having no flaws or loopholes.

water tower. A standpipe or tank used as a reservoir or for maintaining equal pressure on a water system.

wa•ter•way (wô′tər-wā′, wŏt′ər-) *n.* A body of water used for travel or transport, esp. a river or canal.

water wheel. A wheel propelled by falling or running water, primarily for use as a source of power.

wa•ter•works (wô′tər-wûrks′, wŏt′ər-) *pl.n.* **1.** The water system of a city. **2.** A single unit, as a pumping station, within such a system.

wa•ter•y (wô′tə-rē, wŏt′ə-) *adj.* **-ier, -iest. 1.** Wet; moist. **2.** Resembling or suggestive of water; liquid. **3.** Diluted. **4.** Without force; insipid: *watery prose.*

watt (wŏt) *n.* A unit of power equal to one joule per second. [< J. *Watt* (1736–1819), Scottish engineer.]

wat•tage (wŏt′ĭj) *n.* An amount of power, esp. electric power, expressed in watts.

wat•tle (wŏt′l) *n.* **1. a.** Poles intertwined with twigs, reeds, or branches for use in construction, as of walls or fences. **b.** Materials thus used. **2.** A fleshy fold of skin hanging from the neck or throat, as of certain birds. [< OE *watel, watul.*]

wave (wāv) *v.* **waved, waving. 1. a.** To move or cause to move back and forth or up and down in the air. **b.** To signal by such a movement, esp. with the hand. **2.** To curve or curl. —*n.* **1.** A ridge or swell moving along the surface of a body of water. **2.** Often **waves.** The sea or seas. **3.** A moving curve or succession of curves in or upon a surface: *waves of wheat in the wind.* **4.** A curve or curl, as in the hair. **5.** A movement up and down or back and forth. **6.** A surge. **7.** A persistent meteorological condition: *cold wave.* **8.** *Phys.* A disturbance or oscillation propagated from point to point in a medium or in space. [< OE *wafian,* to move back and forth, esp. with the hands, and < OE *wǣg,* motion, wave.] —**wav′er** *n.*

Wave (wāv) *n.* A member of the WAVES.

wave•form (wāv′fôrm′) *n.* The mathematical representation of a wave, esp. a graph of deviation at a fixed point versus time.

wave front. A surface of a propagating wave that is the locus of all points having identical phase.

wave•length (wāv′lĕngth′) *n.* In a periodic wave, the distance between two points of corresponding phase in consecutive cycles.

wa•ver (wā′vər) *v.* **1.** To swing or move back and forth; sway. **2.** To show irresolution or indecision. **3.** To falter. **4.** To tremble or quaver, as a voice. **5.** To flicker or flash, as light. [ME *waveren,* to wander, fluctuate.] —**wa′ver** *n.* —**wa′ver•ing•ly** *adv.*

WAVES (wāvz). The women's reserve of the U.S. Navy. [W(omen) A(ccepted for) V(olunteer) E(mergency) S(ervice).]

wa•vy (wā′vē) *adj.* **-vier, -viest. 1.** Having or rising in waves: *a wavy sea.* **2.** Proceeding in a wavelike motion. **3.** Having curls, curves, or undulations. —**wa′vi•ness** *n.*

waw. Variant of **vav.**

wax[1] (wăks) *n.* **1.** Any of various natural unctuous, viscous or solid heat-sensitive substances, as beeswax, consisting essentially of heavy hydrocarbons or fats. **2.** A waxy substance found in the ears. —*v.* To coat or treat with wax. [< OE *weax, wæx,* beeswax. See **wokso-.**] —**wax′en, wax′y** *adj.*

wax[2] (wăks) *v.* **1.** To become gradually larger, more numerous, stronger, or more intense. **2.** To increase in illumination or progress toward being full. Used of the moon. **3.** To grow or become: *The seas wax calm.* [< OE *weaxan.* See **aug-.**]

wax bean. A variety of string bean with yellow pods.

wax•wing (wăks′wĭng′) *n.* A crested bird with mostly brown plumage and waxy red tips on the wing feathers.

wax•works (wăks′wûrks′) *pl.n.* An exhibition of wax figures.

way (wā) *n.* **1.** A road or path. **2.** Room to proceed: *clear the way.* **3.** A course or route. **4.** Travel along a route. **5.** A manner of doing something. **6.** A mode of living or conduct. **7.** Freedom to do as one prefers. **8.** Distance: *a long way off.* **9.** A specific direction. **10.** An aspect of something. **11.** An individual manner of behaving. **12.** A condition, as of health: *in a bad way.* **13.** A home or neighborhood. —**by the way.** Incidentally. —**by way of. 1.** By route of. **2.** As a means of. —**have a way with.** To have the ability to handle. —**under way.** Making progress. —*adv.* Also **'way.** *Informal.* **1.** At a great distance; far: *way off yonder.* **2.** Away: *go way.* [< OE *weg,* a road, path. See **wegh-.**]

way•far•er (wā′fâr′ər) *n.* One who travels, esp. by foot. —**way′far′ing** *adj.* & *n.*

way•lay (wā′lā′) *v.* **-laid** (-lād′), **-laying. 1.** To lie in wait for and assail from ambush. **2.** To accost or intercept. —**way′lay′er** *n.*

way-out (wā′out′) *adj. Informal.* Strange or unconventional.

-ways. *comb. form.* Manner, direction, or position: **sideways.**

way•side (wā′sīd′) *n.* The side or edge of a road.

way•ward (wā′wərd) *adj.* **1.** Wanting one's own way in spite of the advice or wishes of another; willful. **2.** Erratic; unpredictable. [< ME *awayward,* turned away.] —**way′ward•ly** *adv.* —**way′ward•ness** *n.*

we (wē) *pron.* The 1st person pl. pronoun in the nominative case, used to represent the speaker and one or more others that share in the action of the verb. [< OE *wē,* we. See **we-.**]

weak (wēk) *adj.* **1.** Lacking physical strength. **2.** Liable to fail under pressure; lacking resistance. **3.** Lacking strength of character or will. **4.** Lacking the proper or full strength of some component. **5.** Unsound. **6.** Lacking capacity or capability. **7.** Lacking authority or power to rule. [< ON *veikr,* pliant, flexible.] —**weak′ly** *adj.* & *adv.*

weak•en (wē′kən) *v.* To make or become weak or weaker. —**weak′en•er** *n.*

weak•fish (wēk′fĭsh′) *n.* A marine food and game fish of North Atlantic waters.

weak•ling (wēk′lĭng) *n.* A person of weak constitution or character.

weak•ness (wēk′nĭs) *n.* **1.** The state of being weak. **2.** A defect or failing. **3.** A special fondness.

weal[1] (wēl) *n.* Prosperity; well-being. [< OE *weola,* wealth, well-being.]

weal[2] (wēl) *n.* A welt. [Var of WALE.]

wealth (wĕlth) *n.* **1.** A great quantity of valuable material possessions or resources; riches. **2.** A profusion or abundance. **3.** All goods and resources having economic value. [< WEAL[1].]

wealth•y (wĕl′thē) *adj.* **-ier, -iest.** Prosperous; affluent. —**wealth′i•ness** *n.*

wean (wēn) *v.* **1.** To cause (a young mammal) to give up suckling and accept other food. **2.** To detach (a person) from that to which he is accustomed or devoted. [< OE *wenian,* to accustom, train, wean. See **wen-.**]

weap•on (wĕp′ən) *n.* **1.** Any instrument or possession used in combat. **2.** Any means employed to get the better of another. [< OE *wǣpen* < Gmc **wēpnam.*]

weap•on•ry (wĕp′ən-rē) *n.* Weapons collectively.

wear (wâr) *v.* **wore, worn, wearing. 1.** To be clothed in. **2.** To have on one's person. **3.** To affect or exhibit: *wear a smile.* **4.** To bear or maintain in a particular manner: *wears her hair long.* **5.** To impair or consume by or as by long or hard use, friction, or exposure to elements. **6.** To produce by constant use or exposure: *wore a hole in the steps.* **7.** To fatigue; weary. **8.** To react to use or strain in a specified way. **9.** To pass gradually or tediously: *The hours wore on endlessly.* —**wear off. 1.** To diminish gradually. **2.** To become effaced; rub off. —**wear out. 1.** To make or become unusable through heavy use. **2.** To use up. **3.** To exhaust. —*n.* **1.** The act of wearing or state of being worn; use. **2.** Clothing, esp. of a particular kind: *footwear.* **3.** Gradual impairment or diminution from use or attrition. [< OE *werian,* wear, carry. See **wes-**[1].] —**wear′er** *n.*

wea•ri•some (wîr′ē-səm) *adj.* Causing mental or physical fatigue. —**wea′ri•some•ness** *n.*

wea•ry (wîr′ē) *adj.* **-rier, -riest. 1.** Tired; fatigued. **2.** Expressive of fatigue or resignation. —*v.* **-ried, -rying.** To make or become weary. [< OE *wērig* < Gmc **wōriga.*] —**wear′i•ly** *adv.* —**wear′i•ness** *n.*

wea•sel (wē′zəl) *n.* Any of various carnivorous mammals with a long, slender body, short legs, and a long tail. —*v.* To be evasive; equivocate. [< OE *weosule, wesle.*]

weath•er (wĕ*th*′ər) *n.* **1.** The state of the atmosphere at a given time and place, described by temperature, moisture, wind velocity, and pressure. **2.** Unpleasant or destructive atmospheric conditions, esp. high winds and heavy rain on the seas and in the air. —**under the weather.** *Informal.* Ill; indisposed. —*v.* **1.** To expose to or withstand the action of the weather. **2.** To show the effects of exposure to the weather. **3.** To pass through safely; survive. [< OE *weder.* See **wē-.**]

weath•er-beat•en (wĕ*th*′ər-bēt′n) *adj.* **1.** Worn by exposure to the weather. **2.** Tanned and leathery from being outdoors.

weath•er•board (wĕ*th*′ər-bôrd′, -bōrd′) *n.* Clapboard; siding.

weath•er-bound (wĕ*th*′ər-bound′) *adj.* Delayed, halted, or kept indoors by bad weather.

weath•er•cock (wĕ*th*′ər-kŏk′) *n.* **1.** A weather vane, esp. in the form of a rooster. **2.** One that is fickle.

weath•er•ing (wĕ*th*′ər-ĭng) *n.* Chemical or mechanical processes by which rocks exposed to the weather decay to soil.

weath•er•man (wĕ*th*′ər-măn′) *n.* One who predicts or reports weather conditions.

weath•er•proof (wĕ*th*′ər-pro͞of′) *adj.* Able to withstand exposure to weather without damage. —*v.* To render weatherproof.

weath•er-strip (wĕ*th*′ər-strĭp′) *v.* To fit or equip with weather stripping.

weather stripping. A narrow piece of material installed around doors and windows to protect an interior from external extremes of temperature.

weather vane. A vane for indicating wind direction.

weave (wēv) *v.* **wove, woven, weaving. 1. a.** To make (cloth) by interlacing the threads of the weft and warp on a loom. **b.** To interlace (yarns) into cloth. **2.** To construct by interlacing or interweaving the materials of: *weave a basket.* **3.** To interweave or combine (elements) into a whole: *wove the incidents into a story.* **4.** To run (something) in and out through some material or composition. **5.** To spin, as a web. **6.** *p.t.* **weaved.** To make or move in (a course) by winding in and out or shuttling from side to side. *—n.* The pattern, method of weaving, or construction of a fabric: *a twill weave.* [< OE *wefan.* See **webh-**.] **—weav'er** *n.*

web (wĕb) *n.* **1.** A textile fabric, esp. one woven on a loom. **2.** A latticed or woven structure. **3.** A structure of threadlike strands spun by spiders or certain insect larvae. **4.** Something intricately constructed, esp. something that ensnares. **5.** A complex network. **6.** A fold of skin or membranous tissue, as that connecting the toes of certain water birds. **7.** A metal sheet or plate connecting the heavier sections or ribs of any structural element. *—v.* **webbed, webbing. 1.** To provide with a web. **2.** To cover or envelop with or as with a web. **3.** To ensnare or entrap in a web. [< OE *webb.* See **webh-**.] **—webbed** *adj.*

web•bing (wĕb'ĭng) *n.* Sturdy woven strips of fabric used for seat belts, upholstering, etc.

web-foot•ed (wĕb'fŏŏt'ĭd) *adj.* Having feet with webbed toes.

Web•ster (wĕb'stər). **1. Daniel.** 1782–1852. American statesman and diplomat. **2. Noah.** 1758–1843. American lexicographer.

wed (wĕd) *v.* **wedded, wed** or **wedded, wedding. 1.** To take as husband or wife; marry. **2.** To perform the marriage ceremony for. **3.** To unite. [< OE *weddian,* to engage (to do something), marry. See **wadh-**.]

we'd (wēd). Contraction of *we had, we should,* and *we would.*

Wed. Wednesday.

wed•ding (wĕd'ĭng) *n.* **1.** The ceremony or celebration of a marriage. **2.** The anniversary of a marriage. **3.** A joining or uniting.

wedge (wĕj) *n.* **1.** A piece of metal or wood tapered for insertion in a narrow crevice and used for splitting, tightening, securing, or levering. **2.** Anything in the shape of a wedge. **3.** Something that tends to divide or split associations of people. *—v.* **wedged, wedging. 1.** To split or force apart with or as with a wedge. **2.** To fix in place with a wedge. **3.** To crowd or force into a limited space. [< OE *wecg,* a wedge, ingot of metal.]

wed•lock (wĕd'lŏk') *n.* The state of being married. [< OE *wedlāc,* "pledge-giving," marriage vow.]

Wednes•day (wĕnz'dē, -dā') *n.* The 4th day of the week. [< OE *Wōdnesdæg,* "day of Woden," a Teutonic god.]

wee (wē) *adj.* **weer, weest. 1.** Very small. **2.** Very early: *the wee hours.* [< OE *wǣge,* a weight.]

weed[1] (wēd) *n.* A plant considered troublesome or useless, esp. one growing abundantly in cultivated ground. *—v.* **1.** To remove weeds from. **2.** To eliminate as unsuitable or unwanted: *weed out unqualified applicants.* [< OE *wēod* < Gmc *wiudha.] **—weed'er** *n.*

weed[2] (wēd) *n.* **1.** A token of mourning. **2. weeds.** A widow's mourning clothes. [< OE *wǣd* and *wǣde,* a garment.]

weed•y (wē'dē) *adj.* **-ier, -iest. 1.** Full of weeds. **2.** Resembling a weed; weedlike. **3.** Spindly. **—weed'i•ly** *adv.* **—weed'i•ness** *n.*

week (wēk) *n.* **1. a.** A period of seven days. **b.** A seven-day calendar period, esp. one starting with Sunday and continuing through Saturday. **2.** A week designated by an event occurring within it: *graduation week.* [< OE *wice, wicu.* See **weik-[1]**.]

week•day (wēk'dā') *n.* **1.** Any day of the week except Sunday. **2.** Any day exclusive of the days of the weekend.

week•end (wēk'ĕnd') *n.* The end of the week; usually, the period from Friday evening through Sunday evening.

week•ly (wēk'lē) *adv.* **1.** Once a week. **2.** Every week. **3.** By the week. *—adj.* **1.** Of or pertaining to a week. **2.** Occurring once a week or each week. **3.** Computed by the week. *—n., pl.* **-lies.** A publication issued once a week.

ween (wēn) *v. Archaic.* To think; suppose. [< OE *wēnan.*]

weep (wēp) *v.* **wept, weeping. 1.** To mourn; grieve (with *for*). **2.** To shed (tears). **3.** To emit drops of moisture. [< OE *wēpan.* See **wāb-**.] **—weep'er** *n.*

weep•ing (wē'pĭng) *adj.* **1.** Tearful. **2.** Having slender, drooping branches.

wee•vil (wē'vəl) *n.* Any of numerous destructive beetles characteristically having a downward-curving snout. [< OE *wifel,* a beetle.]

weft (wĕft) *n.* **1.** The horizontal threads interlaced through the warp in a woven fabric; woof. **2.** Woven fabric. [< OE *wefta, weft.*]

weigh[1] (wā) *v.* **1.** To determine the weight of by or as by using a scale or balance. **2.** To measure off an amount equal in weight to. **3.** To determine mentally the worth or significance of; ponder. **4.** To burden (with *down*). **5.** To be a burden. **6.** To have or be of a specific weight. **7.** To carry weight; be considered important. **8.** *Naut.* To raise anchor. [< OE *wegan,* to carry, balance in the scale, weigh. See **wegh-**.] **—weigh'er** *n.*

weigh[2] (wā) *n.* **—under weigh.** In progress. [Var of WAY.]

weight (wāt) *n.* **1.** A measure of the heaviness or mass of an object. **2.** The gravitational force exerted on an object, equal to the product of the object's mass and the local value of gravitational acceleration. **3. a.** A unit measure of this force. **b.** A system of such measures. **4.** Any object used principally to exert a force by virtue of its gravitational attraction to the earth, esp.: **a.** A solid used as a standard in weighing. **b.** An object used to hold something down. **c.** A dumbbell or other object used in weightlifting. **5.** Burden; oppressiveness: *the weight of responsibilities.* **6.** The greatest part or stress; preponderance. **7.** Influence; importance. *—v.* **1.** To add heaviness or weight to. **2.** To load down; burden. [< OE *wiht, gewiht.* See **wegh-**.]

weight•less (wāt'lĭs) *adj.* **1.** Having little or no weight. **2.** Experiencing little or no gravitational force. **—weight'less•ness** *n.*

weight•lift•ing (wāt'lĭf'tĭng) *n.* The lifting of heavy weights as an exercise or in athletic competition.

weight•y (wā'tē) *adj.* **-ier, -iest. 1.** Heavy. **2.** Burdensome. **3.** Of great consequence. **4.** Carrying weight; efficacious. **5.** Solemn. **—weight'i•ly** *adv.* **—weight'i•ness** *n.*

weir (wîr) *n.* **1.** A fence or wattle placed in a stream to catch or retain fish. **2.** A dam placed across a river or canal to raise or divert the water or regulate the flow. [< OE *wer.*]

weird (wîrd) *adj.* **1.** Suggestive of or concerned with the supernatural. **2.** Of an odd and inexplicable character. [< OE *wyrd,* fate, destiny. See **wer-[3]**.] **—weird'ness** *n.*

wel•come (wĕl'kəm) *adj.* **1.** Received with pleasure and hospitality. **2.** Gratifying. **3.** Cordially permitted or invited, as to do or enjoy. *—n.* A cordial greeting to or reception of an arriving person. *—v.* **-comed, -coming. 1.** To greet or entertain cordially or hospitably. **2.** To receive or accept gladly. *—interj.* Expressive of cordial greeting or reception. [< OE *wilcuma,* a welcome guest, and *wilcume,* the greeting of welcome. See **gwā-**.]

weld (wĕld) *v.* **1.** To join (metals) by applying heat, sometimes with pressure. **2.** To bring together as a unit. *—n.* A union or joint produced by welding. [Var of WELL (to surge).] **—weld'er** *n.*

wel•fare (wĕl'fâr') *n.* **1.** Health, happiness, and general well-being. **2.** Work on behalf of the poor. **3.** Public relief. [< ME *wel faren,* to fare well.]

welfare state. A state that assumes primary responsibility for the welfare of its citizens.

wel•kin (wĕl'kĭn) *n. Archaic.* The vault of heaven; sky. [< OE *wolcen,* sky.]

well[1] (wĕl) *n.* **1.** A deep hole or shaft dug or drilled to obtain water, oil, gas, or brine. **2.** Something resembling this in shape or function, as an inkwell. **3.** An opening cut vertically through the floors of a building, as for stairs or ventilation. **4.** A spring or fountain. **5.** A source to be drawn upon. *—v.* **1.** To rise to the surface, ready to flow. **2.** To surge from some inner source. [< OE *wælla, wiella.* See **wel-[3]**.]

well[2] (wĕl) *adv.* **better, best. 1.** Satisfactorily. **2.** With skill: *sing well.* **3.** In a comfortable or affluent manner: *live well.* **4.** Advantageously: *married well.* **5.** With reason or propriety, properly: *I can't very well say no.* **6.** Prudently: *You would do well to say nothing.* **7.** On close or familiar terms: *I know him well.* **8.** Favorably: *speak well of him.* **9.** Thoroughly: *well cooked.* **10.** Entirely: *well worth seeing.* **11.** Far: *well in advance.* **—as well. 1.** In addition; also. **2.** With equal or better effect: *I might as well go.* **—as well as. 1.** In addition to. **2.** As satisfactorily as. *—adj.* **1.** In a satisfactory state: *All is well.* **2. a.** In good health. **b.** Cured or healed. **3. a.** Advisable; prudent. **b.** Fortunate; good. *—interj.* **1.** Expressive of surprise. **2.** Used to introduce a remark or cover a pause. [< OE *wel.* See **wel-[2]**.]

we'll (wēl). Contraction of *we will* and *we shall.*

well-be•ing (wĕl'bē'ĭng) *n.* The state of being healthy, happy, or prosperous; welfare.

well-born (wĕl'bôrn') *adj.* Of good lineage or stock.

well-bred (wĕl'brĕd') *adj.* Of good upbringing; polite; refined.

well-dis•posed (wĕl'dĭs-pōzd') *adj.* Disposed to be kindly or sympathetic.

well-done (wĕl'dŭn') *adj.* **1.** Cooked all the way through. **2.** Properly accomplished.

well-found•ed (wĕl'foun'dĭd) *adj.* Based on sound judgment, reasoning, or evidence.

well-groomed (wĕl'grōōmd') *adj.* **1.** Attentive to details of dress. **2.** Carefully tended.

well-ground•ed (wĕl'groun'dĭd) *adj.* **1.** Adequately versed in a subject. **2.** Having a sound basis.

Wel•ling•ton (wĕl'ĭng-tən). The capital of New Zealand on North Island. Pop. 127,000.

well-mean•ing (wĕl'mē'nĭng) *adj.* Having or prompted by good intentions.
well-nigh (wĕl'nī') *adv.* Nearly; almost.
well-off (wĕl'ôf', -ŏf') *adj.* **1.** In fortunate circumstances. **2.** Wealthy.
well-timed (wĕl'tīmd') *adj.* Occurring or done at an opportune time.
well-to-do (wĕl'tə-do͞o') *adj.* Affluent.
well-turned (wĕl'tûrnd') *adj.* **1.** Shapely. **2.** Aptly expressed.
well-wish•er (wĕl'wĭsh'ər) *n.* One who wishes another well.
well-worn (wĕl'wôrn', -wōrn') *adj.* **1.** Showing signs of much wear. **2.** Trite; hackneyed.
welsh (wĕlsh, wĕlch) *v. Slang.* **1.** To swindle a person by not paying a debt or wager. **2.** To fail to fulfill an obligation. [?] **—welsh'er** *n.*
Welsh (wĕlsh) *n.* **1. the Welsh** *(takes pl. v.).* The people of Wales. **2.** The Celtic language of Wales. **—Welsh** *adj.* **—Welsh'man** *n.*
Welsh rabbit. Also **Welsh rarebit.** A dish made of melted cheese, served hot over toast or crackers.
welt (wĕlt) *n.* **1.** A strip of leather or other material stitched into a shoe between the sole and upper. **2.** A tape or covered cord sewn into a seam as reinforcement or trimming. **3.** A ridge or bump raised on the skin by a blow or an allergic disorder. *—v.* **1.** To reinforce or trim with a welt. **2.** To beat severely. [ME *welte, walt.*]
wel•ter (wĕl'tər) *v.* **1.** To writhe, roll, or wallow. **2.** To lie soaked in blood. **3.** To roll and surge, as the sea. *—n.* **1.** Turbulence; tossing. **2. a.** Confusion; turmoil. **b.** A confused mass. [ME *welteren.*]
wel•ter•weight (wĕl'tər-wāt') *n.* A boxer or wrestler who weighs between 136 and 147 pounds.
wen (wĕn) *n.* A cyst containing sebaceous matter. [< OE *wenn.*]
wench (wĕnch) *n. Archaic.* A young woman or girl. [< OE *wencel,* child, maid.]
wend (wĕnd) *v.* To proceed on or along: *wend one's way.* [< OE *wendan,* to turn away, direct, happen. See **wendh-.**]
went (wĕnt). *p.t.* of **go.** [< ME *wenden,* to wend.]
wept (wĕpt). *p.t.* & *p.p.* of **weep.**
were (wûr). **1.** Pl. & 2nd person sing. of the past indicative of **be. 2.** Past subjunctive of **be.** [< OE *wǣre* (sing), *wǣron* (pl). See **wes-[3].**]
Usage: Were, as a past subjunctive form, occurs principally in clauses expressing conditions that are clearly hypothetical or contrary to fact, as in *if I were you.* Often such clauses are introduced by *if, as if,* or *as though.* Sometimes they express a wish or desire. When the clause expresses a mere condition that is neither purely hypothetical nor contrary to fact, however, *was* is the choice. It is also the choice in indirect questions. In each of the following, *was* (not *were*) is proper: *He said that if Smith was elected, he would resign. I peered out to see whether the way was clear. He inquired whether I was satisfied with the outcome.*
we're (wîr). Contraction of *we are.*
wer•en't (wûrnt, wûr'ənt). Contraction of *were not.*
were•wolf (wîr'wo͝olf', wûr'-, wâr'-) *n.* Also **wer•wolf.** A person capable of assuming the form of a wolf. [< OE *wer(e)wulf*: *wer,* a man + *wulf,* a WOLF.]
wert (wûrt). *Archaic.* 2nd person sing. past indicative and past subjunctive of **be.**
Wes•ley (wĕs'lē, wĕz'-), **John.** 1703–1791. English theologian; founder of Methodism.
west (wĕst) *n.* **1. a.** The direction opposite that of the earth's rotation. **b.** The point on the mariner's compass 270° clockwise from north, directly opposite east. **2.** Often **West. a.** The W part of any country or region. **b.** The W part of the world, esp. Europe and the W Hemisphere; the Occident. **—the West.** In the U.S.: **1.** Formerly, the region lying W of the Alleghenies. **2.** The region W of the Mississippi. *—adj.* **1.** To or from the west. **2. West.** Designating the W part of a country, continent, or other geographic area: *West Germany.* *—adv.* In, from, or toward the west. [< OE. See **wespero-.**]
West Berlin. The W zone of Berlin, associated politically and economically with West Germany. Pop. 2,200,000.
west•er•ly (wĕs'tər-lē) *adj.* **1.** Toward the west. **2.** From the west. **—west'er•ly** *adv.*
west•ern (wĕs'tərn) *adj.* **1.** Toward, in, or facing the west. **2.** Coming from the west. **3.** Often **Western.** Of or characteristic of western regions or the West, esp. Europe and the W Hemisphere; Occidental. *—n.* Often **Western.** A film dealing with frontier or cowboy life.
west•ern•er (wĕs'tər-nər) *n.* **1.** A native or inhabitant of the west. **2.** Often **Westerner.** A native or inhabitant of the W U.S.
Western Hemisphere. The half of the earth that includes North and South America.
west•ern•ize (wĕs'tər-nīz') *v.* **-ized, -izing.** To convert to the ways of Western civilization.
Western Samoa. A nation in the S Pacific. Pop. 122,000. Cap. Apia.
West Germanic. A subdivision of Germanic.
West Germany. The unofficial name for the German Federal Republic. See **Germany.**
West In•dies (ĭn'dēz). An island chain between the SE U.S. and N South America, separating the Caribbean from the Atlantic and including the Bahamas, the Greater Antilles, and the Lesser Antilles. **—West Indian.**
West Virginia. A state of the east-central U.S. Pop. 1,744,000. Cap. Charleston.
west•ward (wĕst'wərd) *adv.* Also **west•wards** (-wərdz), **west•ward•ly** (-wərd-lē). Toward the west. *—adj.* Toward or in the west.
wet (wĕt) *adj.* **wetter, wettest. 1.** Covered or saturated with a liquid, esp. water; moistened; damp. **2.** Not yet dry or firm: *wet plaster.* **3.** Rainy. **4.** Allowing alcoholic beverages to be produced and sold: *a wet county.* *—n.* **1.** Moisture. **2.** Rainy or snowy weather. *—v.* **wetted, wetting.** To make or become wet. [< OE *wǣt, wēt.* See **wed-.**]
wet•back (wĕt'băk') *n.* A Mexican laborer who illegally crosses the U.S. border.
wet blanket. *Informal.* One that discourages enjoyment, enthusiasm, etc.
weth•er (wĕth'ər) *n.* A castrated male sheep. [< OE.]
wet nurse. A woman who suckles another woman's child.
we've (wēv). Contraction of *we have.*
whack (hwăk) *v.* To strike with a sharp blow; slap. *—n.* **1.** A sharp, swift blow. **2.** The sound made by such a blow. **—have** (or **take**) **a whack at.** To attempt; try out. **—out of whack.** Not functioning correctly. [Perh var of THWACK.]
whack•y. Variant of **wacky.**
whale[1] (hwāl) *n.* **1.** Any of various often very large marine mammals having a generally fishlike form. **2.** A superlative example of a thing specified: *a whale of a game.* *—v.* **whaled, whaling.** To hunt whales. [< OE *hwæl.* See **skwalo-.**]
whale[2] (hwāl) *v.* **whaled, whaling.** To thrash; flog. [?]
whale•boat (hwāl'bōt') *n.* A long rowboat, pointed at both ends and formerly used in whaling.
whale•bone (hwāl'bōn') *n.* **1.** The elastic, hornlike material forming plates or strips in the upper jaw of certain whales. **2.** An object made of this material, as a corset stay.
whal•er (hwā'lər) *n.* **1.** One who hunts or processes whales. **2.** A whaling ship.
whal•ing (hwā'lĭng) *n.* The hunting, killing, and processing of whales.
wham (hwăm) *n.* **1.** A forceful, resounding blow. **2.** The sound of such a blow. *—v.* **whammed, whamming.** To strike or smash into with resounding impact.
wham•my (hwăm'ē) *n., pl.* **-mies.** *Slang.* A supernatural spell; hex. [Perh < WHAM.]
wharf (hwôrf) *n., pl.* **wharves** (hwôrvz) or **wharfs.** A landing place at which vessels may tie up and load or unload. [< OE *hwearf.* See **kwerp-.**]
wharf•age (hwôr'fĭj) *n.* **1.** The use of a wharf or wharves. **2.** The charges for this.
what (hwŏt, hwŭt; *unstressed* hwət) *pron.* **1. a.** Which thing or which particular one of many. **b.** Which kind, character, or designation. **c.** A person or thing of how much value or significance: *What are possessions to a dying man?* **2. a.** That which or the thing that. **b.** Whatever thing that: *come what may.* **3. a.** *Nonstandard.* Which, who, or that: *It's the poor what gets the blame.* **b.** *Informal.* Something: *I'll tell you what.* *—adj.* **1.** Which one or ones of many. **2.** Whatever: *repaired what damage had been done.* **3.** How great: *What a fool!* *—adv.* **1.** How: *What does it matter?* **2.** Why (with *for*): *What are you hurrying for?* *—interj.* **1.** Expressive of surprise or incredulity. **2.** *Brit. Informal.* Expressive of agreement: *A fine evening, what?* [< OE *hwæt.* See **kwo-.**]
Usage: What (relative pronoun), used as the subject of a clause, can be either singular or plural in construction, depending on the sense involved. It is construed as singular when it is the equivalent of *that which* or *a* (or *the*) *thing that,* and plural when it stands for *things that* or *those which.* The number of the verb or verbs governed by *what* depends on how it is construed: *He is involved in what seems to be an outright fraud. They are making what appear to be signs of welcome.*
what•ev•er (hwŏt-ĕv'ər, hwŭt-) *pron.* **1.** Everything or anything that. **2.** What amount that. **3.** No matter what. **4.** *Informal.* What. *—adj.* **1.** Of any number or kind; any. **2.** All of. **3.** No matter what. **4.** Of any kind at all.
what•not (hwŏt'nŏt', hwŭt'-) *n.* A set of open shelves for ornaments.
what•so•ev•er (hwŏt'sō-ĕv'ər, hwŭt'-) *pron.* Whatever. **—what'so•ev'er** *adj.*
wheat (hwēt) *n.* **1.** A cereal grass widely cultivated for its commercially important grain. **2.** The grain of such a plant, ground to produce flour. [< OE *hwǣte.* See **kweit-.**]
wheat germ. The vitamin-rich embryo of the wheat kernel, separated before milling for use as a cereal or food supplement.
whee•dle (hwēd'l) *v.* **-dled, -dling.** To persuade, attempt to persuade, or obtain by flattery or guile; cajole. [Perh < G *wedeln,* "to wag the tail."] **—whee'dler** *n.*
wheel (hwēl) *n.* **1.** A solid disk or rigid circular ring connected by spokes to a hub, designed to turn around an axle passed through the center.

2. Anything resembling such a device in appearance or movement. 3. A medieval instrument to which a victim was bound for torture. 4. The steering device on a vehicle. 5. *Informal.* A bicycle. 6. **wheels.** Forces that provide energy, movement, or direction: *the wheels of commerce.* 7. The act or process of turning. 8. *Slang.* One with a great deal of power or influence. —*v.* 1. To roll or move on or as on a wheel or wheels. 2. To revolve; rotate. 3. To turn or whirl around; pivot. [< OE *hwēol.* See **kwel-.**]

wheel•bar•row (hwēl'băr'ō) *n.* A one- or two-wheeled vehicle with handles, used to convey small loads.

wheel•base (hwēl'bās') *n.* The distance from front to rear axle in a motor vehicle.

wheel•chair (hwēl'châr') *n.* Also **wheel chair.** A chair mounted on large wheels for the use of the sick or disabled.

wheel•er-deal•er (hwē'lər-dē'lər) *n. Informal.* A sharp operator.

wheel house. A pilothouse.

wheel•wright (hwēl'rīt') *n.* One whose trade is the building and repairing of wheels.

wheeze (hwēz) *v.* **wheezed, wheezing.** To breathe with difficulty, producing a hoarse whistling sound. —*n.* 1. A wheezing sound. 2. An old joke. [Prob < ON *hvæsa,* to hiss.]

wheez•y (hwē'zē) *adj.* **-ier, -iest.** Given to wheezing. —**wheez'i•ness** *n.*

whelk (hwĕlk) *n.* Any of various large, sometimes edible marine snails. [< OE *weoloc.*]

whelm (hwĕlm) *v.* To overwhelm. [< OE **hwelman,* to turn over.]

whelp (hwĕlp) *n.* 1. A young offspring of a dog, wolf, etc. 2. **a.** A mere child or youth. **b.** An impudent young fellow. —*v.* To give birth to whelps. [< OE *hwelp.*]

when (hwĕn) *adv.* 1. At what time. 2. At which time. —*conj.* 1. At the time that. 2. As soon as. 3. Whenever. 4. While. 5. Whereas. 6. Considering that; since. —*pron.* What or which time. —*n.* The time or date. [< OE *hwanne, hwenne.* See **kwo-.**]

whence (hwĕns) *adv.* 1. From where. 2. From what origin or source. 3. Out of which. —*conj.* By reason of which; from which; wherefore. [< OE *hwanon.* See **kwo-.**]

Usage: *Whence* contains the sense of *from;* consequently, the construction *from whence* is redundant, though it has literary precedent, and *whence* is preferably used alone.

when•ev•er (hwĕn-ĕv'ər) *adv.* 1. At whatever time. 2. When. —*conj.* 1. At whatever time that. 2. Every time that.

when•so•ev•er (hwĕn'sō-ĕv'ər) *adv.* At whatever time at all; whenever. —*conj.* Whenever.

where (hwâr) *adv.* 1. At or in what place. 2. In what situation or position. 3. From what place or source. 4. To what place. —*conj.* 1. At what or which place. 2. **a.** In a place in which. **b.** Wherever. 3. **a.** To a place in which. **b.** To any place or situation in which. —*pron.* Which place. —*n.* The place or occasion. [< OE *hwǣr.* See **kwo-.**]

Usage: *Where* is used with *from* to indicate motion from a place: *Where did they come from?* A preposition is not needed to indicate direction or motion to a place in a construction such as *Where did they go?* (*go to* is redundant); nor is a preposition used to indicate location or position of rest in *Where are they?* (not *Where are they at?*).

where•a•bouts (hwâr'ə-bouts') *adv.* About where; in, at, or near what location. —*n.* The approximate location of someone or something.

where•as (hwâr-ăz') *conj.* 1. It being the fact that; inasmuch as. 2. While at the same time. 3. While on the contrary.

where•at (hwâr-ăt') *adv.* 1. At which place. 2. Whereupon.

where•by (hwâr-bī') *adv.* 1. In accordance with or by means of which. 2. By what means; how.

where•fore (hwâr'fôr', -fōr') *adv. Archaic.* For what purpose or reason; why. —*conj. Archaic.* For which reason. —*n.* A purpose or cause: *whys and wherefores.*

where•from (hwâr'frŏm', -frŭm') *adv. Archaic.* Whence.

where•in (hwâr-ĭn') *adv.* 1. In what; how. 2. In which thing, place, or situation.

where•of (hwâr-ŏv', -ŭv') *adv.* 1. Of what or which. 2. Of whom.

where•on (hwâr-ŏn', -ôn') *adv. Archaic.* On which or what.

where•so•ev•er (hwâr'sō-ĕv'ər) *conj.* In, to, or from whatever place at all.

where•to (hwâr'to͞o') *adv.* 1. To what place or end. 2. To which.

where•up•on (hwâr'ə-pŏn', -pôn') *adv.* 1. *Archaic.* Upon what. 2. On top of which. 3. At which time; after which.

wher•ev•er (hwâr-ĕv'ər) *adv.* 1. In or to whatever place. 2. Where. —*conj.* In or to whichever place or situation.

where•with (hwâr'wĭth', -wĭth') *adv.* With what or which. —*pron. Archaic.* The thing or things with which.

where•with•al (hwâr'wĭth-ôl', -wĭth-ôl') *adv. Archaic.* Wherewith. —*pron. Archaic.* Wherewith. —*n.* The necessary means.

wher•ry (hwĕr'ē) *n., pl.* **-ries.** A light, swift rowboat. [ME *whery.*]

whet (hwĕt) *v.* **whetted, whetting.** 1. To sharpen (a knife or other tool); hone. 2. To stimulate; heighten. [< OE *hwettan.* See **kwed-.**] —**whet'ter** *n.*

wheth•er (hwĕth'ər) *conj.* 1. If it is so that. 2. If it happens that; in case. 3. Either. [< OE *hwæther.* See **kwo-.**]

whet•stone (hwĕt'stōn') *n.* A stone for honing tools.

whew (hw/y/o͞o) *interj.* Expressive of relief, amazement, etc. [ME *whewe.*]

whey (hwā) *n.* The watery part of milk that separates from the curds, as in the process of making cheese. [< OE *hwæg* < Gmc **khwuja-.*] —**whey'ey** *adj.*

which (hwĭch) *pron.* 1. What particular one or ones. 2. The particular one or ones. 3. The thing, animal, group of people, or event previously designated or implied. 4. *Archaic.* The person designated or implied. 5. Whichever. 6. A thing or circumstance that. —*adj.* 1. What particular one or ones. 2. Any one or any number of; whichever. 3. Being the one or ones previously designated. [< OE *hwilc, hwelc.* See **kwo-.**]

which•ev•er (hwĭch-ĕv'ər) *pron.* 1. Any one or ones. 2. No matter which. —*adj.* 1. Any one or any number of a group. 2. No matter what.

which•so•ev•er (hwĭch'sō-ĕv'ər) *pron.* Whichever. —**which'so•ev'er** *adj.*

whick•er (hwĭk'ər) *v.* To whinny. [Imit.] —**whick'er** *n.*

whiff (hwĭf) *n.* 1. A slight, gentle gust of air; a waft. 2. A brief, passing odor carried in the air. 3. An inhalation of air, perfume, smoke, etc. —*v.* 1. To be carried in brief gusts; convey in whiffs. 2. To draw in or breathe out air, smoke, etc. 3. To smell; sniff.

whif•fle•tree (hwĭf'əl-trē) *n.* The pivoted horizontal crossbar to which the harness traces of a draft animal are attached.

Whig (hwĭg) *n.* 1. In England, a member of a political party of the 18th and 19th centuries, opposed to the Tories. 2. In the American Revolution, one who supported the war against England. 3. In the U.S., a political party (1834–55) formed to oppose the Democratic Party. [Prob short for *Whiggamore,* a 17th-century Scottish insurgent.]

while (hwīl) *n.* 1. A period of time: *stay for a while.* 2. The time or effort taken in doing something. —*conj.* 1. As long as. 2. Although. 3. Whereas; and. —*v.* **whiled, whiling.** To spend (time) idly or pleasantly: *while the time away.* [< OE *hwīl.* See **kweyə-.**]

whi•lom (hwī'ləm) *adj.* Former; having once been: *the whilom Miss Smith.* —*adv. Archaic.* Formerly. [< OE *hwīlum.*]

whilst (hwīlst) *conj. Chiefly Brit.* While.

whim (hwĭm) *n.* 1. A sudden or capricious idea; a passing fancy. 2. Arbitrary thought or impulse. [Short for earlier *whim-wham.*]

whim•per (hwĭm'pər) *v.* 1. To cry or sob with soft intermittent sounds; whine. 2. To complain. —*n.* A whine. [Dial *whimp* (imit).]

whim•si•cal (hwĭm'zĭ-kəl) *adj.* 1. Capricious; playful; arbitrary. 2. Unusual; fantastic; odd. —**whim'si•cal•ly** *adv.*

whim•sy (hwĭm'zē) *n., pl.* **-sies.** Also **whim•sey** *pl.* **-seys.** 1. An odd or capricious idea. 2. Anything quaint, fanciful, or odd. [Prob < WHIM.]

whine (hwīn) *v.* **whined, whining.** 1. To utter a plaintive, high-pitched sound, as in pain, fear, complaint, etc. 2. To complain in an annoying fashion. 3. To produce a sustained noise of relatively high pitch. [< OE *hwīnan.* See **kwei-.**] —**whine** *n.* —**whin'y** *adj.*

whin•ny (hwĭn'ē) *v.* **-nied, -nying.** To neigh, esp. softly. [Prob < WHINE.] —**whin'ny** *n.*

whip (hwĭp) *v.* **whipped** or **whipt, whipping.** 1. To strike with repeated strokes, as of a strap; lash; beat. 2. **a.** To punish in this manner; flog; thrash. **b.** To reprove severely. 3. To drive or force by flogging, lashing, etc. 4. To move in a manner similar to a whip; thrash about. 5. To beat (cream or eggs) into a froth or foam. 6. To move or remove in a sudden, rapid manner: *whipped off his cap.* 7. To dart about. 8. To wrap or bind (a robe) with twine to prevent unraveling. 9. To defeat; outdo; beat. —*n.* 1. A flexible instrument, as a rod or thong, used in whipping. 2. A whipping or lashing motion or stroke; whiplash. 3. A blow made by or as by whipping. 4. A member of a legislative body charged by his party with enforcing party discipline and insuring attendance. 5. A dish made of sugar and stiffly beaten egg whites or cream, often with fruit. [Perh < MDu *wippen,* to vacillate, swing.] —**whip'per** *n.*

whip•cord (hwĭp'kôrd') *n.* 1. A ribbed worsted fabric. 2. A strong twisted or braided cord. 3. Catgut.

whip•lash (hwĭp'lăsh') *n.* 1. The lash of a whip. 2. An injury caused by an abrupt jerking motion of the head, either backward or forward. —**whip'lash'** *adj.*

whip•per•snap•per (hwĭp'ər-snăp'ər) *n.* An insignificant and pretentious person.

whip•pet (hwĭp'ĭt) *n.* A swift-running dog resembling the greyhound but smaller. [?]

whip•poor•will (hwĭp'ər-wĭl', hwĭp'ər-wĭl') *n.* Also **whip-poor-will.** A brownish night-flying North American bird having a call of which its

name is imitative.
whip•saw (hwĭp'sô') *n.* A narrow two-man crosscut saw.
whipt (hwĭpt). Alternate *p.t.* & *p.p.* of **whip.**
whir (hwûr) *v.* **whirred, whirring.** To move so as to produce a vibrating or buzzing sound. *—n.* **1.** A sound of buzzing or vibration. **2.** A bustle; hurry. [< Scand.]
whirl (hwûrl) *v.* **1.** To revolve or spin rapidly. **2.** To turn aside or away rapidly; wheel. **3.** To have the sensation of spinning; reel. **4.** To move or drive rapidly. **5.** To move or drive in a circular or curving course, esp. at high speed. *—n.* **1.** The act of whirling. **2.** One that whirls or is whirled. **3.** A state of confusion; tumult. [< ON *hvirfla.*] **—whirl'er** *n.*
whirl•i•gig (hwûr'lĭ-gĭg') *n.* **1.** Any of various spinning toys. **2.** A carousel or merry-go-round. **3.** Something that continuously whirls.
whirl•pool (hwûrl'po͞ol') *n.* Water in rapid rotating movement.
whirl•wind (hwûrl'wĭnd') *n.* **1.** A column of air rotating around a more or less vertical axis and moving forward. **2.** Anything moving forward or whirling with violence and force.
whirl•y•bird (hwûr'lē-bûrd') *n. Slang.* A helicopter.
whisk (hwĭsk) *v.* **1.** To move or cause to move with quick light, sweeping motions. **2.** To whip (eggs or cream). *—n.* **1.** A quick light, sweeping motion. **2.** A small broom. **3.** A small bunch, as of twigs or hair. **4.** A kitchen utensil for whipping. [< Scand.]
whisk•broom (hwĭsk'bro͞om', -bro͝om') *n.* A small short-handled broom used esp. to brush clothes.
whisk•er (hwĭs'kər) *n.* **1. whiskers. a.** The unshaven hair on a man's face; the beard. **b.** *Informal.* The mustache. **2.** One hair from the beard. **3.** One of the bristles or long hairs growing near the mouth of certain animals. [< WHISK.]
whis•key (hwĭs'kē) *n., pl.* **-keys.** Also **whis•ky** *pl.* **-kies.** An alcoholic liquor distilled from grain, such as corn, rye, or barley, and containing approx. 40 to 50% ethyl alcohol by volume. [< Ir Gael *uisce beathadh,* "water of life."] **—whis'key** *adj.*
Usage: *Whiskey* is the usual American spelling, esp. with reference to U.S. and Irish liquor. *Whisky* is the spelling used in *Scotch whisky* and *Canadian whisky.*
whis•per (hwĭs'pər) *v.* **1.** To speak softly, without full voice. **2.** To tell secretly or privately. **3.** To make a soft rustling sound, as leaves. *—n.* **1.** Speech produced by whispering. **2.** Something whispered. **3.** A rumor or hint. [< OE *hwisprian.* See **kwei-.**]
whist (hwĭst) *n.* A game played with 52 cards by two teams of two players each. [?]
whis•tle (hwĭs'əl) *v.* **-tled, -tling. 1.** To produce a clear musical sound by forcing air through the teeth or an aperture formed by pursing the lips. **2.** To produce a similar high-pitched sound. *—n.* **1.** A device for making whistling sounds by means of the breath, air, or steam. **2.** A sound produced by such a device or by whistling through the lips. [< OE *hwistlian.* See **kwei-.**]
whis•tler (hwĭs'lər) *n.* **1.** One that whistles. **2.** *Phys.* An electromagnetic wave of audio frequency produced by atmospheric disturbances such as lightning, having a characteristically decreasing frequency responsible for a whistling sound of descending pitch in detection equipment.
whit (hwĭt) *n.* A particle; least bit; iota. [Var of ME *wight,* thing.]
white (hwīt) *n.* **1.** An achromatic color of maximum lightness. **2.** The white or nearly white part of something, as: **a.** The albumen of an egg. **b.** The white part of an eyeball. **3.** Something or somebody white or nearly white, as: **a. whites.** A white outfit: *tennis whites.* **b.** A white pigment. **c.** A Caucasoid. *—adj.* **whiter, whitest. 1.** Being of the color white. **2.** Pale; weakly colored; almost colorless. **3. a.** Having the comparatively pale complexion typical of Caucasoids. **b.** Of, pertaining to, characteristic of, or dominated by Caucasians. **4.** Not written or printed upon; blank. **5.** Unsullied; pure. **6.** Incandescent: *white heat.* [< OE *hwīt,* white, white of an egg. See **kweit-.**]
white ant. A termite.
white blood cell. A leukocyte.
white•cap (hwīt'kăp') *n.* A wave with a crest of foam.
white-col•lar (hwīt'kŏl'ər) *adj.* Of or pertaining to workers, salaried or professional, whose work usually does not involve manual labor and who are expected to dress with some degree of formality.
white elephant. 1. A rare whitish form of the Asian elephant, often regarded with special veneration locally. **2.** A rare and expensive possession that is financially a burden to maintain. **3.** An article no longer wanted by its owner.
white feather. A sign of cowardice.
white•fish (hwīt'fĭsh') *n.* Any of various silvery freshwater food fishes.
white flag. A white cloth or flag signaling surrender or truce.
White House, The. 1. The executive mansion of the President of the U.S. in Washington, D.C. **2.** The supreme executive authority of the U.S. Government.
white lead. A heavy white poisonous compound of lead, used in paint pigments.
whit•en (hwīt'n) *v.* To make or become white. **—whit'en•er** *n.*
white•ness (hwīt'nĭs) *n.* The condition or quality of being white.
white slave. A woman held unwillingly for purposes of prostitution.
white squall. A sudden squall occurring in tropical or subtropical waters, characterized by the absence of a dark cloud and the presence of white-capped waves or broken water.
white•wall (hwīt'wôl') *n.* A vehicular tire having a white band on the visible side.
white•wash (hwīt'wŏsh', -wôsh') *n.* **1.** A mixture of lime and water, often with whiting added, used to whiten walls, concrete, etc. **2.** A concealing or glossing over of flaws or failures. *—v.* **1.** To paint or coat with or as with whitewash. **2.** To gloss over (a flaw).
whith•er (hwĭth'ər) *adv.* **1.** To what place, result, or condition. **2.** To which specified place, position, etc. **3.** To whatever place, result, or condition. [< OE *hwider.* See **kwo-.**]
whith•er•so•ev•er (hwĭth'ər-sō-ĕv'ər) *adv.* To whatever place.
whit•ing[1] (hwī'tĭng) *n.* A pure white ground chalk used in paints, ink, and putty.
whit•ing[2] (hwī'tĭng) *n.* Any of several marine food fishes. [< MDu *wijting.*]
whit•ish (hwī'tĭsh) *adj.* Somewhat or almost white. **—whit'ish•ness** *n.*
whit•low (hwĭt'lō) *n.* Any inflammation of the area around the nail of a finger or toe.
Whit•man (hwĭt'mən), **Walt.** 1819–1892. American poet.
Whit•ney, Mount (hwĭt'nē). The highest elevation (14,495 ft.) in the U.S., excluding Alaska, in E California.
Whit•sun•day (hwĭt'sən-dē, -dā') *n.* Pentecost. [< OE *hwīta sunnandæg,* "white Sunday."]
whit•tle (hwĭt'l) *v.* **-tled, -tling. 1.** To cut small bits or pare shavings from (a piece of wood). **2.** To fashion or shape in this way. **3.** To reduce or eliminate gradually by or as by whittling: *He whittled down his expenditures.* [< OE *thwītan.* See **twei-.**] **—whit'tler** *n.*
whiz (hwĭz) *v.* **whizzed, whizzing.** Also **whizz. 1.** To make a whirring, buzzing, or hissing sound, as of something rushing through air. **2.** To rush past. *—n., pl.* **whizzes. 1.** The sound or passage of something that whizzes. **2.** *Slang.* One who has remarkable skill. [Imit.]
who (ho͞o) *pron.* The interrogative pronoun in the nominative case. **1.** What or which person or persons. **2.** That. **3.** The person or persons that; whoever. [Who, whose, whom < OE *hwā, hwæs, hwǣm.* See **kwo-.**]
Usage: The distinction between *who* and *whoever,* nominative forms, and *whom* and *whomever,* the corresponding objective forms, is carefully observed in formal usage, esp. in writing. In speech, however, *who* frequently occurs in examples such as the following, in which *whom* is the grammatical choice: *Who did you meet? He wants to know who he should speak to. Who* (or *whoever*) is always the choice when it functions as the subject of a clause: *He saw a girl who he thinks may fit the role. Who shall I say is calling? Choose whoever seems most suitable.*
who•ev•er (ho͞o-ĕv'ər) *pron.* **1.** Anyone that. **2.** No matter who. **3.** Who: *Whoever did it?*
whole (hōl) *adj.* **1.** Containing all component parts; complete: *a whole formal wardrobe.* **2.** Not divided or disjoined. **3.** Sound; healthy. **4.** Constituting the full amount, extent, or duration: *cried the whole trip home.* **5.** *Math.* Integral; not fractional. *—n.* **1.** All of the component parts or elements of a thing. **2.** A complete entity or system. **—on the whole.** In general. [< OE *hāl,* sound, unharmed. See **kailo-.**] **—whole'ness** *n.*
whole•heart•ed (hōl'här'tĭd) *adj.* Without reservation: *wholehearted cooperation.* **—whole'heart'ed•ly** *adv.* **—whole'heart'ed•ness** *n.*
whole note. *Mus.* A note having the value of four quarter notes.
whole number. An integer.
whole•sale (hōl'sāl') *n.* The sale of goods in large quantities, as for resale by a retailer. *—adj.* **1.** Pertaining to or engaged in the sale of goods at wholesale. **2.** Sold in large bulk or quantity, usually at a lower cost. **3.** Made or accomplished extensively and indiscriminately: *wholesale destruction.* *—adv.* **1.** In large bulk or quantity. **2.** Extensively and indiscriminately. [< the phrase *by (the) whole sale.*] **—whole'sal'er** *n.*
whole•some (hōl'səm) *adj.* Conducive to mental or physical well-being; healthy. **—whole'some•ly** *adv.* **—whole'some•ness** *n.*
whole-wheat (hōl'hwēt') *adj.* Made from the entire grain of wheat.
whol•ly (hō'lē, hōl'lē) *adv.* **1.** Entirely. **2.** Exclusively.
whom (ho͞om). The objective case of *who.* See Usage note at **who.**
whom•ev•er (ho͞om-ĕv'ər). The objective case of *whoever.*
whom•so•ev•er (ho͞om'sō-ĕv'ər). The objective case of *whosoever.*
whoop (ho͞op, hwo͞op) *n.* **1.** A loud or hooting

cry, as of exultation or excitement. **2.** The gasp characteristic of whooping cough. **—whoop** *v.* **—whoop'er** *n.*

whooping cough. An infectious disease involving catarrh of the respiratory passages and characterized by spasms of coughing interspersed with deep, noisy inspiration.

whoosh (hwo͞osh, hwo͝osh) *v.* To make a gushing or rushing sound. *—n.* A whooshing sound. [Imit.]

whop•per (hwŏp'ər) *n. Informal.* **1.** Something exceptionally big or remarkable. **2.** A gross untruth. **—whop'ping** *adj.*

whore (hôr, hōr) *n.* One who engages in sexual intercourse for money. [< OE *hōre.* See **kā-.**]

whore•house (hôr'hous', hōr'-) *n.* A brothel.

whorl (hwôrl, hwûrl) *n.* **1.** An arrangement of three or more radiating parts, as leaves or petals. **2.** A coil or convolution, as one of the circular ridges of a fingerprint or a turn of a spiral shell. [ME *whorle.*] **—whorled** *adj.*

whose (ho͞oz). The possessive form of the pronoun *who* and, less commonly, *which.*

Usage: Whose, as the possessive form of a relative pronoun, can refer to both persons and things: *the boy whose arm was broken; the book whose cover was soiled.*

who•so (ho͞o'sō) *pron.* Whoever.

who•so•ev•er (ho͞o'sō-ĕv'ər) *pron.* Whoever.

whse. warehouse.

whsle. wholesale.

why (hwī) *adv.* **1.** For what purpose, reason, or cause. **2.** For which; because of which. *—n.* The cause or intention: *whys and wherefores.* [< OE *hwȳ.* See **kwo-.**]

Wich•i•ta[1] (wĭch'ə-tô') *n., pl.* **-ta** or **-tas.** **1.** A confederacy of Caddoan-speaking North American Indians, formerly living between the Arkansas River and C Texas. **2.** A member of this confederacy. **3.** The language of these Indians.

Wich•i•ta[2] (wĭch'ə-tô). A city of S Kansas. Pop. 255,000.

wick (wĭk) *n.* A cord of fibers, as in a candle, that draws up fuel to the flame by capillary attraction. [< OE *wēoce.*]

wick•ed (wĭk'ĭd) *adj.* **1.** Vicious; depraved. **2.** Harmful. [< OE *wicca,* wizard. See **weik-2.**] **—wick'ed•ly** *adv.* **—wick'ed•ness** *n.*

wick•er (wĭk'ər) *n.* Also **wick•er•work** (-wûrk'). Flexible twigs or shoots, as of a willow, interwoven to make baskets, furniture, etc. [< Scand.] **—wick'er** *adj.*

wick•et (wĭk'ĭt) *n.* **1.** A small door or gate. **2.** *Cricket.* Either of the two sets of three upright sticks that forms the target of the player hurling the ball. **3.** *Croquet.* A small arch, usually made of wire, through which one tries to direct the ball. [< ONF *wiket.*]

wide (wīd) *adj.* **wider, widest.** **1.** Extending over a large area from side to side; broad. **2.** Having a specified extent from side to side. **3.** Having great range or scope: *a wide selection.* **4.** Fully open: *wide eyes.* **5.** Landing or located away from a desired goal. *—adv.* **1.** Over a large area; extensively. **2.** To the full extent; completely. [< OE *wīd.* See **wi-.**] **—wide'ly** *adv.* **—wide'ness** *n.*

wide-a•wake (wīd'ə-wāk') *adj.* **1.** Completely awake. **2.** Alert.

wide-eyed (wīd'īd') *adj.* With the eyes completely opened, as in wonder.

wid•en (wīd'n) *v.* To make or become wide or wider. **—wid'en•er** *n.*

wide•spread (wīd'sprĕd') *adj.* Occurring or accepted widely.

widg•eon (wĭj'ən) *n.* Also *Brit.* **wi•geon.** A wild duck with brownish plumage and a light head patch. [?]

wid•ow (wĭd'ō) *n.* A woman whose husband has died and who has not remarried. [< OE *widuwe.* See **weidh-.**]

wid•ow•er (wĭd'ō-ər) *n.* A man whose wife has died and who has not remarried.

width (wĭdth, wĭth) *n.* **1.** The state of being wide. **2.** The measurement of the extent of something from side to side. **3.** Something having a specified width.

wield (wēld) *v.* **1.** To handle (a weapon, tool, etc.). **2.** To exercise (power or influence). [< OE *wealdan* and *wieldan.* See **wal-.**]

wife (wīf) *n., pl.* **wives** (wīvz). A woman married to a man. [< OE *wīf* < Gmc **wīf,* woman.] **—wife'ly** *adj.*

wig (wĭg) *n.* A piece of artificial or human hair worn on the head as personal adornment, part of a costume, or to conceal baldness. [Short for PERIWIG.]

wi•geon. *Brit.* Variant of **widgeon.**

wig•gle (wĭg'əl) *v.* **-gled, -gling.** To move or cause to move with short irregular motions from side to side. [ME *wiglen.*] **—wig'gler** *n.*

wig•wam (wĭg'wŏm') *n.* A North American Indian dwelling, commonly having an arched or conical framework overlaid with bark or hides. [< Algon.]

wild (wīld) *adj.* **1.** Occurring, growing, or living in a natural state; not domesticated, cultivated, or tamed. **2.** Lacking discipline, restraint, or control. **3.** Full of intense, ungovernable emotion: *wild with jealousy.* **4.** Furiously disturbed or turbulent; stormy. **5.** *Card Games.* Having an arbitrary equivalence or value determined by the holder's needs. *—n.* An uninhabited or uncultivated region. [< OE *wilde.* See **welt-.**] **—wild, wild'ly** *adv.* **—wild'ness** *n.*

wild•cat (wīld'kăt') *n.* **1.** A lynx, bobcat, or other small to medium-sized wild cat. **2.** An oil well drilled in an area not known to yield oil. *—adj.* **1.** Risky or unsound, esp. financially. **2.** Done without official sanction: *a wildcat strike.*

wil•de•beest (wĭl'də-bēst', vĭl'-) *n.* The gnu.

wil•der•ness (wĭl'dər-nĭs) *n.* An unsettled, uncultivated region left in its natural condition. [< OE *wildēor,* wild beast.]

wild-eyed (wīld'īd') *adj.* Glaring in or as in anger, terror, or madness.

wild•fire (wīld'fīr') *n.* A raging fire that travels and spreads rapidly.

wild•fowl (wīld'foul') *n.* A bird, as a duck or goose, hunted as game.

wild-goose chase (wīld'go͞os'). A hopeless pursuit of an unattainable or imaginary object.

wild•life (wīld'līf') *n.* Animals living in a natural, undomesticated state.

wile (wīl) *n.* **1.** A deceitful stratagem or trick. **2.** A disarming or seductive manner, device, or procedure. **3.** Trickery. *—v.* **wiled, wiling.** To entice; lure. [ME *wil.*]

wil•ful. Variant of **willful.**

will[1] (wĭl) *n.* **1.** The mental faculty by which one deliberately chooses or decides upon a course of action; volition. **2.** Deliberate intention or wish: *against his will.* **3.** Free discretion; inclination: *wandered about at will.* **4.** Bearing or attitude toward others; disposition: *full of good will.* **5.** Determination: *the will to win.* **6.** A legal declaration of how a person wishes his possessions to be disposed of after his death. *—v.* **1.** To decide upon; choose; determine. **2.** To bequeath; grant in a legal will. [< OE *will, willa.* See **wel-2.**]

will[2] (wĭl) *v.* past **would,** present **will.** **1.** —Used as an auxiliary followed by a simple infinitive to indicate (often with future reference) willingness, intention, likelihood, requirement, habitual action, or ability. *Will* is used more commonly than *shall* in all persons except (a) in questions with subject *I* or *we,* (b) in formulaic contexts requiring the special prescriptive force of *shall,* and (c) in formal prose as a stylistic device expressing various shades of meaning. **2.** To wish: *Do what you will.* [< OE *wyllan.* See **wel-2.**]

Usage: On all but an expressly formal level, *will* often occurs in all three grammatical persons, including the first, in expressing simple futurity (unstressed intention or normal expectation). *Will,* in all three persons, is now also used more often than *shall* to express any of the forms of emphatic futurity.

willed (wĭld) *adj.* Having a will of a specified kind: *weak-willed.*

will•ful (wĭl'fəl) *adj.* Also **wil•ful.** **1.** Said or done in accordance with one's will; deliberate. **2.** Inclined to impose one's will; obstinate. **—will'ful•ly** *adv.* **—will'ful•ness** *n.*

Wil•liam I (wĭl'yəm). Called the Conqueror. 1027–1087. King of England (1066–87).

William II. 1859–1941. Emperor of Germany and king of Prussia (1888–1918).

will•ing (wĭl'ĭng) *adj.* **1.** Of or resulting from the process of choosing. **2.** Disposed to accept or tolerate; acquiescent. **3.** Acting or ready to act gladly; compliant. **—will'ing•ly** *adv.* **—will'ing•ness** *n.*

will-o'-the-wisp (wĭl'ə-*thə*-wĭsp') *n.* **1.** A phosphorescent light that hovers over swampy ground at night, possibly caused by spontaneous combustion of gases emitted by rotting organic matter. **2.** A delusive or misleading goal. [?]

wil•low (wĭl'ō) *n.* **1.** Any of various trees or shrubs usually having narrow leaves and slender, flexible twigs. **2.** The wood of such a tree. [< OE *welig.*]

wil•low•y (wĭl'ō-ē) *adj.* **-ier, -iest.** Resembling or suggestive of a willow tree, as in suppleness, slenderness, etc.

will power. The ability to carry out one's decisions, wishes, or plans; strength of mind.

wil•ly-nil•ly (wĭl'ē-nĭl'ē) *adv.* Whether desired or not. [Var of *will I nill I,* "be I willing, be I unwilling."]

Wil•ming•ton (wĭl'mĭng-tən). A city of N Delaware. Pop. 96,000.

Wil•son (wĭl'sən), **(Thomas) Woodrow.** 1856–1924. 28th President of the U.S. (1913–21).

Woodrow Wilson

wilt[1] (wĭlt) *v.* **1.** To lose or cause to lose freshness; make or become limp or drooping. **2.** To weaken. [Var of dial *wilk, welk.*]

wilt[2] (wĭlt). *Archaic.* 2nd person sing. present tense of **will.**

wi•ly (wī'lē) *adj.* **-lier, -liest.** Full of wiles; guileful; calculating. **—wil'i•ness** *n.*

wim•ple (wĭm'pəl) *n.* A cloth framing the face and drawn into folds beneath the chin, worn by women in medieval times and as part of certain nuns' habits. [< OE *wimpel.*]

win (wĭn) *v.* **won, winning. 1.** To achieve victory over others in a competition. **2.** To finish first in a race. **3.** To receive as a prize or reward for performance. **4.** To succeed in gaining the support of. *—n.* A victory, esp. in a competition. [< OE *winnan,* to strive. See **wen-.**] **—win'ner** *n.*

wince (wĭns) *v.* **winced, wincing.** To shrink or start involuntarily, as in pain or distress. *—n.* A wincing movement or gesture. [ME *wincen,* to kick, wince.] **—winc'er** *n.*

winch (wĭnch) *n.* **1.** A stationary hoisting machine having a drum around which a rope or chain winds as the load is lifted. **2.** The crank used to give motion to a grindstone or similar device. [< OE *wince,* a pulley. See **weng-.**]

wind[1] (wĭnd) *n.* **1.** Moving air, esp. natural and perceptible movement of air parallel to or along the ground. **2. a.** A movement or current of air blowing from one of the four cardinal points of the compass. **b.** The direction from which such currents come. **3. winds.** The wind instruments in an orchestra or band. **4.** Gas produced in the body during digestion. **5.** Respiration; breath, esp. normal or adequate breathing. **6.** Utterance empty of meaning. **—get wind of.** To receive hints of. *—v.* To cause to be out of or short of breath. [< OE. See **wē-.**]

wind[2] (wīnd) *v.* **wound, winding. 1.** To wrap (something) around an object or center once or repeatedly. **2.** To turn in a series of circular motions, as a crank or handle. **3.** To coil the spring of (a clock or other mechanism) by turning a stem. **4.** To move in or as in a bending or coiling course. **5.** To be coiled or spiraled about something. *—n.* A single turn, twist, or curve. [< OE *windan.* See **wendh-.**]

wind•burn (wĭnd'bûrn') *n.* Skin irritation caused by exposure to wind.

wind•ed (wĭn'dĭd) *adj.* **1.** Having breath or respiratory power: *short-winded.* **2.** Out of breath.

wind•fall (wĭnd'fôl') *n.* **1.** Something that has been blown down by the wind, as a ripened fruit. **2.** A sudden and unexpected piece of good fortune or personal gain.

wind•flow•er (wĭnd'flou'ər) *n.* An anemone.

Wind•hoek (vĭnt'ho͝ok'). The capital of Namibia. Pop. 61,260.

wind•ing (wīn'dĭng) *adj.* **1.** Twisting or turning; sinuous. **2.** Spiral.

wind instrument (wĭnd). Any musical instrument sounded by wind, esp. by the breath, as a clarinet, trumpet, or harmonica.

wind•lass (wĭnd'ləs) *n.* Any of numerous hauling or lifting machines consisting essentially of a drum or cylinder wound with rope and turned by a crank. [< ON *vindāss.*]

wind•mill (wĭnd'mĭl') *n.* A mill that runs on the energy generated by a wheel of adjustable blades or slats rotated by the wind.

win•dow (wĭn'dō) *n.* **1.** An opening constructed in a wall to admit light or air, usually framed and spanned with glass. **2.** A pane of glass; windowpane. **3.** Any opening that resembles a window in function or appearance. [< ON *vindauga,* "wind eye."]

win•dow•pane (wĭn'dō-pān') *n.* A plate of glass in a window.

win•dow-shop (wĭn'dō-shŏp') *v.* To look at merchandise in the windows or showcases of stores without purchasing anything. **—win'dow-shop'per** *n.*

win•dow•sill (wĭn'dō-sĭl') *n.* The horizontal ledge at the base of a window opening.

wind•pipe (wĭnd'pīp') *n.* The trachea.

wind•shield (wĭnd'shēld') *n.* A framed pane of glass or other transparent shielding located in front of the occupants of a vehicle to protect them from the wind.

wind•sock (wĭnd'sŏk') *n.* A large, tapered, open-ended sleeve that indicates the direction of the wind blowing through it.

Wind•sor (wĭn'zər). A city of SE Ontario. Pop. 193,000.

wind•swept (wĭnd'swĕpt') *adj.* Exposed to or moved by the force of wind.

wind up (wīnd). To come or bring to an end.

wind-up (wīnd'ŭp') *n.* **1.** The act of bringing something to a conclusion. **2.** The concluding part of an action, presentation, speech, etc.

wind•ward (wĭnd'wərd) *n.* The direction from which the wind blows. *—adj.* **1.** Of or moving toward the quarter from which the wind blows. **2.** Of or on the side exposed to the wind or prevailing winds. **—wind'ward** *adv.*

wind•y (wĭn'dē) *adj.* **-ier, -iest. 1.** Characterized by or abounding in wind. **2.** Resembling wind in swiftness or force. **3. a.** Characterized by lack of substance; empty. **b.** Characterized by or given to prolonged talk. **—wind'i•ly** *adv.* **—wind'i•ness** *n.*

wine (wīn) *n.* The fermented juice of grapes or sometimes other fruits or plants. [< OE *wīn* < Gmc **wīna-* < L *vīnum.*]

wing (wĭng) *n.* **1.** One of a pair of specialized organs of flight, as of a bird, bat, or insect. **2.** A structure or part resembling a wing. **3.** An airfoil whose principal function is providing lift, esp. either of two such airfoils positioned on each side of the fuselage. **4.** *Theater.* The unseen backstage area on either side of a stage. **5.** A structure attached to the side of a house, building, or fortification. **6.** A section of a party, legislature, or community holding distinct political views. **7.** Either of the forward positions played near the sideline, as in hockey. **8.** A unit of military aircraft. **—under one's wing.** Under one's protection. *—v.* **1.** To fly. **2.** To wound superficially, as in the wing or arm. [< ON *vængr,* bird's wing.] **—winged** *adj.*

wing•span (wĭng'spăn') *n.* The linear distance from wing tip to wing tip of an aircraft or bird.

wing•spread (wĭng'sprĕd') *n.* The distance between the tips of the extended wings, as of an airplane, bird, or insect.

wink (wĭngk) *v.* **1.** To close and open (the eyelid of one eye) deliberately, as to convey a message, signal, or suggestion. **2.** To shine fitfully; twinkle. *—n.* **1. a.** The act of winking. **b.** The time required for a wink. **2.** A gleam; twinkle. **—wink at.** To pretend not to see: *winked at corruption.* [< OE *wincian,* to close one's eyes. See **weng-.**]

win•kle (wĭng'kəl) *n.* A snail, the periwinkle.

win•ning (wĭn'ĭng) *adj.* **1.** Successful; victorious. **2.** Charming: *a winning personality.* *—n.* **1.** The act of one that wins. **2. winnings.** That which has been won, esp. money.

Win•ni•peg (wĭn'ə-pĕg). The capital of Manitoba. Pop. 476,000.

win•now (wĭn'ō) *v.* **1.** To separate the chaff from (grain) by means of a current of air. **2.** To separate (a desirable or undesirable part); sort or eliminate. [< OE *windwian* < *wind,* WIND[1].]

win•some (wĭn'səm) *adj.* Pleasant; charming. [< OE *wynsum.*] **—win'some•ly** *adv.* **—win'some•ness** *n.*

win•ter (wĭn'tər) *n.* The usually coldest season of the year, occurring between autumn and spring. *—adj.* **1.** Pertaining to, characteristic of, or occurring in winter. **2. a.** Capable of being stored for use during the winter: *winter squash.* **b.** Planted in the autumn and harvested in the spring or summer: *winter wheat.* [< OE. See **wed-.**] **—win'try, win'ter•y** *adj.*

win•ter•green (wĭn'tər-grēn') *n.* **1.** A low-growing plant with aromatic evergreen leaves and spicy red berries. **2.** An oil or flavoring obtained from this plant.

win•ter•ize (wĭn'tə-rīz') *v.* **-ized, -izing.** To prepare or equip for winter weather.

win•ter•time (wĭn'tər-tīm') *n.* The winter season.

wipe (wīp) *v.* **wiped, wiping. 1.** To rub, as with a cloth or paper, in order to clean or dry. **2.** To remove by rubbing; brush. **—wipe out.** To destroy; annihilate. [< OE *wīpian.* See **weip-.**] **—wipe** *n.*

wip•er (wī'pər) *n.* A device designed for wiping, as for a windshield.

wire (wīr) *n.* **1.** A usually pliable metallic strand or rod, sometimes clad and often electrically insulated, used chiefly for structural support or to conduct electricity. **2.** A group of such strands bundled or twisted together; a cable. **3.** The telegraph service. **4.** A telegram. **5.** An open telephone connection. **6.** The finish line of a racetrack. *—adj.* Made of or like wire. *—v.* **wired, wiring. 1.** To connect or provide with a wire or wires. **2.** To send by telegraph: *wire congratulations.* **3.** To send a telegram to. [< OE *wīr.* See **wei-**[1].]

wire-haired (wīr'hârd') *adj.* Having a coat of stiff, wiry hair.

wire•less (wīr'lĭs) *n.* **1.** A radio telegraph or telephone system. **2.** *Brit.* Radio.

wire•tap (wīr'tăp') *n.* A concealed listening or recording device connected to a communications circuit. *—v.* To monitor (a telephone line) by means of a wiretap.

wir•ing (wīr'ĭng) *n.* A system of electric wires.

wir•y (wīr'ē) *adj.* **-ier, -iest. 1.** Wirelike; kinky: *wiry hair.* **2.** Slender but tough: *a wiry physique.* **—wir'i•ness** *n.*

Wis•con•sin (wĭs-kŏn'sən). A state of the north-central U.S. Pop. 4,418,000. Cap. Madison.

wis•dom (wĭz'dəm) *n.* **1.** Understanding of what is true, right, or lasting. **2.** Common sense; good judgment. [< OE *wīsdōm.* See **weid-.**]

wisdom tooth. One of four molars, the last on each side of both jaws, usually erupting much later than the others.

wise[1] (wīz) *adj.* **wiser, wisest. 1.** Having wisdom; judicious. **2.** Prudent; sensible. **3.** Shrewd: *a wise move.* **4.** Having knowledge or information. **5.** *Slang.* Arrogant. [< OE *wīs.* See **weid-.**] **—wise'ly** *adv.*

wise[2] (wīz) *n.* Method or manner of doing: *in no wise.* [< OE *wīse, wīs,* manner, condition. See **weid-.**]

-wise. *comb. form.* Used to form adverbs from nouns or adjectives to indicate: **1.** Manner, direction, or position: **clockwise. 2.** *Informal.* With reference to: *taxwise.* See Usage note.

[< OE *wīse*, WISE[2].]
Usage: The practice of attaching *-wise* to nouns, in the sense of *with reference to*, has become so closely associated with commercial jargon in the minds of many writers and speakers that it is dubious usage on any higher level.

wise•crack (wīz′krăk′) *n. Slang.* A flippant, commonly sardonic remark.

wish (wĭsh) *n.* **1.** A desire for some specific thing. **2.** An expression of such a desire. **3.** Something desired. *—v.* **1.** To have or feel a desire; want: *I wish to know.* **2.** To desire (a person or thing) to be in a specified state or condition: *I wish this rug were green.* **3.** To express wishes for; bid: *wished her good night.* **4.** To call or invoke upon: *I wish him luck.* **5.** To express a wish. [< OE *wȳscan.* See **wen-.**] **—wish′ful** *adj.* **—wish′ful•ly** *adv.*

wish•bone (wĭsh′bōn′) *n.* The forked bone in front of the breastbone of most birds.

wishful thinking. Erroneous identification of one's own wishes with reality.

wish•y-wash•y (wĭsh′ē-wŏsh′ē, -wô′shē) *adj.* **-ier, -iest.** Lacking in strength or purpose; indecisive. [Redupl of *washy* < WASH.]

wisp (wĭsp) *n.* **1.** A small bunch or bundle, as of hair. **2.** Someone or something thin, frail, or slight. **3.** A faint streak, as of smoke or clouds. [ME.] **—wisp′y** *adj.*

wis•ter•i•a (wĭ-stîr′ē-ə) *n.* Also **wis•tar•i•a** (wĭ-stâr′ē-ə). A climbing woody vine with drooping clusters of purplish or white flowers. [< C. *Wistar* or *Wister* (1761–1818), American anatomist.]

wist•ful (wĭst′fəl) *adj.* Full of a melancholy yearning; wishful. **—wist′ful•ly** *adv.* **—wist′ful•ness** *n.*

wit (wĭt) *n.* **1.** Often **wits.** Understanding; intelligence; resourcefulness. **2. a.** The ability to perceive and express in an ingeniously humorous manner the relationship or similarity between seemingly incongruous or disparate things. **b.** One noted for this ability. [< OE. See **weid-.**]

witch (wĭch) *n.* **1.** A woman who practices sorcery or is believed to have dealings with the devil. **2.** An ugly, vicious old woman. [< OE *wicce* (fem), witch, and *wicca* (masc), wizard. See **weik-2.**]

witch•craft (wĭch′krăft′, -kräft′) *n.* Black magic; sorcery.

witch doctor. A medicine man among primitive peoples.

witch hazel. 1. A North American shrub with yellow flowers that bloom in late autumn or winter. **2.** An astringent liniment obtained from this shrub.

with (wĭth, wĭth) *prep.* **1.** Accompanying. **2.** Next to. **3.** Having as a possession, attribute, or characteristic. **4.** In a manner characterized by. **5.** In the charge or keeping of. **6.** In the opinion or estimation of. **7.** In support of. **8.** Of the same opinion or belief as. **9.** In the same group as; among. **10.** In the membership or employment of. **11.** By the means or agency of. **12.** In spite of. **13.** In the same direction as. **14.** At the same time as. **15.** In regard to. **16.** In comparison or contrast to. **17.** Having received. **18.** And; plus; added to. **19.** In opposition to; against. **20.** As a result or consequence of. **21.** To; onto. **22.** So as to be separated from. **23.** In the course of. **24.** In proportion to. **25.** In relationship to. **26.** As well as. [< OE, against or in opposition to, together with. See **wi-.**]

with•al (wĭth-ôl′) *adv.* **1.** Besides; in addition. **2.** Despite that; nevertheless. **3.** *Archaic.* Therewith. [< WITH + ALL.]

with•draw (wĭth-drô′, wĭth-) *v.* **-drew** (-drōō′), **-drawn** (-drôn′), **-drawing. 1.** To take back or away; remove. **2.** To move or draw back; retreat. **3.** To remove oneself from activity or a social or emotional environment.

with•draw•al (wĭth-drô′əl, wĭth-) *n.* **1.** The act or process of withdrawing. **2.** The act or physiological effect of terminating use of an addictive drug.

with•drawn (wĭth-drôn′, wĭth-) *adj.* Shy.

withe (wĭth, wĭth, wīth) *n.* A tough, supple twig, as of willow, used for binding things together. [< OE *withthe.*]

with•er (wĭth′ər) *v.* **1.** To dry up or shrivel from or as from loss of moisture. **2.** To lose freshness; fade; droop. **3.** To cause to feel belittled: *withered her with a glance.* [ME *widderen.*]

with•ers (wĭth′ərz) *pl.n.* The high point of the back of a horse or other animal, between the shoulder blades.

with•hold (wĭth-hōld′, wĭth-) *v.* **-held** (-hĕld′), **-holding.** To refrain from giving, granting, or permitting; forbear.

withholding tax. A portion of an employee's wages or salary withheld by his employer as partial payment of his income tax.

with•in (wĭth-ĭn′, wĭth-) *adv.* **1.** Inside. **2.** Indoors. **3.** Inside the body or mind; inwardly. *—prep.* **1.** Inside. **2.** Inside the limits or extent of. **3.** Inside the fixed limits of: *within one's rights.* **4.** In the scope or sphere of.

with-it (wĭth′ĭt′, wĭth′-) *adj. Slang.* Up-to-date; hip.

with•out (wĭth-out′, wĭth-) *adv.* **1.** In or on the outside. **2.** Outdoors. *—prep.* **1.** Not having; lacking. **2. a.** With no or none of. **b.** Not accompanied by. **3.** Free from. **4.** At, on, to, or toward the outside or exterior of. **5.** With neglect or avoidance of.

with•stand (wĭth-stănd′, wĭth-) *v.* **-stood** (-stŏŏd′), **-standing.** To oppose (something) with force; resist or endure successfully.

wit•ness (wĭt′nĭs) *n.* **1.** One who has seen or heard something. **2.** Something that serves as evidence; a sign. **3.** *Law.* **a.** One who is called upon to testify before a court. **b.** One who is called upon to be present at a transaction in order to attest to what took place. *—v.* **1.** To be present at; see. **2.** To serve as or furnish evidence of. **3.** To testify. **4.** To be the setting or site of. **5.** To attest to the authenticity of by signing one's name. [< OE *wit*, knowledge, WIT.] **—wit′ness•er** *n.*

wit•ti•cism (wĭt′ĭ-sĭz′əm) *n.* A witty remark or saying. [< WITTY.]

wit•ting•ly (wĭt′ĭng-lē) *adv.* Intentionally; deliberately.

wit•ty (wĭt′ē) *adj.* **-tier, -tiest.** Having or showing wit; cleverly humorous. **—wit′ti•ly** *adv.* **—wit′ti•ness** *n.*

wives. *pl.* of **wife.**

wiz•ard (wĭz′ərd) *n.* **1.** A sorcerer or magician. **2.** A brilliantly skillful person. [< WISE[1].]

wiz•ard•ry (wĭz′ər-drē) *n.* Sorcery.

wiz•ened (wĭz′ənd) *adj.* Shriveled; withered. [< OE *wisnian*, to dry up. See **wei-2.**]

wk. 1. week. **2.** work.

wkly. weekly.

WNW west-northwest.

WO warrant officer.

woad (wōd) *n.* **1.** An Old World plant with leaves that yield a blue dye. **2.** The dye obtained from this plant. [< OE *wād.*]

wob•ble (wŏb′əl) *v.* **-bled, -bling. 1.** To move or cause to move erratically from side to side. **2.** To waver or vacillate. [Perh < LG *wabbeln.*] **—wob′ble** *n.* **—wob′bly** *adj.*

woe (wō) *n.* **1.** Deep sorrow; grief. **2.** Misfortune. [< OE *wā* (interj). See **wai.**]

woe•be•gone (wō′bĭ-gôn′, -gŏn′) *adj.* Mournful or sorrowful in appearance. [< WOE + ME *be-*, about + *gon*, to GO.]

woe•ful (wō′fəl) *adj.* **1.** Afflicted with woe; mournful. **2.** Pitiful or deplorable.

woke (wōk). *Chiefly Brit. & Regional. p.t.* of **wake.**

wok•en (wō′kən). *Chiefly Brit. & Regional.* Alternate *p.p.* of **wake.**

wolf (wŏŏlf) *n., pl.* **wolves** (wŏŏlvz). **1.** A carnivorous mammal, chiefly of northern regions, related to and resembling the dogs. **2.** *Slang.* A man given to avid amatory pursuit of women. *—v.* To eat voraciously: *wolfed down the hamburger.* [< OE *wulf.* See **wlkwo-.**]

wolf•hound (wŏŏlf′hound′) *n.* A large dog originally trained to hunt wolves.

wolf•ram (wŏŏl′frəm) *n.* Tungsten. [G.]

wol•ver•ine (wŏŏl′və-rēn′) *n.* A carnivorous mammal of northern regions, having dark fur and a bushy tail. [< WOLF.]

wom•an (wŏŏm′ən) *n., pl.* **women** (wĭm′ĭn). **1.** An adult female human being. **2.** Women collectively. **3.** A mistress; paramour. [< OE *wīf*, WIFE + *man*, person, MAN.]

wom•an•hood (wŏŏm′ən-hŏŏd′) *n.* **1.** The state of being a woman. **2.** Womankind.

wom•an•ish (wŏŏm′ə-nĭsh) *adj.* Characteristic of a woman; womanlike.

wom•an•kind (wŏŏm′ən-kīnd′) *n.* Female human beings collectively; women.

wom•an•ly (wŏŏm′ən-lē) *adj.* **-lier, -liest.** Having the becoming qualities of a woman. **—wom′an•li•ness** *n.*

womb (wōōm) *n.* **1.** The uterus. **2.** A place where something is generated. [< OE *wamb* < Gmc **wambō.*]

wom•bat (wŏm′băt′) *n.* An Australian marsupial, resembling a small bear.

wom•en. *pl.* of **woman.**

wom•en•folk (wĭm′ĭn-fōk′) *pl.n.* **1.** Women collectively. **2.** A particular group of women.

won[1] (wôn) *n., pl.* **won. 1.** The basic monetary unit of South Korea. **2.** The basic monetary unit of North Korea.

won[2] (wŭn). *p.t. & p.p.* of **win.**

won•der (wŭn′dər) *n.* **1. a.** That which arouses awe or admiration; a marvel. **b.** The emotion thus aroused. **2.** A feeling of puzzlement or doubt. *—v.* **1.** To have a feeling of awe or admiration. **2.** To be filled with curiosity or doubt. **3.** To have doubts or curiosity about. [< OE *wundor* < Gmc **wundar-.*]

won•der•ful (wŭn′dər-fəl) *adj.* **1.** Capable of exciting wonder; marvelous. **2.** Admirable; excellent. **—won′der•ful•ly** *adv.*

won•der•land (wŭn′dər-lănd′) *n.* **1.** A marvelous imaginary realm. **2.** A marvelous real place or scene.

won•drous (wŭn′drəs) *adj.* Wonderful.

wont (wônt, wōnt, wŭnt) *adj.* **1.** Accustomed: *The poor man is wont to complain.* **2.** Apt or likely. *—n.* Usage or custom. [< OE *wunian*, to dwell. See **wen-.**]

won't (wōnt). Contraction of *will not.*

wont•ed (wôn′tĭd, wōn′-, wŭn′-) *adj.* Accustomed; usual.

woo (wōō) *v.* **1.** To seek the affection of, esp. with intent to marry. **2.** To seek to achieve. **3.** To entreat or importune. [< OE *wōgian.*]

wood (wŏŏd) *n.* **1. a.** The tough, fibrous supporting and water-conducting substance lying beneath the bark of trees and shrubs. **b.** Such a substance used for various purposes, as building material or fuel. **2.** Often **woods.** A dense growth of trees; a forest. **3.** A wooden object. *—adj.* **1.** Wooden. **2.** Associated with, used on, or containing wood. **3.** Growing or living in woods. *—v.* **1.** To cover with trees. **2.** To gather or be supplied with wood. [< OE *wudu.* See **widhu-.**]

wood alcohol. Methanol.

wood•bine (wŏŏd′bīn′) *n.* Any of various climbing vines, esp. an Old World honeysuckle. [< OE *wudu,* WOOD + *bindan,* to BIND.]

wood•carv•ing (wŏŏd′kär′vĭng) *n.* **1.** The art of carving in wood. **2.** An object carved from wood. **—wood′carv′er** *n.*

wood•chuck (wŏŏd′chŭk′) *n.* A common North American rodent, with a short-legged, heavy-set body; a ground hog. [< Algon.]

wood•cock (wŏŏd′kŏk′) *n.* A short-legged, long-billed game bird.

wood•craft (wŏŏd′krăft′, -kräft′) *n.* **1.** Skill in matters pertaining to the woods, as hunting or camping. **2.** The art of working with wood.

wood•cut (wŏŏd′kŭt′) *n.* **1.** A piece of wood with an engraved design for printing. **2.** A print made from such a piece of wood.

wood•cut•ter (wŏŏd′kŭt′ər) *n.* One who cuts wood or trees.

wood•ed (wŏŏd′ĭd) *adj.* Having trees or woods.

wood•en (wŏŏd′n) *adj.* **1.** Made or consisting of wood. **2.** Without life; lifeless. **3.** Clumsy.

wood•land (wŏŏd′lənd, -lănd′) *n.* Land covered with trees.

wood•peck•er (wŏŏd′pĕk′ər) *n.* Any of various birds that cling to and climb trees and have a chisellike bill for drilling through bark and wood.

woods•man (wŏŏdz′mən) *n.* One who works or lives in the woods or is versed in woodcraft.

wood•wind (wŏŏd′wĭnd′) *n.* Any of a group of musical wind instruments that includes the bassoon, clarinet, flute, oboe, and sometimes the saxophone. **—wood′wind′** *adj.*

wood•work (wŏŏd′wûrk′) *n.* Something made of wood, esp. wooden interior fittings.

wood•y (wŏŏd′ē) *adj.* **-ier, -iest. 1.** Consisting of or containing wood. **2.** Suggestive of wood. **3.** Wooded.

woof (wŏŏf, wōōf) *n.* **1.** The threads in a woven fabric at right angles to the warp threads. **2.** The texture of a fabric. [< OE *wefan,* to weave.]

woof•er (wŏŏf′ər) *n.* A loud-speaker designed to reproduce bass frequencies. [< *woof,* the gruff bark of a dog.]

wool (wŏŏl) *n.* **1.** The dense, soft, often curly hair of a sheep and some other animals, valued as a textile fabric. **2.** A material or garment made of wool. **3.** A covering or substance suggestive of the texture of wool. [< OE *wull.* See **wel-[1].**] **—wool** *adj.*

wool•en (wŏŏl′ən). Also **wool•len.** *adj.* Pertaining to or consisting of wool. *—n.* Often **woolens.** Fabric or clothing made from wool.

wool•gath•er•ing (wŏŏl′găth′ər-ĭng) *n.* Absent-minded indulgence in fanciful daydreams.

wool•ly (wŏŏl′ē) *adj.* **-lier, -liest.** Also **wool•y. 1. a.** Pertaining to, consisting of, or covered with wool. **b.** Resembling wool. **2.** Blurry; fuzzy. **3.** Rough and generally lawless: *wild and woolly.* *—n., pl.* **-lies.** Also **wool•y.** A garment, esp. an undergarment, made of wool.

wooz•y (wōō′zē, wŏŏz′ē) *adj.* **-ier, -iest. 1.** Dazed; confused. **2.** Dizzy or queasy. [Perh var of OOZY.] **—wooz′i•ness** *n.*

Worces•ter (wŏŏs′tər). A city of C Massachusetts. Pop. 187,000.

word (wûrd) *n.* **1.** A sound or a combination of sounds, or its representation in writing or printing, that symbolizes and communicates a meaning. **2.** An utterance, remark, or comment. **3. words.** A discourse or talk; speech. **4. words.** Lyrics; text. **5.** An assurance or promise. **6. a.** A command or direction. **b.** A verbal signal. **7. a.** News. **b.** Rumor. **8. words.** A dispute or argument. **9. Word.** The Scriptures or Gospel: *the Word of God.* **—in a word.** In short. **—in so many words.** Exactly. **—word for word.** In the same words. *—v.* To express in words. [< OE. See **wer-[2].**]

word•ing (wûr′dĭng) *n.* The style of expressing in words.

word square. A group of words arranged in a square that read the same vertically and horizontally.

Words•worth (wûrdz′wûrth′), **William.** 1770–1850. English poet.

word•y (wûr′dē) *adj.* **-ier, -iest.** Expressed in or using more words than are necessary. **—word′i•ly** *adv.* **—word′i•ness** *n.*

wore (wôr, wōr). *p.t.* of **wear.**

work (wûrk) *n.* **1.** Effort directed toward the production or accomplishment of something; toil; labor. **2.** Employment. **3.** A trade, craft, business, or profession. **4.** A duty or task. **5.** Something that has been produced as a result of effort. **6. works.** The output of an artist or artisan considered as a whole. **7. works.** Engineering structures. **8.** Any material being processed during manufacture. **9. works** *(takes sing. v.).* A factory, plant, or similar building or system of buildings. **10. works.** Machinery. **11.** The manner or style of working. **12.** *Phys.* The transfer of energy to a body by the application of force. *—v.* **1.** To labor or toil. **2.** To be employed; have a job. **3.** To function or operate. **4.** To prove successful. **5.** To have an influence, result, or effect, as on a person. **6.** To change into a specified state, esp. gradually or by repeated movement. **7.** To force a passage or way. **8.** To move or contort from emotion or pain. **9.** To be processed. **10.** To ferment. **11.** To undergo small motions that result in friction and wear. **12.** To cause or effect; bring about. **13.** To handle or use. **14.** To form or shape; mold. **15.** To solve (an arithmetic problem). **16.** To make productive; cultivate. **17.** To make or force to work. **18.** To excite, rouse, or provoke. **19.** To influence or persuade. **—work up. 1.** To make one's or its way up. **2.** To arouse or excite. **3.** To develop. [< OE *weorc,* act, deed, work. See **werg-.**]

-work. *comb. form.* **1.** A product composed of a (specified) material: **paperwork. 2.** Work produced in a (specified) way or of a (specified) kind: **piecework. 3.** Work performed in a (specified) place: **housework.**

work•a•ble (wûr′kə-bəl) *adj.* **1.** Capable of being worked. **2.** Practicable or feasible.

work•a•day (wûrk′ə-dā′) *adj.* **1.** Pertaining or appropriate to working days. **2.** Mundane; commonplace.

work•bench (wûrk′bĕnch′) *n.* A sturdy table, as one used by a machinist or carpenter.

work•book (wûrk′bŏŏk′) *n.* **1.** A booklet of problems and exercises in which a student may write. **2.** A manual of operating instructions. **3.** A book in which a record of work is kept.

work•day (wûrk′dā′) *n.* **1.** A day on which work is done. **2.** The part of the day during which one works.

work•er (wûr′kər) *n.* **1.** One that works. **2.** One who works for wages. **3.** A sterile female of certain social insects, as the ant or bee, that performs specialized work.

work•horse (wûrk′hôrs′) *n.* **1.** A horse used for labor rather than racing or riding. **2.** One who works tirelessly.

work•house (wûrk′hous′) *n.* **1.** A prison in which limited sentences are served at manual labor. **2.** A former British public institution for the indigent.

work•ing (wûr′kĭng) *adj.* **1.** Employed. **2.** Of, used for, or spent in work. **3.** Sufficient or large enough for using. **4.** Capable of being used as the basis of further work.

work•man (wûrk′mən) *n.* A man who performs some form of labor.

work•man•like (wûrk′mən-līk′) *adj.* Characteristic of a skilled workman or craftsman.

work•man•ship (wûrk′mən-shĭp′) *n.* **1.** The art, skill, or technique of a workman. **2.** The quality of such art, skill, or technique.

work out. 1. To come or make its way out. **2.** To exhaust (a mine, soil, etc.). **3.** To solve. **4.** To formulate or develop. **5.** To have a specified end or result. **6.** To perform exercises.

work•out (wûrk′out′) *n.* **1.** A period of exercise or practice, esp. in athletics. **2.** An exhausting task.

work•room (wûrk′rōōm′, -rŏŏm′) *n.* A room where work is done.

work•shop (wûrk′shŏp′) *n.* **1.** An area, room, or establishment in which manual work is done. **2.** A regularly scheduled seminar in some specialized field.

work•ta•ble (wûrk′tā′bəl) *n.* A table designed for a specific task or activity.

world (wûrld) *n.* **1.** The earth. **2.** The universe. **3.** The earth and its inhabitants collectively. **4.** The human race. **5.** The public. **6.** Often **World.** A particular part of the earth. **7.** Any sphere, realm, domain, or kingdom. **8.** An individual way of life or state of being. **9.** The secular life. **10.** A large amount; much. **11.** A planet or other celestial body. [< OE *world, weorold.* See **wiros.**]

world•ly (wûrld′lē) *adj.* **-lier, -liest. 1.** Not spiritual or religious; secular. **2.** Sophisticated or cosmopolitan; worldly-wise. **—world′li•ness** *n.*

world•ly-wise (wûrld′lē-wīz′) *adj.* Experienced in the ways of the world; sophisticated.

World War I. A war fought from 1914 to 1918, in which Great Britain, France, Russia, the U.S., and other allies defeated Germany, Austria-Hungary, Turkey, and Bulgaria.

World War II. A war fought from 1939 to 1945, in which Great Britain, France, the Soviet Union, the U.S., and other allies defeated Germany, Italy, and Japan.

world•wide (wûrld′wīd′) *adj.* Reaching or extending throughout the world; universal.

worm (wûrm) *n.* **1.** Any of various invertebrates, as an earthworm or tapeworm, having a long, flexible rounded or flattened body. **2.** Any of various insect larvae having a long, soft body. **3.** A contemptible person. **4.** An insidiously tormenting force: *"The worm of conscience still begnaw thy soul!"* (Shakespeare). **5. worms.** Intestinal infestation with worms. *—v.* **1.** To make (one's way) with or as with the sinuous crawling motion of a worm. **2.** To elicit by devious means. **3.** To cure of intestinal worms. [< OE *wyrm,* worm, serpent. See **wer-[3].**] **—worm′y** *adj.*

worm•wood (wûrm'wŏŏd') *n.* An aromatic plant yielding a bitter extract used in making absinthe. [< OE *wermōd* < Gmc **wer-mōd-*.]

worn (wôrn, wōrn). *p.p.* of **wear.** *—adj.* **1.** Affected or impaired by wear or use. **2.** Exhausted; spent. **3.** Trite; hackneyed.

worn-out (wôrn'out', wōrn'-) *adj.* **1.** Worn or used until no longer usable. **2.** Thoroughly exhausted; spent.

wor•ri•some (wûr'ē-səm) *adj.* **1.** Causing worry or anxiety. **2.** Tending to worry.

wor•ry (wûr'ē) *v.* **-ried, -rying.** **1.** To feel uneasy about some uncertain or threatening matter. **2.** To cause to feel anxious, distressed, or troubled. **3. a.** To grasp and tug at repeatedly. **b.** To touch, press, or handle idly. *—n., pl.* **-ries.** **1.** Mental uneasiness or anxiety. **2.** A source of nagging concern. [< OE *wyrgan,* to strangle. See **wer-[3].**] **—wor'ri•er** *n.*

wor•ry•wart (wûr'ē-wôrt') *n. Informal.* One who tends to worry excessively and needlessly.

worse (wûrs). **1.** *compar.* of **bad. 2.** *compar.* of **ill.** *—adj.* **1.** More inferior, as in quality, condition, or effect. **2.** More severe or unfavorable. *—n.* Something that is worse. *—adv.* In a worse way. [< OE *wyrsa.* See **wers-.**]

wors•en (wûr'sən) *v.* To make or become worse.

wor•ship (wûr'shĭp) *n.* **1. a.** The reverent love accorded a deity, idol, or sacred object. **b.** A set of ceremonies or prayers by which this love is expressed. **2.** Ardent devotion. **3.** Often **Worship.** *Chiefly Brit.* A title of honor used in addressing magistrates, mayors, etc. *—v.* **-shiped** or **-shipped, -shiping** or **-shipping.** **1.** To honor and love as a deity. **2.** To love devotedly. **3.** To participate in religious rites of worship. [< OE *weorth,* WORTH + -SHIP.] **—wor'ship•er** *n.*

wor•ship•ful (wûr'shĭp-fəl) *adj.* Given to or expressive of worship; reverent.

worst (wûrst). **1.** *superl.* of **bad. 2.** *superl.* of **ill.** *—adj.* **1.** Most inferior, as in quality, condition, or effect. **2.** Most severe or unfavorable. *—n.* Something that is worst. *—adv.* In the worst manner or degree. *—v.* To gain the advantage over; defeat.

wor•sted (wŏŏs'tĭd, wûr'stĭd) *n.* **1.** Firm-textured, compactly twisted woolen yarn made from long-staple fibers. **2.** Fabric made from such yarn. [< *Worthstede* (now Worstead), a village in England.]

-wort. *comb. form.* A plant: **liverwort.** [< OE *wyrt,* plant, herb.]

worth (wûrth) *n.* **1.** The quality of something that renders it desirable or valuable. **2.** The material value of something. **3.** The quantity of something that can be purchased for a specific sum. **4.** The quality within a person that renders him deserving of respect. *—adj.* **1.** Equal in value to something specified. **2.** Deserving of; meriting. [< OE *weorth.*]

worth•less (wûrth'lĭs) *adj.* Without worth, use, or value. **—worth'less•ness** *n.*

worth•while (wûrth'hwīl') *adj.* Sufficiently valuable or important to justify the expenditure of time or effort.

wor•thy (wûr'*th*ē) *adj.* **-thier, -thiest.** **1.** Having worth, merit, or value. **2.** Honorable; admirable. **3.** Deserving: *worthy of acclaim.* *—n., pl.* **-thies.** A worthy person. **—wor'thi•ly** *adv.* **—wor'thi•ness** *n.*

would (wŏŏd). *p.t.* of **will[2].** See Usage note at **should.**

would-be (wŏŏd'bē') *adj.* Desiring or pretending to be.

would•n't (wŏŏd'ənt). Contraction of *would not.*

wouldst, would•est (wŏŏdst; wŏŏd'ĭst). *Archaic.* 2nd person sing. past tense of **will[2].**

wound[1] (wōōnd) *n.* An injury, esp. one in which the skin is torn, pierced, or cut. *—v.* To inflict a wound or wounds upon. [< OE *wund.* See **wā-.**]

wound[2] (wound). *p.t.* & *p.p.* of **wind[2].**

wove (wōv). *p.t.* & *rare p.p.* of **weave.**

wo•ven (wō'vən). *p.p.* of **weave.**

wow (wou) *interj.* Expressive of wonder, amazement, etc.

w.p.m. words per minute.

wrack (răk) *n.* **1.** Damage or destruction by violent means: *bring to wrack and ruin.* **2.** Seaweed forming a tangled mass. [< OE *wrǣc,* punishment, vengeance, and MDu *wrak,* wreckage, wrecked ship.]

wraith (rāth) *n.* An apparition. [?]

wran•gle (răng'gəl) *v.* **-gled, -gling.** **1.** To dispute noisily or angrily; quarrel. **2.** To win or obtain by argument. **3.** *Western U.S.* To herd horses or other livestock. *—n.* An angry, noisy dispute. [ME *wranglen.*] **—wran'gler** *n.*

wrap (răp) *v.* **wrapped** or **wrapt** (răpt), **wrapping.** **1.** To arrange or fold about in order to cover or protect. **2.** To cover or envelop, as with paper. **3.** To clasp, fold, or coil about or around something. **4.** To immerse in some condition: *wrapped in thought.* *—n.* **1.** A garment to be wrapped or folded about a person. **2.** A wrapping or wrapper. [ME *wrappen.*]

wrap•per (răp'ər) *n.* **1.** One that wraps. **2.** The paper or other material in which something is wrapped. **3.** A loose robe or negligee.

wrap•ping (răp'ĭng) *n.* Also **wrap•pings** (-ĭngz). The material in which something is wrapped.

wrap up. **1.** To work out and complete the details of: *wrap up a business deal.* **2.** To summarize.

wrap-up (răp'ŭp') *n.* A brief summary.

wrath (răth, räth) *n.* **1.** Violent, resentful anger; rage. **2. a.** A manifestation of anger. **b.** Divine retribution. [< OE *wrāth,* angry. See **wer-[3].**] **—wrath'ful** *adj.* **—wrath'ful•ly** *adv.*

wreak (rēk) *v.* **1.** To inflict (vengeance or punishment). **2.** To express or gratify (anger, malevolence, or resentment). [< OE *wrecan,* to drive, expel, vent. See **wreg-.**]

wreath (rēth) *n., pl.* **wreaths** (rē*th*z). **1.** A ring or circlet of flowers or leaves. **2.** Something resembling this: *a wreath of smoke.* [< OE *writha.* See **wer-[3].**]

wreathe (rē*th*) *v.* **wreathed, wreathing.** **1.** To twist or entwine into a wreath. **2.** To crown or decorate with or as with a wreath. **3.** To curl or spiral. **4.** To assume the form of a wreath. [< WREATH.]

wreck (rĕk) *v.* **1.** To destroy accidentally, as by collision. **2.** To tear down or dismantle. **3.** To bring to a state of ruin. *—n.* **1.** The action of wrecking or condition of being wrecked. **2.** The remains of something that has been wrecked or ruined. **3.** Something in a disorderly or worn-out state. [< Scand.]

wreck•age (rĕk'ĭj) *n.* **1.** The act of wrecking or condition of being wrecked. **2.** The debris of anything wrecked.

wreck•er (rĕk'ər) *n.* **1. a.** A member of a wrecking or demolition crew. **b.** One who destroys or ruins. **2.** A vehicle or ship employed in recovering or removing a wreck.

wren (rĕn) *n.* A small, brownish bird usually holding the tail upright. [< OE *wrenna* < Gmc **wrendila-.*]

wrench (rĕnch) *n.* **1.** A sudden, forcible twist or turn. **2.** An injury produced by twisting or straining. **3.** Any of various tools with fixed or adjustable jaws for gripping a nut, bolt, etc., and a long handle for effective leverage. *—v.* **1. a.** To twist or turn suddenly and forcibly. **b.** To twist and sprain. **2.** To pull forcibly. [< OE *wrencan,* to twist. See **wer-[3].**]

wrest (rĕst) *v.* **1.** To obtain by or as by pulling with violent twisting movements. **2.** To usurp: *wrest power.* [< OE *wrǣstan,* to twist. See **wer-[3].**] **—wrest'er** *n.*

wres•tle (rĕs'əl) *v.* **-tled, -tling.** **1.** To contend by grappling and attempting to throw one's opponent, esp. under certain contest rules. **2.** To contend; struggle to master. **3.** To wrestle with. *—n.* An act of wrestling, esp. a wrestling match. [< OE *wrǣstlian.* See **wer-[3].**] **—wres'tler** *n.*

wres•tling (rĕs'lĭng) *n.* A gymnastic contest between two competitors who attempt to throw each other by grappling.

wretch (rĕch) *n.* **1.** A miserable or unfortunate person. **2.** A base or despicable person. [< OE *wrecca,* wretch, exile. See **wreg-.**]

wretch•ed (rĕch'ĭd) *adj.* **1.** Attended by misery and woes. **2.** Of a poor or depressing character: *a wretched building.* **3.** Contemptible. **4.** Inferior in performance or quality. **—wretch'ed•ly** *adv.* **—wretch'ed•ness** *n.*

wrig•gle (rĭg'əl) *v.* **-gled, -gling.** **1.** To turn or twist the body with sinuous motions. **2.** To proceed with sinuous motions. **3.** To insinuate or extricate oneself by sly or subtle means. *—n.* The action or movement of wriggling. [< MLG *wriggeln.*] **—wrig'gly** *adj.*

wrig•gler (rĭg'lər) *n.* The larva of a mosquito.

Wright (rīt). **1. Frank Lloyd.** 1869–1959. American architect. **2. Orville.** 1871–1948. American aviation pioneer and inventor; with his brother, **Wilbur** (1867–1912), made first powered flights in heavier-than-air craft (1903).

wring (rĭng) *v.* **wrung, wringing.** **1. a.** To twist and squeeze. **b.** To compress to extract liquid. **2.** To extract (liquid) by twisting or compressing. **3.** To twist forcibly: *wring one's neck.* **4.** To cause distress to: *wring one's heart.* **5.** To obtain by applying force or pressure to. [< OE *wringan.* See **wer-[3].**]

wring•er (rĭng'ər) *n.* One that wrings, esp. a device in which laundry is pressed or spun to extract water.

wrin•kle[1] (rĭng'kəl) *n.* A small furrow, ridge, or crease on a normally smooth surface. *—v.* **-kled, -kling.** **1.** To make a wrinkle or wrinkles in. **2.** To become wrinkled. [< OE *gewrinclian,* to wind. See **wer-[3].**] **—wrin'kly** *adj.*

wrin•kle[2] (rĭng'kəl) *n. Informal* An ingenious new method; innovation. [< WRINKLE.]

wrist (rĭst) *n.* **1.** The junction between the hand and forearm. **2.** The system of bones forming this junction. [< OE. See **wer-[3].**]

writ (rĭt) *n.* A written order issued by a court, commanding the person to whom it is addressed to perform or cease performing some specified act. [< OE < Gmc **wrītan,* to scratch.]

write (rīt) *v.* **wrote, written, writing.** **1.** To form (letters, words, symbols, etc.) on a surface with a pen, pencil, or other tool. **2.** To compose, esp. as an author or musician. **3.** To relate or communicate by writing. **—write down.** To put into writing. **—write off.** **1.** To cancel from accounts as a loss. **2.** To consider as a failure. [< OE *wrītan* < Gmc **wrītan,* to tear, scratch.]

writ•er (rī'tər) *n.* **1.** One who has written (something specified): *the writer of the note.* **2.** An author.

write-up (rīt'ŭp') *n.* A published account, review, or notice.
writhe (rīth) *v.* **writhed, writhing.** To twist or squirm, as in pain. [< OE *wrīthan.* See **wer-**[3].]
writ•ing (rī'tĭng) *n.* **1.** Written form: *Put it in writing.* **2.** Something written. **3.** Any written work, esp. a literary composition. **4.** The activity, art, or occupation of a writer.
writ•ten (rĭt'n). *p.p.* of **write.**
wrnt. warrant.
wrong (rông, rŏng) *adj.* **1.** Not correct; erroneous. **2.** Contrary to conscience, morality, or law. **3.** Not required, intended, or wanted: *take a wrong turn.* **4.** Not fitting or suitable; improper. **5.** Not in accordance with an established method or procedure. **6.** Out of order; amiss; awry. —*adv.* **1.** In a wrong manner; erroneously. **2.** Immorally or unjustly. —*n.* **1.** That which is wrong; an unjust, injurious, or immoral act. **2.** The condition of being mistaken or to blame: *in the wrong.* —*v.* **1.** To treat unjustly or dishonorably. **2.** To discredit unjustly; malign. [< Scand.] —**wrong'ly** *adv.*
wrong•do•er (rông'dōō'ər, rŏng'-) *n.* One who does wrong. —**wrong'do'ing** *n.*
wrong•ful (rông'fəl, rŏng'-) *adj.* **1.** Wrong; injurious; unjust. **2.** Contrary to law; illegal. —**wrong'ful•ly** *adv.* —**wrong'ful•ness** *n.*
wrote (rōt). *p.t.* of **write.**
wroth (rôth) *adj. Archaic.* Wrathful; angry.
wrought (rôt) *adj.* **1.** Put together: *carefully wrought.* **2.** Shaped by hammering with tools: *wrought iron.* —**wrought up.** Agitated; excited. [< the archaic pt and pp of WORK.]
wrought iron. A very pure easily welded or forged iron containing about 0.2% carbon. —**wrought'-iron'** *adj.*
wrung (rŭng). *p.t.* & *p.p.* of **wring.**
wry (rī) *adj.* **wrier** or **wryer, wriest** or **wryest. 1.** Twisted, as facial features. **2.** Temporarily twisted in an expression of distaste or displeasure: *a wry face.* **3.** Dryly humorous, often with a touch of irony. [< OE *wrigian,* to proceed, turn. See **wer-**[3].] —**wry'ly** *adv.*
WSW west-southwest.
wt. weight.
Wu•han (wōō'hän'). A city of E China. Pop. 2,226,000.
W.Va. West Virginia.
W.W.I World War I.
W.W.II World War II.
Wyc•liffe (wĭk'lĭf), **John.** 1320?–1384. English theologian and religious reformer.
Wy•o•ming (wī-ō'mĭng). A state of the W U.S. Pop. 332,000. Cap. Cheyenne.

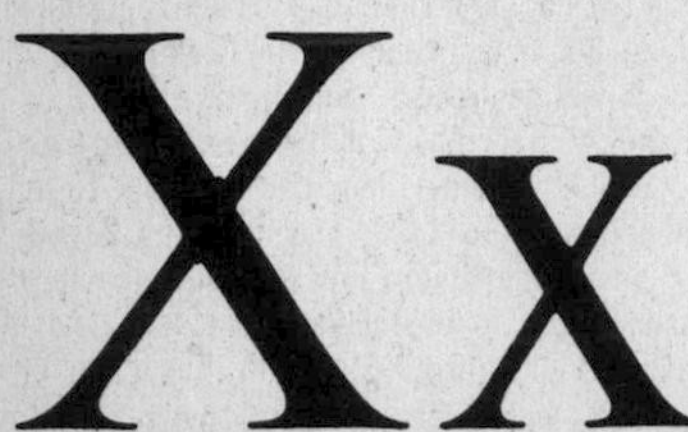

x, X (ĕks) *n.* **1.** The 24th letter of the English alphabet. **2.** Anything shaped like the letter **X.**
x Any unknown or unnamed factor, thing, or person.
X. 1. A symbol for Christ or Christian. **2.** A symbol placed on a map or diagram to mark the location or position of a point.
x-ax•is (ĕks'ăk'sĭs) *n., pl.* **x-axes** (-sēz). The horizontal axis of a two-dimensional Cartesian coordinate system.
X-chro•mo•some (ĕks'krō'mə-sōm') *n.* The sex chromosome associated with female characteristics, occurring paired in the female and single in the male sex-chromosome pair.
Xe xenon.
xe•non (zē'nŏn') *n. Symbol* **Xe** A colorless, odorless, highly unreactive gaseous element found in minute quantities in the atmosphere. Atomic number 54, atomic weight 131.30. [< Gk *xenos,* stranger.]
xen•o•phobe (zĕn'ə-fōb') *n.* One unduly fearful or contemptuous of strangers or foreigners. [< Gk *xenos,* stranger + -PHOBE.] —**xen'o•pho'bi•a** *n.* —**xen'o•pho'bic** *adj.*
xe•rog•ra•phy (zĭ-rŏg'rə-fē) *n.* A dry photographic or photocopying process that transfers images by means of electric charges. [< Gk *xēros,* dry + -GRAPHY.] —**xer'o•graph'ic** (zîr'ə-grăf'ĭk) *adj.*
Xer•ox (zîr'ŏks) *n.* A trademark for a photocopying process or machine using xerography. —*v.* To reproduce by means of a Xerox machine. [< XEROGRAPHY.]
Xerx•es I (zûrk'sēz). 519?–465 B.C. King of Persia (486–465 B.C.).
Xho•sa (kō'sä) *n., pl.* **-sa** or **-sas.** Also **Xo•sa.** One of a Bantu people of the Republic of South Africa.
xi (zī, sī) *n.* The 14th letter in the Greek alphabet, representing *x.*
X•mas (krĭs'məs, ĕks'məs) *n. Informal.* Christmas.
Usage: Xmas occurs principally in commercial writing and is now chiefly appropriate to that level.
x-ra•di•a•tion (ĕks'rā'dē-ā'shən) *n.* **1.** Treatment with or exposure to x rays. **2.** Radiation composed of x rays.
x ray. 1. a. A relatively high-energy photon with a very short wavelength. **b.** Often **x rays.** A stream of such photons. **2.** Also **X ray.** A photograph taken with x rays. —**x'-ray'** *adj.*
x-ray (ĕks'rā') *v.* To examine or photograph by means of x rays.
xy•lo•phone (zī'lə-fōn') *n.* A musical percussion instrument consisting of a mounted row of wooden bars graduated in length to sound a chromatic scale, played with two small mallets. [< Gk *xulon,* wood + -PHONE.] —**xy'lo•phon'ist** *n.*

y, Y (wī) *n.* **1.** The 25th letter of the English alphabet. **2. Y.** Anything shaped like the letter **Y.**
y ordinate.
Y yttrium.
y. year.
-y[1], **-ey.** *comb. form.* **1.** The existence or possession of what is expressed in the root: **cloudy. 2.** A relationship to what is expressed in the root: **watery.** [< OE *-ig, -ǣg* < Gmc **-iga.*]
-y[2]. *comb. form.* **1.** A condition or quality: **jealousy. 2.** An activity, products dealt with, or a place of business: **cookery.** [< L *-ia.*]
-y[3], **-ey.** *comb. form.* **1.** Smallness: **doggy. 2.** Endearment: **daddy.** [ME *-ie.*]
yacht (yät) *n.* A small sailing or mechanically propelled vessel, used for pleasure cruises or racing. —*v.* To race, sail, or cruise in a yacht. [< obs Du *jaght(schip),* "chasing (ship)."]
yachts•man (yäts'mən) *n.* One who owns or sails a yacht. —**yachts'man•ship'** *n.*
ya•hoo (yä'hōō, yā'-) *n.* A crude or brutish person. [< the *Yahoos,* a race of human beings in Swift's *Gulliver's Travels.*]
Yah•weh (yä'wĕ). Also **Jah•weh.** A name for God, commonly rendered Jehovah.
yak (yăk) *n.* A long-haired bovine mammal of the mountains of C Asia. [Tibetan *gyag.*]
yam (yăm) *n.* **1.** The starchy, edible root of a tropical vine. **2.** A sweet potato with reddish flesh. [Port *inhame,* "edible."]
Yang•tze (yăng'tsē'). A river of C China.
yank (yăngk) *v.* To pull or extract suddenly; jerk. —*n.* A sudden vigorous pull; a jerk. [?]
Yank (yăngk) *n. Informal.* Yankee.
Yan•kee (yăng'kē) *n.* **1.** A native or inhabitant

of New England. 2. A native or inhabitant of a N state. 3. A native or inhabitant of the U.S. [Poss < the Du name *Janke.*] —**Yan'kee** *adj.*

Ya•oun•dé (yä-o͞on-dā'). The capital of Cameroon. Pop. 178,000.

yap (yăp) *v.* **yapped, yapping.** 1. To bark sharply or shrilly; yelp. 2. *Slang.* To talk noisily or stupidly; jabber. —*n.* A sharp, shrill bark; yelp. [Imit.] —**yap'per** *n.*

yard[1] (yärd) *n.* 1. A measure of length equal to 3 feet or 0.9144 meter. 2. A long spar slung at right angles to a mast to support a sail. [< OE *gerd, gierd,* staff, measuring rod. See **ghasto-**.]

yard[2] (yärd) *n.* 1. A tract of ground adjacent to a building. 2. An enclosed area used for a specific purpose: *shipyard.* 3. An area where railroad trains are made up and cars are switched, stored, or serviced. [< OE *geard,* enclosure, residence. See **gher-**[2].]

yard•age (yär'dĭj) *n.* The amount or length of something measured in yards.

yard•arm (yärd'ärm') *n.* Either end of a yard of a square sail.

yard•stick (yärd'stĭk') *n.* 1. A measuring stick one yard in length. 2. Any standard used in comparison or judgment.

yar•mul•ke (yä'məl-kə) *n.* Also **yar•mel•ke.** A skullcap worn by male Jews. [Yidd.]

yarn (yärn) *n.* 1. A continuous strand of twisted threads of wool, cotton, etc., used in weaving or knitting. 2. *Informal.* A long story or tale. [< OE *gearn.* See **gher-**[1].]

yaw (yô) *v.* 1. To deviate from the intended course, as a ship. 2. To turn about the vertical axis. —*n.* The action or extent of yawing. [?]

yawl (yôl) *n.* A two-masted fore-and-aft-rigged sailing vessel with a smaller mast aft of the mainmast and tiller. [MLG *jolle.*]

yawn (yôn) *v.* 1. To open the mouth wide with a deep inspiration, from drowsiness or boredom. 2. To open wide; gape. —*n.* An act of yawning. [< OE *geonian.* See **ghēi-**.]

yaws (yôz) *pl.n.* An infectious tropical skin disease characterized by multiple red pimples. [Cariban.]

y-ax•is (wī'ăk'sĭs) *n., pl.* **y-axes** (-sēz). The vertical axis of a two-dimensional Cartesian coordinate system.

Yb ytterbium.

Y-chro•mo•some (wī'krō'mə-sôm') *n.* The sex chromosome associated with male characteristics, occurring with one X-chromosome in the male sex-chromosome pair.

y•clept (ĭ-klĕpt') *adj. Archaic.* Known as; named; called. [< OE *cleopian,* to speak, call.]

yd yard (measurement).

ye[1] (*th*ē) *adj. Archaic.* The. [Incorrect transcription of the runic letter thorn as *th.*]

ye[2] (yē) *pron. Poetic & Archaic.* You (plural). [< OE *gē.* See **yu-**.]

yea (yā) *adv.* Yes; aye. —*n.* 1. An affirmative vote. 2. One who votes affirmatively. [< OE *gēa,* yes.]

yeah (yĕ'ə, yă'ə, yā'ə) *adv. Informal.* Yes. [Var of YEA.]

year (yîr) *n.* 1. The period of time as measured by the Gregorian calendar in which the earth completes a single revolution around the sun, consisting of 365 days, 5 hours, 49 minutes, and 12 seconds of mean solar time divided into 12 months, 52 weeks, and 365 or 366 days. 2. A period of time, usually shorter than 12 months, devoted to some special activity: *the school year.* 3. **years. a.** Age, esp. old age. **b.** A long time. [< OE *gēar.* See **yēro-**.]

year•book (yîr'bo͝ok') *n.* A book published every year, containing information about the previous year.

year•ling (yîr'lĭng) *n.* An animal that is one year old or in its second year.

year•ly (yîr'lē) *adj.* Occurring once a year or every year; annual. —*adv.* Once a year.

yearn (yûrn) *v.* To have a strong or deep desire. [< OE *giernan,* to desire. See **gher-**[5].]

yearn•ing (yûr'nĭng) *n.* A deep longing.

yeast (yēst) *n.* 1. Any of various unicellular fungi capable of fermenting carbohydrates. 2. Froth produced by and containing yeast cells, formed in the production of alcoholic beverages. 3. A commercial preparation containing yeast cells, used esp. as a leavening agent. [< OE *gist, gyst.* See **yes-**.]

yell (yĕl) *v.* To cry out loudly, as in pain, fright, surprise, or enthusiasm. —*n.* A loud cry; a shout. [< OE *giellan,* to sound, shout. See **ghel-**[1].]

yel•low (yĕl'ō) *n.* 1. Any of a group of colors of a hue resembling that of ripe lemons. 2. The yolk of an egg. —*adj.* 1. Of the color yellow. 2. Having yellowish skin. 3. *Slang.* Cowardly. 4. Distorting or exaggerating news sensationally: *yellow journalism.* —*v.* To make or become yellow. [< OE *geolu.* See **ghel-**[2].] —**yel'low•ish** *adj.*

yellow fever. An acute infectious viral disease of subtropical and tropical New World areas, transmitted by a mosquito.

yellow jacket. A small wasp with yellow and black markings.

Yellow Sea. An arm of the Pacific between China and Korea.

yelp (yĕlp) *v.* To utter a sharp, short bark or cry. —*n.* A sharp, short cry or bark. [< OE *gielpan,* to boast, exult. See **ghel-**[1].]

Yem•en (yĕm'ən, yā'mən). 1. Officially, Yemen Arab Republic. A country of S Arabia, at the S entrance to the Red Sea. Pop. 5,237,900. Cap. Sana. 2. Or **Southern Yemen.** Officially, People's Democratic Republic of Yemen. A country of S Arabia. Pop. 1,555,000. Cap. Aden.

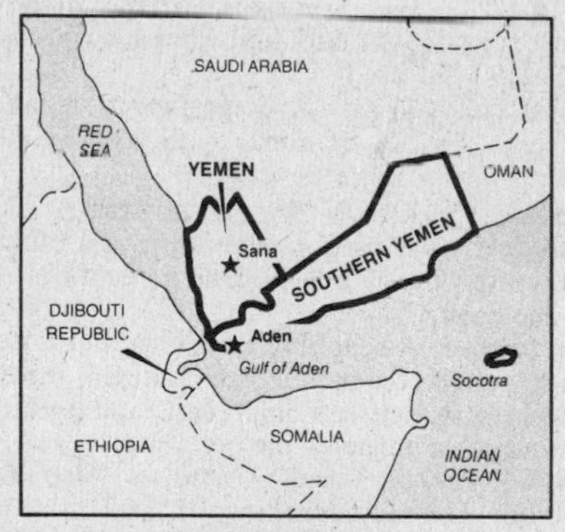

Yemen
Southern Yemen

yen[1] (yĕn) *n. Informal.* A yearning; a longing. [Cant *yan.*]

yen[2] (yĕn) *n., pl.* **yen.** The basic monetary unit of Japan.

yeo•man (yō'mən) *n.* 1. A member of a former class of lesser freeholder farmers, below the gentry, in England. 2. A petty officer performing chiefly clerical duties in the U.S. Navy. [Perh < YOUNG + MAN.]

Ye•re•van (yĭ-ryĭ-vän'). The capital of the Armenian S.S.R. Pop. 767,000.

yes (yĕs) *adv.* It is so; as you say or ask. Expressive of affirmation, agreement, or consent. —*n.* An affirmative reply or vote. [< OE *gēa,* YEA + *sīe,* "may it be" (see **es-**).]

yes•ter•day (yĕs'tər-dā', -dē) *n.* 1. The day before the present day. 2. Time recently past. —*adv.* 1. On the day before the present day. 2. A short while ago.

yet (yĕt) *adv.* 1. At this time; now. 2. Thus far. 3. In the time remaining; still. 4. Besides; in addition. 5. Even; still more: *a yet sadder tale.* 6. Nevertheless: *young yet wise.* 7. At some future time; eventually. —*conj.* Nevertheless; and despite this. [< OE *giet.*]

Usage: *Yet,* as an adverb of time in the sense *up to the present, thus far,* or in the phrase *as yet,* occurs with a perfect tense rather than with the simple past: *They have not started yet.*

yew (yo͞o) *n.* 1. An evergreen tree or shrub with poisonous flat, dark-green needles and scarlet berries. 2. The hard, fine-grained wood of a yew. [< OE *ēow, īw.*]

Yid•dish (yĭd'ĭsh) *n.* A language derived from High German dialects and Hebrew and some Slavic languages.

yield (yēld) *v.* 1. To give forth by a natural process; produce. 2. To furnish or give in return: *an investment that yields 6%.* 3. To relinquish or concede. 4. To surrender; submit. 5. To give way, as to pressure, force, or persuasion. —*n.* 1. The amount yielded. 2. The profit obtained from investment; a return. [< OE *gieldan,* to yield, pay.]

-yl. *comb. form. Chem.* A radical: **ethyl.** [< Gk *hulē,* wood, matter.]

yod (yōd, yo͝od) *n.* Also **yodh.** The 10th letter of the Hebrew alphabet, representing *y.*

yo•ga (yō'gə) *n.* 1. A Hindu discipline aimed at training the consciousness for a state of perfect spiritual insight. 2. A system of exercises practiced as part of this discipline.

yo•gurt (yō'gərt, -go͝ort') *n.* Also **yo•ghurt.** A custardlike food prepared from milk curdled by bacteria. [Turk *yoğurt.*]

yoke (yōk) *n.* 1. A crossbar with two U-shaped pieces that encircle the necks of a pair of draft animals. 2. *pl.* **yoke.** A pair of draft animals joined by such a device. 3. A fitted part of a garment, as at the shoulders, to which another part is attached. 4. Any form or symbol of subjugation or bondage. —*v.* **yoked, yoking.** 1. To fit or join with or as with a yoke. 2. To harness (a draft animal) to something. [< OE *geoc.* See **yeug-**.]

Yo•ko•ha•ma (yō'kə-hä'mə). A city of Japan in C Honshu. Pop. 1,619,000.

yolk (yōk) *n.* The yellow inner mass of nutritive material in the egg of a bird or reptile. [< OE *geolu,* YELLOW.]

Yom Kip•pur (yŏm' kĭp'ər, yōm' kĭ-po͝or'). The holiest Jewish holiday, observed by fasting and prayer for the atonement of sins.

yon•der (yŏn'dər) *adj.* Being at an indicated distance, usually within sight. —*adv.* Over there. [< OE *geond.*]

yore (yôr, yōr) *n.* Time long past: *days of yore.* [< OE *gēara,* formerly, once.]

you (yo͞o) *pron.* The 2nd person sing. or pl. in the nominative or objective case, used to represent the person or persons addressed by the speaker. [< OE *ēow.* See **yu-**.]

you'd (yo͞od). Contraction of *you had* or *you would.*

you'll (yo͞ol). Contraction of *you will* or *you shall.*

young (yŭng) *adj.* 1. In the early period of life or development; not old. 2. Vigorous or fresh. —*n.* 1. Young persons collectively; youth. 2. Offspring. [< OE *geong.* See **yeu-**.]

young•ster (yŭng′stər) *n.* A young person.
Youngs•town (yŭngz′toun). A city of NE Ohio. Pop. 165,000.
your (yŏŏr, yôr, yōr; *unstressed* yər). The possessive form of the pronoun *you,* used attributively. [< OE *ēower.* See **yu-**.]
you're (yŏŏr; *unstressed* yər). Contraction of *you are.*
yours (yŏŏrz, yôrz, yōrz). The possessive form of the pronoun *you,* used as a predicate adjective, a substantive, and in the complimentary closing of letters: *This hat is yours. I like yours better. Yours very truly.* **—of yours.** Belonging to you: *a friend of yours.*
your•self (yŏŏr-sĕlf′, yōr-, yər-) *pron., pl.* **-selves.** A form of the 2nd person pronoun. **1.** Used reflexively: *Did you hurt yourself?* **2.** Used for emphasis: *Do it yourself.* **3.** Used to indicate one's normal or proper state: *You are not yourself today.* **—by yourself. 1.** Alone. **2.** Without help.
youth (yōōth) *n., pl.* **youths** (yōōths, yōōthz). **1.** The condition or quality of being young. **2.** An early period of development or existence. **3. a.** Young people collectively. **b.** A young man. [< OE *geoguth.* See **yeu-**.]
youth•ful (yōōth′fəl) *adj.* **1.** Possessing youth. **2.** Vigorous; active. **3.** Of or belonging to youth. **4.** In an early stage of development; new. **—youth′ful•ness** *n.*
you've (yōōv). Contraction of *you have.*
yowl (youl) *v.* To howl; wail. *—n.* A howl; a wail. [ME *youlen.*]
yr. 1. year. **2.** your.
yt•ter•bi•um (ĭ-tûr′bē-əm) *n. Symbol* **Yb** A soft, bright, silvery rare-earth element used as an x-ray source for portable irradiation devices, in some laser materials, and in some special alloys. Atomic number 70, atomic weight 173.04. [< *Ytterby,* town in Sweden.] **—yt•ter′bic** (ĭ-tûr′bĭk) *adj.*
yt•tri•um (ĭt′rē-əm) *n. Symbol* **Y** A silvery metallic element used to increase the strength of magnesium and aluminum alloys. Atomic number 39, atomic weight 88.905. [< *Ytterby,* town in Sweden.]
yu•an (yü′än′) *n.* **1.** The basic monetary unit of China. **2.** The basic monetary unit of Taiwan.
yuc•ca (yŭk′ə) *n.* Any of various tall New World plants with a large cluster of white flowers. [Span *yuca.*]
Yu•go•sla•vi•a (yōō′gō-slä′vĭ-ə). A republic of SE Europe. Pop. 19,279,000. Cap. Belgrade. **—Yu′go•slav′** *n.* **—Yu′go•sla′vi•an** *adj.* & *n.*

Yugoslavia

Yu•kon River (yōō′kŏn). A river of NW North America.
Yule (yōōl) *n.* Christmas. [< OE *gēol,* originally a twelve-day heathen feast < Gmc **jehwla-.*]
Yule•tide (yōōl′tīd′) *n.* The Christmas season.
yum•my (yŭm′ē) *adj.* **-mier, -miest.** *Informal.* Delightful; delicious.

Zz

z, Z (zē) *n.* The 26th letter of the English alphabet.
z. 1. zero. **2.** zone.
zaire (zä-îr′) *n.* The basic monetary unit of Zaire. [Native word in Zaire.]
Zaire (zä-îr′). Formerly **Democratic Republic of the Congo.** A republic and former Belgian colony in west-central Africa. Pop. 21,638,000. Cap. Kinshasa.

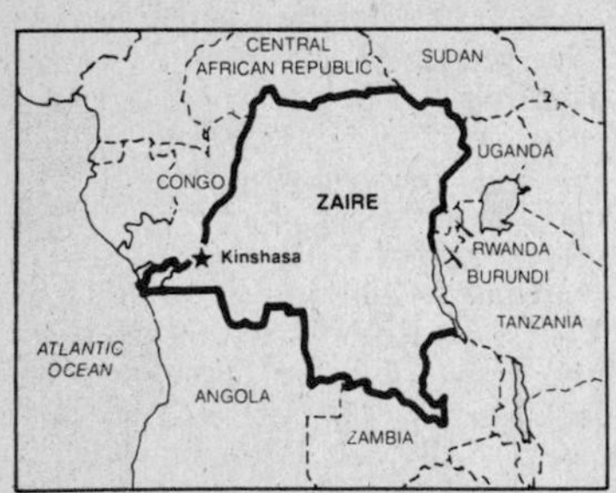

Zaire

Zam•be•zi (zăm-bē′zē). A river of S Africa.
Zam•bi•a (zăm′bē-ə). A republic in south-central Africa. Pop. 3,733,000. Cap. Lusaka.
za•ny (zā′nē) *n., pl.* **-nies.** A clown; buffoon. *—adj.* **-nier, -niest. 1.** Clownish; droll. **2.** Silly; absurd. [It *zani,* buffoon.]
Za•ra•thus•tra (zăr′ə-thōōs′trə, zä′rä-thōōs′-trä). Zoroaster.
za•yin (zä′yĭn) *n.* The 7th letter of the Hebrew alphabet, representing *z.*
zeal (zēl) *n.* Enthusiastic and diligent devotion, as to a cause. [< Gk *zēlos.*]
zeal•ot (zĕl′ət) *n.* One who is fanatically committed, as to a cause.
zeal•ous (zĕl′əs) *adj.* Filled with zeal; enthusiastic; fervent. **—zeal′ous•ly** *adv.*
ze•bra (zē′brə) *n.* A horselike African mammal with conspicuous dark and whitish stripes. [< OSpan, wild ass.]
ze•bu (zē′byōō′) *n.* A domesticated Asian or African bovine mammal with a prominent hump and a large dewlap.
zed (zĕd) *n. Chiefly Brit.* The letter *z.*
Zeit•geist (tsīt′gīst′) *n.* The spirit and outlook characteristic of a period or generation. [G, "time spirit."]
Zen (zĕn) *n.* A school of Buddhism that asserts that enlightenment can be attained through meditation, self-contemplation, and intuition rather than through the scriptures.
Zend-A•ves•ta (zĕnd′ə-vĕs′tə) *n.* Also **Zend** (zĕnd). The sacred writings of the Zoroastrian religion.

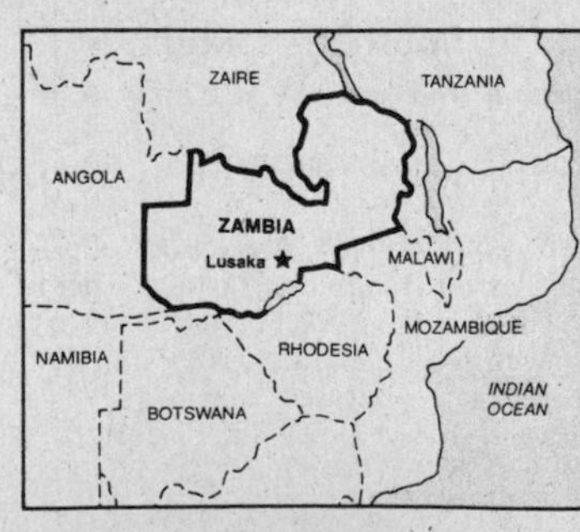

Zambia

ze•nith (zē′nĭth) *n.* **1.** The point on the celestial sphere that is directly above the observer. **2.** The highest point above the observer's horizon attained by a celestial body. **3.** Any culmination or high point. [< Ar *samt,* road.] **—ze′nith•al** (-nə-thəl) *adj.*
Zeph. Zephaniah (Old Testament).
zeph•yr (zĕf′ər) *n.* **1.** The west wind. **2.** A gentle breeze. **3.** Any of various light, soft fabrics or yarns. [< Gk *zephuros.*]
zep•pe•lin (zĕp′ə-lĭn) *n.* Also **Zep•pe•lin.** A rigid airship having a long, cylindrical body supported by internal gas cells. [< Count Ferdinand von *Zeppelin* (1838–1917), German military leader.]
ze•ro (zîr′ō, zē′rō) *n., pl.* **-ros** or **-roes. 1.** The numerical symbol "0"; a cipher; naught. **2.** *Math.* **a.** An element of a set that when added to any other element in the set produces a sum identical with the element to which it is added. **b.** A cardinal number indicating the absence of any or all units under consideration. **c.** An ordinal number indicating an initial point or origin. **3.** The temperature indicated by the numeral 0 on a thermometer. **4.** A nonentity; nobody. **5.** The lowest point. **6.** Nothing; nil. *—v.* **-roed, -roing. —zero in. 1.** To aim or concentrate firepower on an exact target location. **2.** To converge intently; move near; close in. [< Ar *ṣifr,* zero, CIPHER.]
zero hour. The scheduled time for the start of an operation or action, esp. a concerted military attack.
zero population growth. The limiting of population increase to the number of live births needed to replace the existing population,

estimated at 2.11 children per family.

zest (zĕst) *n.* **1.** Piquancy; charm. **2.** Spirited enjoyment; gusto. [Obs F, orange or lemon peel.] **—zest'ful** *adj.*

ze•ta (zā'tə, zē'-) *n.* The 6th letter of the Greek alphabet, representing *z.*

Zeus (zōōs). Supreme god of the Greek pantheon.

zig•zag (zĭg'zăg') *n.* **1.** A line or course that proceeds by sharp turns in alternating directions. **2.** One of a series of such turns. **3.** Something exhibiting one or a series of sharp turns, as a road or design. *—adj.* Having or moving in a zigzag. *—adv.* In a zigzag manner or pattern. *—v.* **-zagged, -zagging.** To form into or move in a zigzag.

zinc (zĭngk) *n. Symbol* **Zn** A bluish-white, lustrous metallic element used to form a wide variety of alloys, including brass, bronze, and various solders, and in galvanizing iron and other metals. Atomic number 30, atomic weight 65.37. [G *Zink.*]

zinc ointment. A salve consisting of about 20% zinc oxide with beeswax or paraffin and petrolatum.

zinc oxide. An amorphous white or yellowish powder, ZnO, used as a pigment and in pharmaceuticals and cosmetics.

zing (zĭng) *n.* A brief high-pitched humming or buzzing sound. [Imit.] **—zing** *v.*

zin•ni•a (zĭn'ē-ə) *n.* A widely cultivated plant with showy, variously colored flowers. [< J. *Zinn* (1727–1759), German botanist.]

Zi•on (zī'ən) *n.* Also **Si•on** (sī'ən). **1. a.** The Jewish people; Israel. **b.** The Jewish homeland as a symbol of Judaism. **2.** A place or religious community regarded as a city of God. **3.** A utopia. [< Heb *Ṣīyōn.*]

Zi•on•ism (zī'ən-ĭz'əm) *n.* **1.** A plan or movement of the Jewish people to return to Palestine. **2.** A movement for the re-establishment of a Jewish national homeland and state in Palestine. **—Zi'on•ist** *adj.* & *n.*

zip (zĭp) *n.* **1.** A brief sharp, hissing sound. **2.** Alacrity; vim. *—v.* **zipped, zipping. 1.** To move or act swiftly. **2.** To fasten or unfasten with a zipper. [Imit.]

zip gun. A crude homemade pistol.

zip•per (zĭp'ər) *n.* A fastening device consisting of rows of teeth on adjacent edges of an opening that are interlocked by a sliding tab.

zir•con (zûr'kŏn') *n.* A brown to colorless mineral, essentially $ZrSiO_4$, that is heated, cut, and polished to form a brilliant blue-white gem. [< Pers *zargūn,* gold-colored.]

zir•co•ni•um (zûr-kō'nē-əm) *n. Symbol* **Zr** A lustrous, grayish-white, strong, ductile metallic element used chiefly in ceramic and refractory compounds, as an alloying agent, and in nuclear reactors. Atomic number 40, atomic weight 91.22. [< ZIRCON.]

zith•er (zĭth'ər) *n.* Also **zith•ern** (-ərn). A musical instrument constructed of a flat sounding box with about 30 to 40 strings stretched over it and played with the finger tips or a plectrum. [< Gk *kithara,* an ancient musical instrument.] **—zith'er•ist** *n.*

zlo•ty (zlô'tē) *n., pl.* **-tys** or **-ty.** The basic monetary unit of Poland.

Zn zinc.

zo•di•ac (zō'dē-ăk') *n.* **1.** A band of the celestial sphere, extending about 8° to either side of the ecliptic, that represents the path of the principal planets, the moon, and the sun. **2.** *Astrol.* This band divided into 12 equal parts called signs each bearing the name of the constellation for which it was named. **3.** A diagram or figure representing the zodiac. [< Gk *zōidiakos (kuklos),* "(circle) of carved figures."] **—zo•di'a•cal** (zō-dī'ə-kəl) *adj.*

-zoic. *comb. form.* A specific geological division: **Mesozoic.** [< Gk *zōion,* animal.]

Zo•la (zō-lä'), **Emile.** 1840–1902. French novelist.

Zom•ba (zŏm'bə). A former interim capital of Malawi. Pop. 20,000.

zom•bie (zŏm'bē) *n.* Also **zom•bi** *pl.* **-bis. 1.** A voodoo snake god. **2. a.** A spell that according to voodoo belief can reanimate a dead body. **b.** A corpse revived in this way. **3.** One who looks or behaves like an automaton.

zo•nal (zō'nəl) *adj.* Also **zo•na•ry** (zō'nər-ē). **1.** Of or associated with a zone or zones. **2.** Divided into zones. **—zo'nal•ly** *adv.*

zone (zōn) *n.* **1.** An area, region, or division distinguished from adjacent parts by some distinctive feature or character. **2.** Any of the five regions of the surface of the earth that are loosely divided according to prevailing climate and latitude, including the Torrid Zone, the N and S Temperate Zones, and the N and S Frigid Zones. **3.** Any section or division of an area or territory. [< Gk *zōnē.*]

zoo (zōō) *n.* Also **zoological garden.** A park or institution in which living animals are kept and exhibited to the public. [Short for zoological garden.]

zoo-. *comb. form.* Animals or animal forms. [< Gk *zōion,* living being, animal.]

zool. zoological; zoology.

zo•o•log•i•cal (zō'ə-lŏj'ĭ-kəl) *adj.* Also **zo•o•log•ic** (-ə-lŏj'ĭk). Of or pertaining to animal life or the science of zoology. **—zo'o•log'i•cal•ly** *adv.*

zo•ol•o•gy (zō-ŏl'ə-jē) *n.* The biological science of animals. **—zo•ol'o•gist** *n.*

zoom (zōōm) *v.* **1.** To move with a buzzing sound. **2.** To climb suddenly and sharply in an airplane. **3.** To move about rapidly; swoop. [Imit.] **—zoom** *n.*

-zoon. *comb. form.* An individual animal or organic unit: **spermatozoon.** [< Gk *zōion, zōon,* living being, animal.]

Zo•ro•as•ter (zôr'ō-ăs'tər). Persian prophet of the 6th century B.C. **—Zo'ro•as'tri•an** *adj.* & *n.* **—Zo'ro•as'tri•an•ism'** (-trē-ən-ĭz'əm) *n.*

zounds (zoundz) *interj.* Expressive of anger, surprise, or indignation. [Euphemism for *God's wounds.*]

Zr zirconium.

zuc•chi•ni (zōō-kē'nē) *n., pl.* **-ni.** A narrow, green-skinned variety of squash. [< It *zucca,* gourd.]

Zu•lu (zōō'lōō) *n., pl.* **-lu** or **-lus. 1.** A member of a large Bantu nation of SE Africa. **2.** The Bantu language of this people. **—Zu'lu** *adj.*

Zu•ñi (zōōn'y/ē, sōō'-) *n., pl.* **-ñi** or **-ñis. 1.** A member of a pueblo-dwelling tribe of North American Indians of W New Mexico. **2.** The language used by this tribe.

Zu•ñi•an (zōōn'yē-ən, sōōn'yē-) *n.* A distinct language family made up of Zuñi alone.

zy•go•mat•ic bone (zī'gə-măt'ĭk). A small quadrangular bone in vertebrates on the side of the face below the eye.

zy•gote (zī'gōt') *n.* **1.** The cell formed by the union of two gametes. **2.** The organism that develops from such a cell. [Gk *zugōtos,* joined, yoked.] **—zy•got'ic** (zī-gŏt'ĭk) *adj.*

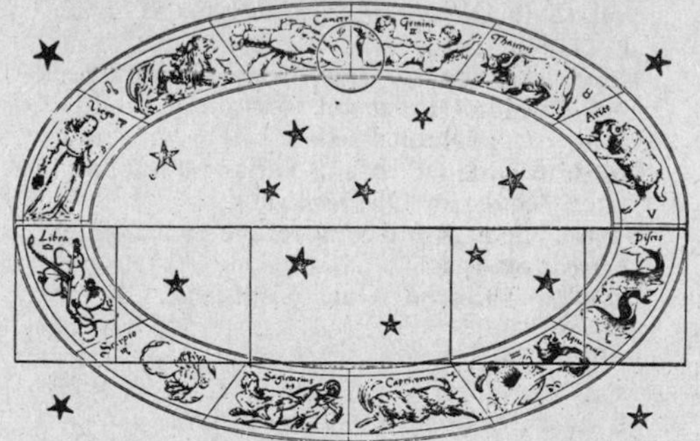

zodiac

APPENDIX OF INDO-EUROPEAN ROOTS

Some of the etymologies in the main body of the Dictionary make cross-references in boldface type to entries in this Appendix, which is drawn from the fully explained Appendix in the hard-bound edition of *The American Heritage Dictionary.*

The Appendix selectively represents the prehistoric ancestry of the English language. English, together with most of the languages of Europe and a number of others (see the chart on pages 362–3), is descended from a reconstructed language called *Indo-European.* This language probably belongs to the neolithic period, but the culture in which it was spoken has not been archaeologically identified. The linguistic reconstruction, however, based on 150 years of scholarly work, is firm and intricate.

The fundamental relationship of Indo-European to English is hereditary. Thus, the Indo-European word (or root) for "field" was **agro-;* this, in the Germanic branch of the family (to which English belongs), changed to **akraz,* which in Old English changed to *æcer,* becoming ACRE in Modern English. This word is thus part of the *native* vocabulary, which has been in unbroken use, though with regularly changing phonetic forms, for at least 6,000 years. This Appendix lists a selection of such native words. The histories of the English words that have been borrowed from other Indo-European languages, chiefly from Germanic and Romance and from Latin and Greek, are not traced here.

Each boldface entry is an Indo-European root, followed by its meaning. If the meaning is enclosed in quotation marks, it is to be taken as an approximate abstraction rather than a precise meaning. Next, usually, comes a Germanic descendant of the root, then an Old English descendant of the Germanic form. Meanings are given to these only if they differ markedly from that of the root. Following the Old English word is the Modern English form in SMALL CAPITALS. Each of these is a cross-reference to the etymology of the word in the main body of the Dictionary.

Homographic roots are given superscript numbers. When one of these numbers differs from the number given in the hard-bound edition of *The American Heritage Dictionary* (abbreviated AHD), the latter is given in brackets at the end of the entry.

An asterisk is placed before every unattested form (one that is not found in documents but has been reconstructed) except for the entry forms. Technical terms have been used as sparingly as possible in this Appendix. An o-grade form is one in which an *e* has changed to an *o,* and a zero-grade form is one in which an *e* has dropped out or an *ā* or an *ē* has been reduced to *ə* (schwa).

abel-. Apple. Gmc **aplu-,* **apal-,* in OE *æppel:* APPLE.

ad-. To, near, at. Gmc **at* in OE *æt:* AT.

agh-[1]. To be depressed or afraid. Gmc **ag-* in OE *eglan,* to afflict: AIL.

agh-[2]. A day. Gmc **dagaz* (initial *d-* obscure) in: **a.** OE *dæg:* DAY; **b.** OE *dagian,* to dawn: DAWN.

agro-. Field. Gmc **akraz* in OE *æcer:* ACRE.

agwesī. Ax. Gmc **akwesī* in OE *æx:* AX.

ais-. To wish. Gmc **aiskōn* in OE *āscian, ācsian:* ASK.

aiw-. Life, long life, eternity. Gmc **aiwi* in: **a.** OE *ā,* ever: NO[1]; **b.** OE *ǣfre,* ever: EVER.

ak-. Sharp. **1.** Gmc **akjō* in OE *ecg,* sharp side: EDGE. **2.** Gmc **ahuz* in OE *ēar, æhher,* ear of grain: EAR[2].

akwā-. Water. Gmc **ahwjō,* **aujō,* "thing on the water," in OE *īegland (land,* LAND*):* ISLAND.

al-[1]. Beyond. Gmc **aljaz* in OE *elles:* ELSE.

al-[2]. To grow. Gmc **alda-,* "grown," in OE *eald,* old: OLD. [AHD *al-[3].*]

alu-. Intoxication. Gmc **aluth-* in OE *ealu,* ale: ALE.

ambhi. Around. Reduced form **bhi* in Gmc **bi* in OE *bī, bi, be:* BY.

an[1]. On. Gmc **ana* in OE *an, on:* ON.

an[2]. Demonstrative particle. Gmc **antharaz* in OE *ōther:* OTHER.

ank-. Also **ang-.** To bend. **1.** Gmc **ank-* in OE *anclēow* (and ON **ankula*): ANKLE. **2.** Gmc **ang-* in OE *angul,* fishhook: ANGLE[1].

anti. Against or in front of; also, an end. **1.** Gmc **andi-* in OE *and-:* UN-[2]. **2.** Gmc **andjō* in OE *ende,* end: END.

apo-. Also **ap-.** Off, away. **1.** Gmc **af* in: **a.** OE *of,* off: OF, OFF; **b.** OE *ebba,* low tide: EBB. **2.** Gmc **aftar-* in OE *æfter:* AFTER. **3.** Variant **ēp-* in Gmc **eben-,* "the after or later time," in OE *ǣfen,* evening: EVENING.

apsā. Aspen. Gmc **aspōn* in OE *æspe:* ASPEN.

arkw-. Bow and arrow. Gmc **arhwō* in OE *arwe, earh:* ARROW.

as-. To burn. Gmc **askōn-* in OE *æsce:* ASH[1].

aug-. To increase. **1.** Gmc **aukan* in OE *ēacan,* to increase: EKE. **2.** Variant forms **wogs-,* **wegs-,* in Gmc **wahsan* in: **a.** OE *weaxan,* to grow: WAX[2]; **b.** OE **wæst,* growth, size: WAIST. [AHD *aug-[1].*]

aukwh-. Also **aukw-.** Cooking pot. Gmc **uhwna-* in **ufna-* in OE *ofen:* OVEN.

awes-. Also **aus-.** To shine. **1.** Gmc **aust-* in OE *ēast:* EAST. **2.** Gmc **austrōn-,* dawn goddess worshiped at the vernal equinox, in OE *ēastre:* EASTER.

ayer-. Day, morning. **1.** Gmc **airiz* in OE *ǣr,* before: EARLY, ERE. **2.** Gmc **airistaz* in OE *ǣrest,* earliest: ERST.

ayos-. A metal. Variant **ayes-* in Gmc **aiz* in OE *ār,* brass: ORE.

bend-. Protruding point. Gmc **pannja,* "structure of stakes," in OE *penn:* PEN[2].

beu-. Also **bheu-.** To swell. **1.** Gmc **puk-* in OE *pocc,* pustule: POCK. **2.** Form **bheu-* in: **a.** OE *bōsm:* BOSOM; **b.** OE *býle:* BOIL[2]. [AHD *beu-[1].*]

bhā-[1]. To shine. Gmc **baukna-,* beacon, signal, in: **a.** OE *bēacen:* BEACON; **b.** OE *bēcnan:* BECKON.

bhā-[2]. To speak. Gmc **banwan,* "to speak publicly," in OE *bannan,* to summon (and ON *banna,* to prohibit): BAN.

bha-bhā-. Broad bean. Variant **bha-un-* in Gmc **baunō* in OE *bēan:* BEAN.

bhad-. Good. Gmc comparative **batizō* in OE *betera:* BETTER.

bhāghu-. Elbow. Gmc **bōguz* in OE *bōg:* BOUGH.

bhāgo-. Beech tree. **1.** Gmc **bōkō,* "beech staff for carving runes on," in OE *bōc:* BOOK. **2.** Gmc **bōkjo* in OE *bēce:* BEECH.

bhar-. Projection, bristle. **1.** O-grade form **bhor-* in Gmc **barsaz,* "spiny fish," in OE *bærs:* BASS[1]. **2.** Zero-grade form **bhr̥-* in Gmc **bursti-* in OE *byrst:* BRISTLE.

bhardhā. Beard. Gmc **bardaz* in OE *beard:* BEARD.

bhares-. Also **bhars-.** Barley. Gmc **barz-* in OE *bære:* BARLEY.

bhau-. To strike. Gmc **bautan* in OE *bēatan:* BEAT.

bhē-. To warm. Zero-grade form **bhə-* in: **a.** Gmc **batham* in OE *bæth:* BATH; **b.** Gmc **bakan* in OE *bacan:* BAKE.

bhedh-[1]. To dig. Gmc **badjam,* "garden plot, sleeping place," in OE *bedd:* BED.

bhedh-[2]. To bend. **1.** Gmc **bidjan* in OE *biddan,* to pray: BID. **2.** Gmc **bidam* in OE *gebed,* prayer: BEAD.

bhei-[1]. Bee. Gmc **bīōn-* in OE *bēo:* BEE.

bhei-[2]. To strike. Gmc **bhi-li-* in OE *bile,* bird's beak: BILL[2].

bheid-. To split. **1.** Gmc **bitiz* in OE *bite,* a bite: BIT[2]. **2.** Gmc **bītō* in OE *bita,* piece bitten off: BIT[1]. **3.** Gmc **bītan,* to bite, in: **a.** OE *bītan:* BITE; **b.** OE *biter,* "biting": BITTER. **4.** Gmc **bait-,* boat (< "split planking"), in OE *bāt* (and ON *bātr*): BOAT.

bheidh-. To persuade, compel. **1.** Gmc **bīdan,* "to trust, to await trustingly, to stay," in OE *bīdan:* BIDE. **2.** Gmc **baidjan* in OE *bǣdan,* to compel: BAD.

bhel-[1]. To shine, flash; shining white; fire. **1.** Gmc **blaikjan* in OE *blǣcan:* BLEACH. **2.** Gmc **blas-* in OE *blæse,* torch: BLAZE[1]. **3.** Gmc **blend-,* "dazzle, blind," in OE *blind:* BLIND. **4.** Gmc **blisk-* in OE *blyscan:* BLUSH. **5.** Variant **bhleg-* in Gmc **blakaz,* "burned," in OE *blæc:* BLACK.

bhel-[2]. To blow, swell; a round object. Zero-grade form **bhl̥-* in Gmc **bul-* in OE *bolla:* BOWL[1].

bhel-[3]. To thrive, bloom. Extended form **bhlē-.* **1.** O-grade form **bhlō-* in Gmc **blō-s-* in OE *blōstma:* BLOSSOM. **2.** Zero-grade form **bhlə-* in Gmc **bladaz* in OE *blæd,* leaf: BLADE.

bhel-[4]. To yell. Gmc **bell-* in: **a.** OE *belle:* BELL; **b.** OE **belgan:* BELLOW.

bheld-. To strike. Zero-grade form **bhl̥d-* in Gmc **bult-* in OE *bolt,* heavy arrow: BOLT[1].

bhelgh-. To swell. **1.** Gmc **balgiz* in OE *belig,* bellows: BELLY. **2.** Gmc **bolgstraz* in OE *bolster:* BOLSTER.

bhen-. To strike. Gmc **banōn* in OE *bana:* BANE.

bhendh-. To bind. **1.** Gmc **bindan* in OE *bindan:* BIND. **2.** O-grade form **bhondh-* in Gmc **band-* in OE *bendan:* BEND. **3.** Celtic **benna* in OE *binne,* basket: BIN.

bher-[1]. To carry. **1.** Gmc **beran* in OE *beran:* BEAR[1]. **2.** Gmc **bērō* in OE *bēr:* BIER. **3.** Gmc **barwōn* in OE *bearwe,* basket: BARROW. **4.** Gmc **bur-* in OE *byrthen:* BURDEN. **5.** Compound root **bhrenk-* in Gmc **brengan* in OE *bringan:* BRING.

bher-[2]. To bore. Gmc **borōn* in OE *borian:*

BORE[1].

bher-[3]. Brown. 1. Variant **bhrū-* in Gmc **brūnaz* in OE *brūn:* BROWN. 2. Redupl form **bhibhru-* in OE *beofor:* BEAVER. 3. Gmc **berō* in OE *bera:* BEAR[2].

bherdh-. To cut. Zero-grade form **bhr̥dh-* in Gmc **burd-* in OE *bord:* BOARD.

bherəg-. To shine; white. 1. Gmc **berhtaz* in OE *beorht:* BRIGHT. 2. Gmc **berkjōn,* "the white tree," in OE *birce:* BIRCH.

bherək-. To shine, glitter, hence to move jerkily. Variant **bhrek-.* 1. Gmc **bregdan* in OE *bregdan:* BRAID. 2. Gmc **brigdil-* in OE *brīdel:* BRIDLE.

bherg-. To growl. Gmc **berk-* in OE *beorcan:* BARK[1].

bhergh-[1]. To hide, protect. 1. Zero-grade form **bhr̥gh-* in: a. Gmc **burgjan* in OE *byrgan:* BURY; b. Gmc **burgisli-* in OE *byrgels* (pl): BURIAL. 2. Gmc **borgēn* in OE *borgian:* BORROW.

bhergh-[2]. High; hill. Zero-grade form **bhr̥gh-* in Gmc **burgs,* hill-fort, in OE *burg:* BOROUGH, BURG.

bheu-. To be, exist, dwell. 1. Extended form **bhwī-* in Gmc **biju* in OE *bēon:* BE. 2. Zero-grade form **bhu-* in Gmc **buthla,* dwelling, in OE *bold:* BUILD. 3. Lengthened form **bhū-* in Gmc **būram* in OE *būr,* a dwelling, and *gebūr,* dweller: BOWER; NEIGHBOR.

bheudh-. To be or make aware. 1. Gmc **biudan,* to proclaim, in OE *bēodan:* BID. 2. Gmc **budōn-* in OE *boda,* messenger: BODE[1]. 3. Gmc **budilaz,* herald, in OE *bydel:* BEADLE.

bheug-. To swell; curved objects. 1. Gmc **bugōn-* in OE *boga:* BOW[3]. 2. Gmc **būgan* in OE *būgan,* to bend: BOW[2], BUXOM. [AHD *bheug-[3]*.]

bhlē-[1]. To howl. Gmc **blē-t-* in OE *blǣtan:* BLEAT.

bhlē-[2]. To blow, swell. Gmc **blē-.* 1. OE *blāwan:* BLOW[1]. 2. OE *blædre:* BLADDER. 3. OE *blǣst:* BLAST.

bhoso-. Naked. Gmc **bazaz* in OE *bær:* BARE.

bhrāter-. Brother. Gmc **brōthar-* in OE *brōthor:* BROTHER.

bhreg-. To break. Gmc **brekan* in OE *brecan:* BREAK.

bhrem-. To project. Gmc **brema* in: a. OE *brōm:* BROOM; b. OE *brǣmbel:* BRAMBLE. [AHD *bhrem-[2]*.]

bhres-. To burst. Gmc **brest-* in OE *berstan:* BURST.

bhreu-[1]. To break up. 1. Gmc **briutan* in OE **brytel:* BRITTLE. 2. Gmc **briuthan* in OE *brēothan,* to deteriorate: BROTHEL.

bhreu-[2]. To boil, burn; also to brew, cook. 1. Gmc **breuwan* in OE *brēowan:* BREW. 2. Gmc **braudam* in OE *brēad:* BREAD. 3. Gmc **brudam* in OE *broth:* BROTH. 4. Variant **bhrē-* in: a. Gmc **brōd-,* "a warming, hatching, rearing of young," in OE *brōd:* BROOD; b. Gmc **brōdjan,* "to rear," in OE *brēdan:* BREED; c. Gmc **brēthaz,* "warm air," in OE *brǣth:* BREATH. 5. Gmc **brenw-* in OE *beornan, byrnan,* and *bærnan:* BURN. 6. Gmc **brandaz* in OE *brand,* piece of burning wood: BRAND.

bhreus-[1]. To swell. Gmc **briustam* in OE *brēost:* BREAST.

bhreus-[2]. To break. Gmc **brūsjan* in OE *brȳsan:* BRUISE.

bhrū-. Eyebrow. Gmc **brūs* in OE *brū:* BROW.

bhudh-. Bottom. OE *botm:* BOTTOM.

bhugo-. Male animal. Gmc **bukkaz* in OE *buc, bucca:* BUCK[1].

dā-. To divide. Variant **dī-.* 1. Gmc **tīdiz,* "division of time," in: a. OE **tīd:* TIDE; b. OE *tīdan,* to happen: BETIDE. 2. Gmc **tīmo* in OE *tīma:* TIME.

dail-. To divide. 1. Gmc **dailiz* in OE *dǣlan:* DEAL[1]. 2. Gmc **dailaz* in OE *dāl,* share: DOLE.

dakru-. A tear. Gmc **tahr-* in OE *tēar:* TEAR[2].

de-. Demonstrative stem. Gmc **tō* in OE *tō:* TO.

deigh-. Insect. Gmc **tīk-* in OE *ticia:* TICK[2].

deik-. To show. Variant *deig-.* 1. Gmc **taikjan* in OE *tǣcan:* TEACH. 2. Gmc **taiknam* in OE *tācen:* TOKEN.

dek-. "Fringe, tail." Gmc **taglaz* in OE *tægel:* TAIL. [AHD *dek-[2]*.]

dekm̥. Ten. Gmc **tehun* in OE *tīen:* TEN.

del-[1]. Long. Prob form **dlon-gho-* in Gmc **langaz* in: a. OE *long:* LONG[1]; b. OE *langian,* "to grow longer, yearn": LONG[2].

del-[2]. To recount. 1. Gmc **taljan* in OE *tellan:* TELL. 2. Gmc **talō* in OE *talu:* TALE. 3. OE *talian:* TALK.

demə-[1]. To build. Gmc **timram,* building material, in OE *timber:* TIMBER.

demə-[2]. To constrain, break in (horses), tame. O-grade form **dom-* in Gmc **tamaz* in OE *tam:* TAME.

denk-. To bite. 1. Gmc **tanhuz,* tenacious, in OE *tōh:* TOUGH. 2. Gmc **tanguz* in OE *tange:* TONGS.

dent-. Tooth. O-grade form **dont-* in Gmc **tanthuz* in OE *tōth:* TOOTH.

der-[1]. To run, walk, step. 1. Gmc **tred-* in OE *tredan:* TREAD. 2. Gmc **trep-,* "something into which one steps, snare," in OE *træppe:* TRAP.

der-[2]. To split. Gmc **teran* in OE *teran:* TEAR[1].

deru-. To be firm, solid; also "wood, tree." 1. Variant **drew-* in: a. Gmc **trewam* in OE *trēow:* TREE; b. Gmc **triuwō* in OE *trēow,* faith: TRUCE. 2. Variant **dreu-* in Gmc **triuwaz* in OE *trēowe:* TRUE. 3. Variant **drou-* in Gmc **traujam* in OE *trīg,* wooden board: TRAY. 4. Form **dru-ko-* in Gmc **trugaz* in OE *trog:* TROUGH. 5. Variant **derw-* in Gmc **terw-,* resin, pitch, in OE *teru:* TAR[1].

deuk-. To lead. 1. Gmc **tiuhan* in OE *tēon:* TUG. 2. Zero-grade form **duk* in Gmc **tugōn* in OE *togian:* TOW[1], TAUT. 3. O-grade form **douk-* in: a. OE *tīgan:* TIE; b. Gmc **tauhmjan,* to beget, in OE *tīeman:* TEEM; c. Gmc **tauhmaz,* descendant, family, in OE *tēam:* TEAM.

dhē-. To set, put. 1. O-grade form **dhō-* in: a. Gmc **dōn* in OE *dōn:* DO; b. Gmc **dōmaz* in OE *dōm:* DOOM; c. Gmc **domjan* in OE *dēman:* DEEM. 2. Gmc **dēdiz* in OE *dǣd:* DEED. [AHD *dhē-[1]*.]

dheigh-. To knead. 1. Gmc **daigjōn* in OE *dǣge,* bread kneader: DAIRY. 2. Gmc **-dīg-* in OE *hlǣfdige,* "bread kneader, mistress of a household" (*hlǣf,* LOAF): LADY. 3. O-grade form **dhoigh-* in Gmc **daigaz* in OE *dāg:* DOUGH.

dhel-. A hollow. 1. Gmc **daljō* in OE *dell:* DELL. 2. Gmc **dalam* in OE *dæl:* DALE.

dhelbh-. To dig. Gmc **delban* in OE *delfan:* DELVE.

dher-[1]. To make muddy; darkness. 1. Gmc **derk-* in OE *deorc:* DARK. 2. Zero-grade form **dhr̥-* in: a. Gmc **drah-sta-* in OE *drōs:* DROSS; b. Gmc **drab-* in OE *dreflian:* DRIVEL.

dher-[2]. To drone, buzz. Gmc **drēn-,* male honeybee, in OE *drān:* DRONE[1]. [AHD *dher-[3]*.]

dhers-. To be bold. Gmc **ders-* and **durs-* in OE *durran:* DARE.

dheu-[1]. "To rise in a cloud as dust"; hence also dark colors, breath, confused perceptions, etc. 1. Extended form **dheus-* possibly in: a. Gmc **dus-* in OE *dysig:* DIZZY; b. Gmc **diuzam,* "breathing animal," in OE *dēor:* DEER. 2. Extended form **dhwens-* in Gmc **duns-* in OE *dūst:* DUST. 3. Extended form **dhus-* in Gmc **duskaz* in OE *dox:* DUSK. 4. Extended form **dhoubh-* in: a. Gmc **daubaz* in OE *dēaf:* DEAF; b. Gmc **dūbōn,* "dark-colored bird," in OE **dūfe:* DOVE[1]. 5. Zero-grade form **dhu-* in Gmc **dumbaz* in OE *dumb:* DUMB. 6. Extended form **dhwel-* in Gmc **dwelan* in OE *dwellan,* to deceive: DWELL.

dheu-[2]. To flow. Gmc **dauwaz* in OE *dēaw:* DEW.

dheu-[3]. To die. 1. O-grade form **dhou-* in Gmc **daudaz* in OE *dēad:* DEAD. 2. Extended zero-grade form **dhwī-* in Gmc **dwīnan* in OE *dwīnan:* DWINDLE.

dheub-. Deep. 1. Gmc **diupaz* in OE *dēop:* DEEP. 2. Gmc **duppjan* in OE *dyppan:* DIP. 3. Gmc **dubjan* in OE *dȳfan* and *dufan:* DIVE.

dheubh-. Wedge. Gmc **dub-* in OE *dubbian:* DUB[1].

dhīgw-. To fix. Gmc **dīk-* in OE *dīc:* DIKE, DITCH.

dhragh-. To drag. Gmc **dragan* in: a. OE *dragan* (and ON *draga*): DRAG, DRAW; b. OE *dræge:* DRAY.

dhreg-. To draw. Variant of **dhragh-.** 1. Gmc **drinkan* in OE *drincan:* DRINK. 2. Gmc **drankjan* in OE *drencan:* DRENCH.

dhreibh-. To drive. Gmc **drīban* in OE *drīfan:* DRIVE.

dhreu-. To fall, drip. 1. Extended form *dhreus-* in Gmc **driusan* in OE *drēosan:* DRIZZLE. 2. O-grade form **dhrous-* in: a. Gmc **drauzaz* in OE *drēor:* DREARY; b. Gmc **drusjan* in OE *drūsian:* DROWSE. 3. Extended zero-grade form **dhrub-* in Gmc **drupan* in OE *dropa:* DROP.

dhreugh-. To deceive. Gmc **draugma-* in OE *drēam:* DREAM.

dhughəter. Daughter. Gmc **dohtēr* in OE *dohtor:* DAUGHTER.

dhwen-. To make noise. Gmc **duniz* in OE *dyne:* DIN.

dhwer-. Door. Zero-grade form **dhur-* in Gmc **durunz* and **duram* in OE *dor:* DOOR.

dn̥ghū. Tongue. Gmc **tungōn* in OE *tunge:* TONGUE.

dwō. Two. 1. Gmc **twai,* two, in: a. OE *twā, tu:* TWO; b. OE *twēgen:* TWAIN; c. Gmc **twalif-,* "two left (over from ten)," in OE *twelf:* TWELVE. 2. Forms **dwis* and **dwi-* in: a. Gmc **twiyes* in OE *twige:* TWICE; b. Gmc **twegentig,* "twice ten," in OE *twēntig:* TWENTY; c. Gmc **twīhna,* "double thread," in OE *twīn:* TWINE; d. Gmc **twisnaz* in OE *getwinn:* TWIN; e. Gmc **twiga,* fork, in OE *twigge:* TWIG.

ed-. To eat. Gmc **itan* in OE *etan:* EAT.

eg. I. Gmc **eg* in OE *ic:* I.

ēik-. To possess. 1. Gmc **aigan* in OE *āgan:* OUGHT[1], OWE. 2. Gmc **aiganaz* in OE *āgen:* OWN.

eis-. Ice. Gmc **īs-* in OE *īs:* ICE. [AHD *eis-[2]*.]

el-[1]. Elbow. O-grade form **ol-* in Gmc **alinobogōn-* in OE *elnboga:* ELBOW.

el-[2]. Red, brown. 1. Gmc **elmo-* in OE *elm:* ELM. 2. Gmc **aliza* in OE *aler:* ALDER.

en. In. Gmc **in* in OE *in, inn:* IN, INN.

er-[1]. To set in motion. 1. O-grade form **or-* in Gmc **arnja-* in OE *eornost:* EARNEST[1]. 2. Variant root **rei-,* to flow, in zero-grade form **ri-* in Gmc **rinwan* in OE *rinnan:* RUN.

er-[2]. Earth. Gmc **erthō* in OE *eorthe:* EARTH. [AHD *er-[3]*.]

erə-. To row. Form **rē-* in: a. Gmc **rō-* in OE *rōwan:* ROW[2]; b. Gmc **rōthra* in OE *rōther:* RUDDER. [AHD *erə-[1]*.]

es-. To be. 1. Gmc **izmi* in OE *eam:* AM. 2. Stem **sī-* in Gmc **sijai-* in OE *sīe:* YES. 3. Form **sont-* in: a. Gmc **santhaz* in OE *sōth:* SOOTH; b. Zero-grade **sn̥t-* in Gmc **sunjō,* sin (< a formula of repentance, "it is true, the sin is real") in OE *synn:* SIN[1].

esen-. Harvest. O-grade form **osn-* in Gmc **aznōn,* to do harvest work, serve as a laborer, in OE *earnian:* EARN.

eu-. Lacking. Extended form **wə-* in Gmc

**wanēn* in OE *wanian:* WANE. [AHD *eu-[2]*.]

eudh-. Udder. Zero-grade form **ūdh-* in Gmc **ūthr-* in OE *ūder:* UDDER.

gal-[1]. Bald. Gmc **kalwaz* in OE *calu,* bald: CALLOW.

gal-[2]. To call, shout. Gmc **klat-* in OE **clatrian:* CLATTER.

gel-[1]. To form into a ball. Gmc **klūd-* in OE *clott,* lump: CLOT.

gel-[2]. Bright. Extended form **glei-* in Gmc **klai-* in OE *clǣne:* CLEAN.

gel-[3]. Cold. **1.** Gmc **kaliz* in OE *ciele:* CHILL. **2.** Gmc **kaldaz* in OE *ceald:* COLD. **3.** Gmc **kōl-* in OE *cōl:* COOL.

gembh-. Tooth. O-grade form **gombh-* in Gmc **kambaz* in OE *comb, camb:* COMB.

genə-. To give birth. Zero-grade form *gn̥-*. **1.** Gmc **kunjam* in OE *cynn:* KIN. **2.** Gmc **kuningaz,* "son of the royal kin," in OE *cyning:* KING. **3.** Gmc **kundjaz* in OE *cynd, gecynd,* birth, nature: KIND[2]. **4.** Gmc **kundiz* in OE *gecynde,* natural: KIND[1].

genu-[1]. Knee. Variant **gneu-* in: **a.** Gmc **kniwam* in OE *cnēo:* KNEE; **b.** Gmc **kniwljan* in OE *cnēowlian:* KNEEL.

genu-[2]. Chin. Form **genw-* in Gmc **kinnuz* in OE *cinn:* CHIN.

geph-. Jaw. Gmc **kabal-* in OE *ceafl:* JOWL[1].

ger-[1]. To gather. Extended form **grem-* in Gmc **kram-* in OE *crammian:* CRAM.

ger-[2]. To cry hoarsely. **1.** Gmc **krē-* in: **a.** OE *crāwe:* CROW[1]; **b.** OE *crāwan:* CROW[2]; **c.** OE *cracian:* CRACK. **2.** Gmc **kranu-* in OE *cran:* CRANE. [AHD *ger-[4]*.]

gerebh-. To scratch. Variant **grebh-* in: **a.** Gmc **krabb-* in OE *crabba:* CRAB[1]; **b.** Gmc **kerban* in OE *ceorfan:* CARVE.

geulo-. A glowing coal. Gmc **kolam* in OE *col:* COAL.

geus-. To choose. Gmc **kiusan* in OE *cēosan:* CHOOSE.

ghabh-. Also **ghebh-.** To give. Gmc **giban* in OE *giefan:* GIVE.

ghaido-. Goat. Gmc **gaitaz* in OE *gāt:* GOAT.

ghalgh-. Branch, rod. Gmc **galgōn-* in OE *gealga:* GALLOWS.

ghans-. Goose. **1.** Gmc **gans-* in OE *gōs:* GOOSE. **2.** Gmc **ganr-* in OE *gandra:* GANDER. **3.** Gmc **ganōtōn* in OE *ganot:* GANNET.

ghasto-. Rod. Gmc **gazdaz* in OE *gierd:* YARD[1].

ghē-. To let go. Gmc **gēn* in OE *gān:* GO.

ghedh-. To unite, join, fit. **1.** Form **ghōdh-* in Gmc **gōdaz,* "fitting, suitable," in OE *gōd:* GOOD. **2.** Gmc **gaduri* in OE *tōgædere:* TOGETHER. **3.** Gmc **gadurōn* in OE *gaderian:* GATHER.

ghēi-. To yawn. Form **ghi-n-ā-* in Gmc **ginōn* in OE *geonian:* YAWN.

gheis-. Fear, amazement. O-grade form **ghois-* in Gmc **gaistaz* in OE *gāst:* GHOST.

ghel-[1]. To call. Gmc **gel-* in: **a.** OE *giellan:* YELL; **b.** OE *gielpan:* YELP.

ghel-[2]. To shine. **1.** Gmc **gelwaz* in OE *geolu:* YELLOW. **2.** Zero-grade form **ghl̥-* in Gmc **gultham* in OE *gold:* GOLD.

ghend-. Also **ghed-.** To seize. Gmc **getan* in: **a.** OE *begietan:* BEGET; **b.** OE *forgietan:* FORGET.

ghengh-. To go. Gmc **gang-* in OE *gang:* GANG.

gher-[1]. Gut, entrail. Gmc **garnō,* string, in OE *gearn:* YARN.

gher-[2]. To enclose. **1.** Zero-grade form **ghr̥-* in Gmc **gurdjan* in: **a.** OE **gyrdan:* GIRD; **b.** OE *gyrdel:* GIRDLE. **2.** O-grade form **ghor-* in Gmc **gardaz,* "enclosure," in OE *geard:* YARD[2].

gher-[3]. To call out. Form **ghrēd-* in Gmc **grōtjan* in OE *grētan:* GREET.

gher-[4]. Gray. Gmc **grēwaz* in OE *grǣg:* GRAY.

gher-[5]. To want. Gmc **gernjan* in OE *giernan:* YEARN. [AHD *gher-[6]*.]

ghēu-. To yawn. Gmc **gō-ma-* in OE *gōma:* GUM[2].

gheu(ə)-. To invoke (as a god). Zero-grade form **ghu-* in: **a.** Gmc **gudam* in OE *god:* GOD; **b.** Gmc **gud-igaz,* "possessed by a god," in OE *gydig:* GIDDY.

ghrē-. To grow, become green. **1.** O-grade form **ghrō-* in: **a.** Gmc **grōwan* in OE *grōwan:* GROW; **b.** Gmc **grōnjaz* in OE *grēne:* GREEN. **2.** Zero-grade form **ghrə-* in Gmc **grasam* in OE *græs:* GRASS.

ghrebh-. To dig, bury. **1.** O-grade form **ghrobh-* in: **a.** Gmc **graban* in OE *grafan:* GRAVE[3]; **b.** Gmc **graba* in OE *græf:* GRAVE[1]. **2.** Gmc **grubjan* in OE **grybban:* GRUB. [AHD *ghrebh-[2]*.]

ghreib-. To grip. **1.** Gmc **grip-* in OE *gripe* and *gripa:* GRIP[1]. **2.** Gmc **grīpan* in OE *grīpan:* GRIPE. **3.** O-grade form **ghroib-* in Gmc **graipjan* in OE *grāpian:* GROPE.

ghrem-. Angry. Gmc **grimmaz* in OE *grim:* GRIM.

ghren-. Also **gwhren-.** To grind. **1.** Gmc **grindan* in OE *grindan:* GRIND. **2.** Gmc **grinst-* in OE *grīst:* GRIST.

ghrēu-. To grind. **1.** Gmc **griut-* in OE *grēot:* GRIT. **2.** Gmc **grautaz,* "coarsely ground," in OE *grēat:* GREAT.

gleubh-. To split. **1.** Gmc **kliuban* in OE *clēofan:* CLEAVE[1]. **2.** Gmc **klub-* in OE *clufu:* CLOVE[2].

gnō-. To know. **1.** Extended form **gnōw-* in Gmc **knōw-* in OE *gecnāwan:* KNOW. **2.** Zero-grade form **gnə-* in: **a.** Gmc **kunnan* in OE *cunnan:* CAN[1], CON[2], CUNNING; **b.** Gmc **kunth-* in OE *cūth:* UNCOUTH.

gras-. To devour. Gmc **krasjōn-* in OE *cresse:* CRESS.

greut-. To compress. Gmc **krūdan* in OE *crūdan:* CROWD.

grə-no-. Grain. Gmc **kornam* in OE *corn:* CORN[1].

gwā-. To come. **1.** Gmc **kuman* in OE *cuman:* COME. **2.** Gmc **kuma-* in OE *wilcuma:* WELCOME.

gwei-. To live. Zero-grade form **gwi-* in Gmc **kwikwaz* in OE *cwic,* living: QUICK.

gwel-[1]. To swallow. Gmc **kel-* in OE *ceolu:* JOWL[2]. [AHD *gwel-[5]*.]

gwel-[2]. To pierce. **1.** O-grade form **gwol-* in Gmc **kwaljan* in OE *cwellan:* QUELL. **2.** Zero-grade form **gwl̥-* in Gmc **kuljan* in OE **cyllan:* KILL.

gwen-. Woman. Lengthened form **gwēn-* in Gmc **kwēniz* in OE *cwēn:* QUEEN.

gwet-. To speak. Gmc **kwithan* in OE *cwethan:* BEQUEATH, QUOTH. [AHD *gwet-[2]*.]

gwou-. Cow. Form **gwōu-s* in Gmc *kōuz* in OE *cū:* COW[1].

gyeu-. To chew. Gmc **kewwan* in OE *cēowan:* CHEW.

gzhyes. Yesterday. Gmc **ges-ter-* in OE *geostran:* YESTER-.

kā-. To like, desire. Gmc **hōraz* in OE *hōre:* WHORE.

kād-. Hatred. Zero-grade form **kəd-* in Gmc **hatōn* in OE *hatian:* HATE.

kadh-. To cover. **1.** Gmc **hattuz* in OE *hætt:* HAT. **2.** Form **kōdh-* in: **a.** Gmc **hōda* in OE *hōd:* HOOD[1]; **b.** Gmc **hōdjan* in OE *hēdan:* HEED.

kagh-. To catch; fence. Gmc **hagjō* in OE *hecg:* HEDGE.

kaghlo-. Hail. Gmc **haglaz* in OE *hagol:* HAIL[1].

kai-. Heat. **1.** Gmc **haitaz* in OE *hāt:* HOT. **2.** Gmc **haitī-* in OE *hǣtu:* HEAT.

kailo-. Whole, uninjured. **1.** Gmc **hailaz* in OE *hāl:* HALE[1], WHOLE. **2.** Gmc **hailithō* in OE *hǣlth:* HEALTH. **3.** Gmc **hailjan* in OE *hǣlan:* HEAL. **4.** Gmc **hailagaz* in OE *hālig:* HOLY. **5.** Gmc **hailagōn* in OE *hālgian:* HALLOW.

kaito-. Forest. **1.** Gmc **haithiz* in OE *hǣth:* HEATH. **2.** Gmc **haithinaz* in OE *hǣthen:* HEATHEN.

kan-. To sing. Gmc **hannī* in OE *hen:* HEN.

kap-. To grasp. **1.** Gmc **habēn* in OE *habban:* HAVE. **2.** Gmc **habukaz* in OE *heafoc:* HAWK[1]. **3.** Gmc **hafigaz,* "having weight," in OE *hefig:* HEAVY. **4.** Gmc **hafjan* in OE *hebban:* HEAVE.

kapho-. Hoof. Form **kāp-o-* in Gmc **hōfaz* in OE *hōf:* HOOF.

kaput. Head. Gmc **haubidam* in OE *hēafod:* HEAD.

kar-. Hard. O-grade form **kor-* in Gmc **harduz* in OE *hard:* HARD. [AHD *kar-[1]*.]

kas-. Gray. Gmc **hasōn-* in OE *hara:* HARE.

kau-. To hew. **1.** Gmc **hawwan* in OE *hēawan:* HEW. **2.** Gmc **haujam* in OE *hīeg:* HAY. [AHD *kau-[2]*.]

keg-. Hook. Gmc **hōka-* in OE *hōc:* HOOK.

kē-. To sharpen. O-grade form **kō-* in Gmc **hainō* in OE *hān,* stone: HONE.

kei-[1]. To lie; home. O-grade form **koi-* in Gmc **haima* in OE *hām:* HOME.

kei-[2]. Color adjective. **1.** O-grade form **koi-* in Gmc **hairaz* in OE *hār:* HOARFROST. **2.** Zero-grade form **ki-* in Gmc **hiwan* in OE *hēo:* HUE[1].

kel-[1]. Warm. Form **klē-* in Gmc **hlēwaz* in OE *hlēo:* LEE.

kel-[2]. To strike. Extended o-grade form **kold-* in Gmc **haltōn* in OE *healtian:* HALT[2].

kel-[3]. To shout. Form **klā-* in Gmc **hlō-* in OE *hlōwan:* LOW[2].

kel-[4]. To cover. **1.** Gmc **haljō,* "concealed place," in OE *hell:* HELL. **2.** Gmc **hallō* in OE *heall:* HALL. **3.** Zero-grade form **kl̥-* in Gmc **hul-* in: **a.** OE *hulu:* HULL; **b.** OE *hol:* HOLE; **c.** OE *holh:* HOLLOW.

kel-[5]. To prick. Gmc **hulin-* in OE *holen:* HOLLY. [AHD *kel-[9]*.]

kel-[6]. Hill. Zero-grade form **kl̥-* in Gmc **hulni-* in OE *hyll:* HILL. [AHD *kel-[8]*.]

kelb-. To help. Gmc **helpan* in OE *helpan:* HELP.

kelp-. To hold. O-grade form **kolp-* in: **a.** Gmc **halb-* in OE *helma:* HELM; **b.** Gmc **half-* in OE *hælftre:* HALTER.

kem-[1]. Hornless. Gmc **hinthjō* in OE *hind:* HIND[2].

kem-[2]. To compress. Gmc **hamjan* in OE *hemm,* a doubling over: HEM[1].

kenəko-. Yellow. Gmc **hunagam* in OE *hunig:* HONEY.

kenk-[1]. Heel. **1.** Gmc **hanha* in OE *hōh:* HOCK[1]. **2.** Gmc **hanhila* in OE *hēla:* HEEL[1]. [AHD *kenk-[3]*.]

kenk-[2]. To be hungry. Zero-grade form **kn̥k-* in Gmc **hungruz* in OE *hungor:* HUNGER.

ker-[1]. Horn, head. **1.** Zero-grade form **kr̥-* in: **a.** Gmc **hurnaz* in OE *horn:* HORN; **b.** Gmc **hurznuta* in OE *hyrnet:* HORNET. **2.** Extended form **keru-* in Gmc **herutaz* in OE *heorot:* HART.

ker-[2]. "Loud noise, bird's cry." Zero-grade form **kr̥-*. **1.** Gmc **hring-* in OE *hringan:* RING[2]. **2.** Gmc **hraik-* in OE *hrǣcan:* RETCH. **3.** Gmc **hraban* in OE *hræfn:* RAVEN.

ker-[3]. Heat, fire. Gmc **herthō* in OE *heorth:* HEARTH. [AHD *ker-[4]*.]

kerd-. Heart. Gmc **hertōn-* in OE *heorte:* HEART. [AHD *kerd-[1]*.]

kerdh-. Herd. Gmc **herdō* in OE *heord:* HERD.

kerp-. To harvest. Variant **karp-* in Gmc **harbistaz* in OE *hærfest:* HARVEST.

kert-. To entwine. Zero-grade form **kr̥t-* in Gmc **hurdiz,* wicker frame, hurdle, in OE *hyrdel:* HURDLE.

keu-. To observe, see, hear. O-grade form

*kou-. 1. Extended form _*kous-_ in Gmc _*hausjan_ in: a. OE _hīeran:_ HEAR; b. OE _*heorcian:_ HARK, HEARKEN. 2. Variant _skou-_ in: a. Gmc _*skauwon,_ to look at, in OE _scēawian:_ SHOW; b. Gmc _*skauniz,_ bright, in OE _sciene:_ SHEEN. [AHD _keu-_[1].]

kēwero-. North (wind). Gmc _*skūra-,_ wind, storm, in OE _scūr:_ SHOWER.

klēg-. To sound, cry out. Variant _*klak-_ in Gmc _*hlahjan_ in OE _hliehhan:_ LAUGH.

klei-. To lean. 1. Zero-grade form _*kli-_ in: a. Gmc _*hlid-,_ "that which bends over," in OE _hlid:_ LID; b. Gmc _*hlinēn_ in OE _hleonian:_ LEAN[1]. 2. O-grade form _*kloi-_ in Gmc _*hlaidr-_ in OE _hlǣdder:_ LADDER.

kleng-. To bend. 1. Gmc _*hlink-_ in OE _hlinc:_ LINKS. 2. Gmc _*hlank-_ in OE _hlanc:_ LANK.

kleu-. To hear. Zero-grade form _*klu-._ 1. Gmc _*hlusinōn_ in OE _hlysnan:_ LISTEN. 2. Lengthened form _*klū-_ in Gmc _*hlūdaz_ in OE _hlūd:_ LOUD. [AHD _kleu-_[1].]

ko-. "This." Variant _*ki-_ in Gmc _*hi-_ in: a. OE _he:_ HE[1]; b. OE _him:_ HIM; c. OE _his:_ HIS; d. OE _hire:_ HER; e. OE _hit:_ IT; f. OE _hēr:_ HERE; g. OE _heonane:_ HENCE; h. OE _hider:_ HITHER.

konk-. To hang. Gmc _*hanhan_ in OE _hangian_ and _hon_ (and ON _hanga_): HANG.

kormo-. Pain. Gmc _*harmaz_ in OE _hearm:_ HARM.

koselo-. Hazel. Gmc _*haselaz_ in OE _hæsel:_ HAZEL.

krapo-. Roof. Gmc _*hrōfam_ in OE _hrōf:_ ROOF.

krep-. Body. Gmc _*hrifiz_ in OE _hrif:_ MIDRIFF.

kreu-[1]. Raw flesh. Form _*krēw-_ in Gmc _*hrēwaz_ in OE _hrēaw:_ RAW.

kreu-[2]. To strike. Gmc _*hrewwan_ in OE _hrēowan:_ RUE[1].

kreut-. Reed. Gmc _*hriuda-_ in OE _hrēod:_ REED.

kus-. A kiss. Gmc _*kussjan_ in OE _cyssan:_ KISS.

kwed-. To sharpen. Gmc _*hwatjan_ in OE _hwettan:_ WHET.

kwei-. To hiss. Gmc _*hwī-n-_ and _*hwis-_ in: a. OE _hwīnan:_ WHINE; b. OE _hwisprian:_ WHISPER; c. OE _hwistlian:_ WHISTLE. [AHD _kwei-_[4].]

kweit-. White. 1. Gmc _*hwītaz_ in OE _hwīt:_ WHITE. 2. Gmc _*hwaitjaz_ in OE _hwǣte:_ WHEAT.

kwel-. To revolve. Redupl form _*kwe-kwel-o-_ in OE _hwēol:_ WHEEL. [AHD _kwel-_[1].]

kwerp-. To turn oneself. Gmc _*hwarb-_ in OE _hwearf,_ wharf (< "place where people move about"): WHARF.

kwetwer-. Four. O-grade form _*kwetwor-_ prob in Gmc _*petwor-_ in: a. OE _fēower:_ FOUR; b. OE _fēowertig:_ FORTY.

kweyə-. Cozy, quiet. Variant _*kwī-_ in Gmc _*hwīlō_ in OE _hwīl:_ WHILE.

kwo-. Stem of relative and interrogative pronouns. 1. Gmc _*hwas, *hwasa, *hwam,_ in OE _hwā, hwæs, hwǣm:_ WHO, WHOSE, WHOM. 2. Gmc _*hwat_ in OE _hwæt:_ WHAT. 3. Gmc _*hwī_ in OE _hwȳ:_ WHY. 4. Gmc _*hwa-līk-_ in OE _hwelc:_ WHICH. 5. Gmc _*hwō-_ in OE _hū:_ HOW. 6. Gmc _*hwan-_ in OE _hwenne_ and _hwanon:_ WHEN and WHENCE. 7. Gmc _*hwithrē_ in OE _hwider:_ WHITHER. 8. Gmc _*hwar-_ in OE _hwǣr:_ WHERE. 9. Gmc _*hwatharaz_ in: a. OE _hwæther:_ NEITHER, WHETHER; b. Gmc _*aiwo gihwatharaz,_ "ever each of two," in OE _ǣghwæther:_ EITHER.

kwon-. Dog. Zero-grade form _*kwn̥-_ in Gmc _*hundaz_ in OE _hund:_ HOUND.

lab-. To lick. Gmc _*lapjan_ in OE _lapian:_ LAP[3].

las-. To be eager or wanton. 1. Gmc _*lustuz_ in OE _lust:_ LUST. 2. Gmc _*lustjan_ in OE _lystan:_ LISTLESS.

leb-. Lip. Gmc _*lep-_ in OE _lippa:_ LIP. [AHD _leb-_[2].]

legh-. To lie, lay. 1. Gmc _*ligjan_ in OE _licgan:_ LIE[1]. 2. Gmc _*lagjan_ in OE _lecgan:_ LAY[1].

legwh-. Light. Gmc _*līhtaz_ in OE _līht:_ LIGHT[2].

lei-. Slimy. Gmc _*lī-_ in: a. OE _slīm:_ SLIME; b. OE _slipor:_ SLIPPERY.

lēi-. To let go. 1. Form _*lēd-_ in Gmc _*lētan_ in OE _lǣtan:_ LET[1]. 2. Form _*ləd-_ in: a. Gmc _*lataz_ in OE _læt, lætra, latost:_ LATE, LATTER, LAST[1]; b. Gmc _*latjan_ in OE _lettan:_ LET[2]. [AHD _lēi-_[2].]

leigh-. To lick. Zero-grade form _*lig-_ in Gmc _*likkōn_ in OE _liccian:_ LICK.

leikw-. To leave. O-grade form _*loikw-_ in Gmc _*laihwnjan_ in OE _lǣnan:_ LEND.

leip-. To stick, adhere; fat. 1. Gmc _*lībam,_ "continuance," in OE _līf:_ LIFE. 2. Gmc _*libēn,_ "to continue," in OE _libban:_ LIVE[1]. 3. Gmc _*laibjan_ in OE _lǣfan:_ LEAVE[1]. 4. Gmc _*librō_ in OE _lifer:_ LIVER.

leis-. Track, furrow. O-grade form _*lois-._ 1. Gmc _*laist-,_ "footprint," in OE _lāst:_ LAST[3]. 2. Gmc _*laistjan,_ "to follow a track," in OE _lǣstan:_ LAST[2]. 3. Gmc _laizō_ in OE _lār:_ LORE. 4. Gmc _*liznōn_ in OE _leornian:_ LEARN.

leit-. To detest. 1. Gmc _*laithaz_ in OE _lāth:_ LOATH. 2. Gmc _*laithōn_ in OE _lāthian:_ LOATHE.

leith-. To go forth. O-grade form _*loit-._ 1. Gmc _*laidjan_ in OE _lǣdan:_ LEAD[1]. 2. Variant _*loid-_ in Gmc _*laidō_ in OE _lād,_ course: LOAD, LODE, LIVELIHOOD.

lem-. Broken. Gmc _*lamōn-_ in OE _lama:_ LAME. [AHD _lem-_[1].]

lendh-. Open land. Gmc _*landam_ in OE _land:_ LAND. [AHD _lendh-_[2].]

lento-. Flexible. Gmc _*linthjaz_ in OE _līthe:_ LITHE.

lep-. To be flat; palm. Form _*lōp-_ in Gmc _*galōfō_ in OE _glōf:_ GLOVE. [AHD _lep-_[2].]

letro-. Leather. Gmc _*lethram_ in OE _lether-:_ LEATHER.

leu-. To cut apart. 1. Gmc _*lausaz_ in OE _los:_ LOSE, LOSS. 2. Gmc _*ferliusan_ in OE _forlēosan:_ FORLORN. [AHD _leu-_[1].]

leubh-. To care; love. 1. O-grade form _*loubh-_ in Gmc _*galaubjan_ in OE _gelēfan, belēfan:_ BELIEVE. 2. Zero-grade form _*lubh-_ in Gmc _*lubō_ in OE _lufu:_ LOVE.

leud-. Small. Gmc _*lūt-_ in OE _lȳtel:_ LITTLE.

leugh-. To lie. Gmc _*liugan_ in OE _lēogan:_ LIE[2].

leuk-. Light. Gmc _*liuhtam_ in OE _līht:_ LIGHT[1].

leup-. To break off. Gmc _*laubaz_ in OE _lēaf:_ LEAF.

lou-. To wash. 1. Gmc _*laugō_ in OE _lēag:_ LYE. 2. OE _lēathor:_ LATHER.

lus-. Louse. Gmc _*lus-_ in OE _lūs:_ LOUSE.

mā-. Damp. Gmc _*mōra-_ in OE _mōr:_ MOOR[2]. [AHD _mā-_[3].]

mad-. Moist (as food). Gmc _*mati-_ in OE _mete:_ MEAT.

mag-. Also **mak-.** To knead, fit. 1. Gmc _*makōn_ in OE _macian:_ MAKE. 2. Gmc _*ga-mak-ōn,_ "fitted together with (another), spouse," in OE _gemæcca:_ MATCH[1]. 3. Gmc _*mangjan,_ to mix, in: a. OE _mengan:_ MINGLE; b. OE _gemang:_ AMONG, MONGREL.

magh-. To be able. 1. Gmc _*mag-_ in OE _magan:_ MAY[1]. 2. Gmc _*mah-ti-_ in OE _miht:_ MIGHT[1]. 3. Gmc _*mag-ena_ in OE _mægen:_ MAIN. [AHD _magh-_[1].]

maghu-. Young person. Form _*magho-_ in Gmc _*magadin-_ in OE _mægden:_ MAIDEN.

mai-[1]. To cut. 1. Gmc _*ā-mait-jon,_ "the biter," in OE _ǣmette:_ ANT. 2. Gmc _*mītōn-_ in OE _mīte:_ MITE[1].

mai-[2]. To soil. Gmc _*mail-,_ a blemish, in OE _māl:_ MOLE[1].

man-. Man. Extended form _*manu-_ in Gmc _*manna-_ in OE _mann:_ MAN. [AHD _man-_[1].]

marko-. Horse. Gmc feminine _*marhjōn_ in OE _mere:_ MARE[1].

māter-. Mother. Gmc _*mōthar-_ in OE _mōdor:_ MOTHER.

me-. First person singular pronoun. 1. Gmc _*mĕ-_ in OE _mĕ:_ ME. 2. Possessive form _*meino-_ in Gmc _*mīn-_ in OE _mīn:_ MINE[2], MY. [AHD _me-_[1].]

mē-[1]. Mind, disposition. O-grade form _*mō-_ in Gmc _*mōthaz_ in OE _mōd:_ MOOD[1].

mē-[2]. To measure. 1. Gmc _*mǣlaz,_ "appointed time," in OE _mǣl:_ MEAL[2]. 2. Extended form _*mēn-_ in: a. Gmc _*mǣnon_ in OE _mōna:_ MOON; b. Gmc _*mǣnōth-_ in OE _mōnath:_ MONTH.

mē-[3]. Big. 1. Gmc comparative _*maizōn-_ in OE _māra_ and _māre:_ MORE. 2. Gmc superlative _*maista-_ in OE _mǣst:_ MOST.

mē-[4]. To cut down grass. Gmc _*mǣ-_ in OE _māwan:_ MOW[1].

med-. To take appropriate measures. Gmc _*metan_ in OE _metan:_ METE.

medhu-. Honey; mead. Gmc _*medu_ in OE _meodu:_ MEAD[1].

medhyo-. Middle. Gmc _*middila-_ in OE _middel:_ MIDDLE.

meg-. Great. Gmc _*mik-_ in OE _mycel:_ MUCH.

mei-. To change, exchange. 1. O-grade form _*moi-_ in Gmc _*ga-maid-az,_ "changed for the worse, abnormal," in OE _gemād:_ MAD. 2. Form _*mit-to-,_ "changed, wrongly," in a. Gmc _*missa-_ in OE _mis-:_ MIS-; b. Gmc _*missjan_ in OE _missan:_ MISS[1]. [AHD _mei-_[1].]

meigh-. To urinate. Gmc _*mih-,_ urine, rain, in OE _mist:_ MIST.

mei-no-. Opinion, intention. 1. Gmc _*main-,_ complaint, in OE _*mān:_ MOAN. 2. Gmc _*mainjan,_ to intend, in OE _mǣnan:_ MEAN[1].

mel-. Soft. 1. Extended form _*meld-_ in: a. Gmc _*meltan_ in OE _meltan:_ MELT; b. Gmc _*malta-_ in OE _mealt:_ MALT. 2. Extended form _*meldh-_ in Gmc _*mildja-_ in OE _milde:_ MILD. [AHD _mel-_[1].]

melə-. To crush, grind. Gmc _*mel-wa-,_ flour, in OE _melu:_ MEAL[1].

melg-. To milk. Gmc _*meluk-_ in OE _milc:_ MILK.

mēlo-. Also **smēlo-.** Small animal. Zero-grade form _*sməlo_ in Gmc _*smal-_ in OE _smæl:_ SMALL.

men-. To think. Zero-grade form _*mn̥-_ in Gmc _*ga-mundi-_ in OE _gemynd:_ MIND. [AHD _men-_[1].]

menegh-. Copious. Gmc _*managa-_ in OE _manig:_ MANY.

menth-. To chew. Form _*mn̥tho-_ in Gmc _*muntha-_ in OE _mūth:_ MOUTH.

mer-[1]. To flicker. Gmc _*murgana-_ in OE _morgen:_ MORN.

mer-[2]. To trouble. Gmc _*marzjan_ in OE _merran:_ MAR. [AHD _mer-_[4].]

merg-. Boundary. Gmc _*mark-_ in OE _mearc:_ MARK[1].

meu-. Damp. Gmc _*meus-_ in OE _mos:_ MOSS.

mōd-. To meet. Gmc _*mōtjan_ in OE _mētan:_ MEET[1].

mon-. Neck. Gmc _*manō_ in OE _manu:_ MANE.

mori-. Body of water. Gmc _*mariska-_ in OE _mersc:_ MARSH.

mozgo-. Marrow. Gmc _*mazgā-_ in OE _mærg:_ MARROW.

mregh-mo-. Brain. Gmc _*brag-na-_ in OE _brægen:_ BRAIN.

mreghu-. Short. Zero-grade form _*mr̥ghu-_ in: a. Gmc _*murja-,_ short, pleasant, in OE _mirige:_ MERRY; b. Gmc _*murgithō_ in OE _myrgth:_ MIRTH.

mū-. Mouse. Gmc _*mūs-_ in OE _mūs:_ MOUSE. [AHD _mū-_[1].]

nas-. Nose. Gmc _*nasō_ in OE _nosu:_ NOSE.

nāu-. To be exhausted. Zero-grade form _*nəu-_ in Gmc _*naudi-_ in OE _nēod, nēd:_ NEED. [AHD _nāu-_[1].]

n̥dher-. Under. Gmc _*under-_ in OE _under:_ UNDER.

ne. Not. 1. Gmc _*ne-_ in OE _ne:_ NO[1]. 2. Zero-

grade form **ṇ-* in Gmc **un-* in OE *un-:* UN-[1].
ned-. To bind, tie. O-grade form **nod-* in: **a.** Gmc **nati-* in OE *net:* NET[1]; **b.** Gmc *nat-ilō* in OE *netle:* NETTLE.
nek-. To attain. O-grade form **nok-* in Gmc **ga-nah-* in OE *genōg:* ENOUGH. [AHD *nek-[2]*.]
nekwt-. Night. O-grade form **nokwt-* in Gmc **naht-* in OE *niht:* NIGHT.
nem-. To take. Gmc **nem-* in: **a.** OE *niman:* NUMB; **b.** OE *nǣmel* and *numol:* NIMBLE. [AHD *nem-[2]*.]
ner-. Under, on the left; north. Zero-grade form **nr̥* in Gmc *north-* in OE *north:* NORTH. [AHD *ner-[1]*.]
nes-. Personal pronoun. Zero-grade form **ṇs-* in: **a.** Gmc **uns* in OE *ūs:* US; **b.** Gmc **un-sara-* in OE *ūre:* OUR. [AHD *nes-[2]*.]
nētr-. Snake. Gmc **nēthrō-* in OE *nǣdre:* ADDER.
newŋ. Nine. Gmc **niwun* in OE *nigon:* NINE.
newo-. New. Gmc **neuja-* in OE *nēowe:* NEW.
ni. Down. **1.** Gmc **nith-* in OE *nithan, neothan:* BENEATH, UNDERNEATH. **2.** Gmc **nitheraz* in OE *nither:* NETHER.
nizdo-. Bird's nest. **1.** Gmc **nist-* in OE *nest:* NEST. **2.** Gmc **nistilōn* in OE *nestlian:* NESTLE.
nobh-. Navel. Gmc **nabalō* in OE *nafela:* NAVEL.
nogh-. Nail. Gmc **nagla-* in OE *nægl:* NAIL.
nogw-. Naked. Gmc **nakweda-* in OE *nacod:* NAKED.
nomen-. Name. Gmc **namōn-* in OE *nama:* NAME.
nu-. Now. Gmc **neuja-* in OE *nū:* NOW.
ōg-. Fruit. Zero-grade form **əg-* in Gmc **akran-* in OE *æcern:* ACORN.
oino-. One. **1.** Gmc **ainaz* in OE *ān:* A, AN, ONE. **2.** Gmc **ain-lif-*, "one left (beyond ten)," in OE *endleofan:* ELEVEN. **3.** Gmc **ainigaz* in OE *ǣnig:* ANY.
oito-. An oath. Gmc **aithaz* in OE *āth:* OATH.
oktō. Eight. Gmc **ahtō* in OE *eahta:* EIGHT.
okw-. To see. Gmc **augōn-* in OE *ēage:* EYE.
ous-. Ear. Gmc **auzan-* in OE *ēare:* EAR[1].
owi-. Sheep. Gmc *awi-* in OE *ēowu:* EWE.
pā-. To feed. **1.** Gmc **fōdram* in OE *fōdor:* FODDER. **2.** Extended form **pāt-* in: **a.** Gmc **fōd-* in OE *fōda:* FOOD; **b.** Gmc **fōdjan* in OE *fēdan:* FEED; **c.** Gmc **fōstra-* in OE *fōstor:* FOSTER.
pag-. To fasten. Form **pa-n-g-* in Gmc **fangiz* in OE *fang:* FANG.
pan-. Fabric. Gmc **fanōn-* in OE *fana:* VANE.
past-. Solid, firm. **1.** Gmc **fastuz* in OE *fæst:* FAST[1]. **2.** Gmc **fastinōn* in OE *fastnian:* FASTEN. **3.** Gmc **fasten,* to hold fast, in OE *fæstan:* FAST[2].
ped-[1]. Foot. **1.** Lengthened o-grade form **pōd-* in Gmc **fōt-* in OE *fōt:* FOOT. **2.** Gmc **feterō* in OE *feter:* FETTER.
ped-[2]. Container. O-grade form **pod-* in Gmc **fatam* in OE *fæt:* VAT.
peig-[1]. Also **peik-**. To cut. Gmc **fihala* in OE *fēol:* FILE[2].
peig-[2]. Also **peik-**. Evil-minded. **1.** Zero-grade form **pig-* in Gmc **fikala-* in OE *ficol:* FICKLE. **2.** O-grade form **poik-* in: **a.** Gmc **gafaihaz* in OE *gefāh:* FOE; **b.** Gmc **faigjaz* in OE *fǣge:* FEY.
peisk-. Fish. Gmc **fiska-* in OE *fisc:* FISH.
pel-[1]. To thrust. Extended form **peld-* in: **a.** Gmc **falt-* in OE *anfealt:* ANVIL; **b.** Gmc **feltaz,* "compressed wool," in OE *felt:* FELT[1]. [AHD *pel-[6]*.]
pel-[2]. Pale. Variant **pal-* in Gmc **falwaz* in OE *fealo:* FALLOW DEER.
pel-[3]. To fold. Extended form **pelt-* in: **a.** Gmc **falthan* in OE *faldan:* FOLD[1]; **b.** Gmc **-falthaz* in OE *-feald:* -FOLD.
pel-[4]. Skin. Gmc **fel-men-* in OE *filmen,* membrane: FILM.
pel-[5]. Also **pelə-**. To fill. Zero-grade form **plə-* in: **a.** Gmc **fullaz* in OE *full:* FULL[1]; **b.** Gmc **fulljan* in OE *fyllan:* FILL. [AHD *pel-[8]*.]
pelə-. Flat; to spread. **1.** Gmc **felthuz* in OE *feld:* FIELD. **2.** Variant **plā-* in Gmc **flōruz* in OE *flōr:* FLOOR. [AHD *pelə-[1]*.]
penkwe. Five. **1.** Gmc **fimfti* in OE *fīf:* FIVE. **2.** Gmc **fimftehun* in OE *fīftēne:* FIFTEEN. **3.** Gmc **fimfton* in OE *fīfta:* FIFTH. **4.** Gmc **fimftig* in OE *fīftig:* FIFTY. **5.** Gmc **fingwraz,* "one of five," in OE *finger:* FINGER. **6.** Form **pn̥ksti-* in Gmc **fūstiz* in OE *fȳst:* FIST.
pent-. To tread, go. Gmc **finthan* in OE *findan:* FIND.
per[1]. "Forward, through, before." **1.** Gmc **ferra* in OE *feor:* FAR. **2.** Zero-grade form **pr̥-* in: **a.** Gmc *for* in OE *for:* FOR; **b.** Gmc **furth-* in OE *forth:* FORTH; **c.** Gmc **furthera-* in OE *furthor:* FURTHER; **d.** Gmc **furma-* in OE *forma:* FORMER; FOREMOST; **e.** Gmc **furista-* in OE *fyrst:* FIRST. **3.** Variant **para* in Gmc **fora* in: **a.** OE *fore:* FORE; **b.** OE *beforan:* BEFORE. **4.** Variant **pro* in: **a.** Gmc **fram* in OE *from:* FROM; **b.** Gmc **framjan,* "to come forward," in OE *framian:* FRAME.
per-[2]. To lead, pass over. **1.** O-grade form **por-* in Gmc **faran* in OE *faran:* FARE. **2.** Zero-grade form **pr̥-* in Gmc **furdu-* in OE *ford:* FORD.
per-[3]. To risk. Gmc **fēraz,* "danger," in OE *fǣr:* FEAR. [AHD *per-[5]*.]
perk-. To dig out. Zero-grade form **pr̥k-* in Gmc **furh-* in OE *furh:* FURROW. [AHD *perk-[3]*.]
perkwu-. Oak. Zero-grade form **pr̥kw-* in Gmc **furhu-* in OE *fyrh:* FIR.
pet-[1]. To fly. Gmc **fethrō* in OE *fether:* FEATHER.
pet-[2]. To spread. O-grade form **pot-* in Gmc **fathmaz* in OE *fæthm:* FATHOM.
peyə-. To be fat. Form **poid-* in Gmc **faitaz* in OE *fǣtt:* FAT.
pəter. Father. Gmc **fadar* in OE *fæder:* FATHER.
phol-. To fall. **1.** Gmc **fallan* in OE *feallan:* FALL. **2.** Gmc **falljan,* "to cause to fall," in OE *fellan:* FELL[1].
plat-. To spread. Variant **plad-* in Gmc **flatjam* in OE *flett,* floor: FLAT[2].
plek-. To plait. O-grade form **plok-* in Gmc **flahsam* in OE *fleax:* FLAX.
plēk-. Also **pleik-**. To tear. **1.** Form **plak-* in Gmc **flahan* in OE *flēan:* FLAY. **2.** Gmc **flaiskaz,* "piece of torn flesh," in OE *flǣsc:* FLESH.
pleu-. To flow. **1.** Extended form **pleuk-* in: **a.** Gmc **fliugan* in OE *flēogan:* FLY[1]; **b.** Gmc **fliugjō* in OE *flēoge:* FLY[2]; **c.** Zero-grade form **pluk-* in Gmc **flug-ti-* in OE *flyht* and **flyht:* FLIGHT[1], FLIGHT[2]; **d.** Gmc **fluglaz, fuglaz,* in OE *fugol:* FOWL. **2.** Extended form **pleud-* in: **a.** Gmc **fliutan* in OE *flēotan:* FLEET[1]; **b.** Zero-grade form **plud-* in Gmc **flut-* in OE *flotian* and *floterian:* FLOAT, FLUTTER. **4.** Forms **plōu-, *plō-,* in: **a.** Gmc **flōwēn* in OE *flōwan:* FLOW; **b.** Gmc **flōdu* in OE *flōd:* FLOOD.
pleus-. Fleece. Gmc **fliusaz* in OE *flēos:* FLEECE.
plou-. Flea. Extended form **plouk-* in Gmc **flauhaz* in OE *flēah:* FLEA.
pneu-. To breathe. Gmc **fniu-* in OE *fnēosan:* SNEEZE.
pōl-. To feel. Gmc **fōljan* in OE *fēlan:* FEEL.
pōu-. Few, little. **1.** Variant **pau-* in Gmc **fawaz* in OE *fēawe:* FEW. **2.** Variant **pu-lo-,* "young of an animal," in Gmc **fulō* in OE *fola:* FOAL.
preu-. To hop. Zero-grade form **pru-* in Gmc **fru-* in OE *frogga:* FROG.
preus-. To freeze. **1.** Gmc **friusan* in OE *frēosan:* FREEZE. **2.** Zero-grade form **prus-* in Gmc **frustaz* in OE *frost:* FROST.
prī-. To love. Extended form **priy-*. **1.** Gmc **frijaz* in OE *frēo:* FREE. **2.** Gmc **frijand-* in OE *frēond:* FRIEND. **3.** Gmc **frije-dagaz* in OE *frīgedæg:* FRIDAY.
pu-. To rot. Form **pū-lo-*. **1.** Gmc **fūlaz* in OE *fūl:* FOUL. **2.** Gmc **fūlithō* in OE *fȳlth:* FILTH. [AHD *pu-[2]*.]
puk-. Bushy-haired. **1.** Gmc **fuhsaz* in OE *fox:* FOX. **2.** Gmc **fuhson* in OE *fyxe:* VIXEN. [AHD *puk-[2]*.]
pûr-. Fire. Gmc **fūri-* in OE *fȳr:* FIRE.
pūro-. Grain. OE *fyrs:* FURZE.
rebh-. To roof over. Gmc **reb-jōn,* "covering of the chest cavity," in OE *rib:* RIB.
reg-[1]. To move in a straight line. **1.** Gmc **rehtaz* in OE *riht:* RIGHT. **2.** O-grade form **rog-* in: **a.** Gmc **rakō* in OE *raca:* RAKE[1]; **b.** Gmc **rak-inaz* in OE *gerecenian:* RECKON; **c.** Lengthened form **rōg-* in Gmc **rōkja-* in OE *rēcelēas:* RECKLESS.
reg-[2]. Moist. Variant **rek-* in Gmc **regnaz* in OE *rēn:* RAIN.
rei-[1]. To scratch, cut. **1.** Form **roig-* in Gmc **raigwa* in OE *rāw:* ROW. **2.** Form **reipp-* in Gmc **raipaz* in OE *rāp:* ROPE. **3.** Form **reib-* in: **a.** Gmc **rīpja-* in OE *rīpe:* RIPE; **b.** Gmc **ripjan* in OE *rīpan:* REAP.
rei-[2]. Flecked. O-grade form **roi-* in Gmc **raihaz* in OE *rā:* ROE[2].
reidh-. To ride. **1.** Gmc **rīdan* in OE *rīdan:* RIDE. **2.** O-grade form **roidh-* in: **a.** Gmc **raid-* in OE *rād:* RAID, ROAD; **b.** Gmc **raid-ja* in OE *rǣde:* READY.
reig-. To reach. O-grade form **roidh-* in Gmc **raikjan* in OE *rǣcan:* REACH. [AHD *reig-[2]*.]
rendh-. To tear up. **1.** Gmc **randjan* in OE *rendan:* REND. **2.** Gmc **rind-* in OE *rinde:* RIND.
rēp-. Stake, beam. Variant **rap-* in Gmc **raftra-* in OE *ræfter:* RAFTER. [AHD *rēp-[2]*.]
rēt-. Post. O-grade form **rōt-* in Gmc **rodd-* in OE *rodd:* ROD.
reudh-. Red, ruddy. **1.** O-grade form **roudh-* in Gmc **raudaz* in OE *rēad:* RED. **2.** Zero-grade form **rudh-* in: **a.** Gmc **rudō* in OE *rudu:* RUDDY; **b.** Gmc **rūst-* in OE *rūst:* RUST.
reug-. To belch, smoke. Gmc **riukan* in OE *rēocan:* REEK.
rewə-. To open; space. Variant **rū-* in Gmc **rūmaz* in OE *rūm:* ROOM.
rezg-. To plait. Gmc **ruski-* in OE *rysc:* RUSH[2].
ruk-. Rough. Form **rūk-* in Gmc **rūhwaz* in OE *rūh:* ROUGH. [AHD *ruk-[2]*.]
sā-. To satisfy. Zero-grade form **sə-*. **1.** Gmc **sadaz* in OE *sæd,* sated: SAD. **2.** Gmc **sadōn* in OE *sadian:* SATE[1].
sab-. Juice. Gmc **sapam* in OE *sæp:* SAP[1].
sāg-. To seek out. **1.** Gmc **sōkjan* in OE *sēcan:* SEEK. **2.** Gmc **sakō* in OE *sacu:* SAKE[1]. **3.** Gmc **sakan* in OE *forsacan:* FORSAKE.
sai-. Suffering. **1.** Gmc **sairaz* in OE *sār:* SORE. **2.** Gmc **sairig-* in OE *sārig:* SORRY.
sal-[1]. Salt. Gmc **saltam* in OE *sealt:* SALT.
sal-[2]. Dirty. Gmc **salwaz* in OE *salo:* SALLOW.
saus-. Dry. Gmc **sausaz* in OE *sēar:* SEAR, SERE.
sāwel-. Sun. Variants **swen-, *sun-*. **1.** Gmc *sunnōn* in OE *sunne:* SUN. **2.** Gmc **sunthaz* in OE *sūth:* SOUTH.
sē-. To sow. **1.** Gmc **sējan* in OE *sāwan:* SOW[1]. **2.** Gmc **sēdiz* in OE *sǣd:* SEED. [AHD *sē-[1]*.]
sed-. To sit. **1.** Gmc **sitan* in OE *sittan:* SIT. **2.** Gmc **setlaz* in OE *setl:* SETTLE. **3.** O-grade form **sod-* in: **a.** Gmc **satjan* in OE *settan:* SET[1]; **b.** Gmc **sadulaz* in OE *sadol:* SADDLE; **c.** Lengthened form **sōd-* in Gmc **sōtam* in OE *sōt:* SOOT. [AHD *sed-[1]*.]
sek-. To cut. **1.** Gmc **segithō* in OE *sīthe:* SCYTHE. **2.** O-grade form **sok-* in Gmc **sagō*

in OE *sagu:* SAW[1].
sekw-[1]. To say. O-grade form **sokw-.* **1.** Gmc **sawjan* in OE *secgan:* SAY. **2.** Gmc **sagō* in OE *sagu:* SAW[2]. [AHD *sekw-[3]*.]
sekw-[2]. To see. **1.** Gmc **sehwan* in OE *sēon:* SEE[1]. **2.** Gmc **sih-th* in OE *sihth:* SIGHT.
sel-[1]. To take. Gmc **saljan,* "to sell" (< "cause to take"), in OE *sellan:* SELL. [AHD *sel-[3]*.]
sel-[2]. Of good mood. Gmc **sēl-* in OE *gesǣlig:* SILLY.
selp-. Fat. Gmc **salb-* in OE *salf:* SALVE.
sem-[1]. Form **sm̥m-o-*in Gmc **sumaz* in OE *sum:* SOME.
sem-[2]. Summer. Form **sm̥m-* in Gmc **sumaraz* in OE *sumor:* SUMMER. [AHD *sem-[3]*.]
sen-. Separated. Zero-grade form **sn̥-.* **1.** Gmc **sundrō* in OE *sunder:* ASUNDER. **2.** Gmc **sundrōn* in OE *syndrian:* SUNDER. **3.** Gmc **sundriga-* in OE *syndrig:* SUNDRY. [AHD *sen-[2]*.]
sendhro-. Crystalline deposit. Gmc **sendra-* in OE *sinder:* CINDER.
sengw-. To sink. Gmc **sinkwan* in OE *sincan:* SINK.
sengwh-. To sing. **1.** Gmc **singan* in OE *singan:* SING. **2.** O-grade form **songwh-* in Gmc **sangwaz* in OE *sang:* SONG.
senk-. To burn. O-grade form **sonk-* in Gmc **sangjan* in OE *sengan:* SINGE.
sent-. To go. O-grade form **sont-* in Gmc **sandjan* in OE *sendan:* SEND.
septm̥. Seven. Gmc **sibum* in OE *seofon:* SEVEN.
seu-[1]. To seethe. Gmc **siuthan* in OE *sēothan:* SEETHE.
seu-[2]. Third person and reflexive pronoun. Form **sel-bho-* in Gmc **selbaz* in OE *self:* SELF.
seu-[3]. To give birth. Gmc **sunuz* in OE *sunu:* SON.
seu-[4]. To take liquid. Form**sūg-.* **1.** Gmc **sūk-* in OE *sūcan:* SUCK. **2.** Gmc **suk-* in OE *socian:* SOAK.
skei-. To cut. **1.** Gmc **ski-nōn-* in OE *scinu:* SHIN. **2.** Extended form **skeit-* in Gmc **skaith-* in OE *scēadan:* SHED[1].
skel-[1]. To cut. **1.** Gmc **skaljō,* "piece cut off," in OE *scell:* SHELL. **2.** Gmc **skelduz* in OE *scield:* SHIELD.
skel-[2]. To be under an obligation. O-grade form **skol-* in Gmc **skal-,* "I owe, I ought," in OE *sceal, sceolde:* SHALL, SHOULD.
skeng-. Crooked. Gmc **skankō* in OE *scanca:* SHANK.
skep-. "To cut, scrape." **1.** Gmc **skap-* in: **a.** OE *gesceap:* SHAPE; **b.** OE *-scipe:* -SHIP. **2.** Gmc **skaftaz* in OE *sceaft:* SHAFT[1]. **3.** Gmc **skabb-* in OE *sceabb:* SHABBY. **4.** Gmc **skab-* in OE *sceafan:* SHAVE.
sker-[1]. To cut. **1.** Gmc **skeran* in OE *sceran:* SHEAR. **2.** Gmc **skar-* in: **a.** OE *scēar:* SHARE[2]; **b.** OE *scearu:* SHARE[1]. **3.** Gmc **skēr-* in OE *scēara:* SHEARS. **4.** Gmc **skardaz* in OE *sceard:* SHARD. **5.** Extended form **skerd-* in Gmc **skurtaz* in: **a.** OE *scort:* SHORT; **b.** OE *scyrte:* SHIRT. **6.** Extended form **skerbh-* in Gmc **skarpaz* in OE *scearp:* SHARP. **7.** Gmc **skrub-* in OE *scrybb:* SHRUB.
sker-[2]. To turn, bend. **1.** Form **skreng-* in Gmc **skrink-* in OE *scrincan:* SHRINK. **2.** Form **skrengh-* in Gmc **hringaz* in OE *hring:* RING[1]. **3.** Form **kreuk-* in Gmc **hrugjaz* in OE *hrycg:* RIDGE. [AHD *sker-[3]*.]
skeru-. To cut. Variant **skreu-.* **1.** Gmc **skraw-* in OE *scrēawa:* SHREW. **2.** Gmc **skraud-* in OE *scrēade:* SHRED. **3.** Gmc **skrūd-,* "piece of cloth," in OE *scrūd:* SHROUD.
skeu-. Also **keu-.** To cover. **1.** Zero-grade form **ku-* in: **a.** Gmc **husōn-* in OE *hosa:* HOSE; **b.** Gmc **huzdam* in OE *hord:* HOARD; **c.** Gmc **hūdiz* in OE *hȳd:* HIDE[2]. **2.** Gmc **hūdjan* in OE *hȳdan:* HIDE[1].
skeubh-. To shove. **1.** Gmc **skiuban* in OE *scūfan:* SHOVE. **2.** Gmc **skub-ilōn-* in OE *scofl:* SHOVEL.
skeud-. To shoot, chase, throw. **1.** Gmc **skiutan* in OE *scēotan:* SHOOT. **2.** Gmc **skutaz* in OE *scot:* SHOT[1]. **3.** Gmc **skuttjan* in OE *scytel:* SHUTTLE.
skeup-. Cluster. Gmc **skauf-* in OE *scēaf:* SHEAF.
skhed-. To split, scatter. Form **skod-* in Gmc **skat-* in OE *sceaterian:* SHATTER.
skī-. To gleam. **1.** Gmc **skīnan* in OE *scīnan:* SHINE. **2.** Gmc **skim-* in OE *scimerian:* SHIMMER.
skot-. Shade. Gmc **skadwaz* in OE *sceadu:* SHADE.
skwalo-. Big fish. Variant **kwal-* in Gmc **hwaliz* in OE *hwæl:* WHALE.
slagw-. Also **lagw-.** To seize. Gmc **lakkjan* in OE *læccan:* LATCH.
slak-. To strike. **1.** Gmc **slahan* in OE *slēan:* SLAY. **2.** Gmc **slagja-* in OE *slecg:* SLEDGEHAMMER.
slēg-. To be slack. Zero-grade form **sləg-* in Gmc **slak-* in OE *slæc:* SLACK.
sleidh-. Slippery. Gmc **slīdan* in OE *slīdan:* SLIDE.
slenk-. To wind. Variant **sleng-* in Gmc **slinkjan* in OE *slincan:* SLINK.
sleubh-. To slide. Gmc **sliub-* in OE *slēf:* SLEEVE.
smē-. To smear. Extended root **smeid-* in Gmc **smītan* in OE *smītan:* SMITE.
smeg-. To taste. Gmc **smak-* in OE *smæc:* SMACK[2].
smei-. To smile. Gmc **smer-* in OE *smearcian:* SMIRK.
smer-[1]. To remember. Zero-grade form **smr̥-* in Gmc **murnōn* in OE *murnan:* MOURN.
smer-[2]. Grease. Gmc **smerwjan* in OE *smerian:* SMEAR. [AHD *smer-[3]*.]
smerd-. Pain. Gmc **smertan* in OE *smeortan:* SMART.
smeug-. Smoke. Gmc **smuk-* in OE *smoca:* SMOKE.
smi-. To cut (as with a sharp instrument). Gmc **smithaz* in OE *smith:* SMITH.
snē-[1]. Also **ne-.** To spin, sew. Gmc **nēthlō* in OE *nǣdl:* NEEDLE.
snē-[2]. "Nose." Gmc **snuf-* in OE *snyflan:* SNIVEL.
sneg-. To creep; creeping thing. O-grade form **snog-.* **1.** Gmc **snag-ila-* in OE *snægel:* SNAIL. **2.** Gmc **snakan-* in OE *snaca:* SNAKE.
sneigwh-. Snow. O-grade form **snoigwh-* in Gmc **snaiwaz* in OE *snāw:* SNOW.
snēu-. Sinew. Variant **senw-* in Gmc **senawō* in OE *sinu:* SINEW.
so-. This. Form **syā* in Gmc **sō* in OE *sēo:* SHE.
spei-. Sharp point. **1.** Gmc **spituz* in OE *spitu:* SPIT[2]. **2.** Gmc **spī-ra-* in OE *spir:* SPIRE[1]. **3.** O-grade form **spoig-* in Gmc **spaikōn-* in OE *spāca:* SPOKE[1].
spēi-. To thrive. O-grade form **spōi-* in Gmc **spōdiz* in OE *spēd:* SPEED.
spel-[1]. To split, break off. Gmc **spilthjan* in OE *spillan:* SPILL.
spel-[2]. To recite. Gmc **spellam* in OE *spell:* SPELL[2]. [AHD *spel-[3]*.]
spen-. To draw, stretch, spin. **1.** Gmc **spinnan* in OE *spinnan:* SPIN. **2.** Gmc **spin-ilōn* in OE *spinel:* SPINDLE. **3.** O-grade form **spon-* in Gmc **spanno-* in OE *span:* SPAN[1].
sper-[1]. Spear. Gmc **speru-* in OE *spere:* SPEAR.
sper-[2]. To strew. Zero-grade form **spr̥-.* **1.** Gmc **spr-* in OE *sprēawlian:* SPRAWL. **2.** Form **spreut-* in Gmc **sprūt-* in: **a.** OE *sprūtan:* SPROUT; **b.** OE *spryttan:* SPURT. **3.** Form *spreit-* in Gmc **spraidjan* in OE *sprǣdan:* SPREAD. [AHD *sper-[4]*.]
sper-[3]. Sparrow. O-grade form **spor-* in Gmc **sparwan-* in OE *spearwa:* SPARROW.
spergh-. To move, spring. Form **sprengh-* in Gmc **springan* in OE *springan:* SPRING.
sphē-. Long, flat piece of wood. **1.** Gmc **spēnu-* in OE *spōn:* SPOON. **2.** Form *spə-dh-* in Gmc **spadan* in OE *spadu:* SPADE[1].
spher-. Ankle. **1.** Gmc **spurōn* in OE *spora:* SPUR. **2.** Gmc **spurnōn* in OE *spurnan,* to kick: SPURN.
sping-. Also **ping-.** Gmc **finki-* in OE *finc:* FINCH.
splei-. To split. Gmc **flī-* in OE *flint:* FLINT.
spoimo-. Foam. Variant **poimo-* in Gmc **faimaz* in OE *fām:* FOAM.
spreg-. To speak. Gmc **sprek-, spek-,* in: **a.** OE *specan:* SPEAK; **b.** OE *spræc:* SPEECH.
spyeu-. To spit. **1.** Gmc **spit-* in OE *spittan:* SPIT[1]. **2.** Gmc **spiu-* in OE *spīwan:* SPEW. **3.** Gmc **spāt-* in OE *spātl:* SPITTLE.
sreu-. To flow. O-grade form **srou-* in Gmc **straumaz* in OE *strēam:* STREAM.
stā-. To stand. Zero-grade form **stə-.* **1.** Gmc **standan* in: **a.** OE *standan:* STAND; **b.** OE *understandan:* UNDERSTAND. **2.** Gmc **stamniz* in OE *stemn:* STEM[1]. **3.** Gmc **stadiz* in OE *stede:* STEAD. **4.** Variant **steu-* in Gmc **stiurjan* in OE *stīeran:* STEER[1].
stāk-. To stand. Zero-grade form **stək-.* **1.** Gmc **staga-* in OE *stæg:* STAY[3]. **2.** Gmc **stahla-* in OE *stēli:* STEEL.
stebh-. Post; to place firmly on. **1.** Gmc **stab-* in OE *stæf:* STAFF. **2.** Form **steb-* in: **a.** Gmc **stap-* in OE *stæpe:* STEP; **b.** Gmc **stamp-* in OE **stampian:* STAMP.
steg-[1]. To cover. Variant o-grade form **tog-* in Gmc **thakjan* in OE *theccan:* THATCH.
steg-[2]. Stick. O-grade form **stog-* in Gmc **stak-* in OE *staca:* STAKE[1].
stegh-. To prick. **1.** Form **stengh-* in Gmc **stengjan* in OE *stingan:* STING. **2.** O-grade form **stogh-* in Gmc **stag-* in OE *stagga:* STAG.
stei-. Stone. O-grade form **stoi-* in Gmc **stainaz* in OE *stān:* STONE.
steig-. To stick. Zero-grade form **stig-.* **1.** Gmc **stik-* in OE *sticca* and *stician:* STICK. **2.** Gmc **stikiz* in OE *stice:* STITCH.
steigh-. To stride, step. **1.** Gmc **stīgan* in OE *stīgan:* STY[2]. **2.** O-grade form **stoigh-* in Gmc **staigri* in OE *stǣger:* STAIR.
steip-. To compress. Gmc **stīfaz* in OE *stīf:* STIFF.
stel-. To put, stand. Gmc **stilli-* in OE *stille:* STILL. [AHD *stel-[1]*.]
stene-. To thunder. Zero-grade form **stn̥ə-* in Gmc **thunaraz* in OE *thunor:* THUNDER.
ster-[1]. Stiff. **1.** O-grade form **stor-* in: **a.** Gmc **staren* in OE *starian:* STARE; **b.** Gmc **starkaz* in OE *stearc:* STARK; **c.** Gmc **starkjan* in OE *stercan:* STARCH. **2.** Zero-grade form **str̥-* in: **a.** Gmc **sturkaz* in OE *storc:* STORK; **b.** Gmc **strūt-* in OE *strūtian:* STRUT. **3.** Extended form **sterd-* in Gmc **stert-* in: **a.** OE *styrtan:* START; **b.** OE *steartlian:* STARTLE. **4.** Gmc **sterban* in OE *steorfan:* STARVE. **5.** Gmc **sternjaz* in OE *stierne:* STERN[1].
ster-[2]. To spread. **1.** Form **streu-* in Gmc **striw-* in OE *strēon:* STRAIN[2]. **2.** Form **strou-* in: **a.** Gmc **strawjan* in OE *strēowian:* STREW; **b.** Gmc **strāwam* in OE *strēaw:* STRAW.
ster-[3]. Star. Gmc **sterrōn-* in OE *steorra:* STAR.
ster-[4]. To steal. **1.** Gmc **stelan* in OE *stelan:* STEAL. **2.** Gmc **stalkōjan* in OE *stealcian:* STALK[2].
stern-. A thorny plant. Form **tr̥-nu-* in Gmc **thurnu-* in OE *thorn:* THORN.
steu-. To push, stick, beat. **1.** Extended forms

steup-, *steub-,* in: **a. Gmc **staup-* in OE *stēap:* STEEP[1]; **b.** Gmc **staupilaz* in OE *stȳpel:* STEEPLE; **c.** Gmc **stūp-* in OE *stūpian:* STOOP[1]; **d.** Gmc **stubb-* in OE *stybb:* STUB. **2.** Extended form **steud-* in Gmc **stuntjan* in OE *styntan:* STINT. **3.** Extended form **steug-* in Gmc **stukkaz* in OE *stocc:* STOCK.

storos. Starling. Gmc **staraz* in OE *stær:* STARLING.

streig-. To stroke, rub, press. **1.** Gmc **strīkan* in OE *strīcan:* STRIKE. **2.** Gmc **strikōn-* in OE *strica:* STREAK. **3.** O-grade form **stroig-* in Gmc **straik-* in OE **strāc:* STROKE.

su-. Pig. **1.** Gmc **swīnam* in OE *swīn:* SWINE. **2.** Celtic **sukko-* in OE *hogg:* HOG. **3.** Lengthened form **sū-* in Gmc **sū-* in OE *sugu:* SOW[2]. [AHD *su-[1]*.]

sūro-. Sour. Gmc **sūraz* in OE *sūr:* SOUR.

swād-. Sweet. Gmc **swōtja-* in OE *swēte:* SWEET.

swei-. To bend, turn. **1.** Gmc **swīp-* in: **a.** OE *swāpan:* SWEEP, SWOOP; **b.** OE *swift:* SWIFT. **2.** Gmc **swīf-* in OE *swīfan:* SWIVEL. **3.** Gmc **swīm-* in OE *swīma:* SQUEAMISH, SWIM[2]. [AHD *swei-[2]*.]

sweid-. To sweat. O-grade form **swoid-* in Gmc **swaidjan* in OE *swǣtan:* SWEAT. [AHD *sweid-[2]*.]

sweks. Six. Gmc **seks* in OE *six:* SIX.

swel-[1]. To eat, drink. Gmc **swelgan* in OE *swelgan:* SWALLOW[1].

swel-[2]. To shine, burn. Gmc **swiltan* in OE *sweltan:* SWELTER.

swel-[3]. Post. Gmc **suljō-* in OE *sylle:* SILL.

swen-. To sound. O-grade form **swon-* in Gmc **swanaz* in OE *swan:* SWAN.

sweng-. To swing. Gmc **swingan* in OE *swingan:* SWING.

swento-. Healthy. Form **sunto-* in Gmc **sunth-* in OE *gesund:* SOUND[2].

swer-[1]. To talk. O-grade form **swor-* in: **a.** Gmc **swarjan* in OE *swerian:* SWEAR; **b.** Gmc **andswaru,* "a swearing against," in OE *andswaru:* ANSWER.

swer-[2]. To buzz. O-grade form **swor-* in Gmc **swarmaz* in OE *swearm:* SWARM.

swer-[3]. To pierce. Gmc **swerdam* in OE *sword:* SWORD. [AHD *swer-[4]*.]

swerbh-. To turn, wipe off. Gmc **swerb-* in OE *sweorfan:* SWERVE.

swergh-. To worry. Gmc **sorg-* in OE *sorh:* SORROW.

swesor-. Sister. Form **swesr̥-* in Gmc **swistr-* in OE *sweostor:* SISTER.

swo-. So. **1.** Gmc **swa-* in OE *swā:* SO. **2.** Gmc **swa-līk-* in OE *swylc:* SUCH.

swordo-. Black, dirty. Gmc **swartaz* in OE *sweart:* SWARTHY.

syū-. To bind, sew. **1.** Gmc **siwjan* in OE *seowian:* SEW. **2.** Form **sū-* in Gmc **saumaz* in OE *sēam:* SEAM.

tā-. To melt. Gmc **thāwōn* in OE *thāwian:* THAW.

tegu-. Thick. Gmc **thiku-* in OE *thicce:* THICK.

ten-. To stretch. Zero-grade form **tn̥-* in Gmc **thunniz* in OE *thynne:* THIN.

ter-[1]. To pass through. Zero-grade form **tr̥-* in Gmc **thurh* in OE *thurh:* THROUGH. [AHD *ter-[3]*.]

ter-[2]. To rub, turn. **1.** Gmc **thersk-* in: **a.** OE *therscan:* THRESH; **b.** OE *therscold:* THRESHOLD. **2.** Form **trē-* in: **a.** Gmc **thrēw-* in OE *thrāwan:* THROW; **b.** Gmc **thrēdu-* in OE *thrǣd:* THREAD.

ters-. To dry. Zero-grade form **tr̥s-* in Gmc **thurs-* in OE *thurst:* THIRST.

teuə-. To swell. **1.** Form **teuk-* in Gmc **thiuham* in OE *thēoh:* THIGH. **2.** Form **teus-* in Gmc **thus-hundi-,* "swollen hundred," in OE *thūsend:* THOUSAND. **3.** Form **tum-* in OE *thūma:* THUMB.

to-. Demonstrative pronoun. **1.** Gmc **thē-* in OE *thē:* THE. **2.** Gmc **thasi-* in OE *thes:* THIS. **3.** Gmc **thana-* in OE *thanne:* THAN, THEN. **4.** Gmc **thanana-* in OE *thanon:* THENCE. **5.** Gmc **thar* in OE *thēr:* THERE. **6.** Gmc **thathro* in OE *thider:* THITHER. **7.** Gmc **thai* in OE *thā* (and ON *their*): THEY. **8.** Gmc **thaim* in OE *thǣm* (and ON *theim*): THEM. **9.** Gmc **that* in OE *thæt:* THAT. **10.** Gmc **thus-* in OE *thus:* THUS.

tong-. To think, feel. **1.** Gmc **thankōn* in: **a.** OE *thancian:* THANK; **b.** OE *thencan:* THINK **2.** Gmc **thauht-* in OE *thōht:* THOUGHT.

trei-. Three. **1.** Gmc **thrijiz* in OE *thrēo, thriga, thrītig,* and *thrēotīne:* THREE, THRICE, THIRTY, THIRTEEN. **2.** Gmc **thrithjaz* in OE *thridda:* THIRD.

treud-. To squeeze. Gmc **thriut-* in OE *thrēat:* THREAT.

trozdos-. Thrush. Gmc **thruskjōn-* in OE *thrysce:* THRUSH.

tu-. You, thou. **1.** Form **tū* in Gmc **thū* in OE *thū:* THOU. **2.** Form **twei-no-* in Gmc **thīnaz* in OE *thīn:* THINE, THY.

twei-. To agitate, toss. Extended form **tweid-* in Gmc **thwīt-* in OE *thwītan:* WHITTLE.

twengh-. To press in on. **1.** Gmc **thwang-* in OE *thwang:* THONG. **2.** Gmc **twangjan* in OE *twengan:* TWINGE.

twer-. To whirl. Variant **stur-*. **1.** Gmc **sturmaz* in OE *storm:* STORM. **2.** Gmc **sturjan* in OE *styrian:* STIR. [AHD *twer-[1]*.]

ud-. Up, out. **1.** Gmc **ūt-* in OE *ūt:* OUT. **2.** Gmc **ūt-era-* in OE *ūtera:* UTTER[2]. **3.** Gmc **bi-ūtana* in OE *būtan:* BUT, ABOUT.

uper. Over. Gmc **uberi* in OE *ofer:* OVER.

upo. Under, up from under, over. **1.** Gmc **upp-* in OE *up, uppe:* UP. **2.** Gmc **upanaz* in OE *open:* OPEN. **3.** Gmc **bi-ufana* in OE *abufan:* ABOVE. **4.** Gmc **ubilaz,* "excessive," in OE *yfel:* EVIL. **5.** Gmc **obaswa,* "that which is above," in OE *yfes:* EAVES.

wā-. To wound. Zero-grade form **wn̥-* in Gmc **wundaz* in OE *wund:* WOUND[1]. [AHD *wā-[2]*.]

wāb-. To cry. Gmc **wōpjan* in OE *wēpan:* WEEP.

wadh-. A pledge. Gmc **wadi-* in OE *weddian:* WED.

wādh-. To go. Gmc **wathan* in OE *wadan:* WADE.

wai. Alas. Gmc **wai* in OE *wā:* WOE.

wal-. To be strong. Form **woldh-* in Gmc **waldan* in OE *wieldan:* WIELD.

we-. We. Gmc **wīz* in OE *wē:* WE.

wē-. To blow. **1.** Gmc **wedram* in OE *weder:* WEATHER. **2.** Gmc **windaz* in OE *wind:* WIND[1].

webh-. To weave. **1.** Gmc **weban* in OE *wefan:* WEAVE. **2.** O-grade form **wobh-* in Gmc **wabjam* in OE *webb:* WEB.

wed-. Water; wet. **1.** O-grade form **wod-* in: **a.** Gmc **watar-* in OE *wæter:* WATER; **b.** Gmc **wat-skan* in OE *wæscan:* WASH. **2.** Form **wēd-* in Gmc **wēd-* in OE *wǣt:* WET. **3.** Form **wend-* in Gmc **wintruz* in OE *winter:* WINTER. **4.** Form **ud-ro-* in Gmc **otraz* in OE *otor:* OTTER. [AHD *wed-[1]*.]

weg-. To be lively. O-grade form **wog-*. **1.** Gmc **waken* in OE *wacian* and **wacan:* WAKE[1]. **2.** Gmc **wakjan* in OE *wæccan:* WATCH. [AHD *weg-[2]*.]

wegh-. To go, transport. **1.** Gmc **wigan* in OE *wegan:* WEIGH[1]. **2.** Gmc **wihti-* in OE *wiht:* WEIGHT. **3.** Gmc **wegaz* in OE *weg:* WAY.

wei-[1]. To twist. Gmc **wī-ra-* in OE *wīr:* WIRE.

wei-[2]. To wither. Gmc **wis-* in OE *wisnian:* WIZENED. [AHD *wei-[3]*.]

weid-. To see. **1.** Gmc **wītan* in OE *wītan:* TWIT. **2.** Gmc **wīssaz* in: **a.** OE *wīs:* WISE[1]; **b.** OE *wīsdōm:* WISDOM. **3.** Gmc **wīssōn-* in OE *wīse:* WISE[2]. **4.** Zero-grade form **wid-* in: **a.** Gmc **wit-* in OE *wit:* WIT; **b.** Gmc **witan* in OE *witan:* UNWITTING.

weidh-. To separate. Zero-grade form **widh-* in Gmc **widewaz* in OE *widuwe:* WIDOW.

weik-[1]. To wind. Variant **weig-*. Gmc **wikōn-,* "a series," in OE *wice:* WEEK. [AHD *weik-[4]*.]

weik-[2]. "Divination, sorcery." Gmc **wikk-* in OE *wicce* and *wicca:* WICKED, WITCH.

weip-. To vacillate. Variant **weib-* in Gmc **wīpjan,* "to move back and forth," in OE *wīpian:* WIPE.

weis-. To flow. Gmc **wisōn* in OE *wāse:* OOZE[2]. [AHD *weis-[1]*.]

wekti-. Thing. Gmc **wihti-* in OE *wiht:* NOT.

wel-[1]. Wool. Gmc **wullō* in OE *wull:* WOOL. [AHD *wel-[5]*.]

wel-[2]. To wish, will. **1.** Gmc **wel-* in OE *wel:* WELL[2]. **2.** Gmc **wiljōn-* in OE *will:* WILL[1]. **3.** Gmc **willjan* in OE *wyllan:* WILL[2].

wel-[3]. To turn, roll. **1.** O-grade form **wol-* in Gmc **wall-* in OE *wælla:* WELL[1]. **2.** Form **welw-* in Gmc **walwōn* in OE *wealwian:* WALLOW.

welt-. Wild. Gmc **wilthigaz* in OE *wilde:* WILD.

wen-. To desire, strive for. **1.** Gmc **winnan* in OE *winnan:* WIN. **2.** Zero-grade form **wn̥-* in: **a.** Gmc **wunēn* in OE *wunian:* WONT; **b.** Gmc **wunsk-* in OE *wȳscan:* WISH. **3.** Gmc **wanjan* in OE *wenian:* WEAN.

wendh-. To turn, wind. **1.** Gmc **windan* in OE *windan:* WIND[2]. **2.** Gmc **wandjan* in OE *wendan:* WEND. **3.** Gmc **wandrōn* in OE *wandrian:* WANDER.

weng-. To bend, curve. **1.** Gmc **wink-* in OE *wincian:* WINK. **2.** Gmc **winkja* in OE *wince:* WINCH. **3.** Gmc **winkil-* in OE *-wincel:* PERIWINKLE[1].

wer-[1]. High, raised spot. Gmc **wartōn-* in OE *wearte:* WART.

wer-[2]. To speak. Zero-grade form **wr̥-* in Gmc **wurdam* in OE *word:* WORD. [AHD *wer-[6]*.]

wer-[3]. To turn, bend. **1.** Form **wert-* in: **a.** Gmc **warth-* in OE *-weard:* -WARD; **b.** Gmc **wurth-,* "that which befalls one," in OE *wyrd:* WEIRD. **2.** Form **wreit-* in Gmc **wrīth-* in: **a.** OE *writha:* WREATH; **b.** OE *wrīthan:* WRITHE; **c.** OE *wrāth:* WRATH. **3.** Form **wergh-*. **a.** Gmc **wurgjan* in OE *wyrgan:* WORRY; **b.** Gmc **wreng-* in OE *wringan:* WRING. **4.** Root **werg-* in Gmc **wrankjan* in: **a.** OE *wrencan:* WRENCH; **b.** OE *gewrinclian:* WRINKLE. **5.** Form **wreik-*. **a.** Gmc **wrīg-* in OE *wrīgian:* WRY; **b.** Gmc **wristiz* in OE *wrist:* WRIST. **6.** Form **wrizd-* in Gmc **wraistjan* in OE *wrǣstan* and *wrǣstlian:* WREST, WRESTLE. **7.** Form **werb-* in Gmc **werp-* in OE *weorpan:* WARP. **8.** Form **wermi-* in Gmc **wurmiz* in OE *wyrm:* WORM.

wer-[4]. To watch out for. O-grade form **wor-*. **1.** Gmc **waraz* in: **a.** OE *wær:* WARY; **b.** OE *gewær:* AWARE. **2.** Gmc **wardaz* in OE *weard:* WARD.

wer-[5]. To cover. O-grade form **wor-* in Gmc **war-n-* in OE *wearnian:* WARN.

werg-. To do. Gmc **werkam* in OE *weorc:* WORK. [AHD *werg-[1]*.]

wers-. To confuse. Gmc **wersizōn-* in OE *wyrsa:* WORSE.

wes-[1]. To clothe. O-grade form **wos-* in Gmc **wazjan* in OE *werian:* WEAR. [AHD *wes-[4]*.]

wes-[2]. Wet. Gmc **wōs-* in OE *wōs:* OOZE[1].

wes-[3]. To delay; "to be." O-grade form **wos-* in Gmc **wos-* in OE *wæs, wǣre, wǣron:* WAS, WERE.

wespero-. Evening, night. Gmc **west-* in OE *west,* WEST.

wi-. Apart, in half. **1.** Gmc **wīdaz* in OE *wīd:* WIDE. **2.** Gmc **withrō* in OE *with:* WITH.

widhu-. Tree. Gmc **widu-* in OE *wudu:* WOOD.

wiros. Man. Gmc **weraldh-,* "life or age of man," in OE *weorold:* WORLD.

wl̥kwo-. Wolf. Variant **wl̥po-* in Gmc **wulfaz*

in OE *wulf:* WOLF.
wokso-. Wax. Gmc **wahsam* in OE *wæx:* WAX.
wopsā. Wasp. Variant **wospā* in Gmc **wosp-* in OE *wæsp:* WASP.
wreg-. To shove, drive. **1.** Gmc **wrekan* in OE *wrecan:* WREAK. **2.** O-grade form **wrog-* in Gmc **wrakjō,* "one pursued," in OE *wrecca:* WRETCH.
wrōd-. To root, gnaw. Gmc **wrōt-* in OE *wrōtan:* ROOT².
wrughyo-. Rye. Gmc **rugi-* in OE *ryge:* RYE.
yeg-. Ice. Gmc **jekilaz* in OE *gicel:* ICICLE.
yēro-. Year. Gmc **jēram* in OE *gēar:* YEAR.
yes-. To bubble. Gmc **jest-* in OE *gist,* yeast: YEAST.
yeu-. Young. **1.** Gmc **juwungaz* in OE *geong:* YOUNG. **2.** Gmc **jugunth-* in OE *geoguth:* YOUTH. [AHD *yeu-²*.]
yeug-. To join. Zero-grade form **yug-* in Gmc **yukam* in OE *geoc:* YOKE.
yu-. You. Gmc **jūz* and **iww-* in OE *gē, ēow, ēower:* YE², YOU, YOUR. [AHD *yu-¹*.]

PICTURE CREDITS

The following list of credits includes the names of many of the organizations and individuals who helped secure illustrations for this Dictionary. The editors wish to thank all of them—as well as others not specifically mentioned—for their invaluable assistance. The credits are arranged alphabetically by entry word, which is printed in boldface type. Unless we have indicated to the contrary, all maps were supplied by Francis & Shaw, Inc., and all human anatomy drawings were supplied by Neil Hardy.

abacus From the Collection of the IBM Corp.; **John Adams** U.S. Bureau of Engraving; **John Quincy Adams** The New-York Historical Society, New York City; **Apollo** Vatican Museum, Photo Alinari; **Chester A. Arthur** U.S. Bureau of Engraving; **Athena** British Museum (Leonard Von Matt); **Augustus** Leonard Von Matt; **bacteria** Prepared from materials in Frobisher's *Fundamentals of Microbiology*, 8th Edition, W.B. Saunders Co., Philadelphia, Pa., 1968; **beef** Jean Erdoes; **Simón Bolívar** Sr. Alfredo Boulton, Caracas; **Brahma** The Metropolitan Museum of Art, Eggleston Fund, 1927; **Braille alphabet** Phoebe McGuire; **Leonid Brezhnev** Pictorial Parade; **James Buchanan** Brown Brothers; **Buddha** Photo Giraudon; **Julius Caesar** Photo Alinari; **Winston Churchill** © Karsh, Ottawa; **Grover Cleveland** Library of Congress; **comet** Yerkes Observatory Photograph; **compass** E.S. Ritchie & Sons, Inc.; **Calvin Coolidge** Library of Congress; **currency** Fundamental Photographs, courtesy American Numismatic Society; **Charles Darwin** Radio Times Hulton Picture Library; **Jefferson Davis** National Archives, Brady Collection; **Charles De Gaulle** French Embassy, Press & Information Division; **Frederick Douglass** Library of Congress; **eclipse** John G. Kirk, Kitt Peak National Observatory; **Albert Einstein** Ernst Haas, © 1966 Magnum Photos; **Dwight David Eisenhower** Burt Glinn, © 1966 Magnum Photos; **Elizabeth I** Detail from National Portrait Gallery, London; **Millard Fillmore** Culver Pictures, Inc.; **fish** Francis & Shaw, Inc.; **flag** (International Code) Phoebe McGuire; **flower** Matthew Kalmenoff; **Benjamin Franklin** Historical Society of Pa.; **Sigmund Freud** Culver Pictures, Inc.; **galaxy** California Institute of Technology—Mount Wilson and Palomar Observatories—(diagrams) After E.P. Hubble from *Sourcebook of Space Sciences* by Samuel Glasstone, © 1965, by Litton Educational Publishing, Inc., by permission of Van Nostrand Reinhold Company; **Mahatma Gandhi** Information Service of India; **James A. Garfield** U.S. Bureau of Engraving; **Geronimo** National Archives; **gill¹** Neil Hardy; **Ulysses S. Grant** The GAF Historical Photo Collection; **Johann Gutenberg** Culver Pictures, Inc.; **Dag Hammarskjöld** United Nations; **Warren G. Harding** Library of Congress; **Benjamin Harrison** U.S. Bureau of Engraving; **William Henry Harrison** The Metropolitan Museum of Art, Gift of I.N. Phelps Stokes, Edward S. Hawes, Alice Mary Hawes, Marion Augusta Hawes, 1937; **Rutherford B. Hayes** Culver Pictures, Inc.; **Adolf Hitler** Wide World Photos; **Ho Chi Minh** Eastfoto; **Herbert Hoover** Fabian Bachrach; **Table of Indo-European Languages** Phoebe McGuire; **Andrew Jackson** The New-York Historical Society, New York City; **Thomas Jefferson** The New-York Historical Society, New York City; **Andrew Johnson** Library of Congress; **Lyndon Baines Johnson** Gerry Cranham, Rapho-Guillumette; **John F. Kennedy** Ted Spiegel, Rapho-Guillumette; **Martin Luther King, Jr.** Wide World Photos; **lamb** Cal Sacks; **Lenin** Tass, from Sovfoto; **Abraham Lincoln** Library of Congress; **Lin Piao** Wide World Photos; **Martin Luther** Uffizi Gallery, Florence, Photo Alinari; **James Madison** U.S. Bureau of Engraving; **manual alphabet** Gallaudet College, Washington, D.C.; **Mao Tse-tung** Eastfoto; **Karl Marx** Sovfoto; **William McKinley** Library of Congress; **James Monroe** The Metropolitan Museum of Art, Bequest of Seth Low, 1929; **Benito Mussolini** United Press International Photo; **Napoleon I** Samuel H. Kress Collection, National Gallery of Art, Washington, D.C.; **Richard M. Nixon** United Press International Photo; **Noah** Pierpont Morgan Library; **note** Cal Sacks; **Pericles** British Museum; **Saint Peter** Vatican Grottoes, Leonard Von Matt; **Franklin Pierce** Library of Congress; **James K. Polk** U.S. Bureau of Engraving; **pork** Cal Sacks; **Quetzalcoatl** Bibliothèque Nationale; **Franklin Delano Roosevelt** Franklin D. Roosevelt Library; **Theodore Roosevelt** The White House Collection; **rune** Alice Koeth; **Sitting Bull** National Archives; **Joseph Stalin** Sovfoto; **William Howard Taft** Library of Congress; **Zachary Taylor** U.S. Bureau of Engraving; **Harry S Truman** Wide World Photos; **John Tyler** The White House Collection; **Martin Van Buren** Library of Congress; **Victoria¹** Radio Times Hulton Picture Library; **Booker T. Washington** Chicago American's Morgue; **George Washington** Pennsylvania Academy of Fine Arts; **Woodrow Wilson** The White House Collection; **zodiac** Zodiac design adapted from zodiac drawn by Hans Holbein and Albrecht Dürer, reproduced with the permission of Charles Scribner's Sons from *Shakespeare's Globe Playhouse* by Irwin Smith, © 1956 Charles Scribner's Sons.

Word Division Dictionary

WORDBREAK RULES

1. Division of words should be minimized in leaded matter and avoided in double-leaded matter.

2. Except in narrow measures, wordbreaks should be avoided at the ends of more than two lines. Similarly, no more than two consecutive lines should end with the same word, symbol, group of numbers, etc.

3. In two-line centerheads, the first line should be centered and set as full as possible, but it is not set to fill the measure by unduly wide spacing. Wordbreaks should be avoided. Flush sideheads are set full measure and wordbreaks are permitted if unavoidable. They are not set ragged unless so indicated on copy.

4. The final word of a paragraph should not be divided.

5. Words should preferably be divided according to pronunciation; and to avoid mispronunciation, they should be divided so that the part of the word left at the end of the line will suggest the whole word: *capac-ity*, not *capa-city; extraor-dinary*, not *extra-ordinary; Wednes-day*, not *Wed-nesday; physi-cal*, not *phys-ical; service-man*, not *serv-iceman*.

6. Although Word Division lists beginning and ending one-letter syllables for pronunciation purposes, under no circumstances are words to be divided on a single letter (e.g., *usu-al-ly*, not *u-su-al-ly; imag-i-nary*, not *i-mag i nar y*).

7. Division of short words (of five or fewer letters) should be avoided; two-letter divisions, including the carryover of two-letter endings (*ed, el, en, er, es, et, fy, ic, in, le, ly, or*, and *ty*); should also be avoided. In narrow measure, however, a sounded suffix (e.g., paint-*ed;* not rained) or syllable of two letters may be carried over—only if unavoidable. (See rule 10.)

8. Words of two syllables are split at the end of the first syllable: *dis-pelled, con-quered;* words of three or more syllables, with a choice of division possible, divide preferably on the vowel: *particu-lar, sepa-rate*.

9. In words with short prefixes, divide on the prefix; e.g., *ac, co, de, dis, ex, in, non, on, pre, pro, re, un*, etc. (e.g. *non-essential*, not *nones-sential; pre-selected*, not *prese-lected*).

If possible, prefixes and combining forms of more than one syllable are preserved intact: *anti, infra, macro, micro, multi, over, retro, semi*, etc. (e.g., *anti-monopoly*, not *antimo-nopoly; over-optimistic*, not *overop-timistic*). (For chemical prefixes, see rule 30.)

10. *Words ending in* -er.—Although two-letter carryovers are to be avoided (rule 7), many *-er* words which are derived from comparatives (*coarse, coarser; sharp, sharper*) have been listed to prevent a wrong wordbreak; e.g., *coars-er*, not *coar-ser*.

Nouns ending in *-er* (*adviser, bracer, keeper, perceiver, reader*) derived from action verbs are also listed to prevent a wrong division; e.g., *perceiv-er*, not *percei-ver*.

Except in narrow measure and if unavoidable, the above *-er* words are not divided unless division can be made on a prefix; e.g., *per-ceiver*.

11. *Words ending in* -or.—Generally, *-or* words with a consonant preceding are divided before the preceding consonant; e.g., *advi-sor* (legal), *fabrica-tor, guaran-tor, interve-nor, simula-tor, tai-lor;* but *bail-or, bargain-or, con-sign-or, grant-or*.

12. The following suffixes are not divided: *ceous, cial, cient, cion, cious, scious, geous, gion, gious, sial, tial, tion, tious*, and *sion*.

13. The suffixes *-able* and *-ible* are usually carried over intact; but when the stem word loses its original form, these suffixes are divided according to pronunciation: *comfort-able, corrupt-ible, manage-able;* but *dura-ble, audi-ble*.

14. Words ending in *-ing*, with stress on the primary syllable, are preferably divided on the base word; e.g., *appoint-ing, combat-ing, danc-ing, engineer-ing, process-ing, program-ing, stencil-ing, trac-ing*, etc. However, present participles, such as *control-ling, forbid-ding, refer-ring*, with stress placed on the second syllable, divide between the doubled consonants (see also rule 16).

15. When the final consonant sound of a word belongs to a syllable ending with a silent vowel, the final consonant or consonants become part of the added suffix: *chuck-ling, han-dler, han-dling, crum-bling, twin-kled, twin-kling;* but *rollick-ing*.

16. When the addition of *-ed, -er, -est*, or of a similar ending, causes the doubling of a final consonant, the added consonant is carried over: *pit-ted, rob-ber, thin-nest, glad-den, control-lable, transmit-table;* but *bless-ed* (adj.), *dwell-er, gross-est*.

17. Words with doubled consonants are usually divided between these consonants: *clas-sic, ruf-fian, neces-sary, rebel-lion;* but *call-ing, mass-ing*.

18. If formation of a plural adds a syllable ending in an *s* sound, the plural ending should not be carried over by itself: *hor-ses, voi-ces;* but *church-es, cross-es*, thus not breaking the base word (see also rule 7).

19. The digraphs *ai, ck, dg, gh, gn, ng, oa, ph, sh, tch*, and *th* are not split.

20. Do not divide contractions: *doesn't, haven't*.

21. Solid compounds are divided preferably between the members: *bar-keeper, hand-kerchief, proof-reader, humming-bird*.

22. Avoid a division which adds another hyphen to a hyphened compound: *court-martial*, not *court-mar-tial; tax-supported*, not *tax-sup-ported*.

23. A word of one syllable is not split: *tanned, shipped, quenched, through, chasm, prism*.

24. Two consonants preceded and followed by a vowel are divided on the first consonant: *abun-dant, advan-tage, struc-ture;* but *attend-ant, accept-ance, depend-ence*.

25. When two adjoining vowels are sounded separately, divide between them: *cre-ation, gene-alogy*.

26. In breaking homonyms, distinction should be given to their relative functions: *pro-ject* (v.), *proj-ect* (n.); *pro-duce* (v.), *prod-uce* (n.); *stran-ger* (n.), *strang-er* (comparative adjective); *rec-ollect* (recall), *re-collect* (collect again); but *proc-ess* (n., v.); *pro-test* (n., v.).

27. *Words ending in* -meter.—In the large group of words ending in *-meter*, distinction should be made between metric system terms and terms indicating a measuring instrument. When it is necessary to divide metric terms, preserve the combining form *-meter;* e.g., *centi-meter, deca-meter, hecto-meter, kilo-meter*. Bu measuring instruments divide after the *m: al-tim-e-ter, ba-rom-e-ter, mi-crom-e-ter, mul-tim-e-ter*, etc. Derivatives of these *-meter* terms follow the same form; e.g., *mul-tim-e-ter, mul-tim-e-try*.

For orthographic reasons, however, several measuring instruments do not lend themselves to the general rule; e.g., *flow-meter, flux-meter, gauss-meter, taxi-meter, torque-meter, volt-meter, water-meter, watt-meter*, etc.

28. *Foreign languages.*—Rules for word division in foreign languages, by language, are printed in the 1967 GPO Style Manual (unabridged), pages 387–492.

29. *Chemical formulas.*—In chemical formulas, the hyphen has an important function. If a break is unavoidable in a formula, division is preferably made after an original hyphen to avoid the introduction of a misleading hyphen. If impractical to break on a hyphen, division may be made after an original comma, and no hyphen is added to indicate a runover. The following formula shows original hyphens and commas where division may be made. No letterspacing is used in a chemical formula, but to fill a line, a space is permitted on both sides of a hyphen.

1-(2,6,6-trimethylcyclohex-1- en -1- yl)-
3,7,12,16

30. *Chemical combining forms, prefixes, and suffixes.*—If possible, and subject to rules of good spacing, it is desirable to preserve as a unit such combining forms as follows:

aceto, anhydro, benzo, bromo, chloro, chromo, cincho, cyclo, dehydro, diazo, flavo, fluoro, glyco, hydroxy, iso, keto, methyl, naphtho, phospho, poly, silico, tetra, triazo.

The following suffixes are used in chemical printing. For patent and narrow measure composition, two-letter suffixes may be carried over.

al, an, ane, ase, ate, ene, ic, id, ide, in, ine, ite, ol, ole, on, one, ose, ous oyl, yl, yne.

31. *Mineral elements.*—When it is necessary to break mineral constituents, division should preferably be made before a center period and beginning parenthesis, and after inferior figures following a closing parenthesis; but elements within parentheses are not separated. In cases of unavoidable breaks, a hyphen is not added to indicate a runover.

$$Mg(UO_2)_2(SiO_3)_2(OH)_2 \cdot 6H_2O$$

32. The em dash is not used at the beginning of any line of type, unless it is required before a credit line or signature, or in lieu of opening quotation marks in foreign languages. (See rules 9.52, 9.53, p. 142, 1967 GPO Style Manual.)

33. Neither periods nor asterisks used as an ellipsis are overrun alone at the end of a paragraph. If necessary, run over enough preceding lines to provide a short word or part of a word to accompany the ellipsis. If a runback is possible, subject to rules of good spacing and word division, this method may be adopted.

34. Abbreviations and symbols should not be broken at the end of a line: *A.F. of L., A.T. & T., C. Cls. R., f.o.b., n.o.i.b.n., R. & D., r.p.m., WMAL.* Where unavoidable in narrow measures and AGO's, long symbols may be broken after letters denoting a complete word. Use no hyphens. COM SUB A C LANT (Commander Submarine Allied Command Atlantic).

35. Figures of less than six digits, decimals, and closely connected combinations of figures and abbreviations should not be broken at the end of a line: *$15,000, 34,575, 31.416, £8 4s. 7d., $10.25, 5,000 kw.-hr., A.D. 1952, 9 p.m., 18° F., NW¼.* If a break in six digits or over is unavoidable, divide on the comma or period, retain it, and use a hyphen.

36. Closely related abbreviations and initials in proper names and accompanying titles should not be separated, nor should titles, such as *Rev., Mr., Esq., Jr., 2d,* be separated from surnames.

37. Avoid dividing proper names, but if inescapable, follow general rules for word division.

38. Divisional and subdivisional paragraph reference signs and figures, such as *§ 18, section (a)(1), page 363(b),* should not be divided, nor should such references be separated from the matter to which they pertain.

In case of an unavoidable break in a lengthy reference (e.g., *7(B)(1)(a)(i)*), division will be made after elements in parentheses, and no hyphen is used.

39. In dates, do not divide the month and day, but the year may be carried over.

40. In case of an unavoidable break in a land-description symbol group at the end of a line, use no hyphen and break after a fraction.

41. Avoid breaking longitude and latitude figures at the end of a line; space out the line instead. In case of an unavoidable break at end of line, use hyphen.

A

Aar-on
Aa-ron-ic
ab-a-ca
ab-a-cus
ab-a-lo-ne
a-ban-don
a-bat-a-ble
ab-a-tis
ab-at-toir
a-bet-ter
a-bet-tor (law)
ab-bre-vi-a-tor
ab-di-ca-tor
ab-do-men
ab-dom-i-nal
ab-dom-i-no-per-i-ne-al
ab-dom-i-nos-co-py
ab-duc-tor
a-be-ce-dar-i-an
A-bed-ne-go
ab-en-ter-ic
ab-er-om-e-ter
ab-er-ra-tion
a-bey-ance
ab-hor-rence
ab-hor-ri-ble
a-bid-ance
ab-i-et-ic
Ab-i-gail
Ab-i-lene
a-bil-i-ty
a-bi-ot-ic
a-bi-ot-ro-phy
ab-ju-ra-tion
ab-jur-a-to-ry
ab-la-tive
a-blep-si-a
ab-ne-ga-tor
ab-nor-mal-i-ty
ab-nor-mi-ty
a-bol-ish
ab-o-li-tion-ist
a-bom-i-na-ble
ab-o-rig-i-nes
a-bor-ti-cide
a-bort-in
a-bor-tive
ab-ra-ca-dab-ra
a-brad-ant
A-bra-ham
a-bran-chi-ate
ab-ra-si-om-e-ter
ab-ra-sion
ab-ra-sive
a-bridg-ment
ab-ro-ga-tive
ab-rupt
ab-scess
ab-scis-sa
ab-scis-sion
ab-scond
ab-sence
ab-sen-tee-ism
ab-sinthe
ab-sin-thin
ab-so-lu-tion
ab-so-lut-ism
ab-so-lu-tive
ab-so-lu-tize
ab-sol-u-to-ry
ab-sol-vent
ab-solv-er
ab-sorb-ate
ab-sorb-ent
ab-sorp-tance
ab-sorp-ti-om-e-ter
ab-ste-mi-ous
ab-sten-tious
ab-ster-gent
ab-sti-nence
ab-stract-er
ab-strac-tive
ab-struse
ab-surd-i-ty
a-bu-lo-ma-ni-a
a-bun-dance
a-bus-age
a-bu-sive
a-but-ting
a-bys-mal
a-byss-al
Ab-ys-sin-i-an
a-ca-cia
ac-a-dem-i-cal
a-cad-e-mi-cian
a-cad-e-my
a-camp-si-a
ac-a-na-ceous
ac-an-tha-ceous
a-can-thoid
ac-an-tho-ma
a-can-thus
a cap-pel-la
a-cap-su-lar
a-ca-pul-co
a-car-dite
ac-a-ri-a-sis
a-car-i-cid-al
ac-a-roid
a-cau-date
ac-ced-ence
ac-cel-er-ans
ac-cel-er-a-tive
ac-cel-er-a-tor
ac-cel-er-om-e-ter
ac-cend-i-ble
ac-cen-tu-a-tor
ac-cept-a-ble
ac-cept-ance
ac-cep-ta-tion
ac-cept-er
ac-cep-tor (law)
ac-ces-si-ble
ac-ces-so-ri-al
ac-ciac-ca-tu-ra
ac-ci-den-tal
ac-cla-ma-tion
ac-clam-a-to-ry
ac-cli-mate
ac-cli-ma-ti-za-tion
ac-cliv-i-ty
ac-cli-vous
ac-co-lade
ac-com-mo-dat-ing
ac-com-pa-ni-ment
ac-com-pa-nist
ac-com-plice
ac-com-plish
ac-cord-ance
ac-cor-di-on-ist
ac-couche-ment
ac-cou-cheur
ac-count-a-ble
ac-count-an-cy
ac-cou-ter
ac-cred-i-ta-tion
ac-cres-cence
ac-cre-tive
ac-cul-tur-ate
ac-cum-bent
ac-cu-mu-la-tive
ac-cu-mu-la-tor
ac-cu-ra-cy
ac-cursed (v.)
ac-curs-ed (adj.)
ac-cus-a-ble
ac-cu-sa-tive
ac-cus-a-to-ry
ac-cus-er
ac-cus-tomed
ac-e-naph-thy-lene
a-ceph-a-lous (adj.)
a-ceph-a-lus (n.)
ac-er-bate
a-cer-bi-ty
ac-er-ose
ac-e-tab-u-lum
ac-et-al-de-hyde
a-cet-a-mide
ac-et-am-i-dine
ac-et-a-mi-do-cin-nam-ic
ac-et-an-i-lide
ac-et-ar-sone
ac-e-tate
ac-e-ta-to-so-da-lite
a-ce-tic
a-ce-ti-fy
ac-e-tin
ac-e-to-ac-et-an-i-lide
a-cet-o-in
ac-e-tol-y-sis
ac-e-tom-e-ter
ac-e-tom-e-try
ac-e-tone
ac-e-ton-yl-i-dene
ac-e-to-phe-net-i-dide
ac-e-to-phe-none
ac-e-to-pro-pi-o-nate
ac-e-to-pur-pu-rine
ac-e-tous
ac-e-tox-yl
a-ce-tum
ac-e-tyl-ac-e-tone
a-cet-y-late
a-cet-y-la-tor
ac-e-tyl-cho-line
a-cet-y-lene
a-cet-y-lide
ac-e-tyl-meth-yl-car-bi-nol
ac-e-tyl-phen-yl-hy-dra-zine
ac-e-tyl-sa-lic-y-late
ac-e-tyl-sal-i-cyl-ic
Ach-il-le-an
A-chil-les
a-chol-ic
ach-ro-mat-ic
ach-ro-ma-tic-i-ty
a-chro-ma-tin
a-chro-ma-tism
a-cic-u-lar
ac-i-dif-er-ous
ac-i-dim-e-ter
ac-i-dim-e-try
a-cid-i-ty
a-cid-o-phil
ac-i-doph-i-lus
ac-i-do-sis
a-cid-u-lous
ac-i-na-ceous
ac-knowl-edge-a-ble
ac-knowl-edg-ment
ac-o-lyte
a-con-ic
ac-o-nite
ac-o-nit-ic
a-con-i-tine
a-cou-me-ter
a-cou-me-try
a-con-ti-um
a-cous-tic
ac-ous-ti-cian
a-cous-ti-con
ac-quaint-ance
ac-quaint-ed
ac-qui-es-cence
ac-quire
ac-qui-si-tion
ac-quis-i-tive
ac-quit-tal
a-cre-age
ac-ri-bom-e-ter
ac-rid
ac-ri-dine
ac-ri-din-i-um
a-crid-i-ty
ac-ri-mo-ni-ous
ac-ro-bat-ic
ac-ro-gen
a-crog-e-nous
a-cro-le-in
ac-ro-lith
ac-ro-nym
a-crop-e-tal
ac-ro-pho-bi-a
a-croph-o-ny
a-crop-o-lis
a-cros-tic
a-crot-ic
ac-ryl-am-ide
ac-ry-late
a-cryl-ic
ac-ry-lo-ni-trile
a-cryl-o-yl
ac-ry-lyl
ac-tin-ic
ac-tin-ism
ac-tin-i-um
ac-ti-no-bac-il-lo-sis
ac-ti-noid
ac-tin-o-lite
ac-ti-nom-e-ter
ac-ti-no-my-cin
ac-ti-no-my-co-sis
ac-ti-nos-co-py
ac-tion-om-e-ter
ac-ti-va-ble
ac-ti-va-tor
ac-tiv-ism
ac-tiv-ist
ac-tiv-i-ty
ac-to-my-o-sin
ac-tor
ac-tress
ac-tu-al-i-ty
ac-tu-ar-y
ac-tu-a-tor
a-cu-i-ty
a-cu-men
a-cu-mi-nate
a-cute-ness
a-cy-clic
ac-yl-ate
ad ab-sur-dum
ad-age
a-da-gio
ad-a-mant
ad-a-man-tine
A-dam-si-a
ad-ams-ite
Ad-am-son
a-dapt-a-ble
a-dapt-a-bil-i-ty
ad-ap-ta-tion
a-dapt-er
a-dapt-ive
ad-ap-tom-e-ter
a-dap-tor
ad-ax-i-al
add-a-ble
add-ed
ad-den-da
add-er (one who adds)
ad-der (snake)

ad-dict-ed
ad-dic-tion
ad-dit-a-ment
ad-di-tion
ad-di-tive
ad-di-to-ry
ad-dress-ee
ad-dress-er
Ad-dres-so-graph
ad-dres-sor (law)
ad-du-cent
ad-duc-i-ble
ad-duc-tor
Ad-e-la
Ad-e-laide
Ad-el-bert
ad-e-nase
a-de-ni-a
a-den-i-form
ad-e-nine
ad-e-ni-tis
ad-e-no-car-ci-no-ma
ad-e-no-fi-bro-ma
ad-e-noi-dal
ad-e-no-ma
ad-e-nom-a-tous
ad-e-nop-a-thy
a-den-o-sine
ad-e-not-o-my
ad-e-nyl
ad-ept
a-dept-ness
ad-e-qua-cy
a-der-min
ad-her-ence
ad-her-ent
ad-he-res-cent
ad-he-sion
ad-he-sive
ad-i-a-bat-ic
ad in-fi-ni-tum
ad-i-nole
a-dip-a-mide
ad-i-pate
a-dip-ic
ad-i-po-ni-trile
ad-i-po-sis
ad-i-pos-i-ty
ad-i-po-so-gen-i-tal
ad-i-po-yl
ad-ja-cent
ad-jec-ti-val
ad-jec-tive
ad-ju-di-cate
ad-junc-tive
ad-ju-ra-tion
ad-jur-er
ad-just-a-ble
ad-just-er
ad-jus-tor (zoology)
ad-ju-tage
ad-ju-tant
ad-ju-vant
Ad-le-ri-an
ad lib-i-tum
ad-min-is-tra-tor
ad-min-is-tra-trix
ad-mi-ra-ble
ad-mi-ral-ty
ad-mi-ra-tion
ad-mir-er
ad-mis-si-ble
ad-mit-tance
ad-mon-ish
ad-mo-ni-tion
ad-mon-i-to-ry
ad nau-se-am
a-do-be
ad-o-les-cent
Ad-olph
A-do-nis
a-dopt-er
a-dop-tive
a-dor-a-ble
ad-o-ra-tion
a-dor-er
a-dorn-ment
ad-re-nal
A-dren-a-lin
a-dren-er-gen
ad-re-ner-gic
a-dre-no-chrome
a-dre-no-cor-ti-co-troph-ic
A-dri-an
A-dri-at-ic
a-droit-ness
ad-sorb-ate
ad-sorb-ent
ad-sorp-tive
ad-u-la-tion
a-dul-ter-a-tor
a-dult-i-cide
ad-um-brate
ad va-lo-rem
ad-vanc-er
ad-van-ta-geous
ad-vec-tive
ad-ven-ience
Ad-vent-ist
ad-ven-ti-tious
ad-ven-tur-er
ad-verb-i-al
ad-ver-sar-y
ad-ver-si-ty
ad-vert-ence
ad-ver-tise-ment
ad-ver-tis-er
ad-vis-a-ble
ad-vis-er
ad-vi-sor (law)
ad-vi-so-ry
ad-vo-ca-cy
ad-voc-a-to-ry
Ae-ge-an
ae-o-li-an
aer-ate
aer-a-tor
aer-i-al
ae-rie
aer-if-er-ous
aer-i-fi-ca-tion
aer-o-bac-ter
aer-o-bat-ics
aer-o-bic
aer-o-dy-nam-ic
aer-ol-o-gy
aer-om-e-ter
aer-o-mo-tor
aer-o-nau-tics
aer-on-o-my
aer-o-scope
aer-os-co-py
ae-rose
aer-o-sol
aer-o-stat
Aes-chy-le-an
af-fa-ble
af-fec-ta-tion
af-fect-er
af-fect-i-ble
af-fec-tion-ate
af-fer-ent
af-fi-anced
af-fi-da-vit
af-fil-i-ate
af-fin-i-ty
af-firm-ance
af-fir-ma-tion
af-firm-a-tive
af-fla-tus
af-flict-ive
af-flu-ent
Af-ghan-i-stan
a-fi-ci-o-na-do
a-for-ti-o-ri
Af-ri-can-ize
af-ter
a-gam-ic
ag-a-ric
a-gar-i-cin-ic
ag-a-rin-ic
Ag-as-siz
ag-ate
Ag-a-thin
a-ga-ve
a-gen-cy
a-gen-da
a-gen-ti-val
a-geu-si-a
ag-er-a-tum
ag-glom-er-ate
ag-glu-ti-nant
ag-glu-ti-noid
ag-gran-dize
ag-gra-vate
ag-gre-gate
ag-gres-sive
ag-gres-sor
ag-griev-ance
ag-ile
a-gil-i-ty
ag-i-ta-tive
ag-i-ta-tor
ag-it-prop
a-glo-mer-u-lar
ag-no-si-a
ag-nos-te-rol
ag-nos-ti-cism
ag-o-niz-ing
ag-o-ra-pho-bi-a
a-grar-i-an
ag-ri-cul-tur-al
ag-ri-mo-ny
ag-ro-nom-ic
a-gron-o-mist
a-gron-o-my
ag-ros-tol-o-gy
ag-ryp-not-ic
a-gu-ish
aide me-moire
ai-grette
ai-le-ron
ai-lu-ro-phobe
air-i-ness
air-om-e-ter
Ak-ti-en-ge-sell-schaft
Al-a-bam-i-an
al-a-bas-ter
a-lac-ri-ty
al-a-me-da
al-a-mo
a-la-mode
al-a-nine
al-a-nyl
a-larm-ist
A-las-kan
Al-ba-ni-an
al-ba-tross
al-be-dom-e-ter
al-be-rene
al-bes-cent
al-bin-ic
al-bi-nism
al-bi-nos
al-bo-lite
Al-bu-quer-que
al-bu-men (egg)
al-bu-min (chemical)
al-bu-mi-nate
al-bu-mi-nom-e-ter
al-bu-mi-no-sis
al-bu-mi-nu-ri-a
al-bur-num
al-ca-mine
al-chem-ic
al-che-mist
al-che-my
al-co-hol-ism
al-co-hol-om-e-ter
al-co-hol-om-e-try
al-co-hol-y-sis
Al-deb-a-ran
al-de-hyd-ic
al-de-hy-drol
al-der-man
Al-der-ney
Al-dine
al-do-fu-ran-o-side
al-dol-ase
al-don-ic
a-le-a-to-ry
a-lem-bi-cate
a-lep-ric
a-lert-ness
al-eu-drin
al-eu-rit-ic
al-eu-rom-e-ter
al-eu-rone
A-leu-tian
a-lex-i-a
a-lex-in
al-ge-bra-i-cal
al-ge-fa-cient
Al-ge-ri-an
al-ge-si-a
al-ge-sim-e-ter
al-gi-nate
al-gin-ic
al-gol-o-gy
al-gom-e-ter
Al-go-rab
al-go-rism
al-gra-phy
a-li-as
al-i-bi
al-i-cy-clic
al-i-dade
al-ien-ate
al-ien-ist
a-lif-er-ous
al-i-men-ta-ry
al-i-mo-ny
a-line-ment
a-lin-er
al-i-phat-ic
al-i-quot
al-i-vin-cu-lar
a-liz-a-rin
al-ka-li
al-ka-lim-e-ter
al-ka-lin-i-ty
al-ka-loi-dal
al-ke-nyl
alk-ox-ide
alk-ox-yl-ate
al-kyl-ate
al-kyl-ene
al-kyl-ic
al-kyl-ize
al-lan-to-in-ase
al-le-ga-tion
Al-le-ghe-ni-an
Al-le-ghe-ny
al-le-giance
al-le-gor-i-cal
al-le-go-ry
al-le-gro
al-ler-gen-ic
al-ler-gic
al-le-vi-ate
al-le-vi-a-tor
al-li-a-ceous
al-li-ga-tor
al-lit-er-a-tive
al-lo-ca-ble
al-lo-ca-tor
al-log-a-my
al-lom-er-ism
al-lom-e-try
al-lo-path
al-lop-a-thy
al-loph-a-nate
al-lo-se-mat-ic
al-lo-troph-ic
al-lot-ro-py
al-lot-ted
al-lot-tee
al-lot-ting
al-lur-ing
al-lu-sive
al-lu-vi-al
al-lu-vi-um
al-lyl-a-mine
al-lyl-ic
al-ma-nac
al-might-y
al-mond
al-mon-er
a-lo-di-um
al-o-et-ic
al-o-gism
al-o-in
al-o-pe-ci-a
Al-o-ys-i-us
al-pac-a
al-pha-bet-i-cal
al-pha-bet-ize
al-pha-mer-ic
al-pha-tron
Al-pine
Al-pin-ism
al-read-y
al-sike
al-tar
al-ter
al-ter-na-tive
al-ter-na-tor
al-tim-e-ter
al-tim-e-try
al-ti-tu-di-nar-i-an
al-to-geth-er
al-trose
a-lu-mi-na
al-u-min-i-um
a-lu-mi-nize
a-lu-mi-nous
a-lu-mi-num
a-lum-nus
a-lun-dum
al-u-nite
al-ve-o-lar
Al-ve-o-li-tes
a-lys-sum
a-mal-ga-mate
a-mal-ga-ma-tor
a-man-u-en-sis
am-a-ranth
am-a-ran-thine
am-a-roid
am-a-ryl-lis
am-a-teur-ish
am-a-tol
am-a-to-ry
a-maze-ment
Am-a-zo-ni-an
am-bas-sa-do-ri-al
am-ber-gris
am-ber-oid
am-bi-dex-trous
am-bi-ent
am-bi-gu-i-ty
am-big-u-ous
am-bip-a-rous
am-bi-tious
am-biv-a-lence
am-bling
am-blys-to-ma
am-bro-si-a
am-bu-lance
am-bu-la-to-ry
am-bus-cad-er
a-me-ba
a-me-bi-a-sis
a-me-bic
A-mel-ia
a-me-lio-ra-tive
am-e-lo-blas-to-ma
a-me-na-ble
a-mend-a-to-ry
a-men-i-ty
a-men-or-rhe-a
am-ent (botany)
am-en-ta-ceous
A-mer-i-can-a
A-mer-i-can-ism
am-er-i-ci-um
ames-ite
am-e-thyst
a-mi-a-ble
am-i-ca-ble
a-mi-cus cu-ri-ae
am-i-dase
am-ide
a-mid-ic
a-mi-do
a-mi-do-gen
am-i-dol
am-i-dox-ime
a-mi-go
am-i-nate
a-mine
a-mi-no
a-mi-no-ben-zo-ic
am-i-nol-y-sis
am-i-nop-ter-in
a-mi-no-sal-i-cyl-ic
am-me-ter
am-mo-ni-a
am-mo-ni-ate
am-mo-nite
Am-mon-ites (Biblical)
am-mo-ni-um
am-mu-ni-tion
am-ne-sia
am-nes-ty
a-mo-le
am-o-rous
a-mor-phism
am-or-ti-za-tion
A-moy-ese
am-per-age
am-pere-me-ter
am-per-o-met-ric
am-per-om-e-try
am-per-sand
am-phet-a-mine
am-phib-i-an
am-phib-i-ol-o-gy
am-phib-i-ous
am-phi-bol-ic
am-phib-o-lite
am-phib-o-lous
am-phi-dip-loi-dy
am-phi-ge-net-ic
am-phig-e-nous
am-phi-kar-y-on
Am-phip-o-da
am-pho-ter-ic
am-phot-er-ism
am-pli-fi-er
am-pli-tude
am-poule
am-pu-ta-tor
Am-ster-dam
am-u-let
a-mu-si-a
a-mus-ing
a-myg-da-la-ce-ae
a-myg-da-lin
a-myg-da-loi-dal
am-y-la-ceous
am-y-lase
am-yl-ene
am-y-loi-dal
am-y-loi-do-sis
am-y-lol-y-sis
am-y-lo-pec-tin
am-y-lose
a-nab-a-sine
an-a-bi-o-sis
an-a-bol-ic
a-nab-o-lism
a-nach-ro-nism
an-a-con-da
A-nac-re-on
a-nad-ro-mous
an-aer-o-bi-a
an-aer-o-bic
a-nag-ly-phy
an-a-glyp-tics
an-a-gog-ic
a-nal-cite
an-a-lep-tic
an-al-ge-si-a
an-al-ge-sic
an-a-log-i-cal
a-nal-o-gous
a-nal-o-gy
a-nal-y-sis
an-a-lyst
an-a-lyt-i-cal
an-a-lyz-er
an-a-mor-pho-sis
An-a-ni-as
an-a-phy-lax-is
an-ar-chism
an-ar-chis-tic
an-ar-chy
a-nas-to-mo-sis
a-nas-to-mot-ic
an-a-tase
a-nath-e-ma
an-a-tom-i-cal
a-nat-o-mist
a-nat-o-my
an-ces-tral
an-chor-age
an-cho-rite (hermit)
an-chor-ite (rock)
an-cho-vy
an-cient
an-cil-lar-y
an-cy-lo-sto-mi-a-sis
An-da-lu-sian
an-da-lu-site
An-da-man
an-de-site
and-i-ron
An-dor-ran
an-dor-ite
An-do-ver
an-dro-gen-ic-i-ty
an-drog-y-nous
An-drom-e-da
An-dro-mede
an-dro-sin
an-dro-stane
an-dros-te-rone
an-ec-dot-al
a-ne-mi-a
a-ne-mic
a-nem-o-gram
an-e-mom-e-ter
a-nem-o-ne
a-nem-o-scope
an-er-oid
an-es-the-sia
an-es-the-sim-e-ter
an-es-the-si-ol-o-gy
an-es-thet-ic
an-es-the-tist
a-neu-ri-a
an-eu-rin
an-eu-rysm
an-ga-ry
an-gel-ic
an-ger
an-gi-i-tis
an-gi-na pec-to-ris
an-gi-o-car-di-og-ra-phy
an-gi-o-cyst
an-gi-om-e-ter
an-gi-op-a-thy
an-gi-o-sis
an-gi-os-to-my
an-gi-o-to-nin
an-gler
An-gli-can
an-gli-cize
An-go-lese
An-go-ra
an-gos-tu-ra
an-gry
ang-strom
an-guish
an-gu-lar-i-ty
an-he-dral
an-hi-dro-sis
an-hi-drot-ic
an-hy-dride
an-hy-dro-bi-o-sis
an-hy-drous
an-i-lide
an-i-line
a-nil-i-ty
an-i-mad-ver-sion
an-i-mal-cule
an-i-mal-ism
an-i-ma-tion
an-i-mism
an-i-mos-i-ty
an-i-on-ic
an-i-on-ot-ro-py
an-is-ate
an-ise
an-i-seed
an-is-ette
a-nis-ic
a-nis-i-dine
an-i-sot-ro-py
an-klet
an-ky-lo-sis
an-ky-los-to-ma
an-nal-ist
An-nam-ese
an-neal-er
an-ni-hi-late
an-ni-ver-sa-ry
an-no-ta-tor
an-nounc-er
an-nu-al
an-nu-i-tant
an-nu-lar
an-nu-let
an-nun-ci-a-to-ry
an-ode
an-od-ic
an-od-ize
an-o-dyne
a-noint-ment
a-nom-a-lis-tic
a-nom-a-lous
a-nom-a-ly
an-o-nym-i-ty
a-non-y-mous
an-o-op-si-a
A-noph-e-les
an-ox-i-a
an-ser-ine
an-swer
ant-ac-id
an-tag-o-nism
Ant-arc-tic
An-tar-es
an-te-ced-ent
an-te-di-lu-vi-an
an-te-lope
an-te-pe-nul-ti-mate
an-te-ri-or
ant-he-lion
ant-hel-min-tic
an-them
an-ther-al
an-tho-cy-an-i-din
an-thog-e-nous
an-tho-log-i-cal
an-thol-o-gy
An-tho-ny
an-thra-cene
an-thra-cif-er-ous
an-thra-cite
an-thra-co-sil-i-co-sis
an-thra-nil-ic
an-thran-o-yl
an-thra-pur-pu-rin
an-thra-qui-no-nyl
an-thrax
an-thro-poi-dal
an-thro-po-log-i-cal
an-thro-pol-o-gy
an-thro-pom-e-ter
an-thro-po-met-ric

an-thro-poph-a-gy
an-ti-bi-ot-ic
an-ti-cal
an-tic-i-pa-to-ry
an-ti-cli-nal
an-ti-dot-al
an-ti-gen-ic
an-ti-ge-nic-i-ty
An-tig-o-ne
An-ti-guan
an-ti-his-ta-min-ic
An-til-le-an
an-til-o-gism
an-ti-mo-ny
an-ti-pas-to
an-ti-pa-thet-ic
an-tip-a-thy
an-tiph-o-nal
an-tip-o-dal
an-ti-pode
an-tip-o-de-an
an-tip-o-des
an-ti-quar-i-an
an-ti-quate
an-tique
an-tiq-ui-ty
an-ti-sep-tic
an-tith-e-sis
an-ti-thet-i-cal
ant-ler
an-to-nym
Ant-werp
an-u-re-sis
anx-i-e-ty
anx-ious
a-or-tic
a-pache (Paris thug)
A-pach-e (Indian tribe)
a-pa-re-jo
a-part-heid
ap-as-tron
ap-a-thet-ic
ap-a-thy
ap-a-tite
Ap-en-nine
a-pe-ri-ent
a-pe-ri-od-ic
a-per-i-tif
ap-er-tom-e-ter
ap-er-tur-al
aph-a-nite
aph-a-nit-ic
a-pha-sia
a-phe-lion
aph-i-cide
aph-o-rism
a-phra-si-a
aph-ro-dis-i-ac
Aph-ro-di-te
a-pi-a-rist
a-pi-ar-y
ap-i-cal
a-pi-ose
ap-ish
a-piv-o-rous
ap-neu-sis
a-poc-a-lyp-tic
a-poc-o-pe
a-poc-ry-phal
Ap-o-des
ap-o-dic-tic
a-pog-a-my
ap-o-ge-an
ap-o-gee
a-pog-e-ny
A-pol-li-nar-is
A-pol-lo
a-pol-o-get-ic
ap-o-lo-gi-a
a-pol-o-gist
ap-o-pho-rom-e-ter
ap-o-phyl-lite
ap-o-plec-tic
ap-o-plex-y
a-pos-ta-sy
a-pos-tate
a-pos-ta-tize
a pos-te-ri-o-ri
a-pos-tle
a-pos-to-late
ap-os-tol-ic
a-pos-tro-phe
ap-os-troph-ic
a-poth-e-car-y
a-poth-e-o-sis
Ap-pa-lach-ian
ap-pall-ing
ap-pa-nage
ap-pa-ra-tus
ap-par-eled
ap-par-ent
ap-pa-ri-tion
ap-pear-ance
ap-pel-lant
ap-pel-la-tion
ap-pend-age
ap-pend-ant
ap-pen-dec-to-my
ap-pen-di-cal
ap-pen-di-ci-tis
ap-pen-dix
ap-per-cep-tion
ap-pet-i-ble
ap-pe-tiz-er
ap-pe-tiz-ing
ap-pli-ca-ble
ap-pli-ca-tor
ap-pli-ca-to-ry
ap-pli-que
ap-pog-gia-tu-ra
ap-point-ee
ap-point-ive
ap-po-site
ap-pos-i-tive
ap-prais-al
ap-pre-ci-a-tive
ap-pre-hen-si-ble
ap-pre-hen-sive
ap-pren-tice
ap-proach-ing
ap-pro-ba-tion
ap-pro-pri-a-tive
ap-prov-al
ap-prox-i-mate
ap-pui
ap-pur-te-nance
a-pri-cot
A-pril
a pri-o-ri
ap-ro-pos
ap-sis
ap-te-ri-um
ap-ter-ous
ap-ti-tude
aq-ua-plane
aq-ua-relle
a-quar-i-um
A-quar-i-us
a-quat-ic
aq-ua-tint
aq-ua-vit
aq-ue-duct
a-que-ous
aq-ui-fer
aq-ui-line
ar-a-besque
A-ra-bi-an
Ar-a-bic
a-rab-i-nose
Ar-ab-ize
ar-a-ble
A-rach-ni-da
ar-ach-noi-dal
Ar-a-go-nese
a-rag-o-nite
ar-al-kox-y
ar-al-kyl-ate
Ar-a-ma-ic
A-rap-a-ho
A-rau-ca-ni-an
ar-bi-ter
ar-bi-tra-ble
ar-bi-trag-er
ar-bit-ra-ment
ar-bi-trar-y
ar-bi-tra-tor
ar-bo-re-al
ar-bo-res-cent
ar-bo-re-tum
ar-bo-ri-cul-tur-al
ar-bo-rize
ar-bor-vi-tae
ar-bu-tus
ar-cade
Ar-ca-di-an
ar-ca-num
ar-cha-ic
ar-che-o-log-i-cal
ar-che-ol-o-gy
arch-er-y
ar-che-typ-al
ar-che-us
Ar-chi-bald
ar-chi-e-pis-co-pa-cy
Ar-chi-me-de-an
ar-chi-pel-a-go
ar-chi-tec-tur-al
ar-chi-trave
ar-chives
ar-chi-vist
Arc-tic
Arc-tu-rus
ar-cu-ate
ar-dent
ar-dor
ar-du-ous
ar-e-al
a-re-na
ar-e-na-ceous
a-re-o-la
ar-gen-tal
ar-gen-te-ous
ar-gen-tif-er-ous
Ar-gen-ti-na
ar-gen-tite
ar-gen-tous
ar-gen-tum
ar-gil-la-ceous
ar-gil-lif-er-ous
ar-gil-lite
ar-gi-nine
ar-gol
ar-gon
Ar-go-naut
ar-go-sy
ar-gu-men-ta-tive
Ar-gy-rol
a-rid-i-ty
Ar-i-el
A-ri-es
A-ri-on
a-ris-tate
ar-is-toc-ra-cy
a-ris-to-crat-ic
Ar-is-to-te-li-an
Ar-is-tot-le
ar-ith-met-ic (adj.)
a-rith-me-tic (n.)
ar-ith-met-i-cal
ar-ith-mom-e-ter
Ar-i-zo-nan
Ar-kan-san
ark-ite (mineral)
ar-ma-da
ar-ma-dil-los
Ar-ma-ged-don
ar-ma-ment
ar-ma-men-tar-i-um
ar-ma-ture
Ar-me-ni-an
ar-mi-stice
ar-mor-er
ar-mo-ri-al
ar-mo-ry
ar-ni-ca
a-ro-ma
ar-o-mat-ic
ar-o-ma-ti-za-tion
a-rous-al
a-rous-ing
ar-raign
ar-range-ments
ar-rear-age
ar-rest-er
ar-res-tive
ar-rhyth-mi-a
ar-riv-al
ar-ro-gant
ar-ron-disse-ment
ar-roy-o
ar-se-nal
ar-se-nate
ar-se-nic (n.)
ar-sen-ic (adj.)
ar-sen-i-cal
ar-se-nide
ar-se-ni-ous
ar-se-ni-o-sid-er-ite
ar-se-no-ben-zene
ar-sine
ar-son-ist
ar-so-ni-um
ars-phen-a-mine
ar-te-ri-al
ar-te-ri-og-ra-phy
ar-te-ri-o-lar
ar-te-ri-o-scle-ro-sis
ar-te-ri-ot-o-my
ar-te-ri-tis
ar-ter-y
ar-te-sian
ar-thrit-ic
ar-thri-tis
ar-thro-dese
ar-throd-e-sis
ar-throg-e-nous
ar-throg-ra-phy
ar-throm-e-ter
ar-throp-a-thy
ar-thro-pod
Ar-throp-o-da
ar-ti-choke
ar-ti-cle
ar-tic-u-la-tor
ar-ti-fact
ar-ti-fice
ar-tif-i-cer
ar-ti-fi-cial
ar-til-ler-y
ar-ti-nite
ar-ti-san
art-ist
ar-tiste
ar-tis-ti-cal
ar-tist-ry
A-run-del (Maryland)
Ar-y-an-ize
ar-yl-am-ine
ar-yl-ate
ar-yl-ene
as-a-fet-i-da
as-bes-to-sis
as-ca-ri-a-sis
as-car-i-dole
as-cend-an-cy
as-cend-ant
as-cend-er
as-cer-tain
as-cet-i-cism
as-cid-i-an
as-ci-tes
a-scor-bic
as-cribe
a-sep-sis
a-sep-tic
Ash-ke-na-zi
A-si-at-ic
as-i-nin-i-ty
a-skance
a-skew
as-pa-rag-i-nase
as-par-a-gine
as-par-a-gus
as-par-tic
as-pect
as-pen
as-per-ate
as-perge
as-per-gil-lus
as-per-i-ty
as-per-sion
as-phal-tene
as-phal-tic
as-phyx-i-ate
As-pi-dis-tra
as-pi-rant
as-pi-ra-tor
as-pir-a-to-ry
as-pi-rin
As-ple-ni-um
as-sail-ant
As-sam-ese
as-sas-si-nate
as-sem-bla-ble
as-sem-bler
as-sem-bly
as-sen-tor
as-sert-i-ble
as-ser-tive
as-sess-ee
as-ses-sor
as-ses-so-ri-al
as-sev-er-ate
as-si-du-i-ty
as-sid-u-ous
as-si-ette
as-sign-a-ble
as-sig-nat
as-sig-na-tion
as-sign-ee
as-sign-or
as-sim-i-la-ble
as-sist-ant
as-so-ci-a-ble
as-so-ci-ate
as-so-nance
as-suage
as-sump-sit
as-sur-ance
As-syr-i-an
as-ta-tine
as-ter
as-te-ri-al
as-ter-isk
as-ter-oid
as-ter-oi-dal
as-the-ni-a
as-then-ic
asth-mat-ic
as-tig-mat-ic
a-stig-ma-tism
as-tig-mom-e-ter
as-ton-ish
as-tound-ing
as-tra-gal
as-trag-a-lus
as-tra-khan
as-tral
as-tric-tion
as-trin-gent
as-tri-on-ics
as-tro-ga-tor
as-trog-o-ny
as-troid
as-tro-labe
as-trol-o-ger
as-tro-log-i-cal
as-trol-o-gy
as-trom-e-try
as-tro-naut
as-tro-nau-tics
as-tron-o-mer
as-tro-nom-i-cal
as-tron-o-my
as-tro-sphere
As-tu-ri-an
as-tute
a-sun-der
a-sy-lum
a-sym-met-ri-cal
as-ymp-tote
as-ymp-tot-ic
a-syn-ap-sis
a-sys-to-le
At-a-brine
at-a-rac-tic
at-a-vism
at-a-vis-tic
a-tax-i-a
at-e-lier
a-the-is-ti-cal
ath-e-ne-um
A-the-ni-an
Ath-ens
ath-er-o-ma
ath-er-om-a-tous
ath-er-o-scle-ro-sis
ath-let-i-cal-ly
a-threp-si-a
ath-ro-cyte
ath-ro-gen-ic
At-lan-tic
at-lan-tite
at-mol-y-sis
at-mom-e-ter
at-mos-pher-i-cal
at-oll
a-tom-ic
a-tom-i-cal
at-o-mic-i-ty
at-om-ism
at-om-is-tic
at-om-iz-er
a-ton-al
a-tone-ment
at-o-ny
at-o-py
a-tre-si-a
a-tri-o-ven-tric-u-lar
a-tri-um
a-tro-cious
a-troc-i-ty
a-troph-ic
at-ro-phy
at-ro-pine
at-ro-pin-ize
at-ta-ché
at-tain-der
at-tem-per-a-tor
at-tend-ant
at-ten-tive
at-ten-u-a-tor
at-test-ant
at-tes-ta-tion
at-test-er
at-ti-tu-di-nize
at-tor-ney
at-tract-ant
at-trac-tive
at-trac-tor
at-trib-ut-a-ble
at-tri-bute (n.)
at-trib-ute (v.)
at-trib-u-tive
at-tri-tus
auc-tion-eer
auc-to-ri-al
au-da-cious
au-dac-i-ty
au-di-ble
au-di-ence
au-di-o-gen-ic
au-di-om-e-ter
au-di-om-e-try
au-di-to-ri-um
au-di-to-ry
Au-du-bon
au-gan-ite
au-ger
au-gite
au-gi-tite
aug-men-ta-tion
aug-ment-a-tive
aug-men-tor
au-gu-ry
au-gust
Au-gus-tin-i-an
au-ral
au-ra-mine
au-re-ate
au-re-li-an
au-re-o-le
Au-re-o-my-cin
au-ri-cle
au-ric-u-lar
au-ric-u-lo-pa-ri-e-tal
au-ro-ra bo-re-al-is
au-rum
aus-cul-tate
aus-pic-es
aus-pi-cious
aus-ten-it-ic
aus-ter-i-ty
Aus-tra-la-sian
Aus-tra-lian
Aus-tri-an
au-tar-chic
au-tar-chy
au-then-ti-cal-ly
au-then-ti-ca-tor
au-then-tic-i-ty
au-thor-i-tar-i-an
au-thor-i-ta-tive
au-thor-i-za-tion
au-thor-iz-er
au-tism
au-toc-ra-cy
au-to-crat
au-to-ge-net-ic
au-to-gen-ic
au-tog-e-nous
au-to-gi-ro
au-to-graph
au-tog-ra-pher
au-tol-y-sate
au-to-mat-i-cal
au-to-ma-tic-i-ty
au-tom-a-tin
au-to-ma-tion
au-tom-a-tism
au-tom-a-tist
au-tom-a-ti-za-tion
au-tom-a-ton
au-tom-a-tous
au-tom-ne-si-a
au-to-net-ics
au-to-nom-ic
au-ton-o-mous
au-toph-a-gous
au-toph-o-ny
au-top-sy
au-tos-co-py
au-tot-o-my
au-tox-i-diz-a-ble
au-tum-nal
aux-a-nom-e-ter
aux-il-ia-ry
aux-in
aux-o-chrom-ic
aux-om-e-ter
av-a-lanche
av-a-ri-cious
av-a-tar
av-e-nue
av-er-age
a-ver-sion
a-vert-i-ble
a-vi-an-ize
av-i-a-rist
a-vi-ar-y
a-vi-a-tor
a-vi-a-trix
av-i-din
a vid-i-ty
A-vi-gnon-ese
a-vi-on-ics
av-o-ca-dos
av-o-ca-tion
a-voc-a-to-ry
a-void-ance
av-oir-du-pois
a-vow-al
a-vun-cu-lar
a-wak-en
awk-ward
awn-ing (n., v.)
ax-i-al-ly
ax-il-lar-y
ax-i-o-mat-ic
Ax-min-ster
ax-o-lotl
ax-om-e-ter
a-za-lea
az-e-la-ic
a-ze-o-trop-ic
a-ze-ot-ro-py
Az-er-bai-ja-ni
az-ide
az-i-do-a-ce-tic
az-i-mi-no
az-i-muth-al
az-ine
az-o-im-ide
az-ole
az-o-meth-ane
a-zo-ni-um
A-zo-to-bac-ter
az-o-tom-e-ter
az-ox-y-ben-zene
Az-tec-an
az-u-lene
az-ure
az-u-rin
az-ur-ite
az-y-gous

B

ba-bas-su
bab-bitt
bab-bling
Ba-bel
bab-i-ru-sa
ba-boon
ba-bush-ka
Bab-y-lo-ni-an
bac-ca-lau-re-ate
bac-cha-na-lian
bac-chant
bac-cif-er-ous
bach-e-lor
bac-il-lar-y
ba-cil-li
ba-cil-lus
bac-i-tra-cin
ba-con
Ba-co-ni-an
bac-te-ri-a
bac-te-ri-cid-al
bac-te-ri-cid-in
bac-ter-id
bac-te-ri-o-log-i-cal
bac-te-ri-ol-o-gy
bac-te-ri-ol-y-sis
bac-te-ri-o-lyt-ic
bac-te-ri-os-co-py
bac-te-ri-um
bac-te-roi-dal
badg-er
bad-i-nage
Bae-de-ker
baf-fling
ba-gasse
bag-a-telle
ba-gel
ba-guette
Ba-ha-i
Ba-ha-ma
bail-ee
bail-er
Bai-ley
bail-iff
bail-i-wick
ba-ke-lite

bak-er-y
bak-sheesh
Ba-la-kla-va
bal-a-lai-ka
bal-anc-er
ba-la-ta
bal-brig-gan
bal-co-ny
bal-der-dash
bal-dric
Bal-e-ar-ic
ba-leen
Ba-li-nese
Bal-kan
balk-y
bal-lad-eer
bal-le-ri-na
bal-lis-tics
bal-lo-net
bal-loon-ist
bal-ma-caan
balm-i-ness
Bal-mor-al
bal-ne-al
ba-lo-ney
bal-sam
Bal-tic
Bal-ti-mor-e-an
bal-us-trade
bam-bi-no
bam-boo-zle
ba-nal (commonplace)
ban-al (governor)
ba-nal-i-ty
ba-nan-a
Ban-bury
ban-dag-er
ban-dan-na
ban-deau
band-er
ban-dit-ry
ban-do-leer
ban-dy-ing
ban-ga-lore
ban-gle
ban-ish
ban-is-ter
bank-er
bank-rupt-cy
ban-quet-er
ban-shee
ban-tam
ban-ter
bant-ling
ban-zai
bap-tis-mal
bap-tis-ter-y
bap-tiz-er
Bar-ab-bas
Bá-rá-ny
bar-a-the-a
Bar-ba-dos
bar-bar-i-an
bar-bar-ic
bar-ba-rism
bar-ba-rous
Bar-ba-ry
bar-be-cue
bar-ber
bar-bette
bar-bi-tal
bar-bi-tu-rate
bar-bi-tu-ric
bar-gain-er
bar-gain-or (law)
bar-ing
bar-ite
bar-i-tone
bar-i-to-sis
bar-i-um
bar-ken-tine
bark-er
Bark-hau-sen
Bar-kis
bark-om-e-ter
Bar-na-bas
bar-na-cle
bar-o-graph
ba-rom-e-ter
bar-o-met-ric
bar-o-met-ro-graph
bar-o-me-trog-ra-phy
ba-rom-e-try
bar-on-ess
bar-on-et
ba-ro-ni-al
ba-roque
bar-o-scope
ba-rouche
bar-ra-cu-da
bar-rage
bar-ra-try
bar-reled
bar-ren
bar-rette
bar-ri-cade
bar-ring
bar-ris-ter
bar-ter
Bart-lett
bar-y-lite
ba-ry-ta
ba-ryt-ic
bar-y-tron

ba-sal
ba-salt
ba-sal-tic
ba-sic
ba-si-cal-ly
ba-sic-i-ty
ba-sid-i-um
bas-il
ba-sil-i-ca
bas-i-lisk
ba-sin
ba-sis
Bas-ker-ville
bas-ket-ry
bas-si-net
bas-tar-dy
bas-tille
bas-ti-na-do
Ba-ta-vi-an
ba-teau
bath-o-lith-ic
ba-thom-e-ter
ba-thos
ba-thym-e-ter
bath-y-met-ric
ba-thym-e-try
bath-y-scaphe
ba-thys-mal
ba-tik
ba-tiste
ba-ton (n.)
bat-on (v.)
ba-tra-chi-um
bat-tal-ion
bau-ble
Bau-mé
baux-ite
baux-it-ic
Ba-var-i-an
bay-ard
bay-o-net
Ba-yonne
bay-ou
ba-zoo-ka
bdel-li-um
bea-con
bead-er
bea-dle
bea-gle
beak-er
bé-ar-naise
beat-er
be-a-tif-ic
be-at-i-fy
be-at-i-tude
Be-a-trice
beau-sé-ant
beau-te-ous
bea-ver
be-bee-rine
Bech-u-a-na-land
beck-on
Bec-que-rel
be-di-zen
Bed-ou-in
Be-el-ze-bub
Be-er-she-ba
Bee-tho-ven
bee-tle
beg-gar-y
be-gin-ning
beg-ohm
be-go-nia
be-hav-ior-al
be-he-moth
be-hold-en
bei-del-lite
be-lat-ed
be-lea-guered
bel-fry
Bel-gian
be-liev-er
bel-la-don-na
bel-li-cos-i-ty
bel-lig-er-ent
Be-na-res
ben-e-fac-tor
be-nef-i-cent
ben-e-fi-cial
ben-e-fi-ci-ar-y
ben-e-fi-ci-ate
ben-e-fit-ed
be-nev-o-lence
be-nign
be-nig-nant
be-ni-to-ite
Ben-ja-min
ben-ton-ite
benz-al-de-hyde
ben-zald-ox-ime
benz-am-ide
Ben-ze-drine
ben-zene-di-a-zo-ni-um
ben-ze-noid
ben-zil-ic
benz-im-id-a-zole
ben-zo-ate
ben-zo-fla-vine
ben-zo-ic
ben-zo-in
ben-zo-i-nat-ed
ben-zo-phe-none
ben-zo-sul-fi-mide
benz-ox-y-a-ce-tic

ben-zo-yl-ate
ben-zyl-ate
ben-zyl-ox-y
ber-ba-mine
ber-ber-ine
be-ret
ber-ga-mot
berg-schrund
ber-i-ber-i
Ber-ing
Berke-ley
berke-li-um
Ber-mu-da
Bern-ese
Ber-noul-li
Ber-tha
berth-ing
Ber-tram
be-ryl-li-um
ber-yl-loid
Bes-sa-ra-bi-an
Bes-se-mer
bes-tial
bes-ti-al-i-ty
be-stride
be-ta-cism
be-ta-ine
be-ta-tron
be-tel
Be-tel-geuse
Be-thes-da
be-troth-al
Beu-lah
bev-a-tron
bev-eled
bev-er-age
be-wil-der
bez-el
Bhu-ta-nese
Bi-a-fra
bi-ased
bi-be-lot
Bi-ble
Bib-li-cal
bib-li-o-graph-ic
bib-li-og-ra-phy
bib-li-o-phile
bib-u-lous
bi-car-bon-ate
bi-ceph-a-lous
bi-chlo-ride
bi-chro-mate
bick-er-ing
bi-cus-pid
bi-cy-clist
bi-cy-clo-al-kane
bi-fur-cat-ed
big-a-mous
big-ot-ry
bi-gua-nide
Bi-ki-ni
bil-i-ar-y
bil-i-cy-a-nin
bil-i-fi-ca-tion
bil-ious
bil-i-ru-bin
bil-i-ru-bi-ne-mi-a
bil-liards
bi-loc-u-lar
bi-met-al-lism
bi-na-ry
bin-au-ral
bind-er-y
bin-na-cle
bin-oc-u-lar
bi-no-mi-al
bi-og-e-ny
bi-o-graph-i-cal
bi-og-ra-phy
bi-o-log-i-cal
bi-ol-o-gist
bi-ol-y-sis
bi-om-e-ter
bi-o-met-ric
bi-om-e-try
bi-on-o-my
bi-op-sy
bi-os-co-py
bi-os-o-phy
bi-os-ter-ol
bi-ot-ic
bi-o-tin
bi-o-tite
bi-o-vu-lar
bip-a-rous
bi-par-ti-ble
bi-par-ti-ent
bi-par-tite
Bir-ming-ham
bis-cuit
bish-op-ric
bis-muth-ate
bis-muth-yl
bi-son
bit-er
bi-tu-men
bi-tu-mi-nous
bi-u-ret
bi-va-lent
biv-ouacked
bi-zarre
black-ened
blad-ed
blam-a-ble

Blan-chard
blanch-er
blan-dish
blan-ket
blar-ney
blas-phe-mous
blas-te-ma
blast-er
blas-tog-e-ny
Blas-to-my-ce-tes
blas-to-my-co-sis
blas-tu-la
bla-tant
blath-er-ing
blaz-er
bla-zon
blem-ish
blend-er
bleph-a-ral
bless-ed (adj.)
blessed (v.)
blind-er
blink-er
blis-ter
bloat-er
block-ade
blon-dine
bloom-er
bloop-er
blu-cher
bludg-eon
bluff-ing
blu-ing
blun-der-er
blus-ter
boat-swain
bob-bi-net
bo-cac-cio
bo-dhi-satt-va
bod-ice
bod-i-ly
bo-gey (golf term)
bo-gie (cart)
bo-gy (specter)
Bo-he-mi-an
boil-er
bois-ter-ous
bo-le-ro
bo-le-tus
Bo-liv-i-an
Bo-lo-gna
bo-lom-e-ter
Bol-she-vi-ki
bol-she-vism
Bol-she-vist
bol-ster
bom-bard-ier
bom-bas-ti-cal
bom-ba-zine
bom-bi-nate
bo-na fi-de
bo-nan-za
Bo-na-parte
bond-age
Bond-er-ize
bo-ni-to
bo-nus
boo-by
boo-dler
Bool-e-an
boo-mer-ang
boor-ish
boost-er
boo-tee
boo-ty
booz-er
bo-rac-ic
bo-ra-cite
bo-rat-ed
bo-rax
Bor-deaux
bor-der
bo-re-al
Bor-ghe-se
bo-ric
bo-ride
Bor-ne-an
bor-ne-ol
born-ite
bor-nyl
bo-ron
bor-ough
Bor-zoi
bos-om
Bos-po-rus
boss-ism
Bos-to-ni-an
bo-tan-i-cal
bot-a-nist
bot-a-ny
both-er-a-tion
bo-tog-e-nin
bot-ry-oi-dal
Bot-swa-na
bot-u-lin-ic
bot-u-lism
bou-cle
bou-doir
Bou-gain-vil-le-a
bouil-la-baisse
bouil-lon
boul-der
bou-le-vard
bound-a-ry

boun-te-ous
bou-quet
Bour-bon-ism
bour-geois
bour-geoi-sie
bou-ton-niere
bo-vine
bowd-ler-ize
bow-ie
boy-sen-ber-ry
bra-ce-ro
brach-i-al
bra-chi-o-la
Brach-i-op-o-da
brach-y-ceph-a-lous
bra-chyp-ter-ous
brach-ysm
bra-chyt-ic
brac-ing
brack-et
brack-ish
brac-te-al
brag-ga-do-ci-o
Brah-man-ism
bram-ble
bran-chi-al
bran-chif-er-ous
Bran-chi-op-o-da
brand-er
bran-dish
bra-se-ro
Bra-si-lia
bras-sid-ic
bras-siere
bra-va-do
brav-er-y
bra-vo
bra-vu-ra
bray-er
bra-zen
bra-zier
braz-il (mining term)
bra-zil (wood, nut)
Bra-zil
Bra-zil-ian
breath-er
brec-ci-a
breez-i-ness
Bre-men
brems-strah-lung
brem-sung
brenn-schluss
breth-ren
Bret-on
bre-vet
bre-vi-ar-y
bre-vier
brev-i-ty
brew-er-y
Brew-ster
brib-er-y
brid-al
bri-dle
bri-dling
bri-er
bri-gade
brig-a-dier
brig-and-age
brig-an-tine
Brigh-ton
bril-liant
brin-dle
Bri-nell
bri-quet-ted
bri-sance
brisk-en
bris-ket
bris-tle
bris-tly
Brit-ain
Bri-tan-ni-a
Brit-ish
broad-cast-er
bro-cade
broc-co-li
bro-chure
broil-er
bro-ken
bro-ker-age
brom-ar-gy-rite
bro-mate
bro-me-lin
bro-mide
bro-mid-ic
bro-mi-dro-sis
bro-min-ate
bro-mi-na-tion
bro-mine
bro-mo-cre-sol
bro-mo-i-o-dide
bro-mo-met-ric
bro-mom-e-try
bron-chi-al
bron-chi-tis
bron-choph-o-ny
bron-chos-co-py
bron-co
bron-tom-e-ter
brood-er
broth-el
broth-er
brows-er
bru-cel-lo-sis
bruc-ine

bruc-ite
bruis-er
bru-tal-ize
brut-ish
bu-bon-ic
buc-ca-neer
buc-ci-na-tor
Bu-chan-an
Bu-cha-rest
buck-et-ful
buck-ler
buck-ling
bu-col-ic
Bu-da-pest
Bud-dha
budg-er-i-gar
budg-et-ar-y
budg-et-eer
Bue-nos Ai-res
buf-fa-lo
buff-er
buf-fet
buff-ing
buf-foon-er-y
bu-gle
bul-ba-ceous
bul-bar
bul-bo-cap-nine
bul-bous
Bul-gar-i-an
bulg-er
bulk-er
bul-late
bull-doz-er
bul-le-tin
bul-lion
bull-ish
bul-lock
bul-ly-ing
bul-rush
bum-bling
bump-er
bump-i-ness
bump-om-e-ter
bump-tious
bun-combe
Bun-des-rat
bun-dler
bun-ga-low
bun-gee
bun-gler
bun-ion
bun-ker-age
bun-kum
bunt-ing (v.)
bun-ting (bird, flag)
buoy-ant
bur-bled
bur-den
bu-reau
bu-reauc-ra-cy
bu-reau-crat-ic
bu-ret
bur-gee
bur-geon
bur-gess
bur-gher
bur-glar-ize
bur-gla-ry
bur-go-mas-ter
Bur-gun-di-an
bur-i-al
bur-ied
bur-lesque
bur-ley
Bur-mese
burn-ers
bur-nish-er
bur-sar
bur-si-tis
Bu-run-di-an
bur-y-ing
bus-es
bush-el
bus-i-ly
busi-ness
bus-kin
bust-er
bus-tling
bu-ta-di-ene
bu-tal-de-hyde
bu-tane
bu-ta-no-ic
bu-ta-nol
butch-er
bu-te-nyl
bu-tox-yl
but-tress
bu-tyl-a-mine
bu-tyl-ene
bu-tyr-a-ceous
bu-tyr-ate
bu-tyr-ic
bu-tyr-in-ase
bu-tyr-o-lac-tone
bu-tyr-om-e-ter
bu-tyr-yl
bux-om
buz-zard
buzz-er
Byel-o-rus-sia
By-ron-ic
bys-si-no-sis
Byz-an-tine

C

ca-bal
cab-a-la
cab-a-lis-ti-cal
ca-ban-a
ca-bane
cab-a-ret
cab-bage
ca-ber-net
cab-e-zon
cab-i-net
ca-bling
cab-o-chon
ca-boose
cab-o-tage
cab-ri-o-let
ca-bu-ya
ca-ca-o
cach-a-lot
ca-chec-tic
ca-chet
cach-in-na-tion
ca-chou
ca-cique
cack-ling
cac-o-dyl-ic
ca-cog-ra-phy
cac-o-mis-tle
ca-coph-o-ny
cad-a-lene
ca-das-tral
ca-dav-er-ous
ca-delle
ca-dence
ca-den-za
ca-det
cad-i-nene
Ca-diz
cad-mi-um
cad-re
ca-du-ca-ry
ca-du-ce-us
Cae-sar
cae-si-ous
caf-e-te-ri-a
caf-feine
Ca-ga-yan
cais-son
ca-jol-er-y
ca-la-di-um
cal-a-mine
ca-lam-i-tous
ca-lan-dri-a
ca-lash
cal-a-ver-ite
cal-car-e-ous
cal-cif-er-ol
cal-cif-er-ous
cal-ci-fi-ca-tion
cal-cim-e-ter
cal-ci-mine
cal-ci-na-tion
cal-cite
cal-ci-um
cal-cu-la-ble
cal-cu-la-tor
cal-cu-la-to-ry
cal-cu-lus
cal-dron
cal-e-fa-cient
cal-en-dar
cal-en-der
ca-len-du-lin
ca-les-cent
cal-i-ber
cal-i-brat-er
cal-i-bra-tor
ca-li-che
Cal-i-for-ni-an
cal-i-for-ni-um
ca-lig-i-nous
cal-i-per
ca-liph
cal-is-then-ics
calk-er
cal-li-graph-ic
cal-lig-ra-phy
cal-li-o-pe
cal-lous (adj.)
cal-lus (n.)
cal-lus-es
cal-o-mel
cal-o-res-cence
ca-lor-ic
cal-o-rie
ca-lor-i-fa-cient
cal-o-rif-ic
cal-o-rim-e-ter
cal-o-ri-met-ri-cal
cal-o-rize
ca-lum-ni-ate
cal-um-ny
Cal-va-ry
Cal-vin-ism
ca-ly-coid
ca-lyp-so
ca-lyp-tra
ca-lyx
ca-ma-ra-de-rie
cam-a-ril-la
ca-ma-ta
cam-ber
cam-bi-um
Cam-bo-di-an
cam-bric
cam-el-eer
ca-mel-o-pard
Cam-em-bert
cam-e-o
cam-er-a
Cam-e-roon
ca-mion
cam-i-sole
cam-o-mile
Ca-mor-ra
cam-ou-flage
cam-pa-ni-le
camp-er
cam-pha-nyl
cam-phoid
cam-pho-len-ic
cam-pho-ra-ceous
cam-phor-ene
cam-phor-ic
cam-pim-e-ter
cam-pus
Ca-naan
Can-a-da
Ca-na-di-an
ca-nai-gre
ca-naille
ca-nal-i-za-tion
ca-na-pe
ca-nard
ca-nar-y
ca-nas-ta
Ca-nav-er-al
can-celed
can-cel-ing
can-cel-la-tion
can-cer-ous
can-croid
can-de-la
can-de-la-brum
can-de-li-lla
can-did
can-di-date
can-died
can-dling
can-dor
ca-nes-cent
ca-nic-o-la
ca-nine
can-is-ter
can-ker
can-na-bi-nol
can-na-bis
can-ner-y
can-ni-bal-ize
can-non-ade
can-nu-lar
ca-noe-ist
can-on
ca-ñon (Spanish form for canyon)
can-on-ess
ca-non-i-cal
can-on-i-za-tion
Ca-no-pus
can-o-py
can-ta-bi-le
can-ta-loup
can-tan-ker-ous
can-ta-ta
can-ter (v.)
cant-er (n.)
can-thar-i-des
can-tha-ris
can-thus
can-ti-cle
can-ti-le-ver
can-ton-ment
Ca-nuck
can-vassed
can-vass-er
caou-tchouc
ca-pa-ble
ca-pa-cious
ca-pac-i-tance
ca-pac-i-tor
ca-par-i-son
cap-e-lin
ca-per
ca-pi-as
cap-il-la-ros-co-py
cap-il-lar-y
cap-i-tal-ist
cap-i-tal-i-za-tion
ca-pi-tan
ca-pit-u-la-tor
cap-no-di-um
ca-pon-ette
ca-pote
cap-ric
ca-pric-cio
ca-price
ca-pri-cious
Cap-ri-cor-nis
cap-ro-ate
ca-pro-ic
cap-ry-late
ca-pryl-ic
cap-ry-lyl
cap-sa-i-cin
cap-si-cum
cap-stan
cap-su-lar
cap-ti-va-tor
cap-u-chin
cap-y-bar-a
car-a-bao
car-a-bi-neer
Ca-ra-cas
car-a-cul
ca-rafe
car-a-mel
car-a-pace
car-at
car-a-van-sa-ry
car-a-way
carb-ac-i-dom-e-ter
carb-alk-ox-yl
car-ba-mate
car-bam-ic
car-bam-ide
carb-am-i-do-hy-dan-to-in
car-ba-mine
carb-am-i-no
car-bam-o-yl
car-ba-nil-ic
car-ba-nil-ide
car-bar-sone
car-baz-ic
car-ba-zole
car-beth-ox-yl
car-bine
car-bi-nol
car-bo-cy-a-nine
car-bo-cy-clic
car-bo-di-i-mide
car-bol-ic
car-bo-lize
Car-bo-loy
car-bo-na-ceous
car-bon-ate
car-bon-ic
car-bon-if-er-ous
car-bo-ni-um
car-bon-ize
car-bon-yl
car-bon-y-late
Car-bo-run-dum
car-box-yl-ase
car-box-yl-ic
car-bun-cle
car-bu-rant
car-bu-ret-ed
car-bu-ret-or
car-bu-riz-er
car-byl-a-mine
car-cass
car-cin-o-gen
car-ci-no-gen-ic
car-ci-noid
car-ci-no-ma
car-ci-no-ma-to-sis
car-ci-nom-a-tous
car-ci-no-sis
car-da-mom
car-di-ac
Car-di-a-zol
car-di-nal
card-ing
car-di-o-gen-ic
car-di-og-ra-phy
car-di-oid
car-di-ol-o-gy
car-di-om-e-ter
car-di-ot-o-my
car-di-tis
ca-reen
ca-reer
ca-ress-ive
car-et
Car-ib-be-an
car-i-bou
car-i-ca-tur-al
car-ies
car-il-lon-neur
ca-ri-na
car-i-nate
car-i-ous
Car-list
Car-mel-ite
car-min-a-tive
car-min-ic
car-nage
car-nal-i-ty
car-nau-ba
Car-ne-gie
car-ne-lian
car-ni-tine
car-ni-val
car-niv-o-rous
car-no-tite
car-oled
Car-o-lin-i-an
car-om
car-o-tene
ca-rot-e-noid
ca-rot-id
ca-rous-al
Car-pa-thi-an
car-pel
car-pen-try
carp-er
car-pho-lite
car-pho-sid-er-ite
car-po-go-ni-um
car-riage
car-ri-on
car-ron-ade
car-rou-sel
cart-age
car-tel-ize
car-ti-lag-i-nous
car-tog-ra-phy
car-ton
car-toon-ist
car-touche
car-tridge
car-un-cle
car-vene
carv-er
Car-ver
car-y-at-id
car-y-op-sis
ca-sa-ba
Ca-sa-blan-ca
cas-car-a
ca-sein-ate
ca-se-ous
cash-ew
cash-ier
cas-ing
ca-si-no
cas-ket
cas-se-role
cas-si-mere
Cas-si-o-pe-ian
cas-sit-er-ite
cas-ta-net
cas-tel-late
cast-er
cas-ti-ga-tor
cas-tile
Cas-til-ian
cas-tle
cas-tor-ite
cas-tra-tive
cas-u-al-ty
cas-u-ist-ry
ca-sus bel-li
cat-a-bol-ic
ca-tab-o-lism
cat-a-clys-mic
cat-a-di-op-tric
cat-a-falque
cat-a-lase
cat-a-lec-tic
cat-a-lep-tic
cat-a-loged
cat-a-log-ing
ca-tal-y-sis
cat-a-lyst
cat-a-lyt-i-cal-ly
cat-a-lyz-er
cat-a-ma-ran
cat-a-me-ni-al
cat-a-pult
cat-a-ract
ca-tarrh-al
ca-tas-tro-phe
cat-a-stroph-ic
Ca-taw-ba
cat-e-che-sis
cat-e-chet-i-cal
cat-e-chism
cat-e-chu-men-al
cat-e-chol
ca-te-na
cat-e-gor-i-cal
cat-e-go-rize
cat-e-nar-y
cat-e-noid
ca-ter-er
cat-er-pil-lar
cat-er-waul
ca-thar-sis
ca-thar-tic
Ca-thar-ti-dae
ca-thec-tic
ca-the-dral
ca-thep-sin
cath-e-ter-i-za-tion
cath-e-tom-e-ter
cath-ode
ca-thod-ic
cath-o-lic-i-ty
ca-thol-i-cism
cat-i-on-ic
Cau-ca-sian
cau-cus
cau-dal
cau-di-llo
cau-li-flow-er
caus-al
cau-sal-i-ty
cau-sa-tion
caus-a-tive
cause ce-le-bre
cau-se-rie
caus-tic-i-ty
cau-ter-i-za-tion
cav-al-cade
cav-a-lier
cav-al-ry
cav-a-ti-na
ca-ve-at
cav-ern-ous
cav-i-ar
cav-iled
cav-il-er
cav-i-ta-tion
Ca-vi-te
cav-i-ty
ca-vort
cay-enne
Ca-yu-ga
Cay-use
ce-cum
ce-dar
ce-drat
ce-drol
ce-du-la
ceil-om-e-ter
Cel-an-ese
Cel-e-bes
cel-e-brate
ce-leb-ri-ty
ce-ler-i-ty
cel-er-y
ce-les-tial
cel-es-tite
ce-li-ac
cel-i-ba-cy
ce-li-ot-o-my
ce-lite
cel-lif-er-ous
cel-lo-phane
cel-lu-lar
cel-lu-loid
cel-lu-lose
cel-lu-los-ic
Cel-si-us
Celt-ic
cel-ti-um
ce-men-ta-tion
ce-ment-er
ce-ment-ite
ce-men-ti-tious
cem-e-ter-y
ce-no-bi-an
cen-o-bite
Ce-no-zo-ic
cen-so-ri-ous
Cen-tau-rus
cen-ta-vo
cen-te-nar-i-an
cen-te-nar-y
cen-ten-ni-al
cen-tes-i-mal
cen-te-si-mo
cent-ge-ner
cen-ti-me-ter
cen-ti-pede
cen-tral-ize
cen-trif-u-gal
cen-tri-fuge
cen-trip-e-tal
cen-troi-dal
cen-tu-ry
ce-phal-ic
ceph-a-lin
ceph-a-lo-di-um
ceph-a-lom-e-ter
ceph-a-lom-e-try
Ceph-e-id
ce-ram-ic
ce-ram-ist
ce-ram-i-um
ce-ra-ti-um
cer-a-to-sau-rus
Cer-ber-us
ce-re-al
cer-e-bel-lo-ru-bral
cer-e-bel-lum
cer-e-bral
cer-e-brate
cer-e-bro-side
cer-e-bro-spi-nal
cer-e-brum
cere-ment
cer-e-mo-ni-al
Ce-ren-kov
Ce-res
cer-e-sin
ce-rise
ce-rite
ce-ri-um
ce-ro-graph
ce-rog-ra-phy
ce-roid
ce-ro-lite
ce-rot-ic
cer-tain-ly
cer-tif-i-cate
cer-ti-fi-ca-tion
cer-ti-o-ra-ri
cer-ti-tude
ce-ru-le-an
ce-ru-men
ce-russ-ite
cer-van-tite
cer-vi-cal
ce-sar-e-an
ce-si-um
ces-sa-tion
Ce-ta-ce-a
ce-tane
ce-tene
ce-tyl
Cha-blis
Chad-i-an
chaf-er
chaff-er (one who chaffs or banters)
chaf-fer (trade term—buying and selling)
Cha-gres
cha-grin
chair-maned
chaise longue
chal-ced-o-ny
chal-ce-don-yx
chal-co-py-rite
chal-dron
cha-let
chal-ice
chal-i-co-sis
cha-lyb-e-ate
cham-ber-lain
cham-bray
cha-me-le-on
cham-fer
cham-ois
cham-pi-gnon
cham-pi-on
chan-cel-ler-y
chan-cel-lor
chan-cer-y
chan-cre
chan-croi-dal
chan-de-lier
chan-delle
chan-dler
change-a-ble
chang-er
chan-neled
chan-teur
chan-ti-cleer
cha-ot-ic
chap-ar-ral
cha-peau
chap-el
chap-er-on
chap-lain
char-a-banc
char-ac-ter-is-tic
cha-rade
charge-a-ble
char-gé d'af-faires
charg-er
char-i-ly
char-i-ness
char-i-ot-eer
cha-ris-ma
char-is-mat-ic
char-i-ta-ble
cha-ri-va-ri
Char-ley
Char-lotte
charm-er
char-nel
char-ter
char-treuse
Cha-ryb-dis
chas-er
chas-sis
chas-ten
chas-tis-er
chas-ti-ty
cha-teau
cha-te-laine
Chat-ham
cha-toy-an-cy
Chau-ce-ri-an
chau-tau-qua
chau-vin-ism
check-ered
chedd-ite
Che-ha-lis
chei-li-tis
Che-ka
che-la-tion
chel-i-do-ni-um
che-li-form
che-lo-ne
Chel-ten-ham
chem-i-at-ric
chem-i-cal
che-mig-ra-phy
che-mise
chem-i-sette
chem-is-try
chem-o-sphere
chem-o-ther-a-py
che-mot-ro-pism
che-mur-gic
chem-ur-gy
che-nille
Che-no-po-di-um
cher-ish
cher-no-zem
Cher-o-kee
che-root
cher-ub
che-ru-bic
cher-u-bim
Chesh-ire
Ches-ter
chev-a-lier
chev-i-ot
chev-ron
Chey-enne
chi-a-ro-scu-ro
chi-ca-ner-y
chick-en
chi-cle
chic-o-ry
chif-fon

chif-fo-nier
chi-gnon
chil-dren
Chil-e-an
chi-me-ra
chi-mer-i-cal
chim-pan-zee
Chi-nese
chi-noi-se-rie
Chi-nook
chin-qua-pin
Chi-ri-qui
chi-ro-graph
chi-rog-ra-pher
chi-ro-man-cy
chi-rop-o-dy
chi-ro-prac-tor
chi-rur-gi-cal
chis-eled
chis-el-ing
chi-tin-oid
chiv-al-rous
chlo-ral
chlor-al-um
chlor-a-lu-mi-nite
chlor-am-ide
chlor-am-ine
chlor-am-phen-i-col
chlo-rate
chlor-az-ide
chlor-co-sane
Chlo-rel-la
chlor-e-mi-a
chlor-en-chy-ma
Chlo-re-tone
chlo-ric
chlo-ride
chlo-ri-dize
chlor-im-ide
chlo-ri-nate (v.)
chlo-rin-ate (n.)
chlo-rine
chlo-rit-ic
chlo-ro-form
chlo-ro-gen-ic
chlo-rom-e-ter
chlo-rom-e-try
Chlo-ro-my-ce-tin
chlo-ro-phyll
chlo-ro-prene
chlo-ro-sis
chlo-ro-then
chlo-rous
choc-o-late
choic-est
chok-er
cho-lan-ic
chol-an-threne
cho-le-ate
cho-le-cal-cif-er-ol
cho-le-cys-tec-to-my
cho-le-cys-ti-tis
cho-le-cys-tog-ra-phy
cho-le-cys-to-ki-nin
cho-le-cys-tos-to-my
cho-le-ic
cho-le-mi-a
chol-er
chol-er-a
cho-le-ret-ic
chol-er-ic
cho-les-tane
cho-les-ta-nol
cho-les-ter-ic
cho-les-ter-ol
cho-lic
cho-lin-er-gic
cho-lin-es-ter-ase
chol-o-ge-net-ic
cho-los-co-py
chon-dri-o-som-al
chon-dri-o-some
chon-drit-ic
chon-dro-dite
chon-dro-dit-ic
chon-dro-ma
chon-drom-a-tous
chon-drot-o-my
chon-drule
cho-ral
cho-rale
chord-al
chor-date
chor-di-tis
chor-dot-o-my
cho-re-a
cho-re-og-ra-pher
cho-ri-o-men-in-gi-tis
cho-ri-sis
cho-ris-ter
cho-roi-dal
cho-roid-i-tis
cho-rol-o-gy
chor-tle
cho-rus
cho-sen
chow-der
chres-tom-a-thy
chris-ten
Chris-tian
Chris-ti-an-i-ty
chro-ma-mom-e-ter
chro-mate
chro-mat-ic

chro-ma-tic-i-ty
chro-ma-tin
chro-mat-o-gram
chro-ma-tog-ra-phy
chro-ma-tol-y-sis
chro-mat-o-lyt-ic
chro-mat-o-scope
chro-ma-to-sis
chro-mic
chro-mif-er-ous
chro-mi-nance
chro-mite
chro-mi-um
chro-mo-gen-ic
chro-mo-i-so-mer-ic
chro-mom-e-ter
chro-mos-co-py
chro-mo-som-al
chro-mo-trop-ic
chro-mous
chron-i-cler
chron-o-graph
chro-nog-ra-pher
chro-nol-o-ger
chron-o-log-i-cal-ly
chro-nol-o-gy
chro-nom-e-ter
chron-o-met-ri-cal
chro-nom-e-try
chron-o-scope
chro-nos-co-py
chrys-a-lis
chrys-a-loid
chrys-an-the-mum
chrys-a-ro-bin
chrys-a-zin
chry-sene
chrys-o-er-i-ol
chrys-o-graph
chry-sog-ra-phy
chry-so-i-dine
chrys-o-lite
chrys-o-phyll
chuck-ling
Church-ill
churl-ish
chut-ist
chy-la-ceous
chy-lo-sis
chy-mi-fy
chy-mo-tryp-sin
ci-ca-da
cic-a-tri-sive
cic-a-trix
cic-a-trize
cic-e-ro-ne (n.)
cic-e-rone (v.)
ci-der
ci-gar
cig-a-rette
cil-i-ar-y
cil-i-um
ci-mi-cid
cim-o-lite
cin-cho-loi-pon
cin-cho-me-ron-ic
cin-cho-na
cin-chon-a-mine
cin-cho-nine
cin-cho-phen
cinc-ture
Cin-der-el-la
cin-e-ma
cin-e-mat-o-graph
cin-e-ma-tog-ra-pher
cin-e-ole
cin-e-rar-i-a
ci-ne-re-ous
cin-na-bar
cin-nam-ic
cin-nam-o-yl
ci-pher
ci-pho-ny
cir-ci-nate
cir-clet
cir-cling
circ-o-var-i-an
cir-cuit-al
cir-cuit-er
cir-cu-i-tous
cir-cuit-ry
cir-cu-lar-ize
cir-cu-la-to-ry
cir-cum-e-ter
cir-cum-fer-en-tial
cir-cum-lo-cu-tion
cir-cum-loc-u-to-ry
cir-cum-scrib-a-ble
cir-cum-stan-tial
cir-rho-sis
cis-tern
cit-a-ble
ci-ta-to-ry
cit-i-fy
cit-i-zen
cit-ral
cit-rate
cit-ric
cit-ri-nin
cit-ron
cit-ron-el-la
cit-rus
civ-et
civ-il

ci-vil-ian
civ-i-li-za-tion
claim-ant
clam-or-ous
clan-des-tine
clang-or
cla-queur
Clar-ence
clar-et
clar-i-fi-ca-tion
clar-i-net
clar-i-on
clas-si-cal
clas-si-fy
clas-tic
claus-tro-pho-bi-a
clav-a-cin
clav-i-cle
cla-vic-u-lar
cleans-er
cleans-ing
clear-ance
cleav-age
Clem-a-tis
clem-en-cy
Clem-en-tine
Cle-o-pat-ra
cler-gy-man
cler-i-cal
clev-er
clev-is
cli-an-thus
click-er
cli-ent-age
cli-en-tele
cli-mac-ter-ic
cli-mac-tic
cli-mat-ic
cli-ma-tize
cli-ma-to-log-i-cal
cli-ma-tol-o-gy
cli-ma-tom-e-ter
cli-max
climb-er
clin-i-cal
cli-ni-cian
clin-i-co-path-o-log-ic
clin-i-co-pa-thol-o-gy
clink-er
cli-no-he-dral
cli-nom-e-ter
cli-quish
clit-o-ris
cloi-son-ne
clois-ter
Clo-rox
Clos-trid-i-um
clo-sure
cloth-ier
clo-ture
clo-ven
clo-ver
clown-ish
clum-si-ness
clus-ter
cne-mi-al
co-ad-ju-tor
co-ag-u-la-tor
co-ag-u-lom-e-ter
co-a-les-cence
co-a-lite (v.)
Coal-ite (n.)
co-a-li-tion
co-arc-ta-tion
coast-al
coast-er
co-bal-a-min
co-bal-tic
co-balt-if-er-ous
co-bal-ti-ni-trite
co-bal-to-cal-cite
co-bal-tom-e-nite
co-bal-tous
cob-bler
co-bra
co-caine
coc-cid-i-oi-dal
coc-cid-i-oi-din
coc-cid-i-o-sis
coc-cin-ic
coc-ci-nite
coc-cyg-e-al
co-chin
coch-i-neal
coch-le-ar
cock-ade
cock-er-el
cock-le-bur
co-coa
co-co-nut
co-coon
co-deine
codg-er
cod-i-cil
cod-i-fy
co-di-mer
cod-ling
co-erc-i-ble
co-er-cive
co-e-val
co-gen-cy
cog-i-ta-tive
co-gnac
cog-na-tus

cog-ni-tive
cog-ni-za-ble
cog-no-men
co-gno-scen-ti
cog-nos-ci-ble
co-her-ence
co-he-si-ble
co-he-sive
co-in-ci-den-tal
col-an-der
col-chi-cine
Col-chi-cum
co-lec-ti-vo
col-ec-to-my
Co-le-op-te-ra
col-ick-y
col-i-se-um
co-li-tis
col-lab-o-ra-tor
col-la-gen-ase
col-lag-e-nous
col-laps-i-ble
col-lat-er-al
col-la-tor
col-league
col-lect-a-ble
col-lec-ta-ne-a
col-lec-tive
col-lec-tor
col-le-gi-ate
col-lier
col-li-ma-tor
col-li-sion
col-lo-di-on
col-loi-dal
col-lo-qui-al-ism
col-lo-quy
col-lu-sive
col-lu-vi-um
co-logne
Co-lom-bi-an
co-lo-met-ric
co-lom-e-try
co-lon
colo-nel
co-lo-ni-al
co-lon-ic
col-o-nize
col-on-nade
col-o-ny
col-o-phon
co-lo-pho-ny
col-or
Col-o-rad-an
Col-o-ra-do
col-or-a-tu-ra
col-or-im-e-ter
col-or-i-met-ric
col-or-im-e-try
co-los-sal
Col-os-se-um
co-los-sus
co-los-to-my
co-los-trum
col-por-teur
Co-lum-bi-a
col-um-bif-er-ous
col-um-bine
co-lum-bite
co-lum-bi-um
col-umn
co-lum-nar
col-um-nist
co-lure
Co-man-che
co-ma-tose
co-mat-u-la
com-bat-ant
com-bat-ed
com-bat-ing
com-bat-ive-ness
com-ba-tiv-i-ty
comb-er
com-bin-a-ble
com-bi-na-tive
com-bu-rim-e-ter
com-bus-ti-ble
com-bus-tor
co-me-di-an
com-e-dy
co-mes-ti-ble
com-e-tar-y
co-met-ic
com-fort-a-ble
com-fort-er
com-i-cal
Com-in-form
com-ing
co-mique
com-i-ty
com-man-dant
com-man-deer
com-mand-er
com-man-do
com-mem-o-ra-tor
com-mend-a-ble
com-men-da-tion
com-mend-a-to-ry
com-men-su-ra-ble
com-men-tar-y
com-men-ta-tor
com-mer-cial
com-mi-na-to-ry
com-min-gle

com-mi-nute
com-mis-er-ate
com-mis-sar-i-at
com-mis-sar-y
com-mis-sion
com-mis-sur-al
com-mis-sur-ot-o-my
com-mit-ta-ble
com-mit-tee
com-mo-di-ous
com-mod-i-ty
com-mon-er
com-mon-sen-si-ble
com-mo-rant
com-mu-nal
com-mu-ni-ca-tive
com-mu-ni-ca-tor
com-mun-ion
com-mu-ni-que
com-mu-nism
Com-mu-nist
com-mu-nis-tic
com-mu-ni-ty
com-mut-a-ble
com-mu-ta-tion
com-mu-ta-tor
com-mut-er
com-pact-er
com-pact-i-ble
com-pac-tor
com-pan-ion
com-pa-ny
com-pa-ra-ble
com-par-a-tive
com-par-a-tor
com-par-i-son
com-par-o-scope
com-part-men-tal-ize
com-pat-i-ble
com-pel-ling
com-pen-di-um
com-pen-sa-ble
com-pen-sat-ing
com-pen-sa-to-ry
com-pe-tent
com-pe-ti-tion
com-pet-i-tor
com-pi-la-tion
com-pil-er
com-pla-cent
com-plain-ant
com-plai-sance
com-ple-men-tal
com-ple-men-ta-ry
com-ple-tive
com-plex-ion
com-pli-cate
com-plic-i-ty
com-pli-men-ta-ry
com-po-nent
com-pos-er
com-pos-ite
com-po-si-tion
com-pos-i-tor
com-po-sure
com-pound-er
com-pre-hend-i-ble
com-pre-hen-si-ble
com-press-i-ble
com-press-ing
com-pres-sive
com-pres-som-e-ter
com-pres-sor
com-pris-al
com-pro-mise
Comp-tom-e-ter
comp-trol-ler
com-pul-so-ry
com-put-er
com-put-ist
co-nal
co-na-tion
con-cat-e-na-tion
con-cav-er
con-ceiv-a-ble
con-cen-tra-tor
con-cen-tri-cal
con-cen-tric-i-ty
con-cep-tu-al
con-cer-ti-na
con-cert-ize
con-ces-sion-aire
con-chi-form
con-choi-dal
con-cho-log-i-cal
con-chol-o-gy
con-chyl-i-um
con-cil-i-a-to-ry
con-clu-sive
con-coct-er
con-com-i-tant
con-cord-ance
con-cord-ant
con-cres-cence
con-cret-er
con-cu-bi-nage
con-cu-pis-cence
con-cu-pis-ci-ble
con-dem-na-to-ry
con-den-sa-ble
con-den-sa-tion
con-dens-er
con-dens-ing
con-de-scen-sion

con-di-ment
con-do-lence
con-do-min-i-um
con-don-ance
con-duc-i-ble
con-du-cive
con-duct-ance
con-duct-ed
con-duct-i-ble
con-duc-tiv-i-ty
con-duc-tom-e-ter
con-duc-tor
con-duit
con-du-ran-gin
con-dy-loid
con-el-rad
Con-es-to-ga
con-fec-tion-er-y
con-fed-er-a-tion
con-fes-sor
con-fi-dant (n.)
con-fi-dent (adj.)
con-fig-u-ra-tion
con-fin-er
con-firm-a-ble
con-fir-ma-tion
con-firm-a-to-ry
con-firm-er
con-fis-ca-to-ry
con-fla-gra-tion
con-flic-tive
con-flux-i-ble
con-form-a-ble
con-for-ma-tion
con-form-i-ty
Con-fu-cian-ism
con-fus-a-ble
con-fut-a-ble
con-fu-ta-tion
con-ge-la-tive
con-gel-i-fract
con-ge-ner
con-ge-nial
con-ge-ni-al-i-ty
con-gen-i-tal
con-ge-ries
con-gest-i-ble
con-glom-er-at-ic
Con-go-lese
con-grat-u-la-to-ry
con-gre-ga-tor
con-gres-sion-al
con-gru-i-ty
con-i-cal
co-nic-e-ine
co-nid-i-um
con-i-fer
co-nif-er-ous
Co-ni-oph-o-ra
co-ni-um
con-jec-tur-al
con-ju-gal
con-ju-gate
con-junc-ti-vi-tis
con-ju-ra-tion
con-jur-er
con-nect-a-ble
con-nect-er
Con-nect-i-cut-er
con-nec-tive
con-niv-ance
con-nois-seur
con-nu-bi-al
co-noi-dal
co-no-phor
con-quer-or
con-quin-a-mine
con-san-guin-e-ous
con-sci-en-tious
con-scion-a-ble
con-scious
con-se-cra-tor
con-sec-u-tive
con-se-nes-cence
con-sen-sus
con-se-quen-tial
con-ser-va-tion
con-serv-a-tive
con-ser-va-tor
con-serv-a-to-ry
con-sid-er-ate
con-sig-na-tion
con-sign-ee
con-sign-or
con-sist-ent
con-sis-to-ry
con-so-la-tion
con-sol-i-date
con-som-me
con-so-nant
con-sor-ti-um
con-spi-cu-i-ty
con-spic-u-ous
con-spir-a-cy
con-spi-ra-tion
con-sta-ble
con-stab-u-lar-y
con-stan-cy
con-stant-an
con-ster-na-tion
con-sti-pa-tion
con-stit-u-ent
con-sti-tu-tive
con-stric-tor

con-struc-tor
con-sul-ar
con-sul-ate
con-sult-ant
con-sul-ta-tion
con-sult-a-tive
con-sult-er
con-sum-er
con-sum-mate
con-sum-ma-to-ry
con-sump-ti-ble
con-tac-tor
con-ta-gious
con-tam-i-na-tor
con-tem-pla-tor
con-tem-po-ra-ne-ous
con-tempt-i-ble
con-temp-tu-ous
con-tend-er
con-ten-tious
con-test-ant
con-tes-ta-tion
con-tex-tur-al
con-ti-gu-i-ty
con-tig-u-ous
con-ti-nence
con-ti-nen-tal
con-tin-gen-cy
con-ti-nu-i-ty
con-tin-u-ous
con-tin-u-um
con-tor-tive
con-tra-band
con-tract-a-ble
con-tract-ile
con-trac-tor
con-tra-dict-er
con-tra-dic-tor
con-tra-dic-to-ry
con-trail
con-tra-ri-e-ty
con-trar-i-wise
con-tras-tive
con-trib-ut-ing
con-tri-bu-tion
con-trib-u-tor
con-triv-ance
con-triv-er
con-trol-la-ble
con-tro-ver-sy
con-tro-vert-i-ble
con-tu-ma-cious
con-tu-me-li-ous
con-tu-me-ly
con-tu-sion
co-nun-drum
co-nus
con-va-les-cence
con-vec-tor
con-ven-ience
con-ven-ien-cy
con-ver-gent
con-verg-ing
con-vers-a-ble
con-ver-sant
con-ver-sive
con-vert-er
con-vert-i-ble
con-vey-or
con-vic-tive
con-vin-ci-ble
con-vinc-ing
con-viv-i-al
con-vo-lute
con-vul-sive
con-y-rine
cool-ant
cool-er
Coo-lidge
coo-lie
coop-er-age
co-op-er-a-tive
co-or-di-na-tor
coot-ie
co-pai-ba
co-pal-ite
Co-pen-ha-gen
Co-per-ni-cus
cop-ies
co-pi-ous
co-pla-nar
co-pol-y-mer
co-po-lym-er-ize
co-pra
cop-ro-por-phy-rin
cop-ro-stane
co-pros-ta-nol
co-pros-ter-ol
cop-u-la-tive
co-quet-ry
co-quet-tish
co-qui-na
cor-al
Cor-a-mine
cord-age
cor-date
cor-dial
cor-dial-i-ty
cor-dil-le-ra
cord-ite
Cor-do-ba
cor-don
cor-do-van
cor-du-roy
cor-dyl-ite
co-re-op-sis
co-re-spond-ent
co-ri-a-ceous
co-ri-an-der
Cor-i-ci-din
Cor-inth
Co-rin-thi-an
cor-i-o-lis
cor-mo-rant
cor-mus
cor-ne-al
cor-nered
cor-net-ist
cor-nice
cor-nif-ic
Cor-nish
cor-nu-co-pi-a
co-rol-la
cor-ol-lar-y
co-ro-na
cor-o-nal
cor-o-nar-y
cor-o-na-tion
cor-o-nene
cor-o-ner
cor-o-net
co-ro-ni-um
cor-po-ral
cor-po-ra-tive
cor-po-re-al
cor-pu-lent
cor-pus-cle
cor-pus-cu-lar
cor-rect-a-ble
cor-rect-ant
cor-rec-tive
cor-rec-tor
cor-re-late
cor-rel-a-tive
cor-re-spond-ence
cor-ri-dor
cor-ri-gen-dum
cor-ri-gi-ble
cor-rob-o-ra-to-ry
cor-rod-i-ble
cor-ro-si-ble
cor-ro-sive
cor-ru-ga-tor
cor-rupt-i-ble
cor-rup-tive
cor-sage
corse-let
cor-tege
cor-ti-cate
cor-ti-cip-e-tal
cor-ti-ci-um
cor-ti-co-ad-re-nal-o-trop-ic
cor-ti-cos-ter-one
cor-ti-sone
co-run-dum
co-rus-cant
cor-us-ca-tion
cor-vus-ite
co-ryd-a-line
cor-ym-bose
cor-y-phee
co-ry-za
co-sa-lite
co-se-cant
co-sine
cos-me-col-o-gy
cos-met-i-cal
cos-me-ti-cian
cos-me-tol-o-gy
cos-mi-cal-i-ty
cos-mism
cos-mo-gon-ic
cos-mog-o-ny
cos-mog-ra-pher
cos-mo-graph-ic
Cos-mo-line
cos-mol-o-gy
cos-mo-naut
cos-mo-pol-i-tan
cos-mop-o-lite
cos-mo-ra-ma
cos-mo-ram-ic
cos-mos-o-phy
cos-mo-tron
Cos-ta Ri-can
cos-tive
cos-tum-er
co-tar-nine
co-te-rie
co-ter-mi-nous
co-til-lion
co-to-ne-as-ter
cot-tag-er
cot-y-le-don
couch-ant
cou-lomb
cou-lom-e-ter
cou-ma-rin
cou-ma-rone
coun-cil-or
coun-seled
coun-sel-or
coun-te-nance
count-er (who counts)
coun-ter (other meanings)
coun-ter-feit
count-ess
coun-try
coun-ty
cou-pler
cou-plet
cou-pling
cou-pon
cour-age
cou-ra-geous
cou-rant
cou-ri-er
cours-er
cour-te-ous
cour-te-san
cour-te-sy
cour-tier
cous-in
cou-tu-ri-er
cou-vert
cov-e-nant-er
cov-e-nan-tor (law)
Cov-en-try
cov-er-age
cov-ert-ly
cov-et-ous
cov-ey
cox-i-tis
Cox-sack-ie
cow-ard-ice
cowl-ing
coy-ote
coz-en
co-zi-ness
crack-ers
crack-ling
cra-dling
cra-nid-i-um
cra-ni-ec-to-my
cra-ni-o-graph
cra-ni-og-ra-pher
cra-ni-ol-o-gy
cra-ni-om-e-ter
cra-ni-os-co-py
cra-ni-um
cra-ter-i-form
cra-tic-u-lar
cra-vat
Cra-ven-ette
crawl-er
cray-on
cra-zy
cream-er-y
creas-er
cre-at-ic
cre-a-tine
cre-at-i-nine
cre-a-tiv-i-ty
crea-ture
cre-den-tial
cre-den-za
cred-i-ble
cred-it-a-ble
cred-i-tor
cre-do
cre-du-li-ty
cred-u-lous
creed-ite
creep-er
cre-ma-to-ry
Cre-mo-na
cre-nate
cren-a-ture
cren-eled
cren-el-lat-ed
cre-nit-ic
cren-u-lat-ed
cre-oph-a-gous
cre-o-sol
cre-o-sote
crep-i-tant
cre-pus-cu-lar
cre-scen-do
cres-cen-tic
cre-sol
cre-sor-ci-nol
cre-sot-ic
cres-o-tine
cres-yl-ate
cre-syl-ic
cre-ta-ceous
cre-tin-ism
cre-tonne
cre-vasse
crev-ice
cre-vic-u-lar
crib-el-late
cri-bel-lum
cri-ce-tus
crick-et-er
cri-coid
Cri-me-an
crim-i-nal-i-ty
crim-i-no-log-ic
crim-i-nol-o-gy
crim-i-not-ic
cring-er
crin-kle
cri-noi-dal
crin-o-line
cri-nos-i-ty
crip-pling
cris-pate
crisp-er
cris-tate
cri-te-ri-a
crit-i-cal
crit-i-cism
cri-tique
croak-er
cro-ce-tin
cro-cheted
cro-chet-ing
cro-cid-o-lite
croc-o-dile
croc-o-ite
cro-con-ic
cro-ny-ism
cro-qui-gnole
cro-ta-lar-i-o-sis
crotch-et-y
cro-ton-ate
cro-ton-o-yl
crou-pi-er
croup-ous
crou-ton
cru-cial
cru-ci-ble
cru-ci-fix
cru-ci-form
cru-di-ty
cruis-er
crul-ler
crum-bling
crum-ple
cru-ral
cru-sad-er
crus-ta-ceous
crust-al
crus-tose
cry-o-gen-ics
cry-om-e-ter
cry-o-phil-ic
cry-oph-o-rus
cry-os-co-py
crypt-a-nal-y-sis
cryp-ta-rithm
cryp-ti-cal
cryp-to-gram-mic
cryp-tog-ra-pher
cryp-to-graph-ic
cryp-tom-e-ter
crys-taled
crys-tal-lin-i-ty
crys-tal-lite
crys-tal-li-za-tion
crys-tal-liz-er
crys-tal-log-ra-phy
crys-tal-loi-dal
cten-o-phore
cte-tol-o-gy
cu-bi-cal
cu-bic-u-lum
cub-ism
cub-ist
cu-bi-tal
cu-bi-tus
cu-boi-dal
cuck-old
cuck-oo
cudg-eled
cui-rass
cui-sine
cul-i-nar-y
cull-ing
cul-mi-na-tion
cu-lotte
cul-pa-ble
cul-prit
cult-ism
cul-ti-va-tor
cul-tur-al
cu-mal-de-hyde
cum-ber-some
cum-brous
cu-mene
cu-me-nyl
cu-mic
cu-mi-dine
cum-in
cu-min-o-in
cu-mi-nol
cu-mi-nyl
cu-mo-yl
cu-mu-la-tive
cu-mu-lene
cu-mu-lo-nim-bus
cu-mu-lus
cu-ne-ate
cu-ne-i-form
cu-no-ni-a-ceous
cu-pid-i-ty
cu-po-la
cu-pram-mo-ni-um
cu-pre-ine
cu-pre-ous
cu-pric
cu-prif-er-ous
cu-prite
cu-pro-cy-a-nide
cu-proid
cu-pro-ri-va-ite
cu-prous
cur-a-ble
Cu-ra-çao
cu-ra-re
cu-rate
cu-ra-tive
cu-ra-tor
cur-cu-min
cur-dle
cu-rette
cur-few
cu-rie
cu-rine
cu-ri-os-i-ty
cu-ri-o-so
cu-ri-ous
cu-rite
cu-ri-um
curl-i-cue
curl-i-ness
cur-mudg-eon
cur-ric-u-lums
cur-sive
cur-so-ry
cur-tain
cur-te-sy
cur-va-ceous
cur-va-ture
cur-vet-ted
cur-vi-lin-e-ar
cur-vom-e-ter
cush-ioned
cus-pa-rine
cus-pi-dal
cus-pi-dor
cuss-ed-ness
cus-tard
cus-to-di-an
cus-tom-ar-i-ly
cus-tom-ar-y
cus-tom-er
cu-ta-ne-ous
cu-ti-cle
cu-tic-u-lar
cy-an-a-mide
cy-a-nate
cy-an-e-ous
cy-an-ic
cy-a-ni-da-tion
cy-a-nide
cy-an-i-din
cy-a-nite
cy-an-o-gen
cy-a-no-ge-net-ic
cy-a-no-gua-ni-dine
cy-a-no-hy-drin
cy-a-nom-e-ter
cy-a-no-met-ric
cy-a-nope
cy-a-no-phy-cin
cy-a-no-sis
cy-a-nu-ric
cy-aph-e-nine
cy-ber-net-ics
cyc-la-mate
cy-cli-cal
cy-clic-i-ty
cy-cling
cy-clist
cy-cli-tis
cy-cli-za-tion
cy-clo-hex-i-mide
cy-clo-hex-yl-a-mine
cy-cloi-dal
cy-clol-y-sis
cy-clom-e-ter
cy-clon-ic
cy-clo-nite
Cy-clo-pe-an
cy-clo-ra-ma
cy-clo-ser-ine
cy-clot-o-my
cy-clo-tron
cyl-in-der
cyl-in-dra-ceous
cy-lin-dri-cal
cyl-in-dric-i-ty
cyl-in-drite
cy-mene
cy-mo-graph
cy-mose
cyn-i-cal
cyn-i-cism
cyn-o-don-tin
cy-no-sure
Cyn-thi-a
cy-press
Cyp-ri-an
Cyp-ri-ot (native of Cyprus)
Cy-prus
Cyr-e-na-ic
Cy-ril-lic
cys-tec-to-my
cys-te-ic
cys-teine
cys-tine
cys-ti-tis
cys-toid
cys-to-ma
cys-tom-e-ter
cys-to-scope
cys-tos-co-py
cy-tase
cyt-i-dine
cyt-i-dyl-ic
cyt-i-sine
cy-toc-i-dal
cy-to-ge-net-ics
cy-tog-e-nous
cy-tol-o-gy
cy-tol-y-sin
cy-tol-y-zate
cy-to-lyze
cy-tom-e-ter
cy-to-sine
czar-ism
Czech-o-slo-vak

D

dachs-hund
Da-cron
dac-tyl-ic
dac-tyl-o-graph
dac-ty-log-ra-phy
dac-ty-loid
dac-ty-lol-o-gy
dac-ty-los-co-py
dac-ty-lus
Dae-da-li-an
daf-fo-dil
da-guerre-o-type
dahl-ia
Da-ho-me-an
dain-ti-ness
Dai-qui-ri
dair-y
dai-sy
Da-kar
Da-kin
Dal-e-car-li-an
dal-li-ance
Dal-ma-tian
dam-a-scene
Da-mas-cus
dam-ask
dam-na-ble
damn-ing
Dam-o-cles
Da-mon
damp-en-er
damp-er
damp-ish
dam-son
danc-ing
dan-de-li-on
dan-druff
dan-ger-ous
dan-gling
Dan-ish
dan-seuse
dark-en
dar-ling
da-sheen
das-tard
da-sym-e-ter
da-tive
da-tum
da-tu-ric
daub-er
daugh-ter
dau-phin
Da-vi-son-ite
da-vit
daw-dler
daz-zling
dea-con-ess
deaf-en-ing
deal-er
de-ba-cle
de-bar-ka-tion
de-bat-a-ble
deb-au-chee
de-bauch-er-y
de-ben-ture
deb-ile
de-bil-i-tate
deb-it
deb-o-nair
de-bris
debt-or
de-but
deb-u-tante
dec-ade
dec-a-dence
dec-a-dent
dec-a-he-dral
dec-a-lage
de-cal-co-ma-ni-a
de-ca-les-cence
Dec-a-lin
dec-a-li-ter
dec-a-log
de-cam-e-ter (verse)
dec-a-me-ter (measure)
dec-a-me-tho-ni-um
de-ca-nal (adj.)
dec-a-nal (n.)
dec-ane
dec-a-no-ic
dec-a-no-yl
De-cap-o-da
de-cap-i-ta-tor
de-cant-er
dec-are
de-cath-lon
de-ce-dent
de-ceiv-er

de-cel-er-a-tor
de-cel-er-om-e-ter
de-cel-er-on
De-cem-ber
de-cen-cy
dec-ene
de-cen-na-ry
de-cen-ni-al
dec-e-nyl
de-cep-tive
dec-i-bel
de-cid-u-ous
dec-ile
dec-i-mal
dec-i-ma-tion
dec-i-me-ter
de-ci-pher
de-ci-sion
de-ci-sive
deck-led
dec-la-ma-tion
de-clam-a-to-ry
de-clar-ant
dec-la-ra-tion
de-clar-a-tive
de-clar-a-to-ry
de-clin-a-ble
dec-li-na-tion
de-clin-a-to-ry
dec-li-nom-e-ter
de-cli-vate
de-cliv-i-ty
de-cli-vous
de-coct-i-ble
de-coc-tive
de-cod-er
de-col-le-te
dec-o-ra-tive
dec-o-rous
de-co-rum
dec-re-ment
de-crem-e-ter
de-crep-i-tude
de-cre-tive
dec-re-to-ry
dec-yl-ene
de-cyl-ic
ded-i-ca-to-ry
de-duc-i-ble
de-duct-i-ble
de-fal-ca-tion
def-a-ma-tion
de-fam-a-to-ry
de-fat-i-ga-ble
de-fea-si-ble
def-e-ca-tor
de-fec-ti-bil-i-ty
de-fec-tive
de-fec-tor
de-fend-ant
de-fend-er
de-fen-si-ble
de-fen-sive
de-fer
def-er-ence
de-fer-ra-ble
de-fer-ves-cence
de-fi-bra-tor
de-fi-cient
def-i-cit
def-i-lade
de-file
de-fin-a-ble
def-i-ni-tion
de-fin-i-tive
def-la-gra-tion
de-fla-tion
de-flec-tive
de-flec-tom-e-ter
de-flec-tor
def-lo-ra-tion
def-lu-ent
de-fo-li-ate
de-form-a-ble
de-for-ma-tion
de-form-a-tive
de-for-me-ter
de-form-i-ty
de-frau-da-tion
de-frost-er
de-gen-er-a-tive
de-glu-ti-tion
deg-ra-da-tion
de-grade
de-guel-in
de-his-cent
de-hy-dra-tor
de-hy-dro-cho-late
de-hy-dro-cho-les-ter-ol
de-hy-dro-gen-ase
de-i-fi-ca-tion
de-is-tic
de-jeu-ner
Del-a-war-e-an
de-lec-ta-ble
del-e-gate
del-e-te-ri-ous
de-le-tion
de-lib-er-a-tive
del-i-ble
del-i-ca-cy
del-i-ca-tes-sen
de-li-cious
De-li-lah
de-lin-e-a-tor
de-lin-quen-cy
del-i-ques-cence
de-lir-i-ous
de-lir-i-um
de-lo-mor-phous
del-phi-nin
del-phin-i-um
Del-sar-ti-an
del-toi-dal
del-uge
de-lu-so-ry
dem-a-gog
dem-a-gog-ic
dem-a-gogu-er-y
de-mand-ant
de-mar-ca-tion
de-mean-or
de-men-tia
de-mer-it
de-mesne
dem-i-monde
de-mise
dem-i-tasse
de-mo-bi-li-za-tion
de-moc-ra-cy
dem-o-crat
de-moc-ra-tize
de-mog-ra-pher
de-mo-graph-ic
dem-oi-selle
de-mol-ish
dem-o-li-tion
de-mon-e-tize
de-mo-ni-a-cal
de-mon-ic
de-mon-stra-ble
dem-on-stra-tion
de-mon-stra-tive
dem-on-stra-tor
de-mor-al-ize
de-mul-cent
de-mur-rage
de-nar-i-us
de-na-ry
den-drit-ic
den-dro-lite
den-drol-o-gy
den-drom-e-ter
Den-eb
de-ner-vate
den-gue
de-ni-er (one who denies)
de-nier (coin; silk)
den-i-gra-to-ry
den-im
den-i-son
de-nom-i-na-tive
de-nom-i-na-tor
de-noue-ment
den-sim-e-ter
den-si-tom-e-ter
den-si-ty
den-tal
den-ti-cle
den-tic-u-lar
den-ti-frice
den-tig-er-ous
den-tist-ry
de-nu-da-tion
de-nun-ci-a-tive
de-nun-ci-a-to-ry
de-o-dor-ant
de-o-dor-iz-er
de-ox-y-ri-bose
de-part-men-tal-ize
de-par-ture
de-pend-a-ble
de-pend-en-cy
de-pend-ent
de-perm-ing
de-phleg-ma-to-ry
dep-i-late
de-pil-a-to-ry
de-plor-a-ble
dep-lo-ra-tion
de-po-nent
de-por-ta-tion
de-port-ee
de-pos-al
de-pos-er
de-pos-i-tar-y
de-pos-it-ed
dep-o-si-tion
de-pos-i-to-ry
de-pot
dep-ra-va-tion
de-prav-i-ty
dep-re-ca-to-ry
de-pre-ci-ate
dep-re-da-tion
dep-re-da-to-ry
de-pres-sant
de-press-i-ble
de-pres-sor
de-priv-al
dep-ri-va-tion
depth-om-e-ter
dep-u-ra-tor
dep-u-tize
de-rac-i-nate
de-re-cho
der-e-lict
de ri-gueur
de-ri-sive
der-i-va-tion
de-riv-a-tive
der-ma-ti-tis
der-mat-o-graph
der-ma-tol-o-gy
der-ma-to-sis
der-moi-dal
der-nier
der-o-gate
de-rog-a-to-ry
der-vish
des-cant
de-scend-ant
de-scend-er
de-scend-i-ble
de-scrib-a-ble
de-scrip-tive
des-cry
des-e-crat-er
des-e-de-ri-um
Des-er-et
de-sert (n., that which is deserved)
des-ert (n., adj., barren tract)
de-sert (v.)
de-sert-er
des-ic-cate
des-ic-ca-tor
de-sid-er-a-tum
des-ig-na-ble
des-ig-nat-a-ble
des-ig-na-tive
des-ig-na-tor
de-sign-ed-ly
des-ig-nee
de-sign-er
de-sip-i-ent
de-sir-a-ble
de-sist-ance
des-mo-di-um
des-mo-lase
des-mol-y-sis
des-mo-trop-ic
des-mot-ro-pism
des-o-la-tion
des-ox-y-cho-lic
des-ox-y-ri-bo-nu-cle-ase
de-spair
des-per-a-do
des-per-ate
des-pi-ca-ble
de-spis-a-ble
de-spis-er
de-spite
de-spoil
de-spo-li-a-tion
de-spond-ence
de-spond-ent
des-pot-i-cal
des-pot-ism
des-pu-ma-tion
des-qua-ma-tion
des-sert
des-ti-na-tion
des-ti-ny
des-ti-tute
de-stroy-er
de-struct-i-ble
de-struc-tive
de-struc-tor
des-ue-tude
des-ul-to-ry
des-yl
de-syn-ap-sis
de-tect-a-ble
de-tec-tive
de-tec-tor
de-ten-tive
de-ter-gent
de-te-ri-o-ra-tive
de-ter-mi-na-ble
de-ter-mi-nant
de-ter-min-er
de-ter-rence
de-test-a-ble
det-o-nant
det-o-na-tor
de-trac-tor
det-ri-men-tal
de-tri-tal
de-tri-tus
deu-ter-ide
deu-te-ri-um
deu-ter-on
Deu-ter-o-nom-ic
Deu-ter-on-o-my
deut-sche
dev-as-ta-tor
de-vel-op-men-tal
de-vi-a-tor
de-vice
dev-il-ish
dev-il-try
de-vi-ous
dev-i-see
de-vis-er
dev-i-sor (legal)
De-vo-ni-an
dev-o-tee
Dew-ar
dex-ter-i-ty
dex-tral-i-ty
dex-trin-ate
dex-trin-o-gen-ic
dex-tro-car-di-a
dex-tro-pi-mar-ic
dex-trorse
dex-trose
dex-trous
di-a-ban-tite
di-a-be-tes
di-a-bet-ic
di-a-bol-i-cal
di-ab-o-lism
di-ac-e-tyl
di-a-dem
di-ag-no-sis
di-ag-nos-ti-cian
di-ag-o-nal
di-a-gramed
di-a-gram-mat-i-cal
di-a-lec-tic
di-a-lec-tol-o-gy
di-a-log
di-a-lu-ric
di-al-y-sis
di-a-lyt-ic
di-a-lyz-er
di-a-man-tine
di-am-e-ter
di-a-met-ri-cal
di-am-i-no-gen
di-a-mond
Di-an-a
di-a-nite
di-a-pa-son
di-a-per
di-aph-a-nom-e-ter
di-aph-a-nous
di-a-phon-ic
di-aph-o-re-sis
di-a-phragm
di-a-phrag-mat-ic
di-ar-rhe-a
di-a-ry
di-as-po-ra
di-a-spore
di-a-stase
di-as-ta-sis
di-a-stat-ic
di-a-stim-e-ter
di-as-to-le
di-a-stol-ic
di-a-sto-mat-ic
di-as-tro-phe
di-a-stroph-ic
di-ath-e-sis
di-a-ther-my
di-a-thet-ic
di-a-tom
di-a-to-ma-ceous
di-at-o-mite
di-at-ro-pism
di-a-zine
di-a-zo-ic
di-az-o-im-ide
di-a-zole
di-az-o-meth-ane
di-a-zo-ni-um
di-az-o-tize
di-az-o-type
di-ba-sic
di-bro-mo-a-ce-tic
di-bu-caine
di-ce-tyl
di-chlone
di-chlo-ro-di-flu-o-ro-meth-ane
di-cho-tom-ic
di-chot-o-mous
di-chot-o-my
di-chro-mat-ic
di-con-dyl-ic
di-cot-y-le-don
di-cou-ma-rol
di-crot-ic
Dic-ta-phone
dic-ta-tor
dic-ta-to-ri-al
dic-tion-ar-y
Dic-to-graph
di-dac-tic
di-dym-i-um
di-er-e-sis
di-e-ret-ic
die-sel-ize
di-e-tar-y
di-e-tet-ic
di-e-ti-tian
dif-fer-en-tial
dif-fi-dence
dif-flu-ent
dif-frac-tion
dif-frac-tom-e-ter
dif-fran-gi-ble
dif-fus-er
dif-fus-i-ble
dif-fu-sive
di-gest-er
di-gest-i-ble
di-ges-tive
dig-i-tal
dig-i-tal-is
dig-i-tal-i-za-tion
dig-i-tal-ose
dig-i-ti-ner-vate
dig-it-iz-er
dig-i-to-gen-in
dig-i-to-nin
dig-ni-tar-y
di-he-dral
di-hy-dro-er-go-cor-nine
di-hy-dro-er-got-a-mine
di-hy-drox-y-a-ce-tic
di-lap-i-dat-ed
di-lat-ant
dil-a-ta-tion
di-la-tion
dil-a-tom-e-ter
di-la-tor
dil-a-to-ry
di-lem-ma
dil-et-tan-te
dil-u-ent
di-lut-ant
di-lut-er
di-me-don
di-men-hy-dri-nate
di-men-si-ble
di-mer-cap-rol
di-mer-ic
di-meth-yl
di-mid-i-ate
di-min-ish
dim-i-nu-tion
di-min-u-tive
dim-i-ty
di-mor-phous
din-ghy
di-ni-tro-tol-u-ene
di-no-saur
di-oc-e-san
di-o-cese
Di-og-e-nes
di-op-side
di-op-ter
di-op-tom-e-ter
di-o-ra-ma
di-o-ram-ic
di-o-rite
di-par-tite
di-phen-yl
diph-the-ri-a
diph-the-rit-ic
diph-the-roid
diph-thong-al
di-pic-o-lin-ic
di-ple-gi-a
di-plex-er
dip-loi-dal
dip-loid-ize
di-plo-ma-cy
dip-lo-mat
di-plo-ma-tist
di-plo-sis
dip-o-dy
dip-so-ma-ni-a
dip-ter-al
di-rec-tiv-i-ty
di-rec-tor-ate
di-rec-to-ri-al
dir-i-gi-ble
dirn-dl
dirt-i-ness
dis-ap-peared
dis-ap-point-ed
dis-as-ter
dis-as-trous
dis-az-o
dis-burs-al
dis-burs-er
dis-cern-i-ble
dis-cerp-ti-ble
dis-ci-ple
dis-ci-pli-nar-i-an
dis-ci-pli-nar-y
dis-ci-plin-er
dis-clo-sure
dis-coi-dal
dis-com-fi-ture
dis-con-so-late
dis-cord-ant
dis-co-theque
dis-cour-sive
dis-crep-an-cy
dis-crete
dis-cre-tion-ar-y
dis-crim-i-na-ble
dis-crim-i-na-tor
dis-cur-sive
dis-cus
dis-cuss-ant
dis-cuss-i-ble
dis-cus-sion
dis-eas-es
di-seuse
dis-ha-bille
di-shev-eled
dis-in-fect-ant
dis-in-te-grate
dis-man-tle
dis-mis-sal
dis-par-ag-er
dis-par-ate
dis-par-i-ty
dis-patch-er
dis-pen-sa-ble
dis-pen-sa-ry
dis-pens-er
dis-per-sal
dis-pers-ant
dis-pers-er
dis-pers-i-ble
dis-per-sive
dis-per-soid
dis-pir-it
dis-pos-al
dis-put-a-ble
dis-pu-tant
dis-pu-ta-tious
dis-pu-ta-tive
dis-put-er
dis-qui-si-tion
dis-quis-i-tive
dis-rep-u-ta-ble
dis-re-pute
dis-rupt-er
dis-sat-is-fied
dis-sect-i-ble
dis-sec-tor
dis-sem-i-na-tive
dis-sen-sion
dis-sent-er
dis-sim-i-la-tive
dis-si-pat-er
dis-sol-u-ble
dis-so-lute
dis-solv-a-ble
dis-sol-vent
dis-so-nance
dis-suad-er
dis-sua-sive
dis-sym-me-try
dis-taff
dis-tant
dis-tem-per
dis-ten-si-ble
dis-ten-tion
dis-til-la-tion
dis-tilled
dis-till-er-y
dis-till-ing
dis-tinc-tive
dis-tin-guished
dis-to-ma-ta
di-sto-ma-to-sis
di-stom-a-tous
dis-tor-tive
dis-tract-er
dis-tract-i-ble
dis-trac-tive
dis-tress-ing
dis-trib-ut-a-ble
dis-trib-u-tar-y
dis-trib-ute
dis-trib-u-tee
dis-tri-bu-tion
dis-trib-u-tive
dis-trib-u-tor
dis-turb-ance
dis-turb-er
di-thi-o-nate
di-thi-o-nous
di-thi-zone
dith-y-ram-bic
di-tol-yl
di-u-re-sis
di-u-ret-ic
di-ur-nal
di-va-ga-tion
di-van
div-er
di-ver-gent
di-vers (several)
di-ver-si-ty
di-vert-er
di-vert-i-ble
di-ver-tic-u-lec-to-my
di-ver-tic-u-lo-sis
di-ver-tic-u-lum
di-ver-tise-ment
di-ver-tisse-ment
di-ver-tive
di-ver-tor (electricity)
di-vest-i-ble
di-ves-ti-ture
di-vid-ed
div-i-dend
di-vid-er
div-i-na-tion
di-vin-a-to-ry
di-vin-i-ty
di-vis-i-ble
di-vi-sion
di-vi-so-ry
di-vor-cee
di-vul-gence
do-blon
do-cent
doc-i-ble
doc-ile
do-cil-i-ty
dock-et
doc-o-sane
doc-tor-al
doc-tor-ate
doc-tri-naire
doc-tri-nal
doc-u-ment-a-ble
doc-u-men-ta-ry
do-de-cane

do-dec-a-no-ic
Do-dec-a-nese
do-dec-ant
do-de-cyl-ene
dodg-er
dog-ger-el
dog-mat-ic
dog-ma-tism
dog-ma-tize
dol-drum
dol-er-ite
dol-i-cho-ce-phal-ic
do-lo-mite
do-lo-rous
dol-phin
do-main
do-mes-ti-cate
do-mes-tic-i-ty
dom-i-cil-i-ar-y
dom-i-nant
dom-i-na-tor
dom-i-neer
Dom-i-ni-ca
do-min-i-cal
Do-min-i-can
dom-i-nie
do-min-ion
dom-i-no
do-na-ble
do-nee
don-keys
do-nor
doo-dle
Dopp-ler
Do-ri-an
Dor-ic
Dor-is
dor-mant
dor-mer
dor-mi-to-ry
Dor-o-the-a
dor-sal
dor-sa-lis
dos-age
do-sim-e-ter
do-sim-e-try
dos-sier
dot-age
dot-ard
dot-ing
dot-ish
dou-ble
dou-blet
dou-bling
dou-bloon
dou-bly
dough-ty
dou-rine
dow-a-ger
dow-eled
down-i-ness
dox-o-log-i-cal
dox-ol-o-gy
doy-en
doz-en
drag-on
dra-goon
drain-age
dra-ma
Dram-a-mine
dra-mat-ic
dra-ma-tis per-so-nae
dram-a-tize
drap-er-y
dream-i-ness
drear-i-ness
dredg-er
dredg-ing
dress-er
dri-er
drift-age
drift-er
drill-ing
drink-om-e-ter
driv-el-er
driv-en
driv-er
droll-er-y
drom-e-dar-y
drop-si-cal
drop-sonde
dro-som-e-ter
dro-ver
drows-i-ness
drudg-er-y
drunk-ard
drunk-en-ness
dru-pa-ceous
du-al-ism
du-ar-chy
du-bi-e-ty
du-bi-ous
du-bi-ta-ble
du-cal
duc-at
duch-ess
du-chesse
duc-ti-ble
duc-tile
dudg-eon
duf-fel-bag
duff-er
du-fre-nite
dul-ci-mer
dul-ci-tol
dul-lard
dull-er
dum-found
dump-er
dump-ling
dump-y
dun-ga-ree
Dun-ge-ness
dun-geon
du-nite
Dun-kard
Dun-stan
du-o-dec-i-mos
du-o-de-nal
du-o-de-ni-tis
du-o-de-nos-co-py
du-o-de-num
du-op-o-ly
du-op-so-ny
du-plex-er
du-pli-ca-tive
du-pli-ca-tor
du-plic-i-ty
du-ra-bil-i-ty
du-ral-u-min
dur-ance
du-ra-tion
du-rene
du-ress
du-rom-e-ter
dur-yl
dusk-i-ness
dust-er
du-te-ous
du-ti-ful
du-ve-tyn
dwarf-ish
dwell-ing
dwin-dling
Dy-cril
dy-nam-e-ter
dy-nam-i-cal
dy-nam-ics
dy-nam-it-er
dy-na-mi-za-tion
dy-na-mom-e-ter
dy-na-mo-met-ric
dy-na-mom-e-try
dy-na-mos
dy-na-mo-tor
Dy-na-Soar
dy-nas-tic
dy-na-tron
Dy-nel
dy-node
dys-cra-site
dys-en-ter-y
dys-pep-si-a
dys-pho-ri-a
dysp-ne-a
dys-pro-si-um

E

ea-ger
ea-glet
ear-li-er
earn-er
ear-nest
earth-en-ware
ea-sel
eas-i-ly
Eas-ter
east-er (storm)
east-ern-er
eb-on-ite
eb-on-y
e-bul-lient
e-bul-li-om-e-ter
e-bul-li-o-scop-ic
e-bul-li-os-co-py
eb-ul-li-tion
ec-cen-tric-i-ty
ec-cle-si-as-ti-cal
ec-dys-i-al
ec-go-nine
ech-e-lon
e-chi-noid
e-chi-nus
ech-o-me-ter
ec-lamp-si-a
ec-lec-ti-cal
e-clip-tic
e-clo-sion
ec-o-log-i-cal
e-col-o-gy
e-con-o-met-ric (adj.)
e-con-o-me-trics (n.)
ec-o-nom-i-cal
ec-o-nom-ics
e-con-o-mist
e-con-o-mize
ec-o-sphere
ec-sta-sy
ec-stat-ic
ec-to-der-moi-dal
ec-tog-e-nous
ec-to-pi-a
ec-top-ic
ec-to-plasm
ec-typ-al
Ec-ua-dor-an
ec-u-men-i-cal
ec-ze-ma
ec-zem-a-tous
e-del-weiss
e-de-ma
e-dem-a-tous
ed-i-ble
ed-i-fi-ca-tion
ed-i-fice
e-di-tion
ed-i-to-ri-al-ize
ed-u-ca-ble
ed-u-ca-tor
e-duc-i-ble
e-duc-tor
ee-ri-ly
ef-fac-ing
ef-fect-i-ble
ef-fec-tive
ef-fec-tu-al
ef-fem-i-nate
ef-fer-ves-cence
ef-fer-ves-ci-ble
ef-fi-ca-cious
ef-fi-ca-cy
ef-fi-cien-cy
ef-fi-cient
ef-fi-gy
ef-flo-res-cence
ef-flu-vi-um
ef-fron-ter-y
ef-ful-gence
ef-fu-si-om-e-ter
ef-fu-sive
e-gal-i-tar-i-an
e-go-cen-trism
e-go-ism
e-go-is-ti-cal
e-go-tism
e-go-tis-ti-cal
e-gre-gious
E-gyp-tol-o-gy
ei-co-sane
ei-der
ei-gen
eight-een
eight-i-eth
ei-ko-nom-e-ter
ein-stein-i-um
eis-e-ge-sis
Ei-sen-how-er
ei-ther
e-jac-u-la-to-ry
e-jec-tive
e-jec-tor
e-lab-o-ra-tive
e-las-tic-i-ty
e-las-to-mer
e-las-tom-e-ter
e-las-to-sis
e-lat-er-in
el-a-te-ri-um
el-der
el-e-cam-pane
e-lec-tion-eer
e-lec-tive
e-lec-tor-al
e-lec-tor-ate
e-lec-tri-cal
e-lec-tric-i-ty
e-lec-tri-fi-ca-tion
e-lec-tro-car-di-o-gram
e-lec-tro-cute
e-lec-trode
e-lec-tro-graph-ic
e-lec-trog-ra-phy
e-lec-trol-y-sis
e-lec-tro-lyte
e-lec-tro-lyt-i-cal
e-lec-trom-e-ter
e-lec-tron-i-cal-ly
e-lec-tron-ics
e-lec-troph-o-rus
e-lec-trot-o-nus
el-ee-mos-y-nar-y
el-e-gant
el-e-gi-ac
el-e-gy
el-e-men-tar-i-ly
el-e-men-ta-ry
el-e-phan-ti-a-sis
el-e-va-tor
e-lev-enth
el-e-von
elf-in
e-lic-it
el-i-gi-ble
e-lim-i-nant
e-lim-i-na-tor
e-lix-ir
E-liz-a-be-than
el-lip-soi-dal
el-lip-som-e-ter
el-lip-ti-cal
el-lip-tic-i-ty
e-lo-gi-um
e-lon-ga-tion
el-o-quent
e-lu-ci-date
e-lud-i-ble
e-lu-so-ry
e-lu-tri-ate
e-lu-vi-um
E-lyr-i-a
E-ly-sian
E-ly-si-um
e-ma-ci-ate
em-a-nate
e-man-ci-pate
em-a-nom-e-ter
e-mar-gi-nate
e-mas-cu-late
em-ba-cle
em-bar-go
em-bar-ka-tion
em-bar-ras (n.)
em-bar-rass (v.)
em-bed-ded
em-bla-zon
em-blem-at-i-cal
em-bod-i-ment
em-bold-en
em-bol-ic
em-bo-lism
em-bo-lus
em-boss-er
em-bou-chure
em-brac-er
em-bra-sure
em-broi-der-y
em-bry-ol-o-gy
em-bry-on-ic
e-mend-a-ble
e-men-da-tion
e-mend-a-to-ry
em-er-al-dine
e-mer-gen-cy
e-mer-i-tus
e-mer-sion
em-er-y
e-met-ic
em-e-tine
em-i-grant
em-i-gree
em-i-nence
em-is-sar-y
e-mis-siv-i-ty
e-mit-ter
em-o-din
e-mol-lient
e-mol-u-ment
e-mot-er
e-mo-tion-al-ize
em-path-ic
em-pa-thy
em-pen-nage
em-per-or
em-pha-sis
em-phat-ic
em-phy-se-ma
em-pir-i-cal
em-pi-ris-tic
em-ploy-ee
em-po-ri-um
em-press
emp-ti-ness
em-py-e-ma
em-py-re-an
em-py-reu-ma
em-u-la-tive
em-u-la-to-ry
em-u-lous
e-mul-si-fi-er
e-mul-sive
e-mul-soi-dal
en-a-bling
en-am-el-er
en-am-o-ra-to
en-am-ored
e-nan-thic
en-ar-gite
en-ar-thro-sis
en-cap-su-late
en-caus-tic
en-ceinte
en-ce-phal-ic
en-ceph-a-li-tis
en-ceph-a-lo-cele
en-ceph-a-lo-gram
en-ceph-a-lo-graph-ic
en-ceph-a-log-ra-phy
en-ceph-a-loid
en-chi-la-da
en-chym-a-tous
en-clos-er
en-clo-sure
en-coi-gnure
en-co-mi-ast
en-co-mi-um
en-coun-ter
en-cour-age
en-cri-nal
en-crin-ic
en-cum-ber
en-cum-brance
en-cyc-li-cal
en-cy-clo-pe-di-a
en-cys-ta-tion
end-ar-te-ri-tis
en-deav-ored
en-de-mi-al
en-dem-i-cal-ly
en-de-mic-i-ty
en-de-mi-ol-ogy
En-der-by
end-er-gon-ic
en-dive
en-do-car-di-tis
en-do-cri-nal
en-do-crine
en-do-crin-o-log-ic
en-do-cri-nol-o-gy
en-do-cri-no-path-ic
en-do-cri-nop-a-thy
en-doc-ri-nous
en-do-ge-net-ic
en-do-ge-nic-i-ty
en-dog-e-nous
en-do-me-tri-tis
en-do-plas-ma
en-dors-a-ble
en-dors-ee
en-dors-er
en-dos-co-py
en-drin
en-dur-a-ble
en-dur-ance
ene-di-ol
en-e-ma
en-er-get-i-cal-ly
en-er-giz-er
en-er-vate
en-fi-lade
en-force-a-ble
en-fran-chise
en-gen-der
en-gi-neer-ing
en-gine-ry
Eng-land
Eng-lish
en-grav-er
e-nig-mat-ic
e-nig-ma-tize
en-join-der
en-liv-en
en-mi-ty
en-nui
e-nor-mi-ty
e-nor-mous
en-rolled
en-roll-ee
en-sem-ble
en-sign
en-si-lage
en-ter-ic
en-ter-i-tis
en-ter-o-cri-nin
en-ter-os-to-my
en-thal-py
en-thu-si-asm
en-thu-si-as-tic
en-tire-ty
en-ti-ty
en-to-mo-log-i-cal
en-to-mol-o-gy
en-tou-rage
en-trails
en-trance
en-tree
en-tre-pre-neur-i-al
en-tro-py
e-nu-cle-ate
e-nu-mer-ate
e-nun-ci-a-tive
en-vel-op (v.)
en-ve-lope (n.)
en-vel-op-ment
en-vi-a-ble
en-vi-ous
en-vi-ron
en-vis-age
en-zy-mat-ic
en-zy-mol-o-gy
e-o-sin-o-phil
e-os-pho-rite
ep-a-go-ge
ep-au-let
ep-en-dy-ma
e-phed-rine
e-phem-er-al
e-phem-er-is
E-phra-im
Eph-ra-ta
ep-i-cal
ep-i-cu-re-an
ep-i-dem-i-cal
ep-i-de-mi-o-log-i-cal
ep-i-de-mi-ol-o-gy
ep-i-der-mis
ep-i-der-moi-dal
ep-i-dote
ep-i-du-ral
ep-i-ge-al
e-pig-e-nous
ep-i-glot-tis
e-pig-ra-pher
ep-i-la-tor
ep-i-lep-tic
ep-i-log
ep-i-mer-i-za-tion
ep-i-neph-rine
Ep-i-nine
E-piph-a-ny
e-piph-y-sis
ep-i-pter-ic
E-pi-rus
E-pis-co-pa-lian
ep-i-sco-tis-ter
ep-i-sod-ic
e-pis-ta-sis
ep-i-stat-ic
e-pis-te-mol-o-gy
e-pis-tle
e-pis-to-lar-y
ep-i-stome
ep-i-taph
ep-i-the-li-um
e-pith-e-sis
ep-i-thet
e-pit-o-me
ep-i-tom-i-cal
e-pit-ro-phy
ep-och-al
ep-ox-y
ep-si-lon
eq-ua-ble
e-qualed
e-qual-iz-er
e-qua-nim-i-ty
e-quat-ive
e-qua-to-ri-al
eq-uer-ry
e-ques-tri-an
e-qui-dis-tant
e-qui-lat-er-al
eq-ui-len-in
e-quil-i-bra-tion
e-qui-lib-rist
e-qui-lib-ri-stat
e-qui-lib-ri-um
e-qui-noc-tial
e-qui-nox
eq-ui-page
eq-ui-poise
e-quipped
eq-ui-ta-ble
eq-ui-ty
e-quiv-a-lent
e-quiv-o-cal
e-quiv-o-ca-tor
e-rad-i-ca-tor
e-ras-er
e-ra-sure
er-bi-um
Er-e-bus
e-rec-tile
e-rec-tor
er-e-ma-cau-sis
er-ga-tive
er-god-ic
er-go-gen-ic
er-gom-e-ter
er-go-no-vine
er-gos-ter-ol
er-got
er-got-a-mine
er-got-ic
er-go-tize
e-rin-e-um
er-in-ite
er-i-nose
er-i-o-dic-ty-ol
er-i-om-e-ter
Er-len-mey-er
er-mine
e-rod-i-ble
e-ro-sive
e-rot-i-cism
err-a-bil-i-ty
er-ra-ta
er-rat-ic
er-ro-ne-ous
er-u-bes-cent
e-ru-cic
e-ruc-ta-tion
er-u-di-tion
e-rup-tiv-i-ty
er-y-sip-e-las
er-y-the-ma
er-y-them-a-tous
er-y-thrine
er-y-thrite
e-ryth-ri-tol
e-ryth-ro-cyte
e-ryth-ro-cy-tom-e-ter
er-y-thro-i-dine
er-y-thro-pi-a
e-ryth-ro-scope
er-y-throse
e-ryth-ro-sin
er-y-thro-sis
e-ryth-ru-lose
es-ca-drille
es-ca-la-tor
es-cal-loped
es-cap-a-ble
es-ca-pade
es-cap-ee
es-cap-ism
es-cap-ist
es-ca-role
es-carp-ment
es-cha-tol-o-gy
es-chy-nite
es-cri-toire
es-crow
es-cu-dos
es-cu-lent
es-cutch-eon
es-er-o-line
Es-ki-mos
e-soph-a-ge-al
e-soph-a-gi-tis
e-soph-a-go-scope
e-soph-a-gos-co-pist
e-soph-a-gus

es-o-ter-ic
es-pal-ier
es-pe-cial
Es-pe-ran-to
es-pi-o-nage
es-pla-nade
es-pous-al
es-pous-er
es-tab-lish
es-ter-ase
es-ter-ize
es-thet-ic
es-ti-ma-ble
es-ti-ma-tor
es-ti-va-tor
Es-to-nian
es-top-pel
es-to-vers
es-tra-di-ol
es-trange
es-tray
es-tro-gen-ic
es-tu-a-rine
es-tu-ar-y
e-ter-ni-ty
eth-ane
eth-a-nol-a-mine
eth-a-nol-y-sis
eth-e-nyl
e-the-re-al
e-the-re-ous
e-ther-ize
eth-i-cal
eth-i-on-ic
e-thi-o-nine
E-thi-o-pi-an
eth-moi-dal
eth-moid-i-tis
eth-ni-cal
eth-nog-e-ny
eth-no-graph-ic
eth-nog-ra-phy
eth-no-log-i-cal
eth-nol-o-gy
eth-ox-y-line
eth-yl-a-mine
eth-yl-ate
eth-yl-ene-di-a-mine
eth-yl-e-nic
eth-yl-e-phed-rine
eth-yl-i-dine
eth-y-nyl-a-tion
e-ti-o-late
e-ti-o-log-i-cal
e-ti-ol-o-gy
e-ti-o-phyl-lin
et-i-quette
et-y-mo-log-i-cal
et-y-mol-o-gy
eu-ca-lyp-tus
Eu-cha-rist
eu-chred
eu-chro-ite
eu-clase
Eu-clid-e-an
eu-da-lene
eu-di-om-e-ter
Eu-ge-nia
eu-gen-ic
eu-gen-ist
eu-ge-nol
eu-lo-gis-ti-cal
eu-lo-gize
eu-lo-gy
eu-nuch
eu-pa-to-rin
eu-pav-er-ine
eu-phe-mism
eu-pho-ni-um
eu-pho-ny
eu-pho-ri-a
Eur-a-sian
eu-re-ka
Eu-ro-pe-an
eu-ro-pi-um
eu-ryth-mics
Eu-sta-chi-an
eu-tha-na-si-a
eu-then-ics
eux-e-nite
e-vac-u-ate
e-vag-i-nate
ev-a-nes-cence
e-van-gel-i-cal
e-van-ge-list
e-van-ge-lize
e-vap-o-ra-tor
e-vap-o-rim-e-ter
e-va-si-ble
e-va-sive
e-ven-ing (making level)
eve-ning (close of day)
e-ven-tu-al-i-ty
e-ver-si-ble
ev-er-y
e-vic-tor
ev-i-denc-ing
ev-i-den-tial
e-vinc-i-ble
e-vis-cer-a-tor
ev-i-ta-ble
e-voc-a-to-ry
ev-o-lu-tion-ar-y
ev-o-lu-tion-ist
ex-ac-er-bat-ing
ex-ac-ti-tude
ex-ag-ger-ate
ex-al-ta-tion
ex-am-i-na-tion
ex-am-in-er
ex-as-per-ate
ex-ca-va-tor
ex-cel-len-cy
ex-cel-si-or
ex-cept-a-ble
ex-cerpt-er
ex-cerpt-i-ble
ex-ces-sive
ex-cheq-uer
ex-cip-i-ent
ex-cit-a-ble
ex-cit-ant
ex-cit-a-tive
ex-cit-er
ex-cla-ma-tion
ex-clam-a-to-ry
ex-clud-a-ble
ex-clu-so-ry
ex-co-ri-a-tion
ex-cre-ment
ex-cres-cence
ex-cre-to-ry
ex-cru-ci-ate
ex-cul-pa-to-ry
ex-cus-a-ble
ex-e-cra-to-ry
ex-ec-u-tant
ex-e-cut-ed
ex-ec-u-tive
ex-ec-u-to-ry
ex-e-ge-sis
ex-e-get-ic
ex-em-pla-ry
ex-empt-i-ble
ex-emp-tive
ex-e-qua-tur
ex-er-cis-er
ex-er-e-sis
ex-ert-ive
ex-hal-ant
ex-ha-la-tion
ex-haust-ed
ex-haust-i-ble
ex-haus-tive
ex-hib-it
ex-hi-bi-tion
ex-hib-i-tive
ex-hib-i-to-ry
ex-hil-a-ra-tive
ex-hor-ta-tion
ex-hort-a-to-ry
ex-hu-ma-tion
ex-i-gen-cy
ex-i-gi-ble
ex-i-gu-i-ty
ex-ig-u-ous
ex-ist-ence
ex-is-ten-tial-ism
ex li-bris
ex-o-don-ti-a
ex-o-dus
ex-og-e-nous
ex-on-er-ate
ex-o-pep-ti-dase
ex-or-bi-tant
ex-or-di-um
ex-o-ter-ic
ex-o-ther-mic-i-ty
ex-ot-ic
ex-pand-a-ble
ex-pand-er
ex-pan-si-ble
ex-pan-sive
ex-pa-ti-ate
ex-pa-tri-ate
ex-pect-an-cy
ex-pect-ant
ex-pec-ta-tion
ex-pect-a-tive
ex-pec-to-ra-tor
ex-pe-di-en-cy
ex-pe-dit-er
ex-pe-di-tious
ex-pel-lee
ex-pel-ling
ex-pend-i-ture
ex-pen-sive
ex-pe-ri-ence
ex-per-i-men-tal
ex-per-i-ment-er
ex-per-tise (n.)
ex-pert-ize (v.)
ex-pi-a-to-ry
ex-pi-ra-tion
ex-pir-a-to-ry
ex-pla-na-tion
ex-plan-a-to-ry
ex-ple-tive
ex-pli-ca-ble
ex-pli-ca-tive
ex-pli-ca-tor
ex-plic-a-to-ry
ex-plic-it-ly
ex-plod-er
ex-ploi-ta-tion
ex-ploit-a-tive
ex-ploit-er
ex-plo-ra-tion
ex-plor-a-to-ry
ex-plo-si-ble
ex-plo-sim-e-ter
ex-plo-sive
ex-po-nen-tial
ex-port-a-ble
ex-por-ta-tion
ex-pose (v.)
ex-po-sé (n.)
ex-po-si-tion
ex-pos-i-to-ry
ex-pos-tu-late
ex-po-sure
ex-press-age
ex-press-er
ex-press-i-ble
ex-pres-sive
ex-pres-sor
ex-pug-na-to-ry
ex-pul-sive
ex-pur-ga-to-ry
ex-quis-ite
ex-sic-cate
ex-tem-po-ra-ne-i-ty
ex-tem-po-re
ex-tem-po-rize
ex-tend-a-ble
ex-tend-er
ex-ten-si-ble
ex-ten-som-e-ter
ex-ten-sor
ex-ten-u-a-tor
ex-te-ri-or-ize
ex-ter-mi-na-tor
ex-ter-nal-i-ty
ex-tinc-tive
ex-tin-guish-er
ex-tir-pa-tor
ex-tract-a-ble
ex-tract-ant
ex-trac-tive
ex-trac-tor
ex-tra-dit-a-ble
ex-tral-i-ty
ex-tra-ne-ous
ex-traor-di-nar-i-ly
ex-trap-o-lat-ed
ex-trap-o-la-to-ry
ex-tra-sen-so-ry
ex-trav-a-gance
ex-trav-a-sa-tion
ex-tre-mism
ex-trem-ist
ex-trem-i-ty
ex-tri-cate
ex-trin-sic
ex-tro-vert-ish
ex-tro-ver-tive
ex-trud-er
ex-tru-si-ble
ex-tu-ber-ance
ex-u-ber-ant
ex-u-da-tion
ex-ult-ant
ex-ul-ta-tion
ex-ur-bi-a
eye-le-teer
ey-ing

F

fa-ba-ceous
Fa-bi-an
fa-bled
fab-ri-ca-tor
Fab-ri-koid
fab-u-lous
fa-cade
face-a-ble
fac-er
fac-et-ed
fa-ce-tious
fa-cial
fa-cient
fa-ci-es
fac-ile
fa-cil-i-ty
fac-ing
fa-con-ne
fac-sim-i-le
fac-tic-i-ty
fac-tious
fac-ti-tious
fac-tor
fac-to-ri-al
fac-to-ry
fac-to-tum
fac-u-la
fac-ul-ty
fa-cun-di-ty
fade-om-e-ter
fad-er
fa-gine
fag-ot
Fahr-en-heit
fa-ience
fail-ure
fai-naigue
fair-y-like
fak-er (one who fakes)
fa-kir (dervish)
Fa-lan-gist
fal-cip-a-rum
fal-con-er
fal-la-cious
fal-la-cy
fall-en
fal-li-bil-i-ty
Fal-lo-pi-an
fal-set-tos
fal-si-fi-ca-tion
fal-si-ty
Fal-staff-i-an
fal-ter
fa-mil-iar
fa-mil-i-ar-i-ty
fa-mil-iar-ize
fam-i-ly
fam-ish
fa-mous
fam-u-lus
fa-nat-i-cal
fa-nat-i-cism
fan-ci-er
fan-ci-ful
Fan-euil
fan-gled
fan-ta-sia
fan-ta-size
fan-tas-tic
fan-ta-sy
far-ad
Far-a-day
fa-rad-ic
far-a-dism
far-ci-cal
fa-ri-na
far-i-na-ceous
far-i-nose
farm-er
far-ther
far-thing
far-thin-gale
fas-ces
fas-ci-cle
fas-cic-u-lar
fas-ci-na-tor
fas-ci-o-li-a-sis
fas-cism
Fas-cist
Fa-scis-ti
fash-ion-a-ble
fas-ten-er
fas-tid-i-ous
fas-tig-i-um
fa-tal-ism
fa-tal-i-ty
fa-ther
fath-om-a-ble
Fa-thom-e-ter
fat-i-ga-ble
fa-tigue
fa-tigu-ing-ly
Fat-i-ma
fa-tu-i-tous
fat-u-ous
fau-cal-ize
fau-cet
fau-nal
fau-vism
fa-ve-o-lus
fa-vism
fa-vor-ite
fa-vor-it-ism
fa-vrile
fa-yal-ite
fe-al-ty
fea-sance
fea-si-bil-i-ty
feath-er-ing
fea-tured
fe-bric-i-ty
fe-bric-u-la
fe-brif-ic
fe-brif-u-gal
feb-ri-fuge
fe-brif-u-gine
feb-rile
fe-bril-i-ty
Feb-ru-ar-y
fe-cal
fec-u-lent
fe-cund
fec-un-date
fe-cun-da-tive
fe-cun-di-ty
fed-er-a-cy
fed-er-al-ese
fed-er-a-tive
fee-ble
Feh-ling
feld-spath-ic
feld-spath-oi-dal
fe-li-cide
fe-lic-i-tate
fe-lic-i-tous
fe-line
fe-lin-i-ty
fel-on
fe-lo-ni-ous
fel-o-ny
felt-er
Felt-ham
fe-luc-ca
fem-i-ne-i-ty
fem-i-nin-i-ty
fem-i-nism
fem-o-ral
fe-mur
fen-chene
fen-chone
fen-chyl
fen-ci-ble
fend-er
fe-nes-tra
fen-es-tra-tion
Fe-ni-an
fe-ra-cious
Fer-di-nand
fer-ment-a-ble
fer-men-ta-tion
fer-ment-a-tive
fer-ment-er
fer-men-tive
fer-mi-um
fe-ro-cious
fe-roc-i-ty
fer-rif-er-ous
fer-ri-na-trite
fer-rit-ic
fer-ri-tin
fer-ro-cene
fer-ro-cy-a-nide
fer-rom-e-ter
fer-ru-gi-nous
fer-rule
fer-til-i-ty
fer-til-iz-a-ble
fer-til-iz-er
fe-ru-lic
fer-va-nite
fer-ven-cy
fer-vor
fes-ter
fes-ti-val
fes-tiv-i-ty
fes-toon
fe-tal
fet-e-ri-ta
fe-ti-cide
fet-id
fe-tid-i-ty
fet-ish-ism
fe-tus
feu-dal-ism
feud-ist
feuil-le-ton
fe-ver-ous
fi-an-ce
Fi-ber-glas
fi-ber-ize
fi-bril-la-tion
fi-brin-o-gen-ic
fi-bri-nog-e-nous
fi-broid
fi-bro-in
fi-bro-sis
fi-bro-si-tis
fi-brous
fib-u-la
fick-le
fic-tile
fic-ti-tious
fid-dler
fi-del-i-ty
fidg-et-y
fi-du-ci-ar-y
field-er
fiend-ish
fi-er-y
fi-es-ta
fight-er
fig-ur-al
fig-u-ra-tion
fig-u-ra-tive
fig-u-rine
fil-a-men-tous
fi-lar-i-al
fil-a-ri-a-sis
fil-bert
fil-i-al
fil-i-bus-ter
fil-i-gree
Fil-i-pi-no
fill-er (filled)
fil-ler (money unit)
fil-let
fil-o-selle
fil-ter-er
filth-i-ness
fil-tra-ble
fil-tra-tion
fin-a-ble
fi-na-gle
fi-nal-e
fi-nal-i-ty
fi-nan-cial
fin-an-cier
fi-nanc-ing
find-er
fin-er-y
fi-nesse
fin-ger
fin-i-cal
fin-ick-y
fi-nis
fin-ished
fi-nite
fin-i-tude
Finn-ish
fir-ing
fir-kin
fir-ma-ment
firm-er
fis-cal
fisch-er-ite
fish-er-y
fis-sion
fis-sip-a-rous
fis-sure
fist-i-cuff
fis-tu-la
fis-tu-lous
fix-a-tive
flac-cid-i-ty
flag-el-lant
flag-el-la-tor
flag-eo-let
fla-gi-tious
flag-on
fla-grant
flam-beau
flam-boy-ant
fla-min-go
flam-ma-ble
flang-er
flank-er
flap-er-on
flar-ing
flat-u-lence
flau-tist
flav-a-none
fla-van-throne
fla-ves-cence
fla-vi-an-ic
fla-vin
fla-vo-nol
fla-vo-pur-pu-rin
fla-vor
fledg-ling
fletch-er-ize
flex-i-bi-lize
flex-om-e-ter
flex-or
flex-ur-al
flick-er-y
flin-ders
flir-ta-tious
float-er
floc-cu-lant (n.)
floc-cu-la-tor
floc-cu-lent (adj.)
flood-om-e-ter
flo-ral
Flor-ence
flor-enc-ite
Flor-en-tine
flo-res-cence
flo-ret
flo-ri-cul-tur-al
Flor-i-da
Flo-rid-i-an
flor-id-ness
flo-rif-er-ous
flo-ri-gen
flor-in
flo-rist
flo-riv-o-rous
flor-u-lent
flo-tage
flo-ta-tion
flo-til-la
flot-sam
floun-der
flour-ish
fluc-tu-ate
flu-en-cy
fluff-i-ness
flu-id-i-ty
flu-mer-in
flu-o-bo-rate
flu-o-bo-rite
flu-o-ran-thene
flu-or-ap-a-tite
flu-o-rene
flu-o-re-nyl
flu-o-res-ce-in
flu-o-res-cence
flu-o-ri-date
flu-o-ride
flu-o-ri-dize
flu-o-ri-nate
flu-o-rine
flu-o-rite
flu-o-ro-a-ce-tic
flu-o-ro-graph-ic
flu-o-rog-ra-phy
flu-o-rom-e-ter
flu-o-ro-scope
flu-o-ros-co-py
flu-o-ro-sis
flu-o-sil-i-cate
flu-o-si-lic-ic
flus-ter
flut-ist
flu-vi-al
flu-vi-ol-o-gy
flux-i-ble
flux-ion-al
flux-me-ter
Foam-ite
fo-cal-ize
fo-com-e-ter
fo-cus-er
fo-cus-ing

foi-ble
fol-de-rol
fo-li-a-ceous
fo-li-age
fo-lic
fo-lin-ic
fo-li-o-late
fol-lic-u-lar
fol-lic-u-li-tis
fo-men-ta-tion
fon-dant
fond-ling
fool-er-y
fool-ish
foo-zle
for-age
fo-ra-men
fo-ram-i-na
Fo-ram-i-nif-er-a
fo-ram-i-nif-er-ous
fo-ram-i-nous
for-ay
for-bear-ance
for-ceps
forc-er
forc-i-ble
forc-ing
fore-clo-sure
for-eign-er
fo-ren-si-cal
fore-see-a-ble
for-est-a-tion
for-est-er
for-est-ry
for-feit-er
for-feit-ure
forg-er
for-ger-y
fo-rint
for-mal
form-al-de-hyde
For-ma-lin
for-mal-ist
for-mal-i-ty
for-mal-ize
form-am-ide
form-am-i-dine
form-ant
for-mate
for-ma-tion
form-a-tive
form-a-zan
form-er (one who forms)
for-mer (previous)
for-mic
For-mi-ca
for-mi-cide
for-mi-da-ble
for-mol-ize
For-mo-san
for-mu-la
for-mu-la-ri-za-ble
for-mu-lar-i-za-tion
for-mu-lar-y
for-mu-la-tor
for-myl-ate
for-ni-ca-tion
for-syth-i-a
for-ti-eth
for-ti-fi-ca-tion
for-ti-fy
for-tis-si-mo
for-ti-tude
for-tress
for-tu-i-tous
for-tu-i-ty
for-tu-nate
for-ty
fo-rum
fos-sil-if-er-ous
fos-sil-ize
fos-so-ri-al
fos-ter
fou-lard
foun-da-tion
found-er (n.)
foun-der (v.; also as n., act of foundering)
found-ling
found-ry
foun-tain
Four-drin-i-er
Fou-ri-er
four-ra-gere
fo-ve-o-late
Fow-ler
fowl-er
fra-cas
frac-tion-ate
frac-tious
frac-tog-ra-phy
frac-tur-al
frag-ile
fra-gil-i-ty
frag-men-tal
frag-men-tar-y
frag-ment-ize
fra-grance
frail-ty
fram-er
fran-chise
fran-ci-um
fran-gi-ble
fran-gi-pan-i
frank-furt-er
fran-kin-cense
fran-ti-cal-ly
fra-ter-nal
fra-ter-ni-ty
frat-er-nize
frat-ri-ci-dal
fraud-u-lent
frau-lein
freck-led
free-dom
freez-er
freight-er
fre-net-ic
fren-zied
fre-quen-cy
fre-quen-ta-tion
fresh-et
Freud-i-an
fric-an-deau
fric-as-see
frig-ate
fright-ened
frig-id
Frig-i-daire
fri-gid-i-ty
frig-o-rim-e-ter
fris-ket
frisk-i-ly
fri-vol-i-ty
friv-o-lous
frizz-ing
frol-icked
fron-des-cence
front-age
fron-tal
fron-ta-lis
fron-tier
fron-tis-piece
fron-to-gen-e-sis
front-o-ly-sis
fron-to-pa-ri-e-tal
frost-i-ness
froth-i-ly
frow-zy
fro-zen
fruc-tif-er-ous
fruc-ti-fy
fruc-tose
fru-gal-i-ty
fruit-age
fru-i-tion
frump-ish
frus-trate
frus-tum
fru-tes-cence
fu-ca-ceous
fuch-sia
fuch-sin-o-phil
fu-coi-dal
fu-cos-ter-ol
fu-el-er
fu-ga-cious
fu-gac-i-ty
fu-gi-tive
ful-crum
ful-fill-ing
ful-gen-ic
ful-gide
ful-gu-rant
ful-gu-ra-tion
ful-gu-rite
fu-lig-i-nous
full-ness
ful-mi-nate
ful-min-ic
ful-min-u-ric
fu-ma-rase
fu-mar-ic
fu-mar-o-yl
fum-bler
fu-mig-a-cin
fu-mi-ga-tor
fu-mu-lus
fu-nam-bu-list
fun-da-men-tal
fun-dus-co-py
fu-ner-al
fu-ne-re-al
fun-gi-ble
fun-gi-ci-dal
fun-giv-o-rous
fun-goid
fun-gous (adj.)
fun-gus (n.)
fu-ni-cle
fu-nic-u-lar
fun-neled
fu-ra-nose
fu-ran-o-side
fur-be-low
fur-bish
fur-fu-ra-ceous
fur-fu-ral
fur-fu-ryl-i-dene
fu-ri-ous
fur-long
fur-lough
fur-nace
fur-nish-er
fur-ni-ture
fu-ro-ic
fu-ror
fur-ring
fur-ther
fur-thest
fur-tive
fu-run-cle
fu-run-cu-lo-sis
fu-ryl
fu-sar-i-um
fu-see
fu-sel
fu-se-lage
fu-si-ble
fu-si-lier
fu-sil-lade
fu-sion
fu-so-spi-ro-chete
fus-tian
fu-tile
fu-til-i-ty
fu-tu-ram-ic
fu-tur-ist
fu-tu-ri-ty
fuzz-i-ness

G

gab-ar-dine (fabric)
ga-ba-rit
gab-er-dine (gown)
ga-bi-on
ga-bling
Ga-bon
Gab-o-nese
Ga-bri-el
gadg-et-eer
gadg-et-ry
gad-o-le-ic
gad-o-lin-i-um
Gael-ic
gaf-fer
gag-er
gai-ner (diving)
gain-er (one who gains)
Gains-bor-ough
gait-er (harness)
gai-ter (overshoe)
ga-lac-ta-gogue
ga-lac-tic
ga-lac-to-lip-id
gal-ac-tom-e-ter
gal-ac-ton-ic
ga-lac-to-poi-e-sis
ga-lac-tos-a-mine
ga-lac-to-sid-ase
gal-ac-to-sis
ga-lac-tu-ron-ic
Ga-la-pa-gos
gal-a-te-a
ga-lax-i-al
gal-ax-y
ga-le-gine
ga-le-na
ga-le-nic (mineral)
ga-len-ic (medicinal)
ga-le-no-bis-mu-tite
Ga-li-cian
Gal-i-le-an
gal-lant-ry
gal-le-in
gal-ler-y
gal-li-na-ceous
gal-li-nule
Gal-lip-o-li
gal-li-vant
gal-lo-cy-a-nine
gal-lop
gal-op
ga-lore
ga-losh
gal-van-ic
gal-va-nism
gal-va-ni-za-tion
gal-va-nom-e-ter
gal-va-no-met-ric
gal-van-o-scope
Gam-bi-an
gam-bling
gam-boled
game-ster
ga-mete
ga-met-ic
ga-me-to-cide
gam-e-toid
gam-in
gam-ing
gam-ut
gan-der
Gan-dha-ra
Gan-dhi
gan-gling
gan-gli-on-at-ed
gan-gli-on-ic
gan-gli-o-side
gan-gre-nous
gang-ster
gan-is-ter
ga-nom-a-lite
gant-let (track)
Gan-tri-sin
gan-try
gap-er
ga-rage
gar-an-cine
Ga-rand
gar-bage
gar-bling
gar-den-er
gar-de-nia
Gar-di-nol
gar-gan-tu-an
gar-gling
gar-goyle
gar-ish
gar-land
gar-lick-y
gar-ner
gar-ni-er-ite
gar-nish-ee
gar-ni-ture
gar-ru-li-ty
gas-con-ade
gas-e-ous
gas-i-fy
gas-ket
gas-o-line
gas-om-e-ter
gas-o-met-ric
gas-sing
gas-ter-o-sto-ma-ta
gas-tral-gi-a
gas-tra-li-um
gas-trec-to-my
gas-tric
gas-tri-tis
gas-tro-cne-mi-us
gas-tro-en-ter-os-to-my
gas-tro-in-tes-ti-nal
gas-trol-o-ger
gas-tro-nom-ic
gas-tron-o-my
gas-tro-pod
Gas-trop-o-da
gas-tros-co-py
gas-tros-to-my
gath-er-ing
Ga-tun
gau-che-rie
gau-chos
gaud-i-ness
gau-lei-ter
Gaull-ist
gaunt-let
ga-vage
gav-el-er
ga-votte
gawk-i-ness
ga-zelle
gaz-er
ga-zette
gaz-et-teer
Gei-ger
gei-sha
gel-a-tin-ase
ge-lat-i-nate
ge-lat-i-ni-za-tion
ge-lat-i-niz-er
ge-lat-i-no-chlo-ride
ge-lat-i-nous
ge-la-tion
geld-ing
ge-lid-i-ty
gel-ig-nite
gel-ling
gel-ose
gel-se-mic
gem-i-na-tive
Gem-i-ni
gem-mif-er-ous
gen-dar-mer-y
gen-der
gen-e-al-o-gist
gen-e-al-o-gy
gen-er-a-lis-si-mo
gen-er-al-i-ty
gen-er-al-ize
gen-er-a-tor
ge-ner-i-cal
gen-er-os-i-ty
gen-e-sis
gen-et
ge-net-i-cal
Ge-ne-va
ge-nial
ge-ni-al-i-ty
gen-ic
ge-nic-u-late
ge-nie
gen-in
ge-ni-o-plas-ty
ge-nis-te-in
gen-i-tal
gen-i-tive
gen-i-to-u-ri-nar-y
ge-nius
Gen-o-a
gen-o-ci-dal
ge-nome
ge-no-mere
gen-o-type
genth-ite
gen-tian-in
gen-tian-ose
gen-til-i-ty
gen-ti-o-bi-ose
gen-tis-ic
gen-ti-sin
gent-ly
gen-try
gen-u-flec-to-ry
gen-u-ine
ge-nus
ge-o-ce-rite
ge-oc-ro-nite
ge-o-des-ic
ge-od-e-sy
ge-o-det-i-cal
ge-od-ic
ge-o-dim-e-ter
ge-og-e-nous
ge-og-nos-tic
ge-og-o-ny
ge-og-ra-pher
ge-o-graph-ic
ge-og-ra-phy
ge-oi-dal
ge-o-log-i-cal
ge-ol-o-gist
ge-ol-o-gy
ge-om-a-lism
ge-om-e-ter
ge-o-met-ri-cal
ge-om-e-triz-er
ge-om-e-try
ge-o-pon-ics
geor-gette
Geor-gian
ge-os-co-py
ge-ot-ri-cho-sis
ge-o-trop-ic
ge-ot-ro-pism
ge-ran-ic
ge-ra-ni-ol
ge-ra-ni-um
ge-ra-nyl
Ge-rard
ge-rat-ic
ger-a-tol-o-gy
ge-rent
ger-i-a-tri-cian
ger-i-at-rics
ger-mane
ger-ma-nite
ger-ma-ni-um
ger-mi-ci-dal
ger-mi-nal
ger-mi-na-tor
Ge-ron-i-mo
ger-on-toc-ra-cy
ge-ron-to-log-i-cal
ger-on-tol-o-gy
Ger-trude
ger-und
ger-un-di-val
ge-run-dive
ge-sell-schaft
Ge-stalt
Ge-sta-po
ges-ta-tion
ges-tic-u-late
ges-ture
Geth-sem-a-ne
gey-ser
Gha-na-ian
gher-kin
ghoul-ish
gibbs-ite
Gi-bral-tar
gi-gan-tic
gi-gan-tism
gild-er
gil-son-ite
gim-baled
gin-ger
ging-ham
gin-gi-val
gin-gi-vi-tis
gink-go
gin-seng
gi-raffe
Gi-rard
gird-er
gir-dling
girl-ish
gi-tal-in
gi-tox-i-gen-in
giv-en
gla-bres-cent
gla-brous
gla-cial
gla-ci-a-tion
gla-cier
gla-ci-ol-o-gy
gla-ci-om-e-ter
glad-i-a-tor
glad-i-o-lus
glam-or-ous
glam-our
glan-ders
glan-du-lar
glar-ing
glass-ine
glass-i-ness
glau-ber-ite
glau-co-cer-i-nite
glau-co-ma
glau-co-ma-tous
glau-co-nite
glau-cous
glaz-er
gla-zier
glis-ten
gloam-ing
glob-al-ism
glo-bal-i-ty
glo-boid
glob-u-lar
glob-ule
glob-u-lif-er-ous
glob-u-lin
glo-mer-u-lar
gloom-i-ly
glo-ri-fy
glo-ri-ous
glos-sa-ry
gloss-i-ness
gloss-me-ter
Glouces-ter
glov-er
glu-ca-mine
glu-car-ic
glu-cin-i-um
glu-ci-tol
glu-ci-tyl
glu-co-nate
glu-con-ic
glu-co-py-ran-o-side
glu-co-sa-mine
glu-cose
glu-co-si-dase
glu-co-side
glu-cu-ron-ic
glu-cu-ron-i-dase
glu-cu-ro-nide
glu-ey-ness
glu-ing
glut-a-con-ic
glu-ta-mate
glu-tam-ic
glu-ta-min-ase
glu-ta-mine
glu-ta-min-ic
glu-tam-o-yl
glu-ta-thi-one
glu-te-al
glu-ten
glu-te-nin
glu-ten-ous
glu-ti-nous
glyc-er-ate
gly-ce-mi-a
gly-ce-mic
glyc-er-al-de-hyde
gly-cer-ic
glyc-er-ide
glyc-er-in
glyc-er-ol
glyc-er-o-phos-phor-ic
glyc-er-yl
glyc-ide
gly-cid-ic
glyc-i-dol
gly-cine
gly-co-cy-a-mine
gly-co-gen
gly-co-gen-ol-y-sis
gly-co-gen-o-lyt-ic
gly-col-y-sis
gly-co-lyt-ic
gly-co-si-dase
glyc-u-re-sis
gly-cyl
gly-ox-yl-ic
glyp-tol-o-gy
gnath-ism
gneiss-oid
gnom-ish
gno-se-ol-o-gy
gno-sis
gnos-tic
goa-tee
gob-ble-dy-gook
gob-bler
Go-be-lin
gob-lin
Goe-thals
goi-ter
goi-tro-gen-ic
goi-tro-ge-nic-i-ty
goi-trous
gold-en
Go-li-ath
go-nad-ec-to-my
go-nad-o-tro-phin
gon-do-la
gon-fa-lon
go-nid-i-al
go-nid-i-um
go-ni-om-e-ter
go-ni-o-met-ric
gon-o-coc-ci
gon-or-rhe-al
goo-gol-plex
go-pher
gor-geous
go-ril-la
gor-ic
Go-shen
gos-pel-er
gos-sa-mer
gos-syp-i-trin
Goth-am-ite
Goth-ic
gour-man-diz-er
gov-ern-ess
gov-ern-men-tal
gov-er-nor
goy-a-zite

Graaf-i-an
grac-ile
gra-cious
gra-da-tion
grad-a-to-ry
grad-er
gra-di-ent
gra-di-om-e-ter
grad-u-al
grad-u-ate
graft-er
gra-ham
grai-ning (fish)
grain-ing (of grain)
gram-i-cid-in
gram-i-na-les
gram-ine
gra-min-e-ous
gram-mar-i-an
gram-mat-i-cal
gra-na-ry
gran-dam
gran-deur
gran-dil-o-quent
gran-di-ose
grang-er
gran-ite
gra-nit-ic
gran-o-blas-tic
gran-o-di-o-rite
grant-ee
grant-er
Grant-ham
grant-or
gran-u-lar-i-ty
gran-u-late
gran-ule
gran-u-lo-ma-to-sis
gran-u-lous
graph-eme
gra phe-mic
graph-i-cal
graph-ite
gra-phit-ic
gra-phol-o-gy
graph-o-met-ric
grap-pling
grasp-er
grat-er
grat-i-cule
grat-i-fy
grat-in
gra-tis
grat-i-tude
gra-tu-i-tous
gra-va-men
grav-eled
grav-el-ly
grav-en
grav-id
gra-vid-i-ty
gra-vim-e-ter
grav-i-met-ri-cal-ly
gra-vim-e-try
grav-i-sphere
grav-i-tat-er
grav-i-tom-e-ter
grav-i-ty
gra-vure
graz-er
greas-er
greas-i-ness
Gre-cian
greed-i-ness
green-sward
gre-gar-i-ous
Gre-go-ri-an
grei-sen
gre-nade
gren-a-dier
gren-a-dine
Gresh-am
grid-i-ron
griev-ance
griev-ous
Gri-gnard
gril-lage
grim-ace
gri-mal-kin
grind-er
grin-gos
griph-ite
gris-e-o-ful-vin
gris-tly
griz-zly
gro-cer-y
gro-per (fish)
grop-er
gro-schen
gros-grain
gro-tesque
gro-tes-que-rie
ground-ling
grou-per (fish)
group-er
grou-ser (timber; cleats)
grous-er
grout-er
grov-el-er
growl-er
grum-bler
gru-mose
grun-ion
Gru-yere
guai-ac
guai-a-col
Gua-ma-ni-an
gua-na-mine
gua-ni-dine
gua-nif-er-ous
gua-nine
gua-nyl-ic
gua-ra-ni
guar-an-tee (n., v.)
guar-an-ty (n.) (legal)
guard-i-an
Gua-te-ma-la
gua-va
gua-yu-le
gu-ber-na-to-ri-al
gudg-eon
guer-don
Guern-sey
guer-ril-la
guid-ance
gui-don
guil-lo-tine
guilt-i-ly
Guin-ea
gui-pure
gui-tar
gul-den
gul-li-ble
gu-lose
Gun-ite
gur-gi-ta-tion
gur-gling
gur-nard
gush-er
gus-set
gus-ta-to-ry
Gu-ten-berg
gut-tur-al
Guy-a-nese
gym-na-si-um
gym-nas-tic
gym-no-sto-ma-ta
gym-no-stom-a-tous
gyn-e-coc-ra-cy
gyn-e-col-o-gy
gyp-se-ous
gyp-sif-er-ous
gy-ra-to-ry
gy-roi-dal
gy-ro-scop-ic

H

ha-be-as
ha-ben-dum
hab-er-dash-er-y
ha-bil-i-ment
hab-it-a-ble
hab-i-ta-tion
ha-bit-u-al
ha-bit-u-e
ha-chure
ha-ci-en-da
hack-ler
Ha-des
haf-ni-um
Ha-ga-nah
hag-i-ol-o-gy
Hai-fa
hai-kwan
Hai-tian
ha-la-tion
hal-a-zone
hal-berd-ier
hal-cy-on
hal-i-but
ha-lide
hal-i-dom
hal-i-eu-tics
hal-i-ste-re-sis
ha-lite
hal-i-to-sis
hal-le-lu-jah
Hal-low-een
hal-lu-ci-na-tion
ha-lo
hal-o-gen-a-tion
ha-log-e-nous
hal-o-hy-drin
ha-lom-e-ter
ha-lot-ri-chite
halt-er (one who halts)
hal-ter (other meanings)
ham-burg-er
Ham-mar-skjold
ham-per
ham-ster
hand-i-cap
hand-i-craft
hand-i-ly
hand-i-work
han-dle-a-ble
han-dler
han-dling
hand-som-est
hang-ar
hang-er
han-ker
Han-o-ver
Ha-nuk-kah
hap-pi-ness
har-a-kir-i
ha-rangued
ha-rangu-er
har-assed
har-bin-ger
har-bor
hard-en-er
har-di-ness
Har-ding
har-dy
ha-rem
har-i-cot
hark-en
har-le-quin
har-ma-line
har-mo-ni-al
har-mon-i-ca
har-mo-ni-ous
har-mo-nize
har-ness
harp-ist
har-poon
harp-si-chord
har-te-beest
Hart-ley
har-um-scar-um
har-vest-er
hash-ish
has-sled
has-tate
has-ten
hast-i-ly
Hast-ings
hatch-er-y
hatch-et
ha-tred
haugh-ti-ness
hau-teur
Ha-va-na
ha-ven
hav-er-sack
hav-oc
Ha-wai-ian
haw-ser
haz-ard-ous
ha-zel
haz-ing
head-quar-ters
health-i-est
heart-i-ly
heat-er
hea-then
heath-er
heav-en
heav-i-ly
Heav-i-side
heb-dom-a-dal
He-bra-ic
He-brew
Heb-ri-des
Hec-a-te
hec-a-tomb
heck-ler
hec-o-gen-in
hec-tare
hec-to-li-ter
hec-to-me-ter
hed-er-in
he-don-ics
he-do-nism
he-do-nis-tic
he-do-nom-e-ter
he-dral
heg-e-mon-ic
he-gem-o-ny
he-gi-ra
heif-er
hei-li-gen-schein
hei-nous
Hel-e-na
hel-e-nin
he-li-a-cal
he-li-an-the-mum
he-li-an-thus
hel-i-cal
hel-i-ces
hel-i-coi-dal
Hel-i-con
hel-i-cop-ter
he-li-o-graph
he-li-og-ra-phy
he-li-om-e-ter
he-li-o-met-ric
he-li-om-e-try
he-li-o-pho-bic
he-li-o-trope
he-li-ot-ro-pism
hel-i-port
he-li-um
he-lix
he-lix-om-e-ter
Hel-len-ic
Hel-le-nism
Hel-les-pont
hel-min-thic
hel-min-tho-spo-rin
hel-ot-ism
hel-ter-skel-ter
hel-vite
hel-vol-ic
he-ma-cy-tom-e-ter
he-ma-fi-brite
he-mag-glu-ti-nin
he-mal-bu-men
he-man-gi-o-ma-to-sis
he-ma-poi-e-sis
he-mar-thro-sis
he-ma-tal
he-ma-te-in
he-mat-ic
hem-a-tin-om-e-ter
hem-a-tite
hem-a-tit-ic
hem-a-to-cele
hem-a-to-crit
hem-a-tog-e-nous
hem-a-to-lite
he-ma-tol-o-gy
he-ma-to-ma
he-ma-tom-e-ter
hem-a-to-por-phy-rin
he-ma-to-sis
he-ma-tox-y-lin
hem-i-ac-e-tal
hem-i-cy-clic
hem-i-he-dral
hem-i-kar-y-on
he-min
he-mip-ter-oid
hem-i-spher-ic
hem-i-stich-al
he-mo-chro-mo-gen
he-mo-chro-mom-e-ter
he-mo-co-ni-o-sis
he-mo-cy-a-nin
he-mo-cyte
he-mo-cy-tol-y-sis
he-mo-glo-bin
he-mo-glo-bi-nom-e-ter
he-mol-y-sin
he-mol-y-sis
he-mo-lyt-ic
he-mom-e-ter
hem-or-rhag-ic
hem-or-rhoi-dal
he-mo-sid-er-in
he-mo-sid-er-o-sis
he-mo-stat-ic
hemp-en
hen-e-quen
hep-a-rin
he-pat-i-ca
hep-a-ti-tis
hep-a-to-cu-pre-in
hep-a-to-fla-vin
hep-a-tos-co-py
hep-ta-dec-yl
hep-tag-o-nal
hep-tam-e-ter
hep-tar-chy
hep-tu-lose
hep-tyl-ene
her-ald
he-ral-dic
her-ba-ceous
herb-age
her-bar-i-um
her-bi-ci-dal
her-biv-o-rous
Her-cu-les
her-e-dit-a-ment
he-red-i-tar-y
Her-e-ford
her-e-sy
her-e-tic
he-ret-i-cal
her-it-age
her-maph-ro-dite
her-me-neu-tics
her-met-i-cal
her-mit-age
her-ne-ar-in
her-ni-a
her-ni-ot-o-my
he-ro-ic
her-o-ine
her-o-ism
her-on
her-pes
her-pe-tol-o-gy
Hertz-i-an
hes-i-tan-cy
hes-i-tat-er
hes-i-ta-tion
hes-per-i-din
Hes-per-is
Hes-sian
hess-ite
het-er-o-aux-in
het-er-o-cy-clic
het-er-o-dox-y
het-er-o-ge-ne-ous
het-er-og-e-nous
het-er-o-ki-ne-sis
het-er-ol-o-gy
het-er-ol-y-sis
het-er-o-ou-si-a
het-er-o-pol-y
het-er-os-co-py
hex-a-chlo-ro-eth-ane
hex-a-gon
hex-ag-o-nal
hex-a-he-dral
hex-am-e-ter
hex-a-no-yl
hex-es-trol
hex-os-a-mine
hex-u-lose
hex-u-ron-ic
hex-yl-ene
hi-a-tus
hi-ber-na-tor
hick-o-ry
hid-e-ous
hi-dro-sis
hi-drot-ic
hi-er-ar-chy
hi-er-o-glyph-ic
high-fa-lu-tin
hi-lar-i-ous
hill-ocked
hi-lus
Hi-ma-la-yan
hin-der (v.)
hind-er (adj.)
hin-drance
Hin-du-stan-i
hint-er
hin-ter-land
Hip-po-crat-ic
hip-po-pot-a-mus
hip-pu-ric
Hir-o-shi-ma
hir-su-tal
His-pa-ni-a
His-pan-ic
his-pa-ni-dad
his-tam-i-nase
his-ta-mine
his-ti-dine
his-to-log-i-cal
his-tol-o-gy
his-tol-y-sis
his-to-ri-an
his-tor-i-cal
his-to-ric-i-ty
his-to-ry
his-tri-on-ic
hith-er-to
hock-ey
hod-o-graph
Hoh-en-zol-lern
hoist-er
hold-er
hol-i-day
ho-li-ness
hol-lan-daise
Hol-land-er
hol-mi-um
hol-o-caust
hol-o-graph
hol-o-he-dral
hol-o-pho-tal
ho-loph-ra-sis
hol-ster
Hol-yoke
hom-age
ho-me-ol-o-gy
ho-me-o-path-ic
ho-me-op-a-thy
ho-me-o-sta-sis
hom-i-ci-dal
hom-i-let-ics
hom-i-ly
hom-ish
hom-o-cys-teine
ho-mog-a-my
ho-mo-ge-ne-i-ty
ho-mo-ge-ne-ous
ho-mog-e-ni-za-tion
ho-mog-e-niz-er
ho-mog-e-nous
hom-o-log
ho-mol-o-gous
ho-mol-y-sis
hom-o-nym-ic
ho-mo-thet-ic
Hon-du-ran
hon-ey
Hon-i-ton
Hon-o-lu-lu
hon-or-a-ble
hon-o-rar-i-um
hon-or-ar-y
hon-or-if-ic
Hoo-ver
ho-ra-ry
ho-ri-zon
hor-i-zon-tal
hor-mo-nal
hor-mon-ic
ho-rol-o-gy
hor-o-scope
ho-ros-co-py
hor-ren-dous
hor-rif-ic
hor-ta-to-ry
hor-ti-cul-tur-al
ho-san-na
ho-sier-y
hos-pi-ta-ble
hos-pi-tal-i-za-tion
hos-tage
host-al
hos-tel-ry
host-ess
hos-til-i-ty
hos-tler
Hou-dry
hous-ing
hov-el
hov-er
how-it-zer
howl-er
how-lite
hua-ra-che
huck-ster
Hue-ne-me
Hu-gue-not
hul-la-ba-loo
hu-man-i-tar-i-an
hu-man-ize
hum-bling
hu-mec-tant
hu-mer-us
hu-mid-i-ty
hu-mil-i-a-tion
hu-min
hum-ite
hu-mi-ture
hu-mor-ous
hu-mous (adj.)
hu-mu-lene
hu-mus (n.)
hun-dred
Hun-gar-i-an
hun-ger
hun-gry
hunt-er
hur-dler
hurl-er
Hu-ron
hur-ried-ly
hur-ter (bumper)
hurt-er
hur-tling
hus-band-ry
husk-i-ness
hus-ting
hus-tler
hy-a-cin-thine
Hy-a-des
hy-a-les-cence
hy-a-lin-i-za-tion
hy-a-li-no-sis
hy-al-o-gen
hy-al-o-phane
hy-a-lu-ro-nate
hy-a-lu-ron-i-dase
hy-brid-ize
hy-dan-to-in-ate
hy-da-tid-o-sis
hy-da-to-gen-ic
hy-drac-ry-late
hy-dra-cryl-ic
hy-dral-a-zine
hy-dra-mat-ic
hy-dra-mine
hy-dran-ge-a
hy-drar-gil-lite
hy-dras-ti-nine
hy-dra-tor
hy-drau-lic
hy-dra-zide
hy-draz-i-dine
hy-dra-zine
hy-dra-zin-i-um
hy-dra-zo-ate
hy-dra-zone
hy-dre-mi-a
hy-dri-od-ic
hy-dri-o-dide
hy-dro-ab-i-et-yl
hy-dro-cal-u-mite
hy-dro-cele
hy-dro-ce-phal-ic
hy-dro-ceph-a-lous (adj.)
hy-dro-ceph-a-lus (n.)
hy-dro-chlo-ric
hy-dro-flu-or-ide
hy-dro-form-ate
hy-dro-gen-a-tion
hy-dro-gen-a-tor
hy-drog-e-nous
hy-drog-no-sy
hy-drog-ra-pher
hy-dro-graph-ic
hy-dro-lase
hy-drol-o-gy
hy-drol-y-sate
hy-drol-y-sis
hy-dro-lyze
hy-drom-e-ter
hy-dro-met-ric
hy-dro-ni-um
hy-drop-a-thy
hy-dro-pho-bi-a
hy-dro-pon-ics
hy-drox-ide
hy-drox-im-i-no
hy-drox-y-am-i-no
hy-drox-y-bu-tyr-ic
hy-drox-yl-a-mine
hy-drox-yl-ate
hy-drox-y-zine
hy-e-tom-e-ter
hy-gi-en-ic
hy-gien-ist
hy-grom-e-ter
hy-gro-met-ric
hy-gro-scop-ic
hy-me-ne-al
hy-me-no-cal-lis

hy-per-bo-la
hy-per-bo-le
hy-per-bol-i-cal
hy-per-bo-loi-dal
hy-per-crit-i-cal
hy-per-e-mi-a
hy-per-go-lic-i-ty
hy-per-i-cin
hy-per-in
hy-per-o-pi-a
hy-per-sthene
hy-per-ten-sive
hy-per-troph-ic
hy-per-tro-phy
hy-phen-ate
hyp-no-sis
hyp-not-ic
hyp-no-tism
hy-po-bro-mous
hy-po-chlo-rous
hy-po-chon-dri-a
hy-poc-ri-sy
hyp-o-crite
hy-po-der-mic
hy-poid
hy-po-i-o-dous
hy-po-mor-pho-sis
hy-pos-ta-sis
hy-pot-e-nuse
hy-poth-e-cate
hy-poth-e-sis
hy-po-thet-i-cal
hy-pox-e-mi-a
hy-pox-i-a
hyp-som-e-ter
hys-taz-a-rin
hys-ter-ec-to-my
hys-ter-e-sis
hys-te-ri-a
hys-ter-i-cal
hys-ter-or-rha-phy
hys-ter-os-co-py
hys-ter-ot-o-my
hy-ther-graph

I

i-at-ro-gen-ic
i-at-ro-ge-nic-i-ty
I-be-ri-an
Ice-land-er
Ice-lan-dic
ich-neu-mon
ich-nog-ra-phy
Ich-thy-ol
ich-thy-o-sis
i-ci-cle
ic-ing
i-con-o-clast
i-co-nog-ra-phy
i-co-nol-a-try
i-co-nom-e-ter
i-con-o-scope
ic-ter-ic
I-da-ho-an
i-de-al-ism
i-de-al-ist
i-de-al-i-za-tion
i-den-ti-cal
i-den-ti-fi-a-ble
i-de-oc-ra-cy
i-de-og-ra-phy
i-de-o-log-i-cal
i-de-ol-o-gy
id-i-o-cy
i-di-o-gram-mat-ic
id-i-om
id-i-o-mat-ic
id-i-om-e-ter
id-i-o-path-ic
id-i-op-a-thy
id-i-o-syn-cra-sy
id-i-ot-i-cal
id-i-tol
i-dol-a-ter
i-dol-a-trous
i-dol-ize
i-dyl-lic
i-dyll-ist
ig-loo
ig-ne-ous
ig-nit-a-ble
ig-nit-er
ig-ni-tron
ig-no-min-i-ous
ig-no-min-y
ig-no-ra-mus
ig-no-rance
Ig-o-rot
il-e-i-tis
il-e-os-to-my
il-e-um
il-leg-i-ble
il-lic-it
il-lim-it-a-ble
Il-li-nois-an
il-lu-mi-nant
il-lu-mi-na-tor
il-lu-min-er
il-lu-mi-nom-e-ter
il-lu-sive
il-lu-so-ry
il-lus-tra-tive
il-lu-vi-al
il-men-ite
I-lo-i-lo
im-age-ry
i-mag-i-na-ble
i-mag-i-nar-y
i-mag-i-na-tive
i-ma-go
im-be-cil-i-ty
im-bri-cate
im-bro-glio
im-id-az-ole
im-id-az-o-line
im-ide
im-i-do
im-in-az-ole
im-i-no
im-i-ta-tive
im-mac-u-late
im-ma-nence
im-mar-gin-ate
im-me-di-a-cy
im-mem-o-ra-ble
im-me-mo-ri-al
im-men-si-ty
im-men-su-ra-ble
im-mers-i-ble
im-mers-ing
im-mer-sion
im-mi-gra-tion
im-mi-nent
im-mis-ci-ble
im-mo-late
im-mu-ni-ty
im-mu-ni-za-tion
Im-mu-no-gen
im-mu-nol-o-gy
im-mu-ta-ble
im-pac-tive
im-pal-pa-ble
im-par-ta-tion
im-part-i-ble
im-pass-a-ble
im-pas-si-ble
im-pas-sive
im-pa-tience
im-pe-cu-ni-ous
im-ped-ance
im-ped-i-ble
im-ped-i-men-tal
im-pe-dom-e-ter
im-pe-dor
im-pel-ling
im-per-a-tive
im-pe-ra-tor
im-per-cep-ti-ble
im-per-fo-rate
im-pe-ri-al
im-per-iled
im-pe-ri-ous
im-per-scrip-ti-ble
im-per-son-a-tor
im-per-sua-si-ble
im-per-turb-a-ble
im-per-vi-ous
im-pe-ti-go
im-pet-u-os-i-ty
im-pe-tus
im-ping-er
im-ping-ing
im-pi-ous
imp-ish
im-plac-a-ble
im-plan-ta-tion
im-plau-si-ble
im-ple-men-tal
im-pli-cate
im-plic-it-ly
im-plo-sion
im-pol-i-tic
im-por-tance
im-por-tant
im-port-er
im-por-tu-nate
im-post-er
im-pos-tor (deceiver)
im-pos-ture
im-po-tence
im-pov-er-ish
im-prec-a-to-ry
im-preg-na-tor
im-pre-sar-i-o
im-pre-scrip-ti-ble
im-press-a-ble
im-press-i-ble
im-pres-sive
im-pri-ma-tur
im-promp-tu
im-prov-i-dent
im-prov-i-sa-tion
im-pro-vise
im-pu-dence
im-pul-sive
im-pu-ni-ty
im-pu-ri-ty
im-put-a-ble
im-pu-ta-tion
in-ad-vert-ent
in-am-o-ra-ta
in-an-i-mate
in-a-ni-tion
in-an-i-ty
in-au-gu-ra-tion
in-cal-cu-la-ble
in-ca-les-cent
in-can-des-cent
in-ca-pac-i-tate
in-car-cer-ate
in-car-nate
in-cen-di-ar-y
in-cen-tive
in-cep-tive
in-ces-tu-ous
in-cho-ate
in-ci-den-tal
in-cin-er-a-tor
in-cip-i-ent
in-ci-sive
in-ci-sor
in-cit-ant
in-ci-ta-tion
in-cit-er
in-clem-ent
in-clin-a-ble
in-cli-na-tion
in-cli-na-to-ry
in-cli-nom-e-ter
in-clud-a-ble
in-clu-sive
in-cog-ni-to
in-com-pa-ra-ble
in-com-pat-i-ble
in-con-cus-si-ble
in-con-gru-ous
in-cor-po-ra-tor
in-cor-ri-gi-ble
in-creas-er
in-cred-i-ble
in-cre-du-li-ty
in-cred-u-lous
in-cre-ment
in-crim-i-nate
in-crus-ta-tion
in-cu-ba-tor
in-cu-bous (adj.)
in-cu-bus (n.)
in-cum-bent
in-cu-nab-u-lum
in-cur-a-ble
in-cur-ra-ble
in-cur-sive
in-da-mine
in-da-zole
in-de-fat-i-ga-ble
in-dem-ni-fi-ca-tion
in-dene
in-den-ta-tion
in-dent-er
in-den-ture
in-de-pend-ent
in-de-struct-i-ble
In-di-an
In-di-an-a
In-di-an-ap-o-lis
In-di-an-i-an
in-di-can
in-di-ca-tion
in-dic-a-tive
in-di-ca-tor
in-di-ci-a
in-dic-o-lite
in-dict-a-ble
in-dict-er
In-dies
in-dig-e-nous
in-di-gent
in-di-gest-i-ble
in-di-go
in-dig-o-lite
In-di-go-sol
in-dig-o-tin
in-di-ru-bin
in-dis-pen-sa-ble
in-dis-pu-ta-ble
in-dis-sol-u-ble
in-di-um
in-di-vid-u-al-ize
in-di-vis-i-ble
in-doc-tri-nate
in-dole-a-ce-tic
in-do-lent
in-do-line
in-do-lyl
in-dom-i-ta-ble
In-do-ne-sian
in-do-phe-nin
in-dox-yl
in-du-bi-ta-ble
in-duc-er
in-duc-i-ble
in-duct-ance
in-duct-ee
in-duc-tive
in-duc-tom-e-ter
in-duc-tor
in-duc-to-ri-um
in-dul-gence
in-du-line
in-du-ra-tive
in-dus-tri-al-i-za-tion
in-e-bri-ate
in-ef-fa-ble
in-ef-face-a-ble
in-e-luc-ta-ble
in-ep-ti-tude
in-ert-ance
in-er-tial
in-ev-i-ta-ble
in-ex-o-ra-ble
in-ex-press-i-ble
in-ex-pres-sive
in-ex-pung-i-ble
in-ex-tir-pa-ble
in-ex-tri-ca-ble
in-fa-mous
in-fan-ti-cide
in-fan-tile
in-fan-try
in-fat-u-ate
in-fect-ant
in-fect-i-ble
in-fec-tious
in-fec-tive
in-fe-lic-i-tous
in-fer-a-ble
in-fer-ence
in-fe-ri-or-i-ty
in-fer-nal
in-fest-ant
in-fes-ta-tion
in-fil-tra-tor
in-fil-trom-e-ter
in-fi-nite
in-fin-i-tes-i-mal
in-fin-i-ti-val
in-fin-i-ty
in-fir-ma-ry
in-fir-mi-ty
in-flat-a-ble
in-flect-i-ble
in-flict-er
in-flo-res-cence
in-flu-en-tial
in-for-mal-i-ty
in-for-ma-lize
in-form-ant
in-for-ma-tion
in-form-a-tive
in-form-er
in-fract-i-ble
in-fran-gi-ble
in-fring-er
in-fun-dib-u-lum
in-fu-ri-ate
in-fu-si-ble
in-fu-so-ri-al
in-ge-nious
in-ge-nue
in-ge-nu-i-ty
in-gen-u-ous
in-ges-tant
in-got
in-gra-ti-ate
in-grat-i-tude
in-gra-ves-cence
in-grav-i-date
in-gre-di-ent
in-gui-nal
in-gur-gi-tate
in-hab-it-a-bil-i-ty
in-hab-it-ant
in-hab-it-er
in-hal-ant
in-ha-la-tion
in-ha-la-tor
in-her-ent
in-her-it-a-ble
in-her-it-ance
in-hib-it-er
in-hi-bi-tion
in-hib-i-tor (chem.)
in-hib-i-to-ry
in-hos-pit-a-ble
in-im-i-cal
in-im-i-ta-ble
in-iq-ui-tous
i-ni-tial
i-ni-ti-a-tive
in-jec-tor
in-junc-tive
in-ju-ri-ous
in-kling
in me-mo-ri-am
in-nas-ci-ble
in-noc-u-ous
in-no-va-to-ry
in-nu-en-do
in-nu-mer-a-ble
in-oc-u-late
in-or-di-nate
i-no-si-tol
in per-so-nam
in-quir-er
in-quir-y
in-qui-si-tion
in-quis-i-tive
in-sa-tia-ble
in-scrib-a-ble
in-scrib-er
in-scru-ta-ble
in-sec-ti-ci-dal
in-sec-tiv-o-ra
in-sec-tiv-o-rous
in-sec-tol-o-gy
in-sem-i-na-tion
in-sen-sate
in-ser-tive
in-sid-i-ous
in-sig-ne
in-sig-ni-a
in-sig-nif-i-cant
in-sip-id
in-si-pid-i-ty
in-sist-ence
in-sist-er
in-so-lence
in-sol-u-ble
in-sol-vent
in-sou-ci-ance
in-sou-ci-ant
in-spec-tor
In-spec-to-scope
in-spir-a-ble
in-spi-ra-tion
in-spir-a-tive
in-stal-la-tion
in-stalled
in-stan-ta-ne-ous
in-sti-ga-tor
in-stinc-tive
in-sti-tu-tor
in-struct-i-ble
in-struc-tive
in-struc-tor
in-stru-men-tal-i-ty
in-su-lar
in-su-la-tor
in-su-lin
in-su-per-a-ble
in-sur-ance
in-sur-er
in-sur-gen-cy
in-tagl-io
in-tan-gi-ble
in-te-ger
in-te-gral
in-te-gra-tor
in-teg-ri-ty
in-teg-u-men-tal
in-tel-lec-tu-al
in-tel-li-gen-tsi-a
in-tend-ant
in-ten-si-fy
in-ten-si-tom-e-ter
in-ten-si-ty
in-ten-sive
in-ter-ca-lar-y
in-ter-cede
in-ter-cep-tor
in-ter-cos-tal
in-ter-est
in-ter-fer-ence
in-ter-fer-om-e-ter
in-ter-im
in-te-ri-or
in-ter-jec-tor
in-ter-jec-tur-al
in-ter-lin-gua
in-ter-loc-u-to-ry
in-ter-lop-er
in-ter-me-di-ate
in-ter-mi-na-ble
in-tern
in-ter-nal
in-ter-ne-cine
in-ter-nist
in-ter-po-lat-er
in-ter-pret-a-ble
in-ter-pre-ta-tive
in-ter-pret-er
in-ter-pre-tive
in-ter-ro-gate
in-ter-rog-a-to-ry
in-ter-rupt-ed
in-ter-rupt-er
in-ter-rupt-i-ble
in-ter-rupt-ing
in-ter-stic-es
in-ter-sti-tial
in-ter-ven-er
in-ter-ve-nor (law)
in-tes-tate
in-tes-ti-nal
in-ti-ma-cy
in-ti-mat-er
in-tim-i-da-tor
in-to-nate
In-tox-im-e-ter
in-trac-ta-ble
in-tran-si-gent (n., adj.)
in-trav-a-sa-tion
in-tra-ve-nous
in-trep-id
in-tre-pid-i-ty
in-tri-ca-cy
in-trigu-er
in-trigu-ing
in-trin-si-cal
in-tro-duc-to-ry
in-tro-spec-tive
in-tro-ver-si-ble
in-trud-er
in-tru-sive
in-tu-i-tive
in-tu-mes-cence
in-u-lase
in-un-da-tor
in-vad-er
in-va-lid (n., v., adj., not well)
in-val-id (adj., not valid)
in-val-i-date
in-va-lid-i-ty
in-var-i-a-ble
in-vec-tive
in-vei-gle
in-vent-a-ble
in-ven-tor
in-ven-to-ry
in-vert-ase
in-ver-te-brate
in-vert-er
in-vert-i-ble
in-ver-tor (muscle)
in-ves-ti-ga-tor
in-ves-ti-ture
in-ves-tor
in-vet-er-ate
in-vid-i-ous
in-vig-o-rate
in-vin-ci-ble
in-vi-o-la-ble
in-vis-i-ble
in-vi-ta-tion
in-vit-er
in-vo-ca-tion
in-voc-a-tive
in-vo-lu-cre
i-o-di-nate
i-o-dine
i-o-din-oph-i-lous
i-o-do-a-ce-tic
i-o-do-form
i-o-do-hy-drin
i-o-dom-e-try
i-o-do-ni-um
i-o-do-phthal-ein
i-o-do-pyr-a-cet
i-o-dox-y-ben-zene
i-od-y-rite
I-o-ni-an
I-on-ic
i-o-ni-um
i-on-i-za-tion
i-o-nom-e-ter
i-o-none
i-on-o-spher-ic
I-o-wan
ip-e-cac
I-ra-ni-an
i-ras-ci-ble
ir-i-dec-to-my
ir-i-des-cence
i-rid-ic
i-rid-i-um
i-ron-i-cal
i-ron-y (of iron)
i-ro-ny (sarcasm)
Ir-o-quois
ir-ra-di-ate
ir-rad-i-ca-ble
ir-rec-on-cil-a-ble
ir-re-duc-i-ble
ir-ref-ra-ga-ble
ir-ref-u-ta-ble
ir-re-me-di-a-ble
ir-rep-a-ra-ble
ir-re-press-i-ble
ir-re-sist-i-ble
ir-re-spon-si-ble
ir-re-vers-i-ble
ir-rev-o-ca-ble
ir-ri-ga-ble
ir-ri-tant
i-sa-go-ge
i-sa-gog-ics
I-sa-iah
i-sa-tin-ic
is-che-mi-a
i-sin-glass
Is-lam-ic
is-land-er
is-let
i-so-am-yl-ene
i-so-bar-ic
i-so-bath-y-therm
i-soch-ro-nal
i-so-chrone
i-soch-ro-nism
i-so-cla-site
i-so-cli-nal
i-so-drin
i-sog-a-mous
i-so-gly-co-sa-mine
i-sog-o-nal
i-so-gon-ic
i-so-lat-a-ble
i-so-leu-cine
i-so-mer-ic
i-som-er-ize
i-so-met-ri-cal-ly
i-som-e-try
i-so-ni-a-zid
i-so-phthal-ic
i-so-pre-noid
i-so-pro-pe-nyl
i-so-pro-pyl
i-sos-ce-les
i-sos-ta-sy
i-so-ther-mal
i-so-top-ic
i-so-to-py
i-so-tron
Is-rae-li
Is-ra-el-ite
Is-tan-bul

isth-mus
it-a-con-ic
I-tal-ian
I-tal-i-cize
i-tem-ize
it-er-ate
i-tin-er-ar-y
i-vo-ry

J

ja-bot
jack-al
jack-a-napes
jack-et
Ja-cob
Jac-o-be-an
Ja-co-bi-an
Jac-o-bin
jac-o-net
jac-quard
Jacque-mi-not
jag-uar
jal-ap
ja-lop-y
jal-ou-sie
Ja-mai-can
jam-bo-ree
jan-gling
jan-i-tor
Jan-u-ar-y
Ja-nus
Ja-pan
Jap-a-nese
ja-panned
ja-pon-i-ca
jar-di-niere
jar-gon-ize
jar-ring
jas-mine
jas-per
jaun-dice
jaunt-i-ly
jav-a-nese
jav-e-lin
jeal-ous-y
Jef-fer-so-ni-an
Je-ho-vah
je-ju-nos-to-my
je-ju-num
Je-kyll
jeop-ard-ize
jeop-ard-y
Je-ru-sa-lem
jes-sa-mine
Jes-u-it
Je-sus
jew-eled
Jez-e-bel
jin-gling
jin-rik-i-sha
jock-ey
jo-cos-i-ty
joc-u-lar
joc-und
jo-cun-di-ty
Jodh-pur
joh-nin
John-ston
join-der
joint-er
join-ture
jok-er
joke-ster
Jo-nah
jon-quil
Jor-da-ni-an
jo-se-ite
Jo-seph
Jo-se-phine
Josh-u-a
jos-tled
jos-tling
jour-nal-ist
jour-ney
jo-vi-al-i-ty
ju-bi-lant
ju-bi-la-tion
Ju-da-ism
judg-ment
ju-di-ca-to-ry
ju-di-ca-ture
ju-di-cial
ju-di-ci-ar-y
ju-di-cious
ju-gal
jug-gler
jug-gling
jug-u-lar
ju-jit-su
ju-jube
Ju-lian
ju-li-enne
Ju-li-et
Ju-lius
jum-bled
jump-er
junc-tur-al
Ju-neau
jun-ior
ju-nior-i-ty
ju-ni-per
Jun-ius
Jun-ker
junk-er
jun-ket-eer
Ju-pi-ter
Ju-ras-sic
ju-rat
ju-rid-i-cal
ju-ri-di-cial (obs.)
ju-ris-dic-tion
ju-ris-pru-dence
ju-ris-tic
ju-ror
jus-tice
jus-ti-ci-a-ble
jus-ti-fi-ca-tion
jus-tif-i-ca-to-ry
ju-ve-nes-cence
ju-ve-nile
ju-ve-nil-i-ty
jux-ta-po-si-tion

K

Kad-iak
Kaf-fir
kai-nite
kai-nos-ite
kai-ser
ka-lei-do-scop-ic
kal-i-bo-rite
ka-lic-i-nite
ka-lig-e-nous
Kal-i-spell
ka-mi-ka-ze
kan-ga-roo
Kan-san
ka-o-lin-ic
ka-o-lin-ite
ka-pok
Ka-rā-chi
kar-y-o-gam-ic
kar-y-og-a-my
kar-y-o-ki-ne-sis
kar-y-ol-o-gy
kar-y-ol-y-sis
kar-y-o-mi-to-sis
kar-y-o-some
ka-tab-a-sis
kat-a-bat-ic
Ka-tan-gan
Kath-a-rine
ka-ty-did
kay-ak
keep-er
ken-o-tron
Ken-tuck-i-an
Ken-yan
ker-a-tin
ke-rat-i-nous
ker-a-ti-tis
Ker-a-tol
ker-a-tol-y-sis
ker-a-to-sis
ker-chiefed
ker-mes-ite
ker-neled
ker-o-gen
ker-o-sene
ker-sey
ke-ta-zine
Ketch-i-can
ke-tene
ke-ti-mine
ke-to-gen-e-sis
ke-to-glu-tar-ic
ke-tol-y-sis
ke-to-lyt-ic
ke-tone
ke-to-side
ke-to-sis
Keynes-i-an
kha-ki
Khar-toum
khe-dive
Khru-shchev
kib-itz
ki-bosh
kid-nap-er
kie-sel-guhr
kill-er
kil-o-cy-cle
kil-o-me-ter
kil-o-ton
kil-o-watt
ki-mo-no
ki-nase
kin-der-gar-ten
kin-der-gart-ner
kind-li-ness
kin-dling
kin-dred
kin-e-mat-ics
kin-e-scope
ki-ne-si-at-rics
ki-ne-sics
kin-e-sim-e-ter
ki-ne-si-o-log-ic
ki-ne-si-ol-o-gy
kin-es-the-si-a
ki-net-ic
ki-ne-to-phone
ki-ne-to-scope
kin-e-to-sis
Kings-ton
Kirch-hoff
Kirsch-ner
kitch-en-ette
Kjel-dahl
Klam-ath (river, etc.)
Klee-nex
klep-to-ma-ni-a
klys-tron
knav-ish
knick-er-bock-er
knock-er
knowl-edge-a-ble
knuck-led
ko-gas-in
Koh-i-noor
kohl-ra-bi
ko-jic
kok-sa-ghyz
ko-lin-sky
kol-khoz
Kom-man-da-tu-ra
ko-nim-e-ter
ko-ni-ol-o-gy
Koo-te-nay
ko-peck
Ko-ran
Ko-re-an
ko-ru-na
ko-sher
kreu-zer
kro-nen
kro-ner
kryp-ton
ku-lak
Kuo-min-tang
kur-to-sis
Ku-wait
Ku-wai-ti
Kwaj-a-lein
kwa-shi-or-kor
ky-mo-graph
ky-mog-ra-phy
kyn-u-ren-ine

L

lab-a-rum
lab-e-fac-tion
la-beled
la-bel-er
la-bi-al
la-bile
la-bi-lize
la-bi-um
lab-o-ra-to-ry
la-bor-er
la-bo-ri-ous
lab-ra-dor-ite
la-bur-num
lab-y-rin-thine
lac-er-ate
lach-es
lach-ry-mose
lack-a-dai-si-cal
la-con-ic
lac-o-nism
lac-quer
lac-ri-mal
la-crosse
lac-tal-bu-min
lac-tase
lac-te-al
lac-tes-cent
lac-tif-er-ous
lac-to-fla-vin
lac-tom-e-ter
lac-tose
la-cu-na
la-cus-trine
lad-en-ing
lad-ing
la-di-no
la-dler
la-drone
La-fay-ette
la-ger
la-gniappe
la-goon-al
la-gu-na
lai-tance
la-lop-a-thy
la-ma-ser-y
lam-bent
lam-bre-quin
la-mel-lar
lam-el-late
la-mel-lose
la-ment
lam-en-ta-ble
lam-en-ta-tion
lam-i-na-graph
lam-i-nag-ra-phy
lam-i-nal
lam-i-nar-in
lam-i-nate
lam-i-na-tor
lam-i-ni-tis
lam-poon
lam-prey
la-nat-o-side
Lan-ce-lot
lan-ce-o-lar
lanc-er
lan-cet
lan-ci-nate
lan-dau-let
Lang-shan
lan-guage
lan-guish
lan-guor-ous
lan-o-ce-ric
lan-o-lin
la-nos-ter-ol
Lan-ston
lan-tern
lan-tha-nide
lan-tha-num
lan-thi-o-nine
lap-a-rot-o-my
la-pel-er
lap-i-dar-y
la-pis
lap-is la-zu-li
La-o-tian
Lar-a-mie
lar-ce-nous
lar-da-ceous
lar-der
larg-er
lar-gess
larg-est
lar-i-at
lar-va
lar-vi-cid-al
lar-vic-o-lous
lar-viv-o-rous
la-ryn-ge-al
lar-yn-gec-to-my
lar-yn-git-ic
lar-yn-gi-tis
la-ryn-go-log-i-cal
lar-yn-gol-o-gy
la-ryn-go-scope
lar-yn-gos-co-py
lar-yn-got-o-my
lar-ynx
las-civ-i-ous
las-si-tude
Lat-a-ki-a
la-teen
la-ten-cy
lat-er
lat-er-al
lat-er-ite
la-tes-cent
lat-est
la-tex
lath-er-ing
lat-i-cif-er-ous
Lat-in-ize
la-tite
lat-i-tu-di-nous
la-trine
laud-a-ble
lau-dan-i-dine
lau-da-nine
lau-dan-o-sine
lau-da-num
laud-a-to-ry
launch-er
laun-der
Laun-der-om-e-ter
laun-dress
Laun-dro-mat
lau-rate
lau-re-ate
lau-reled
Lau-rence
Lau-ren-tian
lau-ric
lau-ro-len-ic
lau-ryl
la-vage
lav-a-liere
lav-a-to-ry
lav-en-der
lav-ish
Law-rence
law-renc-ite
lay-ette
Laz-a-rus
la-zi-ly
laz-u-rite
lead-er
lea-guer
leak-age
learn-ed (adj.)
leath-er-ine
leav-en
Leb-a-nese
le-bens-raum
lech-er-ous
lec-i-thin-ase
lec-tern
lec-tur-er
ledg-er
le-dol
leg-a-cy
le-gal-i-ty
le-gal-ize
leg-ate (n.)
le-gate (v.)
leg-a-tee
le-ga-tion
leg-end-ar-y
leg-er-de-main
le-ger-i-ty
leg-i-ble
le-gion-naire
leg-is-la-tive
leg-is-la-tor
leg-is-la-to-ri-al
le-git-i-ma-cy
leg-ume
le-gu-mi-nous
Leices-ter
leish-ma-ni-a-sis
lei-sure
lem-on-ade
lend-er
length-en
le-ni-en-cy
len-i-ty
Lent-en
len-ti-cel
len-tic-u-lar
len-ti-go
len-til
Leom-in-ster
Leon-ard
Le-o-nar-desque
le-o-nine
leop-ard
lep-er
lep-i-do-cro-cite
le-pid-o-lite
Lep-i-dop-ter-a
lep-i-do-sis
lep-rol-o-gy
lep-ro-sar-i-um
le-pro-sis
lep-ro-sy
lep-rous
lep-to-ceph-a-lus
lep-to-mat-ic
lep-to-spi-ro-sis
le-sion
Le-so-tho
les-pe-de-za
les-see
less-en
less-er
les-son
les-sor
le-thal
leth-ane
le-thar-gic
leth-ar-gy
leu-cite
leu-con-ic
leu-cop-te-rin
leu-co-sin
leu-co-sphe-nite
leu-cot-o-my
leu-cov-o-rin
leu-ke-mi-a
leu-ke-mic
leu-ker-gy
leu-ko-cyte
leu-ko-cyt-ic
leu-ko-cy-to-sis
leu-ko-poi-e-sis
leu-ko-poi-et-ic
leu-kor-rhe-a
leu-ko-sis
lev-an
Le-vant
Le-vant-er
Le-van-tine
le-va-tor
le-vee (reception)
lev-ee (dam)
lev-el-er
le-ver
le-ver-age
le-vi-a-than
lev-i-ga-tor
lev-i-tat-ing
lev-i-ty
le-vo-glu-co-san
lev-u-li-nate
lev-u-lin-ic
lev-u-lose
lev-y-ing
lew-is-ite
lex-i-cog-ra-pher
lex-i-co-graph-ic
lex-i-cog-ra-phy
lex-ig-ra-phy
li-ai-son
li-bel-ant
li-beled
li-bel-ous
lib-er-al-i-ty
lib-er-a-tor
lib-er-tar-i-an
lib-er-tine
lib-er-ty
li-bid-i-nous
li-bi-do
Li-bra
li-brar-i-an
li-bra-to-ry
li-bret-to
Lib-y-an
li-can-ic
li-cens-a-ble
li-censed
li-cens-ee
li-cens-er
li-cen-sor
li-cen-tious
li-chen-in
lic-o-rice
lid-o-caine
Lie-der-kranz
lien-ee
lien-or
lieu-ten-an-cy
lift-er
lig-a-men-tous
li-ga-tion
lig-a-ture
light-ened
light-en-ing (brighten-ing)
light-er-age
light-ning (a flash)
lig-ne-ous
lig-nes-cent
lig-nite
lig-num vi-tae
lig-ro-in
lig-u-lar
lik-a-ble
lik-en
li-la-ceous
lil-li-pu-tian
lim-ber
Lim-burg-er
lime-ade
li-mic-o-lous
lim-i-ta-tion
lim-it-ed
li-miv-o-rous
lim-ner
lim-nim-e-ter
lim-nol-o-gy
Li-moges
lim-o-nene
li-mo-nite
lim-ou-sine
lim-pid-i-ty
lin-a-ble
lin-age
lin-al-o-ol
lin-a-mar-in
Lin-coln
lin-dane
lin-e-age
lin-e-al
lin-e-a-ment
lin-e-ar-i-ty
lin-en
lin-e-o-late
lin-er
lin-ger
lin-ge-rie
lin-gual
lin-guis-tics
lin-guist-ry
link-age
Lin-nae-us
li-no-le-ate
lin-o-le-ic
li-no-le-in
lin-o-le-nic
li-no-le-um
Li-no-type
li-nox-yn
lin-tel
lint-er
li-on-ess
li-on-ize
lip-a-rid
li-pe-mi-a
lip-ide
lip-i-do-sis
lip-o-chon-dri-on
lip-o-fus-cin
li-pog-e-nous
li-po-ic
lip-oi-do-sis
li-pol-y-sis
lip-o-lyt-ic
li-po-ma-to-sis
li-po-si-tol
lip-o-trop-ic
li-qua-tion
liq-ue-fa-cient
liq-ue-fy
li-ques-cent
li-queur
liq-uid
liq-ui-da-tor
li-quid-i-ty
liq-ui-dus
liq-uor
li-roc-o-nite
lis-e-ran
lisp-er
lis-ten-er
lis-ter-el-lo-sis
lis-te-ri-a
lis-ter-ize
lit-a-ny
li-tchi
li-ter
lit-er-al-ly
lit-e-ra-ti
lit-e-ra-tim
lit-er-a-ture
lith-arge
li-the-mi-a
lith-i-a
li-thi-a-sis
li-thid-i-o-nite
lith-i-um

lith-o-cho-lic
lith-o-graph
li-thog-ra-pher
lith-o-graph-ic
li-thog-ra-phy
lith-ol-a-pax-y
lith-o-log-ic
li-thol-o-gy
lith-o-pone
lith-o-sol
li-thot-o-my
li-thot-ri-ty
Lith-u-a-ni-an
li-thu-ri-a
lit-i-ga-ble
lit-i-ga-tor
li-ti-gious
lit-ter-a-teur
lit-to-ral
li-tur-gi-cal
lit-ur-gy
liv-a-ble
live-li-hood
liv-er-y
liv-id
Liv-ing-ston
Li-vo-ni-an
lix-iv-i-ate
liz-ard
lla-ma
load-er
load-om-e-ter
loaf-er
loath-er
lo-bar
lo-bate
lob-bied
lo-bec-to-my
lo-be-li-a
lo-be-line
lo-bot-o-my
lob-u-lar
lob-u-lose
lo-cale
lo-cal-i-ty
lo-cal-iz-er
lo-cant
lo-cat-er
loc-a-tive
lo-ca-tor
lock-age
lock-er
lo-co-mo-tive
loc-u-late
lo-cust
lodg-er
lo-ga-nin
log-a-rith-mic
log-i-cal
lo-gi-cian
lo-gis-ti-cian
lo-gis-tics
log-o-gram-mat-ic
lo-gom-a-chy
log-o-pe-dic
log-o-type
loi-ter
lol-li-pop
Lom-bar-dy
lone-li-ness
long-er
lon-ger (cask)
lon-ge-ron
long-est
lon-gev-i-ty
lon-gi-fo-lene
lon-gi-tu-di-nal
loos-en
loot-er
lo-phine
lop-sid-ed
lo-qua-cious
lo-quac-i-ty
lo-ran
lor-gnette
Los An-ge-les
los-er
los-ing
loss-er
Lo-thar-i-o
Lou-i-si-an-i-an
lous-i-ness
lou-ver
lov-a-ble
lox-o-drom-ic
loy-al-ist
loz-enge
lu-bri-ca-tor
lu-bric-i-ty
lu-cid-i-ty
Lu-ci-fer
lu-cif-er-ase
lu-cite
lu-cra-tive
lu-cu-brate
lu-di-crous
lu-gu-bri-ous
lum-bar
lu-men
lu-miere
lu-mi-fla-vin
lu-mi-naire
lu-mi-nar-y
lu-mi-nes-cence
lu-mi-nif-er-ous
lu-mi-nom-e-ter
lu-mi-nos-i-ty
lu-mi-nous
lu-mis-ter-ol
lu-na-cy
lu-nar-i-an
lu-na-tic
lunch-eon
lu-nette
lu-nik
lu-nu-late
lu-pet-i-dine
lu-pin-ine
lu-pu-lone
lu-rid
lus-cious
Lu-si-ta-ni-a
lus-ter (shine)
lust-er (n.) (one that lusts)
lus-trous
lu-te-in-ize
lu-te-o-lin
lu-te-o-vi-res-cent
lu-te-ti-um
Lu-ther-an
lu-ti-din-ic
Lux-em-bourg-er
lux-u-ri-ant
lux-u-ri-ous
ly-ce-um
ly-co-pene
lydd-ite
lymph-ad-e-ni-tis
lymph-ad-e-nop-a-thy
lym-phan-gi-al
lym-phat-ic
lym-pho-cyte
lymph-oid
lym-pho-ma-to-sis
ly-o-phil-ic
ly-oph-i-lize
lyr-i-cal
ly-ser-gic
ly-sim-e-ter
ly-sine
ly-so-gen-ic

M

ma-ca-bre
mac-ad-am-ize
mac-a-ro-ni
mac-a-ron-ic
mac-a-roon
Ma-cas-sar
ma-caw
Mac-ca-be-an
Mac-e-do-ni-an
mac-er-a-tor
ma-che-te
Mach-i-a-vel-li-an
ma-chi-nal
mach-i-na-tion
ma-chin-er-y
ma-chin-ist
mack-er-el
mack-in-tosh
mac-ro-bi-o-sis
mac-ro-cosm
mac-ro-cy-clic
mac-ro-cy-to-sis
mac-ro-mol-e-cule
ma-cron
ma-crop-si-a
mac-ro-scop-ic
mac-u-la-ture
mad-am
ma-dame
Ma-dei-ra
ma-de-moi-selle
ma-don-na
Ma-dras
Ma-drid
mad-ri-gal
mael-strom
mae-stro
Ma-fi-a
maf-ic
mag-a-zine
Mag-da-len
Mag-de-burg
ma-gen-ta
mag-i-cal
ma-gi-cian
Ma-gi-not
ma-gis-ter
mag-is-te-ri-al
mag-is-tra-cy
mag-na-nim-i-ty
mag-nan-i-mous
mag-ne-sia
mag-ne-si-o-chro-mite
mag-ne-site
mag-ne-si-um
mag-ne-syn
mag-net-i-cal-ly
mag-net-ism
mag-net-ite
mag-net-ize
mag-ne-to-graph
mag-ne-tom-e-ter
mag-ne-to-met-ric
mag-ne-tom-e-try
mag-ne-tos
mag-ne-tron
mag-ni-fi-ca-tion
mag-nif-i-cence
mag-ni-fy
mag-nil-o-quent
mag-ni-tude
mag-no-lia
ma-guey
mah-jong
ma-hog-a-ny
Ma-hom-et
maid-en
mail-er
Main-er
main-te-nance
mai-so-nette
mai-tre d'ho-tel
ma-jes-tic
maj-es-ty
ma-jol-i-ca
ma-jor-i-ty
maj-us-cule
ma-jus-cu-lar
mak-er
mal-a-chite
mal-a-dy
Mal-a-ga
Mal-a-gas-y
mal-a-gue-na
mal-aise
ma-lar
ma-lar-i-al
ma-lar-i-om-e-try
mal-a-thi-on
Ma-la-wi
Ma-lay-an
Ma-lay-sian
ma-le-ate
mal-e-dic-tion
mal-e-fac-tor
ma-lef-i-cent
ma-le-ic
ma-lev-o-lent
mal-fea-sance
Ma-li-an
mal-ic
mal-ice
ma-li-cious
ma-lif-er-ous
ma-lign
ma-lig-nant
ma-lin-ger
mal-le-a-ble
mal-o-nate
ma-lo-nic
malt-ase
Mal-tese
mal-tha
Mal-thu-sian
malt-ose
mam-ma-li-an
mam-ma-lif-er-ous
mam-mal-o-gy
mam-ma-ry
mam-mif-er-ous
man-a-cle
man-age-a-ble
man-ag-er
man-a-ge-ri-al
Ma-na-gua
ma-ña-na
man-a-tee
Man-chu-ri-an
man-da-mus
man-da-rin-ate
man-da-to-ry
man-del-ate
man-di-ble
man-dib-u-lar
man-do-lin-ist
man-drake
man-drel
ma-nege
ma-neu-ver
man-ga-nate
man-ga-nese
man-gan-ic
man-ga-nif-er-ous
man-ga-nin
man-ga-nite
man-ga-no-site
man-ga-nous
man-ger
man-gler
man-gy
ma-ni-ac
ma-ni-a-cal
ma-ni-co-ba
man-i-cur-ist
man-i-fes-tant
man-i-fes-ta-tion
man-i-fold-er
man-i-kin
Ma-nil-a
ma-nil-la
man-i-oc
ma-nip-u-la-tor
man-nu-ron-ic
ma-nom-e-ter
man-o-met-ric
ma-nom-e-try
man-or
ma-no-ri-al
man-o-stat
man-sard
man-tel (arch)
man-tle (garment)
man-tling
man-u-al
man-u-duc-to-ry
man-u-fac-tur-er
ma-nure
ma-quette
ma-quis
mar-a-bou
ma-rac-a
mar-a-schi-no
ma-ras-mus
ma-raud-er
mar-bled
mar-ble-ize
mar-ca-site
mar-che-se
mar-chion-ess
mar-ga-rate
Mar-ga-ret
mar-gar-ic
mar-ga-rin
mar-ga-rite
mar-ga-ro-san-ite
mar-gin-al
mar-gi-na-li-a
mar-gin-ate
mar-gue-rite
Mar-i-an
Mar-i-co-pa
mar-i-gold
mar-i-hua-na
ma-rim-ba
ma-ri-na
ma-rine
mar-i-ner
Ma-ri-nist (of Marin)
ma-rin-ist (sea)
ma-ri-no-ra-ma
mar-i-o-nette
mar-i-tal
ma-rit-i-cide
mar-i-time
mar-jo-ram
Mar-jo-ry
mark-er
mar-ket-er
mar-la-ceous
marl-ite
mar-ma-lade
mar-mo-ra-ceous
mar-mo-re-al
mar-mo-set
ma-roon
mar-que-try
mar-quis
mar-qui-sette
mar-riage-a-ble
Mar-seil-laise
Mar-seilles
mar-shaled
mar-shal-er
mar-su-pi-al-ize
mar-tens-ite
mar-tial
mar-ti-net
mar-tin-gale
Mar-ti-ni
mar-tite
mar-tyr-ize
mar-vel-ous
Mar-y-land-er
Ma-sa-ryk
mas-cu-lin-i-ty
mask-er
mas-och-ism
mas-och-is-tic
Ma-son-ite
ma-son-ry
masqu-er
mas-quer-ade
Mas-sa-chu-setts-an
mas-sa-cred
mas-sag-er
mas-sive
mast-er (with masts)
mas-ter (owner, etc.)
mas-tic
mas-ti-cate
mas-tiff
mas-tit-ic
mas-ti-tis
mas-to-don
mas-toi-dal
mas-toid-i-tis
mas-toid-ot-o-my
ma-su-ri-um
mat-a-dor
mat-er
ma-te-ri-al-ize
ma-te-ri-a med-i-ca
ma-te-ri-el
ma-ter-ni-ty
math-e-mat-i-cal
math-e-ma-ti-cian
math-e-mat-ics
ma-thet-ic
mat-in-al
mat-i-nee
ma-tri-ar-chal
mat-ri-ces
ma-tri-ci-dal
ma-tric-u-late
mat-ri-mo-ni-al
ma-trix
ma-tron
mat-ro-nym-ic
mat-u-ra-tion
mat-u-ra-tive
ma-tu-ri-ty
ma-tu-ti-nal
mat-zoth
maud-lin
maul-er
maun-der
Mau-re-ta-ni-an
Mau-rice
Mau-ri-ti-us (island)
Mau-ser
mau-so-le-um
mau-vine
mav-er-ick
mawk-ish
max-i-miz-er
max-i-mum
may-on-naise
may-or-al-ty
maz-a-rine
ma-zur-ka
mea-con-ing
mead-ow
mea-ger
meal-y-mouthed
me-an-der
mea-sles
mea-sly
meas-ur-a-ble
meas-ured
me-a-tus
me-cap-rine
me-chan-i-cal
mech-a-ni-cian
mech-a-nism
mech-a-ni-za-tion
mech-a-no-mor-phic
me-com-e-ter
me-con-ic
mec-o-nin
me-co-ni-um
med-al-ist
me-dal-lion
med-dler
me-di-an
me-di-as-ti-ni-tis
me-di-as-ti-num
me-di-a-tor
me-di-ca-ble
med-ic-aid
med-i-cal
me-dic-a-ment
med-i-care
Med-i-ci
me-dic-i-nal
med-i-cine
me-di-e-val
Me-di-na
me-di-o-cre
me-di-oc-ri-ty
med-i-ta-tive
Med-i-ter-ra-ne-an
me-di-um
me-dul-la
med-ul-lar-y
meer-schaum
meg-a-lo-ma-ni-a
meg-a-lop-o-lis
meg-a-lo-pol-i-tan
meg-a-phone
meg-a-ton
meg-ohm-me-ter
me-grim
mei-o-nite
mei-ot-ic
mei-ster
me-lac-o-nite
mel-a-mine
mel-an-cho-li-a
mel-an-chol-y
me-lange
me-lan-ger
me-lan-ic
mel-a-nin
mel-a-no-ma-to-sis
mel-a-no-sis
mel-a-no-stib-i-an-
me-lan-ter-ite
me-lee
me-lez-i-tose
mel-i-bi-ose
mel-i-lite
me-lio-ra-tive
Me-lis-sa
mel-i-tose
mel-lif-lu-ous
mel-li-tate
mel-lit-ic
me-lod-ic
me-lo-di-on
me-lo-di-ous
mel-o-dra-ma
mel-o-dy
mel-o-ma-ni-a
mel-o-nite
mel-o-plas-ty
melt-er
mem-bra-nate
mem-bra-nous
me-men-tos
mem-oir
mem-o-ra-ble
mem-o-ran-dums
me-mo-ri-al-iz-ing
mem-o-riz-er
men-ace
men-a-di-one
me-nag-er-ie
me-naph-thone
men-da-cious
men-dac-i-ty
men-de-le-vi-um
Men-de-li-an
men-de-lye-ev-ite
mend-er
men-di-cant
men-dic-i-ty
men-ha-den
me-ni-al
Me-ni-ere
men-i-lite
me-nin-ge-al
me-nin-gi-o-ma
men-in-git-ic
men-in-gi-tis
me-nin-go-cele
me-nin-go-coc-cus
me-nin-go-my-e-li-tis
me-nis-cus
Men-non-ite
Me-nom-i-nee
men-o-pau-sal
me-no-rah
men-ses
men-stru-al
men-su-ra-ble
men-su-ral
men-su-ra-tion
men-tal-i-ty
men-tha-di-ene
men-thane
men-tha-nol
men-the-none
men-tho-lat-ed
men-thyl
men-ti-cide
me-per-i-dine
me-phen-e-sin
Meph-is-to-phe-li-an
me-phit-ic
me-phi-tis
me-pro-ba-mate
mer-al-lu-ride
mer-can-tile
mer-cap-to
mer-cap-tom-er-in
mer-cap-tu-ric
Mer-ca-tor
mer-ce-nar-y
mer-cer-ize
mer-chan-dise
mer-chant-a-ble
mer-cu-rate
mer-cu-ri-al
mer-cu-ric
mer-cu-rous
me-ren-gue
me-re-ol-o-gy
mer-e-tri-cious
mer-gan-ser
mer-gence
Mer-gen-tha-ler
merg-er
me-rid-i-an
me-rid-i-o-nal
me-ringue
me-ri-nos
mer-it-ed
mer-i-to-ri-ous
mer-o-crine
mer-o-gon-ic
me-rog-o-ny
mer-o-he-dral
Mer-o-pe
me-ro-pi-a
me-rot-o-mize
me-rox-ene
mer-sal-yl
Mer-thi-o-late
mes-al-liance
mes-ar-te-ri-tis
mes-en-ce-phal-ic
mes-en-ceph-a-lon
mes-en-chy-ma
mes-en-chym-a-tous
mes-en-chyme
mes-en-ter-ic
mes-en-ter-i-tis
me-sic
mes-i-dine
mes-i-tyl
me-sit-y-lene
mes-mer-ism
mes-o-blast
mes-o-car-di-a
mes-o-ce-phal-ic
mes-o-derm
mes-o-lite
mes-o-mer-ic

me-som-er-ism
mes-on
mes-o-phyll
mes-o-sphere
mes-ox-al-ic
mes-ox-a-lyl
Mes-o-zo-ic
mes-quite
mes-sage
mes-sen-ger
mes-si-an-ic
mes-ti-zos
mes-yl
me-tab-a-sis
met-a-bi-o-sis
met-a-bi-ot-ic
met-a-bol-ic
me-tab-o-lism
me-tab-o-liz-a-ble
met-a-bo-rate
met-a-car-pus
me-tag-ra-phy
met-al-de-hyde
me-tal-lic
met-al-lif-er-ous
met-al-lize
met-al-log-ra-phy
met-al-lur-gi-cal
met-al-os-co-py
met-a-mer-ic
me-tam-er-ism
met-a-mor-phism
met-a-mor-pho-sis
met-a-phor-i-cal
met-a-phys-ics
met-ar-te-ri-ole
met-a-so-ma-to-sis
met-a-sta-ble
me-tas-ta-sis
me-tath-e-sis
me-tem-psy-cho-sis
me-te-or-ic
me-te-or-ite
me-te-or-it-ics
me-te-or-o-graph
me-te-or-og-ra-phy
me-te-or-oid
me-te-or-o-log-i-cal
me-te-or-ol-o-gist
me-te-or-ol-o-gy
me-te-or-om-e-ter
me-te-or-o-scope
me-te-or-os-co-py
me-ter
meth-ac-ry-late
meth-a-cryl-ic
meth-a-done
meth-al-lyl
meth-ane
meth-a-nol
meth-a-no-lic
meth-a-nol-y-sis
meth-a-nom-e-ter
meth-an-the-line
me-the-na-mine
meth-ene
meth-ide
meth-i-on-ic
me-thi-o-nine
me-thi-um
meth-od
me-thod-i-cal
Meth-od-ist
meth-od-ize
meth-od-ol-o-gy
me-tho-ni-um
meth-ox-ide
me-thox-y-car-bon-yl
meth-ox-yl
Me-thu-se-lah
meth-yl-a-mine
meth-yl-ate
meth-yl-ene
meth-yl-en-i-mine
meth-yl-eth-yl-pyr-i-dine
me-thyl-i-dyne
meth-yl-naph-tha-lene
meth-yl-ol-u-re-a
me-tic-u-lous
me-tier
me-ton-y-my
me-top-ic
met-o-pon
met-o-pos-co-py
Met-ra-zol
met-ric
met-ri-cal
me-tri-tis
me-trol-o-gy
met-ro-nome
me-tro-nym-ic
met-ro-pole
me-trop-o-lis
met-ro-pol-i-tan
mev-a-lon-ic
mez-za-nine
mho-me-ter
mi-ar-gy-rite
mi-ca-ceous
mi-cel-lar
mi-celle
Mi-chael
Mich-ael-mas

Mich-i-gan-ite
mi-cri-nite
mi-cro-bi-al
mi-cro-cosm
mi-crog-ra-phy
mi-cro-lite
mi-cro-me-rit-ics
mi-crom-e-ter
mi-cro-met-ri-cal
mi-crom-e-try
mi-cro-mho
mi-cron-ize
mi-cro-phon-ic
mi-crop-si-a
mi-cro-scop-ic
mi-cros-co-py
mi-crot-o-my
mid-dling
midg-et
mi-gnon-ette
mi-graine
mi-grain-oid
mi-grant
mi-gra-tet-ics
mi-gra-to-ry
mi-ka-do
Mi-lan
Mil-a-nese
mil-i-a-ri-a
mil-i-ar-y
mi-lieu
mil-i-tant
mil-i-ta-rism
mil-i-tate
mi-li-tia
milk-er
mil-le-nar-y
mil-len-ni-um
mill-er
mil-les-i-mal
mil-let
mil-li-am-me-ter
mil-li-ner-y
mil-lion-aire
Mim-e-o-graph
mi-met-ic
mim-e-tite
mim-ick-er
mim-ic-ry
mi-mo-sa
mi-mo-sine
min-a-ble
min-a-ret
minc-ing
mi-nen-wer-fer
min-er
min-er-ag-ra-phy
min-er-al-iz-er
min-er-al-og-i-cal
min-er-al-o-gy
Mi-ner-va
min-e-stro-ne
mi-nette
min-gling
min-i-a-ceous
min-i-a-ture
Min-ic
min-i-mize
min-i-mum
min-ion
min-is-te-ri-al
min-is-try
min-i-track
Min-ne-so-tan
mi-nom-e-ter
mi-nor-i-ty
min-strel
mint-age
mint-er
min-u-et
mi-nus-cu-lar
min-us-cule
min-ute (time)
mi-nute (small)
min-ute-ly (every minute)
mi-nute-ly (precisely)
mi-nu-ti-a
mi-o-sis
mi-ot-ic
mi-rab-i-lite
mir-a-cle
mi-rac-u-lous
mi-rage
mis-an-throp-ic
mis-an-thro-py
mis-ceg-e-na-tion
mis-cel-la-ne-ous
mis-cel-la-ny
mis-chie-vous
mis-ci-bil-i-ty
mis-cre-ant
mis-de-mean-or
mis-er-a-ble
Mis-e-re-re
mi-ser-ly
mis-er-y
mis-fea-sance
mis-no-mer
mi-sog-y-nist
mis-pri-sion
mis-sil-eer
mis-sile-ry
Mis-sis-sip-pi-an
mis-sive

Mis-sou-ri-an
mis-spelled
mis-tak-a-ble
mis-tak-en
mis-ter
mis-tle-toe
mis-tral
mis-tress
mi-ter
mit-i-ga-tor
mi-to-chon-dri-a
mi-to-sis
mi-tot-ic
mi-trail-leuse
mi-tral
mix-ture
mne-mon-ic
mo-bile
mo-bil-i-ty
mo-bi-li-za-tion
mo-bil-om-e-ter
mob-oc-ra-cy
moc-ca-sin
mo-cha
mock-er-y
mod-al-ism
mo-dal-i-ty
mod-eled
mod-er-a-tor
mod-ern-is-tic
mod-ern-ize
mod-es-ty
mod-i-cum
mod-i-fy
mod-ish
mo-diste
mod-u-la-bil-i-ty
mod-u-lar
mod-u-la-tor
mod-u-lus
mo-dus op-e-ran-di
Mo-ham-med-an
Mo-ha-ve
moi-e-ty
moi-re
moist-en-er
mois-ture
mo-lar-i-ty
mo-la-ry
mo-las-ses
mold-er
mo-lec-u-lar
mol-e-cule
mo-les-ta-tion
mol-ten
molt-er
mo-lyb-date
mo-lyb-de-num
mo-lyb-do-me-nite
mol-y-site
mo-men-tar-i-ly
mo-men-tar-y
mo-men-tous
mo-men-tum
mom-ism
Mon-a-can
mo-nad
mo-nad-ic
mo-nan-dry
mo-nar-chal
mo-nar-chi-cal
mon-ar-chist
mon-as-te-ri-al
mon-as-ter-y
mo-nas-tic
mon-a-tom-ic
mon-a-zite
mo-nel
mo-ne-sia
mon-e-tar-y
mon-e-tite
mon-e-tize
mon-eys
mon-ger
Mon-go-li-an
Mon-gol-oid
mon-grel
mon-i-ker
mo-nim-o-lite
mon-ism
mo-nis-tic
mon-i-to-ry
mon-keys
monk-ish
mon-o-ac-e-tin
mon-o-ac-id
mon-o-a-cid-ic
mon-o-am-ide
mon-o-a-mine
mon-o-chro-mous
mo-noch-ro-nous
mon-o-cle
mon-o-coque
mo-noc-ra-cy
mon-o-crot-ic
mo-noc-u-lar
mo-nog-a-my
mo-nog-o-ny
mon-o-gramed
mon-o-gram-mat-ic
mo-nog-ra-pher
mon-o-graph-ic
mo-nog-y-ny
mon-o-lith-ic

mon-o-log
mo-nol-o-gist
mo-nom-a-chy
mon-o-ma-ni-a
mon-o-mer
mo-nom-e-ter
mo-no-mi-al
mon-o-nu-cle-o-sis
mon-o-plane
mo-nop-o-lize
mo-nop-so-ny
mon-o-rail
mon-o-the-ism
mon-o-tone
mo-not-o-nous
mo-not-ro-py
mon-ox-ide
mon-sei-gneur
mon-sieur
mon-si-gnor
mon-ster
mon-stros-i-ty
mon-strous
mon-tage
Mon-tan-an
Mon-te-ne-grin
Mon-tes-so-ri
mon-tic-u-lous
mont-mo-ril-lon-ite
Mon-tre-al
mon-troy-dite
mon-u-men-tal
mon-zo-nite
Moor-ish
mo-quette
mo-raine
mor-al
mo-rale
mor-al-ist
mo-ral-i-ty
mor-al-ize
mo-rass-ic
mor-a-to-ri-um
Mo-ra-vi-an
mo-ra-vite
mor-bid-i-ty
mor-bose
mor-da-cious
mor-dac-i-ty
mor-dant
mo-reen
mo-rel-lo
mo-ren-cite
mo-res
mor-ga-nat-ic
mor-i-bund
mo-rin-done
mo-rin-ite
Mor-mon-ite
morn-ing
Mo-roc-co
mo-ron-ic
mo-ros-i-ty
mor-pheme
mor-phe-mics
Mor-pheus
mor-phine
mor-phog-ra-phy
mor-pho-line
mor-pho-log-i-cal
mor-phol-o-gy
mor-phom-e-try
mor-pho-sis
mor-phot-o-my
mor-tal-i-ty
mort-ga-gee
mort-ga-gor
mor-ti-cian
mor-ti-fi-ca-tion
mor-tis-er
mor-tu-ar-y
mo-sa-i-cism
mo-ses-ite
mos-qui-toes
mo-tel
moth-er
mo-til-i-ty
mo-ti-vate
mo-tor
mo-to-ri-al
mou-lage
mou-lin
moun-tain-eer
moun-te-bank
mount-er
mourn-er
mous-er
mous-que-taire
mousse-line
mov-a-ble
mov-ant
mov-er
mov-ie
mu-ce-dine
mu-ced-i-nous
mu-cic
mu-cif-er-ous
mu-ci-lage
mu-ci-lag-i-nous
mu-cin-o-gen
mu-cin-oid
mu-ci-no-lyt-ic
mu-coi-dal

mu-co-i-tin
mu-co-lyt-ic
mu-con-ic
mu-co-sa
mu-cos-i-ty
mu-cous (adj.)
mu-cus (n.)
mud-dled
muf-fler
Muh-len-berg
mu-lat-toes
mulch-er
mu-le-teer
mul-ish
mul-li-ga-taw-ny
mull-ite
mul-ti-far-i-ous
mul-tif-er-ous
Mul-ti-graph
Mul-ti-lith
mul-til-o-quent
mul-tim-e-ter
mul-tim-e-try
mul-tip-a-rous
mul-ti-par-tite
mul-ti-ple
mul-ti-plic-a-ble
mul-ti-pli-ca-tion
mul-ti-plic-i-ty
mul-ti-tu-di-nous
mul-ti-va-lent
mum-bling
Mun-chau-sen
mun-dane
Mu-nich
mu-nic-i-pal
mu-nif-i-cent
mu-ni-tion
mu-ral
mu-rar-i-um
mur-der-ous
mu-ri-at-ic
mu-rine
mu-ri-um
mur-mur-ous
mus-ca-dine
mus-ca-rine
mus-ca-tel
mus-cle
Mus-co-vite
mus-cu-lar
mus-cu-la-ture
mus-cu-lo-trop-ic
mu-se-ol-o-gy
mu-se-um
mu-si-cal
mu-si-col-o-gy
mus-ing
mus-ket-eer
mus-tache
mus-tard
mu-ta-bil-i-ty
mu-ta-gen-ic
mu-tant
mu-tase
mu-ta-tive
mu-ti-late
mu-ti-nous
mut-ism
mu-tu-al-ism
mu-zhik
muz-zling
my-al-gi-a
My-an-e-sin
my-as-the-ni-a
my-as-then-ic
my-ce-li-um
my-ce-to-ma
my-co-my-cin
my-co-sis
myc-ter-ic
my-dri-a-sine
my-dri-a-sis
myd-ri-at-ic
my-e-li-tis
my-e-lo-cyte
my-e-loid
my-e-lo-ma-to-sis
my-e-lom-a-tous
my-e-lop-a-thy
my-e-lo-sis
my-o-car-di-tis
my-op-a-thy
my-o-pi-a
my-op-ic
my-o-sin
my-o-si-tis
my-os-mine
my-ot-o-my
myr-i-ad
myr-i-am-e-ter
my-ric-e-tin
my-ric-i-trin
myr-i-cyl
myr-in-gi-tis
myr-in-got-o-my
my-ris-tate
myr-mi-don
myrrh-ic
myr-tle
mys-te-ri-ous
mys-ter-y
mys-ti-cal
mys-ti-fi-ca-tion

mys-tique
myth-i-cal
myth-o-log-i-cal
my-thol-o-gy
myx-o-bac-te-ri-al
myx-o-ma-to-sis

N

na-bob
na-celle
na-cre-ous
na-crite
na-dir
nad-or-ite
Na-ga-sa-ki
nah-co-lite
nail-er
nain-sook
na-ive
na-ive-te
na-ked
nam-a-ble
na-no-gram
na-palm
na-per-y
na-phaz-o-line
naph-tha
naph-tha-lene
naph-tha-len-ic
naph-thal-ic
naph-thene
naph-the-nic
naph-thi-o-nate
naph-thi-on-ic
naph-thol-ate
naph-tho-res-or-cin-ol
naphth-ox-y-a-ce-tic
naph-tho-yl
naph-thyl-a-mine
naph-thy-lene
Na-ples
Na-po-le-on
na-prap-a-thy
nar-cis-sism
nar-co-lep-sy
nar-co-sis
nar-cot-ic
nar-co-tol-ine
na-res
nar-in-gen-in
na-rin-gin
Nar-ra-gan-sett
nar-rat-a-ble
nar-ra-tor
na-sa-lis
na-sal-i-ty
nas-cent
na-so-scope
nas-ti-ly
nas-tur-tium
na-tal
na-tant
na-ta-to-ri-al
na-ta-to-ri-um
Natch-ez
Na-than-iel
na-tion-al-ist
na-tiv-is-tic
na-tiv-i-ty
na-tri-um
na-tro-lite
na-troph-i-lite
nat-u-ral-ist
nat-u-ral-ize
na-ture
na-tur-o-path
na-tur-op-a-thy
naugh-ti-ness
nau-pli-us
nau-se-ate
nau-seous
nau-ti-cal
nau-ti-lus
nau-to-phone
Nav-a-ho
na-val
nav-ar
na-vel
na-vic-u-lar
nav-i-ga-ble
nav-i-ga-tor
na-vite
Naz-a-rene
na-zism
Ne-an-der-thal
Ne-a-pol-i-tan
near-est
ne-ar-thro-sis
Ne-bras-kan
neb-u-lar
ne-bu-li-um
neb-u-los-i-ty
neb-u-lous
nec-es-sar-i-ly
ne-ces-si-tate
ne-ces-si-tous
nec-ro-bi-o-sis
nec-ro-log-i-cal
ne-crol-o-gy
nec-ro-man-cy
ne-crop-o-lis
ne-crop-sy
ne-cros-co-py
nec-ro-sin

ne-cro-sis
ne-crot-ic
ne-crot-o-my
nec-tar-ine
nec-ta-ry
nee-dler
ne-far-i-ous
ne-ga-tion
neg-a-tive
neg-a-to-ry
neg-a-tron
ne-glect-er
neg-li-gee
neg-li-gence
neg-li-gi-ble
ne-go-ti-a-ble
ne-go-ti-a-tor
Ne-gress
Ne-grit-ic
Ne-gro
Ne-groid
Ne-gus
neigh-bor
nei-ther
ne-mat-ic
nem-a-to-ci-dal
nem-a-tode
nem-a-to-di-a-sis
nem-a-tol-o-gy
Nem-bu-tal
ne-mes-ic
nem-e-sis
ne-moph-i-ly
nem-o-ral
Ne-o-ant-er-gan
ne-o-ars-phen-a-mine
ne-o-dym-i-um
ne-og-a-my
ne-o-lith-ic
ne-o-log-i-cal
ne-ol-o-gy
ne-o-my-cin
ne-on-tol-o-gy
ne-o-phyte
ne-o-pla-si-a
ne-o-prene
ne-o-stig-mine
Ne-o-sy-neph-rine
ne-o-ter-ic
ne-ot-o-cite
Ne-pal
Nep-a-lese
ne-pen-the
neph-e-lin-ite
neph-e-lite
neph-e-lom-e-ter
neph-e-lo-scope
neph-ew
ne-phol-o-gy
neph-o-scope
ne-phrec-to-my
neph-ric
ne-phrid-i-al
neph-rite
ne-phrit-ic
ne-phri-tis
ne-phrol-o-gy
neph-rop-to-sis
ne-phro-sis
ne-phrot-ic
ne-phrot-o-my
nep-i-on-ic
ne-pot-ic
nep-o-tism
nep-tu-ni-um
ne-rit-ic
ne-rol-i-dol
nerv-ate
nerv-ine
ner-von-ic
nerv-ous
ner-vule
ne-science
nest-ling (n.)
nes-tling (v.)
Nes-tor
neth-er
Ne-trop-sin
net-tled
Neuf-châ-tel
neu-ral-gia
neur-as-the-ni-a
neur-as-then-ic
neu-rec-to-my
neu-rine
neu-rit-ic
neu-ri-tis
neu-ro-blas-to-ma
neu-ro-crine
neu-ro-gen-ic
neu-rog-ra-phy
neu-roid
neu-ro-log-i-cal
neu-rol-o-gy
neu-rol-y-sis
neu-ro-path-ic
neu-rop-a-thy
neu-ro-sis
neu-rot-ic
neu-rot-i-cism
neu-rot-o-my
neu-ro-trop-ic
neu-rot-ro-pism
neu-ter
neu-tral-i-ty
neu-tral-iz-er
neu-tri-no
neu-tro-dyne
neu-tron
Ne-vad-an
ne-vus
new-com-er
New-to-ni-an
New Zea-land-er
nex-us
ni-a-cin-a-mide
Ni-ag-a-ra
nib-b'ing
Nic-a-ra-guan
ni-ce-ty
nick-el-if-er-ous
nick-el-ine
nick-el-o-de-on
nic-o-tin-a-mide
nic-o-tin-ate
nic-o-tin-ic
nic-o-ti-no-yl
nic-o-tin-u-ric
ni-dic-o-lous
nid-i-fi-cate
ni-dol-o-gy
Nietz-sche-ism
Ni-ger
Ni-ge-ri-a
ni-ger-ite
night-in-gale
ni-gres-cence
ni-grine
ni-grom-e-ter
ni-gro-sine
ni-grous
ni-hi-list
ni-lom-e-ter
nim-bly
nim-bo-stra-tus
ni-mi-e-ty
Nin-hy-drin
Ni-o-be
ni-o-bic
ni-o-bi-um
nip-e-cot-ic
Nip-pon-ese
Nir-va-na
Ni-sei
ni-sin
ni-ter
ni-tra-mine
ni-trate
ni-tra-tor
ni-tric
ni-trid-ize
ni-tri-fi-ca-tion
ni-trite
ni-tro-an-i-line
ni-tro-fu-ra-zone
ni-tro-gen-ate
ni-tro-gen-ize
ni-trog-e-nous
ni-tro-lic
ni-trom-e-ter
ni-tro-ni-um
ni-tros-a-mine
ni-tro-sate
ni-tro-so
ni-tro-tol-u-ene
ni-tro-tol-u-ol
ni-trous
ni-trox-yl-ene
ni-tryl
No-bel
no-bel-i-um
no-bil-i-ty
no-blesse
no-bly
no-car-di-o-sis
no-cer-ite
no-ci-cep-tor
noc-tam-bu-list
noc-ti-lu-cine
noc-tiv-a-gant
noc-tur-nal
noc-turne
noc-u-ous
nod-al
no-dal-i-ty
nod-u-lar
nod-ule
no-e-ma-ta-chom-e-ter
nois-i-ly
noi-some
no-lo con-ten-de-re
no-mad-ic
no-men-cla-ture
no-mi-al
nom-i-nal-ize
nom-i-nat-ed
nom-i-na-tion
nom-i-na-tive
no-moc-ra-cy
nom-o-gram
nom-o-graph-ic
no-mog-ra-phy
non-a-co-sane
non-a-dec-ane
non-a-ge-nar-i-an
no-nane
non-a-no-ic
no-na-nol
non-cha-lance
non-de-script
no-nene
non-en-ti-ty
no-no-ic
non-pa-reil
non-plused
non pro-se-qui-tur
non se-qui-tur
non-yl-ene
no-nyl-ic
noo-dle
no-ol-o-gy
no-pi-nene
Nor-dic
nor-di-hy-dro-guai-a-ret-ic
nor-mal-i-ty
nor-mal-iz-er
nor-ma-tive
North-amp-ton
north-ern
North-um-ber-land
Nor-we-gian
no-se-lite
no-sog-ra-phy
no-sol-o-gist
nos-tal-gi-a
nos-tril
nos-trum
nos-y
no-ta-ble
no-tam
no-tar-i-al
no-ta-ry
notch-er
noth-ing
no-tice-a-ble
no-ti-fi-ca-tion
no-to-ri-e-ty
no-to-ri-ous
nou-gat
nour-ish
nou-veau
nov-el-ette
nov-el-ist
no-vel-la
nov-el-ty
No-vem-ber
no-ve-na
nov-ice
no-vi-ti-ate
no-vo-cain
nox-ious
Nu-bi-an
nu-cle-ar
nu-cle-ate
nu-cle-in-a-tion
nu-cle-og-o-ny
nu-cle-o-his-tone
nu-cle-o-lar
nu-cle-ol-y-sis
nu-cle-om-e-ter
nu-cle-on-ics
nu-cle-o-tid-ase
nu-cle-us
nu-clide
nu-clid-ic
nudg-er
nud-ism
nu-di-ty
nu-ga-to-ry
nui-sance
nul-li-ty
num-bered
nu-mer-al
nu-mer-a-tive
nu-mer-a-tor
nu-mer-i-cal
nu-mer-ol-o-gy
nu-mis-mat-ics
nu-mis-ma-tist
num-skull
nun-ci-a-ture
nup-tial
nup-ti-al-i-ty
Nur-em-berg
nurs-er
nurs-er-y
nur-tur-al
nu-tri-a
nu-tri-ent
nu-tri-lite
nu-tri-tious
nu-tri-tive
nyc-ta-lo-pi-a
ny-lon
nym-pha
nymph-al
nys-tag-mus
nys-ta-tin
ny-tril

O

oak-en
oa-kum
o-a-sis
ob-bli-ga-to
ob-du-ra-cy
ob-du-rate
o-be-di-ence
o-bei-sance
o-be-li-al
ob-e-lisk
o-be-si-ty
ob-fus-ca-to-ry
o-bit-u-ar-y
ob-jec-tee
ob-jec-tiv-ism
ob-jec-tiv-i-ty
ob-jec-tor
ob-ju-ra-tion
ob-jur-gate
ob-last
ob-la-to-ry
ob-li-ga-tor
o-blig-a-to-ry
ob-li-gee
o-blig-ing
ob-li-gor
o-blique
ob-liq-ui-ty
ob-lit-er-ate
ob-li-ves-cence
ob-liv-i-on
ob-liv-i-ous
ob-long-at-ed
ob-lo-quy
ob-mu-tes-cence
ob-nox-ious
ob-nu-bi-la-tion
ob-o-lus
ob-scen-i-ty
ob-scu-ran-tism
ob-scu-ri-ty
ob-se-qui-ous
ob-seq-ui-ty
ob-se-quy
ob-serv-ance
ob-serv-ant
ob-ser-va-tion
ob-serv-a-to-ry
ob-serv-er
ob-ses-sion
ob-sid-i-an
ob-so-les-cence
ob-so-lete
ob-sta-cle
ob-ste-tri-cian
ob-stet-rics
ob-sti-na-cy
ob-strep-er-ous
ob-struc-tive
ob-struc-tor
ob-tru-sive
ob-tund-ent
ob-tu-ra-tor
ob-tu-si-ty
ob-ver-tend
oc-a-ri-na
oc-ca-sion
oc-ci-den-tal
oc-cip-i-ta-lis
oc-cip-i-to-pa-ri-e-tal
oc-ci-put
oc-clu-sal
oc-clu-sion
oc-cul-ta-tion
oc-cult-ism
oc-cu-pan-cy
oc-cu-pa-tive
oc-curred
oc-cur-rence
o-cea-nar-i-um
o-ce-an-ic
o-cean-o-graph-ic
o-cean-og-ra-phy
oc-el-late
o-ce-lot
o-cher-ous
och-loc-ra-cy
o-chro-no-sis
oc-ta-co-sane
oc-ta-dec-a-di-e-no-ic
oc-ta-dec-ane
oc-ta-dec-a-no-ic
oc-ta-dec-yl
oc-ta-gon
oc-tag-o-nal
oc-ta-he-dron
oc-ta-mer
oc-tam-er-ous
oc-tam-e-ter
oc-tane
oc-tan-gu-lar
oc-ta-no-ate
oc-ta-nol
oc-ta-no-yl
oc-ta-vos
Oc-to-ber
oc-to-ge-nar-i-an
oc-tog-e-nar-y
oc-to-ic
Oc-top-o-da
oc-to-pus
oc-to-roon
oc-tose
oc-tu-ple
oc-tup-let
oc-tyl-ene
oc-u-lar
oc-u-list
oc-u-lo-gy-ric
o-da-lisque
odd-i-ty
o-dif-er-ous
o-di-om-e-ter
o-di-ous
od-ist
o-di-um
o-dom-e-ter
o-don-ti-tis
o-don-to-gen-ic
o-don-tol-o-gy
o-don-tom-e-ter
o-don-tot-o-my
o-dor-ant
o-dor-if-er-ous
o-dor-om-e-ter
o-dor-ous
Od-ys-sey
oed-i-pal
oe-nan-thic
oer-sted
of-fal
of-fend-er
of-fen-sive
of-fer-to-ry
of-fi-cer
of-fi-cial
of-fi-ci-ate
of-fic-i-nal
of-fi-cious
off-ing
of-ten
o-gi-val
o-gre-ish
O-hi-o-an
ohm-ic
ohm-me-ter
oil-er
oi-ti-ci-ca
o-ken-ite
O-ki-na-wan
O-kla-ho-man
ok-o-nite
o-kra
old-en
old-ster
o-le-ag-i-nous
o-le-an-der
o-le-an-drin
o-lec-ra-non
o-le-fin-ic
o-le-ic
o-le-in-ic
o-le-og-ra-phy
o-le-o-mar-ga-rine
o-le-om-e-ter
o-le-o-res-in
o-le-o-yl
ol-fac-tom-e-ter
ol-fac-to-ry
ol-i-gar-chi-cal
ol-i-gar-chy
ol-i-ge-mi-a
ol-i-go-chro-ne-mi-a
ol-i-go-clase
ol-i-go-dy-nam-ic
ol-i-go-nite
ol-i-gop-o-ly
ol-i-gop-so-ny
ol-i-va-ceous
ol-i-var-y
o-liv-en-ite
ol-i-ves-cence
ol-i-vine
O-lym-pi-an
O-ma-ha
om-bro-graph
om-brom-e-ter
om-buds-man
o-me-ga
om-e-let
o-men-ol-o-gy
om-i-cron
om-i-nous
o-mis-si-ble
o-mis-sion
o-mit-ted
om-ni-bus
om-nif-i-cence
om-nim-e-ter
om-nip-o-tence
om-ni-science
om-niv-o-rous
om-pha-li-tis
on-a-ger
on-co-gen-ic
on-cog-e-ny
on-col-o-gy
on-col-y-sis
on-com-e-ter
on-cot-o-my
on-dom-e-ter
on-du-le
O-nei-da
on-er-ous
on-ion
on-o-ma-si-ol-o-gy
on-o-mat-o-poe-ia
On-on-da-ga
On-tar-i-an
on-tog-e-ny
on-to-log-i-cal
on-tol-o-gy
on-y-chol-y-sis
on-y-cho-my-co-sis
on-y-choph-a-gy
on-y-cho-sis
o-ol-o-gy
o-pa-cim-e-ter
o-pac-i-ty
o-pal-es-cent
o-pal-ine
o-paqu-er
o-paqu-ing
o-pei-do-scope
op-er-a
op-er-a-ble
op-er-and
op-er-ate
op-er-at-ic
op-er-a-tive
op-er-a-tor
o-per-cu-lar
oph-i-cleide
o-phid-i-an
o-phi-ol-o-gy
o-phit-ic
oph-thal-mi-a
oph-thal-mic
oph-thal-mo-log-ic
oph-thal-mol-o-gy
oph-thal-mom-e-ter
oph-thal-mo-met-ric
oph-thal-mo-scope
oph-thal-mos-co-py
o-pi-an-ic
o-pi-ate
o-pin-ion-at-ed
o-pin-ion-a-tor
op-i-som-e-ter
o-pis-tho-gas-tric
o-pi-um
o-pos-sum
op-po-nent
op-por-tun-ism
op-por-tun-ist
op-por-tu-ni-ty
op-pos-al
op-po-site
op-press-i-ble
op-pres-sive
op-pres-sor
op-pro-bri-um
op-ti-cal
op-ti-cian
op-ti-mal-ize
op-ti-me
op-tim-e-ter
op-ti-mism
op-ti-mis-tic
op-ti-mum
op-tom-e-ter
op-to-met-ric
op-tom-e-try
op-u-lent
or-a-cle
o-rac-u-lar
o-ral-ly
or-ange
o-ran-ge-lo
or-ange-ry
o-rang-u-tan
o-ra-tion
or-a-tor
or-a-tor-i-cal
or-a-to-ri-o
or-bic-u-lar
or-bit-al
or-bit-ed
or-bit-er
or-bit-ing
or-chard
or-ches-tra
or-chi-da-ceous
or-chid-ol-o-gy
or-cin-ol
or-deal
or-dered
or-di-nal
or-di-nance
or-di-nar-i-ly
or-di-nar-y
ord-nance
Or-do-vi-cian
Or-e-go-ni-an
or-gan-dy
or-gan-ic
or-ga-nism
or-gan-ist
or-ga-niz-a-ble
or-ga-ni-za-tion
or-ga-niz-er
or-gan-o-gel
or-ga-no-gen-ic
or-ga-nog-e-ny
or-ga-nog-ra-phy
or-ga-nos-co-py
or-gan-o-sol
or-gi-as-tic
o-ri-el
O-ri-ent
o-ri-en-tal
o-ri-en-ta-lia
o-ri-en-ta-tor
o-ri-en-tite
or-i-fi-cial
or-i-flamme
or-i-gin
o-rig-i-nal-i-ty
o-rig-i-nat-ing
o-rig-i-na-tive

o-ri-ole
O-ri-on
or-is-mol-o-gy
or-i-son
Or-lan-do
Or-le-ans
Or-lon
or-mo-lu
or-na-men-tal
or-ner-y
or-ni-thine
or-ni-tho-log-i-cal
or-ni-thol-o-gy
or-ni-thop-ter
or-ni-tho-rhyn-chus
or-ni-tho-sis
or-ni-thot-o-my
or-nith-u-ric
o-rog-e-ny
o-rog-ra-phy
o-ro-ide
o-rol-o-gy
o-rom-e-ter
or-o-met-ric
o-ro-tun-di-ty
or-phan-age
or-pi-ment
or-ris
or-sel-lin-ic
or-tha-nil-ic
or-thi-con
or-tho-ar-se-nate
or-tho-ben-zo-qui-none
or-tho-clase
or-tho-don-ti-a
or-tho-don-tist
or-tho-dox-y
or-tho-e-py
or-tho-for-mic
or-thog-o-nal
or-thog-ra-phy
or-thom-e-try
or-tho-pe-dic
or-tho-pe-dist
or-thop-ne-a
Or-thop-ter-a
or-thop-tics
or-tho-sis
or-tho-typ-ic
or-to-lan
o-ryc-tol-o-gy
o-ryc-tog-no-sy
o-sa-zone
Os car
os-cil-la-tor
os cil-la-to-ry
os-cil-lom-e-ter
os-cil-lo-scope
os-ci-tant
os-cu-la-to-ry
os-cu-lom-e-ter
O-si-ris
os-mi-dro-sis
os-mi-rid-i-um
os-mi-um
os-mom-e-ter
os-mo-met-ric
os-mom-e-try
os-mo-sis
os-mot-ic
os-phre-sis
os-prey
os-se-ous
os-si-cle
os-sic-u-lar
os-si-cu-lec-to-my
os-sif-i-ca-to-ry
os-si-fy
os-te-al
os-te-it-ic
os-te-i-tis
os-ten-si-ble
os-ten-ta-tious
os-te-o-chon-dro-sis
os-te-ol-o-gy
os-te-ol-y-sis
os-te-o-ma
os-te-o-ma-tous
os-te-om-e-try
os-te-o-my-e-li-tis
os-te-o-path
os-te-op-a-thy
os-te-ot-o-my
os-tra-cism
os-tra-cize
os-trich
o-tal-gi-a
o-the-o-scope
oth-er
o-ti-ose
o-ti-os-i-ty
o-ti-tis me-di-a
o-tog-e-nous
o-to-lar-yn-go-log-i-cal
o-to-lar-yn-gol-o-gy
o-tos-co-py
o-to-sis
oua-ba-in
ou-bli-ette
ou-ri-cu-ry
oust-er
out-er
out-land-ish
out-law-ry
out-ra-geous
out-rag-er
ou-trance
out-rid-er
out-sid-er
o-val-i-form
o-val-i-ty
o-var-i-an
o-var-i-ec-to-my
o-var-i-ole
o-var-i-ot-o-my
o-va-ri-tis
o-va-ry
ov-en
o-ver-head
o-ver-land-er
o-ver-se-er
o-ver-ture
o-vi-ci-dal
o-vic-u-lar
O-vid-i-an
o-vi-na-tion
o-vip-a-ra
o-vi-par-i-ty
o-vip-a-rous
o-vi-pos-i-tor
o-vu-lar
o-vu-la-to-ry
ow-ing
own-er
ox-a-late
ox-al-ic
ox-al-u-ric
ox-a-lyl
ox-am-ide
ox-am-i-dine
ox-an-i-late
ox-a-nil-ic
ox-a-zine
ox-a-zol-i-dine
ox-i-dant
ox-i-dase
ox-i-da-tion
ox-ide
ox-i-dim-e-try
ox-i-diz-a-ble
ox-i-diz-er
ox-id-u-lat-ed
ox-im-e-ter
ox-i-met-ric
ox-in-dole
ox-o-ni-um
ox-o-phen-ar-sine
ox-y-a-can-thine
ox-y-a-cet-y-lene
ox-y-gen
ox-y-gen-ate
ox-y-gen-ize
ox-y-lu-cif-er-in
ox-y-tet-ra-cy-cline
ox-y-to-cin
oys-ter
Oz-al-id
O-zark-i-an
o-zo-ke-rite
o-zon-ate
o-zon-ide
o-zon-iz-er
o-zon-ol-y-sis
o-zo-no-sphere

P

pab-u-lum
pac-er
pa-chi-si
pach-no-lite
pach-y-der-ma-tous
pa-chym-e-ter
pac-i-fi-a-ble
pa-cif-ic
pac-i-fi-ca-tion
pa-cif-i-ca-to-ry
pac-i-fist
pac-i-fy
pack-ag-er
pack-et
pad-dling
pa-dre
pa-dro-ne
Pad-u-an
pae-an
pa-gan-ism
pag-eant-ry
pag-er
pag-i-nal
pag-i-nate
pag-ing
pa-go-da
pains-tak-ing
paint-er
Pais-ley
Pak-i-stan-i
pal-ace
pa-la-ceous
pal-a-din
pal-an-quin
pal-at-a-bil-i-ty
pal-at-a-ble
pal-a-tal-ize
pal-ate (roof of mouth)
pa-la-tial
pa-lat-i-nate
pal-a-tine
pal-a-ti-tis
pal-a-to-gram
pa-lav-er
pa-le-a-ceous
pa-le-og-ra-pher
pa-le-ol-o-gy
pa-le-on-tol-o-gy
Pa-le-o-zo-ic
Pal-es-tin-i-an
pal-ette (artist's board)
pal-frey
pa-lil-o-gy
pal-imp-sest
pal-in-drome
pal-i-sade
pal-la-di-um
pal-let (a bed)
pal-let-ize
pal-lette (armor)
pal-li-a-tive
pal-mate
palm-er
pal-met-to
palm-is-try
pal-mit-ic
pal-mit-o-le-ic
pal-o-mi-no
pal-pa-ble
pal-pi-tate
pal-sy
pal-try
pal-u-drine
pa-lus-trine
pal-y-nol-o-gy
pam-a-quine
Pam-e-la
pam-pas
pam-pe-an
pam-per
pam-phlet
pam-phlet-eer
pam-phlet-ize
pan-a-ce-a
pa-nache (headdress)
pa-na-che (food)
Pan-a-ma-ni-an
pan-a-ry
pan-a-tel-a
pan-car-di-tis
pan-chro-mat-ic
pan-cre-as
pan-cre-a-tec-to-my
pan-cre-a-tin
pan-cre-a-ti-tis
pan-cre-o-zy-min
pan-dem-ic
pan-de-mo-ni-um
pan-der
pan-e-gyr-ic
pan-e-gy-rize
pan-el-ist
pan-go-lin
pan-icked
pan-i-cle
pa-nic-u-late
pan-mne-si-a
pan-nic-u-li-tis
pan-nier
pa-no-cha
pan-o-ply
pan-o-ram-a
pan-o-ram-ic
pan-soph-ic
pan-tag-a-my
Pan-ta-gru-el
pan-ta-loon
pan-tarch-y
pan-te-the-ine
pan-the-ism
pan-the-on
pan-ther
pant-i-soc-ra-cy
pan-to-chro-mism
pan-to-graph
pan-tog-ra-pher
pan-to-ic
pan-tol-o-gy
pan-tom-e-ter
pan-to-mime
pan-to-then-ic
pan-to-yl
pan-try
pa-pa-cy
pa-pa-in-ase
Pa-pa-ni-co-laou
pa-par-chy
pa-pav-er-ine
pa-paw
pa-pay-a
pa-per
pa-pier ma-che
pa-pil-la
pap-il-lar-y
pap-il-lo-ma-to-sis
pap-il-lom-a-tous
pa-pism
pa-poose
pa-pri-ka
Pap-u-an
pap-u-lar
pap-y-ra-ceous
pap-y-rin
pa-py-rus
par-a-ban-ic
par-a-ba-sic
pa-rab-a-sis
par-a-bi-o-sis
par-a-ble
pa-rab-o-la
par-a-bol-i-cal
pa-rab-o-loi-dal
par-a-chor
par-a-chord-al
pa-rach-ro-nism
par-a-chut-ist
par-a-clete
pa-rad-er
par-a-digm
par-a-dise
par-a-di-si-a-cal
par-a-dox
par-af-fin-ic
par-a-gly-co-gen
par-a-go-ge
par-a-gog-ic
par-a-gon
pa-rag-o-nite
par-a-graph-er
Par-a-guay-an
par-a-keet
par-al-de-hyde
par-al-lac-tic
par-al-leled
par-al-lel-e-pi-ped
par-al-lel-e-pip-e-don
par-al-lel-ing
par-al-lel-om-e-ter
pa-ral-o-gize
pa-ral-y-sis
par-a-lyt-ic
par-a-lyzed
pa-ram-e-ter
par-a-mide
par-a-mi-no-ben-zo-ic
par-a-mor-phism
par-a-mour
par-a-noi-a
par-a-noi-ac
par-a-noi-dal
par-ant-he-lion
par-a-pet-ed
par-a-pha-si-a
par-a-pher-na-lia
par-a-phrase
pa-raph-ra-sis
pa-raph-y-sis
par-a-ple-gi-a
par-a-ple-gic
pa-rap-sis
par-a-se-le-ne
par-a-sit-e-mi-a
par-a-sit-i-cal
par-a-sit-i-ci-dal
par-a-sit-ism
par-a-si-tize
par-a-si-to-sis
par-a-sol
pa-rat-ro-phy
par-celed
par-don-a-ble
par-e-gor-ic
pa-ren-chy-ma
par-en-chym-a-tous
par-ent-age
pa-ren-tal
par-en-ter-al
pa-ren-the-sis
par-en-thet-i-cal
par-er-gon
pa-re-sis
pa-ret-ic
par-he-lion
pa-ri-ah
pa-ri-e-tal
pa-ri-e-to-fron-tal
par-i-mu-tu-el
par-i-nar-ic
par-ing
Par-is
par-ish
pa-rish-ion-er
Pa-ri-sian
Pa-ri-si-enne
par-i-son
par-i-ty
Par-ker
park-er
par-lance
par-lia-men-tar-i-an
par-lia-men-ta-ry
par-lous
pa-ro-chi-al
par-o-dis-tic
par-o-dy
pa-rol
pa-role
pa-rol-ee
par-o-nych-i-a
par-o-nym
pa-ron-y-mous
pa-rot-id
pa-rot-i-dec-to-my
par-o-tit-ic
par-o-ti-tis
par-ox-ysm
par-ox-ys-mal
par-quet-ry
par-ri-ci-dal
par-si-mo-ni-ous
pars-ley
pars-nip
par-son-age
par-tage
par-tak-er
part-er
par-terre
Par-the-non
par-ti-al-i-ty
par-tial-ly
par-ti-bil-i-ty
par-tic-i-pant
par-tic-i-pa-tor
par-ti-cip-i-al
par-ti-ci-ple
par-ti-cle
par-tic-u-lar-i-ty
par-tic-u-late
par-ti-san
par-ti-tion-er
par-ti-tive
par-tridge
par-tu-ri-tion
pa-ru-lis
par-ve-nu
pas-chal
pa-sha
pas-i-graph-ic
pa-sig-ra-phy
pas-quin-ade
pass-a-ble
pas-sa-ca-glia
pas-sage
pas-sé
pas-sen-ger
pas-ser (bird)
pass-er
pas-si-ble
pas-sim-e-ter
pass-ing
pas-sion-ate
pas-si-va-tor
pas-siv-ist
pas-siv-i-ty
pas-som-e-ter
pass-o-ver
pas-tel
past-er
pas-tern
pas-teur-i-za-tion
pas-tiche
pas-tille
pas-time
pas-tor
pas-to-ral
pas-to-rale
pas-tor-ate
pas-tra-mi
pas-try
pas-tur-age
Pat-a-go-ni-an
Pa-taps-co
patch-er-y
patch-ou-li
pa-tel-la
pat-ent-ee
pat-en-tor
pa-ter-fa-mil-i-as
pa-ter-nal
pa-ter-ni-ty
pa-ter-nos-ter
pa-thet-ic
path-o-don-ti-a
path-o-gen-ic
path-o-ge-nic-i-ty
pa-thog-e-ny
pa-thog-no-my
path-o-log-i-cal
pa-thol-o-gist
pa-thol-o-gy
pa-thom-e-ter
pa-thos
pa-tho-sis
pa-tien-cy
pat-i-na
pat-i-o
pa-tois
pa-tri-ar-chal
pa-tri-arch-ate
pa-tri-arch-y
pa-tri-cian
pat-ri-cid-al
pat-ri-mo-ni-al
pat-ri-mo-ny
pa-tri-ot-ic
pa-tri-ot-ism
pa-tris-tic
pa-trolled
pa-trol-ling
pa-tron-age
pa-tron-ess
pat-ro-nite
pa-tron-ize
pat-ro-nym-ic
pa-tron-y-my
pa-troon
pat-terned
pau-ci-ty
Pau-li-na
Pau-line
Paul-ine (of Paul)
Paul-ist
pau-lo-post
pau-per-ize
paus-al
pav-er
pa-vil-ion
Pav-lov-i-an
pav-o-nite
pawn-ee (pledgee)
Paw-nee (Indian)
pay-ee
pay-o-la
peace-a-ble
peaked (topped)
peak-ed (pale)
pearl-es-cent
pearl-ite
peas-ant-ry
pe-can
pec-ca-ble
pec-ca-dil-lo
pec-cant
pec-ca-ry
pec-tin-ase
pec-ti-nate
pec-tin-ic
pec-to-lyt-ic
pec-to-ral
pec-to-ril-o-quy
pec-tous (chemistry)
pec-tus (zoology)
pe-cu-liar
pe-cu-li-ar-i-ty
pe-cu-ni-ar-y
ped-a-gog
ped-a-gog-i-cal
ped-a-gog-y
ped-aled
ped-al-ine
ped-ant
pe-dan-tic
ped-ant-ry
ped-dler
Pe-der-sen
ped-es-tal
pe-des-tri-an
pe-di-at-ric
pe-di-a-tri-cian
ped-i-cel
ped-i-cle
pe-dic-u-lar
Pe-dic-u-lar-is
pe-dic-u-lo-sis
pe-dic-u-lous (adj.)
Pe-dic-u-lus (n.)
ped-i-cure
ped-i-gree
ped-o-cal
pe-dol-o-gy
pe-dom-e-ter
ped-o-met-ri-cal
pe-dun-cu-lar
peel-er
peep-er
peer-age
pee-vish
Peg-a-sus
peg-ma-tite
peg-ma-tit-ic
peign-oir
pei-ram-e-ter
pej-o-ra-tive
Pe-king-ese
pe-koe
pe-lag-ic
pel-ar-go-nate
pel-ar-gon-ic
pel-ar-gon-i-din
pel-ar-go-nin
pel-er-ine
pel-i-can
pe-lisse
pel-la-gra
pel-let-er
pel-lu-cid-i-ty
pel-mat-o-gram
pe-lo-rus
pelt-er (n.)
pel-ter (v.)
pelt-ry
pel-vic
pel-vim-e-ter
pem-mi-can
pe-nal-ize
pen-al-ty
pen-ance
pe-na-tes
pench-ant
pen-ciled
pend-ant (n.)
pend-en-cy
pend-ent (adj.)
pen-du-los-i-ty
pen-du-lum
Pe-nel-o-pe
pen-e-tra-ble
pen-e-tram-e-ter
pen-e-tra-tive
pen-e-tra-tor
pen-e-trom-e-ter
pen-guin
pen-i-cil-lin
pen-i-cil-lin-ase
pen-i-cil-li-o-sis
pe-nin-su-lar
pen-i-tent
pen-i-ten-tia-ry

pen-ni-nite
Penn-syl-va-nian
Pe-nob-scot
pe-no-log-i-cal
pe-nol-o-gy
Pen-sa-co-la
pen-sive
pent-ac-id
pen-ta-cle
pen-tad
pen-ta-dec-ane
pen-ta-dec-yl
pen-ta-e-ryth-ri-tol
pen-ta-gon
pen-tag-o-nal
pen-ta-he-dral
pen-ta-hy-drite
pen-ta-mer
pen-tam-er-al
pen-tam-er-ous (adj.)
pen-tam-er-us (n.)
pen-tam-e-ter
pent-am-i-dine
pen-tane
pen-ta-no-ic
pen-ta-ploi-dic
pen-tarch-y
pen-ta-rone
Pen-ta-teuch
pen-tath-lon
pen-ta-tom-ic
pen-ta-va-lent
Pen-te-cos-tal
pen-te-nyl
pen-ti-tol
pen-to-bar-bi-tal
pen-tode
pen-tom-ic
pen-to-san
Pen-to-thal
pent-ox-ide
pen-tryl
pen-tu-lose
pen-tyl-ene
pen-tyl-i-dene
pe-nul-ti-mate
pe-num-bra
pe-nu-ri-ous
pen-u-ry
pe-on-age
pe-o-ny
peo-ple
Pe-o-ri-a
pe-pi-no
pep-lum
pep-si-gogue
pep-sin-if-er-ous
pep-sin-o-gen
pep-ti-dase
pep-to-nate
pep-to-nize
per-a-ce-tic
per-am-bu-la-tor
per-bo-rate
Per-bu-nan
per-ca-line
per-ceiv-a-ble
per-ceiv-er
per-cent-age
per-cent-ile
per-cep-ti-ble
per-cep-tive
per-cep-tu-al
perch-er
Per-che-ron
per-chlo-rate
per-chlo-ryl
per-cip-i-ent
per-co-la-tor
per cu-ri-am
per-cus-sive
per-e-gri-nate
pe-rei-ra
pe-remp-tive
pe-remp-to-ry
pe-ren-ni-al
per-fect-er
per-fect-i-ble
per-fec-tor
per-fer-vid
per-fid-i-ous
per-fi-dy
per-fo-ra-tor
per-form-ance
per-form-er
per-fum-er-y
per-func-to-ry
per-i-anth
per-i-ar-thri-tis
per-i-as-tron
per-i-car-di-tis
per-i-car-di-um
per-i-cla-site
Per-i-cle-an
pe-ric-o-pe
per-i-cop-ic
pe-rid-i-um
pe-rid-o-tite
per-i-gee
pe-rig-y-nous
per-i-he-lion
per-iled
per-il-ous
pe-rim-e-ter
per-i-met-ri-cal
pe-rim-e-try
per-i-ne-al
per-i-ne-or-rha-phy
per-i-neph-ri-um
per-i-ne-um
pe-ri-od-ic (at intervals)
per-i-od-ic (chemistry)
pe-ri-od-i-cal
pe-ri-o-dic-i-ty
per-i-os-te-um
per-i-pa-tet-ic
pe-riph-er-al-ly
pe-riph-er-y
per-i-phrase
pe-riph-ra-sis
pe-rip-ter-al
pe-rip-ter-y
pe-rique
pe-ris-cil
per-i-scop-ic
per-ish
per-i-som-al
pe-ris-sad
per-i-stal-tic
per-i-sta-sis
per-i-sty-lar
pe-rit-o-my
per-i-to-ne-os-co-py
per-i-to-ne-um
per-i-to-nit-ic
per-i-to-ni-tis
per-i-win-kle
per-jur-er
per-ju-ri-ous
per-ju-ry
per-lite
per-ma-frost
Perm-al-loy
per-ma-nent
per-man-ga-nate
per-me-a-ble
per-me-am-e-ter
Per-mi-an
per-mis-si-ble
per-mit-tee
per-mut-a-ble
per-mu-ta-tor
per-ni-cious
per-ni-o-sis
per-o-ne-al
Pe-ro-nist
per-o-ra-tion
pe-ro-sis
per-ox-i-dase
per-ox-ide
per-ox-y-a-ce-tic
per-ox-y-di-sul-fate
per-pen-dic-u-lar
per-pe-tra-tor
per-pet-u-al
per-pe-tu-i-ty
per-qui-site
per-se-cu-tion
per-se-cu-to-ry
Per-se-id
per-se-i-tol
per-se-ver-ance
per-sev-er-a-tive
Per-shing
Per-sian
per-si-flage
per-sist-ence
per-sist-er
per-snick-e-ty
per-son-a-ble
per-son-al-i-ty
per-son-al-ty
per-son-nel
per-spec-tive
per-spec-tom-e-ter
per-spi-ca-cious
per-spi-cac-i-ty
per-spi-cu-i-ty
per-spic-u-ous
per-spir-a-ble
per-spi-ra-tion
per-spir-a-tive
per-spir-a-to-ry
per-suad-er
per-sua-si-ble
per-sua-sive
perth-ite
per-ti-na-cious
per-ti-nac-i-ty
per-ti-nent
per-turb-a-ble
per-tur-ba-tion
per-turb-er
pe-rus-al
Pe-ru-vi-an
per-va-sive
per-ver-sion
per-ver-si-ty
per-vert-i-ble
per-vi-ca-cious
per-vi-cac-i-ty
per-vi-ous
per-y-lene
pe-se-ta
Pe-sha-war
pes-sa-ry
pes-si-mis-tic
pes-tered
pes-ti-ci-dal
pes-tif-er-ous
pes-ti-lence
pes-tle
pes-tol-o-gy
pet-al-if-er-ous
pet-al-ite
pet-al-ous
pet-al-y
pe-tard
pe-te-chi-al
Pe-ter
pet-i-o-lar
pet-i-ole
pet-it
pe-tite
pe-ti-tion-er
Pe-trar-chan
Pe-trarch-ist
pe-trel
pe-tres-cence
pe-tri
pet-ri-fac-tion
pe-tro-chem-i-cal
pe-trog-e-ny
pe-trog-ra-pher
pet-ro-graph-i-cal
pe-trog-ra-phy
pet-rol
pet-ro-lage
pet-ro-la-tum
pet-ro-lene
pe-tro-le-um
pe-trol-ic
pet-ro-lif-er-ous
pet-ro-lize
pet-ro-log-ic
pe-trol-o-gy
pe-tro-sal
pet-rous
pe-trox-o-lin
pet-u-lant
pe-tu-nia
pe-yo-te
pha-com-e-ter
pha-e-ton
phag-o-cyte
phag-o-cyt-ic
phag-o-cy-to-sis
pha-lange
pha-lan-ge-al
pha-lanx
phal-loi-dine
phan-er-ite
phan-er-o-gam
phan-er-os-co-py
phan-er-o-sis
phan-o-tron
phan-tas-ma-go-ri-al
phan-tas-mal
phan-tom
phan-to-scope
Phar-aoh
phar-i-sa-i-cal
Phar-i-see
phar-ma-ceu-ti-cal
phar-ma-cist
phar-ma-cog-no-sy
phar-mac-o-lite
phar-ma-col-o-gy
phar-ma-co-peia
pha-ryn-ge-al
phar-yn-gi-tis
pha-ryn-go-log-i-cal
phar-yn-gol-o-gy
pha-ryn-go-scope
phar-ynx
phase-me-ter
pha-se-o-lin
phas-er (one who phases)
pha-sic
pha-si-tron
pha-sor (electrical)
pheas-ant
phel-lan-drene
phen-ac-e-tin
phen-a-cite
phen-a-cyl
phen-an-threne
phen-an-thri-dine
phe-nan-thri-din-i-um
phe-nan-thro-line
phe-nan-thryl
phen-ar-sa-zine
phen-a-zine
phe-net-i-dine
phen-e-tole
phe-nic
phen-mi-az-ine
phe-no-bar-bi-tal
phe-no-cop-ic
phe-no-crys-tic
phe-nol
phe-no-lase
phe-no-late
phe-no-lic
phe-no-log-i-cal
phe-nol-o-gy
phe-nol-phthal-ein
phe-nom-e-nal
phe-nom-e-no-log-i-cal
phe-nom-e-nol-o-gy
phe-no-plast
phe-no-type
phen-ox-ide
phe-nox-y-a-ce-tic
phen-tol-a-mine
phen-yl-ac-et-al-de-hyde
phen-yl-ate
phen-yl-ene
phen-yl-eph-rine
phen-yl-eth-yl-ene
phe-nyl-ic
phen-yl-ke-to-nu-ric
phe-nyt-o-in
phe-o-chro-mo-cy-to-ma
phe-o-phor-bide
phe-o-phy-tin
Phil-a-del-phi-an
phi-lan-der
phil-an-throp-ic
phi-lan-thro-pist
phi-lan-thro-py
phil-a-tel-ic
phi-lat-e-list
phi-lat-e-ly
phil-har-mon-ic
phil-i-a-ter
phi-lip-pic
Phil-ip-pine
Phil-is-tine
phil-o-den-dron
phil-o-graph
phi-log-y-ny
phil-o-log-i-cal
phi-lol-o-gy
phil-o-pe-na
phi-los-o-pher
phil-o-soph-i-cal
phi-los-o-phiz-er
phi-los-o-phy
phil-ter
phle-bit-ic
phle-bi-tis
phleb-o-graph-ic
phle-bog-ra-phy
phle-bot-o-my
phleg-mat-ic
phlob-a-phene
phlo-em
phlo-gis-ton
phlog-o-pi-ti-za-tion
phlo-i-on-ic
phlor-e-tin
phlor-i-zin-ize
phlor-o-glu-cin-ol
phlo-rol
phlox-ine
pho-bi-a
pho-bo-tax-is
phoe-be
Phoe-ni-cian
Phoe-nix
phon-as-the-ni-a
phon-au-to-graph
pho-ne-mat-ic
pho-ne-mic
pho-ne-mic-i-ty
pho-nen-do-scope
pho-net-ic
pho-ne-ti-cian
Phone-vi-sion
pho-ni-at-ric
phon-ic
pho-no-gen-ic
pho-no-graph-i-cal
pho-nog-ra-phy
pho-no-lite
pho-nol-o-gy
pho-nom-e-ter
pho-nom-e-try
pho-no-phore
pho-noph-o-rous
pho-ny
phor-bin
pho-re-sis
pho-ret-ic
pho-rom-e-ter
pho-rom-e-try
pho-rone
pho-rop-tor
phos-gen-ite
phos-pham-ic
phos-pha-tase
phos-pha-te-mi-a
phos-phat-ic
phos-phi-nate
phos-phin-ic
phos-pho-a-mi-no-lip-
ide
phos-pho-di-es-ter-ase
phos-pho-nate
phos-phon-ic
phos-pho-rate
phos-pho-re-al
phos-pho-res-cence
phos-phor-ic
phos-phor-o-gen
phos-pho-ro-gen-ic
phos-pho-rol-y-sis
phos-pho-rous (adj.)
phos-pho-rus (n.)
phos-pho-ryl-ase
phos-vi-tin
pho-tics
pho-to-chro-my
pho-to-gen-ic
pho-to-gram-me-try
pho-tog-ra-pher
pho-to-graph-ic
pho-tog-ra-phy
pho-to-gra-vure
pho-tol-y-sis
pho-to-lyt-ic
pho-tom-e-ter
pho-to-met-ric
pho-tom-e-try
pho-ton
pho-to-nas-tic
pho-top-a-thy
pho-to-pho-re-sis
phot-op-tom-e-ter
pho-to-stat-ed
pho-to-trop-ic
pho-tot-ro-pism
pho-tron-ic
phras-a-ble
phra-se-o-gram
phra-se-og-ra-phy
phra-se-ol-o-gy
phras-er
phras-ing
phren-ic
phren-i-cot-o-my
phre-ni-tis
phren-o-log-i-cal
phre-nol-o-gy
phren-o-sin
Phryg-i-an
phtha-lam-ic
phthal-ate
phthal-ein
phthal-ic
phthal-im-ide
phthal-in
phthal-o-ni-trile
phthal-o-yl
phthi-o-col
phthi-ri-a-sis
phthis-ick-y
phthis-i-ol-o-gy
phthi-sis
phy-col-o-gy
phy-lac-tery
phyl-lo-por-phy-rin
phy-lo-ge-net-ic
phy-log-e-ny
phy-lum
phy-ma-to-sis
phys-i-at-rics
phys-ic
phys-i-cal
phy-si-cian
phys-i-cist
phys-i-og-no-my
phys-i-og-ra-phy
phys-i-ol-a-ter
phys-i-o-log-i-cal
phys-i-ol-o-gy
phys-i-om-e-try
phys-i-os-o-phy
phy-sique
phy-so-car-pous
phy-so-stig-mine
phy-tase
Phy-tin
phy-to-flu-ene
phy-tog-a-my
phy-to-gen-ic
phy-tol-o-gy
phy-tom-e-ter
phy-to-met-ric
phy-toph-a-gous
phy-to-sis
phy-tos-te-rol
phy-tyl
pi-a-nis-si-mo
pi-an-ist
pi-a-niste
pi-a-nis-tic
pi-an-o-for-te
pi-as-sa-va
pi-as-ter
pic-a-resque
pic-a-yune
Pic-ca-dil-ly
pic-ca-lil-li
pic-e-in
pi-cene
pick-et-er
pick-led
pick-ling
pic-nick-er
pic-o-line
pic-o-lin-ic
pic-ram-ic
pic-ram-ide
pic-rate
pic-ric
pic-ro-cro-cin
pic-ro-lon-ic
pic-rom-er-ite
pic-ryl
pic-to-graph-ic
pic-tog-ra-phy
pic-to-ri-al
pic-tur-a-ble
pic-tur-esque
pic-ul
pid-dler
pi-ece de re-sis-tance
piec-er
pierc-er
pi-e-ty
pi-e-zom-e-ter
pi-e-zom-e-try
pi-geon-eer
pig-men-tar-y
pi-gnon
pik-er
pi-las-ter
pil-chard
pil-er
pil-fer-age
pil-grim-age
pi-lif-er-ous
pil-lag-er
pil-lo-ry
pi-lo-car-pi-dine
pi-lose
pi-lo-sine
pi-los-i-ty
pi-lot-age
Pil-sner
pil-u-lar
pim-an-threne
pi-mar-ic
pim-e-late
pi-men-ta
pi-men-to
pi-mien-to
pim-ply
pin-a-coi-dal
pin-a-col
pi-nac-o-late
pi-nac-o-lone
pin-a-cy-a-nol
pi-nane
pin-cers
pinch-er
pin-e-al
pi-nene
pin-er-y
pi-nic
pin-ion
pi-nite
pi-ni-tol
pink-er
pin-na-cle
pi-no-cam-phe-ol
pi-noch-le
pi-no-lin
pi-ñon
pi-non-ic
pi-no-syl-vin
pin-tle
pi-nyl
pi-o-neered
pi-os-i-ty
pi-ous
pip-age
pi-pec-o-line
pip-er
pi-per-a-zine
pi-per-ic
pi-per-i-dine
pip-er-ine
pi-per-o-nyl-ic
pip-er-ox-an
pi-per-y-lene
pi-pet
pi-quan-cy
pi-quant
pi-qué (fabric)
pi-quet
pi-ra-cy
pi-ra-nha
pi-rat-i-cal
pi-rogue
pir-ou-ette
pis-ca-to-ri-al
Pis-ces
pis-cine
pi-si-form
pis-tach-i-o
pis-til-late
pitch-er
pit-e-ous
pith-e-can-thro-poid
pith-e-col-o-gy
pith-i-ness
pit-i-a-ble
pi-tom-e-ter
pi-ton
pi-tu-i-tar-y
Pi-tu-i-trin
pi-val-ic
piv-ot-al
piv-ot-er
pix-i-lat-ed
piz-ze-ri-a
plac-a-ble
plac-ard (n.)
pla-card (v.)
pla-cat-er
pla-ca-to-ry
place-a-ble
pla-ce-bo
pla-cen-ta
plac-en-tar-y
plac-en-ti-tis
plac-er
plac-id
pla-cid-i-ty
plack-et
pla-coi-dal

pla-gia-rism
pla-gia-rize
pla-gi-o-clase
pla-gi-o-nite
plagu-ed
pla-gui-ly
pla-guy
plain-tiff
plain-tive
plait-er
pla-nar-i-ty
pla-na-tion
plan-chet
plan-chette
pla-ner (tree)
plan-er
plan-et
plan-e-tar-i-um
plan-e-tar-y
plan-e-tes-i-mal
plan-et-oi-dal
plan-et-o-log-ic
plan-e-tol-o-gy
plan-gen-cy
pla-nig-ra-phy
pla-nim-e-ter
pla-ni-met-ric
plan-i-sphere
plank-tiv-o-rous
pla-no-con-cave
plan-o-graph
pla-nog-ra-phy
pla-nom-e-ter
plan-o-sol
plan-tain
plan-tar
plan-ta-tion
plant-er
pla-num
pla-quette
plas-ma-pher-e-sis
plas-min-o-gen
plas-mo-di-a-sis
plas-mo-di-um
plas-mol-y-sis
plas-mo-lyt-ic
plas-ter
plas-ti-ca-tor
plas-ti-cim-e-ter
plas-tic-i-ty
plas-ti-ciz-er
plas-ti-line
plas-ti-noid
plas-ti-sol
plas-to-mer
plas-tom-e-ter
plas-tron
pla-teau
plat-ed
plat-en
plat-er
pla-ti-na
pla-tin-ic
plat-i-no-type
plat-i-num
plat-i-tu-di-nar-i-an
pla-ton-ic
Pla-to-nist
pla-toon
plat-y-nite
plat-y-pus
plau-dit
plau-si-ble
plead-er
pleas-ant-ry
pleas-ur-a-ble
pleat-er
ple-be-ian
pleb-i-scite
pledg-ee
pledge-or (law)
pledg-er
pledg-et
Ple-ia-des
plei-o-bar
plei-ot-ro-py
Pleis-to-cene
ple-na-ry
plen-i-po-ten-tia-ry
plen-i-tude
plen-te-ous
plen-ti-ful
ple-num
ple-o-nasm
ple-rot-ic
pleth-o-ra
ple-thor-ic
pleu-ral
pleu-ri-sy
pleu-rit-ic
pleu-ro-dont
plex-im-e-ter
plex-us
Pli-o-cene
plom-bage
plov-er
plu-ma-ceous
plum-age
plu-mate
plum-ba-gin
plum-ba-go
plum-bate
plumb-er
plum-bif-er-ous
plum-bite
plum-bous
plu-mose
plump-er
plun-der
plung-er
plu-ral-i-ty
plu-ri-va-lent
plu-tar-chy
plu-toc-ra-cy
plu-to-crat
plu-to-nism
plu-to-ni-um
plu-vi-og-ra-phy
plu-vi-om-e-ter
plu-vi-o-met-ric
plu-vi-ous
Plym-outh
pneu-drau-lic
pneu-mat-ic
pneu-ma-tic-i-ty
pneu-ma-tol-y-sis
pneu-ma-tom-e-ter
pneu-ma-to-sis
pneu-mec-to-my
pneu-mo-coc-cus
pneu-mol-y-sis
pneu-mo-nia
pneu-mon-ic
pneu-mo-ni-tis
poach-er
po-choir
pock-et
po-dal-ic
po-di-a-trist
po-di-a-try
po-di-um
po-do-lite
pod-zol-ize
po-et-as-ter
po-et-i-cal
po-et-ry
po-go-not-ro-phy
po-grom
poign-an-cy
poign-ant
poi-ki-lit-ic
poi-kil-o-cy-to-sis
poin-ci-an-a
poin-set-ti-a
point-er
Poi-ret
pois-er
poi-son-ous
pok-er
po-lar
po-lar-im-e-ter
po-lar-i-met-ric
Po-la-ris
po-lar-i-scope
po-lar-i-stro-bom-e-ter
po-lar-i-ty
po-lar-iz-er
po-lar-o-graph-ic
po-lar-og-ra-phy
Po-lar-oid
po-lar-on
po-lem-ic
pol-e-mize
pol-er
po-li-a-nite
po-lic-ing
pol-i-cy
po-li-o-my-e-li-tis
po-li-o-sis
Pol-ish
pol-ish-er
Po-lit-bu-ro
po-lit-i-cal
pol-i-ti-cian
pol-i-tics
po-litz-er
pol-len-iz-er
poll-er
pol-li-na-tion
pol-li-nif-er-ous
pol-lin-i-um
pol-li-no-sis
pol-lu-cite
pol-lut-ant
pol-lut-er
pol-lu-tion
pol-o-naise
po-lo-ni-um
pol-troon
pol-y-a-cryl-ic
pol-y-am-ide
pol-y-an-dry
pol-y-ar-gy-rite
pol-y-ba-site
pol-y-chro-mat-ic
pol-y-chro-my
pol-y-clin-ic
pol-y-crase
pol-y-cy-the-mi-a
po-lyd-y-mite
pol-y-ene
pol-y-es-ter
pol-y-eth-yl-ene
pol-y-gam-ic
po-lyg-a-my
po-lyg-e-ny
pol-y-glot
pol-y-gon
po-lyg-o-nal
pol-y-graph-ic
po-lyg-ra-phy
pol-y-he-dral
pol-y-hi-dro-sis
pol-y-i-so-bu-tyl-ene
pol-y-i-so-top-ic
pol-y-kar-y-on
pol-y-mer-ic
po-lym-er-i-za-tion
po-lym-er-iz-er
po-lym-er-ous
pol-y-me-ter
pol-ym-nite
pol-y-mor-phous
Pol-y-ne-sian
pol-y-no-mi-al
pol-y-nu-cle-o-sis
pol-yp-ec-to-my
po-lyph-a-gous
po-lyph-o-ny
pol-y-ploi-dic
pol-yp-ous
pol-yp-tych
pol-y-pus
pol-y-so-ma-ty
pol-y-sty-rene
pol-y-tech-ni-cal
pol-y-trop-ic
pol-y-u-ro-nide
pol-y-va-lent
pol-y-vi-nyl
pom-ace
po-made
po-ma-tum
pome-gran-ate
Pom-er-a-ni-an
pom-meled
po-mo-log-i-cal
po-mol-o-gy
pom-pa-dour
pom-pa-no
Pom-pe-ian
pom-pos-i-ty
pomp-ous
Pon-a-pe-an
pon-cho
pond-age
pon-der-o-sa
pon-der-os-i-ty
pon-der-ous
pon-iard
pon-tage
pon-tif-i-cal
pon-tif-i-ca-tor
poo-dle
pop-e-line
pop-lit-e-al
pop-ping
pop-u-lace
pop-u-lar-i-ty
pop-u-lar-ize
pop-u-lous
por-ce-lain
por-ce-la-ne-ous
por-cine
por-cu-pine
po-ri-ci-dal
po-rif-er-ous
po-ri-tes
por-nog-ra-pher
por-no-graph-ic
po-rom-e-ter
po-ro-scope
po-ros-co-py
po-rose
po-ro-sim-e-ter
po-ros-i-ty
po-rot-ic
po-rous
por-phin
por-phy-rin
por-phy-rit-ic
por-phyr-ox-ine
por-phy-ry
por-poise
port-a-ble
por-tage
por-tal
por-ten-tous
por-ter
port-fo-li-o
por-ti-co
por-tiere
port-man-teau
por-trai-ture
Por-tu-guese
por-tu-lac-a
pos-er
po-seur
po-si-tion-er
pos-i-ti-val
pos-i-tiv-ism
pos-i-tri-no
pos-i-tro-ni-um
po-sol-o-gy
pos-sessed
pos-sess-es
pos-ses-sive
pos-ses-sor
pos-si-bil-i-ty
post-age
post-al
post-er
pos-te-ri-or
pos-ter-i-ty
pos-ter-o-dor-sal
post-hu-mous
pos-tu-lant
pos-tur-al
po-ta-ble
po-tage
po-tam-ic
pot-a-mog-ra-phy
pot-a-mom-e-ter
pot-ash
pot-as-sam-ide
po-tas-sic
po-tas-si-um
po-ta-to-ry
Pot-a-wat-o-mi
po-ten-cy
po-ten-tate
po-ten-ti-al-i-ty
po-ten-ti-om-e-ter
po-tom-e-ter
pot-pour-ri
pot-sherd
poul-tice
poul-try
pounc-er
pound-age
pound-er
pour-par-ler
pousse ca-fe
pout-er
pov-er-ty
pow-dered
pow-ered
poz-zo-la-nic
prac-ti-ca-ble
prac-ti-cal-i-ty
prac-tic-er
prac-ti-tion-er
prae-ci-pe
prag-mat-ic
prag-ma-tism
prai-rie
prais-er
pra-line
pranc-er
pran-di-al
prank-ster
pra-se-o-dym-i-um
pras-oid
pra-tique
prat-tler
prax-e-ol-o-gy
pray-er
preach-er
pre-am-ble
pre-car-i-ous
prec-a-to-ry
pre-ced-a-ble
prec-e-dence
pre-ce-dent (adj.)
prec-e-dent (n., v.)
pre-ced-ing
pre-cep-tor
pre-ci-os-i-ty
pre-cious
prec-i-pice
pre-cip-i-tant
pre-cip-i-ta-tor
pre-cip-i-tin-o-gen
pre-cip-i-tous
Pre-cip-i-tron
pre-ci-sion
pre-ci-sive
pre-clu-sive
pre-co-cious
pre-coc-i-ty
pre-cor-di-um
pre-cur-sor
pre-da-ceous
pre-dac-i-ty
pred-a-to-ry
pred-e-ces-sor
pre-den-ta-ry
pre-des-ti-nate
pred-i-ca-ble
pre-dic-a-ment
pred-i-cate
pred-i-ca-to-ry
pre-dict-able
pre-dic-tion
pre-dic-tor
pred-i-lec-tion
pred-nis-o-lone
pred-ni-sone
pre-dom-i-nance
pre-emp-to-ry
pre-fab-ri-ca-tor
pref-ace
pref-a-to-ry
pre-fec-ture
pre-fer
pref-er-a-ble
pref-er-ence
pref-er-en-tial
pre-fer-ment
pre-for-ma-tion
preg-nan-cy
preg-nen-in-o-lone
preg-nen-o-lone
pre-hen-si-ble
pre-hen-sile
prehn-ite
prehn-i-tene
prehn-it-ic
prej-u-di-cial
prel-ate
pre-lim-i-nar-y
prel-ude
pre-lu-di-al
pre-ma-ture
pre-med-i-ta-tive
pre-mier
pre-miere
prem-ise (n.)
pre-mise (v.)
pre-mi-um
pre-mo-ni-tion
pre-mon-i-to-ry
prep-a-ra-tion
pre-par-a-to-ry
pre-par-er
pre-pon-der-ant
pre-po-si-tion (before)
prep-o-si-tion
pre-pos-ter-ous
pre-puce
pre-req-ui-site
pre-rog-a-tive
pres-age (n.)
pre-sage (v.)
pres-by-o-phre-ni-a
pres-by-o-pi-a
Pres-by-te-ri-an
pres-by-ter-y
pre-science
pre-scient
pre-scis-sion
pre-scrib-er
pre-scrip-ti-ble
pre-scrip-tive
pres-ent (adj. and n.)
pre-sent (v.; also as n., military term)
pre-sent-a-ble
pres-en-ta-tion
pre-sen-ta-tive
pre-sent-er
pre-sen-ti-ment
pre-sen-tive
pres-er-va-tion
pre-serv-a-tive
pre-serv-er
pres-i-den-cy
pres-i-den-tial
pre-sid-i-o
pre-sid-i-um
press-er
pres-sor
pres-sur-ize
pres-ti-dig-i-ta-tor
pres-tig-i-ous
Pres-tone
pre-sum-a-ble
pre-sump-tion
pre-sump-tive
pre-sump-tu-ous
pre-tend-er
pre-tense
pre-ten-tious
pret-er-it
pre-ter-i-tal
pre-ter-mit
pre-to-ri-al
pret-ti-ness
pret-zel
pre-vail
prev-a-lence
pre-var-i-ca-tor
pre-vent-a-tive
pre-vent-er
pre-ven-tive
pre-vi-ous
pric-er
prick-ling
pri-ma-cy
pri-ma fa-ci-e
pri-ma-quine
pri-mar-i-ly
pri-mar-y
pri-mate
Pri-ma-tes
pri-ma-tol-o-gy
pri-ma-ve-ral
prim-er
pri-me-val
prim-i-tiv-ism
pri-mo-gen-i-ture
pri-mor-di-al
prim-u-lav-er-in
prim-u-line
pri-mus
prin-cess
prin-ci-pal
prin-ci-ple
print-er-y
pri-or-i-ty
pri-o-ry
pris-mat-ic
pris-ma-toi-dal
pris-moi-dal
pri-som-e-ter
pris-on-er
pris-tine
pri-va-cy
pri-va-teer
pri-va-tion
priv-a-tive
pri-vat-ize
priv-et
priv-i-leged
priv-i-ty
priz-a-ble
prob-a-bil-i-ty
prob-a-ble
pro-ba-tion-er
pro-ba-tive
pro-bi-ty
prob-lem-at-i-cal
prob-o-la
pro-bos-cis
pro-caine
pro-ce-dur-al
pro-ce-dure
proc-ess (n., v.)
proc-ess-ing
pro-ces-sion
proc-es-sor
pro-claim
proc-la-ma-tion
pro-clam-a-to-ry
pro-clit-ic
pro-cliv-i-ty
pro-cli-vous
proc-ne-mi-al
pro-cras-ti-na-tor
pro-cre-a-tor
pro-crus-te-an
proc-ti-tis
proc-to-log-i-cal
proc-tol-o-gy
proc-to-ri-al
proc-to-scop-ic
proc-tos-co-py
pro-cur-a-ble
proc-u-ra-cy
proc-u-ra-to-ry
pro-cur-er
pro-cur-ess
prod-i-gal-i-ty
pro-dig-i-o-sin
pro-di-gious
prod-i-gy
pro-drome
pro-duce (v.)
prod-uce (n.)
pro-duc-er
pro-duc-i-ble
prod-uct (n.)
pro-duct-i-ble
pro-duc-tion
pro-duc-tiv-i-ty
prof-a-na-tion
pro-fan-i-ty
pro-fess-ant
pro-fessed
pro-fes-sion
pro-fes-sor
pro-fes-so-ri-al
prof-fered
pro-fi-cient
pro-fil-er
pro-fil-o-graph
pro-fi-lom-e-ter
prof-it-a-ble
prof-it-eer
prof-it-er
prof-li-ga-cy
prof-li-gate
prof-lu-ence
pro-fun-di-ty
pro-fu-sion
pro-gen-i-tor
prog-e-ny
pro-ges-ter-one
prog-na-thous
prog-no-sis
prog-nos-ti-ca-tor
pro-gramed
pro-gram-er
pro-gram-ing
pro-gram-ist
pro-gram-mat-ic
prog-ress (n.)
pro-gress (v.)
pro-gres-sion
pro-gres-sive
pro-hib-it-er
pro-hi-bi-tion
pro-hib-i-tive
pro-hib-i-to-ry
proj-ect (n.)
pro-ject (v.)
pro-jec-tile
pro-jec-tive
pro-jec-tor
pro-ji-cient
pro-lam-in
pro-la-tive
pro-le-gom-e-non
pro-lep-sis
pro-le-tar-i-an
pro-lif-er-a-tive
pro-lif-ic
pro-li-fic-i-ty
pro-line
pro-lix
pro-log
pro-lon-ga-tion

pro-lu-so-ry
prom-e-nad-er
Pro-me-the-us
pro-me-thi-um
prom-i-nence
prom-is-cu-i-ty
pro-mis-cu-ous
prom-is-ee
prom-i-sor
prom-is-so-ry
Prom-i-zole
prom-on-to-ry
pro-mot-er
prompt-er
promp-ti-tude
pro-mul-ga-tion
pro-mul-ga-tor
pro-na-tor
pro-nom-i-nal
pro-no-tum
pro-nounce-a-ble
pro-nun-ci-a-tion
proof-er
pro-pa-di-ene
prop-a-ga-ble
prop-a-gan-dist
prop-a-ga-tor
pro-pam-i-dine
pro-pa-no-ic
pro-pa-nol
pro-par-gyl
pro-par-ox-y-tone
pro-pel-lant (n.)
pro-pel-lent (adj.)
pro-pel-ler
pro-pe-no-ic
pro-pen-si-ty
pro-pe-nyl
pro-per-din
prop-er-ly
prop-er-ty
proph-e-cy (n.)
proph-e-sy (v.)
proph-et
pro-phet-ic
pro-phy-lac-tic
pro-phy-lax-is
pro-pin-qui-ty
pro-pi-o-late
pro-pi-o-lic
pro-pi-o-nate
pro-pi-on-ic
pro-pi-o-ni-trile
pro-pi-o-nyl
pro-pi-on-y-late
pro-pi-ti-ate
pro-pi-tious
pro-po-de-um
pro-po-nent
pro-por-tion-ate
pro-pos-al
pro-pos-er
prop-o-si-tion
pro-pri-e-tar-y
pro-pri-e-tor
pro-pri-e-ty
pro-pox-y-ac-et-an-i-lide
pro-pul-sive
pro-pul-so-ry
pro-pyl-a-mine
pro-pyl-ene
pro-pyl-ic
prop-y-lite
pro ra-ta
pro-rat-a-ble
pro-rat-er
pro-ro-ga-tion
pro-rogue
pro-sa-i-cal-ly
pro-sce-ni-um
pro-scribe
pro-scrip-tive
pros-e-cu-to-ry
pros-e-cu-trix
pros-e-lyte
pros-e-lyt-iz-er
pro-sod-i-cal
pros-o-dy
pros-o-pite
pros-o-pla-si-a
pros-pect
pro-spec-tive
pros-pec-tor
pro-spec-tus
pros-per-i-ty
pros-per-ous
pro-spi-cience
pros-ta-tec-to-my
pros-tat-ic
pros-ta-ti-tis
pro-sthen-ic
pros-the-sis
pros-thet-ic
pros-the-tist
Pro-stig-min
pros-ti-tute
pros-tra-tor
prot-ac-tin-i-um
pro-ta-gon
pro-tag-o-nist
prot-a-mine
pro-ta-no-pi-a
pro-te-an
pro-te-ase
pro-tect-ant
pro-tec-tive
pro-tec-tor-ate
pro-te-ge
pro-te-ide
pro-tein
pro-tein-a-ceous
pro-tein-ase
pro tem-po-re
pro-te-ol-y-sin
Prot-er-o-zo-ic
pro-test
pro-tes-tant (law)
Prot-es-tant (religion)
prot-es-ta-tion
pro-test-er
pro-thon-o-tar-y
pro-throm-bin
pro-tide
pro-ti-um
pro-to-blast
pro-to-cat-e-chu-al-de-hyde
pro-to-clas-tic
pro-toc-neme
pro-to-col
pro-to-gen
pro-tog-y-ny
pro-ton-ate
pro-to-pine
pro-to-plas-mal
pro-to-trop-ic
pro-tot-ro-py
pro-to-type
pro-to-ver-a-trine
prot-ox-ide
pro-to-zo-a
pro-to-zo-i-a-sis
pro-tract-i-ble
pro-trac-tile
pro-trac-tor
pro-tru-si-ble
pro-tru-sive
pro-tu-ber-ance
proust-ite
prov-a-ble
prov-e-nance
prov-en-der
pro-ve-nience
prov-er
prov-erb
pro-ver-bi-al
pro-vide
prov-i-dence
prov-i-den-tial
pro-vid-er
prov-ince
pro-vin-cial
pro-vi-sion
pro-vi-so-ry
prov-o-ca-tion
pro-voc-a-tive
pro-voc-a-to-ry
pro-vost (military)
prov-ost-al
prow-ess
prowl-er
prox-i-mate
prox-im-i-ty
pru-dence
pru-den-tial
prud-er-y
prud-ish
pru-i-nes-cence
pru-na-sin
pru-nel-la
prun-er
pru-ne-tin
pru-ni-trin
pru-ri-ent
pru-rit-ic
pru-ri-tus
prus-si-ate
psalm-ist
psal-mod-ic
psal-ter-y
pseud-an-dry
pseud-ar-thro-sis
pseu-do-cu-mi-dine
pseu-do-i-o-none
pseu-do-ni-trole
pseu-do-nym
pseu-don-y-mous
pseu-dos-co-py
pseu-dos-to-ma
psil-an-thro-py
psi-lo-mel-ane
psi-lo-sis
psi-lot-ic
psit-ta-co-sis
psit-ta-cot-ic
pso-phom-e-ter
pso-ri-a-sis
pso-ro-sis
Psy-che
psy-che-om-e-try
psy-chi-at-ric
psy-chi-a-trist
psy-chi-a-try
psy-chi-cal
psy-cho-an-a-lyst
psy-cho-an-a-lyt-ic
psy-cho-an-a-lyze
psy-cho-gen-ic
psy-cho-ge-nic-i-ty
psy-cho-graph-ic
psy-chog-ra-phy
psy-cho-log-i-cal
psy-chol-o-gist
psy-chom-e-ter
psy-cho-met-ric
psy-chom-e-tri-cian
psy-chom-e-try
psy-cho-nom-ics
psy-cho-path-ic
psy-chop-a-thy
psy-cho-sis
psy-cho-so-mat-ic
psy-chot-ic
psy-cho-trine
psy-chrom-e-ter
psy-chrom-e-try
psyl-li-um
psyl-lyl
ptar-mi-gan
pter-i-dine
pter-o-dac-tyl
pte-ro-ic
pter-o-pod
Pte-rop-o-da
pter-o-yl
pte-ryg-i-um
pter-y-goid
Ptol-e-ma-ic
pto-maine
pto-sis
pu-ber-ty
pu-ber-u-lent
pu-ber-u-lon-ic
pu-bes-cent
pu-bic
pu-bi-ot-o-my
pub-li-ca-tion
pub-li-cist
pub-lic-i-ty
puck-ered
pu-den-dal
pueb-lo
pu-er-ile
pu-er-per-al
pu-er-pe-ri-um
puff-er
pu-gi-lism
pu-gi-list
pu-gi-lis-tic
pug-na-cious
pug-nac-i-ty
pu-is-sant
pul-chri-tu-di-nous
pu-le-gone
pu-li-cide
pul-ing
pull-er
pul-let
pul-lo-rum
pul-mom-e-ter
pul-mo-nar-y
pul-mon-ic
Pul-mo-tor
pulp-er
pul-pit-eer
pulp-ot-o-my
pulp-ous
pul-que
pul-sa-tance
pul-sa-to-ry
puls-er
pul-sim-e-ter
pul-som-e-ter
pul-ver-iz-er
pul-ver-u-lent
pul-vin-ic
pu-mi-cate
pum-ice
pu-mi-ceous
pump-age
pump-er
pum-per-nick-el
pun-cheon
punch-er
pun-chi-nel-lo
punc-tate
punc-ti-form
punc-til-i-o
punc-til-i-ous
punc-tu-al-i-ty
punc-tu-ate
punc-tur-a-ble
punc-tured
pun-dit
pun-gen-cy
Pu-nic
pu-nic-ic
pun-ish-er
pu-ni-tive
pun-ster
punt-er
Punx-su-taw-ney
pu-pa-tion
pu-pif-er-ous
pu-pil
pu-pil-late
pu-pil-lom-e-ter
pup-pet-eer
pup-pet-ry
pur-chas-er
pu-ree
pur-ga-tive
pur-ga-to-ry
purg-er
pu-ri-fi-ca-tion
pu-rine
pur-ist
pu-ris-tic
pu-ri-tan
pu-ri-ty
Pur-kin-je
pur-lieu
pur-lin
pur-loin
pu-ro-my-cin
pur-ples-cent
pur-plish
pur-pos-ive
pur-pu-ra
pur-pu-rin
pur-pu-rite
pur-pu-ro-gal-lin
pur-pu-rog-e-nous
purs-er
pur-su-ant
pur-suit-me-ter
pur-sui-vant
pur-te-nance
pu-ru-lence
pur-vey-or
pu-sil-la-nim-i-ty
pu-sil-lan-i-mous
pus-tu-lous
pu-ta-tive
pu-tre-fa-cient
pu-tre-fac-tion
pu-tres-cent
pu-tres-ci-ble
pu-tres-cine
pu-trid
put-ter (n., v.)
putt-er (golf club)
Puy-al-lup
puz-zler
pyc-nom-e-ter
pyc-no-sis
pyc-not-ic
py-e-lit-ic
py-e-li-tis
py-e-lo-graph-ic
Pyg-ma-li-on
pyg-my
pyk-rete
py-lor-ic
py-lo-ro-plas-ty
py-lo-rus
py-o-cy-a-nase
py-o-cy-a-nin
py-o-gen-ic
py-or-rhe-a
pyr-a-cene
Pyr-a-lin
pyr-a-mid
py-ram-i-dal
pyr-a-mid-er
pyr-a-mid-i-cal
py-ran
pyr-a-nom-e-ter
py-ran-o-side
pyr-ar-gy-rite
pyr-a-zin-a-mide
pyr-az-ine
pyr-az-ole
py-raz-o-lone
py-raz-o-lyl
py-rene
Pyr-e-ne-an
py-ren-em-a-tous
py-re-thrin
py-re-thrum
Py-rex
py-rex-in
pyr-ge-om-e-ter
pyr-he-li-om-e-ter
pyr-i-bole
py-rid-a-zine
py-rid-ic
pyr-i-dine
pyr-i-din-i-um
pyr-i-done
pyr-i-dyl
py-rim-i-dine
py-rite
py-ri-tes
py-rit-ic
py-rit-if-er-ous
py ri-to-he-dral
py-ro-cat-e-chu-ic
py-ro-gal-lol
py-ro-ge-na-tion
py-rog-ra-phy
py-ro-lu-site
py-rol-y-sis
py-ro-lyze
py-ro-ma-ni-a
py-rom-e-ter
py-rone
py-ro-sis
py-ro-sphere
py-ro-tech-nic
py-rox-ene
pyr-ox-i-dine
py-rox-y-lin
pyr-rhic
pyr-rol-i-dine
pyr-ro-line
pyr-ro-lo-pyr-i-dine
pyr-ro-lyl
pyr-uv-al-de-hyde
pyr-u-vic
py-ryl-i-um
Py-thag-o-re-an
Pyth-i-an
py-thon-ic

Q

quack-er-y
quad-ded
quad-ra-ges-i-mal
quad-ran-gle
quad-ran-gu-lar
quad-rant
quad-rat-ic
quad-ra-ture
quad-ra-tus
quad-ren-ni-al
quad-ric
quad-rille
quad-ril-lion
quad-ri-ple-gic
quad-ri-va-lent
quad-roon
quad-ru-ped
quad-ru-ple
quad-ru-plet
quad-ru-plex
quad-ru-pli-cate
quak-er
qual-i-fi-ca-tion
qua-lim-e-ter
qual-i-ta-tive
qualm-ish
quan-da-ry
quan-tile
quan-tim-e-ter
quan-ti-ta-tive
quan-ti-ty
quan-ti-za-tion
quan-tize
quan-tum
quar-an-tin-er
quar-reled
quar-tan
quar-tered
quar-tern
quar-tet
quar-tile
quartz-ite
quartz-it-ic
quartz-ose
qua-si
quas-si-a
qua-ter-nar-y
qua-ter-ni-on
qua-ter-ni-ty
qua-ter-ni-za-tion
qua-ter-phen-yl
qua-torze
quat-rain
qua-vered
que-brach-i-tol
que-bra-cho
quell-er
quench-er
quen-stedt-ite
quer-ce-tin
quer-ci-mer-i-trin
que-rist
quer-u-lous
que-ry
ques-tion-naire
quet-zal
queu-er
queu-ing
quib-bler
quick-en-ing
qui-es-cent
qui-e-tude
qui-e-tus
quin-a-chrine
quin-al-din-i-um
quin-a-mine
qui-naph-thol
qui-na-ry
quin-az-o-line
quin-i-dine
qui-nine
qui-nin-ic
qui-niz-a-rin
qui-noi-dine
quin-o-line
quin-o-lin-yl
qui-nol-o-gy
quin-o-lyl
qui-none
qui-non-ize
qui-no-nyl
qui-no-va-tan-nic
qui-no-vose
quin-sy
quin-tal
quin-tant
quin-ter-ni-on
quint-es-sence
quin-tet
quin-tile
quin-tu-ple
quin-tu-plet
qui-nu-cli-dine
quip-ster
quiv-ered
quix-ot-ic
quix-o-tism
quiz-zi-cal
quon-dam
quo-rum
quot-a-ble
quo-ta-tion
quot-er
quo-tient

R

rab-bet-ed
rab-bin-ate
rab-id
ra-bid-i-ty
ra-bies
rac-coon
rac-e-mate
ra-ceme
ra-ce-mic
rac-e-mi-za-tion
rac-e-mose
ra-chi-om-e-ter
ra-chis
ra-chit-ic
ra-chi-tis
ra-cial-ism
rac-ing
rac-ist
rack-et-eer
rack-et-y
ra-con
rac-on-teur
ra-dar
ra-di-ac
ra-di-al
ra-di-ant
ra-di-a-tor
rad-i-cal
rad-i-cand
rad-i-cle
ra-di-o
ra-di-o-graph-ic
ra-di-og-ra-phy
ra-di-o-i-so-tope
ra-di-o-log-i-cal
ra-di-ol-o-gy
ra-di-ol-y-sis
ra-di-om-e-ter
ra-di-o-met-ric
ra-di-on-ic
ra-di-o-nu-clide
ra-di-os-co-py
ra-di-o-sonde
rad-ish
ra-di-um
ra-di-us
ra-dome
ra-don
raf-fi-a
raf-fi-nase
raf-fi-nate
raf-fi-nose
raf-fled
raf-ter (roof)
raft-er (worker on rafts)
ra-gout
raid-er
rail-ler-y
rai-ment
rais-er
rai-sin
rais-ing
ra-jah
rak-er
rak-ish
Ra-leigh
ral-ston-ite
ram-bler
ram-bunc-tious
ram-e-kin
ram-ie
ram-i-fi-ca-tion
ra-mose
ram-pa-geous
ram-pag-er
ramp-ant
ram-part
ra-na-les
ranch-er
ran-che-ro
ran-cho
ran-cid-i-ty
ran-cor-ous
ran-dom-ize
rang-er
rang-ette
ra-nine
rank-er
ran-kled
ran-som-er
rant-er
ra-pa-cious
ra-pac-i-ty
ra-pa-ki-vi
rap-er
Raph-a-el

rap-id
ra-pid-i-ty
ra-pi-er
rap-ine
rap-proche-ment
rap-tur-ous
rar-e-fy
rar-i-ty
ras-cal-i-ty
rash-er
rasp-er
ras-ter
rat-a-ble
rat-a-fi-a
ratch-et
rat-er
rath-er
rat-i-fy
ra-tio
ra-ti-oc-i-na-tion
ra-ti-om-e-ter
ra-tion-ale
ra-tion-al-ize
rat-tler
rau-cous
rau-vite
Rau-wol-fi-a
rav-ag-er
rav-eled
rave-lin
rav-el-ing
ra-ven (bird)
rav-en (other meanings)
rav-en-ing
rav-en-ous
ra-vine
rav-ing
rav-ish-er
ra-win-sonde
ra-zon
ra-zor
re-act-ance
re-ac-tion-ar-y
re-ac-tive
re-ac-tor
read-er
read-i-ness
re-a-gent
re-a-gin
re-al-gar
re-al-ism
re-al-is-tic
re-al-ize
re-al-tor
ream-er
reap-er
rea-son-a-ble
Re-au-mur
re-bat-er
re-bel (v.)
reb-el (adj., n.)
re-bel-lious
re-but-ta-ble
re-cal-ci-trant
re-ca-les-cence
re-can-ta-tion
re-ca-pit-u-late
re-ced-ence
re-ced-er
re-ceipt-or
re-ceiv-a-ble
re-ceiv-er
re-cen-sion
re-cep-ta-cle
re-cep-ti-ble
re-cep-tiv-i-ty
re-cep-tor
re-cess-er
re-ces-sion-al
re-ces-sive
re-cher-che
re-cid-i-vist
Re-ci-fe
rec-i-pe
re-cip-i-ent
re-cip-ro-ca-ble
re-cip-ro-cal
rec-i-proc-i-ty
re-ci-sion
re-cit-al
rec-i-ta-tive
reck-on-ing
re-claim
rec-la-ma
rec-la-ma-tion
re-clin-a-ble
rec-li-na-tion
re-clin-er
rec-luse
re-clu-sive
rec-og-ni-tion
re-cog-ni-zance
rec-og-nize
re-cog-ni-zee
rec-og-niz-er
re-cog-ni-zor
re-col-lect (collect again)
rec-ol-lect (remember)
rec-om-men-da-tion
rec-om-mend-a-to-ry
rec-om-pens-er
re-con-cen-tra-do
rec-on-cil-a-ble

rec-on-cil-er
rec-on-cil-i-a-tion
rec-on-dite
re-con-nais-sance
re-con-noi-ter
rec-ord (adj., n.)
re-cord (v.)
re-cord-a-ble
rec-or-da-tion
re-cord-er
re-coup
re-cov-er-y
rec-re-ant
rec-re-ate (refresh)
re-cre-ate (create again)
rec-re-a-tion
re-cre-a-tion
re-crim-i-na-to-ry
re-cru-des-cence
re-cruit-er
rec-tan-gle
rec-tan-gu-lar
rec-tan-gu-lom-e-ter
rec-ti-fi-er
rec-ti-lin-e-ar
rec-ti-tude
rec-tor-ate
rec-to-ry
rec-tum
re-cum-bent
re-cu-per-a-tive
re-cur-rence
re-cur-sive
rec-u-sant
re-dac-tor
re-demp-ti-ble
re-demp-tive
re-demp-tor
red-in-gote
red-o-lent
re-doubt-a-ble
re-dox
re-dress-a-ble
re-dress-er
re-duc-er
re-duc-i-ble
re-duc-tase
re-duc-tone
re-duc-tor
re-dun-dan-cy
reef-er
reel-er
re-fec-to-ry
ref-er-a-ble
ref-er-ee
ref-er-ence
ref-er-en-dum
ref-er-en-tial
re-fer-ring
re-fin-er-y
re-flec-tance
re-flect-i-ble
re-flec-tive
re-flec-tom-e-ter
re-flec-tom-e-try
re-flec-tor-ize
re-flex-iv-i-ty
ref-lu-ent
re-for-est-a-tion
re-form-a-ble
ref-or-ma-tion
re-form-a-to-ry
re-form-er
re-frac-tive
re-frac-tom-e-ter
re-frac-to-met-ric
re-frac-tom-e-try
re-frac-to-ry
re-fran-gi-ble
ref-re-na-tion
re-frig-er-ant
re-frig-er-at-ing
re-frig-er-a-tion
re-frig-er-a-tor
ref-uge
ref-u-gee
re-ful-gent
re-fus-al
ref-use (adj., n.)
re-fuse (v.)
re-fut-a-ble
ref-u-ta-tion
re-fut-er
re-ga-lia
re-gal-i-ty
re-ge-late
re-gen-cy
re-gen-er-a-tive
re-gen-er-a-tor
reg-i-cide
re-gime
reg-i-men
reg-i-men-tal
reg-i-men-ta-ry
Re-gi-na
re-gion-al
reg-is-tered
reg-is-tra-ble
reg-is-trar
reg-is-trate
reg-let
Re-gnault
reg-o-sol

re-gres-sive
re-gret-ta-ble
reg-u-lar-i-ty
reg-u-la-tive
reg-u-la-to-ry
reg-u-lus
re-gur-gi-tate
re-ha-bil-i-ta-tive
re-hears-al
re-hears-er
Re-ho-both
Reichs-tag
re-im-burs-a-ble
Rei-nec-ke
re-in-forced
re-it-er-ate
re-ject-a-ble
re-ject-er (one that rejects)
re-jec-tor (circuit)
re-joic-ing
re-join-der
re-ju-ve-na-tor
re-ju-ve-nes-cence
re-laps-er
re-lat-er
rel-a-tiv-ism
rel-a-tiv-i-ty
re-la-tor (law)
re-lax-om-e-ter
re-leas-er
rel-e-ga-ble
rel-e-vant
rel-ict (n.)
re-lict (adj.)
re-lief-er
re-liev-er
re-li-gion
re-li-gi-os-i-ty
re-li-gious
re-lin-quish
rel-i-quar-y
rel-ish
re-lu-cence
re-luc-tance
rel-uc-tiv-i-ty
re-lu-mine
re-main-der
rem-a-nence
re-mark-a-ble
re-me-di-a-ble
re-me-di-al
rem-e-di-less
rem-e-dy
re-mem-brance
re-mind-er
rem-i-nis-cence
rem-i-nis-cer
re-miss-i-ble
re-mis-sive
re-mit-tee
re-mod-eled
re-mon-strance
re-mon-stra-tive
re-mon-stra-tor
re-mov-al
re-mu-ner-a-ble
re-mu-ner-a-tive
ren-ais-sance
Re-nais-sant
re-nal
re-nas-cence
ren-der (v.)
rend-er (n.)
ren-dez-vous
rend-i-ble
ren-di-tion
ren-dzi-na
ren-e-gade
re-nege
ren-gue
re-nin
ren-o-va-tor
re-nowned
rent-al
rent-er (n.)
ren-ter (v.)
re-nun-ci-a-to-ry
re-pair-a-ble
rep-a-ra-ble
rep-a-ra-tion
rep-ar-tee
re-pa-tri-ate
re-peal-er
re-peat-er
re-pel-lant (n.)
re-pel-lent (adj.)
re-pent-ance
re-per-cus-sion
rep-er-to-ry
rep-e-tend
rep-e-ti-tion
re-pet-i-tive
re-place-a-ble
re-plen-ish-er
re-ple-tive
re-plev-in
re-plev-i-sor
rep-li-ca
rep-li-cate
re-port-er
rep-or-to-ri-al
rep-o-si-tion (n.)
re-po-si-tion (v.)

re-pos-i-to-ry
rep-re-hen-si-ble
rep-re-hen-so-ry
rep-re-sen-ta-tion
rep-re-sent-a-tive
rep-re-sent-er
re-press-er
re-press-i-ble
re-pres-sive
re-priev-al
rep-ri-mand
re-pris-al
rep-ro-ba-cy
rep-ro-bate
re-pro-duc-er
re-pro-duc-i-ble
rep-til-i-an
re-pub-li-can
re-pu-di-a-tor
re-pug-nant
re-pul-sive
rep-u-ta-ble
rep-u-ta-tion
re-pute
re-quest-er
req-ui-em
re-qui-es-cat
re-quir-er
req-ui-site
req-ui-si-tion
re-quit-al
res-az-ur-in
re-scind
re-scis-sion
re-scrip-tive
res-cu-a-ble
re-sect-a-ble
re-sem-blance
re-sem-bler
res-ene
re-ser-pic
Re-ser-pine
res-er-va-tion
re-served
re-serv-ist
res-er-voir
re-side
res-i-dence
res-i-den-tial
re-sid-u-al
re-sid-u-ar-y
res-i-due
re-sid-u-um
re-sign
res-ig-na-tion
re-sil-ience
re-sil-ien-cy
re-sil-i-om-e-ter
rés-in-a-ceous
res-in-ate
res-in-ic
res-in-if-er-ous
re-sin-i-fi-ca-tion
res-in-og-ra-phy
res-in-oid
res-in-ol
res-in-ous
res-i-pis-cence
re-sist-ance
re-sist-er (one that resists)
re-sist-i-ble
re-sis-tiv-i-ty
re-sis-tor (device)
res-ite (resin)
res-i-tol
res ju-di-ca-ta
res-ol
re-sol-u-ble
res-o-lute
re-sol-u-tive
re-solv-ent
re-solv-er
res-o-nance
res-o-na-tor
res-or-cin-ol
res-or-cyl-ic
re-sorp-tive
res-o-ru-fin
re-spect-a-ble
re-spect-er
re-spec-tive
res-pi-ra-ble
res-pi-ra-tion
res-pi-ra-tor
res-pi-ra-to-ry
res-pi-rom-e-ter
res-pite
re-splend-ent
re-spond-ent
re-spond-er
re-spons-er
re-spon-si-ble
re-spon-sive
re-spon-sor
re-spon-so-ry
res-tau-rant
res-tau-ra-teur
res-ti-tu-tion
res-tive
res-to-ra-tion
re-stor-a-tive
re-stric-tive
re-sult-ant

re-sume (v.)
ré-su-mé (n.)
re-sump-tive
re-sur-gent
res-ur-rec-tor
re-sus-ci-ta-ble
re-sus-ci-ta-tor
re-tal-i-a-to-ry
re-tard-ant
re-tar-da-tion
re-tard-ed
re-tene
re-ten-tive
re-ten-tor
ret-ger-site
re-ti-ar-y
ret-i-cence
ret-i-cle
re-tic-u-late
ret-i-cule
re-tic-u-lin
re-tic-u-li-tis
re-tic-u-lo-cy-to-sis
re-tic-u-lose
ret-i-form
ret-i-na
re-tin-a-lite
ret-i-nene
ret-i-ni-tis
ret-i-no-cho-roid-i-tis
ret-i-nop-a-thy
ret-i-nos-co-py
ret-i-nue
re-tir-al
re-tir-ee
ret-o-na-tion
re-tort-er
re-tract-a-ble
re-trac-tile
re-trac-tion
re-trac-tive
re-trac-tor
ret-ri-bu-tion
re-trib-u-tive
re-trib-u-to-ry
re-triev-a-ble
re-triev-al
re-triev-er
ret-ro-ac-tive
ret-ro-cede (v.i.)
re-tro-cede (v.t.)
ret-ro-ced-ence
ret-ro-ces-sion
ret-ro-gra-da-to-ry
ret-ro-gres-sive
ret-ro-ne-cine
re-tror-sine
ret-ro-spec-tive
ret-ro-stal-sis
ret-rous-sé
ret-ro-vert-ed
re-turn-ee
re-un-ion
re-vanche
rev-eil-le
rev-e-la-tion
re-vel-a-to-ry
rev-eled
rev-el-ry
re-veng-er
rev-e-nue
re-ver-a-ble
re-ver-ber-a-to-ry
re-vere
rev-er-ence
rev-er-ie
re-ver-sal
re-vers-er
re-vers-i-ble
re-ver-sion
re-vert-er
re-vert-i-ble
re-vet-ment
re-vil-er
rev-i-res-cent
re-vised
re-vis-er
re-vi-sion
re-vi-so-ry
re-viv-al
re-viv-i-fy
rev-i-vis-cent
re-vi-vor
rev-o-ca-ble
rev-o-ca-tion
rev-o-ca-to-ry
re-vok-a-ble
re-vok-er
re-volt-er
rev-o-lu-ble
rev-o-lu-tion
re-volv-er
re-vul-sive
Rey-kja-vik
rey-nard
Reyn-olds
rhab-do-man-cer
rham-na-zin
rham-ni-nose
rham-no-side
rha-pon-ti-gen-in
rhap-sod-i-cal
rhap-so-dy

rhe-a-dine
rhe-ni-um
rhe-ol-o-gy
rhe-om-e-ter
rhe-o-stat
rhe-sus
rhet-o-ric
rhe-tor-i-cal
rhet-o-ri-cian
rheu-mat-ic
rheu-ma-tism
rheum-ic
rhig-o-lene
rhi-ni-tis
rhi-noc-er-os
rhi-nol-o-gy
rhi-nos-co-py
rhi-zoi-dal
rhi-zom-a-tous
rhi-zome
rhi-zop-ter-in
rhi-zot-o-my
rho-da-mine
rho-da-nate
Rho-de-sian
rho-di-nol
rho-dite
rho-di-um
rho-di-zon-ic
rho-do-chro-site
rho-do-den-dron
rhom-bo-clase
rhom-bo-he-dral
rhom-boi-dal
rhum-ba-tron
rhyme-ster
rhy-o-lite
rhyth-mi-cal
rib-al-dry
ri-bi-tyl
ri-bo-fla-vin
ri-bo-nu-cle-ase
ri-bo-side
ri-bu-lose
ric-er
ri-chell-ite
ric-in-o-le-ic
rick-ett-si-al
ric-o-cheted
rid-dled
rid-er
rid-i-cule
ri-dic-u-lous
rid-ing
ri-ding (political division)
rif-fling
ri-fling
right-cous
right-er
ri-gid-i-ty
rig-id-ly
rig-ma-role
rig-or-ous
ri-mose
rin-der-pest
ring-er
rins-a-ble
rins-er
ri-ot-ous
ri-par-i-an
rip-en
ri-pid-o-lite
rip-pled
ris-er
ris-i-bil-i-ty
ris-ing
ris-que
rit-u-al
ri-valed
ri-val-ry
riv-et-er
Riv-i-er-a
riv-u-let
Ri-yadh
road-ster
Ro-a-noke
roam-er
roast-er
Rob-ert
rob-in (bird)
ro-bin (chemistry)
ro-bi-nose
ro-bust
Ro-chelle
Roch-es-ter
rock-et-eer
rock-et-er
rock-et-ry
rock-oon
ro-co-co
ro-den-ti-ci-dal
Rod-er-ick
roe-bling-ite
roent-gen-o-graph
roent-gen-og-ra-phy
roent-gen-ol-o-gy
roent-gen-om-e-ter
roent-gen-om-e-try
roent-gen-o-scope
roent-gen-os-co-py
rog-a-to-ry
Rog-er
ro-gnon

rogu-er-y
rogu-ish
roist-er-er
Ro-land
roll-er
rol-lick-ing
ro-maine
ro-manc-er
Ro-man-esque
Ro-man-ism
ro-ma-ni-um
ro-man-ti-cism
ro-man-ti-cist
Rom-a-ny
ro-me-ite
Ro-me-o
Rom-ish
romp-er
ron-deau
ro-ne-o-graph
ron-geur
roof-er
rook-er-y
Roo-se-velt
roost-er
rop-er
Roque-fort
ro-rif-er-ous
Ror-schach
ro-sa-ceous
Ros-a-lind
Ros-a-mond
ro-sa-ry
rosch-er-ite
ro-se-ate
ro-se-o-la
ro-sette
Rosh Ha-sha-na
Ros-i-cru-cian
ros-in-ate
ros-i-ness
ro-sol-ic
ros-ter
ros-trum
ros-y
ro-tal
ro-tam-e-ter
Ro-tar-i-an
ro-ta-ry
ro-tat-a-ble
ro-ta-tive
ro-ta-tor
ro-ta-to-ry
ro-te-noid
ro-te-none
Ro-tif-er-a
ro-tis-ser-ie
ro-to-graph
ro-to-gra-vure
ro-tor
ro-tun-da
ro-tun-di-ty
rough-en
rough-er
rough-om-e-ter
rou-lade
rou-leau
rou-lette
roun-del
round-er
rout-er
rou-tine
ro-ver (robber)
rov-er
row-dy-ism
row-eled
roy-al-ist
ru-ba-to
ru-be-an-ic
ru-be-fa-cient
ru-be-o-la
rub-e-ryth-ric
ru-bes-cent
ru-bi-cun-di-ty
ru-bid-i-um
ru-big-i-nous
ru-ble
ru-brene
ru-bric
ru-bri-ca-tor
ru-di-men-ta-ry
ru-fes-cence
ruf-fi-an
ruf-fler
ruf-fling
ru-fos-i-ty
ru-fous
ru-gos-i-ty
ru-gu-lose
ru-ined
ru-in-ing
ru-in-ous
rul-a-ble
rul-er
Ru-ma-ni-an
rum-bler
ru-mi-nant
rum-mag-er
ru-mor
rump-er
rum-pled
rum-pus
run-ci-ble
ru-nic
ru-pee
ru-pic-o-lous
rup-tured
ru-ral
ru-rig-e-nous
Rus-sian
rus-ti-ca-tor
rus-tic-i-ty
rust-i-ness
rus-tler
rus-tling
ru-ta-ba-ga
ru-ta-ceous
ru-te-car-pine
Ru-the-ni-an
ru-then-ic
ru-the-ni-um
ruth-er-ford-ine
ru-tile
ru-tin-ose
ru-ty-lene
Rwan-dan
ry-an-o-dine
Ry-u-kyu-an

S

sab-a-dine
Sab-ba-tar-i-an
sab-bat-i-cal
sa-ber
Sa-bine
sab-ine (pine)
sab-i-nene
sa-bi-no
sab-o-tage
sa-bra
sab-u-lous
sa-bu-tan
sac-cha-rate
sac-char-ic
sac-cha-ride
sac-cha-rif-er-ous
sac-cha-rim-e-ter
sac-cha-rin-ate
sac-cha-rin-ic
sac-cha-rom-e-ter
sac-cha-rose
sac-er-do-tal
sa-chem
sa-chet
sac-ral
sac-ra-men-tal
sac-ra-men-ta-ry
sa-cred
sac-ri-fi-cial
sac-ri-fic-ing
sac-ri-le-gious
sac-ris-tan
sac-ris-ty
sac-ro-il-i-ac
sac-ro-sanct
sac-rum
sad-dler-y
sa-dism
sa-dis-tic
Saeng-er-fest
sa-fa-ri
safe-ty
saf-flor-ite
saf-fron
saf-ra-nine
sa-ga-cious
sa-gac-i-ty
sag-a-more
sag-a-pe-num
sag-e-nite
Sag-it-tar-i-us
Sa-ha-ra
sail-or
sa-laam
sal-a-ble
sa-la-cious
sal-ad
sal-a-man-der
sa-la-mi
sal-a-ried
sal-e-ra-tus
sal-i-cin
sal-i-cyl-am-ide
sa-lic-y-late
sal-i-cyl-ic
sa-lic-y-lide
sal-i-cyl-ize
sal-i-cyl-o-yl
sal-i-cyl-u-ric
sa-lient
sal-i-gen-in
sa-lim-e-ter
sal-i-na-tion
sa-line
sa-lin-i-ty
sa-lin-o-gen-ic
sal-i-nom-e-ter
Salis-bur-y
sa-li-va
sal-i-var-y
sal-i-va-tion
sa-li-vous
salm-on
Sal-mo-nel-la
sal-mo-nel-lo-sis
salm-ons-ite
Sal-ol
Sa-lo-me
sa-lon
sal-pin-gec-to-my
sal-pin-gi-tis
sal-si-fy
sal-ta-to-ri-al
salt-er-y
salt-pe-ter
sa-lu-bri-ous
sa-lu-bri-ty
sal-u-tar-y
sal-u-ta-tion
sa-lu-ta-to-ry
sa-lute
sal-va-ble
Sal-va-dor-an
sal-vage-a-ble
sal-vag-er
Sal-var-san
sal-ver
sal-vi-a-nin
sal vo-la-ti-le
sal-vor
sam-a-ra
Sa-mar-i-tan
sa-mar-i-um
sam-bu-ni-grin
Sa-mo-an
sam-o-var
Sam-o-yed
sam-pler
sa-mu-rai
san-a-to-ri-um
sanc-ti-fi-ca-tion
sanc-ti-mo-ni-ous
sanc-tion-er
sanc-ti-ty
sanc-tu-ar-y
sanc-tum
san-daled
sand-er
sand-i-ness
san-dust
San-for-ize
san-guin-a-rine
san-gui-nar-y
san-guin-e-ous
san-guin-o-lent
San-he-drin
san-i-dine
san-i-tar-i-um
san-i-tar-y
san-i-tiz-er
san-i-ty
San-skrit
san-ta-lene
san-ta-lol
san-te-none
san-to-nin
sa-phe-nous
sap-id
sa-pid-i-ty
sa-pi-ence
sap-o-gen-in
sap-o-na-ceous
sa-pon-i-fi-ca-tion
sap-o-nin
sap-o-rif-ic
sap-phir-ine
sap-ro-gen-ic
sap-ro-ge-nic-i-ty
sa-prog-e-nous
sap-ro-pel-ic
Sar-ah
Sa-ran
sar-casm
sar-cas-tic
sar-coid-o-sis
sar-col-y-sis
sar-co-ma
sar-co-ma-to-sis
sar-com-a-tous
sar-coph-a-gus
sar-cop-side
sar-co-sine
sar-dine
sar-don-ic
sar-don-yx
sar-ki-nite
sar-men-to-gen-in
sa-rong
sar-sa-pa-ril-la
sar-to-ri-al
sar-to-ri-us
Sar-tri-an
sas-sa-fras
sas-so-lite
sa-tan-i-cal
satch-el
sa-teen
sat-el-lit-ed
sat-el-lit-oid
sat-el-lit-o-sis
sat-el-loid
sa-tia-ble
sa-ti-ate
sa-ti-e-ty
sat-in-et
sat-in-ize
sat-ire
sa-tir-i-cal
sat-i-rize
sat-is-fac-to-ri-ly
sat-is-fy
sa-trap
sat-u-ra-ble
sat-u-ra-tor
Sat-ur-day
Sat-urn
sat-ur-na-lian
Sa-tur-ni-an
sat-ur-nine
sat-yr
sa-tyr-ic
sau-cer
sau-ci-ness
Sau-di A-ra-bi-a
sau-er-bra-ten
sau-er-kraut
saun-ter
sau-rel
sau-ri-an
sau-sage
saus-su-rite
sau-ted
sau-terne
sav-a-ble
sav-age-ry
sa-van-na
sa-vant
sav-ing
sav-ior
Sav-iour
sa-voir faire
sa-vor-y
Sa-voy-ard
sax-i-frage
sax-o-phone
scab-bler
sca-bies
sca-bres-cent
scab-rous
sca-lar
scald-er
sca-le-no-he-dral
scal-er
scal-loped
scal-pel
scalp-er
scam-per
scan-dal-ize
scan-dal-ous
Scan-di-na-vi-an
scan-di-um
scan-ner
scant-ling
scap-o-lite
scap-u-la
scar-ab
scar-ci-ty
scarf-er
scar-i-fy
scar-i-ous
scar-la-ti-na
scar-let
scat-o-log-i-cal
sca-tol-o-gy
scat-tered
scav-eng-er
sce-nar-i-o
sce-nar-ist
sce-ner-y
sce-ni-cal
sce-no-graph
sce-nog-ra-phy
scent-er
scep-ter
sched-ule
schee-lite
sche-ma
sche-mat-ic
sche-ma-tist
sche-mat-o-graph
Sche-ring
schiff-li
schis-mat-ic
schist-oid
schist-ose
schis-to-some
schis-to-so-mi-a-sis
schiz-oid-ism
schiz-o-phre-ni-a
schiz-o-phren-ic
schle-miel
schlie-ren
Schnei-der
scho-la can-to-rum
schol-ar
scho-las-tic
schoo-ner
schor-la-ceous
schot-tische
schra-dan
schrei-ner-ize
Schro-ding-er
schroec-king-er-ite
Schweit-zer
schwei-zer
sci-at-i-ca
sci-en-tif-ic
sci-en-tist
scil-i-cet
scil-li-ro-side
scim-i-tar
scin-tig-ra-phy
scin-til-la-tor
scin-til-lom-e-ter
sci-oph-i-lous
sci-re fa-ci-as
scis-sors
sclar-e-ol
scle-rec-to-my
scle-ren-chy-ma
scle-ri-tis
scle-ro-ma
scle-rom-e-ter
scle-ro-sis
scle-ro-tal
scle-rot-ic
scle-rot-o-my
scob-i-nate
scoff-er
scold-er
scol-e-cite
sco-li-o-sis
sconc-i-ble
scoop-er
scoot-er
sco-pa-rin
scoph-o-ny
sco-pine
sco-pol-a-mine
sco-po-le-tin
scop-u-lite
scor-bu-tic
sco-ri-a-ceous
sco-ri-fi-ca-tion
scorn-er
scor-o-dite
scor-per
Scor-pi-o
scor-pi-on
scor-za-lite
sco-to-ma
sco-tom-a-tous
scoun-drel
scourg-er
scrab-bler
scram-bling
scrap-er
scratch-er
scrawl-er
scream-er
screen-er
scrib-bler
scrib-er
scrip-tur-al
scriv-en-er
scrof-u-la
scrof-u-lo-sis
scro-tum
scru-ple
scru-pu-lous
scru-ti-nize
scru-ti-ny
scuf-fling
scul-ler-y
sculp-tor
sculp-tur-al
scum-bled
scur-ril-i-ty
scur-ri-lous
scur-vi-ly
scut-tle-butt
scu-tum
seal-ant
seal-er
seal-ine
seam-stress
se-ance
sea-son-a-ble
seat-er
seb-a-cate
se-ba-ceous
se-bac-ic
seb-or-rhe-a
sec-a-lose
se-cant
se-ced-er
se-clu-sive
Sec-o-nal
sec-ond-ar-i-ly
sec-ond-ar-y
sec-ond-er
se-cre-cy
se-cret
se-cre-ta-gogue
sec-re-tar-i-al
se-cre-tin
se-cre-tive
se-cre-to-ry
sec-tar-i-an
sec-til-i-ty
sec-tion-al-ize
sec-tor-al
sec-to-ri-al
sec-u-lar-ize
se-cund
se-cun-date
se-cu-ri-ty
se-dan
se-date
sed-a-tive
sed-en-tar-y
sed-i-men-ta-ry
se-di-tious
se-duc-er
se-duc-i-ble
se-duc-tive
se-du-li-ty
sed-u-lous
seed-ling
seek-er
seep-age
seg-men-tal
seg-re-ga-ble
Seid-litz
sei-gnior-age
sei-sin
seis-mic-i-ty
seis-mo-graph
seis-mog-ra-phy
seis-mo-log-i-cal
seis-mol-o-gy
seis-mom-e-ter
seis-mo-met-ric
seiz-er
sei-zin
seiz-ing
sei-zor (law)
sei-zure
sel-dom
se-lect-ance
se-lect-ee
se-lec-tiv-i-ty
se-lec-tor
sel-e-nate
se-len-ic
sel-e-nide
se-le-ni-ous
sel-e-nite
se-le-ni-um
se-le-no-bis-muth-ite
se-le-no-graph-ic
sel-e-nog-ra-phy
se-le-no-lite
se-le-no-log-i-cal
sel-e-nol-o-gy
sel-e-no-ni-um
sel-e-no-sis
self-ish
sell-er
sel-syn
Selt-zer
sel-vage
se-man-ti-cist
sem-a-phor-ist
se-ma-si-ol-o-gy
sem-blance
se-mei-ol-o-gy
se-mes-ter
sem-i-dine
sem-i-nal
sem-i-nar-y
sem-i-nif-er-ous
Sem-i-nole
Sem-ite
Se-mit-ic
Sem-i-tism
sem-o-li-na
sen-a-ry
sen-a-to-ri-al
send-er
se-ne-cic
se-ne-ci-o-nine
se-ne-ci-o-sis
Sen-e-gal-ese
se-nes-cence
sen-e-schal
se-nhor (Portuguese)
se-nile
se-nil-i-ty
sen-ior
se-nior-i-ty
se-nor
se-no-ri-ta
sen-sa-tion
sen-si-bil-i-ty
sen-sile
sen-si-tiv-i-ty
sen-si-tiz-er
sen-si-tom-e-ter
sen-so-ri-um
sen-so-ry
sen-su-al-i-ty
sen-su-ous
sen-tence
sen-ten-tious
sen-tience
sen-ti-men-tal
sen-ti-neled
sen-try
se-paled
sep-al-oid
sep-a-ra-ble
sep-a-ra-tee
sep-a-rat-ist
sep-a-ra-tor
se-phar-dic
se-pi-a
Sep-tem-ber
sep-ten-a-ry
sep-ti-ce-mi-a
sep-ti-mal
sep-tu-a-ge-nar-i-an
sep-tu-a-ges-i-ma
sep-tu-ple
sep-tu-plet
sep-tu-pli-cate
sep-ul-cher
se-pul-chral
sep-ul-ture
se-quac-i-ty
se-que-la
se-quen-tial

se-ques-tered
se-ques-tra-tor
se-ra-glio
ser-al
ser-aph
se-raph-ic
ser-a-phim
Ser-bi-an
ser-e-nad-er
ser-en-dip-i-ty
se-rene
se-ren-i-ty
ser-geant
se-ri-al
se-ri-a-tim
se-ri-ceous
ser-i-cin
ser-i-cite
se-ries
ser-i-graph
se-rig-ra-pher
se-rig-ra-phy
ser-ine
se-rin-ga
ser-in-gal
se-ri-ous
ser-mon-ize
se-ro-log-ic
se-rol-o-gy
se-ro-si-tis
se-ro-ton-in
se-rous
ser-pen-tin-ite
ser-pig-i-nous
se-rum
serv-ant
serv-er
serv-ice-a-ble
ser-vi-ent
ser-vile
ser-vil-i-ty
ser-vi-tor
ser-vi-tude
ser-vo-mo-tor
ses-a-me
ses-a-min
ses-a-moid-i-tis
ses-a-mo-lin
ses-qui-pe-da-lian
ses-sile
ses-sion
se-ta-ceous
se-ti-ger
se-tig-er-ous
set-tler
sev-en-ti-eth
sev-er-al
sev-ered
se-ver-i-ty
sew-age
sew-er-age
sex-a-ge-nar-i-an
sex-ag-e-nar-y
sex-tant
sex-tu-ple
sex-tu-plet
sex-tu-pli-cate
sfer-ics
sfor-zan-do
shack-led
shad-er
shad-ow
Sha-drach
sha-green
shak-er
Shake-spear-e-an
sham-bles
shank-er
shap-er
shap-om-e-ter
shar-a-ble
sharp-en-ing
sharp-er
shat-tered
shav-er
sheath-er
sheep-ish
sheet-age
shek-el
shel-lack-ing
shel-tered
shelv-ing
she-nan-i-gan
shep-herd
Sher-a-ton
sher-bet
sher-iff
shib-bo-leth
shield-er
shift-er
shi-kim-ic
shil-le-lagh
shil-ling
shin-er
shin-gled
shirk-er
shirr-ing
shiv-ered
shock-er
sho-far
shoot-er
sho-ran
short-en
short-om-e-ter
Sho-sho-ne
shoul-dered
shov-eled
shov-er
show-er-y
shriev-al-ty
Shrin-er
shrink-age
shrink-er
shriv-eled
shriv-ing
Shrop-shire
shuf-fled
shy-ster
si-a-log-ra-phy
si-al-o-li-thi-a-sis
Si-a-mese
Si-be-ri-an
sib-i-lant
sib-i-la-to-ry
sib-ling
sib-yl-line
Si-cil-ian
sick-en-ing
sick-led
si-de-re-al
sid-er-ite
sid-er-og-ra-pher
sid-er-o-graph-ic
sid-er-o-na-trite
sid-er-o-sis
sid-ing
si-dled
si-er-o-zem
Si-er-ra Le-one
siev-er
sift-er
sight-er
sig-ma-tism
sig-moid-ec-to-my
sig-moid-os-to-my
sig-naled
sig-nal-ize
sig-na-to-ry
sig-nif-i-cant
sig-ni-fi-ca-tion
si-gnor
si-gno-ra
si-lage
sil-ane
si-lenc-er
si-le-si-a
si-lex
sil-hou-ette
sil-i-cate
sil-i-ca-ti-za-tion
sil-i-ca-tor
si-li-ceous
si-lic-ic
sil-i-cide
si-lic-i-dize
sil-i-cif-er-ous
si-lic-i-fy
sil-i-co-mag-ne-sio-flu-o-rite
sil-i-con
sil-i-cone
sil-i-co-sis
sil-i-cot-ic
silk-en
sil-li-man-ite
si-lox-ane
sil-ta-tion
Si-lu-ri-an
sil-ver
sil-vi-cul-tur-al
sim-i-lar-i-ty
sim-i-le (like)
si-mi-le (music)
si-mil-i-tude
si-mon-ize
si-mo-ny
si-moom
sim-pat-i-co
sim-per
sim-pler
sim-plex
sim-plic-i-ty
sim-pli-fy
sim-u-lac-rum
sim-u-la-tor
si-mul-cast
si-mul-ta-ne-ous
Si-na-it-ic
si-nap-ic
sin-a-pine
sin-ar-quism
sin-cer-i-ty
si-ne-cure
sin-ew
sing-er
sin-gly
sin-gu-lar-i-ty
Sin-ha-lese
sin-is-tral
sink-age
sink-er
si-nom-e-nine
sin-ter
sin-u-ous
si-nus-i-tis
si-nus-oi-dal
si-phon-age
si-pid-i-ty
si-ren
si-ri-a-sis
Sir-i-us
si-roc-cos
sir-up
si-sal
sis-y-phe-an
si-tol-o-gy
si-to-ste-rol
sit-u-at-ed
si-tus
siz-a-ble
siz-zled
skat-ole
skeet-er
skel-e-ton-ize
skep-ti-cal
skep-ti-cism
skew-er
ski-am-e-try
ski-as-co-py
skill-ful-ness
skimp-i-ly
skir-mish
skirt-er
skit-tish
skiv-er
skul-dug-ger-y
skulk-er
slack-ened
slak-er
slan-der-ous
slat-tern
slaugh-ter
slav-er-y
slav-ish
Sla-von-ic
sleep-er
slen-der
slic-er
slick-en-side
slick-er
slid-a-ble
slid-om-e-ter
sling-er
slith-er-y
sliv-er
slo-gan
slop-ing
Slo-vak-i-an
slov-en
Slo-ve-ni-an
sludg-er
slum-ber-ous
smart-en
smell-er
smelt-er
smi-la-gen-in
smi-lax
smith-er-eens
Smith-so-ni-an
smok-er
smol-dered
smor-gas-bord
smoth-ered
smudg-er
smug-gler
snarl-ish
snatch-er
sneak-i-ness
sneez-er
snick-er-ing
sniff-er
snif-ter
snip-er
sniv-el-er
snob-ber-y
Sno-ho-mish
snoop-er-y
snor-kel
snort-er
snuf-fled
snug-gled
soak-age
soap-er
so-ber
so-bri-e-ty
so-bri-quet
so-cia-ble
so-cial-is-tic
so-ci-a-try
so-ci-e-ty
so-ci-oc-ra-cy
so-ci-o-log-ic
so-ci-ol-o-gist
so-ci-om-e-try
so-ci-op-a-thy
sock-dol-a-ger
sock-et
Soc-ra-tes
So-crat-ic
so-da-lite
so-dal-i-ty
so-dam-ide
so-dar
so-di-um
sod-om-y
so-far
soft-en-er
soi-gne
soi-ree
so-journ-er
sol-ace
so-lan-der
so-lan-i-dine
so-la-nine
so-la-no
so-lar
so-lar-ism
so-lar-i-um
so-lar-i-za-tion
so-las-o-nine
sol-dered
sol-dier
sol-e-cism
sol-emn
so-lem-ni-ty
sol-em-nize
so-le-noi-dal
sol-fe-ri-no
so-lic-i-ta-tion
so-lic-i-tor
so-lic-it-ous
so-lic-i-tude
sol-id
sol-i-dar-ic
sol-i-da-ris-tic
sol-i-dar-i-ty
so-lid-i-fy
so-lid-i-ty
sol-i-dus
so-lig-e-nous
so-lil-o-quy
so-li-lu-nar
sol-ip-sism
sol-i-taire
sol-i-tar-y
sol-i-tude
so-lod-ize
so-lo-ist
Sol-o-mon
sol-o-netz
so-lo-ni-an
sol-stice
sol-sti-tial
sol-u-bil-i-ty
sol-u-bi-liz-er
so-lum
sol-ute
so-lu-tion
sol-u-tiz-er
solv-a-ble
sol-ven-cy
sol-vent
sol-vol-y-sis
So-ma-li
so-mat-ic
so-ma-ti-za-tion
so-ma-to-gen-ic
som-bre-ro
som-er-sault
som-nam-bu-list
som-nil-o-quy
som-niv-o-len-cy
som-no-lent
so-na-ble
so-nar
so-na-ta
song-ster
son-ic
so-nif-er-ous
son-net-eer
son-o-buoy
so-nom-e-ter
So-no-ra
so-no-rant
son-o-res-cent
son-o-rif-er-ous
so-nor-i-ty
so-no-rous
soon-est
Soph-ist
so-phis-ti-cat-ed
soph-ist-ry
soph-o-mor-ic
sop-o-rif-er-ous
sop-o-rif-ic
so-pra-no
sor-be-fa-cient
sor-bent
sorb-ic
sor-bi-tan
sor-bite
sor-bi-tol
sor-bose
sor-bo-side
sor-cer-er
sor-cer-y
sor-did
sor-ghum
so-ri-tes
so-rit-i-cal
So-rop-ti-mist
so-ror-i-cide
so-ror-i-ty
so-ro-sis
sort-er
sor-tie
sor-ti-lege
so-ste-nu-to
sou-brette
souf-fle
soun-der (herd of swine)
sound-er
sou-tache
south-er-ly
south-ern-er
sou-ve-nir
sov-er-eign
so-vi-et-ism
sov-khoz
Soxh-let
so-zol-ic
spa-cious
spa-cis-tor
spa-ghet-ti
spall-er
span-drel
span-gled
Span-iard
span-iel
spank-er
sparg-er
spark-let
spar-kling
spar-si-ty
Spar-tan
spar-te-ine
spas-mod-ic
spas-mol-y-sis
spas-mo-lyt-ic
spas-tic-i-ty
spa-tial
spa-ti-og-ra-phy
spat-u-la
spav-in
spawn-er
speak-er
spe-cial-ist
spe-ci-al-i-ty
spe-cial-i-za-tion
spe-cial-ty
spe-ci-e (in sort)
spe-cie (coin)
spe-cif-i-cal-ly
spec-i-fi-ca-tion
spec-i-fic-i-ty
spec-i-fi-er
spec-i-men
spe-ci-os-i-ty
spe-cious
speck-led
spec-ta-cle
spec-tac-u-lar
spec-ta-tor
spec-ter
spec-trog-ra-phy
spec-trom-e-ter
spec-trom-e-try
spec-tro-scope
spec-tros-co-py
spec-trum
spec-u-la-tive
spec-u-la-tor
spec-u-lum
speed-er
speed-om-e-ter
speed-ster
spe-le-ol-o-gy
spel-ter
spe-lunk-er
Spen-ce-ri-an
spend-er
Spen-gle-ri-an
sper-ma-ce-ti
sper-mat-ic
sper-ma-tif-er-ous
sper-ma-tin
sper-ma-ti-za-tion
sper-ma-to-cele
sper-ma-to-ci-dal
sper-ma-to-cyte
sper-ma-tor-rhe-a
sper-ma-to-zo-id
sperm-ine
sperm-ism
sphal-er-ite
sphe-nog-ra-phy
sphe-noi-dal
spher-al
spher-i-cal
sphe-ric-i-ty
sphe-roi-dal
sphe-roid-ic-i-ty
sphe-rom-e-ter
spher-u-lite
sphinc-ter-ot-o-my
sphin-gom-e-ter
sphin-go-sine
sphyg-mo-ma-nom-e-ter
sphyg-mom-e-ter
spic-i-ness
spic-u-lar
spi-der
spie-gel-ei-sen
spiel-er
spig-ot
spike-nard
spik-i-ness
spi-lite
spill-er
spil-ler (fish)
spi-lo-ma
spi-lo-site
spi-na-ceous
spin-ach
spi-nal
spi-na-ste-rol
spi-nate
spin-dler
spi-nel
spi-nes-cence
spin-et
spin-or
spi-nose
spi-nos-i-ty
spi-nous
spin-ster
spin-thar-i-scope
spi-nu-les-cent
spir-a-cle
spi-rac-u-lar
spi-raled
spi-re-a
spi-reme
Spi-ri-fer
spi-rif-er-ous
spir-it-ed
spir-it-u-al
spir-i-tu-el
spir-it-u-ous
spi-ro-chete
spi-ro-chet-o-sis
spi-ro-graph
spi-rom-e-ter
spi-ro-met-ric
spi-ro-pen-tane
splanch-ni-cec-to-my
splen-dent
splen-did
splen-dif-er-ous
splen-dor-ous
sple-net-ic
sple-nic
sple-ni-tis
sple-ni-um
splic-er
splin-tered
spo-di-um
spod-u-mene
spoil-age
spoil-er
spo-ken
spo-li-a-tion
spon-dy-li-tis
spong-er
spon-gi-ness
spon-gi-ol-o-gy
spon-si-ble
spon-sor
spon-ta-ne-i-ty
spon-ta-ne-ous
spoon-er-ism
spo-rad-ic
spo-ri-ci-dal
spo-rif-er-ous
spo-ro-gen-ic
spo-ro-phyll
spo-ro-zo-an
spor-tive
spor-u-la-tion
spor-ule
spout-er
spring-er
sprin-kler
sprin-kling
sprint-er
sprock-et
spu-mes-cence
spu-mous
spu-ri-ous
spur-tive
spu-tum
squad-ron
squa-lene
squal-id-i-ty
squal-or
squa-mous
squan-dered
squawk-er
squeal-er
squeam-ish
squee-gee
squeez-er
squint-er
squirt-er
sta-bi-la-tor
sta-bile
stab-i-lim-e-ter
sta-bil-i-ty
sta-bi-li-za-tion
sta-bi-liz-er
sta-bled
stac-ca-to
stach-y-drine
sta-dim-e-ter
sta-di-um
staff-er
stag-mom-e-ter
stain-er
Sta-kha-nov-ite
sta-lac-tite
stal-ac-tit-ic
sta-lag-mite
stal-ag-mit-ic
stal-ag-mom-e-ter
Sta-lin-grad
sta-men
stam-i-na
stam-pede
stamp-er
stan-chion
stand-ard-i-za-tion
stand-ing
sta-nine

stan-nite
sta-pes
Staph-y-lo-coc-cus
staph-y-lot-o-my
sta-pler
starch-er
sta-re de-ci-sis
star-ling
star-lite
start-er
star-tling
star-va-tion
sta-sis
stat-ed
stat-i-cal-ly
sta-tion-ar-y
sta-tion-er-y
sta-tis-ti-cal
stat-is-ti-cian
stat-i-tron
sta-tom-e-ter
sta-tor
stat-o-scope
stat-u-ar-y
stat-u-esque
stat-ure
sta-tus
stat-ute
stat-u-to-ry
stau-ro-lite
stau-ro-scop-ic
stead-i-ness
stealth-i-ness
steam-er
ste-a-rate
ste-ar-ic
ste-a-rin
ste-a-rit-ic
ste-ar-o-yl
ste-a-ryl
ste-a-tite
ste-a-tol-y-sis
ste-a-to-sis
steep-er
stee-ple
steer-age
Ste-fan
Stel-lite
sten-ciled
ste-nog-ra-pher
sten-o-graph-ic
ste-nog-ra-phy
sten-o-ha-line
ste-nom-e-ter
ste-no-sis
sten-o-typ-ist
sten-to-ri-an
Ste-phen
ste-ra-di-an
ster-co-bi-lin-o-gen
ster-co-rite
ster-cu-lic
ster-e-og-no-sis
ster-e-og-ra-pher
ster-e-o-graph-ic
ster-e-om-e-ter
ster-e-om-e-try
ster-e-o-phon-ic
ster-e-oph-o-ny
ster-e-op-ti-con
ster-e-o-scope
ster-e-os-co-py
ster-e-ot-o-my
ster-e-o-typ-er
ster-ic
ster-ile
ste-ril-i-ty
ster-i-li-za-tion
ster-i-liz-er
ster-let
ster-ling
ster-num
ster-nu-ta-to-ry
ste-roi-dal
ste-rol
ster-to-rous
ste-thom-e-ter
steth-o-scope
ste-thos-co-py
Steu-ben
ste-ve-dore
Ste-ven-son
ste-vi-o-side
stew-ard
sthen-ic
stib-a-mine
stib-ine
sti-bin-ic
stib-i-o-pal-la-di-nite
sti-bon-ic
sti-bo-ni-um
stib-o-phen
sti-chom-e-try
stick-ler
stiff-en-er
sti-fling
stig-mas-ter-ol
stig-mat-ic
stig-ma-tism
stig-ma-tize
stil-bene
stil-bes-trol
sti-let-to
stilp-no-mel-ane

stim-u-lant
stim-u-la-tive
stim-u-la-tor
stim-u-lus
sting-er
sting-y (stinging)
stin-gy (close)
stink-er
sti-pend
sti-pen-di-ar-y
sti-pes
stip-i-tat-ic
stip-pled
stip-u-la-tion
stip-ule
stitch-er
stock-ade
sto-gy
sto-i-cal
stoi-chi-o-met-ric
stoi-chi-om-e-try
stok-er
stol-id
sto-lid-i-ty
stom-ach
sto-mach-ic
sto-ma-ti-tis
sto-ma-tol-o-gy
ston-i-ness
stop-pled
stor-age
sto-ried
sto-ri-ette
storm-i-ness
sto-ver
stow-age
stra-bis-mom-e-ter
stra-bis-mus
strad-dler
strag-gler
straight-en-er
strain-er
strait-ened
stra-mo-ni-um
strand-er
stran-ger (n.)
strang-er (adj.)
stran-gler
stran-gu-late
strat-a-gem
stra-te-gi-cal
strat-e-gist
strat-e-gy
strat-i-fi-ca-tion
strat-i-graph-ic
stra-tig-ra-phy
stra-to-cu-mu-lus
strat-o-sphere
strat-o-spher-ic
stra-tum
stra-tus
streak-i-ness
stream-er
strength-en-ing
stren-u-ous
strep-o-gen-in
strep-ta-mine
strep-to-coc-cic
strep-to-coc-co-sis
strep-to-my-cin
strep-to-thri-cin
stretch-er
stri-at-ed
stric-ture
stri-dent
strid-u-lous
stri-gose
strik-er
strin-gent
string-er
strip-er
strob-i-la-ceous
strob-o-scop-ic
strob-o-tron
stro-ga-noff
strok-er
stro-mat-ic
stro-ma-tin
stron-gy-lo-sis
stron-ti-an-if-er-ous
stron-ti-an-ite
stron-ti-um
stro-phan-thi-din
stro-phe
stroph-ic
struc-tur-al
strug-gled
strum-pet
strych-nine
stub-born-ness
stu-dent
stud-ied
stu-di-ous
stul-ti-fy
stum-bling
stump-age
stu-pe-fa-cient
stu-pe-fy
stu-pen-dous
stu-pid-i-ty
stu-por
stur-di-ly
stur-geon
stut-tered

Styg-i-an
sty-let
styl-ish
sty-lis-tic
styl-ize
sty-lo-graph-ic
sty-lom-e-try
sty-lus
sty-mie
styp-tic
sty-rac-i-tol
styr-e-nate
sty-rene
sty-ryl
sua-si-ble
suav-i-ty
su-ber-ate
su-ber-ic
su-ber-in
su-ber-ose
su-ber-yl-ar-gi-nine
sub-jec-tiv-ism
sub-ju-gate
sub-junc-tive
sub-lim-a-ble
sub-li-mate
sub-lime
sub-lim-i-nal
sub-lim-i-ty
sub-li-mize
sub-merged
sub-mer-gence
sub-mer-gi-ble
sub-mer-sal
sub-mersed
sub-mers-i-ble
sub-or-di-nate
sub-or-na-tion
sub-pe-naed
sub-ro-gate
sub-scrib-er
sub-ser-vi-ent
sub-sid-ence
sub-sid-i-ar-y
sub-si-dize
sub-sist-ence
sub-son-ic
sub-stan-tial
sub-stan-tive
sub-stit-u-ent
sub-sti-tut-a-ble
sub-sti-tu-tive
sub-sump-tive
sub-ter-fuge
sub-ti-lin
sub-tle-ty
sub-tract-er
sub-trac-tive
sub-ur-ban
sub-ver-sive
sub-vert-er
sub-vert-i-ble
suc-ce-da-ne-ous
suc-ce-dent
suc-ces-sive
suc-ces-sor
suc-cin-a-mate
suc-ci-nam-ic
suc-cin-a-mide
suc-ci-nate
suc-cin-ic
suc-ci-nyl
suc-cu-lence
suck-ler
su-cre
su-crose
suc-to-ri-al
su-da-men
Su-da-nese
su-da-to-ry
su-do-rif-er-ous
suf-fic-er
suf-fi-cien-cy
suf-fo-ca-tive
suf-fra-gist
suf-fus-a-ble
suf-fu-sive
sug-ar
sug-gest-i-ble
sug-ges-tive
su-i-ci-dal
sui gen-er-is
suit-a-ble
suit-or
su-ki-ya-ki
sul-fa-cet-a-mide
sul-fa-di-az-ine
sul-fa-gua-ni-dine
sul-fa-mer-a-zine
sul-fa-meth-yl-thi-az-ole
sul-fam-ic
sulf-am-ide
sul-fam-o-yl
sul-fa-nil-a-mide
sul-fa-nil-ic
sul-fan-i-lyl
sul-fa-pyr-i-dine
sulf-ars-phen-a-mine
sul-fat-ase
sul-fa-thi-az-ole
sul-fen-ic
sulf-hy-dryl
sul-fide
sul-fi-nyl

Sul-fo-nal
sul-fon-a-mide
sul-fo-nat-ed
sul-fo-na-tor
sul-fon-eth-yl-meth-ane
sul-fon-ic
sul-fo-ni-um
sulf-ox-ide
sul-fu-re-ous
sul-fu-ret-ed
sul-fu-ric
sul-fu-rize
sul-fu-rous
sul-fur-yl
sulk-i-ness
sul-tan-ate
sul-try
su-mac
Su-ma-tran
sum-mar-i-ly
sum-ma-rize
sum-ma-ry
sum-mit-ry
sump-tu-ar-y
sun-der
sun-dry
sunk-en
su-per-a-ble
su-perb
su-per-cil-i-ous
su-per-er-o-gate
su-per-e-rog-a-to-ry
su-per-fi-cial
su-per-flu-ous
su-per-in-tend-ent
su-pe-ri-or-i-ty
su-per-la-tive
su-per-nal
su-per-na-tant
su-per-nat-u-ral
su-per-nu-mer-ar-y
su-per-se-de-as
su-per-se-dure
su-per-sen-si-ble
su-per-son-ic
su-per-sti-tious
su-per-ve-nience
su-per-vis-ee
su-per-vi-so-ry
su-pi-na-tor
sup-ple-men-tal
sup-ple-men-ta-ry
sup-ple-tive
sup-pli-ca-to-ry
sup-port-ive
sup-pos-al
sup-po-si-tion
sup-pos-i-ti-tious
sup-pos-i-to-ry
sup-press-i-ble
sup-pres-sor
sup-pu-ra-tive
su-pra
su-prem-a-cy
sur-a-min
sur-cin-gle
sur-e-ty
sur-fac-er
sur-fac-ing
sur-fac-tant
sur-feit
sur-geon
sur-ger-y
sur-gi-cal
Su-ri-nam-ese
sur-li-ness
sur-mis-a-ble
sur-plice
sur-plus-age
sur-pris-a-ble
sur-re-al-ist
sur-ren-der
sur-rep-ti-tious
sur-ro-gate
sur-veil-lance
sur-viv-al
sur-vi-vor
sus-cep-ti-bil-i-ty
sus-pend-er
sus-pend-i-ble
sus-pen-si-ble
sus-pen-so-ry
sus-pi-cious
sus-pi-ra-tion
sus-te-nance
su-sur-rus
su-tur-al
su-ze-rain
swad-dled
swamp-er
swank-i-ness
swarth-i-ness
swas-ti-ka
sweat-er
Swe-den
Swed-ish
sweep-er
sweet-ened
swel-ter
swift-er
swin-dler
swin-dling
swin-ish
switch-er

Swit-zer-land
swiv-eled
Syb-a-rite
Syb-a-rit-ic
syc-a-more
sych-no-car-pous
syc-o-phan-cy
sy-co-sis
sy-e-nite
syl-la-bar-y
syl-lab-ic
syl-lab-i-fi-ca-tion
syl-la-bize
syl-la-ble
syl-lo-gism
syl-lo-gis-ti-cal
Syl-phon
syl-van-ite
Syl-ves-ter
syl-ves-trene
syl-vite
sym-bi-o-sis
sym-bi-ot-ic
sym-bol-i-cal
sym-bol-ism
sym-bol-ize
sym-bol-o-gy
sym-met-ri-cal
sym-me-trize
sym-me-try
sym-pa-thec-to-my
sym-pa-thet-ic
sym-path-i-co-trop-ic
sym-pa-thin
sym-pa-thiz-er
sym-pa-tho-lyt-ic
sym-pa-thy
sym-phon-ic
sym-pho-ni-ous
sym-pho-nize
sym-pho-ny
sym-phy-sis
sym-phyt-ic
sym-po-si-um
symp-to-mat-ic
symp-tom-a-tize
symp-tom-a-tol-o-gy
syn-a-gogue
syn-apse
syn-ar-thro-sis
syn-chon-drot-o-my
syn-chro-nism
syn-chro-ni-za-tion
syn-chro-niz-er
syn-chron-o-graph
syn-chro-nous
syn-chro-ny
syn-chrop-ter
syn-chro-scope
syn-chro-tron
syn-cli-nal
syn-co-pa-tion
syn-co-pe
syn-des-mo-sis
syn-di-cal-ism
syn-di-cate
syn-drome
syn-ec-do-che
syn-e-col-o-gy
syn-er-e-sis
syn-er-gis-ti-cal
syn-es-the-si-a
syn-ge-nite
syn-od-al
syn-od-i-cal
syn-o-nym
syn-on-y-mous
syn-on-y-my
syn-op-sis
syn-op-tic
syn-o-vi-tis
syn-tec-tic
syn-the-sis
syn-the-siz-er
syn-the-tase
syn-thet-i-cal
syn-thol
syn-to-ni-za-tion
syph-i-lit-ic
syph-i-lol-o-gy
Syr-a-cuse
Syr-i-an
sy-rin-ga
sy-ringe
sy-rin-ge-al
sy-rin-gic
sy-rin-gin
syr-in-gi-tis
syr-in-got-omy
syr-inx
sys-tem-at-i-cal
sys-tem-a-tize
sys-tem-ic
sys-to-le
sys-tol-ic
sy-zyg-i-al
syz-y-gy

T

tab-ard
Ta-bas-co
tab-er-na-cle
tab-er-nan-thine

ta-bes dor-sa-lis
ta-bet-ic
tab-i-net
tab-leaux
ta-ble d'hote
tab-let
ta-bling
tab-loid
ta-boo
tab-o-ret
tab-u-lar
tab-u-la-tor
ta-chis-to-scope
tach-o-graph
ta-chom-e-ter
tach-o-met-ric
ta-chom-e-try
tach-y-car-di-a
tach-y-gen-ic
tach-y-graph-om-e-ter
ta-chyg-ra-phy
ta-chym-e-ter
tach-y-met-ric
ta-chys-ter-ol
tac-it
tac-i-tur-ni-ty
tack-ling
tac-o-nite
tac-ti-cal
tac-ti-cian
tac-tic-i-ty
tac-til-i-ty
tac-tom-e-ter
tac-to-sol
taf-fe-ta
Ta-ga-log
tag-a-tose
tag-e-tone
Ta-hi-tian
tail-er
tai-lored
Tai-wan-ese
tak-ing
talc-ose
tal-ent
ta-les (law)
tal-i-pes
tal-is-man
tal-i-tol
talk-a-tive
talk-er
tal-lage
tall-ate
tal-lith
Tal-mud-ic
tal-on
ta-lon-ic
tal-ose
ta-lus
ta-ma-le
tam-a-rack
tam-a-rind
tam-bour
tam-bou-rine
tamp-er (n.)
tam-per (v.)
Tam-pi-co
tam-pon-ade
tan-a-ce-tin
tan-a-ger
Ta-nan-a-rive
tan-dem
Tan-gan-yi-kan
tan-ge-los
tan-gen-tial
tan-ger-e-tin
tan-ger-ine
tan-gi-ble
tan-gled
tank-age
tan-kard
tank-er
tan-nom-e-ter
tan-ta-lite
tan-ta-liz-er
tan-ta-lum
tan-ta-mount
tan-trum
Tan-za-ni-a
ta-per
tap-er (device; one who tapes)
tap-es-try
ta-pe-tum
tap-i-o-ca
ta-pir
tap-ster
tar-an-tel-la
ta-ran-tu-la
ta-rax-e-in
tar-di-ness
tar-get-eer
tar-iff
tar-nish
tar-pau-lin
tar-pon
tar-sal
tars-ec-to-my
tar-sor-rha-phy
tar-sus
tar-tan
tar-tar-e-ous
tar-tar-ic
tar-tar-ous

tar-tram-ic
tar-tra-mide
tar-trat-ed
ta-sim-e-ter
Tas-ma-ni-an
tas-ma-nite
tas-seled
tast-er
tat-ter-de-ma-lion
tat-too-er
tau-rine
tau-ro-cho-late
tau-rom-a-chy
Tau-rus
tau-ryl
tau-to-log-i-cal
tau-tol-o-gy
tau-to-mer-ic
tau-tom-er-ism
tau-to-met-ric
tau-toph-o-ny
tav-ern
taw-dry
tax-i-der-mist
tax-ied
tax-i-fo-lin
tax-i-ing
tax-i-me-ter
tax-o-nom-ic
tax-on-o-my
Tche-by-cheff
team-ster
tea-seled
teas-er
tech-ne-ti-um
tech-ni-cal
tech-ni-cian
tech-nique
tech-noc-ra-cy
tech-no-log-i-cal
tech-nol-o-gy
tec-ton-ics
tec-ton-ite
te-di-ous
te-di-um
tee-ter
tee-to-tal-er
Tef-lon
teg-men-tal
Te-he-ran
Te-huan-te-pec-er
Tel-Au-to-graph
te-leg-ra-pher
tel-e-graph-ic
tel-e-ki-ne-sis
te-lem-e-ter
tel-e-met-ric
te-lem-e-try
tel-e-mo-tor
tel-e-o-log-i-cal
tel-e-ol-o-gy
tel-e-path-ic
te-lep-a-thy
tel-e-phon-ic
te-leph-o-ny
tel-e-ran
tel-e-scope
tel-e-scop-ic
te-les-co-py
tel-es-the-si-a
tel-e-vi-sion
tel-e-vi-sor
tell-er
tel-lu-ri-an
tel-lu-ride
tel-lu-ri-um
tel-lu-rom-e-ter
tel-lu-ro-ni-um
te-lome
tel-o-mer-i-za-tion
tel-pher-age
tem-blor
te-mer-i-ty
tem-per-a-men-tal
tem-per-ate
tem-per-a-ture
tem-pered
tem-pes-tu-ous
tem-plar
tem-plet
tem-po-ral
tem-po-rar-i-ly
tem-po-rar-y
tem-po-riz-er
tempt-a-ble
tempt-er
tempt-ress
ten-a-ble
te-na-cious
te-nac-i-ty
ten-an-cy
ten-ant-ry
tend-en-cy
tend-er (one who attends; ship)
ten-der (soft; offer)
ten-der-iz-er
ten-der-om-e-ter
ten-di-ni-tis
ten-don
ten-dril
ten-e-bres-cence
ten-e-brous
ten-e-ment

Ten-er-iffe
ten-et
te-nien-te
Ten-ite
Ten-nes-se-an
ten-o-de-sis
ten-on
ten-or
te-not-o-my
ten-si-ble
ten-sil-i-ty
ten-sim-e-ter
ten-si-om-e-ter
ten-so-ri-al
ten-ta-cle
ten-ta-tive
tent-age
ten-ter (drying frame)
tent-er
ten-ter-hook
te-nu-i-ty
ten-u-lin
ten-u-ous
ten-ure
te-pa-che
te-pee
teph-ro-sin
tep-id
te-pid-i-ty
te-qui-la
ter-a-con-ic
ter-a-cryl-ic
ter-a-to-log-i-cal
ter-a-tol-o-gy
ter-a-to-ma
ter-bi-um
ter-cen-te-nar-y
ter-e-ben-thene
te-reb-ic
ter-e-bin-thi-nate
ter-e-bin-thine
ter-eph-thal-ic
ter-gite
ter-gi-ver-sa-tor
ter-ma-gant
term-er
ter-mi-na-ble
ter-mi-nal
ter-mi-na-tor
ter-mi-nol-o-gy
ter-mi-nus
ter-mite
ter-mit-ic
ter-na-ry
ter-op-ter-in
ter-pene
ter-pe-nyl-ic
ter-pi-nene
ter-pin-e-ol
ter-pin-o-lene
ter-pi-nyl
terp-sich-o-re
terp-si-cho-re-an
ter-ra-pin
ter-rar-i-um
ter-raz-zo
terre-plein
ter-res-tri-al
ter-ri-bly
ter-rif-ic
ter-rig-e-nous
ter-ri-to-ri-al
ter-ror-ism
ter-tian
ter-ti-ar-y
ter-tile
tes-sel-lat-ed
test-a-ble
tes-ta-ceous
tes-ta-men-ta-ry
tes-ta-tor
test-er
tes-ter (canopy)
tes-tic-u-lar
tes-ti-fy
tes-ti-mo-ni-al
tes-ti-ness
tes-tos-ter-one
te-tan-ic
tet-a-no-gen-ic
tet-a-nus
tet-a-ny
te-tar-toi-dal
teth-ered
tet-ra-bro-mo
tet-ra-cene
tet-ra-chlo-ro
te-trac-id
tet-ra-co-sa-no-ic
tet-ra-cy-cline
tet-rad
te-trad-ic
tet-ra-eth-yl
tet-ra-gon
te-trag-o-nal
tet-ra-he-dral
tet-ra-hy-dro-fu-ran
tet-ra-kis-a-zo
te-tral-o-gy
tet-ra-mine
tet-ra-ni-tro-meth-ane
tet-ra-ple-gi-a
tet-ra-ploi-dy
te-trar-chic

te-trar-chy
tet-ra-som-a-ty
tet-ra-thi-o-nate
tet-ra-va-lent
tet-ra-zine
tet-ra-zo-li-um
te-traz-o-lyl
tet-ra-zone
tet-ri-tol
te-tron-ic
tet-rose
te-trox-ide
tet-ryl
Teu-ton-ic
Tex-an
tex-tile
tex-tu-al
tex-tur-al
Thai-land
thal-a-mot-o-my
thal-as-som-e-ter
thal-lif-er-ous
thal-line
thal-li-um
than-a-to-sis
thau-ma-site
thau-ma-tur-gy
the-a-ter
the-at-ri-cal
the-mat-i-cal-ly
then-o-yl
the-oc-ra-cy
the-o-crat-ic
the-od-o-lite
The-o-do-si-a
the-o-lo-gian
the-ol-o-gy
the-oph-a-gy
the-o-rem
the-o-re-mat-ic
the-o-ret-i-cal
the-o-re-ti-cian
the-o-rize
the-os-o-phy
ther-a-peu-ti-cal-ly
ther-a-pist
the-ri-at-rics
ther-mal
therm-i-on-ic
therm-is-tor
Ther-mit
ther-mo-chro-mism
ther-mo-du-ric
ther-mog-ra-pher
ther-mo-graph-ic
ther-mol-y-sis
ther-mo-lyt-ic
ther-mom-e-ter
ther-mo-met-ri-cal-ly
ther-mom-e-try
ther-moph-i-ly
ther-mo-scop-ic
ther-mo-stat
ther-mo-ther-a-py
the-sau-rus
the-sis
thes-pi-an
the-tin
the-ve-tin
thi-am-ide
thi-am-i-nase
thi-a-mine
thi-a-naph-thene
thi-an-threne
thi-a-zole
thi-az-o-line
thi-a-zol-sul-fone
thick-en-ing
thiev-ish
thi-mer-o-sal
think-er
thi-o-fla-vine
thi-o-naph-thene
thi-on-ic
Thi-o-nine
thi-o-ni-um
thi-oph-e-nine
thi-o-u-ra-cil
thi-o-u-re-a
thirst-i-ness
thir-ti-eth
this-tle
thith-er
thi-u-ro-ni-um
thix-ot-ro-py
Thom-as
Tho-mism
thon-zyl-a-mine
tho-rac-ic
tho-rac-i-co-lum-bar
tho-ra-co-scope
tho-ra-cos-to-my
tho-ri-ate
tho-rif-er-ous
tho-rite
tho-ri-um
tho-ron
thor-ough
thou-sand
thrash-er
thread-er
threat-en-ing
thre-i-tol
thre-node

thren-o-dy
thre-o-nine
thresh-er
thresh-old
thrift-i-ness
thrill-er
throat-i-ness
throm-bin
throm-bo-an-gi-i-tis
throm-bo-cy-to-sis
throm-bo-plas-tin
throm-bo-sis
throm-bot-ic
throm-bus
throt-tled
thrust-er (one that thrusts)
thrus-tor (machine)
thu-co-lite
thu-ja-pli-cin
thu-jyl
thu-li-um
thump-er
thun-der-ous
thu-ri-ble
thu-rif-er-ous
thy-mi-dine
thy-mi-dyl-ic
thy-mine
thy-mol-phthal-ein
thy-mo-nu-cle-ic
thy-mus
Thy-ra-tron
thy-rite
thy-roi-dal
thy-roid-ec-to-my
thy-roid-i-tis
thy-ro-nine
thy-rot-ro-phin
ti-ar-a
Ti-bet-an
tib-i-al
tick-et-er
tick-i-ci-dal
tick-lish
tid-al
ti-di-ness
ti-ding (news)
tid-ing (tide)
Ti-flis
ti-ger-ish
tight-en-er
tig-lal-de-hyde
ti-gnon
ti-go-nin
ti-gress
ti-grine
ti-grol-y-sis
till-a-ble
till-age
till-er
tilt-er
tim-bered
tim-brel
tim-er
tim-id
ti-mid-i-ty
tim-o-rous
tim-o-thy
tim-pa-nist
tin-cal-co-nite
tinc-to-ri-al
tinc-ture
tin-der
tin-gled
tin-ker
tin-kling
tin-seled
tint-er
tin-tin-nab-u-lous
tint-om-e-ter
tip-ster
ti-queur
ti-rade
ti-rail-leur
Tish-chen-ko
ti-ta-nate
ti-tan-ic
ti-ta-nif-er-ous
ti-ta-ni-um
ti-ter
tith-er
Ti-tian
tit-il-late
ti-tled
ti-trat-a-ble
ti-tra-tion
ti-trim-e-ter
ti-tri-met-ri-cal-ly
tit-u-lar-i-ty
toast-er
to-bac-co-nist
to-bog-gan-er
to-col-o-gy
to-coph-er-ol
toc-sin
tod-dler
to-geth-er
tog-gler
To-go-lese
toil-er
toi-let-ry
to-ken
To-ky-o

tol-bu-ta-mide
tol-er-a-ble
tol-er-a-tion
tol-i-dine
tol-u-ene
to-lu-i-dine
tol-u-ol
to-lu-ric
tol-u-yl-ene
tol-yl-ene
to-mat-i-dine
tom-a-tine
to-men-tose
to-mog-ra-phy
ton-al
to-nal-i-ty
to-neme
ton-er
to-net-ics
tongu-er
tongu-ing
ton-ic
to-nic-i-ty
to-nite (explosive)
ton-neau
ton-o-log-i-cal
to-nom-e-ter
ton-o-met-ric
to-nom-e-try
ton-sil-lec-to-my
ton-sil-li-tis
ton-sil-lot-o-my
ton-so-ri-al
ton-tine
to-nus
tool-er
to-paz-ine
to-pec-to-my
to-per
to-pi-ar-y
top-i-cal
to-pog-ra-pher
top-o-graph-i-cal
to-pog-ra-phy
top-o-log-i-cal
to-pol-o-gy
to-pon-y-my
top-sy-tur-vy
tor-chon
to-re-a-dor
to-ric
to-rin-gin
tor-men-tor
tor-na-do
to-roi-dal
tor-pe-do
tor-pid-i-ty
tor-por-if-ic
torqu-er
torqu-ing
torque-me-ter
tor-ren-tial
tor-si-bil-i-ty
tor-si-om-e-ter
tor-sion-al
tor-til-la
tor-som-e-ter
tor-toise
tor-tu-os-i-ty
tor-tu-ous
tor-tur-ous
tos-yl-ate
tot-a-ble
to-tal-i-tar-i-an-ism
to-tal-i-ty
to-tal-iz-er
to-ta-quine
to-tem-ism
tou-ché
tough-en
tou-pee
tour-ist
tour-ma-line
tour-na-ment
tour-ni-quet
tou-sled
tout-er
tow-age
to-ward
tow-eled
tow-ered
tox-e-mi-a
tox-e-mic
tox-ic-i-ty
tox-i-co-log-i-cal
tox-i-col-o-gist
tox-i-co-sis
tox-if-er-ous
tox-i-ge-nic-i-ty
tox-in
trac-er-y
tra-che-al
tra-che-i-tis
tra-che-ot-o-my
tra-cho-ma
tra-chyt-ic
trac-ing
track-age
trac-ta-ble
trac-tile
trac-tor
trad-er
tra-dev-man
tra-di-tion-al

tra-duc-er
tra-duc-i-ble
traf-fic-a-ble
traf-fick-er
trag-a-can-thin
tra-ge-di-an
tra-ge-di-enne
trag-e-dy
trag-i-cal
trail-er
train-ee
trai-tor-ous
trai-tress
traj-ect (n.)
tra-ject (v.)
tra-jec-tile
tra-jec-to-ry
tram-meled
tramp-er
tram-po-line
tran-quil-iz-er
tran-quil-li-ty
trans-ac-tion
trans-am-i-nase
trans-at-lan-tic
trans-ceiv-er
tran-scend-ent
tran-scen-den-tal
tran-scrib-er
tran-script
trans-duc-er
trans-duc-tor
tran-sect
trans-fer-a-ble
trans-fer-ase
trans-fer-ee
trans-fer-ence
trans-ferred
trans-for-ma-tion
trans-form-er
trans-fus-a-ble
trans-gres-sor
tran-sient
tran-sil-ience
tran-sis-tor
tran-sit-er
tran-si-tion
tran-si-tive
tran-si-to-ry
tran-si-tron
trans-la-tive
trans-la-tor
trans-lit-er-a-tor
trans-lu-cen-cy
trans-mis-si-ble
trans-mis-som-e-ter
trans-mit-ta-ble
trans-mog-ri-fy
trans-mut-a-ble
tran-som
tran-son-ic
trans-par-ent
tran-spir-a-ble
tran-spi-ra-tion
tran-spire
tran-spi-rom-e-ter
trans-plan-ta-tion
trans-pon-der
trans-por-ta-tion
trans-pose
trans-ship
trans-u-da-tion
trans-ver-sal
trans-vers-er
trans-vert-er
trans-vert-i-ble
tra-pe-zi-um
trap-e-zoi-dal
trau-mat-ic
trau-ma-tism
trav-ail
trav-eled
trav-el-er
trav-el-og
tra-vers-a-ble
tra-vers-al
trav-erse (n.)
tra-verse (v.)
trav-er-tine
trav-es-ty
trawl-er
treach-er-ous
treach-er-y
trea-cle
trea-dle
trea-son-a-ble
treas-ur-a-ble
treas-ur-er
treas-ur-y
treat-er
trea-tise
tre-bled
tre-foil
tre-ha-lose
trel-lised
Trem-a-to-da
trem-bling
tre-men-dous
trem-e-tol
trem-o-lo
trem-or
trem-u-lous
trench-ant
tren-cher (board; cap)

trench-er (digger)
tre-pan
tre-phine
treph-o-cyte
treph-one
trep-i-da-tion
tre-pid-i-ty
trep-o-ne-ma-to-sis
trep-o-ne-mi-ci-dal
tres-pass-er
tres-tle
tri-an-gu-lar
tri-ar-yl-meth-ane
tri-a-zine
tri-az-i-nyl
tri-a-zole
tri-az-o-lyl
trib-al
tri-bom-e-ter
tri-bro-mo-eth-yl
trib-u-la-tion
tri-bu-nal
trib-une
trib-u-tar-y
trib-ute
tri-chi-a-sis
tri-chi-na
trich-i-no-sis
tri-chit-ic
tri-chlo-ride
tri-chlo-ro-meth-ane
trich-o-mo-ni-a-sis
tri-cho-sis
tri-chot-o my
trick-er-y
trick-ster
tri-cli-no-he-dric
tri-cy-cle
tri-dec-yl-ene
tri-dent
tri-eth-a-nol-a-mine
tri-far-i-ous
tri-fling
trig-o-nal
tri-go-ni-tis
trig-o-nom-e-ter
trig-o-no-met-ric
trig-o-nom-e-try
tri-ha-lide
tri-he-dral
tri-hy-dric
tri-ke-tone
tri-lo-bite
tri-log-ic
tril-o-gy
tri-mer-ide
tri-mes-ic
tri-meth-yl-ene-tri-ni-tra-mine
tri-met-ro-gon
tri-na-ry
Trin-i-dad
tri-ni-tro-tol-u-ene
trin-i-ty
trin-ket
tri-no-mi-al
Tri-o-nal
tri-part-i-ble
tri-par-tite
tri-phen-yl-ene
tri-phib-i-ous
triph-thong
tri-ple-gi-a
tri-plet
trip-li-cate
trip-loi-dy
tri-pod
trip-o-dal
tri-pod-ic
trip-tych
tri-so-mic
tri-syl-lab-ic
tri-thi-o-nate
trit-i-um
trit-u-ra-tor
tri-tyl
tri-um-phant
tri-um-vi-rate
tri-va-lent
triv-et
triv-i-al
tro-car
tro-chan-ter
tro-che
troch-e-am-e-ter
troch-le-ar
tro-choi-dal
tro-chom-e-ter
trog-lo-dyte
Tro-jan
trom-bi-di-a-sis
tro-mom-e-ter
tro-nom-e-ter
troop-er
tro-pane
tro-pe-ine
troph-ic
tro-phy
trop-i-cal
tro-pism
trop-o-lone
tro-pom-e-ter
tro-po-sphere
trop-tom-e-ter
tro-pyl
trou-ba-dour
trou-bled
trou-blous
trou-sers
trous-seau
tro-ver
trow-eled
tru-an-cy
Truck-ee
truck-ling
truc-u-lent
trump-er-y
trum-pet-er
trun-cat-ed
trun-cheon
trun-dle
truss-ing
trust-ee
tru-xi-llic
tryp-a-no-ci-dal
tryp-a-no-so-ma
tryp-ar-sa-mide
tryp-o-graph
tryp-sin-o-gen
tryp-to-phan
tset-se
tsu-nam-i
tsu-tsu-ga-mu-shi
tu-bec-to-my
tu-ber-cle
tu-ber-cu-lar
tu-ber-cu-lo-sis
tu-ber-cu-lous
tu-ber-os-i-ty
tu-bi-fa-cient
tub-ing
tu-bo-cu-ra-rine
tu-bu-lar
Tuc-son
tu-fa-ceous
tuff-a-ceous
tuft-er
Tui-ler-ies
tu-la-re-mi-a
tu-lip
tum-bler
tum-bling
tum-brel
tu-me-fa-cient
tu-mes-cent
tu-mid
tu-mor
tu-mul-tu-ous
tun-a-ble
tung-sten
tung-stite
tu-nicked
Tu-ni-si-an
tun-neled
tun-nel-er
tu-pe-lo
tu-ran-ose
tur-ban
tur-bi-dim-e-ter
tur-bi-di-met-ric
tur-bid-i-ty
tur-bi-nate
tur-bine
tur-bi-nec-to-my
tur-bo-charg-er
tur-bu-la-tor
tur-bu-lence
tu-reen
tur-ges-cence
tur-gid-i-ty
tur-key
Turk-ish
tur-mer-ic
tur-nip
tur-pen-tine
tur-pi-tude
tur-quoise
tur-tle
tu-te-lage
tu-tored
tu-to-ri-al
Tu-tu-i-lan
tu-yere
tweet-er
tweez-ers
twen-ti-eth
twin-kling
twist-er
Twitch-ell
ty-ing
tym-pan-ic
tym-pa-nist
tym-pa-num
tyn-dall-om-e-ter
typ-a-ble
typh-li-tis
ty-phoi-dal
ty-phoon
ty-phus
typ-i-cal
typ-i-fy
ty-pog-ra-pher
ty-po-graph-ic
ty-pog-ra-phy
ty-po-nym
ty-poth-e-tae
ty-ra-mine
ty-ran-ni-cal
tyr-an-nize
tyr-an-ny
ty-rant
ty-ro-ci-dine
Ty-rode
Ty-ro-le-an
Tyr-o-lese
ty-ro-sin-ase
ty-ro-sine
ty-ro-sin-o-sis

U

u-biq-ui-tous
u-biq-ui-ty
u-dom-e-ter
U-gan-dan
U-krain-i-an
u-ku-le-le
ul-cer-a-tive
ul-nar
ul-na-re
u-lot-o-my
ul-ster
ul-te-ri-or
ul-ti-ma-cy
ul-ti-ma-tum
ul-tra-ma-rine
ul-tra-son-ic
ul-u-late
U-lys-ses
um-bel-lif-er-one
um-ber
um-bil-i-cal
um-bil-i-cus
um-bra-geous
um-brel-la
u-mo-ho-ite
um-pire
u-na-nim-i-ty
u-nan-i-mous
u-na-ry
un-cial
un-ci-na-ri-a-sis
un-ci-nate
un-cle
unc-tu-ous
un-dec-yl-ene
un-dec-y-len-ic
un-der-tak-er
un-du-la-to-ry
un-guen-tous
un-gui-nous
u-ni-bi-va-lent
u-nic-i-ty
u-ni-corn
u-ni-fi-ca-tion
u-ni-form-i-ty
un-ion-ism
u-nip-a-rous
u-nip-o-tent
u-nique-ly
u-ni-son
u-nit-a-ble
u-ni-tar-i-an
u-ni-tar-y
u-nit-ed
u-nit-ize
u-ni-va-lent
u-ni-ver-sal-i-ty
u-ni-ver-si-ty
u-niv-o-cal
un-prec-e-dent-ed
un-re-quit-a-ble
up-heav-al
up-hol-ster-er
Up-per Vol-tan
up-roar-i-ous
u-ra-chus
u-ra-cil
u-ra-nate
U-ra-ni-an
u-ran-ic
u-ra-nif-er-ous
u-ra-nin-ite
u-ra-nite
u-ra-ni-um
u-ra-nog-ra-phy
u-ra-nol-o-gy
u-ra-nom-e-try
u-ra-nos-co-py
u-ra-nous
U-ra-nus
u-ra-nyl
u-ra-zine
ur-ban-i-ty
ur-bi-cul-ture
ur-chin
u-re-am-e-ter
u-re-mi-a
u-re-om e-ter
u-re-ter-i-tis
u-re-thane
u-re-thra
u-re-thri-tis
u-ret-ic
u-re-yl-ene
ur-gen-cy
u-ri-col-y-sis
u-ri-co-lyt-ic
u-ri-nal-y-sis
u-ri-nar-y
u-ri-nate
u-ri-no-cry-os-co-py
u-ri-nol-o-gy
u-ri-nom-e-ter
u-ro-bi-lin-o-gen
u-ro-fla-vin
u-ro-gen-i-tal
u-rog-ra-phy
u-ro-leu-cic
u-ro-li-thi-a-sis
u-ro-li-thol-o-gy
u-ro-log-ic
u-rol-o-gist
u-ro-poi-e-sis
u-ro-poi-et-ic
u-ro-por-phy-rin
u-ros-co-py
u-rot-ro-pine
ur-si-gram
ur-ti-car-i-a
us-a-ble
us-que-baugh
us-ti-la-gin-e-ous
u-su-al-ly
u-su-fruct
u-su-rer
u-su-ri-ous
u-sur-pa-tion
u-surp-er
u-su-ry
U-tah-an
u-ten-sil
u-ter-ine
u-ter-og-ra-phy
u-ter-us
u-til-i-tar-i-an
u-til-i-ty
u-ti-li-za-tion
u-ti-liz-er
u-to-pi-an
u-tri-cle
u-tric-u-lar
u-ve-i-tis
u-vi-ton-ic
u-vu-la
ux-or-i-cide
ux-o-ri-ous
u-zar-i-gen-in
u-za-rin

V

va-can-cy
vac-ci-na-tor
vac-il-la-tion
vac-u-ist
va-cu-i-ty
vac-u-om-e-ter
vac-u-um
va-de me-cum
vag-a-bond-age
va-gar-i-ous
va-gar-y
va-gi-na
vag-i-nal
vag-i-nec-to-my
vag-i-ni-tis
va-got-o-my
va-gran-cy
va-guish
val-ance
val-e-dic-to-ri-an
va-lence
va-len-ci-a
Va-len-ci-ennes
va-lent
val-en-tine
val-er-ate
va-le-ri-an
va-ler-ic
va-le-ryl
val-et
val-e-tu-di-nar-i-an
val-iant
val-i-da-tion
va-lid-i-ty
va-line
va-lise
val-or-i-za-tion
val-or-ous
val-u-a-ble
val-vate
val-vu-lar
val-vu-li-tis
val-vu-lot-o-my
va-nad-ic
van-a-dif-er-ous
va-na-di-um
Van-cou-ver
van-dal-ism
va-nil-la
van-ish
van-i-ty
van-quish-er
van-tage
vap-id
va-pid-i-ty
va-pog-ra-phy
va-por-im-e-ter
va-por-i-za-tion
va-por-iz-er
va-por-ous
var-i-a-bil-i-ty
Var-i-ac
var-i-ant
var-i-at-ed
var-i-a-tion
var-i-co-cele
var-i-cose
var-ied
var-i-e-gat-ed
va-ri-e-tal
va-ri-e-ty
var-i-o-lite
var-i-o-loid
var-i-om-e-ter
var-i-ous
var-is-tor
Var-i-typ-er
var-nish-er
vas-cu-lar
vas-ec-to-my
vas-e-line
vas-o-dil-a-tin
vas-o-di-la-tor
vas-o-mo-tor
vas-sal-age
vas-ti-tude
Vat-i-can
va-tic-i-nal
vaude-ville
vec-to-ri-al
veg-e-ta-ble
veg-e-tar-i-an
veg-e-ta-tive
ve-he-mence
ve-hi-cle
ve-hic-u-lar
vel-lum
vel-o-cim-e-ter
ve-loc-i-pede
ve-loc-i-ty
ve-lom-e-ter
ve-lours
ve-lum
vel-vet-een
ve-nal-i-ty
ve-na-tion
vend-ee
vend-er
ven-det-ta
vend-i-ble
ven-dor
ve-neer-er
ven-e-nif-er-ous
ven-er-a-ble
ve-ne-re-al
ve-ne-re-ol-o-gy
ven-er-y
Ve-ne-tian
venge-ance
ve-ni-al
ve-ni-re fa-ci-as
ven-i-son
ven-om-ous
ve-nous
ven-ter (abdomen)
vent-er (utters)
ven-ti-la-tor
ven-tom-e-ter
ven-tral
ven-tri-cle
ven-tric-u-lar
ven-tri-lo-qui-al
ven-tril-o-quism
ven-tril-o-quist
ven-tur-er
ven-tu-ri
ven-tur-ous
ven-ue
ven-ule
ven-u-lose
Ve-nu-si-an
ve-ra-cious
ve-rac-i-ty
ve-ran-da
ver-a-scope
ver-a-tral-de-hyde
ver-a-tram-ine
ve-rat-ric
ve-rat-ro-yl
Ve-ra-trum
ver-a-tryl-i-dene
ver-bal (adj.)
verb-al (n.) (part of speech)
ver-bal-i-ty
ver-bal-iz-er
ver-ba-tim
ver-be-na
ver-be-na-lin
ver-bi-age
ver-bile
ver-bos-i-ty
ver-bo-ten
ver-dant
ver-di-gris
ver-dur-ous
verg-er
ver-i-fi-a-ble
ver-i-fi-ca-tion
ver-i-si-mil-i-tude
ver-i-ta-ble
Ver-i-tas
ve-ri-tas
ver-i-ty
ver-mi-cel-li
ver-mi-ci-dal
ver-mic-u-lar
ver-mic-u-lite
ver-mi-form
ver-mif-u-gal
ver-mi-fuge
ver-mil-ion
ver-mi-no-sis
ver-min-ous
Ver-mont-er
ver-mouth
ver-nac-u-lar
ver-nal
ver-ni-er
ve-ron-i-ca
ver-ru-co-sis
ver-sa-til-i-ty
ver-sic-u-lar
ver-si-fi-ca-tion
ver-si-fi-er
ver-sus
ver-te-bra
ver-ti-cal
ver-tic-i-ty
ver-tig-i-nous
ver-ti-go
ves-i-cant
ves-i-ca-to-ry
ves-i-cle
ve-sic-u-lar
ves-per-al
ves-tal
vest-ed
ves-tib-u-lar
ves-ti-bule
ves-ti-bu-li-tis
ves-tig-i-al
ves-ti-ture
ves-try
ves-tur-al
Ve-su-vi-us
vet-er-an
vet-er-i-nar-i-an
vex-a-tious
vi-a-bil-i-ty
vi-a do-lo-ro-so
vi-a-duct
vi-bran-cy
vi-bra-to-ry
vib-ri-o-sis
vi-brom-e-ter
vi-bur-num
vic-ar-age
vi-car-i-ous
vice-ge-rent
vice-roy
vi-ce ver-sa
Vi-chy-ite
vi-chys-soise
vi-ci-a-nin
vi-ci-a-nose
vic-i-nage
vic-i-nal
vi-cin-i-ty
vi-cious
vi-cis-si-tude
vic-tim-ize
vic-to-ri-an
vic-to-ri-ous
vict-ualed
vict-ual-er
vi-cu-na
vi-de-li-cet
vid-e-o
Vi-et-nam-ese
vig-i-lance
vig-i-lan-te
vig-i-lan-tism
vi-gnette
vi-gnet-ter
vig-or-ous
vi-king
vi-la-yet
vil-i-fi-er
vil-lag-er
vil-lain-ous
vi-na-ceous
vin-ai-grette
vin-ci-ble
vin-cu-lum
vin-di-ca-ble
vin-di-ca-to-ry
vin-dic-tive
vin-e-gar
vin-er-y
vin-i-cul-tur-al
vi-nif-er-a
vin-ol-o-gy
vin-om-e-ter
vi-nous
vin-tag-er
vint-ner
vi-nyl-a-tion
vi-nyl-ene
vi-nyl-i-dene
Vi-nyl-ite
vi-nyl-o-gous
vi-o-la-ble
vi-o-la-ceous
vi-o-lan-throne
vi-o-la-tor
vi-o-lence
vi-o-les-cent
vi-o-lin-ist
vi-o-lon-cel-lo

vi-o-lu-ric
vi-os-ter-ol
vi-per-ous
vi-ra-go
vi-ral
vi-re-mi-a
vi-res-cence
vir-gin-al
Vir-gin-ian
vir-gin-i-ty
vir-gin-i-um
vir-i-al
vi-ri-ci-dal
vi-rid-i-ty
vir-ile
vi-ril-i-ty
vi-rol-o-gy
vi-ro-sis
vir-tu-al
vir-tu-os-i-ty
vir-tu-o-so
vir-tu-ous
vir-u-lent
vi-rus
vis-aged
vis-cer-al
vis-cid-i-ty
Vis-co-liz-er
vis-com-e-ter
vis-co-scope
vis-cose
vis-co-sim-e-ter
vis-cos-i-ty
vis-cous
vis-i-bil-i-ty
vi-sion-ar-y
vi-sioned
vis-it-ant
vis-it-a-tion
vis-i-tor
vi-sor
vis-ta
vis-u-al
vis-u-al-i-ty
vis-u-al-iz-er
vi-tal-i-ty
vi-tal-ize
vi-ta-min-ol-o-gy
vi-ta-scope
vi-tel-lin
vi-ti-at-ed
vit-i-cul-ture
vit-i-li-go
vit-rain
vit-re-ous
vi-tres-cence
vi-tres-ci-ble
vit-ri-fi-a-ble
vit-ri-fi-ca-tion
vit-ri-ol
vit-ri-o-lat-ed
vit-ri-ol-ic
vi-tu-per-a-tive
vi-va-cious
vi-vac-i-ty
vi-van-dier
vi-vant
vi-var-i-um
vi-va vo-ce
viv-id
vi-vid-i-ty
viv-i-fi-ca-tion
viv-i-par-i-ty
vi-vip-a-rous
viv-i-sec-tion
vix-en-ish
vi-zier
Vlad-i-vos-tok
vo-ca-ble
vo-cab-u-lar-y
vo-cal-ist
vo-cal-iz-er
vo-ca-tion
voc-a-tive
vo-cif-er-ous
voic-ing
void-ance
vol-a-til-i-ty
vol-a-til-i-za-tion
vol-can-ic
vol-ca-no
vo-cod-er
vo-lem-i-tol
vo-li-tion
volt-age
vol-ta-ic
vol-tam-e-ter
volt-am-me-ter
vol-u-bil-i-ty
vol-ume
vol-u-me-nom-e-ter
vo-lu-me-ter
vol-u-met-ric
vo-lu-mi-nous
vol-un-tar-i-ly
vol-un-teered
vo-lup-tu-ar-y
vo-lup-tu-ous
vo-lute
vol-u-tin
vol-vu-lus
vo-mer-ine
vom-it-er
vom-i-tus
voo-doo
vo-ra-cious
vo-rac-i-ty
vor-tex
vor-ti-ces
vor-tic-i-ty
vot-a-ble
vo-ta-ry
vot-er
vo-tive
vouch-er
vow-el
vox po-pu-li
voy-ag-er
voy-a-geur
vul-can-ite
vul-can-i-za-tion
vul-can-iz-er
vul-gar-i-an
vul-gar-ism
vul-gar-i-ty
vul-ner-a-ble
vul-pine
vul-pin-ic
vul-tur-ous
vul-vi-tis

W

wad-dled
wad-er
wa-fer
waf-fle
waft-age
wa-ger (bet)
wag-er (competitor)
wag-es
Wag-ne-ri-an
wag-on-er
wag-on-ette
wain-scot-ing
wait-er
wait-ress
waiv-er
wak-en-er
walk-er
wal-lop-er
Wal-tham
waltz-er
wam-pum
wan-der
wan-gled
wan-ton
wap-i-ti
war-bler
war-den
ward-er
war-fa-rin
war-i-ness
warm-er
warp-age
war-rant-ee
war-rant-er
war-ran-tor (law)
war-ran-ty
war-ri-or
wash-a-ble
Wash-ing-to-ni-an
wasp-ish
was-sail
Was-ser-mann
wast-age
wast-er
was-trel
wa-ter-me-ter
watt-age
wave-me-ter
wa-ver (sway)
wav-er (waving)
Wa-ver-ley
wax-en
weak-ened
weak-ling
weap-on-eer
wear-a-ble
wea-ri-ness
wea-ri-some
wea-seled
weath-ered
weath-er-om-e-ter
weav-er
Web-er
Web-ste-ri-an
Wechs-ler
wed-ding
Wedg-wood
Wednes-day
weed-er
weep-er
wee-viled
weight-i-ness
Weight-om-e-ter
Wei-mar-an-er
weld-er
wel-kin
welsh-er
wel-ter
welt-er (worker on shoes, etc.)
Wes-ley-an
west-er-ly
west-ern-er
West-min-ster
West-pha-li-an
weth-er
whal-er-y
wharf-age
wheat-en
whee-dled
wheel-er
wheez-i-ness
wher-ev-er
wheth-er
whi-lom
whim-pered
whim-si-cal
whim-sy
whirl-er
whirl-i-gig
whisk-ered
whis-kies
whis-ky
whis-pered
whis-tler
whis-tling
whit-en-ing
whith-er
whit-ish
whit-tled
whor-tle-ber-ry
wick-ed-ly
wick-ered
wick-et
wick-i-up
wid-en
widg-eon
widg-et
wid-ow-er
wie-ner schnit-zel
Wies-ba-den
wie-sen-bo-den
wild-er
wil-der-ness
Wil-helms-ha-ven
Wil-helm-stras-se
Wil-lam-ette
will-ful-ness
Wil-liam
Wil-ton
wind-age
wind-er
wind-i-ness
win-dow
wind-row
Wins-low
win-some
win-ter-ize
win-try
wip-er
wir-i-ness
Wis-con-sin-ite
wise-a-cre
wis-tar-i-a
Wis-te-ri-a
witch-er-y
with-al
with-ered
wit-ti-cism
wiz-ard-ry
wiz-ened
wob-bu-la-tor
woe-ful-ness
wolf-ra-min-i-um
wolf-ram-ite
wol-las-ton-ite
wol-ver-ine
wom-an
wom-bat
wom-en
won-dered
won-drous
wood-en
woof-er
wool-en
wool-ly
Worces-ter
word-ster
work-er
wor-ri-some
wor-shiped
wor-ship-er
wor-sted
wor-thi-ly
wor-thy
wo-ven
wran-gler
wreck-age
wres-tler
wres-tling
wretch-ed
wring-er
wrin-kled
wrist-let
writ-er
Wy-an-dotte
Wyc-liffe
Wy-o-ming-ite

X

xan-tha-mide
xan-thate
xan-the-nyl
xan-thine
xan-tho-gen-ate
xan-tho-ma
xan-tho-ma-to-sis
xan-thom-a-tous
xan-thom-e-ter
xan-tho-phyll
xan-thop-ter-in
xan-thous
xan-thox-y-le-tin
xan-thy-drol
Xa-ve-ri-an
xe-ni-al
xen-o-lith
xe-non
xen-o-pho-bi-a
xen-yl
Xe-res
xe-ric
xe-ro-gel
xe-ro-graph-ic
xe-rog-ra-phy
xe-ro-phyte
xe-ro-phyt-ic
xe-ro-sis
xiph-oid
xi-phop-a-gus
xy-lem
xy-lene
xy-le-nol
xy-le-nyl
xy-lic
xy-li-dine
xy-lin-de-in
xy-lo-graph-ic
xy-log-ra-phy
xy-loid
xy-lol-o-gy
xy-lom-e-ter
xy-loph-a-gous
xy-lo-phone
xy-lo-side
xy-lot-o-my
xy-lo-yl
xy-lu-lose
xy-lyl-ene
Xy-ris

Y

Yak-i-ma
Yak-u-tat
ya-men
Yan-kee
Ya-qui
yard-age
yaw-me-ter
Ya-zoo
year-ling
yeast-i-ness
yelp-er
Yem-en-ite
yeo-man
yes-ter-day
yield-a-ble
yo-del-er
yo-gurt
yo-him-bine
yo-kel
yon-der
Yo-sem-i-te
young-ster
y-per-ite
yp-sil-i-form
yt-ter-bi-um
yt-ter-bous
yt-trif-er-ous
yt-tri-um
yt-tro-tan-ta-lite
Yu-go-slav

Z

Zach-a-ri-ah
Zam-bi-an
za-ni-ness
za-pa-te-a-do
zeal-ot
zea-lot-i-cal
zeal-ous
ze-a-xan-thin
ze-bra
ze-nith
ze-nog-ra-phy
ze-o-lite
ze-ol-i-tize
zeph-yr
Zep-pe-lin
ze-ro-ize
ze-ros
zib-el-ine
zinc-ate
zinc-if-er-ous
zin-cog-ra-phy
zinc-oid
zin-ger-one
zin-gi-ber-ene
Zi-on-ism
zirc-ite
zir-con-ate
zir-co-ni-um
zir-co-nyl
zith-er
Ziz-i-phus
zlo-ty
zo-an-thro-py
zo-di-ac
zo-di-a-cal
Zo-is-i-a
zois-it-i-za-tion
Zoll-ver-ein
zon-al
zon-ar-y
zon-ate
zo-nif-er-ous
zo-og-a-my
zo-o-gen-ic
zo-ol-a-ter
zo-o-log-i-cal
zo-ol-o-gy
zo-om-e-ter
zo-on-o-sis
zo-o-phyte
zo-os-co-py
zo-os-ter-ol
zo-ot-o-my
Zo-ro-as-tri-an
Zou-ave
Zo-ys-i-a
zu-mat-ic
zun-yite
zwie-back
zwit-ter-i-on
zyg-a-de-nine
zy-gal
zy-go-mat-ic
zy-gote
zy-got-ic
zy-mase
zy-min
zy-mo-gen-ic
zy-mog-e-nous
zy-mo-hy-drol-y-sis
zy-mol-o-gy
zy-mom-e-ter
zy-mo-sis
zy-mos-ter-ol
zy-mos-then-ic
zy-mur-gy

German/English Dictionary

German is spoken by over 80 million people in Germany, Austria and parts of Switzerland and Czechoslovakia. There are a number of local variations of German and sometimes you will hear people speaking in a way that seems quite different from what is shown in this *Guide*. However, almost everybody also speaks, or at least understands, the form of German given here, which is the one taught in the German schools.

*How to Use the Records and Guide

This *Guide* is not intended to give you a complete command of the language. If you want to embark upon a somewhat extensive study of the spoken language you should obtain the USAFI course, Spoken German—see the current USAFI Catalog for instructions. This *Guide* will, however, enable you to carry on simple conversations in German.

The records that go with this *Guide* give you a number of the most important words and phrases in German. Read the section called *Hints on Pronunciation* and then listen to the records until you know the *Useful Words and Phrases* by heart. Repeat each word out loud right after you hear it and say it exactly the way the German speaker does. Imitate the pronunciation as closely as you can, just as you might mimic someone who has an unusual accent. Try to get every detail of the pronunciation, even the rhythm and the intonation. Follow the words in your *Guide* but use them only as a reminder; if you hear something different from what you see written, go by what you hear. Remember that you can't get the sound of a language from the printed word alone—you have to use your ears even more than your eyes. If you don't have the records and can't get a German speaker to read the words, you will have to rely on the *Hints on Pronunciation* alone.

By the time you have practiced the *Useful Words and Phrases* several times you will know what sound each letter stands for in the *Guide*. You will then be able to pronounce the *Additional Expressions* even though you have not actually heard them and you will be able to form sentences of your own by using the section called *Fill-In Sentences*.

**Hints on Pronunciation

If you have studied German before, you may not need additional practice in pronunciation. However, unless you have had a chance to try out your German and know that you are understood without any difficulty, you had better do a little practicing.

All the words and phrases in this *Guide* are written both in German spelling and in a simplified spelling which you read like English. (Don't use the German spelling, the one given in parentheses, unless you have studied German before.) *Read the simplified spelling as though it were English.* Each letter or combination of letters is used for the sound it usually stands for in English and it *always* stands for that sound. Thus, *oo* is always pronounced as it is in *too*, *boot*, *tooth*, *roost*, never as anything else. Say these words and then pronounce the vowel sound by itself. That is the sound you must use every time you see *oo* in the *Pronunciation* column. If you should use some other sound—for example, the sound of *oo* in *blood*—you may be misunderstood.

Syllables that are accented, that is, pronounced louder than others, are written in capital letters. Curved lines (‿) are used to show sounds that are pronounced together without any break; for example, *P‿FEN-nik* meaning "pfennig," *P‿FEF-fer* meaning "pepper."

Special Points

Here are a few points to note as you listen to the records:

AY	as in *may*, *say*, *play* but don't drawl it the way we do in English. Example: *TAY* meaning "tea."
O or OH	as in *go*, *so*, *oh*, *note*, *joke* but don't drawl it the way we do in English. Example: *VO* meaning "where."
AI	as in *aisle* Example: *AINSS* meaning "one."
EW	stands for a sound we do not have in English. To make it you round your lips as though to say the *oo* in *boo* and at the same time say the *ee* in *bee*. Example: *guh-MEW-zuh* meaning "vegetables."
ER	stands for a sound somewhat like the one in *her* except that you round your lips as you make the sound. Example: *TSVERLF* meaning "twelve."
KH	stands for a sound something like the one you make when you clear your throat to spit. Example: *NAHKH* meaning "toward."

*Records no longer available. ** *ow* as in *now; ai* as in *aisle*

Memory Key

AY	as in *day* but not so drawled.
O or *OH*	as in *go* but not so drawled.
AI	as in *aisle*
EW	for the sound in *bee* said with the lips rounded.
ER	for the sound in *her* said with the lips rounded.
KH	for a sound which is like the one you make when you clear your throat to spit.

USEFUL WORDS AND PHRASES

The following is the exact wording of the German Language Records issued with this *Guide:*

> These records give you a few useful phrases in German. To learn to say these phrases so that you will be understood, imitate the sounds exactly as you hear them. You will hear the English first, followed by the German; then repeat the German out loud, and say it *good and loud.* Remember! Repeat every German phrase right after you hear it.
>
> In the *German Language Guide* which should be used with these records, all the phrases you will hear are written both in German spelling and in a simplified spelling which you read like English. Don't use the German spelling unless you have studied German before.
>
> Listen to the records six or seven times and you will know the phrases by heart.

GREETINGS AND GENERAL PHRASES

English	Pronunciation and German Spelling
Good morning	*GOO-ten MAWR-gen* (Guten Morgen)
Good day	*GOO-ten TAHK* (Guten Tag)
Good evening	*GOO-ten AH-bent* (Guten Abend)
How are you?	*vee GAYT ess ee-nen?* (Wie geht es Ihnen?)
Sir	*main HAYR* (mein Herr)
Madam	*G‿NAY-dig-uh FROW* (gnädige Frau)
Miss	*G‿NAY-dig-ess FROY-lain* (gnädiges Fräulein)

When you address a person by name you say:

Mr. Schmidt	*HAYR SHMIT* (Herr Schmidt)
Mrs. Schmidt	*FROW SHMIT* (Frau Schmidt)
Miss Schmidt	*FROY-lain SHMIT* (Fräulein Schmidt)
Please	*BIT-tuh* (Bitte)
Excuse me	*fayr-TSAI-oong* (Verzeihung)
Thank you	*DAN-kuh* (Danke)

When someone thanks you, you answer with the word for "please."

English	Pronunciation and German Spelling
Please	*BIT-tuh* (Bitte)
Yes	*YA* (Ja)
No	*NAIN* (Nein)
Do you understand?	*fer-SHTAY-en zee?* (Verstehen Sie?)
I understand	*ish fer-SHTAY-uh* (Ich verstehe)
I don't understand	*ish fer-SHTAY-uh nisht* (Ich verstehe nicht)
Speak slowly	*SHPRESH-en zee LAHNK-zahm* (Sprechen Sie langsam)
Please repeat	*BIT-tuh vee-der-HO-len zee* (Bitte wiederholen Sie)

LOCATION

When you need directions to get somewhere you use the phrase "Where is?" and then add the words you need.

English	Pronunciation and German Spelling
Where is	*VO IST* (Wo ist)
a restaurant	*ain ress-to-RAHNG* (ein Restaurant)
Where is a restaurant?	*VO ist ain ress-to-RAHNG?* (Wo ist ein Restaurant?)
a hotel	*ain ho-TEL* (ein Hotel)
Where is a hotel?	*VO ist ain ho-TEL?* (Wo ist ein Hotel?)
a railroad station	*ain BAHN-hohf* (ein Bahnhof)
Where is a railroad station?	*VO ist ain BAHN-hohf?* (Wo ist ein Bahnhof?)
a toilet	*ai-nuh twa-LET-tuh* (eine Toilette)
Where is a toilet?	*VO ist ai-nuh twa-LET-tuh?* (Wo ist eine Toilette?)

DIRECTIONS

The answer to your question "Where is such and such?" may be "To the right" or "To the left" or "Straight ahead," so you need to know these phrases.

To the right	*nahkh RESHTS* (nach rechts)
To the left	*nahkh LINKS* (nach links)

In the word *NAHKH* you heard a sound you must practice. It is written in your *Language Guide* as *kh*. Listen to the word again and repeat: *NAHKH, NAHKH*. It is like clearing your throat when you have to spit. Try just the sound again: *kh, kh*

Straight ahead	*guh-RA-duh-OWSS* (geradeaus)

It is sometimes useful to say "Please show me."

** *ow* as in *now; ai* as in *aisle*

English	Pronunciation and German Spelling
Please show me	*BIT-tuh TSAI-gen zee meer* (Bitte zeigen Sie mir)

If you are driving and ask the distance to another town, it will be given you in kilometers, not miles.

Kilometer	*kee-lo-MAY-ter* (Kilometer)

One kilometer equals ⅝ of a mile.

NUMBERS

You need to know the numbers.

One	*AINSS*	eins
Two	*TSVAI*	zwei
Three	*DRAI*	drei
Four	*FEER*	vier
Five	*FEWNF*	fünf
Six	*ZEKS*	sechs
Seven	*ZEE-ben*	sieben
Eight	*AHKHT*	acht
Nine	*NOYN*	neun
Ten	*TSAYN*	zehn
Eleven	*ELF*	elf
Twelve	*TSVERLF*	zwölf

Notice the sound of *er* in the last word. Listen to the word again and repeat: *TSVERLF, TSVERLF.* We don't have this sound in English, but the sound we have in "her" is close to it. Round your lips as though you were pronouncing the "o" in *go*, and at the same time say the *er* in *her*. Try just the sound again: *er, er*.

Thirteen	*DRAI-tsayn*	dreizehn
Fourteen	*FEER-tsayn*	vierzehn
Fifteen	*FEWNF-tsayn*	fünfzehn
Sixteen	*ZESH-tsayn*	sechzehn
Seventeen	*ZEEP-tsayn*	siebzehn
Eighteen	*AHKH-tsayn*	achtzehn
Nineteen	*NOYN-tsayn*	neunzehn
Twenty	*TSVAHN-tsik*	zwanzig

To say "twenty-one," "twenty-two," etc. you say in German "one and twenty," "two and twenty," etc.

English	Pronunciation and German Spelling	
Twenty-one	*AIN-oont-tsvahn-tsik*	einundzwanzig
Twenty-two	*TSVAI-oont-tsvahn-tsik*	zweiundzwanzig
Thirty	*DRAI-sik*	dreissig
Forty	*FEER-tsik*	vierzig
Fifty	*FEWNF-tsik*	fünfzig
Sixty	*ZESH-tsik*	sechzig
Seventy	*ZEEP-tsik*	siebzig
Eighty	*AHKH-tsik*	achtzig
Ninety	*NOYN-tsik*	neunzig
Hundred	*HOON-dert*	hundert
Thousand	*TOW-zent*	tausend

WHAT'S THIS?

When you want to know the name of something you can say "What's this?" or "What's that?" and point to the thing you mean.

English	Pronunciation and German Spelling
What is	*VAHSS IST* (Was ist)
this	*DEESS* (dies)
What's this?	*VAHSS ist DEESS?* (Was ist dies?)
What's that?	*VAHSS ist DAHSS?* (Was ist das?)

ASKING FOR THINGS

When you want something, use the phrase "I want" and then add the name of the thing wanted. Always use "Please"—*BIT-tuh*.

I want	*ish MERSH-tuh* (Ich möchte)
cigarettes	*tsee-ga-RET-ten* (Zigaretten)
I want cigarettes	*ish MERSH-tuh tsee-ga-RET-ten* (Ich möchte Zigaretten)
to eat	*ESS-sen* (essen)
I want to eat	*ish MERSH-tuh ESS-sen* (Ich möchte essen)

Here are the words for some of the things you may require.

English	Pronunciation and German Spelling
drinking water	*TRINK-vahss-ser* (Trinkwasser)
bread	*BROHT* (Brot)
butter	*BOOT-ter* (Butter)
eggs	*AI-er* (Eier)
cheese	*KAY-zuh* (Käse)
meat	*FLAISH* (Fleisch)
pork	*SHVAI-nuh-flaish* (Schweinefleisch)
mutton	*HAHM-mel-flaish* (Hammelfleisch)
veal	*KAHLP-flaish* (Kalbfleisch)
beef	*RINT-flaish* (Rindfleisch)
chicken	*HOON* (Huhn)
fish	*FISH* (Fisch)
soup	*ZOOP-puh* (Suppe)
vegetables	*guh-MEW-zuh* (Gemüse)

** *ow* as in *now; ai* as in *aisle*

You have just heard another sound you must practice. It is written in your *Guide* as *ew*. Listen to the word again and repeat: *guh-MEW-zuh*, *guh-MEW-zuh*. To make this sound you round your lips as though to say *oo* but say *ee* instead. Try just the sound again: *ew*, *ew*.

English	Pronunciation and German Spelling
potatoes	*kar-TAWF-feln* (Kartoffeln)
beets	*RO-tuh REW-ben* (rote Rüben)
beans	*BO-nen* (Bohnen)
cabbage	*KOHL* (Kohl)
salad	*za-LAHT* (Salat)
fruit	*OHPST* (Obst)
milk	*MILSH* (Milch)
salt	*ZAHLTS* (Salz)
pepper	*P‿FEF-fer* (Pfeffer)
sugar	*TSOOK-ker* (Zucker)
chocolate	*sho-ko-LA-duh* (Schokolade)
tea	*TAY* (Tee)
coffee	*KAHF-fay* (Kaffee)
a cup of coffee	*ai-nuh TAHSS-suh KAHF-fay* (eine Tasse Kaffee)
wine	*VAIN* (Wein)
beer	*BEER* (Bier)
a glass of beer	*ain GLAHSS BEER* (ein Glas Bier)
tobacco	*TA-bahk* (Tabak)
matches	*SHTRAISH-herl-tser* (Streichhölzer)

MONEY

To find out how much things cost, you say

How much	*vee-FEEL*	Wieviel
costs	*KAWSS-tet*	kostet
that	*DAHSS*	das
How much does that cost?	*vee-feel'KAWSS-tet DAHSS?*	(Wieviel kostet das?)

The answer will be given you in marks and pfennigs

mark	*MARK* (Mark)
pfennig	*P‿FEN-nik* (Pfennig)

TIME

When you want to know what time it is, you say really "How late is it?"

English	Pronunciation and German Spelling
What time is it?	*vee SHPAYT ist ess?* (Wie spät ist es?)
Two o'clock	*TSVAI OOR* (zwei Uhr)
Ten past two	*TSAYN nahkh TSVAI* (zehn nach Zwei)
Quarter past five	*FEER-tel nahkh FEWNF* (viertel nach Fünf)

"Half past six" is "six o'clock thirty" or "half seven."

Half past six	*ZEKS oor DRAI-sik* (sechs Uhr dreissig) *or HAHLP ZEE-ben* (halb Sieben).

"A quarter of eight" is "three quarters eight."

Quarter of eight	*DRAI-feer-tel AHKHT* (dreiviertel Acht)

"Five minutes to nine" is "five minutes before nine."

Five minutes to nine	*FEWNF mee-NOO-ten for NOYN* (fünf Minuten vor Neun)

For the hours after 12 noon it is customary to say "thirteen o'clock"—*DRAI-tsayn OOR*, and so on, just as we do in the Army.

If you want to know when a movie starts or when a train leaves, you say:

English	Pronunciation and German Spelling
When	*VAHN* (Wann)
begins	*buh-GINT* (beginnt)
the movie	*dahss KEE-no* (das Kino)
When does the movie start?	*VAHN buh-GINT dahss KEE-no?* (Wann beginnt das Kino?)
leaves	*GAYT* (geht)
the train	*dayr TSOOK* (der Zug)
When does the train leave?	*vahn GAYT dayr TSOOK?* (Wann geht der Zug?)
Yesterday	*GESS-tern* (gestern)
Today	*HOY-tuh* (heute)
Tomorrow	*MAWR-gen* (morgen)

The days of the week are:

Sunday	*ZAWN-tahk* (Sonntag)
Monday	*MOHN-tahk* (Montag)
Tuesday	*DEENSS-tahk* (Dienstag)
Wednesday	*MIT-vawkh* (Mittwoch)
Thursday	*DAWN-nerss-tahk* (Donnerstag)
Friday	*FRAI-tahk* (Freitag)
Saturday	*ZAMSS-tahk* (Samstag) *or ZAWN-ah-bent* (Sonnabend)

OTHER USEFUL PHRASES

The following phrases will be useful.

** *ow* as in *now*; *ai* as in *aisle*

English	Pronunciation and German Spelling
What is your name?	*VEE HAI-sen zee?* (Wie heissen Sie?)
My name is___	*ish HAI-suh___* (Ich heisse___)
How do you say *table* (or anything else) in German?	*vahss ZA-gen zee fewr* table *owf DOYTSH?* (Was sagen Sie für *table* auf Deutsch?)
I am an American	*ish bin ah-may-ree-KA-ner* (Ich bin Amerikaner)
Please help me	*BIT-tuh HEL-fen zee meer* (Bitte helfen Sie mir)
Where is the nearest town?	*VO ist dee NAYSH-stuh AWRT-shaft?* (Wo ist die nächste Ortschaft?)
Good-by	*owf VEE-der-zayn* (Auf Wiedersehen)

ADDITIONAL EXPRESSIONS

English	Pronunciation and German Spelling
I am hungry	*ish HA-buh HOONG-er* (Ich habe Hunger)
I am thirsty	*ish HA-buh DOORST* (Ich habe Durst)
Halt! *or* Stop!	*HAHLT!* (Halt!)
Come here!	*KAWM-men zee HAYR!* (Kommen Sie her!)
Quickly	*SHNEL* (schnell)
Come quickly!	*KAWM-men zee SHNEL!* (Kommen Sie schnell!)
Go quickly!	*GAY-en zee SHNEL!* (Gehen Sie schnell!)
Help!	*HIL-fuh!* (Hilfe!)
Bring help!	*HO-len zee HIL-fuh!* (Holen Sie Hilfe!)
I am lost	*ish HA-buh mish fayr-LOW-fen* (Ich habe mich verlaufen)
I will pay you	*ish VAYR-duh EE-nen GELT GAY-ben* (Ich werde Ihnen Geld geben)
Where are the American sailors?	*VO ZINT dee a-may-ree-KA-nee-shen mah-TROH-zen?* (Wo sind die amerikanischen Matrosen?)
Where is the town?	*VO IST dee SHTAHT?* (Wo ist die Stadt?)
Where is it?	*VO IST ess?* (Wo ist es?)
How far is it?	*vee VAIT ist ess?* (Wie weit ist es?)
Which way is north?	*VO ist NAWR-den?* (Wo ist Norden?)
Which is the road to___?	*VO ist dayr VAYK nahkh___?* (Wo ist der Weg nach___?)
Draw me a map	*TSAISH-nen zee meer ai-nuh KAR-tuh* (Zeichnen Sie mir eine Karte)
Take me there	*BRIN-gen zee mish dawrt HIN* (Bringen Sie mich dort hin)
Take me to a doctor	*BRIN-gen zee mish tsoo AI-nem ARTST* (Bringen Sie mich zu einem Arzt)
Take me to a hospital	*BRIN-gen zee mish tsoo AI-nem la-tsa-RET* (Bringen Sie mich zu einem Lazarett)
Danger!	*guh-FAR!* (Gefahr!)
Watch out!	*OWF-pahss-sen!* (Aufpassen!)
Gas!	*GAHSS!* (Gas!)
Take cover!	*DEK-koong!* (Deckung!)
Wait a moment!	*VAR-ten zee ai-nen OW-gen-blik!* (Warten Sie einen Augenblick!)

FILL-IN SENTENCES

In this section you will find a number of sentences, each containing a blank space which can be filled in with any one of the words in the list that follows. For example, to say "Where can I get some soap?" look for the phrase "Where can I get___?" in the English column and find the German expression given beside it: *VO kahn ish___buh-KAWM-men.* Then look for "soap" in the list that follows; the German word is *ZAI-fuh.* Put the word for "soap" in the blank space and you get *VO kahn ish ZAI-fuh buh-KAWM-men?*

English	Pronunciation and German Spelling
I want___	*ish MERSH-tuh___* (Ich möchte___)
We want___	*veer MERSH-ten___* (Wir möchten___)
Give me___	*GAY-ben zee meer___* (Geben Sie mir___)
Bring me___	*BRIN-gen zee meer___* (Bringen Sie mir___)
Get me___	*HO-len zee meer___* (Holen Sie mir___)
Where can I get___?	*VO kahn ish___ buh-KAWM-men?* (Wo kann ich___ bekommen?)
I have___	*ish HA-buh___* (Ich habe___)
We have___	*veer HA-ben___* (Wir haben___)
Have you___?	*HA-ben zee___?* (Haben Sie___?)

EXAMPLE

I want___	*ish MERSH-tuh___* (Ich möchte___)
food	*ET-vahss tsoo ESS-sen* (etwas zu essen)
I want food	*ish MERSH-tuh ET-vahss tsoo ESS-sen* (Ich möchte etwas zu essen)
apples	*EP-fel* (Äpfel)
bacon	*SHPEK* (Speck)
beefsteak	*BEEF-shtayk* (Beefsteak)
boiled water	*AHP-guh-kawkh-tess VAHSS-ser* (abgekochtes Wasser)
carrots	*GEL-buh REW-ben* (gelbe Rüben)
cucumbers	*GOOR-ken* (Gurken)
grapes	*TROW-ben* (Trauben)
ham	*SHIN-ken* (Schinken)
a meal	*ai-nuh MAHL-tsait* (eine Mahlzeit)
onions	*TSVEE-beln* (Zwiebeln)
oranges	*ahp-fel-ZEE-nen* (Apfelsinen)
peas	*AYRP-sen* (Erbsen)
rice	*RAISS* (Reis)

** *ow* as in *now;* *ai* as in *aisle*

English	Pronunciation and German Spelling
spinach	*shpee-NAHT* (Spinat)
tangerines	*mahn-da-REE-nen* (Mandarinen)
turnips	*VAI-suh REW-ben* (weisse Rüben)
a cup	*ai-nuh TAHSS-suh* (eine Tasse)
a fork	*ai-nuh GA-bel* (eine Gabel)
a glass	*ain GLAHSS* (ein Glas)
a knife	*ain MESS-ser* (ein Messer)
a plate	*ai-nen TEL-ler* (einen Teller)
a spoon	*ai-nen LERF-fel* (einen Löffel)
a bed	*ain BET* (ein Bett)
bedding	*BET-tsoyk* (Bettzeug)
blankets	*DEK-ken* (Decken)
a mattress	*ai-nuh ma-TRA-tsuh* (eine Matratze)
a pillow	*ain KISS-sen* (ein Kissen)
a room	*ain TSIM-mer* (ein Zimmer)
sheets	*BET-la-ken* (Bettlaken)
cigars	*tsee-GAR-ren* (Zigarren)
a pipe	*ai-nuh P‿FAI-fuh* (eine Pfeife)
pipe tobacco	*P‿FAI-fen-ta-bahk* (Pfeifentabak)
ink	*TIN-tuh* (Tinte)
a pen	*ai-nen FAY-der-hahl-ter* (einen Federhalter)
a pencil	*ai-nen BLAI-shtift* (einen Bleistift)
a comb	*ai-nen KAHM* (einen Kamm)
hot water	*HAI-sess VAHSS-ser* (heisses Wasser)
a razor	*ai-nen ra-ZEER-ahp-pa-raht* (einen Rasierapparat)
razor blades	*ra-ZEER-kling-en* (Rasierklingen)
a shaving brush	*ai-nen ra-ZEER-pin-zel* (einen Rasierpinsel)
shaving soap	*ra-ZEER-zai-fuh* (Rasierseife)
soap	*ZAI-fuh* (Seife)
a toothbrush	*ai-nuh TSAHN-bewr-stuh* (eine Zahnbürste)
tooth paste	*TSAHN-kraym* (Zahncreme)
a towel	*ain HAHN-tookh* (ein Handtuch)
a handkerchief	*ain TA-shen-tookh* (ein Taschentuch)
a raincoat	*ai-nen RAY-gen-mahn-tel* (einen Regenmantel)
a shirt	*ain HEMT* (ein Hemd)
shoe laces	*SHNEWR-zen-kel* (Schnürsenkel)
shoe polish	*SHOO-kraym* (Schuhcreme)

English	Pronunciation and German Spelling
shoes	*SHOO-uh* (Schuhe)
undershirt	*OON-ter-hemt* (Unterhemd)
undershorts	*OON-ter-ho-zen* (Unterhosen)
underwear	*OON-ter-vesh-shuh* (Unterwäsche)
buttons	*KNERP-fuh* (Knöpfe)
a needle	*ai-nuh NA-del* (eine Nadel)
pins	*SHTEK-na-deln* (Stecknadeln)
safety pins	*ZISH-sher-haits-na-deln* (Sicherheitsnadeln)
thread	*FA-den* (Faden)
aspirin	*ah-spee-REEN* (Aspirin)
a bandage	*ai-nuh BIN-duh* (eine Binde)
cotton	*VAHT-tuh* (Watte)
a disinfectant	*ain dess-in-fekts-YOHNSS-mit-tel* (ein Desinfektionsmittel)
iodine	*YOHT* (Jod)
a laxative	*ain AHP-fewr-mit-tel* (ein Abführmittel)

I want to___	*ish MERSH-tuh___* (Ich möchte___)

EXAMPLE

I want to___	*ish MERSH-tuh___* (Ich möchte___)
eat	*ESS-sen* (essen)
I want to eat	*ish MERSH-tuh ESS-sen* (Ich möchte essen)
buy it	*ess KOW-fen* (es kaufen)
drink	*TRIN-ken* (trinken)
have my clothes washed	*mai-nuh ZA-khen VA-shen lahss-sen* (meine Sachen waschen lassen)
rest	*mish OWSS-roo-en* (mich ausruhen)
sleep	*SHLA-fen* (schlafen)
take a bath	*BA-den* (baden)
wash up	*mish VA-shen* (mich waschen)

When you want a haircut or shave you say:

Haircut, please!	*BIT-tuh HA-ruh-shnai-den!* (Bitte, Haareschneiden!)
Shave, please!	*BIT-tuh ra-ZEE-ren!* (Bitte, Rasieren!)

Where is___?	*VO ist___?* (Wo ist___?)

EXAMPLE

Where is___?	*VO ist___?* (Wo ist___?)
a barber	*ain free-ZER* (ein Friseur)
Where is a barber?	*VO ist ain free-ZER?* (Wo ist ein Friseur?)
a bridge	*ai-nuh BREWK-kuh* (eine Brücke)

** *ow* as in *now; ai* as in *aisle*

English	Pronunciation and German Spelling
a bus	*ain AWM-nee-booss* (ein Omnibus)
a church	*ai-nuh KEER-shuh* (eine Kirche)
a clothing store	*ain KLAI-der-la-den* (ein Kleiderladen)
a dentist	*ain TSAHN-artst* (ein Zahnarzt)
a doctor	*ain ARTST* (ein Arzt)
a drugstore	*ai-nuh dro-gay-REE* (eine Drogerie)
a fountain (or well)	*ain BROON-nen* (ein Brunnen)
a garage	*ai-nuh ga-RA-shuh* (eine Garage)
a grocery store	*ain LAY-benss-mit-tel-guh-SHEFT* (ein Lebensmittelgeschäft)
a hospital	*ain la-tsa-RET* (ein Lazarett)
a house	*ain HOWSS* (ein Haus)
a laundry	*ai-nuh vesh-shuh-RAI* (eine Wascherei)
a mechanic	*ain may-SHA-nee-ker* (ein Mechaniker)
a pharmacy	*ai-nuh ah-po-TAY-kuh* (eine Apotheke)
a policeman	*ain po-lee-TSIST* (ein Polizist)
a porter	*ain guh-PAYK-tray-ger* (ein Gepäckträger)
a shoemaker	*ain SHOO-ster* (ein Schuster)
a (natural) spring	*ai-nuh KVEL-luh* (eine Quelle)
a tailor	*ain SHNAI-der* (ein Schneider)
a telephone	*ain tay-lay-FOHN* (ein Telephon)
a workman	*ain AR-bai-ter* (ein Arbeiter)
the camp	*dahss TROOP-pen-la-ger* (das Truppenlager)
the city	*dee SHTAHT* (die Stadt)
the highway	*dee LAHNT-shtra-suh* (die Landstrasse)
the main street	*dee HOWPT-shtra-suh* (die Hauptstrasse)
the market	*dayr MARKT* (der Markt)
the nearest town	*dee NAYSH-stuh AWRT-shaft* (die nächste Ortschaft)
the police station	*dahss po-lee-TSAI-ahmt* (das Polizeiamt)
the post office	*dahss PAWST-ahmt* (das Postamt)
the railroad	*dee AI-zen-bahn* (die Eisenbahn)
the river	*dayr FLOOSS* (der Fluss)
the road	*dayr VAYK* (der Weg)
the telegraph window (in post office)	*dayr tay-lay-GRAHM-shahl-ter* (der Telegrammschalter)

I am___	*ish bin___* (Ich bin___)
He is___	*ayr ist___* (Er ist___)
We are___	*veer zint___* (Wir sind___)
They are___	*zee zint___* (Sie sind___)
Are you___?	*zint zee___?* (Sind Sie___?)

EXAMPLE

I am___	*ish bin___* (Ich bin___)
sick	*KRAHNK* (krank)
I am sick	*ish bin KRAHNK* (Ich bin krank)

English	Pronunciation and German Spelling
tired	*MEW-duh* (müde)
wounded	*fer-VOON-det* (verwundet)

Is it___?	*ist ess___?* (Ist es___?)
It is___	*ess ist___* (Es ist___)
It is not___	*ess ist nisht___* (Es ist nicht___)
That is___	*dahss ist___* (Das ist___)
This is___	*deess ist___* (Dies ist___)
That is too___	*dahss ist tsoo___* (Das ist zu___)
That is very___	*dahss ist zayr___* (Das ist sehr___)

EXAMPLE

It is not___ good	*ess ist nisht___* *GOOT* (Es ist nicht___ gut)
It is not good	*ess ist nisht GOOT* (Es ist nicht gut)
bad	*SHLESHT* (schlecht)
expensive	*TOY-er* (teuer)
large	*GROHSS* (gross)
small	*KLAIN* (klein)
clean	*ZOW-ber* (sauber)
dirty	*SHMOO-tsik* (schmutzig)
cold	*KAHLT* (kalt)
hot	*HAISS* (heiss)
few	*VAY-nik* (wenig)
much	*FEEL* (viel)
enough	*guh-NOOK* (genug)
far	*VAIT* (weit)
near	*NA-huh* (nahe)
here	*HEER* (hier)
there	*DAWRT* (dort)

IMPORTANT SIGNS

German	English
Halt!	Stop!
Langsam!	Go slow!
Gefahr!	Danger!
Einbahnstrasse	One Way Street
Einbahnverkehr	One Way Traffic
Keine Durchfahrt	No Thoroughfare
Rechts fahren	Keep To The Right
Strasse im Bau	Road Under Construction
Kurve	Dangerous Curve
Kreuzung	Dangerous Crossing
Bahnübergang	Grade Crossing
Parken verboten	No Parking
Kein Zutritt	No Admittance
Frauen *or* Damen	Women

** *ow* as in *now; ai* as in *aisle*

IMPORTANT SIGNS

German	*English*
Männer *or* Herren	Men
Nichtraucher *or* Rauchen verboten	No Smoking
Eingang	Entrance
Ausgang	Exit

ALPHABETICAL WORD LIST

English	*Pronunciation and German Spelling*
A	
a	*ain* (ein) *or* *ain-en* (einen) *or* *ain-uh* (eine)
am	
I am___	*ish BIN___* (Ich bin___)
American	*ah-may-ree-KA-ner* (Amerikaner)
American sailors	*ah-may-ree-KA-nee-shuh mah-TROH-zen* (amerikanische Matrosen)
I am an American	*ish BIN ah-may-ree-KA-ner* (Ich bin Amerikaner)
and	*oont* (und)
apples	*EP-fel* (Äpfel)
are	*zint* (sind)
Are you___?	*zint zee___?* (Sind Sie___?)
They are___	*zee zint___* (Sie sind___)
We are___	*veer zint___* (Wir sind___)
aspirin	*ah-spee-REEN* (Aspirin)
B	
bacon	*SHPEK* (Speck)
bad	*SHLESHT* (schlecht)
bandage	*BIN-duh* (Binde)
barber	*free-ZER* (Friseur)
bath	
take a bath	*BA-den* (baden)
beans	*BO-nen* (Bohnen)
bed	*BET* (Bett)
bedding	*BET-tsoyk* (Bettzeug)
beef	*RINT-flaish* (Rindfleisch)
beefsteak	*BEEF-shtayk* (Beefsteak)
beer	*BEER* (Bier)
a glass of beer	*ain GLAHSS BEER* (ein Glas Bier)
beets	*RO-tuh REW-ben* (rote Rüben)
begins	*buh-GINT* (beginnt)
blankets	*DEK-ken* (Decken)
boiled water	*AHP-guh-kawkh-tess VAHSS-ser* (abgekochtes Wasser)
bread	*BROHT* (Brot)
bridge	*BREWK-kuh* (Brücke)
bring	
Bring help!	*HO-len zee HIL-fuh!* (Holen Sie Hilfe!)
Bring me___	*BRIN-gen zee meer___* (Bringen Sie mir___)
bus	*AWM-nee-booss* (Omnibus)
butter	*BOOT-ter* (Butter)
buttons	*KNERP-fuh* (Knöpfe)
buy	
buy it	*ess KOW-fen* (es kaufen)
C	
cabbage	*KOHL* (Kohl)
camp	*TROOP-pen-la-ger* (Truppenlager)
can	
Where can I get___?	*VO kahn ish___ buh-KAWM-men?* (Wo kann ich___ bekommen?)
carrots	*GEL-buh REW-ben* (gelbe Rüben)
cheese	*KAY-zuh* (Käse)
chicken	*HOON* (Huhn)
chocolate	*sho-ko-LA-duh* (Schokolade)
church	*KEER-shuh* (Kirche)
cigarettes	*tsee-ga-RET-ten* (Zigaretten)
cigars	*tsee-GAR-ren* (Zigarren)
city	*SHTAHT* (Stadt)
clean	*ZOW-ber* (sauber)
clothing store	*KLAI-der-la-den* (Kleiderladen)
coffee	*KAHF-fay* (Kaffee)
a cup of coffee	*ai-nuh TAHSS-suh KAHF-fay* (eine Tasse Kaffee)
cold	*KAHLT* (kalt)
comb	*KAHM* (Kamm)
Come!	*KAWM-men zee!* (Kommen Sie!)
Come here!	*KAWM-men zee HAYR!* (Kommen Sie her!)
Come quickly!	*KAWM-men zee SHNEL!* (Kommen Sie schnell!)
cost	*KAWST-et* (kostet)
How much does that cost?	*vee-feel KAWSS-tet DAHSS?* (Wieviel kostet das?)
cotton	*VAHT-tuh* (Watte)
cover	
Take cover!	*DEK-koong!* (Deckung!)
cucumbers	*GOOR-ken* (Gurken)
cup	*TAHSS-suh* (Tasse)

** *ow* as in *now; ai* as in *aisle*

English	Pronunciation and German Spelling
a cup of___	*ai-nuh TAHSS-suh___* (eine Tasse___)

D

English	Pronunciation and German Spelling
Danger!	*guh-FAR!* (Gefahr!)
day	*TAHK* (Tag)
Good day	*GOO-ten TAHK* (Guten Tag)
dentist	*TSAHN-artst* (Zahnarzt)
dirty	*SHMOO-tsik* (schmutzig)
disinfectant	*dess-in-fekts-YOHNSS-mit-tel* (Desinfektionsmittel)
Do you understand?	*fer-SHTAY-en zee?* (Verstehen Sie?)
doctor	*ARTST* (Arzt)
Take me to a doctor	*BRIN-gen zee mish tsoo ai-nem ARTST* (Bringen Sie mich zu einem Arzt)
Draw me a map	*TSAISH-nen zee meer ai-nuh KAR-tuh* (Zeichnen Sie mir eine Karte)
drink	*TRIN-ken* (trinken)
drinking water	*TRINK-vahss-ser* (Trinkwasser)
drugstore	*dro-gay-REE* (Drogerie)

E

English	Pronunciation and German Spelling
eat	*ESS-sen* (essen)
something to eat	*ET-vahss tsoo ESS-sen* (etwas zu essen)
I want to eat	*ish MERSH-tuh ESS-sen* (Ich möchte essen)
eggs	*AI-er* (Eier)
eight	*AHKHT* (acht)
eighteen	*AHKH-tsayn* (achtzehn)
eighty	*AHKH-tsik* (achtzig)
eleven	*ELF* (elf)
enough	*guh-NOOK* (genug)
Excuse me	*fayr-TSAI-oong* (Verzeihung)
evening	*AH-bent* (Abend)
Good evening	*GOO-ten AH-bent* (Guten Abend)
expensive	*TOY-er* (teuer)

F

English	Pronunciation and German Spelling
far	*VAIT* (weit)
How far is it?	*vee VAIT ist ess?* (Wie weit ist es?)
Is it far?	*ist ess VAIT?* (Ist es weit?)
few	*VAY-nik* (wenig)
fifteen	*FEWNF-tsayn* (fünfzehn)
fifty	*FEWNF-tsik* (fünfzig)
fish	*FISH* (Fisch)
five	*FEWNF* (fünf)
food	*ET-vahss tsoo ESS-sen* (etwas zu essen)
fork	*GA-bel* (Gabel)
forty	*FEER-tsik* (vierzig)
fountain (well)	*BROON-nen* (Brunnen)
four	*FEER* (vier)
fourteen	*FEER-tsayn* (vierzehn)
Friday	*FRAI-tahk* (Freitag)
fruit	*OHPST* (Obst)

G

English	Pronunciation and German Spelling
garage	*ga-RA-shuh* (Garage)
Gas!	*GAHSS!* (Gas!)
German	*DOYTSH* (Deutsch)
in German	*owf DOYTSH* (auf Deutsch)
get	
Get me___	*HO-len zee meer___* (Holen Sie mir___)
Where can I get___?	*VO kahn ish___buh-KAWM-men?* (Wo kann ich bekommen?)
Give me___	*GAY-ben zee meer___* (Geben Sie mir___)
glass	*GLAHSS* (Glas)
a glass of___	*ain GLAHSS___* (ein Glas___)
Go!	*GAY-en zee!* (Gehen Sie!)
Go quickly!	*GAY-en zee SHNEL!* (Gehen Sie schnell!)
good	*GOOT* (gut)
Good day	*GOO-ten TAHK* (Guten Tag)
Good evening	*GOO-ten AH-bent* (Guten Abend)
Good morning	*GOO-ten MAWR-gen* (Guten Morgen)
Good-by	*owf VEE-der-zayn* (Auf Wiedersehen)
grapes	*TROW-ben* (Trauben)
grocery store	*LAY-benss-mit-tel-guh-SHEFT* (Lebensmittelgeschäft)

H

English	Pronunciation and German Spelling
hair	*HAR* (Haar)
Haircut, please!	*BIT-tuh HA-ruh-shnai-den!* (Bitte, Haareschneiden!)
half	*HAHLP* (halb)
Halt!	*HAHLT!* (Halt!)
ham	*SHIN-ken* (Schinken)
handkerchief	*TA-shen-tookh* (Taschentuch)
have	
Have you___?	*HA-ben zee___?* (Haben Sie___?)
I have___	*ish HA-buh___* (Ich habe___)
We have___	*veer HA-ben___* (Wir haben___)
he	*ayr* (er)
He is___	*ayr ist___* (Er ist___)

** *ow* as in *now*; *ai* as in *aisle*

English	Pronunciation and German Spelling
Help!	*HIL-fuh!* (Hilfe!)
Bring help!	*HO-len zee HIL-fuh!* (Holen Sie Hilfe!)
Please help me	*BIT-tuh HEL-fen zee meer* (Bitte helfen Sie mir)
here	*HEER* (hier)
It is here	*ess ist HEER* (Es ist hier)
Come here!	*KAWM-men zee hayr!* (Kommen Sie her!)
highway	*LAHNT-shtra-suh* (Landstrasse)
hospital	*la-tsa-RET* (Lazarett)
Take me to a hospital	*BRIN-gen zee mish tsoo AI-nem la-tsa-RET* (Bringen Sie mich zu einem Lazarett)
hot	*HAISS* (heiss)
hot water	*HAI-sess VAHSS-ser* (heisses Wasser)
hotel	*ho-TEL* (Hotel)
Where is a hotel?	*VO ist ain ho-TEL?* (Wo ist ein Hotel?)
house	*HOWSS* (Haus)
how	*VEE* (wie)
How are you?	*vee GAYT ess ee-nen?* (Wie geht es Ihnen?)
How do you say *table* in German?	*vahss ZA-gen zee fewr* table *owf DOYTSH?* (Was sagen Sie für *table* auf Deutsch?)
How far is it?	*vee VAIT ist ess?* (Wie weit ist es?)
How much does that cost?	*vee-feel KAWSS-tet DAHSS?* (Wieviel kostet das?)
hundred	*HOON-dert* (hundert)
hungry	
I am hungry	*ish HA-buh HOONG-er* (Ich habe Hunger)

I

English	Pronunciation and German Spelling
I	*ish* (ich)
I am___	*ish bin___* (Ich bin___)
I have___	*ish HA-buh___* (Ich habe___)
I want___ *or* **I want to___**	*ish MERSH-tuh___* (Ich möchte___)
in German	*owf DOYTSH* (auf Deutsch)
ink	*TIN-tuh* (Tinte)
iodine	*YOHT* (Jod)
is	*ist* (ist)
Is it___?	*IST ess___?* (Ist es___?)
It is___	*ess IST___* (Es ist___)
It is not___	*ess ist NISHT___* (Es ist nicht___)

K

English	Pronunciation and German Spelling
kilometer	*kee-lo-MAY-ter* (Kilometer)
knife	*MESS-ser* (Messer)

L

English	Pronunciation and German Spelling
large	*GROHSS* (gross)
laundry	*vesh-shuh-RAI* (Wäscherei)
laxative	*AHP-fewr-mit-tel* (Abführmittel)
leave	*GAYT* (geht)
When does the train leave?	*vahn GAYT dayr TSOOK?* (Wann geht der Zug?)
left	*LINKS* (links)
To the left	*nahkh LINKS* (nach links)
lost	
I am lost	*ish HA-buh mish fayr-LOW-fen* (Ich habe mich verlaufen)

M

English	Pronunciation and German Spelling
madam	*G‿NAY-dig-uh FROW* (gnädige Frau)
main street	*HOWPT-shtra-suh* (Hauptstrasse)
map	*KAR-tuh* (Karte)
Draw me a map	*TSAISH-nen zee meer ai-nuh KAR-tuh* (Zeichnen Sie mir eine Karte)
mark	*MARK* (Mark)
market	*MARKT* (Markt)
matches	*SHTRAISH-herl-tser* (Streichhölzer)
mattress	*ma-TRA-tsuh* (Matratze)
me	*mish* (mich) *or meer* (mir)
meal	*MAHL-tsait* (Mahlzeit)
meat	*FLAISH* (Fleisch)
mechanic	*may-SHA-nee-ker* (Mechaniker)
milk	*MILSH* (Milch)
Miss	*FROY-lain* (Fräulein) *or G‿NAY-dig-ess FROY-lain* (gnädiges Fräulein)
Mister	*HAYR* (Herr)
Monday	*MOHN-tahk* (Montag)
morning	*MAWR-gen* (Morgen)
movie	*KEE-no* (Kino)
When does the movie start?	*VAHN buh-GINT dahss KEE-no?* (Wann beginnt das Kino?)
Mrs.	*FROW* (Frau)
much	*FEEL* (viel)
mutton	*HAHM-mel-flaish* (Hammelfleisch)

N

English	Pronunciation and German Spelling
name	
My name is___	*ish HAI-suh___* (Ich heisse___)
What's your name?	*VEE HAI-sen zee?* (Wie heissen Sie?)

** *ow* as in *now; ai* as in *aisle*

English	Pronunciation and German Spelling
near	*NA-huh* (nahe)
the nearest town	*dee NAYSH-stuh AWRT-shaft* (die nächste Ortschaft)
needle	*NA-del* (Nadel)
nine	*NOYN* (neun)
nineteen	*NOYN-tsayn* (neunzehn)
ninety	*NOYN-tsik* (neunzig)
no	*NAIN* (nein)
north	*NAWR-den* (Norden)
Which way is north?	*VO ist NAWR-den?* (Wo ist Norden?)
not	*nisht* (nicht)

O

English	Pronunciation and German Spelling
one	***AINSS*** **(eins)**
onions	***TSVEE-beln*** **(Zwiebeln)**
oranges	***ahp-fel-ZEE-nen*** **(Apfelsinen)**

P

English	Pronunciation and German Spelling
pay	
I will pay you	*ish VAYR-duh EE-nen GELT GAY-ben* (Ich werde Ihnen Geld geben)
peas	*AYRP-sen* (Erbsen)
pen	*FAY-der-hahl-ter* (Federhalter)
pencil	*BLAI-shtift* (Bleistift)
pepper	*P‿FEF-fer* (Pfeffer)
pfennig	*P‿FEN-nik* (Pfennig)
pharmacy	*ah-po-TAY-kuh* (Apotheke)
pillow	*KISS-sen* (Kissen)
pins	*SHTEK-na-deln* (Stecknadeln)
safety pins	*ZISH-sher-haits-na-deln* (Sicherheitsnadeln)
pipe	*P‿FAI-fuh* (Pfeife)
pipe tobacco	*P‿FAI-fen-ta-bahk* (Pfeifentabak)
plate	*TEL-ler* (Teller)
Please	*BIT-tuh* (Bitte)
police station	*po-lee-TSAI-ahmt* (Polizeiamt)
policeman	*po-lee-TSIST* (Polizist)
pork	*SHVAI-nuh-flaish* (Schweinefleisch)
porter	*guh-PAYK-tray-ger* (Gepäckträger)
post office	*PAWST-ahmt* (Postamt)
potatoes	*kar-TAWF-feln* (Kartoffeln)

Q

English	Pronunciation and German Spelling
quickly	*SHNEL* (schnell)
Come quickly!	*KAWM-men zee SHNEL!* (Kommen Sie schnell!)
Go quickly!	*GAY-en zee SHNEL!* (Gehen Sie schnell!)

R

English	Pronunciation and German Spelling
railroad	*AI-zen-bahn* (Eisenbahn)
railroad station	*BAHN-hohf* (Bahnhof)
Where is a railroad station?	*VO ist ain BAHN-hohf?* (Wo ist ein Bahnhof?)
raincoat	*RAY-gen-mahn-tel* (Regenmantel)
razor	*ra-ZEER-ahp-pa-raht* (Rasierapparat)
razor blades	*ra-ZEER-kling-en* (Rasierklingen)
repeat	*vee-der-HO-len zee!* (Wiederholen Sie!)
Please repeat	*BIT-tuh vee-der-HO-len zee* (Bitte wiederholen Sie)
rest	
I want to rest	*ish MERSH-tuh mish OWSS-roo-en* (Ich möchte mich ausruhen)
restaurant	*ress-to-RAHNG* (Restaurant)
Where is a restaurant?	*VO ist ain ress-to-RAHNG?* (Wo ist ein Restaurant?)
rice	*RAISS* (Reis)
right	*RESHTS* (rechts)
To the right	*nahkh RESHTS* (nach rechts)
river	*FLOOSS* (Fluss)
road	*VAYK* (Weg)
Which is the road to___?	*VO ist dayr VAYK nahkh___?* (Wo ist der Weg nach___?)
room	*TSIM-mer* (Zimmer)

S

English	Pronunciation and German Spelling
safety pins	*ZISH-sher-haits-na-deln* (Sicherheitsnadeln)
sailors	*mah-TROH-zen* (Matrosen)
Where are the American sailors?	*VO ZINT dee a-may-ree-KA-nee-shen mah-TROH-zen?* (Wo sind die amerikanischen Matrosen?)
salad	*za-LAHT* (Salat)
salt	*ZAHLTS* (Salz)
Saturday	*ZAMSS-tahk* (Samstag) *or ZAWN-ah-bent* (Sonnabend)
(to) say	*ZA-gen* (sagen)
How do you say *table* in German?	*vahss ZA-gen zee fewr* table *owf DOYTSH?* (Was sagen Sie für *table* auf Deutsch?)
seven	*ZEE-ben* (sieben)
seventeen	*ZEEP-tsayn* (siebzehn)
seventy	*ZEEP-tsik* (siebzig)

** *ow* as in *now; ai* as in *aisle*

English	Pronunciation and German Spelling
shave	
Shave, please!	*BIT-tuh ra-ZEE-ren!* (Bitte, Rasieren!)
shaving brush	*ra-ZEER-pin-zel* (Rasierpinsel)
shaving soap	*ra-ZEER-zai-fuh* (Rasierseife)
she	*zee* (sie)
sheets	*BET-la-ken* (Bettlaken)
shirt	*HEMT* (Hemd)
undershirt	*OON-ter-hemt* (Unterhemd)
shoemaker	*SHOO-ster* (Schuster)
shoes	*SHOO-uh* (Schuhe)
shoe laces	*SHNEWR-zen-kel* (Schnürsenkel)
shoe polish	*SHOO-kraym* (Schuhcreme)
show	
Please show me	*BIT-tuh TSAI-gen zee meer* (Bitte zeigen Sie mir)
sick	*KRAHNK* (krank)
sir	*main HAYR* (mein Herr)
six	*ZEKS* (sechs)
sixteen	*ZESH-tsayn* (sechzehn)
sixty	*ZESH-tsik* (sechzig)
sleep	*SHLA-fen* (schlafen)
slowly	*LAHNK-zahm* (langsam)
Speak slowly	*SPRESH-en zee LAHNK-zahm* (Sprechen Sie langsam,
small	*KLAIN* (klein
soap	*ZAI-fuh* (Seife)
shaving soap	*ra-ZEER-zai-fuh* (Rasierseife)
soup	*ZOOP-puh* (Suppe)
speak	*SPRESH-en zee!* (Sprechen Sie!)
Speak slowly	*SPRESH-en zee LAHNK-zahm* (Sprechen Sie langsam)
spinach	*shpee-NAHT* (Spinat)
spoon	*LERF-fel* (Löffel)
(natural) spring	*KVEL-luh* (Quelle)
start	*buh-GINT* (beginnt)
When does the movie start?	*VAHN buh-GINT dahss KEE-no?* (Wann beginnt das Kino?)
station	
police station	*po-lee-TSAI-ahmt* (Polizeiamt)
railroad station	*BAHN-hohf* (Bahnhof)
Stop!	*HAHLT!* (Halt!)

English	Pronunciation and German Spelling
store	
clothing store	*KLAI-der-la-den* (Kleiderladen)
drugstore	*dro-gay-REE* (Drogerie)
Straight ahead	*guh-RA-duh-OWSS* (geradeaus)
street	*SHTRA-suh* (Strasse)
main street	*HOWPT-shtra-suh* (Hauptstrasse)
sugar	*TSOOK-ker* (Zucker)
Sunday	*ZAWN-tahk* (Sonntag)

T

English	Pronunciation and German Spelling
tailor	*SHNAI-der* (Schneider)
take	
Take cover!	*DEK-koong!* (Deckung!)
Take me to a doctor	*BRIN-gen zee mish tsoo AI-nem ARTST* (Bringen Sie mich zu einem Arzt)
Take me to a hospital	*BRIN-gen zee mish tsoo AI-nem la-tsa-RET* (Bringen Sie mich zu einem Lazarett)
Take me there	*BRIN-gen zee mish dawrt HIN* (Bringen Sie mich dort hin)
tangerines	*mahn-da-REE-nen* (Mandarinen)
tea	*TAY* (Tee)
telegraph window (in post office)	*tay-lay-GRAHM-shahl-ter* (Telegrammschalter)
telephone	*tay-lay-FOHN* (Telephon)
ten	*TSAYN* (zehn)
Thank you	*DAN-kuh* (Danke)
that	*dahss* (das)
What's that?	*VAHSS ist DAHSS?* (Was ist das?)
the	*dayr* (der) *or dee* (die) *or dahss* (das)
there	*DAWRT* (dort)
Take me there	*BRIN-gen zee mish dawrt HIN* (Bringen Sie mich dort hin)
they	*zee* (sie)
They are___	*zee zint___* (Sie sind___)
thirsty	
I am thirsty	*ish HA-buh DOORST* (Ich habe Durst)
thirteen	*DRAI-tsayn* (dreizehn)
thirty	*DRAI-sik* (dreissig)
this	*DEESS* (dies)
What's this?	*VAHSS ist DEESS?* (Was ist dies?)
thousand	*TOW-zent* (tausend)

** *ow* as in *now*; *ai* as in *aisle*

English	Pronunciation and German Spelling
thread	*FA-den* (Faden)
three	*DRAI* (drei)
Thursday	*DAWN-nerss-tahk* (Donnerstag)
time	
What time is it?	*vee SHPAYT ist ess?* (Wie spät ist es?)
tired	*MEW-duh* (müde)
tobacco	*TA-bahk* (Tabak)
today	*HOY-tuh* (heute)
toilet	*twa-LET-tuh* (Toilette)
Where is a toilet?	*VO ist ai-nuh twa-LET-tuh?* (Wo ist eine Toilette?)
tomorrow	*MAWR-gen* (morgen)
too	*tsoo* (zu)
toothbrush	*TSAHN-bewr-stuh* (Zahnbürste)
tooth paste	*TSAHN-kraym* (Zahncreme)
towel	*HAHN-tookh* (Handtuch)
town	*AWRT-shaft* (Ortschaft) *or SHTAHT* (Stadt)
the nearest town	*dee NAYSH-stuh AWRT-shaft* (die nächste Ortschaft)
train	*TSOOK* (Zug)
When does the train leave?	*vahn GAYT dayr TSOOK?* (Wann geht der Zug?)
Tuesday	*DEENSS-tahk* (Dienstag)
turnips	*VAI-suh REW-ben* (weisse Rüben)
twelve	*TSVERLF* (zwölf)
twenty	*TSVAHN-tsik* (zwanzig)
two	*TSVAI* (zwei)

U

English	Pronunciation and German Spelling
undershirt	*OON-ter-hemt* (Unterhemd)
undershorts	*OON-ter-ho-zen* (Unterhosen)
understand	
Do you understand?	*fer-SHTAY-en zee?* (Verstehen Sie?)
I understand	*ish fer-SHTAY-uh* (Ich verstehe)
I don't understand	*ish fer-SHTAY-uh nisht* (Ich verstehe nicht)
underwear	*OON-ter-vesh-shuh* (Unterwäsche)

V

English	Pronunciation and German Spelling
veal	*KAHLP-flaish* (Kalbfleisch)
vegetables	*guh-MEW-zuh* (Gemüse)
very	*zayr* (sehr)

W

English	Pronunciation and German Spelling
Wait!	*VAR-ten zee!* (Warten Sie!)
Wait a moment!	*VAR ten zee ai-nen OW-gen-blik!* (Warten Sie einen Augenblick!)
want	
I want___ *or* I want to___	*ish MERSH-tuh*___ (Ich möchte___)
We want___	*veer MERSH-ten*___ (Wir möchten___)
wash	*VA-shen* (waschen)
I want to wash up	*ish MERSH-tuh mish VA-shen* (Ich möchte mich waschen)
I want to have my clothes washed	*ish MERSH-tuh mai-nuh ZA-khen VA-shen lahss-sen* (Ich möchte meine Sachen waschen lassen)
Watch out!	*OWF-pahss-sen!* (Aufpassen!)
water	*VAHSS-ser* (Wasser)
boiled water	*AHP-guh-kawkh-tess VAHSS-ser* (abgekochtes Wasser)
drinking water	*TRINK-vahss-ser* (Trinkwasser)
hot water	*HAI-sess VAHSS-ser* (heisses Wasser)
we	*veer* (wir)
We are___	*veer zint*___ (Wir sind___)
We have___	*veer HA-ben*___ (Wir haben___)
We want___	*veer MERSH-ten*___ (Wir möchten___)
Wednesday	*MIT-vawkh* (Mittwoch)
welcome	
You're welcome	*BIT-tuh* (Bitte)
well	
I am well	*es GAYT meer GOOT* (Es geht mir gut)
well (for water)	*BROON-nen* (Brunnen)
what	*VAHSS* (was)
What's that?	*VAHSS ist DAHSS?* (Was ist das?)
What's this?	*VAHSS ist DEESS?* (Was ist dies?)
What is your name?	*VEE HAI-sen zee?* (Wie heissen Sie?)
What time is it?	*vee SHPAYT ist ess?* (Wie spät ist es?)
when	*VAHN* (wann)
When does the movie start?	*VAHN buh-GINT dahss KEE-no?* (Wann beginnt das Kino?)
When does the train leave?	*vahn GAYT dayr TSOOK?* (Wann geht der Zug?)

** *ow* as in *now*; *ai* as in *aisle*

English	Pronunciation and German Spelling
where	*VO* (wo)
Where is___?	*vo ist___?* (Wo ist___?)
Where are___?	*vo zint___?* (Wo sind___?)
Where can I get___?	*vo kahn ish___ buh-KAWM-men?* (Wo kann ich___ bekommen?)
wine	*VAIN* (Wein)
workman	*AR-bai-ter* (Arbeiter)
wounded	*fayr-VOON-det* (verwundet)

Y

English	Pronunciation and German Spelling
yes	*YA* (ja)
yesterday	*GESS-tern* (gestern)
you	
Are you___?	*sint zee___?* (Sind Sie___?)
Have you___?	*HA-ben zee___?* (Haben Sie___?)

***ow* as in *now; ai* as in *aisle*

Spanish/English Dictionary

Spanish is one of the most widespread languages in the world. It is spoken by some 25 million people in Spain and Morocco and over 60 million in South and Central America, Mexico, and the Caribbean. It is also one of the languages of the Philippines.

This *Language Guide* will enable you to ask directions, buy things or order a meal in these Spanish-speaking regions. Knowing a little Spanish will also help you get along with the people, for they will naturally be pleased to see a stranger showing enough interest in them to try to learn their language.

How to Use the Record * and Guide

This Guide is obviously not intended to give you a complete command of the Spanish language. If you want to embark upon a somewhat extensive study of the spoken language you should obtain the USAFI course, *Spoken Spanish*—see the current USAFI Catalog for instructions. This Language Guide will, however, enable you to carry on simple conversations in Spanish.

The records that go with this *Guide* give you a number of the most important words and phrases in Spanish. Read the section called *Hints on Pronunciation* and then listen to the records until you know the *Useful Words and Phrases* by heart. Repeat each word out loud right after you hear it, and say it exactly the way the Spanish speaker does. Imitate the pronunciation as closely as you can, just as you might mimic someone who has an unusual accent. Try to get every detail of the pronunciation, even the rhythm and intonation. Follow the words in your *Guide* but use them only as a reminder; if you hear something different from what you see written, go by what you hear. Remember that you can't get the sound of a language from the printed word alone—you have to use your ears even more than your eyes. If you don't have the records and can't get a Spanish speaker to read the words, you will have to rely on the *Hints on Pronunciation* alone.

By the time you have practiced the *Useful Words and Phrases* several times, you will know what sound each letter stands for in the *Guide*. You will then be able to pronounce the *Additional Expressions* even though you have not actually heard them, and you will be able to form sentences of your own by using the section called *Fill-In Sentences*.

Hints on Pronunciation

If you have studied Spanish before, you may not need any additional practice in pronunciation. However, unless you have had a chance to try out your Spanish and know that you are understood without any difficulty, you had better do a little practicing.

*Records no longer available

You will find all the words and phrases written in a spelling which you read like English. When you see the Spanish word for "one" spelled *OO-no*, give the *oo* the sound it has in the English words *too*, *boot*, etc. and not the sound it has in German or any other language you may happen to know.

Each letter or combination of letters is used for the sound it usually stands for in English and it *always* stands for that sound. Thus, *oo* is always pronounced as in *too*, *boot*, *tooth*, *roost*, never as anything else. Say these words and then pronounce the vowel sound by itself. That is the sound you must use every time you see *oo* in the *Pronunciation* column. If you should use some other sound—for example, the sound of *oo* in *blood*—you might be misunderstood.

Syllables that are accented, that is, pronounced louder than others, are written in capital letters. In Spanish, unaccented syllables are not skipped over quickly, as they are in English. Hyphens are used to divide words into syllables in order to make them easier to read. Curved lines (‿) are used to show sounds that are pronounced together without any break; for example, *K‿YAY-ro* meaning "I want," *D‿YESS* meaning "ten."

Special Points

Here are a few points to note as you listen to the records:

AY	as in *may, say, play* but don't drawl it as we do in English. Since it is not drawled it sounds a little like the *e* in *let*. Example: *ka-FAY* meaning "coffee."
O or OH	as in *go, so, oh, note, joke* but don't drawl it as we do in English. Since it is not drawled it sounds a little like the *aw* in *saw*. Example: *NO* meaning "no."
H	as in *house, hat, hall* but stronger. Example: *free-HO-less* meaning "beans."
RR	stands for a strongly rolled *r*-sound, like the telephone operator's "thuh-r-r-ree" for "three" or like the Scotchman's "burr" in pronouncing *very* as "ver-r-ry." This double *rr* differs from the single *r*, which is made by a quick tap of the tongue against the gums back of the teeth. Example of *rr: see-ga-RREE-yohss* meaning "cigarettes." Example of *r: ah la day-RECH-ah* meaning "to the right."

You will often hear Spanish speakers pronounce the *d* very much like our *th*-sound in "breathe" and "then," the *b* very much like our *v*, and the *v* at the beginning of a word like *b*. Thus, *guisado* meaning "stew" may sound like *ghee-SA-tho* (*th* as in *then*); *sábado* meaning "Saturday" like *SA-va-do;* and *veinte* meaning "twenty" like *BAYN-tay*. If you pronounce a *d* or *v* or *b* according to what you see written you will be understood, but it is of course best to try to imitate the sound you hear.

Regional Differences

If you follow the pronunciation on the records that go with this *Guide*, you will be understood wherever Spanish is spoken. However, if you find yourself in a region where the people have a slightly different pronunciation, it is well to try to speak the way they do. Here are a few of the differences you will find:

About three-fourths of all Spanish speakers pronounce an *s*-sound in words like *SEN-tro* (spelled *centro*) meaning "center," *s‿yoo-DAHD* (*ciudad*) meaning "city" and *PLA-sa* (*plaza*) meaning "plaza." In Central and Northern Spain, however, people use the *th*-sound of *thin* or *breath* in words like these and say *THEN-tro*, *th‿yoo-DAHD*, *PLA-tha*. The *th*-sound is used in words that are written with *c* or *z* in Spanish spelling but not in words spelled with *s;* for example, *SEE* (*sí*) meaning "yes," *sen-YOR* (*señor*) meaning "sir," or *SAHL* (*sal*) meaning "salt."

Most Spanish speakers use a *y*-sound in words that are spelled with *ll*. The word *llama*, for example, in the expression *¿Cómo se llama usted?* meaning "What is your name?" is pronounced *YA-ma*. In Central and Northern Spain, however, a combination sound like the *ly* in *schoolyard* is used instead. Thus, *llama* is pronounced as *L‿YA-ma*. In Argentina and in some other regions the *ll* has a sound something like the *j* in *judge*.

In Southern Spain and much of Latin America, *s*-sounds at the end of syllables are often not pronounced; thus, *ESS-tohss DOHSS OHM-bress* meaning "these two men" may sound like *AY-to DO OHM-bray*.

USEFUL WORDS AND PHRASES

The following is the exact wording of the Spanish language records issued with this *Guide*.

These records give you a few useful phrases in Spanish as spoken in most of Latin America. The phrases and other words which you will need are found also in the pamphlet which should be used with these records.

To learn to imitate the sounds of Spanish you should listen to the records at least six or seven times.

The English will be given first, followed by the Spanish. Then repeat the Spanish out loud and say it good and loud! Remember! Repeat every Spanish phrase right after you hear it.

Words, greetings, and general phrases, which are useful and should be memorized, are given first.

GREETINGS AND GENERAL PHRASES

English	*Pronunciation and Spanish Spelling*
Good day	*BWEN-ohs DEE-ahss* (Buenos días)
Good evening	*BWEN-ahss TAR-dess* (Buenas tardes)
Sir	*sen-YOR* (señor)
Madam	*sen-YO-ra* (señora)
Miss	*sen-yo-REE-ta* (señorita)

Spanish speakers have several words for "please" and they use them often.

Please	*SEER-va-say*___ (Sírvase___)
or	*por fa-VOR* (Por favor)
or	*TEN-ga la bohn-DAHD day*___ (Tenga la bondad de___)
Excuse me	*payr-DO-nay-may* (Perdóneme)
Thank you	*GRAHSS-yahss* (Gracias)

If you have studied Spanish, you probably remember the *th*-sound for the letter *c*, as in *GRAHTH-yahss*, instead of *GRAHSS-yahss*, which you have just heard. Both *GRAHTH-yahss* and *GRAHSS-yahss* are absolutely correct. But *GRAHSS-yahss* with the *s*-sound is used almost entirely in South and Central America as well as in the Philippines and many other places where Spanish is spoken.

Yes	*SEE* (sí)
No	*NO* (no)
Understand me?	*may ent-YEN-day?* (¿Me entiende?)
I don't understand	*NO ent-YEN-do* (No entiendo)
Please speak slowly	*TEN-ga la bohn-DAHD day ah-BLAR dess-PAHSS-yo* (Tenga la bondad de hablar despacio)

LOCATION

When you need directions to get somewhere, you use the phrase "Where is" and add the word you need.

Where is	*DOHN-day ess-TA* (Dónde está)
the restaurant	*el rress-ta‿oo-RAHN-tay* (el restaurante)

In many parts of the Spanish-speaking world, the *s*-sound is frequently left out. Such words as *ess-TA* are often pronounced *ay-TA*. This is particularly true in Cuba and Chile.

the hotel	*el o-TEL* (el hotel)
Where is the hotel?	*DOHN-day ess-TA el o-TEL?* (¿Dónde está el hotel?)
the railroad station	*la ess-tahss-YOHN* (la estación)
Where is the railroad station?	*DOHN-day ess-TA la ess-tahss-YOHN?* (¿Dónde está la estación?)
the toilet	*el rray-TRAY-tay* (el retrete)
Where is the toilet?	*DOHN-day ess-TA el rray-TRAY-tay?* (¿Dónde está el retrete?)

DIRECTIONS

The answer to your question "Where is such and such?" may be "To the right" or "To the left" or "Straight ahead," so you need to know these phrases.

English	*Pronunciation and Spanish Spelling*
To the right	*ah la day-RECH-ah* (a la derecha)
To the left	*ah la eesk-YAYR-da* (a la izquierda)
Straight ahead	*ah-day-LAHN-tay* (adelante)

It is sometimes useful to say "please point."

Please point *SEER-va-say ah-poon-TAR* (Sírvase apuntar)

If you are driving and ask the distance to another town it will be given to you in kilometers, not miles.

Kilometers *kee-LO-met-rohss* (kilómetros)

One kilometer equals ⅝ of a mile.

NUMBERS

You need to know the numbers.

One	*OO-no*	uno
Two	*DOHSS*	dos
Three	*TRESS*	tres

In rapid conversation you will frequently hear these without the *s*-sound: *DO, TRAY*, instead of *DOHSS, TRESS.*

Four	*KWA-tro*	cuatro
Five	*SEEN-ko*	cinco
Six	*SAYSS*	seis
Seven	*S‿YAY-tay*	siete
Eight	*O-cho*	ocho
Nine	*NWEV-ay*	nueve
Ten	*D‿YESS*	diez

For the numbers "eleven" through "fifteen" you add an ending which sounds like *say.*

Eleven	*OHN-say*	once
Twelve	*DO-say*	doce
Thirteen	*TRESS-ay*	trece
Fourteen	*ka-TOR-say*	catorce
Fifteen	*KEEN-say*	quince

For the numbers "sixteen" through "nineteen" you put the word *d‿yess-ee* (diez y) "ten and—" and then add the words for "six" through "nine."

Sixteen	*d‿yess-ee-SAYSS*	dieciséis
Seventeen	*d‿yess-eess-YAY-tay*	diecisiete
Eighteen	*d‿yess-YO-cho*	dieciocho
Nineteen	*d‿yess-een-WEV-ay*	diecinueve
Twenty	*VAYN-tay*	veinte
Twenty-one	*vaynt-YOO-no*	veintiuno
Twenty-two	*vayn-tee-DOHSS*	veintidós
Thirty	*TRAYN-ta*	treinta
Forty	*kwa-REN-ta*	cuarenta
Fifty	*seen-KWEN-ta*	cincuenta

English	*Pronunciation and Spanish Spelling*	
Sixty	*say-SEN-ta*	sesenta
Seventy	*say-TEN-ta*	setenta
Eighty	*o-CHEN-ta*	ochenta
Ninety	*no-VEN-ta*	noventa
One hundred	*S‿YEN*	cien
One thousand	*MEEL*	mil

WHAT'S THIS?

When you want to know the name of something you can say "What's this?" and point to the thing you mean.

What is	*KAY ESS* (Qué es)
this	*ESS-to* (esto)
What's this?	*KAY ess ESS-to?* (¿Qué es esto?)

ASKING FOR THINGS

When you want something you say "I want" and add the name of the thing wanted. Always be sure to say "please"—*SEER-va-say* or *por fa-VOR.*

I want	*K‿YAY-ro* (Quiero)
cigarettes	*see-ga-RREE-yohss* (cigarrillos)
I want cigarettes	*K‿YAY-ro see-ga-RREE-yohss* (Quiero cigarrillos)
to eat	*ko-MAYR* (comer)
I want to eat	*K‿YAY-ro ko-MAYR* (Quiero comer)

Here are the words for some of the things you may require:

bread	*PAHN* (pan)
fruit	*FROO-ta* (fruta)
oranges	*na-RAHN-hahss* (naranjas)
bananas	*PLA-ta-nohss* (plátanos) **or** *ba-NA-nohss* (bananos)
water	*AH-gwa* (agua)
eggs	*WEV-ohss* (huevos)
butter	*mahn-tay-KEE-ya* (mantequilla)
meat	*KAR-nay* (carne)
beefsteak	*beef-TEK* (biftec)
chops	*ko-STEE-yahss* (costillas)
lamb	*kar-NAY-ro* (carnero)
pork	*PWAYR-ko* (puerco)
lamb chops	*ko-STEE-yahss day kar-NAY-ro* (costillas de carnero)
pork chops	*ko-STEE-yahss day PWAYR-ko* (costillas de puerco)
stew	*ghee-SA-do* (guisado)
soup	*SO-pa* (sopa)
potatoes	*PA-pahss* (papas) **or** *pa-TA-tahss* (patatas)
rice	*ah-RROHSS* (arroz)
beans	*free-HO-less* (frijoles)

English	Pronunciation and Spanish Spelling
fish	*pess-KA-do* (pescado)
milk	*LECH-ay* (leche)
ice cream	*ay-LA-do* (helado)
salad	*en-sa-LA-da* (ensalada)
a match	*oon FO-sfo-ro* (un fósforo)
beer	*sayr-VESS-ah* (cerveza)
a glass of beer	*oon VA-so day sayr-VESS-ah* (un vaso de cerveza)
a cup of coffee	*oo-na TA-sa day ka-FAY* (una taza de café)

HOW MUCH?

To find out how much things cost you say:

How much	*KWAHN-to* (Cuánto)
costs	*KWESS-ta* (cuesta)
this	*ESS-to* (esto)
How much does this cost?	*KWAHN-to KWESS-ta ESS-to?* (¿Cuánto cuesta esto?)

KWAHN-to KWESS-ta ESS-to?

TIME

To find out what time it is you say really "What hour is it?"

What time is it? *KAY O-ra ESS?* (¿Qué hora es?)

Ten past one is "it is the one and ten."

Ten past one *ESS la OO-na ee D‿YESS* (es la una y diez)

Quarter past five is "they are the five and a quarter."

Quarter past five *SOHN lahss SEEN-ko ee KWAR-to* (son las cinco y cuarto)

Twenty past seven is "they are the seven and twenty."

Twenty past seven *SOHN lahss S‿YAY-tay ee VAYN-tay* (son las siete y veinte)

Half past six is "six and a half."

Half past six *SOHN lahss SAYSS ee MED-ya* (son las seis y media)

Twenty to eight is "they are the eight minus twenty."

Twenty to eight *SOHN lahss O-cho men-ohss VAYN-tay* (son las ocho menos veinte)

Quarter of two is "they are the two minus a quarter."

Quarter of two *SOHN lahss DOHSS men-ohss KWAR-to* (son las dos menos cuarto)

Ten minutes to three is "they are the three minus ten."

Ten minutes to three *SOHN lahss TRESS men-ohss D‿YESS* (son las tres menos diez)

It is also possible to indicate time before the hour by saying "so many minutes until the hour."

Ten to three *D‿YESS pa-ra lahss TRESS* (diez para las tres)

If you want to know when a movie starts or when a train leaves you say:

English	Pronunciation and Spanish Spelling
At what time	*ah KAY O-ra* (A qué hora)
starts	*emp-YESS-ah* (empieza)
the movie	*el SEE-nay* (el cine)
What time does the movie start?	*ah KAY O-ra emp-YESS-ah el SEE-nay?* (¿A qué hora empieza el cine?)
the train	*el TREN* (el tren)
leaves	*SA-lay* (sale)
What time does the train leave?	*ah KAY O-ra SA-lay el TREN?* (¿A qué hora sale el tren?)
Today	*OY* (hoy)
Tomorrow	*mahn-YA-na* (mañana)
Yesterday	*ah-YAYR* (ayer)

The days of the week are:

Sunday	*do-MEEN-go* (domingo)
Monday	*LOO-ness* (lunes)
Tuesday	*MAR-tess* (martes)
Wednesday	*M‿YAYR-ko-less* (miércoles)
Thursday	*H‿WEV-ess* (jueves)
Friday	*V‿YAYR-ness* (viernes)
Saturday	*SA-ba-do* (sábado)

OTHER USEFUL PHRASES

The following phrases will be useful:

What is your name? *KO-mo say YA-ma oo-STED?* (¿Cómo se llama usted?)

If you have studied Spanish you may have been taught that the *ll* as in *¿Cómo se llama usted?* is pronounced like *l‿y*—*L‿YA-ma*. In most parts of Latin America, it sounds like a simple *y*-sound—*YA-ma*. In Argentina they pronounce it like the *j*-sound of the English word "pleasure"—for example: *¿KO-mo say JA-ma?* instead of *¿KO-mo say YA-ma?*

My name is___ *may YA-mo___* (Me llamo___)

How do you say *table* (or anything else) in Spanish? *KO-mo say DEE-say* table *en ess-pahn-YOHL?* (¿Cómo se dice *table* en español?)

There are many ways of saying "Good-by" in Spanish. The most usual is:

ahd-YOHSS (Adiós)

For "So long" you say in Spanish:

ah-sta L‿WEG-o (Hasta luego)

For "See you soon" you say in Spanish:

ah-sta l‿way-GHEE-to (Hasta lueguito)

For "I'll see you later" you say in Spanish:

ah-sta la VEESS-ta (Hasta la vista)

For "Until tomorrow" you say in Spanish:

ah-sta mahn-YA-na (Hasta mañana)

For "Until tonight" you say in Spanish:

ah-sta la NO-chay (Hasta la noche)

NOTE

The expression given on the record for "please point" may not be understood in some Spanish-speaking regions. If people do not understand you when you say *SEER-va-say ah-poon-TAR*, try saying *SEER-va-say sen-ya-LAR-may-lo*.

ADDITIONAL EXPRESSIONS

English	Pronunciation and Spanish Spelling
I am hungry	*TEN-go AHM-bray* (Tengo hambre)
I am thirsty	*TEN-go SED* (Tengo sed)
Stop!	*PA-ray!* (¡Pare!)
Come here!	*VEN-ga ah-KA!* (¡Venga acá!)
Right away *or* Quickly	*PROHN-to* (Pronto)
Come quickly!	*VEN-ga PROHN-to!* (¡Venga pronto!)
Go quickly!	*VA-ya PROHN-to!* (¡Vaya pronto!)
Help!	*so-KO-rro!* (¡Socorro!)
Bring help!	*TRA‿ee-ga ah-YOO-da!* (¡Tráiga ayuda!)
You will be rewarded	*NO lo ah-RA day BAHL-day* (No lo hará de balde)
I am an American	*SOY nor-tay-ah-may-ree-KA-no* (Soy norteamericano)
I am your friend	*SOY soo ah-MEE-go* (Soy su amigo)
Where are the sailors?	*DOHN-day ess-TAHN lohss mah-REE-nohss?* (¿Dónde están los marinos?)
Where are the American sailors?	*DOHN-day ess-TAHN lohss mah-REE-nohss nor-tay-ah-may-ree-KA-nohss?* (¿Dónde están los marinos norteamericanos?)
Which way is north?	*DOHN-day ess-TA el NOR-tay?* (¿Dónde está el norte?)
Which is the road to__?	*KWAHL ess el ka-MEE-no pa-ra__?* (¿Cuál es el camino para__?)
Draw me a map	*dee-BOO-hay-may oon PLA-no* (Dibújeme un plano)
Take me there	*YEV-ay-may ah-YA* (Lléveme allá)
Take me to a doctor	*YEV-ay-may ah oon MED-ee-ko* (Lléveme a un médico)
Take me to the hospital	*YEV-ay-may ahl o-spee-TAHL* (Lléveme al hospital)
How far is it?	*ah KAY dee-STAHNSS-ya ess-TA?* (¿A qué distancia está?)
Where is it?	*DOHN-day ess-TA?* (¿Dónde está?)
Is it far?	*ess-TA LAY-hohss?* (¿Está lejos?)
It is near	*ess-TA SAYR-ka* (Está cercá)
Danger!	*pay-LEE-gro!* (¡Peligro!)
Careful! *or* Watch out!	*kwee-DA-do!* (¡Cuidado!)
Gas!	*GA-sess!* (¡Gases!)
Take cover!	*ahl ah-BREE-go!* (¡Al abrigo!)
Wait a minute!	*ess-PAY-ray oon mee-NOO-to!* (¡Espere un minuto!)
Good luck!	*BWEN-ah SWAYR-tay!* (¡Buena suerte!)

FILL-IN SENTENCES

In this section you will find a number of sentences, each containing a blank space which can be filled in with any one of the words in the list that follows. For example, in order to say "I want a room," look for the phrase "I want___" in the English column and find the Spanish expression given beside it: *K‿YAY-ro___*. Then look for "a room" in the list that follows; the Spanish is *oon KWAR-to*. Put the word for "a room" in the blank space and you get *K‿YAY-ro oon KWAR-to*.

English	Pronunciation and Spanish Spelling
I want__	*K‿YAY-ro__* (Quiero__)
We want__	*kay-REM-ohss__* (Queremos__)
I need__	*ness-ay-SEE-to__* (Necesito__)
Bring me__	*TRA‿ee-ga-may* (Tráigame__)
Give me__	*DAY-may__* (Déme__)
Where can I get__?	*DOHN-day kohn-SEE-go__?* (¿Dónde consigo__?)
I have__	*TEN-go__* (Tengo__)
We have__	*tay-NEM-ohss__* (Tenemos__)
I don't have__	*NO TEN-go__* (No tengo__)
We don't have__	*NO tay-NEM-ohss__* (No tenemos__)
Have you__?	*T‿YEN-ay oo-STED__?* (¿Tiene usted__?)

EXAMPLE

English	Pronunciation and Spanish Spelling
I want__	*K‿YAY-ro__* (Quiero__)
drinking water	*AH-gwa po-TA-blay* (agua potable)
I want drinking water	*K‿YAY-ro AH-gwa po-TA-blay* (Quiero agua potable)
apples	*mahn-SA-nahss* (manzanas)
bacon *or* salt pork	*to-SEE-no* (tocino)
or	*to-see-NET-ah* (tocineta)
or	*MA-grahss* (magras)
boiled water	*AH-gwa ayr-VEE-da* (agua hervida)
carrots	*sa-na-O-ree-ahss* (zanahorias)
chicken	*PO-yo* (pollo)
chocolate	*cho-ko-LA-tay* (chocolate)
cucumbers	*pay-PEE-nohss* (pepinos)
grapes	*OO-vahss* (uvas)
ham	*ha-MOHN* (jamón)
onions	*say-BO-yahss* (cebollas)
pepper	*peem-YEN-ta* (pimienta)
salt	*SAHL* (sal)
sugar	*ah-SOO-kar* (azúcar)
tea	*TAY* (té)
veal	*KAR-nay day tayr-NAY-ra* (carne de ternera)
a cup	*oo-na TA-sa* (una taza)
a fork	*oon ten-ay-DOR* (un tenedor)
a glass	*oon VA-so* (un vaso)

English	*Pronunciation and Spanish Spelling*
a knife	*oon koo-CHEE-yo* (un cuchillo)
a plate	*oon PLA-to* (un plato)
a spoon	*oo-na koo-CHA-ra* (una cuchara)
a bed	*oo-na KA-ma* (una cama)
blankets	*fra-SA-dahss* (frazadas)

In some regions the word given for "blankets" may not be understood. In that case try one of the following words:
MAHN-tahss (mantas)
ko-BEE-hahss (cobijas)

a mattress	*oon kohl-CHOHN* (un colchón)
a mosquito net	*oon mo-skee-TAY-ro* (un mosquitero)
a pillow	*oo-na ahl-mo-AH-da* (una almohada)
a room	*oon KWAR-to* (un cuarto)
sheets	*SA-ba-nahss* (sábanas)
a towel	*oo-na to-AH-ya* (una toalla)
cigars	*see-GA-rrohss* (cigarros)

In some regions the word *see-GA-rrohss* means "cigarettes." If you don't get what you want try one of the following words for "cigars":

POO-rohss (puros)
ta-BA-kohss (tabacos)

a pipe	*oo-na PEE-pa* (una pipa)
tobacco	*ta-BA-ko* (tabaco)
ink	*TEEN-ta* (tinta)
paper	*pa-PEL* (papel)
a pen	*oo-na PLOO-ma* (una pluma)
a pencil	*oon LA-peess* (un lápiz)
a comb	*oon PAY‿ee-nay* (un peine)
hot water	*AH-gwa kahl-YEN-tay* (agua caliente)
a razor	*oo-na na-VA-ha* (una navaja)
razor blades	*O-hahss day ah-fay-TAR* (hojas de afeitar)
a shaving brush	*BRO-cha day ah-fay-TAR* (brocha de afeitar)
shaving soap	*ha-BOHN day ah-fay-TAR* (jabón de afeitar)
soap	*ha-BOHN* (jabón)
a tooth-brush	*oon say-PEE-yo day D‿YEN-tess* (un cepillo de dientes)
tooth paste	*PA-sta day D‿YEN-tess* (pasta de dientes)
a handker-chief	*oon pahn-yoo‿AY-lo* (un pañuelo)
a raincoat	*oon eem-payr-may-AH-blay* (un impermeable)
a shirt	*oo-na ka-MEE-sa* (una camisa)
shoe laces	*kor-DO-ness day sa-PA-tohss* (cordones de zapatos)
shoe polish	*bay-TOON* (betún)
shoes	*sa-PA-tohss* (zapatos)
underwear	*RRO-pa een-tayr-YOR* (ropa interior)
buttons	*bo-TO-ness* (botones)
a needle	*oo-na ah-GOO-ha* (una aguja)
safety pins	*eem-payr-DEE-bless* (imperdibles)
thread	*EE-lo* (hilo)
adhesive tape	*ess-pa-ra-DRA-po* (esparadrapo)
an antiseptic	*oon ahn-tee-SEP-tee-ko* (un antiséptico)
aspirin	*ah-spee-REE-na* (aspirina)
a bandage	*oon ven-DA-hay* (un vendaje)
cotton	*ahl-go-DOHN* (algodón)
a disin-fectant	*oon dess-een-fek-TAHN-tay* (un desinfectante)
iodine	*YO-do* (yodo)
a laxative	*oon lahk-SAHN-tay* (un laxante)
gasoline	*ga-so-LEE-na* (gasolina)

I want to___	*K‿YAY-ro___* (Quiero___)

EXAMPLE

I want to___	*K‿YAY-ro___* (Quiero___)
eat	*ko-MAYR* (comer)
I want to eat	*K‿YAY-ro ko-MAYR* (Quiero comer)
buy it	*kohm-PRAR-lo* (comprarlo)
eat	*ko-MAYR* (comer)
drink water	*to-MAR AH-gwa* (tomar agua)
wash up	*la-VAR-may* (lavarme)
take a bath	*bahn-YAR-may* (bañarme)
rest	*dess-kahn-SAR* (descansar)
sleep	*dor-MEER* (dormir)
have my hair cut	*kor-TAR-may el PEL-o* (cortarme el pelo)
be shaved	*ah-fay-TAR-may* (afeitarme)

Where can I find___?	*DOHN-day PWED-o ah-YAR___?* (¿Dónde puedo hallar___?)
Where is there___?	*DOHN-day A‿ee___?* (¿Dónde hay___?)

EXAMPLE

Where can I find___?	*DOHN-day PWED-o ah-YAR___?* (¿Dónde puedo hallar___?)

English	*Pronunciation and Spanish Spelling*
a barber	*oon bar-BAY-ro* (un barbero)
Where can I find a barber?	*DOHN-day PWED-o ah-YAR oon bar-BAY-ro?* (¿Dónde puedo hallar un barbero?)
a barber	*oon bar-BAY-ro* (un barbero)
a dentist	*oon den-TEE-sta* (un dentista)
a doctor	*oon MED-ee-ko* (un médico)
a mechanic	*oon may-KA-nee-ko* (un mecánico)
a policeman	*oon po-lee-SEE-ah* (un policía)
a porter	*oon MO-so* (un mozo)
a servant	*oon seerv-YEN-tay* (un sirviente)
a shoemaker	*oon sa-pa-TAY-ro* (un zapatero)
a tailor	*oon SA-stray* (un sastre)
a workman	*oon o-BRAY-ro* (un obrero)
a house	*oo-na KA-sa* (una casa)
a church	*oo-na ee-GLESS-ya* (una iglesia)
a clothing store	*oo-na T‿YEN-da day RRO-pa* (una tienda de ropa)
a drugstore	*oo-na bo-TEE-ka* (una botica)
a filling station	*oo-na ga-so-lee-NAY-ra* (una gasolinera)
or	*oo-na ess-tahss-YOHN day ay-SENSS-ya* (una estación de esencia)
a garage	*oon ga-RA-hay* (un garaje)
a grocery	*oo-na T‿YEN-da day ko-mess-TEE-bless* (una tienda de comestibles)
a laundry	*oo-na la-vahn-day-REE-ah* (una lavandería)
a spring (for water)	*oon ma-nahnt-YAHL* (un manantial)
or	*oon O-ho day AH-gwa* (un ojo de agua)
a well	*oon PO-so* (un pozo)

Where is___?	*DOHN-day ess-TA___?* (¿Dónde está___?)
How far is___?	*ah KAY dee-STAHNSS-ya ess-TA___?* (¿A qué distancia está___?)

EXAMPLE

Where is___?	*DOHN-day ess-TA___?* (¿Dónde está___?)
the bridge	*el PWEN-tay* (el puente)
Where is the bridge?	*DOHN-day ess-TA el PWEN-tay?* (¿Dónde está el puente?)
the bridge	*el PWEN-tay* (el puente)
the bus	*el a‿oo-to-BOOSS* (el autobús)
the city	*la s‿yoo-DAHD* (la ciudad)
the highway	*la ka-rray-TAY-ra* (la carretera)
the hospital	*el o-spee-TAHL* (el hospital)
the main street	*la KA-yay ma-YOR* (la calle mayor)
the market place	*la PLA-sa del mayr-KA-do* (la plaza del mercado)
the nearest town	*el PWEB-lo MAHSS sayr-KA-no* (el pueblo más cercano)
the nearest settlement	*el po-BLA-do MAHSS sayr-KA-no* (el poblado más cercano)
the police station	*el kwar-TEL day la po-lee-SEE-ah* (el cuartel de la policía)
the post office	*el ko-RRAY-o* (el correo)
the railroad	*el fay-rro-ka-RREEL* (el ferrocarril)
the road	*el ka-MEE-no* (el camino)
the river	*el RREE-o* (el río)
the ship	*el BOO-kay* (el buque)
the telephone	*el tay-LEF-o-no* (el teléfono)
the telegraph office	*el tay-LEG-ra-fo* (el telégrafo)
the town	*el PWEB-lo* (el pueblo)

I am___	*ess-TOY___* (Estoy___)
He is___	*ess-TA___* (Está___)
Are you___?	*ess-TA oo-STED___?* (¿Está usted___?)

EXAMPLE

I am___	*ess-TOY___* (Estoy___)
sick	*en-FAYR-mo* (enfermo)
I am sick	*ess-TOY en-FAYR-mo* (Estoy enfermo)
sick	*en-FAYR-mo* (enfermo)
well	*B‿YEN* (bien)
wounded	*ay-REE-do* (herido)
hurt	*less-yo-NA-do* (lesionado)
lost	*payr-DEE-do* (perdido)
tired	*kahn-SA-do* (cansado)

We are___	*ess-TA-mohss___* (Estamos___)
They are___	*ess-TAHN___* (Están___)

EXAMPLE

We are___	*ess-TA-mohss___* (Estamos___)
sick	*en-FAYR-mohss* (enfermos)
We are sick	*ess-TA-mohss en-FAYR-mohss* (Estamos enfermos)
sick	*en-FAYR-mohss* (enfermos)
well	*B‿YEN* (bien)
wounded	*ay-REE-dohss* (heridos)
hurt	*less-yo-NA-dohss* (lesionados)
lost	*payr-DEE-dohss* (perdidos)
tired	*kahn-SA-dohss* (cansados)

Is it___?	*ess-TA___?* (¿Está___?)
It is___	*ess-TA___* (Está___)
This is___	*ESS-to ess-TA___* (Esto está___)

English	*Pronunciation and Spanish Spelling*
That is___	*a-KAY-yo ess-TA*___ (Aquello está___)
It is not___	*NO ess-TA*___ (No está___)
It is too___ / It is very___	*ess-TA MOO‿ee*___ (Está muy___)

EXAMPLE

It is___	*ess-TA*___ (Está___)
clean	*LEEMP-yo* (limpio)
It is clean	*ess-TA LEEMP-yo* (Está limpio)
dirty	*SOOSS-yo* (sucio)
hot *or* warm	*kahl-YEN-tay* (caliente)
cold	*FREE-o* (frío)
here	*ah-KEE* (aquí)
there	*ah-YEE* (allí)
near	*SAYR-ka* (cerca)
far	*LAY-hohss* (lejos)
Is it___?	*ESS___?* (¿Es___?)
It is___	*ESS*___ (Es___)
This is___	*ESS-to ess*___ (Esto es___)
That is___	*a-KAY-yo ess*___ (Aquello es___)
It is not___	*no ESS*___ (No es___)
It is too___ / It is very___	*ess MOO‿ee*___ (Es muy___)

EXAMPLE

This is___	*ESS-to ess*___ (Esto es___)
expensive	*KA-ro* (caro)
This is expensive	*ESS-to ess KA-ro* (Esto es caro)
cheap	*ba-RA-to* (barato)
good	*BWEN-o* (bueno)
bad	*MA-lo* (malo)
big	*GRAHN-day* (grande)
small	*pay-KEN-yo* (pequeño)
enough	*soo-feess-YEN-tay* (suficiente)
much	*MOO-cho* (mucho)

NOTE

The last two sets of Fill-In Sentences are listed separately because there are two different words for "is" in Spanish.

IMPORTANT SIGNS

Spanish	*English*
Alto	Stop
Despacio	Slow
Desviación	Detour
Cuidado *or* Atención	Caution
Dirección de marcha única	One Way
Circulación prohibida *or* No hay paso	No Thoroughfare
Paso a nivel	Grade Crossing
Vía muerta	Dead End
Circulación por la derecha *or* Conserve su derecha	Keep to the Right
Viraje rápido *or* Curva peligrosa	Dangerous Curve
Ferrocarril	Railroad
Puente	Bridge
Cruce	Crossroad
Alta tensión *or* Cables de alta tensión	High Tension Lines
Prohibido el paso	Keep Out
Se prohibe la entrada	No Admittance
Prohibido el estacionamiento	**No Parking**
Prohibido fumar	**No Smoking**
Prohibido escupir	**No Spitting**
Lavatorio *or* Retrete *or* Mingitorio	**Lavatory**
Caballeros *or* Hombres	**Men**
Damas *or* Señoras *or* Mujeres	**Women**
Abierto	**Open**
Cerrado	**Closed**
Entrada	**Entrance**
Salida	**Exit**

ALPHABETICAL WORD LIST

English	*Pronunciation and Spanish Spelling*
	A
a	*oon* (un) *or* *oo-na* (una)
adhesive tape	*ess-pa-ra-DRA-po* (esparadrapo)
am	
I am	*ess-TOY* (Estoy) *or* *SOY* (Soy)
American (North American)	*nor-tay-ah-may-ree-KA-no* (norteamericano)
Americans	*nor-tay-ah-may-ree-KA-nohss* (norteamericanos)
American sailors	*mah-REE-nohss nor-tay-ah-may-ree-KA-nohss* (marinos norteamericanos)
and	*ee* (y)

English	Pronunciation and Spanish Spelling
antiseptic	*ahn-tee-SEP-tee-KO* (antiséptico)
apples	*mahn-SA-nahss* (manzanas)
are	
Are you___?	*ess-TAHN oo-STED-ess___?* (¿Están ustedes___?)
They are___	*ess-TAHN___* (Están___)
We are___	*ess-TA-mohss___* (Estamos___)
aspirin	*ah-spee-REE-na* (aspirina)
B	
bacon *or* salt pork	*to-SEE-no* (tocino)
or	*to-see-NET-ah* (tocineta)
or	*MA-grahss* (magras)
bad	*MA-lo* (malo)
bananas	*ba-NA-nohss* (bananos)
or	*PLA-ta-nohss* (plátanos)
bandage	*ven-DA-hay* (vendaje)
barber	*bar-BAY-ro* (barbero)
bath	
take a bath	*bahn-YAR-may* (bañarme)
be shaved	
I want to be shaved	*K‿YAY-ro ah-fay-TAR-may* (Quiero afeitarme)
beans	*free-HO-less* (frijoles)
bed	*KA-ma* (cama)
beefsteak	*beef-TEK* (biftec)
beer	*sayr-VESS-ah* (cerveza)
a glass of beer	*oon VA-so day sayr-VESS-ah* (un vaso de cerveza)
big	*GRAHN-day* (grande)
blankets	*fra-SA-dahss* (frazadas)
or	*ko-BEE-hahss* (cobijas)
or	*MAHN-tahss* (mantas)
boiled water	*AH-gwa ayr-VEE-da* (agua hervida)
bread	*PAHN* (pan)
bridge	*PWEN-tay* (puente)
bring	
Bring help!	*TRA‿ee-ga a-YOO-da!* (¡Tráiga ayuda!)
Bring me___	*TRA‿ee-ga-may___* (Tráigame___)
brush	*BRO-cha* (brocha)
shaving brush	*BRO-cha day a-fay-TAR* (brocha de afeitar)
bus	*a‿oo-to-BOOSS* (autobús)
butter	*mahn-tay-KEE-ya* (mantequilla)
buttons	*bo-TO-ness* (botones)
buy it	*kohm-PRAR-lo* (comprarlo)
C	
can	
I can	*PWED-o* (puedo)
cheap	*ba-RA-to* (barato)
Careful!	*kwee-DA-do!* (¡Cuidado!)
carrots	*sa-na-O-ree-ahss* (zanahorias)
cheap	*ba-RA-to* (barato)
chicken	*PO-yo* (pollo)
chocolate	*cho-ko-LA-tay* (chocolate)
chops	*ko-STEE-yahss* (costillas)
lamb chops	*ko-STEE-yahss day kar-NAY-ro* (costillas de carnero)
pork chops	*ko-STEE-yahss day PWAYR-ko* (costillas de puerco)
church	*ee-GLESS-ya* (iglesia)
cigarettes	*see-ga-RREE-yohss* (cigarrillos)
cigars	*see-GA-rrohss* (cigarros)
or	*POO-rohss* (puros)
or	*ta-BA-kohss* (tabacos)
city	*s‿yoo-DAHD* (ciudad)
clean	*LEEMP-yo* (limpio)
clothing store	*T‿YEN-da day RRO-pa* (tienda de ropa)
coffee	*ka-FAY* (café)
a cup of coffee	*oo-na TA-sa day ka-FAY* (una taza de café)
cold	*FREE-o* (frío)
comb	*PAY‿ee-nay* (peine)
Come!	*VEN-ga!* (¡Venga!)
Come here!	*VEN-ga a-KA!* (¡Venga acá!)
Come quickly!	*VEN-ga PROHN-to!* (¡Venga pronto!)
cost	
it costs	*KWESS-ta* (cuesta)
How much does it cost?	*KWAHN-to KWESS-ta?* (¿Cuánto cuesta?)
cotton	*ahl-go-DOHN* (algodón)
cover	
Take cover!	*ahl ah-BREE-go!* (¡Al abrigo!)
cucumbers	*pay-PEE-nohss* (pepinos)
cup	*TA-sa* (taza)
a cup of___	*oo-na TA-sa day___* (una taza de___)
D	
Danger!	*pay-LEE-gro!* (¡Peligro!)
day	
Good day	*BWEN-ohs DEE-ahss* (Buenos días)
dentist	*den-TEE-sta* (dentista)
dirty	*SOOSS-yo* (sucio)
disinfectant	*dess-een-fek-TAHN-tay* (desinfectante)
doctor	*MED-ee-ko* (médico)
Take me to a doctor	*YEV-ay-may a oon MED-ee-ko* (Lléveme a un médico)
Draw me a map	*dee-BOO-hay-may oon PLA-no* (Dibújeme un plano)
(to) drink	*to-MAR AH-gwa* (tomar agua)
drinking water	*AH-gwa po-TA-blay* (agua potable)

English	Pronunciation and Spanish Spelling
drugstore	*bo-TEE-ka* (botica)
E	
(to) eat	*ko-MAYR* (comer)
eggs	*WEV-ohss* (huevos)
eight	*O-cho* (ocho)
eighteen	*d‿yess-YO-cho* (dieciocho)
eighty	*o-CHEN-ta* (ochenta)
eleven	*OHN-say* (once)
enough	*soo-feess-YEN-tay* (suficiente)
evening	
Good evening	*BWEN-ahss TAR-dess* (Buenas tardes)
Excuse me	*payr-DO-nay-may* (Perdóneme)
expensive	*KA-ro* (caro)
too expensive	*MOO‿ee KA-ro* (muy caro)
F	
far	*LAY-hohss* (lejos)
How far is it?	*a KAY dee-STAHNSS-ya ess-TA?* (¿A qué distancia está?)
Is it far?	*ess-TA LAY-hohss?* (¿Está lejos?)
fifteen	*KEEN-say* (quince)
fifty	*seen-KWEN-ta* (cincuenta)
a filling station	*oo-na ga-so-lee-NAY-ra* (una gasolinera)
or	*oo-na ess-tahss-YOHN day ay-SENSS-ya* (una estación de esencia)
(to) find	*ah-YAR* (hallar)
Where can I find___?	*DOHN-day PWED-o ah-YAR___?* (¿Dónde puedo hallar___?)
fish	*pess-KA-do* (pescado)
five	*SEEN-ko* (cinco)
fork	*ten-ay-DOR* (tenedor)
forty	*kwa-REN-ta* (cuarenta)
four	*KWA-tro* (cuatro)
fourteen	*ka-TOR-say* (catorce)
Friday	*V‿YAYR-ness* (viernes)
friend	*ah-MEE-go* (amigo)
I am your friend	*SOY soo ah-MEE-go* (Soy su amigo)
fruit	*FROO-ta* (fruta)
G	
garage	*ga-RA-hay* (garaje)
Gas!	*GA-sess!* (¡Gases!)
gasoline	*ga-so-LEE-na* (gasolina)
get	
Where can I get___?	*DOHN-day kohn-SEE-go___?* (¿Dónde consigo___?)
Give me___	*DAY-may___* (Déme___)
glass	*VA-so* (vaso)
a glass of___	*oon VA-so day___* (un vaso de___)

English	Pronunciation and Spanish Spelling
Go!	*VA-ya!* (¡Vaya!)
Go quickly!	*VA-ya PROHN-to!* (¡Vaya pronto!)
good	*BWEN-o* (bueno)
Good day	*BWEN-ohz DEE-ahss* (Buenos días)
Good evening	*BWEN-ahss TAR-dess* (Buenas tardes)
Good luck	*BWEN-ah SWAYR-tay* (Buena suerte)
Good-by	*ahd-YOHSS* (Adiós)
grapes	*OO-vahss* (uvas)
grocery	*T‿YEN-da day ko-mess-TEE-bless* (tienda de comestibles)
H	
hair	*PEL-o* (pelo)
have my hair cut	*kor-TAR-may el PEL-o* (cortarme el pelo)
half	*MED-ya* (media)
half past six	*SAYSS ee MED-ya* (seis y media)
ham	*ha-MOHN* (jamón)
handkerchief	*pahn-yoo‿AY-lo* (pañuelo)
have	
Have you___?	*T‿YEN-ay oo-STED___?* (¿Tiene usted___?)
I have___	*TEN-go___* (Tengo___)
I don't have___	*NO TEN-go___* (No tengo___)
We have___	*tay-NEM-ohss___* (Tenemos___)
We don't have___	*NO tay-NEM-ohss___* (No tenemos___)
he	*EL* (él)
He is sick	*ess-TA en-FAYR-mo* (Está enfermo)
help	*ah-YOO-da* (ayuda)
or	*so-KO-rro* (socorro)
Bring help!	*TRA‿ee-ga ah-YOO-da!* (¡Tráiga ayuda!)
here	
Come here!	*VEN-ga ah-KA!* (¡Venga acá!)
highway	*ka-rray-TAY-ra* (carretera)
hospital	*o-spee-TAHL* (hospital)
Take me to a hospital	*YEV-ay-may ah oon o-spee-TAHL* (Lléveme a un hospital)
hot *or* warm	*kahl-YEN-tay* (caliente)
hot water	*AH-gwa kahl-YEN-tay* (agua caliente)
hotel	*o-TEL* (hotel)
Where is the hotel?	*DOHN-day ess-TA el o-TEL?* (¿Dónde está el hotel?)
house	*KA-sa* (casa)
how	*KO-mo* (cómo)
How are you?	*KO-mo ess-TA oo-STED?* (¿Cómo está usted?)
How do you say___?	*KO-mo say DEE-say___?* (¿Cómo se dice___?)
How far is it?	*a KAY dee-STAHNSS-ya ess-TA?* (¿A qué distancia está?)

English	Pronunciation and Spanish Spelling
how much	*KWAHN-to* (cuánto)
How much does this cost?	*KWAHN-to KWESS-ta ESS-to?* (¿Cuánto cuesta esto?)
hundred	*S͜YEN* (cien)
hungry	
I am hungry	*TEN-go AHM-bray* (Tengo hambre)
hurt	*less-yo-NA-do* (lesionado)

I

English	Pronunciation and Spanish Spelling
I	*YO* (yo)
I am an American	*SOY nor-tay-ah-may-ree-KA-no* (Soy norteamericano)
I am sick	*ess-TOY en-FAYR-mo* (Estoy enfermo)
I have___	*TEN-go___* (Tengo___)
I don't have___	*NO TEN-go___* (No tengo___)
I want___	*K͜YAY-ro___* (Quiero___)
ice cream	*ay-LA-do* (helado)
in Spanish	*en ess-pahn-YOHL* (en español)
ink	*TEEN-ta* (tinta)
iodine	*YO-do* (yodo)
is	
Is it expensive?	*ess KA-ro?* (¿Es caro?)
Is it far?	*ess-TA LAY-hohss?* (¿Está lejos?)
It is expensive	*ess KA-ro* (Es caro)
It is not___	*NO ESS___* (No es___)
What is it?	*KAY ESS?* (¿Qué es?)
Where is it?	*DOHN-day ess-TA?* (¿Dónde está?)
Where is there___?	*DOHN-day A͜ee___?* (¿Dónde hay___?)

K

English	Pronunciation and Spanish Spelling
kilometers	*kee-LO-met-rohss* (kilómetros)
knife	*koo-CHEE-yo* (cuchillo)

L

English	Pronunciation and Spanish Spelling
lamb	*kar-NAY-ro* (carnero)
lamb chops	*ko-STEE-yahss day kar-NAY-ro* (costillas de carnero)
laundry	*la-vahn-day-REE-a* (lavandería)
laxative	*lahk-SAHN-tay* (laxante)
leave	
it leaves	*SA-lay* (sale)
left	
to the left	*ah la eesk-YAYR-da* (a la izquierda)
lost	*payr-DEE-do* (perdido)
luck	*SWAYR-tay* (suerte)
Good luck	*BWEN-ah SWAYR-tay* (Buena suerte)

M

English	Pronunciation and Spanish Spelling
Madam	*sen-YO-ra* (señora)
main street	*KA-yay ma-YOR* (calle mayor) *or* *KA-yay preen-see-PAHL* (calle principal)
map	*PLA-no* (plano)
Draw me a map	*dee-BOO-hay-may oon PLA-no* (Dibújeme un plano)
market place	*PLA-sa del mayr-KA-do* (plaza del mercado)
matches	*FO-sfo-ro* (fósforo)
mattress	*kohl-CHOHN* (colchón)
me	*may* (me)
meat	*KAR-nay* (carne)
mechanic	*may-KA-nee-ko* (mecánico)
milk	*LECH-ay* (leche)
minus	*men-ohss* (menos)
minute	*mee-NOO-to* (minuto)
Wait a minute	*ess-PAY-ray oon mee-NOO-to* (Espere un minuto)
Miss	*sen-yo-REE-ta* (señorita)
Monday	*LOO-ness* (lunes)
mosquito net	*mo-skee-TAY-ro* (mosquitero)
movie	*SEE-nay* (cine)
What time does the movie start?	*ah KAY O-ra emp-YESS-ah el SEE-nay?* (¿A qué hora empieza el cine?)
much	*MOO-cho* (mucho)

N

English	Pronunciation and Spanish Spelling
name	
My name is___	*may YA-mo___* (Me llamo___)
What's your name?	*KO-mo say YA-ma oo-STED?* (¿Cómo se llama usted?)
near	*SAYR-ka* (cerca) *or* *sayr-KA-no* (cercano)
It is near	*ess-TA SAYR-ka* (Está cerca)
the nearest town	*el PWEB-lo MAHSS sayr KA-no* (el pueblo más cercano)
the nearest settlement	*el po-BLA-do MAHSS sayr-KA-no* (el poblado más cercano)
need	
I need___	*ness-ay-SEE-to___* (Necesito___)

English	Pronunciation and Spanish Spelling
needle	*ah-GOO-ha* (aguja)
night	*NO-chay* (noche)
until tonight	*ah-sta la NO-chay* (Hasta la noche)
nine	*NWEV-ay* (nueve)
nineteen	*d‿yess-een-WEV-ay* (diecinueve)
ninety	*no-VEN-ta* (noventa)
no *or* not	*NO* (no)
north	*NOR-tay* (norte)
Which way is north?	*DOHN-day ess-TA el NOR-tay?* (¿Dónde está el norte?)

O

English	Pronunciation and Spanish Spelling
of	*day* (de)
a cup of coffee	*oo-na TA-sa day ka-FAY* (una taza de café)
a glass of beer	*oon VA-so day sayr-VESS-ah* (un vaso de cerveza)
quarter of two	*lahss DOHSS men-ohss KWAR-to* (las dos menos cuarto)
one	*OO-no* (uno)
onions	*say-BO-yahss* (cebollas)
oranges	*na-RAHN-hahss* (naranjas)

P

English	Pronunciation and Spanish Spelling
paper	*pa-PEL* (papel)
past	
half past six	*lahss SAYSS ee MED-ya* (las seis y media)
quarter past five	*lahss SEEN-ko ee KWAR-to* (las cinco y cuarto)
ten past one	*la OO-na ee D‿YESS* (la una y diez)
twenty past seven	*S‿YAY-tay ee VAYN-tay* (siete y veinte)
pen	*PLOO-ma* (pluma)
pencil	*LA-peess* (lápiz)
pepper	*peem-YEN-ta* (pimienta)
pillow	*ahl-mo-AH-da* (almohada)
pins	
safety pins	*eem-payr-DEE-bless* (imperdibles)
pipe	*PEE-pa* (pipa)
plate	*PLA-to* (plato)
please	*por fa-VOR* (por favor) *or* *SEER-va-say___* (Sírvase___) *or* *TEN-ga la bohn-DAHD day___* (Tenga la bondad de___)
Please point	*SEER-va-say ah-poon-TAR* (Sírvase apuntar)
Please point it out to me	*SEER-va-say sen-ya-LAR-may-lo* (Sírvase señalármelo)
Please speak slowly	*TEN-ga la bohn-DAHD day ah-BLAR dess-PAHSS-yo* (Tenga la bondad de hablar despacio)
(to) point	*ah-poon-TAR* (apuntar)
(to) point it out to me	*sen-ya-LAR-may-lo* (señalármelo)
policeman	*po-lee-SEE-ah* (policía)
police station	*kwar-TEL day la po-lee-SEE-ah* (cuartel de la policía)
pork	*KAR-nay day PWAYR-ko* (carne de puerco)
pork chops	*ko-STEE-yahss day PWAYR-ko* (costillas de puerco)
porter	*MO-so* (mozo)
post office	*ko-RRAY-o* (correo)
potatoes	*PA-pahss* (papas) *or* *pa-TA-tahss* (patatas)

Q

English	Pronunciation and Spanish Spelling
quarter	*KWAR-to* (cuarto)
quarter of two	*DOHSS men-ohss KWAR-to* (dos menos cuarto)
quarter past five	*SEEN-ko ee KWAR-to* (cinco y cuarto)
quickly	*PROHN-to* (pronto)
Come quickly!	*VEN-ga PROHN-to!* (¡Venga pronto!)
Go quickly!	*VA-ya PROHN-to!* (¡Vaya pronto!)

R

English	Pronunciation and Spanish Spelling
railroad	*fay-rro-ka-RREEL* (ferrocarril)
railroad station	*ess-tahss-YOHN* (estación)
raincoat	*eem-payr-may-AH-blay* (impermeable)
razor	*na-VA-ha* (navaja)
razor blades	*O-hahss day ah-fay-TAR* (hojas de afeitar)
(to) rest	*dess-kahn-SAR* (descansar)
restaurant	*rress-ta‿oo-RAHN-tay* (restaurante)
Where is the restaurant?	*DOHN-day ess-TA el rress-ta‿oo-RAHN-tay?* (¿Dónde está el restaurante?)
rewarded	
You will be rewarded	*NO lo ah-RA day BAHL-day* (No lo hará de balde)
rice	*ah-RROHSS* (arroz)
right	
to the right	*ah la day-RECH-ah* (a la derecha)
right away	*PROHN-to* (pronto)
river	*RREE-o* (río)
road	*ka-MEE-no* (camino)
room	*KWAR-to* (cuarto)

English	Pronunciation and Spanish Spelling
	S
safety pins	*eem-payr-DEE-bless* (imperdibles)
sailors	*mah-REE-nohss* (marinos)
Where are the American sailors?	*DOHN-day ess-TAHN lohss mah-REE-nohss nor-tay-ah-may-ree-KA-nohss?* (¿Dónde están los marinos norteamericanos?)
Where are the sailors?	*DOHN-day ess-TAHN lohss mah-REE-nohss?* (¿Dónde están los marinos?)
salad	*en-sa-LA-da* (ensalada)
salt	*SAHL* (sal)
Saturday	*SA-ba-do* (sábado)
say	
How do you say___?	*KO-mo say DEE-say___?* (¿Cómo se dice___?)
see	
I'll see you later	*ah-sta la VEE-sta* (Hasta la vista)
See you soon	*ah-sta l‿way-GHEE-to* (Hasta lueguito)
servant	*seerv-YEN-tay* (sirviente)
seven	*S‿YAY-tay* (siete)
seventeen	*d‿yess-eess-YAY-tay* (diecisiete)
seventy	*say-TEN-ta* (setenta)
(to) shave	*ah-fay-TAR* (afeitar)
I want to be shaved	*K‿YAY-ro ah-fay-TAR-may* (Quiero afeitarme)
shaving brush	*BRO-cha day ah-fay-TAR* (brocha de afeitar)
shaving soap	*ha-BOHN day ah-fay-TAR* (jabón de afeitar)
she	*AY-ya* (ella)
sheets	*SA-ba-nahss* (sábanas)
ship	*BOO-kay* (buque)
shirt	*ka-MEE-sa* (camisa)
shoemaker	*sa-pa-TAY-ro* (zapatero)
shoes	*sa-PA-tohss* (zapatos)
shoe laces	*kor-DO-ness day sa-PA-tohss* (cordones de zapatos)
shoe polish	*bay-TOON* (betún)
sick	*en-FAYR-mo* (enfermo)
sir	*sen-YOR* (senor)
six	*SAYSS* (seis)
sixteen	*d‿yess-ee-SAYSS* (dieciséis)
sixty	*say-SEN-ta* (sesenta)
(to) sleep	*dor-MEER* (dormir)
slowly	*dess-PAHSS-yo* (despacio)
small	*pay-KEN-yo* (pequeño)
So long	*ah-sta L‿WEG-o* (Hasta luego)
soap	*ha-BOHN* (jabón)
shaving soap	*ha-BOHN day ah-fay-TAR* (jabón de afeitar)
soon	
See you soon	*ah-sta l‿way-GHEE-to* (Hasta lueguito)
soup	*SO-pa* (sopa)
Spanish	*ess-pahn-YOHL* (español)
in Spanish	*en ess-pahn-YOHL* (en español)
(to) speak	*ah-BLAR* (hablar)
Please speak slowly	*SEER-va-say ah-BLAR dess-PAHSS-yo* (Sírvase hablar despacio)
spoon	*koo-CHA-ra* (cuchara)
spring (for water)	*ma-nahnt-YAHL* (manantial)
start	
it starts	*emp-YESS-ah*
What time does the movie start?	*ah KAY O-ra emp-YESS-ah el SEE-nay* (¿A qué hora empieza el cine?)
station	
police station	*kwar-TEL day la po-lee-SEE-ah* (cuartel de la policía)
railroad station	*ess-tahss-YOHN* (estación)
Where is the railroad station?	*DOHN-day ess-TA la ess-tahss-YOHN* (¿Dónde está la estación?)
steak	
beefsteak	*beef-TEK* (biftec)
stew	*ghee-SA-do* (guisado)
Stop!	*PA-ray!* (¡Pare!)
store	*T‿YEN-da* (tienda)
clothing store	*T‿YEN-da day RRO-pa* (tienda de ropa)
straight ahead	*ah-day-LAHN-tay* (adelante)
street	*KA-yay* (calle)
main street	*KA-yay ma-YOR* (calle mayor)
or	*KA-yay preen-see-PAHL* (calle principal)
sugar	*ah-SOO-kar* (azúcar)
Sunday	*do-MEEN-go* (domingo)
	T
tailor	*SA-stray* (sastre)
take	
Take cover!	*ahl ah-BREE-go!* (¡Al abrigo!)
Take me to a doctor	*YEV-ay-may ah oon MED-ee-ko* (Lléveme a un médico)
Take me to the hospital	*YEV-ay-may ahl o-spee-TAHL* (Lléveme al hospital)

English	Pronunciation and Spanish Spelling
Take me there	*YEV-ay-may ah-YA* (Lléveme allá)
tea	*TAY* (té)
telegraph office	*tay-LEG-ra-fo* (telégrafo)
telephone	*tay-LEF-o-no* (teléfono)
ten	*D‿YESS* (diez)
Thank you	*GRAHSS-yahss* (Gracias)
the	*el* (el)
or	*la* (la)
or	*lohss* (los)
or	*lahss* (las)
there	
Take me there	*YEV-ay-may ah-YA* (Lléveme allá)
they	*AY-yohss* (ellos)
They are sick	*ess-TAHN en-FAYR-mohss* (Están enfermos)
thirsty	
I am thirsty	*TEN-go SED* (Tengo sed)
thirteen	*TRESS-ay* (trece)
thirty	*TRAYN-ta* (treinta)
this	*ESS-to* (esto)
What's this?	*KAY ess ESS-to?* (¿Qué es esto?)
thousand	*MEEL* (mil)
thread	*EE-lo* (hilo)
three	*TRESS* (tres)
Thursday	*H‿WEV-ess* (jueves)
time	
at what time	*ah KAY O-ra* (a qué hora)
What time is it?	*KAY O-ra ESS?* (¿Qué hora es?)
tired	*kahn-SA-do* (cansado)
to	*ah* (a)
to the right	*ah la day-RECH-ah* (a la derecha)
to the left	*ah la eesk-YAYR-da* (a la izquierda)
to a doctor	*ah oon MED-ee-ko* (a un médico)
to the hospital	*ahl o-spee-TAHL* (al hospital)
twenty to eight	*O-cho men-ohss VAYN-tay* (ocho menos veinte)
ten minutes to three	*TRESS men-ohss D‿YESS* (tres menos diez)
or	*D‿YESS pa-ra lahss TRESS* (diez para las tres)
tobacco	*ta-BA-ko* (tabaco)
today	*OY* (hoy)
toilet	*rray-TRAY-tay* (retrete)
Where is the toilet?	*DOHN-day ess-TA el rray-TRAY-tay?* (¿Dónde está el retrete?)
tomorrow	*mahn-YA-na* (mañana)
too expensive	*MOO‿ee KA-ro* (muy caro)
toothbrush	*say-PEE-yo day D‿YEN-tess* (cepillo de dientes)
tooth paste	*PA-sta day D‿YEN-tess* (pasta de dientes)
towel	*to-AH-ya* (toalla)
town	*PWEB-lo* (pueblo)
the nearest town	*el PWEB-lo MAHSS sayr-KA-no* (el pueblo más cercano)
train	*TREN* (tren)
What time does the train leave?	*ah KAY O-ra SA-lay el TREN* (¿A qué hora sale el tren?)
Tuesday	*MAR-tess* (martes)
twelve	*DO-say* (doce)
twenty	*VAYN-tay* (veinte)
twenty-one	*vaynt-YOO-no* (veintiuno)
twenty-two	*vayn-tee-DOHSS* (veintidós)
two	*DOHSS* (dos)

U

English	Pronunciation and Spanish Spelling
understand	
Understand me?	*may ent-YEN-day?* (¿Me entiende?)
I don't understand	*NO ent-YEN-do* (No entiendo)
underwear	*RRO-pa een-tayr-YOHR* (ropa interior)
until	*ah-sta* (hasta)
Until to-morrow	*ah-sta mahn-YA-na* (Hasta mañana)
Until tonight	*ah-sta la NO-chay* (Hasta la noche)

V

English	Pronunciation and Spanish Spelling
veal	*KAR-nay day tayr-NAY-ra* (carne de ternera)

W

English	Pronunciation and Spanish Spelling
Wait!	*ess-PAY-ray!* (¡Espere!)
Wait a minute!	*ess-PAY-ray oon mee-NOO-to!* (¡Espere un minuto!)
want	
I want___ *or* I want to___	*K‿YAY-ro___* (Quiero___)
We want___	*kay-REM-ohss___* (Queremos___)
warm *or* hot	*kahl-YEN-tay* (caliente)
wash up	
I want to wash up	*K‿YAY-ro la-VAR-may* (Quiero lavarme)

English	Pronunciation and Spanish Spelling
Watch out!	*kwee-DA-do!* (¡Cuidado!)
water	*AH-gwa* (agua)
boiled water	*AH-gwa ayr-VEE-da* (agua hervida)
drinking water	*AH-gwa po-TA-blay* (agua potable)
hot water	*AH-gwa kahl-YEN-tay* (agua caliente)
we	*no-SO-trohss*
We are sick	*ess-TA-mohss en-FAYR-mohss* (Estamos enfermos)
We have___	*tay-NEM-ohss___* (Tenemos___)
We don't have___	*NO tay-NEM-ohss___* (No tenemos___)
We want___	*kay-REM-ohss___* (Queremos___)
Wednesday	*M‿YAYR-ko-less* (miércoles)
well (in good health)	*B‿YEN* (bien)
well (for water)	*PO-so* (pozo)
what	*KAY* (qué)
What is it?	*KAY ESS?* (¿Qué es?)
What is your name?	*KO-mo say YA-ma oo-STED?* (¿Cómo se llama usted?)
What time is it?	*KAY O-ra ESS?* (¿Qué hora es?)
What's this?	*KAY ess ESS-to?* (?Qué es esto?)
at what time	*ah KAY O-ra* (a qué hora)
where	*DOHN-day* (dónde)
Where is it?	*DOHN-day ess-TA?* (¿Dónde está?)
Where are they?	*DOHN-day ess-TAHN?* (¿Dónde están?)
Where can I find___?	*DOHN-day PWED-o ah-YAR___?* (¿Dónde puedo hallar___?)
Where can I get___?	*DOHN-day kohn-SEE-go___?* (¿Dónde consigo___?)
Where is there___?	*DOHN-day A‿ee___?* (¿Dónde hay___?)
which	*KWAHL* (cuál)
Which is the road to___?	*KWAHL ess el ka-MEE-no pa-ra___?* (¿Cuál es el camino para___?)
Which way is north?	*DOHN-day ess-TA el NOR-tay?* (¿Dónde está el norte?)
workman	*o-BRAY-ro* (obrero)
wounded	*ay-REE-do* (herido)

Y

English	Pronunciation and Spanish Spelling
yes	*SEE* (sí)
yesterday	*ah-YAYR* (ayer)
you	*oo-STED* (usted)
You will be rewarded	*NO lo ah-RA day BAHL-day* (No lo hará de balde)
Have you?	*T‿YEN-ay oo-STED?* (¿Tiene usted?)
Are you sick?	*ess-TA oo-STED en-FAYR-mo?* (¿Está usted enfermo?)

French/English Dictionary

French is spoken by over 60 million people—about 47 million in France, the rest principally in Belgium, Switzerland, Canada, and the French-speaking African countries.

This *Language Guide* will enable you to ask directions, buy things or order a meal in these French-speaking regions. Knowing a little French will also help you get along with the people, for they will naturally be pleased to see a stranger showing enough interest in them to try to learn their language.

How to Use the Records* and Guide

This *Guide* is not intended to give you a complete command of the French language. For a thorough course in French, write to the United States Armed Forces Institute, Madison, Wisconsin. Even without a thorough course, however, the instructions given in this handbook will enable you to carry on simple conversations in the language.

The records that go with this *Guide* give you a number of the most important words and phrases in French. Read the section called *Hints on Pronunciation* and then listen to the records until you know the *Useful Words and Phrases* by heart. Repeat each word out loud right after you hear it and say it exactly the way the French speaker does. Imitate the pronunciation as closely as you can, just as you might mimic someone who has an unusual accent. Try to get every detail of the pronunciation, even the rhythm and the inflection of the voice. Follow the words in your *Guide* but use them only as a reminder; if you hear something different from what you see written, go by what you hear. Remember that you can't get the sound of a language from the printed word alone—you have to use your ears even more than your eyes. If you don't have the records and can't get a French speaker to read the words, you will have to rely on the *Hints on Pronunciation* alone.

By the time you have practiced the *Useful Words and Phrases* several times you will know what sound each letter stands for in the *Guide*. You will then be able to pronounce the *Additional Expressions* even though you have not actually heard them, and you will be able to form sentences of your own by using the section called *Fill-In Sentences*.

*Records no longer available.

Hints on Pronunciation

You will find all the words and phrases written both in French spelling and in a simplified spelling which you read like English. Don't use the French spelling, the one given in parentheses, unless you have studied French before. *Read the simplified spelling as though it were English*. When you see the French word for "where" spelled *oo*, give the *oo* the sound it has in the English words *too, boot*, etc. and not the sound it has in German or any other language you may happen to know.

Each letter or combination of letters is used for the sound it usually stands for in English and it *always* stands for that sound. Thus, *oo* is always pronounced as it is in *too, boo, boot, tooth, roost*, never as anything else. Say these words and then pronounce the vowel sound by itself. That is the sound you must use every time you see *oo* in the *Pronunciation* column. If you should use some other sound—for example, the sound of *oo* in *blood*—you might be misunderstood.

Syllables that are accented, that is, pronounced louder than others, are written in capital letters. In French, unaccented syllables are not skipped over quickly, as they are in English. The accent is generally on the last syllable in the phrase.

Hyphens are used to divide words into syllables in order to make them easier to pronounce. Curved lines (‿) are used to show sounds that are pronounced together without any break; for example, *day-z‿UH* meaning "some eggs," *kawm-B‿YANG* meaning "how much?"

Special Points

Here are a few points to note as you listen to the records:

AY	as in *may, say, play* but don't drawl it out as we do in English. Since it is not drawled it sounds almost like the *e* in *let*. Example: *ray-pay-TAY* meaning "repeat."
J	stands for a sound for which we have no single letter in English. It is the sound we have in *measure, leisure, usual, division, casualty, azure*. Example: *bawn-JOOR* meaning "Good day."
EW	is used for a sound like *ee* in *bee* made with the lips rounded as though about to say the *oo* in *boot*. Example: *ek-skew-zay MWA* meaning "Excuse me."
U or UH	as in *up, cut, rub, gun*. Examples: *nuf* meaning "nine," *juh* meaning "I."
U̲ or U̲H̲	as in *up, cut*, etc. but made with the lips rounded. Example: *DU̲H̲* meaning "two."

The difference between these two sounds is not too important in French and you will be understood if you use the vowel in *up* in all cases. The *uh* which is pronounced like the vowel in *up* but with the lips rounded is underlined in the *Useful Words and Phrases* so that you can compare the two sounds as you listen to the record.

NG, N or M — are used to show that certain vowels are pronounced through the nose, very much in the way we generally say *huh, uh-uh, uh-huh.* Examples: *lahnt-MAHNG* meaning "slowly," *juh kawm-PRAHNG* meaning "I understand," *NAWNG* meaning "no," *PANG* meaning "bread."

Memory Key

AY	as in *day* but not so drawled.
U *or* UH	as in *up*.
EW	for the sound in *bee* said with the lips rounded.
J	for the sound in *measure, division.*
NG, N *or* M	for vowels pronounced through the nose.

USEFUL WORDS AND PHRASES

The following is the exact wording of the French Language records issued with this *Guide.*

These records give you a few useful phrases in French. To learn to say these phrases so that you will be understood, imitate the sounds exactly as you hear them. You will hear the English first, followed by the French; then repeat the French out loud, and say it *good and loud.* Remember! Repeat every French phrase right after you hear it.

In the *French Language Guide* which should be used with these records, all the phrases you will hear are written both in French spelling and in a simplified spelling which you should read like English. Don't use the French spelling unless you have studied French before.

Listen to the records six or seven times and you will know the phrases by heart.

GREETINGS AND GENERAL PHRASES

English	*Pronunciation and French Spelling*
Hello *or* Good day	*bawn-JOOR* (Bonjour)

Notice the sound of *j* in the word *JOOR.* Listen again and repeat: *JOOR, JOOR.* It is the same sound we have in *measure, usual, division, azure,* etc. We have no single letter for this sound in English, so we write it in your *Language Guide* as *j.* But remember—always pronounce *j* as you heard it in *JOOR,* never as the *j* in *judge.* Try just the sound again: *j, j.*

English	*Pronunciation and French Spelling*
Good evening	*bawn-SWAR* (Bonsoir)
How are you?	*kaw-MAHN-T‿ah-lay VOO?* (Comment allez-vous?)
Sir	*muss-Y<u>UH</u>* (Monsieur)
Madam	*ma-DAHM* (Madame)
Miss	*mad-mwa-ZEL* (Mademoiselle)

English	*Pronunciation and French Spelling*
Please	*SEEL voo PLAY* (S'il vous plaît)
Excuse me	*ek-skew-zay MWA* (Excusez-moi)
You're welcome	*eel nee ah pa duh KWA* (Il n'y a pas de quoi)
Yes	*WEE* (oui)
No	*NAWNG* (non)

In the last word you heard a sound pronounced through the nose. Listen again and repeat: *NAWNG, NAWNG.* In English we often have a somewhat similar sound when we say *huh, uh-uh, uh-huh.* The vowel sounds that must be pronounced through the nose like this are written in your *Guide* with an *ng* or *n,* and in a few cases, *m* after them. Always remember, however, that these letters are there only to remind you to pronounce the vowels through the nose. Try just the sound again: *AWNG, AWNG.*

Do you understand?	*KAWM-pruh-nay VOO?* (Comprenez-vous?)
I understand	*JUH kawm-PRAHNG* (Je comprends)
I don't understand	*juh nuh KAWM-prahng PA* (Je ne comprends pas)
Speak slowly, please	*par-lay LAHNT-mahng, seel voo PLAY* (Parlez lentement; s'il vous plaît)
Please repeat	*RAY-pay-tay, seel voo PLAY* (Répétez s'il vous plaît)

LOCATION

When you need directions to get somewhere you use the phrase "where is" and then add the words you need.

Where is	*oo AY* (Où est)
the restaurant	*luh RESS-to-RAHNG* (le restaurant)
Where is the restaurant?	*oo AY luh RESS-to-RAHNG?* (Où est le restaurant?)
the hotel	*lo-TEL* (l'hôtel)
Where is the hotel?	*oo AY lo-TEL?* (Où est l'hôtel?)
the railroad station	*la GAR* (la gare)
Where is the railroad station?	*oo AY la GAR?* (Où est la gare?)
the toilet	*luh la-va-BO* (le lavabo)
Where is the toilet?	*oo AY luh la-va-BO?* (Où est le lavabo?)

DIRECTIONS

The answer to your question "Where is such and such?" may be "To the right" or "To the left" or "Straight ahead," so you need to know these phrases:

To the right	*ah DRWAT* (à droite)
To the left	*ah GOHSH* (à gauche)
Straight ahead	*too DRWA* (tout droit)

It is sometimes useful to say "Please show me.

Please show me	*seel voo PLAY, mawn-tray-MWA* (S'il vous plaît, montrez-moi)

English	Pronunciation and French Spelling	

If you are driving and ask the distance to another town it will be given you in kilometers, not miles.

Kilometer *kee-lo-METR* (kilomètre)

One kilometer equals ⅝ of a mile.

NUMBERS

You need to know the numbers.

One	*UNG*	un
Two	*DUH*	deux

You have just heard a sound you should practice. It is like the *u*-sound in *up* or *but*, said with the lips rounded. Listen again and repeat: *DUH*, *DUH*. Try just the sound again: *UH*, *UH*.

Three	*TRWA*	trois
Four	*KATR*	quatre
Five	*SANK*	cinq
Six	*SEESS*	six
Seven	*SET*	sept
Eight	*WEET*	huit
Nine	*NUF*	neuf
Ten	*DEESS*	dix
Eleven	*AWNZ*	onze
Twelve	*DOOZ*	douze
Thirteen	*TREZ*	treize
Fourteen	*KA-TAWRZ*	quatorze
Fifteen	*KANZ*	quinze
Sixteen	*SEZ*	seize
Seventeen	*DEESS-SET*	dix-sept
Eighteen	*DEEZ-WEET*	dix-huit
Nineteen	*DEEZ-NUF*	dix-neuf
Twenty	*VANG*	vingt

Three other vowels that are pronounced through the nose have now been used several times. You heard them in *kaw-MAHNG*, *VANG*, *UNG*. Listen again and repeat: *kaw-MAHNG*, *VANG*, *UNG*. Try just the sounds again: *AHNG*, *ANG*, *UNG*.

For "twenty-one," "thirty-one" and so on, you say "twenty and one," "thirty and one," but for "twenty-two," "thirty-two" and so on, you just add the words for "two" and "three" after the words for "twenty" and "thirty," as we do in English.

Twenty-one	*van-t‿ay UNG*	vingt-et-un
Twenty-two	*vant-DUH*	vingt-deux
Thirty	*TRAHNT*	trente
Forty	*KA-RAHNT*	quarante
Fifty	*SAN-KAHNT*	cinquante
Sixty	*SWA-SAHNT*	soixante

"Seventy," "eighty," "ninety" are said "sixty ten," "four twenties" and "four twenties ten."

Seventy	*swa-sahnt-DEESS*	soixante-dix
Eighty	*kat-ruh-VANG*	quatre-vingt
Ninety	*kat-ruh-van-DEESS*	quatre-vingt-dix

English	Pronunciation and French Spelling	
One hundred	*SAHNG*	cent
One thousand	*MEEL*	mille

WHAT'S THIS?

When you want to know the name of something you can say "What is it?" or "What's this?" and point to the thing you mean.

What is it? *kess kuh SAY?* (Qu'est-ce que c'est?)

What's this? *kess kuh suh-SEE?* (Qu'est-ce que ceci?)

What's that? *kess kuh say kuh SA?* (Qu'est-ce que c'est que çà?)

ASKING FOR THINGS

When you want something use the phrase "I want" and then add the name of the thing wanted. Always use "Please"—*seel voo PLAY*.

I want *juh voo-DRAY* (Je voudrais)

some cigarettes *day see-ga-RET* (des cigarettes)

I want some cigarettes *juh voo-DRAY day see-ga-RET* (Je voudrais des cigarettes)

to eat *mahn-JAY* (manger)

I want to eat *juh voo-DRAY mahn-JAY* (Je voudrais manger)

Here are the words for some of the things you may require. Each of them has the French word for "some" before it.

bread	*dew PANG*	(du pain)
butter	*dew BUR*	(du beurre)
soup	*duh la SOOP*	(de la soupe)
meat	*duh la V‿YAHND*	(de la viande)
lamb	*dew moo-TAWNG*	(du mouton)
veal	*dew VO*	(du veau)
pork	*dew PAWR*	(du porc)
beef	*dew BUF*	(du boeuf)
eggs	*day-z‿UH*	(des oeufs)
vegetables	*day lay-GEWM*	(des légumes)

In the last word you heard a sound you must practice. It is written in your *Guide* as *ew*. Listen to the word again: *lay-GEWM*, *lay-GEWM*. To pronounce the sound *ew*, you say *ee* but at the same time round your lips as though about to say *oo*. Try just the sound again: *ew*, *ew*.

potatoes	*day PAWM duh TAYR*	(des pommes de terre)
string beans	*day ah-ree-ko VAYR*	(des haricots verts)
cabbage	*day SHOO*	(des choux)
carrots	*day ka-RAWT*	(des carottes)
peas	*day puh-tee PWA*	(des petits pois)
salad	*duh la sa-LAD*	(de la salade)
sugar	*dew SEWKR*	(du sucre)

English	Pronunciation and French Spelling
salt	*dew SEL* (du sel)
pepper	*dew PWAVR* (du poivre)
milk	*dew LAY* (du lait)
drinking water	*duh LO paw-TABL* (de l'eau potable)
a cup of tea	*ewn TASS duh TAY* (une tasse de thé)
a cup of coffee	*ewn TASS duh ka-FAY* (une tasse de café)
a glass of beer	*ung VAYR duh B‿YAYR* (un verre de bière)
a bottle of wine	*ewn boo-TAY‿ee duh VANG* (une bouteille de vin)
some matches	*day-z‿ah-lew-MET* (des allumettes)

MONEY

To find out how much things cost, you say:

How much? *kawm-B‿YANG?* (Combien?)

The answer will be given in francs, sous, and centimes.

Five centimes equal one sou, twenty sous or one hundred centimes equal one franc.

centime	*sahn-TEEM* (centime)
sou	*SOO* (sou)
franc	*FRAHNG* (franc)

TIME

When you want to know what time it is you say really "What hour is it?"

What time is it? *kel UR ay-t‿EEL?* (Quelle heure est-il?)

For "One o'clock" you say "It is one hour."

One o'clock *eel ay-t‿EWN UR* (Il est une heure)

For "Two o'clock" you say "It is two hours."

Two o'clock *eel ay DUH-Z‿UR* (Il est deux heures)

"Ten past two" is "Two hours ten."

Ten past two *duh-z‿UR DEESS* (deux heures dix)

"Quarter past five" is "Five hours and quarter."

Quarter past five *sank UR ay KAR* (cinq heures et quart)

"Half past six" is "Six hours and half."

Half past six *see-z‿UR ay duh-MEE* (six heures et demie)

"Quarter of eight" is "Eight hours less the quarter."

Quarter of eight *wee-t‿UR mwang luh KAR* (huit heures moins le quart)

When you want to know when a movie starts or when a train leaves, you say:

At what hour	*ah KEL UR* (à quelle heure)
begins	*kaw-MAHNSS* (commence)
the movie	*luh see-nay-MA* (le cinéma)
When does the movie start?	*ah KEL UR kaw-MAHNSS luh see-nay-MA?* (A quelle heure commence le cinéma?)
the train	*luh TRANG* (le train)
leaves	*PAR* (part)
When does the train leave?	*ah KEL UR par luh TRANG?* (A quelle heure part le train?)
Yesterday	*ee-YAYR* (hier)
Today	*o-joord-WEE* (aujourd'hui)
Tomorrow	*duh-MANG* (demain)

The days of the week are:

Sunday	*dee-MAHNSH* (dimanche)
Monday	*LUN-DEE* (lundi)
Tuesday	*MAR-DEE* (mardi)
Wednesday	*MAYR-kruh-DEE* (mercredi)
Thursday	*JUH-DEE* (jeudi)
Friday	*VAHN-druh-DEE* (vendredi)
Saturday	*SAM-DEE* (samedi)

OTHER USEFUL PHRASES

The following phrases will be useful:

What is your name?	*kaw-MAHNG voo-z‿ah-puh-lay VOO?* (Comment vous appelez-vous?)
My name is___	*juh ma-PEL___* (Je m'appelle___)
How do you say *table* in French?	*kaw-MAHNG deet voo* table *ang frahn-SAY?* (Comment dites-vous *table* en français?)
I am an American	*juh SWEE-Z‿ah-may-ree-KANG* (Je suis Américain)
I am your friend	*juh SWEE vawtr ah-MEE* (Je suis votre ami)
Please help me	*ay-day MWA seel voo PLAY* (Aidez-moi s'il vous plaît)
Where is the camp?	*oo ay luh KAHNG?* (Où est le camp?)
Take me there	*muh-nay-z‿ee MWA* (Menez-y moi)
Good-by	*o ruh-VWAR* (Au revoir)

ADDITIONS AND NOTES

Thank you	*mayr-SEE* (merci)
I want	*juh VUH* (Je veux)

The expression given on the record—*juh voo-DRAY*—is a polite way of saying "I want"; it really means "I would like." *juh VUH* is much stronger and should be used only when making a strong request or demand.

ADDITIONAL EXPRESSIONS

I am hungry	*jay FANG* (J'ai faim)
I am thirsty	*jay SWAF* (J'ai soif)

English	Pronunciation and French Spelling
Stop!	*ALT!* (Halte!)
Come here!	*vuh-NAY-Z‿ee-SEE!* (Venez ici!)
Right away	*toot SWEET* (Tout de suite)
Come quickly!	*vuh-nay VEET!* (Venez vite!)
Go quickly!	*ah-lay VEET!* (Allez vite!)
Help!	*o suh-KOOR!* (Au secours!)
Help me!	*ay-day MWA!* (Aidez-moi!)
Bring help!	*ah-lay shayr-SHAY dew suh-KOOR!* (Allez chercher du secours!)
You will be rewarded	*voo suh-RAY ray-kawm-pahn-SAY* (Vous serez récompensé)
Where are the American sailors?	oo SAWNG lay mah-RANG-Z‿ah-may-ree-KANG? (Où sont les marins américains?)
Which way is north?	*duh kel ko-TAY ay luh NAWR?* (De quel côté est le nord?)
Which is the road to___?	*kel ay luh shuh-MANG poor___?* (Quel est le chemin pour___?)
Draw me a map	*fet MWA ung kraw-KEE* (Faites-moi un croquis)
Is it far?	*ess kuh say LWANG?* (Est-ce que c'est loin?)
Take me to a doctor	*kawn-dwee-zay-MWA shay-z‿ung dawk-TUR* (Conduisez-moi chez un docteur)
Take cover!	*met-ay VOO-Z‿ah la-BREE!* (Mettez-vous à l'abri!)
Gas!	*gahz!* (Gaz!)
Danger!	*dahn JAY!* (Danger!)
Watch out!	*pruh-nay GARD!* (Prenez garde!)
Be careful!	*fet ah-tahnss-YAWNG!* (Faites attention!)
Wait!	*ah-tahn-DAY!* (Attendez!)
Good luck	*bawn SHAHNSS* (Bonne chance)

FILL-IN SENTENCES

In this section you will find a number of sentences, each containing a blank space which can be filled in with any one of the words in the list that follows. For example, in order to say "I want a room," look for the phrase "I want___" in the English column and find the French expression given beside it: *juh VUH*___. Then look for "a room" in the list that follows; the French is *ewn SHAHMBR*. Put the word for "a room" in the blank space and you get *juh VUH ewn SHAHMBR*.

English	Pronunciation and French Spelling
I want___	*juh VUH*___ (Je veux___)
We want___	*noo voo-LAWNG*___ (Nous voulons___)
I'd like___	*juh voo-DRAY*___ (Je voudrais___)
I need___	*eel muh FO*___ (Il me faut___)
Bring me___	*ah-pawr-tay MWA*___ (Apportez-moi___)
Give me___	*daw-nay MWA*___ (Donnez-moi___)
Where can I get___?	*oo pweej troo-VAY___?* (Où puis-je trouver___?)
I have___	*jay*___ (J'ai___)
We have___	*noo-z‿ah-VAWNG*___ (Nous avons___)
We don't have___	*noo na-vawng PA*___ (Nous n'avons pas___)
Have you___?	*ah-vay VOO___?* (Avez-vous___?)

EXAMPLE

English	Pronunciation and French Spelling
I want___	*juh VUH*___ (Je veux___)
boiled water	*duh LO boo-YEE* (de l'eau bouillie)
I want boiled water	*juh VUH duh LO boo-YEE* (Je veux de l'eau bouillie)

English	Pronunciation and French Spelling
bacon	*LAR* (lard)
beefsteak	*bif-TEK* (bifteck)
chicken	*poo-LAY* (poulet)
chops	*kawt-LET* (côtelettes)
lamb chops	*kawt-LET duh moo-TAWNG* (côtelettes de mouton)
pork chops	*kawt-LET duh PAWR* (côtelettes de porc)
beans	*ah-ree-KO* (haricots)
rice	*REE* (riz)
spinach	*ay-pee-NAR* (épinards)
turnips	*na-VAY* (navets)
apples	*PAWM* (pommes)
chocolate	*shaw-kaw-LA* (chocolat)
fruit	*frwee* (fruit)
grapes	*day ray-ZANG* (des raisins)
oranges	*o-RAHNJ* (oranges)
a cup	*ewn TASS* (une tasse)
a plate	*ewn ahss-YET* (une assiette)
a glass	*ung VAYR* (un verre)
a knife	*ung koo-TO* (un couteau)
a fork	*ewn foor-SHET* (une fourchette)
a spoon	*ewn kwee-YAYR* (une cuillère)
a room	*ewn SHAHMBR* (une chambre)
a bed	*ung LEE* (un lit)
blankets	*day koo-vayr-TEWR* (des couvertures)
sheets	*day DRA* (des draps)
a mattress	*ung mat-LA* (un matelas)
a pillow	*un‿aw-ray-YAY* (un oreiller)
a mosquito net	*ewn moo-stee-KAYR* (une moustiquaire)
cigars	*day see-GAR* (des cigares)

English	Pronunciation and French Spelling
a pipe	*ewn PEEP* (une pipe)
tobacco	*dew ta-BA* (du tabac)
a pen	*ewn PLEWM* (une plume)
a pencil	*ung kray-YAWNG* (un crayon)
ink	*duh LAHNKR* (de l'encre)
a comb	*ung PEN-yuh* (un peigne)
hot water	*duh lo SHOHD* (de l'eau chaude)
a razor	*ung ra-ZWAR* (un rasoir)
razor blades	*day LAM duh ra-ZWAR* (des lames de rasoir)
a shaving brush	*ung blay-RO* (un blaireau)
shaving soap	*dew sa-VAWNG ah BARB* (du savon à barbe)
soap	*dew sa-VAWNG* (du savon)
a tooth-brush	*ewn BRAWSS ah DAHNG* (une brosse à dents)
tooth paste	*duh la PAHT dahn-tee-FREESS* (de la pâte dentifrice)
a towel	*ewn sayrv-YET* (une serviette)
a handker-chief	*ung moo-SHWAR* (un mouchoir)
a raincoat	*un‿am-payr-may-AHBL* (un imperméable)
a shirt	*ewn shuh-MEEZ* (une chemise)
shoes	*day sool-YAY* (des souliers)
shoe laces	*day la-SAY* (des lacets)
shoe polish	*dew see-RAJ* (du cirage)
underwear	*day soo-vet-MAHNG* (des sous-vêtements)
buttons	*day boo-TAWNG* (des boutons)
needle	*ewn ah-GWEE-yuh* (une aiguille)
pins	*day-z‿ay-PANGL* (des épingles)
safety pins	*day-z‿ay-PANGL duh sewr-TAY* (des épingles de sûreté)
thread	*dew FEEL* (du fil)
aspirin	*duh lah-spee-REEN* (de l'aspirine)
a bandage	*ung pahnss-MAHNG* (un pansement)
cotton	*dew kaw-TAWNG* (du coton)
a disin-fectant	*ung day-zan-fek-TAHNG* (un désinfectant)
iodine	*duh L‿Yawd* (de l'iode)
a laxative	*ung lak-sa-TEEF* (un laxatif)

English	Pronunciation and French Spelling
I want to___	*juh VUH___* (Je veux___)
I'd like to___	*juh voo-DRAY___* (Je voudrais___)

EXAMPLE

English	Pronunciation and French Spelling
I want to___	*juh VUH___* (Je veux___)
eat	*mahn-JAY* (manger)
I want to eat	*juh VUH mahn-JAY* (Je veux manger)
buy it	*lash-TAY* (l'acheter)
drink	*BWAR* (boire)
wash up	*muh la-VAY* (me laver)
take a bath	*prahndr ung BANG* (prendre un bain)
rest	*muh ruh-po-ZAY* (me reposer)
sleep	*dawr-MEER* (dormir)
have my hair cut	*muh fayr koo-PAY lay shuh-VUH* (me faire couper les cheveux)
be shaved	*muh fayr ra-ZAY* (me faire raser)
Where is there___?	*oo ee-ah-t‿EEL___?* (Où y a-t-il___?)
Where can I find___?	*oo pweej troo-VAY___?* (Où puis-je trouver___?)

EXAMPLE

English	Pronunciation and French Spelling
Where is there___?	*oo ee-ah-t‿EEL___?* (Où y a-t-il___?)
a barber	*ung kwa-FUR* (un coiffeur)
Where is there a barber?	*oo ee-ah-t‿EEL ung kwa-FUR?* (Où y a-t-il un coiffeur?)
a dentist	*ung dahn-TEEST* (un dentiste)
a doctor	*ung dawk-TUR* (un docteur)
a mechanic	*ung may-ka-neess-YANG* (un mécanicien)
a policeman	*un‿ah-JAHNG duh paw-LEESS* (un agent de police)
a porter	*ung pawr-TUR* (un porteur)
a servant	*ung daw-mess-TEEK* (un domestique)
a shoemaker	*ung kawr-dawn-YAY* (un cordonnier)
a tailor	*ung ta-YUR* (un tailleur)
a workman	*un‿oov-R‿YAY* (un ouvrier)
a church	*ewn ay-GLEEZ* (une église)
a clothing store	*ung ma-ga-ZANG duh kawn-feks-YAWNG* (un magasin de confection)
a drugstore	*ewn far-ma-SEE* (une pharmacie)
a garage	*ung ga-RAJ* (un garage)
a grocery	*ewn ay-peess-REE* (une épicerie)
a house	*ewn may-ZAWNG* (une maison)
a laundry	*ewn blahn-sheess-REE* (une blanchisserie)
a spring	*ewn SOORSS* (une source)
a well	*ung PWEE* (un puits)

English	Pronunciation and French Spelling
Where is___?	*oo AY___?* (Où est___?)
How far is___?	*ah kel deess-TAHNSS ay___?* (A quelle distance est___?)

EXAMPLE

English	Pronunciation and French Spelling
Where is___?	*oo AY___?* (Où est___?)

English	*Pronunciation and French Spelling*
the bridge	*luh PAWNG* (le pont)
Where is the bridge?	*oo AY luh PAWNG?* (Où est le pont?)
the bus	*lo-to-BEWSS* (l'autobus)
the city	*la VEEL* (la ville)
the highway	*la grahnd ROOT* (la grande route)
the hospital	*lo-pee-TAL* (l'hôpital)
the main street	*la grahng REW* (la grand' rue)
the market	*luh mar-SHAY* (le marché)
the nearest town	*luh vee-LAJ luh plew PRAWSH* (le village le plus proche)
the police station	*luh PAWST duh paw-LEESS* (le poste de police)
the post office	*luh bew-RO duh PAWST* (le bureau de poste)
the railroad	*luh shuh-MANG duh FAYR* (le chemin de fer)
the river	*la reev-YAYR* (la rivière)
the road	*la ROOT* (la route)
the ship	*luh na-VEER* (le navire)
the telegraph office	*luh bew-RO dew tay-lay-GRAF* (le bureau du télégraphe)
the telephone	*luh tay-lay-FAWN* (le téléphone)
the town	*luh vee-LAJ* (le village)

I am	*juh SWEE___* (Je suis___)
He is___	*eel AY___* (Il est___)
We are___	*noo SAWM___* (Nous sommes___)
You are___	*voo-z‿ET___* (Vous êtes___)
They are___	*eel SAWNG___* (Ils sont___)

EXAMPLE

I am___	*juh SWEE___* (Je suis___)
sick	*ma-LAD* (malade)
I am sick	*juh SWEE ma-LAD* (Je suis malade)
wounded	*blay-SAY* (blessé)
lost	*payr-DEW* (perdu)
tired	*fa-tee-GAY* (fatigué)

It is___	*SAY___* (C'est___)
Is it___?	*ess kuh SAY___?* (Est-ce que c'est___?)
It is not___	*suh nay PA___* (Ce n'est pas___)

EXAMPLE

It is not___	*suh nay PA___* (Ce n'est pas___)
good	*BAWNG* (bon)
It is not good	*suh nay pa BAWNG* (Ce n'est pas bon)
bad	*mo-VAY* (mauvais)
expensive	*SHAYR* (cher)
too expensive	*tro SHAYR* (trop cher)
here	*ee-SEE* (ici)
there	*LA* (là)
near	*PRAY* (pres)
far	*LWANG* (loin)

IMPORTANT SIGNS

Stop *or* Halte	Stop
Ralentir	Go Slow
Détour	Detour
Attention	Caution
Sens Unique	One Way
Sens Interdit	No Thoroughfare
Passage à Niveau	Grade Crossing
Impasse	Dead End
Tenez votre Droite	Keep to the Right
Tournant Dangereux	Dangerous Curve
Chemin de Fer	Railroad
Lignes à haute tension	High Tension Lines
Défense d'entrer	Keep Out *or* No Admittance
Défense de Fumer	No Smoking
W.C.	Toilet
Hommes	Men
Dames	Women
Entrée	Entrance
Sortie	Exit

ALPHABETICAL WORD LIST

English	*Pronunciation and French Spelling*
	A
a *or*	*ung* (un) *ewn* (une)
am	
I am	*juh SWEE* (Je suis)
Americans	*ah-may-ree-KANG* (américains)
American sailors	mah-RANG Z‿ah-may-ree-KANG (marins américains)
I am an American	*juh SWEE-Z‿ah-may-ree-KANG* (Je suis américain)
and	*ay* (et)

English	Pronunciation and French Spelling
apples	*PAWM* (pommes)
are	
Are you___?	*et VOO___?* (Etes-vous___?)
They are___	*eel SAWNG___* (Ils sont___)
We are___	*noo SAWM___* (Nous sommes___)
aspirin	*ah-spee-REEN* (aspirine)

B

English	Pronunciation and French Spelling
bacon	*LAR* (lard)
bad	*mo-VAY* (mauvais)
bandage	*pahnss-MAHNG* (pansement)
barber	*kwa-FUR* (coiffeur)
beans	*ah-ree-KO* (haricots)
string beans	*ah-ree-ko VAYR* (haricots verts)
bed	*LEE* (lit)
beef	*BUF* (boeuf)
beer	*b‿yayr* (bière)
a glass of beer	*ung VAYR duh B‿YAYR* (un verre de bière)
blankets	*koo-vayr-TEWR* (couvertures)
boiled water	*o boo-YEE* (eau bouillie)
bread	*PANG* (pain)
bridge	*PAWNG* (pont)
bring	
Bring help!	*ah-lay shayr-SHAY dew suh-KOOR!* (Allez chercher du secours!)
Bring me___	*ah-pawr-tay MWA___* (Apportez-moi___)
brush	
shaving brush	*blay-RO* (blaireau)
bus	*o-to-BEWSS* (autobus)
butter	*BUR* (beurre)
buttons	*boo-TAWNG* (boutons)
buy it	*lash-TAY* (l'acheter)

C

English	Pronunciation and French Spelling
cabbage	*SHOO* (chou)
can	
Where can I find___?	*oo PWEEJ troo-VAY___?* (Où puis-je trouver___?)
careful	
Be careful!	*fet ah-tahnss-YAWNG!* (Faites attention!)
carrots	*ka-RAWT* (carottes)
centime	*sahn-TEEM* (centime)
chicken	*poo-LAY* (poulet)
chocolate	*shaw-kaw-LA* (chocolat)
chops	*kawt-LET* (côtelettes)
lamb chops	*kawt-LET duh moo-TAWNG* (côtelettes de mouton)
pork chops	*kawt-LET duh PAWR* (côtelettes de porc)
church	*ay-GLEEZ* (église)
cigarettes	*see-ga-RET* (cigarettes)
cigars	*see-GAR* (cigares)
city	*VEEL* (ville)
clothing store	*ma-ga-ZANG duh kawn-feks-YAWNG* (magasin de confection)
coffee	*ka-FAY* (café)
a cup of coffee	*ewn TASS duh ka-FAY* (une tasse de café)
comb	*PEN-yuh* (peigne)
Come!	*vuh-NAY!* (Venez!)
Come here!	*vuh-NAY-Z‿ee-SEE!* (Venez ici!)
Come quickly!	*vuh-nay VEET!* (Venez vite!)
cotton	*kaw-TAWNG* (coton)
cover	
Take cover!	*met-ay VOO-Z‿ah la-BREE!* (Mettez-vous à l'abri!)
cup	*TAHSS* (tasse)
a cup of___	*ewn TAHSS duh___* (une tasse de___)

D

English	Pronunciation and French Spelling
Danger!	*dahn-JAY!* (Danger!)
day	*JOOR* (jour)
Good day	*bawng JOOR* (Bonjour)
dentist	*dahn-TEEST* (dentiste)
disinfectant	*day-zan-fek-TAHNG* (désinfectant)
Do you understand?	*KAWM-pruh-nay VOO?* (Comprenez-vous?)
doctor	*dawk-TUR* (docteur)
Take me to a doctor	*kawn-dwee-zay-MWA shay-z‿ung dawk-TUR* (Conduisez-moi chez un docteur)
Draw me a map	*fet-mwa ung kraw-KEE* (Faites-moi un croquis)
(to) drink	*BWAR* (boire)
drinking water	*o paw-TABL* (eau potable)
drugstore	*far-ma-SEE* (pharmacie)

E

English	Pronunciation and French Spelling
(to) eat	*mahn-JAY* (manger)
eggs	*UH* (oeufs)

English	Pronunciation and French Spelling
eight	*WEET* (huit)
eighteen	*DEEZ-WEET* (dix-huit)
eighty	*kat-ruh-VANG* (quatre-vingt)
eleven	*AWNZ* (onze)
excuse me	*ek-skew-zay MWA* (excusez-moi)
evening	*SWAR* (soir)
Good evening	*bawn-SWAR* (Bonsoir)
expensive	*SHAYR* (cher)

F

English	Pronunciation and French Spelling
far	*LWANG* (loin)
Is it far?	*ess kuh SAY LWANG?* (Est-ce que c'est loin?)
How far is it?	*ah kel dee-stahnss ESS?* (A quelle distance est-ce?)
fifteen	*KANZ* (quinze)
fifty	*san-KAHNT* (cinquante)
(to) find	*troo-VAY* (trouver)
Where can I find___?	*oo pweej troo-VAY___?* (Où puis-je trouver___?)
fish	*pwa-SAWNG* (poisson)
five	*SANK* (cinq)
fork	*foor-SHET* (fourchette)
forty	*ka-RAHNT* (quarante)
four	*KATR* (quatre)
fourteen	*ka-TAWRZ* (quatorze)
franc	*FRAHNG* (franc)
French	*frahn-SAY* (français)
in French	*ang frahn-SAY* (en français)
Friday	*VAHN-druh-DEE* (vendredi)
friend	*ah-MEE* (ami)
I am your friend	*juh SWEE vawtr a-MEE* (Je suis votre ami)
fruit	*frwee* (fruit)

G

English	Pronunciation and French Spelling
garage	*ga-RAJ* (garage)
get	
Where can I get___?	*oo pweej troo-VAY___?* (Où puis-je trouver___?)
Give me___	*daw-nay MWA___* (Donnez-moi___)
glass	*VAYR* (verre)
a glass of___	*ung VAYR duh___* (un verre de___)
Go!	*ah-LAY!* (Allez!)
Go quickly!	*ah-lay VEET!* (Allez vite!)
good	*BAWNG* (bon)
Good day	*bawng-JOOR* (Bonjour)
Good evening	*bawn-SWAR* (Bonsoir)
Good-by	*o ruh-VWAR* (Au revoir)
grapes	*ray-ZANG* (raisins)
grocery	*ay-peess-REE* (épicerie)

H

English	Pronunciation and French Spelling
hair	*shuh-VUH* (cheveux)
have my hair cut	*muh fayr koo-PAY lay shuh-VUH* (me faire couper les cheveux)
half	*duh-MEE* (demi)
half past six	*see-z‿UR ay duh-MEE* (six heures et demi)
ham	*jahm-BAWNG* (jambon)
handkerchief	*moo-SHWAR* (mouchoir)
(to) have	*av-WAR* (avoir)
Have you?	*ah-vay VOO?* (Avez-vous?)
I have	*JAY* (J'ai)
I don't have	*juh nay PA* (Je n'ai pas)
We have	*noo-z‿ah-VAWNG* (Nous avons)
We don't have	*noo na-vawng PA* (Nous n'avons pas)
he	*eel* (il)
He is___	*eel AY___* (Il est___)
Help!	*o suh-KOOR!* (Au secours!)
Bring help!	*ah-lay shayr-SHAY dew suh-KOOR!* (Allez chercher du secours!)
Help me!	*ay-day MWA!* (Aidez-moi!)
here	*ee-SEE* (ici)
Come here!	*vuh-NAY-z‿ee-see!* (Venez ici!)
highway	*grahn ROOT* (grande route)
hospital	*o-pee-TAL* (hôpital)
Take me to a hospital	*kawn-dwee-zay-MWA ah lo-pee-TAL* (Conduisez-moi à l'hôpital)
hot water	*o shohd* (eau chaude)
hotel	*o-TEL* (hôtel)
house	*may-ZAWNG* (maison)
how	*kaw-MAHNG* (comment)
How are you?	*kaw-MAHN-T‿ah-lay VOO?* (Comment allez-vous?)
How do you say___?	*kaw-MAHNG deet voo___?* (Comment dites-vous___?)
How far is it?	*ah kel dee-stahnss ESS?* (A quelle distance est-ce?)
How much?	*kawm-B‿YANG?* (Combien?)
hundred	*SAHNG* (cent)
hungry	
I am hungry	*jay FANG* (J'ai faim)

English	Pronunciation and French Spelling
I	
I	*juh* (je)
I have___	*JAY*___ (J'ai___)
I don't have___	*juh nay PA* (Je n'ai pas___)
I am hungry	*jay FANG* (J'ai faim)
I am thirsty	*jay SWAF* (J'ai soif)
I want___ *or* I want to___	*juh VUH*___ (Je veux___)
I would like___	*juh voo-DRAY*___ (Je voudrais___)
ink	*AHNKR* (encre)
iodine	*yawd* (iode)
is	
He is___	*eel AY*___ (Il est___)
It is___	*SAY*___ (C'est___)
It is not___	*suh nay PA*___ (Ce n'est pas___)
Is it___?	*ess kuh SAY___?* (Est-ce que c'est___?)
Is it far?	*ess-kuh SAY LWANG?* (Est-ce que c'est loin?)
What is it?	*kess kuh SAY?* (Qu'est-ce que c'est?)
Where is___?	*oo AY___?* (Où est___?)
Where is there___?	*oo ee-ah-t‿EEL*___ (Où y-a-t-il___?)
K	
kilometer	*kee-lo-METR* (kilomètre)
knife	*koo-TO* (couteau)
L	
lamb	*moo-TAWNG* (mouton)
lamb chops	*kawt-LET duh moo-TAWNG* (côtelettes de mouton)
laundry	*blahn-sheess-REE* (blanchisserie)
laxative	*lak-sa-TEEF* (laxatif)
leave	
When does the train leave?	*ah KEL UR par luh TRANG?* (A quelle heure part le train?)
left	
to the left	*ah GOHSH* (à gauche)
like	
I would like	*juh voo-DRAY* (Je voudrais)
lost	*payr-DEW* (perdu)
luck	*SHAHNSS* (chance)
Good luck	*bawn SHAHNSS* (Bonne chance)
M	
madam	*ma-DAHM* (madame)
main street	*grahng REW* (grand'rue)
map	*kraw-KEE* (croquis)
Draw me a map	*fet MWA ung kraw-KEE* (Faites-moi un croquis)
market	*mar-SHAY* (marché)
matches	*ah-lew-MET* (allumettes)
mattress	*mat-LA* (matelas)
me	*MWA* (moi)
meat	*V‿YAHND* (viande)
mechanic	*may-ka-neess-YANG* (mécanicien)
milk	*LAY* (lait)
miss	*mad-mwa-ZEL* (mademoiselle)
moment	*maw-MAHNG* (moment)
Monday	*LUN-DEE* (lundi)
mosquito net	*moo-stee-KAYR* (moustiquaire)
movie	*see-nay-MA* (cinéma)
When does the movie start?	*ah KEL UR kaw-MAHNSS luh see-nay-MA* (A quelle heure commence le cinéma?)
N	
name	
My name is___	*juh ma-PEL*___ (Je m'appelle___)
What's your name?	*kaw-MAHNG voo-z‿ah-puh-lay VOO?* (Comment vous appelez-vous?)
near	*pray* (près)
the nearest town	*luh vee-LAJ luh plew PRAWSH* (le village le plus proche)
I need___	*eel muh FO*___ (Il me faut___)
needle	*ay-GWEE-yuh* (aiguille)
nine	*NUF* (neuf)
nineteen	*deez-NUF* (dix-neuf)
ninety	*kat-ruh-van-DEESS* (quatre-vingt-dix)
no	*NAWNG* (non)
north	*NAWR* (nord)
Which way is north?	*duh kel ko-TAY ay luh NAWR?* (De quel côté est le nord?)
not	*ne . . . pa* (ne . . . pas)
I do not understand	*juh nuh kawn-prahng PA* (Je ne comprends pas)
O	
of	*duh* (de)
of the *or*	*dew* (du) *duh la* (de la)

English	Pronunciation and French Spelling
one	*UNG* (un)
o'clock	
one o'clock	*eel ay-t‿EWN UR* (il est une heure)
two o'clock	*eel ay DUH-Z‿UR* (il est deux heures)
oranges	*aw-RAHNJ* (oranges)

P

English	Pronunciation and French Spelling
past	
half past six	*see-z‿UR ay duh-MEE* (six heures et demi)
pears	*PWAR* (poires)
peas	*puh-tee PWA* (petits pois)
pen	*PLEWM* (plume)
pencil	*kray-YAWNG* (crayon)
pepper	*PWAVR* (poivre)
pillow	*aw-ray-YAY* (oreiller)
pins	*ay-PANGL* (épingles)
safety pins	*ay-PANGL duh sewr-TAY* (épingles de sûreté)
pipe	*PEEP* (pipe)
plate	*ah-SYET* (assiette)
please	*seel voo PLAY* (S'il vous plaît)
policeman	*ah-JAHNG duh paw-LEESS* (agent de police)
police station	*pawst duh paw-LEESS* (poste de police)
pork	*PAWR* (porc)
pork chops	*kawt-LET duh PAWR* (côtelettes de porc)
porter	*pawr-TUR* (porteur)
post office	*bew-RO duh PAWST* (bureau de poste)
potatoes	*PAWM duh TAYR* (pommes de terre)

Q

English	Pronunciation and French Spelling
quarter	
quarter of eight	*wee-t‿UR mwang luh KAR* (huit heures moins le quart)
quarter past five	*sank UR ay KAR* (cinq heures et quart)
quickly	*VEET* (vite)
Come quickly!	*vuh-nay VEET!* (Venez vite!)
Go quickly!	*ah-lay VEET!* (Allez vite!)

R

English	Pronunciation and French Spelling
railroad	*shuh-MANG duh FAYR* (chemin de fer)
railroad station	*GAR* (gare)
Where is the railroad station?	*oo AY la GAR?* (Où est la gare?)
raincoat	*am-payr-may-ABL* (imperméable)
razor	*ra-ZWAR* (rasoir)
razor blades	*LAM duh ra-ZWAR* (lames de rasoir)
Repeat!	*ray-pay-TAY!* (Répétez!)
rest	
I want to rest	*juh VUH muh ruh-po-ZAY* (Je veux me reposer)
restaurant	*ress-to-RAHNG* (restaurant)
Where is the restaurant?	*oo AY luh ress-to-RAHNG?* (Où est le restaurant?)
rewarded	*ray-kawm-pahn-SAY* (récompensé)
You will be rewarded	*voo suh-RAY ray-kawn-pahn-SAY* (Vous serez récompensé)
rice	*REE* (riz)
right	
to the right	*ah DRWAT* (à droite)
right away	*toot SWEET* (tout de suite)
river	*reev-YAYR* (rivière)
road	*root* (route)
room	*SHAHMBR* (chambre)

S

English	Pronunciation and French Spelling
safety pins	*ay-PANGL duh sewr-TAY* (épingles de sûreté)
sailors	mah-RANG (marins)
Where are the American sailors?	oo SAWNG lay mah-RANG-Z‿ah-may-ree-KANG? (Où sont les marins américains?)
salad	*sa-LAD* (salade)
salt	*SEL* (sel)
Saturday	*SAM-DEE* (samedi)
say	
How do you say___?	*kaw-MAHNG deet voo___?* (Comment dites-vous___?)
servant	*daw-mess-TEEK* (domestique)
seven	*SET* (sept)
seventeen	*deess-SET* (dix-sept)
seventy	*swa-sahnt-DEESS* (soixante-dix)
shave	
I want to be shaved	*juh VUH muh fayr rah-ZAY* (Je veux me faire raser)
shaving brush	*blay-RO* (blaireau)
shaving soap	*sa-VAWNG ah BARB* (savon à barbe)
she	*el* (elle)
sheets	*DRA* (draps)

English	*Pronunciation and French Spelling*
shirt	*shuh-MEEZ* (chemise)
shoes	*sool-YAY* (souliers)
shoe laces	*la-SAY* (lacets)
shoe polish	*see-RAJ* (cirage)
shoemaker	*kawr-dawn-YAY* (cordonnier)
show	
Show me	*mawn-tray-MWA* (Montrez-moi)
sick	*ma-LAD* (malade)
sir	*muss-YUH* (monsieur)
six	*SEESS* (six)
sixteen	*SEZ* (seize)
sixty	*swa-SAHNT* (soixante)
ship	*na-VEER*
Where is the ship?	*oo AY luh na-VEER* (Où est le navire?)
(to) sleep	*dawr-MEER* (dormir)
slowly	*lahnt-MAHNG* (lentement)
soap	*sa-VAWNG* (savon)
shaving soap	*sa-VAWNG ah BARB* · (savon à barbe)
sou	*SOO* (sou)
soup	*SOOP* (soupe)
Speak!	*par-LAY!* · (Parlez!)
Speak slowly	*par-lay lahnt-MAHNG* (Parlez lentement)
spoon	*kwee-YAYR* (cuillère)
spring (for water)	*SOORSS* (source)
starts	*kaw-MAHNSS* (commence)
When does the movie start?	*ah KEL UR kaw-MAHNSS luh see-nay-MA?* (A quelle heure commence le cinéma?)
station	
police station	*PAWST duh paw-LEESS* (poste de police)
railroad station	*GAR* (gare)
Where is the railroad station?	*oo AY la GAR* (Où est la gare?)
steak	
beefsteak	*bif-TEK* (bifteck)
Stop!	*ALT!* (Halte!)
store	*ma-ga-ZANG* (magasin)
clothing store	*ma-ga-ZANG duh kawn-feks-YAWNG* (magasin de confection)
straight ahead	*too DRWA* (tout droit)
street	*rew* (rue)
main street	*grahng REW* (grand'rue)
string beans	*ah-ree-ko VAYR* (haricots verts)
sugar	*sewkr* (sucre)
Sunday	*dee-MAHNSH* (dimanche)

English	*Pronunciation and French Spelling*
	T
tailor	*ta-YUR* (tailleur)
take	
I want to take a bath	*juh VUH prahndr ung BANG* (Je veux prendre un bain)
Take me to a doctor	*kawn-dwee-zay-MWA shay-z‿ung dawk-TUR* (Conduisez-moi chez un docteur)
Take me to the hospital	*kawn-dwee-zay-MWA ah lo-pee-TAL* (Conduisez-moi à l'hôspital)
Take me there	*muh-nay-z‿ee MWA* (Menez-y-moi)
tea	*TAY* (thé)
telegraph office	*bew-ro dew tay-lay-GRAF* (bureau du télégraphe)
telephone	*tay-lay-FAWN* (téléphone)
ten	*DEESS* (dix)
Thank you	*mayr-SEE* (merci)
that	
What's that?	*KESS kuh say kuh SA?* (Qu'est-ce que c'est que ça?)
the	*luh* (le)
or	*lah* (la)
or	*lay* (les)
there	
Take me there	*muh-nay-z‿ee MWA* (Menez-y-moi)
they	*eel* (ils)
They are	*eel SAWNG* (Ils sont)
thirsty	
I am thirsty	*jay SWAF* (J'ai soif)
thirteen	*TREZ* (treize)
thirty	*TRAHNT* (trente)
this	*suh-SEE* (ceci)
What's this?	*KESS kuh suh-SEE?* (Qu'est-ce que ceci?)
thousand	*MEEL* (mil)
thread	*FEEL* (fil)
three	*TRWA* (trois)
Thursday	*JUH-DEE* (jeudi)
time	
at what time	*ah kel UR* (à quelle heure)
What time is it?	*kel UR ay-t‿EEL?* (Quelle heure est-il?)
tired	*fa-tee-GAY* (fatigué)
to	
to the right	*ah DRWAT* (à droite)
to the left	*ah GOHSH* (à gauche)

English	Pronunciation and French Spelling
to a doctor	*o dawk-TUR* (au docteur)
to the hospital	*ah lo-pee-TAL* (à l'hôpital)
tobacco	*ta-BA* (tabac)
today	*o-joord-WEE* (aujourd'hui)
toilet	*la-va-BO* (lavabo)
Where is the toilet?	*oo AY luh la-va-BO?* (Où est le lavabo?)
tomorrow	*duh-MANG* (demain)
too expensive	*tro SHAYR* (trop cher)
toothbrush	*BRAWSS ah DAHNG* (brosse à dents)
tooth paste	*PAHT dahn-tee-FREESS* (pâte dentifrice)
towel	*sayrv-YET* (serviette)
town	*vee-LAJ* (village)
the nearest town	*luh vee-LAJ luh plew PRAWSH* (le village le plus proche)
train	*TRANG* (train)
When does the train leave?	*ah KEL UR par luh TRANG?* (A quelle heure part le train?)
Tuesday	*MAR-DEE* (mardi)
twelve	*DOOZ* (douze)
twenty	*VANG* (vingt)
twenty-one	*van-t‿ay UNG* (vingt-et-un)
twenty-two	*vant-DUH* (vingt-deux)
two	*DUH* (deux)

U

English	Pronunciation and French Spelling
understand	
Do you understand?	*KAWM-pruh-nay VOO?* (Comprenez-vous?)
I understand	*juh kawm-PRAHNG* (Je comprends)
I don't understand	*juh nuh KAWM-prahng PA* (Je ne comprends pas)
underwear	*soo-vet-MAHNG* (sous-vêtements)

V

English	Pronunciation and French Spelling
veal	*vo* (veau)
vegetables	*lay-GEWM* (légumes)

W

English	Pronunciation and French Spelling
Wait!	*ah-tahn-DAY!* (Attendez!)
Wait a moment	*ah-tahn-DAY-Z‿ung mo-MAHNG* (Attendez un moment)
want	
I want__ *or* I want to__	*juh VUH__* (Je veux__)
We want__	*noo voo-LAWNG__* (Nous voulons__)
wash up	
I want to wash up	*juh VUH muh la-VAY* (Je veux me laver
Watch out!	*pruh-nay GARD!* (Prenez garde!)
water	*O* (eau)
boiled water	*O boo-YEE* (eau bouillie)
drinking water	*O paw-TABL* (eau potable)
hot water	*o SHOHD* (eau chaude)
we	*NOO* (nous)
We are__	*noo SAWM__* (Nous sommes__)
We have__	*noo-z‿ah-VAWNG__* (Nous avons__)
We don't have__	*noo na-vawng PA__*(Nous n'avons pas__)
We want__	*noo voo-LAWNG__* (Nous voulons__)
Wednesday	*MAYR-kruh-DEE* (mercredi)
well (for water)	*pwee* (puits)
welcome	
You're welcome	*eel nee ah pa duh KWA* (Il n'y a pas de quoi)
what	
What is it?	*kess kuh SAY?* (Qu'est-ce que c'est?)
What's this?	*KESS kuh suh-SEE?* (Qu'est-ce que ceci?)
What's that?	*KESS kuh say kuh SAH?* (Qu'est-ce que c'est que çà?)
What is your name?	*kaw MAHNG voo-z‿ah-puh-lay VOO?* (Comment vous appelez-vous?)
What time is it?	*kel UR ay-t‿EEL?* (Quelle heure est-il?)
when	*KAHNG* (quand)
When does the movie start?	*ah KEL UR kaw-MAHNSS luh see-nav-MA?* (A quelle heure commence le cinéma?)
When does the train leave?	*ah KEL UR par luh TRANG?* (A quelle heure part le train?)
where	*oo* (où)
Where is__?	*oo AY__?* (Où est__?)
Where are__?	*oo SAWNG__?* (Où sont__?)
Where is there__?	*oo ee-ah-t‿EEL__?* (Où y a-t-il__?)
which	
Which is the road to__?	*kel ay luh shuh-MANG poor__?* (Quel est le chemin pour__?)
Which way is north?	*duh kel ko-TAY ay luh NAWR?* (De quel côté est le nord?)
wine	*vang* (vin)
a bottle of wine	*ewn boo-TAY‿ee duh VANG* (une bouteille de vin)

English	Pronunciation and French Spelling
workman	*oov-R‿YAY* (ouvrier)
wounded	*blay-SAY* (blessé)

Y

English	Pronunciation and French Spelling
yes	*wee* (oui)
yesterday	*ee-YAYR* (hier)
you	*voo* (vous)
You will be rewarded	*voo suh-RAY ray-kawm-pahn-SAY* (Vous serez récompensé)
Have you?	*ah-vay VOO?* (Avez-vous?)
Are you?	*et VOO?* (Etes-vous?)

Medical Dictionary

A

a *abbr.* accommodation; anterior; asymmetric; area; total acidity.

a- *or* **an-** *prefix* without; lacking; wanting: asexual, anesthesia.

Å *abbr.* Ångstrom; Ångstrom unit.

āā *abbr.* (in prescriptions) of each.

ab- *prefix* from; deviating from: *abnormal.*

abactio induced abortion.

abactus venter induced abortion.

abalienated mentally incapable.

abalienation the state of being mentally deranged or incapable.

abapical opposite the extremity or apex.

abaptiston a conical-shaped trephine, designed to minimize damage to the brain tissues while removing a section of the skull.

abarognosis inability to estimate the weight of something.

abarthrosis a movable joint; synovial joint.

abarticular not directly involving a joint; at some distance from a joint.

abarticulation 1. diarthrosis. 2. a dislocated joint.

abasia difficulty in walking owing to faulty motor control.

abaxial 1. not within the axis of any body or part. 2. located at the opposite extremity of some axis.

abdient tending to move away from the point of a stimulus.

abdomen the section of the front part of the body lying between the pelvis and the thorax and containing many major organs; belly. **—abdominal** *adj.*

abdominalgia pain in the abdomen; bellyache.

abdomino- *combining form* relating to or associated with the abdomen.

abdominoscopy examination of the abdominal contents.

abduce abduct.

abduct to draw away from a median or center line.

abduction the manipulation of a limb away from the middle line of the body.

abductor a muscle, as the deltoid, that draws a limb away from the middle line of the body.

aberration deviation from or variation of the normal condition or course.

abiogenesis spontaneous generation of a living organism.

abionarce lack of energy and drive due to chronic illness.

abiotic not compatible with life; nonliving.

abirritant an agent that soothes or relieves irritation.

ablastin an antibody that inhibits the multiplication or growth of certain microorganisms.

ablation the detachment or removal of a bodily part, esp. by cutting.

ablatio retinae detachment of the retina of the eye.

ablepsia blindness.

abluent any agent capable of cleansing.

abortifacient an agent, as a drug, for inducing abortion. **—abortifacient** *adj.*

abortion spontaneous or induced expulsion of a fetus from the uterus, esp. during the first 12 weeks of pregnancy. **—abortive** *adj.*

abortus an aborted fetus.

abrasion a superficial cut or scrape on the skin or mucous membrane.

abreaction the release of tension and anxiety by the reliving of repressed painful experiences and the understanding of their meaning through the psychoanalytic process.

abruptio a tearing away or premature detachment, especially of the placenta (abruptio placentae).

abscess a localized accumulation of pus in a tissue or organ that is surrounded by inflamed tissue.

absinthism a nerve disorder caused by the excessive consumption of absinthe.

absorbefacient 1. causing absorption. 2. an agent that causes absorption.

absorbent taking in or up by capillary action. **—absorbency** *n.*

acalculia the inability or loss of ability to solve even a simple mathematicial problem.

acampsia abnormal stiffness or rigidity of a joint; ankylosis.

acantha the spine or a spinous process of a vertebra.

acanthosis abnormal thickening of the outermost layer of the epidermis.

acapnia a diminished amount of carbon dioxide in the blood.

acardia absence of the heart from birth.

acariasis any disease caused by infestation with mites (acarids).

acaricide an agent that kills mites.

Acarus a genus of mites including those causing scabies.

acatalepsy absence of comprehension or understanding. **—acataleptic** *adj.*

acataphasia a speech disorder characterized by an inability to express thoughts in clear, logical sequence.

acataposis inability to swallow liquids or great difficulty in doing so.

acathexis a mental disorder characterized by the absence of normal emotional reactions towards objects or ideas, esp. those that are subconsciously significant to the patient.

accessorius relating to any of various muscles, glands, nerves, etc., that have an accessory or auxiliary function; assisting.

accommodation the ability of the eye to focus on near and far objects by contraction of the ciliary muscles to control the curvature of the lens.

accouchement childbirth; labor and delivery.

acephaly absence of the head from birth.

acescent slightly acid.

acetabuloplasty an operation on the acetabulum to correct a deformity or treat osteoarthritis.

acetabulum the cuplike socket of the hipbone.

acetic acid the acid contained in vinegar, used esp. in urine testing.

acetone a colorless, volatile solvent liquid produced synthetically and found in minute quantities naturally in the body and in larger amounts in the condition diabetes mellitus.

acetonemia abnormal presence of large amounts of acetone in the blood.

acetonuria abnormal presence of large amounts of acetone in the urine.

acetylcholine a chemical compound released at autonomic nerve endings to aid in the transmission of nerve impulses.

acetylsalicylic acid chemical name for aspirin.

achalasia failure of various visceral openings or sphincters, as the pylorus, to relax normally.

Achilles tendon the large strong tendon joining the muscles of the calf of the leg with the bone of the heel.

achillorrhaphy surgical repair of a ruptured Achilles tendon.

achillotomy surgical division of the Achilles tendon.

achiria 1. absence of the hands from birth. 2. loss of sensation in one or both hands.

achlorhydria lack of hydrochloric acid in the stomach.

achluophobia fear of being in the dark.

acholia a lack of bile secretions.

achondroplasia abnormal development of cartilage leading to dwarfism.

achromasia the absence of normal skin pigmentation.

achylia absence of chyle in the intestinal tract.

acid any of various water-soluble, sour compounds that combine with alkalis to form salts and turn blue litmus paper red.

acidemia an abnormally high acid level of the blood.

acid-fast not decolorized easily by acids.

acidity the quality or degree of being acid.

acidosis a condition of decreased alkalinity of the blood and body tissues below normal levels.

aciduria the condition of an acid urine.

acinus *pl.* **acini** one of the small, secreting, saclike structures lining a compound gland.

acmesthesia sensitivity to a sharp point on the skin, as a pinprick.

acne a disorder of the skin esp. of the face, shoulders, and back that occurs chiefly during adolescence, is marked by pustules and blackheads, and is caused by hyperactivity of the sebaceous glands.

acnemia 1. wasting of the calf muscles. 2. absence of the legs from birth.

acomia baldness.

acoprosis absence or virtual absence of waste matter in the large intestine.

acorea absence of the pupil of the eye at birth.

acoustic of or relating to sound or hearing.

acquired assumed or contracted after birth; not congenital or hereditary.

acriflavine a yellow dye used as an antiseptic esp. on wounds.

acrocentric having the centromere closer to one arm of the chromosome than to the other.

acrocephaly a malformation of the skull in which the crown is pointed.

acrocyanosis a severe form of chilblains, resulting from an inadequate blood supply to the hands and feet.

acrodynia painful inflammation of the nerves of the fingers or toes.

acrogeria premature wrinkling and aging of the skin of the hands and feet.

acromegaly abnormal enlargement of the facial features, hands, and feet owing to hypersecretion of growth hormone by the pituitary gland after puberty. Compare *gigantism.*

acromicria abnormal smallness of the bones of the skull and extremities, thought to be caused by a deficiency of growth hormone secreted by the pituitary gland.

acromion the outward projection of the spine of the scapula forming the high point of the shoulder.

acronyx an ingrown fingernail or toenail.

acroparesthesia an abnormal numbness or tingling sensation in the hands or feet.

acrophobia an abnormally severe dread of being at a great height.

acrosome part of the head of a sperm cell.

ACTH adrenocorticotrophic hormone.

actinism the property of radiant energy that produces chemical changes.

actinodermatitis dermatitis resulting from exposure to radiant energy, esp. sunlight.

Actinomyces a genus of rod-shaped bacteria including disease-producing parasites.

actinomycin an antibacterial agent esp. active against Gram-positive bacteria, obtained from a species of *Actinomyces.*

actinomycosis disease produced by bacteria of the genus *Actinomyces* and characterized chiefly by discharging abscesses.

actinomyoca a swelling caused by infection with bacteria of the genus *Actinomyces.*

actinoneuritis inflammation of nerves caused by chronic exposure to radium or X-rays.

actinophage a virus capable of destroying bacteria of the genus *Actinomyces.*

actinotherapy treatment with infra-red or ultra-violet radiation.

activator a substance serving to effect a physical or chemical change in another substance while remaining itself inactive.

actomyosin a complex of actin and myosin that with ATP is responsible for muscular contraction and relaxation.

acupuncture a technique of Chinese origin of puncturing the body with needles to relieve pain or cure disease.

acute (of a disease) having a sudden onset, swift rise, and brief course.

acystia absence of the bladder from birth.

adactylia absence of fingers or toes from birth. —**adactylous** *adj.*

adamantinoma a highly destructive tumour of the jaw.

Adam's apple a prominence at the front of the neck (esp. in men), formed by the largest laryngeal cartilage.

adaptation an adjustment to environmental conditions or to variations or intensity of stimulation.

addiction compulsive physical or psychological dependency on a habit-forming drug.

Addison's disease a disease resulting from deficient secretions of the adrenal cortical hormone and being typically characterized by weight loss, nausea, low blood pressure, malaise, and brownish pigmentation of the skin and mucous membranes, esp. of the mouth.

adduct to draw (a limb) toward or past the median axis of the body. —**adduction** *n.*

adductor a muscle serving to draw a bodily part toward the median line of the body or toward the axis of a bodily extremity.

adenalgia pain originating in a gland.

adenectomy the surgical removal of a gland.

adenectopia the presence of a gland in an abnormal site.

adenine a purine chemical base coding hereditary data in the genetic code in DNA and RNA.

adenitis inflammation of a gland or a lymph node.

adenocarcinoma a malignant tumor in or composed of glandular cells.

adenocyte one of the cells forming a gland.

adenofibroma a benign tumor of connective tissue composed largely of glandular tissue.

adenoidectomy surgical removal of the adenoids.

adenoids an enlarged mass of glandular tissue in the nasopharynx that can potentially inhibit breathing. —**adenoidal** *adj.*

adenoma a benign tumor of glandular tissue.

adenosine a nucleoside yielding adenine and ribose.

adenosine diphosphate ADP.

adenosine monophosphate AMP.

adenosine triphosphate ATP.

adenovirus any of various DNA-containing viruses that cause infections of the upper respiratory tract.

ADH antidiuretic hormone.

adhesion tissues joined abnormally by fibrous tissue chiefly as the result of inflammation.

adiaphoresis inadequate ability to perspire.

adipoma a lipoma.

adipometer a device for measuring skin thickness.

adiponecrosis necrosis of fatty tissues.

adiposalgia painful areas of fatty tissue beneath the skin.

adipose relating to animal fat; fatty.

adiposis an excessive accumulation of body fat; liposis.

adiposity fatness; obesity.

aditus an anatomical passage or opening for entry.

adjuvant an ingredient that adds to the effectiveness of a remedy.

ad lib. as much as required (of a drug, remedy, etc.).

admedial near the median plane.

adnexa associated anatomical parts; appendages.

adolescence the period of life between puberty and maturity.

ADP adenosine diphosphate; an ester of adenosine converted to ATP for storing energy in the form of a high-energy phosphate bond.

adrenal 1. adjacent to the kidneys. 2. relating to or derived from the adrenal glands.

adrenalectomy surgical removal of one or both adrenal glands.

adrenal glands a pair of endocrine glands adjacent to the anterior medial border of the kidney, consisting of a cortex and a medulla.

adrenaline epinephrine.

adrenalopathy any disease or disorder of the adrenal glands.

adrenergic activated or transmitted by epinephrine (adrenaline).

adrenocorticotrophic hormone a hormone that is secreted by the anterior lobe of the pituitary gland and stimulates the secretion of hormones by the adrenal cortex.

adrenolytic a substance that inhibits the action of epinephrine (adrenaline) or the function of the adrenal glands.

adrenomegaly abnormal enlargement of the adrenal glands.

adrenopause a supposed period of reduced activity of the adrenal glands.

adrenosterone an androgen secreted by the adrenal cortex.

adrenotoxin any substance that is poisonous to the adrenal glands.

adsorbent relating to or characterized by adsorption.

adsorption the adhesion of a thin molecular layer of a substance, as a gas or liquid, to the solid or liquid surface with which it is in contact.

adventitia the outermost covering or coat of a vein, artery or other structure, not forming an integral part of it.

aerogen a bacillus that produces intestinal gas.

afebrile lacking fever; having a normal body temperature.

affect the consciously apprehended aspect of an emotion regarded as distinct from bodily reactions.

afferent carrying toward; said of nerves carrying impulses to a nerve center and of blood and lymph vessels supplying a particular organ or part.

affinity a force of attraction between particles or substances that brings them into a chemical combination.

afterbirth the placenta, umbilical cord, and fetal membranes expelled from the uterus after the birth of the infant.

afterbrain the metencephalon.

aftercare treatment and supervision of a patient discharged from a hospital.

afterdischarge the extension or prolongation of a reflex response after removal of the original stimulus.

afterimage a visual impression that remains after the stimulation causing it has ceased.

afterpain pain arising from uterine contractions following expulsion of the placenta.

aftosa foot and mouth disease.

agalactia the absence of milk secretion following the birth of a child.

agalorrhea the sudden stopping of the flow of milk from the breast.

agamous relating to reproduction by budding, fission or other nonsexual means.

agar *or* **agaragar** a gelatinous, colloidal extractive of a red alga, used esp. in bacteriology as a culture medium.

agenesis failure or lack of development, esp. of a bodily part.

agenosomia the absence or severe malformation of the genital organs in a fetus.

agerasia youthful appearance of an elderly person.

ageusia loss of the sense of taste.

agglutination the clumping together of particles, as blood cells or bacteria, suspended in a liquid.

agglutinin a substance, as an antibody, causing agglutination.

agglutinogen an antigen stimulating the production of an agglutinin.

aggression hostile or destructive behavior or attitude arising chiefly from frustration or feelings of inadequacy.

agitophasia abnormally rapid but impaired speech.

aglutition an inability to swallow.

agnea the inability to recognize objects.

agnosia a disturbance in the ability to comprehend the nature of a sensory impression.

agonist relating to or describing a muscle in a state of contraction, compared with its opposing (antagonist) muscle.

agoraphobia a fear of open spaces or of crossing an open area.

agraffe a device for holding the edges of a wound together without the use of sutures.

agrammatism loss of the ability to use words in a normal or meaningful pattern as the result of brain damage or disease.

agranulocytosis a destructive condition characterized by severe reduction in the number of granulocytes in the blood.

agraphia the psychological loss of the ability to express oneself in writing.

ague a malaria-like condition marked by fever, chills, and sweating recurring in paroxysms at regular intervals.

agyria a congenital defect of the brain in which the normal cerebral folds are undeveloped or absent.

AHG antihemophilic globulin; a blood-coagulating protein factor in which hemophiliacs are deficient.

AID. artificial insemination with donor semen.

AIH. artificial insemination with the husband's semen.

air embolism embolism resulting from air entering the circulatory system.

akathisia a psychological condition marked by restlessness, hyperactivity, and anxiety.

akinesis loss or impairment of movement.

Al *symbol* aluminum.

ala a wing or winglike part or anatomical process.

alalia the inability to talk due to impairment, as by disease, of the organs of speech.

alba the white matter of the brain, composed mainly of the myelinated axons of nerve cells.

albinism congenital deficiency in skin pigment resulting typically in milky skin, white hair, and eyes with red pupils and pink or blue irises.

albino one affected with albinism.

albocinereous relating to both the white and the gray matter of which the brain and spinal cord are composed.

albumin any of various water-soluble proteins found in blood plasma or serum, muscle, and the whites of eggs and other animal substances.

albuminuria the abnormal presence of albumin (or other proteins) in the urine, usually a sign of some kidney disorder.

alcohol a colorless, flammable, volatile liquid constituting the intoxicating agent in distilled and fermented liquors; ethyl alcohol.

alcoholism an abnormal physiologic or psychological dependence on alcoholic drinks, commonly characterized by excessive solitary or secret drinking and various withdrawal symptoms should drinking cease abruptly; poisoning of the body with alcohol.

alcoholophilia an unnatural craving for alcohol.

alcoholuria the presence of alcohol in the urine.

aldehyde an oxidation product of alcohol, being intermediate in composition between an acid and an alcohol.

aldosterone a hormone of the adrenal cortex regulating the body's salt and water balance.

aldosteronism a condition characterized by weakness, tetany, high blood pressure, irregular heartbeat, and excessive secretion of urine, associated with the production by the adrenal cortex of abnormally large amounts of aldosterone.

aleukocytosis a condition of greatly diminished numbers of white blood cells in the circulation or, rarely, their absence.

alexia an inability to read.

alga *pl.* **algae** any of a group of aquatic plants, as seaweeds, containing chlorophyll often with a brown or red pigment.

algesia sensitivity to pain.

algogenic producing or causing pain.

alimentary of or relating to nutrition or nourishment.

alimentary canal a tubular passage from the mouth to the anus serving to digest and absorb food and eliminate bodily waste.

alimentation the process of giving nourishment; the state of being nourished.

alinasal relating to the flaring part of the nostrils (alae nasi).

alinjection the preservation of tissue specimens by hardening with an injection of alcohol.

aliphatic oily or fatty.

aliquot a measured portion of something.

alkalemia excessive alkalinity of the blood.

alkalescence mild alkalinity or the process of becoming alkaline.

alkali a substance that combines with acids to form salts and turns red litmus paper blue.

alkalimeter an instrument for measuring the alkalinity of a mixture or the strength of alkalis alone.

alkaline relating to or having the properties of an alkali.

alkalinity the amount of alkali in a given substance.

alkaloid any of various complex, bitter, nitrogen-containing organic bases, as morphine or quinine, that are derived from plants and have potent pharmacological activities.

alkalosis a condition in which the body fluids become abnormally alkaline due to the withdrawal of acid or chlorides from the blood or an excess of alkalis in the blood or other body fluids.

allele allelomorph.

allelomorph any of a group of genes occurring alternatively at a given locus.

allergen a substance that induces allergy.

allergic relating to, inducing, or showing allergy.

allergist a physician specializing in allergy.

allergy hypersensitive reaction to a substance (allergen), as by the swelling of mucous membranes or sneezing or itching.

allochromasia a change in the color of the skin or hair.

allocortex the part of the cerebral cortex that is phylogenetically oldest.

allopath one who practices allopathy.

allopathy a system of medicine characterized by treating diseases by the induction of a dissimilar morbid reaction in some part of the body.

alloplasty the surgical repair of the human body using nonhuman tissue.

alloy a mixture of two or more metals.

alopecia loss of hair; baldness.

altitude sickness the effects, as nausea or nosebleed, of reduced oxygen in the blood resulting from exposure to rarefied air at high altitudes.

alveolotomy the surgical incision into the socket of a tooth to drain an abscess or gain access for other treatment.

alveolus 1. the socket of a tooth. 2. an air sac in the lungs.

alvine relating to the abdomen or intestines.

alvus the abdomen and its contents.

alymphia lack or deficiency of lymph.

amalgam an alloy of mercury and another metal used esp. for filling dental cavities.

amarillic relating to yellow fever.

amaroidal having a slightly bitter taste.

amastia congenital absence of one or both breasts.

amathophobia fear of dirt, dust or filth.

amaurosis progressive degeneration of sight, esp. in the absence of any pathological change to the eye.

ambidextrous using both hands with equal skill and ease.

ambivalence simultaneous attraction toward and repulsion from a person, object, or goal.

amblyopia dimness of vision not of apparent organic origin and attributed esp. to dietary deficiency or toxic effects. **—amblyopic** *adj.*

ambulant ambulatory.

ambulatory (of a patient) able to walk about.

ameba amoeba.

amebiasis amoebiasis.

amebicide amoebicide.

ameburia the presence of amoebas in voided urine.

ameiosis cell division in which gametes are formed without a reduction in their chromosome number.

amelanotic relating to certain types of growths on the skin that do not contain the pigment melanin.

amelia absence of one or more limbs from birth.

amelification formation of tooth enamel.

amelioration improvement in the condition of a patient or symptom.

amenorrhea abnormal cessation or absence of menstruation.

amentia mental deficiency.

ametria congenital absence of the uterus.

ametropia a defective refractive condition of the eye in which the image received fails to focus on the retina.

amino acid an amphoteric organic acid; esp., any of such acids that are the chief components of proteins and are obtained as essential components of the diet or are synthesized by living cells.

amitosis cell division by simple cleavage of the nucleus and division of the cytoplasm.

ammonia a volatile alkali with an extremely pungent odor.

ammoniemia the abnormal presence in the blood of ammonia or its breakdown products, resulting in various symptoms including weak pulse and coma.

ammoniuria the presence of an excessive amount of ammonia in voided urine.

amnesia loss of memory esp. from shock, brain injury, psychological repression, illness, or fatigue.

amnesiac one who suffers from loss of memory.

amnestic an agent that induces amnesia.

amniocentesis the drawing off of amniotic fluid for diagnostic purposes.

amnioclepsis the unrecognized escape of small amounts of amniotic fluid.

amnion the thin, membranous sac enclosing an embryo.

amniotic fluid the serous fluid surrounding and cushioning the embryo inside the amnion.

amniotomy deliberate rupture of the amnion to induce or facilitate labor.

amobarbital a barbiturate drug used to depress the central nervous system, induce sleep, etc., given by injection or as capsules.

amoeba *also* **ameba** a unicellular microscopic protozoan that moves by extending its membranous walls. —**amoebic, amebic** *adj.*

amoebiasis *also* **amebiasis** disease caused by infection with amoebas.

amoebicide *also* **amebicide** a substance lethal to amoebas.

amor lesbicus lesbianism.

amorphous having no definite shape; formless.

amotio retinae detachment of the retina.

AMP adenosine monophosphate; adenosine containing only one phosphoric acid group.

amphetamine a synthetic drug that is a stimulant to the central nervous system and is potentially addictive, once widely used to suppress appetite.

amphiarthrosis a joint with surfaces connected by disks of fibrocartilage.

amphiblestritis inflammation of the retina; retinitis.

amphicrania neuralgia affecting both sides of the head.

amphigenetic produced by both male and female.

amphodiplopia double vision affecting both eyes simultaneously.

amphoteric capable of acting either as an acid or as a base.

ampule *also* **ampul, ampoule** a small, hermetically sealed glass vial for holding a solution, esp. for hypodermic injection.

ampulla a flask-shaped swelling or pouch esp. of a duct.

amputate to perform an amputation.

amputation the cutting off of a limb or other bodily appendage.

amusia loss of the ability to recognize musical tones.

amyelencephalia congenital absence of both the brain and spinal cord.

amyelia congenital absence of the spinal cord.

amyelination loss of the protective myelin sheath that covers the axon of a nerve.

amyelineuria paralysis of the spinal cord.

amygdaloid resembling a tonsil or an almond in shape.

amygdala a mass of gray matter in the front part of the brain's temporal lobe.

amylase any of the enzymes that aid in the hydrolysis of starch and glycogen.

amyloid 1. a waxy, translucent glycoprotein deposited in some organs under unnatural conditions. 2. resembling starch.

amyloidosis the deposition of amyloid in bodily tissues or organs.

ana (in prescriptions) of each in equal amount.

anabolism constructive metabolism in which an organism synthesizes complex molecules from simpler ones.

anaerobe an organism living, thriving, or occurring in the absence of free oxygen. —**anaerobic** *adj.*

anal relating to or situated near the anus.

analeptic 1. a medication that is restorative or stimulating to the central nervous system. 2. relating to such a medicine or remedy; invigorating.

analgesia insensitivity to pain without loss of consciousness.

analgesic 1. a drug that relieves pain, such as aspirin. 2. relating to analgesia.

analgia freedom from pain.

anallergic 1. not causing the production of hypersensitivity or anaphylaxis. 2. a serum, etc., that is not anaphylactic.

analogous similar or comparable in many respects.

analysand one who is undergoing psychoanalysis.

analysis 1. separation of a whole into its component parts; identification or separation of the ingredients of a substance. 2. psychoanalysis.

analyst 1. one who is skilled in making analyses. 2. psychoanalyst.

ananaphylaxis a condition in which anaphylaxis is neutralized.

anaphase a stage in cell division in which the chromosomes move toward the poles of the cell.

anaphoresis reduction in activity of the sweat glands.

anaphylaxis extreme and sometimes fatal allergic response to the injection of a drug or foreign protein resulting from previous sensitization to the substance; anaphylactic shock.

anaplasia reversion of cells to a more primitive or less differentiated form.

anastate any product or substance formed as the result of anabolism.

anastole the separation, shrinking back or retraction of the edges of a wound.

anastomosis the uniting of blood vessels or tubular internal organs so as to create communication between them.

anatherapeusis treatment characterized by the gradual increase in the dose of a drug.

anatomical snuff-box the natural depression or hollow formed between the index finger and the base of the thumb when the latter is abducted.

anatomy a branch of medical science dealing with the form and structure of organisms, esp. the human body.

ancipital having two edges or heads.

anconad in the direction of the elbow.

androgen a hormone producing male sex characteristics. —**androgenic** *adj.*

androsterone an androgenic hormone occurring in male urine.

anemia *also* **anaemia** a condition in which the blood has a deficiency in red blood cells, in hemoglobin, or in volume. —**anemic, anaemic** *adj.*

anencephaly impaired development of the brain with absence of neural tissue in the cranium.

anergic marked by an abnormal degree of inactivity; unenergetic.

anesthesia *also* **anaesthesia** loss of sensitivity to pain with or without loss of consciousness, achieved through any of various means.

anesthesiologist *also* **anaesthesiologist** a physician specializing in anesthesiology.

anesthesiology *also* **anaesthesiology** a branch of medicine concerned with anesthesia and anesthetics.

anesthetic *also* **anaesthetic** 1. a substance producing anesthesia. 2. relating to or capable of producing anesthesia.

anesthetist *also* **anaesthetist** one who administers anesthetics.

anetic relaxing or soothing.

anetus intermittent fever.

aneuria lack of energy and drive.

aneurine vitamin B_1; thiamine.

aneurysm a permanent, blood-filled, abnormal dilation of the wall of a blood vessel.

aneurysmectomy surgical removal of the sac formed by an aneurysm.

aneurysmotomy surgical incision into the sac of an aneurysm.

anfractuosity a fissure or sulcus in the cerebrum.

angel's wing a deformity in which the shoulder blades project posteriorly.

angialgia pain in a blood vessel.

angiasthenia vascular weakness or instability.

angiectasis dilation of a blood vessel.

angiectomy surgical removal of a section of a damaged or diseased blood vessel, usually followed by suturing together the remaining ends or (in larger vessels) replacement of the segment with a graft.

angiitis *also* **angitis** inflammation of a blood vessel or lymph vessel.

angina a condition marked by spasmodic attacks of suffocating pain.

angina pectoris a condition marked chiefly by brief paroxysmal attacks of chest pains resulting from an insufficient supply of blood to the heart.

angiocardiography X-ray photography of the heart and its blood vessels after injection of a radiopaque contrast medium.

angiocardiopathy any disease that involves both the heart and blood vessels.

angiocarditis inflammation of the heart and blood vessels.

angiocholecystitis inflammation of the gallbladder and bile vessels.

angioclast a surgical instrument for controlling arterial bleeding; arterial forceps.

angioedema angioneurotic edema.

angiofibrosis fibrous thickening of the walls of blood vessels.

angiography X-ray photography of the blood vessels after injection of a radiopaque contrast medium.

angiohypertonia spasm of the blood vessels; angiospasm.

angiology the branch of anatomy concerned with the study of the blood vessels and lymphatics.

angioma a tumor composed of blood vessels or lymph vessels.

angioplasty plastic repair of blood vessels or lymphatic glands.

angiotomy surgical separation of a blood vessel.

anhidrotic an agent that checks sweating.

anhydrase an enzyme that acts in the removal of water from a compound.

anhydrous free from water.

animalcule a minute or microscopic organism.

anion an ion with a negative electric charge.

anisocoria inequality in the pupils of both eyes.

anisogamous marked by the fusion of heterogamous gametes or of gametes differing chiefly in size. —**anisogamy** *n.*

anisometropia marked inequality in refractive power in the two eyes.

ankle 1. the joint between the foot and the leg. 2. the region surrounding this joint.

ankyloblepharon adhesion or fusion of the edges of the eyelids.

ankyloglossia restricted mobility of the tongue resulting from a foreshortened frenum.

ankylosis 1. abnormal stiffness or immobilization of a joint through disease or surgery. 2. fusion of separate bones to form a single bone. —**ankylose** *vb.*

annular *also* **anular** ring-shaped, as a muscle.

annulorrhaphy the closure of the circular opening around a hernia by suturing.

anode the positive pole of a primary cell or of a storage battery that is delivering current.

anodontia the absence of teeth.

anodyne 1. a drug that eases pain. 2. serving to lessen pain.

anomia loss of the ability to recognize objects or recognize names.

anoperineal relating to or situated near the anus and perineum.

Anopheles any member of a large genus of mosquitoes including all those that transmit malaria to man.

anophelicide any agent that kills *Anopheles* mosquitoes.

anophelifuge an insect repellent effective against *Anopheles* mosquitoes.

anophthalmus 1. congenital absence of the eyes. 2. one born without eyes.

anorectal relating to or situated within the anus and the rectum.

anorectic 1. relating to anorexia. 2. a drug that suppresses appetite; anorexiant.

anorexia loss of appetite.

anorexia nervosa prolonged loss of appetite esp. when of neurotic origin.

anorexiant a drug or agent that causes a loss of appetite; anorectic.

anoscope proctoscope.

anosigmoidoscopy medical examination of the anus, rectum and lower part of the large intestine.

anosmia impairment or loss of the sense of smell.

anotia absence of the ear from birth.

anotus one without ears.

anovulant a drug that suppresses ovulation.

anovular *also* **anovulatory** 1. not related to or accompanied by ovulation. 2. without ovulation.

anovulation cessation or suppression of ovulation.

anoxemia a condition of the blood marked by insufficient oxygenation.

anoxia severe lack of oxygen causing permanent damage.

ansa 1. (in bacteriology) a small wire loop used to pick up and transport bacteria, protozoa, etc., suspended in a liquid film. 2. any bodily structure or part shaped like or resembling a loop or arc.

ansate *also* **ansiform** loop-shaped.

ansotomy surgical division of a constricting loop.

antacid 1. neutralizing an acid. 2. a substance that counteracts acidity, such as sodium bicarbonate or aluminum hydroxide.

antagonist 1. a muscle that contracts with and limits the action of another muscle with which it is paired. 2. a drug that counteracts the action of another drug.

antalgesic a drug or agent that eases pain; anodyne.

antalkaline neutralizing or counteracting alkalinity.

antasthmatic 1. preventing asthma or relieving the symptoms of an asthmatic attack. 2. an agent that prevents asthma or relieves its symptoms.

antefebrile occurring before the onset of a fever.

antemortem preceding death.

antenatal of or relating to an unborn child or to pregnancy; prenatal.

antepartum before birth.

anterior situated before or toward the front; reverse from posterior.

anterograde proceeding or pointed forward.

antero-inferior lying or situated in front and below.

antero-interior lying or situated toward the front and internally.

anterolateral lying or situated in front and to the side.

anteromedian lying or situated in front and toward a mid-line.

anteroposterior lying or situated from front to back.

anterosuperior lying or situated in front and above.

anthelmintic *also* **anthelminthic** an agent for expelling or destroying parasitic intestinal worms.

anthema any skin eruption.

anthocyanin any of various blue to red pigments that color plants.

anthracosilicosis a disease of the lungs resulting from prolonged inhalation of carbon dust and fine particles of silica.

anthracosis a disease of the lungs resulting from prolonged inhalation of carbon dust alone.

anthrax an acute, infectious disease chiefly of cattle and sheep that is caused by a spore-forming bacterium, is transmissible to man, and is characterized by external ulcerating nodules or by lesions in the lungs.

anthropoid 1. resembling man. 2. resembling an ape.

anthropology the study of the physical, cultural, and environmental aspects of mankind.

anthropometry the branch of anthropology concerned with comparative physical measurements of the body.

anthropophobia a fear of human companionship or an aversion to people generally.

antiagglutinin a specific antibody that counteracts, inhibits or destroys the activity of an agglutinin.

antianaphylaxis desensitization to the potentially harmful effects of a specific antigen, as by a series of very small but progressively increased doses of the antigen.

antiasthmatic 1. preventing asthma or relieving the symptoms of an asthmatic attack. 2. an agent that prevents asthma or relieves its symptoms.

antibacterial killing or inhibiting the growth of bacteria.

antibiotic 1. tending to or capable of preventing or destroying life. 2. a substance, as penicillin, produced by a microorganism and able to inhibit the growth of or kill another microorganism.

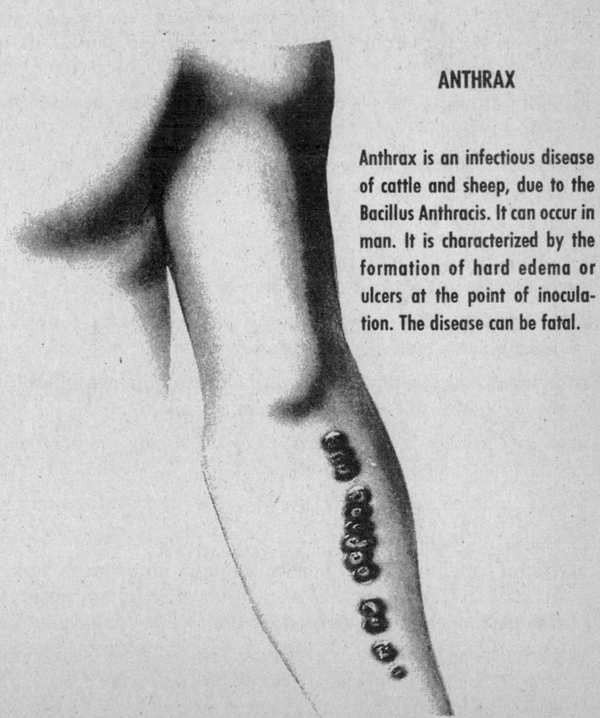

ANTHRAX

Anthrax is an infectious disease of cattle and sheep, due to the Bacillus Anthracis. It can occur in man. It is characterized by the formation of hard edema or ulcers at the point of inoculation. The disease can be fatal.

antibody a specific protein substance produced by the body to attack invading bacteria or other foreign matter.

anticholinergic repelling or annulling the physiologic action of acetylcholine.

antidiuretic 1. relating to the reduction of urinary excretion. 2. an agent that acts to reduce the excretion of urine.

antidote an agent that counteracts the effects of a poison or neutralizes the poison before it takes effect.

antiepileptic relating to a drug that prevents or relieves the severity of an epileptic seizure.

antifebrile reducing fever or relieving its symptoms.

antigen a substance, as a foreign protein or microorganism, that stimulates the production of an antibody when introduced into the body. —**antigenic** *adj.* —**antigenicity** *n.*

antihistamine any drug that counteracts the effects of histamine, used in the symptomatic treatment of various allergies.

antitoxin an antibody formed in response to the presence of a specific toxin and able to neutralize that toxin. —**antitoxic** *adj.*

aorta main artery of the trunk.

apastia failure to eat.

aphasia loss or impairment of the faculty of speech, due to some disease of or injury to the brain.

aphonia loss of the voice, esp. caused by laryngitis or some disease of the vocal cords or their nerve supply.

apnea breathlessness; inability to catch one's breath.

apneumia congenital absence of the lungs.

apodal without feet.

apodia congenital absence of the feet.

apoplexy stroke.

appendectomy surgical removal of the vermiform appendix.

appendicitis inflammation of the vermiform appendix.

appendix 1. any bodily appendage. 2. the wormlike (vermiform) appendage attached to the blind pouch at the beginning of the large intestine.

appestat the part of the brain (thought to be in the hypothalamus) responsible for governing the sensations of hunger and satiety.

aqueous humor the watery fluid filling the space between the cornea and lens of the eye.

arachnoid one of the three membranes (meninges) that cover the brain and spinal cord, lying between the pia mater below and the dura mater above.

areola the pigmented circular area surrounding the nipples.

arrhythmia any abnormal rhythm, esp. of the heartbeat.

arteriography X-ray photography of the arteries following injection of a radiopaque contrast medium.

arterioles the smallest vessels of the arterial system, linked by the capillaries to the venous system.

arteriosclerosis a disease marked by thickening and hardening of arterial walls. —**arteriosclerotic** *adj.*

artery a blood vessel that carries blood away from the heart.

arthritis inflammation of a joint.

artificial insemination the fertilization of an ovum by means other than coitus, such as the introduction of spermatozoa into the vagina with a syringe.

artificial respiration any of various means of forcing air into and out of the lungs of a person who has stopped or nearly stopped breathing.

THE AORTA

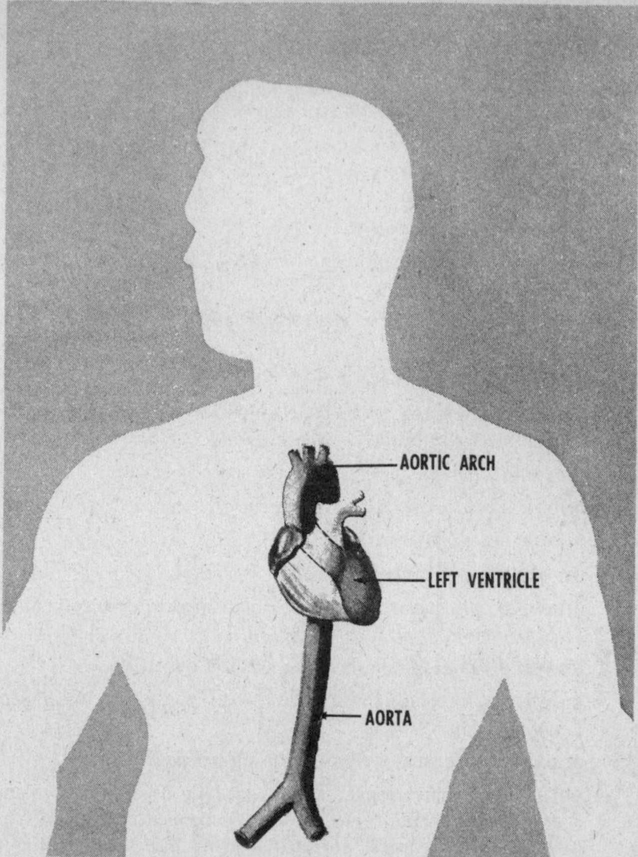

asbestosis a lung disease caused by chronic inhalation of tiny particles of asbestos.

ascariasis intestinal infestation with parasitic roundworms of the species *Ascaris lumbricoides.*

ascorbic acid vitamin C.

asepsis a germ-free condition.

Asian flu a severe epidemic of influenza that took place in 1957, caused by a virus strain that is thought to have originated in Singapore.

aspermia inability to produce or ejaculate semen.

asphyxia loss of consciousness from too little oxygen and overabundance of carbon dioxide in the blood.

aspirate to draw off fluid or gas (as from a body cavity) by means of suction.

aspirator an instrument for drawing off fluid or gas by means of suction.

aspirin a drug used to reduce pain and fever; acetylsalicylic acid.

astasia the inability to stand due to loss of motor coordination.

asteatosis loss of activity of the sebaceous glands or gross diminution of their secretions.

astereognosis loss of the ability to recognize shapes by the sense of touch.

asterixis involuntary jerking movements of various muscle groups caused by advanced liver disease or some disturbance of cerebral metabolism.

asternia absence of the breastbone (sternum).

asthenia loss of strength or stamina; debility. —**asthenic** *adj.*

asthenocoria retarded reaction of the pupil when stimulated by light, caused by a disorder of the adrenal glands.

asthenopia eyestrain; weak sight, caused by fatigue of the muscles that control the eyeball.

asthenospermia loss of movement or impaired motility of sperm cells.

asthma a condition that is marked by severely labored breathing, wheezing, and sensations of chest constriction along with periods of respite and is often thought to be of allergic origin.

astigmatism a defect of vision in which light rays entering the eye are abnormally bent before reaching the retina, thus producing a blurred image.

astatine a radioactive halogen element.

astomia congenital absence of the mouth.

astragalus former term for the ankle bone (talus).

astraphobia fear of lightning and thunder.

astringent 1. causing contraction of soft tissues. 2. an agent that causes contraction of tissues, used to check hemorrhage, arrest secretion, etc.

astrocyte a star-shaped cell of nervous tissues.

astrocytoma a tumor of nerve tissue composed of astrocytes.

asymmetry lack of symmetry; imbalance.

asystole cessation of the heartbeat; cardiac standstill.

atactilia loss of the sense of touch.

ataraxia calmness of mind; total relaxation; imperturbability.

atavism recurrence in an organism of a characteristic typical of its distant ancestors.

ataxia an inability to coordinate voluntary muscular movement.

ataxiophemia impaired coordination of the muscles concerned with speech production.

atelectasis 1. collapse or incomplete expansion of a lung. 2. defective expansion of the pulmonary alveoli at birth.

atelocardia incomplete development of the heart.

atelochilia harelip.

atelochiria incomplete or imperfect development of the hands.

athelia congenital absence of the nipples.

atherogenic of or relating to the production of degenerative changes in arterial walls.

atheroma degeneration of arterial walls resulting from the deposit of fatty esters.

atheromatosis widespread vascular disease characterized by atheroma.

atherosclerosis abnormal thickening of arterial walls resulting from fatty deposits and fibrosis. **—atherosclerotic** *adj.*

athetosis a nervous disorder chiefly of children that is usually the result of brain lesion and is characterized by continuous slow movements of the hands and feet. **—athetotic, athetosic** *adj.*

athlete's foot a fungus infection (ringworm) of the feet, typically of the areas between the toes, characterized by itching, cracking and scaling of the skin and the formation of watery blisters.

atlas the first vertebra of the neck, shaped like a ring and supporting the skull.

atom the smallest particle of an element existing either alone or in combination. **—atomic** *adj.*

atomizer an instrument for dispensing a liquid in a spray of fine droplets.

atony lack or insufficiency of muscular tone.

ATP adenosine triphosphate; an adenosine ester derivative supplying energy for many biochemical cellular processes.

atresia absence or closure of a natural bodily passage.

atrium *pl.* **atria** either of the two upper chambers of the heart. Also called *auricle.* **—atrial** *adj.*

atrophy the wasting away or decrease in size of a body part or tissue; degeneration.

atropine a white, poisonous, crystalline compound derived chiefly from belladonna and used to control spasms and dilate the pupil of the eye.

audiogram a graph tracing the relationship between frequency of vibration and the minimal level at which a person can hear.

audiometer an instrument for measuring keenness of hearing. **—audiometric** *adj.* **—audiometry** *n.*

auditory relating to or experienced through the sense of hearing.

aura a subjective sensation sometimes experienced before the onset of a neurological attack, as of epilepsy.

aural relating to the ear or the sense of hearing.

auricle 1. pinna. 2. atrium.

auricular 1. of or relating to the sense of hearing. 2. of or relating to the auricles (atria) of the heart.

auriscope an instrument for examining the ear; otoscope.

auscultation the diagnostic technique of listening to and analyzing sounds produced by organs within the body.

autism an emotional disorder found chiefly in young children and marked by alternating periods of extreme withdrawal and irrational violence. Also called *infantile autism.* **—autistic** *adj.*

autoclave 1. an electric appliance using superheated steam under pressure to sterilize dental or surgical instruments and other operating room equipment. 2. to subject to the action of an autoclave.

autoerotism *also* **autoeroticism** sexual desire and the seeking for its gratification directed toward oneself.

autogenous 1. originating within an organism. 2. produced independently of external influences or aid. **—autogenic** *adj.* **—autogeny** *n.*

autograft an organ or tissue transplanted from one part to another part of the same body.

autohypnosis hypnosis that is self-induced.

autoimmunity a condition in which the body is abnormally sensitive to some of its own tissues as the result of forming antibodies against them.

autoinfection reinfection resulting from the presence of pathogenic microorganisms already present in the body.

autointoxication poisoning resulting from toxins already within the body.

autolysis the disintegration of cells or tissues by enzymes produced within the body.

automatism repetitive, unconscious motor activity, as that sometimes following an epileptic seizure.

automyosophobia fear of being dirty or of smelling bad.

autonomic 1. acting independently: *autonomic reflexes.* 2. resulting from internal influences or causes.

autonomic nervous system the part of the nervous system that supplies smooth and cardiac muscle and glandular tissue and regulates involuntary actions.

autonomotropic acting on the autonomic nervous system, as a drug.

autophagia 1. the self-consumption of a cell. 2. the biting of one's own flesh.

autophilia love of self; narcissism.

autopsy a post-mortem examination; necropsy.

autoradiograph a photographic image produced by the radiation of a radioactive substance contained in a subject in close contact with the emulsion. —**autoradiography** *n.*

avascular 1. lacking blood vessels. 2. relating to an inadequate blood supply.

avirulent not virulent.

avitaminosis disease resulting from a dietary deficiency of any of various vitamins.

avulsion the tearing away or separation of a bodily structure or part either accidentally or surgically.

axanthopsia inability to see yellow hues or tints.

axenic (of a culture) free from contamination by foreign organisms.

axilla armpit.

axis *pl.* **axes** the second vertebra of the neck, serving as the pivot for turning the head.

axon a long nerve cell process that conducts impulses away from the cell body.

azoospermia inability to produce spermatozoa; absence of live sperm cells in the semen.

azotemia the abnormal accumulation of urea in the blood; uremia.

B

Babinski reflex *or* **Babinski's reflex** a reflex movement of the foot in which when the sole is tickled the great toe turns upward, indicative of organic lesion of the brain or spinal cord.

baccate resembling a berry; berrylike.

bacciform having the shape of a berry.

bacillary 1. rod-shaped. 2. relating to or produced by bacilli.

bacillemia the presence in the blood of rod-shaped bacteria.

bacilli *pl. of* bacillus.

bacillicide any agent capable of killing bacilli.

bacilliform rod-shaped; resembling a bacillus in form.

bacilliparous producing bacilli.

bacillogenic *or* **bacillogenous** 1. of bacillary origin; originating in bacilli. 2. producing bacilli; bacilliparous.

bacillophobia abnormal fear or dread of bacilli.

bacillosis a condition caused by infection with bacilli.

bacilluria the presence of bacilli in the urine.

bacillus *pl.* **bacilli** 1. any of a genus (*Bacillus*) of rod-shaped, aerobic bacteria including saprophytes and some parasites. 2. a disease-producing bacterium.

bacteremia the presence of bacteria in the blood.

bacteria *pl. of* bacterium.

bacterial relating to or caused by bacteria.

bactericholia the presence of bacilli in the bile.

bactericidal destructive of bacteria.

bactericide a drug or agent that destroys bacteria.

bacteriogenous 1. caused by bacteria or of bacterial origin. 2. producing bacteria.

bacteriology a science concerned with bacteria and their importance to medicine, agriculture, and industry.

bacteriolytic destroying or dissolving the cellular structure of bacteria.

bacteriopathology the study of diseases caused by bacteria or their toxic products.

bacteriophage a bacteriolytic virus.

bacteriophobia an abnormal fear of bacteria and other microorganisms.

bacteriosis widespread bacterial infection.

bacteriostasis prevention of the growth and multiplication of bacteria. —**bacteriostatic** *adj.*

bacteriostat any agent that inhibits the growth or multiplication of bacteria.

bacterium *pl.* **bacteria** any of a class of microscopic plantlike organisms lacking chlorophyll that have single-celled bodies, live in water, soil, organic matter, or in the bodies of animals and plants, and are significant as pathogens or for their chemical effects.

BAL British anti-lewisite; dimercaprol.

balanitis inflammation of the glans penis.

balanoplasty plastic surgery involving repair or reconstruction of the glans penis.

balanoposthitis inflammation of the glans penis and foreskin (prepuce).

balanorrhagia a constant discharge from the glans penis.

balanorrhea inflammation of the glans penis accompanied by the discharge or formation of pus.

balanus glans penis.

ball-and-socket joint enarthrosis.

balm 1. a soothing ointment or other application. 2. balsam.

balneology the branch of medical science concerned with balneotherapy.

balneotherapy the therapeutic use of baths, esp. using natural mineral waters, in treating disease or pain.

balsam 1. a fragrant, resinous exudate obtained from various trees. 2. balm.

bandage a strip of cloth or plastic fabric for binding and dressing wounds.

Band-Aid a trademark for a small adhesive bandage with a gauze pad affixed to the center of the adhesive side.

baragnosis inability to sense the weight of a hand-held object.

barbiturate any of various derivatives of barbituric acid used extensively as antispasmodics, sedatives, and hypnotics.

barbituric acid a synthetic crystalline acid that is derived from pyrimidine.

barbiturism chronic poisoning by derivatives of barbituric acid, characterized by fever, chills and headache.

barbula hirci the hairs that grow in the outer part of the external ear in men.

baresthesia the sense of pressure.

baresthesiometer a delicate instrument for measuring the sense of pressure.

barium a silver-white bivalent toxic metallic element.

barium enema a procedure for rendering the rectum and lower part of the large intestine visible on X-ray photographs by first introducing barium sulfate into the rectum under gentle pressure.

barium meal a procedure for rendering the esophagus and upper part of the digestive tract visible on X-ray photographs by first swallowing a quantity of barium sulfate.

barium sulfate a colorless insoluble compound used esp. as an opaque medium in X-ray photography of the alimentary canal.

baroreceptor a nerve ending, as in the arterial walls, responsive to changes in pressure.

bartholinitis inflammation of Bartholin's glands.

Bartholin's gland either of two glands, located one on each side of the vagina, that secrete a mucous lubricating fluid.

basad toward a base.

basal metabolic rate the rate at which an organism at rest releases heat.

base 1. the lowest or underlying part; foundation. 2. a chemical compound capable of reacting with an acid to form a salt.

basement membrane a thin single-layered membrane of connective tissue cells underlying the epithelium of many organs.

basic reacting as an alkali.

basiphobia fear of walking.

basophil *or* **basophile** a white blood cell with basophilic granules.

basophilia 1. an increased number of basophils in the blood. 2. a tendency to stain with basic dyes.

basophilic susceptible to staining with basic dyes.

bathmotropic affecting the excitability of nerves or muscles in response to stimuli.

bathophobia fear of looking down into deep places or a fear of being in a deep place.

bathycardia a condition in which the heart is located abnormally low in the thoracic cavity.

bathyesthesia sensation in muscles and other deep structures.

bathyhyperesthesia abnormal sensitivity of muscles and other deep structures.

bathyhypesthesia impairment or partial loss of sensation in muscles and deeper structures.

battered child syndrome the complex of severe physical harm to a child resulting from the brutality of a parent or other adult guardian.

BCG vaccine Bacillus Calmette-Guérin; a vaccine from living tubercle bacilli used to vaccinate against tuberculosis.

B complex vitamin B complex.

bdelygmia nausea.

bear down to contract the abdominal muscles and diaphragm during childbirth.

bedbug a wingless bloodsucking bug that feeds on human blood and sometimes infests houses.

bedpan a shallow receptacle used for urination or defecation by someone confined to bed.

bedsore an ulcerated lesion of tissue, esp. that overlying bony prominences, resulting from deprivation of nutrition through prolonged pressure.

behavior the conduct and response of an organism to outside stimuli.

behaviorism the psychological study of human behavior exclusive of the study of the mind and consciousness.

belch to raise gas or air from the stomach; eructate.

belladonna 1. a poisonous plant of the nightshade family that yields atropine. Also called *deadly nightshade.* 2. a medical extract, as atropine, of the belladonna plant.

belly 1. the thick central area of a muscle. 2. the abdomen.

belonephobia fear of sharp-pointed objects, such as needles or pins.

Benadryl a trademark for diphenhydramine hydrochloride (an antihistamine).

bends caisson disease; decompression sickness.

benign not malignant or a threat to life; innocent.

Benzadrine a trademark for amphetamine.

beriberi a vitamin deficiency disease affecting the nerves, heart, and digestive system and resulting from a lack of thiamine.

berylliosis poisoning from prolonged exposure to the element beryllium, as by direct contact or inhalation.

beryllium a white metallic bivalent element.

bestiality sexual intercourse between a human being and an animal.

betacism a relatively rare speech defect in which the sound of the letter B is given to other consonants.

beta globulin a globulin of plasma or serum with electrophoretic mobilities between alpha globulin and gamma globulin.

between-brain the diencephalon.

bhang a powdered preparation of cannabis which is smoked or chewed for its intoxicating effects in some Eastern countries.

bi- *prefix* 1. two. 2. twice. 3. double.

bicarbonate an acid salt of carbonic acid.

bicarbonate of soda sodium bicarbonate.

biceps either of two two-headed muscles, situated at the front of the upper arm or at the back of the upper leg.

bicornuate having two horn-shaped processes: *a bicornuate uterus.*

bicuspid 1. ending in or having two points: *bicuspid teeth.* 2. a premolar tooth.

bifid divided into two sections or parts by a median cleft: *a bifid chin.*

biforate having two openings.

bifurcate divided into two branches or parts. —**bifurcation** *n*

bigeminal paired or consisting of two parts.

bilabe delicate forceps for removing calculi, as those lodged in the urethra.

bilateral having or affecting two sides.

bile a greenish or yellowish alkaline viscid fluid secreted by the liver and serving chiefly as an aid to digestion.

bilharziasis *pl.* **bilharziases** schistosomiasis.

biliary relating to bile.

bilious 1. of or relating to bile. 2. suffering from or marked by disordered liver function.

bilirachia the presence of bile in the spinal fluid.

bilirubin a reddish-yellow pigment found in bile, urine, and blood.

bilirubinemia the presence of abnormally large amounts of bilirubin in the blood.

bilirubinuria the presence of bile in the urine.

biliverdin a green pigment found in bile.

bimanual using or requiring both hands.

binary fission the division of a cell into two daughter cells.

binaural relating to or using both ears.

binocular relating to, using, or designed for use by both eyes.

binomial having two names, esp. for both genus and species.

bioassay analysis of the strength of a substance by comparing its effect on a test organism with the effect of a standard preparation.

bioastronautics the branch of science concerned with the effects of space travel on biological processes.

biochemistry chemistry that deals with life processes and compounds. —**biochemical** *adj.*

bioelectricity electrical activity in living organisms or tissues.

biogenesis the development of life from life already in existence. —**biogenetic** *adj.*

biogravics the branch of science concerned with studying the effects on living organisms of weightlessness and excessive gravitational force.

biology the scientific study of living organisms and their life processes. —**biologic, biological** *adj.*

biometry the statistical analysis of biological problems. —**biometric** *adj.*

biophage a parasite.

biophagous (of certain parasites) feeding on living organisms.

biophysics the application of the principles and methods of physics to biological problems. —**biophysical** *adj.*

biopsy the examination of tissues, fluids, or cells removed from the living body.

biosynthesis the production by a living organism of a chemical compound. —**biosynthetic** *adj.*

biotin a member of the vitamin B complex found in all forms of life.

biotoxicology the branch of science concerned with the study of toxins produced by living organisms.

biotoxin a toxin formed and shown to be present in the tissues of a living animal.

biparous having given birth to two young.

birth the emergence of a new individual from the body of its parent; parturition.

birthmark any skin blemish present at birth; nevus.

bisexual 1. having characteristics of both sexes; hermaphroditic. 2. erotically attracted to both sexes.

bisferious (of the pulse) beating twice.

bistoury a long knife-like instrument for draining abscesses, etc.

biventer (of a muscle) having two bellies.

blackhead comedo.

bladder a membranous sac functioning as a receptacle for a liquid, esp. the urinary bladder.

blain a sore or blister on the skin; blotch.

bland non-irritating; mild: *a bland diet.*

blastin a substance that stimulates the growth of cells.

blastogenesis 1. reproduction by budding. 2. embryonic development during cleavage and the formation of the germ layers.

blastoma a tumor composed mainly of undifferentiated or immature cells.

blastomere any of the cells into which the ovum divides after fertilization.

blastomycosis a skin disease caused by a yeast-like fungus.

blastula *pl.* **blastulas** *or* **blastulae** an early stage in the cleavage of a fertilized ovum.

bleeder a hemophiliac.

blennadenitis inflammation of the mucus-secreting glands.

blennemesis the vomiting of mucus.

blennogenic forming mucus.

blennoid resembling mucus; having a viscid consistency.

blennostatic relating to a reduction in mucus secretion.

blennothorax accumulation of mucus in the bronchi.

blennuria the presence of excessive amounts of mucus in the urine.

THE BLADDER AND THE PROSTATE GLAND

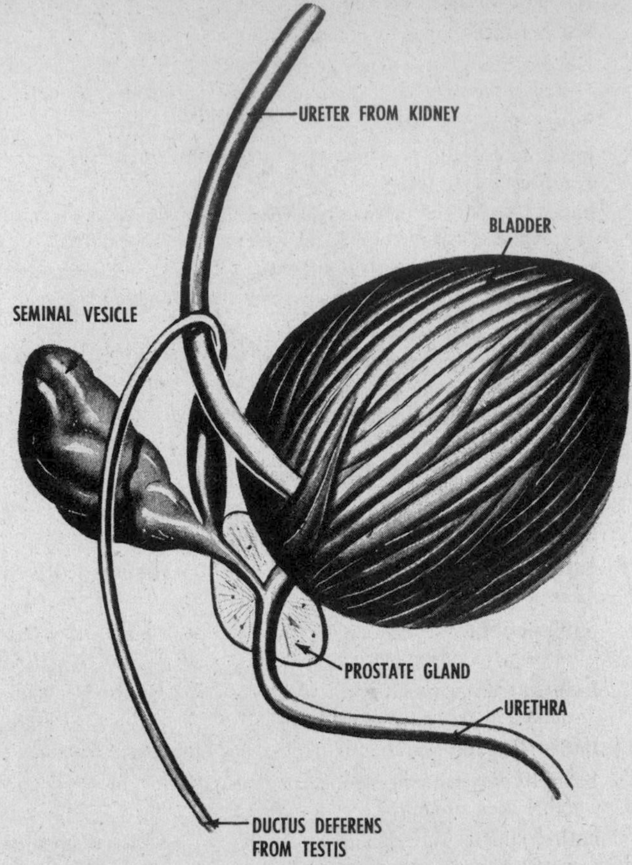

blepharal relating to the eyelids.

blepharectomy surgical removal of part of the eyelid.

blepharedema swelling of the eyelids.

blepharism twitching of the eyelid.

blepharitis inflammation of the eyelid, esp. the margin.

blepharoadenoma a glandlike tumor of the eyelid.

blepharoatheroma a sebaceous cyst of the eyelid.

blindness lack of visual perception; loss of sight.

blind spot a point in the retina of the eye that is insensitive to light.

blister a usually circular elevation of the epidermis containing a watery liquid. —**blistery** *adj.*

blood the fluid circulating in the heart, arteries, veins and capillaries and carrying oxygen and nourishment to all parts of the body and bringing away waste products.

blood bank an establishment for storing blood or plasma.

blood cell a cell present normally in blood; a white blood cell, red blood cell or platelet.

blood count the determination of the number and type of blood cells present in a specific volume of blood.

blood group any of various classes into which human beings are grouped according to the presence or absence in their blood of certain antigens. Also called *blood type.*

blood poisoning septicemia.

blood pressure the pressure exerted by the blood flowing through the blood vessels, esp. the arteries.

blood sugar glucose present in the blood.

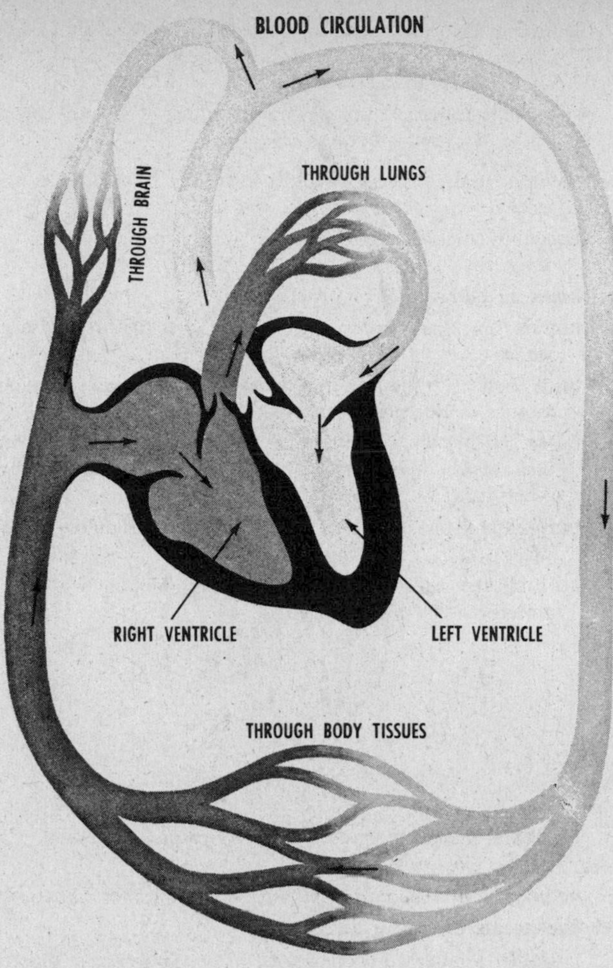

blue baby an infant with a circulatory defect that imparts a bluish tint to the skin.

boil the common name for a furuncle.

bolus a soft, rounded mass of chewed food.

bone one of the hard structures forming the skeleton of a vertebrate. —**bony** *or* **boney** *adj.*

boric acid a white powder used in solution as a mild antiseptic.

boss a rounded swelling.

bosselated characterized by or having several rounded protuberances. —**bosselation** *n.*

botulin a toxin sometimes occurring in imperfectly canned food.

botulism acute food poisoning caused by the presence of botulin.

bougie a tapering surgical instrument for introduction into a bodily passage.

bougienage the use of a bougie in the examination or treatment of a bodily passage or canal.

bouton a knoblike swelling or structure.

bowel the intestine or one of its divisions.

bowleg a leg that bows outward at the knee. —**bowlegged** *adj.*

B.P. blood pressure.

brachialgia intense pain in the arm.

brachiocyllosis the condition of having a crooked arm.

brachiotomy incision into or removal of an arm.

brachium the upper part of the arm. —**brachial** *adj.*

brachycephalic having an abnormally short head or skull. —**brachicephaly** *or* **brachycephalia** *n.*

brachycnemic having abnormally short legs.

brachydactylic having abnormally short fingers.

brachydont having short teeth.

brachygnathia a receding lower jaw. —**brachygnathous** *adj.*

brachypodous having short feet.

bradycardia relatively slow heartbeat.

brain the part of the central nervous system located within the skull and serving as the organ of thought and neural and muscular coordination.

brain stem the part of the brain consisting of the pons, medulla oblongata and midbrain; all of the brain except the cerebrum and cerebellum.

breast either of two protuberant, glandular, milk-secreting organs on the front of the female chest; mammary gland.

bregma the point on the skull where the coronal and sagittal sutures meet.

Bright's disease a kidney disease marked by albumin in the urine; a form of nephritis.

Brill's disease an acute infectious disease similar to but milder than typhus.

broad-spectrum effective against many microorganisms or insects: *broad-spectrum antibiotics; broad-spectrum insecticides.*

Broca's area the speech center in the brain.

bromide a salt of hydrobromic acid, esp. one used as a depressant drug.

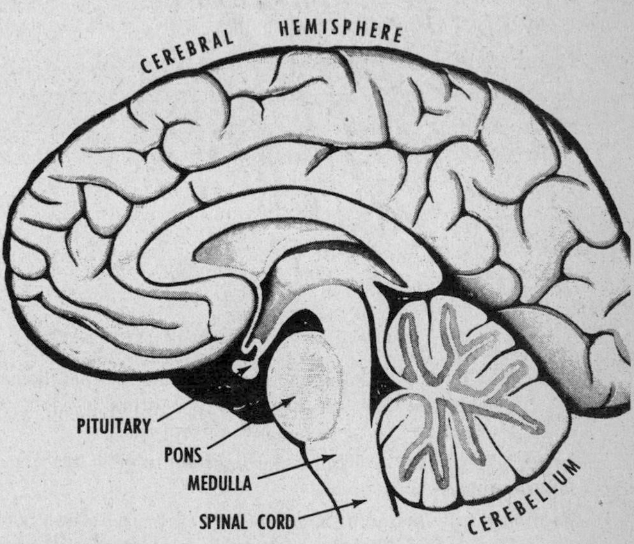

bromine a liquid nonmetallic element obtained from sea water and natural brines, whose compounds are of medical use.

bromism *also* **brominism** poisoning caused by the chronic use of bromides.

bronchi *pl. of* bronchus.

bronchi- *or* **bronchio-** *prefix* bronchial tubes.

bronchiectasis *also* **bronchiectasia** dilation of a bronchus or of the bronchi.

bronchiogenic originating in or coming from the bronchi.

bronchiole *also* **bronchiolus** one of the smallest divisions of the bronchial tree, having no cartilaginous walls and being less than 1 mm in diameter.

bronchiostenosis the abnormal narrowing of a bronchial tube.

bronchitis inflammation of the bronchi.

BRONCHIAL TUBES

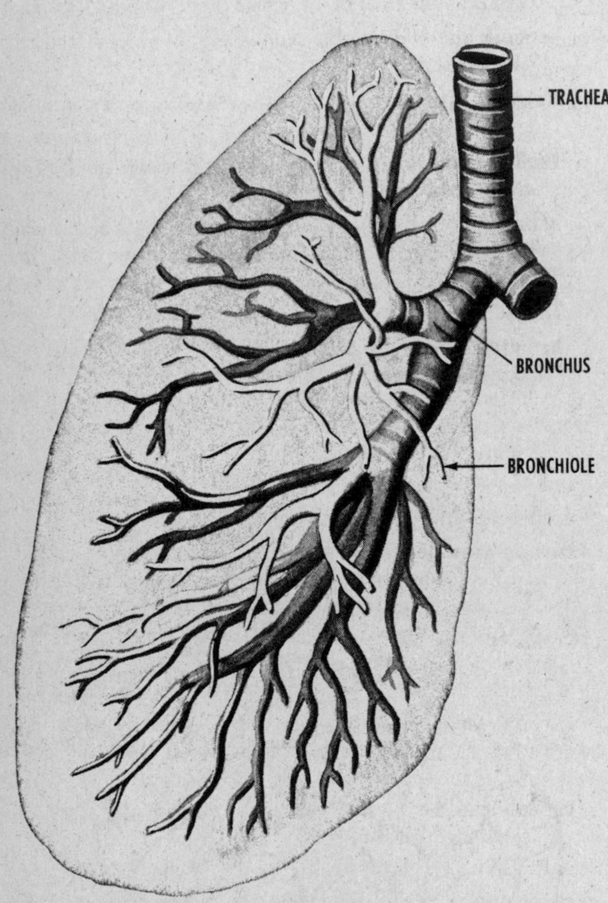

bronchodilator 1. causing an increase in the internal diameter of a bronchial tube or bronchus. 2. a drug or agent that causes dilation of a bronchial tube or bronchus.

bronchoscope an instrument for insertion to view the bronchi. **—bronchoscopy** *n.*

bronchus *pl.* **bronchi** either of two primary tubes of the trachea leading to the right and left lung respectively. **—bronchial** *adj.*

brontophobia an abnormal fear of thunder.

brucellosis undulant fever.

bruise an epidermal injury with discoloration from ruptured blood vessels but without a break in the skin.

bruit any abnormal sound discovered during auscultation, such as a gurgling or splashing sound heard when both fluid and air are present in the pericardium.

bubo *pl.* **buboes** an inflammatory swelling of a lymph gland, esp. in the groin. **—bubonic** *adj.*

bubonic plague plague marked especially by buboes of the groin.

buccal relating to, occurring in, or situated in the cheeks or the oral cavity.

bulla *pl.* **bullae** blister; vesicle.

bunion an inflammation with swelling over the first bursa of the big toe.

burn damage to the skin from exposure to fire, heat, radiation, caustics, or electricity. **—burn** *vb.*

bursa *pl.* **bursas** *or* **bursae** a small sac filled with serous fluid between movable parts, as between a bone and a tendon. **—bursal** *adj.*

bursitis inflammation of a bursa, esp. of the shoulder or the elbow.

buttock the back of the hip forming one of two fleshy protuberances on which one sits.

C

cachexia malnutrition and physical wasting associated with chronic disease.

cadaver a dead body; corpse, esp. one intended for dissection.

caesarean *or* **caesarian** cesarean.

caffeine a bitter compound used as a stimulant and diuretic and found in coffee, tea, and kola nuts.

caffeinism chronic poisoning by caffeine, characterized by irritability, insomnia, and palpitations.

caisson disease a condition marked typically by pain, paralysis, asphyxia, and collapse, caused by too rapid a shift from a high-pressure atmospheric environment to a normal environment, which results in the release of nitrogen bubbles in the bloodstream and tissues. Also called *bends.*

calamine a pink powder used in lotions, ointments, etc., to relieve itching and as an astringent.

calcaneal *or* **calcanean** relating to the heel bone or calcaneus.

calcaneus a tarsal bone forming the major bone of the heel.

calcanodynia pain in the heel on walking or standing.

calcar a spurlike projection.

calcareous containing calcium or calcium carbonate.

calcarine spurlike.

calcariuria the presence of calcium salts in the urine.

calcaroid resembling lime salts.

calcemia the presence of abnormally large amounts of calcium in the blood.

calcicosis a lung disease caused by the inhalation of limestone dust.

calciferol vitamin D_2.

calcification the deposit of insoluble lime salts in tissue.

calciphilia a condition in which the tissues tend to absorb an abnormally large amount of calcium salts, leading to their calcification.

calciprivia lack of dietary calcium.

calciprivic deprived of calcium.

calcitonin a thyroid hormone important in the metabolism of calcium.

calcium a metallic element occurring only in combination, forming about 85 per cent of the mineral matter of bones.

calcium carbonate a compound used in medicine as an antacid.

calcodynia pain in the heel.

calcoid a tumor of the dental pulp.

calculary relating to a calculus or to the formation of calculi.

calculosis the tendency or predisposition to form calculi.

calculus *pl.* **calculi** *or* **calculuses** a concretion of mineral salts in a hollow organ or a duct; stone.

calicectomy surgical removal of a calyx.

caligo dimness of vision.

calipers an instrument with two adjustable legs for measuring the distance, diameter, or thickness between surfaces.

callosal relating to the corpus callosum.

callosity a callus.

callous thickened and hardened esp. from friction and pressure.

callus 1. a thickening of or hard thickened area of the skin; callosity. 2. a mass of tissue forming around a break in a bone and converted to bone during healing.

calor heat, one of the signs of inflammation.

Calorie a unit of heat; the amount of heat required to raise the temperature of one kilogram of water one degree centigrade: used to express heat- or energy-producing value of food oxidized in the body. Also called *kilocalorie.* **—caloric** *adj.*

calorifacient producing or generating heat.

calorimeter a device for the measurement of the amount of heat given off by a body.

calvarium the upper, domelike part of the skull.

calvities baldness; alopecia.

calyx one of the cuplike divisions of the renal pelvis.

canaliculus *pl.* **canaliculi** a small channel or passage.

cancer a malignant tumor of potentially limitless growth. **—cancerous** *adj.*

cancerocidal able to destroy cancer cells; cytotoxic.

cancerophobia an abnormal fear of getting cancer.

cancriform resembling cancer or the manifestations of a malignant growth.

cancroid 1. resembling a crab. 2. resembling a cancer.

candida any of a genus of yeast-like fungi that are the causative agents of thrush.

canine any of four pointed, conical teeth situated between the lateral incisors and first premolars in the upper and lower jaws.

canker a small ulcer of the lips, mouth, or tongue.

cannabis the dried flowering spikes of the hemp plant (*Cannabis sativa*), which yield hashish; marijuana.

cannabism severe hallucinations and other symptoms associated with cannabis poisoning.

cannula a small tube for insertion into a body cavity.

cannulation insertion of a cannula.

canthal relating to a canthus.

cantharides a counterirritant drug prepared from the dried bodies of the blister beetle (*Cantharis vesicatoria*), now no longer in use because of its dangerous irritant effects on the urinary tract; Spanish fly.

canthectomy surgical incision into a canthus to increase the width of the slit between the lids.

canthus *pl.* **canthi** either of the angular junctures of the eye formed by the meeting of the upper and lower eyelids.

capiat an instrument for removing foreign objects from the uterus or other body cavities.

capillarectasia dilation of the capillaries.

capillaritis inflammation of the capillaries.

capillarity the spontaneous rise or depression of liquids placed in very narrow tubes; an effect of surface tension.

capillary *pl.* **capillaries** any of the very small blood vessels forming a network throughout the body and connecting arterioles and venules.

capitate 1. having a round or head-shaped extremity. 2. one of the carpal bones.

capitium a special bandage made to fit the head.

capitopedal relating to both the head and feet.

capnogram a record of the amount of carbon dioxide in exhaled air.

caprizant denoting a bounding pulse beat.

capsule 1. an enveloping membrane around an organ, joint or other structure. 2. a small container made of soluble material, such as gelatin, for enclosing powdered drugs, medicated pellets, etc. 3. any bodily structure or part resembling a capsule.

capsulitis inflammation of an anatomical capsule.

caput *pl.* **capita** 1. the head. 2. any structure or part resembling a head; the rounded end of an organ or part.

carbohydrate any of various compounds of oxygen, hydrogen, and carbon, as sugars and starches, that are the principal energy-producing foods in the diet.

carbolic acid a disinfectant and poison derived from coal tar; phenol.

carbolize to mix with or add carbolic acid.

carboluria the presence of carbolic acid in the urine.

carbon dioxide a colorless, heavy gas, CO_2, that is noncombustible, is absorbed from the air by plants, and is formed in the tissues during respiration and expelled by the lungs.

carbon monoxide a colorless, odorless gas, CO, that is formed by incomplete combustion of carbon and is lethal in sustained amounts.

carbon monoxide poisoning poisoning by inhalation of carbon monoxide, marked by dizziness, headache, convulsions, paralysis, coma, and, eventually, death.

carbonuria the presence of carbon compounds, esp. carbon dioxide, in the urine.

carbophilic requiring carbon dioxide for efficient growth.

carbuncle a painful staphylococcal inflammation of the skin and subcutaneous tissue characterized by necrosis of the deeper tissues and multiple openings for the discharge of pus.

carbunculosis the presence of multiple carbuncles.

carcinectomy the surgical removal of a malignant tumor.

carcinogen an agent or substance producing or conducive to cancer. **—carcinogenesis** *n.* **—carcinogenic** *adj.* **—carcinogenicity** *n.*

carcinoma *pl.* **carcinomas** *or* **carcinomata** a malignant tumor of epithelial tissue. **—carcinomatous** *adj.*

carcinomatosis a condition marked by the spreading of carcinomas from a primary source.

carcinosarcoma a mixed malignant growth exhibiting features of both carcinoma and sarcoma.

carcinostatic 1. arresting the growth of a carcinoma. 2. an agent that arrests or inhibits the growth of a carcinoma.

cardi- *or* **cardio-** *prefix* heart; cardiac.

cardiac 1. of, near, or acting on the heart. 2. relating to the part of the stomach into which the esophagus opens.

cardialgia a burning sensation in the stomach or seeming to come from the region of the heart, usually caused by indigestion; heartburn.

cardiasthenia a condition in which the action of the heart is weak.

cardiataxia severe abnormalities or irregularities in the heart action.

cardiatelia failure of the heart to develop normally.

cardiectasia dilation of the heart.

cardiectopia abnormal location of the heart within the thoracic cavity.

cardioangiology the branch of science concerned with the heart and blood vessels.

cardioaortic relating to both the heart and aorta.

cardioarterial relating to the heart and the arteries.

cardiocele protrusion of the heart through a space in the diaphragm or other opening, such as a wound.

cardiocentesis a surgical procedure involving puncture of the heart.

cardiodynamics the forces, movements and actions of the beating heart.

cardiodynia pain originating in the heart.

cardiogenesis the embryonic formation of the heart.

cardiogenic originated by the heart; of cardiac origin.

cardiogram a tracing made by a cardiograph.

cardiograph an instrument that traces graphically the electrical events and movements taking place within the heart. —**cardiographer** *n.* —**cardiography** *n.*

cardiohepatomegaly abnormal enlargement of both the heart (cardiomegaly) and the liver (hepatomegaly).

cardioinhibitory slowing down or inhibiting the normal action of the heart.

cardiokinetic influencing the heart action.

cardiology the branch of medicine concerned with the heart and its disorders. —**cardiological** *adj.* —**cardiologist** *n.*

cardiomegaly abnormal enlargement of the heart.

cardiomuscular relating to the heart muscle.

cardiomyopathy a chronic disease of heart muscle.

cardiomyotomy surgical incision into the heart muscle.

cardionecrosis necrosis of part of the heart muscle, as in severe myocardial infarction.

cardiopalmus palpitation of the heart.

cardiopathy any disease of the heart.

cardiopericarditis inflammation of both the heart muscle and its surrounding sac (pericardium).

cardiophobia abnormal fear of heart disease.

cardiophone a specially adapted stethoscope for listening to heart sounds, usually consisting of a microphone and amplifier.

cardiospasm painful spasm of the stomach at its upper (cardiac) part or of the esophagus near the point where it joins the stomach, typically causing regurgitation.

cardiothrombus a blood clot within a heart chamber.

cardiotomy 1. surgical incision into the heart muscle. 2. surgical incision into the upper (cardiac) part of the stomach in the area of the esophageal opening.

cardiotoxic exerting a toxic or harmful effect on the action of the heart or its tissues.

cardiovalvulitis inflammation of the heart valves.

cardiovascular relating to or involving the heart and blood vessels.

caries 1. tooth decay (dental caries). 2. bone decay.

cariogenesis the process or mechanism of producing caries.

cariogenic (of certain dietary constituents, esp. sugar) producing tooth decay; causing caries.

carminative a substance, as oil of peppermint, aiding in the expulsion of gas from the alimentary canal.

carotene a yellow or red pigment occurring in some plants that is convertible to vitamin A.

carotenemia the presence in the blood of unusually large quantities of carotene, sometimes resulting in a yellowish-red pigmentation of the skin resembling jaundice; pseudo-jaundice.

carotenoid 1. any one of a group of plant pigments that includes carotene. 2. resembling carotene; yellowish.

carotid either of two great arteries passing up the neck and supplying the head with blood.

carpoptosia dropping of the wrist; wrist drop.

carpus the eight bones between the hand and the forearm; wrist.

carrier an agent who harbors pathogenic microorganisms transmittable to others while remaining personally immune to the disease.

cartilage translucent elastic tissue which, with bone, comprises the basic structure of the skeleton. —**cartilaginous** *adj.*

caruncle a small fleshy protuberance often of abnormal origin.

caseation necrosis in which damaged tissue is converted into a cheesy soft substance.

casein a phosphoprotein derived from milk.

cassette a special holder for photographic or X-ray film.

cast a mass of fibrous matter that takes the shape of the organ in which it is formed and is ejected from the body.

castration removal of the testes or the ovaries. —**castrate** *vb.*

catabolism a destructive phase of metabolism resulting in the breakdown of complex materials within the organism. —**catabolize** *vb.*

catalepsy a condition marked by suspended animation and a tendency for the limbs to remain in whatever position they are placed.

catalyst an agent or substance that speeds up a chemical reaction without itself taking part of it. —**catalysis** *n.*

catamenia menses. —**catamenial** *adj.*

catamnesis the medical history or follow-up of a patient after treatment of an illness.

cataphasia a speech disorder characterized by involuntary repetition of the same word.

cataphoresis electrophoresis.

cataplasm a poultice.

cataplexy a sudden loss of muscular strength following an emotional crisis.

cataract a clouding of the lens of the eye that obstructs the transmission of light.

catarrh inflammation of the mucous membranes and especially those of the nose and respiratory passages. —**catarrhal** *adj.*

catatonia a schizophrenic condition marked chiefly by stupor and immobility with occasional attacks of hyperactivity and excitability. —**catatonic** *adj.*

catgut a tough cord made from sheep intestines and used chiefly for absorbable sutures and ligatures.

catharsis 1. purgation. 2. the psychoanalytic resolution of an emotional conflict through verbal release.

cathartic 1. relating to catharsis. 2. an agent used to purge the bowels; purgative.

catheter a tubular instrument for introduction into a body cavity or passage esp. to permit withdrawal of fluids or maintain an opening.

catheterize to introduce a catheter into.

cat scratch fever *also* **cat scratch disease** a mild disease thought to be typically caused by the scratch of a cat and marked by malaise, fever, and swelling of the lymph glands.

cauda a structure or part resembling a tail or having a tapering extremity. —**caudal** *adj.*

cauda equina a bundle of nerve roots that extend downward from the spinal cord.

caudalis toward the tail; caudal.

caul the inner fetal membrane sometimes covering the head at birth.

caustic a chemical substance, as a strong acid or alkali, that has a corrosive action on other substances.

cauterization the application of a caustic agent to sear or destroy tissue and esp. to stop hemorrhage. —**cauterize** *vb.* —**cautery** *n.*

cavernous relating to or filled with hollow spaces: *cavernous tissue.*

cavitation the development of cavities in bodily tissue or organs esp. as a result of disease.

cavum a hole or hollow; cavity.

cecectomy surgical removal of the cecum of the large intestine.

cecitis inflammation of the cecum.

cecocolostomy the surgical formation of an artificial connection between the cecum and colon.

cecoptosis an abnormal downward displacement of the cecum.

cecotomy surgical incision into the cecum.

cecum the blind pouch forming the first part of the large intestine, to which the vermiform appendix is attached.

celiac *also* **coeliac** related to, situated in, or affecting the abdominal cavity.

celiac disease a chronic disease of young children marked by defective digestion and absorption of gluten and by persistent diarrhea.

celialgia abdominal pain; colic.

celiodynia celialgia; colic.

celiopathy the branch of pathology concerned with the study of abdominal diseases.

celiotomy laparotomy.

celitis peritonitis.

cell a microscopic mass of protoplasm containing a nucleus and other elements and constituting the basic reproducible structural unit of living organisms.

cellulitis a spreading inflammation of cellular or connective tissue, resulting from a failure of the body's immune mechanism to contain an originally localized infection.

celluloneuritis inflammation of nerve cells.

cellulose a polysaccharide that constitutes the chief structural part of the cell walls of plants.

celology the branch of surgery concerned with the study and repair of hernias.

celoscopy examination of any body cavity.

Celsius centigrade; relating to or having a thermometric scale divided into 100 degrees, with 0° representing freezing point and 100° representing boiling point. Abbreviated *C*

centesis surgical puncture of a body cavity, as for the draining off of contained fluid.

centigrade Celsius. Abbreviated *C*

central nervous system the part of the nervous system consisting of the brain and spinal cord and serving to coordinate the entire nervous system of the body.

centrifuge a machine that uses centrifugal force to separate substances, as the cellular components of blood from plasma, having different densities.

centriole either of a pair of cellular organelles near the nucleus and during mitosis forming the poles of the spindle.

centromere the clear cytoplasm containing a centriole.

centrum the center of any structure or part, as the body of a vertebra.

cephalalgia headache.

cephalic relating to or situated on or near the head.

cephalitis inflammation of the brain; encephalitis.

cephalogenesis the embryonic formation of the head.

cephalomegaly abnormal enlargement of the head.

cephalometry the science of measuring the head.

cephalomyitis inflammation of the muscles of the head and scalp.

cercus *pl.* **cerci** any stiff structure resembling a hair.

cerebellitis inflammation of the cerebellum.

cerebellospinal relating to both the cerebellum and spinal cord.

cerebellum one of the major divisions of the brain, situated underneath the rear part of the cerebrum and controlling muscular coordination and (together with the inner ear) bodily equilibrium. —**cerebellar** *adj.*

cerebral of or relating to the cerebrum.

cerebral accident sudden, severe injury within the cerebrum, esp. the rupture of a blood vessel.

cerebral cortex the topmost layer of gray matter that covers the cerebrum.

cerebral palsy a disorder resulting from brain damage before or during birth and marked typically by muscular incoordination and speech difficulties.

cerebration mental activity, conscious or subconscious.

cerebrifugal (of efferent nerve fibers or impulses) proceeding away from the cerebrum.

cerebripetal (of afferent nerve fibers or impulses) proceeding toward the cerebrum.

cerebritis a general, nonpurulent inflammation of the cerebrum or brain.

cerebromeningitis inflammation of both the brain and its covering membranes (meninges).

cerebropontile relating to the brain and pons.

cerebrospinal of or relating to the brain and spinal cord.

cerebrospinal fluid a watery, clear fluid surrounding the spinal cord and brain and filling the lateral ventricles of the brain.

cerebrovascular relating to or affecting the cerebrum and the blood vessels that supply it.

cerebrum the largest division of the brain, overlying the cerebellum and brain stem (medulla oblongata, midbrain and pons).

cerumen a yellowish waxy substance secreted by the glands of the external ear; earwax.

cervical relating to or affecting the neck or a cervix, esp. of the uterus.

cervicitis inflammation of the cervix of the uterus.

cestode any of a subclass of flatworms comprising the tapeworms.

chalk calcium carbonate.

chancre an initial lesion, esp. of the primary stage of syphilis. **—chancrous** *adj.*

chancroid a venereal disease characterized by an initial genital lesion resembling that of the primary stage of syphilis. **—chancroidal** *adj.*

change of life menopause; climacteric.

charas hashish.

cheilitis inflammation of the lips.

chem- *or* **chemo-** *or* **chemi-** *prefix* chemical; chemistry; chemically.

chemopallidectomy chemical destruction of part of a structure in the brain (globus pallidus), once widely used in the treatment of parkinsonism and related diseases.

chemoprophylaxis the prevention of disease by the administration of drugs.

chemoreceptor a sensory nerve-ending that receives chemical stimuli. **—chemoreception** *n.* **—chemoreceptive** *adj.*

chemotherapy the use of chemical agents in controlling or treating disease.

chest thorax.

chiasma a crossing of two tendons, nerves or other structures.

chickenpox an acute, contagious viral disease marked chiefly by low-grade fever and the formation of vesicles and occurring usually in children.

chilblain an inflammatory sore occurring esp. on the hands or feet as the result of exposure to cold.

chilitis *also* **cheilitis** inflammation of the lips.

chilophagia chronic biting of the lips.

chiropodist podiatrist. **—chiropody** *n.*

chiropractic a system of treating disease by manipulation, esp. of the spinal column.

chloramphenicol a broad-spectrum antibiotic.

chloroform a clear, volatile, toxic liquid that has an odor like ether and is used as a solvent and (esp. formerly) as a general anesthetic.

Chloromycetin a trademark for chloramphenicol.

chlorophyll *also* **chlorophyl** the green pigment of plants, preparations of which are used for their ability to soothe and remove odors.

chloropsia a rare visual defect in which everything appears to have a green or yellowish-green hue.

chlortetracycline a broad-spectrum antibiotic.

chloruretic relating to the action or effect of increasing the excretion of chloride in the urine.

cholagogue 1. an agent that causes contraction of the gallbladder, thereby stimulating the flow of bile into the duodenum. 2. relating to an agent that stimulates the flow of bile.

cholalic relating to bile.

cholangiography X-ray examination of the bile ducts. **—cholangiographic** *adj.*

cholangiotomy surgical incision into a bile duct.

cholangitis inflammation of a bile duct.

cholecyst a rare name for the gallbladder.

cholecystectomy surgical removal of the gallbladder.

cholecystitis inflammation of the gallbladder.

cholecystostomy surgical formation of an artificial opening into the gallbladder.

cholecystotomy surgical incision into the gallbladder.

cholelithiasis the presence or production of gallstones.

cholemesia the vomiting of bile.

cholemia the abnormal presence of bile salts in the bloodstream.

choleperitonitis inflammation of the peritoneum caused by the presence of bile in the abdominal cavity.

cholera an acute, infectious bacterial disease usually caused by drinking contaminated water and marked by vomiting and severe gastrointestinal disturbance.

choleriform resembling cholera; choleroid.

cholerrhagia the excessive flow of bile into the small intestine.

cholestasia *also* **cholestasis** cessation of the flow of bile.

cholesterol a steroid alcohol found in animal cells and body fluids and implicated as a contributing factor in arteriosclerosis and atherosclerosis.

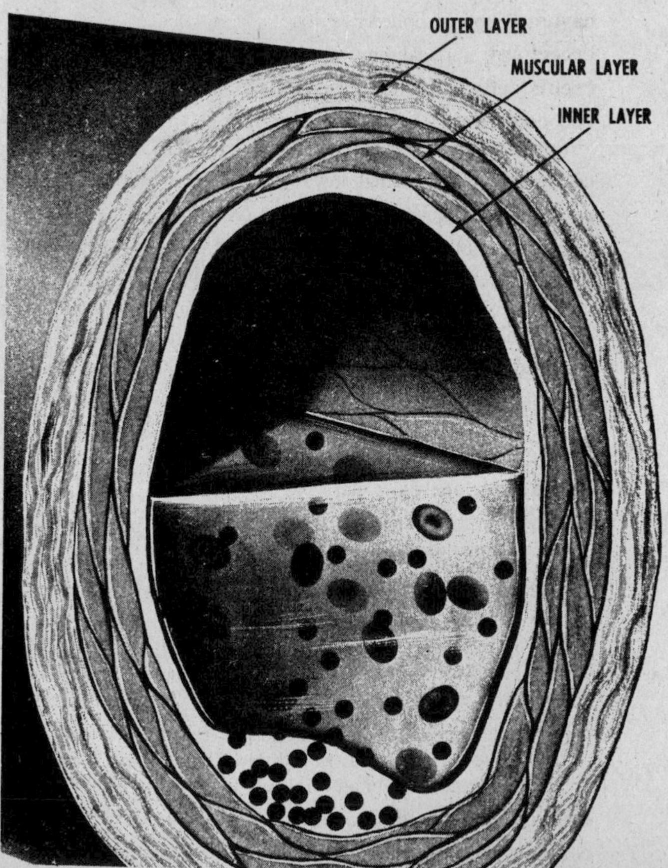

BLOOD CHOLESTEROL

This is a cross section of a blood vessel showing the cholesterol (fat) particles invading the inner wall. A hard yellowish plaque forms which may eventually impede the blood flow.

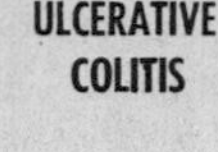

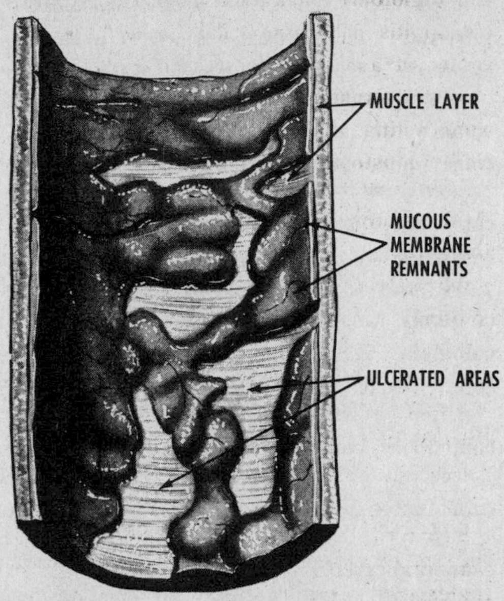

Colitis is an inflammation of the mucous membrane and walls of the large intestine, in the pathologic picture of which ulceration predominates. Ulceration generally begins in the rectum and spreads upward, eventually involving the entire colon. The symptoms are fever, malaise, prostration, persistent diarrhea, and the passage of blood, mucus, and pus.

cholesterolemia the presence in the bloodstream of unusually large amounts of cholesterol.

cholic relating to the bile.

choline an organic base that is a B-complex vitamin vital to liver function.

cholinergic relating to nerve endings that release acetylcholine.

choloplania the abnormal presence of bile salts in the tissues or bloodstream.

cholopoiesis the formation of bile.

cholorrhea excessive secretion of bile into the small intestine.

chondr- *or* **chondri-** *or* **chondro-** *prefix* cartilage.

chondral relating to cartilage.

chondrectomy surgical removal of a piece of cartilage.

chondritis inflammation of cartilage.

chondrodynia pain in cartilage.

chondrogenesis the formation of cartilage.

chondromalacia the abnormal softening of cartilage.

chondrosarcoma a malignant tumor derived from cartilage cells, usually near the extremities of long bones.

chondrotome a strong knife used to cut cartilage.

chondrotomy surgical separation or division of a cartilage.

chondrotrophic influencing the growth and development of cartilage.

chorda a tendon or tendinous structure or part.

chordee painful erection of the penis, often with a downward curvature, usually occurring as a symptom of gonorrhea.

chorditis inflammation of a cord, esp. a vocal cord.

chorea a disease marked by spastic movements of the muscles of the limbs and face and progressive mental deterioration.

chorioangioma a benign tumor of blood vessels, esp. those of the placenta.

chorion the outer embryonic membrane, part of which contributes to the placenta. —**chorionic** *adj.*

chorionitis inflammation of the outermost of the fetal membranes (chorion).

chorioretinitis inflammation of the choroid and retina of the eye.

choroid a vascular membrane between the retina and the sclerotic coat of the eye that contains pigment cells.

chromatid either of the paired complex strands of a chromosome.

chromaturia any abnormal discoloration of the urine.

chromesthesia 1. the stimulation of taste, smell, etc., by the perception of color. 2. color sense.

chromophobe *also* **chromophobic** (of certain tissues or cells) resistant to stain or incapable of receiving stains.

chromophobia an abnormal aversion to colors.

chromopsia incomplete or partial color blindness.

chromoscopy the procedure of testing for color perception.

chromosome one of the rod-shaped bodies of a cell nucleus containing the genes (each human cell has 46 chromosomes). —**chromosomal** *adj.* —**chromosomic** *adj.*

chromotrichial relating to colored hair.

chronognosis time sense; the ability to appreciate the passage of time.

chronotaraxis the inability to appreciate the passage of time; impaired time sense.

chyle a milky fluid found in lymph vessels and formed in the small intestine during the digestion of fats.

chyme a virtually liquid mass of partially digested food and secretions that is formed in the stomach and passes to the small intestine during the process of digestion.

cicatricial of or relating to a cicatrix.

cicatrix a scar remaining from a healed wound.

cilium *pl.* **cilia** a minute protoplasmic thread projecting from the surface of a cell and capable of lashing movements. —**ciliary** *adj.*

cimex *pl.* **cimices** a bedbug.

cinchona the dried bark of a tree (cinchona tree) from which quinine can be obtained, formerly used in the treatment of malaria; Peruvian bark.

cinchonism poisoning by cinchona, quinidine or quinine, characterized by headache, ringing in the ears or loss of hearing, and sometimes a severe allergic reaction.

circadian involving or based on 24-hour periods or intervals.

circinate (of certain structures or parts) shaped like a ring; circular.

circulation the movement of blood through the vessels resulting from the pumping action of the heart.

circulus a circular or ringlike structure or part.

circumcision the surgical removal of all or part of the foreskin. —**circumcise** *vb.*

cirrhosis disease of the liver marked by fibrosis and hardening.

cirsectomy surgical removal of a varicose vein.

cirsodesis the tying off or ligation of varicose veins.

cirsoid varicose.

cirsotome a surgical instrument for removing varicose veins.

clamp a device designed to constrict a vessel or to provide a secure hold on a structure.

clap (colloquial) gonorrhea.

claudication the condition of being lame; limping.

claustrophobia an abnormal fear of being in narrow or enclosed spaces.

clavicle a bone of the shoulder; collarbone.

cleft palate fissure of the roof of the mouth occurring congenitally.

climacteric 1. menopause. 2. a period in the male corresponding to the menopause in the female and marked by reduced sexual interest and activity.

climatotherapy treatment of a disease or disorder by moving to a different climate, as to a warm and dry climate in treating bronchitis.

clinic 1. medical instruction based on the examination and discussion of patients. 2. a medical facility supplementary to a hospital and specializing in the treatment of outpatients. 3. a group practice of several physicians working cooperatively. —**clinical** *adj.*

clinician a physician, psychiatrist, or psychologist specializing in clinical practice rather than in laboratory or research work.

clitoris a small organ homologous to the penis and located at the upper part of the vulva.

clitorism a rare, painful condition in which the clitoris remains erect for prolonged periods.

clonus a sequence of muscular spasms in which rigidity is followed by relaxation. —**clonic** *adj.*

club foot talipes; a deformed foot twisted out of normal position: a congenital defect.

coagulate to cause to become or to become thickened into a coherent mass; clot; curdle. —**coagulation** *n.*

coarctotomy surgical division of a stricture.

cobalt a hard, gray metallic element related to nickel and iron.

cocaine an alkaloid from coca leaves that is used as a local anesthetic and can become addictive.

coccus *pl.* **cocci** a spherical bacterium.

coccygectomy surgical removal of the coccyx.

coccygodynia pain in the coccyx.

coccyx the terminal bone of the spinal column formed by the fusion of four rudimentary vertebrae.

cochlea the spiral cavity of the internal ear that is the seat of the hearing organ. —**cochlear** *adj.*

coconsciousness two streams of consciousness existing simultaneously.

codeine a morphine derivative that is found in opium and is used as an analgesic and in cough suppressant remedies.

coition sexual intercourse.

coitus sexual intercourse.

colectasia distention of the colon.

colectomy surgical removal of a section of the colon or (rarely) its complete removal.

coleocele a vaginal hernia.

colic severe abdominal pains resulting from spasms of a hollow organ and chiefly affecting infants. —**colicky** *adj.*

colitis inflammation of the colon.

collagen an insoluble fibrous protein forming the major part of intercellular connective tissue.

collapse a state of acute prostration and physical depression.

collarbone clavicle.

colliculus any small anatomical elevation.

colloid a mucinous or gelatinous substance found in the thyroid and in certain other tissues. —**colloidal** *adj.*

collyrium a fluid for cleansing the eyes; eyewash.

colon the part of the large intestine between the cecum and the rectum. —**colonic** *adj.*

coloproctitis inflammation of both the colon and rectum.

color blindness inability to perceive or distinguish one or more colors. —**color-blind** *adj.*

colostomy surgical formation of an artificial anus.

colostrum milk, rich in protein and antibodies, secreted from the breasts directly after parturition.

colotomy surgical incision into the colon.

colpalgia vaginal pain.

coma a state of profound unconsciousness, as from injury, poison, or disease. —**comatose** *adj.*

comedo *pl.* **comedones** a small plug of sebum blocking a sebaceous gland esp. on the face, chest, or back; blackhead.

comminuted (of a fractured bone) broken into several small fragments.

commotio cerebri brain concussion.

compensation correction of an organic defect or loss by inceased functioning of another organ or part.

complement the substance in normal blood serum and plasma that combines with antibodies to combat bacteria and other antigens.

complex a group of repressed desires and memories that exert a powerful influence on a personality.

complication a secondary disorder or disease developing in consequence of a primary disease or injury.

compos mentis of sound mind, understanding, and memory.

compound a substance formed by the chemical union of two or more elements in strict proportion by weight.

compound fracture open fracture.

compress a folded pad or cloth, as of gauze, for applying local pressure to a bodily part.

conceive to become pregnant.

conception the act of becoming pregnant; the impregnation of an ovum.

concha *pl.* **conchae** 1. the largest and deepest cavity of the outer ear. 2. one of three thin bones in the nasal cavity.

concretion a hardened mass; calculus.

concussion a jarring injury to the brain that temporarily or permanently impairs its normal functioning.

condom a thin rubber sheath worn over the penis to prevent conception or venereal disease during sexual intercourse.

condyle a rounded prominence at the end of a bone.

condyloma a warty growth in the area of the anus and genitals.

confabulation the invention of events esp. to compensate for episodes of memory loss, as in chronic alcoholism.

confinement the state of preparing for childbirth; lying-in.

congenital existing at the time of birth: *congenital deformity.*

congestion an abnormal accumulation of blood in a bodily part.

conjunctiva *pl.* **conjunctivas** *or* **conjunctivae** the mucous membrane lining the inside of the eyelid and the forepart of the eyeball.

conjunctivitis inflammation of the conjunctiva.

connective tissue tissue that supports and binds together other tissues and forms ligaments and tendons.

consolidation an alteration in lung tissue in pneumonia in which air spaces become filled with exudate.

constipation abnormally delayed or difficult passage of feces.

consumption tuberculosis. —**consumptive** *adj.*

contact a person who has been exposed to or transmits an infectious disease.

contact lens a thin lens fitted over the cornea of the eye.

contagion the transmission of a disease by contact.

contagious communicable by direct or indirect contact; catching: *contagious disease.*

contraception the voluntary prevention of impregnation or conception.

contraceptive 1. relating to or used for contraception. 2. a contraceptive device or agent.

contraindication a caution against the advisability of using a particular medication or medical treatment. —**contraindicate** *vb.* —**contraindicative** *adj.*

contusion bruise. —**contuse** *vb.*

convalesce to regain one's health at a gradual pace. —**convalescence** *n.*

convolution any of the irregular ridges on the surface of the brain; gyrus.

convulsion an abnormal, violent muscular contraction or series of contractions. —**convulse** *vb.* —**convulsive** *adj.*

coprolalia a rare condition in which obscene or vulgar words are uttered involuntarily.

copulation sexual intercourse.

cordate heart-shaped.

cordectomy surgical removal of a cord.

corn a localized hardening and thickening of the skin, as on a toe, from pressure or friction.

cornea the transparent part of the eyeball coat that covers the pupil and iris and admits light.

coronary vessel any of the arteries and veins that carry the blood supply of the heart muscle.

corpulence *also* **corpulency** the state of being extremely fat. —**corpulent** *adj.*

corpuscle a cell, esp. a red or white blood cell.

cortex the outer layer of an organ or bodily structure. —**cortical** *adj.*

corticipetal (of nerve fibers) conveying nerve impulses toward the cerebral cortex.

corticothalamic relating to nerve fibers that connect the cerebral cortex with specific areas of the thalamus.

coryza an upper respiratory infection, esp. the common cold.

costal of or relating to the ribs.

costive affected with or causing constipation; constipated. —**costiveness** *n.*

costotome a surgical instrument for cutting through a rib.

costotomy surgical division of a rib.

cotyledon a nodule of the placenta.

counterdepressant 1. relating to the action of any drug or agent that prevents or inhibits the potential depressant action of another drug. 2. a drug or agent with this effect.

counterirritant an agent producing localized, superficial inflammation in order to reduce inflammation in adjacent, deeper structures or tissues. —**counterirritation** *n.*

courses menses.

couvercle a blood clot that forms outside of a vessel.

Cowper's gland either of two small glands that discharge into the male urethra.

coxalgia pain or inflammation involving the hip joint.

coxotomy surgical incision into the hip joint.

Coxsackie virus any of various viruses associated with human diseases.

c.p. *abbr.* chemically pure.

c.p.s. *abbr.* cycles per second; counts per second.

crab louse a louse that infests the pubic region of humans.

crabs infestation with crab lice.

cramp 1. a painful, spasmodic contraction of a muscle. 2. usually **cramps,** sharp abdominal pain.

crani- *or* **cranio-** *prefix* skull; cranial.

cranial of or relating to the skull.

cranial index the ratio of the maximum breadth of the skull to its maximum height, multiplied by 100.

cranialis toward the head; cranial; superior (in humans); anterior (in quadrupeds).

cranial nerve any of the twelve pairs of nerves arising from the brain to the periphery of the body.

craniectomy surgical removal of a piece of the skull, as in preparation for a brain operation.

craniology a science dealing with the variations in size and shape of the skulls of different races.

craniomalacia abnormal softening of the bones of the skull.

craniomeningocele the protrusion of the covering membranes of the brain (meninges) through a defect in the bones of the skull.

craniometry a science dealing with the measurement of skulls.

craniopathy any disease or disorder of the skull.

cranioplasty surgical repair of a skull defect or deformity.

craniopuncture surgical puncture of the skull.

craniosclerosis an abnormal thickening of the bones of the skull.

cranium the skull, esp. the part enclosing the brain.

crapulent *also* **crapulous** drunk; intoxicated with alcohol.

crater the depressed central portion of something, such as the recessed portion of an ulcer.

crateriform having a depressed center; hollowed.

c.r.d. *abbr.* chronic respiratory disease.

creatine a nitrogenous, energy-storing substance found in muscles.

crena a cleft or notch.

crena ani the cleft between the buttocks.

crenate *also* **crenated** indented or notched.

crepitant (of a sound heard from the lungs in pneumonia or certain other pulmonary diseases) crackling.

crepitation *also* **crepitus** 1. the fine grating sound heard when two ends of a broken bone rub together. 2. the crackling chest sound heard in pneumonia and other lung infections.

crest a bony ridge or prominence.

cretinism a congenital, abnormal condition caused by thyroid deficiency and marked by mental retardation and small stature. —**cretin** *n.* —**cretinous** *adj.*

cribriform pierced with small holes.

crisis the turning point in a disease or fever after which the patient either improves or declines rapidly.

croup inflammation of the larynx, esp. in infants, marked by periods of difficult breathing and hoarse cough. **—croupous** *adj.* **—croupy** *adj.*

crural relating to the thigh; femoral.

cry- *or* **cryo-** *prefix* cold; freezing.

cryalgesia pain caused by exposure to cold.

cryanesthesia the inability to sense or perceive cold.

cryesthesia the sensation of cold or the state of being especially sensitive to low temperatures.

cryohypophysectomy the surgical destruction of all or part of the pituitary gland (hypophysis cerebri) by cold.

cryotherapy the therapeutic use of cold, as that produced by liquid nitrogen.

crystalluria the presence of crystals in the urine.

cuneiform wedge-shaped: *cuneiform bone.*

cunnilingus *or* **cunnilinctus** oral stimulation of the vulva and clitoris. **—cunnilingual** *adj.*

cupula a cuplike or dome-shaped structure or part.

curare an extract of a vine used by South American Indians as an arrow poison and in medicine (in very small amounts) as a muscle relaxant.

curettage surgical cleaning or scraping using a curette.

curette *or* **curet** a surgical loop or scoop used in performing curettage. **—curette** *or* **curet** *vb.*

curie a unit of radioactive quantity.

cutaneous relating to or affecting the skin.

cuticle 1. the horny outer layer of the skin, esp. at the margins of the nail beds. 2. epidermis.

cyanocobalamin vitamin B_{12}.

cyanosis a bluish discoloration of the skin resulting from inadequate oxygenation of the blood.

cyclamate an artificially prepared sodium or calcium salt used as a sweetener.

cyst a fluid-filled, membranous sac developing abnormally in a bodily cavity or structure.

cystic fibrosis a hereditary disease of infants, children, and young adults that is attributable to dysfunction of the exocrine glands and is marked by pancreatic deficiency, respiratory problems, and loss of salt in the sweat.

cystine an amino acid that is a metabolic source of sulfur.

cystitis inflammation of the urinary bladder.

cystolith a calculus in the urinary bladder.

cystoscope an instrument for visual examination of the bladder and the introduction of exploratory instruments.

cyt- *or* **cyto-** *prefix* 1. cell: *cytology.* 2. cytoplasm.

cytochrome any of several iron-containing proteins that play an important role in cell oxidations.

cytogenetics the branch of biology dealing with the study of heredity (genetics) in relation to that of cells (cytology).

cytology the biological study of the structure, function, and life history of cells.

cytolysis the disintegration of cells.

cytoplasm the protoplasm of a cell excluding the nucleus.

cytotoxin a substance having a toxic effect on cells. **—cytotoxic** *adj.* **—cytotoxicity** *n.*

cytotropic attracted to cells.

D

dacryocystitis inflammation of the tear sac.

dacryocystotome a small knife for making incisions in the tear sac.

dacryolith a calculus in the tear duct.

dacryops the chronic presence of an accumulation of tears in the eye.

dacryopyorrhea the discharge of pus from the tear duct.

dacryopyosis the formation of pus in the tear sac or duct.

dacryorrhea the excessive flow of tears.

dactyl a finger or toe.

dactylalgia pain in a finger or toe.

dactyledema edema of the finger.

dactylology the science or practice of using the finger alphabet in communicating.

dactylomegaly abnormal enlargement of one or more fingers.

daltonism color blindness, esp. involving the color red.

dandruff small whitish flakes of desquamated cells forming chiefly on the scalp; scurf.

Darwinism a theory of the origin and evolution of new species of animals and plants stressing that natural selection favors the survival of some offspring over others; biological evolution.

DDT *abbr.* dichlorodiphenyltrichloroethane: a very powerful insecticide which can be poisonous if ingested with DDT-sprayed food that has not been properly washed.

deaf-mute a person who can neither hear nor speak.

deallergize desensitize.

deaminate to remove the amino group from (a compound). **—deamination** *n.*

deaquation dehydration.

debilitate to impair the strength of; enfeeble. **—debilitation** *n.*

debility loss of strength; feebleness; weakness.

debridement the surgical removal and cleansing of damaged or contaminated tissue.

decaffeinate to remove the caffeine from.

decalcify to remove calcium or calcium compounds from. **—decalcification** *n.*

decalvant making bald; removing the hair.

decapitate to sever the head of; behead. **—decapitation** *n.* **—decapitator** *n.*

decerebrate 1. having the cerebrum removed or rendered inactive. 2. to remove the cerebrum of or make incapable of cerebral activity.

decerebrize to remove the brain of.

dechloridation removal of salt (sodium chloride) from the body fluids and tissues by restricting the dietary intake of salt.

decidua *pl.* **deciduae** the mucous membrane lining the uterus that thickens and becomes modified in preparation for pregnancy and is cast off during parturition and menstruation. **—decidual** *adj.*

deciduitis inflammation of the decidua.

deciduoma a tumor of the uterus believed to arise from decidual tissue left behind following a miscarriage or abortion.

deciduous falling off or out at a certain stage in the life cycle: *deciduous teeth.*

deciliter one tenth of a liter.

decimeter one tenth of a meter.

decinormal (denoting the strength of a solution) one tenth that of normal or standard values.

decipara a woman who has given birth to ten children.

declinator a surgical instrument for retracting certain parts out of the immediate operative field.

decompensation failure of compensation, esp. inability of the heart to maintain adequate circulation.

decompose to undergo breakdown by hydrolytic enzymes; rot; putrify. —**decomposability** *n.* —**decomposable** *adj.* —**decomposition** *n.*

decompression the relieving of pressure or compression, esp. surgery to release internal bodily pressure. —**decompression** *n.*

decongestant a drug or agent that relieves congested blood vessels, esp. those of the mucous membrane of the nose.

decorticate to remove the outer covering or cortex from (an organ). —**decortication** *n.* —**decorticator** *n.*

decrudescence the lessening or easing of the symptoms of a disease or illness.

decubitus ulcer an ulcer formed by constant pressure on the skin over a bony prominence while lying in bed; bedsore; pressure sore.

decussate to intersect; cross, as nerve fibers. —**decussation** *n.*

defecation the discharge of feces from the bowels. —**defecate** *vb.*

defemination the loss of secondary sexual characteristics or femininity, esp. as the result of a hormonal disorder.

deferens a duct that conveys spermatozoa from each testicle; vas deferens; ductus deferens.

deferent downward; away from; carrying away.

deferentectomy vasectomy.

deferential relating to the vas deferens or ductus deferens.

deferentitis inflammation of the vas deferens.

defervescence the falling or lessening of a fever or the period during which this occurs.

defibrillate to restore the normal rhythm of (a fibrillating heart) with electrical shocks. —**defibrillation** *n.* —**defibrillator** *n.* —**defibrillatory** *adj.*

deficiency disease a disease, as rickets, beriberi, scurvy, resulting from a dietary deficiency, as of an essential vitamin or mineral.

deflorescence the disappearance of a skin eruption or the period during which a skin rash begins to abate.

defluxio sudden loss of hair.

deganglionate to deprive of ganglia.

degeneration progressive deterioration in the structure or function of organs or tissues. —**degenerate** *vb.*

deglutition the act or process of swallowing.

degustation the sense of taste; tasting.

dehiscence the bursting open of the edges of a wound, esp. after they have been sutured or sewn together.

dehydration loss of water; an abnormal depletion of body fluids. —**dehydrate** *vb.* —**dehydrator** *n.*

déjà vu the illusion of remembering events and scenes actually being experienced for the first time; paramnesia.

deleterious harmful; injurious.

deliquesce (of certain salts) to become liquid or damp as the result of atmospheric water absorption. —**deliquescence** *n.*

delirifacient 1. causing delirium. 2. a toxic agent capable of causing delirium.

delirium a mental condition characterized by hallucinations, disordered speech, and extreme confusion.

delirium tremens a violent psychotic delirium with tremors and hallucinations that is induced by prolonged and excessive use of alcohol. Also called *D.T.'s.*

delivery parturition; childbirth.

delomorphous of definite shape and form.

deltoid a large triangular muscle covering the shoulder joint and serving to raise and lower the arm laterally.

delusion a false conviction about the self, other persons, or the environment that persists despite the demonstrable facts. —**delusional** *adj.*

dementia a condition of impaired or deteriorated mentality; insanity; madness.

dementia praecox an obsolete term for schizophrenia.

demilune a small body shaped like a crescent or half-moon, such as certain cells.

demineralization a loss or progressive diminution of mineral constituents, esp. of calcium from bone.

demorphinization 1. the process or technique of removing morphine from an opiate drug. 2. a method of curing morphine addiction by the gradual withdrawal of the drug.

demulcent a substance capable of soothing or protecting an irritated mucous membrane.

demyelination loss or destruction of the fatty insulating sheath (myelin) that surrounds most nerve fibers.

denarcotize to deprive an opitate drug of its narcotic properties; to remove narcotic properties from.

denature 1. to alter the structure of a protein molecule by physical or chemical action. 2. to make (alcohol) unfit for drinking without otherwise impairing its usefulness. —**denaturation** *n.*

dendriform branching out; tree-shaped.

dendrite any of the branching processes of a nerve cell that conveys impulses toward the cell body. —**dendritic** *adj.*

dendroid branching; like a tree.

dendron dendrite.

denematize deworm; free from infestation with nematodes.

denervate to deprive of a nerve supply. —**denervation** *n.*

dengue an acute viral disease chiefly of the tropics characterized by fever, headache, joint pains, and rash.

denitrify to remove nitrogen from. —**denitrification** *n.*

dens 1. a tooth. 2. a toothlike structure or part.

densimeter an instrument for measuring the density of a liquid.

dental of, relating to, affecting, or used for the teeth.

dentalgia toothache.

dentate notched; having teeth or cogs.

dentes teeth.

denticle 1. a small toothlike projection from a surface. 2. a small tooth.

denticulate notched; having fine teeth; serrated.

dentiform shaped like a tooth.

dentifrice any preparation used to clean the teeth, including toothpaste, tooth powder and special washes.

dentigerous having or containing teeth.

dentilabial relating to both the teeth and lips.

dentilingual relating to both the teeth and tongue.

dentinalgia pain or tenderness of the dentine.

dentine *or* **dentin** the calcareous substance that forms the body of a tooth.

dentiparous bearing teeth.

dentition 1. the development and cutting of teeth. 2. the form and arrangement of the teeth in the mouth.

dentoalveolar relating to the bony sockets surrounding the teeth.

dentulous containing teeth.

denture a partial or complete set of false teeth.

denucleated deprived of a nucleus.

deodorant a preparation that ameliorates or disguises unpleasant odors.

deodorize to eliminate or mask the unpleasant odor of.

deossification the removal of minerals from bone.

deoxidize to remove the oxygen from. —**deoxidation** *n.*

deoxyribonucleic acid a nucleic acid localized chiefly in cell nuclei that is the hereditary material of many organisms; DNA.

depigmentation partial or total loss of pigment or color.

depilate to remove hair. —**depilation** *n.*

depilatory 1. an agent for removing body hair. 2. able to remove hair.

deplumation loss or falling out of the eyelashes as the result of disease.

deprecusis loss of the ability to hear external sounds while eating, as the result of otosclerosis.

depressant an agent that reduces functional bodily activity esp. by inducing muscular relaxation.

depressed marked by or suffering from depression.

depression a condition marked by pessimism, inactivity, dejection, lack of concentration, and often insomnia.

depressomotor 1. inhibiting motor activity. 2. an agent that inhibits or slows motor activity.

depuration purification; removal of waste products.

deradenitis inflammation of the lymph nodes in the neck; cervical adenitis.

derma dermis.

dermatalgia pain restricted to the skin.

dermatitis any of various forms of inflammation of the skin.

dermatochalasis loose skin.

dermatoconiosis inflammation of the skin caused by the irritant effects of dust, usually affecting those who work in certain environments where an unusual amount of dust is generated.

dermatodynia pain restricted to the skin; dermatalgia.

dermatoid resembling skin.

dermatology a branch of medicine dealing with the structure, functions, and diseases of the skin. —**dermatologic, dermatological** *adj.* —**dermatologist** *n.*

dermatolysis a congenital defect in which the skin is abnormally loose.

dermatoma an overgrowth or thickening of the skin in a circumscribed area.

dermatome an instrument for removing very thin sections of skin, as in skin grafting.

dermatomegaly a congenital defect in which the skin hangs in heavy folds.

dermatoneurosis any skin eruption caused by emotional stimuli.

dermatopathology the microscopic study of skin lesions.

dermatopathy any disease or disorder of the skin.

dermatophobia an abnormal fear of skin diseases.

dermatophyte a fungus that is parasitic on the skin, hair, or nails. —**dermatophytic** *adj.*

dermatoplasty surgical repair of skin defects; skin grafting.

dermatosis any disease of the skin.

dermatozoon any skin parasite of the animal kingdom.

dermatozoonosis any skin eruption caused by an animal parasite.

dermatrophia *also* **dermatrophy** an abnormal wasting away or thinning of the skin.

dermis the inner mesodermic layer of the skin.

dermitis dermatitis; inflammation of the skin.

dermoid *or* **dermoidal** resembling or made up of skin.

dermoidectomy the surgical removal of a cyst on the skin.

dermology dermatology.

dermotropic attracted to or entering through the skin.

desensitize to render (a hypersensitive individual) insensitive to an aggravating agent. —**densensitization** *n.*

desiccant an agent that absorbs or dries, such as one placed in a bottle of tablets to prevent them from deteriorating in environmental moisture.

desiccate to dry up. —**desiccation** *n.* —**desiccative** *adj.*

desmitis inflammation of a ligament.

desmoenzymes enzymes that exist within cells; intracellular enzymes.

desmology the branch of anatomy concerned with the ligaments.

desmopathy any disease or disorder of the ligaments.

desmotomy the surgical separation of a ligament.

desquamate to peel off in scales. —**desquamation** *n.*

detoxicate detoxify.

detoxify to remove a poison or toxin or the effects of a poison or toxin from. —**detoxification** *n.*

deuteranopia color blindness limited to the inability to perceive green hues.

deviated septum a congenital or acquired (as by injury) deflection of the cartilaginous separation between the nostrils.

dexter relating to or located on the right.

dextroamphetamine amphetamine.

dextrose a glucose used esp. as an intravenously supplied nutrient replenisher.

diabetes any of various diseases marked esp. by excessive excretion of urine; (commonly) short for diabetes mellitus.

diabetes insipidus a metabolic disorder of the pituitary gland marked by intense thirst and the passage of large quantities of urine.

diabetes mellitus a metabolic disorder marked by insufficient secretion or utilization of insulin, polyuria, large amounts of sugar in the urine and blood, and by weight loss, thirst, and hunger.

diabetic 1. of, relating to, or affected with diabetes. 2. a person suffering from diabetes.

diacid an acid with two acid hydrogen atoms. —**diacid** *or* **diacidic** *adj.*

diagnosis the skill or act of identifying a disease from its symptoms and signs. —**diagnose** *vb.*

diagnostic of or relating to diagnosis.

diagnostics the branch of medicine dealing with the diagnosis of disease. —**diagnostician** *n.*

dialysis *pl.* **dialyses** the separation of substances in solution by means of their unequal diffusion through a semipermeable membrane.

dialyze to undergo dialysis. —**dialyzability** *n.* —**dialyzable** *adj.* —**dialyzer** *n.*

diapedesis the passage of blood or blood cells through vessel walls into the tissues. —**diapedetic** *adj.*

diaphanometer an instrument for measuring the relative transparency of fluids.

diaphoresis perspiration, esp. when profuse.

diaphoretic an agent that promotes diaphoresis.

diaphragm 1. the muscular partition separating the chest from the abdomen. 2. a circular cap usually of thin flexible rubber fitted over the cervix of the uterus as a barrier to conception.

diaphysectomy surgical removal of part of the shaft of a long bone.

diaphysis the shaft of a long bone.

diapiresis diapedesis.

diapyesis the formation of pus; suppuration.

diapyetic 1. relating to or causing suppuration. 2. anything that causes the production of pus.

diarrhea *also* **diarrhoea** frequent loose emptying of the bowels.

diarthric relating to two joints.

diarthrosis a joint that permits free movement, such as a ball-and-socket joint.

diastase an enzyme in plant cells and in digestive juice which acts in the conversion of starch into sugar.

diastasis *pl.* **diastases** 1. the rest period of the cardiac cycle occurring before systole. 2. separation of the epiphysis from the shaft of a long bone, as through injury.

diastole the dilation of the heart cavities during which they become filled with blood. —**diastolic** *adj.*

diathermy the therapeutic generation of heat in tissues by means of electric currents. —**diathermic** *adj.*

diathesis a constitutional predisposition toward a particular disease or abnormality.

diatomic having two atoms in the molecule.

dibromide a bromide (such as calcium bromide) that contains two bromine atoms in each molecule.

dichromasia a form of color blindness in which only two of the three primary colors are perceived, those usually perceived being red and blue or blue and green.

dichromat a person affected with dichromasia.

Dick test a test for susceptibility or immunity to scarlet fever by injection of scarlet fever toxin.

dicrotic of or relating to a pulse that beats twice for each single beat of the heart. —**dicrotism** *n.*

didelphic relating to or having a double uterus.

didymalgia pain in the testicles; orchialgia.

didymitis inflammation of the testicles; orchitis.

diencephalon the part of the brain that includes the thalamus, hypothalamus and related structures; between-brain.

dietetics the science of applying the principles of nutrition to balanced feeding.

diethylstilbestrol a synthetic preparation that is more powerful than natural estrogens, used to treat estrogen deficiencies and menopausal problems; stilbestrol.

dietician *or* **dietitian** a specialist in dietetics.

digest to convert (food) into absorbable form. —**digestibility** *n.* —**digestible** *adj.* —**digestion** *n.*

digestant 1. relating to or stimulating digestion. 2. something that aids or promotes digestion.

digestive 1. relating to or promoting digestion. 2. an agent that aids in or stimulates digestion.

digit a finger or toe. —**digital** *adj.*

digitalis the dried leaf of the common foxglove that when ground to powder acts as a powerful cardiac stimulant.

diiodide a compound that has two atoms of iodine in each molecule.

dilatation the condition of being stretched or expanded beyond normal dimensions: *dilatation of the abdomen.*

dilate to enlarge or widen in extent or degree. —**dilation** *n.*

dilator an instrument for enlarging a bodily opening, as the anus or urethra.

dilute to make thinner, more fluid, or less potent by addition of another substance. —**dilute** *adj.* —**dilution** *n.*

diopter *also* **dioptre** a unit of measurement of the refractive power of the lens.

dioptometer an instrument for measuring the refractive power of the eyes. —**dioptometry** *n.*

dioptroscopy the use of an ophthalmoscope to determine the degree of refraction.

diose the most simple sugar; glycolaldehyde.

diovulatory releasing two ova during one menstrual cycle.

dioxide an oxide containing two atoms of oxygen in the molecule.

diphtheria an acute infectious bacterial disease characterized by the formation of a false membrane in the throat or larynx.

diplacusis the hearing of two sounds from a single source due to a difference in perception by the two ears, either in pitch or time.

diplegia paralysis affecting both sides of the body in like areas. —**diplegic** *adj.*

diplococcus any of a genus of often pathogenic bacteria occurring chiefly in pairs.

diploë osseous tissue between the two layers of the skull. —**diploic** *adj.* —**diploetic** *adj.*

diploid having the basic (haploid) chromosome number doubled.

diplomyelia the abnormal presence of a longitudinal fissure in the spinal cord which divides it into distinct halves.

diplopia double vision.

dipsogen any agent that stimulates thirst.

dipsomania an uncontrollable craving for alcohol; alcoholism. —**dipsomaniac** *n.* —**dipsomaniacal** *adj.*

disaccharide a sugar that yields two monosaccharide molecules.

disarticulation the condition of being disjointed.

disc disk.

discharge the release of something contained, as of pus from a boil.

dischronation a disturbance in the ability to recognize the passage of time; loss of time sense.

discography X-ray of an intervertebral disk.

discoid resembling or shaped like a disk.

discopathy any disease involving an intervertebral disk.

disease a condition that impairs some function of the body or one of its parts. —**diseased** *adj.*

disinfectant an agent, as a chemical, that destroys certain harmful microorganisms: usually for external use only. —**disinfect** *vb.*

disk *or* **disc** any of various flattened and rounded anatomical structures, as one of the fibro-cartilaginous, articulating plates between vertebrae of the spinal column.

dislocation the displacement of a bone from its normal position in relation to another bone. —**dislocate** *vb.*

disorientation loss of a sense of time, identity, or place.

dispensary a place, as an outpatient clinic, providing medical and dental aid.

dispense to prepare and distribute (medication).

dispermy the penetration of an ovum by two sperm cells.

dissect to cut apart or open for scientific examination. —**dissection** *n.*

distal remote from the point of attachment or origin.

distemper any of certain specific infectious diseases of dogs, cats and horses, caused by infection with a virus (dogs and cats) or bacteria (horses).

districhiasis the growth of two hairs from a single hair follicle.

distrix the splitting of the ends of hairs.

diuresis an increased secretion of urine.

diuretic 1. relating to or tending to increase the flow of urine. 2. a drug or agent that increases the urinary output.

diurnal daily.

diverticulitis inflammation of a diverticulum.

diverticulosis an intestinal disorder marked by the presence of many diverticula.

diverticulum *pl.* **diverticula** a pouch or sac protruding abnormally from a hollow organ, as the bladder or intestine.

divulsion 1. the forcible dilation of the walls of a bodily cavity or passage. 2. the crude removal of a part by tearing or ripping it out.

divulsor an instrument used to force apart the walls of a bodily cavity or passage such as the urethra.

dizygotic *also* **dizygous** fraternal: *dizygotic twins.*

DNA deoxyribonucleic acid.

dolichocephalic having an unusually long head. —**dolichocephaly** *n.*

dolor pain, one of the signs of inflammation.

dolorific producing or causing pain.

dominant relating to or exerting genetic dominance.

donor a person used as the source of biological material, as for an organ transplant or blood transfusion.

dopa dihydroxyphenylalanine; an amino acid used in treating Parkinson's disease.

doraphobia an abnormal fear of petting animals or of touching their fur or skin.

dorsabdominal relating to both the back and the abdomen.

dorsad toward the back or posterior.

dorsal relating to or located near, on, or at the back.

dorsalgia pain in the back.

dorsiflexion an upward turning of the toes or foot.

dosage 1. the administration of drugs or other therapeutic agents in prescribed amounts. 2. the determination of the correct quantity of a drug to be administered or taken at one time.

dose the exact amount of a drug or therapeutic agent to be administered or taken at one time or at prescribed intervals.

double vision a disorder of vision in which two images of the same object are seen simultaneously because of unequal action of the eye muscles; diplopia.

douche 1. a stream of water, with or without medication or other additives, directed so as to irrigate or cleanse a body cavity. 2. a device for giving a douche. —**douche** *vb.*

Down's syndrome mongolism.

drastic acting quickly and powerfully: *a drastic purgative.*

dropsy the excessive accumulation of clear fluid in body tissues or cavities; edema; ascites.

drug 1. a substance used in diagnosing, curing, mitigating, treating, or preventing disease. 2. a narcotic. —**drug** *vb.*

druggist a pharmacist.

D.T.'s delirium tremens.

duct a tube or vessel of the body esp. for the passage of secretions or excretions.

duodenum the first part of the small intestine extending from the pylorus to the jejunum. —**duodenal** *adj.*

dura mater the tough outer membrane enveloping the brain and spinal cord.

dwarf a person of unusually or abnormally small stature. —**dwarfish** *adj.* —**dwarfism** *n.*

dys- *prefix* abnormal; difficult.

dyscrasia an abnormal condition of the body: *blood dyscrasia.*

dysentery a disease that is characterized by intestinal inflammation, abdominal pain, and the passage of mucus and bloody stools and is caused by bacteria or protozoa.

dysfunction abnormal or impaired functioning. —**dysfunctional** *adj.*

dyslexia a disturbance in the ability to read; word blindness. —**dyslexic** *adj.*

dysmenorrhea difficult or painful menstruation. —**dysmenorrheal** *adj.* —**dysmenorrheic** *adj.*

dyspepsia indigestion. —**dispeptic** *adj.*

dysphagia difficulty in swallowing. —**dysphagic** *adj.*

dysphasia impairment of the ability to use or understand spoken language coherently owing to injury or brain disease. —**dysphasic** *adj.*

dysplasia abnormality of development, as of organs or cells. —**dysplasic** *adj.*

dyspnea difficult or labored respiration. —**dyspneic** *adj.*

dystrophy a disorder resulting from faulty nutrition. —**dystrophic** *adj.*

dysuria difficult or painful urination.

E

ear the organ of hearing and equilibrium, consisting of a sound-collecting outer ear separated by a membranous drum (tympanic membrane) from a sound-transmitting middle ear that is itself separated by a membranous fenestra from a sensory inner ear.

eardrum tympanic membrane.

earlobe the pendent part of the outer ear.

ebonation removal of bony fragments from a wound.

ebrietas *also* **ebriety** the state of being intoxicated with alcohol; drunkenness.

ebullism the formation at high altitudes of bubbles of water vapor in the tissues.

ebur tissue resembling ivory in appearance or consistency.

eburnation a degenerative change in bone in which it becomes hard and dense like ivory.

eburneous resembling ivory; having the color of ivory.

ecaudate without a tail; tailless.

ecbolic 1. hastening childbirth or accelerating the termination of pregnancy. 2. any agent that speeds up delivery or produces abortion; oxytocic.

eccdemic (of a disease) brought into a region or community; not epidemic or endemic.

eccentropiesis pressure exerted outwards.

ecchondroma a tumor formed as an outgrowth of cartilaginous tissue and usually protruding from the surface of a bone within a joint.

ecchymoma a small mass of clotted blood formed as the result of a bruise.

ecchymosis a bruise appearing on the skin or mucous membrane and resulting from the escape of blood into the tissues from ruptured blood vessels. —**ecchymotic** *adj.*

eccoprotic having the properties of a laxative; cathartic.

eccrine exocrine.

eccrisis 1. removal from the body of waste matter. 2. waste matter; excrement.

eccritic 1. acting to expel waste matter. 2. an agent that acts to excrete waste matter.

eccyesis the development of a fertilized ovum outside the uterus; extrauterine pregnancy.

ecdemomania an abnormal desire to wander.

ecdysiasm an abnormal erotic desire or tendency to remove one's clothes in the presence of strangers.

ECG electrocardiogram.

ecgonine an alkaloid derived from cocaine.

echeosis mental suffering and emotional upset caused by prolonged exposure to loud or disturbing noises.

echidnin snake venom.

echidnotoxin a toxic protein in snake venom.

echinococcus *pl.* **echinococci** any of a genus of tapeworms that in the larval stage invade tissues esp. of the liver and constitute a dangerous pathogen.

echinosis an abnormal condition of red blood cells characterized by the loss of their smooth outlines.

echis a highly poisonous snake occurring in parts of Africa and the Middle East; carpet viper.

echoacousia subjective impairment of hearing in which a sound seems to be repeated.

echoencephalography the diagnostic technique of using ultrasound in examining the cranial contents.

echokinesia the involuntary mimicking of a sign or gesture made by another person.

echolalia the often pathological echoing of the words spoken by other people. —**echolalic** *adj.*

echomatism the involuntary and automatic repetition of an observed act.

echophotony the phenomenon of mentally associating a musical tone or tones with a specific color or colors.

echophrasia echolalia.

echopraxia the involuntary repetition or imitation of movements made by someone else; echomatism.

eclabium the eversion of a lip.

eclampsia an attack of convulsions sometimes occurring during pregnancy. —**eclamptic** *adj.*

eclaptogenous convulsive or causing convulsions.

ecmnesia the failure to recall recent events; short-term loss of memory.

ecphoria the ability to remember; recall of memory.

ecphyma a wartlike growth or elevation.

ECT electroconvulsive therapy.

ectacolia dilation of the large intestine.

ectad toward the surface; outward or externally.

ectal outer or external.

ectasia *also* **ectasis** dilation of a tubular passage.

ecthyma a pus-generating bacterial infection of the skin caused by staphylococci or streptococci.

ectiris the outermost layer of the iris.

ecto- *prefix* on the outside; outer.

ectoderm the outermost germ layer of an embryo. —**ectodermal** *adj.* **ectodermic** *adj.*

ectoglobular not within a red blood cell or other globular body.

ectomorphic having a light, slender body. —**ectomorph** *n.*

-ectomy *suffix* surgical removal: *mastectomy.*

ectoparasite any parasite that lives on the outer surface of the body.

ectoperitonitis inflammation of the layer of peritoneum that lines the abdominal cavity.

ectopic occurring or appearing in an abnormal place, position, or manner.

ectopic pregnancy gestation occurring elsewhere than in the uterus, as a fallopian tube.

ectoplasm the outermost layer of the protoplasm of a living cell.

ectoplastic formed at the outside or periphery.

ectopotomy surgical removal of a fetus developing outside the uterus.

ectopy *also* **ectopia** abnormal displacement of an organ or part.

ectoretina the outermost layer of the retina.

ectosteal relating to the external surface of a bone.

ectotoxemia blood poisoning caused by the introduction of a poison into the body.

ectozoon an animal parasite that lives on the surface of the body.

ectrimma an ulcer caused by constant friction.

ectrogeny the congenital absence of any structure or part.

ectrotic preventing or inhibiting the development of a disease.

eczema inflammation of the skin characterized initially by redness, itching, and oozing vesicles and later by scaling and crusting. —**eczematous** *adj.*

ED effective dose.

ED_{50} a dose which has the desired effect in half of the subjects or laboratory animals.

edeitis inflammation of the external genitals in the female; vulvitis.

edema any condition in which the tissues contain an excessive amount of fluid, such as the result of the inflammatory process, kidney disorders, or increased permeability of the capillary walls.

edematous characterized or marked by edema.

edentate without teeth; toothless.

edulcorate to make sweet or sweeter; sweeten. —**edulcorant** *n.*

EEG electroencephalogram.

effector 1. a muscle or gland that becomes active upon being stimulated. 2. a motor or secretory nerve ending in a muscle or gland.

efferent conveying impulses, blood, etc., outward: *efferent nerves.*

effuse (of the surface appearance of a bacterial culture) widely spreading; thin.

egersis the condition of being unusually alert or attentive; abnormal wakefulness.

egesta any waste matter discharged from the body, esp. feces.

egg the female sex cell; ovum.

eglandulous without glands.

ego (in psychoanalytic theory) the part of the mind or psyche that is conscious and serves to mediate between the id and the superego and react to the outside world.

egotropic self-centered.

egrotogenic (of an illness) induced by the patient.

eidetic 1. relating to or possessing a photographic memory; having total recall of what has been seen before. 2. a person with total recall of what he has seen.

eiloid resembling a loop, coil or roll.

ejaculate 1. to eject (semen) in orgasm. 2. the semen ejaculated in orgasm. **—ejaculation** *n.* **—ejaculatory** *adj.*

ejaculatio precox premature ejaculation of semen; extremely rapid male orgasm at the start of sexual intercourse.

EKG *also* **ECG** electrocardiogram.

elastosis degenerative changes in elastic tissue, esp. the skin.

elbow the joint of the arm between the upper arm and the forearm.

Electra complex the female equivalent of the Oedipus complex; symptoms caused by a daughter's suppressed sexual love for her father.

electroanesthesia anesthesia induced by means of an electric current.

electrobiology the branch of biology concerned with the study of electrical phenomena in living organisms.

electrocardiogram a tracing made by an electrocardiograph.

electrocardiograph an instrument for recording variations in the electrical current of the heartbeat and used esp. to diagnose abnormalities in heart function. **—electrocardiographic** *adj.* **—electrocardiography** *n.*

electrocatalysis the breakdown of compounds or chemical decomposition by means of electricity.

electrocauterization *also* **electrocautery** cauterization by means of an electrically heated wire.

electrochemistry the branch of science concerned with the study of chemical changes brought about by electricity.

electrocoagulation the use of high frequency currents to harden growths and diseased tissues.

electrocontractility the ability of a muscle to contract when stimulated electrically.

electroconvulsive therapy electroshock therapy.

electrode a conductor for establishing electrical contact with a nonmetallic part of a circuit.

electroencephalogram a tracing made by an electroencephalograph.

electroencephalograph an instrument for recording brain waves. **—electroencephalographic** *adj.* **—electroencephalography** *n.*

electrohemostasis the arrest of bleeding by the use of electrocauterization.

electrohysterograph an instrument for recording the electrical activity of the uterus.

electrolysis 1. the destruction of the roots of hair by means of an electric current. 2. chemical change, esp. ionization, of a substance when an electric current is passed through it.

electrolyte a solution or a substance in solution that is decomposed into ions by the passage through it of an electric current, such as certain acids, bases and salts.

electromyograph an instrument for recording the contraction of muscles following their electrical stimulation. **—electromyogram** *n.* **—electromyographic** *adj.* **—electromyography** *n.*

electronarcosis the use of electricity to produce sleep or loss of consciousness.

electroshock therapy the treatment of psychiatric disorders by use of short bursts of an electric current to induce a brief therapeutic coma.

electrosurgery the surgical use of electricity.

electrothanasia death by means of electricity; electrocution.

elephantiasis a chronic filarial disease caused by infestation of the lymphatics by nematodes and marked by gross enlargement of the limbs or scrotum and leathery hardening of the skin.

eliminate to expel (waste matter) from the body. **—elimination** *n.* **—eliminative** *adj.*

elinguation the surgical removal of the tongue.

elixir a usually alcohol-containing, sweetened liquid used as a vehicle for a medication, as a cough suppressant.

emaciation the condition of becoming very thin or of wasting away. **—emaciate** *vb.*

emaculation the removal of skin blemishes.

emasculation loss of masculinity by castration of the male. **—emasculate** *vb.*

embolectomy the surgical removal of an embolus.

embolism the sudden obstruction by an embolus of a blood vessel.

embololalia the periodic interjection of nonsense words in a sentence while talking.

embolus an abnormal body, as an air bubble or blood clot, floating in the blood.

embrocate to moisten and massage with a lotion. **—embrocation** *n.*

embryo *pl.* **embryos** the developing human being from the time of fertilization to the end of the eighth week after conception.

embryology the branch of biology dealing with embryos and their development. **—embryologist** *n.*

embryoplastic relating to the formation of an embryo.

emesis *pl.* **emeses** an act or instance of vomiting.

emetic an agent that induces vomiting. **—emetic** *adj.*

emetine hydrochloride a drug used in the treatment of amoebiasis.

emetology the scientific study of the causes and mechanisms responsible for vomiting.

EMF electromotive force; voltage.

-emia *suffix* blood.

emission a discharge of semen esp. when involuntary.

emmenagogic causing or increasing menstrual flow.

emmenia menses. **—emmenic** *adj.*.

emmenology the branch of medical science concerned with the study of normal and disordered menstruation.

emolient something that is soft and soothing to the skin or mucous membranes.

emotiovascular relating to vascular changes such as blushing and pallor induced by emotional stimuli.

emphysema a condition marked by air-filled expansion of tissues of the body esp. those of the lungs. —**emphysematous** *adj.*

empyema *pl.* **empyemata** the collection of pus in a body cavity. —**empyemic** *adj.*

emulsion a suspension of minute globules of one fluid within another. —**emulsive** *adj.*

enamel the hard thin calcareous substance forming the outer layer of a tooth.

enanthesis the skin eruption or rash associated with a specific internal disease, such as typhoid fever.

enarthrosis the ball-and-socket articulation of a joint in which the rounded extremity of one bone fits into the cuplike cavity of the other to permit movement in any direction.

encanthis a tiny growth at the inner angle of the eye.

encapsulated surrounded by a membranous capsule or sheath.

encarditis endocarditis; inflammation of the membrane that lines the chambers of the heart.

enceinte pregnant.

encelitis *also* **enceliitis** inflammation of any abdominal organ.

encephal- *or* **encephalo-** *prefix* brain: *encephalitis.*

encephalalgia headache.

encephalatrophy a wasting away of brain tissue; atrophy of the brain.

encephalic lying or situated within the cranial cavity.

encephalitis inflammation of the brain. —**encephalitic** *adj.*

encephalodialysis abnormal softening of the brain.

encephalodynia headache.

encephalogram an X-ray picture of the brain.

encephalography X-ray photography of the brain, esp. after air has been introduced into the lateral ventricles by lumbar puncture or directly into an area at the base of the brain.

encephalolith a calculus within the brain or one of its ventricles.

encephalomalacia softening of the brain.

encephalomeningitis inflammation of the brain and its covering membranes (meninges).

encephalomyelitis inflammation of the brain and spinal cord simultaneously.

encephalomyelopathy any disease involving both the brain and spinal cord.

encephalomyocarditis an acute febrile disease marked by inflammation, degeneration, and lesions of the skeletal and cardiac muscles and the central nervous system.

encephalon the brain of a vertebrate.

encephalopathy disease of the brain. —**encephalopathic** *adj.*

encephalospinal cerebrospinal.

encephalothlipsis brain compression.

encyst to form or become enclosed in a cyst. —**encystation** *n.*

end- *or* **endo-** *prefix* inside; within.

Endamoeba a genus of amoebas, usually distinguished from *Entamoeba,* that are parasitic in the intestines of invertebrates but do not affect man.

endangeitis *also* **endangiitis** inflammation of the inner coat of a blood vessel.

endangeitis obliterans inflammation of the inner coat of a blood vessel resulting in obstruction of the vessel.

endangium the inner coat of a blood vessel.

endaortitis inflammation of the inner coat of the aorta (the largest artery in the body).

endarterectomy the surgical removal of fatty deposits from the inner coat of a large artery.

endarterial within an artery or relating to its inner coat.

endarteritis inflammation of the inner coat of an artery.

endarterium the inner coat of an artery.

endaural within the ear.

endemia any endemic disease.

endemic peculiar or restricted to a particular area: *endemic diseases.*

endepidermis the inner layer of the epidermis.

endo- *prefix* within; inner.

endoangiitis inflammation of the inner coat of a blood vessel.

endocarditis inflammation of the lining of the heart.

endocardium *pl.* **endocardia** the thin membrane lining the inside of the heart.

endoceliac within a body cavity.

endocervicitis inflammation of the mucous membrane that lines the neck of the womb (cervix of the uterus).

endocolpitis inflammation of the mucous membrane that lines the vagina.

endocrine gland a gland, as the thyroid, producing secretions (hormones) that are circulated through the body in the bloodstream.

endocrinology a science dealing with endocrine glands and the hormones they secrete. —**endocrinologic** *or* **endocrinological** *adj.*

endocystitis inflammation of the mucous membrane that lines the urinary bladder.

endoderm the innermost layer of cells of an embryo. —**endodermal** *adj.*

endodontology the branch of dentistry concerned with the diagnosis and treatment of diseases that affect the dental pulp.

endoenteritis inflammation of the mucous membrane that lines the intestines.

endoenzyme any enzyme that is active within a cell.

endoesophagitis inflammation of the mucous membrane that lines the esophagus.

endogenous *or* **endogenic** growing from or produced within the body.

endolymph the fluid in the membranous labyrinth of the ear. —**endolymphatic** *adj.*

endometrium *pl.* **endometria** the mucous membrane lining the uterus.

endomorphic having a heavy rounded body with a tendency to become fat. —**endomorph** *n.*

end organ a structure forming the end of a neural path.

endoscope an instrument for viewing the inside of a hollow bodily organ. —**endoscopic** *adj.* —**endoscopy** *n.*

endothelium *pl.* **endothelia** the membrane lining blood vessels, serous cavities, and lymphatics.

endotracheal placed within or applied through the trachea.

enema introduction of a fluid into the rectum by way of the anus to help evacuate the lower bowel, introduce medicine, etc.

enervate 1. to lessen the strength or vitality of. 2. to remove or cut through a nerve.

engorge to congest with blood. —**engorgement** *n.*

engram (in the theory of memory mechanisms) a trace left in the brain following any experience, which is activated in the recall of that experience.

Entamoeba a genus of amoebas parasitic in the human digestive tract one species of which (*Entamoeba histolytica*) is responsible for causing amoebic dysentery. Compare *Endamoeba.*

enter- *or* **entero-** *prefix* intestine: *enterocolitis.*

enteralgia severe abdominal pain and cramps.

enterectasis dilation of the small intestine.

enterelcosis ulceration of the intestine.

enteric of or relating to the intestines.

enteric-coated (of tablets) having a coating unaffected by the digestive juices of the stomach but which dissolves to release the medication beneath on reaching the small intestine.

enteritis inflammation of the intestines, esp. of the small intestine.

enterobiasis infestation with pinworms (*Enterobius vermicularis*).

enterococcus streptococcus present normally in the intestine.

enterocolitis inflammation of both the large and small intestine.

enterohepatitis inflammation of both the intestine and liver.

enteromycosis any fungal disease of the intestines.

enteron the alimentary canal system esp. of the human embryo.

enteropathy any disease of the intestine. —**enteropathic** *adj.*

enterorrhagia bleeding into or from the intestines.

enterostomy surgical formation of an artificial opening into the intestine through the abdominal wall.

enterozoon any animal parasite inhabiting the intestine.

entoptic within the eyeball.

enuresis involuntary release of urine, esp. during sleep. —**enuretic** *adj.* & *n.*

enzyme a complex protein produced by living cells and capable of inducing chemical changes without itself being changed or destroyed in the process. —**enzymatic** *or* **enzymic** *adj.* —**enzymology** *n.*

enzymology the branch of science concerned with the study of the structure and function of enzymes.

eosin a red acid dye used for staining.

ephedrine an alkaloid used in the form of a salt to relieve asthma, hay fever, and nasal congestion.

epicanthic fold either of the extended folds of the skin of the upper eyelids over the inner or both angles of the eyes. Also called *Mongolian fold.*

epicardium the inner layer of the pericardium.

epicranium the muscles and skin that cover the cranium; the scalp.

epidemic affecting many individuals of the same community, region, or population simultaneously. —**epidemic** *n.* —**epidemical** *adj.*

epidemiology the scientific study of the distribution and occurrence of diseases. —**epidemiological** *or* **epidemiologic** *adj.* —**epidemiologist** *n.*

epidermis the outermost layer of the skin. —**epidermal** *adj.*

epidermitis inflammation of the outer layers of the skin.

epididymectomy surgical removal of the epididymis.

epididymis *pl.* **epididymides** an extended, convoluted mass of efferent tubes through which the sperm pass from the testis to the vas deferens. —**epididymal** *adj.*

epididymitis inflammation of the epididymis.

epigastric lying upon or over the stomach.

epiglottis the thin cartilaginous plate that folds back and protects the glottis during swallowing. —**epiglottal** *adj.*

epilepsy any of various diseases distinguished by disturbance of the electrical rhythms of the central nervous system with characteristic convulsive episodes and clouding of consciousness. —**epileptic** *n.* & *adj.*

epinephrine *or* **epinephrin** an adrenal hormone used medicinally as a bronchiole relaxant, heart stimulant, and vasoconstrictor. Also called *adrenaline.*

epiphysis *pl.* **epiphyses** the end of a long bone developing separately from the shaft (from which it is originally separated by an area of cartilage) with which it eventually unites.

episioplasty plastic surgery involving the vulva.

episiorrhagia bleeding from the vulva.

episiotomy surgical incision of the perineum to facilitate childbirth.

epispadias a congenital defect of the penis in which the urethra opens on the back surface.

epistaxis *pl.* **epistaxes** nosebleed.

epithelium *pl.* **epithelia** a membranous, protective tissue forming the outermost layer of the skin and lining tubes, cavities, and other free surfaces of the body. —**epithelial** *adj.*

erectile tissue tissue that becomes rigid when filled with blood, such as the penis, clitoris and nipples.

erection the condition of being rigid and elevated, as the penis or clitoris when filled with blood.

eremophobia the abnormal fear of being alone; fear of solitude.

ereuthophobia the abnormal fear of blushing.

ergasiophobia the abnormal fear of working or of work.

ergot 1. the dried sclerotium of a fungus replacing the seeds of a grass, as rye. 2. a disease of rye and other grasses caused by ergot fungus. 3. a derivative alkaloid of ergot used medicinally for its contractile action on smooth muscle.

ergotamine an alkaloid derivative from ergot, used esp. in treating migraine.

ergotism a toxic condition produced chiefly by eating grain or grain products infected with ergot fungus.

erogenous *also* **erogenic** producing or gratifying feelings of sexual excitement: *erogenous zones of the body.*

erosion the wearing away of the surface of a structure or part.

erotic of or arousing sexual desire.

erotophobia the abnormal fear of sexual intercourse or of physical contact associated with sexual arousal.

eruct to release stomach gas through the mouth; belch. —**eructation** *n.*

eruption the breaking out of a skin inflammation; rash. —**erupt** *vb.*

erysipelas an acute streptococcal inflammatory disease of the skin.

erythema acute, abnormal redness of the skin. —**erythematous** *adj.*

erythralgia a condition in which the skin is red and painful.

erythroblast an immature red blood cell.

erythroblastosis the abnormal presence in the bloodstream of large numbers of immature red blood cells.

erythrocyte a mature red blood cell.

erythrocytosis an abnormal increase in the number of circulating red blood cells; polycythemia.

erythropoiesis the production of red blood cells.

eschar a slough formed esp. after a burn.

esophagitis inflammation of the esophagus.

esophagus the part of the digestive tract between the pharynx and the stomach; gullet.

estrinase a liver enzyme that inactivates estrogens.

estrogen any of the female sex hormones, produced by the ovaries or prepared synthetically.

estrus the receptive phase of the sexual cycle of female animals; heat.

ethyl alcohol alcohol.

etiolate to make or become pale from lack of light. —**etiolation** *n.*

etiology the study of the causes of disease or the cause of a specific disease or abnormal condition. —**etiologic** *or* **etiological** *adj.*

eugenics a science dealing with methods to improve the hereditary qualities of a race or breed. —**eugeneticist** *n.* —**eugenic** *adj.*

eunuch a man or boy deprived of the testes; castrated male. —**eunuchoid** *adj.*

euphoria an exaggerated sense of elation and general well-being. —**euphoric** *adj.*

Eustachian tube the tube connecting the throat to the ear and serving to equalize air pressure on both sides of the eardrum.

eustachitis inflammation of the mucous membrane that lines a Eustachian tube.

euthanasia the act or practice of killing individuals considered hopelessly sick or injured or permitting them to die for reasons of mercy.

evacuate to discharge (waste products) from the body. —**evacuation** *n.*

evert to turn or fold outward or inside out. —**eversible** *adj.* —**eversion** *n.*

eviscerate to remove the bowels or entrails of. —**evisceration** *n.*

exacerbation an increase in the severity of a disease or an aggravation of its signs and symptoms.

exanthem any skin eruption associated with a general disease, such as measles.

exarteritis inflammation of the outer coat of an artery.

excipient an inert substance that is used as a vehicle for a drug.

excision the act of removing something by cutting; surgical removal. —**excise** *vb.*

excoriate to remove the skin of; abrade. —**excoriation** *n.*

excrement waste matter discharged from the alimentary canal; fecal matter.

excrescent forming an abnormal or useless outgrowth or enlargement. —**excrescence** *n.*

excreta waste matter.

excrete to discharge (waste matter) from the body. —**excretion** *n.*

exfoliate to cast off in flakes or scales. —**exfoliation** *n.*

exhale to breathe out.

exhibitionism an abnormal urge to expose one's body and genitals to others without warning. —**exhibitionist** *n.* —**exhibitionistic** *adj.*

exhumation disinterment of a dead body. —**exhume** *vb.*

exobiology the branch of science concerned with examining evidence and investigating the possibility of life on other planets.

exogenous originating from or due to external causes.

exophthalmos *also* **exophthalmus** protrusion of the eyeballs, esp. as a consequence of overactivity of the thyroid gland (hyperthyroidism or thyrotoxicosis).

expectorant an agent that promotes the discharge of mucus from the respiratory tract. —**expectorant** *adj.*

expectorate to eject from the throat or lungs esp. by coughing; spit. —**expectoration** *n.*

extrasystole premature contraction of the heart.

extravasation the passage of a fluid, esp. blood, from its proper channel or vessels into surrounding tissues. —**extravasate** *vb.*

extravert *or* **extrovert** one whose interests are directed primarily outside the self. —**extraverted** *or* **extroverted** *adj.* —**extraversion** *or* **extroversion** *n.*

extremity a limb of the body; an arm or leg.

extrinsic originating or being on the outside; external.

extrovert extravert.

exudate 1. to exude matter; ooze. 2. matter exudated. —**exudation** *n.*

eye the organ of sight, consisting of a round structure with a clear outer covering (cornea) and a biconvex transparent lens to focus incoming light through the central gelatinous substance (vitreous humor) and onto the back light-sensitive surface (retina), situated as one of a pair in bony frontal orbits of the skull.

eyeball the approximately globular capsule of the vertebrate eye.

eyelid a movable lid of skin and muscle that can be lowered over the eye.

eyestrain fatigue or discomfort of vision esp. from overuse of the eyes.

THE EYE
(CROSS SECTION)

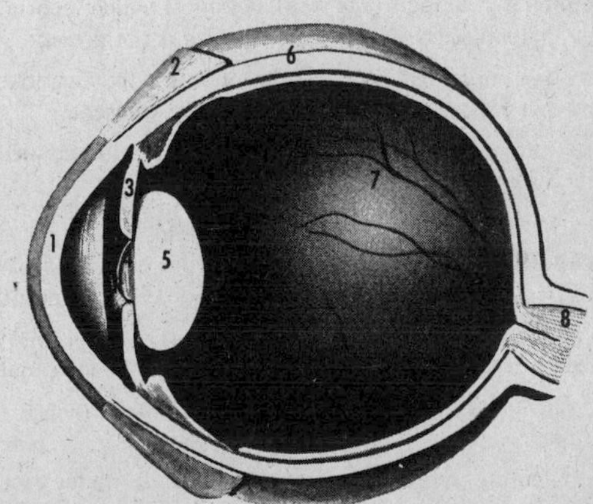

1 CORNEA
2 CONJUNCTIVA
3 IRIS
4 PUPIL
5 LENS
6 SCLERA
7 RETINA
8 OPTIC NERVE

F

face the front part of the human head that includes the forehead, eyes, nose, cheeks, mouth, and chin.

facial relating to the face or situated on the lower anterior part of the head.

facies *pl.* **facies** 1. an appearance or expression of the face indicating a particular condition; countenance. 2. the surface of a structure or part.

faciobrachial relating to or involving both the face and arm, as in the manifestations of juvenile muscular dystrophy.

faciocephalalgia pain in the face and head along the course of one or more nerves; neuralgia of this region.

faciocervical relating to or involving both the face and neck, as in a form of progressive muscular dystrophy.

faciolingual relating to or involving both the face and the tongue, as in a certain form of paralysis.

facioplasty plastic surgery involving the soft tissues of the face.

facioplegia palsy or paralysis of the facial muscles, usually with a loss of sensation in the skin of the face.

factitious fever fever produced artificially, as to fake an illness.

faecal fecal.

faeces feces.

falcial relating to a falx.

falcate *also* **falciform** shaped like a crescent or sickle.

fallacia an optical illusion or hallucination.

fallectomy surgical removal of a section of a fallopian tube; salpingectomy.

falling sickness a former popular term for epilepsy or an epileptic condition.

falling womb protrusion of the body of the uterus into the vagina.

fallopian tube either of a pair of tubes through which an ovum, released during ovulation, travels from the ovary to the uterus.

fallostomy surgical opening of a fallopian tube; salpingostomy.

fallotomy surgical separation of a fallopian tube; salpingotomy.

false-negative relating to the results of a test which incorrectly suggest that a disease or specific condition is not present.

false-positive relating to the results of a test that incorrectly suggest that a disease or specific condition is present.

false ribs the lower five pairs of ribs, which are not connected directly with the breastbone (sternum).

falx any structure or part shaped like a sickle.

falx cerebelli a fold or short process of the outermost of the meninges (dura mater) which forms a vertical partition between the two halves of the cerebellum.

falx cerebri a fold of dura mater that dips into the longitudinal fissure between the two halves of the cerebrum.

fames hunger.

familial affecting more members of a family than can be attributed to chance: *familial illnesses.*

family 1. parents and their children. 2. close blood relatives. 3. (in biologic classification) a division between order and genus.

fantasy mental images created in response to psychological need: *sexual fantasies of adolescence.*

faradic relating to induced electricity.

faradism the therapeutic use of an induced electric current. —**faradize** *vb.*

farinaceous starchy.

farsightedness the inability to focus on objects relatively close to the eye; hypermetropia; hyperopia.

fascia *pl.* **fasciae** a sheath of connective tissue enclosing muscle.

fascial relating to or resembling fascia.

fascicle fasciculus.

fascicular arranged in a bundle or rodlike collection.

fasciculation 1. the formation of fasciculi. 2. the involuntary twitching of groups of muscle fibers.

fasciculus *pl.* **fasciculi** a small bundle of fibers, esp. of muscles or nerves.

fasciectomy the surgical removal of strips of fascia.

fasciola a small group of fibers.

Fasciola a genus of flukes.

fascioplasty plastic surgery involving fascia.

fasciotomy surgical incision and separation of fascia.

fat animal tissue composed of cells enlarged with greasy or oily matter. —**fatty** *adj.*

fatigue 1. physical or emotional exhaustion. 2. to weary with labor or exertion.

fauces the passage between the soft palate and the base of the tongue that links the mouth and the pharynx.

faucitis inflammation of the fauces.

faveolus a small depression, esp. on the skin.

favus a contagious fungal disease of the skin, esp. of the scalp, characterized by the formation of round cup-shaped yellow crusts having a musty odor.

febrifacient causing or producing fever.

febrile of or relating to fever; feverish.

febrious conducive to the development of fever.

fecal *also* **faecal** of, relating to, or constituting feces.

feces *also* **faeces** solid waste matter formed in the large intestine and expelled through the anus.

fecund fruitful in offspring; prolific. —**fecundity** *n.*

feebleminded mentally incapable or deficient. —**feeblemindedly** *adv.* —**feeblemindedness** *n.*

fellatio *also* **fellation** oral stimulation of the penis.

felo de se 1. a person who commits suicide. 2. the act of suicide.

felon a whitlow.

feminism the abnormal development or condition in a male of feminine characteristics, usually as the result of a hormonal disorder.

femorotibial relating to both the femur and tibia.

femur *pl.* **femurs** *or* **femora** the bone extending from the pelvis to the knee; thighbone. —**femoral** *adj.*

fenestra *pl.* **fenestrae** an anatomical aperture, frequently one closed by a membrane.

fenestrated having openings suggestive of or resembling windows.

fenestration the presence of window-like openings in a structure or part.

ferment 1. to decompose or undergo fermentation. 2. a substance capable of bringing about fermentation.

fermentation the breakdown of complex substances by means of certain enzymes (ferments) produced by microorganisms such as bacteria, molds and yeasts, as in the production of alcohol.

fermentative causing or able to cause fermentation.

ferrous relating to iron or a salt containing iron (such as ferrous sulfate).

ferruginous relating to or containing iron.

fertile producing or capable of producing young; fecund. —**fertility** *n.*

fertilize to cause (a human egg) to become impregnated. —**fertilization** *n.*

fester to become inflamed and produce pus.

fetal *also* **foetal** of or relating to a fetus.

fetal position a resting position in which the body is curved with the legs drawn up, the arms are bent around the chest, and the head is inclined forward.

feticide the destruction of the fetus in induced abortion.

fetid having an offensive smell.

fetish *or* **fetich** an object or body part that becomes psychologically necessary for sexual gratification and may interfere with normal or complete sexual gratification.

fetishism *also* **fetichism** the pathological displacement of erotic interest to a fetish. —**fetishist** *n.*

fetor an extremely foul odor.

fetus *also* **foetus** a developing human being usually from three months after conception to birth.

fever an abnormal rise in body temperature. —**feverish** *adj.* —**feverishness** *n.*

fiber *or* **fibre** a threadlike structure, esp. a strand of nerve or muscle tissue. —**fibrous** *adj.* —**fibrousness** *n.*

FERTILIZATION

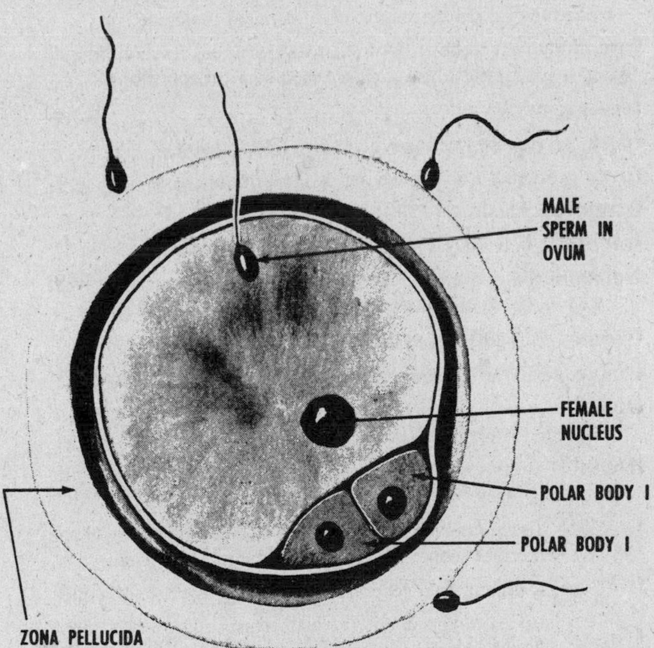

THE EVENTS OF FERTILIZATION

The female ovum (egg), surrounded by a thick, transparent Zona Pellucida, divides unequally, producing Polar Body I. At this point, a single sperm penetrates the Zona. The ovum again divides, producing Polar Body II. The female nucleus migrates toward the male sperm. The union of the two completes fertilization.

fiberscope an instrument for examining body cavities and passages and composed of flexible bundles of glass fibers through which light is transmitted.

fibr- *or* **fibro-** *prefix* fiber; fibrous.

fibril a very small fiber.

fibrillation 1. irregular and uncoordinated contractions of the heart. 2. muscular twitching resulting from the spontaneous contraction of muscle fibers.

fibrin an insoluble component of blood, created by chemical conversion from fibrinogen, that forms the matrix of blood clots.

fibrinogen a clotting factor in solution in the bloodstream from which fibrin is made.

fibroblast a cell forming connective tissue. —**fibroblastic** *adj.*

fibroid 1. resembling or constituting fibrous tissue. 2. a benign tumor esp. when occurring in the uterine wall.

fibroma any fibrous tumor of connective tissue.

fibromatosis a condition characterized by the formation of many fibromas.

fibrosarcoma a malignant tumor derived from fibrous connective tissue.

fibrosis the reactive formation of fibrous tissue, as in the healing of a wound.

fibrositis rheumatic inflammation of fibrous tissue.

fibrotic relating to or characterized by fibrosis.

fibrous composed of or containing fibers.

fibula a slender bone that extends from the knee to the ankle on the outer side of the leg.

ficin an enzyme isolated from figs that is capable of dissolving proteins, used in the treatment of worm infestation.

field of vision visual field.

filaria *pl.* **filariae** any of various parasitic nematodes that infest the blood and tissues of mammals.

filariasis disease caused by infestation with filariae.

filariform resembling small threadlike worms or filariae.

filioparental relating to the relationships between parents and their children.

filterable virus a virus of such minute size that a fluid in which it is contained remains virulent even when passed through the pores of a special filter which can trap bacteria and the larger viruses.

filtrate the fluid that has been passed through a filter.

filtration the act or process of passing a fluid through a filter.

filum a threadlike structure; filament.

fimbria *pl.* **fimbriae** any structure or part resembling a fringe or having fringelike attachments, such as the upper part of the fallopian tubes nearest the ovaries.

fimbriate *also* **fimbriated** having fimbriae.

finger a digit of the hand, esp. any of the four digits of the hand other than the thumb.

fissure a cleft between two structures or parts; sulcus.

fissure of Rolando the central fissure of the cerebrum, dividing the parietal from the frontal lobe in each hemisphere; central sulcus.

fissure of Sylvius the lateral fissure of the cerebrum, dividing the temporal lobe from the frontal and parietal lobes in each hemisphere.

fistula *pl.* **fistulas** *or* **fistulae** an abnormal passage from an abscess to the surface of the body or from one organ to another. —**fistulous** *adj.*

flaccid lacking in firmness; soft; limp. —**flaccidity** *n.* —**flaccidly** *adv.*

flagellum *pl.* **flagella** a long, slender, tapering process providing the means of locomotion for certain cells, as spermatozoa and some protozoa.

flatfoot a condition of the feet in which the arches of the insteps are flattened so that the soles rest entirely on the ground.

flatulent marked by, affected with, or likely to cause gas within the stomach or intestinal tract. —**flatulence** *n.* —**flatulency** *n.*

flatus gas generated in the bowels or stomach.

flavedo yellowness of the skin; jaundice.

fletcherism a dietary system characterized by eating very small quantities of food each day which is to be excessively chewed before swallowing.

fletcherize to practice the dietary system (fletcherism) devised by the American dietician Horace Fletcher (1849-1919).

flexion 1. a bending of a joint between adjacent bones. 2. the condition or state of being bent.

flexor a muscle that produces flexion.

flooding profuse bleeding from the uterus, esp. following childbirth or in severe menstrual disorders.

fluke any of various species of parasitic flatworms (trematodes) which can infest the liver, blood, intestines or lungs.

fluor albus leukorrhea.

fluorescein a yellow or red dye that produces a vivid green fluorescence in solution, used in the diagnosis of disorders of the cornea and in intravenous injections for studying the rate of blood flow (circulation time).

fluorescent having the ability to become luminous when exposed to light rays, X-rays, or other forms of radiant energy.

fluoridate to add a fluoride to (as drinking water). —**fluoridation** *n.*

fluoride a compound of fluorine.

fluorine a nonmetallic, gaseous, halogenic element.

fluoroscope a device with a fluorescent screen for examining the movement and condition of deep structures of the body by means of X-rays. —**fluoroscopic** *adj.* —**fluoroscopy** *n.*

fluorosis a condition mainly characterized by discoloration of the teeth, caused by the chronic intake of excessive amounts of fluorine in the drinking water.

flutter 1. abnormal, spasmodic, muscular movement of a part of the body. 2. to move in irregular spasms. —**fluttery** *adj.*

focus *pl.* **focuses** *or* **foci** a point at which rays, as of light, converge.

folic acid a crystalline acid of the B complex found naturally in liver, yeast and green leafy vegetables and used in synthetic form to treat nutritional anemias and sprue.

folie à deux a condition in which two persons in an intimate relationship share the same delusional ideas.

follicle a small narrow-mouthed cavity or depression. —**follicular** *adj.* —**folliculate** *also* **folliculated** *adj.*

fomentation the application of a moist, hot substance to the skin to ease pain.

fomites articles, as items of clothing, that have been in contact with a person having a contagious disease and may themselves be agents of transmission.

fontanelle *or* **fontanel** a soft membrane-covered space at the top of an infant's skull before the bones have completely merged.

food poisoning acute gastrointestinal distress caused by ingestion of food containing toxic bacteria or chemical residues.

foot *pl.* **feet** the terminal part of a vertebrate leg that serves as support for standing; the part of the leg below the ankle.

foot-and-mouth disease an acute, contagious, febrile disease of viral origin affecting chiefly cloven-footed animals and marked by ulcerating vesicles in the mouth and about the hoofs. Also called *hoof-and-mouth disease.*

foramen *pl.* **foramina** a natural opening or hole, esp. in bone, for the passage of nerves, blood vessels, etc.

foramen magnum the large opening at the base of the skull for the passage of the spinal cord.

forceps *pl.* **forceps** any of various instruments used esp. in surgery for lifting, grasping, or holding.

forcipate resembling or shaped like forceps.

forebrain the part of the embryonic brain that develops into the cerebrum and closely related structures.

forensic medicine the branch of medicine concerned with the application of medical information to legal problems, as in proving criminal responsibility in a sudden death or death under unusual circumstances.

foreskin a retractable fold of skin that covers the glans of the penis; prepuce.

formaldehyde a pungent gas used in solution as a disinfectant and tissue preservative for anatomical specimens.

formalin an aqueous solution containing 37 per cent formaldehyde.

formication an abnormal sensation of insects creeping over the skin.

formula *pl.* **formulas** *or* **formulae** 1. prescription. 2. a nutritive mixture for feeding an infant. 3. the symbolic or alphanumeric representation of a chemical molecule.

formulary any collection of chemical formulas for compounding or listing the constituents of medicinal preparations.

fornix an arch.

fossa *pl.* **fossae** an anatomical pit or depression.

fovea a small pit or cuplike depression; minute fossa.

foxglove digitalis.

fracture the breaking of hard tissue, as bone. —**fracture** *vb.*

frenulum *pl.* **frenula** a membranous fold of tissue, as that under the tongue, serving as a support or restraint; frenum.

frenum *pl.* **frenums** *or* **frena** frenulum.

friable easily broken or reduced to powder; dry and brittle.

frigidity sexual unresponsiveness or indifference on the part of a woman. —**frigid** *adj.*

frontal 1. anterior. 2. relating to or situated on or near the forehead.

frostbite tissue damage resulting from freezing of a part of the body, esp. parts such as the ears, nose, fingers and toes.

frottage sexual arousal generated by rubbing against someone.

frotteur a person who obtains sexual pleasure by means of the sense of touch, esp. by rubbing against someone.

fructose a sugar occurring in honey and in many fruits.

full-term (of a fetus) retained in the uterus for the entire normal duration of pregnancy.

fulminating sudden and severe in onset: *fulminating infections.*

fundus *pl.* **fundi** the part or section of a hollow organ furthest from the natural opening.

fungicide an agent that destroys fungi. —**fungicidal** *adj.*

fungiform (of a structure or part) having a narrow base and a broad or branched upper free area; shaped like a mushroom.

fungus *pl.* **fungi** any of various primitive forms of plant life (including the mushrooms, molds and mildews) characterized by the absence of chlorophyll and living off organic matter.

funiculus any structure shaped like a cord; cordlike.

furuncle a swollen inflammation of the skin; boil.

fusiform spindle-shaped.

G

gag 1. a surgical device for holding the mouth open. 2. to hold (the mouth) open with a gag. 3. to retch.

gait a characteristic manner or style of walking.

galact- *or* **galacto-** *prefix* milk: *galactopoiesis.*

galactacrasia an abnormal composition of breast milk.

galactemia an abnormal condition in which the blood appears milky or cloudy.

galactophagous subsisting on milk.

galactophore a milk duct.

galactophoritis inflammation of a milk duct.

galactopoiesis the production and secretion of milk. —**galactopoietic** *adj.*

galactorrhea the excessive flow of milk.

galactoschesis the retention or inhibition of milk secretion.

galactostasis 1. the inhibition or suppression of milk secretion. 2. an abnormal accumulation of milk within the breast.

galacturia whiteness or milkiness of the urine due to the abnormal presence of chyle or lymph.

galea any structure or part shaped like or resembling a helmet.

galenical 1. relating to or resembling the philosophy and medical teaching of the Greek physician Galen (2nd century A.D.). 2. any therapeutic preparation derived from plants.

galeophilia the abnormal and excessive love of cats.

galeophobia the abnormal fear of cats.

gall secretion of the liver; bile.

gallbladder a pear-shaped membranous sac in which bile from the liver is stored until its release into the small intestine.

gallery the subcutaneous burrow occupied by some metazoan parasites.

galloping consumption a form of tuberculosis that has a rapid course ending in death.

gallop rhythm a sequence of three sounds heard on auscultation of the heart, usually caused by an excessively fast rate of contraction of the ventricles.

gallstone a calculus formed in the gallbladder or in a bile duct.

galvanic relating to or caused by galvanism.

galvanic battery a battery that produces electricity by means of chemical action.

galvanic current the direct current produced by a galvanic battery.

galvanism the therapeutic use of direct current produced by chemical energy in a galvanic battery. —**galvanization** *n.* —**galvanize** *vb.*

galvano- *prefix* direct current electricity.

galvanocautery electrocautery.

galvanochemical electrochemical.

galvanocontractility the ability of a muscle to contract when stimulated by a galvanic current.

galvanolysis electrolysis.

gamete a male or female reproductive cell; spermatozoon or ovum. —**gametic** *adj.*

gametogenesis the production of sperm or ova.

-gamic *suffix* relating to or resulting from sexual union.

gammacism a speech disorder characterized by difficulty in pronouncing correctly words or syllables that contain the letter *g.*

gamma globulin a globulin of serum or plasma that is involved in antibody production.

gamogenesis sexual reproduction.

gamophobia an abnormal fear of marriage.

gangliectomy *also* **ganglionectomy** the surgical removal of a ganglion or of ganglia.

gangliform resembling a ganglion; having the appearence or form of a ganglion or of ganglia.

ganglion *pl.* **ganglia** a mass of nerve tissue esp. if located outside the spinal cord or the brain. 2. a cystic swelling or tumor on a tendon. —**ganglial** *adj.* —**gangliate** *adj.*

ganglioneure a cell in a nerve ganglion.

ganglionitis inflammation of a ganglion or of ganglia.

gangrene necrosis of soft tissues of the body resulting from loss of blood supply.

gargle 1. a liquid for clearing or soothing the throat. 2. to rinse the throat with a gargle.

gas a basic state of matter characterized by free movement of its molecules, which permits it to expand indefinitely or to occupy the entire volume of a container holding it, or to be compressed until it assumes a liquid or eventually solid state.

gaseous relating to or having the properties or nature of gas.

gastr- *or* **gastro-** *or* **gastri-** *prefix* stomach; belly: *gastrectomy.*

gastralgia pain in the stomach; stomach ache.

gastrectomy surgical removal of part or all of the stomach, as in the treatment of severe gastric ulcers.

gastric of, relating to, or affecting the stomach.

gastric ulcer a peptic ulcer of the stomach.

gastritis inflammation of the mucous lining of the stomach.

gastroatonia loss of normal muscle tone in the stomach.

gastrocardiac relating to or involving both the stomach and the heart.

gastrocele a hernia of the stomach.

gastrocolitis inflammation of both the stomach and the colon.

gastrocolostomy the surgical formation of an artificial opening between the stomach and the colon.

gastrocolotomy surgical incision into the stomach and the colon.

gastroduodenal relating to or involving both the stomach and duodenum.

gastroenteritis inflammation of the stomach and intestines.

gastroenterology the branch of medical science concerned with the study and treatment of diseases of the stomach and intestines. —**gastroenterologist** *n.*

gastrointestinal of, relating to, or affecting the stomach and intestines.

gastrology the branch of medical science concerned with the study and treatment of diseases of the stomach (a part of gastroenterology).

gastromalacia abnormal softening of the walls of the stomach.

gastroscope an instrument for viewing and examining the interior of the stomach. —**gastroscopist** *n.* —**gastroscopy** *n.*

gastrosplenic relating to or involving both the stomach and the spleen.

gastrostomy the surgical formation of an artificial opening through the wall of the stomach.

gather (of a boil or furuncle) to form or ooze pus; come to a head.

gathering 1. the formation and accumulation of pus in a boil or abscess. 2. a localized collection of pus in a boil or abscess.

gauss a unit of the intensity of a magnetic field.

gauze a loosely woven fabric used for dressing wounds.

gavage feeding by means of a tube inserted through the nose and into the stomach; direct gastric feeding.

gene a tiny particle usually occurring in pairs on a chromosome and responsible for transmitting hereditary traits and characteristics from one generation to the next.

genetic *also* **genetical** of or relating to genetics.

genetics the branch of science concerned with the various aspects of heredity and the natural development of an organism. —**geneticist** *n.*

geniculate *also* **geniculated** (of a structure or part) bent like a knee.

geniculum any small structure bent like a knee or having a knotlike appearance.

genioplasty plastic surgery involving the chin or cheek.

genital relating to reproduction or the organs of reproduction: *genital organs.*

genitalia the reproductive organs; genitals.

genitals the reproductive organs: the penis and testes in the male and the vulva (external genitals), vagina, uterus, fallopian tubes and ovaries in the female.

genitourinary relating to reproduction and urination or to the organs responsible for these functions; urogenital.

genu 1. the knee. 2. any structure or part resembling a bent knee.

genu valgum knock knee (knees that bend inward).

genu varum bowleg (knees that bend outward).

genus *pl.* **genera** a group of related species, the distinct members of which are not usually able to interbreed.

geopathology the study of diseases in relation to different geographical characteristics, such as climate and terrain.

geriatric relating to old age or to the elderly.

geriatrician a physician who specializes in the practice of geriatrics.

geriatrics the branch of medical science concerned with the study and treatment of diseases in the elderly.

germ any microorganism, esp. one capable of causing disease; microbe.

German measles a viral infection common in children and accompanied by a typical skin eruption, milder than true measles (morbilli) but potentially dangerous to the developing fetus of a pregnant woman not previously exposed to the disease. Compare *measles.*

germ cell an ovum or spermatozoon.

germicide an agent capable of destroying germs. —**germicidal** *adj.*

gerontology the branch of medical science concerned with the study of the process of aging and the social and health problems of the elderly.

gestation the developmental period within the womb from conception (fertilization of the ovum) until birth, averaging 266 days. Also called *gestation period.*

gigantism enlargement of the entire body or a limb as the result of overproduction of growth hormone by the pituitary gland before puberty, rarely producing a human giant up to eight feet tall. Compare *acromegaly.*

gingiva the gums.

gingivectomy surgical removal of some of the tissues of the gums, as in the management of severe infection (pyorrhea).

gingivitis inflammation of the gums.

gland a cell or collection of cells that produces specialized substances (secretions) from materials in the blood which are either used by the body or eliminated as waste matter.

glandular fever an acute infectious disease caused by a virus. Also called *infectious mononucleosis.*

glans *pl.* **glandes** the bulbous, vascular extremity of the penis or the clitoris.

glaucoma an eye disease marked by increased pressure within the eyeball and gradual loss of vision.

globulin any of a group of simple proteins occurring in animal and plant tissue, the best known of which is gamma globulin (important in the production of antibodies).

glossal of or relating to the tongue.

glossitis inflammation of the tongue.

glottis the two vocal cords and the space between them, concerned with sound production.

glucose a colorless, soluble sugar that occurs widely in nature and is produced naturally in the body by the breakdown of dietary starch.

gluteal of or relating to the buttocks or the gluteus muscles.

gluten a protein substance in cereals, responsible for a digestive disease (celiac disease) in children who are hypersensitive to it.

gluteus muscle any of the large muscles forming the buttocks.

glycerin *also* **glycerol** a sweet syrupy alcohol produced by the saponification of fats and used esp. as a solvent.

glycogen the carbohydrate that provides the body with a reserve of energy and heat, stored in the liver and converted into glucose on demand by active muscles.

glycosuria the abnormal presence of sugar in the urine, one sign of diabetes mellitus.

goiter *also* **goitre** abnormal enlargement of the thyroid gland.

gonad one of the sex glands; an ovary or testis. —**gondal** *adj.*

gonadotrophin any of several hormones that stimulate the ovaries or testes.

gonococcus a bacterium that causes gonorrhea. —**gonococcal** *or* **gonococcic** *adj.*

gonorrhea a contagious bacterial disease typically characterized by inflammation of the urethra, urinary frequency, a burning sensation during urination and a discharge of pus from the penis or vagina, transmitted mainly during sexual intercourse with an infected partner (venereal disease). Also called *clap.*

gout a metabolic disorder characterized by excessive deposits of crystals of uric acid (urate) in the tissues and marked by painful swelling of the joints, esp. of the big toe. Also called *gouty arthritis.* —**gouty** *adj.*

Graafian follicle a small sac in an ovary that contains an ovum, one follicle rupturing each month during menstruation to release a mature ovum.

grand mal the most severe form of epilepsy.

granuloma a nodule or mass of chronically inflamed tissue.

gravel a mass of small concretions in the kidneys or bladder.

gravid pregnant.

gray matter *or* **grey matter** unmyelinated nerve cells and fibers of the brain and spinal cord, having a grayish color.

greenstick fracture a bone fracture in which the bone is partially fractured and partially bent.

grippe influenza. —**grippy** *adj.*

groin the area of the lower abdomen at the juncture of the legs with the trunk.

growing pains nonspecific pains often occurring in the legs of children.

gullet esophagus.

gumma a rubbery tumor that can appear anywhere on the body during the third stage of syphilis.

gut intestine.

gynecology the branch of medical science concerned with the diagnosis and treatment of diseases that affect women, esp. those involving the female reproductive system. —**gynecologist** *n.* —**gynecological** *adj.*

gynecomastia abnormal enlargement of the male breasts.

H

habena *pl.* **habenae** a restricting fibrous band. —**habenular** *adj.*

habit an act or response that has become virtually automatic and is thus difficult to break or interrupt. —**habitual** *adj.*

habituation a psychological dependence, esp. on drugs for which the user has an abnormal or compulsive craving or desire.

habitus the physical characteristics of an individual that are thought to play a role in the tendency to be affected by certain diseases or disorders.

hacking cough a short, frequent and usually dry (nonproductive) cough.

haem- *or* **haemo-** *prefix* hem-.

hagiotherapy therapy that depends on religious convictions, as when a sick person submits to religious rituals, goes on pilgrimages, touches sacred relics, etc.

hairball trichobezoar.

halation blurring of vision by strong light coming directly in front of or behind the viewed object or scene.

halethazole an antiseptic agent that is also effective against some species of fungus.

half-life the period of time taken for a radioactive isotope to lose half of its activity through disintegration.

half-way house a center or institution for housing patients who no longer require intensive medical or psychiatric care but who are not yet ready to resume normal social activities or employment within the community.

halide a salt or compound of a halogen.

haliphagia the ingestion of abnormally large quantities of a salt or salts, esp. of sodium chloride (common table salt) or sodium bicarbonate (a common antacid).

halisteresis a deficiency of calcium in the bones; osteomalacia. —**halisteretic** *adj.*

halitosis a condition of having foul breath.

halitus an expired breath; exhaled vapor.

hallex hallux.

hallucination 1. the perception of objects or sounds having no basis in reality and commonly arising from a nervous disorder, fatigue, or the use of a drug. 2. the objects or sounds so perceived. —**hallucinate** *vb.* —**hallucinatory** *adj.*

hallucinogen a drug, as LSD, inducing hallucinations. —**hallucinogenic** *adj.*

hallucinosis a severe mental disorder characterized by persistent or recurring hallucinations.

hallux *pl.* **halluces** the great toe; first digit of the foot. —**hallucal** *adj.*

hallux valgus a deformity of the big toe in which it bends over or beneath the adjacent toe.

hallux varus a deformity of the big toe in which it bends toward the inner side of the foot away from the adjacent toe.

haloderma a skin disorder caused by the ingestion of halides such as iodides and bromides.

halogen any of the elements fluorine, chlorine, bromine and iodine that combine with metals to form salts and with hydrogen to form acids. —**halogenous** *adj.*

halogenation the altering of the physical and therapeutic properties of a molecule by the incorporation of halogen atoms in its structure.

haloid resembling salt or a halogen.

halophil *also* **halophile** any microorganism that needs a high concentration of salt for enhanced growth. —**halophilic** *adj.*

haloprogin an antifungal agent.

halothane a general anesthetic developed by British chemists in the 1950s for its nonirritant and nonflammable properties.

ham the buttock and posterior part of the thigh.

hamartophobia an abnormal fear of error or of committing a sin.

hamate having a hook; hooked.

hammer malleus; one of the three small conducting bones of the middle ear.

hammertoe a deformity of a toe characterized by permanent angular flexion.

hamstring either of two groups of tendons at the back of the knee.

hamstring muscle any of the three muscles at the back of the thigh that extend the thigh when the leg is flexed.

hamular having the shape of a hook; hook-shaped.

hamulus any hooklike structure or part.

hangnail a small piece of partially detached skin at the base of a nail, esp. of a fingernail.

Hansen's disease leprosy.

hapalonychia lack of firmness or rigidity of the nails.

haphalgesia abnormal sensitivity of the skin to pain when touched lightly.

haphephobia abnormal dislike or fear of being touched by another person.

haplopia normal, single vision. Compare *diplopia.*

hapten *also* **haptene** an incomplete antigen capable of stimulating antibody formation only when covalently linked to protein.

haptodysphoria an unpleasant tactile sensation.

haptometer an instrument for measuring a person's sensitivity to touch.

harelip a congenital deformity in which the center of the upper lip is marked by a vertical fissure like that of a hare, often associated with cleft palate.

Hashimoto's disease chronic inflammation of the thyroid gland.

hashish resin obtained from the flowering tops of the female hemp plant (*Cannabis sativa*) and chewed or smoked for its hallucinogenic effect. Also called *charas, hash.*

haustus a medicinal potion.

hay fever acute allergic rhinitis and sometimes conjunctivitis caused typically by exposure of a hypersensitive person to pollens and dust.

headache pain or aching in the head. —**headachy** *adj.*

headshrinker *Slang* psychiatrist; psychoanalyst.

heal to make or become sound and whole.

health the condition of being sound in body and mind; freedom from pain or illness. —**healthy** *adj.*

health officer an official responsible for health and sanitation laws.

heart a hollow muscular organ that acts by rhythmic contraction to pump the blood through the circulatory system of the body.

heart attack an acute episode of dysfunctioning of the heart.

heart block irregularity in the rhythm of the heart resulting in decreased cardiac output.

heartburn a burning sensation at the lower end of the esophagus; pyrosis.

heart failure a condition in which the heart cannot pump blood at an adequate rate or in adequate volume to sustain life.

heart-lung machine a machine used for maintenance of oxygenation and circulation of the blood while the heart is stopped during heart surgery.

heart murmur an abnormal murmuring sound heard through the chest wall.

heat exhaustion a condition marked by nausea, weakness, dizziness, and sweating that results from exertion in a very warm climate and from the loss of sodium chloride from the body.

heat prostration heat exhaustion.

heatstroke heat exhaustion.

hebephrenia schizophrenia marked chiefly by childish behavior, hallucinations, and regressive response. —**hebephreniac** *n.* —**hebephrenic** *adj.*

hebetic relating to youth.

hebetude emotional disinterest; lethargy.

hebosteotomy surgical enlargement of the opening of the bony pelvis to facilitate childbirth.

hederiform (of specific sensory nerve endings in the skin) ivy-shaped.

hedonophobia an abnormal fear of pleasure or of having fun.

hedrocele prolapse of part of the intestine through the anus; proctocele.

helcoid resembling an ulcer.

helcoplasty the repair of ulcers by the use of skin grafts, being a form of dermatoplasty.

helcosis the development of an ulcer; ulceration.

helicine relating to a coil or helix; spiral.

helicoid resembling a helix or spiral.

heliencephalitis inflammation of the brain as a consequence of sunstroke.

helioaerotherapy treatment involving exposure to sunlight and fresh air.

heliopathy any injury incurred as a result of exposure to sunlight.

heliophobia an abnormal fear of being exposed to the rays of the sun.

heliosis sunstroke.

heliotherapy treatment by exposure to sunlight.

helix *pl.* **helices** *also* **helixes** 1. the inward-curving rim of the outer ear. 2. one of the two coiled strands forming the structure of DNA.

THE HEART

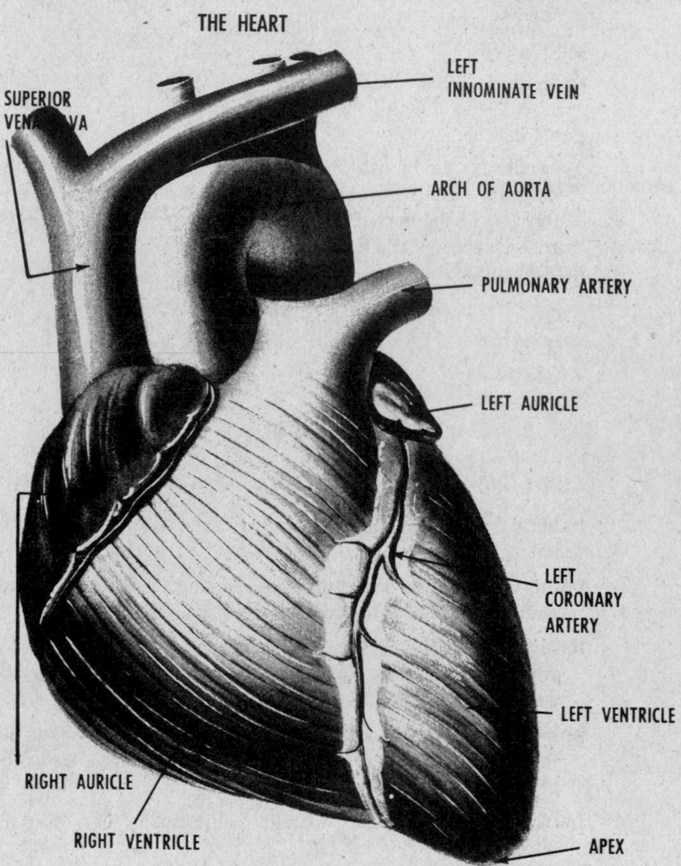

helminth a parasitic worm esp. of the intestine. —**helminthic** *adj.*

helminthiasis infestation with parasitic worms.

helminthoid wormlike.

helminthology the study of parasitic worms.

heloma a corn.

helosis the condition of having corns on the feet or toes.

helotomy the surgical removal of a corn or corns.

hem- *or* **hemo-** *or* **haem-** *or* **haemo-** *prefix* blood.

hema- *or* **haema-** *prefix* blood.

hemachrosis unusual redness of the blood.

hemadostenosis a narrowing or contraction of the arteries.

hemagglutinate to cause agglutination of red blood cells. —**hemagglutination** *n.*

hemagglutinin an agent that causes hemagglutination.

hemagogue 1. promoting or enhancing the flow of blood. 2. an agent that promotes the flow of blood.

hemal relating to, involving, or affecting the blood or blood vessels.

hemanalysis laboratory examination or analysis of a sample of blood.

hemangio- *prefix* relating to or involving the blood vessels.

hemangioma a benign tumor made up of blood vessels.

hemarthrosis the abnormal presence of blood in a joint.

hematemesis the vomiting of blood or food mixed with blood.

hemathermal *also* **hemathermous** warm blooded.

hemathidrosis *also* **hematidrosis** an abnormal condition in which a person's sweat contains traces of blood.

hematic 1. relating to the blood. 2. any drug used in the treatment of anemia.

hematimeter a device used to count the number of blood cells in one cubic millimeter of blood.

hematin the portion of the hemoglobin molecule containing iron in the ferric state.

hematinemia the presence of heme in the circulating blood.

hematinic 1. relating to the blood. 2. any agent that increases the concentration of hemoglobin or the number of red blood cells in the circulating blood, used in the treatment of anemia.

hematinuria the abnormal presence of heme in the urine.

hematischesis the control or arrest of bleeding.

hematobium any parasite that lives in the blood.

hematoblast an immature or primitive cell from which all blood cells are derived. Also called *hemocytoblast.*

hematocele 1. a blood cyst. 2. the abnormal accumulation of blood within a bodily canal or cavity. 3. a swelling caused by effusion of blood into the sheath surrounding a testicle.

hematocelia bleeding into the peritoneal cavity.

hematochezia the passage of feces containing blood.

hematochyluria the abnormal presence of both blood and chyle in the urine.

hematocolpometra the accumulation of menstrual blood in the uterus and vagina, usually due to an obstruction of normal outflow by an intact hymen.

hematocrit 1. a centrifuge for separating the solid constituents of a blood sample from the plasma. 2. the percentage (by volume) of red blood cells in a sample of blood that has been centrifuged (which causes the cells to become packed in one end of the test tube or other container).

hematocystis an abnormal effusion of blood into the urinary bladder.

hematocyturia the presence of red blood cells (rather than just hemoglobin) in the urine. Compare *hemoglobinuria.*

hematogenesis the production of blood cells; hemopoiesis. **—hematogenic** *adj.* **—hematogenous** *adj.*

hematoglobin *also* **hematoglobulin** hemoglobin.

hematoid resembling blood; bloody; sanguineous.

hematology the study of the structure, functions, and diseases of blood and blood-forming tissues. **—hematologist** *n.*

hematoma *pl.* **hematomas** *or* **hematomata** a swelling or tumor composed of clotted blood.

hematometra an accumulation of blood within the cavity of the uterus.

hematomyelia bleeding into the substance of the spinal cord, usually as a response to injury.

hematopenia a deficiency in the size or number of the blood cells.

hematophagous (esp. of certain insects) surviving on a diet of blood.

hematophagia 1. (esp. of leeches or animals such as vampire bats) subsistence on the blood of other animals. 2. the drinking of blood as a supposed means of curing a disease or disorder.

hematopsia bleeding into the eye.

hematorrhachis bleeding of or into the spine; spinal hemorrhage.

hematosalpinx the abnormal accumulation of blood within a bodily tube, esp. a fallopian tube.

hematoscheocele the abnormal accumulation of blood within the cavity of the scrotum.

hematospectroscopy the examination of a sample of blood with the use of a spectroscope.

hematuria the presence of blood or blood cells in the urine.

heme the portion of hemoglobin that carries oxygen and gives the blood its characteristic color.

hemeralopia reduced visual capacity in the presence of bright light.

hemi- *prefix* one half.

hemiopalgia pain in one eye, usually associated with migraine.

hemiplegia paralysis of one side of the body. **—hemiplegic** *adj.*

hemochromatosis an iron metabolism disorder characterized by bronzing of the skin from iron-containing pigments deposited in the tissues.

hemodialysis purification or filtration of the blood, as with an artificial kidney, through dialysis.

hemoglobin an iron-containing respiratory pigment in the red blood cells.

hemoglobinemia the presence of free hemoglobin in the blood plasma.

hemoglobinuria the presence of free hemoglobin in the urine. **—hemoglobinuric** *adj.*

hemolysin a substance causing the breakdown of red blood cells.

hemolysis the breakdown or destruction of red blood cells. **—hemolytic** *adj.*

hemophilia a hereditary blood defect of males marked by delayed clotting of the blood and a tendency to hemorrhage after the slightest injury. **—hemophiliac** *n. & adj.* **—hemophilic** *adj.*

hemopoiesis the production of blood or blood cells in the body.

hemoptysis the coughing or spitting up of blood or sputum mixed with blood.

hemorrhage a heavy outpouring of blood from the blood vessels. **—hemorrhage** *vb.* **—hemorrhagic** *adj.*

hemorrhoids varicose dilation of veins near or at the anal sphincter. Also called *piles.* **—hemorrhoidal** *adj.*

hemostasis 1. the arresting of bleeding. 2. stagnation of the blood.

hemostat a surgical clamp for compressing a blood vessel that is bleeding.

hemostatic 1. stopping hemorrhage. 2. an agent that stops hemorrhage.

hemotoxin any substance, esp. one of biological origin, that causes destruction of red blood cells.

hemp a plant, *Cannabis sativa,* whose dried flower heads yield the drug hashish.

heparin a polysaccharide acid ester occurring esp. in the liver and useful in prolonging blood clotting time, as in the treatment of thrombosis and embolism.

hepat- *or* **hepato-** *prefix* 1. liver. 2. hepatic.

hepatalgia pain in the liver.

hepatatrophia *also* **hepatatrophy** a wasting away or atrophy of the liver.

hepatectomy surgical excision of part of the liver. **—hepatectomize** *vb.*

hepatic relating to, resembling, or affecting the liver.

hepatitis inflammation of the liver.

hepatocele herniation of part of the liver through the diaphragm or the abdominal wall.

hepatography X-ray photography of the liver.

hepatolithiasis the presence of calculi in the liver.

hepatologist an expert on the liver and the treatment of diseases that affect it.

hepatology the branch of medical science concerned with the liver and the diagnosis and treatment of diseases that affect it.

hepatoma a tumor of the liver.

hepatomegaly abnormal enlargement of the liver.

hepatopathy any disease of the liver.

hepatosplenomegaly abnormal enlargement of both the liver and spleen.

hepatotoxic capable of causing toxic damage to the liver. **—hepatotoxicity** *n.*

hereditary genetically transmittable or transmitted from generation to generation; inheritable or inherited.

heredity the sum of the genetic characteristics transmitted from one generation to the next chiefly through the chromosomes of the germ cells.

hermaphrodite one having sexual tissues or genitals of both sexes. **—hermaphroditic** *adj.* **—hermaphroditism** *n.*

hernia *pl.* **hernias** *or* **herniae** the protrusion of an organ or part through the wall or cavity within which it is normally contained. Also called *rupture.* **—hernial** *adj.*

herniate to develop a hernia.

heroin a narcotic drug obtained from morphine, formerly used as an antitussive but now rendered illegal in the U.S. because of its addictive properties and potential for abuse.

herpes any of various inflammatory viral diseases marked by clusters of vesicles. **—herpetic** *adj.*

herpes simplex a viral disease marked by clusters of watery vesicles on the mucous membranes chiefly of the lips, mouth, or genitals.

herpes zoster shingles.

hexachlorophene an antibacterial agent used in some soaps and detergents.

hexylresorcinol a broad-spectrum drug used in the treatment of worm infestations.

hiatus any gap, opening or fissure.

hiatus hernia *also* **hiatal hernia** an abnormal condition in which a portion of the top part of the stomach protrudes up through a gap in the diaphragm.

hiccup *also* **hiccough** repeated spasmodic inhalation of the breath accompanied by closure of the glottis and by a characteristic explosive sound. **—hiccup** *or* **hiccough** *vb.*

hidrosis the secretion of sweat; perspiration. **—hidrotic** *adj.*

high *Slang* intoxicated with drugs or alcohol. **—high** *n.*

hindbrain the division of the embryonic brain that develops into the cerebellum, pons, and medulla oblongata.

hip the upper part of the thigh.

hip joint the articulation between the innominate bone and the femur.

Hippocratic oath an oath traditionally taken by those entering medical practice that embraces a code of medical ethics attributed to the Greek physician Hippocrates, born about 460 B.C. and known as the "Father of Medicine".

hirsute 1. having hair; hairy. 2. relating to hirsutism.

hirsutism pronounced or excessive growth of hair esp. on the body.

histamine a compound found esp. in animal tissue and in ergot that causes dilation of the blood vessels in many allergic reactions. **—histaminic** *adj.*

histogenesis the formation and differentiation of animal tissues. **—histogenetic** *adj.*

histology a branch of anatomy dealing with the microscopic study of tissues. **—histological** *adj.*

histolysis the disintegration or degeneration of tissues.

hives urticaria.

Hodgkin's disease a neoplastic disease that is marked chiefly by enlargement of the lymph glands, liver, and spleen and by progressive anemia.

homeopath a practitioner of homeopathy.

homeopathy the treatment of a disease by administering minute doses of a substance or agent that in large doses in a healthy person would produce symptoms of the disease itself. **—homeopathic** *adj.*

homeostasis the automatic self-regulation of bodily functions under environmental variations, resulting in a basic balance or equilibrium of temperature, blood pressure, water content, blood sugar, etc.

homoerotic homosexual. **—homoeroticism** *n.*

homologous having the same relative position, structure, or function.

homosexual relating to or practicing homosexuality. **—homosexual** *n.*

homosexuality sexual desire toward or sexual activity practiced with members of one's own sex.

hookworm a parasitic nematode worm that attaches to the intestinal wall of the host and is a serious bloodsucking pest.

hormone a chemical substance secreted directly into the bloodstream by the endocrine glands which has a specific effect on cells remote from its point of origin. **—hormonal** *adj.*

housemaid's knee a swelling of the knee due to enlargement of the bursa in front of the patella and caused typically by prolonged kneeling on a hard surface or substance.

humerus the bone of the upper arm.

hydr- *or* **hydro-** *prefix* water.

hydrocephalus *also* **hydrocephaly** an abnormal increase in the amount of cerebrospinal fluid in the cranium resulting in enlargement of the skull and atrophy of the brain.

hydrophobia rabies.

hydrotherapy the scientific use of water in treating disease. **—hydrotherapeutic** *adj.*

hygiene the science and practice of maintaining good health. **—hygienic** *adj.*

hymen a membranous fold partially closing the entrance to the vagina; maidenhead. **—hymeneal** *adj.*

hyper- *prefix* excessive; above.

hyperacidity excessively acid. **—hyperacid** *adj.*

hypersensitive abnormally susceptible to a drug, antigen, or other agent. **—hypersensitivity** *n.*

hypertension blood pressure exceeding normal limits.

hypnosis a state resembling sleep that is induced by a hypnotist and in which the subject readily responds to suggestion. —**hypnotist** *n.* —**hypnotize** *vb.*

hypnotic 1. tending to induce sleep; soporific. 2. an agent that induces sleep.

hypo- *or* **hyp-** *prefix* 1. under; down. 2. less than normal.

hypochondria a depressed state of mind often centering on concern for imaginary illnesses. —**hypochondriac** *n.* & *adj.* —**hypochondriacal** *adj.*

hypochondriasis hypochondria.

hypodermic 1. relating to the parts beneath the skin. 2. adapted for injection beneath the skin: *hypodermic needle.*

hysterectomy surgical removal of the uterus.

hysteria a psychoneurotic disorder marked by extreme excitability and disturbances of various psychic and physical functions.

I

iatrology medical science.

ichthyoid shaped like a fish.

ichthyophagy the habit or practice of subsisting on fish.

ichthyophobia an abnormal fear of fish, whether living or dead.

ichthyosis a dry, scaly skin condition.

ichthyotoxin a toxic substance found in the roe of certain fishes.

ichthyotoxism poisoning caused by eating toxic fish roe, characterized by disorders of the nervous system and gastrointestinal tract.

ICSH *abbr.* interstitial cell-stimulating hormone.

ictal relating to or caused by a seizure or stroke.

icteric relating to or characterized by jaundice (icterus).

ictero- *prefix* relating to jaundice (icterus).

icterogenic causing jaundice.

icterohematuric relating to jaundice associated with blood in the urine.

icterohepatitis inflammation of the liver (hepatitis) marked by jaundice.

icterus jaundice.

id (in Freudian theory of psychoanalysis) one of the three basic divisions of the psyche, considered to be the most primitive part of the personality and accounting for simple drives and instinctive behaviour. Compare *ego, superego.*

identical twins monozygotic twins.

idiocy a condition of severely marked low intellectual capacity, typically with a functional IQ below 75.

idiopathic relating to any state or condition of unknown cause: *idiopathic disease.*

idiot one marked with idiocy.

ileitis inflammation of the ileum.

ileostomy the surgical construction of a communicating passage through the abdominal wall to the ileum.

ileum the distal section of the small intestine.

ilium the upper part of the innominate bone.

imbecility a condition of marked mental incapacity. —**imbecile** *n.*

immunity a condition of resistance to infection.

immunization the procedure or technique of bringing about or increasing a state of immunity in an individual, as by the injection of a vaccine or other agent into the body or taking an oral substance that provides protection against a specific disease.

immunosuppressive 1. relating to any of various drugs that act to suppress the body's natural immune response, used esp. to permit the surgical transplant of a foreign organ or tissue by inhibiting its biological rejection. 2. a drug with this action.

immunotherapy therapy aimed at the production of immunity in the patient.

immunotoxin any antitoxin.

impacted pressed or jammed together or against something else: *impacted teeth.*

impaction the state or condition of being impacted.

impalpable incapable of being detected by means of the sense of touch.

impaludism malaria.

imparidigitate possessing an odd number of toes or fingers.

impatent not open or patent; closed.

imperception the inability to form a mental image of an object subjected to the senses; inadequate or insufficient perception.

imperforate lacking an opening; closed. —**imperforation** *n.*

impermeable not capable of being penetrated; impervious to fluids.

impetigo a contagious skin rash.

implant 1. to graft or insert. 2. the material grafted or inserted. —**implantation** *n.*

impotence *also* **impotency** inability in the male to achieve erection of the penis. —**impotent** *adj.*

impotentia impotence.

impregnate 1. to cause to conceive. 2. to fill or permeate with some other substance; saturate. —**impregnation** *n.*

impressio *pl.* **impressiones** an indentation or impression apparently made by the pressure of one structure or part upon another.

impulsive relating to actions or behavior actuated by an impulse rather than conscious thought or reason.

imus (or a structure or part compared with a similar neighbor) lowermost; being most caudal or inferior.

inanition extreme weakness or lack of strength and drive due to dietary insufficiency or failure of the digestive system to assimilate food.

inappetence absence of craving or desire; lethargy.

inarticulate unable to speak or communicate clearly or intelligibly.

in articulo mortis at the time of death.

incise to cut with a knife or knife-like instrument.

incision 1. a separation or division of soft tissue with a scalpel or other knife-like instrument. 2. a cut or surgical wound.

incisura incision.

incisure a notch or incision.

incontinence inability of the body to control the elimination of urine (urinary incontinence) or feces (fecal incontinence). —**incontinent** *adj.*

incrustation the formation over a healing wound of a crust or scab.

incubation 1. the technique or practice of maintaining tissue cultures or microorganisms at a controlled temperature that favors their growth or development. 2. care of a premature baby in an incubator. 3. the period of time from exposure to an infecting microorganism to the first appearance of the signs or symptoms of the disease it causes.

incubator 1. an apparatus in which premature babies are placed and maintained at the optimum temperature and humidity. 2. any container or receptacle for the incubation of tissue cultures or microorganisms.

incubus a nightmare.

incus one of the three tiny conducting bones of the middle ear; anvil.

indigestion difficulty in digesting food or imperfect digestion, characterized by a burning sensation in the stomach or lower part of the esophagus (heartburn) and the formation of gas in the stomach, usually relieved by taking antacids; dyspepsia. **—indigestible** *adj.*

indomethacin a powerful anti-inflammatory drug used in the treatment of rheumatoid arthritis and other forms of joint inflammation.

indurated (of the normally soft tissues of the body) hardened; becoming firm or firmer. **—indurative** *adj.*

inebriant 1. intoxicating. 2. a drug or agent able to cause intoxication or drunkenness. **—inebriation** *n.*

inebriety the chronic consumption of excessive amounts of alcoholic beverages.

inert 1. slow; sluggish. 2. not active. 3. having no therapeutic or pharmacologic properties or action: *an inert chemical.*

in extremis at the point of death.

infant a baby, esp. one less than a year old. **—infancy** *n.*

infanticide the murder of a child.

infantile paralysis poliomyelitis.

infarct a necrotic area in an organ or tissue resulting from circulatory blockage. **—infarction** *n.* **—infarcted** *adj.*

infection invasion of the body by pathogenic organisms or the clinical signs and symptoms of such an invasion. **—infectious** *adj.*

infectious hepatitis an acute viral inflammation of the liver marked by fever, jaundice, and nausea.

infectious mononucleosis an acute infectious viral disease primarily affecting the lymph glands, which become swollen and tender. Also called *glandular fever.*

infecundity the inability of a woman to conceive; female sterility or barrenness.

inferior (of a structure or part) situated lower or below another structure or part; caudal.

inferiority complex acute feelings of lack of personal worth typically manifested in timidity or in overagressiveness resulting from overcompensation.

infertility the inability to conceive or father offspring. **—infertile** *adj.*

infirm weak or feeble, esp. as the result of old age or a debilitating illness. **—infirmity** *n.*

infirmary a small hospital or medical center for the care and treatment of the ill or infirm, esp. one attached to a school or college.

inflammation the changes that take place in tissues in response to local damage, typically characterized by pain, heat, swelling, reddening and an interruption of function in the affected area.

inflammatory relating to or characterized by inflammation: *inflammatory disease.*

influenza an acute contagious viral disease affecting esp. the respiratory tract. **—influenzal** *adj.*

infraction *also* **infracture** a fracture, esp. one in which the broken bones are not displaced.

infrahyoid (of certain muscles) situated below the hyoid bone.

infundibulum any funnel-shaped structure or part, esp. the stalk-like extension by which the pituitary gland is attached to the base of the brain.

ingest to introduce food or drink into the stomach through the mouth. **—ingestion** *n.* **—ingestive** *adj.*

inguinal relating to or located near the groin.

inhale to breathe in; take air or gas into the lungs. **—inhalation** *n.*

inhalation therapy the therapeutic use of a nebulized solution of drugs or other therapeutic agents which the patient breathes in.

inject to introduce (fluid) into the body by means of a syringe. **—injection** *n.*

innervate to supply with nerves. **—innervation** *n.*

inquest a judicial inquiry into the causes of a death.

insanity a deranged state of the mind; madness. **—insane** *adj.*

inseminate to introduce semen into the vagina or uterus of.

insemination the deposition of semen within the vagina during sexual intercourse or introduced artificially (artificial insemination).

insensible 1. not appreciable by the senses. 2. not conscious.

insidious developing for a period before being detected: *insidious disease.*

in situ in a natural or original position.

insomnia inability to fall or stay asleep. **—insomniac** *n.*

inspiration the act of inhaling; inhalation.

insulin a hormone secreted by the islets of Langerhans in the pancreas and crucial to the metabolism of carbohydrates, also used in the treatment and control of diabetes mellitus.

insulinemia the presence of an abnormally large amount of insulin in the circulating blood.

insulin shock coma resulting from excessive amounts of insulin in the system.

insuloma a tumor of the islets of Langerhans of the pancreas (an adenoma).

integument an enveloping membrane or skin.

intelligence quotient a number indicating the apparent intelligence level of a person and arrived at by dividing the mental age by the chronological age and multiplying by 100. Also called *IQ.*

inter- *prefix* between; among.

intergyral between the convolutions (gyri) of the cerebral cortex.

intern a recent graduate of a medical school undergoing training at a hospital, usually for a period of one year, before becoming fully qualified to practice.

internal medicine a branch of medicine dealing with the diagnosis and treatment of diseases not requiring surgery, esp. those involving the internal organs of the chest and abdomen.

internist a physician specializing in internal medicine.

internuncial (of a neuron) connecting two other neurons.

interstitial situated between the cellular components of an organ or part.

intestinal relating to, affecting, or occurring in the intestine.

intestine the tubular section of the alimentary canal extending from the stomach to the anus.

intima *pl.* **intimae** *or* **intimas** the innermost coat of an organ or artery.

intimitis inflammation of an intima.

intolerance exceptional sensitivity, as to a drug or medication.

intra- *prefix* 1. between. 2. during. 3. inward; within.

intracardiac occurring or existing within the heart.

intracranial occurring or existing within the cranium.

intradermal occurring, accomplished, or situated within the layers of the skin.

intrauterine device a device, as a metal or plastic coil or loop, inserted and left in the uterus to prevent conception. Also called *intrauterine contraceptive device; IUCD; IUD.*

intravenous within a vein: *intravenous injection.*

introvert one whose interests and concerns center primarily on the self. —**introverted** *adj.* —**introversion** *n.*

intubation the insertion of a tube into a hollow organ, as the trachea. —**intubate** *vb.*

intussusception the abnormal infolding of one segment of the intestine within another segment. —**intussusceptive** *adj.*

in utero within the uterus.

involution 1. a turning inward or rolling over of a rim. 2. any backward or retrograde change. 3. the shrinking back to normal size of the uterus after childbirth. 4. a physical decline in bodily vigor, as that associated with menopause in women.

iodide a compound, as a salt, of iodine.

iodinate to combine or treat with iodine.

iodine a nonmetallic element of the halogen group, essential in minute amounts in the diet (as in iodized table salt) for the proper development and functioning of the thyroid gland.

iodize to impregnate or treat with iodine.

ion an atom or atom group containing a positive or negative charge of electricity.

IQ intelligence quotient.

iridectomy surgical removal of part of the iris of the eye.

iridemia bleeding from the iris.

iris the pigmented diaphragm surrounding the pupil of the eye.

iritis inflammation of the iris of the eye.

iron a metallic element essential in the diet for the prevention of iron-deficiency anemia, the production of hemoglobin, and as an essential component of certain enzymes.

irrigation the washing out or cleansing of a structure or part with water or other fluid. —**irrigate** *vb.*

irritant 1. tending to produce physical irritation. 2. something that irritates.

irritation a state of soreness or inflammation or irritability or overexcitation.

ischemia *also* **ischaemia** inadequate blood supply to an organ or part due to obstruction or constriction of the blood vessels. —**ischemic** *adj.*

ischium *pl.* **ischia** the posterior dorsal bone of the pelvis.

islets of Langerhans any of the groups of endocrine cells within the pancreas that secrete insulin.

isometrics a system of exercises stressing the contraction of opposing muscles in such a way that shortening is minimal but the increase in muscle fiber tone is great.

isthmus a contracted or restricted anatomical part connecting two larger bodily parts.

itching a persistent irritation of the cutaneous tissues that causes an urge to scratch and that is often held to result from mild stimulation of pain receptors. —**itch** *vb. & n.*

IUCD intrauterine contraceptive device.

IUD intrauterine device.

J

jactitation extreme restlessness; tossing from one side to the other.

jargon terms or expressions peculiar to a specific activity or field of interest: *medical jargon.*

jaundice yellowing of the skin, body fluids, and tissues resulting from the deposit of bile pigments. —**jaundiced adj.**

jaw either of the two bony structures within the mouth into which the teeth are set, forming an upper and immovable structure (maxilla) and a lower movable structure (mandible).

jejunectomy surgical removal of all or part of the jejunum.

jejunitis inflammation of the jejunum.

jejuno- *also* **jejun-** *prefix* relating to the jejunum.

jejunocolostomy the surgical formation of an artificial opening between the jejunum and the colon.

jejunoileal relating to both the jejunum and the ileum.

jejunoileitis inflammation of both the jejunum and the ileum; inflammation of the small intestine.

jejunojejunostomy the surgical formation of an artificial junction between two portions of the jejunum, as to bypass a diseased or permanently obstructed area.

jejunostomy the surgical formation of an artificial opening between the jejunum and the wall of the abdomen.

jejunotomy surgical incision into the jejunum.

jejunum the part of the small intestine between the duodenum and the ileum. —**jejunal** *adj.*

joint a point of articulation between two or more bones.

jugular 1. of or relating to the throat or the neck. 2. a jugular vein.

jugular vein either of two large veins in the neck that return blood from the head.

jugulum the neck or throat.

jugum *pl.* **juga** 1. a ridge connecting two points. 2. a type of surgical forceps.

junctura a joint; articulation.

K

kabure a form of schistosomiasis occurring in Asia, esp. in Japan.

kainophobia an abnormal fear of things unfamiliar or new; neophobia.

kala-azar a tropical or subtropical infectious disease caused by a species of protozoa (*Leishmania donovani*) and transmitted by the bite of infected sandflies (*Phlebotomus* species).

kaliemia the presence of potassium in the blood.

karyogenesis the formation and development of the nucleus of a cell.

karyokinesis equal division of the nucleus during cell division. —**karyokinetic** *adj.*

karyolysis the dissolution or destruction of the nucleus of a cell or its loss of ability to be stained by basic dyes. —**karyolytic** *adj.*

karyomitosis changes in the nucleus of a cell during cell division or mitosis.

karyomorphism the shape or form of the nucleus of a cell.

karyophage a parasitic protozoan within a cell that destroys its nucleus.

katabolism catabolism.

kathisophobia an abnormal fear of sitting down and remaining still.

kation cation.

keloid a dense scar resulting from growth of connective tissue.

kenophobia an abnormal fear of empty spaces.

keratectomy surgical removal of a portion of the cornea of the eye.

keratiasis the formation on the skin of horny warts.

keratic relating to horn or horny substances.

keratin a sulfur-containing fibrous protein constituting the basis of horny epidermal material, including the hair.

keratinize (of tissues) to make or become horny or hard.

keratitis inflammation of the cornea of the eye.

kerato- *also* **kerat-** *prefix* 1. the cornea. 2. a horny substance.

keratodermatitis inflammation of the horny layer of the skin.

keratogenous producing or causing the development of horny tissue.

keratohelcosis ulceration of the cornea.

keratoiritis inflammation of both the cornea and the iris.

keratolysis 1. periodic shedding of the skin. 2. a loosening of the skin's horny layer. —**keratolytic** *adj.*

keratoma a callus or horny growth.

keratomalacia a result of vitamin A deficiency of early childhood characterized by a softening of the cornea of the eye. Also called *xerotic keratitis.*

keratome a surgical knife for making incisions into the cornea of the eye.

keratometer a special instrument for measuring the curves of the cornea of the eye.

keratomycosis a fungal infection involving the cornea of the eye.

keratonyxis surgical puncture of the cornea.

keratoplasty surgical repair of the cornea.

keratosis any disorder characterized by overgrowth of horny material on the skin. —**keratotic** *adj.*

ketogenesis the generation of ketone bodies, as in diabetes.

ketone an organic compound having a carbonyl group linking two carbon atoms. —**ketonic** *adj.*

ketone body one of the three compounds acetoacetic acid, beta-hydroxybutyric acid, and acetone found in the urine and blood esp. in diabetes mellitus.

ketosis an abnormal increase of ketone bodies, as in diabetes mellitus.

ketosteroid a steroid containing a ketone group.

Kg *abbr.* kilogram.

kidney *pl.* **kidneys** either of a pair of bean-shaped organs, located near the spinal column behind the peritoneum, that excrete waste products of metabolism in the form of urine.

kilo- *prefix* one thousand.

kilogram one thousand grams. Abbr. *kg.*

kinaesthesia *or* **kinaesthesis** kinesthesia.

kinesia motion sickness.

kinesialgia pain caused by muscular activity.

kinesiology the branch of science concerned with the study of muscles, muscle groups, and muscular activity.

kinesioneurosis any functional disorder characterized by muscular spasms or tics.

-kinesis *suffix* movement.

kinesthesia *or* **kinesthesis** sensory awareness of bodily movements, as of muscles. —**kinesthetic** *adj.*

Klebsiella a genus of gram-negative bacteria associated with infections of the respiratory tract.

kleptomania a neurotic compulsion to steal without any economic need. —**kleptomaniac** *n.*

klieg eyes a condition of the eyes characterized by conjunctivitis and excessive watering and caused by prolonged exposure to very bright light.

knee a joint in the mid-part of the leg that connects the femur, tibia, and patella.

kneecap patella.

knee jerk an involuntary forward kick of the lower leg that results normally when the tendon below the patella is tapped lightly.

knock-knee a condition in which the legs turn inward at the knee. —**knock-kneed** *adj.*

knuckle a rounded prominence formed at the joining of two adjacent bones, esp. of a finger.

Koplik's spots a diagnostic sign of measles consisting of the development of tiny white spots on a red base on the inner surface of the cheeks, typically seen just before the appearance of the characteristic skin rash.

Korsakoff's syndrome *or* **Korsakoff's psychosis** an abnormal mental condition that is usually induced by chronic alcoholism and is marked chiefly by disorientation, hallucinations, and amnesia compensated for by confabulation.

kwashiorkor acute malnutrition in the young as the result of a diet low in protein and high in carbohydrates.

kyphosis abnormal curvature of the spine in a backward direction. —**kyphotic** *adj.*

L

labia *pl. of* labium.

labial of or relating to the lips or the labia.

labia majora the two fleshy, fatty outer lips that form the boundaries of the vulva.

labia minora the inner vascular lips of the vulva.

labio- *prefix* relating to lips.

labiochorea a chronic spasm of the lips, frequently presenting difficulty in producing clear speech sounds.

labioclination abnormal inclination of a tooth toward the lips.

labioglossolaryngeal relating to a paralysis affecting the lips, tongue and larynx.

labiomental relating to the lower lip and the extremity of the chin.

labiomycosis any fungal infection involving the lips.

labiopalatine relating to both the lips and the palate or roof of the mouth.

labioplacement (of a tooth or teeth) abnormal positioning toward the lips.

labor 1. the physiological activities that take place in the process of giving birth. 2. the period during which this takes place.

labrum *pl.* **labra** a lip or any structure or part shaped like or resembling a lip or lips.

labyrinth the bony and membranous structures that constitute the inner ear.

labyrinthectomy surgical removal of the labyrinth of the inner ear.

labyrinthitis inflammation of the labyrinth of the inner ear.

labyrinthotomy surgical incision into the labyrinth of the inner ear.

lacerate to tear roughly or jaggedly.

laceration a ragged, torn wound.

lacertus 1. any band of muscles or fibers. 2. the muscular part of the arm.

lachrymal *or* **lacrimal** of or relating to tears or to the glands that produce tears.

lacrimation the excessive formation and secretion of tears.

lacrimator any agent or substance that produces tears by its irritant effects on the eyes, such as tear gas.

lacrimatory causing the production of tears.

lacrimotomy surgical incision into the glands that produce tears.

lact- *or* **lacti-** *or* **lacto-** *prefix* milk.

lactate to secrete milk. **—lactation** *n.*

lacteal 1. relating to or like milk; milky. 2. a lymphatic vessel in which chyle is conveyed from the intestine.

lactescent resembling milk; milky.

lactic relating to milk.

lactiferous conveying or secreting milk: *lactiferous ducts.*

lactifuge any agent that arrests the flow of milk from the mammary glands.

lactigenous producing milk.

lactogen an agent that stimulates the production or secretion of milk.

lactogenesis milk production. **—lactogenic** *adj.*

lactovegetarian a vegetarian who includes dairy products in his diet, such as milk and cheese, as well as eggs.

lacus *pl.* **lacus** any very small collection or accumulation of fluid.

lacus lacrimalis a small space at the medial angle of the eye where tears collect after bathing the surface of the eyeball.

lagneia 1. sexual intercourse; coitus. 2. lust; sexual urge.

lagnesis *also* **lagnosis** excessive and persistent sexual desire in a man or woman; nymphomania or satyriasis.

lake (of blood in hemolysis) to change so that the hemoglobin is dissolved in the plasma.

-lalia *suffix* speech disorder.

laliophobia an abnormal fear of speaking or stuttering.

lallation a speech defect characterized by difficulty in enunciation of words that contain the letter *l*.

lalochezia psychological or emotional relief obtained by swearing or speaking obscene or vulgar words.

lalognosis the understanding of speech or spoken communication.

THE LACRIMAL APPARATUS

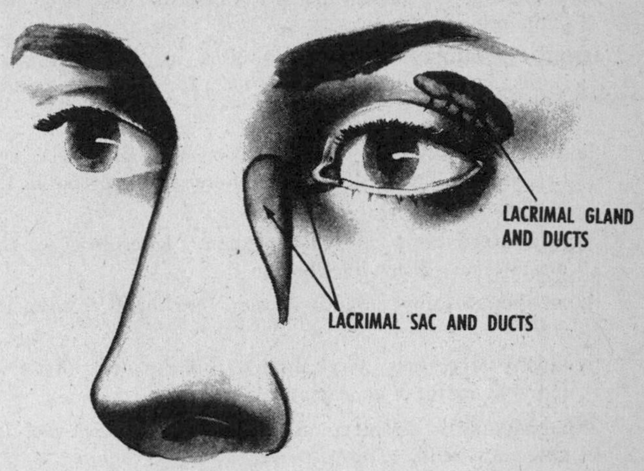

The lacrimal gland secretes tears which are poured over the eyes through small ducts. The tears collect in the inner corner of the eye and pass through two small openings into the lacrimal ducts and into the lacrimal sac. The sac empties into the nose.

lalopathology a branch of science concerned with disorders of speech production and their treatment.

lalopathy any type of speech defect.

laloplegia paralysis of the muscles required in the production of speech sounds.

lalorrhea an excessive flow of words and phrases.

lambdacism 1. difficulty in or inability to pronounce or articulate the letter *l*. 2. pronunciation of the letter *l* as the letter *r*.

lamella *pl.* **lamellae** any thin layer or sheet. **—lamellar** *adj.*

lamina *pl.* **laminae** 1. any flat layer or thin plate. 2. the flattened part on either side of a vertebral arch. **—laminar** *adj.*

laminectomy surgical removal of a vertebral lamina, esp. the posterior arch of a vertebra.

laminitis inflammation of a lamina.

laminotomy surgical incision into a vertebral lamina.

lance 1. to incise an abscess, boil, etc., as to permit the release of pus. 2. a lancet.

lancet a small, pointed, two-edged knife used in surgery.

lancinating (of pain) piercing, cutting, or extremely sharp; tearing.

Langerhans' islets islets of Langerhans.

laniary (of the canine teeth) adapted for tearing.

lanolin wool grease refined esp. for use as the base of various ointments.

lanosterol a sterol found in wool fat.

lanthanides the rare earth elements.

lanthionine an amino acid obtained from wool.

lanuginous covered with soft hair; downy.

lanugo soft, downy hair covering the body.

lapactic laxative; purgative.

laparocele an abdominal hernia.

laparocolostomy the surgical formation of an artificial anus by creating a permanent opening between the colon and the abdominal wall.

laparocolotomy surgical incision through the abdominal wall to the colon; colotomy.

laparocystectomy surgical removal of an ovarian cyst or cystlike tumor through an incision made in the abdominal wall.

laparocystotomy removal of the contents of an ovarian cyst or cystlike tumor by means of a surgical incision in the abdominal wall.

laparoenterostomy surgical formation of an artificial anus by means of an incision into the loin.

laparohepatotomy surgical incision into the liver from the side.

laparohysterectomy surgical removal of the uterus (hysterectomy) by means of an abdominal incision.

laparomyositis inflammation of the lateral muscles of the abdominal wall.

laparonephrectomy surgical removal of the kidney by means of an incision in the loin.

laparosalpingectomy surgical removal of a fallopian tube by means of an abdominal incision.

laparosplenectomy surgical removal of the spleen by means of an incision in the abdominal wall.

laparosplenotomy surgical incision into the spleen through the abdominal wall.

laparotomize to subject (a patient) to laparotomy.

laparotomy *pl.* **laparotomies** surgical section of the abdominal wall.

laryngeal of or relating to the larynx.

laryngectomy *pl.* **laryngectomies** surgical removal of all or part of the larynx.

laryngitic relating to or caused by inflammation of the larynx.

laryngitis inflammation of the larynx.

laryngo- *also* **laryng-** *prefix* relating to the larynx.

laryngograph an instrument for measuring the movements of the larynx by means of a tracing (laryngogram).

laryngology a branch of medicine dealing with diseases of the larynx and nasopharynx.

laryngomalacia an abnormal softening of the cartilages of the larynx.

laryngoparalysis paralysis of the muscles of the larynx.

laryngopathy any disease or disorder affecting the larynx.

laryngopharyngectomy surgical removal of part of the larynx and pharynx, as in the treatment of cancer.

laryngopharyngitis inflammation of both the larynx and pharynx.

laryngoscope an instrument for visual examination of the larynx. —**laryngoscopic** *adj.* —**laryngoscopist** *n.* —**laryngoscopy** *n.*

laryngostenosis abnormal narrowing or stricture of the lumen of the larynx.

laryngostomy the surgical formation of a permanent opening from the neck into the larynx.

laryngotome a surgical knife for making incisions into the larynx.

larynx *pl.* **larynges** the upper part of the trachea that contains the vocal cords.

Lassa fever a viral disease first noted in Nigeria in 1969, characterized by high fever, headache, facial flushes, vomiting and bleeding from the skin and mucous membranes, thought to be transmitted by a species of rat.

lassitude a feeling of profound weakness; fatigue.

latent present but not active or visible: *latent infection.* —**latency** *n.*

lateral relating to, situated on, or coming from the side. —**laterally** *adv.*

lateralis lateral; at the side.

laudanum a tincture that contains opium, formerly widely used as a pain killer.

laughing gas nitrous oxide.

lavage the therapeutic irrigation of a hollow organ, such as the stomach or lower intestine.

laxative any agent serving to relieve constipation; cathartic.

L.E. *abbr.* 1. left eye. 2. lupus erythematosus.

lead poisoning chronic poisoning that is the result of ingestion or absorption of lead and is characterized by colic, a dark line along the gums, and muscular paralysis.

leg either of the lower limbs, used for standing and moving.

leiodermia the condition of having abnormally smooth or glossy skin.

leiomyoma a benign tumor derived from smooth or nonstriated muscle.

leiomyomatosis the condition of having several leiomyomas in different parts of the body.

leiomyosarcoma a malignant tumor derived from smooth or nonstriated muscle.

leiotrichous having hair that is straight; straight-haired.

Leishmania a genus of parasitic protozoa.

leishmaniasis infection with protozoa of the genus *Leishmania,* one species of which causes the disease kala-azar.

leishmaniosis leishmaniasis.

leishmanoid any pathological condition that resembles the signs of leishmaniasis.

lemic relating to any epidemic disease, esp. the plague.

lens a transparent, nearly spherical body in the eye that focuses light rays upon the retina.

lenticular having the shape of or resembling a lens.

lenticulopapular (of a skin eruption) having papules that are shaped like a tiny dome or convex lens.

lentiform lenticular; shaped like a lens.

leprology the branch of medical science concerned with the study and treatment of leprosy.

leprosy a chronic, communicable disease that is caused by a bacillus and is marked by the formation of granules on the skin that enlarge and spread, eventual paralysis of muscle, and the development of deformities. —**leprous** *adj.*

-lepsy *suffix* seizure: *catalepsy.*

lepto- *prefix* thin, slender or light; frail.

leptocephalous having an abnormally small head. —**leptocephalus** *n.*

leptochroa the condition of having skin that is abnormally delicate.

leptodermic characterized by or having abnormally thin skin.

leptomeninges the two inner membranes that envelop the brain and spinal cord; pia mater and arachnoid (as distinguished from the dura mater).

leptomeningitis inflammation of the pia mater and arachnoid; inflammation of the leptomeninges.

leptophonia the condition of having an abnormally weak

voice. **—leptophonic** *adj.*

leptopodia the condition of having unusually narrow or slender feet.

leptoprosopia the condition of having an unusually narrow face.

lesion an abnormal change in a part or tissue resulting from disease or injury.

Lesbian *or* **lesbian** a female homosexual. **—lesbianism** *n.*

lethal relating to or causing death; deadly; fatal. **—lethality** *n.* **—lethally** *adv.*

lethargy abnormal drowsiness, fatigue, or indifference. **—lethargic** *adj.*

lethe loss of memory; amnesia. **—letheral** *adj.*

leuk- *or* **leuko-** *or* **leuc-** *or* **leuco-** *prefix* white; colorless: *leukocyte.*

leukemia *also* **leukaemia** a malignant, progressive disease marked by an abnormal increase in the number of white blood cells in the tissues and in the blood. **—leukemic** *adj.*

leukocyte *or* **leucocyte** a white blood cell. **—leukocytic** *adj.*

leukocytoblast any immature cell that eventually develops into one of the white blood cells (leukocytes).

leukocytogenesis the formation and development of white blood cells; leukocytopoiesis.

leukocytoid resembling a white blood cell.

leukocytolysin any of various substances that cause the destruction or dissolution of white blood cells.

leukocytolysis the destruction or dissolution of white blood cells. **—leukocytolytic** *adj.*

leukocytoma the local accumulation of white blood cells in a dense mass.

leukocytopoiesis the formation and development of white blood cells; leukocytogenesis.

leukocytosis *or* **leucocytosis** an increased number of white blood cells in the circulating blood. **—leukocytotic** *adj.*

leukocytotoxin any toxic substance that causes the degeneration or destruction of white blood cells.

leukocyturia the presence of white blood cells in the urine.

leukoderma a partial or total absence of pigment in the skin. **—leukodermatous** *adj.*

leukodontia the desirable condition of having white teeth.

leukodystrophy the degeneration or destruction of the white matter of the brain, thought to be caused by a disorder of fat metabolism.

leukoencephalitis the inflammation of the white matter of the brain.

leukoma *or* **leucoma** a dense white opacity of the cornea of the eye.

leukopenia a condition in which there is an abnormally small number of white blood cells in the bloodstream. Also called *leukocytopenia.*

leukorrhea a whitish discharge from the vagina resulting from inflammation of its mucous membranes. **—leukorrheal** *adj.*

leukotomy the surgical division of nerve fiber tracts in the white matter of the frontal lobe of the cerebrum.

leukotrichia the state or condition of having white hair.

levator a muscle that raises a body part.

levulose fructose; fruit sugar.

libido, emotional or psychic energy, esp. sexual drive. **—libidinal** *adj.* **—libidinous** *adj.*

lichen any of various skin diseases marked by patches of small, firm papules.

lid eyelid.

life-span 1. an individual's duration of existence. 2. the average duration of existence of the members of a particular species.

ligament a tough band of tissue that connects bones together at the joints or supports an organ in place. **—ligamentary** *adj.* **—ligamentous** *adj.*

ligation ligature.

ligature any of various threads or wires used in surgery to tie off or constrict a vessel or part.

light adaptation adaptation of the eye to intensified light through contraction of the pupil and a decrease in visual purple.

limbus the region forming a margin between the cornea and sclera of the eye.

liminal of or relating to a sensory threshold; barely perceptible.

limitrophic (of the sympathetic nervous system) governing or controlling nutrition.

limosis abnormal and persistent hunger.

linea any long, narrow strip or mark anatomically distinguished from the surrounding areas by its elevation, color or texture.

lingua *pl.* **linguae** the tongue or a structure or part that resembles the tongue.

lingual of, relating to, or lying near the tongue.

lingually in the direction of the tongue; toward the tongue.

linguo- *prefix* relating to the tongue.

liniment a liquid preparation used for soothing irritated skin or as a counterirritant or cleansing agent.

linolenic acid a liquid, fatty acid held to be essential to nutrition.

lip 1. either of the two fleshy folds forming the margins of the mouth. 2. labium.

lip- *or* **lipo-** *prefix* fat; fatty.

lipase any of various enzymes that dissolve or split fat.

lipectomy the surgical removal of fatty tissue.

lipemia the presence in the bloodstream of an abnormally large amount of fatty material.

lipid any type of fat (such as fatty acids) or fatlike substance (such as cholesterol).

lipidosis any disorder of fat metabolism.

lipoarthritis inflammation of the fatty tissues of joints.

lipoblast an immature fat cell.

lipoblastoma a tumor of fatty tissue; lipoma.

lipocardiac 1. relating to fatty degeneration of the heart. 2. a person who suffers from fatty degeneration of the heart.

lipochondroma a tumor that contains both fat and cartilage.

lipoclasis lipolysis; the splitting up of fat.

lipocyte a fat cell.

lipodystrophy a disorder of metabolism of fat that affects chiefly women and is marked by obesity of the buttocks and legs.

lipofibroma a fatty tumor that contains a relatively large amount of fibrous tissue. Also called *fibrolipoma.*

lipogenesis the formation and development of fats or fatty tissue. **—lipogenetic** *adj.*

lipogenic fat producing; lipogenetic.

lipogenous producing fat.

lipoid 1. resembling fat. 2. a lipid.

lipoidemia the presence in the bloodstream of an abnormally large quantity of lipids; lipemia.

lipoiduria lipids in the urine.

lipolysis the decomposition or dissolution of fat. **—lipolytic** *adj.*

lipoma *pl.* **lipomas** *or* **lipomata** a tumor of fatty tissue. —**lipomatous** *adj.*

lipomatosis a condition characterized by the excessive deposition of fat in the tissues.

lipostomy congenital absence of the mouth.

Lippes loop an S-shaped plastic intrauterine device.

liquor an aqueous solution of a drug.

lithiasis *pl.* **lithiases** the formation of stony concretions in the body.

lithotomy *pl.* **lithotomies** surgical incision into the bladder to remove a stone.

liver a large vascular organ in the upper right part of the abdomen that secretes bile, maintains the composition of the blood, and regulates many important metabolic processes.

lobar of or relating to a lobe.

lobe a rounded protuberance of a bodily part or organ.

lobotomize to perform a lobotomy on.

lobotomy *pl.* **lobotomies** surgical incision of some or all of the fibers of a lobe of the brain performed for the relief of some mental disorders.

lobule a small lobe or a subsection of a lobe. —**lobular** *adj.*

localized restricted to a limited region or spot.

lockjaw 1. an initial symptom of tetanus in which spasms of the jaw muscles prevents opening of the jaws. 2. tetanus.

locomotor ataxia impairment in the coordination of bodily movements and irregularity of gait often occurring as a late symptom of syphilis.

locum tenens a person who substitutes for another, esp. a physician who temporarily takes over the responsibilities of another physician.

loin 1. the section on each side of the spinal column between the hipbone and the false ribs. 2. *pl.* the abdominal region about the hips including the pubic region. 3. *pl.* genitals.

long bone any of the large, elongated bones supporting a limb.

longevity a long duration of individual life.

lordosis abnormal curvature of the spine in a forward direction. —**lordotic** *adj.*

lotion a liquid preparation for cosmetic use or medicinal soothing of the skin.

louse *pl.* **lice** any of several small wingless insects that are parasitic on warm-blooded animals.

LSD lysergic acid diethylamide; an organic compound sometimes used experimentally in treating mental disorders and often having as side effects hallucinating and psychotic behavior.

lucid having full command of one's faculties; sane.

lues syphilis.

lumbago painful muscular rheumatism of the lumbar region.

lumbar of or relating to the loins or to the region of the back between the hipbone and the false ribs.

lumen *pl.* **lumina** *or* **lumens** the cavity within the tube of an organ or vessel.

lung either of two thoracic organs that are the chief functional organs of respiration.

lunule a crescent-shaped part of the body, as the light-colored area at the base of a nail.

lupus any of various diseases marked by skin lesions, as lupus erythematosus.

luxate to throw out of joint; dislocate. —**luxation** *n.*

lying-in the state or period attending childbirth; confinement.

lymph a transparent, slightly yellowish liquid occurring in the lymphatic vessels, bathing the tissues, and carrying away wastes.

lymphadenitis inflammation of the lymphatic glands.

M

maceration the softening of a solid by soaking it in a fluid substance. —**macerate** *vb.*

macies emaciation.

macrencephaly *also* **macrencephalia** extensive growth of the brain; the condition of having an unusually large brain.

macro- *or* **macr-** *prefix* large; long.

macrobiosis longevity; an unusually long span of life.

macrobiote any organism that is relatively long-lived.

macrobiotic 1. long-lived. 2. tending to extend or prolong life.

macrobiotics the scientific study of factors that influence the prolongation of life.

macroblast a large immature red blood cell (erythroblast).

macroblepharia the state or condition of having unusually large eyelids.

macrobrachia the condition of having unusually long or large arms.

macrocardia the state or condition of having an abnormally enlarged heart. Also called *cardiomegaly*.

macrocardius a person with an abnormally large heart.

macrocephalous *or* **macrocephalic** having an abnormally large head or cranium. —**macrocephaly** *n.*

macrocephalus a fetus with an abnormally large head.

macrocheilia abnormal enlargement of the lips. Also called *macrolabia*.

macrocyte an abnormally large red blood cell occurring in various forms of anemia. —**macrocytic** *adj.*

macroscopic *also* **macroscopical** sufficiently large to be visible to the naked eye.

macula *pl.* **maculae** *or* **maculas** macule. —**macular** *adj.*

macule a discolored but not elevated spot on the skin.

mal any disease or disorder.

mal- *prefix* bad; ill.

malabsorption ineffective or faulty absorption of nutrient materials from the alimentary canal.

malacia an abnormal softening of an organ, structure or part.

-malacia *suffix* abnormal softening.

malaco- *prefix* soft; softening.

malacoma malacia.

malacosis malacia.

malacosteon abnormal softening of the bones; osteomalacia.

malacotic relating to or characterized by an abnormal softening of an organ, structure or part; relating to malacia.

malacotomy surgical incision into soft structures or parts, esp. those of the abdominal wall.

maladie malady; illness; disease.

malady any illness or disease, esp. one of a potentially serious nature.

malaise a general feeling of ill health or torpor often accompanying the onset of a determinable illness.

malar of or relating to the cheek or to the side of the head.

malaria an infectious, febrile protozoal disease transmitted by female *Anopheles* mosquitoes and characterized chiefly by intermittent attacks of chills and fever. —**malarial** *also* **malarian** *adj.*

malariology the branch of medical science concerned with the study and treatment of malaria.

malarious relating to or characterized by the presence or prevalence of malaria.

malassimilation inadequate, incomplete or faulty assimilation of food.

mal comitial epilepsy. See *grand mal* and *petit mal.*

maldigestion inadequate or incomplete digestion.

malemission the failure of semen to be ejaculated from the penis during sexual intercourse.

maleruption imperfect or faulty eruption of a tooth or teeth.

malformation irregular or faulty structure or formation.

malignant tending to produce severe deterioration or death: *malignant disease.* —**malignancy** *n.*

malinger to feign illness so as to avoid duty or work. —**malingerer** *n.* —**malingering** *n.*

malleation a nervous disorder characterized by the repeating hammering or beating of the hands against the thighs.

malleolus *pl.* **malleoli** *or* **malleoluses** a rounded protuberance, as that on either side of the ankle joint.

malleotomy surgical division of the malleus.

malleus the largest of the three conducting bones of the middle ear; hammer.

malnutrition inadequate or faulty nutrition caused by a disorder of assimilation, insufficient dietary intake, or chronic imbalance of the diet.

malocclusion incorrect alignment of the teeth when the jaws are closed, as caused by loss of teeth, imperfect development, or abnormal growth and development of the jaw bones.

maloplasty plastic surgery involving the cheek or cheeks.

malpractice negligent, improper or careless treatment of a patient by physicians, nurses or other qualified medical personnel.

maltase an enzyme active in the hydrolysis of maltose to glucose.

maltose a sugar obtained by the hydrolysis of starch.

malum any disease.

malum caducum epilepsy.

malum cordis heart disease.

malus venereum syphilis.

mamma *pl.* **mammae** a mammary gland; breast. —**mammate** *adj.*

mammal any individual belonging to the class Mammalia, characterized by being warm-blooded vertebrates that suckle their offspring.

mammalogy the branch of biological science concerned with the study of mammals.

mammaplasty *also* **mammoplasty** plastic reconstruction of a breast.

mammary of, relating to, or located near the breasts.

mammary gland either of two large, compound glands situated on the chest of female mammals and modified to secrete milk for the feeding of young.

mammectomy *pl.* **mammectomies** mastectomy; surgical removal of the breast.

mammiform having the shape of a breast; breast-shaped; resembling a breast or mammary gland.

mammill- *or* **mammilli-** *prefix* 1. relating to the nipple or nipples. 2. relating to any small, rounded elevation resembling a nipple.

mammilla *pl.* **mammillae** 1. the nipple. 2. any structure or part that resembles a nipple.

mammillary relating to or resembling a nipple.

mammillated possessing projections or elevations that resemble a nipple.

mammillation 1. the condition of possessing projections or elevations that resemble a nipple. 2. any elevation or projection that resembles a nipple.

mammilliform shaped like a nipple.

mammillitis inflammation of a nipple.

mammitis inflammation of a breast or mammary gland; mastitis.

mammo- *prefix* relating to the breasts or mammary glands.

mammogram an X-ray photograph of the breast or mammary gland.

mammography X-ray examination of the breasts.

mammoplasty mammaplasty.

mammose 1. resembling or shaped like a breast or mammary gland. 2. possessing unusually large breasts.

mammotomy surgical incision into the breast or mammary gland. Also called *mastotomy.*

mammotropic having a direct effect on stimulating the formation, development or growth of the breasts.

mandible the lower jaw.

mandibula *also* **mandibulum** the lower jaw or mandible.

mandibular relating to the lower jaw or mandible.

mandibulectomy surgical removal of part or all of the lower jaw.

mandibulofacial relating to both the lower jaw and the face.

maneuver any specific procedure or movement, esp. in surgery or obstetrics.

mania an abnormal psychic state marked chiefly by elation, disorganized behavior, and physical hyperactivity.

maniac madman; lunatic. —**maniacal** *adj.*

manic affected with or resembling mania.

manic-depressive marked by psychotic alternation between seizures of mania and depression. —**manic-depressive** *n.*

manifestation (in medicine) the exhibition or development of specific diagnostic signs or symptoms of a disease or disorder.

maniphalanx any bony segment of a finger.

manometer any of various instruments for measuring gas or vapor pressure. —**manometric** *adj.* —**manometry** *n.*

mantle any layer that covers a structure or part.

manubrium *pl.* **manubria** an anatomical part or process shaped like a handle, esp. the upper part of the breastbone.

manus the hand.

manustupration masturbation.

marasmus progressive emaciation, esp. in the very young, resulting from malnutrition. —**marasmic** *adj.*

marcid wasting away or emaciating.

marcor marasmus.

margo margin or border; edge.

marihuana *or* **marijuana** cannabis.

mariposia the ingestion or drinking of sea water.

marmorated (of the skin) having a streaked or marble-like appearance.

marrow the soft, vascular substance that fills the cavities of most bones.

martial relating to or containing iron.

maschaladenitis inflammation of the axillary glands.

maschale axilla.

maschalephidrosis sweating in the armpits (axillae).

maschaloneus a tumor in the armpit or axilla.

maschalyperidrosis excessive sweating in the armpits.

masculine relating to or having male characteristics.

masculinity the sexual characteristics (primary and secondary) of the male.

masculinization the normal or (in women) abnormal development of male characteristics. **—masculinize** *vb.*

masculinus masculine.

masochism a form of sexual deviation in which pleasure is gained through being punished or humiliated. **—masochist** *n.* **—masochistic** *adj.*

masque mask.

massa a lump or mass; an accumulation of coherent material.

massage therapeutic stroking or kneading of the body, esp. to promote circulation of the blood or to relax muscles.

masseter a large, powerful muscle that raises the lower jaw and assists in chewing. **—masseteric** *adj.*

masseur a man skilled in massage and physiotherapy.

masseuse a woman skilled in massage and physiotherapy.

massotherapy the therapeutic use of massage.

mast- *or* **masto-** *prefix* breast; mammary gland.

mastadenitis inflammation of a breast or mammary gland; mastitis.

mastadenoma a benign tumor of the breast.

mastalgia pain in the breast. Also called *mastodynia.*

mastatrophy *also* **mastatrophia** a wasting away or atrophy of breast tissues; degeneration of the mammary glands.

mastauxe excessive growth of breast tissues; hypertrophy of the breasts.

mast cell a large cell occurring in connective tissue.

mastectomy *pl.* **mastectomies** surgical removal of a breast; mammectomy.

masthelcosis the formation of ulcers of the breasts; ulceration of the breast.

mastication the process of moving the jaws in chewing, esp. in preparation for swallowing food. **—masticate** *vb.* **—masticatory** *n.*

masticatus chewed or masticated.

mastitis inflammation of the breast or udder. **—mastitic** *adj.*

masto- *or* **mast-** *prefix* relating to or involving the breast.

mastodynia pain in the breast. Also called *mastalgia.*

mastoid 1. relating to or being a process of the temporal bone behind the ear. 2. resembling or shaped like a breast. **—mastoidal** adj.

mastoidectomy *pl.* **mastoidectomies** surgical removal of the mastoid process.

mastoiditis inflammation of the mastoid process.

mastoidotomy surgical incision into the mastoid process.

mastology the branch of medical science concerned with the anatomy, physiology and pathology of the breasts or mammary glands.

mastoncus a swelling or tumor of the breasts.

mastoparietal relating to the suture that unites the mastoid process and the parietal bone of the skull or to the bones themselves.

mastopathy any disease or disorder that involves the breasts or mammary glands.

mastopexy a surgical procedure for correcting excessively sagging breasts.

mastoplasia abnormal or excessive enlargement of the breasts.

mastoplasty any form of plastic surgery that involves the breasts.

mastoptosis a sagging of the breasts.

mastorrhagia bleeding from a breast or mammary gland.

mastosyrinx a fistula of the breast.

mastotomy surgical incision of the breast or mammary gland.

masturbation stimulation of the genitals exclusive of sexual intercourse and typically with the purpose of inducing orgasm. **—masturbate** *vb.* **—masturbatory** *adj.*

mater 1. anything that nourishes or forms. 2. mother.

materia substance; matter.

materia medica the branch of medical science dealing with drugs and medicines.

materies morbi any substance that is the direct cause of a disease.

maternal relating to or coming or derived from a mother.

maternity 1. relating to the obstetrical ward or department of a hospital or medical center. 2. the state or condition of being a mother; motherhood.

matrical relating to a matrix.

matricide 1. the murder of one's mother. 2. one who kills their own mother.

matrix 1. the intercellular substance of a tissue. 2. a mold in which something is cast. 3. the formative portion of a nail or a tooth. 4. the uterus or womb.

matter 1. any substance. 2. pus.

maturate (of a wound) to exude pus; suppurate.

maturation the process of becoming fully developed.

maxilla *pl.* **maxillae** *or* **maxillas** the upper jaw. **—maxillary** *adj.*

maxillitis inflammation of the upper jaw.

maxillodental relating to the upper jaw and the teeth it contains.

maxillofacial relating to the jaws and face.

maxillomandibular relating to both the upper and lower jaws.

maximus (in anatomical nomenclature) greatest.

mayidism pellagra.

MBC *abbr.* maximum breathing capacity.

M.C. *abbr.* 1. Medical Corps. 2. Master of Surgery (*Magister Chirurgiae*).

M.D. *abbr.* Doctor of Medicine (*Medicinae Doctor*).

M.D.S. *abbr.* Master of Dental Surgery.

measles a contagious viral disease, esp. of childhood, marked chiefly by the eruption of red circular spots on the skin and by infection of the respiratory tract.

meato- *prefix* relating to a meatus.

meatotomy surgical incision to enlarge the meatus of the urethra.

meatus *pl.* **meatuses** *or* **meatus** an opening to a body passage or organ. **—meatal** *adj.*

mechanophobia an abnormal fear of machines or machinery.

meconism addiction to or poisoning from the prolonged use of opium.

meconium 1. fecal matter accumulated in the bowel during fetal development and evacuated shortly after birth. 2. opium.

mediad toward the middle line.

medial relating to or located at or near the middle; median.

medialis medial.

median situated in the middle of the body or a part; central; medial.

medianum *or* **medianus** medial.

mediastinitis inflammation of the cellular components of the mediastinum.

mediastinography X-ray photography of the mediastinum.

mediastinum *pl.* **mediastina** a septum or space between two parts, esp. the space between the lungs containing the heart and other thoracic organs.

medic one who is engaged in medicine, esp. an assistant to a physician.

medicable capable of being treated; admitting of treatment and possible cure.

medical of, relating to, or involving the practice of medicine or physicians.

medical examiner a public official who performs post mortems to determine the cause of death.

medicament a substance or agent used to ease physical discomfort or treat disease.

medicate 1. to treat with medicine. 2. to infuse with a medication. —**medicated** *adj.*

medication 1. the process or act of medicating. 2. a substance or agent that promotes healing or soothes pain.

medicinal used to cure disease or relieve pain.

medicine 1. a preparation, substance, or drug used in treating disease. 2. the science of maintaining good health and of the alleviating, preventing, or curing of disease or injury.

medico *pl.* **medicos** a physician or medical student.

medico- *or* **medi-** *prefix* medical.

medicobiologic *also* **medicobiological** relating to the biological aspects of medicine or medical science.

medicochirurgical 1. relating to both medicine and surgery. 2. relating to both physicians and surgeons.

medicolegal relating to or concerning both medicine and the law.

medicomechanical (of therapy) relating to the use of both medical and mechanical measures.

medicus a physician or medical doctor.

mediocarpal relating to the central part of the wrist (carpus).

medulla *pl.* **medullas** *or* **medullae** 1. marrow. 2. the central part of an organ. 3. medulla oblongata.

medulla oblongata the lower portion of the brainstem continuous posteriorly with the spinal cord.

medullary *also* **medullar** of or relating to marrow or to a medulla.

mega- *or* **meg-** *prefix* large; great.

megabacterium a bacterium of unusually large size.

megacardia an abnormally enlarged heart. Also called *cardiomegaly.*

megacephaly the condition of having an abnormally large head.

megacolon a condition in which the colon is abnormally large and dilated.

megacycle one million cycles.

megadactyl having or characterized by unusually large fingers. —**megadactyly** *n.*

megadolichocolon a condition in which the colon is unusually long and dilated.

megakaryocyte a large cell found chiefly in bone marrow and regarded as being the source of blood platelets.

megal- *or* **megalo-** *prefix* large; giant; enormous.

megalgia extremely severe pain.

megalocardia an abnormally enlarged heart; megacardia. Also called *cardiomegaly.*

megaloencephalic relating to a brain of unusually large size. —**megaloencephaly** *n.*

megaloenteron the state or condition of having an unusually large intestine.

megalogastria the state or condition of having an unusually large stomach.

megalomania a delusional disorder marked by infantile convictions of one's own worth, importance, power, or greatness. —**megalomaniac** *n.* —**megalomaniacal** *or* **megalomanic** *adj.*

megalosplenia splenomegaly.

megalourethra a congenital dilation of the urethra.

megarectum extreme dilation of the rectum.

megavolt one million volts.

megohm one million ohms (a measure of electrical resistance).

megrim migraine.

meiosis the process of cell division resulting in the number of chromosomes in gamete-producing cells being reduced to one-half. —**meiotic** *adj.*

melalgia pain in an arm or leg, esp. pain that radiates from the foot to the upper leg or thigh (possibly caused by a disease related to vitamin deficiency).

melan- *or* **melano-** *prefix* dark; black.

melancholia an abnormal mental condition marked by extreme depression, impaired bodily and mental activity, loss of appetite, and insomnia. —**melancholiac** *n.* —**melancholic** *adj.*

melanin the dark brown pigment of the skin and hair.

melanism an excessive amount of dark pigmentation of the skin and hair. —**melanistic** *adj.*

melanoderma an abnormal deposition of melanin or metallic substances (such as iron or silver) in the skin causing severe darkening.

melanodermatitis the deposit of excessive amounts of melanin in an inflamed area of skin.

melanoid a dark pigment resembling melanin.

melanoma *pl.* **melanomas** *or* **melanomata** a dark-pigmented, usually malignant tumor.

melanomatosis a condition characterized by the widespread occurrence of melanomas.

melanonychia discoloration of the nails with a black pigment.

melanoplakia an abnormal condition characterized by the deposition of pigmented patches on the tongue and the inner surfaces of the cheeks.

melanosis a condition marked by abnormally intense dark pigmentation of the tissues of the body.

melanosity a dark complexion.

melanotic relating to or characterized by melanosis.

melanotrichous possessing black hair.

melanous having a dark complexion; brunette.

melanuria a condition in which the excreted urine has an abnormally dark color, caused by the presence of various pigments and the derivatives of products containing coal tar.

melasma gravidarum the unusual but often temporary discoloration of the skin during pregnancy.

melasma universale a patchy pigmentation of the skin occurring in old age.

melena the passage of dark, tarry stools as the result of traces of blood in the intestinal secretions and juices.

membrana *pl.* **membranae** a membrane.

membrana abdominis the peritoneum.

membranaceous membranous.

membrana cordis the pericardium.

membranate resembling a membrane; having the nature of a membrane.

membrane a thin, pliable layer of tissue. —**membranous** *adj.*

membraniform having the characteristics of appearance of a membrane.

membrum *pl.* **membra** a member or limb.

membrum muliebre the clitoris.

membrum virile the penis.

menarche the beginning of menstruation. —**menarcheal** *adj.*

mendelism the body of hereditary and genetic principles derived from Mendel's laws.

Mendel's laws laws of genetics stating that characteristics are determined by pairs of factors (genes); one member of each pair is dominant to the other; the members of each pair separate during gamete formation so that the gametes contain only one factor for each characteristic.

Menière's disease a dysfuntion of the membranous labyrinth of the inner ear marked by attacks of tinnitis, dizziness, and deafness. Also called *Menière's syndrome.*

meningeal of or relating to the meninges.

meninges the three membranes that surround the brain and spinal cord; the pia mater, arachnoid and dura mater.

meningioma *pl.* **meningiomas** *or* **meningiomata** a slow-growing tumor arising from the meninges and often exerting pressure on the brain.

meningism a condition that simulates meningitis but is characterized by irritation rather than true inflammation.

meningitis inflammation of the meninges. —**meningitic** *adj.*

meningo- *or* **mening-** *prefix* relating to the meninges.

meningocele protrusion of the covering membranes of the brain or spinal cord through a gap or defect in the skull or vertebral column.

meningocortical relating to both the meninges of the brain and the cerebral cortex.

meningoencephalitis inflammation of both the brain and its covering membranes (meninges). Also called *cerebromeningitis.*

meningomyelocele protrusion through a defect in the vertebral column of a part of the spinal cord and its covering membranes.

meningopathy any disease or disorder of the covering membranes of the brain or spinal cord.

meningoradiculitis inflammation of both the spinal meninges and the roots of the spinal nerves.

meningorhachidian relating to both the spinal cord and its covering membranes.

meningorrhagia bleeding into or beneath the covering membranes of the brain or spinal cord.

meninx *pl.* **meninges** any of the three membranes surrounding the brain and spinal cord.

meniscectomy surgical removal of a meniscus, esp. one from the knee joint.

meniscotome a knife-like instrument used in the surgical removal of a meniscus.

meniscus any crescent-shaped structure or part, esp. the crescentic cartilage of the knee joint (*meniscus medialis*).

meno- *prefix* relating to menstruation or to the menses.

menolipsis a temporary interruption or cessation of menstruation.

menopause the period, usually occurring between the ages of 45 and 50, during which menstruation ceases. —**menopausal** *adj.*

menorrhagia abnormally heavy menstrual flow. —**menorrhagic** *adj.*

menosepsis a relatively rare form of blood poisoning caused by the absorption of septic material from retained menstrual blood.

menostasis *also* **menostasia** the absence of menstruation. Also called *amenorrhea.*

menostaxis an unusually prolonged flow of menstrual blood.

menothermal relating to hot flushes experienced as one symptom of the menopause.

menouria an abnormal condition in which some of the menstrual blood flows into the urinary bladder as a result of a fistula between the uterus and the bladder.

menoxenia any disorder or abnormality of menstruation.

menses the menstrual flow.

menstruant menstruating.

menstruation a discharge of tissue debris, secretions, and blood from the uterus in nonpregnant females from puberty occurring at approximately monthly intervals. —**menstrual** *adj.* —**menstruate** *vb.*

mental 1. of or relating to the mind. 2. of or relating to the chin.

mental defective one who has mental deficiency.

mental deficiency inadequate mental development usually attributed to a brain disorder or defect and thought to be incurable; feeblemindedness.

meprobamate a mild tranquilizer used in the relief of anxiety states and emotional tension.

meralgia pain in the upper part of the leg or thigh.

mes- *or* **meso-** *prefix* mid; middle; intermediate.

mesaortitis inflammation of the middle coat of the aorta.

mesarteritis inflammation of the middle coat of any artery.

mescaline a poisonous alkaloid derived from the dried tops of the mescal cactus and used as an antispasmodic and as a stimulant and hallucinogen. Also called *peyote.*

mescalism addiction to mescaline or psychological dependence on its effects (exotic or beautiful visions).

mesencephalon the middle part of the brain; midbrain. —**mesencephalic** *adj.*

mesencephalotomy surgical interruption of any of the fiber tracts or section of any of the tissues in the midbrain, as in the relief of intractable pain.

mesenteric of or relating to a mesentery.

mesenteritis inflammation of a mesentery.

mesenterium mesentery.

mesentery a membrane in the form of a double fold serving as attachment for various bodily organs, esp. the peritoneal fold connecting the small intestine to the back wall of the body.

mesmerism hypnotism. —**mesmeric** *adj.*

mesoderm the middle of the three primary germ layers of an embryo that develops into bone, muscle, connective tissue, and other structures. —**mesodermal** *or* **mesodermic** *adj.*

mesomorph one having a husky, muscular body build. —**mesomorphic** *adj.*

mesothelium *pl.* **mesothelia** epithelium derived from the mesoderm and lining serous body cavities. —**mesothelial** *adj.*

metabolism the chemical changes in living cells through which energy is provided for vital activities and processes by the breakdown of molecules and new molecules are synthesized to replace them. —**metabolic** *adj.*

metabolite any product of metabolism, such as an intermediate substance or waste product, esp. as produced during catabolism.

metabolize to subject to or perform metabolism.

metacarpal 1. of or relating to the metacarpus. 2. a bone of the metacarpus.

metacarpus the skeletal part of the hand between the carpus and the phalanges that is made up of the five elongated bones of the palm.

metaplasia the transformation of one kind of tissue into another form of tissue.

metastasis *pl.* **metastases** the transfer of a malignancy or a disease-producing agent from the original site to another part of the body. —**metastatic** *adj.* —**metastasize** *vb.*

metatarsal 1. of or relating to the metatarsus. 2. a bone of the metatarsus.

metatarsus the part of the foot between the tarsus and the phalanges.

methylcellulose a tasteless powder that swells when mixed with water, used in antiobesity therapy as a bulk substitute in foods.

metopodynia pain in the forehead, or toward the front of the head; frontal headache.

metra the uterus.

metra- *or* **metr-** *prefix* relating to or denoting the uterus.

metralgia pain in the uterus. Also called *hysteralgia.*

metratonia the lack of muscular tone in the walls of the uterus following childbirth.

metritis inflammation of the uterus.

metrocystosis the formation of cysts in the uterus.

metropathy any disease or disorder involving the uterus.

metrorrhagia profuse bleeding from the uterus at times other than during the normal menstrual period. —**metrorrhagic** *adj.*

mg. *abbr.* milligram.

mho the unit of electrical conductivity (the reciprocal of ohm, the unit of electrical resistance).

miasmology the branch of ecology concerned with the study and control of air pollution.

microbe germ; microorganism. —**microbial** *or* **microbic** *adj.*

microbicide any agent that kills microorganisms; an antiseptic.

microbiology a branch of biology concerned with microscopic forms of life. —**microbiological** *also* **microbiologic** *adj.* —**microbiologist** *n.*

microcephalic having an abnormally small head. —**microcephaly** *n.*

micrococcus *pl.* **micrococci** a small, rounded bacterium. —**micrococcal** *adj.*

microcyte a small red blood cell. —**microcytic** *adj.*

microorganism an organism of microscopic size.

microscope an optical instrument for viewing minute objects through magnification. —**microscopy** *n.*

microscopic *also* **microscopical** 1. of or relating to a microscope or to the use of a microscope. 2. invisible without the aid of a microscope.

microsome a minute structural part of a cell, consisting of ribosomes associated with endoplasmic reticulum. —**microsomal** *adj.*

microtome a special knife-like instrument for cutting sections of tissue for microscopic examination.

micturition the act or process of urinating; urination. —**micturate** *vb.*

midbrain the part of the vertebrate brain between the forebrain and hindbrain.

midgut the central part of the embryonic alimentary canal.

midline the median line or plane of the body or of some part of the body.

midriff the middle section of the human torso, esp. the diaphragm.

midwife a woman who assists another woman in childbirth. —**midwifery** *n.*

migraine severe headache often accompanied by nausea, vomiting, and distortion of vision. —**migrainous** *adj.*

miliaria an eruptive, itching inflammation of the skin, as prickly heat.

miliary consisting of a profusion of projecting lesions or tubercles.

milium *pl.* **milia** a small whitish protrusion of the skin resulting from blockage of the duct of an oil gland.

milk the fluid secreted by the mammary glands of females for the nourishment of their young.

milk tooth any of a set of initial, deciduous teeth replaced by permanent teeth.

miosis *pl.* **mioses** marked smallness or contraction of the eye pupil. —**miotic** *adj.*

miscarriage abortion, esp. when spontaneous.

mitochondrion *pl.* **mitochondria** a long, slender, membranous intracellular body producing energy for a cell. —**mitochondrial** *adj.*

mitosis *pl.* **mitoses** the process of division of the nucleus of a cell. —**mitotic** *adj.*

mitral valve the valve between the left ventricle and the left atrium of the heart. Also called *biscupid valve.*

molar a tooth with a flattened or rounded surface adapted for grinding food. —**molar** *adj.*

mole a pigmented protuberance or mark on the human skin.

molecule the smallest particle of a substance, composed of one or more atoms. —**molecular** *adj.*

mongolism *also* **mongolianism** a form of congenital idiocy marked by the formation of a broad, short skull, slanting eyes, and broad, short-fingered hands.

mongoloid *or* **mongolian** of or relating to mongolism.

moniliasis *pl.* **moniliases** thrush.

monocular of, relating to, or affecting a single eye.

monomania abnormally pronounced concentration on a single idea or object. —**monomaniac** *n.* —**monomaniac** *or* **monomaniacal** *adj.*

mononucleosis an acute, infectious, disease marked by fever, inflammation of the mucous membranes, and swelling of the lymph glands. Also called *infectious mononucleosis* and *glandular fever.*

monosaccharide the simplest form of a sugar, as glucose.

monozygotic twin one of two individuals developing originally from a single egg.

mons pubis the rounded, fleshy mound over the female pubic bones. Also called *mons veneris.*

monster one grotesquely malformed during fetal development.

morbid relating to, characteristic of, or affected with disease. —**morbidity** *n.*

morbus disease.

morgue a place where bodies of persons found dead are kept until they are identified or released for burial.

moribund being in a state approaching death; dying. —**moribundity** *n.*

morning sickness nausea and vomiting occurring during the early months of pregnancy, esp. on arising in the morning.

moron a mentally defective adult with a mental age of between 8 and 12 years.

morphine a bitter, addictive narcotic base that is the chief alkaloid of opium and is used as a sedative and painkiller.

morphinism a state of ill health resulting from the habitual use of morphine.

morphocytology the branch of biology concerned with the study of the size, shape, structure and other physical properties of cells.

morphology a branch of science dealing with the structure and shape of organisms. —**morphological** *adj.* —**morphologically** *adv.* —**morphologist** *n.*

mortality the ratio of the number of deaths to the total population; death rate.

mortuary *pl.* **mortuaries** a place in which dead bodies are kept until burial.

morula *pl.* **morulae** a solid mass of cells constituting an early stage of a fertilized ovum. —**morulation** *n.*

mosaic an organism composed of cells of different genetic types, caused by mutation or an anomaly of chromosome division. —**mosaicism** *n.*

motile capable of independent movement. —**motility** *n.*

motion sickness nausea induced by the movements of travel, as by plane, ship, or car.

motor 1. relating to a nerve that transmits impulses from a nerve center to a muscle or gland. 2. of or relating to movement of the muscles.

mountain sickness sickness resulting from insufficient oxygen at high altitudes.

mucoid resembling or constituting mucus.

mucous 1. secreting or containing mucus. 2. covered with mucus.

mucous membrane a bodily membrane that secretes and is protected by mucus.

mucus a slippery, viscous, glandular secretion produced by mucous membranes.

multiparous having undergone one or more previous childbirths.

multiple myeloma a disease of the bone marrow marked by many myelomas.

mumps a contagious viral disease marked chiefly by fever and swelling of the parotid glands.

mural relating to the wall of any bodily cavity.

murmur an abnormal sound heard on auscultation of the heart, lungs or blood vessels.

muscae volitantes cells and cell fragments in the vitreous humor and lens of the eye that appear as floating spots.

muscicide any agent that kills flies.

muscle body tissue that consists of long cells and expands or contracts a bodily part when stimulated. —**muscular** *adj.*

musculature the muscular structure of the body.

musculus *pl.* **musculi** a muscle.

mutation a change in hereditary genetic material or the resulting morphological or organic change transmitted to a subsequent generation.

mute a person who is unable to speak. —**mute** *adj.*

my- *or* **myo-** *prefix* muscle.

myalgia muscular pain. —**myalgic** *adj.*

myasthenia gravis a disease marked by progressive weakening of the muscles without atrophy.

mycosis *pl.* **mycoses** disease caused by a fungus. —**mycotic** *adj.*

mydriasis prolonged or marked dilation of the pupil of the eye.

mydriatic 1. causing dilation of the pupil. 2. an agent with this action.

myelitis inflammation of bone marrow or of the spinal cord.

myeloid of or relating to the spinal cord or to bone marrow.

myeloma a bone marrow tumor. —**myelomatous** *adj.*

myelopathy disease of the spinal cord or of the bone marrow. —**myelopathic** *adj.*

myocardiograph an instrument for making a traced recording of heart-muscle action. —**myocardiographic** *adj.*

myocarditis inflammation of the myocardium.

myocardium the muscular tissue of the heart.

myogenic relating to or originating from muscle tissue.

myoglobin an oxygen-binding protein in muscles, similar to hemoglobin in blood.

myology the study of muscles. —**myologic** *or* **myological** *adj.*

myoma *pl.* **myomas** *or* **myomata** a tumor composed of muscle tissue. —**myomatous** *adj.*

myopathy any abnormal condition of muscle or muscle tissue. —**myopathic** *adj.*

myope one having myopia.

myopia a condition of the eyes in which a visual image is focused in front of the retina, resulting in imperfect perception of distant objects; nearsightedness. —**myopic** *adj.* —**myopically** *adv.*

myotonia a tonic muscular spasm. —**myotonic** *adj.*

myxedema a hypothyroid condition marked by dry skin and hair, swelling of tissues, and decline of mental and physical vigor. —**myxedematous** *adj.*

myxoma *pl.* **myxomas** *or* **myxomata** a tumor of connective tissue cells. —**myxomatous** *adj.*

N

NAD *abbr.* no appreciable disease.

nail a horny sheath covering and protecting the outer end of each finger and toe.

nalorphine a drug used in the treatment of some types of overdose with narcotics and, since it induces severe withdrawal symptoms in morphine addicts, as a means of diagnosing morphine addiction.

nanism dwarfism.

nano- *prefix* (in the metric system of measurement) one-billionth (10^{-9}).

nanometer one-billionth of a meter; 10^{-9} meter.

nape the back of the neck.

narcissism 1. erotic interest in and attraction to one's own body. 2. egocentricity; egotism. —**narcissist** *n.* —**narcissistic** *adj.*

narcohypnosis deep sleep or unconsciousness induced by hypnosis.

narcolepsy an abnormal condition marked by frequent, sudden periods of deep sleep. —**narcoleptic** *n. & adj.*

narcomania 1. an intense desire or craving for narcotics. 2. severe mental disability caused by addiction to narcotic drugs.

narcosis a condition of unconsciousness or stupor induced by drugs or chemicals.

narcotic a drug, as opium or morphine, that is used in small amounts to ease pain or cause sleep but that in large amounts may cause addiction and death. —**narcotic** *adj.*

naris *pl.* **nares** either of the openings of the nose; nostril.

nasal of or relating to the nose or the nostrils.

THE NASAL CAVITY
(CROSS SECTION)

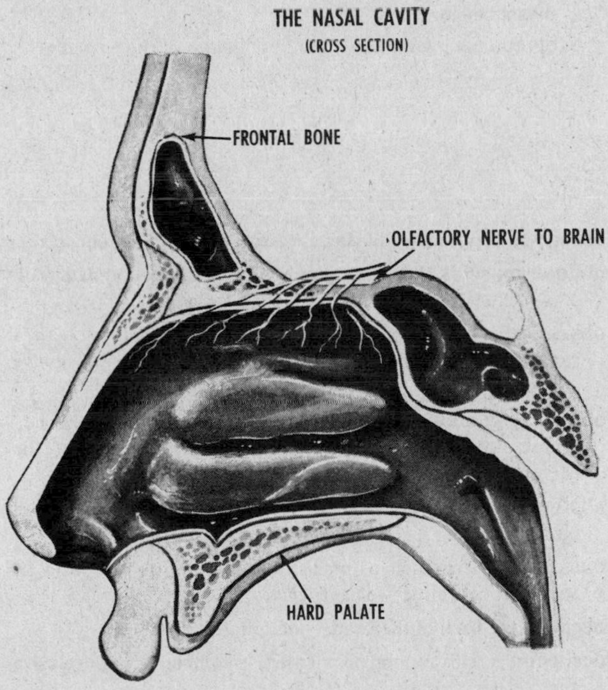

OLFACTORY SENSE
Specialized sensory neurons, capable of being stimulated by airborne odor particles, are located in the roof of the nasal cavity. The neurons collect into numerous small nerves which form the olfactory nerve. The odors most recognized are floral, fruity, herbal or spicy, resinal, and smoky.

nasopharynx the nasal passages in continuation with the upper pharynx. —**nasopharyngeal** *adj.*

nates buttocks.

nausea a sensation of queasiness in the stomach, often associated with an urge to vomit. —**nauseate** *vb.*

navel a small depression in the center of the abdomen marking the former point of attachment of the umbilical cord; umbilicus.

ne- *or* **neo-** *prefix* 1. new; recent. 2. new and different in form.

neck 1. the part of an animal that connects the head with the body. 2. a necklike structure or part; cervix.

necrophilia obsessive and usually erotic interest in dead bodies. —**necrophilic** *adj.*

necrophobia an abnormal fear of dead bodies.

necropsy the detailed examination of a body and its organs and parts after death. Also called *post mortem, autopsy.*

necrosis *pl.* **necroses** the localized death of living tissue. —**necrotic** *adj.*

neisseria any of a genus of microorganisms including those causing gonorrhea.

nematode any of various cylindrical parasitic worms; esp. hookworm.

Nembutal a trademark for the sodium salt of pentobarbital.

neomycin a broad-spectrum antibiotic.

neonatal relating to or affecting a newborn infant, esp. during the first month after birth.

neonate a newborn child or one less than a month old.

neoplasia the formation of tumorous tissues. —**neoplastic** *adj.*

neoplasm new and abnormal tissue having no organic function; tumor. —**neoplastic** *adj.*

neph- *or* **nephro-** *prefix* kidney.

nephrectomy *pl.* **nephrectomies** the surgical removal of a kidney.

nephremorrhagia bleeding into or from the kidney.

nephritic renal; relating to the kidney.

nephritis inflammation of the kidney.

nephrogenic developing in the kidney or produced or originating in kidney tissue. —**nephrogenically** *adv.*

nephron the functional unit of the kidney which filters the blood of its waste products, numbering approximately one million in each kidney.

nephropathy an abnormal state of the kidney. —**nephropathic** *adj.*

nephrosis *pl.* **nephroses** degeneration of the kidneys without inflammation. —**nephrotic** *adj.*

nerve a filamentous band or bundle of nerve fibers outside the central nervous system that connects the brain and spinal cord with various organs and tissues of the body.

nerve gas a war gas that interrupts normal nerve transmission and induces intense respiratory spasm.

nervous 1. relating to or composed of neurons. 2. relating to or affecting the nerves. 3. easily excited or irritated; edgy.

nervous breakdown 1. neurasthenia, esp. when incapacitating. 2. emotional despair, esp. when intense and severe enough to require medical or psychiatric treatment.

nervous system the central nervous system or autonomic nervous system.

nervus *pl.* **nervi** nerve.

nervy excitable; irritable; nervous. —**nerviness** *n.*

nettle rash urticaria; hives.

neural of, relating to, or affecting the nerves or the nervous system. —**neurally** *adv.*

neuralgia acute pain radiating paroxysmally along the course of one or more nerves. —**neuralgic** *adj.*

neurasthenia a fundamentally neurotic condition marked chiefly by exhaustion, feelings of inadequacy, depression, loss of concentration and of appetite, insomnia, and often gastrointestinal disturbance. —**neurasthenic** *adj.* —**neurasthenically** *adv.*

neuritis *pl.* **neuritides** *or* **neuritises** painful inflammation of a nerve. —**neuritic** *adj.*

neuroblastoma *pl.* **neuroblastomas** *or* **neuroblastomata** a malignant tumor of nerve ganglia.

neurodynia neuralgia.

neuroleptanalgesia *or* **neuroleptoanalgesia** the administration of an analgesic agent and a tranquilizing drug jointly, esp. as an adjunct to surgery. —**neuroleptanalgesic** *or* **neuroleptoanalgesic** *adj.*

neuroleptic a drug used to alleviate mental disturbance; tranquilizer.

neurologist a physician specializing in the diagnosis and treatment of disease of the nervous system. —**neurology** *n.* —**neurologically** *adv.*

neuroma *pl.* **neuromas** *or* **neuromata** a tumor or new growth arising from a nerve or from nerve fibers.

neuromuscular relating to or involving the nervous system and muscles jointly.

neuron a nerve cell and its processes (axon and dendrites), being the chief unit of the nervous system. —**neuronal** *adj.* —**neuronic** *adj.*

neuropathy *pl.* **neuropathies** an abnormal and often degenerative condition of the nervous system. —**neuropathic** *adj.* —**neuropathically** *adv.*

neuropharmacology a branch of medicine concerned with the effects of drugs on the nervous system. —**neuropharmacologic** *or* **neuropharmacological** *adj.* —**neuropharmacologist** *n.*

neuropsychiatry a branch of medicine dealing with the relationships of mental and physical aspects of mental disorders. —**neuropsychiatric** *adj.* —**neuropsychiatrically** *adv.* —**neuropsychiatrist** *n.*

neurosis *pl.* **neuroses** any of various emotionally based, disabling, functional nervous disorders lacking a related physical lesion. —**neurotic** *adj.* & *n.* —**neurotically** *adv.*

neurosurgery surgery involving any part of the spinal cord, brain, or peripheral nerves. —**neurosurgeon** *n.* —**neurosurgical** *adj.* —**neurosurgically** *adv.*

neurotoxin a poisonous protein complex that acts on the nervous system. —**neurotoxic** *adj.*

nevus *pl.* **nevi** a pigmented area of the skin; mole; birthmark.

Newcastle disease a viral disease transmittable to humans that involves respiratory and nervous symptoms.

niacin nicotinic acid.

nicotine a poisonous alkaloid that is the active principle of tobacco.

nicotinic acid an acid of the vitamin B complex used in the treatment of pellagra. Also called *niacin.*

nictitate to blink the eyelids; wink. —**nictation** *n.* —**nictitation** *n.*

night blindness impaired visual capacity in faint light or in darkness. Also called *nyctalopia.*

nipple the pigmented protuberance in the center of each breast that in the female serves as the outlet for the secretion of milk in nursing.

nit the egg of a parasitic insect, esp. of a louse.

nitrate a salt of nitric acid.

nitric acid a chemical used as a local caustic agent, the fumes from which can be dangerous to health.

nitroglycerin a highly explosive oily liquid, the main constituent of dynamite, used medically as a vasodilator, esp. in the symptomatic relief of pain caused by angina pectoris.

nitrous oxide a colorless gas used chiefly as an anesthetic in dentistry and often producing laughter and exhilaration before the onset of insensibility. Also called *laughing gas.*

node a thickened or swollen enlargement of a part; a circumscribed mass of tissue: *lymph node.*

nodus *pl.* **nodi** node.

noetic relating to the mental processes.

nose the part of the face bearing the nostrils and constituting the chief vehicle for olfactory sensations.

nosology the branch of medical science concerned with the classification or description of diseases. —**nosologic** *adj.*

noxious physically harmful to living organisms: *noxious gases.*

nucleic acid an acid composed of sugar or a derivative of a sugar, a base, and phosphoric acid that is found chiefly in cell nuclei.

nucleolus *pl.* **nucleoli** a small spherical body within the nucleus of a cell, being occasionally one of two to five such bodies within a single cell nucleus.

nulliparous describing a female who has never borne offspring.

nutation the act of nodding the head, esp. involuntarily.

nyctalopia night blindness.

nymphomania abnormally intense sexual desire on the part of a female, esp. when unresolved by sexual intercourse. —**nymphomaniac** *n.* & *adj.*

nystagmus an involuntary, rapid oscillation of the eyeballs.

O

obesity a condition of having excessive bodily fat. —**obese** *adj.*

oblique muscles 1. two large muscles of the abdominal wall. 2. two external muscles of the eyeball.

obsession a persistent, often upsetting preoccupation with a particular idea, object, or person. —**obsess** *vb.* —**obsessive** *adj.* & *n.*

obsessive compulsive neurosis a mental disorder characterized by compulsive behavior known or recognized by the patient himself to be absurd.

obstetric *or* **obstetrical** of, relating to, or dealing with obstetrics.

obstetrics the branch of medicine dealing with birth and its attendant concerns. —**obstetrician** *n.*

occiput the back of the head. —**occipital** *adj.*

occlusion a closing up; obstruction. —**occlude** *vb.* —**occlusive** *adj.*

occult blood blood passed in the stools and detectable, because of the very small amounts, only by means of special laboratory tests.

occupational disease disease or disability arising from one's regular occupation.

ocular of or relating to the eyes or to sight. —**ocularly** *adv.*

oculomotor nerves the third pair of cranial nerves which act to help move the eyeball.

odontalgia toothache.

-odontia *suffix* of the teeth.

odontolith dental tartar; calcareous material deposited on a tooth.

odontology dentistry.

ohm the unit of electrical resistance. Compare *mho.*

oesophagus esophagus.

olfactory of or relating to the sense of smell.

olig- *or* **oligo-** *prefix* few; deficient; a little.

oligemia lack of blood.

oligospermia abnormally few spermatozoa in the semen.

omentum a free fold supporting or connecting structures within the abdominal cavity.

onychia inflammation of the matrix of a nail.

onychocryptosis an ingrowing nail.

onychomycosis a fungal infection of the nails or a nail.

oogenesis *pl.* **oogeneses** the production of ova within the ovary.

oophorectomy the surgical removal of an ovary.

ophthalm- *or* **ophthalmo-** *prefix* eyeball; eye.

ophthalmia inflammation of the eye and usually the conjunctiva.

ophthalmologist a physician or surgeon specializing in diseases of the eye. **—ophthalmological** *adj.* **—ophthalmology** *n.*

ophthalmoscope a small illuminated instrument for examining the interior of the eye, esp. the retina.

optic of or relating to the eyes or to sight. **—optically** *adv.*

optic disc the point at which the optic nerve enters the eye.

optician a maker of optical instruments and devices.

optometry the profession of examining the eyes for defects of structure and refraction and prescribing corrective lenses. **—optometrist** *n.*

oral of, relating to, or affecting the mouth. **—orally** *adv.*

THE ORAL CAVITY

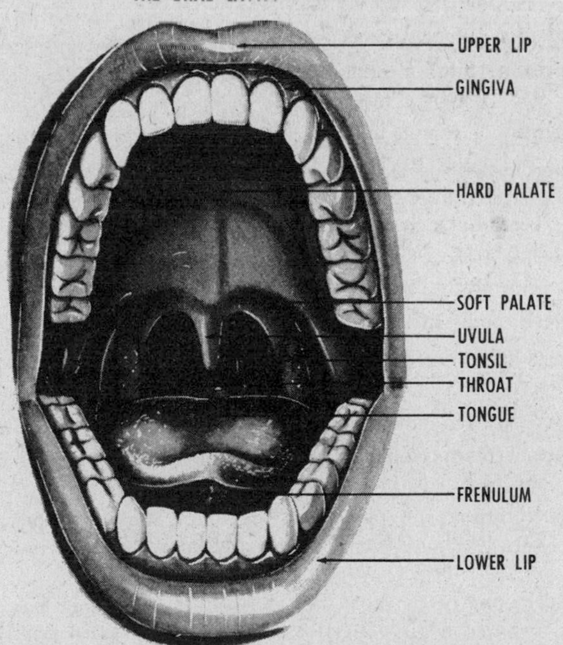

orbit the bony cavity of the skull containing the eyeball.

orchis testicle.

orchitis inflammation of a testicle.

organ a differentiated bodily structure performing specific functions within the body.

organic relating to or affecting the organs of the body: *organic diseases.*

orgasm the climax of sexual excitement, which in the male leads to ejaculation of semen. **—orgasmic** *or* **orgastic** *adj.*

orifice an opening, esp. a natural opening of the body.

os *pl.* **oses** 1. bone. 2. mouth; orifice.

osseous resembling or composed of bone; bony.

ossicle a small bone or bony structure, esp. any of the three sound-conducting bones of the middle ear. **—ossicular** *adj.* **—ossiculate** *adj.*

ossification 1. the formation of bone. 2. the abnormal change into bone, as of connective tissues. **—ossify** *vb.*

oste- *or* **osteo-** *prefix* bone.

osteitis inflammation of bone.

osteoarthritis degenerative arthritis chiefly of the larger joints.

osteomyelitis inflammation of bone marrow.

osteopathy medical practice that ascribes the source of many diseases to be loss of structural integrity and uses the manipulation of joints as a healing technique. **—osteopath** *n.* **—osteopathic** *adj.*

otalgia earache.

otitis inflammation of the ear.

ovarian relating to or affecting the ovaries.

ovariectomy *pl.* **ovariectomies** the surgical removal of an ovary. **—ovariectomized** *adj.*

ovaritis inflammation of an ovary.

ovary *pl.* **ovaries** either of two female reproductive organs that produce eggs and female sex hormones.

ovulation the monthly development and discharge of a mature ovum from an ovary. **—ovulate** *vb.*

ovum *pl.* **ova** a female gamete; egg.

oxygenation to saturate or supply with oxygen. **—oxygenate** *vb.*

P

pacemaker 1. an area in the wall of the heart (sino-atrial node) where the impulse is generated that governs the rhythm of the heart's activity. 2. an electrical device for steadying or stimulating the action of the heart or for re-establishing the action of an arrested heart. Also called *artificial pacemaker.*

pachydermatous having an abnormal thickening of the skin.

pachydermia thickening of the skin.

pachylosis a condition characterized by an abnormally rough, dry and thick skin, esp. of the legs.

pachymeningitis inflammation and thickening of the outermost membrane (dura mater) that covers the brain and spinal cord.

paediatrics pediatrics.

pain a usually localized physical suffering associated with a bodily disorder, injury, or disease. **—painful** *adj.* **—painfully** *adv.* **—painfulness** *n.*

painter's colic lead poisoning.

palliative 1. a medicine or method of treatment that eases symptoms of a disease. 2. relating to the relief of symptoms; mitigating.

pallor deficiency of natural color of the skin, esp. of the face; paleness.

palm the flexible surface of the hand between the wrist and the base of the fingers.

palmar relating to or located on the palm.

palpation medical examination by means of the sense of touch. —**palpate** *vb.*

palpebra *pl.* **palpebrae** eyelid.

palpebral relating to an eyelid or to the eyelids.

palpebrate 1. having eyelids. 2. to open and close the eyelids very quickly; wink.

palpebration the act of winking.

palpitation a pronounced throbbing or pulsation of the heart that is perceptible to the patient. —**palpitate** *vb.*

palsy paralysis or partial paralysis; paresis.

paludism malaria.

panacea a remedy that is claimed to cure all ills.

pancreas a large gland that secretes digestive enzymes and insulin. —**pancreatic** *adj.*

pancreatic juice a clear, alkaline fluid produced by the pancreas and important to the digestive process.

pancreatitis, inflammation of the pancreas.

pandemic occurring over a large area and affecting large numbers of people: *pandemic diseases.*

papilla *pl.* **papillae** a small, nipple-shaped structure.

papilloma a benign tumor composed of epithelial tissue and characterized by one or more outward projections or outgrowths.

papule a small, conical elevation of the skin. —**papular** *adj.*

para- *or* **par-** *prefix* 1. alongside. 2. abnormal; faulty.

paracentesis withdrawal of fluid from a bodily cavity by means of surgical puncture and aspiration. —**paracentetic** *adj.*

paradenitis inflammation of the tissues that surround or are adjacent to a gland.

parageusia an impairment of the sense of taste.

paralysis *pl.* **paralyses** loss of function in part of the body, esp. when involving sensation or motion. —**paralytic** *adj.* —**paralyze** *vb.*

paramedian near the middle line of an organ, structure or part.

paramedical supplementing the work of professional medical personnel. —**paramedic** *n. & adj.*

paranoia a psychosis characterized chiefly by delusions of persecution or grandeur. —**paranoiac** *adj. & n.* —**paranoid** *adj. & n.*

paranoid schizophrenia a psychosis characterized by paranoia along with hallucinations and often characterized by mental deterioration.

paraplegia paralysis of the lower half of the torso and of both legs. —**paraplegic** *adj. & n.*

parasympathetic nervous system a part of the autonomic nervous system.

paresis partial or incomplete paralysis.

paresthesia an unaccountable numb, creeping, tingling, or prickling sensation of the skin.

parietal relating to the parietal bone of the skull.

parietal bone either of the two bones that together form the sides and roof of the skull.

Parkinson's disease a progressive disease, esp. of late life, marked by tremors and rigidity of resting muscles and by an shuffling gait when walking. Also called *parkinsonism, Parkinson's syndrome.*

parolfactory related to or associated with the sense of smell or the olfactory system.

parotid gland either of a pair of large salivary glands located below and in front of the ear.

parotitis 1. inflammation of a parotid gland. 2. mumps (properly, *infectious parotitis*).

paroxysm 1. the sudden flare-up of the symptoms of a disease. 2. a fit or convulsion. —**paroxysmal** *adj.*

pars *pl.* **partes** a part.

parturient giving or about to give birth.

parturition the act of giving birth to young; childbirth.

partus parturition; childbirth.

parvus small.

pasteurization exposure of a substance, as milk, to controlled heat to kill certain organisms without altering the chemical structure. —**pasteurize** *vb.*

patella *pl.* **patellae** *or* **patellas** a thick, triangular, movable bone at the front of the knee; kneecap.

pathogenic capable of causing disease: *pathogenic bacteria.* —**pathogenesis** *n.*

pathology the branch of medicine dealing with the nature of diseases and the bodily changes they cause. —**pathologic** *or* **pathological** *adj.* —**pathologist** *n.*

pathophobia an abnormal fear of disease.

pectoral of or relating to the chest or its muscles.

pediculosis the state or condition of being infested with lice.

pelvis *pl.* **pelvises** *or* **pelves** 1. the bony cavity outlined by the hips and lower bones of the spine and holding the lower intestine, bladder and (in females) the internal genital organs. 2. any bodily cavity resembling a basin or cup, such as that at the base of the kidney (renal pelvis). —**pelvic** *adj.*

penicillin any of several antibiotics produced by molds or synthetically and used esp. against cocci.

penile of or relating to the penis.

penis the male organ of copulation, composed of erectile tissue and containing the urethra.

penitis inflammation of the penis.

pentobarbital a barbiturate used as an antispasmodic, sedative, and hypnotic.

peptic of, relating to, or affecting the stomach or digestion.

percussion the technique of tapping the surface of the body to diagnose from the resultant sound the condition of the parts beneath. —**percuss** *vb.*

perforation a hole in an organ produced by disease or injury. —**perforate** *vb.*

peri- *prefix* all around; about.

perianal located around the area of the anus; surrounding the anus.

pericarditis inflammation of the pericardium.

pericardium *pl.* **pericardia** the membranous sac surrounding the heart. —**pericardial** *adj.*

pericranium *pl.* **pericrania** the thick, fibrous membrane covering the surface of the bones of the skull; the periosteum of the skull.

perineum *pl.* **perinea** the region of the pelvic floor between the anus and the anterior portion of the external genitalia. —**perineal** *adj.*

peristalsis the involuntary muscular waves of the intestine that move the contents onward. —**peristaltic** *adj.* —**peristaltically** *adv.*

peritoneum *pl.* **peritoneums** *or* **peritonea** the transparent membrane that lines the abdominal cavity. —**peritoneal** *adj.*

pernicious highly destructive or injurious; deadly: *pernicious anemia.*

PEPTIC ULCER

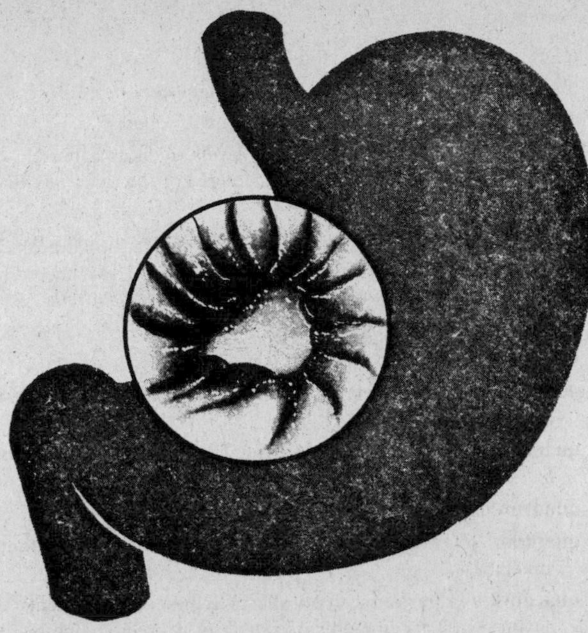

A peptic ulcer is a benign crater in the mucous membrane of the stomach or duodenum, caused by the action of the acid gastric juice.

peroral occurring through or taken by way of the mouth. **—perorally** *adv.*

pertussis whooping cough.

perversion an aberrant sexual practice.

pes *pl.* **pedes** foot.

pessary *pl.* **pessaries** 1. a device placed in the vagina to support the uterus or prevent conception. 2. a vaginal suppository.

pestilence an epidemic disease.

petit mal a mild form of epilepsy.

phagocyte a white blood corpuscle that typically consumes and destroys debris and foreign bodies.

phalanx *pl.* **phalanxes** *or* **phalanges** one of the digital bones of the hand or foot.

phallus *pl.* **phalluses** *or* **phalli** 1. the penis. 2. anything resembling or suggestive of a penis. **—phallic** *adj.*

phantom limb the sensation sometimes experienced after amputation of a limb that the limb is still there.

pharmaceutical 1. of or relating to pharmacy or to pharmacists. 2. of or relating to a drug or drugs. 3. a medicinal drug. **—pharmaceutically** *adv.*

pharmaco- *prefix* medicine; drug.

pharmacology the science dealing with medicinal drugs and their action on the body. **—pharmacological** *adj.* **—pharmacologist** *n.*

pharmacopoeia an official book describing drugs, medicinal preparations, and chemicals.

pharmacy *pl.* **pharmacies** 1. the practice of preparing, compounding, and dispensing drugs. 2. a place where drugs and medicines are compounded and dispensed. **—pharmacist** *n.*

pharyngeal of or relating to the pharynx.

pharyngitis inflammation of the pharynx.

pharynx the part of the alimentary canal between the mouth and the esophagus; the lower back part of the throat.

phimosis severe contraction of the foreskin usually requiring circumcision.

phlebectomy *pl.* **phlebectomies** excision of a vein.

phlebitis inflammation of a vein.

phlebotomy *pl.* **phlebotomies** the bleeding of a patient by the opening of a vein, as in the treatment of polycythemia.

phlegm a thick mucus produced in abnormal quantities by the respiratory passages.

phosphoprotein any of various proteins combined with a compound containing phosphorus.

phrenic 1. of or relating to the diaphragm. 2. relating to the mind.

phthisis an older name for tuberculosis of the lungs.

physiology a branch of biology dealing with the structure and function of living organisms. **—physiological** *adj.* **—physiologist** *n.*

physiotherapy therapy involving the use of heat, massage and exercise rather than medication. **—physiotherapist** *n.*

piles the informal name for hemorrhoids.

pimple a small, inflamed, pus-filled elevation of the skin; pustule. **—pimpled** *adj.* **—pimply** *adj.*

pink eye infectious conjunctivitis.

pituitary gland an endocrine gland at the base of the brain producing various essential hormones.

placebo a chemically inactive agent given to reassure a patient or used in the double-blind or single-blind evaluation of active drugs, where one group of patients receives the test drug and another the inactive agent.

placenta the vascular organ surrounding the fetus within the uterus. **—placental** *adj.*

plague an acute, infectious bacterial disease transmitted to man by rat fleas.

plantar relating to, affecting, or occurring on the sole of the foot: *plantar wart.*

plasma the liquid portion of the blood, in which the corpuscles are suspended.

plastic surgery surgical repair or restoration of damaged or deformed tissue. **—plastic surgeon.**

pleura *pl.* **pleurae** *or* **pleuras** a thin membrane lining the lungs and the inner surface of the chest cavity.

pleurisy inflammation of the pleura.

plexus a network of interlacing nerves or blood vessels.

pneumoconiosis fibrosis of the lungs from prolonged inhalation of irritant dust particles.

pneumonia a disease marked by severe inflammation of the lungs.

pockmark a cavity of the skin caused by a pustule, as from smallpox or acne.

podiatrist a physician specializing in the care and treatment of the feet. **—podiatry** *n.*

poliomyelitis a viral disease marked by inflammation of the nerve cells of the spinal cord, deformity, and paralysis. Also called *infantile paralysis, polio.*

polycythemia an abnormal increase in the total number of circulating red blood cells.

polyp a small projecting tumor, esp. in a body cavity or passage.

pons the bridge of tissue at the base of the brain that connects the medulla oblongata with the cerebral hemispheres and the cerebellum. Also called *pons Varolii.*

post mortem necropsy; autopsy.

postpartum following parturition.

postprandial following meals: *postprandial medication.*

poultice a moist bandage applied over a wound.

prepuce foreskin.

pressure point a point at which pressure may be applied to check hemorrhage.

prickly heat inflammation around the sweat ducts causing redness and itching.

primipara a woman who has borne only one child.

probe a slender instrument for exploring wounds.

proctology a branch of medicine dealing chiefly with the structure and diseases of the lower bowel. **—protological** *adj.* **—proctologist** *n.*

proctoscope an instrument for examining the interior of the rectum.

prostatectomy *pl.* **prostatectomies** surgical removal of the prostate gland.

prostate gland a muscular gland at the base of the male urethra that secretes the viscid fluid that is a major constituent of semen. **—prostatic** *adj.*

prostatitis inflammation of the prostate gland.

prosthesis replacement of an absent organ or limb with an artificial one. **—prosthetics** *n.*

pruritis an itching of the skin.

psittacosis a viral disease of birds, as parrots, transmittable to man.

psoriasis a skin disease marked by the formation of red scaly patches.

psychiatrist a physician who specializes in psychiatry.

psychiatry a branch of medicine that deals with mental, emotional, or behavioral disorders. **—psychiatric** *adj.* **—psychiatrically** *adv.*

psychoanalysis a method of treating emotional disorders in which the patient talks freely about himself and esp. about his dreams and childhood to an analyst. **—psychoanalytic** *adj.*

psychology the science concerned with the mind and human behavior. **—psychological** *adj.* **—psychologist** *n.*

psychopath a mentally deranged person. **—psychopathic** *adj.*

psychosis severe, disabling mental derangement marked esp. by a loss of contact with reality. **—psychotic** *n. & adj.*

psychosomatic relating to or involving both psychological and physical factors: *psychosomatic illness.*

puberty the age at which a person becomes capable of reproducing sexually and during which the genitals mature and the secondary sex characteristics appear; generally between the ages of 12 and 14.

pubes 1. the hair that appears just above the external genital organs at puberty. 2. the two bones forming the front of the pelvis. **—pubic** *adj.*

pupil the round, contractive area in the center of the eye.

purgative a medicine for inducing evacuation of the bowels.

pus a thick, opaque whitish fluid containing cellular debris and being a product of inflammation or infection.

pustule a small elevation of the skin containing pus. **—pustular** *adj.*

pyelitis inflammation of the pelvis of the kidney.

pylorus *pl.* **pylori** the valve-like opening of the stomach into the duodenum. **—pyloric** *adj.*

Q

q.i.d. *abbr.* quater in die: four times daily.

quack a pretender to medical skills. **—quackery** *n.*

quadrate having four sides that are equal; square.

quadriceps a muscle having four heads, such as a muscle of the thigh (*musculus quadriceps femoris*) or the calf (*musculus quadriceps surae*).

quadricepsplasty a surgical procedure to repair the quadriceps muscle of the thigh.

quadricuspid having four cusps. Also called *tetracuspid.*

quadridigitate having four digits.

quadriplegia paralysis of both legs and arms.

quadriplegic 1. relating to quadriplegia. 2. one with paralysis of all four limbs.

quadrisect to divide or separate into four parts. **—quadrisection** *n.*

quadruplet one of four children born at one birth.

quantum *pl.* **quanta** 1. a unit of radiant energy. 2. a definite amount.

quarantine a restraint upon the activities or movements of anyone with a communicable disease in order to inhibit its spread; detention and isolation from others for a given period of anyone with a contagious disease.

quartan recurring every fourth day.

quater in die (in prescription writing) four times daily.

quaternary 1. (of a chemical compound) containing four elements. 2. coming fourth in a series.

quick 1. pregnant with a child whose movement can be felt within the uterus. 2. any sensitive part that is particularly painful to touch. 3. the part of a finger or toe to which the nail is attached.

quickening the first indications of movement of the fetus within the uterus, usually noted within the first 16 to 20 weeks of pregnancy.

quicksilver mercury.

quin- *or* **quino-** *prefix* relating to or containing quinoline or quinine.

quinine a white, crystalline alkaloid derived from cinchona bark and used as an analgesic, antipyretic and antimalarial agent.

quinoline a substance derived from coal tar and used medically as an analgesic, antipyretic and in the treatment of amoebic dysentery and related infections.

quinsy inflammation of the throat with swelling and fever.

quintan recurring every fifth day.

quinti- *prefix* fifth.

quintipara a woman who has given birth five times.

quintuplet one of five children born at one birth.

quotidian occurring each day; recurring daily.

quotidian fever a malarial fever that flares up every day during the illness.

R

rabbit fever tularemia.

rabiate suffering from rabies.

rabic relating to or concerning rabies.

rabicidal destructive to the virus that causes rabies.

rabid affected with rabies.

rabies an acute and inevitably fatal viral disease transmitted by the bite of a rabid animal.

racemose (esp. of a gland) resembling a bunch of grapes.

rachi- *or* **rachio-** *prefix* relating to or indicating the spinal column.

rachialgia pain in the spine. Also called *rachiodynia.*

rachianalgesia spinal anesthesia.

rachidian relating to the spinal column.

rachiodynia pain in the spine. Also called *rachialgia.*

rachis *pl.* **rachises** *also* **rachides** spinal column.

rachitic relating to or affected with rickets; rickety.

radectomy surgical removal of all or part of the root of a tooth.

radiad in the direction of a radius or the radial side of a structure or part.

radical 1. (in chemistry) a group of atoms that act as a single unit, capable of passing unchanged from one chemical compound to another. 2. relating to or being anything that attacks or reaches an origin or root of something else.

radiobiology a branch of biology dealing with the effects on living organisms of radioactive materials or ionizing radiation. **—radiobiological** *adj.* **—radiobiologist** *n.*

radiograph a picture of internal structures of the body using X-rays or gamma rays on a sensitive photographic surface. **—radiographic** *adj.* **—radiography** *n.*

radiology the use of radiant energy, as X-rays, in the diagnosis and treatment of disease. **—radiological** *adj.* **—radiologist** *n.*

radiosensitive sensitive to the effects of radiant energy.

radiotherapy the treatment of disease by the use of radioactive substances or X rays. **—radiotherapist** *n.*

radium a radioactive and fluorescent metallic element, used in the treatment of various tumors esp. by implantation or insertion into the tissues.

radium therapy the therapeutic use of radium, esp. in controlling the spread of tumors.

radius *pl.* **radii** *or* **radiuses** the outer and shorter bone of the forearm.

radix the root of anything, such as the root portion of a spinal or cranial nerve.

rale an abnormal respiratory sound.

ramus *pl.* **rami** a secondary branch of a bodily structure, as a nerve or vessel.

ranula a cyst formed in a mucous membrane, as that under the tongue. **—ranular** *adj.*

rape sexual intercourse with a female without her consent or when she is legally under age or mentally incapable of making moral decisions.

raphe a ridge, crease or fibrous junction uniting two parts of an organ or part.

rash a usually minor eruption on the skin.

rat-bite fever a febrile, bacterial disease transmitted by the bite of an infected rat.

reaction a bodily response to a stimulus. **—reactive** *adj.*

recalcitrant resistant to treatment: *a recalcitrant disease.*

receptor an organ that receives stimuli.

recessive tending to recede or be of minor importance.

recipient one who receives.

recrudescence a recurrence of symptoms after an abatement. **—recrudesce** *vb.* **—recrudescent** *adj.*

rectal relating to, being near, or involving the rectum.

rectum *pl.* **rectums** *or* **recta** the part of the intestine from the sigmoid flexure to the anus.

rectus *pl.* **recti** a straight muscle, as one sustaining the abdomen.

recumbent lying down.

recuperate to recover health; become well. **—recuperative** *adj.* **—recuperation** *n.*

recurrent 1. turning back in an opposite direction. 2. repeated; returning after an intermission: *a recurrent head cold.*

red blood cell any of the hemoglobin-containing cells that carry oxygen to the tissues and give redness to the blood; erythrocyte.

reduction the correction of a hernia, fracture, or luxation.

reflex an automatic response to a stimulus that involves a nerve impulse passing to a nerve center and outward again, producing an automatic reaction. Also called *reflex act, reflex action.*

refractory resistant to cure or treatment: *a refractory wound.*

regeneration renewal or restoration of a structure or part of the body, esp. after injury. **—regenerate** *vb.*

regimen a strict plan of diet, medication, or exercise for the purpose of maintaining or restoring health.

regression 1. the decline of a symptom of a disease. 2. gradual loss of function of a body part, esp. as the result of the process of aging.

regurgitation 1. the casting up of incompletely digested food. 2. the backward flow of blood from a defective heart valve. **—regurgitate** *vb.*

Reiter's syndrome *or* **Reiter's disease** arthritis, conjunctivitis, and urethritis occurring simultaneously and of unknown cause.

rejection an immune reaction against grafted tissue or a transplanted organ.

relapse the recurrence of the symptoms of a disease after a period of recovery. **—relapse** *vb.*

relapsing fever any of various acute infectious diseases marked by recurrent high fever for periods of about a week and caused by various spirochetes.

remission a condition or period during which the symptoms of a disease subside.

renal relating to, affecting, or located in the area of the kidneys; nephritic.

resection the surgical excision of part of an organ or structure. **—resect** *vb.* **—resectable** *adj.*

resolution the diminution of inflammation.

resonance the sound produced by percussion of the chest.

respiration the intake of oxygen and expulsion of carbon dioxide from the lungs; breathing. **—respiratory** *adj.*

respirator 1. a device covering the mouth and nose for protecting the respiratory tract. 2. a device for aiding in artificial respiration.

respiratory system the system or organs, as the lungs, their circulatory and nervous supply, and their connecting channels, by which air is conducted to and from the body.

resuscitation the action of reviving a person from apparent death or from unconsciousness. **—resuscitate** *vb.*

retardation a less than normal degree of intellectual development. **—retard** *vb.* **—retardant** *adj & n.*

retch to strain in an effort to vomit. **—retch** *n.*

retention abnormal holding in of a secretion or fluid of the body.

reticular of or resembling a net or network: *reticular tissues.*

retina *pl.* **retinas** *or* **retinae** a sensory membrane that lines the interior of the eye, contains the light-sensitive receptors, receives the optical image formed by the lens, and is connected by the optic nerve to the brain. —**retinal** *adj.*

retinitis inflammation of the retina.

retinol vitamin A.

retinopathy any noninflammatory disorder of the retina.

retinoscopy the projection of a beam of light into the eye to observe abnormalities of the retina.

retractor 1. an instrument used in surgery to hold back the edges of a wound. 2. a muscle that draws back or in an organ or part.

retro- *prefix* back; behind.

retroflexion *or* **retroflection** the turning back of a bodily organ upon itself.

retroperitoneal located behind the peritoneum.

retroversion a bending backward of the cervix and uterus.

rheum a watery discharge from the eyes. —**rheumy** *adj.*

rheumatic relating to, affected with, or associated with rheumatism.

rheumatic fever an acute febrile disease marked chiefly by pain and inflammation of the joints and inflammation of the heart valves and the endocardium.

rheumatism inflammation or pain in joints, fibrous tissues, or muscles.

rheumatoid arthritis a progressive disease marked by inflammation, swelling, and sometimes deformation of the joints.

Rh factor a substance present in the red blood cells capable of producing antigenic reactions.

rhinal of, relating to, or affecting the nose; nasal.

rhinitis inflammation of the mucous membranes of the nose.

rhinopharyngitis inflammation of the nose and pharynx.

rhinoscope a speculum for examining the nasal passages.

rhinoscopy examination of the nasal passages.

rhodopsin a red photosensitive pigment in the rods of the retina of the eye.

rhonchus *pl.* **rhonchi** a hoarse whistling sound heard upon ausculation of the chest and caused by obstruction of the air passages.

rib any one of the twelve pairs of curved bones that enclose the lungs and protect the viscera of the chest.

riboflavin vitamin B.

ribonuclease an enzyme active in catalyzing the hydrolysis of RNA.

ribonucleic acid RNA.

ribosome any of the cytoplasmic granules that are rich in RNA and are central to protein synthesis. —**ribosomal** *adj.*

rickets a disease of childhood caused by insufficient assimilation of calcium and phosphorus from inadequate vitamin D and sunlight and marked by softening and deformation of the bones.

rickettsia *pl.* **rickettsias** *or* **rickettsiae** any of a family of microorganisms, intermediate in size between bacteria and viruses, that cause various diseases, as typhus and Rocky Mountain spotted fever. —**rickettsial** *adj.*

rigor mortis stiffening of the muscles in a dead body.

ringworm any of several diseases of the skin or scalp caused by fungi and marked by ring-shaped, scaly, pigmented patches.

risus sardonicus a fixed, grinning expression caused by spasm of the facial muscles and associated chiefly with tetanus.

RNA ribonucleic acid; any of various nucleic acids found mainly in the nucleolus and mitochondria of cells and being important to the control of cellular chemical action, as protein synthesis.

rod any of the rod-shaped, photosensitive receptors in the retina of the eye.

roentgen 1. of or relating to X-rays. 2. the international unit of X-radiation or gamma radiation.

roentgenology a branch of radiology using X-rays for the diagnosis and treatment of disease. —**roentgenologic** *or* **roentgenological** *adj.* —**roentgenologist** *n.*

roentgenoscope fluoroscope. —**roentgenoscopic** *adj.* —**roentgenoscopy** *n.*

roentgen ray X-ray.

root 1. the basal, enlarged part of a hair within the skin. 2. the part of a tooth within the socket. 3. either of the two bundles of nerve fibers that emerge from the spinal cord, joining to form a single spinal nerve.

roseola a rose-colored rash, as that occurring as a symptom of German measles.

roughage food containing dietary fiber that is not readily digestible and therefore stimulates peristalsis and is considered essential to maintain the health of the intestinal tract.

rubefacient a substance that causes the skin to redden. —**rubefacient** *adj.*

rubella an infectious viral disease that is less severe than measles but is harmful to the fetus during pregnancy. Also called *German measles.*

ruga *pl.* **rugae** an anatomical wrinkle or fold, as one of the many folds of mucous membrane that lines the stomach.

rugose full of wrinkles; wrinkled.

rupture hernia.

S

Sabin vaccine an orally administered vaccine for protection against poliomyelitis, containing attenuated strains of live polio virus.

sabulous gritty or sandy; resembling coarse sand.

sac a small, internal, usually fluid-containing pouch. —**sacular** *adj.* —**saculated** *adj.*

saccharin a white crystalline compound that is much sweeter than cane sugar and is used in food and liquid as a calorie-free sweetener.

saccharine relating to sugar or sweetness; sweet.

saccharo- *or* **sacchar-** *or* **sacchari-** *prefix* relating to sugar.

saccus *pl.* **sacci** a sac.

sacrad in the direction of or toward the sacrum.

sacralgia pain in the region of the sacrum. Also called *sacrodynia.*

sacro- *or* **sacr-** *prefix* relating to the sacrum.

sacrococcygeal relating to both the sacrum and the coccyx.

sacrodynia pain in the region of the sacrum. Also called *sacralgia.*

sacroiliac 1. relating to both the sacrum and the ilium. 2.

(informal) the lower part of the back, including the base of the spine.

sacrolumbar relating to both the sacrum and the lumbar region. Also called *lumbosacral.*

sacrum *pl.* **sacra** the lower part of the vertebral column that connects with and forms part of the pelvis. —**sacral** *adj.*

sadism sexual pleasure derived from inflicting physical or mental pain on others; delight in cruelty. —**sadist** *adj.* & *n.* —**sadistic** *adj.* —**sadistically** *adv.*

sadomasochism sexual pleasure derived from both inflicting pain and cruelty on others and being the recipient of cruelty or physical pain.

sagittal relating to or located in the median plane of the body. —**sagittally** *adv.*

Saint Vitus's dance chorea.

sal *pl.* **sales** salt.

salify to convert or change into a salt.

saline consisting of or containing salt: *a saline solution.*

saliva the clear, alkaline, somewhat viscid liquid secretion of the salivary glands.

salivary of or relating to saliva or the salivary glands.

salivary gland any of the glands of the oral cavity that secrete saliva.

salivate to produce marked quantities of saliva.

salivation the production of saliva.

Salk vaccine a vaccine that contains three types of polio viruses that have been inactivated for inoculation against poliomyelitis.

salmonella *pl.* **salmonellae** *or* **salmonellas** any of a genus of microorganisms causing food poisoning, diseases of the genital tract, and inflammation of the gastrointestinal tract.

salmonellosis infection with salmonellae.

salpingectomy surgical removal of a fallopian tube.

salpingemphraxis obstruction of a eustachian or a fallopian tube.

salpingian relating to the eustachian or the fallopian tube.

salpingioma any tumor or growth developing in a fallopian tube.

salpingitis inflammation of a eustachian tube or a fallopian tube. —**salpingitic** *adj.*

salpingo- *or* **salping-** *prefix* relating to or denoting a tube, usually a fallopian or eustachian tube.

salpingocele hernia involving a fallopian tube.

salpingolysis the surgical or manual freeing from adhesions of a fallopian tube.

salpingo-oophor- *or* **salpingo-oophoro-** *prefix* relating to a fallopian tube and ovary.

salpingo-oophorectomy surgical removal of a fallopian tube and ovary.

salpingo-oophoritis inflammation of both a fallopian tube and ovary.

salpingoplasty plastic surgery involving the fallopian tubes.

salpingorrhagia bleeding from a fallopian tube.

salpingorrhaphy the procedure of suturing a fallopian tube.

salpinx *pl.* **salpinges** a eustachian or fallopian tube.

saltpeter potassium nitrate.

salubrious favoring health or healthy conditions; healthful. —**salubrity** *n.*

saluresis the excretion in the urine of sodium.

saluretic enhancing or favoring the excretion of sodium by the kidneys.

salutarium sanitarium.

salutary wholesome or healthful.

salve an adhesive, unctuous ointment for soothing wounds or sores.

sanative healing or curative.

sanatorium *pl.* **sanatoriums** *or* **sanatoria** an institution for the convalescent or for the chronically ill.

sandfly fever a febrile, viral disease transmitted by any of various biting, two-winged flies. Also called *phlebotomus fever.*

sanguine of, relating to, or filled with blood. —**sanguinary** *adj.* —**sanguineous** *adj.*

sanitarium *pl.* **sanitariums** *or* **sanitaria** sanatorium.

sanitary of or relating to health. —**sanitation** *n.*

sanitary napkin a soft, disposable, absorbent pad worn to absorb blood flow during the menstrual period.

sanitize to make sanitary.

sanity soundness of mind; rationality. —**sane** *adj.*

saphenous relating to or being either of the two chief superficial veins of the leg.

sapo- *or* **sapon-** *prefix* relating to soap.

saponaceous relating to or resembling soap; soapy.

saponify to convert into soap.

sapphic lesbian. —**sapphism** *n.*

sarapus one who has flatfoot.

sarcoid 1. relating to or resembling flesh; fleshy. 2. a tumor resembling a sarcoma.

sarcoidosis a chronic, progressive disease of unknown origin that is marked chiefly by the appearance of nodules on various bodily organs or tissues or on parts of the body.

sarcolemma a thin membrane enclosing a striated muscle fiber.

sarcoma *pl.* **sarcomas** *or* **sarcomata** an often malignant tumor of connective tissue, striated muscle, bone, or cartilage. —**sarcomatous** *adj.*

sarcomatosis *pl.* **sarcomatoses** a disease marked by the development and spreading of sarcomas.

sartorius a long muscle that crosses the front of the thigh.

sawbones *Slang.* physician; surgeon.

scab a crust over a wound formed of hardened blood, pus, and serum. —**scabby** *adj.*

scabies a contagious skin disease caused by mites and marked by intense itching. —**scabietic** *adj.*

scald a burn caused by hot liquid or steam. —**scald** *vb.*

scale a thin, dry aggregation of cells shed from the skin in some skin diseases. —**scale** *vb.*

scalp the skin covering the top of the head, normally covered with hair.

scapula *pl.* **scapulae** *or* **scapulas** either of the flat triangular bones forming the back of the shoulder; shoulder blade.

scar a mark on the skin remaining after the healing of a wound.

scarification the making of small incisions in the skin, as for a vaccination. —**scarify** *vb.*

scarlatina scarlet fever. —**scarlatinal** *adj.*

scarlet fever an acute, contagious disease marked by fever, extensive skin rash, tonsillitis, and generalized toxemia.

Schick test a test for susceptibility to diphtheria by skin injection of a dilution of diphtheria toxin.

schistosomiasis *pl.* **schistosomiases** a parasitic disease caused by infestation with blood flukes and marked by loss of blood and damage to tissues caused mainly by the deposition in the vessels and tissues of the worms' eggs. Also called *bilharzia.*

schizophrenia a psychotic condition marked chiefly by withdrawal from reality, hallucinations, delusions, and bizarre behavior. Also called (informal) *split personality.* —**schizophrenic** *adj. & n.*

sciatica pain radiating from the lower back to the buttocks and the lower extremities. —**sciatic** *adj.*

sciatic nerve either of a pair of large nerves of the posterior limb and pelvic region passing down the back of the thigh.

scissura 1. a fissure; cleft. 2. a splitting.

sclera the hard white outer coating of the eyeball excluding the cornea. —**scleral** *adj.*

scleradenitis inflammation and hardening of a gland.

sclerema a hardening of subcutaneous fat.

sclero- *or* **scler-** *prefix* 1. hard. 2. relating to the sclera.

scleroderma a skin disease marked by the hardening and thickening of the skin. —**sclerodermatous** *adj.*

sclerosis hardening of tissue. —**sclerotic** *adj.*

scolecoiditis appendicitis.

scolex *pl.* **scolices** the head of a tapeworm.

scoliosis *pl.* **scolioses** lateral curvature of the spine. —**scoliotic** *adj.*

scopolamine an alkaloid derived from the roots of plants of the nightshade family and used as a sedative and as a so-called truth serum.

scorbutic relating to or suffering from scurvy.

scorbutus scurvy.

scotoma *pl.* **scotomas** *or* **scotomata** a blind spot in the field of vision. —**scotomatous** *adj.*

scotophobia an abnormal fear of the dark.

scrotum *pl.* **scrotums** *or* **scrota** the external pouch that holds the testes. —**scrotal** *adj.*

scurf dry thin scales shed from the epidermis esp. in some skin diseases. —**scurfy** *adj.*

scurvy a disease caused by deficiency of ascorbic acid and marked chiefly by sponginess of the gums and loosening of the teeth.

sebaceous relating to, resembling, or secreting fatty material; fatty: *sebaceous glands.*

seborrhea abnormally profuse production and discharge of sebum. —**seborrheic** *adj.*

sebum a lubricant, fatty substance secreted by the sebaceous glands of the skin.

secondary sex characteristic a physical characteristic, as the appearance of facial hair in boys, that appears at the time of puberty but is not directly related to reproduction.

secondary syphilis the second stage of syphilis that appears from 2 to 6 months after the primary stage and is marked by lesions in the skin, organs, and tissues and has a duration of 3 to 12 weeks.

section 1. a surgical division of a structure or part; cut. 2. a cut surface. 3. an extremely thin slice of tissue taken for microscopic examination.

secundigravida a woman who is pregnant for the second time.

sedative 1. tending to calm or neutralize nervousness or excitement. 2. an agent or drug that has a sedative effect. —**sedate** *vb.* —**sedation** *n.*

segmentum *pl.* **segmenta** 1. a section or part of a structure. 2. the part or region of an organ that has an independent function, separate nerve or vascular supply, etc.

semen a whitish, viscid fluid produced by the male reproductory tract that serves as the vehicle for spermatozoa.

semicircular canal a loop-shaped canal of the inner ear associated with maintenance of the sense of equilibrium.

seminal of, relating to, or consisting of semen.

senescence the condition or process of aging.

senility the loss of mental faculties owing to old age. —**senile** *adj.*

sensation a mental process, as seeing or smelling, that is a direct response to bodily stimulation.

sense organ a structure of the body, as an eye or ear, that receives stimuli and transmits the excitation to nerve fibers continuous with the central nervous system where the stimuli are interpreted as sensations.

sensitive highly susceptible; hypersensitive: *sensitive to ragweed pollen.*

sensitization the condition of being sensitive or hypersensitive to an antigen or drug. —**sensitize** *vb.*

sensory carrying nerve impulses from the sense organs to the nerve centers; afferent. —**sensorial** *adj.*

sepsis *pl.* **sepses** a toxic condition resulting from the spread of bacteria or the products of bacteria from an infection. —**septic** *adj.*

septicemia circulation of virulent microorganisms in the bloodstream. Also called *blood poisoning.*

septum *pl.* **septa** a dividing wall or membrane between two bodily cavities.

sequestrum *pl.* **sequestrums** *or* **sequestra** a fragment of dead bone; bony necrosis.

serosa a serous membrane. —**serosal** *adj.*

serous relating to or resembling serum; watery and thin.

serum *pl.* **serums** *or* **sera** the watery part of a fluid, as blood, remaining after coagulation or removal of the other parts.

serum sickness an allergic reaction following an injection of foreign serum and marked by skin rash, pain in the joints, swelling, fever, and prostration.

sesamoid of or relating to a mass of cartilage or bone at a joint or bony prominence. —**sesamoid** *n.*

sessile attached to a base; not free to move: *sessile polyps.*

sex 1. either of two divisions of living organisms distinguished as male or female respectively. 2. the functional, structural, and behavioral characteristics of the male or female sex. 3. sexual activity. 4. (informal) sexual intercourse.

sex chromosome a chromosome inherited differently in the two sexes and concerned with the determination of sex.

sexual 1. relating to or associated with sex or the sexes. 2. erotic in nature or character. —**sexually** *adv.*

sexual intercourse sexual connection esp. between human beings; penetration of the vagina by the penis, usually leading to orgasm; coitus.

sexuality sexual feelings and interests.

shinbone tibia.

shingles an acute viral inflammation of the spinal and cranial nerves marked by neuralgic pains and vesicular eruptions; herpes zoster.

shock severe circulatory disturbance with markedly reduced blood pressure and volume caused typically by a severe injury, burn, or the like.

show (informal) a discharge of bloodstained mucus from the vagina occurring chiefly at the beginning of labor.

sibling one of two or more individuals having the same parent.

sick bay an infirmary on a naval ship or at a naval station.

sick call a military formation at which individuals can report if in need of medical attention.

sickle to form into a crescent.

sickle-cell anemia an inherited anemia occurring chiefly among people of Negro ancestry and in which a large proportion or the majority of the red blood cells tend to sickle.

sigmoid curved like the letter *S*.

sigmoid flexure the contracted and crooked part of the colon just above the rectum.

silicon a nonmetallic element that is the most abundant element (25 per cent) next to oxygen in the earth's crust.

silicone an organic compound in which the carbon has been replaced by silicon.

silicosis a disease of the lungs marked by shortness of breath and caused by prolonged inhalation of silica dust.

simple fracture a bone fracture having no secondary complications.

sinciput the upper and fore part of the cranium. —**sincipital** *adj.*

sinew a tendon connecting a muscle to a bone. —**sinewy** *adj.*

sinistral relating to or situated on the left side.

sinus 1. a passage leading from an abscess to an external opening of the body. 2. a dilated channel for venous blood. 3. an air-filled passage communicating from the bones of the skull to the nostrils.

sinusitis inflammation of a sinus of the skull.

sinusoid 1. resembling a sinus. 2. a blood channel in certain organs. —**sinusoidal** *adj.* —**sinusoidally** *adv.*

skeleton the rigid, supportive bony framework of the body. —**skeletal** *adj.* —**skeletally** *adv.*

skin the outer integument of the body.

skull the bony skeleton of the head protecting the brain and the major sense organs.

sleeping sickness an acute infectious protozoal disease chiefly of Africa that is marked by fever, tremors, intense lethargy and is transmitted by tsetse flies.

slough dead tissue cast off from the body or a bodily part.

smallpox a highly infectious viral disease marked by fever and scarring skin eruptions with pustules.

smegma a cheesy sebaceous substance collecting between the glans penis and the foreskin or around the labia minora and clitoris.

snare a surgical instrument consisting of a wire loop contracted by a mechanism in the handle and used for removing masses of tissue, such as the tonsils.

snow blindness inflammation and photophobia of the eyes resulting from exposure to ultraviolet light reflected from snow or ice. —**snow-blind** *adj.*

sodium pentobarbital a sodium salt of pentobarbital used esp. as a sedative and as an adjunct to other anesthesia.

solar plexus a nerve plexus in the abdomen.

soleus a muscle in the calf of the leg.

solvent a liquid capable of dissolving a substance.

somatic of, relating to, or affecting the body, esp. as distinct from the psyche.

somnambulism the habit of walking while asleep. —**somnambular** *adj.* —**somnambulist** *n.* —**somnambulistic** *adj.*

soporific an agent that tends to induce sleep; hypnotic. —**soporific** *adj.*

sore throat inflammation of the lining of the throat, esp. caused by a bacterial infection.

spasm an involuntary, abnormal muscular contraction. —**spasmodic** *adj.* —**spasmodically** *adv.*

spasmolytic capable of relieving spasms.

spastic 1. relating to or characterized by spasms. 2. marked by spastic paralysis. —**spastic** *n.*

spectroscope an instrument for forming and examining optical spectra. —**spectroscopy** *n.*

speculum *pl.* **specula** *or* **speculums** an instrument for insertion into a body passage for inspection or applying medication.

speech center the part of the brain controlling speech.

sperm 1. semen. 2. a spermatozoon; male sex cell.

spermatic cord a cord that suspends the testis within the scrotum and contains the vas deferens.

spermatozoon *pl.* **spermatozoa** a motile male gamete having a flagellum for propulsion and being the means for fertilizing the human egg.

spermicide *also* **spermatocide** a substance that destroys spermatozoa.

sphincter an annular muscle for contracting a body opening.

sphygmomanometer an instrument for measuring blood pressure. —**sphygmomanometry** *n.*

spinal column the backbone; vertebral column; spine.

spinal cord the cord of nerve tissue extending from the brain through the spinal column.

THE SPINAL CORD
(CROSS SECTION)

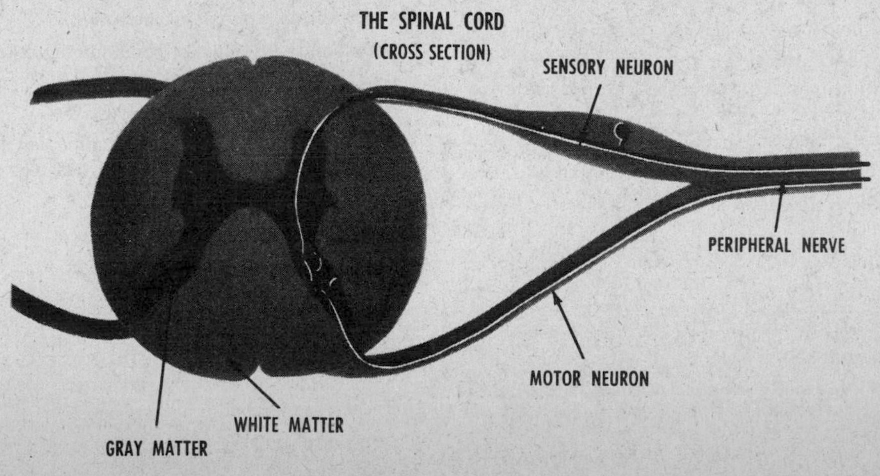

spine the backbone; spinal column; vertebral column.

spirochete *also* **spirochaete** any slender, spirally undulating bacterium.

spleen a vascular organ involved with destruction of blood cells, storage of blood, and production of lymphocytes. —**splenic** *adj.*

splenectomy *pl.* **splenectomies** surgical removal of the spleen.

spotted fever any of various eruptive fevers, as typhus.

sprain a wrench of a joint with stretching or tearing of the ligaments.

sprue a chronic disease with chronic diarrhea, soreness of the tongue and mouth, and anemia.

sputum *pl.* **sputa** expectorated matter composed chiefly of mucus but sometimes also of discharge from the respiratory passages.

stapes *pl.* **stapes** *or* **stapedes** the innermost of the three conducting bones of the middle ear; stirrup.

staph staphylococcus.

staphylococcus *pl.* **staphylococci** any of various round (coccal) bacteria that include parasites of the skin and mucous membranes. —**staphylococcal** *adj.*

stasis *pl.* **stases** a slowing or stopping of the normal flow of body fluids.

steat- *or* **steato-** *prefix* fat.

steatopygia an abnormal development of fat on the buttocks. —**steatopygic** *or* **steatopygous** *adj.*

sterile unable to produce offspring. —**sterility** *n.*

sterilization deprivation of the ability to produce offspring, esp. by removal of the ovaries or by vasectomy. —**sterilize** *vb.*

sternum *pl.* **sternums** *or* **sterna** the breastbone.

stertor rasping, wheezing respiration during deep sleep; a snore. —**stertorous** *adj.*

stethoscope an instrument for listening to and diagnosing sounds produced within the body, esp. those of the heart and lungs.

stillborn dead at birth. —**stillborn** *n.*

stimulant a substance that produces alertness and a temporary increase in functional activity. —**stimulant** *adj.* —**stimulate** *vb.* —**stimulation** *n.*

stomach an expansion of the alimentary canal, extending from the esophagus to the duodenum, in which food is first digested before entering the small intestine.

stomachic an agent that stimulates the digestion of food in the stomach.

stool a discharge of fecal matter.

strabismus an inability of one eye to focus in conjunction with the other through muscle weakness.

strangulated constricted so as to be cut off from a supply of blood: *strangulated hernia.*

streptococcus any of a genus of parasitic bacteria that includes many important pathogens. —**streptococcal** *adj.*

stroke cardiovascular accident, often causing sensory or motor impairment.

sty *or* **stye** an inflamed swelling at the margin of an eyelid.

styptic tending to arrest bleeding.

subcutaneous beneath the skin.

sunstroke heat exhaustion.

suppository a medication in the form of a small capsule, etc., that melts at body temperatures and is administered esp. by means of the rectum or vagina.

suppuration the formation or discharge of pus. —**suppurate** *vb.* —**suppurative** *adj.*

surgery 1. the branch of medical science concerned with diseases and conditions requiring operations. 2. a specially equipped room where surgical operations are performed.

surgical of, relating to, or used in surgery. —**surgically** *adv.*

suspensory *pl.* **suspensories** a fabric supporter for the testicles.

suture a fiber or strand used to sew parts of the body that are wounded or have undergone surgery. —**suture** *vb.*

swab a wad of absorbent material, as cotton, used alone or wrapped around the end of a small stick to cleanse a wound or remove material from an area. —**swab** *vb.*

sweat to exude moisture through the skin, esp. profusely; perspire. —**sweat** *n.*

sycosis inflammation of the hair follicles esp. of the beard.

symphysis *pl.* **symphyses** an articulation of various bones joined together by fibrous cartilage.

symptom a bodily change experienced by a patient that is indicative of a disease or disorder. —**symptomatic** *adj.*

syncope temporary loss of consciousness; faint.

syndrome the aggregate of signs and symptoms characteristic of a particular disease.

synovia a transparent fluid secreted by a membrane of a joint or bursa. —**synovial** *adj.*

synovitis inflammation of the synovial membrane of a joint.

syphilis a chronic disease usually transmitted during sexual intercourse with an infected partner, caused by a spirochete and characteristically marked by three sequential degenerative stages occurring over the course of many years. —**syphilitic** *n & adj.*

syringe 1. an instrument for injecting a drug or medication and consisting of a hollow barrel with a plunger to hold the substance and a hollow needle. 2. an instrument with a nozzle and compressible bulb used for irrigation of a cavity.

systemic involving or affecting the entire body.

systole the contraction of the heart by which the blood is forced through the circulatory system.

T

tabella *pl.* **tabellae** a medicated mass of compressed material such as a tablet or lozenge.

tabes *pl.* **tabes** wasting of the body associated with a chronic disease, as syphilis. —**tabetic** *adj.*

tabescence the state or condition of wasting away.

tablespoon (as a unit of measure) one-half fluid ounce; 15 milliliters.

tache a small area of discoloration on the skin or a mucous membrane, such as a freckle or macule. —**tachetic** *adj.*

tachycardia increased heart beat.

tactile relating to the sense of touch.

tactus the sense of touch; touch.

taenia *also* **tenia** 1. any bandlike structure or part. 2. a tapeworm.

Taenia saginata the beef tapeworm, acquired by humans as the result of eating inadequately cooked infected beef and causing the condition known as teniasis.

taeniasis teniasis.

Taenia solium the pork tapeworm, acquired by humans as the result of eating inadequately cooked infected pork and causing the conditon known as cysticercosis.

talipes club foot.

tarsus 1. the seven bones that together constitute the articulation between the foot and leg; ankle. 2. the cartilaginous connective tissue supporting the eyelids. —**tarsal** *adj.*

tartar a calcium deposit forming on the teeth in combination with saliva and food particles.

taste bud an end organ lying chiefly on the surface of the tongue and conveying the sense of taste.

tear a drop of saline fluid secreted by the lacrimal glands. —**tear** *vb.* —**teary** *adj.*

teeth *pl. of* tooth.

tegument the skin; integument.

temperature degree of heat.

temple the flattened area on each side of the forehead. —**temporal** *adj.*

tendinitis inflammation of a tendon.

tendon a tough band or cord of dense connective tissue that joins a muscle with some other part. —**tendinous** *adj.*

tenesmus ineffectual, painful straining to evacuate the bowel or bladder.

teniasis *also* **taeniasis** the presence of tapeworms in the body; infestation with tapeworms.

tenorrhaphy suture of the cut ends of a tendon. Also called *tenosuture.*

tenosynovitis inflammation of both a tendon and its enclosing sheath. Also called *tendosynovitis.*

tenotomy surgical incision of a tendon, as in the treatment of a deformity caused by abnormal shortening of a muscle.

teratogenic tending to cause malformation of a fetus. —**teratogen** *n.* —**teratogenesis** *n.*

ter in die (in prescription writing) three times daily. Abbr. *t.i.d.*

tertiary syphilis the third degenerative and usually fatal stage of syphilis.

testicle testis.

testis *pl.* **testes** either of two male reproductive glands suspended in the scrotum.

testosterone a male hormone produced in the testes or synthetically and responsible for male secondary sex characteristics.

tetanus an acute infectious disease characterized by spasms of the muscles esp. of the jaw and caused by a bacillic toxin introduced through a wound.

tetany muscular spasms caused by mineral deficiency.

tetracycline a broad-spectrum antibiotic.

thalamus a mass of nerve cells at the base of the brain that is the main receptor for sensory impulses, which it transmits to the cerebral cortex.

thalidomide a hypnotic, sedative drug that was discovered in the early 1960s to produce malformation of the fetus when taken during pregnancy.

theca *pl.* **thecae** an enveloping sheath of a bodily part. —**thecal** *adj.*

therapeutics a branch of medical science dealing with methods of treating disease. —**therapeutic** *adj.*

thermography a technique for measuring the heat in various parts of the body and transforming the signals received into a diagnostic photographic record. —**thermograph** *n.* —**thermographic** *adj.*

thermometer an instrument, typically a liquid-filled glass tube with a numbered scale, used for recording variations in temperature. —**thermometric** *adj.*

thiamine *also* **thiamin** a B vitamin essential to metabolism and nerve function.

thigh the part of the leg between the pelvis and the knee.

thighbone femur.

thoracic relating to, involving, or located within the thorax.

thorax *pl.* **thoraxes** *or* **thoraces** the part of the body between the neck and the abdomen including the heart and lungs contained within it; chest.

thromb- *or* **thrombo-** *prefix* blood clot; relating to a blood clot or to clotting.

thromboembolism the blocking of a blood vessel by an embolus.

thrombophlebitis inflammation of a vein with thrombosis.

thrombosis *pl.* **thromboses** the formation of a clot within a blood vessel. —**thrombotic** *adj.*

thrombus *pl.* **thrombi** a blood clot formed within a blood vessel and remaining attached to its point of origin. Compare *embolus.*

thrush a fungus disease marked by the formation of white patches in the mucous membranes esp. of the mouth.

thymus a glandular structure of uncertain function that is present in the upper chest or base of the neck of the young and tends to atrophy with age.

thyroid 1. a large endocrine gland at the base of the neck producing the hormone thyroxine. Also called *thyroid gland.* 2. of or relating to the thyroid gland.

thyroidectomy *pl.* **thyroidectomies** surgical removal of tissue of the thyroid gland.

thyroiditis inflammation of the thyroid gland.

THE THYROID GLAND

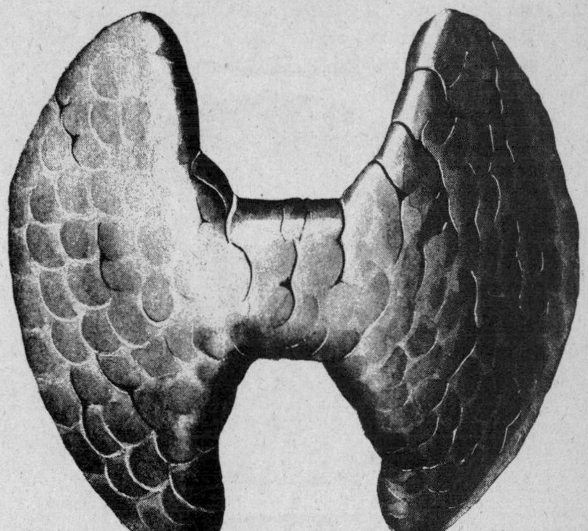

The thyroid is a large reddish, endocrine (ductless) gland located in front of, and on either side of, the trachea. It consists of two lateral lobes and a connecting isthmus.

tibia the larger of the two bones of the lower leg extending from the knee to the ankle; shin bone.

tic spasmodic, habitual twitching of a muscle, esp. of the face.

tic douloureux trigeminal neuralgia.

t.i.d. *abbr.* ter in die: three times daily.

tincture a medicinal substance diluted with alcohol. —**tincture** *vb.*

tinea any of various fungal skin diseases. Also called *ringworm.*

tinnitus a sensation of noise, as roaring or ringing, in the ears.

tissue an aggregate of cells of a particular kind together with its intercellular substance forming part of the body's structural material.

tissue culture the method of causing tissue to grow in a medium outside of the parent source.

tolerance 1. the ability to endure the effects of a drug, food, or other agent without adverse reaction. 2. the development of a decreased effect of a particular drug at a given dose, requiring that the dose be increased in order to achieve the original effect. —**tolerable** *adj.* —**tolerant** *adj.* —**tolerate** *vb.* —**toleration** *n.*

tone the condition of the body or any of its parts in relation to a standard of vigorous health.

tongue the muscular organ on the floor of the mouth equipped with the end organs providing the sense of taste and functioning as an organ of speech.

tongue-tie shortening of the frenum of the tongue resulting in restricted mobility. —**tongue-tied** *adj.*

tonic 1. any remedy that is considered to be invigorating. 2. relating to or characterized by tonus.

tonsil either of two masses of lymphoid tissue that lie one on each side of the throat.

tonsillectomy surgical removal of the tonsils.

tonsillitis inflammation of the tonsils.

TONSILLITIS

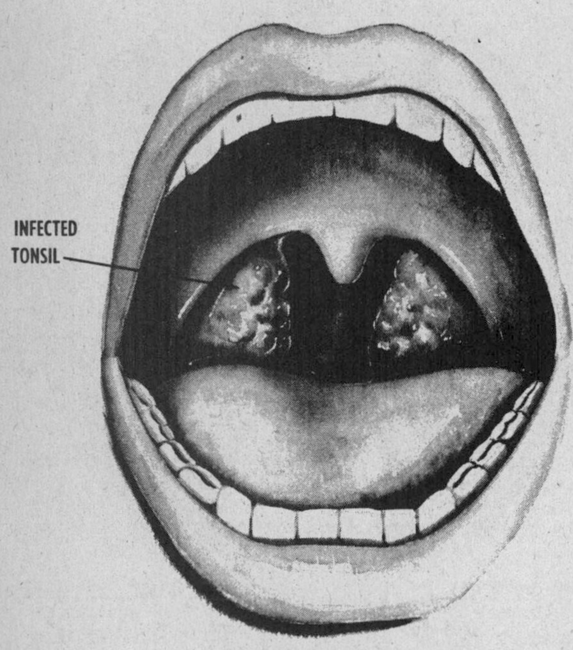

tonus a condition of mild contraction characteristic of normal muscle.

tooth *pl.* **teeth** one of the hard bony appendages lining the jaws and used in mastication.

tophus *pl.* **tophi** deposits of urate or crystals of uric acid in tissue characteristic of advanced or chronic gout, typically seen in the fleshy folds of the external ear.

topical intended for external application to a local area: *a topical anesthetic.*

torpor extreme sluggishness; lethargy.

torsion the act of twisting or the state of being twisted.

torso *pl.* **torsoes** *or* **torsi** the trunk of the body.

torticollis contraction of the neck muscles resulting in a twisted, unnatural carriage of the head. Also called *wryneck.*

tourniquet an instrument or device, as a bandage twisted and held fast with a stick, formerly recommended to check the flow of arterial bleeding.

toxemia the presence of a toxic substance in the blood. —**toxemic** *adj.*

toxic of, relating to, or caused by poison.

toxic- *or* **toxico-** *prefix* poison.

toxicant a toxic agent. —**toxicant** *adj.*

toxicology a branch of science dealing with poisons and their effects. —**toxicological** *or* **toxicologic** *adj.*

toxicosis *pl.* **toxicoses** a disease caused by poisoning.

toxigenic producing toxin. —**toxigenicity** *n.*

toxin a poisonous substance of bacterial or other origin that is capable of causing antibody formation.

toxoid a toxin that has had its toxicity neutralized so as to be functional as an antitoxin for injection.

toxoplasma any of a genus of parasitic protozoal microorganisms that are pathogens of vertebrate organisms. —**toxoplasmic** *adj.*

toxoplasmosis *pl.* **toxoplasmoses** a disease caused by infection with toxoplasmas and marked by severe damaging effects on the central nervous system.

trabecula *pl.* **trabeculae** *or* **trabeculas** a strand of connective tissue in the structure of a bodily part or organ.

trachea *pl.* **tracheae** *or* **tracheas** the main trunk of the air passages from the larynx to the bronchi. —**tracheal** *adj.*

tracheitis inflammation of the trachea.

tracheotomy *pl.* **tracheotomies** surgical incision of the trachea through the muscles and skin of the neck.

trachoma a chronic, contagious form of conjunctivitis.

traction a constant pulling force exerted on a skeletal part as a means of achieving proper alignment of bones.

tragus *pl.* **tragi** the cartilaginous prominence central to the opening of the outer ear.

trance an abnormal, profound state of sleep.

tranquilizer *also* **tranquillizer** a drug used to reduce or modify tension or anxiety. —**tranquilize** *also* **tranquillize** *vb.*

transfusion the transference of a fluid, as blood, into a vein.

transplant an organ or tissue used for transplantation. —**transplant** *vb.*

transplantation the transfer of an organ or tissue from one part of the body to another or from one individual to another.

transsexual one having a psychological urge to be a member of the opposite sex and often seeking surgical and hormonal remedy to alter gender. —**transsexualism** *n.*

transudation the passage of a fluid from a tissue or through a membrane. —**transude** *vb.*

transvestism the adoption of the attire and often the behavior of the opposite sex. —**transvestite** *n.*

trapezium *pl.* **trapeziums** *or* **trapezia** a wrist bone at the base of the thumb.

trapezius a large triangular muscle at each side of the back.

trauma *pl.* **traumas** *or* **traumata** physical or psychological injury. —**traumatic** *adj.* —**traumatically** *adv.*

treatment any of various means of curing or alleviating the signs and symptoms of a disease or disorder.

tremor a physical trembling caused typically by neurological disease, debility, or emotional stress. —**tremulous** *adj.*

trench mouth Vincent's angina.

trephine 1. a circular incision, as one made surgically on the skull or a cornea. 2. a surgical instrument for performing a trephine. —**trephination** *n.*

triceps a muscle arising from three heads, esp. the large muscle of the back of the upper arm.

tricuspid valve a valve of three flaps preventing the return of blood from the right ventricle to the right auricle of the heart.

trigeminal nerve either of two major nerves supplying motor and sensory fibers chiefly to the face.

trigeminal neuralgia intense paroxysmal pain of the trigeminal nerves. Also called: *tic douloureux.*

triplet any of three children born at one birth.

trismus a spasm of the muscles of the jaw; lockjaw.

trocar *also* **trochar** a sharp-pointed instrument used with a cannula for drawing off body fluids.

trochlear of, relating to, or affecting a trochlear nerve.

trochlear nerve a cranial nerve supplying motor fibers to the eye muscles.

trophic of, relating to, or involving nourishment. —**trophically** *adv.*

trunk the part of the body exclusive of the head or limbs; torso.

truss a device worn to retain a hernia by external pressure. —**truss** *vb.*

trypanosome any of a genus of parasitic protozoans that infest the blood, are usually transmitted by the bite of an insect, and cause serious disease, as sleeping sickness.

trypanosomiasis *pl.* **trypanosomiases** disease caused by trypanosomes.

tsetse fly a two-winged fly of Africa, south of the Sahara, that is a vector of trypanosomes. Also called *tsetse.*

tubal of or involving a tube, esp. a fallopian tube.

tubercle a small knobby excrescence or prominence; nodule.

tubercle bacillus a bacterium causing tuberculosis.

tubercul- *or* **tuberculo-** *prefix* tubercle; tubercle bacillus.

tubercular relating to or affected by tuberculosis.

tuberculin a sterile liquid extracted from the tubercle bacillus and used in the diagnosis of tuberculosis.

tuberculin test a test for hypersensitivity to tuberculin.

tuberculosis *pl.* **tuberculoses** a communicable disease caused by infection with the tubercle bacillus and characterized by toxic symptoms partly affecting the lungs. —**tuberculous** *adj.*

tubule a small, slender, anatomical channel.

tularemia an infectious plague-like disease transmitted by the bite of blood-sucking insects.

tumefaction the process or action of becoming swollen. —**tumefactive** *adj.*

tumescence the condition or process of becoming swollen. —**tumesce** *vb.* —**tumescent** *adj.*

tumor an abnormal growth or mass of tissue that is not inflammatory and may be either benign or malignant; neoplasm. —**tumorous** *adj.*

turgid marked by a state of swollenness; distended. —**turgidity** *n.* —**turgor** *n.*

tussive of, relating to, or involved in coughing.

twin either of two children born at one birth.

tympanic membrane a membrane that separates the external ear and the middle ear and serves in the reception and transmission of sound waves; eardrum.

tympanites distension of the abdomen caused by retention of abdominal gas.

tympanum *pl.* **tympana** *or* **tympanums** tympanic membrane; eardrum.

typhoid typhoid fever. —**typhoid** *adj.*

typhoid fever an acute, infectious bacterial disease marked by fever, headache, diarrhea and prostration.

typhus a severe febrile rickettsial disease marked by stupor and delirium in alternation, body rash, and violent headache and transmitted by body lice.

U

ulcer a break in mucous membrane or skin resulting in the development of an open sore. —**ulcerate** *vb.* —**ulceration** *n.* —**ulcerative** *adj.*

ulcerous relating to or marked by an ulcer.

ulcus *pl.* **ulcera** ulcer.

ulcus hypostaticum a bedsore; decubitus ulcer.

ulectomy surgical removal of scar tissue.

uletic relating to a scar; scarred.

uletomy surgical incision of a scar to relieve tension.

ulna the inner of two bones of the forearm between the elbow and the wrist. —**ulnar** *adj.*

ulnad toward the ulna.

ulo- *or* **ule-** *prefix* relating to or denoting a scar or scarring.

ulosis scar formation; cicatrization.

ultrafiltration filtration of a colloidal substance through a semipermeable membrane or other filter to separate it from its dispersion medium and crystalloids.

ultramicroscope a device using scattered light to make visible those particles too small for viewing by an ordinary microscope.

ultramicroscopic smaller than can be perceived with an ordinary microscope.

ultrasonics the diagnostic or therapeutic use of extremely high-frequency sound waves. —**ultrasonic** *adj.*

ultrasonogram a record obtained from the use of ultrasonography.

ultrasonography the diagnostic use of ultrasonic waves to locate, delineate or measure deep structures of the body by measuring their relative ability to reflect or transmit these extreme high-frequency sound waves.

ultraviolet ray a light ray beyond the visible spectrum at its violet end but having a wavelength longer than that of an X-ray.

umbilical of, relating to, or situated at the navel.

umbilical cord a cord from the navel of a fetus that connects with the mother's placenta.

umbilicus *pl.* **umbilici** *or* **umbilicuses** a small depression (or sometimes a slight elevation) in the center of the abdomen marking the original connective point of the umbilical cord.

uncinariasis infection with hookworms.

uncinate shaped like or resembling a hook; hook-shaped.

unconscious 1. not conscious; unable to perceive or respond to external stimuli. 2. (in psychoanalytic theory) the part of the mind that influences impulses, thoughts, desires, etc., but of which the individual is not aware.

undulant fever an acute, infectious, febrile disease marked by recurring attacks of fever and weakness; brucellosis.

unguent a healing or soothing ointment or salve.

unicellular consisting of a single cell: *unicellular microorganism.*

uniparous having borne only one child.

ur- *or* **uro-** *prefix* urine; urinary.

urea a white, crystalline substance found in urine, constituting the chief nitrogenous waste product of metabolism.

uremia a severe toxic condition caused by retention in the blood of high levels of the waste product urea, which is normally eliminated in the urine. —**uremic** *adj.*

ureter the long, narrow tube that carries the urine from the kidney to the bladder. —**ureteral** *adj.*

urethr- *or* **urethro-** *prefix* urethra: *urethritis.*

urethra *pl.* **urethras** *or* **urethrae** the canal that carries the urine from the bladder for excretion and in the male also serves as the conduit for semen. —**urethral** *adj.*

urethritis inflammation of the urethra.

urethroscope an instrument for viewing the interior of the urethra.

uric acid a waste product normally present in small quantities in urine, but which in larger amounts can form crystals of urate in the joints and give rise to the painful symptoms of gout or gouty arthritis.

urinalysis *pl.* **urinalyses** a chemical analysis of the constituents of urine.

urinary relating to or involving urine or the urinary bladder.

urinary bladder a membranous sac for retaining urine.

urination the act of excreting urine. —**urinate** *vb.*

urine fluid waste material secreted by the kidneys, temporarily stored in the urinary bladder, and eventually discharged from the body through the urethra.

urinometer a small hydrometer for determining the specific gravity of urine. —**urinometric** *adj.*

urogenital of, relating to, or involving the urinary and genital organs. —**urogenitally** *adv.*

urography X-ray examination of the urinary tract. —**urographologist** *n.*

urolith a calculus in the urinary tract.

urologist a specialist in urology.

urology a branch of medicine concerned with diseases or problems of the urinary or urogenital tracts. —**urologic** *or* **urological** *adj.*

urticaria an allergic reaction marked by an eruptive skin rash; nettle rash; hives.

uterus *pl.* **uteri** *or* **uteruses** an organ of the female for containing and nourishing the developing fetus; womb. —**uterine** *adj.*

uvea the posterior, pigmented layer of the iris of the eye.

uveitis inflammation of the uvea.

uvula *pl.* **uvulas** *or* **uvulae** a pendant lobe at the back of the soft palate. —**uvular** *adj.*

uvulectomy *pl.* **uvulectomies** surgical removal of the uvula.

uvulitis inflammation of the uvula.

V

vaccination 1. the inoculation with a vaccine to prevent smallpox. 2. inoculation with any bacterial vaccine. 3. the scar left by a vaccination. —**vaccinate** *vb.*

vaccine a suspension made from killed or attenuated organisms for inoculation to establish resistance to an infectious disease.

vaccinia cowpox.

vacciniform resembling cowpox (vaccinia).

vagal of or relating to the vagus nerve.

vagina a canal leading in the female from the external genital orifice to the uterus. —**vaginal** *adj.*

vaginectomy surgical removal of all or part of the vagina.

vaginismus painful contraction of the vaginal muscles, often associated with a psychological aversion to sexual intercourse and preventing insertion or withdrawal of the penis.

vaginitis inflammation of the vagina.

vaginopathy any disease or disorder of the vagina.

vaginoplasty plastic surgery involving the vagina.

vagus *pl.* **vagi** either one of the tenth pair of cranial nerves which supply chiefly the viscera with sensory and motor fibers.

valgus an abnormal outward turning or twisting of a joint.

valva *pl.* **valvae** valve. —**valval** *adj.* —**valvar** *adj.*

valve a fold of membranous tissue in a passage or channel that permits the flow of a fluid in just one direction. —**valvular** *adj.*

valvula *pl.* **valvulae** a small fold or valve.

valvulitis inflammation of the valves of the heart.

varicella chickenpox.

varicocele varicose enlargement of the veins of the spermatic cord.

varicose *also* **varicosed** abnormally swollen or dilated: *varicose veins.* —**varicosity** *n.*

variola smallpox. —**variolous** *adj.*

varioloid 1. resembling smallpox. 2. a mild form of smallpox occurring chiefly in persons who have previously had smallpox or who have been vaccinated.

varix *pl.* **varices** an abnormally dilated vein, artery or lymphatic vessel.

varus an abnormal condition of inward turning of a joint.

vas *pl.* **vasa** an anatomical duct.

vas- *or* **vaso-** *prefix* 1. vessel; blood vessel. 2. vas deferens.

vascular relating to or being a channel for the conveyance of a body fluid. —**vascularity** *n.*

vas deferens the excretory duct of the testis, through which semen is conveyed during ejaculation.

vasectomy *pl.* **vasectomies** surgical incision of the vas deferens chiefly as a permanent method of male contraception.

vasoconstriction narrowing of the diameter of blood vessels.

vasodilatation widening of the diameter of blood vessels.

vasomotor relating to or being nerves controlling the inner diameter of blood vessels.

vasoparalysis paralysis or lack of tone of blood vessels.

vasoparesis a slight degree of vasoparalysis.

vasopressin a hormone secreted by the posterior lobe of the pituitary gland that acts to elevate blood pressure and inhibit the excretion of urine.

vasospasm spasmodic contraction of a blood vessel. **—vasospastic** *adj.*

vastus one of three large muscles of the thigh.

vector an organism, as an insect, that transmits disease. **—vectorial** *adj.*

vegan a strict vegetarian who not only excludes meat but all animal products from the diet.

vegetation an abnormal concretion or outgrowth upon part of the body, as the valves of the heart.

vein any of the tubular vessels that branch throughout the body and carry oxygen-depleted blood to the heart (except the pulmonary veins, which convey oxygen-rich blood from the lungs to the heart).

vena cava *pl.* **venae cavae** either one of the two large veins (inferior and superior venae cavae) that carry the blood to the right atrium of the heart.

venepuncture venipuncture.

venereal 1. contracted or transmitted during sexual intercourse: *venereal disease.* 2. relating to or resulting from sexual intercourse.

venereal disease an infectious disease, esp. gonorrhea or syphilis, contracted through sexual intercourse or other sexual contact with an infected partner.

venereology *or* **venerology** a branch of medicine dealing with venereal diseases. **—venereological** *or* **venerological** *adj.* **—venereologist** *or* **venerologist** *n.*

venesection the opening of a vein for the letting of blood, as in the treatment of polycythemia.

venipuncture *also* **venepuncture** puncture of a vein, esp. for the withdrawal of a sample of blood for laboratory analysis.

venography X-ray examination of a vein after injection with a radiopaque substance.

venous relating to or affecting the veins.

ventral of or relating to the belly; abdominal. **—ventrally** *adv.*

ventricle 1. a chamber of the heart from which blood is forced into the arteries. 2. any one of the cavities of the brain that contain cerebrospinal fluid. **—ventricular** *adj.*

ventriculus *pl.* **ventriculi** a digestive cavity; stomach. **—ventricular** *adj.*

venule a small vein.

vermicide an agent for destroying intestinal worms. **—vermicidal** *adj.*

vermifuge causing worms to be expelled or destroyed. **—vermifuge** *n.*

verminosis *pl.* **verminoses** infestation with parasitic worms.

verruca *pl.* **verrucae** a wart.

version manual alteration in the uterine position of a fetus to achieve normal delivery.

vertebra *pl.* **vertebrae** *or* **vertebras** any of the thirty-three bony and cartilaginous segments that make up the spinal column. **—vertebral** *adj.*

vertex *pl.* **vertexes** *or* **vertices** the crown of the skull; top of the head.

vertigo *pl.* **vertigoes** *or* **vertigos** a state of disorientation in which an individual or his surroundings seem to be whirling; giddiness; dizziness. **—vertiginous** *adj.*

vesical of or relating to the urinary bladder.

vesicant an agent, as a gas, that induces blistering. **—vesicant** *adj.*

vesicate to blister.

vesicle a small, often painful elevation on the skin filled with watery fluid; blister. **—vesicular** *adj.*

vesiculate 1. covered with or containing vesicles. 2. to form or become covered with vesicles.

vestibule 1. the bony cavity of the labyrinth of the inner ear. 2. the opening between the labia minora of the vulva. **—vestibular** *adj.*

vestige the remnant of a bodily structure formerly having a functional purpose. **—vestigial** *adj.*

viable born in a fully normal and developed condition; fit for life: *viable fetus.* **—viability** *n.*

vibrio *pl.* **vibrios** any of a genus of bacteria in the form of an *S* or a comma, one of which causes cholera.

villus *pl.* **villi** a small, protruding, cellular process found on the surface of certain membranes. **—villous** *adj.*

Vincent's angina a mildly contagious bacterial disease marked chiefly by ulceration of the mucous membrane of the mouth and adjacent parts.

viremia the presence of viruses in the blood. **—viremic** *adj.*

viricide *or* **virucide** an agent that inactivates or destroys viruses. **—viricidal** *or* **virucidal** *adj.*

virilism 1. the development in a female of male secondary sex characteristics. 2. early development of secondary sex characteristics in a male.

virology a branch of science concerned with the study of viruses and the diagnosis and treatment of diseases they cause. **—virologic** *or* **virological** *adj.* **—virologically** *adv.* **—virologist** *n.*

virulence the ability of microorganisms to produce a disease with a rapid, severe, and malignant course. **—virulent** *adj.*

virus any of a large group of infective, submicroscopic agents that are capable of growing only in living cells and are the cause of many significant diseases.

viscera *pl. of* viscus.

viscid sticky in quality; adhesive; glutinous: *a viscid fluid.*

viscous viscid.

viscus *pl.* **viscera** an internal bodily organ.

vision the act or state of perceiving with the eyes.

visual of or relating to vision.

vital relating to life; essential to maintaining life: *the vital organs are the heart, lungs, brain, kidneys and liver.*

vital signs the body temperature, pulse and respiratory rates, and blood pressure, the existence of which indicates a person is alive.

vitamin any of various organic substances that are essential in the diet in very small quantities to maintain health; they act as metabolic regulators and are present chiefly in natural foodstuffs.

vitamin A any of various fat-soluble vitamins found typically in the oils of fish liver, in egg yolk, and in milk, deficiency of which results in impaired vision.

vitamin B complex a group of water-soluble vitamins that include niacin, riboflavin, thiamine, and niacinamide.

vitamin B_1 thiamine.

vitamin B_2 riboflavin; a vitamin of the B complex concerned with oxidative processes and found in kidney, liver, milk, grass, eggs, and other sources.

vitamin B_6 pyridoxine; a vitamin of the B complex that is necessary for protein metabolism.

vitamin B_{12} a complex compound containing cobalt, found in liver, and essential to blood formation, growth, and the functioning of the nervous system.

vitamin C a vitamin found esp. in fruits and leafy vegetables and used in the prevention and treatment of scurvy and as a nutritional additive.

vitamin D a vitamin essential to the development of bones and teeth and found chiefly in milk, egg yolk, and the oil of fish liver.

vitamin E any of various vitamins important to the development of muscle and to fertility.

vitamin G riboflavin; vitamin B_2.

vitamin H biotin.

vitaminize to supplement with vitamins. —**vitaminization** *n.*

vitamin K either of two vitamins (vitamins K_1 and K_2) essential to the ability of the blood to clot.

vitiligo a skin condition marked by white, depigmented spots or patches on the body.

vitreous relating to or constituting the vitreous humor of the eye.

vitreous humor the transparent, clear, colorless substance between the lens and the retina of the eye.

vivisection surgery performed on living animals chiefly for purposes of research. —**vivisect** *vb.* —**vivisectionist** *n.*

vocal cords either of two pairs of folds of mucous membranes extending into the cavity of the larynx, which when vibrated by the passage of air act in the production of the voice.

voluntary functioning under conscious control: *voluntary muscles.*

volvulus a twisting of the intestine upon itself causing obstruction.

vomer a bone forming part of the septum of the nose.

vomit 1. to disgorge (the contents of the stomach) through the mouth. 2. the matter disgorged by vomiting.

vomiturition repeated, ineffectual attempts to vomit.

vomitus matter ejected by vomiting.

vulva *pl.* **vulvae** the external parts of the female genital organs; pudendum. —**vulval** *or* **vulvar** *adj.*

vulvitis inflammation of the vulva.

vulvovaginitis inflammation of the vulva and vagina.

W

wadding surgical dressing of carded cotton or sheets of wool.

waddle a swaying or side-to-side walk seen in some forms of muscular dystrophy or nervous disorders.

wale a linear weal, as one produced by the sharp blow of a stick or whip.

walk 1. the manner in which one moves; gait. 2. to move about on foot.

ward a room or area in a hospital equipped with beds for patients: *surgical ward.*

wart an epithelial tumor occurring typically as a horny projection on the skin of the extremities and caused by a virus. Also called *verruca.* —**warty** *adj.*

wash a lotion.

Wassermann reaction a test for the detection of syphilis. Also called *Wassermann, Wassermann test.*

waste 1. to lose tissue bulk; grow thin; emaciate. 2. excrement.

wasting emaciation.

waterborne carried by water: *waterborne infections.*

water brash a burning sensation in the stomach and esophagus with acid regurgitation; heartburn.

waters (colloquial) amniotic fluid.

Watson-Crick helix the double-stranded helical structure of deoxyribonucleic acid (DNA).

watt the unit of electrical power.

weal a lump or ridge raised on the skin, usually by a blow; welt.

wean to accustom (a child) to take nourishment other than by nursing. —**weaning** *n.*

webbing a congenital condition marked by the abnormal existence of a sheet or band of tissues joining two adjacent structures or parts.

welt a weal.

wen a cyst formed by obstruction of a sebaceous gland; a sebaceous cyst.

wheal a slightly elevated, reddened, itching patch on the skin typically associated with an insect bite or urticaria.

wheatgerm oil an oil rich in vitamin E, obtained from the germs of wheat seeds.

whiplash injury injury to the vertebrae and soft tissues of the neck produced by a sudden and violent jerking backward or forward of the head, as can occur to passengers involved in a rear-end collision of a motor vehicle.

whipworm a parasitic worm of the human intestine.

white blood cell leucocyte.

whitlow an abscess or purulent infection of the bed of a nail or the distal end of a finger. Also called *felon.*

whooping cough an infectious disease typically of children marked by paroxysms of violent coughing followed by a shrill, whooping drawing in of the breath. Also called *pertussis.*

Wilson's disease a rare hereditary disease marked by toxic deposits of copper in tissues, organs and the central nervous system and characterized esp. by symptoms of severe mental disorder.

windburn irritation and redness of the face caused by prolonged exposure to strong wind.

windpipe trachea.

wink 1. to open and close the eyelids very quickly, either as a conscious action or (usually) as an involuntary response. 2. the act or movement of opening and closing the eyelids quickly.

winter itch itching associated with exposure to cold, dry weather, thought to be caused by the drying of skin that is deficient in natural oils.

wisdom tooth the rearmost molar tooth in each half of each jaw, typically being the final teeth to erupt (as late as age 25 or so).

withdrawal 1. a pathological retreat from objective reality. 2. the complex of symptoms attending an addict following abstention from addictive drugs.

wolfram tungsten.

womb uterus.

wood alcohol an alcohol obtained from the distillation of wood, being poisonous and capable of causing blindness if ingested.

wood tick a species of tick occurring in North America and responsible for transmitting the micoorganisms that cause tularemia and Rocky Mountain spotted fever.

wool fat a fatty substance obtained from the wool of sheep, used as a base in the preparation of various ointments.

woolsorter's disease pulmonary anthrax caused by handling wool contaminated with the infecting microorganism *Bacillus anthrax.*

wound 1. an injury to the body involving piercing or laceration of the skin. 2. a surgical incision. 3. to injure; inflict a wound or wounds (on or upon).

W.r. *abbr.* Wassermann reaction.

wrinkle any crease or fold in the skin.

wrist the joint between the hand and the forearm; carpus.

writer's cramp muscular spasm of the hand induced by prolonged writing.

wryneck torticollis; stiff neck.

wuchereriasis infestation with threadlike worms of the genus *Wuchereria.* Also called *filariasis.*

X

xanthic 1. yellow or yellowish. 2. relating to xanthine.

xanthine a precursor of uric acid sometimes forming renal or urinary calculi.

xanthinuria the excretion of abnormally large quantities of xanthine in the urine.

xantho- *or* **xanth-** *prefix* yellow or yellowish.

xanthochromatic yellow-colored.

xanthochromia a condition characterized by the abnormal formation of yellow patches in the skin. Also called *xanthopathy.*

xanthochroous having a light or fair complexion; blond.

xanthocyanopsia a type of color blindness in which red and green are not distinguished but yellow and blue are; red-green blindness.

xanthoderma any yellowish discoloration of the skin. Also called *xanthoplasty.*

xanthodont a person with a yellowish discoloration of the teeth.

xanthoma a yellowish nodule or plaque in the skin caused by the deposition of certain lipids. **—xanthomatous** *adj.*

xanthomatosis a condition characterized by the multiple occurrence of xanthomas, esp. on the knees and elbows.

xanthone an agent that kills moth eggs.

xanthopathy xanthochromia.

xanthoplasty xanthoderma.

xanthopsia a visual defect in which all objects appear to be colored yellow.

xanthopsydracia a skin eruption characterized by the formation of small yellowish pustules.

xanthosis a yellowish discoloration seen in some malignant tumors and degenerating tissues.

xanthous yellow.

xanthylic relating to xanthine.

X chromosome a sex chromosome occurring paired in each female cell and zygote and singly in each male cell and zygote.

xenophobia an abnormal fear of meeting strangers.

xenophthalmia inflammation of the eye caused by the presence of a foreign particle.

Xenopsylla a genus of fleas, including the rat flea (*Xenopsylla cheopis*) which transmits the bacteria that cause the plague.

xenopus test a test for pregnancy in which the patient's urine is injected into the dorsal lymph sac of a toad.

xer- *or* **xero-** *prefix* dry.

xeransis a loss of moisture in the tissues.

xerantic causing dryness.

xerasia a condition characterized by abnormally dry and brittle hair.

xerochilia dryness of the lips.

xeroderma a dry, rough condition of the skin.

xeroma xeroph thalmia.

xeromycteria a condition characterized by abnormal dryness of the mucous membranes of the nose.

xeronosus xerosis.

xerophagia subsisting on a diet that is dry or lacking in moisture.

xerophthalmia a dry, thickened condition of the eyeball resulting from a deficiency of vitamin A.

xerosis severe dryness of the skin, mouth, or eye.

xerostomia excessive dryness of the mouth.

xerotes dryness.

xiphisternum *pl.* **xiphisterna** the posterior segment of the sternum.

xiphoid of, relating to or being the xiphisternum.

X ray a photon having a frequency distribution that is higher than the ultraviolet range of the electromagnetic spectrum and has the ability of penetrating various thicknesses of all solids.

x-ray to photograph, examine, or treat with X rays.

X-ray therapy treatment of a disease, as cancer, with the use of X rays.

Y

yaws an infectious tropical disease with symptoms resembling syphilis and caused by a spirochete. Also called *frambesia.*

Y chromosome a sex chromosome that is characteristic of male cells.

yeast any of various true fungi that are active fermenters of carbohydrates.

yellow fever an acute viral disease transmitted by a mosquito and marked by fever, prostration, jaundice, and occasionally bleeding. Also called *yellow jack.*

yerba a herb.

yolk the stored nutrient portion of an ovum.

yperite a type of mustard gas.

ytterbium a metallic element of the rare earth group.

yttrium a metallic element.

Z

zein a protein present in corn (maize).

zelotypia pathologically excessive zeal in the support or advocacy of a cause.

zero gravity *also* **zerogravity** the phenomenon or state of weightlessness resulting from the absence of the pull of gravity as occurs during flights into outer space.

zestocausis cautery achieved by the use of hot steam.

zinc a metallic element.

zincoid resembling or relating to zinc.

zingiber ginger.

zoanthropy a mental delusion of being a lower animal, such as a dog or cat.

zoetic relating to life.

zona *pl.* **zonae** an encircling area, as in shingles. —**zonal** *adj.*

zonula any small zone. —**zonular** *adj.*

zonula ciliaris suspensory ligament of the lens of the eye.

zoo- *prefix* relating to or denoting animal life or an animal.

zooblast any animal cell.

zooerastia human sexual gratification involving a lower animal.

zoograft a tissue graft obtained from a lower animal.

zoology the branch of science concerned with the study of animal life and its classifications. —**zoological** *adj.* —**zoologist** *n.*

zoomania an abnormal or exaggerated fondness or love of animals.

zoopathology the branch of pathology concerned with lower animals; veterinary pathology.

zoophagous eating the flesh of animals; carnivorous.

zoophobia an abnormal fear of animals.

zoster herpes zoster; shingles.

zygoma *pl.* **zygomata** *also* **zygomas** zygomatic arch.

zygomatic relating to or situated near the zygomatic arch.

zygomatic arch an arch of bone of the side of the face below the eyes; cheekbone. Also called *zygomatic bone.*

zygote a cell developing from the union of two gametes. —**zygotic** *adj.*

Heart Terms Dictionary

A

ADRENAL GLANDS *(ah-dre'nal)*
A pair of endocrine (hormone-secreting) glands that sit atop the kidneys. The inner portion of each—the adrenal medulla—secretes norepinephrine and epinephrine. Epinephrine is a heart stimulant and norepinephrine is a powerful blood vessel constrictor. The outer shell—the adrenal cortex—secretes aldosterone, cortisone, and other steroid hormones that influence the body's handling of salt, water, carbohydrates and other aspects of metabolism.

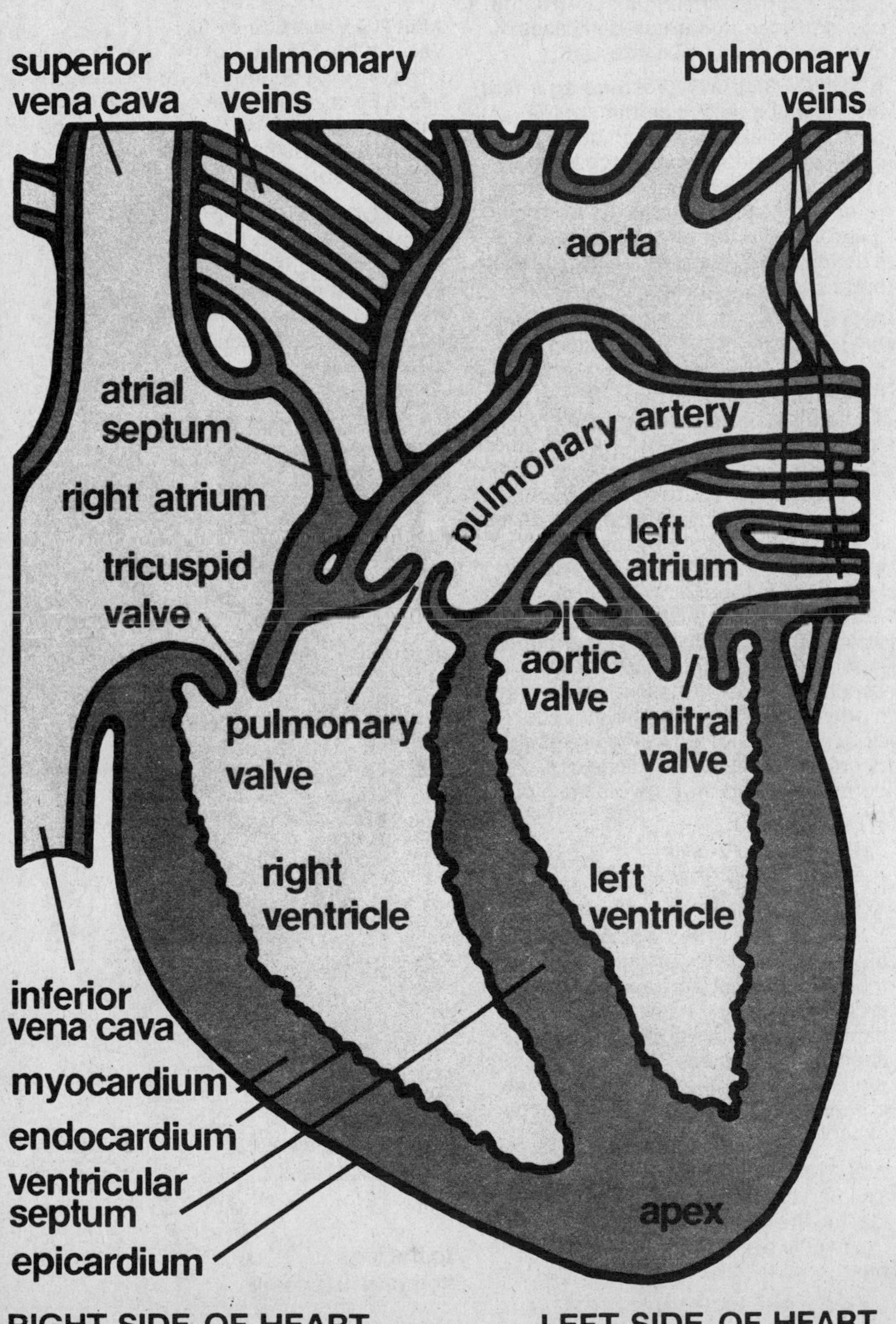

ADRENALIN *(ah-dren'ah-lin)*
See Epinephrine.

ADRENERGIC BLOCKING AGENTS *(ad"ren-er'jik)*
Drugs which block the normal response of an organ or tissue to nerve impulses transmitted by the adrenergic nervous system (more or less the same as the sympathetic nervous system). Blocking adrenergic nerves to the heart and blood vessels tends to decrease heart rate and the vigor of heart contraction and to suppress the constriction of blood vessels. Adrenergic blocking agents are often used to treat angina pectoris (since by reducing heart work they reduce its need for oxygen). Some are also used to treat arrhythmias and to control high blood pressure, especially when it is accompanied by a hyperactive heart.

There are two classes of these drugs, alpha- and beta-adrenergic blocking agents. Both can be used in cardiovascular disorders, although beta-adrenergic blocking agents are used more often; of these, propranolol is the most common.

AGE-ADJUSTED DEATH RATE
See Mortality Rate, Age-Adjusted.

AGE-SPECIFIC DEATH RATE
See Mortality Rate, Age-Specific.

ALDOSTERONE *(al-dos'ter-on OR al"do-ster'on)*
A hormone secreted by the adrenal cortex that promotes the retention of salt and water by the kidneys. Aldosteronism, or excessive secretion of this hormone, may cause an increase in blood pressure. In this case drugs known as aldosterone antagonists can be given; one example is spironolactone.

ALDOSTERONISM *(al"do-ster'on-izm")*
See Aldosterone.

AMINE *(ah-meen' OR am'in)*
An organic compound that may be derived from ammonia by the replacement of one or more of the hydrogen atoms by hydrocarbon fractions.

ANEURYSM *(an'u-rizm)*
A ballooning-out of the wall of a vein, an artery or the heart due to weakening of the wall by disease, traumatic injury or an abnormality present at birth.

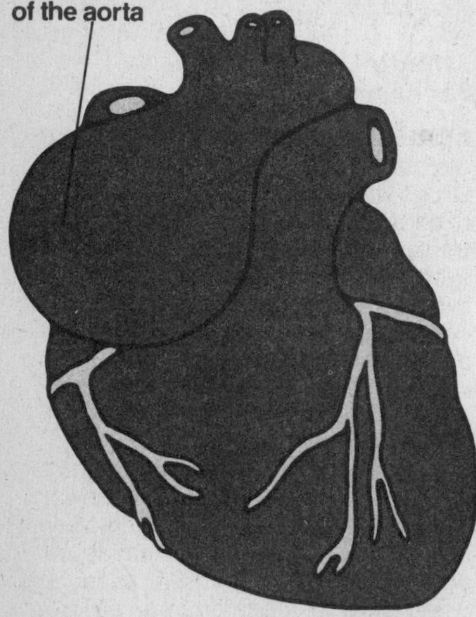

ANGINA PECTORIS *(an-ji'nah OR an'ji-nah pek'tor-is)*
An episode of chest pain due to a temporary discrepancy between the supply and demand of oxygen to the heart. This may be due to low oxygen levels in the blood (from smoking or respiratory disease), to a restricted bloodflow to the heart (coronary insufficiency) or to an increase in heart work beyond normal levels. Most often, angina pectoris is a chronic condition caused by a blood supply restricted by hardening and narrowing of the coronary arteries supplying the heart muscle (coronary atherosclerosis).

An angina attack is not to be confused with a heart attack (myocardial infarction), which results from a severe and prolonged lack of oxygenated blood to a part of the heart.

ANGIOCARDIOGRAPHY *(an"je-o-kar"de-og'rah-fe)*
A diagnostic method involving injection of an x-ray dye into the bloodstream. Chest x-rays taken after the injection show the inside dimensions of the heart and great vessels outlined by the liquid. **See Cineangiography.**

ANOREXIA *(an"o-rek'se-ah)*
Lack or loss of appetite for food.

ANOXIA *(an-ok'se-ah)*
Literally, no oxygen. This condition most frequently occurs when the blood supply (and hence the oxygen supply) to a part of the body is completely cut off. This results in the death of the affected tissue. For example, a specific area of the heart muscle may die when the blood supply has been blocked, as by a clot in the artery supplying that area.

ANTIARRHYTHMIC DRUGS *(an"ti-ah-rith'mic)*
Drugs which are used to treat disorders of the heart rate and rhythm. The drugs lidocaine, procaine amide, quinidine, digitalis, and propranolol are often given to correct arrhythmias. Atropine and isoproterenol are used in cases of abnormally slow heart rates.

ANTICOAGULANT *(an"ti-ko-ag'u-lant)*
A drug which delays clotting of the blood (coagulation). When given in cases of a blood vessel plugged up by a clot, it tends to prevent new clots from forming, or the existing clots from enlarging, but does not dissolve an existing clot. Examples are heparin and coumarin derivatives.

ANTIHYPERTENSIVE DRUGS *(an"ti-hi"per-ten'siv)*
Drugs which can be used to control high blood pressure (hypertension). Those most often given are the diuretics (primarily the thiazides), which promote the natural elimination of excess fluids in the tissues and circulation. Some of the other major antihypertensive drugs lower blood pressure by their direct or indirect dilating effect on the arteries. Hydralazine, for example, directly relaxes the tiny muscles in the artery walls. Other drugs block or damper the nerves which signal the arteries to constrict. Some of these are reserpine, methyldopa and guanethidine. The drug propranolol slows the heartbeat, decreases the force of the heart's contraction and thus lowers the blood pressure.

ANXIETY *(ang-zi'e-te)*
A feeling of apprehension.

AORTA *(a-or'tah)*
The main trunk artery which receives blood from the left ventricle of the heart. It originates from the base of the heart, arches up over the heart like a cane handle, and passes down through the chest and abdomen in front of the spine. It gives off many lesser arteries which conduct blood to all parts of the body except the lungs.

AORTIC ARCH *(a-or'tik)*
The part of the aorta, or large artery leaving the heart, which curves up like the handle of a cane over the top of the heart.

AORTIC INSUFFICIENCY *(a-or'tik in"su-fish'en-se)*
An improper closing of the valve between the aorta and the left ventricle of the heart permitting a backflow of blood.

AORTIC STENOSIS *(a-or'tik ste-nos'sis)*
A narrowing of the valve opening between the left ventricle of the heart and the large artery called the aorta. The narrowing may occur at the valve itself or slightly above or below the valve. Aortic stenosis may be the result of scar tissue forming after a rheumatic fever infection, or may have other causes.

AORTIC VALVE *(a-or'tik)*
Valve at the junction of the aorta, or large artery, and the left ventricle of the heart. Formed by three opposing cup-shaped membranes, it allows the blood to flow from the heart into the aorta and prevents a backflow. **See Valve.**

AORTOGRAPHY *(a"or-tog'rah-fe)*
X-ray examination of the aorta (main artery conducting blood from the left ventricle of the heart to the body) and its main branches. This is made possible by the injection of a dye which is opaque to x-rays.

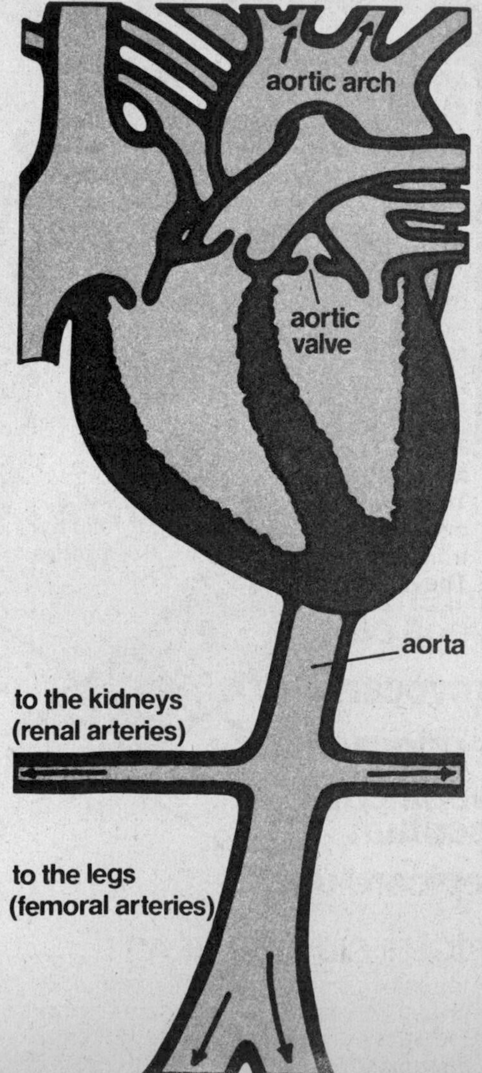

APEX *(a'peks)*
The blunt rounded end of the heart, normally directed downward, forward, and to the left.

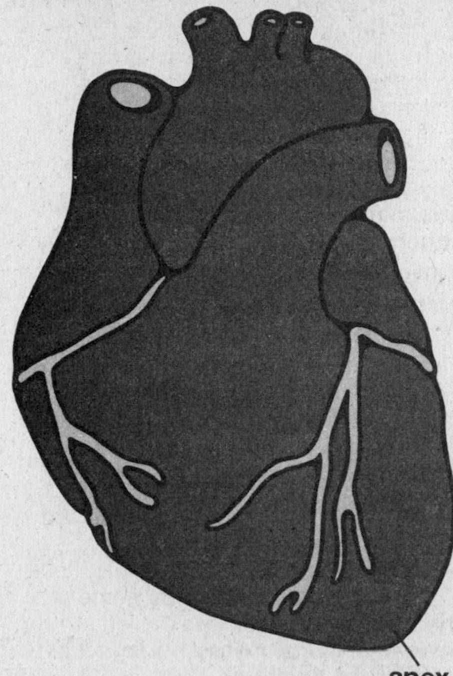

ARCUS *(ar'kus)*
A curved or bowlike structure. **See Corneal Arcus.**

ARRHYTHMIA *(ah-rith'me-ah)*
Any variation from the normal rhythm of the heartbeat.

ARTERIAL BLOOD *(ar-te're-al)*
Oxygenated blood. The blood is oxygenated in the lungs and passes from the lungs to the left side of the heart via the pulmonary veins. It is then pumped by the left side of the heart into the arteries which carry it to all parts of the body. **See Venous Blood.**

ARTERIOLES *(ar-te're-ols)*
The smallest arterial vessels (about 0.2 mm. or 1/125 inch in diameter) resulting from repeated branching of the arteries. They conduct the blood from the arteries to the capillaries.

ARTERIOSCLEROSIS *(ar-te"re-o-skle-ro'sis)*
A group of diseases characterized by thickening and loss of elasticity of artery walls. This may be due to an accumulation of fibrous tissue, fatty substances (lipids) and/or minerals. **See Atherosclerosis.**

ARTERITIS *(ar"te-ri'tis)*
A general term for inflammation of arteries. This may be secondary to some underlying condition (such as an infectious disease) or it may be the primary phenomenon. Primary arteritis includes polyarteritis nodosa (which is disseminated throughout the body), temporal arteritis (occurring at the temples) and aortitis (arteritis of the aorta and its major branches).

ARTERY *(ar'ter-e)*
Blood vessels which carry blood away from the heart to the various parts of the body. They usually carry oxygenated blood except for the pulmonary artery which carries unoxygenated blood from the heart to the lungs for oxygenation. **See Vein.**

ASCHOFF BODIES *(ash'of)*
Spindle-shaped nodules, occurring most frequently in the tissues of the heart, often formed during an attack of rheumatic fever. Named after Ludwig Aschoff (1866-1942), a German pathologist who described them.

ASSIST DEVICES
Special mechanical devices used to provide pumping assistance to a heart weakened by acute heart attack or heart failure.

ASYMMETRIC SEPTAL HYPERTROPHY (ASH) *(a"sim-met'rik sep'tal hi-per'tro-fe)*
Also called idiopathic hypertrophic subaortic stenosis (IHSS). A disease of the heart muscle (cardiomyopathy) in which there is an asymmetric enlargement (hypertrophy) of the walls of the left ventricle—the interventricular septum thickens more than the outer wall does. This makes the contraction of the left ventricle less effective and obstructs bloodflow to the aorta (and therefore to all parts of the body including the heart muscle itself). This condition is fairly common, is sometimes hereditary, and can create such symptoms as chest pain and dizziness. Treatment, when necessary, includes surgery, drugs or reduced physical exertion.

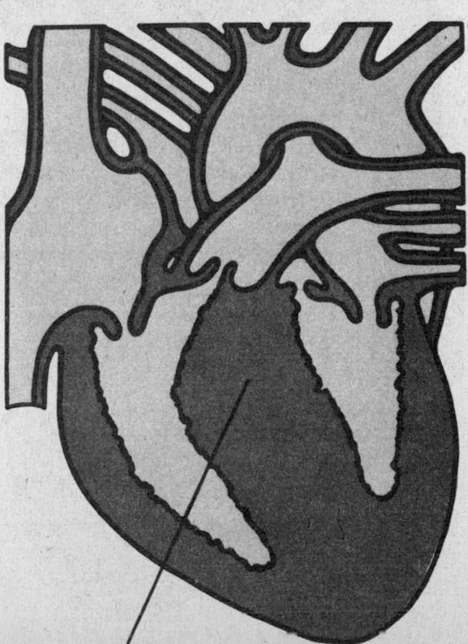

abnormal, thickened septum (asymmetric septal hypertrophy)

ATHEROMA *(ath"er-o'mah)*
Also called plaque. A deposit of fatty (and other) substances in the inner lining of the artery wall, characteristic of atherosclerosis. Plural is **Atheromata** *(ath"er-o-mah'ta).* **See Atherosclerosis.**

ATHEROSCLEROSIS *(ath"er-o"skle-ro'sis)*
A kind of arteriosclerosis in which the inner layer of the artery wall is made thick and irregular by deposits of a fatty substance. These deposits (called atheromata or plaques) project above the surface of the inner layer of the artery, and thus decrease the diameter of the internal channel of the vessel. **See Arteriosclerosis.**

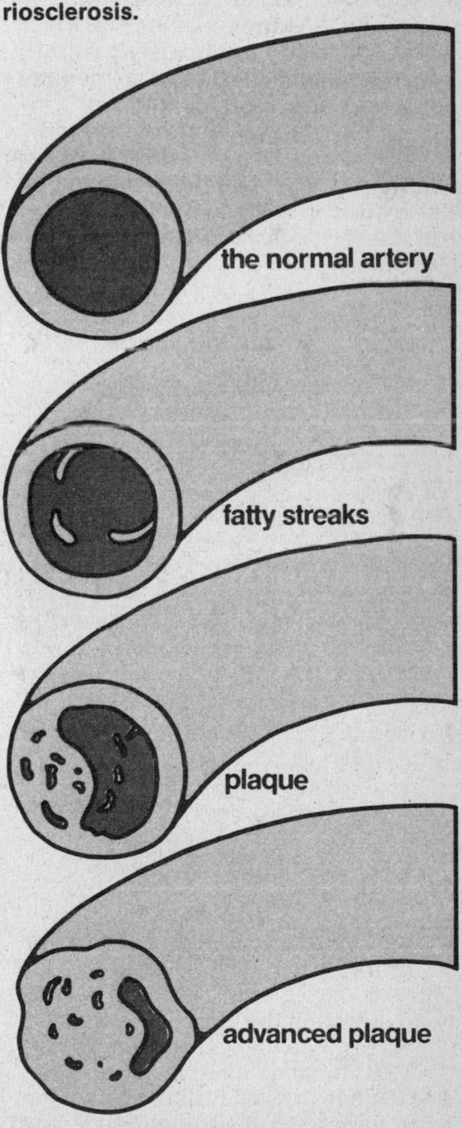

ATRIAL FIBRILLATION *(a"tre-al fi-bri-la'shun)*
See Fibrillation.

ATRIAL FLUTTER *(a'tre-al flut'er)*
An arrhythmia which occurs occasionally in healthy hearts, but more commonly in diseased hearts. It results in a

rapid regular heartbeat. Drugs are often used to slow the rate.

ATRIAL SEPTUM *(a'tre-al sep'tum)*
Sometimes called interatrial septum. Muscular wall dividing left and right upper chambers of the heart which are called atria. **See Septum.**

ATRIOVENTRICULAR BUNDLE *(a"tre-o-ven-trik'u-lar)*
See Bundle of His.

ATRIOVENTRICULAR NODE *(a"tre-o-ven-trik'u-lar)*
A small mass of special muscular fibers at the base of the wall between the two upper chambers of the heart. It forms the beginning of the Bundle of His which is the only known normal direct muscular connection between the upper and the lower chambers of the heart. The electrical impulses controlling the rhythm of the heart are generated by the pacemaker, conducted through the muscle fibers of the right upper chamber of the heart to the atrioventricular node, and then conducted to the lower chambers of the heart by the Bundle of His. **See Bundle of His and Pacemaker.**

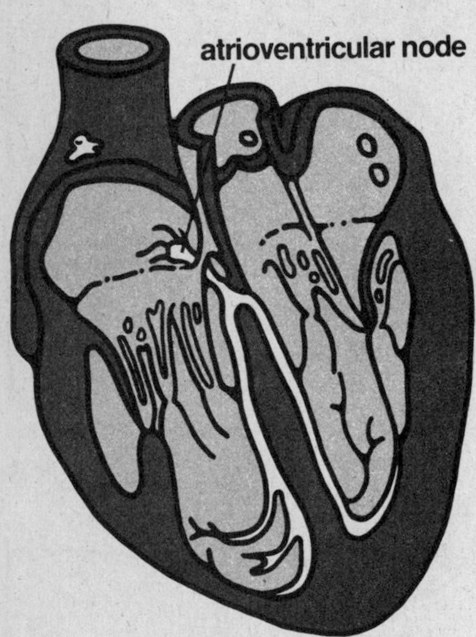

ATRIOVENTRICULAR VALVES *(a"tre-o-ven-trik'u-lar)*
The two valves, one in each side of the heart, between the upper and lower chambers. The one in the right side of the heart is called the tricuspid valve, and the one in the left side is called the mitral valve. **See illustration inside front cover.**

ATRIUM *(a'tre-um)*
Formerly "auricle." One of the two upper chambers of the heart. The right atrium receives unoxygenated blood from the body. The left atrium receives oxygenated blood from the lungs.

ATROPINE *(at'ro-peen)*
A drug used to treat, among other things, an abnormally slow heart rate; an antiarrhythmic drug.

AUENBRUGGER, LEOPOLD JOSEPH (1722-1809)
Austrian physician who invented the technique of tapping the surface of the body to determine the condition of organs beneath. The technique is called percussion.

AURICLE *(aw're-kl)*
Archaic term for atrium.

AUSCULTATION *(aws"kul-ta'shun)*
The act of listening to sounds within the body, usually with a stethoscope.

AUTONOMIC NERVOUS SYSTEM *(aw"to-nom'ik)*
Sometimes called the involuntary nervous system. The nerves of this system regulate tissues and functions not normally under conscious control (heartbeat, blood pressure, etc.). It consists of two divisions, the sympathetic and parasympathetic, which usually have opposing effects on the cardiovascular system: the sympathetic nerves, when stimulated, tend to increase heart rate, constrict blood vessels, and raise blood pressure; the parasympathetic tend to slow the heart rate, relax blood vessels, and lower blood pressure.

A-V BUNDLE
See Bundle of His.

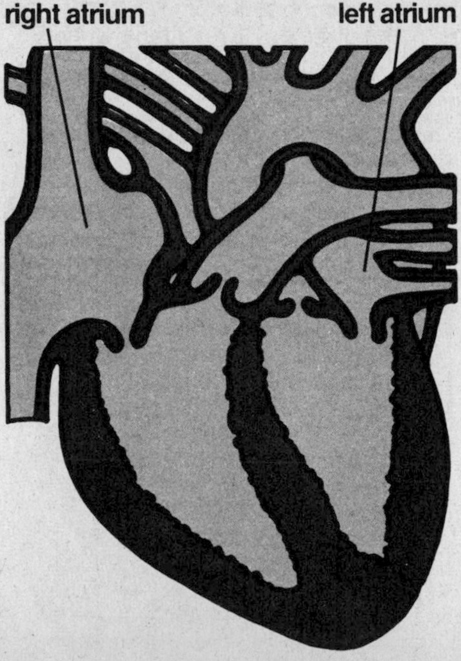

B

BACTERIAL ENDOCARDITIS *(bak-te're-al en"do-kar-di'tis)*
An inflammation of the inner layer of the heart caused by bacteria; it may be a complication of another infectious disease, an operation or injury. The lining of the heart valves is most frequently affected, most commonly valves with previous damage from rheumatic disease or congenital abnormality.

BARLOW'S SYNDROME *(bar'loz)*
Also called floppy mitral valve syndrome as well as systolic click-murmur syndrome, billowing mitral leaflet syndrome, and prolapsed mitral valve leaflet syndrome (among other terms). A structural alteration of the mitral valve (which normally permits a one-way flow of blood from the left atrium down to the left ventricle of the heart) leading to stretching and weakness of the cusps or valve leaflets. Thus when the heart pumps, some of the blood leaks back into the left atrium instead of being pushed through the aorta to the body.

This syndrome is associated with unusual chest discomfort and arrhythmias.

BARORECEPTORS *(bar"o-re-sep'torz)*
Sensory nerve endings which respond to changes in pressure, as those in the walls of blood vessels.

BEHAVIOR, TYPE A AND TYPE B
Two kinds of behavior patterns, as recognized in medicine. Type A behavior is characterized by high degrees of competitiveness, aggressiveness and feelings of the pressure of time. This type of behavior is thought by some cardiologists to be a risk factor in the development of coronary heart disease. Individuals with the converse Type B behavior are more easygoing and contemplative and more easily satisfied.

BENZOTHIADIAZIDES *(ben"zo-thi"ah-di'ah-sidz)*
See Thiazides.

BETA-BLOCKING AGENTS *(bay'tah)*
Also called beta-adrenergic blocking agents. **See Adrenergic Blocking Agents.**

BICUSPID VALVE *(bi-kus'pid)*
Usually called mitral valve. A valve of two cusps or triangular segments, located between the upper and lower chambers in the left side of the heart. However, in cardiology a "bicuspid valve" usually refers to the common congenital abnormality of the aortic valve's having two cusps instead of its usual three.

BIOFEEDBACK *(bi"o-feed'bak)*
A technique using instrumentation to provide moment-to-moment information about bodily processes which a person is not normally aware of, so that he or she can learn to control them. For example, one setup may include a blood pressure measuring device and colored lights to indicate whether the blood pressure is in the high or normal range. Evidence indicates that biofeedback may be used to teach a person to regulate his or her heart rate, blood pressure, bloodflow, skin temperature, and the activity of the gastrointestinal tract.

This term also refers to the normal and physiologic mechanisms the body uses to regulate myriad physiologic phenomena.

BLOOD PRESSURE
The force the flowing blood exerts against the artery walls. Two pressures are usually measured:

1. The upper, or **systolic**, pressure occurs each time the heart contracts (systole) and pumps blood into the aorta.
2. The lower, or **diastolic**, pressure occurs when the heart relaxes (diastole) and refills with blood flowing in from the large veins, the venae cavae.

The blood pressure is therefore expressed by two numbers, with the upper one over the lower one; for example, 120/80, which is spoken as "120 over 80."

BLUE BABIES
Babies having a blueness of skin (cyanosis)caused by insufficient oxygen in the arterial blood. This often indicates a heart defect, but may have other causes such as premature birth or impaired respiration.

BRADYCARDIA *(brad-e-kar'de-ah)*
Abnormally slow heart rate. Generally, anything below 60 beats per minute is considered bradycardia.

BRIGHT, RICHARD (1789-1858)
English physician who demonstrated the association of heart disease to kidney disease.

BUERGER'S DISEASE *(ber'gerz)*
A disease of the blood vessels which is more commonly called thromboangiitis obliterans. **See Thromboangiitis Obliterans.**

BUERGER'S SYMPTOM *(ber'gerz)*
In thromboangiitis obliterans (Buerger's disease), the pain in the affected leg when the patient is lying down is relieved only by letting the leg hang over the side of the bed. **See Thromboangiitis Obliterans.**

BUNDLE OF HIS *(hiss)*
Also called atrioventricular bundle or A-V bundle. A bundle of specialized muscle fibers running from a small mass of muscular fibers (atrioventricular node) between the atria of the heart down to the ventricles. It is the only known normal direct muscular connection between the atria and the ventricles, and serves to conduct impulses for the rhythmic heartbeat from the atrioventicular node to the heart muscle. Named after Wilhelm His, German anatomist.

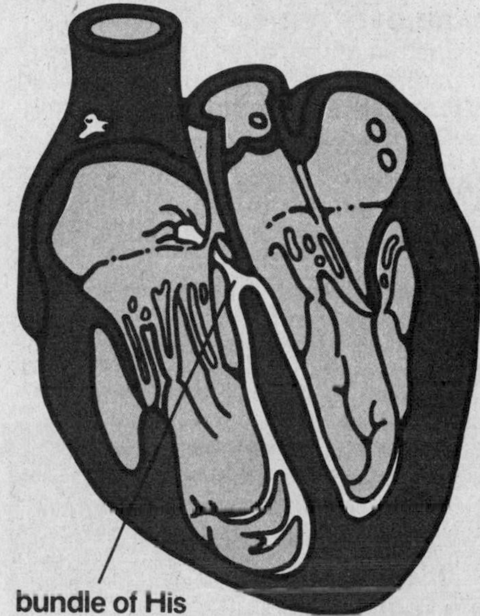

C

CAESALPINUS, ANDREAS (1519?-1603)
First to use the term "circulation" in connection with the movement of the blood. However, he still believed in many of the classical theories taught by Galen.

CALORIE *(kal'o-re)*
Sometimes called large or kilocalorie. Unit used to express food energy. The amount of heat required to raise the temperature of 1 kilogram of water 1 degree Centigrade.

A high caloric diet has a prescribed caloric value above the total daily energy requirement. A low caloric diet has a prescribed caloric value below the total energy requirement.

CAPILLARIES *(kap'i-lar"ez)*
The tiniest blood vessels. Capillary networks connect the arterioles and venules. Capillary walls are composed of a single layer of cells through which oxygen and nutritive materials pass out to the tissues, and carbon dioxide and waste products are admitted from the tissues into the bloodstream.

CARBON DIOXIDE *(kar'bon di-ox'ide)*
A waste product of chemical reactions in the cells. It passes from the cells to the blood which eventually releases it in the lungs to be breathed out.

CARDIAC *(kar'de-ak)*
Pertaining to the heart. Sometimes refers to a person who has heart disease.

CARDIAC ARREST
Cessation of the heartbeat. As a result, blood pressure drops abruptly and the circulation of the blood ceases. Until recently, this was always fatal. Today, the heart can be stimulated to start beating again and death averted under certain circumstances. **See Cardiopulmonary Resuscitation.**

CARDIAC CYCLE
A cardiac cycle is the series of mechanical and electrical events associated with one heartbeat. One cycle or beat lasts about 0.9 seconds and includes contraction and pumping, relaxation and filling actions.

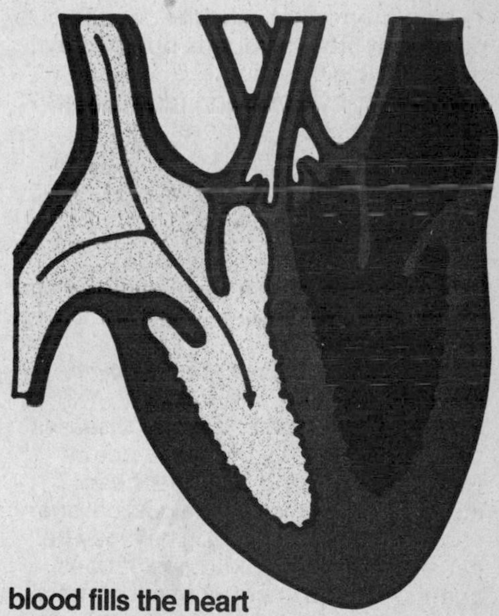

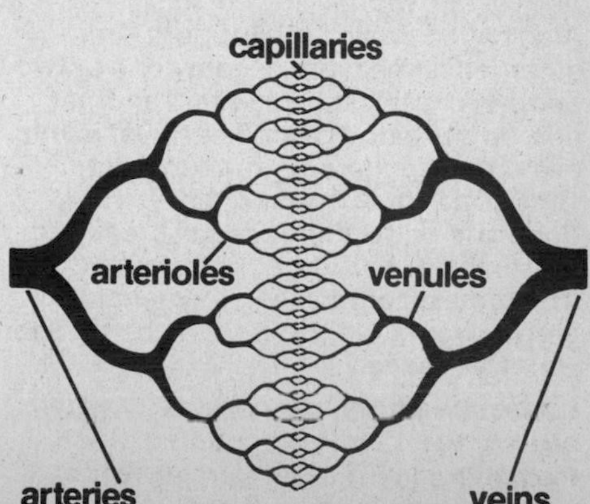

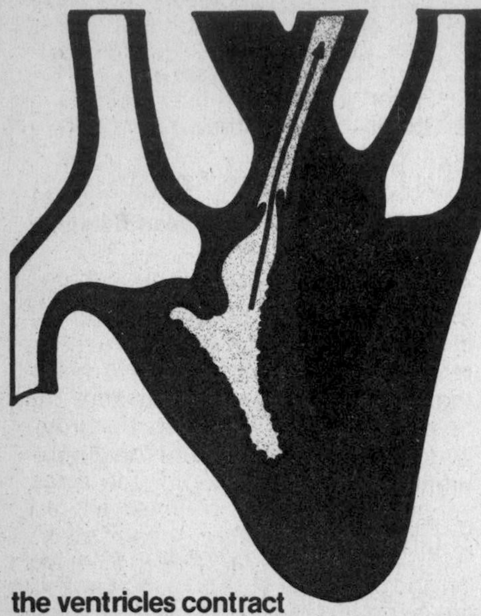
the ventricles contract and pump the blood out

CARDIAC OUTPUT
The amount of blood pumped by the heart per minute.

CARDIAC RESERVE
The difference between the cardiac output at rest (about 5 quarts pumped by one ventricle per minute) and at the maximum physical effort (as much as 25 quarts per minute or more).

CARDIOLOGIST *(kar-de-ol'o-jist)*
A specialist in the diagnosis and treatment of heart disease.

CARDIOLOGY *(kar"de-ol'o-je)*
The study of the heart and its functions in health and disease.

CARDIOMYOPATHY *(kar"de-o-mi-op'ah-the)*
A general diagnostic term for diseases that involve mainly the myocardium (heart muscle) and not other heart structures (such as the valves, coronary vessels or pericardium). They may be caused by known toxic or infectious agents. For the majority of cases, however, the cause is not known.

CARDIOPULMONARY RESUSCITATION (CPR) *(kar"de-o-pul'mo-ner-e re-sus"i-ta'shun)*
Also called Basic Life Support. An emergency measure used by one or two people to artificially maintain another person's breathing and heartbeat in the event these functions suddenly stop. CPR consists of keeping the airway open and performing rescue breathing and external cardiac compression (heart massage) to keep oxygenated blood circulating through the body. **See Heart Massage.**

CARDIOVASCULAR *(kar"de-o-vas'ku-lar)*
Pertaining to the heart and blood vessels.

CARDIOVASCULAR-RENAL DISEASE *(kar"de-o-vas'ku-lar re'nal)*
Disease involving the heart, blood vessels, and kidneys.

CARDIOVERSION *(kar'de-o-ver"zhun)*
The application of very brief discharges of direct-current electricity across the intact chest and into the heart muscle in order to stop a cardiac arrhythmia (rhythm disorder) and allow the normal heart rhythm to take over. This technique is most often used as an emergency measure, but can also be used to correct chronic conditions.

CARDIOVERTER *(kar'de-o-ver"ter)*
An instrument capable of delivering a brief direct-current electric shock. Used to terminate certain cardiac arrhythmias. **See Cardioversion.**

CARDITIS *(kar-di'tis)*
Inflammation of the heart.

CAROTID ARTERIES *(kah-rot'id)*
The left and right common carotid arteries are the principal arteries supplying the head and neck. Each has two main branches, the external carotid artery and the internal carotid artery.

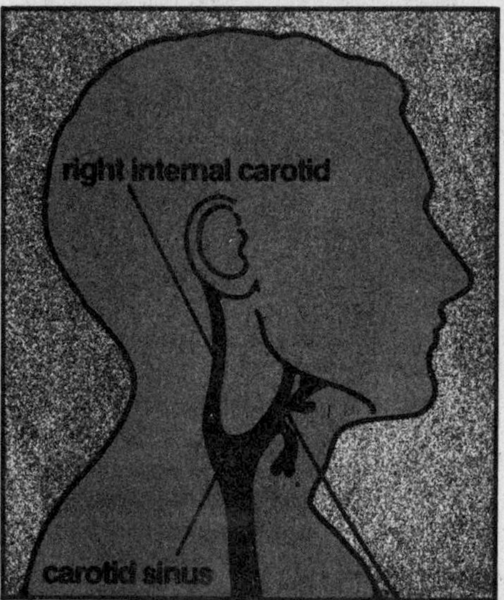

right common carotid artery / right external carotid

CAROTID BODY *(kah-rot'id)*
A tiny (5 mm. or 1/5 inch) oval mass of cells located in each carotid sinus, that is, at the branching point in the arteries supplying the head and neck. The carotid bodies contain nerve endings known as chemoreceptors which are sensitive to oxygen and carbon dioxide content and to pH of the blood. For example, when the oxygen content of the blood is reduced, the carotid bodies cause an increase in respiration rate.

CAROTID SINUS *(kah-rot'id si'nus)*
On either side of the neck, a slight dilation at the point where the internal carotid artery branches from the common carotid artery. These arteries supply the head and neck with blood. The carotid sinus contains the carotid body and many baroreceptors, special nerve endings sensitive to changes in blood pressure to keep it relatively constant. For example, if blood pressure starts to rise, baroreceptors in the carotid sinuses are stimulated to reduce the rate and force of heart contraction and to dilate the arteries—thus lowering the blood pressure. **See Carotid Arteries and Carotid Body.**

CATHETER *(kath'e-ter)*
A thin, flexible tube which can be guided into body organs. A cardiac catheter is made of woven plastic, or other material to which blood will not adhere, and is inserted into a vein or artery (usually of an arm or a leg) and gently threaded into the heart. Its progress can be watched on a fluoroscope.

Cardiac catheters can be used for diagnosis (to take samples of blood or pressure readings in the chambers of the heart) or for treatment (to implant the electrodes of a pacemaker or to administer a drug).

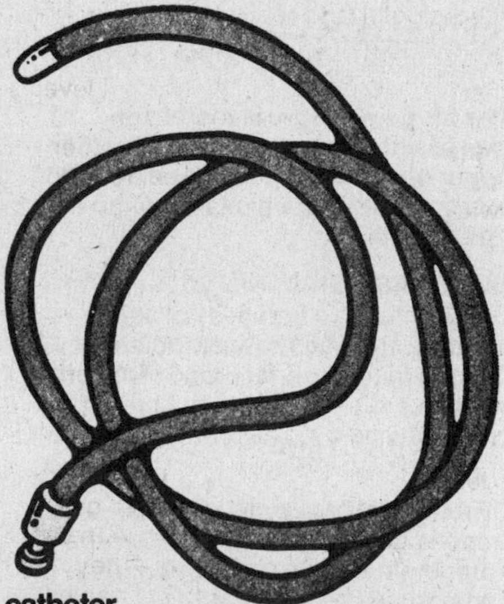
catheter

CATHETERIZATION *(kath"e-ter-i-za'shun)*
In cardiology, the process of introducing a thin, flexible tube (a catheter) into a vein or artery and guiding it into the heart for purposes of examination or treatment.

CEREBRAL VASCULAR ACCIDENT *(ser'e-bral OR se-re'bral vas'ku-lar)*
Sometimes called cerebrovascular accident, apoplectic stroke, or simply stroke. An impeded blood supply to some part of the brain, generally caused by one of the following four conditions:

1. A blood clot forming in the vessel (cerebral thrombosis).

2. A rupture of the blood vessel wall (cerebral hemorrhage).
3. A piece of clot or other material from another part of the vascular system which flows to the brain and obstructs a cerebral vessel (cerebral embolism).
4. Pressure on a blood vessel as by a tumor.

For illustration see Stroke.

CEREBROVASCULAR *(ser"e-bro-vas'ku-lar)*
Pertaining to the blood vessels in the brain.

CHAGAS HEART DISEASE *(chag'as)*
A form of heart disease resulting from an infection by a microscopic parasite found in South America.

CHEMOTHERAPY *(ke"mo-ther'ah-pe)*
The treatment of disease by administering chemicals. Frequently used in the phrase "chemotherapy of hypertension," i.e., the treatment of high blood pressure by the use of drugs.

CHLOROTHIAZIDE *(klo"ro-thi'ah-zid)*
One of the thiazide diuretics (drugs which promote the excretion of urine). Sometimes used to treat high blood pressure and edema (waterlogged tissues).

CHOLESTEROL *(ko les'ter ol)*
A fat-like substance found in animal tissue. In blood tests the normal level for Americans is assumed to be between 180 and 230 milligrams per 100 cc. A higher level is often associated with high risk of coronary atherosclerosis.

CHOLESTYRAMINE *(ko"les-ti'rah-meen)*
A drug used to lower blood levels of the lipid cholesterol. **See Lipid-Lowering Drugs.**

CHORDAE TENDINEAE *(kor'di ten'dun-i)*
Fibrous chords which serve as guy ropes to hold the valves between the upper and lower chambers. They stretch from the cusps of the valves to muscles called papillary muscles in the walls of the lower heart chambers.

CHOREA *(ko-re'ah)*
Involuntary, irregular twitching of the muscles, sometimes associated wth rheumatic fever. Also called St. Vitus Dance, or Sydenham's Chorea.

CINEANGIOCARDIOGRAPHY *(sin"e-an"je-o-kar"de-og'rah-fe)*
A diagnostic method similar to angiocardiography except that instead of still x-ray pictures, motion pictures of the heart are made by fluoroscopy, as an injected opaque liquid is carried through the heart and blood vessels. **See Angiocardiography.**

CIRCULATORY *(ser'ku-lah-to"re)*
Pertaining to the heart, blood vessels, and the circulation of the blood.

CLAUDICATION *(klaw"di-ka'shun)*
Pain and lameness or limping. Can be caused by defective circulation of the blood in the vessels of the limbs. **See Intermittent Claudication.**

CLOFIBRATE *(klo-fi'brat)*
A drug generally used to lower elevated levels of triglyceride lipids in the blood. **See Lipid-Lowering Drugs.**

CLUBBED FINGERS *(klubd)*
Fingers with a short broad tip and overhanging nail, somewhat resembling a drumstick. This condition is sometimes seen in children born with certain kinds of heart defects and in adults with heart, lung or gastrointestinal diseases. It may also be familial and insignificant.

COAGULATION *(ko-ag"u-la'shun)*
Process of changing from a liquid to a thickened or solid state. The formation of a clot.

COARCTATION OF THE AORTA *(ko"ark-ta'shun of the a-or'ta)*
Literally a pressing together or narrowing of the aorta, the main trunk artery which conducts blood from the heart to the body. One of several types of congenital heart defects.

COLLATERAL CIRCULATION *(ko-lat'er-al ser"ku-la'shun)*
Circulation of the blood through nearby smaller vessels when a main vessel has been blocked up.

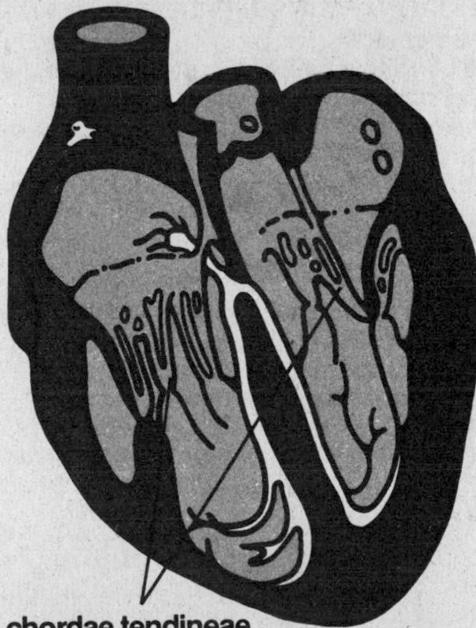
chordae tendineae

COMMISSUROTOMY *(kom"e-shur-ot'o-me)*
An operation to widen the opening in a heart valve which has become narrowed by scar tissue. The individual flaps of the valve are spread apart along the natural lines of their closure by a blunt instrument. This operation was developed to correct rheumatic heart disease. **See Mitral Valvulotomy.**

CONGENITAL ANOMALY *(kon-jen'i-tal ah-nom'ah-le)*
An abnormality present at birth.

CONGESTIVE HEART FAILURE *(kon-jes'tiv)*
"Heart failure" is a condition in which the heart is unable to pump its required amount of blood.

Heart failure is often congestive because loss of pumping power by the heart leads to congestion in the body tissues; fluid accumulates in the abdomen and legs and/or in the lungs (pulmonary edema). Congestive heart failure often develops gradually over several years, although it can be acute (short and severe). It can be treated by drugs or in some cases by surgery. **See Heart Failure.**

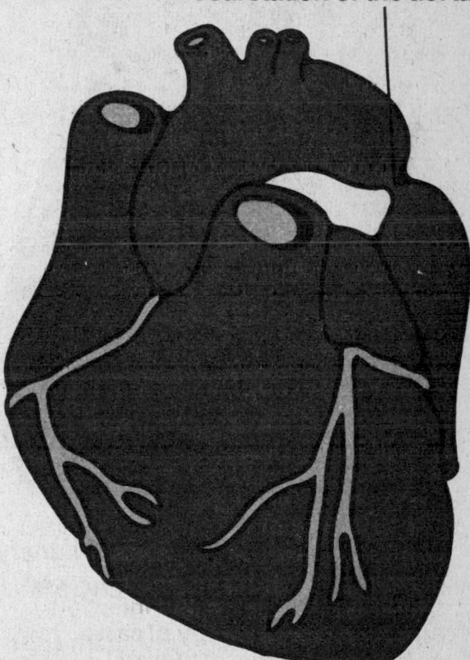

CONSTRICTIVE PERICARDITIS *(kon-strik'tiv per"i-kar-di'tis)*
A thickening of the outer sac of the heart which prevents the heart muscle from expanding and filling normally.

CONTRACTILE PROTEINS *(kon-trak'til pro'te-ins)*
Proteins which occur within all muscle fibers, including those of the heart muscle. Contractile proteins are responsible for shortening the muscle fibers and therefore causing the muscle to contract. There are several kinds of contractile proteins.

CORNEAL ARCUS *(kor'ne-al ar'kus)*
A hazy ring around the edge of the

cornea (the transparent covering over the front of the eye). It can have a variety of causes, including exposure to irritating chemicals, viral or bacterial infections, and old age. It can also be a normal finding in certain racial backgrounds.

In addition, corneal arcus can be a sign of Type II or Type IV hyperlipoproteinemia, blood-lipid disorders associated with premature development of atherosclerosis (hardening of the arteries).

CORONARY ARTERIES *(kor'o-na-re)*
Arteries, arising from the base of the aorta, which conduct blood to the heart muscle. These arteries, and the network of vessels branching off from them, come down over the top of the heart like a crown (corona).

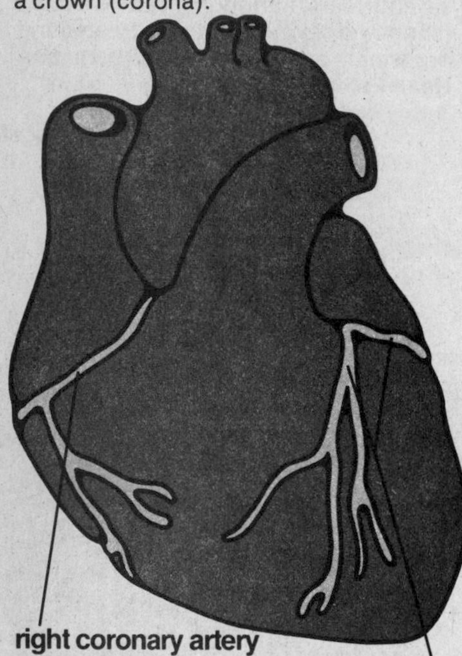

CORONARY ARTHEROSCLEROSIS *(ath"er-o"skle-ro'sis)*
Commonly called coronary heart disease. An irregular thickening of the inner layer of the walls of the arteries which conduct blood to the heart muscle. The internal channel of these arteries (the coronaries) becomes narrowed and the blood supply to the heart muscle is reduced. **See Atherosclerosis.**

CORONARY BYPASS SURGERY *(kor'o-na-re bi'pas)*
Surgery to improve the blood supply to the heart muscle when narrowed coronary arteries reduce flow of the oxygen-containing blood which is vital to the pumping heart. This reduction in bloodflow causes chest pain and leads to increased risk of heart attack. Thus coronary bypass surgery involves constructing detours through which blood can bypass narrowed portions of coronary arteries to keep the heart muscle supplied. Veins or arteries taken from other parts of the body where they are not essential are grafted onto the heart to construct these detours.

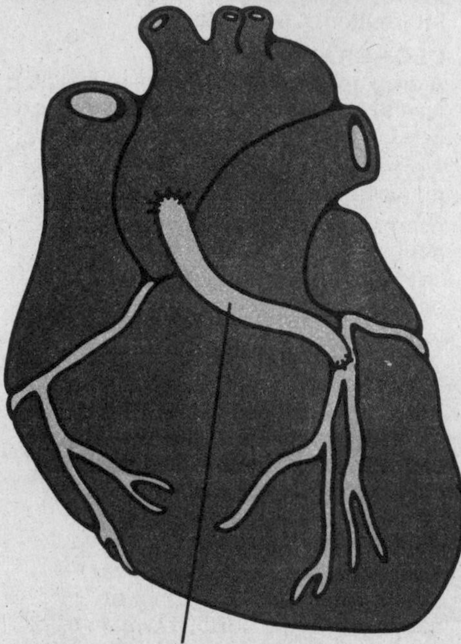

a bypass graft from the aorta to one of the coronary arteries

CORONARY HEART DISEASE
Also called coronary artery disease and ischemic heart disease. Heart ailments caused by narrowing of the coronary arteries and therefore a decreased blood supply to the heart (ischemia).

CORONARY INSUFFICIENCY *(in"su-fish'en-se)*
A condition which occurs whenever the coronary arteries (which supply the heart muscle with blood) do not provide oxygen adequate to the needs of the pumping heart. This may produce chest pain (angina pectoris) or a heart attack, or no pain may occur at all.

"*Acute* coronary insufficiency" is a term used to describe chest pain that is more severe than that of angina pectoris, but in which no heart muscle damage is done (as there would be in a heart attack).

CORONARY OCCLUSION *(o-kloo'zhun)*
An obstruction in a branch of one of the coronary arteries which hinders the flow of blood to some part of the heart muscle. This part of the heart muscle then dies because of lack of oxygen supply. Sometimes called a coronary heart attack or simply a heart attack. **See Heart Attack.**

CORONARY THROMBOSIS *(throm-bo'sis)*
Formation of a clot in a branch of one of the arteries which conduct blood to the heart muscle (coronary arteries). A form of coronary occlusion. **See Coronary Occlusion.**

COR PULMONALE *(kor pul-mo-nal'e)*
Heart disease resulting from disease of the lungs or the blood vessels of the lungs. The lung problems cause high blood pressure in the pulmonary vessels (pulmonary hypertension). Thus the right ventricle enlarges because it must work harder to pump blood through the lungs.

CORVISART, JEAN NICOLAS (1755-1821)
One of the earliest of the modern cardiologists, and the first person to call him or herself a "heart specialist." Favorite physician to Napoleon.

COUMARIN *(koo'mah-rin)*
A class of chemical substances which delay clotting of the blood. An anticoagulant.

CPR
See Cardiopulmonary Resuscitation.

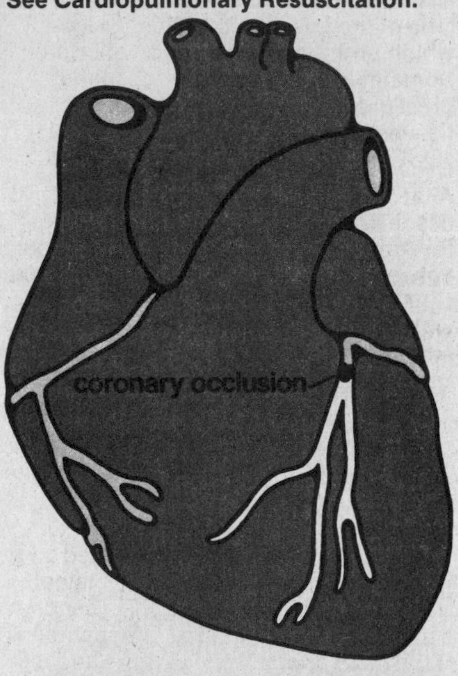

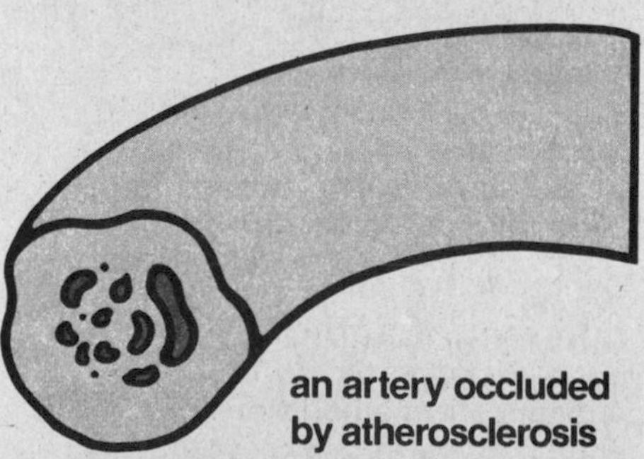

an artery occluded by atherosclerosis

CRUDE DEATH RATE
Also called crude mortality rate. The ratio of total deaths to total population during a given period of time, such as a

year. It is calculated by dividing the total number of deaths during the year by the mid-year population (estimated population on July 1) of the same year.

CYANOSIS *(si"ah-no'sis)*
Blueness of skin caused by insufficient oxygen in the blood. Oxygen is carried in the blood by hemoglobin, which is bright red when saturated with oxygen. When hemoglobin is not carrying oxygen, it is dark burgundy and is called reduced hemoglobin. The blueness of the skin occurs when the amount of reduced hemoglobin exceeds 5 grams per 100 cc. of blood.

D

DECOMPENSATION *(de"kom-pen-sa'shun)*
Inability of the heart to maintain adequate circulation, usually resulting in a waterlogging of tissues. A person whose heart is failing to maintain normal circulation is said to be "decompensated."

DEFIBRILLATION *(de-fib"ri-la'shun)*
Termination of atrial or ventricular fibrillation. Usually refers to treatment by the application of electric shock (cardioversion). **See Fibrillation and Cardioversion.**

DEPRESSANT *(de-pres'ant)*
Any drug which decreases functional activity.

DESCARTES, RENE (1596-1650)
Author of the first physiology textbook which accepted the theory of the circulation of the blood as described by William Harvey.

DEXTROCARDIA *(deks"tro-kar'de-ah)*
Two different types of congenital phenomena are often described as dextrocardia. The first is a condition more correctly termed "dextroversion" in which the heart is slightly rotated and lies almost entirely in the right (instead of the left) side of the chest. The second is a condition in which the left chambers of the heart are on the right side and the right chambers are on the left side, so that the heart and great vessels present a mirror image of the normal heart.

DIASTOLE *(di-as'to-le)*
In each heartbeat, the period of the relaxation of the heart. Atrial diastole is the period of relaxation of the atria, or upper heart chambers. Ventricular diastole is the period of relaxation of the ventricles, or lower heart chambers. **See Cardiac Cycle.**

DIET *(di'et)*
Daily allowance or intake of food and drink.

DIETETICS *(di-e-tet'iks)*
The science and art dealing with the application of principles of nutrition to the feeding of individuals or groups under different economic or health conditions.

DIETITIAN *(di-e-tish'an)*
One skilled in the scientific use of diet in health and disease.

DIGITALIS *(dij"e-tal'is)*
A drug prepared from leaves of the foxglove plant. Its main effect is cardiotonic, that is, it causes the heart muscle to pump more forcefully and effectively, thereby improving the circulation of the blood and promoting the normal elimination of excess fluid. Digitalis is often used to treat heart failure because it can relieve one of the early effects of the condition—buildup of fluid in the body tissues.

Digitalis is the most frequently used cardiotonic drug; other examples are ouabain and strophanthidin.

DILATION *(di-la'shun)*
A stretching or enlargement of the heart or blood vessels beyond the norm.

DIURESIS *(di"u-re'sis)*
Increased excretion of urine.

DIURETIC *(di"u-ret'ik)*
A medicine which promotes the excretion of urine. These drugs are often used to treat conditions involving excess body fluid such as hypertension and congestive heart failure. One important class of diuretics is the thiazides.

DUCTUS ARTERIOSUS *(duk'tus ar-te"re-o'sis)*
A small duct in the heart of the fetus between the artery leaving the right side of the heart (pulmonary artery) and the artery leaving the left side of the heart (aorta). Normally this duct closes soon after birth. If it does not close, the condition is known as patent or open ductus arteriosus. **See Patent Ductus Arteriosus.**

DYSPNEA *(disp'ne-ah)*
The uncomfortable sensation or awareness of shortness of breath.

E

ECG
See Electrocardiogram

ECHOCARDIOGRAPHY *(ek"o-kar"de-og'rah-fe)*
A diagnostic method by which pulses of sound (ultrasound) are transmitted into the body and the echoes returning from the surfaces of the heart and other structures are electronically plotted and recorded. Stop-action or real-time images of the heart can be made into a record of the heart's movements.

ECHOGRAM *(ek'o-gram)*
An image of the heart and great vessels, as would be produced by echocardiography.

ECTOMORPH *(ek'to-morf)*
Wiry body type.

EDEMA *(e-de'mah)*
Swelling due to abnormally large amounts of fluid in the tissues of the body.

EFFORT SYNDROME *(sin'drom)*
A group of symptoms (quick fatigue, rapid heartbeat, sighing breaths, dizziness) that do not result from disease of organs or tissues and that are out of proportion to the amount of exertion required. Often called functional heart disease.

EISENMENGER'S SYNDROME *(i'sen-meng"erz)*
A condition in which there is a large congenital shunting defect complicated by high blood pressure in the vessels of the lungs (pulmonary hypertension). A shunting defect is an abnormal opening between heart chambers (septal defect) or between the great vessels (such as patent ductus arteriosus) such that some oxygen-poor blood gets pumped to the body and some oxygen-rich blood gets pumped to the lungs.

The syndrome is also called Eisenmenger's Reaction. The term **Eisenmenger's Complex** is used only when the defect is in the ventricular septum.

EKG
See Electrocardiogram.

ELECTROCARDIOGRAM *(e-lek"tro-kar'de-o-gram")*
Often referred to as ECG or EKG. A graphic record of the electric currents generated by the heart.

The word "electrocardiogram" most often refers to a resting electrocardiogram, that is, the patient is lying at rest while the recording is being made. The recording can also be made during exercise. **See Exercise Electrocardiogram.**

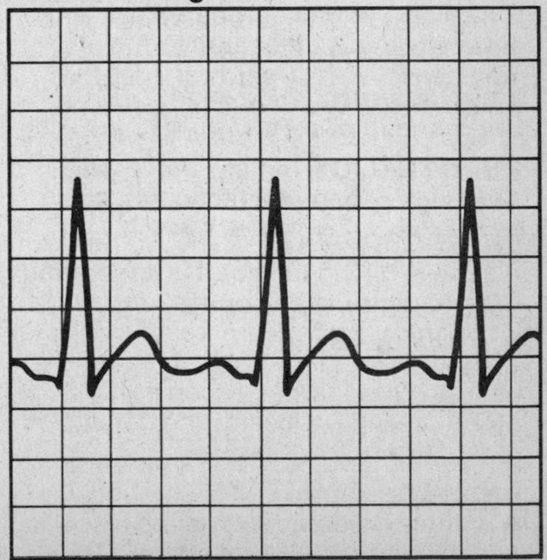

electrocardiogram

ELECTROLYTE *(e-lek'tro-lit)*
A substance which, when dissolved in a liquid, dissociates into ions (positively and negatively charged particles). A solution of electrolytes is capable of conducting an electrical current.

Electrolytes, especially sodium and potassium, occur naturally in the body fluids. Heart disease and medications to treat it can cause abnormal electrolyte concentrations in the body fluids. Physicians sometimes prescribe diet and medications to correct these disordered concentrations.

EMBOLISM *(em'bo-lizm)*
The blocking of a blood vessel by a clot or other substance carried in the bloodstream.

EMBOLUS *(em'bo-lus)*
A blood clot (or other substance such as an air bubble, fat or tumor) which drifts unattached in the bloodstream until it becomes lodged in a small vessel and obstructs circulation. **See Thrombus.**

ENDARTERECTOMY *(end"ar-ter-ek'to-me)*
Surgical removal of the innermost lining (intima) of an artery when it is thickened by fatty deposits (atheroma) and blood clots (thromboses).

ENDOCARDIAL FIBROELASTOSIS *(en"do-kar'de-al fi"bro-e"las-to'sis)*
A heart disease of unknown cause occurring in adults, but mostly in infants. It involves thickening of the lining of the heart chambers (endocardium) with elastic tissue. The thickening is most pronounced in the left ventricle and greatly impairs cardiac function.

ENDOCARDITIS *(en"do-kar-di'tis)*
Inflammation of the inner lining of the heart (endocardium) usually associated with acute rheumatic fever or some infectious agents.

ENDOCARDIUM *(en"do-kar'de-um)*
A thin smooth membrane forming the inner surface of the heart.

ENDOMORPH *(en'do-morf)*
Short and thickset body type.

ENDOTHELIUM *(en"do-the'le-um)*
The thin lining of the blood vessels.

ENLARGED HEART
A state in which the heart is larger than normal. This may be due to heredity, a large amount of exercise over a period of time, or conditions which cause the heart to work harder—such as high blood pressure, obesity and defects of the heart or great vessels.

ENZYME *(en'zim)*
A complex organic substance which is capable of speeding up specific biochemical processes in the body. Enzymes are universally present in living organisms.

EPICARDIUM *(ep"e-kar'de-um)*
The outer layer of the heart wall. Also called the visceral pericardium.

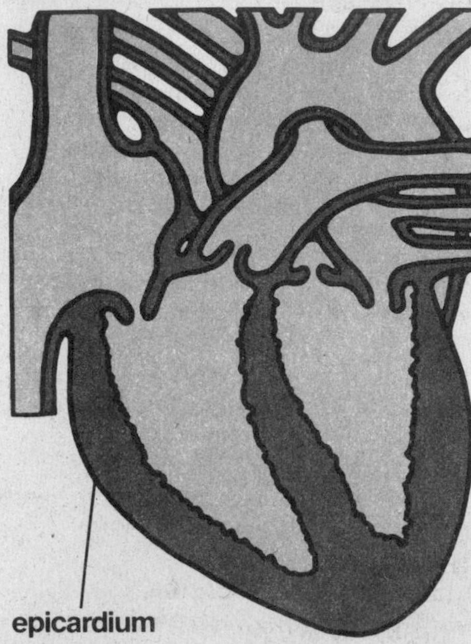

EPIDEMIOLOGY *(ep'e-de"me-ol'-o-je)*
The science dealing with the factors which determine the frequency and distribution of a disease in a human community.

EPINEPHRINE *(ep"e-nef'rin)*
One of the secretions of two small glands, called adrenal glands, located just above the kidneys. This secretion, also called adrenalin, and sometimes prepared synthetically, constricts the small blood vessels (arterioles), increases the heart rate, and raises blood pressure. It is a vasoconstrictor or vasopressor substance.

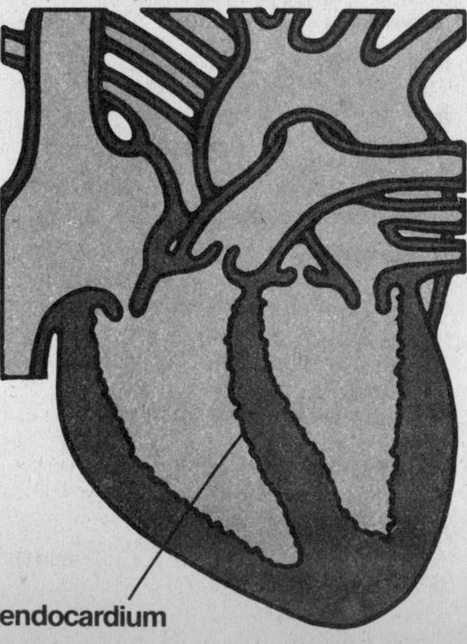

ERYTHROCYTE *(e-rith'ro-site)*
Red blood cell.

ESOPHOGEAL VARICES *(e-sof"ah-je'al var'i-seez)*
Varicosed or swollen veins in the wall of the esophagus, the tube connecting the mouth and the stomach. These are dangerous because they may rupture and bleed profusely. Esophageal varices are often associated with cirrhosis of the liver. **See Varix.**

ESSENTIAL HYPERTENSION *(e-sen'shal hi"per-ten'shun)*
Sometimes called primary hypertension, and commonly known as high blood pressure. An elevated blood pressure of unknown cause.

ETIOLOGY *(e"te-ol'o-je)*
The sum of knowledge about the causes of a disease.

EXERCISE ELECTROCARDIOGRAM *(e-lek"tro-kar'de-o-gram")*
Often referred to as a "stress test." An electrocardiogram taken while the patient is exercising—usually jogging on a treadmill, walking up and down a short set of stairs, or pedaling on a stationary bicycle. **See Electrocardiogram.**

EXTRACORPOREAL CIRCULATION *(eks"trah-kor-po're-al)*
The circulation of the blood outside the body as by a mechanical pump or pump-oxygenator. This is often done while surgery is being performed on the heart.

EXTRASYSTOLE *(eks"trah-sis'to-le)*
A contraction of the heart which occurs prematurely and interrupts the normal rhythm.

EYEGROUND *(i'ground)*
The inside of the back part of the eye seen by looking through the pupil. Examining the eyeground is one means of assessing changes in the blood vessels. Also called fundus of the eye.

F

FABRICIUS AB AQUAPENDENTE, HIERONYMUS (1560-1634)
Italian anatomist, a teacher of William Harvey at Padua. He studied the valves of the veins. Harvey is reported to have credited the work of Fabricius with leading to his own concept of the circulation of the blood.

FALLOT, ETIENNE LOUIS ARTHUR (1850-1911) *(fal-o')*
French physician who gave an important description of a congenital heart defect known as the Tetralogy of Fallot (more accurately, *Tetrad* of Fallot). **See Tetralogy of Fallot.**

FEMORAL ARTERY *(fem'or-al ar'ter-e)*
Main blood vessel supplying blood to the leg.

FIBRILLATION *(fi-bri-la'shun)*
A kind of cardiac arrhythmia. Uncoordinated contraction of the heart muscle occurring when the individual muscle fibers take up independent irregular contractions. **Atrial fibrillation** involves very rapid, irregular contractions of the atria, followed irregularly by contractions of the ventricles. This may occur suddenly and for a short time, or, if there is an existing heart disease, can become chronic. Treatment is usually by drugs and sometimes by cardioversion (brief electric shock). **Ventricular fibrillation** involves contractions of the ventricles which are irregular, haphazard and ineffective, resulting in a rapid decline of blood circulation and death. Emergency treatment may include external cardiac massage (cardiopulmonary resuscitation—CPR), electrical defibrillation (cardioversion) or drugs. **See Cardiopulmonary Resuscitation and Cardioversion.**

FIBRIN *(fi'brin)*
An elastic, threadlike protein which forms the essential portion of a blood clot.

FIBRINOGEN *(fi-brin'o-jen)*
A protein dissolved in the blood which, by the action of certain enzymes, is converted into the insoluble threadlike protein of a blood clot (fibrin).

FIBRINOLYSIN *(fi"bri-no-li'sin)*
An enzyme which can cause coagulated blood to return to a liquid state.

FIBRINOLYTIC AGENTS *(fi"bri-no-lit'ik)*
Also called thrombolytic agents. Substances which dissolve blood clots. Two examples are streptokinase and urokinase.

FLOPPY MITRAL VALVE SYNDROME
See Barlow's Syndrome.

FLUORESCENT ANTIBODY TEST *(floo"o-res'ent an'te-bod"e)*
A rapid and sensitive laboratory test. Among other things, it can be used to detect the disease-causing bacteria known as streptococci, especially those that cause rheumatic fever and therefore rheumatic heart disease. The test consists of "tagging" with a fluorescent dye the antibodies, i.e., substances in blood serum that have been built up to defend the body against bacteria. This dyed antibody is then mixed with a smear taken from the throat of the patient. If there are streptococci present in the smear, the glowing antibodies will attach to them, and they can be clearly seen through a microscope. **See Rheumatic Fever and Rheumatic Heart Disease.**

FLUOROSCOPE *(floo'o-ro-skop)*
An instrument for observing the internal body organs at work. X-rays are passed through the body onto a fluorescent screen where the shadows of the beating heart and other organs can be seen and studied.

FLUOROSCOPY *(floo"or-os'ko-pe)*
The examination of structures within the body by means of a fluoroscope.

FLUTTER
See Atrial Flutter.

FORAMEN OVALE *(fo-ra'men o-va"le)*
An oval hole between the left and right upper chambers of the heart which normally closes shortly after birth. Its failure to close is one of the congenital defects of the heart, called a patent (open) foramen ovale.

FUNDUS OF THE EYE *(fun'dus)*
The inside of the back part of the eye seen by looking through the pupil. Examining the fundus of the eye is used as a means of assessing changes in the blood vessels. Also called the eyeground.

G

GALEN (CLAUDIUS GALENUS) (c. 130-200 A.D.)
Renowned Greek physician whose theory that life and health depended upon the balance of four "humors" in the body dominated medical practice for 1500 years. His concept of the ebb and flow of the blood (which transported the humors to various parts of the body) was not refuted until William Harvey's discovery of the circulation of the blood in 1628.

GALLOP RHYTHM
An extra heart sound which, when the heart rate is rapid enough, resembles a horse's gallop. It may or may not be significant.

GANGLION *(gang'gle-on)*
A mass of nerve cells which serves as a center of nervous influence.

GANGLIONIC BLOCKING AGENTS *(gang"gle-on'ik)*
Drugs which block the transmission of a nerve impulse at the nerve centers (ganglia) rather than at the nerve endings (as would adrenergic blocking agents). Some of these drugs, such as hexamethonium and mecamylamine hydrochloride, may be used in the treatment of high blood pressure.

GENETICS *(je-net'iks)*
The study of heredity.

GUANETHIDINE *(gwa-ne'thi-deen)*
One of the drugs used to control high blood pressure. **See Antihypertensive Drugs.**

H

HARVEY, WILLIAM (1578-1657)
English physician who discovered the circulation of the blood and described his theory in 1628 in his classic work *De Motu Cordis.*

HEART ATTACK
The death of a portion of heart muscle which may result in disability or death of the individual, depending on how much of the heart is damaged. A heart attack occurs when an obstruction in one of the coronary arteries prevents an adequate oxygen supply to the heart. Symptoms may be none, mild or severe and may include chest pain (sometimes radiating to the shoulder, arm, neck or jaw), nausea, cold sweat, and shortness of breath.

Doctors often refer to a heart attack in terms of the obstruction (i.e., coronary occlusion, coronary thrombosis, or simply "coronary") or of the heart muscle damage (myocardial infarction, "infarct," or "M.I."). In common usage, the term "heart attack" often incorrectly refers to irregular heartbeats or attacks of angina pectoris.

HEART BLOCK
A condition in which the electrical impulse which travels through the heart's specialized conduction system to trigger the events of the heartbeat is slowed or blocked along its pathway. This can result in a dissociation of the rhythms of the upper and lower heart chambers, and is the major disorder for which artificial pacemakers are used. **See Sinoatrial Node and Pacemaker.**

HEART DISEASE
A general term used to mean ailments of the heart or blood vessels. Some of these are present at birth (congenital) and are either inherited or are the result of environmental influences on the embryo as it develops in the womb. The majority of cases of heart disease, however, are acquired later in life, for example, through the development of atherosclerosis.

HEART FAILURE
A condition in which the heart is unable to pump the amount of blood required to maintain a normal circulation. It can be isolated to either the left or the right side of the heart, or can involve the whole heart. Heart failure can develop from many heart and circulatory disorders, especially high blood pressure (an increased resistance to

bloodflow in the arteries), heart attack, rheumatic heart disease and birth defects.

Heart failure often leads to congestion in the body tissues; fluid accumulates in the abdomen and legs and/or in the lungs (pulmonary edema). Congestive heart failure often develops gradually over several years, although it can be acute (short and severe). It can be treated by drugs or in some cases by surgery.

HEART-LUNG MACHINE
A machine through which the bloodstream is diverted for pumping and oxygenation, for example, during heart surgery. **See Extracorporeal Circulation.**

HEART MASSAGE
Also called cardiac massage. An emergency technique using compression of the heart to keep the blood pumping through the body in the event the heart stops pumping effectively. **External heart massage** involves pressing on the chest to compress the heart between the breast-bone and the spine. Also, raising the pressure inside the chest by external compression may aid the heart's emptying as well. **Internal cardiac massage** is usually done in the operating room where the heart is directly compressed by the surgeon's hand through an incision in the chest.

HEMIPLEGIA *(hem"e-ple'je-ah)*
Paralysis of one side of the body caused by damage to the opposite side of the brain. Nerves cross in the brain, and one side of the brain controls the opposite side of the body. Such paralysis is sometimes caused by a blood clot or hemorrhage in a blood vessel in the brain. **See Stroke.**

HEMODYNAMICS *(he"mo-di-nam'iks)*
The study of the flow of blood and the forces involved.

HEMOGLOBIN *(he"mo-glo'bin)*
The oxygen-carrying red pigment of the red blood cells (corpuscles). When it has absorbed oxygen in the lungs, it is bright red and is called oxyhemoglobin. After it has given up some of its oxygen load in the tissues, it is dark burgundy in color and is called reduced hemoglobin.

HEMORRHAGE *(hem'or-ij)*
Loss of blood from a blood vessel. In external hemorrhage blood escapes from the body. In internal hemorrhage blood passes into tissues surrounding the ruptured blood vessel.

HEMORRHOIDS *(hem'o-roidz)*
Varices or excessively distended veins in the lower rectum and anus caused by a persistent increase in pressure within or against these veins. They are painful and often complicated by inflammation, bleeding, and clotting blood. **See Varix.**

HEPARIN *(hep'ah-rin)*
A naturally occurring substance which tends to prevent blood from clotting. Sometimes used in cases of an existing clot in an artery or vein to prevent enlargement of the clot or the formation of new clots. An anticoagulant.

HIGH BLOOD PRESSURE
An unstable or persistent elevation of blood pressure above the normal range. Uncontrolled, chronic high blood pressure strains the heart, damages arteries, and creates a greater risk of heart attack, stroke, and kidney problems. Also known as hypertension. **See Primary Hypertension and Secondary Hypertension.**

HIS, WILHELM (1831-1904) *(hiss)*
German anatomist who discovered the bundle of specialized muscle fibers running from the upper to lower chambers of the heart. These fibers are known as the "Bundle of His."

HYDRALAZINE *(hi-dral'ah-zeen)*
One of the drugs used to control high blood pressure. **See Antihypertensive Drugs.**

HYDROGENATED *(hi'dro-jen-a"tid)*
Combined with more hydrogen; more saturated.

HYPERCHOLESTEREMIA *(hi"per-ko-les"ter-e'me-ah)*
An excess of a fatty substance called cholesterol in the blood. Sometimes called hypercholesterolemia or hypercholesterinemia. **See Cholesterol.**

HYPERLIPEMIA *(hi"per-li-pe'me-ah)*
An excess of fats or lipids in the blood. Also called hyperlipidemia.

HYPERLIPOPROTEINEMIA *(hi"per-lip"o-pro"te-in-e'me-ah)*
The name for several types of blood-lipid disorders involving high blood levels of lipoproteins (complexes of lipids—either cholesterol or triglycerides—and certain kinds of proteins). Some types of hyperlipoproteinemia (Type II and Type IV) are associated with the premature development of atherosclerosis (hardening of the arteries) and therefore with increased risk of heart attack and stroke.

HYPERTENSION *(hi"per-ten'shun)*
Commonly called high blood pressure. **See High Blood Pressure, Primary Hypertension, and Secondary Hypertension.**

HYPERTENSIVE *(hi"per-ten'siv)*
A person with high blood pressure (hypertension).

HYPERTHYROIDISM *(hi"per-thi'roid-izm)*
A condition in which the thyroid gland is overly active. This may eventually result in a speeded up rate of heartbeat.

HYPERTROPHY *(hi-per'tro-fe)*
The enlargement of a tissue or organ due to increase in the size of its constituent cells. This may result from a demand for increased work.

HYPOCHOLESTEREMIC DRUGS *(hi"po-ko-les"te-re'mik)*
See Lipid-Lowering Drugs.

HYPOLIPEMIC DRUGS *(hi"po-li-pe'mik)*
Also called hypolipidemic drugs. **See Lipid-Lowering Drugs.**

HYPOTENSION *(hi"po-ten'shun)*
Commonly called low blood pressure. Blood pressure below the normal range. Most commonly used to describe an acute fall in blood pressure, as occurs in shock or syncope (fainting).

HYPOTHALAMUS *(hi"po-thal'ah-mus)*
A part of the brain which exerts control over activity of the abdominal organs, water balance, temperature, etc. Damage to the hypothalamus may cause abnormal gain in weight, among other things.

HYPOTHERMIA *(hy"po-ther'me-ah)*
Also called hypothermy. The state of low body temperature. Often induced (usually to 86-88 degrees F) during heart surgery in order to slow the metabolic processes. In this cooled state body tissues require less oxygen, and are therefore less likely to be damaged by oxygen deprivation.

HYPOTHYROIDISM *(hi"po-thi'roid-izm)*
A condition in which the thyroid gland is underactive, resulting in the slowing down of many of the body processes including the heart rate.

HYPOXIA *(hi-pok'se-ah)*
Less than normal content of oxygen in the organs and tissues of the body. At very high altitudes a healthy person experiences hypoxia because of insufficient oxygen in the air.

I

IATROGENIC HEART DISEASE *(i"at-ro-jen'ik)*
Literally means "caused by the doctor." A heart ailment inadvertently caused by the doctor or simply by the patient's belief that he has heart disease inferred from the manner and actions of his physician or other member of the medical team.

IDIOPATHIC HYPERTROPHIC SUBAORTIC STENOSIS (IHSS) *(id"e-o-path'ik hi"per-tro'fik sub"a-or'tik ste-no'sis)*
See Asymmetric Septal Hypertrophy.

ILIAC ARTERY *(il'e-ak ar'ter-e)*
A large artery which conducts blood to the pelvis and the legs.

INCIDENCE *(in'si-dens)*
The number of new cases of a disease developing in a given population during a specified period of time, such as a year.

INCOMPETENT VALVE *(in-kom'pe-tent)*
Any valve which does not close tight and leaks blood back in the wrong direction. Also called valvular insufficiency.

INFARCT *(in'farkt)*
The area of tissue which is damaged or dies as a result of receiving an insufficient blood supply. Frequently used in the phrase "myocardial infarct," referring to the area of heart muscle injury due to the interrupted flow of blood through the coronary artery which normally supplies it.

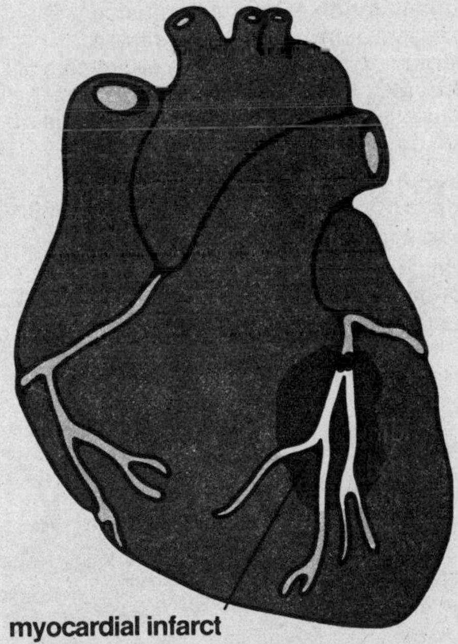

INFARCTION *(in-fark'shun)*
The occurrence of an infarct.

INNOMINATE ARTERY *(in-nom'i-nat)*
One of the largest branches of the aorta. It arises from the arch of the aorta and divides to form the right common carotid artery and the right subclavian artery.

INTERATRIAL SEPTUM *(in"ter-a'tre-al sep'tum)*
Sometimes called atrial septum. Muscular wall dividing left and right upper chambers (the atria) of the heart. **For illustration see Septum.**

INTERMITTENT CLAUDICATION *(in"ter-mit'ent klaw"di-ka'shun)*
Pain in the muscles of a limb which, similar to angina pectoris, occurs intermittently—during stress but not at rest. This condition frequently accompanies diseases of the peripheral blood vessels, such as thromboangiitis obliterans. The resting muscle has an adequate blood supply, but when the need for blood increases (as during exercise), the disease impairs the circulation. An inadequate blood supply and the buildup of waste products of metabolism in the tissues cause pain. "Claudication" means lameness.

INTERVENTRICULAR SEPTUM *(in"ter-ven-trik'u-lar sep'tum)*
Sometimes called ventricular septum. Muscular wall, thinner at the top, dividing the left and right lower chambers of the heart which are called ventricles. **For illustration see Septum.**

INTIMA *(in'ti-mah)*
The innermost layer of a blood vessel (it includes the endothelium).

IN VITRO *(in vee'tro)*
Literally means "in glass," hence in a laboratory vessel. Describes a phenomenon studied outside a living body under laboratory conditions. **See In Vivo.**

IN VIVO *(in vee'vo)*
In a living organism. Describes a phenomenon studied in a living body. **See In Vitro.**

ISCHEMIA *(is-ke'me-ah)*
A local, usually temporary, deficiency of oxygen in some part of the body, often caused by a constriction or an obstruction in the blood vessel supplying that part.

ISCHEMIC HEART DISEASE *(is-kem'ik)*
Also called coronary artery disease and coronary heart disease. Heart ailments caused by narrowing of the coronary arteries and therefore a decreased blood supply to the heart (ischemia).

ISOPROTERENOL *(i"so-pro"te-re'nol)*
A drug which can be used as a cardiac stimulant to treat an abnormally slow heartbeat.

ISOTOPE *(i'so-top)*
Any of two or more species of a chemical element. The isotopes of one element are chemically identical, but differ by some physical property such as mass or radioactivity. Radioactive isotopes (radioisotopes) are often used in medicine to trace the fate of substances in the body. **See Radioisotopic Scanning.**

J

JUGULAR VEINS *(jug'u-lar)*
Veins which return blood from the head and neck to the heart.

L

LAENNEC, RENE THEOPHILE HYACINTHE (1781-1826)
French physician who invented the stethoscope.

LEEUWENHOEK, ANTONY VAN (1632-1723)
Dutch microscopist who, among other scientific contributions, discovered the interwoven structure of the muscle fibers of the heart.

LEUKOCYTES *(lu'ko-sitz)*
See White Blood Cells.

LIFESTYLE
An individual's typical way of life, including diet, kinds of recreation, job, home environment, location, temperament, and smoking, drinking and sleeping habits.

LINOLEIC ACID *(lin-o-lay'Ik)*
An important component of many of the unsaturated fats. It is found widely in oils from plants. A diet with a high linoleic acid content tends to lower the amount of cholesterol in the blood.

LIPID *(lip'id)*
A fatty substance.

LIPID-LOWERING DRUGS
Drugs used to treat the various types of hyperlipoproteinemia, that is, abnormally high concentrations of lipids (fats) in the blood. Also called hypolipemic and hypolipidemic drugs; those drugs that lower blood levels of the lipid cholesterol are called hypocholesteremic.

The most common lipid-lowering drugs used are cholestyramine, clofibrate and nicotinic acid.

LIPOPROTEIN *(lip"o-pro'te-in)*
A complex consisting of lipid (fat) and protein molecules bound together. Lipids do not dissolve in the blood, but must circulate in the form of lipoproteins.

LUMEN *(lu'men)*
The passageway inside a tubular organ. The vascular lumen is the passageway inside a blood vessel.

M

MALIGNANT HYPERTENSION *(mah-lig'nant hi"per-ten'shun)*
Severe high blood pressure that may run a rapid course and cause damage to the blood vessel walls in the kidney,

eye, and other organs. Its cardinal feature is central nervous system impairment, for example, coma, seizures, etc.

MALPIGHI, MARCELLO (1628-1694)
Italian anatomist who, among other discoveries, demonstrated the existence of capillary connections between the arteries and veins in the lungs.

MESOMORPH *(mes'o-morf)*
Muscular body type.

METABOLISM *(me-tab'o-lizm)*
A general term designating all chemical changes which occur to substances within the body.

METHYLDOPA *(meth"il-do'pah)*
One of the drugs used to control high blood pressure. **See Antihypertensive Drugs.**

MITRAL INSUFFICIENCY *(mi'tral in"su-fish'en-se)*
An incomplete closing of the mitral valve between the upper and lower chamber in the left side of the heart which permits a backflow of blood in the wrong direction. Sometimes the result of scar tissue forming after a rheumatic fever infection.

MITRAL STENOSIS *(mi'tral ste-no'sis)*
A narrowing of the valve (called the mitral valve) opening between the upper and lower chamber in the left side of the heart. Sometimes the result of scar tissue forming after a rheumatic fever infection.

MITRAL VALVE *(mi'tral)*
A valve of two cusps or triangular segments, located between the upper and lower chamber in the left side of the heart. **See Valve.**

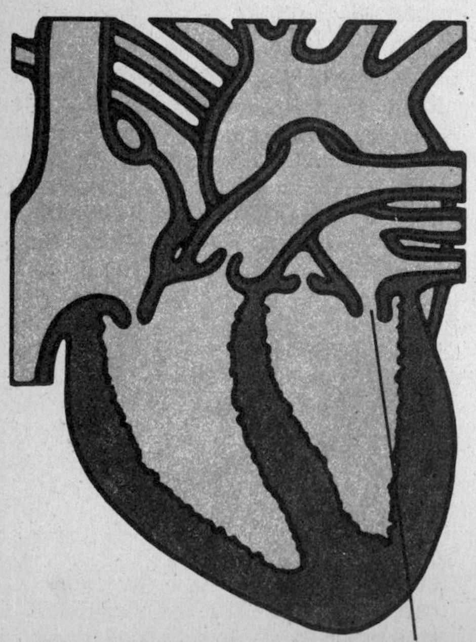

MITRAL VALVULOTOMY *(mi'tral val"vu-lot'o-me)*
An operation to widen the opening of the mitral valve by means of surgery with a knife. Usually performed when the valve opening is so narrowed as to obstruct bloodflow, which sometimes happens as a result of rheumatic fever. **See Commissurotomy.**

MONO-UNSATURATED FAT *(mon"o-un-sat'u-rat-ed)*
A fat so constituted chemically that it is capable of absorbing additional hydrogen but not as much hydrogen as polyunsaturated fat. These fats in the diet have little effect on the amount of cholesterol in the blood. One example is olive oil. **See Polyunsaturated Fat.**

MORBIDITY RATE *(mor-bid'i-te)*
The ratio of the number of cases of a disease to the number of well people in a given population during a specified period of time, such as a year. The term "morbidity" involves two separate concepts:

a. **Incidence** is the number of new cases of a disease developing in a given population during a specific period of time, such as a year.
b. **Prevalence** is the number of cases of a given disease existing in a given population at a specified moment of time.

MORTALITY RATE, AGE-ADJUSTED *(mor-tal'i-te)*
Also called age-adjusted death rate. Death rates which have been standardized for age for the purpose of making comparisons between different populations or within the same population at various intervals of time. The age-specific death rates of the populations being compared are applied to a population that is arbitrarily selected as standard, to determine what would be the crude death rate in the standard population if it were exposed first to the rates of one population and then to the rates of the other.

MORTALITY RATE, AGE-SPECIFIC *(mor-tal'i-te)*
Also called age-specific death rate. The ratio of deaths in a specific age group to the population of the same age group during a given period of time, such as a year. It is calculated by dividing the deaths that occurred among the specific age group during the year by the mid-year population in the same group (estimated population in the age group on July 1) of the same year.

MORTALITY RATE, CAUSE-SPECIFIC *(mor-tal'i-te)*
The ratio of deaths from a specific cause to total population during a given period of time, such as a year.

MORTALITY RATE, CRUDE *(mor-tal'i-te)*
The ratio of total deaths to total population during a given period of time, such as a year. Sometimes called crude death rate. It is calculated by dividing the total number of deaths during the year by the mid-year population (estimated population on July 1) of the same year.

MORTALITY RATE (SPECIFIC-CAUSE-OF-DEATH) *(mor-tal'i-te)*
The number of deaths from a specific cause that occurred in a unit of population (such as per 100,000 or per 10,000 or per 1,000) in a specified time, such as a year.

MURMUR *(mur'mur)*
An extra heart sound, sounding like fluid passing an obstruction, heard between the normal heart sounds.

MYOCARDIAL INFARCTION *(mi"o-kar'de-al in-fark'shun)*
The damaging and death of an area of heart muscle (myocardium) resulting from an interruption in the blood supply reaching that area. **See Heart Attack.**

MYOCARDITIS *(mi"o-kar-di'tis)*
Inflammation of the heart muscle (myocardium). It may be due to a variety of diseases, certain chemicals or drugs, trauma (e.g. electric shock or excessive x-ray treatment), or may be of unknown origin.

MYOCARDIUM *(mi"o-kar'de-um)*
The muscular wall of the heart. The thickest of the three layers of the heart wall, it lies between the inner layer (endocardium) and the outer layer (epicardium).

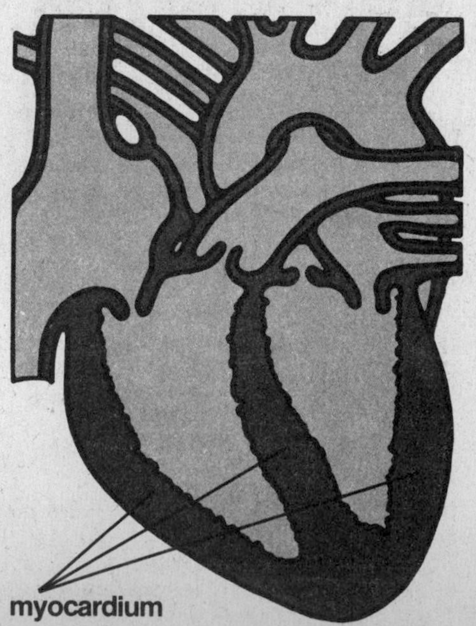

N

NEUROCIRCULATORY ASTHENIA *(nu"ro-cir'cu-lah-to"re as-the'na-ah)* Sometimes called soldier's heart, effort syndrome, or functional heart disease. A complex of nervous and circulatory symptoms, often involving a sense of fatigue, dizziness, shortness of breath, rapid heartbeat, and nervousness. **See Effort Syndrome.**

NEUROGENIC *(nu"ro-jen'ik)* Originating in the nervous system.

NICOTINIC ACID *(nik'o-tin"ik)* A lipid-lowering drug which can be used to lower elevated levels of both cholesterol and triglycerides in the blood. **See Lipid-Lowering Drugs.**

NITRITES *(ni'trits)* A group of chemical compounds, many of which cause dilation of the small blood vessels and thus lower blood pressure. Examples are amyl nitrite, sodium nitrite, nitroprusside and nitroglycerin.

NITROGLYCERIN *(ni-tro-glis'er-in)* A drug (one of the nitrites) which relaxes the muscles in the blood vessels. Often used to relieve attacks of angina pectoris and spasm of coronary arteries. It is one of the vasodilators.

NORADRENALIN *(nor"ad-ren'ah-lin)* **See Norepinephrine.**

NOREPINEPHRINE *(nor"ep-e-nef'rin)* An organic compound which produces a rise in blood pressure by constricting the small blood vessels. Sometimes used in the treatment of shock. Also called noradrenalin.

NORMOTENSIVE *(nor"mo-ten'siv)* Characterized by normal blood pressure.

NUTRITIONIST *(nu-trish'un-ist)* One professionally engaged in investigating and solving problems of nutrition.

O

OBESITY *(o-bees'i-te)* An increase in body weight beyond physical and skeletal requirements due to an accumulation of excess fat. This puts a strain on the heart and increases the chance of developing two major heart attack risk factors—high blood pressure and diabetes.

OCCLUSIVE *(o-kloo'siv)* Closing or shutting off. A coronary occlusion is a closing off of a coronary artery (which supplies the heart muscle with blood).

OPEN-HEART SURGERY Surgery performed on the opened heart. This phrase is also often used to refer to all heart surgery—whether or not the heart itself is opened.

ORGANIC HEART DISEASE Heart disease caused by some structural abnormality in the heart or circulatory system.

OXYGEN *(ok'si-jen)* A gas which is the most important component of the air we breathe. It is vital to energy-producing chemical reactions in the living cells of the body. Breathed into the lungs, it enters the bloodstream and is carried by the blood to the body tissues.

P

PACEMAKER *(pas'mak-er)* A small mass of specialized cells in the right atrium of the heart which gives rise to the electrical impulses that initiate contractions of the heart. Also called sinoatrial node or S-A node of Keith-Flack. Under abnormal circumstances, other cardiac tissues may assume the pacemaker role by initiating electrical impulses which stimulate contraction.

The term "artifical pacemaker" is applied to an electrical device which can substitute for a defective natural pacemaker and control the beating of the heart by a series of rhythmic electrical discharges. If the electrodes which deliver the discharges to the heart are placed on the outside of the chest, it is called an "external pacemaker." If they are placed within the chest wall, it is called an "internal pacemaker."

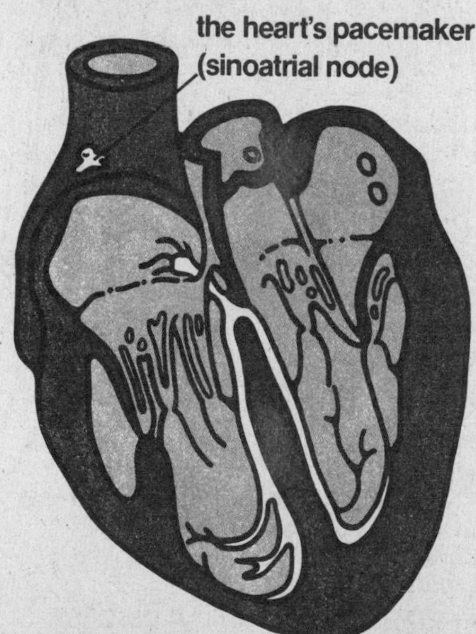

PALPITATION *(pal"pi-ta'shun)* A sensation of fluttering of the heart or abnormal rate or rhythm of the heart as experienced by the person.

PAPILLARY MUSCLES *(pap'i-ler"e)* Small, cone-shaped muscles projecting from the walls of the lower heart chambers (the ventricles) to which are attached fibrous cords (chordae tendineae) stretching up to the flaps of the valves between upper and lower chambers. When the ventricles fill with blood and contract, the papillary muscles also contract and tighten the cords, allowing the valves to be pressed shut, but preventing them from being pushed back and open into the upper chambers (the atria) by the surging blood.

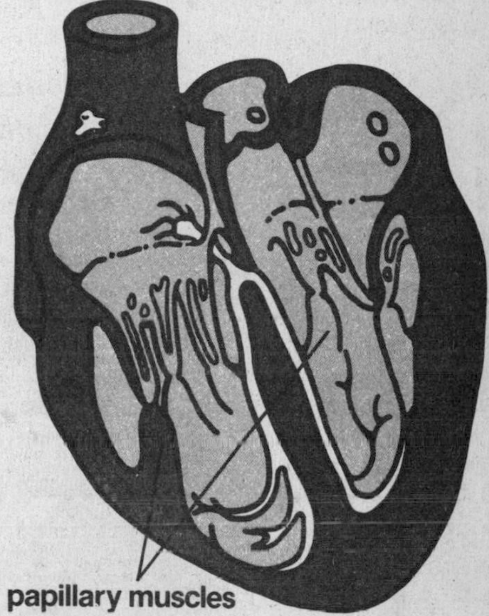

PARASYMPATHETIC NERVOUS SYSTEM *(par"ah-sim"pah-thet'ik)* One of the two divisions of the autonomic nervous system. **See Autonomic Nervous System.**

PARIETAL PERICARDIUM *(pah-ri'e-tal per"e-kar'de-um)* A thickened protective membrane which is the outer wall of the pericardium, the double-walled sac surrounding the heart. **For illustration see Pericardium.**

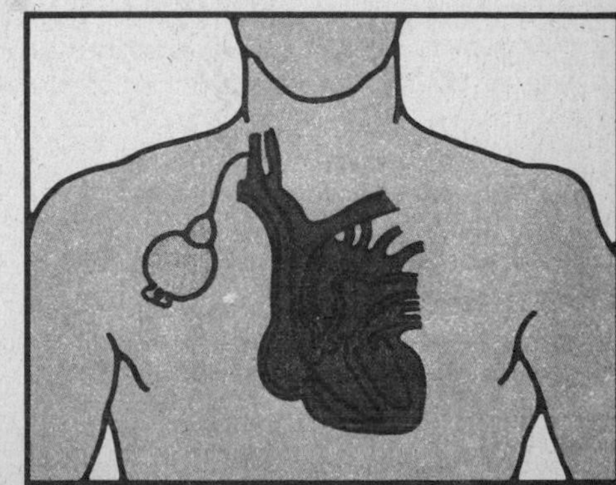
an implanted artificial pacemaker

PAROXYSMAL TACHYCARDIA *(par"ok-siz'mal tak"e-kar'de-ah)* A period of rapid heartbeats which begins and ends suddenly.

PATENT DUCTUS ARTERIOSUS *(pa'tent duk'tus ar-te"re-o'sis)* A congenital heart defect in which a small duct between the artery leaving the left side of the heart (aorta) and the artery leaving the right side of the heart (pulmonary artery), which normally closes soon after birth, remains open. As a result of this duct's failure to close, blood from both sides of the heart is pumped into the pulmonary artery and into the lungs. This defect is sometimes called simply patent ductus. Patent means open.

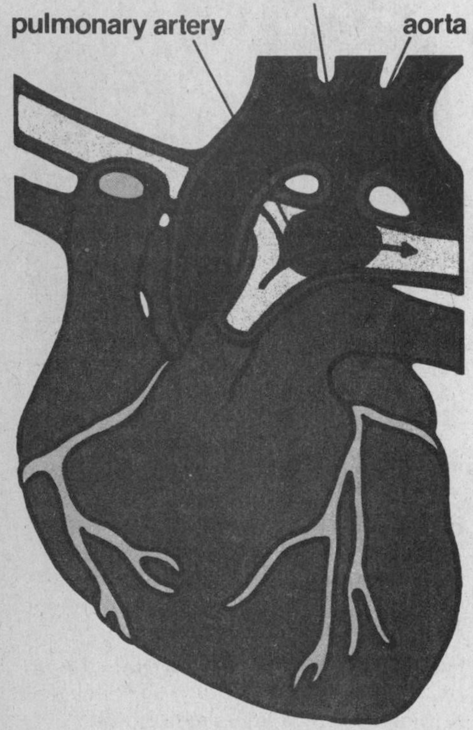

PATENT FORAMEN OVALE *(pa'tent fo-ra'men o-va'le)* One type of congenital heart defect. An oval hole (the foramen ovale) between the left and right upper chambers of the heart, which normally closes shortly after birth, remains open.

PERCUSSION *(per-kush'un)* Tapping the body as an aid in diagnosing the conditions of parts beneath by the sound obtained. A physician will often tap the chest to determine the state of the heart and lungs—for instance, whether there may be a fluid accumulation or an enlarged heart.

PERIARTERITIS NODOSA *(per"e-ar"te-ri'tis no-do'sa)* **See Polyarteritis Nodosa.**

PERICARDIAL TAMPONADE *(per"i-kar'de-al tam"pon-ad')* An accumulation of excess fluid between the two layers of the membrane sac surrounding the heart (the pericardium). This can happen rapidly or gradually and impairs the normal functioning of the heart. **See Pericardium.**

PERICARDITIS *(per"e-kar-di'tis)* Inflammation of the membrane sac (pericardium) which surrounds the heart.

PERICARDIUM *(per"e-kar'de-um)* A closed sac surrounding the heart and roots of the great vessels. The sac is formed by two walls:
The **visceral pericardium** is on the inside, closely adhering to the heart. It forms the outermost layer of the heart wall and is also called the epicardium. The **parietal pericardium** is on the outer side of the sac and is anchored to other chest structures such as the breastbone. It is a protective membrane.

The space inside the sac (the **pericardial cavity**), between the two walls, contains a fluid which provides for smooth movements of the heart as it beats.

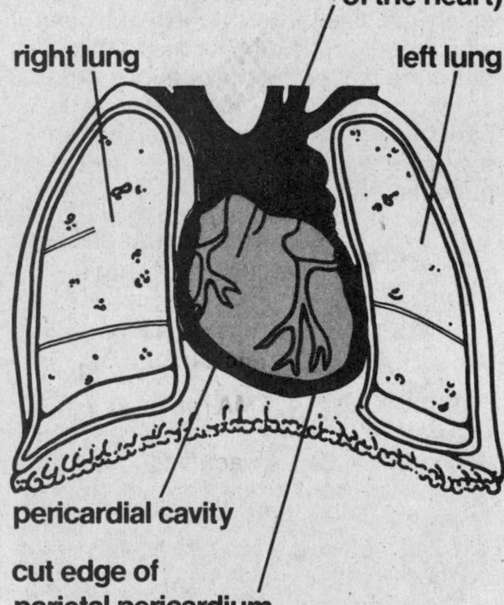

PERIPHERAL RESISTANCE *(pe-rif'er-al)* The resistance offered by the arterioles to the flow of blood. An increase in peripheral resistance causes a rise in blood pressure.

PERIPHERAL VASCULAR DISEASE *(pe-rif'er-al vas'cu-lar)* A term which, in its broadest sense, refers to diseases of any of the blood vessels outside of the heart and to diseases of the lymph vessels. These are circulation disorders caused by changes in the caliber of the vessels. **Functional** peripheral vascular diseases are not structural or organic in cause, but are transient and reversible. An example is Raynaud's disease, which can be triggered by cold temperatures, emotional stress, work with vibrating machinery or smoking. The term **organic** describes circulation disturbances which are caused by structural changes in the vessels (such as inflammation and tissue damage). An example is Buerger's disease (thromboangiitis obliterans).

PERSONALITY, TYPE A AND TYPE B **See Behavior, Type A and Type B.**

PHEOCHROMOCYTOMA *(fe-o-kro"mo-si-to'mah)* A tumor which arises in the adrenal glands. It produces and releases into the bloodstream large quantities of norepinephrine and epinephrine. These powerful natural stimulants may then create such symptoms as high blood pressure, elevated heart rate, headaches, anxiety, and excessive sweating.

PHLEBITIS *(fle-bi'tis)* Inflammation of a vein, often in the leg. Sometimes a blood clot is formed in the inflamed leg. **See also Thrombophlebitis.**

PHOSPHOLIPIDS *(fos"fo-lip'idz)* One of the three major classes of lipids (fatty substances) in the blood. Unlike the other two classes—cholesterol and triglycerides—phospholipids are *not* known to be associated with atherosclerosis (hardening of the arteries).

PLAQUE *(plak)* **See Atheroma.**

PLASMA *(plaz'mah)* The cell-free liquid portion of uncoagulated blood. It is different from serum which is the fluid portion of the blood obtained after coagulation.

PLATELETS *(plat'letz)* One of the three kinds of formed elements found in the blood. Literally "little plates," they are small, colorless, disk-shaped bodies which are involved in the formation of blood clots. Also called thrombocytes. **See Red Blood Cells and White Blood Cells.**

PLETHYSMOGRAPHY *(pleth"iz-mog'rah-fe)* The recording of changes in the size of an organ, part, or limb as blood circulates through it. However, lung volumes can also be measured with the technique.

POLYARTERITIS NODOSA *(pol"e-ar"te-ri'tis no-do'sa)* A disease of unknown cause characterized by inflammation and destruction along segments of small and medium-sized arteries, creating lumps or nodes of scar tissue. This leads to functional impairment of the tissues supplied by the affected vessels.

POLYCYTHEMIA *(pol"e-si-the'me-ah)*
An abnormal condition of the blood characterized by an excessive number of red blood cells.

POLYUNSATURATED FAT *(pol"e-un-sat'u-rat-ed)*
A fat so constituted chemically that it is capable of absorbing additional hydrogen. These fats are usually liquid oils of vegetable origin, such as corn oil or safflower oil. A diet with a high polyunsaturated fat content tends to lower the amount of cholesterol in the blood. These fats are sometimes substituted for saturated fat in a diet in an effort to lessen the hazard of fatty deposits in the blood vessels. **See Mono-unsaturated Fat.**

PRESSOR *(pres'or)*
Tending to increase blood pressure, as a pressor substance.

PREVALENCE *(prev'ah-lens)*
The number of cases of a given disease existing in a given population at a specified moment of time.

PRIMARY HYPERTENSION *(hi"per-ten'shun)*
Also called essential hypertension. High blood pressure of unknown origin (as opposed to secondary hypertension, which is caused by some primary disease, such as kidney disease). Most people who have high blood pressure have primary hypertension. **See Secondary Hypertension.**

PROCAINE AMIDE *(pro'kane am'id)*
A drug sometimes used to treat abnormal rhythms of the heartbeat; an antiarrhythmic drug.

PROPRANOLOL *(pro-pran'o-lol)*
A member of the group of drugs known as beta-blocking agents. Propranolol is used to treat angina pectoris, cardiac arrhythmias, high blood pressure, and other disorders of the cardiovascular system. **See Adrenergic Blocking Agents.**

PROSTAGLANDINS *(pros"tah-glan'dinz)*
Hormone-like substances made from fatty acids which are found throughout the body tissues. They are thought to have important roles in tissue metabolism and bloodflow, among other things.

PROSTHESIS *(pros-the'sis)*
An artificial substitute for a body part, such as a leg, tooth, heart valve or blood vessel. The plural form is **Prostheses.**

PSYCHOSOMATIC *(si"ko-so-mat'ik)*
Pertaining to the influence of the mind, emotions, fears, etc., upon the functions of the body, especially in relation to disease.

PULMONARY *(pul'mo-ner"e)*
Pertaining to the lungs.

PULMONARY ARTERY
The large artery which conveys unoxygenated (venous) blood from the lower right chamber of the heart to the lungs. This is the only artery in the body which normally carries unoxygenated blood, all others carrying oxygenated blood to the body.

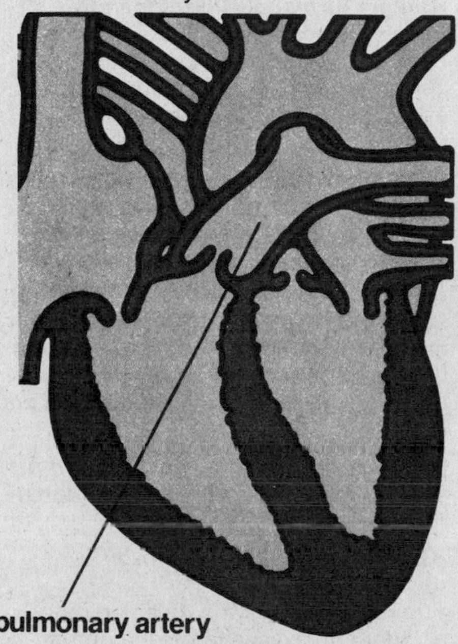

pulmonary artery

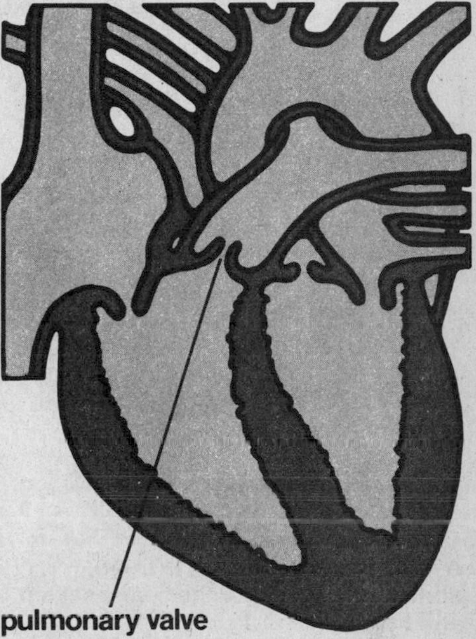

pulmonary valve

PULMONARY CIRCULATION
The circulation of the blood through the lungs, the flow being from the right lower chamber of the heart (right ventricle) through the lungs, back to the left upper chamber of the heart (left atrium). **See Systemic Circulation.**

PULMONARY EDEMA *(pul'mo-ner"e e-de'mah)*
A condition, usually acute (sudden and severe) but sometimes chronic, marked by an excess of fluid in the extravascular (outside the vessels) spaces in the lungs. It may be confined to the interstitial spaces or may appear in the alveoli (the millions of tiny air sacs in each lung). Pulmonary edema occurs most often as a complication of left ventricular failure due to ischemic heart disease, high blood pressure or disease of the aortic valve. **See Congestive Heart Failure and Heart Failure.**

PULMONARY EMBOLISM *(em'bo-lizm)*
A condition in which a blood clot (embolus), usually one formed in a vein of the leg or pelvis, breaks loose and becomes lodged in one of the arteries of the lungs. This may produce no symptoms at all or may create very serious impairment of pulmonary circulation.

PULMONARY HYPERTENSION *(hi"per-ten'shun)*
High blood pressure (hypertension) in the blood vessels of the lungs. The two most common causes are chronic obstructive lung diseases (such as emphysema) and septal defects (holes in the wall which separates the left and right sides of the heart).

PULMONARY VALVE
Valve formed by three cup-shaped membranes at the junction of the pulmonary artery and the right lower chamber of the heart (right ventricle). When the right ventricle contracts, the pulmonary valve opens and the blood is forced into the artery leading to the lungs. When the chamber relaxes, the valve is closed and prevents a backflow of the blood. **See Valve.**

PULMONARY VEINS
The veins which conduct oxygenated blood from the lungs into the left upper chamber of the heart (left atrium).

PULSE *(puls)*
The expansion and contraction of an artery which may be felt with the finger.

PULSE PRESSURE
The difference between the blood pressure in the arteries when the heart is in contraction (systole) and when it is in relaxation (diastole).

PULSUS ALTERNANS *(pul'sus awl-ter'nanz)*
A pulse in which there is regular alternation of weak and strong beats.

PURKINJE FIBERS *(pur-kin'je)*
Specialized muscular fibers forming a

network in the walls of the lower chambers of the heart and believed to be involved in conducting electrical impulses to the muscular walls of the two lower chambers (ventricles). These electrical impulses are responsible for the contractions of the heart.

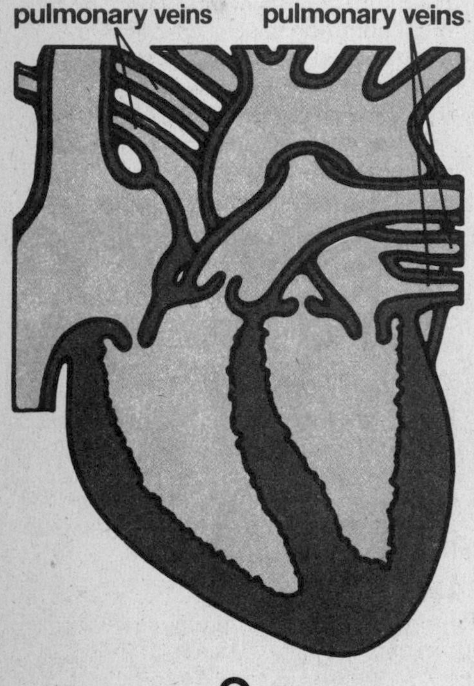

Q

QUINIDINE *(kwin'i-deen)*
A drug sometimes used to treat abnormal rhythms of the heartbeat; an antiarrhythmic drug.

R

RADIOISOTOPE *(ray"de-o-i'so-top)*
A radioactive form ("isotope") of an element. **See Isotope.**

RADIOISOTOPIC SCANNING *(ray"de-o-i'so-top-ik skan'ning)*
A diagnostic technique involving radioactive labelling of tissues and organs by the injection of radioisotopes into the bloodstream. The emitted radioactivity is detected by a scanner and a record or "scan" of the labelled area is made. Used by cardiologists to visualize the heart and great vessels, it can often reveal areas of heart damage. **See Isotope and Radioisotope.**

RAUWOLFIA *(raw-wol'fe-ah)*
A drug consisting of powdered whole root of a plant (Rauwolfia serpentina) which lowers blood pressure and slows the heart rate. Sometimes used in treatment of high blood pressure. An antihypertensive agent. **See Reserpine.**

RAYNAUD'S DISEASE *(ray-noz')*
Also called Primary Raynaud's Phenomenon. A disorder characterized by occurrences of Raynaud's Phenomenon, but not known to have an underlying cause.

RAYNAUD'S PHENOMENON *(ray-noz')*
Short episodes of pallor and numbness in the fingers, toes and, rarely, the nose and ears, due to temporary constriction of the arterioles in the skin. Pallor in the affected area is followed by blueness (due to insufficient oxygen supply), then occasionally by redness as oxygenated blood rushes in. These episodes may be triggered by cold temperatures, emotional stress, working with vibrating machinery or cigarettes.

Primary Raynaud's Phenomenon is called **Raynaud's Disease**, is generally benign, and has no known cause. **Secondary Raynaud's Phenomenon** is a symptom of one of several serious disorders, which, if not detected and treated, may have serious consequences.

RED BLOOD CELLS (CORPUSCLES)
One of the three kinds of formed elements found in the blood. Their most important function is to carry oxygen by means of hemoglobin, the red pigment these cells contain. Also called erythrocytes. **See White Blood Cells and Platelets.**

REGURGITATION *(re-gur"ji-ta'shun)*
The backward flow of blood through a defective valve.

REHABILITATION *(re"hah-bil"i-ta'shun)*
The return of a person disabled by accident or disease to the maximum attainable physical, mental, emotional, social and economic usefulness, and, if employable, to an opportunity for gainful employment.

RENAL *(re'nal)*
Pertaining to the kidney.

RENAL CIRCULATION
The circulation of the blood through the kidneys. Important in heart disease because of its functon in the elimination of water, certain chemical elements, and waste products from the body.

RENAL HYPERTENSION *(re'nal hi"per-ten'shun)*
High blood pressure caused by damage to or disease of the kidneys or their blood vessels.

RESERPINE *(res'er-peen OR re-ser'peen)*
One of the organic substances found in the root of the Indian snake root plant (Rauwolfia serpentina) which lowers blood pressure, slows the heart rate, and has a sedative effect.

REVASCULARIZATION *(re-vas"ku-lar-i-za'shun)*
Restoration of sufficient bloodflow to body tissues when supplying arteries are narrowed or blocked by injury or disease. Such surgery can be done on the legs, kidneys, brain, neck or (most commonly) the heart.

One procedure for cardiac revascularization is endarterectomy, removal of the thickened inner lining of a narrowed coronary artery. Other procedures may involve the use of additional blood vessels, either artificial ones or ones from elsewhere in the body. Vessels from other parts of the body may either be rerouted from nearby structures (for example, the internal mammary artery) or by grafting whole sections of vessels onto the heart (as is done with the saphenous vein in coronary bypass surgery). **See Endarterectomy and Coronary Bypass Surgery.**

RHEUMATIC FEVER *(roo-mat'ik)*
A disease, usually occurring in childhood, which may follow a few weeks after a streptococcal infection. It is sometimes characterized by one or more of the following: fever, sore swollen joints, a skin rash, occasionally by involuntary twitching of the muscles (called chorea or St. Vitus Dance) and small nodes under the skin. In some cases the infection affects the heart and may result in scarring the valves, weakening the heart muscle, or damaging the sac enclosing the heart. **See Rheumatic Heart Disease.**

RHEUMATIC HEART DISEASE *(roo-mat'ik)*
The damage done to the heart, particularly the heart valves, by one or more attacks of rheumatic fever. The valves are sometimes scarred so they do not open and close normally. **See Rheumatic Fever.**

RISK FACTORS
In cardiology, characteristics which are associated with an increased risk of developing coronary heart disease. These include high blood pressure (hypertension), elevated blood levels of cholesterol and other lipids (hyperlipoproteinemia), cigarette smoking, obesity, diabetes and a family history of heart disease. A competitive, aggressive lifestyle (Type A Behavior) is also thought to predispose a person to heart disease.

S

S-A NODE
See Sinoatrial Node.

SAPHENOUS VEIN *(sah-fe'nus)*
A large vein in the leg which can be removed and grafted onto the heart in coronary bypass surgery to provide adequate coronary circulation. **See Coronary Bypass Surgery.**

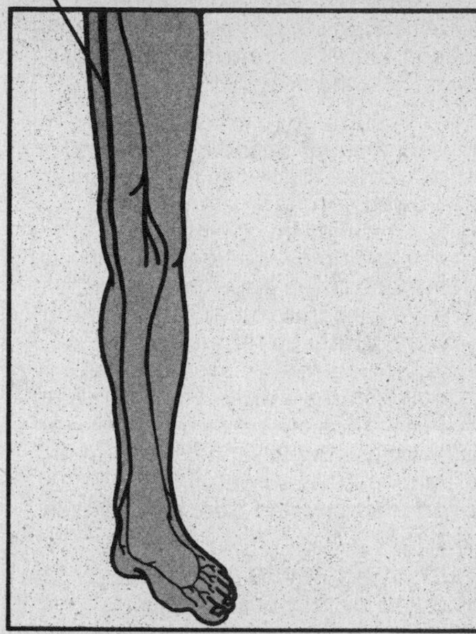

SATURATED FAT *(sat'u-rat"ed)*
A fat so constituted chemically that it is not capable of absorbing any more hydrogen. These are usually the solid fats of animal origin such as the fats in milk, butter, meat, etc. A diet high in saturated fat content tends to increase the amount of cholesterol in the blood. Sometimes these fats are restricted in the diet in an effort to lessen the hazard of fatty deposits in the blood vessels.

SCLEROSIS *(skle-ro'sis)*
Hardening, as in the term "arteriosclerosis," hardening of the arteries.

SECONDARY HYPERTENSION *(hi"per-ten'shun)*
High blood pressure caused by (i.e. secondary to) certain specific diseases or infections. **See Pheochromocytoma and Renal Hypertension.**

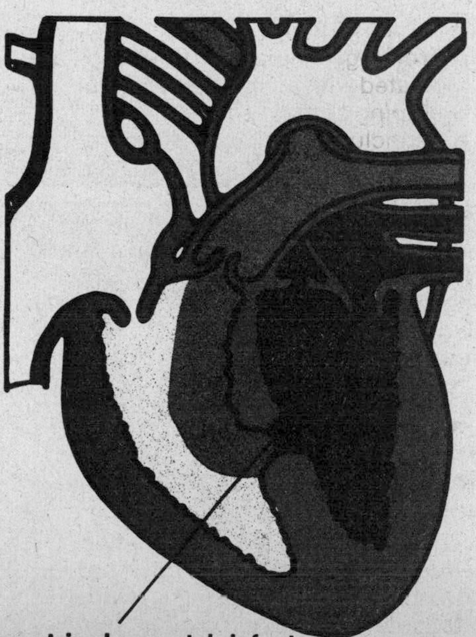

SEMILUNAR VALVES *(sem"e-lu'nar)*
Cup-shaped valves. The aortic valve at the entrance to the aorta and the pulmonary valve at the entrance to the pulmonary artery are semilunar valves. They consist of three cup-shaped flaps which prevent the backflow of blood.

SEPTAL DEFECT *(sep'tal)*
An abnormal opening in the wall (septum) that normally divides the right and left sides of the heart. There are both atrial and ventricular septal defects, depending on whether the upper or lower heart chambers are involved.

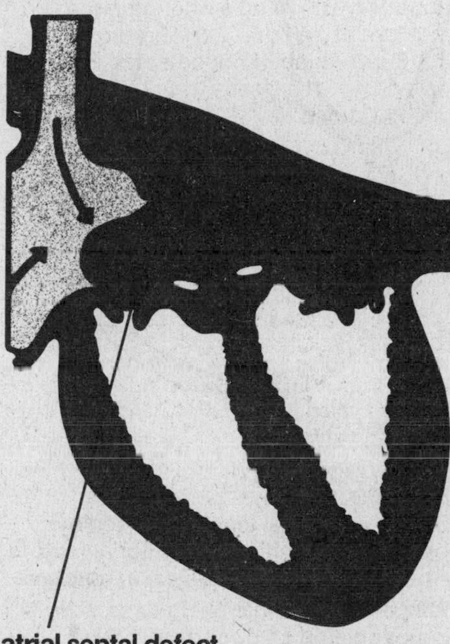

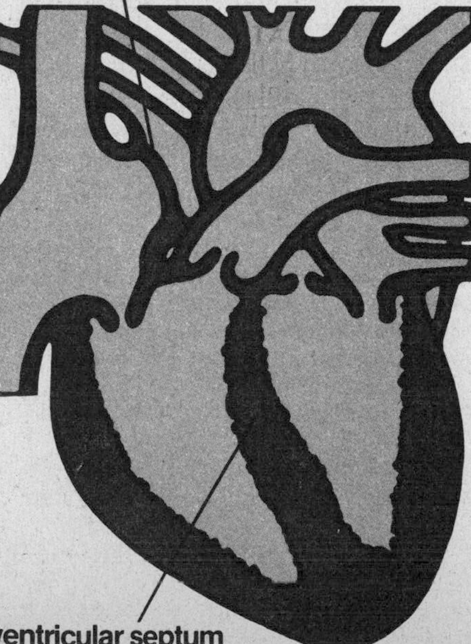

SEPTUM *(sep'tum)*
A dividing wall.

1. Atrial or interatrial septum. Muscular wall dividing left and right upper chambers (atria) of the heart.
2. Ventricular or interventricular septum. Muscular wall, thinner at the top, dividing the left and right lower chambers (ventricles) of the heart.

SEROTONIN *(ser"o-to'nin)*
A naturally occurring compound, found mainly in the gastrointestinal tract and in lesser amounts in the blood, which has a stimulating effect on the circulatory system.

SERUM *(se'rum)*
The fluid portion of blood which remains after the cellular elements have been removed by coagulation. It is different from plasma which is the cell-free liquid portion of uncoagulated blood.

SERVETUS, MICHAEL (1509-1553)
Spanish physician who discovered the circulation of the blood through the lungs. Burned at the stake in Geneva for his religious doctrines.

SHOCK
The collection of symptoms resulting from an inadequate volume of fluid circulating through the body to maintain normal metabolism. This may be due to a large loss of blood or to some derangement of circulatory control. Shock is marked by hypotension (low blood pressure), pale, cold skin, usually tachycardia (weak, rapid pulse), and often anxiety. Cardiogenic shock is shock resulting from a greatly diminished cardiac output, such as may occur in a large heart attack.

SHUNT
A passage between two blood vessels or between the two sides of the heart, as in cases where an opening exists in the wall which normally separates them. In surgery, the operation of forming a passage between blood vessels to divert blood from one part of the body to another.

SIGN
Any objective evidence of a disease. **See Symptom.**

SINOATRIAL NODE *(si"no-a'tre-al)*
A small mass of specialized cells in the right upper chamber of the heart which give rise to the electrical impulses that initiate contractions of the heart. Also called S-A node or pacemaker. **For illustration see Pacemaker.**

SINUS RHYTHM *(si'nus rith'm)*
Normal heart rhythm as initiated by electrical impulses in the sinoatrial node or pacemaker. **See Pacemaker.**

SINUSES OF VALSALVA *(si'nus-sez of val-sal'vah)*
Three pouches in the wall of the aorta behind the three cup-shaped membranes of the aortic valve.

SODIUM *(so'de-um)*
A mineral essential to life, found in nearly all plant and animal tissue. Table salt (sodium chloride) is nearly half sodium. In some types of heart disease the body retains an excess of sodium and water, and therefore sodium intake is restricted.

SPHYGMOMANOMETER *(sfig"mo-mah-nom'e-ter)*
An instrument for measuring blood pressure in the arteries.

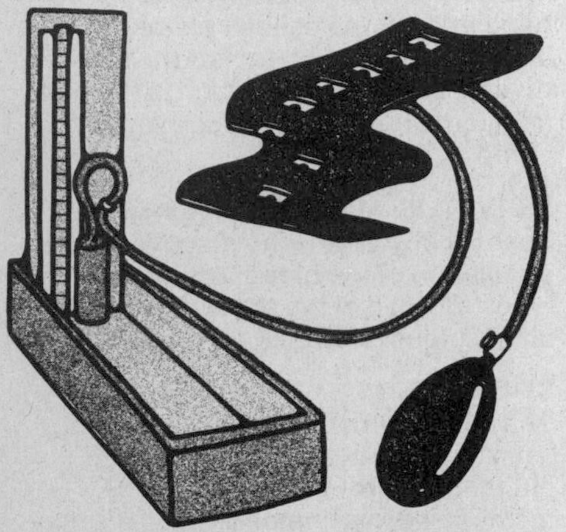

mercury column sphygmomanometer

dial or aneroid sphygmomanometer

STARLING'S LAW OF THE HEART
A law which states that the more the heart muscle is stretched when an increased amount of blood fills the ventricles, the more vigorous its contraction will be, resulting in a greater amount of blood pumped out of the heart.

STASIS *(sta'sis)*
A stoppage or lessening of the flow of blood or other body fluid in any part.

STENOSIS *(ste-no'sis)*
A narrowing or stricture of an opening. Mitral stenosis, aortic stenosis, etc., mean that the valve indicated has become so narrowed that it does not function normally.

STETHOSCOPE *(steth'o-skop)*
An instrument for listening to sounds within the body.

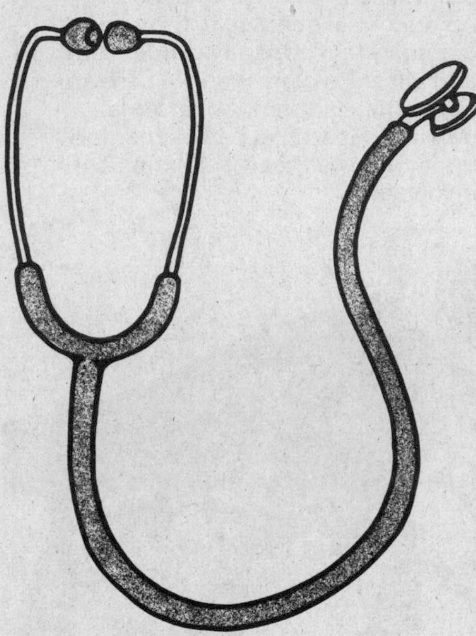

stethoscope

STRESS
Bodily or mental tension caused by physical, chemical or emotional factors. Stress can refer to physical exertion as well as mental anxiety.

STRESS TEST
A diagnostic method used to determine the body's response to physical exertion (stress). Usually involves taking an ECG and other physiological measurements (such as breathing rate and blood pressure) while the patient is exercising—usually jogging on a treadmill, walking up and down a short set of stairs, or pedaling on a stationary bicycle.

STROKE *(strok)*
Also called cerebral vascular accident. An impeded blood supply to some part of the brain, generally caused by:

1. A blood clot forming in the vessel (cerebral thrombosis).
2. A rupture of the blood vessel wall (cerebral hemorrhage).
3. A blood clot or other material from another part of the vascular system which flows to the brain and obstructs a cerebral vessel (cerebral embolism).
4. Pressure on a blood vessel, as by a tumor.

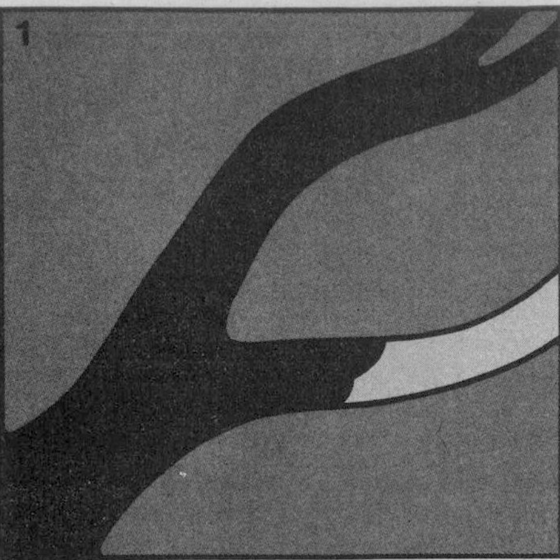

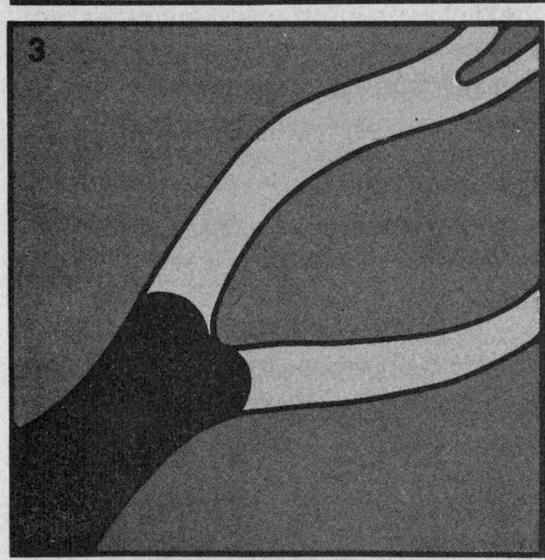

STROKE VOLUME *(strok)*
The amount of blood which is pumped out of the heart at each contraction of the heart.

SYMPATHECTOMY *(sim"pah-thek'to-me)*
An operation which interrupts some part of the sympathetic nervous system. The sympathetic nervous system is a part of the autonomic or involuntary nervous system which normally regulates tissues not under voluntary control, e.g., glands, heart, and smooth muscles. Sometimes the interruption is accomplished by drugs, in which case it is called a chemical sympathectomy.

SYMPATHETIC NERVOUS SYSTEM *(sim"pah-thet'ik)*
One of the two divisions of the autonomic nervous system. **See Autonomic Nervous System.**

SYMPTOM *(simp'tum)*
Any subjective evidence of a patient's condition. **See Sign.**

SYNCOPE *(sin'ko-pe)*
A faint. One cause for syncope can be an insufficient blood supply to the brain.

SYNDROME *(sin'drom)*
A set of symptoms which occur together and are therefore given a name to indicate that particular combination.

SYSTEMIC CIRCULATION *(sis-tem'ik)*
The circulation of the blood through all parts of the body except the lungs, the flow being from the left lower chamber of the heart (left ventricle) through the body, back to the right upper chamber of the heart (right atrium). **See Pulmonary Circulation.**

SYSTOLE *(sis'to-le)*
In each heartbeat, the period of contraction of the heart. Atrial systole is the period of the contraction of the upper chambers of the heart, called the atria.

Ventricular systole is the period of the contraction of the lower chambers of the heart, called the ventricles. **See Cardiac Cycle.**

T

TACHYCARDIA *(tak"e-kar'de-ah)*
Abnormally fast heart rate. Generally, anything over 100 beats per minute is considered a tachycardia.

TETRALOGY OF FALLOT *(te-tral'o-je of fal-o')*
A congenital malformation of the heart involving four distinct defects (hence tetralogy). Named for Etienne Fallot, French physician who described the condition in 1888. The four defects are:

1. An abnormal opening in the wall between the lower chambers of the heart (ventricular septal defect).
2. Misplacement of the aorta, "overriding" the abnormal opening, so that is receives blood from both the right and left lower chambers instead of only the left.
3. Pulmonary outflow obstruction usually below or at the valve.
4. Enlargement of the right ventricle.

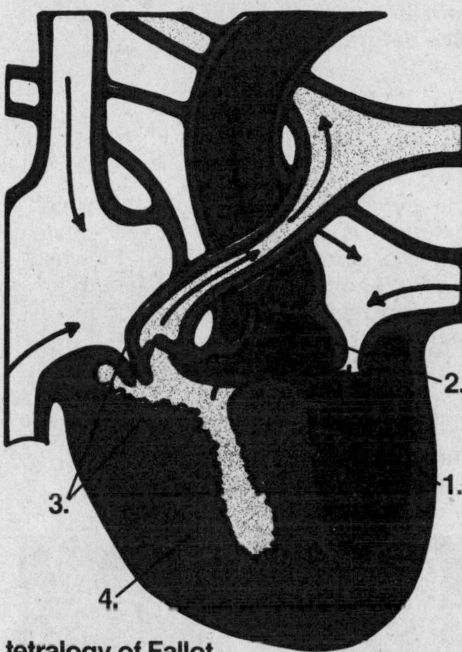

tetralogy of Fallot

THIAZIDES *(thi'a-sidz)*
Also called thiazide diuretics or benzothiadiazides. A class of diuretics (drugs which promote excretion of urine) which includes chlorothiazide. The thiazides are often used to treat high blood pressure and for the relief of edema, or waterlogged tissues. **See Antihypertensive Drugs.**

THORACIC *(tho-ras'ik)*
Pertaining to the chest (thorax).

THROMBECTOMY *(throm-bek'to-me)*
An operation to remove a blood clot from a blood vessel.

THROMBOANGIITIS OBLITERANS *(throm"bo-an"je-i'tis ob-lit'er-anz)*
Also called Buerger's disease. A disease of the blood vessels of the extremities, primarily the legs, which occurs most commonly in men and is associated with tobacco use. It is characterized by inflammation of the veins, arteries and nerves and by thrombosis in the vessels (blood clot formation). This leads to poor circulation and gangrene. **See Buerger's Syndrome.**

THROMBOEMBOLISM *(throm"bo-em'bo-lizm)*
Obstruction (embolism) of a blood vessel by a blood clot (thrombus) formed elsewhere in the circulatory system and carried along by the bloodstream to plug a smaller vessel.

THROMBOLYTIC AGENTS *(throm"bo-lit'ik)*
Substances which dissolve blood clots. Also called fibrinolytic agents. Two examples are streptokinase and urokinase.

THROMBOPHLEBITIS *(throm"bo-fle-bi'tis)*
Inflammation and blood clotting in a vein.

THROMBOSIS *(throm-bo'sis)*
The formation or presence of a blood clot (thrombus) inside a blood vessel or cavity of the heart.

THROMBUS *(throm'bus)*
A blood clot which forms inside a blood vessel or cavity of the heart. **See Embolus.**

TOXIC *(tok'sik)*
Poisonous,

TRANSPLANTATION, HEART
The replacement of a healthy heart from a recently deceased donor into the chest of a person whose own heart can no longer function adequately. The donor's heart then replaces or assists the failing heart.

TRANSPOSITION OF THE GREAT VESSELS *(trans"po-zish'un)*
A congenital heart defect in which the two largest arteries occur in the wrong places: the aorta arises from the right (rather than left) ventricle and the pulmonary artery arises from the left (rather than right) ventricle. Thus the right heart pumps used blood from the body through the aorta and back to the body, and the left heart pumps oxygenated blood from the lungs back

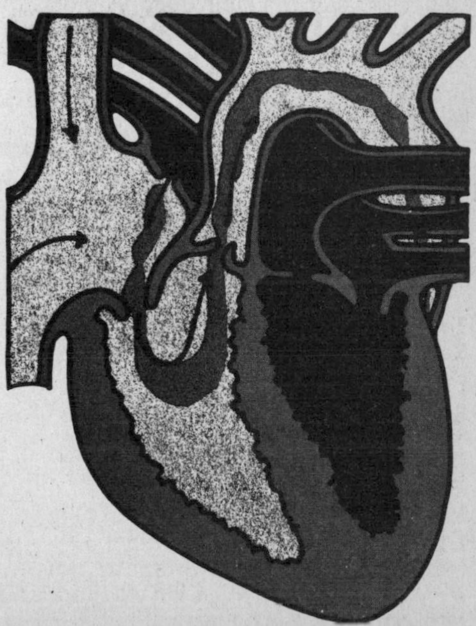
transposition of the great vessels with atrial septal defect

to the lungs. Only if there is a sizeable hole between right and left chambers (a septal defect) or a channel between the aorta and pulmonary artery (patent ductus arteriosus) will enough oxygenated blood get pumped to the body to sustain life for the infant.

TRICUSPID VALVE *(tri-kus'pid)*
A valve consisting of three cusps or triangular segments located between the upper and lower chamber in the right side of the heart. Its position corresponds to the mitral valve (which is bicuspid) in the left side of the heart. **See Valve.**

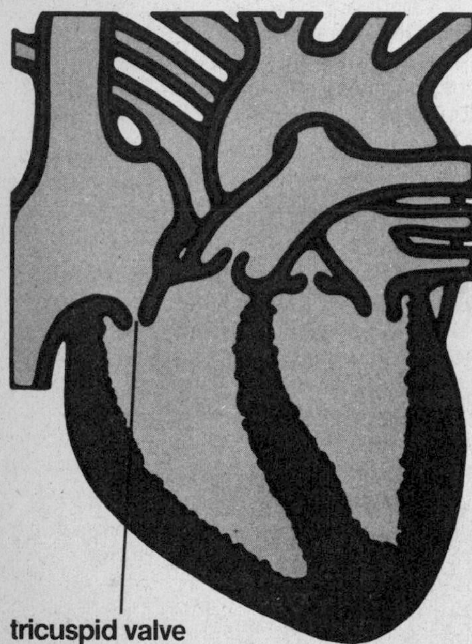

tricuspid valve

TRIGLYCERIDE *(tri-glis'er-id)*
The main type of lipid (fatty substance) found in the adipose (fat) tissue of the body and also the main dietary lipid. High levels of triglycerides in the blood may be associated with a greater risk of coronary atherosclerosis.

TRUNCUS ARTERIOSUS *(trun'kus ar-te"re-o'sus)*
An arterial trunk arising from the fetal heart which develops into the aorta and pulmonary artery. It is a congenital defect if it persists past the birth of the infant.

TYPE A BEHAVIOR
See Behavior, Type A and Type B.

TYPE B BEHAVIOR
See Behavior, Type A and Type B.

U

ULTRASOUND *(ul'tra-sownd)*
High frequency sound vibrations, not audible to the human ear. In a sonar-like application, it can be used by cardiologists for diagnosis. **See Echocardiography.**

UNSATURATED FAT *(un-sat'u-rat"ed)*
A fat whose molecules have one or more double bonds, so that it is capable of absorbing more hydrogen. **Monounsaturated fats**, such as olive oil, have only one double bond (the rest are single) and seem to have little effect on blood cholesterol. **Polyunsaturated fats**, such as corn oil and safflower oil, have two or more double bonds per molecule and tend to lower blood cholesterol. **See Saturated Fat.**

V

VAGUS NERVES *(va'gus)*
Two of the nerves of the parasympathetic nervous system which extend from the brain, through the neck and thorax into the abdomen. Known as the inhibitory nerves of the heart, they slow the heart rate when stimulated.

VALVE
A flap of tissue which prevents backflow of blood to keep it moving through the heart and circulatory system in the right direction. There are tiny valves along the inside of the veins and four large valves at the entrances and exits of the ventricles in the heart. **See Aortic, Mitral, Pulmonary, and Tricuspid Valves.**

how a one-way valve works

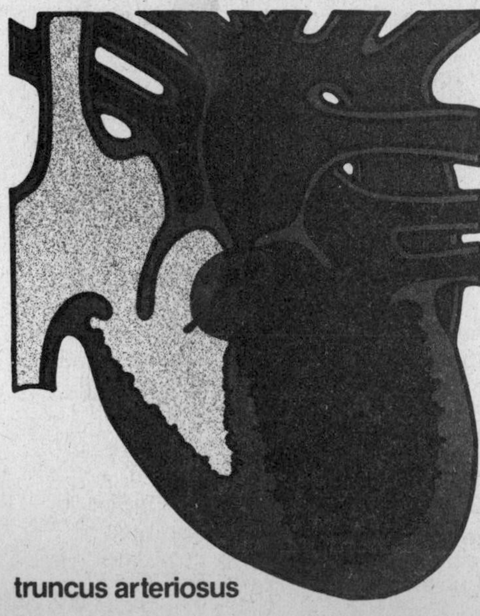

truncus arteriosus

the heart valves seen from above (atria removed)

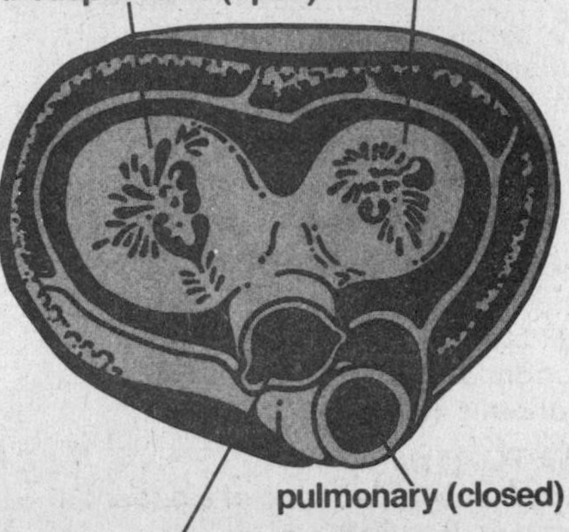

DIASTOLE (relaxation phase)

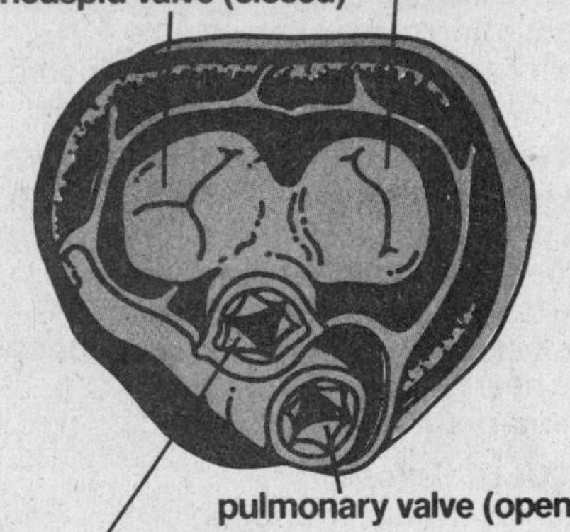

SYSTOLE (contraction phase)

right side left side

VALVULAR INSUFFICIENCY *(val'vu-lar)*
Valves which close improperly and permit a backflow of blood in the wrong direction. **See Incompetent Valve.**

VARICOSE VEINS *(var'i-kos)*
Also called "varicosities" and "varices," they are swollen veins found most frequently on the legs, especially the calves. **See Varix.**

VARIX *(var'iks)*
A varicosity or abnormally swollen vein, artery, or lymph vessel. The plural form is "varices." Varices can occur in such locations as the esophagus, the anus, or the legs (where they are more

commonly called "varicose veins"). **See Esophageal Varices, Hemorrhoids, and Varicose Veins.**

VASCULAR *(vas'ku-lar)*
Pertaining to the blood vessels.

VASO- *(vas'o)*
A combining form meaning vessel or duct.

VASOCONSTRICTOR *(vas"o-kon-strik'tor)*
Vasoconstrictor nerves are a part of the involuntary nervous system. When these nerves are stimulated, they cause the muscles of the arterioles to contract, narrowing the arteriole passage, increasing the resistance to bloodflow, and raising the blood pressure.

Vasoconstrictor agents (or vasopressors) are chemical substances which stimulate the muscles of the arterioles to contract. An example is norepinephrine (noradrenalin).

VASODILATOR *(vas"o-di-lat'or)*
Vasodilator nerves are certain nerve fibers of the involuntary nervous system which cause the muscle of the arterioles to relax, thus enlarging the arteriole passage, reducing resistance to the flow of blood, and lowering blood pressure.

Vasodilator agents are chemical compounds which cause a relaxation of the muscles of the arterioles. Examples are nitroglycerin and other nitrites, hydralazine, and many others.

VASOINHIBITOR *(vas"o-in-hib'i-tor)*
An agent which inhibits the action of the vasomotor nerves, that is, an agent which prevents the blood vessels from a normal response (constriction or dilation) to stimuli.

VASOMOTOR *(vas"o-mo'tor)*
Any agent (nerve or substance) that affects the caliber of a vessel, especially of a blood vessel, that is, any agent that is either a vasoconstrictor or a vasodilator.

VASOPRESSOR *(vas"o-pres'or)*
A vasoconstrictor agent. **See Vasoconstrictor and also Pressor.**

VECTORCARDIOGRAPHY *(vek"tor-kar"de-og'rah-fe)*
Determination of the direction and magnitude of the electrical forces of the heart by using electrocardiography in three dimensions.

VEIN *(vain)*
Any one of a series of vessels of the vascular system which carries blood from various parts of the body back to the heart. All veins in the body conduct unoxygenated blood except the pulmonary veins which conduct freshly oxygenated blood from the lungs back to the heart.

VENA CAVA *(ve'nah ka'vah)*
One of the two great veins which conduct unoxygenated blood from the body to the right atrium of the heart. The superior vena cava brings blood from the upper part of the body (head, neck and chest). The inferior vena cava brings blood from the lower part of the body (legs and abdomen). Plural form is **Venae Cavae** *(ve'ni ka'vi).*

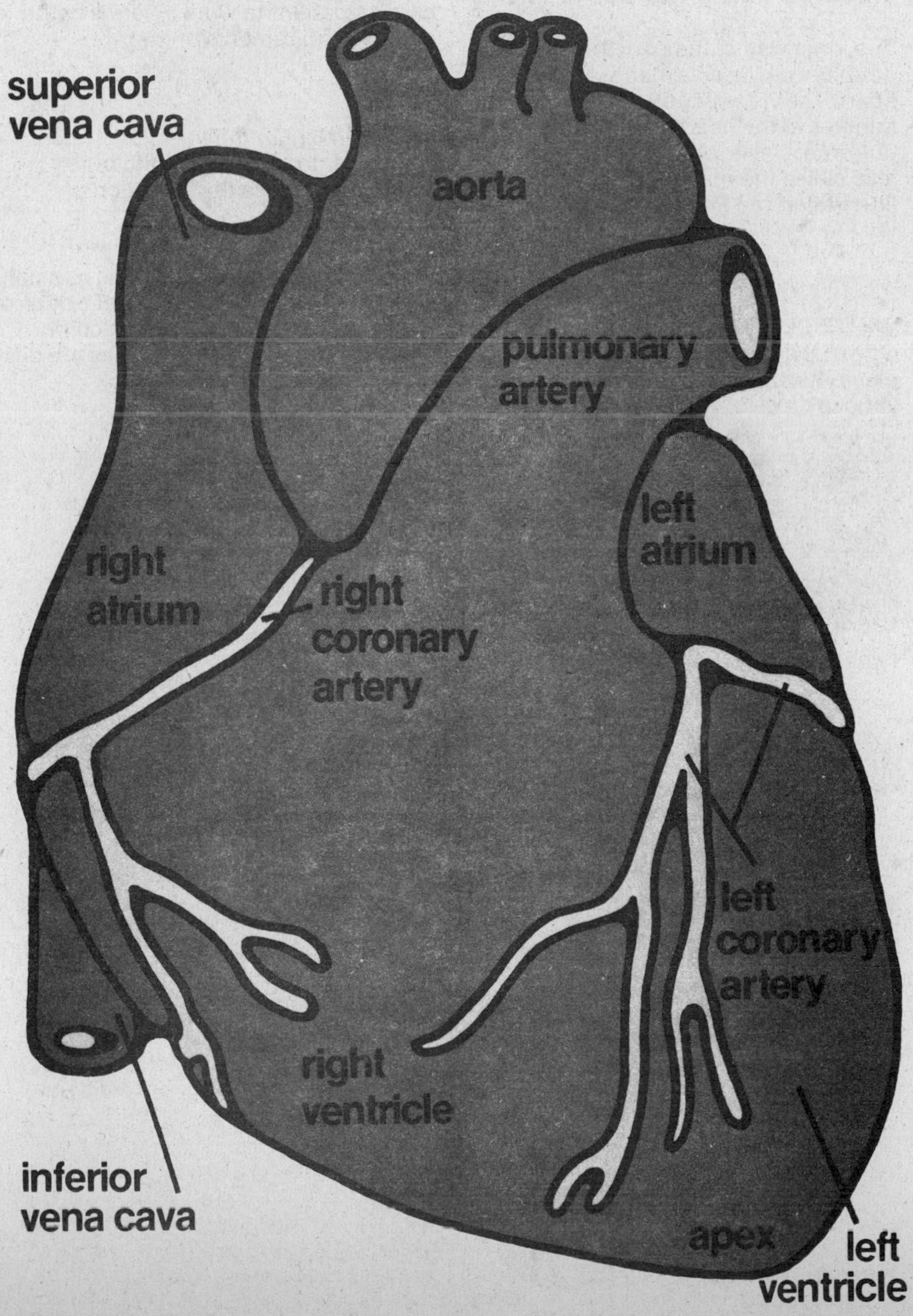

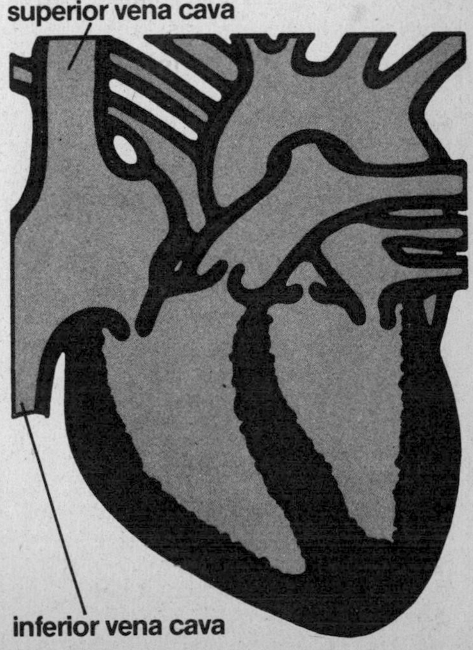

VENOUS BLOOD *(ve'nus)*
Unoxygenated blood. The blood, with hemoglobin in the reduced state, is carried by the veins from all parts of the body back to the heart and then pumped by the right side of the heart through the pulmonary artery to the lungs where it is oxygenated.

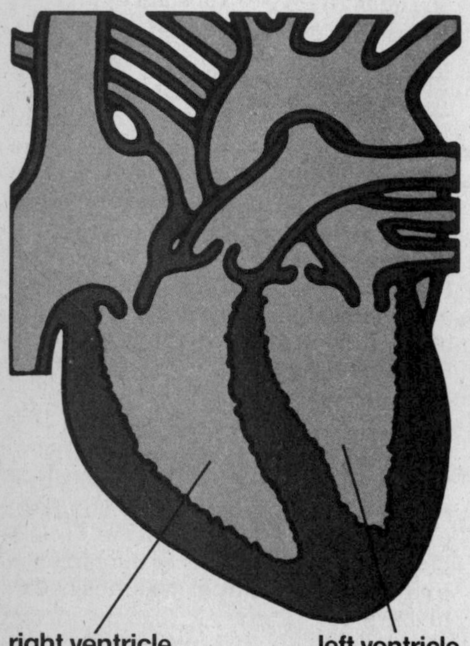

VENTRICLE *(ven'tre-kl)*
One of the two main pumping chambers of the heart. The left ventricle pumps oxygenated blood through the arteries to the body. The right ventricle pumps unoxygenated blood through the pulmonary artery to the lungs. Capacity of each ventricle in an adult averages 85 cc. or about 3 ounces.

VESALIUS, ANDREAS (1514-1564)
Belgian anatomist who questioned many of the then current theories of the circulatory system as taught by Galen, chiefly the existence of openings in the wall dividing the left from the right side of the heart through which blood was believed to pass.

VISCERAL PERICARDIUM *(vis'er-al per"i-kar'de-um)*
The inner wall of the pericardium, the double-walled sac which surrounds the heart. The visceral pericardium closely adheres to the heart and forms the outermost layer of the heart wall and is also called the epicardium. **For illustration see Pericardium.**

W

WHITE BLOOD CELLS
One of the three kinds of formed elements found in the blood. There are various types of white blood cells. Their best-known function is defense: they destroy foreign bodies, such as bacteria, in areas of infection. Also called leukocytes. **See Red Blood Cells and Platelets.**

WITHERING, WILLIAM (1741-1799)
Eminent English clinician who discovered the use and proper dosage of digitalis in the treatment of heart disease. By analyzing the effective herbal mixture used by an old woman in Shropshire, he identified foxglove leaves as the active ingredient which influenced the function of the heart and kidneys.

WORK CLASSIFICATION UNIT
A community facility involving a team approach to assessing the ability of the cardiac patient to work in terms of the energy requirements of the job.

X

XANTHINE *(zan'theen)*
A class of drugs used among other things to increase the excretion of urine. A diuretic.

XANTHOMA *(zan-tho'mah)*
A new growth of skin occurring as small flat or slightly raised patches or nodules which are yellowish-orange in color. The various types of xanthomas are due to blood lipid disorders (hyperlipoproteinemias).

Bible Dictionary

A

Aa'ron
The elder brother of and often the spokesman for Moses. From him descended, through his eldest son Eleazer, the hereditary class of priests in Israel.

Ab
The 5th month of the Hebrew year. *See* Calendar.

Ab'ba
A name addressed to God in Jewish and early Christian prayers. It occurs three times in the NT, with its Greek equivalent placed after it (Mk 14.36; Rom 8.15; Gal 4.6).

A·bed'ne·go
The Babylonian name of one of the companions of Daniel, his Hebrew name being Azariah. *See* Shadrach.

A'bel
(Heb. "vanity," "breath"; Akkad. "son") 1. The second son of Adam, who was murdered by his brother Cain (Gen 4.2ff). He was God-fearing and righteous, and in contrast with Cain is a pattern of a worshiper pleasing to God, who on that account has to suffer (1 Jn 3.12). He is described as righteous by our Lord (Mt 23.35), and in Heb 11.4 he stands at the head of the heroes of faith.

2. Part of the name of several places in Israel; it probably signifies "plain" or "meadow." *Abel of Beth-maacah,* a fortified city, identified with the mound Tell Abil, 12 mi. N of Lake Huleh, extreme north of Israel (2 Sam 20.14-19). *Abel-keramim,* the plain of the vineyards, in Ammonite territory, probably near modern Amman (Judg 11.29-33). *Abel-meholah,* probably east of the Jordan on Wadi el-Yabis, modern Tell el-Maqlub (Judg 7.22; 1 Kings 4.12; 19.16). *Abel-mizraim,* possibly between Jericho and the Dead Sea (Gen 50.11). *Abel-shittim,* in the plains of Moab NE of the Dead Sea; possibly the present Tell el Hammam. Early name for Shittim (Num 33.49).

A·bi'a·thar
(Heb. "the Father [God] gives abundantly") A priest who became the priest of David.

A'bib
(Heb. "young head of grain") The 1st month of the Hebrew year; Nisan. *See* Calendar.

Ab'i·gail
(Heb. "my father rejoices") Wife of Nabal and after Nabal's death the wife of David.

A·bim'e·lech
(Heb. "Melek is Father") 1. A king of Gerar who appears in similar accounts of Isaac and Rebecca and of Abraham and Sarah (Gen 20–21; 26).

2. Son of Jerubbaal (Gideon), king of Shechem (Judg 8.31; 9.1-57).

Ab'ner
(Heb. "father is Ner") Commander of the Israelite army under Saul.

a·bom·i·na'tion
Anything ritually or ethically repugnant or loathsome to God and men.

A'bra·ham, A'bram
(Heb. "Father of a multitude"; "exalted Father") One of the greatest OT characters, and possibly the story of two persons combined into one (Gen 11.27–25.8). Abraham was born in Ur of the Chaldees, in what is now Iraq. Terah, his father, migrated with Abraham and Sarah, Abraham's wife, and Lot, his nephew, as far as Haran, now Harran, in Turkey. There Terah died. The others, with flocks and herds, moved on to Palestine (Canaan).

Abraham stopped near ancient Shechem, a short distance E of Nablus and now extensively excavated; he moved on to Egypt for a time, then returned to Palestine for the remainder of his life. Lot settled at Sodom and became a Canaanite. When the Canaanites rebelled against Babylon and Lot was taken captive, Abraham recovered the captives and the booty.

Throughout his life, Abraham was in contact with the many peoples about him, carrying on various negotiations with them. He talked with God, to whom he was always faithful. And he doubted God when he and his wife Sarah were in their old age promised a son. This son was Isaac. However, Abraham's relationship with God was such that when he was called upon to sacrifice his only son he responded without question. God released him from the sacrifice and promised him many descendants and land, which promises were fulfilled.

At Sarah's death he arranged the purchase of a burial place at Machpelah, where he also was buried after a long life of constant activity and great drama.

Ab'sa·lom
(Heb. "father of peace") Son of David and Maachah, through popular arts alienating the people from his father, at length raised a revolt against him, but was defeated by Joab and slain by him, to the great sorrow of David (2 Sam 3.3, 13.20–19.10).

a·ca'cia
A tree providing a hard wood, useful in building.

Ac'cad
(Gen 10.10) One of the four cities of Nimrod in Shinar (Babylonia). Land of Sumer and Accad (or Akkad) is in the Assyrian inscriptions the common designation of Babylonia as a whole. *See* Akkad; Babylonia.

A·cel'da·ma, A·kel'da·ma
A burial ground outside the Jerusalem wall.

Acts of the A·pos'tles, The
Written by the author of the Gospel according to Luke, Acts is the account of what Jesus' disciples did after His resurrection. It tells about the early Christian church and its missionaries, the baptism of Cornelius, the Council in Jerusalem, and about the conversion of Paul and his journeys to establish churches and to teach. Acts emphasizes that the church is guided continually by the Holy Spirit.

Ad'am
("earthy," "a human") 1. The Hebrew word for man, specifically applied to the first man.

Created on the same day as the animals, he is not semi-divine but has the ability for spiritual growth.

2. A city east of the Jordan, now Tell ed-Damiyeh (Josh 3.9-17).

ad'a·mant

It is not known what is meant by this word; it is something impenetrably hard (Ezek 3.9; Jer 17.1; Zech 7.12).

A'dar, Ad'dar

The 12th Hebrew month. *See* Calendar.

Ad·on·i'

A Hebrew name for God.

Ad·o·ra'im

(Heb. "two threshing floors"?) A city identified with modern Dura, 5 mi. W-SW of Hebron (2 Chron 11.9).

A·dul'lam

(Heb. "retreat, refuge") Extensive ruins in the Wadi es-Sur, 9½ mi. ENE of Beit Jibrin, perhaps mark the site of Adullam, to which there are many biblical references.

a·ga'pe, the

(Gr. agape, "love") Love feasts, the common meals of the early Christians, which expressed the brotherly love that bound them together as one family, and culminated in the Lord's Supper. Gross abuses of this beautiful custom, such as are condemned in 1 Cor 11.17ff, and Jude 12, led to the separation of the Lord's Supper from the love feast in the post-apostolic church.

ag'ate

The agate is one of the many varieties of minutely crystalline silica, denoting those arranged more or less in bands of different tints. From a very early period it has been used as a gem, and was often engraved.

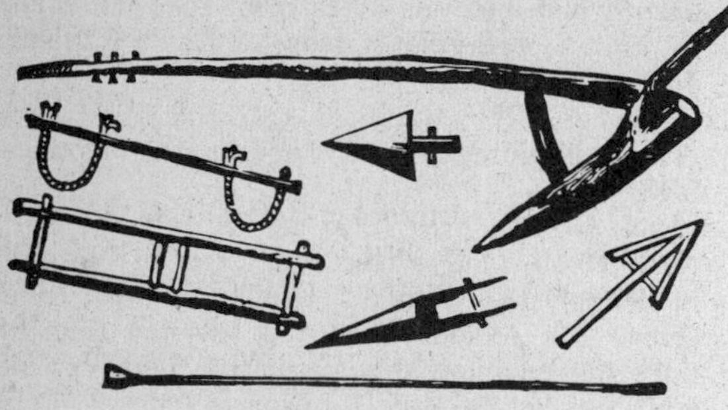

Plow and other implements

ag'ri·cul·ture

Excavations reveal a developed agriculture in Bible lands as early as 8000-7000 B.C.; flint sickles for harvesting and basalt mortars and pestles for grinding grain are found in abundance. The religious year of the Israelites was adjusted to the cultivation cycle, and many memorable passages of the Bible have reference to the life of seedtime and harvest.

The patriarchs and their descendants down to the conquest of Canaan were herdsmen of cattle (sheep, oxen, goats, asses, and camels). After the settlement, the western tribes learned agriculture, and the culture of the vine, olive, and fig tree, from the Canaanites. Among the crops raised were wheat, barley, rye, spelt, flax, cummin, fitches or vetch, beans, lentils, and millet.

A'hab

(Heb. "father's brother") Son of Omri, king of the northern kingdom of Israel in the time of Elijah, reigned 22 years. He defeated Benhadad, King of Damascus, twice, destroyed his capital, and shut him up in Aphek, afterward forming a treaty with him against Assyria. Shalmaneser II, King of Assyria, in his monolith inscription claims to have defeated Ahab and Benhadad with other kings at Karkar in 854 B.C. A year after this, Ahab met his death in a battle before Ramothgilead, in which Benhadad overcame both him and his ally, Jehoshaphat of Judah. The worship of Baal and Ashtoreth, introduced by his wife, the Tyrian princess, Jezebel, with the religious struggle this called forth in the country, and his robbery and judicial murder of Naboth, left in Israel a dark shadow on the memory of Ahab (1 Kings 16.29–22.40).

A·has·u·e'rus

The Persian king (485-465 B.C.?) in Ezra 4.6 and Esther. The Ahasuerus of Dan 9.1 is the father of Darius the Mede.

A'haz

(Heb. "possessor" or "he has grasped") Eleventh king of Judah, remembered for his wicked reign (2 Kings 16, 23.12; 2 Chron 28; Is 7,8,9).

A·ha·zi'ah

(Heb. "Yah has grasped") 1. Eighth king of Israel.

2. Sixth king of Judah.

A·hi'jah, A·hi'ah

(Heb. "brother of Yah") Name of 9 persons in the OT, one of whom was a priest in the time of Saul; another a prophet of Shiloh who foretold Jeroboam's kingship.

A·him'a·az

(Heb. "brother is counselor"?) Name of 3 persons in the OT, one of whom was a priest devoted to David.

A·hin'o·am

(Heb. "pleasantness") 1. Wife of Saul, daughter of Ahimaaz.

2. A wife of David, from Jezreel.

A·hith'o·phel

The royal counselor to David.

Ai'ja·lon, Aj'a·lon

(Heb. "place of the deer") 1. Modern Yalo, with remains of a fortified town.

2. A place in Zebulun, probably Tell el-Butneh in the Plain of Asochis.

Ak'kad, Ak·ka'di·an

The Akkadians were the first Semitic people to move into Mesopotamia; the first Akkadian names to appear among Babylonian rulers are found in the period 1200-1100 B.C. Their language had spread widely and had become the common usage for commerce and trade some 750 years earlier. Assyrian and Babylonian are considered dialects of Akkadian.

Alabaster vessels

al'a•bas•ter
A soft stone, often veined; light cream in color. Much used for perfume flasks.

Al•ex•an'dri•a
The great seaport at the mouth of the Nile, founded by Alexander the Great about 332 B.C. He gave the Jews a quarter in it; in the early Christian age it was the chief trade center of East and West, and the home of literature and Greek philosophy.

al'gum
(2 Chron 2.8, 9.10, 11) or **al'mug** (1 Kings 2.8, 10.11, 12) A wood brought from Lebanon, as in 2 Chron 2.8, or from Ophir (1 Kings; 2 Chron 9.10, 11). Probably either pine or sandalwood.

Almond tree and blossoms

al'mond
(Heb. "waking") The common almond, whose beautiful pink-white flowers appear in January, the first of the year; hence its name. It grows wild on the higher lands of Palestine. There are frequent references to this tree in the Bible.

alms
(Gr. "pity"; "relief of the poor") Frequently mentioned and their giving practiced in many ways. Laws were written, tithes were taken with the poor in mind. Gleaning was usual. Passersby might gather as they walked. And the giving of alms meant merit for the donor.

al'mug
See Algum.

Courtesy of *The Interpreter's Dictionary of the Bible*

Aloes

al'oes
1. An aromatic substance, probably an aromatic wood, such as white sandalwood, from which was made incense and perfume. It was an import, not native.

2. The true aloe, a succulent, provided a bitter and evil-smelling purgative and may have been used with myrrh in embalming.

al'pha and o•me'ga
The names of the first and last letters in the Greek alphabet. "Alpha and Omega" often indicates the whole extent, not merely the beginning and the end, of an act or a concept.

Al•phae'us
A Greek name appearing in the NT only. 1. The father of Levi, who may also have been called Matthew (Mk 2.14).

2. The father of James (the Less) (Mt 10.3; Mk 3.18; Lk 6.15; Acts 1.13).

al'tar
An artificial erection for the offering of sacrifices and prayers, originally of earth, turf, and unhewn stones. The law ordained that sacrifices should be offered only in the sanctuary; but the Hebrews continued to erect altars upon the high places until the Temple at Jerusalem, with its altar of incense in the sanctuary and its altar of burnt-offering in the forecourt, became under the reformation of Josiah universally recognized as the only place where sacrifices could be legitimately offered. The "horns" of the altar, placed at its four corners, were its most sacred parts. The blood of the sacrifices was smeared on them, and they were clasped by fugitives who claimed the right of asylum.

Am'a•lek•ites
A nomadic tribe, descendants of Esau, wandering from Sinai across the Negev, below the Sea of Galilee, as far as the Gulf of Aqabah. They warred with the Israelites over the centuries. Saul and David defeated them, but neither suc-

ceeded in exterminating them. At the time of Hezekiah they seem to have been completely defeated. In the Tell el-Amarna letters, they are classed as plunderers.

Am'a•sa
(Heb. "a burden") 1. A nephew of David.
2. An Ephraimite chief.

Am•a•zi'ah
(Heb. "Yah is strong") The name of 4 persons in the OT, one a king of Judah, presumably for 29 years.

am'ber
The word thus rendered is almost certainly not the familiar fossil resin of orange-yellow, which bears this name, but some metallic compound; possibly the mixture of gold and silver now called electrum, or bronze.

a'men'
A Hebrew word meaning "truth," used adverbially to express strong confirmation. It is used as a confirmatory response at the close of prayer ("May it be so").

am'e•thyst
A purplish variety of quartz (crystallized silica), often used for ornamental purposes. It looks like a pale purple glass, but is somewhat harder.

Am'mon•ites
A Semitic people settled NE of the Dead Sea. They warred with Israel, were vassals under David and Solomon, subsequently vassals of Assyria. Origen mentioned them in the 3rd century A.D., after which they seem to have disappeared among the Arabs. Excavations near Amman show a well-developed culture.

A'mon
(Heb. "reliable") Name of 3 persons in the OT, one a king of Judah; also the imperial god of Egypt.

Am'o•rites
An ancient people who may have occupied Syria and N Palestine; their language was probably the forerunner of Aramean. They refused the Israelites passage through their land. The Tell elAmarna letters give information of them at the period of a number of city states; excavations at Mori show a high state of civilization.

A'mos
(Heb. "burden bearer") One of the minor prophets, he was a shepherd of Tekoa, in Judah, and prophesied at Bethel in the reigns of Uzziah, King of Judah, and Jeroboam II, King of Israel. The priests accused him of treason, and expelled him from the northern kingdom, to which his prophecies mainly refer, and whose downfall he foretold.

A'mos, The Book of
The book of the herdsman from Tekoa. He received a direct call from God to prophesy against the unrighteousness of both Judah and Israel. Amos was the first prophet to proclaim that God was the ruler of the whole universe.

An'a•kim
(Heb. "people of the neck") A race of giants who, when driven from the mountains of Hebron by Caleb or Joshua, found refuge in Philistia.

An•a•ni'as
(Heb. "Yah is gracious") Name of 3 NT persons, one of whom was the high priest before whom Paul was tried in Jerusalem. Another lost his life for attempting deceit regarding the price received for property he sold.

a•nath'e•ma
(Gr. "something set up") One form of the word developed a special meaning, "devoted to a divinity or to the lower world so as to be destroyed," and so came to mean accursed.

An'a•thoth
The birthplace of Jeremiah. The name is preserved in Anata, a town 3 mi. N of Jerusalem. The ancient city was at Ras el-Karrubeh, ½ mi. SW.

An'cient of Days
God Himself, of great dignity and wisdom.

an'cients
See Elders.

An'drew
(Gr. "manly") One of the 12 disciples of Jesus, brother of Simon Peter, son of Jonas or John, was born at Bethsaida on the Sea of Galilee. He was one of the first among the disciples of John the Baptist to become a follower of Jesus who called him, along with Peter, while fishing at the Sea of Galilee, to become a fisher of men. He appears to have been one of those disciples who, after Peter, James, and John, stood nearest to his Master. Acts mentions him only in 1.13. According to tradition, he suffered martyrdom in Achaia on a cross shaped in the form of the letter X (Mt 4:18, 10.2-4, 16.17; Mk 1.16-20, 29; 3.16-19, 13.3; Jn 1.35-42, 44; 6.5-9; 12.20-22; 21.15-17; Lk 5.10, 6.14-16; Acts 1.13).

an'gel
(Gr. "messenger") A messenger of God, with the evolving concept of a spiritual being.

an'ise
Seeds of this plant are used for flavoring, and have some use in medicine.

An'nas
See Caiaphas.

ant
Ants are proverbial for the marvelous instinct that guides them in the economy, work, and discipline of their communities. They are small insects, but have wonderful muscular strength. Harvester ants of Palestine store corn for winter (Prov 16.6-8; 30.25).

an'te•lope
The Hebrew word of the OT is also translated "wild bull," "wild ox." The gazelle, a species of antelope, lived in Palestine in biblical times. The antelope is often depicted on Egyptian monuments. It is a beautiful creature, standing about four feet high, very wild and fleet, and fierce when hard pressed by the hunter.

an'ti•christ
This word is used in the NT by John (1 Jn 2.18, 22; 4.3; 2 Jn 7) but the idea, variously expressed, appears as in Dan 7, Ezek 38 and 39, 2

Thess 2.3–10. As used in the NT the name may mean "one who usurps the place of Christ," or "one who sets himself up as a substitute for Christ." The principle of his opposition consists in the denial of the incarnation, which revealed the will of God to unite man with Himself through Christ, and in the assertion of man's divinity apart from God in Christ. St. Paul teaches that Antichrist will appear as a single adversary of Christ, "the man of sin," who, furnished by Satan "with all power, and signs, and wonders of falsehood," will sit "in the sanctuary of God, setting himself forth as God," and will be brought to nought by the manifestation of the coming of the Lord. As Moses was the type of Christ, so Balaam, the "Anti-Moses," was a type of Antichrist (2 Pet 2.15; Jude 11; Rev 2.14).

an'ti·mo·ny
Stibnite (antimony sulphide) was and still is in the East a pigment employed for darkening the outer part of the eye, as when Jezebel "painted" her eyes.

An'ti·och
1. In Syria, on the river Orontes, a great city, ranking next after Rome and Alexandria, where the name Christian was first used (Acts 11.26).

2. In Pisidia, visited by St. Paul and Barnabas (Acts 13.14-52).

An·tip'a·tris
A city 10 mi. NE of Jaffa (Joppa) named after Antipater, father of Herod the Great (Acts 23.31).

apes
Imported by Solomon (1 Kings 10.22). Baboons, apes, and monkeys are represented in the Assyrian and Egyptian monuments.

A'phek
(Heb. "fortress"?) The name of 4 places in the OT. Each location has been identified.

Ap·ol·lo'ni·a
A Greek city in Macedonia, S of Lake Balbe (Acts 17.1).

A·pol'los
An Alexandrian Jew who became a prominent teacher in the Apostolic ages. "Eloquent," "fervent in spirit," and "mighty in the Scriptures" (of the OT), he had been a disciple of John before Priscilla and Aquila at Ephesus "expounded to him the way of God more perfectly." After Paul's departure from Corinth he preached the gospel there. Though one of the parties in the Corinthian church named itself after him, he appears to have stood in a friendly relation to Paul, with whom he afterwards labored at Ephesus. He is last mentioned in Tit 3.13. Luther was the first to suggest that Apollos was the author of the Epistle to the Hebrews (Acts 18.24-28, 19.1; 1 Cor. 1.12, 3.3-10, 22; 4.6, 16.12).

a·pos'tle
(Gr. "to send off") The word appears about 80 times in the NT, limited to certain men of the first generation of the church and missionaries of the gospel. The first twelve apostles sent out by Jesus are named in Mk 3.14-19 and elsewhere. Others also are considered apostles, including Paul, James, Barnabas, Matthias, and in some groupings Junias, Andronicus, and Silvanus. Subsequently many claimed the title, which the church desired to limit to those who had seen Jesus and had firsthand knowledge of the Resurrection, who had the attributes called the signs of an apostle, and were fully committed to the church.

ap'ple
Since the apple grows poorly if at all in Bible lands, an attempt has been made to identify the fruit so called. The apricot seems best to fit the biblical text.

Aq'ui·la and Pris·cil'la
Friends in Corinth and Ephesus of the Apostle Paul, and his assistants in evangelism. In Ephesus they instructed the Alexandrian Apollos.

A·ra'bi·a, A·ra'bi·ans
(Gr. "desert") In biblical times there was no single name for the vast Arabian peninsula. Its peoples were nomads. They traded with Egypt and other countries, selling frankincense and other perfumes, and had camels, sheep, goats, and horses. They may have been dealers in the pet monkeys Solomon had brought from Ophir, of still unknown location. The peoples included Ishmaelites, Midianites, Dedanites, Sabeans, among others. At times they raided and plundered in Israel, at times carried on peaceful commerce. There was a marked difference in the peoples of the N and the S. Whether the Queen of Sheba came from N or S is not definite; more probably she was from the N. There was a certain amount of intermingling, too: for example, David's head camel keeper was an Ishmaelite, and his sister married an Ishmaelite. Moses had friendly contacts with them. Bible references to the peoples of what is now Arabia are plentiful.

A'ram
(Akkad. *Aramu*) The OT name of Syria and Mesopotamia (sometimes used of Syria alone).

Ar·a·ma'ic
The Aramaic language is properly the speech of the people of Aram, an area NE of Syria. They may have learned alphabetic writing from the Canaanites. After the Assyrian conquest Aramaic spread widely as a language of commerce and is found in conjunction with cuneiform on weights and clay tablets from distant regions of the empire. A form of Aramaic influenced the Greek alphabet, and other forms influenced scripts of Asia. It is noteworthy that Dan 2.4-7, 28; Ezra 4.8-6,18 and 7.12-26 are found originally in Aramaic. The language was used in Egypt, and it was spoken familiarly instead of Hebrew in Palestine; Jesus and his followers spoke one of its many dialects.

Eventually Aramaic was displaced by Arabic in much of the old Assyrian empire, even though in some regions it persisted for centuries.

Ar·a·me'ans
A Semitic people, traditionally descendants of Shem, they apparently were in early times

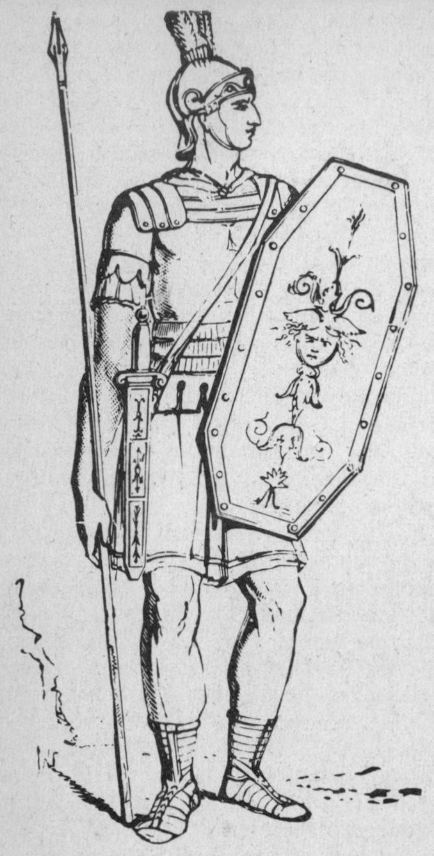

Roman soldier

among the nomads along the W side of the Syrian Desert. For a considerable time they were an active and expanding people, and their culture, particularly their language, spread over the Middle East. The Assyrians conquered and scattered them, and they vanished as a political power.

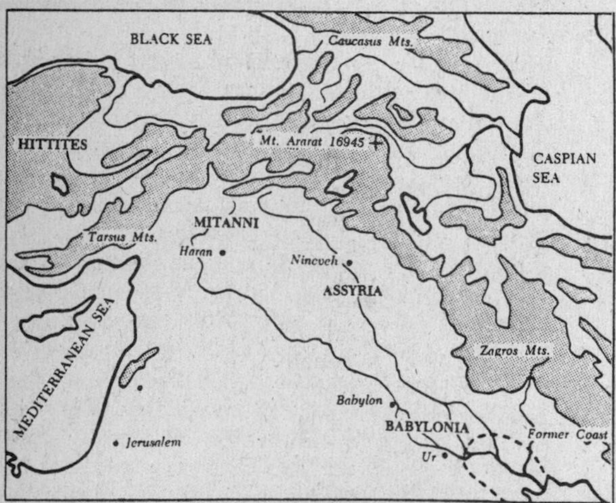

location of Mt. Ararat.

Ar'a•rat
The country of the river Aras in Armenia; also the mount of Ararat, on which the ark rested after the Flood (Gen 8.4), 16,900 ft. elevation.

Ar•is•tar'chus
A Macedonian Gentile arrested with Paul in Ephesus. He traveled with Paul and was a fellow prisoner in Rome.

Ark of the Cov'e•nant
The ark may have been a container for the Mosaic tablets and other sacred objects, or a throne for the invisible God; on it was a slab of gold to support the cherubim, the mercy seat. It probably goes back to the time of Moses, and was a focus for the religious life of the people. In Ex 25 are precise instructions for the construction of an ark. The OT has some 200 references to it: it was captured in battle, left in the homes of individuals, reverenced, sometimes ignored. After Solomon placed it in the sanctuary of the temple it dropped from history. A possibility is that it was destroyed during Nebuchadnezzar's invasion.

Ar•ma•ged'don
The place of the final great struggle between the forces of good and evil. It is linked to Megiddo.

arm'lets
See Frontlets.

arms, ar'mor
Down to the age of David the army of Israel consisted exclusively of foot soldiers. These were probably divided into two classes: the heavy-armed, wearing helmet, coat of mail, and greaves, and carrying a sword, one or two javelins, and a spear; and the light-armed, wearing helmet and corselet of leather, and carrying sword, bow, and sling. The metal earliest employed in the manufacture of weapons was probably an alloy of copper and tin. The use of imported iron followed later.

A sling

Ar'o•er
(Heb. "juniper"?) 1. A city on the N rim of the Arnon Gorge, 3 mi. SE of Dhiban. The ancient city is a mound beside modern 'Ara'ir.

2. A town of Gilead, possibly S of 'Amman near es-Sweiwina.

3. A town in S country of Judah, modern 'Ar'arah, 12 mi. SE of Beer-sheba.

Ar•tax•erx'es
The first Artaxerxes is mentioned in Ezra 7 and Neh 2 and 13. His grandson, Artaxerxes II, may have been the builder of the palace described in Esther 1.

Ar'te•mis
The virgin huntress of Greek classical mythology, called Diana by the Romans, was widely worshiped throughout the Greek world. Artemis or Diana of the Ephesians mentioned in Acts 19 was a fertility goddess, worship of whom was also widespread and elaborate.

As'ca•lon, Ash'ke•lon
One of the Philistine chief cities, on the seacoast. It may have been the birthplace of Herod the Great.

As•cents', Songs of
See Degrees, Songs of.

Ash'dod
("fortress"?) A Philistine chief city, 10 mi. N of Ascalon (Ashkelon), and 3 mi. inland; now called Esdud. It was to Ashdod that the Ark was taken when captured by the Philistines.

A•she'rah
A Semitic fertility goddess and the goddess' cult object, a sacred tree (for which a pole was often substituted) which, with the Masseba or sacred stone pillar, stood near the altar on every Canaanite high place. The deity was believed to be present in the Asherah. There are many OT references to the trees and the groves on the high places.

Ash'ke•lon
See Ascalon.

Ash'to•reth, pl. **Ash'ta•roth, Ash'to•roth**
A Canaanite fertility goddess.

As•mo•de'us
The prince of demons, also called Abaddon, Apollyon, Beelzebul.

asp
A viper or adder; a poisonous snake.

ass
The domesticated ass, which is traced by Darwin to the wild ass of Abyssinia, is depicted in the earliest Egyptian records, and also on the oldest Assyrian monuments. The ass is much more highly prized in the East than in the West. From early times, white (albino) asses were reserved for dignitaries. The ass was the animal of peace as the horse was of war. It was forbidden to plough with an ass and an ox together. *Ass, Wild* Most of the Biblical references are to the wild ass of Syria, especially the descriptions in Job and the Prophets. The wild ass is untamable, and in fleetness far surpasses the horse. The allusions to its habits in Scripture are most accurate. The hunting of the wild ass is

Ashtoreth

frequently represented in the Assyrian sculptures.

as•sas'sin
(Arab, *hashashin* "those addicted to hashish, hemp") A numerous body of desperadoes that arose in Judea during the procuratorship of Felix, and afterward took a leading part in the Jewish war. Their name Sicarii was derived from the curved dagger (Lat. *sica*), which they carried under their clothes, and with which they stabbed their opponents secretly in the crowds at festivals.

As'shur, As'sur
See Assyria.

As•syr'i•a
After the decline of the great kingdom of Sumer, two Semitic-language peoples developed in its region. Babylonia gradually rose in the former Central Sumer area. To the N of it Assyria developed, early unstable and unaggressive, borrowing heavily from Babylonia, but with sharp distinctions in social and intellectual concepts. Several strong personalities built up successive Assyrian empires, which in turn broke up on the death of the particular person. This was the Assyrian history for hundreds of years. They gradually conquered the mountain peoples N and E of them, and turned to the W. From the time of Omri (876-869 B.C.) to Manasseh (687-642 B.C.) the people of Israel were under pressure from Assyria: paying tribute to, fighting against, being conquered by Assyria; Tiglath-pileser II (966-935 B.C.), a contemporary

of Solomon, was known to Israel, as was Shalmaneser III (858-824 B.C.), the first Assyrian king to have contact with the kings of Israel. Tiglath-pileser III (745-727) B.C.) began large-scale deportations of the conquered. Esarhaddon (680-669 B.C.) attacked Egypt. The over-extended Assyrian empire fell with the destruction of Asshur, its old capital, in 614 B.C. and of Nineveh in 612 B.C. by a coalition of Babylonia and the Medes. A vast quantity of historical, artistic, and literary material has been found in the excavations of the ancient Assyrian cities in what is now Iraq, Turkey, and Syria, and many previously unsuspected links between the ancient peoples have been revealed.

Ath′ens

The capital of Attica, the chief division of ancient Greece, and the seat of Greek literature, art, and civilization. Paul visited it in his second journey and delivered a famous address on the Areopagus, or Hill of Mars.

Ath′ter

See Molech.

A·tone′ment, Day of

This was the annual day of humiliation and expiation for the sins of the nation, when the high priest made atonement for the sanctuary, the priests, and the people. It was celebrated on the 10th day of Tishri, the 7th month, by abstinence from ordinary labor, by a holy convocation, and by fasting. It was the only fast enjoined by the Mosaic law, and hence was called "the fast." The high priest, laying aside his official ornaments, first offered a sin-offering for himself and for the priesthood, entering into the Holy of Holies with the blood. He afterwards took 2 he-goats for the nation. One was slain for Jehovah. On the head of the other the sins of the people were typically laid; it was made the sin-bearer of the nation; and, laden with guilt, was sent away into the wilderness. The idea of atonement was never at any time remote.

Sin offering

a·veng′er

Hebrew custom, like that of many other early peoples, authorized and even required the next of kin to avenge a murdered person by killing his murderer. The Mosaic legislation aimed at mitigating its effects by providing cities of refuge to which a homicide might escape, and where he might claim a fair trial. Blood vengeance is mentioned often in the OT.

Az·a·ri′ah

(Heb. "Yah has helped") Name of 24 persons in the OT, one of whom was the prophet who encouraged Asa, king of Judah, to reform of religion. In 2 Chron 22.6, KJV, it is used instead of Ahaziah.

A·za′zel

The evil spirit of the wilderness to whom on the Day of Atonement the goat laden with the sins of the people is said to be sent.

B

Ba′al

The fertility gods of Canaan. There were many local Baals.

Ba′al·ze′bub

A god of the city of Ekron of the Philistines of whom King Ahaziah of Israel asked an oracle.

Ba′bel (Heb.), **Bab′y·lon** (Gr.)

Capital of Babylonia, or Shinar, also called Chaldea. Its ruins are near the present city of Hilla SW of Baghdad, on a small tributary of the Euphrates. Its temple of Bel (Marduk), the city God, a ziggurat or stepped tower, is the biblical Tower of Babel. It was a splendid and magnificent city, and became to the people of Israel a symbol of all that was wicked. In NT times it became the symbolic name for Rome.

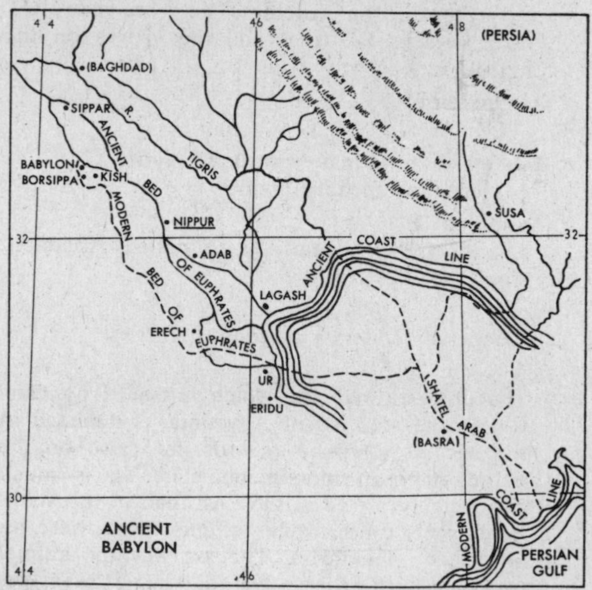

Bab·y·lo′ni·a

The downfall of Sumer brought Babylonia into being. The great Hammurabi (c. 1800-1750 B.C.) extended the power of his city-state, Babylon, making it a capital over other city-states. He was an effective administrator and established an enduring political plan; even so, the history of Babylonia is as that of Assyria, of war and destruction, advance and retreat. The complexities of the histories of both countries are slowly being resolved through excavations and subsequent interpretations of the records found. The aggressions of Babylon are woven through the history of the Israelites; there were the sorrowful days of the exiles, when thousands of the people of Israel were deported eastward, never to return. There were such happenings as the three young men in the fiery furnace (Dan 3). Lying as Israel did, between Egypt and the Tigris-Euphrates powers, Assyria and Babylonia, it was a buffer or a pawn in the multiple strife of the larger powers. But Babylon emerged as the most hated. Babylon was synonymous with all that was evil. It eventually became a part of the empire of the Medes and Persians.

Bab·y·lo′ni·an Cap·tiv′i·ty or Ex′ile

The period in Jewish history from the carrying away of the people to Babylon in 597 and 586 to their return in 538 B.C.

badg′er

A small mammal; a coney.

Ba′laam

("the clan brings forth"?) A seer, possibly from the neighborhood of Carchemish, summoned by the Moabite King Balak to pronounce a curse on Israel before its entrance into Canaan. Instead he spoke a series of blessings (Num 22–24). There are many references to Balaam in both OT and NT; in the NT he becomes the false prophet.

Baker, from an ancient marble

balm

An aromatic gum or resin used in healing and in cosmetics as well as for embalming. It is not fully identified.

bal′sam

See Mulberry.

bap′tism

(Gr. "dip" or "immerse") A rite using water as a symbol of religious purification.

Ba′rak

(Heb. "lightning-flash") Son of Abinoam, who, encouraged by the prophetess Deborah to take the lead in the struggle against the Canaanites, seized Mount Tabor with 10,000 men and, rushing down the mountain, defeated Sisera's army at its foot and along the right bank of the Kishon, near Megiddo. A splendid "song of Deborah and Barak" celebrates the victory (Judg 5).

bar′ley

Extensively cultivated in Palestine and neighboring countries from the earliest times.

Bar′na·bas

The surname given by the apostles to Joses or Joseph, a Levite of Cyprus, who was sent by them to Antioch to confirm the church there. From Antioch he "went forth to Tarsus to seek for Saul," whom he had introduced at Jerusalem to Peter and James as a new convert. When he had brought him to Antioch, they remained there together for a year, and "taught much people." Barnabas accompanied Paul on his first missionary journey, and on his journey to the council at Jerusalem, and afterward at Antioch. When Paul, starting on his second missionary journey, refused to take John Mark, the cousin of Barnabas, the two apostles separated, Barnabas taking Mark with him to Cyprus. Paul refers to him in 1 Cor 9.6; Gal 2.13; Col 4.10. The authorship of the Epistle to the Hebrews was attributed to Barnabas by Tertullian The Codex Sinaiticus includes an "Epistle of Barnabas," which was regarded as canonical by many in the ancient church, but is held to date from the beginning of the 2nd century A.D. (Acts 4.36, 37; 8.1; 9.1, 27; 11.19-27, 30; 13.2, 3, 9, 13; 14.12, 14; 15).

Bar·thol′o·mew

(Aram. "son of Talmai"). One of the twelve apostles of Jesus (Mt 10.3; Mk 3.18; Lk 6.14; Acts 1.13). He is identified with Nathanael of Cana of Galilee (John 1.45-51; 21.2) on the ground that (1) Bartholomew is not mentioned in John, nor is Nathanael in the other three gospels; and (2) Philip in the first three gospels is associated with Bartholomew, and in John with Nathanael.

Ba′shan

A high tableland, 1600 to 2300 ft., sometimes considered coextensive with the Kingdom of Og.

bat

Classed among unclean winged creatures. It swarms in the numberless ravines, caves, and ruins of Palestine (Lev 11.19; Deut 14.19; Is 2.20).

bay tree

Does not refer to a particular kind of tree, but to a tree growing luxuriantly in its native soil, and is thus translated by the revisers (Ps 37.35). There is no ground for identifying the tree with the bay or noble laurel.

bdel′li·um

What is meant is uncertain, possibly a gem, but some have suggested a vegetable gum, others pearls (Gen 2.12; Num 11.7).

bean
Used both as a vegetable and as flour by the Jews.

bear
The Syrian brown bear was found in the N of Palestine as recently as the early 20th century. It is mentioned frequently in the OT.

beard
Full beards were common among Hebrews. Egyptians and Romans shaved the beard. Assyrians are portrayed with beards. Hebrews were forbidden to trim the beard; its removal or plucking was an insult, except in cases of leprosy.

Ancient types of beards

beat'en oil
Oil produced by crushing fully ripe olives, without pressing, was of the first quality, used for the lamp of the sanctuary.

bed
The poorer people in Palestine slept upon the bare floor, wrapped in their cloaks, or upon a mattress or quilt, which was rolled up and put away in the daytime. The wealthy used a wooden framework covered with cushions as a divan by day and a bed at night, and the more luxurious had bedsteads carved and inlaid with ivory. The bed of Og (Deut 3.11) was probably a sarcophagus of ironstone.

bee
Canaan was described as a land of milk and honey, which indicates that bees were plentiful. Honey entered into commerce with Tyre (Ezek 27.17).

Be·el'ze·bub, Be·el'ze·bul
The names used by Jesus and others for the chief or prince of devils.

bee'tle
Possibly the long-horned grasshopper.

be·he'moth
(Heb. "dumb beast") A name for the hippopotamus; sometimes, a mythical creature.

Bel
(Akkad. "he who possesses") The state god of Babylon (Marduk).

Be'li·al
(Heb. "worthless, useless") A liar; an iniquitous, wicked person.

Bel·shaz'zar
Babylonian prince, co-regent with his father Nabonidus.

Be·na'iah
(Heb. "Yah has built") The name of 9 persons in the OT, one of whom was a son of Jehaida, a valiant warrior under David, and commander of Solomon's army.

Ben'ja·min
The youngest son of Jacob; Rachel, his mother, died at his birth. Joseph, his brother, demanded that he be brought to Egypt before he would help his brothers. The tribe of Benjamin was the smallest of the tribes.

Ber'o·dach-bal'a·dan
See Merodach-Baladan.

ber'yl
A silicate of beryllium and aluminum; the crystals are usually green. The emerald is of the same type.

Beth'a·ny
A village on the E slope of the Mount of Olives. It is 1⅝ mi. E of Jerusalem, and is now called el-'Aziriyeh.

Beth·az'ma·veth
A town identified with modern Hizmeh, 5 mi. NNE of Jerusalem.

Beth'el
(Heb. "house of God") More frequently mentioned than any city except Jerusalem, Bethel (now Beitin) lies 14 mi. N of Jerusalem. It was founded before 2000 B.C., has been destroyed several times despite being heavily fortified, and has been excavated. Near here Abraham built his altar. The Ark of the Covenant rested here, and the place is associated with Jacob and Elijah and with the tabernacle. Jeroboam made it a place of idolatry.

Be·thes'da, Beth·za'tha
A spring, possibly with medicinal properties, near the sheep gate or market in Jerusalem. The precise location is not now known.

Beth'le·hem
(Heb. "house of bread"?) A very old town, about 6 mi. SSW of Jerusalem, associated with David, Ruth, and many other persons of the OT, and the birthplace of Jesus.

Beth'shan, Beth·she'an
(Heb. "house of safety") A fortress city at the N end of the Jordan Valley, dating back to the 4th millennium B.C. It was along the route between Egypt, Damascus, and Arabia. Excavations there have provided much information on life in Bible times.

Beth·she'mesh
(Heb. "house of the seen") The name of 4 places mentioned in the OT, one of which, 24 mi. W of Jerusalem, was first settled in the 3rd millennium B.C., as shown by excavations there.

Beth-za'tha
See Bethesda.

bier
The Israelites, like the later Jews, buried the bodies of their dead. The burial was within a few hours after death. Probably the wooden framework of a bed served for a bier, as the same word is used for both.

birds
There are in Palestine about 350 species of birds,

26 of which are peculiar to that country. In the Law, 19 or 20 species of birds, mostly carnivorous, are (with the addition of the bat) declared to be unclean. The birds caught for food were chiefly pigeon, partridge, and quail. The dove is mentioned in the Bible more than 50

Birds perched in a mimosa tree, from an Egyptian wall painting of about the time of Abraham

times, and was the bird with which the Israelites were most familiar. Turtledoves and young pigeons were the only birds used for sacrifices; hence there was a busy trade in them in the neighborhood of the Temple. There are many Scriptural allusions to the habits of pigeons. Dovecots made of pots imbedded in clay are numerous in Palestine. They are often placed inside the walls in the houses of the poor. At the present day partridges abound, and also wild ducks, especially near the Dead Sea. There is, on the whole, a deficiency of singing birds, though blackbirds, larks, finches, cuckoos, and Palestine nightingales are heard in spring. There are many birds of prey.

birth'right
A position of peculiar honor and privilege assigned to the eldest son. The birthright could be parted with or lost through misconduct.

bish'op
(Gr. "overseer") In the NT one of the overseers of a Christian congregation, synonymous with presbyter (elder).

bi·tu'men
("asphalt," "slime") The name includes several compounds of carbon and hydrogen, from which pitch, asphalt, etc., are obtained. Bitumen is often washed up on the shores of the Dead Sea. It is found near Nineveh and at the base of Hermon, and there are springs of it in the Euphrates Valley. This substance is not necessarily connected with volcanic disturbances. Also called *slime.*

boar, wild
Wild boars are especially numerous in the thickets and brakes of the Jordan Valley, whence, when the river rises just before harvest, they are driven out, and play havoc with the cornfields and cultivated ground of the uplands. They are equally common in the southern wilderness, where they plough the ground for the bulbs that abound there.

Bo'az
A virtuous and wealthy man of Bethlehem, who married the widow Ruth of Moab.

Booths, Feast of
An autumn festival, one of the 3 great annual festivals in Israel.

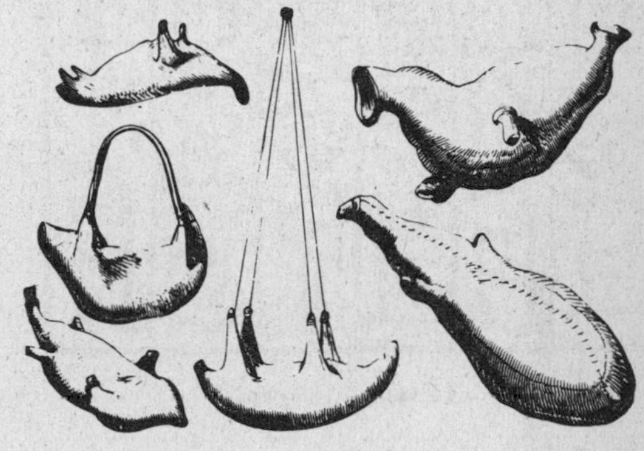

Leather bottles

box
The box shrub has been found in Palestine. *See* Pine.

bram'ble, bri'er, this'tle, thorn
About 20 biblical words imply thorny or spiny flora. Spine-bearing plants form a considerable portion of the flora of Palestine.

brass
Copper alloy. *See* copper.

bread
Commonly of wheat meal, sometimes of barley. The meal was kneaded in wooden troughs; the dough was then mixed with yeast or leaven, pressed or cut into thin, round cakes, then baked over hot stones or in an oven.

breth'ren of Jesus
Four in number (Mt 13.55; Mk 6.3), during His life unbelieving (Jn 7.3-7), were among the earliest members (Acts 1.14) and missionaries (1 Cor. 9.5) of the church. One of them, James the Lord's brother, had the authority of an Apostle (Gal 1.19; 2.9 and 12).

brick
Sun-dried brick made from muddy clay was widely used in the ancient world, but in Babylonia it was kiln dried. Often bricks were stamped with seals or names. Mortar in most areas was the same material as the bricks; in Assyria and Babylonia bitumen was used.

bri'er
See Bramble.

brim'stone
See Sulphur.

broom
A desert shrub.

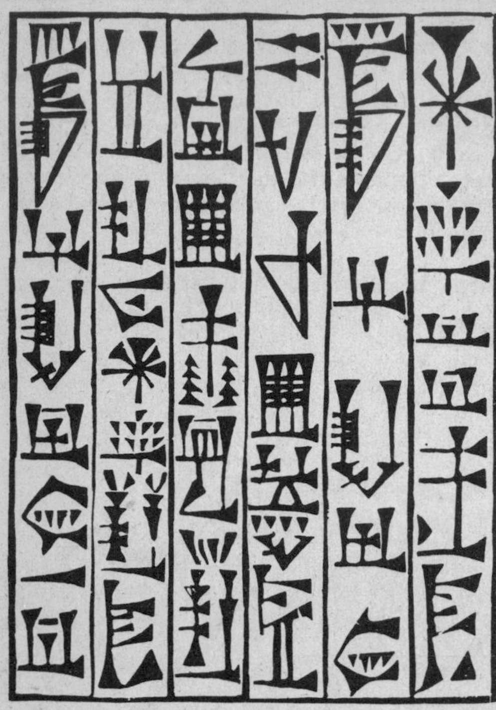

Babylonian brick

bronze
Copper alloy. *See* copper.

Bul
The 8th month in the Hebrew calendar.

bul'rush
The papyrus, which formerly grew in the Nile, rooting itself in the river mud. It is now extinct in Egypt, though still found higher up the Nile valley. It covers acres of the shallow water in Lake Merom. The papyrus has a triangular stem 8 to 10 feet high, terminating in a bush of slender leaves. Paper is made by pressing the pith into sheets.

bur'i·al
Probably, as it now is in Palestine, on the day of death, or next day. As soon as death had taken place, the eyes of the dead were closed. The body was washed, anointed, and swathed in linen. There is no mention of the Egyptian custom of embalming as having ever been followed by Israelites. In OT times the dead appear to have been buried in the clothes worn in life. The dead body was carried to the grave on an open bier, followed by the mourners and professional wailing-women. Burning of the dead was resorted to only in the case of criminals guilty of the most hateful of crimes and was regarded with horror. It was the greatest calamity to be deprived of burial. Many passages of the OT prove the desire of Israelites to be buried in the family burying-place ("with their fathers"), an evidence of their belief that the communion of kindred subsisted after death. The burial places were graves dug in the earth, caves, or chambers hewn in the rock, and closed with large stones to secure them from wild beasts. Such rock sepulchers abound in the neighborhood of Jerusalem. In later times the custom arose of whitewashing every year after the rainy season the stones enclosing the sepulchers, to prevent passersby from being accidentally defiled by touching them.

burnt of'fer·ings
Sacrifices in which the victim was wholly burnt with fire, to express the entire surrender of the offerer to God.

bush, burn'ing
The bush that flamed as the angel called Moses may have been an acacia or a thorn bush. It has not been identified.

C

Caes·a·re'a
A city founded as Straton in the 4th century B.C., on the coast of Palestine 23 mi. S of Mt. Carmel. It was given to Herod by Augustus; Herod renamed it Caesarea in honor of Augustus and rebuilt it as a seaport.

Caes·a·re'a Phi·lip'pi
The name given by Philip the Tetrarch to Paneas, at the main Jordan source, and at the foot of Hermon; now the village of Banias.

Ca'ia·phas
Jewish high priest in the time of Jesus. His proper name was Joseph, Caiaphas being his surname. He was a son-in-law of Annas, high priest (A.D. 7-14). Under the Roman dominion the high priests were frequently changed; but Caiaphas held the office long. He was appointed by Pilate's predecessor, Valerius Gratus, probably about A.D. 18, and not removed till after the deposition of Pilate by Vitellius, governor of Syria, in A.D. 36. The statement (John 11.49; 18.13) that Caiaphas was "high priest that year" has led some to suppose wrongly that the high priests were at that time changed every year. The usage of Josephus in extending the title high priest to all those still living who had held the office explains how Annas is so styled in Acts 4.6 and probably John 18.19, 22.

cal'a·mus
Sweet flag was imported from a far country, possibly India, and sold in the markets of Tyre, and is still brought to the Damascus market from Arabia. Its root stock is aromatic. It was a chief ingredient of the holy anointing oil.

cal'en·dar
The Hebrews early used the equinox as the beginning of the new year, the agricultural year beginning in the spring and the civil or religious year in the autumn. The month was related to the lunar month, and seems to have been counted from the spring new year even when the autumnal new year was used; the use of the lunar month provided only 354¼ days instead of the necessary 365¼ between successive spring equinoxes, so that every few years an extra month had to be provided. The months were first given Canaanite names; then they came to be known by number and eventually, after the Exile, some of the Babylonian names were adopted. Various ways of adjusting the

year were suggested by various persons, the added days sometimes early in the year, sometimes late. The 12-month sequence was not otherwise disturbed, and corresponded roughly with our contemporary calendar as follows: *Abib* or *Nisan,* April; *Ziv* or *Iyyar,* May; *Sivan,* June; *Tammuz,* July; *Ab,* August; *Elul,* September; *Ethanim* or *Tishri,* October; *Bul* or *Marchewan,* November; *Chislev,* December; *Tebeth,* January; *Shebat,* February; *Adar,* March.

Cal'va•ry

The place of the Crucifixion. Tradition places it where the Church of the Holy Sepulchre now stands. Other places in Jerusalem have been suggested.

Camels

cam'el

The camel, usually the Arabian, single-humped, has been the beast of burden and means of travel in the Near and Middle East for more than 3 millenniums. There is the slower burden-bearing camel and the swifter dromedary. The two-humped camel appears less often. The camel can go without water for several days, and its flat feet make it capable of traveling over sand. In biblical times, trade caravan travel across the deserts was commonplace; during warfare the camels carried supplies. Camel's milk was used, and the hair was woven into cloth used for tents and coarse robes such as that worn by John the Baptist.

cam'phire, cam'phor

See Henna.

Ca'naan, Ca'naan•ites

(Hurrian? "reeds"? "red purple"?) Canaan included the land between the Jordan River and the sea and the portion of Syria along the coast. The Canaanites were an advanced people, with a written language of 80 characters by 2000 B.C. It was an agricultural society, probably including merchants and seamen. The Hebrews learned writing from them, were sometimes attracted by their gods, intermarried with them, warred with them, and merged with them, seemingly in the 14th century B.C.

can'dle•stick

The candlestick of biblical times is properly called a *lampstand.* Many have been found in excavations. The earliest lamps were pottery saucers of olive oil, into which was laid a twisted thread as a wick. As early as 3000 B.C. the rims were pinched into lips to hold the thread wicks. Herod's temple had a seven-branched lampstand, called the Menorah, with a cup of oil at the top of each branch.

Ca•per'na•um

Excavations have shown Capernaum to be the present Tell Hum, on the NNW coast of the Sea of Galilee.

The seven-branched candlestick, representing that taken from the temple of Herod in the sack of Jerusalem in A.D. 69-70.

Caph'tor

The traditional homeland of the Philistines; Caphtor has been identified as Crete. It has also been considered possible that the Philistines originated in the Aegean area and had sufficient contact with Cretans to have adopted dress and customs from them.

Cap•pa•do'ci•a

The area W of the Euphrates, S of the Black Sea, N of the Taurus Mountains, E of Galatia.

cap•tiv'i•ty

See Exile.

car'bun•cle

A red stone, garnet or ruby. Error in translation has in a few instances made it a green stone, such as emerald or beryl.

Car'che•mish, Char'che•mish

An ancient and important city on the Euphrates, an objective in warfare between Assyria and Egypt. Excavation has revealed its great antiquity. The present name is Jerablus.

Car'mel

(Heb. "garden," "orchard") A high headland on the coast of Palestine. The modern city of Haifa lies below.

cart

Goods were transported for the most part on the backs of men or of animals; but a cart, probably with 2 solid wheels, was also in use for carrying grain or other produce.

Courtesy of *The Interpreter's Dictionary of the Bible*

Upper: an ancient Egyptian cart; lower: a cart with captured women; from Lachish

cas′sia

A coarser kind of cinnamon.

cat

Apparently not commonly known in W Asia in biblical times. The cat was domesticated in Egypt 13 centuries before Christ. It was there a sacred animal, and thousands of mummified cats have been found.

cat′er•pil•lar

(Heb. "to peel off," "finish") Also translated as "destroying locust," "destroyer."

cat′tle

Words meaning cattle appear in the oldest languages. The Hebrews had oxen, asses, horses, sheep, and goats, and were familiar with camels.

ce′dar

Lebanon cedar grows also on the Taurus and Atlas Mountains. It was the king of trees, the symbol of grandeur, might, loftiness, and continuous expansion. Its wood was used in the successive temples at Jerusalem and in the palace of Nebuchadnezzar.

Ce′dron

See Kidron.

Cen′chre•a

Seaport 7 mi. E of Corinth.

chal•ced′o•ny

(Gr. *chalkedon*) One of the many varieties of minutely crystalline silica, of a light, translucent color, related to agate.

Chal•de′a, Chal•dea′a

The plain of Babylon, or lower Mesopotamia; a region of swamps and lakes. One of its great cities was Ur of the Chaldees.

Chal•de′ans

The early people of Chaldea were fishermen and small-scale herdsmen and farmers, opposed to urbanized life. They were not willing to perform any kind of military service and avoided taxes. They were at times under the control of Babylonia or Assyria; later, Chaldea controlled Babylonia and a wide empire, gradually changing the name from Babylonia to Chaldea. During this period Chaldea assisted in the conquest of Nineveh, the capital of Assyria. Thereafter Chaldea declined, and the Chaldeans went into the world as astrologers, magicians, fortune tellers, and diviners. As such they were famous throughout the Egyptian, Greek, and Roman worlds. The name is still associated with magic.

cha•me′le•on

A lizardlike creature.

cham′ois

A mountain sheep; a small, goat-like antelope.

Char′che•mish

See Carchemish.

char′i•ot

There were disk-wheeled vehicles drawn by asses in the 4th millennium B.C. in Mesopotamia. The first spoked wheels appeared about the time of Hammurabi. The vehicle was two-wheeled, closed in front and open behind, arranged to carry arrows and battle axes, and had a crew of 2, warrior and driver. Usually 2 horses were used. Around 1800 B.C. the chariot was the most powerful of weapons. With it, the Hyksos conquered most of Syria and Egypt. There were also gold and silver chariots and others painted and decorated for pleasure and display by royalty and the wealthy. When the Hebrews first entered Canaan, the Canaanites were using iron chariots; the Hebrews themselves apparently did not have chariots until the time of David. They traded grain to the Egyptians for horses.

Courtesy of *The Interpreter's Dictionary of the Bible*

Assyrian relief of a royal chariot

Ched•or•la′o•mer

An Elamite king with whom Abraham contended.

Che′mosh

God of the Moabites.

che′rub (pl. **cher′u•bim**)

A symbolical winged creature with a human face. Two cherubim were placed on the mercy seat or covering of the Ark of the Covenant in the Tabernacle and in the Temple, and figures representing cherubim were wrought into the hangings of the Holy of Holies.

chest′nut tree

A tall and majestic tree, growing near water in Palestine. From the globular form of the flowers and fruits it is often called button-tree. *See* Plane tree.

Chin'ne·roth, Cin'ne·roth

An early name of the Sea of Galilee. Also the name of a district in Naphtali and of a fortified city in the district, now Tell el-'Oreimeh. Some excavation has been carried on at this site.

Chis'lev

The 9th month in the Hebrew calendar.

Chit'tim, Kit'tim

Greek Kition, the Phoenician port of Cyprus; the modern Larnaka. *See* Cyprus.

Christ

The coming of a Christ (Messiah) was foretold often in the OT, perhaps the most notable prophecy being in Is 9–11. He was to be of the House of David; justice and righteousness never ending would be established on His coming. This was not universally accepted; there were many unbelievers when Jesus was born, who remained unbelievers throughout His life. The believers accepted Him as God the Son, the second member of the Trinity, Christ (meaning the Anointed One), the Messiah, the One foretold: Jesus the Christ, Christ Jesus. His complete acceptance of Himself as the Son of God had its influence in winning many doubters, and the incomparable beauty and power of His preaching influence constantly increasing numbers of mankind.

Chron'i·cles

The two *Books of Chronicles* have much in common with the books of Samuel and Kings. They contain genealogical tables from Adam to the death of Saul, the reign of Solomon, the division of the kingdom, the exile, and the proclamation of Cyrus.

chro·nol'o·gy

It is doubtful that the authors of the books of the Bible were in any way conscious of writing history as history is known today. The calendar developed as they developed. They knew seasons rather than days, and periods of war or of peace or succession of rulers rather than years. Consequently a tidy arrangement by years is difficult for either OT or NT. Records of then contemporary governments, which have been and still are being revealed through excavations in the Near and Middle East, are constantly being checked against the gaps and uncertainties of the biblical record. It is possible that in time a complete chronology can be determined.

chrys'o·lite

(Gr. "chrysolithus") Properly this is a greenish-yellow gem, a variety of olivine, a ferromagnesian silicate. In early times the name was usually applied to the Oriental topaz, a yellow variety of corundum.

chrys'o·prase

(Gr. "chrysoprasos") An apple-green variety of chalcedony.

church

(Gr. *Ekklesia,* "an assembly") In the NT it is used in the following senses:

1. An ordinary public meeting (Acts 19.32, 39, 41).

2. The congregation of the Israelites under the Old Testament.

3. A meeting of Christians for worship.

4. The company of Christians associated for the worship and service of God in a particular locality or region.

5. The whole body of Christians throughout the world.

6. In the widest sense, the whole body of the redeemed.

Cin'ner·roth

See Chinneroth.

cir·cum·cis'ion

Removal of the foreskin. Circumcision was widely practiced; of the neighbors of the Hebrews, only the Philistines did not practice it.

cith'ern

A lyre-like instrument with 11 or 12 strings.

cit'ies

There were many ancient cities. Carbon-14 dating shows a wall and fortification at Jericho before 7000 or 8000 B.C. Cities had surrounding villages, whose inhabitants went inside the city walls in times of danger. The population of Ur of the Chaldees, where Abraham was born, has been estimated at a quarter to a half million.

cit'y of ref'uge

Crimes of violence were in ancient civilizations often avenged by the injured person himself or by a relative. But the accused person could be sure of trial according to the laws of the time and country if he could get to a city of refuge. In Palestine there were 6, 3 of them across the Jordan. The cities in Canaan were Kedesh, Shechem, and Hebron. The trans-Jordan cities were Bezer, Ramoth-Gilead, and Golan. Biblical law restricted refuge to the accidental homicide.

cloke, cloak

Originally a long strip of coarse cloth thrown over the shoulders. Later it became elaborated, of finer material, fitted, even embroidered. A creditor might seize this garment, but not the inner one. Sometimes called a *robe,* a *mantle,* a *garment.*

cloud

See Pillar of cloud and of fire.

coat

A garment worn under the mantle, usually tied by a girdle.

coat of mail

A sleeveless armor made (1) of skin or leather; or (2) of small plates of bronze or iron, sewn on leather or fastened together in rows.

coins

See Money.

Co·los'si·ans

The Letter (Epistle) of Paul to the Colossians was written by Paul, while he was a prisoner in Rome, to the Christians at Colossae in Asia Minor. Paul writes to encourage them with real truth—that through Christ they have the everlasting love of God.

com'fort·er

A paraclete. One who stands by to aid, to counsel, to strengthen; an advocate.

com·mand′ments
See Ten Commandments.

co′ney
(Heb. "the hider") A small animal, sometimes called a rock rabbit or rock badger. It is forbidden as food.

cop′per, brass, bronze
The name copper derives ultimately from Cyprus, the famous copper source of the ancient world. Egyptians, Edomites, and others mined copper in the Arabah, the area between the Dead Sea and the Gulf of Aqabah; Solomon's copper mines have been identified. Some articles made of copper have been found in excavations in the Holy Land. More bronze articles have been found; bronze is an alloy of copper and tin. The Phoenicians brought in tin ore as an article of commerce, and the Hebrews knew smelting and metallurgy. Brass, made of copper and zinc, has not been found, and seems not to have been made, nor have zinc deposits or worked-out mines been found.

cor′al
The red coral of the Mediterranean, used for beads and ornaments, was an article of commerce, and was considered a precious stone.

cor′ban
A Hebrew word, which is translated "offering" or "oblation," hence referring to any article or possession solemnly dedicated to God. Our Lord rebuked those who adopted this device to escape the necessity of supporting their parents.

co·ri·an′der
An annual plant, with seeds used as a spice.

Cor′inth
A city of Southern Greece, 40 mi. SW of Athens. Cenchreae was its eastern harbor. Destroyed by the Romans in 146 B.C., it was rebuilt by Julius Caesar in 46 B.C., and peopled by a colony of veterans and others. Situated on the isthmus which had always formed the highway of commerce between Asia and Italy, it became the metropolis of the Roman province of Achaia, the meeting-place of all the social forces of the age, and a center of licentiousness, much of it in the form of pagan religion and rites. The city was the home of Aquila and Priscilla, who became great friends of Paul and his assistants in evangelism in both Corinth and Ephesus; Paul was their frequent visitor.

Co·rin′thi·ans
The *Letters of Paul to the Corinthians* were written from Ephesus about 57 A.D. The Christians of Corinth found it hard to live as they knew they should and questioned Paul about their difficulties. In *First Corinthians* Paul answers their question, points out to them what they have done wrong, and encourages them with his message. "You are Christ's." *Second Corinthians* contains Paul's message of thanksgiving and love. Then he goes on to describe his tribulations as he went about preaching the gospel of Christ.

cor′mo·rant
A bird not positively identified.

corn
This is a general term, meaning grain. The grains grown in Palestine are wheat, barley, millet, and spelt. *See* Wheat.

cor′net
(Lat. *cornu*) A horn, a wind instrument made of horn, wood, or metal.

cos·met′ics
Ointments were used to counteract the dry heat of the climate, and perfumes were added to the ointments. Eye paint, usually black, was also used, and there is doubtful reference to henna, used in some cultures not only as a perfume but as a dye for hair, palms, soles of the feet, and nails.

cot′ton, hang′ings, net′work
Cotton was used in the Middle East from very early times. It is probable that the colored hangings in the palace of Susa (Esther 1.6) and the networks woven in Egypt (Is 19.9) were of cotton.

court
See Temple.

cov′e·nant
The religion of Israel rested on a covenant between Jehovah and that people. God founded the covenant by His promise, and His people's part in it was the fulfillment of the divine command. Entrance into it was marked by the sign of circumcision. A New Covenant was promised by the prophets; and this is established in Christ.

Cov′e·nant, Ark of the
See Ark of the Covenant.

Cov′e·nant, the Book of the
This is taken to refer to Ex 20.23–23.33.

crafts, crafts′men
Many craftsmen worked in their homes or had shops; sometimes a single craft occupied a special area in a town. Their number and diversity were increased notably by contact with the Canaanites and with the Babylonians during the Exile. Crafts included boatbuilders, netmakers, carpenters, wood carvers, furniture makers, carvers of ivory and alabaster, weavers, tanners, goldsmiths, silversmiths, bronzesmiths, leatherworkers, tentmakers, carpetmakers, ropemakers, basketmakers, fullers, dyers, jewelers, glassworkers, lampmakers, potters.

cre·a′tion
Cuneiform tablets have been discovered that give the different accounts of the creation current in Babylonia. One of them, in the form of a long poem, resembles in many respects the account in Gen 1. It commences with the statement that "in the beginning" all was chaos of waters. Then the Upper and Lower Firmaments were created, and the gods came into existence. After that comes a long account of the struggle between Bel-Marduk and the "Dragon" of Chaos, "the serpent of evil," with her allies, the forces of anarchy and darkness. It ended in the victory of the god of light, who thereupon created the present world by the power of his "word." The fifth tablet or book of the poem

describes the appointment of the heavenly bodies for signs and seasons, and the sixth (or perhaps the seventh) the creation of animals and reptiles.

Crete
An island in the Mediterranean SE of Greece. Center of Minoan civilization in the time of Abraham. Paul passed along the coast on his way to Rome. There was a Jewish colony on Crete; a Christian group was also established there. The people of the island were not well regarded (Tit 1.12).

crick'et
This may be the long-horned grasshopper.

crim'son, scar'let
Red coloring matter of many shades, extracted from cochineal insects; used for dyeing.

cross
The cross as a means of inflicting death in the most cruel and shameful way was used by the

Crosses

Phoenicians, from whom it passed to the Greeks and the Romans. It consisted of two beams of wood nailed one to the other in the form of X, or T, or +. The last, which is most familiar to us in art, was in all probability the shape of Christ's cross.

cu'cum•ber
Long cultivated in Syria and Egypt.

cum'min
The aromatic seed of an umbelliferous plant, used as a condiment.

curse
In the ancient warfare of the Israelites, as of the neighboring nations, the enemy and all his belongings were placed under a ban or curse. Thus on the Moabite stone we read, "I destroyed all the people of the city to delight the eyes of Chemosh and Moab."

Cush, Cu'shan, Cu'san
1. The Cushites in Ethiopia, the Kassites of Babylonia, or a Midianite tribe near Edom.
2. A king of Aram.

cut'ter
See Locust.

cym'bals
These were used in pairs, only by men, as signaling instruments and as accompaniments to the trumpet and lyre.

cy'press
The Hebrew word has been variously translated as pine or larch, box (box shrub), or holm (a form of oak; holly). *See* Holm tree; Pine.

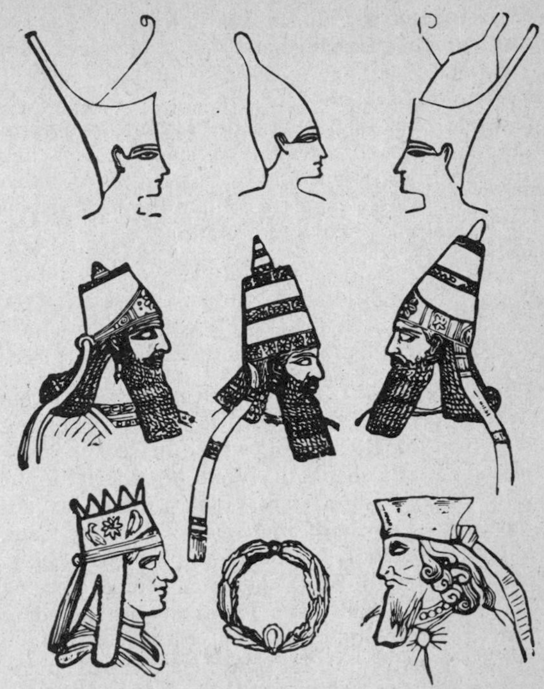
Ancient crowns

Cy'prus
A large island in the Mediterranean, 41 mi. from the Coast of Asia Minor and 60 mi. from Syria, also called Chittim or Kittim. In ancient times it was famous as a source of copper, and a particular pottery made there has been found in widely scattered excavations. It was the home of Barnabas, and was visited by Paul.

Cy'rus
A Persian king, founder of the Achaemenian dynasty.

D

Da•mas'cus
The first mention of Damascus in an inscription is dated in the 16th century B.C. It claims to be the oldest continuously occupied city site in the world, and is now the capital of Syria. In ancient times it was a widely known caravan center. The city was captured and plundered many times, by Assyria, Babylonia, David of Israel, Persia, Alexander the Great, and Rome.

Dan
1. The fifth son of Jacob.
2. A city in the N of Palestine, identified with Tell el-Qadi, to which the Danites migrated. Jeroboam established idolatry there.

Dan'iel
(Heb. "God has judged") The name of 3 persons in the OT, one of whom is the author of the 4th of the prophetic books. He was taken as a captive to Babylon, where he was trained in the king's palace. Among other triumphs he interpreted the king's dreams and the handwriting on the wall, looked after his own friends, Shadrach, Meshach, and Abednego, and then was cast into a den of lions for refusing to acknowledge Darius

the Mede as a god. He was saved by God, and subsequently Darius made him a governor of a province.

Dan'iel, the Book of

The OT book of Daniel is divided into two parts. The first six chapters tell of Daniel's faith and the greatness of his God over the idols of Babylon. The last six chapters contain the four visions of Daniel and their interpretations.

dar'ic

See Money.

Da·ri'us

Darius I and Darius II, rulers of Persia.

Da'vid

(Heb. "beloved") The second and greatest king over Israel, was the youngest son of Jesse, and was born at Bethlehem, where his early youth was spent as a shepherd. While still a stripling he slew the Philistine giant Goliath, and was admitted to the court and service of King Saul, whose melancholy he soothed by his skilful playing on the harp. Saul's daughter Michal became his wife, and Saul's son Jonathan was united to him in a lifelong friendship. Fleeing from the deadly jealously of Saul, he first escaped to the country of the Philistines. Then, gathering at the cave of Adullam a band of 400 (afterward 600) men, he contrived to avoid Saul by moving hither and thither in the S country. For 16 months he lived at Ziklag, as a vassal of the king of Gath. After the death of Saul and Jonathan at Gilboa, David reigned over Judah at Hebron for 7½ years, and after the death of Saul's son Ishbosheth he became king over all Israel. He took the stronghold Jebus, on the hill of Zion (the "city of David"), from the Jebusites, and built a palace there, with a tent beside it, in which the Ark of the Covenant was placed until a temple should be built for it by his successor. In addition to his old guard of 600 gibborim (or "heroes"), now largely recruited from foreigners, especially "Cherethites and Pelethites" (most probably Cretans and Philistines), he had, according to Chronicles, 288,000 fighting men, of whom 24,000 were under arms each month in the year. Several years of successful war made David master of the whole territory from the Euphrates to the Egyptian frontier. In the latter part of his reign of 32 years in Jerusalem, his favorite son Absalom rebelled against him and was slain, to his father's great sorrow; and shortly before his death, which has been variously dated 1015, 980, and 977 B.C., another son, Adonijah, attempted by means of a revolt to frustrate his father's choice of Solomon as successor.

David, while he was the hero of the people, refused to lift his hand against "the Lord's anointed," even in his own defense, contenting himself with an appeal to the Divine judgment. In contrast to Saul, he is "the man after God's own heart." Heroic confidence in God sustained him in all the difficulties of his life and of his reign. "He executed judgment and justice unto all his people," and established the monarchy on a sound civil and religious basis. The greatest stain upon his character was his foul wrong done to Uriah, whose wife he wanted, followed by his indirect murder, by sending him into battle and arranging to have him deserted, sins of which he bitterly repented. The last song of "the sweet psalmist of Israel" expresses the spirit of his life and of his rule. In the darkest days of the nation's history, men felt that the promises of God could only be fulfilled under another David. The memory of the "sure mercies of David" and the "everlasting covenant" God made with him quickened their Messianic hope of One who should be given "for a witness to the people, a leader and commander to the people."

day

The word may mean the time from sunrise to sunset; or the civil day of 24 hours, from sunrise to sunrise or from sunset to sunset; or in a poetic sense of "in the time of" as in the phrase "in the day of . . ."

Day of A·tone'ment

See Atonement, Day of.

day star

See Lucifer.

dea'con

(Gr. "servant") In the NT, the name of a class of congregational office-bearers, first mentioned about A.D. 63. Their work seems chiefly to have been the visiting and relief of the poor. The early church appointed 7 in every church, and assigned to them the special care of the sick and of the poor.

dea'con·ess, serv'ant

Women especially charged with the care of the poor and sick women. Widows may have constituted a special case.

Dead Sea

This body of water at the mouth of the Jordan River is called in the Bible the Salt Sea, the Sea of the Arabah, the Sea of the Plain. It is about 53 mi. long and 10 mi. wide, 1500 ft. deep, and its surface is 1292 ft. below sea level. It is about 25 per cent salt, 5 times as salty as the ocean. Its mineral compounds are chlorides of magnesium, sodium, calcium, and potassium, as well as magnesium bromide.

Deb'o·rah

1. Rebekah's nurse and her lifelong companion.

2. An early judge of Israel. She roused opposition to Canaanite oppression of Israel, and Judg 5.2-31 is her Song of Victory over Canaan. It is one of the oldest Hebrew poems in existence, dating from the 12th century B.C., and it has been described as one of the most magnificent.

De·cap'o·lis

A federation of 10 Greek cities in Palestine, some of which lay along the trade routes of the day, and several of which were founded by soldiers from the armies of Alexander the Great. Most of them have been identified, and some have been extensively excavated.

Ded·i·ca'tion, Feast of

The principal feast of Dedication was that of the reconsecration of the temple after its desecration by the Greeks, an 8-day celebration today called Hanukkah, in mid-December. Sometimes it is called the Feast of Lights.

De·grees', Songs of, or As·cents', Songs of

The titles of 15 psalms. The degrees or ascents are believed to be the steps between the men's and women's courts of the temple. The Levites stood on these steps to sing these psalms.

De·li'lah

Samson's beloved. She was bribed by the Philistines to get for them the secret of his strength, which she did.

del'uge

See flood.

De·struc'tion, Cit'y of

See City of the Sun.

Deu·ter·on'o·my

A sequel to Numbers. Narrated in it are three speeches and two poems, supposedly spoken by Moses in Moab before the crossing of Jordan, in which he gives the Ten Commandments to the chosen people. A minor narrative in three of the chapters tells of the last days of Moses.

Di·a'na of the E·phe'si·ans

This is the Latin name of the ancient goddess of the region of Ephesus; some 300 years after the first Greek settlers had arrived in the area they had adopted this local mother-goddess or fertility goddess as their own, calling her Artemis. By 800 B.C., they had begun to build a magnificent temple for her. Worship of her was widespread and conducted in magnificent rituals and surroundings. The primary image, probably a meteorite, is believed to have been placed in the temple at Ephesus.

Di·as'po·ra, Dis·per'sion

At the time of the Exile the Jewish people scattered widely and settled permanently in Mesopotamia, particularly in Babylonia, and in Alexandria, Asia Minor, and as far away as Cyrenaica.

Di'bon

A Moabite city 13 mi. E of the Dead Sea, 3 mi. N of the Arnon River. The famous Moabite Stone was found in Dibon. It tells of a Moabite victory over Israel at the time of Omri.

dill

Both the plant and the seeds are used as flavoring and have some use in medicine.

Dis·per'sion

See Diaspora.

di·vorce'

The Hebrew name for husband, baal, meant "owner," and in primitive Israel dissolution of marriage might take place at the husband's will. The Book of the Covenant shows that the wife so put away retained the right to be fed and clothed by the husband (Ex. 21.7-11), unless she was redeemed by her own relatives, and thus set free to marry another man. In Deut. 24.1–4 it is enacted that the husband must give a dismissed wife a "bill of divorcement," a document releasing her from all claims on his part and setting her free to marry again.

Our Lord teaches that marriage rests on the original creative ordinance of God, making the bond between man and wife indissoluble, and that the Mosaic legislation with regard to divorce was a concession to natural hardness of heart, and did not correspond to its divine idea (Mt 19.4-9; 5.31 ff). Divorce was permissible only in the case of unfaithfulness (Mt 5.32; 19.9).

dog

Mentioned about 40 times in Scripture, almost always in a tone of contempt. The Jews, not being a hunting people, did not train the dog, except to guard their flocks (Job 30.1). They had not the noble mastiffs and wolfhounds we find carved on Assyrian monuments, nor the varied breeds of hunting dogs portrayed on the Egyptian walls. Their dogs were, doubtless, as they are still in Palestine, pariah or ownerless dogs, of a type not unlike the Scottish collie. Their nocturnal habits are referred to in Ps 59.14, 15. In the East they are the scavengers of the towns. The term dog is still hurled in reproach by the Jew at the Gentile and by the Moslem at the Christian. Christians also use it.

Do'than

The place where Joseph found his brothers. Now called Tell Dotha, excavations show it to have been a city from about 3000 B.C. to A.D. 300 or 400.

drach'ma

The unit of silver coinage of Greece; spoken of as a piece of silver.

drag'on

This seems to have been a fabulous monster of tremendous strength. It is called leviathan, sea monster, Rahab (in poetic passages only) and sea serpent. *See* Whale.

dress

The outermost garment of men may have been a rectangular piece of cloth, a mantle, cloak, cloke, wrapped about the body. Under that was a garment called a coat, tunic, robe or chiton (Greek), which might have been baglike, with openings for arms and head and of various lengths. A loincloth or girdle might be worn; the priests had breeches. The girdle and the tunic might be made of skins of animals. Cloth woven of wool, linen, animal hair, or fine linen (probably cotton) was used, of varying degrees of beauty and elegance. The draped or wrapped garments were tied around by a girdle, a long folded wool cloth, through which a sword might be thrust; also, it might be folded in such a way as to provide a money belt. Sandals were worn, fastened by leather straps. Men of importance wore a ring or rings. There was elaborate jewelry for men of rank or wealth. Women's clothing was similar, sometimes more elaborate, being decorated with fringe or other ornamentation. Women had more head dresses, veils, and ornaments than men. A number of dyes were used.

drom'e·da·ry

A finer and swifter race of camel, differing from the ordinary camel as a race horse does from a cart horse. According to an Arabic proverb, "Men are like camels—not one in a hundred is a dromedary."

E

ea′gle, gier, vul′ture
The largest flying birds of Palestine, all unclean for food. The vulture is a carrion-eating bird. The same Heb. word has been thus variously translated.

ear of grain
The individual head of grain.

ear′ring
These ornaments seem usually to have been circular in shape, made of gold. Men may have worn a single earring.

E′bal
A mountain N of Mount Gerizim and forming the N side of an E to W pass with Gerizim on the S.

eb′on•y
The core wood of several varieties of ebony, imported from Ceylon, S India, and possibly from Ethiopia. Egyptians, Babylonians, Greeks, Romans, and Phoenicians made furniture of ebony inlaid with ivory. Idols were also carved from ebony.

Ec•cle•si•as′tes
The book of *Ecclesiastes* contains the writings of a wealthy Jew who suffered from the sorrows and disappointments of life and now tries to discover the true value and meaning of life through God. The author of this book calls himself "The Preacher," "The son of David," and "king in Jerusalem." But whether this was Solomon or a later "son of David" is uncertain.

E′den
The root of the Hebrew word is uncertain, and the location of Eden has not been determined. The plain of the Tigris-Euphrates rivers has been most favored.

E′dom
(Heb. "the red region") Edom extended from the Brook Zered about 70 mi. toward the Gulf of Aqabah, with an approximate 15-mi. width. Excavations show a busy civilization there between the 23rd and 20th centuries, after which the only inhabitants were wandering Bedouins. In the 13th century the Edomites, a Semitic people, arrived. They were at war much of the time with the Israelites; David conquered them, making possible trade with Arabia and access to the copper mines of Edom. Later, Amaziah and his successor Azariah again conquered the country. After the Exile, the Edomites moved into Palestine. Eventually, Rome conquered the entire area.

E′gypt
The name applied since the time of Homer to the land of the Nile, in the NE of Africa. Egypt consists geographically of 2 halves, the N being the Delta, and the S, Upper Egypt, between Cairo and the First Cataract. The Hebrews called it Mizraim, the land of Ham, or Rahab. The Egyptians belonged to the Mediterranean race and their original home is still a matter of dispute. The ancient Egyptian language, of which the latest form is Coptic, is distantly connected with the Semitic family of speech.

The civilization of Egypt goes back to a remote antiquity. The two kingdoms, the north and the south, were united by Menes, founder of the first historical dynasty of kings. The first 6 dynasties, lasting until 2200 B.C., constitute what is known as the Old Kingdom, which had its capital at Memphis, S of Cairo (the Old Testament Moph or Noph). The native name was Mennofer, "the good place." The Pyramids were tombs of the monarchs of the Old Kingdom, those of Gizeh being erected in the time of the Fourth Dynasty.

After the fall of the Old Kingdom came a period of decline and obscurity, followed by the Middle Kingdom, the most powerful dynasty of which was the Twelfth. The Faiyum was rescued for agriculture by the kings of the Twelfth Dynasty, and 2 obelisks were erected in front of the temple of the Sun-god at On or Heliopolis (near Cairo), one of which is still standing. The capital of the Middle Kingdom was Thebes, in Upper Egypt.

The Middle Kingdom was overthrown by the Hyksos (*haq schas,* Bedouin chieftains) or Shepherd princes from Asia, whose three dynasties ruled over Northern Egypt for several centuries. They had their capital at Zoan or Tunis (now San), in the NE part of the Delta. In their time Abraham, Jacob, and Joseph entered Egypt. The Hyksos were finally expelled about 1600 B.C. by the hereditary princes of Thebes, who founded the Eighteenth Dynasty, and carried the war into Asia. Canaan, Syria, and Cyprus were subdued, and the boundaries of the Egyptian Kingdom were fixed at the Euphrates. The Sudan, which had been conquered by the kings of the Twelfth Dynasty, was again annexed to Egypt, and the eldest son of the Pharaoh took the title of prince of Cush. One of the later kings of the dynasty, Amen-hotep IV (1369-1353 B.C.), taking the name Akh-en-Aton (spirit of the sun), endeavored to supplant the ancient state religion of Egypt by a pantheistic monotheism derived from Asia, the one supreme god being adored under the image of the solar disk. The attempt led to religious and civil war, and the Pharaoh retreated from Thebes to Central Egypt, where he built a new capital, on the site of the present Tel el-Amarna. The cuneiform tablets that were found here in 1887 represent his foreign correspondence. He surrounded himself with officials and courtiers of Asiatic and more especially Canaanitish extraction; but the native party succeeded eventually in overthrowing the government; the capital of Amenhotep was destroyed, and the foreigners were driven out of the country—those that remained being reduced to serfdom.

The national triumph was marked by the rise of the Nineteenth Dynasty, in the founder of which, Ramses I, we must see the "new king, who knew not Joseph." His grandson, Ramses II. reigned 67 years (1290-1224 B.C.), and was an indefatigable builder. Pithom, excavated by Naville in 1883, was one of the cities he built; he may have been the Pharaoh of the Oppres-

Egyptian standards

sion. The Pharaoh of the Exodus may have been one of his immediate successors, whose reigns were short. Under them Egypt lost its empire in Asia, and was itself attacked by barbarians from Libya and the north.

The Nineteenth Dynasty soon afterward came to an end, Egypt was distracted by civil war, and for a short time a Syrian, Irsu, ruled over it.

Then came the Twentieth Dynasty, the 2nd Pharaoh of which, Ramses III (1195-1164 B.C.), restored the power of his country. In one of his campaigns he overran the S part of Palestine, where the Israelites had not yet settled. They must at the time have been still in the wilderness. But it was during the reign of Ramses III that Egypt finally lost Gaza and the adjoining cities to the Philistines.

After Ramses III, Egypt fell into decay. Solomon married the daughter of one of the last kings of the Twenty-first Dynasty, which was overthrown by Sheshonk or Shishak I, the general of the Libyan mercenaries, who founded the Twenty-second Dynasty (940-745 B.C.). A list of the places he captured in Palestine is engraved on the outside of the S wall of the temple of Karnak.

In the age of Hezekiah, Egypt was conquered by Ethiopians from the Sudan, who constituted the Twenty-fifth Dynasty. The 3rd of them was Tirhakah (689-664 B.C.). In 671 B.C. it was conquered by the Assyrians, who divided it into 20 satrapies, and Tirhakah was driven back to his ancestral dominions. Fourteen years later it successfully revolted under Psamtik or Psammetichus I (663-609 B.C.) of Sais, the founder of the Twenty-sixth Dynasty. Among his successors were Neco of Necho and Hophra, or Apries. The dynasty came to an end in 525 B.C. when the country was subjugated by Cambyses. Soon afterward it became a Persian satrapy.

The title of Pharaoh, given to the Egyptian king, is the Egyptian for Great House. The name is found in very early Egyptian texts.

Egyptian religion was a strange mixture of pantheism and animal worship, the gods being adored in the form of animals. While the educated classes resolved their many deities into manifestations of one omnipresent and omnipotent divine power, the lower classes regarded the animals as incarnations of the gods. Under the Old Kingdom, Ptah, the Creator, the god of Memphis, was at the head of the Pantheon; afterward Amon, the god of Thebes, took his place. Amon, like most of the other gods, was identified with Re, the sun god of Heliopolis.

The Egyptians believed in a resurrection and a future state of rewards and punishments. The judge of the dead was Osiris, who had been slain by Set, the representative of evil, and afterward restored to life. His death was avenged by his son Horus, whom the Egyptians invoked as their Redeemer. Osiris and Horus, along with Isis, formed a trinity, representing the sun god under different forms.

The Pyramids, the temples, and the obelisks of Egypt have been described in all ages, but it was not until early in the 19th century, through the finding of the Rosetta stone, that the key to reading the hieroglyphic texts was discovered by the French scholar Champollion. The work of Brugsch and Birch then led to the recovery of history contained on the monuments or in papyri. The exacavations of Mariette followed; and those of Petrie and De Morgan further increased our information about the religion, social customs, and history of Egypt. In 1896, among the ruins of a temple of Mer-ne-Ptah at Thebes, Petrie found a large granite stele, on which is engraved a hymn of victory commemorating the defeat of Libyan invaders who had overrun the Delta. At the end other victories of Mer-ne-Ptah are glanced at, and it is said that "the Israelites (I-s-y-r-a-e-l-u) are minished (?) so that they have no seed." This statement of an Egyptian poet is a remarkable parallel to Ex 1.10-22.

E'lah, Val'ley of

(Heb. "valley of the terebinth"?) A valley identified as Wadi es-Sant, 14 mi. WSW of Bethlehem.

E'lam, E'lam•ites

Elam occupied the area of the Zagros Mountains and present-day Luristan and Khuzistan. Its capital was Susa. Its history through about 2 millennia was warfare first with Sumer and subsequently with Babylonia and Assyria. Darius completed the conquest of the country.

el'ders, an'cients

Heads of families and tribes, among the early Hebrews as among other primitive peoples, administered justice within their own circles in time of peace and were the leaders in time of war (cf. the Arabian sheikh, or elder). The "elders of the city" afterward took the place of the elders of tribes and families, retaining their judicial functions. The "judges" and "officers" were probably those among the elders who acted respectively as administrators and executors of justice. When the synagogue became an established institution, the elders who were the civil authorities of a place were also the elders of its synagogue.

The elders or presbyters (Gr. "elders") of Christian churches were local overseers chosen after the model of the synagogue. They appear from the first to have been elected by the people, and, on their being approved by the apostles, to have been instituted to their office by prayer and the laying on of hands. Their duties were to exercise spiritual oversight over the people as pastors, visiting the sick and caring for the poor and for strangers, to maintain order in the religious assemblies, to teach, and to administer the affairs of the congregation, in concurrence with the deacons. The word elder or presbyter was interchangeable with the word bishop in NT times, and the offices were one and the same till about A.D. 150, when the presbyters first became subordinate to the bishops.

el'e·phant

The elephant is not mentioned in the OT, but Solomon imported ivory (1 Kings 10.22; 2 Chron 9.21) so there must have been knowledge of the animal. The Persians used elephants in warfare in the 4th century B.C., and they were used in war against Palestine by the Seleucids in 163 B.C.

E'li

(Heb. "exalted") A judge in Israel, he held that office and the high-priesthood for 40 years at Shiloh. His sons, Hophni and Phinehas, through gross misconduct, disgraced their priestly descent and position; and a great defeat, in which they and many Israelites were slain by the Philistines and the Ark of the Covenant was captured, was regarded as a divine judgment. Eli died of horror at the news and was succeeded by Samuel (1 Sam 1–4).

E·li'hu

(Heb. "he is my God") The name of 5 persons in the OT, one of whom argued with Job and his friends (Job 32–37).

E·li'jah, E·li'as

(Heb. "Yah is God") Elijah the Tishbite was of the inhabitants or sojourners of Gilead. His prophetic ministry belongs to the Northern Kingdom, in the reigns of Ahab and Ahaziah. When Ahab, under the influence of his Tyrian wife Jezebel, threatened to suppress the worship of Jehovah, and made Baal worship the court religion, Elijah suddenly appeared before the king to announce a long drought, in punishment of the apostasy of the covenant nation. While this lasted (3 years) he was at first miraculously fed by ravens at the brook Cherith and afterward lived at Zarephath, a Tyrian city, in the house of a widow, whose son he restored to life. Elijah now appears before Ahab, and challenges the prophets of Baal to a contest between Baal and Jehovah, in which it shall be shown by fire from heaven which is the true God. The fire consumes the sacrifice and altar of Jehovah; the people acknowledge that Jehovah is God, and fall upon the priests of Baal and slay them; and before evening there is a tempest of rain. But this victory is soon followed by defeat; and, despairing of man, Elijah journeys to Horeb to meet God. There a vision passes before him, and reveals to him that God establishes His kingdom not by the violence of earthquake and tempest, but in gentleness and stillness. He returns with new faith to carry out God's commands, on his way to Damascus anointing Elisha to be his successor. Elijah again met Ahab to announce the ruin of his house for his heartless robbery of Naboth, whose death had been compassed by Jezebel. Wonderful as Elijah's whole career was, its completion in which the Enoch miracle was repeated was its most remarkable event. There appeared chariots of fire and horses of fire, and Elijah was taken up to heaven in a whirlwind. Elijah was the leader of the reaction of spiritual religion of Jehovah against the nature religion of Baal, and through his efforts Baal worship was effectually checked in Israel. He was held in high esteem by the later Jews. No other prophet is so often mentioned in the NT. The last prophet, Malachi, prophesies his return before the day of the Lord. This prophecy was literally interpreted in Israel. The evangelists and Jesus show that it was fulfilled in John the Baptist. In the transfiguration of our Lord, Elijah appears as the representative of the prophets, beside Moses, the representative of the law (1 Kings 17–19, 21; 2 Kings 1, 2).

E·li'phaz

(Heb. "God crushes"?) One of Job's friends.

E·li'sha

(Heb. "God is salvation") The son of Shaphat of Abel-Meholah, Elisha was the disciple and successor of Elijah, to whom he is related much as Joshua is to Moses. His prophetic work belonged to the reigns of Jehoram, Jehu, and Jehoahaz. As the spiritual guide of the people, he showed the same spirit of opposition to the idolatrous court and priesthood that had inspired Elijah, and was to the faithful servants of Jehovah what his great teacher had been before him, "the chariot of Israel, and the horsemen thereof," Israel's strength and protection. Many miracles are recorded as having been wrought by him. He died early in the reign of Joash, at an extreme old age (2 Kings 2-9, 12).

elm

An erroneous translation of ela (Hos 4.13), elsewhere rendered oak, teil tree, or terebinth. The elm is not found in Palestine.

E'lul

The 6th month in the Hebrew calendar.

em·balm'ing

A mode of preserving a dead body from decay by the use of aromatic spices. The art was practiced by the Egyptians from the very earliest times, and was by them brought to great perfection. It probably originated in the belief in the future reunion of the soul and the body. It was rarely practiced by the Jews. The Jewish process required 40 days, and that of the Egyptians 70 days. An embalmed body is a mummy.

em'er·ald

A variety of beryl of rich green color.

Em·ma′us
(Gr. "warm wells") A Judean town, not definitely identified. Four modern towns have been suggested.

En′dor
(Heb. "spring of *dor*") A city in Manasseh, home of a medium or witch consulted by King Saul. Near Endor, Sisera and Jabin were destroyed. Located at the modern Endor.

En·ro′gel
(Heb. "spring of the fuller") A spring in the valley of the Kidron, near Jerusalem.

E·phe′sians
The Letter of Paul to the Ephesians, written about A.D. 62, seems to be a general letter to the churches of Asia Minor. Paul presents God's eternal purpose to save men through faith in Christ; "the dividing wall of hostility" between Jews and Gentiles has been broken down through the cross of Christ. Paul exhorts us to live as worthy, true Christians.

Eph′e·sus
A famous city of Lydia, in Asia Minor, and the capital of Proconsular Asia, it is noted for its Temple of Artemis or Diana and its great theater. It was visited by Paul in his second journey when he left Aquila and Priscilla there to carry on the work; and in his third journey, when Demetrius raised an uproar against him.

eph′od
A priestly garment.

E′phra·im
(Heb. "fruitful") The most powerful of the tribes of Northern Israel, extended from Benjamin to Manasseh W of Jordan.

E′phra·im, Mount
The tribe of Ephraim lived in hill country; Joshua (an Ephraimite) was buried on Mount Ephraim, but which hill is intended is not known.

E·sar·had′don
King of Assyria and Babylonia (681-669 B.C.).

Es·dra·e′lon
Greek name for the W portion of the Valley of Jezreel, including the Valley of Megiddo. It is a well-watered and fertile valley, which separates Galilee from Samaria. The River Kishon drains it.

Es′dras, First and Sec′ond Books of
In the Vulgate these books appear as 3 and 4 Esdras, because Ezra and Neh have been counted as two books of Ezra. Counting them in this way, *Third Esdras* is a new version of the events relating to the return from the Captivity, the chief incident being a contest before the king by the young wits of the court. Zerubbabel wins with the well-known maxim, *Magna est veritas, et praevalebit,* "Truth is great, and will prevail." In consequence, he obtains concessions for the Jewish captives.

Fourth Esdras has perished in the Greek, but is extant in other versions. Its major part is a series of revelations to Ezra regarding the fortunes of Israel and of Jerusalem. Its date is probably after A.D. 70.

Es·senes′
An ascetic order, known to have existed from about 150 B.C. In the time of our Lord they were settled in monastic communities near the Dead Sea and in villages throughout the country. The Dead Sea Scrolls (found in 1947 and after) constitute a major part of the literature of the Qumran monastery. The name is probably from the root of a Hebrew word meaning "pious." The Essenes endeavored to reach absolute religious purity through strict abstemiousness and cleanliness. Their common meals were regarded as sacrificial feasts. Their lives were divided between religious exercises, lustrations (purification ceremonies), and labor at tillage and handicrafts. They had a community of goods and disapproved of marriage. They forbade trading, swearing of oaths, and anointing with oil. They sent gifts of incense to the Temple at Jerusalem, but differed from orthodox Judaism in their rejection of all animal sacrifices, in praying daily at sunrise, and in their view of the body as essentially evil and incapable of resurrection. The principles in which they differed from Judaism may have been derived from the East. They are not mentioned in the NT, and by the time of our Lord appear to have had little or no influence on the life of their nation.

Es′ther
A Jewess of Susa who became the queen of Ahasuerus, and frustrated a plot to destroy all Jews. This is commemorated in the Jewish festival of Purim.

Es′ther, the Book of
The last of the OT historical books, it contains an early example of pre-Christian anti-Semitism. Esther, a Jewess, was chosen as the new queen for Ahasuerus, the king of Persia. Her uncle Mordecai had incurred the enmity of Haman, the evil court favorite, and so brought the threat of death to his people. Esther, through her position, was able to avert the tragedy and save her people.

Eth′a·nim
The 7th month in the Hebrew calendar, later called Tishri.

E·thi·o′pi·a
An ancient name of the territory S of Egypt, also called Cush, and including what was subsequently called Sudan. From about 2000 B.C. there was sporadic warfare with Egypt. For some hundreds of years the area was independent of Egypt as the Kingdom of Nubia, with Napata as its capital. Later it was subdued in the expansion of the Assyrian empire.

Eu·phra′tes
The largest river in W Asia, called "the river" and "the great river." It flows from the mountains of Armenia to the Persian Gulf, 1700 mi.; 140 mi. above the Gulf, it is joined by the Tigris. The region between the rivers is thence called Mesopotamia.

ex′ile
Israel's geographical position made the country a buffer between Egypt to the W and the Assyrians and Babylonians to the E, involved in their

almost constant warfare. In 721 B.C. the Assyrian Sargon II captured Samaria, the capital of the Northern Kingdom, and recorded in his inscriptions that he deported 27,290 Israelites to the E. With this deportation the identity of the N ten tribes disappeared; they were assimilated into the Assyrian population. People from the E were moved into Palestine. A century and a half later, after Babylonia had defeated Assyria, Jerusalem was captured; in 578 B.C. King Jehoiachin and some 10,000 of the population were deported to Babylon. An abortive rebellion led to further deportations in 587 B.C., and a reprisal deportation as a penalty for the assassination of the Babylon-appointed governor of Judah occurred in 582 B.C. Many of those deported were absorbed into the population of Babylonia, but following 538 B.C., the return from exile began, and with it the rebuilding of the temple.

Ex'o•dus

The return of the Hebrew people from Egypt to Israel is called the exodus from Egypt. The easy route had Egyptian fortifications scattered along the way, hence was avoided. It was for them, as a consequence, a journey of immense difficulty through wilderness and wild terrain, related in the Book of Exodus.

Ex'o•dus, the Book of

The second book of the OT relates the history of the Israelites from after the death of Joseph to the erection of the Tabernacle by Moses. It includes an account of the wanderings in the wilderness of Sinai and the giving of the law to the nation.

ex'or•cists

Persons who professed to expel evil spirits by adjuration or the performance of certain rites. Strolling exorcists were very numerous in the first century, especially in Asia Minor. Some of them undertook, instead of their usual formulas, to employ the name of Jesus (Acts 19.13).

E•ze'ki•el

(Heb. "God strengthens") A Jewish prophet, some of a priest Buzi, was among the captives whom Nebuchadnezzar carried with king Jehoiachin in 598 B.C. to Babylonia, where he settled near the river Chebar. His prophetic work extended over not less than 22 years (592-570).

E•ze'ki•el, the Book of

This OT book is written by the prophet of the exile. It is divided into two sections; the first denounces the sins and abominations of Jerusalem and the second looks to the future with the hope that the city will be restored after it has been cleansed. This latter section contains passages strongly messianic in nature.

Ez'ra, Ez'rah

(Heb. "Yahweh helps") The name of 3 persons in the OT, one of whom, a priest and scribe, was the organizer of the post-Exilic community. With the favor and support of Artaxerxes Longimanus, he led a band of 1800 male Israelites from Persia to Palestine in 458 B.C. to strengthen Zerubbabel's colony. He carried out a drastic reform by casting out the foreign wives and their children, and established a regular synagogue service, in which the chief place was given to reading and exposition of the Law. For this service he founded the special class of Scribes. Ezra exercised a most powerful influence on the development of Judaism. The complete subjection of the people under the Law was the fruit of his work (Ezra 7–10; Neh 8–10, and 12).

Ez'ra, the Book of

Ezra and Nehemiah are companion OT books, continuing the narration of Chronicles. Ezra details the first return of the Jews from their captivity in Babylon and the rebuilding of the Temple.

F

fal'low deer, roe'buck

More than one variety of deer can be found in the Near and Middle East, but the precise species to which reference is made has not been identified (Deut 4.5; 1 Kings 4.23).

fast'ing

Complete or partial abstinence from food is an expression of religious humiliation in the OT, often described by the phrase, "to afflict the soul." It was regarded as the natural sign of sorrow, especially of penitence; and where this mood, which gives fasting its value, is wanting, the prophets condemn it as displeasing to God (Jer 14.12). The only regularly recurring fast prescribed by the law is "from even till even" on the great Day of Atonement. After the Exile the days of national calamity were commemorated with fasting: the 10th day of the 10th month (Tebeth), the day of the beginning of the siege by Nebuchadnezzar; the 9th day of the 4th month (Tammuz), when the city was taken: the 7th day of the 5th month (Ab), when the Temple was destroyed, and in the 7th month (Tishri), the day of Gedaliah's murder. Fasting came to be regarded as meritorious in itself. The Pharisees fasted twice a week; on the 5th day of the week, when Moses was believed to have gone up to Mount Sinai and on the 2nd, when he was supposed to have descended. John's disciples fasted often. Our Lord imposed no fasting on His disciples while He was with them, but did not condemn the practice when followed in a right spirit, and He fasted before the beginning of His ministry. The first Christians fasted, in particular before the mission of Apostles and the appointment of elders. Paul's fastings appear to have been involuntary. The RSV excludes, on the evidence of the MSS, the references to fasting in Mt 17.21; Mk 9.29; Acts 10.30; 1 Cor 7.5.

fa'ther

The title of the First Person in the Godhead. God was revealed and known as the Father of His chosen people under the Old Testament dispensation and in a fatherly relation to individuals; but it was peculiarly the function of Christ to reveal the Fatherhood of God, and to bring men back to this relationship, as it is the function of the Spirit to seal and testify to this relationship of God and the believer.

feasts

The 3 annual festivals of the sanctuary were: (1) the Passover, (2) The Feast of Weeks, (3) the Feast of Tabernacles.

1. *The Passover* commemorated the deliverance of the Israelites from Egypt. It began on the 14th of Abib or Nisan in the evening, i.e. in the beginning of the 15th day, with a sacrificial meal, when a lamb or kid was roasted whole, and was eaten with bitter herbs and unleavened bread by the members of every family, and the head of the household recited the history of the redemption from Egypt. The sacrifices denoted expiation and dedication; the bitter herbs recalled the bitterness of the Egyptian bondage; unleavened bread was an emblem of purity.

2. *The Feast of Weeks* or of Harvest, or Day of Firstfruits or Pentecost (Gr. "fiftieth"), held on the 50th day or 7 weeks after the second day of the Passover, was the 2nd of the 3 annual festivals of the Sanctuary. It was limited to a single day, for only a portion of the products of the year had been garnered. Two loaves of leavened bread, representing the firstfruits of the grain harvest, were offered to the Lord. Ten suitable animals were sacrificed as a burnt offering, a kid for a sin offering, and 2 lambs for a peace offering.

3. *The Feast of Tabernacles,* or Ingathering, was the last of the 3 annual festivals. It was appointed to take place in the 7th month, at the close of the agricultural season, when all the products of the year had been gathered. It was celebrated during 7 days: The daily burnt offering included a total of 70 bullocks, distributed by a decreasing scale over the 7 days, and in addition 2 rams and 14 lambs daily, and as a sin offering a he-goat was daily sacrificed. During its celebration the people dwelt in booths made of the boughs of trees.

fer'ret, geck'o

A lizard such as the gecko is probably intended. A ferret is related to the weasel.

fig

This fruit is frequently mentioned in Scriptures, and indigenous to Palestine. These figs appear in February before the leaves, which do not cover the tree until a month or six weeks later. When the leaves are fully out, the fruits should be ripe.

fir

See Pine.

fish'es

The fishes of Palestine include several different species. The fishes of the Jordan and Lake Tiberias are extremely like those of the Nile. They are carplike, large-scaled fishes, barbels, dace and bleak, loaches, etc. The Phoenicians engaged in sea-fishing.

fitch'es

An archaic spelling for vetch, a legume. It probably should be translated as the word *spelt* rather than as any variety of vetch.

flax

This fiber was grown in Egypt and Palestine from very early times. The tabernacle hangings and the high priest's dress were of linen (Ex 27–29).

flea

This insect is only twice mentioned in the Bible, where David compares himself to a flea, a thing too insignificant for Saul to pursue. Fleas are, however, a real pest in the Holy Land, as in most other Mediterranean countries, the huts and camps of the natives swarming with them (1 Sam 24.16; 26.20).

flood

There are among native tribes of the Americas, the Pacific Islands and Australia and the early peoples of Mesopotamia, many stories of floods resembling that of the time of Noah. As related in Gen 6–9, God found the mankind He had created to be wicked, and decided upon its destruction. Noah was a righteous man and was to be spared, he was instructed to build an ark, and to take into it 2 of every species of animal, with provisions, and with his wife, their 3 sons, and the sons' wives. God closed the ark and the rains came, flooding the entire earth. Some time after the rains stopped, Noah sent forth successively a raven and a dove to learn whether or not the waters had gone down. When on its 3rd flight the dove did not return, Noah knew that the bird had found a resting

Coin of Apamea depicting Noah and ark.

Flood tablet from Nippur, Babylonia, bearing one of the earliest stories of the flood, and the fall of man. The language is Sumerian.

place, and the ark was again opened. The biblical statement is that the ark rested on Ararat. Archaeologists have been refused permission to search for it, as Ararat overlooks Soviet territory.

fly

Two Hebrew words are taken to mean fly, one the ordinary housefly, the other the large horsefly. The stinging fly, the 4th of the plagues visited on the Egyptians, is a separate word in the Hebrew.

food, laws regarding

In the law all animals are divided into the clean, which might be eaten, and the unclean, which are forbidden. It distinguishes as clean the beasts which both chew the cud and have parted hooves; fishes with fins and scales; all birds except 19 or 20, mostly carnivorous; and among creeping things, the locust. Laws more or less similar are found among the Egyptians, Hindus, Persians, and Muslims. The distinction between clean and unclean food before it was established in God's name in the law was a settled custom and tradition among the Jews, perhaps originally derived from the natural repugnance and loathing at the sight, or touch, or smell of many animals, from ill effects on health traced to various meats, and from the place which, e.g., swine's flesh, had in the customs of heathen idolatry. The purpose for which this traditional distinction of clean from unclean meats was elevated into a formal law is distinctly expressed; it was to form a part of the partition wall that should separate from the Gentiles the people chosen by Jehovah for His own possession. All those parts of animals which, according to the sacrificial ritual, were consecrated to the altar, were forbidden under severe penalties; especially blood, for (1) "the life of all flesh is the blood thereof," and must be given back to the Lord of life; and (2) blood was set apart to make atonement for the soul. Contrast the practice of the heathen, e.g., the Philistines, who in their idolatry drank the blood reeking in the sacrificial basin. Certain pieces of the fat of such animals as were suitable for sacrifices (oxen, sheep, and goats) were not to be eaten, but were consecrated to the Lord. It was forbidden also "to seethe a kid in his mother's milk," which might possibly be taken as equivalent to eating flesh with the blood, and thus forbidden to the Hebrews along with the blood sacraments of the heathen; present-day Arabs sometimes stew a lamb or kid in milk. The flesh of animals that had been strangled or killed without being bled in the regular manner and flesh that had been sacrificed to heathen idols were likewise forbidden. Except in times of great distress or of religious decline these laws were well observed. The scrupulousness of the Jews in regard to these laws of food rendered it difficult for Jewish Christians and Gentile Christians to eat together and enjoy full religious fellowship; a compromise was therefore agreed to by the Gentile Christians to meet the Jewish Christians on this point. Christ declared the whole of this legislation to be morally indifferent.

fox

In Ps 63.10 and Lam 5.18 the translation should be jackal rather than fox.

frank'in·cense

A fragrant gum resin imported into Palestine from Arabia.

freed'men

See Libertines.

frog

Frogs are mentioned in the OT only in connection with the second Egyptian plague.

front'lets and arm'lets

The same as phylacteries (Ex 13.16; Deut 6.8). To carry out the injunction of the Law literally, four passages (Ex 13.1-10, 11-16; Deut 6.4-9; 11.13-21) were copied on strips of parchment, enclosed in a leather case, and bound by a strap around the head or around the left arm.

G

Ga·la'tia

A Roman province in central Asia Minor. Its S portion was in Paul's missionary field.

Ga·la'tians

The Letter of Paul to the Galatians, written in A.D. 57 or 58, probably from Antioch, is the cornerstone of Christian freedom. In Galatians Paul tells of his own conversion and of how he stood firm in his belief that Christ was the Savior of people everywhere, not just those who observed every detail of the Jewish law.

gal'ba·num

A resinous juice used for the sacred incense.

Gal·i·le'ans

The people of Galilee being little under the influence of Jerusalem, the center of Jewish piety and culture, were looked down upon as ignorant rustics. They bitterly resented, however, the Roman yoke and supplied a large proportion of the Zealots.

Gal'i·lee

The region between Samaria on the W, the river Leontes on the S, the maritime plain on the N, and the Sea of Galilee, including its E coast, on the E. Exclusive of the lake, it measured about 50 mi. N and S, by 25 to 35 E and W. It included the plain of Esdraelon; Lower Galilee, a series of parallel ranges, none over 1,850 ft.; and Upper Galilee in the N, a series of plateaus surrounded by hills from 2,000 to 4,000 ft. high. The line between the two Galilees ran from the N end of the lake, W to Acre. Galilee is well watered and wooded, with stretches of good grain land. Earthquakes are frequent. The greatest thoroughfare is the so-called Way of the Sea, connecting Damascus with the Levant.

Gal'i·lee, the Sea of

In a great ditch 680 ft. below the level of the sea is the Sea of Galilee, 13 mi. long by 8 broad. On the W lay Tiberias; Magdala and Taricheae, where the fish were cured, were probably to the S. On the NW are Capernaum and Chorazin. Bethsaida is on the E of Jordan. On the eastern shore lay Gergesa. Gadara was about 5 mi. from the SE corner of the lake, about 2300 ft. above it.

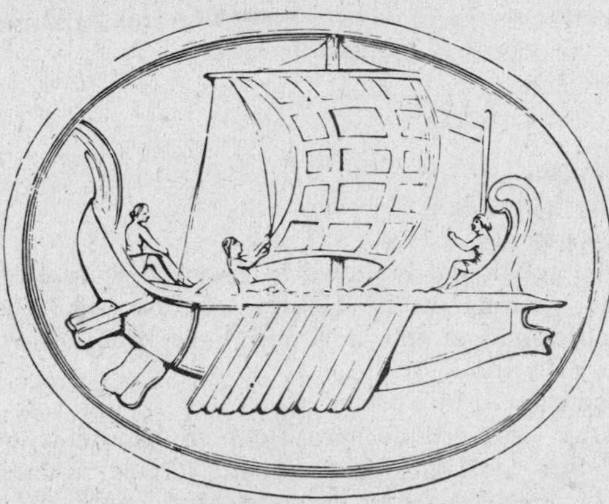

Roman galley

gall
A bitter, poisonous herb, possibly the same as the hemlock of Socrates.

gar'lic, gar'lick
A bulb of the lily family. Egyptian inscriptions list it, and during their wandering in the wilderness the Hebrews longed for it.

gate
In most Hebrew towns the only open space was just within the gate or gates. There the market was held, disputes were decided, and business of all kinds was transacted. The gate was the center of the social life of the place.

Ga'za
A famous Philistine city in SW Palestine, close to the sea. It retained its importance as a caravan depot in all ages. Little excavating has been done because of the modern city on the site of the old. *See also* Gezer.

geck'o
A lizard. *See* Ferret.

gems
Three lists of gems occur in the Bible: the high priest's breastplate (Ex 28); the ornaments of the king of Tyre (Ezek 28); the foundations of the heavenly Jerusalem (Rev 21).

Gems do not occur naturally in Palestine, and no great numbers have been found in excavations there, as compared with Egypt and Mesopotamia where many jewels have been found in tombs and temples. Faceted cutting was not understood, or at least not practiced, in the ancient world, but their engraving of jewels was fully as expert as anything done today.

Gen'e·sis
The first book of the OT; a collection of the earliest Israelite traditions concerning the origin of things. The book has two main divisions. The first is the history of early mankind, narrating the events of the Creation, the Fall, the Flood, and the Dispersion. The second section concerns the lives of Abraham, Isaac, Jacob, and Joseph.

Gen·nes'a·ret
A fertile plain on the shore of the Sea of Galilee. Also, an early name for the Sea of Galilee.

Ger'i·zim, Mount
Modern Jebel el-Tor, 2900 ft., directly S of Mount Ebal.

Geth·sem'a·ne
A garden at the foot of the Mount of Olives, where Judas betrayed Jesus. Its exact position is not known.

Ge'zer, Ga'zer, Ga·za'ra, Ga·ze'ra, Ga'za
Now called Tell el-Jazari, this site was excavated at the beginning of the 20th century. It had been a settlement at least since 4000 B.C.

Gid'e·on
(Heb. "hewer," "slasher") He tore down the Baal altar of his family and destroyed the Asherah. He was answered regarding his fitness to save Israel by having his fleece remain dry while the floor around it was wet with dew, and vice versa; he had other miraculous experiences. By a ruse he routed the Midianites. He was liberator and reformer but refused to be made king.

gier
See Eagle.

Gi'hon
An intermittent spring in the Kidron Valley beneath the City of David.

Gil·bo'a, Mount
Modern Jebel Fuqu'ah, at the E end of the Valley of Jezreel 6 mi. W of Beth-shean; elevation 1737 ft.

Gil'e·ad
(Heb. "monument of stones") 1. The name of 2 persons and a family in the OT.

2. A region E of the Jordan between the Yarmuk and Arnon rivers. It is a well-watered and fertile region, suitable for grapes and olives. Well forested, it is the source of balm of Gilead, an aromatic resin regarded as having medicinal properties and exported to Egypt and Phoenicia.

Gil'e·ad, Mount
There is no single Mount Gilead; the entire area is rugged, above the Jordan Valley, at this point 700 ft. below sea level.

Gil'gal
(Heb. "circle of stones") The name of several places in the OT. One lies E of Jericho, in the Jordan Valley. Possibly it is the modern Khirbet Mefjir. Another is probably the modern Jiljulieh, on the top of a high hill 7 mi. N of Bethel. This is the Gilgal of Elijah and Elisha. Another Gilgal has been compared with Harosheth-ha-Goiim but has not been definitely identified. It has been placed in Samaria, in Sharon, and elsewhere. One Gilgal near Shechem has been suggested and another is said to be on the road from Jericho to Jerusalem.

gnats, lice
Being among the smallest of insects they are used in metaphors to emphasize contrast, for example, to a bulky animal such as the camel.

goats
An important item in the pastoral wealth of the Near East since biblical times. They are

reared alongside of but not with the sheep. The sheep close graze the tender herbage; the goats browse on the twigs of the bushes. Goats' milk is preferred to any other.

goat, wild
The Sinaitic ibex. The Hebrew is translated always by "wild goat," except in Prov 5.19, where the feminine form is rendered "roe." Another word, akko, occurs only in Deut 14.5, where it is translated "wild goat." The Sinaitic ibex is a very beautiful creature, of a light fawn color, with very long recurved and regularly knotted horns, smaller and more slender than the Alpine and Himalayan species.

Gog and Ma'gog
Gog, prince of Meshech, who came from a land called Magog, is in Ezek 38–39 the leader of the forces of evil in a battle with Yahweh. In Rev 20.8 Magog is a leader with Gog of the forces of Satan in the battle of Armageddon.

gold
This metal apparently was not obtained in Palestine; some was imported from Sheba (part of Arabia), some from Ophir. The last district has been identified both with the W coast of India and with some part of the E coast of Africa. Some came from Nubia by way of Egypt. Gold, as we know from the contents of ancient graves, was in use for ornamental purposes at a very early date, even when stone held the place of metal for weapons and tools. It was no doubt obtained (and this is still a source of supply) by washing the river sands and other alluvial deposits.

Gol'go•tha
(Heb. "skull") The place of the crucifixion of Jesus.

Go•mor'rah
One of the 5 cities of the Valley mentioned with Sodom, Admah, Zeboim, and Zoar. Believed to be under the water of the S end of the Dead Sea.

go'pher wood
Not definitely identified.

Go'shen
The name of 3 places in the OT. One is presumably the area between Hebron and the Negev. Another is sometimes identified with modern Zahariyeh, 12 mi. SW of Hebron. The 3rd is the area of Egypt where the Israelites were from the time of Joseph until the Exodus.

gourd
The bottle gourd is used for booths and trellises in the Near East, and may be the plant mentioned in Jonah 4. The castor bean has also been suggested. The wild gourd has a poisonous fruit. At Gilgal during a famine, men were poisoned by it and appealed to Elisha for help. The vine of Sodom was probably the wild gourd.

grass' hop•per, lo'cust
"Locust" is sometimes used for the gregarious phase of certain short-horned grasshoppers. The grasshopper destroys vegetation at all stages of its life.

Grasshopper

Gre'cians
Greek-speaking Hebrews.

grey' hound
The greyhound is shown in Assyrian sculptures; the meaning of the Hebrew of Prov 30.31 is uncertain, but this dog may have been known in Palestine.

grind'ing
Grain was ground into flour in handmills or querns consisting of two hard circular stones, one revolved upon the other by means of a peg or handle. The labor was commonly performed by women. The Law forbade any one to take another's millstone in pledge.

grove
See Asherah.

H

Ha•bak'kuk
A prophet of Judah in the last days of Josiah (640-609 B.C.) and the reign of Jehoiakim (609-598 B.C.).

Ha•bak'kuk, the Book of
An OT book of prophecy concerned with the problem of unpunished evil in the world. It was revealed to Habakkuk that the Chaldean armies were to be God's means of punishing the wicked and that evil would destroy itself. The book concludes with a poem of thanksgiving and great faith.

Hag•ga'da, Hag•ga'dah
(Heb. "narration") The name for that part of the traditions of the Jewish scribes consisting of the elaboration of the historical and didactic portions of Scripture. As contrasted with the Halacha, which confined itself to the exposition and application of the text, its handling of the Scripture is unrestrained. It freely admits additions and interpolations, including legends.

Hag'ga•i
A Jewish prophet who came forward at Jerusalem, in 529 B.C., to urge the rebuilding of the Temple.

Hag'ga•i, the Book of
This OT book is a report on the utterances of the prophet Haggai during the second year of the reign of Darius, king of the Persian Empire, in the post-exilic period. The prophet is singularly concerned with the rebuilding of the Temple, which was essential to restoring the nation's religious purity. Haggai also believed that a great messianic age was at hand.

Hag•i•og'ra•pha
(Heb. "writings") The third division of the books included in the Hebrew Canon have a

more diversified character than either Law or Prophecy, and they have never received a more definite designation.

hair
The Hebrews regarded a strong growth of hair both on the head and on the chin as an ornament to a man. By many it was worn hanging down to the shoulder. To cut off a man's beard was to offer him the grossest insult. Only in times of mourning was the head shaved. That the hair was also worn in locks or ringlets is shown by the case of Samson.

Ha·la·cha'
(Heb. "that which is current") The Rabbinical law of custom, which was developed beside the written Torah or Law of Moses. It was distinguished from the Haggada as being the legal part of the oral tradition of the scribes, including their expositions of the Torah, and all the additional laws which were recognized as binding by the Jews after the Exile.

Hal·lel', Hal·le·lu'jah
(Heb. "praise ye the Lord") Probably sung in unison by the Temple choir.

Ham
1. The name of Noah's second son.
2. A city E of the Jordan, attacked by Chedorlaomer. Tell Ham, the ruin of the ancient city, is near modern Ham on the Wadi er-Rejeilah.
3. A poetic synonym for Egypt, used several times in the Psalms.

Ha'math
A town on the Orontes in Syria, the modern Nahr el Asi. Excavation revealed 12 layers, going back to Neolithic times. It is one of the important centers of Hittite inscriptions. It made alliance with David, and in 740 B.C. with Azariah (against Assyria). Conquered by the Assyrians in 720 B.C., the people of Hamath were transported to Samaria.

hang'ings
See Cotton.

Ha'ran
Now Harran, in Turkey, a city devoted to the moon cult, where Abraham stopped on his journey from Ur to Canaan.

hare
Though the name occurs only in the lists of Leviticus and Deuteronomy, there is no question about the translation, the hare being very common, and the Arabic name the same as the Hebrew. It was forbidden as food to the Israelites because it does not divide the hoof, even though (Moses parenthetically adds) it chews the cud, i.e., re-chews.

harp
A 10-string harp has been found in an Egyptian tomb of 1000 B.C., an earlier wooden one of 1550 B.C., and a golden lyre at Ur. The harp, lute and cithern are similar; David's harp, however, seems to have been more properly a lyre.

hart, hind
Fallow deer, habitat Syria, now almost if not altogether extinct in Palestine, must have been very common in ancient times. Deer are often depicted on the monuments both of Egypt and Assyria. The bones of the red deer have been found in caverns in Lebanon.

Har'vest, Feast of
One of the 3 great annual festivals, held at the end of the agricultural year. Also called the *Feast of Ingathering. See* Feasts.

hawk
The bird mentioned is not positively identified.

head-dress
The common head-dress of the people was probably like that of the modern Bedouin—a colored handkerchief bound round the head with a cord so as to shade both neck and ears from the sun. In later times the rich wore a turban formed of a long strip of fine linen rolled many times round the head. Yet another "headtire" was worn on festive occasions, especially by brides or bridegrooms.

heath
See Juniper.

He'brews
The descendants of Eber (Gen 10.21). They may have been a separate ethnic group, but were closely related to the Israelites; the names in some circumstances became interchangeable.

He'brews, the Let'ter to the
An anonymous NT book which urges the Hebrew Christian community not to fall back into Judaism and argues for Christian superiority.

He'bron
An ancient city in the high mountains of Judah, 19 mi. S of Jerusalem. The modern town, el-Khalil, surrounds the cave of Machpelah.

hedge'hog
The Hebrew word has also been translated "bittern" and "porcupine." Porcupines are found in modern Palestine.

Hel'len·ists
Greek-speaking Jews, in Judea or abroad, many of whom had adopted a measure of Greek (Hellenic) culture and manners.

hem'lock
A poisonous plant or one with a bitter root, also translated gall or wormwood. The plant most probably meant grows in waste places in Palestine, a perennial 3 to 4 ft. tall, with leaves resembling a carrot's.

hen'na, cam'phire
A fragrant flowering shrub. A dye prepared from the crushed leaves mixed with water is used to color the soles of the feet, palms, and nails.

Her'mon, Mount
The S spur of the anti-Lebanon, elevation 9100 ft., and frequently snow-covered. It is visible from many places in Palestine.

Her'od the Great
The founder of the dynasty that ruled Palestine 37 B.C.-A.D. 70, was the son of Antipater, an Idumaean, who had been Asmonaean governor in Edom, and who rose to a position of great influence as the minister of Hyrcanus II, the last Asmonaean king and high-priest. Antipater saw that the future of Judaea was in the

hands of Rome and cunningly ingratiated himself first with Pompey, then, after his death, with Julius Caesar (who rewarded his assistance with men and money in Egypt in 48 B.C. by making him governor of Judaea, Samaria, and Galilee, under the nominal sovereignty of Hyrcanus), and after Caesar's assassination in 44 B.C., with Cassius, Antonius and Augustus. Herod consistently followed his father's policy and took advantage of all the vicissitudes of Roman affairs. He saw himself at last the "confederate king" (*rex socius*) of the Roman emperor. A decree of the Roman senate made him king of Judaea in 40 B.C. In 37 B.C. he married Mariamne, granddaughter of Hyrcanus, and with the help of two Roman legions, captured Jerusalem. The next 9 years he spent in strengthening his position. He executed 45 members (the Sadducee majority) of the Sanhedrin and murdered every member of the Asmonaean house, including his wife Mariamne. The next 14 years (28-14 B.C.) were chiefly devoted to the erection of public buildings, including a theater in Jerusalem and a great amphitheater outside the gates, as well as numerous heathen temples and new cities, the chief of which was Caesarea, named after the emperor. His greatest work was the rebuilding of the Temple. But the golden eagle, the symbol of Roman supremacy, which he placed over its chief entrance, was to the people a continual reminder of his subservience to Rome. All the material advantages of his despotic rule, the tranquility of the country, his remissions of taxation and encouragement of trade and agriculture, his provision for the poor in time of scarcity, were forgotten. His life was constantly threatened by conspiracies, which he fought with secret police and the most cruel torture. In the year 7 B.C. he caused Alexander and Aristobulus, his 2 sons by Mariamne, to be strangled at Samaria, a crime which led Augustus to remark that he would rather be one of Herod's swine than one of his sons. Another son, Antipater, who had tried to assassinate his father, was executed 5 days before the death of Herod in 4 B.C. His sons shared his dominions according to his will. The elder, Archelaus, ethnarch of Judaea, Samaria, and Idumaea, was deposed by Augustus for misgovernment in A.D. 6, and died in Gaul. The eastern and northern provinces fell to Philip, who died in A.D. 34. Herod Antipas, who received Galilee and Peraea, was deposed by Caligula in A.D. 39. The Herod of Acts 12 was a grandson of Herod "the Great," and was surnamed Agrippa. He obtained from Caligula the inheritance of Philip, and also that of Antipas, to which Claudius added Judaea and Samaria, so that from A.D. 41 to 44, he ruled over the whole of Palestine. He succeeded by cunning and hypocrisy in gaining the confidence of the people. His son, Herod Agrippa II (Acts 25, 26), after doing all in his power to dissuade the Jews from making war against the Romans, took their side against his countrymen, and after Jerusalem was taken, lived chiefly at Tiberias as a Roman vassal prince till he died childless in A.D. 100.

He·ro'di·ans

A political and nonpatriotic minority, in the main a court party, which stood to the Idumaean dynasty of the Herods in Galilee much as the Sadduceean nobility stood to the Roman procurator in Judaea. They made less pretense, however, of aiming higher than at worldly prosperity. Their natural enemies were the strict Pharisees; and it is a mark of the shifts to which both parties were driven in their hatred of Jesus that they united to work His ruin. The "leaven of Herod" (Mk 8.15) was worldly wisdom.

Hez·e·ki'ah

(Heb. "Yah is my strength") The name of 4 persons in the OT, one of whom was King of Judah 715–687 B.C.

Hid'de·kel

The Hebrew name of the Tigris River.

high place, sanc'tu·ar·y

The Canaanites were worshiping their gods on high places when Abraham appeared in their country. Usually there were groves of trees associated with these hilltops and other sites. The sanctuary was a temple with an altar or an altar alone, with the altar often elevated. The Israelites were instructed by God to destroy the Canaanite high places and the groves and the altars, usually dedicated to a local god, but in this they were frequently remiss. At times the high places were simply taken over. Hezekiah was diligent in their destruction, but many of the kings were indifferent. The sanctuary won recognition only after a long period.

high priest

The chief in the priestly hierarchy. At times in Israel's history, the chief priest shared full honors with the king.

hind

See Hart.

Hin'nom

A deep valley S of Jerusalem, called variously the Valley of the Sons of Hinnom, Valley of the Children of Hinnom, Valley of Ben-Hinnom, and usually identified with the modern Wadi er-Rababi.

Hit'tites

First mentioned by Sargon of Agade about the end of the 3rd millennium, the Hittites came from N of the Taurus Mountains, and at an early date conquered part of N Syria. They made Carchemish on the Euphrates one of their capitals, and established themselves in Kadesh near Emesa. After years of war, Ramses II of Egypt made a treaty of peace with the Hittite king, probably between 1290 and 1280 B.C. Hittites had previously settled in the south of Palestine, at Hebron, and at Jerusalem. They had a number of small kingdoms, and seem to have extended over the greater part of Asia Minor as well as over N Syria. The westward conquest by the Assyrians overcame the Hittite kingdoms and their independent history ended with the capture of Carchemish by Sargon in 717 B.C. The Hittites used a peculiar hieroglyphic writing, not deciphered until after 1925. The Egyptian monuments agree with their own in representing them as short, thick-limbed, with protrusive jaw and nose, beardless face, high cheekbones, yellow skin, and black hair and eyes. Their language was of the Indo-European group.

Hi′vites
A nation in Canaan before the Israelites.

holm tree, cy′press
Sometimes identified with the evergreen holm oak; since the root of the word means "to be lean," sometimes translated "cypress."

Ho•ly Ghost′, Ho•ly Spir′it
The third person of the Trinity, through whom the entire Godhead works with man.

Hor, Mount
This may be a mountain on the border of Edom, or a mountain near Petra, now called Jebel Harun, elevation 4800 ft.

hor′net
(Heb. "depression") Hornets belong to the same order of insects as bees and wasps and are closely allied to the latter. All these insects have four wings; they wound by a sting lodged in the end of the abdomen, and inject a poisonous fluid into the wound.

horse
The horse was introduced in the Near East about the middle of the 2nd millennium B.C. Solomon brought the horse to Israel. The principal use was in warfare; the Israelites looked upon horses as a pagan luxury and a symbol of dependence on physical power rather than upon God. Nevertheless the use of the horse did increase, not only for war chariots but for transport. Israel's horses came from Egypt.

horse′leech
The horseleech (*haemopis sanguisuga*) and the medicinal leech (*hirudo medicinalis*) are both common in Palestine, as are several other kinds of leeches. The leeches abound in waters and damp places of hot countries and frequently become a regular pest, attacking men and animals alike.

Ho•se′a
(Heb. "salvation") The last of the great prophets of the Northern Kingdom.

Ho•se′a, the Book of
The first book of the twelve minor prophets in the OT. Because the times were outwardly prosperous, idolatry prevailed and immorality was rampant. Hosea urges a return to God in order that He may show mercy and forgiveness.

Ho•she′a
(Heb. "may Yah save") The name of 4 persons in the OT, one of whom was the last king of Israel.

house
(Heb. beth, common in compound names of places, as Beth-el) The nomad's house was his tent. The settled Hebrew dwelt generally in a one-story building with few and small windows, built of mud bricks or sun-dried brick, and flat-roofed. Here both the family and the animals found shelter, a raised dais separating the two. But, except in bad weather, the family spent their day either in the open field or on the roof, where they also slept.

Hur′ri•ans
The name of an ancient people referred to variously as Horites, Hivites, Jebusites.

hy•e′na
The Hebrew word has also been translated "wild beast" and "speckled bird." The hyena has been the commonest of the carnivores of Palestine.

Hyk′sos kings
The Egyptian word for "rulers of foreign countries" was applied to the 15th and 16th dynasties in the Egyptian Delta. These foreigners, sometimes called the Shepherd Kings, had entered from the NE. The last ruler of the 17th dynasty at Thebes drove the Hyksos northward, and the first of the 18th dynasty expelled them from Egypt entirely in about 1550 B.C.

hys′sop
A bushy small plant, probably orégano or Syrian marjoram. The entire plant was used as a brush to sprinkle sacrificial blood. This use of the plant seems to have followed upon its use to mark the lintels of Hebrew homes at the 1st Passover.

I

I′bex
See Pygarg.

i′bis
The ibis is found in Egypt, but not in Palestine; it may have been native to Palestine in biblical times. The translation may be erroneous; the word has also been translated "great owl."

Im•man′u•el
(Heb. "God is with us") The name of the child whose birth was prophesied by Isaiah; in the NT it becomes a prophecy of the birth of Jesus.

In′gath•er•ing, Feast of
The Feast of Harvest. *See under* Feasts.

i′ron
It is probable that smelting iron ore and working iron began with the Hittites in the middle of the 2nd millennium B.C. The Philistines may have brought it to Palestine, but they permitted no Hebrew smiths. All iron work had to be taken to the Philistines. But gradually a supply of iron was imported, and iron slag is found in the Arabah, indicating that there was some native iron industry.

I′saac
(Heb. "he laughs") The son of Abraham and Sarah and half-brother of Ishmael was born when his parents were advanced in age. By his wife Rebekah he was the father of Jacob and Esau. He died at Hebron at the age of 180.

I•sa′iah
(Heb. "Yahweh is salvation") The son of Amoz, he prophesied in the reigns of Uzziah, Jotham, Ahaz, and Hezekiah, kings of Judah. Tradition says that he survived into the reign of Manasseh and was martyred by him. He advocated the policy of the separateness of Israel, opposing the Assyrian alliance of Ahaz and equally opposing all alliances with the neighboring peo-

ples, with Egypt, or with the Babylonian-Elamitic combination against Assyria. During his life, the Assyrian and Babylonian empires were part of the time identical, the great oppressing power; and part of the time Babylon was a dangerous seducer, striving to lead the chosen people into disastrous hostilities with Assyria.

I·sa'iah, the Book of
This OT book is the first collection of prophecy of the five major Hebrew prophets. Judgment to come is fundamental to Isaiah's teaching. Israel and Judah are to perish but a remnant will survive and a new Jerusalem will rise up as a city of the faithful. It is also in Isaiah that memorable prophecies of Christ's coming are found.

Ish'ma·el
(Heb. "may God hear") The name of 6 persons in the OT, one of whom is Abraham's son, by Hagar. He is Isaac's half brother.

Ish'ma·el·ite
The wandering people of N Arabia, descendants of Ishmael, who were found in that region from the early 2nd millennium B.C. to the 7th century B.C.

Ish'tar
The Babylonian fertility goddess, Ashtoreth, in Palestine.

Is'ra·el
(Heb. "he who striveth with God," or "God striveth") The new name that Jacob received after his mysterious struggle at the Jabbok and hence the name of the whole people descended from him. The name "Hebrews" was mostly applied to them by foreigners, as was also the name "Jews," which arose at the time when Judah, after the fall of the Northern Kingdom, represented the entire people. After the separation under Jeroboam, the name Israel was confined to the kingdom of the ten tribes, also called Ephraim after the chief of these. Moral and religious degeneracy, with frequent revolutions and changes of rulers, prepared its fall (722 B.C.). The Assyrians led the best of the people into exile, from which they never returned, and the remnant left was included in the mixed people known as the Samaritans.

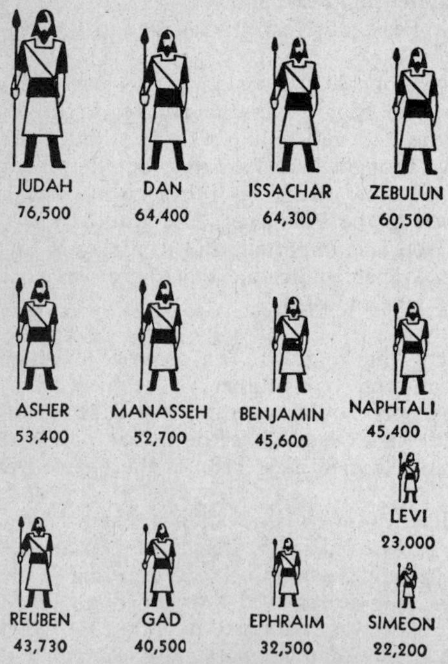

Relative size of the 12 tribes of Israel, based on the number of men of military age

It'a·ly
The peninsula in the middle of Southern Europe. The name was applied at different periods to the whole peninsula and to the southern part.

Iy'yar
A name of the 2nd month of the Hebrew year. It is also called Ziv.

J

ja'cinth, lig'ure
A variety of zircon, a reddish-orange stone.

Ja'cob
(Heb. "he overreaches") The son of Isaac and Rebekah and father of the people of Israel, he gained by craft the birthright and blessing that his father meant for his brother Esau. He fled to his uncle Laban, who treated him with cunning equal to his own. Yet he enriched himself in Laban's service and Laban's daughters, Leah and Rachel, became his wives. On his return, after a mysterious struggle in the darkness of night at the Jabbok, his name was changed to Israel and he was reconciled to Esau. His old age was made sorrowful by evil deeds of his sons, till at last he found a refuge in Egypt with his favorite, Joseph.

James
The name of 5 persons in the NT.

1. "The elder," son of Zebedee and brother of John, one of the Twelve, was martyred under Herod Agrippa.
2. James "the younger," son of Alphaeus, was also an Apostle.
3. James "the brother of the Lord" was a pillar in the church at Jerusalem and had probably been led to believe by a special appearance of our Lord to him. His judgment prevailed in the council at Jerusalem. For his piety he was called James the Just. According to Josephus, he was stoned to death by order of Ananus the high priest, between the departure of Festus and the arrival of the new procurator Albinus.
4. A son of Mary.
5. The father of Judas.

James, the Let'ter of
This NT book, according to tradition written by the brother of our Lord, provides ethical instruction for all Jewish people who have become Christians. It is clear and practical in its dealing with Christian behavior.

Ja'pho
See Joppa.

jas'per
A green chalcedony.

Jeb'u·sites
The tribe that occupied Jerusalem at the time

of the Israelitish conquest of Canaan. They seem to have been of the Amorite race.

Je•ho'a•haz
(Heb. "Yah has grasped") The name of 3 persons in the OT, one the King of Israel (815-801 B.C.) and one King of Judah (609-608 B.C.).

Je•ho'ram
See Joram.

Je•hosh'a•phat
(Heb. "Yah judges") The name of 4 persons in the OT, one of whom was King of Judah for 25 years, c. 850 B.C.

Je•ho'vah
The Hebrews did not commonly use the sacred name, in the fear that it might be profaned. The consonants of the name are four, called the tetragrammaton. To these vowels may be added, with the result that for a period of their history the spoken name was Adoni, Lord, arrived at by adding the vowels of that name to the consonants YHWH (JHVH). Misinterpretation of this eventually led to Jehovah.

Je'hu
(Heb. "he is Yah") The name of 4 persons in the OT, one of whom was King of Israel 842-815 B.C.

Jeph'thah
(Heb. "he opens") A warrior of Gilead, a judge in Israel and an illegitimate son, he was driven from home by his father's heirs. He lived the life of a freebooter in the land of Tob, east of Jordan, until the elders of the tribes summoned him to their help against the Amorites, who had oppressed them for 18 years. Returning a conquerer, he sacrificed his daughter, his only child, in fulfilment of a thoughtless vow.

Jer•e•mi'ah
(Heb. "may Yah lift up") The name of 10 persons in the OT, one of whom was Jeremiah the Prophet. Jeremiah's prophesying began in the 13th year of Josiah, 626 B.C., and covered the time following to the Exile. He was of priestly descent. His prophetic career began at an early age. In later years he was the leader of a small minority in Judah against 3 great wrongs: the religious apostasies of his people, their neglect of justice, and the false patriotism that led them to break faith by repeated revolts against Babylon. His services in this last matter were recognized by the Babylonian authorities.

Jer•e•mi'ah, the Book of
An OT account of the writing of certain of Jeremiah's prophecies, from dictation, by his friend Baruch. This seems to imply that these prophecies had been originally uttered without writing. As the roll of Baruch included "all" the prophecies for 23 years, besides "many like words," we are compelled to infer that most of the prophecies it contained were very briefly sketched. Jeremiah's mission was to testify to a doomed people, and then to witness their obduracy and their doom; but common opinion probably exaggerates the sorrowful element in the career of the "weeping prophet." It should be noticed that he prophesied concerning the return from the Exile, as well as concerning the Exile itself. It was especially his prophecies that actually led the exiles to the movement for return. Jeremiah insists especially upon the Lord's unfailing covenant with Israel and with David. He gives shape to the doctrine of a righteous "Branch" to grow up unto David. Like the other prophets, Jeremiah is a prophet not merely of rebuke and warning, but also of the Messianic promise and hope.

Jer'i•cho
An ancient city at the S end of the Jordan Valley, famous for its palms and gardens of balsam, which have now disappeared. It has been extensively excavated; carbon dating shows its oldest walls to date from 8000 to 7000 B.C.

Jer•o•bo'am
(Heb. "may the people grow numerous") The name of 2 kings of Israel, one of them Israel's 1st king, the son of Nebat, the founder of the N kingdom of Israel. He took advantage of the other tribes' envy of Judah and Jerusalem, and the general discontent with Solomon's oppressive taxation, to revolt against him. After the death of Solomon, on his son Rehoboam's blunt refusal to lighten the people's burdens, Jeroboam became the leader of the 10 northern tribes in their separation (922 B.C.). The reestablishment of the high places served to lend the political change a religious consecration. Golden calves and ox images, similar to those Aaron made in the wilderness, were set up at Dan in the north and Bethel on the southern frontier of Jeroboam's kingdom, to win the people away from the Temple at Jerusalem, where God was worshiped without images.

Jeroboam II ruled the kingdom of Israel from 786 to 746 B.C. He conquered in the N and E all the lands that had belonged to David and Solomon, and encouraged trade with the Phoenicians; but in his reign the Baal worship that Jehu had extirpated again arose, bringing with it the moral corruption in which Amos and Hosea foresaw the ruin of the king's house and of the nation.

Je•ru'sa•lem
(Heb. "foundation of Shalem") The chief city of Palestine, mentioned in Egyptian texts as early as the 19th and 18th centuries B.C., the 3rd most holy city of the Muslims and the most important to the Christians and Jews, the name of Jerusalem appears in more than 25 of the

Damascus Gate, the principal entry through the north wall of Jerusalem

Sketch of a Roman medal commemorating the capture of Jerusalem.

books of the OT and in more than a dozen books of the NT.

Flints found in excavations in the area indicate very early inhabitants, and pottery from the 4th millennium B.C. has been found at Jerusalem itself. Abraham was once and quite possibly twice at Jerusalem, then called Salem or Shalem. The Jebusites were there before Abraham had entered Palestine; David captured the city and made it his capital, and Solomon built the Temple and made the city splendid.

In the almost incessant warfare of the last 2 millennia B.C., Jerusalem was often besieged and captured. It was at various times possessed by Assyria, Egypt, Babylonia, Persia, and Greece. Nebuchadnezzar sacked and destroyed the city, and took its people into exile. When they returned, they rebuilt the Temple and much of the city, but in A.D. 70 the Romans captured Jerusalem and devastated it so thoroughly that almost nothing of the time of Jesus remained. However, a city grew again on the ruins. The Crusaders held it for a time, as did the Turks. At present, Jerusalem is divided between Jordan and the State of Israel.

Excavation has not been complete or thorough, because of the impossibility of carrying on such work in a densely populated area. Even so, a great number of the locations mentioned in the Bible have been identified and the life of Jerusalem in biblical times can be reconstructed.

Je·ru'sa·lem, the New

The principal city of God's new world that is to come, its spiritual capital, beautiful and adorned; an expression of the church of those who are of the people of God.

Jesh'u·a

See Joshua.

Je'sus

The coming of Jesus, the Christ, the Messiah, was anticipated in the OT; of His life on earth the Gospels are the source of what we know. Secular contemporary accounts are fragmentary. Calendars were not stabilized as today, and the precise date of His birth is not recorded. The earliest Church did not concern itself with the facts of His physical life on earth. He was Jesus, the man, and Christ, the Anointed One, a person of the Triune God. But by the 5th century the Church had concerned itself sufficiently to have set December 25 as the date of His birth. This had been the date of the festival of the sun god Mithra, and to the Christians a greater light was come, Jesus Christ, the true Light of the World.

Jesus was born in Bethlehem to Mary, the betrothed wife of Joseph, a carpenter. The genealogy is traced in the Gospels to David and to Abraham. The Gospels further tell of the flight of the family to Egypt to avoid the slaughter of the Innocents by Herod the King, but say little of His early boyhood. The family lived the life of consecrated and pious Jews; Jesus must have had careful education and training, for at age 12 he talked on fully equal terms with the rabbis in the Temple.

Then follows another unrecorded period in His life. When a man of about 30 He was baptized by John the Baptist, who testified that this Jesus was the Son of God. After a great temptation to which He did not yield, He began His ministry, first calling His disciples. He was known by His works throughout Galilee and in adjacent areas, and attracted many followers, Jews and Greeks. But He disturbed many. He was arrested, tried, and crucified. There followed the Resurrection, the triumph over death. *See also* Christ.

Jew

The Bible provides definitions: 1. The members of the State of Judah (Neh 1.2; Jer 32.12; 40.11).

2. The post-exilic people of Israel in contrast to the Gentiles (Esther 9.15-19; Dan 3.8; Zech 8.23; John 4.9; Acts 14.1).

3. The adherents of worship of Yahweh as done at Jerusalem after the Exile (Esther 3.4-6; Dan 3.8). In contrast to Gentiles, Samaritans, proselytes (John 2.6, 4.9, 22; Acts 2.10, 14.1). The term is now highly fluid. It covers religion and birth, religion only, or birth only.

Jewish history between the Testaments

The whole period falls into four epochs.

1. *Persian Period* (537-330 B.C.). Nehemiah (444 B.C.) had been a favorite at the court to which, 90 years before, the Jews had owed their return from Exile; and, on the whole, the restored remnant remained loyal to the "great king," in spite of the tribute and other galling features of their subjection. Many Jews, however, were removed to Babylonia and elsewhere by Artaxerxes Ochus, about 350 B.C., for taking part in a revolt. To the last century of Persian rule belong the final breach between the Jews and the Samaritans, the gradual replacement among the Jews of Hebrew by the widespread Aramaic dialect, and the beginning of the recovery of Galilee to the faith of Jehovah.

2. *Greek Period* (330-167 B.C.). Alexander the Great, who ushers in this period, besides granting special privileges to Jerusalem, bestowed marks of favor upon the Jews settled by him in his new city, Alexandria. It was here that Judaism entered into its most intimate relations with the Greek world of thought and literature. On Alexander's death (323 B.C.) his conquests passed into the hands of his generals and, during the struggles that ensued, Palestine shared in the confusion, until the battle of Ipsus (301

B.C.) made the kings of Egypt (the Ptolemies) its overlords for a full century, in spite of several attempts on the part of the rival kings of Syria (the Seleucids) to overthrow them. The new sovereign power was both stronger and juster than the Persian; and under it the government at Jerusalem in the hands of the high-priestly dynasty, assisted by a sort of senate including the higher ranks of the priesthood, grew and consolidated. Outside Palestine, too, the Jews waxed influential, not only in Alexandria, but also in Libya, Cyrene, Asia Minor, and all parts of Syria, where they settled either by the compulsion or favor of Ptolemies and Seleucids. From the other side also foreign intercourse was fostered by Greek settlements in Northern Palestine, especially about the Sea of Galilee.

The most momentous outcome of all this was the Greek version of the Hebrew Scriptures, called the Septuagint, which did much to break down Jewish isolation, and fixed the type of language in which the NT is written. The influence of Hellenic culture was at work in both the life and the literature of the Jews during the Ptolemaic supremacy (320-198 B.C.), but its effects became clearer after 198 B.C., when Antiochus the Great brought Judea under Seleucid or Syrian sway.

The priestly nobility grew more worldly in spirit as Hellenism advanced. The high-priesthood became an object of base intrigue. Under Antiochus Epiphanes it became the fashion among the upper classes to turn their names into Greek forms, e.g., Menelaus for Menahem, and in other ways to obscure their Jewish origin. At length the folly of Antiochus and his high-priestly tools led to a violent crisis and revolt.

3. *Maccabean or Asmonaean Period* (167-63 B.C.). The outrages upon the national religion which stung the Maccabees into revolt stirred the people to realize the value of their distinctive faith. From their ranks had arisen a party called the Chasidim, distinguished for piety. The Maccabean movement carried these with it, and became a rally of the whole nation to the faith of its fathers. By the wars of liberation from the yoke of Syria the religious end was attained. The Temple was restored and solemnly rededicated (165 B.C.), the rival temple on Mount Gerizim razed along with the Samaritan capital itself (129 B.C.), and the Maccabean leader recognized as "Governor and High Priest for ever, until there should arise a faithful prophet."

But the mass of the nation was now possessed by the spirit of foreign aggression; and against this the successors of the quiet Chasidim, whose expectation was from God and not from human agency, constantly protested. "The idea of Judaism" was in danger in the eyes of this growing party of religious protest, which in the last years of Hyrcanus (135-106 B.C.) became known as Pharisees (Perushim, or "Separatists"). These men, whose stronghold was among the Scribes or professed students of the Law, by degrees gained the ear of the people. They indeed suffered a severe check under Alexander Jannaeus (105-78 B.C.), in whose favor a revulsion of popular feeling took place. But the lost ground was more than made up under his widow Salome (78-69 B.C.), who separated the secular and sacred headship (her son Hyrcanus II was high-priest). About this time the Sanhedrin came more under the influence of the Scribes than heretofore; and so it remained henceforth. On the death of Salome, internal dissensions, centering round Hyrcanus and his brother Aristobulus, gave the Romans their chance. Under Pompey they occupied Jerusalem, abolished the kingship, and restored the high-priestly dignity to Hyrcanus.

4. *Roman Period*. While the Pharisees gained by the change, which robbed the Sadducees of political power, it sharpened the contrast between the Pharisaic ideal and the popular hope of the restoration of the kingdom. It was especially galling when Antipater, of the hated Idumaean race, became the real power in the state under Rome till his death in 43 B.C., and when in 37 B.C. his son Herod the Great became by Rome's aid king of Judea.

"By birth an Idumaean, by profession a Jew, by necessity a Roman, by culture and by choice a Greek," this unscrupulous monarch maintained himself only by inspiring fear. He filled the chief offices with obscure men of priestly descent from Babylon and Alexandria and abolished the life tenure of the high-priesthood. He tried to overcome the national feeling against him by diverting attention to a great national object, the building of a new Temple, begun in 18 B.C. His death in 4 B.C. was the signal for an insurrection, which the Romans sternly repressed, handing over the country to 3 sons of Herod. Of these, Philip had the land east of Jordan; Antipas, Galilee and Perea; Archelaus, Judea and Samaria. After A.D. 6, Archelaus' kingdom passed under the direct rule of Rome, Pontius Pilate being procurator from A.D. 26 to 36.

Jo'ab

(Heb. "Yah is father") The name of 3 persons in the OT, one of whom was commander of David's army.

Jo'ash, Je·ho'ash

(Heb. "Yah gives") The name of 8 persons in the OT, one of whom was king of Judah (837-800 B.C.).

Job

1. The author of the Book of Job; unknown otherwise.

2. The name of the third son of Issachar, Iob, is sometimes written Job.

Job, the Book of

The first of the OT poetical books deals with the problem of suffering. God allows Satan to afflict Job, a prosperous and pious Jew, with many hardships in order to test his faith. Job loses his children and his worldly goods, and is afflicted by a terrible disease. Finally when God questions Job, he is forced to admit to the limits of human wisdom, and bows humbly before the will of God. With this new humility his faith is strengthened and Job finds peace.

Jo'el

(Heb. "Yah is God") The name of 13 persons in the OT, one of whom is the author of the Book of Joel. Nothing is known of him.

Jo'el, the Book of

This OT prophetical book was written during a locust plague, a time of great distress for the people. The prophet sees in the devastation of the locusts an indication of the coming day of the Lord. Therefore all must repent with fasting and mourning. With repentance, however, there is a promise for relief and God's blessing for Israel.

John

The name of 5 persons in the NT; one is John the Baptist, another John the Apostle.

John the A•pos'tle

A son of Zebedee and brother of James, a fisherman, he has been called the Beloved Disciple. At the time of the Crucifixion, Jesus committed His mother to John's care. There is tradition that he was banished to Patmos, and that he was bishop at Ephesus for many years. He is considered the author of the Fourth Gospel, the Letters of John, and the book of Revelation.

John the Bap'tist

The son of Elizabeth, who was related to Mary, the Mother of Jesus, a prophet and descended from priests. He has been called the forerunner of Jesus, and was heeded by many for his own message of the need for repentance. He was arrested by Herod and beheaded in prison.

John Mark

See Mark.

John, the Gos'pel according to

The Fourth Gospel, written by "the disciple whom Jesus loved," tells us who Jesus was and what He is; what He can always mean to those who love Him. This Gospel contains more than the other Gospels about the stories of Lazarus and Nicodemus and Jesus' trial, crucifixion, and resurrection, and about the disciples Andrew, Philip, and Thomas.

John, the Let'ters of

These three NT epistles, traditionally assigned to the writer of the Fourth Gospel and Revelation, testify that God is love and that love is the test of religion. *Second John* is written to "the elect lady and her children," probably a church; *Third John* is addressed "to the beloved Gaius."

Jo'nah, Jo'nas

(Heb. "dove") The name of 2 persons in the OT, one of whom is the central figure of the Book of Jonah.

Jo'nah, the Book of

This OT book is the story of a prophet sent by God to Nineveh. Jonah was fearful of the call and tried to flee by sea to Tarshish. During the sea voyage he was thrown overboard by his fellow passengers and swallowed by a great fish sent by God. The prophet was saved and went on to Nineveh to successfully convert the people of that city.

Jon'a•than

(Heb. "Yah has given") The name of 15 persons in the OT, one of whom was the eldest son of Saul and David's friend. To David he gave his own robe and armor. He was a man of great strength and courage. He fell, with his father and 2 brothers, at the battle of Gilboa, leaving a son 5 years old, Meribbaal or Mephibosheth. He was lamented by David in the elegy called the Song of the Bow (2 Sam. 1.17-27).

Jop'pa, Ja'pho

(Heb. "beautiful") At this seaport for Jerusalem little excavation has been possible, because the site is a rock hill on which one city after another has been built. It first appears as a city in about 1500 B.C. when it was captured by Egyptians. Rafts of cedar logs for the Temple were floated to Joppa from Lebanon. Now it has become a part of the city of Tel Aviv.

Jo'ram, Je•ho'ram

(Heb. "Yah is high") The name of 5 persons in the OT, one of whom, Jehoram, was king of Judah (849-842 B.C.).

Jor'dan

The chief river of Palestine, flowing S for 100 miles through a deep valley. Its 3 sources are at the foot of Hermon. In its course are 2 lakes, Lake Huleh and the Sea of Galilee. From the Sea of Galilee to the Dead Sea the Jordan Valley (Ghor) is 65 mi. falling from 682 to 1292 ft. below sea level. The average width of the river is not more than 30 yds., and it varies in depth from 3 ft. at the fords to 7, 8, and 10 ft. The current is very rapid. The river was miraculously crossed by the Israelites and by Elijah and Elisha. In its waters Jesus was baptized by John the Baptist.

Jo'sech

See Joseph.

Jo'seph, Jo'se•phus, Jo'sech, Jo'ses

(Heb. "may Yah add") The name of 14 persons in the Bible. Included are Joseph the son of Jacob, Joseph the husband of Mary the mother of Jesus, and Joseph of Arimathea.

1. *Joseph, husband of Mary.* A carpenter, resident of Nazareth, descended from David. It is presumed that he died in Jesus' youth because there is little mention of him after Jesus was 12.

2. *Joseph, the son of Jacob and Rachel.* He was father of Ephraim and Manasseh, and thus ancestor of the people of the Northern Kingdom. Sold into Egypt by his brothers, he was imprisoned on a false accusation by his master's wife. (A similar incident occurs in a story, written in the time of Ramses II, preserved in a papyrus now in the British Museum.) Yet his skill in interpreting dreams brought him Pharaoh's favor and the first place next to the throne. Gen 42–47 relates how, during a famine, his father and brothers came to settle in Goshen.

3. *Joseph of Arimathea.* A member of the Sanhedrin. He buried the body of Jesus in a tomb on his own property.

Josh'u•a, Jesh'u•a
(Heb. "Yah is salvation") The name of 11 persons in the OT, one of whom is Joshua, son of Nun. Of the tribe of Ephraim, he led the people into the Promised Land. He died at age 110.

Josh'u•a, the Book of
This OT book tells the story of Moses' successor as leader of the Israelites, Joshua, son of Nun, and narrates the conquest of Canaan and the division of the country among the twelve tribes of Israel.

Jo•si'ah
(Heb. "let Yah give") The son of Amon, king of Judah from 639 to 608 B.C. In the 18th year of his reign the Book of the Law was discovered and thereafter the high places throughout the country were suppressed. He was defeated and slain by Pharaoh-Neco at Megiddo. Under his sons Jehoahaz (609), Jehoiachim (608-598) and Zedekiah (597-586) the kingdom of Judah was by turns under Egyptian and Babylonian domination, till its extinction in 586 B.C.

jot
A transliteration of iota, the name of the smallest letter in the Greek alphabet; used metaphorically for the smallest thing.

Jo'tham
(Heb. "may Yah complete") The name of 3 persons in the OT, one of whom was king of Judah 742-735 B.C.

Ju'bi•lee
The final year in a cycle of 50 years.

Ju•dae'a, Ju'dah
See Judea.

Ju'da•iz•ers
A name given to those among the early Jewish Christians who could not believe that all that had once been conveyed to man through the Law was now made available in far greater fullness in the Gospel. Thus they insisted on circumcision as giving a man the right to believe on Jesus as Israel's Savior. The Judaizers were a dwindling body among Palestinian Christians, and they have left no real record of themselves in the New Testament. When they appear in history later on, it is under the title of Ebionites, representing, as their predecessors had done, the "poor" (Heb. *ebion*) and oppressed classes in Jewish society.

Ju'das
The name of 6 persons in the NT, one of whom was Judas Iscariot, the betrayer of Jesus.

Ju'das Mac•ca•be'us
See Maccabees.

Jude, the Let'ter of
This NT epistle designates its author as "a servant of Jesus Christ and brother of James." Its message was for Christians wherever unity was threatened by heretical teaching and where Christian doctrinal and moral standards were questioned.

Ju•de'a, Ju'dah, Ju•dae'a
The land of the Jews, a name applied sometimes to the whole land of Palestine, sometimes to the S division only. It was used in the wider sense at the close of the Captivity, most of those who returned having belonged to the ancient kingdom of Judah. Under the Romans, and in the time of Christ, the name was restricted to the S division; the N being Galilee, and the middle, Samaria; but even then it sometimes denoted the whole country. In its limited sense, it formed part of the kingdom of Herod the Great, and included part of Idumaea, or the land of Edom. As a Roman province, it was annexed to the proconsulate of Syria, and was governed by a procurator. "The wilderness of Judea," in which John began his preaching, and where the temptation of Christ took place, was the E part of Judah, near the Dead Sea, and stretching toward Jericho. It was, and is still, a dreary and desolate region.

Judg'es, the Book of
This OT book is so called because it relates of the times of various rulers, or judges, of Israel from the possession of Canaan until the time of Samuel. Also found in Judges is the recounting of the adventures of Samson.

Ju'dith
1. This Apocryphal book is a story that was originally in Hebrew, but is not now extant in that language. It relates that when Nebuchadnezzar's general, Holofernes, was besieging the Jewish fortress of Bethulia, the besieged were rescued from their peril by the self-sacrifice of Judith, a Jewish woman, who surrendered herself to the camp of Holofernes, and by a stratagem succeeded in cutting off Holofernes' head. The story was probably written to inflame patriotic feeling at the time of some invasion.

2. Esau had a foreign wife named Judith.

ju'ni•per, heath
An almost leafless broom found in the Jordan Valley and the wilderness of Sinai. The Lebanon juniper is a timber-producing tree.

K

Ka'desh, Ka•desh-bar'ne•a, Mer•i•bah-ka'desh
Ancient Canaanite cities with the name Kadesh were sanctuaries. Two of them have been identified.

Kad'mon•ites
(Heb. "easterners") The people inhabiting the Syro-Arabian Desert between Palestine and the Euphrates.

Ke'nites
(Heb. "belonging to the smiths") A gypsylike nomadic or seminomadic tribe. As early as 1300 B.C., they were doing metal work in the areas they roamed over. They lost their identity shortly after 1000 B.C.

Ke'ri•oth
(Heb. "cities") The name of 2 cities in the OT. One of them, Kerioth-Hezron, has been identified with Khirbet el-Qaryatein.

Kid'ron, Ce'dron
A valley E of Jerusalem, through which an intermittent brook still flows. At one time the

waters of a spring, Gihon, were allowed to flow through this valley. The stream was often used for irrigation.

Kings, First and Sec'ond
The two OT books follow the monarchy to its summit under Solomon and the nation's division, decline, and fall under Jeroboam and Rehoboam. Kings also gives an outline of the double captivity of Israel under the Assyrians and Judah under the Chaldeans.

Kir
(Heb. "wall") The name of 2 places in the OT, one of which is identified as Kerak, 11 mi. E of the Dead Sea, 17 mi. S of the Arnon.

Kir·i·ath-se'pher, Kir·jath-se'pher
(Heb. "city of the Scribe") An older name for Debir, the modern Tell Beit Mirsin, which has been partially excavated. It is possible that Abraham visited here.

Ki'shon, Ki'son
A river draining the Valley of Jezreel and the Plain of Acco, and emptying into the Mediterranean.

Kit'tim
See Chittim.

L

Lam·en·ta'tions
This OT book consists of five poems occasioned by the fall of Jerusalem and the Babylonian captivity. The first three elegies describe the terrible plight of the nation, the fourth compares the past history of Zion with her present state, and the last is a prayer for compassion and deliverance.

lamp'stand
See candlestick.

Ancient lamps used in the Near East.

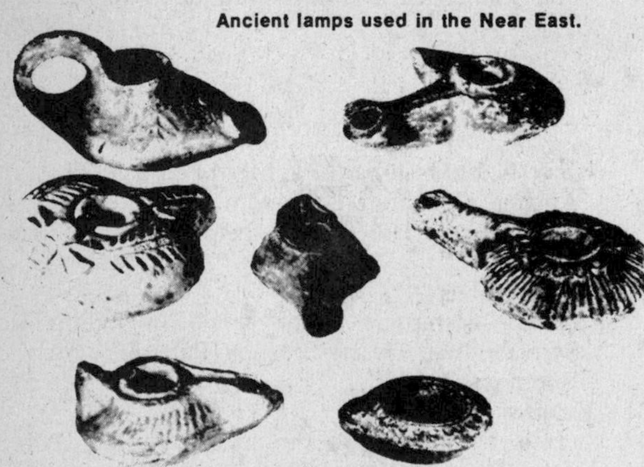

La·od·i·ce'a
A city on the Lycus River in Phrygia, one of the richest in Asia. It struck its own coins, traded wisely, and was an early Christian center. When destroyed by an earthquake in A.D. 60, it was affluent enough to arrange its own reconstruction.

lap'is laz'u·li, sap'phire
Both are blue stones, lapis being semiprecious and sometimes substituted for sapphire. *See* Sapphire.

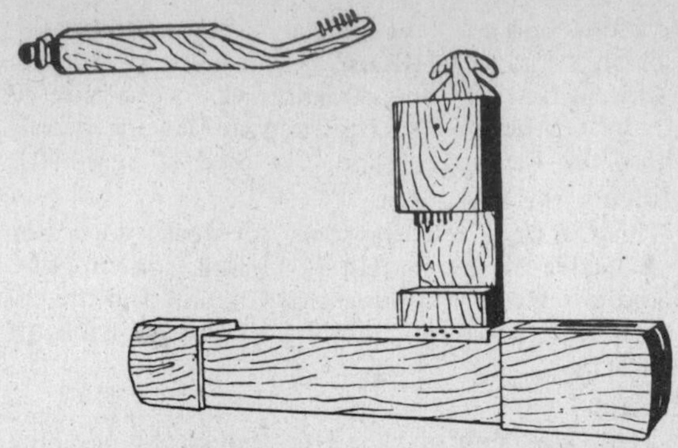

Ancient wooden lock, showing the bolt with its pins, and also the lift key to release it

la'ver
A vessel used in ceremonial rites of purification in the tabernacles and temples, and particularly in Solomon's Temple at Jerusalem. The concept is carried over to the container for the water of baptism.

law, the
The earliest collection of laws so far discovered is that of Ur, earlier than 2000 B.C. Several almost equally early codes have been found, including the code of Hammurabi. All these show evidence of being much earlier in actuality than the incised inscriptions found and translated. What has been called the law of Moses, found in the Pentateuch, may also be much earlier than its actual date of transcription. It is instruction and direction for moral, judicial, and ceremonial conduct, called the Torah by the Jewish people. The code of the Pentateuch is more humane in its judicial sections than other early codes, and much finer in its moral sections. In NT times Jesus recognized and accepted the divine origin and authority of these phases of the law. Though discussion of their extension and interpretation still continues, they are the basis of much of the code of the civilized world today. *See* Torah.

law'yers, scribes
Those skilled in the interpretation of the laws set down by Moses. *See* Scribes.

Laz'a·rus
1. Lazarus, the beggar in the parable of the beggar and the rich man, was taken to Abraham's bosom when he died. But the rich man was in torment after death and he wanted his brothers to be warned of what might befall them. He was denied.

2. Lazarus of Bethany, brother of Mary and Martha, was raised to life after being four days dead. This may have been a major factor in the decision to kill Jesus: their inability to explain the raising of Lazarus was infuriating to the high priests and the Pharisees.

lead
The metal was imported into Palestine, apparently from Tyre. There are, however, mines in the Lebanon, as well as in Sinai and parts of Egypt.

Leb'a·non
(Heb. "white") A mountain range to the N of Palestine, with summits of more than 11,000 ft. For a part of the year they are snow-capped.

leeks
These are included with onions and garlic as among the good things of Egypt for which the Israelites lusted in the wilderness.

len'tils
A legume used for food; a member of the pea family.

leop'ard
A large carnivorous animal found in Palestine as late as the 20th century. The Cheetah, a hunting leopard, was also widely familiar and is found in ancient sculptures.

lep'ro·sy
The Hebrew name means "a stroke," the disease being regarded as the sorest affliction by the hand of God. Its description is given in Lev 13, 14, along with the regulations connected with it. The "botch of Egypt" was probably elephantiasis, which, it is generally agreed, was the disease that afflicted Job, and which is quite distinct from leprosy. Lepers were required to live outside the camp or city and to warn passersby with cries of "Unclean! Unclean!"

le·vi'a·than
(Heb. "coiled one") The primeval dragon, and by extension a sea monster; the crocodile. *See* Whale.

Le'vites
The persons charged with the care of the Tabernacle and the Temple. They embraced all the men of the tribe of Levi, exclusive of the sons of Aaron, though the latter were also Levites and could perform any Levitical service. They were set apart for this service on behalf of the children of Israel. On the settlement of Canaan they were assigned to 48 cities, scattered over the whole country, and were provided with fields for the pasture of their cattle. In David's reign they were divided into 4 classes: (1) Assistants of the priests in the work of the sanctuary; (2) Judges and Scribes; (3) Gate-keepers; (4) Musicians. Each of these classes, with the possible exception of the 2nd, was subdivided into 24 courses, or families, to serve in rotation.

Le·vit'i·cus, the Book of
This 3rd book of the OT can also be called "The Book of the Law of the Priests" as it contains very little historical matter, concerning itself with priestly legislation and the practice of the law among the people. In Leviticus much importance is placed upon Israel's separation from all heathen influences so that the nation may retain its religious purity.

Lib'er·tines, freed'men
(Lat. "freedmen") These were probably descendants of Jews who had been taken to Rome or elsewhere by Pompey as prisoners of war, and had afterward received their freedom there. They did not speak Aramaic, then the language of Jerusalem, and separate synagogues for them were established.

lice
Lice were sent upon the Egyptians as the third plague.

lign·al'oe, al'oes
Lignum aloes, or wood of aloes. *See* aloes.

lig'ure, ja'cinth
This is the gem generally called in Greek lyncurion, from a singular notion as to its origin, which is identified with the true jacinth.

lil'y
This may have meant the scarlet martegon lily or the scarlet anemone, or have been used poetically for the lion; a beautiful flower.

li'on
Mentioned in the OT about 130 times, the animal was well known throughout W Asia as late as 500 B.C. The lion, Judah's emblem, was in all lands the symbol of royal power and strength. It was taken by pitfalls in its tracks, or by nets.

liz'ard
(Heb. "clinger"?) A reptile with scaly body, long tail, and usually 4 legs. A number of species occur in Palestine, including geckoes, skinks, and chameleons, and larger spiny lizards.

lo'custs
These insects are often referred to, and under 9 different names:

1. *Arbeh,* generally and rightly translated "locust." The record of the 8th plague in Egypt gives a true account of a typical severe invasion of locusts; an E wind brought them from the other side of the isthmus of Suez, and a W wind hurled them back into the Red Sea, where they perished. They are placed among the clean creatures.

2. *Sal'am,* occurring once only, and translated "bald locust." The word seems to have the same root as *selu,* which means rock; hence we may think of certain species of grasshoppers, which delight in basking on sun-exposed rocks, and translate the word "rock locust."

3. *Chargol.* In the vernacular, these are called katydids or long-horned grasshoppers.

4. *Chagab,* generally used for and translated "grasshoppers," many of which are much smaller than locusts.

5. *Gazam,* translated "palmerworm," is interpreted either as the locust in its larval stage or as the larva of butterflies or moths. "Palmerworm" should not apply to locusts.

6. *Yelek,* very difficult to interpret, the more so since there is no evidence that the different authors meant the same creature. It is translated "cankerworm" and caterpillar." Etymologically, the word means a creature that licks up the grass. It is evidently intended to express some insect pest.

7. *Tzelatzal.* The word *tzelatzal* means a tinkling, musical instrument, and is hence applied to a creature able to produce musical sounds. Thus the author may have used it as the name of one of the grasshoppers, the chirping notes of which are frequently loud enough to be heard at some distance, or for the well-

known cicada, which is found in abundance all around the Mediterranean.

8. *Gob* appears several times, and is translated "grasshoppers"; it cannot be referred to any particular kind.

9. *Chasil,* generally mentioned together with the locust, and therefore believed to signify the locust in its larval stage. But in some versions it is translated "caterpillar." *See* grasshopper.

Egyptian locust

Lord's Prayer

The model prayer which our Lord taught His disciples. According to the text of Luke it consists of 5 petitions, according to that of Matthew of 6 (or 7). The Reformed churches count 6; 3 with "Thy," and 3 with "our"; the Roman Catholics and Lutherans 7, regarding "Lead us not into temptation" and "Deliver us from evil" as separate petitions. The concluding doxology (occurring only in Matthew, and omitted in some versions), is wanting in the best MSS., and is a later addition, based on 1 Chron 29.11, and 2 Tim 4.18. It accords with the first 3 petitions.

Lord's Sup′per

(Cor 11.20), called also "breaking of bread" (Acts 2.42), "cup of blessing," "communion of the blood of Christ," and "of the body of Christ" (1 Cor 10.16), and "the Lord's table" (10.21). It is a holy ordinance, which Christ initiated as the last meal (the Passover) with His disciples, on the night before His death, and appointed to be observed in remembrance of Him. In it, by the giving and receiving of bread and wine, Christ's death is showed forth "till He come." As the Passover commemorated Israel's deliverance from the "house of bondage," and election to be a covenant-people, the Lord's Supper marks the establishment of a new covenant in His blood, His death being the foundation of a new relation of His church to God, and of the communion of His people with one another.

Lot

The nephew of Abraham, who came with Abraham to Canaan. The story of Lot is found in Gen 11.27–14.29; 19.

love ap′ple

The mandrake, a perennial herb, related to the poisonous nightshade. It is superstitiously considered an aphrodisiac.

Lu′ci•fer, day star

(Lat. "light bringer") The day star was a name applied by the prophet to the king of Babylon in his pride and splendor and glory before his fall, when he said, "I will ascend into heaven, I will exalt my throne above the stars of God" (Is 14.12-13).

Luke

A Gentile, a physician, an educated man, familiar with the E Mediterranean and adjacent countries, who in Acts appears as the companion of Paul from Troas to Philippi, where he probably remained from A.D. 52 to 58, rejoining the Apostle at that place, and continuing with him to the time when the narration closes (A.D. 58-63). In 2 Tim. 4.11 he is referred to as being with Paul. Hence the evangelist must have been in Palestine during the 2 years of Paul's imprisonment at Caesarea (A.D. 58-60).

Luke, the Gos′pel according to

This NT book, the 3rd Gospel, was written by "The beloved physician," the companion of the apostle Paul. Only in Luke are found the Magnificat, the story of the birth of John the Baptist, the Christmas story of the shepherds, the parables of the good Samaritan, the lost sheep, and the prodigal son, and the great hymns—the *Gloria in Excelsis* and *Nunc Dimittis.* Jesus is presented as the compassionate Savior, healer, redeemer, and friend of the weak. From this Gospel comes a special feeling of the mercy of God as Jesus made men understand it.

lute

An instrument resembling the harp and the cithern; examples have been found of the period of 1500 B.C.

LXX

See Septuagint.

lye

See Nitre.

lyre

An early stringed instrument found in Egyptian and Assyrian relief, the "harp" played by David. Played especially in the Temple by the Levites.

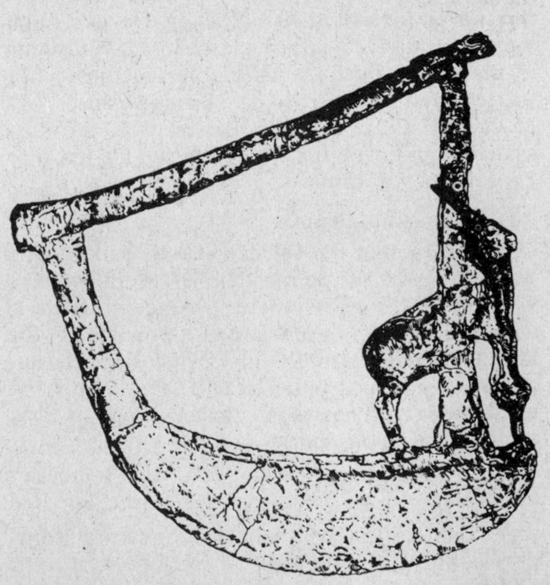

Lyre frame of silver, from Ur, dated previous to the time of Abraham

M

Mac'ca·bees
The family of priestly descent that freed the Jewish people from the Syrian yoke. The name Makkaba ("hammer") belongs properly to Judas, the third of the five sons of Mattathias, who from his father's death in 166 B.C. to his own death at the battle of Elasa or Adasa in 161 led the defenders of their country and faith in one of the most heroic struggles in history. His work was completed by his brothers, who founded the Asmonaean Dynasty. The Maccabees are included among the heroes of faith in Heb 11.

Mac·e·do'ni·a
In NT times, the northern Roman province of Greece, the southern being Achaia. Paul was summoned thither by the vision of the "man of Macedonia" and he visited it a 2nd time. Philippi was one of its chief cities, and there Lydia was converted.

Ma'gi
In the NT, the wise men from the East who came to worship the infant Christ. The name Magos is also given to Elymas in Acts 13.6, 8, and is there translated "sorcerer"; and to Simon who "used sorcery" (Acts 8.9).

Mal'a·chi
(Heb. "My messenger") An OT prophet.

Mal'a·chi, the Book of
The last book of the OT belongs to the period of Nehemiah. The prophet's message is to the priests and the people, charging them with indifference, doubt, and immorality. Malachi tells of the coming day of the Lord and closes the book with a prophecy of John the Baptist.

mal'low
Probably the shrubby orache, eaten only when nothing else is available.

Ma·nas'seh
(Heb. "one who causes to forget") The name of 2 persons in the OT, one the eldest son of Joseph and ancestor of one of the 12 tribes; the other was Judah's king (687-642 B.C.).

Ma·nas'seh, Prayer of
It is mentioned in the statement by the Chronicler, 2 Chron 33.18, 19. The extant Prayer of Manasseh found in the Apocrypha is a noble monument of devotion. The early Christian church placed it as one of the 9 canticles at the head of the Psalter.

man'drake
See Love apple.

man'na
(Heb. "What is that?") The food supplied to the Israelites in the wilderness. Studies in the Sinai region indicate that it is the honeydew secretion of two scale insects on the tamarisk bushes abundant there, very sweet and high in carbohydrates.

mar'ble
The name is properly applied to a completely crystalline limestone, such as is used for statuary, but is commonly extended to any ornamental limestone that can be polished. In Palestine, probably the latter was meant.

Mar'che·wan
A name of the 8th month of the Hebrew year. It is also called Bul.

Mark, John Mark
He was the son of Mary, at whose house in Jerusalem the early Christians seem to have found a home. He was a cousin of Barnabas, and the attendant of the 2 Christian preachers in Paul's first missionary journey. But he became the occasion of sharp contention between Paul and Barnabas in consequence of his leaving them at Perga. Afterward, however, he was with the Apostle Paul during his first imprisonment at Rome. The Apostle Peter refers to Mark as with him when he wrote his 1st epistle, probably at Babylon. Evidently the evangelist made a journey to the E about A.D. 63, and he was at Ephesus with Timothy shortly before the death of Paul. Reliable details of his later life are wanting. He is spoken of as the interpreter of Peter, and, according to tradition, was the founder of the church at Alexandria. His Gospel may have been written at Rome, between A.D. 63 and 66.

Mark, the Gos'pel according to
The earliest of the Gospels, this NT book contains much of the teaching of Peter. This Gospel presents Jesus as the man of power, the strong and active Son of God; its climax is reached when Peter makes his great confession, "You are the Christ."

Ma'ry
The name of 7 persons in the NT, one of them the mother of Jesus. Another Mary was the sister of Lazarus; a third is the mother of James the Younger; and a fourth, Mary Magdalene.

Mas'o·retes
Down to the close of the 5th century A.D., the tradition of the accepted pronunciation of the bare consonantal text of the OT was kept alive by the oral teaching of the Rabbis and by the recitation of the Scriptures in the synagogues. The reduction to writing of this exegetical tradition was the work of the scholars called the Masoretes, (from Masora, "tradition"), whose chief center was the Rabbinical school of Tiberias. They took great pains that the texts should be kept entire, for this purpose counting up the number of words, and even the number of letters in the different books, noting expressions that occurred but once or rarely, drawing attention to peculiar modes of writing, and the like. One great service rendered by the Masoretes was their devising a system of dots and strokes (vowel points), which are placed above, below, or in the heart of the consonants, and denote precisely how the words were read by the scholars of the time. These are regarded as forming no part of the sacred text, and the Pentateuch rolls used in the Synagogue are written in the bare consonants as originally received. Closely connected with the vowel system is the system of accents, which indicate the manner in which the words and clauses were

separated or conjoined, and also form a kind of musical notation, according to which the Scriptures are to be melodiously recited. The text, with this array of symbols, is called the Masoretic text; and it gives us what was the traditional reading at the time the work was accomplished.

The Masoretic text, with its complete equipment, cannot be placed earlier than the 7th century of the Christian era. But it gives us a tradition reaching back to a much earlier time; and it is a cause of thankfulness that, in the handing down of the text, the Masoretes did not allow themselves to deviate in the smallest details from what they had received. There remain in the text, as they have handed it down, evident indications of what had been slips of the pen or mistakes of the eye of the transcribers, but the Masoretes allowed even these to stand, contenting themselves with drawing attention to their presence.

mas•se′ba
A sacred pillar.

Mat′thew
(Heb. "gift of Yah") Also called "Levi the son of Alphaeus." When called to become a disciple he was a publican, or tax gatherer, probably a collector of tolls and custom duties at the Sea of Galilee. His call is narrated in the 3 Gospels, but while he refers to the feast that Mark and Luke distinctly place at his house, he makes no allusion to that fact. Papias and Irenaeus, writing in the 2nd century, state that Matthew wrote in Hebrew (Aramaic). The earliest citations, some of them in works of the earlier half of the 2nd century, give the exact words of the Greek Gospel we now have, and no certain traces of a previous Aramaic Gospel have been discovered. If there was an Aramaic original, it was superseded very soon by a Greek version. The very early date often assigned (A.D. 45) may be correct if applied to an Aramaic original; but the Greek Gospel we have may have been written about A.D. 60.

Mat′thew, the Gos′pel according to
This first NT book has been pre-eminently the Gospel of the church. It tells us of God's love for Israel and of the fulfillment in Christ of God's promise to the nation. It gives the complete story of Jesus' ministry, death, and resurrection. The Sermon on the Mount, and some of the most precious of Jesus' parables are contained in this Gospel.

meals
In Palestine there were two meals, one late in the morning and the other, the chief one, in the evening.

meas′ures
Bath (liquid) = 5½ gallons.
Cor (liquid or dry) = 10 baths (liquid) = 55 gals. (dry).
Cubit (length) = 21.8 inches English (or 20.24 inches for the ordinary cubit).
Ephah (dry) = ½ bushel.
Hin (liquid) = 4 quarts.
Homer (dry) = 5.16 bushels.
Kab (dry) = 1.16 quarts.
Log (liquid or dry) = 0.67 pint.
Omer (dry) = 2.09 quarts.
Seah (dry) = ⅔ peck.

Medes
An Aryan or Indo-European people who inhabitated the country to the SW of the Caspian, whence they extended S to the Persian Gulf. One of the offshoots was the tribe of Persians. Called also Madai.

Me•gid′do, Me•gid′don, Ar•ma•ged′don
A Canaanite and later Israelite city identified as the modern Tell el-Mutesellim, overlooking the Plain of Esdraelon, 20 mi. SSE of Haifa. As an inhabited area it has a history of more than 3500 years. Both Egyptians and people from the E destroyed it. Thut-mose III of Egypt about 1450 B.C., Tiglath-pileser III the Assyrian in 733 B.C., and Neco of Egypt in 609 B.C. destroyed it completely. During its long history it has been a walled city, a royal chariot city, a city of great splendor, the site of many battles. It is believed to be the place of Armageddon, the final struggle. *See* Armageddon.

Mel•chiz′e•dek
(trad. "King of righteousness") A worshiper of the Supreme God, to whom, as priest and king of Salem or Jerusalem, Abraham gave tithes. In Heb 7 he is shown to be a type of Christ.

mel′on
A fruit known to them in Egypt for which the Israelites longed when in the wilderness. Both muskmelons and watermelons are common in Egypt.

Mer•i•bah-ka′desh
See Kadesh.

Mer′o•dach-bal′a•dan, Ber′o•dach-bal′a•dan
Ruler of a Chaldean tribe and twice (721-710, 704 B.C.) king of Babylon (Jer 50.2).

Me′sha
The name of 2 persons and a place in the OT, and of the king of Moab who erected the Moabite Stone, which chronicled his story.

Me′shach
The Babylonian name of one of the friends of Daniel. *See* Shadrach.

Mes•o•po•ta′mi•a
The land between the rivers, the Tigris and the Euphrates.

Mes•si′ah, Mes•si′as
(Heb. the "Anointed," same as Gr. *Christos*) Though in the OT sometimes applied to such divinely appointed agents as the high priest, the prophets, and even King Cyrus (Is 45.1), chiefly designates the promised Deliverer and Saviour whom prophecy foretold, and in whom all the promises of God are fulfilled.

Mi′cah
(Heb. "who is like Yah?") Micah the prophet, a contemporary of Isaiah.

Mi′cah, the Book of
The prophecy of the fourth in the great quartet of eighth-century B.C. prophets, with Amos, Hosea, and Isaiah, who preached against the idolatrous and unjust nations of their genera-

tion. Micah's message was stern and uncompromising; judgment was to come soon for Judah.

Mi'chael
(Heb. "who is like God?") One of the archangels.

Mid'i·an·ites
A tribe living in NW Arabia, descendants of Keturah and Abraham. They were nomads and traders with Egypt, and pillaged the Israelites until conquered by Gideon.

Mil'com
See Molech.

mill
The handmill consisted of 2 stones, between which the grain was ground. A rectangular and slightly concave stone might be rubbed over a larger stone, or 2 round stones, the lower convex and the upper concave, might have grain for grinding poured through a hole in the center of the top stone. These mills were used by women in the home. Larger round millstones turned on a flat lower stone by animal power were community enterprises. No part of a handmill could be taken for debt.

mil'let
The smallest of the grass seeds grown for food; usually mixed with other seeds or grains.

mil'lo
A part of the fortification of Jerusalem, erected by David.

mi'na
See Weights.

Mi'nor Proph'ets
The last 12 books of the OT. Because of their brevity, they are frequently called the minor prophets.

mint
(Gr. "sweet odor") An herb, the oil of which was used as a condiment and as medicine. Several species are found in Palestine. The Pharisees required the tithing even of mint, but neglected law and justice, mercy and faith.

Mint

mir'a·cle
(Lat. "wonderful thing") Defined as an event, whether natural or supernatural, in which one sees an act or revelation of God.

mite
See Money.

Miz'pah, Miz'peh
(Heb. "watchtower") The name of 4 towns and 1 region in the OT; 2 towns and the region have been tentatively identified.

Miz'ra·im
The Hebrew word for Egypt; it also applies to a land of Musri, from which Shalmaneser III got double-humped camels. Solomon imported horses from a place of this name.

Mo'ab·ites
A people allied to the Israelites, settled from before the time of Moses SE of the Dead Sea. Like the Ammonites, from whom they were separated by the river Arnon, they were descendants of Lot, and mortal enemies of Israel. They were subdued by Saul and David, and after Ahab's death cast off the yoke of the N kingdom. To this period belongs the Moabite Stone. Jeroboam II again made them tributary.

Mo'ab·ite Stone
In 1868 an inscription was found among the ruins of Dibon, giving an account by the Moabite king Mesha of his successful revolt from Samaria, and of his buildings in Moab. "Omri, king of Israel, oppressed Moab many days, for Chemosh was angry with his land." Then Mesha revolted in the time of Ahab. He overthrew the Israelites, took Medeba, Ataroth, Jahaz, and Nebo, where there had been an altar to "Yahweh" (Jehovah), and he rebuilt Korkhah, Aroer, Bezer, and other fortresses. It is clear from 2 Kings 3.5 that the chief successes of Mesha were gained after Ahab's death. The language of the inscription hardly differs from Hebrew.

mole
(Heb. "digger"?) The moles of Is 2.20 perhaps included the rat, ground squirrel, and similar animals. The U. S. mole is unknown in Palestine, but the mole-rat is very abundant.

Mo'lech, Mo'loch, Mil'com, Ath'ter
A deity to whom human sacrifices were made, and worshiped by Ammonites, Edomites, Moabites, and others. The Valley of Hinnom, outside Jerusalem, was a place of sacrifice to this god.

mon'ey
In the sense of stamped coin, money did not exist in Israel before the Exile. Of coined money, an invention of the Greeks, there is some trace in Western Asia in the 7th century B.C. in the Greek colonies and in Lydia. Gold and silver earlier were "weighed to" the seller by the buyer. The name of the common unit, the shekel, means "weight" (cf. English pound sterling; also Old French livre, and Italian lira, from Latin libra, "a pound"). The pieces of metal were in the form of bars (cf. the "wedge" of 50 shekels' weight in Josh 7.21), larger pieces in that of rings, as the Hebrew name for talent

Silver quarter-shekel

Copper coin of Cyprus

Daric

Mite of Herod the Great

Shekel of the sanctuary

Copper coin of Herod Agrippa II.

("circle") shows. The weighing of ring money is represented on the Egyptian monuments. The balance and the weights (of stone) were carried along with the precious metal in a bag attached to the girdle.

Recent investigations have proved that the ratio of the value of gold to that of silver fixed in Babylon and Assyria, 1:13½, prevailed over all Western Asia (in Greece it was 1:12). The whole monetary system of the Hebrews, as of their neighbors, was based on the Babylonian system of weights. The Babylonian weight-talent was equal to 60 minas of 60 shekels each; but the Babylonian money-talent was equal to 60 minas of 50 shekels each, or 3000 shekels. The unit, the shekel, was the same in both.

Darius I, Darius Hystaspes, extended the circulation of coins, but a gold coin called the daric was used earlier by King Cyrus (550-530 B.C.). After the Exile, Persian money was current. After the fall of the Persian monarchy, talents and drachmas came in. Simon Maccabaeus struck (141 B.C.) silver and bronze coins, of which a number are still extant, but the Greek money was still current, and in the time of our Lord they counted by drachmas and staters. The smallest copper coin in use is translated mite.

Coins of the Bible

Assarion, a Roman bronze coin, 1/10 denarius to 1/20 denarius. *See penny.*

Aureus, a Roman gold coin. Its weight was changed several times.

Beka, Bekah, half a shekel, 0.201 ounce.

Daric or *Dram,* a Persian gold coin, 8.424 grams.

Denarius, a Roman silver coin, 3.8 grams.

Drachma, a Greek silver coin, nearly equal to the Roman denarius.

Dram. See daric.

Gerah, 1/20 shekel, 8.71 grams.

Gold, the Roman aureus = 25 denarii, was of pure gold, and weighed 126¼ grains.

Lepton, the smallest Greek bronze coin; possibly 1/100 drachma. *See mite.*

Mite, the smallest Jewish coin.

Money, pieces of, in Gen 33.19; Job 42.11; Josh 24.32, are of unknown value. In the NT, piece of money, Gr. stater (only in Mt 17.27; R. V. shekel), a silver coin, the Attic silver tetradrachma (four drachmas), officially tariffed by Pompey 63 B.C. for purposes of exchange, at 4 denarii.

Penny in the NT represents a Roman silver coin, the denarius. It was the daily wage of a laborer or of a common soldier in the time of our Lord.

Pound (only occurring in Lk 19.13-25) is the mina = 100 drachmas.

Shekel (Heb. "weight," only in OT), 0.403 ounce. The "holy" shekel, mentioned in parts of Exodus, Leviticus, and Numbers, means the full weight shekel, as contrasted with that which had deteriorated in weight.

Denarius with image and superscription of Tiberius Caesar.

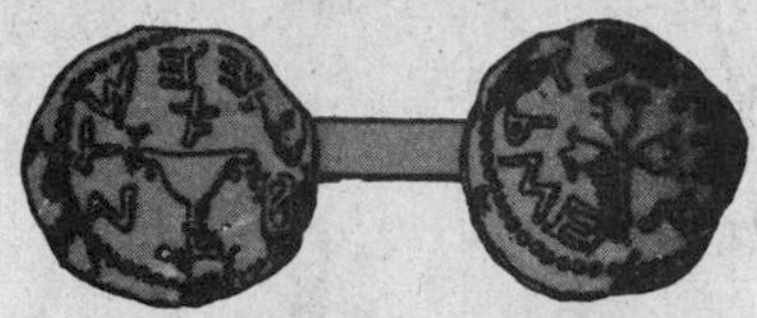
Silver half shekel of Year 1.

Procurator's copper coin.

Silver coin of Vespasian, commemorating the capture of Jerusalem.

Silver, piece of. Here probably shekels are meant. In the NT "piece of silver" represents the Gr. drachma or the silver shekel.

Silverlings. Silver shekels.

Talent, about 75 pounds.

Copper coin of Herod Antipas, Tetrarch of Galilee.

Silver Drachma of Alexander the Great found at the Treasury, Persepolis, Iran.

mon'ey chang'ers

The money changers at the Temple sat in the court of the Gentiles, and were not allowed within the inner precincts or naos. Here they acted as bankers, and gave Jewish money in exchange for foreign, as only Jewish money could be used to pay the Temple tax. The practices of the money changers must have been so bad as to warrant their expulsion by our Lord, who "overthrew the tables of the money changers."

Weighing money

Mor'de•cai

The name of 2 persons in the OT, one of them the important character of the Book of Esther.

Mo•ri'ah

A region near Beer-Sheba, mentioned in the OT. Also, a rocky hill of Jerusalem N of the City of David, and the site of the Temple.

Mo'ses

The great deliverer and law-giver of Israel was the son of Amram and Jochebed, of the tribe of Levi, and younger brother of Miriam and Aaron. Born during the oppression of the Israelites in Egypt, he was placed while an infant child in an ark of bulrushes among the reeds of the river Nile, where he was found by the daughter of Pharaoh. Brought up in Pharaoh's house, he became learned in "all the wisdom of the Egyptians." In his 40th year he fled to Midian, "fearing the wrath of the king" for his killing an Egyptian whom he had found ill-treating a Hebrew. In Midian he married Zipporah, daughter of a priest and sheikh, and lived 40 years. Then God revealed Himself to Moses as Jehovah in a bush that burned and was not consumed, and commissioned him to return to Egypt and be the deliverer of Israel. After 10 miracles of judgment or "plagues" wrought by Moses, the greatest and last of these being the death of the first-born, Pharaoh consented, and the children of Israel set forth for Canaan. Thenceforward for 40 years he was their leader through the wilderness; at Sinai, where he received the law from Heaven; at Kadesh; and in the land of Moab, where he died, after viewing the promised land from the top of Pisgah. Moses, "the mediator of the old covenant," is one of the greatest figures in history. He made the children of Israel a nation, and established the national life of Israel on the basis of a religious covenant that determined the whole future of that people and of the world.

moth

(Heb. "consumer") The moth mentioned in the Bible is the clothes moth, of which several species are very destructive to fur and wool and the garments made of them. It is only the larvae that feed upon the hairs. In Is 51.8 we read, "For the moth shall eat them up like a garment, and the worm (Heb. sas) shall eat them like wool"; the word sas, translated "worm," is interpreted as the larva.

mourn'ing

Signs of mourning were: rending the outer garments, wearing sackcloth, strewing earth or ashes, cutting or shaving beard or hair, fasting, and in some cases, even cutting the hands and the body.

mouse

Doubtless a generic term, including all the small rodents. The mouse was forbidden as food by the Mosaic law.

mul'ber•ry, syc'a•mine, bal'sam

The black mulberry is common in Palestine. The Heb. word has also been translated as sycamine and as balsam.

A bough of the mulberry tree.

mur'der•ers

See Assassins.

mur'rain

An infectious disease of animals.

mu'sic

According to 1 Chron 15.17, David, credited as the originator of liturgical music, instituted an orchestra, with 3 leaders: Heman, Asaph, Ethan or Jeduthun, all of them Levites. These pioneers founded schools of musical performance. The instruments played were percussion, cymbals and timbrels or tambourines; stringed psalteries and harps; wind instruments, the pipe and the trumpet or cornet. There was antiphonal singing by Temple choirs and singing by the congregations.

Ancient musical instruments

The Temple priests used trumpets and cornets on special occasions, and the priestly family made up an orchestra as well.

mus'tard

An annual plant with very small seeds. It grows to a considerable size in Palestine.

Courtesy of *The Interpreter's Dictionary of the Bible*

Mustard

myrrh, per'fume
A general term for fragrant gums or resins from various trees and shrubs, most frequently the rockrose, the ladanum. It was an article of commerce as early as the 2nd millennium B.C.

myr'tle
A shrub indigenous to Western Asia and common on hillsides in Palestine, flourishing especially by watercourses. It has dark glossy leaves, marked with transparent dots, the result of the presence of a volatile aromatic oil. The flowers are small, white, and fragrant, and when dried are used as a perfume.

N

Na'a•man
(Heb. "pleasantness") A Syrian army commander, healed of leprosy by Elisha.

Na'hum, Na'um
The name of a person of the OT and one of the NT. Nahum of the OT and prophet of the Book of Nahum was born at Elkosh in SW Judah and prophesied in the period between 633 and 612 B.C.

Na'hum, the Book of
This OT book consists of two poems. The prophet tells of the fall of Nineveh, the capital of the Assyrian nation. God is depicted as revengeful to those who conspire against Him. The book of Nahum also contains a classic rebuke against warfare and militarism.

Na'in
(Heb. "pleasant") A town of SW Galilee, now called Nein, on the NW side of Nebi Dahi and 2 mi. SW of Endor.

nard
See Spikenard.

Na'than
(Heb. "gift") The court prophet who denounced David for planning Uriah's death and stealing his wife; he also assisted in securing the throne for Solomon.

Na•than'a•el
(Heb. "gift of God") A man of Cana of Galilee, often identified with Bartholomew.

Naz'a•reth
(Heb. "watchtower") The village in Lower Galilee where Jesus was brought up. It is not mentioned in the OT. It is now a flourishing town. The "brow of the hill" is probably the cliff to the N.

Naz'i•rites
(Heb. "one consecrated") These were not members of a party or brotherhood, but individuals "separated" to God's special service by a personal vow of longer or shorter duration. Of this nature was probably the vow of the men named in Acts 21.23-26, and even of Paul (Acts 18.18). The typical Nazirite of the NT is John the Baptist.

Ne'bo
The name of a Babylonian deity, and of 2 towns mentioned in the OT, one probably Kirbeh Mekhayyet, 5 mi. SW of Heshbon, and the other Nuba, 15 mi. SW of Jerusalem.

Ne'bo, Mount
Probably a mountain of the Abarim range, modern Jebel en-Neba, 2740 ft. above sea level, 12 mi. E of the mouth of the Jordan River.

Neb•u•chad•nez'zar, Neb•u•chad•rez'zar
(Akkad. "Nabu protect my boundary stone") King of Babylonia for 43 years, he records in an inscription his defeat of the Pharaoh Amasis in 567 B.C., verifying the prophecy of Jeremiah (43.10-13); and a contract tablet, dated in his 40th year, proves that he had by that time conquered Tyre, confirming Ezek (28.7-14).

Ne•he•mi'ah
(Heb. "Yah has comforted") The name of 3 persons in the OT, one of whom was the restorer (with Ezra) of Judaism after the Babylonian exile and cupbearer to the Persian king Artaxerxes I, who gave him permission to return with a colony to Jerusalem in 445 B.C. Appointed governor of Judea, he rebuilt the city walls in spite of the opposition of the Samaritans and others, and organized the service of God, returning to Persia in 430.

Ne•he•mi'ah, the Book of
Ezra and Nehemiah are companion OT books. *Nehemiah* (or *Second Book of Ezra*) gives an account of the rebuilding of Jerusalem and of the efforts to bring religious reform to the people, covering the history of the Jews from the Exile to the time of Darius II.

net'works
See cotton.

New Je•ru'sa•lem
See Jerusalem, New.

Nic•o•de'mus
(Gr. "conqueror of the people") A member of the Sanhedrin, who came at night to talk with Jesus; he provided the spices for and helped to embalm the body of Jesus.

Nic•o•la'i•tans, Nic•o•la'i•tanes
The name of a sect of Gentile Christians in Ephesus and Pergamum, who rejected the decision of the Jerusalem council with regard to food, and its prohibition of unchastity.

Nile
The great fertilizing river of Egypt. The name, which means "dark" or "blue," is not found in the Bible, but it is understood to be referred to as Shihor or the black stream and as "the river." It is formed by 2 rivers: the White Nile, which flows from the Victoria Nyanza; and the Blue Nile, which flows from the Abyssinian Mountains. These streams unite at Khartoum. To the annual overflowing of the Nile, caused by periodic rains in the southern regions around its sources, Egypt owes its fertility. Below Cairo the river is divided into channels through the Deltas. The names and locations of these shift and the precise patterns in antiquity are not known.

Nim'rod
A legendary hero of the Mesopotamian region. The legends may have grown around the Baby-

lonian war god Ninurta, or a historical figure, the Assyrian king Tukulti-Ninurta (1246-1206 B.C.), the first Assyrian to rule over all Babylonia. Nimrod son of Cush has the legendary greatness.

Nin'e•veh
The later capital of Assyria after the kingdom had been extended north along the Tigris from Assur, the great city on the Upper Tigris, which has yielded almost a complete monumental history of Assyria. An inscription of the Akkad Dynasty (23rd to 21st century B.C.) has been found

Winged bull from the palace of Sargon near Nineveh

in the excavations. It was destroyed about 612 B.C. by the allied Medes, Persians, and Babylonians, after having been ruined by the Scythians.

Nip'pur
A city about 100 mi. S of Baghdad, founded around 4000 B.C.

Ni'san
The 1st month of the Hebrew year. Also called Abib. It falls in March-April.

ni'tre, lye
Native sodium carbonate, nitre, is found in Egypt about 50 mi. W of Cairo. The reference in Prov 25.20 and Jer 2.22, a substance used for cleaning, may be potassium carbonate, which in Palestine could be made from wood ashes. The addition of vinegar would destroy its action.

No'ah, No'e
Tenth generation from Adam, son of Lamech, and a righteous man, whose story is told in Gen 6–9. To Noah God gave the promise after the Flood that never again would he send such a catastrophe, and the rainbow was declared the reminder of His promise. *See* Flood.

Noph
The city of Memphis in Egypt.

Num'bers, the Book of
The 4th book of the OT, it is a continuation of Exodus, recording the stay of the Israelites in the wilderness of Sinai until their arrival at Moab. The title of the book is derived from the two numberings of the people recorded here.

O

oak, ter'e•binth
Three species of oak are found in Palestine. The terebinth is now identified as distinct from the oak. Symbolism of the oak includes long life and grandeur.

O•ba•di'ah
The name of 11 persons in the OT.

O•ba•di'ah, the Book of
This is the shortest book of the OT, containing only one chapter. In it is given a prophetic interpretation of a great calamity that has already occurred in Edom and a prediction of a universal judgment.

oil tree
This term can include the olive, wild olive, oleaster, and some pines.

ol'ive
Grafted on wild stock, the olive is extensively cultivated in Palestine for its valuable fruit and oil. The cherubim, the doors of the oracle, and the doorposts of the Temple were made of its finely grained wood.

Ol'ives, Mount of; Ol'i•vet, the Mount called
A mountain with 3 summits E of Jerusalem; the highest summit, sometimes called Mount Scopus, is 2963 ft. Gethsemane is on its lower slope. The Mount of Olives is closely associated with the last days of the life of Jesus.

o•me'ga
The last letter in the Greek alphabet, used in Revelation as a title for Christ as the One in whom all things find their consummation.

Om'ri
(Heb. "worshiper of Yah") The name of 4 persons in the OT, one of whom was king of Israel 876-968 B.C.

O•ni'as
The name of 5 priests, 2 of whom were high priests. The family descended from Zadok, appointed high priest by Solomon.

on'y•cha
An ingredient, possibly obtained from marine mollusks, of incense to be burned on the altar.

o'nyx
A chalcedony with bands of alternate milk-white and black. It is sometimes translated as a color rather than black.

O'phir
A place from which gold was obtained. The location has been placed in India, Africa, and Arabia; it seems probable that it was on the coast of Somaliland. The imports from Ophir, other than gold, seem characteristically African, such as monkeys and ivory.

or'gan, pipe
A pipe or perforated wind instrument, perhaps in a group or cluster.

or'na•ments
A list of feminine ornaments is given in Is 3.18-24. They included rings for the fingers, the ears, and the nose; bangles round the arms and the ankles; bracelets and necklaces; pomander boxes, and mirrors. Cosmetics were also

used, both to blacken the nails and the eyelids, and to color the cheeks (2 Kings 9.30; Ezek 23.40).

Egyptian bracelets.

ouch'es
Settings for jewels.

P

Pa·dan-a'ram, Pad·dan-a'ram
The area in what is now S central Turkey, including the city of Haran, now Harran.

Pal'es·tine
The Greek and Roman name for Canaan, together with the country of Jordan occupied by the Jews (the Bible itself confines this name to the territory of the Philistines). Palestine is 140 mi. long, 40 to 50 mi. broad, some 8500 sq. mi. in area: about the size of Massachusetts or of Wales. It is shut off from Egypt by 100 mi. of desert; has the Arabian desert on the E, and the Mediterranean on the W; and is bounded on the N by the mountain chains of Lebanon and Anti-Lebanon. Palestine lies midway between the valleys of the Euphrates and the Nile, two of the earliest seats of civilization and of empire. The traffic between Mesopotamia and Egypt passed through it. Of these empires Palestine was the battlefield down to 500 B.C. Then others followed: the Persians under Cambyses, Greeks under Alexander, Seleucus and the Ptolemies, the Romans under Pompey, the Parthians, the Romans again and again, then in A.D. 634 the Arabs, in the 11th century the Turks and Crusaders, in the 13th and 14th, the Mongols, and in the 19th, Napoleon.

Israel came originally from the desert, and Midianites, Ishmaelites, Amalekites, Arabs, and other Semitic tribes kept pouring into the land; hence the population is in the main Semitic to this day.

The kingdom of Herod the Great embraced all the country won by the tribes under Joshua, except the tribe of Asher in the N, and a small part in the SW. It included: (1) W of Jordan, Galilee, Samaria, Judea, and Idumea; (2) E of Jordan, Perea, Gaulanitis, Auranitis, and Trachonitis, with Decapolis (part in Perea, part in Gaulanitis). The part E of Jordan thus comprehended the ancient kingdoms of Moab and Ammon; the earlier divisions of Gilead (from the Dead Sea to the Yarmuk), and Bashan (a volcanic plateau 2000 ft. above the sea), extending from the Yarmuk to Hermon; and the regions of Golan, E of the Sea of Galilee, and Hauran, still farther E.

Palestine is laid down from N to E in 4 long lines: the Maritime Plain, the Western (or Central) Range, the Jordan Valley, and the Eastern Range. Palestine W of Jordan is an upland carved out of masses of limestone, 2000 to 3000 ft. above the sea. The Ghor, or great trench of the Jordan Valley, descends from ocean level at Huleh to 682 ft. lower at the Sea of Galilee, and to 1292 ft. at the Dead Sea. The Western Range is broken by the Plain of Esdraelon, which opens a way from the Maritime Plain to the Jordan Valley. At its S end it declines into a broad plateau named the Negev, or Parched Land. The lower hills, known as the Shephelah, are between Judea and the Maritime Plain, which, farther N, is broken by Carmel. Thus the leading features of the country are: (1) the Maritime Plain, interrupted by (2) Carmel; (3) the Low Hills or Shephelah; (4) the Western Range, cut in two by (5) Esdraelon, and running S into the (6) Negev; (7) the Jordan Valley; (8) the Eastern Range.

The rivers of Palestine are the Jordan with its lakes, Huleh (Waters of Merom) and Gennesaret (Sea of Galilee), and its E tributaries, the Yarmuk and the Jabbok; the Arnon, flowing into the Dead Sea; and the Kishon, into the Mediterranean.

N of Carmel are natural harbors, large enough for the ships of the Phoenicians, whose chief seats were Accho (Ptolemais), and (farther N) Tyre, Sarepta, Sidon, and Byblus (Beirut); S of Carmel the shores are level to the mouths of the Nile. The seaports Caesarea, Joppa, Ascalon, and Gaza have no natural harbors.

The 4 long lines above described, with their breaks and additions, render Palestine a marvelous mixture of hilly and level country, with all kinds of climate from the tropical oasis of the Jordan plain to the sub-Alpine slopes of Hermon (9150 ft.). The subtropical coastland has a mean annual temperature of 69° F. In the Ghor in May a temperature has been observed of 110° F. in the shade at noon, and 88° F. in the shade at 8 A.M. Jerusalem (3167 ft. above the sea) has an average temperature of 63° F., ranging from 39° in January to 102° in August (the greatest extremes observed since 1860); the average variation of temperature within 24 hours being no less than 51° F. These changes are characteristics of the whole of Syria.

The brokenness of the land, and especially the mixture of hill and plain, predisposed Palestine to be a land of tribes and clans. The Western Range, both S and N of Esdraelon, with Gilead on the Eastern Range, comprised Israel's proper territory. This confinement to the hills secured Israel's independence and purity. The plains and the valleys were the portions of the country open to the traffic and the war of foreign empires. Though the ancient highways of trade between the Euphrates and the Nile, and from Tyre to the Arabian Gulf, passed through the entire length of Palestine, Israel was planted aloof from all these in mountain isolation; long after her neighbors had succumbed to Assyrian war or Greek culture, Judah preserved her independence and her loyalty to the law of her God.

palm′er•worm
A name more properly applied to certain insects other than the locust (particularly butterflies and moths), but the locust is intended where the translation is used.

palm tree
The date palm. Phoenicia means "land of palm"; Bethany "house of dates."

pan′nag
Possibly a place name; other possible translations are early figs; a kind of confection.

pa•py′rus
An aquatic reed, used as a writing material in Egypt from the early 3rd millennium B.C.

par′a•ble
(Gr. "comparison") The statement of a spiritual truth, a law or principle of the kingdom of God, by means of a description or narration of facts in the world of nature or in human experience, which are represented in such a way as to illuminate facts in the world of spirit.

par′a•clete
A Greek word, applied to Jesus Christ to indicate His function in making intercession for the people with God the Father. It implies one who pleads for, counsels, strengthens, comforts.

Par′thi•a
A country on the SE of the Caspian Sea. The kingdom of Parthia, founded 248 B.C. by Arsaces II, grew into an empire, and contended on equal terms with Rome.

Palm tree

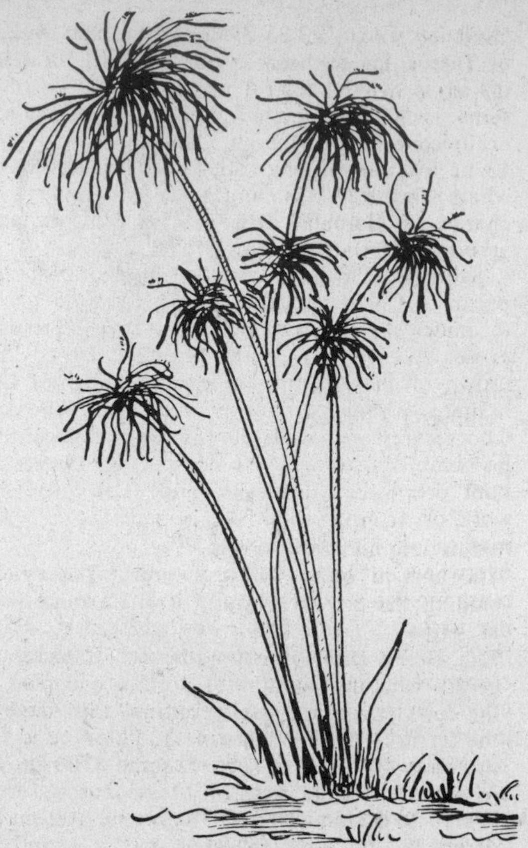

The papyrus, or paper reed, from the pith of which one of the principal writing materials of ancient time was made

Pass′o•ver
The feast commemorating the deliverance from Egypt. It is one of the 3 annual great festivals, and occurs in the spring; also called the Feast of Unleavened Bread. *See* Feasts.

pas′to•ral let′ters, pas′to•ral e•pis′tles
The 3 epistles of Paul in which he gives instructions to Timothy and Titus for their ministry. It is believed that 1 Tim and Tit were written after the imprisonment mentioned in Acts 28, 30, 31, and 2 Tim during a 2nd imprisonment at Rome.

Pat′mos
A very rugged island south of Samos, where John wrote the Apocalypse, having, according to tradition, been banished to it during the reign of Domitian.

pa′tri•archs
The forefathers of the Israelites. Its strictest application is to the forefathers mentioned in Genesis. A few later names are added, such as David and Daniel.

Paul
Saul of Tarsus was the son of Hebrew parents, and belonged to the tribe of Benjamin. He was above his brethren in intellect and influence, as his namesake, the king, had been in mere physique. He was born to the privilege of Roman citizenship, and is best known by his Roman name of Paul; and he used his birthright for his own protection when persecuted as a

Christian (Acts 22.25-29). He thought highly of Tarsus, his birthplace, where he was brought up as a strictly Jewish child, getting possibly some insight into pagan literature, but mainly occupied with the Hebrew Canon. At the age of 13 he was most likely transferred to Jerusalem, where his sister was, and there put under the charge of Gamaliel, the son of Simeon, and grandson of the renowned Hillel.

Saul seems to have been led into deep antagonism to Christ and His cause and stood ready to undertake a crusade against the Christian cause. Accordingly, when Stephen earned the crown of martyrdom, the young Saul did not hesitate to hold the raiment of the witnesses who secured his condemnation and stoned him; he obtained authority from the chief priests to hunt down the Christians, and prosecuted his work of extermination. As he approached Damascus on his mission of persecution, he was overwhelmed by a dazzling splendor such as outshone the Syrian sun, and heard a voice saying to him, "Saul, Saul, why persecutest thou me?" Most probably the stricken persecutor recognized the voice; but to make sure, he cried, "Who art thou, Lord?" and received an answer, "I am Jesus, whom thou persecutest." He is directed to go on to Damascus, where he will receive further light. Here his lost sight is restored, he is baptized by Ananias, and receives the gift of the Holy Ghost.

He is now driven by the Spirit, as Christ had been before him, into the wilderness, and in Arabia he spends a considerable season in meditation. Three years enabled him to elaborate that view of Christianity now usually called Paulinism. The young rabbi at Gamaliel's feet becomes, at the feet of Christ, the great teacher of the church, translating Christianity into a universal religion.

On his 1st missionary journey he went to Antioch, where he and Barnabas were "set apart" for the work. They went then with John Mark to Salamis and Paphos on Cyprus, then to the mainland to Perga, where John Mark left them, and to Antioch in Pisidia; Iconium, Lystra, and Derbe. They reversed the route to return, and sailed from Atalia to Seleucia, the seaport of Antioch in Syria.

After a journey to Jerusalem and a conference there, Paul set off on his 2nd journey, which took him, with Silas and later with Timothy, into Syria and Cilicia, Derbe and Lystra, into Phrygia and Galatia, and into Macedonia, where new churches were established at Philippi, Thessalonica, and Beroea. There had been many stops along the way. Then he went into Athens, where he spoke in the market place, the Agora. From there he went to Corinth and Ephesus, and continued by boat to Caesarea in Palestine.

He went to Jerusalem and from there to Antioch where he lingered for some time, writing and resting. Then he set out on a 3rd journey, going again to Galatia and Phrygia, then on to Ephesus, where he stayed for more than 2 years. It was at Ephesus that there was a great riot against the new religion that Paul was preaching, instigated by those whose living was threatened, as they felt, by the threat to the great temple of Artemis, visited by worshipers from far and near. From Ephesus Paul went to Macedonia and Achaia, then to Troas to take ship for Caesarea, again with many stops along the way. He then went to Jerusalem.

In Jerusalem he was accused of taking Greeks into the inner Temple, and soldiers broke up the crowd that attacked him. His statement of Roman citizenship prevented his being scourged. He was turned over to Felix the procurator, who kept him imprisoned for 2 years. His successor, Festus, also found himself embarrassed by his prisoner, but Paul's appeal to Caesar, the right of a Roman citizen, led to his being sent to Rome. This too was an eventful voyage. Paul was allowed to visit friends along the way, and was not chained when the ship was wrecked at Malta. At Rome he was detained for 2 years under a sort of house arrest, then freed. He visited a number of the churches, but was again arrested and returned to Rome. The former tolerance was gone, and Christians were being prosecuted, having been blamed for the great fire in Rome. It is presumed that Paul was beheaded, following this 2nd trial.

Paul, the E·pis'tles (Let'ters) of

Of these we possess thirteen. They were written by amanuenses, and authenticated by the addition of a paragraph in Paul's own writing or by his signature. With the exception of the letters to Timothy and Titus, which are still questioned by some critics, those ascribed to Paul are generally received as his.

These 13 letters all belong to the later half of Paul's ministry. In A.D. 52 or 53, the 2 letters to the Thessalonians were written. Then follows another blank period till 57 or 58, when, within the space of a year, the 4 great epistles to the Corinthians, Galatians, and Romans were produced. Again there occurs an interval of 5 years till 63, when the 4 "prison epistles" appeared; and finally, yet another gap, until 66-68, when he sent the pastoral letters to Timothy and Titus.

In the earliest group the second coming and the kingdom of Christ are in the foreground. The 2nd group exhibits the doctrines of grace in conflict with Judaism, and also shows us in detail the difficulties Christianity had to overcome in the social ideas and customs of the Roman world. The 3rd group is characterized by a calmer spirit, a higher reach of Christian thought, more constructive statements regarding Christ's person. In the 4th group we have chiefly instructions regarding church order, interspersed with passages of remarkable beauty and richness.

pearl

Also translated ruby, crystal. Pearls were found in the Red Sea.

pel'i·can, vul'ture

Identification of the bird intended is not definite.

Pen'ta·teuch
(Gr. "five books") The 5 books of Moses in the OT. The Jews named these, from their chief contents, Torah Law; and the Greek translators gave each book its distinctive title; hence the names in our Bible: Genesis, origin, of the world and of men; Exodus, departure of the Israelites from Egypt; Leviticus, the book of the law of the priests; Numbers, from the numbering of the people related in it; Deuteronomy, second Law. The authorship of the Pentateuch has been the subject of much controversy.

Pen'te·cost
(Gr. "fiftieth") The 50th day after the ceremony of the barley sheaf in the Passover observances. On this day occurred the gift of the Holy Spirit to the church, and for this is observed by the Christian church.

per'fume
Perfume was important in the rites of worship and as a luxury item. Moreover, perfumes were important articles of commerce, originating as they did in India, Somaliland, Persia, Ceylon, Palestine, and the Red Sea. They were manufactured and blended, and in addition to Temple incense were used in spicing wine, on clothing and furniture, and in embalming.

Per'ga·mos, Per'ga·mum
A town of Mysia in Asia Minor, in the valley of the Caicus. Near the top of its acropolis hill, 1,000 ft. above the valley, are the ruins of many temples and a great theater. It is called the most spectacular Hellenistic city in Asia Minor.

Per'iz·zite, Pher'ez·ite
(Heb. "dweller of the open country"?) One of the peoples found in Canaan when the Israelites arrived.

Per'sians
The Persians were originally a Median tribe which settled in Persia, on the E side of the Persian Gulf. They were Aryans, their language belonging to the eastern division of the Indo-European group. One of their chiefs, Teispes, conquered Elam in the time of the decay of the Assyrian Empire, and established himself in the district of Anshan. His descendants branched off into 2 lines, one line ruling in Anshan, while the other remained in Persia. Cyrus II, king of Anshan, finally united the divided power, conquered Media, Lydia, and Babylonia, and carried his arms into the far E. His son, Cambyses, added Egypt to the empire, which, however, fell to pieces after his death. It was reconquered and thoroughly organized by Darius, son of Hystaspes, whose dominions extended from India to the Danube. Scripture mentions Cyrus, who released the captive Jews (Ezra 1.1); Darius, who confirmed the decree of Cyrus (Ezra 6.1); and Artaxerxes (Ezra 4.7; 7.1).

Pe·shit'ta
The Syriac version of the Bible, otherwise called the Peshitta (which means either simple or vulgate), belongs to the 3rd century. The OT part was made direct from the Hebrew, with occasional reference to the Septuagint, as early as the 1st century. It was very likely made in the first instance for Jewish proselytes. There is another Syriac version made directly from the Septuagint as it stood in the Hexapia.

Pe'ter
(Gr. "rock") Surname of that Simon, son of John, and brother of Andrew, who, originally a fisherman near Capernaum, became the first apostle of Jesus. His character vacillates between obstinate resolution and momentary cowardice, as is shown in the story of his denial of his Master. In Paul's letters he appears as a "pillar" of the primitive church and the "Apostle of the Circumcision." He was married and was accompanied by his wife on his journeys. Papal claims of primacy for Peter have appealed for support to Mt 16.17-19; Lk 22.32; and Jn 21.15-17; but are set aside by such passages as Mt 20.20-28; Mk 9.35; 10.35-45; Lk 9.48; 22.26.

Peter is not mentioned in Acts after the council of Jerusalem, A.D. 50, but Gal 2.11 refers to a subsequent visit by him to Antioch. His history after that incident has been overlaid with legends. It is impossible for him to have spent 25 years in Rome, though it is probable that his last years were passed there, and that he there suffered martyrdom. It is less probable that he and Paul were put to death at the same time. If "Babylon" is not, as some suppose, a mystical name for Rome, Babylon was the scene of his labor at some period after the visit to Antioch.

Pe'ter, the First and Sec'ond Let'ters of
Two NT epistles. *The First Letter of Peter* was probably written by the apostle Peter from Rome between A.D. 64 and 67 to Christians who had fled Asia Minor. It admonishes the pilgrims to have hope and courage and to trust in the power of God. *The Second Letter of Peter* was written by an unknown Christian leader, perhaps a disciple of Peter's, in the middle of the 2nd century. It warns of false teachers who had come into the early church and urges Christians to be brave and patient.

Pe'tra
The Roman name of the Nabataean city close to Mount Hor. No evidence of an Edomite settlement has been found. It seems to have been begun about the 4th century B.C.

pha'raoh
(Egyp. "the great house") One of the designations of the royal palace was "the Great House," as early as 2500 B.C. By 1500 B.C. it had become the designation or title of the ruler who lived in the palace.

Phar'i·sees
(Heb. "separated") The name given by their opponents to the party that arose among the Jewish scribes after the victory of the Maccabees, and devoted themselves to the most scrupulous fulfilment of the Law as expounded by the scribes.

Phe·ni'ce, Phe·ni'ci·a
See Phoenicia.

Pharaoh Ramses II, thought to have been the pharaoh of the oppression of Israel

Phi·le′mon
The receiver of the short letter of Paul which bears his name. He lived at Colossae, where his house was the meeting place of the Christian community.

Phi·le′mon, the Let′ter of Paul to
This NT epistle is a personal letter in which the apostle beseeches Philemon to take back a runaway slave, Onesimus. The slave had come to Rome, where Paul was being held prisoner, and there had been converted by Paul.

Phil′ip
(Gr. "lover of horses") The name of 4 persons in the NT.

1. Philip the Apostle, born in Bethsaida, one of the first to be called, and mentioned in the feeding of the 5000 from 5 loaves and 2 fishes, which Jesus blessed and broke.

2. Philip the Evangelist, a Greek-speaking Christian in Jerusalem, who following the martyrdom of Stephen fled to Samaria, where he became a successful missionary.

3. Philip the Tetrarch, son of Herod the Great and Cleopatra of Jerusalem, who ruled Batanea, Trachonitis, Auranitis, Gaulanitis, and Panias with justness and benevolence. He founded and built the city of Caesarea.

4. Herod, a half-brother of Philip the Tetrarch, son of Herod the Great and Mariamne, first husband of Herodias, who in Mk 6.17 and elsewhere is also called Philip.

Other persons of this name important in the history of biblical times are Philip II, king of Macedonia, 359-336 B.C., father of Alexander the Great; Philip V, king of Macedonia 220-179 B.C.; a Phrygian appointed, probably in 169 B.C., to be governor of Jerusalem; a regent of the Seleucid state appointed by Antiochus Epiphanes at his death (164 B.C.) and quickly overthrown by Lycias.

Phi·lip′pi·ans, the Let′ter of Paul to the
Written while Paul was in prison in Rome. Philippi was an important town of Macedonia on the great highway from E to W. Philip II of Macedonia had named it after himself. In Paul's time it was a Roman "colony," a settlement of veteran soldiers. From Philippi, where he had been at first grievously maltreated, he "once and again" received pecuniary aid. The letter was written to acknowledge the receipt of such a gift. It is the most "epistolary of all the epistles;" in it the apostle pours out his heart to his friends, and entreats them to be "of one accord, one mind."

Phi·lis′tines
One of the "People of the Sea," the possessors of Philistia, the coastland from Joppa to the Wadi Ghazzeh, with its 5 cities, Gaza, Ashkelon, Ashdod, Ekron, and Gath. Though not of the Semitic race, they adopted the Semitic language of Canaan. They came from Caphtor (Crete). They were repulsed by Ramses III of Egypt after their arrival at the coast and capture of the 5 cities, until then controlled by Egypt. The Israelites warred with and defeated them, and they disappeared as a separate people.

Phoe•ni′ci•a, Phe•ni′ci•a, Phe•ni′ce

A country stretching 120 mi. along the coast N of Palestine, averaging 20 mi. E to W. It was the great trading nation of its time, its sailors going to distant lands and often establishing colonies such as Carthage. The most valuable and profitable of many items of commerce was purple dye made from the sea snail murex. As cities were rebuilt in the same site after destruction and the sites are still occupied, excavation has been difficult. However, Egyptian objects of 3000 B.C. have been found, indicating active trade at that date. The country was prosperous at the time of Christ.

The Phoenicians are closely linked with the development of writing and the alphabet.

Phryg′i•a, Phryg′i•ans

An area and people of Asia Minor. Their boundaries shifted constantly under pressure of aggressive neighbors.

phy•lac′te•ries

Small containers, in which were placed quotations from Scripture, bound on the arm and forehead during prayer, and sometimes called amulets.

Pi′late, Pon′ti•us

Procurator of Judea from A.D. 26 to 36. Jesus was taken before him, accused of stirring up the people, but Pilate was not impressed and tried to avoid action by referring the matter to Herod Antipas. Herod also failed to act, and Jesus was returned to Pilate. Again Pilate found no fault with Him, washed his hands, and turned Jesus over to the mob to be crucified, after having Him scourged.

Unverified reports exist to the effect that Pilate himself became a Christian, and Eusebius quoted earlier reports that Pilate committed suicide.

pil′lar of cloud and fire

The cloud by day and the fire by night led the Israelites through the wilderness. The image may be that of cressets such as were used in Solomon's temple, which burned with flame and smoke.

pine, pine tree, cy′press, fir, wild ol′ive, box

The identification of evergreens and cone-bearing trees is uncertain. It is probable that authors of the Bible were not interested in precise botanical classification, and may not have been able to make such classifications.

Pis′gah, Mount

This is probably the present Ras es-Siyaghah, in the Abarim mountain range, and stands opposite Jericho.

Plowing with cattle, and with a camel

plane tree, chest′nut

As the chesnut or chestnut is very rare in the countries of the Bible, this is probably an error of translation. The plane tree does grow there.

Ple′ia•des, sev′en stars

A configuration of 7 stars in the constellation Taurus (Job 9.9; 38.31).

pome′gran•ate

A fruit found in Palestine. It is prominent in ancient art and in mythology.

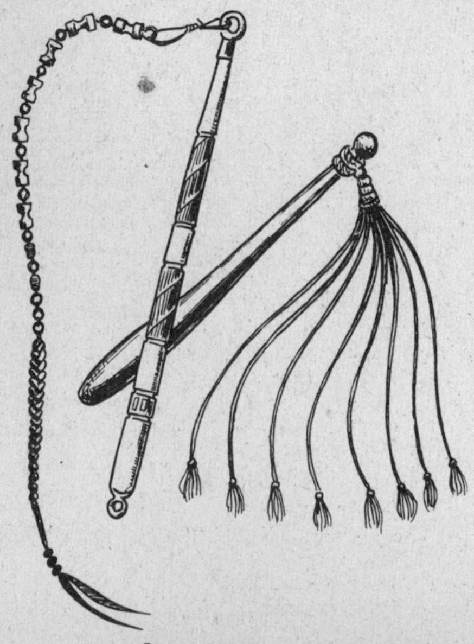

Roman scourges.

Pomegranate

pound, mi'na
Greek measures, mina and lipta, and the Latin libra apparently were measures of capacity and also of weight, 12 ounces, as is the Troy pound. *See* Weights.

priests
Ministers at the altar, descendants of Aaron, to whose family the priestly office was restricted by the Levitical legislation. In later times they traced their descent from the priestly family of Zadok, the contemporary of David. The priest was subject to special laws. His duties were mainly three: to minister at the Sanctuary, to teach the people, and to communicate the divine will. His dress, of white linen, consisted of short breeches; a coat without seam, reaching to the ankles; a girdle; a cap shaped like a cup. The priests were divided by David into 24 courses, each course usually officiating for a week at a time. The "second priest" was probably the same as the "ruler of the house of God" and the "captain of the Temple." As teachers of the people the priests were superseded, first by the prophets, afterward by the scribes. The "chief priests" of the NT were the acting high priest, former high priests still living, and members of these privileged families.

The High Priest was the spiritual chief of the nation. The head of the house of Aaron held this office. He was subject to special laws. His special duties were to oversee the Sanctuary, its service, and its treasures; to perform the service of the Day of Atonement, when he was required to enter the Holy of Holies; and to consult God by Urim and Thummim. It was after the Exile, and when Israel was under foreign domination, that the High Priest became also the political representative of the nation. His official garments, besides those common to the priests, were: the ephod, of blue, purple, scarlet, and fine linen, interwoven with gold thread, not otherwise identified; the breastplate, of the same material, which had, outside, twelve precious stones set in gold in four rows, each bearing the name of a tribe of Israel, and, inside, in a pocket, the Urim and Thummim; the sleeveless robe of the ephod, of dark blue, with a fringe of pomegranates and bells; the miter, a turban.

Pris·cil'la
See Aquila.

prod'i·gal son
A dramatic and vivid parable of repentance (Lk 15.11-32).

proph'ets
The books which, in the Hebrew Bible, immediately follow the Pentateuch, are Joshua, Judges, Ruth (by some considered an adjunct of Judges), Samuel, and Kings, which give a connected history of the nation from the death of Moses to the Babylonian Captivity, and all the books that we call prophetical, with the exception of Daniel.

The "former prophets" are so called simply from their position.

Among the latter prophets, the "Twelve," often termed minor prophets, have been placed together and reckoned as one book, owing to their being written on one roll.

Daniel, though a prophetical or rather apocalyptical book, is not put along with the other prophets; the most probable explanation being that it did not exist, at least in its present form, when the other prophetical books were included in the OT Canon.

Pottery from Tell-el-Obeid, near Ur, an ancient settlement in Babylonia

pros'e·lyte
(Gr. "newcomer, visitor") This word in OT times meant a person in a community not his own; perhaps a refugee, a stranger, an alien. In NT times it had come to mean a convert. Some of these embraced Judaism completely, accepting circumcision, the rite of baptism, and sacrifice. Others were of the persuasion of the Hellenists: they were admitted to worship without circumcision or acceptance of the Jewish law.

Prov'erbs, the Book of
The Book of Proverbs is included with the OT Wisdom literature, and it has customarily been attributed to Solomon. Contained in the book are short, pithy sayings of common sense and sound advice that relate to all ways of life; in short, a practical, everyday philosophy of living.

Psalms, the Book of
The first book in the group known as the Writings. These are hymns of both Judaism and Christianity. Psalms is a collection of poems written over a long period of time by various authors. They express the heart of humanity in all generations through a variety of religious experiences. Originally the poems were chanted or sung to the accompaniment of a stringed instrument. One of the characteristics of this Hebrew poetry is parallelism; that is, the second line reiterates the idea of the first line.

psal'ter·y
This instrument is found on Assyrian reliefs. Strings are drawn over a box resonator and struck with a rod.

pub'li·cans, tax col·lec'tors
The alien government, whether of Rome or of its deputy princes, the Herods, collected its taxes and customs through speculators, who bought

up the right of collecting the revenue (publicum) for their own advantage. These men were called *publicani* by the Romans. The corresponding word in the NT covers not only the tax-farmer but also his collectors. These were often natives and were classed by the Jews not only with the social outcasts but also with the heathen, as if outside Israel altogether. Christ's gracious attitude to them was therefore specially criticized and his hopeful sympathy went to their hearts.

Pul, Put
King of Assyria, Tiglath-pileser III. Also an unidentified region.

pulse, veg'e•ta•ble
Things sown.

pur'ple
This dye was obtained from a species of mollusk abundant on the Phoenician coast and produced colors in the red-purple field. Garments so dyed were of great price.

py'garg, i'bex
A white-rumped antelope.

Q

Queen of Heav'en
Jeremiah censured the Jews for burning incense to and worshiping the Queen of Heaven. Precisely what goddess was so called by Jeremiah is not clear. Ishtar, goddess of love and fertility, was so designated as was Ashtoreth, the Canaanite fertility goddess. The Egyptians had a goddess Antit, called in Canaan Anat, also a fertility goddess, and all were called Queen of Heaven.

R

Ra'hab
(Heb. "wide, broad") 1. In the OT, the name of the woman who sheltered Joshua's men sent out as spies to Jericho.

2. A mythological dragon conquered by Yahweh, as mentioned in several poetic passages of the OT. The dragon Rahab was used figuratively to designate Egypt.

3. In the NT a woman in the genealogy of Jesus.

rain
Rain falls in Palestine from December to March. The beginning of the rainy season is called the "early," the end of it the "latter" rain. The summers are almost rainless.

reap'ing
Harvesting grain by hand. Barley ripened in April and May. The grain was cut halfway down the stalk by a sickle made of flints and tied in sheaves, or cut close to the head. After the 10th century B.C. the sickle blade was curved. The harvesting of all the grains required 6 or 7 weeks and the law forbade careful gleaning so there might be a share for the poor.

Re'chab, Re'chab•ites
(Heb. "rider"?) The Rechabites were a seminomadic people, roaming in the wilderness.

Red Sea
A body of water between Arabia and Africa, about 1200 mi. in length and from 130 to 250 mi. in width. The water has depths of 7200 ft. The Israelite crossing must have been at the bend of the Red Sea or through the lakes between it and the Nile Delta and the Mediterranean; there are several possible routes, but that used has not been determined.

ref'uge
See City of Refuge.

Reph'a•im
1. The dead, the Shades.

2. The pre-Israelite people in Palestine, reputed to be giants.

3. A valley near Jerusalem.

Rev•e•la'tion to John, the
This is the only prophetic book in the NT. Generally presumed to have been written by John, one of the apostles of Christ, about A.D. 95 or 96, the book is addressed to the seven Christian churches in Asia Minor, whose members were being persecuted by Roman officials. The images and illusions of Revelation are difficult for us to understand today, but to the persecuted members of the seven churches John's message was clearly one of hope, courage, and faith in times of trouble; and that on the Lord's day the faithful would be greatly rewarded. It is characterized by the use of symbolical visions as the vehicle of prophecy. The model for this mode of prophecy was set by the Book of Daniel. The theme of the Book is the gradual triumph of the kingdom of God, culminating in the Second Advent.

rie, rye
This is a grain of colder climates than Palestine. It is now believed that spelt is the grain to which this word refers.

riv'ers
In Mesopotamia the Euphrates and the Tigris and in Egypt the Nile were important to the agriculture and commercial life of the countries. Palestine had the Jordan, the Sea of Galilee, and the Dead Sea, but the people were not dependent on their river to the same degree as were the Egyptians and Mesopotamians. Palestine also had smaller streams, some of which at least ceased to flow in the dry season.

rocks
Clay, dust, earth, flint, lime, stone, and sand are words of more or less frequent occurrence in the Bible; but, as they are employed in their ordinary sense, they require no comment. It may, however, be observed that the first-named was used in making bricks, which very commonly, as in Egypt and in Assyria, were not burnt but sun-dried. In this case, straw was often added to increase the tenacity of the material. Some of the limestones of Palestine and the adjacent regions, as well as those of Egypt, afford excellent building stones, and certain varieties can be polished. The former are generally of a very pale cream-color.

rod, staff
The "rod and staff" of Ps 23.4 probably refer

to two instruments still used by Eastern shepherds, the first a heavy-headed club for driving off wild animals, the second a curved stick for guiding the sheep.

roe'buck

See fallow deer.

roll

Long strips of leather or papyrus that were written upon and then wound upon a spindle from which they could be wound off onto a second spindle as read (Ezek 2.9).

Ro'man cit'i·zen·ship

A prized possession in the time of Christ, conferring certain privileges; obtained by birth, grant, reward, or purchase. Since Paul was free born, he must have inherited his citizenship (Acts 22.27, 28).

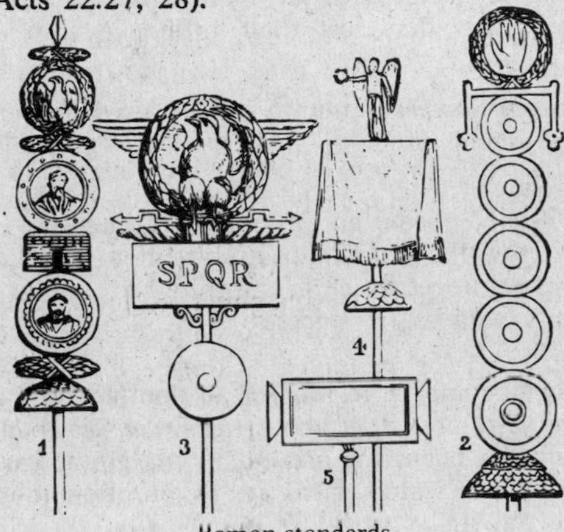

Roman standards

Ro'mans, the Let'ter of Paul to the

This book stands first among the Pauline letters, partly owing to its doctrinal importance, partly on account of its being addressed to the metropolis of the world. It was written from Corinth about 58 A.D. The purpose of the letter is to secure the active support of the church in Rome for his missionary program. Paul stresses the universality of man's sin but that God saves all men through faith in Christ. He discusses the place of Israel in God's plan of salvation and how Christians should conduct themselves.

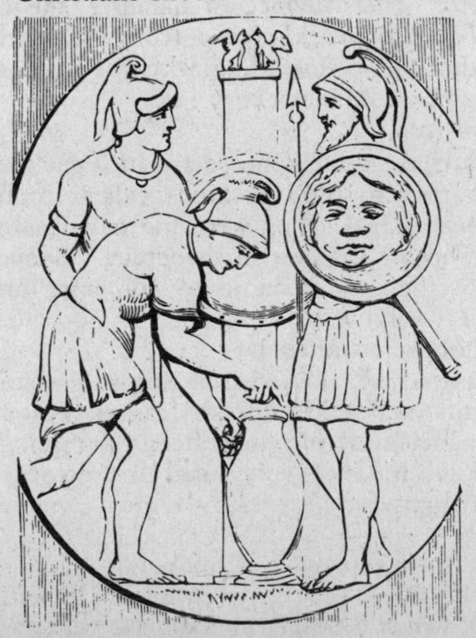
Roman soldiers

Rome

A city in Italy, founded some 700 years after the entrance of Israel into the Promised Land, and at about the beginning of the ministry of Isaiah. By the time of Christ it had become the capital of an empire reaching from Britain to the Euphrates, and from the Black Sea into Africa. Christianity had reached to Rome, and there was a thriving church there previous to Paul's visit. The Jews were expelled from Rome about A.D. 50, but were soon allowed to return. It was here that Paul and Peter presumably suffered martyrdom about A.D. 64.

roof

In the East the roof is flat and usually surfaced with a 10-inch layer of tamped clay, in which grass grows in the rainy season (Ps 129.6). It is extensively used for drying, storage, and even for sleeping in the warmer months, thus needing a protecting wall about its edges (Deut 22.8).

rose

The context indicates that the true rose is not always intended; probably the word is at times used figuratively as well. The crocus may have been intended in some cases, and the oleander, the rose of Sharon. The rose of Jericho is a dried weed, which opens when put in water.

Ro·set'ta Stone

Found in 1799 in the Nile Delta, this stone had inscribed upon it the same decree in 3 languages: hieroglyphic Egyptian, Demotic, and Greek. With this key the hieroglyphic and Demotic scripts were deciphered within 35 years.

ru'by

The true ruby has not been found in excavated sites in the Near East. The red stone may possibly be red coral, or of the nature of the garnet.

rue, dill

Rue is a heavily scented perennial shrub widely used as a condiment and in medicines. Some early manuscripts have in Lk 11.42 dill instead of rue, and dill may have been intended.

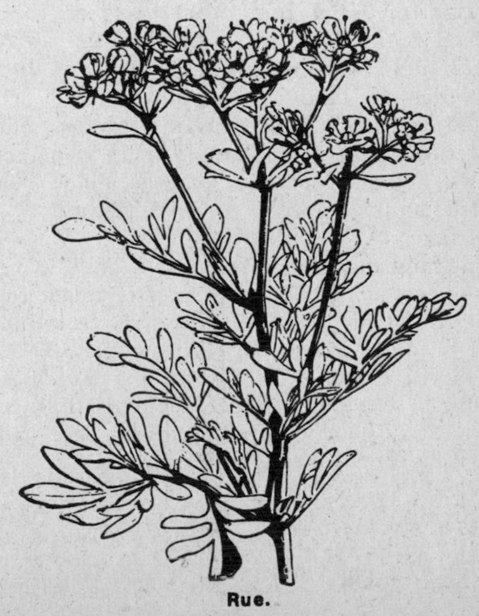
Rue.

rush
Reedlike plants, found in swampy areas and along river banks.

Ruth, the Book of
The story of Ruth, a Moabitess who, after her husband's death, accompanied her mother-in-law Naomi to Bethlehem, there married Boaz, and was thereby an ancestress of David. The book is an idyll of family life, often regarded as a supplement to the book of Judges, but possibly of a later date.

rye
See rie.

S

Sab'bath
(Heb. "cessation") The Israelites apparently adopted the calendar of the Canaanites about them, related to the Babylonian Calendar described below, before the giving of the Ten Commandments established the Sabbath as an ordinance forever. After the resurrection of Christ on the 1st day of the week, that day came to replace the 7th as the Christian Sabbath. The Babylonians observed a day of rest, called Sabattu, described as "a day of rest for the heart." On that day it was forbidden to eat cooked meat, to put on fresh clothes, to offer sacrifices, to ride in a chariot, and the like. It fell on the 7th, 14th, 19th, 21st, and 28th days of the lunar month, the 19th day being the 49th day, or 7th week, from the 1st of the preceding month. The Babylonian account of the Creation makes the Creator say to the moon: "On the 7th day halve thy disk; stand upright with its first half on the Sabbath (Sabattu)."

sab·bat'i·cal year
Every seventh year, during which, according to the law, the fields and vineyards were to be uncultivated, and their produce to be shared with the poor and the stranger and the beasts of the field. Debts of Israelites to Israelites, were to be remitted. Alexander the Great and Julius Caesar freed the Jews from taxes on the sabbatical years. After seven times seven sabbatical years there was appointed a Year of Jubilee, in which all lands that had been sold or forfeited returned to their original owners, and all slaves were set free. Though there is no record of the actual observance of the Jubilee Year, it is frequently referred to in Scripture.

sac'ri·fice
Something of value offered to a deity in return for expected favors, or as an atonement for sin or wrongdoing. Such a custom is very ancient, and is found among all early peoples. The laws of sacrifice and offerings for the Israelites are found in Leviticus. The OT rituals of sacrifice were abolished in Christ's death, the perfect sacrifice for all through all time.

Sad'du·cees
Zadokites, a party attached to the aristocratic priests who traced their lineage to the sons of Zadok, the chief ministers of the Temple from the time of Solomon. They were an exclusive caste, drawn from men of wealth and position. While the Pharisees found their strongholds in the synagogues and schools of the towns and villages, the Sadducees had their center in the Temple at Jerusalem. They were open to worldly influences of all kinds, including in later times Greek culture and Roman statecraft. Their main interest was political, and their guiding principle was to keep in with any power that secured to them their monopoly of office. They acknowledged as binding only the written Law, rejecting the traditions of the scribes; ignored the Messianic hope and the doctrine of the resurrection; and denied alike the existence of angels and spirits and the overruling or cooperating hand of God in the actions of men. After the fall of Jerusalem they lost their influence (A.D. 70).

saf'fron
Purple-flowered autumn crocus, used in cooking and medicines.

Sa·lo'me
Wife of Zebedee and mother of James and John. She saw the crucifixion and went to our Lord's grave on resurrection morning to anoint His body with sweet spices.

salt
Not uncommon in more than one part of Palestine, and abundant about the Dead Sea, beds of rock-salt occurring around its margin at various levels. Its waters also, on evaporation, deposit the mineral.

sal·u·ta'tions
Among the Jews the salutation was "Peace be with thee" and the like. The reply was, "The Lord bless thee." It was only in great haste or intense absorption that they were omitted.

Sa·ma'ri·a
A city in Palestine 42 mi. N of Jerusalem and 25 mi. E of the Mediterranean, founded by Omri about 920 B.C. as his capital. It was taken by Sargon in 722 B.C., and rebuilt by Herod the Great, who named it Sebaste. Excavation has revealed a magnificently built city, beautifully designed. The province of Samaria, the central part of Palestine, stretched from the sea to the Jordan Valley, coinciding with the land of the half-tribe of Manasseh.

Sa·mar'i·tans
The mixed population, partly of Israelitish descent, which the restored exiles found in Northern Israel. They were the hated neighbors and rivals of the Jewish theocracy. "Samaritan" was to the Jew a name of contempt and reproach (John 8.48).

Sa·mar'i·tan Pen'ta·teuch
A Qumran MS (Dead Sea Scrolls) verifies its antiquity and faithfulness of transmission, and other ancient scrolls indicate its antiquity. It is extant in MSS of very nearly as great age as the Hebrew.

Sam'son
(Heb. "sun's man") A judge or hero of the tribe of Dan, the son of Manoah, a native of Zorah, which belonged to Dan. He was a "Naza-

rite unto God" from his birth, the first Nazarite mentioned in Scripture. The narrative does not represent him as a leader of the people, either in war or peace; it consists of personal exploits against the Philistines.

Sam'u•el
The last of the Judges, an Ephraimite, a prophet of the 11th century B.C., who by wise administration in war and peace gained great authority in Israel, but had at last to yield to the popular wish, and resign his leadership to a king. He spent his later years at Ramah, founding and directing schools of the prophets.

Sam'u•el, the First and Sec'ond Books of
The two books of Samuel are one in the Hebrew. First and Second Samuel contain the history of Israel from Eli to the old age of David, particularly material concerning the religious and moral conditions of the period. Samuel is the great prophet-judge who helps to unite the scattered tribes under one king, Saul. The history of the reigns of Saul and David is also recorded.

san'dal
A sole of leather fastened to the foot by a strap or thong, a latchet. On the ancient monuments many types are shown, but most persons are usually depicted barefoot.

San'he•drin
The senate, or supreme Jewish court of justice for enforcing the Mosaic system of sacred law in national and civic life. It existed as early as the Grecian period. It sat under the presidency of the high priest, and consisted of some 71 members (chief priests, elders, scribes), among whom the priestly aristocracy generally had the upper hand, or a lower council of 23 members. It lost the power of life and death under the Romans though in moments of special excitement this limit was not always respected.

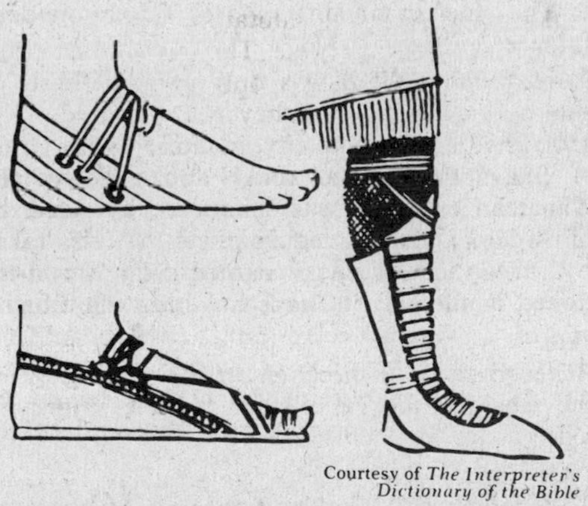

Courtesy of *The Interpreter's Dictionary of the Bible*

Assyrian sandals fastened to the foot by means of thongs (latchets)

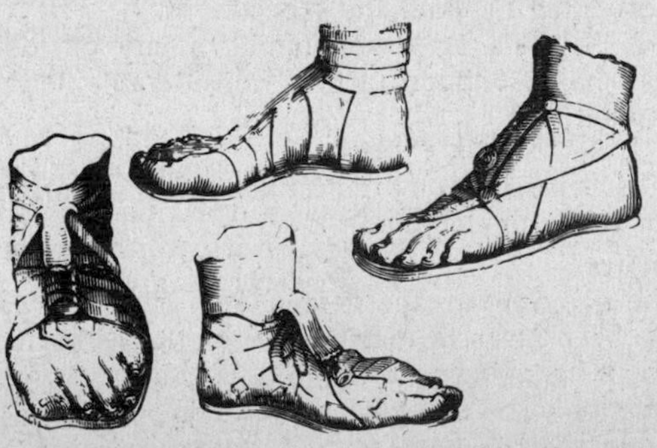

Sandals

sap'phire, lap'is laz'u•li
Properly a blue variety of corundum but in ancient times the name may have denoted the beautifully mottled blue stone now called lapis lazuli. This is a silicate of various bases, softer than steel and still much valued for ornaments. It was obtained in Ethiopia and Persia. *See* Jacinth.

Sar'dis
Capital of Lydia. It was a wealthy commercial town, with a strong citadel.

sar'di•us, sar'dine
A reddish translucent variety of chalcedony darker than carnelian.

sar'do•nyx
A banded form of chalcedony.

Sar'gon
(Akkad. "the king is legitimate") Sargon I (1850 B.C.?) was a king of Assyria, listed on tablets and monuments as the 27th. Sargon II (722-705 B.C.) ended the kingdom of Israel by the conquest and destruction of Samaria, and deported more than 27,000 of its people; they disappeared or were absorbed in Media. Other conquered peoples were moved into Samaria to replace them.

Sa'ron
See Sharon.

sa'tyrs
(Heb. "hairy ones") Elsewhere the word means he-goats; but in some passages it means demons in the shape of goats, to whom the heathen sacrificed. Such satyrs are depicted on the Egyptian monuments.

Saul
Son of Kish, of the tribe of Benjamin, the first king over Israel. He fought successfully against Moab, Ammon, Edom, Zobah, the Philistines, and the Amalekites. Wilfulness in preferring sacrifice to obedience to the divine command before entering on the war against the Philistines, and violation of the curse against the Amalekites, proofs of his failure in allegiance to Jehovah, the true king of Israel, led to his rejection from the kingship. In wild fury he sought to take the life of David and massacred the Gibeonites and the priests of Nob. In the disastrous battle of Gilboa, where the brave Jonathan and two other sons of Saul were slain by the Philistines, he fell in despair upon his sword, and perished.

Stately in presence and demeanor, generous in impulse, upright in character, heroic in action, he yet showed that one act of disobedience, one instance of unfaithfulness, may be the beginning of a fall from a divine call to the highest service.

Saul of Tar'sus
See Paul.

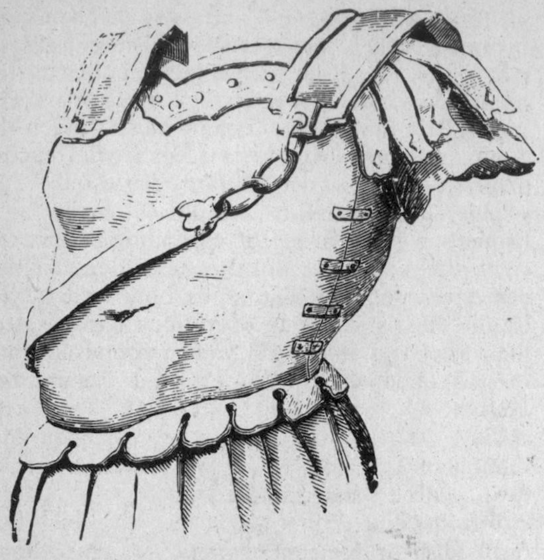

Saul's coat of mail

scape'goat

The goat laden with the sins of the people, and driven away into the wilderness on the Day of Atonement.

scar'let

A costly dye made from an insect similar to the cochineal and found in the Ararat valleys.

scor'pi·on

A lobster-shaped invertebrate with 8 legs, and a poisonous sting in the tail.

Scorpion

scribes

The "scholars" or men of letters to whom belonged the professional study of the Mosaic Law. This special class of non-priestly Jews, beginning in the time of Ezra, had by the Maccabaean period taken this duty under their own peculiar care, and formed a body of traditional law, which, though ever growing by discussion as fresh cases arose, was regarded as equally binding with the written Mosaic Law. Their work included a theoretic development of the Law to cover fresh cases; the teaching of it gratuitously to "disciples," its practical administration in the courts, in which they sat as judges or assessors. They were addressed as "master," "lord," "sir" (Rabbi or Rabboni), "father."

Scrip'ture, Scrip'tures

This first was a general term, meaning simply "writing" or "writings." Then came the more precise designation "The Scripture" or "The Scriptures," as we find these terms employed in the NT to denote what were the sacred books of the Jews at the time, and we now speak of Scripture, Scriptures, or Holy Scripture when we mean the collected writings held sacred by the Christian Church.

Scyth'i·a

The country N of the Euxine and Caspian.

Scyth'i·ans

The Scythians, also called Ashkenaz, moved through the Caucasus into Asia Minor, and made raids of extreme savagery until the Medes defeated and almost destroyed them.

seal, sig'net

Like other Eastern peoples (Babylonians, Egyptians), the Hebrews carried a ring or stamp, or in later times a cylinder engraved with certain figures or characters. This being impressed on a tablet of clay or soft wax served as a signature in a country where very few could write. Sealing with such a signet was also applied to the tomb of Jesus, and to the book in Revelation. Metaphorically, it is used of circumcision, of the Holy Spirit, and of converts as the attestation of Paul's ministry.

sea mon'ster

See Whale.

Se'ir, Mount

1. The chief mountain range of Edom; modern Jabel esh-Shera.

2. A mountain 9 mi. W of Jerusalem.

Se'la

1. A fortified Edomite city, identified with Umm el Bagyarah, on the rocks above Petra, the Nabatean city. Sela was conquered by Amaziah of Judah, and renamed Joktheel.

2. Two other places named Sela are mentioned in the OT but have not been identified.

se'lah

Believed to be a direction to the conductor of the music in the Temple for clash of the cymbals.

Se·leu'ci·a

The name of 9 ancient towns, 4 of them of interest to readers of the Bible.

1. Seleucia in Syria, the port of Antioch, frequented by Paul the Apostle.

2. Seleucia in Mesopotamia, a city of more than half a million, with a considerable Jewish population.

3. Seleucia in Cilicia.

4. Seleucia in N Palestine, once important, but today unidentified.

Sem'ites

The name means the descendants of Shem, and has been given to that portion of the white race which has spoken the Semitic languages: Assyro-Babylonian, Aramaic, Hebrew, Canaanite, Arabic Syrian, Samaritan, Palmyrene, Nabatean,

Phoenician, Moabite, Sabean, Minean, and Ethiopic.

Semitic man, possibly a Hebrew, from a wall painting in Egypt of about the time of Abraham. The man plucks his lyre; the donkey bears a pack, a spear, and a throwing stick

Sen•nach'e•rib
King of Assyria and Babylonia (705-681 B.C.).

Sep'tu•a•gint
The name of the oldest Greek version of the OT, made in Alexandria, which is called after the 70 interpreters who are supposed to have made it, the Septuagint (Lat. "seventy"), and commonly abbreviated by using the Roman numeral LXX. The legend of its formation is as follows. Ptolemy Philadelphus, king of Egypt, at the suggestion of his librarian, Demetrius Phalereus, sent an embassy to Eleazar, the high priest at Jerusalem, to obtain copies of the sacred books of the Jewish law, in order to translate them into Greek. Superb copies were sent, and a body of translators, 70 or 72 in number, were assigned quarters on the island of Pharos. A later tradition says that the translators were all shut up in separate cells, and that when they had finished their work, the translations were found to tally exactly.

There is no doubt that the Pentateuch was translated into Greek in Alexandria as early as the time of Ptolemy Philadelphus (284-246 B.C.). The true account of its origin is that, as there were in Alexandria many Jews who could not read the OT in the original, a Greek version was gradually produced for their use in the 3rd and 2nd centuries B.C.; probably the whole work was completed by 150 B.C. It is, as a translation, very unequal, and it has come down to us in a state of great corruption.

Ser'mon on the Mount
The address which in Mt 5–7 opens the public ministry of Jesus as the Messiah, while in Lk 6.17-49 it appears in a shorter form and at a later stage. The "mount of beatitudes," supposed to have been near the Sea of Galilee, has not been located. The Sermon on the Mount is an exposition of the nature of the kingdom of God and His righteousness. It sets forth in the beatitudes the character, and then, under the figures the "salt of the earth" and "the light of the world," the duty to the world of the citizens of the Kingdom. After showing that the better righteousness of the Kingdom comes to fulfil and carry to perfection, not to destroy, what was good in the past, it proceeds to unfold the true righteousness with regard to the 6th, 7th, and 3rd commandments. Obedience should carry beyond the language of the commandments. Ch. 6 deals with the religious exercises of almsgiving, prayer, and fasting, and shows that the Christian's relation to his worldly property is to be without greed and avarice, without pursuit of by-ends, but with a single eye, and without anxiety. Ch. 7 forbids rash judgment and profanation of that which is holy, gives encouragement to prayer, lays down the "golden rule" of love, and enforces the necessity of religious decision; then, after describing the test which will distinguish false prophets from true, and false disciples from true, concludes with the double parable of the house and its foundation.

ser'pent
In Palestine more than 30 different kinds of serpents are known, of which some are poisonous. All snakes were considered unclean.

serv'ant
See Deaconess.

sev'en stars
See Pleiades.

Sha'drach, Me'shach, A•bed'ne•go
The Babylonian names of the 3 companions of Daniel, the Hebrew names being Hananiah, Michael, and Azariah. The 4 young men demonstrated the strength of Jewish faith at the hostile Babylonian court.

Shal•ma•ne'ser
(Akkad. "Salmanu is leader") The name of 5 kings of Assyria. The last Shalmaneser V (727-722 B.C.), besieged Samaria and died or was assassinated during the siege.

Shar'on, Sa'ron
(Heb. "plain or level country") From Carmel to some low hills S of Joppa extends the plain or level of Sharon, once covered in the N by a considerable forest, but more cultivated in its southern part.

She'ba
The name of 2 persons and a place, Beer-Sheba, mentioned in the OT, in addition to the queen of Sheba.

She'bat
The 11th month in the Hebrew calendar.

She'chem, Si'chem, Sy'chem
(Heb. "shoulder"?) An ancient Canaanite city near Mount Gerizim, 40 mi. N of Jerusalem. Abraham, Jacob, and Joshua visited Shechem, and Jereboam made it his capital. A small group of Samaritans lives in the modern town, with their synagogue on the S slope of Nablus. Excavations indicate the presence of a town as early as 4000 B.C.

sheep
The first animal mentioned in the Bible. The plains on the coast, the wilderness of the south, the rolling downs of Moab and eastern Bashan,

were and are pasture lands. Sheep were used for sacrifice; otherwise slain only for feasts, or to entertain guests. Ewe's milk was the most valued product of the flock; next in value was the wool. The common breed of today, with the enormous development of fat on the tail, seems to have been the ancient breed of Israel. The Eastern shepherd's life was one of ceaseless watchfulness. At evening the flocks are folded in caves, or in enclosures on the open plain.

shek'el
See Money.

She'lah, Si•lo'ah
(Heb. "pool of the aqueduct") A reservoir of the King's garden in Jerusalem; the lower pool. *See* Siloam.

She'ma
(Heb. "hear") "Hear, O Israel, the Lord our God is one. . . ." The central confession of Jewish faith (Deut 6.4-9; 11.13-21; Num 15.37-41).

She'ol
The abode of the dead.

shep'herd
The patriarchs lived a nomadic and pastoral life and the children of Israel to a large extent continued to be shepherds after their settlement in Canaan. Mount Carmel, Sharon, the hill country S of Hebron, Gilead and Bashan were noted for their pastures. The laborious life of the shepherd is referred to by Jacob. Its characteristic features

A shepherd's scrip, sling, and pipes

are the same to this day. The dress of a Syrian shepherd consists of a shirt of unbleached cotton, with a leathern girdle, and a large cloak of sheepskin, or wool, or hair, which also serves for a blanket at night. He carries a scrip or provision-pouch of kidskin, a gourd for holding water or milk, an oak staff six feet long, and a weapon in the form of an oak club two feet long, the thick end of which is studded with nails. The shepherd stays with his sheep night and day. In the morning he counts them under his staff. Obedient to his call, they follow him to their pasture. At sunset they are led into caves or enclosures made of rough stones and the shepherd stays at night in a booth made of branches near the entrance, to be ready to protect his flock from thieves and from wild beasts.

shew'bread, Bread of the Pres'ence
The continual offering of bread in the Temple; 12 loaves, arranged in 2 rows.

shib'bo•leth
A Gilead password, mispronunciation of which by Ephraimites led to their detection.

Shi•lo'ah
An aqueduct in Jerusalem. *See* Siloam.

Shi'loh
A town of Ephraim, now Khirbet Seilum, 10 mi. NE of Bethel, the site of the Tabernacle from the time of Joshua to that of Samuel.

Shi'nar
A name for Babylonia.

Shi'shak
An Egyptian pharaoh (940-915 B.C.), the founder of the Egyptian Twenty-second Dynasty, has given, on the S wall of the temple of Karnak, a list of the places he captured in Palestine. Most of them were in Judah; a few, Megiddo and Taanach, belonged to the northern kingdom.

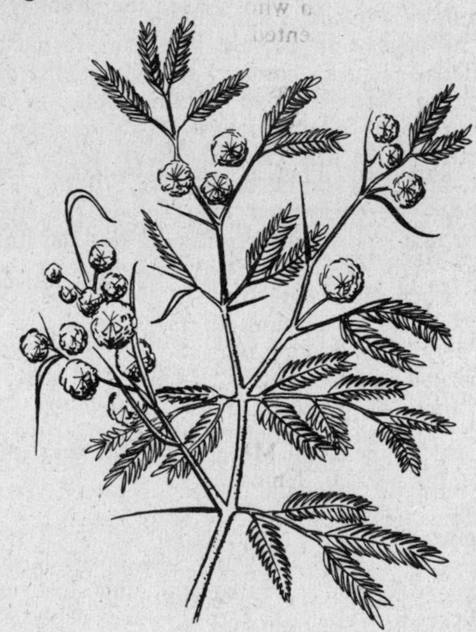

Shittah tree.

shit'tah tree, shit'tim wood
A kind of acacia tree.

Shu'nem
A village in Issachar, identified with modern Solem, first mentioned earlier than 1400 B.C. It lies 9 mi. N of Jenin. Saul fought the Philistines there, and Elijah revived the dead son of a woman of Shunem.

Shu'shan, Su'sa
The ancient capital of Elam, in SW Iran. Its history as a city for more than 5000 years has been revealed by excavation.

Si'chem
See Shechem.

Si'don
Now Saida, a very ancient Canaanite city with a good port, center of Phoenician trade, north of Tyre. Its name is set down on monuments as early as 1500 B.C. The sarcophagus of Eshmunazar, who ruled Phoenicia and Sharon in the 3rd century B.C., was found here.

sig'net
See Seal.

Si·lo'am, Si·lo'ah
A pool in Jerusalem, also called The Pool Between the Two Walls.

sil'ver
An imported metal in Palestine, though some may have been obtained in Lebanon from an ore of lead (the sulphide), which is frequently silver-bearing. Spain appears to have been one of the chief sources of supply in ancient times. Silver was used for money and for ornamental purposes, and was well known to the Egyptians in patriarchal ages.

Sim'e·on, Sym'e·on, Si'mon
(Heb. "[the deity] has heard") 1. The second son of Jacob, ancestor of one of the 12 tribes.
2. A devout man who blessed the infant Jesus when he was presented in the Temple.

Si'mon
(Heb. "[the deity] has heard")
1. Simon Peter. *See* Peter.
2. Simon the Zealot, also one of the Twelve.
3. Simon the Pharisee in whose house Jesus was anointed.
4. Simon of Cyrene, who carried the cross.

Si'mon Mac·ca·be'us
Brother of Judas Maccabeus. *See* Maccabees.

Si'mon Ma'gus
A Samaritan magician who, impressed by early Christian miracles, offered money to Peter and John for the power of the Holy Spirit.

Si'nai, Mount
Believed to be Jebel Musa, 7500 ft., near the S end of the Sinai Peninsula.

sing'ing
Singing and chanting were a part of the Temple service. The people had such folk music as work songs, songs for weddings and other festivities, and probably knew the fertility songs of the people among whom they lived.

Si'on
See Zion.

Si'van
The 3rd month in the Hebrew calendar.

slime
See Bitumen.

Smyr'na
The modern Izmir, originally a Greek colony. The old city was destroyed in the early 6th century B.C., and refounded early in the 3rd century B.C. On the slope of Mount Pagus are the remains of the great theater and the stadium, close to which Polycarp, the first bishop, suffered martyrdom.

Sod'om
One of the Cities of the Plain. *See* Gomorrah.

Sol'o·mon
(Heb. "peaceful") Son of David and Bathsheba, the 3rd king of Israel. His history is narrated in 1 Kings 1–11 and 2 Chron 1–9. Under his brilliant reign the power of the kingdom reached its zenith. He stood on friendly terms with Egypt, and married a daughter of the Pharaoh. He maintained his authority over all the lands won by David and subjugated all the non-Israelite inhabitants of Palestine. His greatest achievement was the building of the Temple. He built a palace for himself, and another for his Egyptian queen; also the "House of the forest of Lebanon," an arsenal on Zion made of wood from Lebanon, and completed the fortification of Jerusalem. Not until all these works had been finished, in the 24th year of his reign, was the Temple consecrated. Solomon completed the transition of the kingdom which his father had consolidated into an Oriental despotism, establishing fortresses, increasing the army, introducing cavalry, and entering into great undertakings for the furtherance of trade with foreign nations. He formed an enormous harem, and was led away into idolatry under the influence of his heathen wives. The magnificence of his court was maintained by oppressive taxation, which, in the end, exasperated his subjects. The latter part of his reign did not fulfil the promise of its beginning, when, in the famous vision of Gibeon, he chose wisdom before long life, gold, or victory, and God gave him, besides riches and honor, "a wise and understanding heart." Along with an extraordinary power of discerning human motives, he had the gift of expressing his thoughts in pregnant sayings, which were famous even beyond his own country. There was nothing in the realm of nature of which he could not speak. He was pre-eminently skilled in that practical wisdom which, based on religion, embraced all the moral problems of life, and was the founder of the Wisdom Literature. Proverbs, Ecclesiastes, Song of Songs, the 72nd and 127th Psalms are ascribed to him. The collection of 18 poems called the Psalms of Solomon, also called the "Psalms of the Pharisees," were written in Hebrew in the 1st century B.C., and are now extant only in a Greek translation. The "Wisdom of Solomon" was also attributed to him.

Song of Sol'o·mon, the
The matchless poem of the OT is also called "Song of Songs" and "Canticles." This collection of love songs has long been an enigma and many interpretations have been offered for it. This love-relationship could signify the relation between God and His people, or that between Christ and the Church.

South Ra'moth
Ramoth of the Negev.

spelt
A coarse and inferior wheat.

spi'ces
Vegetable products used for fragrance or flavor. They were an important item of trade and of wealth, necessary for the worship in the Temple, and used in embalming.

spi'der
There are hundreds of species of spider in Palestine; that one mentioned in Prov 30.28 is more probably a lizard.

spike'nard, nard
A perennial herb with an aromatic root; a member of the Valerian family and native in India. The ointment was very expensive.

stac'te
Possibly an exudate from the storax tree or the opobalsamum; one of the aromatic ingredients of the Temple incense.

staff
See Rod.

Ste'phen
(Gr. "crown") The first Christian martyr, one of the Seven who were chosen for the special service of tables, the distribution of food to the poor. His gifts of inspired speech and miracle made him preeminent among the Seven. Accused of blasphemy against Moses and against God, he was condemned on the evidence of false witnesses. In his defense he showed by historical proof that the Jews had always resisted God's prophets, at last had murdered the Messiah, and that the Temple was not an indispensable and indestructible institution of the religion of revelation. He was stoned to death, and "fell asleep" with a prayer on his lips which was an echo of our Savior's upon the cross. Saul of Tarsus (later Paul) was standing by, consenting to the death, and he held the raiment of those who stoned him. The death of Stephen was the signal for the beginning of a general persecution of the Christians.

Suc'coth
A city of Gad, identified as Tell Deir'alla, 2 mi. N of the Jabbok. There is evidence of very early settlement. Succoth in Egypt has been identified with Tell el-Maskhutah.

sul'phur, brim'stone
Sulphur springs and encrustations of sulphur are not uncommon near the Dead Sea.

Su'mer, Su·me'ri·an
The Sumerians came into the Mesopotamian area about 3500 B.C., absorbing, driving out, or being absorbed by the Ubaid people, who had been there from 4000 B.C. Sumer developed elaborate irrigation systems, worked out rather complicated mathematical tables and algebraic problems, had a pharmacology, a pantheon, cylinder seals, and a system of cuneiform writing. Semitic nomads, the Amorites, gradually conquered the cities and introduced their language, Akkadian. Sumer was extinct as a people and a government, and Babylonia and Assyria arose in its place.

Sun, Cit'y of the; Cit'y of De·struc'tion
Probably a city in Egypt.

Su'sa
See Shushan.

swine
Regarded by Jews (and Muslims) as the most unclean and polluting of animals.

syc'a·mine
Possibly the mulberry tree.

syc'a·more, syc'o·more
A type of fig with a leaf like a mulberry leaf.

Sy'char
A village about a mile east of Shechem, near Joseph's tomb and Jacob's well, the modern Tell Balatah.

Sy'chem
See Shechem.

syn'a·gogue
(Gr. "a meeting") A Jewish meeting-house for worship. It served for church, law-court, and school, and was governed by local elders or "rulers" who had power to inflict various penalties, including scourging and excommunication (temporary and permanent). Meetings were held in the synagogue every Sabbath, and on the 2nd and 5th days of the week. Worship was conducted by any one selected by the ruler on each occasion. The synagogues, first instituted after the Exile, were the chief means by which religious knowledge and spiritual fellowship were maintained among the people. The organization of the early Christian communities was largely molded on the lines of the synagogue.

Syr'i·a
(Heb. "plain") The region extending from Mount Taurus to Tyre, and from the Mediterranean to the Tigris. In NT times Syria included Western Aram only. It was under a Roman proconsul.

T

tab'er·na·cle
The tabernacle and its furnishings, prepared according to the instructions of Ex 25–31 and carried by the Israelites during their wandering in the wilderness, and for a considerable period after that, was the place of the presence of God. It was a portable sanctuary, financed by voluntary gifts, that served until Solomon built the Temple. The materials to be used were available and in use for somewhat similar purposes in the lands round about; the colors to be used for the skins and hangings were also available. The tabernacle was designed to provide a suitable housing for the Ark of the Covenant and a meeting place for the rituals and worship of the people of Israel. It was surrounded by a court, also as specified, 150 x 75 ft., and enclosing in addition to the tabernacle an altar of burnt offering and a laver.

Tab'er·na·cles, Feast of
Also called the Feast of Booths, this is the celebration of the harvest. It begins on the day of

the full moon of the 7th month; that is, in early October.

Ta'bor, Mount
In the NE corner of the Valley of Jezreel, 6 mi. ESE of Nazareth, Mount Tabor rises 1843 ft.

tal'ent
A weight used in Mesopotamia, Canaan, and Israel. Although it varied, it was in the neighborhood of 75 pounds. It was equivalent to 6000 drachmas (a silver coin) in NT times.

Tal'mud
(Heb. "to study, to learn") The fundamental code of the civil and canonical law of Rabbinical Judaism. It consists of the Mishna ("repetition"), i.e., the Halacha, or traditional law, as it was committed to writing by Rabbi Judah the Holy (who died A.D. 219) and his disciples, divided into 6 parts comprising 63 treatises, or 524 chapters. A supplementary work called Tosephta was completed about A.D. 400. The second part of the Talmud is the Gemara (completion), which originated in the school of Tiberias in Palestine about A.D. 250 and was completed about 400; and the Babylonian, which was developed in the school of Sura in Babylonia, and completed at 550. For the two methods of interpretation followed in the Talmud, *see* Halacha and Haggada.

Tam'muz
The 4th month in the Hebrew calendar.

Tam'muz, Tham'muz
The Sumerian god of spring vegetation.

Tares, left compared with wheat, right.

tares
Weeds.

Tar'gums
When the Biblical Hebrew was no longer understood by the Aramaic-speaking peoples, just as Wycliffe's English version would be unintelligible to a modern English congregation, it became necessary for a qualified translator to give the equivalent Aramaic when the Hebrew was read. This oral interpretation or Targum was at first of the simplest kind, but it gradually became more elaborate and was reduced to writing. The Targum of Onkelos on the Pentateuch, perhaps as old as the 2nd or 3rd century A.D., became official, as did the Targum of Jonathan Ben Uzziel on the Prophets and Historical Books, which is of later date.

Tar'shish, Thar'shish
(Heb. "yellow jasper"?) The name of Taurus, a port, far off and not identified, a distant paradise, in the OT.

tax col·lec'tors
See Publicans.

tax'es
Every Hebrew who had reached the age of 20 had to pay a half shekel for the upkeep of the sanctuary. Under Nehemiah a third of a shekel was raised from every Israelite for the building of the temple. In later times the regular temple tax was a half shekel. Civil taxes were at first unknown, but Samuel shows that they would be exacted under the monarchy. Large contributions in kind were required by Solomon; the first cutting of grass is called "the king's mowing." Money taxes were demanded only in times of extraordinary necessity. Under the Persians the Jews were required to pay not only excise and land-tax, but also a capitation tax, a direct levy on each person; and their condition under the Egyptian and Syrian rule became still harder when Antiochus demanded 1000 talents. The taxes now began to be farmed, and this system was universal under the Roman domination, during which the Jews had to pay capitation and land taxes, as well as customs.

Te'beth
The 10th month of the Hebrew calendar.

teil
Obsolete name for lime or linden tree. *See* Terebinth.

Tell el-A·mar'na Tab'lets
A collection of 296 clay tablets found at Tell el-Amarna, in Egypt, in 1887. They consist of letters to Amen-hotep IV and his father, Amen-hotep III, from various kings of Western Asia, from Phoenician and Canaanite princes, written in cuneiform characters, and almost entirely in the Babylonian language, though only 1 or 2 of their writers were Babylonians. Their date is uncertain, but may be about 1400 B.C. and earlier. Israel is identified by some with the Khabiri of these letters, who invaded Egypt some 150 years before.

tem'ple
Solomon's Temple took its plan from the Tabernacle; but its general dimensions were double those of the Tabernacle, and its furniture and decorations were on a grander scale. The Temple proper was 90 x 30 ft., and 45 ft. high. It was built of stones dressed at the quarry, and roofed with cedar. The floors were of cypress overlaid with gold and the walls were lined with cedar overlaid with gold. No stone was seen. The Holy of Holies was a cube of 30 ft. In it were 2 cherubim of olive wood, overlaid with gold, each 15 ft. high, and with wings 7½ ft. long. It was separated from the Sanctuary by a curtain and by chains of gold and 2 doors of olive wood. The Holy Place, or Sanctuary, was 60 ft. long, 30 ft. wide, and 45 ft. high. There

were windows in its walls, probably near the roof. It contained the altar of incense, which was of cedar overlaid with gold, 10 candlesticks, and 10 tables, and was entered from the vestibule by doors of cypress. Against the 2 sides and rear of the Temple were 3 stories of rooms for officials and for storage; in front was a portico 15 ft. wide before which stood the brass

Courtesy of *The Interpreter's Dictionary of the Bible*

Solomon's temple, front view, after Schick (1896)

pillars called Boaz and Jachin, 27 ft. high with lotus-shaped capitals, or column heads. The courts of the Temple were the great court for Israel, and the inner or upper court of the priests, walled off by a parapet, and containing a brass altar, a brass sea standing on 4 groups of 3 oxen each, and 10 lavers (vessels for ablutions) of brass. The Temple was burned by Nebuzar-adan, Nebuchadnezzar's general, 587 B.C.

Zerubbabel's Temple was erected by the Jews under Zerubbabel on their return from captivity. It had the same general plan as the old, though with different proportions, and on a scale of less magnificence. Begun September 24, 520, it was finished on March 3, 515 B.C.

Herod's Temple superseded Zerubbabel's. It was begun about 19 B.C., and was not finished till A.D. 63-64. The area was enlarged to twice the former dimensions. The Temple proper reproduced the old plan, except that the height was 60 instead of 45 ft. The Holy of Holies was separated from the Holy Place by a veil and was empty. The exterior eastern end was flanked by two wings, making the front 150 ft. long. Beyond the court of the priests lay a large court, of which the part nearest the Sanctuary was reserved for men of Israel, the E portion for women. These were enclosed by a strong wall. The grand portal in the E wall was probably the Beautiful Gate. Beyond these precincts was the large court of the Gentiles, where money changers sat and traders displayed cattle for sale.

Ten Com·mand′ments
The covenant requirements of Yahweh and the Israelites, covering prohibitions in man's relations with his God and his neighbor.

ter′a·phim
Small, portable household gods.

ter′e·binth
Also called the turpentine tree; a kind of sumac, yielding Chian turpentine. It has been translated as elm, but the elm does not occur in Palestine.

Tham′muz
See Tammuz.

thar′shish
See Tarshish.

Thes·sa·lo′ni·ans, the Let′ters of Paul to the
These two epistles written by Paul at Corinth in A.D. 50 or 51 are the earliest writings of the NT. They were occasioned by his interest in the church that he had founded within 18 months before at Thessalonica, and persecution had compelled him to leave. Paul tells these Christians what sort of persons they must be, and that they must do their duty every day and not stand idle, waiting for the Second Coming.

Thes·sa·lo·ni′ca
Now Salonika, in Macedonia, at the head of the Thermaic Gulf. It was in Paul's time a free city governed by 7 politarchs. Its public assembly of Demas is mentioned in Acts 17.5. It was rebuilt by Cassander (315 B.C.), and renamed after his wife, sister of Alexander the Great, and from 146 B.C. was the seat of the Roman governors of Macedonia. A great seaport and the center of the Via Egnatia (the great high road from the Adriatic to the Hellespont), it was, after Corinth, the second commercial city of the European Greeks, and it is now Salonika, or Thessaloniki in Greece.

this′tle
See Bramble.

Thom′as
One of the 12 disciples of Jesus, in the Gospel of John called Didymus ("twin"), which is the Greek rendering of the Aramaic name. The passages in John's Gospel, 11, 14, and 20, in which Thomas appears, reveal the intense love that bound him to his Master. The image of the crucifixion filled his mind, and his sorrow would not be comforted by others' testimony; he must himself see before he could believe that his Lord was risen. Jesus, tenderly reproving him, granted him all that he desired; "and Thomas answered and said unto Him 'My Lord and my God.' "

There is an early tradition that Thomas preached the gospel in Parthia and was buried at Edessa. The Christians of Malabar, the "Thomas-Christians," regarded him as the founder of their community.

thorn
See Bramble.

thresh′ing
Lighter grain, such as spelt and cummin, was beaten out with rods and flails; other kinds were threshed either by the feet of cattle or by a

threshing instrument, made either of planks studded with stones or iron or of rollers spiked with iron teeth.

Thy·a·ti′ra
An important city of ancient Lydia, on the Lycus, with a large Greek population and a probable Jewish population, and noted for purple-dyeing and weaving. An inscription found there mentions its dyers' guild, among others.

thy′ine wood
The hard, fragrant wood of a North African cypress; also translated as scented wood.

Ti·be′ri·as
Built by Herod Antipas, on the W shore of the Sea of Galilee, and famous in the 2nd century A.D. for its schools of rabbis, and as the seat of the Sanhedrin, it is now a popular resort. It lies 700 ft. below sea level.

Tig·lath-pi·le′ser, Til·gath-pil·ne′ser III
King of Assyria (745-727 B.C.) and, with the name Pul, of Babylonia, 729-727 B.C. He invaded Palestine, and Hoshea, the king of Israel, paid him tribute.

tim′brel
A small drum or a tambourine.

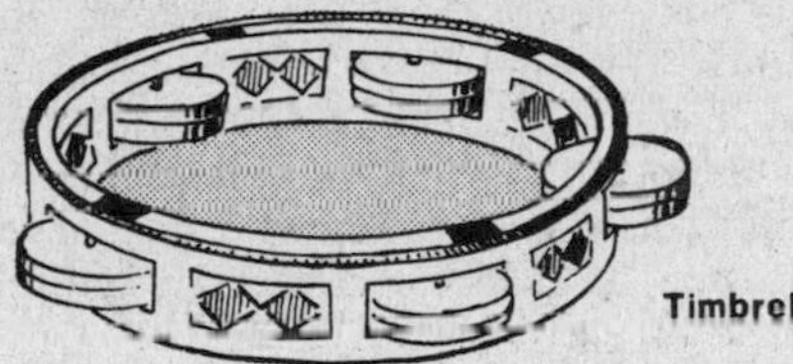
Timbrel.

time
Man early recognized the year, the seasons, and the lunar month, and the calendar, made with varying degrees of accuracy, is also ancient. It was easy to halve the lunar month into 14-day periods, and halve those into weeks. Then came the jockeying of time to make the week-and-lunar-month fit the cycle of the equinox. But the division of the single day into fixed segments of time was long in coming: the hour was of variable length until the 18th century. Hence the smaller divisions indicated for Bible times are approximations only. *See also* Calendar.

OLD TESTAMENT	
Morning	until about 10 a.m.
Heat of the Day	until about 2 p.m.
Cool of the Day	until about 6 p.m.
First Night Watch	until midnight.
Second Night Watch	until 3 a.m.
Third Night Watch	until 6 a.m.

NEW TESTAMENT	
Third Hour of the Day	6 to 9 a.m.
Sixth Hour of the Day	9 to 12 midday.
Ninth Hour of the Day	12 to 3 p.m.
Twelfth Hour of the Day	3 to 6 p.m.
First Watch, Evening	6 to 9 p.m.
Second Watch, Midnight	9 to 12 p.m.
Third Watch, Cockcrow	12 to 3 a.m.
Fourth Watch, Morning	3 to 6 a.m.

Tim′o·thy, Ti·mo′the·us
(Gk. "one who honors God") An assistant and companion of Paul who had been trained in piety by his Jewish-Christian mother Eunice and grandmother Lois. A convert of Paul's, he traveled in Macedonia and Greece, sometimes with the Apostle, sometimes commissioned by him. He appears afterward as the Apostle's representative at Ephesus and was at Rome while Paul was in prison there.

Tim′o·thy, the Let′ters of Paul to
Two epistles, written by the apostle to his friend Timothy at Lystra, tell of the conditions in the church and describe the qualifications and duties of church officers. *Second Timothy* contains Paul's request that Timothy come to Rome to see him. *First Timothy,* which has been compared with pearls of varied size and color loosely strung on one thread, must have been written between A.D. 64 and 67; *Second Timothy* was written about 67, and is the last of Paul's extant writings.

tin
The metal (obtained only from the oxide) has not been found in Palestine. It was, however, in use, chiefly as a constituent of bronze. It was brought to the Near East by the Phoenicians and was probably procured from the Caucasus.

Tir′ha·kah
A king of Ethiopia and Egypt (689-664 B.C.) who was defeated in the Nile Delta by the Assyrians and driven S. He set up his capital in Thebes.

tish′ri
The 7th month of the Hebrew calendar.

Ti′tus
As an assistant of Paul in his apostolic work, Titus accompanied him to the council at Jerusalem as a Gentile Christian who had remained uncircumcised. He afterward appears as Paul's commissioner in Corinth.

Ti′tus, the Let′ter of Paul to
This NT epistle mentions that Titus was left by Paul in Crete to organize the work there, and sets forth the duties of the pastoral office and the virtues of domestic and social life. It can scarcely have been written earlier than Nero's persecution (A.D. 64).

To′bit
The Book of Tobit may have been written in Aramaic about 200 B.C. It is the story of the reward of a good Jew and his son for their piety and good deeds. It is placed in the Apocrypha by Protestants.

tongues, speaking with
Glossolalia, which may range from unintelligible babbling to a possible higher language, opened to the Apostles in their ecstasy when, as it seemed, the Messianic age had come and they were the people of the New Covenant, with Jesus as the Anointed.

to′paz
The topaz is a fluosilicate of aluminum, generally of a resin-yellow color.

treas'ure, treas'ur·er, treas'u·ry
All wealth is treasure. The worldly wealth, the treasure of the Temple is listed in Ezra 1.9-11, 2.69-70. The royal treasures are listed in 2 Chron 32.27-29, and Solomon's in 1 Kings 10.10-29. But the teaching of Jesus was that worldly treasure was to be given up in order to have treasure in heaven. Treasuries, places where treasure might be kept, have been found in excavations, chests, grain pits in the rock, store-cities. Personal treasure might be carried on the body or buried in a secret place. The treasurer was the custodian of the treasure.

Fluted bowl and tumbler, and a spouted pitcher, all in gold, from Ur, and about the time of Abraham

trib'ute
A payment by one ruler or nation to another as acknowledgment of submission, for protection, or in fulfillment of a treaty. Some neighboring countries paid tribute to David and Solomon, and Omri also succeeded in exacting tribute, but during much of her history Israel was in the position of paying tribute to Syria and the Mesopotamian countries to the E and Egypt to the W.

The temple tax was sometimes called tribute, because of the covenant of God and the Israelites. Census of the population with a subsequent tax was also sometimes called tribute or civil tribute.

trump'et
The trumpets found are made of gold, silver, bronze, copper, bones, or shell, with an air column somewhat less than 2 ft. In the Dead Sea Scrolls are directions for blowing a number of complicated signals. The shofar or ram's horn is not a true trumpet.

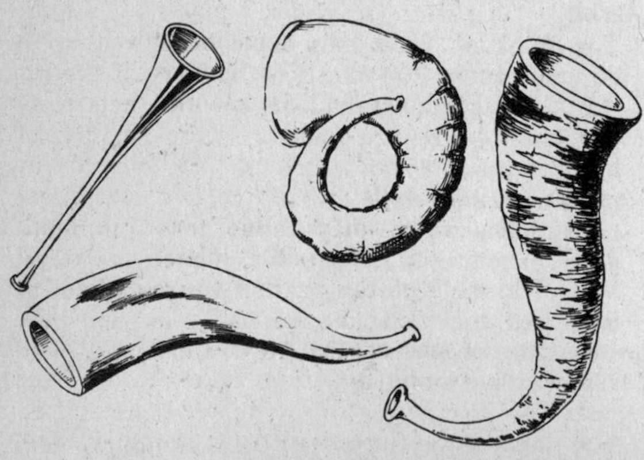

Ancient horns and trumpets.

Tyre
A famous Phoenician city which, according to Herodotus, dates to the 28th century B.C. It does appear as an already famous city in the 14th century, in the Tell el-Amarna Letters. King Hiram (981-947 B.C.), who traded with Solomon and sent workmen to help in the building of the Temple, built a great breakwater that gave Tyre one of the best harbors of the E Mediterranean; it can still be seen, now under 50 ft. of water. The city was famous for its purple dye, glassware, and other manufactures, and traded throughout the Mediterranean, founding many colonies; that at Carthage dates from 850 B.C. It was often attacked by Egypt and Assyria, and was at times forced to pay tribute to one or the other. It was Alexander who destroyed it, selling 30,000 of its people as slaves, and hanging 2000 of the leaders. Tyre never regained its former prestige, and is now a city of a few thousand, called Sur.

U

u'ni·corn, wild ox
This may have been the aurochs, the extinct wild ox; the single horn of the legendary unicorn may have been derived from some account of the rhinoceros, which was mentioned in the 4th century B.C. by a writer who had never seen it. The wild ox does not appear in sculptures later than 800 B.C.

Ur of the Chal·dees'
A city in present-day Iraq, now known as al-Mugayyer, some of which has been excavated. As early as 3000-2500 B.C. it was a magnificent city, with vast temples and palaces and fine works of art.

U'rim and Thum'mim
The sacred lots placed within the pocket of the breastplate of the high priest, used in question-and-answer communication with God. The answer was usually expected as "yes" or "no." The Urim and Thummim are not mentioned after the time of David.

Uz·zi'ah
(Heb. "Yah is my might") The name of 3 persons in the OT, one of whom was king of Judah (788-742 B.C.).

V

veg'e·ta·ble
Something sown.

ver·mil'ion
Red ocher, the hematite iron ore, was used for enamel and as a paint.

vine, vine'yard
The grapevine is one of the most characteristic plants of Palestine. Noah is credited with being the father of its culture; the manner of planting, usually on a hill, is described in Is 5.1-6. A watchman was maintained, and nonbearing vines were pruned away. The harvested crop of ripe grapes were eaten at once, dried as raisins, boiled

into a thick syrup, or made into wine. Gleanings in the vineyard were left for widows and orphans, and for strangers. *See* Wine.

vows

In the OT, vows are solemn promises to offer sacrifices, etc., to God in return for His help, or to abstain from some legitimate enjoyment for His sake. Such vows are voluntary and are not to be lightly made; once made, they are to be inviolate. Our Lord only once mentions vows (Mt 15.5-9; Mk 7.11-13), condemning those who give to God what should go to support their parents. Paul, at Jerusalem, took part in a Nazarite vow (Acts 21.24-26), and made or fulfilled a similar vow at Cenchreae (Acts 18.18).

Vul'gate

(Lat. *versio vulgata,* "common version") The great work of Jerome, who about A.D. 382 was commissioned by Pope Damasus to revise the Latin Bible. The result of his labors is the Latin Vulgate, of which a vast number of MSS. are extant. Probably the best text of all for determining the text of the Vulgate as Jerome left it is the Codex Amiatinus, which was written shortly before A.D. 716 either at Wearmouth or at Jarrow in Northumberland, by the command of Ceolfrid the Abbot, as a votive offering for the Pope of Rome. Ceolfrid died on the journey to Rome, and the fortunes of the book after his death are unknown; it was probably presented to the Pope in due course, and ultimately found its way to the monastery of Monte Amiata, after which it is named. It is now in Florence.

The revision of the OT was made by Jerome in Palestine between 392 and 404, by direct reference to the Hebrew, of which language he had made himself master somewhat late in life. The work of revision is very unequally done; some books underwent very little change, others were much more carefully treated. In particular, the Psalter, which Jerome translated afresh from the Hebrew, had already been twice revised by him on the basis of the Septuagint; these revisions are known as the Roman and Gallican Psalters. The new Hebrew translation found very slow acceptance, and the old Psalter from the Septuagint was not displaced from ecclesiastical use until the 16th century. A curious parallel to the Roman conservatism over the Psalter will be found in the Psalter of the English Prayer-book, which does not follow the text of the Authorized Version, but that of the Great Bible of 1539-1541, though frequent efforts have been made to change it.

vul'ture

See Eagle.

W

wea'sel

(Heb. "to crawl, creep, burrow") Weasels, and also polecats, are common in Palestine, and perhaps others of the genus. The weasel is included in the list of unclean beasts.

Weeks, Feast of

The Day of First Fruits, the 2nd of the 3 great festivals of the year. It is also called the Feast of Pentecost. *See* Feasts.

weights, meas'ures of ca·pac'i·ty

Weights are notable for their inexactness. Excavations have yielded some inscribed weights, and the figures offered are averages only. As throughout Western Asia, the shekel is the basic weight; there are light and heavy shekels, common and royal. A light royal shekel is heavier than a light common shekel: this in addition to the variations in weights identically marked. The averages follow.

Stone weights used by ancient tradesmen in Nineveh. Often weights were made in the shape of a duck or a lion.

gerah, 1/20 shekel	8.71 grains
1/3 shekel	0.134 ounce
beka, 1/2 shekel	0.201 ounce
pim, 2/3 shekel	0.268 ounce
shekel	0.403 ounce
mina, 50 shekels	1.26 pounds
talent, 3000 shekels	75.6 pounds

Measures of capacity were never finally fixed and discrepancies are greater than with weights. The averages:

Dry Measures	
kah	1.16 quarts
omer, issaron, 1/10 ephah	2.09 quarts
seah 1/3 ephah	2/3 peck
lethech, 1/2 homer	2.58 bushels
homer, cor	5.16 bushels

Liquid Measures	
log	0.67 pint
hin	1 gallon
bath	5½ gallons
cor, homer	55 gallons

wells

In a land of few rivers, where rain fell only at certain seasons, wells were of the utmost importance. They were artificial ponds or pits sunk in the ground, in which the rainwater collected and was stored. Springs were often supplemented with wells.

whale, sea mon'ster, drag'on, le·vi'a·than

The whale is an air-breathing, warm-blooded sea mammal. The great fish of Jonah is not otherwise identified. Large sharks are found, as well as dolphins and whales, in the Red Sea and the

Mediterranean. The mythological dragon and the leviathan, or sea monster, persisted in the folk lore.

wheat, corn

Wheat has been cultivated for food in the Near East since Neolithic times or longer. "Corn" as a name for a grain has in modern times been used for maize, discovered in the Western Hemisphere.

wil'der·ness

In Scripture wilderness generally denotes open, uncultivated ground, suitable for pasture, as well as desert, arid areas, and wild and rocky terrain. The wilderness of Judea, the Jeshimon, lies between the Dead Sea and the district of Hebron. The "wilderness of the wanderings" is the N part of the Sinaitic Peninsula, the W region of which is named the "wilderness of Shur" and the E the "wilderness of Paran."

wild ol'ive

See Pine.

wild ox

See Unicorn.

wil'low

Of this there are several species in Palestine. It is sometimes confused with the oleander and the poplar.

wine

Grapes were occasionally pressed by heavy stones, but usually they were trampled in vats. The quickly fermenting juice was put into jars or new skins. Water was scarce in Palestine, and the use of wine increased accordingly. It was abundant in the country, and was drunk, partly as sweet must, partly after fermenting and settling on the lees. It was an old custom to add spices. Wine before being drunk was commonly filtered, to remove dregs and insects. The vice of drunkenness is frequently referred to, and there are many emphatic warnings against it in Scripture. The Rechabites and Nazarites abstained from wine. The priests were forbidden to use it when engaged in their sacred duties. A drink-offering of wine was presented with the daily sacrifice, with the offering of the first fruits, and with various other sacrifices.

win'now·ing

After the grain was threshed, it was winnowed by being tossed in the air with shovels or forks after the nightwind had begun to blow. The grain then fell to the ground and the chaff was blown away.

wis'dom

The Book of Proverbs is the earliest extensive wisdom document. Many strains of source material can be traced in it, and it expresses a wisdom accumulated from all. It contains a number of short homilies, many similies, and balanced-line proverbs. The structure is poetic and impressive.

Wis'dom of Sol'o·mon

This book, together with the Wisdom of the Son of Sirach, or Ecclesiasticus, belongs to the class of what are called the sapiential books, represented within the limits of the Canon by Job, Proverbs, and Ecclesiastes.

The Wisdom of Solomon has nothing to do with Solomon, and is not older than the first (or perhaps second) century B.C. It was probably written in Greek by an Alexandrian Jew. It is a noble work, and was so highly esteemed by the Christian church that it came nearer to canonical acceptance than any other part of the Apocrypha. Some portions of it, which discuss the praise of wisdom, and the rewards and punishments attached respectively to the just and the unjust, have always been much admired, and some of its sentences have become proverbial: "In all ages wisdom entereth into holy souls, and maketh them friends of God and prophets"; "The souls of the righteous are in the hands of God, and there shall no torment touch them."

wolf

The wolf is everywhere known as the terror of the sheepfold. The wolf of Syria is the same as that of Europe, and formerly of Britain. The wolf is often spoken of in Scripture as the emblem of ferocity and bloodthirstiness.

worm

Included among the worms of the Bible are earthworms, larvae of moths, leaf-eating insects, maggots, beetles.

worm'wood

Several species of Artemesia are found in Palestine, all with a bitter taste.

writ'ing (He'brew)

From notices in the OT we learn that the Jews wrote their books with ink on rolls of smoothed sheepskin or goatskin, with a staff attached to each end. The rolls were not written across, but from end to end, the writing being arranged in columns. When a roll was read, the beginning of it was at the reader's right hand, the end at his left. When a column had been read, it was rolled round the right-hand staff, and a new column was unrolled from the left-hand one. According to Jewish tradition, the square character now in use was introduced by Ezra. Subsequent to the Restoration, the scribes transcribed from the old character to the new such books as were written in the former. This was a task of great delicacy, because of the condition of the texts and the dangers of error. In Hebrew writing originally only the consonants of the words were written, the vowels being supplied by the reader. In such a mode of writing, the same combination of consonants may be pronounced differently. Thus, to take an English example, the consonants BRD may be read bird, bard, broad, bread, etc., and the appropriate pronunciation must in each case be determined by the context. The danger in copying such a text was that the mind of the scribe would be continually engaged on the sense while his hand and eye were engaged on the form, or else that he would slavishly copy the letters without regarding the sense; and on either hand there was the risk of mistake, all the more that several letters in both scripts closely resembled one another, and that there was no system of punctuation, nor clear spacing between words. There are many readings in the Septuagint which appear to be due to variations in the Hebrew original from which it was translated.

Y

yoke
Animals engaged in ploughing were united to one another and to the shaft of the plough by a yoke, which was a framework of wood, or wood and leather, passing round the breast of each. The yoke was always double.

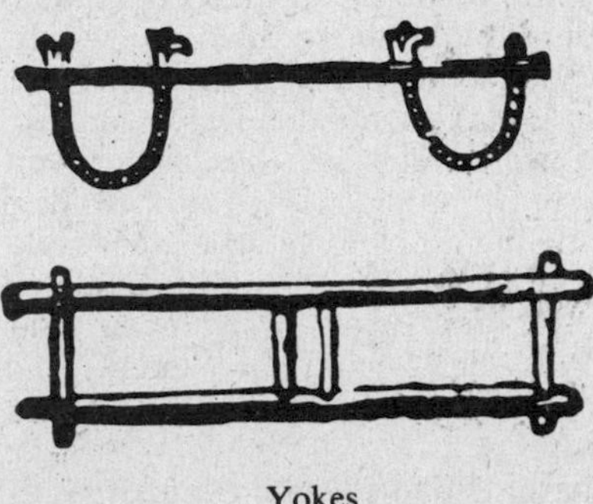

Yokes

Z

Zeal'ots
The extreme wing of the national party, in which the Pharisees represented the policy of passive resistance. From Herod the Great's time to the fall of Jerusalem in A.D. 70 they were in a constant state of ferment. Their headquarters were in Galilee. "Cananaean" is the Hebrew equivalent of Zealot.

Zech·a·ri'ah, Zach·a·ri'ah, Zach·a·ri'as, Ze'cher, Za'cher
(Heb. "Yah has remembered") The name of 33 persons in the Bible, one of whom was the son of Berechiah, a coadjutor of Haggai in promoting the rebuilding of the Temple, who prophesied in 520 and 518 B.C.

Zech·a·ri'ah, the Book of
This OT book of prophecy consists chiefly of visions presenting motives for confidence and effort. Chs. 9–14 have a different historical setting, and refer to conquests of Tiglath-pileser III (745-727 B.C.), and may have been written by the Zechariah of Is 8.2.

Zed·e·ki'ah, Zid·ki'jah
(Heb. "Yah is my righteousness") The name of 4 persons in the OT, one of whom was the last king of Judah.

Zeph·a·ni'ah
(Heb. "Yah has sheltered") The name of 4 persons in the OT, one of whom prophesied in the time of Josiah and before the fall of Nineveh (606 B.C.).

Zeph·a·ni'ah, the Book of
In this OT book the prophet Zephaniah warned Judah and Jerusalem that the great day of the Lord's judgment is near, the neighboring nations are about to fall. He urged Jerusalem to repent, prophesied that the faithful remnant will be gathered, and the peoples will serve Jehovah with one consent. The hymn of the world's judgment, *Dies irae, dies illa* ("That day of wrath, that dreadful day"), was taken by Thomas of Celano (13th century) from Zephaniah 1.14-18.

Ze·rub'ba·bel
(Akkad. "scion of Babylon) A descendant of the kings of Judah, who was permitted by Cyrus to lead back the Jews from exile in 538 B.C. He saw the completion of the new Temple in 515 B.C.

Zi'on, Si'on
Originally the name of the fortified hill of pre-Israelite Jerusalem and poetically extended to become the religious capital of Israel.

Ziv
Second month in the Hebrew calendar.

Zo'an
A city in NE Egypt, the capital of the Hyksos and now San el-Hajar. It was once called per-Ramses, and is the area from which the Exodus began.

Zo'phar
One of Job's friends.

WHAT IS THE BIBLE?

The name "Bible" is derived from the Greek word *biblos*, meaning "book." This "Book," actually composed of sixty-six separate books, is a collection of ancient Hebrew and Christian writings, each complete in itself. The order of these sixty-six books in the Old Testament and New Testament is a logical one, giving, in general, a consecutive history of mankind—from the story of creation in the first chapter of Genesis to the visionary future of the book of Revelation.

The order of Old Testament books in the English Bible differs somewhat from the order of the books of Hebrew Scriptures. The sacred writings of the Jews were divided into three parts: (1) the Law, five books setting forth the laws which God gave through Moses; (2) the Prophets, including the four "Former Prophets," Joshua, Judges, Samuel, and Kings, and the four "Latter Prophets," Isaiah, Jeremiah, Ezekiel, and the Twelve (the Twelve consisting of twelve brief prophetical books contained in a single scroll, thus looked upon as a single book); and (3) the Writings, which are divided into four sections: (a) Psalms, Proverbs, Job; (b) Song of Solomon, Ruth, Lamentations, Ecclesiastes, Esther; (c) Daniel; and (d) Ezra, Nehemiah, Chronicles. The relative importance of the scriptural writings according to Jewish thinking is shown by this order: The Law, standing first, was considered the most important; second, the Prophets; and third, the Writings, which were truly inspired and to be treasured but were not as important as the Law and the Prophets.

In English translations of the Old Testament, the thirty-nine books may be regarded as falling into four categories: (1) History, the books from Genesis to Esther, including the Pentateuch; (2) Poetry, the books from Job to the Song of Solomon; (3) the Major Prophets, the books of Isaiah, Jeremiah, Ezekiel, and Daniel (with Lamentations, a brief and largely poetical book, regarded as an appendix to the book of Jeremiah); and (4) the Minor Prophets, the same brief prophetical books spoken of by the Jews as "The Twelve."

The word "pentateuch," derived from the Greek, means "five books," and is used to designate the first five books of the Old Testament. This section is also called "The Law" or "The Books of Moses," following the Jewish tradition that these five books were written by Moses.

The twenty-seven New Testament books are also divided into four categories: (1) History, including the four Gospels (i.e. books proclaiming the good news) and the book of Acts; (2) Paul's Epistles, the books of Romans through Philemon; (3) the General Epistles, the books of Hebrews through Jude; and (4) the Apocalypse, the book of Revelation.

Original Languages of the Bible

Nearly all the Old Testament was originally written in Hebrew; the small remaining portion was written Aramaic, sometimes called Syriac. The Aramaic section comprises three passages (Ezra 4:8—6:18; 7:12—26; Dan. 2:4—7:28), one verse of Jeremiah (10:11), and two words in Genesis (31:47, a place name meaning "heap of witness"). Aramaic was the language spoken by the people and was the language spoken by Jesus during His public ministry. However, the New Testament was written in Greek, the language used in letters and other writings. Greek was the language understood practically everywhere throughout the Roman Empire, even in the remote provinces, and was recognized as the language of culture.

Since few persons can easily read the ancient languages of the Scriptures, many versions and translations of the Bible have been made. It has been translated, either in whole or in part, into nearly every language of the world today; but, because the spoken languages change from generation to generation, the work of translation continues.

Hebrew.—All of the Old Testament manuscripts which have been found are written in square, black letters which resemble the printed Hebrew of today. These square characters came into use some years prior to the birth of Christ.

Two facts made the translator's task difficult. First, Hebrew then was written without any spaces separating the words. For this reason, the translator sometimes was puzzled to know where one word ended and the next began. Second, the Hebrew alphabet consisted of twenty-two letters, all of them consonants. (Four of these consonants, however, were sometimes used to represent vowels.) In writing, only the consonants were put down. The reader was expected to know what vowels should be added. Evidently it was believed that the reader would be sufficiently familiar with the sacred text to be able to supply from memory the omitted vowels, or else it was thought that the context in which each word occurred would suggest the proper vowel or vowels to be inserted. If we may use English to illustrate the problem, let us suppose one came upon the consonants *m* and *n*. Could one tell with certainty what word was intended? Would it be "man" or "men," "main," "mean," "mien," "moan," "moon," or even "omen."

In the sixth and seventh centuries A.D., when Hebrew as a spoken language was beginning to die out, it was observed that the rabbis were not always agreed as to the proper reading of passages in the synagogue scrolls. As a result, there was danger of confusion and misunderstanding. Accordingly, Jewish scholars of that period, who became known as the Massoretes, undertook to determine and to indicate the proper vowel or vowels for every word in the Hebrew Scriptures. They indicated these vowels by means of small marks above, within, or below the consonants. They did not regard these vowel points as a part of the sacred text, and for that reason they refrained from marking them on the synagogue scrolls. They did insert them, however, on other scrolls and in their commentaries on the Scriptures.

Furthermore, in Hebrew there are no capital letters to distinquish proper nouns from common nouns and to mark the beginning of each new sentence. Finally, Hebrew is read from right to left, rather than from left to right as in English. The lines of Hebrew follow naturally down the page, from top to bottom. In the case of a scroll or book, one begins to read at what we would consider the end or back, and continues his reading till he reaches what we would consider the beginning or front.

Greek.—The Greek in which the New Testament books were written differs somewhat from the classical Greek of a few centuries earlier. It is the *koine*, that is to say, the everyday speech of the common people (and of the aristocrats also) in the first century A.D. Greek is like English in that it is read from left to right. The vowels are included in the Greek alphabet, and they appear in all Greek words except a few frequently used abbreviations. The oldest and most important New Testament manuscripts are written entirely in capital letters, and for this reason are called uncials. As a rule, there are no spaces separating the words.

Later Greek manuscripts are written in a running hand (cursives). Both capital letters and small letters are employed. The latter frequently are joined together, much as in handwriting today. In the later manuscripts there are spaces between the words and some punctuation is employed. These manuscripts come from the ninth to fifteenth century A.D., and they are called miniscules. The name means "rather small"; they take that name from the fact that they are written in small letters rather than in capitals.

Although much writing in Old Testament times was done on papyrus (a kind of paper), important documents were written on carefully prepared skins (vellum or parchment), because of their greater durability and permanence. In the case of a long roll, the skins were stitched together. The New Testament manuscripts doubtless were written originally on papyrus. Later, when their great value had been perceived, they were copied on vellum. It is not possible to state precisely when the change from scrolls to books took place. It did not happen all at once. It is now known that there were papyrus books much earlier than had been supposed. For several centuries both scrolls and books were in common use. Important books were made of vellum rather than the more fragile papyrus. A manuscript which is in the form of a book, rather than a roll, is called a codex. The word codex means "book."

The History of the Chapter Divisions

In the Hebrew manuscripts there were some indications of where the major divisions of the text began and ended. Because these sections sometimes were rather long, it was inevitable that someone eventually would make marks of one sort or another in the margins. Perhaps these marks at first merely indicated the point at which he had stopped reading. Later, they may have been added for the guidance of the reader in the synagogue, and were meant to show him appropriate points at which his reading might begin and end.

In the case of the New Testament, sections were marked off at an early date. These sections were shorter than the present day chapter divisions.

The chapter divisions usually are attributed to Stephen Langton, Archbishop of Canterbury, in England. Langton died in 1228. Cardinal Hugo, who died in 1263, used these chapter divisions in a concordance which he prepared for use with the Latin Vulgate. Chapter divisions are found in Wyclif's versions of the New Testament (1382), and all subsequent English versions.

These chapter divisions proved so convenient when referring to passages of Scripture that Jewish scholars borrowed the idea and employed it in editions of the Hebrew Scriptures. Thus, the present-day Hebrew Old Testament has the same chapter divisions as does our English Old Testament.

The Origin of the Verse Divisions

The material within each chapter is further divided into verses, numbered in regular order throughout each chapter. Although these verse divisions are helpful, they should not be emphasized, for they are not properly a part of the Holy Scriptures. They should not be permitted to interrupt the connected reading of the Scriptures, especially when the passage is of a narrative or poetical character.

Most authorities hold that the verse divisions for the Old Testament were first worked out by Rabbi Nathan in 1448. A Greek New Testament, which was published in 1551 by Robert Stephanus, a printer of Paris, contains the same verse divisions and numbers which we have now in the New Testament. His Latin Vulgate, published in 1551, was the first complete Bible to contain the verse numbers with which we are familiar. The first English Bible to contain them was the Geneva Bible, published in 1560. Since then, all English Bibles have contained the verse numbers.

The Words in Italics

Readers of the King James Version now and again come upon words printed in italics; that is to say, with slanting letters. Some have supposed, mistakenly, that these words were printed in this fashion for emphasis. This is not the case. The explanation, really, is quite simple. The words in italics are words which do not have any equivalents in the Hebrew or Greek text. They are words which have been supplied by the translators in order to make the meaning of the sentence clearer, or in order to make the passage read more smoothly in English. Numerous italicized words are found in the fifth chapter of Matthew, and they occur with almost equal frequency in other parts of the Scriptures.

The Geneva Bible, which was a pioneer version in many different ways, was the first to use italics in this fashion.

HOW TO STUDY THE BIBLE

The Bible is the greatest book that has ever been written. In it God Himself speaks to men. It is a book of divine instruction. It offers comfort in sorrow, guidance in perplexity, advice for our problems, rebuke for our sins, and daily inspiration for our every need.

The Bible is not simply one book. It is an entire library of books covering the whole range of literature. It includes history, poetry, drama, biography, prophecy, philosophy, science, and inspirational reading. Little wonder, then, that all or part of the Bible has been translated into more than 1,200 languages, and every year more copies of the Bible are sold than any other single book.

The Bible alone truly answers the greatest questions that men of all ages have asked: **"Where have I come from?" "Where am I going?" "Why am I here?" "How can I know the truth?"** For the Bible alone reveals the truth about God, explains the origin of man, points out the only way to salvation and eternal life, and explains the age-old problem of sin and suffering.

The great subject of all the Bible is the Lord Jesus Christ and His work of redemption for mankind. The person and work of Jesus Christ are promised, prophesied, and pictured in the types and symbols of the Old Testament. In all of His truth and beauty, the Lord Jesus Christ is revealed in the gospels; and the full meanings of His life, His death, and His resurrection are explained in the epistles. His glorious coming again to this earth in the future is unmistakably foretold in the book of Revelation. The great purpose of the written Word of God, the Bible, is to reveal the living Word of God, the Lord Jesus Christ (read John 1:1-18).

Dr. Wilbur M. Smith relates seven great things that the study of the Bible will do for us:

1. **The Bible discovers and convicts us of sin.**
2. **The Bible helps cleanse us from the pollutions of sin.**
3. **The Bible imparts strength.**
4. **The Bible instructs us in what we are to do.**
5. **The Bible provides us with a sword for victory over sin.**
6. **The Bible makes our lives fruitful.**
7. **The Bible gives us power to pray.**

You do not need a whole library of books to study the Bible. The Bible itself is its own best commentator and explanation.

I. PERSONAL BIBLE STUDY

A. Devotional Bible Study

The Bible is not an end in itself but it is a means to the end of knowing God and doing His will. God has given us the Bible in order that we might know Him and that we might do His will here on earth.

Therefore devotional Bible study is the most important kind of Bible study. Devotional Bible study means reading and studying the Word of God in order that we may hear God's voice personally and that we may know how to do His will and to live a better Christian life.

For your devotional reading and study of the Bible, here are several important, practical suggestions:

1. Begin your Bible reading with prayer. **(Ps. 119:18; John 16:13, 14, 15).**
2. Take brief notes on what you read. Keep a small notebook for your Bible study (see no. 4).
3. Read slowly through one chapter, or perhaps two or three chapters, or perhaps just one paragraph at a time. After reading, ask yourself what this passage is about. Then reread it.
4. It is often very helpful in finding out the true meaning of a chapter or passage to ask yourself the following questions, and then write the answers simply in your notebook:
   - **a.** What is the main subject of this passage?
   - **b.** Who are the persons revealed in this passage: Who is speaking? About whom is he speaking? Who is acting?
   - **c.** What is the key verse of this passage?
   - **d.** What does this passage teach me about the Lord Jesus Christ?
   - **e.** Is there any sin for me to confess and forsake in this passage?
   - **f.** Is there any command for me to obey in this passage?
   - **g.** Is there any promise for me to claim?
   - **h.** Is there any instruction for me to follow?
   - **i.** Is there any prayer that I should pray?

Not all of these questions may be answered in every passage.

5. Keep a spiritual diary. Either in your Bible study notebook mentioned above (no. 2), or in a separate notebook entitled, "My Spiritual Diary," write down daily what God says to you through the Bible. Write down the sins that you confess or the commands you should obey that are mentioned above.
6. Memorize passages of the Word of God. Write verses on cards with the reference on one side and the verse on the other. Carry these cards in your pocket and review them while you're waiting for a train, standing in lunch line, etc.

   Other person prefer to memorize whole passages or chapters of the Bible. A small pocket Bible will help you to review these passages when you have spare moments. One of the best ways is to spend a few minutes every night before going to sleep, in order that your subconscious mind may help you fix these passages of God's Word in your mind while you're asleep. **(Ps. 119:11).**

   To meditate means "to reflect, to ponder, to consider, to dwell in thought,"

Through meditation the Word of God will become meaningful and real to you, and the Holy Spirit will use this time to apply the Word of God to your own life and its problems.

7. Obey the Word of God. As Paul said to Timothy in 2 Tim. 3:16, "All scripture is inspired of God and profitable for teaching, for reproof, for correction, and for training in righteousness." The Bible has been given to us that we may live a holy life, well-pleasing unto God.
8. The Navigators, a group of men banded together just before World War II to encourage. Bible study among Christian servicemen, has developed a splendid plan for a personal, devotional study.
   a. After prayer, read the Bible passage through slowly once silently, and then read it again aloud.
   b. In a large notebook divide the paper into columns and head each column as follows: Chapter title, Key verse, Significant truth, Cross-references, Difficulties in this passage (personal or possible), Application to me, and Summary or outline of the passage. In each of these columns write the information desired.

Do not try to adopt all of these methods at once, but start out slowly, selecting those methods and suggestions which appeal to you. You will find, as millions of others have done before you, that the more you read and study the Word of God, the more you'll want to read it. Therefore the following suggestions of Bible study are made for those who wish to make a more intensive study of the Bible truths.

B. Study for Bible Knowledge

There are many valuable methods of Bible study. One may study the Bible to see the great truths which stand out in every book. Or one may study the Bible to find all of the marvelous details which are in this mine of spiritual riches. In this section there are several proven methods by which a person may do more intensive Bible study. The most important thing is to follow faithfully some systematic method of Bible study.

1. *Bible Study by Chapters.*

   In the Bible there are 1,189 chapters in the Old and New Testaments. In a little over three years a person could make an intensive study of the whole Bible, just taking a chapter a day. It is usually a good practice to start your Bible study in the New Testament.

   a. Read through the chapter carefully, seeking to find its main subject or subjects.
   b. As you read each chapter, give it a title which suggests its main content.
   c. Reread the chapter again and make a simple outline of it which will include its main thoughts.
   d. Concerning each chapter, ask and answer the questions suggested in item number 4 of devotional Bible study hints above. Especially take note of any practical or theological problems in this chapter. Then using your concordance look up the key words in those verses and find out what other portions of the Bible will have to say about this question or problem. Compare Scripture with Scripture to find its true meaning. Very often to understand an important Bible chapter, one must study it together with the preceding or following chapters.

2. *Bible Study by Paragraphs.* A paragraph is a unit of thought in writing, usually containing several sentences. When an author changes his subject of emphasis in his writing, he usually begins a new paragraph. Studying the Bible by paragraphs like this is often called analytic Bible study.
   a. Read the paragraph carefully for its main thought or subject.
   b. In order to find the relation of the important words and sentences in this paragraph, it is often helpful to rewrite the text in paragraph form.
   c. From the text which you've now rewritten so that you can see the relationship of the various parts of the paragraph, it is easy to make a simple outline
   d. It is helpful also to look up important words in the concordance that occur in this paragraph.

3. *Bible Study by Verses.* In studying the historical passages of the Bible, such as much of the Old Testament or parts of the gospels, each verse may have only one simple meaning.

   But many verses in both the Old and New Testaments are rich with many great Bible truths which will demand more detailed study. There are many ways that you can study a single Bible verse.
   a. Study it by the verbs in the verse. For example, if you were studying **John 3:16,** you would find the following verbs: "loved, gave . . . should not perish . . . hath . . ."
      Or simply take the nouns in this wonderful verse: "God . . . world . . . only begotten Son . . . whosoever . . . everlasting life."
   b. Study a verse through the personalities revealed. For example, once again taking John 3:16, these very simple but significant points are brought to light: "God . . . only begotten Son . . . whosoever . . . Him."
   c. Study a verse by looking for the great ideas revealed in it.

d. Sometimes a combination of these various ideas applied to a verse will bring the richest results.

4. *Bible Study by Books.* After you have begun to study the Bible by chapters or paragraphs or verses, you will be ready to study the Bible by books.

a. There are several methods of Bible book study.

(1) One is called the inductive method of studying in detail the contents of a Bible book and then drawing from these details general conclusions or principles concerning the contents and purpose of the book.

(2) Another method of book study is called the synthetic method. By this method, one reads the Bible book over several times to receive the general impressions of the main ideas and purpose of the book without attention to the details. (It is sometimes hard to distinguish these two methods.)

(3) In some case the study of a Bible book becomes a historical study, if that book relates the history of a nation or a man in a particular period of time. For example, the book of Exodus tells the history of the children of Israel from the death of Joseph in Egypt until the erection of the tabernacle in the wilderness under Moses. This covers approximately 400 years.

The principles for Bible book study, whether inductive or synthetic, are very similar. Such study will require more time than the previous methods mentioned, but it will be amply rewarding to you.

b. Here are some methods for Bible study by books:

(1) Read the book through to get the mood, the sweep, and the general emphasis of the book.

(2) Reread the book many times, each time asking yourself one main question and jotting down the answers you find as you read. Here are the most important questions to ask:

First Reading

What is the central theme or emphasis of this book? What is the key verse in this book?

Second Reading

Remembering the theme of the book, see how it is emphasized and developed in the book. Look for any special problems or applications to this theme.

Third Reading

What does this book tell me about the author and his circumstances when he wrote?

Fourth Reading

What does the book tell me about the people to whom the book was written and their circumstances, need, or problems?

Fifth Reading

What are the main divisions of the book? Is there any outline apparent in the logical organization and development of the book? During this reading, it is now time to divide the text into the paragraphs as you see them and then give a title to each paragraph.

Sixth and Successive Readings

Look for other facts and/or information that your earlier reading has suggested. By now certain words will stand out in the book. See how often they recur.

As you read and reread a book, you'll find soon that you begin to see its structure and its outline very clearly. It is true, however, that there are many more than one possible outline for any given book. It depends on the principle of division that you select.

5. *Bible Study by Words.* There are two profitable and helpful ways of studying great words or subjects in the Word of God.

a. Word study by Bible books. Certain words have special significance in certain Bible books. For example, after studying the Gospel of John as a book and by chapters, you'll find it instructive and inspiring to trace the word "believe" or "belief." It occurs almost 100 times.

b. General word study. The fine index and concordance which you'll find in this Bible will be a great help. By the study of great Bible words anyone can soon become familiar with the great doctrines of the Bible and understand the great theological principles which the Bible reveals.

6. *Bible Study by Topics.* Closely related to the method of study by words, is the study according to great topics or subjects: Bible prayers, Bible promises, Bible sermons, Bible songs, Bible poems, etc.

Or one might study Bible geography by reading rapidly through and looking for rivers, seas, mountains, etc., highlighted in Scripture. For example, the mountain top experiences in the life of Abraham are a thrilling study.

Another challenging study is to read rapidly through the Gospels and epistles looking for the commands of the Lord to us. The list of Bible topics is unlimited.

First, for a topical study on prayer, look up the word "prayer," "pray," etc., in your concordance. Look up every form of these words and such related words as "ask," "intercession," etc. After you have looked up these verses, study them and bring together all the teaching on prayer that you find. You will find: conditions of prayer, words to be used in prayer, results to expect from prayer, when to pray, where to pray, etc.

7. *Bible Study Through Biography.* The Bible is a record of God's revealing Himself to men and through men. The Old Testament as well as the New is rich in such biographical studies.

   Let us summarize various methods for studying the great Bible biographies:

   a. Read the Bible book or passages in which this person's life is prominent, e.g., Abraham in **Gen. 12-25**, plus references to Abraham in **Heb. 11** and **Rom. 4.**
   b. Trace character with your concordance.
   c. Be careful to note indirect references to the man or his life in other portions of Scripture.

8. *Conclusion.* There are many other methods of studying the Bible: the psychological method, the sociological method, the cultural method, the philosophical method, etc. However, the methods given above largely include all these other methods.

Use all the Bible study methods suggested above. From time to time change your method so that you'll not become too accustomed to any one method, or tired from delving too deeply into one type of study.

The great thrill of Bible study is discovering these eternal truths of God's Word for yourself and embarking on the adventure of obeying them and experiencing the blessing in your personal life.

II. FAMILY BIBLE STUDY

Nothing is more important in a Christian home than the family altar. At a convenient time when all members of the family are home, father or mother should lead them in worship of God and in reading His Word. A simple program for family worship includes singing a hymn, an opening prayer by a family member, a brief Bible study and a concluding period of prayer in which all members take part.

The family altar and Bible study will bind the family togetrher, eliminate juvenile delinquency, foster deeper love, and enable each member to become a stronger, better Christian.

Since family Bible study usually includes small children, it is wise to avoid deep, difficult topics and study something of interest and help to all. Such subjects might be Bible biographies as outlined above, stories of miracles and deeds of Jesus as revealed in the Gospels, miracles in the Old Testament, and other narrative portions of the Bible. It is wise to keep the study brief and concentrate on a short passage of Scripture. For example, if the family is going to study the life of Moses, it could be divided into units like this:

First day: The birth of Moses: Exodus 2:1-10
Second day: Moses' great choice and great mistake: Heb. 11:24-27; Ex. 2:11-15
Third day: Moses' wilderness training: Ex. 2:16-25
Fourth day: Moses' call to serve God: Ex. 3:1-22
Fifth day: Moses' argument with God: Ex. 4:1-17
Sixth day: Moses' return to Egypt: Ex. 4:18-31, etc.

Here are several practical hints on how to make your family Bible study interesting and profitable to all:

1. Keep your family Bible study reasonably short: one brief chapter or several paragraphs a day.
2. Have each member read a verse.
3. Appoint one family member to lead in worship each day and select the passage to read. This one may appoint others to help in the family worship.
4. Read through a Bible book, a chapter or several paragraphs each day. As you read, together decide on a name or a title for each chapter and memorize this.
5. After reading the passage, have each member in the family explain one verse or one paragraph.
6. Let the leader (or the father or mother) prepare five or ten questions on the Bible passage and ask various members of the family to answer these questions after the passage has been read.
7. Study the maps in your Bible together and trace Paul's journeys, or the wandering of the children of Israel in Egypt.
8. Study Bible topics together. Assign verses concerning a topic or great word to each member of the family. Let each read this verse and tell what his verse teaches about his topic or word.
9. After the Bible reading, have each member tell what this verse means to him or how he believes it can be applied to his life.
10. Make up Bible games by having each member make up questions to try to stump the others.
11. Study a Bible book together, using the hints given above. There are many wonderful ways to make the Bible the heart of your home.

III. PRINCIPLES OF BIBLE INTERPRETATION

Since the Bible was written by many men over a period covering 1,500 years; and since the last author of the Bible has been dead 1,900 years, there are definite problems in understanding the exact meaning of certain passages of the Bible.

There is a need to interpret clearly certain passages of the Bible because there is a gap between the way we think and the words we use today and the way of thinking and the words that these Bible writers used thousands of years ago. Bible scholars have pointed out that there are language gaps—differences in words that we use; there are cultural gaps—different customs were in vogue then. There are geographical gaps—certain rivers that are spoken of in the Bible have long since dried up. Some places that are spoken of frequently in the Bible are not on our modern maps. And then there are historical gaps—the Bible speaks of kings and empires which existed years ago.

Therefore there is a need for Bible interpretation. This is a fascinating study in itself, but I want to give you just a few principles of interpretation of the Bible that will keep you from error and help you to understand the difficult passages of the Word of God.

1. Always remember that the Bible is God's infallible, inerrantly inspired word. There are no mistakes in the Bible. God has included everything in the Bible that He wants you to know and that is necessary for you to know concerning salvation and your Christian life.
2. The second principle of interpretation is to interpret the Bible in the light of its historical background. There are three aspects of this:
   a. Study the personal circumstances of the writer.
   b. Study the culture and customs of the country at the time that the writing or story was taking place.
   c. Study and interpret the Bible in the light of the actual historical situation and events that were taking place at the time of the story.
3. Interpret the Bible according to the purpose and plan of each book.

   Every Bible book has its specific purpose intended by the Holy Spirit to bring some special message to man.
4. One of the most important principles of interpretation is always to interpret according to the context of a verse.

   The "context" is the verses immediately preceding and immediately following the verse you are studying. If you do not take care to interpret the verse according to the context, you could make the Bible teach atheism. For the Bible itself says, "there is no God" **(Psalms 14:1)**. But the context makes very clear what this verse means: The immediately preceding sentence says, "the *fool* hath said in his heart, 'there is not God.' "

   Always study the passage immediately preceding and immediately following any verse, word, or topic to make sure that you see this truth in the setting which God intended.
5. Interpret always according to the correct meaning of words. You can find the correct meaning of a word in several ways. First of all look up the usage of the word in other parts of the Bible to find how it was used in that generation. Another way is to look up its background or its root. You could do this with the use of a dictionary. Still another way is to look up the synonyms—words that are similar in meaning but slightly different: for example, "prayer," "intercession," "supplication."
6. Interpret the Bible also according to all of the parallel passages which deal with the subject, and according to the message of the entire Bible.

   The more you read the Bible, the more you will understand that in it God is revealing His way of salvation to men from beginning to end. And when you come to a difficult passage, think of it in the light of the overall purpose of the Bible. For example, the animal sacrifices of the Old Testament are meant to be a picture of the perfect sacrifice of Jesus Christ on the cross.

If you will follow these simple rules, you will be kept from error and extremes, and you will be helped to understand correctly the teachings of even the more difficult passages in God's Word.

Business Terms Dictionary

BUSINESS AND INVESTMENT

ASSETS—those items, property, and services that reflect the total financial value of a person, business, or estate. Assets include the value of all real property and personal property you own.

BALANCE SHEET—a statement of the financial condition of an individual or business at any given time.

BETTER BUSINESS BUREAU—a nonprofit organization that gives information about companies and corporations to the public. In many instances, it provides information you will need when purchasing or using these specific products. The bureau patrols the advertising and marketing methods used by various companies. It may also provide business speakers for different school and civic groups.

BOND—a certificate evidencing a debt of a corporation. In other words, it is the corporation's promise to repay an amount of money that it has borrowed, usually with added interest; the bond holder simply lends his money to the corporation for repayment at a later date. When a corporation issues a bond without any security behind it, the bond is called a *debenture*. When there is security, it is called a *secured bond*.

BOOK VALUE—the assets of a business as shown on its account books. As used in the stock market, the term generally refers to a company's book value for each share of common stock. This value is obtained by dividing the company's total book value by the number of outstanding shares.

BROKER'S COMMISSION—a fee paid to a person for acting as an agent in a contract of sale. This fee is generally decided prior to the transaction and confirmed in writing.

CAPITAL—the total amount of property or assets an individual or business owns.

CAPITAL GAINS/LOSSES—In general, a *capital gain* is the excess of capital assets over the appraised value or cost of an asset. For example, if you've sold a share of stock at a higher price than what you paid for it, the excess is called a capital gain. A *capital loss* exists when an asset costs more than its appraised value, or if the asset is sold at a price less than it originally costs.

Under present tax laws, if an asset is held at least six months and then sold, the gain is considered to be a long-term capital gain and is charged at a lower tax rate.

CHARITABLE CONTRIBUTIONS—An individual or a corporation is allowed to give away a limited amount of money or property and deduct it from taxable income. Many organizations are allowed to receive these contributions.

COMMERCIAL PAPER—a piece of paper used to convey value in a business transaction.

COMMON STOCK—shares of stock that receive equal dividends from a corporation. When a company issues different classes of stock, the shares without special rights are *common*. Most of the stock issued by corporations is common.

COMPOUND INTEREST—interest paid upon interest, as well as upon principal. That is, the interest earned upon the principal is added to the principal, thereby raising the amount of the return to the lender. For example, D promises to repay $100 to C at the end of the year with interest at six percent per annum, compounded quarterly. At the end of the first quarter, the interest earned would be added to the principal. At the end of the second quarter, interest would be computed on the principal plus the preceding quarter's interest. This pattern would continue for the last two quarters as well. Thus, interest would be paid upon interest, as well as upon principal.

CONSUMER PROTECTION AGENCY—an organization created by the federal government to insure a customer's rights in business transactions. This agency offers information about truth in advertising, franchises, business rights, fair debt collection, label information, credit reporting, equal credit opportunity, and truth in lending.

CONVERTIBLE BOND—a bond that may be exchanged for stock in the corporation, under the conditions stated in the bond.

CORPORATION—an association of individuals that has its own distinct legal identity. A corporation has certain legal advantages for carrying on commercial activities. Among these advantages are: (1) continuity of the business. Its work will not be stopped if a member dies or withdraws from the corporation. (2) transferability of its property interest. This is done when the corporation sells stock. In this way, the corporation shares its financial obligations with people outside the corporation. (3) centralization of business control in the hands of its board of directors. (4) little or no individual liability for the debts of the corporation.

A corporation is a separate entity in the eyes of the law. Individuals who own an interest in the corporation (evidenced by their shares or certificates of stock) are called *stockholders*. By owning a share of stock, the stockholder generally enjoys three basic rights: (1) a right to share in the profits, (2) a right to vote upon major business decisions of the corporation, and (3) a right to share in the remaining assets if the corporation is dissolved.

The shares of stock may be given away, traded, or sold. This is generally done at a stock exchange. The exchange simply acts as a place where the various shares of stock can be traded.

DEPRECIATION—the decrease in the value of an asset or property due to wear and tear, obsolescence, and so on.

EX-DIVIDEND—A corporation may declare that it will pay a dividend to everyone who owns shares of its stock at a given date, and pay the dividends at a future date. The shares traded between the given dates will be marked *Ex-Dividend,* meaning they do not entitle the buyer to the new dividend.

FAIR MARKET VALUE—the price arrived at by a buyer and seller who are ready, willing, and able to buy and sell an asset.

FIRST-IN, FIRST-OUT—a method of pricing goods, based on the assumption that a merchant sells or uses goods in the same order in which they are received.

GIFT TAX—a tax upon the transfer of property, rather than on the property itself. This tax is levied during the lifetime of the person making the gift, rather than after his death. The federal gift tax applies only to the transfer of property by individuals, and not to transfers by corporations.

The gift must be made by a taxpayer, and it may be deducted only in the year the gift was made. The Internal Revenue Service has many lengthy rules governing this type of charitable contribution, especially gifts to corporations.

GOOD WILL—an intangible asset of every successful business. A business is said to have "good will" if its customers will probably return to make additional purchases.

INTANGIBLE ASSETS—the powers of a person or business that will allow continuing business success. Intangible assets would include a variety of privileges such as good will, secret processes, patents, and copyrights.

INTEREST—payment that a lender receives for the use of his money. It is usually a fixed percentage of the amount loaned (called *principal*), and it is to be paid at an agreed time.

INVENTORY—a list of the goods or property held by an individual or business.

INVESTMENT TRUST—an organization that accepts money from subscribers and invests it for them. The organization attempts to earn profits that can be distributed to the various subscribers.

LAST-IN, FIRST-OUT—a method of pricing goods, based on the assumption that the goods last received are the goods first sold or used.

LIABILITIES—the debts and obligations of an individual, business, or state.

LISTED STOCK—a stock of a corporation that is listed on the national stock exchange, such as the New York Stock Exchange or the American Stock Exchange. A stock that is not listed on one of the national exchanges is known as *unlisted.* It is sometimes referred to as stock "sold over the counter," or *over-the-counter* stock.

LOAN SHARK—a person who lends money at an exorbitant or illegal rate of interest. This is often called a "shirt-pocket loan." Usually it is for a short time (30 days or less) and its interest rate will be very high—perhaps 40 or 50 percent. Loan sharks often use severe techniques for making loans and collecting them, sometimes resorting to violence.

MONTHLY INVESTMENT PLAN—a plan in which an investor makes monthly payments to his stock broker. With this money, the broker buys as many shares as possible of certain stocks for the investor. If stock prices are low, the investor receives more stocks; if prices are high, he receives less stock. The investor may discontinue his monthly payment at any time.

MUNICIPAL BOND—a city's promise to repay a certain amount of money at a predetermined date and at a stated rate of interest. Federal and state governments levy no income tax on the interest paid by municipal bonds, so this is a very popular source of financing. A city or a county often uses this type of bond to finance large capital improvements.

MUTUAL FUND—an investment company that sells shares to the public, usually at a price determined by supply and demand. The proceeds of the sale are invested to make a profit. As the fund earns higher profits, its shares become more valuable.

NET WORTH—what remains after liabilities or obligations are subtracted from assets. As used in stock-market trading, the term means the net worth of each outstanding share of a company. It is obtained by dividing a company's total net worth by the number of its outstanding shares (i.e., the shares owned by persons outside the corporation).

NO-LOAD MUTUAL FUND—a mutual fund that charges no commission for the shares you buy. It may be hard to purchase shares of a no-load fund; most brokers do not like to sell them because they do not make any money on the sale. Investors usually buy these shares directly from the company that manages the no-load fund.

PREFERRED STOCK—stock that is given priority in the sharing of profits (called *dividends*). The holder of preferred stock is entitled to receive dividends out of the profits of a company at a fixed annual rate, before any profits are distributed to the common stockholders. With some preferred stocks, the fixed dividend is *cumulative*. In that case, if the fixed dividend is not paid within a given year, it must be paid the following year before any profits are distributed to common stockholders. If the preferred stock is *noncumulative,* no such accumulations take place.

PRICE-EARNINGS RATIO—the earnings of a corporation, divided by the number of shares. This ratio is a handy index to the financial condition of the corporation. Generally, as the company becomes more profitable, its price-earnings ratio increases.

PROBATE—official proof that a certain document is valid. For example, a probate court must determine whether a will is valid before the will can take legal effect. Witnesses who have signed the will are usually asked to appear; but it can be probated without their presence. After the court probates a will, it issues a certificate that declares the will legal and official.

PUTS and CALLS—A *put* is an option to sell a fixed amount of a certain stock or commodity at a specified price within a limited amount of time. A *call* is the privilege to buy a stock or commodity at a fixed price within a limited amount of time.

RECEIVABLES—the unpaid claims, bills, and notes of services or merchandise that other merchants have received from a company. These are carried on the company's books as being "due."

RULE OF 78's—the method for computing a refund of interest when a loan contract is paid before maturity. Another name for the Rule of 78's is the *Sum of the Digits*. The number *78* is the sum of the digits 1–12, which stand for the months of the year.

For example, let's say a person borrows $1,000 for 12 months. After two months, he decides to repay the loan. He should be charged only for the amount of time he used the money, so the rule of 78's says this figure would be 24/78 of the interest that would have been charged for the entire year. The borrower can get back 54/78 of the finance charge. *Note:* The rule of 78's applies only to a 12-month contract period.

SAVINGS BOND—a borrowing device that the federal government originated after World War II. The government was heavily in debt and needed a way to raise large amounts of money in a hurry. So it issued savings bonds to attract small loans from private citizens.

Today you can buy a Savings Bond for an amount smaller than its face value and turn it in for the full amount in cash at the end of a seven-year period. The savings bond earns about six percent interest during that time. Savings bonds are not as popular today as they were several years ago, because most banks and savings-and-loan companies pay a higher rate of return.

SECURITY—something given as a promise of repayment. A security may be any note, stock, treasury stock, bond, or debenture. It also includes any document that shows a person's membership or ownership in an organization that has borrowed money from him.

SHORT SALE—a contract to sell shares of stock that the seller does not own, or that are not under his control. The seller hopes that when he has to deliver the stock to the purchaser, its price will be lower than when he made the contract. If it is, he can buy the stock on the open market, deliver it, and make a profit.

SIMPLE INTEREST—interest paid only on the principal balance, and not figured on the accumulated interest. Simple interest is paid simply for the use of the money borrowed.

STOCK SPLIT—A corporation with 100,000 shares outstanding (i.e., owned by private investors) may decide to recall them and issue 200,000 shares, giving each shareholder two shares for one. This is known as a *stock split*. It does not increase or reduce the value of the shareholder's assets; his interest in the corporation remains the same. But if the price of the stock rises after a split, the value of the investor's holdings will increase more rapidly.

STRAIGHT-LINE METHOD—the most common way of figuring depreciation of an asset for tax purposes. Another name for it is *fixed percentage*. It is based on the theory that an asset will loose value at the same rate each year.

To use the straight-line method, estimate the ultimate salvage value of the item and subtract this from its original cost. Divide the result by the number of years you expect to use the item. This will give you the amount of straight-line depreciation for each year.

TREASURY BILL—an obligation of the United States Government to pay the bearer a fixed amount of money after a certain number of days. The Treasury Bill is the most important investment in today's money market. The most common Treasury Bills are the three- and six-month bills; they can be purchased at any Federal Reserve Bank. These bills raise new cash for the federal government. The biggest buyers of Treasury Bills are banks, corporations, and state and local government.

UNIFORM GIFT TO MINORS ACT—a federal law that allows an adult to make a gift to a minor without the minor's having to pay a gift tax. This gift may be in the form of money, security, proceeds from a life insurance policy, or annuities.

The gift can only be made to one minor, and only one person can act as custodian of the gift for the minor. The gift must be final, and the person who gives it must convey its legal title to the minor.

USURY—the act of lending money at an illegally high rate of interest. Usury laws vary from state to state. In some states, a violator of the usury law is required to refund the entire amount of interest paid; in other states, only the amount of excess interest is given back.

WARRANTS AND OPTIONS—A *warrant* confers the right to purchase stock in a corporation at a later date, under stated terms and conditions. A corporation may sell warrants much like it sells common stock. An *option* is similar, except that it is not necessarily sold. The corporation may give an option to a stockholder or friend of the company as a special privilege.

BANKING

BANKER'S ACCEPTANCE—a bank's agreement to accept a bill of exchange or bank draft. Since the bank becomes responsible to pay on the instrument, a person would prefer to exchange a bill or draft for an acceptance.

BILL OF EXCHANGE—a written order to pay a stated amount out of a bank account. A bill of exchange must conform to the following requirements: (1) It must be in writing and signed by the *drawer*—the person issuing the order; (2) It must contain an unconditional order to pay a certain sum in money; (3) It must be payable on demand or at a fixed time; (4) It must state that the amount is payable to a designated person or company, or to the person who holds the bill.

A bank will not honor a bill that does not conform to these requirements. If the bill does conform, it can move about quite freely in business transactions. There is an obvious risk involved in purchasing a bill of exchange that does not conform to any of these requirements, because it may not be honored by the bank that holds the drawer's account. Such a bill would be called a *non-negotiable* instrument.

Many of the common bills of exchange are checks, drafts, trade acceptances, and banker's acceptances. They involve a *drawer* (the person who draws up the bill), a *drawee* (the person who keeps the drawer's account), and a *payee* (a person to whom the bill is paid); so bills of exchange are referred to as *three-party* instruments. Promissory notes are known as *two-party* instruments, since they involve a *maker* (the person who makes the promise to pay) and a *payee* (the person to whom the note is payable).

The drawee is not responsible for the document until he accepts it. He may do this by writing the word *accepted* on the face of the document, followed by his name or initials.

CERTIFICATE OF DEPOSIT—a certificate issued by a bank to acknowledge the deposit of a specific sum of money. The bank promises to pay the depositor the face amount, along with an agreed amount of interest. Most certificates of deposit have an established expiration date; in all cases, the full payment is made only when the depositor gives the certificate back to the bank.

CERTIFIED CHECK—a bank's written promise to pay a specific amount of money on behalf of one of the bank's account holders. In effect, the bank takes funds out of the account and assumes the duty of paying the check when it is negotiated. Thus, it has been said that "a certified check is as good as cash."

CHECK—a bill of exchange drawn on a bank and payable on demand. It is the most common negotiable instrument.

When a depositor opens up a deposit account with a bank, he becomes a lender and a bank becomes his borrower. Under their contract, the bank must surrender the funds of a depositor whenever the depositor gives an order in the form of a check. The check must be presented to the bank within a reasonable time after it is issued.

A bank is not primarily responsible to pay the check; the person who wrote the check is. Therefore, a bank may refuse to honor a check. But if it refuses to pay a valid check, the bank has breached its contract with the depositor, and may be held liable for any losses the depositor incurs because the check was not honored.

COLLATERAL—a pledge of real or personal property to secure the payment of a loan or the extension of credit. Collateral can be in many forms, but it should have enough value to secure the loan. Also, it should be in a form that the lender can convert to cash, if the need arises. Many banks use only the borrower's signature as collateral for small loans. But each lending institution must decide the amount and type of collateral it will accept.

DISCOUNTING—a bank's practice of charging a fee for converting credit instruments into cash. A bank may advance money to the person who holds the instrument and charge him its usual discount rate. Then the bank holds the documents until maturity. If the person or institution that issued the document pays the bank, the transaction is closed. If not, the bank will expect the depositor to return its money.

FEDERAL RESERVE BANK—The Federal Reserve System was established in 1913 by President Woodrow Wilson when he signed the Federal Reserve Act. This act created 12 regional banks across the nation, controlled by the Federal Reserve Board of governors in Washington, D.C. These banks regulate the flow of credit and money. Any bank that wants to use money from the Federal Reserve Bank in its region must become a member of the Federal Reserve System. The Federal Reserve Bank provides many services for its member banks; it handles their reserve accounts, furnishes currency and coins, clears and collects checks, transfers funds by wire, and acts as a depository for the funds handled by government agencies.

INDEPENDENT RETIREMENT ACCOUNT —a bank account for accumulating money that a person will use during retirement. Each year the depositor can put up to fifteen percent of his earned income in the account, up to a maximum of $1,750 each year. This money is not charged Federal income taxes during the current year; it is taxed only when an individual starts withdrawing money. He can do this as early as age 59½, and he must begin withdrawing the money by age 70½. He can take out the deposit in one lump sum or in a certain amount per month.

If both husband and wife are working, each of them can have an Individual Retirement Account. They can set aside a maximum total of $3,000 for these accounts each year. The bank pays interest to these accounts while the money is on deposit; the rate of interest varies from bank to bank.

INTEREST PENALTY—an amount of interest that you forfeit to the bank if you withdraw the money in a time certificate of deposit before it matures. The federal law states that when you cash a certificate of deposit before maturity, you will earn the regular passbook savings rate *minus* 90 days' interest. This means that if you cash a time certificate of deposit early, the bank will not pay interest for 90 days of the time you had the certificate in effect. The bank would pay you the regular passbook rate for the rest of the time you had the money on deposit.

JOINT TENANTS—the partners who jointly own an asset. In banking, this term usually refers to two or more people who jointly own a bank account. If one of the partners dies, his interest or ownership is automatically transferred to the remaining owner(s). Married couples often establish bank accounts as joint tenants.

LINE OF CREDIT—the amount of money that any one person, corporation, or organization can borrow with a certain amount of collateral. Different lending institutions have different ways of arriving at this figure.

For example, let us say that a certain bank has a policy of financing only 75 percent of the value of an automobile. A certain vehicle is valued at $10,000. The bank would loan up to $7,500 for this car; that's the line of credit available.

NONTAXABLE TRUST—an account that an employer uses to provide a stock bonus, pension, or profit-sharing plan for the benefit of his employees. The money deposited in this trust account will not be taxed if it meets all the requirements imposed by federal and state governments.

PRINCIPAL—the original amount of debt, or the initial amount a person owes to another. A bank charges interest only on the principal.

PROMISSORY NOTE—a written promise to pay. A promissory note must conform to the following: (1) It must be in writing and signed by the maker; (2) It must contain an unconditional promise to pay a certain sum of money; (3) It must be payable on demand or at a fixed future time; (4) It must be payable to a designated person or to the bearer.

The payee does not need to hold the note until the maturity date. He may decide to sell it to someone else; in that case, if the instrument is *order paper* (i.e., written to pay a designated person), he endorses the instrument and gives it to the buyer. If it is *bearer paper* (i.e., written to pay the bearer), he simply gives it to the buyer.

PROXY—authorization to allow another person to vote in your absence at a business meeting. In banking, this term usually refers to the proxies that an account holder in a savings-and-loan company may give to the officers of his company.

REDISCOUNTING—If a bank wants to convert some of its holdings into cash, it would submit its bills and notes to its local Federal Reserve Bank for rediscounting. After charging a *rediscount fee,* the Federal Reserve Bank would dispense the cash and hold the instruments until maturity. If all of the debtors pay their notes, the transaction is completed. If not, the Federal Reserve Bank will demand payment from the borrowing bank, which in turn will demand payment from the debtor(s).

SECURED LOAN—a loan that requires the borrower to make a pledge of collateral. Many institutions make only this type of loan. The greater the risk that the loan will not be repaid, the more security the lending institution will require. A good example might be an automobile loan. The bank will hold the title to the car as collateral until the debt has been paid. If the debt isn't paid, the bank may sell the car and recover the money it lended.

SIGNATURE LOAN—a loan that requires only the signature of the borrower as collateral. The lending institution relies on the integrity of the person who borrows the money. In most cases, this type of loan is for a short term and for a low amount.

TENANTS IN COMMON—ownership of an asset by two or more persons, in which each person has an individual interest. In banking, this term usually refers to the common ownership of a bank account. When one of the owners dies, his ownership passes to his heirs or to whomever he has named in his will; the surviving owners do not automatically inherit the account. Tenants in common do not necessarily have equal interests in the account. If one member wishes to dispose of his portion of the account and the others do not, he may force them to convert the account to cash so that he can receive his share.

TRADE ACCEPTANCE—a bill of exchange that arises out of a merchant's purchase of goods. The seller of goods (*drawer*) signs over the debt of the buyer *(drawee),* to a designated agent *(payee).* When the buyer accepts this document, he agrees to pay his debt to the agent.

Let us say that ABC Company has purchased a shipment of goods on credit. The company that sold the goods to ABC issues a trade acceptance. When ABC Company receives the trade acceptance, one of its officers will write the word *accepted* across the face of the document with the date and place of payment, followed by his signature. ABC Company then becomes liable to pay the bill as stated.

TRUST OFFICER—one who manages a trust for someone else. The trust officer may also be called *trustee.*

INSURANCE

ACCIDENT INSURANCE—insurance covering such risks as death, dismemberment, loss of eyesight, or loss of time as a result of accidents. An *accident* is generally defined as an unlooked-for mishap; if someone intentionally cuts off his arm or leg, it would not be an accident. Accident insurance would cover death from accidental means, but no other kind of death.

DOUBLE INDEMNITY—an insurance company's practice of giving twice the amount of insurance benefits when an insured person dies. Double indemnity is most commonly given when the insured person dies in an accident. Many insurance companies do not give double indemnity if the death occurred through suicide, service in time of war, air travel, or disease.

FIRE INSURANCE—insurance that guards against the loss of property by fire. The person who owns a fire insurance policy must have an *insurable interest* in the property involved. In other words, the insured must have a lawful, economic interest in the safety or preservation of the property from loss or destruction. (For example, the average citizen couldn't buy fire insurance on the White House.)

FLOOD INSURANCE—insurance against loss caused by cloudbursts and floods, tidal waves or overflowing streams and rivers. This type of insurance is usually available in low-lying areas and in the vicinity of rivers and dams.

HEALTH INSURANCE—insurance to cover losses caused by illness or sickness.

INCONTESTABILITY—protection against having a life insurance policy cancelled by the insurance company. Most policies state that they are incontestable after two years, unless you fail to pay your premium.

INCREASE OF HAZARD—taking unnecessary or unusual risks. Usually a fire insurance policy will state that the insurance company is not liable for loss or damage if the likelihood of fire is increased by any means within your control. For example, the company may not pay for a fire if you keep fireworks, explosives, gasoline, kerosene, or other highly flammable materials on your property.

INDUSTRIAL LIFE INSURANCE—a fairly small amount of life insurance, for which you pay premiums at weekly or other frequent intervals. Generally, this kind of life insurance policy offers the least amount of protection for the dollars you spend.

INSURABLE INTEREST—Usually a person takes out a life insurance policy on himself. However, you can take out a life insurance policy on someone else and make yourself the beneficiary, if you have an insurable interest in the life of that person. The term *insurable interest* generally means: (1) In the case of persons related by blood or law, an interest that arises from love and affection, or (2) In the case of other persons, a lawful economic interest in protecting the life of the insured person.

LIFE INSURANCE—a form of insurance that pays benefits in the event of death. An insurance company will pay an agreed sum of money to a designated person (called a *beneficiary*) when the insured person dies. The beneficiary may be the estate of the insured, a member of his family, a business associate, or even a stranger. The policy will state whether you can change the name of the beneficiary. If you can't, the beneficiary has what is called a *vested interest*—that is, his interest in the policy may not be stripped from him without his consent. Thus, you may take out a life insurance policy on a member of your family or upon the life of another person who owes you a debt. A business partnership may take out a policy on the lives of its partners. Likewise, a corporation may obtain a life insurance policy for each of its corporate officers. But if you have no insurable interest in the life of the person insured, the law considers it to be a *contract of wager*. Even if an insurance company issues a policy under these circumstances, it is illegal and unenforceable.

MARINE INSURANCE—insurance that covers losses connected with marine activities. This contract may also protect against losses on inland waters or on land, if the losses are connected with a sea voyage. The person or firm obtaining this kind of insurance must have an insurable interest in the subject of the policy (e.g., the boat or the cargo carried by the boat).

MUTUAL INSURANCE—a form of insurance in which the policyholders make up the insurance company. (The *policyholders* are those who buy insurance policies.) Mutual insurance companies only insure the lives and property of their members. When the annual premiums that members pay exceed the amount of losses covered by the company, the company often pays a *dividend* (i.e., a small refund) to the policyholders.

PAID-UP and ENDOWMENT OPTIONS—the opportunity to convert a life insurance policy to another form of insurance, so that you do not have to pay premiums. The original policy may state that when you do this you can keep the same amount of insurance in force *(paid-up option)*, or that you will have a declining amount of insurance *(endowment option)*. Usually these options require that: (1) The money you've invested in the policy must be earning interest equal to the amount of your premium. (2) You must ask the company to convert the policy. (3) Your request will be subject to the company's approval. (4) The company will determine how much insurance you can buy under the new plan. (5) If you've borrowed money against your present policy, your new policy will become the collateral for the loan. Not all life insurance policies carry these options.

UNOCCUPANCY—a clause that states that the insurance company will not pay for loss or damage that occurs while an insured building is vacant or unoccupied beyond a certain period of time—usually ten days.

WAIVER OF PREMIUM—a provision that allows you to stop paying premiums on a life insurance policy if you become disabled. Your policy would remain in force, and when your disability ends you resume making the payments.

REAL ESTATE

ABSTRACT OF TITLE—a legal document that shows the history of ownership for a certain piece of property. In most states, the abstract of title passes from the seller to the buyer with each sale of property, and the buyer's name is added to the permanent record. The seller must pay the expense of bringing the abstract up to date. The buyer must have an attorney check the abstract to be sure it is complete.

APPRECIATION—a property's increase in value over a length of time. It is the opposite of *depreciation*. For example, let us say that a tract of land was purchased for $500 per acre five years ago. Today the same land would probably be worth at least $1,000 per acre.

ASSESSMENT—a government's charge against a certain parcel of real estate. This charge is usually made to cover the property owner's share of the cost of a public improvement such as a street or sewer.

BREACH OF CONTRACT—a situation in which one or both parties fail to perform a legal contract. Both parties must accept the breach. If one doesn't accept it for any reason, he may sue the other party to regain what was lost.

EARNEST MONEY—a down payment that a purchaser of real estate makes to show his good faith in the transaction. Earnest money shows the seller that the buyer really means to follow through with the agreement. Sometimes the seller refunds the money if the transaction fails to go through; sometimes he doesn't. This decision is up to the seller.

ESCROW—an account where money is held until a contract has been fulfilled. This type of arrangement is most often used in the sale of real estate. An escrow agent holds the buyer's down payment until the title search is completed and the transaction is closed. The seller receives none of the money until all the legalities are in order. Banks and lawyers are the most common escrow agents.

FEE SIMPLE—the transfer of property to someone and his heirs without limitations. An estate or inheritance that you own completely and without restrictions is called an estate in *fee simple*. You may use it in any way you choose during your life time or after your death (through your will). If you have not made any plans for the distribution of this estate, it must pass to your heirs without any future limitations.

FIRST/SECOND MORTGAGE—a lender's claim to a piece of property that the owner has used as collateral on a loan. If the property owner fails to repay his loan, the lender can force him to sell the property to repay the debt. The only difference between a first and second mortgage is the order in which the lenders file their claim on the property. A second mortgage would only be good after the first mortgage had been satisfied. A lender would prefer to have a first mortgage rather than a second mortgage, since he would be more likely to get his money back.

LIEN—a claim that a person or institution has upon the property of another. The borrower must keep the property as security for the debts. In other words, a lien puts a "hold" on a certain item until its borrower has paid the debt. A lender may hold a lien on real estate, an automobile, or any other item of personal property.

PRORATED TAXES—taxes that are split between the buyer and the seller of a piece of property. When property is sold, the taxes are usually divided according to the time the sale takes place. The buyer should only be expected to pay taxes for the time after he receives title to the property, and not for the entire year.

QUIT-CLAIM DEED—a deed that gives a buyer whatever right, title, or interest that the seller has in a piece of property. It does not indicate whether other persons have an interest in the property, too.

SURVEYOR'S REPORT—a report from a licensed surveyor, which is used to determine limits and boundaries of a piece of property. The surveyor checks legal descriptions of the tract and usually drives stakes at the corners of the property to aid anyone else determining the boundaries at a later time. A surveyor's report should include the measurements of the land in terms of acres, square miles, or square feet. It should also give definite boundaries, the corner locations, and a definite point of beginning the measurement.

The cost of this report varies upon the time required for the research. This fee is customarily paid by a person who is purchasing the property.

TITLE INSURANCE—a contract to protect the owner of real estate against loss arising from defective property titles, hidden liens, or other encumbrances.

Usually title insurance losses are very small, because title insurance companies examine all legal papers very carefully before they will insure them. The premiums paid for title insurance are quite high, because of the amount of time it takes to research the documents. The title company must examine many records of land titles involving many previous owners, deeds, mortgages, and so on. A title insurance policy remains in effect until some further change of ownership takes place, or until a claim is made against a property.

WARRANTY DEED WITH FULL COVENANTS—the most complete form of property title that a seller can give. In this type of deed, a seller guarantees: (1) that he has the right to give the purchaser the title as designated in the contract; (2) that the buyer shall enjoy the premises without having to dispute claims from others; (3) that the premises are free from encumbrances such as tax debts; (4) that the seller will provide any further necessary assurances of the title; and (5) that the seller will forever guarantee the buyer's title to the premises. This is the most valuable form of protection, from the purchaser's viewpoint.

Of course, a buyer can obtain title insurance from a title insurance company for even more protection.

BIOGRAPHICAL DICTIONARY

It would be impossible to name all of the people who have played an important role in the history of the United States. But in this chapter we list some of the leading Americans from all walks of life, both living and dead, who have left their mark on American society.

AARON, HENRY L. "HANK" (1934–   ), baseball player. Born in Mobile, Alabama, Aaron began playing for the Indianapolis Clowns of the Negro League in 1952. He joined the Milwaukee Braves as shortstop in 1954 and soon moved to an outfield position. The next year he emerged as top batter of the National League with a .328 average. When the Braves won the World Series in 1957, Aaron was voted the league's Most Valuable Player. He moved with the Braves to Atlanta in 1966, and broke Babe Ruth's home-run record when he hit run number 715 on April 8, 1974 in Atlanta.

ABBOTT, BUD (1896–1974), associated in comedy with Lou Costello. A son of Harry Abbott who served with Ringling Brothers' Circus, he organized a network of burlesque houses in the generation of the Ziegfeld Follies. Abbott starred in several movies, including *One Night in the Tropics, Hold That Ghost,* and *Abbott and Costello Meet Frankenstein.* He promoted the sale of millions of war bonds in World War II and entertained troops during the war. His efforts on behalf of radio, stage, and screen performance made him a well-known entertainer in an age that placed a premium on slapstick.

ABBOTT, LYMAN (1835–1922), an ordained minister of the Congregational Church; prominent journalist and exponent of the "social gospel." Abbott was associated with *Harper's Magazine* and *The Christian Union* (also known as *The Outlook*). He authored *The Life and Literature of the Ancient Hebrews* and other titles that sought to integrate religion and science. After the publication of Charles Darwin's theories of evolution, he became involved with liberal writers and thinkers. Abbott rarely opposed the theological trends of his day. He believed that man was constantly improving, and he affirmed the essential goodness of man. Ira Brown has written an excellent biography titled *Lyman Abbott* (1953).

ABERNATHY, RALPH DAVID (1926–   ), civil rights leader of the Southern Christian Leadership Conference. Abernathy was closely identified with Dr. Martin Luther King and the human rights revolution of the 1960s. A deliberative preacher committed to nonviolence, he was a member of the Atlantic Ministers Union and Operation Breadbasket. This gave him a unique sensitivity to the religious applications of human needs. During the Montgomery (Alabama) bus boycott he demonstrated strength of purpose and determination that helped to change the social order. He was ordained into the Baptist ministry in 1948.

ACHESON, DEAN (1893–1971), Secretary of State under President Truman; a diplomat in the early stages of the Cold War between the United

States and the Soviet Union. Acheson wrote *Power and Diplomacy,* among other titles. He was largely responsible for the establishment of the North Atlantic Treaty Organization (NATO). During the period of McCarthyism, Acheson refused to testify against his friend Alger Hiss, who had been charged with espionage. He received many honors during his lifetime, including honorary degrees from Yale University and Wesleyan University. He was affiliated with the Democratic Party.

ACUFF, ROY (1903–), born Maynardsville, Tennessee, a noted country-music singer and bandleader. Acuff organized the Smokey Mountain Boys and has been closely associated with Nashville's Grand Ole Opry. He has achieved international fame for his songs, "Wabash Cannon Ball," "That Lonely Mountain of Clay," and "The Great Judgment Morning." He produced a succession of recording classics for Columbia Records and was elected to the Country Music Hall of Fame. An automobile accident in 1965 left him severely injured, but he recovered sufficiently to record "Roy Acuff Sings Famous Opry Favorites" in 1967. He toured college campuses and received considerable recognition for his courage and determination in the face of his injuries.

ADDAMS, JANE (1860–1935), with Ellen Gates Starr organized Hull House in Chicago, Illinois, as a social and humanitarian center. Miss Addams was an early feminist and shared a Nobel Peace Prize. She authored *The Spirit of Youth* and *The City Streets.* Miss Addams was a leader of the Progressive Party and the Women's International Peace and Freedom. She sought legislation to end the corruption of political life in Chicago, and she served as an adviser to several Presidents.

ALI, MUHAMMAD (1942–), a significant figure in American boxing history, known for his colorful and poetic use of language. Born as Cassius M. Clay, he became associated with the Black Muslims and adopted his Muslim name. He refused to be drafted into the military in 1967 and became the center of legal controversies. He won numerous Golden Gloves awards, the Olympic Championship, and the Heavyweight Championship of the world. He has engaged in limited screen roles and frequently appears on television. Leon Spinks won the Heavyweight championship from Ali at Las Vegas, Nevada on February 15, 1978.

ALLEN, ETHAN (1738–1789), author and military figure from the Revolutionary period. During the American Revolution, Allen was captured by the British and was held as a prisoner of war. He organized a militia group in Vermont known as the Green Mountain Boys, and he asked the Continental Congress to raise similar units among the other colonies. He authored a book titled *Reason the Only Grade of Man* (1784), an apology for deism.

ALLPORT, GORDON (1897–1967), outstanding psychologist and teacher. Allport wrote *The Individual and His Religion.* He was associated with Harvard University and produced several new theories of personality and social psychology. Allport was involved in many different organizations, including the British Psychological Society and the National Research Council. He received numerous honors and recognitions, and served as editor of the *Journal for Abnormal and Social Psychology* from 1937 to 1949.

ANDERSON, MARIAN (1902–), black contralto recognized as an outstanding singer within concert and operatic circles. Honored in many countries for her musical excellence, she is a native of South Philadelphia. Miss Anderson authored *My Lord, What a Morning* and has travelled extensively, giving concerts in Great Britain, Scandinavia, Germany, and the Soviet Union. She has worked with Paul Robeson and others to achieve greater freedoms for black Americans. Miss Anderson has received special recognition from the National Association for the Advancement of Colored People (NAACP) and was honored by Howard University and 20 other colleges and universities with honorary doctorates.

Muhammad Ali lands a right to George Foreman during their title bout in Kinshasa, Zaire, on Oct. 29, 1976.

ANTHONY, SUSAN B. (1820–1906), an early proponent of women's rights, identified with the leadership of the American Suffrage Association and several temperance associations. Miss Anthony organized support for the enactment of the fourteenth and fifteenth amendments to the United States Constitution. She was involved in the publication of *The History of Woman's Suffrage* and worked with Ida Harper on *The Life and Work of Susan B. Anthony.*

ARBUCKLE, ROSCOE "FATTY" (1887–1933), American actor and producer born in Smith Center, Kansas. Mr. Arbuckle was identified with numerous motion picture roles in *Moonshine, The Bell Boy,* and *The Sheriff,* among others. He organized the Comique Film Corporation.

ARMSTRONG, LOUIS (1900–1971), jazz trumpeter and vocalist, also known as "Satchmo." Mr. Armstrong appeared in numerous movies, including *Pennies from Heaven, New Orleans, The Glenn Miller Story,* and *Hello Dolly.* Born in New Orleans, he revolutionized American Jazz. After touring the United States with his band, he played at the London Palladium and made numerous appearances before royalty in Sweden, Belgium, Holland, and Denmark. Mr. Armstrong's performance in *High Society* and numerous other recordings have made him an enduring part of the American scene.

ARMSTRONG, NEIL (1930–), veteran astronaut; the first man to set foot on the moon. Born near Wapakoneta, Ohio, he graduated from Purdue University. As a test pilot he was chosen to serve with Edwin Aldrin and Michael Collins on the historic moon flight of July 16, 1969. He also served as the command pilot for the later Gemini 8 program. Mr. Armstrong was an aviator for the United States Naval Reserve from 1949 to 1950. His name will always be associated with the famous words he spoke as he set foot on the moon: "One small step for man; one giant step for mankind."

ARNAZ, DESI (1917–), Latin American musician, comedian, and television producer. Born in Santiago, Cuba, he was associated in comedy with Lucille Ball during the early stages of television. Mr. Arnaz starred in several lesser-known movie musicals until he organized Desilu Productions with his wife, Lucille Ball. He co-starred with Lucille Ball in other movie productions, such as *The Long, Long, Trailer* and *Forever Darling.* He hosted *Desilu Playhouse.* After 1962, he became an independent producer and president of Desi Arnaz Productions. He served during World War II in the United States Army.

ARNOLD, BENEDICT (1741–1801), a patriot and traitor from the Revolutionary period. Arnold organized an army early in the Revolutionary War, but escaped to the British in 1781. His name is synonymous with treachery. In the winter of 1776–1777, he was accused of misconduct and of stealing property from merchants in Montreal during the Canadian campaign. In anger, he resigned his commission in 1777. He conceived the idea of turning over the command of West Point to the English for a ransom; the plot was uncovered and he was forced to seek sanctuary with the English army.

ASBURY, FRANCIS (1745–1816), an early bishop in the Methodist Episcopal Church, associated with John Wesley. Asbury came to America as a missionary and remained to become a leading spokesman for the Independent Methodist Episcopal Church of America. He preached in the Pennsylvania, Maryland, Delaware, and Virginia colonies with a vigor and effectiveness that attracted popular notice. He developed a feud with rival church leader, Thomas Rankin, and during the American Revolution, they were asked to return to England. Rankin left but Asbury remained and became a leading force in the development of religious independence. He authored *Journals and Letters,* edited by Elmer T. Clark (1958).

ASTAIRE, FRED (1899–), American dancer and entertainer. His more famous screen performances include *Easter Parade* (1948), *On the Beach* (1959), and *The Pleasure of His Company* (1961). Mr. Astaire authored *Steps in Time.* His dancing abilities were emphasized in most of his screen performances, such as *The Ziegfeld Follies.* He starred on numerous television specials and occasionally appeared on *The Alcoa Premier.*

ASTOR, JOHN JACOB (1763–1848), American capitalist and entrepreneur. Born in Germany, he immigrated to America and became involved in fur-trading. He organized the American

Fur Company. Mr. Astor's life was characterized by the amassing of incredible wealth. Following the Louisiana Purchase, his trading activities penetrated the Northwest Territories; his traders would collect furs and sell them in the Far East. The town of Astoria was named after the family. After 1800, he became more interested in New York City real estate.

ATTUCKS, CRISPUS (1723–1770), among the group that precipitated the Boston Massacre. Attucks was among the first to die in the struggle that led to the American Revolution. Attucks has been described as a mulatto owned by Deacon William Browne of Framingham, Massachusetts. Although little is known about his life before the Boston Massacre, he has achieved stature as a martyr and patriot. J. B. Fisher, in the *American Historical Record,* Volume I (1872), sought to analyze the deeper meaning of Crispus Attucks' life.

AUDUBON, JOHN J. (1785–1851), a popular naturalist and *ornithologist* (one who studies birds). A man of science, he was responsible for the classification of numerous bird species. Audubon authored *Birds of America,* a classic in the study of birds. His fame extended to Europe. Audubon's earliest research was completed in the wilderness of Kentucky; he travelled to Henderson, Kentucky, to study rare birds. His famous bird drawings evolve from this period. His work is judged as excellent art and science.

AUTRY, GENE (1907–   ), singer, actor, and entertainer born in Tioga, Texas. Autry made his first record in 1929, singing cowboy songs. He starred in over eighty movies and owns several radio stations in the Southwest and on the West Coast. He has written many songs, including "You're the Only Star in My Blue Heaven" and "Here Comes Santa Claus." He has also produced several television specials.

BAEZ, JOAN (1941–   ), folk singer and political activist identified with the anti-war protests of the 1960s. Her musical style reflects melancholy and sadness. Miss Baez was a student at Boston University Fine Arts School. Early in her career, she appeared in Ballard Room and Club 47, and she attracted attention at the Newport (R.I.) Folk Festival. She toured college campuses and in 1962 had a successful Carnegie Hall concert. She established the Institute for the Study of Non-violence in Carmel, California.

BAILEY, F. LEE (1933–   ), defense attorney born in Waltham, Massachusetts. Bailey achieved early fame in the second murder trial of Dr. Sam Sheppard, in which he won Dr. Sheppard's acquittal. He has been described as the most significant criminal lawyer in contemporary America. After Albert DeSalvo's revelations regarding the Boston Strangler Case, he fought for DeSalvo's acquittal but lost. The DeSalvo trial has been regarded as a classic episode in American legal history.

BAILEY, PEARL (1918–   ), female singer born in Newport News, Virginia. Miss Bailey attended various public schools until she achieved early fame as a popular vocalist with stage bands in New York. She has performed in several Broadway musicals, including *The House of Flowers.* She played significant roles in several screen plays, including *Carmen Jones* and *Variety Girl.*

BALL, LUCILLE (1911–   ), actress, television personality, producer, and director. Born in Jamestown, New York, she achieved early fame with her first husband, Desi Arnaz, in the successful television comedy series, *I Love Lucy.* She organized the Desilu Production Company and achieved additional successes in several film productions, including *Forever Darling* and *Love From a Stranger.* Miss Ball has been regarded as the most significant personality from the "situation comedy" programs of American television. Her programs have been syndicated around the world.

BALL, THOMAS (1819–1911), sculptor born in Boston, Massachusetts. Ball achieved early fame at the New England Museum. He travelled to Florence, Italy, at the end of the American Civil War, and received several significant commissions. His more famous creations include *Christmas Morning, St. John the Evangelist* and *Love Memories.* He authored an autobiography titled *My Threescore Years and Ten.* He returned to America in 1897. His most famous work done in the United States is the statue of President Washington.

BARNUM, PHINEAS T. (1810–1891), showman and organizer of circus performances. In 1844, Barnum engaged the services of Tom

Thumb, a dwarf, and travelled to Europe for a series of shows. Barnum was responsible for the early and successful appearances of Jenny Lind in America. He ran for Congress and was defeated. He then organized what came to be called "The Greatest Show on Earth," launching the circus firm of Barnum and Bailey in 1881. Barnum authored the *Life of P. T. Barnum Written by Himself* in 1855.

BASIE, WILLIAM "COUNT" (1904–1984), jazz musician, band leader, and composer. Born in Red Bank, New Jersey, Basie has been featured in concerts at Carnegie Hall and Lincoln Center. He has given command performances before the Queen of England and was featured at the Kennedy Inaugural Ball. Basie has also performed on numerous television programs. His new jazz styles and themes have achieved distinction.

BEAN, ROY (1825–1904), rough-and-ready judge of the American frontier. Born in Mason County, Kentucky, Bean worked as teamster and saloonkeeper in the Southwest until he settled in San Antonio, Texas. In 1882, he moved up the Pecos River and established a saloon for workers who were building the Southern Pacific Railroad. Appointed justice of the peace, he made his saloon in Vinegaroon, Texas his courtroom. Bean was noted for his humor. He became known as "the law west of the Pecos."

BEECHER, HENRY WARD (1813–1887), clergyman and public figure born in Litchfield, Connecticut. Beecher attended Amherst College and became a minister. He sought to effect a moral change in the lives of his audience. He edited the *Western Farmer and Gardener,* based in Indianapolis. In 1847, he was called to Park Street Church as minister; he rejected the invitation and launched a public speaking campaign against slavery in the United States.

BEECHER, LYMAN (1775–1863), clergyman and father of Henry Ward Beecher. Born in New Haven, Connecticut, the elder Beecher was instrumental in organizing the American Bible Society. He served as president of Lane Theological Seminary in Cincinnati, and became embroiled in controversies of the General Assembly of the Presbyterian Church in Ohio.

BELL, ALEXANDER GRAHAM (1847–1922), prolific American inventor born in Edinburgh, Scotland. Although the telephone is his most famous invention, Bell developed many early electronic devices for the deaf. His long-time assistant was Thomas Watson. The first words transmitted by telephone on April 3, 1877 were "Mr. Watson, come here; I want you." Bell received many honors, including the Volta Prize awarded by the French Government. He wrote *Duration of Life* and *Condition Associated with Longevity* (1918).

BENNY, JACK (1894–1974), violinist, vaudeville star, radio and motion-picture personality. Born in Waukegan, Illinois, as Benjamin Kubelsky, he took the stage name of Jack Benny. He achieved significant fame through his television program, *The Jack Benny Show.* He entertained the troops during World War II, and was honored by the National Academy of Television Arts and Science in 1957 for his contributions to the world of entertainment.

BERLIN, IRVING (1888–), composer and musician. Born in Russia and migrated to the United States in 1893, Berlin transformed American popular music with his relaxing themes and topical lyrics. Among his famous song titles are: "All Alone," "Remember Reaching for the Moon," and "When I Lost You." His most famous composition was "God Bless America." Berlin composed the stage musicals *Annie Get Your Gun, Call Me Madam,* and *Mr. President.*

BERNSTEIN, LEONARD (1918–), conductor, pianist, and composer. Born in Lawrence, Massachusetts, he became a student of Fritz Reiner and Serge Koussevitsky. He was appointed musical director of the New York Philharmonic, where he achieved worldwide recognition. Among his more famous musical creations have been *West Side Story* (1957) and music for *On the Waterfront* (1954). Bernstein wrote *The Joy of Music* (1959) and *Leonard Bernstein's Young People's Concerts for Reading and Listening* (1962).

BETHUNE, MARY MCLEOD (1875–1955), black educator. Born in Mayesville, South Carolina, she studied at Moody Bible Institute of Chicago and later served as president of Bethune-Cookman College. She was appointed as special adviser for minority affairs to President

Franklin Roosevelt and was associated with the National Association for the Advancement of Colored People (NAACP). For a time, she was president of the Central Life Insurance Company and served with the United Negro College Fund. Mrs. Bethune received many honors and degrees from colleges and universities, including Howard University, Wilberforce University, Atlanta University, and the Tuskegee Institute.

BLACK HAWK (1767–1838), Indian war chief. Born in a Sauk village on the Rock River in Illinois, Black Hawk opposed a treaty negotiated by William Henry Harrison with the Sauk nation in 1804; the treaty gave the United States all Sauk country east of the Mississippi River. Black Hawk assisted the British forces in the War of 1812. During the Black Hawk War, he was taken prisoner and jailed at Fort Armstrong in 1832. In 1833, he dictated the *Autobiography of Black Hawk* to a journalist, J. B. Patterson.

BLACK, HUGO L. (1886–1971), jurist and United States Senator. Born in Harlan County, Alabama, Black attended law school at the University of Alabama. He served as prosecuting attorney for Jefferson County from 1915 to 1917, and was in general law practice from 1919 to 1927. He was elected the United States Senator from Alabama for 1927–1931. He served as an associate justice on the United States Supreme Court from 1937 until his death in 1971. Black favored a liberal interpretation of the United States Constitution. He aided the Earl Warren court rulings in the area of civil rights.

BLOCK, HERBERT "HERBLOCK" (1909–), editorial cartoonist born in Chicago, Illinois. Block has served as a cartoonist with the *Washington Post* and the *Chicago Daily News.* He received the Pulitzer Prize, 1942 and 1954. He has been associated with various civil-liberty causes. Block wrote *The Herblock Book* (1952) and *Straight Herblock* (1964), among others. He was commissioned to design the United States postage stamp to commemorate the 175th anniversary of the Bill of Rights.

BOGART, HUMPHREY (1899–1957), actor and film producer. Born in New York City, Bogart portrayed outstanding screen roles without sentimentality. Among his best-known films were *African Queen, Caine Mutiny,* and *Casablanca.* He was married to Lauren Bacall. Bogart's characterization of Captain Queeg in *Caine Mutiny* received an Academy Award.

BOONE, DANIEL (1734–1820), frontier explorer and Indian fighter. Born near Reading, Pennsylvania, Boone moved to Kentucky in 1767. There he was involved with several expeditions against the Shawnee Indians, and served as captain of the local militia when Kentucky became organized as part of Virginia. Stuart Edward White's *Daniel Boone, Wilderness Scout* (1922) is regarded as the best biography of Boone.

BOOTH, EDWIN T. (1833–1893), actor of international fame. Born in Bel Air, Maryland, Booth played minor roles in *Richard III* (1849) and *The Iron Chest* (1851). Then he travelled west to California, settled in San Francisco, and appeared in leading roles as Richard III, Macbeth, and Hamlet. He went to Australia on tour in 1854 and then to New York, where he obtained a major role in *The Fool's Revenge* in 1864. His younger brother John Wilkes Booth assassinated President Abraham Lincoln.

BOOTH, JOHN WILKES (1838–1865), actor and assassin of President Abraham Lincoln. Born in Bel Air, Maryland, Booth had considerable promise as an actor. He performed with great success at the Boston Museum in 1863. His sympathies were with the South during the Civil War, and he served as a member of the Virginia militia that arrested and executed John Brown. Booth organized the conspiracy that led to the assassination of President Lincoln on April 14, 1865.

BRADY, MATTHEW B. (1823–1896), pioneer photographer. Born in Warren County, New York, Brady began making portraits with the daguerreotype, an early photographic technique developed by S.F.B. Morse and J.W. Draper. Brady published *The Gallery of Illustrious Americans* in 1850. With the approval of President Lincoln, he photographed many historic scenes during the Civil War. His innovations had far-reaching significance in the development of photography.

BRINKLEY, DAVID (1920–), broadcast journalist. Born in Wilmington, North Carolina, Brinkley served as a reporter with Wilmington *Star-News* and then as Washington correspondent for the National Broadcasting Company (NBC). With Chet Huntley, he established a reputation as news analyst and co-anchor for *The NBC News*. Brinkley has received the du Pont and Peabody Awards for outstanding journalism.

BROOKS, PHILLIPS (1835–1893), clergyman, author, and composer. Born in Boston, Massachusetts, Brooks became an outstanding leader in American Protestantism. He came from a family that treasured piety and learning; scholarship and eloquence in preaching were the characteristics of his ministry in Boston. Brooks was a leading voice in the Episcopal Church in America. He delivered several noted lectures on preaching before the Divinity School of Yale College in 1877. Alexander U.G. Allen's *Life and Letters of Phillips Brooks* is the most useful biography.

BROWN, JOHN (1800–1859), abolitionist leader. Brown was born in Tourington, Connecticut. He is remembered for his attack on Harpers Ferry, Virginia before the Civil War. Brown hoped to start a wider revolt among black people by seizing the arsenal and distributing arms among the blacks. But the attack failed; John Brown was indicted on three counts of treason and executed.

BRYAN, WILLIAM JENNINGS (1860–1925), lawyer, editor, orator, and political figure. Born in Salem, Illinois, Bryan ran unsuccessfully for President on three occasions. He was described as "The Great Commoner" because of his policies that favored farmers and common laborers. In 1913, he was named Secretary of State by President Woodrow Wilson. He opposed the United States' entry into World War. Later Bryan defended the anti-evolution educational laws passed by the State of Tennessee. He successfully prosecuted a teacher named Thomas Scopes for violating the anti-evolution statutes.

BUNCHE, RALPH (1904–1971), diplomat and human rights leader. Bunche was born in Detroit, Michigan. He attended the University of California and Harvard University, as well as the London School of Economics. He studied anthropology and colonial policy. Bunche participated in several study projects on race relations and international understanding. He attended the San Francisco Conference of the United Nations as a member of the United States delegation. Later he served as a member of the United Nations' Palestine Commission. He received the Nobel Prize, the Presidential Medal of Freedom, and the Spingarn Medal awarded by the National Association for the Advancement of Colored People (NAACP).

BURBANK, LUTHER (1849–1926), plant breeder and agricultural innovator. Burbank was born in Lancaster, Massachusetts. He was deeply influenced by Charles Darwin's views regarding plants and animal life. With an inheritance of 17 acres, he began a series of experiments that developed the "Burbank potato." He authored a significant publication titled *The Training of the Human Plant*. Burbank received an honorary degree from Tufts University. He was a fellow of the American Association for the Advancement of Science and the Royal Horticultural Society.

BURGER, WARREN (1907–), lawyer and Chief Justice of the United States. Born in St. Paul, Minnesota, Burger was appointed to the Supreme Court by President Nixon. Under his leadership, the Supreme Court has been less activist in legal sentiments than was the Earl Warren court. Burger has been involved with the Mayo Foundation. Prior to his appointment to the Supreme Court, he was a law partner in the firm Fairicy, Burger, Moore, & Costello.

BURR, AARON (1756–1836), lawyer and political figure, Vice-President under Thomas

Aaron Burr

Jefferson. Burr was born in Newark, New Jersey. After his term as Vice-President, he conspired to invade Spanish Territories in the Southwest and organize a separate nation. He killed Alexander Hamilton in a duel, which ended Burr's active involvement in politics until the conspiracy was discovered. He was tried for treason and acquitted on a legal technicality.

BURROWS, ABE (1910–), playwright and director born in New York City. Burrows wrote for the CBS and NBC radio networks. He was writer and star of *The Abe Burrows Show*. He co-authored *Guys and Dolls, Three Wishes for James,* and *How to Succeed in Business without Really Trying,* and he received a Pulitzer Prize for the last. Burrows' music achieved significance in recording with Decca Records.

BUSHNELL, HORACE (1802–1876), Congregational clergyman, author, and educator. Bushnell was born in Bantam, Connecticut. He rejected rigid Puritanism for liberal religious views. He authored *Christian Nurture* (1847), *God in Christ* (1848), and *Nature and the Supernatural* (1858). More conservative Christian thinkers regarded his views as heretical. He denied that religious conversion was necessary.

CAESAR, SID (1922–), actor and comedian born in Yonkers, New York. With the emergence of television, Sid Caesar achieved wide recognition. *Caesar's Hour* and *Sid Caesar Invites You* became popular TV programs. Mr. Caesar often appeared on *The Jackie Gleason Show* and *The Carol Burnett Show*. He starred in the motion picture, *It's a Mad, Mad, Mad, Mad World*. For his work in television, he received the Emmy Award and was named to the United States Hall of Fame.

CALDER, ALEXANDER (1898–1976), sculptor and illustrator. Born in Philadelphia, Pennsylvania, Calder studied at the Stevens Institute of Technology. He built animated wire performers called "the miniature circus" and travelled to Europe with the exhibit. As a result, he developed kinetic sculptures, or mobiles. His designs can be seen at the Lincoln Center, New York, Massachusetts Institute of Technology in Cambridge, and at the UNESCO Gardens in Paris.

CALHOUN, JOHN C. (1782–1850), American statesman and political theorist. Born in South Carolina, he served as a member of both houses of Congress and as Secretary of War in the administration of James Monroe. He served as Vice-President in 1825–1829. Calhoun authored the *South Carolina Exposition* that was a response to the so-called Tariff of Abominations. By 1830, Calhoun was promoting the theory of states' rights embraced in the Nullification Doctrine, which held that states could nullify acts of Congress. Calhoun also wrote *Disquisition on Government* and *Government of the United States,* both published posthumously.

CANTOR, EDDIE (1892–1964), comedian and humanitarian leader. Born in New York City, Mr. Cantor began his career in vaudeville and was later associated with burlesque. He toured as Sam Beverly Moon and starred in the stage productions *Broadway Brevities* (1920), *Make It Snappy* (1922), and *Whoopee* (1929). His first motion picture appearance was in 1926. Mr. Cantor was active in Jewish and Christian charities. He authored *Take My Life: The Way I See It* (1959). He received numerous recognitions for his charity work; Temple University honored him with a Doctor of Humane Letters degree.

CAPONE, ALPHONSE "AL" (1899–1947), gangster; perhaps the most notorious criminal in American history. Born in Naples, Italy, he came

Al Capone is led aboard a train to start his journey to the federal penitentiary in Atlanta, Georgia.

to the United States with his family and settled in Brooklyn, New York. In high school, he took charge of the Five Points gang. In a gang fight, he was slashed across the face with a razor blade, and carried the nickname of "Scarface Al" ever after. In 1920, gang leader Johnny Torrio summoned Capone to Chicago to supervise the sale of bootleg whiskey. Torrio retired in 1925, leaving Capone in charge of Chicago's largest crime racket. "Scarface Al" used murder, bombings, and torture to drive out his competitors. In 1927, he exerted his powers to elect "Big Bill" Thompson as mayor of the city. Capone's henchmen executed seven members of a rival gang in the infamous St. Valentine's Day Massacre of 1929. The United States Treasury Department arrested Capone in 1933 on charges of income-tax evasion. After serving 11 years in Alcatraz Prison, he retired to his Miami Beach estate.

CAPP, AL (1909–1979), newspaper cartoonist. Born in New Haven, Connecticut, Capp attended the Pennsylvania Academy of Fine Arts and the Museum of Fine Arts in Boston. He created the comic strip titled "Li'l Abner," which was widely syndicated throughout the United States. United Feature Syndicate distributed "Li'l Abner." He also served as columnist for the *New York Herald Tribune.* Capp was associated with the People to People program of the United Nations.

CARNEGIE, ANDREW (1835–1919), American industrialist, businessman, and philanthropist. Carnegie was born in Scotland. He became one of the so-called "Captains of Industry" at the turn of the century. In 1848, his family settled in the Allegheny region of Pittsburg. Carnegie was a self-educated lover of books, theater, and classical music. In the 1850s, he took advantage of the rising importance of steel. With his capital, Carnegie constructed the Bessemer Steel Rail Company. Toward the close of the century, he completely dominated the United States steel industry. He authored the article entitled "Wealth," which became the core of what sociologists called the Gospel of Wealth. He believed the rich should spend their fortunes for the welfare of the community. He supported the extensive construction of libraries that bear his name.

CARROLL, JOHN (1735–1815), first bishop of the Roman Catholic Church in America. Born in Upper Marlborough, Maryland, he supported the educational and political integration of the Roman Catholic Church with early America. Carroll sought to unify the several Catholic groups in America, and he obtained religious toleration for Catholics. Regulations developed by his associates became the first canon law in America. Carroll encouraged the establishment of parochial education, secular schools, and colleges at Georgetown (1788) and Baltimore (1799).

CARSON, KIT (1809–1868), soldier, Indian agent, and hunter. Born in Madison County, Kentucky, Carson had no formal education and remained illiterate all his life. He travelled to Arizona and southern California and married an Arapaho woman. He served as John C. Frémont's guide and helped Frémont plan expeditions to Wind River Mountains, the Oregon Trail, the Dalles River, and Klamath Lake. He guided Frémont through the Sierra Nevadas to the Great Salt Lake. Carson served in the Office of Indian Affairs and died in Fort Lyon, Colorado.

CARVER, GEORGE WASHINGTON (1861–1943), black botanist, chemist, and educator. Carver was born in Kansas Territory and attended school in Minneapolis, Kansas, and San Francisco. At Booker T. Washington's invitation, he came to the Tuskegee Institute, where he established an international reputation in horticulture and farming. He became a close friend of Henry A. Wallace, who ran for the United States Presidency. He also developed enduring friendships with Thomas Edison, Luther Burbank, and Harvey Firestone.

CHAMBERLAIN, WILT (1936–), professional basketball player. Born in Philadelphia, Pennsylvania, Chamberlain attended Kansas State University. He then served as star center for the Los Angeles Lakers, the Philadelphia 76ers, and the Philadelphia Warriors. In 1967, he led the National Basketball Association in points scored per season. He has achieved stature as an all-time great in the National Basketball Association.

CHANCELLOR, JOHN (1927–), broadcast journalist. Born in Chicago, Illinois, he attended DePaul Academy and became a reporter with the *Chicago Sun-Times.* From 1950 to 1965, he was on the staff of NBC News as a newswriter and served as a correspondent in Vienna, London, and Moscow. He served briefly on the NBC *Today* program. Under President Kennedy, Chancellor served as director of the Voice of America. In recent years, he has been anchorman with David Brinkley on the *NBC Nightly News*.

CHANNING, WILLIAM ELLERY (1780–1842), Unitarian theologian and minister. Channing was born in Newport, Rhode Island. He served as minister to the Federal Street Church in Boston most of his life. He held the view that God was merciful and would save all mankind; thus Channing established the basic tenets of Unitarianism and fathered the American Unitarian Association. Through his writings, he sponsored the movement for cultural independence from England. *The Importance and Means of a National Literature* (1830) is the most significant of his writings.

CHAPMAN, JOHN "JOHNNY APPLESEED" (1774–1845), planter of apple orchards on the American frontier. We cannot determine his parentage and place of birth; he was simply known as "Johnny Appleseed." He enjoyed long trips for the study of birds. Chapman's orchards of apple trees became legendary, particularly around Ashland County near Mansfield, Ohio. He said he was a primitive Christian. In 1838, he travelled into Allen County, Indiana. The legend of Johnny Appleseed is closely identified with the Westward expansion.

CHAVEZ, CESAR (1927–), union organizer among migrant farm workers. Chavez was born near Yuma, Arizona. His early activities in the California Community Service Organization established his abilities as an activist and organizer. He became director of the Organized National Farm Workers Association, which then merged with the Agricultural Workers Organizing Committee of the AFL-CIO. Chavez' ability to organize boycotts and strikes made the growers in the Modesto and Sacramento Valleys of California hostile toward his work. Chavez served in the United States Navy Reserve during World War II.

CHISHOLM, SHIRLEY (1924–), black Congresswoman and outspoken political leader born in Brooklyn, New York. She attended Brooklyn College and Columbia University; she has received honorary degrees from Pratt Institute, Hampton Institute, William Patterson College, and Capital University, among others. The Congresswoman has served in numerous organizations that deal with social programs and public policy. In 1972, she made an unsuccessful bid for the United States Presidency. She has written numerous books and pamphlets, including *Unbought and Unbossed* (1970) and *The Good Fight* (1973).

CLARK, WILLIAM (1770–1838), frontier explorer and Indian fighter born in Caroline County, Virginia. Clark served with "Mad" Anthony Wayne in his campaign against the Indians. He joined Meriwether Lewis for expeditions to the Pacific Northwest. Clark was skilled in dealing with Indians and making maps. His diaries of the Lewis and Clark expeditions are essential to our early knowledge of the Northwest Territories. Clark was appointed as superintendent of Indian affairs for the Louisiana Territories. He was a highly regarded soldier and explorer.

CLAY, HENRY (1777–1852), Secretary of State and political leader for a generation (1812–1852). Born in Hanover County, Virginia, Clay fathered the "American System"—a legislative program to unite the industrial East with the farming West. Clay's plan established protective tariffs and provided federal money for public improvements. Clay ran for the Presidency in 1844 as candidate of the Whig Party and lost. He was the

Henry Clay addressing the U.S. Senate

architect of the Compromise of 1850, which delayed the controversies that erupted in Civil War a decade later.

COBB, TY (1886–1961), regarded by many as the greatest offensive player in baseball history; called "the Georgia Peach." He was born in Narros, Georgia. Cobb was a fierce competitor; he appeared in more games (3,033), batted more times (11,429), with more hits (4,191), finished with a higher lifetime average (.367) than any other major league player. Cobb achieved his reputation with the Detroit Tigers, with which he spent 22 seasons. He was elected into the Baseball Hall of Fame in 1936.

CODY, WILLIAM F. "BUFFALO BILL" (1846–1917), Indian fighter whose fame became part of literature and legend; he established a Wild West show that achieved international standing. Cody was born in Scott County, Iowa. After serving in the Civil War, he worked as a civilian scout for the United States Army. He is said to have slaughtered 4,280 buffalo in an eight-month period to provide food for the Army. His reputation in marksmanship was equalled only by his memory of terrain and geography. Cody engaged in over sixteen Indian battles; his popularity as a showman developed later in life.

COFFIN, HENRY SLOANE (1877–1954), clergyman, author and educator. Born in New York City, Coffin became a leader of liberal evangelicalism. He served as president of Union Theological Seminary and was an effective preacher. Coffin sought to apply Christianity to social problems and tried to improve theological education. He served as a fellow of the Corporation of Yale University. He was moderator of the General Assembly of the Presbyterian Church in the U.S.A. Coffin wrote numerous books, including the *Meaning of the Cross* (1931).

COLE, NAT "KING" (1919–1965), singer, entertainer, and jazz pianist. Cole was born in Montgomery, Alabama. He organized the King Cole Trio and later he achieved prominence as a singer. His musical style was relaxed. Cole's most successful recordings included "Nature Boy" and "Walking My Baby Back Home." His name and voice are associated with the song "Unforgettable." He appeared in several motion pictures without distinction.

COPLEY, JOHN SINGLETON (1738–1815), American painter in the realist tradition, born in Boston, Massachusetts. Copley completed several portraits of outstanding Americans, including Paul Revere and Samuel Adams. In 1774, he travelled to Europe to avoid problems of the Revolutionary era. He was elected to the Royal Academy and painted several massive historical scenes, including *Siege of Gibraltar* (1791) and *The Death of the Earl of Chatham* (1781). Copley died in London.

COSTELLO, LOU (1906–1959), film and radio comedian associated with Bud Abbott in comedy. Born in Paterson, New Jersey, Costello worked as a common laborer at Metro-Goldwyn-Mayer Studios and then as a stunt man. After his comic talents emerged, he appeared on the *Kate Smith Hour.* Costello starred in several movies, including *Hold That Ghost, Abbott and Costello in Hollywood,* and *Abbott and Costello Meet the Mummy.* He is best known for his work in the comedy of errors.

CROCKETT, DAVID (1786–1836), political figure, Indian fighter, and celebrity of the American frontier. Born in Hawkins County, Tennessee, Crockett was involved with the so-called Creek War against Creek Indians in Alabama. He was elected to the Tennessee legislature and later won a seat in the United States House of Representatives. After three terms in Congress, he returned to Tennessee to organize an expedition to Texas, looking for new land and challenge. He died in the Battle of the Alamo.

CRONKITE, WALTER (1916–), broadcast journalist. Born in St. Joseph, Missouri, Cronkite began his career with the *Houston Post,* where he served as reporter. After a succession of assignments, he became a news correspondent with the American forces in World War II. He began his association with Columbia Broadcasting System (CBS) in 1950 and was assigned to develop the news department. In 1953, he began the narration of a series titled *You Are There;* in 1952, he inaugurated national television coverage of the political conventions; and in 1962, he became anchorman for the *CBS Evening News.* His name is synonymous with television news.

CROSBY, FRANCES J. "FANNY" (1820–1915), Christian composer born in New York City.

She wrote over five thousand hymns, including "Safe in the Arms of Jesus" and "There's Music in the Air." When six weeks old, she lost her eyesight. She entered an institution for the blind at age 15, and taught there from 1847 to 1858. She authored numerous publications that included *The Blind Girl and Other Poems* (1844), *A Wreath of Columbia's Flowers* (1859), and *Autobiography* (1906).

CROSBY, HARRY "BING" (1904–1977), singer, songwriter, and actor. Born in Tacoma, Washington, Crosby's easygoing manner suited the emerging style of popular music. He studied law for a period of time, then entered show business. The songs "Ghost of a Chance" and "When the Blue of the Night" became associated with his voice. He appeared in a series of filmed musical comedies with Bob Hope and Dorothy Lamour. He received an Academy Award for his performance in the film, *Going My Way* (1944). "I'm Dreaming of a White Christmas" is the song commonly associated with Crosby. His autobiography was entitled *Call Me Lucky*.

CURTIS, CYRUS H. K. (1850–1933), magazine publisher. Born in Portland, Maine, Curtis was educated in the public schools. He moved to Philadelphia, where he joined the staff of the *Tribune*. His success in publishing the *Ladies' Home Journal* achieved national recognition, and he became president of the newly organized Curtis Publishing Company. There he pursued other magazine enterprises, including *Country Gentleman* and the *Saturday Evening Post*. Under Curtis' direction, the *Post* achieved a national audience. He acquired the *New York Evening Post* in 1923 in an effort to compete with the Hearst papers and the *New York Times*.

CUSTER, GEORGE (1839–1876), soldier commonly known for his military operations against hostile Sioux and Cheyenne Indians. Custer was born in New Rumley, Ohio. In 1876, he was defeated in an epochal battle at the Little Big Horn in Wyoming. He and his entire army of 655 men were killed by a far superior force of Indians. Custer wrote an interesting commentary titled *My Life on the Plains;* his *War Memoirs* give a useful recollection of the Civil War.

DALEY, RICHARD (1902–1976), leading political figure of the Democratic Party. Born in the Bridgeport district of Chicago, Mr. Daley studied law at De Paul University. He was admitted to the bar in 1933. Through patronage and appointment power, he organized the Illinois Democratic Party with ultimate loyalty to himself. In 1955, he became mayor of Chicago and retained that post until his death, directing one of the most powerful political structures in American history. In 1960, he supported John F. Kennedy's bid for the Presidency and delivered his state for the Democratic presidential contender. In 1968, he was criticized for his treatment of anti-war protesters during the Democratic National Convention in Chicago. In spite of the criticism, political writers considered him the most effective mayor of a large metropolitan city.

DANA, CHARLES A. (1819–1897), newspaper editor and publisher. Dana was born at Hinsdale, New Hampshire. After a series of newspaper jobs, Dana used his friendship with Horace Greeley to secure the position of city editor at the *New York Tribune*. After the Civil War, he acquired the *New York Sun,* which he built into one of New York's greatest daily papers. He was described as a man of wide intellectual interests. Dana wrote *Recollections of the Civil War* (1898), *The Art of Newspaper Making* (1899), and other books.

DANIELS, JOSEPHUS (1862–1948), journalist and statesman, ambassador to Mexico, and Secretary of the Navy under President Woodrow Wilson. Daniels was born in Washington, North Carolina. He became a close friend of William Jennings Bryan and devoted his energies to the Democratic Party. Daniels used considerable restraint in his dealings with the Mexican government; he was a man of great diplomacy and political skill. Daniels authored several books, including *Tar Heel Editor, The Wilson Era: Years of War and After,* and *The Cabinet Diaries of Josephus Daniels.*

DAVIS, JEFFERSON (1808–1889), President of the Confederate States of America. Born in Todd County, Kentucky, Davis attended West Point Military Academy and graduated in 1828. He served with distinction in the Black Hawk Indian War of 1832. He then served as Secretary of War and as a Senator before the outbreak of the Civil War. After the Civil War broke the Confederacy, he lived a sad and helpless existence. Davis wrote *The Rise and Fall of the Confederate Government.*

DE FOREST, LEE (1873-1961), an inventor who pioneered in radio and broadcasting. De Forest was born at Council Bluffs, Iowa. He worked with the Western Electric Company in Chicago, where he invented the audio amplifier. This was the single most significant contribution to the advance of radio, and De Forest is often regarded as the father of radio. He held major responsibilities in the De Forest Wireless Telegraph Company and the Radio Telephone Company. He wrote *Father of Radio* (1950). William R. Maclaurin's *Invention and Innovation in the Radio Industry* explains De Forest's contributions.

DeMILLE, CECIL B. (1881-1959), motion picture producer and director who established a reputation for his spectacular portrayals of biblical themes. DeMille was born in Ashfield, Massachusetts. *The Ten Commandments, The King of Kings, The Sign of the Cross,* and *Samson and Delilah* were some of his best-known films. His screen productions cost millions, yet he was able to produce films that were highly profitable. DeMille rejected criticism that his productions were garish and unartistic by saying that public taste determines the standards of artistry. In later years, he developed movies that reflected historical themes, including *The Greatest Show on Earth, Union Pacific,* and *The Plainsman.*

DEMPSEY, JACK (1895-), champion heavyweight boxer. Because Dempsey was born in Manassa, Colorado, he was called the "Manassa Mauler." Initially he won the heavyweight championship from Jess Willard in 1919. The most controversial aspect of his career was the "long count" during the second fight between Dempsey and Gene Tunney. In the seventh round, Dempsey floored Tunney but failed to go to a neutral corner. The count was delayed; Tunney recovered and subsequently won the fight. After retirement, he became a restauranteur in New York City. With Bob Considine and Bill Slocum he co-authored the book, *Dempsey.*

DEWEY, GEORGE (1837-1917), first Admiral of the Navy; hero of the Spanish-American War. Dewey served under Admiral David G. Farragut during the Civil War. In 1897, he requested sea duty in the Pacific as commodore of the new American fleet. He led his six boats into Manila Bay on May 1, 1898, and destroyed the Spanish fleet of 10 ships. In August, he used the American navy to assist General Wesley Merritt's capture of Manila. He returned to a hero's welcome in the United States, where Congress named him Admiral of the Navy. Dewey published his autobiography in 1913.

DEWEY, JOHN (1859-1952), educator and pragmatic philosopher who advocated traditional values of education. Dewey was born in Burlington, Vermont. He believed that science was the highest manifestation of human intelligence. He established his reputation through articles in the *Journal of Speculative Philosophy.* Dewey studied at the University of Vermont, Johns Hopkins, the University of Michigan, and the University of Chicago. At Chicago, he turned to pedagogy and educational philosophy. He authored many books, including *Democracy and Education* (1916) and *Reconstruction in Philosophy* (1920).

DIMAGGIO, JOE (1914-), noted baseball player born in Martinez, California. DiMaggio played as an outfielder with the San Francisco Seals until 1934, when he was purchased by the New York Yankees. In his first year the Yankees recognized him as a potential star; he batted an average of .323, fielded .978, and established the

Admiral Dewey with President McKinley and Cardinal Gibbons, 1899

longest consecutive hitting record by hitting safely in 56 consecutive games. Fans called DiMaggio the "Yankee Clipper." On December 11, 1951, he announced his retirement from baseball. His subsequent marriage to actress Marilyn Monroe drew national attention.

DISNEY, WALTER E. "WALT" (1901–1966), filmmaker, cartoonist, and entertainment entrepreneur. A native of Chicago, Disney developed the cartoon characters Mickey Mouse and Donald Duck in the 1920s. He developed the first feature-length animated cartoons in *Snow White* (1938). Disney's later films *Pinocchio, Bambi, Fantasia,* and *Mary Poppins* achieved spectacular success. The amusement parks named Disneyland and Disney World bear his genius. *The Disney Version: The Life, Times, Art, and Commerce of Walt Disney,* by Richard Schickel (1968) is the most comprehensive study on Disney.

DIX, DOROTHEA L. (1802–1887), humanitarian associated with Dr. William Ellery Channing. Born in Hampden, Maine, Miss Dix became the tutor to Dr. Channing's children. Under Channing's influence, she initiated significant reforms in mental institutions. During the Civil War, she served as a superintendent of nurses; after the war, she continued her efforts on behalf of the mentally ill. Her reforms attracted international attention, particularly in Europe. Francis Tiffany's *The Life of Dorothea Lynde Dix* (1890) is the most definitive biography.

DOOLITTLE, JAMES H. "JIMMY" (1896–), aviator, oil company executive, and war hero. A native of Alameda, California, Doolittle became one of the most famous of American heroes during World War II. He led the first bombing of Japan and commanded thousands of planes in attacks on North Africa, Italy, and Germany. He commanded attacks upon German cities from 1944 to the end of the war in Europe. Doolittle then joined General Douglas MacArthur's command in the Far East until the end of the war in the Pacific. He became an executive of the Shell Oil Company after the war. In the 1950s, he became involved with NACA, which later became the National Aeronautics and Space Administration.

DOUGLAS, STEPHEN A. (1813-1861), United States Senator and candidate for the Presidency, identified with the Democratic Party. Born in Brandon, Vermont, Douglas spearheaded the new Democratic Party in Chicago. He sponsored efforts to make Chicago a significant rail center. The senatorial campaign of 1858 between Douglas and Abraham Lincoln was a rehearsal for the 1860 presidential campaign, even though Lincoln lost. In the famous Lincoln-Douglas debates, Lincoln established his national reputation. Many argue that if Douglas had become President, he could have prevented a Civil War. For a review of this argument, see Gerald M. Capers, *Stephen A. Douglas, Defender of the Union,* edited by Oscar Handlin (1959).

DOUGLAS, WILLIAM O. (1898–1980), liberal justice of the United States Supreme Court. Douglas was born in Yakima, Washington, and attended Columbia Law School. He served briefly as a professor at the Yale Law School, worked on legal matters for the Securities and Exchange Commission. In 1939, he was appointed to the Supreme Court and became the leader of the liberal wing of the court. He challenged tradition in his opinions on obscenity, religion, desegregation, and the rights of criminals. He wrote several books, including *Points of Revolution* (1970). The best study of Douglas' career is *Douglas of the Supreme Court: A Selection of His Opinions,* edited by Vern Countryman (1959).

DOUGLASS, FREDERICK (1817–1895), abolitionist, journalist, and orator. He was born at Tuckahoe, Maryland with the name of Frederick Augustus Washington Bailey. After he escaped from slavery he changed his name to Frederick Douglass. Greatly influenced by William Lloyd Garrison's *The Liberator,* Douglass joined the Massachusetts Anti-Slavery Society. He wrote *The Narrative of the Life of Frederick Douglass, an American Slave* (1845), which some abolitionists thought was too inflammatory. Douglass disagreed with William Lloyd Garrison on proper abolitionist procedures.

DREW, CHARLES RICHARD (1904–1950), a black surgeon who developed the blood bank and new methods for training surgeons. A native of Washington, D.C., Dr. Drew implemented the blood bank in World War II as director of the American Red Cross Bank. He chaired the department of surgery at Howard University and recommended new surgical standards to the National Medical Association. Dr. Drew received the

Spingarn Medal of the National Association for the Advancement of Colored People. He was awarded numerous honorary degrees from colleges and universities.

DU BOIS, WILLIAM E. B. (1868–1963), major black scholar and leader of black protest and panafricanism. Born in Great Barrington, Massachusetts, he received the Master of Arts degree and a doctorate from Harvard University. Dr. Du Bois organized the Niagara group, an all-black protest organization of scholars and professionals. He was one of the founders of the National Association for the Advancement of Colored People (NAACP) in 1909. He edited *Crisis,* a publication of the NAACP, and regarded himself as a Socialist. Dr. Du Bois authored numerous books and pamphlets.

DULLES, JOHN FOSTER (1888–1959), foreign diplomat and Secretary of State under President Dwight D. Eisenhower. Born in the nation's capital, Dulles served at the Paris Peace Conference in 1919. He was legal adviser to the United States delegation at the San Francisco conference on the United Nations. He supported General Eisenhower during the 1952 election. As Secretary of State, Dulles developed the broader aspects of North Atlantic Treaty Organization (NATO). He dealt courageously with the Suez Crisis of 1956 by compelling President Nasser of Egypt to withdraw. Louis L. Gerson's *John Foster Dulles* (1967) is a good biography of Dulles.

DURANTE, JIMMY (1893–1980), entertainer and songwriter born in New York City. Durante began his career in the Bowery district of New York, where he organized a five-piece jazz band for Club Alamo in Harlem. At this time, he was only known as a pianist. In 1923, he opened Club Durante. Other entertainers were attracted to his comedy and musical routines. He wrote many songs after 1923, including "I'm Jimmy, That Well-Dressed Man" and "Did You Ever Have the Feeling That You Wanted to Go?" He appeared in several Broadway musicals, including *Red, Hot and Blue* with Ethel Merman, *Keep off the Grass, Stars in Your Eyes.* He was nicknamed the "Schnozzle" for the generous proportions of his nose. Durante was regarded with great affection as an entertainer.

DUROCHER, LEO (1906–   ), professional baseball manager. Born in West Springfield, Massachusetts, he played for a time as a second baseman for the New York Yankees. Then he was shortstop for the Cincinnati Reds and St. Louis Cardinals. His fame comes from his management of the Brooklyn Dodgers, who won the National League pennant in 1951 and 1954. He became a television announcer for a short time, then returned as a manager for the Chicago Cubs 1966-1972 and the Houston Astros in 1972-1973. He co-authored a book entitled, *Nice Guys Finish Last* with Ed Linn. That phrase became synonymous with his name.

DWIGHT, TIMOTHY (1752–1817), Congregationalist minister and president of Yale College. Dwight was born in Northhampton, Massachusetts, and received his education at Hopkins Grammar School in New Haven, Connecticut. Dwight served in the Massachusetts Legislature, then taught Latin and Greek. He wrote "The Conquest of Canaan," an epic poem. In 1795, he became the president of Yale College; he administered the affairs of the college, taught moral philosophy, and served in the college pulpit on Sundays. Kenneth Silverman's *Timothy Dwight* is a significant study of his life.

EARHART, AMELIA (1898–1937), aviatrix. A native of Atchison, Kansas, Miss Earhart attended Columbia University and taught extension courses for the Commonwealth of Massachusetts. She was the first woman to cross the Atlantic in an airplane. Miss Earhart became the aviation editor of *Cosmopolitan Magazine* and vice-president of National Airways. She received numerous honors and recognitions, including the Distinguished Flying Cross and the gold medal of the National Geographic Society. She wrote *20 Hours, 40 Minutes* (1928) and *The Fun of It* (1931). Miss Earhart's plane went down in the Pacific Ocean as she was completing a round-the-world flight.

EASTMAN, GEORGE (1854–1932), inventor, industrialist, and mass producer of photographic equipment. Eastman was born in Waterville, New York. He made photography available to the general public. Eastman's discoveries in chemical processing were essential to the United States war effort during World War I. He developed an innovative system of profit-sharing that allowed his employees to enjoy the Eastman Company's profits. Eastman was a lonely man who took his own life. The best single work on Eastman is Carl W. Ackerman's *George Eastman* (1930).

EDDY, MARY BAKER (1821–1910), established the Church of Christ—Scientist in an effort to apply religion to health. She was born at Bow, New Hampshire. Her nervous condition in early life brought several illnesses, which led to her study of science and health. In 1908, she established the *Christian Science Monitor*. Her book, *Science and Health,* became the basis for her religious and scientific theories. Her most significant impact remained in Boston and the East Coast. *The Life of Mary Baker Eddy* by Sibyl Wilbur is the official biography.

EDDY, NELSON (1901–1967), screen star and entertainer, a native of Providence, Rhode Island. Mr. Eddy's baritone voice was matched with the soprano voice of Jeanette MacDonald for several filmed musicals. He starred in popular stage musicals during the 1930s and 1940s, including *Naughty Marietta* (1935), *Rose Marie* (1936), *Girl of the Golden West* (1938), and *Bittersweet* (1940). After his screen career, he entered radio and nightclub entertaining. Eddy made famous the songs, "Ah, Sweet Mystery of Life" and "Indian Love Call." His rich voice singing "Stouthearted Men" was his radio trademark.

EDISON, THOMAS A. (1847-1931), inventor who made outstanding contributions in electric light and electrical devices; his greatest contribution is the incandescent lamp. Born in Milan, Ohio, Edison made significant advances in organized research. Because of deafness, he was exempt from military service. Edison made major contributions to the development of the phonograph, lighting, electric-powered plant, and the movie industry. The Edison Company produced hundreds of movies, and Edison laid the basis for "talking" movies. He also contributed to the development of synthetic rubber. Edison sponsored the early work of Charles Steinmetz and other budding inventors. The best biography of Thomas A. Edison is Matthew Josephson's *Edison: A Biography* (1959).

EDWARDS, JONATHAN (1703–1758), New England minister and missionary, commonly regarded as America's finest preacher and theologian of the eighteenth century. He was born in East Windsor, Connecticut, the son and grandson of clergymen. Edwards' *Personal Narrative* (1740) reflects a close affection for God. He is associated with the Great Awakening, an intense period of revivalism in colonial America. He wrote the influential book entitled, *The Great Christian Doctrine of Original Sin Defended* (1758). His writings and sermons changed the outlook of his entire generation. He became president of the College of New Jersey, now Princeton University.

EINSTEIN, ALBERT (1879–1955), physicist, born in Ulm, Germany, and known for his theory of relativity. Einstein's general and special theories of relativity revolutionized the world of science. He approached President Roosevelt with his theories regarding the development of atomic energy for military purposes. This resulted in the "Manhattan Project" for the development of an atomic bomb. He was expelled from Nazi Germany because of his Jewish heritage, and this had a profound impact on his life. Einstein regarded himself a pacifist and humanitarian. Carl Seelig's biography, *Albert Einstein: A Documentary Biography* (1956), is one of the best portraits of Einstein.

Albert Einstein
This photograph is considered to be the last one made of the physicist. The occasion was Professor Einstein's 76th birthday on Mar. 14, 1955.

Douglas Fairbanks, Sr. (right) and son Douglas, (ca.) 1933

FAIRBANKS, DOUGLAS SR. (1883–1939), distinguished American actor born in Denver, Colorado. His marriages attracted national attention, particularly to Mary Pickford (divorced in 1935) and Lady Ashley. He made his first stage appearance in New York City; among other plays, he appeared in *All For a Girl, The Cub,* and *Show Shop*. He also appeared in motion pictures, such as *His Majesty the American, When the Clouds Roll By, The Mark of Zorro, Robin Hood,* and *The Taming of the Shrew*. He organized his own production company and achieved national attention for his somber portrayals.

FARRAGUT, DAVID G. (1801–1870), naval officer who carried significant assignments during the American Civil War. Born at Campbells Station, Tennessee, he opposed the Southern cause and migrated north to Hastings-on-the-Hudson. His initial assignment was to open the Mississippi to Union battleships. He stationed his gunboats in the Gulf of Mexico, which gave him a more direct striking capability between 1861 to 1864. In 1864, he was assigned to strike at Confederate defenses in Mobile Bay. His success led to the command to strike defenses at Wilmington, North Carolina, which he also accomplished. Farragut was regarded as among the outstanding heroes of the Civil War. A. T. Mahan's *Admiral Farragut* (1892) is still a classic.

FIELD, MARSHALL (1834-1906), merchant and chain-store retailer. Born near Conway, Massachusetts, Field served as a travelling salesman before he was admitted to partnership in the retail firm of Farwell, Field and Company. Unlike A. T. Stewart, John Wanamaker, and other leading retailers of his day, Field was not interested in political activity nor philanthropy; but he did give money to the newly established University of Chicago and fostered the establishment of the Chicago Manual Training School. He was also associated with the establishment of the Field Museum of Natural History in Chicago, and his will provided for the construction of the building in Chicago, and that houses the Field Museum.

FIELDS, W. C. (1879–1946), comedian of the stage, motion pictures, and radio. Fields was born in Philadelphia, Pennsylvania. His first appearances were in vaudeville productions and the Ziegfeld Follies. His fame developed from his movie appearances, in films such as *So's Your Old Man, It's the Old Army Game, One in a Million, David Copperfield, Never Give a Sucker an Even Break,* and his most popular *My Little Chickadee*. He also reached a national audience through his radio broadcast, *The Chase and Sanborn Hour*. Fields was highly regarded for his wry humor.

FINNEY, CHARLES G. (1792–1875), revivalist and educator. Finney was born in Warren, Connecticut. His term as president of Oberlin College gave Presbyterianism a significant voice in educating the ministry. His preaching style contained substance and eloquence. Finney was a strong advocate of temperance; he opposed the use of tobacco, tea, and coffee. Although a Mason, he opposed masonry. Among his more significant book titles: *Sermons on Important Subjects* (1836), *Lectures to Professing Christians* (1837), and *Lectures on Systematic Theology* (1846, 1847). His revivals reached wide audiences and had significant impact on the religious patterns of nineteenth-century America.

FITZGERALD, ELLA (1918–), jazz vocalist with an international reputation. Born in Newport News, Virginia, at age fifteen she entered an amateur contest at the Apollo Theatre in New York City. She was hired by Chick Webb for his band. In 1938, she gained worldwide fame with her recording of "A Tisket, a Tasket." Among her more famous recordings are "Love You Madly," "Hard-Hearted Hannah," and "He's My Guy."

Miss Fitzgerald is recognized as an outstanding performer and recording artist. She has received considerable respect in the black community for her civil rights concerns.

FORD, HENRY (1863–1947), automobile manufacturer born in Dearborn Township, Michigan. Ford learned the machinist trade and was the chief engineer for the Edison Illuminating Company. In 1903, he organized the world's largest automobile corporation. In 1914, he announced plans to involve all his workers in a profit-sharing plan, distributing millions of dollars back to his workers. His plan to mass-produce the Model T and Model A made the automobile readily available to the American public at competitive prices. He constructed assembly plants at Highland Park, Michigan, and River Rouge, Michigan; the latter was regarded as the largest single factory in the world. Ford was also active in political and humanitarian efforts. He built the Henry Ford Hospital; in 1918, he ran for the Senate and lost. Ford authored *My Life and Work* (1925) among other titles.

FOSDICK, HARRY EMERSON (1878–1969), clergyman and author who established the Riverside Church in New York, which was distinctive for its interdenominational character. Fosdick was born in Buffalo, New York. His *National Vespers* radio program brought his ideas into the national arena. He was ordained as a Baptist minister, but his theological perspective is associated with a liberal interpretation. Fosdick wrote numerous books, including *The Modern Use of the Bible* (1924) and *A Faith for Tough Times* (1952). His autobiography is contained in *The Living of These Days* (1956). He also wrote numerous hymns.

FOSTER, STEPHEN C. (1826–1864), composer of musical sketches and minstrel songs. At Jefferson College, Foster's musical capacities became evident to his teachers; he continued his education under tutors; his Negro ballads, "O Susanna" and "Away Down South," achieved instant success. In 1851, he began his work with E. P. Christy, who would sing Foster's songs. Each assisted the other. Foster's more famous songs were "The Old Folks at Home," "My Old Kentucky Home," and "Massa's in the Cold, Cold Ground." He remained in Pittsburgh, Pennsylvania most of his life; but his music gave a nostalgic reflection of Negro life in the Old South.

Benjamin Franklin
Signer of the Declaration of Independence

FRANKLIN, BENJAMIN (1706–1790), author, printer, inventor, diplomat, and scientist. Born in Boston, Massachusetts, he began a writing sequence on self-improvement at an early age. These efforts are best reflected in *Poor Richard's Almanack,* which contained slogans on personal improvement, such as: "Necessity never made a good bargain" and "It is hard for an empty sack to stand upright." Franklin became interested in electricity; he initiated projects for community improvement that included the lighting of streets with natural gas. He established police forces and circulating libraries. He also established the American Philosophical Association. Franklin served in the second Continental Congress. He travelled to France in 1776 to negotiate a treaty with the French Government, and negotiated the peace treaty with Great Britain. He served as a member of the Constitutional Convention. The best biography of Franklin is Carl Van Doren's *Benjamin Franklin* (1938).

FREMONT, JOHN C. (1813–1890), soldier and politician born in Savannah, Georgia. His explorations of Minnesota and Dakotas added to his knowledge of science and topography. He travelled the Oregon Trail with Kit Carson and explored the Columbia River. Fremont was regarded as the "Great Pathfinder." He travelled to California and wintered (1845) in Oregon. He then returned to California and served a short term as United

States Senator from California. He ran as a Presidential candidate of the newly formed Republican Party. His autobiographical sketch titled, *My Life* (1887), is a useful overview of the era.

FRIEDMAN, MILTON (1912–), foremost economist in the United States reflecting the conservative perspective. A native of Brooklyn, New York, he served as economic adviser to President Richard Nixon. He wrote *A Monetary History of the United States, 1867–1960* (1963). Friedman advocates the competitive free-market economy, and he originated the negative tax-credit idea. He is a professor at the University of Chicago; his economic theories are commonly associated with the Chicago School. Friedman has received numerous honors and awards, including the Nobel Prize for economics.

FULBRIGHT, J. WILLIAM (1905–), distinguished American political figure. Born in Sumner, Missouri, he attended the University of Arkansas and won a Rhodes scholarship to Oxford University. Fulbright received his law degree from George Washington University. From 1939 to 1941, he served as president of the University of Arkansas. In 1942, he began a political career as Representative to the United States House from the Third District. He called for the creation of the United Nations during World War II. In 1944, he was elected to the United States Senate; he sponsored laws that established an educational exchange program known as the Fulbright-Hays program. Fulbright served on the Senate Banking Committee. He criticized the war in Vietnam from his position as chairman of the Senate Foreign Relations Committee.

FULLER, R. BUCKMINSTER (1895–1983), architect, designer, and inventor. Born in Milton, Massachusetts, his earliest work was the Dymaxion House, a design that blends "dynamism" and "maximum utilization." Dymaxion House, like Fuller's Dymaxion Car, had interest but little direct use in production. He is described as a "catalyst to change." By mid-century some of his more enduring creations were taking form. The United States Pavilion at the Montreal Expo in 1967 was designed by Fuller; he was responsible for the geodesic dome that was built in Dearborn, Michigan for the Ford Motor Company. Fuller's influence is discussed by Roystan Landau, *New Directions in British Architecture* (1968).

FULTON, ROBERT (1765–1815), inventor and engineer born in Lancaster County, Pennsylvania. He built the first successful steamboat. Fulton and Robert R. Livingston designed the steamboat, which came to be called the *Clermont*. In 1807, the *Clermont* made its first trip. H. W. Dickinson's *Robert Fulton: Engineer and Artist: His Life and Works* (1913) is still a classic biography.

GALLUP, GEORGE H. (1901–), public opinion researcher. Born in Jefferson, Iowa, Gallup established his reputation as director of the American Institute of Public Opinion. He graduated from State University of Iowa, then served as a professor of journalism at Drake University and Northwestern University. His work in public opinion surveys evolved from reader-interest surveys that Gallup developed for the Des Moines *Register & Tribune*, the Cleveland *Plain Dealer* and the St. Louis *Post-Dispatch*. He established the American Institute of Public Opinion "impartially to measure and report public opinion." His surveys have become standards for political action or popularity. He has received honorary degrees from many universities, including Northwestern University and Tufts University.

GARFUNKEL, ART (1941–), singer and actor, associated in his early career with Paul Simon. Simon's acoustic guitar and Garfunkel's voice became a national standard of music during the 1960s. In 1964 they cut their first album titled, *Wednesday Morning*. One song that appeared on that album achieved national attention—"The Sound of Silence"; it eventually sold over one million copies. A succession of musical hits brought them international recognition. They composed and performed the music for the film entitled, *The Graduate*. "Bridge Over Troubled Waters" was another significant music success; in 1970, the two parted to pursue their separate careers. Garfunkel was born in Forest Hills, New York.

GARLAND, JUDY (1922–1969), actress and singer. Born in Grand Rapids, Michigan, she achieved instant success in her early portrayal of Dorothy in the film, *The Wizard of Oz*. Her singing of "Somewhere over the Rainbow" in that movie has become an American classic. She was also associated with Mickey Rooney in the Andy Hardy series of films. Her musical successes were highlighted by her performance in the film, *Easter*

Parade (with Fred Astaire); her performance in *A Star Is Born* was also widely acclaimed. In the 1960s, she made a spectacular return by appearances at the London Palladium and Carnegie Hall in New York. She received an Oscar nomination for her dramatic role in *Judgment at Nuremburg*.

GARRISON, WILLIAM L. (1805–1879), editor, reformer, and leader of abolition. In Garrison's day, the anti-slavery movement was split into two camps: those who sought gradual elimination of slavery and those who wanted immediate reform and abolition. Garrison called for the more immediate formula through his newspaper, *The Liberator*. He opposed slaveholders in his book, *Thoughts on Colonization* (1832). He criticized the New England clergy for their reluctance to condemn the broader aspects of slavery. He viewed the Civil War as a means of destroying the institution of slavery, and he wanted to disband the American Anti-Slavery Society after the Civil War. George M. Frederickson's *William Lloyd Garrison* (1969) is an excellent study of his life. Garrison was born in Newburyport, Massachusetts.

GERONIMO (1829–1909), leader of the Apache Indians. He was born with the name *Goyathlay,* and saw his family killed by Mexican troops in 1859. Taking the name *Geronimo* ("Jerome"), he led raids of revenge against white settlements in Arizona and New Mexico until he was confined to a reservation. In 1876, he led his warriors into Mexico, where he plundered white settlers for the next 10 years. He finally agreed to move to a reservation in Florida, but escaped en route. General Nelson A. Miles captured him after 18 months of pursuit. Later, Geronimo was converted to Christianity and lived peaceably with white people. He appeared in President Theodore Roosevelt's inaugural parade in 1905. *Geronimo's Story of His Life* (1906), by S. M. Barrett, gives Geronimo's own account of his experiences.

GERSHWIN, GEORGE (1898–1937), musical composer, distinguished in classical and popular fields. He was born in Brooklyn, New York. With lyricist Irving Caesar, Gershwin composed "Swanee," made famous by Al Jolson in *Sinbad*. In the 1920s he established many successes with his brother Ira: "Oh Kay," "Funny Face," "Rosalie," and "Strike Up the Band." His most distinguished efforts included *Rhapsody in Blue* (1924) for piano and jazz, and *An American in Paris* (1928). He had a fondness for jazz forms and black musical expression, and Gershwin's music reflected the current American scene. The most outstanding biography is David Ewen's *George Gershwin: His Journey to Greatness*. Gershwin's opera, *Porgy and Bess* (1935), was a stinging social commentary on racial prejudice.

Geronimo (center) and his braves shortly before surrendering.

GIBBONS, JAMES (1834–1921), Roman Catholic Cardinal born in Baltimore, Maryland. Gibbons supported the Catholic Church in a generation of change. He wrote *The Faith of Our Fathers* (1875), in which he underscored the practical applications of Catholicism. Known for his religious toleration, Gibbons supported labor organizations such as the Knights of Labor. He had considerable administrative skills, and he blended a profound affection for the church with his deep regard for America. Robert D. Cross gives a masterful summary of his contributions in *The Emergence of Liberal Catholicism in America* (1958).

GLADDEN, WASHINGTON (1836–1918), Congregationalist clergyman who sought to apply Christian principles to social problems. Gladden was born in Norwich, Connecticut. In 1866, he accepted the parish in North Adams, Massachusetts. His writings appeared in the *New York Independent* and *Scribner's Monthly,* usually on ethical themes of everyday living. He served as moderator to the National Council of Congregational Churches, where his scholarship reflected less depth and more of the conventional. He wrote several books on biblical criticism, including *Who Wrote the Bible* (1891), *How Much Is Left of the Old Doctrines* (1899), and *Social Salvation* (1902). Gladden addressed his later writings to municipal reform; he served with some distinction in interchurch associations.

GLENN, JOHN (1921–), aviator, astronaut, and United States Senator. Born in Cambridge, Ohio, he attended Muskingum College and trained as a naval air cadet. During World War II he flew 59 fighter bomber missions in the Pacific; he flew 90 missions in the Korean War. Glenn received the Flying Cross on five occasions and was awarded the Air Medal 19 times. He was the oldest of seven astronauts selected in April 1959 for Project Mercury program; but he was selected to make the first orbital flight in 1961. He was the first man to fly at supersonic speeds from Los Angeles to New York. In more recent years, Glenn has distinguished himself in political life as a United States Senator from Ohio.

GODDARD, ROBERT H. (1882–1945), established rocketry and the science of astronautics. Goddard's reputation was established while he was at Clark University, where the focus of his study was rocketry. He was able to perfect a system for liquid-propelled rockets. During World War II he addressed his attention to the potential of rockets in war; he concluded his life as a researcher in the employ of the Curtiss-Wright Corporation. Goddard's importance to the development of aerospace technology and interplanetary travel is great. Milton Lehman's *This High Man: The Life of Robert H. Goddard* is the only definitive biography available. *The Papers of Robert H. Goddard,* edited by Esther C. Goddard and G. Edward Pendray, is a collection of his writings.

GOLDBERG, RUBE (1883–1970), newspaper cartoonist whose funny drawings became world famous. Goldberg's political cartoons reached a wide audience through syndication. He worked for the *San Francisco Chronicle,* the *San Francisco Bulletin,* and the *New York Evening Mail.* He created the characters Lala Palooza, Mike, and Ike before he was offered the position of political cartoonist for the *New York Sun.* His reputation was established from that perspective. His cartoon, "Peace Today," was awarded a Pulitzer Prize in 1948.

GOLDWATER, BARRY M. (1909–), United States Senator and candidate for the Presidency in 1964. He suffered a heavy defeat in his quest for the Presidency against President Lyndon Johnson. Born in Phoenix, Arizona, Goldwater attended the University of Arizona but left to manage his family's department stores. During World War II, he served in the Army Air Forces; he helped to organize the Arizona Air National Guard. He was first elected to the Senate in 1952 and was reelected in 1958. After his defeat in 1964, he returned to Arizona for a brief period away from the Senate. The voters sent him back to the Senate in 1966. He has written numerous articles and books on his political philosophy and issues of national importance.

GOODSPEED, EDGAR J. (1871–1962), Greek scholar and Bible translator. Goodspeed studied at Denison, Ohio, Yale, and Chicago universities. In 1898, he came to the University of Chicago as a lecturer, then professor of Patristic Greek. He served as secretary to the president of the university. He devoted considerable work to developing a more readable version of the Bible. He wrote *The Conflict of Severus, The Story of the New Testament, The New Testament—an Ameri-*

can Version, The Complete Bible–an American Version. He was born in Quincy, Illinois.

GOODYEAR, CHARLES (1800–1860), inventor and noted rubber manufacturer. Goodyear was born in New Haven, Connecticut. His father was a hardware manufacturer, and Charles became associated with his father's hardware store in Philadelphia. When the store went bankrupt, he began experiments with rubber products. His fascination with inflated rubber life preservers led to his acquaintance with the American Indian Rubber Company. Goodyear wrote *Gum-Elastic and Its Varieties* and began experiments of treating rubber with sulfur and turpentine. By mid-century, the rubber industry was established in the United States and he migrated to Europe. He was honored by Napoleon III of France for his contributions to the Paris Exposition of 1855.

GOULD, CHESTER (1900–), cartoonist famous for his "Dick Tracy" series. Born in Pawnee, Oklahoma, Gould attended Oklahoma A & M and graduated from Northwestern University. He served as cartoonist for the Hearst Newspapers from 1924 to 1929; in 1931, he began working with the *Chicago Tribune* and created the cartoon character Dick Tracy. The character was a serious detective whose primary task was to reckon with criminal elements. "Dick Tracy" reached wide circulation through the Chicago Tribune-New York News Syndicate. The cartoon strip reached hundreds of newspapers throughout the country.

GOULD, JAY (1836–1892), builder of railroads, stock manipulator, and industrial capitalist. Born in Roxbury, New York, Gould began his career as a leather merchant. He established himself as a stock market speculator and helped the Erie Railroad compete against railroad baron Cornelius Vanderbilt. Through unscrupulous practices, he accumulated wealth at the expense of Erie Railroad and many unsuspecting investors. Later he bought an interest in the Wabash and Union Pacific Railroads. His influence extended to Manhattan's rapid transit system and the Western Union Telegraph Company. Louis M. Hacker's *The World of Andrew Carnegie* places Gould and this era into perspective.

GRAHAM, WILLIAM F. "BILLY" (1918–), evangelist and religious thinker. Born in Charlotte, North Carolina, he studied at Wheaton College. After a brief tenure as a pastor in Western Springs, Illinois, Graham became an evangelist. He served with Youth for Christ, then as president of Northwestern College in Minneapolis. He organized the Billy Graham Evangelistic Association for massive evangelism efforts. Through the radio program *Hour of Decision,* he is heard worldwide. He has written *My Answer, World Aflame,* and *Angels,* among many other titles. He has spoken to millions through crusades and television. John C. Pollock's *Billy Graham: The Authorized Biography* is a helpful view of Billy Graham's life.

GREELEY, HORACE (1811–1872), journalist, reformer, and editor. He was an early partner with the *New Yorker,* but the paper lacked profitability. In 1841, he began a more successful experiment known as the *New York Tribune.* Greeley urged social reform and resisted revolutionary approaches. He opposed the pro-slavery Compromise of 1850. Greeley was instrumental in the establishing of the Republican Party; after the Civil War, he became identified with the Radical Republicans. Soon frustrated with that group, he established the Liberal Republican Party. He wrote *Recollections of a Busy Life.* G.G. Van Deusen's *Horace Greeley: Voice of the People* places the man within the context of his generation.

GUGGENHEIM, MEYER (1828–1905), industrialist who established a mining empire. Born in Lengnau, Switzerland, he came to the United States in 1848. He obtained interests in silver-mining in Colorado. Guggenheim later expanded his smelting and mine acquisitions to Mexico. With the establishment of the Guggenheim Exploration Company and the American Smelting Company, his family obtained control of the broader aspects of mining and smelting in the United States. With his seven sons he was able to establish a force that dominated the American industrial scene for generations. The dated but authoritative *The Guggenheims: The Making of an American Dynasty* (1937) by Harvey O'Conner is still an outstanding overview.

HALE, GEORGE ELLERY (1868–1938), noted astronomer and astro-physicist. Born at Chicago, Illinois, Hale attended the Massachusetts Institute of Technology, the Harvard College Observatory, and the University of Berlin. He served as director of the Kenwood Astro-Physical Observatory in Chicago from 1890 to

1896. He invented the spectroheliograph, which was first used in 1892 to discover solar vortices and magnetic fields of sun spots. Hale achieved an international reputation among scientists. He wrote many books, including *The Study of Stellar Evolution, Beyond the Milky Way,* and *The New Heavens.*

HAMILTON, ALEXANDER (1757–1804), political leader and financial advisor. He was born on the island of Nevis in the British West Indies, the illegitimate son of James Hamilton and Rachel Fawcett Lavien. During the early stages of the American Revolution, Hamilton served as a close confidante of General George Washington. He became a member of the Federalist Party after the Revolution and was a co-author of the Federalist Papers. Hamilton served as Secretary of the Treasury under President Washington. He supported the concept of a central banking authority as the United States Bank and authored numerous studies on banking. Hamilton drafted the basic text of Washington's "Farewell Address." He died in a duel with Aaron Burr.

HAMMERSTEIN, OSCAR II (1895–1960), lyricist, theatrical producer, and songwriter. Born in New York City, Hammerstein was a student at Columbia University and received a law degree in 1918. His first musical success was as lyricist with "Wildflower" (1923). He then wrote "Rose Marie" (1924), "Sunny" (1925) and "Desert Song" (1926). With Jerome Kern, he achieved success with *Showboat* (1927). With Richard Rodgers his success became phenomenal. Together they wrote *Oklahoma* (1943), *Carousel* (1945), and *South Pacific* (1949), which received a Pulitzer award. Other successes included *The King and I* (1951), *Flower Drum Song* (1958), and *The Sound of Music* (1959). His more famous musical themes include "The Last Time I Saw Paris," which received an Academy Award, and "Ol' Man River."

HANCOCK, JOHN (1737–1793), first signer of the Declaration of Independence. A Colonial merchant and patriot, Hancock opposed Great Britain's efforts to restrict colonial trade. He resisted the Stamp Act by engaging in smuggling; by 1773, his name was identified with rebellion. Hancock was disappointed when the Continental Congress appointed George Washington to command the armies around Boston as the Revolution mounted. As an accountant for Harvard College, he engaged in erratic bookkeeping that brought embarrassment to him and his family. Hancock later served as president of the States Convention where Massachusetts ratified the United States Constitution. He also served as governor of Massachusetts.

John Hancock
Signer of the Declaration of Independence

HANDY, W. C. (1873–1958), black songwriter regarded as the "Father of the Blues." Born in Florence, Alabama, Handy grew up in a home where both parents were ministers and secular music was regarded with disdain. Yet he organized tours and minstrel performances. His fame grew out of the Mahara Minstrels, a group he led. He travelled to Memphis, Tennessee, where his "Memphis Blues" became famous among musical circles. He also published the classic "St. Louis Blues." Handy was accused of plagiarism on certain musical themes, but he resisted those claims. He organized the W. C. Handy Foundation for the Blind. His book entitled, *Blues: An Anthology* contains some material about his life. He also wrote his autobiography titled *Father of the Blues,* published in 1941.

HARDY, OLIVER (1892–1957), actor and comedian. He was the senior member of a comic team with Stan Laurel. Laurel and Hardy made their first movie in 1926; in their career they were responsible for over two hundred movie features. In the 1950s, they expanded their comedy to the medium of television. The overweight Hardy and the lean Laurel developed a comedy style that reflected the anxieties of life situations. Their slapstick humor was popular in America at the time. Hardy's line, "Another fine mess that you got us into," became associated with the routine.

HATFIELD, MARK O. (1922–), modern political figure. Born in The Dalles, Oregon, Hatfield graduated from Stanford University. He served as instructor and dean of students at Willamette University. From 1950 to 1956, he served as the Secretary of State for Oregon, and as governor from 1959 to 1967. He won election as United States Senator in 1967. Hatfield's involvement in the anti-war movement during the 1960s generated discontent within the Republican Party; he has been identified with the liberal Republicans. Hatfield is a significant leader in evangelical Protestantism. He has written several books, including *Between a Rock and a Hard Place.*

HEARST, WILLIAM RANDOLPH (1863–1951), newspaper publisher and editor. Born in San Francisco, California, Hearst grew up in a wealthy family. He was expelled from Harvard College in 1885, and received permission from his father to work with *The Daily Examiner.* There he sensationalized and fabricated the news in irresponsible fashion. After his father's death, he moved to New York where he used the *New York Morning Journal* to compete against Joseph Pulitzer's *New York World.* In an era of "yellow journalism," Hearst's irresponsible reporting generated a newspaper boom. He established the *Chicago American* in 1900, along with other newspapers in Boston and Los Angeles. Eventually he retired on the Hearst estate at San Simeon in southern California. Ferdinand Lundberg's *Imperial Hearst: A Social Biography* (1936) is an unflattering portrait.

HENRY, CARL F. H. (1913–), minister and educator. Henry was born in New York City. He received the Ph.D. from Boston University and the Th.D. from Northern Baptist Theological Seminary. He established *Christianity Today,* a journal for evangelical Protestantism. Dr. Henry has held faculty positions with Gordon, Fuller, Wheaton Colleges, and numerous other colleges and universities as visiting lecturer. He has authored a number of publications in systematic theology; but his most significant views were shared through his editorials for *Christianity Today,* which he edited from 1956 to 1968.

HENRY, PATRICK (1736–1799), orator and noted political figure born in Hanover County, Virginia. As a member of the Virginia House of Burgesses, Henry spoke against the Stamp Act and opposed the power of Parliament to tax Virginians. He was described as the "Demosthenes of America." His name is synonymous with rebellion, through his impassioned cry, "I know not what course others may take; but as for me, give me liberty or give me death." After the Revolution, he served as governor of Virginia. He opposed the American Constitution because he believed it would concentrate too much power in the central government.

HOFMAN, HANS (1880–1966), cubist and abstract painter. Born in Weissenberg, Germany, Hofman suffered under the political difficulties of postwar Germany. He decided to emigrate to America and accept an appointment at the University of California. During the 1940s, he exhibited his paintings in New York, where his work received wide attention. With exhibitions at the Whitney Museum during the decade of the 1960s, his reputation as a German-American master was assured. His more famous paintings are *Fantasia* (1943), *Liberation* (1947), *The Gate* (1959), and *Agrigento* (1961).

HOGAN, BEN (1912–), an outstanding golfer. Born in Dublin, Texas, Hogan attended Fort Worth public schools. In his professional career as a golfer, he won the United States Open championship on four occasions; the United States Masters twice; won the British Open once. In 1946 and 1948, he won the Professional Golfers Association championship. He has received numerous awards including the Ryder Cup. Hogan was named Golfer of the Year in 1948, 1950, 1951, and 1953. He has written several books on the game of golf, including *Power Golf.*

HOMER, WINSLOW (1836–1910), a well-known American painter in the naturalist tradition. A native of Boston, Massachusetts, Homer began his career by working for *Harper's Weekly* as an illustrator. He proceeded to painting adult subjects in their natural settings; and in 1873, he began his work with watercolors in a graphic style. He moved from New York to the coast of Maine, where he sought a balance in his perspective. Late in life, he moved to the Bahamas, Bermuda, and Florida. At his death, he was regarded as the most significant American painter. *The World of Winslow Homer,* by James Thomas Flexner (1966) gives a good analysis of the man and his generation.

HOOVER, J. EDGAR (1895–1972), first director of the Federal Bureau of Investigation. Upon his initial appointment as acting director in 1924, Hoover established a fingerprint collection and national crime laboratory. The bureau was the center of Prohibition controversies and organized crime. Hoover opposed the emerging menace of Communism, particularly after World War II; he became involved in the McCarthy campaigns, writing books and articles that dealt with the themes of organized crime and Communism. *Masters of Deceit* (1958) is his most famous publication. Hoover was born in Washington, D.C.

HOPE, BOB (1903–   ), comedian and film star. Born in Eltham, England, Hope developed an instinct for comedy during his early days in vaudeville. He appeared in 1935 in the Ziegfeld Follies with Fanny Brice. He starred in the musical, *Red, Hot, and Blue* with Jimmy Durante and Ethel Merman; he developed a close partnership with Bing Crosby and Dorothy Lamour in a series of films titled *Road to. . . .* During World War II, he entertained troops, particularly during the Christmas holiday season. In 1950, he appeared on the television show, *Star Spangled Revue,* and in October of 1950, he embarked on an entertainment tour for the United States Armed Forces in the Pacific. These tours were continued for over twenty-five years. His television specials draw large audiences. He authored *They've Got Me Covered* (1941), *I Never Left Home* (1944), and *So This Is Peace* (1946).

HOPKINS, JOHNS (1795–1873), merchant and philanthropist. He entered business in partnership with his brothers. In exchange for groceries, the Hopkins Brothers would receive whiskey; then they would sell the whiskey as "Hopkins Best" brand. He developed banking interests by buying up overdue notes. His primary investment was the Baltimore & Ohio Railroad; he became director of it in 1847. He advanced money to the City of Baltimore during periods of financial crisis; he established a hospital and a university that later adopted his name. His biographies have suggested that "he knew how to be generous in large matters."

HOUDINI, HARRY (1874–1926), circus entertainer and escape artist. His real name was Robert Housini. He was born soon after his parents left Budapest, Hungary for Appleton, Wisconsin. In his career as a magician, he took the name Harry Houdini; he learned his magic tricks from a variety of sources—sideshows, circuses, books. His wife Beatrice assisted him in magical routines; they worked the Orpheum circuit. After a sensational escape from Scotland Yard as a publicity stunt, he attracted great attention. Houdini toured the European continent, where he was able to extricate himself from many difficult situations. His return to America was received enthusiastically. He wrote *The Unmasking of Robert Housini* (1908) and starred in three motion pictures after World War I.

HOUSTON, SAMUEL (1793–1863), American statesman and soldier born in Rockbridge County, Virginia. Houston was a Jacksonian Democrat with great oratorical skills and military abilities. He was a lawyer with political ambitions. As a member of Congress and then governor of Tennessee, he became involved with the westward expansion. President Jackson asked Houston to negotiate treaties with various Indian tribes in the Southwest. He moved to Texas, where he advocated statehood for the territory. Houston directed military operations against Mexican president Antonio Lopez dé Santa Anna; from 1845–1859, he served as Senator from Texas. A good biography of Houston was written by Marquis James, *The Raven: A Biography of Sam Houston* (1929).

HOWARD, ROY W. (1883–1964), newspaper publisher who served as director of the Scripps-Howard newspaper chain from 1953 to 1964. Born in Gano, Ohio, his newspaper career began with the *Indianapolis News* in 1902. After he was appointed as general news manager for the United Press, he achieved a broader recognition among publishing circles. While covering World War I, he prematurely reported the signing of the Armistice. Howard negotiated the purchase of the *New York Telegram,* the *New York World,* and the *New York Sun.*

HOWE, ELIAS (1819–1867), inventor who designed the first sewing machine, which revolutionized the garment industry. With ingenuity and persistence, Howe developed a workable sewing machine by 1845 and applied for the appropriate patents. He travelled to England to sell his machine, fell into difficult times, and sold his patents. He returned to America nearly penniless. Through legal proceedings, he was able to get the appropriate license fees on machines that had been produced from 1849 to 1854 in violation of his valid patents. With this newfound wealth, his personal life was stabilized. After the Civil War, sewing machines became major items for mass production.

HUBBLE, EDWIN P. (1889–1953), noted astronomer. Hubble was born in Marshfield, Massachusetts, and pursued a doctorate at the Yerhes Observatory near Pasadena, California. He determined the distances to several galaxies and studied their composition. He led in the development of Mount Palomar's telescope. Hubble wrote an autobiograpical sketch in *The Realm of Nebulae* and *Observational Approach to Cosmology* (both published in 1937). Harlow Shapley's *Through Rugged Ways to the Stars* places Hubble in the context of modern astronomy.

HUGHES, CHARLES EVANS (1862–1948), statesman and chief justice of the United States. After a 20-year period as a lawyer, Hughes became governor of New York State. As governor, he introduced historic reform legislation. President William Taft appointed him to the Supreme Court. In 1916, he was the Presidential candidate for the Republican Party; but he lost to Woodrow Wilson. After World War I, he supported President Wilson's proposal to join the League of Nations. He served as Secretary of State in the scandal-ridden Harding Administration, and gave excellent service. He called the Washington Conference on the limitation of Armaments and dealt with German war reparations. President Herbert Hoover appointed him as Chief Justice of the United States, where his progressive rulings foreshadowed those of the Earl Warren court.

HUGHES, HOWARD R. (1905–1976), business tycoon who achieved great renown through his efforts in aviation technology. After the death of his parents, he took control of the Hughes Tool Company. There he established his reputation and his wealth. Hughes produced motion pictures, and owned hotels, gambling casinos, an airline, television networks, and mines for precious metals. His complex personality contributed to his problems. He required privacy and developed a secretive manner. When Clifford Irving wrote a fraudulent biography on Hughes, the recluse telephoned news reporters to expose the hoax. At his death, many acquaintances of Hughes produced documents that claimed to be his will.

HULL, CORDELL (1871–1955), Congressman, Secretary of State under President Franklin D. Roosevelt. Hull generated the "Good Neighbor" policy toward Latin America. He signed the far-reaching agreement of Montevideo that made it illegal for military powers to intervene in the affairs of nations in the New World. He called for lower tariffs and opposed the expansionism of Japan that preceded World War II. He worked toward the establishment of the United Nations and earned a Nobel Peace Prize in 1945. *The Memoirs of Cordell Hull* (2 vols., 1948) provide a useful overview of the man and his era.

HUMPHREY, HUBERT H. (1911–1978), political figure, United States Senator, and Vice-President of the United States under President Lyndon Johnson. Humphrey was recognized as a spokesman for liberal political views. He was born in Wallace, South Dakota, and attended the University of Minnesota, graduating as a pharmacist from the Denver (Colorado) School of Pharmacy. His father served in the South Dakota state legislature. Hubert studied political science at the University of Minnesota while he served as pharmacist in the family drugstore. He became fascinated by the New Deal of President Franklin Roosevelt. He campaigned for mayor of Minneapolis in 1945 and won. He pursued vigorous reform of urban politics in Minneapolis, and advocated civil rights. Humphrey favored medical insurance through Social Security, the National Defense Education Act, the Peace Corps, and countless other programs of Lyndon Johnson's "Great Society."

HUNTLEY, CHET (1911–1974), television newscaster who achieved national recognition as co-anchorman with David Brinkley on the *Huntley-Brinkley Report,* featured by the National Broadcasting Company. He served as a correspondent on the West Coast for all three television networks. In 1956, he was brought to New York to co-anchor the national political conventions with Brinkley. Their partnership continued until 1970, and their news reporting received every award in broadcasting. Their famous sign-off—"Good night, Chet; Good night, David"—was immediately associated with the report. Huntley returned to Big Sky, Montana, after 1970.

IVES, BURL (1909–), singer and actor. Ives worked with the Columbia Broadcasting System as a folk song artist on radio and travelled throughout the states as a troubadour. He has appeared on numerous television programs. Ives' appearances on stage and film reflect a form of character acting. He has been featured in several films, including *East of Eden, Our Man in Havanna,* and *Cat On A Hot Tin Roof.* His television appearances on *The Bold Ones* from 1970 to 1972 developed a new character form—the lawyer. He has received numerous awards and recognitions. His autobiography is titled *Wayfaring Stranger* (1948).

IVES, CHARLES E. (1874–1954), pioneer in musical expression. Born in Danbury, Connecticut, Ives received initial musical training from his father. He graduated from Yale College in 1898 as a skilled musician and organist. He sold insurance for a time, but continued to compose music. He blended opposite musical forms, using familiar themes within his compositions. He wrote four symphonies, four separate theme works, chamber works, piano sonatas, violin sonatas, hundreds of songs, as well as piano and organ works. Peter Yates' *Twentieth Century Music* (1967) gives particular reference to Ives.

JACKSON, JESSE (1941–   ), clergyman and civic leader. Born in Greenville, North Carolina, he attended the University of Illinois and did postgraduate work at the Chicago Theological Seminary. He was ordained to the ministry of the Baptist Church and worked with Dr. Martin Luther King and the Southern Christian Leadership Conference in civil rights efforts. Jackson established Operation Breadbasket and Operation PUSH (People United to Save Humanity). He has been active in the Coalition for United Community Action, and is recognized as a fiery speaker.

JACKSON, MAHALIA (1911–1972), black singer and civil rights activist born in New Orleans, Lousiana. Miss Jackson symbolized black protest by associating with the civil rights movement. She became famous through her singing of "He's Got the Whole World in His Hands" and other popular songs. She achieved recognition in the white community after a widely acclaimed concert at Carnegie Hall in 1950. She was regularly featured in the Newport Jazz Festival after 1958.

JACKSON, THOMAS "STONEWALL" (1824–1863), Civil War general and Confederate hero. Jackson attended the United States Military Academy and served in the Mexican War. In the 1860 election, he supported John C. Breckinridge for the Presidency. After Virginia seceded from the Union he was commissioned to defend Harpers Ferry. At the First Battle of Bull Run, he earned the name "Stonewall" through his determined strategy. He was less successful in the battle to protect Richmond from Union Forces under General McClellan, but he scored a great victory for the South at the Second Battle of Bull Run. At the Battle of Fredericksburg, he was mistaken for a Union soldier and accidentally shot. This proved fatal. In strategy and audacity, Jackson remained unequalled in the Confederate ranks.

JAMES, WILLIAM (1842–1910), philosopher and psychologist. James was educated at Harvard, and his educational interests reflected a composite of the Renaissance mind. He was a determined advocate of the evolutionary theories of Charles Darwin. He wrote *Principles of Psychology* (1890), in which he underscored the human qualities of habit, emotion, consciousness of self, stream of thought, and will. His concern for individual freedom was reflected in his lectures on "The Will to Believe." His book, *Varieties of Religious Experience,* remains a classic study of the psychology of religion. Bernard P. Brennan's *William James* (1968) is a useful biography.

JAY, JOHN (1745–1829), diplomat, politician, Chief Justice of the United States. Jay served as President of the Continental Congress in 1778; after the American Revolution, he served as the new nation's Secretary for Foreign Affairs. He was a co-author of the *Federalist Papers,* which made him an advocate of the American Constitution. With James Madison and Alexander Hamilton, he called for a more centralized authority. Jay proposed the early outlines of a national judiciary. The treaty that ended the war with Great Britain bears his name; although it was written by Alexander Hamilton, it bore the diplomatic skills of John Jay.

JOLSON, AL (1886–1950), singer and star of motion pictures and radio. Born in St. Petersburg, Russia, his real name was Asa Yoelson and he was the son of a Jewish cantor. In 1909, he joined a minstrel group and entertained in the New York Garden. His role in the motion picture entitled *The Jazz Singer* (1927) is regarded as the first talking

Al Jolson in a scene from the *Jazz Singer* (ca.) 1927

picture. In 1928, he appeared in the film, *The Singing Fool.* His renditions of such songs as "Mammy" and "April Showers" became a permanent part of the American musical scene. He produced George Gershwin's *Rhapsody in Blue,* and the film entitled *The Al Jolson Story* was a phenomenal success.

JONES, E. STANLEY (1884–1973), missionary, author, and spiritual leader. Jones served as a missionary to India. His writings give a balanced, positive expression of Christian experience. He wrote several books, including *A Song of Ascents* (1968), which is his spiritual autobiography. He worked with the Ashram movement in India to communicate a religious message of love and understanding. Jones stressed the need for conversion, transformation, and the abundant life.

JONES, JOHN PAUL (1747–1792), distinguished American Revolutionary officer. His naval operations during the Revolution contributed greatly to the American victory. Historians believe the duel between Jones' ship, the *Bon Homme Richard,* and the British ship *Serapis,* was a significant episode of the war. He managed to seize the copper-bottom ship from the British. Jones received a gold medal and numerous honors for his naval successes. He served a brief period in the Russian navy, and most of his later years were spent in Paris. Alfred Thayer Mahan's book, *The Major Operations of the Navies in the American War of Independence* (1913), remains the classic on John Paul Jones and the Revolution.

JONES, RUFUS M. (1863–1948), college professor and religious leader. Born in South China, Maine, Jones attended Haverford College and the University of Heidelberg. He received his graduate degrees from Harvard and Oxford universities. In 1889, he became instructor at the Oak Grove Seminary in Maine; he taught at Haverford College from 1904 to 1934. Jones served as chairman of the American Friends Service Committee and of the European Relief in 1917–1927 and 1934–1944. He wrote numerous books, including *Autobiography of George Fox: The Story of George Fox* (1919); *The Faith and Practise of the Quakers* (1927); *Re-thinking Religious Liberalism* (1936); and *The Radiant Life* (1944).

JUDSON, ADONIRAM (1788–1850), Baptist missionary to Burma and founder of the American Board of Commissioners for Foreign Missions (1810). Judson was a Congregationalist when he travelled to India under the sponsorship of the board. There he adopted Baptist beliefs and received support from the American Baptist Missionary Union. He then went to Rangoon, Burma, to begin the translation of Scripture into Burmese. His linguistic abilities brought him into contact with broader levels of Burmese royalty. He completed an English-Burmese dictionary.

KEATON, BUSTER (1895–1966), comedian and film star. Born in Piqua, Kansas, Keaton performed in vaudeville before his appearances in Hollywood. He made comic use of pantomime, his portrayals in silent movies established his reputation as a classic performer. Keaton achieved fame in television and as a motion picture actor and director. His performances in *A Funny Thing Happened on the Way to the Forum, Around the World in 80 Days,* and *It's a Mad, Mad, Mad, Mad World* were received with acclaim. He achieved a new standard of excellence in the film, *When Comedy was King.*

KELLER, HELEN (1880–1968), author and humanitarian. Miss Keller was born in Tuscumbia, Alabama. An early illness left her blind and deaf by the age of 18 months. Her tutor Anne Sullivan helped her gain an education; and by age 16, she matriculated at Radcliffe College. She graduated *cum laude.* Her life was dedicated to the broader aspects of education and assistance to the blind and deaf. Miss Keller knew Alexander Graham Bell, whose experiments became essential to her work with the deaf and blind. She authored *Helen Keller's Journal, Out of the Dark,* and *The Story of My Life,* among other works.

KELLY, EMMETT (1898–1979), renowned pantomime clown. Born in Sedan, Kansas, he served as cartoonist for the Advertizing Film Company, where he created the "Wearie Willie" pen-and-ink cartoon. In 1921, he joined the circus as a clown; he worked as a trapeze artist and clown from 1924 to 1931. He appeared in several pictures, including *The Fat Man, The Greatest Show on Earth,* and others. He appeared on television with Ed Sullivan, Garry Moore, Jackie Gleason, Captain Kangaroo, and others.

KELLY, GENE (1912–), dancer, actor, and motion-picture celebrity. Born in Pittsburg, Pennsylvania, he appeared in the New York productions *Leave It To Me* (1938), *Time of Your Life* (1940), *Pal Joey* (1941), and others. Kelly directed the dancers for several movies: *Anchors Aweigh* (1944), *The Pirate* (1948), *An American in Paris* (1950), and *Brigadoon* (1954). Between 1944 and 1946, he served in the United States Naval Reserve. He authored *Take Me Out to the Ballgame* (1948).

KELLY, GRACE (1929–1982), actress, model, and (since 1956) princess of Monaco. Born in Philadelphia, Pennsylvania, she attended the Raven Hall Academy and Stevens School in that city. After early stage productions, she appeared in several motion pictures: *High Noon, Dial M For Murder, Rear Window, The Country Girl, To Catch A Thief,* and *High Society.* She received the Academy award for her role in *Country Girl.* Her marriage to Prince Rainier III of Monaco received considerable attention in America and Europe.

KELLY, WALT (1913–1973), newspaper cartoonist. His fame grew out of the comic strip "Pogo," with the classic line: "We have seen the enemy, and he is us." Kelly's characters reflected an innocent satire on society. Pogo was an opossum who spoke garbled language and had a community of animal friends, such as Howland Owl and the other inhabitants of Okefenokee Swamp. Kelly first worked as an animator for Walt Disney Productions. His comic strip appeared first in the *New York Star;* it reached syndication in over four hundred newspapers. Kelly was named Cartoonist of the Year in 1952.

KENNEDY, EDWARD M. (1932–), United States Senator born in Brookline, Massachusetts. Educated at Harvard and the University of Virginia Law School, he won election to the Senate in 1962 to complete the unexpired term of his brother, John F. Kennedy. In 1964, he was reelected. Mary Jo Kopechne, a campaign worker, died in an automobile accident at Chappaquiddick, Massachusetts that cast shadows on Kennedy's personal integrity. Yet he won reelection in 1970 and 1976. In the Senate, he has established a national health insurance program and favored tax reform. During the 1960s, he loudly opposed the war in Vietnam.

KENNEDY, ROBERT F. (1925–1968), United States Senator assassinated in a Los Angeles hotel after he won the 1968 California Democratic Presidential primary. Kennedy served in the United States Navy during World War II. He graduated from Harvard and received his law degree from the University of Virginia Law School in 1951. He served as assistant counsel to Senator Joseph McCarthy's Permanent Subcommittee on Investigations; and in 1957, he was chief counsel to the Senate Select Committee conducting investigations into labor racketeering. In 1960, he conducted the campaign of his brother, John F. Kennedy, for the Presidency. From 1961 to 1964, he served as Attorney General. From 1965 to his death, he was Senator from New York. Kennedy authored *The Enemy Within* (1960), *Just Friends and Brave Enemies* (1962), and *Pursuit of Justice* (1964).

KETCHAM, HANK (1920–), cartoonist. Born in Seattle, Washington, his real name is Henry King. He worked with Universal Studios and Walt Disney Productions from 1938 to 1942. He created Dennis the Menace and related cartoon characters after 1951. His "Dennis the Menace" cartoon strip was distributed through Field Newspaper Syndicate. He has received numerous awards, including the Billy de Beck Award for Outstanding Cartoonist (1952). He wrote several *Dennis the Menace* cartoon book collections, beginning in 1954, and *I Wanna Go Home* (1965).

KING, MARTIN LUTHER, JR. (1929–1968), civil rights leader who developed and practiced nonviolence as a strategy in dealing with racial prejudice and segregation. King organized a bus boycott to deal with segregation on transportation facilities. He was active in the National Association for the Advancement of Colored Peoples (NAACP); later he organized the Southern Christian Leadership Conference. King participated in the "sit-ins" to integrate lunch counters. The apex of the civil rights movement was achieved in a rally in Washington, D.C., where King delivered his speech, "Let Freedom Ring." In December of 1964, King was nominated for the Nobel Prize. He became involved in the anti-war movement shortly before he was assassinated in Memphis, Tennessee. He authored numerous publications; his most famous was, *I Have a Dream* (1968).

KISSINGER, HENRY (1923-), diplomat and Secretary of State. Born in Furth, Germany, he emigrated to the United States in 1938. Kissinger served during World War II. He received his doctorate from Harvard in 1954. Kissinger received national attention through publication of *Nuclear Weapons and Foreign Policy* (1957). He became a political advisor to Nelson Rockefeller in 1957. In 1968, Richard Nixon named him Presidential Assistant for National Security. Kissinger arranged the visits made by President Nixon to China and the Soviet Union. He was the architect of the treaty that ended the United States involvement in Vietnam. He also began *détente* with the Soviet Union and limited disengagement in the Middle East. Kissinger was recognized as an outstanding Secretary of State.

KOUFAX, SANDY (1935-), baseball pitcher and sportscaster. Born in Brooklyn, New York, he attended the University of Cincinnati. In 1955, he began his professional baseball career with the Brooklyn Dodgers (later the Los Angeles Dodgers). He appeared in World Series championships in 1959, 1963, 1965, and 1966. From 1963 to 1966, he was named to the National League All-Star Team. He was named Major League Player of the Year in 1963 and 1965. In 1963, 1965, and 1966, he received the Cy Young Award. From 1966 to 1972, he was associated with the National Broadcasting Company (NBC) as a sportscaster.

KRESGE, S. S. (1867–1966), merchandiser and businessman who established a network of "five and dime" stores throughout the country to make less expensive merchandise available to a broader market. Kresge was the founder of the S. S. Kresge stores; and from 1907 to 1925, he served as president of the company. From 1913 to 1966, he was chairman of the board; at its peak, over nine hundred thirty general merchandise stores throughout the country bore his name.

KUIPER, GERARD (1905–1973), astronomer. Born in Harencarspel, Netherlands, he analyzed early lunar photos and determined the exact sites where Apollo space craft would land. As chief scientist for the Ranger spacecraft program, he augmented United States efforts in the NASA space projects. The lunar landing of 1969 would not have been possible without his efforts.

LaFARGE, CHRISTOPHER GRANT (1862–1938), modern architect. Born in New York City, LaFarge studied at the Massachusetts Institute of Technology, 1880–1881. He obtained the Master of Fine Arts degree from Princeton University and became a partner in the firm Heins & LaFarge. LaFarge was the architect for the Cathedral of St. John the Divine in New York; St. Matthew's in Washington, D.C.; St. Patrick's in Philadelphia; as well as numerous other churches, hospitals, and governmental structures. He served as general manager of the United States Housing Corporation; also, director of the American Institute of Architects.

LaFOLLETTE, ROBERT M. (1855–1925), political reformer. LaFollette graduated from the University of Wisconsin in 1879 and was admitted to the bar one year later. He served as a member of the United States House of Representatives from

Senator Robert La Follette (left) and Senator Burton K. Wheeler, presidential and vice-presidential candidates of the League for Progressive Political Action

1885 to 1891. He campaigned against political corruption in his own state and was elected governor of Wisconsin in 1900. During his two terms there, he enacted new laws enabling voters to nominate candidates by direct primary elections, regulating government employment, and levying more reasonable taxes on business. LaFollette won election to the United States Senate in 1906 and was reelected twice thereafter. He ran for the Presidency on three occasions—the most successful being in 1924, when he and his running mate Burton K. Wheeler polled five million votes for the League for Progressive Political Action. LaFollette's ideas influenced national policy. He published his *Autobiography: A Personal Narrative of Political Experiences,* in 1913.

LANDON, ALFRED "ALF" (1887–   ), political leader and presidential candidate. Born in West Middlesex, Pennsylvania, Landon graduated from the University of Kansas in 1908. In 1912 and 1914, he worked for the Progressive Party; in 1932, he was elected governor of Kansas. He brought major governmental reform in state finance, water conservation, and utility rate regulation. In 1936 he won the Republican nomination for President, but he carried only Maine and Vermont. He opposed the United States' entry into World War II; after the war, he assumed an independent position and sought recognition of Communist China.

LAUREL, STAN (1890–1965), motion picture comedian. Born in Ulverson, England, he was part of the famous comedy team with Oliver Hardy. The Laurel and Hardy duo made slapstick comedy popular in the 1920s and 1930s. After 1926, he starred with Hardy in a succession of comedies, including *Air Raid Wardens* (1943), *Jitterbugs* (1943), *The Dancing Masters* (1943), *The Big Noise* (1944), *Nothing But Trouble,* and *The Bullfighters* (1945). He also appeared in numerous television roles after 1950; with his partner, he became an enduring part of America.

LAWRENCE, DAVID (1888–1973), editor and columnist. Born in Philadelphia, Pennsylvania, Lawrence began his career as a columnist with the *New York Evening Post* in 1916. His columns were syndicated in over three hundred daily newspapers. In 1947, he became editor of the *U.S. News and World Report.* He wrote numerous books, including *Diary of a Washington Correspondent.* He received the Presidential Medal of Freedom in 1970.

LEE, ROBERT E. (1807–1870), general of the Confederate armies and one of the greatest military strategists of history. Lee was born in

Jefferson Davis and his Cabinet with General Lee in the Council Chamber at Richmond.

Westmoreland County, Virginia, and graduated from the United States Military Academy. He fought in the Mexican War. When the Civil War began, his blood ties in Virginia affirmed his allegiance to the South. He accepted a commission as colonel in the Confederate army; within a month, he was given command of all the Southern armies. The battles of the war revealed his abilities as a strategist and diplomat—from Manassas where he achieved victory, to Fredericksburg where Stonewall Jackson fell. Gettysburg and Vicksburg were overwhelming losses for Lee. Historians of war agree that Lee had better strategic than tactical sense. *Lee's Dispatches,* revised by Grady McWhiney (1957), gives a useful perspective.

LEWIS, JERRY (1926–), comedian and television personality. Educated in the public schools of Irvington, New Jersey, Lewis began his career as an entertainer by appearing in the hotels and clubs of the Catskills. He formed a highly successful comedy routine with Dean Martin from 1946–1956. The Martin-Lewis comedy routine appeared on television until an embittered quarrel terminated the association. Lewis appeared in zany roles on screen, including *Sad Sack* (1957), *The Nutty Professor, Big Mouth,* and others. He has appeared on television and has developed a national relationship with the Muscular Dystrophy Association. His yearly telethons have raised millions of dollars for medical research in muscular dystrophy.

LEWIS, JOHN L. (1880–1969), labor leader who organized the Congress of Industrial Organizations (CIO) and was head of the United Mine Workers of America (UMWA). Born in Lucas, Iowa, Lewis worked as a miner in Montana and Utah. After a mine disaster in Wyoming, he dedicated his life to mine safety and defending miner's causes. He used the UMWA as a political base to launch his labor programs in Congress. During the Great Depression and Franklin Roosevelt's New Deal, he differed with the leadership of the American Federation of Labor and organized the CIO. He confronted the steel industry and the automobile industry and gained political leverage. In the 1940 election, he supported the Republican Wendell Willkie in preference to Roosevelt. Saul Alinsky's *John L. Lewis* (1949) is a useful biography.

LEWIS, MERIWETHER (1774–1809), frontier explorer. Born in Albemarle County, Virginia, he explored the territories of the Northwest with William Clark. President Thomas Jefferson, a friend and associate, commissioned their westward expedition. With considerable difficulty, they moved westward into territories inhabited by Indians and wildlife. Lewis' skills in dealing with the Indians proved essential to avoiding war. Upon his return, he was made governor of the Upper Louisiana Territory. However, his journals about the expedition were less persuasive than were those of William Clark, and it is agreed that Clark was an essential component of the expedition. See Bernard DeVoto, *The Journals of Lewis and Clark* (1953).

LINDBERGH, CHARLES A. (1902–1974), aviator who made the first solo non-stop flight across the Atlantic Ocean. Lindbergh was competing for a $25,000 prize posted by Raymond Orteig. He assembled the necessary financial backing to construct the plane he called *Spirit of St. Louis.* On May 20, 1927, he left New York, and in 33½ hours he arrived in Paris. He received numerous awards for the feat. In 1932, he and his wife were horrified at the kidnapping of their infant son; they paid a ranson of $50,000, but the baby was found dead. Lindbergh organized the America First Organization to prevent United States' entry into World War II; after the Japanese attack on Pearl Harbor, he joined the war effort. He wrote *We* (1927) and *The Spirit of St. Louis* (1953); he received a Pulitzer Prize for the latter.

Lindbergh stands under the wing of his plane, the *Spirit of St. Louis,* before taking off on his transatlantic flight.

LINDSAY, JOHN V. (1921–), political leader and news commentator. Born in New York City, Lindsay graduated from Yale in 1944 and served in the Navy during World War II. He represented New York's seventeenth Congressional District in the House of Representatives from 1959 until his election as mayor of New York in 1965. He began his political career as a Republican, but later changed his party affiliation to Democrat. His years as mayor of New York saw a succession of labor difficulties and conflicts. After leaving office, he turned his attention to television and broadcast interests; he has appeared on ABC's *Good Morning, America* program as political and public affairs commentator.

LODGE, HENRY CABOT, JR. (1902–), Senator, government official, author, and lecturer. Lodge graduated from Harvard and Northwestern University, and was elected to the U.S. Senate from Massachusetts in 1936. He resigned the Senate for military service during World War II; he was reelected in 1946. In 1960, he ran with Richard Nixon as the Vice-Presidential candidate for the Republican Party. From 1953 to 1960, he served as the United States representative to the United Nations. He was United States Ambassador to South Vietnam from 1963 to 1964 and 1965 to 1967; there he served a significant diplomatic function. Lodge authored *The Storm Has Many Eyes;* he has received numerous honors and recognitions.

LOUIS, JOE (1914-1981), American boxer and world heavyweight champion. Louis demonstrated his boxing abilities by his successes in the Golden Gloves competition of 1933. Also called the "Brown Bomber," his successes became legendary—particularly over boxers like Billy Conn, Rocky Marciano, and "Jersey Joe" Walcott. During World War II, he boxed on behalf of Army and Navy Relief. He authored *My Life Story* (1947). Jack Olsen's *The Black Athlete: A Shameful Story* (1968) places Louis within the generation of black athletes and racial discrimination.

LUCE, HENRY R. (1898–1967), magazine publisher. Born in Tenchow, China of Presbyterian missionary parents, Luce graduated *summa cum laude* from Yale University. With Briton Hadden, he founded *Time* magazine in 1922; the success of *Time* ushered in a new form of magazine journalism. In 1930, he launched *Fortune,* designed for the business executive. His marriage to playwright Clare Boothe Brokaw was much publicized. In this same period was launched *Life,* a venture into photographic journalism. At the time of his death, the combined circulation of *Life* and *Time* was in the millions. The most definitive study on the man and his ventures is John Kobler's *Luce: His Time, Life, and Fortune* (1968).

MacARTHUR, DOUGLAS (1880–1964), American general with distinguished service in the Far East during the occupation and reconstruction of Japan after World War II. MacArthur graduated from West Point with the highest scholastic average in the history of the academy. His rise within the military was spectacular. In 1936, he was dispatched to the Philippines by President Roosevelt to devise a strategy of defense; MacArthur mistakenly thought that the Japanese

Max Schmeling hangs on the ropes as he is pummeled by Joe Louis in their championship fight on June 22, 1938.

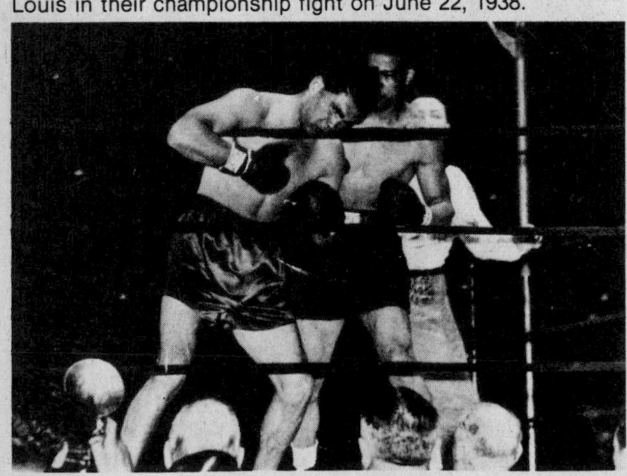

General Douglas MacArthur strides ashore during the landing on Leyte on Oct. 20, 1944.

wouldn't engage in such an attack. During World War II, he reclaimed the Philippines. After the war, he sought to expand American military efforts in the Korean War; because this strategy disagreed with President Truman's, he was dismissed. MacArthur returned to the United States in the midst of sympathy for the military hero. He authored *Reminiscences* (1964), an autobiography.

McCORMICK, CYRUS H. (1809–1884), inventor and manufacturer. He was primarily interested in farm machinery. In 1832, he took out a patent for a horizontal plow. He built a factory in Chicago for manufacturing reapers, and by mid-century he had a national market for reapers. Throughout his life, he competed with Obed Hussey for advantage in the farm machinery market. A contest in London pitted the McCormick reaper against the Hussey, and McCormick won. He expanded his factories in the United States; he developed steam-powered, self-propelled combines. He gave large sums of money to religious causes, and he received numerous honors from governments and organizations. William T. Hutchinson's *Cyrus Hall McCormick* is the standard biography.

MacDONALD, JEANETTE (1907–1965), actress and singer. With Nelson Eddy, she starred in several outstanding musical productions, including *Naughty Marietta* (1935), *Rose Marie* (1936), *Maytime* (1937), *Sweethearts* (1938), and *New Moon* (1940). She appeared in Broadway musicals such as *Love Me Tonight* (1932) and *One Hour With You* (1932). She starred with Clark Gable in *San Francisco* (1936).

McGUFFEY, WILLIAM H. (1800–1873), author of early elementary-school readers. McGuffey served as president of Cincinnati College and sought to promote public education. In 1836, he wrote the *Eclectic Readers;* the last of the now-famous *McGuffey Readers* was completed in 1854. Each of his books contained readings, aphorisms, messages on thrift and initiative. Within the emerging public schools, the readers were popular for several generations. McGuffey became president of Ohio University, and later professor of natural and moral philosophy at the University of Virginia. Richard D. Mosier's *Making the American Mind: Social and Moral Ideas in the McGuffey Readers* (1947) describes the impact of McGuffey's books.

MACHEN, J. GRESHAM (1881–1937), theologian and Bible scholar. Born in Baltimore, Maryland, Machen studied at Johns Hopkins University, Princeton University, and Princeton Theological Seminary. He then became professor and lecturer at Princeton. Machen was ordained as a Presbyterian minister; he became a leading voice of orthodox Protestantism in the early twentieth century. His books include *The Origin of Paul's Religion* (1921), *Christianity and Liberalism* (1923), *New Testament Greek for Beginners* (1923), and *The Virgin Birth of Christ* (1930).

McNAMARA, ROBERT S. (1916–), banker, automobile executive, public servant. McNamara was born in San Francisco, California, and received his undergraduate education at the University of California. He received his graduate degree in business administration from Harvard University. McNamara served for a brief period as a professor at Harvard. He became an executive with the Ford Motor Company in 1946 and president of that firm in 1960. President John Kennedy named him as Secretary of Defense in 1961. His eight years in that office were the most difficult years of the war in Vietnam. In 1968, he became president of the World Bank. McNamara has received numerous honors and recognitions. He authored *The Essense of Security* (1968) and other titles.

MADDOX, LESTER (1915–), segregationist leader and Georgia politician. Born in Atlanta, Georgia, he engaged in various business relationships—real estate, furniture, and a restaurant. As owner of a restaurant, he was told to comply with an integration order. He refused to comply and the restaurant was closed. He subsequently ran for political office and was elected governor of Georgia from 1967 to 1971. He served as lieutenant-governor under Governor Jimmy Carter in 1971–1975.

MALCOLM X (1925–1965), black religious leader. He was born as Malcolm Little in Omaha, Nebraska. Influenced by his father and the "back to Africa" ideas of Marcus Garvey, he resolved to defend the cause of black people. As a child, he saw his father murdered. In Boston, he worked in various menial jobs and was arrested for burglary. While in prison, he was converted to the Black Muslim religion; this provided a new forum for his ideas on race. He became an assistant minister of the Detroit Mosque. After the Kennedy assassination he made certain remarks that caused his suspension from the Black Muslims. He left the Nation of Islam to join the Organization of Afro-American Unity, and was assassinated at a public rally. His experiences were included in *The Autobiography of Malcolm X* by Alexander Haley.

MANCINI, HENRY (1924–), popular composer. Born in Cleveland, Ohio, Mancini attended the Juilliard Institute of Music. He served as pianist and arranger for the Tex Beneke Orchestra. As staff composer for Universal Pictures, he wrote scores for *The Glenn Miller Story, The Benny Goodman Story, The Great Waldo Pepper,* and other films. His recordings have achieved national attention. Among them are "Days of Wine and Roses" and "Moon River" (with Johnny Mercer). Mancini has received over twenty Grammy awards; he received Academy Awards for his music in *Breakfast at Tiffany's, Moon River,* and *Days of Wine and Roses.*

MANN, HORACE (1796–1859), educational reformer who promoted education throughout the United States. After graduating as valedictorian from Brown University, he pursued the study of law. His legal studies were interrupted by an interest in tutoring Latin and Greek; but later he returned to his legal studies, graduated from Tapping Reeve, and was admitted to the bar in 1823. He regarded education as "the great equalizer" of society. He abandoned a political career for a position as First Secretary of the State Board of Education. His admiration for Prussian education and non-sectarian study made his views controversial. Mann served as a member of the United States House of Representatives and president of Antioch College. *The Republic and the School: The Education of Free Men* (1957) is the most comprehensive collection of his writings.

MANTLE, MICKEY (1931–), baseball player born in Spavinaw, Oklahoma. In 1949, he signed with the New York Yankees. He has appeared with the New York Yankees in numerous World Series and All-Star games. Mantle is regarded as an outstanding baseball player. He was inducted into the Baseball Hall of Fame in 1974.

MARSHALL, GEORGE C. (1880–1959), soldier, statesman, architect of United States foreign policies after World War II. Marshall graduated from Virginia Military Institute and served in World War I under General John Pershing. Appointed Chief of Staff of the Army, he helped to prepare the United States for World War II. He received criticism for his failure to alert our Far East bases of the impending attack by the Japanese; but he directed military operations throughout the war and served as advisor to President Roosevelt. After the war he was named Secretary of State. The Marshall Plan set up a framework for the reconstruction of war-devastated Europe; actually, the plan combined the wisdom of George Kennan and Dean Acheson. Marshall encouraged the formation of the North Atlantic Treaty Organization (NATO). He was Secretary of Defense during the Korean War. The best work on Marshall is Forrest C. Pogue's *George C. Marshall* (2 vols., 1963, 1967).

MARSHALL, JOHN (1755–1835), the fourth Chief Justice of the United States. Marshall consolidated the principle of judicial review and strengthened the powers of the Supreme Court. Marshall was named to the court in 1801; he authored a definitive five-volume biography of George Washington. In 1803, his ruling in the celebrated case of *Marbury* vs. *Madison* established the principle of declaring acts of Congress unconstitutional. In *United States* vs. *Peters* he established the Supreme Court as the final interpreter of Federal law. In *McCulloch* vs. *Maryland* and *Gibbons* vs. *Ogden,* he upheld the principle that allowed the chartering of the Second Bank of the United States and the credit structure for interstate currency. Marshall was one of the truly outstanding Chief Justices in American history. *The Life of John Marshall,* by Albert J. Beveridge (2 vols., rev. ed. 1947) is a significant biography.

MARSHALL, THURGOOD (1908–), civil rights lawyer, Associate Justice of the United States Supreme Court. A native of Baltimore, Maryland, Marshall developed techniques for civils rights litigation during his early career as a lawyer. He served as counsel for the Baltimore chapter of the National Association for the Advancement of Colored People (NAACP). In 1938, he was admitted to practice before the United States Supreme Court. He achieved a phenomenal success ratio in his cases before the high court. For example, he argued the successful *Brown* vs.

Board of Education, which overturned segregation in public education. In 1964, President Johnson appointed him Solicitor General; in 1967, he was named to the Supreme Court. He has received numerous honors. An excellent biography is Lewis H. Fenderson's *Thurgood Marshall* (1969).

MARTIN, DEAN (1917–), actor, singer, and comedian. Born in Steubenville, Ohio, Martin became associated with Jerry Lewis in a successful comedy routine. The television series titled *The Martin-Lewis Comedy Hour* achieved considerable attention. His disagreement with Lewis resulted in the break-up of the comedy team. His screen roles have varied from the *Matt Helm* series to *The Bells Are Ringing* (1960), *Oceans II* (1960), *Silences* (1970), and *Airport.* His weekly television program on the National Broadcasting Company was widely received.

MARTIN, MARY (1913–), actress and singer born in Weatherford, Texas. Miss Martin was the singer in *Leave It to Me* (1938). She then starred in numerous musical productions, including *The Great Victor Herbert, Kiss the Boys Goodbye, Birth of the Blues,* and *Night and Day.* She starred in Noel Coward's *Pacific 1860.* Her role as entertainer in tours of United States military forces received acclaim. Her roles in *Annie Get Your Gun* (1948), the stage production of *South Pacific* (1949–1952), *Peter Pan* (1954–1955), and *The Sound of Music* (1959–1961) were widely acclaimed.

MARX, JULIUS "GROUCHO" (1890–1977), comedian and entertainer. In his early days, he joined his brothers Harpo and Chico in comic routines; the vaudeville circuit became the arena for the Marx comedy. With a cigar in hand, Groucho perfected comedy of the lunatic fringe. His scandalous humor was in comedy revues such as *Monkey Business* (1929), *Horsefeathers* (1932), and *Duck Soup* (1933). After the war, he became the host of a radio quiz show, *You Bet Your Life,* which achieved remarkable television success. The last movie effort starring Harpo and Chico was *The Incredible Jewel Robbery* (1959). A useful study of Groucho and his brothers is by Allen Eyles: *The Marx Brothers: Their World of Comedy* (second edition, 1969).

MATHER, COTTON (1663–1728), a leading author from the Puritan era, associated with the Salem witchcraft trials. Mather's youth was as remarkable as his life. At twelve, he was a student at Harvard College. He studied medicine, philosophy, and science in his teens. With his father, Increase Mather, he became a guiding force in the emerging Puritan society. The Salem witchcraft mentality was generated by Cotton Mather; his ill-fated efforts to become president of Harvard College or Yale brought serious disappointments in his later life. He was honored by other means—through election to the Royal Society of London. The best biography on Cotton Mather is Barrett Wendell's *Cotton Mather: The Puritan Priest* (rev. ed., 1963).

MAULDIN, BILL (1921–), editorial cartoonist. Born in Mountain Park, New Mexico, he studied at the Chicago Academy of Fine Arts. Mauldin served as cartoonist for the *St. Louis Post-Dispatch* until 1962, when he joined the staff of the *Chicago Sun-Times.* During World War II, he served with the United States Army; his military service earned him The Purple Heart and Legion of Merit award. Mauldin received the Pulitzer Prize for cartoons in 1944 and 1958. He authored numerous books, including *Bill Mauldin's Army* (1951), *Bill Mauldin in Korea* (1953), and *The Brass Ring* (1972).

MAYS, WILLIE (1931–), professional baseball player born in Westfield, Alabama. In 1950, he joined the New York Giants, which later moved to San Francisco. From 1951 to 1972, he was characterized as a "superstar" of baseball because he held numerous records: National League home run record; National League's Most Valuable Player of 1954 and 1965; and the Sporting News Player of the Year 1954. He wrote *Willie Mays: My Life In and Out of Baseball* (1966).

MEAD, MARGARET (1901–1978), anthropologist and author. Her early studies in Samoa provided new insights into tension, social organization, and adulthood; she authored *Coming of Age in Samoa.* She served as curator of ethnology at the American Museum of National History, then returned to her anthropological studies in New Guinea and wrote *Growing up in New Guinea* (1930). In later writings, she applied her findings to issues of public policy. After World War II, she authored *The Study of Cultures at a Distance* (1953) on cultural integration and analysis. In the 1960s and 1970s, her studies concerned the need for population control.

MEANY, GEORGE (1894–1980), labor leader associated with the American Federation of Labor (AFL). In his early career, Meany was associated with the building trades unions in New York. He promoted the pro-labor legislation of the New Deal; and during World War II, he served on the War Labor Board. In 1952, he was chosen as president of the AFL; later, he became president of the combined AFL and Congress of Industrial Organizations (CIO). Meany committed the organization to social reform and civil rights. Most Presidents since Eisenhower have had to reckon with the labor movement led by George Meany.

MELLON, ANDREW W. (1855–1937), businessman and United States Secretary of the Treasury. While associated with T. Mellon & Sons, he assisted in forming the Aluminum Corporation of America and organized the Gulf Oil Corporation. He then formed the Mellon National Bank of Pittsburgh, which identified him with significant banking and investment leaders. During the 1920s, he assisted the Harding, Coolidge, and Hoover Administrations in planning their monetary policies. His tax policies contributed to the unequal distribution of income that culminated with the Great Depression. Mellon wrote *Taxation: The People's Business* (1924).

MENNINGER, KARL (1893–), psychiatrist and author. Born in Topeka, Kansas, Menninger attended the University of Wisconsin and Harvard, receiving his medical degree *cum laude* from Harvard University. In 1946, he established the Menninger School of Psychiatry; he has been involved in the treatment, education, and rehabilitation of mental disorders. Menninger's books include *The Vital Balance* and *Love Against Hate*.

MILLER, GLENN (1904–1944), band leader of the "swing" era. Born in Chicago, Miller attended schools in Colorado and graduated from the University of Colorado. He began his musical career as a trombone player and as arranger for various orchestras. In 1933, he organized the Glenn Miller Band. The band played on several radio programs, but regularly appeared on the *Chesterfield Radio Program*. He composed many songs that achieved national popularity, including "Moonlight Serenade." Miller died in a plane crash over Holland shortly before the end of World War II.

MONDALE, WALTER (1928–), Vice-President of the United States and former United States Senator. In 1948, he worked in Hubert Humphrey's campaign for the Senate. He left Minnesota to work in Washington, D.C., for the student wing of Americans for Democratic Action; then he returned to Minnesota and graduated from college in 1951. In 1956, he obtained his law degree. In 1964, while serving as attorney general for Minnesota, he was appointed to finish Humphrey's Senate term when Humphrey became Vice-President; he was reelected in 1966 and 1972. On January 20, 1977, he became the forty-second Vice-President of the United States. Mondale has projected the image of a political liberal.

MONROE, MARILYN (1926–1962), motion picture star who built her reputation on a frivolous and sexual image. She was an illegitimate child with the name of Norma Jean Mortenson. Raised by foster parents, she had an unsuccessful marriage to an aircraft worker named James Dougherty. Then she became a photographer's model. In 1954, she married baseball star Joe DiMaggio, but the marriage lasted less than a year. She married playwright Arthur Miller but again was divorced in four years. Her most famous screen roles were in *Gentlemen Prefer Blondes* (1953), *How to Marry a Millionaire* (1953), *The Seven-Year Itch* (1955), *Some Like It Hot* (1959), and *The Misfits* (1961).

MOODY, DWIGHT L. (1837–1899), revivalist and evangelist. While Moody worked as a shoe salesman in Chicago, he became interested in the Young Men's Christian Association (YMCA). He organized "Sunday Schools" for slum families, supported through the YMCA. In 1872, he teamed up with Ira D. Sankey to hold revivals throughout England and Scotland; he then returned to America where he conducted revivals in New York, Philadelphia, Chicago, and Boston. Moody established schools for ministers in Northfield, Massachusetts, and Chicago. Chicago Bible Institute (named after Moody upon his death) achieved a great reputation. James Findlay's *Dwight L. Moody; American Evangelist* (1969) is a good biography.

MORGAN, J. PIERPONT (1837–1913), banker and financier who was instrumental in the financial reorganization of the railroads. During a severe economic crisis in 1893, Morgan managed to sell government bonds for gold. He organized the House of Morgan investment and banking corporation; established United States Steel as the largest corporation of its day; and gained control of major rail routes to the West. He was an avid collector of art; through a personal interest, he provided the funds to make the Metropolitan Museum of Art in New York among the finest museums in the world. Frederick Lewis Allen's *The Great Pierpont Morgan* (1949) is the most readable biography on the man.

MORRIS, GOUVERNEUR (1752–1816), statesman and diplomat. Born in Morisania, New York, he served in the New York provisional congress during the early stages of the American Revolution. He was elected in 1778 as a delegate to the Continental Congress and served as an assistant to Robert Morris, who was Superintendent of Finance. Morris was a significant delegate to the Constitutional Convention in 1787; he helped to draft the American Constitution, which he also signed. Morris served as foreign minister to France from 1792 to 1794. He also served as Senator from New York, and was critical of Jeffersonian Democrats. The diary of Morris is contained in *A Diary of the French Revolution* (2 vols., 1939) edited by B. C. Davenport.

MORSE, SAMUEL F. B. (1791-1872), inventor and designer of the first telegraph system. Morse was born in Charlestown, Massachusetts, the son of a clergyman. He graduated from Yale College. As an artist and painter, his work attracted little attention. Then he developed an interest in electricity. He combined the existing technology of sender, receiver, and code to invent telegraphy. Congress authorized the construction and development of a telegraphic line between Washington, D.C., and Baltimore, Maryland. By 1844, he was able to send the message "What hath God wrought" over this line. Robert L. Thompson's book, *Wiring a Continent* (1947) places Morse within the broader framework of technology.

MOSES, ANNA MARY ROBERTSON "GRANDMA" (1860-1961), painter of the primitive style. Born in Greenwich, New York, she held her first show in New York City in 1940. Subsequently her paintings were exhibited in shows throughout the United States, including the Museum of Modern Art in New York, the Metropolitan Museum in New York, and the Carnegie Institute. From 1950 to 1957, her paintings were exhibited in Europe. She received the Certificate of Merit (1956), the Woman's National Press Club Award (1949), and others. She wrote *My Life's History: Autobiography of Grandma Moses* (1952).

MUHAMMAD, ELIJAH (1897–1975), leader of the black Nation of Islam. Born in Sandersville, Georgia, he became Minister to the Nation of Islam in 1934. He molded the Nation of Islam into an organization of social, economic, and religious importance. Muhammad preached a message of black nationalism and imposed a standard of strict morality. He called for separation from white America and rejected the notion of racial integration. Malcolm X and boxer Muhammad Ali were among the more influential converts to the Nation of Islam.

MURROW, EDWARD R. (1908–1965), broadcast journalist. Born near Greensboro, North Carolina, Murrow spent his early youth in Washington State. He worked in logging camps as he attended Washington State College. In 1935, he joined the Columbia Broadcasting System. He travelled to London in 1937, and there he developed the dramatic "on the spot" style of radio news journalism. He won renown for his broadcasts describing the bombing raids on the city of London. After the war he developed television news journalism through the *See It Now* program; his most famous program was *Person to Person*. In 1961, he was appointed director of the United States Information Agency. Alexander Kendrick's *Prime Time* (1969) is a biography of Murrow.

NADER, RALPH (1934–   ), consumer advocate. Born in Winsted, Connecticut, Nader graduated *magna cum laude* from Princeton University. He later graduated from Harvard Law School. He was appointed as a consultant to the Department of Labor in his initial work on auto safety; served with Senator Abraham A. Ribicoff's Government Operations Subcommittee as a resource expert on safety. Nader wrote *Unsafe at Any Speed: The Designed-In-Dangers of the American Automobile* (1965) and became a bitter foe of the automobile industry. General Motors admitted spying on him, and he sued the company for $26 million in 1966. Nader organized the Center for the Study of Responsive Law in 1969. He has become identified with the consumer protection movement.

The Third-Term Panic, by Thomas Nast.
(The first use of the elephant as the symbol of the Republican Party.)

NAST, THOMAS (1840–1902), caricaturist, painter, and political cartoonist. Nast was born in Ludwig, Bavaria. As a youth he emigrated to the United States. In 1862, he began working for the *Harper's Weekly;* his initial cartoon attacks dealt with the Andrew Johnson Administration. His caricatures of Boss Tweed and the Tammany Hall political machine of New York City achieved national attention. He was offered a $200,000 bribe to stop the series, but he refused the bribe. Nast invented the symbols now associated with the Democratic and Republican parties—the donkey and elephant.

NATION, CARRY (1846–1911), temperance reformer, agitator, and an early leader in the Prohibition movement. Born in Garrard County, Kentucky, she married Dr. Charles Gloyd in 1867. He became an alcoholic and brought considerable hardship to his wife. In 1877, she married David Nation; and in 1890, she began her work with the Women's Christian Temperance Union (WCTU). Mrs. Nation and her associates organized prayer groups outside saloons and bars. In her campaign on behalf the WCTU, she carried a hatchet for breaking up saloon furniture. She displayed an aggressive character in achieving her moral ends.

NEUMANN, JOHN N. (1811–1860), religious leader; first male American saint of the Roman Catholic church. Born in Prachatice (now in Czechoslovakia), Neumann studied at the University of Prague and came to the United States as a Catholic missionary in 1836. After several years of missionary and pastoral work, he was named Bishop of Philadelphia in 1852. Neumann established about one hundred parochial schools and a Catholic seminary; he was well known for his deep personal faith in God. He was declared venerable in 1896, beatified in 1963, and canonized as a saint in 1977.

NICKLAUS, JACK (1940–), professional golfer born in Columbus, Ohio. Nicklaus attended Ohio State University. His career as a professional golfer included winning these major tournaments: United States Open 1962, 1967, 1972; United States Masters 1963, 1965, 1966, 1972, 1975; the British Open 1968, 1970; the Professional Golfer's Association (PGA) 1963, 1971, 1973, 1974. He has won more tournament championships than any other person in the history of professional golf. Nicklaus has authored numerous publications, such as *Ways to Lower Your Golf Score* (1962) and *The Best Way to Better Golf* (1974).

NIEBUHR, H. RICHARD (1894–1962), theologian and sociologist of religion. Born in Wright City, Missouri, Niebuhr graduated from Elmhurst College (1912) and Eden Theological Seminary (1915). He received his Bachelor of Divinity degree and doctorate from Yale University. Niebuhr authored *The Social Sources of Denominationalism* (1929), in which he discusses the relationships of social groups to denominations. His *Kingdom of God in America* (1937) discusses the concept of "Kingdom" in the transformation of Puritan thought to Protestant ideas in American history. He participated in study groups that led to the major assemblies of the World Council of Churches. He was instrumental in the merger between the United Church of Christ, Congregational, and Evangelical and Reformed Churches.

NIEBUHR, REINHOLD (1892–1971), distinguished theologian within the Neo-Orthodox movement. Born in Wright City, Missouri, Niebuhr attended Elmhurst College and Eden Theological Seminary. He received his master's degree from Yale University. Niebuhr pastored a church in Detroit, Michigan, from 1915 to 1928. In 1927, he wrote *Does Civilization Need Religion?* This book criticized the capitalistic values of the American industrial order. In 1928, he joined the faculty of Union Theological Seminary in New York City. There he wrote an attack on liberal Protestantism titled *Moral Man in Immoral Society* (1932). His many books and articles underscored the social and cultural applications of theology. He opposed the expansion of United States military power in Asia during the 1960s.

OAKLEY, ANNIE (1860–1926), an outstanding figure from America's Wild West. Born in Drake County, Ohio, she teamed up with Frank E. Butler in vaudeville and later married him. In spite of her abilities in marksmanship, she was a modest woman. Her exploits inspired the modern musical, *Annie Get Your Gun*. Miss Oakley's religious views were fundamentalist. She was generous with her wealth, and many legends grew out of her reputation after she died. Annie Fern Swarthout's *Missie: An Historical Biography of Annie Oakley* (1947) is a very interesting study.

OCHS, ADOLPH S. (1858–1935), newspaper publisher and philanthropist. Born in Cincinnati, Ohio, Ochs bought and published the *Chattanooga Dispatch* and the *Chattanooga Times*. Then he moved to New York City where, in 1896, he acquired control of the *New York Times*. In an age of "yellow journalism," he sought to establish a newspaper that reflected dignity and trust. He established the *New York Times Index of Current History* (a topical journal) and funded the development of the *Dictionary of American Biography*. Ochs tried to make editorial opinion more objective. Gay Talese's, *The Kingdom and the Power* (1969) is a massive overview of Ochs and the *New York Times*.

President John F. Kennedy, Governor Connally, and Mrs. Jacqueline Kennedy stand under the wing of the presidential plane moments after arriving in Dallas, Texas, on Nov. 22, 1963.

ONASSIS, JACQUELINE KENNEDY (1929–), former wife of John F. Kennedy, the thirty-fifth President of the United States. Born in Southampton, New York, she attended Vassar College and The Sorbonne in Paris, France. After the assassination of President Kennedy, she received national consolation and regard. In 1968, she married Aristotle Onassis, wealthy Greek shipbuilder; the marriage attracted considerable notice. Since Onassis' death she has served as a publishing consultant. In earlier years, she was photographer for the *Washington Times-Herald*. Mrs. Onassis is a trustee of the Whitney Museum of American Art; she has received an Emmy Award for public service.

OPPENHEIMER, J. ROBERT (1904–1967), physicist; director of the atomic energy research project at Los Alamos, New Mexico. Born in New York City, Oppenheimer attended Harvard University and Cambridge University. He joined the staff of the California Institute of Technology in Pasadena, where he established a reputation in quantum mechanics and research in the continuous spectrum. Oppenheimer served as director of the project to develop the atomic bomb. After the development of the bomb, he regretted its devastation. He became the focus of attacks by Senator Joseph McCarthy, who alleged that Oppenheimer had communist sympathies; the allegations were unfounded. In the 1960s, he received the Fermi Award and was appointed director of the Institute for Advanced Study at Princeton University.

OWENS, JESSE (1913–1980), Olympic track star. He was born in Oakville, Alabama, the son of a sharecropper. He soon became an outstanding athlete. In 1935, he competed in the National Intercollegiate Track and Field Championships, where he established new records in broad jump and track. As a member of the United States Olympic team, he won four gold medals and served to refute Adolf Hitler's concept of "Aryan superiority." After several unsuccessful enterprises, Owens was appointed national director of physical education for blacks by the Office of Civilian Defense. He served as director of personnel for Ford Motor Company in Detroit from 1942 to 1946. He has received numerous recognitions and appointments. His autobiography is entitled, *Blackthink: My Life as a Black Man and White Man* (1970).

PALEY, WILLIAM S. (1901–), television network executive. Born in Chicago, Illinois, he attended the University of Chicago and the University of Pennsylvania. In 1928, he joined the staff of the Columbia Broadcasting System, where he rose from president to chairman of the board. He has served on numerous federal commissions, including the White House Conference on Education, Resources for Freedom, and others. He served in the military in World War II and was decorated with the Legion of Honor and Legion of Merit.

PALMER, ARNOLD (1929–), professional golfer born in Youngstown, Pennsylvania. Palmer attended Wake Forest College. As a golfer, he won the Masters Tournament in 1958, 1960, 1962, and 1964; the United States Open in 1960; the British Open in 1961 and 1962; and others. His friendship with President Dwight Eisenhower (and the President's affection for golf) established Palmer as a national celebrity. He is the president of Arnold Palmer Enterprises.

PATTERSON, FLOYD (1935–), boxer and former heavyweight champion, born in Waco, North Carolina. In 1952, Patterson began his boxing career as an Olympic middleweight champion; later in 1952, he fought his first professional fight. In 1956, he won the World Heavyweight Championship by defeating Archie Moore (the title had been vacated by the retirement of Rocky Marciano). After several defenses of the title, he lost it to Ingemar Johansson in 1959. He regained the title from Johansson in 1960, then lost it to Sonny Liston in 1962.

PATTERSON, JOSEPH MEDILL (1879–1946), newspaper publisher. Born in Chicago, Patterson attended the Groton School and Yale University. He began a journalistic career with the *Chicago Tribune* in 1901. In 1919, he founded the *New York Daily News* and remained as editor and publisher of that newspaper from 1919 to 1946. He served during World War I and wrote several books, including *The Fourth Estate* (with J. Keeley and Harriet Ford), *By-Products,* and *Rebellion.* His *New York Daily News* emphasized sensationalism, sex, and crime. After the financial crash of 1929, he addressed the newspaper to social reform and New Deal legislation. Although he supported President Franklin Roosevelt on most items, he felt that the United States should not enter World War II.

PATTON, GEORGE S. (1885–1945), general and military strategist. Born in San Gabriel, California, Patton graduated from the United States Military Academy at West Point. He distinguished himself as a tactician and commander of mobile tank warfare. His strict discipline and colorful language earned him the nickname "Old Blood and Guts." Patton was a student of United States Civil War strategy. Between World Wars, he learned tank warfare. He established his reputation in the North African campaign and the capture of Palermo. His sweep across France with the Third Army was marked by ruthlessness and drive. Patton was strategically involved in the Battle of the Bulge. He authored *War as I Knew It.*

PAULING, LINUS (1901–), atomic chemist. Born in Portland, Oregon, Pauling studied at Oregon State University and California Institute of Technology. He headed the Gates and Crellin Laboratories. His studies involved hemoglobin and protein structures. He is a member of the National Academy of Sciences and numerous other associations. In 1954, he received the Nobel Prize in Chemistry and the Nobel Peace Prize in 1962. Pauling has written numerous articles; his most famous appeared in 1931 and was entitled "The Nature of the Chemical Bond." Pauling advocated military disarmament, as described in *Quest for Peace* (1966) by Mortimer Lipsky.

PEABODY, GEORGE (1795–1869), merchant, financier, and philanthropist. Peabody dealt in securities in London after 1837; he generated capital for American industries. His firm, George Peabody and Company, specialized in foreign exchange. Peabody's international banking earned him a considerable personal fortune. After the Panic of 1837, he purchased several securities that were depressed. His company brought large supplies of capital investment to the United States. His wealth was distributed in various programs of educational reconstruction and poor relief. Franklin Parker's *George Peabody: A Biography* (1971) is highly informative and readable.

PEALE, NORMAN VINCENT (1898–), influential Protestant clergyman. Peale obtained his undergraduate degree from Ohio Wesleyan College in 1920. He was torn between a career in journalism or the ministry; he worked for the *Morning Republican* in Findlay, Ohio, and the *Detroit Journal.* He returned to study at Boston University and was ordained into the Methodist Episcopal Church in 1921. In 1932, he became pastor of the Marble Collegiate Church in New York. He has written numerous books, including *The Art of Living* (1932), *A Guide to Confident Living* (1948), *The Art of Real Happiness* (1950), and his phenomenally successful book, *The Power of Positive Thinking* (1952). Peale also began a radio program titled *The Art of Living,* which began in 1935 on NBC. He has been criticized for his moral pragmatism.

PEALE, REMBRANDT (1778–1860), painter best known for his portraits of Revolutionary heroes. Born in Bucks County, Pennsylvania, Peale was a son of the renowned painter, Charles Willson Peale. He made several trips to France, where he met Jacques Louis David and other leading artists. Peale established the Pennsylvania Academy of Fine Arts. His portrait of George Washington (1822) achieved considerable fame. He was elected president of the American Academy of the Fine Arts in 1825. Peale wrote *Graphics: The Art of Accurate Delineation* (1835). He developed a massive series of paintings on death that reflected several allegorical figures. In an era that emphasized romanticism, Peale's realistic work achieved considerable fame, particularly in Europe.

PEARSON, DREW (1897–1969), controversial newspaper columnist. His syndicated news column "Washington Merry-Go-Round" first appeared in 1932; he shared the writing with Jack Anderson after 1959. Pearson reported President Franklin Roosevelt's plan to pack the Supreme Court; he was generally disliked among Presidents and other public officials. He sponsored humanitarian causes; for example, he organized the Friendship Train to collect food for the people of Europe. He authored several books, including *Washington Merry-Go-Round* (1931) and (with Jack Anderson) *The Case Against Congress* (1968).

PEARY, ROBERT E. (1856–1920), Arctic explorer, famous for his discovery of the North Pole. Peary was born in Cresson, Pennsylvania. After his studies in civil engineering, he served as a county surveyor and draftsman. He was commissioned in the United States Navy in 1881. His early travels to Greenland were a prelude to his subsequent discovery of the North Pole. He reached the North Pole on April 6, 1909; but controversy surrounded Frederick A. Cook's claims that he reached the North Pole in 1908. In later life, Peary became identified with the development and expansion of aviation. John Edward Weems *Race to the Pole* (1960) details the controversy between Cook and Peary.

PENN, WILLIAM (1644–1718), Quaker leader and founder of Pennsylvania. Penn was born in London, where he became associated with the development of Quakerism and the Society of Friends. At Oxford, he was influenced by Puritanism and was expelled from the university. In 1672, he became a Quaker advocate. After the Glorious Revolution of 1688, he came to establish the colony of Pennsylvania. In 1712, he sold the colony to England. His last years were filled with disappointment. Mary M. Dunn's *William Penn: Politics and Conscience* (1967) is a useful analysis of the man.

PENNEY, JAMES C. (1875–1971), business executive and philanthropist born in Hamilton, Ohio. In 1902, he established the J.C. Penney Company, which operated on the principle of the Golden Rule and Christian morality. The department stores that he opened were called Golden Rule Stores; his first store was in Kemmerer, Wyoming. By 1971, his chain of stores numbered 1,660 outlets with gross sales of $4.1 billion. Penney exhibited a deep religious perspective in his personal manner and corporate leadership.

PERRY, OLIVER H. (1785–1819), naval officer and hero of the War of 1812. Born in South Kingston, Rhode Island, Perry held the command of a flotilla at Newport, Virginia, at the outbreak of the War of 1812. Commander Robert H. Barclay challenged Perry on September 10, 1813 in a battle between Perry's *Niagra* and Barclay's *Detroit.* Barclay was defeated, and Perry sent his superiors the famous message: "We have met the enemy and they are ours." This decisive victory strengthened United States claims in the Northwest. Perry retired and received honors from Congress. He later travelled to the Mediterranean, where he died of yellow fever.

PERSHING, JOHN J. (1860–1948), distinguished American commander during World War I. After graduation from West Point in 1886, Pershing was assigned to the campaign against the Apache Indians in the Southwest United States. He was also involved in the Spanish-American War and served as military attache in Tokyo during the Russo-Japanese War (1904–1905). Pershing's most significant service came during World War I, when he called for an independent American army. The Allies questioned his strategy during the last years of the war. Congress awarded him the title General of the Armies, a title given previously to George Washington. He authored *My Experiences in the World War* (1948), which was awarded the Pulitzer Prize.

PICKFORD, MARY (1893-1979), actress and movie star born in Toronto, Canada. Her acting career began at age eight, when she appeared in various melodramas and as a child actress on Broadway. At age 13, she took the name Mary Pickford. She appeared in various roles between 1910 and 1916, when she established the Mary Pickford Film Company. She joined Douglas Fairbanks, Charlie Chaplin, and the United Artists Corporation in 1919. She starred in numerous productions on the silent screen. She aided the work of numerous philanthropic and charity organizations.

PINKERTON, ALLAN (1819–1884), founder of a famous detective agency that bears his name; prototype of the modern crime investigator. Born in Glasgow, Scotland, he migrated to Dundee, Illinois. He supported abolitionists and the Underground Railroad in the years leading up to the Civil War. In 1850, he served as the director of police in Chicago; he then organized his private agency. He worked with the United States Post Office and the Illinois Central Railroad to solve robberies. He prevented an assassination of President Lincoln during the first inaugural. He organized the framework of the most comprehensive detective agency.

POCAHONTAS (ca. 1595–1617), early symbol of the American Indians. The daughter of an Indian chief, her real name was Matoaka; *Pocahontas* means "playful one." According to tradition, she played at the fort at Jamestown. She was taken as a prisoner by Captain Samuel Argall to guarantee the safety of Englishmen who had fallen into Indian hands. She was brought to Jamestown, instructed in Christianity, and baptized. She married colonial leader John Rolfe, and the marriage brought a period of peace between the colonists and the Indians. During a trip to England, she contracted smallpox and died in 1617.

POLLOCK, JACKSON (1912–1956), painter within the abstract, expressionist tradition. Born in Cody, Wyoming, he studied with Thomas Hart Benton between 1929 and 1931. He worked with the Depression-inspired Federal Arts Project from 1938 to 1942. During World War II, his art was influenced by European developments in cubism and surrealism. His paintings attracted the attention of Peggy Guggenheim; and under the Guggenheim influence, his art was shown throughout Europe. Pollock's international reputation became established in this period. During the last years of his life, his work was seen at the Sidney Janis Gallery in New York. In 1956, he was honored by a special exhibition at the New York Museum of Modern Art.

POPE, JOHN RUSSELL (1874–1937), architect; best known for designing the National Gallery of Art in Washington, D.C. Pope was born in New York City and trained at the American Academy at Rome. He was able to duplicate historic architectural styles through his studies. Pope began his architectural career in New York. He designed the Scottish Rite Temple in Washington, D.C., and was chosen to design memorials for Theodore Roosevelt in Washington and Abraham Lincoln in Hodgenville, Kentucky.

POST, ELIZABETH L. "EMILY" (1872–1960), well-known authority on social manners.

Born in Baltimore, Maryland, she began writing short stories and novels in 1904. Her book, *Etiquette,* appeared in 1922 and went through 10 revisions and 89 printings. It served as a guide to proper behavior and manners for ordinary people. Miss Post regarded etiquette as the science of proper living. She also wrote a nationally syndicated newspaper article on etiquette and authored numerous other publications, including *The Personality of a House* (1930), *Children Are People* (1940), and the *Emily Post Cook Book* (1949).

PRESLEY, ELVIS (1935–1977), singer commonly recognized as the father of "rock and roll" music. Presley's performances were filled with emotion and intensity. His gyrating hips and suggestive stage movements became a trademark, and he was idolized by teenagers throughout the world. He signed a recording contract with RCA Victor in 1956; he then recorded success after success. His first 45 records sold over a million copies each. Presley appeared in *Love Me Tender* and a succession of movies. He grossed over $4.3 billion in his 21-year career. His more famous musical titles included "Love Me Tender," "All Shook Up," and "Are You Lonesome Tonight?" His Graceland Mansion in Memphis, Tennessee, was a mecca for his fans.

PULITZER, JOSEPH, SR. (1847–1911), newspaper publisher and editor. Born in Mako, Hungary, he grew up in Budapest and pursued an active interest in military affairs. After being rejected by the French Foreign Legion, he was recruited by the Union forces for the Civil War and obtained passage to Boston. He quickly became identified with journalism through the *Westliche Post* in 1871. He purchased the *St. Louis Post-Dispatch,* which had shaky finances until about 1881. He served as a delegate to the National Democratic Convention and was elected as a member of Congress from New York in 1885. He then purchased the *New York World,* which added strength to his emerging influence. He used the *World* to promote sensational journalism and scandal. Its fiery reports from Cuba drew the United States into the Spanish-American War.

PYLE, ERNEST T. "ERNIE" (1900–1945), outstanding newspaper correspondent of World War II. Born near Dana, Indiana, Pyle studied journalism at Indiana University. After varied assignments, he received permanent appointment with the Scripps-Howard newspaper chain. Pyle developed a column that was syndicated through two hundred daily newspapers. He received a Pulitzer Prize for his coverage of the campaigns in North Africa, Sicily, Italy, and France. Pyle was with United States forces in Iwo Jima, where he died. He authored *Ernie Pyle in England* (1941), *Here Is Your War* (1943), *Brave Men* (1944), and *Last Chapter* (1946).

RAUSCHENBUSCH, WALTER (1861–1918), clergyman associated with the "social gospel." Born in Rochester, New York, Rauschenbusch graduated from Rochester Theological Seminary and assumed a pastorate in the area of New York City known as "Hells Kitchen." His experiences in New York led him to question the capitalistic ethic, and he formulated a theology of Christian socialism. He authored several books, including *Christianity and the Social Crisis, Christianizing the Social Order,* and *A Theology of Social Gospel.*

RAYBURN, SAM (1882–1961), political leader and long-time Speaker of the House of Representatives. Born in Roane County, Texas, Rayburn graduated from Mayo Normal School (now East Texas State University). He taught in rural schools, then ran for the Texas House of Representatives. He attended law school and passed the state bar in 1908. In 1910, he won a seat in the United States House of Representatives; he was subsequently reelected for 23 terms. He served as Speaker of the House for many years. Clearly identified with the Democratic Party and its leadership, he managed the Presidential campaign of Lyndon Baines Johnson in 1960. An interesting analysis of Rayburn's impact on national politics is included in William Leuchtenburg's *Franklin D. Roosevelt and The New Deal, 1932–1940* (1963).

REAGAN, RONALD (1911–), Hollywood actor and political figure. Reagan appeared in over fifty movies. In 1966, he ran for governor of California against incumbent Edmund G. "Pat" Brown and was victorious. He became an important force in the Republican Party. Although he was viewed as a radical conservative because he supported Barry Goldwater for the presidency in 1964, Reagan resisted such labeling. He opposed federally funded welfare programs and the expansion of big government. He was elected President of the United States in 1980.

Presidential candidate Ronald Reagan waves to an enthusiastic crowd on his arrival on Aug. 15, 1976, in Kansas City.

REASONER, HARRY (1923–), broadcast journalist. Born in Dakota City, Iowa, Reasoner began a writing career in 1946 with the *Minneapolis Times*. In 1948, he began an association with radio station WCCO in Minneapolis, a CBS radio affiliate. After a period of time with the United States Information Agency in the Far East, he returned to CBS with a television assignment in New York. He covered the racial crisis in Little Rock, Arkansas, in 1958. During the 1960s, he had numerous assignments with *CBS Reports* and narrated special documentaries on smoking, taxation, and federal aid to schools. He was seen as the weekly anchorman for *CBS Sunday News* until 1970, when he left CBS to join ABC News. He co-anchored news broadcasts at ABC with Howard K. Smith and Barbara Walters, then returned to the staff of CBS News in 1978.

REED, WALTER S. (1851–1902), military surgeon who is credited with having conquered yellow fever. Reed received two medical degrees, one from the University of Virginia and another from Bellevue Hospital Medical College. He served as a professor at the Army Medical School in Washington. He was able to determine the mode of transmission of yellow fever through many controlled experiments. He developed a way to immunize soldiers against the disease. In 1901, he resumed his teaching responsibilities at the Army Medical School. Reed received many honors, including honorary degrees from Harvard University and the University of Michigan. For more information about his life and times, read Albert E. Truby's, *Memorial of Walter Reed: The Yellow Fever Episode* (1943).

REMINGTON, FREDERIC (1861–1909), author and sculptor; painter and illustrator. Remington attended several schools, including Yale School of Fine Arts. His early work reflected his fascination with the West. He often painted horses in action. His work contained a high degree of realism. He represented the cowboy, Indian, and the Western landscape with native color. Remington wrote many significant books, including *Pony Tracks* (1895), *Stories of War and Peace* (1899), and *The Way of an Indian* (1906). A significant collection of his work can be found in the New York Public Library.

RENWICK, JAMES, JR. (1818–1895), architect most famous for St. Patrick's Cathedral in New York City. Born in the Bloomingdale section of New York, Renwick got his abilities in design from his father, James Renwick. He graduated from Columbia College. His designs for several churches brought him to national prominence—Grace Church, Church of the Puritans on Union Square, Church of the Covenant, and St. Patrick's Cathedral. Renwick also designed the New Smithsonian Institution in Washington. He taught a generation of apprentices and draftsmen and was a collector of art objects from his trips abroad.

RESTON, JAMES (1909–), author and journalist born in Clyde-Bank, Scotland. Reston attended the University of Illinois and began his journalistic career with the *Springfield Daily News*. In 1934, he joined the staff of the Associated Press in London. In 1939, he came back to the United States to work with the *New York Times*—first as reporter for the London bureau, then with the Washington bureau, finally as Chief Washington Correspondent (1953–1964). From 1964 to 1968, he was associate editor of the *Times*. He received the Pulitzer Prize in 1945 and 1957. Reston has received numerous other awards, recognitions, and honorary degrees.

RICKENBACKER, EDWARD "EDDIE" (1890–1973), World War I flying ace, racing driver, and executive of a major airline. Rickenbacker worked with the Frayer-Miller company as a race driver and he achieved numerous records. During World War I, he shot down more than twenty-two enemy planes, and became the most decorated pilot of the war. As general manager and later president of Eastern Airlines, he brought innovative promotions to the industry. After World War

II, he supported conservative McCarthyism and the anti-communist crusade. His autobiography is titled, *Rickenbacker—An Autobiography.*

RIDDLE, NELSON (1921–), composer, conductor, and arranger of popular musical themes. He was associated with numerous bands early in his career, including the Tommy Dorsey Band. He served as staff arranger for the National Broadcasting Company in Hollywood, 1947–1950; then he was musical director for Capitol Records, 1951–1962. Riddle has been guest conductor with the Hollywood Bowl and the Atlanta Symphony. He received the Emmy nomination in 1954, 1955, 1956, and 1957, and an Oscar nomination in 1960. Riddle received a Grammy award for *Come Blow Your Horn* and other musical scores. He composed theme music for the television series *Untouchables, Naked City, Route 66,* and others.

ROCKEFELLER, JOHN D., JR. (1874–1960), business entrepreneur and philanthropist. Born in Cleveland, Ohio, Rockefeller was educated at Brown University. After graduation, he became involved in the business affairs of Standard Oil Company, which his father had founded. He disliked the world of business and became involved in philanthrophy. He established the Rockefeller Institute for Medical Research and the Rockefeller Foundation. He supported the education of black people in the South. The last quarter-century of his life was devoted to conservation, the national parks system, and the restoration of Williamsburg. His modesty was in direct contrast to the image that his father projected.

ROCKEFELLER, NELSON A. (1908–1979), former governor of New York and Vice-President of the United States under President Gerald R. Ford. He was a son of John D. Rockefeller, Jr. His government service began as Assistant Secretary of State in 1944–1945. After the war, he chaired the Development Advisory Board. From 1958 to 1973, he was governor of New York, where he inaugurated a major construction program in the state capital of Albany. After President Richard Nixon's resignation, he was named by President Ford to become Vice-President. He was a trustee of the Rockefeller Brothers fund.

ROCKWELL, NORMAN (1894–1978), painter and illustrator of covers for the *Saturday Evening Post* and numerous other magazines, including the *Ladies' Home Journal, Look,* and *McCall's.* Rockwell's *Paintings of Four Freedoms* is represented in the Metropolitan Museum of Art in New York City. During World War I, he served as a first-class painter with the United States Navy. He received numerous recognitions and honorary degrees, and wrote *Norman Rockwell: My Adventures as an Illustrator* (1959), *The Norman Rockwell Album* (1961), *Norman Rockwell: Artist and Illustrator* (1970), and *Norman Rockwell's America* (1975).

RODGERS, RICHARD (1902–1979), noted composer of music. Born near Arverne, New York, Rodgers worked with Lorenze Hart and Jerome Kern in his early years. With Lorenze Hart, he produced a succession of musicals that captured national attention; among their more successful productions were: *On Your Toes* (1936), *Babes in Arms* (1937), and *Pal Joey* (1940). His more popular music with Hart included *My Funny Valentine, With a Song in My Heart, This Can't Be Love,* and *The Lady Is a Tramp.* His association with Oscar Hammerstein resulted in such musical successes as *Carousel* (1945), *South Pacific* (1949), *The King and I* (1951), and *The Sound of Music* (1959). Rodgers' most popular songs include "If I Loved You," "Hello Young Lovers," and "Climb Every Mountain."

ROGERS, WILL (1879–1935), entertainer and newspaper columnist. Rogers was born in Cologah, Oklahoma, of Indian descent; as a young man he was a cowboy—panhandling, twirling rope, and herding steers. In 1902, he joined a Wild West show in Australia. In 1912, he played in his first Broadway musical, *The Wall Street Girl,* and in 1922, he appeared in the Ziegfeld Follies. That same year, he began writing a column that wedded political humor with wit; the column appeared daily in 1926 and was widely syndicated. He authored *Letters of a Self-Made Diplomat to His President* (1926) and *There's Not a Bathing Suit in Russia* (1927). He was an early enthusiast of air travel and was killed in a plane crash en route to Alaska.

ROONEY, MICKEY (1920–), actor and star of films. Born in Brooklyn, New York, he first appeared in vaudeville with his parents. Rooney starred in numerous television and film productions, including *Hold That Kiss, Babes in Arms, National Velvet, Breakfast at Tiffany's, Requiem* *for a Heavyweight,* and the entire *Andy Hardy* series. He starred in the television spectacular *Pinocchio* (1957). Rooney wrote *An Autobiography* (1965).

ROOSEVELT, ELEANOR (1884–1962), author, diplomat, and wife of President Franklin Delano Roosevelt, thirty-second President of the United States. After her husband contracted polio in 1921, she became increasingly involved with his career. She rejected her mother-in-law's notion that Franklin should surrender to his condition. During the Great Depression, she led several New Deal programs for work relief. During World War II, she became involved with several efforts on behalf of the Red Cross and war relief. After the death of her husband in 1945, she assumed international stature in connection with her work on the United Nations. She was a leading voice in the Democratic Party, particularly on behalf of Adlai Stevenson's campaigns for the Presidency. Mrs. Roosevelt authored numerous books, including *On My Own* (1958).

ROOT, ELIHU (1845–1937), Secretary of War and Secretary of State; Senator from New York. Mr. Root attended Hamilton College and graduated from New York University with a law degree. He served as Secretary of War under President William McKinley during the Spanish-American War, and created the Army War College. He was highly regarded by President Theodore Roosevelt; and in 1905, he was named Secretary of State. He was awarded the Nobel Peace Prize in 1912. As Senator from New York (1909–1915), he opposed the progressive program of the Taft Administration, Root authored numerous titles. Richard Jessup's *Elihu Root* (2 vols., 1938) is the official biography.

ROSS, BETSY (1752–1836), legendary maker of the first American flag. Born in Philadelphia, Pennslyvania, she attended the Friends School in Philadelphia and demonstrated a great skill for needlework. In 1773, she eloped with John Ross, whom she married. She was a loyal member of the Society of Free Quakers. The story that George Washington commissioned her to make the first Stars and Stripes is based on tradition; but the flag was adopted as the national flag on June 14, 1777. There is considerable romance and legend associated with her making of the flag.

ROZELLE, PETE (1927–), football figure, flamboyant commissioner of the National Football league. Born in South Gate, California, Rozelle, was educated at the University of San Francisco. From 1948 to 1950, he served as the news director of the University of San Francisco; from 1952 to 1955, he was the public relations director for the Los Angeles Rams. Rozelle was general manager of the Los Angeles Rams from 1955 to 1957. In 1960, he was appointed commissioner of the National Football League.

RUBINSTEIN, ARTUR (1887-1982), concert pianist. Born in Lodz, Poland, he made his concert debut in Berlin at the age of twelve. He studied under I. J. Paderewski and began his concert tours with appearances in Paris, London, and the United States in 1905–1906. After World War II, Rubinstein came to live in the United States and continued a hectic pace of concert playing. He is noted for his stirring renditions of classical and patriotic themes.

RUSK, DEAN (1909–), Secretary of State during a turbulent era of American-Soviet relations. Appointed by President John Kennedy, he was loyal to the Kennedy-Johnson program of war in Vietnam. He personally confronted the Senate with the Administration's policies in Southeast Asia. Rusk had been president of the Rockefeller Foundation and became identified with foreign policy during the post-World War II period. However, he was unable to chart a course different from the John Foster Dulles policies of the 1950s.

RUTH, GEORGE HERMAN "BABE" (1895–1948), legendary sports figure called the

Babe Ruth hits his 60th home run.

"sultan of swat" for his ability to hit home runs. Ruth began his baseball career as a pitcher for the Boston Red Sox. Because of his reputation as a hitter, he was transferred to the outfield. He became a national celebrity and the perennial home-run king. In 1927, he hit 60 home runs, a record that remained until Roger Maris hit 61 in an extended game. His 714 lifetime home runs remained the record until Hank Aaron surpassed that mark. He is regarded as the game's greatest player. He died of cancer in 1948.

SALK, JONAS (1914–   ), developed the first vaccine to combat polio. After his study at the College of Medicine of New York, Salk interned at New York's Mount Sinai Hospital. During his stay at the University of Michigan he developed a vaccine for influenza. Working with the National Foundation for Infantile Paralysis, he developed the successful vaccine for polio. Controversies surrounded his achievements; the Sabin oral vaccine competed with his. In 1963, he established the Salk Institute for Biological Studies. For more information, see Richard Carter's *Breakthrough: The Saga of Jonas Salk* (1966).

SALOMON, HAYM (1740–1785), financier, merchant, and banker of the Revolutionary period. Salomon was born in Poland and emigrated to New York in the early 1770s. During the British occupation of New York in 1776, he was arrested as a spy. He induced Hessians to desert the British army, which established his identity among the revolutionaries. Salomon's business and commercial dealings brought him unusual successes in the area of securities. He worked with Robert Morris to maintain a flow of finance and credit during the crucial "last days" of the American Revolution. Following the war, he suffered heavy financial losses.

SARNOFF, DAVID (1891–1971), pioneer radio technician and chairman of the Radio Corporation of America. His early work with John Wanamaker's station in New York allowed him to develop his interests in radio; he was the first to receive the distress call of the S.S. *Titanic* in 1912. Sarnoff became inspector and instructor for the Marconi Institute, which was then merged with the Radio Corporation of America owned by Owen D. Young. Sarnoff supervised the manufacture of radio sets and the expansion of radio programming. RCA became a leader in radio and television broadcast and electronics manufacture. Sarnoff served as communications consultant to President Dwight Eisenhower. He received numerous honors.

SCHECHTER, SOLOMON (1847–1915), a leading voice in Judaism in the United States. Born in Focsani, Romania, his career began as a reader in rabbinics at Cambridge University. During this period, he wrote several books on rabbinic theology. In 1902, he became president of the Jewish Theological Seminary of America in New York and emerged as the leader of conservative Judaism. He became a spokesman for American Zionism. Schechter's numerous writings are contained in his *Seminary Addresses and Other Papers* (1969). He served as co-editor of the *Jewish Quarterly Review*.

SCHLESINGER, ARTHUR, JR. (1917–   ), distinguished historian and author. His father, Arthur Schlesinger, Sr. was also a historian and professor. The younger Schlesinger graduated from Harvard in 1938, and the following year his thesis was published under the title *Orestes Brownson: A Pilgrim's Progress*. During World War II, he served as a member of the Office of Strategic Services. His book entitled *The Age of Jackson* brought him into national prominence. *The Vital Center* (1949) was his third book. His study of the Roosevelt Presidency resulted in three volumes: *The Crisis of the Old Order, The Coming of the New Deal,* and *The Politics of Upheaval*. He was appointed special adviser to President John Kennedy. His study of the Kennedy Presidency, titled *A Thousand Days,* received national attention.

SCHULLER, ROBERT (1926–   ), popular clergyman, proponent of "church growth." Born in Alton, Iowa, Schuller attended Hope College and Western Theological Seminary. He established the Garden Grove (California) Community Church in 1955 and began a television and radio ministry. In 1970, he established the Robert H. Schuller Institute for Successful Church Leadership. His leadership has made a national impact. He has authored numerous titles, including *God's Way to the Good Life* (1963), *Your Future Is Your Friend* (1964), *You Can Become the Person You Want to Be* (1973), and others. Dr. Schuller's weekly television broadcast is entitled *The Hour of Power*.

SCHULZ, CHARLES (1922–), newspaper cartoonist, famous for his "Peanuts" series. Born in Minneapolis, Minnesota, he served as cartoonist for the *St. Paul Pioneer Press* and the *Saturday Evening Post* (1948–1949). In 1950, he created the comic strip "Peanuts," with characters Charlie Brown, Lucy, Linus, and Snoopy. Schulz has received the Outstanding Cartoonist Award from the National Cartoonist Association (1956) and an Emmy Award for the television special, *A Charlie Brown Christmas* (1966). His collected cartoons have appeared in books under numerous titles: *Peanuts; More Peanuts; Good Grief, More Peanuts; A Charlie Brown Christmas,* and others.

SCOTT, GEORGE C. (1927–), actor and star of motion pictures. Born in Wise, Virginia, Scott attended Redford High School in Detroit. During World War II, he enlisted in the Marines. Later he entered the School of Journalism of the University of Missouri; there he appeared in several dramatic performances. During the 1950s, he achieved very little. But during his performance in *Comes the Day* on Broadway, Otto Preminger observed Scott's abilities and offered him the lead in the film, *Anatomy of a Murder.* He received an Academy nomination for that role. *The Hustler* (1961) was his next role, followed by *Patton* (1970). Scott has made numerous television appearances in *Playhouse 90, Armstrong Theatre,* and *Hallmark Hall of Fame,* among others.

SEABURY, SAMUEL (1729–1796), the first bishop of the Episcopal Church in America. He was born in Groton, Connecticut as the son of a Congregational minister. He attended Yale College. Seabury worked diligently to maintain union with the British crown; he called for orderly change and petition. His pamphlets were answered by Alexander Hamilton and others who called for revolution. After the Revolution, Anglican officials in Great Britain consecrated him to serve the church in the now-independent colonies. Seabury's sermons and writings were published in *Discourses on Several Subjects* (1793) and *Discourses on Several Important Subjects* (1798).

SELZNICK, DAVID O. (1902–1965), motion picture producer, whose greatest work was the epic *Gone with the Wind* (1939). Selznick's name is associated with other outstanding screen productions, including *A Star is Born* (1937) and *A Farewell to Arms* (1957). He was rated Outstanding Producer for 22 consecutive years. Selznick received Academy Awards for the best production of the year in 1939 and 1940.

SENNETT, MACK (1884–1960), producer of silent movies. In 1912, he organized the Keystone Company; and within the first year, he produced over one hundred forty comedies under the *Keystone* label. Sennett's movies lacked logic or cohesion; they offered a succession of "slapstick" episodes instead. Gloria Swanson added a sexual delight to the Keystone series. In 1928, Sennett was awarded an honor by the Academy of Motion Picture Arts and Sciences for his "contributions to comedy techniques of the screen."

SETON, ELIZABETH B. (1774–1821), first American to be named a saint by the Roman Catholic church. The Seton family travelled to Italy in 1803 to visit the Filicchi family, prominent in banking. There Miss Seton was converted to Catholicism. Upon returning to the United States, she established a boarding school in Baltimore called Sisters of the Charity of St. Joseph. After 1814, she opened orphanages and schools under the same order in New York and Philadelphia. She was declared venerable in 1959, beatified in 1963, and canonized as a saint in 1975.

SEVAREID, ERIC (1912–), broadcaster, news commentator, and author. Born in Velva, North Dakota, Sevareid studied at the University of Minnesota and then travelled to France and enrolled at the Alliance Francaise. After a brief period as a reporter for the *Minneapolis Star,* he joined the staff of the *New York Herald Tribune* in Paris. In 1939, he became a European correspondent for the Columbia Broadcasting System, and broadcast the fall of France to the Nazis. After the war, he became a national correspondent for CBS News. In the 1960s, his editorial commentaries appeared on the *CBS Evening News with Walter Cronkite.* Sevareid received numerous awards, including the George Foster Peabody award in 1949, 1964, and 1968. He authored *Not So Wild a Dream* (1946) and *This Is Eric Sevareid* (1964), among others.

DeSEVERSKY, ALEXANDER P. (1894–1974), aeronautic engineer born in Tiflis (now a part of the U.S.S.R.). DeSeversky served as an aviator for Tzarist Russia and engaged in combat action during World War I. He then served as a lower-level diplomat in America. When Russia closed its Washington embassy in 1918, he decided to remain in the United States. After World War I, he became a strong advocate of strategic air power. He contributed greatly to modern aircraft technology, and developed the first automatic bombsight.

SEWARD, WILLIAM HENRY (1801–1872), Secretary of State under President Abraham Lincoln. Seward graduated from Union College and was admitted to the bar in 1822. He was elected as the Whig candidate for governor of New York; as a two-term governor, he came into conflict with governors from Southern states. Seward wrote *Argument in Defense of William Freeman,* the account of his legal defense of two Negroes. As Secretary of State, Seward was a strong defender of Lincoln. He is considered to be among the greatest Secretaries of State; his most famous action was the purchase of Alaska from Russia.

SHEPARD, ALAN B., JR. (1923–   ), the first American to travel in space. Born in East Derry, New Hampshire, Shepard graduated from the United States Naval Academy and the Naval War College. He served as a test pilot with the United States Navy Test Pilot School and joined the Project Mercury space program of NASA in 1959. He was the first American in space with a sub-orbital flight on May 5, 1961. He was selected to command the Apollo 14 Lunar Landing Mission in 1971 and became the fifth man to walk on the moon. Shepard has received numerous honors and awards, including a Presidential Citation, the NASA Distinguished Service Award, and the Lungley Award of the Smithsonian Institution.

Apollo 14 astronauts (left to right) Stuart Roosa, Alan Shepard, and Edgar Mitchell

SHRIVER, R. SARGENT (1915–   ), lawyer and public figure, candidate for the Vice-Presidency with George McGovern in 1972. Shriver graduated from Yale College, *cum laude,* in 1938. He married Eunice Kennedy, sister of the future President John Kennedy. His work as the first director of the Peace Corps in the Kennedy Administration drew international attention. Shriver served as director of the Office of Economic Opportunity under President Johnson and was appointed Ambassador to France. Presently he practices law in Washington, D.C.; he has received numerous honors and awards. His efforts on behalf of the Peace Corps brought him into contact with world leaders in developing countries.

SIKORSKY, IGOR (1889–1972), aeronautical engineer who designed the first multi-motored airplane and the first practical helicopter (in 1939). Sikorsky served as engineering manager and consultant to the Sikorsky Aircraft Division of the United Aircraft Corporation. He designed the S-42 Clipper Ship for Pan American Airlines. United Aircraft developed Sikorsky's helicopter designs, and the V5-300 was the first helicopter to go into mass production. Although helicopters were not used in World War II, they became vital military tools in Korea and Vietnam. Frank J. Delear's *Igor Sikorsky: His Careers in Aviation* is a useful biography.

SIMON, PAUL (1941–   ), musician and composer who became famous for his compositions with Art Garfunkel. Born in Newark, New Jersey, Simon met Garfunkel in the sixth grade. They began singing together in the mid-1950s as teenagers. Simon entered Queens College to study literature and then went to law school. He and Garfunkel continued singing together, and recorded an album titled, *Wednesday Morning, 3 A.M.* The album achieved success through a song titled "The Sounds of Silence." Simon's success is evident in his musical score for *The Graduate,* for "Bridge Over Troubled Water" and other titles. In 1970, the two singers parted company. On his own, Simon has composed and performed numerous musical selections.

SINATRA, FRANK (1915–   ), singer and actor. Born in Hoboken, New Jersey, Sinatra began his career by touring with the Henry James and Tommy Dorsey Bands. He played leading roles in the movies, *Guys and Dolls, The Tender Trap, Pal Joey, Can Can,* and *Oceans II*. Sinatra received an Academy Award for best supporting role in *From Here to Eternity* (1953). He has received numerous additional awards, including the Peabody and Emmy Awards in 1965, and the Sylvania TV Award.

SIRICA, JOHN (1904–   ), judge who presided over the trials of Watergate scandal, which ousted President Richard Nixon from office. Born in Waterbury, Connecticut, he attended George Washington University Law School. Sirica found the work difficult and had to drop his studies. Later he enrolled at Georgetown University Law School. He graduated and was admitted to the bar in 1926. In 1930, he became Assistant United States Attorney for the District of Columbia; he later built a private law practice and entered Republican politics. In 1957, President Dwight Eisenhower appointed him to the United States District Court for the District of Columbia. By virtue of seniority, he became the chief judge of the District Court. He presided over the case that involved the seven Watergate defendents, including Presidential aides H. R. Haldeman and John Erlichman.

SITTING BULL (1831–1890), a Hunkpapa Sioux medicine man and Indian chief, leader of his tribe at the time of George Custer's massacre. The battle at the Little Bighorn River wiped out Custer and 265 men at the hands of Crazy Horse and his warriors. After 1879, the United States government offered amnesty to Indians who would surrender. Sitting Bull had left for Canada after the episode at Little Bighorn, so he accepted government amnesty. He was placed on a reservation in the Dakota Territory. In 1890, he was arrested on rumors that he would lead the Sioux on the warpath again; he was fatally shot in a struggle that ensued. Robert M. Utley's *The Last Days of The Sioux Nation* (1963) contains a scholarly analysis of Sitting Bull's life.

SLOAN, ALFRED P., JR. (1875–1966), business executive; first president of General Motors. Born in New Haven, Connecticut, Sloan attended public schools and the Polytechnic Institute. He graduated from the Massachusetts Institute of Technology with a bachelor's degree in 1895. His work with the Hyatt Rolling Bearing Company provided steel roller bearings for the automobile industry. Sloane's work came to the attention of William C. Durant, the builder of General Motors. Durant made Sloan the president of United Motors Corporation, which was eventually merged with General Motors. When the control of General Motors passed to the Dupont family, Sloan assumed greater influence. At his retirement, GM controlled 52 percent of the automobile market. He endowed the Alfred P. Sloan Foundation, whose primary contributions have been to the Sloan-Kettering Cancer Research.

SMITH, JOSEPH (1805–1844), religious leader; founder of the Church of Jesus Christ of Latter Day Saints (Mormons). In 1830, he published the *Book of Mormon*. Smith stressed the need for a restored church, and he suggested that he had special revelations from God. He organized a Utopian community of followers and led them westward to Nauvoo, Illinois. Smith admonished his followers against the use of tobacco, alcohol, and hot drinks. Through the theory of the "Hamitic Curse," Smith excluded blacks from the Mormon faith. Smith was murdered on June 27, 1844, while in jail, awaiting trial.

SMITH, HOWARD K. (1914–   ), newscaster and commentator. Born in Louisiana, he attended Tulane University and travelled in Europe after graduation. There Smith accepted a Rhodes scholarship to study at Merton College, Oxford University. During World War II, he served as a reporter with United Press. In 1940, he joined the CBS editorial team. In 1942, Smith wrote *Last Train from Berlin*. After the war, he served as the chief European correspondent for CBS and worked with Edward R. Murrow on the television series, *See It Now*. In 1957, he returned to America, where he became moderator for *The Great Challenge, Face the Nation,* and other programs of public policy. Smith also moderated the first of the Kennedy-Nixon Presidential debates. In October 1961, he resigned his position with CBS over a policy dispute. He moderated ABC's *Issues and Answers* program, and later he was co-anchor with Harry Reasoner on the *ABC Evening News*.

SNEAD, SAM (1912–   ), professional golfer born in Hot Springs, Virginia. Snead became a golfing professional in 1935. He won the Professional Golfer's Association (PGA) Championship in 1942, 1949, and 1951; the British Open in 1946; and the Master's Golf Tournament in 1949, 1952, and 1954. He was inducted into the Professional Golfer's Association Hall of Fame. Snead has written several books, including *How to Hit a Golf Ball* (1940), *How to Play Golf* (1946), and (with Al Stump) *Education of a Golfer* (1962).

SOUSA, JOHN PHILIP (1854–1932), America's foremost composer of music for marching bands. Born in Washington, D.C., he enlisted in the Marine Band. During the Centennial Exposition in Philadelphia, he played in the orchestra conducted by Jacques Offenbach. In 1880, he became the Director of the Marine Band; and in 1892, he organized what he called the New Marine Band. Sousa made several trips to Europe and was widely acclaimed. Some of his compositions achieved an international reputation: "The Stars and Stripes Forever," "The High School Cadets," "The Washington Post," and "The Gladiator." Sousa also wrote comic operas, including *The Bridge Elect.*

SPOCK, BENJAMIN (1903–   ), physician and educator, noted for his principles of child-rearing. Born in New Haven, Connecticut, Spock received his medical degree from the College of Physicians and Surgeons of Columbia University. As a pediatrician, he authored the *Common Sense Book of Baby and Child Care* (1946), which has gone through numerous printings. Spock's views on child-rearing influenced a generation of parents. In the decade of the 1960s, his opposition to the war in Vietnam brought prestige to the movement of protest and dissent. He authored other books, including *Decent and Indecent* (1970) and *A Teenagers' Guide to Life and Love* (1970). Spock has served on the faculty of the University of Pittsburg and Case Western Reserve, and on the staff of the Mayo Clinic.

STASSEN, HAROLD (1907–   ), lawyer and controversial candidate for President. A native of West St. Paul, Minnesota, Stassen attended the University of Minnesota and Hamlin University. From 1938 to 1945, he was the governor of Minnesota; and in 1948, he became president of the University of Pennsylvania. In 1953, he left the university to take assignments with the Disarmament Commission and as Special Assistant to the President. During World War II, he served in the South Pacific, where he earned the Legion of Merit and the Bronze Star. He authored *Where I Stand* (1947). Stassen's liberal views made him an unsuccessful contender for the Republican Presidential nomination in 1948, 1964, and 1968. But his ideas affected Republican foreign policy.

Charles Steinmetz

STEINMETZ, CHARLES (1865–1923), mathematician and electrical engineer. Born in Breslau, he came to Yonkers, New York, to work with the electrical inventor Rudolph Eickemeyer in developing alternating-current devices. General Electric hired Steinmetz to do industrial research, and he gave GE a reputation for research and development. Steinmetz perfected the incandescent and arc lights. He also worked on new batteries and other electrical problems. As a consulting engineer with GE, he had freedom to explore projects and problems that were to his liking.

STEVENSON, ADLAI E. (1900–1965), diplomat, governor, and candidate for the United States Presidency. He was the grandson of Adlai E. Stevenson, who served as Vice-President in 1893–1897. He graduated from Princeton University, attended Harvard Law School, and graduated from the Northwestern Law School in 1926. During World War II, he was assistant to the Secretary of the Navy. He served as an adviser to the United States delegation at the San Francisco Conference, which chartered the United Nations. In 1948, he was elected governor of Illinois. He ran for President in 1952 and 1956 and lost. In 1960, President John Kennedy named Stevenson as United States Ambassador to the United Nations.

STOKES, CARL (1927–   ), the first black mayor of a major American city. Born in Cleveland, Ohio, he passed the bar examination in 1957 and established a law firm with his brother.

Elected to the Ohio House of Representatives in 1962, he became mayor of Cleveland in 1967. *The Cleveland Plain Dealer* lauded his election; he showed a balance in his administration. In 1969, he won reelection; but chose to enter broadcasting instead of attempting another campaign in 1971.

STONE, MELVILLE E. (1848–1929), newspaper executive. Born in Hudson, Illinois, Stone became a newspaper reporter for the *Chicago Republican* in 1867. In 1875, he organized the first penny daily in the United States, the Chicago *Daily News*. He sold out his interests in 1888 and became associated with the Globe National Bank. In 1893, he became the general manager of the Associated Press and moved the AP to New York to compete with the United Press. Stone developed a close relationship between the AP and Reuter Telegram Company of Great Britain for sharing foreign news. His autobiography is titled *Fifty Years a Journalist* (1921).

STRAUS, ISIDOR (1845–1912), merchant and chain-store president born in Otterburg, Bavaria. Educated in public schools, Straus was not able to attend West Point, due to the American Civil War. After the war, he established the enterprise of L. Straus & Son. In 1874, the basement of R. H. Macy and company became the center of Straus merchandising. Throughout Boston, Chicago, and Philadelphia, the Straus family established department stores. Isidor and brother Nathan made R. H. Macy the largest department store in the world. Through underselling, advertising and odd pricing, they controlled the merchandising market. Straus described himself as a Gold Democrat and a friend of President Grover Cleveland. He served as a United States Congressman from 1893 to 1895.

STREISAND, BARBRA (1942–), singer, actress, and film producer. A native of Brooklyn, New York, she began her career playing in summer stock theater. She appeared in numerous clubs, including Bon Soir and The Blue Angel. Miss Streisand starred in the Broadway roles of *I Can Get It For You Wholesale* (1962) and *Funny Girl* (1964–65). As a recording artist for Columbia Records, she became nationally popular. Miss Streisand has appeared in numerous screen roles, including *Funny Girl, Hello Dolly, On a Clear Day You Can See Forever, The Owl and the Pussycat, What's Up Doc? The Way We Were, A Star Is Born* (which she produced), and others. She received the Academy Award as best actress for her role in *Funny Girl* (1968).

STUART, GILBERT (1755–1828), painter and portraitist of the early Republic. During the Revolutionary period, his family moved to London, where he met fellow American exile, Benjamin West. During his London period, Stuart was regarded among the great artists, equal with Joshua Reynolds and Thomas Gainsborough. In 1792, he returned to America and achieved fame through his portraits of Washington. Although Stuart painted President Washington during the later years of his life, little of age is reflected in the portrait of the man. Stuart's portraits of other Revolutionary figures reveal a style that transcends age. He used few colors, but his mixtures reflected shadows and illusions. He set the standard for American portrait painting that prevailed in the nineteenth century.

SUNDAY, WILLIAM A. "BILLY" (1863–1935), preacher and revivalist who introduced America to the "sawdust trail." Born in Ames, Iowa, Sunday began his career as a baseball player with the Chicago White Sox in 1883. He later played with teams in Pittsburgh and Philadelphia. He embraced Christianity and left baseball in 1891 to begin working with the Young Men's Christian Organization. Sunday's preaching reflected the fundamentalist tradition. He opposed Sabbath-breaking and the use of alcohol, and he stirred religious enthusiasm. Sunday wrote several books that coincided with his athletic integration of Christianity, such as *Burning Truths from Billy's Bat* (1914).

SUSSKIND, DAVID (1920–), producer for television, motion pictures, and theatre. Susskind was born in New York City and graduated from Harvard University. He worked with the publicity department of Warner Brothers and Universal Pictures from 1946 to 1948. From 1952, he produced several Broadway plays, including *A Very Special Baby* (1956) and *Brief Lives* (1967). He produced a number of motion pictures: *Raisin in the Sun* (1960), *Requiem for a Heavyweight* (1961), *All Things Bright and Beautiful* (1976), and others. Susskind has been involved in producing several television programs, such as *The du Pont Show of the Month, Kaiser Aluminum Hour, Hallmark Hall of Fame,* and *Kraft Theatre*. He has received the Peabody Award, Academy Awards, and numerous other recognitions and honors.

SWANSON, GLORIA (1899–1983), actress and film celebrity. Born in Chicago, Illinois, she began working with Essanay Studios in Chicago. She later formed her own production company, called Gloria Swanson Productions. From 1971, she organized the Facial Fitness Clinics. Miss Swanson starred in numerous screen productions, including *Airport 1975* and *Sunset Boulevard* (1950). The first picture that recorded her speaking and singing was *The Trespasser* (1929). She appeared in the Broadway production, *Butterflies Are Free* (1970–1972). Miss Swanson is recognized for her acting abilities and business perception.

TAYLOR, ELIZABETH (1932–), actress and movie personality born in London, England. Miss Taylor's first major screen role was in *National Velvet* (1944). She also starred in *A Place in the Sun* (1950), *The Last Time I Saw Paris, Cat on a Hot Tin Roof, Butterfield 8, Cleopatra, The Sand Piper,* and *Who's Afraid of Virginia Wolf?* She received Academy Awards for her roles in *Butterfield 8* and *Who's Afraid of Virginia Wolf?* She has authored *Nibbles and Me* (with Richard Burton) and *World Enough and Time.* She has become notorious for her numerous marriages—to Conrad Nicholas Hilton, Jr.; to Michael Wilding; to Mike Todd; to Eddie Fisher; to Richard Burton (twice); and to John Warner.

TAYLOR, KENNETH (1917–), religious publishing executive. Taylor attended Wheaton (Illinois) College and began his publishing career with Moody Press. In 1963, he became president of his own company, Tyndale Press. He has served as an officer with numerous other organizations, including Living Bibles International and Coverdale Publishers. He has authored numerous titles, including *Is Christianity Credible?* (1946), *Living Letters: The Paraphrased Epistles* (1962), and *The Living Bible* (1971).

TEMPLE, SHIRLEY (1928–), actress, popular child star of movies in the 1930s, and politician. At the age of seven, she was Hollywood's greatest box-office attraction. She is remembered for her singing of "The Good Ship Lollipop." She portrayed a child who was capable of dealing with adult ego and hatred. Her films included *Baby Burlesks, Stand Up and Cheer, Little Miss Marker, Wee Willie Winkie,* and *The Little Princess.* In later life, she married a civic leader in San Francisco and became affiliated with the Republican Party. She ran unsuccessfully for the office of United States Representative to Congress. In 1969, President Nixon appointed her a member of the United States delegation to the United Nations General Assembly.

TESLA, NIKOLA (1856–1943), electrical engineer and inventor born in Smiljan, Croatia (now Yugoslavia). He devised an electrical transformer known as the Tesla coil. He worked briefly with Thomas Edison, designing electrical dynamos; in 1887, he established his own laboratory in New York. Tesla sided with engineers who favored alternating electrical current, rather than direct current (which Edison advocated). The alternating current system was adopted by George Westinghouse and became the basis for power generation from the Niagara Falls to Chicago's Columbian Exposition. Tesla produced motors, transformers, electrical coils, and other devices that contributed greatly to the emerging world of electrical technology.

THOMAS, LOWELL (1892–), radio news commentator, born in Woodington, Ohio. Thomas attended the University of Northern Indiana, University of Denver, Kent College, and Princeton University. In 1915, he made the first of a series of filmed travelogues; he toured extensively and lectured on his travels. President Woodrow Wilson appointed him to the civilian commission on World War I. In 1930, he made his debut on CBS radio; he would regularly conclude his nightly news broadcasts with the words, "So long until tomorrow." He continued producing *Lowell Thomas and the News* until 1976. He was the voice of Movietone News and served in the development of Cinerama movie features. Among his numerous publications are *Beyond the Khyber Pass* (1925), *The Untold Story of Exploration* (1936), and *With Allenby in the Holy Land* (1938).

THURMOND, STROM (1902–), former governor of South Carolina, Presidential candidate, and United States Senator. In 1948, Thurmond launched a Presidential campaign under the "states' rights" banner of the Dixiecrats. He attended Clemson College and was admitted to the bar in 1930. His public career has been identified with the concept of "states' rights" and racial segregation. In 1964, he broke with the Democratic Party and became a Republican. He has served in the United States Senate for over two decades. During World War II, he served in the United States Army during the invasion of Europe. He received the Bronze Star, the Purple Heart, and the Legion of Merit.

TILLICH, PAUL (1886–1965), theologian, religious scholar, and author. Born in Starzeddel, Prussia, Tillich attended the Universities of Berlin, Tübingen, and Halle. He received the Ph.D. from the University of Breslau. Ordained a minister in the Evangelican Lutheran Church, he taught at Marburg, Dresden, and Leipzig before becoming professor at the University of Frankfurt am-Main in 1929. He opposed the Nazis and was dismissed from the university, so he emigrated to the United States. Tillich taught at Union Theological Seminary (1933–1955), Harvard University (1955–1962), and the University of Chicago (1962–1965). He wrote numerous books, including a three-volume *Systematic Theology* (1951–1963).

TRUMBULL, JOHN (1756–1843), painter of historic scenes from the Revolutionary War. Trumbull was born in the Connecticut colony, where his father was governor. He took private painting lessons from John Singleton Copley and graduated from Harvard at age 17. During the Revolution, he served as aide-de-camp to General Washington. In 1780, he sailed to London, where he studied with Benjamin West. A controversy with Thomas Jefferson in 1793 damaged his later career. His art is in the tradition of Peter Paul Rubens; it deals exclusively with the American Revolution. Trumbull's works include the famous *Battle of Bunker Hill* and *Capture of the Hessians at Trenton.* He achieved fame in later life with commissions from Congress for paintings of the *Signing of the Declaration of Independence, Surrender of Cornwallis at Yorktown,* and others that decorate the rotunda of the Capitol in Washington.

TRUTH, SOJOURNER (1797–1883), abolitionist leader whose real name was Isabella Baumfree. Born in Ulster County, New York, she was the daughter of an African couple. After New York had passed an emancipation act, she asked for freedom from her master John J. Dumont. He refused and she ran away with one of her five children. She worked menial jobs and came under the influence of a religious fanatic named Mathias. Eventually she left Mathias and travelled to speak on her own, with the name of Sojourner Truth. She was the first person to test the legality of segregation on Washington, D.C., street cars.

TUBMAN, HARRIET (ca. 1820–1913), black agent for the Underground Railroad. Tubman helped hundreds of slaves flee captivity. She was born a slave herself, in Dorcester County, Maryland. In 1848, she ran away with her two brothers, leaving her husband John Tubman behind. A bounty of $40,000 was placed on her. Before the Civil War, she returned to the South 20 times to help over three hundred slaves to escape. She supported John Brown's insurrection at Harpers Ferry, Virginia. Tubman spoke against slavery and in support of women's rights. During the war, she served as a scout and nurse for the Union forces.

TUNNEY, JAMES J. "GENE" (1898–1978), professional boxer; corporation director. Born in New York City, Tunney won the light heavyweight championship at Paris in 1919. In 1926, he won the heavyweight championship from Jack Dempsey. He retained that title in a return engagement at Chicago in 1927. He retired from boxing in 1928 undefeated. He has served as director to many corporations, including the Bank of Commerce of New York and the Penobscot Building in Detroit. He wrote *A Man Must Fight* (1932) and *Arms for Living* (1941). In later years, Jack Dempsey became Tunney's close personal friend.

TURNER, NAT (1800–1831), black slave leader born in Southampton County, Virginia. He was a restless young man who turned to the Bible for guidance on slavery and freedom. He believed he was appointed of God to deliver his people from slavery, and he understood a solar eclipse to be a sign from God that he was supposed to lead a rebellion. Turner and his friends killed many whites in the rebellion that bears his name. By August of 1831, the tide had turned, and blacks were executed in large numbers. After a brief escape, Turner was caught, tried, and executed. His rebellion galvanized the abolitionist movement. William Styron's *Confessions of Nat Turner* (1968) is an analysis of the man and the movement.

VALENTINO, RUDOLPH (1895–1926), actor and matinee idol of the silent-film era. Born in Castellanetz, Italy, he attended the Dante Alighieri College and the Royal Academy. He came to the United States in 1913 and began his career as a dancer. Valentino joined the Musical Comedy Company and travelled to San Francisco. He entered motion pictures during a stay in Los Angeles, and scored a remarkable triumph as Julio in *The Four Horsemen.* His other performances included *The Conquering Power, Blood and Sand, The Sainted Devil,* and others.

VALLEE, RUDY (1901–), orchestra leader, vocalist, and popular radio personality. In 1929 he starred in the film, *Vagabond Lover;* a succession of screen performances followed: *George White's Scandals* (1934), *Sweet Music* (1935), *Gold Diggers in Paris* (1938), and *Too Many Blondes* (1941). Vallee had a weekly radio program for Standard Brands from 1929 to 1939. He has made frequent nightclub appearances and starred in the musical comedy *How to Succeed in Business Without Really Trying* (1961). During World War I, he served in the United States Navy.

VAN BUREN, ABIGAIL (1918–), writer, lecturer, and newspaper columnist. Born in Sioux City, Iowa, she attended Morningside College. Miss Van Buren has engaged in volunteer activities on behalf of better mental health and the National Foundation for Infantile Paralysis. In 1956, she began writing a column for the *San Francisco Chronicle* titled "Dear Abby." Her column was syndicated through the *Chicago Tribune-New York News Syndicete.* It now appears in foreign press as well, including Brazil, Australia, Japan, Germany, and Holland. In 1963, she established a *Dear Abby* radio program on CBS. She authored *Dear Abby* (1957), *Dear Teen Ager* (1959), and *Dear Abby on Marriage* (1962).

VANDERBILT, CORNELIUS (1794–1877), wealthy builder of railroads and steamship companies. After the success of Robert Fulton and Robert Livingston with steamboats, Vanderbilt became involved with steamboat operations. In a competitive war against Daniel Drew, Vanderbilt was able to establish steamship service between New York and Peekskill. He then opened service between New York, Providence, and Boston. His primary success was achieved in connection with the expansion of railroads after the Civil War. Commodore Vanderbilt again challenged Daniel Drew in pursuit of the Erie Railroad. Illegal maneuvers by Drew, Jay Gould, and James Fisk almost destroyed Vanderbilt in his pursuit of the Erie. He turned his attention to acquiring the Lake Shore, Illinois, and Michigan Central rail companies, which he did.

VAUGHN, SARAH (1924–), jazz vocalist born in Newark, New Jersey. In 1942, she joined the Earl Hines Orchestra; and in 1943, she sang with the Billy Eckstein Band. She has served as vocalist for Mercury Records. In 1942, she won the Apollo Theatre amateur contest. She received the annual Vocalist Award from *Down Beat,* 1946 to 1952; and she has appeared on numerous television programs.

WALLACE, GEORGE (1919–), political leader, governor, and candidate for President. Born at Clio, Alabama, Wallace studied law at the University of Alabama. As governor, he defied a Supreme Court integration order at the University of Alabama. In 1968, his challenge to the Democratic Party resulted in the formation of the American Independent Party. He captured much of the South and nationally obtained 14 percent of the popular vote in that election. In 1972, he became the object of an assassination attempt, which left him paralyzed. He was reelected governor of Alabama, but declining health made him discard plans for another term.

WARHOL, ANDY (1931–), pioneer in pop art and filmmaking. Warhol attended the Carnegie Institute of Technology and received a degree in pictorial design. He began work as a designer with *Glamour* magazine, then *Vogue* and *Harper's Bazaar.* He used the comic-strip characters Dick Tracy, Popeye, and Superman for colorful effects, and he painted Campbell Soup cans in endless rows to show the monotony of American society. After 1965, he concentrated on filmmaking. *The Chelsea Girls* (1966) and *Trash* (1970) received considerable public notice.

WARING, FRED (1900–), musical conductor and entertainer born in Tyrone, Pennsylvania. Waring attended Pennsylvania State College. He composed numerous songs and appeared in several musical shows on Broadway and in motion pictures. He organized an ensemble called "The Pennsylvanians" and began a radio program of the same title in 1933. In 1948, he organized the Fred Waring Music Workshops for Choral Directors. He conducted musical groups for *The Fred Waring Show* on television and produced numerous television programs.

WASHINGTON, BOOKER T. (1856–1915), black educator who was born a slave in Franklin County, Virginia. Booker overheard talk about a school for blacks called the Hampton Institute; the institute had been founded by a Union general and emphasized trades and manual training. In 1881, he was invited to go to Tuskegee to head up the institute, which he discovered had no buildings or program. Under his leadership, the institute became a vital force in education of black youth. In 1895, he delivered the famous "Atlanta Compromise" speech, in which he renounced protest and agitation as a means of achieving educational reform. His views were in contrast to those of Frederick Douglass, who called for racial agitation.

WAYNE, ANTHONY (1745–1796), military hero of early America. Born at Easttown, Pennsylvania, he attended local schools and learned surveying. When the Revolution began, Wayne organized a regiment of infantry and joined General George Washington at Morristown, New Jersey. He gave distinguished service in several battles; he also served with Marquis de Lafayette in Virginia until the British surrender at Yorktown. In 1792, Wayne was asked to serve as Commander-in-Chief of the Army. At Full Timbers, Ohio, he defeated Indians in the first of several battles. Indian tribes recognized his military superiority and signed the treaty of Greenville in 1795.

WAYNE, JOHN (1907–1979), actor and movie personality, noted for his character portrayals from the Old West. Born in Winterset, Iowa, his name was Marian Michael Morrison; but early in life he received the nickname "Duke." On an athletic scholarship, he studied at the University of Southern California. His career as a screen actor began as a stunt man and with bit parts in Westerns. He made two Westerns with Columbia: *Girls Demand Excitement* (1931) and *Three Girls Lost.* Over the next few years he made low-budget Westerns. During and after World War II, he emerged as an actor of some renown; his role in *True Grit* won an Academy Award nomination. During the War in Vietnam, he projected the image of a loyalist to the Administration's expanding of the war. Mike Tomkies' *Duke* (1971) is a useful biography.

WEBSTER, DANIEL (1782–1852), celebrated lawyer and politician. Webster was born in Salisbury, New Hampshire. He graduated from Dartmouth College and then studied law. Identified as a leading spokesman for the Federalists, he was elected to the House of Representatives in 1813. In 1816, his political career temporarily ended, but he achieved prominence in arguing several significant cases before the Supreme Court. For example, Webster defended the Bank of the United States in *McCulloch* vs. *Maryland.* In 1823, he returned to the House of Representatives; and from 1825 to 1829, he supported the Federalist President John Quincy Adams. Webster's Senate record achieved historic importance. He supported President Andrew Jackson on the nullification controversy. His last debate was on behalf of the unpopular Fugitive Slave Law in 1850. He served as Secretary of State in Millard Fillmore's administration.

WEBSTER, NOAH (1758–1843), lexicographer who compiled a dictionary of American usage. Webster was an active literary man; he read widely and was admitted to the bar in 1781. He authored *A Grammatical Institute of the English Language: Part I* in 1783. His grammar book sold over seventy million copies. Webster toured the United States selling his textbooks. As a Federalist, he wrote *Sketches on American Policy* (1785); he authored numerous books and pamphlets, his most famous being *The Effects of Slavery on Morals and Industry* (1793). His dictionaries became his most enduring contribution to American thought and learning.

WEISSMULLER, JOHNNY (1904–1984), Olympic swimmer and movie star as "Tarzan." Born in Windber, Pennsylvania, Weissmuller became a skilled free-style swimmer. In the 1920s, he established world records in over sixty-seven events. Weissmuller was trained as a swimmer at the Illinois Athletic Club in Chicago. In the 1924 and 1928 Olympic games, he won five gold medals; he also won a bronze medal as a member of the United States water polo team. In his acting role as "Tarzan," his abilities as a free-style swimmer made him world famous.

WELCH, RAQUEL (1942–), model, movie actress, and renowned sex symbol. She was born Raquel Tejada in Chicago, Illinois, of Castilian Spanish parents. The family moved to LaJolla, California, where her father worked for General Dynamics. After graduating from high school, she served temporarily as a weather girl for a San Diego television station while attending San Diego State College. After marriage in 1959, she had two children and became a householder. Divorced in 1964, she travelled to Texas where she modeled for Neiman-Marcus department stores. She then returned to Hollywood, where she received minor roles until she appeared in *Life* magazine (October 2, 1964). She soon obtained a contract with Twentieth Century-Fox. She then appeared in *Fantastic Voyage, Bandolero, Lady in Cement, The Magic Christian,* and *Myra Breckinridge,* among others.

WEST, BENJAMIN (1738–1820), noted painter of the Revolutionary era. Born in Springfield Township, Pennsylvania, West was among the most outstanding of America's new artists. He reflected the neo-classical tradition. He lived for a time in Italy, where he attracted numerous patrons. West received encouragement from Joshua Reynolds and won numerous portrait commissions. He became a close friend of King George III; and after the death of Reynolds, he was named president of the Royal Academy. West's more famous paintings include *Death on the Pale Horse* (1802) and *Christ Healing the Sick* (1811). West helped many young artists who visited his studio.

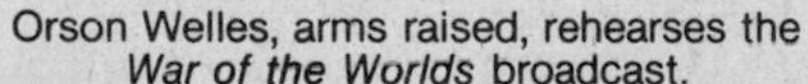
Orson Welles, arms raised, rehearses the *War of the Worlds* broadcast.

WEST, MAE (1892–1980), stage and film actress; her sensuality established her stage presence in early vaudeville days. Miss West made her debut with the Keith vaudeville circuit. When she starred in a sensational Broadway play titled *Sex* (1926), she was jailed for her role and attracted national publicity. She starred in several movies, including *Diamond Lil* (1928); *The Constant Sinner* (1931) and *Night after Night* (1932). During World War II, her name was attached to the inflatable life jackets that were used by Allied soldiers. Her autobiography was titled *Goodness Had Nothing to Do With It* (1959). In 1970, she starred in the screen production of *Myra Breckinridge.*

WELK, LAWRENCE (1903–), famed orchestra leader of the "big band" era. Born in Strasburg, North Dakota, he appeared on radio station WNAX of Yankton, South Dakota in 1920. In 1927, he organized an orchestra that appeared throughout the country. Welk's orchestra appeared on television in Los Angeles from 1950 to 1955, when the American Broadcasting Company syndicated the Lawrence Welk show nationally. The program achieved considerable popularity until it was cancelled in 1971. Welk was a recording artist for Ranwood Records; he has received numerous awards and recognitions, including the Top Dance Band of America award in 1955. His program is now syndicated by the National Broadcasting Company.

WELLES, ORSON (1915–), motion picture actor, director, producer, writer, and photographer. His various theatrical roles have placed him among the outstanding actors of his generation. Born in Kenosha, Wisconsin, he studied at the Art Institute of Chicago. Welles' acting debut was made at Gate Theatre, Dublin, in the fall of 1931. He made his Broadway debut in Shakespeare's *Romeo and Juliet* (1934); he had toured with the Katherine Cornell Company in *Candida* (1933) and *The Barretts of Wimpole Street.* His radio career began with narrating the series, *The March of Time.* His simulation of a Martian invasion in 1938 created a panic among his radio listeners. He has directed numerous Shakespearean plays and has appeared on television.

WESTINGHOUSE, GEORGE (1846–1914), distinguished American inventor and manufacturer; developed the transmission of electrical power. He served with the Union Army in the Civil

War and attended Union College. His fortune came from the patents on his air-brake invention. In 1882, he formed the Union Switch and Signal Company and directed his attention to the orderly transmission of natural gas. In 1886, he formed the Westinghouse Electric Company. In the 1890s, Westinghouse received contracts to develop power from the Niagara Falls. During the 1880s, he received an average of one patent per month for his inventions; his truly significant inventions include the geared turbine and air springs.

WESTMORELAND, WILLIAM C. (1914–), commander of American forces in Vietnam and chief military adviser to President Lyndon Johnson. Westmoreland was born in Spartanburg County, South Carolina, and graduated from West Point in 1936. He commanded the Thirty-Fourth Field Artillery Battalion of the Ninth Infantry Division in Europe during World War II. He served as an instructor at the Command and General Staff College and the Army War College. Between 1960 and 1963, he was superintendent of the U.S. Military Academy, where his effectiveness contributed to his elevation to general. He was assigned to the Military Assistance Program in Vietnam, where he advocated increased bombing and "search and destroy" missions. By 1967, he had over 500,000 men under his command. In 1968, he became Army Chief of Staff. He ran unsuccessfully for governor of South Carolina.

WHISTLER, JAMES A. McNEILL (1834–1903), lithographer and painter; emphasized "art for art's sake." Born in Lowell, Massachusetts, Whistler moved to St. Petersburg, Russia, early in his life when his father worked on a Russian rail project commissioned by Tsar Nicholas I. He returned to America in 1849 and studied at the United States Military Academy. Because he could not conform to the rules, he was dismissed in 1854. He travelled to Europe and studied for a time at the Louvre. In 1859, his first painting appeared; it was titled *At the Piano*. In 1871, he began certain themes titled *Nocturnes* in etchings, including *The Artist's Mother* (1872). His views on aesthetics were summarized in "Ten O'Clock," a lecture delivered at Prince's Hall.

WHITE, WILLIAM ALLEN (1868–1944), prize-winning journalist and author. Born in Emporia, Kansas, he attended Emporia College. He began his journalistic career with work on various newspapers. He purchased the *Emporia Gazette* in 1895 and continued working with that paper until his death. His progressive views ran contrary to conservative political trends. He backed Teddy Roosevelt and the Bull Moose party in 1912; in the 1930s he supported the New Deal of Roosevelt. White worked enthusiastically with "The Committee to Defend America by Aiding the Allies" in generating hostility for Nazism. He received the Pulitzer Prize for *The Autobiography of William Allen White*.

WHITNEY, ELI (1765–1825), inventor who perfected the cotton gin. Whitney was born in Westboro, Massachusetts, and graduated from Yale college. Although a number of cotton gins were in operation in the 1790s, only Whitney's design made practical sense. He manufactured small arms for the federal government, but his delivery of these small arms was hopelessly behind schedule. He substituted machines for hand labor, made uniform parts, and accelerated production. Whitney gave substance to the concept of mass production.

WILKINS, ROY (1901–1981), important civil rights leader. Wilkins was born in St. Louis, Missouri, and attended the University of Minnesota. He served in the local chapters of the National Association for the Advancement of Colored People (NAACP) and edited *Call,* a militant weekly newspaper. In 1931, he joined the executive staff of the NAACP at its national headquarters. He worked on numerous internal studies for the NAACP, and in 1955, became the Executive Director of the organization. He enthusiastically supported the Kennedy Civil Rights program. His organizing abilities, articulate speech, and incisive writing made him a significant leader in the black community. He received the Medal of Freedom from President Nixon in 1969, the Spingarm Award from the NAACP, as well as many other honors and awards.

WILLARD, FRANCES E. (1839–1898), prominent temperance leader. Born in Churchville, New York, she sought independence from her parents at an early age. She attended Northwestern Female College and graduated as class valedictorian. After a brief teaching career, she authored a book titled, *Nineteen Beautiful Years* (1864). Miss Willard toured Europe from 1869 to 1870 and studied at the Sorbonne. She was appointed president of Northwestern Female College in 1871. After 1874, she resigned and accepted the presidency of the Women's Christian Temperance Union (WCTU). She is best known for her work with the WCTU. Miss Willard helped establish the Prohibition Party in 1884; she became president of the World Women's Temperance Union in 1891.

WILLIAMS, ROGER (1603-1683), Puritan clergyman; spokesman for religious toleration and separation of church and state. Williams believed that sinful mankind was hopeless until Christ's return. He refused to serve the Massachusetts Church because it maintained close ties with civil authority. He was banished to Rhode Island in 1635, and there he authored a dictionary titled *A Key into the Language of America* (1643). His quest for perfection made him first a Baptist and then a Seeker. In 1643, he travelled to England and wrote *Queries of Highest Consideration* (1644). Williams opposed the Christian persecution of other Christian groups. He returned to Providence and sought to unify the colony; he disagreed with the local Quakers but granted them toleration nonetheless.

WILLIAMS, TED (1918-), baseball player born in San Diego, California. Williams was professionally associated with the Boston Red Sox of the American League; he compiled a lifetime batting average of .344. Williams' career spanned the years 1939 to 1960. He hit a total of 521 homeruns and won the triple crown of baseball (best average, most home runs, most runs batted in) twice. He was elected to the Baseball Hall of Fame in 1966. He managed the Washington Senators; in his initial year as manager he received the American League Manager of the Year Award.

WINCHELL, WALTER (1897–1972), newspaper columnist and newscaster. Winchell began his radio program with the familiar words, "Good evening, Mr. and Mrs. America and all ships at sea; let's go to press." At first he was a performer in vaudeville. His journalistic career began in 1920 with the *New York Evening Graphic;* later he was associated with the Hearst *New York Mirror.* Winchell introduced a variety of items—political and theatrical—in his column "On Broadway." His column was syndicated in over eight hundred newspapers; his radio career began in 1932. His easily recognized voice narrated the popular television series *The Untouchables*. Later in life, he wrote for the *New York Journal Tribune*.

WINTHROP, JOHN (1588–1649), political leader and historian; a dominant figure in the early development of the Massachusetts Bay Colony. Born in Suffolk County, England, he agreed to go to America in 1629. Winthrop called for a covenant Christian community in his famous sermon, "A Model of Christian Charity." He was the political leader of the colony. New England society in the seventeenth century bore the enduring stamp of John Winthrop.

WOOD, GRANT (1892–1942), regional painter of the 1930s. A native of Anamosa, Iowa, Wood took painting lessons during the family stay at Cedar Rapids, Iowa. During World War I, he took classes in fresco painting at the Chicago Art Institute. He left for Europe in 1923 and spent time at the Academie Julian in Paris. On his return to America, he worked at a factory in Cedar Rapids while painting various subjects. In 1927, he received a commission for a stained-glass window for the Cedar Rapids City Hall. Wood was most famous for his homespun themes. His painting titled *American Gothic* (1930) attracted widespread notice; his satiric sense was evident in *Daughters of the American Revolution*. He opposed conservative political tendencies and directed several projects for the Works Project Administration (WPA).

WOOLWORTH, FRANK (1852–1919), chain-store executive; originator of the "five and dime" store concept. Born in upstate New York, Woolworth opened his first store with a modest three hundred dollars inventory. The growth of his chain stores was spectacular; he derived capital for new stores from profits. He relocated his headquarters in Brooklyn, New York, which brought him into close contact with suppliers and wholesalers. Woolworth emphasized window and counter displays. His enterprises grew rapidly between 1890 and 1910, until his gross business revenue exceeded sixty million dollars annually. In 1913, he began erecting the structure in New York that became the Woolworth Building. At his death, there were over one thousand stores nationwide.

WRIGHT, FRANK LLOYD (1867-1959), the most innovative architect of the twentieth century. Wright's work reflects his fertile imagination. He worked at the firm of Dankmar Adler and Louis Sullivan of Chicago in 1887. He was greatly influenced by Louis Sullivan; and in 1893, he opened his own office. The houses Wright built in Chicago and elsewhere gained particular attention for their innovative spirit. His international fame brought him Japanese and European projects; for example, he designed the Imperial Hotel in Tokyo. Wright blended radical and traditional concepts of architecture. His most famous creations are the Guggenheim Museum in New York, the Administration Building for the Johnson Wax Company, and the Greek Orthodox Church in Milwaukee. Wright was an authentic giant in American architecture and design.

WRIGHT BROTHERS, ORVILLE (1871–1948); WILBUR (1867–1912), aviation pioneers born in Millville, Indiana. In 1892, they opened the Wright Cycle Shop in Dayton, Ohio. The efforts of Otto Lilienthal, glider pilot, attracted the interest of the Wright Brothers. The Wrights were acquainted with the combustion engine, aerodynamics, and basic engineering. Together they developed double-winged gliders and applied motor techniques to the glider. On December 17, 1903, they made the first "heavier-than-air craft" flight (which lasted twelve seconds) at Kitty Hawk, North Carolina. On May 22, 1906, they received a patent for their machine. The federal government demonstrated an interest in the machine, and they received bids for construction and development. The brothers formed the American Wright Company to produce aircraft. The death of Wilbur Wright greatly affected Orville; in 1915, he sold his rights to the company and left manufacturing. He served as a member of the National Advisory Committee for Aeronautics (NACA), the predecessor to NASA. His efforts contributed greatly to the subsequent advances made in aerospace technology.

WYETH, ANDREW (1917–   ), the most significant American painter of his generation. His father was the book illustrator for great American classics such as *Treasure Island.* The most famous of his paintings is *Christina's World.* Wyeth used his neighbors as his subjects; he utilized high and low points of emphasis. He received numerous awards, including the Medal of Freedom. In 1970, Wyeth held a one-man exhibit at the White House. His professional technique and graphic ability have become his legacy to American art.

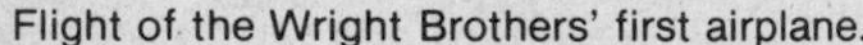
Flight of the Wright Brothers' first airplane.

YOUNG, BRIGHAM (1801–1877), pioneer leader of the Mormons. In 1832, he read Joseph Smith's *Book of Mormon* and was baptized into the new faith. He formed a Mormon church in Kirkland, Ohio, in 1833. In 1835, he was selected as a member of the Quorum of Twelve Apostles to assist Joseph Smith; he became the fiscal agent for the emerging church in 1841. On December 5, 1847, he was elected president of the Quorum of Twelve Apostles, a position he retained until his death. After Smith was murdered, Young led the Mormons to Utah and established Mormon communities around the Great Salt Lake. He encouraged polygamy and opposed the use of liquor, stimulants, and tobacco. Young established the University of Deseret (now the University of Utah) in 1850.

YOUNG, CHIC (1901–1973), newspaper cartoonist who created the popular feature, "Blondie." Born in Chicago, Illinois, his real name was Murat Bernard. He developed "Blondie," her husband Dagwood, and associated characters. The comic strip was syndicated nationally through King Features. At the time of his death, it was appearing in over sixteen hundred newspapers in 60 countries.

YOUNG, DENTON T. "CY" (1867–1955), baseball player from Gilmore, Ohio. Young began playing for the Cleveland team of the National League in 1890. During his career, he pitched for the St. Louis Cardinals, the Boston Red Sox, the Cleveland Indians, and the Boston Braves. He pitched 751 complete games, winning 511 of them. He also pitched baseball's first "perfect" game (in which no batters reached base) on May 5, 1904. After his death, the major baseball leagues established the Cy Young Award for the best pitcher of the year.

YOUNG, WHITNEY M. (1921–1971), civil rights leader. Born in Lincoln Ridge, Kentucky, he graduated from Kentucky State College and the University of Minnesota. Young was associated with the Urban League in St. Paul, Minnesota, and Omaha, Nebraska. He became dean of the school of Social Work at Atlanta University in 1954. After a period of study at Harvard University, he was named executive director of the Urban League; there he introduced the concept of preferential treatment of blacks in jobs and educational facilities. He tried to mediate between militant civil rights groups and those who advocated more orderly processes. President Richard Nixon awarded him the Medal of Freedom in 1969. Young authored *To Be Equal* (1964) and *Beyond Racism* (1969).

ZAHARIAS, MILDRED DIDRIKSON "BABE" (1914–1956), Olympic athlete; regarded as the greatest woman golfer of all time. She appeared in the Olympic Games at Los Angeles in 1932, where she was the top performer in the 80-meter hurdle and the javelin throw. She excelled in athletic endeavors such as baseball, basketball, swimming, and diving. But her greatest achievements were in golf. From 1935 to 1950, she won every major women's golf championship—the United States National Open in 1948, 1950, and 1954; the national amateur tournament in 1946; and the World Championship four times. In 1947, she became a professional golfer. Stricken with cancer in 1953, she waged a battle to overcome the disease. She continued her athletic successes until her death in 1956. She wrote *This Life I've Led,* her autobiography.

"Babe" Didrikson Zaharias won The AP Award six times, once for starring in track and field and the five others for golfing brilliance. Later, the award was named in her honor.

ZENGER, JOHN PETER (1697–1746), colonial newspaper publisher. Born in the Rhine Country of Germany, he became an apprentice printer to William Bradford. He moved to Chestertown, Pennsylvania, to establish his reputation. Zenger became involved in New York political controversies after he arrived there in 1732. He used his *New York Weekly Journal* to support the political faction of Lewis Morris. Zenger was arrested in 1734 and charged with printing seditious and libelous material. His lawyers were disbarred, so Alexander Hamilton came from Philadelphia to defend Zenger. He was acquitted, and the case became a classic in constitutional law.

ZIEGFELD, FLORENZ (1869–1932), theatrical manager who made burlesque famous. Ziegfeld was born in Chicago, Illinois. In 1906, he developed "The Parisian Model," a revue that attracted popular notice. After viewing the Follies Bergere in Paris, he returned to the United States to assemble the Ziegfeld Follies. He developed several stars; Fanny Brice, Marilyn Miller, W. C. Fields, Eddie Cantor, and Will Rogers were under contract to Ziegfeld. He attempted musical comedy with such productions as *Show Boat, Rio Rita,* and *Bittersweet.* But in 1927, he abandoned the Follies because the Great Depression made it seem inappropriate.

Roget's Thesaurus

Plan of Classification

(following the original Roget plan)

Class I. ABSTRACT RELATIONS

Section I.	Existence	Nos. 1-8
II.	Relation	9-24
III.	Quantity	25-57
IV.	Order	58-83
V.	Number	84-105
VI.	Time	106-139
VII.	Change	140-152
VIII.	Causation	153-179

Class II. SPACE

Section I.	Generally	180-191
II.	Dimensions	192-239
III.	Form	240-263
IV.	Motion	264-315

Class III. MATTER

Section I.	Generally	316-320
II.	Inorganic	321-356
III.	Organic	357-449

Class IV. INTELLECT

Section I.	Formation of Ideas	450-515
II.	Communication of Ideas	516-599

Class V. VOLITION

Section I.	Individual	600-736
II.	Intersocial	737-819

Class VI. AFFECTIONS

Section I.	Generally	820-826
II.	Personal	827-887
III.	Sympathetic	888-921
IV.	Moral	922-975
V.	Religious	976-1000

Tabular Synopsis of Categories

Class I. ABSTRACT RELATIONS

I. EXISTENCE

1. existence	2. nonexistence
3. substantiality	4. unsubstantiality
5. intrinsicality	6. extrinsicality
7. state	8. circumstance

II. RELATION

9. relation	10. nonrelation
11. consanguinity	
12. correlation	
13. identity	14. contrariety
15. difference	
16. uniformity	16a. lack of uniformity
17. similarity	18. dissimilarity
19. imitation	20. nonimitation
20a. variation	
21. copy	22. prototype
23. agreement	24. disagreement

III. QUANTITY

25. quantity	26. degree
27. equality	28. inequality
29. mean	
30. compensation	
31. greatness	32. smallness
33. superiority	34. inferiority
35. increase	36. decrease
37. addition	38. deduction
39. adjunct	40. remainder
	40a. decrement
41. mixture	42. simpleness
43. junction	44. disjunction
45. link	
46. coherence	47. incoherence
48. combination	49. decomposition
50. whole	51. part
52. completeness	53. incompleteness
54. composition	55. exclusion
56. component	57. extraneousness

IV. ORDER

58. order	59. disorder
60. arrangement	61. derangement
62. precedence	63. sequence
64. precursor	65. sequel
66. beginning	67. end
68. middle	
69. continuity	70. discontinuity
71. term	
72. assemblage	73. dispersion
74. focus	
75. class	
76. inclusion	77. exclusion
78. generality	79. specialty
80. regulation	81. multiformity
82. conformity	83. unconformity

V. NUMBER

84. number	
85. numeration	
86. list	
87. unity	88. accompaniment
89. duality	
90. duplication	91. bisection
92. triality	
93. triplication	94. trisection
95. quaternity	
96. quadruplication	97. quadrisection
98. five, etc.	99. quinquesection
100. plurality	100a. fraction
	101. zero
102. multitude	103. fewness
104. repetition	
105. infinity	

VI. TIME

106. time	107. absence of time
108. period	109. course
110. durability	111. transience
112. perpetuity	113. instantaneousness
114. chronometry	115. anachronism
116. antecedence	117. posteriority
118. present time	119. different time
120. contemporaneousness	
121. the future	122. the past
123. newness	124. oldness
125. morning; noon	126. evening; midnight
127. youth	128. age
129. infant	130. veteran
131. adolescence	
132. earliness	133. lateness
134. opportuneness	135. unopportuneness
136. frequency	137. infrequency
138. regularity	139. irregularity

VII. CHANGE

140. change	141. permanence
142. cessation	143. continuance
144. conversion	
	145. reversion
146. revolution	
147. substitution	148. interchange
149. changeableness	150. stability
151. present events	152. future events

VIII. CAUSATION

153. cause	154. effect
155. attribution	156. chance
157. power	158. impotence
159. strength	160. weakness
161. production	162. destruction
163. reproduction	
164. producer	165. destroyer
166. parentage	167. posterity
168. productiveness	169. unproductiveness
170. agency	
171. energy	172. inertness
173. violence	174. moderation
175. influence	175a. absence of influence
176. tendency	
177. liability	
178. concurrence	179. counteraction

Class II. SPACE

I. SPACE IN GENERAL

180. space (indefinite)	180a. inextension
	181. region (definite)
	182. place
183. situation	
184. location	185. displacement
186. presence	187. absence
188. inhabitant	189. habitation
190. contents	191. receptacle

II. DIMENSIONS

192. size	193. littleness
194. expansion	195. contraction
196. distance	197. nearness
198. interval	199. contiguity
200. length	201. shortness
202. breadth, thickness	203. narrowness, thinness
204. layer	205. filament
206. height	207. lowness
208. depth	209. shallowness
210. summit	211. base
212. verticality	213. horizontality
214. suspension	215. support
216. parallelism	217. obliquity
218. inversion	
219. crossing	
220. exteriority	221. interiority
222. centrality	
223. covering	224. lining
225. dress	226. undress
227. environment	228. interspersion
229. circumscription	
230. outline	
231. edge	
232. enclosure	
233. limit	
234. front	235. rear
236. side	237. opposition
238. right	239. left

III. FORM

240. form	241. formlessness
242. symmetry	243. distortion
244. angularity	
245. curvature	246. straightness
247. circularity	248. convolution
249. rotundity	
250. convexity	252. concavity
251. flatness	
253. sharpness	254. bluntness
255. smoothness	256. roughness
257. notch	
258. fold	
259. furrow	
260. opening	261. closure
262. perforator	263. stopper

IV. MOTION

264. motion	265. rest
266. journey	267. navigation
268. traveler	269. mariner, flier
270. transference	
271. carrier	
272. vehicle	273. ship
274. velocity	275. slowness
276. impulse	277. recoil
278. direction	279. deviation
280. precedence	281. sequence
282. progression	283. regression
284. propulsion	285. traction
286. approach	287. recession
288. attraction	289. repulsion
290. convergence	291. divergence
292. arrival	293. departure
294. ingress	295. egress
296. reception	297. ejection
298. eating	299. excretion
300. insertion	301. extraction
302. passage	
303. infringement	304. shortcoming
305. ascent	306. descent
307. elevation	308. depression
309. leap	310. plunge
311. circular motion	
312. rotation	313. evolution
314. oscillation	
315. agitation	

Class III. MATTER

I. MATTER IN GENERAL

316. materiality	317. immateriality
318. world	
319. gravity	320. levity

II. INORGANIC MATTER

321. density	322. thinness
323. hardness	324. softness
325. elasticity	326. inelasticity
327. tenacity	328. brittleness
329. structure	
330. granularity	
331. friction	332. lubrication
333. fluidity	334. gaseity
335. liquefaction	336. vaporization
337. water	338. air
339. moisture	340. dryness
341. ocean	342. land
343. gulf, lake	344. plain
345. marsh	346. island
347. stream	
348. river	349. wind
350. conduit	351. air-pipe
352. semiliquidity	353. bubble, cloud
354. pulpiness	355. unctuousness
	356. oil
	356a. resin

III. ORGANIC MATTER

357. animate matter	358. inanimate matter
359. life	360. death
	361. killing
	362. corpse
	363. interment
364. animality	365. vegetation
366. animal	367. vegetable
368. zoology	369. botany
370. ranching	371. agriculture
372. mankind	
373. man	374. woman
375. sensibility	376. insensibility
377. pleasure	378. pain
379. touch	
380. sensations of touch	381. numbness
382. heat	383. cold
384. calefaction	385. refrigeration
386. furnace	387. refrigerator

388. fuel	
389. thermometer	
390. taste	391. tastelessness
392. pungency	
393. condiment	
394. savoriness	395. unsavoriness
396. sweetness	397. sourness
398. odor	399. inodorousness
400. fragrance	401. fetor
402. sound	403. silence
404. loudness	405. faintness
406. snap	407. roll
408. resonance	408a. nonresonance
	409. sibilation
410. stridency	
411. cry	412. ululation
413. melody, concord	414. discord
415. music	
416. musician	
417. musical instruments	
418. hearing	419. deafness
420. light	421. darkness

422. dimness

423. luminary	424. shade
425. transparency	426. opacity
	427. semitransparency
428. color	429. colorlessness
430. whiteness	431. blackness
432. gray	433. brown
434. red	435. green
436. yellow	437. purple
438. blue	439. orange
440. variegation	
441. vision	442. blindness
	443. dimsightedness
444. spectator	
445. optical instruments	
446. visibility	447. invisibility
448. appearance	449. disappearance

Class IV. INTELLECT

I. FORMATION OF IDEAS

450. intellect	450a. absence of intellect
451. thought	452. absence of thought
453. idea	454. topic
455. curiosity	456. incuriosity
457. attention	458. inattention
459. care	460. neglect
461. inquiry	462. answer
463. experiment	
464. comparison	
465. discrimination	465a. indiscrimination
466. measurement	
467. evidence	468. counter-evidence

469. qualification

470. possibility	471. impossibility
472. probability	473. improbability
474. certainty	475. uncertainty
476. reasoning	477. intuition, sophistry
478. demonstration	479. confutation
480. judgment	481. misjudgment
480a. discovery	
482. overestimation	483. underestimation
484. belief	485. disbelief, doubt
486. credulity	487. incredulity
488. assent	489. dissent
490. knowledge	491. ignorance
492. scholar	493. ignoramus
494. truth	495. error
496. maxim	497. absurdity
498. intelligence, wisdom	499. imbecility, folly
500. sage	501. fool
502. sanity	503. insanity
	504. madman
505. memory	506. oblivion
507. expectation	508. nonexpectation
	509. disappointment
510. foresight	
511. prediction	
512. omen	
513. oracle	
514. supposition	
515. imagination	

II. COMMUNICATION OF IDEAS

516. meaning	517. meaningless
518. intelligibility	519. unintelligibility

520. equivocalness

521. figure of speech	
522. interpretation	523. misinterpretation
524. interpreter	
525. manifestation	526. latency
527. information	528. concealment
529. disclosure	530. ambush
531. publication	
532. news	533. secret
534. messenger	
535. affirmation	536. negation, denial
537. teaching	538. misteaching
	539. learning
540. teacher	541. learner

542. school

543. veracity	544. falsehood
	545. deception
	546. untruth
547. dupe	548. deceiver
	549. exaggeration
550. indication	
551. record	552. obliteration
553. recorder	
554. representation	555. misrepresentation
556. painting	
557. sculpture	
558. engraving	
559. artist	
560. language	
561. letter	
562. word	563. neology
564. nomenclature	565. misnomer
566. phrase	
567. grammar	568. solecism
569. style	
570. perspicuity	571. obscurity
572. conciseness	573. diffuseness
574. vigor	575. feebleness
576. plainness	577. ornament
578. elegance	579. inelegance
580. voice	581. muteness
582. speech	583. inarticulateness
584. loquacity	585. taciturnity
586. public address	587. response
588. conversation	589. soliloquy
590. writing	591. printing
592. correspondence	593. book
594. description	
595. dissertation	
596. compendium	
597. poetry	598. prose
599. the drama	

Class V. VOLITION

I. INDIVIDUAL VOLITION

600. will	601. necessity
602. willingness	603. unwillingness
604. resolution	605. irresolution
604a. perseverance	
606. obstinacy	607. recantation
	608. caprice
609. choice	609a. neutrality
	610. rejection
611. predetermination	612. impulse

613. habit	614. disuse
615. motive	615a. absence of motive
	616. dissuasion
617. plea	
618. good	619. evil
620. intention	621. chance
622. pursuit	623. avoidance
	624. relinquishment
625. business	
626. plan	
627. method	
628. mid-course	629. circuit
630. requirement	
631. instrumentality	
632. means	
633. instrument	
634. substitute	
635. materials	
636. store	
637. provision	638. waste
639. sufficiency	
640. insufficiency	641. redundance
642. importance	643. unimportance
644. utility	645. inutility
646. expedience	647. inexpedience
648. goodness	649. badness
650. perfection	651. imperfection
652. cleanness	653. uncleanness
654. health	655. disease
656. salubrity	657. insalubrity
658. improvement	659. deterioration
660. restoration	661. relapse
662. remedy	663. bane
664. safety	665. danger
666. refuge	667. pitfall
668. warning	
669. alarm	
670. preservation	
671. escape	
672. deliverance	
673. preparation	674. nonpreparation
675. essay	
676. undertaking	
677. use	678. disuse
	679. misuse
680. action	681. inaction
682. activity	683. inactivity
684. haste	685. leisure
686. exertion	687. repose
688. fatigue	689. refreshment
690. agent	
691. workshop	
692. conduct	
693. direction	
694. director	
695. advice	
696. council	
697. precept	
698. skill	699. unskillfulness
700. expert	701. bungler
702. cunning	703. artlessness
704. difficulty	705. facility
706. hindrance	707. aid
708. opposition	709. cooperation
710. opponent	711. auxiliary
712. party	
713. discord	714. concord
715. defiance	
716. attack	717. defense
718. retaliation	719. resistance
720. contention	721. peace
722. warfare	723. pacification
724. mediation	
725. submission	

726. combatant	
727. arms	
728. arena	
729. completion	730. noncompletion
731. success	732. failure
733. trophy	
734. prosperity	735. adversity
736. mediocrity	

II. INTERSOCIAL VOLITION

737. authority	738. laxity
739. severity	740. lenience
741. command	
742. disobedience	743. obedience
744. compulsion	
745. master	746. servant
747. scepter	
748. freedom	749. subjection
750. liberation	751. restraint
	752. prison
753. keeper	754. prisoner
755. commission	756. abrogation
	757. resignation
758. consignee	
759. deputy	
760. permission	761. prohibition
762. consent	
763. offer	764. refusal
765. request	766. deprecation
767. petitioner	
768. promise	
769. compact	
770. conditions	
771. security	
772. observance	773. nonobservance
774. compromise	
775. acquisition	776. loss
777. possession	777a. exemption
778. participation	
779. possessor	
780. property	
781. retention	782. relinquishment
783. transfer	
784. giving	785. receiving
786. apportionment	
787. lending	788. borrowing
789. taking	790. restitution
791. stealing	
792. thief	
793. booty	
794. barter	
795. purchase	796. sale
797. merchant	
798. merchandise	
799. market	
800. money	
801. treasurer	
802. treasury	
803. wealth	804. poverty
805. credit	806. debt
807. payment	808. nonpayment
809. expenditure	810. receipt
811. accounts	
812. price	813. discount
814. dearness	815. cheapness
816. liberality	817. economy
818. prodigality	819. parsimony

Class VI. AFFECTIONS

I. AFFECTIONS IN GENERAL

820. affections	
821. feelings	
822. sensibility	823. insensibility
824. excitation	
825. excitability	826. inexcitability

II. PERSONAL AFFECTIONS

827. pleasure	828. pain
829. pleasurableness	830. painfulness
831. content	832. discontent
	833. regret
834. relief	835. aggravation
836. cheerfulness	837. dejection
838. rejoicing	839. lamentation
840. amusement	841. weariness
842. wit	843. dullness
844. humorist	
845. beauty	846. ugliness
847. ornament	848. blemish
	849. simplicity
850. taste	851. vulgarity
852. fashion	
	853. ridiculousness
	854. fop
	855. affectation
	856. ridicule
	857. laughing-stock
858. hope	859. hopelessness
	860. fear
861. courage	862. cowardice
863. rashness	864. caution
865. desire	867. dislike
866. indifference	
	868. fastidiousness
	869. satiety
870. wonder	871. expectance
872. prodigy	
873. repute	874. disrepute
875. nobility	876. commonalty
877. title	
878. pride	879. humility
880. vanity	881. modesty
882. ostentation	
883. celebration	
884. boasting	
885. insolence	886. servility
887. blusterer	

III. SYMPATHETIC AFFECTIONS

888. friendship	889. enmity
890. friend	891. enemy
892. sociality	893. seclusion, exclusion
894. courtesy	895. discourtesy
896. congratulations	
897. love	898. hate
899. favorite	
	900. resentment
	901. irascibility
	901a. sullenness
902. endearment	
903. marriage	904. celibacy
	905. divorce
906. benevolence	907. malevolence
	908. malediction
	909. threat
910. philanthropy	911. misanthropy
912. benefactor	913. evildoer
914. pity	914a. pitilessness
915. condolence	
916. gratitude	917. ingratitude
918. forgiveness	919. revenge
	920. jealousy
	921. envy

IV. MORAL AFFECTIONS

922. right	923. wrong
924. claim	925. unrightfulness
926. duty	927. dereliction of duty
	927a. exemption
928. respect	929. disrespect
	930. contempt
931. approbation	932. disapprobation
933. flattery	934. detraction
935. flatterer	936. detractor
937. vindication	938. accusation
939. probity	940. improbity
	941. knave
942. disinterestedness	943. selfishness
944. virtue	945. vice
946. innocence	947. guilt
948. good man	949. bad man
950. penitence	951. impenitence
952. atonement	
953. temperance	954. intemperance
	954a. sensualist
955. asceticism	
956. fasting	957. gluttony
958. sobriety	959. drunkenness
960. purity	961. impurity
	962. libertine
963. legality	964. illegality
965. jurisdiction	
966. tribunal	
967. judge	
968. lawyer	
969. lawsuit	
970. acquittal	971. condemnation
	972. punishment
973. reward	974. penalty
	975. scourge

V. RELIGIOUS AFFECTIONS

976. deity	
977. angel	978. devil
979. fabulous spirit	980. demon
981. heaven	982. hell
983. theology	
983a. orthodoxy	984. heterodoxy
985. revelation	986. religious writings
987. piety	988. impiety
	989. irreligion
990. worship	991. idolatry
	992. sorcery
	993. spell
	994. sorcerer
995. churchdom	
996. clergy	997. laity
998. rite	
999. canonicals	
1000. temple	

Thesaurus

Class I

Words Expressing Abstract Relations

I. Existence

1 existence *n* being, entity, subsistence, reality, actuality, presence, fact, matter of fact, truth. science of existence: ontology.

v exist, be, subsist, live, breathe; occur, happen, take place; consist in, lie in; endure, remain, abide, survive, last, stay, continue.

adj existent, extant; prevalent, current, afloat; real, actual, true, positive, absolute; substantial, substantive; well founded, well grounded.

adv actually, in fact, in reality.

2 nonexistence *n* inexistence; insubstantiality, nonentity; blank, *tabula rasa*, void, emptiness, nothingness; potential, possibility; annihilation, extinction, obliteration, total destruction.

v not exist; pass away, perish, die, die out, disappear, dissolve; annihilate, destroy, obliterate, wipe off the face of the earth; nullify, void; take away, remove.

adj nonexistent, inexistent; blank, void, empty; unreal, baseless, unsubstantial, intangible, ineffable, spiritual, spectral; unborn, uncreated, unbegotten, unconceived; potential, possible; exhausted, gone, lost, departed, extinct, defunct; fabulous, visionary, imaginative, ideal, conceptual, abstract.

3 substantiality *n* materiality, corporality, tangibility, material existence, bodiliness, matter, stuff; creature, being, person, body, flesh and blood, substance; thing, object, article.

adj substantive, substantial, corporeal, material, bodily, physical, concrete, tangible, palpable, corporal, materialistic.

4 unsubstantiality *n* nothingness; nothing, naught, nil, nullity, zero; shadow, phantom, apparition, dream, illusion; fallacy, inanity, frivolity; hollowness, blank, void; flimsiness, thinness, slightness.

v vanish, evaporate, fade, dissolve, melt away, disappear.

adj unsubstantial, baseless, groundless, ungrounded, without foundation, fallacious, erroneous, untenable; insignificant, slight, thin, trifling, frivolous; imaginary, visionary, dreamy, shadowy, ethereal, airy, immaterial, spectral, illusory, incorporeal, intangible, bodiless, abstract; vacant, vacuous, empty, blank, hollow.

5 intrinsicality *n* ego, essence, quintessence, gist, pith, marrow, sap, lifeblood, backbone, heart, soul, core; principle, nature, constitution, construction, character, type, quality; habit, temper, temperament, personality, spirit, humor, grain, moods, features, peculiarities, aspects, idiosyncrasies, tendencies, bents; inbeing, inherence, essentiality.

v be intrinsic, be inherent.

adj intrinsic, inherent, implanted, innate, inborn, inbred, ingrained; essential, fundamental, basic, normal; inherited, congenital, hereditary, indigenous, in the blood, in the genes; instinctive, instinctual, internal, personal, subjective; characteristic, peculiar, idiosyncratic; fixed, set in one's ways, invariable, unchangeable, incurable, ineradicable.

adv intrinsically, at bottom, in effect, practically, virtually, substantially.

6 extrinsicality *n* extraneousness, externals.

adj extrinsic, extraneous, external, adventitious; collateral, accidental, incidental, objective.

adv extrinsically.

7 state *n* condition, case, circumstances, situation, status, surroundings, pass, plight, pickle; mood, temper, frame; constitution, structure, form, phase, frame, fabric, stamp, set, fit, mold; mode, style, fashion, light, complexion, character; tone, tenor, turn.

v be in a state.

8 circumstance *n* situation, phase, position, condition, posture, attitude, place, point; footing, standing, status; occasion, happening, event, juncture, conjunction; predicament, exigency, emergency, crisis, pinch, plight, pass; climax, apex, turning point.

adj circumstantial, conditional, provisional; contingent, incidental, adventitious; critical, climactic.

adv under the circumstances, under the conditions; thus, in such wise; accordingly, that being the case, since, seeing that, as matters stand; conditionally, provided, if, in case; if so, if it so happen, in the event of, provisionally, unless.

II. Absolute Relation

9 relation *n* connection, concern, bearing, reference; correlation, analogy; similarity, affinity, homogeneity, alliance, association, nearness; approximation, relationship; comparison, ratio, proportion; link, tie, bond.

v relate to, refer to; bear upon, regard, concern, touch, affect, have to do with, pertain to, appertain to, belong to; bring into relation with, associate, connect, parallel; link, bind, tie.

adj relative, relative to, relating to, referable to, with reference to; belonging to; related, connected, associated, affiliated, allied; in the same category, relevant.

adv as regards, about, concerning, with relation to, with reference to, with regard to, with respect to, in connection with, under the head of, in the matter of.

10 [absence of relation] **non-relation** *n* irrelation, dissociation, lack of connection; disconnection, disjunction; inconsequence, irreconcilability, disagreement, heterogeneity; independence.

v have no relation to, have no bearing upon, have nothing to do with, have no connection with.

adj unrelated, irrespective, unallied, unconnected, disconnected, heterogeneous, independent; adrift, insular, isolated; extraneous, strange, alien, foreign, outlandish, exotic; irrelevant, inapplicable, not pertinent, beside the mark, off base; remote, farfetched, out-of-the-way, forced, detached, distanced; incidental, parenthetical.

adv parenthetically, by the way, by the by; incidentally.

11 [relations of kindred] **consanguinity** *n* relationship, kindred, blood; parentage, paternity, maternity, lineage, heritage; filiation, affiliation, connection, alliance, tie; family, blood relation, ties of blood, kinsman, kinfolk, kith and kin, relation, relative, one's own, one's own flesh and blood; fraternity, sorority, brotherhood, sisterhood; race, stock, generation.

v be related to, claim relationship with.

adj related, akin, consanguineous, allied, affiliated, connected; kindred, familial.

12 [double or reciprocal relation] **correlation** *n* correspondence, reciprocity, reciprocation, interdependence, mutuality, interchange, exchange.

v reciprocate, alternate, interchange, interact, interdepend; interchange, exchange; correlate, correspond, relate.

adj reciprocal, mutual, correlative, corresponding, analogous, complementary; equivalent, interchangeable, alternate.

adv reciprocally.

13 identity *n* sameness, exactness, equality, correspondence, parallelism, unity, convertibility, resemblance, similarity; self, oneself, name, personality; facsimile, duplicate, replica, copy, reproduction.

v be identical, coincide, coalesce.

adj identical, self, the same, selfsame; coincident, coinciding, coalescent, indistinguishable; one, equal, equivalent.

adv identically.

14 contrariety *n* contrast, foil, antithesis, oppositeness, opposition, contradiction, antipathy, antagonism; the reverse, the inverse, the converse, inversion, subversion, reversal, the opposite, antipodes.

v be contrary, contrast with, differ from, oppose; invert, revert, turn upside down; contradict, contravene; antagonize.

adj contrary, opposite, counter, converse, reverse; opposed, antithetical, contrasted, antipodean, antagonistic, opposing; conflicting, inconsistent, contradictory; negative, hostile.

15 difference *n* discrepancy, disparity, dissimilarity, inconsistency, variance, variation, diversity, imbalance, disagreement, inequality, inequity, divergence, contrast, contrariety; discrimination, distinction, nice distinction, shade, nuance, subtlety.

v differ, vary; diversify, modify, change, alter; contrast, mismatch; discriminate, distinguish.

adj different, diverse, heterogeneous, unlike, divergent, altered, changed, deviant, deviating, variant, varied, modified; diversified, various, divers, miscellaneous, manifold; other, another, not the same, unequal, unmatched, wide apart; distinctive, characteristic, discriminative.

16 uniformity *n* homogeneity, permanence, continuity, consistency, stability, accordance, standardization, conformity, agreement; regularity, constancy, evenness, sameness; monotony, routine, invariability.

v be uniform, accord with; conform to, assimilate; level, smooth, even.

adj uniform, homogeneous, of a piece, consistent; consistent, regular, constant, even, level; invariable, unchanging, unvarying, unvaried, unchanged, constant, regular; undiversified, solid, plain, dreary, monotonous, routine.

adv uniformly; always, invariably, without exception; ever, forever.

16a lack of uniformity *n* diversity, irregularity, unevenness, inconsistency, nonconformity, heterogeneity.

adj diversified, varied, irregular, inconsistent, motley, patchwork, uneven, rough; multifarious, of various kinds.

17 similarity *n* resemblance, likeness, similitude, semblance, affinity, approximation, parallelism; agreement, correspondence, analogy; brotherhood, family likeness; repetition, sameness, uniformity, identity; the like, fellow, match, pair, mate, twin, double, counterpart; alter ego, chip off the old block, birds of a feather, like two peas in a pod; simile, parallel, type, image, representation.

v be similar, resemble, look like, bear a resemblance, take after, approximate, parallel, match, rhyme with.

adj similar, resembling, like, alike; twin; analogous, parallel, of a piece; allied to, akin to, corresponding; approximate, much the same, near, close, something like; imitative, mock, pseudo, simulating, representing, representative; exact, true, lifelike, faithful, true to life, identical.

adv as if, so to speak; as it were, as if it were; quasi, just as.

18 dissimilarity *n* dissimilitude, unlikeness, difference; diversity, disparity, divergence; novelty, originality, uniqueness.

v be unlike, differ from, bear no resemblance; vary, diversify, differentiate.

adj dissimilar, unlike, different, disparate; unique, new, novel, unprecedented, unmatched, unequaled; diversified.

19 imitation *n* copying; copy, duplication, reproduction, replica; mocking, mimicry, aping; simulation, impersonation, representation, semblance, approximation, paraphrase, parody; plagiarism, forgery.

v imitate, copy, mirror, reflect, impersonate, duplicate, reproduce, simulate, counterfeit; mock, take off, mimic, ape, personate, parody, caricature, travesty; follow, emulate, pattern after, model oneself on, parallel, follow, take after.

adj imitative, modeled after, modeled on, based on; fake, phony, counterfeit, false, imitation, mock; duplicate, second hand.

adv literally, word for word, to the letter.

20 nonimitation *n* originality, uniqueness.

adj unimitated, uncopied; unmatched, unparalleled; inimitable, original, unique, special, one of a kind, rare, exceptional.

20a variation *n* alteration, change, modification; divergency, deviation, aberration, innovation.

v vary, change; deviate, diverge, alternate, modify.

adj varied, modified, diversified, altered, changed.

21 [result of imitation] **copy** *n* facsimile, counterpart, effigy, form, likeness, similitude, semblance, cast, mold, model, representation, image, portrait; reflexion, shadow, echo; transcript, transcription, reproduction, imitation, carbon, ditto, stencil, duplicate, reprint, transfer, replica; parody, caricature, burlesque, travesty, paraphrase; counterfeit, forgery, deception.

adj faithful, lifelike, exact, similar.

22 [thing copied] **prototype** *n* original, model, pattern, precedent, standard; type, archetype, exemplar, paradigm, module, example; text, copy, design; die, mold; matrix, mint, seal, punch, intaglio, negative, plate, stamp.

v be an example, set an example.

23 agreement *n* unanimity, harmony, accord, accordance, concord, union, unity, understanding, settlement, treaty, pact; uniformity, conformity, consistency, congruity, logic, correspondence, parallelism, apposition; consent, assent, concurrence, cooperation.

v agree, accord, harmonize; correspond, tally, (*informal*) jibe; meet, suit, fit, befit, square with, dovetail, match; adapt, fit, accommodate, adjust.

adj agreeing, accordant, correspondent, congenial, harmonious; reconcilable, comfortable, compatible, congruous, consistent, logical, consonant, commensurate; in accordance with, in harmony with, in keeping with; apt, apposite, pat, pertinent; agreeable, happy, felicitous.

24 disagreement *n* discord, dissonance, dissidence, disunion, discrepancy, nonconformity, incongruity, dissension, conflict, opposition, antagonism, difference; disparity, disproportion, mismatch, variance, divergence, inequity, inequality.

v disagree, clash, jar, argue, quarrel, dispute.

adj disagreeing, discordant, dissonant, inharmonious; at variance, hostile, conflicting, antagonistic, clashing, disputing, factious, dissenting, irreconcilable, incompatible, inconsistent with; incongruous, disproportionate, disparate, divergent; disagreeable, uncongenial, mismatched; out of joint, out of step, out of tune.

III. Simple Quantity

25 [absolute quantity] **quantity** *n* size, mass, volume, amount, measure, measurement, substance, strength; mouthful, spoonful, handful; stock, batch, lot, dose.

adj quantitative, some, any, more or less.

26 [relative quantity] **degree** *n* grade, extent, measure, amount, ratio, standard, height, pitch; reach, range, scope, rate, caliber; gradation, shade, tint; tenor, tone, compass; sphere, station, rank, standing; point, mark, stage, level; intensity, strength.

adj comparative, gradual, shading off.

adv by degrees, gradually, step by step, bit by bit, little by little, inch by inch, drop by drop; in some degree, to some extent; up to a point.

27 [sameness of quantity or degree] **equality** *n* parity, symmetry, balance, counterbalance; evenness, monotony, level; equivalence, equipoise, equilibrium; par, even keel, quits; identity, similarity; tie, dead heat, draw, drawn game, neck and neck race; match, peer, equal, mate, fellow, brother; equivalent.

v equal, match, reach, keep pace with, run abreast; come up to; balance, even the score; equalize, level, trim, adjust; strike a balance; restore equilibrium.

adj equal, even, level, monotonous, coequal, symmetrical, balanced; on a par with, on a level with, on an equal footing with, up to the mark; equivalent, tantamount, synonymous, quits, even, much the same, all one, one and the same; drawn, half and half, six of one and half a dozen of another.

adv equally, to all intents and purposes.

28 [difference of quantity or degree] **inequality** *n* disparity, dissimilarity, difference, odds; unevenness, imbalance; inferiority, shortcoming, deficiency, imperfection, inadequacy; mediocrity; superiority.

v be unequal, have the advantage, turn the scale, turn the tide; topple, overmatch; not come up to, fall short of, not come up to snuff.

adj unequal, uneven, imbalanced; disparate, partial, inferior, insufficient, deficient, inadequate, mediocre, short.

29 mean *n* medium, average, balance, middle, mid-point, center, median, golden mean; compromise, neutrality.

v split the difference, take the average, move to the center.

adj mean, intermediate, middle, average, standard, normal, neutral; mediocre, middle class, bourgeois, commonplace, run of the mill, egalitarian.

adv on the average, in the long run.

30 compensation *n* equation; indemnification, requital; compromise, measure for measure, tit for tat, eye for an eye, retaliation, equalization; setoff, off-set, counterpoise, ballast; indemnity, equivalent, *quid pro quo*, amends, reparation.

v compensate, indemnify, recompense, remunerate; counterbalance, counterpoise, countervail, offset, counteract, balance, balance out, make up for, square, even out, equalize; cover, neutralize, nullify; redeem, atone, make amends.

adj compensatory, compensating, equivalent, equal.

adv but, however, yet, still, notwithstanding, nevertheless, although, though, nonetheless; howbeit, albeit; at all events, at any rate, be that as may, even so, on the other hand, at the same time.

31 greatness *n* magnitude, size, bulk, dimensions, vastness; multitude; enormousness, immensity, might, strength, intensity, fullness; importance, distinction, eminence, renown; quantity, store, volume, mass, bulk, heap; abundance, sufficiency.

v be great, soar, tower, rise above, transcend; enlarge, increase, expand.

adj great, large, considerable, big, huge, mammoth, gigantic; ample, abundant, sufficient; full, intense, strong; widespread, extensive, wholesale; goodly, noble, precious, mighty; utter, uttermost, arch, profound, intense, consummate; extraordinary, important, unsurpassed, supreme; complete, total; vast, immense, enormous, extreme, inordinate, excessive, extravagant, exorbitant, outrageous, monstrous; towering, stupendous, prodigious, marvelous; unlimited, infinite; absolute, positive, stark, decided, unequivocal, essential, perfect; remarkable, notable, noteworthy.

adv [in a positive degree] truly; decidedly, unequivocally, absolutely, essentially, fundamentally, downright; [in a complete degree] entirely, completely, totally, wholly; abundantly, fully, amply, widely; [in a great or high degree] greatly, much, indeed, very, very much, most, pretty, pretty well, enough, in a great measure, to a large extent; richly, on a large scale, ever so much; mightily, powerfully; extremely, exceedingly, intensely, exquisitely, consummately, acutely, indefinitely, immeasurably, beyond compare, beyond measure, beyond all bounds, incalculably, infinitely; [in a supreme degree] pre-eminently, superlatively, supremely, incomparably; [in a too great degree] immoderately, inordinately, exorbitantly, excessively, enormously, preposterously, monstrously, out of all proportion, with a vengeance; [in a marked degree] particularly, remarkably, singularly, curiously, uncommonly, unusually, peculiarly, notably, signally, strikingly, pointedly, mainly, chiefly; famously, egregiously, prominently, glaringly, emphatically, strangely, wonderfully, amazingly, surprisingly, astonishingly, incredibly, marvelously, stupendously; [in a violent degree] violently, furiously, severely, desperately, tremendously, extravagantly; [in a painful degree] painfully, sadly, sorely, bitterly, piteously, grievously, miserably, cruelly, woefully, lamentably, shockingly, frightfully, fearfully, dreadfully, terribly, horribly.

32 smallness *n* littleness, tininess, diminutiveness; slenderness, thinness, paltriness, slightness; paucity, fewness, sparseness, scarcity; unimportance, triviality, inconsequentiality, pettiness, insignificance; meanness, sordidness, selfishness, narrow-mindedness; small quantity, modicum, atom, particle, molecule, point, speck, dot, dab, mote, jot, iota; minutiae, details, *soupçon*, scintilla, granule; drop, droplet, drizzle, sprinkling, dash, smack, tinge; dole, scrap, shred, splinter; mite, bit, morsel, crumb, seed; snippet, snatch, slip; chip, sliver; nutshell, thimbleful, spoonful, handful, mouthful; fragment, fraction, drop in the ocean; trifle.

v be small.

adj small, little, tiny, diminutive, petite, miniature, minuscule, minute, microscopic, infinitesimal, fine; unimportant, trivial, minor, secondary, trifling, inconsequential, petty, paltry, insignificant; slender, thin, slight, scanty, scant, meager, insufficient; few, sparse, scarce; low, so-so, middling, tolerable, inconsiderable, inappreciable; mean, sordid, selfish, narrow, narrow-minded, illiberal, ungenerous; feeble, weak, faint.

adv [in a small degree] to a small extent; a wee bit; slightly, imperceptibly, faintly; miserably, wretchedly;

insufficiently, imperfectly; passably, pretty well, well enough; [in a certain or limited degree] partially, in part, to a certain degree; some, rather, to some degree; simply, only, purely, merely, at the least; ever so little; almost, nearly, well nigh, short of, not quite, all but, near the mark; scarcely, hardly, barely, only just, no more than; [in an uncertain degree] about, thereabouts, somewhere about; [in no degree] noway, nowise, not at all, not in the least, not a bit, not a jot, not a whit, in no respect, by no means, on no account.

33 superiority *n* supremacy, pre-eminence, ascendancy, transcendence; excellence, greatness, nobility, eminence, worthiness, preponderance, predominance, prevalence, advantage; majority; quality, high caliber.
v be superior, exceed, excel, transcend, outdo, outweigh, outrival, outrank; pass, surpass; top, cap, outstrip, eclipse, predominate, prevail; take precedence, come first.
adj superior, greater, major, higher, exceeding; supreme, greatest, utmost, paramount, pre-eminent, foremost, crowning; first-rate, important, excellent, unrivaled, matchless, priceless, unparalleled, unequaled, unsurpassed, inimitable, incomparable, superlative, beyond compare, transcendent.
adv beyond, more, over, over and above, at its height; [in a superior or supreme degree] eminently, pre-eminently, prominently, surpassingly, superlatively, supremely, above all, to crown all, *par excellence;* principally, especially, particularly, peculiarly.

34 inferiority *n* low quality, deficiency, imperfection, shortcoming, inadequacy; mediocrity, commonalty, commonness, poorness, meanness; minority, subordination, subjection.
v be inferior, fall short of, come short of, not come up to, not pass muster; want, lack.
adj inferior, minor, less, lesser, deficient; poor, indifferent, mean, base, bad, shabby, paltry, humble, imperfect, mediocre, common, commonplace, second-rate; poorer; secondary, minor, subordinate, lower; diminished, reduced, unimportant.
adv less, subpar; short of, under.

35 increase *n* growth, augmentation, enlargement, extension, expansion, addition, increment, accretion, aggrandizement; development, rise, ascent.
v increase, grow, dilate, enlarge, expand, multiply; augment, add to, enlarge, greaten; extend, spread out, prolong; advance, rise, sprout, ascend; raise, exalt, deepen, heighten, intensify, magnify, redouble; aggrandize.
adj increasing, growing; additional, incremental; developmental.

36 decrease *n* diminution, abatement, decline, reduction, wane, falling-off, contraction, dwindling, shrinking, lessening, ebb, ebbing; subtraction, abridgment, shortening; depreciation, deterioration.
v decrease, lessen, abate, fall off, decline, contract, shrink, dwindle, wane, ebb, subside; diminish, deteriorate, depreciate, languish, decay; abridge, shorten, subtract.
adj decreased, decreasing, on the wane.

37 addition *n* increment, increase, enlargement, aggrandizement, accession; supplement, adjunct, attachment, addendum; annexation, interposition, insertion; uniting, joining.
v add, annex, affix, subjoin, tack on, append, attach, join, supplement, increase, augment, make an addition to; accrue, accumulate, pile up; total, sum, add up; reinforce.
adj additional, supplemental, supplementary; extra, accessory, auxiliary.
adv in addition, more, plus; and, also, likewise, too, further, furthermore, besides, to boot, etc., and so on, and so forth; over and above, moreover; with, as well as, together with, along with, in conjunction with.

38 deduction *n* subtraction, retrenchment, withdrawal, removal; mutilation, amputation, curtailment; shortening, abbreviation; decrease, cutback.
v deduct, subtract, retrench, withdraw, remove; take from, take away; shorten, abbreviate, cut back, pare down, reduce, decrease, diminish, curtail, eliminate, deprive of; mutilate, amputate, cut off, cut away, excise; pare, thin, thin out, prune, scrape, file.
adj subtracted, subtracting; removable, reducible; deductible.
adv less, short of; minus, without, excepting, except, with the exception of, save, exclusive of.

39 [thing added] **adjunct** *n* addition, affix, suffix, appendage, annex, augmentation, increment, reinforcement, accessory, accompaniment, sequel; addendum, complement, supplement, appendix, attachment; rider, offshoot, episode, corollary.
adj additional.

40 [thing remaining] **remainder** *n* residue, remains, remnant, leftover, excess, superfluity, balance, surplus, rest, relic; leavings, odds and ends, residuum, dregs, refuse, crumbs, stubble, ruins, skeleton, stump.
v remain, survive, be left; be left over.
adj remaining, left, left over, residual; over, odd, spare, unused; superfluous; surviving.

40a [thing deducted] **decrement** *n* discount, defect, loss, deduction.

41 mixture *n* admixture, mix, combination, mingling, amalgamation, junction; infusion, suffusion, transfusion; infiltration, interlarding, interpolation; adulteration. thing mixed: tinge, tincture, touch, dash, sprinkling, spice, seasoning, infusion. compounds: alloy, amalgam, mélange, pastiche, miscellany, medley, patchwork, hotchpotch, gallimaufry, conglomeration, jumble, potpourri, farrago; cross, hybrid, mongrel.
v mix, join; combine, blend, mingle, commingle, confuse, jumble, unite, compound, amalgamate, adulterate; interlard, interlace, intertwine, interweave, interpolate; conjoin, associate, consort; instill, imbue, infuse, suffuse, transfuse, infiltrate, dash, tinge, tincture, season, blend, cross.
adj mixed, composite, half-and-half, hybrid, cross, mongrel, heterogeneous; motley, variegated, miscellaneous, promiscuous, indiscriminate.
adv among, amongst, amid, amidst, with; in the midst of.

42 [freedom from mixture] **simpleness** *n* purity, homogeneity; elimination, sifting, purification.
v simplify, sift, winnow, eliminate, strain, clean, purify; disentangle.
adj simple, uniform, homogeneous, single, pure, clear; unmixed, unadulterated, elemental, elementary, basic.

43 junction *n* joining, union; connection, conjunction, annexation, attachment; coupling, marriage, wedlock; confluence, communication, concatenation; meeting, assemblage, assembly, reunion; joint, joining, juncture, pivot, hinge, articulation; seam, stitch, linkage, link.
v join, unite, connect, link up, link; associate; put together, piece together, bind together; attach, fix, affix, fasten, bind, secure, clinch, twist, tie, string, strap, sew, lace, stitch, hem, knit, button, buckle, hitch, lash, splice, gird, tether, picket, moor, harness, leash; chain; fetter, lock, hook, couple, link, yoke, bracket; marry, wed, bridge over, span; pin, bolt, clasp, clamp, screw, rivet; solder, weld, fuse; entwine, interlace, intertwine, interweave; entangle.
adj joined, joint; corporate, compact; firm, fast, close, tight, taut, secure, set, inseparable, indissoluble.
adv jointly, in conjunction with; fast, firmly; intimately.

44 disjunction *n* disconnection, disunion, disengagement, dissociation, discontinuity; isolation, insularity, insulation, separateness; dispersion; separation, parting; detachment, segregation; divorce; division, subdivision, break, fracture, rupture; dismemberment, dislocation, severance; fissure, breach, rent, split, rift, crack, cut, slit, incision.
v disjoin, disconnect, disengage, disunite, dissociate, divorce, part, detach, separate, disentangle, cut off, rescind, discontinue; segregate, set apart, keep apart, isolate, insulate; cut adrift, loose, set free, liberate; divide, subdivide, sever, dissever, cut, saw, snip, chop, ax, cleave, rive, rend, slit, split, splinter, chip, crack, snap, break, tear, burst, rend; wrench, rupture, shatter; hack, hew, slash, slice, cut up, carve, dissect, tear to pieces; disband, disperse, dislocate, break up, apportion, divide; part, part company, separate, leave.
adj disjoined, discontinuous, disjunctive; isolated, insular; separate, apart, asunder, loose, adrift, free; unattached, unconnected.
adv separately, one by one, severally, apart, adrift, asunder.

45 link *n* connective, connection, vinculum, copula, tie, bond, bridge; junction, bracket.
v link, bond, join, connect, conjoin, fasten, pin, bind, tie; bridge, span.

46 coherence *n* cohesion, cohesiveness, adherence, adhesion, adhesiveness; connection, union, conglomeration, aggregation, consolidation; stickiness, inseparability.
v cohere, adhere, stick, cling, cleave, hold, take hold, clasp, hug; hang together, stay together; glue, cement, paste, solder, weld; consolidate, solidify, agglomerate.
adj cohesive, adhesive, adhering, sticky; tenacious, tough; united, unified, inseparable, inextricable, (*informal*) together, (*informal*) tight.

47 incoherence *n* looseness, laxity, relaxation, nonadhesion; loosening, disjunction, disconnection; disagreement, inconsistency, incongruity.
v loosen, make loose, slacken, relax; detach, disjoin.
adj nonadhesive, noncohesive, detached, loose, slack, lax, relaxed, segregated, unconsolidated; inconsistent, incongruous, illogical, absurd, rambling.

48 combination *n* mixture; junction; union, unification, synthesis, incorporation, amalgamation, coalescence, fusion, blend, blending, mix, centralization; compound, alloy, amalgam, composition, composite.
v combine, unite, incorporate, amalgamate, absorb, blend, mix, merge, fuse, marry, consolidate, coalesce, centralize, cement, harden, solidify.
adj combined, unified.

49 decomposition *n* analysis, dissection, dissolution, breaking down; disjunction; corruption, decay, rot, putrefaction.
v decompose, analyze, dissolve; resolve into its elements, dissect, disperse, crumble; decay, rot, turn.
adj decomposed.

50 [principal part] **whole** *n* totality, entirety, total, sum, aggregate; unity, completeness, integrity, indivisibility; bulk, mass, lump; body, trunk.
v form a whole, integrate, embody, amass, aggregate, assemble; amount to, come to, add up to.
adj whole, total, full, entire, undiminished, undivided, integral, complete, unimpaired, unbroken, faultless, sound, intact; indivisible, indissoluble.
adv wholly, altogether; totally, completely, entirely, all, all in all, wholesale, in a body, collectively, in the main, on the whole.

51 part *n* division, portion, piece, fragment, fraction, lump, bit, component, constituent, ingredient, element, section, segment, subdivision; member, limb, branch, bough, offshoot, ramification; compartment, department, class.
v part, divide, break, disjoin; partition, apportion, allot.
adj fractional, fragmentary, sectional; divided, split up.
adv partly, in part, partially; piecemeal, bit by bit, by installments, in dribs and drabs, in drips and snatches; in detail.

52 completeness *n* wholeness, entirety, totality, solidarity, fullness, intactness, unity, perfection; thoroughness.
v complete, accomplish, fulfill, finish; fill, charge, load, replenish; fill up, fill in; saturate.
adj complete, entire, whole, full, intact, undivided, one, perfect, fulfilled; full, good, absolute, thorough, solid; exhaustive, radical, sweeping, thoroughgoing; consummate, unmitigated, sheer, unqualified, unconditional; brimming, brimful, chock-full, saturated, crammed, replete, fraught.
adv completely, altogether, outright, wholly, totally, quite, utterly; fully, thoroughly, in all aspects, in every respect, out and out, to all intents and purposes; throughout, from first to last, from beginning to end, from top to bottom, from head to foot, every whit, every inch.

53 incompleteness *n* deficiency, shortcoming, insufficiency, imperfection; immaturity; noncompletion.
[part wanting] defect, deficit, omission, interval, break; discontinuity, missing link.
v be incomplete, fall short of; lack; neglect.
adj incomplete, imperfect, unfinished, uncompleted; defective, deficient, wanting, lacking, failing, short, short of; meager, lame, limp, perfunctory, sketchy, crude, immature; in progress, in preparation, going on, ongoing, proceeding.
adv incompletely.

54 composition *n* constitution, make-up, form; combination, compilation, incorporation, inclusion, synthesis.
v be composed of, be made up of, consist of; include, contain, hold, comprehend, take in, admit, embrace, embody; compose, constitute, form, make.
adj constituting.

55 exclusion *n* omission, exception, rejection, repudiation; exile, seclusion, segregation, separation, elimination, prohibition; restraint, keeping out.
v exclude, bar, leave out, shut out, keep out; reject, repudiate, blackball, throw out; lay aside, put aside, set aside; relegate, segregate, separate, seclude, banish, exile; pass over, omit, eliminate, weed out, winnow.
adj exclusive, not included in; inadmissible.

56 component *n* component part, integral part, element, constituent, ingredient; contents, feature, member, part; personnel.
v enter into, be part of, form part of; merge in, share in, participate; belong to, appertain to; form, make, constitute.
adj inclusive, comprehensive.

57 extraneousness *n* extrinsicality, externality; superfluousness; foreign body, foreign substance; intrusion.
v be extraneous, be unnecessary.
adj extraneous, foreign, alien, extrinsic, external; not germane, nonessential, superfluous; excluded.

IV. Order

58 order *n* regularity, uniformity, arrangement, harmony, symmetry; course, routine, method, methodology; disposition, array, arrangement, system, economy, discipline, orderliness; gradation, progression, series, sequence, continuity; rank, place, grade, class, degree.
v order, regulate, manage, adjust, arrange, systematize, standardize, rank.
adj orderly, regular, systematic, methodical; in order, neat, tidy, well-regulated, well-organized, organized, uniform, symmetrical, businesslike, shipshape.
adv in order, methodically, in turn, in its turn; step by step, at regular intervals, systematically.

59 disorder *n* derangement, disarray, untidiness, irregularity, anomaly; anarchy, anarchism, disunion, discord; confusion; jumble, mess, muddle, hash, hodgepodge, chaos; perplexity, labyrinth, wilderness, jungle; raveling, entanglement, complication, convolution; turmoil, ferment, agitation, trouble, row, disturbance, convulsion, tumult, uproar, riot, rumpus, ruckus, scramble, fracas, melee, pandemonium.
v disorder, put out of order, derange, ruffle, rumble; confuse, jumble, mess up.
adj disorderly, out of order, out of place, irregular, desultory; anomalous, disorganized, straggling, unsystematic, untidy, slovenly, messy; indiscriminate, chaotic, confused, deranged; anarchic, inverted, convoluted, topsy-turvy; complex, complicated, perplexed, involved, raveled, entangled, knotted, tangled; troublesome, problematical; riotous, violent, turbulent, tumultuous.
adv irregularly, helter skelter; at cross purposes, (*informal*), after the flood.

60 [reduction to order] **arrangement** *n* plan, method, organization; preparation, groundwork, planning; sorting, disposal, disposition, distribution, assortment, allotment, apportionment, graduation, groupings; analysis, classification, division, ordering, systematization.
v arrange, dispose, place, form; set out, marshal, range, array, rank, group, parcel out, allot, apportion, assign, dole out, distribute; sort, sift, put into shape; plan, prepare, organize, lay the groundwork; classify, divide, file, register, catalog, record, tabulate, index, graduate, rank; regulate, systematize, coordinate, organize, settle, fix; unravel, disentangle, straighten out.
adj arranged, ordered; methodical, orderly, regular, systematic.

61 [subversion of order] **derangement** *n* disorder, mess, disarray, disorganization; discomposure, disturbance, dislocation, perturbation, interruption.
v derange, disarrange, discompose, displace, misplace; mislay, disorder, disorganize; embroil, disconcert, convulse, unsettle, disturb, confuse, trouble, perturb, jumble, muddle, fumble; unhinge, dislocate, throw out of gear, throw out of whack; invert, turn upside down, turn topsy-turvy; complicate, confound, tangle, entangle; litter, scatter, mix.

62 precedence *n* coming before, the lead, superiority; precursor, antecedence; importance, consequence; priority, preference.
v precede, come before, forerun, come first; head, lead the way, usher in, introduce; set the fashion, influence, establish; have precedence, take precedence; place before, prefix, preface.
adj preceding, precedent, antecedent, anterior, prior, before; former, foregoing; preliminary, prefatory, introductory; preparatory.
adv before; in advance.

63 sequence *n* coming after, following, succession, order, series; posteriority; continuation; order of succession; outcome, consequence, result, sequel.
v succeed, come after, follow, ensue; replace.
adj succeeding, following; consequent, subsequent; proximate, next; sequential, consecutive.
adv after, subsequently; behind.

64 precursor *n* antecedent, precedent, predecessor, forerunner, pioneer, leader, bellwether; herald, harbinger; prelude, preamble, preface, prolog, proem, prefix, foreword, introduction; heading, frontispiece, groundwork; preparation.
adj prefatory, introductory, preliminary, precursory.

65 sequel *n* continuation, extension, supplement, outgrowth, offshoot, result, consequence, inference, deduction; result, consequence, aftermath, outcome, effect; conclusion, end, culmination, dénouement, finale, finish; appendage, suffix, epilog, postscript, tag, train, trail, wake; afterthought, afterpiece, second thoughts.

66 beginning *n* commencement, opening, outset, start, initiation, inauguration, introduction, prelude; outbreak, onset, brunt; initiative, first move; origin, cause, source, bud, germ, genesis, birth, nativity, cradle; starting point, first step, square one; title page, head, heading; rudiments, basics, elements.
v begin, commence, open, start, initiate, inaugurate; conceive; set out, embark, depart; usher in, lead the way, take the lead, take the initiative, head, stand at the head, launch, set in motion, get going, take the first step, break ground; burst forth, break out; begin at the beginning, start again, start over, make a fresh start; originate, conceive, think up.
adj initial, introductory, inaugural; incipient; embryonic, rudimental, primal, essential, natal, nascent; first, foremost, leading; maiden, virgin.
adv first, in the first place, first and foremost; in the bud, in its infancy; from the beginning.

67 end *n* close, termination, conclusion, finale, finish, last word; consummation, climax, apex, dénouement; goal, destination; expiration, death, finality; limit, extreme, extremity; breakup, last stage, final stage, turning point, death blow.
v end, close, finish, terminate, conclude; expire, die, come to a close, draw to a close, run its course, run out, pass away; bring to an end, put an end to, make an end of, wrap up; get through, complete, consummate; stop, desist, call it quits.
adj final, terminal, concluding; conclusive, crowning, definitive, last, ultimate, consummate; ended, settled, decided, over, concluded, played out.
adv finally, at last, once and for all, over and done with.

68 middle *n* center, midpoint, midst; mean, midcourse, middle ground, compromise; core, kernel, heart, nucleus, nub; equidistance, bisection; equator, diaphragm, midriff.
adj middle, medial, mean, mid, median, midmost; intermediate, equidistant, central, halfway.
adv midway, halfway, in the middle.

69 [uninterrupted sequence] **continuity** *n* continuousness, consecutiveness, progression, constant flow, succession, train, series, chain, string, scale, gradation; round, suite; procession, column, retinue; pedigree, genealogy, lineage; rank, file, line, row, range, tier.

v follow in a line; arrange in a series, string together, file, thread, graduate, tabulate.

adj continuous, progressive, successive, serial, consecutive, unbroken, uninterrupted, gradual; linear, in a line; perennial, constant.

adv continuously, in succession, consecutively; gradually, step by step, in a column.

70 [interrupted sequence] **discontinuity** *n* disjunction, disconnectedness; interruption, break, fracture, fault, flaw, crack, cut; gap, interval, caesura, pause, (*informal*) breather, rest, intermission, parenthesis, episode.

v alternate; discontinue, break, interrupt, intervene; pause, rest, take a breather, stop; break in upon, interpose; disconnect.

adj discontinuous, disconnected, unconnected, broken, interrupted; fitful, spasmodic, desultory, intermittent, irregular; alternate, recurrent, periodic.

adv at intervals, in snatches, by fits and starts.

71 term *n* rank, station, stage, step, phase; scale, grade, degree, status, position, place, point, mark, period, limit; stand, standing, footing.

72 assemblage *n* collection, levee, gathering, ingathering, muster; concourse, conflux, congregation; meeting, reunion; assembly, congress, convention, conclave, council; miscellany, compilation, menagerie; crowd, throng, mob, flood, rush, rash, deluge, press, crush, horde, body, tribe, crew, gang, squad, band, party, swarm, flock, bevy; company, troop, regiment, squadron, army; host, multitude, populace, clan, brotherhood, sisterhood, association; group, cluster, clump, batch, pack, assortment; accumulation, heap, lump, pile, mass, conglomeration, conglomerate, aggregation, aggregate; quantity.

v assemble, come together, collect, gather, muster; meet, unite, join, rejoin; cluster, flock, swarm, surge, stream, herd, crowd, throng, associate; congregate, concentrate, huddle; bring together, draw together, place together, lump together; convene, invoke; compile, group, assemble, unite; amass, accumulate, store.

adj assembled; closely packed, dense, crowded, teeming, swarming, populous.

73 dispersion *n* divergence, spreading, radiation, dissemination, diffusion, dissipation, distribution, apportionment, division.

v disperse, scatter, sow, disseminate, diffuse, shed, spread, dispense, disband, distribute, apportion, divide; break up, dispel, cast forth, strew, cast, sprinkle; issue, deal out, dole out.

adj dispersed, spread, scattered, strewn, diffuse, diffusive; sparse, widespread, broadcast; adrift, stray, disheveled.

74 [place of meeting] **focus** *n* center, gathering place, haunt, rendezvous, rallying point, headquarters, club, retreat.

v focus, bring to a point, bring to a focus; center on, bring out, clarify, elucidate.

75 class *n* division, subdivision, category, heading, order, section; department, province, domain; type, kind, sort, genus, species, variety, family, race, tribe, cast, clan, breed, sect.

76 inclusion *n* admission, acceptance into, incorporation, comprehension, reception.

v include, comprise, comprehend, contain, admit, embrace, receive, accept; inclose, circumscribe, encircle, encompass, embody, incorporate; number among, count among, fall under.

adj inclusive, comprehensive, extensive, all-embracing, compendious, sweeping; including, incorporating.

77 exclusion *n* (see 55).

78 generality *n* universality, catholicity, miscellany, miscellaneousness; generalization, simplification, oversimplification; prevalence, common run:

v be general, be universal, prevail, be true for everyone; render general, generalize, universalize; make a generalization, abstract, simplify.

adj general, universal, catholic, common, ecumenical, egalitarian, worldwide; prevalent, prevailing, rife, current; generic, collective, all-encompassing, comprehensive, all-inclusive, broad, widespread.

79 specialty *n* speciality, skill, ability, talent; individuality, singularity, distinctive feature, particularity, personality, characteristic, mannerism, idiosyncrasy, nonconformity; particulars, details, items; special feature.

v specify, particularize, individualize, specialize; designate, determine, single out, isolate, differentiate; be specific, come to the point, detail, get down to particulars.

adj special, particular, especial, individual, specific, proper, personal, original, private, respective, definite, certain, endemic, peculiar, characteristic, marked, appropriate, exclusive, singular, exceptional, idiomatic, unique.

adv specially, especially, in particular; each, apiece, severally, respectively, each to each, each to his own; in detail.

80 regulation *n* regularity, uniformity, constancy, clockwork, precision, exactness; routine, custom, formula, rule, form, procedure; standard, model, precedent, prototype; conformity, convention; nature, law, principle; normal state, ordinary condition, normalcy; hard and fast law.

adj regular, uniform, constant, steady; customary, conventional, formal, formulaic, procedural.

81 multiformity *n* variety, diversity.

adj multifold, multifarious, manifold, many-sided; heterogeneous, motley, mosaic; indiscriminate, irregular, diversified, diverse; of every description, all manner of kinds.

82 conformity *n* observance, compliance, assent; conventionality, customariness, agreement; example, instance, specimen, sample, illustration, exemplification, case in point.

v conform to, accommodate oneself to, adapt to; be regular, conform, follow the rules, obey the rules, go by the rules, comply, assent, agree, yield, give in, accept, harmonize; illustrate, stand as an example, embody.

adj conformable to rule, adaptable, agreeable, compliant, malleable; conventional, customary, standard, ordinary, common, habitual, usual, natural, normal, typical; formal, orthodox, strict, rigid, uncompromising; exemplary, illustrative.

adv by rule, in conformity with, in accordance with, in keeping with, consistent with; for the sake of conformity, as a matter of course, for form's sake; invariably, uniformly.

83 unconformity *n* nonconformity, unconventionality, nonobservance, informality; anomaly, variation, inconsistency, irregularity, incongruity, oddity, eccentricity, peculiarity, aberration, abnormality, exception; violation of custom, infraction, infringement; individuality, originality, mannerism, idiosyncrasy, quirk.

v be unconformable.

adj unconformable, unconventional; unnatural, odd, eccentric, peculiar, aberrant, abnormal, exceptional; anomalous, inconsistent, irregular, incongruous, arbitrary, whimsical, wanton; unusual, uncustomary, uncommon, rare, singular, unique, extraordinary; queer, quaint, strange; original, fantastic, newfangled, bizarre, outlandish, exotic, esoteric.

adv unless, except, save, beside.

V. Number

84 number *n* numeral, symbol, figure, cipher, digit, integer, round number, whole number, fraction; sum, total, product.

adj numeral; prime, fractional, decimal; positive, negative.

85 numeration *n* numbering; tallying, enumeration, reckoning, computation, calculation; arithmetic, calculus, algebra; statistics, poll, census, roll call; arithmetic operations.

v number, count, tell, tally, enumerate, add up, sum, reckon, compute, calculate, take account; muster, poll, recite; add, subtract, multiply, divide.

adj numeral, numerical; arithmetical, analytic, algebraic, statistical, numerable, computable, calculable.

86 list *n* catalog, index, listing, inventory, schedule, register, record, ledger, tally, file, table, calendar; directory, gazette, atlas, dictionary, thesaurus; roll, checklist.

87 unity *n* oneness, singleness, singularity, individuality; unification, unison, uniformity.

v unite, join, combine; isolate, insulate, seclude.

adj one, sole, single, solitary, lone; individual, apart, alone; unaccompanied, unattended, singlehanded, solo; singular, odd, unique; isolated, insular.

adv singly.

88 accompaniment *n* association, partnership, company; accessory, adjunct, concomitant, attachment, complement, attendant, fellow, associate, coexistence.

v accompany, join, escort, convoy, wait on; coexist with, consort with; associate with, couple with.

adj accompanying, fellow, twin, joint; associated with, coupled with; accessory, concomitant, attendant.

adv with, together with, along with, in company with, hand in hand, side by side; therewith, herewith.

89 duality *n* dualism, doubleness, polarity, biformity, duplexity; two, deuce, couple, brace, pair, twins.

v pair, mate, couple, bracket, pair off, yoke.

adj two, twain; dual, twin, two-sided, binary, binomial, duplex; coupled, both.

90 duplication *n* doubling, reduplication; iteration, repetition; renewal.

duplicate, double, copy, carbon, facsimile.

v double; redouble, reduplicate; repeat, renew; duplicate.

adj double; doubled, duplicated; twin, duplicate, second.

adv twice, once more, over again.

91 bisection *n* halving, bifurcation, twofold division, forking, dichotomy, (*informal*) fifty-fifty split.

v bisect, divide in two, halve, divide, split, cut in two, cleave, fork, bifurcate; split down the middle, (*informal*) go halves.

adj bisected, cloven, cleft, halved; bipartite; bifurcated; semi-, demi-, hemi-.

92 triality *n* trinity; three, triad, triplet, trio.

adj three, threefold, triform, tertiary.

93 triplication *n* tripling; triplicity.

v triple, treble, cube.

adj triple, treble; threefold, triplicate; third.

adv three times, thrice; in the third place, thirdly; triply, trebly.

94 trisection *n* tripartition, threefold division, third, third part.

v trisect, divide into three parts.

95 quaternity *n* four, tetrad, quartet, quarter.

v square, reduce to a square.

adj four, fourfold, quadrilateral.

96 quadruplication *n* quadrupling, multiplying by four.

v multiply by four, quadruplicate.

adj four, fourfold, quadruple; fourth.

adv four times, in the fourth place, fourthly.

97 quadrisection *n* quartering, quadripartition, fourfold division; fourth part, quarter.

v quarter, divide into four parts.

adj quartered, quadripartite.

98 five, etc. *n* five; six, half a dozen; seven; eight; nine; ten, decade; eleven; twelve, dozen; thirteen, baker's dozen, long dozen; twenty, score; twenty-five, quarter of a hundred; fifty, half a hundred; hundred, century, centenary; thousand.

99 quinquesection *n* fivefold division.

adj quinquepartite.

100 [more than one] **plurality** *n* two or more, couple, few, several; majority, multitude.

adj plural, more than one, upwards of, some, several, many, numerous.

100a [less than one] **fraction** *n* fractional part, segment, subdivision, part, portion.

101 zero *n* nothing, naught, (*informal*) zip; none, shutout; nobody.

102 multitude *n* multitudinous, multiplicity, profusion, mass, quantity, volume, abundance, amplitude, enormity; numbers, array, scores, droves, host, throng, collection; mob, crowd, assemblage.

v be numerous, swarm with, teem with, crowd, swarm, outnumber, multiply; people, populate.

adj multitudinous, manifold, profuse, multiple, teeming, populous, crowded, thick; many, several, sundry, various, numerous; endless, infinite.

103 fewness *n* paucity, scarcity, sparseness, scantiness; small number, small quantity; infrequency.

diminution of number: reduction, weeding, elimination.

v render few, reduce, diminish, weed, thin, eliminate, eradicate.

adj few, not many, scanty, scarce, sparse, rare, few and far between, limited, meager; sporadic, occasional, infrequent; reduced, diminished, pared back.

104 repetition *n* iteration, reiteration, recapitulation, restatement; sameness, monotony, harping, recurrence, tautology; redundance; rhythm, beat, echo, reverberation; reappearance, reproduction, duplication.

v repeat, iterate, reiterate, recapitulate, restate, rehash, go over again, harp on, hammer; reproduce, duplicate, echo; recur, revert, return, reappear; resume, return to, go back to; rehearse, go over the same ground.

adj repeated, repetitious, recurrent, recurring, frequent, incessant, never-ending, unceasing; repetitive, redundant, tautological; rhythmic, reverberant, reverberating; monotonous, harping, iterative; habitual.

adv repeatedly, often, again, anew, afresh, over again, once more; over and over, again and again, year after year; ditto, encore.

105 infinity *n* infinitude, infiniteness, perpetuity, endlessness, boundlessness, inexhaustibility, immeasurability, limitlessness, vastness, expanse.

v be infinite, have no limits, know no bounds, go on forever.

adj infinite, countless, numberless, limitless, boundless, measureless, unlimited, interminable, inexhaustible, incalculable; immense, vast, endless, perpetual; incomprehensible; eternal, perfect, omnipotent, absolute.

adv infinitely, *ad infinitum*.

VI. Time

106 time *n* duration, extent; period, interval, spell, term, space, span, season, stage; course; interim, interlude; interregnum, intermission; respite, break, timeout; era, epoch, season, age, year, date.

v time, measure, pace; continue, last, endure, go on, remain, persist, stand; pass time, spend time, while away the time, waste time, kill time, fill up the time.

adj permanent, lasting, durable; timely.

adv while, whilst, during, in the course of, for the time being, in due time; meantime, meanwhile, in the meantime, in the interim; till, until, up to, yet; the whole time, all the time, throughout, for good, (*informal*) for keeps.

107 absence of time *n* no time; outside time.

adv never, at no time; on no occasion, nevermore.

108 [definite duration or period of time] **period** *n* interval, age, era, eon, epoch, term, time; year, decade, century, millennium; lifetime, generation.

109 [indefinite duration] **course** *n* march of time, course of time, flux, passing time.

v elapse, lapse, flow, run, proceed, advance, pass, flit, fly, slip, slide, drag, creep, crawl; run its course; expire, go by, pass by.

adv in due time, in due course, in due season, in time.

110 [long duration] **durability** *n* permanence, persistence, continuance, lastingness, standing, stability; survival, longevity; protraction, prolongation.

v last, remain, stand, endure, abide, continue, persist; tarry, drag on, drag out, prolong, protract, eke out, draw out, lengthen; outlive, outlast, survive.

adj permanent, durable, lasting, longstanding, stable, immutable, invariable, constant; enduring, abiding, perpetual; lingering, protracted, prolonged, spun-out.

adv long, for a long time, ever so long; long ago; all day long, all the livelong day.

111 [short duration] **transience** *n* impermanence, evanescence, ephemerality, transitoriness, mortality; suddenness, swiftness, changeableness, vicissitude, uncertainty.

v be transient, flit, pass away, fly, gallop, vanish, fade, evaporate, melt.

adj transient, transitory, evanescent, ephemeral, fleeting, flitting, flying, passing; impermanent, temporal, temporary, provisional, short-lived; perishable, precarious, vulnerable, mortal; brief, quick, brisk; sudden, momentary, instantaneous.

adv temporarily, for the moment, for a time; awhile, soon; briefly.

112 [endless duration] **perpetuity** *n* eternity, timelessness, everlastingness, endlessness, infinity; constancy, endurance, durability, ceaselessness.

v last forever, endure, go on forever; perpetuate, immortalize, eternalize.

adj perpetual, eternal, timeless, everlasting, endless; unceasing, ceaseless, interminable, neverending, continuous, incessant, uninterrupted; unfading, imperishable, unvulnerable, immortal.

adv perpetually, always, ever, evermore, forever; constantly, continuously.

113 [point of time] **instantaneousness** *n* suddenness, abruptness; moment, instant, second, twinkling, trice, flash, crack, burst.

v be instantaneous, twinkle, flash.

adj instantaneous, momentary, sudden, instant, abrupt.

adv instantaneously, in no time, (*informal*) in two shakes (of a lamb's tail), presto, suddenly, like a shot, in a moment, all of a sudden, in a jiffy; immediately, on the spur of the moment, on a moment's notice.

114 [estimation, measurement and record of time] **chronometry** *n* chronology, timetable; almanac, calendar, register, chronicle, log, annal(s), journal, diary; clock, watch, stopwatch, timepiece, chronometer.

v fix the time, mark the time; date, register, chronicle; measure time, mark time, beat time.

adj chronological.

115 [false estimate of time] **anachronism** *n* misdate, misplacement, chronological error; disregard of time.

v misdate, antedate, postdate, anticipate; take no note of time.

adj misdated; undated, overdue; anachronistic, out of place, misplaced.

116 antecedence *n* priority, anteriority, precedence, pre-existence; antecedent, predecessor, precursor, forerunner.

v precede, antedate, come before; go before, lead, forerun; dawn, presage, herald, break the ground.

adj antecedent, prior, previous, anterior, preceding, pre-existent; former, foregoing, aforementioned; precursory, introductory.

adv before, prior to; earlier, previously, ere, already, yet, beforehand.

117 posteriority *n* succession, sequence; subsequence, following, continuance; successor, sequel, follower; future, futurity.

v follow after, come after, go after, succeed, be subsequent to.

adj posterior, subsequent, following, after, later, succeeding, successive, ensuing, resulting; posthumous.

adv subsequently, after, afterwards, since, later; next, close upon, thereafter, thereupon; ultimately.

118 present time *n* the present juncture, the present day; the times, the time being, right now.

adj present, actual, instant, current, existing.

adv at this time, at this moment; at the present time, now, at present, nowadays.

119 different time *n* other time; another time.

adv at that time, at that instant; then, on that occasion; when, whenever, whensoever; at some other time, at a different time, at some time or other.

120 contemporaneousness *n* simultaneousness, synchronism, simultaneity, coincidence, concurrence, coexistence, concomitance.

v coexist, concur, accompany, go side by side, keep pace with; synchronize.

adj simultaneous, coincident, concurrent, concomitant, coexisting; contemporary, contemporaneous, coeval.

adv simultaneously, concurrently, together, at the same time.

121 the future *n* futurity, hereafter, time to come, tomorrow, morrow; millennium, doomsday, day of judgment, crack of doom, flood; advent, eventuality; destiny, fate; heritage, heirs, posterity; prospect, expectation, anticipation.

v look forward, anticipate, expect, foresee; approach, await, threaten, impend, come near, draw near, come on.

adj future, to come; coming, impending, near, close at hand, in prospect; eventual, ulterior.

adv prospectively, hereafter, in future, in course of time, tomorrow; eventually, ultimately, sooner or later; henceforth, from this time; soon, early, on the eve of, on the point of, on the brink of.

122 the past *n* past time, days of old, days of yore, days gone by, yesterday, yesteryear, former times, ancient times; retrospection, memory; antiquity, history, time immemorial, remote past; ancestry, lineage, forbears; heritage.

v run its course, pass away, pass, lapse, blow over.

adj past, gone, gone by, passed away, bygone, elapsed, lapsed, expired, extinct, forgotten, irrecoverable, obsolete; former, pristine, late; foregoing, last, latter, recent; looking back, retrospective; retroactive.

adv formerly, of old, of yore, ago, over; long ago, years ago, a long while back, some time ago; lately, of late; retrospectively, ere now, before now, hitherto, heretofore; already, yet, up to this time.

123 newness *n* novelty, recentness, freshness; immaturity, greenness, youth, juvenility; innovation, uniqueness, originality; renovation, restoration; modernity, modernism, stylishness, fashionableness, newfangledness, fashion, faddishness, the latest thing, futurism, trendiness.

v renew, renovate, restore; modernize.

adj new, novel, recent, fresh; green, immature, unripe, young, youthful, untried, untested, virgin, virginal; modern, late, new, newfangled, stylish, fashionable, faddish, trendy, brand-new, up-to-date; renovated, restored, spick and span.

adv newly, afresh, anew, lately, just now, of late.

124 oldness *n* age, antiquity; maturity, ripeness; decline, decay, old age, senility, superannuation; archaism, antiquarianism, relic, thing of the past; tradition, custom, common law.

v be old, have had its day, have seen its day; become old, age, fade.

adj old, ancient, antique; time honored, venerable, traditional, vintage, of long standing; elderly, aged, hoary, decayed, senile, decrepit; primeval, primitive, aboriginal, primordial, antediluvian, prehistoric, archaic; traditional, prescriptive, customary, immemorial, inveterate, rooted; antiquated, outdated, outmoded, of other times; out of date, obsolete, out-of-fashion, out-of-style, gone by, stale, old-fashioned, timeworn, crumbling, ramshackle, run-down, wasted.

125 morning. noon *n* morning, morn, dawn, daybreak, sunrise, sunup, forenoon, break of day, peep of day, prime of day, morningtide, matins, cockcrow, first blush, antemeridian, A.M.

noon, midday, noonday, noontide, meridian, prime, height, noontime.

spring, springtime; summer, summertime, midsummer.

126 evening. midnight *n* evening, eve, eventide, dusk, vespers, nightfall, sundown, sunset, twilight, curfew, bedtime; afternoon, post meridian, P.M.

midnight, end of the day, close of the day, witching hour, dead of night.

autumn, fall, harvest time; winter.

127 youth *n* juvenility, infancy, childhood, boyhood, girlhood; minority, tender years, young years, formative years, next generation, tender age; cradle, nursery; puberty.

adj young, youthful, juvenile, green, callow, budding, immature, developing, underage, formative; younger, junior.

128 age *n* old age, advanced age, senility, years, gray hairs, declining years, golden years, mature years, decrepitude, anility, superannuation, longevity, ripe age, ripe old age; maturity, seniority, eldership.

adj aged, old, advanced, gray, elderly; senile, decline, failing, waning, ripe, overripe, mellow, venerable, wrinkled, wizened; older, elder, eldest.

129 infant *n* baby, babe, babe in arms, nursling, little one, tot, toddler, chick, kid, lamb, cherub; youth, youngster, child, minor; girl, lass, maiden, miss, schoolgirl; boy, lad, stripling, master, schoolboy.

adj infantile, infantlike, puerile, girlish, boyish, childish, babyish; newborn, young.

130 veteran *n* old man, old woman, patriarch, matriarch, grandmother, grandfather, grandsire, seer, graybeard, forefather, elder.

adj aged, old.

131 adolescence *n* majority, adulthood, manhood, womanhood, maturity, ripeness, fullness, puberty, pubescence; teenage years, prepubescence.

v come of age, grow up, attain majority.

adj adolescent, teenage, pubescent, of age, grown up, full grown, adult, womanly, manly, marriageable, nubile.

132 earliness *n* punctuality, promptitude, speediness, readiness, expedition, alacrity, quickness, haste; suddenness; prematurity, precocity, precipitation, anticipation.

v be early, be beforehand; anticipate, forestall, steal a march on, get a head start; bespeak, secure, engage, pre-engage; accelerate, expedite, quicken, hasten, make haste, make time, hurry.

adj early, timely, punctual, on time, prompt; premature, precipitate, precocious, anticipatory; sudden, instantaneous, immediate, expeditious; unexpected.

adv early, soon, anon, betimes, before long; punctually, to the minute, on time, on the dot; beforehand, prematurely, precipitately, too soon, hastily, in anticipation, unexpectedly; suddenly, instantaneously, at short notice, on the spur of the moment; at once, on the spot, on the instant, at sight, straight, offhand, straightway; forthwith, summarily, immediately, shortly, quickly, speedily; presently, by and by, directly.

133 lateness *n* tardiness, slowness, sloth, tarrying, dilly-dallying, loitering; delay, procrastination, postponement, adjournment, retardation, protraction, prolongation; respite, reprieve, suspension, moratorium, stop, stay.

v be late, tarry, wait, stay, bide, take time, linger, loiter, dawdle, shilly-shally, dilly-dally; put off, defer, delay, lay over, suspend; retard, postpone, adjourn; procrastinate, prolong, protract, drag out, draw out, lengthen, table, shelve, stall.

adj late, tardy, slow, dilatory, backward, unpunctual; delayed, overdue, belated.

adv late; backward, at the eleventh hour, at length, at last, ultimately, behind time; too late; slowly, leisurely, deliberately, at one's leisure, on one's own time.

134 opportuneness *n* timeliness, opportunity, occasion, suitable time, proper time, suitability, high time; crisis, turn, juncture; turning point, given time; nick of time, golden opportunity; clear stage, open field.

v be opportune, be suitable; seize the opportunity, seize the time, seize the day, *carpe diem*, use the occasion; suit the occasion, be expeditious, strike while the iron is hot.

adj opportune, timely, well-timed, seasonable, suitable, appropriate; providential, lucky, fortunate, happy, favorable, fortuitous, propitious, auspicious.

adv opportunely, in due time, in the nick of time, just in time, now or never; by the way, by the by, speaking of, while on the subject; on the spot, on the spur of the moment, since the occasion presents itself.

135 inopportuneness *n* untimeliness, unseasonableness, improper time, unsuitable time; (*informal*) bad timing; intrusion; anachronism.

v be ill timed, mistime, intrude, break in upon, (*informal*) butt in; lose an opportunity, waste an occasion, (*informal*) blow one's chance, let the opportunity slip by; waste time.

adj inopportune, untimely, unpropitious, unseasonable, unsuitable, inauspicious, unfavorable, unfortunate, unsuited, untoward, unlucky; ill-timed, mistimed, poorly timed; unpunctual, premature.

136 frequency *n* repetition, recurrence, iteration, reiteration.

v recur, repeat, reiterate; keep on, continue; attend regularly, visit often, patronize.

adj frequent, oft-repeated, recurring, incessant, constant, continual, perpetual; habitual, customary.

adv often, oft, oftentimes, frequently, repeatedly, day after day; daily, hourly, every day; perpetually, continually, constantly, incessantly, at all times; commonly, habitually, customarily; sometimes, occasionally, at times, now and then, every once in a while, from time to time.

137 infrequency *n* rarity, rare occurrence; long shot, surprise, (*informal*) mindblower.

v be rare, be infrequent.

adj infrequent, occasional, sporadic, rare, uncommon, unusual, unheard of, unprecedented; few, scant, scarce.

adv infrequently, rarely, seldom, scarcely, hardly; not often, hardly ever.

138 regularity [of recurrence] *n* periodicity, intermittence; beat, pulse, pulsation, rhythm; alternation, oscillation, vibration; bout, round, turn, revolution, rotation, rpm; cycle, period, routine; punctuality, regularity, steadiness.

v recur, revolve, return, come in its turn, come round again; beat, pulsate, alternate.

adj regular, periodic, periodical; serial, recurrent, cyclical, cyclic, recurring, rhythmical, rhythmic; intermittent, alternate, every other; regular, steady, punctual, continual, constant, regular as clockwork.

adv regularly, periodically, serially, cyclically; intermittently, alternately; by turns, in turn, in rotation, off and on, round and round.

139 irregularity [of recurrence] *n* uncertainty, unpredictability, haphazardness, fitfulness, capriciousness.

v be irregular, be haphazard.

adj irregular, uncertain, unpredictable, haphazard, fitful, capricious, flickering; spasmodic, sporadic.

adv irregularly, fitfully, capriciously, by fits and starts.

VII. Change

140 change *n* alteration, modulation, modification, variation, mutation, permutation, qualification, deviation, turn, shift, innovation; diversion, break; transformation, transfiguration, transmutation, metamorphosis; conversion, revolution, inversion, reversal; displacement, transference, transposition; changeableness.

v change, alter, vary, modulate, qualify, diversify, tamper with, play with, experiment with; turn, shift, veer, tack, swerve, warp, deviate, turn aside; turn, take a turn, (*informal*) hang a turn; modify, revamp, transform, transfigure, transmute, metamorphose, convert; innovate, restructure, give a new turn to, recast, redesign, remodel.

adj changed, newfangled; changeable, variable, transformable; innovative.

141 permanence *n* stability, invariability, unalterability, immutability, constancy, endurance, durability, persistence; maintenance, preservation, conservation; obstinacy, immovability, inflexibility, immobility, rigidity.

v endure, bide, abide, stay, remain, last, persist, stand, stand fast; maintain, keep, keep up, preserve; subsist, live, outlive, survive.

adj permanent, lasting, unchanged, unchanging, fixed, stable, invariable, constant; enduring, durable, abiding, everlasting; intact, inviolate; persistent.

adv permanently, for good, for good and all.

142 cessation *n* discontinuation, discontinuance, halt, stoppage, termination, suspension, interruption, stopping; pause, rest, lull, respite, truce, break; interregnum, abeyance; completion, end, finish; stop, death.

v cease, discontinue, terminate, desist, stay; break off, leave off, hold, stop, pull up, stop short, halt, pause, rest; suspend, interrupt, delay, cut short, arrest, bring to a standstill; complete, end, finish, close up shop; wear away, go out, die out, pass away, die.

143 continuance [in action] *n* continuation, continuity, protraction, prolongation, maintenance, perpetuation; persistence, perseverance, repetition.

v continue, persist, go on, keep on, hold on; abide, keep, pursue, stick to; maintain course, carry on, keep up; sustain, uphold, hold up, keep going, maintain, preserve, perpetuate, prolong.

adj continuing, uninterrupted, unvarying; continuous, persistent, perpetual.

144 conversion *n* transformation, transmutation, reduction, change, changeover, resolution, assimilation; passage, transit, transition, shifting, flux; growth, progress, development; chemistry, alchemy.

v be converted into, become, turn into, lapse, shift; pass into, grow into, ripen into, merge into; melt, grow, ripen, mature, mellow; convert into, resolve into; make, render; mold, form, model, remodel, remake, do over, reform, reorganize; assimilate, bring into, reduce to.

adj convertible, transmutable, changeable.

145 reversion *n* return, revulsion, reverting, returning; alternation, rotation; inversion; recoil, reaction, reflex, repercussion, rebound, boomerang, ricochet, backlash, repulse; retrospection, retrogression, retrogradation, falling back; restoration, going back; turning point, turn of the tide.

v revert, return, turn back, reverse; relapse, regress, fall back; recoil, rebound; retreat; restore; undo, unmake; turn the tide.

146 [sudden or violent change] **revolution** *n* revolt, rebellion, overthrow, overturn, coup, *coup d'état*, rising, uprising, mutiny, counterrevolution; breakup, destruction, subversion, clean sweep; spasm, convulsion, throe, revulsion.

v revolt, rebel, rise, rise up; revolutionize, remodel, recast, change.

adj revolutionary, rebellious; new.

147 substitution *n* replacement, supplanting, commutation, exchange, change, shift.

substitute, expedient, makeshift, stopgap, equivalent, double, alternative, representative.

v substitute, put in the place of, change, exchange, interchange; replace, supplant, supersede, take the place of, stand for, represent, pinch hit, substitute for, sub; redeem, commute, alternate.

adv instead, in place of, in lieu of.

148 [double or mutual change] **interchange** *n* exchange, commutation, permutation, transposition; reciprocation, reciprocity, intercourse; barter, swap, trade; interchangeability; retaliation, reprisal, requital, retort, crossfire.

v interchange, exchange, barter, trade, swap, bandy, transpose, commute, reciprocate; give and take, battle with words; retort, requite, retaliate.

adj interchangeable, all-purpose, multi-purpose; reciprocal; mutual.

adv in exchange, vice versa, turn and turn about.

149 changeableness *n* mutability, inconstancy, volatility, instability; malleability, adaptability, versatility, mobility; vacillation, irresolution, indecision, capriciousness, oscillation, alternation, fluctuation, vicissitude; restlessness, fidgetiness, disquiet, disquietude; unrest, agitation.

v fluctuate, oscillate, vary, waver, flounder, shuffle, hem and haw, vacillate, tremble, alternate.

adj changeable, mutable, variable, malleable, adaptable, adjustable, versatile, mobile, transformable, convertible; inconstant, unsteady, unstable, unreliable, vacillating, oscillating, fluctuating; volatile, fitful, fickle, capricious, mercurial, indecisive, irresolute, flighty, impulsive, fanciful, erratic, wayward, wanton; restless, fidgety, tremulous, agitated; unfixed, unsettled.

150 stability *n* immutability, unchangeableness, constancy; firmness, fixity, solidity, steadiness, soundness, balance, stabilization, equilibrium, quiescence; immobility, immovability, fixedness; steadfastness, reliability, resolution, determination, obstinacy, stubbornness, pertinacity, tenacity, doggedness, will, pluck, resoluteness; permanence, endurance, perseverance, durability; continuity, uniformity, changelessness.

v be firm, stick fast, stand firm; settle, establish, fix, set, stabilize; retain, keep hold; make sure, fasten, make solid.

adj stable, fixed, rigid, firm, steady, established, strong, sturdy, immovable, invariable, unvarying, permanent, unchangeable, unchanging, unalterable, immutable; enduring, constant, durable, lasting, abiding, secure, fast, perpetual; unwavering, steadfast, staunch, reliable, steady, solid, sound, balanced; resolute, obstinate, dogged, willful, stubborn, pertinacious, tenacious.

151 present events *n* event, occurrence, incident, affair, eventuality, happening, proceeding, transaction, fact; phenomenon; circumstance, situation, particular; adventure, episode, thrill; crisis, pass, emergency, contingency, impasse; things, doings, affairs, matters, issues; the world, life, the times.

v happen, occur, take place, come to pass, take place, come about, come round, fall out, turn out, befall, chance, prove, eventuate; turn up, crop up, arise, arrive, issue, ensue, start, hold; take its course, pass off; experience, meet with, meet up with, fall to, be one's lot, be one's fortune, find, encounter, undergo, go through, live through, endure, put up with.

adj happening, going on, doing, current; eventful, stirring, bustling, busy, full of incident.

adv eventually, finally; as things go, in the course of things, as it happens.

152 future events *n* destiny, luck, lot, chance, fortune, karma, doom, end; future, futurity, next world, hereafter; prospects, expectations, tomorrow.

v impend, hang over, hover, threaten, loom, await, come on, approach; foreordain, preordain; destine, predestine, doom, have in store for.

adj impending, destined; coming, in store, to come, at hand, near, close by, imminent, brewing, forthcoming; in the wind, in the cards, in prospect, looming, on the horizon.

adv in time, in the long run, in good time, in its own sweet time, eventually.

VIII. Causation

153 cause *n* origin, source, principle, element; prime mover, first cause; author, producer, creator; mainspring, agent, catalyst; groundwork, foundation, support; spring, fountain, well, fount, font; genesis, descent, remote cause, influence; pivot, hinge, axis, turning point; egg, germ, embryo, root, nucleus, seed; causality, causation, origination, production.

v cause, originate, give rise to, occasion, sow the seeds of, kindle, bring to pass, bring about; produce, create, set up, develop; found, broach, institute; induce, evoke, elicit, draw, provoke; determine, decide; conduce to, contribute, have a hand in, influence, effect.

adj causal, generative, productive, formative, creative; primal, primary, original, embryonic.

adv because.

154 effect *n* consequence, issue, derivation, upshot, outgrowth, development, fruit, crop, harvest, product, outcome, end, conclusion; offspring, offshoot; complications, concomitants, side effects.

v be the effect of, be due to, be owing to; originate in, originate from, rise from, spring from, proceed from, emanate from, come from, grow from, issue from, flow from, result from; depend upon, hinge upon.

adj owing to, resulting from, due to, derivable from, caused by; derived from, evolved from; derivative, hereditary.

adv consequently, as a consequence, necessarily.

155 [assignment of cause] **attribution** *n* theory, ascription, assignment, rationale, reference to, accounting for; imputation, derivation; explanation, interpretation, reason why.

v attribute to, ascribe to, impute to, refer to, point to, trace to, assign to; account for, derive from; theorize, speculate.

adj attributed, attributable, referable, due to, owing to.

adv hence, thence, therefore, *ergo*, for, since, on account of, because; why? wherefore? whence? how come? how so?

156 [absence of assignable cause] **chance** *n* fortune, fate, accident, hap, hazard, luck, fluke, (*informal*) freak; gamble, lottery, tossup, fifty-fifty chance, throw of the dice, heads or tails; probability, possibility, contingency, odds; speculation, gaming, gambling.

v chance, hap, turn up; fall to one's lot; stumble on, light on; take one's chances.

adj chancy, causal, fortuitous, accidental, (*informal*) iffy, adventitious, haphazard, random, indeterminate, flukey, (*informal*) freaky.

adv by chance, by accident; at random; perchance, as chance will have it.

157 power *n* potency, strength, puissance, might, force, energy, vigor; control, command, dominion, authority, rule, sway, ascendancy, sovereignty, omnipotence; ability, capability, capacity, facility, competence, competency, efficacy; validity, cogency.

v be powerful, control, command, rule; confer power, empower, invest, endow; arm, strengthen, authorize; compel, force.

adj powerful, potent, strong, mighty, energetic; able, capable, competent, efficacious, equal to, up to, effective, efficient, adequate; omnipotent, almighty; influential, forceful.

adv powerfully.

prep by virtue of, by dint of.

158 impotence *n* inability, incapability, incapacity, infirmity, debility, disability; inefficacy, inefficiency, incompetence, ineptitude, feebleness, weakness, frailty, powerlessness; helplessness, prostration, paralysis, collapse, exhaustion; decrepitude, senility; sexual failure, barrenness.

v be impotent; collapse, faint, swoon, drop; render powerless, disable, disarm, incapacitate, disqualify, invalidate; cramp, tie the hands, paralyze, muzzle, cripple, maim, laim, hamstring, throttle, strangle, tie up in knots; unman, unnerve, enervate; shatter, exhaust, weaken; emasculate.

adj impotent, powerless, incapable, unable, incompetent, ineffective, inefficient, ineffectual, inept, unfit, unfitted, unqualified; disabled, incapacitated, crippled, paralyzed, paralytic; decrepit, senile, exhausted, worn out, used up, limp, spent; weak, frail, infirm, feeble, helpless; harmless; sterile, barren, frigid; emasculated, inadequate, inoperative; futile, fruitless, bootless, vain.

159 strength *n* power, force, might, vigor, health, stoutness, hardiness, lustihood, stamina, energy, potency, capacity; spring, bounce, tone, elasticity, tension; virility, vitality, nerve, verve; strengthening, invigoration, refreshment.

v strengthen, invigorate, brace, nerve, fortify, sustain, harden, steel; vivify, revivify, refresh, reinforce, restore.

adj strong, mighty, vigorous, forceful, hard, stout, robust, sturdy, hardy, powerful, potent, puissant; irresistible, invincible, indomitable, unconquerable, impregnable, inextinguishable incontestable; able-bodied, athletic, muscular, sinewy, strapping, gigantic, Herculean.

adv strongly, by force.

160 weakness *n* debility, relaxation, languor, enervation; impotence, infirmity, fragility, flaccidity; frailty, delicacy, softness; senility, decrepitude.

v be weak, drop, crumble, give way, teeter, totter, tremble, shake, halt, limp, fade, languish, decline, flag, fail; weaken, enfeeble, cramp, debilitate, shake, enervate, unnerve; relax; dilute, water down.

adj weak, feeble, infirm, sickly; languid, faint, dull, slack, spent; limp, flaccid, powerless, impotent; relaxed, unstrung, unnerved; frail, fragile, delicate, flimsy; rickety, drooping, teetering, tottering, withered, shaky, shattered; palsied, decrepit, lame; decayed, rotten, worn, seedy, wasted, laid low.

161 production *n* creation, formation, fabrication, construction, manufacture; building, architecture, erection; organization, establishment; workmanship, craftsmanship, performance; achievement, product, end result; flowering, fructification, fruition, fulfillment; gestation, evolution, development, growth; genesis, generation, procreation; authorship, publication, works, *oeuvre*.

v produce, perform, operate, do, make, form, construct, fabricate, frame, contrive, manufacture; build, raise, rear, erect, put up; set up, establish, constitute, compose, organize, institute; achieve, accomplish, fulfill; bud, flower, blossom, bloom, bear fruit, bring forth; propagate, beget, generate, procreate, engender; breed, hatch, develop, bring up; induce, cause.

adj productive, constructive, formative, creative; generative; prolific, blooming.

162 [nonproduction] **destruction** *n* waste, dissolution, breaking up, disruption; consumption; fall, downfall, ruin, perdition; breakdown, wreck, wrack, havoc, mess, chaos, cataclysm; desolation, extinction, annihilation; demolition; overthrow, subversion, suppression; dilapidation, devastation, road to ruin.

v perish, fall, tumble, topple, fall to pieces, break up, crumble, go to the dogs, go to wrack and ruin; destroy, do away with, demolish, tear up, overturn, overthrow, wipe out, (*informal*) waste; upset, subvert, undo; waste, squander, dissipate, dispel, dissolve; smash, squash, squelch, shatter, crumble, batter, crush, pull to pieces; fell, sink, scuttle, wreck, swamp, ruin, raze, level, expunge, erase, sweep away; lay waste, ravage, gut; disorganize, dismantle, take apart; devour, devastate, desolate, sap, exterminate, extinguish, stamp out, trample out, crush out, eradicate.

adj destructive, subversive, ruinous, incendiary, deadly, lethal, fatal; destroyed, wiped out, extinct.

163 reproduction *n* renovation, restoration, renewal, revival, regeneration, revivification, resuscitation, reanimation, resurrection; reappearance; generation, childbirth.

v reproduce, renovate, restore, renew, revive, regenerate, revivify, resuscitate, breathe new life into, reanimate, refashion, resurrect, bring back to life; give birth to, multiply, people the world.

adj reproductive; regenerative, restorative; renascent, reappearing, resurgent.

164 producer *n* originator, inventor, author, founder, generator, mover, creator, maker, architect; backer, angel.

165 destroyer *n* spoiler, waster, ravager, wrecker, killer, assassin, executioner; cankerworm, bane; iconoclast, rebel, pessimist, cynic, nihilist, misanthrope.

166 parentage *n* family, ancestry, lineage, genealogy; procreator, progenitor.

paternity: fatherhood, fathership; father, dad, pop, sire, papa, (*informal*) old man; grandfather, grandsire.

maternity: motherhood; mother, mom, ma, mamma, mummy, mum, (*informal*) old lady; grandmother.

adj parental, familial, ancestral, lineal, paternal, maternal; patriarchal, matriarchal.

167 posterity *n* progeny, breed, issue, offspring, brood, litter, family, children, grandchildren, heirs; child, son, daughter; descendant, heir, scion, (*informal*) chip off the old block; heredity.

adj filial.

168 productiveness *n* fecundity, fertility, fruitfulness, productivity; multiplication, propagation, procreation; creativity, inventiveness, originality.

v make productive, fructify, fulfill; procreate, generate, conceive, impregnate, fertilize; teem, multiply, produce, reproduce.

adj productive, prolific, fruitful, copious; teeming, fertile, fecund; procreative, generative, life-giving.

169 unproductiveness *n* infertility, sterility, barrenness, unfruitfulness, impotence; unprofitableness, wastefulness.

v be unproductive, do nothing, produce nothing, come to nothing.

adj unproductive, unfruitful, infertile, barren, sterile, arid; unprofitable, useless.

170 agency *n* operation, force, working, function, office, maintenance, exercise, work, play; causation, instigation, instrumentality, influence.

v operate, work, do; act, perform, play, support, sustain, maintain, take effect, quicken, strike; come into play, have free play; bring to bear upon, influence.

adj operative, efficient, efficacious, effectual, practical; at work, on foot, in operation, in force, in play, in action.

adv through the agency of, by means of.

171 energy *n* force, power, strength, intensity, vigor, zeal, dynamism, pep, fire, spirit, ebullience, life; activity, agitation, exertion, effervescence, ferment, fermentation, ebullition, bustle.

v give energy, energize, stimulate, kindle, excite, inflame, exert; strengthen, invigorate; sharpen, intensify.

adj energetic, strong, forcible, potent, forceful, active, powerful, intense, vigorous, zealous, dynamic, ebullient, spirited, animated, keen, vivid, sharp, acute, incisive, trenchant, biting; invigorating, rousing, stimulating; energized.

172 inertness *n* inertia, inactivity, torpor, languor, dullness, immobility, passivity, passiveness, lifelessness; quiescence, latency; inexcitability, sloth, indolence, irresolution, indecisiveness, cowardice, spinelessness.

v be inert, be inactive.

adj inert, inactive, immobile, unmoving, motionless, lifeless, passive, dead; sluggish, dull, heavy, flat, slack, tame, slow, blunt, torpid, languid; latent, dormant, sleeping, smoldering, quiescent.

adv in suspense, in abeyance.

173 violence *n* vehemence, fury, ferocity, impetuosity, boisterousness, turbulence, ebullition, effervescence, intensity, severity, acuteness; energy, force, might; fit, paroxysm, orgasm, spasm, convulsion, throe; exacerbation, exasperation, hysterics, excitability, passion; outbreak, outburst, uproar, riot, explosion, blow-up, blast, eruption; turmoil, disorder, ferment, agitation, storm, tempest; destruction, brutality, fighting, combat, warfare, hostilities; injury, wrong, outrage, injustice.

v be violent, ferment, effervesce; romp, rampage, run wild, run riot, rush, tear, run headlong, run amuck, go wild, kick up a row, (*informal*) flip out, go beserk; bluster, rage, roar, riot, storm, boil, boil over, fume, foam; explode, go off, detonate, thunder, blow up, flare, burst; render violent, sharpen, stir up, quicken, excite, incite, urge, lash, whip up, stimulate; irritate, inflame, kindle, accelerate, aggravate, exasperate, exacerbate, convulse, infuriate, madden, fan the fire, whip into a frenzy.

adj violent, vehement, acute, sharp; rough, rude, bluff, boisterous, brusque, abrupt, wild, impetuous, rampant; disorderly, turbulent, blustering, raging, riotous, tumultuous, obstreperous; raving, frenzied, (*informal*) freaked, mad, unhinged, insane; desperate, furious, frantic, hysterical; savage, fierce, ferocious, physical, brutal, combative; uncontrollable, ungovernable, irrepressible, excited; spasmodic, convulsive, orgasmic; explosive, volcanic, stormy.

adv violently; by storm, by force.

174 moderation *n* temperateness, temperance, reasonableness, judiciousness, deliberateness, fairness; gentleness, mildness, calmness, peacefulness; quiet, calm, composure; lenity, lenience; relaxation, assuagement, tranquilization, pacification, mitigation; measure, middle ground, middle of the road.

v moderate, ally, meliorate, calm, pacify, assuage, lull, smooth, compose, still, calm, quiet, hush, sober, mitigate, soften, mollify, temper, qualify, alleviate, appease, lessen, abate, diminish; slake, curb, tame; arbitrate, referee, umpire, regulate.

adj moderate, temperate, reasonable, judicious, deliberate, fair, gentle, mild, calm, cool, sober, measured, unruffled, quiet, tranquil, still, peaceful, pacific; unexciting, even, smooth, bland, palliative; lenient, relaxed, easy going.

adv moderately, in moderation, within reason.

175 influence *n* importance, weight, pressure, preponderance, prevalence, sway; predominance, ascendancy; dominance, reign, rule, authority, power, control, capability; input, (*informal*) say, persuasion, play, leverage, vantage ground; patronage, protection, auspices.

v be influential, have a say, have input, carry weight, affect, sway, impress, bias, direct, control; move, activate, incite, impel, rouse, arouse, induce, persuade; dominate, predominate, outweigh, override, prevail.

adj influential, important, weighty; prevalent, rife, rampant, dominant, predominant; potent, powerful, effective, authoritative.

175a absence of influence *n* impotence, powerlessness; unimportance, irrelevancy.

adj uninfluential, unpersuasive, weak, impotent, (*informal*) wishy-washy.

176 tendency *n* aptness, aptitude, disposition, predisposition, proclivity, proneness, propensity, susceptibility, inclination, leaning, bias, drift, trend, bent, turn; quality, nature, temperament; idiosyncrasy, cast, vein, mood, humor.

v tend, contribute, conduce, lead, dispose, incline, verge, bend to, gravitate toward, lean, drift, tend, affect; promote, influence.

adj tending, leaning; conducive, working toward, in a fair way to; liable, likely; influential, instrumental, useful, subsidiary, subservient.

177 liability *n* susceptibility, penchant, vulnerability, predilection, propensity, tendency; drawback, hindrance, obstacle, difficulty, impediment; responsibility, obligation, debt, debit, indebtedness, pledge.

v be liable, incur, lay oneself open to, run the risk of, stand a chance, expose oneself to.

adj liable, subject, exposed, likely, open, in danger of; obliged, responsible, accountable, answerable; contingent, incidental, possible.

178 concurrence *n* accordance, accord, agreement, consent, assent; cooperation, collaboration, partnership, alliance, concert, union.

v concur, conduce, conspire, contribute; agree, unite, combine, hang together, pull together, cooperate, collaborate; keep pace with, run parallel, go hand in hand with.

adj concurrent, cooperative, collaborative, joint, allied with, of one mind, at one with, in concert with.

179 counteraction *n* opposition, antagonism, contrariety, polarity; clashing, collision, interference, resistance, friction; reaction, response, counterblast, counter maneuver; neutralization, check, curb, hindrance; repression, restraint.

v counteract, run counter to, clash, cross, interfere with, conflict with; jostle, run up against, oppose, antagonize, withstand, resist, hinder, impede, check, curb, repress, restrain; recoil, react; neutralize, nullify, cancel out, undercut, undermine, undo; counterpoise, offset, balance out, compensate.

adj counteracting, antagonistic, conflicting, contrary, reactionary.

adv although.

prep in spite of, against.

Class II

Words Relating to Space

I. Space in General

180 [indefinite space] **space** *n* extension, extent, expanse, span, stretch, scope, range, latitude, spread, proportions, sweep, capacity, play, swing, expansion; elbowroom, room, breathing space, leeway; open space(s), free space, waste, desert, wild, wilderness; unlimited space, wide world, heavens, universe, solar system, outer space, abyss, the void, infinity.

adj spacious, roomy, extensive, expansive, capacious, ample; widespread, vast, worldwide, boundless, limitless, unlimited, infinite.

adv extensively, far and wide, right and left, from the four corners of the world, all over, from pole to pole, under the sun, on the face of the earth, from all points of the compass, to the four winds.

180a inextension *n* nonextension, point, atom.

181 [definite space] **region** *n* sphere, ground, soil, area, realm, quarter, orb, hemisphere, circuit, circle; domain, tract, territory, country, county, province; clime, climate, zone, meridian, latitude.

adj regional, provincial, territorial.

182 [limited space] **place** *n* spot, point; niche, nook, hole, pigeonhole; locality; locale, situation.

adv somewhere, in some place, here and there, in various places.

183 situation *n* position, locality, locale, latitude and longitude, location; footing, standing, standpoint; aspect, attitude, posture, perspective, pose; place, site, station, post, predicament, whereabouts; bearings, direction; topography, geography; map, chart.

v be situated, be located, lie, have its seat in; situate, locate.

adj situated, located; local, topical, topographical.

adv here and there, hereabouts, thereabouts, in such and such a place.

184 location *n* place, situation; establishment, settlement, installation; anchorage, mooring, encampment.

v locate, place, situate, put, lay, set, make a place for, seat; station, lodge, quarter, house, post, install; establish, fix, settle, root; graft, plant; inhabit, domesticate, colonize, take root, establish roots, come to rest, settle down, take up quarters, locate oneself, relocate; squat, perch, bivouac, burrow, get a footing, encamp.

adj located, placed, ensconced, rooted, settled, moored.

185 displacement *n* dislocation, misplacement, derangement, transposition; ejection, expulsion, banishment, removal, exile.

v displace, dislodge, disestablish; misplace, disturb, disorder, unsettle, derange, confuse; transpose, set aside, transfer, remove, unload, empty, eject, expel, banish, exile; vacate, depart, leave.

adj displaced; unplaced, unhoused, unsettled, unestablished; homeless, out of place, misplaced, out of its element.

186 presence *n* attendance, company; occupancy, occupation; ubiquity, omnipresence, permeation, pervasion, pervasiveness, diffusion, dispersion; nearness, vicinity, proximity, closeness.

v be present; look on, attend, stand by, remain, find oneself; occupy, inhabit, dwell, stay, sojourn, live, abide, lodge, nestle, roost, perch, tenant; fill, pervade, permeate, run through.

adj present, attending; occupying, inhabiting, resident, moored; ubiquitous, omnipresent, pervasive, diffused; near, close, in proximity.

adv here, there, and everywhere; in presence of.

187 absence *n* nonappearance, nonattendance, absenteeism, nonresidence; emptiness, void, vacuum, vacancy, vacuity.

v be absent; keep away, play truant, absent oneself, stay away.

adj absent, not present, away, out, not here, not in, not present, off; wanting, lacking, missing, nonexistent; vacant, empty, void, vacuous, devoid.

adv without, minus, nowhere, *sans*; elsewhere.

188 inhabitant *n* resident, dweller, occupant; tenant, inmate, boarder, lodger; native, townsman, villager, citizen; population, community, society, state, people, race, nation.

v inhabit, live, reside, dwell.

adj indigenous, native, domestic.

189 habitation *n* abode, residence, domicile, lodging, dwelling, address, habitation, housing, quarters; home, homestead, motherland, fatherland, country; nest, lair, den, cave, hole, hiding place, cell, hive, haunt, habitat, perch, roost, retreat, (*informal*) pad, (*informal*) crashpad.

v inhabit, take up one's abode.

190 [things contained] **contents** *n* stuffing, cargo, lading, freight, shipment, haul, load, bale, burden.

v load, lade, ship, haul, charge, fill, stuff.

191 receptacle *n* container, holder, repository, vessel, receiver, depository, reservoir; storage areas; bulk containers; liquid containers; wrapping.

II. Dimensions

192 size *n* proportions, dimensions, magnitude, bulk, volume; largeness, greatness; expanse, amplitude, mass; capacity, tonnage; corpulence, obesity, plumpness; hugeness, enormousness, immensity; monstrosity, enormity; giant, monster, mammoth, behemoth, leviathan, elephant; lump, bulk, block, mass, clod, thumper, whopper, strapper, (*informal*) mother, mountain, mound, heap.

v be large; become large, expand.

adj sizable, large, big, great, considerable, bulky, voluminous, ample, massive, massy; capacious, comprehensive, spacious; mighty, towering, magnificent; corpulent; stout, fat, plump, obese, portly; full-grown, stalwart, brawny; hulky, unwieldy, bulky, lumpish, whopping, thundering, thumping; overgrown; huge, immense, enormous, mighty, vast, amplitudinous, stupendous; monstrous, gigantic, colossal.

193 littleness *n* smallness, diminutiveness, tininess; epitome; microcosm; vanishing point.

v be little; become little, decrease.

adj little, small, minute, diminutive, microscopic, submicroscopic; tiny, puny, wee, miniature, pigmy, dwarf, undersized, underdeveloped, dwarfish, stunted, dumpy, squat; imperceptible, invisible, infinitesimal.

194 expansion *n* increase, enlargement, extension, growth, development; augmentation, aggrandizement, increment, amplification; spreading, swelling, distention, puffiness, dropsy.

v expand, widen, enlarge, extend, grow, increase, swell, fill out; dilate, stretch, spread; bud, sprout, shoot, germinate, open, burst forth; outgrow, overrun; spread, extend, aggrandize; distend, develop, amplify, spread out, magnify; inflate, puff up, blow up, stuff, pad, cram, fatten; exaggerate.

adj expanded, larger; swollen, expansive, widespread, overgrown, exaggerated, bloated, fat, turgid, tumid, dropsical; pot-bellied, chubby, corpulent, obese, heavy; full-blown, full-grown.

195 contraction *n* reduction, diminution; decrease, lessening, shrinking; collapse, emancipation, attenuation, atrophy; condensation, compression, compactness, compendium, squeezing.

v contract, become small, lessen, decrease, dwindle, shrink, narrow, shrivel, collapse, wither, wizen, fall away, waste, wane, ebb, decay, deteriorate; diminish, contract, draw in, constrict, condense, compress, squeeze, crush, crumple up, pinch, squash, cramp; pare, reduce, attenuate, scrape, file, grind, chip, shave, shear, cut down; circumscribe, limit, restrain, confine.

adj contracting, astringent; shrunk, shrunken, contracted; wizened, stunted, waning; compact.

196 distance *n* remoteness, farness, background, offing, far cry to, horizon, elongation; interval, remove, gap, span, reach, range; outpost, outskirts, foreign parts.

v be distant; extend to, stretch to, reach to, spread to; range.

adj distant, far off, far away, remote, far, afar, outlying, removed, at a distance, away, yonder, yon; inaccessible, out of the way, unapproachable.

adv far off, far away, afar, away, a long way off.

197 nearness *n* closeness, propinquity, proximity, proximation; vicinity, neighborhood, contiguity; short distance, earshot, close quarters, stone's throw, gunshot, hair's breadth; approach, access.

v be near, adjoin, neighbor, border upon, touch, stand next to; approximate, come close to, resemble; converge, crowd.

adj near, nigh, close, neighboring, adjoining, adjacent, bordering; proximate, approximate; at hand, handy; intimate.

adv near, nigh, hard by, close to, close upon, within reach, at one's fingertips.

198 interval *n* separation, space, break, gap, caesura, interspace, interstice, distance; hiatus, skip, division, opening; pause, recess, interim, respite, interlude, interregnum, interruption, term, spell, period; cleft, crevice, chink, cranny, crack, slit, fissure, rift, flaw, breach, rent, gash, cut, leak; ditch, dike, gorge, ravine, abyss, gulf.

v gape, open; intervene, interrupt.

199 contiguity *n* contact, contiguousness, proximity, apposition, juxtaposition, touching, abutment, meeting.

v be contiguous, join, adjoin, abut on, border, touch, meet, graze, adhere; coincide, coexist.

adj contiguous, touching, in contact, end to end; close, near.

200 length *n* distance, extent, longitude, span, reach, range; lengthiness, elongation, size; duration, continuance, term, period.

v be long, stretch out, sprawl; extend to, reach to, stretch to; lengthen, stretch, elongate, extend; prolong, protract, draw out, spin out.

adj long, lengthy, extended, outstretched; lengthened, interminable; linear, lineal, longitudinal; tall, stringy, protracted, lanky.

adv lengthwise, at length, longitudinally.

201 shortness *n* brevity, littleness; shortening, abridgment, abbreviation, conciseness, condensation; retrenchment, curtailment, reduction.

v be short; shorten, abridge, abbreviate, condense, compact, compress, epitomize; retrench, cut short, reduce, pare down, clip back, cut back, prune, shear, shave, crop, chop up, hack up, truncate.

adj short, brief, curt; compendious, compact, compressed, condensed; stubby, stunted, stumpy, squat, dumpy; concise, pointed; curtailed, cut back, reduced, shortened, abbreviated, abridged.

202 breadth. thickness *n* breadth, width, latitude, amplitude, extent, diameter.

thickness, density, denseness, heaviness, bulk, body.

v be broad; expand, widen. be thick; thicken.

adj broad, wide, ample, extended, expansive, large; outspread, outstretched.

thick, dense, heavy, bulky, solid, compact; dumpy, squat, thickset.

203 narrowness. thinness *n* narrowness, slenderness, exiguity, closeness, straitness, scantiness, slightness, slimness.

thinness, slenderness, slimness, leanness, lankness, meagerness, skinniness.

v be narrow; narrow, taper. be thin; thin, slenderize, slim; dilute, water down.

adj narrow, close, slender, thin, fine, threadlike, slim, delicate; restricted, confined, limited; thin, emaciated, lean, skinny, meager, gaunt, spindly, lanky, scrawny, haggard, pinched, skeletal, wasted; frail, unsound, fragile; weak, shrill, faint, feeble; watery, waterish, diluted, unsubstantial.

204 layer *n* stratum, substratum, bed, zone, floor, stage, story, tier, slab, tablet, board, sheet, platter; scale, coat, peel, membrane, film, leaf, slice.

v slice, shave, pare, peel; plate, coat, veneer; cover; layer.

adj layered, stratified, tiered; scaly, filmy, membranous, flaky.

205 filament *n* thread, fiber, strand, hair, cilia, tendril, gossamer, wire, strand, vein.

adj fibrous, threadlike, wiry, stringy, ropy; capillary.

206 height *n* altitude, stature, elevation, tallness; prominence, eminence, pre-eminence, loftiness, sublimity; top, peak, pinnacle, acme, summit, zenith, culmination.

v tower, soar, hover, cap, command; mount, bestride, surmount, overhang; heighten, elevate, raise up, rise up.

adj high, tall, elevated, towering, skyscraping, gigantic, huge, colossal; distinguished, prominent, eminent, pre-eminent, exalted, lofty, sublime; overhanging, overlying.

207 lowness *n* depression, debasement, prostration; flatness, proneness; lowlands, flatlands.

v be low; lie low, lie flat, crouch, slouch, wallow, grovel; underlie; lower, depress.

adj low, flat, level, low-lying; crouched, squat, prone, supine, prostrate, depressed; groveling, abject, sordid, mean, base, lowly, degraded, debased, ignoble, vile.

adv under, beneath, underneath, below, down, downward; underfoot, underground; downstairs, belowstairs.

208 depth *n* deepness, profundity, obscurity; depression, bottom, unfathomable space; pit, hollow, shaft, well, crater, chasm, abyss, bottomless pit; central part, midst, middle, bosom, womb, base, heart, core; soundings, draft, submersion, dive.

v deepen, hollow, plunge, sink, dig, excavate; sound, have the lead, take soundings.

adj deep, deep-seated, profound, mysterious, obscure, unfathomable; sunk, buried, submerged; bottomless, soundless, fathomless, unfathomed, abysmal, yawning, gaping.

adv beyond one's depth, out of one's depth, over one's head.

209 shallowness *n* superficiality, banality, triviality, frivolity, flimsiness, emptiness, vacancy; shallow, shoal, sand bar.

adj shallow, superficial, slight, cursory, trivial, banal, trashy, flimsy, substanceless, empty, vacuous, vacant; skin deep, ankle-deep, knee-deep.

210 summit *n* top, peak, apex, pinnacle, vertex, acme, culmination, zenith; height, pitch, maximum, climax; crowning point, turning point, watershed.

v culminate, climax, crown, top.

adj highest, top, topmost, uppermost, tiptop; capital, head, polar; supreme, supernal.

211 base *n* bottom, stand, rest, pedestal, dado, understructure, substructure, foot, basis, foundation, ground, groundwork; principle, touchstone, fundamental part, element, ingredient; bottom, nadir, foot, sole, heel.

adj bottom, undermost, nethermost; fundamental, basic, elemental; based on, founded on, grounded on, built on; base, vile, venal.

212 verticality *n* perpendicularity, erectness; wall, precipice, cliff.

v be vertical, stand up straight, stand upright, stand erect, stand straight and tall.

adj vertical, upright, erect, perpendicular, straight, bolt upright, plumb.

adv vertically, on end, endwise.

213 horizontality *n* flatness; level, plane, stratum; horizon; recumbency, lying down, reclination, proneness, supination, prostration.

v be horizontal, lie, recline, lie down, lie flat, sprawl; render horizontal, flatten, level, prostrate, knock down, floor, fell.

adj horizontal, level, even, plane, flat, smooth; prone, supine, prostrate.

adv horizontally, on one's back.

214 suspension *n* hanging down, free swinging; pendant, tail, train, flap, pendulum.

v suspend, hang, swing, dangle; flap, trail, flow; depend.

adj suspended, pendent, hanging, swinging, dangling, pendulous; dependent.

215 support *n* foundation, base, basis, ground, footing, hold; supporter, prop, brace, stay, rib, truss, stalk, stilts, splint; bar, rod, boom, outrigger; staff, stick, crutch; bracket, ledge, shelf, trestle, buttress.

v support, bear, carry, hold, sustain, shoulder, bolster; shore up, hold up, prop up, brace; help, aid, maintain, sustain; base, found, ground.

adj supporting, supported; fundamental.

216 parallelism *n* coextension; comparison, affinity, correspondence, semblance, likeness, resemblance, analogy, equation.

v parallel, compare, relate, associate, connect, correspond to, equate.

adj parallel, coextensive, collateral, aligned, equal; like, similar, allied, corresponding, correlative, analogous, equivalent.

217 obliquity *n* incline, inclination, slope, slant, leaning, tilt, list, bend, curve; acclivity, rise, ascent, grade, rising ground, hill, bank; declivity, decline, downhill, dip, fall; steepness.

v be oblique, slope, slant, lean, incline, stoop, decline, descend; bend, careen, slouch, sidle; render oblique, sway, bias, slant, warp, incline, bend, crook, tilt, distort.

adj oblique, inclined; sloping, tilted; askew, asquint, awry, crooked; uphill, rising, ascending; downhill, falling, descending; declining, declivitous; steep, abrupt, sharp, precipitous; diagonal, transverse.

adv obliquely, on one side; askew, askance, edgewise, at an angle; sidelong, sideways, slantwise.

218 inversion *n* subversion, reversion, contraposition, transposition, transposal, conversion; contrariety, contradiction, opposition, polarity, antithesis; reversal, overturn, somersault, turn of the tide, revulsion, revolution.

v be inverted, turn about, wheel about, go about, turn over, go over, tilt over; invert, subvert, reverse, overturn, upturn, upset, turn topsy-turvy; transpose.

adj inverted, inside out, wrong side out, upside down, topsy-turvy; inverse, reverse, obverse, opposite.

adv inversely.

219 crossing *n* intersection, grade crossing, crossroad, interchange; network, reticulation; net, netting, network, web, mesh, wicker, lace; mat, matting, plait, trellis, lattice, grating, grille, gridiron, tracery, fretwork, filigree; knot, entanglement.

v cross, intersect, interlace, intertwine, interweave, interlink, crisscross; twine, intwine, weave, twist, wreathe; dovetail, splice, link, link up; mat, plait, plat, braid; tangle, entangle, ravel; net, knot, twist.

adj crossing; crossed, matted, transverse; weaved, woven, intertwined, interlaced.

220 exteriority *n* outside, exterior; surface, superficies; covering, skin, face, appearance, façade, aspect, facet.

v be exterior, lie around, encircle.

adj exterior, external, outer, outside, outward, superficial; outlying, extraneous, foreign, extrinsic.

adv externally, out, over, outwards.

221 interiority *n* interior, inside, inner part, center, interspace; subsoil, substratum, contents, substance, pith, marrow, backbone, heart, bowels, belly, guts, lap, womb; recesses, innermost recesses, hollows, nook, niche, cave.

v be interior, be inside; inclose, circumscribe; intern; embed, insert.

adj interior, internal, inside, inner, inward, inmost, innermost; deep-seated, inlaid, embedded, ingrained, innate, inherent, intrinsic, inborn; private, secret, intimate, confidential; home, domestic.

adv internally; inward, within, indoors, withindoors.

222 centrality *n* center, middle, midst; core, kernel, nucleus, heart, pole, axis, pivot, navel, nub, hub; centralization; center of gravity.

v be central; centralize, concentrate; focus on, bring into focus, get to the heart of.

adj central, middle, pivotal, focal, concentric; middlemost.

adv centrally; middle, midst.

223 covering *n* cover; canopy, awning, tent, marquee; umbrella, parasol, sunshade; shade, screen, shield; roof, ceiling, thatch, shed; top, lid; bandage, wrappings; coverlet, blanket, sheet, quilt, tarpaulin; skin, fleece, fur, hide; clothing, mask; peel, crust, bark, rind; veneer, coating, facing, varnish.

v cover, superimpose, overlay, overspread; wrap, encase, face, case, veneer, paper; conceal, cover over.

adj covered, clothed, wrapped; protected.

224 lining *n* inner coating, coating; filling, stuffing, padding, wadding.

v line, stuff, wad, pad, fill; coat, incrust, face, cover.

adj lined.

225 dress *n* clothing, covering, raiment, drapery, costume, attire, garb, apparel, wardrobe, outfit, clothes; equipment, livery, gear, rigging, trappings, togs, accouterments; uniforms, regimentals, suit.

v dress, clothe, drape, robe, array, fit out, deck out, garb, rig out, apparel; equip, harness, outfit, uniform; cover, wrap, wrap up, sheathe, swathe, swaddle.

adj dressed, clothed, clad, invested.

226 undress *n* nudity, nakedness, bareness, dishabille.

v undress, uncover, divest, expose, disrobe, strip, bare, doff, peel, take off, put off, lay open.

adj undressed, nude, naked, bare, stark-naked, exposed, in the buff, *au naturel*, in the altogether, in one's birthday suit; undressed, unclad, undraped, disrobed.

227 environment *n* environs, surroundings, outskirts, suburbs, purlieus, precincts, neighborhood.

v environ, surround, encompass, compass, inclose, enclose, circle, encircle, gird, twine round, hem in.

adj surrounding, circumjacent.

adv around, about; without; on every side, on all sides, right and left, every which way.

228 interspersion *n* interjacence, interlocation, interpenetration, permeation; interjection, interpolation, interlineation, intercalation; intervention, interference, interposition, intrusion; insinuation; insertion.

v intervene, come between, get between, interpenetrate; intersperse, permeate, introduce, throw in, work in, interpose, interject, interpolate, insert; interfere, intrude, obtrude.

adj intervening, interjacent; parenthetical, episodic; intrusive.

adv between, betwixt, among, amid, amongst; in the thick of, betwixt and between, parenthetically.

229 circumscription *n* limitation, enclosure; confinement, restraint.

v circumscribe, limit, bound, confine, inclose; surround, hedge in, fence in, wall in; imprison, restrain; enfold, bury, incase.

adj circumscribed, confined, restrained, imprisoned; buried in, immersed in, embosomed, embedded.

230 outline *n* circumference, perimeter, periphery; circuit, lines, contour, profile, silhouette.

v outline, draw, sketch, trace, profile.

231 edge *n* frame, fringe, trimming, trim, edging, skirting, hem; verge, brink, brim, lip, margin, border, skirt, rim, mouth; threshold, door, porch, portal; coast, shore.

v edge, skirt, border; trim, hem.

232 enclosure *n* envelope, case, wrapper; girdle; pen, fence, fold, cote, corral, stockyard, paddock, yard, pound, compound; fence, pale, paling, balustrade, rail, railing; hedge; wall, barrier, barricade; gate, gateway, door, doorway; boundary, border.

v enclose, circumscribe.

233 limit *n* boundary, bounds, extent, confine, term, pale, verge; termination, terminus; frontier, marches, outer edges, unknown; boundary line, border, edge; turning point, flood gate.

v limit, restrain, restrict, confine, check, hinder, bound, circumscribe, define.

adj limited, definite; terminal.

adv thus far, only so far, thus far and no further.

234 front *n* forefront, foreground, lead; face, frontage, façade, frontispiece, proscenium; vanguard, front rank, first rank, head of the column, advanced guard.

v front, face, confront; be in front, stand in front; come to the front.

adj fore, foremost; front, frontal, anterior, forward.

adv before, in front, in advance; ahead, right ahead, in the foreground; in the lead.

235 rear *n* back, background, rearguard, rear rank; distance, hinterland; rump, buttocks, posterior, rear, backside, hindquarters; wake, train; reverse, other side of the coin, (*informal*) flipside.

v be behind, bring up the rear; rear, bring up, nurture, raise; elevate, lift, loft, lift up, hold up; build, put up, erect.

adj rear, back, hindmost; posterior.

adv behind, in the rear, in the background, at the heels; after, aft, rearward.

236 side *n* laterality, flank, quarter, lee, hand; cheek, jowl, shoulder; profile, lee side, broadside.

v be on the side; be side by side, be cheek to cheek; flank, skirt, outflank, sidle.

adj sidelong, lateral; flanking, skirting; flanked.

adv sideways, sidelong; broadside, on one side, abreast, alongside, beside, side by side, cheek by jowl; laterally.

237 opposition *n* opposite, contraposition, opposite side, opposite poles, polarity, antithesis, reverse, inverse; counterpart, companion piece, complement.

v be opposite; stand as opposites, oppose.

adj opposite, reverse, inverse, converse; antipodal, antithetical, countering, opposing; fronting, facing, diametrically opposite; complementary.

adv over, over the way, over against; poles apart; face to face.

238 right *n* right hand, right side; offside, starboard.

adj right-handed, dextral.

239 left *n* left hand, left side; near side, port.

adj left-handed, sinistral.

III. Form

240 form *n* shape, outline, mold, appearance, cast, cut, configuration; make, formation, frame, construction, cut, set, build, trim; mold, model, pattern; posture, attitude, convention, rule, formality, formula, ceremony, conformity.

v form, shape, figure, fashion, carve, cut, chisel, hew, cast; shape, model, mold, fashion, cast, construct, build; stamp, cast, type.

adj formal, ceremonial, ceremonious, conventional; regular, set, fixed, stiff, rigid.

241 formlessness *n* shapelessness, amorphism, asymmetry; disorder, chaos; misproportion, deformity, disfigurement, defacement, mutilation, truncation.

v deface, disfigure, deform, mutilate, truncate.

adj formless, shapeless, amorphous, asymmetrical, unformed, unshaped, unfashioned, unshapely, misshapen, out of proportion, disordered, chaotic; rough, rude, coarse, barbarous, rugged.

242 [regularity of form] **symmetry** *n* shapeliness, finish, comeliness, gracefulness, grace, beauty; proportion, uniformity, parallelism; regularity, evenness, balance, order, harmony, agreement.

adj symmetrical, shapely, well set, finished; beautiful, lovely; classic, classical, formal, chaste, severe; regular, uniform, balanced, harmonious, ordered; even, parallel, equal.

243 [irregularity of form] **distortion** *n* contortion, warp, buckle, screw, twist; crookedness, obliquity; deformity, malformation, misproportion, disfigurement, monstrosity, ugliness; asymmetry.

v distort, contort, warp, buckle, screw, twist, wrest; writhe, grimace, make faces; deform, disfigure, misshape.

adj distorted, out of shape, irregular, unsymmetrical, awry, askew, crooked; not true, not straight, uneven; misshapen, ill-made, ill-fashioned, ill-proportioned, malformed, deformed.

244 angularity *n* bifurcation, bend, fork, crook, notch, angle; elbow, knee, knuckle, crotch; right angle, acute angle, obtuse angle; corner, nook, niche, recess.

v angle, tilt, bend, fork, bifurcate.

adj angular, bent, crooked, jagged, serrated; forked, bifurcate, cornered, V-shaped, hooked; akimbo.

245 curvature *n* curve, incurvature, bend; flexure, bending, crook, hook;

deflection, turn, deviation, detour, sweep, curl, winding; curve, arc, arch, arcade, vault, bow, crescent, half-moon, horse-shoe, loop; parabola, hyperbola.

v be curved, sweep, sag; deviate, turn; render curved, bend, curve, deflect, inflect, crook; turn, round, arch, arch over, bow, curl, coil, recurve.

adj curved, bowed, vaulted, hooked, arched, arced; circular, nonlinear, semi-circular, rounded, crescent, crescent-shaped, lunar, demi-lune.

246 straightness *n* directness; inflexibility, stiffness; straight line, direct line, bee line.

v be straight, go straight; render straight, straighten, rectify, correct, right; put right, put straight, unbend, unfold, uncurl, unravel.

adj straight, even, true, unbent, direct, rectilinear, linear, not curved, uncurved; square, erect, perpendicular, vertical, upright; candid, forthright, definite, reliable, plain, blunt, frank, sure, positive, irrefutable, certain, unequivocal, inescapable; honest, honorable, fair, just, equitable, impartial, aboveboard, reputable, scrupulous, worthy, lawful, licit, conscientious, decent, ethical; correct, sound, sane, accurate, true; sober, conventional, provincial, (*informal*) unhip, (*informal*) square, (*informal*) not with it.

247 [simple circularity] **circularity** *n* roundness, rotundity; circle, ring, hoop, areola; bracelet, armlet; eye, loop, wheel, cycle, orb, orbit; zone, belt, cord, band, sash, girdle, circuit; wreath, garland, crown, corona, coronet; necklace, collar; ellipse, oval.

v round; go around, encircle, circle.

adj round, rounded, circular, oval, elliptic, elliptical, egg-shaped.

248 [complex circularity] **convolution** *n* involution, winding, wave, undulation, sinuosity, meandering, twist, twirl; coil, roll, curl, buckle, spiral, corkscrew, worm, tendril; serpent, snake, eel; maze, labyrinth.

v wind, twine, entwine, twirl, wave, undulate, meander, turn; twist, coil, roll; wrinkle, curl, frizz, frizzle; wring, contort.

adj convoluted, winding, twisted; wavy, undulating, circling, snaky, serpentine; involved, intricate, complex, complicated, labyrinthine, tortuous, mazy; spiral, coiled.

adv in and out, round and round.

249 rotundity *n* roundness, cylindricality, sphericity, globularity; cylinder, barrel, drum; roll, roller, rolling pin; sphere, globe, ball, spheroid, globule; bulb, pellet, pill, marble, pea, knob, pommel.

v sphere, form into a sphere, roll into a ball, round.

adj rotund, round, circular, ball-shaped; cylindrical, spherical, globular; egg-shaped, pear-shaped, ovoid.

250 convexity *n* prominence, projection, swelling, bulge, protuberance, protrusion; hump, hunch, bunch; knob, node, nodule, bump, clump; pimple, pustule, pock, growth, polyp, blister, boil; nipple, teat, pap, breast; nose, beak, snout, nozzle; peg, button, stud, ridge; cupola, dome, arch; relief, high relief, low relief; hill, mountain, cape, ness, promontory, headland; jetty, ledge, spur.

v project, bulge, protrude, jut out, stand out, stick out, stick up, start up, shoot up, swell up; raise; emboss.

adj convex, prominent, protuberant; bossed, nodular, bunchy, hummocky, bulbous, swollen, swelling, bloated, bowed, arched, bellied; salient, in relief, raised.

251 flatness *n* smoothness, evenness; plane, level; plate, platter, table, tablet, slab.

v flatten, level, even off.

adj flat, plane, even, smooth; level, smooth, horizontal; flat as a pancake.

252 concavity *n* depression, dip, hollow, indentation, dent, cavity, dint, dimple; excavation, pit, trough; cup, basin, crater; valley, vale, dale, dell, glade, grove, glen, cave, cavern.

v render concave, depress, hollow, scoop, scoop out, gouge; dig, delve, excavate, mine, stave in, tunnel.

adj concave, hollow, hollowed out; indented, dented, sunken, cupped; cavernous, rounded inward, incurved.

253 sharpness *n* acuteness, pointedness; point, spike, spine, needle, pin, prick, prickle, spur, barb, thorn; knife edge, cutting edge, razor edge.

v be sharp, taper to a point; sharpen, point, whet, barb, strop, grind, whittle.

adj sharp, keen, acute, trenchant; pointed, peaked, conical, spiked, spiky, tapering; studded, prickly, barbed, spiny, thorny, bristling, thistly; craggy, snaggy; cutting, sharp edged, razor sharp.

254 bluntness *n* dullness; obtuseness, roughness.

v be blunt; render blunt, dull, take off the point, round the edge.

adj blunt, dull, obtuse, dimwitted; rough, gruff; rounded, round, unsharpened, unpointed.

255 smoothness *n* polish, gloss; lubrication, lubricity.

v smooth, plane, file, scrape, shave, sand, sandpaper; level, press, flatten, roll; iron, steam press; polish, burnish, rub, wax, sleek, buff, glaze; lubricate, oil, grease.

adj smooth, polished, glossy, shiny, sleek, silken, silky; even, level, sanded; soft, downy, velvety; slippery, glassy, oily.

256 roughness *n* asperity, irregularity, corrugation, nodulation; grain, texture, pile, nap.

v roughen, rough up, crinkle, ruffle, rumple, crumple.

adj rough, uneven, irregular, rugged, scabrous, knotted, craggy, gnarled; shaggy, coarse, hairy, bristly, hirsute; scraggly, prickly, bushy; unpolished, unsmooth, rough-hewn, textured; downy, velvety, fluffy, woolly.

adv against the grain.

257 notch *n* dent, nick, cut, scratch, indentation; saw, tooth, scallop.

v notch, nick, cut, scratch, indent, jag, scarify, scallop.

adj notched, toothed, serrated.

258 fold *n* plait, ply, crease, pleat, tuck; wrinkle, ripple, rimple, pucker, ruffle.

v fold, double, plait, crumple, crease, pleat, wrinkle, crinkle, ripple, curl, rumple, frizzle, rimple, ruffle, pucker, corrugate; tuck, hem, gather.

adj folded.

259 furrow *n* groove, rut, scratch, streak, cut, crack, score, incision, slit; channel, gutter, trench, gulley, ditch, dike, moat, trough; ravine, valley.

v furrow, dig, plow; channel, flute, groove, incise, cut, engrave, etch, seam, cleave, score; wrinkle, knit, pucker.

adj furrowed, ribbed, striated, fluted.

260 opening *n* hole, gap, aperture, orifice, perforation, pinhole, peephole, keyhole; slot, slit, rift, breach, cleft, chasm, fissure, rent; outlet, inlet, vent; portal, porch, gate, hatch, door, doorway, gateway; way, path, channel, passage.

v open, ope, gape, yawn; perforate, pierce, tap, bore, drill; mine, tunnel, dig to daylight; impale, spike, spear, gore, spit, stab, puncture, lance, stick, prick, riddle; uncover, unclose, lay bare, expose, bare, reveal; lay open, cut open, rip open, throw open.

adj open, unclosed, uncovered, exposed; ajar, wide-open, gaping, yawning; perforated, porous, reticulated, permeable; accessible, available, public.

261 closure *n* blockade, shutting up, obstruction, stoppage, clogging, sealing, plugging; contraction; constipation; culmination; cessation, completion, termination, windup; lid, top, cap, stopper, plug, barrier.

v close, plug, block up, stop up, fill up, cork up, cork, button up, stuff up, shut up, dam up; blockade, obstruct, hinder; bar, bolt, stop, seal, choke, throttle, shut.

adj closed, shut, unopened; unpierced, impervious, impermeable; impenetrable, impassable, pathless; tight, snug, airtight, unventilated, watertight, hermetically sealed.

262 perforator *n* piercer, borer, auger, drill, awl, scoop, corkscrew, probe, lancet, scalpel, needle, pin, stiletto, puncher, hole puncher, gouge; knife, spear, bayonet.

263 stopper *n* lid, cap, cover; cork, spike, stopcock, pin, plug, tap, faucet, valve, spigot, rammer, ramrod; wadding, stuffing, padding, stopping, bandage, tourniquet.

IV. Motion

264 motion *n* movement, action, activity, move, going; progress, locomotion; mobilization, mobility, movableness, motive power; unrest, restlessness; stream, flow, flux, run, course, stir; rate, pace, step, tread, stride, gait; velocity, speed.

v move, go, hie, budge, stir, pass, flit; hover around, hover about; shift, slide, glide, roll, roll on, flow, drift, stream, run, sweep along; wander, meander, browse, stroll, walk, perambulate; dodge, keep on one's toes, keep moving, hit the road, (*informal*) truck; move, impel, propel; mobilize.

adj moving, in motion, traveling, on the road; transitional, shifting, mobile, movable; mercurial, restless, unquiet, nomadic, transient.

adv under way; on the move, on the go, on the march.

265 rest *n* quiescence, stillness, quietude, calm, calmness, tranquillity, repose, serenity, peace, silence; pause, lull, cessation; stagnation, immobility, fixity.

v rest, be still, stand still, lie still, stand immobile, keep quiet, repose; remain, stay, pause, wait, mark time, hold, halt, stop short, cease, desist, discontinue, stop; stagnate, be inactive, immobilize; dwell, settle, settle down, establish roots; alight, arrive; stand fast, stand firm, stick fast; quell, becalm, hush, stay, lull, lull to sleep, tranquilize.

adj restful, quiescent, still, calm, tranquil, peaceful, undisturbed, unruffled, serene, silent; motionless, fixed, stationary; unmoved, stable, at rest, at a standstill, stock-still, sleeping, dormant, inactive, stagnant.

266 [locomotion by land] **journey** *n* traveling, travel, excursion, tour, trip, expedition, jaunt, pilgrimage; wayfaring, roving, gadding about, (*informal*) bumming around, nomadism, vagabondism; migration, immigration, moving; walk, promenade, constitutional, stroll, peregrination, perambulation, march, stroll, saunter, jaunt, outing, hike, airing; horsemanship, horseback riding; drive, driving, motoring, ride, spin; cycling, biking; procession, cavalcade, caravan, file, cortege, column.

v journey, travel, tour, take a trip; flit, take wing, (*informal*) hit the road, rove, ramble, roam, prowl, (*informal*) bum, (*informal*) bum around, range, traverse, scour the country, wander, meander, saunter, gad about; move, migrate, immigrate.

adj journeying, traveling, on the road; itinerant, peripatetic, rambling, roving, gadding, flitting, vagrant, nomadic, migratory, wayfaring.

267 [locomotion by water or air] **navigation** *n* voyage, sail, cruise, passage, boat ride; aquatics, boating, yachting, sailing, shipping.

flight, air travel, flying, gliding; aeronautics, aviation.

v navigate; sail, put to sea, embark, shove off, spread the sails, make sail, take oar; go boating, cruise, float, drift, coast; row, paddle, pull, scull, punt, steam; ride the waves.

fly, take off, take wing, take to the skies; aviate, soar, glide, fly over, plane, jet.

adj sailing, nautical, naval, maritime, seagoing, seafaring, ocean-going; afloat; navigable.

flying, jetting; aloft, in flight; aviational, aeronautical, aerial.

268 traveler *n* wayfarer, journeyer, rover, rambler, wanderer, free spirit, nomad, vagabond, bohemian, gypsy, itinerant, vagrant, tramp, hobo, straggler, waif; pilgrim, palmer, seeker, quester; voyager, passenger, tourist, sightseer, excursionist, vacationer, globe-trotter, jet-setter; immigrant, emigrant, refugee, fugitive; pedestrian, walker, cyclist, biker, rider, horsewoman, horseman, equestrian, driver.

269 mariner, flier *n* mariner, sailor, seaman, seafaring man, sea dog; pilot, skipper, captain, commander, helmsman, steersman; crew, hands, mates; navigator, flier, airman, aviator, aviatrix, pilot, skipper; astronaut, cosmonaut, spaceman.

270 transference *n* transfer, move, shift, transit, transition, passage, transmission, transport, transplantation, transposition; removal, relegation, deportation, extradition.

v transfer, transmit, transport, convey, carry, bear, pass; move, shift, conduct, convey, bring, fetch, reach; send, delegate, consign, turn over, hand over, deliver; transpose, transplant, displace, remove, relegate, deport, extradite; shovel, ladle.

adj transferable, transmittable, transmissible, transportable, movable, portable.

271 carrier *n* porter, bearer, messenger, runner, courier; postman, letter carrier; conductor, conveyor, transporter; freighter, ship, barge; train, locomotive; truck, vehicle, carriage; beast of burden.

272 vehicle *n* conveyance, carriage, transportation, rig; car, motorcar, automobile, (*informal*) wheels, truck; wagon, cart, coach, chaise, buggy; bicycle, bike, motorcycle, motorscooter; train, sleeping car, cattle car, boxcar.

273 ship *n* vessel, boat, liner, freighter, steamer, schooner, sailboat, motorboat, merchant ship, barge, tugboat, tanker, trawler, yacht, cruiser, yawl, ketch, brig, brigantine, square-rigger, sloop, cutter, launch; navy, fleet.

airplane, plane, jet, jumbo jet, aircraft, glider, helicopter, dirigible, blimp, balloon, spaceship, capsule, module, space station.

274 velocity *n* rapidity, quickness, swiftness, celerity, speed, alacrity; acceleration, pickup; spurt, rush, dash, race, flying, flight.

v move quickly, speed, hie, hasten, post, scamper, run, race, shoot, tear, whisk, sweep, rush, dash, dash off; bolt, bound, spring, dart, flit; hurry, hasten, haste, accelerate, (*informal*) turn on the juice, quicken, speed up, take off like a shot.

adj fast, speedy, swift, rapid, quick, brisk, fleet; nimble, agile, expeditious, light-footed, fast as a bullet, quick as lightning.

adv swiftly, apace, at full speed, at full gallop, posthaste.

275 slowness *n* languor, sluggishness, slackness, sloth, indolence; deliberateness, moderation, leisureliness; tardiness.

v move slowly, creep, crawl, lag, drawl, linger, loiter, saunter, trail, drag, dawdle; plod, trudge, lumber; grovel, sneak, steal, worm one's way, inch; waddle, wobble, shuffle, hobble, limp, shamble, amble, traipse, slouch, mince, mince steps, halt; flag, totter, teeter, stagger; retard, hinder, impede, obstruct; slacken, check, relax, moderate; brake, curb, slow, put on the brakes.

adj slow, slack, late, tardy; gentle, easy, unhurried, deliberate, gradual, moderate, leisurely; languid, sluggish, indolent, lazy; tedious, humdrum, dull, boring; dense, stupid.

adv slowly, leisurely; at half speed, at a snail's pace; gradually, little by little, step by step, inch by inch, bit by bit, one step at a time.

276 impulse *n* impetus, implosion, push, thrust, shove; propulsion; sudden impulse, yearning, craving; reaction, response, reflex; collision, clash, encounter, shock, bump, crash; impact; blow, stroke, knock, rap, tap, slap, smack, pat, dab; hit, whack, thwack, slam, punch, belt, kick, thump, cut, thrust, lunge.

v impel, push, urge, thrust, shove, heave, prod, shoulder, jostle, hustle, hurtle, jog, jolt; start, give a start to, set going, get going, drive; run against, bump against, butt against; collide with, run into, bang into, butt; strike, knock, bang, hit, thump, beat, slam, dash, punch, thwack, whack; batter, pelt, buffet, butt; hit, rap, slap, tap, pat, dab.

277 recoil *n* reflex, rebound, ricochet, boomerang, backfire, backlash; snap, elasticity; reverberation, resonance; reaction, response, rebuff, repulse, revulsion.

v recoil, rebound, ricochet, boomerang, snap back, spring back, fly back; react, respond; reverberate, echo, quiver.

adj reactionary; elastic, backfiring.

278 direction *n* bearing, course, set, drift, tenor, trend, tendency, inclination; tack, aim, determination, intention; points of the compass, cardinal points; line, path, road, range, line of march; alignment.

v direct, point, aim; tend toward, point toward, conduct to, go to; bend, tend, verge, incline, determine; steer for, make for, aim at, level at, set one's sights on, take aim, hold a course for, be bound for.

adj direct, straight; bound for; undeviating, unswerving.

adv toward, on the road to; hither, thither, whither; directly, straight, straightforward, point-blank, on a line with.

279 deviation *n* diversion, digression, departure from, aberration; divergence, zigzag, detour, circuit; warp, refraction; swerving.

v deviate, alter one's course, turn, bend, curve, swerve, heel, bear off; divert, deflect, shift, shunt, draw aside, crook, warp; stray, straggle, digress, ramble, rove, drift, go astray, go adrift; wander, wind, twist, meander; veer, turn aside, change direction, steer clear of, dodge.

adj deviating, errant, aberrant; discursive, desultory, loose, rambling, digressive, stray, erratic, undirected; circuitous, indirect, zigzag, roundabout, crooked.

adv astray, roundabout, wide of the mark; circuitously.

280 [going before] **precedence** *n* priority; leading, heading, the lead, van, vanguard; precursor, coming beforehand.

v precede, go before, forerun; usher in, introduce, herald; head, take the lead, lead the way; take precedence, have priority, come first, come before.

adv in advance, before, ahead, in the vanguard, in front.

281 [going after] **sequence** *n* coming after, following, sequel; shadow, dangler, train.

v follow, come in sequence, go after; attend, be attendant on, follow in the steps of, follow in the wake of, trail, shadow; pursue; lag, fall behind.

adj following; sequential.

adv behind, after; in the rear.

282 [motion forward] **progression** *n* progress, improvement, proceeding, advance, advancement, headway; growth, rise, increase, development.

v proceed, advance, progress, get on, get along, gain ground, press onward, forge ahead, make headway, make progress, make strides, stride forward; grow, develop, increase, improve.

adj advancing; progressive, advanced.

adv forward, onward; forth, on, ahead.

283 [motion backward] **regression** *n* retrogression, retreat, recession, retirement, withdrawal; reflux, backwater, return, recoil; backsliding; deterioration, decrease, fall.

v regress, recede, return, revert, retreat, back out, back down, turn back, fall back, drop out, retire, withdraw; lose ground, drop off, fall behind; ebb, shrink, shy.

adj retrograde, retrogressive; regressive, refluent, reflex.

adv backwards; aboutface.

284 propulsion *n* propulsive force, impulse, push, projection, thrust, drive, impulsion, impetus; throw, fling, toss, shot, discharge.

v propel, project, throw, fling, cast, pitch, chuck, toss, heave, hurl; drive, sling, push, shove; send off, fire off, discharge, shoot, launch, let fly; put in motion, set in motion, start, get going, impel; expel.

adj propulsive.

285 traction *n* drawing, hauling, pulling, towing, towage; yank, tug, drag, jerk.

v draw, pull, haul, lug, drag, tug, tow, trail, train, take in tow; wrench, jerk, yank.

adj tractile; in tow.

286 [motion towards] **approach** *n* access, advent, advance; nearness, approximation.

v approach, near, draw near, move towards, get close to; gain on, get closer to; pursue, trail.

adj approaching; approximate; impending, imminent.

287 [motion from] **recession** *n* retirement, withdrawal; flight, removal, retreat; regression, return, falling back, regress; reaction, reversal, recoil; departure, leave-taking.

v recede, move back, go back, move away from, retire, withdraw; drift, abate, fade, wane, ebb, subside, drift away, fall back, shrink; react, revert, relapse, recoil, regress; run away, fly, avoid.

288 attraction *n* attractiveness, inclination, affinity; pull, magnetism, gravity.

v attract, draw, drag, pull, magnetize, exert force; interest, invite, engage, fascinate, lure, allure, charm, decoy, bait.

adj attractive, attracting, enticing, seductive, alluring; have pull, magnetic, gravitational.

289 repulsion *n* aversion, antipathy, dislike; repulse, rebuff.

v repel, push back, drive away, chase away, rebuff, beat back; repulse, revolt, offend, sicken, disgust, displease, irritate.

adj repulsive, repellent, averse, repelling.

290 convergence *n* confluence, conflux, concurrence, concourse, congress, coming together, meeting, joining.

v converge, concur, come together, meet, join, unite; gather together, concentrate, center.

adj convergent, confluent, concurrent.

291 divergence *n* division, radiation, spread, severance, separation, refraction, deflection; ramification, furcation, branching, forking, detachment; deviation, aberration, disparity, difference, variance, heterogeneity.

v diverge, ramify, radiate, branch off, fork, spread, swerve, scatter, disperse; divide, separate, part, sever; vary, deviate, dissent, disagree.

adj divergent, radial, radiant, centrifugal.

292 arrival *n* advent, coming; reaching, attainment, landing, debarkation, disembarkation; reception, welcome, welcoming.

v arrive, get to, come to, reach a point, attain, complete; light, alight, dismount; land, disembark, debark, deplane, detrain.

293 departure *n* embarkation; outset, start, starting point, place of departure, point of departure; removal, exit; exodus, flight; leave-taking, valediction, *adieu*, farewell, goodbye.

v depart, go away, take one's leave, start, set out, leave, retire, quit, withdraw, absent, go, (*informal*) split, take off, (*informal*) cut out, move off, move out, ship out, pack it up; vacate, evacuate, abandon; sally, set forth, set forward, go forth; embark, set sail, put out to sea, shove off, get under way, enplane, entrain.

294 [motion into] **ingress** *n* entrance, entry; influx, intrusion, inroad, incursion, invasion, irruption, penetration, infiltration; insinuation, insertion.

v enter, come in, pour in, flow in; burst in, break in, invade, intrude; penetrate, infiltrate, insinuate oneself.

adj incoming, inbound.

295 [motion out of] **egress** *n* exit, issue; emergence, emanation; outbreak, outburst, eruption; evacuation, leakage, percolation, oozing, drainage, drain; outpouring, gush, effluence, effusion, discharge.

v emerge, emanate, issue; pass out of, come out of, pour out of, flow out of; exude, leak, ooze, drain, drip, trickle, dribble; gush, gush out, pour out, spout, flow out, discharge; escape, find vent.

adj outgoing, outward, outbound.

296 [motion into, actively] **reception** *n* admission, admittance, entry, entrée; importation, introduction, initiation, induction, absorption; ingestion, eating, drinking; suction, sucking; insertion, injection.

v give entrance to, admit, introduce, usher, initiate, induct; receive, import, bring in, ingest, absorb, imbibe.

297 [motion out of, actively] **ejection** *n* rejection, expulsion, eviction, dislodgment, banishment, exile; emission, effusion, discharge, evacuation, regurgitation, elimination.

v reject, eject, expel, evict, dislodge, banish, exile; push aside, push away, turn away, brush aside; empty, drain, clear out, clean out, purge, void, evacuate; vomit, spew, regurgitate, throw up, (*informal*) puke, retch, (*informal*) barf, belch out, burp out; discharge, eliminate, discard, get rid of, do away with, cast off, cut adrift, turn out, throw out, oust.

298 eating *n* dining, supping, taking nourishment; ingestion, chewing, mastication; imbibition, drinking. food, nourishment, nutrition, nutriment, sustenance, subsistence, provender, provisions, rations, keep, board, fare; drink, beverage, potion, draught.

v eat, feed, breakfast, lunch, dine, sup, break bread; taste, devour, wolf, swallow, gulp, bolt, gulp down, fall to, dig in; chew, masticate, bite, bite into, chomp, munch, crunch, gnaw, nibble, peck at; live on, live off, fatten, feast on.

drink, drink up, drink one's fill, quaff, (*informal*) down, chug, empty, sip.

adj eatable, edible, digestible; drinkable, potable; nutritious, nutritive.

299 excretion *n* discharge, emanation, exhalation, secretion, effusion, perspiration, sweat; evacuation, elimination, urination; hemorrhage, bleeding.

v excrete; emanate, exhale; secrete, perspire, sweat; eliminate, evacuate; urinate.

300 [forcible ingress] **insertion** *n* implantation, injection, inoculation, infusion, importation, insinuation, interpolation; immersion, submersion, dip, plunge.

v insert, introduce, put in; inject, infuse, instill, inoculate, impregnate, imbue; graft, ingraft, implant, plant, bud; thrust in, stick in, shove in, ram in, stuff in, tuck in, press in, drive in; immerse, merge; dip, plunge.

301 [egress] **extraction** *n* removal, elimination, extrication, eradication, extirpation, extermination, ejection; wrench, squeezing, pulling.

v extract, draw, draw out, take out, pull out, tear out, rip out, pluck out; wring from, wrench, pull; root out, weed out, rake out, eradicate, uproot, pull up, extirpate; evolve, elicit, draw forth; extricate, remove, eliminate; squeeze out.

302 [motion through] **passage** *n* transmission; permeation, penetration, infiltration; ingress, egress; voyage, trip, tour, excursion, journey; way, route, channel, avenue, road, path, way, thoroughfare, conduit.

v pass, pass through; penetrate, permeate, thread, go through, cut across; ford, traverse, cross; go, move, proceed; leave, go away, depart.

303 [motion beyond] **infringement** *n* transgression, trespass, encroachment, infraction.

v infringe, transgress, trespass, encroach; surpass, go beyond, shoot ahead of, overrun; overstep, overreach, overshoot; outstrip, outrun, outride, outdo; exceed, surmount, transcend, soar.

adv beyond the mark, ahead.

304 [motion short of] **shortcoming** *n* failure, falling short; default, defalcation; incompleteness, imperfection, deficiency, insufficiency, noncompletion.

v fall short, come up short, come short of, not reach; want, lack; fail, break down, collapse, come to nothing; fall through, cave in.

adj deficient, lacking, insufficient; incomplete, imperfect.

305 ascent *n* ascension; rising, rise, upgrowth; leap, jump; acclivity, hill, grade.

v ascend, rise, mount, climb upward, climb, arise; clamber, mount, scale, go up, get up; tower, soar, hover, surmount, scale the heights.

adj ascendant; rising, acclivitous.

306 descent *n* declension, inclination, declination, slope, declivity, grade, decline, drop, cliff, precipice, dip, hill; fall, falling, descending, sinking; downfall, tumble, slip, tilt, trip, lurch.

v descend, go down, drop down, come down, drop, fall, gravitate, slip, slide, settle; decline, set, sink, droop, wilt, slump; dismount, alight, get down; swoop down, stoop; tumble, trip, stumble, lurch, pitch, topple, tilt, sprawl.

adj declivitous, sloping, precipitous, steep; descending.

307 elevation *n* raising; erection, lift; upheaval; sublimation, exaltation; prominence, height.

v elevate, heighten, raise, lift, lift up, erect; set up, tilt up, rear, hoist, heave; uplift, upraise, uprear; exalt, enhance, advance; take up, drag up, fish up, drag, dredge.

adj elevated, stilted, rampant.

308 depression *n* lowering; dip, concavity; upset, overturn, overthrow; prostration, abasement, debasement, degradation; bow, curtsy, genuflection, kowtow, obeisance.

v depress, lower, let down, take down, cast down, let drop, let fall; sink, debase, bring low, abase, degrade, reduce; overthrow, overturn, upset, prostrate, level, fell; bow, curtsy, genuflect, kowtow, kneel, bend over, make obeisance.

adj depressed; at a low ebb; prostrate, horizontal.

309 leap *n* jump, hop, spring, bound, vault; dance, caper, frisk, buck.

v leap, jump, hop, spring, bound, vault, hurtle, hurdle; dance, caper, trip, skip, frisk, bob, flounce, start; trip the light fantastic toe, dance all night.

adj leaping; frisky, lively, springy.

310 plunge *n* dip, dash, rush, dive, leap; ducking, dunking, submersion, immersion.

v plunge, immerse, submerge, douse, souse, dunk, dip; dash, rush, hasten, hurry; dive, leap, jump; descend, drop, fall, hurtle over.

311 circular motion *n* circulation, circularity; turn, excursion; circumvention, circumnavigation, circling; turning; coil, corkscrew, spiral; full circle, full turn, turn, circuit, lap.

v turn, bend, wheel, turn a circle, turn around, make a U-turn, put about, make a complete circle; circle, go around, circuit, circumnavigate; whisk, twirl, twist.

adj circuitous, roundabout; circular.

312 rotation *n* revolution, gyration, circulation, roll; spinning, pirouette, convolution; whir, whirl, eddy, vortex, whirlpool, maelstrom; cyclone, tornado.

v rotate, turn, spin, revolve, wheel, whirl, twirl, spin around; pivot, swivel, circle around.

adj rotating, rotary, gyratory, revolving.

313 evolution *n* evolvement, unfolding, development.

v evolve, unfold, unfurl, unroll, unwind, develop.

adj evolutionary, evolutional.

314 [motion to and fro] **oscillation** *n* vibration, pulsation, undulation; pulse, beat, (*informal*) vibes, ripple, wave; alternation, coming and going, ebb and flow, ups and downs, flux and reflux; fluctuation, vacillation, irresolution.

v oscillate, vibrate, vacillate, swing, fluctuate, vary; undulate, wave; pulsate, beat, throb, ripple; reel, quake, quiver, quaver, shake; roll, toss, pitch; flounder, stagger, totter.

adj oscillating; undulatory; pulsating.

adv to and fro, up and down, back and forth, seesaw, zigzag, in and out, from side to side.

315 [irregular motion] **agitation** *n* stir, ripple, tremor, shake, jog, jolt, jar, jerk, shock, quiver, quaver, twitter, flicker, flutter; disquiet, perturbation, commotion, turbulence, turmoil, tumult; hubbub, bustle, fuss, ado, racket, fits; spasm, throe, throb, palpitation, convulsion, fit; disturbance, disorder, restlessness, hypertension; ferment, fermentation, ebullition, effervescence, hurly-burly; tempest, storm, groundswell, whirlpool, vortex; whirlwind, tornado, cyclone, twister.

v be agitated, shake, tremble, quiver, quaver, quake, shiver, twitter, writhe, toss, shuffle, tumble, stagger, bob, reel, sway; waggle, wriggle, dance, prance, stumble, shamble, flounder, totter, teeter, flounce, flop; throb, pulsate, beat, palpitate, go pit-a-pat; flutter, flicker, bicker, bustle; ferment, effervesce, foam, boil, bubble, simmer; agitate, shake, convulse, toss, tumble, bandy, flap, whisk, jerk, hitch, jolt, joggle, jostle, buffet, hustle, disturb, stir, shake up, churn, jounce, wallop, whip.

adj agitated, shaking, pulsating, tremulous, convulsive, jerky, shaky, throbbing.

adv by fits and starts; in convulsions, in fits.

Class III

Words Relating to Matter

I. Matter in General

316 materiality *n* corporeality, substantiality, flesh and blood, physicality; matter, body, substance, brute matter, physical elements, material; object, article, thing, materials.

science of matter: physics, natural philosophy, physical science, materialism.

materialist, physicist.

v materialize, embody, body in.

adj material, bodily, corporeal, physical, somatic; sensible, tangible, palpable, touchable, substantial, unspiritual, materialistic.

317 immateriality *n* incorporeality, insubstantiality, spirituality, ineffability.

adj immaterial, incorporeal, unsubstantial, intangible, ineffable, untouchable, bodiless, unreal, unearthly, spiritual, psychical, otherworldly.

318 world *n* creation, nature, universe, solar system, galaxy, globe, earth, wide world, sphere, macrocosm; heavens, firmament, vault, celestial spaces, space, sky; heavenly bodies, planets, asteroids, comets, meteors, constellations.

adj worldly, mundane, terrestrial, earthly, sublunary; cosmic, celestial, heavenly, astral, solar, lunar.

adv in all creation, on the face of the earth, under the sun, here below.

319 gravity *n* gravitation, weight, heaviness, pull, pressure, load, burden.

v gravitate, weigh, pull, press, encumber, load, be heavy.

adj weighty, heavy, heavy as lead, ponderous, lumpish, cumbersome, burdensome, cumbrous, massive, unwieldy, like a ton of bricks.

320 levity *n* lightness, buoyancy, volatility; ferment, leaven, yeast.

v be light, float, swim, waft; lighten, leaven.

adj light, subtle, airy, weightless, ethereal, volatile, buoyant, feathery.

II. Inorganic Matter

321 density *n* solidity, solidness, impenetrability, impermeability; condensation, solidification, consolidation, concretion, coagulation, petrification, hardening, crystallization, thickening; solid body, mass, block, knot, lump, conglomerate.

v be dense; solidify, condense, consolidate, coagulate, congeal, set, cohere, crystallize, petrify, harden; condense, compress, thicken.

adj dense, solid, compact, close, thick, substantial, massive; impenetrable, impermeable, coherent, cohesive; indivisible, indissoluble, insoluble.

322 thinness *n* rarity, tenuity; rarefaction, expansion, dilation, inflation.

v thin, rarefy, expand, dilate, inflate.

adj thin, rare, fine, tenuous, compressible, flimsy, slight, light; unsubstantial.

323 hardness *n* rigidity, firmness, inflexibility, temper; induration, petrification, ossification, crystallization.

v harden, stiffen, cement, petrify, temper, ossify.

adj hard, solid, firm, inflexible, rigid, resistant, adamantine, impenetrable, strong, hard as a rock, hard as nails, tough.

324 softness *n* pliability, flexibility, pliancy, malleability, ductility, tractility, plasticity, flaccidity, elasticity; mollification, softening.

v soften, mollify, mash, knead, temper, bend, yield, give, relent, relax.

adj soft, tender, supple, pliant, pliable, flexible, limber, plastic, ductile, tractile, tractable, plastic, malleable, moldable, impressible, elastic; flabby, limp, flimsy, flaccid, doughy, mushy, squishy, waxy, soft as butter.

325 elasticity *n* springiness, spring, resilience, resiliency, give.

v be elastic, spring, give, bend, stretch; spring back, recoil.

adj elastic, tensile, springy, resilient, buoyant, rubbery.

326 inelasticity *n* want of elasticity, flaccidity, limpness, softness, mushiness.

adj inelastic, flaccid, limp.

327 tenacity *n* toughness, strength, cohesiveness, cohesion; stubbornness, obstinacy, grit.

adj tenacious, cohesive, tough, strong, resistant, gristly, stringy, gummy, adhesive, sticky, viscous, glutinous; stubborn, obstinate.

328 brittleness *n* fragility, frailty, breakability.

v be brittle; break, crack, snap, split, shiver, splinter, crumble, burst, fly, fly to pieces, shatter, give way.

adj brittle, fragile, breakable, frangible, delicate, frail, splintery, crisp.

329 structure *n* organization, constitution, anatomy, frame, framework, mold, form, architecture, construction. texture: tissue, grain, web, surface; coarseness; fineness.

adj structural, organizational, anatomical, anatomic, architectural textural: fine, delicate, subtle, gossamery, filmy; coarse, homespun, rough, woolly.

330 granularity *n* pulverulence, sandiness, graininess, friability; powder, dust, sand, grit, grain, particle, crumb, fine powder.

reduction to powder; pulverization, granulation, disintegration, abrasion, attenuation, filing.

tools for pulverization: mill, grater rasp, file, mortar and pestle, grinder, grindstone.

v grind, pulverize, granulate, grate, scrape, file, abrade, rasp, pound, beat, crush, crumble, disintegrate.

adj granular, powdery, mealy, floury, branny, dusty, sandy, arenose, gritty, crumbly.

331 friction *n* attrition, rubbing, abrasion, elbow-grease.

v rub, scratch, scrape, scrub, fray, rasp, curry, scour, polish, rub out, erase, grind.

332 [absence or prevention of friction] **lubrication** *n* anointment, oiling, greasing, coating, lathering.

v lubricate, oil, grease, lather; anoint.

333 fluidity *n* liquidity, liquefaction, solubility, fluency.

v be fluid, flow, run, pour, stream; liquefy.

adj fluid, liquid, watery, serous, sappy, juicy, soluble; fluent, unstable.

334 gaseity *n* gaseousness, vaporousness, volatility.

adj gaseous, vaporous, airy, etheric, voluble, evaporable; flatulent, windy.

335 liquefaction *n* liquefying, deliquescence, melting, thawing, solubleness, dissolution.

v liquefy, melt, thaw, dissolve.

adj deliquescent, soluble, dissolvable, solvent.

336 vaporization *n* atomization, steaming, boiling, distillation, gasification, evaporation.

v vaporize, atomize, distill, evaporate, gasify, boil, steam.

adj vapory, vaporous, volatile, evaporable, gaseous.

337 water *n* liquid, serum, lymph, fluid, aqua.

v add water, water, wet, moisten, dip, immerse, submerge, plunge, douse, dunk, drown, soak, steep, wash, sprinkle, splash, souse, drench; dilute; deluge, inundate.

adj watery, aqueous, liquid, fluid, wet, moist, humid, soggy, sodden, rheumy, hydrous, juicy, lush, succulent; waterish, adulterated, transparent, thin, weak, tasteless, insipid, vapid, flat, feeble, dull.

338 air *n* atmosphere, stratosphere, the open, open air, blue sky, sky; weather, climate, clime; ventilation, current, breath of air, wind, breeze.

v air, ventilate, fan, aerate, freshen, refresh, cool.

adj airy, open, exposed, breezy, windy; flatulent; effervescent; atmospheric, aerial, ethereal, aeriform.

adv in the open air, out in the open, out of doors, in the wide open spaces, under the stars.

339 moisture *n* dampness, humidity, dankness, dew, wetness, condensation; perspiration.

v moisten, sponge, damp, bedew, wet, soak, saturate, sodden, sop, drench; perspire.

adj moist, damp, watery, humid, dank, dewy, muggy, juicy, wet; soggy, mushy, marshy, muddy.

340 dryness *n* drought, aridity; dessication, drainage, evaporation.

v dry, dry up, soak up, sponge, swab, wipe; drain, parch, evaporate.

adj dry, arid, parched, juiceless, sapless, dry as a bone.

341 ocean *n* sea, main, deep, brine, salt water, waters, high seas, waves, billows, great waters, tides.

adj oceanic, marine, maritime, seagoing, oceanographic.

342 land *n* earth, ground, dry land, mother earth, *terra firma;* continent, inlands, interior, shore, coast, terrain, dirt, soil, rock, chalk; real estate, lands, grounds, acres, acreage.

v land, alight, arrive, disembark, come ashore, go ashore, tie up, set foot on dry land.

adj earthy, terrestrial, earthly, alluvial, landed, territorial, continental.

adv ashore, on land, on dry land.

343 gulf, lake *n* gulf, bay, inlet, estuary, bayou, arm, fjord, firth, lagoon, cove, mouth, natural harbor, sound, straits.

lake, loch, lough, mere, tarn, basin, reservoir, lagoon, pond, pool.

344 plain *n* plateau, champaign, grassland, pasture, pasturage, meadow, flat, moor, heath, tundra, prairie, lowland, steppe, field, desert, basin, fields, grounds.

345 marsh *n* swamp, morass, moss, fen, bog, quagmire, slough, wash, mud.

adj marshy, swampy, boggy, quaggy, soft, muddy, sloppy, squashy.

346 island *n* isle, islet, atoll, reef, ait, key, bar, holm, ridge, eyot, archipelago.

adj insular, sea-girt.

347 [fluid in motion] **stream** *n* stream, etc. (of water) **348**; (of air) **249.**

v flow, etc., 348; blow, etc., **349.**

348 [water in motion] **river** *n* running water, jet, spurt, squirt, spout, splash, rush, gush, torrent; fall, cascade, inundation, deluge; rain, rainfall, storm; trickle, drizzle, shower; stream, course, flux, flow, flowing, current, tide, race; spring, rill, rivulet, stream, river, tributary; rapids, flood, whirlpool, maelstrom, vortex, eddy; wave, billow, surge, swell, ripple, surf, breaker, white caps, rough seas, rolling seas, choppy seas; irrigation, pump, hose.

v flow, run, gush, pour, spout, roll, jet, well issue; drop, drip, dribble, drizzle, trickle, stream, overflow, inundate, deluge, flow over, splash, swash; gurgle, murmur, babble, bubble, sputter, spurt, regurgitate; ooze, flow out, squeeze; rain, rain hard, rain cats and dogs, rain in torrents, rain in buckets; flow into, open into, drain into; pour, pour out, shower down, irrigate, drench, spill.

adj fluent, tidal, streamy, showery, rainy, trickly, drizzly, bubbly.

349 [air in motion] **wind** *n* draft, air, breath of air, puff, whiff, zephyr, drift, blow; fresh wind, stiff breeze, keen blast, trade wind, gust, blast, breeze, squall, gale, storm, tempest, hurricane, whirlwind, tornado, twister, cyclone, monsoon.

v blow, waft, blow hard, blow great guns, stream, gust, blast, storm; respire, breathe, pant, puff, gasp, wheeze, cough; fan, ventilate, inflate, pump, blow up.

adj windy, drafty, breezy, stormy, tempestuous, cyclonic.

350 [channel for the passage of water] **conduit** *n* channel, duct, aqueduct, canal, trough, gutter, dike, main, gully, moat, ditch, drain, sewer, culvert, sough, siphon, pipe, tube, hose, funnel, tunnel, artery, spout, floodgate, watergate, sluice, lock, valve.

351 [channel for the passage of air] **air-pipe** *n* tube, shaft, flue, chimney, funnel, vent, hole, windpipe, duct.

352 semiliquidity *n* viscosity, adhesiveness, stickiness, glutinosity, pastiness.

v thicken, mash, squash, churn, beat up, blend.

adj semiliquid, semifluid; milky, muddy, creamy, slushy, starchy, gummy, gluey, sticky, slimy, oozy, thick, succulent, viscous, viscid, glutinous, adhesive, clammy.

353 [mixture of air and water] **bubble, cloud** *n* bubble, foam, froth, head, lather, suds, spray, surf, yeast; effervescence, fermentation, bubbling, boiling, gurgling, foaming.

cloud, vapor, fog, mist, haze, steam; nebula, nebulosity, cloudiness, opacity, dimness.

v bubble, boil, foam, froth, gurgle, lather, effervesce, ferment, fizzle.

cloud, fog, mist, steam, shadow, darken, cast over, steam up.

adj bubbly, foamy, frothy; effervescent.

cloudy, foggy, misty, hazy, steamy.

354 pulpiness *n* pulp, paste, dough, curd; fleshiness, fattiness, sponginess.

v pulp, mash, squeeze, juice, squash.

adj pulpy, pasty, doughy, fleshy, meaty, fatty.

355 unctuousness *n* unctuosity, oiliness, greasiness, lubricity; lubrication, ointment, grease, oil, anointment.

v oil, grease, lubricate.

adj unctuous, oily, greasy, oleaginous, slippery, slimy, slick.

356 oil *n* fat, butter, cream, grease, tallow, suet, lard, dripping, blubber; soap, wax; petroleum, gasoline, kerosene, propane, naphtha; vegetable oil, salad oil, olive oil, linseed oil; ointment, unguent, liniment, salve, balm.

356a resin *n* rosin, gum, wax, amber, ambergris, bitumen, pitch, tar, asphalt; varnish, lacquer, shellac, mastic, sealing wax, putty.

v resin, rosin; varnish, shellac, lacquer, overlay.

adj resinous, gummy, waxy.

III. Organic Matter

357 animate matter *n* nature, natural world, animated nature, living beings, organisms, organic remains, animal life, plant life, fauna, flora; protoplasm, cell.

science of living beings: biology, natural history, zoology, botany, anatomy, physiology, organic chemistry.

naturalist, biologist, zoologist, botanist.

adj animate, organic.

358 inanimate matter *n* mineral world, mineral kingdom, inorganic matter, brute matter.

science of the mineral kingdom: mineralogy, geology, metallurgy.

adj inanimate, inorganic, mineral.

359 life *n* existence, being; animation, vigor, vivacity, vitality, energy, vital spark, vital flame, lifeblood, spirit, soul; respiration, breath, breath of life; nourishment, nutriment, staff of life.

v be alive, live, breathe, respire, exist, subsist; be born, come into the world, see the light; quicken, revive, come to; give birth to, bring to life, vitalize; vivify, reanimate; keep alive, *(informal)* keep going, *(informal)* hang in there.

adj alive, live, vigorous, vivacious, vital, energetic, lively, alive and kicking, active.

360 death *n* decease, demise, expiration, passing, dissolution, departure, release, rest, quietus, fall; end, cessation, loss of life, extinction, dying, mortality, doom, finale, stop; last breath, final gasp, death rattle, death agonies, hand of death, dying day, *rigor mortis;* decay, fatality, natural causes, death blow.

v die, decease, pass away, pass on, perish, expire, depart, dissolve; cease, end, vanish, disappear; fail, subside, fade, sink, fall, decline, wither, decay; be taken, yield, give in, breathe one's last, end one's days, depart this life, be no more, drop off, pop off, drop dead, drop down dead, break one's neck, give up the ghost, shuffle off the mortal coil, go the way of all flesh, turn to dust, *(informal)* kick the bucket, *(informal)* go out like a light, *(informal)* croak.

adj dead, lifeless, extinct, defunct, late, gone, no more, dead and gone, dead as a door nail; deadly, fatal, lethal.

361 [destruction of life; violent death] **killing** *n* murder, homicide, assassination, slaughter, bloodshed, carnage, butchery, massacre, holocaust; suffocation, strangulation, garrote, hanging, electrocution, gassing, drawing and quartering; suicide, regicide, parricide, matricide, fratricide, infanticide; death blow, finishing stroke, *coup de grace,* execution; suicide; slaughtering, hunting, coursing, shooting, fishing; butcher, slayer, murderer, executioner, assassin, cutthroat, thug, guerilla, saboteur, garroter.

v kill, put to death, murder, slaughter, butcher, massacre, execute, behead, decapitate, guillotine, dispatch, *(informal)* waste; *(informal)* wipe out, strangle, garrote, hang, throttle, choke, stifle, suffocate, smother, asphyxiate, drown, gas, electrocute, stab, bayonet, cut, cut to pieces, cut to ribbons, mutilate, run through, put to the sword, shoot, gun down, do away with, *(informal)* blow away; hunt, spear; cut off, nip in the bud, cut down, give no quarter, decimate; commit suicide, destroy oneself, blow one's brains out, put an end to oneself.

adj murderous, homicidal, bloodthirsty, bloody, gory; mortal, fatal, lethal, deadly, deathly; suicidal.

362 corpse *n* body, remains, carcass, corse, cadaver, empty vessel, bones, skeleton, relics, mortal remains, mortal coil, clay, dust, ashes, earth, carrion, fodder, food for worms, shade, ghost.

adj corpselike, cadaverous.

363 interment *n* burial, sepulture, entombment, inhumation; cremation; funeral, funeral rites, obsequies, wake; knell, death bell, dirge, elegy; shroud, winding sheet, grave clothes; coffin, shell, sarcophagous, urn, pall, bier, catafalque, hearse; grave, pit, sepulchre, tomb, vault, crypt, catacomb, mausoleum, cemetery, burial ground, mortuary, graveyard, charnel house, morgue; monument, gravestone, tombstone, headstone, *memento mori;* exhumation, disinterment, autopsy, post mortem examination.

v inter, bury, lay in the grave, lay to rest, lay in the ground, consign to the grave, entomb; lay out, mummify, embalm; cremate; exhume, disinter, unearth.

adj burial, funereal, funeral, mortuary, sepulchral, cinerary.

364 animality *n* corporality, animal life, living being, flesh, flesh and blood; physique, strength, vigor, vitality.

adj animalistic, bodily, corporeal, fleshly.

365 vegetation *n* vegetable life, growth, plant life.

adj vegetative; rank, dense, lush, fecund.

366 animal *n* animal kingdom, brute creation, fauna; beast, brute, creature, living thing, creeping thing, dumb animal; mammal, quadruped, bird, reptile, fish, crustacean, shellfish, mollusk, worm, insect; flocks and herds, wild animals, domestic animals, livestock, game, beasts of the field, fowls of the air.

adj animal, animalistic, zoological.

367 vegetable *n* vegetable kingdom, flora, plant life, flowerage, herbage, shrubbery, foliage, leafage, leaves, foliation, verdure, greens; tree, shrub, bush, creeper, herb, fruit, grass.

v vegetate, germinate, shoot, sprout, shoot up, grow, swell, spring up, develop, increase, flourish, blossom, bloom.

adj vegetable, vegetal, vegetative, leguminous, herbal, herbaceous, botanic, verdant.

368 [science of animals] **zoology** *n* morphology, zoography, embryology, anatomy; comparative anatomy, animal physiology, comparative physiology, anthropology, ornithology, icthyology, paleontology, entomology.

adj zoological.

369 [science of plants] **botany** *n* phytology, vegetable physiology, dendrology; flora, botanic garden.

adj botanical, herbal, horticultural.

370 [management of animals] **ranching** *n* breeding, raising; taming, domestication; veterinary science.

v ranch, raise, breed; tame, domesticate, train, housebreak; cage, bridle, restrain.

adj bred; tame, domestic, domesticated, housebroken.

371 [management of plants] **agriculture** *n* farming, cultivation, husbandry, tillage; agronomy, agrobiology, agrology, agronomics; gardening, horticulture, floriculture, landscaping, arboriculture; forestry.

v cultivate, till, till the soil, work the land, farm, garden, sow, seed, plant; reap, mow, cut; plow, plough, harrow, rake, weed, hoe, lop; garden, landscape.

adj agricultural, agrarian; arable, fertile.

372 mankind *n* human race, man, woman, humankind, human species, humanity, mortality, people, human being, person, personage, individual, creature, fellow creature, fellow man, mortal, body, soul, somebody, someone, one, party, head, hand, heart.

people, persons, folk, public, society, community, group, general public, society of men, civilization, commonwealth, commonweal, body politic, human community, population, millions, multitudes.

adj human, mortal, personal, individual; social, national, civic, public; cosmopolitan, humanitarian.

373 man *n* male, manhood, masculinity, he him; gentleman, sir, mister, Mr., master, swain, fellow, chap, boy.

male animal: cock, drake, gander, dog, boar, stag, hart, buck, stallion, tomcat, billygoat, ram, bull, ox; gelding, steer.

adj male, masculine, manly.

374 woman *n* female, womanhood, femininity, she, her; lady, gentlewoman, madam, madame, miss, *(informal)* ma'am, Ms., Mrs., matron, girl.

female animal: hen, bitch, sow, doe, roe, mare, nannygoat, ewe, cow.

adj female, feminine, womanly.

375 sensibility *n* sensation, sensitiveness, feeling, responsiveness, impressibility; sensation, impression, touch; consciousness.

v be sensible, be sensitive to, feel, touch, perceive; render sensible, sharpen, cultivate, stir, excite, sensitize; cause sensation, impress, excite an impression, stir.

adj sensitive, sensible, sensuous; perceptive, sentient, responsive, susceptible, conscious, aware, alive, acute, sharp, keen, vivid, lively.

adv to the quick.

376 insensibility *n* lack of feeling, obtuseness, paralysis, numbness, anesthesia; insusceptibility, unresponsiveness, unconsciousness.

v be insensible; render insensible, blunt, pall, numb, benumb, paralyze, deaden, freeze, anesthetize; cloy, stuff, satiate, drown; stupefy, stun.

adj insensible, senseless, unsusceptible, unresponsive, insensitive, numb, hard, dead; dull, dense, thick, obtuse, unperceptive; anesthetic, paralytic.

377 pleasure *n* bodily pleasure, sensuality, sensuousness, physical gratification, sex, sexuality, sensual delight, ecstasy, orgasm, climax; titillation, teasing; comfort, ease, relish, delight, joy, luxury, luxuriousness, pleasure, lap of luxury.

v feel pleasure, receive pleasure, enjoy, relish, revel in, bask in, swim in, luxuriate, feast on, wallow in, gloat over, *(informal)* dig, *(informal)* get off on, *(informal)* be turned on, *(informal)* get into; give pleasure, *(informal)* turn on, thrill, excite.

adj pleasurable, sensual, sensuous, sexual, voluptuous, luxurious, ecstatic, orgasmic, climactic; agreeable, comfortable, cordial, delightful, joyful; palatable, sweet, tasty; fragrant; melodious, lovely.

adv in comfort, in ecstasy, on a bed of roses.

378 pain *n* suffering, dolor, ache, aching, smart, shoot, shooting, twinge, twitch, gripe, grip, hurt, cut, sore, soreness, tenderness, discomfort, malaise, disease; spasm, cramp, crick, stitch, convulsion, throe, throb, pang; torment, torture, rack, anguish, agony.

v feel pain, suffer, undergo pain, ache, smart, bleed, tingle, shoot, twinge, twitch, writhe, wince, hurt; inflict pain, hurt, chafe, sting, bite, gnaw, gripe, pinch, tweak, grate, gall, fret, prick, pierce, wring, convulse; torment, torture, wrack, agonize.

adj painful, dolorous, sore, tender, raw, uncomfortable; convulsive, torturous.

379 touch *n* contact, feeling, tactility, palpability, impact, feel, sensation; manipulation, handling, rubbing, massaging, fondling, fingering, kneading, stroking, brushing, grazing over.

v touch, feel, handle, finger, fondle, thumb, paw, grab, rub, massage, knead, stroke, brush, manipulate, run the fingers over, graze over.

adj tactual, tactile, palpable.

380 sensations of touch *n* itching, tickling, titillation, scratching, pricking, stinging.

v itch, tingle, creep, thrill, prick, scratch, sting.

adj itching; ticklish, scratchy, itchy.

381 numbness *n* physical insensibility, lack of feeling, deadness.

v benumb, anesthetize, deaden, dull, drug.

adj numb, dull, benumbed, insensible, unfeeling, frozen, drugged, dead, deadened, dulled.

382 heat *n* warmth, caloricity, caloric, temperature; glow, flush, warmth, intensity, ardor, passion, fever, fervor, zeal; fire, spark, flame, blaze.

v be hot, glow, flush, sweat, swelter, smoke, stew, simmer, seethe, boil, burn, broil, blaze, flame; smolder, parch, fume, pant; heat, warm, thaw, defrost; stimulate, stir, animate, arouse.

adj hot, warm, mild, genial, tepid, lukewarm, unfrozen; heated, torrid, sultry, burning, fiery; sunny, tropical, suffocating, stifling, sweltering, oppressive, reeking, baking; fiery, incandescent, ebullient, glowing, smoking, blazing, on fire, afire, in flames, aflame, ablaze; ardent, fervent, fervid, angry, furious, vehement, intense, excited, excitable, irascible, animated, violent, passionate.

383 cold *n* coldness, iciness, frigidity, chilliness, coolness.

v be cold, shiver, quake, shake, tremble, shudder, quiver; chill, freeze, refrigerate.

adj cold, chilly, chill, cool, frigid, gelid, frozen, freezing, bitter, bitter cold, numbing, nipping, cutting, shivering, bleak, raw, frost-bitten, icy, glacial, frosty, wintry, hibernal, arctic, polar; impassionate, unemotional, apathetic, unresponsive, unsympathetic, stoical, unfeeling, indifferent, cold-blooded, heartless, imperturbable; polite, formal, reserved, hostile; deliberate, depressing, dispiriting, disheartening.

adv coldly, bitterly.

384 calefaction *n* heating, melting, fusion, liquefaction, combustion; cauterization; calcination; incineration, cremation; carbonization.

v heat, warm, chafe; fire, set fire to, set on fire, kindle, light, ignite, rekindle; melt, thaw, fuse, liquefy; burn, inflame, roast, broil, toast, cook, fry, grill, singe, parch, bake, scorch; brand, cauterize, sear, burn in; boil, digest, stew, sauté, cook, scald, parboil, simmer; take fire, catch fire.

adj heated, warmed, fired, burnt, scorched; molten; flammable, combustible, volcanic.

385 refrigeration *n* cooling, congelation, glaciation, icing; solidification, hardening.

v refrigerate, keep cold, chill, ice, congeal, freeze; cool, fan, refresh; benumb, starve, pinch, nip, cut, pierce, bite; quench, put out, stamp out, extinguish.

adj cooled, frozen, chilled; incombustible, inflammable, fireproof.

386 furnace *n* oven, stove, range; hearth, heater, kiln, oil burner, space heater, blast furnace, forge, fire place, fiery furnace.

387 refrigerator *n* ice box, fridge, ice chest, frigidaire, cold storage, freezer, ice house.

388 fuel *n* firing, combustible; coal, hard coal, anthracite, bituminous coal, soft coal, carbon, coke, charcoal; wood, firewood, kindling, brushwood, log, cinder, ember, ash; turf, peat, fuel oil, fossil fuel, petroleum, gasoline, kerosene; gas, natural gas, propane; electricity; nuclear power; solar energy; waterpower; windpower.

v fuel, feed, stoke, fire; power.

adj carbonaceous; combustible, flammable, burnable.

389 thermometer *n* thermometograph, thermoscope, thermostat, telethermometer, pyrometer, calorimeter, glass, mercury.

390 taste *n* flavor, savor, sensation, gusto, relish; smack, smatch, tang, aftertaste; morsel, bit, sip.

v taste, flavor, savor, smatch, smack; tickle the palate, tickle the tastebuds; smack the lips.

adj tasty, savory, flavory, flavorful, flavored; palatable, digestible, *(informal)* edible.

391 tastelessness *n* insipidity, blandness, flatness, unsavoriness.

v be tasteless.

adj tasteless, insipid, bland, flat, weak, mild, vapid, wishy-washy, *(informal)* plastic, pasty.

392 pungency *n* piquancy, poignancy, tang, bite, nip, sharpness, acridity, bitterness, hotness, sourness, unsavoriness.

v be pungent; make pungent, season, spice, salt, pepper, pickle, brine, devil, smoke, curry.

adj pungent, strong, full-flavored, seasoned, highly seasoned, spiced; sharp, biting, nippy, acrid, bitter, sour, stinging, spicy, salty, peppery, piquant, hot; unsavory.

393 condiment *n* seasoning, flavoring, sauce, spice, relish; salt, pepper.

v season.

394 savoriness *n* flavor, flavorfulness, taste, tastiness, relish, piquancy, zest, tang, delectability, palatability.

v be savory, tickle the palate, taste good, taste great; savor, enjoy, appreciate, relish, like, taste.

adj savory, good, tasty, palatable, nice, dainty, delectable, flavorful, appetizing, delicate, delicious, exquisite, rich, luscious, full-flavored, pungent, ambrosial.

395 unsavoriness *n* tastelessness, flavorlessness, blandness; acridness, sourness.

v be unsavory, be unpalatable, taste bad, sicken, disgust, pall, nauseate, turn the stomach, make one sick.

adj unsavory, tasteless, flavorless, bland, flat; bad tasting, ill-flavored, acrid, bitter, sour, unpalatable, inedible, offensive, repulsive, nasty, vile, sickening, nauseous, loathsome, unpleasant, awful.

396 sweetness *n* sugariness, saccharinity, syrupiness, stickiness.

v sweeten, sugar, candy.

adj sweet, sugary, syrupy, honeyed, saccharine, candied, sticky, gooey, luscious, lush, cloying; sweetened.

397 sourness *n* acridity, tartness, sharpness, vinegariness, acerbity, acidity.

v sour, acidify, acerbate, curdle, acidulate, ferment, spoil.

adj sour, acid, bitter, tart, sharp, vinegary, acidulous, astringent, acerbic, acrid; fermented, rancid, bad, spoiled, turned, curdled, gone bad; styptic, hard, rough.

398 odor *n* smell, scent; effluvium; exhalation, emanation; fume, essence, redolence.

v have an odor, smell, smell of, give out a smell; smell, scent, sniff, snuff, inhale.

adj odorous, odoriferous, smelly, strong smelling, redolent, pungent.

399 inodorousness *n* absence of

smell, odorlessness.

v be inodorous, not smell, have no odor, be odorless.

adj odorless, scentless, unsmelling.

400 fragrance *n* aroma, redolence, perfume, sweet smell, sweet scent, smell.

v be fragrant, smell sweet, have a perfume, scent, perfume.

adj fragrant, aromatic, redolent, spicy, scented, perfumed, sweet scented, sweet smelling, odoriferous, odorific.

401 fetor *n* bad smell, bad odor, foul smell, offensive smell, stink, stench, fume, foulness, fetidness, rancidity, rankness, fustiness, mustiness.

v have a bad smell, smell bad, smell rotten, smell, stink, reek.

adj fetid, strong smelling, bad, strong, fulsome, offensive, rank, rancid, noisome, mephitic, miasmic, musty, fusty, foul, rotten, putrid, reeking, stinking, stinky, suffocating, nauseating, nauseous, *(informal)* gross.

402 sound *n* noise, tone, pitch, sound vibrations, strain, sonority, sonorousness, twang, intonation, cadence; audibility, resonance, voice.

science of sound: acoustics, phonology, phonetics, electronic sound reproduction.

v sound, make a noise; give out sound, emit sound; resound, echo.

adj sounding, sonorous, resonant, audible, distinct.

403 silence *n* stillness, quiet, peace, hush, lull, quiescence, dead silence; muteness, speechlessness, taciturnity.

v silence, still, hush, stifle, muffle, stop, muzzle, gag; be silent, hold one's tongue, shut up, keep quiet, be still.

adj silent, quiet, still, calm, noiseless, soundless, hushed, quiescent; mute, speechless, taciturn; solemn, soft, deathlike, awful, silent as the grave.

adv silently.

404 loudness *n* loud noise, power, resonance, thunderousness, roaring, vociferousness, clamorousness; din, clang, clangor, clamor, noise, roar, uproar, hubbub, boom, racket, outcry; blast, peal, swell, flourish of trumpets, boom; thunder, explosion.

v be loud, peal, swell, clang, boom, thunder, fulminate, roar, resound, bellow, scream, holler, shout; ring in the ears, pierce the ears, split the eardrums, stun, deafen; shake, awake.

adj loud, noisy, vociferous, resounding, clamorous, deafening, stentorian, boisterous, tumultuous, sonorous, deep, full, powerful, thundering, ear-splitting, piercing, uproarious, obstreperous, shrill, sharp.

adv loudly, noisily, at the top of one's voice, at the top of one's lungs, aloud.

405 faintness *n* faint sound, whisper, breath, undertone, murmur, hum; inaudibility; hoarseness.

v whisper, breathe, murmur, hum, mutter, speak softly, speak in low tones.

adj faint, whispered, indistinct, dim, inaudible, barely audible, low, stifled, muffled, murmured, muted; gentle, soft, languid, floating, flowing; hoarse, husky.

406 [sudden and violent sounds] **snap** *n* rap, thud, burst, explosion, detonation, discharge, firing, salvo, pop, bang, blast.

v rap, snap, tap, knock, click, clash, crack, crackle, crash, beat.

407 [repeated and protracted sounds] **roll** *n* drumming, tapping, rumbling, grumbling; dingdong, whirring, droning; ratatat, rubadub, pitapat; quaver, quiver, clutter, racket; peal of bells; reverberation.

v roll, drum, rumble, grumble, rattle, clatter, patter, clack; hum, trill, shake; chime, peal, toll; tick, beat.

408 resonance *n* ring, ringing, chime, clang, clangor, boom, roll, roar, rumble, thunder, vibrato, timbre, twang, vibration, reverberation, tintinnabulation, booming, quaver, dingdong, echoing, sonorousness.

v resound, reverberate, re-echo; ring, jingle, chink, clink; gurgle, echo, ring in the ear.

adj resonant, resounding, reverberant, reverberating; deep-toned, deep-sounding.

408a nonresonance *n* dead sound, thud, thump, muffled drums, cracked bell; damper, mute, muffler.

v sound dead, thud, thump; muffle, dampen, mute.

adj nonresonant, dampened, muted, muffled, deadened; dead.

409 [hissing sounds] **sibilation** *n* hissing, wheezing, buzzing, zipping, whooshing; high note.

v hiss, buzz, whiz, wheeze, whoosh, zip, rustle, whistle, fizzle; squash, sneeze.

adj sibilant; hissing, wheezy.

410 [harsh sounds] **stridency** *n* discord, dissonance, harshness, raucousness, atonality, clashing, grinding, grating, rasping, sharpness, creaking, shrillness.

v creak, grate, jar, jangle, clank, clink, grind, grate; scream, yelp.

adj strident, sharp, high, acute, shrill, atonal, unharmonious, unmusical, dissonant, discordant, cacophonous; piercing, ear-piercing, cracked; creaking, harsh, coarse, hoarse, rough, gruff, grating, jarring, guttural, squawking, acute, scratching, croaking, rasping, sour, clashing.

411 cry *n* shout, scream, yell, shriek, roar, howl, wail; exclamation, outcry, clamor, vociferation; hubbub, hullabaloo, chorus, hue and cry; entreaty, appeal, solicitation, plea, plaint, prayer, crying, weeping, wailing, sobbing, lament, whimper, whimpering, tears, moaning.

v cry, roar, shout, bawl, brawl, hoop, whoop, yell, bellow, howl, scream, screech, shriek, squeak, squeal, whine, whimper, wail, weep, sob, moan, lament; cheer, hoot; grumble, groan, complain; vociferate, raise one's voice, sing out, cry out, yell out, exclaim, holler, shout at the top of one's lungs.

adj crying, clamorous; vociferous; solicitous; stentorian.

412 [animal sounds] **ululation** *n* howling, crying, belling, screeching, singing, growling, purring.

v cry, roar, bellow, bark, yelp, yap, growl, snarl, howl, bay, grunt, snort, neigh, bray, mew, purr, caterwaul, bleat, low, moo, squeak, oink, baa, crow, croak, screech, caw, coo, gobble, quack, cackle, gaggle, chuck, cluck, clack, chirp, chirrup, twitter, cuckoo, hum, buzz, hiss, blatter.

413 melody, concord *n* melodiousness, tunefulness, sweet sounds, mellifluence, musicalness, euphony; timbre, tone color, pitch; tune, song, aria, theme, measure, plainsong, canticle, strain, lay.

harmony, harmoniousness; rhythm, meter; symphony, euphony, consonance, attunement, modulation, syncopation; counterpoint, polyphony; concordance, pleasing combination.

v harmonize, chime, symphonize, blend; tune, accord.

adj melodious, musical, tuneful, melodic, lyrical, euphonious, singing, ringing, sweet-sounding, euphonic, mellifluous, dulcet, mellow, clear, sweet, rich, soft, silvery, agreeable, pleasing.

concordant, harmonious, agreeing, symphonious, suiting, congenial, blending, synchronized, consistent, in rapport, in unison, confluent, conjoined, symmetrical, proportionate, consonant, compatible.

414 discord *n* dissonance, atonality; harshness; racket, noise, inharmoniousness.

v be discordant; jar, grate.

adj discordant, dissonant, atonal, harsh; out of tune, tuneless, unmelodious, inharmonious, unmusical; jarring, grating, cacophonous, screeching.

415 music *n* sweet sounds, pleasing sounds, harmonious sounds, melody, song, tune, strain, air, harmony; classical music, popular music, folk music, jazz, electronic music; orchestral music, instrumental music, symphonic music, chamber music; ragtime, reggae, swing, bebop, bop, barrelhouse, rock; pop music, vocal music, choral music, solo, duet, duo, sonata, trio, quartet, quintet, sextet, septet, octet.

v make music, perform; compose.

adj musical, lyrical; instrumental, orchestral, symphonic, vocal, choral, operatic.

416 musician [performance of music] *n* artist, performer, concert artist, player, soloist, instrumentalist, vocalist, accompanist, singer, minstrel; symphony orchestra, orchestra, chamber orchestra, band, rock and roll band, group, combo, ensemble, chamber group, quartet, trio; chorus, choir, vocal group.

v make music, play, perform, strike up, concertize, execute, accompany, present the music, solo, improvise, play the notes; sing, croon, warble, vocalize, spin a melody.

adj musical, instrumental, vocal, choral, operatic; lyrical, harmonious, brilliant, sharp, incisive.

417 musical instruments *n* orchestra, band, brass band, marching band, military band, ensemble, group; strings, plucked instruments, bowed instruments, hammered instruments; woodwinds, winds, tubed instruments, reed instruments, brass instruments; percussion; synthesizer.

418 hearing *n* audition, auscultation, listening, perception, audibility, ear; regarding, attending, heeding.

hearer, auditor, listener; eavesdropper.

v hear, listen, attend, lend an ear, bend an ear, *(informal)* tune in, give a hearing to, give audience to, prick up one's ears, be all ears; overhear, eavesdrop; heed, regard.

adj hearing, auditory, auricular.

419 deafness *n* hardness of hearing, inaudibility.

v be deaf, not hear; turn a deaf ear to, plug up one's ears; deafen, stun, split the eardrums.

adj deaf, stone-deaf, hard of hearing; deafened, stunned; unheeding, inattentive.

420 light *n* ray, beam, stream, gleam, streak; sunbeam, moonbeam, aurora, dawn, sunrise, day-break, day, daylight, light of day, sunshine, broad daylight, glow, glint, glimmering; sun, moon; flush, halo, glory, aureole; spark, scintilla, scintillation, flash, blaze, coruscation; flame, lightening, flare; luster, sheen, shimmer, reflection, refraction; brightness, brilliancy, splendor, effulgence, radiance, illumination, radiation; luminosity, lucidity.

science of light: optics, photography, radioactivity.

v shine, glow, glitter, glisten, gleam, beam, flare, flare up, glare, flash, glimmer, shimmer, flicker, sparkle, scintillate, coruscate, flash, blaze; light, reflect, dazzle, bedazzle, daze, radiate; lighten, enlighten, light, irradiate, shed light upon, cast light upon, illuminate, illumine, kindle, fire.

adj luminous, lucent; light, bright, vivid, splendid, resplendent, lustrous, shiny, radiant; sheeny, glossy, glassy, sunny, burnished; cloudless, clear, unclouded; effulgent, blazing, ablaze, phosphorescent, aglow; iridescent.

421 darkness *n* blackness; obscurity, doom, murkiness, murk; duskiness, dusk, dimness; night, midnight, dead of night; shade, shadow, umbra, penumbra; obscuration; adumbration, extinction, eclipse, total eclipse.

v be dark; darken, obscure, shade, dim, shadow, overcast, cloud, becloud; extinguish, put out, blow out, snuff out.

adj dark, obscure, black, pitch black, nocturnal, overcast, cloudy, darkened; dingy, lurid, murky, gloomy, oppressive; shadowy, shady, umbrageous.

422 dimness *n* duskiness, shadowiness, gloominess, cloudiness, mist, mistiness, haze, haziness, fogginess, paleness, shade, nebulosity, gray, grayness.

v be dim, grow dim, darken, obscure, adumbrate, becloud, cloud, shadow, shade, eclipse, cloud over; blur, dull, fade, pale; glimmer, twinkle, flutter, flicker, waver.

adj dim, dull, dingy, lackluster, darkish, darkened, gray, dark, faint, pale, cloudy, misty, murky, overcast, nebulous, shadowy, umbrageous, blurry, hazy, opaque, foggy, bleary, gloomy, lurid, leaden.

423 [source of light] **luminary** *n* natural light, sun, moon, stars, flame, fire, spark, phosphorescence; artificial light, lamp, gas lamp, oil lamp, kerosene lamp, electric light, lantern, torch, candle, taper, light bulb.

v light, illuminate.

adj self-luminous; phosphorescent, radiant.

424 shade *n* cover, awning, umbrella, parasol, sunshade; screen, curtain, shutter, blind, gauze, veil, mantle, mask, sunglasses, *(informal)* shades; cloud, mist, fog, shadow.

v shade, veil, cover, screen, curtain, veil, draw a curtain, pull the shade, cast a shadow.

adj shady, shadowy, cloudy.

425 transparency *n* transparence, transluscence, diaphanousness, clearness, lucidity, limpidity, thinness, sheerness, gauziness, flimsiness.

v be transparent, transmit light.

adj transparent, pellucid, lucid, diaphanous, translucent, limpid, clear, crystalline, see-through, sheer, gauzy, flimsy.

426 opacity *n* opaqueness, darkness, cloudiness, filminess, haziness, mistiness, nontransparency.

v be opaque, obstruct the passage of light.

adj opaque, impervious to light, impenetrable to light, dim, filmy, thick, smoky, misty, smoggy, shady, murky, cloudy, hazy, obscure, clouded, foggy, unclear, frosted, nontransparent, nontranslucent.

427 semitransparency *n* opalescence, milkiness, pearliness; film, mist.

v let in partial light.

adj semitransparent, semipellucid, semiopaque, opalescent, pearly, nacreous, milky.

428 color *n* hue, tint, tinge, dye, complexion, shade, tincture, cast, coloration, tone, key; primary color, secondary color, complementary color; coloring; spectrum, prism, spectroscope; pigment, paint, dye, wash, stain.

v color, dye, tinge, stain, tint, paint, wash; illuminate, emblazon.

adj colored, dyed, tinted; prismatic, chromatic; bright, vivid, intense, deep, rich, gorgeous; fresh, unfaded; gaudy, florid, garish, showy, flashy, glaring; mellow, harmonious, pearly, sweet, delicate, tender, refined; dull, gray.

429 [absence of color] **colorlessness** *n* neutral tint, black and white, chiaroscuro, monochrome; etiolation, pallor, paleness, discoloration.

v lose color, fade, turn pale, become colorless, pale; deprive of color, bleach, wash out, blanch, tarnish, etiolate, tone down, whiten.

adj uncolored, colorless, hueless, pale, pallid, faint, dull, dun, wan, sallow, dingy, ashy, gray, ashen, lackluster; discolored; light-colored, fair, blond, white.

430 whiteness *n* milkiness, frostiness, silveriness, pearliness; etiolation, albification, decoloration, colorless ness; albinism.

v whiten, bleach, blanch, etiolate, whitewash.

adj white, snowy, frosted, snow-white, milk-white, milky, chalky, pearly, ivory, silver, silvery, opaline, whitish, albinistic, etiolated, bleached, blanched, fair, light, wan, pallid, pale, lackluster, colorless, anemic, sallow, faint.

431 blackness *n* darkness, swarthiness, lividness; ink, ebony, coal, charcoal, pitch; obscurity.

v black, blacken, darken; blot, smutch, smut, smirch.

adj black, sable, somber, livid, dark, inky, ebony, pitchy, swarthy, sooty, dingy, dusky, murky; jet-black, pitch-black, black as coal, coal-black, kohl-black, black as night.

432 gray *n* grayness, neutral tint, silver, salt and pepper, dove color.

adj gray, iron-gray, silver, silvery, silverish, grayish, dun, drab, ashy, ashen, dove colored, dapple-gray; grizzly, grizzled, hoary.

433 brown *n* brownness, beige, khaki.

adj brown, bay, dapple, auburn, nutbrown, chocolate, chestnut, cinnamon, russet, tawny, tan, brunette, mahogany, khaki, beige, ochre, sepia, hazel, brownish, coffee, cocoa, rust, roan, sorrel.

434 red *n* redness; blush, color.

v redden, blush, flush, get red in the face, turn color.

adj red, reddish, scarlet, crimson, blood red, bloody, cherry-colored, vermilion, carmine, maroon, pink, hot pink, rosy, ruby, salmon, wine-colored; red-faced, blushing, embarrassed, red as beet, red as a lobster, flushed, burning, fuming, flaming, inflamed; ruddy, glowing, blooming, warm, hot.

435 green *n* greenness, verdure, blue and yellow.

adj green, greenish, verdant, olive, pea-green, emerald, apple, Kelly green, blue-green, aquamarine, sea-green; grassy, verdurous; fresh, new, recent, young, innocent, naive, raw, unseasoned, immature, inexperienced, ignorant; sickly, wan, pale, livid; jealous, envious.

436 yellow *n* yellowness, jaundice.

v yellow, age, turn color, dry up.

adj yellow, yellowish, gold, golden, ocher, lemon, citrine, saffron, aureate, creamy, straw-colored, flaxen, blond, tawny, sallow; sordid, cheap; cowardly, *(informal)* chicken, craven, lily-livered, contemptible, despicable, mean, cringing, groveling; jaundiced.

437 purple *n* blue and red.

adj purple, purplish, lavender, lilac, magenta, orchid, violet, plum-colored, mauve.

438 blue *n* blueness.

adj blue, bluish, azure, marine blue, navy, aquamarine, greenish blue, sapphire, turquoise, cobalt, baby blue; depressed, down in the dumps, *(informal)* in the pits, *(informal)* down, low.

439 orange *n* red and yellow; flame.

adj orange, orangy, orangish, brass, copper, apricot, tangerine, gold, flame-colored.

440 variegation *n* striation, spottiness, streakiness, iridescence, play of colors.

v variegate, diversify, streak, stripe, checker, speckle, bespeckle, fleck, dapple; dot, striate, tattoo, inlay; embroider, quilt.

adj variegated, multi-colored, many-colored, kaleidoscopic; iridescent, prismatic, opaline, nacreous, pearly; pied, piebald, mottled; dappled, salt and pepper, marbled, flecked, speckled, spotty, studded, freckled, flecky, spotted, diversified; striped, veined, lined, striated, streaked, brindled, banded, checked, checkered, plaid, mosaic, inlaid.

441 vision *n* sight, optics, eyesight; view, look, glance, ken, glimpse, peep, peek, gaze, stare, leer; contemplation, regard, survey; point of view, outlook, viewpoint, perspective, standpoint; perspicacity, discernment, perception, penetration.

v see, behold, discern, perceive, have in sight, descry, sight, make out, discover, distinguish, recognize, spy, espy, catch a glimpse of, command a view of, witness; envision, contemplate; look, view, eye, survey, scan, inspect, run the eye over, glance around; observe, watch, watch for, peep, peer, peek, pry, take a peep, leer, ogle, glare.

adj visual, ocular, optic; clear-sighted, eagle-eyed, discerning; visionary, farsighted.

adv on sight, at first sight, at a glance.

442 blindness *n* sightlessness; cataract; ignorance.

v be blind, not see; grope in the dark; blind, hoodwink, dazzle; screen, hide, mask.

adj blind, eyeless, sightless, unseeing, dark, purblind, stone-blind; dim-sighted, undiscerning, ignorant.

adv blindly, blindfold, darkly.

443 [imperfect vision] **dimsightedness** *n* nearsightedness, farsightedness, purblindness, presbyopia, myopia, astigmatism, color blindness, cataract, ophthalmia; squint, cross-eye, strabismus, lazy eye, cockeye, swivel eye, goggle eyes.

fallacies of vision: refraction, distortion, illusion, mirage, phantasm, vision, specter, apparition, ghost; mirror, lens.

v be dimsighted, see double, wink, blink, squint, look askance, screw up the eyes.

adj dimsighted, purblind, myopic, astigmatic, nearsighted, farsighted, colorblind; blear-eyed, goggle-eyed, cockeyed, crosseyed.

444 spectator *n* beholder, observer, looker-on, onlooker, witness, eyewitness, bystander, passerby; sightseer, audience, crowd; spy, sentinel.

v witness, behold, look on.

445 optical instruments *n* lens, magnifying glass, microscope; spectacles, monocle, eyeglasses, glasses, contact lens, goggles, pince-nez; telescope, lorgnette, binoculars, spyglass, opera glasses; mirror, looking glass, reflector; prism, kaleidoscope, stereoscope.

446 visibility *n* perceptibility, discernibleness, distinctness, clearness, clarity, perceivability, conspicuousness, definition, sharp outline; appearance, manifestation.

v be visible, appear, open to the view, present itself, show itself, reveal itself, peep up, show up, turn up, start up, pop up, crop up; glimmer, loom; burst forth, burst upon the view, come into sight, come into view, come forth, come forward, attract attention.

adj visible, perceptible, discernible, perceivable, apparent, obvious, manifest, plain, clear, distinct, definite, well-defined, outlined, well-marked; recognizable, palpable, glaring, conspicuous, in full view, in full sight, in front of one's nose, under one's nose, before one's eyes.

447 invisibility *n* indistinctness, imperceptibility, invisibleness, indefiniteness; mystery, obscurity, delitescence, haziness, cloudiness; concealment; latency.

v be invisible; be hidden; escape notice; render invisible, conceal, hide.

adj invisible, imperceptible; not in sight, out of sight, out of view, unseen; inconspicuous, covert; dim, faint, mysterious, dark, obscure, confused, indistinct, indistinguishable, shadowy, indefinite, undefined, unmarked, blurry, blurred, unfocused, out of focus, misty, veiled; concealed, hidden.

448 appearance *n* phenomenon, sight, show, scene, view; prospect, vista, perspective, lookout, outlook, bird's-eye view, scenery, landscape, picture, tableau; display, exposure; pageant, spectacle; aspect, phase, seeming, shape, form, manifestation, guise, look, complexion, color, image, mien, air, cast, carriage, comportment, demeanor; presence; feature, trait, lines, outline, contour, face, countenance, physiognomy, visage, profile, outsides.

v appear, be visible, seem, look, show, present; figure, cut a figure; present to the view.

adj apparent, seeming, ostensible.

adv apparently, to all appearance, ostensibly, seemingly, on the face of it, at first sight, to the eye.

449 disappearance *n* evanescence, eclipse; departure, exit; loss.

v disappear, vanish, dissolve, melt, melt away, fade, pass, pass out, go, depart, leave no trace, be gone.

adj disappearing, evanescent; departed, left; missing, lost, vanished.

Class IV

Intellectual Faculties

I. Formation of Ideas

450 intellect *n* rationality, mind, understanding, reason, faculties, judgment, sense, common sense, wits, brains, (*informal*) smarts; brain, head, pate, (*informal*) noodle, skull, (*informal*) upstairs.

v intellectualize, reason, understand, realize, ruminate; note, notice, mark, be aware of, take cognizance of.

adj intellectual, mental, cerebral, rational, sensical, commonsensical.

450a absence of intellect *n* want of intellect; inanity, imbecility, brutishness, brute instinct.

adj unintellectual, unintelligent, unrational, nonrational, empty-headed.

451 thought *n* abstraction, concept, conception, opinion, judgment, belief, idea, notion, tenet, conviction, speculation, consideration, contemplation; meditation, pondering, reflection, musing, cogitation, thinking; intention, design, purpose, intent; anticipation, expectation; consideration, attention, care, regard; trifle, mote.

v think, cogitate, meditate, reflect, muse, ponder, ruminate, contemplate; consider, regard, suppose, look upon, judge, esteem, deem, count, account; bear in mind, recollect, recall, remember; intend, mean, design, purpose; believe, suppose; anticipate, expect.

adj thoughtful, contemplative, meditative, reflective, pensive, deliberate; lost in thought, absorbed, engrossed in; careful, heedful, mindful, regardful, considerate, attentive; discreet, prudent, wary, cautious, circumspect.

452 absence of thought *n* incogitancy, vacancy of mind, thoughtlessness, fatuity, vacuity, emptiness; inattention.

v not think, make the mind a blank, (*informal*) turn off the brain, (*informal*) tune out.

adj vacant, unoccupied, empty; unthinking; inattentive, absent, (*informal*) turned off, (*informal*) tuned out; thoughtless, inconsiderate, unmindful, unheedful, imprudent; unreflective.

453 idea *n* thought, conception, theory, notion; observation, impression, apprehension, perception, brainstorm, brainchild, fancy, (*informal*) flash; opinion, view, belief, sentiment, judgment, supposition; plan, object, objective, aim.

adj ideational.

454 topic *n* subject, theme, thesis, subject-matter, food for thought; business, affair, argument.

adj topical, thematic.

adv under consideration, in question.

455 curiosity *n* interest, inquisitiveness, inquiring mind, thirst for knowledge; spying, prying, meddlesomeness, spy, eavesdropper, gossip.

v be curious, take an interest in, stare, gape, spy, pry.

adj curious, inquisitive, inquiring, prying, spying, peeping, meddlesome, interested.

456 incuriosity *n* lack of interest, incuriousness, indifference, unconcern.

v have no curiosity, take no interest in.

adj incurious, uninquisitive, uninquiring, uninterested, indifferent, impassive, bored, apathetic.

457 attention *n* attending to, attentiveness, intentiveness, care, consideration, observation, heed, regard, mindfulness, notice, watchfulness, alertness; study, scrutiny; civility, courtesy, respect, politeness.

v be attentive, attend, observe, look, see, notice, remark, regard, pay attention, heed; examine, study, scrutinize.

adj attentive, observant, mindful, heedful, thoughtful, alive, alert, awake, on the watch, wary, circumspectful, watchful, careful; polite, courteous, respectful, deferential.

458 inattention *n* inattentiveness, inconsideration, heedlessness, unmindfulness, disregard, unconcern.

v be inattentive, overlook, disregard, pay no attention to, gloss over.

adj inattentive, unobservant, unmindful, unheeding, thoughtless, blind to, deaf to, napping, asleep, lost.

459 care *n* heed, caution, prudence, pains, anxiety, regard, attention, vigilance, carefulness, solicitude, circumspection, alertness, watchfulness, wakefulness; accuracy, exactness.

v be careful, take care.

adj careful, cautious, circumspect, watchful, vigilant, guarded, wary, prudent, tactful; painstaking, meticulous, discerning, exact, thorough, concerned, scrupulous, particular, finical, conscientious, attentive, heedful, thoughtful.

460 neglect *n* disregard, dereliction, negligence, remissness, carelessness, failure, omission, default, inattention, heedlessness, recklessness.

v neglect, disregard, ignore, slight, overlook, omit, be remiss, be negligent.

adj neglectful, disregardful, remiss, careless, negligent, unmindful, inattentive, indifferent, heedless, inconsiderate, thoughtless, imprudent; unwary, unguarded; neglecting, neglected, unheeded, uncared for, unobserved, unnoticed, unattended to.

461 inquiry *n* investigation, examination, study, scrutiny, exploration, research, search, pursuit; inquiring, questioning, interrogation; query, question.

inquirer, investigator, inquisitor, inspector.

v inquire, ask, question, interrogate, query, investigate, examine, seek, search, look for, study, consider.

adj inquiring, inquisitive, curious, scrutinizing, questioning, exploring; inquisitorial, exploratory, interrogative.

462 answer *n* reply, response, retort, rejoinder; discovery, solution; rationale.

v answer, reply, respond, rebut, retort, rejoin; explain, interpret, discover, solve; satisfy, set at rest, atone for.

adj responsive; answerable, discoverable, soluble.

463 experiment *n* test, trial, examination, proof, assay, procedure; experimentation, research, investigation, analysis.

experimenter, analyzer, adventurer.

v experiment, try, test, examine, analyze, prove, assay, essay.

adj experimental, probative, analytic.

464 comparison *n* collation, association, relating, likening, correlation, comparative relation, setting side by side, juxtaposition.

v compare, collate, confront, place side by side, pit one against another, juxtapose, relate, correlate.

adj comparative, metaphorical, compared with; comparable.

465 discrimination *n* distinction, differentiation, diagnosis; appreciation, estimation, discernment, critique, judgment; nicety, refinement, taste.

v discriminate, distinguish, set apart, differentiate.

adj discriminating, critical, distinguishing, discriminative, discriminatory, choosy, picky; discerning, perceptive; tasteful, refined.

465a indiscrimination *n* indistinction, indistinctness, lack of discernment.

v be indiscriminate, not discriminate, confound, confuse.

adj indiscriminate, miscellaneous, undiscriminating.

466 measurement *n* survey, valuation, appraisement, assessment, estimate, estimation, reckoning, gauging; measure, standard, rule, gauge, scale.

v measure, survey, assess, rate, value, appraise, estimate.

adj measurable.

467 [on one side] **evidence** *n* facts, indication, sign, signal; ground, grounds, proof, testimony; information, deposition, affidavit, exhibit, citation, reference, confirmation, corroboration.

v be evident, evince, show, tell, cite, signal, indicate, imply, argue, bespeak; give evidence, testify, depose, witness.

adj evident, evidential, indicative, inferential, referential, corroborative, confirmatory.

468 counter-evidence *n* disproof, refutation, rebuttal, conflicting evidence, negation.

v rebut, refute, check, weaken, contravene, contradict, deny.

adj countervailing, contradictory, conflicting, unsupportive, uncorroborative.

469 qualification *n* modification, limitation, mitigation, narrowing, restriction, coloring, allowance, consideration, extenuation, extenuating circumstances, condition, proviso, exception.

v qualify, modify, limit, mitigate, restrain, narrow, restrict, color, allow, allow for, make allowance for, consider, extenuate, except, make an exception, take into account, take into consideration.

adj qualified, qualifying, provided, conditional, extenuating, mitigating, admitting, supposing, with the proviso, provided that.

470 possibility *n* feasibility, practicality, likelihood, potentiality; contingency, chance.

v be possible, stand a chance, admit of, (*informal*) could be.

adj possible, imaginable, conceivable, credible, feasible, practical, performable, achievable, within reach, within the bounds of possibility, potential.

adv possibly, perhaps, perchance, peradventure, maybe.

471 impossibility *n* impracticality, unfeasibility, hopelessness.

v be impossible, have no chance.

adj impossible, not possible, inconceivable, incredible, unimaginable, unreasonable, unfeasible, impractical, unobtainable, unperformable, unachievable, beyond the bounds of reason, absurd, (*informal*) fat chance, (*informal*) no way.

472 probability *n* likelihood, likeliness, plausibility, tendency, prospect, good chance, reasonable chance, expectation.

v be probable, point to, tend, imply, bid fair.

adj probable, likely, plausible, reasonable, presumable, well-founded, hopeful.

adv probably, in all probability, in all likelihood, most likely, presumably.

473 improbability *n* unlikelihood, bare possibility, implausibility, doubtfulness, questionableness.

v be improbable, not have much of a chance.

adj improbable, unlikely, implausible, doubtful, questionable, beyond all reasonable expectation.

474 certainty *n* fact, truth; infallibility, reliability, unquestionableness, inevitability, certitude, assurance, confidence, conviction.

v be certain, stand to reason, render certain, clinch, make sure; know.

adj certain, confident, sure, assured, convinced, satisfied, indubitable, indisputable, unquestionable, undeniable, incontestable, unimpeachable, irrefutable, unquestioned, incontrovertible, absolute, positive, plain, patent, obvious, clear; sure, inevitable, infallible, unfailing; fixed, agreed upon, settled, prescribed, determined, determinate, constant, stated, given; definite, particular, special, especial; reliable, trustworthy, dependable, trusty.

adv certainly, for certain, no doubt, doubtless, undoubtedly, (*informal*) sure enough.

475 uncertainty *n* insecurity, instability, unreliability, fallibility, danger; incertitude, doubt, doubtfulness, ambiguity, vagueness, questionableness, dubiousness; haziness, fogginess, obscurity; undependability, changeableness, variability, capriciousness, irregularity, fitfulness, chanciness.

v be uncertain, hesitate, flounder, waver; render uncertain, pose, puzzle, perplex, confuse, confound, bewilder; doubt, question.

adj uncertain, insecure, precarious, unsure, doubtful, unpredictable, problematical, unstable, unreliable, unsafe, fallible, perilous, dangerous; unassured, undecided, indeterminate, undetermined, unfixed, unsettled, indefinite, ambiguous, questionable, dubious; doubtful, vague, indistinct; undependable, changeable, variable, capricious, unsteady, irregular, fitful, desultory, chance, (*informal*) chancy.

476 reasoning *n* ratiocination, rationalism, dialectics; discussion, comment, argumentation, debate, disputation.

logic, induction, deduction, chain of thought, analysis, synthesis, syllogistic reasoning.

argument, case, proposition, terms, premises, postulate, data; inference, *argumentum ad hominem, paralipsis, a priori, a posteriori, reductio ad absurdum*, enthymeme, dilemma, on the horns of a dilemma.

reasoner, logician, dialectician, disputant, wrangler, arguer, debater, polemicist, casuist, rationalist.

arguments, reasons, pros and cons.

v to reason, discuss, argue, debate, dispute, wrangle; deduce, induce, infer, analyze, synthesize, postulate, propose, contend, demonstrate.

adj reasoning, rationalistic, dialectical, dialectic, argumentative, disputatious; logical, inductive, deductive, analytical, synthetic, syllogistic, inferential; demonstrable.

477 [the absence of reasoning] **intuition.**

[false reasoning] **sophistry** *n* intuition, instinct, hunch, presentiment; insight, discernment, inspiration.

casuistry, jesuitry, perversion, equivocation, evasion, chicanery, quiddity, speciousness, (*informal*) bull, (*informal*) malarkey, bunk; false statement; fallacy, sophism.

sophist.

v intuit; reason falsely, pervert, quibble, equivocate, evade, mislead, gloss over, cavil, refine, subtilize, misrepresent, fence, beg the question.

adj intuitive, instinctive, instinctual, sophistical, equivocal, evasive, specious, fallacious, illogical, unsound, false, incorrect, untenable; inconsequential, weak, feeble, poor, flimsy, vague, nonsensical, absurd, foolish; frivolous, pettifogging, trifling, quibbling, nit-picking, subtle, over-refined.

adv intuitively, by intuition; illogically.

478 demonstration *n* proof, conclusiveness, example, verification, explanation.

v demonstrate, prove, establish, verify; evince, show, explain.

adj demonstrative, demonstrable, probative, conclusive, convincing; demonstrated, proven, proved, shown.

479 confutation *n* refutation, answer, disproof, invalidation, exposure.

v confute, refute, disprove, expose the error, overturn, invalidate.

adj confutable, refutable.

480 judgment *n* verdict, decree, decision, determination, conclusion, result, upshot, deduction, inference, assessment, opinion, estimate, criticism, critique; understanding, discrimination, discernment, perspicacity, sagacity, wisdom, intelligence, prudence, brains, taste, penetration, discretion, common sense.

judge, assessor, reviewer, critic, commentator; connoisseur.

v judge, estimate, consider, regard, esteem, appreciate, appraise, reckon, value; decide, determine, conclude, form an opinion, pass judgment; criticize, rate, rank; try, pass sentence upon, rule.

adj judicious, judicial, judgmental, determinate, conclusive; critical, discriminating, penetrating, perspicacious.

480a discovery *n* detection, determination, disclosure, trove, find.

v discover, learn of, ascertain, unearth, uncover, determine, ferret out, flush out, dig up; find out, detect, espy, descry, discern, see, notice, hit upon, stumble onto.

481 misjudgment *n* miscalculation, miscomputation, misconception, misinterpretation, misapprehension.

v misjudge, misconjecture, misconceive, misunderstand, misconstrue, misinterpret; overestimate, underestimate.

adj misjudging, ill-judging, wrongheaded, (*informal*) off base, wrong, in error.

482 overestimation *n* exaggeration, overvaluation, optimism; miscalculation.

v overestimate, overrate, overprize, overpraise, exaggerate, magnify, attach too much importance to, set too high a value on; miscalculate.

adj overestimated, overrated, inflated, pompous, pretentious.

483 underestimation *n* undervaluation, depreciation, detraction; modesty, self-depreciation; pessimism.

v underestimate, undervalue, underrate, depreciate, disparage, detract, slight, minimize, make light of, make little of, disregard.

adj underestimating, depreciating, depreciative, deprecatory; underestimated, depreciated, unvalued, unprized; modest, pessimistic.

484 belief *n* opinion, view, tenet, doctrine, dogma, creed; certainty, conviction, assurance, confidence, persuasion, believing, trust, reliance; credence, credit, acceptance, faith, assent.

believe, credit, give credence to, accept, have faith in, give assent, accept; know, see, realize, assume, presume; think, opine, hold, conceive, consider; rely on, put one's trust on, have confidence in.

adj certain, sure, assured, positive, cocksure, satisfied, confident, convinced, secure; believing, trusting, confiding, credulous; believed, accredited, trusted, accepted; believable, credible, trustworthy.

485 disbelief, doubt *n* disbelief, incredulity; dissent, change of mind, retraction.

uncertainty, irresolution, hesitation, hesitancy, vacillation, misgiving, suspense; scruple, qualm, mistrust, distrust, suspicion, skepticism.

unbeliever, nonbeliever; skeptic.

v disbelieve, discredit, dissent, doubt, distrust, mistrust, suspect, have qualms; hesitate, waver, demur.

adj unbelieving, incredulous, doubtful, disputable, questionable, suspicious; uncertain, unsure; doubting, hesitating, hesitant, wavering, irresolute, dubious, skeptical.

486 credulity *n* credulousness, gullibility, infatuation, superstition, self-deception, self-delusion.

gull, dupe, (*informal*) sucker.

v be credulous, swallow.

adj credulous, believing, trusting, unsuspecting, gullible; simple, silly, childish, stupid; infatuated, superstitious.

487 incredulity *n* incredulousness, caution, wariness, suspicion, doubt, skepticism, disbelief.

nonbeliever, skeptic, heretic.

v be incredulous, distrust, doubt, suspect.

adj incredulous, cautious, wary; suspicious, dubious, doubtful, skeptical, unbelieving.

488 assent *n* acknowledgment, agreement, concurrence, acquiescence, consent, allowance, approval, concord, accord, approbation.

v assent, acquiesce, accede, concur, agree, fall in, acknowledge, admit, yield, allow; own, avow, confess.

adj assenting, agreeing, concurring, consenting, of one accord, of the same mind; agreed, acquiescent.

489 dissent *n* difference, discordance, dissension, disagreement, dissatisfaction; opposition, protest; nonconformity, separation.

dissenter, protester, rebel, radical, dissident, nonconformist.

v dissent, differ, disagree, protest, contradict; repudiate.

adj dissenting, negative; dissident, contradictory, disagreeing, opposing; nonconformist.

490 knowledge *n* enlightenment, erudition, wisdom, science, letters, information, learning, scholarship, lore; understanding, discernment, perception, apprehension, comprehension, judgment.

v know, be aware of; understand, discern, perceive, realize, fathom, apprehend, comprehend, (*informal*) dig; (*informal*) be hip; learn, discover.

adj knowing, aware of, cognizant of, acquainted with, privy to; discerning, perceptive, (*informal*) sharp, shrewd; knowledgeable, educated, enlightened, erudite, wise, instructed, learned, well-educated, bookish, well-read; known, recognized, received.

491 ignorance *n* illiteracy, unenlightenment, unawareness, unlearnedness, unacquaintance, unconsciousness, inexperience, darkness, blindness, incomprehension, simplicity, stupidity.

v be ignorant, know nothing, have no idea, be blind to.

adj ignorant, illiterate, unlettered, uneducated, uninstructed, untaught, untutored, uninformed, unenlightened, nescient; shallow, superficial; stupid, dumb, thick, dull.

492 scholar *n* savant, wise man, sage, academician, thinker, intellectual, bibliomaniac, bookworm, pedant; student, pupil, disciple, learner.

493 ignoramus *n* illiterate, know-nothing, blockhead, numskull, dullard, simpleton, dunce, ass, fool, bonehead, duffer, dolt, turkey, twerp, idiot, imbecile, cretin, moron, dimwit, (*informal*) jerk.

494 truth *n* fact, reality, verity, veracity; accuracy, precision, exactness.

v be true, be the case, have a true ring.

adj true, factual, actual, real, authentic, genuine, veracious, truthful, veritable; pure, natural; accurate, exact, faithful, correct, precise; agreeing; right, proper; legitimate, rightful; to the point, (*informal*) right on, (*informal*) where it's at, (*informal*) on target.

495 error *n* fallacy, misconception, misapprehension, misunderstanding, misinterpretation, misjudgment; aberration, inexactness, laxity; mistake, fault, blunder, slip, oversight, flaw, stumble, bungle; delusion, false impression.

v err, be in error, mistake, blunder, slip, go astray, trip up; misconceive, misapprehend, misunderstand, misinterpret, miscalculate, misjudge.

adj erroneous, in error, fallacious, mistaken, incorrect, inaccurate, false, wrong, untrue, (*informal*) off base, (*informal*) off the mark.

496 maxim *n* proverb, aphorism, dictum, saying, adage, apothegm, motto, epigram, *mot juste*, truism, words of wisdom, axiom.

adj proverbial, aphoristic, axiomatic, truistic, (*informal*) corny, trite.

adv as they say, as the saying goes.

497 absurdity *n* nonsense, imbecility, foolishness, silliness, inanity, stupidity; farce, rhapsody, farrago, blunder, bathos; inconsistency, paradox, *non sequitur*, jargon, extravagance, exaggeration.

v be absurd, talk nonsense, play the fool.

adj absurd, nonsensical, ridiculous, silly, preposterous, foolish, inane, asinine, stupid, senseless, unreasonable, irrational, incongruous, self-contradictory, paradoxical; farcical, rhapsodic, bathetic, extravagant, exaggerated, bombastic, fantastic, meaningless.

498 intelligence, wisdom *n* intelligence, intellect, mind, capacity, understanding, discernment, reason, acumen, aptitude, penetration, brains, (*informal*) smarts; knowledge, news, information, tidings.

discretion, reasonableness, judgment, discernment, insight, sense, common sense, sagacity, insight, understanding, prudence; knowledge, information, learning, sapience, erudition, enlightenment.

v be intelligent; understand, discern, reason; be wise, discriminate.

adj intelligent, understanding, intellectual, quick, bright; astute, clever, sharp, alert, bright, apt, discerning, canny, shrewd, nimble, penetrating, piercing, on the ball.

wise, discerning, judicious, sage, sapient, sensible, sound, penetrating, sagacious, intelligent, perspicacious, profound, rational, prudent, cautious, politic, reasonable, thoughtful, reflective; learned, educated, erudite, schooled.

499 imbecility, folly *n* imbecility, want of intelligence, incompetence, incapacity, vacancy, dull understanding, meanness, simplicity, shallowness, stolidity, hebetude, puerility, fatuity, silliness, foolishness, driveling, stupidity, idiocy.

frivolity, irrationality, trifling, ineptitude, silliness, eccentricity, extravagance; rashness.

v be imbecilic.

be foolish, trifle, drivel, dote, ramble.

adj imbecile, imbecilic, idiotic, fatuous, driveling; vacant, mindless, witless, brainless, weak-headed, addle-brained, muddle-headed, dull-witted, feeble-minded, half-witted, dull, shallow, stolid, dim-witted, thick-skulled; shallow, weak, wanting, soft, sappy, stupid, obtuse, blunt, stolid, doltish, thick as a brick, asinine; childish, childlike, infantile, puerile, simple.

foolish, silly, senseless, irrational, insensate, nonsensical, inept, frivolous, trifling; eccentric, crazed, rash, thoughtless, giddy, obstinate, bigoted, narrow-minded; foolish, unwise, injudicious, improper, unreasonable, ridiculous, stupid, asinine; ill-conceived, ill-advised, ill-judged, inexpedient, extravagant, frivolous, trivial, useless.

500 sage *n* wise man, master mind, thinker, philosopher, oracle, luminary, man of learning, expert, authority.

501 fool *n* simpleton, dolt, dunce, blockhead, nincompoop, ninny, numskull, ignoramus, booby, sap, dunderhead, dunderpate, idiot, natural, oaf, lout, loon, dullard; jester, buffoon, droll, zany, harlequin, clown; imbecile, moron, idiot, cretin.

502 sanity *n* soundness, mental balance, rationality, reason, sense, clear-headedness, lucidity, coherence, normality, sobriety, (*informal*) good head.

v be sane, (*informal*) have one's act together.

adj sane, rational, reasonable, sensible, clearheaded, level-headed, logical, sober, lucid, self-possessed, (*informal*) together.

503 insanity *n* disorder, imbalance, derangement, dementia, lunacy, madness, craziness, aberration; frenzy, raving, incoherence, delirium, delusion; (*informal*) oddity, eccentricity, twist, mania.

v be insane, become insane, lose one's senses, go mad, rave, rant, (*informal*) lose it

adj insane, deranged, demented, lunatic, crazed, crazy, maniacal, mad, touched, cracked, unhinged, unsettled, daft, frenzied, possessed, delirious, far gone, wild, flighty, distracted, frantic, mad as a hatter, (*informal*) crackers, (*informal*) zonkers, (*informal*) nuts, (*informal*) zonko, (*informal*) weird, (*informal*) bananas, (*informal*) kaput.

504 madman *n* lunatic, maniac, bedlamite, raver, (*informal*) nut, (*informal*) weirdo, (*informal*) crazy; dreamer, romantic, rhapsodist, enthusiast, visionary, seer, fanatic.

505 memory *n* retention, retentiveness, remembrance, recollection, reminiscence, retrospect; recognition; reminder, hint, suggestion, keepsake, souvenir, memento, token, memorial.

v remember, recall, recollect, call up, call to mind, bring to mind, think back upon, haunt one's thoughts, (*informal*) flash on; remind, suggest, hint, prompt, summon up, reminisce; retain, keep in mind, bear in mind, memorize, engrave in the mind, learn by heart; keep the memory alive.

adj reminiscent (of), mindful (of); fresh, alive, vivid; unforgotten, enduring, indelible, memorable, never to be forgotten, unforgettable, stirring, eventful.

506 oblivion *n* forgetfulness, short memory, slippery memory, untrustworthy memory, obliteration of the past, amnesia.

v forget, be forgetful, have a short memory, lose sight of, sink into oblivion; unlearn, efface from the memory, think no more of, consign to oblivion, banish from one's thoughts.

adj oblivious, forgetful, heedless, deaf to the past, insensible; out of mind, unremembered, forgotten, past recollection, buried, sunk into oblivion.

507 expectation *n* expectancy, anticipation, prospect, reckoning, calculation; suspense, waiting; hope, trust, assurance, confidence, reliance, presumption.

v expect, look for, look out for, look forward to, anticipate, await, hope for, wait for, foresee, prepare for, count on, rely on; predict, prognosticate, forecast.

adj expectant, watchful, vigilant, open-eyed, on tenterhooks, on one's toes, ready, in readiness, prepared, (*informal*) all set for; foreseen, long expected, prospective, in view, in sight, on the horizon, impending.

adv expectantly, on the watch, on edge, with bated breath.

508 nonexpectation *n* unforeseen occurrence, surprise, shock, blow, wonder, bolt out of the blue, astonishment; miscalculation, false expectation.

v not expect, be taken by surprise, catch unawares; burst upon, come out of nowhere, drop from the clouds; surprise, startle, stun, stagger, throw off one's guard, astonish.

adj nonexpectant, surprised, unwarned, unaware, off one's guard; unanticipated, unexpected, unlooked for, unforeseen; unheard of, startling; sudden.

adv unexpectedly, abruptly, suddenly, without warning.

509 [failure of expectation] **disappointment** *n* failure, defeat, frustration, unfulfillment, blighted hope, vain expectation, disillusion, (*informal*) come-down.

v be disappointed; disappoint, dash one's hopes, dash one's expectations, balk, jilt, tantalize; dumfound, disillusion, let down.

adj disappointed; disgruntled, disconcerted, aghast.

510 foresight *n* prudence, forethought, prevision, anticipation, precaution; forecast; prescience, fore-knowledge, prospect.

v foresee; look forward to, look ahead, look beyond; look into the future; see one's future, catch the lay of the land; anticipate, expect, assume, surmise, predict, forewarn.

adj anticipatory, prescient; far-sighted, prudent, provident; prospective, expectant.

511 prediction *n* prophecy, forecast, augury, prognostication, foretoken, portent, divination, soothsaying, presage.

v predict, foretell, prophesy, foresee, forecast, presage, augur, prognosticate, foretoken, portend, divine.

adj prophetic, oracular, portentous, premonitory.

512 omen *n* portent, foreboding, augury, sign, harbinger; sign of the times, symbol, warning.

513 oracle *n* prophet, prophetess, seer, soothsayer, augur, fortune-teller, witch, sibyl, necromancer, sorcerer, clairvoyant, interpreter.

514 supposition *n* assumption, presumption, condition, hypothesis, theory, postulate, proposition, thesis, theorem; conjecture, suggestion, guess, guesswork, suspicion, inkling, speculation.

v suppose, conjecture, surmise, suspect, guess, divine; theorize, speculate, presume, presuppose, assume, predicate; believe, take for granted; propound, put forth, propose, advance, hazard a suggestion, suggest.

adj assumed, given; conjectural, hypothetical, presumptive, theoretical, speculative, suggestive.

515 imagination *n* imaginativeness, fancy, invention, inspiration, creativity, originality, fiction, vision, fantasy, illusion, ideality, castles in the air, dreaming, dream, golden dreams; mental image, conception, idea, notion, thought, conceit, fancy, whim, figment, romance, vision, dream, chimera, shadow, illusion, phantasm, supposition, delusion; verve, vivacity, liveliness, animation.

v imagine, fancy, conceive, dream, idealize; create, originate, think up, devise, invent, coin, fabricate.

adj imaginative, fanciful, original, inventive, creative, visionary, ideal, unreal, illusory, unsubstantial, dreamy, dreamlike, romantic, fantastic, fabulous, chimerical, fantastical; vivacious, lively, animated; imaginable, conceivable, possible, believable; imagined.

II. Communication of Ideas

516 [idea to be conveyed] **meaning** *n* tenor, spirit, gist, trend, idea, purport, significance, signification, sense, import, denotation, conotation, interpretation; intent, intention, aim, object, purpose, design.

thing signified: matter, subject matter, substance, gist, argument.

v mean, signify, denote, conote, express, import, purport; convey, imply, indicate, point to, allude to, touch on, drive at, involve; declare, affirm, state; intend, aim, design, purpose.

adj meaning; meaningful, pointed, poignant, significant, expressive.

517 meaninglessness *n* unmeaningness, absence of meaning, senselessness, emptiness, empty words, rhetoric, platitude, nonsense, jargon, gibberish, jabber, rant, bombast, (*informal*) hot air; inanity, rigmarole, absurdity, ambiguity.

v mean nothing, jabber, rant, say nothing.

adj meaningless, senseless, nonsensical, inexpressive, vague, trivial, insignificant.

518 intelligibility *n* comprehensibility, clarity, clearness, lucidity, coherence, explicitness, perscicuity, precision, plain-speaking.

v be intelligible; render intelligible, clear up, simplify, elucidate, explain; understand, comprehend, take in, catch on, grasp, follow, master.

adj intelligible, understandable, comprehensible, clear, clear as day, lucid, luminous, transparent; plain, distinct, pointed, clear-cut, obvious, explicit, precise; graphic, illustrative, expressive.

519 unintelligibility *n* incomprehensibility, vagueness, obscurity, ambiguity, uncertainty, confusion.

v be unintelligible; render unintelligible, conceal, darken, confuse, perplex, mystify, bewilder.

adj unintelligible, incomprehensible, indecipherable, unfathomable, inexplicable, inscrutable, insoluble, impenetrable; puzzling, enigmatic, obscure, muddy, dim, nebulous, mysterious, (*informal*) strange, (*informal*) weird; inexpressible, incommunicable, ineffable, unutterable.

520 equivocalness *n* ambiguity, uncertainty, questionableness, dubiousness, indeterminateness; double-meaning, word-play, double entendre, pun, play on words, conundrum, riddle, quibble; equivocation, duplicity, prevarication, white lie.

v be equivocal; have two meanings; equivocate, prevaricate.

adj equivocal, ambiguous, uncertain, doubtful, questionable, dubious, indeterminate; duplicitous, enigmatic, double-edged, deceptive, misleading.

521 figure of speech *n* phrase, expression, euphemism, manner of speaking, colloquialism, idiom, image; metaphor, simile, imagery, poetic device, poetics, figures of beauty.

v employ figures of speech; image, speak prettily.

adj figurative, idiomatic, colloquial, colorful, imagistic, poetic, expressive, allusive.

522 interpretation *n* definition, explanation, explication, elucidation, translation; exegesis, exposition, comment, commentary, gloss; solution, answer, meaning.

v interpret, define, explain, explicate, elucidate, translate, shed light on, cast light on, decipher, decode, unravel, disentangle, gloss, annotate, expound, comment upon; construe, understand.

adj explanatory, expository, exegetical, interpretative, interpretive; interpretable, explicable, intelligible.

adv in explanation, that is to say, namely.

523 misinterpretation *n* misapprehension, misconception, misunderstanding, misreading, misconstruction, mistake; misrepresentation, perversion, exaggeration, false coloration, falsification, travesty.

v misinterpret, misapprehend, misconceive, misunderstand, misread, misconstrue, misapply, mistake; misrepresent, pervert, misstate, garble, falsify, distort, travesty, stretch the meaning, twist the meaning.

524 interpreter *n* translator, explainer, expounder, expositor, commentator, annotator, guide, critic; spokesman, speaker, representative.

525 manifestation *n* indication, expression, exposition, demonstration, showing, display, exhibition, declaration; materialization; openness, candor.

v make manifest, show, display, reveal, disclose, open, exhibit, evince, evidence, demonstrate, declare, express, make known; appear, be plain, come to light, materialize; indicate, point out.

adj manifest, evident, obvious, apparent, plain, clear, distinct, patent, open, palpable, visible, unmistakable, conspicuous, explicit; unreserved, downright, frank, plain spoken; barefaced, bold; manifested.

adv manifestly, openly, plainly, above board, in broad daylight, in plain sight.

526 latency *n* dormancy, latentness, quiescence, obscurity, darkness, hidden meaning, obscure meaning, undercurrent, suggestion, concealment; potentiality.

v be latent, lurk, smolder, underlie.

adj latent, dormant; lurking, secret, cryptic, veiled, hidden; potential; implied, implicit; allusive.

527 information *n* enlightenment, knowledge, news, data, facts, circumstances, situations, intelligence, advice; communication, notification, announcement, record; hint, suggestion, innuendo, inkling, whisper, insinuation.

informant, authority, intelligencer, reporter; informer, eavesdropper, detective, newsmonger; messenger.

guide, guidebook, handbook, manual, map, chart.

v inform, tell, acquaint with, impart to, make acquainted with, apprize, advise, enlighten; communicate, make known, express, mention, let fall, intimate, hint, insinuate, allude to, suggest; announce, report, give an account, disclose; know, learn, find out, get the scent of.

adj informed, communicated, reported, advised, apprized of, acquainted with, enlightened, published, (*informal*) filled in; declarative, expository, communicative.

528 concealment *n* hiding, secretion, ensconcing, sheltering, covering, burying, screening; keeping secret, secrecy, hiding, disguising, veiling, camouflaging, obscuring, dissembling, obfuscation, evasiveness; reticence, reserve, reservation, suppression, silence, secretiveness.

v conceal, hide, secrete, cover, put away, ensconce, bury, screen, shelter, keep out of sight, stow away; keep secret, hide, disguise, veil, cloak, mask, camouflage, obscure, obfuscate, dissemble, be evasive.

adj concealed, hidden, secret, private, privy, confidential, in secret, close, undercover, in hiding, in disguise, covert, mysterious; furtive, stealthy, surreptitious, secretive, evasive, clandestine; reserved, reticent, suppressed, uncommunicative.

adv secretly, in secret, in private, behind closed doors, on the sly; confidentially; stealthily.

529 disclosure *n* revelation, divulgence, exposition, exposure; exposé, uncovering, muckraking; acknowledgment, avowal, confession.

v disclose, discover, uncover, lay open, expose, bring to light, unmask; reveal, make known, divulge, show, tell, unveil, unmask, communicate; let slip, let drop, betray, blurt out; acknowledge, allow, concede, grant, admit, own up, confess.

adj disclosed, revealed.

530 [means of concealment] **ambush** *n* ambuscade, lurking place, trap, snare, pitfall; hiding place, secret place, recess, hole, cubbyhole; screen, cover, shade, blinker, veil, curtain, cloak, cloud; mask, visor, disguise, masquerade.

v ambush, lie in wait for, set a trap for.

531 publication *n* issuance, distribution; announcement, proclamation, promulgation, propagation, pronouncement, declaration, disclosure, divulgence, advertisement, publicity; edition.

v publish, issue, distribute, print; make public, make known, announce, proclaim, promulgate, propagate, circulate, spread, disseminate, declare, disclose, divulge, advertise, publicize, get into print.

adj published; current, public, in circulation, in print, in black and white.

532 news *n* information, intelligence, tidings, report, rumor, scuttlebutt, hearsay, gossip, (*informal*) the word; newsstory, headlines, copy.

reporter, newsmonger, talebearer, gossip, tattler, informer.

v transpire, make news, make headlines; be rumored.

adj in the news, in the headlines, current, in circulation, in print.

533 secret *n* mystery; problem, question, difficulty, a confidence; unintelligibility.

adj secret, hidden, concealed, unrevealed, unknown, mysterious; reticent, secretive; private.

534 messenger *n* envoy, emissary, representative, intermediary, go-between, delegate, courier, runner, errand boy; intelligencer, reporter, newsmonger, spokesman, informant; forerunner, harbinger, herald, precursor.

535 affirmation *n* statement, profession, pronouncement, deposition, assertion, declaration; confirmation, ratification, endorsement; swearing, oath, affidavit; emphasis, dogmatism.
v affirm, state, assert, aver, avow, maintain, declare, swear, asseverate, depose, testify, say, pronounce; establish, confirm, ratify, approve, endorse, assent, acknowledge; swear, emphasize.
adj affirmative, declaratory, declarative, positive, assertive, emphatic, dogmatic; confirmative, corroborative, affirming, acquiescent.

536 negation, denial *n* nullification, invalidation.
disputation, confutation, contradiction, qualification; repudiation, rejection, abjuration, disavowal, disclaimer, recantation, retraction, rebuttal.
v negate, nullify, cancel, invalidate.
deny, dispute, controvert, contravene, oppose, gainsay, contradict, rebut; reject, renounce, abjure, disclaim, disavow; recant, revoke; refuse, repudiate, disown.
adj contradictory; negative.

537 teaching *n* instruction, education, pedagogy, pedagogics, edification, tutelage, tutorship; guidance, direction, preparation, schooling, learning, discipline; lesson, lecture, disquisition, discourse, explanation, harangue, homily, sermon, lore; doctrine, dogma, tenet, principle, rule, maxim, article of faith, creed, credo, belief, opinion.
v teach, instruct, edify, educate, inform, enlighten, prepare, discipline, train, drill, tutor, prime, coach, guide, direct, school, indoctrinate, inculcate, infuse, instill, imbue; expound, interpret, lecture, discourse, hold forth, sermonize, moralize.
adj educational, scholastic, academic, pedagogic, pedagogical, didactic; edifying, instructive.

538 misteaching *n* misinformation, misdirection, misguidance, perversion, sophistry, error.
v misteach, misinform, misinstruct, misdirect, misguide, pervert, mislead, misrepresent, confuse, bewilder, lie.

539 learning *n* acquisition of knowledge, acquirements, attainment, mental cultivation, scholarship, erudition. study, inquiry, questioning, search, pursuit of knowledge.
apprenticeship, tutelage, matriculation.
v learn, acquire, gain knowledge, memorize, master, study, grind, cram, (*informal*) book, read, peruse, pore over, wade through, ingest, burn the midnight oil, (*informal*) pull an all-nighter.
adj studious, industrious; scholarly, scholastic, well-read, learned, erudite.

540 teacher *n* instructor, tutor, lecturer, professor, don, master, schoolmaster, guide, counselor, adviser, mentor; preacher, missionary, propagandist.

541 learner *n* scholar, student, pupil, apprentice, novice, neophyte, beginner; disciple, acolyte, follower.

542 school *n* academy, educational institution, college, university, institute, seminary, place of learning.
schoolbook, textbook, text, primer, grammar, reader, workbook.
adj scholastic, academic, collegiate.

543 veracity *n* truthfulness, frankness, truth, sincerity, candor, honesty, probity, fidelity, accuracy.
v speak the truth, (*informal*) level with, (*informal*) be straight with.
adj veracious, true, truthful, sincere, honest, honorable, candid, frank, open, straightforward, honest, scrupulous, punctilious, trustworthy.

544 falsehood *n* falsification, lie, fib, untruth, distortion, deception, misrepresentation, fabrication, fiction, sham; untruthfulness, lying, prevarication, duplicity, double dealing, deceitfulness, equivocation, dissembling, cunning, guile, insincerity, dishonesty, inaccuracy.
v lie, fib, falsify, prevaricate, misrepresent, deceive, (*informal*) come on to, doctor, feign, pretend, play false, dissemble, counterfeit, fabricate.
adj false, untrue, wrong, mistaken, incorrect, erroneous; untruthful, lying, mendacious, dishonest, deceitful, treacherous, faithless, insincere, hypocritical, disingenuous, unfaithful, cunning, perfidious, two-faced, recreant; deceptive, misleading, fallacious, spurious, fraudulent, bogus, phony, sham, counterfeit.

545 deception *n* deceiving, guiling, falseness, untruthfulness; artifice, sham, cheat, imposture, deceit, treachery, subterfuge, stratagem, ruse, hoax, fraud, trick, wile, snare, trap, illusion, delusion.
v deceive, mislead, lead astray, take in, delude, cheat, cozen, dupe, gull, fool, bamboozle, hoodwink, (*informal*) con, trick, double-cross, defraud, outwit; entrap, ensnare, betray.
adj deceptive, misleading, delusive, illusory, fallacious, specious, untrue, false, deceitful; tricky, cunning, insidious.

546 untruth *n* falsehood, fib, lie, fiction, story, tale, tall tale, fabrication, fable, forgery, invention.
v make believe, pretend, feign, sham, fib, lie.
adj untrue, false, trumped up, unfounded, invented, fictitious, fabulous.

547 dupe *n* gull, pigeon, laughingstock, greenhorn, fool, sucker, puppet, (*informal*) nebbish.
v be deceived, be the dupe of, fall into a trap, go for the bait, bite, swallow.
adj credulous, gullible, unsuspecting, trusting.

548 deceiver *n* dissembler, hypocrite, sophist, liar, (*informal*) fast talker, storyteller, (*informal*) faker, (*informal*) phony, fraud, (*informal*) four-flusher, (*informal*) shyster, confidence man, con man, cheat, swindler, imposter, pretender, humbug, adventurer, adventuress, serpent, snake in the grass.

549 exaggeration *n* overstatement, hyperbole, extravagance, coloring, coloration, embroidery; yarn, tale, (*informal*) shaggy dog story, (*informal*) fish story; tempest in a teacup, much ado about nothing, puffery, rant.
v exaggerate, magnify, amplify, expand, overestimate, overstate; heighten, color, embroider, puff up, fill out.
adj exaggerated, overwrought, bombastic, magniloquent, hyperbolic, fabulous, extravagant, preposterous.

550 [means of communication] **indication** *n* symbolism, semiology; sign, symbol, index, indicator, pointer, note, token, symptom; type, mark, figure, emblem, insigne, cipher, device, representation; signal, beacon, alarm; feature, trait, characteristic, peculiarity, quality, earmark, cast; gesture, gesticulation, motion, cue, hint, clue, scent.
v indicate, denote, betoken, designate, signify, represent, stand for, typify, symbolize; note, mark, stamp; label, ticket; make a sign, signalize, signal, gesture, gesticulate; sign, seal, attest, underline, underscore, call attention to.
adj indicative, indicatory; connotative, denotative, typical, representative, symbolic, symbolical, characteristic, significant, emblematic.

551 record *n* trace, vestige, relic, remains; monument, achievement; account, chronicles, annals, history, note, register, memorandum, document, diary, log, journal, ledger.
v record, set down, place in the record, chronicle, enter, register, enter, list, enroll; commemorate, celebrate.

552 [suppression of sign] **obliteration** *n* erasure, cancelation, deletion, blot, effacement, extinction.
v obliterate, efface, expunge, erase, cancel, delete, blot out, rub out, strike out, wipe out, leave no trace.
adj obliterated, erased, blotted out; unrecorded.

553 recorder *n* notary, clerk, registrar, register, secretary, scribe, bookkeeper; annalist, historian, historiographer, chronicler, biographer, journalist, antiquarian, memorialist.

554 representation *n* depiction, imitation, illustration, delineation, expression, imagery, portraiture, figuration.
v represent, delineate, depict, portray, picture, figure, describe, trace, copy, illustrate, symbolize; personate, personify, play, mimic.
adj representative, imitative, illustrative, figurative, symbolic, descriptive.

555 misrepresentation *n* distortion, exaggeration, misfiguration, falsification; bad likeness, caricature.
v misrepresent, distort, overdraw, exaggerate, falsify, caricature, daub.

556 painting *n* fine art, picture, depiction, representation, pictorialization, delineation, design, drawing, likeness, copy, imitation, fake, image.
art gallery, picture gallery, studio.
v paint, design, limn, draw, sketch, pencil, color; depict, represent.
adj pictorial, picturesque.

557 sculpture *n* carving, modeling, statuary; ceramics, potting.
statue, statuette, bust; cast, mold.
v sculpt, fashion, cast, mold, model, chisel, carve, cut, shape, form, figure, hew.

558 engraving *n* etching, chiseling, incising, plate engraving, photoengraving.
v engrave, grave, carve, incise, chisel, hatch, etch, stipple, print.

559 artist *n* painter, drawer, sketcher, designer, draftsman, cartoonist, caricaturist, sculptor, engraver.

560 language *n* speech, phraseology, style, expression, diction, jargon, dialect, terminology, vernacular, lingo, tongue.
literature, letters, belles lettres, humanities, classics, dead language.
linguist.
v express, say, express by words.
adj lingual, linguistic; dialectic, vernacular, current, colloquial, slangy, polyglot, literary.

561 letter *n* character, hieroglyph, symbol, alphabet, consonant, vowel.
syllable, monosyllable, dissyllable, polysyllable.
spelling, orthography; phonetics; cipher, code; monogram, anagram.
v spell.
adj literal; alphabetical; syllabic; phonetic.

562 word *n* term, symbol, name, part of speech.
dictionary, vocabulary, lexicon, index, thesaurus, glossary.
etymology, derivation, philology, terminology, lexicography.
adj literal, verbal.

563 neology *n* neologism, new-fangled expression, (*informal*) hip expression, barbarism, corruption.
neologist, word coiner.
v coin words.
adj neologic, neological; colloquial, slang, (*informal*) hip, cant, barbarous.

564 nomenclature *n* naming; name, appellation, designation, epithet, nickname, (*informal*) moniker, (*informal*) handle, label, title, head, heading; style, proper name, surname, namesake.
v name, call, term, designate, denominate, style, entitle, dub, christen, baptize, nickname, characterize, specify, label.
adj titular, nominal.

565 misnomer *n* misnaming, malapropism; sobriquet, nickname, assumed name, alias, pen name, stage name, pseudonym, nom de plume, nom de guerre.
v misname, miscall, misterm; take an assumed name.
adj misnamed; soi-disant, self-styled; so-called.

566 phrase *n* expression, set phrase, turn of speech, idiom, tag phrase, figure of speech, euphemism, motto; phraseology.
v phrase, express, put into words, find the right words, arrange in words, voice, vocalize.

567 grammar *n* rules of language, usage, forms, style, formal features, constructions, parts of speech; accidence, syntax, inflection, case, declension, conjugation; grammar book, primer, rulebook.
grammarian.
adj grammatical, syntactic, syntactical.

568 solecism *n* ungrammatical usage, bad grammar, faulty grammar, error, slip, inconsistency, impropriety.
v solecize.
adj ungrammatical, incorrect, inaccurate, faulty, inconsistent, improper.

569 style *n* diction, phraseology, wording; composition, mode of expression, choice of words, command of language, mode, manner, method, approach; kind, form, appearance, character, touch, characteristic, mark, signature, imprint, (*informal*) name.
v style, compose, express by words; write.
adj stylistic; characteristic; expressive.

570 perspicuity *n* clearness, clarity, lucidity, plainness, plain-speaking, distinctness, explicitness, exactness, intelligibility.
adj perspicuous, pellucid, clear, lucid, intelligible, plain, distinct, explicit, exact, definite, unequivocal.

571 obscurity *n* unintelligibility, involution, confusion, indistinctness, indefiniteness, ambiguity, vagueness, inexactness, impenetrability.
adj obscure, involved, confused, unintelligible, impenetrable, indefinite, vague, inexact, hidden, dark.

572 conciseness *n* brevity, summary, abridgment, terseness, pithiness, compression, tightness.
v be concise, condense, abridge, abstract, compress, tighten; come to the point.
adj concise, brief, compendious, short, terse, laconic, pithy, trenchant, succinct, compact, tight.
adv concisely, briefly, summarily, in short.

573 diffuseness *n* long-windedness, verbosity, wordiness, verbiage, looseness, exuberance, redundancy, profuseness, richness.
v be diffuse, enlarge, amplify, expand, inflate; meander, digress, ramble, run on and on.
adj diffuse, profuse, wordy, verbose, copious, exuberant; lengthy, long-winded, protracted, prolix, diffusive, roundabout; digressive, discursive, loose.

574 vigor *n* power, force, boldness, spirit, verve, heart, ardor, enthusiasm, raciness, glow, fire, warmth; loftiness, elevation, gravity, sublimity; eloquence, strong language.
adj vigorous, nervous, powerful, forcible, forceful, trenchant, biting, incisive, impressive; spirited, lively, glowing, sparkling, racy, bold, pungent, pithy; lofty, elevated, sublime, grand, weighty; eloquent, vehement, impassioned, passionate.

575 feebleness *n* weakness, enervation, frailty, faintness.
adj feeble, tame, weak, meager, vapid, insipid; trashy, poor, dull, dry, languid; prosy, prosaic, slight; careless, loose, slip-shod, wishy-washy, sloppy, slovenly; puerile, childish.

576 plainness *n* simplicity, homeliness, restraint, severity.
v speak plainly, speak directly, come straight to the point, be straightforward, not beat around the bush.
adj plain, simple, homely, homey, unadorned, unvarnished, neat, homespun; severe, chaste, pure.
adv in plain terms, in plain English; point-blank.

577 ornament *n* floridness, ornateness, elegance, grandiloquence, magniloquence, rhetorical flourish, declamation, rhetoric, flourish, fancy talk, (*informal*) big words; pretention, inflation, bombast, fustian, rant, fine writing, fine speaking.
v ornament, overcharge, talk big, talk fancy.
adj ornate, ornamented, beautified, florid, rich, flowery, fancy; euphuistic, euphemistic; sonorous, high sounding, inflated, swelling, turgid, pompous, pedantic, stilted, high-flown, sententious, rhetorical, declamatory, grandiose, grandiloquent, magniloquent, bombastic, flashy.

578 elegance *n* taste, good taste, propriety, correctness; lucidity, purity, grace, ease; gracefulness, euphony, gentility, cultivation, polish, refinement.
purist, classicist.
adj elegant, polished, classic, classical, fine, tasteful, proper, correct; chaste, pure, graceful, easy, readable, fluent, flowing, unaffected, natural, mellifluous, euphonious, felicitous, neat, well put.

579 inelegance *n* tastelessness, vulgarity, impropriety; bad diction, awkwardness, stiffness, turgidity, abruptness; barbarism, solecism, slang, mannerism, affectation, formality.
adj inelegant, graceless, ungraceful, harsh, abrupt, dry, stiff, cramped, formal, forced, labored, awkward, ponderous, turgid; artificial, mannered, affected, euphuistic; tasteless, barbarous, uncouth, rude, crude, vulgar.

580 voice *n* vocality, intonation, articulation, enunciation, distinctness, clearness, delivery; accent, accentuation, emphasis, stress; utterance, vocalization.
v voice, speak, utter; articulate, enunciate, vocalize, intone, pronounce, accent, accentuate, deliver.
adj vocal, oral; articulate, distinct, euphonious, melodious.

581 muteness *n* dumbness, silence, speechlessness; aphasia.
v be mute, be silent, be dumb; silence, muzzle, muffle, suppress, smother, gag, strike dumb, dumfound.
adj mute, silent, dumb, mum, tongue-tied; voiceless, speechless.

582 speech *n* talk, parlance, locution, conversation, parley, communication, prattle; talk, oration, address, discourse, lecture, recitation, sermon, harangue, tirade; oratory, eloquence, rhetoric, declamation.
speaker, spokesman, mouthpiece, orator, rhetorician.
v speak, utter, talk, voice, converse, communicate, pronounce, say, articulate; declaim, harangue, stump, spout, rant, lecture, sermonize, discourse, expatiate, soliloquize, address.
adj oral; talkative, conversational; declamatory.

583 [imperfect speech] **inarticulateness** *n* stammering, hesitation, muttering, mumbling, stuttering; reticence, taciturnity; speech impediment, aphasia.
v be inarticulate, stammer, hesitate, mutter, mumble, slur one's words, garble, sputter, hem and haw, whisper, croak, crack.
adj inarticulate, tongue-tied, speechless, voiceless, hesitant, reticent, taciturn.

584 loquacity *n* loquaciousness, volubility, talkativeness, verbosity, garrulity, volubility; chatter, jabber, prattle, twaddle.
talker, chatterer, chatterbox, babbler, ranter.
v be loquacious, talk a mile a minute, pour forth, prate, chatter, babble, gab, run off at the mouth, jabber, jaw, gush.
adj loquacious, voluble, talkative, verbose, wordy, garrulous, chatty, chattering, glib, fluent, effusive.

585 taciturnity *n* silence, muteness, reserve, reticence, uncommunicativeness.
v be silent, keep silence, keep quiet, hold one's tongue, say nothing.
adj taciturn, silent, mute, mum, reserved, reticent, guarded, uncommunicative, close-mouthed, quiet.

586 public address *n* allocution, speech, formal speech, address, invocation.
v speak to, address; invoke, hail, salute; lecture, pronounce.

587 response *n*. See **answer 462.**

588 conversation *n* interlocution, colloquy, confabulation, talk, (*informal*) rap, discourse, verbal interchange, dialog, oral communication; chat, chit, chit-chat, small talk, table talk, idle talk, prattle, gossip; conference, parley, interview, audience, *tête-à-tête*, council, congress; palaver, debate, discussion.
v converse, confabulate, talk together, hold a conversation, carry on a conversation, engage in a discussion; bandy words, chat, chit-chat, gossip, tattle, prate; discourse with, confer with; talk it over, (*informal*) rap, (*informal*) chew the fat.
adj conversational, conversable; chatty, gossipy.

589 soliloquy *n* monolog, apostrophe, aside.
v soliloquize, talk to oneself, think out loud, apostrophize.

590 writing *n* chirography, penmanship, calligraphy, hand, script, longhand, shorthand, stenography; handwriting, signature, mark, hand; manuscript, MS., document, script, writ, author's copy, copy, original; composition, authorship, work, opus, book, volume, tome, publication, article, poetry, verse, literature.
writer, author, scribe, scrivener, clerk, copyist, secretary.
v write, pen, copy, transcribe; print, scribble, scrawl, scratch; compose, draw out, write down, set down, put pen to paper, take up the pen, take pen in hand.
adj written, in writing, in black and white.

591 printing *n* lettering, typography; type; composition, print, letterpress, text, matter; copy, impression, proof.
printer, compositor, reader, proofreader, copyeditor.
v print, compose; go to press, publish, bring out, issue.
adj typographical, printed.

592 correspondence *n* letter, epistle, missive, note, post card; communication, dispatch, bulletin, circular.
v correspond, communicate, write to, send a letter.

adj epistolary; in touch with, in communication with.

593 book *n* booklet; writing, work, volume, tome, opus, tract, treatise, brochure, handbook; novel, story; script, libretto; publication.

writer, author, essayist, editor; bookseller, publisher; librarian, bibliophile, bookworm.

594 description *n* narration, account, recounting, telling, recital, relation, statement, report, record; delineation, portrayal, characterization, representation, depiction, sketch, vignette.

v describe, set forth, narrate, account, recount, recite, rehearse, tell, relate, detail; picture, delineate, portray, characterize, limn, represent, depict.

595 dissertation *n* treatise, essay, thesis, theme, tract, discourse, disquisition, investigation, study, discussion, exposition; commentary, critique, criticism, review, article, commentator, critic, essayist, reviewer.

v discuss a subject, treat, examine, comment, criticize, explain.

596 compendium *n* abstract, précis, epitome, analysis, digest, compendium, brief, abridgment, abbreviation, condensation, summary; draft, note, synopsis, outline, syllabus, contents, prospectus; compilation, collection, album, anthology; extracts, cuttings, fragments, pieces; list, inventory, survey.

v abridge, abstract, précis, epitomize, summarize; abbreviate, shorten, condense, compress; compile, collect, note; list, inventory, survey.

adj compendious, synoptic, analytic, analytical.

597 poetry *n* poetics; verse, poesy, versification, rhyming, rhymes, making verses, metrics; doggerel.

poet, laureate, bard, troubadour, minstrel, versifier, rhymer, sonneteer, rhapsodist, poetaster.

v poeticize, sing, versify, rhyme, make verses, compose.

adj poetic, poetical, rhythmic, metrical, lyrical, tuneful, musical; beautiful, lovely, tender, sensitive.

598 prose *n* writing, fiction, imaginative writing, narrative prose.

v write prose.

adj prosy, unpoetic, rhymeless, prosaic, dull, flat, matter-of-fact, unimaginative, commonplace, humdrum, pedestrian, trite, hackneyed, mediocre, stock, ordinary; fictional.

599 the drama *n* the stage, the theater; theatricals, dramaturgy, playwriting; play, drama, stage-play, opera.

performance, acting, representation, impersonation, stage business, actor, actress, player, performer, thespian.

theater, playhouse, operahouse, amphitheater.

dramatist, playwriter, playwright.

v dramatize, act, play, perform, personate, act a part, put on the stage, enact.

adj dramatic, theatrical, histrionic, stagy.

Class V

Voluntary Powers

I. Individual Volition

600 will *n* volition, free will, freedom; choice, wish, desire, pleasure, disposition, inclination; intent, purpose, option; determination, resolution, resoluteness, decision, forcefulness; force of will, will power, self-control.

v will, see fit, think fit, decide, decree, determine, direct, command, bid.

adj willful, voluntary, volitional, intentional; free, optional, discretionary; autocratic, obdurate, adamant.

adv willfully, voluntarily, at will; of one's own accord, intentionally, deliberately.

601 necessity *n* obligation, compulsion, subjection; fate, destiny, fatality; inevitability, inevitableness, unavoidability, unavoidableness, irresistibility; requirement, requisite, demand; instinct, impulse.

v be obligated, be obliged, be fated; necessitate, compel, subject; require.

adj necessary, essential, requisite, needful; inevitable, unavoidable, ineluctable, irresistible, inexorable; compulsory; involuntary, instinctive, automatic, blind, mechanical.

adv necessarily, of necessity, willy nilly.

602 willingness *n* disposition, inclination, leaning, propensity, frame of mind, liking, humor, mood, vein, bent, penchant, aptitude; geniality, cordiality, good will; alacrity, readiness, eagerness, enthusiasm; assent, compliance, agreement.

v be willing, incline, lean to, mind, hold to, cling to; desire; acquiesce, assent, comply; find one's way to, give it a shot, *(informal)* take a swing at, *(informal)* lay into.

adj willing, fain, favorable, content, well disposed; ready, earnest, eager, desirous; genial, cordial.

adv willingly, freely, with pleasure, with all one's heart, graciously.

603 unwillingness *n* indisposition, disinclination, reluctance, dislike; aversion, indifference, slowness, lack of readiness, obstinacy; scrupulousness, hesitation, qualm, shrinking, holding back, recoil; averseness, dissent, refusal.

v be unwilling, dislike; demur, hesitate, shrink from, swerve, recoil; dissent, refuse.

adj unwilling, loath, reluctant, averse; laggard, backward, slow, slack, indifferent; scrupulous, hesitant.

adv unwillingly, grudgingly, against one's will, under protest.

604 resolution *n* determination, will, decision, strength of mind, resolve, firmness, energy, manliness, vigor, resoluteness; pluck, zeal, devotion; self-control, self-command, self-possession, self-reliance, self-restraint, self-denial; tenacity, perseverance, obstinacy, *(informal)* gumption.

v be resolute, resolve, will, determine, decide, make a resolution, conclude, fix, bring to a crisis, take a decisive step; stand firm, insist upon, make a point of, not give an inch.

adj resolute, firm, steadfast, resolved, purposeful, fixed, inflexible, bold, game, indomitable, relentless, tenacious, gritty, stern, irrevocable, obstinate.

adv resolutely, in earnest, earnestly, manfully.

604a perseverance *n* persistence, tenacity, resolution, doggedness, determination, steadfastness, indefatigability, pluck, stamina, backbone.

v persevere, persist, continue, keep on, last, stick it out, hang in there.

adj persevering, constant, steady, steadfast, persistent, tenacious, resolute, dogged, indefatigable, indomitable, staunch, true, game, *(informal)* tough.

605 irresolution *n* indecision, indetermination, instability, uncertainty; hesitation, hesitancy, vacilllation, oscillation, changeableness, fluctuation, fickleness, weakness, frailty, timidity, cowardice.

v be irresolute, dawdle, dilly-dally, shilly-shally, hesitate, falter, waver, vacillate, change, fluctuate, blow hot and cold.

adj irresolute, indecisive, indeterminate, unstable, uncertain; hesitant, changeable, capricious, fickle, frail, feeble, weak, timid, *(informal)* soft, cowardly.

606 obstinacy *n* doggedness, persistence, pertinacity, resolution, intractability, firmness, immovability, inflexibility, obduracy, willfulness, perversity, stubborness, mulishness; uncontrollability, wildness.

fixed idea, *idée fixe*, fanaticism, zealotry, infatuation, monomania; bigotry, intolerance, dogmatism.

bigot, dogmatist, zealot, fanatic.

v be obstinate, persist, die hard, fight, stick to an idea.

adj obstinate, dogged, persistent, pertinacious, resolute, intractable, firm, refractory, headstrong, willful, inflexible, immovable, perverse, stubborn, mulish, pig-headed; wayward, unruly, incorrigible, uncontrollable, wild; fanatic, zealous, monomaniacal; intolerant, dogmatic, arbitrary.

607 recantation *n* tergiversation, renunciation, abjuration, retraction, defection, apostasy, disavowal, revocation, reversal.

turncoat, apostate, renegade, deserter.

v recant, change one's mind, abjure, retract, renounce, disavow, revoke, defect, change sides.

adj changeful, irresolute, slippery, timeserving.

608 caprice *n* fancy, humor, whim, quirk, freak, fad, vagary, prank.

v be capricious.

adj capricious, erratic, eccentric, fitful, inconsistent, fanciful, whimsical, crotchety, freakish, wayward, wanton; contrary, captious, unreasonable, arbitrary, fickle; frivolous.

609 choice *n* selection, decision, pick, choosing, election, option, alternative, preference, predilection, desire.

v choose, select, elect, make a choice, prefer, pick, cull, decide.

adj optional, discretional, preferential.

609a neutrality, absence of choice *n* neutrality, indifference; indecision, irresolution.

no choice, first come first served.

v be neutral, have no preference, waive, abstain.

take what's offered.

adj neutral, indifferent; indecisive, irresolute.

610 rejection *n* refusal, repudiation, renunciation; exclusion, elimination.

v reject, refuse, repudiate, decline, deny, rebuff, repel, renounce; discard, throw away, exclude, eliminate; jettison.

611 predetermination *n* premeditation, predeliberation, foregone conclusion; resolve, intention; fate, predestination, destiny.

v predetermine, predestine, premeditate, resolve beforehand, calculate.

adj aforethought; foregone.

adv advisedly, deliberately, intentionally.

612 impulse *n* sudden thought, flash, spurt, inspiration, improvisation.

v improvise, extemporize; flash on, hit on, come up with, pull out of a hat, pull out of the air; say what comes to mind.

adj impulsive, impromptu, spontaneous; extemporaneous.

adv extempore, extemporaneously; impromptu, offhand, impulsively.

613 habit *n* addiction, disposition, tendency, bent, wont; custom, prescription, practice, way, usage, wont, manner; prevalence, observance; conventionalism, conventionality, mode, fashion, vogue, conformity; rule, precedent, routine, rut, groove.

v habituate, inure, harden, season; accustom, familiarize; acclimate, accommodate; cling to, adhere to, acquire a habit, fall into a rut; be habitual, come into use, become a habit, take root.

adj habitual, customary, prescriptive, usual, general, ordinary, common, frequent, everyday, familiar, trite, commonplace, conventional, regular, set, stock, fixed, permanent; prevalent, current, fashionable; addictive.

adv habitually, as usual, as things go, as the world goes; as a rule, for the most part, generally.

614 disuse *n* desuetude, disusage, lack of practice.

v be unaccustomed, break a habit; disuse.

adj unaccustomed; unusual, original.

615 motive *n* reason, ground, principle, mainspring, purpose, cause, occasion, influence, impulse, instigation, spur, stimulus, incitement, incentive, inducement, consideration, temptation, motivation; intention, ulterior motive.

v motivate, induce, move, inspire, put up to, prompt, stimulate, spur, excite, arouse, rouse, incite, instigate; influence, sway, incline, dispose, lead, persuade, prevail upon, enlist, engage, invite, court, tempt, charm.

adj suasive, persuasive, seductive, attractive, provocative.

615a absence of motive *n* caprice, chance, absence of design.

v have no motive.

adj capricious, without rhyme or reason.

adv capriciously.

616 dissuasion *n* expostulation, remonstrance, deprecation, discouragement, damper, restraint, curb, check.

v dissuade, cry out against, remonstrate, expostulate, warn, disincline, indispose, shake, discourage, dishearten, disenchant; deter, hold back, restrain, repel, turn aside, wean from, damp, cool, chill, blunt.

adj dissuasive.

617 [ostensible motive, ground, or reason] **plea** *n* pretext, allegation, excuse; pretense, shallow excuse, lame excuse, makeshift.

v plead, allege, excuse, make a pretext of, pretend.

adj ostensible, alleged.

adv ostensibly, under the pretense of.

618 good *n* benefit, interest, service, behalf, advantage, improvement, gain, boot, profit, harvest; boon, blessing, good luck, prize, good fortune, windfall, godsend; prosperity, happiness, goodness.

v benefit, serve, profit, advantage.

adj commendable; useful, good, beneficial, advantageous.

619 evil *n* ill, harm, hurt, mischief, nuisance; damage, loss; disadvantage, drawback; disaster, accident, casualty, mishap, misfortune; calamity, catastrophe, tragedy, ruin, destruction, adversity; mental suffering, pain, anguish; outrage, wrong, injury, foul play.

v be in trouble; harm, hurt, injure, ruin, destroy, torture.

adj evil, hurtful, injurious, harmful; disastrous, catastrophic, cataclysmic, tragic, ruinous.

620 intention *n* intent, purpose, project, undertaking, design, ambition, contemplation, view, proposal, meaning; object, aim, end, destination, mark, point, goal, target, prey, quarry, game; decision, determination, resolve, resolution, settled purpose.

v intend, mean, design, purpose, propose, contemplate, plan, expect, mediate, calculate, project, aim for, aim at, aspire at.

adj intentional, advised, express, determinate, bound for, bent upon, in view, in prospect.

adv intentionally, advisedly, wittingly, knowingly, purposely, on purpose, by design, pointedly; deliberately.

621 [absence of design] **chance** *n* destiny, lot, fate, luck, good luck, turn, *(informal)* break, *(informal)* jinx, fortune; speculation, venture, stake, shot in the dark, fluke; wager, gambling, betting.

gambler, gamester, adventurer.

v chance, chance it, tempt fate, speculate, risk, venture, hazard, stake, wager, bet, place a bet, gamble, play for.

adj unintentional, accidental, random; fortuitous, lucky; speculative, venturesome.

adv unintentionally, unwittingly.

622 pursuit *n* pursuance, enterprise, undertaking, business, adventure, essay, quest, search.

v pursue, prosecute, follow, do, engage in, undertake, endeavor, seek, aim at, fish for, press on, go after, chase.

adj in quest of, in pursuit of.

623 avoidance *n* evasion, flight, escape, retreat, recoil, departure; abstention, abstinence, forbearance, inaction.

avoider, shirker, quitter, truant; fugitive, refugee, runaway, deserter.

v avoid, shun, steer clear of, keep clear of, evade, elude, shirk, fly from, turn away from; abstain, refrain, eschew, leave alone, not get involved; shrink, hold back, retire, recoil, flinch, blink, shy, dodge, beat a retreat, turn tail, run for one's life, head for the hills, take flight, beat it out; desert, sneak off, shuffle off, slink away, steal away, slip, sneak, bolt, abscond.

adj elusive, evasive, escapist, fugitive.

624 relinquishment *n* surrender, resignation, yielding, waiver, waiving, abdication, leaving, desertion, withdrawal, secession, abandonment, renunciation.

v relinquish, surrender, give up, resign, yield, cede, waive, forswear, forgo, abdicate, leave, forsake, desert, renounce, quit, abandon, let go, resign, *(informal)* throw in the towel, call it quits, *(informal)* hang it up.

625 business *n* occupation, trade, craft, profession, calling, employment, vocation, pursuit; affair, matter, concern, transaction, undertaking; function, duty, office, position, part, role, capacity.

v employ oneself, undertake, turn one's hand to; be at work on, be engaged in, be occupied with.

adj businesslike; workaday, professional, official, functional; busy.

626 plan *n* scheme, plot, stratagem, policy, procedure, project, formula, method, system, organization, design, contrivance, device; drawing, sketch, draft, map, chart, diagram, representation; intrigue, cabal, conspiracy.

planner, designer, organizer, schemer, strategist, intriguer.

v plan, arrange, frame, scheme, plot, design, devise, contrive, invent, concoct, hatch; project; forecast; systematize, organize, cast, recast, lay groundwork.

adj procedural, formulaic, methodological, systematic, organizational; conspiratorial; strategic.

627 [path] **method** *n* road, procedure, way, means, manner, fashion, technique, process, course, route, track, beat, tack; door, gateway, channel, passage, avenue, means of access, approach.

adv how, in what way, in what manner; by what mode; one way or another, after this fashion.

628 mid-course *n* middle way, middle course, mean, golden mean; compromise, *(informal)* six of one and half a dozen of another, half measures, neutrality.

v steer a middle course, go straight; compromise, go half way, make a compromise.

adj moderate, midway; neutral, impartial.

629 circuit *n* roundabout way, digression, detour, loop, winding.

v go round about, make a circuit, detour, wind around, circle around; deviate, digress.

adj circuitous, indirect, roundabout; zigzag.

adv in a roundabout way, by an indirect course, indirectly.

630 requirement *n* requisite, requisition, need, necessity, wants, claim, demand, prerequisite; mandate, order, command, directive, injunction, charge, claim, precept.

v require, need, call for, have occasion for, necessitate, obligate; demand, request, need, order, enjoin, direct, ask.

adj requisite, necessary, essential, indispensable, needful; urgent, exigent, instant, crying.

adv of necessity.

631 instrumentality *n* mediation, intervention, medium, intermedium, vehicle, hand; aid; subservience.

go-between, intermediary, minister.

v mediate, minister, intervene; be instrumental, aid.

adj instrumental, useful, serviceable; intermediary, intermediate.

adv through, by, whereby, thereby, by the agency of, by dint of, by means of.

632 means *n* resources, wherewithal, way, ways and means, know how, ability; agency, method, approach; capital, provisions.

v have the means, find the means, possess the means.

adj instrumental.

adv by means of; herewith, therewith; wherewithal.

633 instrument *n* tool, implement, utensil, machinery, equipment.

adj instrumental; mechanical.

634 substitute *n* deputy, alternate, understudy, stand-in, proxy, *(informal)* sub, replacement.

v to substitute for, sub.

635 materials *n* raw materials, resources, stuff, stock, staples, supplies.

636 store *n* stock, fund, mine, supply, reserve, reservoir, *(informal)* stash; accumulation, hoard, storing, storage.

v store, put aside, lay away; store up, put up, hoard away, accumulate, amass, garner; reserve, husband, *(informal)* stash, hold back.

adj in store, in reserve, spare.

637 provision *n* supply, grist, resources, store, provender, stock, food; catering, providing, purveying, purveyance, supplying.

v make provision, provide, lay in, lay in a stock, lay in a store; supply, furnish, purvey, provision, cater, stock, store, replenish.

638 waste *n* consumption, expenditure, dissipation, diminution, decline, emaciation, exhaustion, loss, destruction, decay, impairment; misuse, prodigality, wasting; ruin, devastation, spoilation, desolation.

v waste, consume, spend, throw out, expend, squander, misuse, misspend, dissipate; destroy, wear away, erode, eat away, reduce, wear down, exhaust, enfeeble, wear out.

adj wasteful, prodigal, spendthrift; destructive; wasted, gone to waste.

639 sufficiency *n* adequacy, enough, competence.

v be sufficient, suffice, do, just do, satisfy; have enough.

adj sufficient, enough, adequate, ample, up to the mark, competent, commensurate, satisfactory.

adv sufficiently, amply.

640 insufficiency *n* inadequacy, incompetence, incompleteness, deficiency, imperfection, shortcoming; paucity, scarcity, dearth; dole, pittance; emptiness, poorness, depletion, flaccidity.

v be insufficient, not suffice, not do, fall short of, *(informal)* not cut it; want, lack, need, require, be in want.

adj insufficient, inadequate, too little, not enough, incomplete, deficient, imperfect, wanting, short, scarce, meager, poor, thin, sparse, scant; incompetent, perfunctory.

641 redundance *n* superfluity, superabundance, too much, too many, exuberance, profuseness, profusion, plenty, repletion, plethora, congestion, surfeit, overdose, overflow; excess, surplus; repetition, verbosity.

v superabound, overabound, swarm, overflow, run over, run riot, overrun, overdose, overload, overdo, overwhelm; supersaturate, gorge, glut, load, drench, inundate, deluge, flood; choke, cloy, suffocate, pile on, lay on thick, lavish.

adj redundant, exuberant, inordinate, superabundant, excessive, overmuch, replete, profuse, lavish; exorbitant, extravagant, overweening, *(informal)* much; superfluous, unnecessary, needless, over and above, spare, duplicate; repetitious, verbose.

adv over and above, over much, out of proportion, beyond bounds, over one's head.

642 importance *n* consequence, substance, weight, moment, prominence, consideration, significance, import, concern, emphasis, interest, momentousness, weightiness; gravity, seriousness, solemnity; pressure, urgency, stress.

v be important, deserve consideration, be worthy of notice, merit attention; attach importance, ascribe importance, value, care for, set store by; import, signify, matter, boot, carry weight; accentuate, emphasize, lay stress on; mark, underline, underscore.

adj important, consequential, weighty, momentous, prominent, considerable, significant, notable, salient; grave, serious, earnest, grand, solemn, impressive, commanding, imposing; urgent, pressing, critical, crucial, paramount, essential, vital, prime, primary, principal, all-important, capital, foremost, of vital importance; superior, considerable; significant, telling, trenchant, emphatic.

643 unimportance *n* insignificance, immateriality, triviality, paltriness, indifference, nothing, trifling; trumpery, trash, rubbish, frippery, chaff, bauble, trifle.

v be unimportant, not matter, matter little, signify little; make light of.

adj unimportant, of little account, of small importance, immaterial, unessential, nonessential, inconsequential, insignificant, inconsiderable, so-so; commonplace, ordinary, uneventful, mere, common; trifling, trivial, slight, slender, light, flimsy, shallow; frivolous, petty, niggling, piddling; poor, paltry, pitiful, sorry, mean, meager, shabby, beggarly, worthless, cheap, tawdry, trashy, gimmicky; unworthy of consideration, unworthy of notice; useless, of no account.

644 utility *n* usefulness, efficacy, helpfulness, service, use, stead, avail, help, aid; applicability, value, worth, productiveness.

v be useful, avail, serve, perform, help, aid, benefit; act a part, discharge a function, stand one in good stead.

adj useful, serviceable, functional, advantageous, valuable, productive, profitable, helpful, effectual, effective, efficacious, beneficial, salutary; applicable, available, practical, practicable, workable.

645 inutility *n* uselessness, inefficacy, ineptitude, inaptitude, inadequacy, inefficiency, unfruitfulness, futility, worthlessness, hopelessness.

v be useless, be of no help.

adj useless, unavailing, futile, inutile, fruitless, vain, ineffectual, profitless, bootless, valueless, worthless, hopeless; unserviceable, unusable, inoperative.

646 expedience *n* expediency, fitness, utility, suitability, profitability, advisability, propriety, appropriateness, desirability; opportunism, pragmatism, realism.

v be expedient, suit, befit, suit the occasion.

adj expedient, advantageous, opportune, fit, suitable, convenient, profitable, worthwhile, advisable, meet, proper, becoming, appropriate, desirable.

647 inexpedience *n* inexpediency, impropriety, unfitness, unsuitability, inappropriateness, undesirability; inconvenience, impracticality.

v be inexpedient, be inconvenient, hinder.

adj inexpedient, inopportune, unfit, unsuitable, disadvantageous, discommodious, unadvisable, unseemly, improper, unworkable, impractical, inconvenient, unprofitable, useless, worthless.

648 [good qualities] **goodness** *n* virtue, excellence, merit, value, worth; perfection, eminence, superiority, masterpiece, *chef d'oeuvre*, prime, flower, cream, elite, pick, pick of the litter, salt of the earth, *(informal)* A-1, *(informal)* tops, second to none; gem, jewel, treasure, one in a million; beneficence.

v be good, excel, transcend, stand the test, pass muster, challenge comparison, vie, emulate, rival, *(informal)* dwarf the competition; be beneficial, do good, profit, benefit, improve, be the making of, do a world of good, produce a good effect, do a good turn.

adj good, excellent, better, superior, above par, fine, genuine, true; best, choice, select, rare, invaluable, priceless, inestimable, superlative, perfect, inimitable, first-rate, first-class, very best, crack, prime, tip-top, capital, *(informal)* tops; beneficial, valuable, advantageous, profitable, edifying, salutary, serviceable; favorable, propitious.

649 [bad qualities] **badness** *n* harmfulness, hurtfulness, virulence, painfulness, abomination, pestilence, guilt, depravity, vice, evil, malignity, malevolence; bane, plague, evil star, ill wind, bad omen, *(informal)* jinx, *(informal)* whammy; snake in the grass, skeleton in the closet, *(informal)* ghosts, *(informal)* demons; ill-treatment, annoyance, molestation, abuse, oppression, persecution, outrage, misusage, injury, damage.

v hurt, harm, injure, damage, pain; wrong, aggrieve, oppress, persecute, trample upon, tread upon, walk over, overburden, weigh down, run down; victimize, maltreat, molest, abuse, ill-use, bruise, scratch, maul, smite, do violence, do harm, stab, pierce.

adj hurtful, harmful, baleful, injurious, deleterious, detrimental, noxious, pernicious, mischievous; oppressive, burdensome, onerous, malign, malevolent; virulent, venomous, corrosive, poisonous, deadly, destructive; bad, ill, dreadful, horrid, horrible, dire, rank, foul, rotten, as low as one can go, *(informal)* the pits; evil, wrong, reprehensible, hateful, abominable, detestable, execrable, damnable, infernal, diabolical; vile, base, villainous, cruel, mean, low; deplorable, wretched, sad, grievous, lamentable, pitiable, pitiful, woeful, painful.

650 perfection *n* ideal, summit, paragon, model, standard, pattern, mirror; impeccability, faultlessness, excellence; masterpiece, master stroke; transcendence, superiority.

v perfect, bring to perfection, ripen, mature, complete, finish; be perfect, transcend.

adj perfect, faultless, immaculate, spotless, unblemished, impeccable, exquisite, consummate; in perfect condition, sound, intact; best, model, standard, inimitable, beyond all praise.

651 imperfection *n* deficiency, inadequacy, insufficiency, immaturity; fault, defect, weak point, weak spot, flaw, taint, blemish, weakness, shortcoming, drawback.

v be imperfect, have a defect, not pass muster, fall short.

adj imperfect, deficient, inadequate, insufficient, immature, defective, faulty, unsound, out of order, out of tune, warped, lame, frail, weak, crude, incomplete, below par, found wanting; indifferent, middling, ordinary, mediocre, average, so-so, tolerable, fair, passable, decent, not bad, bearable, better than nothing; inferior, secondary, second-rate, poor substitute.

652 cleanness *n* purity, purification, purgation, cleanliness; ablution, lavation; neatness, tidiness, orderliness; cathartic, purgative, laxative; detergent, disinfectant.

v clean, cleanse, purify, purge, expurgate, clarify, refine; wash, launder, scour, scrub, disinfect, fumigate, deodorize, ventilate; rout out, clear out, sweep out, make a clean sweep of, start fresh; neaten, tidy up, order, put things in order.

adj clean, pure, immaculate, spotless, stainless, unsullied, sweet; neat, spruce, tidy, trim, kempt.

653 uncleanness *n* impurity, defilement, contamination, taint; decay, putrefaction, corruption, mold, mildew, rot, dry rot; squalor, slovenliness, filth, dirt, smut, grime, mud, mire, muck, quagmire, slime.

v be unclean, rot, putrefy, fester, rankle, reek, stink, mold, go bad; dirty, soil, tarnish, spot, smear, blot, blur, smudge, smirch; besmear, befoul, splash, stain, sully, pollute, defile, debase, contaminate, taint, corrupt.

adj unclean, dirty, filthy, grimy, soiled; dusty, smutty, sooty, slimy; slovenly, untidy, sluttish, dowdy, unkempt, unscoured, squalid; nasty, coarse, foul, impure, offensive, abominable, beastly, reeky, fetid; moldy, musty, moth-eaten, bad, gone bad, rancid, rotten, corrupt, putrid, carious, fecal; gory, bloody; gross.

654 health *n* soundness, well-being, vigor, good health, bloom, color, vitality, robust health.

v be in health, be healthy, bloom, flourish, feel fine, feel good.

adj healthy, healthful, in health, well, sound, hearty, hale, strong, hardy, robust, vigorous, fit as a fiddle, in top shape, chipper, *(informal)* all together.

655 disease *n* illness, sickness, ill health, ailment, infirmity, indisposition, complaint, disorder, malady; delicacy, delicate condition, decline, deterioration, decay.

v ail, suffer, be affected with, droop, flag, languish, sicken, pine, gasp, waste away, fail; take sick, take ill, come down with, contract a disease, catch a bug.

adj ill, sick, indisposed, not well, unwell, in poor health, in bad health, ailing, poorly, laid up, bed-ridden, out of sorts, under the weather, *(informal)* in bad shape; sickly, infirm, unsound, unhealthy, *(informal)* falling apart, weak, lame, decrepit; diseased, morbid, mangy, corrupt, contaminated, leprous.

656 salubrity *n* healthiness, healthfulness, wholesomeness.

v be salubrious, be good for, agree with.

adj salubrious, healthy, healthful, salutary, wholesome, sanitary, bracing, invigorating, benign, nutritious, tonic, hygienic.

657 insalubrity *n* unhealthiness, unsoundness.

v be unhealthy, not be good for, disagree with.

adj insalubrious, unhealthy, unwholesome, noxious, noisome, deleterious, pestilential, bad, harmful, virulent, venomous, poisonous, septic, toxic, deadly.

658 improvement *n* amelioration, amendment, emendation, correction, revision, reformation, restoration, repair, betterment, gain, advancement, elevation, increase, refinement, elaboration; acculturation, cultivation, civilization.

reformer, radical.

v improve, mend, amend, get better; ameliorate, better, amend, emend, correct, right, rectify, revise, reform, restore, repair; advance, progress, ascend, increase, fructify, ripen, mature; refine, enrich, elaborate; promote, cultivate, foster, enhance.

adj better, better off, all for the better; emendatory, corrective, reformative, restorative, improving, progressive, improved.

659 deterioration *n* debasement, recession, retrogradation, degeneracy, degeneration, degradation, depravation, depravity, retrogression; detriment, damage, loss, injury, impairment, contamination, spoilage, corruption, adulteration; decline, declension, senility, decrepitude; decadence, decay, dilapidation, falling off, wear and tear, erosion, corrosion, rottenness, blight, atrophy, collapse.

v deteriorate, degenerate, fall off, wane, ebb, decline, droop, go down, go downhill, sink, go to seed, go to waste, lapse, break down, crack, shrivel, fade, wither, molder, rot, rankle, decay, go bad, rust, crumble, shake, totter, perish, die; taint, infect, contaminate, poison, canker, corrupt, pollute, vitiate, debase, degrade, adulterate; injure, impair, damage, harm, hurt, spoil, mar, despoil, dilapidate, waste, ravage; wound, maim, cripple, scotch, mangle, mutilate, disfigure, blemish, deface, warp; blight, rot, corrode, erode, wear away, wear out, sap, mine, undermine, shake the foundations of, break up, destroy, decimate.

adj deteriorated, unimproved, injured, degenerate, imperfect; battered, weathered, weather-beaten, all the worse for wear, stale, dilapidated, faded, shabby, threadbare, worn, far gone, *(informal)* had it; decayed, moth-eaten, worm-eaten, mildewed, rusty, moldy, seedy, time-worn, wasted, crumbling, moldering, rotten, blighted, tainted; decrepit, broken down, worn-out, used up, out of commission, in a bad way, past cure, past hope, *(informal)* long gone.

660 restoration *n* reestablishment, replacement, reinstatement, renewal, rehabilitation, reconstruction, reproduction, rebuilding, renovation, revival; refreshment, resuscitation, revivification; renaissance, renascence, new birth, regeneration, reconversion; redress, retrieval, reclamation, recovery, resumption; repair, reparation, restitution, relief, deliverance, rectification, cure, healing; redemption.

v restore, recover, rally, revive, come round, pull through, get well, get over; reestablish, replace, rehabilitate, reinstate; reconstruct, rebuild, reproduce, reorganize, reconstitute, renew, renovate; redeem, reclaim, recover, retrieve, rescue, deliver; redress, recure; cure, heal, remedy, doctor, bring round; resuscitate, revive, reanimate, revivify, reinvigorate, refresh; recoup, make good, square, set to rights, correct, put in order; repair, retouch, patch up, fix.

adj restorative, recuperative, curative, remedial; restorable, remediable, retrievable, curable; restored, convalescent, renascent, reborn.

661 relapse *n* lapse, falling back, retrogradation, deterioration, backsliding.

v relapse, lapse, fall back, slip back, sink back, suffer a relapse, fall again.

adj retrograde.

662 remedy *n* help, redress, solution, answer, panacea; cure, relief, medicine, treatment, restorative, specific, medication, ointment, balm; antidote, corrective, antitoxin, counteractive.

doctor, physician, surgeon.

v remedy, cure, heal, set right, put right, doctor, nurse, restore, recondition, repair, redress; counteract, remove, correct, right, solve.

adj remedial, restorative, corrective, palliative; medicinal, therapeutic, curative; soluble.

663 bane *n* curse, evil, plague, scourge, pain, nuisance, thorn in the side, pain in the neck; poison, virus, venom; fungus, mildew, dry rot, canker, cancer; sting, fang, thorn, bramble, briar, nettle.

adj baneful, bad, sinister, pernicious, evil, baleful, poisonous, venomous, ruinous, unwholesome, harmful, deadly.

664 safety *n* security, surety, impregnability, invulnerability; safeguard, safety valve, precaution, custody, safe keeping, preservation, protection.

protector, guardian, warden, preserver, custodian, watchdog, sentinel, scout.

v be safe; protect, take care of, care for, preserve, cover, screen, shelter, shroud, guard, defend, secure, house, garrison; watch, patrol, look out, take precautions.

adj safe, secure, snug, warm, sure, sound, on the safe side, out of danger; dependable, trustworthy, sure, reliable; cautious, wary, careful; defensible, tenable, invulnerable, impregnable, unassailable, safe and sound.

665 danger *n* hazard, insecurity, instability, precariousness, slipperiness, risk, peril, jeopardy, liability, exposure; injury, evil; warning, alarm, apprehension.

v be in danger, run into trouble, lay oneself open to, hang by a thread, totter; endanger, expose to danger, imperil, jeopardize, adventure, venture, risk, hazard, threaten.

adj dangerous, hazardous, risky, perilous, precarious, unsafe, insecure, unstable, untrustworthy, unsteady, shaky, slippery, ominous, fearful, explosive, fraught with danger; defenseless, vulnerable, open, liable.

666 refuge *n* sanctuary, retreat, asylum, hiding place, stronghold, fortress, shelter, cover; anchor, mainstay, support, check, last resort, safeguard.

v seek refuge, take refuge, find refuge, take shelter, find safety.

667 pitfall *n* snare, trap, snag, ambush, snake in the grass, wolf in sheep's clothing, menace, complication, danger; slippery ground, weak foundation, rocks, reefs, sunken rocks, sand, quicksand, breakers, shoals, shallows, precipice, maelstrom.

668 warning *n* caution, notice, premonition, prediction, admonition, advice, lesson; alarm, omen, sign, signal, augury, portent, presage.

sentinel, sentry, watch, watchman, watchdog, patrol, scout, spy.

v warn, caution, admonish, forewarn; give notice, notify, appraise, inform; menace, threaten, portend.

adj premonitory, cautionary, advisory; ominous, portentous.

669 [indication of danger] **alarm** *n* alarum, alarm bell, tocsin, distress signal, siren, danger signal, hue and cry, SOS, cry, scream.

v alarm, sound the alarm, warn, cry out.

670 preservation *n* safekeeping, conservation; guarding, safeguard, shelter, protection, defense; maintenance, support, sustenance, continuance, retention, salvation.

v preserve, keep, conserve; guard, safeguard, shelter, shield, protect, defend, rescue; keep up, maintain, continue, support, uphold, sustain; retain; store, husband; cure, pickle, bottle, can.

adj preserved, unimpaired, uninjured, unhurt, safe, sound, intact; conservative, preservative.

671 escape *n* flight, evasion, loophole, retreat; reprieve, release, liberation; narrow escape, close call, near miss.

v escape, flee, abscond, fly, steal away, run away, *(informal)* take off, *(informal)* split; shun, fly, elude, evade, avoid.

adj stolen away, fled, *(informal)* cut out.

672 deliverance *n* extrication, disentanglement, rescue, reprieve, respite; liberation, release, emancipation, freedom; redemption, salvation.

v deliver, extricate, disentangle, rescue, reprieve, save, redeem; set free, liberate, release, emancipate, free; come to the rescue.

673 preparation *n* provision, plan, arrangement, anticipation, precaution, forecast, rehearsal; groundwork, homework, foundation, scaffolding; training, education, dissemination; readiness, ripeness, maturity.

v prepare, get ready, make ready, prime, arrange, make preparations, plan, devise, anticipate, lay the foundations, provide, order; mature, ripen, mellow, season, nurture; equip, arm, fit out, furnish; train, teach, prepare for, rehearse, make provision for, take steps, provide against.

adj prepatory, precautionary, provident, preparative, preparatory; provisional, preliminary; prepared, ready, available, all ready, handy; ripe, mature, mellow.

674 nonpreparation *n* unpreparedness, unreadiness; improvidence.

v be unprepared; extemporize, improvise.

adj unprepared, incomplete, premature, rudimental, embryonic, immature, unripe, raw, green, coarse, crude, rough, unhewn, untaught, fallow, unready; out of order, nonfunctional, *(informal)* on the fritz, in disrepair, *(informal)* out of whack; shiftless, improvident, thoughtless, careless, slack, remiss, happy-go-lucky.

675 essay *n* trial, endeavor, effort, attempt, struggle, venture, adventure, speculation, experiment.

v essay, try, experiment; endeavor, strive, tempt, attempt, venture, adventure, speculate, tempt fortune, *(informal)* give it a go, *(informal)* take a shot at.

adj experimental, tentative, probationary; venturesome, adventurous, speculative.

adv experimentally, on trial.

676 undertaking *n* task, job, venture, engagement, compact, contract, enterprise; pilgrimage, quest.

v undertake, engage in, embark on, launch into, plunge into, volunteer; engage, promise, contract, take upon onself, devote onself to, determine, take up, take in hand; tackle, set about, fall to, begin, broach.

677 use *n* employ, exercise, application, appliance; disposal; consumption; agency, usefulness; benefit, recourse, resort, avail; utilization, utility, service, wear; usage.

v use, make use of, employ, put to use, put into operation, apply, set in motion, set to work; ply, work, wield, handle, manipulate; exert, exercise, practice, avail oneself of, profit by; resort to, have recourse to, recur to, take up, try; utilize, bring into play, press into service; use up, consume, expend, tax, task, wear.

adj useful, instrumental, utilitarian, subservient, employable, applicable, beneficial.

678 disuse *n* forbearance, abstinence; relinquishment, abandonment; desuetude.

v not use, do without, dispense with, let alone, forbear, abstain, spare, waive, neglect; keep back, reserve; disuse, lay up, shelve, set aside, put aside, leave off, have done with; supersede, discard, throw aside, relinquish, dismantle.

adj not in use, unemployed, unapplied; disused, unused, done with.

679 misuse *n* misusage, misemployment, misapplication, misappropriation; abuse, profanation, prostitution, desecration; waste.

v misuse, misemploy, misapply, misappropriate; abuse, profane, prostitute, desecrate; waste, squander, destroy; overwork, overtask, overtax.

680 action *n* movement, work, labor, performance, moving, working, performing, operation; deed, act, feat, exploit; conduct, behavior, procedure, execution; energetic activity, exercise, exertion, energy, effort; affair, encounter, meeting, engagement, conflict, combat, fight, battle.

actor, doer, worker.

v act, do, perform, execute, achieve, transact, enact; commit, perpetrate, inflict; exercise, prosecute, carry on, work, function, labor, operate, exert energy, be active; behave, conduct oneself, comport oneself; play, feign, fake, imitate.

adj in action, in operation, operative.

681 inaction *n* passivity, inactivity, idleness, slothfulness; waiting, mulling around, killing time; rest, repose.

v not act, not do, be inactive, abstain from doing, do nothing, let alone, let things take their course; stand aloof, refrain, pause, wait, bide one's time, cool one's heels, waste time, lie idle.

adj inactive, passive, idle, slothful; out of work.

682 activity *n* movement, hustle, bustle, stir, fuss, flurry, action, business; industry, assiduity, assiduousness, laboriousness, drudgery; diligence, perseverance, vigilance, wakefulness, restlessness, fidgetiness; briskness, liveliness, animation, life, vivacity, spirit, dash, energy; eagerness, zeal, ardor, vigor, abandon, exertion; earnestness, intentness, devotion.

v be active, busy oneself in, stir about, rouse oneself, speed, hasten, bustle, fuss, *(informal)* raise a ruckus; push, push ahead, *(informal)* step on it, *(informal)* move it, make progress; toil, plod, persist, persevere, hustle, *(informal)* hustle it, *(informal)* push; look sharp, keep moving, seize the opportunity, *carpe diem*, lose no time, dash off, make haste; have a hand in, trouble oneself about.

adj active, brisk, lively, busy as a bee, vivacious, alive, frisky; quick, prompt, ready, alert, spry, sharp, smart, awake, wide awake, eager, zealous; industrious, assiduous, diligent, vigilant; businesslike; restless, fussy, fidgety, busy.

683 inactivity *n* inaction, inertness, lull, quiescence; idleness, remissness, sloth, indolence, dawdling, laziness; dullness, languor, sluggishness, torpor, stupor, lethargy; procrastination.

idler, drone, dawdler, moper, lounger, loafer, sluggard, laggard, slumberer.

v be inactive, do nothing, dawdle, lag, hang back, slouch, loll, lounge, loaf, loiter, take it easy; fritter away time, idle, piddle, putter, dabble, dally, dilly-dally; languish, flag, relax; kill time, waste time.

adj inactive, motionless; indolent, lazy, slothful, idle, remiss, slack, inert, torpid, sluggish, languid, supine, heavy, dull, listless; laggard, slow, rusty, lackadaisical, irresolute; drowsy, lethargic, soporific, dreamy, dreamy-eyed.

684 haste *n* urgency, need, hurry, flurry, bustle, spurt, rush, dash, scramble, bustle, ado, precipitancy, precipitation; swiftness, celerity, alacrity, quickness, rapidity, dispatch, speed, expedition, promptitude, timeliness, promptness.

v haste, hasten, make haste, hurry, dash, push on, press on, press forward, scurry, bustle, scramble, rush, accelerate, urge, expedite, quicken, speed, precipitate, dispatch.

adj hasty, speedy, quick, hurried, swift, rapid, fast, fleet, brisk; precipitate, rash, foolhardy, reckless, indiscreet, thoughtless, headlong; testy, touchy, irascible, petulant, waspish, fretful, fiery, excitable, irritable, peevish.

685 leisure *n* spare time, free time, convenience, liberty, pause, stay, halt, lull, breather, *(informal)* letup, breathing spell, break, *(informal)* time out; interlude, vacation, holiday.

v have leisure, take one's time; rest, relax, repose.

adj leisure, spare, free; leisurely, slow, deliberate, quiet, calm, restful, peaceful, languid, easy, gradual.

686 exertion *n* effort, action, activity, endeavor, struggle, attempt, strain, trial, stress; labor, work, toil, travail; trouble, pain; energy.

v exert, exert oneself, labor, work, toil, sweat, drudge, strive, strain; work hard, rough it, buckle to, take pains, concentrate, spare no effort.

adj laborious, wearisome, burdensome, *(informal)* tough, *(informal)* rough, strenuous, herculean, Sisyphean.

687 repose *n* rest, sleep, slumber; relaxation, breathing spell; halt, pause, respite, cessation; day of rest, Sabbath; holiday, vacation, recess.

v repose, rest; relax, unbend, slacken, catch one's breath, get one's wind, take a breather, pause; recline, lie down, go to bed, take a nap, go to sleep; take a holiday, go on vacation, shut up shop.

adj reposing, resting.

adv at rest.

688 fatigue *n* weariness, lassitude, tiredness, exhaustion, faintness; ennui, boredom, tedium, languor, yawning, drowsiness.

v be fatigued, yawn, droop, sink, flag, *(informal)* give out; gasp, pant, puff, blow, drop, swoon, faint; fatigue, tire, weary, exhaust, wear out; tax, task, strain; bore, tire, irritate, annoy.

adj fatigued, weary, drowsy, haggard, faint, exhausted, spent, tired, tired to death, worn out, *(informal)* gone; breathless.

689 refreshment *n* recovery of strength, restoration, revival, repair, relief.

v refresh, brace, strengthen, reinvigorate, revive, stimulate, freshen, cheer, enliven, reanimate; restore, repair, renew.

adj refreshing, restoring.

690 agent *n* doer, actor, performer, perpetrator, operator; practitioner, executioner, executor, executrix, minister, representative, deputy, servant, worker; participant, party to.

691 workshop *n* laboratory, factory, mill, mint, forge, studio, hive, beehive, seat of activity.

692 conduct *n* behavior, demeanor, action, actions, deportment, bearing, carriage, mien, manners; process, ways, practice, procedure, method; policy, tactics, strategy, plan; direction, management, execution, guidance, leadership, administration.

v conduct, behave, deport, act, bear; transact, execute, dispatch, discharge, proceed with, enact; direct, manage, carry on, supervise, regulate, administer, guide, lead.

adj procedural, practical, methodical, tactical, strategical, businesslike; directive, managerial, administrative, executive.

693 direction *n* guidance, advice, regulation, conduct, management, disposition, supervision, auspices, steerage, stewardship, ministration, administration, control, leadership, government, rule, command; order, command, instruction.

v direct, guide, advise, regulate, conduct, manage, control, dispose, supervise, overlook, steer, steward, pilot, minister, administer, legislate, lead, rule, govern, have charge of, command; order, instruct, prescribe.

adj directing, guiding, supervisory, managing, administering.

694 director *n* manager, governor, controller, superintendent, supervisor, overseer, inspector, foreman, surveyor, taskmaster, master, leader, boss; adviser, guide, pilot, captain, helmsman, driver; head, chief, principal, president, minister, official, functionary.

695 advice *n* counsel, opinion, recommendation, guidance, suggestion, persuasion, urging, exhortation; instruction, charge, injunction; admonition, warning, caution.

adviser, council, counselor, mentor.

v advise, give counsel to, suggest, recommend, prescribe, advocate, exhort, persuade; enjoin, enforce, charge, instruct; admonish, caution, warn; take counsel, confer, deliberate, discuss, consult, refer to; give counsel, offer counsel.

adj advisory, suggestive, persuasive, suasive; admonitory.

696 council *n* committee, court, chamber, cabinet, board, board of directors, advisory board, staff, syndicate, chapter; assembly, caucus, conclave, meeting, conference, session.

697 precept *n* direction, instruction, charge, prescript, prescription; golden rule, maxim, canon, law, code, act, statute, regulation, formula, form, technicality, rubric; order, command.

698 skill *n* skillfulness, dexterity, adroitness, expertness, proficiency, competence, facility, knack, mastery; accomplishment, acquirement, attainment, ability, craft; knowledge, wisdom, *savoir faire*, tact, wit, sagacity, discretion, finesse, craftiness, cunning, management; cleverness, ingenuity, capacity, talent, talents, faculty, endowment, *forte*, turn, gift, genius; intelligence, sharpness, readiness, invention, inventiveness, aptness, aptitude, proclivity, capacity for, genius for, felicity, capability, qualification.

v be skillful, excel in, be master of, have a knack for; take advantage of.

adj skillful, dextrous, adroit, adept, expert, apt, handy, quick, deft, proficient, masterly, crack, first-rate, conversant; skilled, experienced, practiced, competent, efficient, qualified, capable, fit, fit for, trained, prepared, finished; clever, able, ingenious, felicitous, inventive; shrewd, sharp, smart, intelligent, cunning, tactful, discreet, wise, knowledgeable.

adv skillfully, artistically, with consummate skill.

699 unskillfulness *n* want of skill, incompetence, inability, inexpertness, maladroitness, ineptitude, clumsiness, awkwardness, carelessness, bumbling, bungling; indiscretion.

v be unskillful, blunder, bungle, boggle, fumble, botch, stumble.

adj unskillful, unskilled, inexpert, incompetent, unable, inapt, bungling, inept, maladroit, awkward, clumsy, gawky; unfit, ill-qualified, unhandy, not conversant; raw, rusty, out of practice.

700 expert *n* specialist, authority, master, professional, connoisseur, veteran, old hand, old soldier; genius, mastermind, wizard, prodigy, *(informal)* pro.

701 bungler *n* blunderer, blunderhead, fumbler, duffer, clown, *(informal)* turkey, butter-fingers, greenhorn, amateur, rookie, novice, *(informal)* Sunday driver, *(informal)* armchair quarterback.

702 cunning *n* craftiness, skillfulness, shrewdness, artfulness, wiliness, subtlety, finesse, artifice, device, stratagem, intrigue, craft, guile, chicanery, duplicity, subterfuge, deceit, deceitfulness, slyness, deception; ability, skill, adroitness, expertness.

v be cunning, maneuver, contrive, manipulate, intrigue, finesse, surprise.

adj crafty, shrewd, artful, wily, subtle, tricky, foxy, politic, insidious, stealthy, Machiavellian, deceitful, duplicitous, sly, deceptive; canny, astute; ingenious, clever, skillful, sharp.

703 artlessness *n* simplicity, innocence, naivete, unworldliness, inexperience, inexposure, plainness, plain speaking, sincerity, honesty, openness, candor, matter of factness, bluntness.

v be artless, speak one's mind, come to the point, pull no punches.

adj artless, natural, simple, innocent, naive, childlike, unsuspicious, unworldly, unartificial, plain; sincere, frank, open, candid, honest, ingenuous, guileless, straightforward, aboveboard, point-blank, plain spoken, outspoken, blunt, direct, matter of fact.

adv in plain English, in simple words, without mincing words.

704 difficulty *n* dilemma, predicament, quandary, fix, exigency, emergency, crisis, trouble, problem, scrape, entanglement, strait, pass, pinch; reluctance, unwillingness, obstinacy, stubbornness; demur, objection, obstacle; labor, task, hard task, herculean task.

v be difficult, pose, perplex, bother, nonplus, hinder; encumber, embarrass, entangle.

adj difficult, hard, arduous, troublesome, irksome, laborious, formidable; awkward, unwieldy, unmanageable; fastidious, particular, stubborn, intractable, perverse; obscure, complex, intricate, delicate, uncertain, ticklish, critical; unfeasible, impracticable, impossible, hopeless; austere, rigid.

705 facility *n* ease, easiness, capability, feasibility, practicability; flexibility, pliancy, smoothness, child's play.

v be easy, run smoothly, work well; facilitate, smooth, ease, lighten, free, clear, disencumber, disentangle, extricate, unravel.

adj easy, facile; feasible, practicable, within reach, accessible; manageable, tractable, pliant, smooth.

adv easily, readily, smoothly.

706 hindrance *n* impediment, deterrent, hitch, encumbrance, obstruction, check, stricture, restraint, hobble, obstacle, stumbling block; interruption, interference; impeding, stopping, stoppage, preventing.

v hinder, interrupt, check, impede, retard, encumber, delay, hamper, obstruct, trammel, cramp, handicap; block, thwart, frustrate, disconcert, prevent.

adj obstructive, intrusive; onerous, burdensome, cumbersome, obtrusive.

707 aid *n* help, support, succor, assistance, service, furtherance; relief, rescue, charity; assistant, helper, supporter, servant; patronage, championship, advocacy, favor, interest.

v aid, support, help, succor, assist, serve, abet, back, second; spell, relieve, rescue; sustain, uphold, prop, hold up, bolster; promote, facilitate, ease, advocate; be of help, give help, give assistance, oblige, accommodate, humor, encourage.

adj aiding, auxiliary, helpful, supportive; charitable; friendly, amicable, well-disposed, neighborly.

708 opposition *n* antagonism, hostility, resistance, counteraction; competition, enemy, foe, adversary, antagonist; opposing, resisting, combating.

v oppose, resist, combat, withstand, thwart, confront, contravene, interfere; hinder, obstruct, prevent, check; contradict, gainsay, deny, refuse, dissent.

adj adverse, antagonistic, contrary, at variance, at odds, anti, at issue, in opposition; unfavorable, unfriendly, hostile, inimical, resistant.

adv against, versus, counter to, in conflict with, at cross purposes; in spite, in defiance.

709 cooperation *n* concert, concurrence, agreement, concord, togetherness, harmony, unanimity; complicity, collusion, participation, combination, union, team-work; association, partnership, alliance, pool, coalition, confederation, fusion, fellowship, fraternity; unanimity, partisanship, spirit, party spirit, *esprit de corps*.

v cooperate, concur, combine, unite, pool, share, band together, pull together; act in concert, join forces, fraternize; conspire, be in league with; side with, go along with, join hands with, throw in one's lot with, rally round; participate, have a hand in.

adj cooperating, cooperative, participatory; in league, party to.

adv cooperatively, unanimously, shoulder to shoulder.

710 opponent *n* adversary, antagonist, competitor, rival, opposition; enemy, foe.

711 auxiliary *n* helper, aid, ally, assistant, confederate, collaborator, colleague, associate, partner, mate, friend.

712 party *n* group, gathering, assembly, assemblage, company, crew, band; clan, family, fellowship, community; body, faction, side, circle, clique, set, gang, claque, coterie, combination, ring, league, alliance, association.

v unite, join, band together, cooperate, assemble.

adj clannish, cliquish, communal, familial, fraternal.

713 discord *n* dissidence, dissonance, disagreement, clash, shock; variance, difference, dissension, misunderstanding, cross-purposes, odds, division, split, rupture, disruption, breach, schism, feud, conflict, struggle, argument, contention, quarrel, dispute, tiff, squabble, altercation, words; strife, outbreak.

v be discordant, disagree, clash, jar, conflict, differ, dissent, fall out, quarrel, dispute, squabble, wrangle, bicker, have words with; split, break, disunite, feud.

adj discordant, dissident, dissonant; divisive, disruptive; contentious, argumentative, quarrelsome, disputatious, fractious; at variance, at cross purposes.

714 concord *n* accord, harmony, sympathy, agreement, union, unison, unity, peace; amity, friendship, alliance, *detente*, understanding, togetherness, conciliation.

v agree, accord, harmonize with, fraternize, understand one another, concur, pull together; side with, sympathize with.

adj concordant, congenial, in accord; harmonious, sympathetic, friendly, fraternal, conciliatory.

adv with one voice, unanimously, in concert with.

715 defiance *n* daring, courage, courageousness, bravery, boldness; assertiveness, aggressiveness; antagonism, insubordination, recalcitrance, rebelliousness, insolence, resistance.

v defy, challenge, resist, dare, brave, flout, scorn, despise.

adj defiant, daring, courageous, brave, bold; resistant, insolent, rebellious, recalcitrant, contumacious, insubordinate, antagonistic.

adv in the face of, under one's very nose.

716 attack *n* onslaught, assault, offense, battery, onset, charge, encounter, aggression, incursion, invasion, sally, sortie, raid, foray; criticism, blame, censure, abuse.

assailant, aggressor, invader, attacker.

v assail, assault, molest, threaten, storm, charge, set upon, invade, bombard, beset, besiege, lay siege, storm; criticize, impugn, blame, censure, abuse; declare war, begin hostilities.

adj aggressive, offensive; critical, abusive.

adv on the offensive.

717 defense *n* guard, garrison, fortification, shield, shelter, screen, preservation, protection, guardianship, safeguard, security; justification, pleading, vindication.

v defend, guard, fortify, shield, shelter, screen, preserve, protect, keep safe, guard against, watch over, safeguard, secure; parry, repel, put to flight; uphold, maintain, justify, vindicate.

adj defensive, protective.

718 retaliation *n* reprisal, requital, retort, counterstroke, counterattack, retribution, reciprocation, reciprocity, recrimination, revenge, vengeance, reaction.

v retaliate, requite, retort, counterattack, revenge, repay, return, avenge.

adj retaliatory, vengeful, revengeful, retributive, reciprocal, reactive.

adv in retaliation.

719 resistance *n* opposition, withstanding, front, stand, oppugnance, reluctance, repulsion; interference, friction; insurrection, insurgence, rebellion.

v resist, withstand, stand up, stand; confront, oppose, grapple with, rise up, revolt, rebel, repel, repulse.

adj resistant, refractory, recalcitrant, repulsive, repellent; stubborn, indomitable, obstinate.

720 contention *n* struggling, struggle, strife, discord, dissention, quarrel, disagreement, squabble, feud; rupture, break, falling out; opposition, belligerency, combat, conflict, competition, rivalry, contest; disagreement, dissension, debate, wrangle, altercation, dispute, argument, controversy.

v contend, struggle, strive, fight, battle, combat, vie, compete, rival; debate, dispute, argue, wrangle; assert, maintain, claim.

adj contentious, combative, belligerent, bellicose, warlike, quarrelsome, pugnacious; competitive.

721 peace *n* treaty, truce, accord, amity, harmony, concord; calm, quiet, tranquillity, peacefulness, calmness; order, security.

v be at peace; keep the peace; make peace.

adj peaceful, tranquil, placid, serene, calm, complacent; mellow, halcyon, pacific; peaceable, amicable, friendly, amiable, mild, gentle.

722 warfare *n* fighting, hostilities, war, combat, battle, ordeal; tactics, strategy, generalship.

v war, make war, wage war, fight, give fight, battle, do battle, combat, contend, cross swords.

adj warlike, contentious, belligerent, combative, bellicose, martial, military, militant.

adv to arms.

723 pacification *n* conciliation, reconciliation, accommodation, arrangement, adjustment, compromise; amnesty, peace offering, truce, armistice, suspension of hostilities.

v pacify, reconcile, propitiate, placate, conciliate, accommodate, appease, make peace; quiet, calm, tranquilize, assuage, still, smooth, moderate, ameliorate, mollify, meliorate, soothe, bury the hatchet.

adj pacific, concilatory.

724 mediation *n* negotiation, arbitration, parley; intervention, intercession, interposition.

mediator, arbiter, arbitrator, peacemaker, go-between, negotiator, moderator, diplomat.

v mediate, intercede, intervene, interpose, interfere; step in, negotiate, arbitrate.

adj mediatory.

725 submission *n* nonresistance, obedience, compliance, acquiescence, yielding, submissiveness, pliancy; surrender, cessation, capitulation; resignation, passivity, docility.

v succumb, submit, yield, bend, acquiesce, resign, agree, obey, comply, bow, surrender, capitulate.

adj submissive, obedient, compliant, acquiescent, passive, docile, tame, humble.

726 combatant *n* fighter, contestant, disputant, battler, litigant, contender, competitor, militarist, soldier, warrior, polemic, candidate; antagonist, foe, enemy, opponent, rival, adversary, assailant, opposition, assailer, assailant, assaulter, opposer, opponent.

727 arms *n* weapons, weaponry, armaments, armor, ammunition, munitions, deadly weapons.

v arm, outfit, ready for battle, prepare for battle.

728 arena *n* battleground, battlefield, field of battle, theater, ring, lists; playhouse, amphitheater, stage, boards; Colosseum, gymnasium, playing field.

729 completion *n* culmination, finish, conclusion, close, termination, end, finale; upshot, result; final touch, crowning touch; consummation, accomplishment, achievement, fulfillment; performance, execution; perfection, thoroughness.

v complete, finish, end, conclude, close, terminate, finalize; consummate, perfect, accomplish, do, fulfill, achieve, effect, execute, enact, dispatch, discharge.

adj whole, entire, full, intact, unbroken, one, perfect; done, consummate, perfect, thorough, through-and-through.

adv completely, thoroughly; perfectly.

730 noncompletion *n* incompleteness, nonfulfillment, nonperformance; neglect, shortcoming.

v not complete, leave unfinished, leave undone; neglect, let alone, let slip; fall short of.

adj incomplete, unfinished, sketchy.

731 success *n* progress, advance; hit, stroke, trump card; good fortune, good luck, luck, break; prosperity, achievement, fulfillment, accomplishment; ascendancy, mastery, conquest, victory, triumph; proficiency, skill, mastery.

v succeed, attain an end, secure an objective; progress, advance; accomplish, achieve, effect, complete; prosper, find fulfillment, fulfill oneself; master, conquer, triumph, surmount, overcome.

adj successful, prosperous, well-to-do; victorious, triumphant; masterful, proficient.

adv successfully, with flying colors, in triumph.

732 failure *n* unsuccessfulness, miscarriage, abortion, failing; neglect, omission, dereliction, non-performance; deficiency, insufficiency, defectiveness; blunder, mistake, fault, slip, mishap, scrape, mess, fiasco, breakdown; decline, decay, deterioration, loss; bankruptcy, insolvency, bust, dud.

v fail, come short, fall short, disappoint, miss the mark, miscarry, abort, blunder, botch, make a mess of, *(informal)* blow it, founder, flounder, sink, go amiss, go wrong, go hard with; fall off, dwindle, decline, fade, weaken, wane, give out, cease; desert, forsake.

adj unsuccessful, abortive, stillborn, fruitless, bootless, ineffectual, inefficient, insufficient, useless; lost, undone, bankrupt; wide of the mark, erroneous; frustrated, thwarted, foiled, defeated; defective, faulty.

adv unsuccessfully, in vain, to little purpose.

733 trophy *n* medal, prize, palm, laurel, honor, accolade, decoration, reward, recognition, triumph, celebration.

734 prosperity *n* well-being, success, fortune, wealth, affluence.

v prosper, thrive, flourish, rise, make one's way, flower, grow, blossom, bloom, fructify, succeed, *(informal)* make it.

adj prosperous, successful, wealthy, rich, well-to-do, well-off; favorable, propitious, fortunate, lucky, auspicious, golden, bright.

735 adversity *n* calamity, distress, catastrophe, crisis, disaster, failure; bad luck, hard times, misfortune, *(informal)* downers, *(informal)* bummers, trouble, hardship, pressure, affliction, wretchedness.

v go downhill, go to the dogs, decay, sink, decline, come to grief, *(informal)* hit the pits, fall on evil days.

adj adverse, unfavorable, unlucky, unfortunate; calamitous, disastrous, critical, dire, catastrophic; unprosperous, hapless, in a bad way, under a cloud, in adverse circumstances, down in the mouth.

adv adversely; if worst comes to worst.

736 mediocrity *n* average capacity, ordinariness, commonplaceness, insignificance, passableness, tolerableness, indifference, inferiority, paltriness, triviality; moderation, golden mean.

v jog on, get along.

adj mediocre, average, normal, ordinary, commonplace, run-of-the-mill, insignificant, tolerable, unimportant, indifferent, inferior, poor, slight, paltry; moderate, reasonable, temperate, respectable.

II. Intersocial Volition

737 authority *n* control, influence, jurisdiction, command, rule, sway, power, dominion, supremacy; expert, adjudicator, arbiter, judge, sovereign, ruler; warrant, justification, permit, permission, sanction, liberty, authorization.

v authorize, empower, commission, allow, permit, sanction, approve; warrant, justify, legalize, support, back; rule, sway, control, administer, govern.

adj authoritative, peremptory, magisterial, imperative, dogmatic, masterful; executive, administrative, sovereign, regnant, supreme, dominant, paramount, predominant, preponderant, influential, official, decisive, valid, absolute.

738 [absence of authority] **laxity** *n* laxness, looseness, slackness, lenience, toleration, relaxation, loosening, licence, freedom.

v be lax, tolerate, relax, give a free rein.

adj lax, loose, slack, remiss, lenient, negligent, careless, weak.

739 severity *n* seriousness, gravity, sternness, harshness, austerity, rigidity, rigorousness, strictness, stringency, relentlessness, abruptness, curtness; arbitrariness, absolutism, despotism, dictatorship, autocracy, tyranny, oppression; strength, force, brute force, coercion.

tyrant, disciplinarian, despot, taskmaster, oppressor, inquisitor.

v be severe, tyrannize, domineer, dominate, bully, inflict, wreak, be hard on, ill-treat, maltreat, oppress, trample on, crush, coerce.

adj severe, serious, grave, stern, harsh, austere, rigid, stiff, dour, rigorous, strict, strait-laced, stringent, relentless, hard, inexorable, abrupt, peremptory, curt, short; arbitrary, absolute, despotic, dictatorial, autocratic, tyrannical, oppressive, coercive, inquisitorial, ruthless, cruel, malevolent, arrogant.

adv severely, with a high hand, with a heavy hand.

740 lenience *n* leniency, tolerance, toleration, moderation, mildness, gentleness, favor, indulgence, forbearance, quarter, compassion, clemency, mercy.

v be lenient, tolerate, bear with, favor, indulge, allow.

adj lenient, tolerant, mild, easy, easy-going, gentle, tender, indulgent, compassionate, sympathetic, merciful.

741 command *n* order, ordinance, direction, bidding, injunction, charge, mandate, behest, ukase, commandment, requisition, requirement, instruction, dictum, act, fiat; demand, exaction, claim, request; control, mastery, disposal, rule, sway, power, domination.

v command, order, direct, bid, demand, charge, instruct, enjoin, require, impose; decree, enact, ordain, dictate, prescribe, appoint; claim, lay claim to.

adj commanding, authoritative.

742 disobedience *n* noncompliance, nonobservance, insubordination, contumacy, infraction, infringement, defiance, unruliness, rebelliousness, obstinacy, stubbornness, resistance, mutinousness, mutiny, rebellion.

insurgent, mutineer, rebel, revolutionary, rioter, traitor, *(informal)* radical.

v disobey, transgress, violate, disregard, defy, infringe, shirk, resist, mutiny, rebel, revolt.

adj disobedient, insubordinate, contumacious, defiant, refractory, unruly, fractious, rebellious, mutinous, obstinate, stubborn, unsubmissive, uncompliant, recalcitrant, insurgent, riotous.

743 obedience *n* observance, compliance, docility, tractability, deference, respect, duty, subservience, submissiveness, obsequiousness; allegiance, loyalty, fealty, homage, devotion.

v obey, comply, submit, follow, attend to, serve.

adj obedient, submissive, compliant, tractable, docile, deferential, respectful, dutiful, loyal, subservient.

adv obediently, in compliance with, in obedience to.

744 compulsion *n* coercion, constraint, duress, enforcement, conscription, force; impulse, necessity.

v compel, force, make, drive, coerce, constrain, enforce, impel, require, necessitate, oblige, motivate; subdue, subject, bend, bow, overpower.

adj compelling, compulsory, coercive, forcible, constraining; obligatory, necessary, unavoidable, inescapable, ineluctable, irresistible, inexorable.

adv by force, forcibly, on compulsion.

745 master *n* lord, commander, commandant, chief, head, leader, director, ruler, boss, authority.

746 servant *n* subject, retainer, follower, henchman, domestic, menial, help, helper, employee, worker, laborer.

v serve, function, answer, assist, help, aid, provide, cater, satisfy; wait on, attend.

747 [insignia of authority] **scepter** *n* regalia, staff, symbol, emblem, flag, badge; title.

748 freedom *n* liberty, independence, autonomy, noninterference; immunity, franchisement, franchise, privilege, latitude, scope; ease, facility; frankness, openness; familiarity, license, looseness, laxity.

v be free, have scope, do as one likes, do what one wants; free, liberate, permit, allow, set free.

adj free, independent, at large, loose, scot free; unconstrained, unconfined, unchecked, unhindered, unobstructed, unbound, uncontrolled, ungoverned, unchained, unfettered, unshackled, uncurbed, unbridled, unmuzzled; unrestricted, unlimited, unconditional; absolute; discretionary; wanton, rampant, irrepressible, unvanquished; immune, exempt, freed; autonomous.

adv freely.

749 subjection *n* dependence, subordination, thrall, thralldom, subjugation, bondage, serfdom, slavery, servitude, enslavement; service, employ, tutelage, constraint, yoke, submission, obedience.

v be subject, be at the mercy of, depend upon, fall prey to, play second fiddle to, serve, submit; subject, subjugate, master, tame, tread down, weigh down, enslave, enthral, rule.

adj subject, dependent, subordinate; under control, in harness.

750 liberation *n* disengagement, release, enlargement, emancipation, enfranchisement, deliverance, extrication, discharge, dismissal, acquittal, absolution.

v liberate, set free, free, disengage, release, emancipate, enfranchise, deliver, extricate, discharge, dismiss, unfetter, disenthrall, set loose, loose, let out, acquit, absolve.

adj liberated, freed.

751 restraint *n* restriction, circumscription, limitation, control, confinement, curb, check, suppression, constraint, repression.

v restrain, check, keep down, repress, curb, bridle, suppress, compel, hold, keep, constrain; restrict, circumscribe, confine, hinder.

adj restrained, constrained, restrictive, suppressive, repressive; imprisoned, pent up, under restraint.

752 prison *n* jail, gaol, cage, coop, pen, penitentiary, jailhouse, cell, block, dungeon, lock-up, stir, irons, *(informal)* calaboose, *(informal)* hoosegow, *(informal)* the joint, *(informal)* the big house.

753 keeper *n* custodian, guard, *(informal)* screw, jailer, gaoler, warder; escort, body-guard; protector, guardian, governor, governess, teacher, tutor, nurse.

754 prisoner *n* captive, convict, con, jailbird.

v be imprisoned, stand convicted.

adj in prison, in custody, in chains, under wraps, in stir.

755 [vicarious authority] **commission** *n* delegation, consignment, assignment, deputation, legation, mission, embassy, agency, special committee; errand, charge, permit; appointment, nomination, charter.

v commission, delegate, consign, assign, charge, entrust, authorize; appoint, name, nominate, ordain; install, induct, invest, employ, empower.

756 abrogation *n* abolition, cancelation, annulment, repeal, retraction, revocation, remission, recision, nullification, invalidation.

v abrogate, abolish, cancel, annul, repeal, retract, revoke, rescind, nullify, void, invalidate.

adj null and void.

757 resignation *n* abjuration, renunciation, abdication, abandonment, desertion, relinquishment, retirement.

v resign, quit, give up, abjure, renounce, forgo, disclaim, abrogate, abandon, desert, relinquish, retire.

758 consignee *n* trustee, nominee, committee, delegation, delegate, commission; functionary, agent, representative, messenger.

759 deputy *n* substitute, proxy, delegate, representative, surrogate, alternate, second, assistant.

v stand for, represent, answer for.

760 permission *n* authorization, warrant, sanction, liberty, license, enfranchisement, franchise, leave, permit, liberty, freedom, allowance, consent, concession, tolerance, sufferance, indulgence, favor.

v permit, allow, let, tolerate, bear with, agree to, suffer, concede, accord, favor, humor, indulge; grant, empower, franchise, charter, confer, license, authorize, warrant, sanction.

adj permitted, permissive, indulgent, libertarian, tolerant; permissible, allowable, legal, legalized, lawful, legitimate.

761 prohibition *n* interdiction, injunction, prevention, embargo, ban, restriction, disallowance.

v prohibit, forbid, interdict, veto, disallow, bar, restrict, limit; prevent, hinder, preclude, obstruct.

adj prohibitive, proscriptive, restrictive; preventive.

762 consent *n* assent, acquiescence, acceptance, acknowledgment, permission, compliance, concurrence, agreement, approval; accord, concord, consensus, settlement, ratification, confirmation.

v consent, assent, agree, concur, permit, allow, let, yield, grant, comply, accede, acquiesce.

adj compliant, agreeable, amenable.

763 offer *n* proposal, proposition, overture, tender, bid; offering, gift.

v offer, present, proffer, tender; propose, give, move, put forward, advance, invite, hold out, make a motion; hawk, merchandise, offer for sale.

adj for sale, in the open market.

764 refusal *n* rejection, spurning, denial, rebuff, repulse, repudiation; abnegation, protest, renunciation, disclaimer.

v refuse, decline, reject, spurn, turn down, deny, rebuff, repulse, repudiate; resist, repel, repudiate, renounce, disclaim, rescind, revoke.

adj noncompliant, dissident, recalcitrant, reluctant.

765 request *n* claim, demand, application, appeal, solicitation, petition, suit, entreaty, supplication, prayer.

v request, ask, ask for, beg, sue, petition, entreat, supplicate, solicit, beseech, plead, implore, require, demand, importune, clamor for.

adj importunate, clamorous, solicitous.

766 [negative request] **deprecation** *n* expostulation, intercession, mediation, protest, disapproval, remonstrance.

v deprecate, protest, expostulate, enter a protest, disapprove, remonstrate.

adj deprecatory, expostulatory, remonstrative; unsought.

767 petitioner *n* claimant, aspirant, postulant, seeker, solicitor, suitor, applicant, suppliant, supplicant; competitor, bidder; beggar, mendicant, panhandler, *(informal)* bum, *(informal)* streetwalker.

768 promise *n* undertaking, word, covenant, commitment, pledge, assurance, profession, vow, oath, guarantee, warranty, obligation, contract.

v promise, undertake, engage, enter into, bind oneself, commit oneself, pledge, agree, assure, warrant, guarantee, covenant, swear, give one's word; secure, give security, underwrite.

adj promissory, upon one's oath, on one's honor; promised, pledged, committed, bound, sworn.

769 compact *n* covenant, pact, contract, treaty, agreement, negotiation, bargain, arrangement, *(informal)* deal.

v contract, negotiate, bargain, stipulate, make terms; agree, engage, promise; complete, settle, confirm, subscribe, endorse.

adj compactual, contractual, promissory.

770 conditions *n* terms, articles, clauses, provisions, provisos, stipulations, promises, obligations, covenants.

v condition, stipulate, insist upon, contract, provide, bind, tie, oblige.

adj conditional, provisional.

adv conditionally, provisionally, on condition.

771 security *n* guarantee, warranty, bond, tie, pledge, promise, contract; mortgage, lien, pawn; stake, deposit, collateral, *(informal)* IOU, *(informal)* mark, promissory note; deed, bill of sale, receipt, certificate, title; sponsorship, surety, bail.

v give security, post bail, pawn, mortgage; guarantee, warrant, assure, promise; accept, endorse, underwrite, sponsor, stand for.

772 observance *n* performance, compliance, obedience, execution, discharge, acquittance, fulfillment, satisfaction; adhesion, acknowledgment, fidelity, faithfulness.

v observe, comply with, respect, abide by, acknowledge, adhere to, be faithful to, obey, act up to; meet, fulfill; carry out, execute, perform, satisfy, discharge.

adj observant, compliant, faithful, obedient, true, honorable; punctilious, scrupulous, as good as one's word.

adv faithfully.

773 nonobservance *n* evasion, failure, omission, noncompliance, neglect, negligence, laxity, laxness, carelessness, irresponsibility, disobedience; infringement, infraction, violation, transgression.

v fail, neglect, evade, omit, elude, ignore, disregard, discard, set at naught; infringe, transgress, violate, break.

adj nonobservant, lax, loose, disdainful, evasive, elusive, negligent, irresponsible, disobedient.

774 compromise *n* adjustment, negotiation, concession; compensation.

v compromise, bend, give and take, split the differences, come to an agreement, opt for the mean, adjust, arrange, settle.

775 acquisition *n* procurement, appropriation, gain, attainment, purchase, gift, find; profit, earnings, wages, winnings, income, proceeds, produce, crop, harvest, benefit.

v acquire, appropriate, gain, win, earn, attain, gather, collect; take over, take possession of, procure, secure, obtain, get, come into, receive, get hold of; profit, turn to profit.

adj profitable, advantageous, gainful, remunerative.

776 loss *n* damage, injury, privation, lapse, forfeiture, deprivation.

v lose, incur a loss, miss, mislay, let slip, forfeit; waste, get rid of.

adj lost, bereft, minus, deprived of, cut off, rid of; long lost, irretrievable.

777 possession *n* ownership, occupancy, holding, proprietorship, tenure, tenancy, control, custody; belonging.

v possess, own, have, hold, occupy, control, command, have to oneself, have in hand, belong to.

adj possessing, possessed of, in possession of, master of, in hand, at one's disposal; possessive, custodial.

777a exemption *n* exception, immunity, impunity, release.

v exempt, excuse, release; not have, be without.

adj exempt from, immune from, devoid of, without.

778 [joint possession] **participation** *n* partnership, co-ownership, joint tenancy, common holding, communion, community of possessions; communism, socialism, collectivism; cooperation.

participant, sharer, partner, copartner, shareholder; communist, socialist.

v participate, partake, share, share in, go halves, split up, divide, have in common, own in common.

adj participatory, joint, common, collective, communal, communist, communistic, socialist, socialistic.

779 possessor *n* holder, occupant, tenant, lessee; proprietor, proprietress, master, mistress, owner.

780 property *n* possession, possessions, goods, effects, chattels, estate, belongings, assets, means, resources, land, real estate, acreage; ownership, right; attribute, quality, characteristic, feature.

781 retention *n* keeping, holding, detention, custody, preservation, maintenance.

v retain, keep, hold, hold fast, secure, withhold, preserve, detain, reserve, maintain.

adj retentive.

782 relinquishment *n* renunciation, surrender, resignation, yielding, waiver, abdication, desertion, abandonment, quitting.

v relinquish, renounce, surrender, give up, resign, yield, cede, waive, forswear, forgo, abdicate, leave, forsake, desert, quit, abandon, let go, discard, cast off, dismiss, divest oneself.

adj cast off, done away with, left, forsworn, given up, left behind.

783 transfer *n* sale, lease, release, exchange, interchange; transference, transmission, changing hands.

v transfer, convey, assign, grant, consign, make over, hand over, pass, transmit, change, exchange, interchange, change hands; devolve, succeed.

adj transferable, conveyable, transmissive, exchangeable.

784 giving *n* bestowal, presentation, concession, delivery, consignment, dispensation, endowment, investiture, award; charity, almsgiving, liberality, generosity, philanthropy; gift, donation, present, boon, favor, grant, offering; allowance, contribution, donation, bequest, legacy; alms, largesse, bounty, help, gratuity; bribe, bait.

giver, granter, donor.

v give, bestow, confer, grant, accord, award, assign, entrust, consign; invest, allow, settle upon, donate, bequeath, leave; furnish, supply, help; afford, spare, favor with, lavish; deliver, hand, pass, turn over, present, give away, dispense, dispose of, give out, deal out, dole out, mete out, fork out; pay, render, impart.

adj charitable, beneficent, tributary, liberal, generous, philanthropic.

785 receiving *n* acquisition, reception, acceptance, admission, recipient, receiver, legatee, grantee, donee, beneficiary, pensioner.

v receive, take, acquire, admit, take in, accept; come into, fall to one, accrue.

adj receiving; received.

786 apportionment *n* allotment, consignment, assignment, allocation, distribution, dispensation, division, partition; portion, lot, share, measure, dose, dole, ration, ratio, proportion, quota, allowance.

v apportion, divide, distribute, dispense, allot, share, mete, portion out, parcel out, dole out, deal, carve, administer; partition, assign, appropriate, appoint.

adj distributive; respective.

787 lending *n* loan, advance, accommodation, mortgage, investment.

v lend, loan, advance, accommodate, lend on security, pawn; let, lease.

788 borrowing *n* pledging, pawning; appropriating, stealing, theft.

v borrow, pledge, pawn, borrow money; hire, rent, lease; appropriate, use, steal from, imitate.

789 taking *n* appropriation, capture, apprehension, seizure, abduction, dispossession, deprivation, expropriation, divestment, confiscation, eviction; extortion, theft; reprisal, recovery.

v take, catch, hook, nab, bag, pocket, receive, accept; reap, cull, pluck, gather; appropriate, assume, possess oneself of, help oneself to, commandeer, make free with; take away, abduct, steal, seize, snatch, snap up, capture, get hold of, take from, take away from, dispossess, expropriate, oust, eject, divest, confiscate, usurp, strip, fleece; retake, resume, recover.

adj predatory, rapacious, parasitic, greedy, ravenous.

790 restitution *n* return, restoration, reinvestment, rehabilitation, reparation, atonement, compensation, recovery.

v return, restore, give back, render, give up, let go; recoup, reimburse, compensate, reinvest, remit, rehabilitate, repair, make good, settle up; recover, get back, redeem, take back again.

adj compensatory, redemptive, recouperative.

791 stealing *n* theft, thievery, robbery, swindling, fraud, appropriation.

v steal, take, thieve, rob, pilfer, purloin, *(informal)* swipe, filch, embezzle, swindle, appropriate, fleece, defraud, *(informal)* rip off, *(informal)* screw.

adj thievish, light-fingered, piratical, predatory.

792 thief *n* robber, pilferer, filcher, rifler, crook, *(informal)* rip-off artist, cheat; burglar, house-breaker, second-story man, safecracker.

793 booty *n* spoils, plunder, prize, loot, catch, pickings, stolen goods, *(informal)* haul.

794 barter *n* exchange, trade, traffic, commerce, business, bargain; dealing, transaction, negotiation.

v barter, trade, exchange, traffic, bargain, swap, buy and sell, give and take, deal, haggle, negotiate, drive a bargain, transact.

adj commercial, mercantile, interchangeable, in trade, for sale, marketable.

795 purchase *n* buying, purchasing, acquisition; bargain, buy.

buyer, purchaser, shopper, customer, client, patron, clientele.

v purchase, buy, acquire, get, obtain, procure; shop, market, go shopping.

796 sale *n* selling, vendition, commerce, mercantilism, transaction, exchange, auction, trade.

seller, vendor, merchant.

v sell, trade, barter, vend, exchange, deal in, dispose, merchandise, hawk.

adj salable, marketable, vendible, for sale.

797 merchant *n* trader, dealer, seller, salesman, saleswoman, tradesman, shopkeeper, retailer, hawker, huckster, peddler, broker.

798 merchandise *n* goods, wares, commodity, articles, stock, produce, product, staple commodity, store, cargo.

v merchandise, sell.

799 market *n* mart, marketplace, fair, bazaar, business district, mall, shopping center, store, department store, establishment, place of business, office.

800 money *n* finance, accounts, funds, assets, wealth, supplies, ways and means, wherewithal, capital, almighty dollar, cash, currency, hard cash, *(informal)* bucks, change, small change, *(informal)* green, greenbacks; sum, amount, balance.

adj monetary, pecuniary, financial, fiscal.

801 treasurer *n* bursar, banker, purser, receiver, steward, trustee, accountant, paymaster, cashier, teller, financier.

802 treasury *n* bank, exchequer, strongbox, stronghold, coffer, chest, depository, purse, moneybag, safe, vault, cash box, cash register, till; securities, stocks, bonds, notes.

803 wealth *n* riches, fortune, opulence, affluence, easy circumstance, *(informal)* silver spoon, independence, competence, sufficiency, solvency; provision, livelihood, maintenance, means, resources, substance; income, capital, money.

v be wealthy, be rich.

adj wealthy, rich, affluent, well-off, well-to-do, comfortable.

804 poverty *n* indigence, penury, pauperism, destitution, want, need, neediness, lack, privation, distress, difficulties, straits, bad straits.

v be poor, want, lack, starve, live from hand to mouth, go to the dogs.

adj poor, indigent, destitute, poverty-stricken, needy, penniless, broke, *(informal)* bust, hard up, insolvent, seedy, beggarly.

805 credit *n* trust, score, tally, account, *(informal)* tab, bill.

creditor, lender, usurer.

v credit, accredit, entrust, keep an account with.

806 debt *n* obligation, liability, debit, score, duty, due.

debtor, borrower.

adj liable, answerable for, in debt; unpaid, in arrear.

807 payment *n* discharge, settlement, clearance, liquidation, satisfaction, reckoning, arrangment; acknowledgment, release, receipt, voucher; installment, remittance.

v pay, settle, liquidate, discharge, quit, acquit oneself of, reckon up, satisfy, compensate, reimburse, remunerate, recompense, make payment, square accounts, balance accounts, pay in full.

adj out of debt, solvent; straight, clear.

808 nonpayment *n* default, protest, repudiation; insolvency, bankruptcy, failure.

v not pay, default, fail, stop payment; run up bills.

adj in debt.

809 expenditure *n* outlay, expenses, disbursement, payment, costs, fees.

v expend, spend, pay out, disburse, *(informal)* fork out, lay out.

810 receipt *n* value received, acknowledgment of payment.

v receive, take, get, bring in.

adj profitable, remunerative.

811 accounts *n* money matters, finance, budget, bill, score, reckoning, account; statement, ledger, inventory, register, book, books, sheet; balance.

accountant, auditor, bookkeeper, financier.

v keep accounts, enter, post, book, credit, debit, balance.

812 price *n* amount, cost, expense, charge, figure, demand, damage, fare, hire, wages; worth, rate, value, valuation, appraisal; market price, quotation; bill, invoice.

v price, set a price, fix a price, appraise, assess, charge, demand, ask, require, exact; fetch, sell for, bring in, yield, accord.

813 discount *n* abatement, reduction, depreciation, allowance, qualification, rebate, sale.

v discount, put on sale, reduce, take off, allow, deduct, abate, rebate.

814 dearness *n* expensiveness, costliness, high price; overcharge, extravagance, exorbitance.

v be expensive, cost a lot; overcharge, bleed, fleece, extort.

adj dear, expensive, costly, precious; extravagant, exorbitant, unreasonable; priceless.

815 cheapness *n* low price, depreciation, bargain, value, *(informal)* steal, *(informal)* great buy.

v be cheap, cost little.

adj cheap, moderate, reasonable, inexpensive, dirt cheap.

816 liberality *n* generosity, munificence, bounty, bounteousness, hospitality, charity.

v be liberal, spend freely, give, spare no expense.

adj liberal, free, generous, bountiful, hospitable, munificent, beneficient, princely, charitable.

817 economy *n* frugality, thrift, thriftiness, saving, care, husbandry, retrenchment, parsimony.

v economize, save, retrench, husband.

adj economical, frugal, careful, thrifty, chary, parsimonious.

818 prodigality *n* unthriftiness, waste, wastefulness, profusion, profuseness, extravagance, profligacy, lavishness, squandering.

prodigal, spendthrift, squanderer.

v be prodigal, squander, lavish, misspend, waste, dissipate, fritter one's money.

adj prodigal, profuse, unthrifty, improvident, wasteful, profligate, extravagant, lavish.

819 parsimony *n* stinginess, illiberality, avarice, rapidity, rapacity, venality, cupidity, selfishness.

miser, niggard, churl, skinflint, codger, scrimp, *(informal)* tightwad, usurer, Scrooge.

v be parsimonious, grudge, begrudge, stint, pinch, hold back, withhold, starve, famish.

adj parsimonious, penurious, stingy, cheap, miserly, mean, pennywise, niggardly, tight, ungenerous, churlish, mercenary, venal, covetous, usurious, avaricious, greedy, rapacious, selfish.

Class VI

Words relating to the Sentient and Moral Powers

I. Affections in General

820 affections *n* character, qualities, disposition, nature, spirit, temper, temperament, idiosyncracy, habit, bent, bias, predisposition, proclivity, propensity, humor, mood, sympathy; soul, heart, inner man, essence; passion, driving spirit, ruling passion.

adj affected, characterized, formed, cast, molded, tempered, predisposed, prone, inclined, imbued; inborn, ingrained, deep-rooted.

adv at heart.

821 feeling *n* consciousness, impression; emotion, passion, sentiment, sensibility; sympathy, empathy; fervor, ardor, zeal, warmth, tenderness, sensitivity, sentimentality, susceptibility, pity; sentiment, opinion.

v feel, receive an impression, respond to.

adj feeling, emotional, sensitive, tender; sympathetic; emotional, impassioned, passionate, fervent, tender, sensitive; heart-felt, thrilling, rapturous, soul-stirring; moved, touched, affected.

adv heart and soul, from the bottom of one's heart.

822 sensibility *n* responsiveness, sensitiveness, awareness, susceptibility, impressibility, tenderness, sentimentality, sentimentalism; excitability; appreciation, understanding, moral sensibility.

v be sensitive, have a soft spot in one's heart.

adj sensitive, impressionable, susceptible, tender, warm-hearted, sentimental; excitable; aware, understanding, appreciative.

823 insensibility *n* insensitiveness, impassivity, apathy, coldness, callousness; imperturbable; dullness, boorishness.

v be insensitive, not care, be unaffected, have no interest in.

adj insensitive, unconscious, unaware; inattentive, indifferent, lukewarm; apathetic, impassive, unimpressionable; cold-blooded, cold-hearted, unmoved, unaffected, callous, thick-skinned, uncaring.

adv in cold blood.

824 excitation *n* excitation of feeling; mental excitation; galvanism, stimulation, provocation, inspiration, infection; animation, agitation, perturbation; fascination, intoxication, ravishment; irritation, anger, passion, thrill.

v excite, affect, touch, move, impress, interest, animate, inspire, infect, awake; evoke, provoke; stir up, wake up, light up; rouse, arouse, stir, fire, kindle, inflame; stimulate, quicken, sharpen, whet, wet the appetite, fan the fire, raise to a fervor; absorb, rivet, intoxicate, fascinate, enrapture; agitate, perturb, ruffle, fluster, disturb, startle, shock, stagger, astound, electrify, galvanize; irritate.

adj excited, excitable, wrought up, overwrought, upset, hysterical, hot, red-hot, flushed, feverish, boiling, ebullient, seething, fuming, raging, raving, frantic, mad, distracted, beside oneself; exciting, warm, glowing, fervid, soul-stirring, thrilling, overwhelming, overpowering, sensational.

825 [excess of sensitiveness] **excitability** *n* impetuosity, vehemence, boisterousness, impatience, intolerance, irritability, restlessness, agitation; passion, excitement, fever, tumult, ebullition, tempest, fit, paroxysm, explosion, outburst, agony; violence, rage, fury, furor, desperation, madness, distraction, delirium, frenzy, hysterics.

v be impatient, lose patience, fuss, fidget; lose one's temper, flare up, burn, boil over, foam, fume, rage, rant, run wild, go mad, go into hysterics.

adj excitable, high-strung, nervous, irritable, impatient, intolerant; feverish, hysterical, delirious, mad; hurried, restless, fidgety, fussy; vehement, violent, wild, furious, fierce, fiery, hotheaded; overzealous, enthusiastic, impassioned, fanatical; rabid, clamorous, turbulent, tumultuous, boisterous; impulsive, impetuous, passionate, uncontrolled, uncontrollable, ungovernable, irrepressible, volcanic.

826 inexcitability *n* imperturbability, even temper, dispassion, patience, impassivity; coolness, calmness, composure, placidity, serenity, quietude; self-possession, self-restraint, stoicism; resignation, submission, sufferance, endurance, forbearance, fortitude, moderation, restraint.

v bear, endure, tolerate, suffer, put up with, reconcile oneself to, resign oneself to, brook, swallow, make the best of, stomach; compose, appease, propitiate, repress, calm down, cool down.

adj inexcitable, imperturbable, unsusceptible, dispassionate, enduring, stoical, staid, sober, sedate; easygoing, peaceful, placid, calm, cool; composed, collected, unruffled, content, resigned, subdued.

II. Personal Affections

827 pleasure *n* happiness, gladness, delectation, enjoyment, delight, joy, glee, cheer, cheerfulness, well-being, satisfaction, gratification, comfort, ease; felicity, bliss, enchantment, transport, rapture, ravishment, ecstasy, luxury, sensuality, voluptuousness.

v be pleased, joy, enjoy oneself, have one's head in the clouds, fall into raptures; be pleased with, derive pleasure from, take pleasure in, *(informal)* get into, delight in, rejoice in, indulge in, luxuriate in, relish, love, enjoy, like, *(informal)* dig, take a fancy to, take a shine to.

adj happy, blissful, joyful, gladsome, cheerful; comfortable, at ease, content; ecstatic.

adv happily, with pleasure.

828 pain *n* suffering, distress, torture, misery, dolor, anguish, agony, torment, throe, pang, ache, smart, twinge, stitch; displeasure, dissatisfaction, discomfort, discomposure, disquiet, malaise, inquietude, uneasiness, vexation, discontent, dejection, weariness; annoyance, irritation, worry, affliction, bore, bother, mortification, plague, care, solicitude, trouble, trial, ordeal, burden, load, fret; prostration, desolation, despair.

v suffer, afflict, torture, torment, distress, despair; hurt, harm, injure, trouble, grieve, disquiet, discomfort, discompose, worry, irritate, vex, mortify, plague.

adj uncomfortable, uneasy, weary; unhappy, infelicitous, poor, wretched, miserable, woebegone, careworn, cheerless, sorry, sorrowful, stricken, in tears, in despair.

829 pleasurableness *n* pleasantness, agreeableness, delectability, delight, congeniality; sprightliness, cheer, cheerfulness, liveliness; attraction, attractiveness, charm, fascination, enchantment, witchery, seduction, winning ways, amenity, amiability; loveliness, beauty, brightness; goodness.

v be pleasurable, afford pleasure, offer pleasure, please, charm, delight, gladden, cheer; attract, invite, allure, stimulate, interest, captivate, fascinate, enchant, entrance, enrapture, bewitch, ravish, enravish, transport; agree with, satisfy, gratify; slake, satiate, quench; regale, refresh, treat, amuse.

adj pleasurable, pleasant, agreeable, enjoyable, delightful, congenial, amiable; comfortable, cordial, genial, gladsome, sweet, delectable, nice, dainty, delicate, delicious, luscious, luxurious, voluptuous, sensual; attractive, lovely, beautiful, seductive, rapturous, ecstatic, beatific, heavenly; fair, sunny, bright; gay, sprightly, merry, cheery, cheerful, lively, vivacious.

830 painfulness *n* trouble, care, trial, affliction, blow, burden, curse, mishap, misfortune, adversity; annoyance, nuisance, grievance, bore, bother, vexation, mortification; wound, sore, sore subject, thorn in the side, skeleton in the closet; sorry sight, heavy news, bad news; affront, insult, offense.

v pain, hurt, wound, sadden, displease, annoy, trouble, disturb, cross, perplex, irk, vex, mortify, worry, plague, bother, pester, harass, badger, bait, heckle, irritate, anger, persecute, provoke; harrow, torment, torture; affront, insult, give offense, offend.

maltreat, mistreat; sicken, disgust, revolt, nauseate, repel, shock, horrify, appal.

adj painful, hurtful, dolorous; unpleasant, disagreeable, unpalatable, bitter, distasteful; unwelcome, undesirable, obnoxious; dismal, dreary, melancholy, grievous, piteous, woeful, rueful, mournful, deplorable, pitiable, lamentable, pathetic; invidious, vexatious, troublesome, irksome, wearisome, worrisome; intolerable, insufferable, unsupportable, unbearable, unendurable, grim, dreadful, fearful, frightful, dire, odious, hateful, repulsive, repellant, abhorrent, horrid, horrible, offensive, nauseous, loathsome, vile, hideous; sore, severe, grave, hard, harsh, cruel; ruinous, disastrous, calamitous, tragic; burdensome, onerous, oppressive, cumbersome.

adv painfully.

831 content *n* contentment, complacency, satisfaction, ease, serenity, comfort; conciliation, resignation.

v gratify, satisfy, set at ease, comfort, appease, conciliate, reconcile.

adj contented, complacent, satisfied, sanguine, comfortable; assenting, acceding, resigned, willing, agreeable.

adv to one's heart's content.

832 discontent *n* discontentment, dissatisfaction, uneasiness, disquietude, restlessness, displeasure.

v be discontented, repine, regret, fret, chafe, grumble; dissatisfy, disappoint, disconcert.

adj discontented, dissatisfied, displeased, uneasy, restless, dejected, malcontent, regretful, down in the dumps.

833 regret *n* sorrow, lamentation, grief; remorse, penitence, contrition, repentance.

v regret, deplore, lament, feel sorry about, grieve at, bemoan, bewail, rue, mourn for, repent.

adj regretful, sorry, lamentable, rueful; penitent, contrite.

834 relief *n* deliverance, alleviation, ease, assuagement, mitigation, comfort, solace, consolation; help, assistance, aid.

v relieve, ease, alleviate, assuage, mitigate, allay, comfort, soothe, lessen, abate, diminish; cheer, comfort, console; aid, help, assist, succor, refresh, remedy, support.

adj soothing, consoling, assuaging, comforting, palliative, curative.

835 aggravation *n* worsening, heightening, intensification, exaggeration; (*informal*) annoyance, irritation, vexation.

v aggravate, worsen, intensify, heighten, increase, make serious, make grave.

adj worse, intensified, irritated.

adv from bad to worse, out of the frying pan and into the fire.

836 cheerfulness *n* geniality, high spirits, liveliness, vivacity, joviality, jocularity, mirth, merriment, exhilaration.

v cheer, gladden, enliven, inspirit, delight, rejoice, exhilarate, animate, encourage; shout, applaud, acclaim, salute.

adj cheery, gay, blithe, happy, lively, spirited, sprightly, joyful, joyous, mirthful, buoyant, sparkling, vivacious, gleeful, sunny, jolly; pleasant, bright, gay, winsome, gladdening, cheery, cheering, inspiring, animating, hearty, robust.

adv cheerfully.

837 dejection *n* depression, heaviness, heavy heart, melancholy, sadness, dumps, doldrums, despondency, gloom, weariness, disgust, despair, hopelessness.

v be dejected, lose heart, frown, mope, droop, despond, brood over, sink, despair.

adj unhappy, depressed, dispirited, disheartened, discouraged, despondent, (*informal*) down, downhearted, sad, melancholy, lugubrious, heartsick, dismal, gloomy, miserable, desolate; pessimistic, cynical.

adv with a long face, with tears in one's eyes.

838 rejoicing *n* exaltation, triumph, jubilation, reveling, merrymaking, celebration, paean; smile, smirk, grin, giggle, titter, laughter, guffaw, shout, peal of laughter.

v rejoice, congratulate oneself, clap one's hands, dance, skip, sing, hurrah; cry for joy, leap with joy, exalt, triumph; smile, smirk, grin, giggle, titter, chuckle, cackle, laugh, crow, burst out, shout, split, roar, shake one's sides, split one's sides.

adj jubilant, exultant, triumphant, flushed, (*informal*) high, elated, laughing, convulsed with laughter.

839 lamentation *n* lament, howl, wail, wailing, complaint, moan, moaning, groan, sob, sigh; dirge, elegy, monody, threnody.

v lament, bewail, bemoan, deplore, grieve, scream, sob, cry, weep, mourn over, sorrow over.

adj lamenting, in mourning, sorrowful, mournful, lamentable, tearful, plaintive.

840 amusement *n* enjoyment, entertainment, recreation, diversion, relaxation, pastime, pleasure, playing, festivity.

v amuse, entertain, cheer, divert, enliven, interest; amuse oneself, play, sport, make merry.

adj amusing, entertaining, diverting, relaxing, pleasant, witty, jovial, jolly, playful.

841 weariness *n* ennui, lassitude, fatigue, exhaustion, boredom; tedium, monotony, dullness.

v weary, tire, fatigue, bore, exhaust.

adj wearisome, tiresome, boring, tedious, irksome, monotonous, humdrum, dull, prosaic, trying; weary, drowsy, exhausted, tired, wearied, fatigued; uninterested, impatient, dissatisfied.

842 wit *n* drollery, facetiousness, pleasantry, repartee, cleverness, humor, fun; understanding, intelligence, sagacity, wisdom, intellect, mind, sense.

v joke, jest, banter, pun.

adj witty, quick, quick-witted, nimble, sharp, clever, facetious, whimsical, pleasant, humorous, playful, sparkling, scintillating; intelligent, sagacious, wise, perceptive, insightful.

843 dullness *n* heaviness, flatness, stupidity, obtuseness, lack of originality, banality.

v be dull, blunt, deaden, benumb.

adj dull, uninteresting, unimaginative, dry, prosaic, matter-of-fact, commonplace, boring, tedious, dreary, vapid; stupid, stolid, slow, flat.

844 humorist *n* wit, wag, comedian, comedienne, joker, jester, wisecracker, epigrammatist, punster, buffoon, clown, fool, satirist, lampooner, cutup, funnyman.

845 beauty *n* loveliness, pulchritude, elegance, grace, gracefulness, comeliness, seemliness, fairness, attractiveness, brilliance, radiance, splendor, gorgeousness, magnificence, sublimity.

v beautify.

adj beautiful, handsome, comely, seemly, attractive, lovely, pretty, fair, fine, elegant, beauteous, graceful, pulchritudinous, brilliant, radiant, gorgeous, magnificent; artistic, aesthetic, picturesque.

846 ugliness *n* homeliness, inelegance, unsightliness, distortion, disfigurement, deformity, frightfulness.

v deface, disfigure, distort.

adj ugly, displeasing, hard-featured, unlovely, unsightly, unseemly, homely; hideous, gruesome, repulsive, offensive, revolting, terrible, base, vile, squalid, gross, monstrous, heinous; disagreeable, unpleasant, objectionable.

847 ornament *n* ornamentation, adornment, decoration, embellishment, frills, finery.

v ornament, embellish, adorn, decorate, beautify.

adj ornamental, decorative; ornamented, ornate, embellished, beautified.

848 blemish *n* disfigurement, deformity, defect, flaw, fault, taint, blot, spot, speck.

v stain, sully, spot, taint, tarnish, injur, mar, damage, deface, impair.

adj disfigured, injured, imperfect, discolored, freckled, pitted.

849 simplicity *n* plainness, homeliness; clarity, chasteness, restraint, severity, lack of adornment, lack of affectation.

v simplify, uncomplicate, clarify, strip to essentials, get back to basics.

adj simple, plain, homely, natural, unadorned, unaffected, unembellished, neat, unassuming, unpretentious; chaste, severe; clear, straightforward, lucid.

850 [good taste] **taste** *n* good taste, delicacy, refinement, polish, elegance, grace, discrimination, culture, cultivation.

v show taste, appreciate, judge, criticize, discriminate.

adj tasteful, in good taste, decorous, attractive, cultivated, cultured, refined, discriminative, polished, felicitous, appropriate, suitable, apt, becoming, pleasing.

adv tastefully, elegantly.

851 [bad taste] **vulgarity** *n* bad taste, barbarism, coarseness, lack of decorum, ill-breeding, boorishness; gaudiness, tawdriness, finery, frippery, tinsel.

v be vulgar; vulgarize.

adj vulgar, in bad taste, unrefined, boorish, common, coarse, ill-bred, ill-mannered, ignoble, mean, plebeian, crude, rude, shabby; gaudy, tawdry, flashy, garish, crass, showy, (*informal*) tacky.

852 fashion *n* custom, style, vogue, mode, rage, craze; conventionality, conformity; society, polite society, beau monde; manners, breeding, air, demeanor, savoir-faire, gentility, decorum, propriety, etiquette.

v be fashionable, be the rage; fashion, adapt, suit, fit, adjust; make, shape, frame, form, mold.

adj fashionable, in vogue, à la mode, all the rage; modish, stylish, conventional, customary; well-bred, well-mannered, civil, polite, courteous, polished, refined, genteel, decorous.

853 ridiculousness *n* outrageousness, silliness, absurdity.

v be ridiculous, make a fool of oneself, play the fool.

adj absurd, preposterous, extravagant, asinine, laughable, nonsensical, silly, funny, ludicrous, droll, comical, farcical, outlandish, outrageous, fantastic.

854 fop *n* fine gentleman, dandy, (*informal*) dude, coxcomb, beau, man about town, prig, jackanapes.

855 affectation *n* affectedness, pretense, pretention, airs, mannerisms, unnaturalness, display, show, sham, feigning, simulation, foppery.

v affect, act a part, put on airs, pretend, assume, feign, counterfeit, simulate, pose, attitudinize.

adj affected, pretentious, ostentatious, feigned, artificial, stilted, mannered, stagey, theatrical, modish, unnatural.

856 ridicule *n* derision, scoffing, mockery, gibes, jeers, taunts, raillery; satire, burlesque, sneer, banter, wit, irony.

v ridicule, deride, banter, chaff, twit, mock, taunt, make fun of, sneer at, burlesque, satirize, rail at, lampoon, jeer at, scoff at, (*informal*) put down.

adj derisory, derisive, sarcastic, ironic, ironical, burlesque, mocking.

857 [object and cause of ridicule] **laughing-stock** *n* butt, game, fair game, fool, dupe, original, oddity, queer fish, square, straight, buffoon.

858 hope *n* confidence, trust, reliance, faith, assurance; expectation, expectancy, anticipation, aspiration, longing, desire, dream, wish.

v hope, trust, rely on, lean on, have faith in; hope for, expect, presume, anticipate; long for, desire.

adj hopeful, expectant, sanguine, optimistic, confident; probable, promising, propitious, reassuring, encouraging, cheering, inspiriting.

859 hopelessness *n* despair, desperation, despondency, dejection, pessimism.

v despair, give up hope, despond.

adj hopeless, despairing, desperate, despondent, forlorn, disconsolate; irremediable, remediless, unremedial, incurable.

860 fear *n* apprehension, consternation, dismay, alarm, trepidation, dread, terror, fright, horror, panic; anxiety, solicitude, suspicion, misgiving, concern; awe, reverence, veneration.

v fear, be afraid of, apprehend, distrust, dread; revere, venerate, reverence.

adj fearful, afraid, apprehensive, dismayed, alarmed, frightened, terrified, horrified, aghast, terror-stricken, horror-stricken, panic-stricken; anxious, concerned, solicitous, suspicious; fearful, awesome, awe-inspiring; awful, dreadful, terrible.

861 courage *n* fearlessness, dauntlessness, intrepidity, guts, fortitude, pluck, spirit, nerve, heroism, daring, audacity, bravery, mettle, valor, hardihood, bravado, gallantry.

v dare, venture, look danger in the face, take heart, take the bull by the horns.

adj courageous, fearless, dauntless, intrepid, (*informal*) gutsy, spirited, stout-hearted, resolute, bold, heroic, daring, audacious, brave, valorous, enterprising, adventurous, gallant.

862 cowardice *n* fear, poltroonery, dastardliness, faint-heartedness, yellow streak, dread, timidity, baseness, abject fear.

coward, poltroon, craven, sneak, lily-liver, (*informal*) chicken.

v be cowardly, cower, skulk, quail, hide.

adj cowardly, fearful, craven, dastardly, pusillanimous, recreant, timid, timorous, faint-hearted, lily-livered, chicken-hearted, fearful, afraid, scared, spineless, (*informal*) chicken.

863 rashness *n* haste, impetuosity, recklessness, impulsiveness, heedlessness, thoughtlessness, imprudence, indiscretion, audacity, carelessness, foolhardiness.

v be rash, plunge.

adj rash, hasty, impetuous, reckless, headlong, precipitate, impulsive, thoughtless, heedless, imprudent, indiscreet, careless, unwary, foolhardy, presumptuous, audacious.

864 caution *n* prudence, discretion, circumspection, heed, care, wariness, heedfulness, vigilance, forethought; warning, admonition, advice, injunction, counsel.

v be cautious, take care; warn, admonish, advise, counsel.

adj cautious, prudent, heedful, careful, watchful, discreet, wary, vigilant, alert, provident, chary, circumspect, guarded.

865 desire *n* longing, fancy, craving, yearning, wish, want, need, hunger, appetite, thirst; request, wish, ambition, aspiration; love, passion, lust.

v desire, wish for, long for, crave, want, wish, covet, fancy; ask, request, solicit; lust for.

adj desirous, desiring, craving, wishful, hungry, thirsty, covetous, fervent, ardent, lustful.

866 indifference *n* unconcern, listlessness, apathy, insensibility, coolness, insensitiveness, inattention.

v be indifferent, take no interest in, have no heart for, spurn, disdain.

adj indifferent, unconcerned, listless, apathetic, cool, cold, lukewarm, insensitive, inattentive.

867 dislike *n* disinclination, disrelish, distaste, disgust, repugnance, antipathy, antagonism, aversion, hatred, horror, loathing.

v dislike, disrelish, be averse to, be disinclined, be reluctant, have no taste for; disgust, repel, nauseate, hate, loathe.

adj disliking, disinclined, averse, loath; dislikable, distasteful, disagreeable, offensive, repulsive, repugnant, repellent, abhorrent, nauseating, disgusting, loathsome.

868 fastidiousness *n* nicety; hypercriticism; discernment, discrimination, judiciousness, keenness, perspicacity.

v be fastidious, split hairs.

adj fastidious, nice, dainty, delicate; hard to please, finicky, hypercritical, fussy, querulous, meticulous, exacting, scrupulous, proper, priggish, prim; discerning, discriminative, judicious, keen, sharp, perspicacious, sagacious.

869 satiety *n* repletion, saturation, glut, surfeit; disgust, weariness.

v sate, satiate, saturate, cloy, glut, stuff, gorge, surfeit; gall, disgust, bore, tire, weary.

adj satiated, glutted, stuffed, gorged, surfeited; disgusted, bored, tired, weary.

870 wonder *n* surprise, marvel, astonishment, stupefaction, amazement, awe, admiration, bewilderment, puzzlement.

v wonder, think, speculate, conjecture, meditate, ponder, question; marvel, admire, be surprised, start, stare, startle, astonish, amaze, astound, stagger, stupefy, bewilder, dumfound.

adj marvelous, wonderful, extraordinary, remarkable, awesome, startling, wondrous, miraculous, astonishing, amazing, astounding, unique, curious, strange, odd, peculiar; astonished, surprised, aghast, agog, startled, breathless, awe-struck, spell-bound, lost in wonder, amazed, fascinated, bewildered.

871 expectance *n* expectancy, expectation.

v expect, foresee, assume, not be surprised, make nothing of.

adj expecting, expectant, relied on, expected, figured on, foreseen.

872 prodigy *n* phenomenon, wonder, marvel, miracle; freak, monstrosity, spectacle, curiosity; genius, intellectual giant, wizard, mastermind, expert, sage, child genius, wunderkind.

873 repute *n* estimation, reputation, account, regard, report; name, standing, distinction, credit, respect, respectability, dignity, greatness, eminence, honor, renown.

v consider, esteem, account, hold, regard, deem, reckon; be held in high repute, be distinguished.

adj reputed, regarded, accounted; reputable, respected, respectable, esteemed, celebrated, distinguished, dignified, honored, renowned, eminent.

874 disrepute *n* disgrace, dishonor, disfavor, discredit, ill repute, low repute, bad name, shame, degradation, obloquy, debasement, ignominy, infamy, stain, spot, blot, tarnish, taint.

v disgrace oneself, have a bad name, shame, disgrace, dishonor, tarnish, stain, taint, blot.

adj disreputable, base, low, unsavory, shady, unworthy, disgraced, vile, ignominious, dishonorable, opprobrious, shameful, disgraceful, infamous, tainted, tarnished.

875 nobility *n* distinction, eminence, stateliness, majesty, grandeur, dignity, loftiness, profundity, highmindedness; rank, condition, high birth, gentility, quality, royalty, aristocracy, lord, lady.

v be noble; ennoble.

adj noble, exalted, honorable, dignified, imposing, stately; titled, aristocratic, patrician, high-born.

876 commonalty *n* the common people, the lower classes, commoners, multitude, proletariat, populace, rank and file, bourgeoisie, general public, citizenry, peasantry, crowd, herd, rabble.

adj common, mean, low, base, ignoble, vulgar, homely, plebeian, proletarian, low-born, obscure, rustic, boorish, uncivilized.

877 title *n* honor, name, designation, decoration.

adj titled.

878 pride *n* self-respect, self-assurance, self-esteem, conceit, vanity, egotism, arrogance, vainglory, self-importance; insolence, haughtiness, superciliousness, presumption.

v be proud, presume, swagger, give oneself airs.

adj proud, high-minded, dignified, stately, noble, imposing, honorable, creditable; self-assured, self-satisfied, contented, egotistical, vain, conceited, arrogant, haughty, smug, overbearing, over-confident, snobbish, supercilious, presumptuous.

879 humility *n* modesty, humbleness, meekness, lowliness, submissiveness.

v lower, abase, debase, degrade, humiliate, mortify, shame, subdue, crush, break.

adj humble, low, lowly, unassuming, plain, common, poor, meek, modest, submissive, unpretentious; respectful, polite, courteous.

adv with downcast eyes, on bended knee.

880 vanity *n* pride, conceit, self-esteem, self-complacency, egotism, self-admiration, self-love, self-glorification; hollowness, emptiness, sham, triviality.

v be vain, have too high an opinion of oneself, inflate, puff up.

adj vain, conceited, egotistical, self-complacent, proud, vainglorious, arrogant, overweening, inflated; useless, hollow, trifling, trivial.

881 modesty *n* humility, diffidence, timidity, bashfulness; moderation, decency, propriety, simplicity, chastity, prudery, prudishness.

v be modest, retire, give way to, stay in the background.

adj modest, humble, diffident, timid, timorous, bashful, sheepish, shy; moderate, humble, unpretentious, decent, becoming, proper, inextravagant, unostentatious, retiring, unassuming, unobtrusive; demure, prudish, chaste, pure, virtuous.

adv modestly, humbly, quietly, privately, without ceremony.

882 ostentation *n* pretention, pretentiousness, semblance, show, showiness, pretense, display, pageantry, pomp, pompousness, flourish, splendor.

v show off, parade, display, exhibit, blazon forth, emblazon, flaunt.

adj ostentatious, pretentious, showy, flashy, grand, pompous, garish, gaudy, flaunting, high-sounding, sumptuous, theatrical, dramatic, solemn, majestic, ceremonious, punctilious, over-blown.

adv with a flourish.

883 celebration *n* ceremony, ceremonial, commemoration, solemnization, observance, memorialization, festival, festivity.

v celebrate, commemorate, observe, keep; proclaim, announce; praise, extol, laud, glorify, honor, applaud, commend; solemnize, ritualize.

adj celebrational, commemorative, honorific, commendatory; celebrated, famous, renowned, illustrious, eminent, famed.

adv in honor of, in commemoration of, in celebration of.

884 boasting *n* bragging, swaggering, braggadocio, bravado.

boaster, braggart, blusterer, (*informal*) windbag.

v exaggerate, brag, vaunt, swagger, crow, strut, talk big.

adj boasting, boastful, pretentious, vainglorious, elated, exultant, jubilant, triumphant.

885 [undue assumption of superiority] **insolence** *n* boldness, rudeness, disrespect, impertinence, impudence, haughtiness, arrogance, audacity, abusiveness, contemptuousness.

v be insolent, swagger, assume, presume, take liberties, ride roughshod over.

adj insolent, bold, rude, disrespectful, impertinent, impudent, brazen, brassy, haughty, arrogant, audacious, presumptuous, overbearing, abusive, contemptuous, insulting.

886 servility *n* submissiveness, obsequiousness, abasement, slavishness, cringing, fawning, meanness, baseness, groveling, sycophancy, slavery.

toady, sycophant, boot-licker, (*informal*) apple-polisher, (*informal*) brown-noser.

v be servile, cringe, bow, stoop, kneel, toady, fawn, lick the boots of; sneak, crawl, crouch, cower.

adj servile, obsequious, slavish, cringing, fawning, sycophantic, groveling, sniveling, mealy-mouthed, abject, base, mean.

887 blusterer *n* swaggerer, braggart, boaster, windbag, bully, ruffian, rowdy, redneck.

III. Sympathetic Affections

888 friendship *n* amity, friendliness, harmony, concord, fellow-feeling, sympathy, good will, affection; companionship, comradeship, fellowship, fraternity, intimacy.

v be friendly, have an acquaintance with, keep company with, know, sympathize with, befriend, make friends with.

adj friendly, kind, kindly, amiable, neighborly, brotherly, cordial, genial, well-disposed, benevolent, kind-hearted, affectionate; helpful, advantageous, propitious; acquainted, familiar, intimate.

adv amicably, with open arms.

889 enmity *n* unfriendliness, dislike, discord, ill will, antagonism, animosity, hostility, malevolence, hatred.

v be at odds with.

adj inimical, unfriendly, alienated, estranged, hostile.

890 friend *n* companion, acquaintance, crony, chum, pal, mate, fellow, bosom buddy, intimate, confidant; well-wisher, patron, supporter, backer, advocate, partisan, defender, sympathizer; ally, associate.

891 enemy *n* foe, adversary, opponent, antagonist, attacker.

892 sociality *n* sociableness, gregariousness, social interaction, social intercourse, comradeship, camaraderie, companionship, cordiality, good fellowship, conviviality.

v be sociable, consort with, fraternize, welcome.

adj sociable, gregarious, social, warm, genial, cordial, friendly, convivial, amicable, clubbish, chummy, neighborly, hospitable.

893 seclusion, exclusion *n* privacy, retirement, withdrawal, solitude, sequestration, retreat, isolation, hiding, secrecy, elimination, prohibition, exception, omission, preclusion, rejection, ejection, expulsion, banishment, ostracism, exile.

recluse, hermit, cenobite, outcast, castaway, pariah, wastrel, foundling.

v seclude oneself, retire, withdraw, retreat, sequester, isolate, hide, exclude, eliminate, prohibit, reject, eject, expel.

adj secluded, retired, withdrawn, sequestered, private, isolated, solitary, excluded, eliminated, prohibited, omitted, precluded, rejected, ejected, repulsed, banished, ostracized, exiled.

894 courtesy *n* civility, sociability, politeness, good manners, good behavior, affability, gentility, graciousness, courtliness, respect.

v be courteous, behave well.

adj courteous, civil, polite, well-mannered, well-bred, gentlemanly, gallant, urbane, debonair, affable, gracious, courtly, respectful, obliging.

895 discourtesy *n* disrespect, ill-breeding, bad manners, tactlessness, rudeness, impudence, vulgarity.

v be discourteous.

adj discourteous, ill-bred, ill-mannered, ill-behaved, ungentlemanly, uncivil, impolite, ungracious, vulgar, crude, disrespectful, rude.

896 congratulations *n* felicitation, compliment, salute, salutation.

v congratulate, offer congratulations, salute.

adj congratulatory; complimentary.

897 love *n* affection, liking, regard, friendliness, kindness, kindliness, tenderness, fondness, devotion, warmth, attachment, yearning, passion, rapture, adoration, idolatry.

lover, admirer, suitor, adorer, wooer; beau, sweetheart, flame, love, truelove, paramour, boyfriend, girlfriend, ladylove, idol, darling, angel, beloved.

v love, like, be fond of, have affection for, be enamored of, be in love with, cherish, adore, revere, adulate, idolize.

adj loving, smitten, affectionate, tender, fond, attached, enamored, devoted, amorous, passionate, adoring; lovable, adorable, winning, enchanting, bewitching.

898 hate *n* dislike, aversion, animosity, hatred, antipathy, detestation, loathing, abhorrence, odium, horror, repugnance.

v hate, dislike, detest, abhor, loathe, despise, execrate, abominate.

adj hateful, detestable, odious, abominable, loathsome, abhorrent, repugnant, invidious, obnoxious, offensive, disgusting, nauseating, revolting, vile, repulsive; hating, averse from, set against, bitter, spiteful, malicious.

899 favorite *n* pet, minion, idol, jewel, spoiled child, apple of one's eye, man after one's own heart; love, dear, darling, honey, sweetheart.

900 resentment *n* displeasure, pique, umbrage, animosity, bitterness, envy, jealousy, anger, wrath, indignation.

v resent, take offense, bristle over, chafe, fume, frown, pout, snarl, gnash, growl, scowl, glower, grouch, bear a grudge.

adj resentful, offended, bitter, worked up, angry, wrathful, irate, indignant; envious, jealous.

901 irascibility *n* irritability, excitability, sensitivity.

v be irascible, quick to fly off the handle, have a temper.

adj irascible, testy, short-tempered, hot-tempered, quick-tempered, touchy, temperamental, irritable, snappish, petulant, overly sensitive, choleric.

901a sullenness *n* moodiness, moroseness, churlishness, sluggishness.

v be sullen, frown, scowl, sulk, pout.

adj silent, reserved, sulky, morose, moody, ill-humored, sour, vexatious, bad-tempered, surly, cross, grumpy, peevish, perverse; gloomy, dismal, cheerless, overcast, somber, mournful, dark; slow, sluggish, dull, stagnant.

902 [expression of affection or love] **endearment** *n* embrace, caress, hug, kiss, blandishment, dalliance, love token.

v endear, embrace, caress, blandish, flirt, dally.

adj endearing.

903 marriage *n* wedding, nuptials, matrimony, wedlock; union, alliance, association, confederation.

married man, married woman, husband, wife, spouse, mate, partner, consort, better half, (*informal*) old man, (*informal*) old lady.

v marry, tie the knot, take to the altar, wive, couple.

adj married, wed, united.

904 celibacy *n* sexual abstinence; bachelorhood.

celibate, unmarried man, bachelor, unmarried woman, spinster, old maid, virgin, maiden; priest.

adj celibate, unmarried.

905 divorce *n* marital separation, legal separation; separation, disunion, isolation.

v divorce, (*informal*) split up, separate, isolate.

adj divorced, separated, (*informal*) split up.

906 benevolence *n* kindness, kindliness, humanity, tenderness, kindheartedness, unselfishness, generosity, liberality, charity, philanthropy, altruism.

good Samaritan, sympathizer, altruist.

v wish well, take an interest in, treat well, comfort, benefit, assist, aid.

adj benevolent, kind, kindly, well-disposed, kind-hearted, humane, tender, tender-hearted, unselfish, generous, liberal, benevolent, obliging, charitable, philanthropic, altruistic.

907 malevolence *n* ill will, enmity, rancor, resentment, malice, maliciousness, spite, spitefulness, grudge, hate, hatred, venom.

v bear ill will.

adj malevolent, malicious, resentful, spiteful, begrudging, hateful, venomous, vicious, hostile, ill-natured, evil-minded, rancorous.

908 malediction *n* curse, swear, imprecation, denunciation, cursing, damning, damnation, execration; slander.

v curse, swear, imprecate, denounce, damn, execrate; slander.

909 threat *n* menace, danger, indication, portent, foreboding, prognostication; intimidation.

v threaten, menace, endanger, indicate, presage, impend, portend, augur, forebode, foreshadow, prognosticate; frighten, denounce, intimidate, cow, badger.

adj threatening, menacing, endangering, impending, auguring, foreshadowing, foreboding, ominous, inauspicious, sinister, frightening, intimidating.

910 philanthropy *n* humaneness, compassion, humanitarianism, benevolence, helpfulness, munificence, public spirit, charity.

philanthropist, humanitarian, patriot.

adj philanthropic, humanitarian, benevolent, munificent, altruistic, public spirited, civic minded, charitable.

911 misanthropy *n* hatred of mankind, incivism.

misanthrope, man-hater; misogynist, woman-hater.

adj misanthropic, antisocial, uncivil.

912 benefactor *n* succorer, patron, supporter, contributor, friend.

913 evildoer *n* wrongdoer, troublemaker, subversive, oppressor, destroyer.

914 pity *n* sympathy, compassion, commiseration, condolence, mercy.

v pity, commiserate, feel sorry for, be sorry for, sympathize with, feel for.

adj pitying, compassionate, sympathetic, touched, moved, affected, feeling.

914a pitilessness *n* cruelty, meanness, ruthlessness, hard- heartedness.

v have no pity for.

adj pitiless, merciless, cruel, mean, unmerciful, ruthless, implacable, relentless, inexorable, hard-hearted, stony.

915 condolence *n* lamentation, sympathy, consolation.

v condole with, console, sympathize, lament.

916 gratitude *n* thanks, thankfulness, appreciation, indebtedness.

v be grateful, thank, appreciate.

adj grateful, appreciative, thankful, obliged, beholding, indebted, in one's debt.

917 ingratitude *n* thanklessness, unthankfulness.

ingrate.

v be ungrateful.

adj ungrateful, unthankful, unmindful, thankless.

918 forgiveness *n* pardon, excuse, indulgence, remission, reprieve, amnesty, grace, absolution.

v forgive, pardon, excuse, absolve, reprieve, acquit.

adj forgiving.

919 revenge *n* vengeance, retaliation, requital, reprisal, retribution, vindictiveness, vengefulness.

avenger, vindicator, nemesis.

v revenge, avenge, retaliate, requite, vindicate.

adj revengeful, vengeful, vindictive, spiteful, malevolent, resentful, malicious, malignant, unforgiving, implacable.

920 jealousy *n* envy, resentment; suspicion; watchfulness, vigilance.

v be jealous.

adj jealous, envious, resentful; suspicious; solicitous, watchful, vigilant.

921 envy *n* jealousy, enviousness, grudge, covetousness.

v envy, covet, begrudge, resent.

adj envious, covetous, jealous, begrudging.

IV. Moral Affections

922 right *n* virtue, justice, fairness, integrity, equity, equitableness, uprightness, rectitude, morality, morals, goodness, honor, lawfulness; accuracy, truth.

v be right; do right.

adj right, just, good, equitable, moral, fair, upright, honest, lawful; correct, proper, suitable, fit; correct, true, accurate; genuine, legitimate, rightful.

adv righteously, rightfully, lawfully, rightly, justly, fairly, equitably.

923 wrong *n* evil, wickedness, misdeed, sin, vice, immorality, iniquity, inequity, injustice, unlawfulness.

v wrong, injure, harm, maltreat, abuse, oppress, cheat, defraud, dishonor.

adj wrong, bad, evil, wicked, sinful, immoral, iniquitous, reprehensible, unjust, crooked, dishonest; erroneous, inaccurate, incorrect, false, untrue, mistaken; improper, unappropriate, unfit; awry, amiss, out of order.

adv wrongly, wickedly, sinfully.

924 claim *n* due, right, privilege, prerogative, prescription, demand, sanction, warrant, license.

claimant, appellant.

v claim, deserve, have the right, be entitled.

adj claiming, having a right to, privileged, prescribed, sanctioned, allowed, licensed, authorized, due.

925 [absence of right] **unrightfulness** *n* impropriety, illegitimacy, presumption.

usurper, pretender.

v be unentitled.

adj unrightful, having no right to, unentitled, unauthorized, unwarranted, illegitimate, not licensed.

926 duty *n* obligation, function, responsibility, onus, burden, business; conscience, moral imperative, sense of duty; homage, respect, reverence.

v do one's duty, behoove, become, befit, beseem; observe, perform, fulfill, discharge.

adj obligatory, binding, imperative, incumbent, under obligation, obliged, bound, tied, duty bound; dutiful, respectful, docile, submissive, deferential, reverential, obedient.

927 dereliction of duty *n* nonobservance, nonperformance, neglect, failure, carelessness, fault, infraction, violation, transgression.

v neglect, slight, fail, violate.

adj undutiful, negligent, careless, at fault, failing, in violation.

927a exemption *n* immunity, impunity, privilege, freedom, exception, excuse, dispensation.

v exempt, excuse, release, acquit, discharge, free.

adj exempt, immune, privileged, freed, excepted, excused, unbound.

928 respect *n* esteem, deference, regard, consideration, estimation, veneration, reverence, homage, honor, admiration, approbation, approval, affection, feeling; respects, regards, duty; regard, consideration, attention, devotion.

v honor, revere, reverence, esteem, venerate, regard, consider, defer to, admire, adulate, adore, love; regard, heed, attend, notice, consider.

adj respectful, courteous, polite, well-mannered, well-bred, civil, deferential; respected, estimable, venerable, admirable; respecting, heeding, considering, regarding, attending.

929 disrespect *n* discourtesy, impoliteness, rudeness, crudeness, incivility, impudence, impertinence, irreverence, derision.

v hold in disrespect, be disrespectful, insult, deride, scoff, mock, sneer, jeer, deride, ridicule, scorn.

adj disrespectful, discourteous, impolite, rude, crude, uncivil, impudent, impertinent, irreverent, insulting, derisive, scornful.

930 contempt *n* scorn, disdain, derision, contumely; dishonor, disgrace, shame.

v feel contempt for, contemn, scorn, disdain, deride, despise.

adj contemptible, despicable, mean, low, miserable, abject, base, vile; contemptuous, scornful, disdainful, derisive; dishonorable, disgraceful, shameful.

931 approbation *n* approval, sanction, esteem, admiration, commendation.

v approbate, approve, esteem, value, honor, admire, appreciate, sanction, endorse, commend, praise.

adj commendatory, complimentary, laudatory; approved, praised, in high esteem, in favour; praiseworthy, commendable, good, meritorious, estimable, creditable.

932 disapprobation *n* disapproval, dislike, disesteem, odium, disparagement, deprecation, denunciation, censure.

v disapprove, dislike, object to, frown upon, censure, blame, reproach, reprove, admonish, berate.

adj disapproving, disparaging, reproachful, defamatory, denunciatory, condemnatory.

933 flattery *n* adulation, charming, lip-service, (*informal*) brown-nosing, fawning, flunkeyism, sycophancy.

v flatter, curry favor, slobber over, (*informal*) lay it on thick, wheedle, fawn, court, (*informal*) brown-nose, pander to, overpraise.

adj flattering, adulatory, honey-mouthed, smooth-tongued, servile, sycophantic.

934 detraction *n* detracting, disparagement, belittling, defamation, vilification, calumny, abuse, slander, aspersion, deprecation.

v detract, run down, criticize, decry, disparage, blacken, belittle, depreciate, cast aspersions, defame, malign, abuse, slander, vilify.

adj detracting, disparaging, belittling, derogatory, depreciating, calumnious, abusive, slanderous, vilifying, scurrilous.

935 flatterer *n* adulator, toady, flunkey, (*informal*) apple-polisher, fawner, sycophant, (*informal*) brown-noser, bootlicker, opportunist, courtier.

936 detractor *n* reprover, critic, carper, slanderer, (*informal*) hatchet man, backbiter, defamer, castigator, satirist, cynic, reviler.

937 vindication *n* exoneration, exculpation, acquittal; justification, warrant, support, defense.

apologist, vindicator, defender.

v vindicate, exonerate, acquit, clear; uphold, justify, maintain, defend, support.

adj vindicating, vindicated, exonerated, exonerating, exculpatory, acquitted; justified, warranted, supported.

938 accusation *n* arraignment, indictment, charge, incrimination, impeachment; accusal, blaming, inculpation, charging, imputation.

accuser, prosecutor, plaintiff; relator, informer; appellant.

v charge; arraign, indict, charge, incriminate, impeach; blame, inculpate, charge, involve, point to, impute.

adj accused, accusing, accusatory, accusative, incriminatory, imputative.

939 probity *n* honesty, uprightness, virtue, rectitude, integrity.

v be honorable.

adj honest, honorable, virtuous, upright, scrupulous, high-principled.

940 improbity *n* dishonesty, wickedness, immorality, evil.

v be dishonest, play false.

adj dishonest, dishonorable, unscrupulous, immoral, wicked, evil.

941 knave *n* rogue, rascal, blackguard, sneak, villain, scoundrel.

942 disinterestedness *n* impartiality, fairness, lack of bias, unselfishness, generosity, liberality.

v be disinterested.

adj disinterested, unbiased, unprejudiced, unselfish, impartial, fair, generous, liberal.

943 selfishness *n* self-interest, self-seeking, self-love, egoism, egotism, solipsism, illiberality, parsimony, stinginess, meanness.

v be selfish, cultivate one's own garden, look after oneself, feather one's own nest.

adj selfish, self-centered, self-indulgent, self-interested, self-seeking, egotistical, solipsistic, illiberal, parsimonious, stingy, cheap, mean.

944 virtue *n* virtuousness, goodness, uprightness, morality, ethics, probity, rectitude, integrity; excellence, merit, quality, asset; innocence, chastity, purity.
v be virtuous, have the virtue of.
adj virtuous, right, upright, moral, righteous, good, chaste, pure.

945 vice *n* fault, sin, depravity, iniquity, immorality, wickedness; blemish, blot, imperfection, defect.
v sin, err, transgress, trespass.
adj vicious, immoral, depraved, profligate, wicked, sinful, sinning, corrupt, bad, iniquitous; reprehensible, blameworthy, censurable, wrong, improper; spiteful, malignant, malicious, malevolent; faulty, defective; ill-tempered, bad-tempered, refractory.

946 innocence *n* purity, virtue, virtuousness, faultlessness, spotlessness; guiltlessness, blamelessness; uprightness, honesty; naïveté, simplicity, artlessness, guilelessness, ingenuousness.
v be innocent.
adj innocent, pure, untainted, sinless, virtuous, virginal, blameless, faultless, impeccable, spotless, immaculate; guiltless, blameless; upright, honest, forthright; naïve, simple, unsophisticated, artless, guileless, ingenuous.

947 guilt *n* guiltiness, culpability, criminality; sinfulness.
v be guilty.
adj guilty, culpable, to blame, in fault.

948 good man *n* model, paragon, hero, soldier, saint, salt of the earth, (*informal*) ace.

949 bad man *n* wrong-doer, evildoer, sinner, scoundrel, miscreant, villain, wretch, monster, devil, demon, scum of the earth.

950 penitence *n* contrition, atonement, compunction, repentance, remorse, regret.
penitent, prodigal son.
v be penitent, repent, rue, regret.
adj penitent, sorry, contrite, repenting; repentant, atoning, amending, remorseful, regretful; penitential.

951 impenitence *n* irrepentance, obduracy, hardness of heart.
v be impenitent, show no remorse.
adj impenitent, uncontrite, not sorry, obdurate, unrepentant, remorseless; unrepenting, unrepented, unatoned; irreclaimable.

952 atonement *n* satisfaction, reparation, compensation, amends, quittance; redemption, expiation, reclamation, conciliation, propitiation.
v atone, atone for; give satisfaction, satisfy, make amends; expiate, propitiate, reclaim, redeem, repair, absolve, purge, shrive, do penance, repent.
adj atoning, propitiating, propitiatory, redemptive, expiating, expiatory.

953 temperance *n* moderation, self-restraint, self-control, continence; sobriety, even-temperedness, calmness, coolness, detachment, dispassion.
vegetarian; teetotaler; abstainer.
v be temperate, abstain, forbear, restrain.
adj temperate, moderate, self-controlled, self-restrained, frugal, sparing; sober, calm, cool, detached, dispassionate.

954 intemperance *n* excess, exorbitance, inordinateness, extravagance; indulgence, high living, self-indulgence, epicurism, epicureanism, sybaritism; inabstinence, alcoholism.
v be intemperate, indulge, wallow in.
adj intemperate, excessive, exorbitant, inordinate, extravagant; indulgent, self-indulgent, epicurean.

954a sensualist *n* sybarite, voluptuary, pleasure-seeker, epicure, epicurean, libertine, hedonist.

955 asceticism *n* puritanism, austerity, abstemiousness, self-abnegation, self-denial, total abstinence, self-motification.
ascetic, anchorite, puritan, martyr; hermit, recluse.
v abstain, deny oneself, fast, starve.
adj ascetic, puritanical, austere, abstemious, rigorous, rigid, stern, severe, harsh, strict, self-denying, self-mortifying.

956 fasting *n* day of fasting; going hungry, starving oneself, starvation.
v fast, starve, famish.
adj fasting, starving, unfed; starved, half-starved, hungry.

957 gluttony *n* greed, greediness, voracity; epicurism, gormandizing, gulosity, crapulence, over-eating, (*informal*) piggishness.
glutton, epicure, cormorant, hog, (*informal*) pig.
v be gluttonous, hog; overeat, gorge, stuff oneself, make a pig of oneself, guzzle, bolt, devour, engorge, gobble up.
adj gluttonous, greedy, voracious; epicurean, gormandizing, crapulent, swinish, (*informal*) piggish.

958 sobriety *n* abstinence, teetotalism.
teetotaler, abstainer.
v be sober, abstain, take the pledge.
adj sober, unintoxicated, on the wagon, (*informal*) straight, (*informal*) dry, dry as a bone.

959 drunkenness *n* intemperance, drinking, inebriety, insobriety, intoxication, alcoholism.
drunkard, sot, tippler, drinker, inebriate, dipsomaniac, alcoholic, (*informal*) boozer, (*informal*) lush, (*informal*) juicer.
v be drunk, drink, imbibe, booze, guzzle, swill, soak, sot, lush, drink like a fish, hit the bottle.
adj drunk, drunken, sotted, intoxicated, inebriated, tipsy, tight, (*informal*) potted, (*informal*) stewed, (*informal*) stewed to the gills, dead drunk, (*informal*) plowed, (*informal*) plastered, (*informal*) tanked, (*informal*) wasted, (*informal*) juiced, (*informal*) blown away, (*informal*) high, (*informal*) flying, (*informal*) feeling no pain.

960 purity *n* cleanness; decency, decorum, delicacy; continence, chastity, innocence, modesty, virtue, virginity; simplicity, genuineness, faultlessness, perfection; guiltlessness, honesty, uprightness.
virgin, vestal virgin.
v be pure.
adj pure, decent, delicate; innocent, continent, chaste, viginal, modest, virtuous, undefiled, unsullied, unstained, untainted, uncorrupted, clean, spotless, immaculate; simple, genuine, faultless, perfect; honest, upright; unmixed, unadulterated, uncontaminated.

961 impurity *n* indecency, indelicacy; incontinence, immodesty, lewdness, concupiscence, prurience, lechery; grossness, obscenity, ribaldry, smut, bawdry; uncleanness, adulteration, contamination, defilement; fault, flaw, imperfection; guilt, sin, sinfulness.
v be impure.
adj impure, indecent, indelicate; incontinent, immodest, unchaste, concupiscent, lewd, prurient, lecherous; gross, obscene, ribald, dirty, smutty, bawdy; unclean, sullied, defiled, contaminated, adulterated, tainted, stained, corrupted, jaded; faulty, flawed, imperfect; guilty, sinning, sinful, wicked.

962 libertine *n* rake, roué, debauchee, lecher, sensualist, voluptuary, profligate, seducer, deceiver, courtesan, prostitute, strumpet, harlot, whore, street-walker, trollop, hussy, bitch, slut, minx.

963 legality *n* legitimacy, legitimateness, lawfulness; duty, obligation.
law, code, constitution, charter, statute, regulation, decree, order.
v legalize; legislate, enact, ordain, decree, codify, formulate, pass a law.
adj legal, legitimate, authorized, licit, lawful, legalized, legislated; constitutional.

964 illegality *n* illegitimacy, unlawfulness, illicitness, lawlessness.
v be illegal, offend against the law, violate the law.
adj illegal, unlawful, illegitimate, illicit, contraband, unconstitutional, unchartered, unwarranted, unauthorized, unlicensed, proscribed, prohibited, outlawed, criminal; lawless, arbitrary, despotic, unanswerable, unaccountable.

965 [executive] **jurisdiction** *n* judicature, authority, power, right, control; territory, range, magistracy.
v judge, sit in judgment; administer.
adj jurisdictive, judicial, administrative; inquisitorial.

966 tribunal *n* court, courtroom, board, bench, court of law, court of justice, bar of justice, judgment seat, dock, forum, witness-chair.

967 judge *n* justice, judiciary, magistrate, judicator, adjudicator, jurist, juror; moderator, arbiter, arbitrator, umpire, referee.
v judge, adjudge, determine, hear a cause, try a case, pass sentence.
adj judicial, judicious, juridical, legal, juristic, judicatory, jurisdictive.

968 lawyer *n* attorney, attorney-at-law, counselor, barrister, solicitor, pleader, counsel, advocate, counselor-at-law, legal adviser; prosecutor, prosecuting attorney, district attorney, public prosecutor, attorney general.
bar, legal profession.
v practice law, be called to the bar, plead, read the law.
adj learned in the law.

969 lawsuit *n* suit, action, cause, dispute, contention; case, debate, litigation, legal proceedings, legal action, legal process, trial, debate, pleadings, argument, argumentation, disputation, prosecution; writ, summons, subpoena, affidavit, suitor, party to a suit, litigant, verdict, decision; precedent.
v go to the law, sue, file a claim, bring to trial, put on trial, serve, serve with a writ, cite, arraign, prosecute, bring an action against, indict, impeach, attach, summon.
adj litigious.

970 acquittal *n* clearance, exculpation, exoneration, absolution, discharge, pardon; impunity, immunity.
v acquit, exculpate, exonerate, clear, absolve, pardon; discharge, release, liberate, set free.
adj acquitted, cleared, exculpated, exonerated; discharged, released, set free.

971 condemnation *n* conviction, guilty verdict, proscription.
v condemn, convict, find guilty, damn, doom, proscribe; stand condemned.
adj condemned, condemnatory, convicted.

972 punishment *n* sentence, judgment, penalty, retribution, discipline, chastisement, castigation, reproof, correction.
v punish, inflict punishment, correct, discipline, penalize, reprove, castigate, chasten, administer correction, scold, berate, jail, incarcerate, execute, torture, banish, flog, whip, lash, scourge.
adj punishing, punitive, castigatory, penalized, penalizing; punished, castigated.

973 reward *n* recompense, prize, desert, compensation, pay, remuneration, requital, merit; bounty, premium, bonus; reparation, redress; retribution, reckoning, amends.
v reward, recompense, requite, compensate, pay, remunerate.
adj rewarding, remunerative, compensatory, retributive, reparatory; rewarded.

974 penalty *n* punishment, retribution, pain, pains, penance; fine, forfeit, damages, sequestration, incarceration, confiscation.
v penalize, punish; fine, confiscate, sequester; penalized, punished.

975 scourge *n* punishment, flogging; affliction, calamity, plague, bane, pest, nuisance; whip, lash, strap, thong, rod, cane, stick; prison, house of correction.
gaoler, jailer, executioner, hangman.

976 deity *n* divinity, god, godhead, omnipotence, providence, lord, the almighty, supreme being, first cause, prime mover, author, creator, the infinite, the eternal, the all-powerful, the all-merciful, omnipresence.
adj divine, godly, almighty, holy, hallowed, sacred, heavenly, celestial, sacrosanct; superhuman, supernatural, spiritual, ghostly, unearthly.

977 angel *n* glorified spirit, beneficent spirit, ministering spirit, heavenly spirit, winged being, seraph, cherub, archangel, helper, spirit, guardian; (*informal*) friend, patron, protector, guardian angel, love.
adj angelic, seraphic, cherubic, spiritual, ethereal; pure, good, righteous, ideal, beautiful; (*informal*) adorable, entrancing, transporting, rapturous, lovely, enrapturing.

978 devil *n* Satan, Lucifer, Beelzebub; tempter, evil one, evil spirit, serpent, prince of darkness, demon, evil incarnate.
diabolism, satanism.
adj devilish, satanic, diabolic, infernal, hellish.

979 fabulous spirit *n* god, goddess, fairy, fay, sylph, faun, nymph, nereid, dryad, sea-maid, oread, naiad, mermaid, kelpie, nixie, sprite, pixie, elf.
adj fabulous, mythological, imaginary, sylphic.

980 demon *n* demonology; devil, fiend, evil spirit, incubus, monster, succubus, succuba, fury, harpy, ghoul, vampire, ogre, gnome, imp, kobold, dwarf, urchin, troll, sprite, bad fairy, leprechaun; ghost, specter, apparition, spirit, shade, shadow, vision, hobgoblin, wraith, spook, banshee, siren, satyr.
adj demonic, supernatural, weird, uncanny, unearthly, spectral, ghostly, ghostlike, elfin, fiendish, impish, haunted.

981 heaven *n* kingdom of heaven, kingdom of god, heavenly kingdom, paradise, nirvana; celestial bliss, glory.
adj heavenly, celestial, supernal, unearthly, paradisaic, paradisical, beatific, elysian, blissful, beautiful, divine, blessed, beatified, glorified.

982 hell *n* Gehenna, inferno, Hades, Erebus, pandemonium, abyss, limbo; [*informal*] torment, torture, pain, agony, suffering.
adj hellish, infernal, stygian, satanic, diabolic, devilish; [*informal*] painful, agonizing, excruciating, horrifying, unendurable.

983 theology *n* theosophy, divinity, hagiography, theologics,theism,monotheism, religion, religious persuasion, dogma, creed, credo, doctrine, tenet, articles of faith.
theologian, theologue, divine.
adj theological, religious, theosophical, hagiological.

983a orthodoxy *n* soundness; strictness, faithfulness, adherence, observance; truth, true faith, religious truth.
adj orthodox, sound, strict, faithful, catholic, doctrinal, authoritative, official, traditional; scriptural, divine, Christian; conventional, established, approved, prescriptive, prevailing, customary.

984 heterodoxy *n* unorthodoxy, nonconformity, iconoclasm, doubt, skepticism, recusancy, dissent, misbelief, error, heresy, schism, apostasy.
pagan, heathen, dissenter, nonconformist, skeptic, heretic, atheist.
adj heterodox, nonconformist, nonconforming, iconoclastic, doubting, skeptical, unscriptural, unorthodox, uncanonical, recusant, dissenting, misbelieving, heretical, schismatic.

985 revelation *n* disclosure, discovery, expression, declaration, expression, utterance, publication, admission, confession, acknowledgment; enlightenment, proclamation, announcement; Christian Revelation, Scriptures, word of god.
adj revelatory; instructive; confessional.

986 religious writings *n* Scriptures, *Bible*, Old Testament, New Testament, The Vedas, Upanishads, Bhagavad Gita, Koran, Alcoran, Avesta.

987 piety *n* godliness, devoutness, devotion, humility, veneration, sanctity, grace, holiness; reverence, regard, respect.
believer, devotee, pietist, righteous man.
v be pious, have faith; believe, revere, venerate, sanctify, consecrate.
adj pious, devout, godly, reverent, religious, holy, sacred, pietistic, saintly; devoted, humble, reverential.

988 impiety *n* irreverence, irreligion, scoffing, profaneness, profanity, blasphemy, desecration, sacrilege, sin, sinfulness; hypocrisy, cant, sanctimony, sanctimoniousness.
sinner, scoffer, blasphemer, sacrilegist, hypocrite.
v be impious, scoff, swear, profane, blaspheme, desecrate, revile, commit sacrilege.

989 irreligion *n* ungodliness, laxity, impiety, indifference, apathy, skepticism, doubt, disbelief, incredulity, agnosticism, freethinking, atheism, infidelity.
skeptic, doubter, nonbeliever, agnostic, cynic, freethinker, atheist, infidel, heathen.
v be irreligious, doubt, disbelieve, lack faith, question.
adj irreligious, godless, ungodly, unholy, unhallowed, undevout; skeptical, doubting, unbelieving, indifferent, apathetic, incredulous, freethinking, agnostic, atheistic, faithless; worldly, earthly, unspiritual.

990 worship *n* reverence, homage, adoration, honor; regard, idolizing, idolatry, deification; prayer, supplication, petition; service, celebration, rites.
worshiper, congregation, suppliant, communicant, celebrant.
v worship, adore, adulate, idolize, deify, love, like; pray, kneel, bow, fall on one's knees; invoke, supplicate, offer prayers, petition; praise, bless, laud, glorify, magnify, sing praises.
adj worshiping, revering, adoring, honoring; worshipful, reverential, honorific, celebrational.

991 idolatry *n* idolism, idolatrousness, idolization, fetishism, idol-worship, deification, demonology; blind adoration, extravagant love, fervor, ardency, enchantment, hero worship.
idol, image, icon, symbol, statue, false god, pagan deity.
v idolize, worship idols, idolatrize, worship, glorify, put on a pedestal, canonize, deify, apotheosize; dote upon, treasure, prize.
adj idolatrous, idol-worshiping, pagan, fetishistic; adoring, impassioned, lovesick.

992 sorcery *n* occultism, magic, witchery, enchantment, witchcraft, spell, necromancy, divination, charm, conjuration, bewitchery, spiritualism.
v practice sorcery, conjure, charm, enchant, bewitch, divine, entrance, mesmerize, cast a spell, call up spirits, raise spirits.
adj magic, magical, bewitching, enchanting, charming, incantory, weird, cabalistic, talismanic; charmed, bewitched, enchanted.

993 spell *n* charm, incantation, exorcism, voodoo, trance, rapture, suggestion, jinx, hocus-pocus, mumbo-jumbo, abracadabra.

994 sorcerer *n* magician, conjuror, necromancer, wizard, witch, exorcist, charmer, medicine man, shaman, medium, clairvoyant, mesmerist, soothsayer, guru.

995 churchdom *n* church, ministry, priesthood, sisterhood, prelacy, hierarchy.
v call, ordain, consecrate, bestow, elect.
adj ecclesiastical, clerical, priestly, pastoral, ministerial, hierarchical.

996 clergy *n* clerical, ministry, priesthood, the cloth, clergyman, divine, ecclesiastic, churchman, pastor, shepherd, minister, preacher, parson, father, reverend, priest, rabbi.
v receive the call, take orders.
adj clerical; ordained.

997 laity *n* fold, flock, congregation, assembly, brethren, people; layman, parishioner.
v secularize.
adj lay, laical, secular, civil, temporal.

998 rite *n* ceremony, observance, function, service, procedure, form, usage.
v perform a rite.
adj ritualistic, ceremonial.

999 canonicals *n* religious garments, vestments, robe, gown, surplice.

1000 temple *n* place of worship, house of god, cathedral, church, chapel, meetinghouse, synagogue, tabernacle, mosque, shrine, pantheon; monastery, priory, abbey, friary, convent, nunnery, cloister; parsonage, rectory, vicarage.
adj churchly, cloistered, monastic.

Index

C

D

G

I

J

Q

R

T

Dictionary of Occupational Titles

000.000-000 MUSEUM INTERN (museum)
A term applied to individuals who perform curatorial, administrative, educational, conservation, or research duties in museum or similar institution, to assist professional staff in utilization of institution's collections and other resources and to gain practical experience and knowledge to enhance personal qualifications for career. Classifications are made according to assignment which is usually based upon academic specialization as CRAFT DEMONSTRATOR (museum), PAINTINGS RESTORER (profess. & kin.), RESEARCH ASSISTANT (profess. & kin.), or RESEARCH ASSOCIATE (museum).

000.000-000 RESEARCH ASSOCIATE (profess. & kin.)
A term applied to persons who conduct independent research in scientific, legal, medical, political, academic, or other specialized fields. Individuals working at this level are required to have a graduate degree. Classifications are made according to field of specialization as AERODYNAMIST (aircraft-aerospace mfg.); METALLURGIST, PHYSICAL (profess. & kin.); MICROBIOLOGIST (profess. & kin.); PATHOLOGIST (medical ser.); POLITICAL SCIENTIST (profess. & kin.).

002.167-018 AERONAUTICAL PROJECT ENGINEER (aircraft-aerospace mfg.)
Directs and coordinates activities of personnel engaged in designing landing gear, flight control equipment, and armaments of military aircraft, applying knowledge of engineering theory and technology: Reviews request from military services or formulates idea for design and capability changes of aircraft. Analyzes proposals for engineering feasibility, design, production time, and advantages and disadvantages of proposals, using knowledge of engineering theory and technology. Discusses proposals with engineering and military personnel, and assigns and directs personnel to design proposals. Examines and reviews drawings, design specifications, reports, tests, photographs, and finished parts for accuracy and quality control. Coordinates production of parts by subcontractors. GOE 05.01.08 PD L56 EC I56 M6 L6 SVP 9 SOC 1622

003.281-018 DRAFTER, ELECTRO-MECHANICAL (profess. & kin.)
Drafts engineering details and plans of electrical components, assemblies, and systems, working from sketches, conceptual drawings, and notes, utilizing knowledge of standard drafting practices: Receives engineering notes, conceptual drawings, and sketches from engineer. Computes drafting specifications, such as spacing and configuration dimensions to determine drawing data for draft, using calculator and engineering notes and utilizing knowledge of specifications determined by standard manufacturing practices and routine arithmetic, algebraic, and geometric procedures. Drafts detailed documents, such as wiring diagrams, layout drawings, mechanical details, and intermediate and final assemblies of products. GOE 05.03.02 PD S46 EC I M4 L4 SVP 7 SOC 372

005.061-042 WASTE-MANAGEMENT ENGINEER, RADIOACTIVE MATERIALS (profess. & kin.)
Designs, implements, and tests systems and procedures to reduce volume and dispose of nuclear waste materials and contaminated objects: Identifies objects contaminated by exposure to radiation, such as trash, workers' clothing, and discarded tools and equipment. Analyzes samples of sludge and liquid effluents resulting from operation of nuclear reactors to determine level of radioactivity in substances and potential for retention of radioactivity, using radioactivity counters and chemical and electronic analyzers. Refers to State and Federal regulations and technical manuals to determine disposal method recommended for prevention of leakage or absorption of radioactive waste. Compares costs of transporting waste to designated nuclear waste disposal sites and reducing volume of waste and storing waste on plant site. Confers with equipment manufacturers' representatives and plant technical and management personnel to discuss alternatives and to choose most suitable plan on basis of safety, efficiency, and cost-effectiveness. Designs and draws plans for systems to reduce volume of waste by solidification, compaction, or incineration. Oversees construction, testing, and implementation of waste disposal systems, and resolves operational problems. Develops plans for modification of operating procedures to reduce volume and radioactive level of effluents, and writes manuals to instruct workers in changes in work procedures. Advises management on selection of lands suitable for use as nuclear waste disposal sites and on establishment of effective safety, operating, and closure procedures. GOE 05.01.03 PD L456 EC I6 M5 L5 SVP 8 SOC 1628

005.261-010 ENGINEERING TECHNICIAN (profess. & kin.)
Conducts surveys and studies and inspects existing water and wastewater treatment systems and those under construction to insure that pollution control requirements are met: Reviews plans and specifications for details concerning construction or repair of sewage systems, sewage and water treatment facilities, and water supply systems for conformance to pollution control requirements. Reviews information, such as size of unit, capacities, length of pipe, reinforcements, unit locations, and other data to insure adherence to requirements. Conducts stream surveys and comprehensive basin studies to gather data. Sets up and maintains water monitoring equipment to obtain samples, flow measurements, and other data. Tabulates data and prepares sketches, diagrams, and graphs for evaluation by engineering staff. Inspects existing systems and construction, in progress and upon completion, to insure pollution control requirements are met. Performs various other duties, such as filing plans and other documents, answering inquiries, and assisting engineering personnel, or assisting and training personnel operating equipment. GOE 05.03.08 PD L46 EC I M4 L4 SVP 7 SOC 3719

007.161-038 SOLAR-ENERGY-SYSTEMS DESIGNER (profess. & kin.)
Designs solar domestic hot water and space heating systems for new and existing structures, applying knowledge of energy requirements of structure, local climatological conditions, solar technology, and thermodynamics: Estimates energy requirements of new or existing structures, based on analysis of utility bills of structure, calculations of thermal efficiency of structure, and prevailing climatological conditions. Determines type of solar system, such as water, glycol, or silicone, which functions most efficiently under prevailing climatological conditions. Calculates onsite heat generating capacity of different solar panels to determine optimum size and type of panels which meet structure's energy requirements. Arranges location of solar system components, such as panel, pumps, and storage tanks, to minimize length and number of direction changes in pipes and reconstruction of existing structures. Studies engineering tables to determine size of pipes and pumps required to maintain specified flow rate through solar panels. Specifies types of electrical controls, such as differential thermostat, temperature sensors, and solenoid valves, compatible with other system components, using knowledge of control systems. Completes parts list, specifying components of system. Draws wiring, piping, and other diagrams, using drafting tools. May inspect structures to compile data used in solar system design, such as structure's angle of alinement with sun and temperature of incoming cold water. May inspect construction of system to insure adherence to design specifications. GOE 05.03.07 PD L46 EC I M4 L4 SVP 5 SOC 1635

007.267-010 DRAWINGS CHECKER, ENGINEERING (profess. & kin.)
Examines engineering drawings of military and commercial parts, assemblies, and installations to detect errors in design documents: Compares figures and lines on production drawing or diagram with production layout, examining angles, dimensions, bend allowances, and tolerances for accuracy. Determines practicality of design, material selection, available tooling, and fabrication process applying knowledge of drafting and manufacturing methods. Confers with design personnel to resolve drawing and design discrepancies. May specialize in checking specific types of designs, such as mechanical assemblies, microelectronic circuitry, or fluid-flow systems. GOE 05.03.02 PD S46 EC I M4 L4 SVP 6 SOC 1635

008.061-030 NUCLEAR-DECONTAMINATION RESEARCH SPECIALIST (profess. & kin.)
Conducts research into problems of decontaminating radioactive equipment and work areas in nuclear plants, laboratories, and other facilities: Examines and tests machinery and equipment to determine type and cause of radioactive contamination, using electron microscope, Geiger counter, and scintillation counter. Develops new decontamination processes, using knowledge of nuclear chemistry. Invents and constructs models of equipment to achieve specific objectives in decontamination processes, devising ways to minimize radiation risk to operative personnel. Devises wash and leach procedures and designs electropolishing equipment to clean and decontaminate metals. Invents regenerative-dilute decontamination process to reduce volume of radioactive liquid waste generated from wash and leach procedures. Prepares technical report to explain research and development of improved techniques and equipment for decontamination of radioactive equipment and work areas. GOE 05.01.01 PD L456 EC I M6 L6 SVP 8 SOC 1626

011.261-018 NONDESTRUCTIVE TESTER (bus. ser.)
Conducts radiographic, penetrant, ultrasonic, and magnetic particle tests on metal parts in commercial testing laboratory to determine if parts meet nondestructive specifications: Reviews test orders to determine type of tests requested, test procedures to follow, and part acceptability criteria. Applies agents such as cleaners, penetrants, developers, and couplant (light oil which acts as medium) to parts, or heats parts in oven, to prepare parts for testing. Determines test equipment settings according to type of metal, thickness, distance from test equipment, and related variables, using standard formulas. Calibrates test equipment, such as magnetic particle, X-ray, and ultrasonic contact machines, to standard settings, following manual instructions. Sets up equipment to perform tests, and conducts tests on parts, following procedures established for specified tests performed. Examines surface-treated materials when conducting penetrant and magnetic particle tests to locate and identify flaws, cracks, and related defects, using black light. Moves transducer probe across part when conducting ultrasonic tests and observes CRT (cathode ray tube) screen to detect and locate discontinuities in metal structure [ULTRASONIC TESTER (bus. ser.)]. Examines film when conducting radiographic tests to locate structural or welding flaws. Marks tested parts to indicate areas where flaws were detected. Evaluates test results against designated standards, utilizing knowledge of metals and testing experience. Prepares reports outlining findings and conclusions. May perform similar tests on parts or structures composed of materials other than metals. GOE 05.07.01 PD H346 EC B M3 L3 SVP 6 SOC 399

015.061-026 NUCLEAR-FUELS RECLAMATION ENGINEER (profess. & kin.)
Plans, designs, and oversees construction and operation of nuclear fuels reprocessing systems: Performs research and experiments to determine acceptable methods of reclaiming various types of nuclear fuels. Designs nuclear fuel reclamation systems and equipment for pilot plants. Communicates with vendors and contractors, and computes cost estimates of reclamation systems. Writes project proposals and submits them to company review board. Studies safety procedures, guidelines, and controls, and confers with safety officials to insure that safety limits are not violated in design, construction, or operation of systems and equipment. Oversees nuclear fuels reprocessing system construction and operation, conferring with construction supervisory and operating personnel. Tests system equipment and approves equipment for operation. Monitors operations to detect potential or inherent problems. Initiates corrective actions and orders plant shutdown in emergency situations. Identifies operational and processing problems and recommends solutions. Maintains log of plant operations, and prepares reports for review by plant officials. GOE 05.01.03 PD L456 EC I6 M5 L5 SVP 7 SOC 1627

015.061-030 NUCLEAR-FUELS RESEARCH ENGINEER (profess. & kin.)
Studies behavior of various fuels and fuel configurations in differentiated reactor environments to determine safest and most efficient usage of nuclear fuels, applying theoretical and experiential knowledge of reactor physics and thermal and metallurgical characteristics of nuclear fuels and fuel cell claddings: Analyzes available data and consults with other scientists to determine parameters of experimentation and suitability of analytical models. Designs fuels behavior tests and coordinates activities of experimental research team in performance and analysis of test operations. Monitors test reactor indicators of factors such as neutron power level, coolant level, and vital pressure, temperature and humidity readings, and changes or modifies procedures to meet test goals. Synthesizes analyses of test results and prepares technical reports to disseminate findings and recommendations. Formulates equations that describe phenomena occurring during fissioning of nuclear fuels and develops analytical models for nuclear fuels research. GOE 05.01.03 PD L456 EC I M6 L6 SVP 8 SOC 1627

015.067-010 NUCLEAR-CRITICALITY SAFETY ENGINEER (profess. & kin.)
Conducts research and analyzes and evaluates proposed and existing methods of transportation, handling, and storage of nuclear fuel to preclude accidental nuclear reaction at nuclear facilities: Reviews and evaluates fuel transfer and storage plans received from nuclear plants. Studies reports of nuclear fuel characteristics to determine potential or inherent problems. Reads blueprints of proposed storage facilities and visits storage sites to determine adequacy of storage plans. Forecasts nuclear fuel criticality (point at which nuclear chain reaction becomes self-sustaining), given various factors which may exist in fuel handling and storage, using knowledge of nuclear physics, calculator, and computer terminal. Determines potential hazards and accident conditions which may exist in fuel handling and storage and recommends preventive measures. Summarizes findings and writes reports. Confers with project officials to resolve situations where hazard is beyond acceptable levels. Prepares proposal reports for handling and storage of fuels to be submitted to government review board. Studies existing procedures and recommends changes or additions to guidelines and controls to insure prevention of self-sustaining nuclear chain reaction. GOE 05.01.02 PD L456 EC I67 M6 L5 SVP 8 SOC 1627

015.137-010 RADIATION-PROTECTION ENGINEER (gov. ser.)
Supervises and coordinates activities of workers engaged in monitoring radiation levels in water and detecting corrosion of equipment used to produce nuclear energy for generation of power: Evaluates data concerning chemical analysis of water in primary and supportive plant systems to determine compliance with regulations governing radiation content and corrosion control. Investigates problems concerning excessive radiation or corrosion of equipment, applying knowledge of radiation protection techniques and principles of chemistry and engineering to correct conditions. Confers with other supervisory personnel, representatives of equipment manufacturing firms, and regulatory agency staff members to discuss problems and develop plans for safe and efficient monitoring program. Supervises workers who test and analyze water samples and monitor operation of processing system. Prepares reports of environmental monitoring operation and radioactive waste release and shipment activities for review by administrative personnel and submission to regulatory agency. GOE 05.01.02 PD S5 EC I M4 L5 SVP 8 SOC 1627

015.167-010 NUCLEAR-PLANT TECHNICAL ADVISOR (light, heat, & power)
Monitors plant safety status, advises operations staff, and prepares technical reports for operation of thermal-nuclear reactor at electric-power generating station: Observes control-room instrumentation systems and confers with operating personnel to insure safe operation of plant. Walks throughout plant and observes machinery, equipment, and operating procedures to identify potential hazards. Examines locations of accidents and transients (sudden changes of voltage or load) and obtains data to formulate preventive measures. Implements changes in systems, procedures, structure, or equipment to improve safety. Compares critical parameters with plant transient predictions and accident analysis and determines whether response of plant safety systems is sufficient. Formulates corrective actions, calculates critical parameters from raw data, and computes rate of control rod withdrawal during reactor startup. Confers with operating personnel to provide technical assistance and to discuss maintenance activities, abnormal conditions, and safe operation of plant. Prepares reports to inform management officials of any proposed changes or irregularities in plant operation or systems. GOE 05.01.02 PD L56 EC I M5 L5 SVP 8 SOC 1627

015.167-014 NUCLEAR-TEST-REACTOR PROGRAM COORDINATOR (profess. & kin.)
Evaluates, coordinates, and oversees testing of nuclear reactor equipment: Analyzes test proposal to insure that test is valid and feasible. Identifies and resolves problems, such as incompatibilities between proposal and nuclear test-reactor system. Coordinates technical and financial agreements involving feasibility, scope, purpose, and cost of project in nuclear test facility. Assists engineering personnel in interpretation of test language, mathematical formulas, and computer codes used in test. Writes operational instructions. Inspects general condition of nuclear test-reactor vessel and related systems. Verifies setup of nuclear test-reactor for compliance with specifications. Observes control room instrumentation to insure that performance factors such as neutron power level, chemical composition of coolant, and reactor temperatures and pressures are carried out as prescribed. Evaluates and resolves operational problems. Coordinates activities directed toward removal of test specimens from reactors and subsequent chemical, metallurgical, or mechanical analysis. Compiles report of test results. GOE 05.01.04 PD L456 EC I6 M5 L5 SVP 8 SOC 1627

015.261-010 CHEMICAL-RADIATION TECHNICIAN (gov. ser.)
Tests materials and monitors operations of nuclear-powered electric generating plant, using specialized laboratory equipment and chemical and radiation detection instruments: Collects samples of water, gases, and solids at specified intervals during production process, using automatic sampling equipment. Analyzes materials, according to specified procedures, to determine if chemical components and radiation levels are within established limits. Records test results and prepares reports for review by supervisor. Assists workers to set up equipment and monitors equipment that automatically detects deviations from standard operations. Notifies personnel to adjust processing equipment, quantity of additives, and rate of discharge of waste materials, when test results and monitoring of equipment indicate that radiation levels, chemical balance, and discharge of radionuclide materials are in excess of standards. Carries out decontamination procedures to insure safety of workers and continued operation of processing equipment in plant. Calibrates and maintains chemical instrumentation sensing elements and sampling system equipment, using handtools. Assists workers in diagnosis and correction of problems in instruments and processing equipment. Advises plant personnel of methods of protection from excessive exposure to radiation. GOE 11.10.03 PD L4 EC I M3 L3 SVP 6 SOC 389

017.261-042 DRAFTER, COMPUTER-ASSISTED (profess. & kin.)
Drafts layouts, drawings, and designs for application in such fields as aeronautics, architecture, or electronics, according to engineering specifications, using computer: Reviews engineering drawings and supporting documents to verify freedom of movement between parts and adherence to company or industry standard practices and adequacy of parts identification. Analyzes design and confers with engineering staff to resolve details not completely defined. Locates file relating to projection data base library and loads program into computer. Retrieves information from file and displays information on cathode-ray-tube (CRT) screen, using required computer language. Types commands to rotate or zoom-in on display to redesign, modify, or otherwise edit existing design. Traces over face of photosensitive screen to redraw details or rewrite text. Displays final drawing on screen to verify completeness, clarity, and accuracy of drawing. Types command to transfer drawing dimensions from computer onto hardcopy, using peripheral equipment, such as digitizer or plotter controlled by computer. Submits completed drawings to supervisor for review. GOE 05.03.02 PD S46 EC I M4 L4 SVP 7 SOC 372

019.167-018 RESOURCE-RECOVERY ENGINEER (gov. ser.)
Plans and participates in activities concerned with study, development, and inspection of solid-waste resource recovery systems and marketability of solid-waste recovery products: Conducts studies of chemical and mechanical solid-waste recovery processes and system designs to evaluate efficiency and cost-effectiveness of proposed operations. Inspects solid-waste resource recovery facilities to determine compliance with regulations governing construction and use. Collects data on resource recovery systems and analyzes alternate plans to determine most feasible systems for specific solid-waste recovery purposes. Prepares recommendations for development of resource recovery programs, based on analysis of alternate plans and knowledge of physical properties of various solid-waste materials. Confers with design engineers, management personnel, and others concerned with recovery of solid-waste resources to discuss problems and provide technical advice. Coordinates activities of workers engaged in study of potential markets for reclaimable materials. Lectures civic and professional organizations and provides information about practices to

media representatives to promote interest and participation in solid-waste recovery practices. GOE 05.01.02 PD S56 EC I M6 L5 SVP 8 SOC 1628

020.224-010 CUSTOMER-SUPPORT SPECIALIST (whole. tr.)
Converts clients' manual accounting systems to computerized systems, trains clients' employees to program systems, and diagnoses computer hardware malfunctions: Reviews and evaluates client's manual accounting and bookkeeping systems, using established accounting procedures to convert from manual system to computerized system. Contacts computer software vendor to order initial supply of forms. Teaches client's employees to program computer, using standardized programing methods and observing hands-on practices. Reviews client's operational procedures to implement improvements. Troubleshoots computer hardware malfunctions, using electronic test meter and tools, and repairs simple malfunctions or writes service order for use of repair personnel. GOE 11.01.01 PD L456 EC I M4 L4 SVP 7 SOC 1719

020.262-010 SOFTWARE TECHNICIAN (profess. & kin.)
Analyzes problems, plans and develops software programs, transfers programs to memory chips, installs chips on printed circuit boards (PCB), and tests and corrects operation of chips and boards, using computer equipment: Assembles units into logical sequence and translates charts into programed computer language to develop detailed flow charts. Enters coded commands into computer, tests printer for system errors, and corrects errors by altering commands until desired results are attained, using keyboard. Transfers program data onto disk, using terminal keyboard, mounts disk onto cathode-ray-tube (CRT) unit, checks screen for errors, and corrects errors as necessary. Mounts disk and blank chips in device which imprints program onto erasable memory chip. Writes specifications and instructs operator how to input data to obtain required results. Installs chips on printed circuit board and connects lead wires to board circuitry, utilizing diagrams and knowledge of electric circuitry and electronics. Observes operation of chip in terminal, changes sequence of program commands if necessary, and submits data specifications on tested chip to engineering department. GOE 11.01.01 PD L456 EC I M4 L4 SVP 7 SOC 3971

022.081-010 TOXICOLOGIST (drug. prep. & rel. prod.)
Conducts research on toxic effects of cosmetic products and ingredients on laboratory animals for manufacturer of cosmetics: Applies cosmetic ingredient or cosmetic being developed to exposed shaved skin area of test animal and observes and examines skin periodically for possible development of abnormalities, inflammation, or irritation. Injects ingredient into test animal, using hypodermic needle and syringe, and periodically observes animal for signs of toxicity. Injects antidotes to determine which antidote best neutralizes toxic effects. Tests and analyzes blood samples for presence of toxic conditions, using microscope and laboratory test equipment. Dissects dead animals, using surgical instruments, and examines organs to determine effects of cosmetic ingredients being tested. Prepares formal reports of test results. GOE 02.04.02 PD L456 EC I M4 L5 SVP 8 SOC 382

022.261-018 CHEMIST, INSTRUMENTATION (profess. & kin.; sanitary ser.)
Conducts chemical analyses of wastewater discharges of industrial users of municipal wastewater treatment plant to determine industrial waste surcharge assessments and to insure that users meet pollution control requirements: Conducts chemical analyses of samples, using special instrumentation, such as gas chromatograph with electron capture, flame ionization, and thermal conductivity detectors, ultraviolet-visible recording spectrophotometer with photometry attachments, and infrared spectrophotometer. Compares findings with industry declared data and legal requirements and notes variations to be used in determining industrial waste surcharge assessments and to regulate industrial waste discharges. Develops new procedures in use of equipment and procedures for analyzing samples. Directs subordinate laboratory personnel in routine tests. GOE 02.01.01 PD L46 EC I7 M5 L4 SVP 7 SOC 3831

022.261-022 CHEMIST, WASTEWATER-TREATMENT PLANT (profess. & kin.; sanitary ser.)
Analyzes samples of streams, raw and treated wastewater, sludge, and other byproducts of wastewater treatment process to determine efficiency of plant processes and to insure that plant effluent meets water pollution control requirements, using standard laboratory equipment: Conducts tests for settleable solids, suspended solids, total solids, volatile solids, volatile acids, alkalinity, pH, dissolved oxygen demand, turbidity, and other substances. Initiates changes in laboratory procedures and equipment in order to increase efficiency of laboratory. Directs laboratory personnel in prescribed laboratory techniques and performance of routine tests. GOE 02.04.02 PD L46 EC I7 M5 L4 SVP 7 SOC 3831

024.267-010 GEOLOGICAL AIDE (petrol. production)
Examines and compiles geological information to provide technical data to GEOLOGIST, PETROLEUM (petrol. production), using surface and subsurface maps, oil and gas well activity reports, and sand and core analysis studies: Studies geological reports to extract well data and posts data to maps and logs. Draws subsurface formation contours on charts to lay out and prepare geological cross section charts. Compiles information regarding well tests, completions, and formation tops to prepare oil or gas well records. Records net sand and sand percentage counts and calculates isopachous values to compile sand analysis data. Studies directional logs and surveys to calculate and plot formation tops. Reads well activity reports and records key well locations in drilling activity book. Assembles and distributes prepared charts, maps, and reports to geologist requesting material. Maintains file record systems and geological library. Attends SCOUT (petrol. production) meeting to compile information on well activity. Contacts competitors to acquire oil and gas samples from wells. Operates computer terminal for input and retrieval of geological data. GOE 02.04.01 PD L456 EC I M5 L5 SVP 8 SOC 3833

040.261-010 SOIL-CONSERVATION TECHNICIAN (profess. & kin.)
Provides technical assistance to land users in planning and applying soil and water conservation practices, utilizing basic engineering and surveying tools, instruments, and techniques and knowledge of agricultural and related sciences, such as agronomy, soil conservation, and hydrology: Analyzes conservation problems of land and discusses alternative solutions to problems with land users. Advises land users in developing plans for conservation practices, such as conservation cropping systems, woodlands management, pasture planning, and engineering systems, based on cost estimates of different practices, needs of land users, maintenance requirements, and life expectancy of practices. Computes design specification for particular practices to be installed, using survey and field information technical guides, engineering field manuals, and calculator. Submits copy of engineering design specifications to land users for implementation by land user or contractor. Surveys property to mark locations and measurements, using surveying instruments. Monitors projects during and after construction to insure projects conform to design specifications. Periodically revisits land users to view implemented land use practices and plans. GOE 03.02.02 PD L456 EC B M4 L4 SVP 7 SOC 1852

041.061-094 STAFF TOXICOLOGIST (gov. ser.)
Studies effects of toxic substances on physiological functions of human beings, animals, and plants to develop data for use in consumer protection and industrial safety programs: Designs and conducts studies to determine physiological effects of various substances on laboratory animals, plants, and human tissue, using biological and biochemical techniques. Interprets results of studies in terms of toxicological properties of substances and hazards associated with misuse of products containing substances. Provides information concerning toxicological properties of products and materials to regulatory agency personnel and industrial firms. Reviews toxicological data submitted by others for adequacy, and suggests amendment or expansion of data to clarify or correct information. Confers with governmental and industrial personnel to provide advice on precautionary labeling for hazardous materials and products and on nature and degree of hazard in cases of accidental exposure or ingestion. Prepares and maintains records of studies for use as toxicological resource material. Testifies as expert witness on toxicology in hearings and court proceedings. GOE 02.02.01 PD L456 EC I6 M6 L5 SVP 8 SOC 1854

041.067-010 MEDICAL COORDINATOR, PESTICIDE USE (gov. ser.)
Studies human health-and-safety aspects of pesticides and other agricultural chemicals: Studies long-term health implications of low-dose pesticide exposure and determines safe worker reentry intervals. Reviews and provides recommendations on medical regulations governing use of pesticides. Reviews information and recommendations pertaining to safe levels of pesticide residues on agricultural products. Recommends specifications for safe working conditions for workers exposed to pesticides or their residues, and makes recommendations on public safety aspects of pesticide exposure. Confers with health department personnel to develop programs to improve ability of physicians and other medical personnel to diagnose, treat, and report pesticide-related illnesses. Confers with government agency representatives, physicians, university staff members, and other research workers to develop health and safety standards related to pesticide exposure. Advises industry representatives on organization of adequate medical supervision programs for employers. Prepares reports on research studies. Addresses interested groups as requested. GOE 02.02.01 PD S5 EC I M5 L6 SVP 9 SOC 1855

041.167-010 ENVIRONMENTAL EPIDEMIOLOGIST (gov. ser.)
Plans, directs, and conducts studies concerned with incidence of disease in industrial settings and effects of industrial chemicals on health: Confers with industry representatives to select occupational groups for study and to arrange for collection of data concerning work history of individuals and disease concentration and mortality rates among groups. Plans methods of conducting epidemiological studies and provides detailed specifications for collecting data to personnel participating in studies. Develops codes to facilitate computer input of demographic and epidemiological data for use by data processing personnel engaged in programing epidemiological statistics. Compares statistics on causes of death among members of selected working populations with those among general population, using life-table analyses. Analyzes data collected to determine probable effects of work settings and activities on disease and mortality rates, using valid statistical techniques and knowledge of epidemiology. Presents data in designated statistical format to illustrate common patterns among workers in selected occupations. Initiates and maintains contacts with statistical and data processing managers in other agencies to maintain access to epidemiological source materials. Evaluates materials from all sources for addition to or amendment of epidemiological data bank. Plans and directs

activities of clerical and statistical personnel engaged in tabulation and analysis of epidemiological information to insure accomplishment of objectives. GOE 02.02.01 PD L56 EC I M6 L5 SVP 8 SOC 1854

041.384-010 HERBARIUM WORKER (profess. & kin.)
Fumigates, presses, and mounts plant specimens, and maintains collection records of herbarium maintained by botanical garden, museum, or other institution: Records identification information concerning incoming plants. Places specimens in fumigation cabinet and turns valves to release toxic fumes that destroy insects, fungus, or parasites adhering to specimens. Arranges specimens between sheets of unsized paper so that upper and under portions of leaves, blossoms, and other components are visible, and pads paper with layers of felt and newsprint to protect specimens and form stacks. Places specified number of stacks in pressing frame and writes identification information on top layer of paper on each stack. Secures frame around stacks by tightening frame section with screws, fastening with leather straps, or tying with twine, to compress stacks and press and dry specimens in desired configuration. Mounts dried specimens on heavy paper, using glue, adhesive strips, or needle and thread, taking care to prevent distortion or breakage of specimens. Writes identification information on papers and inserts mounted specimens in labeled envelopes or folders. Files folders in drawers or cabinets according to standard botanical classification system. Maintains card files of specimens in herbarium collection and records of acquisitions, loans, exchanges, or sales of specimens. GOE 02.04.02 PD L46 EC I M3 L4 SVP 5 SOC 399

045.107-046 PSYCHOLOGIST, CHIEF (profess. & kin.)
Plans psychological service programs, and directs, coordinates, and participates in activities of personnel engaged in providing psychological services to clients in psychiatric center or hospital: Reviews reports, case management reviews, and psychiatric center's or hospital's procedural manual to assess need for psychological services. Plans psychological treatment programs that meet standards of accreditation. Plans utilization of available staff, assigns staff to treatment units, and recruits professional and nonprofessional psychological staff. Develops, directs, and participates in training programs. Directs testing and evaluation of new admissions and re-evaluation of present clients. Participates in staff conferences to evaluate and plan treatment programs. Interviews clients that present difficult and complex diagnostic problems and assesses their psychological status. Reviews management of cases, assignments, case problems, issues, and methods of treatment. Works with community agencies to develop effective corrective programs and to arrange to provide psychological services. Plans and supervises psychological research. Collaborates with psychiatrists and other professional staff to help develop comprehensive program of therapy, evaluation, and treatment. GOE 10.01.02 PD S56 EC I M5 L6 SVP 8 SOC 1915

049.364-014 VECTOR CONTROL ASSISTANT (gov. ser.)
Assists public health staff in activities concerned with identification, prevention, and control of vectors (disease-carrying insects and rodents): Carries and sets up field equipment to be used in surveys of number and type of vectors in area. Sets traps and cuts through brush and weeds to obtain specimens of vector population for use in laboratory tests, using sweep. Prepares, mounts, and stores specimens, following instructions of supervisor. Prepares reports of field surveys and laboratory tests based upon information obtained from personnel involved in specific activities, for use in planning and carrying out projects for prevention and control of vectors. GOE 02.04.02 PD L4 EC B M2 L3 SVP 5 SOC 382

054.107-010 CLINICAL SOCIOLOGIST (profess. & kin.)
Develops and implements corrective procedures to alleviate group dysfunctions: Confers with individuals and groups to determine nature of group dysfunction. Observes group interaction and interviews group members to identify problems related to factors such as group organization, authority relationships, and role conflicts. Develops approaches to solution of group's problems, based on findings and incorporating sociological research and study in related disciplines. Develops intervention procedures, utilizing techniques such as interviews, consultations, role playing, and participant observation of group interaction, to facilitate resolution of group problems. Monitors group interaction and role affiliations to evaluate progress and to determine need for additional change. GOE 11.03.02 PD S56 EC I M4 L5 SVP 6 SOC 1916

070.107-018 DIRECTOR, DIAGNOSTIC-AND-EVALUATION CLINIC (medical ser.)
Plans, coordinates, and participates in activities of diagnostic clinic serving suspected mental retardates: Establishes procedures for admitting and examining suspected retardates and providing related services, such as home visits, parent counseling, and followup evaluations. Directs and coordinates activities of staff engaged in clinical, maintenance, and clerical services. Arranges for treatment and specialized diagnostic services performed outside clinic. Conducts conferences with staff to arrive at diagnostic conclusions, resolve administrative problems, and inform staff of changes in responsibilities or procedures. Interprets clinic program to parents and visitors, and explains diagnostic findings and patient-care or rehabilitation recommendations to parents. Represents clinic at professional meetings and in contacts with other agencies. Prepares or directs preparation of records, recommendation, and reports for budgetary approval and for use by public health, welfare, and school officials. Examines patients and provides emergency or inpatient treatment. Participates in research activities. Instructs clinic staff, medical and nursing students, residents, and interns in diagnosis and treatment of retarded persons. GOE 02.03.01 PD L56 EC I M5 L6 SVP 8 SOC 261

070.117-010 CHIEF OF NUCLEAR MEDICINE (medical ser.)
Directs activities of nuclear technology laboratory, performs nuclear medical research, determines treatment for patients, and instructs medical students in theory and techniques of nuclear medicine in hospital: Formulates policies and directs operation of nuclear laboratory. Coordinates activities of nuclear laboratory with other hospital departments and medical staff. Performs and directs research to develop new uses for nuclear medicine in diagnosis and treatment of patients. Examines patients, evaluates results of tests, confers with physicians, and recommends treatment for patients. Instructs medical students in theory and techniques of nuclear medicine. Attends conferences, seminars, and workshops, and and reads professional and technical journals to acquire knowledge of current information and research in nuclear medicine. GOE 02.03.01 PD L56 EC I M5 L6 SVP 9 SOC 261

070.117-014 DIRECTOR OF RADIOLOGY (medical ser.)
Administers radiology programs and directs and coordinates department activities in accordance with accepted national standards and administrative policies: Plans, organizes, and oversees radiology program in cooperation with hospital officials and other departments. Participates with personnel of other departments to plan joint administrative and technical programs and recommends methods and procedures to coordinate radiological services with other departments. Investigates and studies trends and developments in radiologic practices and techniques. Develops manuals to assist staff members to keep abreast of current methods, procedures, and techniques. Develops and oversees safety programs to insure safe and acceptable use of X-ray equipment and radioactive materials used in diagnosis and therapy. Prepares and submits budgets, reports, records, and statistical data to ADMINISTRATOR, HOSPITAL (medical ser.). Presents lectures, seminars, and on-the-job training to instruct students and interns in theory and practice of radiology. Recommends course of action following diagnosis to provide technical assistance and guidance. Oversees activities of subordinates and uses X-ray equipment to diagnose symptoms and conditions of patients. GOE 02.03.01 PD L56 EC I6 M5 L6 SVP 8 SOC 261

072.117-010 DIRECTOR, DENTAL SERVICES (medical ser.)
Administers dental program in hospital and directs departmental activities in accordance with accepted national standards and administrative policies: Confers with hospital administrators to formulate policies and recommend procedural changes. Establishes training program, using lectures and seminars, to advance skill levels of students and interns involved in dentistry practice. Implements procedures for hiring of professional staff and approves hiring and promotion of all staff members. Establishes work schedules and assigns staff members to duty stations to maximize efficient use of staff. Observes and assists staff members at work to insure safe and ethical practices and to solve problems and demonstrate techniques. Confers with ADMINISTRATOR, HOSPITAL (medical ser.) to submit budget and statistical reports used to justify expenditures for equipment, supplies, and personnel. GOE 02.03.02 PD S56 EC I M5 L5 SVP 8 SOC 262

073.101-018 ZOO VETERINARIAN (medical ser.)
Maintains zoo veterinary clinic and plans, supervises, and participates in all phases of health care program for zoo animal collection: Establishes and conducts effective quarantine and testing procedures for all incoming animals to insure health of collection, prevent spread of disease, and comply with government regulations. Conducts regularly scheduled immunization and preventive care programs to maintain health of animals and guard against spread of communicable diseases. Provides immediate medical attention to diseased or traumatized animals. Participates with other personnel in planning and executing zoo nutrition and reproduction programs for animals in collection. Develops special programs to encourage reproduction among animals designated as belonging to endangered species, based on knowledge of native habitats and instincts. Participates in employee training in handling and care of animals in collection. Conducts postmortem studies and analyses. Develops medical record system and supervises workers engaged in maintenance of records. GOE 02.03.03 PD M3456 EC I6 M5 L5 SVP 8 SOC 27

073.361-014 LABORATORY ASSISTANT, ZOO (medical ser.)
Assists professional veterinary workers in examination and treatment of animals and performance of research: Prepares treatment room for examination of animals and holds or restrains animals during examination, treatment, or innoculation. Hands instruments and materials to professional workers as directed. Sterilizes and cleans instruments. Administers immunization innoculations to animals to comply with quarantine regulations or assist in preventive medicine program. Performs routine laboratory tests, such as urinalyses and blood counts according to established procedures. Prepares vaccines and serums according to standard laboratory methods, and bottles and stores materials for future use. Assists professional workers in performance of autopsies. Maintains records of preventive and therapeutic treatment administered. Assists professional personnel in perform-

ance of tests and maintenance of records associated with various research projects. GOE 02.04.02 PD L46 EC I6 M3 L4 SVP 5 SOC 369

074.131-010 DIRECTOR, PHARMACY SERVICES (medical ser.)
Supervises and coordinates activities of personnel in hospital pharmacy: Plans, establishes, and implements procedures in hospital pharmacy according to standard practices, hospital policies, and legal requirements. Directs pharmacy personnel programs, such as hiring, training, and intern program. Establishes work schedules and assigns pharmacy personnel to work stations, such as research or dispensary. Supervises personnel engaged in maintenance of records, formularies, and reports of drugs and other supplies dispensed, for drug control and budgetary purposes. Analyzes records to indicate prescribing trends and excessive usage. Prepares pharmacy budget, newsletters, and other reports required by hospital administrators. Attends staff meetings to advise and inform hospital medical staff of various drug applications and characteristics. Supervises and assists pharmacy personnel to prepare and dispense drugs. Observes pharmacy personnel at work to insure safe, legal, and ethical practices. Maintains master files of formulas and procedures for stock drugs prepared in pharmacy. Oversees preparation and dispensation of experimental drugs which are in clinical stage of development. Contacts drug wholesalers to order drugs and chemicals to maintain adequate drug stock levels. GOE 02.04.01 PD S456 EC I M6 L6 SVP 8 SOC 301

074.161-014 RADIOPHARMACIST (medical ser.)
Prepares and dispenses radioactive pharmaceuticals used for patient diagnosis and therapy, applying principles and practices of pharmacy and radiochemistry: Receives radiopharmaceutical prescription from PHYSICIAN (medical ser.) and reviews prescription to determine suitability of radiopharmaceutical for intended use. Verifies that specified radioactive substance and reagent will give desired results in examination or treatment procedures, utilizing knowledge of radiopharmaceutical preparation and principles of drug biodistribution. Calculates volume of radioactive pharmaceutical required to provide patient with desired level of radioactivity at prescribed time, according to established rates of radioisotope decay. Compounds radioactive substances and reagents to prepare radiopharmaceutical, following radiopharmacy laboratory procedures. Assays prepared radiopharmaceutical, using measuring and analysis instruments and equipment, such as ionization chamber, pulse-height analyzer, and radioisotope dose calibrator, to verify rate of drug disintegration and to insure that patient receives required dose. Consults with PHYSICIAN (medical ser.) following patient treatment or procedure to review and evaluate quality and effectiveness of radiopharmaceutical. Conducts research to develop or improve radiopharmaceuticals. Prepares reports for regulatory agencies to obtain approval for testing and use of new radiopharmaceuticals. Maintains control records for receipt, storage, preparation, and disposal of radioactive nuclei. Occasionally conducts training for students and medical professionals concerning radiopharmacy use, characteristics, and compounding procedures. GOE 02.04.01 PD M456 EC I6 M5 L5 SVP 7 SOC 301

075.127-030 NURSE SUPERVISOR, EVENING-OR-NIGHT (medical ser.)
Plans, organizes, and directs activities for evening or night shift of hospital nursing department: Establishes policies and procedures for nursing department, following directions of hospital administrators. Observes techniques of and services rendered by nursing staff to insure adherence to hospital guidelines. Demonstrates techniques for nursing students and new personnel to provide training and direction. Identifies problem areas in nursing department, such as understaffing, absenteeism, and wastefulness, and takes corrective action. Monitors use of supplies and equipment to avoid abuses and requistions supplies. Responds to various departments requesting emergency assistance and assigns staff accordingly during emergencies. Prepares work schedule and assigns duties to nursing staff in department for efficient use of personnel. GOE 10.02.01 PD L456 EC I M4 L5 SVP 8 SOC 29

076.124-018 HORTICULTURAL THERAPIST (medical ser.)
Plans, coordinates, and conducts therapeutic gardening program to facilitate rehabilitation of physically and mentally handicapped patients: Confers with medical staff and patients to determine patients' needs. Evaluates patients' disabilities to determine gardening programs. Conducts gardening sessions to rehabilitate, train, and provide recreation for patients. Revises gardening program, based on observations and evaluation of patients' progress. GOE 10.02.02 PD L3456 EC B M4 L5 SVP 7 SOC 3039

076.127-018 DANCE THERAPIST (medical ser.)
Plans, organizes, and leads dance and body movement activities to improve patients' mental outlooks and physical well-beings: Observes and evaluates patient's mental and physical disabilities to determine dance and body movement treatment. Confers with patient and medical personnel to develop dance therapy program. Conducts individual and group dance sessions to improve patient's mental and physical well-being. Makes changes in patient's program based on observation and evaluation of progress. Attends and participates in professional conferences and workshops to enhance efficiency and knowledge. GOE 10.02.02 PD L2456 EC I M3 L5 SVP 8 SOC 3039

076.264-010 PHYSICAL-INTEGRATION PRACTITIONER (per. ser.)
Conducts physical integration program to improve client's muscular function and flexibility: Determines client's medical history regarding accidents, operations, or chronic health complaints to plan objectives of program, using questionnaire. Photographs client to obtain different views of client's posture to facilitate treatment, using camera. Instructs client to demonstrate arm and leg movement and flexion of spine to evaluate client against established program norms. Determines program treatment procedures and discusses goals of program with client. Applies skin lubricant to section of body specified for treatment and massages muscles to release subclinical adhesions either manually or using handheld tool, utilizing knowledge of anatomy. Demonstrates and directs client's participation in specific exercises designed to fatigue desired muscle groups and release tension. Observes client's progress during program through such factors as increased joint movement, improved posture, or coordination. Records client's treatment, response, and progress. GOE 10.02.02 PD L456 EC I M1 L2 SVP 6 SOC 3033

078.161-014 CARDIOPULMONARY TECHNOLOGIST, CHIEF (medical ser.)
Coordinates activities of CARDIOPULMONARY TECHNOLOGISTS (medical ser.) engaged in performing diagnostic testing and treatment of patients with heart, lung, and blood vessel disorders: Establishes methods for conducting tests and treatments, applying knowledge of medical requirements and laboratory procedures. Schedules patients for tests and treatment by staff members. Reviews reports to insure compliance with test and treatment procedures. Develops and modifies training program for assigned personnel. Evaluates worker performances and recommends promotions, transfers, and dismissals. GOE 02.04.02 PD L456 EC I M4 L5 SVP 7 SOC 369

078.161-018 CHIEF TECHNOLOGIST, NUCLEAR MEDICINE (medical ser.)
Supervises and coordinates activities of NUCLEAR MEDICAL TECHNOLOGISTS (medical ser.): Assigns workers to prepare radiopharmaceuticals, perform nuclear medicine studies, and conduct in vitro and ex vivo laboratory tests, and monitors activities to insure efficiency and accuracy of procedures. Develops protocols for new or revised procedures and trains department workers and other personnel in treatment theory, management of patient, and calibration and use of equipment. Administers radiopharmaceuticals under direction of PHYSICIAN (medical ser.) or other qualified medical personnel. Assists in coordinating activities with other departments and in resolving operating problems. GOE 02.04.02 PD L456 EC I6 M4 L5 SVP 8 SOC 365

078.221-010 IMMUNOHEMATOLOGIST (medical ser.)
Performs immunohematology tests, recommends blood problem solutions to doctors, and serves blood bank and community as consultant and instructor: Visually analyzes blood in specimen tubes to determine temperature and speed of centrifuge for starting hematology tests. Centrifuges blood specimen to separate red cells from serum and examines separated cells to detect presence of antibodies. Interprets evidence observed to devise experiments and suggest techniques that will resolve patient's blood problems. Combines known and unknown serums with red cells in test tubes and selects reagents, such as albumin, protolytic enzymes, and antihuman globulin, for individual tests to enhance and make visible reactions of agglutination and hemolysis. Processes various combinations in centrifuge and examines resulting samples under microscope to identify evidence of agglutination or hemolysis. Repeats and varies tests until normal suspension of reagents, serum, and red cells is attained. Writes blood specifications to meet patient's need, on basis of test results, and applies knowledge of blood classification system to locate donor's blood. Performs hematology tests on donor's blood to confirm matching blood types. Requisitions and sends blood to supply patient's need, and prepares written report to inform physician of test results and of required volume of blood to administer. Forwards copy of report to furnish data input for computer files. Studies worksheets to evaluate completeness of hematology tests and reads labels of related specimen tubes to identify known patients. Instructs MEDICAL LABORATORY TECHNICIANS (medical ser.) in classroom, in work situations, and over telephone to teach techniques of microscopic identification of precipitation, agglutination, or hemolysis in blood that leads to resolutions of problems. Writes notes on worksheets of MEDICAL LABORATORY TECHNICIANS (medical ser.) to suggest possible solutions for specific problems and returns worksheets and specimens to aid personnel in blood bank reference library. GOE 02.04.02 PD L3456 EC I M3 L5 SVP 8 SOC 369

078.262-010 PULMONARY-FUNCTION TECHNICIAN (medical ser.)
Performs pulmonary-function, lung-capacity, and blood-and-oxygen tests to gather data for medical evaluation, following instructions of supervisor: Confers with patient in treatment room to explain test procedures. Explains specified methods of breathing to patient and conducts pulmonary-function tests, such as helium dilution and gross spirometry tests, and lung-capacity tests, such as vital capacity and maximum breathing capacity tests, using spirometer. Activates co-oximeter and injects blood specimen into co-oximeter to perform blood analysis tests, such as oxygen saturation and red cell count. Collects and analyzes contents of expired air of patient, using oxygen analyzer. Observes and records readings on metering devices of analysis equipment, and conveys findings of tests and analyses to supervisor for evaluation. GOE 10.03.01 PD L456 EC I6 M4 L4 SVP 6 SOC 369

078.361-034 RADIATION-THERAPY TECHNOLOGIST (medical ser.)
Operates radiation therapy equipment to treat patients with prescribed doses of ionizing radiation: Positions patient under equipment to expose necessary areas to treatment and adjusts equipment according to instructions. Calculates exposure time and intensity required, using mechanical and electronic regulating controls. Turns controls to operate and adjust equipment and regulate application. Observes dials to monitor duration and intensity of treatment. Prepares and maintains records for review by medical staff. GOE 02.03.04 PD L46 EC I M4 L4 SVP 6 SOC 365

078.362-030 CARDIOPULMONARY TECHNOLOGIST (medical ser.)
Performs diagnostic tests of cardiovascular and pulmonary systems of patients in hospital, using variety of laboratory machines and other work devices, to aid physicians in diagnosis and treatment: Conducts electrocardiogram, phonocardiography, vectorcardiography, ultrasound, stress, cardiac catherization, blood pressure, and other vascular tests to diagnose disorders of cardiovascular system, using variety of laboratory equipment, such as electrocardiograph and phonocardiograph machines, stethoscope, and catheter. Conducts tests of pulmonary system to diagnose pulmonary disorders, using respiratory equipment. Analyzes and interprets test findings and furnishes results to physician. GOE 10.03.01 PD L456 EC I M4 L4 SVP 7 SOC 369

078.362-034 PERFUSIONIST (medical ser.)
Sets up and operates heart-lung machine in hospital to take over functions of patient's heart and lungs during surgery or respiratory failure: Consults with surgeon or physician to obtain patient information needed to set up heart-lung machine. Assembles, sets up, and tests heart-lung machine to insure that machine functions according to specifications. Operates heart-lung machine to regulate blood circulation and composition and oxygen and carbon dioxide levels, to administer drugs, and to control body temperature during surgery or respiratory failure of patient. Changes quantities administered at direction of physician, surgeon, or anesthesiologist. Cleans, repairs, and adjusts malfunctioning parts of heart-lung machine. GOE 10.03.02 PD L456 EC I M3 L4 SVP 7 SOC 369

079.131-010 DIRECTOR, SPEECH-AND-HEARING (medical ser.)
Directs and coordinates activities of personnel in hospital speech and hearing department engaged in research and in testing and treating patients according to established policies: Organizes and establishes personnel procedures, including hiring and training, counsels employees, and evaluates work performance. Confers with ADMINISTRATOR, HOSPITAL (medical ser.) and committee members to request expenditures for equipment, supplies, and personnel. Meets with ADMINISTRATOR, HOSPITAL (medical ser.), department officials, and staff members to explain new techniques and procedures or to demonstrate new and innovative equipment. Plans and directs research and treatment programs to provide direction and assistance to staff members. Conducts workshops and seminars to develop staff expertise and knowledge. Analyzes data and maintains records of research and treatment programs. GOE 11.07.02 PD S56 EC I M5 L5 SVP 8 SOC 131

079.137-010 UTILIZATION-REVIEW COORDINATOR (medical ser.)
Supervises and coordinates activities of utilization review staff and develops policies, standards, and procedures governing admissions and treatment of patients of health-care facility: Analyzes individual patient records to determine legitimacy of admission and continued stay in health-care facility, reviews patient treatment plans to insure adherence to established criteria and standards, and supervises activities of utilization review staff. Reviews and analyzes governmental and accrediting agency standards governing admissions, treatment, and continued stay of patients to develop policies, procedures, and criteria for facility center. Reviews application for patient admission and determines necessity of each admission, applying established admission criteria. Aproves admission or refers case to facility Utilization Review Committee for review and course of action when case fails to meet criteria. Reviews inpatient medical records to determine necessity of continued stay or discharge. Reviews physician treatment plans for inpatients to determine appropriateness of plan to patient manifested conditions and to insure consistency with standard medical practice and facility policies. Makes clinical judgment regarding correctness of physician directed care. Determines next review date in accordance with established diagnostic criteria. Abstracts data from records. Assists review committee in planning and holding federally mandated quality assurance reviews, periodic medical reviews, and professional reviews. Serves as review committee liaison with other committees within facility in development of policies and procedures. Participates in facility orientation and training programs. Supervises and coordinates activities of utilization review staff in maintenance of policy and procedure manuals, file, records, and correspondence. GOE 11.07.02 PD L56 EC I M4 L5 SVP 7 SOC 131

079.224-010 HOME HEALTH TECHNICIAN (medical ser.)
Provides patient care, assistance, and instructions in household management and inhome medical care techniques to patients and families in home or homelike environment: Assists ambulatory and bedridden patient with dressing, bathing, grooming, and elimination. Transfers patient to and from wheelchair, and helps patient to walk to and from bed, shower, tub, and lavatory. Performs procedures and treatments as directed by professional staff, such as massages, hot and cold applications, dressing changes, wound irrigation, enemas, douches, catheterizations, and ostomy care, utilizing knowledge of body structures and function and aseptic techniques. Administers oral medications and injections under medical supervision. Measures and records patient temperature, pulse, and respiration rates, blood pressure, fluid intake and output, and performs throat inspection and urine tests to provide data for health-care team assessment. Teaches patients and family members approved medical techniques, such as mobility training in use of walkers, crutches, and other range-of-motion and supportive devices, to enable continuing home care, utilizing knowledge of physical rehabilitation techniques. Demonstrates basic home management techniques, such as housekeeping, nutrition, meal planning and preparation, and adapts techniques to patient's physical limitations. Guides and encourages patient and family to obtain optimal adjustment to illness or disability. GOE 10.03.02 PD M456 EC I6 M3 L4 SVP 6 SOC 369

079.271-014 ACUPRESSURIST (medical ser.)
Examines patients and analyzes findings to diagnose and treat physical problems according to knowledge and techniques of acupressure: Directs patient to lie on treatment couch and positions patient's arms and legs in relaxed position to facilitate examination and treatment. Examines patient's muscular system visually and feels tissue around muscles, nerves, and blood vessels to locate knots and other blockages which indicate excessive accumulations of blood, water, and other substances in tissue. Determines cause of accumulations and treatment procedures, according to knowledge of acupressure and experience. Feels tissue around muscles, nerves, and blood vessels to locate pressure points and presses at pressure points, using thumbs, fingers, and elbows to redirect accumulated body fluids into normal channels according to acupressure knowledge, techniques, and experience. Discusses findings with patient and explains relationship to internal organs. Outlines course of treatment for patient and advises patient regarding methods and diet for prevention of problem recurrence. Uses specific method or combination of acupressure methods, such as Ghi Ahp, Jin Shin Do, or Shiatsu, and may be known accordingly. GOE 10.02.02 PD M45 EC I M3 L4 SVP 7 SOC 289

079.361-014 ANIMAL HEALTH TECHNICIAN (medical ser.)
Assists veterinary staff to diagnose and treat animals for injury and illness, applying knowledge of veterinary medical assisting procedures and techniques and following directions of veterinary staff: Soothes and quiets patients prior to examination or treatment and restrains patients during examination and treatment to facilitate procedures. Measures and records patient temperature, pulse rate, and respiration as directed. Applies bandages, dressings, and splints, and administers oxygen and oral and injected medications as prescribed. Administers treatments, cleans teeth, removes sutures, and inserts catheters, endotracheal tubes, and related devices as instructed. Draws patient blood and collects specimens as directed. Gathers and positions surgical packs and related instruments and materials for use by veterinary staff during surgery. Administers prescribed preanesthetic drugs to patient, and washes, shaves, and applies antiseptic solution to surgical site to prepare patient for surgery. Monitors patient's vital signs and reflexes during and after surgery and informs veterinary staff of changes. Observes patients in hospital to monitor eating and elimination and to detect abnormal conditions. Conducts test and microscopic examinations of specimens, following standard test and examination procedures and using various laboratory equipment and materials. Dispenses prescribed drugs, maintains prescription records, and inventories supplies of drugs, instruments, and related items. Cleans and sterilizes instruments and materials and maintains equipment and machines. Sets up and operates radiological equipment to conduct X-ray examinations of patients, utilizing knowledge of radiological techniques and procedures. GOE 02.03.03 PD M456 EC I M3 L4 SVP 6 SOC 27

079.364-022 PHLEBOTOMIST (medical ser.)
Draws blood from patients or donors in hospital, blood bank, or similar facility for analysis or other medical purposes: Assembles equipment, such as tourniquet, needles, blood collection devices, gauze, cotton, and alcohol on work tray, according to requirements for specified tests or procedures. Verifies or records identity of patient or donor and converses with patient or donor to allay fear of procedure. Applies tourniquet to arm, locates accessible vein, swabs puncture area with disinfectant, and inserts needle into vein to draw blood into collection tube or bag. Withdraws needle, applies treatment to puncture site, and labels and stores blood container for subsequent processing. May prick finger to draw blood. May conduct interviews, take vital signs, and draw and test blood samples to screen donors at blood bank. GOE 02.04.02 PD L456 EC I M2 L4 SVP 3 SOC 5233

079.374-026 PSYCHIATRIC TECHNICIAN (medical ser.)
Provides nursing care to mentally ill, emotionally disturbed, or mentally retarded patients in psychiatric hospital or mental health clinic and participates in rehabilitation and treatment programs: Helps patients with their personal hygiene, such as bathing and keeping beds, clothing, and living areas clean. Administers oral medications and hypodermic injections, following physician's prescriptions and hospital procedures. Takes and records measures of patient's general physical condition, such as pulse, temperature, and respiration, to provide daily information. Observes patients to detect behavior patterns and reports observations to medical staff. Intervenes to restrain violent or potentially violent or suicidal patients by verbal or physical means as required. Leads prescribed individual or

group therapy sessions as part of specific therapeutic procedures. May complete initial admittance forms for new patients. May contact patient's relatives by telephone to arrange family conferences. May issue medications from dispensary and maintain records in accordance with specified procedures. May be required to hold State license. GOE 10.02.02 PD M45 EC I6 M3 L4 SVP 6 SOC 366

090.222-010 INSTRUCTOR, BUSINESS EDUCATION (education)
Instructs students in commercial subjects, such as typing, filing, secretarial procedures, business mathematics, office equipment use, and personality development, in business schools, community colleges, or training programs: Instructs students in subject matter, utilizing various methods, such as lecture and demonstration, and uses audiovisual aids and other materials to supplement presentations. Prepares or follows teaching outline for course of study, assigns lessons, and corrects homework and classroom papers. Administers tests to evaluate students' progress, records results, and issues reports to inform students of their progress. Maintains discipline in classroom. GOE 11.02.01 PD M456 EC I M4 L5 SVP 8 SOC 2233

099.117-030 DIRECTOR, EDUCATION (museum)
Plans, develops, and administers educational program of museum, zoo, or similar institution: Confers with administrative personnel to decide scope of program to be offered. Prepares schedules of classes and rough drafts of course content to determine number and background of instructors needed. Interviews, hires, trains, and evaluates work performance of education department staff. Contacts and arranges for services of guest lecturers from academic institutions, industry, and other establishments to augment education staff members in presentation of classes. Assists instructors in preparation of course descriptions and informational materials for publicity or distribution to class members. Prepares budget for education programs and directs maintenance of records of expenditures, receipts, and public and school participation in programs. Works with other staff members to plan and present lecture series, film programs, field trips, and other special activities. May teach classes. May speak before school and community groups and appear on radio or television to promote institution programs. May coordinate institution educational activities with those of other area organizations to maximize utilization of resources. May train establishment volunteers to assist in presentation of classes or tours. May develop and submit program and activity grant proposals and applications and implement programs funded as result of successful applications. GOE 11.07.03 PD S56 EC I M4 L5 SVP 7 SOC 1283

099.167-030 EDUCATIONAL RESOURCE COORDINATOR (museum)
Directs operation of educational resource center of museum, zoo, or similar establishment: Maintains collections of slides, video tapes, programed texts, and other educational materials related to institution specialty, storing or filing materials according to subject matter, geographic or ethnic association, or historical period. Composes or directs others in composition of descriptions of materials, and prepares catalog listing materials for use of museum staff members, area school teachers, and others. Compiles list of books, periodicals, and other materials designed to augment items available in resource center. Explains storage and cataloging systems to teachers and others who visit center and suggests materials for various projects, such as preparing school classes for tour of institution or presentation of lecture for community group. Issues loan materials to teachers or lecturer, or schedules and coordinates delivery of materials to designated locations. Maintains records of loans and prepares circulation reports for review by administrative personnel. Conducts workshops to acquaint educators with use of institution's facilities and materials. Attends teacher meetings and conventions to promote use of institution services. GOE 11.07.03 PD L56 EC I M2 L5 SVP 7 SOC 1283

099.227-038 TEACHER (museum)
Teaches classes, presents lectures, conducts workshops, and participates in other activities to further educational program of museum, zoo, or similar institution: Plans course content and method of presentation, and prepares outline of material to be covered and submits it for approval. Selects and assembles materials to be used in teaching assignment, such as pieces of pottery or samples of plant life, and arranges use of audiovisual equipment or other teaching aids. Conducts classes for children in various scientific, history, or art subjects, utilizing museum displays to augment standard teaching methods and adapting course content and complexity to ages and interests of students. Teaches adult classes in such subjects as art, history, astronomy, or horticulture, using audiovisual aids, demonstration, or laboratory techniques appropriate to subject matter. Presents series of lectures on subjects related to institution collections, often incorporating films or slides into presentation. Conducts seminars or workshops for school system teachers or lay persons to demonstrate methods of using institution facilities and collections to enhance school programs or to enrich other activities. Conducts workshops or field trips for students or community groups and plans and directs activities associated with projects. Plans and presents vacation or weekend programs for elementary or preschool children, combining recreational activities with teaching methods geared to age groups. Conducts classes for academic credit in cooperation with area schools or universities. Teaches courses in museum work to participants in work-study programs. Works with adult leaders of youth groups to assist youths to earn merit badges or fulfill other group requirements. Maintains records of attendance. Evaluates success of courses, basing evaluation on number and enthusiasm of persons participating and recommends retaining or dropping course in future plans. When course is offered for academic credit, evaluates class member performances, administers tests, and issues grades in accordance with methods used by cooperating educational institution. GOE 11.02.01 PD L456 EC I M4 L5 SVP 7 SOC 2216

100.117-014 LIBRARY CONSULTANT (library)
Advises administrators of public libraries: Analyzes administrative policies, observes work procedures, and reviews data relative to book collections to determine effectiveness of library service to public. Compares allocations for building funds, salaries, and book collections with statewide and national standards, to determine effectiveness of fiscal operations. Gathers statistical data, such as population and community growth rates, and analyzes building plans to determine adequacy of programs for expansion. Prepares evaluation of library systems based on observations and surveys, and recommends measures to improve organization and administration of systems. GOE 11.07.04 PD S5 EC I M4 L6 SVP 8 SOC 251

102.117-014 DIRECTOR, MUSEUM-OR-ZOO (museum)
Administers affairs of museum, zoo, or similar establishment: Confers with institution's board of directors to formulate policies and plan overall operations. Directs acquisition, education, research, public service, and development activities of institution, consulting with curatorial, administrative, and maintenance staff members to implement policies and initiate programs. Works with members of curatorial and administrative staffs to acquire additions to collections. Confers with administrative staff members to determine budget requirements, plan fund raising drives, prepare applications for grants from government agencies or private foundations, and solicit financial support for institution. Establishes and maintains contact with administrators of other institutions to exchange information concerning operations and plan, coordinate, or consolidate community service and education programs. Represents institution at professional and civic social events, conventions, and other gatherings to strengthen relationships with cultural and civic leaders, present lectures or participate in seminars, or explain institution's functions and seek financial support for projects. Reviews materials prepared by staff members, such as articles for journals, request for grants, and reports on institution programs, and approves materials or suggests changes. Instructs classes in institution's education program or as guest lecturer at university. Writes articles for technical journals or other publications. GOE 11.02.01 PD S56 EC I M4 L6 SVP 8 SOC 252

102.167-014 HISTORIC-SITE ADMINISTRATOR (museum)
Manages operation of historic structure or site: Discusses house or site operation with governing body representatives to form or change policies. Oversees activities of building and grounds maintenance staff and other employees. Maintains roster of volunteer guides, and contacts volunteers to conduct tours of premises according to schedule. Conducts tours, explaining points of interest and answers visitors' questions. Studies documents, books, and other materials to obtain information concerning history of site or structure. Conducts classes in tour presentation methods for volunteer guides. Accepts group reservations for house tours and special social events. Arranges for refreshments, entertainment, and decorations for special events. Collects admission and special event fees, and maintains records of receipts, expenses, and numbers of persons served. Assists in planning publicity, and arranges for printing of brochures or placement of information in media. Inspects premises for evidence of deterioration and need for repair, and notifies governing body of such need. GOE 11.02.01 PD L46 EC I M4 L5 SVP 5 SOC 252

102.167-018 REGISTRAR, MUSEUM (museum)
Maintains records of accession, condition, and location of objects in museum collection, and oversees movement, packing, and shipping of objects to conform to insurance regulations: Observes unpacking of objects acquired by museum through gift, purchase, or loan to determine that damage or deterioration to objects has not occurred. Registers and assigns accession and catalog numbers to all objects in collection, according to established registration system. Composes concise description of objects, and records descriptions on file cards and in collection catalogs. Oversees handling, packing, movement, and inspection of all objects entering or leaving establishment, including traveling exhibits, and confers with other personnel to develop and initiate most practical methods of packing and shipping fragile or valuable objects. Maintains records of storage, exhibit, and loan locations of all objects in collection for use of establishment personnel, insurance representatives, and other persons utilizing facilities. Prepares acquisition reports for review of curatorial and administrative staff. Periodically reviews and evaluates registration and catalog system to maintain applicability, consistency, and operation. Recommends changes in recordkeeping procedures to achieve maximum accessibility to and efficient retrieval of collection objects. Arranges for insurance of objects on loan or special exhibition, or recommends insurance coverage on parts of or entire collection. GOE 07.01.02 PD S56 EC I M4 L5 SVP 6 SOC 252

102.361-014 RESTORER, CERAMIC (museum)
Cleans, preserves, restores, and repairs objects made of glass, porcelain, china, fired clay, and other ceramic materials: Coats excavated objects with surface-active agents to loosen adhering mud or clay and washes objects with clear water. Places cleaned objects in dilute hydrocholoric acid

or other solution to remove remaining deposits of lime or chalk, basing choice of solution on knowledge of physical and chemical structure of objects and destructive qualities of solvents. Cleans glass, porcelain, or similar objects by such methods as soaking objects in lukewarm water with ammonia added, wiping gilded or enameled objects with solvent-saturated swab, or rubbing objects with paste cleanser. Rubs objects with jewelers' rouge or other mild cleanser, soaks objects in distilled water with bleach or solvent added, or applies paste or liquid solvent, such as magnesium silicate or acetone, basing choice of method and material on age, condition, and chemical structure of objects, to remove stains from objects. Recommends preservation measures, such as control of temperature, humidity, and exposure to light, to curatorial and building maintenance staff to prevent damage to or deterioration of object. Impregnates surfaces with diluted synthetic lacquers to reduce porosity of material to increase durability of ancient earthenware. Restores or simulates original appearance of objects by such methods as polishing surfaces to restore translucency, removing crackled glaze and applying soluble synthetic coating, grinding or cutting out chipped edges and repolishing surfaces, or applying matt paints, gold leaf, or other coating to object, basing methods and materials used on knowledge of original craft and condition of objects. Repairs broken objects, employing such techniques as bonding edges together with adhesive, inserting dowel pins in sections and cementing together, or affixing adhesive coated strips to inner portions of broken objects. Replaces missing sections of objects by constructing wire frames of missing sections, shaping plasticene or other materials over frames, affixing modeled sections to objects with dowels or adhesive, and painting attached sections to reproduce original appearance. Constructs replicas of archaeological artifacts or historically significant ceramic ware, basing construction design on size, curvature, and thickness of excavated shards or pieces of objects available and knowledge of techniques and designs characteristic of period. GOE 01.06.02 PD L46 EC I M5 L5 SVP 7 SOC 252

109.067-014 RESEARCH ASSOCIATE (museum)
Plans, organizes, and conducts research in scientific, cultural, historical, or artistic field for use in own work or in project of sponsoring institution: Develops plans for project or studies guidelines for project prepared by professional staff member to outline research procedures to be followed. Plans schedule according to variety of methods to be used, availability and quantity of resources, and number of subordinate personnel assigned to participate in project. Conducts research, utilizing institution library, archives, and collections, and other sources of information, to collect, record, analyze, and evaluate facts. Discusses findings with other personnel to evaluate validity of findings. Prepares reports of completed projects for publication in technical journals, for presentation to agency requesting project, or for use in further applied or theoretical research activities. GOE 11.03.03 PD S56 EC I M6 L6 SVP 7 SOC 252

109.361-010 RESTORER, PAPER-AND-PRINTS (library; museum)
Cleans, preserves, restores, and repairs books, documents, maps, prints, photographs, and other paper objects of historic or artistic significance: Examines or tests objects to determine physical condition and chemical structure of paper, ink, paint, or other coating, in order to identify problem and plan safest and most effective method of treating material. Cleans objects by such methods as sprinkling crumbled art gum or draft powder over surface and rotating soft cloth over cleaning agent to absorb soil (dry cleaning), immersing objects in circulating bath of water or mild chemical solution (wet cleaning), or applying solvent to remove rust, fly specks, mildew, or other stains, basing choice of method on knowledge of physical and chemical structure of objects and effects of various kinds of treatment. Preserves or directs preservation of objects by such methods as immersing paper in deacidification baths to remove acidity from papers and ink to prevent deterioration, sealing documents or other papers in cellulose cases and passing sealed objects through heated rollers to laminate them, spraying objects, storage containers, or areas with fungicides, insecticides, or pesticides, and controlling temperature, humidity, and exposure to natural or artificial light in areas where objects are displayed or stored. Restores objects to original appearance by such methods as immersing papers in mild bleach solution to brighten faded backgrounds, removing old varnish from such art works as engravings and mezzotints, or strengthening papers by resizing in bath of gelatin solution. Repairs objects by such methods as mending tears with adhesive and tissue, patching and filling worm holes, torn corners, or large tears by chamfering, inserting, affixing, and staining paper of similar weight and weave to simulate original appearance, or retouching stained, faded, or blurred watercolors, prints, or documents, using colors and strokes to reproduce those of original artist or writer. GOE 01.06.03 PD S46 EC I M5 L5 SVP 7 SOC 252

109.364-010 CRAFT DEMONSTRATOR (museum)
Demonstrates and explains techniques and purposes of handicraft or other activity, such as candle dipping, horseshoeing, or soap making, as part of display in history or folk museum, or restored or refurbished farm, village, or neighborhood: Studies historical and technical literature to acquire information about time period and lifestyle depicted in display and craft techniques associated with time and area, to devise plan for authentic presentation of craft. Drafts outline of talk, assisted by research personnel, to acquaint visitors with customs and crafts associated with folk life depicted. Practices techniques involved in handicraft to insure accurate and skillful demonstrations. Molds candles, shoes horses, operates looms, or engages in other crafts or activities, working in appropriate period setting, to demonstrate craft to visitors. Explains techniques of craft, and points out relationship of craft to lifestyle depicted to assist visitors to comprehend traditional techniques of work and play peculiar to time and area. Answers visitor questions or refers visitor to other sources for information. GOE 09.01.02 PD L456 EC B M2 L4 SVP 4 SOC 252

109.367-010 MUSEUM ATTENDANT (museum)
Conducts operation of museum and provides information about regulations, facilities, and exhibits to visitors: Opens museum at designated hours, greets visitors, and invites visitors to sign guest register. Monitors visitors' viewing exhibits, cautions persons not complying with museum regulations, distributes promotional materials, and answers questions concerning exhibits, regulations, and facilities. Arranges tours of facility for schools or other groups, and schedules volunteers or other staff members to conduct tours. Examines exhibit facilities and collection objects periodically and notifies museum professional personnel or governing body when need for repair or replacement is observed. GOE 07.04.04 PD L56 EC I M3 L4 SVP 3 SOC 252

129.027-010 CANTOR (profess. & kin.)
Chants and reads portions of ritual during religious services, and directs congregants in musical activities: Arranges musical portion of religious services in consultation with leader of congregation. Chants or recites religious texts during worship services or other observances and trains and leads congregants in musical responses. May create variations of traditional music or compose music for services. May train and direct choir or teach vocal music to youth or other groups of congregants. GOE 11.07.03 PD L5 EC I M1 L4 SVP 8 SOC 2049

141.137-010 PRODUCTION MANAGER, ADVERTISING (profess. & kin.)
Coordinates activities of design, illustration, photography, paste-up, and typography personnel to prepare advertisements for publication, and supervises workers engaged in pasting-up advertising layouts in art department or studio: Determines arrangement of art work and photographs and selects style and size of type, considering factors such as size of advertisement, design, layout, sketches, and method or printing specified. Submits copy and typography instructions to printing firm or department for typesetting. Reviews proofs of printed copy for conformance to specifications. Assigns personnel to mount printed copy and illustration on final layouts, coordinating assignments with completion of art work to insure that schedules are maintained. Writes instructions for final margin widths and type sizes, and submits layout for printing. Examines layout proofs for quality of printing and conformance to layout. GOE 01.02.03 PD S456 EC I M3 L4 SVP 7 SOC 322

142.061-058 EXHIBIT DESIGNER (museum)
Plans, designs, and oversees construction and installation of permanent and temporary exhibits and displays: Confers with administrative, curatorial, and exhibit staff members to determine theme, content, interpretative or informational purpose, and planned location of exhibit, to discuss budget, promotion,, and time limitations, and to plan production schedule for fabrication and installation of exhibit components. Prepares preliminary drawings of proposed exhibit, including detailed construction, layout, and special effect diagrams and material specifications, for final drawing rendition by other personnel, basing design and specifications on knowledge of artistic and technical concepts, principles, and techniques. Submits plan for approval, and adapts plan as needed to serve intended purpose or to conform to budget or fabrication restrictions. Oversees preparation of artwork and construction of exhibit components to insure intended interpretation of concepts and conformance to structural and material specifications. Arranges for acquisition of specimens or graphics or building of exhibit structures by outside contractors as needed to complete exhibit. Inspects installed exhibit for conformance to specifications and satisfactory operation of special effects components. Oversees placement of collection objects or informational materials in exhibit framework. GOE 01.02.03 PD S456 EC I M4 L5 SVP 7 SOC 322

143.260-010 OPTICAL-EFFECTS-CAMERA OPERATOR (motion pic.)
Sets up and operates optical printers and related equipment to produce fades, dissolves, superimpositions, and other optical effects required in motion pictures, applying knowledge of optical effects printing and photography: Reads work order and count sheet to ascertain optical effects specifications and location of subject material on original photography film. Analyzes specifications to determine work procedures, sequence of operations, and machine setup, using knowledge of optical effects techniques and procedures. Loads camera of optical effects printer with magazine of unexposed film stock. Mounts original photography film in transport and masking mechanism of optical-printer projector and moves film into designated position for optical effect, using counter and film markings to determine placement. Adjusts camera position, lens position, mask opening, lens aperture, focus, shutter angle, film transport speed, and related controls, using precision measuring instruments and knowledge of optical effects techniques to determine settings. Selects designated color and neutral density filters and mounts in filter holder to control light and intensity. Sets controls in automatic or manual mode, moves control to start camera, and observes printer operation and footage counter during film-

ing. Adjusts controls during filming operation when operating in manual mode, and stops camera when designated counter reading is observed. Moves controls to rewind camera film and original photography film and repeats select portions or entire operation number of times necessary to produce designated effect. Sets up and operates animation and matte cameras and related equipment to photograph artwork, such as titles and painted mattes. Sets up and operates single pass optical printers when enlarging or reducing film or performing related operations. Sets up and operates subtitle camera and related equipment to photograph film subtitles. Examines frames of film exposed with different combinations of color filters (wedges) to select optimum color balance based on experience and judgment. GOE 01.02.03 PD L46 EC I M3 L3 SVP 7 SOC 326

149.261-010 EXHIBIT ARTIST (museum)
Produces artwork for use in permanent or temporary exhibit settings of museum, zoo, or similar establishment, performing any combination of following duties to prepare exhibit setting and accessories for installation: Confers with professional museum personnel to discuss objectives of exhibits and type of artwork needed. Makes scale drawing of exhibit design, indicating size, position, and general outlines of artwork needed for use of installation and other fabrication personnel. Paints scenic, panoramic, or abstract composition on canvas, board, burlap, or other material to be used as background or component of exhibit, following layout prepared by designer. Paints or stencils exhibit titles and legends on boards, or cuts letters from plastic or plywood to form title and legend copy, and mounts letters on panel or board, using adhesives or handtools. Photographs persons, artifacts, scenes, plants, or other objects, and develops negatives to obtain prints to be used in exhibits. Enlarges, intensifies, or otherwise modifies prints, according to exhibit design specifications. Fashions exhibit accessories, such as human figures, tree parts, or relief maps, from clay, plastic, wood, fiberglass, papier mache, or other materials, using hands, handtools, or molding equipment to cut, carve, scrape, mold, or otherwise shape material to specified dimensions. Brushes or sprays protective or decorative finish on completed background panels, informational legends, and exhibit accessories. Maintains files of photographs, paintings, and accessories for use in exhibits. GOE 01.02.03 PD L46 EC I M3 L4 SVP 6 SOC 325

159.042-010 LASERIST (amuse. & rec.)
Creates optical designs-and-effects show for entertainment of audiences, using control console and related laser projection and recording equipment: Sets up and operates console to control laser projection, recording equipment, and house lights. Presses switches and turns dials to dim house lights, cue opening music, and begin programed laser sequence. Moves controls to orchestrate colors, patterns, and movements in concert with musical accompaniment. Tests, repairs, and adjusts laser and sound systems, using circuit schematics and test equipment. Examines, cleans, and maintains system cooling, optical, and sound equipment according to preventive maintenance schedule. Discusses show concepts and laser equipment operation with press representatives to promote public relations. GOE 05.03.05 PD L456 EC I M3 L4 SVP 6 SOC 328

161.267-030 BUDGET ANALYST (gov. ser.)
Analyzes current and past budgets, prepares and justifies budget requests, and allocates funds according to spending priorities in governmental service agency: Analyzes accounting records to determine financial resources required to implement program and submits recommendations for budget allocations. Recommends approval or disapproval of requests for funds. Advises staff on cost analysis and fiscal allocations. GOE 11.06.05 PD S45 EC I M3 L4 SVP 7 SOC 1419

164.117-018 MEDIA DIRECTOR (profess. & kin.)
Plans and administers media programs in advertising department of food corporation: Confers with representatives of advertising agencies, product managers, and corporate advertising staff to establish media goals, objectives, and strategies within corporate advertising budget. Confers with advertising agents or media representatives to select specific programs and negotiate advertising to insure optimum use of budgeted funds and long-term contracts. Adjusts broadcasting schedules due to program cancellations. Studies demographic data and consumer profiles to identify target audiences of media advertising. Reads trade journals and professional literature to stay informed of trends, innovations, and changes that affect media planning. GOE 11.09.01 PD S456 EC I M4 L5 SVP 8 SOC 125

165.117-014 DIRECTOR, FUNDS DEVELOPMENT (profess. & kin.)
Plans, organizes, directs, and coordinates ongoing and special project funding programs for museum, zoo, or similar institution: Prepares statement of planned activities and enlists support from members of institution staff and volunteer organizations. Develops public relations materials to enhance institution image and promote fundraising program. Identifies potential contributors to special project funds and supporters of institution ongoing operations through examination of past records, individual and corporate contracts, and knowledge of community. Plans and coordinates fund drives for special projects. Assigns responsibilities for personal solicitation to members of staff, volunteer organizations, and governing body according to special interests or capabilities. Organizes direct mail campaign to reach other potential contributors. Plans and coordinates benefit events, such as banquets, balls, or auctions. Organizes solicitation drives for pledges of ongoing support from individuals, corporations, and foundations. Informs potential contributors of special needs of institution, and encourages individuals, corporations, and foundations to establish or contribute to special funds through endowments, trusts, donations of gifts-in-kind, or bequests, conferring with attorneys to establish methods of transferring funds to benefit both donors and institution. Researches public and private grant agencies and foundations to identify other sources of funding for research, community service, or other projects. Supervises and coordinates activities of workers engaged in maintaining records of contributors and grants and preparing letters of appreciation to be sent to contributors. GOE 11.09.02 PD S5 EC I M4 L5 SVP 7 SOC 139

166.167-050 PROGRAM SPECIALIST, EMPLOYEE-HEALTH MAINTENANCE (profess. & kin.)
Coordinates activities of area employers in setting up local government funded program within establishments to help employees who are not functioning at satisfactory levels of job performance due to alcoholism or other behavioral medical problems: Writes and prepares newspaper advertisements, newsletters, and questionnaires and speaks before community groups to promote employee assistance program within business community. Analyzes character and type of business establishments in area, and compiles list of prospective employers appropriate for implementing assistance program. Contacts prospective employers, explains program and fees, points out advantages of program, and reaches agreement with interested employers on extent of proposed program. Develops program within establishment. Establishes committee composed of company officials and workers to develop statement of employee assistance program and policy and procedures. Plans and conducts training sessions for company officials to develop skills in identifying and handling employees troubled by alcoholism or other personal problems. Assists employer in setting up in-plant educational program to prevent alcoholism, using posters, pamphlets, and films, and establishes referral network providing for in-plant and out-of-plant group or individual counseling for troubled employees. Confers with team member of assistance program who provides counseling regarding planning and progress of counseling components. Confers with staff of employee assistance program regarding progress and evaluation of current programs and proposals for developing new programs. GOE 11.05.02 PD S5 EC I M3 L5 SVP 6 SOC 123

166.257-010 EMPLOYER RELATIONS REPRESENTATIVE (profess. & kin.)
Establishes and maintains working relationships with local employers to promote use of public employment programs and services: Contacts employers new to area or company requiring revisit and arranges appointment to visit company representative or employer responsible for hiring workers. Establishes rapport between Employment Service and company to promote use of agency programs and services. Confers with employer to resolve problems, such as local employment office effectiveness, employer complaints, and alternative employer actions for recruiting qualified applicants. Answers employer questions concerning Employment Service programs or services available. Solicits employers to list job openings with Employment Service. Receives job orders from employers by phone or in person and records information to facilitate selection and referral process. GOE 11.09.03 PD L45 EC I M2 L4 SVP 6 SOC 332

166.267-034 JOB DEVELOPMENT SPECIALIST (profess. & kin.)
Promotes and develops employment and on-the-job training opportunities for disadvantaged applicants: Assists employers in revising standards which exclude applicants from jobs. Demonstrates to employers effectiveness and profitability of employing chronically unemployed by identifying jobs that workers could perform. Establishes relationships with employers regarding problems, complaints, and progress of recently placed disadvantaged applicants and recommends corrective action. Assists employers in establishing wage scales commensurate with prevailing rates. Promotes, develops, and terminates on-the-job training program opportunities with employers and assists in writing contracts. Identifies need for and assists in development of auxiliary services to facilitate bringing disadvantaged applicants into job-ready status. Informs business, labor, and public about training programs through various media. GOE 11.03.04 PD S5 EC I M3 L4 SVP 5 SOC 143

166.267-038 PERSONNEL RECRUITER (profess. & kin.)
Seeks out, interviews, screens, and recruits job applicants to fill existing company job openings: Discusses personnel needs with department supervisors to prepare and implement recruitment program. Contacts colleges to set up oncampus interviews. Provides information on company facilities and job opportunities to potential applicants. Interviews college applicants to obtain work history, education, training, job skills, and salary requirements. Screens and refers qualified applicants to company hiring personnel for followup interview. Arranges travel and lodging for selected applicants at company expense. Performs reference and background checks on applicants. Corresponds with job applicants to notify them of employment consideration. Files and maintains employment records for future references. Projects yearly recruitment expenditures for budgetary control. GOE 11.03.04 PD S5 EC I M3 L5 SVP 7 SOC 143

168.161-014 INDUSTRIAL-SAFETY-AND-HEALTH TECHNICIAN (any ind.)
Plans and directs safety and health activities in industrial plant to evaluate and control environmental hazards: Tests noise levels and measures air quality, using precision instruments. Maintains and calibrates instruments. Administers hearing tests to employees. Trains forklift operators to qualify for licensing. Enforces use of safety equipment. Lectures employees to obtain compliance with regulations. Develops and monitors emergency action plans. Investigates accidents and prepares accident reports. Assists management to prepare safety and health budget. Recommends changes in policies and procedures to prevent accidents and illness. GOE 11.10.03 PD L456 EC I M4 L4 SVP 6 SOC 1473

168.167-086 SAFETY MANAGER (medical ser.)
Plans, implements, coordinates, and assesses hospital accident, fire prevention, and occupational safety and health programs under general direction of hospital officials, utilizing knowledge of industrial safety-related engineering discipline and operating regulations: Develops and recommends new procedures and approaches to safety and loss prevention based on reports of incidents, accidents, and other data gathered from hospital personnel. Disseminates information to department heads and others regarding toxic substances, hazards, carcinogens, and other safety information. Assists department heads and administrators in enforcing safety regulations and codes. Measures and evaluates effectiveness of safety program, using established goals. Conducts building and grounds surveys on periodic and regular basis to detect code violations, hazards, and incorrect work practices and procedures. Develops and reviews safety training for hospital staff. Maintains administrative control of records related to safety and health programs. Prepares and disseminates memos and reports. Maintains required records. Assists personnel department in administering worker compensation program. GOE 11.10.03 PD L56 EC I M5 L5 SVP 7 SOC 1473

168.261-010 RADIATION-PROTECTION SPECIALIST (gov. ser.)
Tests X-ray equipment, inspects areas where equipment is used, and evaluates operating procedures to detect and control radiation hazards: Visits hospitals, medical offices, and other establishments to test X-ray machines and fluoroscopes and to inspect premises. Tests equipment to determine that kilovolt potential, alinement of components, and other elements of equipment meet standards for safe operation, using specialized instruments and procedures. Operates equipment to determine need for calibration, repair, or replacement of tubes or other parts. Measures density of lead shielding in walls, using radiometric equipment. Computes cumulative radiation levels and refers to regulations to determine if amount of shielding is sufficient to absorb radiation emissions. Examines license of equipment operator for authenticity and observes operating practices to determine competence of operator to use equipment. Confers with physicians, dentists, and X-ray personnel to explain procedures and legal requirements pertaining to use of equipment. Demonstrates exposure techniques to improve procedures and minimize amount of radiation delivered to patient and operator. Reviews plans and specifications for proposed X-ray installations for conformance to legal requirements and radiation safety practices. Contacts organizations submitting inadequate specifications to explain changes in shielding or layout needed to conform to regulations. GOE 11.10.03 PD L456 EC I M4 L5 SVP 8 SOC 1473

168.267-082 AGRICULTURAL-CHEMICALS INSPECTOR (gov. ser.)
Inspects establishments where agricultural service products, such as livestock feed and remedies, fertilizers, and pesticides, are manufactured, sold, or used to insure conformance to laws regulating product quality and labeling: Visits processing plants, distribution warehouses, sales outlets, agricultural pest control service organizations, and farmers to collect product samples for analysis and to examine fresh and dried produce for spray residue. Inspects product label information concerning ingredients and advertising claims for conformance to chemical analysis of ingredients and documented effects of use. Investigates suspected violations of product quality and labeling laws. Interviews farmers, merchants, and others to determine nature of suspected violations and to obtain documented evidence to be used in legal action against violators. Calls on dealers to determine that licensing requirements have been met, and calls on manufacturers and distributors to collect delinquent tonnage reports. Prepares reports of all inspections and investigations for review by supervisory personnel and for use as evidence in legal action initiated by others. GOE 11.10.03 PD L5 EC B M2 L3 SVP 7 SOC 1473

168.267-086 HAZARDOUS-WASTE MANAGEMENT SPECIALIST (gov. ser.)
Conducts studies on hazardous waste management projects and provides information on treatment and containment of hazardous waste: Participates in developing hazardous waste rules and regulations to protect people and environment. Surveys industries to determine type and magnitude of disposal problem. Assesses available hazardous waste treatment and disposal alternatives, and costs involved, to compare economic impact of alternative methods. Assists in developing comprehensive spill prevention programs and reviews facility plans for spill prevention. Participates in developing spill-reporting regulations and environmental damage assessment programs. Prepares reports of findings concerning spills and prepares material for use in legal actions. Answers inquiries and prepares informational literature to provide technical assistance to representatives of industry, government agencies, and to general public. Provides technical assistance in event of hazardous chemical spill and identifies pollutant, determines hazardous impact, and recommends corrective action. GOE 11.10.03 PD S5 EC I M3 L5 SVP 7 SOC 1473

168.267-090 INSPECTOR, WATER-POLLUTION CONTROL (gov. ser.)
Inspects sites where discharges enter State waters and investigates complaints concerning water pollution problems: Inspects wastewater treatment facilities at sites, such as mobile home parks, sewage treatment plants, and other sources of pollution. Inspects lagoons and area where effluent enters State waters for such features as obvious discoloration of water, sludge, algae, rodents, and other conditions. Informs owner when unacceptable or questionable conditions are present and recommends corrective action. Notifies mobile laboratory technicians when sampling is required. Advises property owners, facility managers, and equipment operators concerning pollution control regulations. Investigates complaints concerning water pollution problems. Compiles information for pollution control discharge permits. Prepares technical reports of investigations. GOE 11.10.03 PD L5 EC I M4 L5 SVP 7 SOC 1473

168.267-094 MARINE-CARGO SURVEYOR (bus. ser.)
Inspects cargoes of seagoing vessels to certify compliance with national and international health and safety regulations in cargo handling and stowage: Reads vessel documents that set forth cargo loading and securing procedures, capacities, and stability factors to ascertain cargo capabilities according to design and cargo regulations. Advises crew in techniques of stowing dangerous and heavy cargo, such as use of extra support beams (deck bedding), shoring, and additional stronger lashings, according to knowledge of hazards present when shipping grain, explosives, logs, and heavy machinery. Inspects loaded, secured cargo in holds and lashed to decks to ascertain that pertinent cargo handling regulations have been observed. Issues certificate of compliance when violations are not detected. Recommends remedial procedures to correct deficiencies. Measures ship holds and depth of fuel and water in tanks, using sounding line and tape measure, and reads draft markings to ascertain depth of vessel in water. Times roll of ship, using stopwatch. Calculates hold capacities, volume of stored fuel and water, weight of cargo, and ship stability factors, using standard mathematical formulas and calculator. Analyzes data obtained from survey, formulates recommendations pertaining to vessel capacities, and writes report of findings. Inspects cargo handling devices, such as boom, hoists, and derricks, to identify need for maintenance. GOE 11.10.03 PD L456 EC B6 M4 L4 SVP 9 SOC 1473

168.267-098 PESTICIDE-CONTROL INSPECTOR (gov. ser.)
Inspects operations of distributors and commercial applicators of pesticides to determine compliance with government regulations on handling, sale, and use of pesticides: Inspects premises of wholesale and retail distributors to insure that registered pesticides are handled in accordance with State and Federal regulations. Determines that handlers possess permits and sell restricted pesticides only to authorized users. Evaluates pesticides for correct labeling, misbranding, misrepresentation, or adulteration, and confiscates or quarantines unacceptable pesticides. Inspects operations of commercial applicators of pesticides and observes application methods to insure correct use of equipment, application procedures, and that applicators possess valid permits. Determines that accurate records are kept to show pesticides used, dosage, times, places, and methods of applications. Inspects premises to insure that storage and disposal of pesticides conform to regulations. Investigates complaints concerning pesticides and uses. Identifies insect or disease, recommends treatment, and authorizes emergency use of suitable restricted pesticides to respond to emergency situations, such as insect infestations or outbreaks of plant disease. GOE 11.10.03 PD L5 EC I M2 L3 SVP 7 SOC 1473

168.267-102 PLAN CHECKER (gov. ser.)
Examines commercial and private building plans and inspects construction sites to insure compliance with building code regulations: Reviews building plans for completeness and accuracy. Examines individual plan components to insure that all code mandated items are included. Calculates footage between building components, such as doors, windows, and parking areas and amount of area occupied by components to insure compliance with code. Notes instances of noncompliance on plans and correction sheet and suggests modifications to bring plans into compliance. Approves and signs plans meeting code requirements. Inspects building sites and buildings to insure construction follows plans. Submits reports detailing items of noncompliance to builder for correction. Provides code information to individuals planning buildings. Issues occupancy certificates to building owners when completed buildings are in compliance with codes. Tours jurisdictional area to detect unapproved or noncompliance construction. Proposes studies to improve or update building codes. Testifies at appeal hearings regarding buildings alleged to be not in compliance with codes. GOE 05.03.06 PD L456 EC I M4 L4 SVP 7 SOC 1472

168.267-106 REGISTRATION SPECIALIST, AGRICULTURAL CHEMICALS (gov. ser.)
Reviews and evaluates information on applications for registration of products containing dangerous chemicals for compliance with statutory regulations: Reads registration applications from manufacturers and distributors of pesticides, fertilizers, and other products containing dangerous

chemicals. Evaluates label information to determine that directions for use and claims for effectiveness of product are stated clearly and accurately. Reviews statements concerning product ingredients, effects of misuse, and administration of antidotes for adequacy of information and conformance to regulatory requirements for substances. Forwards approved applications to other personnel for registration. Contacts manufacturers and distributors of products not meeting standards to clarify regulations and to suggest changes in label information to permit registration. Prepares, organizes, and maintains records to document activities and provide reference materials. Conducts studies and investigations of faulty labeling or use of products as directed by agricultural agency personnel. GOE 11.10.03 PD S5 EC I M3 L4 SVP 7 SOC 1473

168.267-110 SANITATION INSPECTOR (gov. ser.)
Inspects community land areas and investigates complaints concerning neglect of property and illegal dumping of refuse to insure compliance with municipal code: Inspects designated areas periodically for evidence of neglect, excessive litter, and presence of unsightly or hazardous refuse. Interviews residents and inspects area to investigate reports of illegal dumping and neglected land. Locates property owners to explain nature of inspection and investigation findings and to encourage voluntary action to resolve problems. Studies laws and statutes in municipal code to determine specific nature of code violation and type of action to be taken. Issues notices of violation to land owners not complying with request for voluntary correction of problems. Issues notices of abatement to known violators of dumping regulations and informs other municipal agencies of need to post signs forbidding illegal dumping at designated sites. Prepares case materials when legal action is required to solve problems. Conducts informational meetings for residents, organizes neighborhood cleanup projects, and participates in campaigns to beautify city to promote community interest in eliminating dangerous and unsightly land use practices. GOE 11.10.03 PD L5 EC B M2 L3 SVP 5 SOC 1473

168.367-018 CODE INSPECTOR (gov. ser.)
Inspects existing residential buildings and dwelling units, visually, to determine compliance with city ordinance standards and explains ordinance requirements to concerned personnel: Obtains permission from owners and tenants to enter dwellings. Visually examines all areas to determine compliance with ordinance standards for heating, lighting, ventilating, and plumbing installations. Measures dwelling units and rooms to determine compliance with ordinance space requirements, using tape measure. Inspects premises for overall cleanliness, adequate disposal of garbage and rubbish, and for signs of vermin infestation. Prepares forms and letters advising property owners and tenants of possible violations and time allowed for correcting deficiencies. Consults file of violation reports and revisits dwellings at periodic intervals to verify correction of violations by property owners and tenants. Explains requirements of housing standards ordinance to property owners, building contractors, and other interested parties. GOE 05.03.06 PD L56 EC I6 M2 L3 SVP 5 SOC 1473

169.117-014 GRANT COORDINATOR (profess. & kin.)
Develops and coordinates grant-funded programs for agencies, institutions, local government, or units of local government, such as school systems or metropolitan police departments: Reviews literature dealing with funds available through grants from governmental agencies and private foundations to determine feasibility of developing programs to supplement local annual budget allocations. Discusses program requirements and sources of funds available with administrative personnel. Confers with personnel affected by proposed program to develop program goals and objectives, outline how funds are to be used, and explain procedures necessary to obtain funding. Works with fiscal officer in preparing narrative justification for purchase of new equipment and other budgetary expenditures. Submits proposal to officials for approval. Writes grant application, according to format required, and submits application to funding agency or foundation. Meets with representatives of funding sources to work out final details of proposal. Directs and coordinates evaluation and monitoring of grant-funded programs, or writes specifications for evaluation or monitoring of program by outside agency. Assists department personnel in writing periodic reports to comply with grant requirements. Maintains master files on all grants. Monitors all paper work connected with grant-funded programs. GOE 11.05.02 PD S456 EC I M4 L6 SVP 7 SOC 149

169.167-062 COORDINATOR, SKILL-TRAINING PROGRAM (gov. ser.)
Plans and arranges for cooperation with and participation in skill training program by private industry, agencies, and concerned individuals: Organizes and coordinates recruiting, training, and placement of participants. Contacts various service agencies on behalf of trainees with social problems and refers trainees to appropriate agencies to insure trainees receive maximum available assistance. Prepares periodic reports to monitor and evaluate progress of program. GOE 07.01.02 PD L5 EC B M4 L4 SVP 6 SOC 139

169.167-066 LEGISLATIVE ASSISTANT (gov. ser.)
Assists legislator in preparation of proposed legislation: Conducts research into subject of proposed legislation and develops preliminary draft of bill. Analyzes pending legislation and suggests to legislator action to be taken. Briefs legislator on policy issues. Attends committee meetings and prepares reports of proceedings. Speaks with lobbyists, constituents, and members of press to gather and provide information on behalf of legislator. Analyzes voting records of other legislators and political activity in legislator home district to derive data for legislator consideration. Maintains liaison with government agencies affected by proposed or pending legislation. Assists in campaign activities and drafts speeches for legislator. GOE 11.05.03 PD S5 EC I M3 L5 SVP 7 SOC 1139

169.262-010 CASEWORKER (gov. ser.)
Performs research into laws of United States and procedures of Federal agencies and prepares correspondence in office of Member of Congress to resolve problems or complaints of constituents: Confers with individuals who have requested assistance to determine nature and extent of problems. Analyzes U. S. Code to become familiar with laws relating to specific complaints of constituents. Researches procedures and systems of governmental agencies and contacts representatives of Federal agencies to obtain information on policies. Contacts Congressional Research Service to collect information relating to agency policies and laws. Contacts colleges and universities to obtain information relating to constituent problems. Determines action to facilitate resolution of constituent problems. Composes and types letters to Federal agencies and Congressional committees concerning resolution of problems of constituents. Prepares memoranda to inform Member of Congress of problems which require legislative attention. Confers with personnel assisting Member of Congress to discuss introduction of legislation to solve constituent problems. Calculates Social Security benefits, veterans' benefits, tax assessments, and other data concerning constituent complaints, using desk calculator. GOE 07.01.06 PD S456 EC I M3 L4 SVP 5 SOC 1139

169.267-030 PASSPORT-APPLICATION EXAMINER (gov. ser.)
Approves applications for United States passports and related privileges and services: Reviews information on applications, such as applicant's birthplace and birthplaces of applicant's parents, to determine eligibility according to nationality laws and governmental policies. Examines supporting documents, such as affidavits, records, newspaper files, and Bibles, to evaluate relevance and authenticity of documents. Queries applicants to obtain additional or clarifying data. Forwards approved applications to designated official, and prepares summaries for cases not approved indicating points of law. Answers questions of individuals concerning passport applications and related services. GOE 07.01.05 PD L56 EC I M3 L4 SVP 5 SOC 1473

180.161-014 SUPERINTENDENT, HORTICULTURE (museum)
Plans, coordinates, and directs activities concerned with breeding, growing, and displaying ornamental flowers, shrubs, and other plants in botanical garden, arboretum, park, or similar facility: Confers with administrative, technical, and maintenance staff members to plan activities for maintenance of growing stock and production of plants for display on grounds, installation in special exhibits, sale to public, or use in research projects. Discusses plans for renovation or additions to facility with administrative personnel and devises designs for floral exhibits to complement theme of new or renovated sections. Prepares scale drawings of outdoor or greenhouse exhibits for use of gardening staff members. Issues instructions to supervisory personnel in charge of plant growing, greenhouse, and display activities. Inspects greenhouse, hothouses, potting sheds, experimental growing areas, and other areas to determine need for repair and to observe activities of workers. Maintains inventory of propagation and growing equipment and supplies, and orders additional materials as needed. Arranges purchase, sale, or exchange of plants with representatives of similar institutions. Confers with research personnel to discuss development of new strains of plants and to devise methods to exhibit, publicize, or market new products. Represents establishment at civic or professional meetings. Participates in radio or television shows or prepares articles for newspapers to provide horticultural information to public. GOE 02.02.02 PD L456 EC I M4 L5 SVP 8 SOC 5525

187.117-058 DIRECTOR, OUTPATIENT SERVICES (medical ser.)
Supervises and directs activities of outpatient clinic and coordinates activities of clinic with those of other hospital departments: Establishes clinic policies and procedures in cooperation with other hospital officials. Interprets and administers personnel policies and provides for training program. Reviews clinic activities and recommends changes in, or better utilization of, facilities, services, and staff. Establishes and maintains work schedules and assignments of resident professional staff members. Authorizes purchase of supplies and equipment. Prepares and submits budget, records, reports, and statistical data to ADMINISTRATOR, HOSPITAL (medical ser.). Meets with personnel of other local institutions and organizations to promote public health and educational services. Oversees operation of clinic and recommends procedures, treatments, or other course of action to assist medical staff. GOE 11.07.02 PD S56 EC I M5 L6 SVP 8 SOC 131

187.117-062 RADIOLOGY ADMINISTRATOR (medical ser.)
Plans, directs, and coordinates administrative activities of radiology department of hospital medical center: Conducts studies and implements changes to improve internal operations of department. Advises staff and supervisors on administrative changes. Assists hospital officials in preparation of department budget. Conducts specified classes and provides training material to assist in student training program. Directs and coordinates

personnel activities of department. Recommends cost saving methods and hospital supply changes to effect economy of department operations. Interprets, prepares, and distributes statistical data regarding department operations. GOE 11.07.02 PD S56 EC I M5 L5 SVP 7 SOC 137

187.134-010 SUPERVISOR, CONTRACT-SHELTERED WORKSHOP (nonprofit organ.)
Supervises and coordinates activities of handicapped individuals in sheltered workshop to train and improve vocational skills for gainful employment through productive work: Assigns individual to specific tasks, such as cleaning, sorting, assembling, repairing, or hand packing products or components. Demonstrates job duties to handicapped individual and observes worker performing tasks to insure understanding of job duties. Monitors work performance at each individual's work station to insure compliance with procedures and safety regulations and to note behavior deviations. Examines work piece visually to verify adherence to specifications. Confers with individuals to explain or to demonstrate task again to resolve work related difficulties. Reassigns individual to simpler tasks when worker cannot perform assigned tasks, or to tasks containing higher degrees of complexity as level of competence is reached. Performs other duties described under SUPERVISOR (any ind.). GOE 11.07.03 PD L45 EC I M2 L2 SVP 7 SOC 127

187.167-202 DIRECTOR, CRAFT CENTER (profess. & kin.)
Plans, organizes, and directs activities of craft center operated by folk or history museum, historic or ethnic area or community, or historic or regional theme park: Consults with administrative personnel to plan activities, such as craft classes, exhibits, and other projects conducted in cooperation with sponsoring institution. Orders supplies needed for basketry, leatherwork, candlemaking, macrame, tole painting, beadwork, or other crafts compatible with institution theme. Plans and writes publicity material for craft classes, and coordinates presentation of craft shows and exhibits, arranging for participants, and overseeing installation of exhibit booths, distribution of publicity materials, and scheduling of craft demonstrations. Maintains inventory, personnel, and accounting records. Arranges for consignment of craft items for sale, directs sales personnel, and maintains records of operation. Reports operational activities to institution administrative staff or governing body, and confers with staff to plan and implement changes in operation of facilities. GOE 11.07.04 PD L456 EC I M4 L5 SVP 7 SOC 1352

188.117-030 COURT ADMINISTRATOR (gov. ser.)
Administers nonjudicial functions of court: Coordinates activities such as jury selection, notification, and utilization, case scheduling and tracking, personnel assignment, and space and equipment allocation to accomplish orderly processing of court cases. Investigates problems that affect caseflow and recommends or implements corrective measures. Compiles and analyzes data on court activity to monitor management performance and prepare activity reports. Conducts research to analyze current and alternative personnel, facilities, and data management systems and consults with judicial staff of court to evaluate findings and recommendations. May oversee accounting of revenues and expenditures and prepare and justify budget. May resolve questions and complaints raised by court personnel, attorneys, and members of other organizations and public. GOE 11.05.03 PD L56 EC I M4 L5 SVP 8 SOC 1131

188.167-110 PLANNER, PROGRAM SERVICES (gov. ser.)
Conducts studies, prepares reports, and advises public and private sector administrators on feasibility, cost-effectiveness, and regulatory conformance of proposals for special projects or ongoing programs in such fields as transportation, conservation, or health care: Consults with administrators or planning councils to discuss overall intent of programs or projects, and determines broad guidelines for studies, utilizing knowledge of subject area, research techniques, and regulatory limitations. Reviews and evaluates materials provided with proposals, such as environmental impact statements, construction specifications, or budget or staffing estimates, to determine additional data requirements. Conducts field investigations, economic or public opinion surveys, demographic studies, or other appropriate research to gather required information. Organizes data from all sources, using appropriate statistical methods to insure validity of materials. Evaluates information to determine feasibility of proposals or to identify factors requiring amendment. Develops alternate plans for program or project, incorporating recommendations, for review of officials. Maintains collection of socioeconomic, environmental, and regulatory data related to agency functions, for use by planning and administrative personnel in government and private sectors. Reviews plans and proposals submitted by other governmental planning commissions or private organizations to assist in formulation of overall plans for region. GOE 11.03.02 PD L56 EC I M5 L6 SVP 7 SOC 192

189.117-038 USER REPRESENTATIVE, INTERNATIONAL ACCOUNTING (electronics)
Directs activities of information systems group engaged in designing, developing, implementing, and maintaining worldwide integrated finance and accounting system utilized by multi-national organization: Studies and analyzes general plan proposal, confers with corporate officials to obtain details of general plan, and obtains systems requirements from corporate and international accounting and management personnel to compile raw data for plan development. Develops methods and procedures for project accomplishment, applying knowledge of foreign monetary and tax systems and international accounting conventions. Prepares specifications documenting systems and project requirements, including time frame, staffing, activity schedule, and methods and procedures. Interprets international finance and accounting policies and procedures to provide coding assistance to others engaged in systems design and coding. Oversees entering of base data and programs into computer, analyzes output to identify existence and nature of problems, and orders indicated corrections to design or program. Writes procedures manuals for users, reflecting and adapting individual accounting conventions and monetary and tax systems into overall integrated system. Prepares training plan and trains user staff prior to implementation of system. Edits and audits financial and accounting reports to identify problems in installed system and initiates corrective measures. GOE 11.05.02 PD S56 EC I M5 L5 SVP 8 SOC 139

189.167-054 SECURITY CONSULTANT (bus. ser.; per. ser.)
Plans, directs, and oversees implementation of comprehensive security systems for protection of individuals and homes, and business, commercial, and industrial organizations, and investigates various crimes against client: Inspects premises to determine security needs. Studies physical conditions, observes activities, and confers with client's staff to obtain data regarding internal operations. Analyzes compiled data and plans and directs installation of electronic security systems, such as closed circuit surveillance, entry controls, burglar alarms, ultrasonic motion detectors, electric eyes, and outdoor perimeter and microwave alarms. Directs installation and checks operation of electronic security equipment. Plans and directs personal security and safety of individual, family, or group for contracted period. Provides bulletproof limousine and bodyguards to insure client protection during trips and outings. Suggests wearing bulletproof vest when appropriate. Plans and reviews client travel itinerary, mode of transportation, and accommodations. Travels with client and directs security operations. Investigates crimes committed against client, such as fraud, robbery, arson, and patent infringement. Reviews personnel records of client staff and conducts background investigation of selected members to obtain personal histories, character references, and financial status. Conducts or directs surveillance of suspects and premises to apprehend culprits. Notifies client of security weaknesses and implements procedures for handling, storing, safekeeping, and destroying classified materials. Reports criminal information to authorities and testifies in court. GOE 04.02.02 PD L56 EC I6 M3 L5 SVP 7 SOC 5144

195.107-042 CORRECTIONAL-TREATMENT SPECIALIST (social ser.)
Provides casework services for inmates of penal or correctional institution: Interviews inmate and confers with attorneys, judges, and probation officers to compile social history reflecting such factors as nature and extent of inmate criminality and current and prospective social problems. Analyzes collected data and develops and initiates treatment plan. Interviews inmate and consults with employees of institution, such as supervisory personnel, PSYCHOLOGIST, CLINICAL (profess. & kin.), and CHAPLAIN (profess. & kin.), to evaluate inmate social progress, and counsels inmate concerning perceived problems. Reports inmate progress and makes recommendations to parole officials. Assists inmate with matters concerning detainers, sentences in other jurisdictions, and writs. Confers with inmate family to identify family needs prior to inmate release. Occasionally conducts collective counseling for small groups of inmates. Lectures groups of newly admitted inmates to inform them of institution rules and regulations. GOE 10.01.02 PD S5 EC I M3 L5 SVP 7 SOC 2032

195.107-046 PROBATION-AND-PAROLE OFFICER (profess. & kin.)
Counsels juvenile or adult offenders in activities related to legal conditions of probation or parole: Reviews social history of institutionalized offenders due for parole, and talks with offenders regarding development of release plans by parole commission. Determines which juvenile cases fall within jurisdiction of courts and which should be adjusted informally or referred to other agencies. Confers with legal representatives, family, and other concerned persons to conduct prehearing or presentencing investigations. Compiles reports and testifies in courts when requested. Reviews file folders on assigned offenders to determine violation committed and legal stipulation of release. Explains legal requirements to offender, such as visits to office, payment of restitution, and employment requirements to inform offender of release conditions. Interviews offender to formulate release plan and to identify specific problems that hinder probation or parole, such as family indifference, need of employment, and health conditions in need of attention, utilizing interviewing and counseling techniques. Refers offender to other agencies to correct problems, such as drug addiction, educational deficiency, and personality adjustments. Visits and telephones business firms to develop jobs for unemployed offenders. Evaluates offender progress during release with visits to home and place of work. Secures remedial action, or requests leniency by courts, if necessary, when offender behavior justifies such action. GOE 10.01.02 PD L456 EC I6 M3 L5 SVP 7 SOC 2032

195.167-042 ALCOHOL-AND-DRUG-ABUSE-ASSISTANCE PROGRAM ADMINISTRATOR (gov. ser.)
Coordinates government programs dealing with prevention and treatment of alcohol and drug abuse problems affecting work performance of employees in private and public sectors of work force: Studies composi-

tion of industrial and business communities and state agencies to determine methods of promoting information concerning alcohol and drug abuse prevention and treatment programs to executives and administrators in industry and government. Confers with management personnel to explain purpose and benefits of Employee Assistance Program, and attempts to establish programs in establishments, organizations, and agencies. Consults with representatives of Area Service Providers (professionals in health care, counseling, and other special services) to develop participation in prevention and treatment programs. Instructs personnel in methods of recognizing and identifying employee problems, referring employee to community Area Service Providers, and maintaining records of program-related activities. Consults with management and administrators of participating organizations and Area Service Providers to evaluate progress of program and identify administrative problems. Implements corrective action plan to solve problems. Develops training materials to be used by participating organizations and Area Service Providers. Prepares articles for newspaper and other media to explain purpose of program. Lectures and participates in workshops, radio and television interviews, community meetings, and other organizational functions to promote acceptance and support of program. Prepares grant proposals and reports for submission to department supervisor. GOE 11.07.01 PD L45 EC I M3 L5 SVP 7 SOC 1139

195.267-018 PATIENT-RESOURCES-AND-REIMBURSEMENT AGENT (gov. ser.)

Investigates financial assets, properties, and resources of hospitalized retarded and brain-damaged clients to protect financial interests and provide reimbursement of hospital costs: Visits and interviews or contacts by mail or telephone relatives, friends, former employers, pension funds, fraternal and veterans organizations and government agencies. Records documentation of financial resources in patient files. Analyzes data accumulated, such as disability allowances, medicare, medicaid, social security pension, dividends, interest, and insurance, and determines ability to pay for hospitalization. Determines additional sources from which reimbursements can be obtained. Prepares reports and enumerates amounts and sources of reimbursements, including public assistance from social agencies in behalf of patients and families. Reviews patients records to insure that reimbursements are maintained. Applies for appointment of conservators to financially protect patients with assets over statutory limits and submits names of appointees to courts. Occasionally attends court hearings to protect patient interests. GOE 10.01.02 PD L456 EC I M3 L5 SVP 7 SOC 2032

195.367-018 COMMUNITY WORKER (gov. ser.)

Investigates problems of residents of assigned neighborhood to determine needs of those disadvantaged because of income, age, or other economic or personal handicaps: Seeks out and assists persons in need of agency services, under direction of professional staff. Visits individuals and families, and addresses neighborhood groups to publicize supportive services available to the unemployed, parolees, or others needing special assistance. Follows-up all contacts and prepares and submits reports of activities. GOE 10.01.02 PD L5 EC B M4 L4 SVP 6 SOC 2032

195.367-022 FOOD-MANAGEMENT AIDE (gov. ser.) nutrition aide.

Advises low income family members how to plan, budget, shop, prepare balanced meals, and handle and store food, following prescribed standards: Advises clients of advantages of food stamps, how to obtain stamps, and use of stamps during shopping trips. Transports clients to shopping area, using automobile. Observes clients' food selections. Recommends alternate economical and nutritional food choices. Observes and discusses meal preparation. Suggests alternate methods of food preparation. Assists in planning of food budget, utilizing charts and sample budgets. Advises clients on preferred methods of sanitation. Consults with supervisor concerning programs for individual families. Maintains records concerning results of family visits. GOE 10.01.02 PD L5 EC I M2 L3 SVP 3 SOC 2032

195.367-026 PREPAROLE-COUNSELING AIDE (gov. ser.)

Provides individual and group guidance to inmates of correctional facility, who are eligible for parole, and assists in developing vocational and educational plans in preparing inmates for reentry into community life: Conducts inmate orientation sessions to explain programs and resources available to inmates and to induce inmates to join programs. Interviews inmates to record data on individual problems, needs, interests, and attitude. Holds individual and group counseling sessions to discuss programs available that affect inmate's reentry into community life, such as housing and financial aid, veteran's benefits, work release programs, vocational rehabilitation, and job search assistance. Prepares and maintains case folder for each inmate and discusses findings with supervisor to obtain assistance in establishing goals and plan of action for inmates. Conducts followup interview to ascertain inmate progress. Prepares correspondence and applications for medicare, medicaid, veteran benefits, food stamps, and housing. Telephones and corresponds with persons and agencies outside facility to insure that family and/or business matters are attended to. Meets with family members at facility to discuss and resolve problems prior to release of inmate. Develops and prepares informational packets for inmate, listing outside agencies and programs that could assist ex-offender upon release. GOE 10.01.02 PD S5 EC I M2 L4 SVP 6 SOC 5133

195.367-030 RECREATION AIDE (social ser.)

Assists RECREATION LEADER (social ser.) in conducting recreation activities in community center or other voluntary recreation facility: Arranges chairs, tables, and sporting or exercise equipment in designated rooms or other areas for scheduled group activities, such as banquets, wedding receptions, parties, group meetings, or sports events. Welcomes visitors and answers incoming telephone calls. Notifies patrons of activity schedules and registration requirements. Monitors spectators and participants at sports events to insure orderly conduct. Receives, stores, and issues sports equipment and supplies. May keep attendance records or scores at sporting events, operate audiovisual equipment, monitor activities of children during recreational trips or tours, or perform other duties as directed by RECREATION LEADER (social ser.). GOE 09.01.01 PD M456 EC I M2 L3 SVP 2 SOC 5269

195.367-034 SOCIAL-SERVICES AIDE (social ser.)

Assists professional staff of public social service agency, performing any combination of following tasks: Interviews individuals and family members to compile information on social, educational, criminal, institutional, or drug history. Visits individuals in homes or attends group meetings to provide information on agency services, requirements, and procedures. Provides rudimentary counseling to agency clients. Oversees day-to-day group activities of residents in institution. Meets with youth groups to acquaint them with consequences of delinquent acts. Refers individuals to various public or private agencies for assistance. May care for children in client's home during client's appointments. May accompany handicapped individuals to appointments. GOE 10.01.02 PD L5 EC I M3 L5 SVP 6 SOC 2032

199.167-018 ENERGY-CONTROL OFFICER (education)

Monitors energy use and develops, promotes, implements, and coordinates energy conservation program in county school district facilities: Compiles monthly energy report on consumption of electricity, fuel, oil, coal, LP gas, and water in school facilities, listing units consumed and costs. Sets up energy monitoring devices in school facilities that graphically plot energy usage and temperature changes during extended periods of time. Visits school facilities on regular basis to inspect monitoring devices and utilities usage. Determines areas in which energy conservation measures are needed, and compiles needs-assessment report of all school facilities. Monitors energy usage of extracurricular activities in school facilities. Coordinates energy conservation activities in areas with those of local, State, and Federal conservation groups. Recommends energy conservation policies to board of education. Presents lectures on resource conservation at teachers' meetings and to civic groups. GOE 05.03.08 PD L56 EC I M4 L4 SVP 7 SOC 399

199.167-022 ENVIRONMENTAL ANALYST (gov. ser.)

Directs, develops, and administers State governmental program for assessment of environmental impact of proposed recreational projects: Directs assessment of environmental impact and preparation of impact statements required for final evaluation of proposed actions. Directs identification and analysis of alternative proposals for handling projects in environmentally sensitive manner. Plans for enhancement of environmental setting for each proposed recreational project. Designs and directs special studies to obtain technical environmental information regarding planned projects, contacting and utilizing various sources, such as regional engineering offices, park region laboratories, and other governmental agencies. Prepares and controls budget for functions of impact-statement preparation program. Attends meetings and represents department on subjects related to program. GOE 11.05.03 PD S5 EC I M3 L4 SVP 8 SOC 1133

199.261-014 PARKING ANALYST (gov. ser.) engineering technician, parking.

Develops plans for construction and utilization of revenue-producing vehicle parking facilitites: Plans and conducts comprehensive field surveys to locate sites for new parking facilities. Analyzes factors such as capacity, turnover, rates, and required property changes relative to proposed sites, and prepares maps, graphs, tracings, and diagrams to illustrate findings. Designs parking lot facilities, including spaces, aisles, driveways, lighting, gates, landscaping, cashier booths, storm drains, grades, and paving details, and prepares cost estimates. Evaluates work performed by contractors to verify conformity to specifications. Keeps log of construction projects and prepares final reports. Reports maintenance problems occurring at facilities to supervisor. Prepares replies to public suggestions and complaints. GOE 05.03.06 PD L456 EC B M4 L5 SVP 7 SOC 399

199.267-034 RESEARCH ASSISTANT (profess. & kin.) II researcher.

Compiles and analyzes verbal or statistical data to prepare reports and studies for use by professional workers in variety of areas, such as science, social science, law, medicine, or politics: Searches sources, such as reference works, literature, documents, newspapers, and statistical records, to obtain data on assigned subject. Analyzes and evaluates applicability of collected data. Prepares statistical tabulations, using calculator or adding machine. Writes reports or presents data in formats, such as abstracts, bibliographies, graphs, or maps. May interview individuals to obtain data or draft correspondence to answer inquiries. When conducting studies to assist lawmakers may be designated LEGISLATIVE AIDE (gov. ser.). GOE 11.08.02 PD S56 EC I M3 L5 SVP 6 SOC 399

203.362-022 WORD-PROCESSING-MACHINE OPERATOR (clerical) word processor.
Operates word processing equipment to record, edit, store, and revise correspondence, reports, statistical tables, forms, and other materials, utilizing clerical skills and knowledge of word processing functions: Reads instructions to determine procedures to be followed regarding material to be prepared or revised and required format for finished copy. Depresses keys on word processing equipment to adjust controls for spacing, margins, and tabulation, and places tape cassette, diskette, or other magnetic recording medium in holder. Keyboards (types) original material into machine memory, typing from printed copy, machine dictation, or related sources. Reads proof copy of material entered into machine memory, and depresses keys to correct typographical errors, print out final copy, and record material onto magnetic medium. Locates medium in file when revisions are required, places medium in holder and presses keys to insert (type), delete, correct, reposition, or reformat designated material. May operate equipment that extends word processing capabilities, such as cathode ray tube displays (CRT's), single or multiple printers, or optical character recognition (OCR). Important variations are kinds (trade names) of word processing equipment operated. May operate electronic typewriters with limited editing capabilities. GOE 07.06.02 PD S456 EC I M1 L3 SVP 4 SOC 4624

203.582-074 ELECTRONIC-TYPESETTING-MACHINE OPERATOR (print. & pub.)
Operates terminal keyboard of electronic typesetting machine and auxiliary equipment, such as photocomposing and developing machines, to produce hard copy of text such as inhouse publications: Measures lines of copy and size of type to be input to determine machine settings required, using printer's rule. Loads disk or tape into electronic typesetting machine and depresses keys to set length and thickness of printed lines. Depresses keys to input material and scans video screen to monitor input. Depresses keys to move cursor (indicator) to point where error occurs and to delete or correct error. Loads completed disk or tape and magazine of photosensitive paper into photocopying machine. Sets font selector controls to select type of specified face and size and starts machine that automatically prints text from disk or tape onto photosensitive paper. Removes magazine of photosensitive paper from photocopying machine at end of cycle, inserts magazine in developing machine, and starts machine. Proofreads developed copy to detect additional errors. Corrects errors on disk or tape, using typesetting machine and video screen, to prepare disk or tape to produce error-free copy. GOE 07.06.02 PD S46 EC I M3 L4 SVP 6 SOC 4793

203.582-078 NOTEREADER (clerical)
Operates typewriter to transcribe stenotyped notes of court proceedings, following standard formats for type of material transcribed: Reads work order to obtain information, such as type of case, case number, number of copies required, and spelling of participant's names. Reviews form books to ascertain format required for specified document, and adjusts typewriter settings for indentation, line spacing, and other style requirements. Operates typewriter to transcribe contractions and symbols of stenotyped text into standard language form. Proofreads typed copy to identify and correct errors and to verify format specifications. Copies typed documents, using copying machines. May use automatic or manual stenotype noteholder. GOE 07.06.02 PD S46 EC I M1 L3 SVP 5 SOC 4624

205.367-062 REFERRAL CLERK, TEMPORARY-HELP AGENCY (clerical) staffing clerk.
Compiles and records information about temporary job openings and refers qualified applicants from register of temporary help agency: Receives call from hospital, business, or other type of organization requesting temporary workers and obtains and records information regarding job requirements. Reviews records to locate registered workers who match organization requirements and are available for scheduled work shift. Notifies selected workers of job availability and records referral information on agency records. Sorts mail, files records, and performs related clerical duties. May give employment applications to applicants, schedule interviews with agency registration interviewers, or administer standard agency skill tests. May specialize in referring specific types of workers, such as nurses. GOE 07.05.03 PD S56 EC I M3 L3 SVP 3 SOC 4692

209.362-030 CONGRESSIONAL-DISTRICT AIDE (gov. ser.)
Provides information and assistance to public and performs variety of clerical tasks in office of congressional legislator: Answers requests for information and assistance from constituents and other members of public, by phone or in person, using knowledge of governmental agencies and programs and source materials, such as agency listings and directories. Transcribes reports and types letters, using electric typewriter. Operates telecopier to receive and send messages, reports, and other documents. Opens and sorts mail according to addressee or type of assistance or information requested. Maintains record of telephone calls. Files correspondence, reports, and documents. Occasionally composes correspondence in response to written requests. Occasionally contacts other governmental or private agencies to act as liaison on behalf of constituents. GOE 07.04.04 PD S46 EC I M3 L4 SVP 5 SOC 463

209.567-022 OFFICE CLERK (clerical)
Performs any combination of following and similar clerical tasks in office where typing is not required: Copies information from one record to another. Sorts, files, and retrieves records or other documents. Addresses and stuffs envelopes. Sorts and distributes mail. Proofreads records and reports. Duplicates records, using copying machine. Answers telephone and records or relays messages. GOE 07.07.03 PD L456 EC I M2 L3 SVP 2 SOC 463

213.582-010 DIGITIZER OPERATOR (bus. ser.; petrol. production)
Operates encoding machine to trace coordinates on documents, such as maps or drawings, and to encode document points into computer: Reads work order to determine document points to be digitized (encoded). Positions document on digitizer (encoding machine) table. Guides digitizer cursor over document to trace coordinates, stops at specified points, and punches cursor key to digitize points into computer memory unit. Observes monitor screen periodically to verify completeness of encoding. Types command on keyboard to transfer encoded data from memory unit to magnetic tape. Keeps record of work orders, time, and tape production. GOE 07.06.01 PD S46 EC I M3 L2 SVP 5 SOC 4613

214.362-042 BILLING CLERK (clerical)
Operates calculator and typewriter to compile and prepare customer charges, such as labor and material costs: Reads computer printout to ascertain monthly costs, schedule of work completed, and type of work performed for customer, such as plumbing, sheetmetal, and insulation. Computes costs and percentage of work completed, using calculator. Compiles data for billing personnel. Types invoices indicating total items for project and cost amounts. GOE 07.02.04 PD S46 EC I M3 L3 SVP 4 SOC 4715

219.362-070 TAX PREPARER (bus. ser.) income-tax-return preparer; tax form preparer.
Prepares income tax return forms for individuals and small businesses: Reviews financial records, such as prior tax return forms, income statements, and documentation of expenditures to determine forms needed to prepare return. Interviews client to obtain additional information on taxable income and deductible expenses and allowances. Computes taxes owed, using adding machine, and completes entries on forms, following tax form instructions and tax tables. Consults tax law handbooks or bulletins to determine procedure for preparation of atypical returns. Occasionally verifies totals on forms prepared by others to detect errors of arithmetic or procedure. Calculates form preparation fee according to complexity of return and amount of time required to prepare forms. GOE 07.02.02 PD S56 EC I M4 L3 SVP 4 SOC 4712

221.387-054 BATCH-RECORDS CLERK (fabric. plastics prod.)
Compiles and maintains plastic-mixing and ingredient records, and prepares daily mixing instructions for use by MATERIAL MIXERS (fabric. plastics prod.): Compiles and maintains daily mixing and perpetual inventory records from work orders, mixing logs, and formula cards that indicate production information, such as type and quantity of plastic ingredients mixed, ingredient formulas, number of products molded, and identification numbers of molds and molding machines utilized. Copies formula for each plastic mixture from specified formula card onto display card for use by MATERIAL MIXER (fabric. plastics prod.). Determines and records amount of plastic mixture required for each molding machine in daily mixing log, based on amount of mixture stored at each machine and knowledge of machine's consumption rate. GOE 05.09.02 PD S46 EC I5 M2 L2 SVP 3 SOC 4752

222.387-066 SAMPLE CLERK (fabric. plastics prod.)
Receives and fills requisitions for samples of fabricated plastic products and inspects samples for conformance to company standards: Collects sample products from production lines and inspects samples for conformance to company standards, using specification sheets, gages, and color standard chart. Stores selected samples in sample room, pending requests for samples from sales representatives and customers. Wraps and packs samples, upon request, for shipment. Maintains records of requests received and filled. Maintains perpetual inventory of samples and replenishes sample stock to maintain required levels. GOE 05.09.01 PD L46 EC I M3 L3 SVP 5 SOC 4757

222.387-070 TYPE-LIBRARY CLERK (mach. mfg.)
Issues and stores prints of type characters used in type photography: Reads work order specifications to determine type character prints required and selects prints from files. Examines prints for clarity and sharpness of characters, and measures characters to insure correctness of size and accuracy of dimensions, using millimeter rule. Notifies SUPERVISOR, TYPE PHOTOGRAPHY (mach. mfg.) of prints needing correction or replacement. Sorts and collates prints in order indicated on work order and forwards prints to photographer for processing. Examines letters on prints returned from photographer and adds precut adhesive-backed corners to letters as necessary to compensate for shrinkage of photographed image. Refiles prints in designated files. GOE 05.09.01 PD S46 EC I M2 L2 SVP 3 SOC 4754

230.647-010 SINGING MESSENGER (bus. ser.)
Performs song and dance routines to deliver messages and entertain specified individuals for customers of message delivery service: Practices song and dance routines with experienced worker to become familiar with routines offered by service. Receives customer instructions from dispatcher, selects standard message supplied by service, or records customer's

personalized message on form, using typewriter or pen. Applies theatrical makeup and dresses in costume, when necessary, and travels to destination, using vehicle, maps, and customer instructions. Locates recipient of message and performs routine, basing time frame of routine on recipient's reaction. May play musical instruments, such as kazoo or finger cymbals, during routine. May present gift items at conclusion of performance. GOE 07.07.02 PD L2456 EC I M2 L3 SVP 2 SOC 4745

238.367-034 SCHEDULER (museum) education department registrar; museum service scheduler.

Makes reservations and accepts payment for group tours, classes, field trips, and other educational activities offered by museum, zoo, or similar establishment: Provides information regarding tours for school, civic, or other groups, suggests tours on institution calendar, and contacts group leaders prior to scheduled dates to confirm reservations. Provides information regarding classes, workshops, field trips, and other educational programs designed for such special groups as school or college students, teachers, or handicapped persons. Registers groups and individuals for participation in programs, enters registration information in department records, and contacts participants prior to program dates to confirm registration and provide preparatory information. Prepares lists of groups scheduled for tours and persons registered for other activities for use of DIRECTOR, EDUCATION (museum) or other personnel. Collects and records receipts of fees for tours, classes, and other activities. Maintains records of participating groups, fees received, and other data related to educational programs for use in preparation of department reports. May take reservations and sell advance tickets to exhibits, concerts, and other events sponsored by institution, prepare periodic summaries of department activities for review by administrative personnel, or arrange for various support services to facilitate presentation of special activities. GOE 07.05.01 PD S456 EC I M3 L3 SVP 3 SOC 4649

39.367-030 DISPATCHER, STREET DEPARTMENT (gov. ser.)

Receives and records public requests for street maintenance services and lays work orders to maintenance crews, using telephone and two-way dio: Receives telephone requests from public for services, such as street pair, repair of traffic signals, erection of traffic barricades, and snow removal. Relays work orders, messages, and information to or from work ews, supervisors, and field inspectors. Answers routine questions from blic and directs requests for other information to designated personnel. aintains daily log of work orders, messages, or reports received and reyed. GOE 07.04.05 PD S5 EC I M1 L2 SVP 3 SOC 4751

1.367-038 INVESTIGATOR, DEALER ACCOUNTS (finan. inst.)

Visits dealers to verify purchases financed by bank against physical inntory of merchandise, using bank records: Reviews computer printouts ing customer names, addresses, and descriptions of merchandise finced through bank credit and chattel mortgage accounts to plan itiner of unannounced visits to dealer premises. Explains purpose of visit and ates merchandise in areas, such as showroom, storage room, or car lot. serves features of merchandise, such as size, color, model, and serial nber, to verify item against computer printout. Examines records and stions dealer to determine disposition of items missing from inventory to elicit information on dealer arrangement for payment to bank for rchandise sold. Records findings on printout and notifies supervisor of usual findings. GOE 07.05.02 PD L56 EC I M3 L4 SVP 2 SOC 4783

1.367-042 PROPERTY-ASSESSMENT MONITOR (gov. ser.)

Gathers property assessment data at owner premises, verifies data against previously recorded data, and records discrepancies: Visits property, observes premises, and confers with owner to collect and verify property assessment data, using data cards (property assessment records) as guides. Measures and records size of land boundaries and house, using tape measure. Records type of exterior coverings and physical condition of exterior and interior of house. Counts and records number of bathrooms, stoves, and fireplaces. Verifies findings against recorded data and notes discrepancies. Occasionally attends town meetings to answer taxpayer questions regarding use of information contained on data cards. GOE 07.05.02 PD L456 EC I M4 L4 SVP 3 SOC 4799

249.366-010 COUNTER CLERK (photofinish.)

Receives film for processing, loads film into equipment that automatically processes film for subsequent photo printing, and collects payment from customers of photofinishing establishment: Answers customer's questions regarding prices and services. Receives film to be processed from customer and enters identification data and printing instructions on service log and customer order envelope. Loads film into equipment that automatically processes film, and routes processed film for subsequent photo printing. Files processed film and photographic prints according to customer's name. Locates processed film and prints for customer. Totals charges, using cash register, collects payment, and returns prints and processed film to customer. Sells photo supplies, such as film, batteries, and flashcubes. GOE 07.03.01 PD L456 EC I M2 L2 SVP 2 SOC 4363

249.367-082 PARK AIDE (gov. ser.) park technician; ranger aide.

Assists PARK RANGER (gov. ser.) or PARK SUPERINTENDENT (gov. ser.) in operation of State or national park, monument, historic site, or recreational area through performance of any combination of clerical and other duties: Greets visitors at facility entrance and explains regulations. Assigns campground or recreational vehicle sites and collects fees at park offering camping facilities. Monitors campgrounds, cautions visitors against infractions of rules, and notifies PARK RANGER (gov. ser.) of problems. Replenishes firewood and assists GROUNDSKEEPER, PARKS AND GROUNDS (gov. ser.) to maintain camping and recreational areas in clean and orderly condition. Conducts tours of premises and answers visitors' questions when stationed at historic park, site, or monument. Operates projection and sound equipment and assists PARK RANGER (gov. ser.) in presentation of interpretive programs. Provides simple first-aid treatment to visitors injured on premises and assists persons with more serious injuries to obtain appropriate medical care. Participates in carrying out fire-fighting or conservation activities. Assists other workers in activities concerned with restoration of buildings and other facilities, or excavation and preservation of artifacts when stationed at historic or archeological site. GOE 07.04.03 PD L56 EC B M3 L4 SVP 3 SOC 4645

249.367-086 SATELLITE-INSTRUCTION FACILITATOR (education) satellite-project site monitor.

Monitors training programs transmitted by communication satellite from institution of higher learning to remote educational institution or facility: Registers students for satellite communication courses and sells and distributes textbooks and other classroom materials. Activates audiovisual receiver and monitors classroom viewing of live or recorded courses transmitted by communication satellite. Stimulates classroom discussion immediately after broadcast, following standardized format. Monitors live seminar transmittals from institute of higher learning, elicits responses from classroom students, and consolidates and transmits students' questions by teletype or telephone to seminar participants for direct response via satellite. Distributes homework assignments and test blanks to students. Collects completed assignments and tests and mails them to institute of higher learning. Maintains class attendance records. GOE 07.01.02 PD S456 EC I M2 L3 SVP 3 SOC 4795

249.587-018 DOCUMENT PREPARER, MICROFILMING (bus. ser.)

Prepares documents, such as brochures, pamphlets, and catalogs, for microfilming, using paper cutter, photocopying machine, rubber stamps, and other work devices: Cuts documents into individual pages of standard microfilming size and format when allowed by margin space, using paper cutter or razor knife. Reproduces document pages as necessary to improve clarity or to reduce one or more pages into single page of standard microfilming size, using photocopying machine. Stamps standard symbols on pages or inserts instruction cards between pages of material to notify MICROFILM-CAMERA OPERATOR (bus. ser.) of special handling, such as manual repositioning, during microfilming. Prepares cover sheet and document folder for material and index card for company files indicating information, such as firm name and address, product category, and index code, to identify material. Inserts material to be filmed in document folder and files folder for processing according to index code and filming priority schedule. GOE 07.05.03 PD S46 EC I M1 L2 SVP 2 SOC 4759

251.157-014 SALES REPRESENTATIVE, DATA-PROCESSING SERVICES (bus. ser.)

Contacts representatives of government, business, and industrial organizations to solicit business for data-processing establishment: Calls on prospective clients to explain types of services provided by establishment, such as inventory control, payroll processing, data conversion, sales analysis, and financial reporting. Analyzes data-processing requirements of prospective client and draws up prospectus of data-processing plan designed specifically to serve client's needs. Consults SYSTEMS ANALYST, ELECTRONIC DATA PROCESSING (profess. & kin.) and SYSTEMS ENGINEER, ELECTRONIC DATA PROCESSING (profess. & kin.) employed by data-processing establishment to secure information concerning methodology for solving unusual problems. Quotes prices for services outlined in prospectus. Revises or expands prospectus to meet client's needs. Writes order and schedules initiation of services. Periodically confers with clients and establishment personnel to verify satisfaction with service or to resolve complaints. GOE 08.01.02 PD L56 EC I M5 L5 SVP 7 SOC 4152

261.357-074 SALESPERSON, LEATHER-AND-SUEDE APPAREL-AND-ACCESSORIES (ret. tr.)

Sells suede and leather apparel and accessories: Advises customer on selection of apparel and on coordination of accessories, such as handbags, belts, and boots. Answers questions regarding cleaning requirements, color fastness, and durability of article. Packs or wraps customer purchase. Checks merchandise deliveries against packing slips. Tickets merchandise, using ticket gun. Inventories stock. Posts daily sales from sales slips onto inventory sheet. Performs other duties as described under SALESPERSON (ret. tr.; whole. tr.). GOE 08.02.02 PD L456 EC I M3 L3 SVP 5 SOC 4346

295.357-018 FURNITURE-RENTAL CONSULTANT (ret. tr.) decorator consultant; rental clerk, furniture.

Rents furniture and accessories to customers: Talks to customer to determine furniture preferences and requirements. Guides or accompanies customer through showroom, answers questions, and advises customer on compatibility of various styles and colors of furniture items. Compiles list of customer-selected items. Computes rental fee, explains rental terms, and presents list to customer for approval. Prepares order form and lease agreement, explains terms of lease to customer, and obtains customer signature. Obtains credit information from customer. Forwards forms to credit office for verification of customer credit status and approval of order. Collects initial payment from customer. Contacts customers to encourage followup transactions. May visit commercial customer site to solicit rental contracts, or review floor plans of new construction and suggest suitable furnishings. May sell furniture or accessories [SALESPERSON, FURNITURE (ret. tr.)]. GOE 09.04.02 PD L456 EC I M2 L2 SVP 2 SOC 4363

295.367-026 STORAGE-FACILITY RENTAL CLERK (bus. ser.; ret. tr.)
Leases storage space to customers of rental storage facility: Informs customers of space availability, rental regulations, and rates. Assists customers in selection of storage unit size according to articles or material to be stored. Records terms of rental on rental agreement form and assists customer in completing form. Photographs completed form and customer to establish identification record, using security camera. Computes rental fee and collects payment. Maintains rental status record and waiting list for storage units. Notifies customers when rental term is about to expire or rent is overdue. Inspects storage area periodically to insure storage units are locked. Observes individuals entering storage area to prevent access to or tampering with storage units by unauthorized persons. Loads film into security and surveillance cameras, records dates of film changes, and monitors camera operations to insure performance as required. Cleans facility and maintains premises in orderly condition. GOE 09.04.02 PD L46 EC I M3 L3 SVP 2 SOC 4363

299.677-014 SALES ATTENDANT, BUILDING MATERIALS (ret. tr.) yard salesperson.
Assists customers and stocks merchandise in building materials and supplies department of self-service general store: Answers questions and advises customer in selection of building materials and supplies. Cuts lumber, screening, glass, and related materials to size requested by customer, using powersaws, holding fixtures, and various hand cutting tools. Assists customer in loading purchased materials into customer's vehicle. Moves materials and supplies from receiving area to display area, using forklift or handtruck. Marks prices on merchandise or price stickers, according to pricing guides, using marking devices. Straightens materials on display to maintain safe and orderly conditions in sales areas. Covers exposed materials when required to prevent weather damage. Counts materials and records totals on inventory sheets. GOE 09.04.02 PD H3456 EC I M2 L2 SVP 3 SOC 4362

309.367-010 HOUSE SITTER (dom. ser.)
Occupies and oversees house to maintain order and security of property and conduct necessary business transactions during temporary absence of owner, renter, or other occupant: Monitors entrances to property and secures locks and other devices to prevent access of unauthorized persons. Answers telephone and doorbell, takes messages, and forwards information to employer as requested. Forwards or files mail. Pays current bills from designated funds and makes deposits to accounts as required. Cleans, vacuums, and dusts house, using vacuum cleaner and other housecleaning aids. Feeds and waters pets and takes ill pets to veterinarian for treatment. Inspects utilities, such as plumbing and air conditioning, to detect problems requiring services of repairer and contacts repair establishment to arrange for necessary repairs. May care for swimming pool or grounds or perform other related duties. GOE 09.05.06 PD L46 EC I M2 L2 SVP 2 SOC 509

311.472-010 FAST-FOODS WORKER (hotel & rest.) cashier, fast foods restaurant.
Serves customer of fast food restaurant: Requests customer order and depresses keys of multi-counting machine to simultaneously record order and compute bill [FOOD TABULATOR, AUTOMATED SYSTEMS (hotel & rest.)]. Selects requested food items from serving or storage areas and assembles items on serving tray or in takeout bag. Notifies kitchen personnel of shortages or special orders. Serves cold drinks, using drink-dispensing machine, or frozen milk drinks or deserts, using milkshake or frozen custard machine. Makes and serves hot beverages, using automatic water heater or coffeemaker. Presses lids onto beverages and places beverages on serving tray or in takeout container. Receives payment. May cook or apportion french-fries or perform other minor duties to prepare food, serve customers, or maintain orderly eating or serving areas. GOE 09.04.01 PD L456 EC I M2 L2 SVP 2 SOC 5216

319.464-014 VENDING-MACHINE ATTENDANT (hotel & rest.)
Stocks machines and assists customers in facility where food is dispensed from coin-operated machines: Places food or drink items on shelves of vending machines and changes shelf labels as required to indicate selections. Makes change for customers and answers questions regarding selections. Adjusts temperature gages to maintain food items at specified temperatures. Performs minor repairs or adjustments on machines to correct jams or similar malfunctions, using handtools. Prepares requisitions for food and drink supplies. Cleans interior and exterior of machines, using damp cloth. Maintains eating area in orderly condition. May sell precooked foods from hot table. May remove money from vending machines and keep records of receipts. GOE 09.04.01 PD L56 EC I M2 L2 SVP 2 SOC 5219

331.674-014 FINGERNAIL FORMER (per. ser.)
Forms artificial fingernails on customer's fingers: Roughens surfaces of fingernails, using abrasive wheel. Attaches paper forms to tips of customer's fingers to support and shape artificial nails. Brushes coats of powder and solvent onto nails and paper forms with handbrush to extend nails to desired length. Removes paper forms and shapes and smooths edges of nails, using rotary abrasive wheel. Brushes additional powder and solvent onto new growth between cuticles and nails to maintain nail appearance. May soften, trim, or cut cuticles, using oil, water, knife, or scissors, to prepare customer's nails for application of artificial nails. GOE 09.05.01 PD S46 EC I M1 L2 SVP 3 SOC 5253

349.477-010 JINRIKISHA DRIVER (amuse. & rec.) rickshaw driver.
Conveys passengers to destinations, using three-wheeled vehicle: Pumps pedals and turns handlebars to propel and steer vehicle along roadway to attract and convey passengers for novelty rides. Assists passengers into carriage of vehicle and asks their destination. Records time or odometer reading at start of trip. Conveys passengers to specified destination. Computes fare according to miles traveled or time expended and collects payment. GOE 01.07.03 PD M456 EC O M2 L2 SVP 1 SOC 5269

349.677-018 CHILDREN'S ATTENDANT (amuse. & rec.)
Monitors behavior of unaccompanied children in children's section of theater to maintain order: Escorts children who are unaccompanied by adult between theater entrance and children's section when children enter or leave theater. Maintains order among children and searches for lost articles. Notes when each child enters section and reminds child to go home after witnessing complete performance. GOE 09.05.08 PD L56 EC I M1 L1 SVP 2 SOC 5256

355.374-014 MEDICATION AIDE (medical ser.) pharmacy technician.
Administers prescribed medications to patients and maintains related medical records under supervision of NURSE, GENERAL DUTY (medi[illegible] cal ser.), PHARMACIST, HOSPITAL (profess. & kin.), or similar pe[illegible] sonnel: Receives supply of ordered medications and apportions, mixes, [illegible] assembles drugs for administration to patients. Verifies identity of patie[illegible] receiving medication and records name of drug, dosage, and time of a[illegible] ministration on specified forms or records. Presents medication to patie[illegible] and observes ingestion or other application, or administers medicati[illegible] using specified procedures. Takes vital signs or observes patient to det[illegible] response to specified types of medications and prepares report or notif[illegible] designated personnel of unexpected reactions. Documents reasons, such [illegible] discharge of patient, prescribed drugs are not administered. May rec[illegible] and restock medication inventories. May give direct patient care such [illegible] bathing, dressing, and feeding patients, and assisting in examinations a[illegible] treatments [NURSE AIDE (medical ser.)]. GOE 10.03.02 PD L456 E[illegible] M3 L3 SVP 4 SOC 5233

355.377-018 MENTAL-RETARDATION AIDE (medical ser.) resi[illegible] care aide.
Assists in providing self-care training and therapeutic treatments to r[illegible] dents of mental retardation center: Demonstrates activities such as bath[illegible] and dressing to train residents in daily self-care practices. Converses [illegible] residents to reinforce positive behaviors and to promote social interact[illegible] Serves meals and eats with residents to act as role model. Accompa[illegible] residents on shopping trips and instructs and counsels residents in [illegible] chase of personal items. Aids staff in administering therapeutic activ[illegible] such as physical exercises, occupational arts and crafts, and recreati[illegible] games, to residents. Restrains disruptive residents to prevent injury [illegible] themselves and others. Observes and documents residents' behaviors, su[illegible] as speech production, feeding patterns, and toilet training, to facilitate a[illegible] sessment and development of treatment goals. Attends to routine health[illegible] care needs of residents under supervision of medical personnel. May giv[illegible] medications as prescribed by PHYSICIAN (medical ser.). May train par[illegible] ents or guardians in care of deinstitutionalized residents. GOE 10.03.02 PD M456 EC I M3 L3 SVP 6 SOC 5233

355.674-022 RESPIRATORY-THERAPY AIDE (medical ser.)
Assists personnel in Respiratory Therapy Department of hospital, performing any or all of following tasks: Cleans, disinfects, and sterilizes equipment and supplies used in administration of respiratory therapy, using sponges, brushes, and cleaning solutions, and placing items in sterilization chamber for designated time period to insure absence of contamination. Examines equipment to detect indications of disrepair, such as worn tubes or loose connections, and notifies supervisory staff when such indications are noted. Actuates equipment and observes gages measuring pressure, rate of flow, and continuity to test equipment, and notifies supervisor when malfunctions are observed. Assists supervisory personnel in maintenance of inventory records. Delivers oxygen tanks and other equipment and supplies to specified hospital locations. Answers phone and takes and relays messages regarding department operations. Assists in administration of gas or aerosol therapy to patients. GOE 10.03.02 PD M456 EC I M3 L3 SVP 4 SOC 5233

359.363-010 HEALTH-EQUIPMENT SERVICER (medical ser.)
Delivers, installs, demonstrates, and maintains rental medical equipment, such as respirator, oxygen equipment, hospital beds, and wheel chairs, for use in private residences: Loads medical equipment on truck and delivers equipment to renter's or patient's residence. Unloads, installs, and sets up equipment, using handtools. Inspects and maintains rental oxygen equipment, performing such tasks as inspecting hoses and water traps to detect leaks and condensation; observing gages of oxygen analyzer, pressure

gages, and other monitoring equipment to determine pressure and oxygen content of air output of compressors and concentrators; and changing filters. Maintains record on oxygen equipment by hours of usage to determine need for maintenance. GOE 10.03.02 PD H456 EC I6 M2 L3 SVP 5 SOC 5233

359.367-014 WEIGHT-REDUCTION SPECIALIST (per. ser.) nutrition educator.

Assist clients in devising and carrying out weight-loss plan, using established dietary programs and positive reinforcement procedures: Interviews client to obtain information on weight development history, eating habits, medical restrictions, and nutritional objectives. Weighs and measures client, using measuring instruments, and enters data on client record. Discusses eating habits with client to identify dispensable food items and to encourage increased consumption of high nutrition, low calorie food items, or selects established diet program which matches client goals and restrictions. Explains program and procedures which should be followed to lose desired amount of weight, and answers client questions. Reviews client food diary at regular intervals to identify eating habits which do not coincide with established or agreed upon dietary program, and reviews weight loss statistics to determine progress. Counsels client to promote established goals and to reinforce positive results. May photograph client during therapy to provide visual record of progress. May conduct aversion therapy, utilizing electric shock, rancid odors, and other physical or visual stimulus to promote negative association with food designated for elimination from diet. May conduct positive conditioning therapy sessions, utilizing physical and visual stimulus to promote positive association with foods designated for increase in diet. May give client weight-loss aids, such as calorie counters, or sell nutritional products to be used in conjunction with diet program. GOE 09.05.01 PD 456 EC I M2 L3 SVP 3 SOC 5269

359.677-030 RESEARCH SUBJECT (any ind.) subject, scientific research.

Submits to scientifically conducted research relating to such fields as medicine, psychology, or consumer-product testing: Participates in activities such as performing physical tasks, taking psychological tests, or using experimental products, following instructions of researcher. Replies verbally or records responses to questionnaire to provide researcher with data or evaluation. GOE 09.05.06 PD L5 EC I M2 L3 SVP 1 SOC 5269

377.267-010 DEPUTY UNITED STATES MARSHALL (gov. ser.)

Enforces law and order under jurisdiction of Federal courts: Receives prisoners into Federal custody. Escorts prisoners to and from jails and courts and guards prisoners during hospitalization. Provides protection to court personnel, jurors, and witnesses or their families. Serves civil and criminal writs. Reviews records, gathers information, and traces and arrests individuals named in criminal warrants. Assists Federal agencies in matters such as investigations, raids, and arrests as directed. Seizes property pursuant to court orders. GOE 04.01.02 PD M456 EC B6 M2 L3 SVP SOC 5134

[illegible]9.263-014 PUBLIC-SAFETY OFFICER (gov. ser.)

Patrols assigned beat and responds to emergency calls to protect persons or property from crimes, fires, or other hazards: Patrols assigned area on foot or horseback or using vehicle to regulate traffic, control crowds, prevent crime, or arrest violators. Responds to crimes in progress, initiating actions such as aid to victims and interrogation of suspects. Attends public gatherings to maintain order. Responds to fire alarms or other emergency calls. Forces openings in buildings for ventilation of fire or for entry, using ax or crowbar. Controls and extinguishes fires, using water and chemicals. Administers first aid and artificial respiration to injured persons. Participates in drills and emergency precautionary demonstrations. May inspect establishments for compliance with local regulations. May drive and operate firefighting and other emergency equipment. GOE 04.01.02 PD V2456 EC B4567 M3 L3 SVP 7 SOC 5149

379.364-014 BEACH LIFEGUARD (amuse. & rec.)

Patrols public beach area to monitor activities of swimmers and prevent illegal conduct: Observes activities in assigned area on foot, in vehicle, or from tower or headquarters building with binoculars to detect hazardous conditions, such as swimmers in distress, disturbances, or safety infractions. Cautions people against use of unsafe beach areas or illegal conduct, such as drinking or fighting, using megaphone. Rescues distressed persons from ocean or adjacent cliffs, using rescue techniques and equipment. Examines injured individuals, administers first aid, and monitors vital signs, utilizing training, antiseptics, bandages, and instruments, such as stethoscope and sphygmomanometer. Administers artificial respiration, utilizing cardiopulmonary or mouth-to-mouth methods or oxygen to revive persons. Compiles emergency and medical treatment report forms and maintains daily information on weather and beach conditions. Occasionally operates switchboard or two-way radio system to maintain contact and coordinate activities between emergency rescue units. GOE 04.02.03 PD V456 EC O M2 L2 SVP 4 SOC 5149

379.367-010 SURVEILLANCE-SYSTEM MONITOR (gov. ser.)

Monitors premises of public transportation terminals to detect crimes or disturbances, using closed circuit television monitors, and notifies authorities by telephone of need for corrective action: Observes television screens that transmit in sequence views of transportation facility sites. Pushes hold button to maintain surveillance of location where incident is developing, and telephones police or other designated agency to notify authorities of location of disruptive activity. Adjusts monitor controls when required to improve reception, and notifies repair service of equipment malfunctions. GOE 04.02.03 PD S56 EC I M1 L3 SVP 2 SOC 5149

383.684-010 EXTERMINATOR HELPER (any ind.) pest control worker helper.

Assists EXTERMINATOR (any ind.) in destroying and controlling field rodents, noxious weeds, or other pests in or around buildings, performing any combination of following tasks: Sets traps and places poisonous bait in rodent infested areas. Fumigates burrows, using toxic gas, or kills rodents, using firearms. Secures tarpaulins over building to be fumigated, using ladder. Applies insecticides to buildings and grounds, using spray pumps and other equipment. Digs up, sprays with herbicides, or burns noxious weeds. Identifies and reports evidence of pest infestation. May drive service vehicles or equipment. Performs other duties as described under HELPER (any ind.).. GOE 05.10.09 PD M234 EC B37 M2 L2 SVP 4 SOC 5246

406.684-018 GARDEN WORKER (agric.; museum) gardener-florist.

Cultivates and cares for ornamental plants and installs floral displays in indoor or outdoor settings through performance of any combination of following duties as directed by supervisory personnel: Conditions and prepares soils and plants seeds, seedlings, or bulbs in greenhouse or outdoor growing area, using spades, trowels, sprayers, sprinklers, cultivators, and other gardening handtools and equipment. Fertilizes, waters, weeds, transplants, or thins plants in growing areas. Mixes and applies pesticides to maintain health of plants and prepare plants for installation in greenhouse or outdoor display areas. Lays sod or artificial grass and builds framework for indoor floral displays, or prepares outdoor display beds according to work plan. Transplants plants from growing area to display beds, or places potted plants in beds according to work plans. Attends display beds to maintain health of plants and beauty of display. Maintains and repairs gardening handtools and equipment and structures, such as greenhouses and hot beds, using maintenance and carpentry tools. May mow lawns, prune trees, and perform other duties to maintain grounds. GOE 03.04.04 PD M346 EC B M2 L3 SVP 4 SOC 5622

408.364-010 PLANT-CARE WORKER (agric.) interior horticulturist; plant tender.

Cares for ornamental plants on various customer premises, applying knowledge of horticultural requirements, and using items such as insecticides, fertilizers, and gardening tools: Reads work orders and supply requisitions to determine job requirements, and confers with supervisor to clarify work procedures. Loads plants and supplies onto truck in order of scheduled stops, using handtruck. Drives truck to premises and carries needed supplies to work area. Examines plants and soil to determine moisture level, using water sensor gage, and waters plants according to requirements of species, using hose and watering can. Sponges plant leaves to apply moisture and remove dust. Observes plants under magnifying glass to detect insects and disease, and consults plant care books or confers with supervisor to identify problems and determine treatments. Selects and applies specified chemical solutions to feed plants, kill insects, and treat diseases, using hose or mist-sprayer. Transplants rootbound plants into larger containers. Pinches and prunes stems and leaves to remove dead and diseased leaves, to shape plants, and to induce growth, using shears. Removes diseased and dying plants from premises and replaces them with healthy plants. Informs customer of plant care needs. Enters record of actions taken at each stop in route book and prepares requisitions for materials needed on subsequent visit. Returns diseased, dying, and unused plants and supplies to employer premises. GOE 03.04.05 PD M456 EC I67 M2 L3 SVP 3 SOC 5619

410.161-022 HOG-CONFINEMENT-SYSTEM MANAGER (agric.)

Breeds and raises swine in confinement buildings for purpose of selling pork to meatpacking establishments: Selects and breeds swine according to knowledge of animals, genealogy, characteristics, and offspring desired. Regulates breeding of sow herd to produce maximum number of litters. Attends sows during farrowing and helps baby pigs to survive birth and infancy. Castrates and docks pigs. Notches ears to identify animals. Determines weaning dates for pigs based on factors such as condition of sows, cost of feed, and available space in nursery. Vaccinates swine for disease and administers antibiotics and iron supplements, using syringes and hypodermic needles. Formulates rations for swine according to nutritional needs of animals and cost and availability of feeds. Grinds and mixes feed and adds supplements to satisfy dietary requirements. Stores and periodically examines feeds to insure maintenance of appropriate temperatures and moisture levels. Operates water foggers, air conditioners, fans, and heaters to maintain optimal temperature in swine confinement buildings. Flushes hog wastes into holding pit. Repairs and maintains machinery, plumbing, physical structures, and electrical wiring and fixtures in swine farrowing, nursery, and finishing buildings. May hire and supervise worker to assist in swine production activities. GOE 03.01.01 PD M456 EC I M4 L4 SVP 7 SOC 5514

er-
or
ent
d-
ent
on,
ect
ies
as
ord
as
nd
C I

ent

esi-
ing
with
ion.
nies
pur-
ities,
onal
to
ch
s-
n-
e

gages, and other monitoring equipment to determine pressure and oxygen content of air output of compressors and concentrators; and changing filters. Maintains record on oxygen equipment by hours of usage to determine need for maintenance. GOE 10.03.02 PD H456 EC I6 M2 L3 SVP 5 SOC 5233

359.367-014 WEIGHT-REDUCTION SPECIALIST (per. ser.) nutrition educator.

Assist clients in devising and carrying out weight-loss plan, using established dietary programs and positive reinforcement procedures: Interviews client to obtain information on weight development history, eating habits, medical restrictions, and nutritional objectives. Weighs and measures client, using measuring instruments, and enters data on client record. Discusses eating habits with client to identify dispensable food items and to encourage increased consumption of high nutrition, low calorie food items, or selects established diet program which matches client goals and restrictions. Explains program and procedures which should be followed to lose desired amount of weight, and answers client questions. Reviews client food diary at regular intervals to identify eating habits which do not coincide with established or agreed upon dietary program, and reviews weight loss statistics to determine progress. Counsels client to promote established goals and to reinforce positive results. May photograph client during therapy to provide visual record of progress. May conduct aversion therapy, utilizing electric shock, rancid odors, and other physical or visual stimulus to promote negative association with food designated for elimination from diet. May conduct positive conditioning therapy sessions, utilizing physical and visual stimulus to promote positive association with foods designated for increase in diet. May give client weight-loss aids, such as calorie counters, or sell nutritional products to be used in conjunction with diet program. GOE 09.05.01 PD 456 EC I M2 L3 SVP 3 SOC 05269

359.677-030 RESEARCH SUBJECT (any ind.) subject, scientific research.

Submits to scientifically conducted research relating to such fields as medicine, psychology, or consumer-product testing: Participates in activities such as performing physical tasks, taking psychological tests, or using experimental products, following instructions of researcher. Replies verbally or records responses to questionnaire to provide researcher with data for evaluation. GOE 09.05.06 PD L5 EC I M2 L3 SVP 1 SOC 5269

377.267-010 DEPUTY UNITED STATES MARSHALL (gov. ser.)

Enforces law and order under jurisdiction of Federal courts: Receives prisoners into Federal custody. Escorts prisoners to and from jails and courts and guards prisoners during hospitalization. Provides protection to court personnel, jurors, and witnesses or their families. Serves civil and criminal writs. Reviews records, gathers information, and traces and arrests individuals named in criminal warrants. Assists Federal agencies in matters such as investigations, raids, and arrests as directed. Seizes property pursuant to court orders. GOE 04.01.02 PD M456 EC B6 M2 L3 SVP SOC 5134

379.263-014 PUBLIC-SAFETY OFFICER (gov. ser.)

Patrols assigned beat and responds to emergency calls to protect persons or property from crimes, fires, or other hazards: Patrols assigned area on foot or horseback or using vehicle to regulate traffic, control crowds, prevent crime, or arrest violators. Responds to crimes in progress, initiating actions such as aid to victims and interrogation of suspects. Attends public gatherings to maintain order. Responds to fire alarms or other emergency calls. Forces openings in buildings for ventilation of fire or for entry, using ax or crowbar. Controls and extinguishes fires, using water and chemicals. Administers first aid and artificial respiration to injured persons. Participates in drills and emergency precautionary demonstrations. May inspect establishments for compliance with local regulations. May drive and operate firefighting and other emergency equipment. GOE 04.01.02 PD V2456 EC B4567 M3 L3 SVP 7 SOC 5149

379.364-014 BEACH LIFEGUARD (amuse. & rec.)

Patrols public beach area to monitor activities of swimmers and prevent illegal conduct: Observes activities in assigned area on foot, in vehicle, or from tower or headquarters building with binoculars to detect hazardous conditions, such as swimmers in distress, disturbances, or safety infractions. Cautions people against use of unsafe beach areas or illegal conduct, such as drinking or fighting, using megaphone. Rescues distressed persons from ocean or adjacent cliffs, using rescue techniques and equipment. Examines injured individuals, administers first aid, and monitors vital signs, utilizing training, antiseptics, bandages, and instruments, such as stethoscope and sphygmomanometer. Administers artificial respiration, utilizing cardiopulmonary or mouth-to-mouth methods or oxygen to revive persons. Compiles emergency and medical treatment report forms and maintains daily information on weather and beach conditions. Occasionally operates switchboard or two-way radio system to maintain contact and coordinate activities between emergency rescue units. GOE 04.02.03 PD V456 EC O M2 L2 SVP 4 SOC 5149

379.367-010 SURVEILLANCE-SYSTEM MONITOR (gov. ser.)

Monitors premises of public transportation terminals to detect crimes or disturbances, using closed circuit television monitors, and notifies authorities by telephone of need for corrective action: Observes television screens that transmit in sequence views of transportation facility sites. Pushes hold button to maintain surveillance of location where incident is developing, and telephones police or other designated agency to notify authorities of location of disruptive activity. Adjusts monitor controls when required to improve reception, and notifies repair service of equipment malfunctions. GOE 04.02.03 PD S56 EC I M1 L3 SVP 2 SOC 5149

383.684-010 EXTERMINATOR HELPER (any ind.) pest control worker helper.

Assists EXTERMINATOR (any ind.) in destroying and controlling field rodents, noxious weeds, or other pests in or around buildings, performing any combination of following tasks: Sets traps and places poisonous bait in rodent infested areas. Fumigates burrows, using toxic gas, or kills rodents, using firearms. Secures tarpaulins over building to be fumigated, using ladder. Applies insecticides to buildings and grounds, using spray pumps and other equipment. Digs up, sprays with herbicides, or burns noxious weeds. Identifies and reports evidence of pest infestation. May drive service vehicles or equipment. Performs other duties as described under HELPER (any ind.).. GOE 05.10.09 PD M234 EC B37 M2 L2 SVP 4 SOC 5246

406.684-018 GARDEN WORKER (agric.; museum) gardener-florist.

Cultivates and cares for ornamental plants and installs floral displays in indoor or outdoor settings through performance of any combination of following duties as directed by supervisory personnel: Conditions and prepares soils and plants seeds, seedlings, or bulbs in greenhouse or outdoor growing area, using spades, trowels, sprayers, sprinklers, cultivators, and other gardening handtools and equipment. Fertilizes, waters, weeds, transplants, or thins plants in growing areas. Mixes and applies pesticides to maintain health of plants and prepare plants for installation in greenhouse or outdoor display areas. Lays sod or artificial grass and builds framework for indoor floral displays, or prepares outdoor display beds according to work plan. Transplants plants from growing area to display beds, or places potted plants in beds according to work plans. Attends display beds to maintain health of plants and beauty of display. Maintains and repairs gardening handtools and equipment and structures, such as greenhouses and hot beds, using maintenance and carpentry tools. May mow lawns, prune trees, and perform other duties to maintain grounds. GOE 03.04.04 PD M346 EC B M2 L3 SVP 4 SOC 5622

408.364-010 PLANT-CARE WORKER (agric.) interior horticulturist; plant tender.

Cares for ornamental plants on various customer premises, applying knowledge of horticultural requirements, and using items such as insecticides, fertilizers, and gardening tools: Reads work orders and supply requisitions to determine job requirements, and confers with supervisor to clarify work procedures. Loads plants and supplies onto truck in order of scheduled stops, using handtruck. Drives truck to premises and carries needed supplies to work area. Examines plants and soil to determine moisture level, using water sensor gage, and waters plants according to requirements of species, using hose and watering can. Sponges plant leaves to apply moisture and remove dust. Observes plants under magnifying glass to detect insects and disease, and consults plant care books or confers with supervisor to identify problems and determine treatments. Selects and applies specified chemical solutions to feed plants, kill insects, and treat diseases, using hose or mist-sprayer. Transplants rootbound plants into larger containers. Pinches and prunes stems and leaves to remove dead and diseased leaves, to shape plants, and to induce growth, using shears. Removes diseased and dying plants from premises and replaces them with healthy plants. Informs customer of plant care needs. Enters record of actions taken at each stop in route book and prepares requisitions for materials needed on subsequent visit. Returns diseased, dying, and unused plants and supplies to employer premises. GOE 03.04.05 PD M456 EC I67 M2 L3 SVP 3 SOC 5619

410.161-022 HOG-CONFINEMENT-SYSTEM MANAGER (agric.)

Breeds and raises swine in confinement buildings for purpose of selling pork to meatpacking establishments: Selects and breeds swine according to knowledge of animals, genealogy, characteristics, and offspring desired. Regulates breeding of sow herd to produce maximum number of litters. Attends sows during farrowing and helps baby pigs to survive birth and infancy. Castrates and docks pigs. Notches ears to identify animals. Determines weaning dates for pigs based on factors such as condition of sows, cost of feed, and available space in nursery. Vaccinates swine for disease and administers antibiotics and iron supplements, using syringes and hypodermic needles. Formulates rations for swine according to nutritional needs of animals and cost and availability of feeds. Grinds and mixes feed and adds supplements to satisfy dietary requirements. Stores and periodically examines feeds to insure maintenance of appropriate temperatures and moisture levels. Operates water foggers, air conditioners, fans, and heaters to maintain optimal temperature in swine confinement buildings. Flushes hog wastes into holding pit. Repairs and maintains machinery, plumbing, physical structures, and electrical wiring and fixtures in swine farrowing, nursery, and finishing buildings. May hire and supervise worker to assist in swine production activities. GOE 03.01.01 PD M456 EC I M4 L4 SVP 7 SOC 5514

or
nt
ld-
ent
on,
ect
ies
as
ord
as
nd
C I

ent

esi-
king
with
ion.
anies
pur-
ities,
onal
to
ch
as-
h-
e

find
Look before, or you'll / youself behind.
–*Poor Richard's Almanac*

The caret itself has to be written in by hand. Write the caret as an inverted *v*. Since it is such a conspicuous mark, the caret should be made small and in light, not heavy, lines.

s
We visited the capitol in Boston, Ma^sachusetts.

upon
All experience is an arch, to build^.–*Henry Brooks Adams*

DITTO MARKS

Ditto marks ('') are pairs of inverted commas, used where considerable repetition occurs, to take the place of words and groups of words. Ditto itself is derived from the Latin *dicere* (to say) and means "the aforementioned thing." The marks are restricted chiefly to lists and tabulations.

The ditto is another mark that does not appear on standard typewriter keyboards. Quotation marks are the acceptable substitute.

Grammar

Few words can be classified absolutely as one or another of the eight parts of speech traditionally distinguished in our language. Most of us would automatically say that *swim* is a verb; yet in the sentence *He went for a swim,* it is clearly a noun. An even more confusing example is *up:*

> The proposal was on the *up* and up. (noun)
>
> The auctioneer encouraged us to *up* our bid. (verb)
>
> His time was *up*. (adjective, modifying *time*)
>
> We flew *up* and over the clouds. (adverb, modifying *flew*)
>
> He went *up* the stairs. (preposition)

It is clear that we may assign a word to a grammatical class only by considering its use, or *function,* in its context. Grammar is a way of talking about the relationship of words.

NOUNS

A *noun* is a name. It indicates a person, place, or thing.

> The *fireman* climbed to the *top* of the *ladder*.

Not all "things" are concrete objects. A noun may also name a quality, an action, or a concept.

> The *brutality* of the *murder* underlined its *injustice*.

Nouns may be further classified according to five types:

1. A *common* noun names a class or group of persons, places, or things. A title is ordinarily treated as a common noun.

   My *father* is a *history professor*.

   But if it used as a specific name or as part of one it is considered a proper noun.

   I introduced *Father* to *Professor White* of the *Department of History*.

2. A *concrete* noun names a particular or specific member of a class or group that can be seen, heard, touched, smelled, or tasted–one that can be perceived by the senses.

   Naomi Swift, the famous contralto, sang a fourth *aria*. In her *hair* the *rose* glowed as red as *wine*.

3. An *abstract* noun names a quality or concept.

   Continued *apathy* will compromise the *freedom* we enjoy under *democracy*.

4. A *proper* noun names a specific person, place, or thing; it is capitalized.

   After *President Jefferson* returned from *Monticello* he addressed *Congress*.

5. A *collective* noun is a proper or common noun which names a group of persons or things.

   group crowd pack

Note: Nouns can belong to more than one type.

Concrete, common, and collective: He joined a *brotherhood* to meet friends.

Concrete, proper, and collective: He was a member of the *Brotherhood* of RR Engineers.

Abstract, common, and collective: He believed in the *brotherhood* of man.

A noun may be a single word:

The *attorney* is Adams;

or a compound word:

Richard Adams became *attorney general;*

or a phrase:

Hunting the elusive fox was strenuous sport;

or a clause:

That he could have been lying was out of the question.

Gender

The *gender* of a noun presents no problem in English. *Masculine nouns* refer to males (boy, father), *feminine* to females (woman, girl). All others are *neuter.* A number of nouns have masculine and feminine forms clearly marked by differences of pronunciation or of spelling (aviator, aviatrix; alumnus, alumna; fiancé, fiancée). Except in the case of the last example, the tendency seems to be toward using masculine forms in place of the feminine (aviator, etc.).

Number

The *number* of a noun is a way of indicating how many persons, places, and things it refers to. A noun is *singular* if it names one, and *plural* if it names two or more.

Case

The *case* of a noun is determined by what it does in a sentence. If it is *doing* something, it is in the nominative (or subjective) case, as in "The *teacher* graded my paper." If something is *being done to it,* the noun is usually in the objective (or accusative) case, as in "The teacher graded my *paper.*" If the noun is said to own something, it is in the possessive (or genitive) case, as in "the *dog's* tail."

Since the forms of nominative and objective nouns are identical, there is no problem in English of writing them correctly. Even the genitive case causes little difficulty in its grammatical relationships.

Use of Nouns

As *subject* (nominative case): The subject of a sentence is the person, place, or thing about which the statement is made or question asked.

The *girl* enjoyed dancing.

Didn't the *boy* know how to dance?

As *object* (objective, or accusative, case): The *direct object* of a sentence is the person, place, or thing directly affected by the action of a transitive verb.

The car crossed the *bridge.*

The college announced *that tuition would go up again.* (clause as object)

The *indirect object* is indirectly affected by the action of a transitive verb. It precedes the direct object, unless it is a prepositional phrase.

He sent *his mother* a birthday present.

He sent a birthday present *to his mother.*

As *subjective complement* (nominative case), also called the *predicate nominative.* The complement is a noun related directly to the subject, not the verb.

He is the heaviest *player* on the team.

Jenny seemed the last *person* you'd expect to get into trouble.

A linking verb (see page 21) connects subject and subjective complement.

As *objective complement* (objective case): Completes the sense of a transitive verb, related directly to the direct object, not the verb.

She called her best friend a green-eyed *monster.*

Linus considers Beethoven the only *composer.*

As *appositive:* An appositive is a noun that usually follows another noun with the same meaning. It takes the same case as the noun with which it is in apposition.

Our next-door neighbor, a *veteran* of World War II, refuses to join the American Legion. (*Veteran* is in apposition with *neighbor;* both are nominative.)

He finally joined the VFW, a livelier *organization.* (*Organization* is in apposition with *VFW,* both are objective.)

In *direct address:*

Darling, I agree.

Be good, my *dear,* and let who will be clever.

PRONOUNS

A *pronoun* refers to a person, place, or thing without naming it.

She bit *his* arm. Wash *it* with *this.*

Everyone who wants to come is welcome.

There are *four,* you say?

The noun (or pronoun) for which a pronoun substitutes is called its *antecedent.* Thus, in the first example above, *arm* is the antecedent of *it.* The antecedents of *she, his,* and *this* are implied; both speaker and hearer (or writer and reader) know who *she* and *he* are, and *this* refers to an object physically present. The antecedent of *who* in the second example, is *Everyone.* Pronouns may be classified according to seven types:

1. *Personal* pronouns substitute for the name of the person speaking, the person spoken to, or the person or object spoken of. Personal pronouns can be troublesome because, unlike nouns (which rarely change their forms except in the possessive case), most pronouns take a different form for each of the three cases: nominative, objective, and possessive.

	NOMINATIVE	OBJECTIVE	POSSESSIVE
1ST PERSON			
singular	I	me	my, mine
plural	we	us	our, ours
2ND PERSON			
singular	you	you	your, yours
plural	you	you	your, yours
3RD PERSON			
singular			
masculine	he	him	his
feminine	she	her	her, hers
neuter	it	it	its, of it
either gender	one	one	one's
plural	they	them	their, theirs

2. *Relative* pronouns link a subordinate clause with an independent one, referring to a noun or pronoun in the independent clause.

We smiled at the clerk *who* had been so pleasant.

The batter hit a line drive *which* sent two men home.

There is no difficulty of declension with most relative pronouns; only *who* and *whom* (and their related compound forms) present problems. The distinction between these has virtually disappeared in speech, but is still maintained in writing.

NOMINATIVE	OBJECTIVE	POSSESSIVE
who	whom	whose
whoever	whomever	whosever
which	which	of which
that	that	whose
what	what	——
as	as	——

Who and its related forms refer to people, *which* to other living creatures and to things; *that* may be used for either persons or things. *What* is the equivalent of *that which* when used as a relative pronoun. *As* appears in a dependent clause, when *such* or *the same* has appeared in the independent clause.

Ours is the same *as* yours.

Note: Except for the word *one's,* the possessive case of both personal and relative pronouns has no apostrophe.

3. *Interrogative* pronouns introduce questions. They include *who* (objective, *whom;* possessive, *whose*), *which,* and *what.*

Who saw him leave?
Whom do you mean?
Which are the best roads from here?
What is the direction you want to take?

Who (and its related forms) inquires about a person, *which* about a person or thing in a group, *what* about anything.

Note: Remember that the objective form *(whom):* is the object of a verb or a preposition.

Whom did Petrarch love?
Whom do you get them from?

Whose, which, and *what* also function as interrogative adjectives, when instead of substituting for a noun they modify it.

Which roads are best?
What direction are you taking?

4. *Demonstrative* pronouns point out specific persons or things. Principal ones are *this* (plural, *these*) and *that* (plural, *those*).

This is the least flattering of all the photos.
Have you seen *those?*

Note: Demonstrative pronouns may also function as demonstrative adjectives.

This photo is more flattering than *those others.*

5. *Indefinite* pronouns point out persons or things, but less specifically than demonstrative pronouns. A great number in this classification include the following:

SINGULAR INDEFINITE PRONOUNS

another	everything
anyone	somebody
each	such
either	

PLURAL INDEFINITE PRONOUNS

both	many
few	several

SINGULAR OR PLURAL INDEFINITE PRONOUNS

all	most
any	none
more	some

The only problem likely to arise with the use of the indefinite pronoun is that of number; see *Agreement,* page 19.

Note: Except for the words *none* and *plenty,* indefinite pronouns can function as adjectives as well.

6. *Reflexive* pronouns refer back to the subject. A reflexive pronoun is usually the direct object of a verb.

   We dressed *ourselves* hastily.

Reflexive pronouns may also be used for emphasis.

   Many feared the Senate *itself* was discredited.

In formal English the reflexive form is not used as a substitute for either subject or object; this is likely to be a practical problem only in the first person.

   Myrna and I (not: *myself*) made all the arrangements.

   They asked Myrna and *me* (not: *myself*) to chaperone the dance.

7. *Reciprocal* pronouns are compound indefinite pronouns which indicate some mutual relationship between two or more persons and things.

   The lovers lived only for *each other.*

   All members of the company saw *one another* every day.

Case of Pronouns

The case rules that apply to nouns apply also to pronouns. Unlike nouns, however, pronouns frequently change their form according to whether they are in the nominative, objective, or possessive case. For this reason the case rules for pronouns are given separately below. A pronoun used as the subject of a verb takes the nominative case.

Right John and *I* are invited, aren't *we*?

When a verb is omitted but understood, be sure to supply it mentally in order to determine whether the pronoun is used as its subject.

Wrong John knows more than *her.*
You are as good a player as *me.*

Right John knows more than *she* (does). (*She* is the subject of the omitted verb *does.*).

Right You are as good a player as *I* (am).

A pronoun used as a predicate nominative takes the nominative case. A predicate nominative is a noun or pronoun that follows *am, is, are, was, were, be, been,* and that refers back to the subject.

Wrong Knock. Knock. Who's there? It's *me.*
Could that be *her* already?
It might have been *him.*

Right Knock. Knock. Who's there? It's *I.* (*I* is the predicate nominative after the verb *is.*)
Could that be *she* already?
It might have been *he.*

Do not permit such interrupting expressions as *do you suppose, believe, think, say,* etc., to affect the case of *who* and *whom.*

Wrong *Whom* do you believe was the guilty person?

Right *Who* do you believe was the guilty person? (*Who* is the subject of *was,* not the object of *believe.*)

Be careful not to confuse the subject of a verb with the object of a preposition.

Wrong I will vote for *whomever* is the best candidate.

Right I will vote for *whoever* is the best candidate. (*Whoever* is the subject of *is.* The object of the preposition *for* is the whole clause *whoever is the best candidate.*)

A pronoun that is the subject of an infinitive takes the objective case. The infinitive is the form of the verb preceded by *to: to be, to dance,* etc.

Wrong Do you expect John and *I* to be ready?

Right Do you expect John and *me* to be ready? (*Me* is the subject together with *John* of the infinitive *to be.*)

A pronoun that follows the infinitive *to be* takes the objective case.

Wrong Mary took John to be *I*.

Right Mary took John to be *me*.

A pronoun used as the object of a verb, of an infinitive, or of a preposition, or as the indirect object, takes the objective case.

Wrong *Who* did you ask to the party?

Right *Whom* did you ask to the party? (*Whom* is the object of the verb *ask*.)

Wrong The time has come for *we* students to get to work.

Right The time has come for *us* students to get to work. (*Us* is the object of the preposition *for*.)

Wrong The coach gave John and *I* a briefing.

Right The coach gave John and *me* a briefing. (*John* and *me* are the indirect objects of the verb *gave*.)

A pronoun used in apposition with a noun takes the same case as the noun.

Wrong The instructor wants us all–Harry, Sam, and *I*–to stay after class.

Right The instructor wants us all–Harry, Sam, and *me*–to stay after class. (*Harry, Sam,* and *me* are in apposition with *us* and therefore take the same case.)

A pronoun used before a gerund takes the possessive case. A *gerund* is a verbal used as a noun. It has the same form as the verb's present or perfect participle.

Wrong I was sure of *him* winning the prize.

Right I was sure of *his* winning the prize. (*Winning* is the gerund. It is the object of the preposition *of*.)

The case form of the relative pronouns *who* and *whoever* depends upon how the pronoun is used in the clause it introduces.

Right I already know *who* will come to the party. (*Who* is the subject of the verb *come* and is therefore in the nominative case.)

The captain, *whom* I have never met, has asked to see me. (*Whom* is the direct object of the verb *met* and is therefore in the objective case.)

Agreement

Since pronouns are substitute words for other words, there must be agreement between them; otherwise the meaning of the substitute word will not be clear. The word for which a pronoun substitutes and to which it refers is its antecedent. A pronoun does not necessarily agree with its antecedent in case; but it must always agree with it in gender, number, and person.

The problem words are *each, either, neither, every, everyone, anybody, nobody, everybody, somebody.* In informal speech, we generally treat these words as collectives and we make the pronouns that refer to them singular or plural according to sound or whim. In formal writing, these words are treated as singular; therefore, a pronoun that has any one of these words as an antecedent should also be singular.

Informal Each of us knew what *we* were doing.

Formal Each of us knew what *he* was doing.

Informal Everybody should know what *they* want out of life.

Formal Everybody should know what *he* wants out of life.

Informal Will everyone please open *their* book to page 56.

Formal Will everyone please open *his* book to page 56.

Informal Every city and town had a large increase in *their* population.

Formal Every city and town had a large increase in *its* population.

When an antecedent includes mixed sexes and calls for a singular number, the use of *their* as an all-inclusive pronoun is wrong. The use of the double pronouns *he or she, his or her, him or her* is also undesirable. The pronoun that should be used for both sexes is *he, his, him*.

Wrong Every man, woman, and child should wear *their* life jacket.

Undesirable Every man, woman, and child should wear *his or her* life jacket.

Right Every man, woman, and child should wear *his* life jacket.

Use the pronoun *who* to refer to people, *which* to animals other than humans and to things, and *that* for either persons or things.

Wrong *Which* is that person?

Right *Who* is that person?

There are two exceptions to the above rule. *Which* may be used to refer to persons considered as a group. Also, when a reference to an animal results in the awkward *of which* construction, the acceptable alternative is *whose*.

Right Anthropologist believe that the race *which* gave America its first settlers was Mongoloid.

Awkward I claim that the cheetah, the speed *of which* has been timed at seventy miles an hour, is the world's fastest four-legged animal.

Right I claim that the cheetah, *whose* speed has been timed at seventy miles an hour, is the world's fastest four-legged animal.

When two antecedents are joined by *or* or *nor,* the pronoun should agree with the nearer antecedent.

Wrong Neither the President nor the members of the Cabinet could foresee *his* fate.

Right Neither the President nor the members of the Cabinet could foresee *their* fate.

Reference

A pronoun may be grammatically correct. It may agree in every way–in person, number, and gender–with its antecedent, and it may have just the right case form. Yet if the antecedent is not immediately clear, all the effort will be utterly wasted. The reader must be able to tell at a single glance exactly what your pronoun refers to. One of the worst writing sins you can commit is to force your reader to reread the sentence or refer back to a previous sentence to find your meaning. This sin is frequently caused by an ambiguous or misplaced pronoun. A pronoun should have a clearly defined antecedent and should be placed as near the antecedent as possible.

Indefinite I had a fascinating time in Mexico. *They* are a colorful people. (The antecedent of the pronoun *They* may be obvious to the writer, but not to the reader. Who are *They?*)

Definite I had a fascinating time on my trip to Mexico. Mexicans are a colorful people.

Definite I had a fascinating time on my trip to Mexico. It is a colorful country.

Shun the indefinite use of the pronoun *it*. In certain idiomatic phrases the indefinite use of *it* is acceptable. (*It is a fine day. It is a fact. It is necessary. It is likely. It is true.*) But when *it* is not part of an accepted idiom, avoid the indefinite use altogether.

Indefinite In the chapter on the second voyage, it reveals that Columbus sent five hundred Indian slaves as a gift to Queen Isabella.

Definite The chapter on the second voyage reveals that Columbus sent five hundred Indian slaves as a gift to Queen Isabella.

Avoid the use of the impersonal *it* and the pronoun *it* in the same sentence.

Indefinite The car is in rough shape, and it will probably cost more to repair it than the price of a new one.

Definite The car is in rough shape, and the cost of repairing it will probably be more than the price of a new one.

Shun the indefinite use of the pronouns *you* and *they.* The indefinite use of these pronouns is acceptable in informal speech, but not in formal writing. In formal writing use *one* and *everyone.*

Informal In this class *you* are not permitted to take notes.

Formal In this class *one* (or *a student*) is not permitted to take notes.

Informal *They* greet tourists warmly in Holland.

Formal *Everyone* greets tourists warmly in Holland.

VERBS

A *verb* is a word or group of words that indicates action, condition (being), or process.

> They *began* the boat race this morning; by six this evening they *will have sailed* halfway to the island.
>
> He *was* a good dog. The house *seems* empty without him.
>
> The rose *had become* an even deeper crimson.

Types of Verbs

Verbs may be classified according to four types:

1. A *transitive* verb requires a direct object to complete its meaning.

   Hilda *bathed* the *baby*. (The subject, *Hilda*, performs the action upon the direct object, *baby*.)

   Ulysses *plunged* the *stake* into the Cyclops' eye. (The verb *plunged* is transitive and the direct object is *stake*.)

2. An *intransitive* verb is complete within itself and does not require a direct object.

   Let us *pray*.
   We *felt* relieved.
   We *plunged* into the pool and *swam*. Then we *lay* in the sun.

Most verbs, like *plunge*, can be either transitive or intransitive. But *lie* is intransitive only. It is a troublesome verb because its past tense *lay* is frequently confused with the present tense of transitive *lay*.

	TRANSITIVE	INTRANSITIVE
PRESENT TENSE	lay (something down)	lie (on my bed)
PAST TENSE	laid (something down)	lay (on my bed)
PAST PARTICIPLE	have laid (something down)	have lain (on my bed)

3. A *linking* verb or *copula* joins the subject to its complement, which is a predicate noun or adjective. The more common ones are:

appear	look
be	seem
become	smell
feel	taste
grow	turn

Most of these verbs are not exclusively linking verbs.

USED AS LINKING VERBS	USED AS OTHER VERBS
It *grew* colder.	He *grew* a beard. (Transitive verb)
That *tasted* bad.	They *will taste* their soup. (Transitive verb)
He *turned* pirate.	She stopped and *turned*. (Intransitive verb)

4. An *auxiliary* verb helps the main verb of the sentence. It may be formed from *have, can, may, be, shall, will, might, must,* and *do,* and appears before the main verb in a verb phrase.

   We *can* go if we like.

   She *might have been* told earlier.

   I *am* finishing my letter.

Principal Parts

Verbs in English have three principal parts:

INFINITIVE OR BASIC FORM	to walk to sleep	to go to bite
PAST TENSE, USED IN THE SIMPLE PAST	walked slept	went bit
PAST PARTICIPLE, "USED TO" FORM COMPOUND TENSES	(has) walked (has) slept	(has) gone (has) bitten

Regular (or *weak*) verbs form their principal parts by adding *-ed, -d,* or *-t* to the infinitive.

wanted placed dealt

Irregular (or *strong*) verbs change or retain the vowel of the infinitive and do not add *-ed, -d,* or *-t*.

throw, threw, thrown

choose, chose, chosen

Intransitive sit, sat, sat

Transitive set, set, set

Sometimes a verb may have more than one form:

shine, shone (or shined), shone (or shined)

dream, dreamed (or dreamt), dreamed (or dreamt)

Consult a recent dictionary if there is any question of a form's being nonstandard:

see, saw (*not standard:* seen), have seen

Person and Number

Person and number present few problems in English verbs; the verb form usually changes only in the third person singular of the present tense, where an *s* is added (*I jump, he jumps; I cry, she cries*). A notable exception is the highly irregular verb *be*, but this is so frequently used it presents no practical difficulty.

Tense

The tense of a verb indicates the time of its action. There are six tenses in English:

1. The *present* tense uses three forms for positive statements.

SIMPLE PRESENT:	We *know,* you *say,* he *rides*
PROGRESSIVE:	I *am rushing,* you *are moving,* he *is standing* still
EMPHATIC:	I *do move,* he *does ride*

In questions or in negative statements, the progressive or emphatic form is generally used.

PROGRESSIVE:	*Are* you *coming?* She *is* not *coming*
EMPHATIC:	*Does* he *swim?* They *do* not *swim*

2. The *past* tense indicates past time not continuing to the present. It uses three forms for positive statements.

SIMPLE PAST: I *took,* you *jumped,* she *sank*

PROGRESSIVE: He *was flying,* we *were laughing*

EMPHATIC: You *did believe,* they *did prove*

   In questions or in negative statements, the progressive or emphatic form is generally used.

3. The *perfect* (or *present perfect*) tense indicates past time continuing to the present. It is formed by adding the past participle to *have* or *has.*

   I *have shown* her the ring.

   Have you *been* here long?

   He *has filled* the tub.

4. The *past perfect* tense indicates past time occurring before a definite time in the past. It is formed by adding the past participle to *had.*

   We *had been* in the new house for a week.

   You *had come* to visit us.

   Had she *set* the table yet?

Note: In the examples immediately above, any subsequent actions would still be in the past (She *set* the table when I arrived). But an action subsequent to those in the examples for the present perfect would naturally be in the present (He has filled the tub. He *is washing* now).

5. The *future* tense indicates future time continuing from the present. It has three forms.

   We *will* not *leave.*

   You *will be having* dinner.

   Is he *going to tell* us?

The old distinction between *shall* (simple futurity) and *will* (future of determination) has virtually disappeared except in formal writing. It may also be used in the first person, to make clear an important difference in attitude.

   I *shall* do it. (compliance)

   I *will* do it. (desire)

6. The *future perfect* tense indicates future time occurring before a definite time in the future. It is formed by adding the past participle to the future tense of *have.*

   He *shall have seen* them before you do.

   Will they *have escaped* (before the house burns down)?

Note: The present tense may be used for future time (I *leave* for home tomorrow); past time, especially to add immediacy to a narrative (It *is* dark, this Christmas Eve, as Washington *approaches* Trenton); to make a statement that is presumably true at any time (Too many cooks *spoil* the broth); or to discuss a fictional past (When Huck *sneaks* ashore from the raft, we *see* intrepidity at its height).

Voice

A verb is in the *active voice* when its subject performs the action.

   Tennyson published *In Memoriam* in 1850. (*Tennyson* is the subject and the verb *published* is in the active voice.)

A verb is in the *passive voice* when its subject is acted upon.

   In Memoriam was published by Tennyson in 1850. (*In Memoriam* is the subject and the verb *published* is in the passive voice.)

Except for a reason of deliberate emphasis, choose the active voice in preference to the passive voice. It will make your writing more lively and vigorous. *Betty gave a party for all the children* is livelier than *A party was given by Betty for all the children.*

Mood

The *mood* of a verb refers to the manner in which a statement is expressed. There are three moods in English.

1. The *indicative* mood states a fact.

   I *spent* the holiday in New York.

   He *knew* you *had come.*

2. The *imperative* mood gives a command.

   Stop!

   Try and *make* me.

3. The *subjunctive* mood expresses a wish, a doubt, or a condition contrary to fact.

   I wish he *were* somewhere else.

   We wondered if we *were* going to get away with it.

Note: The past subjunctive of the verb *be,* which is *were* in all three persons and both numbers, is the only subjunctive of any real importance in English. In informal writing and in speech, the indicative *was* is an acceptable substitute. Other uses of the subjunctive are consciously formal (We request that this *be* omitted from the report; if this *prove* false I shall resign), or preserved in automatic phrases (*come* what may, whatever it *cost*). The subjunctive mood has largely disappeared.

Finite and Infinite Verbs (Verbals)

A *finite* verb is capable of making a complete and independent assertion.

She *finished* the book.

You *have done* a good job.

A finite verb is limited to a specific person, by a noun or a pronoun (the bear *roars;* he *climbs*). It is also limited in number, either singular or plural (she *laughs;* they *laugh*). And it is limited in time, by a tense form (we *sit;* we *sat*). A finite verb serves as a main verb in a sentence or clause.

She *had eaten* before we *began.*

An *infinite* verb, or *verbal,* is not thus limited. It cannot be used to make a sentence of the typical subject-verb pattern, but is characteristically used in subordinate constructions. (A clear understanding of the difference between a finite verb and a verbal will eliminate most careless sentence fragments from your writing.) There are three classes of verbals:

1. The *infinitive* is one of the present forms of a verb, with *to* either present or understood.

	ACTIVE	PASSIVE
PRESENT	(to push)	(to) be pushed
PERFECT	(to) have pushed	(to) have been pushed

Most versatile of the verbals, the infinitive may be used as a noun:

To ride is good sport. (subject)

She wanted *to play* with the puppies. (object of a verb)

They wanted nothing but *to be left* alone. (object of a preposition)

His intention was *to have kissed* her. (subjective complement)

as an adjective:

Ned Creeth is my choice *to represent* us. (modifies *choice*)

It was courageous *to volunteer.* (modifies *courageous*)

as an adverb:

I am sorry *to disappoint* you. (modifies *sorry*)

To find work, he moved to the city. (modifies *moved*)

with an auxiliary as part of a finite verb:

We must *find* a way. (*to* understood)

2. The *participle* is one of the present or past participle forms of a verb.

	ACTIVE	PASSIVE
PRESENT	trying	being tried
PAST	having tried	having been tried

It may be used as an adjective:

He shot the *leaping* deer.

The *broken* vase lay near the window.

Having paid our respects, we left.

as part of a finite verb:

We were *playing* leapfrog.

I have *had* enough for now.

in an absolute construction (a phrase grammatically independent of any other part of the sentence):

The city *having been taken,* Caesar moved on. (The entire phrase *The city having been taken* is the absolute construction.)

3. The *gerund* is one of the present participial forms of a verb, and is used as a noun.

Kissing is pleasant, but *being kissed* is a perfect joy. (subject, active and passive)

Many prefer *going* to the movies. (object of a verb)

Others waste their time in *bowling.* (object of a preposition)

Uncle Jack's favorite recreation is *sleeping.* (subjective complement)

Problems in Use

The following are some persistent problems in the use of verbs and verbals:

SHALL (SHOULD) and WILL (WOULD)

In questions, *will* is properly used in all persons. However, *shall* is often used to convey a sense of propriety or obligation. *Won't* is the regular negative form.

Shall I write to thank her?

What *shall* I do to avoid it?

What *won't* you do?

Do not overuse *shall*. It is neither more correct nor more elegant than *will*.

Should and *would* suggest doubt or uncertainty.

That *should* be all right. (contrast: That *will* be all right.)

In polite requests, *would* and *should* are used for the first person, *would* for the second.

I *would* (or *should*) be very grateful for your help.

Would you please pass the hominy grits?

CAN and MAY

Can and *may* are used to show ability and possibility, respectively.

You *can* do it if you try.

We *may* arrive in time.

Can is used increasingly to express permission.

Can I come in?

You *can* choose the one you want.

This use of *can* is still not considered formally correct. In writing, and even in speaking, it is preferable to use *may*.

May I come in?

You *may* choose the one you want.

LIE, SIT, RISE

Lie, sit, and *rise* are intransitive verbs. They should not be confused with their transitive counterparts *lay, set,* and *raise*. The best way to avoid difficulty with these troublesome pairs is simply to memorize their principal parts, and then to decide whether a construction calls for a transitive or intransitive verb.

	TRANSITIVE	INTRANSITIVE
PRESENT	lay, set, raise (something)	lie, sit, rise
PAST	laid, set, raised (something)	lay, sat, rose
PAST PARTICIPLE	(have) laid, set, raised (something)	(have) lain, sat, risen

Remember that a hen *sets* on her eggs, and the sun *sets* in the west.

GET

The past participle of the verb *get* is either *got* or *gotten*. The latter seems the more common. (The only past participle of *forget* is *forgotten*.) Avoid *have got* and *have got to* (meaning *must*) where *have* and *have to* are sufficient.

Wrong I have got some here.

I haven't got any more.

I have got to leave soon.

Right I have some here.

I haven't any more.

I have to leave soon.

AIN'T

Ain't is a contraction of *am not, are not,* and occasionally *have not;* despite its long history in English, it is a nonstandard form. Use the equally convenient contractions *I'm not, aren't,* and *haven't*. However, there is no completely satisfactory form for the first person singular negative interrogative: *am I not* is too formal for most speakers, and the clumsy *aren't I* is not everywhere accepted.

Misuse of Past Tense

One of the most common verb errors is to use the past tense instead of the past participle. Use the past participle whenever there is an auxiliary or helping verb.

Wrong It wasn't until I left the house that I noticed I had *forgot* my books.

Right It wasn't until I left the house that I noticed I had *forgotten* my books. (The auxiliary verb *had* demands the past participle.)

Sequence of Tenses

Avoid unnecessary shifts from one tense to another in the same sentence. Make a verb in a subordinate clause (or an infinitive or a participle) agree in time with the verb in the main clause.

Wrong Whenever he *said* yes, she *says* no. (The verb *said* in the subordinate clause does not agree in time with the verb *says* in the main clause.)

Right Whenever he *says* yes, she *says* no. (Both verbs agree.)

Whenever he *said* yes, she *said* no. (Both verbs agree.)

An exception to the above rule applies when one states a universal truth (a statement that is true regardless of time).

Sally *said* that it *is* better to be wise than virtuous. (Disagreement between verbs is acceptable because a universal truth requiring the present tense is stated.)

When two past actions are stated in the same sentence, use the past perfect tense for the earlier action.

Wrong Fred realized just in time that he already *drank* too much.

Right Fred realized just in time that he *had* already *drunk* too much. (The action of the second verb occurred before that of the first verb.)

After *if,* use the auxiliary verb *had* instead of *would have.*

Wrong If you would have used your head, you wouldn't be in this mess.

Right If you had used your head, you wouldn't be in this mess.

The past infinitive is often used to express action not yet completed at the time of the main or preceding verb. This is wrong. The present infinitive is demanded in such constructions.

Wrong We wanted *to have finished* the job by tonight.

Right We wanted *to finish* the job by tonight. (The present infinitive *to finish* is demanded because its action has not yet taken place at the time of the main verb *wanted.*)

Agreement of Subject and Verb

A verb must always agree with its subject in person and number. It is often difficult to tell which is the true subject, or whether a subject is considered singular or plural. The rules below govern the agreement of subject and verb.

The following pronouns, often taken to be plural, are singular and therefore require a singular verb: *each, everyone, everybody, either,* and *neither.*

Wrong Each of the candidates *are* competent.

Neither of us *are* ready.

Right Each of the candidates *is* competent.

Neither of us *is* ready.

The following nouns, plural in form, are considered singular in meaning and therefore require a singular verb: *news, economics, mathematics, politics, mumps,* and *measles. The United States* also takes a singular verb.

Wrong The economics of the plan *are* hazardous.

Right The economics of the plan *is* hazardous.

The United States *has* treated the American Indians abominably.

A collective noun generally takes a singular verb. However, when the individuals of the group are considered, the verb is plural.

Our team always *wins.*

The family *is* worried about my late hours. (Family regarded as a single unit–more usual.)

The family *have* gone about their chores. (Individuals of the family considered–less usual.)

The words *there* and *here* are not subjects. In constructions introduced by *there* and *here,* look for the true subject to ascertain the number of the verb.

Wrong *There's* several ways to skin a cat.

Right There *are* several ways to skin a cat.

Fractions take a singular verb when bulk or a total number or amount is considered, a plural verb when individuals are considered. This rule applies also to words such as *all, any, none, some, more,* and *most.*

Two-thirds of the student body *was* present.

Two-thirds of the students *were* present.

All the money *has* somehow vanished.

All the members of the team *are* on the honor list.

When the word *number* is preceded by the definite article *the,* it usually takes a singular verb. When it is preceded by the indefinite article *a,* it takes a plural verb.

The number on the team who can be counted on in a tight spot *is* small.

A number of the team *have* proved their worth.

When subjects are contrasted, the verb agrees with the affirmative subject.

Wrong She, not I, *am* responsible.

Right She, not I, *is* responsible.

When the subject is a relative pronoun, look for the pronoun's antecedent to determine whether the verb is singular or plural. Relative pronouns are *who, which,* and *that.*

Wrong Joe is one of the few students who *has* maintained an A average.

Right Joe is one of the few students who *have* maintained an A average. (The antecedent of the relative pronoun *who* is *students,* hence it takes a plural verb.)

Words joined to a subject by *as well as, in addition to, with, together with, including,* and *rather than* do not affect the verb.

Wrong The entire student body, as well as most of the members of the faculty, *have* denounced President Green's decision.

Right The entire student body, as well as most of the members of the faculty, *has* denounced President Green's decision.

A compound subject joined by *and* generally takes a plural verb.

Wrong Her arrival and departure *was* not even noticed.

Right Her arrival and departure *were* not even noticed.

Do not use a plural verb when the subject is a compound that is regarded as a single entity.

The long and short of the matter *is* that our front line is weak.

Spaghetti and meat balls *is* my favorite.

Bread and butter *is* all that we have for supper.

Singular subjects joined by *and* but preceded by *every* take a singular verb.

Wrong Every man, woman, and child *are* accounted for.

Right Every man, woman, and child *is* accounted for.

Singular subjects joined by *or, either . . . or, nor,* or *neither . . . nor,* take a singular verb.

Wrong Neither Adams nor Williams *are* present.

Right Neither Adams nor Williams *is* present.

When a verb has two or more subjects differing in person or number and connected by *or, either . . . or, nor,* or *neither . . . nor,* the verb agrees with the subject nearer it.

Wrong Either he or you *is* wrong.

Right Either he or you *are* wrong. (The verb agrees in person with the pronoun nearer it.)

Wrong Either new players or a new play *are* needed.

Right Either new players or a new play *is* needed. (The verb agrees in number with the noun nearer it.)

Irregular Verbs

To find the proper form of irregular verbs, consult a reliable dictionary. It is important to know how dictionaries enter the forms of irregular verbs. The main entry for all verbs is the infinitive (without the *to*) or present tense form. Following the verb's phonetic respelling comes, first, the past tense form, next, the past participial form, and finally, the present participial form. Acceptable variant forms are given. However, if any one form is the same as the one immediately preceding it, that form is not repeated. For verbs that are not irregular, the past tense and the past participle, when not given, are assumed to be formed in the usual way by adding *-d* or *-ed*.

ADJECTIVES AND ADVERBS

Adjectives and adverbs are *modifiers,* words which change the meaning of other words to make them clearer, more exact, weaker, or stronger.

An *adjective* modifies a noun or pronoun. It may answer the questions How many? What kind? Which one?

HOW MANY?

three brothers   *one* dollar   *many* men

WHAT KIND?

early bird   *whole* truth   *beautiful* girl

WHICH ONE?

this visit   *whose* jug?   *her* book

Note that *this, whose,* and *her*–often used as pronouns–here function as *pronominal adjectives.* A pronominal adjective always accompanies a noun.

Also note that the indefinite article *a* (*an*) identifies something as one of its kind (*a* boy, *an* apple), or serves as a substitute for *each* or *every* (once *a* week). The definite article *the* identifies one or more persons or objects by separating them from all others of their kind. Both articles are therefore adjectives.

An *adverb* modifies a verb, adjective, or other adverb. It may answer the questions How? When? Where? How much?

HOW?

Come *quickly.*   It moves *clockwise.*

WHEN?

They arrived *yesterday.*

WHERE?

They went *home.* *Here* it is.

HOW MUCH?

We are more active now, but *only partly* happy.

In addition, there are the conjunctive adverbs *(however, moreover, nevertheless, therefore),* and adverbs of assertion and concession (*yes, no, not, maybe, probably).*

Many adverbs may be distinguished from adjectives by their *-ly* ending *(happy, happily; hard, hardly; particular, particularly).* But some of the more common adverbs do not end in *-ly: now, quite, there, then, up, down, for.* The last four of these can also be adjectives; there is a long list of adjectives and adverbs with identical forms, including *better, early, fast, much, straight,* and *well.*

Some adverbs have two forms: *loud, loudly; slow, slowly; soft, softly; quick, quickly; wrong, wrongly.* Sometimes there is a clear difference of meaning between the two.

He tried *hard.*	He *hardly* tried.
She came *late.*	*Lately* she has been coming at dinner time.

With others, choice depends on sound or on level of usage. The *-ly* ending is more common in formal writing. It is almost invariably used when the adverb precedes the verb *(Tightly* he gripped the narrow ledge). The short form is used especially in commands (hold on *tight;* go *slow).* Do not drop the *-ly* from the adverbs *considerably, really, sincerely,* and the like. For any question of the standard form consult a dictionary.

Adjectives and adverbs in English do not change their forms to indicate person, number, or case. However, they do change their forms to indicate degrees of comparison. They are compared in three degrees, frequently by adding *-er* and *-est.*

	POSITIVE	COMPARATIVE	SUPERLATIVE
ADJECTIVE	long	longer	longest
ADVERB	far	farther	farthest

Some have irregular comparisons, but these rarely cause difficulty:

	POSITIVE	COMPARATIVE	SUPERLATIVE
ADJECTIVE	good	better	best
	bad	worse	worst
	many, much	more	most
ADVERB	well	better	best
	best	worse	worst

Words of two syllables may have comparisons in *-er* and *-est,* or may use *more (less)* and *most (least);* the choice is determined by rhythm and emphasis. Words of three or more syllables are compared only with *more (less)* and *most (least).*

	POSITIVE	COMPARATIVE	SUPERLATIVE
ADJECTIVE	lovely	lovelier; more (less) lovely	loveliest; most (least) lovely
	beautiful	more (less) beautiful	most (least) beautiful
ADVERB	beautifully	more (less) beautifully	most (least) beautifully

In informal speech, or for reasons of emphasis, the superlative is often used in place of the comparative. But the general rule in formal writing is to use the comparative in comparing two things, the superlative for three or more.

Informal Put your *best* foot forward.
May the *best* team win.

Formal The *better* team won decisively.
Rome is the *oldest* of European capitals.

Absolute adjectives cannot, strictly speaking, be compared; something is either *dead, possible, full, perfect, unique,* or it isn't. But in informal usage absolute adjectives are often modified by comparisons, either for emphasis ("*deader* than a doornail") or because some of them have virtually lost their absolute meaning ("this box is *emptier* than that"). In formal usage, "more nearly empty" would be preferable.

Things compared should be of the same kind.

Wrong Marlowe's plays are not so highly regarded as Shakespeare.

Right Marlowe's plays are not so highly regarded as those of Shakespeare (or *as Shakespeare's).*

Other is used only when the things compared are of the same class.

Wrong Helen is more intelligent than any *other* boy.

Right Helen is more intelligent than any boy.
She reads more widely than any *other* student.

Do not use *other* with superlative comparisons.

Wrong Helen was the most intelligent of all the *other* students.

Right Helen was the most intelligent of all the students.

An adjective may precede a noun (or pronoun), or follow one. Or an adjective may follow a linking verb (copula).

The *tired* nations sought a peace, one *secure* and *permanent*. (*Tired* precedes and modifies the noun *nations*. *Secure* and *permanent* follow and modify the pronoun *one;* this word order is not common but completely acceptable.)

They hoped it would not prove *illusory*. (*Illusory* follows the linking verb *prove* and modifies the pronoun *it.)*

Notice in the example immediately above that an adjective, like a noun, may serve as subjective complement. This is not true of adverbs:

Wrong It seems *truly*.
Right It seems *true*.

Through frequent use, *I feel badly* is now sometimes acceptable in informal speech; but to be formally correct, say:

I feel *bad*.

I feel *ill*.

I feel *well*. (meaning: I do not feel ill.)

I feel *good*. (meaning: I feel positively happy, *or* healthy.)

PREPOSITIONS

A *preposition* connects a noun or pronoun with another word in the sentence, and establishes the relationship between them.

Peter walked *to* the store. (connecting *walked* and *store*)

He returned *with* them. (connecting *returned* and *them*)

Since word relationships are more difficult concepts to handle than "plain facts," prepositions are probably the most difficult parts of speech to make satisfactory rules for. Many are used in expressions that are impossible to analyze logically, the meaning of which is usually clear to the native speaker of English: *compare with* and *compare to,* for instance, or *differ from* and *differ with*. Rules in such cases are cumbersome and possibly misleading. The best way to learn proper use of prepositions is by paying attention to the speech and writing of people who use English accurately. Some of the more common prepositions:

about	beneath	in
above	beside	of
along	between	on
among	by	over
at	during	to
before	except	with
behind	for	without
below	from	

The noun or pronoun introduced by the preposition is called *the object of the preposition* and must be in the objective case. This rule gives trouble only in the case of coordinated pronouns. Thus,

The waiter brought some *for her and me*. (NOT: *she and I*)

A preposition with its object is called a *prepositional phrase* and is used as an adjective or an adverb.

The boy *with the dog* is my brother. (adjective, modifying noun *boy)*

They are all playing *with the dog*. (adverb, modifying verb *are playing)*

He threw his hat *over the fence*. (adverb, modifying verb *threw)*

In informal conversation, prepositions are sometimes doubled, though this is not really necessary to the meaning of the sentence. Double prepositions are rarely used in writing.

Informal We left *at about* nine o'clock.

Formal We left *about* nine o'clock.

Never repeat the same preposition near the beginning and at the end of a sentence: She is the person *for* whom I took all that trouble *for*. This is a mark of carelessness. However, contrary to a frequent yet mistaken belief, a preposition may be used at the end of a sentence, whenever it sounds natural to the rhythm of the sentence.

Where does she come *from?*

Whom did she go *with?*

The first example below is obviously a much more natural (and effective) sentence, despite the two prepositions with which it ends, than the second example.

That's the kind of stupidity I won't put *up with*.

That's the kind of stupidity *up with which* I will not put.

One classic example ends with no fewer than five prepositions:

What did you put the book you were being read *to out of away for?*

This sentence, too clumsy for formal, written English, is perfectly clear (though not very elegant) as spoken language.

Problem Prepositions

As already stated, the major problem with most prepositions is their idiomatic use. The following prepositions often pose problems in general usage.

AMONG, BETWEEN
Among is used when more than two persons or things are considered. *Between* is used when only two are considered. This rule, which may be relaxed in informal conversation, must be rigidly followed in written English.

Divide the money *among* Frank, John, and Bill.

We must choose *between* Frank and John.

An exception to this rule occurs when a mutual or reciprocal relationship is indicated. In this event, *between* is used for more than two.

A treaty was concluded *between* the three nations.

Frank, John, and Bill agreed *between* them that they would divide the prize.

AT, IN
At and *in* may often be used interchangeably. However, certain rules govern their usage when they indicate place or locality.

In is used when the reference to the interior of a building is stressed; *at,* when the site itself is stressed.

Please meet me *in* the reception room of the dean's office.

Classes will be held *at* Judson Hall.

In is used before the names of countries; *at* before the names of business firms, office buildings, schools, universities, etc.

The International Conference will be held next year *in* Switzerland.

I was educated *at* Princeton.

In is used before the name of a city to give the impression of permanence; *at,* to indicate a temporary stay.

John goes to school *at* Trenton, but he lives *in* Philadelphia.

Following a brief stay *at* Mexico City, we spent a month *in* Oaxaca.

In is used before the name of a city in local addresses; *at,* before the street number.

Bill lives *in* Newark *at* 562 Kensington Avenue.

BELOW, BENEATH, UNDER, UNDERNEATH
These prepositions are generally used interchangeably, and in most cases one will be as grammatically correct as the other. Choice is usually determined by courtesy. Thus, the use of *beneath* may imply inferiority or contempt where *below* would be more courteous. The example below implies inferiority:

Mary is in the class *beneath* me.

To substitute the word *below* does not make the construction more grammatically correct; however, it does make it more courteous and more in accord with accepted usage.

Mary is in the class *below* me.

BESIDE, BESIDES
Beside is used to mean *next to. Besides* (ordinarily an adverb) is used to mean *in addition to* or *moreover.*

Please sit *beside* me.

Besides a dog, I have three cats. (*Besides* modifies the verb *have.*)

IN, INTO
In refers to position. *Into* denotes motion from without to within.

We ate a buffet supper *in* the living room.

We marched *into* the dining room.

ON, ONTO, ON TO
On refers to position upon something; *onto* denotes motion toward the upper surface of something; the two-word form *on to* is used when *on* belongs to the verb.

I rode *on* the horse.

I got *onto* the horse.

I hung *on to* the horse.

ITEMS IN A SERIES
Items in a series must always be parallel in form. This means that when a preposition is used to introduce a series, it should be either repeated before each ensuing item or dropped before each ensuing item.

Wrong I shall send invitations to John, Bill, and to Mary.

Right I shall send invitations to John, to Bill, and to Mary.

Right I shall send invitations to John, Bill, and Mary.

CONJUNCTIONS

A *conjunction* connects words, phrases, or clauses.

black *and* blue (words)

with the group *but* not part of it (phrases)

He agreed, *though* he had reservations. (clauses)

Conjunctions may be classified according to four types:

A *coordinating conjunction* connects equal words, phrases, or clauses. There are six coordinating conjunctions. These are: *and, but, for, nor, or, yet.*

We didn't walk, *nor* did we drive.

It rained, *yet* we enjoyed the farm.

A coordinating conjunction may occasionally introduce a sentence closely related in thought to the preceding one.

We managed to win the first game. *But* we never had a chance for the championship.

Correlative conjunctions are used in pairs to connect equal elements that are parallel in form. They replace a coordinating conjunction for greater emphasis.

We will go to Yellowstone Park *or* Yosemite. (coordinating conjunction)

We will go *either* to Yellowstone Park *or* Yosemite. (correlative conjunctions)

The most common correlative conjunctions are *both . . . and, neither . . . nor, either . . . or, whether . . . or,* and *not only . . . but (also).*

I didn't care *whether* we went *or* stayed home.

At the party we met *not only* the Jacksons *but* the Blairs.

Not only the husbands came *but also* the children.

A *conjunctive adverb* connects clauses in addition to modifying a verb (or clause). The most common are:

accordingly	however	nevertheless
also	indeed	still
besides	likewise	then
furthermore	meanwhile	therefore
hence	moreover	thus

A group of words may also serve as a conjunctive adverb:

in fact	for that reason
in the first place	on the contrary
in the meantime	on the other hand

The conjunctive adverb always has a semicolon before it when it is used between independent clauses.

I hadn't set the clock; *hence*, I was late.

The search may have ended; *indeed*, it's likely.

We tried the engine; but *in the meantime*, the tire had gone flat.

A *subordinating conjunction* introduces a dependent clause and subordinates it to an independent clause. It establishes the relation between the two clauses. This relation may be one of

CAUSE: *as, because, inasmuch as, since*

We went indoors, *as* it had grown quite dark.

Since he likes animals, they like him.

COMPARISON: *as . . . as, so . . . as, than*

Chaucer's language is not *so* difficult *as* you may think.

There was more smoke *than* (there was) fire.

CONCESSION: *although, though, while*

Although he works hard, he's not very efficient.

He doesn't write well, *though* he tries.

CONDITION: *if, provided that, unless*

She'll come *provided that* you do.

Unless you run you won't catch her.

MANNER: *as, as if, as though*

Do *as* you would be done by.

It seemed *as though* he would win.

PLACE: *where, wherever, whence, whither*

Where one is good, two are better.

"And *whence* they come and *whither* they shall go
The dew upon their feet shall manifest."

PURPOSE: *in order that, so that, that*

So *that* there will be enough for all, take no more than you need.

They died *that* we may live.

RESULT: *so that, so . . . that, such . . . that*

He studied hard, *so that* finally he was the recognized expert in the field.

Such was his optimism *that* we all were prepared for success.

TIME: *after, as, before, since, till, until, when, while*

Ruth arrived *as* they were leaving.

Until you spoke I didn't know you were there.

Troublesome Conjunctions

The following are troublesome conjunctions:

AND, ALSO

Also should not be used in place of *and* to connect items in a series.

Wrong I study English, French, Spanish, *also* Russian.

Right I study English, French, Spanish, and Russian.

AND, ETC.

The abbreviation *etc.* means "and so forth." It is incorrect to use *and* to connect the last item in a series when the last item is followed by *etc.*

Wrong We need eggs, bacon, and bread, etc.

Right We need eggs, bacon, bread, *etc.*

AND WHICH, AND WHO

These should not be used unless preceded in the same sentence by *which* or *who.*

Wrong I am looking for a course with four credits *and which* holds classes on Wednesday mornings.

Right I am looking for a course *which* offers four credits *and which* holds classes on Wednesday mornings.

AND, BUT

And is used to show addition; *but,* to show contrast.

Wrong Mary and I have been invited to a party, *and* I have to take care of my younger brother.

Right Mary and I have been invited to a party, *but* I have to take care of my younger brother.

AS, AS IF, LIKE

As and *as if* are respectably used as conjunctions to introduce clauses of various kinds and to connect comparisons. *Like,* which is gaining respectability as a conjunction in informal usage, is treated only as a preposition in formal writing. Grammarians shudder when they see *like* usurping the role of *as* and *as if.*

Informal You act *like* you're hurt.

Formal You act *as if* you were hurt.

AS, BECAUSE, SINCE

Any one of these may be used to introduce clauses of cause or reason, that is, to connect the stated cause with a fact already given.

I came *because* I was worried.

As you won't go, I will stay.

Since I can, I will.

However, *because* is limited to introducing clauses of cause or reason. *As* and *since* are also used to introduce clauses involving time. To introduce duration of time, use *as.* To introduce sequence of time, use *since.*

I worked less and less *as* each day passed. (time duration)

I haven't done any work *since* last you were here. (time sequence)

BECAUSE, FOR

Because is used when the reason it introduces is based upon fact. *For* is used when the reason it introduces is based upon opinion or speculation.

Come inside, *because* it is raining. (The reason given is an established fact.)

We are going to have a storm, *for* there is a ring around the moon. (The reason given is based on speculation.)

IF, WHETHER

If introduces clauses of supposition or condition involving uncertainty or doubt.

If I had known you were coming, I would have prepared a feast. (implies uncertainty)

If may also stand for *even though* or *whenever.*

If I am wrong, you are not right. (implies *even though*)

If I do not know, I try to find out. (implies *whenever*)

On the other hand, *whether* introduces clauses which involve an alternative. The alternative may be stated or understood. (*Whether* is the conjunction most likely to be used when followed by *or*.)

It will not make any difference *whether* I know or not. (alternative stated)

Please let me know *whether* I am right. (alternative implied)

WHEN, WHERE
When should not be used to introduce a definition unless the definition involves a time element; *where* should not be used unless the definition involves place or location.

Wrong A foul is *when* (or *where*) the ball leaves the court.

Right A foul is made *when* the ball leaves the court during the playing period. (time involved)

Right A foul is made at the place *where* the ball crosses the foul line. (place involved)

WHEN, WHILE
When refers to a fixed period of time; *while* to duration of time.

When you are willing to talk, I will listen. (fixed time: as soon as you are ready to talk)

While you talk, I will listen. (time duration: during the time that you talk)

WHILE, ALTHOUGH, BUT, WHEREAS
While is often used colloquially to mean *although, but,* and *whereas.*

Colloquial I like Mary, *while* I like Jeanne better.

Formal I like Mary, *but* I like Jeanne better.

Colloquial Mary is fat, *while* Jeanne is slim.

Formal Mary is fat, *whereas* Jeanne is slim.

INTERJECTIONS

An interjection is a word of exclamation which expresses emotion, but which has no grammatical relation to the rest of the sentence.

Oh! Hey! Whoa! Ouch! Ha, ha! Boo!

Many words that generally serve as other parts of speech may be used as interjections:

Well! Heavens! Nuts! Run! Good!

SENTENCES

The division of words into eight main parts of speech–a useful way to point out their individual characteristics–is technically termed *accidence.* But words are seldom used alone; how they are put together in sentences is termed *syntax.*

A *sentence* is a group of words expressing a complete thought. It may make a statement, ask a question, give a command, or express an exclamation.

Antarctica is the seventh continent.

Are Europe and Asia separate continents?

See America first!

So this is Africa!

However, a complete thought may be expressed by a single word: a man entering an elevator and saying, "Down"; the answers ("Are you going?") "No," ("Where is it?") "Here," or ("How do you feel?") "Happy." The concept of a *complete thought* is satisfied by such limited sentences as the telegraphic ARRIVING LAGUARDIA FRIDAY. HOME BEFORE SIX. LOVE STANLEY; or the journalistic headline LABOR UNIONS/HIT JOB LOSSES. But in addition, readers expect most sentences to be *grammatically complete.*

Grammatical Completion

The grammatically complete *simple sentence* consists of a subject and a predicate. The *subject* is a noun or a noun equivalent (pronoun in the nominative case, noun clause, gerund, infinitive) naming the person, place, or thing with which the sentence is chiefly concerned. The *predicate* is the verb or verb phrase asserting something about the subject.

Children (subject) *play* (predicate).

This simple sentence may be expanded and made more complicated (or significant) in various ways.

The subject may be modified:

Happy children play.

The predicate may be modified:

Children play *hard*.

Or the verb may be given a complement:

Children play *games*.

It becomes a *compound sentence* when two or more subjects attach to a single predicate:

Children and *adults* play.

or when two or more predicates follow from a single subject:

Children *play* and *sleep*.

or when two or more simple sentences closely related in thought are joined by commas, semicolons, or coordinating conjunctions:

Children play, men work, and women manage.

However complicated it may become, the sentence rests on the solid base of subject and predicate. This is true in the *declarative sentence* (above), the *interrogative sentence:*

Do children play?

the *exclamatory sentence:*

How happily the children play!

and the *imperative sentence:*

Play, children! (the subject, *you,* is understood)

The sentence may be made more flexible and expressive by the use of phrases and clauses.

Phrases

A *phrase* is a group of words used as a single part of speech (noun, adjective, adverb, or verb). It does not contain a subject and a predicate.

NOUN PHRASE: It is impossible *not to pity him; trying to help* him is a problem.

ADVERBIAL PHRASE: *By Monday* they were gone. I hung it *on the wall.*

ADJECTIVE PHRASE: A man *of honor,* a name *to admire.*

VERB PHRASE: He *has asked* for you; he *must have forgotten* already.

Phrases may also be classified by form:

A *prepositional phrase* consists of a preposition and its object, and any accompanying modifiers. It is used as an adjective or adverb.

At once they left *for the big town.* (prepositional phrases used as adverbs)

The man *with the hoe.* (used as adjective)

He felt lost *in the impersonal clamor* (used as adverb) *of the advertising industry.* (used as adjective)

An *infinitive phrase* consists of an infinitive (and its object, if present), and any accompanying modifiers. It is used as a noun, adjective, or adverb.

I want *to see* (infinitive) *the moon* (object). (infinitive phrase used as noun)

Professor Thomson is the man *to know.* (used as adjective)

A diplomat must be able *to make* (infinitive) *the most* (object) *of the existing situation.* (prepositional phrase, adjective modifying *the most,* used as adverb)

A *participial phrase* consists of a participle (and its object, if present), and any accompanying modifiers. It is used as an adjective.

Thinking quickly, he regained his poise.

The plane *carrying* (participle) *the serum* (object) arrived in time.

Shirley, *earnestly* (adverb modifying the next word, *talking*) *talking* (participle) *to the group* (prepositional phrase, adverb modifying *talking*), signaled Carrie to wait.

A *gerund phrase* consists of a gerund (and its object, if present), and any accompanying modifiers. It is used as a noun.

Daily *swimming* kept him in trim.

Flying (gerund) *a kite* (object) can be hard work.

His editor advised *writing* (gerund) *on a totally new subject.* (prepositional phrase, adjective modifying *writing*)

A *verb phrase* consists of a verb and its auxiliaries.

I *will have seen* him by then.

The Senate *could* hardly *have foreseen* the result of its action.

Clauses

A *clause* is a group of words containing a subject and a predicate. It may be independent or dependent. An *independent clause* is, essentially, a sentence; it differs only in its capitalization and/or punctuation. In the following example the independent clause can stand alone by capitalizing *he* and adding a period after *plotters*.

> Mindful of his honor, *he avoided every contact with the plotters* and refused to listen to their schemes.

A *dependent clause* cannot stand alone. It is connected to an independent clause by a relative pronoun, present or implied (*who, which, that*), or by a subordinating conjunction (*after, because, since, while,* etc.) and functions as a part of the sentence–as noun, adjective, or adverb.

> *That everyone was against him* was his constant complaint. (noun clause, subject)
>
> He estimated *which of the problems he could solve.* (noun clause, object of verb)
>
> In the afternoon we came to *what was evidently the main road.* (noun clause, object of preposition *to*)
>
> The man *who fails at everything he tries* may not be trying. (adjective clause, modifying *man*)
>
> He may succeed *if he tries a completely new approach.* (adverbial clause, modifying *succeed*)

A dependent clause need not be so complete as these examples. Often, especially in spoken language and informal writing, the connective between independent clause and dependent adjective clause is merely implied and not expressed.

> The man *he said was coming* never showed up. (*Who* or *that* is understood.)

Sometimes in informal speech or writing a dependent clause contains neither subject nor verb.

> *When crossing,* look both ways. (*When you are crossing* is understood.)
>
> His clothes were old *though clean.* (*Though they were clean* is understood.)

Constructions such as these are called *elliptical clauses.* When properly related to the main clause, an elliptical clause adds economy and punch to writing. The dependent clause used as an adjective (*adjective clause*) is called *restrictive* if it adds information necessary to identify the subject, or restricts it to a special case.

> The boy *you met last Friday* telephoned again.
>
> The man *who can plan ahead* is automatically at an advantage.
>
> Rebellions *that are successful* are recorded as revolutions.

If the subject requires no further identification after being named, the clause is *nonrestrictive,* and simply adds additional information.

> Jaspar, *who never gave up,* finally hit on a way to catch the chipmunk.

There is only one Jaspar being discussed, and the reader presumably knows who he is; the nonrestrictive clause is not essential to the meaning of the sentence, though it enriches it. Here are two more examples of nonrestrictive clauses.

> He sat on the table, *which could barely support him.*
>
> She was sure that the man, *whom she had not met,* must be her long-lost brother.

Who (whom) and *which* may introduce either restrictive or nonrestrictive clauses, but *that* introduces only restrictive clauses. Relative pronouns may be omitted only in restrictive clauses.

> The man *we hoped to see* has left. (Restrictive *who* is understood.)
>
> We all liked the pie *she baked.* (Restrictive *that* is understood.)

Nonrestrictive clauses are set off by commas, and often the various choices of punctuation can give the sentence radically different meanings.

RESTRICTIVE CLAUSE: Engineers who have little understanding of theory are rarely put in charge of a program.

NON-RESTRICTIVE CLAUSE: Engineers, who have little understanding of theory, are rarely put in charge of a program.

The first is a warning; the second is a sneer. (For the specific rules on punctuating restrictive and nonrestrictive clauses, see page 6.)

Kinds of Sentences

A *simple sentence* contains only one independent clause, however modified.

> In times of economic expansion almost any investor may seem a financial wizard by his luck on the stock market.

Stripped of the adverbial prepositional phrases *in times of economic expansion* and *by his luck,* the adjective phrase *on the stock market,* the adverb *almost,* the adjective *financial,* this example reveals itself as basically the simple sentence *(almost any) investor may seem a wizard.*

A *compound sentence* contains two or more coordinate independent clauses, joined by a coordinating conjunction:

> He tried hard, but he simply had no talent.

or by a conjunctive adverb preceded by a semicolon:

> It had begun to rain; however, they had brought umbrellas.

or by a semicolon (or colon) alone:

> He was tired of life; he was afraid to die.

> The Greeks made their decision: They would resist the Persian invasion.

A *complex sentence* contains one independent clause and one or more dependent clauses.

> However fast we ran, the ball ran faster.

> He whispered that he was sure (that) he had recognized one of the men who had come in. (three dependent clauses, the second with *that* understood)

A *compound-complex* sentence contains two or more independent clauses, and one or more dependent clauses.

> Atlhough the weather forecast promised rain, the sky was cloudless, and the dry spell continued.

Spelling and Vocabulary

Spelling is not the horrendous problem that many students think it is. By the time they have reached senior high school, and certainly by the time they finish college, most people have learned most of the words they will ever use, and they spell most of them correctly. The problem is caused by those few words which are misspelled over and over again. Another, but quite separate, problem is the rapid rate at which new words are added to our vocabularly, notably those emerging from enlarging technology and from areas of professional specialization.

For the average person afflicted with habits of bad spelling, corrective measures are not difficult to determine or apply. If you fall in this category, you probably spell most words quite correctly, and only fall down, with depressing recurrence, on certain kinds of words. To improve, you need not relearn how to spell, but only ferret out and concentrate on those specific areas where you have trouble. You will probably find that your problems are confined to certain special areas. Perhaps you are confused by words with *-able* or *-ible* endings, or by the question of whether to double final consonants or not. Once you have a list of such troublesome words–and the real job is running them down–you can take effective curative measures. Brief but regular periods devoted to memorizing the correct spellings will quickly produce results, particularly if the memorizing period is just before you go to bed.

BUILDING A VOCABULARY

We tend to avoid words we do not know how to spell, and in so doing we forget them by nonuse. With the spelling handicap reduced we can explore the various ways of acquiring a large and useful vocabulary.

In school the teacher advises, "Look up in the

dictionary every word you don't know and write it, with its definition, in a notebook. Then examine the meaning of its root, or roots, also possible suffix and/or prefix. Pronounce the word over to yourself, and finally use it in speaking and writing." This remains the surest technique, but it is slow, and demands more conscientious application than most people are prepared to bring to it.

The best way to build a vocabulary is to broaden one's intellectual horizons. An interest and a delight in words and the ideas they convey will bring about attentive listening and wide and thorough reading. It can give impetus to frequent use of the dictionary, memorization of selected vocabulary lists, and the study of the origin and development of words (etymology).

We all possess three basic vocabularies–a speaking, a writing, and a reading vocabulary. Of the three, the reading vocabularly contains by far the largest number of words. As we read extensively, all three vocabularies will expand, but at surprisingly different rates. The reading vocabulary increases the fastest. Only relatively few words will seep down into the speaking and writing vocabularies. We recognize any number of words when we see them in print, but they are neither on the tips of our tongues nor on the points of our pens–ready for us to use when they are applicable.

The main problem is to make the newly learned words accessible when we are speaking–but more especially when we are writing. The words we have learned must become familiar friends; not only should they be recognizable when we see and hear them again, but they should be instantly available.

A much surer way than the list method for making a new word your very own is to use the word in a sentence of your own construction. Don't attempt to do this with every new word you come upon. Be selective. Take the words that appeal to and interest you–words that you think you may want to use again in the future. When a word does appeal to you, go to the dictionary for help in defining it precisely. When you have the definition (or, rather, definitions, for most words have a number of meanings), don't simply accept the dictionary example of how it is used. Compose your own illustrative sentence to fix the new-found word in your mind. Let the sentence express something that is essentially *you*–some interest of yours. Perhaps the word can be used in relation to some hobby or to a friend.

A few words of caution: Don't be too quick to flaunt the new words in public. Don't insist on forcing them into your very next composition or report. You may have a fair idea of the meaning of a word; you may have a good sentence in mind. At the same time, you may not be using the word in precisely its right context. A good idea is to wait a bit before exposing the word to public hearing or view. For example, if the word has to do with biology, try the sentence out on a friend who is at home in this field, and make sure from him that you are using it correctly. This is the most creative way of fixing new words in your mind. It can be guaranteed to work, and even more important, the new words will be ready for recall and use when the occasion arises.

PRONUNCIATION

Just as important as the written word is the spoken or sounded word. The sounded word precedes the written word by thousands of years, and of course without the one there could not be the other. And just as there are correct ways to use words in writing, so are there correct ways to sound them in speaking.

English is supposedly a phonetic language. That is, the letters of our alphabet stand for sounds, and the way words are spoken or pronounced is supposed to correspond to the way they are spelled. In practice it doesn't always work out that way. In the early years, English was more or less phonetic, but time has brought drastic changes in pronunciation, while changes in spelling have not kept pace. (It is an interesting paradox that the language has been remarkably liberal in the matter of pronunciation yet remarkably conservative in the matter of spelling.) It is the gulf that has been created between pronunciation and spelling–widened during the last several centuries by the invention of the printing press–that has transformed English from a phonetic to a most unphonetic language.

To fill this gulf, our dictionaries respell countless thousands of words according to the way they are actually sounded in practice, and they construct elaborate phonetic alphabets that correspond to the true sounds (see page 38). The dictionaries don't always succeed, however, since there is considerable difference in the way people speak. Still, the dictionaries are our only guide, and if you follow the phonetic respellings of a reputable dictionary, you will be sure of pronouncing words correctly in most instances.

In the United States, there are three more or less distinct types of pronunciation–the northeastern, the southern, and the northwestern. Even when pronunciation differs from the norm or standard as given in dictionaries, it is nevertheless considered correct and proper as long as the pronunciation is used by the educated people of any one of these regions.

Common Errors

Do not sound the *t* in most words ending in *-sten* and *stle*.

fasten
wrestle
chasten

Do not sound the *t* in the following words:

often
soften

Beware of dropping the *g* in words that end in *-ing* and in *-ength*.

believing *not* believin'

thinking *not* thinkin'

Beware of dropping the letters *d, t,* and *l*. Even in the South, the practice of dropping these letters is regarded as vulgar by educated Southerners.

old *not* ol'

just *not* jus'

self *not* se'f

Beware of dropping the letter *r*. In New England and the South, correct pronunciation sanctions the substitution of the short *a* for the letter *r* in certain words. But to drop the *r* altogether in these words is regarded as vulgar (not *do'* for *door* or *fo'* for *for*). In these same regions, on the other hand, it is perfectly proper to drop the *r* in words such as *car* and *farther*.

Beware of the so-called intrusive *r*. Do not insert an *r* in a word where it does not belong, nor between two words when one word ends with a vowel and the following word begins with a vowel.

spoil *not* spurl

law and order *not* lawr and order

the idea (*not* idear) of it

USE OF THE DICTIONARY

Do you prize the dictionary as the most valuable tool in your possession to help you choose and use words properly? If you answer no, you are among a majority of students who feel the same way. If you answer yes, you are in a minority who understand what the dictionary is–and who also know how to use it. For the chief reason most people neglect the dictionary is that they just don't know what it's all about. The following pages show how to use the dictionary the way it should be used.

Meanings of Words

A word sometimes has as many as fifty or sixty different meanings or shades of meaning. This is not common, but the point to remember is that a word doesn't necessarily have just one meaning. Most words have several meanings, according to the ways they are used in a sentence. Moreover, the same word changes its form, usually its spelling, and often its pronunciation, according to the part of speech it takes. Therefore, never take the definition immediately following an entry as final. You must read–or at least scan–all its definitions. Different meanings are usually numbered.

Spelling

Occasionally an entry will have two or more different spellings of the same word. This means that all given spellings are in general use. All are acceptable, but the one given first is usually the preferred form. Irregular spellings of the plural form of a word are also given. Regular formations, however, are not given. Thus, when a plural spelling is omitted we can take it for granted that the word forms its plural in the regular way, by adding *s* to the singular and by adding *-es* to words ending in *s, x, z, ch,* and *sh*. Plurals of compound words are also generally omitted when they are formed in the same way as the plurals of the main word. British spelling variations are preceded by the abbreviation *Brit.* Such forms are acceptable in Great Britain, not in the United States.

Inflectional Forms

Often a word is spelled in various ways according to its use; we call these various spellings the *inflectional forms* of the word. For example, plurals of nouns are infiectional forms of the nouns, various tenses of verbs are inflectional forms of the verbs, while comparative and intensive forms of adjectives are their inflectional forms.

A good dictionary lists the inflectional forms that are irregular or that give trouble in spelling. When two inflected forms are listed for a verb, the first is the form for both the past tense and the past participle. When three forms are given, the first is the form for the past tense, the second the past participle, and the third the present participle.

Inflections formed in the regular way are seldom given, even in good dictionaries. In addition to the spelling of plurals, forms regarded as regular inflections include, for verbs, present tenses formed by adding *-s* or *-es,* past tenses and past participles formed by adding *-ed,* and present participles formed by adding *-ing*. Comparatives and superlatives formed in the regular way (by adding *-er* and *-est* to the positive form) are also omitted in most entries.

Usage Labels

Various labels signify a word's status in actual usage. These labels are extremely important. They indicate under what circumstances a word may properly be used. The conventional labels are: *colloquial* (used in conversation but not in formal writing), *slang* (restricted to rare occasions in informal conversation and informal writing), *obsolete* (no longer used), *archaic* (used only in special contexts, as in church ritual, but no longer in general use), *poetic* (restricted to poetry), *dialect* (restricted to special geographical areas), and *British* (characteristically British rather than American). Words that have more than one meaning are generally treated as follows: when the label follows the number introducing a definition, it applies to that definition only; when it precedes a number, it applies to all the definitions that follow.

Syllable Division

The division of all words into syllables is a universal practice of dictionaries. This is done partly as an aid to pronunciation and word derivation, and partly to show how a word is divided at the end of a line when there isn't enough space to write the full word on the same line. Syllable division is indicated by centered dots or small dashes. Some dictionaries divide the word's main entry into syllables, others indicate them in the phonetic respelling (see below) that immediately follows the entry. Many persons confuse the dot (·) or short dash (-) with the longer, heavier dash (–) that indicates a hyphen in compound words. The following is a sample compound word entry in Webster's *New World Dictionary* (note the difference between the syllable dot and the hyphen):

hel·ter–skel·ter

Accent Marks

Dictionary entries also carry accent marks (ʹ) to indicate which particular syllable or part of the word should be stressed. Some dictionaries place the accent marks in the entry itself, others in the respelling that follows the entry. The important thing to remember is that the accent mark appears immediately *after* the syllable to be stressed. When two syllables in a word are to be accented, the syllable that receives the lighter stress is marked by a light accent mark (ʹ). It should be pronounced with less stress than syllables marked with the dark accent mark, but with more stress than syllables that carry no accent mark at all. Words of one syllable have no accent marks. Instead of light and dark marks, some dictionaries use single and double accent marks. The single mark indicates heavy stress; double marks, light stress.

Phonetic "Respelling"

A wide gulf often exists between how words are spelled and how they are pronounced (see page 36). For this reason, all good dictionaries give the phonetic spelling of troublesome words, in addition to the way they are conventionally spelled. The phonetic spelling indicates how to sound out the various parts of a word in actual speech. It is termed the "respelling." Surprisingly few people know how to handle a respelling, but it is very simple.

A word respelling may consist of a simple rearrangement or substitution of vowels and consonants. It may also consist of symbols called "diacritical marks," which appear over the vowels. These marks indicate when a vowel is to be pronounced long, short, etc. It is not necessary to know the names of these marks, and it is not even necessary to memorize how to make the sounds of any particular mark. For they appear in a key at the bottom (or top) of each page (or alternate page) of all good dictionaries. And next to each mark is a short word that anyone can readily pronounce and that shows just what sound is called for. Sometimes the mark is contained in the short word instead of appearing separately. The marks appear in alphabetical order for ready reference. All you need to pronounce a word is to refer to this key listing. You find the vowel with the diacritical mark that corresponds to the mark in the respelling of the word given in the main entry. You pronounce it just as it is sounded in the short word given in the key.

Suppose that we want to be sure of the proper pronunciation of the name of the composer Wagner. The entry in Webster's *New World Dictionary* (Compact Desk Edition) gives the following respelling after the main entry:

vägʹnẽr

Now we immediately know that the beginning letter *W* is pronounced as a *V*. But how about the *ä* and the *ẽ*? These are termed "two-dot *a*" and "tilde *e*" respectively, but we don't need to know this. At the bottom of the page is the following key list:

> **fat**, **āpe**, **bâre**, **cär**; **ten**, **ēven**, **ovẽr**; **is**, **bīte**; **lot**, **gō**, **hôrn**, **tōōl**, **look**; **oil**, **out**; **up**, **ūse**, **fũr**; **ə** for *a* in *ago*; ***th***in, ***th***en; **zh**, leisure; η, ring; **ë**, Fr. leur; **ö**, Fr. feu; Fr. mo*n;* **ü**, Fr. duc; **kh**, G. ich, doch. ‡ foreign; < derived from

We can see that the *a* with the two dots above it is in the short word *cär,* so we know that the *a* in *Wagner* is pronounced as the *a* in *car*. Similarly, the *e* is contained in the short word *ovẽr,* which is how the *e* in *Wagner* should be sounded.

A comprehensive version of the phonetic key appears in the front pages of your dictionary. Ordinarily the simpler key on the pages with the entries is sufficient. Phonetic alphabets vary somewhat between dictionaries, but when you are acquainted with the markings of one, you will be able to interpret the others easily.

One mark that may give some trouble is the so-called *schwa,* or inverted *e* (ə). Not all dictionaries employ the schwa, but it is coming into increasing use, and you should know about it.

When the schwa (ə) appears in a respelling, it always takes the place of a vowel. It is a sign that the vowel is reduced in strength of stress. It has an enfeebled *uh* sound, as the *a* has in the words *ago* and *about.* The schwa can present difficulties, as you can't be sure just how to sound it in every case. You will soon get the knack of it, however, after you see it used a number of times in a dictionary. Its purpose, to repeat, is to reduce, almost to ignore, the vowel's stress. The schwa's importance will be apparent when you realize how dull and unpleasant English would sound if every vowel were clearly stressed and enunciated. To relieve the monotony of vowel enunciation, there are times when vowels should lose their force, and the schwa tells us just when to pass quickly over them.

Word Derivation

The chief languages upon which English is founded are Anglo-Saxon, Old Norse, Old French, Middle English, Latin, and Greek. The abbreviations used by dictionaries to specify the language (or languages) from which a word is derived are, in order of their appearance above: AS., ON., OF., ME., L., and Gk. Additional language abbreviations are listed in the front of the dictionary. The symbol > means "derived from." Generally, word derivation information appears in brackets, either at the beginning or at the end of the entry. A question mark following the derivation signifies that it is only a guess and at best is uncertain.

Frequently Misspelled Words

Words shown with an asterisk below also have an alternate correct spelling. See any good dictionary for the alternate spelling.

A
abominable
abridgment
absence
abundance
abundant
academic
academically
academy
accelerating
accentuation
acceptable
acceptance
accepting
accessible
accessory*
accidental
accidentally
acclaim
accommodate
accompanied
accompanies
accompaniment
accompanying
accomplish
accountant
accuracy
accurate
accurately
accuser
accuses
accusing
accustom
achievement
achieving
acknowledgment*
acquaintance
acquire
across
actuality
actually
acutely
adequately
adhering
admirable
admissible*
admission
admittance
adolescence
adolescent
advancement
advantageous
adversaries
advertisement*
advertiser*
advertising*
advice
advise
aerial
aesthetic
affect
affiliate
afraid
against
ageless
aging
aggravate
aggressive
alibis
allegedly
allergies
alleviate
allotment
allotted
allowed
allows
all right*
all together
already
altar
alter
alternate
alternative
altogether
amateur
amenable
amiable
amicably
among
amount
amplified
amusing
analogies
analysis
analyze
anarchy
anecdote
angrily
annihilate
announcing
annually
anonymous
another
anticipated
antique
anxieties
apiece
apologetically
apologized
apology
apostrophe
appall*
apparatus
apparent
appearance
applies
applying
appraise
appreciate
appreciation
apprehend
approaches
appropriate
approval
approximate
apropos
aptly
aquarium
arbitrary
arduous
area
aren't
arguing
argument
arise
arising
armies
arouse
arousing
arrangement
arrears
arriving
artfully
article
artificial
ascent
ascetic
asinine
asphalt
asphyxiation
aspiration
assassin
assemblies
assertiveness
assiduous
assignment
assimilate
assistance
associating
assortment
assuming
asthma
astonish
astronaut
astute
asylum
atheist
athlete
athletic
atrocious
atrocity
attachment
attack
attempts
attendance
attendant
attended
attirement
attitude
attractive
attribute
audacious
audacity
audience
augment
auspicious
authenticity
author
authoritarian
authoritative
authority
authorization
authorize
autumn
available
awareness
awesome
awfully

B
babbling
balancing
ballerina
balminess
bankruptcy
bare
barely
bargain
barrenness
barrier
barroom
bashfulness
basically
basis
battling
bawdiness
bazaar
bearable
beauteous
beautified
beautiful
beautifying
beauty
become
becoming
before
began
beggar
beginner
beginning
begrudging
beguile
behaving
behavior
belatedly

belief
believe
belittling
belligerence
beneath
benefactor
beneficent
beneficial
benefited*
benevolence
benign
biannual
bicycle
bicycling
bigamy
bigger
biggest
binoculars
biscuit
biting
bitten
blameless
bluing
blurred
blurry
boastfully
bohemian
boisterous
boloney
booby trap
boring
born
borne
bossiness
botanical
bottling
boulevard
bouncing
boundary
bounties
braggadocio
breath
breathe
breezier
brief
brilliance
brilliant
brimming
Britain
Britannica
brochure
bronchial
brutally
budget
bulging
bulletin
bumptious
buoy
buoyant
buried
bursar
bury
bushiness
business
busy

C

cabaret
cafeteria
caffeine
calamity
calculation
calendar
callous
callus
calves
camaraderie
canceled*
candescence
canniness
canning
canoeing
capably
capacity
capitalism
capital
capitol
capricious
captaincy
captivity
careen
career
careless
cargoes
caribou
caricature
caring
carnally
carousing
carpentry
carpeted
carried
carrier
carries
carrousel*
carrying
cascade
casserole
casually
cataclysmal
cataloged*
catalyst
catastrophe
category
caught
causally
causing
caustic
cautious
ceaseless
celibacy
celluloid
cemetery
centrifugal
centuries
ceramics
cerebellum
certainly
certificate
certified
cessation
chafe
chagrined
chalice
challenge
chancing
changeable
changing
chaotic
characteristic
characterized
charging
charlatan
chastise
chatty
chauffeur
chauvinism
cheerier
chief
children
chilliness
chiseling*
chivalry
choice
choose
choosing
chose
choreography*
Christianity
chronically
chronicle
cigarette
cinema
cipher
circling
circuit
circulating
circumstantial
cite
citizen
claimant
clairvoyance*
clamorous
clarify
classification
claustrophobia
cleanly
cleanness
cleanse
clemency
climactic
climatic
closely
clothes
cloudiest
coarse
cocoa
coerce
cognizance*
cohort
coincidence
collaborate
collectively
collegiate
collision
colloquial
colossal
combining
comfortable
coming
commentary
commercial
commiserate
commission
commitment
committee
commodities
commotion
communicate
companies
comparative
comparing
compassion
compatible
compel
compelled
competition
competitive
competitor
complacence
complement
completely
compliment
comprehendible
comprehensible
compromising
concede
conceit
conceive
conceivable
concentrate
concern
concession
condemn
condescend
conditionally
conferred
confidentially
confuse
confusion
congenial
conniving
connotation
connote
conquer
conscience
conscientious
conscious
consciousness
consequence
consequently
conservatively
considerably
considerately
consistency
consistent
conspicuous
constancy
consul
contagious
contemporary
contemptible
contemptuous
continuing
continuously
contrarily
contritely
contrivance
controlled
controlling
controversial
controversy
convalesce
convenience
convenient
conveyance
convincingly
coolly
cooperate
cooperative
coordinate
coordination

corporal
correlate
correspondent
corroborate
corruption
council
counsel
counselor*
countenance
countries
courtesy
cowardice
cozier
crazily
create
credibility
crescendo
crescent
crevice
criminally
cringing
criticism
criticize
crucially
crudely
cruelly
cruelty
crystal
cultivating
cultural
cunning
curing
curiosity
curious
curriculum
cycle
cynicism

D
dahlia
dallying
dauntless
dazedly
debatable*
deceased
deceitfully
deceive
decent
decided
decision
dedicating
deductible
defenseless
deferred
deficiency
define
definitely
definition
degeneracy
deliberating
delicately
delightfully
delinquency
demoralize
denied
denominational
denouncement
department
dependent*
deplorable
depreciate
depressant
depression
derangement
derisive
descend
describe
description
desert
deservedly
desirability
desire
desolately
despair
desperate
desperation
despising
despondency
desert
dessert
destitution
destruction
detach
deteriorate
determining
detriment
deuce
devastating
development*
deviation
device
devise
dexterity
diabolic
diagonally
dialogue
dictionary
difference
different
difficult
dilapidated
dilemma
diligence
diminutive
diner
dinghy
dining
dinner
dinosaur
diphthong
dipsomania
direness
disagreeable
disappear
disappoint
disapproval
disarray
disastrous
disbelief
discernible*
disciple
discipline
disconsolately
discourteous
discreditable
discrimination
discussion
disease
disguise
disgusted
dishevelment
disillusioned
disintegrate
dismally
dismissal
disparaging
disparity
dispersal
dispirited
dispossess
disprove
disqualified
disreputable
dissatisfied
dissension
dissoluteness
dissolve
dissuading
distraught
distressingly
disuse
diversely
divide
divine
divisible
docilely
doesn't
dolorous
dominant
dormitories
double
doubtfulness
drastically
dropped
drudgery
dually
during
duteous
dye
dyed
dyeing
dying

E
eager
easel
easily
eccentric
echelon
ecstasy*
eczema
edified
educating
eerily
effect
efficiency
efficient
effortlessly
egotistical
eighth
eightieth
either
elaborate
elapse
elegy
element
elementary
eligible
eliminate
emaciate
embarrass
embarrassment
embellish
embitter
emergencies
emerging
eminence
emperor
emphasize
employment
emptiness
emulate
enabling
enamel
enamored
encourage
encyclopedia
endeavor
energies
engaging
enjoy
enormous
enough
enrapture
enroute
ensconce
ensuing
enterprise
entertain
entertainment
enthusiastic
enthusiastically
enticement
entirely
entrance
enumerate
enunciate
envelop
envelope
enviable
environment
epitome
equable
equally
equipment
equipped
erratic
erroneous
escapade
escape
especially
essence
et cetera*
ethical
etiquette
eulogy
evacuate
evaporate
eventful
everything
evidently
exaggerate
exceed
excellence
excellent
except
excessive
excising
excitable

excruciating
excusing
exercise
existence
existent
expelled
expense
experience
experiment
explanation
expulsion
extensively
extenuate
extremely

F

fabricator
facetious
facility
facing
facsimile
factually
fallacy
falsely
falsified
familiar
families
fanatical
fancied
fantasies
fantasy
farewell
fascinate
fashions
fastidious
fatally
fatigue
favorable
favorite
feasible
ferocity
fertility
fetish
fiancé
fiancée
fickleness
fictitious
fidelity
field
fierce
fifteenth
figuring
finally
financially
financier
finesse
fitfully
flamboyant
flammable
flatterer
flexible
flimsiness
flippancy
flourish
fluidity
fluorescent
forbearance
forbidding
foreigners
forfeit
forgotten
formally
formerly
formidable
fortieth
fortitude
fortunately
forty
forward
fourth
freer
frequency
friendliness
frightfully
frivolous
fulfill
fundamentally
furrier
further

G

gaiety
galvanizing
gamble
gambol
garish
garnishee
garrulous
gaseous
gauche
gauging
gazette
generally
generating
generic
geniality
genius
gentlest
gesticulating
ghastliest
gladden
glamorous
glamour*
glorified
gluttony
government
governor
gradually
grammar
grammatically
grandeur
grandiloquence
grandiose
graphically
gratefully
gratification
gratuitous
greasing
grieving
grimacing
group
grudgingly
gruesome
guaranteed
guidance
guiding
guileless
guillotine
gullible
gutturally
gypped

H

habitable
hackneyed
hallucination
halving
hamster
handicapped
handled
handsomely
happen
happened
happiness
harangue
harassment
harmfully
harmonizing
hear
height
heinous
hemorrhage
hereditary
heresy
heretofore
heroes
heroic
heroine
hesitancy
heterogeneity
heuristic
hibernate
hierarchy
hilarity
hindrance
hirable
hoarsely
holocaust
homage
homely
homilies
homogeneous
hopeful
hopeless
hoping
horizontally
horrendous
horrified
hospitality
hospitalization
huge
human
humane
humanistic
humidified
humiliating
humorist
humorous
hundred
hundredth
hunger
hungrily
hungry
hydrophobia
hygiene
hygienic
hyphenation
hypnotizing
hypocrisy
hypocrite
hypothesis
hysterical

I

icicle
ideally
ideologies
idiocy
idiomatic
idiosyncrasy
ignoramus
ignorance
ignorant
illegible
illiteracy
illuminate
illusory
imagery
imaginary
imagination
imagine
imbibing
imitating
immaculate
immanent
immediately
immense
immigrant
imminent
immobilized
impartially
impasse
impeccable
impeding
imperceptible
impersonally
impinging
implausible
imploring
impoliteness
importance
impresario
impressionistic
improbability
improvement
inadequacy
inappeasable
inattentively
incalculable
incessantly
incidentally
incomparable
incomprehensible
inconceivable
inconsequential
inconstancy
incorrigible
increase
indefinite
independence
independent
indeterminate
indexes*
indispensable
individually
industries
inebriation
inefficiency
inevitable
inexcusable
inferred
infinitely
inflame

inflammation
inflammatory
influence
influential
informally
infringement
infuriating
ingenious
ingenuity
ingenuous
ingratiate
ingredient
inimitable
initiative
injurious
innervate
inoculate
inquiries
inscrutable
inseparable
insincere
insouciance
installment
instinctive
insuperable
insusceptible
intangible
intellect
intelligence
intelligent
interceding
interchanging
interest
interference
interim
interlining
intermediary
intermittent
internally
interpretation
interrogator
interrupt
intervening
intimately
intricately
intrigue
intuition
involve
invulnerability
irascible
ironical
irrationality
irrefutable
irrelevant
irreproachable
irresistible
irreverence
irreversible
irritable
irritating
irruptive
issuing
itinerary
its
it's

J

jauntily
jealousy
jeopardy
jettison
jocundity
jolliness
jovially
judgment*
judicially
juiciness
juvenile

K

kaleidoscope
keenness
khaki
kidnaped*
kindlier
kinescope
knowledge

L

laboratory
laborer
laboriously
labyrinth
laconic
laid
lamentable
languorous
largess*
laryngitis
lascivious
lassitude
lately
later
laureate
lazier
lead (v.)
lead (n.)
leafy
learnedly
legacy
legality
legibility
leisurely
lengthening
leniency
lenses
lesion
lethally
lethargy
letup
levying
libelous*
liberally
libidinous
license*
licentious
liege
likelihood
likely
likeness
limousine
linage
lineage
listener
literally
literary
literate
literature
litigation
liveliest
livelihood
liveliness
lives
lodging
loneliness
lonely
longitudinal
looniness
loose
lose
losing
loss
lugubrious
luminosity
lustfulness
luxury
lyricism

M

macabre*
macaroni
mademoiselle
magazine
magnanimity
magnificence
magnificent
maintenance
malefactor
malleable
manageability
management
maneuver
manful
manginess
maniacal
manifesto
manner
manning
manually
manufacturers
marauder
marionette
marriage
marveled
masquerade
massacre
massacring
material
maternally
mathematics
matriculating
matter
maturely
maturing
mausoleum
maybe
meant
measurement
mechanics
medallion
medical
medicine
medieval*
mediocrity
melancholia
melancholy
melee
meltable
memorability
memorizing
menacingly
mentally
merchandise
mere
merely
methods
microscopic
middling
mien
mightily
mileage
milieu
millennium
millionth
mimicker
mincingly
miniature
minority
minuscule
minutes
miraculous
mirrored
misalliance
misanthrope
miscalculation
miscellaneous
mischief
mischievous
misconstruing
mismanagement
misshapen
misspell
mistakable
moderately
moisturize
mollification
momentarily
monetary
monitor
monopolies
monosyllable
monotonous
monstrosity
moodily
moral
morale
morally
morbidity
morosely
mortally
mortifying
mosaic
mosquitoes
motif
mottoes*
mousiness
movable*
mucilage
multiplicity
multitudinous
mundanely
munificent
musically
musing
mutuality
mysterious

N

naïve*
naïveté*
namely
narcissus
narrative
natively

naturalistic
naturally
naughtily
nauseate
nearly
necessary
needlessly
nefarious
negativism
negligence
negligible
Negroes
neighbor
neither
neurotic
nevertheless
nicety
niggardly
nihilism
nimbly
nineteen
ninetieth
ninety
ninth
noble
noisily
nominally
noncombustible
normally
nostalgia
noticeable
noticing
notifying
notoriety
nourishment
nudity
nuisance
nullify
numerous
nuptial

O

obedience
objectively
obliging
obliquely
obliterate
obsequious
observance
obsess
obsolescent
obstacle
obstinately
obtuseness
occasion
occupancy
occupying
occur
occurred
occurrence
occurring
o'clock
oculist
oddly
odoriferous
odyssey
Oedipus
off
offense
offensively
officially
officiating
officious
omission
omit
omitted
oncoming
opaque
operate
opinion
opponent
opportunely
opportunity
oppose
opposite
oppression
optimism
optionally
oracular
orating
orderliness
ordinarily
ordinary
organization
original
ornamental
ornateness
orthodoxy
oscillate
ostentatious
ostracism
outrageous
outweigh
overdevelopment
overrun

P

pacified
pageant
paid
painstaking
palatable
palladium
palpitating
pamphlets
pancreas
panicky
pantomime
papier-mâché*
parable
parading
paradoxically
parallel
paralleled
paralyzed
parental
parentheses
parenthesis
parliament
paroxysm
parsimonious
partaking
partiality
participating
participial
participle
particular
passable
passed
passionately
passivity
past
pasteurize
pastime
pastoral
pastorale
pastries
pathetically
pathologist
patriarch
patriotically
patrolling
patronize
paunchy
pausing
peace
pealing
peculiar
pecuniary
pedagogue
pedagogy
pedantic
pedestrian
peeve
peignoir
penetrate
penicillin
penitent
penniless
penology
penury
perambulating
perceive
perceptible
percipience
peremptorily
perfidious
performance
perfunctory
perilous
periodic
permanent
permit
perpetually
persevering
persistent
personal
personally
personnel
perspicacity
persuade
pertain
perversely
pessimism
pestilence
petticoat
petulancy
pharmaceutical
phase
phenomenon
philosophy
phlegmatic
phobia
phonetically
phosphoric
photogenic
phraseology
phrasing
physical
physician
physique
pianos
picayune
piccolo
picnicked*
pictorially
piece
piecing
piling
pinnacle
piquancy
pirouette
piteous
pitifulness
placating
placidity
plagiary
plaintively
planetarium
planned
platitude
plausible
playwright
pleasant
pleasurable
plebeian
plenteous
pliability
poetically
poignant
politely
political
politician
polyethylene
pontifical
popularize
populous
pornographic
porosity
portable
portfolios
positively
possession
possibility
possible
postponement
potentiality
practicability
practical
practically
practice
precautionary
precede
precipice
precipitous
precisely
precursor
predecessor
predictable
predominant
preexistence
preferred
prejudice
prematurely
prepare
preposterous
presence
preservable
prestige
presumedly
pretension
prettily

prevalent
primitive
principal
principle
prisoners
privilege
probably
procedure
proceed
producible
profession
professor
proficient
prognosticating
progressively
prominent
promissory
pronounce
pronunciation
pronouncing
propaganda
propagate
prophecy*
prophesy*
psychoanalysis
psychology
psychopathic
psychosomatic
ptomaine
puerile
pugnacity
punctilious
purposeless
pursue

Q
quadruplicate
quantity
quarreled*
queasiness
querulous
questionnaire
queue
quiescent
quintessence
quipster
quixotic
quotable
quotient

R
rabies
raconteur
radiating
raising
ramification
rapidity
rarely
rarity
rationalize
readily
readmitted
reality
realize
really
reasonable
rebel
receive
receiving
receptacle
recipient
recognize
recollect
recommend
reconciling
recoup
recoverable
recreation
rectangular
rectified
recurrence
redoubling
reexamining
referring
refrigerate
regard
registrant
regretful
regulating
rehearsal
reimbursement
reissuing
reiterate
rejuvenate
relative
relevant
reliability
relieve
religion
remarkable
remember
reminisce
remotely
renaissance
repeatedly
repelled
repentance
repetition
replacement
reprehensible
represent
reprieve
reproachfully
reproducible
repudiating
repulsion
reputable
requisite
rescind
resembling
resignedly
resources
respectful
response
responsible
restaurant
resurrect
resuscitate
retaliating
retrieve
revealed
revenging
reverence
revering
reversible
revising
revocable
revolutionize
rhapsodies
rhinoceros
rhyming
rhythm
ricochet
ridicule
ridiculous
rigidity
risqué
ritualistic
rogue
rollicking
romantically
roommate
rottenness
rudely

S
sabbatical
sacrifice
sadistically
safety
salacious
salutary
sanatorium*
sanitarium*
sapphire
sarsaparilla
satellite
satiety
satisfied
satisfy
saturating
sauerkraut
saxophone
scandalous
scared
scarred
scene
schedule
schemer
scintillating
scissors
sclerosis
scoundrelly
scrupulous
scurrilous
scurrying
secretive
secureness
sedentary
seducible*
seemingly
seize
self-abasement
self-conscious
semantics
senatorial
sensitivity
sensuality
sentence
sentience*
sentimentality
separable
separate
separation
sergeant*
serviceable
seventieth
sexually
Shakespearean*
shamefacedly
shellacked*
shepherd
shining
short circuit
short-lived
shredded
shrinkage
shrubbery
shyly
sibilance
sickliness
sidesplitting
sideways
siege
significance
silhouette
similar
simile
sincerely
situating
skied
skyscraper
slatternly
sleepily
sleigh
sleight of hand
sliest
slipperiness
slurred
smoky*
smuggest
snobbery
snowcapped
sobriety
sociability
socialistic
sociology
solemnity
solicitude
solidity
solitaire
solvable
somnambulist
soothe
sophomore
soporific
sorcery
sorely
sorrier
source
souvenir
spaghetti
sparing
sparsely
speaking
spectrum
speech
speedometer
spirituality
spitefulness
sponsor
spontaneity
spurious
squalid
squarely
squaring
stabilization
starry
startling
stationary
stationery
statuary

stealthy
stepped
stiffen
stimulating
stodginess
stoically
stolidity
straight
strangely
strategy
strength
stretch
stretchable
stubborn
studying
stultify
stupefaction
stylistic
suavely
subjectivity
sublimity
submissiveness
submitted
subsidiary
subsistence
substantial
substituting
subterranean
subtle
succeed
succession
sufficient
suggestible
suitable
summary
summed
superannuate
superficially
superintendent
superlatively
supersede*
superstitious
suppress
supremacy
surcease
surfeited
surreptitious
surrounding
surveillance
susceptible
suspense
suspicious
sustenance
swimming
syllabication
syllable
symbol
sympathetic
symphonic
synonymous
synthesis
systematically

T

tableau
tabooed*
taciturn
tactically
talkativeness
tangible
tassel
tasteless
taught
taut
tawdriness
technique
tedious
telepathy
temperament
temporarily
tenacious
tendency
tentatively
tenuous
terminology
terrifically
terrifying
testicle
thankfully
thatched
themselves
theories
theory
therapeutic
therefore
thesaurus
theses
thesis
thieve
thinkable
thirstily
thirties
thorough
thought
thriving
through
ticklish
timidity
timing
tiresomely
titillate
to
tobaccos
together
tolerable
tomato
tomatoes
tomorrow
too
topography
tormentor
torpedoes
torrential
totally
tousled*
tragedy
tragically
tranquillity*
transcendental
transferred
translucence
transmitter
transparent
treachery
tremendous
trichinosis
tricycle
trivially
tropical
truculence
tubular
tumultuous
tuneful
turmeric*
turquoise
tying
typewriter
tyranny

U

ugliness
ukulele*
ultimately
umbrella
unaccountable
unanimous
unconcernedly
unctuous
undeniable
undoubtedly
unfortunately
uniformity
uniquely
unlikely
unnecessary
unoccupied
unprincipled
unruliness
unusually
urbanely
useful
useless
using
utterly

V

vacating
vacillate
vacuum
validity
valuable
vanquish
vaporous
variegated
varies
various
velocity
venerable
vengeance
ventriloquist
veracity
veritable
vernacular
versatility
vicarious
vicissitude
villain
vinegar
virtually
virulence
visibility
visitor
visualize
vitally
vivacity
vocalist
vociferous
voicing
voluminous
voluntarily
voluptuous
voracity
voucher
vulnerable

W

wakefully
wantonness
wariness
warrant
watery
weakened
wearisome
weather
weighty
weird
weren't
wheeze
where
whether
whistling
whole
wholly
whose
wieldy
wiliness
willfully*
winery
wintry
wireless
wishful
witticism
woeful
wonderfully
wondrous
workable
worrying
wrathfully
wrench
wretchedness
writhe
writhing
writing
wryly

Misuse of the Word

FAULTY DICTION

Aggravate, *to increase,* does not mean *to irritate.*

Ain't, a contraction of *am not,* should be avoided.

Alternative, *one of two things,* may not correctly be applied to more than two.

Among should be applied to more than two persons or things; *between* to two.

Any (every, no, some) place should not be used adverbially for *anywhere (everywhere, nowhere, somewhere).*

And which should be used only when preceded by *which.*

As should not take the place of *that* or *whether,* and preferably not of *because.*

As . . . as are correlatives to be used with positive; with negative use *so . . . as.*

As good as and **better than** are idioms. If they are used in the same sentence, neither *as* nor *than* may be omitted. The following sentence is, therefore, incorrect: *Brazil is as good, if not better, than Argentina in climate.*

As yet is redundant. Omit *as.*

Awful means *profoundly impressive.* It should not be used loosely to mean *very bad.*

Badly should not be used for *very much.*

Balance should not be used for *remainder* except in connection with a financial statement.

Barefoot is preferred to *barefooted.*

Because should not be used instead of *that* if preceded by *the reason why . . . is.* Nor should it be used instead of *the fact that.*

Blame it on him should not be used for *place the blame for it on him* or *blame him for it.*

Bring up or **rear** is preferable to *raise* in speaking of children.

Bursted, bust, and **busted** should not be used for *burst.*

But should not be used with a negative in expressions like *isn't but.*

But what is less desirable than *but that.*

Cannot but should not be confused with *can but.*

Certainly should not be overused.

Claim is a strong word. It should not be used for *maintain.*

Common, meaning *shared similarly,* should not be confused with *mutual,* meaning *reciprocal.* The expression *a friend in common* is naturally preferable to *a common friend.*

Comparison. Two standards should not be combined in one sentence. *Largest (tallest, best)* should be followed by a singular; if preceded by *one of,* by a plural. It is, therefore, incorrect to say, *The* Paul Revere *is New England's fastest, and one of America's best, planes.*

Considerable is overused. It may not be used as a noun.

Contact, used as a verb in business, should be avoided.

Could of is illiterate for *could have.*

Cute is used colloquially to mean *clever.* The word should be avoided.

Criticize, in literature, means *to judge.*

Date may not be used as a verb to mean *make an appointment,* or as a noun to mean *the one with whom an appointment has been made;* it is colloquial for *appointment.*

Different from is the preferred idiom.

Don't, a contraction of *do not,* may not be used in the third person singular.

Drownded is illiterate.

Each other should be used only with two persons or things; *one another* with more than two.

Either and **neither** should be used only with two persons or things. The elements of the correlatives *either . . . or* and *neither . . . nor* may not be interchanged.

Enthuse, a colloquialism, may not be used in formal writing.

Etc. is an overused and almost meaningless abbreviation. It should not be used, especially with *and.*

Every bit is colloquial.

Except, which is not a conjunction, should not be used for *unless.*

Expect should not be used for *think* or *suppose.*

Extra means *beyond that which is usual,* not *extraordinarily.*

Feel bad (not *badly*) is correct but confusing; *feel ill* is preferable. *Feel good* refers to a moral, not a physical, state.

Fellow is colloquial when it means *person* or *fiancé.*

Fewer is used with number; *less* with degree or quantity.

Fine means *finished, refined,* or *perfect.* It should not be used loosely.

Fix (up) is colloquial for *to arrange* or *to repair.*

Former may be used with only two persons or things; likewise *latter.*

Get to go is provincial for *to be able to go.*

Goings on is a vulgar expression.

Good may not be used as an adverb to mean *well.*

Got is an abused word: it is colloquial for *possess,* as is *have got* for *must.*

Gotten, except in a few crystallized expressions, has now been supplanted by *got.*

Grand means *magnificent* or *impressive.* It should be used with care.

Guess, when used to mean *believe* or *suppose,* although possessing a long history in that sense, should be used infrequently if at all.

Had ought is illiterate.

Hardly should not be used with a negative in expressions like *couldn't hardly.*

Have got is both colloquial and redundant. Omit *got.*

Heap(s) is colloquial when meaning *much* or *many.*

Hear to it is vulgar.

Honorable should be preceded by *the* and followed by the first name or *Mr.*

If is less desirable than *whether* after *ask, doubt,* and similar words.

Inside of for *within* is colloquial; in other cases, *of* should be omitted.

Kind and **sort** are singular: *this kind* or *these sorts.*

Kind of and **sort of** are colloquial when meaning *rather.* These phrases in sentences like *You plan to create a kind of game preserve?* should not be followed by the indefinite article, for the noun is used generically.

Lady is correctly applied to one of culture or social distinction; *woman* is, however, entirely correct and is preferred in compounds like *saleswoman.*

Learn means *to gain knowledge; teach* means *to give instruction.* These words must not be confused.

Let's, a contraction of *let us,* should not be followed by *we, don't,* or any other illogical words.

Like, never a conjunction, may not be followed by a clause, thus taking the place of *as* or *as if.*

Line is slang for *kind,* as in *line of work.*

Literally means *true to the fact.* It should not be used untruly for intensification.

Locate means *to place;* it is colloquial when it means *to take up residence.*

Lose out is redundant; omit *out.*

Lovely means *delicate* or *exquisite.* It should not be overused colloquially to mean *very pleasing.*

Mad means *insane* or *enraged,* not *angry.*

Mean, as an adjective, is a synonym for *humble* or *ignoble;* it is colloquial for *ill-tempered* or *selfish.*

Mighty means *powerful* or *wonderful. Mighty tired* is, therefore, incorrect.

Miss, Ms., Mr., Dr., Professor, and similar titles must be followed by the name.

More than means *in a greater number* or *amount;* it should not be confused with *over,* meaning *beyond.*

Mrs. should never be followed by the title or profession of the husband or a married woman: *Mrs. Judge Watson, Mrs. Lawyer Williams, Mrs. Major Wilkinson, Mrs. Director of Public Works Warren.*

Nice means *discriminating, pleasing, or scrupulous.* A more precise word is preferred.

No good is colloquial when used to modify a noun.

Notorious means *discreditably known; noted* means *celebrated.*

No use, except in informal speech, should be preceded by *of.*

Nowhere near is colloquial for *not nearly.*

Of is redundant when preceded by *outside (the house)* or *off;* it is illiterate when used for *have,* as in *could of.*

On account of is not a conjunction and may not be followed by a clause.

One repeated is stiff: *One may earn one's living if one tries.* The shift from *one* to *he* or *his* is sometimes awkward. *A person . . . his . . . he* is perhaps preferable to either.

One of, followed by a group into which it falls, does not govern the number of the verb which follows the group. Thus it is correct to say, *Black Beauty is one of the horses which run at Havre de Grace.*

Only should be placed properly in a sentence. Note the difference in meaning: *Only America won the war. American only won the war. America won the only war. America won the war only.*

Out loud, a colloquialism, should be replaced by *aloud.*

Outside of, meaning *besides* or *except for,* is objectionable.

Over with is redundant; omit *with.*

Overly is unknown to good usage.

Party means one person on one of two sides of a cause, or one entire group. It does not mean *any person.*

Per, coming from the Latin, should be used only with Latin words like *annum, capita, cent,* not with *acre, dozen,* and similar words.

Per cent should be used only after numbers; otherwise *percentage* should be used.

Perfectly is an abused and often unnecessary adjective, as in *perfectly darling* or *perfectly beautiful.*

Piano, voice, violin, vocal, and **instrumental** should not be used alone when speaking of instruction: *lessons* or *instruction* should follow.

Plan on is redundant; omit *on.*

Proven, except in the law, is archaic; *proved* is the modern past participle.

Quite means *completely;* when used to mean *to a great extent,* it is colloquial. It should not be used as by the English, excessively and often absurdly, as a meaningless ejaculation.

Quite a (bit, few, little, number) is colloquial.

Rarely ever and **seldom ever** should be avoided as confusions of *hardly ever* or *rarely (seldom) if ever.*

Real is an adjective or a noun; *really* is an adverb. *I was real happy* is, therefore, incorrect.

Render means *to give, to yield, to extract,* or *to inflict.* One may *render lard,* but one should not *render a vocal selection.*

Reverend should be preceded by *the* and followed by the first name or *Mr.*

Right, meaning *precisely (right here and now)* or *to a large degree (right nice girl)* is colloquial. *Right smart* is dialectal.

Right along (away, off) is colloquial.

Run, when meaning *to conduct* or *to manage,* is colloquial.

Said, when meaning *previously mentioned,* should be avoided except in the law. *Aforesaid* is permissible.

Same, except in the law, should not be used as a pronoun.

Says is the third person singular of *say;* it may not be used with *I. Says* should not be used when the past tense, *said,* is required.

See where is a misuse of *see that.*

Show is colloquial for *drama* or *concert.*

Show up is colloquial for *appear.*

So should not be used as a mere intensive in an incomplete construction: *I am so angry. Because* is preferable to the colloquial *so* in joining coordinate clauses: *He came; so we held a reception* should be rephrased: *Because he came, we held a reception. So* should not be used instead of *so that.* The correlative *as . . . as* are used positively; *so . . . as* are used negatively.

Some is colloquial for *somewhat.*

Stop means *to arrest progress.* A person *stays* at a hotel.

Such should not be used as a mere intensive in an incomplete construction: *I have heard such good things about you* is incomplete. A clause of result following *such* should be introduced by *that,* not *as: There was such a noise that I could not hear.* A relative clause following *such* should be introduced by *as: He will follow such directions as the governor may give.*

Superlatives should not be used for intensification in an incomplete construction, as in *I had the best time.*

Sure is slang when it means *certainly. Surely* should be used.

Suspicion may never be used as a verb.

Take or **take it** should not be used to introduce an example.

The should not take the place of *a: Bittersweet candy is fifty cents the pound* is incorrect because a specific pound is not intended.

That is used colloquially to mean *to such a degree: I am not that tired that I must rest. So* should be used.

There as an expletive should be avoided.

This here *(these here, that there, those there)* is a vulgarism.

These should not be used loosely without any feeling of the demonstrative: *He is one of these modern cowboys who broadcast.*

Those should be followed by a relative clause: *He is one of those militarists* should be completed by adding a clause like *who would involve us in war;* or *He is a militarist.*

Through should not be used before a gerund: *I am through working* should be changed to *I have finished my work.*

Try and should be replaced by *try to.*

Ugly means *hideous* or *offensive morally.* It is used colloquially to mean *unpleasant.*

Up is redundant when preceded by a verb. It may not be used as a verb to mean *to increase,* as in *He upped the price ten dollars.*

Used to could is illiterate.

Verse, when used with the indefinite article, means *a line of poetry.* It should not be confused with *stanza,* a group of verses.

Very much is preferred to *very* when followed by a past participle not yet recognized as an adjective.

Way must be preceded by a preposition if used adverbially: *He works in that way.*

Who is this? when spoken over the telephone is both illogical and impolite.

Which as a relative pronoun should be used if the antecedent is inanimate or an animal; *who* if the antecedent is a person.

Without may not be used as a conjunction.

WORDS COMMONLY CONFUSED

accept, to receive
except, to exclude

access, approach
excess, superfluity

affect, to influence
effect, to execute

aisle, passage
isle, island

alley, lane
ally, associate

all ready, entirely prepared
already, at this time

all together, grouped
altogether, completely

allusion, indirect reference
illusion, deceptive appearance

altar, table
alter, vary

anachorism, violation of geography
anachronism, violation of time

angel, spiritual being
angle, corner

barbarous, almost savage
barbaric, showy, lacking restraint

berth, sleeping compartment
birth, beginning

beside, by the side of
besides, in addition to

boarder, one who takes meals
border, margin

Calvary, site of Christ's crucifixion
cavalry, horsemen

canvas, cloth
canvass, to solicit

capital, principal
capitol, statehouse

censor, examine
censure, condemn

centrifugal, proceeding from center
centripetal, proceeding toward center

chord, combination of tones
cord, small rope

cite, summon, quote
site, position

clothes, garments
cloths, fabrics

coarse, common, harsh
course, route

complement, addition, to add
compliment, to praise

congenial, kindred in taste
genial, cheerful

conscience, moral faculty
conscious, cognizant

consul, commercial representative
council, assembly
counsel, advice, attorney

contemptible, despicable
contemptuous, insolent

continual, in close succession
continuous, uninterrupted

corps, unit of organized establishment
corpse, dead body

credible, trustworthy
creditable, deserving of praise
credulous, inclined to believe

currant, raisin
current, motion

dairy, place for milk and its products
diary, daily record

desert, arid region; v. t., to leave, to abandon
dessert, course at end of meal

disinterested, uninfluenced by personal advantage
uninterested, apathetic

dual, twofold
duel, combat

elegy, lament
eulogy, commendatory oration

emigrant, one who leaves
immigrant, one who enters

enormity, wickedness
enormousness, immensity

euphemism, softened statement
euphony, pleasant sound
euphuism, artificial statement

exceptional, uncommon
exceptionable, objectionable

factious, dissentient
factitious, artificial
fictitious, feigned
fractious, unruly

faint, swoon
feint, pretense

farther, applied to distance, space
further, applied to extent, degree

forceful, possessing power
forcible, violent

feat, deed
feet, terminals of legs

formally, conventionally
formerly, heretofore

forth, onward
fourth, ordinal of *four*

hanged, executed
hung, suspended

healthful, wholesome
healthy, well, vigorous

ingenious, clever
ingenuous, candid

indict, to charge
indite, to write

inhumane, lacking in human kindness
inhuman (also *unhuman*), savage

later, afterward
latter, the second of two

lay (also past of *lie*), to place
lie, to recline

liable, obliged
likely, probably

lightening, relieving
lightning, flashing of light

loose, unattached
lose, to miss

luxuriant, profuse
luxurious, costly, ornate

mantel, shelf
mantle, cloak

misogamist, marriage hater
misogynist, woman hater

noted, renowned
notorious, disgraceful

O, used in invocation
oh, exclamation

observance, act of custom
observation, attentive consideration

passed, crossed
past, bygone

persecute, to afflict
prosecute, to carry on

personal, private
personnel, group collectively employed

plain, level land
plane, level surface

practical, useful, skillful
practicable, feasible

precedence, priority
precedents, antecedents

principal, chief
principle, doctrine

prodigy, wonder
progeny, offspring

propose, to offer
purpose, to resolve

prophecy, prediction
prophesy, to predict

quiet, undisturbed
quite, wholly

raise, to erect (in good use, not a noun)
rise, to ascend

recipe, formula
receipt, written acknowledgment

respectful, deferential
respective, individual

sciolist, pretender
scholiast, commentator

sensual, fleshly
sensuous, pertaining to the senses

sentiment, feeling
sentimentality, excessive feeling

stationary, fixed
stationery, paper

statue, image
stature, height
statute, law

stimulant, alcoholic beverage
stimulus, incentive

specie, coin
species, variety

suit, apparel
suite, set

their, possessive of *they*
there, in that place

therefor, for that
therefore, hence

to, toward
too, also
two, the number

troop, a collection
troupe, company of actors

venal, mercenary
venial, excusable

waive, to relinquish
wave, to swing

weather, condition of atmosphere
whether, if

who's, contraction of *who is* or *who has*
whose, possessive of *who*

your, possessive of you
you're, contraction of *you are*

USING THE TOOLS

Effective Sentences

To write effective sentences, you must learn not only to avoid certain basic errors, but also how to employ the tools of good writing. Often the "tool" to be used is simply on the other side of the coin from the error to be avoided. For example, to correct a *wordy* sentence, you take all unnecessary words out of the sentence; however, you should try to avoid wordiness by writing concisely, by writing no unnecessary words in the first place. Below you will find some constructive suggestions on how to write effective sentences.

Note the word *effective*. It carries the implication that, in writing, we wish to *do* something to our reader, to have an "effect" on him. If we don't take the time and make the necessary effort to determine what this effect is to be, our sentences will be ineffective. On the other hand, if we do assign a purpose to everything we write, something specific that we want to say–a "point of view"–we will have found one pathway toward errorless and effective writing.

MAKING SENTENCES EFFECTIVE

Use Concrete Language

A good writer uses concrete and definite words frequently, and avoids vague or abstract words. Concrete language gives the reader a specific picture rather than a general statement. It builds images that the reader can readily grasp.

General The lovely sounds of nature woke me.

Specific The wind in the trees and a bird's chirping woke me.

Be Positive

Good writing makes direct, positive statements; it avoids indirect, non-committal language. Use the word "not" only when the negative idea is emphatic; otherwise express what you want to say in the positive form.

Indirect He did not like Mr. Harvey's approach to grammar.

Direct He disliked Mr. Harvey's approach to grammar.

Indirect I did not think the trip would be very interesting.

Direct I thought the trip would be a bore.

Indirect Mr. Alexander was perhaps our best committee chairman. He was not long-winded, he was never biased, and he never failed to get the business before us covered.

Direct Mr. Alexander was the best committee chairman we ever had. He was direct, unbiased, and efficient.

Use the Active Voice

A careless writer uses the passive voice when there is no specific reason for doing so, and thereby weakens his effectiveness. Use the passive voice only when the subject is unknown or when the fact that something was *done to* the subject is of primary importance. Otherwise use the active voice. (See *Verbs: Voice*.)

Vary Your Sentences

A good stylist avoids monotonous writing by keeping his sentences varied, in both structure and length. To achieve a varied style one must keep one's ear open to the *sound* of his writing. (See *Basic Sentence Errors: Monotony*.)

Use a Climactic Order

Gain emphasis by placing important words or ideas at the important positions in the sentence–at the beginning or at the end, especially at the end. Sentences which state supporting ideas first and which withhold the important idea until the end are known as "climactic" or "periodic" sentences. Sentences which state the important idea first and then add supporting ideas are called "loose" sentences. Either kind of sentence is effective, but a preponderance of one or the other is decidedly ineffective and artificial. Whatever kind of sentence you select to express an idea, be sure to tuck away illustrative details and parenthetical expressions in the middle of the sentence. As a rule, loose sentences are preferred in informal writing; periodic sentences are more common in formal writing.

Periodic The alternative we must avoid at all costs is armed conflict.

Loose Armed conflict is the alternative we must avoid at all costs. (Important idea expressed first and followed by explanatory comment)

Periodic Against the spangled backdrop of a dark night sky filled with unending stars shone the moon, white and fluorescent.

Loose A white, fluorescent moon shone against the spangled backdrop of a dark night sky filled with unending stars.

Euphony and Rhythm

Euphony is the smooth, pleasant flow of agreeable sounds. An experienced writer chooses and arranges his words so that they form patterns of sound that are rhythmical and euphonious when read aloud. The more experienced and skillful the writer, the more pleasant are the sounds he produces. The ability to produce these sound effects comes only from experience.

Do not repeat words that have the same sound. Do not alliterate. Do not confuse rhythm with rhyme. An alliteration is the repetition of an initial sound in two or more words in the same phrase or clause. It is an eye-catching device used by advertising copy writers, but it has no place in formal prose writing. Rhyme, the repetition of end sounds, is a device of verse, not of prose. The first example below illustrates how euphony can be destroyed by alliteration; the second, by rhyme.

Alliteration In a fury I flew into the fray.

Rhyme I yearn to learn who she is.

Figures of Speech

A prevalent belief among students is that figures of speech are old-fashioned and should be confined to rhetoric and poetry. This is a false belief. We all use figurative language every day, and more often than not, without realizing it. *Hungry as a bear, quick as lightning, time flies, drive a bargain*–these are common figurative expressions. A figure of speech is any deviation from the literal meaning or ordinary use of words designed to make a thought clearer or more forceful. Suppose we express how a girl sings by comparing her with a nightingale. *May sings like a nightingale.* We do not say literally how May sings. We suggest the image of the nightingale and leave it to the reader's imagination to know the quality of May's voice. This is communication in figurative language. The example of May's voice is a figure of speech known as a *simile.* The simile expresses a figurative resemblance or comparison between essentially different things. One thing is said to be like another, and the resemblance is usually introduced by *like* or *as. Hungry as a bear* and *quick as lightning* are also similes. Actually, the best similes compare things which are in most respects unlike, but which have at least one point of striking resemblance.

The "Intentional Fragment"

The grammatical structure of the sentence has been analyzed. We have already stated that a sentence need not necessarily contain a subject and a verb, although by far the majority of our written sentences do. Expressions such as "Why not?" or a conversational colloquialism such as "Me, too" are considered to be sentences. In writing, the sentence that intentionally lacks a subject or a verb is called an "intentional fragment." Professional writers use intentional fragments for stylistic effect. Beginning writers, however, are best advised not to use fragments of any kind.

Idioms

In every language, combinations of words have developed which appear completely proper to the natives of the country where the language is spoken, but which sound peculiar to a foreign visitor. Such expressions are known as *idioms.*

Sometimes idioms conform to grammatical rules, and at other times they may conflict with such rules, but idiomatic usage has established the expression as proper.

The prepositional idiom is a type of expression that gives even the native some difficulty. A seemingly well-written sentence will be ruined by a careless use of a prepositional idiom. The trouble arises in determining the correct preposition. For example: Is it *faced with* or *faced by*? Idiomatic usage has established *faced by* as the proper expression. To determine which preposition an idiom takes, see a good dictionary.

Synonyms

Synonyms are good words to become familiar with. They help give variety to sentences, and their proper use avoids repetitious phrases. A *synonym* actually is a word that means the same or nearly the same as another word. Practical students often resort to synonyms as a device to avoid using words they do not know how to spell. A student may want to use *lugubrious* on his essay examination but, unsure of the spelling, resorts to the word *dismal*. Careless substitution can change the subtle meaning of a sentence, even if it would appear that the two words are almost identical. To *plagiarize* and to *copy* often mean the same thing; there is, however, a distinct difference. To *plagiarize* definitely means to steal another person's literary effort and pass it off as one's own, whereas one may *copy* another person's work, with or without intent to steal it.

Antonyms

This is a word that means the opposite of another word. But even antonyms can be useful in giving sentences a greater variety if properly used. *Happy* and *sad* are antonyms. Seemingly, it would appear they are not interchangeable in a sentence, yet the writer may feel that the word *happy* is too strong, and he may decide, despite the admonition against the use of the negative, that *not sad* is just the right state he is trying to describe.

BASIC SENTENCE ERRORS

The Fragment

The *fragment* is a statement that fails to state a complete thought; it is an incomplete sentence. Generally, the error can be corrected by simply attaching the fragment to the sentence before or after it, as in each of the corrections below. Unintentional fragments used as complete sentences generally consist of phrases, appositives, or dependent clauses.

Fragment The soldiers stood stoically in the rain. *Cursing quietly over their wretched luck.* (verbal phrase incorrectly used as a complete sentence)

Complete The soldiers stood stoically in the rain, cursing quietly over their wretched luck.

Fragment He was an unbelievable person. *A man as well read and as outspoken as any I've ever met.* (an appositive incorrectly used as a complete sentence)

Complete He was an unbelievable person, a man as well read and as outspoken as any I've ever met.

Fragment The settlers were careful to place twenty-four-hour guards around the encampment. *So that they would not be caught off guard by an Indian attack at any time.* (dependent clause used incorrectly as a complete sentence)

Complete The settlers were careful to place twenty-four-hour guards around the encampment, so that they would not be caught off guard by an Indian attack at any time.

The Run-on Sentence

The *run-on sentence* occurs when the writer has failed to separate properly two sentences or independent clauses, with the result that the two "run into" each other. Two major types of run-on sentences occur. The first type contains no punctuation at all between the sentences. Such sentences are known as "fused sentences" or "stringiness." The second type of run-on sentence is one in which a comma has been improperly used. This is often called a "comma splice."

Run-on Let us be wary but let us not fall prey to fear. (fused: failure to use punctuation between independent clauses)

Improved Let us be wary, but let us not fall prey to fear.

Run-on A soft answer turns away wrath, grievious words stir up anger. (comma splice: comma incorrectly used to separate independent clauses)

Improved A soft answer turns away wrath; grievous words stir up anger.

To avoid writing run-on sentences, one must know the four possible ways of connecting independent clauses. (See also *Punctuation: The Comma.*) As a general rule, if the ideas are to receive equal emphasis, use the period and place the ideas in different sentences, or use the semicolon alone. If one idea is more important than the other, use the comma and a coordinating conjunction, or the semicolon and a conjunctive adverb.

Mixed Constructions

A *mixed construction* results when one part of a sentence does not agree grammatically with another part of the sentence. The two major types of mixed construction involve subject and verb disagreement, and pronoun and antecedent disagreement.

Wrong A series of lectures were given by Mr. Olsen. (Plural verb *were* does not agree with singular subject *series*.)

Right A series of lectures was given by Mr. Olsen. (Verb agrees with subject.)

Wrong Sometimes circumstantial evidence will convict a person of a crime they did not commit. (Plural pronoun *they* does not agree with singular antecedent *person*.)

Right Sometimes circumstantial evidence will convict a person of a crime he did not commit. (Pronoun agrees with antecedent.)

Dangling Modifiers

The *dangling modifier* is a verbal phrase that either has no word in the sentence to modify or is placed in such a way that it appears to modify unintended words in the same sentence.

Dangling Making a flying tackle, Sam's shoe came off. (The participial phrase is *Making a flying tackle,* but the subject of the clause that follows is *shoe. Making a flying tackle* cannot possibly refer to a shoe.)

Improved Making a flying tackle, Sam lost his shoe. (*Sam* is now the subject to which the participial phrase properly refers.)

Dangling To be sure of a good seat, your tickets must be bought far in advance. (The understood subject of the infinitive phrase *To be sure* is not the same as the subject of the clause that follows.)

Improved To be sure of a good seat, you must buy your tickets far in advance. (The infinitive phrase modifies *you,* the subject of the sentence.)

Dangling After waiting an hour, the train finally came. (The train waited an hour? Obviously not. *After waiting an hour* has no word in this sentence to modify.)

Improved After waiting an hour, we finally caught our train. *(After waiting an hour* refers to *we,* the subject of the sentence.)

Squinting Modifiers

A *squinting modifier* is one that is carelessly placed so that it appears to modify both the words preceding and the words following it. The reader has to stop reading to figure out what is being modified.

Squinting The man who shoved his way to the platform angrily addressed the crowd. (What does *angrily* modifiy? The way the man made his way to the platform? Or the way he addressed the crowd?)

Improved The man who angrily shoved his way to the platform addressed the crowd. *OR* The man who shoved his way to the platform addressed the crowd angrily.

There are two types of verbal phrase constructions that are independent of the rest of the sentence and that need not modify the subject of the clause that follows it. The first type is the *absolute phrase* consisting of a noun or pronoun followed by a participle.

The play having finished, the audience left.

The second type of verbal phrase that can be independent of the rest of the sentence is a phrase that states a general truth. A general truth does not refer to the action of a specific person or thing. Such expressions as *taking everything into consideration* and *to put it another way* are verbal phrases that can stand apart from the rest of the sentence.

Monotony

The most common form of this fault is the dull repetition of a subject-verb sentence pattern. Monotony also occurs when the writer fails to vary the length of his sentences. Monotony results, in fact, from any continued, dull repetition of sentence structure or length.

Not Varied He opened the car door. He stepped out. He walked towards the store. He tried to remember all the things his wife had told him to buy. He hated shopping!

Varied Opening the car door, he stepped out and walked towards the store, trying to remember all the things his wife had told him to buy. How he hated shopping!

Faulty Parallelism

A series of related ideas of equal importance can often be most effectively expressed by writing them in what is called "parallel form." Parallelism, which treats like ideas in like form, balances words, phrases, and clauses against one another. In a series, for example, words should be in the same class and in the same parts of speech. One may begin a series of parallel forms, then lose the parallelism, and thus commit the error known as "faulty parallelism."

Not Parallel Although very good-looking, Ted was modest, shy, and didn't talk much. (The parallel adjectives *modest* and *shy* demand a third adjective rather than a clause to follow them, in order that the sentence should read smoothly and clearly.)

Parallel Although very good-looking, Ted was modest, shy, and quiet.

Not Parallel The man at the desk ordered me to be silent, to sit down, and that I should wait until I was spoken to. (The two infinitives and the phrase beginning *and that* constitute unparallel form.)

Parallel The man at the desk ordered me to be silent, to sit down, and to wait until I was spoken to. (A third infinitive has been added to complete the parallelism begun by the first two.)

Correlative Conjunctions and Parallelism

The use of the correlative conjunctions can lead the writer to make mistakes in parallelism. These conjunctions–*either . . . or, neither . . . nor, not only . . . but also*–help tighten sentence structure and strength expression, but they must be used logically. That is, the same kinds of words and the same grammatical structure must appear on both sides of the correlatives, otherwise, parallelism and sense and effectiveness will be lost.

Not Parallel Al is both a marvelous athlete and he dresses very well. (A modifying phrase on one side and an independent clause on the other)

Parallel Al is both a marvelous athlete and a fine dresser. (Modifying phrase on either side)

Not Parallel Your grandmother has not only a sharp mind but also her humor is lively.

Parallel Your grandmother has not only a sharp mind but also a lively humor.

Mixed Metaphor

Combining two different comparisons or figures of speech that are inconsistent or incongruous with each other, produces the "mixed metaphor." The writer must be careful to maintain logic as he adds color with images and comparisons; he must make sure his comparisons "fit" one another. A "ship of state" cannot get "lost in the woods of diplomatic entanglements" (ships don't sail in the woods); "her eyes" could not be "glistening pebbles in the twilight sky" (pebbles do not glisten in the sky).

Mixed With determination Ellen dug into the sea of work before her.

Logical With determination Ellen dug into the pile of work before her. *OR* With determination Ellen plunged into the sea of work before her.

Mixed Now, friend, chew upon this branch of my thoughts: all good looks are a snare that no man should let himself be drowned in.

Logical Now, friend, chew upon this morsel of my thoughts: all good looks are a snare that no man should let himself be trapped in.

Inadequate Subordination

Immature minds seldom use subordination. It takes maturity to select one idea over another and to subordinate it to the important one. A child, for example, is likely to give new facts equal importance. Learning about Columbus, the child is likely to say: "Columbus was born in Portugal. He was given three ships by the Queen of Spain. He became famous as the discoverer of America. He died in poverty and neglect." A more mature version of these facts would be: "Columbus, who was born in Portugal, was given three ships by the Queen of Spain. He became famous as the discoverer of America; however, he died in poverty and neglect." Two simple words, the relative pronoun *who* and the conjunctive adverb *however*, place the facts about Columbus in truer perspective, by subordinating the less important facts to the more important ones.

Inadequate subordination is the sign not only of immaturity but of ineffective writing. It results in short, choppy sentences. The writer who combines ideas in sentences without proper subordination inevitably is guilty of an excessive number of *and* and *so* clauses. The rule to remember is: Put subordinate ideas in subordinate (dependent) clauses (or phrases), and main ideas in main (independent) clauses.

Inadequate Subordination Tom was tired of listening to the lecture, and no one could see him, and so he slipped quietly out of the room. (Three ideas are placed in independent clauses, thereby giving each idea equal importance and resulting in no subordination at all.)

Improved Tom was tired of listening to the lecture, and since no one could see him, he slipped quietly out of the room. (One idea has been made subordinate to the other two, by putting it in a dependent clause.) *OR* Since Tom was tired of listening to the lecture and as no one could see him, he slipped quietly out of the room. (two ideas made subordinate)

Faulty Subordination

When combining several ideas in one sentence, be sure not to make the mistake of subordinating the main idea. The less important of two ideas should always be in a dependent clause or phrase. Never introduce the main idea of a sentence with a conjunctive adverb.

Weak Although he easily won the club tennis championship, he showed some signs of fatigue. (The main idea of the sentence is weakly introduced by the subordinating conjunction *Although*. The subordinate idea is in an independent clause.)

Improved Although he showed some signs of fatigue, he easily won the club tennis championship. (The subordinate idea is properly placed in a subordinate clause, and the main idea is properly placed in the independent clause.)

"Fine" Writing

"Fine" writing is a ruse to cover up absence of knowledge. It is the use of big, pretentious words for simple, direct words. It is word exhibitionism at its worst. Students often resort to "fine" writing to impress, to make the reader think that they know what they are talking about. "Fine" writing is a puerile, sophomoric device, and it impresses nobody. Of course, writers often inject pretentious words into the speech of teenage delinquents, race track touts, and hoodlums of diverse sorts. This they do for comic irony, and the results can be hilarious. But it is pathetic to hear the same words uttered by high school and college students.

There is nothing wrong with big words, but they should normally be used only to express meanings and shades of meaning for which simpler words do not exist.

Split Infinitives

To split an infinitive is to insert an expression between the *to* and the verb. The inserted expression is usually an adverb (to *entirely* comprehend). The reason that split infinitives used to be condemned is that *to* is historically a preposition. Grammarians at one time insisted that a preposition should never be separated from its object by any other words. The rule now generally accepted sanctions the split infinitive when it results in a clearer meaning or a pleasanter sound. In the illustrations of acceptable split infinitives below, note how a transposition of the *to* would affect the meaning and the rhythm of the sentences.

Do you want us to really enjoy ourselves?

The judge refused to summarily dismiss the case.

He failed to entirely comprehend the charge.

The Double Negative

Avoid the double negative. Use a single negative to express a negative idea.

Wrong I haven't no money left.

Right I have no money left.

The following are troublesome words. They are all negative, or negative by implication, so should not be accompanied by a second negative word.

barely	no one
hardly	none
neither	not
never	nothing
nobody	only

Unneeded Words

Beware of repeating ideas already expressed.

Repetitious	Repeat what you said again.
Concise	Repeat what you said.
Repetitious	The reason I didn't do my homework was on account of the fact that I forgot the assignment.
Better	The reason I didn't do my homework was that I forgot the assignment.
Concise	I didn't do my homework because I forgot the assignment.

Let us go one step further. We don't simply say that May has a voice *like* a nightingale, but we say that her voice *is* the voice of a nightingale. *May has the voice of a nightingale.* The two voices are equated. This is a *metaphor.* It is simply an expanded simile. A simile states that one thing is *like* another; a metaphor, that one thing *is* another.

Simile	He mouths a sentence as curs mouth a bone.
Metaphor	All the world's a stage, And all the men and women merely players.

Similes and metaphors are the most common figures of speech. Other common figures of speech are: *hyperbole* (extravagant but deliberate and fanciful exaggeration), *litotes* (deliberate understatement), *personification* (infusing life into inanimate things), and *metonymy* (naming one thing in terms of another which is part of it or associated with it).

Hyperbole	Thanks a million.
Litotes	Faulkner is not a bad writer (meaning he is a great writer).
Personification	Time flies.
Metonymy	She set a good table (meaning she prepared a good meal).

Weak Words

The weakest words in the English language are the intensives *very, little, rather,* and *pretty.* An *intensive* is a word that supposedly makes another word more forceful and emphatic. But the use of an adjective (as an adverb) to intensify another adjective often has the opposite effect. This is especially true of adjectives that have been used so often with so little regard for their true meanings that they have lost all the force they once had. Take the words *awful, dreadful, fearful,* and *horrible.* These are potent words when used to mean "to inspire awe" *(awful),* "to inspire dread" *(dreadful),* "to instill fear" *(fearful),* "to excite horror" *(horrible).* However, when these words are loosely used as intensives, they languish into impotence. They are especially absurd when they intensify words that contradict their own meanings. Expressions such as *awfully nice* and *horribly sorry* are not only feeble and placid but absurdly contradictory. The following is a list of words that should not be used as intensives. Unless you know the true meanings of these words, do not use them at all.

amazing	gorgeous	splendid
awful	grand	stunning
colossal	horrible	stupendous
devastating	huge	superb
dreadful	little	terrible
enormous	magnificent	terrific
fabulous	marvelous	tremendous
fearful	pretty	very
frightful	rather	wonderful

Slang

Slang is unacceptable in either ordinary conversation or formal writing. If it belongs anywhere, it is in light banter in an informal setting–but only if it is original and lively. Effective slang usually is a cleverly humorous or dramatically surprising play on words, achieved by taking words out of context, juxtaposing unexpected words, using very compressed metaphors, and the like. Unfortunately, slang ages quickly and becomes stale.

Why, then, is it so popular? Its chief attraction is that it makes a single word do so much. In an instant, a word of slang can communicate a reasonably exact meaning, suggest a humorous comparison, arouse emotion, and suggest personality. Think of how much more is said in the single word "Scram!" than in the sentence, "You may go now." In this very flexibility of slang lies one of its chief dangers: It may be used for so many things that it becomes a crutch for one's vocabulary. One may, for example, use the slang word "dig" in a variety of contexts: "I don't dig (understand) this equation"; "I dig (feel satisfied with) the mark I got in English"; "Baby, I dig (am attracted to) you." With so handy a word available the lazy or obtuse person will overuse it, quite failing to make distinct the various meanings he actually intends. Such dependence on slang prevents the development of a good vocabulary.

In sum, therefore, if you wish to inject slang into the dialogue of your fictional characters, by all means do so–with care and with a sparing hand. Incidentally, never enclose slang words within quotation marks, either single or double.

Solecisms

A *solecism* is the violation of correct grammatical structure. It is considered a blunder, not an illiteracy or a barbarism, and is usually the result of carelessness.

Colloquialisms

The chances are you have only a vague idea of what a colloquialism is. Most students confuse it with provincialisms or localisms and think it refers to sectional peculiarities of speech. Most students also attach some sort of stigma to the word and try to avoid using words or expressions that are labeled colloquial in the dictionary. A colloquialism really has nothing to do with sectional peculiarities, and there is nothing "bad" or improper about using it–under certain circumstances. The word simply labels expressions that are more acceptable in familiar or ordinary conversation than in formal speech and writing. For example, the president of a college, or the principal of a school, when talking with his colleagues, may quite properly use colloquialisms. However, when he dons cap and gown to deliver an address at the annual commencement exercises, he scrupulously avoids colloquialisms. The difference is in the setting.

It is perfectly all right to use colloquialisms when you are talking with members of your family, with friends, and when writing friendly letters and informal reports. An example of a colloquialism and its equivalent formal form is given below.

Colloquialism What a close shave!

Formal What a narrow escape!

Jargon

Dictionaries define *jargon* as language that is "unintelligible." This is an unfortunately broad definition. We usually associate the term with the "bureaucratic jargon" of officialdom, now widely referred to as *governmentese*. In this sense *jargon* has partly derisive, partly humorous connotations. In a stricter sense, *jargon* is the specialized vocabulary of persons who are engaged in the same trade or profession. The intelligibility of the specialized vocabularly naturally excludes the outsider, but for the insider it is loaded with meaning. A single expression can stand for a thought or idea that might otherwise take ten, twenty, or even a hundred words to express with a standard vocabulary. As long as the expression is kept within the specialized group, it is perfectly necessary and legitimate. It is only when the expression is employed outside the field in contexts where other vocabulary is available that it becomes jargon in the commonly accepted sense of the term. Thus, the expression "relate to" is a favorite in the vocabulary of psychologists. Employed by a psychologist outside his professional setting, or by the layman, this same expression loses its specialized meaning and becomes absurd jargon.

Trite Expressions and Clichés

A trite expression is an overused expression. It has been used so much that when the reader sees the first word or two, he can anticipate what follows. And when the reader can anticipate your words, you cannot hold his attention. "A good time was had by all" is a trite expression. A cliché is a figure of speech or turn of words that may have been original and clever once upon a time but that has become trite and stale through overuse. Like an oft-repeated joke, *it wears its welcome thin* (the expression in italics is a cliché). How do you tell when a cliché is a cliché? As happens with jokes, you hear one and you think it is original, or you think one up yourself. You hasten to tell it to your friends. But they have already heard it countless times. So it is with clichés. You must consciously be on the lookout for them in whatever you read or hear. Whenever you spot a cliché, make a mental note not to use it in your own writing.

Provincialisms and Localisms

A *provincialism* is a word, phrase, or idiom peculiar to a major geographical section or region. A *localism* is peculiar to a limited locality. When used in speech by persons who live in a particular section or locality, they are legitimate and proper. Since provincialisms and localisms are not in national usage, however, they do not appear in formal, expository writing. Obviously, both are essential to the speech of characters in fiction.

Barbarisms

Barbarism is the name grammarians give to the gross misuse of words. To use *eats* for *food,* as in "Pass me the eats," would be termed a barbarism. Another example of a barbarism is the use of *learn* for *teach,* as in "That will learn you a lesson."

Effective Paragaraphs

Any reader is aware that an indented sentence means a new paragraph. In dialogue, such indentation shows merely that a new speaker is being quoted. But the indentation at the beginning of the paragraph always indicates some change of subject or approach–in the description, the narration, the argument–whatever the type of the writing may be.

The new paragraph, however, does more for us than indicate a change in thought. For the paragraph is the real building block of any prose writing. The casual letter-writer, the student, the professional journalist, the novelist–all use paragraphing in their letters, essays, articles, or novels. In order to function correctly, that is, to fit neatly among the other blocks as well as help to hold them up, the paragraph must, itself, be a carefully completed and finely shaped unit. Perhaps the best definition of a *paragraph* might be: *the carefully rounded development of a single impression or idea.*

The reader should bear in mind that no absolute criteria exist for determining a good paragraph. There is agreement that a paragraph should contain the stylistic elements which effectively convey the writer's idea, or purpose. Such a paragraph is effective–it is good.

Paragraphs may be purely descriptive, or narrative, or expository, or they may include any mixture of these major types of writing. The principles of good paragraph-writing discussed below can be applied to all types of paragraphs.

PRINCIPLES

The Topic Idea

A good writer knows exactly why he is starting a new paragraph and why he is ending it. Within that one paragraph he is trying to say essentially *one thing* as clearly and as completely as he possibly can. That one thing we call the "topic idea" of a paragraph. Often this topic idea is expressed in a *topic sentence* that generally comes at or near the beginning of the paragraph. The topic sentence, however, need not come at the beginning, nor does the paragraph have to have a topic sentence, so long as the single idea is clear.

Adequate Development

The topic idea can be conveyed only if the writer makes sufficient effort to "show what he means" to his reader. The different methods of "showing" are enumerated below, but it is important to remember that no matter how you construct your paragraph, it must give enough details, facts, examples, or reasons to hold and convince the reader.

Inadequate Everyone should play some sport from which he gets both enjoyment and physical toughening. Sports have always been considered important. They make you strong and you can have a lot of fun with them. Furthermore, friendships can be made through sports. Nobody can deny that for many reasons, sports are a "must."

In the above paragraph, note that most of the sentences are mere restatements of the topic sentence or of each other, and that they are extremely general. The way to construct your paragraphs well consists of your ability to give details, facts, specifics, in concise and *concrete* language.

Unity

The well-written paragraph sticks relentlessly to its topic idea and departs from that idea only to bring in closely related material. A careless writer, on the other hand, "wanders" from his topic, and thereby loses the concentrated focus, or "unity," that writing must have if it is to be effective. The best way to keep each paragraph unified is to make the subject of most of your sentences the same as the subject of your topic sentence; hold on to your subject, and you will hold on to your topic idea.

Transition

Transition is "going across" or–in writing–getting the reader smoothly from one thought to another, one image to another, one sentence to the next. You can achieve good transition by practicing these two important principles:

a) *Arrange the sentences of each paragraph in logical order so that each follows the one before it as naturally as possible.*

Failure to build the paragraph on such a predetermined order can result in confusion and lack of transition. Presenting images or events simply in their *order of occurrence in time* or in their "narrative order" is one of the most common methods of developing a paragraph logically.

You could also arrange the ideas or arguments in a predetermined "order of importance."

b) *Wherever necessary, use words and phrases that tie your ideas together as closely as possible.*

These words and phrases, sometimes called "transitional devices," can be categorized under three headings: pronouns, key (or "echo") words, and connectives.

1) Pronouns

Using pronouns whose antecedents are the subject of the paragraph makes transition stronger. The most useful of these for transitional purposes are the demonstratives: *this, that, these, those.*

> Nothing in the way of equipment was overlooked. It was because of *this* preparation that the expedition was so successful.

2) Key words

These are words that relate to or "echo" the topic idea, and their inclusion holds the paragraph–and the reader–to the subject.

> The men fought the *fire* mightily for three days. However, the *blaze* was too much for them; the *flames* would not be extinguished. Such *holocausts* cost Americans millions of acres in valuable forest every year.

3) Connective words and phrases

This group of transitional devices is extensive, and we use many of them quite naturally in our everyday speech. The group includes all conjunctions–subordinate, correlative, and coordinate–plus a large number of "connective" adverbs and adverb phrases.

The following paragraph has employed transitional words and phrases. Note that the "flow" is smooth and its thought easy to follow.

> My black, furry poodle, Totor, is a real problem to me. *Ever since* I bought him from a pet shop, he has caused me nothing but trouble. *However,* I do like him, *because* he has such a charming, lively personality. *But* this liveliness is also the source of my problem, *for* it leads him to do the most dreadful things. *For instance,* he hops up on the kitchen table and eats a whole ham. *Then* he chews the caps off the milk bottles and drinks all the cream. *And* he is always stealing shoes and chewing them apart. *Nevertheless,* he is worth it, *mostly because* I have learned how to outfox him–most of the time.

Necessary Design

The good paragraph is organically dependent upon its topic sentence or topic idea for its overall construction. It has a logical design that arises out of the purpose of the paragraph. Thus, if your purpose is to describe a room by putting the reader into the scene, your details would be arranged in an order in which he might see them, were he standing in the room. If, in another paragraph, your purpose is to convince your reader of a certain fact, you would list your points in such a way that they would have maximum effect on him (perhaps in an ascending or "climactic" order of importance).

DEVELOPING A PARAGRAPH

The way the writer develops his topic idea in any single paragraph must always be determined by the topic idea and the purpose that the writer has in mind for the paragraph. The six major ways in which a writer can develop a topic idea within any paragraph are described below:

Enumerate Examples or Illustrations

Sometimes we may be saying something that we cannot explain clearly, and our listener may suggest, "Well, suppose you give me an example." Examples, or illustrations, provide us with a way of putting something abstract and perhaps difficult to comprehend into images or pictures that are easy to understand. Examples are almost exactly the same as details, except that they are used for the specific purpose of making a general point. You give an example of something; you make an illustration of a point. Hence, this method of developing a paragraph is especially useful in *expository* and *argumentative* writing.

Use a Single Illustration

Often the easiest way to "say what you mean" is to tell a simple story that says it for you. Such a method of developing a topic idea can help you define a word, make a point clear, or explain an idea. Hence, the "single-illustration paragraph" is used most frequently in *expository* and *argumentative* writing.

Explain by Definition

In *expository* writing, we can sometimes more clearly discuss an idea or concept by *defining* the word that embodies the idea. The definition should expand the basic idea by presenting other ideas with which the reader is already familiar.

Explain by Analogy

An *analogy* is a single illustration that describes or explains one thing by describing something quite different, but at the same time similar, so that there is a clear parallel between the two. George Orwell's much-discussed novel *Animal Farm* is an analogy in the form of a novel. In this book, Orwell presents his attitude toward the aftermath of the Russian Revolution by telling a story of a group of very human animals on a farm. The analogy is often more dramatic than a simple illustration because of its suggestive powers. Thus, for example, Orwell's use of animals immediately suggests that the historical figures whom they represent were somewhat less than human in their behavior.

Illustrate by Comparison and/or Contrast

This method of developing a paragraph can take one of three forms, depending on the topic idea and the purpose of the writer:

a) showing comparisons or similarities
b) showing contrasts or dissimilarities
c) showing both comparisons and contrasts

As you can see, the third is a combination of the first two methods. This approach is especially useful when describing abstract ideas.

Give Reasons

The paragraph that uses reasons to develop its topic idea will be more effective if the reasons are listed in some logical or dramatic order, not haphazardly. The reasons are listed in increasing order of importance. Since the end of the paragraph–like the end of a sentence, or of an essay, or of a speech–is a high point of emphasis, this order is commonly used and is very effective. A "clincher" sentence is used at the end of the paragraph to restate the topic sentence for greater emphasis.

The Total Composition

Every composition has a clearly defined introduction, body, and conclusion, but these are not labeled as such or set apart when the paper is written.

The introduction should (1) arouse the reader's interest; (2) state the main idea of the composition; and (3) possibly preview the main topics. It contains your thesis statement (see "The Research Paper") and a number of other sentences designed to introduce your topic and let the reader know what the paper is about. This is your road map, guiding you through the rest of your paper until you reach your destination.

The body of the composition must develop, support, and explain the main ideas stated in your introduction, or thesis paragraph. It should include appropriate, specific examples and details to back up your thesis. An outline is essential for a well-constructed paper.

The conclusion of the paper should clinch the main points made in the body of the composition. It pulls together the details of the paper into a final statement, giving a feeling of completeness. It should not contain any new evidence. Depending on your objective, the conclusion may simply summarize your position, emphasize a main point, draw a conclusion, or even spur the reader to action.

However, the best ideas and the most detailed research are all to no avail if the end product, the written paper, is not *well* written, if it does not communicate effectively to the reader. Therefore, the mechanics of composition are of paramount importance to you. The three key words to consider in writing are *unity, coherence,* and *emphasis.*

The principle of unity applies to all components of the paper, to the paragraphs which are the building blocks of the paper like bricks in a wall, and to the paper as a whole. Each paragraph should contain only one thought, with the topic sentence controlling the idea of the whole paragraph. By the same token, each paragraph should develop, explain, or expand on the main point of the composition. Do not wander off on tangents; eliminate anything that does not fulfill your thesis statement.

Following the principle of coherence makes the paper understandable. It has to do with arranging your ideas in a clear order according to a definite plan, with the ideas linked together clearly and expressed in vivid, interesting language. Paragraphs should flow naturally from one to another with ideas arranged in logical order. Smooth transitions from one paragraph to the next are essential for the reader to understand the relationship between the ideas expressed in the individual paragraphs. Therefore transitions could be likened to the mortar holding together the separate building blocks of a wall.

Here are some linking expressions to bridge gaps between paragraphs.

To go from one point to another: finally, moreover, besides, in addition to, another, in the next place, also, furthermore, to sum up.

To indicate another time: next, soon, meanwhile, then, later, finally.

To indicate results: therefore, thus, consequently, as a result. .

To show contrast: nevertheless, however, on the other hand, instead, in spite of.

To show relationships: accordingly, similarly, likewise.

To introduce examples: for instance, for example.

Style, the way words are put together, is extremely important in getting ideas across from your mind to your reader's mind. We all use our language in different ways. In everyday conversation we use contractions, slang, colloquialisms, even dialect. This is fine. In addition to our spoken language, we have our written language. When we write letters to friends, or even informal papers, we write in a chatty, informal style. This is fine too. Then there is formal written language. For serious papers informality is totally out of place, so do not use contractions, slang, or colloquial expressions. While avoiding being stodgy or flowery, do be formal or objective in expression, and refrain from using second person (you) or first person (I).

A writer must also be very careful not to be guilty of plagiarism, which is using another person's ideas, words, or even sentence structure as one's own without giving proper credit to the original author.

The third principle of writing concerns emphasis, meaning devoting more space to the more important points and explaining what needs to be explained fully. Put yourself in the reader's place and try to see if another person would have any unanswered questions after reading the paper. Would they really understand what you are trying to say?

It has been said that there is no such thing as good writing, only rewriting. All really great authors polish their works many times. After you have gotten your thoughts down on paper the first time, read it aloud to yourself and listen to what it has to say. Get another person to read it to see if it is understandable to an outsider. After you have reworked the paper for sense and style of writing, go over it again checking your grammar and punctuation. Make a third check just for spelling. After you have copied your paper in its final form, always go over it again proofreading for any copying errors.

Typed papers are always double spaced. If you write by hand, use blue or black ink on one side only of standard notebook paper.

Put the title in the center of the first line. Do not underline it or put it in quotes. Skip a line and begin the paper proper, indenting paragraphs one-half inch. Leave a margin on the left side to coincide with the red line of the notebook paper (about one and one-half inches). Leave a margin on the right side half the width of the left-hand margin. Do not skip lines between paragraphs and do not write on the last blue line at the bottom of the page. On all pages except the first, begin writing on the first blue line. Do not number the first page of the paper but number all other pages of the paper proper in the upper right-hand corner. Outline, end notes, and bibliography pages are not numbered. Never turn in a paper containing crossed-out words. For an example of a title page, see the model at the end of "The Research Paper."

SPECIAL COMPOSITIONS

Written communication falls into four kinds of writing: exposition, argument, description, and narration. Expository writing is to inform or explain. Argument is used to persuade by reason and/or emotion. Description paints a picture appealing to the five senses. Narration gives an account of action or events.

Probably more than 95 percent of contemporary writing is expository for it includes most scientific and technical books, textbooks, philosophical and political tracts (when not contentious), much of biography and history, the bulk of magazine writing, recipes and formulas, essays and editorials, and reviews and criticism, whether of art, music, or literature. Patches of exposition may be found also in argumentation, narration, and description. When a debater pauses to explain or clarify a situation, the temporary digression may serve to strengthen his case. He is then no longer contending for a point but is engaging in exposition. If the author of a detective story pauses to discuss the layout of the apartment in which the crime occurs he is similarly engaged in exposition. In a book like Rachel Carson's *The Sea Around Us,* the text is about evenly divided among narration, description, and exposition.

Since expository writing is so important, we will go into detail about some specific kinds: the research paper, the book report (or review), the précis, and the science project report.

THE RESEARCH PAPER

A research (or library or term) paper is a documented prose work resulting from an organized analysis of a subject. It presents the results of careful investigation of some chosen topic in an interesting, orderly, and clear manner. It is an original paper by a student who has searched with intelligence through varied sources, selecting facts that he recognizes as essential to his stated subject. The student takes a relevant idea from one author, a telling quotation from another and, having gathered together a body of such information, will then, by using his imagination and knowledge, create something new. It is written in his own words unless a direct quotation is attributed to its original author.

STEPS TO FOLLOW

1. CHOOSE, THEN LIMIT YOUR SUBJECT. You will do best with a subject that interests you, that you can understand, that has sufficient information available about it, that is limited in its scope so that it can be covered adequately in a paper of the assigned length.

2. SURVEY YOUR RESOURCES. Check the card catalog of the library for books dealing with

your proposed topic. Determining the key word to look under is a basic problem in library research. No matter what library tool you use—card catalog, *Reader's Guide,* indexes to books—you must ask yourself this question: "What key word will lead me to the information I seek?" The same key word does not always apply to every reference tool. For instance, the *Reader's Guide* may use "Impeachment," while the card catalog may use "Presidents—U. S.—Impeachment." Remember the topic may encompass many subject headings. For instance, the broad subject of "Crime and Criminals" would include these subject headings and many more: Crime prevention; Criminal law; Administration of justice; Juvenile deliquency; Murder; Organized crime; Police; Prisons; Punishment; Racketeering; Social ethics, etc.

Write down the call numbers for books you think you could use, then go to the shelves to find them. Look at books with similar call numbers. Scan tables of contents to see what the books are about. In the card catalog also note references to pamphlets and clippings in the library's Vertical File and to nonbook materials such as filmstrips and multimedia kits. Consider knowledgeable people in the field to interview. Systematically look at the various issues of the *Reader's Guide,* checking off each volume as you finish it.

3. MAKE A PRELIMINARY STATEMENT OF OBJECTIVE (THESIS STATEMENT). At some point during your survey of resources, you may find there is not enough information on your topic. Change topics immediately. If you find much information, you will need to narrow it very soon, but surveying your resources helps you see the different facets of the topic, to help with your narrowing decision. But very soon you must hone in on your chosen objective in order to find all you need to know about it and not to waste time on information not essential to it. Making a preliminary thesis statement helps keep you on track.

Possible topics:

The Supreme Court—No! Impossibly broad!

Recent Supreme Court Decisions—No! Still impossible!

Supreme Court Decisions Pertaining to School Desegration—Still too big!

The Effect of Supreme Court Decisions on Nashville Schools—OK

Thesis Statement: Dramatic changes in the structure of Nashville's school system occurred in the 1950s, in 1971, and in 1983 as a result of Supreme Court decisions.

4. MAKE A WORKING BIBLIOGRAPHY. Once you have settled on what you are looking for, it is time to begin gathering material in earnest. Set up a Working Bibliography on a sheet of notebook paper listing everything that might possibly be of use to you. Here you copy all magazine articles exactly as the information is given you in the *Reader's Guide.* Make notations of those unavailable in your school library so you can check the public library. Scratch off those that prove useless. Enter all books, pamphlets, nonbook materials, people. The Working Bibliography is a good place to list all the varied subject headings you need to check to find available material. This is a valuable tool, so preserve it carefully until you have finished your paper.

5. SCAN YOUR MATERIAL. As you find information, glance through it quickly to see if it contains information you want. You must understand the material and then translate it into an intelligible presentation of your own. Ask yourself, "What is the author trying to say?" "What are the main points he is trying to make?" If the answers to these questions have a bearing on your thesis, prepare to go over the material more thoroughly.

6. MAKE A BIBLIOGRAPHY CARD, separate, complete, and accurate, for each source of information you consult. Do this before you take any notes from that source and keep your master bibliography cards separate from your note cards.

For a book, get your information from the title page and, if no date is listed there, the copyright date from the back of the title page. Book information includes author (full name, last name first), title, place of publication, publisher, and date.

For a magazine you must have the author of the article (if any); name of magazine; its volume number in arabic numerals; its date; and the pages the article is found on, such as pp. 37–41.

7. TAKE GOOD NOTES. If they are prepared properly, writing the paper is relatively easy, and you should not have to consult your sources again. Follow this procedure:

(a) write on 3 x 5 or 4 x 6 cards;

(b) write on one side of the card only;

(c) put only one idea from one source to a card;

(d) include on each card four things—(1) a slug, identification of the specific subject treated on the card; (2) the source, shortened title or author's name so you can tell where the information came from; (3) your notes; (4) the exact page where the material appears.

Do not write down obvious, easily remembered,

well known, or general information. As you read, stop to think what the main idea is. Close your eyes and say it in your own words. Write the notation on the notecard. Check back to see that you have understood the idea correctly. Be careful to avoid misrepresentation by lifting material out of context or by twisting the interpretation to suit your own conclusion. Put the information in your own words, never using words in the book. However, if you think you would like to quote the material from your source, copy it exactly and enclose it in quotation marks.

Here are samples of a bibliography card and a note card made from it.

Muir, Frank
Christmas Customs & Traditions
New York, Taplinger Publishing Company
1975

Preparations – Cookery Muir
Stir Up Sunday – Sun. before Advent
last time to make Christmas
pudding to be ready in time.
p.22 Gets name from Church Collect for
that day which begins "Stir up
we beseech thee, O Lord, the wills of
thy faithful people...."

8. During this reading process, MAKE A PRELIMINARY OUTLINE, so you can see exactly what information you need on various points and how much you will need. (See "Outlining.") Outline topics make good slugs for notecards.

9. CONTINUE READING AND NOTE TAKING. Remember the outline is like a skeleton which your paper will flesh out. The preliminary outline may show that your skeleton lacks an arm, or one arm is much smaller than the other. Your reading and note taking now can fill in what the outline revealed was needed.

10. MAKE UP AN INTERESTING TITLE.

11. WRITE YOUR THESIS STATEMENT IN ITS FINAL FORM. Remember the thesis tells exactly what your paper is about, what it is to cover; and the outline shows how you accomplish the objective of the thesis. In the preliminary stages you may need to adjust both the original thesis and the original outline. Now is the time to get your thesis in precise final form. Play with words, work to express your thesis so it will convey exactly the ideas you want it to in an interesting manner.

12. REVISE OUTLINE into its final form.

13. WRITE AN INTERESTING INTRODUCTION that (1) attracts the reader's attention; (2) states what the paper is about; and (3) previews the main topics. Incorporate your thesis in the introduction.

14. SORT YOUR NOTE CARDS to conform to your outline. Write the paper in your words using formal, objective style. Avoid the use of "you" and "I." The research paper is not an informal essay, although you need to make it interesting and may use imagination in making deductions and drawing conclusions.

Have your end note page beside you and make your end notes as you write. Be specific but do not worry about exact form at this time, as you can go back and set your end notes in precise form later. Just be sure your numbers coincide. End note[1] in your paper must refer to [1]on your end note page.

Even though you are writing in your own words, you have used information supplied by others. You will also want to use direct quotations (but only sparingly, to emphasize an important point or as proof of your conclusions). These must be acknowledged. Use a footnote or an end note to give credit for a direct quotation; to give credit for an original or unusually interesting opinion or interpretation which you have put in your own words; to give credit for all statistics, figures, definitions, illustrations. The question always arises, "Since I knew nothing about this subject before researching it, do I have to footnote every piece of information used?" Obviously that would be impractical. If the ideas seem to be general knowledge of authorities in the field, do not footnote unless you are quoting exactly. (See "Endnoting/Footnoting" for exact details.)

Direct quotations are handled in two different ways. For a short quotation (one that would be four typed lines or less) enclose it in quotation marks and "work it in smoothly as part of your own sentence."[1]

A long quotation (one that is five lines or more of type) should be handled this way:

Double-space (or skip a line of notebook paper) above and below the quotation. Single-space the quotation if you are typing. Indent the quoted material an extra half-inch on each side. Do not use quotation marks around it. Remember always at the end of a quotation, whether it is short or long, that you must put a number slightly above the line to refer to the same number in your footnotes.[2]

15. WRITE A GOOD CONCLUSION that rounds out your paper, sums it up, gives a feeling of completeness.

16. REVISE YOUR PAPER.

17. COPY YOUR PAPER, then proofread for copying errors. Doublecheck footnotes for accuracy and for form.

18. MAKE YOUR BIBLIOGRAPHY. Arrange your bibliography cards alphabetically according to the author's last name. If there is no author, alphabetize by the first word of the title (skipping "A," "An," and "The." If the reference is published by an organization with no author, use the organization as author. Make your bibliography according to the prescribed forms. Often teachers want you to include in your bibliography only the sources you actually used in writing the paper, not a complete listing of sources you may have consulted. (See "Bibliography.")

19. MAKE THE TITLE PAGE. (See form.)

20. ASSEMBLE THE PAPER. The usual order is: (1) title page; (2) outline, which substitutes for a table of contents in a school paper; (3) the paper itself; (4) end notes; (5) bibliography.

ABBREVIATIONS

Common abbreviations found in doing research are:

ca., c.	about (circa)
ch., chs.	chapter, chapters
cf.	compare, confer
et al.	and others (**et alii** or **alibi**)
ed.	edited, edition, editor
e.g.	for example (**exempli gratia**)
f., ff.	and the following page, pages
illus.	illustrated
ibid.	in the same place (**ibidem**) (obsolete)
id.	the same (**idem**)
l., ll.	line, lines
i.e.	that is (**id est**)
loc. cit.	in the place cited (**loco citato**) (obsolete)
lit.	literally
MS, MSS	Manuscript, Manuscripts
N.B.	note well (**nota bene**)
n.d.	no date given
no., nos.	number, numbers
op. cit.	in the work cited (**opere citato**) (obsolete)
p., pp.	page, pages
trans.	translator/translation
viz.	namely
vol., vols.	volume, volumes

OUTLINING

An outline is to a paper what a road map is to a journey. The thesis statement states your destination, and the outline shows you how to get there. Thesis: I am going to Yazoo City, Mississippi, from Nashville, Tennessee. Outline: Take I-40 to Memphis; then I-55 toward Jackson; at Exit 181 go west on Highway 16. . . . The purpose of outlining is to prevent wandering off the subject; to give a quick overall view of the essay; to insure proportionate space to each part; to aid in organizing and giving order to the essay; to enable you to spot missing or irrelevant matter. Some ways to organize are: by time, by space, by likenesses and differences, in order of importance, by cause and effect.

An outline includes only main ideas and important details. Flesh in the outline when you write the paper.

There must always be under any topic more than one subtopic. Subtopics are divisions of the topic above them, and you cannot divide anything into fewer than two parts. If you find yourself wanting to use a single subtopic, rewrite the topic above it so that this "sub idea" is included in the main topic.

Wrong: C. Hostesses
    1. Those who nag
Right: C. Nagging Hostesses

A subtopic must belong under the main topic beneath which it is placed. It must be closely related to the topic above it.

Wrong: A. Dull games
    1. Bingo
    2. Not enough refreshments

Terms such as "Introduction," "Body," and "Conclusion" should not be included in the outline. Of course, you should have them as definite parts of your paper (though never so designated) but these are not topics that you intend to discuss.

There are two kinds of outlines, the topic and the sentence. The topic is composed of words or phrases throughout all divisions. It is used for conciseness and brevity, and no end punctuation is needed. A sentence outline uses sentences throughout its divisions, so end punctuation is needed. It is fuller, clearer, and more exact than a topic outline.

How to Prepare an Outline

To outline a chapter in a book is easy because the information was outlined before it was written. The difficult part of outlining is taking a large body of information and organizing it into a logical, coherent form. Here are some tips to help you do this for your research paper. Notice it is in sentence outline form.

I. Select the subject of your paper.
  A. Decide on a general topic.
    1. Survey available resources.
    2. Note the various aspects of the subject.
  B. Limit your topic to a narrow aspect that can be adequately covered in a paper of your designated length.
  C. Write a thesis statement that exactly pinpoints your objective.

II. Make a rough draft of your outline.
  A. Jot down at random all the points about your paper that come to mind.
  B. Group similar ones together.
  C. Decide what pattern would be best to follow.
    1. It could be chronological.
    2. It could be spatial (geographical).
    3. It could be a study of contrasts or comparisons.
    4. It could be cause-and-effect.
    5. It could be a study of influences.
  D. Write a simple topic outline.
    1. Choose two to four most important points for the major divisions.
    2. Place remaining ideas as subtopics under them.
  E. Assess the result.
    1. Consider if you are fulfilling your thesis statement.
    2. Consider if you have covered the subject adequately.
    3. Check to see that each subtopic falls logically under its larger topic.
    4. Eliminate any material that does not fit.
      (a) This means irrelevant matter.
      (b) This means unnecessary (too detailed) matter for an outline.
    5. Determine if you need to look for additional information.
      (a) Should this information be for an added topic?
      (b) Should it be to expand on an existing topic?

III. Write the outline in final sentence form.
  A. Word the main topics to make them concise, clear, and parallel.*
  B. Fill in the subtopics by the same criteria.
  C. See that the outline is in correct outline form.

* Parallelism means using similar wording for various divisions of equal rank. Here is a topic outline illustrating this.

Wrong
How to Do the Laundry
  I. Sorting by colors
  II. To start the machine
  III. Proper water temperature
  IV. How to handle delicate fabrics

Right
How to Do the Laundry
  I. Sorting by colors
  II. Starting the machine
  III. Choosing proper water temperature
  IV. Handling delicate fabrics

Picture of an Outline

Title of Paper
Thesis Statement: ....
I. Major division
  A. Subdivision
    1. Sub-subdivision
      a.
        (1)
          (a)
          (b)
        (2)
      b.
    2.
  B.
II.

FOOTNOTING/ENDNOTING

The distinction has been made that footnotes are properly used in dissertations and end notes are to be used in research papers. The difference is that footnotes appear at the bottom of the page containing the cited material, while end notes are arranged on one or two pages at the end of the paper. It is much easier to do end notes because in footnotes the writing has to be spaced very carefully to allow sufficient room at the bottom of the page. Teachers vary in which they require. People generally speak of footnotes to mean both those at the foot of the page and those at the end of the paper.

These instructions are for end notes.

* Number them consecutively throughout the paper.

* In the body of your paper put a number slightly above the line *at the end* of the material to be acknowledged. No period follows an end note number.

* On your end note page put the same number as its corresponding number in the paper (again above the line and without a period). Indent the first line of each end note and start the second line even with the left margin.

* The author's *given name* should be written *first.*

When the same source is repeated, it is not necessary to give the full information about that source a second time. Use a shortened form to identify the reference. Formerly Latin terms such as "ibid.," "op. cit.," and "loc. cit." were used. These are now considered obsolete. When the same source is used a second or subsequent time, simply write the end note number, then the author's last name, and then the page number on which the material can be found.

If you have made your bibliography cards properly, you will have there all the information you will need for your end notes, except for the exact page on which that bit of material was found, which will be on your note card. Never end note for several pages in a source; the only time you would indicate two pages is when the sentence on the source page runs over onto a second page.

Examples of End Notes

(First use of book by one author)

[1]Robert W. Kirk, *First Aid for Pets* (New York: E. P. Dutton, 1978), p. 40.

(Second and subsequent uses of preceding book)

[2]Kirk, p. 41.

(First use of book by two authors)

[3]Mary Bray Wheeler and Genon Hickerson Neblett, *Hidden Glory: The Life and Times of Hampton Plantation, Legend of the South Santee* (Nashville: Rutledge Hill Press, 1983), pp. 21-22.

(For a book with no author)

[4]*Webster's Geographical Dictionary* (Springfield: G. & C. Merriam Co., 1981), p. 535.

(For an organization as author)

[5]U.S. Department of Commerce, Bureau of the Census, *Statistical Abstract of the United States 1982–83* (Washington, D.C., Government Printing Office, 1982), p. 1065.

(For a book with an editor)

[6]Lois Decker O'Neill, ed., *The Women's Book of World Records and Achievements* (New York: Doubleday, 1979), p. 84.

(For a magazine article with an author; note the volume number before the date.)

[7]Michael M. Lombardo, "The Intolerable Boss," *Psychology Today,* 18(Jan., 1984), p. 45.

(For the same article, second and subsequent quotings)

[8]Lombardo, p. 46.

(For a magazine article with no author)

[9]"The Muffin-Mix Scare," *Time,* 123(Feb. 13, 1984), p. 20.

(For the same article, second and subsequent quotings)

[10]*Time,* p. 22*

* If you are quoting from several *different* issues of *Time,* include the date in parentheses: *Time,* (Feb. 13, 1984), p. 22. This will indicate which issue you refer to.

(For a newspaper article with a by-line)

[11]Patricia McCormack, "Special Diet Urged to Thwart Cancer," *Nashville Tennessean,* (Feb. 11, 1984), Sec. D, p. 2.

(For a newspaper article with no by-line)

[12]"Moslems Take West Beirut," *Nashville Banner,* (Feb. 8, 1984), Sec. A, p. 1.

(For an encyclopedia article)

[13]"Jet Propulsion," *World Book Encyclopedia,* (1979 ed.), vol. 11, p. 386.

(For an interview)

[14]Richard Fulton, Mayor of Nashville, interviewed by Mary Smith (Metropolitan Courthouse, Nashville, Tenn.), 10 A.M., Jan. 15, 1984.

(For a personal letter)

[15]Personal letter from Lamar Alexander, Governor of Tennessee, to Jason Jones, Feb. 16, 1984.

(For material from one source quoted in another)

[16]James Boswell, *The Life of Samuel Johnson,* quoted by Robert Byrne in *Cat Scan* (New York: Atheneum, 1983), p. 7.

If there are two or more works by the same author, or two or more authors with the same name, a shortened title of the cited work is used after the author's last name. Let us assume you are quoting from two books by Louise Davis, *Nashville Tales* and *Frontier Tales.*

(First citation)

[17]Louise Littleton Davis, *Nashville Tales* (Gretna, LA: Pelican Publishing Co., 1981), p. 35.

(Second citation)

[18]Davis, *Nashville,* p. 4.

Notice the differences between the pattern of end notes and of a bibliography. In end notes the arrangement is strictly numerical in the order the material is cited from the work; the author's first name comes first; the first line is indented and the second line is flush with the left-hand margin. In a bibliography the arrangement is alphabetical by the author's last name and the first line is flush with the left-hand margin with the second line being indented. Here is a bibliography of the works cited in the example of footnotes.

BIBLIOGRAPHY

Alexander, Lamar, Governor of Tennessee, to Jason Jones, Feb. 16, 1984.

Byrne, Robert. *Cat Scan.* New York: Atheneum, 1983.

Davis, Louise Littleton. *Frontier Tales.* Gretna, LA: Pelican Publishing Co., 1980.

———, *Nashville Tales.* Gretna, LA: Pelican Publishing Co., 1981.

Fulton, Richard, Mayor of Nashville, interviewed by Mary Smith, Metropolitan Courthouse, Nashville, Tenn., 10 A.M., Jan. 15, 1984.

"Jet Propulsion." *World Book Encyclopedia,* 1979 ed., vol. 11, p. 386.

Kirk, Robert W. *First Aid for Pets.* New York: E. P. Dutton, 1978.

Lombardo, Michael M. "The Intolerable Boss." *Psychology Today,* 18 (Jan., 1984), pp. 45–48.

McCormack, Patricia. "Special Diet Urged to Thwart Cancer." *Nashville Tennessean,* (Feb. 8, 1984), Sec. D, p. 2.

"Muffin-Mix Scare." *Time,* 123 (Feb. 13, 1984), pp. 20-21.

O'Neill, Lois Decker, ed. *The Women's Book of World Records and Achievements.* New York: Doubleday, 1979.

U. S. Department of Commerce, Bureau of the Census, *Statistical Abstract of the United States 1982#83.* Washington, D.C.: Government Printing Office, 1982.

Webster's Geographical Dictionary. Springfield: G. & C. Merriam Co., 1981.

Wheeler, Mary Bray, and Neblett, Genon Hickerson. *Hidden Glory: The Life and Times of Hampton Plantation, Legend of the South Santee.* Nashville: Rutledge Hill Press, 1983.

You will find slight variations, especially in punctuation, among the many handbooks available showing forms for footnotes and bibliographies. The important thing for you to do is to choose one source as your model and then be scrupulous in following it exactly so your paper is consistent throughout.

(Sample of Title Page)

RAIN OF DEATH: THE IMPACT OF ACID RAIN

ON NATURAL RESOURCES IN THE UNITED STATES

by

Nathan Elliott

American History, Fourth Period

February 21, 1984

Argumentative Writing

That category of writing which attempts to strengthen a view already held, to weaken or undermine such a view, or to persuade the reader to adopt another is called argumentation. The name, though well established, is unfortunate, for one immediately infers that it involves a contentious type of discussion. Persuasion would be a better name, for the aim is to incline another's will to one's own view rather than to controvert it or break it. The writer who conceives his task as persuasion must also assume (even though he may suspect the contrary to be true) that his reader has not taken a firm position, and, as a reasonable man, would be delighted to follow him into his stand. Therefore, from the very start, he tries to confine his attack, so far as he must attack, to issues rather than to persons. The attitude of the persuader must be understanding and generous. He writes, "It would appear . . . ," "It seems . . ." rather than "It is . . ." or "It must be. . . ."

Analysis of the Question

1. DEFINITION OF TERMS

Should a writer wish to contend that New York City is the true capital of America, he would have to define what he means by his terms. Does he mean "Greater New York," or does he mean the financial district? Does "true" have the same sense as "real"? Is "capital" used as "the governing political center" or the "dominant financial center"? By "America" does he mean the United States, North America, or the Western Hemisphere? It will be observed that until these terms are clarified the issue is confused. The process of clarification which must be undertaken by the writer at the outset is known as "defining the terms."

2. HISTORY OF THE QUESTION

Many issues are of long standing and have been discussed before. If the previous discussion has swayed public opinion in any discernible way, the writer may possibly profit by rehearsing previous discussions if their results favor him. Such a presentation is known as "giving the history of the question." If, on the other hand, he can show that his view has in the past received scant attention, has been rudely treated or suppressed, he may actually profit from rehearsing this history.

3. DETERMINING THE ISSUES

Whenever there is a difference of opinion, the holders of opposing views frequently find themselves separated on a multiplicity of issues, many of which may be extremely trivial. If one urges trivial issues, even successfully, when major issues are decisive, his power to persuade will fail. The best way to determine the major issues is to set up the chief issues for each side and to select the ones that collide most sharply; these are the major issues.

Planning Persuasive Measures

Once he has determined the issues, the writer plans the order in which he will present them. He will have to decide on one of two approaches, depending on whether he feels he can easily overcome opposition or will have to work hard to be persuasive. In the former situation he should choose and present his strongest point first, with the intent of putting his opposition to rout; in the latter, he should study the issues to see if there is not one that may be conceded to him without too great a struggle, and use that as an entering wedge. To persuade successfully one must consider every possible factor that can be turned to advantage, but yet must avoid seeming to do so. The tone of persuasion should be concessive, generous.

Briefing

If the issue involves grave consequences or the opposition is entrenched and well armed, it is wise to prepare a formal brief, covering the major issues and indicating the proof to be supplied. The practice of briefing, incidentally, provides an excellent discipline for the reasoning faculties. The form is well established and should be conscientiously adhered to:

The United States should support the U.N., *for*

I. It is the major instrument for world peace, *for*
    A. Balance of power is impossible, *for*
        1. Unilateral action can undermine the balance, *for*
            a. China does not accept Russian leadership in the East.
            b. France is uncooperative in the West.

B. Treaties are good only so long as the parties will honor them.
C. Neutral nations within the organization are a deterrent to immoral action.

II. It is a major instrument for social betterment, *for*

A. Its agencies combat disease and crime, etc.

Proof

1. TESTIMONIAL EVIDENCE

Once the writer has outlined his case, either in his own mind or in a formal brief, his next step is to muster the best proofs of his arguments that he can summon. Such proof is called evidence, and of evidence there are two kinds, testimonial and circumstantial. The first is the evidence of persons or witnesses; the second is that of the facts in the case.

Testimonial evidence is persuasive to the degree that the fairness and credibility of the witness may not be impugned. If the witness has something to gain from his testimony, its value is greatly reduced; in fact, it may be disproportionately reduced if the fact is discovered first by the opposition. The best witness is one who has no personal motivation in his testimony. In certain instances, in order to be judged reliable a witness should have no physical or mental handicaps. If a motorist has driven through a red light, and it can be shown that the only witness to his act is color blind, the case against him may be dismissed. Witnesses may be called upon to estimate the alleged speed of a traveling car, but if they cannot judge distances approximately in the courtroom their evidence may be impugned. The testimony of a witness may be impaired by showing that his morality is suspect because of some past dereliction, for while it is open to question whether a man who has stolen will lie, the world is all too ready to suspect that he will.

Whenever an issue involves special technical or scientific knowledge, it is customary to solicit the testimony of experts. In technical language, this is known as *the appeal to authority*. If responsibility in a boiler explosion is an issue, the testimony of an engineer is obviously worth more than that of a ribbon clerk, but if the quality of yardgoods is in question, the clerk, particularly if he is also a buyer for the store, is the better witness. The appeal to authority may also be invoked to summon the expert testimony of those dead and revered, as for example that of John Marshall (Chief Justice of the United States, 1801-1935) on constitutional questions. But so far as the expert testimony is concerned, it must be remembered that it is good only in the field of competency.

2. CIRCUMSTANTIAL EVIDENCE

Circumstantial evidence is evidence from the facts, but it is evidence from the facts as determined by human reasoning. One car, out of control, collides with another, catapulting its occupant into the street. An eyewitness may testify that the victim is a casualty of reckless driving, but it is disclosed that the victim, an elderly man and quite ill, was being driven to a hospital, and an autopsy reveals that he had been dead some time when the accident occurred. The facts of the autopsy, especially the blood clot closing the aorta, are interpreted as more convincing than the testimony of the eyewitness, though they are all circumstantial facts. (The illustration is a mixed one, for here the facts are presented by a physician and are reinforced by his authority; nevertheless, the court acts on his arrangement of them.) A man caught near the scene of a crime with a recently fired revolver of the same caliber as that of a bullet extracted from the body of the slain man has an impressive array of facts against him, despite a lack of any witness to the shooting. If we conclude he is guilty of the crime, our conclusion is based wholly on our reasoning from the facts. There may be others, however, that we have not taken into consideration. What if he was a friend of the victim who had picked up the murderer's gun and was searching for him? It must ever be kept in mind that in large areas of human experience circumstantical evidence at best produces only a "reasonable certainty."

3. TESTING CAUSAL RELATIONSHIPS

The initial presumptions that both the driver of the car out of control and the friend with the murderer's weapon in his hand were guilty are based upon one of the most fundamental tenets of all human thinking; namely, that nothing takes place without a cause. When the mind deals with an effect (natural death, in the first instance, and violent death, in the second) and searches for its cause, it is likely to commit certain well-known errors. The situation may be searched from the other direction, that is, from cause to effect. First, we may ask if the assumed cause was adequate to produce the effect. In both instances that we have hypothesized, it was; hence, the ready conclusion of guilt. Second, we may ask if the assumed cause is the only cause that could have operated. We have seen that, in each instance, it was not. When we are arguing that a certain cause will produce a "known" effect, we have these variants of the common errors to consider: Is the cause strong enough in this instance to produce the effect? May not some other cause intervene in the relationship?

The Argument from Analogy

Nothing is more enticing to a thinker bent on persuasion than the argument from analogy. It is based on the presumption that if two things have some elements in common, they have others also–a presumption which, of course, does not necessarily follow. Just as persons are always seeing family resemblances, they are quick to apprehend resemblances between things or situations.

There are two tests of real value with an analogy: (1) Are the resemblances really essential or vital resemblances? and (2) Despite the resemblances between the things compared, are there still more important differences between them? Dissenting from the relief measures that Franklin D. Roosevelt put into effect, William Allen White wrote, "If I was the underdog, I should bury my bones against the day of hunger." Mr. White believed that Roosevelt did not understand the "underdog" and, hence, would abandon him. Unfortunately for his analogy, many of the underdogs had no bones to bury, save those that Roosevelt's measures provided.

Generalizing Processes

1. INDUCTION

Every person who reasons inevitably generalizes. After discovering that a law operates in several examples of a kind, the mind finds it an enormous convenience to assume that it operates in all examples of that kind. When a scientist draws a conclusion from a reasonable number of cases, it is called an *induction*. We must remember, however, that there are few perfect inductions, that is, not *all* cases have been surveyed or could be surveyed.

There are four tests that an induction may be subjected to: Is the relative number of the instances observed, as compared with those unobserved, sufficiently large? Are the observed instances fair examples? Are there no invalidating exceptions? Is there an initial probability that the generalization is true?

2. DEDUCTION

It is a general assumption that all science is a product of the inductive method, but scientists frequently imply that the discovery or law was a "hunch" or generalization for which the proof had later to be found by laborious investigation. Be that as it may, there is an almost equal tendency to assume generalizations and to find the assumed law operating in the instance under discussion. This process is called deduction. It is possible to state all deductions in this form, known as a *syllogism:*

All iron objects are subject to oxidation.
A steel rail is an iron object.
Therefore, a steel rail is subject to oxidation.

In the above syllogism, the statement "All iron objects are subject to oxidation" is called *the major premise;* "A steel rail is an iron object," *the minor premise;* and "Therefore, a steel rail is subject to oxidation," *the conclusion*. Mere ability to put a deduction in syllogistic form, however, does not guarantee its validity. Thus, for example:

All men are liars *(major premise)*.
Green is a man *(minor premise)*.
Therefore, Green is a liar *(conclusion)*.

This syllogism is completely correct *if* we accept the major premise. But the major premise is the result of a previous faulty induction.

The ancients discovered that the syllogistic statement could be readily tested for its validity. It must conform to these rules:

a. Every syllogism has three, and only three, terms.

b. Every syllogism contains three, and only three, propositions or statements.

c. The middle term must be distributed (that is, universally applied), once at least, and must not be ambiguous.

d. No term must be distributed in the conclusion which was not distributed in one of the premises.

e. From negative premises nothing can be inferred.

f. If one premise is negative, the conclusion must be negative; and vice versa, to prove a negative conclusion one of the premises must be negative.

g. From two particular premises no conclusion can be drawn.

h. If one premise be particular, the conclusion must be particular.

A *term* denotes an individual or group of individuals or an attribute or a group of attributes. Thus in the syllogism attempting to show Green a liar, the terms are men (man), liars (liar), and Green. The *middle term* is the term which does not appear in the conclusion. With the help of a book on logic, or without it by trial and error, one may discover the complete validity of these rules.

The Common Fallacies

Thus far we have examined errors which occur in logical processes of reasoning, but a person engaged in the process of persuasion may adopt one of two illogical processes of reasoning and be quite unaware that they are illogical processes. Indeed, in practice they may each prove quite effective until an opponent exposes them. They are the common fallacies of *ignoring the question* and of *begging the question*.

1. IGNORING THE QUESTION

A writer ignores the question by substituting an issue which appears to be the same as the one under discussion. Because every writer becomes identified with the cause for which he stands, one of the commonest exhibitions of this fallacy occurs whenever an opponent attacks the writer, rather than his cause or the real issue under discussion.

2. BEGGING THE QUESTION

Whenever a reasoner assumes as true the thing which he is trying to establish, he is said to beg the question. Two forms of this fallacy are common: first, using question-begging epithets, and second, arguing in a circle. The first of these errors is regularly indulged in by impassioned or dishonest propagandists. When one writes, "In the *decadent* South a Negro can expect *no* justice from the *brutal* police," he is really begging the question; purged of these epithets, the proposition should read: In Chicago, Detroit, New York, or the South, the Negro can expect little justice from the police.

Refutation

In formal debate, replying to an opponent is usually left to the rebuttal speeches, though in presenting his case the debater may anticipate counterarguments. In a persuasive article there is no opportunity for rebuttal; hence the anticipation must be complete. Experienced writers know, as a rule, what may be offered in opposition to their views. Yielding an unimportant issue creates an impression of a judicious, a reasonable mind. It is in refutation that the reasoner probably should be most conscious, not of his ability to contend, but of his ability to persuade. Even if there is no chance of this with a dogmatic opponent, the persuasive attitude may win over more undecided listeners and readers than the dogmatism of the opponent. The successful reasoner treats his opponent with respect.

Narrative Writing

That form of writing which presents an event or a sequence of events involving animate beings is called narrative writing. While usually the actors in such a narrative are human beings, narrative writing is not restricted to their participation. The range of actors may be from insects and animals to trolls and fairies, to mechanical creatures and visitors from other planets. One thinks of the fat spider which disturbed little Miss Muffet, the boll weevil, Br'er Rabbit, Donald Duck, the Three Bears, the Rat-Wife, the Snow Princess, Superman, Tommy Tractor, Frankenstein, and the Man from Mars, whose antics may, or may not, bear some resemblance to human behavior. They do, however, have the capacity to carry the reader through an event or series of episodes, a characteristic which represents the primary function of characters in narrative writing.

Simple Narrative

The simplest event that can occur presents an actor in a role that is to some slight degree worth remarking. The commonest form of this narrative is the anecdote; the more familiar the actor, the less the writer has to supply by way of characterization. In repeating the legend of Newton's discovery of the law of gravitation from the falling apple which struck him on the head, the writer can count on persons' generally knowing who Newton was. Elaboration turns an anecdote into a narrative allusion or after-dinner story. A narrative anecdote–it need not be true–that strikes at some foible in human behavior or belief is usually well received.

Fictional Narrative

Characters

To assure plausibility in a fictional narrative, start with the persons to be involved in the action. Ivan Turgenev, the Russian novelist, told the young Henry James that his fictions began "*always* with the vision of some person or persons, who hovered before him, soliciting him, as the active or passive figure, interesting him and appealing to him *just as they were and by what they were*" [italics ours]. That is, Turgenev started with a real person and transferred that person with his or her potentialities to his book. No procedure more surely guarantees plausibility than this one, for once the character is established he or she can do nothing "out of character"–both the artist and his reader would be instantly aware of the inconsistency. An axiomatic statement in fiction is, "Character governs action."

Plot

The persons in a work of fiction should determine the action; if they do not, it will not move. If three persons are placed together and two of them have traits that clash, the third is either bound to take sides or disintegrate, either through his effort to remain neutral or shift sides–and a "plot" is born. Imposing a plot on characters already assembled leads to distortion, unnaturalness, and eventually to implausibility. Increasing the number of characters usually multiplies the possibility of plot intricacy because of the alignment of loyalties. There are only two restrictions on the ramifications of plot: (1) The behavior of the characters must be wholly consistent with their natures, and (2) the high cost of typesetting limits the extent of any story. For the latter reason, three-volume novels and twenty-thousand-word short stories are not the fashion of the twentieth century, though they were common enough in the nineteenth.

All conflicts in life move toward either stalemate or some sort of resolution, but in fiction they must move toward resolution. The ultimate clash of forces we term the *climax* of the tale; the results or consequences of this collision we call the *dénouement.* It is the highest art to make this as brief as possible.

Setting

The leisurely novel of the nineteenth century took much pains to set the stage fully for the action of its story. Frequently these novels began with a descriptive passage on which the author expended much conscious art.

But few writers could afford it today. Forced to economize, they have done so by eliminating extended descriptions of their stages. Instead they give the details of their settings as they proceed with their narratives. Scattering graphic bits of description through the narrative seems the best way to impress upon the reader with the greatest economy of means the setting for modern narrative. In order to impart a real sense of the scene, the writer should prepare a good many notes on his setting in order to select from among them.

Point of View

After a writer has chosen his characters, determined the nature of the conflict among them (even perhaps imagined the course of his plot), and determined where the events of his narrative will take place, he still must ask himself an important question: From what point of view shall I tell this story? He must follow this in his mind by other questions: Should the narrator be outside the tale? Should he know everything that takes place?

Should he be a participant in the action? Should he be a major figure or a minor figure? Should he be a limited or prejudiced observer?

If the narrator is to be outside the tale, he may definitely be identified with the author. Both Fielding and Thackeray do this and are frankly partisan in the conflicts which they imagine. The advantage of this point of view is that converts are more readily made to the author's views; but the limitations are those of partisanship–the intruding voice, the sense of manipulated characters. Because of these intrusions the narrative is always fiction–it loses a degree of verisimilitude; it becomes something less than life, whereas, if art is selective, it should be something more than life. Another choice from outside the action is to adopt what is known as the "omniscient" point of view. Still another choice remains–to plant a spectator on the periphery of the tale to report what goes on.

The recent tendency of writers of fiction seems to be to locate the point of view "in" one of the participants in action in the tale, either a major or a minor character. The author may identify with the hero of the tale and become this "I" narrator of his own adventure. The merit of this is its immediacy; it has, however, the grave limitation of closing to the reader the emotions and thoughts (save as they are overt) of other characters in the tale. And what is more boring than one who talks all the time?

Dialogue

Just as character determines the action in a narrative, so also character determines the dialogue. Relations between characters define what they will express and what they will repress. The talk must advance the story, and it does this either by revealing hidden motives or by suggesting aims and devices. The author has to remember also that a character can divine more than is said from what is unskillfully repressed. To expose the play of mind on mind is one of the most exciting challenges of a writer's career. No talk in good narrative should be pointless.

Description

That form of writing which depicts objects, living things, and the static elements in fantasies is called *description*. It is the vehicle through which we become acquainted with the world, its animals and machines, and the furnishings of its dreams and visions.

Independent Description

Required to write a description of a given thing, the writer should ask himself for whom he is describing it. If he is a professional writer preparing material for a wholesale hardware magazine distributed to retailers, he may assume some knowledge of his object or device, but if he is the same writer describing the same device for the general catalog of a mail order house, he can assume very little; he also has the limitation of space since so many objects are presented through his medium. The amount of description will be further reduced if the catalog uses illustrations and formulas, but his familiarity must include these to compensate for what is not depicted or formularized. The householder without experience may write as good an advertisement of the home he wishes to sell as would the real estate agent (he should; he knows it better) but he does not know so well the purchaser or what will appeal to that purchaser.

Contributory Description

Skill in descriptive writing makes for interest in horticultural books, pleas for the preservation of wildlife, travel literature, and adventure stories, though these works may be chiefly narrative or persuasive. As with independent description, it is helpful to the reader to discover in an involved description a familiar image that will help him to see the scene with his mind's eye.

Long descriptive passages in fictional narrative are not so frequent today as they once were. The fiction writer manages to weave more of his descriptive detail into his narrative as it proceeds. The device is an old one; it is merely utilized more commonly now.

The Book Report/Review

Three conventional ways of writing about books are: (1) book reports, (2) book reviews, and (3) literary criticism. The book report is the traditional method whereby a teacher checks to see that an assignment has been completed and understood. It is the most elementary form. The third type, literary criticism, is an analysis, evaluation and judgment, presupposing critical knowledge on the part of the critic and the reader. You can work up to this.

The second type, the book review, is about halfway between the two, combining elements of both of the other types. Its purpose is (a) to inform the readership that a certain book is available; (b) to tell enough about the book to whet the appetite for someone to want to read it or to allow the reader to decide that he does not want to read it; (c) to make some judgment about its merit, although many reviewers are not acknowledged literary critics.

Students in elementary and middle schools need a lot of practice in doing book reports so when they reach high school they can move up into reviewing and make a good start toward real critiquing.

The way to approach writing a standard book report varies depending on the kind of book and the teacher's objective in making the assignment, so the teacher will often give specific guidelines to follow. However, there are many helpful hints the wise student will utilize which can make the difference between an "A" and a "C" report.

Keep in mind always that a book report is a hybrid, part fact and part fancy. It gives hard information about the book, yet it is your own creation, giving your opinion and judgment of it. Any report should tell at the beginning the author's full name, the title, the publisher, and the date of publication. It also makes very clear exactly what kind of book is being reviewed (fiction, or biography, or factual book about science, current events, history, etc.). Each type is judged by different standards which will be discussed later.

But no matter what kind of book is read, good book reporters and good book reviewers always read with the review constantly in the back of their minds. They mark in the book (if it belongs to them) or they make notes as they read to help them remember important things they want to say about the book and to help them find pertinent passages to quote in the review.

And they read imaginatively which is a skill that is necessary to complete the act of writing, for the greatest work ever written is only a piece of paper until a reader reacts to it. The reader actually helps create literature by responding to what the writer has to say. A thoughtful and imaginative reader considers both what the writer tries to say and how he says it. This gives him or her greater enjoyment in reading, and the critical skills develop with use, just as muscles do.

Usually when you finish a book you have a feeling. It may be of sorrow that the book has ended, or of satisfaction, or even of exhilaration. It may be a let-down feeling or plain indifference. Before you lose these emotions, before they fade away, jot down random notes capturing these reactions to the book. Then let your thoughts simmer on the back burner before actually writing the review.

REVIEWING FICTION

Most likely the majority of your class assignments for review will be in fiction, so you need to keep in mind these elements of literature as you read. First there is *characterization*. A writer may want to describe actions or ideas, but he must also describe the people who do the acting or have the ideas.

Then there is *motivation*, which means the reasons for the characters' actions. The writer should try to make his characters act like real people.

The *setting* is the place in which a character's story occurs. Literary characters, like the persons who read about them, do not exist in a vacuum. They act and react with one another, responding to the world in which they live.

The *plot* tells what happens to the characters in the story. It is built around a series of events that take place within a definite period of time. The leading character has a problem, he faces the problem, he overcomes it or is overcome by it.

Theme is what the author is trying to say, the basic idea behind writing the novel, the statement the author wants to make to the world. Seldom is it expressed in direct words; more often it is implied by the entire work. The mark of a sophisticated reader is being able to understand from the book what the author is trying to say above and beyond the simple story line of who did what to whom. The author may be saying that he thinks life is meaningless, that animals are superior to people, that love is the greatest power on earth, that all people need other people and cannot live alone, or whatever, *ad infinitum.*

Style is the way a writer uses words to create literature, to evoke emotions, to describe beauty or ugliness, to make characters come to life, to make events seem real.

As a mature reader you will understand these elements of literature and will assess them as you read, for they will color your evaluation.

You are now ready to plan your review. You have your notes made during the reading and your notes taken when you finished, and you have allowed your thoughts to take form. Ask yourself these questions:

* What was the author's real goal in writing the book? What was his theme? What was he trying to make me see, feel, or think? Did he accomplish his objective?

* Was the plot convincing? Did the incidents follow one another logically so I felt the story really could have happened?

* Did the characters seem human? Did I really care what happened to them? Did they act like real people or like puppets on a string? Did I learn anything about human nature after meeting these characters?

* Was the dialogue believable? Was it in keeping with the personalities of the characters? Did the dialogue move the story along or hinder it?

* Did the setting come to life? Could I actually see in my mind's eye the places described? Did the author fill in with vivid details?

* Was the style suitable to the plot and theme? Did it blend with the book or was I conscious of inept wording so it detracted from the story?

Make notes of your answers to these questions giving specific details to justify your reasons. Criticize where criticism is justified, but do not feel you must be critical to sound smart.

Summarize the plot briefly, never going into lengthy detail nor revealing an unexpected ending which would spoil the suspense if someone else were to read it. Never, never give a blow-by-blow account of the action; you are not rewriting the book but are judging the elements of the book and evaluating it as a whole. You may describe one particular scene in detail to try to capture the flavor of the book for your audience.

Take into consideration the exact nature of the book. If it is an historical novel, it is set in some specific place and period, so be sure to note the time, place, events, and historical persons involved. For instance, if you read the book *Tituba of Salem Village,* look up Tituba in an encyclopedia and point out that she was a real person and tell how the book followed (or did not follow) the actual events in her life. Read a little about the witchcraft trials in Salem, Massachusetts, so you can fix the book knowledgeably in its historical background.

Sometimes the title of the book needs explanation. If you read *The Magnificent Mutineers,* you should certainly include a paragraph about how mutineers, who are usually thought of as criminals, could be considered "magnificent."

Now ask yourself, What information do I want to get across to my readers about this book, what will *my* theme be? Take all your notes and form them into a logical outline that covers all that you want to say. Begin with the most factual parts and end with your own personal impressions.

Necessary for any good writing is a good introduction which entices the reader to read on and gives an overview of what is to come. Then the body of the work presents all the points the writer wishes to make. Equally critical is the conclusion that wraps up the writing, giving a feeling of completeness to the work.

The reviewer's own style of writing is important, with one word following another logically and interestingly, and with good paragraphs leading from one to the other smoothly. Use of transitional words or phrases between paragraphs helps the reader to follow the writer's meaning. All writing must be grammatically correct, with no misspelled words, and properly proofread.

Revise and polish your rough draft. Read the review over objectively. How do you think a reader of *your* work would evaluate it? Does it make a point? Does it give sufficient information for an outsider to form a valid opinion of the book? Is it dull? Is it a trustworthy evaluation? Be as thorough and critical of your own work as you were of the author's work!

REVIEWING A BIOGRAPHY

In reviewing a biography you must do much more than just tell the facts of the person's life which anyone can look up in an encyclopedia. Do summarize the person's life, telling when and where he lived and why he was worthy of having a book written about him.

A main factor to consider is what the author was trying to say about the person, what area of his life the author stressed. For instance, a biography about Thomas Jefferson might focus on Jefferson the president and what he did during his administration, such as enlarging the country through the Louisiana Purchase. Or the author might aim at showing how multitalented he was in the sciences and the arts. Or the concentration could be on his role in the Revolution as the author of the Declaration of Independence. Perhaps the main thrust was on the personality of Jefferson and his relationships with the people he loved.

Ask yourself these questions:

* Is the biographee presented as a real human being, with good traits and faults, or is he made into a stereotype, someone who is not quite real?

* Do the times and places come alive? Is the setting made real?

* Does the author explain what factors influenced the person? What conditions, or events, or people helped make the person what he became?

* Are the conversations as recorded believable?

* How does the author's style help or hinder the reading of the book?

* Would I have liked to have known the main character?

REVIEWING A SCIENCE BOOK

Here are some questions to ask yourself:

* Was the material easily understood? Did the author explain things clearly? Did I need more background to understand it or did the author write in too simple a manner?

* Were the facts accurate as far as I can tell?

* Were there enough illustrations, pictures, diagrams, and charts to help explain things?

* What are the author's qualifications? Is he a recognized authority in the field? How did he get his information, by actual experience or by research?

* What new sort of knowledge did I learn from reading the book? Is it just new to me or is it brand new scientific information? If it is new, does everyone agree with the author in his assessment of it? For instance, a book detailing how some scientists believe that birds are the direct descendants of dinosaurs would require relating this theory to older theories. Or a book about the discovery of "Lucy," a seven-million-year-old skeleton, would require fitting this information into opinions held by other scientists about how long man has been on this earth. But a book describing the life cycle of a butterfly might present nothing new or controversial although the information in it was new to you and helped enlarge your knowledge of the world about you.

REVIEWING HISTORY AND CURRENT EVENTS

* This type of book often deals with subjects from one point of view alone. What was the author's point of view? What was his purpose in writing it? Does he present only one side of a controversial question or did he look at it from many angles? For instance, a book about nuclear weapons can be slanted to the author's feeling or it can show different perspectives.

* Did my attitude change as I read the book?

* Was the book written in a clear manner so I could understand the various implications discussed?

* Did I feel the author distinguished fact from interpretation? Could I tell when hard facts were being given, those that can be checked elsewhere, and when the author was giving his assessment of the facts? Did he tell all the facts or did he distort or omit any? (This is a difficult thing to pinpoint, but reading a book with this possibility in mind helps open your eyes to the insidious nature of propaganda.)

* What are the author's qualifications for writing the book, his personal background?

A Précis

A précis is a concise summary of the essential points of a longer piece of writing in your own words, usually one-fourth to one-third as long as the original. Learning how to do this provides excellent training in reading for comprehension and in mastering the technique of clear, concise, and accurate writing. It is a useful skill, if mastered, and will be a valuable tool both for school work and later in the business world.

Fully recognize first of all that a précis is not a paraphrase, which is a restatement in different words of what the original said, often of the same length as or longer than the original. A précis, unlike a paraphrase, cuts wordage to the minimum, simplifying and getting to the essential meaning in very few words. It contains no details, examples, or illustrations, and it does not allow any comment or interpretation on your part. The French meaning of the word, "exact," "terse," describes it accurately.

Follow these steps:

* Read the selection quickly for a general overview.

* Reread it paragraph by paragraph several times very thoughtfully.

* In each paragraph look for the topic sentence and restate it, first to yourself, then write it down in your own words.

* Combine these ideas into a statement of the whole. Eliminate any that do not directly bear on the main idea of the paper.

* Revise your version checking to see that it is absolutely accurate in accordance with the author's version and that it follows the original in the same sequence of thoughts and facts.

* Go through your précis and cut it to one-fourth or one-third of the original length by tightening each sentence, cutting any extra words. Substitute a phrase for a clause or one word for a phrase.

Examples:

Wordy: If you do your studying right after school, you will be able to watch television at night.

Terse: Afternoon studying leaves night time free for TV watching.

Wordy: Miss Brown spoke to me in a pleasant manner.

Terse: Miss Brown spoke to me pleasantly.

Science Project Report

Writing a science project report involves a special format, although not all of the items listed below must be included for every project, as the nature of the investigation sometimes imposes limitations. However, knowing what can be required helps the student in planning and executing a successful project conducted according to approved scientific methods.

The writing must be clear and concise, using formal style, which means no colloquial expressions, no contractions, and in the third person (avoiding the words "you" and "I.") Define all terms that might need clarification.

1. *Title:* This should convey exactly what the report is about, being very specific and factual in wording. Cute or catchy titles are out of place. For example, "Sit, Lie Down, Play Dead" would not be a suitable title for a research report about how to train a dog. Instead, "Training a Dog to Follow Simple Commands," would be better.

2. *Abstract:* A one-paragraph summary of the report should introduce the paper telling the purpose of the project, general methods or procedures used, and the main results produced or conclusions reached. The reason for writing the abstract is to allow another busy scientist to decide if he/she wishes to study the entire report.

3. *Introduction:* This includes the importance of

the area under investigation, why you chose it, something of the historical background, and an overview of what other people have done in the field. This literary support requires using the *Readers' Guide* or other indexes to find references to what has already been done on the subject. You will need to document (give credit to) the sources you consulted. Either use conventional footnotes or put in parentheses after a statement a shortened version of the source (Jones, *Science Reports,* 1984) to refer to the work in a bibliography which you will include following the paper itself.

4. *The Problem:* Clearly state what it is you planned to do. Tell if you were testing several hypotheses, were looking for a hypothesis, were suggesting a theory, or were reporting some observations made under certain specific, controlled conditions. If possible, include how your problem relates to other theories. A hypothesis is a tentative assumption made in order to draw out and test its logical consequences.

5. *Hypotheses:* State all hypotheses that you were testing and, if possible, what the results of your experiments will mean as to the acceptance or rejection of these hypotheses.

6. *Procedures:* Describe in detail exactly how you did your experiments so other people can do the same thing with the same results. List all equipment you used, a step-by-step account of procedures followed, an exact description of the conditions influencing the results. Include all failures as well as successes so others will not waste time doing things that will not work. Diagrams and drawings can be used.

7. *Observations and Interpretations:* Record chronologically, perhaps in diary form, the facts you observed as you were conducting your experiments. Compile tables or graphs to present statistics, measurements, and other numerical data. Explain what your observations mean in connection with the hypothesis that was being tested.

8. *Conclusions:* Each hypothesis should be examined in light of your observations and interpretations so that the hypothesis may be rejected outright or accepted with reservations for more testing. Rarely does student work result in a fully accepted hypothesis.

9. *Generalizations:* Here you tell the implication or meaning of your research in relation to its larger field of science. Perhaps your study can suggest some new problems or further areas of study.

10. *Summary:* Write a brief summary of your investigation, listing the principal findings of the project.

Mechanical Details

TYPING TIPS

1. Use good quality bond paper, white, 8½ x 11 inches in size.
2. Use black ribbon and type on one side of the paper only.
3. Always make a carbon copy or photocopy your manuscript.
4. Double space the body of the manuscript, following the single spacing rules for long quotations, footnotes, endnotes, and bibliography entries.
5. The left margin should be 1½ inches wide; the right margin, as nearly as possible 1 inch wide; and the bottom margin, 1½ inches. This results in a page of 25 lines averaging about 10 words each, or a total of 250 words to a page.
6. On the first page, 12 spaces below the top of the paper, type the title, centered, in all capital letters.
7. Begin the paper proper three spaces below the title.
8. Indent each paragraph five spaces.
9. Do not number the first page, but do place a page number on each page of the paper beginning with page 2. Do not number outline, endnote, bibliography, or any appendix pages. The page number should be placed 1 inch from the top of the paper and 1 inch from the right margin. Do not use any punctuation with the number.

10. On all pages after the first continue the body of the text two spaces below the page number.
11. One reason for dividing words at the ends of lines is to keep the right margin as even as possible. However, correct syllabication must be observed. Consult the dictionary.
12. Leave one space after a comma or a semicolon. Leave two spaces after any punctuation mark that ends a sentence. Leave two spaces after a colon when the next word or sentence begins with a capital letter.
13. Center any columns. Figures are usually aligned so the right margin will be in block form.
14. Do not "x" out mistakes. Correct neatly with a whitening agent.
15. Always proofread for typographical errors.
16. Enclose your paper in a folder or stiff paper cover.

HANDWRITTEN MANUSCRIPTS

One of the most valuable skills a student can possess is to be able to type. If you have not had typing and must handwrite your paper, follow these rules.

1. Use standard notebook paper with wide-spaced lines, not paper torn from a spiral notebook.
2. Follow the typing rules as closely as possible.
3. Use the red line for the left margin space.
4. Write very legibly in blue-black or black ink.

Letters and Employment Resumes*

Whenever you write a letter–whether personal or business–those lines of writing become *you* in the mind of your reader. Your letters will, of course, vary in purpose and formality, as the occasion requires, yet each letter you write is, for your reader, like a face-to-face meeting with you. Let your letters be a credit to you in appearance, appropriateness, and good taste; make them also carry something of the naturalness and vitality your reader would experience in a person-to-person visit. Practically all letters can be included within three general classifications:

1. *The social "duty" letter,* a type of letter–formal or informal–demanded by good manners

2. *The personal letter,* a type of informal letter written to share the pleasures of life with friends and relatives

3. *The business letter,* a type of letter written in the conduct of commercial, professional, or administrative affairs

THE SOCIAL "DUTY" LETTER

Social "duty" letters are used as invitations, to acknowledge invitations, to thank friends for favors and gifts, to console relatives and friends in times of trouble. You will want to know how to write them.

Formal Social Letters

Very formal affairs–weddings, receptions, and formal dinners–still require a formal correspondence ritual. Guests are invited in a nonpersonal, formal manner, as is to be seen in the example below. The invitations are usually engraved or printed; they may be written in longhand. Guests responding to such invitations employ the same formal, nonpersonal language that they find in the invitation, but the responses are always handwritten.

*The acute accent over the final *e* in resumé has been omitted in the text of this chapter as this seems to be the rule in most United States business correspondence. In formal writing, the acute accent should be included even if the mark has to be inserted by hand. The Merriam–Webster *Third New International Dictionary* also carries the accent over the first *e*.

INVITATION

Mr. and Mrs. Eugene Parsons
request the honor of your presence
at the marriage of their daughter
Sue Ellen
to
Mr. Harvey Henderson
on Saturday, the first of June
at ten o'clock
Saint Mark's Church
New York

ACCEPTANCE

Thomas Olderbach
accepts with pleasure
the kind invitation of
Mr. and Mrs. Eugene Parsons
to the marriage of their daughter
Sue Ellen
to
Mr. Harvey Henderson
on Saturday, the first of June
at ten o'clock
Saint Mark's Church
New York

Informal Social Letters

Most social occasions that require letters are informal. When a hostess wants a few friends to attend a small dinner party, she does not send out engraved invitations. She writes a short personal note to each of them or she may even telephone. When a weekend guest returns home, he writes a so-called bread-and-butter thank-you note to his hostess.

Dear Mrs. Parsons,

That Saturday morning sunrise over the valley, those gay voices of the twins, and that stimulating table talk are still with me. Every moment of the weekend was perfect, but one–departure. How I hated to have it end!

I loved every moment at Oakridge Manor and I want to thank you very much for a wonderful time.

Sincerely,
Harvey Henderson

Gifts, favors, congratulations, and condolences–all are acknowledged in short notes which are set up like letters, rather than formal announcements. These social letters are written in natural, everyday language, with a friendliness of style appropriate to the relationship between writer and reader. Although a telephone call, greeting card, bouquet, or telegram may substitute for social letters on some occasions, letters are to be written:

Whenever you receive gifts, courtesies, favors, congratulations, or good wishes

Whenever you stay overnight as a guest in someone's home

Whenever you receive an invitation to a dinner or luncheon

Whenever you express or acknowledge condolence

In addition to such "duty" letters, there are innumerable kinds of social notes which it is always becoming to write. There are "cheer-up" notes which you send to the sick. There are "well-done," "best-wishes," "happy-journey," and "welcome-home" notes you can write on other occasions.

Stationery for the Social Letter

Formal social letters should be written on a good quality, white, side-folded letter sheet approximately 5¼ inches x 7½ inches, in black or blue-black ink. Informal social letters may also be written on this type of stationery, on greeting cards, or on any of the personal stationery used in friendly correspondence. Less formal social letters may be typed, including the following, which at one time were handwritten only: letters of sympathy and replies to letters of sympathy, letters expressing and letters acknowledging good wishes, and letters acknowledging wedding gifts.

THE PERSONAL LETTER

Those letters which help us share with friends and relatives the joys of living are called *personal letters*. There is a single test for evaluating the personal letter: Does it provide the writer and the reader with shared satisfaction of friendship? The few principles of personal letterwriting that do exist are designed to help writer and reader enjoy to the full the pleasures of correspondence.

1. Note how Thackeray's daughter achieves the vividness of face-to-face contact in a letter:

I have been imagining you in my favorite corner of my favorite city. Have you opened your windows and looked out, does it smell–rumble–taste–Paris? I'm sure it does. Even the little tin water cans are unlike anything anywhere else.

2. Make your letters as cheerful and constructive as you can; nobody likes a complaining, gloomy, nagging letter.

3. Avoid any statement or hint that writing is a chore. It is impolite to tell a correspondent that you just could not get around to writing, that there is nothing to say, or that you are hastily dashing off a few lines.

4. Avoid putting into a letter any statement that could prove unbecoming if the letter were to fall into the hands of another. Remember, letters are permanent records.

Stationery for the Personal Letter

Close friends may correspond on any kind of stationery available, the only restrictions rising from personal choice and consideration for the reader. Untidy, blotted, scratched-out, or soiled letters are unbecoming to the writer and a discourtesy to the reader. Legibility is only common politeness. Writing in pencil, writing around the edges of the sheet, or writing on lined paper may also be resented, even among friends.

THE BUSINESS LETTER

The importance of the letter as a tool in business, government, the professions, and other administrative activities has developed the type known as *the business letter*.

For all practical purposes, the great variety of business letters may be classified under four basic headings:

1. *Letters that handle routine business.* Most business letters have a simple, routine mission; they carry needed details and short statements of information from businessman to businessman. Letters that order goods, acknowledge orders, and handle remittances make up the bulk of mail interchanged by business organizations. The main qualities these routine letters must possess are brevity and clearness. They must be complete in supplying all details as to style, color, price, conditions, procedures, and the like.

2. *Letters that grant requests.* Many business letters are written to grant requests; they supply information sought by other businessmen and the public; they send out samples and booklets; they open charge accounts; they make adjustments. When a request is granted, it should be done graciously and with good will, usually in the opening sentence of the letter:

> We are pleased to send the samples of Kioba Fabric requested in your letter of January 23.

The middle of the letter can then supply the necessary detail. The ending is usually a further statement of good will.

3. *Letters that deny requests.* Many business letters have to deny requests. The best tactics for making a denial are (a) open with a statement that the reader will find agreeable–*we appreciate very much your detailed description of your recent experience with our Toast-Browner;* (b) give reasons for the denial; (c) make the denial; (d) seek the good will of the reader.

4. *Letters that persuade and sell.* Many business letters have a persuasive mission; they must move the minds and wills of their readers. Some of them must assist in selling goods and services; some of them must collect money; some of them must debate issues. All of them must employ techniques of persuasion.

The sales letter is usually constructed on a patterning of steps which lead to the sale–attention, desire, conviction, and action.

DEAR MR. JONES:

Attention Did you ever wish that your typewriter had an eraser key–one that could correct the original and all copies with a stroke of the finger? Well, here's your chance to get something even better–TYPERASO*–the magic insert and carbon pack that is self-erasing.

Desire With TYPERASO an error can be corrected with the flick of a key. All you have to do is slip the TYPERASO mounting over the error, pull up the TYPERASO carbon, and strike any key. In an instant, the error is gone. What a saving to you in time, money, and nerves.

Conviction TYPERASO has been approved by all leading banks, insurance companies, and typewriter manufacturers. We will give you double your money back if you are not delighted with your TYPERASO pack.

Action Pick up a TYPERASO pack at any office supply store. There's a pack waiting for you right now.

Sincerely,

*This is an imaginary product.

FORMATS OF THE LETTER

The general setup of a letter on a page is called its *format*. Formal invitations and replies, as already noted, are set up like announcements; their formats are different from the more usual letter formats.

Parts of the Letter

There are seven basic parts of a letter. Business and other "official" letters require all seven, and often several additional ones. Social and personal letters usually omit one or two of these parts, as explained below.

1. HEADING. The writer's address, engraved, printed, or written at the top of the sheet, constitutes the heading of the letter. As noted, personal stationery may have the writer's monogram, or name and address, or name alone, or address alone, imprinted upon the letter sheet. If the address does not appear on personal stationery, it must be written or typed at the top of the sheet. This same practice is followed in preparing a business letter when an individual (say, a job applicant) does not have printed letterhead stationery. Business firms and most other organizations have their names and addresses imprinted at the top of their letter sheets.

2. DATE LINE. All letters must be dated. The usual place for a letter date is to the top and right, on a lower line than the heading. Informal social letters, however, often carry their dates as a last element of the letter, at the left margin. The most usual form of date employed in letters is *January 23, 1965,* but social letters often omit the year; sometimes they are dated with a mere *Monday,* or *At home.* Never use such forms as January 23rd, 1965 or 1/23/65.

3. INSIDE ADDRESS. Business and other "official" letters always carry the name and address of the recipient of the letter. This *inside address* is generally placed four or five lines below the date line, beginning flush with the left margin.

4. SALUTATION. The greeting, *Dear Tom* or *Dear Sir,* so characteristic of the letter format, is called the *salutation.* In social and personal letters the salutation is followed by a comma and is generally informal–*Dear Tom, Tom dear,* etc. In business letters the salutation is followed by a colon and is generally formal, unless the writer and reader enjoy a close acquaintanceship–*Dear Mr. Smith:, Dear Sir:.* The formality of the salutation must always match the formality of the complimentary close. See table on Forms of Address, pp. 73-74.

5. BODY. The part of the letter which carries the message is called the *body.*

6. COMPLIMENTARY CLOSE. The closing, *Sincerely yours* or *Very truly yours,* is called the *complimentary close.* In social and personal letters the complimentary close may take such forms as *Affectionately* or *With love,* but in business letters more formal complimentary closes are employed–*Cordially, Sincerely, Yours very truly,* or (to superiors) *Respectfully, Respectfully yours.*

7. SIGNATURE. All letters, typed and handwritten, must be signed by the writer. In social and personal letters the signature may be very informal, consisting of a first name or even a nickname. In business letters the written signature is often followed by a typed signature and an indication of the writer's position in the firm. Titles such as *Mr.* or *Dr.* are never written as part of a signature.

Additional letter parts, often found in business letters are (a) the subject line, (b) the attention line, (3) the identification initials. The subject line identifies the topic of the letter. The attention line (used only in letters addressed to a firm) directs the letter to a particular person within the firm, when the writer feels that the person has a special interest in the subject discussed. The identification initials indicate the person who dictated the letter and the secretary who typed it. The placement of these additional letter parts will be found in a letter model provided later.

Setup of the Letter

The informal social "duty" letter and the personal letter employ the same format with one exception: The date of the informal social "duty" letter may follow the signature, at the left margin.

Typed business letters are usually set up in a *block* format. Parts like the inside address are not staggered as they are in many handwritten letters.

Envelopes must always match letter pages in quality and color, and in style of addressing. In handwritten letters, the envelope address is usually indented. In business letters the envelope address is usually blocked, matching in detail the inside address. The return address is placed in the upper left corner of the envelope, following post office preference; but many writers of social and personal letters place the return address on the back flap of the envelope.

Forms of Address

PERSON	INSIDE ADDRESS	SALUTATION	COMPLIMENTARY CLOSE
President	The President The White House Washington, D.C.	Sir: *or* My dear Mr. President:	Most respectfully yours, *or* Respectfully yours,
Senator	The Honorable John Doe The United States Senate Washington, D.C.	Sir: *or* My dear Senator:	Very truly yours,
Congressman	The Honorable John Doe The House of Representatives Washington, D.C.	Sir: *or* My dear Mr. Doe:	Very truly yours,
Governor	The Honorable John Doe Governor of New York Albany, New York	Sir: *or* Dear Governor Doe:	Very truly yours,
Mayor	The Honorable John Doe Mayor of the City of Troy City Hall Troy, Colorado	Sir: *or* Dear Mayor Doe:	Very truly yours,
College Registrar	The Registrar Finn University Tobin City, N.J.	Dear Sir:	Very truly yours,
Rabbi	Rabbi John Doe	My dear Sir: *or* Dear Rabbi Doe:	Respectfully yours, *or* Very truly yours,
Protestant Clergyman	The Reverend John Doe	Reverend Sir: *or* My dear Mr. Doe:	Respectfully yours, *or* Very truly yours,
Priest	The Reverend John Doe	Reverend and dear Father: *or* Dear Father Doe:	Respectfully yours, *or* Very truly yours,
Nun	Sister Lioba, O.S.B.* .... (*Indicate order)	Reverend and dear Sister: *or* Dear Sister Lioba:	Respectfully yours, *or* Faithfully yours,
Woman Formally in a Business Letter	Miss Mary Doe *or* Mrs. John Smith	My dear Madam: *or* My dear Miss Doe:	Very truly yours,
Man Formally in a Business Letter	Mr. John Doe	My dear Sir: *or* My dear Mr. Doe:	Very truly yours,
Man or Woman in Less Formal Business Letters	Mr. John Doe *or* Miss Mary Doe	Dear Sir: *or* *more usually* Dear Mr. Doe: Dear Miss Doe:	Sincerely yours, *or* Sincerely,

PERSON	INSIDE ADDRESS	SALUTATION	COMPLIMENTARY CLOSE
Business Firm	Perfect Corporation	Gentlemen:	Very truly yours,
Man or Woman in a Social or Personal Letter	(No inside address needed, but be certain to use Mr., Mrs., Miss, Dr., or other title of courtesy before name on the envelope.)	Dear Mr. Jones, Dear Mrs. Doe, Dear Tom, Dear Jane, *or in friendly letters any familiar salutation in good taste*	Sincerely, *or any more intimate closing in good taste, such as* Affectionately yours, Lovingly,

SOLVING THE SEX QUESTION IN LETTER WRITING

With more and more women holding prominent career positions, the question constantly arises about the use of the traditional "Dear Sir" when the identity of the recipient of a business letter is unknown. Many sources suggest using "Dear Sir or Dear Madam," but this is cumbersome. The time-honored "Gentlemen" could be increased to "Gentlemen and Ladies" but this is stilted, and both retain the masculine precedence. A reversal of order might be employed.

However, a simpler solution is to use the title of the person addressed: "Dear Personnel Director"; "Dear Registrar"; "Dear Principal"; "Dear Public Service Commissioners." The same idea can be used in writing to a company: "Dear Jones Bookstore"; "Dear Executive Tax Service."

If it is known that the addressee is a woman, and her preference of titles is known, then address her as "Miss Mary Alston," or "Mrs. Joan Krantz," or "Ms. Sara Ledbetter." However, in many cases the correct choice is unknown and a wrong choice can sour a good relation before it has a chance to develop. If in doubt, simply write "Dear Eunice Reynolds." Or better still, incorporate her title in the salutation as "Dear Professor Caffey" or "Dear Director Smith."

With so many single parents these days, teachers have discarded the former "Dear Mother," in favor of "Dear Parent or Guardian."

COMMUNICATING IDEAS IN A LETTER

A successful letter is one that wins a favorable response. When you write a social "duty" letter, you seek a specific response–*I want Ann to realize how much I appreciate the silver tray she sent.* When you write a business letter, you also seek a specific response–*I want the bookkeeper at Greynolds, Inc., to understand that the 2% discount he took is not justified and that a check for $5.64 must be sent to me.* When you write a personal letter, you seek a much less tangible and much less specific response of friendship shared–*I want Tom to get pleasure and knowledge from the news I send and a deepened appreciation of our friendship.* In all of these types of letters, the success of the letter is judged by the response.

The Response Desired

So important is this response that the first principle of effective letter writing is: *Let the response you desire be your guide throughout the letter.*

A good practice is to pause a moment before beginning to write and answer the following questions:

Just why am I writing this letter?

Just how do I want my reader to feel when he finishes this letter?

In a particularly important letter, you may want to write out for yourself in a sentence or two the response you desire. But in most letters it will be enough if you get the response desired clearly in your own mind before you start writing.

The You-Attitude

When you have determined the desired response, you must next consider that goal from your reader's point of view. Imagine yourself the reader. Then select a plan for your letter, a set of ideas, a tone of approach, and a phrasing that would move *you* to the response desired.

This tactic of viewing a letter problem through the reader's eyes may be called the *you-attitude.* So important is the you-attitude that the second principle of effective letter writing is: *Let your reader's interests be your guide in the selection and phrasing of ideas.*

A letter which concentrates on the selfish interests of the writer is apt to be dull, and generally ineffective. Readers respond best when their own interests are being considered. In writing personal letters, you should stick to subjects that will give pleasure to your reader. Respond to the main points of his last letter to you. Involve him as much as possible in what you say. Instead of saying: "I found the view from the bridge over the rushing waters very impressive," say: "If only you could have shared that view from the dam with me. I know you would have thought, as I did, 'It's just like the Ausable River.' "

When you write business letters, you are always concerned with the advancement of some interest–getting a job, making a sale, collecting an account. Yet, these letters as well must be written with the you-attitude if they are to gain the response desired and win good will for the writer and his firm. A job applicant should tell how his training and experience will benefit the reader. The writer of a collection letter should stress the advantage his reader will gain through prompt payment–satisfaction in knowing his debts are paid or the protection of his credit standing.

Expression Skill

With the exception of formal correspondence, letters are best written in a natural conversational tone. After all, as already mentioned, the letter substitutes for a person-to-person meeting and should employ language appropriate to such meetings. Stilted language, artificiality, or phrases designed to impress have no place in a letter.

Writing skill, however, is very important to the letter writer. Actually, a letter is *not* a person-to-person meeting, and it requires skill to convey an idea and a set of feelings precisely and naturally through the written word.

The need to write well leads to a further principle of effective letter writing: *Let your ideas and feelings find expression in language that is clear, persuasive, natural, thoughtful, and interesting.*

The basic method of improving your ability to express yourself in writing is to read good writing and to practice as much writing as possible. As you read good writing notice how logical and constructive is the thought behind it. Notice how the writer phrases his ideas precisely. Notice how easily and naturally the writer expresses himself. Such attention to the techniques of skillful writing will enhance your own writing skill.

When you practice writing, concentrate on the ideas and feelings you want your writing to convey, rather than on techniques and style. Think hard until you have an idea worthy of expression. Make yourself feel the mood you want to convey–cheeriness, sympathy, friendliness, or whatever that mood may be. Concentrate on that idea and feeling until the right phrasing comes to you. With an increase of experience, you will discover that you are acquiring skill, that the right words and phrasing come more and more readily.

When you concentrate on the ideas and feelings you want to convey, language will begin to flow; the trick is to keep it flowing. Your first attempt to express a business-letter idea may be, "Please do something about this." Obviously, this idea needs more definite thought and expression. If you concentrate upon it, you will gain not only a clearer thought but also more precise expression of that thought, and you will be writing, "Please pick up the damaged table on Saturday morning."

You can speed up this skill-building process further if you bear in mind the writing principles discussed in other chapters of this book.

WATCH THESE EXPRESSIONS

accept, except Do not confuse. *I shall accept* (receive) *the letter. I shall except* (exclude) *this sum from the list.*

affect, effect Do not confuse. *The news will affect* (influence) *his mood. The manager will effect* (bring about) *a new schedule. The effect* (the noun form) *of television is obvious.*

busy In personal letters never write *I would have answered sooner but I was too busy* or any similarly rude expression.

beside, besides Do not confuse. *The wastebasket is beside* (alongside of) *the desk. Who is going besides* (in addition to) *you?*

due to Do not use *due to* in place of *because of* or *owing to. Due* is an adjective and makes a questionable preposition.

favor Do not refer to a letter as a *favor* in such trite expressions as *Your favor of June 1 received.*

good, well Do not use *good* as an adverb. *This program works well* (not *good*).

hoping Avoid such letter endings as *hoping to hear from you.*

I am, I remain Avoid these old-fashioned phrases in your letter closings.

its, it's Do not confuse. *Every machine has its* (possessive) *own cover. It's* (it is) *going to be warm today.*

said Avoid such expressions as *the said program* or *the said matter.*

thanking you Avoid such expressions as *thanking you for your interest* followed by a complimentary close.

AVOID THESE EXPRESSIONS

anticipating
as per, as regards
at your earliest convenience
awaiting, we await
beg
duly noted
esteemed
recent date
trusting that this is satisfactory
valued
we are, we remain
we trust
we wish to
with due regard
with reference to the matter
yours

THE LETTER OF APPLICATION

A particularly important kind of sales letter is the *letter of application,* the letter a job seeker sends to a prospective employer requesting a job interview. The application letter is apt to get attention when it is written or typed neatly upon good, white, bond paper and opens with a statement that is distinctive. Far too many application letters begin with a trite, "I am writing this letter to apply for the job advertised in today's *Herald.*" Much better would be an opening like the following:

> My basic training in computer programing and my two years of part-time experience in data processing are the work advantages I can best offer in a letter. But if I could call upon you, in response to your advertisement in today's *Herald,* I know that I could show you why I am the young man you need in your new automated division.

The application letter builds desire by outlining details of experience, education, and skill which will be useful in the job that is being sought. With desire built, the applicant can provide proof in the form of references and possibly samples of his work. Finally, the applicant moves his reader to action by requesting an interview, making himself available at any time convenient to the prospective employer.

Here are a few *do's* and *don'ts* on application letters:

DO'S

Write or type neatly on one side only of good quality, white paper.

Write large numbers of application letters. Write to firms that advertise, and write to firms that don't. Keep writing.

Learn as much as possible about your prospective employer and gear your letter to the way your education and experience will help him.

Exhibit confidence in your background and ability.

Request an interview at the end of the letter.

Write follow up letters.

DON'TS

Don't write on letterheads of other business firms, hotel or club stationery.

Don't limit your job-seeking efforts to openings provided you by friends, relatives, and the local press. Don't wait for an answer from one firm before writing to another.

Don't make a vague offer to do anything.

Don't be timid and apologetic or conceited and boasting. Don't end vaguely at one extreme or attempt to pressure your reader into action at the other.

Don't neglect to thank the prospective employer for the courtesy of the interview he granted, even when you don't get the job.

How Businessmen Evaluate Applications

Today's business executive has very little time to read long letters. Most executives stress that they are more likely to reply to a short, well-written letter that makes the applicant's point quickly.

A vice president of a large chemical company submits the following letter as an example of a good application. It was received by his company in reply to a blind-box advertisement:

For your review I enclose a copy of my current resume which describes my qualifications for the position advertised in the March 25 issue of the New York Times.

My background and experience closely parallel the requirements outlined in your advertisement. I am, therefore, reasonably sure that I can make a valuable contribution to your company. Won't you call me at 586-3657 to arrange for an interview.

The vice president of a school-supply company received the following letter from a college student. He considers it to be an excellent letter of application:

In answer to my inquiry, the Atlanta Chamber of Commerce sent me your name as one of the firms in your city that hires college students for temporary summer work.

Although my home is San Francisco, and I attend Stanford University, I plan to take a one-day-a-week course at Georgia Tech this summer. This course will be given on Monday of each week and will run for six weeks.

It was a fortunate coincidence for me that your firm's name was submitted, because you are engaged in the type of business in which I hope to make my future.

At present, I am a sophomore at Stanford University, majoring in economics. Scholastically, I am in the top 10 per cent of my class, and I am a reporter on our college newspaper.

I realize that for the first six weeks of my twelve-week vacation, I will be able to work only four days a week. However, since I do not have to be back to school until the end of September, I will be able to work a full week for the last six weeks of my summer vacation.

I wish to learn every aspect of the writing-paper and school-supply business; therefore, I am willing to work in any phase of it–stockroom, manufacturing, sales, or office administration.

I will be in Atlanta on June 12. May I then call you and present myself for an interview?

Very truly yours,

The vice president of marketing of a business machine manufacturing company received the following letter, which accompanied a well-organized resume:

I am presently attending the University of Pennsylvania and will be graduated in June. I have decided that my educational background and experience in summertime and part-time employment is such that selling offers me the best opportunity for personal advancement and financial success. I have been impressed with your ads in recent issues of the Wall Street Journal *and I want to investigate the opportunities in your organization for a selling-trainee opening.*

Please write to me if I may phone for an interview.

Here's an example that the personnel manager of one of the largest merchandising corporations considers to be an effective letter-resume combination:

Your very fine company has impressed me for some time as the type of organization with which I would like to become associated. Your progressive merchandising policies and steady growth provide the type of opportunity I am seeking.

You will note from the attached resume that I am presently employed. I find working for my employer and my relationships with my associates most enjoyable. However, the firm is small and presents little in the way of opportunity for either personal growth or advancement.

I know I do not have much in the way of experience which could be utilized by a company such as Sears. However, I can assure you I would take an enthusiastic approach to learning. I would display mature judgment in viewing business problems after a limited amount of training. Above all, I have considerable ambition and am willing to sacrifice in order to obtain an opportunity.

My plans are such that I will be in Chicago the week of August 10, during which time I would like to have an interview at your convenience. May I call you for an appointment?

Very truly yours,

AN EMPLOYMENT RESUME

The employment resume is designed to introduce you to a prospective employer. You are looking for a job; he is looking for someone to fill the job; it goes without saying that you want the introduction to be a favorable one. So it is up to you to supply him, *briefly and clearly,* with the facts about yourself, your background, your education, and your work experience, in such a way that he will want to hire *you* instead of another applicant.

RULE NUMBER ONE: Be as brief as possible, yet include all pertinent facts.

RULE NUMBER TWO: Present yourself in the best possible light.

Some employment applicants have their employment resumes made up in quantity, either by mimeographing or multigraphing, and send them out with a covering letter to prospective employers. Some carry their resumes about with them when they go to answer advertisements that have appeared in newspapers or periodicals. Some resumes are supposed to be filled out on forms provided by the employment agency to which you have applied for help in finding a job. Whichever way your employment resume is used, it is obvious that it should present you most favorably. Use a typewriter and be sure the copy is letter perfect–no misspellings, no mistakes in grammar; also, no corrections, no strike-overs, no noticeable erasures. And see to it that your typewriter ribbon is dark and legible.

Most employment agencies will require you to fill out their form in ink while you are in their office. In such cases, before starting on the rounds of the agencies, take time and thought to prepare in advance, and to bring with you, a typed employment resume. Even if it is not possible for you to use this resume in its exact form, it is still likely that a great deal of what you have thought out can be used to good advantage.

In gathering material for this section, a number of employment agency directors were interviewed. Without exception they emphasized the point that the employment resume should be *brief, inclusive, and factual.* There is no place in an employment resume for attempts to be funny or clever.

Some employers will be interested in having, in addition, such personal information as:

Height
Weight
Marital Status
Number of Dependents
Military Experience
Present Military
Status, etc.

A good resume has the following advantages over the overly comprehensive resumes so popular a number of years ago: It is brief, which assures that it will be read; it cites the essential information that the applicant wants the prospective employer to know at present; it shows, by its conciseness and organization, that the applicant is a methodical individual who knows how to bring out essential facts.

Below is an example of a resume described in the previous paragraph:

RESUME OF CHARLES DEERING, JR.

PERSONAL DATA: Married, One Child
Excellent Health

MILITARY SERVICE: U.S. Navy–Two years
Lt. Jr. Grade

EDUCATION: DePauw University, Indiana
B.A.–Economics (major)
Speech (minor)

PREVIOUS EXPERIENCE:

Trainee	One year
Merchandise and Operating Assistant Manager	One year

RETAIL EXPERIENCE:
Approximately two years experience in retail stores ranging in sales volume from $500,000 to $1,200,000. Responsibilities included department management, merchandising, advertising, personnel and operating assignments.

The Library: Indispensable Aid

A crucial skill for a literate person is the ability to use the library effectively. Not only is it essential for any organized research project, but it enhances the caliber of all other kinds of writing, and it provides a basis for the fullest enjoyment of pleasure reading.

Since the core of the library is the book collection, people need to know how to find and use books most effectively.

PARTS OF A BOOK: In addition to the main body of printed matter, each book contains some or all of the following parts. Every book has a *title page*, the right-hand page near the front on which are printed the title, the author, the publisher, and the place of publication. Sometimes there is a subtitle printed beneath the title which is added to give a better idea of the scope of the book.

The date on the title page may merely indicate when the book was printed, so the date on the reverse side of the title page is more important, as it tells the *copyright date,* near the time when the book was actually completed. The listing of more than one copyright date often means that additions or revisions were made to the original book. In a bibliography use the latest copyright date.

The *foreword* and *preface* are very similar. They tell something about the purpose of the book, how it can be used, or they acknowledge people who have helped prepare it. An *introduction,* written by the author or an authority on the subject, can summarize the book or introduce the subject.

The *Table of Contents* appears in the front and lists the chapters in order of their appearance, while the *index* is found on the last few pages and is an alphabetical arrangement listing specific persons, places, and topics with the exact page numbers where they are found.

Lists of maps, illustrations, charts are usually found immediately after the Table of Contents. Many books have an appendix near the back containing material that is not really part of the text but which is closely related to it. A United States history book, for example, may have in its appendix a copy of the Constitution.

Many books containing scientific, foreign, or other words that people may not understand have a *glossary* to define these terms.

TYPES OF BOOKS: To help people find books libraries classify, or arrange, books according to a clearly defined plan so that those which are similar in some way stand together on the shelves. They usually first divide the books into *fiction, biography,* and *non-fiction* categories. Fiction is a made-up story, although it can have much truth in it in the way of factual details, real-life characters, and actual settings. Novels such as *The Outsiders,* and short stories, are fiction.

A *biography* is the account of someone's life, and an *autobiography* is the account of one's own life. *Amos Fortune, Free Man* by Elizabeth Yates is a biography, while *The Story of My Life* by Helen Keller is an autobiography.

All other books in the library are usually designated non-fiction, or factual books, although this also includes such special types as folklore, mythology, poetry, drama, and essays.

DEWEY DECIMAL SYSTEM: In school and public libraries non-fiction is cataloged by the *Dewey Decimal System,* named for Melvil Dewey who in 1876 divided all knowledge into ten main classes and assigned numbers to each. Here is a listing of the Dewey class numbers:

CLASS NUMBER	MAIN CLASS
000—099	General Works
100—199	Conduct of Life (Philosophy)
200—299	Religion
300—399	Social Sciences
400—499	Language
500—599	Pure Sciences
600—699	Applied Science/Technology
700—799	Fine Arts and Recreation
800—899	Literature
900—999	History, Geography, Biography

Each of the main classes is subdivided into ten subdivisions. For instance, Pure Science is broken down this way:

510—Mathematics
520—Astronomy
530—Physics
540—Chemistry
550—Earth Sciences
560—Fossils
570—Biology
580—Botany
590—Zoology

Each subdivision is further broken down. For example, within the subclass 790—799 (Recreation), there is 796, outdoor sports; 797, water and air sports; 798, horse and other animal racing; 799, fishing. Further subdivision comes after the decimal. Thus 796.3 is for ball games, while 796.32 is for basketball; 796.33 is for football; 796.34 is for racquet games; and 796.35 is for baseball, etc.

CALL NUMBERS: In addition to the class number, each book also has an author designation which is placed under the class number. These two lines make up the call number which appears on the spine of the book and the catalog card. The call number for *The Many Faces of the Civil War* by Werstein:

973.7 = Dewey # for U. S. history, Civil War period
W498m = W498 for Werstein, the "m" for first word of title.

READING SHELVES: You "read" shelves of books just as you read pages in a book, left to right, line by line (or row by row), with shelf dividers setting off the different "pages." Dewey numbers range from lower numbers on the left to higher on the right, with authors alphabetized within the same number. This is the correct placement of books on a shelf:

155	155.03	155.1	155.1	155.12	155.22
N36g	B42k	M32q	N19h	K14b	A12n

CLASSIFYING FICTION/BIOGRAPHY: Although fiction can fall within the 800s of the Dewey system, and biography in the 900s, most school and public libraries pull these books out and arrange them separately. Fiction is arranged alphabetically by the author's last name. If two authors have the same last name, then the first name is alphabetized, so books by Elizabeth Allen come before those by Merritt Allen. Novels by the same author are alphabetized by title, so Stevenson's *Kidnapped* comes before his *Treasure Island.*

Many libraries give fiction an "F" classification for the first line of the call number, with an author code below it for the second line. A library might have this call number for *Little Women* and *Little Men,* both by Louisa May Alcott: F = Fiction
Alc = Alcott

Biographies are arranged alphabetically by *the person being written about,* so all the books about a person will stand together on the shelf. Often libraries give these books a "B" classification, or sometimes a 92 (part of the Dewey number for biographies.) Thus two biographies of Abraham Lincoln, one by Judson and one by Nolan, would have almost identical call numbers:

B B (The only difference is the author designation
L63j L63n at the end of the number representing Lincoln)

A collective biography, containing the lives of several people, is placed in the Dewey category for biography, 920–928, and has a regular author number.

SPECIAL COLLECTIONS: Sometimes there are other special collections that are housed separately. Short stories may be pulled out of their regular 800 number and put in a place designated S. C. (for story collection). Reference books are routinely shelved by themselves. Here is the call number for the reference book *Twentieth Century Authors* by Kunitz:

R
928
K96t

It is interesting how books from all these sections can be brought together for a special use. A teacher of American history preparing for a class unit on colonial life and the Revolution might go to the library and choose books from every single Dewey class number plus the other designations. Here are some books she might pick, with their broad class numbers: (Notice every class number is used.)

Subject	Class Number
Schools in colonial times	300
Signers of the Declaration (collected biography)	900
Development of constitutional government	300
Revolutionary war weapons	600
Sports and games in colonial days	700
A biography of George Washington	B
Johnny Tremain, a novel laid in Revolutionary days	F
The poem "Paul Revere's Ride"	800
How to embroider a sampler	700
A U. S. history book	900
Slavery	300
Tools used to build a log cabin	600
Foods and recipes	600
Story behind the song "Yankee Doodle"	700
Indian words adopted into our language	400
A description of Monticello, Jefferson's home	900
Colonial costumes	300
The founding of Pennsylvania by Quakers	200
Witchcraft in Salem village	100
Skits from American history	800
An encyclopedia article	000
Native birds painted by Audubon	500

LIBRARY OF CONGRESS CLASSIFICATION SYSTEM: A classification system especially suited to very large libraries or those with large collections of books on one subject find that the Library of Congress System suits their needs better because it can be divided into more precise categories than the Dewey Decimal System. Major classes are indicated by letters rather than by numbers, subdivided then by other letters and numbers. A book, *The Loch Ness Monster* by Cooke would have the L.C. number QL89.C65, while its Dewey call number would be: 001.94
C772l

THE CARD CATALOG is the file for the library

containing alphabetized cards for every book in the library. For each book there is an author card, a title card, and as many subject cards as are necessary to cover the subjects dealt with in the book. Books of fiction have subject cards only if they contain authentic information about a location, a time period, specific events or people. Subject cards are distinguished because they are typed either in red or all capital letters. Here are examples of catalog cards.

USING THE CARD CATALOG: How do you look up a person in the card catalog? Do it as you do someone in the telephone book, last name first. This is true if the person is the author of a book or if the person is the subject of the book.

To find a title, look up the first word of the title unless the first word is "A," "An," or "The." If the first word is an article, go to the second word.

Numbers and abbreviations are filed as though they were spelled out.

Author Card

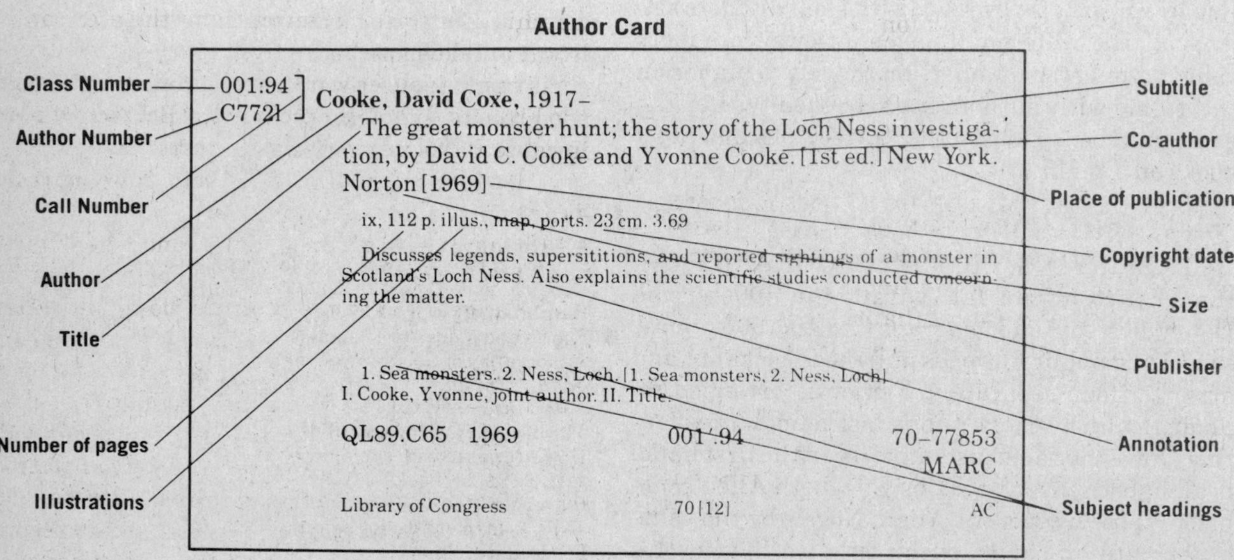

001:94
C772l
Cooke, David Coxe, 1917–
The great monster hunt; the story of the Loch Ness investigation, by David C. Cooke and Yvonne Cooke. [1st ed.] New York. Norton [1969]

ix, 112 p. illus., map, ports. 23 cm. 3.69

Discusses legends, supersititions, and reported sightings of a monster in Scotland's Loch Ness. Also explains the scientific studies conducted concerning the matter.

1. Sea monsters. 2. Ness, Loch. [1. Sea monsters. 2. Ness, Loch]
I. Cooke, Yvonne, joint author. II. Title.

QL89.C65 1969 001'.94 70–77853
MARC

Library of Congress 70 [12] AC

Title Card

The great monster hunt

001:94
C772l
Cooke, David Coxe, 1917–
The great monster hunt; the story of the Loch Ness investigation, by David C. Cooke and Yvonne Cooke. [1st ed.] New York. Norton [1969]

ix, 112 p. illus., map, ports. 23 cm. 3.69

Discusses legends, supersititions, and reported sightings of a monster in Scotland's Loch Ness. Also explains the scientific studies conducted concerning the matter.

1. Sea monsters. 2. Ness, Loch. [1. Sea monsters. 2. Ness, Loch]
I. Cooke, Yvonne, joint author. II. Title.

QL89.C65 1969 001'.94 70–77853
MARC

Library of Congress 70 [12] AC

Subject Card

Sea Monsters

001:94
C772l
Cooke, David Coxe, 1917–
The great monster hunt; the story of the Loch Ness investigation, by David C. Cooke and Yvonne Cooke. [1st ed.] New York. Norton [1969]

ix, 112 p. illus., map, ports. 23 cm. 3.69

Discusses legends, supersititions, and reported sightings of a monster in Scotland's Loch Ness. Also explains the scientific studies conducted concerning the matter.

1. Sea monsters. 2. Ness, Loch. [1. Sea monsters. 2. Ness, Loch]
I. Cooke, Yvonne, joint author. II. Title.

QL89.C65 1969 001'.94 70–77853
MARC

Library of Congress 70 [12] AC

All names beginning "Mc," "Mac," "M'" are filed as though they were spelled "Mac."

In parentheses are the first three letters of the word you would look behind for the following titles: *Mr. Roberts* (Mis); *McGregor Strikes Back* (Mac); *1001 Questions about Birds* (One); *A Moveable Feast* (Mov); *Jane Eyre* (Jan); *The Count of Monte Cristo* (Cou); *And Now Tomorrow* (And because the first word is not "An").

Cards for books by a person come before cards for books about that person: Irving, Washington (author of "Rip Van Winkle") precedes IRVING, WASHINGTON (subject of a biography).

Periods in history are arranged chronologically, factual books first, then fiction.

U. S.–History
U. S.–History-Revolution
U. S.–History-Revolution-Fiction
U. S.–History-Civil War
U. S.–History-Civil War-Fiction
U. S.–History-20th Century

ALPHABETIZING: Most people think they know how to arrange in correct alphabetical order, yet they still have trouble finding things in the card catalog. One reason is that there is more than one system of alphabetical arrangement. The library uses the "word-by-word" system, meaning alphabetizing by letters to the end of each word, short words before long words. The other system, used by many encyclopedias and people who index books, is the letter-by-letter system, which is a strict alphabetical arrangement of all letters disregarding the ending of words.

LIBRARY SYSTEM	OTHER SYSTEM
New Amsterdam	New Amsterdam
New Delhi	Newark
New Zealand	New Delhi
Newark	New Zealand

SUBJECT HEADING: The most difficult part of library research seems to be establishing the key word or phrase that will lead you to the information you seek—finding the right subject heading. This is true not only for the card catalog but also for any other index, in books, encyclopedias, the *Reader's Guide*, etc.

One help is the existence of cross references, "See" and "See also" cards. A "See" card means there is nothing here, that you must look elsewhere. A "See also" card means there is something here but the information you seek may be listed under another heading. For instance, if you look up "Child abuse," you may be told to see the correct subject heading which is "Cruelty to children." Or if you look up "Energy," there may be a "See also" reference which tells you that "Energy" is a valid subject heading (for books about the physics of force and energy) but if you want something about energy as a fuel you should "See also" the alternative heading, "Power resources."

Here are some questions to ask yourself if you are having trouble with subject headings:

* Is there a larger subject that might include it? (U. S.—History—Civil War, rather than Gettysburg, Battle of).

* Is there a smaller subject? (American poetry, rather than Poetry).

* Does your subject overlap another? (Are you searching for the entertainment or the electronics aspect of television?)

* Is there another way to spell it or say it? (Cookery, French vs. French cookery; or Balzac, Honoré de vs. de Balzac, Honoré).

* Does it have a prefix? (U. S. Supreme Court instead of just Supreme Court).

* If your topic is a person, where and when did he live? What was he famous for? (For a report on Michelangelo you would probably do much better not reading a full-length biography but using information under Art—History; European history; Painting—History; Renaissance; Sculpture.

OTHER SOURCES: While today's libraries still find books the most useful sources of information, do not overlook the many non-book materials in its collection. Catalog cards will direct you to recordings, tapes, filmstrips, microfilm, microfiche, pictures, etc. The Vertical File contains pamphlets, clippings, maps, and other materials arranged alphabetically by subject matter in a filing cabinet or pamphlet boxes.

OTHER INFORMATION RETRIEVAL SOURCES: We have discussed at length using the card catalog, for it is a comprehensive index to materials in the library. However, there are additional useful indexes to help you out. Indexes are lists (or catalogs) of subjects, authors, or titles with information about where to find more material.

* Computers, besides storing information can tell where it is located, both within a library and in other places.

* Indexes to books and to encyclopedias are a useful aid to finding material in a book or encyclopedia. Too many people commonly ignore the index volume of an encyclopedia set (usually the last volume), but it is an invaluable tool, as it locates all the information in the entire set and often pinpoints where material is found that has no sepa-

rate article in the alphabetical listing. It can save time, also, as different encyclopedias head the same information differently, i.e. Man, Prehistoric; Prehistoric man; Fossil man; Evolution of Man.

Here is a typical index listing:

Newton, Sir Isaac (English physicist) N:306 with picture
Aerodynamics A: 78-79
Calculus (History) C:22
Color Ci:666
Dynamics D: 321
Gravitation G:320
(Specific information about Newton's Theory of Gravity will be found in volume G on page 320).

* Reference books, such as *Play Index, Short Story Index, Poetry Index* tell in which books specific plays, stories, and poems are located.

* Some magazines and newspapers, such as *National Geographic* and the *New York Times* have indexes to back issues of their publications. Larger libraries index the local newspaper and put it on microfilm or microfiche.

* One of the most valuable indexing tools is the *Reader's Guide to Periodical Literature,* which indexes almost two hundred magazines of general interest. Paperback supplements are published twice a month, which are combined into three-month supplements. Then a full year's guide is bound in a single hardcover volume. There is also an *Abridged Readers' Guide* covering fewer magazines. This service is especially useful for finding recent, current information. Here is a typical entry, with explanation:

Under "Libraries" there are four sub-heads in one issue: Automation; Circulation; Federal aid; and Fines. Under "Fines" is found this entry:

A librarian throws the book at overdue borrowers.
L. Giuliano. il por People Wkly 17:133 Ap 5 '82

This means L. Giuliano has written an article titled "A librarian throws the book at overdue borrowers" which is found in the magazine *People Weekly,* dated April 5, 1982, on page 133. The volume number for that issue is 17. The article also contains pictures (il) and a portrait (por).

A HOME REFERENCE LIBRARY: Reference books, which are usually expensive, are not intended for straight-through reading, but are designed to impart specific information quickly. The reference collection in a library is usually extensive and is not available to be checked out. Everyone should make a survey of what is available at their favorite library, but most people like to build a small home collection which can prove to be very useful at odd times of the day or night. Many of these books can be purchased in paperback so they fit into the average family's budget.

Indispensable in the home is a good *dictionary* which defines words, gives correct spelling and syllable division, and contains a great deal of additional front and back matter. An unabridged dictionary contains almost all the words in the language, while an abridged one is shortened.

Equally important for the home is a multi-volume general *encyclopedia* containing information about people, places, things, ideas, and events. Annual yearbooks keep it up-to-date. While a one-volume encyclopedia is ideal for quick reference, the more comprehensive multi-volume set is naturally better for detailed information such as school reports.

A handy tool is an *almanac,* such as the *World Almanac,* which is published yearly in paperback and is chock full of lists, tables, statistics, and all kinds of facts and figures.

For anyone who writes anything a *thesaurus* is most helpful. Also available in paperback, it is a dictionary of synonyms, to help the writer find the exact word needed.

Quotation books, again in paperback, allow the reader and writer to identify a quotation, to cite it in full, and to find an apt one on a particular theme.

Also useful in the home is an *atlas,* a book of maps, which is indispensable for planning trips as well as for obtaining information on political divisions, population, climate, resources, etc.

If a family has special hobbies or students pursuing special interests, there are innumerable handbooks covering single subjects and other reference books that could be purchased. It is always advisable to make friends with the local librarian, who can direct you to almost any information you seek.

Foreign Words and Phrases

In a language like English, whose vocabulary is at least 80 per cent borrowed from other language sources, it is not always easy to judge whether a word or expression should be considered as "foreign" or "naturalized." The choice is easier when it comes to full sentences and sayings. The chief sources of our foreign words and phrases are French and Latin. Other heavy contributors are Italian (particularly for musical terms), German, Greek, and Spanish. But English is a ready borrower and adapter, and we find in our list contributions from other European languages (Russian, Dutch, Scandinavian, Portuguese, etc.); from Semitic tongues, such as Hebrew and Arabic; from languages of Asia, such as Japanese, Chinese, Persian, and Turkish; from the tongues of the American Indians; and even from languages of the far Pacific, notably Hawaiian.

In each case, we have given the pronunciation of the word or expression with an approximation to the language of origin, even where usage has established a current English pronunciation; for instance, while there is a current English pronunciation of a Latin term like *bona fide,* our transcription approximates the sound of the original Latin because the current pronunciation is already commonly known.

The system of transcription is for the most part self-explanatory. Place the stress on the syllable that appears in capitals. Pronounce: AH like the *a* in *father;* EH like the *e* in *met;* EYE as in *eye;* OH like the *o* in *or;* OO as in *fool;* EE as in *seen;* OW as in *fowl;* ZH like the *s* in *pleasure;* AW as in *awe;* AY as in *lay*. In French words, ÃH, ẼH, ÃW, ŨH represent the four French nasal sounds of *an, vin, on, un,* respectively; shut off completely the passage between nose and mouth, so that your breath-stream is forced into the nose, and pronounce at the same time AH, EH, AW, UH. The transcription Ö represents a sound halfway between the *e* of *met* and the *o* of *or* (for which the French spelling is *eu* or *oeu*); the transcription Ü represents a sound intermediate between the *oo* of *fool* and the *ee* of *seen* (purse lips for *oo,* and try to say *ee*). In German words, KH represents the sound of *ch* in *ach,* Ç the sound of *ch* in *ich* (the nearest English approximation is the *h* of *huge).* Abbreviations for the names of the source language are as follows:

F	French	Jap	Japanese
L	Latin	Ch	Chinese
It	Italian	Du	Dutch
Sp	Spanish	Pers	Persian
G	German	Swed	Swedish
Pt	Portuguese	Yid	Yiddish
R	Russian	Arab	Arabic
Gk	Greek	Turk	Turkish
Sk	Sanskrit	Hind	Hindi
Heb	Hebrew	Norw	Norwegian

Other languages of rare occurrence (Hungarian, Irish, Welsh, Icelandic, Basque, Egyptian, Hawaiian, etc.) are left unabbreviated.

The translations given are sometimes literal, but more often aim at rendering the meaning of the foreign word or expression.

The italicized words and expressions are still considered "foreign." These words should be underlined in the original manuscript and italicized when printed. Not all authorities will agree with this list. When you "naturalize" a word or phrase, be prepared to defend your act. A quick rule to follow is: If the word or phrase does not appear in one of the major dictionaries, then it is still "foreign."

India—Hall of Special Audience in Red Fort, Delhi

A

ab initio (ahb ee-NEE-tee-oh), from the beginning (L)

à bon marché (a bāw mar-SHAY), cheap, a bargain (F)

ab ovo (ahb OH-woh), from the egg, from the very start (L)

absinthe (ap-SĒHT), wormwood, absinth (F)

a cappella (ah kahp-PEHL-lah), church style, without accompaniment (It)

accelerando (ah-chay-lay-RAHN-doh), with increasing speed (It)

Achtung (AKH-toong), attention (G)

adagio (ah-DAH-joh), slowly (It)

ad astra per aspera (ahd AH-strah pehr AH-speh-rah), to the stars through difficult places (L)

addendum (ahd-DEHN-doom) (pl. addenda, ahd-DEHN-dah), to be added (L)

Adeste Fideles (ah-DEHS-teh fee-DEH-lehs), Come, ye faithful (L)

ad hoc (ahd HOHK), for this, for this purpose (L)

adieu (a-DYÖ), farewell, good-bye (F)

ad infinitum (ahd een-fee-NEE-toom), to infinity, on and on (L)

adiós (ah-DYOHS), farewell, good-bye (Sp)

ad lib(itum) (ahd Lee-bee-toom), at pleasure (usually abbr. ad lib) (L)

ad nauseam (ahd NOW-seh-ahm), to the point of disgust (L)

ad valorem (ahd wah-LOH-rehm), in proportion to value or valuation (L)

affaire de coeur (a-FEHR duh KÖR), love affair (F)

affaire d'honneur (a-FEHR daw-NÖR), matter involving honor (F)

aficionado (ah-fee-thyoh-NAH-doh), fan, enthusiast (Sp)

a fortiori (ah fohr-tee-OH-ree), with greater reason, all the more (L)

agenda (ah-GHEHN-dah), things to be done (L)

agent provocateur (a-ZHĀH praw-vaw-ka-TÖR), one who provokes others into unlawful actions (F)

agio (AH-joh), ease; currency differential (It)

Agnus Dei (AHG-noos DEH-ee), Lamb of God (L)

agora (AH-goh-rah), marketplace (Gk)

aguardiente (ah-gwahr-DYEHN-teh), firewater, brandy (Sp)

aide-de-camp (EHD duh KĀH), field aide (F)

aigrette (eh-GREHT), egret, spray of feathers (F)

aiguillette (eh-ghee-YEHT), shoulder-knot (F)

à la (a la), in the–fashion (à la française, French style) (F)

à la carte (a la KART), according to the menu, picking out individual items (F)

alameda (ah-lah-MEH-dah), poplar grove (Sp)

à la mode (a la MAWD), in the fashion (F)

alcázar (ahl-KAH-thahr), fortress, fortified palace (Arab-Sp)

al fresco (ahl FRAYS-koh), in the open air (It)

alias (AH-lee-ahs), otherwise, at another time (L)

alibi (AH-lee-bee), elsewhere (L)

allegro (ahl-LAY-groh), quick, lively, merry (It)

alma mater (AHL-mah MAH-tehr), fostering mother, school or college (L)

aloha oe (ah-LOH-hah OH-eh), farewell to you (Hawaiian)

Alpenstock (AHL-pen-shtok), iron-tipped staff used in mountain climbing (G)

alpha-omega (AHL-fah OH-may-gah), beginning and end (Gk)

alter ego (AHL-tehr EH-goh), another I, close and inseparable friend (L)

alto (AHL-toh), low female voice (used for *contralto,* "counter high") (It)

alumnus, alumna (ah-LOOM-noos, ah-LOOM-nah), graduate of an institution (L)

amabile (ah-MAH-bee-lay), amiable, pleasing (It)

amanuensis (ah-mah-noo-EHN-sees), clerk, secretary (L)

amicus curiae (ah-MEE-koos KOO-ree-eye), friend of the court (L)

amour propre (a-MOOR PRAW-pruh), self-love, pride (F)

ancien régime (ãh-SYẼH ray-ZHEEM), old, prerevolutionary regime (F)

animato (ah-nee-MAH-toh), animated, with spirit (It)

anno Domini (AHN-nob DOH-mee-nee), in the year of our Lord (abbr. A.D.) (L)

Anschluss (AHN-shloos), annexation, union (G)

ante bellum (AHN-teh BEHL-loom), before the war (L)

ante meridiem (AHN-teh meh-REE-dee-ehm), before noon, morning (abbr. A.M.) (L)

antipasto (ahn-tee-PAH-stoh), appetizer, hors d'oeuvre (It)

apartheid (a-PART-hayt), South African policy of racial segregation (Du)

apéritif (a-pay-ree-TEEF), appetizer, before-meal drink (F)

aplomb (a-PLÃW), self-possession, poise (F)

a posteriori (ah pohs-teh-ree-OH-ree), with hindsight, reasoning backwards from observed facts (L)

appassionato (ahp-pahs-syoh-NAH-toh), passionately (It)

Après moi le déluge! (a-PREH MWAH luh day-LÜZH), after me the deluge, I don't care what happens after I'm gone (F)

a priori (ah pree-OH-ree), reaching conclusions before gathering facts (L)

apropos (a praw-POH), opportunely, by the way, with regard to (F)

aquavit (ah kwah-VEET), brandy (Swedish, from Latin *aqua vitae,* water of life)

arbiter elegantiarum (AHR-bee-tehr eh-leh-gahn-tee-AH-room), arbiter of style or taste (L)

argot (ar-GOH), slang, thieves' cant (F)

argumentum ad hominem (ahr-goo-MEHN-toom ahd HOH-mee-nehm), diversion of a discussion to the personality of the opponent (L)

aria (AH-ryah), vocal solo passage in an opera (It)

arista (AH-rees-tah), the best, honors group in a high school (Gk)

arpeggio (ahr-PAY-joh), notes of chord played in harplike succession (It)

arrière-pensée (a-RYEHR pãh-SAY), mental reservation, afterthought (F)

arroz con pollo (ahr-ROHTH kohn POH-lyoh), chicken with rice and condiments (Sp)

ars amandi (AHRS ah-MAHN-dee), the art of loving (L)

ars gratia artis (AHRS GRAH-tee-ah AHR-tees), art for art's sake (L)

ars longa, vita brevis (AHRS LOHN-gah, WEE-tah BREH-wees), art is long, but life is fleeting (L)

attaché (a-ta-SHAY), diplomatic official attached to an embassy (F)

au courant (oh koo-RÃH), posted, informed (F)

auf Wiedersehen (owf VEE-duhr-zayn), good-bye, till we meet again (G)

France—The Sacré Coeur, Paris

au gratin (oh gra-TẼH), baked with crumbs or cheese on top (F)

au jus (oh ZHÜ), in its natural juice or gravy (F)

aurea mediocritas (OW-ray-ah meh-dee-OH-kree-tahs), the golden mean (L)

au revoir (oh ruh-VWAHR), good-bye, till we meet again (F)

auri sacra fames (OW-ree SAH-krah FAH-mehs), sacred lust for gold (L)

aurora borealis (ow-ROH-rah boh-ray-AH-lees), the northern lights (L)

Aut Caesar aut nullus (owt KEYE-sahr owt NOOL-loos), either everything or nothing (L)

Autobahn (OW-toh-bahn), automobile highway (G)

auto da fé (OW-toh dah FEH), burning at the stake on a charge of heresy (Pt)

Aux armes! (oh-ZAHRM), to arms! (F)

avant-garde (a-VÃH-GAHRD), in the van or forefront (F)

Ave atque vale! (AH-weh AHT-kweh WAH-leh), hail and farewell (L)

Ave Caesar, morituri te salutamus (AH-weh KEYE-sahr, moh-ree-TOO-ree teh sah-loo-TAH-moos), Hail, Caesar, we who are about to die salute you (L)

Ave Maria (AH-weh mah-REE-ah), Hail, Mary (L)

à votre santé! (a VAW-truh SÃH-tay), to your health! (F)

B

baba (bah-BAH), light cake (F)

babu (BAH-boo), gentleman, Mr. (Hindi)

babushka (BAH-boosh-kuh), scarf over the head, tied under the chin "little grandmother" fashion (R)

baklava (or *paklava*) (bah-KLAH-vah), Turkish pastry made with nuts and honey (Turkish)

bakshish (BAHK-sheesh), tip, money (Persian)

balalaika (buh-luh-LEYE-kuh), three-stringed triangular guitar (R)

bambino (bahm-BEE-noh), baby, child (It)

banderilla (bahn-deh-REE-lyah), dart with streamer used in bullfight (Sp)

banditti (bahn-DEE-tee), incorrect spelling for *banditi*, "bandits" (It)

banzai (BAHN-zeye), cheer or battle cry, "ten thousand years" (Jap)

bar mitzva (BAHR-MEETS-vah), confirmation ceremony (Heb)

baroque (ba-RAWK), irregular in shape, over-ornamental (F)

bas bleu (BAH BLÖ), blue-stocking, over-intellectual woman (F)

bas-relief (bah-ruh-LYEHF), sculpture with figures projecting from background (F)

basso profundo (BAHS-soh proh-FOON-doh), deep bass voice (It-L)

bathos (BAH-thos), false pathos; an anti-climax (Gk)

beau geste (BOH ZHEHST), fine gesture or deed (F)

beau monde (BOH MÃWD), high society (F)

beaux arts (BOH-ZAHR), fine arts (F)

béchamel (bay-sha-MEHL), rich white sauce (F)

beige (BEHZH), undyed, grayish tan (F)

Beiheft (BEYE-heft), supplement, supplementary volume (G)

bel canto (behl KAHN-toh), fine singing (It)

belladonna (behl-lah-DAWN-nah), lovely lady, poisonous plant, eye-drug (It)

belles-lettres (behl-LEH-truh), literature, the humanities (F)

Bel Paese (behl pah-AY-say), beautiful country, a creamy cheese (It)

berceuse (behr-SÜZ), cradle-song, lullaby (F)

béret (bay-REH), flat, round cap (F)

bête noire (BEHT NWAHR), black beast, pet abomination (F)

bêtise (beh-TEEZ), foolish act or word (F)

beurre noir (BÖR NWAHR), black butter sauce (F)

billet-doux (bee-YEH DOO), love note or letter (F)

bis (BEES), twice, encore (L)

bisque (BEESK), rich soup (F)

bistro (bee-STROH), cabaret, wine-shop (F)

blanc mange (BLÃH MÃHZH), white pudding (F)

blasé (bla-ZAY), jaded, satiated, bored (F)

blintzi (BLEEN-tsy), cheese or meat wrapped in pancake (R)

Blitzkreig (BLITZ-kreek), lightning war; swift, sudden attack (G)

Blut und Boden (BLOOT unt BOH-duhn), blood and soil (G)

Blut und Eisen (BLOOT unt EYE-zuhn), blood and iron (G)

B'nai B'rith (BNEYE BREETH), sons of the covenant, Jewish service organization (Heb)

bocce (BAW-chay), an Italian bowling game (It)

boeuf á la mode (BÖF a la MAWD), larded and pot-roasted beef (F)

Boer (BOOR), peasant or settler in South Africa (Du)

Bohême (boh-EHM), gypsy-like, unconventional living (F)

bolero (boh-LEH-roh), a Spanish dance (Sp)

Bolsheviki (buhl'-shuh-vee-KEE), Maximalists, Lenin-led Communists (R)

bombe glacée (BÃWB gla-SAY), frozen dessert (F)

bona fide (BOH-nah FEE-day), in good faith (L)

bon ami (BÃW-na-MEE), good friend (F)

bonanza (boh-NAHN-thah), windfall, run of luck (Sp)

bonbon (Bãw-BÃW), candy (F)

bon gré mal gré (bãw-GRAY mal-GRAY), willy-nilly (F)

bon marché (baw mar-SHAY) (*see* à bon marché)

bon mot (bãw MOH), witticism (F)

bonne (BAWN), maid, nursemaid (F)

bonus (BOH-noos), extra payment (L)

bon vivant (bãw-vee-VÃH), one who likes to live well (F)

bon voyage (bãw-vwa-YAHZH), a happy trip (F)

borsch (BAWRSHCH), Russian beet soup, usually with sour cream (R)

boudoir (boo-DWAHR), lady's private sitting-room (F)

bouffant (boo-FÃH), puffed out, full (F)

bouillabaisse (boo-ya-BEHS), seafood soup (F)

bouillon (boo-YÃW), clear beef or chicken broth (F)

bourgeoisie (boor-zhwah-ZEE), middle class (F)

boutonnière (boo-taw-NYEHR), buttonhole, flower for a buttonhole (F)

bravo, brava (BRAH-voh, BRAH-vah), cry of approval; hired killer (It)

Brie (BREE), a creamy French cheese (F)

brio (BREE-oh), vivacity, liveliness (It)

brioche (bree-AWSH), bun, light roll (F)

Iran—Street Scene, Teheran

broccoli (BRAWK-koh-lee), green variety of cauliflower (It)

brochure (braw-SHÜR), pamphlet (F)

brut (BRÜ), raw, unadulterated (F)

Bund (BOONT), league; union, organization (G)

Bundesrepublik (BOON-duhs-reh-poo-bleek), West German Federal Republic (G)

burro (BOOR-roh), donkey (Sp)

bushido (BOO-shee-doh), code of honor of *samurai* class (Jap)

C

ca. See *circa*

cabala, kabala (kahb-ah-LAH), Hebrew occult religious philosophy (Heb)

cacciatora (kah-chah-TOH-rah), hunter style (It); more properly *alla cacciatora*

caciocavallo (kah-choh-kah-VAHL-loh), piquant Italian cheese (It)

cacique (kah-THEE-kay), American Indian chief, political leader (Carib-Sp)

caesura (keye-SOO-rah), break in line of poetry (L)

café (ka-FAY), coffee shop, saloon (F);—**au lait** (oh LEH), coffee with milk;—**noir** (NWAHR), black coffee

caffè espresso (kah-FEH ays-PREHS-soh), strong black coffee, machine-made (It)

Calvados (kal-va-DOHS), apple brandy from the French region of the same name (F)

camaraderie (ka-ma-rad-REE), loyalty, comradeship, good fellowship (F)

camarilla (kah-mah-REE-lyah), clique, group of special advisors (Sp)

Camembert (ka-māh-BEHR), a soft French cheese (F)

camino real (kah-MEE-noh reh-AHL), royal or main highway (Sp)

camorra (kah-MAWR-rah), Neapolitan secret society (It)

campanile (kahm-pah-NEE-lay), bell tower (It)

campo santo (KAHM-poh SAHN-toh), graveyard, cemetery (It)

canaille (ka-NA-yuh), rabble (F)

canapé (ka-na-PAY), open sandwich served as appetizer (F)

canard (ka-NAHR), duck, hoax (F)

canasta (kah-NAHS-tah), basket, card game (Sp)

can can (kāh-KĀH), kicking dance (F)

cannelloni (kahn-nayl-LOH-nee), large hollow macaroni stuffed with meat (It)

cantabile (kahn-TAH-bee-lay), singable, in singing style (It)

cantata (kahn-TAH-tah), musical composition for solos or choruses (It)

canton (kāh-TĀW), political subdivision of Switzerland (F)

cap-à-pied (ka-pa-PYEH), head-to-foot armor (F)

capias (KAH-pee-ahs), "you may take"; arrest warrant (L)

capriccio (kah-PREE-choh), free musical composition, caprice (It)

carabiniere (kah-rah-bee-NYEH-ray), Italian military policeman (It)

carioca (kah-RYOH-kah), native of Rio; Brazilian dance (Pt)

carpe diem (KAHR-peh DEE-ehm), "seize the day"; make hay while the sun shines (L)

carte blanche (KART BLĀHSH), free hand; authorization to act as one will (F)

cartel (kar-TEHL), monopoly trust; organized group of business interests (F)

Carthago delenda est (kahr-TAH-goh deh-LEHN-dah EHST), Carthage must be destroyed (L)

cartouche (kar-TOOSH), cartridge; oval space for inscription of name of Egyptian Pharaoh (F)

casserole (kas-RAWL), clay saucepan for cooking and serving; contents thereof (F)

casus belli (KAH-soos BEHL-lee), occurrence giving rise to war (L)

caudillo (kow-DEE-lyoh), chief, leader (Sp)

cause célèbre (KOHZ say-LEH-bruh), famous or sensational trial (F)

causerie (kohz-REE), chat, informal talk (F)

cavatina (kah-vah-TEE-nah), short song (It)

caveat (KAH-weh-aht), let (him) beware (L);—**emptor** (EHMP-tohr), let the buyer beware

cave canem (KAH-weh KAH-nehm), beware of the dog (L)

cello (CHEHL-loh); abbr. of *violoncello*, musical instrument (It)

certiorari (kehr-tee-oh-RAH-ree), "to be ascertained"; writ to procure records (L)

c'est-à-dire (seh-ta-DEER), that is to say (F)

c'est la vie (seh-la-VEE), that's life (F)

ceteris paribus (KEH-teh-rees PAH-ree-boos), other things being equal (L)

chacun à son goût (sha-KŪH a-sāw-GOO), everyone to his taste (F)

chacun pour soi (sha-KŪH poor SWAH), every man for himself (F)

chaise longue (SHEHZ LĀWG), reclining chair or sofa (F)

champagne (shāh-PA-nyuh), French sparkling wine (F)

champignon (shāh-pee-NYĀW), mushroom (F)

chanteuse (shāh-TÖZ), female singer (F)

chargé d'affaires (shar-ZHAY da-FEHR), minor government official temporarily replacing a higher diplomat (F)

charivari (sha-ree-va-REE), mock serenade or raucous music (F)

chasseur (sha-SÖR), hunter; light-infantryman; footman (F)

château (sha-TOH), castle, palace (F)

chef (de cuisine) (SHEF duh kwee-ZEEN), head cook (F)

chef d'oeuvre (SHEH DÖ-vruh), masterpiece (F)

Cherchez la femme! (shehr-SHAY la FAM), look for the woman in the case (F)

chérie (shay-REE), dearie, sweetheart (F)

chetnik (CHET-neek), Yugoslav resistance fighter (Serbo-Croatian)

chevaux-de-frise (shuh-VÖH duh FREEZ), barrier of spikes in timber (F)

chez (SHAY), at the home of (F)

Chianti (KYAHN-tee), Italian wine (It)

chiaroscuro (kyah-roh-SKOO-roh), light and dark effect (It)

chic (SHEEK), elegant, elegance (F)

chiffon (shee-FÃW), rag; silk crepe, whipped ingredients in pie (F)

chile con carne (CHEE-leh kohn KAHR-neh), Mexican dish consisting of kidney beans, ground meat, and red peppers (Sp)

chop suey (TSAH SOO-ee), Chinese-American dish of meat and vegetables (Ch)

chow mein (CHOW MYEHN), Chinese dish of fried noodles, with meat or vegetables (Ch)

Cid (THEED), chieftain, leader (Sp, from Arab *sayyid*)

ci-gît (see-ZHEE), here lies (F)

cinquecento (cheen-kway-CHEHN-toh), 16th century (It)

circa (KEER-kah), about, approximately; abbr. ca. (L)

Civis Romanus sum (Kee-wees roh-MAH-noos SOOM), I am a Roman citizen (L)

Civitas Dei (KEE-wee-tahs DEH-ee), the City of God (L)

clair de lune (KLEHR duh LÜN), moonlight (F)

claret (kla-REH), light red wine (F)

clef (KLAY or KLEHF), key (F)

cliché (klee-SHAY), stereotype; hackneyed expression (F)

clientèle (klee-āh-TEHL), customers or patrons (F)

clique (KLEEK), set; group (F)

clôture (kloh-TÜR), closure of debate (F)

cocido (koh-THEE-doh), Spanish stew (Sp)

coda (KOH-dah), tail; concluding musical passage (It)

Code Napoléon (KAWD na-poh-lay-ÃW), code of civil law of France of 1804, applied with modifications in Louisiana (F)

codex (KOH-dehks), body of laws; manuscript on parchment (L)

Cogito, ergo sum (KOH-ghee-toh, EHR-goh SOOM), I think, therefore I exist (L)

cognac (kaw-NYAK), French brandy (F)

cognoscenti (erroneous for *conoscenti*, koh-noh-SHEHN-tee), experts (It)

coiffeur (kwa-FÖR), hairdresser (F)

coiffure (kwa-FÜR), hairstyle (F)

coloratura (koh-loh-rah-TOO-rah), embellishment in vocal music; soprano (It)

commando (koh-MAHN-doh), raiding troops (Du. from Pt)

comme ci, comme ça (kawm SEE, kawm SA), so-so (F)

comme il faut (kawm eel FOH), proper; properly; in the right fashion (F)

***commedia* dell'arte** (kohm-MEH-dyah dayl-LAHR-tay), guild players' comedy, often improvised (It)

commissar (kuhm-mee-SAHR), government official (R, from F *commissaire*)

commune (kaw-MÜN), self-governing town; French revolutionary movement (F)

communiqué (kaw-mü-nee-KAY), official statement or dispatch (F)

compote (kāw-PAWT), stewed fruit (F)

compte rendu (KÃWT rāh-DÜ), book review; report (F)

con amore (kohn ah-MOH-ray), lovingly (It)

concerto (kohn-CHEHR-toh), musical composition for solo instrument(s) with orchestral accompaniment (It)

concierge (kāw-SYEHRZH), janitor, superintendent (F)

concordat (kāw-kawr-DAH), pact, agreement (F from Latin *concordatus*)

condottiere (kohn-doht-TYEH-ray), Italian Renaissance leader of mercenary troops (It)

confer (KOHN-fehr), compare; see; abbr. cf. (L)

confetti (kohn-FEHT-tee), candies; plaster or paper imitations used at feasts (It)

confrère (kāw-FREHR), colleague; associate (F)

conga (KAWN-gah), Latin-American dance (Sp or Pt)

con moto (kohn MAW-toh), with movement; fast (It)

connoisseur (kaw-neh-SÖR), expert; one who knows (F)

conquistadores (kohn-kees-tah-DOH-rehs), conquerors (Sp)

console (kāw-SAWL), ornamental bracket for supporting shelf; table with ledges (F)

consommé (kāw-saw-MAY), concentrated meat broth (F)

consortium (kohn-SOHR-tee-oom), international finance control group (L)

contra (KOHN-trah), against (abbr. con; L)

contrabasso (kohn-trah-BAHS-soh), double-bass viol (It)

copula (KOH-poo-lah), connective; the verb "to be" or a similar verb (L)

coq au vin (KAWK oh VÊH), chicken braised in wine (F)

coquetterie (kaw-keht-REE), flirtatiousness (F)

coram populo (KOH-rahm POH-poo-loh), publicly (L)

cordillera (kohr-dee-LYEH-rah), mountain range (SP)

cornu copiae (KOHR-noo KOH-pee-eye), horn of plenty (L)

corona (koh-ROH-nah), crown (L)

corps de ballet (KAWR duh ba-LEH), ballet troupe (F)

corpus (KOHR-poos), body; collection (L)

corpus delicti (KOHR-poos deh-LEEK-tee), the body or tangible evidence of a crime (L)

corpus juris (KOHR-poos YOO-rees), the body of the law; collection of laws (L)

corrida (kohr-REE-dah), bullfight (Sp)

corrigenda (kohr-ree-GHEHN-dah), things to be corrected (L)

corsage (kawr-SAHZH), bodice; flowers worn on bodice (F)

cortège (kawr-TEHZH), procession (F)

corvée (kawr-VAY), forced labor (F)

cosi cosi (koh-SEE koh-SEE), so-so (It)

coterie (kawt-REE), small, intimate group or circle (F)

coup de grâce (KOO duh GRAHS), death-blow (F)

coup de main (KOO duh MÊH), sudden blow (F)

coup d'état (KOO day-TAH), seizure of government by sudden stroke (F)

couturier (koo-tü-RYAY), dressmaker (F)

crèche (KREHSH), crib, manger, public nursery (F)

credenza (kray-DEHN-tsah), small table or cupboard (It)

credo (KREH-doh), belief, article of faith, creed (L)

crème de menthe (KREHM duh MÂHT), peppermint liqueur (F)

crêpe (KREHP), thin cloth of silk, rayon, wool, etc. (F)

crêpe suzette (KREHP sü-ZEHT), thin pancake (F)

crescendo (kray-SHEHN-doh), gradual increase in loudness or intensity (It)

critique (kree-TEEK), criticism (F)

croissant (krwa-SÂH), crescent-shaped roll (F)

Croix de Guerre (KRWAH duh GHEHR), war cross, French military decoration (F)

croquette (kraw-KEHT), fried meat or fish, covered with bread crumbs (F)

croupier (kroo-PYAY), man who rakes in stakes at gambling table (F)

crux (KROOKS), cross; main point at issue (L)

cucaracha (koo-kah-RAH-chah), cockroach (Sp)

cui bono? (KOO-ee BOH-noh), to whose advantage? (L)

cuisine (kwee-ZEEN), cookery, cooking (F)

cul-de-sac (KÜL-duh-SAHK), blind alley, dead end (F)

cum grano salis (koom GRAH-noh SAH-lees), with a grain of salt (L)

cum laude (koom LOW-deh), with praise, with honor (L)

curé (kü-RAY), parish priest (F)

curriculum (koor-REE-koo-loom), year's course of studies (L);—**vitae** (WEE-teye), outline of one's life

czar (more precisely *tsar*, TSAHR), Russian emperor, autocrat (R)

czardas (more precisely *csárdás*, CHAHR- dahsh), Hungarian dance (Hungarian)

D

da capo (dah KAH-poh), from the start (It)

Dachshund (DAHKS-hoont), short-legged dog (G)

dal segno (dahl SAY-nyoh), from the sign (It)

data (DAH-tah) (sg. **datum**), information at one's disposal (L)

débâcle (day-BAH-kluh), disaster, collapse (F)

débris (day-BREE), wreckage, rubbish (F)

début (day-BÜ), coming out, first appearance (F)

débutante (day-bü-TÂHT), girl making first social appearance (F)

décolleté (day-kawl-TAY), low-necked (F)

décor (day-KAWR), stage setting, room setting (F)

de facto (deh FAHK-toh), in existence, in actuality (L)

deficit (DEH-fee-keet), amount less than what is needed (L)

de gustibus non est disputandum (deh GOOS-tee-boos nohn EHST dees-poo-TAHN-doom), there is no arguing about tastes (L)

Dei gratia (DEH-ee GRAH-tee-ah), by the grace of God (L)

déjeuner (day-zhö-NAY), lunch, breakfast (F)

de jure (deh YOO-reh), legally, legitimately (L)

dele (DEH-leh), erase, strike out, delete; abbreviation (L)

delenda est Carthago (deh-LEHN-dah EHST kahr-TAH-goh), Carthage must be destroyed (L)

delicatessen (day-LEE-kaht-EHS-suhn), prepared foods (G)

delirium tremens (deh-LEE-ree-oom TREH-mehns), alcoholic brain disease (L)

de luxe (duh LÜKS), luxurious, very fancy (F)

démarche (day-MAHRSH), diplomatic approach, step (F)

dementia praecox (deh-MEHN-tee-ah PREYE-kohks), adolescent mental illness (L)

demi-tasse (duh-MEE-TAHS), small cup of coffee (F)

demi-monde (duh-MEE-MAWD), fringe of society (F)

de mortuis nihil nisi bonum (deh MOHR-too-ees NEE-heel NEE-see BOH-noom), say nothing but good about the dead (L)

denarius (deh-NAH-ree-oos), Roman silver coin (L)

denier (duh-NYAY), small coin, unit of weight for hosiery (F)

dénouement (day-noo-MÂH), unraveling, solution of plot (F)

de novo (deh NOH-voh), anew, again from the start (L)

Deo volente (DEH-oh woh-LEHN-teh), God willing (L)

de profundis (deh proh-FOON-dees), out of the depths (L)

de rigueur (duh ree-GÖR), indispensable, required (F)

dernier cri (dehr-NYAY KREE), latest style, last word (F)

derrière (deh-RYEHR), back part, buttocks (F)

descamisado (dehs-kah-mee-SAH-doh), shirtless, follower of Evita Perón (Sp)

déshabillé (day-za-bee-YAY), in state of informal undress (F)

desideratum (deh-see-deh-RAH-toom; pl. **desiderata,** deh-see-deh-RAH-tah), what is desired (L) *détente* (day-TÃHT), release of strained relations (F)

de trop (duh TROH), in excess, superfluous, not wanted (F)

deus ex machina (DEH-oos ehks MAH-kee-nah), outside intervention to solve a crisis (L)

Deus vobiscum (DEH-oos woh-BEES-koom), God be with you (L)

diaspora (dee-AHS-poh-rah), dispersion, scattering (particularly of Jews after destruction of Jerusalem) (Gk)

dictum (DEEK-toom), saying, pronouncement (L)

diminuendo (dee-mee-noo-EHN-doh), diminishing in volume (It)

Dirndl (DEERNDL), peasant-girl dress (G)

diseur (fem. diseuse; dee-ZÖR, dee-ZÖZ), monologist (F)

diva (DEE-vah), female opera singer (It)

divertissement (dee-vehr-tees-MÃH), lively piece between acts (F)

divide et impera (dee-WEE-deh eht EEM-peh-rah), divide and conquer (L)

doge (DAW-jay), medieval ruler of Venice (It)

dogma (DOHG-mah), belief, article of faith (Gk)

dolce far niente (DOHL-chay FAHR NYEHN-tay), sweet idleness (It)

dolce stil nuovo (DOHL-chay STEEL NWAW-voh), sweet new literary style of 14th century (It)

Dominus vobiscum (DOH-mee-noos woh-BEES-koom), the Lord be with you (L)

don (DOHN), tutor at English universities; Spanish and Italian title of respect; Mafia leader (It, Sp)

donna (DAWN-nah), lady, woman (It)

Doppelgänger (DOH-pehl-gheng-uhr), ghostly double (G)

dossier (daw-SYAY), file (F)

double entendre (DOO-blãh-TÃH-druh), expression with double meaning (F)

dramatis personae (DRAH-mah-tees pehr-SOH-neye), cast of characters (L)

droshky (DRAWSH-kee), cab, carriage (R)

duce (DOO-chay), leader (It)

dueña (DWEH-nyah), chaperone (Sp)

duomo (DWAW-moh), cathedral (It)

dybbuk (DEE-book), bewitched person; evil spirit entering living body (Heb)

E

eau de vie (OH duh VEE), brandy (F)

ecce homo (EHK-keh HOH-moh), behold the man (L)

échelon (aysh-LÃW), steplike formation of troops, any hierarchical arrangement (F)

éclair (ay-KLEHR), pastry filled with cream (F)

éclat (ay-KLAH), success, prestige (F)

Edda (EHD-dah), old Scandinavian poetry (Icelandic)

Edelweiss (AY-duhl-veyes), white Alpine flower (G)

editio princeps (eh-DEE-tee-oh PREEN-kehps), original edition (L)

eisteddfod (ay-STETH-vohd), musical or poetic contest (Welsh)

élan (ay-LÃH), sparkle, liveliness (F)

el dorado (ehl doh-RAH-doh), fabulous South American land of gold (Sp)

Eli (EH-lee), my God (Heb)

élite (ay-LEET), select few (F)

Elohim (eh-loh-HEEM), God, Supreme Being (Heb)

embarras du choix (ãh-ba-RAH dü SHWAH), trouble making up one's mind (F)

embonpoint (ãh-baw̃-PWẼH), plumpness (F)

emeritus (eh-MEH-ree-toos), retired with honor (L)

émigré (ay-mee-GRAY), emigrated, exiled (F)

en bloc (ãh BLAWK), together; as a unit (F)

en brochette (ãh braw-SHEHT), on a skewer (F)

enceinte (ãh-SẼHT), pregnant, with child (F)

en coquille (ãh kaw-KEE-yuh), served in a shell (F)

encore (ãh-KAWR), again; repeat (F)

enfant gâté (terrible) (ãh-FAH gah-TAY, teh-REE-bluh), spoiled child, brat (F)

en masse (ãh MAHS), all together, in a mass (F)

ennui (ãh-NWEE), boredom (F)

en passant (ãh pa-SÃH), incidentally; by the way (F)

ensemble (ãh-SÃH-bluh), together, in a group (F)

entente (ãh-TÃHT), understanding; international agreement, alliance (F)

entourage (ãh-too-RAHZH), surrounding company (F)

entr'acte (ãh-TRAKT), between the acts (F)

entrée (ãh-TRAY), entrance; main dish (F)

entre nous (ãh-truh-NOO), between us (F)

entrepreneur (ãh-truh-pruh-NÖR), one who undertakes or manages (F)

envoi (ãh-VWAH), postscript (F)

épater le bourgeois (ay-pa-TAY luh boor-ZHWAH), to bedazzle and befuddle people (F)

epaulette (ay-poh-LEHT), shoulder piece (F)

e pluribus unum (eh PLOO-ree-boos OO-noom), one out of many (L)

ergo (EHR-goh), therefore, consequently (L)

Erin go bragh (EH-reen goh BRAH), Ireland forever (Ir)

errare humanum est (ehr-RAH-reh hoo-MAH-noom EHST), to err is human (L)

erratum (pl. **errata;** ehr-RAH-toom, ehr-RAH-tah), error, mistake (L)

ersatz (EHR-zatz), substitute, synthetic replacement (G)

escargots (ehs-kar-GOH), snails (F)

espada (ehs-PAH-dah), sword; the matador who kills the bull with a sword (Sp)

esprit de corps (ehs-PREE duh KAWR), spirit of loyalty to one's group (F)

et alii (eht AH-lee-ee); abbr. et al., and others (L)

Sweden—River front, Stockholm

et cetera (eht KEYE-teh-rah); abbr. etc., and others, and other things (L)

ethos (EH-thos), custom, national character (Gk)

et passim (eht PAHS-seem), abbr. et pass., and everywhere, scattered throughout a work (L)

et tu Brute? (eht TOO, BROO-teh), you, too, Brutus? (L)

étude (ay-TÜD), study; short musical composition (F)

et uxor (eht OOK-sohr), abbr. et ux., and wife (L)

eureka! (EH-OO-reh-kah), I have found it! (Gk)

ewig Weibliche (AY-vik VEYEB-li-çe), eternal feminine (G)

ex cathedra (ehks KAH-theh-drah), authoritatively, pontifically (L)

excelsior (ehks-KEHL-see-ohr), ever higher (L)

exempli gratia (ehk-SEHM-plee GRAH-tee-ah), abbr. e.g., for instance (L)

ex libris (ehks LEE-brees), from among the books of (L)

ex officio (ehks ohf-FEE-kee-oh), by virtue of his office (L)

exposé (ehks-paw-ZAY), statement, explanation, revelation (F)

ex post facto (ehks pohst FAHK-toh), after the fact (L)

extempore (ehks-TEHM-poh-reh), without previous preparation (L)

extra (EHKS-trah), beyond, in addition (L)

ex voto (ehks WOH-toh), as a vow; tablet or inscription recording an accomplished vow (L)

F

facsimile (fahk-SEE-mee-leh), exact reproduction (L)

fait accompli (FEH-ta-kolaw-PLEE), thing already done (F)

falsetto (fahl-SAYT-toh), excessively high tone (It)

fandango (fahn-DAHN-goh), Spanish dance (Sp)

farina (fah-REE-nah), flour or meal (L)

fatti maschi, parole femmine (FAHT-tee MAHS-kee, pah-RAW-lay FAYM-mee-nay), deeds are masculine, words feminine (It)

faute de mieux (FOHT duh MYÖ), for lack of anything better (F)

faux pas (FOH PAH), false step, blunder (F)

feis (FAYS), Irish song festival (Ir)

femme de chambre (FAM duh SHÃH-bruh), chambermaid (F)

femme fatale (FAM fa-TAL), enchantress, "vamp" (F)

festina lente (fehs-TEE-nah LEHN-teh), make haste slowly (L)

Festschrift (FEHST-shrift), memorial or commemorative volume (G)

fiacre (FYA-kruh), cab (F)

fiancé, fiancée (fyãh-SAY), betrothed (F)

fiasco (FYAHS-koh), failure (It)

fiat (FEE-aht), administrative order without legislative authorization (L)

fiesta (FYEHS-tah), festival (Sp)

filet mignon (fee-LEH mee-NYÃW), tenderloin steak (F)

financière (fee-nãh-SYEHR), spicy stew (F)

fin de siècle (FẼH duh SYEH-kluh), end of the century; decadence (F)

fine champagne (FEEN shãh-PAH-nyuh), brandy (F)

fines herbes (FEEN ZEHRB), minced chives, parsley, etc. (F)

finis (FEE-nees), end (L)

finocchio (fee-NAWK-kyoh), fennel (It)

fleur de lis (FLÖR duh LEE), lily emblem of France (F)

foie gras (FWAH GRAH), goose liver (F)

fondue (fãw-DÜ), melted cheese (F)

force majeure (FAWRS ma-ZHÖR), superior force (F)

fortissimo (fohr-TEES-see-moh), very loud (It)

foulard (foo-LAHR), neckerchief of silk fabric (F)

franc-tireur (frãh-tee-RÖR), sniper, guerrilla fighter (F)

frappé (fra-PAY), whipped, semifrozen (F)

Frau (FROW), lady, madam, Mrs. (G)

Fräulein (FROY-leyen), Miss, young lady (G)

fresco (FRAYS-koh), mural painting (It)

fricassé (free-ka-SAY), diced meat in thick sauce (F)

frijoles (free-HOH-lehs), kidney beans (Sp)

friseur (free-ZÖR), hairdresser (F)

fritos (FREE-tohs), fried potatoes, etc. (Sp)

fromage (fraw-MAZH), cheese (F)

Führer (FÜ-ruhr), leader (G)

G

gabelle (ga-BEHL), salt tax (F)

gaffe (GAF), bad blunder (F)

gala (GAH-lah), festive (It)

garbanzos (gahr-BAHN-thohs), chick-peas (Sp)

garçon (gar-SÃW), boy, waiter (F)

garni (gar-NEE), garnished (F)

gâteau (gah-TOH), cake (F)

gaucherie (gohsh-REE), awkward or tactless action (F)

gaucho (GOW-choh), South American cowboy (Sp)

gaudeamus igitur (gow-deh-AH-moos EE-ghee-toor), let us therefore rejoice (L)

Gauleiter (GOW-leye-tuhr), Nazi district leader (G)

gazpacho (gath-PAH-choh), Spanish cold soup (Sp)

gefilte fish (guh-FEEL-tuh FISH), stuffed fish (Yiddish)

geheime Staatspolizei (guh-HEYE-muh SHTATS-poh-lee-tseye), abbr. Gestapo, secret state police (G)

geisha (GAY-shah), Japanese professional girl entertainer (Jap)

Gemütlichkeit (guh-MÜT-liç-keyet), congeniality, coziness (G)

gendarme (zhãh-DARM), policeman, constable, state trooper (F)

generalissimo (jay-nay-rah-LEES-see-moh), general in chief (It)

genre (ZHÃHR), kind, sort, species (F)

Gestalt (guh-SHTAHLT), shape, form, pattern (G)

Gestapo (guh-STAH-poh), see geheime Staatspolizei

Gesundheit (guh-ZOONT-heyet), (good) health (G)

ghetto (GAYT-toh), restricted section for Jews or others (It)

gigolo (zhee-goh-LOH), man paid to be dancing partner or companion (F)

glacé (gla-SAY), iced, sugared (F)

Gleichschaltung (GLEYEÇ-shahlt-ung), coordination, assimilation (G)

glissando (glees-SAHN-doh), gliding (F-It)

Glockenspiel (GLOK-uhn-shpeel), carillon (G)

gloria in excelsis Deo (GLOH-ree-ah een ehks-KEHL-sees DEH-oh), glory to God on high (L)

gnocchi (NYAWK-kee), flour or potato small dumplings (It)

golem (GOH-lehm), robot created for an evil purpose (Heb)

goniff (GOH-nif), thief (Yiddish)

gorgonzola (gohr-gohn-TSAW-lah), Italian green mold cheese (It)

Gott mit uns! (GAWT mit OONS), God is with us! (G)

Gott sei dank! (GAWT zeye DAHNK), thanks be to God (G)

goulash (more properly *gulyás*, GOO-LYAHSH), Hungarian meat stew (Hungarian)

gourmet (goor-MEH), epicure, lover of good food (F)

goy (GOY), Gentile, non-Jewish (Heb)

Graf (GRAHF), count (G)

graffiti (grahf-FEE-tee) scratched inscriptions (It)

grande dame (GRÃHD DAHM), great lady (F)

grand prix (GRÃH PREE), first prize (F)

granita (grah-NEE-tah), ice pudding (It)

gratin (gra-TẼH), dish prepared with cheese or bread crumbs (F)

gratis (GRAH-tees), free, without charge (L)

gringo (GREEN-goh), U.S. American (Sp)

gruyère (grü-YEHR), Swiss cheese (F)

guerrilla (ghehr-REE-lyah), warfare by irregulars (Sp)

guru (GOO-roo), teacher (Hindi)

gusto (GOOS-toh), taste, enjoyment (It)

H

habeas corpus (HAH-beh-ahs KOHR-poos), you may have the body; writ to bring someone into court (L)

hacienda (ah-THYEHN-dah), plantation (Sp)

Hadassah (hah-DAHS-sah), Jewish women's organization (Heb)

hallelujah (hah-lay-LOO-yah), praise the Lord (Heb)

hanukkah (HAH-nook-kah), dedication, feast of lights (Heb)

hapax legomenon (HAH-pahks leh-GOH-meh-non), something said only once (Gk)

hara-kiri (HAH-rah-kee-ree), belly-cutting, ceremonial suicide (Jap)

haricots verts (ah-ree-KOH VEHR), green beans (F)

Hasenpfeffer (HAH-zehn-pfef-fuhr), marinated hare (G)

Hasidim (khah-SEE-deem), Jewish religious sect (Heb)

haute couture (OHT koo-TÜR), group of high class dress designers (F)

Heft (HEHFT), volume (G)

hegira (more properly *hijra*, HEEJ-rah), Mohammed's flight; escape; moving day (Arab)

Heimweh (HEYEM-vay), homesickness (G)

Heimwehr (HEYEM-vehr), home guard, militia (G)

Herrenvolk (HEHR-ren-folk), master race (G)

hetaira, **hetaera** (HEH-teye-rah), courtesan (Gk)

hiatus (hee-AH-toos), split, break in line, pause between vowels (L)

hic jacet (HEEK YAH-keht), here lies (L)

hidalgo (ee-DAHL-goh), nobleman, man of gentle birth (Sp)

hierba maté (YEHR-bah mah-TEH), Paraguayan tea (Sp)

hodie mihi, cras tibi (HOH-dee-eh MEE-hee, KRAHS TEE-bee), today to me, tomorrow to you (L)

hoi polloi (hoy pohl-LOY), the many, rabble (Gk)

homard (aw-MAHR), lobster (F)

hombre (OHM-breh), man (Sp)

homo homini lupus (HOH-moh HOH-mee-nee LOO-poos), man is a wolf to his fellow-man (L)

homo sapiens (HOH-moh SAH-pee-ehns), man as a thinking animal or as a genus (L)

honni soit qui mal y pense (aw-NEE SWAH kee MAHL ee PÃHS), evil to him who evil thinks (F)

honoris causa (hoh-NOH-rees KOW-sah), bestowed in recognition of merit (L)

horribile dictu (hohr-REE-bee-leh DEEK-too), horrible to relate (L)

hors de combat (AWR duh kõh-BAH), disabled, out of the fight (F)

hors d'oeuvres (AWR DÖ-vruh), appetizers, relishes (F)

hôtel de ville (hoh-TEHL duh VEEL), town hall (F)

houri (HOO-ree), Mohammedan nymph of paradise (Persian)

hukilau (hoo-kee-LAH-OO), feast (Hawaiian)

hula-hula (HOO-lah-HOO-lah), Hawaiian dance (Hawaiian)

humanum est errare (hoo-MAH-noom EHST ehr-RAH-reh), to err is human (L)

hybris (HOO-brees), transgression of moral law; act of defiance (Gk)

hysteron proteron (HOOS-teh-rohn PROH-teh-rohn), putting the cart before the horse (Gk)

I

ibidem (ee-BEE-dehm), abbr. ibid., in the same place (L)

idée fixe (ee-DAY FEEKS), preconceived notion (F)

id est (EED EHST), abbr. i.e., that is (L)

Iesus Nazarenus Rex Iudaeorum (YEH-soos nah-zah-REH-noos REHKS yoo-deye-OH-room), abbr. I.N.R.I., Jesus of Nazareth King of the Jews (L)

ignis fatuus (EEG-nees FAH-too-oos), will-of-the-wisp (L)

illuminati (eel-loo-mee-NAH-tee), enlightened ones, deep thinkers (L)

imbroglio (eem-BRAW-lyoh), mix-up, mess (It)

impedimenta (eem-peh-dee-MEHN-tah), baggage, hindrances (L)

imprimatur (eem-pree-MAH toor), license to print, sanction (L)

in absentia (een ahb-SEHN-tee-ah), in one's absence (L)

in articulo mortis (een ahr-TEE-koo-loh MOHR-tees), on the point of death (L)

in camera (een KAH-meh-rah), in chambers; in private (L)

incognito (een-KAW-nyee-toh), in disguise, not revealing one's identity (It)

Japan—Ginza by night, Tokyo

incomunicado (een-koh-moo-nee-KAH-doh), cut off from communication with the outside (Sp)

index expurgatorius (EEN-dehks ehks-poor-gah-TOH-ree-oos), list of forbidden books (L)

in esse (een EHS-seh), in being, existing (L)

in extenso (een ehks-TEHN-soh), in full (L)

in extremis (een ehks-TREH-mees), on the point of death (L)

influenza (een-floo-EHN-tsah), respiratory disease, flu (It)

in folio (een FOH-lee-oh), once folded sheet of printing (L)

infra (EEN-frah), below (L)

ingénue (ẽh-zhay-NÜ), innocent feminine character (F)

in hoc signo vinces (een hohk SEEG-noh WEEN-kehs), in this sign you will conquer (L)

in loco parentis (een LOH-koh pah-REHN-tees), in the place of a parent (L)

in medias res (een MEH-dee-ahs REHS), into the thick of things, without introduction (L)

in memoriam (een meh-MOH-ree-ahm), in memory of (L)

innamorato (een-nah-moh-RAH-toh), lover (It)

innuendo (een-noo-EHN-doh), hint, insinuation (L)

in primis (een PREE-mees), among the first (L)

in quarto (een KWAHR-toh), printing sheet folded twice (L)

in re (een REH), in the matter of (L)

in rem (een REHM), proceedings against a thing rather than a person (L)

in saecula saeculorum (een SEYE-koo-lah seye-koo-LOH-room), for ever and ever (L)

insignia (een-SEEG-nee-ah), distinguishing marks (L)

insouciance (ẽh-soo-SYÃHS), indifference, studied carelessness (F)

intaglio (een-TAH-lyoh), decoration cut into a stone (It)

integer vitae scelerisque purus (EEN-teh-ghehr WEE-teye skeh-leh-REES-kweh POO-roos), upright in life and free of guilt (L)

intelligentsia (een-tehl-lee-GHEHN-tsyah), informed intellectual people collectively (R)

inter alia (EEN-tehr AH-lee-ah), among other things (L)

inter alios (EEN-tehr AH-lee-ohs), among others (L)

interim (EEN-teh-reem), meanwhile (L)

intermezzo (een-tayr-MEH-dzoh), music played during intermission (It)

inter nos (EEN-tehr NOHS), between us (L)

in toto (een TOH-toh), completely, entirely (L)

intra muros (EEN-trah MOO-rohs), within the walls (L)

in vino veritas (een WEE-noh WEH-ree-tahs), in wine is the truth (L)

ipse dixit (EEP-seh DEEK-seet), he himself said it; the master has spoken (L)

ipso facto (EEP-soh FAHK-toh), by the very fact (L)

item (EE-tehm), likewise (L)

ite, missa est (EE-teh, MEES-sah EHST), go, the service is finished (L) *izvestiya* (eez-VYEHS-tee-yuh), news, information (R)

J

jai-alai (HAH-ee ah-LAH-ee), Basque ball game (Basque)

jardinière (zhar-dee-NYEHR), mixed vegetables; ornamental flower pot (F)

je ne sais quoi (zhuh nuh SEH KWAH), I don't know what (F)

jeu d'esprit (ZHÖ dehs-PREE), witticism (F)

jeunesse dorée (zhö-NEHS daw-RAY), gilded youth, elegant young people (F)

jihad (JEE-hahd), holy war (Arab)

jinni (JEEN-nee), supernatural being that can take human shape (Arab)

jinrickisha (JEEN-REEK-shah), mandrawn two-wheeled cab (Jap)

jodhpur (JOHD-poor), a kind of riding breeches (Hind)

joie de vivre (ZHWAH duh VEE-vruh), joy of being alive (F)

jongleur (zhaw̃-GLÖR), minstrel, juggler (F)

judo (JOO-doh), Japanese system of wrestling (Jap)

jujutsu (JOO JOO-tsoo), see judo (Jap)

junta (HOON-tah), administrative council or committee (Sp)

Jupiter Pluvius (YOO-pee-tehr PLOO-wee-oos), Jupiter of the rain (L)

jus gentium (YOOS GHEHN-tee-oom), law of nations, international law (L)

K

ka (KAH), the soul (Egypt)

kabuki (KAH-boo-kee), Japanese form of drama (Jap)

Kaddish (KAHD-deesh), prayer for the dead (Heb)

Kaffeeklatsch (kahf-FAY-klahtch), gathering for coffee and chatting (G)

kamikaze (KAH-mee-kah-zeh), divine wind; suicide dive bomber (Jap)

Kapellmeister (kah-PEHL-MEYE-stuhr), orchestra or chorus leader (G)

kaput (kah-POOT), finished, done for (G)

Katzenjammer (KAHT-suhn-yahm-muhr), hangover (G)

kibbutz (keeb-BOOTS), Israeli collective farm settlement (Heb)

kibitzer (KIB-its-uhr), onlooker at game, offering unwanted advice; meddler (Yid)

kimono (KEE-moh-noh), Japanese outer garment with sash and loose sleeves (Jap)

Kirschwasser (KEERSH-VAHS-suhr), cherry brandy (G)

Kismet (KEES-meht), fate, lot, will of Allah (Turk)

Knesset (KNEHS-seht), unicameral Israeli parliament (Heb)

koine (koy-NAY), language common to a large area (Gk)

koinos topos (koy-NOHS toh-POHS), commonplace (Gk)

kolkhoz (kuhl-KHAWS), collective farm (R)

Kol Nidre (KOHL NEE-dray), all vows; prayer of atonement; melody to which prayer is sung (Heb)

Kommandatura (kohm-mahn-dah-TOO-rah), command headquarters (G)

Komsomol (KOHM-suh-muhl), Communist youth organization (R)

Konzertmeister (kohn-TSEHRT-MEYE-stuhr), chief violinist of orchestra (G)

kopek (more properly *kopeika*, kuh-PYEY-kuh), small Russian coin (R)

kraal (KRAHL), South African village or enclosure (Du, from Pt *curral*)

Krasnaya Zvezda (KRAHS-nuh-yuh zviz-DAH), Red Star, Soviet Army organ (R)

Kremlin (more properly *kreml'*, KRYEHML'), citadel of Moscow, seat of government (R)

Kriegspiel (KREEK-shpeel), war game (G)

kulak (koo-LAHK), fist, tight-wad, well-to-do peasant (R)

Kultur (kool-TOOR), civilization, culture German style (G)

Kulturkampf (kool-TOOR-KAHMPF), Prussia's struggle to dominate Catholic Church (G)

kummerbund (KUM-muhr-buhnd), man's sash for waist (Pers)

Kuomintang (GWOH-meen-tahng), national people's party (Ch)

L

la belle dame sans merci (la BEHL DAM SÃH mehr-SEE), the beautiful lady without mercy (F)

labor omnia vincit (LAH-bohr OHM-nee-ah WEEN-keet), labor overcomes everything (L)

lagniappe (la-NYAP), small present to purchaser with purchase (F from Sp from Quechua)

laissez faire (leh-SAY FEHR), let things alone, noninterference (F)

Landwehr (LAHNT-vehr), home guard, militia (G)

lapsus calami (LAHP-soos KAH-lah-mee), slip of the pen (L)

lapsus linguae (LAHP-soos LEEN-gweye), slip of the tongue (L)

largo (LAHR-goh), broad, slow tempo (It)

lasagne (lah-SAH-nyay), broad, flat macaroni (It)

laudator temporis acti (low-DAH-tohr TEHM-poh-rees AHK-tee), one who praises the good old days (L)

lb. (abbr. for *libra*, LEE-brah), pound (L)

Leben Sie wohl (LAY-buhn ZEE VOHL), good-bye, be well (G)

Lebensraum (LAY-buhns-rowm), living space (G)

legato (lay-GAH-toh), bound, with no pause between notes (It)

Légion d'Honneur (lay-ZHÃW daw-NÖR), military and civil order (F)

lei (LAY), wreath of flowers worn around the neck (Hawaiian)

leitmotiv (LEYET-moh-teef), guiding theme (G)

lento (LEHN-toh), slow tempo (It)

lèse-majesté (LEHZ-ma-zhehs-TAY), treason, offense against ruler (F)

l'état, c'est moi! (lay-TAH seh MWAH), *I* am the state! (F)

liaison (lyeh-ZǍW), linking, connection (F)

libido (lee-BEE-doh), psychic drive associated with the sexual instinct (L)

Liederkranz (LEE-duhr-krahnts), singing society; type of cheese (G)

Limburger (LEEM-boor-guhr), type of cheese (G)

lingerie (lĕh-zhuh-REE), women's underwear (F)

lingua franca (LEEN-gwah FRAHN-kah), international or common language in multilingual area (L or It)

lira (LEE-rah), Italian unit of currency (It)

literati (lee-teh-RAH-tee), educated or cultured people, literary men (L)

loggia (LAWJ-jah), portico projecting from a building (It)

logos (LOH-gohs), word (Gk)

luau (loo-AH-oo), Hawaiian banquet (Hawaiian)

Luftwaffe (LOOFT-vahf-fuh), German air force (G)

lycée (lee-SAY), high school (F)

M

macabre (ma-KAH-bruh), gruesome (F)

macédoine (ma-say-DWAHN), mixture of fruits or vegetables (F)

mademoiselle (mad-mwah-ZEHL), young lady, Miss (F)

Madonna (mah-DAWN-nah), my Lady; the Virgin Mary (It)

maestoso (mah-ays-TOH-soh), majestic (It)

maestro (mah-AYS-troh), master, teacher (It)

Mafia (MAH-fyah), Sicilian secret organization (It)

Magna Charta (MAHG-nah KAHR-tah), Great Charter; English Bill of Rights (L)

magna cum laude (MAHG-nah koom LOW-deh), with great praise or distinction (L)

magnifico (mah-NYEE-fee-koh), magnificent; great man (It)

magnum bonum (MAHG-noom BOH-noom), great good; great benefit (L)

magnum opus (MAHG-noom OH-poos), great work, masterpiece (L)

maharajah (mah-hah-RAH-jah), great king (Hind)

maharani (mah-hah-RAH-nee), great queen (Hind)

Mahatma (mah-HAHT-mah), great soul, teacher (Sk)

mais où sont les neiges d'antan? (MEH-ZOO sāw lay NEHZH dāh-TĀH), but where are the snows of yesteryear? (F)

maître d'hôtel (MEH-truh doh-TEHL), head steward, head butler (F)

major domo (MAH-yohr DOH-moh), chief steward, head servant (L)

maladroit (ma-la-DRWAH), awkward, tactless (F)

malaria (mah-LAH-ryah), illness transmitted by mosquito bite (It)

mal de mer (MAL duh MEHR), seasickness (F)

malentendu (ma-lāh-tāh-DÜ), misunderstanding (F)

malgré lui (mal-GRAY LWEE), in spite of himself (F)

mañana (mah-NYAH-nah), tomorrow (Sp)

mandamus (mahn-DAH-moos), we order; legal writ (L)

manicotti (mah-nee-KAWT-tee), stuffed pasta rolls (It)

manifesto (mah-nee-FEHS-toh), declaration (It)

maquis (ma-KEE), French freedom fighters (F)

maraca (mah-RAH-kah), gourd used as musical instrument (Sp)

mardi gras (mar-DEE GRAH), Shrove Tuesday (F)

mare nostrum (MAH-reh NOHS-troom), our sea (L)

mariage de convenance (ma-RYAZH duh kāw-vuh-NĀHS), marriage of convenience (F)

marimba (mah-REEM-bah), wooden xylophone (Sp)

marina (mah-REE-nah), settled and landscaped seashore (It)

marrons glacés (ma-RŌH gla-SAY), candied chestnuts (F)

Marsala (mahr-SAH-lah), Sicilian sweet wine (It)

masseur, masseuse (ma-SÖR, ma-SÖZ), male, female massage expert (F)

matador (mah-tah-DOHR), bullfighter who kills bull with sword (Sp)

maté (mah-TEH), see hierba maté

materia medica (mah-TEH-ree-ah MEH-dee-kah), drugs, pharmacology (L)

matsoth (MAH-tsoth), Passover unleavened bread (Heb)

maxixe (mah-SHEE-shuh), Brazilian dance (Pt)

mazuma (mah-ZOO-mah), money (Yid)

mazurka (mah-ZOOR-kah), Polish dance (Pol)

mazzeltov (MAH-zuhl-tohv), good luck (Heb)

mea (maxima) culpa (MEH-ah MAHK-see-mah KOOL-pah), my (greatest) fault (L)

Meerschaum (MEHR-showm), mineral substance for making smoking pipes (G)

Mein Kampf (meyen KAHMPF), my battle, my struggle (G)

Meistersinger (MEYE-stuhr SING-uhr), master singer (G)

mélange (may-LĀHZH), mixture (F)

mêlée (meh-LAY), mix-up, fight, brawl (F)

memorabilia (meh-moh-rah-BEE-lee-ah), things worth remembering (L)

memorandum (meh-moh-RAHN-doom), something to be remembered, a note to that effect (L)

ménage (may-NAHZH), household (F)

Menorah (meh-NOH-rah), Jewish seven-candle candelabrum (Heb)

mens sana in corpore sano (MEHNS SAH-nah een KOHR-poh-reh SAH-noh), a sound mind in a sound body (L)

menu (muh-NÜ), bill of fare (F)

meringue (muh-RĚHG), beaten and baked egg whites (F)

mesa (MEH-sah), tableland, plateau (Sp)

mésalliance (may-za-lee-ÅHS), marriage with a person of inferior social position (F)

mestizo (mehs-TEE-thoh), half-breed (Sp)

métier (may-TYAY), trade, craft (F)

Métro (may-TROH), Paris subway (F)

mezzo (MEH-dzoh), half (It)

midi (mee-DEE), south (F)

migraine (mee-GREHN), headache (F)

miles gloriosus (MEE-lehs gloh-ree-OH-soos), braggart, swaggerer (L)

minestrone (mee-nehs-TROH-nay), vegetable soup (It)

mirabile dictu (mee-RAH-bee-leh DEEK-too), wonderful to relate (L)

mirabile visu (mee-RAH-bee-leh WEE-soo), wonderful to see (L)

mirabilia (mee-rah-BEE-lee-ah), wonderful things (L)

mise en scène (MEE-zãh-SEHN), stage setting (F)

miserere (mee-seh-REH-reh), have mercy (L)

modicum (MOH-dee-koom), proper or small measure (L)

modus operandi (MOH-doos oh-peh-RAHN-dee), way of working (L)

modus vivendi (MOH-doos wee-WEHN-dee), way of living (together) (L)

mores (MOH-rehs), customs, folkways, conventions (L)

mot juste (MOH ZHÜST), the right word for the occasion (F)

moue (MOO), pout, grimace (F)

mousse (MOOS), frozen whipped dessert (F)

Moyen Age (mwa-YĚH-NAHZH), Middle Ages (F)

mufti (MOOF-tee), civilian judge; civilian garb (Arab)

mutatis mutandis (moo-TAH-tees moo-TAHN-dees), with the appropriate changes (L)

muzhik (moo-ZHEEK), Russian peasant (R)

N

naive (na-EEV), innocent, guileless (F)

naiveté (na-eev-TAY), innocence, guilelessness (F)

née (NAY), born; having as a maiden name (F)

négligée (nay-glee-ZHAY), loose indoor robe for women (F)

ne plus ultra (neh PLOOS OOL-trah), no further (L)

nihil obstat (NEE-heel OHB-staht), there is no impediment (L)

nil admirari (NEEL ahd-mee-RAH-ree), be surprised at nothing (L)

nil desperandum (NEEL dehs-peh-RAHN-doom), never despair (L)

n'importe (něh-PAWRT), it doesn't matter (F)

Nirvana (neer-VAH-nah), extinction; oblivion; Buddhist paradise (Sk)

Nisei (NEE-say), second-generation Japanese-Americans (Jap)

nisi (NEE-see), unless (L)

noblesse oblige (naw-BLEHS aw-BLEEZH), high rank involves responsiblitity (F)

Noël (naw-EHL), Christmas (F)

nolle prosequi (NOHL-leh PROH-seh-kwee), I will prosecute no further (L)

nolo contendere (NOH-loh kohn-TEHN-deh-reh), no contest (L)

nom de guerre (NŌH duh GHEHR), pseudonym (F)

nom de plume (NŌH duh PLÜM), pen name (F)

non compos mentis (nohn KOHM-pohs MEHN-tees), insane, not sound in mind (L)

non sequitur (nohn SEH-kwee-toor), it does not follow; logical inconsistency (L)

nota bene (NOH-tah BEH-neh; abbr. n.b.), note well (L)

note verbale (NAWT vehr-BAHL), verbal communication on diplomatic matter (F)

novella (noh-VEHL-lah), short story (It)

nuance (nü-ÅHS), shade, delicate degree of difference (F)

nuncio (NOON-chyoh), Papal envoy (It)

O

obbligato (ohb-blee-GAH-toh), solo passage, not to be omitted (It)

obit (OH-beet), he died (L)

obiter dictum (OH-bee-tehr DEEK-toom), spoken incidentally (L)

objet d'art (awb-ZHEH DHAR), object of art (F)

odium (OH-dee-oom), hatred; blame (L)

olla podrida (OH-lyah poh-DREE-dah), stew, hodgepodge (Sp)

omnia mutantur, nos et mutamur in illis (OHM-nee-ah moo-TAHN-toor NOHS eht moo-TAH-moor een EEL-lees), all things change, and we change with them (L)

omnia vanitas (OHM-nee-ah WAH-nee-tahs), all is vanity (L)

omnia vincit amor (OHM-nee-ah WEEN-keet AH-mohr), love overcomes everything (L)

omnium gatherum (OHM-nee-oom-GA-ther-um), miscellaneous collection (L and mock L)

onus probandi (OH-noos proh-BAHN-dee), the burden of proof (L)

opera (OH-peh-rah), works (L); musical drama (It)

opéra bouffe (oh-pay-RAH BOOF), comic opera, musical comedy (F)

opera omnia (OH-peh-rah OHM-nee-ah), all the works (L)

operetta (oh-pay-RAYT-tah), light opera, musical comedy (It)

opus (OH-poos), work (L)

opus citatum (OH-poos kee-TAH-toom), abbr. op. cit.; the work previously cited (L)

ora et labora (OH-rah eht lah-BOH-rah), pray and work (L)

ora pro nobis (OH-rah proh NOH-bees), pray for us (L)

oratorio (Oh-rah-TAW-ryoh), musical drama on sacred topic (It)

osso buco (AWS-soh BOO-koh), marrow bone of veal (It)

o tempora! o mores! (OH TEHM-poh-rah OH MOH-rehs), O, times and customs! (L)

outré (oo-TRAY), extreme, excessive (F)

oyer and terminer (oh-YEHR tehr-mee-NEHR), higher criminal court (Old F)

oyez (oh-YEHTS), hear ye! (Old F)

P

paella (pah-EH-lyah), South Spanish dish of rice and meat or fish (Sp)

palette (pa-LEHT), artist's color-mixing board (F)

palio (PAH-lyoh), Siena horse-race (It)

pampa (PAHM-pah), grassy plain in Argentina (Sp, from Quechua)

panache (pa-NASH), plume (F)

panem et circenses (PAH-nehm eht keer-KEHN-sehs), bread and games (L)

Panzer (PAHN-tsuhr), armored car, tank (G)

papier-mâché (pa-PYAY-mah-SHAY), paper pulp, cardboard (F)

par excellence (pa-rehk-seh LÃHS), to a superlative degree (F)

parfait (par-FEH), ice cream with syrup or fudge (F)

pariah (PAH-ree-ah), outcast, rejected (Tamil)

pari passu (PAH-ree PAHS-soo), side by side, evenly (L)

parmigiana (pahr-mee-JAH-nah), Parma style, with melted cheese and tomato (It)

parmigiano (pahr-mee-JAH-noh), Parma cheese, usually for grating (It)

parti pris (par-TEE PREE), preconceived idea (F)

paso doble (PAH-soh DOH-bleh), two-step; Spanish dance (Sp)

passacaglia (pahs-sah-KAH-lyah), slow Italian dance or music (It)

passim (PAHS-seem), abbr. pass.; scattered everywhere (L)

pasta (PAHS-tah), dough; any macaroni product (It)

pâté (pah-TAY), paste (F);—***de foie gras*** (duh FWAH GRAH), goose-liver paste

pater familias (pah-tehr-fah-MEE-lee-ahs), head of family (L)

Pater Noster (PAH-tehr NOHS-tehr), Our Father, Lord's Prayer (L)

pater patriae (PAH-tehr PAH-tree-eye), father of his country (L)

patio (PAH-tyoh), courtyard, inner courtyard (Sp)

pâtisserie (pah-tees-REE), pastry (F)

patois (pa-TWAH), local dialect (F)

Italy—Amphitheatre, Pompeii

pax romana (PAHKS roh-MAH-nah), Roman peace, enforced peace (L)

pax vobiscum (PAHKS woh-BEES-koom), peace be with you (L)

peineta (pay-NEH-tah), tall comb (Sp)

penchant (pãh-SHÃH), leaning, inclination (F)

per annum (pehr AHN-noom), by the year (L)

per capita (pehr KAH-pee-teh), by the head, apiece (L)

per diem (pehr DEE-ehm), by the day (L)

per se (pehr SEH), in itself, inherently (L)

persona non grata (pehr-SOH-nah nohn GRAH-tah), not acceptable diplomatic representative (L)

Pesach (PAY-sakh), Passover (Heb)

peseta (peh-SEH-tah), Spanish coin (Sp)

peso (PEH-soh), Latin American unit of currency (Sp)

petit bourgeois (puh-TEE boor-ZHWAH), lower middle class (F)

petite (puh-TEET), small, trim in figure (F)

petitio principii (peh-TEE-tee-oh preen-KEE-pee-ee), begging the question (L)

petits fours (puh-TEE FOOR), little sponge or pound cakes (F)

petits pois (puh-TEE PWAH), green peas (F)

phobia (FOH-bee-ah), fear, hatred (Gk)

pianissimo (pyah-NEES-see-moh), very softly (It)

piano (PYAH-noh), softly (It)

pibroch (PEE-brokh), bagpipe (Gaelic)

picador (pee-kah-DOHR), mounted bullfighter with lance (Sp)

piccolo (PEEK-koh-loh), small flute (It)

pièce de résistance (PYEHS duh ray-zees-TÃHS), main course (F)

pilaf (pee-LOW), Oriental rice dish (Persian)

piroshki (pee-RAWSH-kee), stuffed puffcakes (R)

pirouette (pee-roo-EHT), spin on one foot or in air (F)

più (PYOO), more (It)

pizza (PEE-tsah), pie, pancake (It)

pizzicato (pee-tsee-KAH-toh), plucking the strings of a musical instrument (It)

placebo (plah-KEH-boh), pacifier, medicine of no efficacy (L)

plaza de toros (PLAH-thah deh TOH-rohs), bullring (Sp)

plus ça change, plus c'est la même chose (PLÜ sa SHÄHZH PLÜ seh la mehm SHOHZ), the more it changes, the more it's the same thing (F)

pogrom (puh-GRAWM), devastation, massacre (R)

point d'appui (PWÊH da-PWEE), fulcrum, support point (F)

polenta (poh-LEHN-tah), thick gruel of corn, chestnuts, etc. (It)

polka (POHL-kah), fast Slavic dance (Czech)

pollice verso (POHL-lee-keh WEHR-soh), thumbs down (L)

Poltergeist (POHL-tuhr-geyest), racketing or prank-playing ghost (G)

pommes frites (PAWM FREET), fried potatoes (F)

poncho (POHN-choh), blanket with opening for head (Sp)

pons asinorum (POHNS ah-see-NOH-room), bridge of donkeys; hard problem for beginners (L)

portico (PAWR-tee-koh), covered gallery open on one side (It)

portmanteau (PAWRT-māh-TOH), traveling bag (F)

posada (poh-SAH-dah), inn (Sp)

posse (comitatus) (POHS-seh koh-mee-TAH-toos), force of a county, sheriff and assistants (L)

post bellum (pohst BEHL-loom), after-war (L)

post hoc, ergo propter hoc (pohst HOHK EHR-goh PROHP-tehr HOHK), after, therefore in consequence of something else (L)

post meridiem (pohst meh-REE-dee-ehm), abbr. p.m., P.M.; after noon (L)

post-mortem (pohst MOHR-tehm), after death, autopsy (L)

post scriptum (pohst SKREEP-toom), abbr. P.S.; written after main letter (L)

potage (paw-TAHZH), soup (F)

potpourri (poh-poo-REE), mixture, medley (F)

pourparler (poor-par-LAY), talk, negotiations (F)

pravda (PRAHV-duh), truth (R)

préciosité (pray-syoh-zee-TAY), excessive refinement (F)

première (pruh-MYEHR), first showing (F)

première danseuse (pruh-MYEHR dāh-SÖZ), first female dancer (F)

prestissimo (prays-TEES-see-moh), very fast (It)

prima donna (PREE-mah DAWN-nah), female opera star; anyone who wants to be first (It)

prima facie (PREE-mah FAH-kee-eh), at first glance, on the face of it (L)

primus inter pares (PREE-moos EEN-tehr PAH-rehs), first among equals (L)

prix fixe (PREE FEEKS), fixed price (F)

pro bono publico (proh BOH-noh POO-blee-koh), for the public good (L)

pro et con(tra) (PROH eht KOHN-trah), for and against (L)

profanum vulgus (proh-FAH-noom WOOL-goos), the fickle crowd (L)

pro forma (proh FOHR-mah), as a matter of form (L)

propaganda (proh-pah-GAHN-dah), that which is to be spread (L)

pro rata (proh RAH-tah), in proportion, in accordance with fixed rate (L)

prosciutto (proh-SHOOT-toh), salted Italian-style ham (It)

prosit (PROH-seet), to your health or success (L)

protégé (praw-tay-ZHAY), one taken under another's sheltering wing (F)

pro tempore (proh TEHM-poh-reh), abbr. pro tem; temporarily (L)

provolone (proh-voh-LOH-nay), spicy Italian cheese (It)

puchero (poo-CHEH-roh), South American stew (Sp)

pudenda (poo-DEHN-dah), genital organs (L)

pueblo (PWEH-bloh), village, town (Sp)

puissance (pwee-SÄHS), power (F)

pulque (POOL-kah), alcoholic beverage of Mexico (Sp from Nahuatl)

pundit (PUN-deet), man of learning (Hind)

purdah (PUR-dah), veil, feminine seclusion (Hind)

purée (pü-RAY), thick cream soup (F)

Purim (POO-reem), Jewish feast of deliverance (Heb)

Putsch (POOCH), abortive revolutionary attempt (G)

Q

qua (KWAH), considered as, in the capacity of (L)

quantum (KWAHN-toom), how great, how much (L)

quasi (KWAH-see), as if, as though (L)

que será será (KEH seh-RAH seh-RAH), what will be will be (Sp)

quidnunc (KWEED-nunk), what now, gossip, newsmonger (L)

quid pro quo (KWEED proh KWOH), something in return for something else (L)

¿quién sabe? (KYEHN SAH-veh), who knows? (Sp)

qui s'excuse s'accuse (KEE sehks-KÜZ sa-KÜZ), he who excuses himself accuses himself (F)

qui vive (KEE VEEV), on the alert, watchful (F)

qui va là? (KEE va LA), who goes there? (F)

quod erat demonstrandum (KWOHD EH-raht deh-mohn-STRAHN-doom), which was to be proved (L)

quod vide (KWOHD WEE-deh); abbr. q.v.; which see (L)

quondam (KWOHN-dahm), former, formerly (L)

quorum (KWOH-room), majority of legislative body for voting purposes (L)

quot homines, tot sententiae (KWOHT HOH-mee-nehs TOHT sehn-TEHN-tee-eye), as many opinions as there are people (L)

quo vadis? (KWOH WAH-dees), where are you going? (L)

R

ragoût (ra-GOO), spicy stew (F)

raison d'état (reh-ZÕH day-TAH), reason of state (F)

raison d'être (reh-ZÕH DEH-truh), reason for existing (F)

rajah (RAH-jah), king, ruler (Sk)

rallentando (rahl-layn-TAHN-doh), slowing up (It)

rani (RAH-nee), queen (Sk)

rapprochement (ra-prawsh-MÃH), reestablishing of friendly relations (F)

rara avis (RAH-rah AH-wees), rare bird (L)

Rathskeller (RAHTS-KEHL-luhr), basement restaurant and bar (G)

ravioli (rah-VYAW-lee), dumplings stuffed with meat or cheese (It)

re (REH), in the matter of (L)

realia (reh-AH-lee-ah), materials for teaching foreign cultures (L)

Reconquista (reh-kohn-KEES-tah), reconquest of Spain from the Moors (Sp)

recto (REKH-toh), on the right-hand page (L)

regata (ray-GAH-tah), Venetian gondola race (It)

Reich (REYEÇ), German state; empire (G)

Reichstag (REYEKS-tahk), German Parliament (G)

rendezvous (rãh-day-VOO), appointment, assignation (F)

répondez s'il vous plait (ray-põh-DAY seel voo PLEH), abbr. R.S.V.P.; please reply (F)

requiem (REH-kwee-ehm), rest; prayer for dead (L)

requiescat in pace (reh-kwee-EHS-kaht een PAH-keh), abbr. r.i.p.; may he rest in peace (L)

residuum (reh-SEE-doo-oom), remnant, residue (L)

résumé (ray-zü-MAY), summary (F)

ricksha (REEK-shaw), see jinrickisha

ricochet (ree-kaw-SHEH), bounce, rebound (F)

ricotta (ree-KAWT-tah), soft white Italian cheese (It)

rigor mortis (REE-gohr MOHR-tees), stiffness of death (L)

Rinascimento (ree-nah-shee-MAYN-toh), rebirth (It)

ris de veau (REE duh VOH), sweetbreads (F)

Risorgimento (ree-sohr-jee-MAYN-toh), Italian movement for unity (It)

risotto (ree-SAWT-toh), Italian rice dish (It)

rissolé (ree-saw-LAY), golden brown (F)

ritardando (ree-tahr-DAHN-doh), slowing up (It)

robot (ROH-boht), automaton trained to do man's work (Czech)

rodeo (roh-DEH-oh), roundup (Sp)

Roma caput mundi (ROH-mah KAH-poot MOON-dee), Rome, head of the world (L)

Rosh Hashanah (ROHSH hah-shah-NAH), head of year, New Year's Day (Heb)

rota (ROH-tah), wheel, Papal court (L)

rôti (roh-TEE), roast (F)

rôtisserie (roh-tees-REE), grill restaurant (F)

rotunda (roh-TOON-dah), circular building with dome (L)

roulette (roo-LEHT), gambling wheel (F)

rubaiyat (ROO-beye-yaht), quatrains, poems (Arab)

Rucksack (RUK-zahk), knapsack (G)

rupee (ROO-pee) Indian currency (Hind)

S

sabotage (sa-baw-TAHZH), intentional damage to arrest production (F)

sabra (SAH-brah), native Israeli (Heb)

sachet (sa-SHEH), small bag of perfume (F)

safari (sah-FAH-ree), hunting trip in Africa (Arab)

sahib (SAH-heeb), sir, master, title of respect (Arab)

salaam (sah-LAHM), peace, form of greeting (Arab)

salame (sah-LAH-meh), spiced sausage (It)

salmagundi (sal-ma-GOON-dee), spicy mixture (doubtful origin)

salon (sa-LAW̃), drawing room, exhibition room (F)

salus populi suprema lex (SAH-loos POH-poo-lee soo-PREH-mah LEHKS), the welfare of the people is the supreme law (L)

salve (SAHL-weh), hail (L)

samba (SAHM-bah), Brazilian dance (Pt. from Am. Indian)

samovar (suh-muh-VAHR), Russian tea urn (R)

samurai (SAH-moo-reye), Japanese feudal nobleman (Jap)

sanctum sanctorum (SAHNK-toom sahnk-TOH-room), holy of holies (L)

sangfroid (sãh-FRWAH), coolness in the face of danger (F)

Yugoslavia—Dubrovnik

sans façon (sãh fa-SÃW), unceremoniously (F)

sans gêne (sãh ZHEHN), without embarrassment, nervy (F)

sans souci (sãh soo-SEE), carefree, free from worry (F)

sarape (sah-RAH-peh), Mexican blanket (Sp)

sari (SAH-ree), Hindu female costume (Hindi)

sartor resartus (SAHR-tohr reh-SAHR-toos), tailor re-tailored, tit for tat (L)

Saturnalia (sah-toor-NAH-lee-ah), Roman December festival (L)

Sauerbraten (ZOW-uhr-BRAH-tuhn), marinated roast (G)

Sauerkraut (ZOW-uhr-krowt), pickled cabbage (G)

sauté (soh-TAY), fried in small amount of fat (F)

sauve qui peut (SOHV kee PO), every man for himself (F)

savoir faire (sa-VWAHR FEHR), tact, ability to do the right thing (F)

savoir vivre (sa-VWAHR VEE-vruh), knowledge of how to behave and get along (F)

sayonara (SAH-yoh-nah-rah), good-bye (Jap)

scherzo (SKAYR-tsoh), lively, jesting musical composition (It)

schlemiel (shluh-MEEL), easy mark, dumbbell (Yid)

Schmalz (SHMAHLTS), fat; silly sentimentality (G)

Schnapps (SHNAHPS), brandy, whiskey (G)

Schnitzel (SHNIT-suhl), cutlet (G)

schnorrer (SHNOHR-ruhr), beggar (Yid)

Schrecklichkeit (SHREHK-liç-keyet), frightfulness, policy of deliberate atrocity (G)

scilicet (SKEE-lee-keht), that is to say, to wit (L)

séance (say-ÃHS), session, sitting (F)

sec (SEHK), dry (F)

Sehnsucht (ZEHN-zookht), longing, nostalgic feeling (G)

semper fidelis (SEHM-pehr fee-DEH-lees), forever faithful (L)

semper paratus (SEHM-pehr pah-RAH-toos), ever ready (L)

senatus populusque romanus (seh-NAH-toos poh-poo-LOOS-kweh roh-MAH-noos), abbr. S.P.Q.R., the Roman Senate and people (L)

se non è vero, è ben trovato (say nohn eh VAY-roh, eh behn troh-VAH-toh), if it isn't true, it's a good lie (It)

sforzando (sfohr-TSAHN-doh), with force or vigor (It)

shah (SHAH), king of Persia (Persian)

shalom (shah-LOHM), peace, form of Hebrew or Israeli greeting (Heb)

shashlik (SHAHSH-leek), meat on skewer (R)

sheikh (SHEYEKH), old man, religious leader (Arab)

shekel (SHEH-kehl), unit of weight or money (Heb)

shillalagh (shil-LAY-lee), cudgel (Irish)

Shinto (SHEEN-toh), way of the gods; Japanese religion (Jap)

shish kebab (SHEESH keh-BAHB), lamb on skewer (Turk)

sic (SEEK), thus, precisely as it appears (L)

sic semper tyrannis (SEEK SEHM-pehr tee-RAHN-nees), may it always go thus with tyrants (L)

sic transit gloria mundi (SEEK TRAHN-seet GLOH-ree-ah MOON-dee), thus passes away the world's glory (L)

Siglo de Oro (SEE-gloh deh OH-roh), golden century (Sp)

s'il vous plaît (seel voo PLEH), please (F)

similia similibus curantur (see-MEE-lee-ah see-MEE-lee-boos koo-RAHN-toor), like is cured with like (L)

sine die (SEE-neh DEE-eh), without assigning a day (L)

sine qua non (SEE-neh KWAH NOHN), indispensable requisite or condition (L)

Sinn Fein (SHIN FAYN), we ourselves; Irish revolutionary movement (Irish)

si vis pacem, para bellum (see wees PAH-khem, PAH-rah BEHL-loom), if you want peace, prepare for war (L)

skoal (SKOHL), to your health (Norw)

slalom (SLAH-lum), downhill skiing race (Norw)

smörgasbord (SMOR-gus-boord), table of appetizers and other foods (Swed)

soi-disant (swah-dee-ZÃH), self-styled (F)

soirée (swah-RAY), evening gathering (F)

solfeggio (sohl-FAY-joh), singing by notes (It)

solitaire (saw-lee-TEHR), alone, single (F)

solo (SOH-loh), alone, musical piece for one person (It)

sombrero (sohm-BREH-roh), hat (Sp)

sotto voce (SOHT-toh VOH-chay), in an undertone (It)

soubriquet (soo-bree-KEH), nickname (F)

soufflé (soo-FLAY), puffed up, baked custard (F)

soupçon (soop-SÃW), suspicion, dash, trace (F)

soviet (suh-VYEHT), council of delegates (R)

spa (SPAH), watering place (Belgian place name)

spoor (SPOHR), track of animal (Du)

Sprachgefühl (SHPRAHKH-guh-FUL), feeling for language (G)

spumone (spoo-MOH-nay), Italian ice cream (It)

sputnik (SPOOT-neek), co-traveler, space satellite (R)

staccato (stahk-KAH-toh), having short notes (It)

Stakhanovite (stuh-KHAHN-uhv), champion speed worker in USSR (R)

stanza (STAHN-tsah) room; subdivision of poem (It)

status quo (STAH-toos KWOH), existing or previously existing state of affairs (L)

stet (STEHT), let it stand; disregard correction (L)

Strudel (SHTROO-duhl), type of cake (G)

stucco (STOOK-koh), mixture of lime and pulverized stone (It)

Stück (SHTUK), piece; selection (G)

studio (STOO-dyoh), study; place for studying or working (It)

Sturm und Drang (SHTOORM oont DRAHNG), storm and stress (G)

sub judice (soob YOO-dee-keh), not yet decided (L)

Ireland—Ashford Castle, County Mayo

subpoena (soob-POY-nah), under penalty; required appearance in court (L)

sub rosa (soob ROH-sah), under cover; in secret (L)

succès d'estime (sük-SEH dehs-TEEM), favored by critics and experts, but not by mass (F)

sui generis (SOO-ee GEH-neh-rees), in a class by itself; unique (L)

sukiyaki (SKEE-yah-kee), Japanese dish of meat and vegetables (Jap)

summa cum laude (SOOM-mah koom LOW-deh), with the highest praise (L)

summum bonum (SOOM-moom BOH-noom), the supreme good (L)

suo nomine (SOO-oh NOH-mee-neh), in his own name (L)

sûreté (sür-TAY), security; French security police (F)

suum cuique (SOO-oom kwoo-EE-kweh), to each his own (L)

svaraj (SVAH-rahj), self-rule, independence (Sk)

T

table d'hôte (TA-bluh DOHT), regular menu, no choice (F)

tabula rasa (TAH-boo-lah RAH-sah), clean slate (L)

tamale (tah-MAH-leh), Mexican dish of corn, meat, and red pepper (Sp)

tant mieux (pis) (TÃH MYÖ PEE), so much the better (worse) (F)

tarantella (tah-rahn-TEHL-lah), swift Italian dance (It)

Te Deum Laudamus (TEH DEH-oom low DAH-moos), hymn of thanksgiving (L)

tempo (TEHM-poh), time, rate, rhythm, beat (It)

tempus fugit (TEHM-poos FOO-gheet), time is fleeting (L)

terminus (a quo, ad quem) (TEHR-mee-noos ah KWOH, ahd KWEHM), limit or boundary from which or to which (L)

terra cotta (TEHR-rah KAWT-tah), baked clay, earthenware (It)

terra firma (TEHR-rah FEER-mah), solid ground, mainland (L)

terra incognita (TEHR-rah een-KOHG-nee-tah), unknown land (L)

tertium quid (TEHR-tee-oom KWEED), a third factor (L)

tête-à-tête (TEH-ta-TEHT), face to face; intimate conversation (F)

thé dansant (TAY dãh-SÃH), afternoon tea and dance (F)

thesaurus (teh-SOW-roos), treasure trove; idea dictionary (L)

timbale, timballo (teh-BAL, teem-BAHL-loh), baked in a mold (F, It)

timeo Danaos et dona ferentes (TEE-meh-oh dah-NAH-ohs eht DOH-nah feh-REHN-tehs), I fear the Greeks even when they bear gifts (L)

toga (TOH-gah), loose, flowing robe of Romans (L)

toreador, torero (toh-reh-ah-DOHR, toh-REH-roh), bullfighter (Sp)

torso (TOHR-soh), upper part of body without head (It)

Totentanz (TOH-tuhn-tahnts), dance of death (G)

touché (too-SHAY), touched; remark that strikes home (F)

toujours (too-ZHOOR), always, forever (F)

toupet (too-PEH), wig, false hair (F)

tour de force (TOOR duh FAWRS), special feat of dexterity (F)

tournure (toor-NUR), roundness, gracefulness of line (F)

tout de suite (TOO duh SWEET), at once (F)

tovarishch (tuh-VAH-reeshch), comrade (R)

traduttore, traditore (trah-doot-TOH-ray, trah-dee-TOH-ray), a translator is a traitor (It)

trauma (TROW-mah), blow, wound, injury (Gk)

tricolore (tree-kaw-LAWR), French Flag, red, white, and blue (F)

Trimurti (tree-MOOR-tee), Hindu trinity, Brahma, Vishnu, and Shiva (Sk)

trio (TREE-oh), group of three (It)

trivia (TREE-vee-ah), commonplace things (L)

troika (TROY-kuh), vehicle drawn by three horses (R)

troppo (TRAWP-poh), too much (It)

trouvère (troo-VEHR), minstrel (F)

tsar (see czar)

tu quoque (TOO KWOH-kweh), you, too (L)

tutti-frutti (TOOT-tee FROOT-tee), all fruits, mixed fruits (It)

U

ubique (oo-BEE-kweh), everywhere (L)

ukaze (oo-KAHS), imperial edict (R)

ukulele (oo-koo-LEH-leh), Hawaiian guitar (Hawaiian)

ultima Thule (OOL-tee-mah TOO-leh), faraway, mythical locality (L)

ultimo (OOL-tee-moh), last (month; abbr. ult.) (L)

ultra (OOL-trah), beyond, outside of (L)

ultra vires (OOL-trah WEE-rehs), beyond one's strength or capacity (L)

und so weiter (oont ZOH VEYE-tuhr), and so forth; etc. (G)

uno animo (OO-noh AH-nee-moh), with one mind (L)

Untergang des Abendlandes (OON-tuhr-gahng dehs AH-buhnt-LAHN-duhs), decline of the West (G)

urbi et orbi (OOR-bee eht OHR-bee), to the city and to the world (L)

ut supra (OOT SOO-prah), as above (L)

V

vade mecum (WAH-deh MEH-koom), a book carried as a constant companion, a handbook (L)

vae victis (WEYE WEEK-tees), woe to the vanquished (L)

vale (WAH-leh), good-bye, farewell (L)

valuta (vah-LOO-tah), currency, foreign exchange (It)

vaquero (bah-KEH-roh), cowboy (Sp)

Veda (VEH-dah), knowledge, book of knowledge (Sk)

veld (FEHLT), open grassy country (Du)

veni, vidi, vici (WEH-nee WEE-dee WEE-kee), I came, I saw, I conquered (L)

verbatim (wehr-BAH-teem), word for word (L)

verbum sat sapienti (WEHR-boom SAHT sah-pee-EHN-tee), a word to the wise is sufficient (L)

Verein (fehr-EYEN), union, club (G)

vermicelli (vayr-mee-CHEHL-lee), thin spaghetti (It)

versus (WEHR-soos), abbr. vs.; against (L)

veto (WEH-toh), I forbid; executive prohibition (L)

Via Crucis (WEE-ah KROO-kees), the Way of the Cross (L)

vibrato (vee-BRAH-toh), with vibration (It)

vice versa (WEE-keh WEHR-sah), the other way around (L)

vide (WEE-deh), see (L)

videlicet (wee-DEH-lee-keht), abbr. viz.; to wit, namely (L)

vignette (vee-NYEHT), illustration, short essay (F)

vinaigrette (vee-neh-GREHT), seasoned with vinegar (F)

vin ordinaire (VĒH nawr-dee-NEHR), common table wine (F)

viola da gamba (VYAW-lah dah GAHM-bah), large viol (It)

virtuoso (veer-too-AW-soh), master performer or singer (It)

vis-à-vis (vee-za-VEE), face to face (F)

vista (VEES-tah), view, panorama (It)

viva voce (WEE-wah WOH-keh), orally, by word of mouth (L)

vive (VEEV) long live (F)

vodka (VAWT-kuh), grain spirits (R)

volaille (vaw-LA-yuh), fowl (F)

vol-au-vent (VAW-loh-VĀH), large, light patty; baked pastry shell (F)

Volkswagen (FOHLKS-vah-guhn), people's car; German automobile (G)

volte-face (VAWLT-FAS), about face; reversal (F)

vomitorium (woh-mee-TOH-ree-oom), exit of large public building (L)

von (FUN), of, from, prefix to noble family name (G)

voortrekker (FOHR-TREHK-kuhr), early settler, pioneer (Du)

vox clamantis in deserto (WOHKS klah-MAHN-tees een deh-SEHR-toh), the voice of one shouting in the wilderness (L)

vox populi, vox Dei (WOHKS POH-poo-lee, WOHKS DEH-ee), the voice of the people is the voice of God (L)

vraisemblance (vreh-sāh-BLĀHS), likelihood, verisimilitude (F)

vulgo (WOOL-goh), commonly, popularly (L)

W

wagon-lit (va-GŌH-LEE), sleeping car (F)

wahini (wah-HEE-nee), woman (Hawaiian)

wanderlust (VAHN-duhr-loost), desire for travel (G)

Wehrmacht (VEHR-makht), armed forces (G)

Weinstube (VEYEN-SHTOO-buh), wine tavern (G)

Weltanschauung, Weltansicht (VEHLT-ahn-show-ung, VEHLT-ahn-ziçt), general outlook, conception of things (G)

Weltschmerz (VEHLT-shmehrts), sorrow for the world, pessimism (G)

wunderbar (VOON-duhr-bahr), wonderful (G)

Wurst (VOORST), sausage (G)

X

xenophobia (KSEH-noh-FOH-bohs), fear or hatred of the foreign (Gk roots)

Y

Yahweh (YAH-veh), Jehovah, God (Heb)

Yoga (YOH-gah), yoking; restraint; Indian philosophy (Sk)

Yogi (YOH-ghee), follower of Yoga (Sk)

Yom Kippur (YOHM keep-POOR), day of atonement, Hebrew holiday (Heb)

Z

zabaione (dzah-bah-YOH-nay), custard mixed with Marsala wine (It)

Zeitgeist (TSEYET-gheyest), spirit of the times (G)

zucchini (dzook-KEE-nee), green squash (It)

Zwieback (TSVEE-bahk), toasted biscuit (G)

Spain—Patio de la Acequia, Granada

READING SKILLS

It is important for student and nonstudent alike to be able to read well and quickly. Every student must be able to master without undue delay the contents of the textbooks or other materials that form a part of his course. The good student is an efficient reader. He reads rapidly with good comprehension, he is able to read critically, and he retains what he has read.

PREVIEWING

A good way for a reader to approach a new text is to devote a few minutes to *previewing* the material. This is a useful reading technique by which the reader familiarizes himself with the general contents of the text before he begins the actual reading. To preview a selection:

1. *Read the title and subtitles.* If the titles have been well prepared, they will indicate the main ideas of the material. The subtitles generally indicate the various points that go logically under the main idea. To read subtitles in order is apt to provide you with a good outline of the material.

2. *Examine the diagrams, charts, and other visual aids.* These visual aids are included to help explain difficult concepts or to repeat essential points.

3. *Pay attention to the length of paragraphs,* and let them determine the speed at which you will read the selection. Long paragraphs are apt to mean more detailed texts; short ones give fewer details and constitute easier texts. Read the long ones more slowly, the short ones more quickly.

Here is an example of the preview technique, making use of a feature story that appeared in a newspaper, with its headline, subheadline, and subtitles. Note that in textbooks, chapter titles and subtitles perform the same function.

Headline	KEY PROBLEMS IN FOREIGN POLICY
Subheadline	How can the President alert the nation to this many-angled crisis?
Subtitles	More "Fireside Chats" Reform of the Press Conference Continuation of the Forums Less Consideration of "World Opinion"

In its original form the story had additional subtitles, but it is apparent that the four subtitles listed are most pertinent. In a very short time the reader has learned the basic theme of the article and the various points the author suggests. The article goes into greater detail, but the preview has provided the reader, in a nutshell, with the essential points. Since the paragraphs in this particular selection are fairly long, the reader will do well to proceed with caution and allow sufficient time for the comprehension of the material.

It is a good idea to preview everything you read–textbooks, newspapers, magazines, technical journals, essays, and so on. This applies especially to material that has a title, subtitles, and visual aids. The few minutes it will take you will pay off in time saved and greater reading efficiency.

FINDING MAIN IDEAS

In presenting factual-type material, the author has set out to convey to you, the reader, in as logical and lucid a manner as possible, the ideas he wishes to impart. In a single paragraph he usually presents the one basic idea; this may be contained in a single sentence, or it may be implied in various sentences in the paragraph. Further, in any given paragraph, most sentences will contain details that explain, illustrate, amplify, or in some way develop the main idea.

You, as the reader, will want to command those skills that will help you to pick out as quickly as possible the central thought of a paragraph. This implies the ability to understand the relationship between the main idea and the supporting details.

Here are some guides to finding the main idea:

1. The main idea may be directly stated in the first sentence of the paragraph.

> *The President tells the visitor that he is giving three-fourths of his time to international affairs.* The White House staff works unclocked hours on problems ranging from Cambodia to the Common Market, from Mongolia to megatons. The foreign callers come to consult and to be feted in a seemingly endless procession–some, seventy-five times since the President took office.

Note the central thought in the first sentence; note also how the following sentences amplify the thought by providing examples of how the President devotes most of his time to the consideration of foreign affairs problems.

2. The main idea may be directly stated in the first sentence and repeated, for emphasis, in the last sentence of the paragraph.

> Many people think that whisky is a good cure for *rattlesnake bites, but scientists claim that whisky is the worst possible medicine.* It acts as a stimulant and therefore makes the heart beat faster. As a result, the heart pumps blood more rapidly all over the body. Rattlesnake poison is dangerous because it gets into the blood stream. If the blood is forced to travel rapidly over the body, then so does the rattlesnake poison that is in the blood. *"Send for the doctor–not for the whisky bottle" is good advice if you're bitten by a rattler.*

Note how the main idea is stated in the first sentence and repeated, for emphasis and as a summary, in the last. The remaining sentences *explain* the main idea.

The above-quoted paragraph illustrates another common technique for presenting the main thought of a paragraph. Often, as here, only a *part of a sentence* contains the main thought. Textbook writers, because paragraphs in textbooks are short, often employ this technique.

3. The main thought may be directly stated in a sentence located in the middle of a paragraph.

> In spite of the disapproval of a number of community organizations, New York State is considering undertaking vast fall-out shelter construction. State officials have been urging comparable projects for years. *However, opinion is divided over the necessity for fall-out shelters.* Local pacifist groups are condemning such projects. Many well-known scientists consider it futile. The federal government has condoned construction of shelters but has not taken positive steps to implement their construction.

Again, note how the main thought appears in a single sentence, and how the remaining sentences explain this main thought.

Of course, not all writers prepare their material in precisely this way. Individual styles of writing and the nature of the material often suggest other ways of presenting one's thoughts.

There may be paragraphs that contain sentences only *implying* the main thought; they do not specifically state it in any one sentence. Other paragraphs may be so short that it becomes difficult to determine the central thought. Or a paragraph may contain two equally important ideas.

Here is a suggestion for finding the main thought in a paragraph, regardless of the type of paragraph construction. Ask yourself two questions in regard to the paragraph; then put together the two answers to these questions into a single sentence. This sentence will provide the main idea. Thus:

a. Ask yourself who or what the paragraph is about.

b. Ask yourself what this paragraph says about the subject.

c. Combine the answers to these two questions into a single sentence, and you will have the main idea.

This technique can be applied whether the main idea is definitely stated, or whether it is implied. The same technique can be used in determining the basic theme of an essay, a chapter, or a short story.

Using this technique, see if you can find the main idea of the following paragraph:

> The room was entirely carpeted with a thick, soft rug. Drapes, spun of gold thread, bedecked the large picture windows. Sterling silver candlesticks flanked a gold clock on the mantelpiece. Crimson velvet covered the large sofa. A Steinway grand piano stood in the center of the room.

What is the subject? *A room.*

What is distinctive about this room? *It is richly or expensively decorated.*

The main idea: The room was expensively decorated.

In stressing main ideas, you are not to infer that they alone are important, and that the details are useless. The sentences containing the details often furnish the "substance" of the story. Details can provide nuances of meaning; they can involve the reader's imagination.

CRITICAL READING

Reading quickly with adequate comprehension is not enough. The efficient reader must also be able to read critically, to evaluate what he reads. Such critical reading is a refinement of skill in reading. It requires that the reader be aware of the sources of the author's information; that he recognize the possible use of propaganda techniques; that he be able to differentiate between fact and opinion. Once you realize you are reading an opinion, accord it only the value you consider it to be worth. This does not mean that all opinion should be arbitrarily dismissed. Not at all. But not all opinion is worth accepting. Before you accept an opinion, evaluate it.

First, consider the author. Who is he? Is he or is he not an expert on the subject he is dealing with? You would not be very likely to accept the opinion of your neighbor, a carpenter, if he were to write an article on the causes of heart disease. But the chances are that you would believe implicitly the statements on heart disease made by Dr. Paul Dudley White, the eminent cardiologist. The critical reader does not blindly accept what he reads without knowing something about the author and his qualifications.

Guard against accepting overgeneralizations. Remember, things are not all white or all black. Don't let yourself be taken in by language that is emotionally tinged.

RATE OF READING

Most readers can improve their rate of reading without losing the essential ability to comprehend. (Obviously, there is no value or virtue in speed without comprehension.) Let your rate be determined by the purpose for which you read, and by the difficulty of the material.

For difficult factual reading, a reader's rate should be only two-thirds as fast as his most rapid reading. It is all very well to race through a popular magazine article or a book of light fiction; in reading *Moby Dick* or *Macbeth*, you will have to go more slowly if you wish to explore the deep meaning of these classics and to enjoy the beauty of the language. Nor should the student try to rush through a chapter of his physics or history text. What he wants to do is to absorb and digest, and make a part of his mental make-up, every fact and idea he comes upon in his reading.

Some of the more important rate-of-reading skills are skimming, skim-reading, and reading for key words.

Skimming

Skimming and reading are not one and the same. Skimming is a subskill in the reading process. Most readers who claim that they can "read" five or ten thousand words an hour are probably skimming, not reading at all.

In skimming you leave out whole sentences, whole paragraphs, even whole pages. When you glance at the headlines and subheadlines of your morning newspaper, you are skimming, not reading. The basic rule is to *skim for a definite purpose.* You will skim for a specific answer to a question, and you will skim when you want to get a general idea of the contents of some printed material.

1. SKIMMING FOR AN ANSWER TO A QUESTION. It may be a telephone number, or some general's middle initial, or the birth date of a President. Here is what you do:

a. *Preview the material* to find the answer you are looking for.

b. *Use guide words or phrases* to help direct you to the answer. For example, for George Washington's date of birth, turn to "Washington, George" in the encyclopedia, almanac, or other source book. Try to locate the words *birth, birthday, born,* or the like.

c. In skimming, *let your eyes move rapidly and*

efficiently over the text. You will not be moving your eyes from left to right from line to line as you do in ordinary reading; instead, there are two different ways you can let your eyes move. When the printed column is narrow (as in most newspapers, some textbook chapters, some magazine articles, etc.), your eyes can follow a vertical path down the center of the column. They will be able to see words to the left and to the right. As soon as you come upon the guide word or words, stop and read carefully. Another procedure is to let your eyes move in a left-to-right, then a right-to-left progression, taking in two or three lines of print as you go along, somewhat like an automobile going downhill, careening from side to side and so on down the hill. You can with this procedure observe words near the center of the zigzag path your eyes are taking.

In skimming, speed is essential. Go ahead as fast as you can.

2. Skimming in order to get a general idea of the contents. This can be a valuable procedure, for most of us just do not have the time to read thoroughly every bit of reading material that comes to our attention. The procedure is simple: First *preview* the article; then *read* the *first paragraph;* next *read* the *first sentence* of each following *paragraph;* last, *read* the *last paragraph* thoroughly.

Skim-Reading

This is a combination of reading and skimming. You read the important sections and skim the less important ones.

You can increase your rate of reading by reading the key words in sentences. Utilizing what may be called the "telegram style," perhaps 50 percent or more of a sentence is left out, without the reader's losing the meaning of the sentence. In the following paragraph, the key words have been italicized. By reading them, and them only, the reader will get the sense of the material.

> Our *forefathers fought* bloody *wars* and *suffered torture* and *death* for the *right to worship God according* to the varied *dictates* of *conscience.* Complete *religious liberty* has been *accepted* as an unquestioned personal *freedom* since our *Bill of Rights* was *adopted.* We have insisted only that *religious freedom* may *not* be pleaded as an *excuse for criminal* or clearly *antisocial conduct.*

A word of caution: Such words as *no, not, only,* and *less* are extremely important; so watch out!

Finally, your attitude when reading is important. Don't be afraid of the printed page! With material that is not especially difficult or technical, read on just as fast as you can without losing comprehension. Enter every reading situation with confidence and enthusiasm, and you will find this frame of mind will be a great help.

For further material on reading skills, refer to the books listed below:

1. Liddle, William, *Reading for Concepts* (New York: McGraw-Hill, 1977). Books "A" through "H" of this series are designed for readers in the seventh through twelfth grades.

2. Pauk, Walter, *How to Read Factual Literature* (Chicago: Science Research Associates, 1970). This book was written for readers in the seventh and eighth grades.

3. Pauk, Walter and Wilson, Josephine M., *How to Read Creative Literature* (Chicago: Science Research Associates, 1970). This book was written for readers in the ninth grade through adult level.

Where To Write for Vital Records

Introduction

This publication, *Where to Write for Vital Records: Births, Deaths, Marriages, and Divorces,* supersedes and incorporates three publications: *Where to Write for Birth and Death Records: United States and Outlying Areas* (DHEW Pub. No. (PHS) 80-1142, revised 1979), *Where to Write for Marriage Records: United States and Outlying Areas* (DHEW Pub. No. (PHS) 80-1144, revised 1979), and *Where to Write for Divorce Records: United States and Outlying Areas* (DHEW Pub. No. (PHS) 80-1145, revised 1979).

An official certificate of every birth, death, marriage, and divorce should be on file in the locality where the event occurred. The Federal Government does not maintain files or indexes of these records. These records are filed permanently either in a State vital statistics office or in a city, county, or other local office.

To obtain a certified copy of any of the certificates, write or go to the vital statistics office in the State or area where the event occurred. Addresses and fees are given for each event in the State or area concerned.

To ensure that you receive an accurate record for your request and that your request be filled with all due speed, please follow the steps outlined below for the event in which you are interested:

- Write to the appropriate office to have your request filled.
- For all certificates send a money order or certified check because the office cannot refund cash lost in transit. All fees are subject to change.
- Type or print all names and addresses in the letter.
- Give the following facts when writing for BIRTH OR DEATH RECORDS:

1. Full name of person whose record is being requested.
2. Sex and race.
3. Parents' names, including maiden name of mother.
4. Month, day, and year of birth or death.
5. Place of birth or death (city or town, county, and State; and name of hospital, if any).
6. Purpose for which copy is needed.
7. Relationship to person whose record is being requested.

- Give the following facts when writing for MARRIAGE RECORDS:

1. Full names of bride and groom (including nicknames).
2. Residence addresses at time of marriage.
3. Ages at time of marriage (or dates of birth).
4. Month, day, and year of marriage.
5. Place of marriage (city or town, county, and State).
6. Purpose for which copy is needed.
7. Relationship to persons whose record is being requested.

- Give the following facts when writing for DIVORCE RECORDS:

1. Full names of husband and wife (including nicknames).
2. Present residence address.
3. Former addresses (as in court records).
4. Ages at time of divorce (or dates of birth).
5. Date of divorce or annulment.
6. Place of divorce or annulment.
7. Type of final decree.
8. Purpose for which copy is needed.
9. Relationship to persons whose record is being requested.

Place of event	*Cost of copy*	*Address*	*Remarks*
ALABAMA			
Birth or Death	$5.00	Bureau of Vital Statistics State Department of Public Health Montgomery, AL 36130	State office has had records since January 1908. Additional copies at same time are $2.00 each. Fee for special searches is $5.00 per hour.
Marriage	$5.00	Same as Birth or Death	State office has had records since August 1936.
	Varies	See remarks	Probate Judge in county where license was issued.
Divorce	$5.00	Same as Birth or Death	State office has had records since January 1950.
	Varies	See remarks	Clerk or Register of Court of Equity in county where divorce was granted.

Place of event	Cost of copy	Address	Remarks
ALASKA			
Birth or Death	$3.00	Department of Health and Social Services Bureau of Vital Statistics Pouch H-02G Juneau, AK 99811	State office has had records since 1913.
Marriage	$3.00	Same as Birth or Death	Records since 1913.
Divorce	$3.00	Same as Birth or Death	Records since 1950.
	Varies	See remarks	Clerk of the Superior Court in judicial district where divorce was granted. Juneau and Ketchikan (First District), Nome (Second District), Anchorage (Third District), Fairbanks (Fourth District).
AMERICAN SAMOA			
Birth or Death	$1.00	Registrar of Vital Statistics Vital Statistics Section Government of American Samoa Pago Pago, AS 96799	Registrar has had records since 1900.
Marriage	$1.00	Same as Birth or Death	
Divorce	$1.00	Same as Birth or Death	
ARIZONA			
Birth or Death	$3.00	Vital Records Section Arizona Department of Health Services P.O. Box 3887 Phoenix, AZ 85030	State office has had records since July 1909 and abstracts of records filed in counties before then.
Marriage	Varies	See remarks	Clerk of Superior Court in county where license was issued.
Divorce	Varies	See remarks	Clerk of Superior Court in county where divorce was granted.
ARKANSAS			
Birth **Death**	$2.00 $3.00	Division of Vital Records Arkansas Department of Health 4815 West Markham Street Little Rock, AR 72201	State office has had records since February 1914 and some original Little Rock and Fort Smith records from 1881.
Marriage	$2.00	Same as Birth or Death	Records since 1917.
	$2.00	See remarks	Full certified copy may be obtained from County Clerk in county where license was issued.
Divorce	$2.00	Same as Birth or Death	Coupons since 1923.
	Varies	See remarks	Full certified copy may be obtained from Circuit or Chancery Clerk in county where divorce was granted.
CALIFORNIA			
Birth or Death	$3.00	Vital Statistics Branch Department of Health Services 410 N Street Sacramento, CA 95814	State office has had records since July 1905. For earlier records, write to County Recorder in county where event occurred.
Marriage	$3.00	Same as Birth or Death	State office has had records since July 1905. For earlier records, write to County Recorder in county where event occurred.
Divorce	$3.00	Same as Birth or Death	Fee is for search and identification of county where certified copy can be obtained. Certified copies are not available from State Health Department.

Place of event	Cost of copy	Address	Remarks
	Varies	See remarks	Clerk of Superior Court in county where divorce was granted.
CANAL ZONE			
Birth or Death	$2.00	Panama Canal Commission Vital Statistics Clerk APO Miami 34011	Records available from May 1904 to September 1979.
Marriage	$1.00	Same as Birth or Death	Records available from May 1904 to September 1979.
Divorce	$0.50	Same as Birth or Death	Records available from May 1904 to September 1979.
COLORADO			
Birth or Death	$2.00	Vital Records Section Colorado Department of Health 4210 East 11th Avenue Denver, CO 80220	State office has had death records since 1900 and birth records since 1910. State office also has birth records for some counties for years before 1910.
Marriage	See remarks	Same as Birth or Death	Statewide index of records for all years except 1940-75. Inquiries will be forwarded to appropriate office. Certified copies are not available from State Health Department.
	Varies	See remarks	County Clerk in county where license was issued.
Divorce	See remarks	Same as Birth or Death	Statewide index of records for all years except 1940-67. Inquiries will be forwarded to appropriate office. Certified copies are not available from State Health Department.
	Varies	See remarks	Clerk of District Court in county where divorce was granted.
CONNECTICUT			
Birth or Death	$3.00	Department of Health Services Vital Records Section Division of Health Statistics 79 Elm Street Hartford, CT 06115	State office has had records since July 1897. For earlier records, write to Registrar of Vital Statistics in town or city where event occurred.
Short form	$2.00		
Marriage	$3.00	Same as Birth or Death	Records since July 1897.
	$3.00	See remarks	Registrar of Vital Statistics in town where license was issued.
Divorce	See remarks	Same as Birth or Death	Index of records since 1947. Inquiries will be forwarded to appropriate office. Certified copies are not available from State office.
	$3.00	See remarks	Clerk of Superior Court in county where divorce was granted.
DELAWARE			
Birth or Death	$2.50	Bureau of Vital Statistics Division of Public Health Department of Health and Social Services State Health Building Dover, DE 19901	State office has records for 1861 to 1863 and since 1881 but no records for 1864 to 1880.
Marriage	$2.50	Same as Birth or Death	Records since 1847.
Divorce	See remarks	Same as Birth or Death	Records since 1935. Inquiries will be forwarded to appropriate office. Fee for search and verification of essential facts of divorce, $2.50. Certified copies are not available from State office.
	$2.00	See remarks	Prothonotary in county where divorce was granted up to 1975. For divorces granted after 1975 the parties concerned should contact Family Court in the county where the divorce was granted.

Place of event	Cost of copy	Address	Remarks
DISTRICT OF COLUMBIA			
Birth or Death	$3.00	Vital Records Branch 615 Pennsylvania Avenue, NW Washington, D.C. 20004	Office has had death records since 1855 and birth records since 1871, but no death records were filed during the Civil War.
Marriage	$3.00	Same as Birth or Death	Records since January 1, 1982.
	$5.00	Marriage Bureau 515 5th Street, NW Washington, D.C. 20001	Fee for proof of marriage, $2.50; proof of age, $2.50.
Divorce	$3.00	Same as Birth or Death	Records since January 1, 1982
	Varies	Clerk, Superior Court for the District of Columbia, Family Division 500 Indiana Avenue, NW Washington, D.C. 20001	Records since September 16, 1956.
	Varies	Clerk, U.S. District Court for the District of Columbia Washington, D.C. 20001	Records before September 16, 1956.
FLORIDA			
Birth or Death	$2.00	Department of Health and Rehabilitative Services Office of Vital Statistics P.O. Box 210 Jacksonville, FL 32231	State office has had some birth records since April 1865 and some death records since August 1877. The majority of records date from January 1917. (If the exact date is unknown, the fee is $2.00 for the first year searched and $1.00 for each additional year up to a maximum of $25.00. Fee includes one copy of record if found.)
Marriage	$2.00	Same as Birth or Death	Records since June 6, 1927. (If the exact date is unknown, the fee is $2.00 for the first year searched and $1.00 for each additional year up to a maximum of $25.00. Fee includes one copy of record if found.)
	$2.00	See remarks	Clerk of Circuit Court in county where divorce was granted.
Divorce	$2.00	Same as Birth or Death	Records since June 6, 1927. (If exact date is unknown, the fee is $2.00 for the first year searched and $1.00 for each additional year up to a maximum of $25.00. Fee includes one copy of record if found.)
	Varies	See remarks	Clerk of Circuit Court in county where divorce was granted.
GEORGIA			
Birth or Death	$3.00	Georgia Department of Human Resources Vital Records Unit Room 217-H 47 Trinity Avenue, SW Atlanta, GA 30334	State office has had records since January 1919. For earlier records in Atlanta or Savannah, write to County Health Department in county where event occurred. Additional copies of same record ordered at same time are $1.00 each.
Marriage	See remarks	Same as Birth or Death	Centralized State records since June 9, 1952. Certified copies are not issued at State office. Inquiries will be forwarded to appropriate office.
	$3.00	See remarks	Probate Judge in county where license was issued.
Divorce	See remarks	Same as Birth or Death	Centralized State records since June 9, 1952. Certified copies are not issued at State office. Inquiries will be forwarded to appropriate office.
	Varies	See remarks	Clerk of Superior Court in county where divorce was granted.

Place of event	Cost of copy	Address	Remarks
GUAM			
Birth or Death	$2.00	Office of Vital Statistics Department of Public Health and Social Services Government of Guam P.O. Box 2816 Agana, GU, M.I. 96910	Office has had records since October 26, 1901.
Marriage	$2.00	Same as Birth or Death	
Divorce	Varies	See remarks	Clerk, Superior Court of Guam, Agana, GU, M.I. 96910.
HAWAII			
Birth or Death	$2.00	Research and Statistics Office State Department of Health P.O. Box 3378 Honolulu, HI 96801	State office has had records since 1853.
Marriage	$2.00	Same as Birth or Death	
Divorce	$2.00	Same as Birth or Death	Records since July 1951.
	Varies	See remarks	Circuit Court in county where divorce was granted.
IDAHO			
Birth or Death	$4.00	Bureau of Vital Statistics, Standards, and Local Health Services State Department of Health and Welfare Statehouse Boise, ID 83720	State office has had records since 1911. For records from 1907 to 1911, write to County Recorder in county where event occurred.
Marriage	$4.00	Same as Birth or Death	Records since 1947.
	Varies	See remarks	County Recorder in county where license was issued.
Divorce	$4.00	Same as Birth or Death	Records since January 1947.
	Varies	See remarks	County Recorder in county where divorce was granted.
ILLINOIS			
Birth or Death	$3.00	Office of Vital Records State Department of Public Health 535 West Jefferson Street Springfield, IL 62761	State office has had records since January 1916. For earlier records and for copies of State records since January 1916, write to County Clerk in county where event occurred. ($3.00 fee is for search of files and one copy of record if found. Additional copies of same record ordered at same time are $2.00 each.)
Marriage	See remarks	Same as Birth or Death	Records since January 1962. All items may be verified (fee $3.00). Inquiries will be forwarded to appropriate office. Certified copies are not available from State office.
	$3.00	See remarks	County Clerk in county where license was issued.
Divorce	See remarks	Same as Birth or Death	Records since January 1962. Some items may be verified (fee $3.00). Certified copies are not available from State office.
	Varies	See remarks	Clerk of Circuit Court in county where divorce was granted.
INDIANA			
Birth or Death	$4.00	Division of Vital Records State Board of Health 1330 West Michigan Street P.O. Box 1964 Indianapolis, IN 46206	State office has had birth records since October 1907 and death records since 1900. Additional copies of same record ordered at same time are $1.00 each. For earlier records, write to Health Officer in city or county where event occurred.

Place of event	Cost of copy	Address	Remarks
Marriage	See remarks	Same as Birth or Death	Marriage Index since 1958. Inquiries will be forwarded to appropriate office. Certified copies are not available from State Health Department.
	Varies	See remarks	Clerk of Circuit Court or Clerk of Superior Court in county where license was issued.
Divorce	Varies	See remarks	County Clerk in county where divorce was granted.
IOWA			
Birth or Death	$4.00	Iowa State Department of Health Vital Records Section Lucas State Office Building Des Moines, IA 50319	State office has had records since July 1880.
Marriage	$4.00	Same as Birth or Death	State Office has had records since July 1880.
Divorce	See remarks	Same as Birth or Death	Brief statistical record only since 1906. Inquiries will be forwarded to appropriate office. Certified copies are not available from State Health Department.
	$4.00	See remarks	Clerk of District Court in county where divorce was granted.
KANSAS			
Birth or Death	$3.00	Bureau of Registration and Health Statistics Kansas State Department of Health and Environment 6700 South Topeka Avenue Topeka, KS 66620	State office has had records since July 1911. For earlier records, write to County Clerk in county where event occurred. Additional copies of same record ordered at same time are $2.00 each.
Marriage	$3.00	Same as Birth or Death	Records since May 1913.
	Varies	See remarks	Probate Judge in county where license was issued.
Divorce	$3.00	Same as Birth or Death	Records since July 1951.
	Varies	See remarks	Clerk of District Court in county where divorce was granted.
KENTUCKY			
Birth or Death	$4.00	Office of Vital Statistics Department for Human Resources 275 East Main Street Frankfort, KY 40621	State office has had records since January 1911 and some records for the cities of Louisville, Lexington, Covington, and Newport before then.
Marriage	$4.00	Same as Birth or Death	Records since June 1958.
	Varies	See remarks	Clerk of County Court in county where license was issued.
Divorce	$4.00	Same as Birth or Death	Records since June 1958.
	Varies	See remarks	Clerk of Circuit Court in county where decree was issued.
LOUISIANA			
Birth or Death	$3.00	Division of Vital Records Office of Health Services and Environmental Quality P.O. Box 60630 New Orleans, LA 70160	State office has had records since July 1914. Birth records for City of New Orleans are available from 1790, and death records from 1803.
Short Form	$2.00		
Marriage	See remarks	Same as Birth or Death	Certified copies are not available from State Health Department. Inquiries will be forwarded to appropriate office.
Orleans Parish	$3.00	Same as Birth or Death	

Place of event	Cost of copy	Address	Remarks
Other Parishes	Varies	See remarks	Certified copies are issued by Clerk of Court in parish where license was issued.
Divorce	Varies	See remarks	Clerk of Court in parish where divorce was granted. For Orleans Parish, copies may be obtained from State office for $2.00.
MAINE			
Birth or Death	$2.00	Office of Vital Records Human Services Building Station II State House Augusta, ME 04333	State office has had records since 1892. For earlier records, write to the municipality where event occurred.
Marriage	$2.00	Same as Birth or Death	
	$2.00	See remarks	Town Clerk in town where license was issued.
Divorce	$2.00	Same as Birth or Death	Records since January 1892.
	$5.00	See remarks	Clerk of District Court in judicial division where divorce was granted.
MARYLAND			
Birth or Death	$2.00	Division of Vital Records State Department of Health and Mental Hygiene State Office Building P.O. Box 13146 201 West Preston Street Baltimore, MD 21203	State office has had records since August 1898. Records for City of Baltimore are available from January 1875.
Marriage	$2.00	Same as Birth or Death	Records since June 1951.
	See remarks	See remarks	Clerk of Circuit Court in county where license was issued or Clerk of Court of Common Pleas of Baltimore City (for licenses issued in City of Baltimore).
Divorce	See remarks	Same as Birth or Death	Records since January 1961. Certified copies are not available from State office. Some items may be verified. Inquiries will be forwarded to appropriate office.
	Varies	See remarks	Clerk of Circuit Court in county where divorce was granted.
MASSACHUSETTS			
Birth or Death	$3.00	Registry of Vital Records and Statistics Room 105, McCormack Building 1 Ashburton Place Boston, MA 02108	State office has had records, except for Boston, since 1841. For earlier records, write to the City or Town Clerk in place where event occurred. Earliest records available in the Boston office are for 1848.
Marriage	$3.00	Same as Birth or Death	Records (except for Boston) since 1841. Earliest Boston records are for 1848.
Divorce	See remarks	Same as Birth or Death	Index only since 1952. Inquirer will be directed where to send request. Certified copies are not available from State office.
	$3.00	See remarks	Registrar of Probate Court in county where divorce was granted.
MICHIGAN			
Birth or Death	$10.00	Office of Vital and Health Statistics Michigan Department of Public Health 3500 North Logan Street Lansing, MI 48914	State office has had records since 1867. Copies of records since 1867 may also be obtained from County Clerk in county where event occurred. Detroit records may be obtained from the City Health Department for births occurring since 1893 and for deaths since 1897.

Place of event	Cost of copy	Address	Remarks
Marriage	$10.00	Same as Birth or Death	Records since April 1867.
	Varies	See remarks	County Clerk in county where license was issued.
Divorce	$10.00	Same as Birth or Death	Records since 1897.
	Varies	See remarks	County Clerk in county where divorce was granted.
MINNESOTA			
Birth or Death	$5.00	Minnesota Department of Health Section of Vital Statistics 717 Delaware Street SE Minneapolis, MN 55440	State office has had records since January 1908. Copies of earlier records may be obtained from Clerk of District Court in county where event occurred or from the Minneapolis or St. Paul City Health Department if the event occurred in either city.
Marriage	See remarks	Same as Birth or Death	Statewide index since January 1958. Inquiries will be forwarded to appropriate office. Certified copies are not available from State Health Department.
	$5.00	See remarks	Clerk of District Court in county where license was issued.
Divorce	See remarks	Same as Birth or Death	Index since January 1970. Certified copies are not available from State office.
	$5.00	See remarks	Clerk of District Court in county where divorce was granted.
MISSISSIPPI			
Birth	$10.00	Vital Records State Board of Health P.O. Box 1700 Jackson, MS 39205	State office has had records since 1912. Full copies of birth certificates obtained within 1 year after the event are $5.00. Additional copies of same record ordered at same time are $1.00 each.
Short Form	$5.00		
Death	$5.00		
Marriage	$5.00	Same as Birth or Death	Statistical records only from January 1926 to July 1, 1938, and since January 1942.
	$3.00	See remarks	Circuit Clerk in county where license was issued.
Divorce	See remarks	Same as Birth or Death	Records since January 1926. Certified copies are not available from State office. Inquiries will be forwarded to appropriate office.
	$2.00	See remarks	Chancery Clerk in county where divorce was granted.
MISSOURI			
Birth or Death	$1.00	Division of Health Bureau of Vital Records State Department of Health and Welfare Jefferson City, MO 65101	State office has had records since January 1910. If event occurred in St. Louis (city), St. Louis County, or Kansas City before 1910, write to the City or County Health Department. Copies of these records are $3.00 each in St. Louis City and County. In Kansas City, $6.00 for first copy and $3.00 for each additional copy ordered at same time.
Marriage	No fee	Same as Birth or Death	Indexes since July 1948. Correspondent will be referred to appropriate Recorder of Deeds in county where license was issued.
	Varies	See remarks	Recorder of Deeds in county where license was issued.
Divorce	See remarks	Same as Birth or Death	Indexes since July 1948. Certified copies are not available from State Health Department. Inquiries will be forwarded to appropriate office.
	Varies	See remarks	Clerk of Circuit Court in county where divorce was granted.
MONTANA			
Birth or Death	$3.00	Bureau of Records and Statistics State Department of Health and Environmental Sciences Helena, MT 59601	State office has had records since late 1907.

Place of event	Cost of copy	Address	Remarks
Marriage	See remarks	Same as Birth or Death	Records since July 1943. Some items may be verified. Inquiries will be forwarded to appropriate office. Apply to county where license was issued if known. Certified copies are not available from State office.
	Varies	See remarks	Clerk of District Court in county where license was issued.
Divorce	See remarks	Same as Birth or Death	Records since July 1943. Some items may be verified. Inquiries will be forwarded to appropriate office. Apply to county where license was issued if known. Certified copies are not available from State office.
	Varies	See remarks	Clerk of District Court in county where divorce was granted.
NEBRASKA			
Birth or Death	$3.00	Bureau of Vital Statistics State Department of Health 301 Centennial Mall South P.O. Box 95007 Lincoln, NE 68509	State office has had records since late 1904. If birth occurred before then, write the State office for information.
Marriage	$3.00	Same as Birth or Death	Records since January 1909.
	Varies	See remarks	County Court in county where license was issued.
Divorce	$3.00	Same as Birth or Death	Records since January 1909.
	Varies	See remarks	Clerk of District Court in county where divorce was granted.
NEVADA			
Birth or Death	$4.00	Division of Health - Vital Statistics Capitol Complex Carson City, NV 89710	State office has had records since July 1911. For earlier records, write to County Recorder in county where event occurred. Additional copies of Death Records ordered at the same time are $4.00 for second and third copies, $3.00 each for the next three copies, and $2.00 each for any additional copies.
Marriage	See remarks	Same as Birth or Death	Indexes since January 1968. Certified copies are not available from State Health Department. Inquiries will be forwarded to appropriate office.
	Varies	See remarks	County Recorder in county where license was issued.
Divorce	See remarks	Same as Birth or Death	Indexes since January 1968. Certified copies are not available from State Health Department. Inquiries will be forwarded to appropriate office.
	Varies	See remarks	County Clerk in county where divorce was granted.
NEW HAMPSHIRE			
Birth or Death	$3.00	Bureau of Vital Records Health and Welfare Building Hazen Drive Concord, NH 03301	State office has had some records since 1640. Copies of records may be obtained from State office or from City or Town Clerk in place where event occurred.
Marriage	$3.00	Same as Birth or Death	Records since 1640.
	$3.00	See remarks	Town Clerk in town where license was issued.
Divorce	$3.00	Same as Birth or Death	Records since 1808. Fee includes search and one copy if found.
	$3.00	See remarks	Clerk of Superior Court where divorce was granted.

Place of event	Cost of copy	Address	Remarks
NEW JERSEY			
Birth or Death	$2.00	State Department of Health Bureau of Vital Statistics CN 360 Trenton, NJ 08625	State office has had records since June 1878. Additional copies of same record ordered at same time are $1.00 each. If the exact date is unknown, the fee is an additional $0.50 per year searched.
		Archives and History Bureau State Library Division State Department of Education Trenton, NJ 08625	For records from May 1848 to May 1878.
Marriage	$2.00	Same as Birth or Death	If the exact date is unknown, the fee is an additional $0.50 per year searched.
	No fee	Archives and History Bureau State Library Division State Department of Education Trenton, NJ 08625	Records from May 1848 to May 1878.
Divorce	$2.00	Superior Court, Chancery Division State House Annex, Room 320 CN 971 Trenton, NJ 08625	The fee is for the first four pages. Additional pages cost $0.50 each.
NEW MEXICO			
Birth or Death	$4.00	Vital Statistics Bureau New Mexico Health Services Division P.O. Box 968 Santa Fe, NM 87503	State office has had records since 1920 and delayed records since 1880.
Marriage	Varies	See remarks	County Clerk in county where license was issued.
Divorce	Varies	See remarks	Clerk of District Court in county where divorce was granted.
NEW YORK (Except New York City)			
Birth or Death	$5.00	Bureau of Vital Records State Department of Health Empire State Plaza Tower Building Albany, NY 12237	State office has had records since1880. For records before 1914 in Albany, Buffalo, and Yonkers or before 1880 in any other city, write to Registrar of Vital Statistics in city where event occurred. For the rest of the State, except New York City, write to State office.
Marriage	$5.00	Same as Birth or Death	Records from January 1880 to December 1907 and since May 1915.
	Varies	See remarks	Records from January 1908 to April 1915. County Clerk in county where license was issued.
	$5.00	See remarks	Records from January 1880 to December 1907. Write to City Clerk in Albany or Buffalo or Registrar of Vital Statistics in Yonkers if marriage occurred in one of these cities.
Divorce	$5.00	Same as Birth or Death	Records since January 1963.
	Varies	See remarks	County Clerk in county where divorce was granted.
NEW YORK CITY			
Birth or Death	$3.50	Bureau of Vital Records Department of Health of New York City 125 Worth Street New York, NY 10013	Office has had birth records since 1898 and death records since 1920. For Old City of New York (Manhattan and part of the Bronx) birth records for 1865-1897 and death records for 1865-1919 write to Municipal Archives and Records Retention, 52 Chambers St., New York, NY 10038.

Place of event	Cost of copy	Address	Remarks
Marriage	$7.00	See remarks	Records from 1847 to 1865. Municipal Archives and Records Retention Center, New York Public Library, 23 Park Row, New York, NY 10038, except Brooklyn records for this period, which are filed with County Clerk's Office, Kings County, Supreme Court Building, Brooklyn, NY 11201. Additional copies of same record ordered at same time are $2.00 each.
	$7.00	See remarks	Records from 1866 to 1907. City Clerk's Office in borough where marriage was performed.
	$7.00	See remarks	Records from 1908 to May 12, 1943. New York City residents write to City Clerk's Office borough of bride's residence; nonresidents write to City Clerk's Office in borough where license was obtained.
	$7.00	See remarks	Records since May 13, 1943. City Clerk's Office in borough where license was issued.
Bronx Borough	$7.00	Marriage License Bureau 1780 Grand Concourse Bronx, NY 10457	
Brooklyn Borough	$7.00	Marriage License Bureau Municipal Building Brooklyn Borough Hall Brooklyn, NY 11201	
Manhattan Borough	$7.00	Marriage License Bureau No. 1 Center Street Municipal Building New York, NY 10007	
Queens Borough	$7.00	Marriage License Bureau Queens Borough Hall 120-55 Queens Boulevard Kew Gardens, NY 11424	
Staten Island Borough (no longer called Richmond)	$7.00	Marriage License Bureau Staten Island Borough Hall St. George Staten Island, NY 11201	
Divorce			See New York State
NORTH CAROLINA			
Birth or Death	$3.00	Department of Human Resources Division of Health Services Vital Records Branch P.O. Box 2091 Raleigh, NC 27602	State office has had birth records since October 1913 and death records since January 1, 1930. Death records from 1913 through 1929 are available from Archives and Records Section, State Records Center, 215 North Blount Street, Raleigh, NC 27602.
Marriage	$3.00	Same as Birth or Death	Records since January 1962.
	$3.00	See remarks	Registrar of Deeds in county where marriage was performed.
Divorce	$3.00	Same as Birth or Death	Records since January 1958.
	Varies	See remarks	Clerk of Superior Court where divorce was granted.
NORTH DAKOTA			
Birth or Death	$2.00	Division of Vital Records State Department of Health Office of Statistical Services Bismarck, ND 58505	State office has had some records since July 1893. Years from 1894 to 1920 are incomplete.
Marriage	$1.00	Same as Birth or Death	Records since July 1925. Requests for earlier records will be forwarded to appropriate office.
	Varies	See remarks	County Judge in county where license was issued.

Place of event	Cost of copy	Address	Remarks
Divorce	See remarks	Same as Birth or Death	Index of records since July 1949. Some items may be verified. Certified copies are not available from State Health Department. Inquiries will be forwarded to appropriate office.
	Varies	See remarks	Clerk of District Court in county where divorce was granted.
OHIO			
Birth or Death	$3.00	Division of Vital Statistics Ohio Department of Health G-20 Ohio Departments Building 65 South Front Street Columbus, OH 43215	State office has had records since December 20, 1908. For earlier records, write to Probate Court in county where event occurred.
Marriage	See remarks	Same as Birth or Death	Records since September 1949. All items may be verified. Certified copies are not available from State Health Department. Inquiries will be referred to appropriate office.
	Varies	See remarks	Probate Judge in county where license was issued.
Divorce	See remarks	Same as Birth or Death	Records since September 1949. All items may be verified. Certified copies are not available from State Health Department. Inquiries will be referred to appropriate office.
	Varies	See remarks	Clerk of Court of Common Pleas in county where divorce was granted.
OKLAHOMA			
Birth or Death	$2.00	Vital Records Section State Department of Health Northeast 10th Street & Stonewall P.O. Box 53551 Oklahoma City, OK 73152	State office has had records since October 1908.
Marriage	Varies	See remarks	Clerk of Court in county where license was issued.
Divorce	Varies	See remarks	Clerk of Court in county where divorce was granted.
OREGON			
Birth or Death	$5.00	Oregon State Health Division Vital Statistics Section P.O. Box 116 Portland, OR 97207	State office has had records since January 1903. Some earlier records for the City of Portland since approximately 1880 are available from the Oregon State Archives, 1005 Broadway, N.E., Salem, OR 97310.
Marriage	$5.00	Same as Birth or Death	Records since January 1906.
	Varies	See remarks	County Clerk in county where license was issued. County Clerks also have some records before 1906.
Divorce	$5.00	Same as birth or Death	Records since 1925.
	Varies	See remarks	County Clerk in county where divorce was granted. County Clerks also have some records before 1925.
PENNSYLVANIA			
Birth Short Form **Death**	$4.00 $5.00 $3.00	Division of Vital Statistics State Department of Health Central Building 101 South Mercer Street P.O. Box 1528 New Castle, PA 16103	State office has had records since January 1906. For earlier records, write to Register of Wills, Orphans Court, in county seat where event occurred. Persons born in Pittsburgh from 1870 to 1905 or in Allegheny City, now part of Pittsburgh, from 1882 to 1905 should write to Office of Biostatistics, Pittsburgh Health Department, City-County Building, Pittsburgh, PA 15219. For events occurring in City of Philadelphia from 1860 to 1915, write to Vital Statistics, Philadelphia Department of Public Health, City Hall Annex, Philadelphia, PA 19107.

Place of event	Cost of copy	Address	Remarks
Marriage	See remarks	Same as Birth or Death	Records since January 1941. Certified copies are not available from State Health Department. Inquiries will be forwarded to appropriate office.
	Varies	See remarks	Marriage License Clerks, County Court House, in county seat where license was issued.
Divorce	Varies	Same as Birth or Death	Records since January 1946. Certified copies are not available from State Health Department. Inquiries will be forwarded to appropriate office.
	Varies	See remarks	Prothonotary, Court House, in county seat where divorce was granted.
PUERTO RICO			
Birth or Death	$0.50	Division of Demographic Registry and Vital Statistics Department of Health San Juan, PR 00908	Central office has had records since July 22, 1931. Copies of earlier records may be obtained by writing to local Registrar (Registrador Demografico) in municipality where event occurred or by writing to central office for information.
Marriage	$0.50	Same as Birth or Death	
Divorce	$0.60	See remarks	Superior Court where divorce was granted.
RHODE ISLAND			
Birth or Death	$4.00	Division of Vital Statistics State Department of Health Room 101, Cannon Building 75 Davis Street Providence, RI 02908	State office has had records since 1853. For earlier records, write to Town Clerk in town where event occurred. Additional copies of the same record ordered at the same time are $2.00 each.
Marriage	$4.00	Same as Birth or Death	Records since January 1853. Additional copies of the same record ordered at the same time are $2.00 each.
	$4.00	See remarks	City or Town Clerk in place where marriage was performed.
Divorce	$1.00	Clerk of Family Court 1 Dorrance Plaza Providence, RI 02903	
SOUTH CAROLINA			
Birth or Death	$3.00	Office of Vital Records and Public Health Statistics S.C. Department of Health and Environmental Control 2600 Bull Street Columbia, SC 29201	State office has had records since January 1915. City of Charleston births from 1877 and deaths from 1821 are on file at Charleston County Health Department. Ledger entries of Florence City births and deaths from 1895 to 1914 are on file at Florence County Health Department. Ledger entries of Newberry City births and deaths from late 1800's are on file at Newberry County Health Department. These are the only early records obtainable.
Marriage	$3.00	Same as Birth or Death	Records since July 1950.
	Varies	See remarks	Records since July 1911. Probate Judge in county where license was issued.
Divorce	$3.00	Same as Birth or Death	Records since July, 1962.
	Varies	See remarks	Records since April 1949. Clerk of county where petition was filed.
SOUTH DAKOTA			
Birth or Death	$3.00	State Department of Health Health Statistics Program Joe Foss Office Building Pierre, SD 57501	State office has had records since July 1905 and access to other records for some events that occcurred before then. Additional copies requested at the same time are $1.00 each.
Marriage	$3.00	Same as Birth or Death	Records since July 1905. Additional copies requested at the same time are $1.00 each.

Place of event	Cost of copy	Address	Remarks
	$2.00	See remarks	County Treasurer in county where license was issued.
Divorce	$3.00	Same as Birth or Death	Records since July 1905. Additional copies requested at the same time are $1.00 each.
	Varies	See remarks	Clerk of Court in county where divorce was granted.
TENNESSEE			
Birth or Death	$3.00	Division of Vital Records State Department of Public Health Cordell Hull Building Nashville, TN, 37219	State office has had birth records for entire State since January 1914, for Nashville since June 1881, for Knoxville since July 1881, and for Chattanooga since January 1882. State office has had death records for entire State since January 1914, for Nashville since July 1874, for Knoxville since July 1887, and for Chattanooga since March 6, 1872. Birth and death enumeration records by school district are available for July 1908 through June 1912. For Memphis birth records from April 1874 through December 1887 and November 1898 to January 1, 1914, and for Memphis death records from May 1848 to January 1, 1914, write to Memphis-Shelby County Health Department, Division of Vital Records, Memphis, TN 38105.
Marriage	$3.00	Same as Birth or Death	Records since July 1945.
	Varies	See remarks	County Court Clerk in county where license was issued.
Divorce	$3.00	Same as Birth or Death	Records since July 1945.
	Varies	See remarks	Clerk of Court in county where divorce was granted.
TEXAS			
Birth or Death	$5.00	Bureau of Vital Statistics Texas Department of Health 1100 West 49th Street Austin, TX 78756	State office has had records since 1903. Additional copies of same *death* record ordered at same time are $2.00 each.
Marriage	See remarks	Same as Birth or Death	Records since January 1966. Certified copies are not available from State office. Fee for search and verification of essential facts of marriage is $1.00.
	Varies	See remarks	County Clerk in county where license was issued.
Divorce	See remarks	Same as Birth or Death	Records since January 1968. Certified copies are not available from State office. Fee for search and verification of essential facts of divorce is $1.00.
	Varies	See remarks	Clerk of District Court in county where divorce was granted.
TRUST TERRITORY OF THE PACIFIC ISLANDS			
Birth or Death	$0.25 plus $0.10 per 100 words	Director of Medical Services Department of Medical Services Saipan, Mariana Islands 96950	Clerk of Court in district where event occurred. (If not sure of district in which event occurred, write to Director of Medical Services to have inquiry referred to the correct district.) Courts have had records since November 21, 1952. Beginning 1950, a few records have been filed with the Hawaii Bureau of Vital Statistics.
Marriage	Varies	See remarks	Clerk of Court in district where marriage was performed.
Divorce	Varies	See remarks	Clerk of Court in district where divorce was granted.
UTAH			
Birth or Death	$5.00	Bureau of Health Statistics Utah Department of Health 150 West North Temple P.O. Box 2500 Salt Lake City, UT 84110	State office has had records since 1905. If event occurred from 1890 to 1904 in Salt Lake City or Ogden, write to City Board of Health. For records elsewhere in the State from 1898 to 1904, write to County Clerk in county where event occurred.

Place of event	Cost of copy	Address	Remarks
Marriage	$5.00	Same as Birth or Death	State office has had records since 1978. Only short form certified copies are available.
	Varies	See remarks	County Clerk in county where license was issued.
Divorce	$5.00	Same as Birth or Death	State office has had records since 1978. Only short form certified copies are available.
	Varies	See remarks	County Clerk in county where divorce was granted.
VERMONT			
Birth or Death	$3.00	Vermont Department of Health Vital Records Section Box 70 115 Colchester Avenue Burlington, VT 05401	Town or City Clerk of town where birth or death occurred.
Marriage	$3.00	Same as Birth or Death	
	$3.00	See remarks	Town Clerk in town where license was issued.
Divorce	$3.00	Same as Birth or Death	
VIRGINIA			
Birth or Death	$3.00	Division of Vital Records and Health Statistics State Department of Health James Madison Building P.O. Box 1000 Richmond, VA 23208	State office has had records from January 1853 to December 1896 and since June 14, 1912. For records between those dates, write to the Health Department in the city where event occurred.
Marriage	$3.00	Same as Birth or Death	Records since January 1853.
	Varies	See remarks	Clerk of Court in county or city where license was issued.
Divorce	$3.00	Same as Birth or Death	Records since January 1918.
	Varies	See remarks	Clerk of Court in county or city where divorce was granted.
VIRGIN ISLANDS (U.S.)			
Birth or Death			
St. Croix	$2.00	Registrar of Vital Statistics Charles Harwood Memorial Hospital St. Croix, VI 00820	Registrar has had birth and death records on file since 1840.
St. Thomas and St. John	$2.00	Registrar of Vital Statistics Charlotte Amalie St. Thomas, VI 00802	Registrar has had birth records on file since July 1906 and death records since January 1906.
Marriage	See remarks	Bureau of Vital Records and Statistical Services Virgin Islands Department of Health Charlotte Amalie St. Thomas, VI 00801	Certified copies are not available. Inquiries will be forwarded to appropriate office.
St. Croix	$2.00	Chief Deputy Clerk Territorial Court of the Virgin Islands P.O. Box 929 Christiansted St. Croix, VI 00820	
St. Thomas and St. John	$2.00	Clerk of the Territorial Court of the Virgin Islands P.O. Box 70 Charlotte Amalie St. Thomas, VI 00801	
Divorce	See remarks	Same as Marriage	Certified copies are not available. Inquiries will be forwarded to appropriate office.

Place of event	Cost of copy	Address	Remarks
St. Croix	$2.00	Same as Marriage	
St. Thomas and St. John	$2.00	Same as Marriage	
WASHINGTON			
Birth or Death	$3.00	Vital Records P.O. Box 9709, LB11 Olympia, WA 98504	State office has had records since July 1907. For King, Pierce, and Spokane counties copies may also be obtained from county health departments. County Auditor of county of birth has registered births prior to July 1907.
Marriage	$3.00	Same as Birth or Death	State office has had records since January 1968.
	$2.00	See remarks	County Auditor in county where license was issued.
Divorce	$3.00	Same as Birth or Death	State office has had records since January 1968.
	Varies	See remarks	County Clerk in county where divorce was granted.
WEST VIRGINIA			
Birth or Death	$2.00	Division of Vital Statistics State Department of Health State Office Building No. 3 Charleston, WV 25305	State office has had records since January 1917. For earlier records, write to Clerk of County Court in county where event occurred.
Marriage	$2.00	Same as Birth or Death	Records since 1921. Certified copies have been available since 1964.
	Varies	See remarks	County Clerk in county where license was issued.
Divorce	See remarks	Same as Birth or Death	Index since 1968. Some items may be verified (fee $2.00). Certified copies are not available from State Office.
	Varies	See remarks	Clerk of Circuit Court, Chancery Side, in county where divorce was granted.
WISCONSIN			
Birth or Death	$4.00	Bureau of Health Statistics Wisconsin Division of Health P.O. Box 309 Madison, WI 53701	State office has scattered records earlier than 1857. Records before October 1, 1907, are very incomplete. Additional copies of the same record ordered at the same time are $2.00 each.
Marriage	$4.00	Same as Birth or Death	Records since April 1836. Records before October 1, 1907, are incomplete. Additional copies of the same record ordered at the same time are $2.00 each.
Divorce	$4.00	Same as Birth or Death	Records since October 1907. Additional copies of the same record ordered at the same time are $2.00 each.
WYOMING			
Birth or Death	$2.00	Vital Records Services Division of Health and Medical Services Hathaway Building Cheyenne, WY 82002	State office has had records since July 1909.
Marriage	$2.00	Same as Birth or Death	Records since May 1941.
	Varies	See remarks	County Clerk in county where license was issued.
Divorce	$2.00	Same as Birth or Death	Records since May 1941.
	Varies	See remarks	Clerk of District Court where Divorce took place.

Where To Write for Birth and Death Records of U.S. Citizens Who Were Born or Died Outside of the United States and Birth Certifications for Alien Children Adopted by U.S. Citizens

Births Records of Persons Born in Foreign Countries Who Are U.S. Citizens at Birth

Births of U.S. citizens in foreign countries should be reported to the nearest American consular office as soon after the birth as possible on the Consular Report of Birth (Form FS-240). This report should be prepared and filed by one of the parents. However, the physician or midwife attending the birth or any other person having knowledge of the facts can prepare the report.

Documentary evidence is required to establish citizenship. Consular offices provide complete information on what evidence is needed. The Consular Report of Birth is a sworn statement of facts of birth. When approved, it establishes in documentary form the child's acquisition of U.S. citizenship. Filing a Consular Report of Birth is not authorized for children 5 years of age or older.

A $6.00 fee is charged for reporting the birth. The original document is filed in the Passport Services, Correspondence Branch, U.S. Department of State, Washington, D.C. 20524. The parents are given a certified copy of the Consular Report of Birth (Form FS-240) and a short form, Certification of Birth (Form DS-1350 or Form FS-545).

To obtain a copy of a report of the birth in a foreign country of a U.S. citizen, write to Passport Services, Correspondence Branch, U.S. Department of State, Washington, D.C. 20524. State the full name of the child at birth, date of birth, place of birth, and names of parents. Also include any information about the U.S. passport on which the child's name was first included. Sign the request and state the relationship to the person whose record is being requested and the reason for the request.

The fee for each copy is $4.00. Enclose a check or money order made payable to the U.S. Department of State.

The Department of State issues two types of copies from the Consular Report of Birth (Form FS-240):

- A full copy of Form FS-240 as it was filed.
- A short form, Certification of Birth (Form DS-1350), which shows only the name and sex of child and the date and place of birth.

The information in both forms is valid. The Certification of Birth may be obtained in a name subsequently acquired by adoption or legitimation after proof is submitted to establish that such an action legally took place.

Birth Records of Alien Children Adopted by U.S. Citizens

Birth certifications for alien children adopted by U.S. citizens and lawfully admitted to the United States may be obtained from the Immigration and Naturalization Service (INS), U.S. Department of Justice, Washington, D.C. 20536, if the birth information is on file.

Certification may be issued for children under 21 years of age who were born in a foreign country. Requests must be submitted on INS Form G-641, which can be obtained from any INS office. (Address can be found in a telephone directory.) For Certification of Birth Data (INS Form G-350), a $5.00 search fee, paid by check or money order, should accompany INS Form G-641.

Certification can be issued in the new name of an adopted or legitimated child after proof of an adoption or legitimation is submitted to INS. Because it may be issued for a child who has not yet become a U.S. citizen, this certification (Form G-350) is not proof of U.S. nationality.

Certificate of Citizenship

U.S. citizens who were born abroad and later naturalized or who were born in a foreign country to a U.S. citizen (parent or parents) may apply for a certificate of citizenship pursuant to the provisions of Section 341 of the Immigration and Nationality Act. Application can be made for this document in the United States at the nearest office of the Immigration and Naturalization Service (INS). The INS will issue a certificate of citizenship for the person if proof of citizenship is submitted and the person is within the United States. The decision whether to apply for a certificate of citizenship is optional; its possession is not mandatory.

Death Records of U.S. Citizens Who Die in Foreign Countries

Reports of deaths of U.S. citizens who die in foreign countries are made to the nearest U.S. consular office. The reports are permanently filed in the U.S. Department of State. (See exception given below.)

To obtain a copy of a report, write to Passport Services, Correspondence Branch, U.S. Department of State, Washington, D.C. 20524. The fee for a copy is $4.00.

Exception: Reports of deaths of members of the Armed Forces of the United States are made only to the branch of the service to which the person was attached at the time of death—Army, Navy, Air Force, or Coast Guard. In these cases, requests for copies of records should be directed as follows.

For members of the Army, Navy, or Air Force:

Secretary of Defense
Washington, D.C. 20301

For members of the Coast Guard:

Commandant, P.S.
U.S. Coast Guard
Washington, D.C. 20226

Records of Births and Deaths Occurring on Vessels or Aircraft on the High Seas

When a birth or death occurs on the high seas, whether in an aircraft or on a vessel, the determination of where the record is filed is decided by the direction in which the vessel or aircraft was headed at the time the event occurred.

a. If the vessel or aircraft was outbound or docked or landed at a foreign port, requests for copies of the record should be made to the U.S. Department of State, Washington, D.C. 20520.

b. If the vessel or aircraft was inbound and the first port of entry was in the United States, write to the registration authority in the city where the vessel or aircraft docked or landed in the United States.

c. If the vessel was of U.S. registry, contact the U.S. Coast Guard facility at the port of entry.

Records Maintained by Foreign Countries

Most, but not all, foreign countries record births and deaths. It is not feasible to list in this publication all foreign vital records offices, the charges they make for copies of records, or the information they may require to locate a record. However, most foreign countries will provide certifications of births and deaths occurring within their boundaries.

U.S. citizens who need a copy of a foreign birth or death record may obtain assistance by writing to the Office of Special Consular Services, U.S. Department of State, Washington, D.C. 20520.

Aliens residing in the United States who seek records of these events should contact their nearest consular office.

WORLD HISTORY

CULTURE AND CIVILIZATION

Only man is capable of producing a culture and his history is inseparable from it. **Culture (in the broadest sense of the term) is the whole of social experience—the knowledges, technics, moral codes, customs and traditions that are transmitted by human groups from generation to generation. Each social group has a unique culture, but cultural anthropologists do distinguish these common elements in culture: the basic patterns are stable but with the years change in details; culture is conservative in its ends, but flexible in its means; it is greater and more enduring than any individual within it, but is realized only through individuals; and it is transmitted by symbols in the form of language, myth, art, religion, etc.** When does a "culture" become a "civilization"? The answer to this question is quantitative. **Culture becomes civilization when it produces an economic surplus, develops mastery over the environment, and has a relatively complex economic organization, a class-system, urban communities, recognized government, systematized law, a form of writing and elevated thought and esthetic patterns.**

Tool Culture. Cultural anthropologists have learned to make a virtue of necessity. The most numerous material remains of prehistoric cultures are the tools and weapons that prevailed. Considerable information about a culture can be derived from a tool. Nor can the importance of the tool in man's development be underestimated. It sharpened his cortico-motor reflexes, developed his sense of spatial relationships, increased his creative powers, extended his muscle power, introduced his first concepts of the possible mechanization of work, expanded his speech powers in order to transmit the tool-heritage and began the important process of division of labor and specialization of work. That this is no exaggeration can be judged by examining the importance of the tool or machine in our own civilization.

THE AGES OF MAN

Tools provide us with the basis for periodizing the cultural history of mankind.

The Eolithic or Dawn Stone Age. The **Eolithic** or Dawn Stone Age covered the first half million years of proto-human history. It was the time of Java or Peking Man. Its primary tool and weapon was a multiple-purpose ealith (a stone shaped by nature and unaltered by man) which fitted the hand and could be used to stab, cut or hack. In these first days the economy was **collectional**—the gathering of berries, roots, small animals and larvae for food. There is some evidence that spoken language and control of fire appeared at the end of Eolithic—but this is not certain. Nor is there any certainty about the grouping of men. It is assumed that the family was the basic unit of social organization and that kinship groups roamed as hunting packs or herds under the leadership of the strongest and craftiest. Nothing at all is known of the clothing or type of habitation used for shelter.

The Paleolithic or Old Stone Age. Since the **Paleolithic** or the Old Stone Age extended from ca. 500,000 B.C. to 10,000 B.C., and since material remains increase abundantly as times become more recent, it has been necessary to divide Paleolithic into **Upper** which ends about 130,000 B.C.,

Middle which ends about 70,000 B.C. and **Lower** which brought the age to an end about 10,000 B.C. While Java and Peking men may have continued on from Eolithic into Paleolithic, the epoch is predominantly that of Heidelberg and Neanderthal and Cro-Magnon men. Spurred by economic and defense needs, Paleolithic men invented the **manufactured tool.** Two types of stone-tool "industries" flourished during Lower and Middle Paleolithic—the "core" and the "flake." Core tools were produced by knocking chips off a large lump of flint or volcanic glass until it was reduced to a standard form, the *coup de poing* or "fist-hatchet." Flakes were produced by the Levalloisian technique: the shape of the tool desired was etched on the core; then, by either percussion or spatula-pressure, a flake was detached; the detached pieces were then shaped to desired sharpness by chipping. Earliest Paleolithic tools were undifferentiated. Over the years, however, the core tool became a primary one, that is, designed to produce secondary or specialized tools for perforating, chopping, cutting, scraping or sawing. By the time of Upper Paleolithic, highly specialized tools appeared and took the forms of bone needles, harpoons, pronged fishhooks, dart-throwers and bows and arrows.

Advances. Tooling revolutionized the food industry of primitive men. The mode of economy now became that of fishing and hunting. The fist-hatchet made the stalking and capture of animals safer and more certain. With the invention of the sling, the dart and the bow and arrow, man could capture animals at a distance; he was now provided with a relatively permanent food supply. With the further invention of the harpoon and fishhook, an increase in the food supply took place. Mastery of fire, moreover, gave Paleolithic men a varied food diet—as well as defense, heat and light. Now began an increase in creature comforts. Paleolithic men donned sewn clothing made from animal skins; they initiated the permanent residence, first in caves and then in crudely constructed shelters; and their men and women began to ornament themselves with beads, necklaces and pendants.

Cultural Advances. During Paleolithic, the family grouping of men expanded into larger kinship groups tracing their origin, either matri- or patrilinearly, from a common ancestor. Out of this kinship grouping came the first cultural institutions—economic, political, educational and religious. Men assumed all the duties of the hunt; women concerned themselves with the collectional and household manufacturing activities. Government was probably concerned with the maintenance of internal peace; and the mightiest hunters and the older men probably arbitrated conflicts, enforced taboos and distributed food equitably. Protection of the hunting lands turned the hunters, on occasion, into warriors. All strangers were, therefore, suspect. But good relations existed among neighboring groups of necessity. Often flint supplies gave out and had to be secured outside the locality by trade; or animals were forced by sudden climatic change to new grazing lands; or population decline caused by an imbalance of males and females may have threatened the survival of the group.

Education was for individual survival. Until puberty the child's education was in the hands of the women of the family. Thereafter, men took over the boy's training. He now underwent a severe initiation which included fasting, keeping long vigils and even mutilation; he was instructed in proper behavior to people and to things in the world about him; finally, he was taught to hunt safely and efficiently. Religious guidance was fundamental to the education of both girls and boys for there were many prescriptions and proscriptions to be heeded. Remains of burial and funerary practices make clear that late in Paleolithic men began to experience religious thought and feeling. It would seem that their religious outlook included concepts of a soul or spirit belonging to each individual, and of its persistence after death. Natural forces were regarded as being motivated by a mysterious, supernatural power or "mana." Later this undifferentiated supernatural force took the shape of spirits or ghosts present unseen, everywhere, and in all things in the universe (**animism**). These spirits or ghosts were capable, as was perfectly obvious from the great insecurity in which men lived, of inflicting great harm unless propitiated. To placate these unseen powers, paleolithic men introduced religious rites. They carved female figurines as symbols of fertility with exaggerated sexual organs and worshipped them. They invented sympathetic magic or the practice of destroying an enemy by first mutilating his spirit resident in some effigy of him. They warded off evil by wearing amulets and talismans of beads or pendants. Finally, they created a class of professional religious practitioners called **shamans** who were possessed of powers of healing, divining and casting magical spells.

Though he accepted fully a supernatural explanation of the world of nature, paleolithic man was a close observer of things that mattered most to him. This was evident in his art work. For example, on the walls of caves he carved and painted reproductions of the animals which his band hunted—bison, mammoth, stags, reindeer, wolves. The realism, the naturalistic modeling, the use of light and dark masses, the employment of harmonious or agitated rhythms, the rigorous attention to detail, the ability to suppress detail to create a center of interest, the accuracy and sureness of drawing, the arresting of movement and action, the use of polychromatic effects—any or all of these characteristics of Cro-Magnon art establish the paleolithic artist as a very accomplished one. Nor was his skill limited to murals. He decorated his tools with small sculptures that never interfered with the function of the tool and made etchings that again illustrate his sense of realistic design. Paleolithic art was unquestionably functional in that it served the purposes of sympathetic magic; it was a form of religious ritual. But its esthetic values are timeless and universal.

The Neolithic or New Stone Age. Neolithic men exhausted the possibilities of stone technology. Since surface flint deposits were nearly depleted by 10,000 B.C., a mining industry was begun. Shafts were sunk and chalk veins were tapped with deerhorn picks for the flint they might yield. When required, Neolithic men burrowed long transverse tunnels in their mine pits. All tools were highly specialized now. In addition they were smoothed down to fine cutting edges on whetstones. Handles were attached to all chopping tools and they assumed distinctively modern appearances.

Toolmaking did not account for the profound revolution which occurred during the Neolithic Age. Discovery of agriculture and the domestication of animals did. When or how these two epoch-making discoveries took place is not known. There is some evidence for the prevailing belief that women first hit upon the art of cultivation; for many years it was they who farmed the land with picks, digging sticks and hoes while the men continued to hunt and fish. Domestication of animals lessened the need to hunt and fish and permitted the man to settle down as a cultivator.

What were the effects of this agricultural revolution? Permanent settlements along river valleys made their appearance; men experienced with new forms of durable housing—mud and thatch affairs or lake dwellings on high piles. Diets were enriched with large varieties of grains, fruits and vegetables; where rivers overflowed, large scale drainage and irrigation projects were begun; grain surpluses led to increased trade and this, in turn, effected a revolution in transportation on land and water—the wheeled vehicle and the sail were invented. Mankind developed new, civilized habits—a sense of property ownership, patience, industry and planning; soil-rootedness made him conscious of the seasons and the stars; new scientific curiosities led him to inventions such as pottery (for storage and cooking purposes) from baked clay, stone mills to grind grain, etc.

Animals continued, of course, to serve as sources of food, but they also provided man with a new source of motive power, new supplies of raw materials for textiles and a new means of transportation. Because of the availability of animals, plows and wheeled carts were invented; the textile industries of spinning and weaving took root. Civilization, clearly, was beginning to take shape.

Social reorganization followed upon economic revolution. Population increased rapidly and lived longer as the result of more abundant and more reliable food supplies. Though kinship grouping persisted in Neolithic times, it had become a fiction; the reality was the large tribe centered in a fixed locality. Tribal organization took on concrete form. Members of the tribe delegated to either strong men or elders authority to adjudicate an increasing number of disputes over property rights, to interpret tradition in changing circumstances, to defend the village against raids by hungry nomads, etc. This delegation of authority was the rudiment of formal government. Near the end of Neolithic times, representative governments gave way to absolute monarchies, out of necessity. An increase in the number, intensity and dire consequences of war was directly responsible. A lost war resulted in either annihilation, dispersal, subjugation or slavery. To prevent this, Neolithic groups submitted themselves to the authoritative leadership of war-chiefs.

Neolithic men carried religious belief forward from its state of a generalized animism to that of **polytheism.** The vague spirits of Paleolithic belief now became numerous specific gods possessing immortal but human or anthropomorphic personalities. These gods resided in stones, animals, springs, trees, caves and mountains. Methods for appeasing angry gods proliferated and took the forms of human sacrifice, animal slaughter, self-mutilation or torture, sacramental sexual relations or ritual cannibalism. Belief in an after-life also grew more concrete. Burials as a result became more elaborate: chambered tombs were constructed above the graves; into the tombs were piled furniture, weapons, clothing and food for the spirit of the departed. The first form of temple worship was that of worship at monumental stone structures—dolmens or trilithons (two upright stones with a covering slab, post-and-lintel style); or just megaliths, tremendous stones set individually in long rows (some were 70 feet high!); or cromlechs, like the famous one at Stonehenge, England, combining dolmens and megaliths in a circle.

Art declined during the Neolithic Age. Naturalism disappeared and was replaced by abstract representations of concentric lines, zigzags, spirals, dots and chevrons which were scratched or painted as decorative motifs on pottery.

ANCIENT EGYPT

The Land. As history recedes into the remoter past, geography emerges as a dominating, if not quite the dominant, factor. Ancient Egypt was, to a considerable extent, the product of a river, cataracts, delta and desert. "Egypt," said the Greek historian, HERODOTUS, "is the gift of a river." It lay along the Nile and annually that river overflowed to provide Egypt with the only moisture it had and with rich deposits of alluvial soil. Egypt proved equal to the challenge and evolved political, economic and social institutions that enabled her to capture, store and distribute the floodwaters. Canals, dikes and reservoirs appeared early in the history of civilization. The cataracts were in the southern Nilotic waters and created a natural boundary there which acted as a barrier both to expansion and invasion. The desert, too, was a formidable barrier. Geography kept Egypt at peace for centuries. The mouth of the Nile spread into a fertile delta; this region made Egypt the granary of the ancient world and gave her a valuable trading link to the Mediterranean world when she finally emerged from her isolation.

Predynastic Egypt. No written records exist from the period prior to the first families of **pharaohs** (called **dynasties**). Excavations reveal, however, that predynastic Egyptians had made important strides toward civilization. Stone was being abandoned for copper, and Egyptians had already mastered the art of smelting and casting this metal. As a people, the Egyptians were racially mixed, lived in villages as farmers and animal herders, fashioned stone, wood and copper tools, decorated pottery and wove linen goods. They had reclaimed swamplands and had begun local irrigation projects. Political units called **nomes** existed and were ruled by local nomarchs. Powerful nomarchs had effected early union of Upper and Lower Egypt. Some form of preternatural belief existed, for the dead were buried in graves along with their implements and with symbolic figurines.

THE PERSIANS

Persia lay on the Iranian plateau stretching eastward from the Tigris River to the Indus River. About 1800 B.C. an Aryan-speaking people occupied the northeastern edge of this plateau. For centuries they were subject to the rule of the Elamites; but Ashurbanipal, the Assyrian, devastated Elam and its capital at Susa (ca. 640 B.C.). When the Assyrians were destroyed in turn, the Medes under Cyaxeres (625–593 B.C.) took over the former Elamite Kingdom. But the Persians now made their bid for power. In 550 B.C. CYRUS THE GREAT took over the Median Kingdom and then continued westward to conquer Lydia and Chaldea. Cyrus's son, Cambyses (530–521 B.C.) added the Egyptian Empire to the Persian. At this point, the empire of the Persians was the largest of all those of the ancient world.

Darius I (521–485 B.C.) added little new territory to this vast empire but devoted his high intelligence to organizing it for efficient administration. His basic principle of organization was centralization through the monarch. Thus he built for himself four capitals with royal residences at Susa, Persepolis, Ecbatana and Babylon. These were interconnected with modernized highways over which flowed normal trade, postal communication and military patrols. The King made a regular circuit of his capitals and while in each he disposed of accumulated local problems. Reporting to him regularly were twenty *satraps* or governors appointed by and responsible solely to himself. (The empire had been divided into twenty *satrapies* or administrative divisions.) Each governor was responsible for the imperial tax and the army levies. In all other matters local autonomy was permitted and everywhere native cultures were tolerated. (Under the Persians, for example, the Hebrews were permitted to return from Babylon to Palestine.) But, to guarantee efficiency and to ward off the evils of bureaucratic corruption, the King appointed official spies known as "The King's eyes and the King's ears" who traveled about the empire incognito and reported back to the King the evils they observed or heard about. The Persian government itself was an absolute hereditary monarchy "by the grace of Ahura-Mazda." There were important limitations on the King's absolutism: he was expected to consult with the nobility, to base his law-making upon the Law of the Medes and the Persians and to be guided by precedents in the law. This was the empire that persisted in the Middle East until 333 B.C. It received its first important setback at the hands of the Greeks at the Battle of Marathon in 490 B.C.; and it was destroyed by Alexander the Great. Its influence, however, continued long after its demise.

CRETE

Between Persia and Ancient Greece lay the Aegean Sea and around that sea there flourished a number of civilizations which became transitional to the Greek. Earliest of these was the **Minoan** civilization which flourished on the island of Crete and which was revealed to the modern world by the brilliant excavations about 1900 (A.D.) of SIR ARTHUR EVANS. Knowledge of the Minoan civilization is still limited because its language is still undeciphered; what is known is due to archaeological discoveries. From these it is known that Minoan civilization flourished between 3000 and 1200 B.C. In this period, they dominated the Mediterranean sea with their trade and military power.

Their power was manifest in the mighty cities which they built at Cnossus and Phaestus on the island itself. Cnossus, for example, was dominated by the king's palace which was at least two stories high, contained a maze of living rooms, store rooms, workshops, offices, etc., was equipped with plumbing that provided running water and efficient sewage. Attached to the palace were factories which turned out articles for export—pottery, textiles and metal goods.

Unearthed figurines indicate that Minoan worship centered about a snake goddess, a symbol of fertility and of destruction. The dead were buried with their implements of war and livelihood; gods were appeased by sacrifice. There were, however, no temples. Minoan murals are exceptionally revealing: they show the people as unusually sports-loving and engaging in bull fights, boxing, races, etc. Women held an exceptionally high position; they play and work side by side with the men. All this is shown by the archaeological record. This record also reveals that about 1400 B.C. Minoan civilization took root in northwestern Asia Minor about the site of Troy and in a group of Greek islands centered about Mycenae on the mainland. Similar pottery, artistic design and "beehive" tombs prove this. Esthetic analysis of Mycenaean remains, however, shows that the creative flame was gone by 1400 B.C. Minoan art, at its height, is a rare combination of naturalism and spontaneity combined with exquisite delicacy; Mycenaean art is derivative and dull by comparison. The Minoan artist was master of the miniature: the figurine, the painted dagger, jewelry, inlay; Mycenaean is large and crude by comparison. The real influence of the Minoan Cretans was not upon the rough Trojans and Mycenaeans but upon those that conquered them, the ancient Greeks of Dorian and Ionian stock.

Greece

ORIGINS

Greek civilization did not spring full-blown from the soil of Greece. It took a millenium before the Greeks cast off their original barbarism. The earliest Greeks lived in the valley of the Danube; they spoke a common Indo-European tongue. By 2000 B.C., however, their language had become differentiated enough to enable us to divide them into Achaeans, Aeolians, Ionians, Illyrians, Boetians, Dorians, etc. About that time, too, they were uprooted from their homeland and began a folk-wandering southward into the Balkan peninsula; they came, that is, as conquerors.

The first to enter may have been the Achaean Hellenes (ca. 2000 B.C.). Over a period of 700 years these people filtered into central and southern Greece and then into the Aegean islands. They seem to have assimilated with the indigenous Greeks, and absorbed their superior culture; but they imposed upon them the Achaean language and rule. Ionians are found in western Greece as early as 1500 B.C. They, too, settled down, absorbed and assimilated with the natives. But about 1300 B.C. a barbarous tribe of Illyrians swept down into Thessaly and uprooted the Achaeans and the Ionians and forced them to scatter into the remoter regions of the peninsula and overseas to Asia Minor. It is quite likely that this upheaval, rather than the legendary kidnapping of Helen, brought the Achaeans under Agamemnon into collision with the Trojans in Asia Minor. This Illyrian conquest was followed by an even more devastating **Dorian invasion** which re-scattered the Achaeans and Ionians. After 1000 B.C. the invasions ended and Greece entered a period of incubation.

Invasion and dispersion were not without positive results. The decadent remnants of Minoan-Mycenean culture were destroyed, paving way for a new culture; the Greek nation differentiated into varied and conflicting types each occupying a fixed territory, and this spurred the growth of individualism; Greek culture became Mediterranean rather than Balkan; overseas, the Greeks came into contact with the civilizing ways of the Near East; and passage over the seas required that the Greeks become "maritime-minded" and oriented to a life of trade and commerce.

The Land. Trade and commerce were vital preconditions for the development of Greek civilization for the Balkan peninsula was a singularly barren land. Criss-crossing mountain ranges covered two-thirds of the land surface; arable plains made up a bare one-sixth. The rivers were non-navigable and varied between winter flood and summer dry-bed. Lakes were rare and inclined, because of poor drainage, to become malarial swampland. Scrubby pasture supported meager flocks of sheep and goats. Deforestation was acute; and there were only thin veins of metals basic to the ancient civilizations—gold, silver, lead, iron and copper. The historian HERODOTUS defined it accurately when he said that poverty was foster-sister to the Greeks. But while geography was, in the main, a barrier to civilization, it did open some opportunities. For example, there were rich deposits of stone and marble and potter's clay; natural harbors abounded along the eastern shore; the Aegean islands were natural stepping-stones to the Asiatic mainland and by occupying them, the Greeks made the Aegean Sea into a Grecian Lake.

The "Homeric" Greeks. Homer's *Iliad* and *Odyssey* are timeless masterpieces of epic poetry; they qualify as such by every standard of literary criticism—by clear, vivid and natural diction; by **epithets** that serve as haunting refrains and impress the *dramatis personae* upon the memory; by an **"heroic" meter, the hexameter;** by suspenseful beginnings *in media res* (in the middle of things) to avoid tedious or interruptive background material; by the music of their language; and by their wide range of human emotions, their varieties of style to fit the scenes, their plenitude of imagery and matchless rhetoric. They are "things of beauty," of "Attic shapes" in motion and as such their influence has not waned in the 2800 years of their lives. In a study of Greek and Roman influences on western civilization (*The Classical Tradition*), Gilbert Highet was compelled to make more than 250 references to Homer's epics. Here we can do no more than note Homer's literary impact. Our interest must be in what he revealed about the "dark age" in the preliterary history of Greece.

Homer's interest was in his own past; but he

was unable to escape his present. So, from between his lines, we are able to piece out that part of Greek history which is called the **"Homeric Age."**

Primitive Society. Homer's Greeks lived in a relatively primitive society. Their methods of wealth-gathering centered upon crude agriculture, herding and plundering on land and sea. Technologically they had passed from the Bronze to the threshold of the Iron Age. Some specialization of craft had begun for the epics speak of **freemen** who were smiths, potters, saddlers, masons, carpenters and cabinetmakers. Costlier goods, however—objects of art, weapons, fancy raiment and gold beakers—seen to have been imported. Trading was very limited and conducted by means of primitive barter. There was no coinage and wealth was estimated in flocks. The ox served as a medium of exchange. Most manufactured goods were produced in the home by slaves with the assistance of their masters and mistresses.

Private ownership, as an institution, had not yet appeared; landed property was owned by the family with the father as chief administrator. While the father could determine the use of the land, he could not sell it. He had to transmit it, by the common law of **primogeniture,** to his eldest son who became head of the household upon his father's death. The family unit was patriarchal; it was, in fact, a patriarchal despotism for the father could, if he wished, take concubines for himself or offer them to his guests, or commit infanticide, or slaughter his children as sacrifices to the gods. Fathers, however, rarely employed such practices. Homeric families are, for the most part, monogamous; intimacy and affection exist between husband and wife and between father and children; the position of the woman in the household is high and free even though marriage was by purchase. (Women were to lose this high status as Greek society developed.)

Homeric men could and did commit unspeakable barbarities upon one another; but concepts of a common humanity tempered their crudities. They are never far from tenderness, sentiment and tears; deep friendships are common; they show rare hospitality to strangers for they bathe them, clothe them, wine-dine-and lodge them, and then send them off with gifts; slaves have a rare position of equality in the household. On the other hand, they are never far from what we would consider immoralities either. Women are offered as prizes in athletic contests; wanton, cruel sacrifices are made upon funeral pyres; slavery and concubinage follow upon conquest; piracy is an honorable profession and pillage a necessary one; they admire unabashed lying, deceit and treachery. This was their response to an insecure world in which human life was cheap; to survive, a man must have the qualities of Ares, the God of War—strength, guile and deception. Fair was foul, and foul was fair. (These, in fact, are among Odysseus' most conspicuous traits.)

Politics. Political institutions were equally primitive though considerably advanced over Oriental forms as no divine-right absolute monarch existed in Homeric Greece. There was a **basileus or dynastic king** who served as commander in chief, high priest and chief justice. He was, however, a chief among equals. His equals were a landed aristocracy who claimed, as did the basileus, divine descent. They met on important occasions as a council and through this agency they checked any exercise of arbitrary power by the basileus. Within the council the nobility enjoyed complete freedom of speech. As a further check on absolutism there existed an assembly of all freemen who could, in a crisis of war or peace, approve or reject proposals made by the king or nobles. Government was completely decentralized; the power of the king extended, on a "feudal" basis, only as far as his noble retainers obeyed him. For example, while his anger was upon him and he did not choose to fight, Achilles ignored every demand and plea to do so made by King Agamemnon. There was no fixed law but custom; justice was administered by the family-feud—though there is some evidence that justice by trial was beginning to take root.

Religion. Homeric Greeks conceived the ideas that they lived on an earth that was a flat disk floating on Oceanus. Above them was the solid dome of heaven kept aloft by Atlas. Around them the seas abounded with marvels and foreign lands with freaks. Natural forces resulted from the actions of unseen gods who dwelt on Mt. Olympus. Gods were distinguished from men only by their immortality and their extraordinary powers; otherwise they had the shape of humans and all of the virtues and vices of mankind. They fought, feasted, made love, played tricks, lied, deceived, made music, roared with laughter, fell in love with mortals and produced thereby generations of illegitimate progeny. They were, indeed, a capricious lot and therefore had to be cajoled, persuaded or "bought off" by prayers, votive offerings and sacrifices. The head of each Greek family was qualified to conduct these religious rites and therefore there were, among the Homerics, no temples, no organized priesthood. Relations between these Greeks and their gods were earthbound for the Greeks seemed not to believe in underworld ghosts, or spirits, or, in fact, in any last judgment and afterlife punishment. Hence they had only the most rudimentary sense of sin. Life was to be lived on earth and religious devotion was centered upon extending it as long as possible with the aid of favoring gods or by outwitting unfavoring ones through developing the gift of prophecy or omen-reading.

THE WARS OF ANCIENT GREECE

The Greek nations were forced to fight their way to freedom because they were caught between the Persian Empire expanding westward from Asia Minor and Carthage expanding eastward from North Africa. The Persian menace first struck the Ionian Greeks who were resident in Asia Minor; by 546 B.C. Cyrus had subdued all the Greek cities there. Mainland Greece was now faced with the possibility that the Persians would cross over the Hellespont into Europe. Already the Persians were seeking to dominate the sea trade on the Mediterranean. When, therefore, Aristagoras in 499 B.C. led the Ionian cities in revolt against DARIUS, Athens risked the fury of the Persians by sending them naval assistance; Sparta refused to send aid. Darius gathered tremendous land and naval forces for an assault on Greece itself.

The Persians first landed at **Marathon** (490 B.C.). This direct threat to the independence of all the Greeks failed to unify them; the Athenian army was left to face the Persians alone. Under the military leadership of Miltiades and Callimachus the Persians were routed and driven into the sea. The results of this victory were immense: it showed that the Persians were not invincible; it delayed a second Persian attack for ten years; it began the Athenian leadership of Greece; it spelled the end of the tyranny as a form of government (for the Persians were fostering this form on the Ionian shore); it inspired the great classics of Aeschylus and Herodotus; it ensured that "western civilization" as opposed to "oriental civilization" would prevail in Europe. Of more immediate value, it forced the Greek cities to unite against the certainty of the second attack.

This attack came in 480 B.C. XERXES, the son of Darius, had gathered a force of 200,000 men for the attack and had selected **Thermopylae** as the battleground. LEONIDAS made his immortal stand against the Persians here and delayed them long enough to permit the evacuation of Athens. The Greeks were unable to prevent the destruction of Athens; nor did they make strenuous efforts to defeat the Persians on land. Greek strategy was to achieve a decisive victory on the sea. They met the Persians, as planned, at Salamis and wiped out the Persian fleet and army there. On the same day Persia's Carthaginian allies were routed. One year later, at Platea, the Persians were defeated on land and driven out of Europe.

The Peloponnesian Wars (431–404 B.C.) The unity finally achieved in the war against the Persians did not last. Capitalizing upon her leadership, Athens, in 478 B.C., organized the **Delian League,** a confederacy of about 200 city-states; then, led by Themistocles and Aristides, Athens converted this League into an imperialist grab-bag for herself. She intervened by occupation and threat of occupation in the internal affairs of the League members; she forced them to pay a tribute to Athens for "protection"; she dominated all their commercial activities. Athenian imperialism forced Sparta, in alliance with Corinth, to take steps against the possible loss of their own independence by strengthening the Peloponnesian League.

Thus matters stood when Pericles came to power in Athens. Democratic at home, Pericles pursued an aggressive imperialist policy abroad; he broke a long-standing alliance with Sparta; he allied with the enemies of Sparta and Corinth (Argos, the landed nobility of Thessaly, Megara, etc.); he helped a group of rebellious helots to colonize in Athenian territory; he began a policy to drive Corinthian trade out of the Aegean. Anticipating the reaction of the Spartans, Pericles completed the fortification of Athens by building the Long Walls connecting Athens with the port of Peiraeus, a distance of four and a half miles.

These preparations were made none too soon for in 431 B.C. Sparta and her allies declared war on Athens. The war lasted 27 years. It was featured, as Thucydides pointed out, by "calamities such as Hellas had never known."

After years of stalemate, the Athenians were

defeated at **Syracuse** in the west (413 B.C.) and ultimately at Athens in 404 B.C. The results of the Peloponnesian wars were calamitous in the extreme: the great age of Athens ended; Spartan hegemony was destroyed by the city-state of Thebes under the leadership of Epaminondas; war and confusion prepared the way for a new power rising in the north and readying itself to spring southward.

THE RISE OF MACEDONIA

Philip. At the beginning of the fourth century B.C. Macedonia was a semi-barbarian state on the northern fringe of Greece. PHILIP came to the Macedonian throne in 359 B.C. As a youth he had been taken as a hostage to Grecian Thebes; there he learned to hold Greek culture in great reverence and to disdain Greek politics, which had deteriorated.

Philip, it seems, determined to save Greece from itself by a liberating Macedonian conquest. He would unite her under his single rule and spread her culture abroad. His policy of conquest was to be by devious political fracturing of whatever Greek unity existed and then by direct military assault. With this goal before him, he developed a powerful army and seized the gold mines of Grecian Amphipolis. When the opportunity presented itself he entered a "sacred war" against Phocis on the side of ruling Thebes and this netted him Greek citizenship and a place on the Amhyctyonic Council.

At this time, only one Greek saw through Philip's maneuvering—DEMOSTHENES, and in his **"Philippics"** he warned of conquest to come and urged unity—military and political—upon the Greek city-states. His passionate and eloquent words went unheeded, even laughed at—Philip was such a cultured gentleman who lived so far away! With this advantage Philip defeated Olynthus and neutralized Athens herself. Against the advice of Demosthenes Athens permitted Macedonia to cooperate with her in a second "sacred war" against Amphissa. In the course of this campaign Philip took over all of central Greece. Thoroughly alarmed, Athens and Thebes permitted Demosthenes to organize a counter-Macedonian **Pan-Hellenic League**—which Philip crushed. He was now sole ruler in Greece. His policy toward the conquered Greeks was one of firm kindness; he even offered them an honored place in an expedition against the Persians that he was now planning. But in 336 B.C. he was murdered. His son Alexander succeeded.

Alexander. ALEXANDER THE GREAT was tutored by the great Greek philosopher Aristotle; and no more thoughtful world conqueror ever existed. Better than most, Alexander knew and appreciated the glory of Greek culture. But he knew that no Greek was safe from barbarian conquest until Greece had conquered all the world. He brought all his genius for military tactics, propaganda and political strategy to bear upon the realization of this goal.

First, Alexander crushed an uprising of Spartans in Greece itself; then, with half his army he went to meet the Persians in Asia Minor. He met them at Granicus in 334 B.C. and at Issus in 333 B.C. and routed them each time. Choosing not to pursue Darius, Alexander turned south and subdued the Phoenican coast; he then descended deeper into Egypt. Here his purpose was revealed fully for he launched a huge public works program to restore all things Egyptian and then recruited thousands of Greek intellectuals and workingmen to build for him a huge Greek city in Egypt itself; this city became **Alexandria,** the first cosmopolitan city in the world, a meeting-place for people from all over the world.

This done, Alexander now returned to meet Darius who had regrouped and enlarged his armed forces until they far outnumbered Alexander's; at Arbela, in 331 B.C., Darius was defeated again. Though Darius escaped, he was murdered by his own men; Alexander then assumed for himself the Persian title of the "Great King." He took over Persia's capitals and its treasuries; he assumed Oriental mannerisms and even his Macedonians had to now prostrate themselves before him. In pursuit of the murders of Darius Alexander now pushed on to conquer Bactria and India; but exhaustion had set in.

Alexander moved on to Babylon, where he contracted the swamp fever and died. He was thirty-three years old; but in his brief lifetime he had changed the face of the world. Alexander's empire died with him. PTOLEMY, a follower, seized Egypt and instituted a pharaonic rule; Seleucus took Syria and the lands of the Persian Empire; Greece degenerated into an internecine war between an Aetolian League and an Achaean League and Macedonia. The world awaited a new unifier and a new peace. In Italy one such was coming slowly to life and power.

Though chaos succeeded Alexander's efforts, what his conquest accomplished was incalculable. He broke down the barriers which had persisted for three millenia between Oriental and Occidental; out of the intermixture of cultures came a new, brilliant Hellenistic civilization; hieroglyphic and cuneiform fell to superiority of the Greek tongue; release of the Persian treasures stimulated trade and commerce to new heights; trade lanes now began to extend from the Pacific Ocean to the Atlantic; new cities grew up and old ones were revitalized all along the trade lanes. He had decisively altered his world.

Rome

THE BASES OF ROMAN CIVILIZATION

Geography. The mountains of Italy were not obstacles to political unification as were those of Greece; while precipitous, they terminated in the broad plains of Latium—large and fertile areas capable of intensive cultivation. The Appenines, however, forced the Romans to face westward, away from the civilizations of the eastern Mediterranean; and this gave the Romans the isolation they needed for independent development. Italy's peninsular form made it inevitable that, when able, the Romans would concentrate upon domination of the Mediterranean Sea. The open land areas, the easy invasion of Italy from northern lands and surrounding seas, forced the Romans on the defensive from their earliest days; militarism became synonymous with survival. Finally, the situation of Rome itself atop seven hills commanding the Tiber River gave her a powerful position on the peninsula.

People. The original Italian peoples are lost in the mists of the past. When the Romans emerged they were a linguistic, cultural and racial mixture of Samnites, Umbrians, Latins, Gauls, Greeks and Etruscans. Greek influence was particularly strong; but most profound was that of the **Etruscans,** an Oriental people whose high civilization was absorbed by the Romans. The earliest Romans were subject for many years to the overlordship of these Etruscans. Etruscan practices of many kinds seeped into Roman life and remained long after the Etruscans themselves had vanished.

Political Institutions. Because they began as a conquered people under absolute monarchy, the Romans created political institutions to defend themselves from the exercise of arbitrary power. When they became a free people, they placed supreme power in the hands of two political bodies —the **Assembly** and the **Senate.** The Assembly included all male citizens of military age. It was basically a ratifying body and as such had an absolute veto on executive decrees in matters of war, peace and justice. The Senate was a council of elders whose membership derived from traditional clans. Senators comprised, for the most part, a conservative, landowning aristocracy; they were charged with choosing successors to the monarchy and with safeguarding the **law of custom** from invasion by either the King or the Assembly. Such were the **checks and balances** that characterized the Roman government when it began its independent existence in 509 B.C.—the year the Etruscan kings were finally expelled.

Socio-Economic Institutions. The family was the basic unit in primitive Roman society. Its sole legal personality was the *pater* (father) who had the power of life and death within the family. Custom and the position of the Roman matron acted as restraints on the absolutism of this *paterfamilias.* The social group was separated by rigid class divisions: there were **patricians** or large landowners of noble birth, a privileged class who served in the Senate, monopolized army offices, and conducted public religious ceremonials. Then there were the **plebeians,** a free citizenry drawn from the the small farming and artisan classes. They served in the Assembly and enjoyed the right of trading, property holding, and judicial self-defense. But they were barred from entry into the Senate, they could not intermarry with the patricians, and had no recorded bill of rights. **Clients** or tenant farmers and slaves completed the class structure; they were without freedom or rights.

Religion. Religion cemented Romans of all classes. There were no priestly castes; religion was related to civic activities. However, specialists in religious knowledge did exist: *haruspices* who inspected the vital organs of sacrificed animals; *augurs* who interpreted omens.

Household and farm deities predominated: Janus, the Spirit of the Doorway; Vesta, The Spirit of the Hearth; the Penates, the Guardians of Household Stores; the Lares, The Guardians of Family Property; and the Genius or Guardian Spirit.

Religious devotion was quite materialistic: it was based on bargaining and contracting with the gods and such bargains and contracts were enforced by law, duty and taboo. Late in the monarchical period national gods made their appearance: **Jupiter,** the sky-god and chief over all; **Juno,** Jupiter's spouse and protector of matrons; **Minerva,** the artisan's divinity; and **Mars,** god of war. With national deities asserting themselves, the gods left the Roman household and entered into temples; worship became cultish.

The Roman Ideal. Where the Greeks found their ideal within themselves, the Romans looked back to their founding ancestors for theirs. For it seemed to Romans that these founders were worthy of worship. They had set the ideal of "sterling integrity, stern dignity, stoic endurance, rugged simplicity, hard economy and sturdy industry" for all posterity. They were unselfish patriots, austere puritans, practical utilitarians—without philosophy, imagination or culture.

FROM CITY-STATE TO NATION-STATE

From 509 to 265 B.C. the small city-state of Rome expanded its dominion until it was master of the whole Italian peninsula. This 250 year expansion was piecemeal and resulted from the efforts of the Romans to make themselves defensively secure against hostile neighbors and to solve their problem of a landless population at the expense of their neighbors.

The Fifth Century B.C. Etruscan power declined steadily during the fifth century B.C. and released a large number of Italian tribes for war and expansion. Rome was threatened by engulfment by any one or all of them. Cities in Latium had formed a **Latin League** and were pressing upon Rome. After many years of defensive battling, Rome brought the Latin League to terms by a tremendous victory at **Lake Regillus** (486 B.C.). Members of the Latin League were forced into an offensive-defensive alliance with Rome, an alliance that held for 150 years in wars against the Etruscans, the Aequi, and the Volsci. Aggressive advances by the northern Sabellians had set the Aequi and Volsci in motion against Rome. Under the leadership of CORIOLANUS the Aequi were vanquished; and under that of CINCINNATUS, the Volsci. Momentarily secure on her farther borders, Rome attacked and eliminated an Etruscan stronghold at Veli—twelve miles to her North across the Tiber. This latter victory enabled Rome to double her territory and to emerge as the leader of the Latin League.

The Fourth Century B.C. The fourth century B.C. opened with a disastrous invasion by barbarous **Gauls** which ended in the sack of Rome and the impoverishment of its people. Under Camillius the Romans painfully rebuilt their razed city, built strong walls around it, reorganized their army into more flexible units, introduced iron weapons, and revised their requirements for Roman citizenship.

Chastened and strengthened, the Romans were occupied for most of the rest of the century with eliminating the strong threat of the Samnites, war-like mountaineers who were threatening Rome's fertile lands in Campania. A victory over the Samnites had the effect of stirring Rome's allies in the Latin League to attack her; she was becoming too big and powerful for the security of other Italian states on the peninsula. But Rome defeated their combined effort. The Latin League was dissolved; its cities were isolated by separate treaties; some were made colonies; others were given a suffrageless Roman citizenship.

Rome became the capital of all Latium and the protector of all under her dominion. Colonies of Roman citizens were settled within the conquered territories to relieve the pressure of the landless upon Rome's land. The Samnites, defeated but not conquered, now (327 B.C.) attempted to organize all of the conquered people into a federation for independence. To meet this new threat, Appius

Claudius made further reforms in the army, built a navy, broadened the base for both military and tax levies, and constructed the first of the great Roman military highways (**The Appian Way**). The result was the complete defeat of the Samnites and their allies at the Battle of **Sentium** (296 B.C.). All Italy was within the grasp of the Romans.

The Conquest of Italy. The remainder of Italy was taken in the third century B.C. This was southern Italy where Greek cities predominated. When war between the Greek cities and Rome threatened, the city of Tarentum called upon King Pyrrhus of Epirus (in Greece) for aid. Pyrrhus responded and at Heraclea (280 B.C.) won a bitter and costly victory—hence the phrase "Pyrrhic victory." Pyrrhus's advantage came from the use of terror-spreading elephant cavalry. Rome now allied with her powerful North African neighbor, Carthage, in a defensive alliance against Pyrrhus. By 275 B.C. Pyrrhus was forced to leave Italy, and Tarentum fell; all of southern Italy now succumbed. Rome occupied Italy from the toe to the Po River.

Why Rome Conquered. Many reasons are given for Rome's success. Her enemies were disunited and Rome's policy of divide and rule was effective; Rome's allies were weakened by continual wars with *Rome's* enemies; Roman statesmen kept internal strife at a minimum by generous land grants, liberal division of the spoils of war and extension of democratic rights. Rome's victims were forced to place their armies at her disposal. Highway trunklines were built with each new conquest, colonies and garrisons were placed at all strategic outposts, bilateral treaties militated against new combinations against Rome.

Most important, however, was the use made of Roman citizenship.

Conquered peoples fell into four classes: **citizens, municipia, Latin Allies** and **Italian Allies.**

Roman citizens had full rights and privileges of citizenship.

Municipia had Roman citizenship *without* suffrage rights; they enjoyed local autonomy and the rights of trade; they served in the army and paid taxes.

The Latin Allies had no citizenship but still enjoyed the rights of trade; they furnished Rome with foreign legions and had some local autonomy.

The Italian Allies were Roman protectorates; they sent troop levies to Rome, levies that were supported at Roman expense and shared in the war booty.

Though the bulk of the Italians thus lost their independence, were bound to do Roman military service and had to pay numerous special taxes to their Roman rulers, Roman rule brought them many advantages: a *pax Romana* (Roman peace), an end to inter-tribal warfare, defense against external aggression, partial freedom and the possibility of full citizenship, economic unity, the use of Roman public works (aqueducts, roads, bridges, etc.) and a share in the new prestige that Rome had won for Italy.

Effects on Rome—Military, Economic, Cultural. The Roman army took on permanent form. It was a paid, national militia based on universal conscription of all property holders for service at home or abroad. The military unit was the phalanx of heavy and light infantry; the sub-unit was the centuriate (100 men). During the fourth century a more flexible form of legion (4000 infantry) was adopted. It was divided into 120 maniples for maneuverability. Larger units of cavalry were added and by the middle of the fourth century the Romans had a navy as well.

The Italian conquest extended the importance of agriculture in Rome's economy, since large tracts of arable soil were added to her holdings. Labor power for these expanded estates was provided by the slaves who were taken as war-prisoners. From the conquered people new techniques of farming were borrowed and applied (particularly in wine and olive production). War profits increased the demand for foreign luxury goods; trade expanded and with trade there came a money economy. Trade brought the trader—a new class of rich men that began to press for a larger share in government.

Latin translations of Greek works began to spread through Italy. Greek gods were adopted and given Roman "citizenship." Hellenistic philosophies began to capture the imagination of the intellectuals and to undermine the traditional beliefs.

THE ROMAN EMPIRE

Rise. Caesar had willed his rule to his nephew OCTAVIUS. Octavius had to fight for his bequest against MARC ANTONY and LEPIDUS—both Caesar's friends and both commanding effective military power. All three, however, had a common enemy in the republican forces led by Cassius and Brutus. **A Second Triumvirate** was therefore formed which consisted of Octavius, Antony and Lepidus. At **Philippi** the republicans were overwhelmed. Antony moved on to Egypt and to Cleopatra while Octavian (Octavius) returned to Rome to consolidate his position. When Antony divorced Octavia (Octavian's sister) to marry Cleopatra, Octavian declared war. At the **Battle of Actium,** 39 B.C., his fleet won a decisive victory over Antony and Cleopatra. Octavian was now without opposition.

The Principate. Julius Caesar had sought to transform Roman society; Octavian sought to reestablish it — within a new order. Octavian, for example, forced Caesar's appointees from the Senate if they were not descended from the highest Roman nobility. He decreed that no Roman citizen could marry a freeman, or outside his rank. Old Temples were restored—in marble. Republican forms were scrupulously observed. When Octavian acted it was *through* the Senate and Assembly. In 27 B.C. Octavian laid down all his extraordinary powers and it was the Senate that granted them to him anew by popular acclaim. Thus by senatorial proclamation Octavian became

Princeps—the head of the Senate and first citizen of the State

Imperator Caesar Divi filius—commander-in-chief of the armed forces and son of the Divine Julius (hence he could become the object of religious worship)

Augustus—restorer and augmenter of the state (a title formerly bestowed on certain gods).

In these bestowals the Senate recognized that the old order was gone; new times, new governmental forms. After a century of civil war the great desire of all Romans was peace and order. And Augustus Caesar was the one to give it to them.

Reforms. Augustus brought the *Pax Romana* to the Romans and to the world. The Roman army, recruited from the ranks of Roman citizens and officered by men from the aristocratic classes, stood guard at all the frontiers and within all troubled areas in the Empire. In Rome Augustus kept for himself a small praetorian guard. A standing navy was added to the armed forces. Military affairs were made the exclusive perogative of Augustus himself. Competence over the provinces was divided: those pacified and near at home were granted to the Senate; others were administered by the Imperator.

Within all provinces Augustus decided upon all military matters. To meet the rise in state expenditures for the military, for public works, for grain distribution and the like, Augustus made tax collection a state function; taxes were now collected efficiently and new import taxes were introduced. To keep expenses down, no new foreign conquests were undertaken—particularly after the resounding defeat suffered by the Romans under Varus at the hands of Arminius, a Germanic barbarian.

Height. Augustus died in 14 A.D. and his stepson TIBERIUS was nominated by the Senate as his successor. Tiberius abolished the *comitia tributa,* transferred certain provinces from the Senate to himself in order to reform them, suppressed two great mutinies in the ranks of the legionnaires and many personal plots against himself. He died unpopular in 37 A.D.

CALIGULA (37–41 A.D.) who succeeded him was insane and managed to dissipate the treasury in drunken revels and bizarre celebrations. The Praetorian Guard disposed of him. It was they who named Claudius as successor.

CLAUDIUS (41-54 A.D.) ruled well. He reoccupied Britain; reformed the bureaucracy by instituting special divisions; he completed the construction of two aqueducts and improved the great harbor at Ostia. Because she plotted against him, Claudius had his wife, Messalina, executed. He then married his niece, Agrippina, who bore him a son Nero. Agrippina then disposed of Claudius by poisoning him.

NERO (54-70 A.D.) was probably insane. His administration was filled with plot and counterplot, with assassination and execution, with persecution of the Christians who were made the scapegoat for a fire that swept Rome in 64 A.D., and with border revolts extending from Britain to Judea. When the Senate finally condemned Nero, he committed suicide.

VESPASIAN (70-79 A.D) proved a wise choice: he reformed the tax structure, recovered large tracts of public lands from extortionists, introduced rigid governmental economy, increased the income of the state, restored discipline in the ranks of the army and kept the peace. His successor, TITUS, ruled for two years only (79-81 A.D.) and was followed by Domitian.

DOMITIAN (81-96 A.D.) built the lines of forts between the Germanic and Roman lands where no natural boundaries existed. This established peace in the northeast. Murder and assassination, including his own, featured Domitian's rule.

NERVA'S (96-98 A.D.) brief rule produced an interesting agricultural scheme: to encourage agriculture in Italy a revolving fund was set up by the state; farmers could borrow from the fund at low interest rates; upon repayment, the principal was returned to the fund, and the interest was used for relief for indigent widows and orphans. Nerva began the adoptive system of imperial succession when he adopted Trajan as his son and successor.

TRAJAN (98-117 A.D.) was the first provincial to become an emperor. He was a brilliant military commander and during his rule he brought the Roman Empire to the Tigris and Euphrates Rivers—its widest extent. He also made important reforms in the imperial administration. He adopted Hadrian as his son.

HADRIAN (117-138 A.D.) was a most unmilitary ruler. His interests were in languages, literature, philosophy and art. To avoid the bother of empire, he ceded Mesopotamia and Assyria to the Parthians; granted independence to Dacia; completed the northern forts; built a wall in Britain between Roman and Celtic lines; destroyed Jerusalem and scattered the Jews far and wide through the Empire. Internal administration was reformed and the praetorian edicts were codified. Hadrian's Tomb (The Castle of Saint Angelo) on the banks of the Tiber is a most fitting memorial of this most esthetic of the Roman emperors.

ANTONINUS PIUS (139-161) ruled long and peacefully; his successor MARCUS AURELIUS (161–180) ruled long, was a man of peace, but lived through troubled times. There were local wars against the Parthians, Germanic tribes and others; there were severe persecutions of the Christians. These external exertions were in direct contradiction to the inner life of Marcus who, in his famous *Meditations,* a treatise on Stoicism, revealed himself as simple, conscientious, retiring, philosophical and ascetic.

COMMODUS (180-192) was a true son of Marcus Aurelius, at least in the flesh. The spirit of Commodus—cruel, sensuous and cowardly—was far removed from that of his father. With Commodus begins the decline of Rome.

THE DECLINE OF ROME

Rome's decline extended over centuries; it had no sudden fall. Many factors contributed to the decline. Science and technology did not keep pace with Roman expansion and Romans found that they were unable to handle efficiently the food, tools and transport problems that arose. The immense size of the empire was also a factor. It was impossible for the best-intentioned emperor to cope with the ceaseless problems of rising nationalisms, border attacks, graft and corruption in the provinces, inefficient bureacracy, gross waste of limited resources. The drain on the public treasury was continuous. The wider the empire became, the less intense became the degree of patriotism; loss of patriotism engendered corrupt political behavior. The army was sensitive to the decline particularly as it lost its Roman character and became increasingly provincial. With decline in emperor character, the army became a prime political force. It began to make and unmake emperors so frequently that one can say accurately that between the rule of Commodus (d. 192 A.D.) and the rise of DIOCLETIAN (284 A.D.) military anarchy prevailed in the Empire.

Political decline hastened the factors making for economic decline. Small farmers, the backbone of the Roman Republic, virtually disappeared or rather were absorbed into the immense estates as semi-slaves. The purchasing power represented by these small farmers disappeared and helped to ruin the city artisans who had produced manufactured goods for sale to the small farmers; besides, an important source of tax revenue also disappeared. With the ruin of the small farming and artisan classes, the state became the primary producer of goods, a factor which destroyed the initiative of the Romans. Resulting shortages of goods produced a steady inflation. Coinage began to disappear; what remained was debased and became worthless. The result was a reversion to barter. This had a tremendous impact upon the trading or middle classes who had become the backbone of the Empire. Foolish imperial decrees hastened the decline of this group. They were made responsible for the collection of taxes in the municipalities. Whatever they did not raise of the quota assigned them, they had to pay out of their own pockets. They could not meet their quotas because the artisans had been ruined with the decline of the small farmers. Soon the middle class followed the artisans into ruin.

Some social factors entered the picture too. Population declined all during the imperial period. War, epidemic and plague were chiefly responsible; and, as times grew harder, natural birth rates declined among the poor as well as the rich. Of equal importance was the failure of nerve which accompanied physical decline. This was revealed in the search for security above enterprise, in the widespread superstitions that developed, in the rush to join mystical cults that guaranteed, at least, some reward in the hereafter, in the loss of patriotism, in the wild and bestial indulgences of the rich, etc.

The Fall. Several strenuous efforts were made to halt the decline of the empire. Most notable was that of DIOCLETIAN (284-305 A.D.). Diocletian tried to augment the powers of the Emperor by introducing Oriental features of absolutism into his rule. He reformed the army; tried to halt inflation by instituting both price and wage controls; and made significant changes in imperial administration. This latter was most important for the future of European history. The Empire was divided in two, a western and eastern half and Diocletian ruled from the east. This division became permanent when CONSTANTINE (306-337) made Constantinople into a second Rome. When the fall came, it was the western half that collapsed; **the eastern half continued for more than a thousand years to preserve and disseminate the culture of the Roman Empire.**

The Foundations of Medieval Civilization

The **Medieval** or **Middle Ages** of European History are those that lie between the Greco-Roman Age and the Age of the Renaissance—approximately from 476 A.D. to about 1350. These Middle Ages reached their height between the 11th and 13th centuries. Our concern in this chapter is with Medievalism at its height and with only the broadest aspects of its civilization and culture.

FEUDALISM

A distinguishing feature of the Middle Ages was the **Feudal System,** a system that pivoted upon a **personal, contractual relationship** between two nobles—**a lord and a vassal.** A nobleman became a **lord** when he made a grant of a **fief** (a section of land with its peasant inhabitants) to another nobleman in exchange for the latter's services, chiefly military. A nobleman became a **vassal** when he accepted the fief and swore homage and fealty to his lord. It is important to remember that both the lord and the vassal were noblemen and freemen.

Origins of the Feudal System. Both Roman and German influences contributed to the creation of the Feudal System. It was not unusual in Roman times for a freeman to attach himself to a wealthy or influential man as a "client." In exchange for services, the client received protection. In more troubled times the practice of **commendation** arose. A client would "commend" both himself and his land to a patron in exchange for protection. In reverse, it was also a common practice for a wealthy landed patron to grant a client a *precarium* (land with precarious or uncertain tenure); in time this became a *beneficium* or a grant of land for a fixed period of time, say, a lifetime or two generations, in exchange for services. This land-services practice became merged with the Germanic practice of establishing a personal military relationship between a chief and his freeman-warriors. The Germans also introduced a practice of "immunity-grants" whereby powerful noblemen were granted free, unsupervised sovereignty over fixed territorial areas.

The Fief. In the tenth century the practice became fixed to **invest** a warrior-vassal with a fief. The fief might be a single, small holding or an entire duchy of many holdings. It was an *hereditary* holding and was transmitted by succession through the eldest son. Within the boundaries of the fief the vassal exercised sovereign rights: he collected taxes, coined money, exploited the resources, raised armies, provided for the public defense, administered justice, established and regulated markets and the like. The investiture of a fief was often recorded in a written contract. In the written contract was also included a listing of the services which the vassal would render to his lord. A fief could be *sub-infeudated* or divided among sub-vassals.

The Services of the Vassal. The basic obligation of the vassal to his lord was military service; in time this came to be limited to about forty days of military action. The number of fully equipped men that each vassal contributed depended upon the number of sub-vassals that he controlled. Vassals were also expected to help garrison the lord's fortress or castle and to engage in administrative activities. A vassal, then, might be chief administrative agent of fief and household; a constable or commander of the castle; a marshal or supervisor of the horses; a butler or supervisor of the wine supplies. Vassals were expected to attend the lord's court and to serve as judges in inter-vassal disputes, thus giving rise to a "trial by one's peers."

Feudal aids or monetary payments accompanied the personal services of the vassal; occasions for such payments were numerous. If the lord was captured in battle, the vassal had to contribute to ransom him back; if the lord planned an expensive undertaking in the nature of a pilgrimage or crusade, the vassal had to provide monetary assistance; if a vassal died, the inheriting son had to pay an inheritance tax. To protect himself against the possibility that an enemy would take legal possession of a fief, the lord secured the right to himself to veto a marriage proposal made to the vassal's daughter or widow; to assign custody over minors, who had inherited a fief, to a male regent. If a vassal failed to deliver his services, he could be forced to forfeit his fief and if he died without an heir, the fief would revert to the lord.

Feudal Hierarchy. Medievalism was patterned on the needs of these broad social groups: the peasants, the military nobility, and the clergy. These three groups formed **estates** and the first was the clergy, the second, the nobility, and the third, the peasantry and other producers (the townsmen did not fit easily into this medieval pattern—as we shall see).

In theory, the feudal hierarchy was carefully pyramided. At the top, as lord of all vassals, was the king; counts, dukes, and viscounts followed; beneath them were the barons or seignors; and knights or chevaliers made up the lowest rank. The Church held a special position in the hierarchy. In the 9th and 10th centuries many churchmen gave military service for feudal allotments and when this was prohibited on moral grounds, church fiefs were usually sub-infeudated among lay knights who could fulfil by proxy the Church's military duties.

Within the hierarchy, the king was potentially powerful but actually limited in his power to his own estate. Theoretically he owned all the land; in reality it was in the inalienable possession of the powerful nobility. Theoretically—as in Germany—the king ruled by divine right (The Holy Roman Emperor); in reality, he was an *elective* monarch chosen by the nobility and the clergy. Theoretically, the king commanded the allegiance of all his subjects; in reality, they obeyed him to the extent of their oath of allegiance and feudal contract. The point of this comparison is that the seeds of royal absolutism were buried in the medieval order and could be released the moment the power of the feudality weakened. This is precisely what happened by the 15th century.

Feudal Life. While feudalism prevailed, violence and turbulence characterized the life of the nobility as they contended over matters of inheritance and succession, of lay and ecclesiastical supremacy, of infractions of the feudal contract and the like. With war as an almost constant condition, feudal lords were forced to convert their homes into fortresses. The castle was a fortress. Its thick walls, crenelated towers, deep donjons, inner and outer battlements, surrounding moat, iron-toothed portcullis and drawbridge made it virtually unassailable by feudal armies except by seige and starvation.

The state of permanent war conditioned the education of youth. Feudal youth were trained to become knights or warriors. Like his Spartan prototypes, the feudal youth was removed from parental care at the age of seven or eight and sent to another feudal household for upbringing. He served as a page until he was sixteen and as a squire until he was twenty-one. Throughout these early years, he was made to live a hard life in the course of which he was taught the use and care of arms and horses. When he was battle-ready, he became a knight. This occasion was an impressive religio-feudal ceremony during which the knight-to-be knelt before another knight and received an *accolade* which was originally a sharp blow with the flat of a sword intended to knock the initiate out but was later modified to a slight tap on the head or shoulder. Once knighted, the warrior spent his time in war or warlike games which took the forms of hunting and tournaments or jousts.

ENGLAND

England was brought into the compass of European civilization by the Romans. In the fifth century A.D., however, the Romans had to retire before the onslaughts of the barbarian Angles, Saxons, Jutes and Frisians. The chaos which resulted was brought into some kind of order as a result of the missionary work of the Irish and Roman clergy. In 664, at the Synod of Whitby, Roman Catholic Christianity was officially adopted by the ruling tribes.

These tribes were divided into seven kingdoms, the so-called **Heptarchy.** By the ninth century, the kingdom of Wessex rose to power and produced one of England's great leaders, ALFRED THE GREAT (871-901). Alfred was able to establish a working relationship with the Danes who were threatening Anglo-Saxon England with extinction and then to initiate in England something of a "renaissance" of learning. He established schools and fostered the translation of Latin classics (e.g., Boethius' *Consolation of Philosophy,* Venerable Bede's *Ecclesiastical History of the English Nation*). He himself helped produce the *Anglo-Saxon Chronicle* and inspired the work of CAEDMON and CYNEWULF, founders of English literature. By codifying the laws and by remarkable defense of his realm, Alfred gave the English a tradition of strong kingship that soon became legendary. His work was undone by weak successors and by the conquest of England by KING CANUTE, the Dane (1016-1035). Canute's invasion forced many of the Anglo-Saxon nobility to flee to Normandy in France.

William the Conqueror. One such who fled was EDWARD THE CONFESSOR who in 1042 returned from Normandy to the throne of England. Edward brought with him many Norman advisers. Great rivalry developed between the Anglo-Saxon earls and these Norman nobles. When Edward died, the Witan (Council) selected Harold the Saxon (of Wessex) as king. WILLIAM, DUKE OF NORMANDY opposed this selection saying that Edward had promised the kingdom to him. In 1066 William invaded England and at the **Battle of Hastings** defeated Harold and his Anglo-Saxon forces. All of England fell as a feudal fief to the Conqueror.

Showing rare wisdom, William kept the government institutions he found in England and infused them with a new life. William destroyed the Anglo-Saxon earldoms, dividing them into smaller administrative units; over them he placed officials directly responsible to himself. Thus he merged Anglo-Saxon institutions with Norman institutions.

William's intention was to build a strong, centralized monarchy in England. His position was unique for he held all of England as a fief and could therefore make every landholder his vassal; every landholder had to serve in William's army. To further strengthen his position William kept a private standing militia for his use and prohibited private warfare. He issued a uniform royal currency. Even more remarkable for his time, William based his taxation upon the Domesday Survey (1085-1086), a national census of property holders and property! To defend his realm, William built castles everywhere and armed them with his own retainers.

Henry I (1100-1135). When William died the nobles tried to disrupt his plans for centralization. HENRY I consolidated his position by creating a permanent council of advisers—a bureaucracy of professional civil servants—and a group of "circuit" judges who traveled about the kingdom bringing the king's justice to all parts.

Henry II (1154-1189). Following Henry I's death, feudal and civil wars reduced England to a state of anarchy. Order was eventually restored by HENRY II, one of the greatest of all English kings. Henry was founder of the **Plantagenet dynasty** and ruled a land that extended from Scotland to the Pyrenees; his wife was the brilliant Eleanor of Aquitaine.

During the course of his reign, the English monarchy was considerably strengthened, particularly in the arena of judicial control. Henry's judicial reforms entered not only into the blood stream of the English nation, but into that of the United States as well. In the Assize of Clarendon of 1166 Henry did more than strengthen the king's justice. He initiated the participation of the people in the law-making process. The Clarendon Assize established the circuit judge as a permanent part of the English judicial system. When the circuit came to town, it was the duty of the sheriff to call up witnesses to give the judges information of existing wrongs. This practice created the **grand jury** which made "presentments" to the judges. In time these presentments were turned over to a **petit jury** ("twelve good men and true") to hear the presentments and pass judgment. He enlarged the jurisdiction of the King's Bench by permitting—contrary to feudal practice—civil as well as criminal cases to come before the circuit judges. This reduced considerably the power of the local, feudal baronial court.

Henry also resolved to reduce the power of the church courts by limiting the claim of "benefit of clergy" to major officials of the church. In this he was opposed by THOMAS A BECKET, the Archbishop of Canterbury. When Henry promulgated in 1164 the **Constitutions of Clarendon** which ordered that church officials accused of a crime should be taken before a royal court, Becket ordered churchmen to ignore the decree. After six years of dispute, at Henry's instigation a group of his followers murdered Becket.

The church and baronial courts having been curbed, the king's justices were free to consolidate English law and practice and out of their procedures there grew up the great system of **English Common Law.** Unlike Roman Law, the Common Law was never codified; it consisted of **customs and precedents.** In spite of this, it is wholly proper to call Henry II the "English Justinian."

Magna Carta (1215). Centralization of monarchical power suffered greatly under the rules of RICHARD THE LIONHEARTED and KING JOHN. Richard spent his father's bequest fighting as a knight errant in the Holy Land. John, whose goals of a centralized monarchy were consistent with Henry's but whose abilities and character were far inferior, became involved in a war with the feudal nobility and in a terrible quarrel with Pope Innocent III. As a result of his quarrel with Innocent, he lost all of his kingdom to the pope as a fief; and as a result of his war with the nobility, having been defeated in the **Battle of Runnymede,** he was compelled to sign the **Magna Carta** which placed severe restrictions on the power of the king in matters of taxation and judicial trial. At the time it was signed, Magna Carta served the interests of the feudal system. Only later did it become the **"charter of English liberties."** To cap this sad climax to the efforts of Henry II to establish the royalty in England, John proceeded to lose all of England's French possessions.

Edward I (1272–1307). When he came to the throne, EDWARD I resumed the reforms that were begun by the two Henrys. He further weakened the baronial and church courts; he strengthened the civil service; he gave strong impetus to a new institution, the English Parliament; he began the union of all the British Isles under one crown by conquering Wales (and creating a post of Prince of Wales as successor to the Crown) and Ireland. His work with Parliament deserves special mention since herein was the "wave of the future."

The Development of Parliament. Parliament is traced to the Anglo-Saxon Witan, a council of prominent nobles. William the Conqueror converted this into a Grand Council of nobles which served him in a judicial and advisory capacity.

Parliaments became popular in Europe during the second half of the thirteenth century as kings sought for revenues outside feudal dues to carry out their programs of national aggrandizement. It became customary to convene an assembly of three "estates," the lords, the clergy and townsmen (bourgeoisie) as a means of raising money. Spain had its **cortes,** France its **Estates General,** Germany its **diet** and England its **Parliament.** In 1265 SIMON DE MONTFORT had convened, on behalf of the feudal lords, the first British Parliament. But it was Edward I who convened the "Model Parliament."

Edward's purpose was to reduce his dependence upon the nobility for moneys and he therefore agreed, in 1297, that certain taxes would be levied only with the consent of Parliament. By the 14th century, this Parliamentary "power of the purse" was ingrained in English practice—to the considerable regret of the monarchs who followed Edward. Not only had this custom begun to prevail, but it also became a custom for the lords temporal and lords spiritual to sit together as the House of Lords, while the others sat separately as the House of Commons.

Furthermore, when Parliament met, it became the practice of the House of Commons to submit to the king a "list of grievances" which had to be taken care of before any money was voted. When England became involved in the Hundred Years War, and the financial drain became severe, the House of Commons began to insist on directing how the funds should be spent. For this to be legal, it became further necessary for the Commons to draw up a law which stipulated the way the money should be spent. Thus, in the Middle Ages, grew up one of the primary forms of modern democracy.

The Hundred Years War (1337–1450). The wars between England and France in the years between 1337 and 1450 were largely inspired by the desire of the kings of England who followed Edward to repossess their French holdings. As a result of these wars, England was driven permanently off the continent and forced to concentrate upon the British Isles. British kings became more and more independent in such matters as freedom of Parliamentary debate, extension of suffrage for Parliamentary members, the right of all money bills to originate in the House of Commons and not the House of Lords. The kings' power having been weakened by war and parliament, the power of the nobility rose.

The Wars of the Roses (1453–1485). The English baronial class split into two factions, **Lancaster** and **York**—Lancaster of the "Red Rose," and York of the "White Rose." (their emblems). Both factions struggled for control of the monarchy and of Parliament. The result was a lengthy civil war known as the **Wars of the Roses** (celebrated in Shakespeare's History Plays). As a result of this civil war, the feudal nobility virtually exterminated one another and permitted Henry VII of the **House of Tudor** to gain power. With Henry VII, England moves from the Middle Ages to modern history.

THE HOLY ROMAN EMPIRE

While other European nations took the path of national unity, Germany and Italy did not become united nations until the nineteenth century. The reasons for this failure were numerous. German emperors dissipated their energies in an effort to unite Germany and Italy, a policy that was opposed, as we have seen, by the papacy and the powerful Italian towns. The popes were particularly effective in preventing this union. They openly interfered in imperial elections within Germany and kept that nation split in perpetual war between Guelph and Ghibelline, they used their extensive powers of excommunication and interdict against such strong rulers as Barbarossa, Henry VI and Frederick II, and, when these failed, they invited foreigners like Charles of Anjou (1265) to make war on the Germans.

The Germans themselves made a unified nation nearly impossible by measures continually adopted to weaken the Emperor. For five hundred years thereafter there was no Germany—just a series of archduchies, margravates, counties, duchies and free cities known as the Germanies.

Italy suffered the same fate. The lead in preventing the unification of the Italian states was taken once more by the popes who feared for their vast possessions in Italy and by the short-sighted Italian cities. Constant invasion plagued the Italians as well. Following the decline of the Carolingian power Italy was invaded by the Normans who settled in Sicily. The Normans provided Italy with models of intelligent rule: laws were codified; a parliament was created (1225); trade and commerce were fostered. Because it threatened their power, the popes invited the French Angevins into Italy as conquerors. So bitter was the Italian resentment against the French that in 1282 at Palermo they rose up, at the house of vespers, and murdered every Frenchman they could find. (This massacre is known in history as the "Sicilian Vespers.") When the French left it became the turn of the Spaniard Alfonso of Aragon to conquer Sicily and Naples (1443). In 1494 Charles the VIII of France invaded Italy . . . but by this time Italy's will to exist as a nation was destroyed.

Out of this failure in government a new state was born—Switzerland. While Frederick II was King he permitted two Swiss cantons to become self-governing—subject to his overlordship. A habit of independence was born. When in 1291 Rudolph of Hapsburg, the German ruler decided to remove their independent rights, the Swiss cantons formed a Perpetual Compact or alliance directed against Rudolph. Their resistance was successful. In 1315 the frustrated Hapsburgs moved an army against the Swiss and were soundly beaten by boulders rolled down the declivities of the cantons. Their success encouraged the Swiss to organize a confederation. In 1394 the Hapsburgs compromised with necessity and recognized Swiss independence. Out of this struggle came the legend of **William Tell.**

The Economic Transition to Modern Times

THE COMMERCIAL REVOLUTION

Statistics of the growth of European commerce between 1350 and 1650 are not available; but some indication of the growth is reflected in the fact that by the latter date there were an estimated 2,000,000 tons of shipping afloat. We are concerned with this fact because with each increase in Europe's trade **the power and position of the middle class grew.** Fixed capital such as landed property began to take second place to fluid capital in the form of money. Manufacturing was becoming a competitor of agriculture for available investment capital. There still were many medieval shackles upon the free flow of trade—feudal tolls and tariffs, religious prohibitions, guild restrictions, and the like. But these were being shaken loose by the rise of **national states** under *national* monarchies, by the wave of humanism and new learning sweeping Europe, and by the religious reformation. Taking advantage of these dissolvents of the medieval order, the middle class began to develop forms of manufacturing that evaded the boundaries set down by the guilds. In the mainstream of all these charges, however, was the revolution in commerce that made itself felt by the fifteenth century.

Trade and Commerce. By 1400 European markets were no longer restricted to the luxury trade from the Near East. These still commanded an imposing position in the trade picture, but trading was as much concerned now with new European foodstuffs, textiles, shipbuilding materials and tools. Markets were no longer restricted to a few favored areas since goods could now travel along the king's roads protected by the king's police and the king's courts. The supply of money had increased; European deposits of gold and silver were dug with intensified fervor and North African mineral sources were tapped. When the Americas were discovered—just as European deposits were almost exhausted—a flood of gold and silver bullion re-entered the trade stream.

Manufacturing. Traders clamored for manufactured products to be sold abroad in exchange for luxury goods and for foodstuffs. Throughout these early years, in fact, the drain of gold and silver out of Europe was very heavy. Europe suffered from an almost continual unfavorable balance of trade which kept her prices low (deflation) and her debts high. When the political power of the guilds declined, entrepreneurs (early capitalists) appeared who discovered and invested in a new mode of production of manufactured goods, the **domestic** or "putting out" system.

Under this system the entrepreneur contracted with many craftsmen to supply them with raw materials and to pay them for the goods they manufactured out of the raw materials. The entrepreneur then disposed of the manufactured goods in the local or international market. This was a very attractive offer to the craftsman. He already owned his own tools, he could do the work at home (hence domestic), he did not have to worry about purchasing raw materials and selling his products, he could keep a garden patch and do some farming to supplement his income from manufacture.

To the entrepreneur this system was still not ideal: the cost was high since the craftsman made the whole product and insisted in producing quality goods, the entrepreneur depended upon the craftsman who owned the tools, the small number of craftsmen kept wages high, production was limited, invention of new tools was discouraged since craftsmen could not afford to finance them, etc. Over the years, the attractiveness of the craftsman's position brought many new workers into the field. Entrepreneurs took advantage of this situation by lowering wages considerably. The lowering of wages had the effect of increasing the dependence of the craftsman upon the entrepreneur. To get more money, the craftsman had to give up his farming and put his wife and children to work. Under pressure to make more, the craftsman became less concerned with the quality of the product. The entrepreneur, in turn, got poorer goods and found it increasingly difficult to supervise many workers in their homes. The time soon came when a more radical innovation in manufacturing processes would have to be made. For this period, however, the domestic system served admirably to build up the quantity of trade, the wealth of the entrepreneurs and to destroy effectively the power of the guilds.

Finance. Financing by means of money grew side by side with commerce and manufacturing.

Professional money lending was an old practice by 1400. As early as the 10th century monasteries began to engage in extensive money lending, generally to local peasants and landlords. Political loans were on occasion made to Emperors, Popes and high feudal lords. Later, the knightly orders (Templars, Hospitalers, etc.) played the part of kings of finance and supplied credit needs.

In the medieval cities the role of professional lenders fell to the Lombards, Jews and money changers. Medieval Jews, prohibited from becoming farmers or artisans, had been among the first to engage in commerce. The rise of Christian merchants forced them out of this business and into the business of money-lending since they were not subject to church prohibitions and money-lending was a necessary function in an expanding economy. Christians permitted them to settle in specified areas *only if they would make loans;* Jews paid with their lives *if they refused to make a loan when security was offered.* Jews, then, won "toleration" so that Christians might evade the church's prohibition of "usury"—though the latter of course reaped the rewards of usury.

Soon, however, the Italian Lombards became active competitors of the Jews. Their loans went out to the urban merchants, feudal lords and handicraftsmen. The Lombards discovered that they might lend out more money than they had (since some was always being paid back)—but not safely. Therefore, they began to solicit interest-bearing deposits (a practice forbidden to the Jews). This was the origin of commercial banking. Other methods—such as bills of exchange, bank drafts and bank acceptances—were soon instituted.

Business Organization. Forms of **partnership,** family and non-family, had developed in the Middle Ages and were continued into the modern period. So too was the **regulated company**—an association of merchants created to monopolize and exploit some branch of trade. It received its charter from the government. Each associated merchant worked as an individual entrepreneur but contributed to a common treasury to finance a central body which maintained foreign trade centers, gave protection to the membership and laid down the rules for the proper conduct of business.

But the most modern of the forms developed in this period was the **joint stock company.** The others were a union of persons; this was a union of capital. A number of investors put their money into a venture and then chose a board of directors to conduct the venture; they then shared the profits and the risks.

When joint stock companies came to be linked to regulated companies, they were called **chartered commercial companies.** A good example of one such was the famous English **East India Company.** Its capital was derived from shareholders but it did more than engage in commercial ventures. Its charter granted it monopoly rights to trade anywhere in the Pacific and Indian Oceans; to buy land in unlimited quantity; to deal with foreign potentates; to wage war and to make peace treaties. With these freedoms permitted to it, chartered companies began to colonize the world on behalf of the mother country.

DISCOVERY AND COLONIZATION

Colonization was first attempted, unsuccessfully, by the Crusaders. The germ of the colonial concept was also present in the trading posts which were set up in Europe and the Near East by the Venetians and the Hanseatic League in the 13th and 14th centuries. But these ventures were in relatively settled and civilized areas. Modern colonization began when a vast new world of either sparsely settled or barbarous regions were suddenly discovered, explored and found more than useful. The first burst of such exploration and discovery came in the half century between 1450 and 1500. Why at that time?

Causes. Many factors combined to produce the burst of overseas exploration in 1450–1500. Nations along the Atlantic coast were growing desperate for gold and silver with which to offset the unfavorable balance of trade with the Near East. They resented more and more bitterly the stranglehold which the free cities of Italy had upon that area and upon the Mediterranean Sea. Momentarily the Italian monopoly had been threatened when the Ottoman Turks in 1453 had captured Constantinople and overthrown the Byzantine Empire. (Indeed, they had advanced deep into Europe itself and had overrun Serbia, Wallachia, Bosnia and Greece.) The Turks, however, anxious to keep the favorable balance of trade with Western Europe, had renewed Venice's privileges in the Near East. Even had there not been this political domination of the Near East, the price of Far

Eastern commodities was extremely high since the price reflected the great distances by sea and overland that the goods had to come, the tariff that had to be paid en route, the brigandage that lined the whole trade route, etc. It was clear to thoughtful merchants that there was but one answer to this distressing problem: some all-water route to the Far East—either around Africa or by a westward sailing.

Successes. MARCO POLO and other travelers had returned to Europe with the news that Far Eastern lands were washed by some mighty water. Why could it not be the same mighty water that washed the Atlantic shores of Europe? Europeans became convinced that it was and began the systematic conquest of this water—which held so many terrors for the uninformed.

By 1450 improvements in seafaring were far advanced. The magnetic compass was in general use; the astrolabe to measure latitude out at sea was perfected; new scientific maps were in circulation; shipbuilding had advanced toward larger and more powerful vessels. With the invention by JOHANN GUTENBERG of the printing press, geographical, maritime and astronomical information was diffused over wide areas. In particular it became better and better known that the earth was a sphere and that one could reach east by sailing west.

Southward and westward sailing were in the minds of many men by 1450. National states were well advanced by that time and the monarchs hungered for more revenue with which to counter the feudal nobility; dispossessed nobles hungered for a new chance to recoup their fortunes. Individuals stirred by the Renaissance stress on man sought new adventures and new glories. Men looked to Africa and to the Far East as vast potential fields of conquest.

Now Europe needed bold and fearless navigators to try the dangers of the unknown sea. One who did not fear the sea was Prince HENRY THE NAVIGATOR, son of King John I of Portugal. Motivated by a zealot's hatred for the Moslems and a desire to conquer them by outflanking them in the south of Africa, Henry organized a navigational center on the southern tip of Portugal facing the Atlantic. Here captains were trained in the making of maps, the reading of them, the use of navigational instruments, etc.

Their training completed, Portuguese navigators began to edge cautiously down the western coast of Africa. In 1488 (twenty years after Henry's death) BARTHOLOMEW DIAZ reached the Cape of Good Hope. Ten years later VASCO DA GAMA sailed around Africa to India. The southward route had been breached. Six years before da Gama's feat, however, the Western route was opened by the world-shaking voyage of CHRISTOPHER COLUMBUS (1492). Some years had to pass before Europeans came to realize that Columbus had discovered a huge continent that blocked the way to the Far East. The first to see the ocean on the other side of the New World was VASCO NUNEZ DE BALBOA; and the first to circumnavigate the globe by sailing westward was FERDINAND MAGELLAN and his crew (Magellan having been killed in the Philippines). By 1522 the Mediterranean Sea route to the luxury items of the Far East had been circumvented in two directions. Hegemony over Far Eastern Trade now passed to the nations on the Atlantic shores. The Commercial Revolution was complete.

The Renaissance

For many years historians took their understanding of the historical period known as the **Renaissance** from a book written by the great Swiss historian, JAKOB BURCKHARDT—*The Civilization of the Renaissance in Italy.* According to Burckhardt, the Renaissance was a spontaneous creation of the Italian people in the fifteenth century (the quattrocento); it was something new that had no roots in the past. From nowhere came a new birth of individuality; from nowhere, an outburst of genius that took the forms of great art and literature. Several concepts distorted Burckhardt's view of the Renaissance: he was primarily concerned with culture and ideas; he, therefore, paid insufficient attention to other factors—religious, political, social or economic; he believed in the "great man theory of history" which blinded him to large movements involving lesser people. In spite of these weaknesses, Burckhardt's study remains a major classic of historical research.

Historians still do not agree on all that the Renaissance was, but most will accept the statement that it was not a "rebirth" so much as a **transitional period between medieval and modern times.** As a transitional period the roots of the Renaissance derive from the medieval outlook; its tentacles stretch toward the dawning era of modern science; in itself it was neither medieval nor modern. Because it was an in-between period it was characterized by criticism of the *status quo,* by restless curiosity about all things, by the raising of questions rather than the answering of them. Such intellectual attitudes inevitably led the men of the Renaissance to place man himself under more intensive examination and it was out of this emphasis upon *man* that the distinctive features of the Renaissance emerged. In this matter, Burckhardt cannot be denied; the Renaissance did burst with creativity and the artists of that period were great men even if they were not the *sole* determinants of the course of history during the Renaissance.

Renaissance Versus Medievalism. There was much in medieval life that Renaissance men openly rejected or disagreed with. While medieval men revered some of the Greco-Roman classics, Renaissance men hailed them all, no matter how pagan, how un-Christian. They made war against medieval Latin and 14th century vernacular and sought to return to the "pure Latin" of Cicero—a virtually unknown tongue. They were optimistic, worldly, and individualistic. They rejected "Gothic" architecture as "barbaric"; they no longer gave unthinking credence to Ptolemaic astronomy which placed man at the center of the universe; they pursued knowledge for knowledge's sake without fearing for their faith; they mocked at chivalry, scholastic philosophy, medieval economics; in short, they affirmed life with enthusiasm and joy.

Causes of the Renaissance. What forces accelerated this drive toward a "new birth?" Many of them lay in earlier developments: contact with Moslem and Byzantine civilizations; the Commercial Revolution with its interchange of goods and ideas; the new learning of the thirteenth century that flowered in scholasticism; the rise of national monarchies bolstered by the Bolognese revival of Roman law; the spread of universities; the near-scientific emphasis of the Nominalist movement within scholasticism; the growth of a wealthy, leisured middle-class seeking prestige as patrons of the arts. These might very well be designated **fundamental causes.** (It is worth re-emphasizing that most of these causes lay, chronologically, *within* the medieval period.) For the more immediate causes, we must turn to the history of Italy in the fourteenth and fifteenth centuries.

IDEAS OF THE RENAISSANCE

The rise of the Renaissance dictators was accompanied by a rationalization of their activities and behavior. One such rationalization was the ideal of *virtù.* A man was to be judged by the bravery and skill with which he achieved his personal goals and by the subtlety and finesse of the means he employed. In pursuit of virtù, conscience was irrelevant. So wrote MACHIAVELLI in *The Prince.*

Machiavellanism. Machiavelli wrote *The Prince* out of a deep sense of frustration with the political condition of Italy—its helplessness before the might of Spanish and French invaders, its lack of patriotism, its dependence upon mercenary soldiers, its state of warring disunity. His dream was of a unified Italy, completely sovereign, untrammeled by church, religion or morals, free to undertake whatever was necessary to bolster its unlimited sovereignty over the lives of its subjects. The end of unity could only be achieved by a patriotic and ruthless prince, possessed of virtù, who by craft and force would reduce the peninsula of Italy to a single sway.

Such a prince, thought Machiavelli, was CESARE BORGIA. Why was Cesare qualified? He took the world as it was and men for what they were—as motivated primarily by evil purposes. He therefore planned to make evil his ally. He did not scruple to break his word when his promise no longer served his purpose; he strove to make himself both loved and feared by giving the appearance of being virtuous but doing all the evil required to maintain himself in power. All means are justified, argued Machiavelli, that serve the end of attaining and retaining political power. Ruse, cunning, artifice, conspiracy—these were the methods of the prince with grandeur of soul, strength of body and mind. Poison to the prince were such Christian ideals as humility, lowliness and contempt of worldly objects.

Such goals were not confined during the Renaissance to princes alone. They can be seen operating in the interesting lives of such Renaissance figures as Pope Alexander VI, Machiavelli, himself, the utterly unscrupulous critic Pietro Aretino, the adventurer Castagno, the braggart Benvenuto Cellini and even in the youth of Leonardo da Vinci.

The Perfect Courtier. The ideal of the "very perfect knight" of chivalry had decomposed by the time of the Renaissance; in its place appeared the ideal of the "very perfect gentleman." BALDASSARE CASTIGLIONE (1478–1529) established this ideal in his book *Il Cortigiano* (*The Courtier*). Who was the gentleman? He was born to a family of good manners or gentility, artistocrats in mind and body, standards and taste. In such an environment he would grow up skilled in sport and the use of arms, a graceful dancer and skilled musician, a master of several languages including Latin, familiar with great works of literature and art, and completely at ease in the company of accomplished women.

Women, said Castiglione, are a necessary part of the environment that makes the gentleman for they refine whatever brute instincts are the natural endowment of man. But women have to be trained in their role of complement to the gentleman and the first requirement was to be feminine in carriage, manners, speech and dress. To be the conversational equals of men, women, too, must undergo the studies that would provide them with ideas on literature, art and statecraft, with facility in many languages. Compared, then, with the medieval ideal of womankind, Renaissance woman was a real woman—rather than an ethereal ideal —and was celebrated as such in paintings of artists like Raphael and Andrea del Sarto both of whom used *live* models for their Madonnas. Gentlemen and gentlewomen, pursuing the ideal of *cortesia* (gentility) inevitably became patrons of the arts.

Art Patronage. Responding to the heightened interest in the remains of classical antiquity, the nobility and wealthy merchants began to collect antiques, to finance projects designed to spread classical, learning, and to give support to local, native artists who possessed unusual talent. The Medici, for example, built a museum for the study of antique art, financed diggings among Etruscan and Roman ruins, invited and supported artists like Bertoldo, Michelangelo, Leonardo and Verrochio to work in the museum on original projects. Lorenzo de Medici was himself exceptionally gifted as a poet and composer.

Artistic Individualism. While the artists appreciated these endowments and made much use of them, they resisted all efforts to form them into guilds or corporations so characteristic of the medieval outlook. The earliest of the great artists worked in guild workshops under the usual guild regulations and restrictions. Gradually the cult of individualism developed; artists of genius established themselves in individual studios and assumed an independent role. They still depended on commissions from the aristocracy and the church, but the subject matter and form of the artwork was to be exclusively their own. The result was that fine art was separated from the crafts; painting, sculpture and architecture became individual liberal arts, each with its own esthetic, or canons of taste and judgment.

As individual artists became recognized, there flocked about them groups of worshipping and imitating students. To bring some kind of order into art instruction, some of the masters began to organize art academies. From the art academies sprang the various schools of art which characterized the Renaissance.

The Protestant Reformation

FUNDAMENTAL CAUSES

Between 1517 and 1648 the "universality" of the Roman Catholic Church was shattered beyond repair. Roman Catholicism now had to share its leadership of Christians with a large number of national churches and private sects, each with its dogma, doctrine, ritual and sacramental acts. This momentous schism began as a reformation within the Roman Church but ended as a series of transformations outside it. The political, economic, social and cultural consequences of this schism in Christian thought and practice were explosive in the days of its origin and remain so in our own day, 300 years later. Reform movements within the Catholic fold had occurred previously, as we have seen; they were part of the evolution of the church's structure to meet changing social conditions. Why, then, should the reform inaugurated by MARTIN LUTHER have had such drastic consequences?

Church abuses. The number of church abuses had multiplied, but not significantly, over those that existed at the time of the Cluniac Reform. Many clergymen were ignorant and ineffective as priests; many led scandalous lives and in so doing broke their vows of poverty and chastity. The papal office was held by a number of Renaissance popes notorious for their loose and indulgent living and who were incredibly corrupt. They made a business out of the sale of religious offices and benefices; church offices and dispensations were placed on the auction block and those who won the bids and became church officers got their money back by charging outrageous fees for priestly services.

Still other venerated church practices were converted into profit-making enterprises. Two that figured largely in Luther's protest were the sale of relics and the sale of indulgences. Relics were objects believed to have been used by Christ, the Virgin and the saints and therefore possessed of miraculous power to cure the afflicted and to protect the threatened. Unrestrained and unreproved, relic-hawkers traveled through Europe selling unlimited quantities of holy splinters from the "true" cross or from the "bones" of saints. When the fantastic proportions reached by this traffic were exposed by the Humanists, a great revulsion followed. Even more controversy centered about the sale of indulgences.

An indulgence was a remission of all or part of the punishment for sinning in this life; it was effective in purgatory but not in hell. The practice was an ancient one and in the beginning granted after works of charity, fasting and the like. Church teaching held that Christ and the saints had accumulated a large "treasury of merit" while they were on earth; this treasury was deposited in heaven and the Pope, possessed of "the power of the keys and the authority to bind and loose," could draw upon the treasury to remit punishment both on earth and in purgatory. No indulgence was valid unless the recipient was truly contrite, confessed his sins and was absolved. Since canonical penalties often inflicted hardships and inequities upon helpless people, the church began the practice of commuting penalties into almsgiving. From almsgiving to the sale of indulgences was a natural step for the Renaissance popes who cared little for the spiritual significance of the indulgence and much for its possibilities for fund-raising. In fact, one of the popes turned over the traffic in indulgences to a banking firm which collected one-third of the "take" as their share of the "profits." When exposed, this, too, caused great indignation among the faithful.

All these things had been before and had brought on reform movements; why should these series of abuses have brought on a schism? The reason must lie deeper. Old abuses gather new force when they occur in a changed environment.

Waves of Doctrine. Disgust with the Pope's exercise of temporal power had stirred JOHN WYCLIFFE (1324?–1384) to denounce it, and to follow this denunciation with demands that the Scriptures be elevated above papal power, and that the clergy be permitted to live secular lives (marriage, etc.) to reduce the amount of corruption that prevailed among them. He thought, too, that the Bible ought to be translated into the vernacular so that all who could would read it.

The fall of the papacy into the "Babylonian Exile" revived Wyclifism after it had been suppressed and found an eloquent spokesman and martyr in the person of JOHN HUS (1369-burned 1415). Humanism added to the amount, not the depth, of anti-clericalism for it did so from within the church. Valla, Mirandola, Le Fevre, Colet, Reuchlin, von Hutten and Erasmus were merciless in their exposure of hair-splitting scholasticism, monkish practices of celibacy, poverty and obedience, church practices like worship of saints and relics, confession and absolution (on the ground that research did not reveal these practices among the first Christians). Humanists generally favored a return to a simpler form of Christian practice.

What the Humanists favored the Mystics in the Church (Thomas à Kempis, Meister Eckhart, Heinrich Suso, Johann Tauler, and others) practiced. In "imitation of Christ" they rejected mechanical schemes of salvation for more direct and personal ones. By contemplation, prayer and fasting they tried to come into direct communion with God without any intermediary—that is, without the church. These men were placing considerable reliance upon justification by faith alone and not upon St. James's, doctrine of "good works." Emphasis upon man's corruptibility and his need of faith caused a revival of interest in the epistles of St. Paul; Jacques Le Fevre made a translation of them into Latin and John Colet delivered a popular series of lectures upon them. The very bases of church practice were being challenged.

Religion and Nationality. While the Church's power prevailed, criticism had, perforce, to be cautious; why did it suddenly become bold and clamorous? When church critics found secular powers to support them by force of arms, they ceased to be fearful and did not hesitate to draw the conclusions from their criticisms.

Everywhere in Europe, save Germany and Italy, new national states had arisen and were making a strong assertion of secular sovereignty. In France, by the Pragmatic Sanction of Bourges (1438) and the Concordat of Bologna (1516), the kings succeeded in winning for themselves the right to dictate ecclesiastical appointments, jurisdiction and tax levies; by the Statute of Provisors (1351, 1390) and the Statute of Praemunire (1353, 1390), the English kings had made a similar assertion; nor were the Spanish kings far behind the French and English in their demands. These gains against the church stimulated rather than appeased royal appetites. They eyed enviously the vast domains of the church; and they resented the flow out of their countries of vast sums collected by the church in the form of annates, "Peter's Pence," indulgence fees, church court fines, income from vacant benefices, fees for bestowing the pallium upon bishops, etc. They felt that every effort of the church to excommunicate or to interdict was a violation of their sovereignty; they even turned hostile eyes upon the presence in their lands of church courts sharing judicial power with royal courts.

The bourgeoisie (middle class) fully supported the kings, for different reasons. They viewed the vast church holdings as immobilized capital that, if freed, could be used as a base for a great credit expansion; and they bitterly resented being deprived of the fluid capital they had in the form of countless payments to the church. And, since the chief burden of payment fell upon the lowly backs of the peasantry, they, too, echoed the bitter resentment of the kings and the bourgeoisie.

In such an atomosphere, church abuses became the sparks of a revolutionary movement to transform the church. This movement found its voice in Martin Luther whose career is a clear illustration of the causes at work in the Protestant Reformation.

The French Revolution

Revolution is a product of national paralysis. Between 1788 and 1789 the French monarchy entered into a period of crisis, chiefly financial. War, royal extravagance, reckless borrowing, inefficient taxation and the short-sighted inflexibility of the ruling groups had emptied the royal treasury; existing revenues were inadequate to meet obligations of the national debt; existing taxes on the peasantry and bourgeoisie were already crushing.

Potentially prosperous, the French nation was experiencing widespread poverty. Prices had risen because of crop failures; wages lagged far behind prices; business failures were increasing as a result of a British invasion of the French markets; large numbers of wage earners (which included part-time peasant workers) were unemployed. Economists like Turgot, Necker and Calonne, called in to solve the financial crisis did their best to delay collapse by minor economies and major loans. Each realized that France's salvation lay in opening the untaxed wealth of the privileged classes to taxation as the only solution; and for recommending this as national policy, each was dismissed.

At Calonne's suggestion, Louis XVI convened in 1787 an Assembly of Notables. These privileged groups were asked to tax themselves. They refused but did suggest that an Estates General or parliament of the three estates (clergy, nobility and the Third Estate) be called to consider the matter of taxation. The current finance minister, Archbishop de Brienne, coldly dismissed the suggestion of the Notables and undertook to float a new loan.

Popular Reaction. Encouraged by vocal popular support, the *parlement* (court) of Paris (on whose bench sat spokesmen for the bourgeoisie) refused to register de Brienne's new loan, or any loan or tax, unless it was approved by an Estates General. This was subversion and the king moved against the court with troops. But the soldiers refused to arrest the judges and in this act they were supported by menacing mobs in Paris. Uncomprehending and bewildered, Louis was compelled to summon the Estates General. Neither he, nor any Frenchman, foresaw the consequences of this act.

The Estates General. In 1789 the Estates General was only an historical memory since it had not met since 1614. At that time it consisted of three estates—the clergy, the nobility and the Third Estate, each meeting and voting as separate bodies. The least of the three had been the Third Estate. That this was no longer possible was clearly stated in an influential pamphlet written by the Abbé Sieyès. "What is the Third Estate?" asked the Abbé. And he answered: "It is everything. What has it been hitherto in the political order? Nothing! What does it desire? To be something!" Advisers of Louis accepted the truth of the Abbé's formulation and in assigning delegates, the Third Estate was permitted to choose 600 out of a total of 1200.

Elections were held in the early months of 1789 on the basis of almost universal male suffrage. In the course of electoral gathering local communities drew up *cahiers*—lists of grievances which the delegates were instructed to correct. It is interesting to note how un-revolutionary national sentiment was on the eve of the Revolution. The cahiers almost universally proclaimed the delegates loyal to the king and to the idea of hereditary succession. But they did propose hundreds of reforms. In general these reforms centered upon limiting by constitution the powers of the king and the bureaucracy; upon no taxation without representation; upon increased elective local autonomy; upon *universal* taxation; upon humane reformation of the criminal law and its procedures; upon immediate relief of the economic crisis.

Paralysis and Revolution. On May 5th the delegates gathered into a temporary structure called (ironically) the Hall of the (King's) Lesser Pleasures. The first important dispute was on a procedural question: How should the delegates vote? The first two estates insisted on each estate casting a single vote, as in the traditional manner. Realizing that this would place them at the mercy of the privileged groups, the Third Estate insisted on voting by head (one delegate—one vote) in a single body. Third Estate strategy rested on the knowledge that some nobility and many parish priests would vote with the Third Estate to give it a majority.

The result was a temporary paralysis; the first two estates met as separate orders and organized for action; the Third Estate refused to organize until its demands for meeting as a single body were met. The impasse lasted for five weeks. Then, on June 12, the Third Estate organized itself and invited the others to join it. To distinguish itself from the others, the Third Estate, on June 17, assumed the title of **National Assembly** and declared that it had sovereign power to act for the nation. The king's government was set aside. The Revolution had begun.

The National Assembly. On the same day (June 17) the National Assembly began quietly but ominously to reform the state of France. All of the royal taxes were abolished; committees were created to draw up a reformed financial structure and to take steps to relieve the distress among the poor. Louis had not yet acted. On the 20th of June Louis suspended the sessions of the Estates General. The Third Estate, in the form of the National Assembly, withdrew to a neighboring tennis court and there took an oath (The "Tennis Court Oath") not to disband until France had a constitution. This was done with great confidence because by this time many of the parish priests and nobility had joined the National Assembly.

On the 27th of June, Louis seemed to capitulate to the National Assembly by ordering the first two estates to sit with it; he began, however, to gather mercenary troops and to station them in Paris for a showdown. With each new detachment of troops, popular indignation and violence grew. It came to a head when, on July 14, the populace stormed and took the Bastille. Violence now rolled out of Paris into the countryside as enraged peasantry attacked the chateaux of the landed nobility. By the late summer of 1789, France was in the hands of the people; the authority of the crown had vanished. All eyes were turned to the National Assembly which in August had begun to reform France.

The Reforms of the National Assembly. Abolition of feudal privileges. In abolishing the survivals of the feudal past, the nobility in the National Assembly itself took the leadership. One after another the nobles rose to propose destruction of such privileges as exemption from taxation, collection of feudal taxes, monopoly rights, distinctions of rank, vested interests, hunting and fishing rights and the like.

The Declaration of the Rights of Man. Taking its lead from the example of the American Revolution, the French Revolutionists turned to a statement of general principles as a guide to further and more permanent reform. They drew up a **Declaration of the Rights of Man and of the Citizen.**

Three pillars of freedom were erected in the ideological structure. One was **property rights:** men were to be protected in their right to private ownership of property; no one could be deprived of property except in case of public necessity; anyone deprived of property had a basic right to compensation. A second was **personal rights:** these included the basic freedoms; religious toleration; equality before the law; due process of law . . . and the like. A third was **democracy:** sovereignty resided with the people; only the people could delegate sovereignty to government; and the people reserved the right of revolution against tyranny.

Secularization of the church. Church lands were confiscated and were sold in parcels to impoverished peasantry and were also used as backing for a new currency issued to meet the financial crisis. A Civil Constitution of the Clergy was then drawn up which made the priesthood elective civil servants of the state. All clergy were forced to take an oath of allegiance to the state to qualify for the priesthood. The Pope, of course, condemned this feature and prohibited oath-taking. The result was that the French clergy were divided into those who did (juring) and those who did not (non-juring) take the oath.

The Constitution of 1791. To complete their essentially conservative revolution, the French Revolutionists drew up a constitution for France which established a limited monarchy on the principle of the separation of powers. A Legislative Assembly was created with full power to make the law; it was to be indirectly elected by electoral colleges. The executive power was given to the king. As a check upon absolutism the king was shorn of control of the army, church and local government and was removed from the legislative process by being given a veto that could be overridden by the Legislative Assembly.

The Radical Phase. By 1791 the conservative phase of the Revolution was complete. Events soon propelled the Revolution into a more radical phase. To begin with, the economic demands of the impoverished wage-earners were not met; if anything, the situation grew worse due to a currency inflation. Restless, hungry workers had become organized mobs directed by leaders of radical clubs which had begun to flourish in Paris. These clubs reflected the political spectrum which early made its appearance in the National Assembly. Conservatives, those who favored a status quo, concentrated in the **Girondist Party;** Radicals, those who favored complete abolition of the monarchy and a sharp limitation on the rights of the bourgeoisie as well as the clergy and nobility, gravitated to the **Jacobin Party.**

Emigres—those who managed to flee from France to the more hospitable lands of Prussia and Austria and England—had created enough anxiety there to cause the monarchs of these countries to issue an ultimatum to the French Revolutionists to desist in their persecution of church and nobility. National irritation with this unwarranted interference resulted in a declaration of war by the Legislative Assembly on Prussia and Austria. Invasion of France by these two nations created a national emergency. National mobilization of a citizen army to meet the threat of foreign invasion followed. The king and queen actively cooperated with the emigres abroad and, on one occasion, even attempted escape. To the Radicals in France, it seemed that the very Revolution was at stake. In 1792 they moved to take over the government.

THE RADICAL PHASE OF THE FRENCH REVOLUTION

Terror. The radical phase of the French Revolution was distinguished by increased use of terrorization as political policy. "Madame Guillotine" became the symbol of this period. Under the loose designation of "enemies of the people" thousands of people were slaughtered. Some were, of course, guilty of treasonable activity, of conspiracy with the emigres abroad and the instigators of civil war at home; some were guilty of no more than association by birth with suspected elements in the population; others were victims of spite, revenge, rivalry and the like. Terror, like power, corrupts; and corruption was no more evident than in the popular jubilation which attended the ceremonies of execution.

Those who used terror were themselves victimized by it. In January 1793 Louis XVI and Marie Antoinette were executed. Only the Girondists opposed this decision. DANTON and ST. JUST, by brilliant oratory, turned the National Convention to this decision. It was not long before the Girondists were made the victims of the terror by the Jacobins led by Danton, ROBESPIERRE and others. This done, it was Danton's turn and he was executed because he felt that it was time to call halt to the terror. Under Robespierre, the guillotine was employed with increasing frequency. But in 1794 he too lost his head though he was almost dead of bullet wounds.

Dictatorship. In September 1792 the monarchy was deposed and the First French Republic declared. An election was then held for a National Convention to frame a new constitution. In 1793 the constitution was published. It was democratic to the core and provided for universal male suffrage, an elected legislature, an executive elected by the legislature, annual elections and the like. But it was not put into effect.

Arguing that the national situation of civil war, foreign war and economic depression was too dire to permit the processes of democracy, the Jacobins set aside the constitution and created instead a dictatorial Committee of Public Safety composed of nine members. This Committee assumed all the powers of government; it sent its agents abroad to check on the loyalty of Frenchmen and to negotiate with foreign governments; it created revolutionary tribunals with virtually unlimited power to try and execute "enemies of the people"; it raised armies and fought the foreign enemies; it nationalized economic enterprise much more effectively than the absolute monarchs of France. For two years there was little but the outer trappings to distinguish Robespierre from Louis XVI.

The fall of Robespierre brought a reaction to terror and dictatorship (the **Thermidorean Reaction**). A new constitution was written in 1795 which returned France to a moderate course. Power was divided between a bicameral legislature and a Directory or executive of five members. Voting was restricted to property owners; age-limits for holding office were raised; two-thirds of the membership of a new legislature had to be chosen from the old. Terror had made men suspicious of democracy.

Reforms. Under the dictatorship some permanent reforms were effected. Price controls stopped the inflation; the metric system was adopted; a commission to revise the law code of France began its work by providing for prison reforms, abolition of imprisonment for debts, abolition of slavery in the colonies; public education was expanded with the creation of Normal schools and Polytechnical institutes; a national library was set up; confiscated land was sold to peasants and made France into a nation of small farmers. Above all, the civil war was suppressed and foreign enemies were forced into signing the peace treaties of 1795 which declared an end to foreign efforts to suppress the French Revolution and French efforts to spread it abroad. These accomplishments left permanent effects.

Not so were the efforts of the radical Jacobins to abolish *Monsieur* and *Madame* in favor of *Citizen;* to introduce a new calendar with 1792 as the Year I and with the months renamed to celebrate nature and her wonders; to institute and enforce the worship of the goddess Reason; to inaugurate an official Reign of Virtue and the like.

NAPOLEON BONAPARTE

The Directory ruled France for four years (1795–1799) and then succumbed to a bloodless *coup d'état* unleashed by NAPOLEON BONAPARTE who then ruled France until 1815.

In those five years the Directory so alienated the affections of the French people that they accepted Napoleon as their savior. The Directory was unable to cope with renewed inflation; when it issued a new currency, it could not force popular acceptance of it. Nor could it cope with increasing pressure by the clergy, widely supported by the people, for some restoration of their property and rights. Unbelievable corruption characterized the Directors, each of whom ruled for a price. Peace had been concluded with Prussia, Holland and Spain; but negotiations with England and Austria had fallen through because the Directory insisted upon an extension of France's boundaries to the Rhine.

On October 5, 1795 a Paris mob attacked the Directory and only the quick and ruthless wit of an artillery officer named Napoleon Bonaparte, a Corsican, saved it. On this "whiff of grapeshot" Napoleon marched into history as the prototype of the modern dictator.

What Makes A Dictator? No man in history has been more analyzed than Napoleon, who rose from complete obscurity to become European conqueror. A boundless ambition seems a first requirement. Napoleon had this in abundance.

Recognition of opportunity or rank opportunism coupled with unscrupulous and amoral actions speeded him. He did not hesitate to use artillery against an unarmed crowd, or to enter into a loveless marriage for advancement or to cajole the support of any group that could be useful to him. He permitted himself loyalty to no man; he was his own cause; and this limitless egotism seems a requisite for the temperament of a dictator. Ability, too, is needed; genius is preferable. Napoleon had both military and administrative genius.

The Rise To Power. Having saved the Republic and won the hand of Josephine Beauharnais who had great influence in the Directory, Napoleon in 1796 secured command of the Army of Italy; his instructions were to use his ragged force of 30,000 men to divert the Austrians from the south while the main thrust was made in the North. Napoleon turned this diversionary movement into a major thrust and virtually marched north on Vienna. The Austrians were forced to sue for peace. Acting on the principle that what is done can often not be undone, Napoleon, *without consent of the Directory,* negotiated the Treaty of Campo Formio which forced Austria to recognize French claims to the Rhine, to release her Italian possessions and to surrender Lombardy and Belgium to the French.

This done, Napoleon proceeded with political reorganization of the Italian states into the Cisalpine and Ligurian Republics. He announced himself as the liberator of Italy, the son of the French Revolution and imposed "liberty and equality" on the occupied lands. Beneath this role of liberator lay the more obvious role of terrorist; opposition to French booty-taking was punished with shocking brutality. Napoleon returned to Paris as a conquering hero. What could the Directory do? The army worshipped their commander.

The Egyptian Maneuver. It was clear to Napoleon that the Directory could not long survive. He, Napoleon, must not lend his strength to support their weakness. With keen political astuteness Napoleon therefore proposed that he undertake an Egyptian Campaign as a first step to deprive England of her life-line to Italy. Anxious to get rid of this rising menace, the Directory gave its ungrudging consent to the campaign. In July of 1798 Napoleon evaded the watchful British navy led by Admiral Nelson and landed in Egypt. In the Battle of the Nile, Nelson destroyed Napoleon's fleet and trapped him inside Egypt. Though Egypt fell an easy prey, Napoleon was unable to remove his army from Egypt. He therefore deserted it when news came that France was his for the taking.

A new coalition of powers (England, Russia, Austria, Portugal, Turkey and Naples) had been formed for an attack on France; along the Rhine and in the Italies the French armies were steadily being pushed back. Leaving his scruples in Egypt to follow his star, Napoleon barely evaded Nelson's fleet and returned to Paris as the conqueror of Egypt, as another Caesar. A conspiracy to overthrow the Directory was effected with the aid of three directors and the upper house of the legislature. On November 9, 1799 Napoleon's armed force took possession of the state.

Dictators prefer to act constitutionally. Having seized power, Napoleon wrote a new constitution establishing an elected **Consulate** with himself as First Consul. He created a legislative apparatus but made it impotent. By 1802, Napoleon was ready to throw off the disguise of democracy. He was elected consul for life. Two years later he became Emperor of the French with rights to hereditary succession.

Wherever possible he remained close to popular acceptance. After each coup he submitted the accomplished fact to a popular vote. Since these votes were conducted without free discussion, with no possible alternatives and under army rule, they were overwhelmingly for each of Napoleon's acts. (There is little doubt, on the other hand, that as long as he was successful, Napoleon did command the loyalty of the French people.)

Conqueror. In 1810 Napoleon ruled France, the eastern half of Italy, Belgium, Holland, the Rhineland—directly; indirectly he controlled the vast Confederation of the Rhine (the Germanies), the Grand Duchy of Warsaw (Poland), the Kingdom of Italy, the Kingdom of Naples, Switzerland and the Kingdom of Spain. Within the French orbits lay Denmark and Norway, Prussia and Austria. This overlordship was achieved by conquest in war.

Napoleon's victories at Ulm, Austerlitz, Jena, Friedland are classics of military strategy and are still studied in military academies. His military principles included: simplicity, rapidity, superiority of forces in localized areas, concentration, quick decision on the spot, meticulous study of positions and alternatives, keen perception of the psychology of the opponent, judicious use of all information, material and moral, attention to the most insignificant of details, obedient officers who took no initiative, rigid discipline and self-confidence. Yet, within five years of his position in 1810, his armies were defeated and his kingdom gone. What brought this conqueror so low?

Decline and Fall. Many factors served to bring about the collapse of Napoleon. None was more important than England's dogged resistance and her command of the seas and her ability to inspire and to supply opposition to Napoleon. England's chief weapon was her shops and her chief warrior shopkeepers who produced manufactured goods that were far more durable and cheap than any produced on the continent.

Napoleon hoped to choke off all British trade with the continent. By a series of decrees he placed a paper blockade around Europe and around England; no English ship could deliver goods to Europe; and no non-English ship could deliver goods to England. England retorted with her own blockade on French ships and on foreign ships trading with the French. Europeans felt severely the prohibition on entry into Europe of British goods and evaded Napoleon's **Continental System** by widespread smuggling.

It was the Continental System that led to Napoleon's disastrous Spanish campaign and march into Russia. In Spain Napoleon had to fight a species of guerilla warfare that drained men and supplies and could not be brought to a decision. In Russia he encountered similar warfare accompanied by a "scorched earth" policy and then by bitter winter fighting for which the French were unprepared. Half-a-million men were lost in the **Russian Campaign of 1812.** Moreover, willingness to fight the French resulted from the insurgence of nationalism that arose out of disillusionment with Napoleon's promises of liberation and out of national humiliation resulting from constant defeat at Napoleon's hands. Freedom proved a double-edged sword for the conqueror.

So, too, did Napoleon's efforts to unify such countries as Italy, Germany and Poland. Napoleon's aim was efficiency in French domination. But having tasted the sweets of unification, these countries now demanded the fruits—independence from French domination.

Finally, continual war exhausted the French materially and spiritually. Only a few Frenchmen reaped the benefits of war profits; on most fell the burdens of French taxation and the loss and mutilation of their loved ones. All of these factors collected at Leipzig in 1814 and in the **Battle of Nations** Napoleon suffered total defeat. He was sent to **Elbe** in exile but escaped and for "100 Days" gave Europe a fright until in 1815 he was finally destroyed at **Waterloo.** Once more he was sent into exile on the island of **St. Helena** in the mid-Atlantic. There he "ruled" until he died on May 5, 1821.

The Industrial Revolution

The Industrial Revolution spread out of England slowly; in 1850 the primary productive pattern in the western world was still agriculture and it was not until 1870 that manufacturing began to overtake agriculture.

There are many explanations for this slow progress. Europe, for example, spent the first quarter of the 19th century recovering from the Napoleonic Wars. Many of the countries lacked some one or more of the basic factors required for industrial progress. Social or cultural lag existed in mental outlook and educational system. In the United States wide stretches of free or almost free land acted as a deterrent and prevented large capital accumulation. England's initial superiority gave her a competitive advantage that handicapped other nations. In spite of these many handicaps, however, the Industrial Revolution spread into Europe, particularly into France, Belgium and Germany; Italy and Russia lagged until the very end of the 19th century.

Stages In The Industrial Revolution. Primary concentration in the first stage (ca. 1750–1850) was upon elaboration of the productive process: discovery of required raw materials, refinement of processes in the extraction of raw materials, extensions of the uses of the steam engine, construction of factories and the development in workers of factory discipline, laying the groundwork for an improved system of transportation and solving the problem of maximizing profits (capital accumulation).

In the second stage of the Industrial Revolution (1850–1900) productive inventiveness continued at a rapid pace; but the other factors of labor, distribution and exchange became the center of concentration. To reduce labor costs and the growing "threat" of labor organization, manufacturers began to invest in machines that would break down production into minute processes and destroy the basis of skilled labor. Symbolic of this trend was the work of the American, FREDERICK WINSLOW TAYLOR (1856–1915), in the field of scientific management. Taylor began experimental studies ("time-and-motion" studies) to set standards of efficient working performance. During this period the corporative form of business organization was elaborated as was the relation of business to banking.

In the field of invention a revolution was effected in transportation and communication. By 1850 the railroad had proved its effectiveness and a rush was begun in all countries to lay track. Problems involved in railroad transport were soon overcome by invention of high powered locomotives, air brakes, standard gauges, signal systems, refrigeration cars, sleepers and the like. Steamboating kept pace with railroading.

More and more industrialism, in this period, began to rely upon pure science. This was nowhere more true than in the field of communications. Out of the work of such men as Franklin, Galvani, Volta, Ampere, Ohm, Maxwell and Faraday came the possibility of communication by electrical impulses. An electric telegraph was invented independently by Carl Steinheil, a German, Charles Wheatstone, an Englishman, and Samuel Morse an American. The telegraph, however, was landbound until Cyrus W. Field solved the oceanographic problems required to lay a trans-Atlantic cable; this was accomplished in 1866.

Important advances were registered, too, in the field of lighting. The kerosene lamp was perfected in 1784. More useful, however, was the gaslighting device perfected by Murdock, Bunsen and Welsbach in the mid-nineteenth century. Toward the end of this period, electric lighting made its appearance as a result of the researches of Davy, Marks, Edison and many others.

The third stage of the Industrial Revolution had little unity—expansion occurred in every imaginable direction. Invention itself was systematized and accelerated through creation of subsidized laboratories. Of special note was the rise of the chemist as an adjunct to industry. Upon him fell the responsibility of discovering new uses for old resources and the manufacture of synthetic resources as substitutes for natural products.

Out of the invention of the internal combustion engine and the electric motor whole new worlds appeared: the automobile industry, the industries of radio and television, great hydroelectric plants, the airplane industry and the like. Of equal importance was the development of the precision instrument—a development that gave to the physicist the same status as the chemist in the industrial world. The engineer, of course, became a key figure as the demand for roads, bridges, communications, building structures, electrical appliances and the like rose.

Mass production became a startling reality when the factory was rationalized through use of assembly lines and standardized parts. Of primary importance was the distribution of this mass production. Problems of transport were solved through further developments of railroad and steamship and the introduction of trucks and airplanes. But the sale of goods required the transformation of advertising into a national industry. This in turn put pressure on the creation of mass media of communication. The linotype machine, typewriter, and rotary press accommodated this need; radio and television enhanced it. Along with the revolution in advertisement of products, came a revolution in the financing of the purchase of goods—installment buying. With exhaustion of resources at home began a worldwide search for raw materials such as rubber, tin, nitrates, manganese, magnesium, chromium, nickel, lead, copper, hardwoods, etc.

With the discovery of thermonuclear power a new and fourth stage in the Industrial Revolution loomed. This stage brought the physicist to the fore. It is too early to project the transformations that will be made as a result of this discovery of a new power-source. The peaceful uses of atomic energy have been probed—chiefly in the areas of medical research, agricultural production, new sources of power and the like. The world is waiting for a new dawn.

RESULTS OF THE INDUSTRIAL REVOLUTION

General. In essence, the Industrial Revolution was a transfer from hand tool to machine process; from muscle-wind-and-water power to steam-gas-electricity-and-atomic power. Manufacturing became a way of life emphasizing compulsory centralization of the labor force around the machine, complete dependence of the labor force upon the machine for a livelihood, impersonalization of the relations between worker and employer and regimentation of the life of the worker to the demands of production. From the factory flowed ever-increasing production and this was reflected in expanding commerce, accumulated capital, national and international corporations, business combinations in the forms of merger, trust, holding company, interlocking directorates, cartels and the like. Increased standards of living resulted and this was followed by rapid increases of population for the most part gathered into urban areas where cultural life blossomed on the nurture provided by increased educational facilities. But culture, too, followed the pattern of standardization; mass media threatened to produce mass minds, mass behavior.

Machine Culture. Mankind came to depend upon invention for innovation; progress was equated with multiplication of gadgets. There was no limit to inventiveness. In the wake of the mechanization of society came many problems affecting human welfare: overcrowded cities, indebtedness, increasing destructiveness of wars, labor-management conflict, and the like.

The Workingman. The brunt of the inhumanity in the machine civilization fell upon the workingman. Skilled workers of the late 18th and early 19th centuries resented and resisted the introduction of the factory system; they became, in fact, "machine-wreckers." Factory processes reduced the workingman to a mechanical unit engaged in some small specialized task that produced fatigue and boredom.

Moreover, in the early period of capital accumulation working conditions were abominable. Factories were hastily and cheaply built; no provisions were made for the health or safety of the employees in matters of ventilation, lighting or provisions for creature comforts. Child labor was brutally exploited in the form of pauper apprentices. Hours of work ranged between 14 and 16 a day. Wages were miserably low.

From impoverished conditions in the factory, workers moved to even worse conditions at home. Slums made up the bulk of dwelling quarters in factory towns. Crime and epidemic disease were the consequences of these miserable hovels in which workers dwelt. Added to these inadequate conditions of work was the continuous insecurity that hung over the heads of the working people. They were completely unprotected in the face of unemployment produced by technological change or depressions, of illness and accident for which there was no compensation, and of old age—a variable figure depending on the supply of workers available. This, then, was the social lag behind industrial progress.

Overcoming The Social Lag. To overcome the social lag to industrial progress, a humanitarian revolution in the minds of the rulers of mankind had to be effected. Horrible conditions had first to be seen as horrible, and felt as such. This required intensive education through propaganda and agitation, a campaign that was launched by workers' organizations, philosophers like Jeremy Bentham and William Godwin, poets like Shelley and Thomas Hood, novelists like Charles Dickens and George Eliot and politicians like Benjamin Disraeli, William Gladstone, Otto von Bismarck, Andrew Jackson. These men helped to transform the problem of working conditions into a *moral* question.

The result of all this agitation and propaganda was a series of social laws passed by interested governments which set out to reform the conditions under which men labored in factories and mines. In England, for example, between 1802 and 1860, a large number of factory acts were passed. These had the effect of reducing by law the number of hours of work, of discouraging the employment of child labor, of limiting the employment of women, of compelling the introduction of health, sanitation and safety devices in factories. Later legislation in England (1870–1920) freed workers to organize into labor unions and to strike for increased wages and improved working conditions.

Germany, under OTTO VON BISMARCK, took the leadership in framing the first social security laws, laws providing for workman's compensation in the event of accident on the job, for old age pensions, for sickness and unemployment insurance. These laws were eventually introduced into all the industrialized nations of the world.

The Capitalist System. Capitalism came to full growth under the impetus of the Industrial Revolution. It was the primary agency in the transformation of society from a low-producing to a high-producing level. In the course of its development, capitalism moved through several stages. The earliest was the stage of industrial capitalism—where individual capitalists owned the factories as single proprietorships or as partnerships. To a great extent these capitalists relied upon their own resources for expansion. As business grew, however, the single proprietorship and partnership proved to be inadequate as financial vehicles. The result was that capitalists began to depend more and more on the corporation—and the sale of stocks and bonds—as a means for gathering in wealth. Increasingly, in this second stage of capitalist development, industrialists began to turn to the banks for loans for expansion.

This led to the third stage, that of finance capitalism. In this stage industrial and banking elements in the economic process merged to provide industry with a virtually unlimited capital expansion base. In this area, as in the area of mechanization, a social lag appeared.

Ownership and management were divorced, a divorce that produced the possibilities of mismanagement. Mismanagement resulted in practices which strangled free competition by monopolization; which defrauded stockholders through issuance of "watered" stock, or failure to declare dividends; which practiced fraud on consumers through price fixing, adulteration of product and the like; which encouraged corrupt political practices like bribery of legislators. The social lag was somewhat remedied in most countries by government intervention that resulted in anti-trust laws, laws regulating the issuance of corporate securities, pure food and drug laws, income and corporate tax laws and the like.

Abandonment of Laissez Faire. Government intervention in the economic process is the antithesis of laissez faire, the system of ideas under which capitalism grew to maturity. As taught by Adam Smith in his *Wealth of Nations*, the doctrine of laissez faire assumed that there were rational, natural laws that governed economic behavior. Men left alone to pursue selfish ends in the use of their capital and labor would ultimately produce social good. The laws of free trade and of competition, of supply and demand, would determine success and failure in the economic struggle for existence; but the end result would be an increase in the total national wealth.

Smith founded the school of liberal or **classical economists,** members of which searched for "natural laws" in the economy of capitalism. Thus THOMAS MALTHUS proposed an "iron law" of population and demonstrated that famine, war, disease and population control are advantageous since population increases geometrically while food supply increases arithmetically. DAVID RICARDO "proved" that wages sink to the mere level of subsistence. Nassau Senior "demonstrated" that hours of work could not be lowered without disastrous consequences to profits. McCulloch "proved" on the basis of and existing "wages-fund" that wage increase to one group had to result in wage decrease for another.

All of this theorizing resulted in a pattern of beliefs that called for abolition of tariffs and subsidies, free contracting, treatment of labor organization as conspiracy, free competition, and no government restraint upon economic free choice. Between 1800 and 1860 the English government, for example, followed this doctrine to the letter. The "corn laws (tariffs)" were repealed, mercantilist regulations concerning the granting of monopolies were removed from the legislative books, laws protecting apprentices were abrogated. We have seen the abuses that followed upon this adoption of the complete policy of laissez faire. (There is little doubt that if we ignore humanitarian considerations, laissez faire did accomplish miracles in production at a time when the resources for such productive effort were limited.)

No country followed England in its application of the policy of laissez faire. From their inception, the classical economists were challenged on theoretical lines. From America and Germany came economic doctrines defending protectionism as a means for hastening industrial advance. Population theorists challenged Malthus when it became obvious that the industrial revolution would extend to the farm and result in fabulous increases in food production. The most serious challenge, however, came from the "socialists" who took the abuses of the capitalist as their starting point and ignored the many efforts being made by governments to correct these abuses.

Socialism. Socialism was as much an *ethical* as an economic discipline; its theories were in part formed out of a preconceived utopian dream in which all men were economically equal and lived in the midst of abundance.

Early socialists like SAINT-SIMON (1760–1825), FOURIER (1772–1837) and ROBERT OWEN (1772–1858) were labelled "Utopians" by later socialists like KARL MARX (1818–1883). This derogatory label was not directed against the ultimate plans of the Utopians, for these plans envisaged the abolition of the capitalist class and the substitution of some form of workingclass ownership and control of the means of production (as socialism is defined). Derogation was directed against the means by which these theoreticians proposed to eliminate the capitalist class.

Saint-Simon hoped to bring socialism by the arts of persuasion and appeal to Christian doctrine; Fourier proposed that workers and others form voluntary socialist societies which he called "phalanxes" where all would work for all; Owen hoped to convince capitalists by his own example to build model socialist communities with their capital. (Fourierism caught on somewhat in the United States in the 1830's and '40's where experiments like Brook Farm and Oneida were tried and failed. Owen went bankrupt after his ventures in capitalist socialism at New Harmony, Indiana.) LOUIS BLANC (1813–1882)—an influential figure in the Revolution of 1848 in France—advanced the concept of government financed socialist communities, a scheme for turning over factories to workers and financing them until they were able to stand on their own feet. In practice this system turned out to be a huge financial dole that almost bankrupted the government.

Karl Marx (author of *Capital* and co-author with Frederick Engels of *Communist Manifesto*) condemned all of these efforts and proposed instead his own brand of "scientific" socialism. He advocated both peaceful and violent waging of a "class war" to overthrow capitalism. His followers, who believed in peaceful "class war" became latter-day socialists; those who favored force and violence to establish a "dictatorship of the proletariat" became communists. Marxism, then, was both a theory about capitalist society and a blueprint for its replacement.

Imperialism and World War I

IMPERIALISM

About 1875 territorial aggrandizement became the dominant drive of the large European powers, and of the United States of America. No one cause can account for this phenomenon. The Industrial Revolution was certainly a most important factor. As industry expanded so did the need for raw materials, many of them unavailable in the industrialized lands. This caused a search for basic materials, particularly for such materials as rubber, tin, petroleum, tungsten, etc.

As mass production mounted, nations began to seek potential "outlets" for surplus goods; colonies could be excellent dumping grounds for these goods and in many cases imperialized markets were the "margin of profit" for manufacturers. Similarly with surplus capital that now began to accumulate. Investments at home rarely brought the rate of return that could be gained by investment in colonial areas where labor was cheap and monopoly assured by government fiat.

Accompanying these economic motives for imperialism were equally strong political, social, psychological and religious ones. Nationalism virtually dictated that each nation should seek some "place in the sun"; national pride was fostered by each new splatter of color on the map that showed national expansion; national propaganda led to widespread belief that each nation was engaged in a civilizing mission. Very popular, though little founded in fact, was the prevailing argument that all nations, riding the crest of tremendous population increases, needed outlets for "surplus" population. Enough people did emigrate to the colonies to make this fiction seem a fact. Also there was the revival in this period of missionary activities that opened wide new worlds to the West.

Finally, imperialist expansion was strongly advocated by military leaders in all nations as the best means for securing naval bases and an adequate supply of strategic raw materials. To the support of these military men came the geographers who developed anew the doctrines of geopolitics, the science of national security that determined what heartland and fringelands were vital to "defense"—even though they were inhabited by other peoples. Geopolitics became power-politics, politics supported by military force. In reality, it was a "scientific" rationale for world conquest or domination.

Methods and Forms of Imperialism. International trade, investments and loans are not imperialistic but are part of a normal process of international intercourse. They become imperialistic when they are used as excuses for territorial conquest or for establishing exclusive economic control. During the late nineteenth century it often happened that rulers of undeveloped areas borrowed heavily from the investment bankers of the west. In exchange for such loans favored concessions were made to European investors. If such rulers defaulted on their debts or were unable to protect the investments in railroads, mines, etc., it often happened that the rulers of the powerful investor nations sent troops into that area to "protect" the lives and property of their nationals. It was at this point that imperialism began. Under foreign control these areas lost their political freedom and the right to exploit their own national wealth.

Out of this pattern emerged four forms of imperialist control: the **colony** or direct political control where the powerful nation openly ruled the undeveloped area as a possession; the **protectorate** or indirect political control where the powerful nation ruled the undeveloped area through a native puppet; the **concession** or exclusive direct control over some particular resource; and the **sphere of influence** or indirect economic control over the whole of the undeveloped area. These basic forms intermingled freely. The imperialist test for any of them was the degree of freedom retained by the undeveloped area.

THE FIRST WORLD WAR

The basic causes of the first World War were the rival imperialist ambitions among the western powers, their excessive nationalistic pride, the armaments race that developed in the face of political and economic rivalry, the struggle of suppressed peoples for independence, the geopolitical drive to reach "natural boundaries" and the absence in the world of any effective world organization that might have prevented war through peaceful settlement of disputes. These fundamental causes worked themselves out in a series of international events the primary effect of which was to create two great systems of alliances that opposed each other in a menacing **balance of power.**

The Triple Alliance vs. The Triple Entente. The **Triple Alliance** of Germany, Austria-Hungary and Italy (and allied satellites) was born from Bismarck's desire to isolate France so that she could never wage a war of revenge against Germany after her ignominious defeat in the Franco-Prussian War. By promise and perfidy Bismarck secured a secret defensive alliance with Austria-Hungary, a "gentleman's agreement" with Russia, an alliance with Italy directed against France, English neutrality, Serbian and Rumanian allegiance, and Turkish friendship.

To each of these nations Germany promised diplomatic support for nationalist aspiration—no matter how contradictory these promises were. Thus Russia and Austria-Hungary were bitter rivals in the Balkans as were Serbia and Austria-Hungary; Italy had many grievances against Austria-Hungary with respect to *Italia Irridenta;* Rumania and Turkey could not be friends. Yet Bismarck accomplished the impossible as long as Germany pursued a non-imperialist policy of its own. When William II overrode Bismarck and began an aggressive policy of imperialism, economic rivalry and arms supremacy, the grand alliance fell apart. Out of its pieces was born the **Triple Entente.**

Russia was the first to leave and to join France in a Dual Alliance in 1894. When Germany rejected Russia's request for large modernization loans, France granted them in exchange for a military convention that amounted to a defensive alliance. (This agreement, incidentally, was as much directed against England as against Germany, for England was threatening France in the Sudan and Russia in Persia and the Far East.)

By 1900 a number of factors compelled England to reconsider her policy of "splendid isolation" from continental affairs. Germany had begun to construct a formidable navy and to challenge England's markets in all parts of the world. She was the chief obstacle to the union of British territories in east Africa. Now she proposed to construct a Berlin to Baghdad Railroad through Turkey which would possibly destroy England's trade advantage in the Near East and India. The result was the **Entente Cordiale** with France (1904), a settlement of all territorial differences and an implied defensive alliance. Russian-English differences over Persia and the Far East were finally settled in an entente that settled differences in Persia and Afghanistan by division of those territories. By 1907 the Triple Entente was complete and faced the Triple Alliance in a delicate balance of power.

International Crises. War approached by a series of international crises in North Africa and the Balkans. In 1905 France began a series of familiar maneuvers westward from Algeria into Morocco, an area that Germany had selected as her own hunting grounds. The Kaiser promised the Moroccan ruler support if he resisted French overtures and then went on to demand that the "Moroccan Question" be submitted to an international conference. Such a conference was held in 1906 at Algeciras and Germany forced through a policy of the "open door" in Morocco to France's chagrin.

In 1911 an uprising in Morocco gave the French an excuse to move in with troops. The Germans sent the "Panther," a gunboat, to challenge French occupation. War hung in the balance. At that moment English warships began to maneuver around the "Panther," and Germany decided that the time was not ripe for a challenge. In exchange for a part of the French Congo Germany gave France a "free hand" in Morocco.

Attention was now focused on the Balkans. In 1908 a group of humiliated **Young Turks,** resentful of the slow disintegration of the Turkish Empire, undertook a revolution. Austria-Hungary took advantage of this situation to annex Balkan territory. Russia, fearful of Austro-Hungarian moves, had secured a promise from her that she would support Russian moves in the Dardenelles area in exchange for Russian support for Balkan seizures by Austria-Hungary. This was the infamous "Buchlau Bargain."

Austria-Hungary violated the bargain by annexing Bosnia and Herzegovina without support for Russia's territorial ambitions. Russia was infuriated and resolved to make war on the first occasion that presented itself. She began to provoke Serbia into anti-Austrian activities. At the same time Russia continued maneuvering against Turkey by organizing a Balkan League (Montenegro, Serbia, Bulgaria and Greece) for an assault on Turkey. This assault came in 1912 and 1913 in two Balkan Wars. Once again Austria frustrated Russian ambitions by creating the buffer state of Albania. Europe became a "powder magazine."

The spark that blew it up occurred in Sarajevo, Bosnia when the Austrian Archduke Ferdinand was assassinated by a member of a secret society for the creation of a greater Serbia. Austria delivered an ultimatum to Serbia to stop all anti-Austrian propaganda, to suppress all anti-Austrian publications, to dismiss Serbian officials implicated in the assassination plot, to permit Austrian police forces to enforce the ultimatum. Serbia temporized and on July 28, 1914 Austria declared war on Serbia. On July 30 Russia mobilized. On July 31 Germany warned Russia to cease mobilizing; Russia refused. On August 1 Germany declared war on Russia and sent an ultimatum to France to remain neutral. France temporized. On August 3 Germany declared war on France and began to pass through Belgium whose neutrality had been guaranteed by all the European powers. On August 4, when Germany refused to respect Belgian neutrality, England declared war. The holocaust was on. Who was responsible?

The Military Phase. From 1914 to 1918 the greatest war in history to that date was fought. Before it was over, thirty nations had become participants, 65,000,000 men bore arms, 8,500,000 soldiers were killed, 29,000,000 were wounded, an inestimable number of civilians were destroyed and some $200,000,000,000 had been expended.

After initial German successes, the war settled down to a stalemate fought in "no-man's lands" from fixed trenches along the western front. Following an initial push to Paris, the Germans were stopped at the Marne; thereafter they were held in spite of such mighty pushes as the one at Verdun.

Allied counter-attacks came similarly to grief. Efforts of the Allies to take Turkey in the Gallipoli campaign were repulsed. The Austrians were checked in the Balkans. Italy deserted the Triple Alliance for the Allied cause but proved more of a handicap than an aid particularly following her defeat at Caporetto. In only one direction did the war move to a completion, that of Germany's assault on Russia. Then came the Russian revolution, and the Bolsheviks, who seized power from the democratic liberals in November of 1917, decided to seek peace. In 1918 they signed the **Treaty of Brest-Litovsk** which ceded Poland, Lithuania, Courland, Bessarabia, the Caucasus, Finland, Estonia, Latvia and the Ukraine to the Central Powers.

Germany did not win the war chiefly as a result of the entry of the United States in 1917. Provoked by unrestricted submarine warfare, sabotage, plots with Mexico and German sabre rattling, and led by economic stakes in the Allied cause and effective Allied propaganda in the United States, America declared war on April 6, 1917, resolved to make the world safe for democracy and to fight a war to end all wars. So did Woodrow Wilson frame the goals of the Allied cause. Entry of men and material from America in 1918 gave the Allied powers the strength to mount a final offensive in 1918, one that broke through German lines and forced the Germans to sue for peace on November 11, 1918.

The Versailles Treaty. Vision and reality met in battle on January 18, 1919 when the victorious powers met to determine the fate of their conquered enemies. The vision was in the person of Woodrow Wilson, President of the United States, who had boldly announced in January 1918 his **Fourteen Points** for an enduring peace. Wilson foresaw a post-war world where secret diplomacy would be outlawed; where the seas would be free; where all economic barriers to international trade would be removed; where armaments races would end; where imperialism would be eliminated on moral grounds; where national aspirations would be respected; where closed waters, such as the Dardenelles, would be forever open; and where a league of nations would be established to settle once for all all international disputes by conciliation, arbitration and judicial settlement. It was a splendid vision, one that captured the imagination of people all over the world.

The reality was in the persons of LLOYD GEORGE of England, CLEMENCEAU of France and ORLANDO of Italy who comprised a "Big Three" determined to make the Peace of Versailles a vengeful and profitable one at the expense of the conquered nations. What emerged was in the nature of a compromise between the vision and the reality.

Germany, Austria-Hungary, Turkey and Bulgaria were punished. Germany ceded Alsace-Lorraine back to France, Eurpen and Malmedy to Belgium and a corridor through West Prussia for Poland to reach the sea. Schleswig was returned to Denmark; Lithuania secured Memel; Danzig became an internationalized "free city"; the Saar was placed under the political control of the League of Nations and the economic control of France for fifteen years after which there was to be a plebiscite held in which the Saarlanders could vote for a permanent political settlement of their fate. Germany lost all of her Pacific holdings to the League of Nations which received them as "mandates" and which distributed them to the victorious powers for education and eventual release as independent states. (Such was Wilson's plan for the eventual elimination of imperialism.)

Germany was then stripped of all military power—armed forces, navy, fortifications—and had to submit to occupation of her territory to ensure enforcement of the terms of the treaty. At the same time, Germany was declared to be guilty of having provoked the war and was therefore made to bear the expense of repairing the damage. Reparations costs ran to some sixty billion dollars. As immediate payments on this reparations bill, Germany was stripped of railroads, capital equipment, livestock and coal. Out of the treaties of St.

Germain, Neuilly and Serves with Austria, Hungary and Turkey respectively came the birth of many new nations and additional mandated territories to be granted to the victorious powers.

The League of Nations. In exchange for many concessions to the nationalist and imperialist aims of the victorious allied powers, Wilson demanded that as Article I of the Versailles Treaty appear a covenant for a League of Nations to which all the victorious powers would belong and which would be given sufficient power to end all future wars.

To some degree this was accomplished. An international organization was framed which would include an Assembly of all the member nations, each with a single vote; an executive Council of permanent big-power members and non-permanent elected members to enforce decrees of the Assembly; a World Court for the judicial settlement of disputes; a Secretariat for arranging meetings and recording results. The covenant also provided for a mandate system to eliminate imperialism. It was projected, too, that the League would form committees to alleviate some of the basic economic, health, education and communication problems of the world.

That there would be an end to war seemed a realizable hope in the year 1919. Countries were already projecting a series of disarmament conferences that would reduce the burden of maintaining powerful armed forces. Nationalism had been satisfied in the creation of the "succession states" of Poland, Czechoslovakia, Austria, Hungary, Yugoslavia and others. Imperialism would end as mandatory nations fulfilled their obligations to their territories and prepared them for the status of independent nations who would then join the League. International anarchy was to end with the establishment and growth in the power of the League of Nations and the World Court. International cooperation was to replace economic rivalry. What causes for any future war were possible?

But twenty years later came a second, and even more terrible, war. What went wrong with the vision?

The Shaping of the Modern World

SOVIET RUSSIA

In March 1917 the Tsar was overthrown and a liberal democratic state set up under the leadership of Prince Lvov and Professor Miliukov. Instrumental in this overthrow were the numerous "soviets" or local government that had made their appearance during the stages of the first revolution. In the elected Soviets the Bolsheviks (communists) led by Lenin had no control.

In the first All-Russian Congress of Soviets held in June of 1917 Kerensky Social Revolutionaries and Menshevik socialists-groups favoring democratic processes of government—were voted control of the government. Even after the Bolsheviks had seized control of the government of Petrograd in November 7th they could not secure approval from a constitutional assembly called in January 1918 to confirm the seizure. This constitutional assembly was freely and democratically elected. However, when it voted down Bolshevik proposals with respect to making peace, distributing land and disarming all of the Russians but the workers, it was abruptly dismissed and in its place was created a dictatorship under the leadership of Nicolai Lenin, Leon Trotsky and Joseph Stalin.

Many circumstances played into the hands of the Bolsheviks to enable them to maintain and to consolidate their power. They voluntarily signed the Treaty of Brest-Litovsk with Germany in which they surrendered a considerable portion of European Russia. Moreover, they published secret treaties that revealed many of the imperialist aims of the warring allied powers.

Frightened by the success of the Bolsheviks, the Allied powers dispatched an international force to aid the "White Russians" in their effort at a counter-revolution. Since these "White Russians" contained many of the elements of the hated Old Regime the Allied intervention was strongly opposed.

Meanwhile, the Bolsheviks set up the Cheka—

secret police and revolutionary tribunals—which destroyed not only elements of the old regime but *all* opposition to Bolshevism. At the same time, to give meaning to their "socialist" revolution, the Bolsheviks temporarily turned factories over to workers' committees, distributed land to the peasants, as much as each could work, nationalized all industry without compensation, confiscated all Tsarist obligations to domestic and foreign lenders and removed money as a means of exchange.

Consolidation. In 1919 a Supreme Economic Council was created to make plans for the eventual creation of complete state ownership and operation of the means of production. The productive system collapsed and in 1921 there was desperate poverty.

In 1921, therefore, Lenin ordered a "new economic policy" to be instituted. The base of the new economic policy was state ownership of about 85 per cent of the means of production. In the remaining 15 per cent the Communists permitted foreign investors to invest funds at high rates of interest. Opposition abroad was considerably disarmed by this maneuver; Western nations were led to believe that Russia would some day return to the family of capitalist nations. In 1924 Communist Russia was officially recognized by Great Britain, France and Italy. Not until 1934 did the United States follow suit.

The "Plan" was fulfilled in a series of "five-year plans" launched by JOSEPH STALIN in 1928. All foreign influence in Russian industry was abolished. A state planning commission drew up goals for a five-year increase in industrialization, mechanization and electrification of state owned industries. Every type of incentive was used to increase worker productivity; this was needed, for productivity increase was linked to a decrease in consumption—the surplus being used to purchase basic machinery abroad. Meanwhile, the process of forcible collectivization of farms was begun.

Thus straitjacketed the Russian economy did move into the high gear of production. Opposition to collectivization was so strong, however, that Russia suffered another severe food famine in 1934. A second five-year plan eased the consumption picture somewhat; a third was just begun when Russia was attacked by the Nazi forces. Her industrialization, considerably aided by American "lend-lease," stood her in good stead and enabled her to make a rapid recovery after the war.

Dictatorship. Protest in Russia could find no effective means of expression once the Bolsheviks had imposed their dictatorship. All political opposition was suppressed. The "purge" and staged trials became an institution by which Joseph Stalin periodically eliminated potential rivals.

Yet the Communists could not forever ignore the need for some form of national consent. In 1936 they granted a constitution which constructed a tremendous facade of republican institutions that were designed to conceal the dictatorship. A bicameral legislature representing all the people and their nationalist divisions was created; an elective ministry headed by a premier was set up as executive. An extensive "bill of rights" was added. But the realities in these political forms are evident in the facts that in Soviet elections only one party is permitted, that only members of the Communist Party may hold high office, in the control which the state holds over all means of communication, in the secret police, in the use of secret trials and summary executions, in the absence of all debate at the meetings, when called, of the legislature, in the rigid control of ingress and egress from Russia itself, in anti-religious official attitudes and propaganda, in the strict control of education.

FASCIST ITALY

BENITO MUSSOLINI, founder of Italian Fascism, came to power by a coup d'etat on October 28, 1922. He and his "Black Shirts"—a private army—"marched on Rome" and took possession of the state apparatus. Only the complete breakdown of the democratic apparatus of the Italian government could have permitted this to take place. This breakdown was due to Italy's multi-party system that, at the crucial moment, was unable or unwilling to form a government to counteract this coup. A breakdown in government was the result of accumulating difficulties resulting from widespread postwar depression, unemployment, radical efforts to seize factories, peasant revolts, etc.

Once in power, Mussolini destroyed all opposition and civil liberty, ruled by terror and secret police, resorted to political assassination and prepared Italy for a series of wars that would make the Mediterranean an Italian lake. Both industry and labor were harnessed to state purposes. Industrialists had no choice but to produce what the state required; labor was denied every form of free action on its own behalf. Both were organized into "corporations" (hence the "corporate state") and these were directed by state-appointed bureaucrats. Propaganda and militarization took the place of education. From earliest age, the youth were organized as military cadres and taught implicit obedience to the dictates of *Il Duce* ("The Leader").

The economy felt the artificial stimulation of increased war production and Mussolini was able to secure a surplus which enabled him to make Italy somewhat more self-sufficient by the draining of marshes, improvement of railroads, large hydroelectric and reclamation projects, subsidies for overseas trade, construction of a merchant marine, etc. But the intent of this program of reform was war and renewed imperialistic attacks on those powers which held territories overseas particularly England and France.

NAZI GERMANY

ADOLPH HITLER'S coup came in January 1933. As in Italy, the normal process of democratic government had broken down when the major parties in the Reichstag were unable to agree on a government bloc. Few governments were more democratically oriented than Germany under the Weimar Republic, a government created to replace that of the German Kaiser. When faced with large scale unemployment and dissatisfaction resulting from the world depression in 1933, the radical and liberal parties were unable and unwilling to combine to suppress the threat of the author of *Mein Kampf* and his private army of Brown Shirts.

Adolph Hitler was a master of vicious propaganda; he exploited every grievance of the Germans by centering them upon a few scapegoats—the Treaty of Versailles, the Jews, the German need for *lebensraum* (living space). To justify the use of these scapegoats, he constructed out of a long history of racist theorizing (DE GOBINEAU, HOUSTON STEWART CHAMBERLAIN) the doctrine of the racial superiority of the German Nordic. He convinced the German people by ceaseless dinning through every means of communication that they were the only source of civilization, that they stood in dread danger of corruption and bestialization through intermingling with inferior race, that they must save the world by conquering it for humanity and civilization, etc.

At best one might say that the German people had little inkling—though the unspeakable brutality of the Nazi Storm Troopers must have been evident to them from the day Hitler took power—that these false and vicious doctrines were soon to be translated into furnaces that would burn up more than 6,000,000 people whose only crime was that they were of different religions and nationalities from the ruling German cliques.

After 1934 Hitler became *Der Führer* ("the Leader"). The German state was completely totalitarianized. Industry and labor were organized in similar fashion to that of Mussolini. Capitalism was retained but placed at the beck and call of state needs. War production was immediately begun in preparation for a series of adventures to test the democracies' will to resist and eventually for a bid for world conquest. German freedom disappeared and the Gestapo and the Storm Troopers combined to produce absolute terror.

THE WEAKENING OF THE DEMOCRACIES

World War I proved to be empty victories for the democracies. In 1921 and again in 1931 they suffered depressions of unparalleled dimensions. England, in particular, found that economically she was slipping into the place of a second rate power in the face of American and Japanese competition. Unemployment, exhaustion of native resources, mounting taxes which destroyed considerable investment capital, the failure of Germany to produce any sizeable reparations, widespread strikes among the transport workers and coal miners—all of these factors helped keep successive British governments reeling. In 1923 the first Labor government, under Ramsey Macdonald, was elected; but it was no more able to manage the various crises than the Conservatives.

With the onset of the Great Depression England experimented with a coalition government of Conservative and Laborites. The great achievement of this government was the final abandonment of England's free trade policy for a policy of imperial preference and the Statute of Westminster. The latter was virtually a declaration of independence for all British dominions. It created the British Commonwealth of Nations for the dominions, a system which permitted any dominion to leave the Empire when it wished and if it stayed within the Empire to enjoy absolute local autonomy. (No dominion has left the Commonwealth except Ireland, which in 1922 became Eire, a free state without any political ties to England.)

As the Fascist menace rose to challenge England's position, England began a rearmament program that stimulated the economy to slow revival. Out of the general feeling of helplessness that England felt, however, was generated her policy of "appeasement"—a policy associated particularly with Prime Minister Neville Chamberlain. This policy had as its central aim the strengthening of Fascism to a point where it could successfully attack Communism. In the struggle which ensued, England hoped, both would destroy each other.

French difficulties were similar to those of England with this addition—under the impact of economic crisis the normally unstable French Governments became even more so. France felt keenly Germany's inability to meet her reparations payments since France had been the chief sufferer among the western powers of the first World War. High taxes and shortages of goods produced an astronomical inflation in France in 1926. Unemployment, loss of foreign markets, colonial difficulties and the threat of both Germany and Italy to her security kept France off balance throughout the two decades and made her a leading exponent of appeasement. She, more than any, sought to direct Hitler's power eastward toward Russia.

Finally, the United States withdrew completely from the arena of international responsibility. She rejected the League of Nations, refused to enter the World Court and adopted a series of neutrality laws that were designed to remove her physically from direct or indirect participation in any future European conflict. The world depression of 1931 struck the United States with especial force. Unemployment mounted to 16,000,000, factory production fell by fifty per cent, emergency relief drained the treasury and forced the policy of government borrowing that was to become the greatest government debt in history following the second world war. These difficulties intensified America's desire to remove itself from the arena of world affairs and to concentrate upon her own revival.

Finally, the hope of the democracies resided in the League of Nations; but it proved to be a weak vessel. Weakened by the requirement of unanimity for any decisive action, by the provision in the convenant permitting an aggressor to leave the League after two years' notice, by the absence from the membership rolls of both the United States and the Soviet Union—the League had proved itself incapable of coping with any threat to the peace involving a major power. Its successes were on the fringes of international politics.

Lack of confidence in the League was reflected in the successive disarmament conferences that were held outside League auspices. Though none of these conferences was an unqualified success, the earliest ones—particularly the Washington Arms Conference of 1921–1922—did manage to provide for a cessation in the armaments race for a ten-year period. Japanese ambitions in the Far East were effectively curbed by a Nine-Power Treaty and a Four-Power Treaty which made her sign support for the open door policy, for preservation of China's territorial integrity and for the integrity of the Pacific island possessions of the western powers. (Japan freely violated all these commitments since no effective check was provided for to ensure that she fulfilled them.) Even the idealist Kellogg-Briand Peace Pact which "outlawed war" was negotiated by America and France outside the League. Moreover, both France and England placed their reliance on the construction of a wide system of security alliances (the Little Entente, the Locarno Pacts, etc.) rather than on the force of the League. International anarchy was as prevalent with the League as in the days before the League. With this state of affairs in the world there was no reason for the aggressive fascist nations to hesitate in their new imperialist policy . . . the second factor leading to World War II.

THE NEW IMPERIALISM

The old imperialism was, for the most part, directed against helpless, undeveloped areas; the new imperialism unleased by the powers of the Rome-Berlin-Tokyo Axis was directed against strong, advanced nations. In 1931 Japan began what she called a punitive expedition against Chinese bandits, an expedition that ended with the conquest of all of Manchuria. When the League investigated this aggression through the Lytton Commission and condemned the actions of Japan, Japan left the League, and converted Manchuria into the puppet state of Manchukuo. From this as a base, Japan in 1933 spilled over into the province of Jehol.

It was now Hitler's turn. In 1935, Hitler ordered general conscription and then marched his troops into the Rhineland. Both these actions had been forbidden in the Treaty of Versailles. The French met this threat with the construction of an "impassable" Maginot Line; Hitler built the "Siegfried Wall" opposite it.

In 1936, Generalissimo Francisco Franco, aided and equipped by both Mussolini and Hitler, began an assault on the Spanish Republic with the avowed purpose of setting up a fascist regime in Spain. Spain became an experimental laboratory for the use of Axis weapons and troops; pursuing the policy of "non-intervention" the democratic nations stood aside while these tactics were being employed. After a gallant but hopeless defense, the Spanish Republic collapsed in 1939. Once again the democracies gave evidence that they would not resist fascist aggression until it was directed against themselves.

In 1936, Mussolini began his assault on Ethiopia to revenge the defeat at Adowa and to outflank England on the east coast of Africa. Worried now, England attempted to force the League to adopt sanctions against Italy, particularly sanctions on the sale of oil. But United States oil companies took this as an opportunity to capture the Italian market. As a result, Italy proceeded unchecked until Ethiopia was hers.

Meanwhile, Hitler's "Fifth Column" of Nazi Austrians had begun to agitate for *anschluss* (union) of Germany and Austria. The Austrian Chancellor Schussnigg resisted Hitler's demands. As European eyes focussed on this crisis, the Japanese, in 1937, began their plunge into the deep south of China, a plunge that Chiang Kai shek—China's President and Generalissimo—could do no more than delay. With attention shifted to the Far East, Hitler on March 11, 1938, simply walked in and took over Austria without a struggle. Within weeks Austria was nazified by the well-organized fifth column which had been in secret preparation for many years.

A few months later Hitler, at a Nuremberg Conference, began agitating for the Sudetenland of Czechoslovakia—a section of Czechoslovakia that contained many German-speaking people. This demand led to a remarkable series of meetings in which England's Chamberlain and France's Daladier granted to Hitler his demands upon Czechoslovakia because this was the only way to achieve "peace in our time" and because this was to be Hitler's "last request!" In the face of this complete acquiescence, Hitler took over all of Czechoslovakia and permitted Poland and Hungary small slices bordering their lands.

Italy, early in 1939, took over Albania. This was no sooner done, than Hitler began to agitate for a return of the Polish Corridor to Germany. This was absolutely his last demand. But in August of 1939 came a "diplomatic revolution" that changed the international situation overnight.

THE SECOND WORLD WAR

Poland was crushed by Hitler in five weeks; the Nazis unleashed the *Blitzkreig* tactic, a combined bombing and armored vehicle attack that was both mobile and paralyzing. Poland's allies lent her no assistance. Russia now moved to collect its dividends on the Nazi-Soviet pact. Lithuania, Latvia, Estonia, the Rumanian provinces of Bessarabia and Bukowina, and (1940) Finland were conquered by the Red Army.

In April 1940 the Nazis overran Denmark and Norway. British failure forced Chamberlain out of office and Winston Churchill became Prime Minister on May 10, 1940. On that very day came the Nazi attack on the Low Countries and France. France fell in one of the most ignominious defeats in military history on June 21, 1940. Collaborationists like Laval set up a new French government at Vichy; Italy formally entered the war by an assault on British positions in North Africa; England was without allies; the United States began to drop its aloofness as Roosevelt began his campaign to win Americans to the support of England. Such were the consequences of the fall of France.

Germany now began its air assault on England and against meager opposition. Hitler's air blitz on England failed. The small Royal Air Force proved marvelously effective and destroyed 3,000 German planes; British morale grew sturdier with each attack; supplies, protected by the British navy, began to pour in; American aid grew mountainously especially after the passage of the Lend-Lease Act; Hitler was forced to pull his Italian ally out of difficulties in North Africa and the Balkans and this diverted his energies eastward.

In June 1941 Hitler attacked Russia without warning in a hope to break through the Caucusus into India and to join there with the Japanese who had already advanced far into Southeast Asia in the direction of eastern India. Initial successes brought the Nazis to the gates of Moscow and far south to the city of Stalingrad. On December 7, 1941, Japan attacked the U.S. naval base at Pearl Harbor. America now entered the conflict.

In 1942 the counteroffensive against the Axis powers began. Russia destroyed the Nazi army at Stalingrad and began an offensive that carried her to Berlin in 1945. England defeated the Nazi-Fascist forces deep in Egypt at El Alemain and took the offensive that ended only when the British met the American forces who had landed in western North Africa to spring a trap on the Nazis. The U.S. began its island-hopping campaign that brought her to the perimeter of the Japanese Islands. No assault had to be made on these islands for the dropping of atom bombs on Hiroshima and Nagasaki convinced the Japanese military that further resistance was useless. Russia completed the demolition of the Japanese by destroying its Manchurian armies.

From North Africa Anglo-American forces crossed over to Italy and began a northward assault on German-held positions. But the greatest water-borne assault in history came on D-day—June 6, 1944—when Anglo-American forces invaded Normandy and continued rolling until all of western Germany had fallen. Victory in Europe came on May 7, 1945; Victory in Japan came on August 14, 1945. The most devastating war in the history of mankind was over. Its total cost in money, lives, disease, broken bodies, broken minds will probably never be fully calculated; its effects upon the political, social, economic, psychological and cultural institutions of the civilized world are as yet incalculable. Yet it, more than any other phenomenon, shaped the frame and features of the world today. We can do no more than indicate some of the vectors that have revealed themselves since 1945 and wait for their unraveling in the future.

THE POST-WAR WORLD

"One World." World War II was fought on a high ideological level. In August 1941 Churchill and Roosevelt met to frame the "Atlantic Charter." The nobility of the cause of the united nations was framed in the words of this document, words that bear repetition especially today. The allied nations agreed that

- they will seek no aggrandizement, territorial or otherwise;
- territorial changes will be made in accord with the freely expressed wishes of the people concerned;
- people will choose the form of government under which they will live;
- they will see to it that people who have forcibly lost their self-government will get it back;
- with due respect for existing obligations, they will see to it that all States have access, on equal terms, to the trade and raw materials of the world;
- they will get all nations to collaborate to improve labor standards, economic advancement, and social security;
- they will establish a peace in which men may live out their lives free from fear and want;
- they will assure freedom of the seas; and
- they will disarm aggressors and will remain armed themselves until permanent security is established.

Out of this drive for world peace came the United Nations organization.

THE UNITED NATIONS

A United Nations Organization had been projected simultaneously with the issuance of the Atlantic Charter. At the Moscow Conference—and other military meetings during the war—the need for such an organization was officially proclaimed and the basic principle of the equality of states was announced (1943).

At Teheran (1943) a planning committee was projected. It met at Dumbarton Oaks (1944) and consisted of the Big Four—the United States, the United Kingdom, the Soviet Union and China. Ninety percent of the Charter of the United Nations was hammered out at Dumbarton Oaks. The remainder was completed at Bretton Woods (N.H.) where an International Bank for Reconstruction and Development and an International Monetary Fund to stabilize world currencies were set up; at Yalta where the formula on the voting procedures in the Security Council was agreed upon and each of the great powers was granted an absolute veto on all matters except procedure; and at San Francisco (April-June 1945) where the addition of the important Article 51 was made, the article that provided for regional pacts for individual or collective self-defense pending action by the Security Council.

Purposes. Article I of the Charter of the UN sets forth its major goals: "To maintain international peace and security, and to that end: to take effective collective measures for the prevention and removal of threats to the peace . . ."; and "To achieve international cooperation in solving international problems of an economic, social, cultural or humanitarian character . . ."

Membership. All independent, peace-loving nations are eligible if they accept the obligations of the UN and are willing and able to carry them out. On January 1, 1957 there were over eighty member nations.

Structure. There are six main organs of the UN: **The General Assembly** composed of all member states. Each state may send five delegates but each state is entitled to only one vote. On most matters a two-thirds vote prevails. The Assembly must meet at least once a year but may meet in special session. After the creation in 1947 of an interim committee called the "Little Assembly" one may now say that the General Assembly is in continuous session.

The Security Council. This was to have been the leading organ of the UN. It consists of eleven members, five (U.S., U.K., USSR, France and China) with permanent seats and six elected by the General Assembly for two-year terms. It is in continuous session and has the primary responsibility for maintaining peace and security; all other members of the UN are bound to carry out its decisions. But its decisions have been few since each of the permanent members has an absolute veto on all substantive matters. Its *potential* power remains virtually limitless.

The Economic and Social Council (ECOSOC). ECOSOC's 18 member council is chosen for staggered three-year terms by the General Assembly. It is charged with carrying out programs of international and social improvement. The most spectacular accomplishments of the UN have been in the work of this organ through its many specialized agencies whose titles clearly indicate their functions: The International Labor Organization (ILO), the Food and Agricultural Organization (FAO), the United Nations Educational Scientific and Cultural Organization (UNESCO), the International Civil Aviation Organization (ICAO), The International Bank for Reconstruction and Development (IBRD), the International Monetary Fund (IMF), the International Telecommunications Union (ITU), the World Health Organization (WHO), the International Trade Organization (ITO). Through these organizations particularly does the light of "one world" shine through.

The Trusteeship Council. This organ supervises territories previously administered by the League of Nations as mandates as well as such territories that nations have voluntarily placed under trusteeship with the UN. Six UN members are at present charged with advancing the political and economic development of 20,500,000 people in eleven African and Pacific areas. The Council sends out questionnaires, hears reports, listens to complaints from natives and sends out on-the-spot investigating committees—unless the trust-holding power designates its trust territory as "strategic."

U.N. Successes and Limitations. Since 1945, the United Nations has scored many successes. It caused Russian withdrawal of troops from Iran (1946); it halted Civil War in Greece and set up the U.N. Balkan Commission; it created the independent states of Israel, Indonesia and Libya; it fought the Korean War to a truce; it halted intense religious battles between India and Pakistan over the disputed territory of Kashmir; it halted similar strife in the Israeli-Arab War of 1948–9; it stopped a tripartite invasion of Egypt by England, France and Israel in 1956 (caused these nations to withdraw from Egyptian territory). In 1948, the General Assembly adopted the Declaration of Human Rights, a world charter of human civil liberty; and in the same year approved the Genocide Convention to protect any ethnic group from extinction. The U.N. sponsored GATT., a general agreement on tariffs and trade to limit world economic nationalism.

U.N. limitations, however, were evident in the rapid increase of regional agreements for collective security (NATO and the WARSAW PACT); the constant use of the veto power by the Soviet Union in the Security Council; inability of the U.N. to establish a permanent international armed force; existence within the U.N. of political blocs (American, Soviet, Afro-Asian), inability to act on such matters as suppression of the Hungarian revolt, etc.

THE COLD WAR

Communist Imperialism. By 1947, the "One World" built during the war was replaced by a so-called Cold War between two power blocs: a Western bloc headed by the United States and an Eastern bloc headed by the Soviet Union. Conflicting military and economic goals were the basic causes of the Cold War. Russian satellite states were created in Albania, Bulgaria, Hungary, Rumania, Czechoslovakia, Poland and East Germany. Yugoslavia, under Marshall Tito, broke from her satellite status but retained a Communist form of government. Estonia, Latvia, Lithuania, the Karelian Isthmus of Finland, Finnish Petsamo, Bessarabia and the eastern provinces of Poland were absorbed into the U.S.S.R. itself. The Chinese Communists drove Chiang Kai shek off the mainland on to Taiwan (Formosa) and assumed control of China; later, the Chinese Communists conquered Tibet. Chinese Communists aided in the formation of Communist North Korea. In each of these conquered or absorbed territories, the Communists instituted political dictatorship and economic totalitarianism modeled after the Soviet state. Efforts at protest or revolt in Czechoslovakia, Poland, East Germany, Hungary and Tibet were crushed. The Communists inspired hostilities in Greece, the Philippines and Malaya; and major wars in Korea and Indo-China. They were constantly active in the Middle East and Latin America, and important inroads were made in Indonesia and Africa. Meanwhile Russia's military power was enhanced by the successful firing of a thermonuclear bomb and by the launching of a 3000-pound space missile. Soviet diplomats combined the diplomacy of threat with an increased program of foreign aid to backwood nations. Through shipments of military equipment, Communist prestige increased in the Middle East and in Africa.

Counterattack. The Western counterattack to Soviet-bloc expansion evolved with events and took three forms.

Containment. In 1947, President Truman called for an end to Communist expansion and in the **Truman Doctrine** offered American military, economic and financial aid to any nation under attack or threat of attack by Communist-bloc nations. Subsequently, the United States intervened directly and unilaterally to counter Communist attacks or threats in Greece, Turkey, Korea, Indo-China, the Philippines and Malaya. This was followed by the formation of a series of defensive military alliances designed to "contain" Communist expansion.

On April 4, 1949, the North Atlantic Treaty Organization (NATO) was formed. Original members included Belgium, Canada, Denmark, France, Greenland, Iceland, Italy, Luxemburg, the Netherlands, Norway, the United Kingdom and the United States; subsequently Greece, Turkey and West Germany were added to the alliance to form a community embracing more than 400,000,000 people. NATO, located in Paris, is composed of a ruling Civilian Council and a Military Council, with a Supreme Commander who controls motorized infantry divisions, air and naval fleets, complex and instantaneous communication systems, suppliers and, of course, conventional and atomic weapons. In its first decade NATO was able to overcome difficulties created by the failure of member nations to meet personnel quotas, forces withdrawn from non-NATO operations (French withdrawal of troops for use in Indo-China and Algeria), competition among members for favored posts and commands and non-NATO rivalries among members (England vs. Greece vs. Turkey over Cyprus; England vs. Iceland over North Atlantic fisheries). The most serious threat to NATO, however, was the demand by President De Gaulle of France for complete parity with the United States and England in Mediterranean commands and over control of atomic weapons (the latter forbidden by the United States without the consent of Congress). As a result, the United States was forced to move all its French-based atomic equipment to other sites.

Less effective than NATO was the alliance formed in Southeast Asia (SEATO) among Australia, New Zealand, Pakistan, the Philippines, Thailand, France, England and the United States. This alliance is purely consultative and it suffers considerably from the absence of India, Burma, Indonesia, Taiwan (the Republic of China) and Japan.

Least effective is the Middle East Treaty Organization (METO) organized by England but financed by the United States. It includes only Turkey, Iran, Pakistan and England (Iraq having dropped out in 1959) and is merely consultative; moreover, Egypt and the Arab League are violently opposed to it. Because these multilateral alliances have been strengthened by bilateral agreements between the United States and countries across the world, American troops are provided with military bases along the fringe of the Communist world. That the United States has not abandoned unilateral action is evident in the 1957 adoption of the **Eisenhower Doctrine** which provides for armed assistance to repel Communist aggression in the Middle East, if requested by a Middle Eastern nation.

Strengthening Europe's Economic Defenses. The United States launched its Marshall Plan (1948–1952) to remove the ruins of war, to rebuild Europe's economy and to reduce the effectiveness of the Communists throughout Europe. This economic and financial aid was distributed in Europe by the **Organization of European Economic Cooperation** (OEEC). European cooperation within the OEEC was the first step in a move toward European integration. In 1946 Belgium, the Netherlands and Luxemburg organized a tariff union (Benelux) within the OEEC. In 1949 a Council of Europe was formed to examine the possibilities of political unity of the OEEC powers. Then in 1952, France, Italy, West Germany and the Benelux nations adopted the Schuman Plan which integrated the economies of these six countries into a coal and steel community under a unified high authority which planned the production, the distribution and the labor forces available for the making of steel. In 1957, Euratom was created to promote common production of nuclear energy; and in 1959, the Schuman Plan nations began Euromarket designed to eliminate all tariffs within the community and to adopt a common tariff against all nations outside the community. England proposed a wider free-trade area to embrace all Western Europe. Finding no approval for this plan by Euromarket, England began to organize its own free-trade area to include itself, Sweden, Norway, Denmark, Austria, Switzerland and Portugal.

Strengthening Non-European Economic Defenses. To offset Communist inroads into the more backward areas of the world, the United States and its allies have begun large-scale programs of economic aid to these areas. Technical assistance to improve control over natural resources was made available under President Truman's Point Four program and a similar United Nation's project. Loans and grants-in-aid were provided for Southeast Asia in the British-sponsored and American-financed Colombo Plan; and to all the rest of the world in the United States' **Development Loan Fund** and **Agricultural Trade and Development Loan Funds** (which distributes America's farm surpluses to needy nations). Other sources of loans for approved projects were the **American Export-Import Bank** and the **International Bank for Reconstruction and Development.** Billions of dollars and pounds poured into these backward areas have successfully halted important Communist gains, and have kept the governments of these nations, generally inclined to Communism, on a neutral path.

Support for Former Enemies. Since enemies of Communism are not necessarily friends of democracy, the Western powers have taken active steps to obtain necessary allies. Thus, Marshall Tito, heading a Communist state in Yugoslavia, was aided by loans and military support to defy the Soviet bloc and retain his independence; Generalissimo Franco, heading a Fascist state in Spain, was encouraged to be friendly to the Western powers by a defense agreement with the United States in which air bases were exchanged for military and economic aid. Similarly, Japan, having been effectively democratized, was permitted to rearm, admitted to the United Nations, granted large sums of rehabilitory aid, and made a defense bastion in the Far East. Most significant, however, was the treatment accorded to Germany.

The Yalta and Potsdam agreements of 1945 provided that both Germany and its historic capital, Berlin, were to be partitioned until the country was completely demilitarized, denazified and democratized. When this was accomplished Germany was to be reunited as a minor power. Unilateral Russian action, however, in changing Germany's boundaries within the eastern zone, in blockading Berlin, and in converting the Russian zone into the satellite nation of East Germany, caused the Western powers to take positive steps. West Germany became an independent state; the German General Staff was recreated; West Germany was militarized and admitted to NATO. The Western powers maintained their position in West Berlin despite the efforts of Russian Premier Khrushchev who threatened to turn West Berlin, located well within the territory of the East German state, over to East Germany, and conclude a separate peace treaty with East Germany.

East and West met at the conference table at Geneva in 1959 in an attempt to solve the problem of a united Berlin and a united Germany.

Decade of Turmoil. The 1960s brought internal strife to many countries of the world as new political groups fought to gain more personal freedoms.

Civil war gave birth to several new nations in Africa, while others claimed their independence from the rule of Great Britain and France. Military leaders vied for control of Greece, Portugal, and a number of countries in Latin America.

The National Association for the Advancement of Colored People (NAACP) led by Roy Wilkins and the Southern Christian Leadership Conference (SCLC) led by Martin Luther King, Jr., championed the cause of racial equality in the United States. Their protest marches and boycotts in the early 1960s won some changes in the law. Later more radical groups stirred up violent riots in the large urban areas, reacting against the bitter plight of blacks and similar minorities.

In Northern Ireland the age-old conflict between (middle-class) Protestants and (lower-class) Catholics erupted again when Catholics called for total independence from Great Britain. Tempers flared and terrorist groups roamed the streets, frightening and murdering their opponents in the cause. The conflict worsened as the decade rolled on.

In Czechoslovakia the democratic policies of President Alexander Dubcek earned the scorn of nearby Russia. To make sure the reforms didn't spread to other Communist satellites, the Soviet government sent its army into Czechoslovakia in August 1968 to sweep Dubcek from power.

Military Challenges. During the 1960s the powers of East and West tested their strength in several crucial showdowns.

When Cuban Premier Fidel Castro brought Russian missiles onto his island fortress in 1962, President John F. Kennedy placed a naval blockage against the shipments. He said Castro and his Russian partners had violated the Monroe Doctrine–the policy which President James Monroe laid down over a hundred years earlier, when he declared that the United States would not allow foreign powers to stake new claims in the Western Hemisphere.

In Southeast Asia, Communist super-powers supported the government of North Vietnam as it tried to take South Vietnam. The United Nations sent military advisors to South Vietnam, then troops. The conflict spread to the neighboring countries of Cambodia, Laos, and Thailand. The United States pledged to defend South Vietnam if the conflict became a full-scale war; Russia and China did the same for North Vietnam. But both sides wanted to keep the conflict from growing into another world war. The United States committed over 500,000 soldiers to the contest, but by the end of the sixties most American leaders knew the effort would fail. At home, college students demonstrated against America's role in Asia and many young men burned their draft cards to show their contempt for what they called an "immoral war."

DÉTENTE

Richard M. Nixon took office as President of the United States in 1969 with two goals for his administration: (1) to settle the unrest in America's streets, and (2) to establish a more peaceful climate on the world scene. He knew the first goal depended on reaching the second. He also realized that if America was to find world peace, it had to melt the ice of its "cold war" with the Communist powers. Mr. Nixon called this process *détente,* using a French term that means "to relax tension."

The United States began a round of Strategic Arms Limitation Talks (SALT) with the Soviet Union. At these conferences the diplomats from both nations agreed to limit the number of new weapons they made–especially atomic weapons. At the same time the United States invited Chinese athletes to visit North America for what newspaper columnists jokingly called "ping-pong diplomacy." Relations grew more friendly between the two nations and climaxed with President Nixon's courtesy trip to China in early 1972. A treaty between the United States and North Vietnam ended the long stand-off in Southeast Asia with American troops leaving the area at the end of 1972. In April 1973, North Vietnamese troops took the last major cities in South Vietnam and united the country with their own.

Economic Problems. Israel and its Arab rivals called for military aid in their long-time dispute, but the spirit of *détente* led major world powers to keep "hands off." Arab nations banded together to resist this policy, and in the fall of 1973 they refused to ship oil to the United States. They ended the boycott several months later, but the Arab-controlled group of Oil Producing and Exporting Countries (OPEC) doubled the price of crude oil. This triggered a new surge of inflation in the United States and other Western countries. China, Russia, and most Communist countries in Eastern

Europe produced enough oil for their own needs, so the price hike did little to harm their economies.

By the time James Earl (Jimmy) Carter became President in 1977, the cost of living in the United States was rising by about eight percent each year. The United States imported much more than it sold to other nations, and had to borrow billions of dollars' worth of credit to cover the difference. This **balance of payments deficit** loomed as a primary concern of the Western world. It meant that the American dollar was worth less than it was a year earlier–or even a month earlier. Because the United States was so active in the business of the Western world, its growing debt threatened to disrupt international economy. President Carter proposed new programs to make the United States able to produce more of its own energy. In early 1978 he met in Munich, West Germany with other Western leaders to seek ways of strengthening the international system of trade. Ironically, by this time the European continent and Japan had bounced back from World War II even better than the United States and Great Britain.

Détente seemed threatened by President Carter's demand for human rights in Communist countries. He cited the Helsinki pact of 1973, in which the Soviet Union pledged to give its citizens freedom of speech, freedom of worship, and other concessions. Carter and his aides criticized the Soviet Union for putting political and religious dissenters on trial: the Soviet government warned the United States to stop meddling in Russia's domestic affairs.

Yet the period of *détente* had real benefits. Because of easing tensions in the Middle East, President Carter could invite President Anwar Sadat of Egypt and Prime Minister Menachem Begin of Israel to a summit conference at Camp David, in the Maryland hills near Washington, D.C. On September 17, 1978, the three men signed a "Framework for Peace in the Middle East," which outlined steps for ending the 30-year dispute between Israel and its Arab neighbors.

AMERICAN HISTORY

Origins

The origins of American history may be found in developments in Europe. The fourteenth and fifteenth centuries saw extraordinary developments taking place in Europe. These included the rise of a middle class, the appearance of independent nations, the growth of industry and commerce, the invention of printing, a new interest in science, the development of religious conflict. These changes led Europeans to explore the world. Columbus' discovery of America in 1492 was but one of many attempts on the part of Europeans to find an all-water route to the Far East.

A year after Columbus' first voyage on behalf of Spain, the Pope gave Spain title to all of the New World, with the exception of the eastern part of South America, known today as Brazil, which was awarded to Portugal. Spain ruled her vast empire despotically. There was no religious freedom, Indians were treated harshly, and self-government was denied to the colonists.

In 1608, the French founded Quebec. For a century afterward, they continued to explore North America, following the great waterways of the continent–the St. Lawrence River, the Great Lakes, and the Mississippi River. However, by 1750 only about 80,000 settlers had come to New France. Like Spain, France denied her colonies the right of self-government. Furthermore, since France was interested mainly in the fur trade, settlers who wished to farm the land were discouraged from migrating to the colonies.

In 1607, the English founded Jamestown in Virginia, and in 1620, what was to become Plymouth in Massachusetts. In 1664, they forced the Dutch to surrender their colony of New Netherlands, which included what is now New York, New Jersey, Pennsylvania, and Delaware. The English flag now floated from Maine to the border of Florida. The English colonies, unlike those of Spain and France, attracted large numbers of settlers. By 1750 there were nearly 1,500,000 people living in the thirteen colonies strung along the Atlantic coast.

These settlers had come for many reasons. Some hoped to find religious freedom; some sought political liberty; others hoped to improve their economic lot. The prospect for the small farmer was far brighter in the English colonies because land ownership was widespread, especially in New England and in the middle colonies. England granted more political, religious, and economic freedom than either Spain or France.

English colonists came to believe that all men were equal and should have equal opportunities. They insisted that the political rights won by their fellow countrymen in England over the centuries were also rightfully theirs. Building upon their heritage of the Magna Charta (1215), the Petition of Rights (1628), and the Bill of Rights (1689), the English colonists developed their own democratic institutions. In Virginia the House of Burgesses, established in 1619, was the first elected legislature in the New World. In 1639, Connecticut drew up the Fundamental Orders, the first written constitution in America. New England town meetings involved the participation of qualified citizens in making local decisions and choosing their officials. By 1750 most of the colonial legislatures had some measure of control over the royal governors by virtue of "the power of the purse," that is, the right to grant or withhold taxes.

Religious freedom also developed in the English colonies. Roger Williams founded Rhode Island as a colony affording complete religious freedom for all, with separation of church and state. Maryland's Act of Toleration granted freedom of worship to all Christians. William Penn, in 1682, granted religious freedom in Pennsylvania.

Beginning in 1689, England and France were engaged in a worldwide struggle for colonies and commerce. In 1754, the fourth and most decisive of these wars broke out. In the New World it was known as the French and Indian War. Its outcome was a complete defeat for the French. The Treaty of Paris (1763) gave to England Canada and all of the French territory east of the Mississippi, with the exception of New Orleans.

The victory proved to be a mixed blessing for England. Before 1763, she had paid little attention to the colonies which had had virtual self-government. The Navigation Acts, which had been designed to compel the colonies to trade almost entirely with the mother country, in accordance with the mercantilist theory, had not been enforced. After the French and Indian War, England's attitude changed. To protect the colonists from Indians, England needed an army of 10,000 in the colonies, at a cost of one million dollars a year. Added to this sum was the huge debt with which the English were saddled as a consequence of the war. She determined to make the colonies pay part of the cost of maintaining the army as well as the interest on the war debt. Furthermore, British officials began to collect customs duties, which had long been evaded by colonial smugglers.

There followed a series of British enactments which became increasingly objectionable to the colonists. The lands west of the Appalachians were closed to colonial settlers. The Sugar Act, the Stamp Act, and the Townshend Acts, all designed to increase revenue for Britain, aroused anger among the colonists. Committees of Correspondence succeeded in organizing opposition to Britain, coordinating the efforts of patriots in the various colonies.

On April 19, 1775, fighting broke out at Lexington, Massachusetts. The news spread quickly. Harsh measures by the British convinced many colonists that independence was the next logical step. On July 4, 1776, the Second Continental Congress adopted the Declaration of Independence, written chiefly by Thomas Jefferson, which expressed the democratic ideals of the American Revolution.

The war between England and her American colonies was a long and a bitter one. Under the inspiring leadership of George Washington, the colonists, with the help of France, scored a series of remarkable victories. The Treaty of Paris (1783) ended the war, granting full independence to the colonies.

Once free, the colonies became thirteen independent states, loosely bound together under the Articles of Confederation. The period from 1781 to 1789 has been called the Critical Period, because it seemed that the weak central government would fail to solve its economic and political problems. In 1787, the representatives of twelve of the thirteen states met in Philadelphia to strengthen the powers of the central government. Instead of merely revising the Articles of Confederation, however, they drew up an entirely new plan of government for the nation and wrote a new constitution. This document, the Constitution of the United States, has remained the basis of our federal system of government.

A task which was uppermost in the minds of the representatives was the prevention of tyranny. They agreed with the famous French philosopher Montesquieu that there could be no liberty when the powers to make the laws and to enforce the laws were given to the same person or group or when the power of judging was not separated from legislative and executive powers. Accordingly, they decided to set up a system in which no one person or agency could make a law, arrest a violator, find him guilty, and punish him.

In the section "American Government," we shall examine the three main branches of our Federal Government in order to understand the responsibilities of each, as well as the relationships among the branches.

Development

During the quarter century between the inauguration of President Washington and the end of the War of 1812, the new nation achieved maturity and general recognition from the international community.

It was first necessary to learn whether the Constitution could adequately provide guidance in transforming the sovereign states into a federal nation. Some leaders were at least as strongly devoted to their state–Jefferson always called Virginia his "country"–as to the Union. Others considered that the United States relegated the states to subdivisions. This division appeared to some extent in the platforms of political leaders and, as they developed, of political parties. As the nation evolved, the aggregation of states, the region–New England, the South, the West–tended to replace the state in its capacity to attract primary loyalties, especially when the region could be identified with a minority position. Nevertheless, political regionalism invariably was disguised as the doctrine of states' rights, because under the Constitution the state was a political entity that had specific rights, whereas the region had no standing of any kind.

POLITICAL PARTIES

Nor did the Constitution recognize the existence of political parties, or factions (the term in vogue in the eighteenth century), and all the Constitution-builders professed an aversion to factionalism. At first only one's opponents were described as forming a faction. Those who favored the strengthening of the new central government described themselves as Federalists. Their opponents, who preferred minimal government administered locally, were therefore dubbed Antifederalists, or simply Antis. But the latter, choosing to emphasize positive concepts, such as liberty, professed to see a trend toward monarchism among the Federalists, and so called themselves Democratic-Republicans, soon shortened to Republicans. With polarization, the factional names acquired symbolic value, and by the time John Adams became President a two-party system was operative.

It then became necessary for that system to develop effective mechanisms. The election in 1796 of an Executive team of antithetical politicians, the Federalist President John Adams and the Republican Vice President Thomas Jefferson, disclosed the absurdity and the need for reform. When the electoral process in the election of 1800 returned a tie vote for two Republican candidates, Jefferson and Aaron Burr, that was resolved under Constitutional procedures only after 36 ballots in Congress just a week before inauguration day, reform became imperative. The result was the Twelfth Amendment, ratified in 1803 and operative in 1804, which required a separate ballot for the President and Vice President.

Once the legitimacy of party organization was accepted, the Congressional members of the several parties (known as *caucuses*) assumed the prerogative of selecting candidates. Federal caucuses nominated John Adams, Charles Pinckney, DeWitt Clinton, and Rufus King in the elections from 1800 through 1816, while Republican caucuses named Thomas Jefferson, James Madison, and James Monroe. After three successive two-term Republican administrations, the Federalist Party ceased to exist nationally in 1820. Four years later the Republican Party, lacking external opposition, was internally in turmoil. Only one-third of the Republicans in Congress attended the caucus that named William Crawford to run for the Presidency. Three competitors found it expedient to announce their candidacies through the sponsorship of state legislatures: Andrew Jackson, John Quincy Adams, and Henry Clay. When the two-party system began to function once more in the 1830s, the caucus had lost its nominative function. It was replaced by the party convention, which had nominated candidates for state office since the 1790s. The first Democratic national convention met in 1832, but two minor parties, the Anti-Masonic and National Republican parties, nominated Presidential candidates in 1831.

FOREIGN RELATIONS

The confrontation between Federalists and Republicans had been well defined during President Washington's Administration, from 1789 to 1797, when Alexander Hamilton and Thomas Jefferson

A cartoon satirizes the 1836 presidential election campaign.

Another cartoon looks at the presidential campaign of 1856.

The Resignation of George Washington (detail).

were their recognized spokesmen. Both foreign and domestic policy were matters of partisan controversy. The French Revolution and the Napoleonic Wars had an impact because interested parties abroad sought support within the United States.

The Republicans considered the early phases of the French Revolution a continuation of the American Revolution. Thomas Paine, Thomas Jefferson, and James Monroe were ardent advocates of the French republic, whereas such Federalists as Alexander Hamilton, John Adams, and John Jay supported a counterrevolutionary backlash. Washington was initially neutral, but gradually turned toward the Federalist position. As the Terror of 1793 was succeeded by the general warfare of the Napoleonic period, even the Republicans were disillusioned.

The break in the alliance between France and the United States was a direct result of the "XYZ Affair" of 1797, a demeaning and unsuccessful attempt by the French Directory to browbeat President Adams' administration by insulting American negotiators. A state of undeclared war in 1798 was accompanied by the establishment of an American navy, while France under Napoleon embarked on full-scale war against Great Britain and neighboring European countries. As the tempo of the European war accelerated, the two major belligerents alternately wooed and abused the United States. Under such conditions, Napoleon unexpectedly sold Louisiana to the United States in 1803. American merchant shipping throve on risky but profitable wartime ventures. After 1805 the attempts of three American Presidents to enforce neutrality through "nonintercourse" and embargoes aroused resentment on the part of American commercial interests and retaliation at the hands of the belligerents. The practice that most outraged Americans was that of "impressment"–removing sailors from United States ships under the pretext that they were British deserters, as was often the case.

THE WAR OF 1812

The years of frustration ultimately played into the hands of a new generation of political leaders from the West, who welcomed an excuse to advocate an offensive foreign policy. Known as the War Hawks, they proposed to smite the Spanish in the Floridas and the British in Canada, to secure the southern and northern borders of the United States. The ensuing War of 1812 proved militarily indecisive, despite moments of naval glory and the spectacular victory for the United States at New Orleans. The political significance of the war makes the Treaty of Ghent, signed in 1814, a landmark in United States history. The world was impressed that a hitherto untried nation could hold to a standstill Europe's foremost naval power, the conqueror of Napoleon.

The development of American internal politics was no less dramatic. The Republicans in 1798 and 1799 had sponsored the Kentucky and Virginia Resolutions, proclaiming the concept that the Union was a revocable compact among sovereign states. Now they had become a nationalist party of militant expansionists. The Federalists, on the other hand were virtually insulated in New England. They compromised their original position by considering, at the Hartford Convention of 1814, whether their region might not be more prosperous outside than within the Union. The Treaty of Ghent made such notions irrelevant, and enabled the country to devote its full energies to the consolidation of the vast territories it now controlled.

ORGANIZING AN EMPIRE

The United States had undergone a remarkable physical change between the treaties of 1783 and 1814. At the end of the Revolutionary War, the thirteen original states claimed a hinterland extending to the Mississippi, with undefined and insecure borders south and north. Spain claimed the entire Gulf coast. British troops continued to occupy strategic points that admittedly belonged to the United States, pending France's fulfillment of all the terms of the Treaty of Paris. Jay's Treaty of 1794 with Great Britain settled some of the disputes with Britain, and Thomas Pinckney's Treaty of San Lorenzo with Spain in 1795 gave Georgia a disputed strip in the hinterland of Florida. These were holding operations, maintaining instability.

Meanwhile, Congress under the Articles of Confederation and later under the Constitution established a pattern of organization for the trans-Appalachian territories. Georgia west of the Chattahoochee was ceded to the Federal Government in 1802 and became Mississippi Territory. The Territory Southwest of the River Ohio, originally the western sections of Virginia and North Carolina, became the states of Kentucky and Tennessee in 1792 and 1796 respectively. The Territory North of the River Ohio (Northwest Territory for short) was organized in 1787 with the provision that it would be formed into states, each of which would be admitted to the Union upon attaining a population of 60,000. A further provision prohibited the institution of slavery throughout the entire area. The authority of the Federal Government to organize and legislate for territories that would be guaranteed statehood was thus established even before the Constitution was ratified.

THE NEW WEST

In 1803, Ohio–the first state carved out of the Northwest Territory–was admitted to the Union. That same year, the total area of the United States was doubled by the acquisition of Louisiana. This vast tract extended the sovereignty of the United States west to the Rocky Mountains. Some questioned the authority of the Federal Government to acquire territory by purchase (as in this instance) or by conquest; but Jefferson set a precedent that met with general approval. The Louisiana Purchase–soon renamed Missouri Territory–was expected to evolve into states and be added to the Union. However, it was not so generally conceded that the Federal Government could legislate concerning the extension of the institution of slavery into the Missouri Territory.

It was anticipated that this territory would be settled mostly by small farmers, who would adhere to the Republican ideals of Jefferson. Within the agrarian South itself, however, planters already prevailed over yeomen, and cotton plantations were taking the place of tobacco plantations to such an extent that the region had virtually developed a one-crop economy: cotton was "king." This resulted in the rejuvenation of the institution of slavery, the narrowing of trade relations to the

The Aaron Burr—Alexander Hamilton Duel (detail)

BRITISH NORTH AMERICA
Boundary undefined
Area disputed with Great Britain
Quebec
Boundary in dispute
LAKE SUPERIOR
CANADA
Ottawa R.
Fort Michilimackinac
Mississippi River
L. HURON
L. MICHIGAN
VT. in dispute
N.H.
Portland
Concord
MASSACHUSETTS
Boston
Connecticut R.
L. ONTARIO
NEW YORK
Albany
Hudson
CONN.
Providence
R.I.
New Haven
Detroit
L. ERIE
Delaware R.
PENNSYLVANIA
New York City
Pittsburgh
Trenton
Philadelphia
NEW JERSEY
Illinois R.
Wabash R.
VIRGINIA
Marietta
Potomac R.
Baltimore
Alexandria
MARYLAND
DEL.
Missouri River
St. Louis
Cahokia
Vincennes
Kaskaskia
OHIO RIVER
Lexington
James R.
Richmond
Yorktown
Williamsburg
Norfolk
Cumberland R.
Nashville
APPALACHIAN MOUNTAINS
MISSISSIPPI RIVER
NORTH CAROLINA
Raleigh
Cape Fear R.
Charlotte
New Bern
Tennessee River
Arkansas Post
Coosa R.
SOUTH CAROLINA
Wilmington
Augusta
Savannah R.
Chattahoochee R.
GEORGIA
Charleston
Boundary in dispute
Area Claimed by Spain
Natchez
Mobile
Alabama R.
Savannah
SPANISH FLORIDA
Pensacola
St. Augustine
SPANISH LOUISIANA
Atlantic Ocean
Gulf of Mexico
THE UNITED STATES
After Treaty of Sept. 3, 1783
0 100 200 300
Scale of miles
Jaber

export of cotton, and the substitution of South Carolina for Virginia as the regional headquarters. Nor were the interests of the cotton South identical with those of the new West on such questions as the protective tariff (which the South abhorred) or the need to build roads or canals.

THE CHANGING EAST

The East–or the North, by which was meant New England and the Middle states–was also changing, largely as a result of the War of 1812 and the introduction from England of the technology of the Industrial Revolution. Commerce and finance, including speculation, had accounted for the earlier prosperity of the East and its prevailing political pattern of Federalism. But now the country had abandoned colonial habits and discovered the function of new devices behind which a manufacturing industry could flourish. While traders needed a strong navy and merchant marine, favored commercial treaties with foreign countries, and valued an expanding hinterland for its investment possibilities (especially in cheap land), manufacturers needed sources of raw materials, markets for finished goods, treaties that would permit selective import discrimination, and a strong and controlled financial structure. The West needed ample credit, free or cheap land for those who would live on it, internal improvements to assure access to and from markets, a militia to control or expel the Indians, and removal of property restrictions on the exercise of the franchise.

Expansion before the Civil War (1814-1861)

Three regional patterns were taking form. The South and the East were in competition for an alliance with the new West. The South and West shared an essentially agrarian base and trust in local rather than in central government; but only central government could provide roads and canals and organize effective armed forces for security against Indians, the Spanish, or the British. Both the East and the West wanted the National Road and the Erie Canal, and tariff schedules to protect the crops of the farmers and the manufactures of the townsmen; but they parted company on the issue of the Bank of the United States. Borrowing homesteaders hated it, while the rising tycoon depended on it. The West could accept neither the Southern version of Republicanism nor the Eastern brand of revived Federalism. Henry Clay, a true son of the West, offered his "American system" that combined roads and canals, protective tariffs, and a strong financial structure, but he never gained the political following of two other Westerners, Andrew Jackson and John C. Calhoun.

JACKSONIANS AND WHIGS

After a period of fluidity two new major parties emerged. One, a Jacksonian (not Jeffersonian) version of Republicanism, became the Democratic Party from 1828 to the eve of the Civil War. This movement was supported generally in the West and among the disfranchised in the East, particularly the emerging urban working class. Jackson's enemies tried to insult him by calling him "King Andrew," and by depicting the Democrats as American-style Tories. In the current jargon, the converse of a Tory was a Whig, and this was the name adopted by the anti-Jacksonians. They included followers of Calhoun, who switched his allegiance from West to South; devotees to Clay's American system; and ex-Federalists who aligned themselves with Daniel Webster of New England, spokesmen for the merchant and manufacturing class. The Whigs, a coalition in the guise of a party, had no platform. Webster supported the protective tariff, but Calhoun didn't. Calhoun reformulated the concept of nullification, while Webster demanded loyalty to the Union. The Whigs finally elected a President after the issueless campaign of 1840. He was the picturesque but nonpolitical William Henry Harrison, who died within a month and was succeeded by an anti-Jacksonian Democrat, John Tyler.

THE ISSUE OF SLAVERY

One issue that did not appear crucial to the major political figures in the decades after the War of 1812 was that of slavery, although such discerning experts as Jefferson and John Quincy Adams suspected its potential gravity early on. The point became controversial in national politics rather indirectly, in connection with the procedure for admitting new states. Eight of the 16 states that comprised the Union in 1803 were "slave" states; that is, their economy significantly depended on the use of slave labor. They shared power in the Senate with an equal number of "free" states, while in the House of Representatives the ratio of delegates was 49 "slave" to 57 "free." However, some of the slave-state Congressmen held office only because the Constitution gave every five blacks as much representation in the House of Representatives as every three whites (although the blacks had no other political existence). Whatever resentment the North felt against this advantage exercised by the slave interests was mitigated by the fact that only three more territories open to slavery remained east of the Mississippi, whereas at least four territories would be formed out of the Northwest Territory, where slavery was prohibited under the Ordinance of 1787. In spite of an initial proslavery handicap, the slave power would soon inevitably be a minority in both Houses.

The trans-Mississippi acquisition postponed the doom of the slave power. In 1820 the 22 states then in the Union were evenly divided, and the "slave" minority in the House had slipped only from 44 percent to 42 percent. The pending admission of Missouri as a slave state would tip the balance against the free-soil power. Henry Clay, known as a compromiser, proposed that the District of Maine in Massachusetts, having long sought statehood, should be matched with Missouri to maintain equilibrium. He also proposed that henceforth a line be extended westward along Missouri's southern border, north of which slavery would be banned just as it had previously been banned in the Northwest Territory. This Missouri Compromise of 1820 was forthwith adopted, and a crisis was averted for a decade or so. But the South did not fail to observe the shape of the remaining territory, of which only a relative sliver remained potential slave territory. The only solution for the slave power was to annex additional land south of the slave-free border: the Spanish Southwest.

ANNEXATION, SOUTH AND NORTH

The notion of annexing contiguous territory was neither novel nor unexplored. As soon as it had become clear that the Louisiana deal did not include any part of Spanish Florida, frontiersmen began to infiltrate their neighbor's domain. West Florida between the Mississippi and Pearl rivers was occupied in 1810 and two years later was annexed to the new state of Louisiana. The process–settlement of Americans on foreign territory, liberation of the area, annexation–was to be repeated on almost every occasion, from Texas to Hawaii. In Florida, the next step was the invasion of Mobile and the extension of American claims eastward to the Perdido in 1813. The rest of Florida was bought in 1819 for a minimal price from Spain, which was in no position to defend its holdings; for much of Spanish America was authentically in a state of revolution. The Adams-Onís Treaty of 1819 not only added Florida to the United States; it also defined for the first time the southern border of the Louisiana Purchase.

Meanwhile, the northern border was also subject to negotiation. There was no question that the United States had hoped to annex part of Canada during the War of 1812. The Treaty of Ghent with Great Britain ended this prospect, and a series of agreements culminated in the Convention of 1818, which made the forty-ninth parallel the permanent boundary between the United States and British North America from the Lake of the Woods to the Rocky Mountains. Between the Rockies and the Pacific Ocean, north of the present northern border of California and south of the still undefined Russian border, was a vast tract known as the Oregon country, still the preserve of fur traders and mountain men. British and American claims to Oregon remained unresolved by mutual agreement, and the region was in effect open to all.

THE MONROE DOCTRINE

These border problems having been settled, the United States asserted a sphere of influence. As the Spanish possessions in South America became independent during the years 1810 to 1825, they sought approval and recognition from the United States. Until pending disputes between the United States and Spain were resolved, these appeals from South America were ignored, but with the ratification of the Adams-Onís Treaty in 1821, the United States took steps to enter into relations with the ex-colonies. When it appeared that a league of European powers (the Holy Alliance) proposed to help Spain recover these colonies, President James Monroe proclaimed his doctrine: "The American continents . . . are henceforth not to be considered as subjects for future colonization by any European powers."

THE MEXICAN WAR

This proclamation, which in fact required the British navy for its enforcement, was not a self-denying ordinance. For an American colony had already infiltrated Spanish Mexico in 1821, and continued to enlarge after Mexico had achieved its independence. The initial step toward acquiring the Mexican state of Texas was undertaken by President Jackson in 1829. Thereafter it was only a matter of time until the sequence of revolution, liberation, and annexation was pursued. This time it required a full-scale war between the United States and Mexico to confirm the objective, but in 1848, under the terms of the Treaty of Guadalupe Hidalgo, the Mexican territories became the American Southwest, adding New Mexico and California to the already admitted state of Texas. In 1846 an agreement had been concluded with Great Britain that extended the forty-ninth parallel westward from the Rocky Mountains through the Oregon country. The ultimate shape of the United States was virtually attained, fulfilling the dogma of Manifest Destiny "to overspread the continent allotted by Providence for the free development of our yearly multiplying millions"–which by 1848 exceeded 20 million.

COMPROMISE OF 1850

The organization of all this territory again raised the problem that had vexed the country in 1820 and had brought about the Missouri Compromise. The Presidential election of 1848 was the first in which the question of slavery, or at least its extension into the territories, was the principal issue. During the Mexican War, the House of Representatives had passed the Wilmot Proviso that would have excluded slavery from any ceded territory, but the South mustered enough support in the Senate to beat back this offensive. In 1848 both parties were split on the question of slavery extension. In the very week during which Wisconsin's admission restored a balance of 15 states on each side, the Democrats picked Lewis Cass for their Presidential candidate. Cass had developed the concept of "popular sovereignty." He wanted to discard the old principle of a demarcation between free and slave territories; he believed that the settlers should vote their preferences on the issue. Inasmuch as hardly any of the remaining unorganized territory would support the use of slave labor, the North could accept popular sovereignty in principle. The South might well endorse a pro-

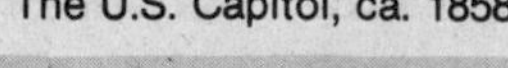
The U.S. Capitol, ca. 1858

gram that would remove the thorny issue from Congress, where they could no longer hope to break even.

The Whigs again nominated a nonpolitical general, Zachary Taylor, taking no stand on the crucial questions–and won. Their victory was made possible, however, by the swing vote of the Free-Soil Party, composed of antislavery Democrats and Whigs, who won enough votes in New York to deprive Cass of the Presidency.

The gold rush that swelled the population of California indirectly canceled the truce, for it was imperative to provide law and order on the West Coast. California applied for immediate statehood in 1849 under a free-soil constitution, although most of the proposed state was on the "slave" side of the Missouri Compromise line. Congress delayed the admission of California despite President Taylor's plea for prompt action, and the Californians set up "vigilantes" to assume the police role. In 1850 Clay again came to the rescue with a compromise. Its basic elements were (for the North) the admission of a free-soil California and (for the South) a strict law enforcing the return of fugitive slaves to their masters. Moreover, two other proposed territories (Utah and New Mexico) north and south of the line of demarcation would be organized under the concept of popular sovereignty. The Compromise of 1850 was unenthusiastically adopted.

THE FAILURE OF COMPROMISE

The nation now attempted to consolidate its acquisitions. During the next decade there was a great leap forward of immigration, homesteading, railroad building. The peopling of the Great Plains inevitably hastened the development of territories into states, and again the slavery issue appeared. In 1854 the Kansas-Nebraska Bill proposed to apply the principle of popular sovereignty to the next tier west of Iowa and Missouri, extending from British North America south to the territory reserved for the Indians, and west to Utah and New Mexico. Under the Missouri Compromise, these territories were both destined for free soil; the new dispensation would give the slave power a chance. Once the bill was signed, partisans with strong convictions and guns were sent into the territories to frame constitutions.

The pro-slavery forces showed special capacity for organization in Kansas Territory (where rival constitutions appeared), accompanied by terrorist campaigns that gave rise to the popular allusion to "bleeding Kansas." By the time of the election of 1856, a national Republican Party had succeeded the transitory Free-Soilers. It held its first convention and nominated John C. Frémont for President. Frémont, with 33 percent of the popular vote, brought the Republicans to the rank of a major party. The Whigs joined the Federalists in the archives of history.

The stroke that ended all possibility of compromise on slavery was applied by the U.S. Supreme Court. The judiciary, under the brilliant and durable guidance of Federalist John Marshall, had established beyond question its role as stabilizer and sustainer of balance between the Executive and Legislative branches. Often upholding the Federal government against the states, sometimes protecting states' rights, only once had the Supreme Court (in *Marbury v. Madison* in 1803) declared an act of Congress unconstitutional. Now, more than half a century later (in *Dred Scott v. Sandford* in 1857), the Court declared that no legislature–national, state, or territorial–could prohibit the institution of slavery. Where the Kansas-Nebraska Act had removed the thorny controversy from Congress to territorial conventions, the Court now forced it to the battlefield. The moderates who had hoped to contain the institution or to control its spread, were driven from contention, leaving as contestants only those who refused to limit slavery or those who would abolish it.

As so many grave issues had taken on the aspect of a clash between Federal and states' rights, so the issue of slavery was transformed into a contest between (1) those who would secede rather than compromise on slavery and (2) those who identified hostility toward slavery with loyalty to the Union. Their predicament was personalized by the Republican candidate for the Presidency in 1860, Abraham Lincoln. Within a few years, on taking office and under the stress of Civil War, Lincoln passed from a free-soil to an abolitionist position. The war was essentially a defense of the Union, as Lincoln and most in the North understood it. But in Southern eyes it was a defense not only of the right of states to leave the Union, but a defense of an institution vital to the economy of the South.

Jefferson Davis

Thomas J. ("Stonewall") Jackson

The Civil War—Black Union soldiers

THE CIVIL WAR

The population of the United States at the outbreak of the Civil War was about thirty-one million, of whom more than 60 percent lived in the North. One-third of the Southern minority were slaves. The economy of the South had long since ceased to compete with that of the North. The South was in effect a colonial supplier of cotton to British and Northern factories. The North, on the other hand, had embraced industrialization and was capable of supplying the potential market of the West and drawing upon its untapped resources. The West had already received more free immigrants than the entire servile labor force of the South. An economic alliance between the West and the North awaited only the building of railroads to link the two regions.

Under these circumstances, few people could expect the South to stave off the Northern military offensive for more than four years. Even during the Civil War, the Union lacked actual unity. The exigencies of war brought a boom to Western farmers, fortunes to profiteers, and a decline in the real income of workers and artisans. It irreversibly altered the economy of the nation.

Readjustment and Reconstruction (1864–1876)

The first postwar decade was devoted to Reconstruction. The Federal Government had to restructure the relationships between the states of the defeated Confederacy and the triumphant Union. President Lincoln and (after his assassination) President Andrew Johnson proposed to bind the nation's wounds by restoring autonomy to the South consistent with the termination of slavery, as formulated in the Thirteenth Amendment ratified in December 1865. This charitable policy would have to be achieved at the expense of the ex-slaves.

THE SOUTH IS READMITTED

A spate of "black codes" enacted by the first popular legislatures throughout the South angered the Republicans who controlled Congress. A Freedmen's Bureau, with the function of protecting the interests of the blacks, had been set up temporarily in March 1865, and was given permanent status over Johnson's veto in July 1866. Inasmuch as the Southern representation in the House of Representatives would increase when the blacks achieved full (rather than three-fifths) representation, Congress refused to readmit the former states until they accepted the Fourteenth Amendment, which spelled out the civil rights of blacks. When all of the "sinful ten" states had "flung back into our teeth the magnanimous offer of a generous nation" (in the words of Congressman James A. Garfield), Congress passed in March 1867 a Reconstruction Act that instituted martial law throughout the South.

By the end of 1869 most of the Southern states were in the fold and the Fifteenth Amendment ratified in March 1870 gave voting privileges to all male blacks, North and South. For the next five or six years the Republican Party closely supervised the legislatures of the Southern states, imposing civil rights through a series of so-called Force Acts. Under this umbrella a combination of freedmen, white Republicans of Northern origin (derisively called "carpetbaggers"), and white Southern Republicans (who were ridiculed as "scalawags") enacted social legislation that was unacceptable to the white supremacists. When the Northern Republicans chose to relax their supervision, the unreconstructed Southern whites resumed their opposition to blacks, both through the underground Ku Klux Klan and an official Democratic Party. Around this party a political structure known as the "solid South" was firmly established.

THE NEW NORTH

The same administration that presided over Reconstruction in the South was responsible for the transformation of the North. There the main drive of the Republican Party was to serve the industrialists and financiers who were building railroads, operating steel mills, mining coal, iron, and the recently discovered petroleum, and in general developing an industrial plant suitable for a powerful modern nation. The legislation to encourage these activities, forming the essential Republican platform, included high tariffs and sound currency. Other ingredients that did not appear in party manifestoes included subsidies for the railroads, relaxation of free enterprise in favor of various patterns of monopoly, and tolerance of corruption. In this era politicians such as William Tweed were able to plunder cities of millions of dollars, slums appeared in large urban centers, and scandals on a large scale demeaned the Presidency.

The first railway from New York to Chicago had been completed in 1865, and four years later the Union Pacific and Central Pacific met in Utah Territory. Railroads had given the Union the edge in the Civil War, and they determined which communities in the West would survive to become cities. In earlier times, commerce and enterprise exemplified in the career of John Jacob Astor had built the great fortunes, but the capital accumulation that followed the Civil War was in the hands of such pioneers as the railroad builder, Cornelius Vanderbilt. Railroads also introduced coolie labor to the United States, and the first serious confrontation between capital and labor alarmed the nation when the railroad workers of the Baltimore and Ohio struck in 1877. Finally, in reaction against the ruthless power exercised in rural areas by the railroads, the Grange (a farmers' social and welfare society) turned toward lobbying for antirailroad legislation on a state level.

The Urbanization of America (1876–1917)

The Reconstruction program formally ended as a result of the Presidential election of 1876. A depression in 1873 and 1874, revulsion against the spread of corruption, firm resistance to civil rights in the South, and even the humiliating defeat of General George Custer by the Sioux in Montana Territory combined to bring about a state of general discontent. The time had come for an understanding between the Democrats (who wished to assume political jurisdiction in the South) and the Republicans (who were frightened when the Democrats gained control of the House of Representatives in 1874, for the first time since the Civil War). In 1876 the Democratic Presidential candidate, Samuel J. Tilden, won a popular majority but was one vote short in the electoral college. A deal was made whereby the Democrats would deprive Tilden of the Presidency in favor of the Republican candidate, Rutherford B. Hayes, if Hayes would withdraw Federal troops from the South. Immediately after the withdrawal the Democrats took over the state governments in the former Confederacy, and within a few years the blacks were tenant farmers, or sharecroppers. They were excluded by economic pressure and by force from exercising civil and political rights they had briefly acquired. The economy of the South continued to produce mainly cotton, recovering from wartime collapse but remaining outside the mainstream of postwar prosperity.

END OF THE FRONTIER

In the North and in the West that prosperity was neither under control nor equitably distributed. At the beginning of this period, which comprised the last quarter of the nineteenth century, about one-fourth of the population lived in communities exceeding twenty-five hundred inhabitants. The total population rose, with the help of some nine million immigrants, from about fifty million in 1880 to about seventy-five million in 1900. Most of the newcomers settled in rural areas and the West was settled so thoroughly that no discernible frontier existed after 1890. The plains proved as fertile as anticipated, once the range was largely enclosed and made arable; and crops were so abundant that their prices fell steadily and farmers could not live on what they produced.

PROBLEMS OF RISING REVENUES

At the same time huge fortunes were accumulated, private enterprise was short-circuited to permit the reckless manipulation of public resources. Financial crises (called "panics") recurred and credit was kept tight. Small entrepreneurs found it difficult to finance a grubstake, but magnates such as John D. Rockefeller and Andrew Carnegie organized industrial empires. The accumulation of private capital was exceeded only by that in the United States Treasury. With revenues constantly exceeding expenditures, the Federal Government no longer needed high tariffs to provide income. Tariffs favored manufacturers and made manufactured goods expensive for farmers and workers, so tariff reduction became a perennial slogan of reformers. Another catchphrase was "cheap money," which usually meant the coinage of silver, a metal increasingly produced in the West and therefore a significant commodity. Groups in every part of the country were for or against high tariffs or free coinage, and geographical sectionalism was giving way to confrontations between the Establishment–big business and big politics–and its victims.

THE 1880s AND 1890s

In three consecutive Presidential elections, 1880 through 1888, the Democratic and Republican candidates evenly shared the electorate, with less than one percentage point separating their popular votes. The Democrat, Grover Cleveland, won the Presidency in 1884. The prize went to Republicans James A. Garfield and Benjamin Harrison respectively in the preceding and following campaigns. But issues played a negligible role in each instance. During the 1890s, however, the monetary system and tariffs began to arouse interest and as tariffs rose, so did passion concerning the imposition of the "cross of gold." After the McKinley Tariff of 1890 and the Panic of 1893, the fervor of the cheap-money partisans was expressed when an eloquent Democratic politician, William Jennings Bryan, reminded the urban gold advocates "that the great cities rest upon our broad and fertile prairies."

LABOR UNIONS

Both workers and farmers attempted to organize in the late nineteenth century. The unions, speaking for an abused minority, were suppressed or controlled by the most powerful segments of society. The mushroom growth of the Knights of Labor in the 1880s was stifled by the thrust of the American Federation of Labor as organization by craft, a narrow but more intensive base, proved more successful than organization by class. After several violent confrontations between labor and management in this period, notably at Haymarket Square in Chicago in 1886 and at the Homestead, Pennsylvania, plant of the Carnegie corporation in 1892, unionism made little progress before the turn of the century.

FARM ORGANIZATIONS

The farmers who were an abused majority, made impressive political progress. Within the Democratic Party, the Farmers' Alliances that developed from the Grange elected nine Congressmen and two Senators in 1890 and began to consider forming an independent party. The convention of the People's Party in 1892 picked a Presidential candidate who won 8.5 per cent of the popular vote and the ballots of 22 electors from four states. Their platform was based on the free coinage of silver, national ownership of rail, telegraph, and telephone facilities, a graduated income tax, an eight-hour day, and the popular election of Senators–several of which proposals were eventually adopted by the traditional parties and enacted into law. The Populists increased their strength in 1894, but in 1896 they were persuaded to endorse the Democratic candidate, Bryan. His defeat terminated third-party efforts for many decades and prolonged the ascendancy of the Republican alliance with big business.

The Spanish-American War—The Battle of Manila Bay, Philippine Islands, May 1898

THE NATION REACHES FULL GROWTH

Through a combination of aggressive enterprise, indulgent government, enormous resources, and geographical isolation, the United States emerged into the twentieth century as a major power. The gold standard and a record tariff were on the books. Farm production began to satisfy an expanding domestic market. The United States produced more steel than any country in the world. For a quarter-century the trade balance was increasingly favorable, and soon after the turn of the century the United States became a creditor rather than a debtor in the international market. The circumstances favored a new manifestation of expansionism, which had been almost dormant in the second half of the nineteenth century; only the purchase of Alaska from the Russians in 1867 significantly added to the national domain. Just before the end of the century the contagion of European imperialism spread to the Western Hemisphere. The vigorous economy would soon require new markets, new sources of raw material, new fields for the investment of capital.

THE SPANISH-AMERICAN WAR

In such an environment, the plight of the offshore island of Cuba proved to be a catalyst. The drive to annex Cuba to the United States had diminished once the island was no longer potential slave territory. But Spain's poor administration of Cuba, in which American capital was heavily invested after the Civil War, provided a reason for intervention. More dramatic justification developed–according to some sources, was provided–when the U.S. battleship *Maine* was blown up in Havana harbor in February 1898. The Spanish-American War began in April; by August, Spain sought peace; and the treaty signed in Paris in December transferred to the United States possession of the Philippine Islands, Puerto Rico, and Guam, as well as the mandate of Cuba. In that year the annexation of the Hawaiian Islands, governed as a "republic" by Americans since 1893, was also consummated. Thus the United States found itself responsible for the administration of widely scattered dependencies inhabited by large populations whose integration into the existing American system was not contemplated.

The Spanish-American War—Wreck of the *Maine*

Emergence as a World Power (1896–1917)

The United States adopted its colonial role vigorously. The attempt by the Filipinos to assert their independence from foreign dominion was suppressed over a period of two years. Cuba was recognized as sovereign only after accepting a constitution that permitted arbitrary American intervention and after ceding Guantánamo for use as a United States military base. In the Insular Cases of 1901, the U.S. Supreme Court ruled that the acquisitions from Spain were not part of the United States, but were to be administered without representation. Hawaii, on the other hand, became a territory and received as its first governor Sanford B. Dole, its erstwhile president. The interests of the United States in China were safeguarded by the unilateral declaration of the Open Door Policy, which won international acceptance in 1900. The United States, in turn, participated in the joint effort by Western powers to suppress the Boxer Rebellion against the Chinese government.

THE BIG STICK

Assured of its status as a Caribbean and Pacific power, the United States planned to protect its interests by building a canal across Central America between the Caribbean Sea and the Pacific Ocean. This was made possible in 1903 when the province of Panama withdrew from Columbia, under the protection of the U.S. Navy. The new republic of Panama then leased a canal zone to United States in perpetuity. United States armed forces were used to protect the interests of businessmen and investors in Santo Domingo in 1905, in Cuba from 1906 through 1909, in Nicaragua in 1909, and in Haiti in 1915.

Perhaps more significant than the establishment of Caribbean protectorates was the extension of the Monroe Doctrine by the so-called Roosevelt Corollary of 1904, which proclaimed the intention of the United States to intervene anywhere in Latin America when local authorities appeared incapable of maintaining law and order. Mexico was a target of this policy during its revolution that began in 1911. President Wilson announced that he would recognize only a chief executive who had been legally elected. In 1914 he dispatched a force to seize Veracruz on a pretext. When Francisco Villa, one of the generals contending for the Mexican presidency, led raids across the border in 1916 to retaliate against the incursion into his country, Wilson sent an American contingent on a counterraid that provoked the indignation of Villa's opponent, President Venustiano Carranza.

PROGRESSIVE POLITICS

The display of energy in foreign policy during the first decade of the twentieth century was matched by a zeal to loosen the ties between big business and the government. The change in policy was a reaction to abuses by such tycoons as J. P. Morgan, John D. Rockefeller, and the railroad magnates James J. Hill and E. H. Harriman, all of whom combined to create a massive trust known as Northern Securities. The Progressive movement led by Congressman Robert M. La Follette weakened monopolies on the state level, and national leaders presented themselves as enemies of corporate arrogance. In 1902 President Theodore Roosevelt used the Sherman Antitrust Act to break up Northern Securities, which gave him the reputation of a "trust-buster." Other accomplishments of his Administration included regulative agencies and legislation, such as the Interstate Commerce Commission and the Pure Food and Drug Act, both in 1906. The succeeding Administration of William Howard Taft attempted to stem the Progressive trend in the Republican Party, driving Roosevelt into opposition.

The political feud within the Republican camp gave the Presidency in 1912 to Woodrow Wilson, the first Democrat other than Cleveland to achieve that office since the Civil War. Wilson rode the Progressive tide under the slogan of the New Freedom. The major domestic achievement during his first term was the ratification in 1912 of the Sixteenth Amendment, which imposed an income tax and thus met a major objective of the Populist movement. Wilson convinced Congress to strengthen the drive against monopoly in 1914 by passing the Clayton Antitrust Act, which specifically exempted trade unions from classification as a "trust," and by creating the Federal Trade Commission. Other reforms and changes in direction under Wilson's purposeful leadership included reorganization of the banking system under the Federal Reserve Act of 1913. Wilson provided Federal aid in the building of highways in 1916 as it became evident that the automobile was here to stay.

DRIFT TOWARD WAR

The course of developing the New Freedom was interrupted by events in Europe, where rival blocs were competing for control of the world's markets. In the approaching showdown between the long-established colonial powers–Great Britain, France, and Russia (the Allies) and the less stable empires of Germany and Austria-Hungary (the Central Powers)–the United States had little interest. But as in the nineteenth-century contest between Great Britain and Napoleonic France, neutrality was difficult to maintain. British conduct toward neutral shipping was often as high-handed as that of the Germans, yet the German embargo of the British Isles threatened the flourishing commerce between Great Britain and the United States. Britain's status as a major customer made it possible for the United States to overlook minor breaches. On the other hand, the Germans had no weapons other than submarines to enforce its blockade, so it inevitably brought about innocent American deaths on the high seas. This swept the United States into the camp of the Allies. Wilson, who was reelected in 1916 because "he kept us out of war," asked Congress for a declaration of war in April 1917; and the United States entered the First World War–not as an "ally," but as an "associated power."

FIRST WORLD WAR

The nation met its responsibilities as a belligerent with efficiency; it accepted unprecedented restrictions on its economy and liberty. The War Industries Board concentrated the forces of industry, agriculture, and manpower. Civilians were conscripted into the armed forces, and the Committee on Public Information mobilized public opinion. Once the war was over, the American people found them so uncomfortable that they rallied around the slogan of a "return to normalcy."

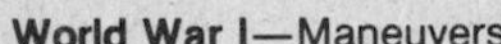

World War I—Maneuvers

World War I—Capt. Eddie Rickenbacker and his Spad Airplane

Between World Wars (1918–1945)

Nevertheless the First World War transformed the United States into a world power, and President Wilson became for a season the hero of the victorious Allies. The Fourteen Points proposed by Wilson to Congress in January 1918 as a peace platform became the framework for peace negotiations in which he participated personally at Versailles in 1919, winning the Nobel Prize for peace en route. He was responsible for formulating a Covenant for a League of Nations that was incorporated into the proposed peace treaty. Its purpose was to set up a forum where a stabilized world could conduct international business without recourse to arms. When the treaty, with its Covenant, was brought to the Senate for ratification in March 1920, it was passed by a majority short of the required two-thirds. Wilson was unable to convert either the Senate or the electorate to his vision. The United States recoiled from the possibility of compromising a particle of its sovereignty. In 1921 a relatively unknown Republican Senator, Warren G. Harding, became the first "dark horse" of the century to achieve the Presidency in the first election in which women were eligible to vote. The country turned back to business as usual.

DECADE OF PROSPERITY

The relaxation of discipline was sudden. The armed forces were demobilized, the railroads were returned to private control, tariffs were raised to peak levels and extended to protect industries that had not existed in prewar days and crops never before shielded. Taxes that confiscated fortunes

The *Question Mark*, a Fokker C-2, with the help of a refueling plane sets an endurance record of almost 151 hours in 1929.

were repealed and monopolistic practices were revived. These changes brought a decade of unprecedented prosperity. Among the contributing factors were a population of well over one hundred million, more than half of whom were urban; advances in technology, particularly in chemistry and the use of electric power; above all the development of the automobile, which paralleled in its economic and social influence the development of the railroad in the mid-nineteenth century. Just as the automobile increased the mobility of persons and goods, so the new medium of radio increased the spread of information. The broadcasting network exemplified the complex modern enterprise, just as the marketplaces of the land were being forged into linked chains. Transportation, communications, and merchandising assumed their modern characteristics, and in turn stimulated such industries as steel, glass, rubber, oil, and advertising. Only the liquor industry was depressed, for during the war the temperance movement convinced the American people of the evils of alcohol. Prohibition became effective one year after the ratification of the Eighteenth Amendment in January 1919.

DRIFT TOWARD DEPRESSION

The United States did not cut itself off entirely from the world. The nation's role on the world stage required its involvement in international trade. Although production and credit were expanding rapidly within the United States after the war, these activities were disrupted on the world scene by maneuvers around the war debt and reparations. Perhaps the inequitable distribution of wealth aggravated the difficulties. In any case, the world's consuming market could no longer profitably absorb the abundance produced. A panic in the stock exchange in September and October 1929, preceded a rapid decline in business activity and employment. The ensuing depression spread from the United States throughout the world. Its effects were profound. It altered the course of American economy and internationally contributed to the political circumstances that led directly to the Second World War.

The Wall Street "crash" occurred seven months after President Herbert Hoover's inauguration, at which he predicted the final victory over poverty. The remainder of Hoover's Administration was engaged in an effort to achieve recovery in a manner consistent with Republican policies. Government could intervene in the private economy sector only if it benefited business, for prosperous industry was considered the prerequisite to general prosperity. Accordingly, the Reconstruction Finance Corporation (RFC) was created in January 1932, with the mission of distributing Federal funds where they would presumably do the most good. Banks and big business received help. Direct relief to victims of the economic disaster was not within the jurisdiction of the RFC.

THE NEW DEAL

This program did not appeal to the stricken electorate. They returned the Democratic Party to power by voting for Franklin D. Roosevelt as Pres-

World War I—U.S. soldiers going over the top

World War I—U.S. soldiers with gas masks in the trenches ident. The crisis of bank failures in 1933 coincided with his inauguration, but Roosevelt told his countrymen that they had "nothing to fear but fear itself." In this spirit of indomitable optimism, a series of bold, innovative measures were directly addressed to the catastrophe. Roosevelt's program, known as the New Deal, included relief for the farmer in the Agricultural Adjustment Act (AAA), for small as well as big business in the National Industrial Recovery Act (NIRA), for the youthful unemployed in the Civilian Conservation Corps (CCC) and the National Youth Administration (NYA), and for jobless adults in the Public Works Administration and successively in the Civil Works, Works Progress, and Work Projects administrations (CWA, WPA). Insurance against bank failures was guaranteed by the Federal Deposit Insurance Corporation (FDIC); and insurance against the effects of severed income was provided in the Social Security system, which also fostered the passage of state unemployment insurance laws. Collective bargaining between management and labor was encouraged by the National Labor Relations Act. The proliferation of what became known as "alphabet agencies" continued. Most of them survived the constitutional test, although the Supreme Court struck down NIRA and AAA. This led to a logistic attack against the Court by Roosevelt, usually referred to as "packing" the Court. Although neither the Constitution nor tradition limited the number of Justices, Roosevelt's lunge proved unpopular. After a series of Court rulings more favorable to the New Deal, the "packing" attempt was abandoned.

At first the business community supported the New Deal. But when the safety of the capitalist system was assured, Roosevelt began to lose business approval. On the other hand, a powerful new labor organization, the Committee for (later Congress of) Industrial Organization (CIO), arose within the established American Federation of Labor (AFL). The CIO organized workers by industry rather than according to craft in the AFL tradition. Spurred by favorable legislation and a friendly government, the unions almost tripled their membership in the eight years after 1933, and could be numbered safely in the Democratic fold. Most of the voting blacks were in Northern working-class precincts and were likely to find more in common with the party of Roosevelt than with the Republicans, whose ties with Lincoln appeared tenuous. Additional support for Roosevelt was gained when, in 1933, the Twenty-First Amendment repealed Prohibition; this reform had been in the Democratic platform. The Depression lingered on despite the best efforts of the first two Administrations of Franklin Roosevelt; yet the New Deal remained popular and even the Republican candidate in 1940, Wendell Willkie, did not attack it in principle. Roosevelt easily won an unprecedented third term. To a great degree, however, his foreign policy accounted for his victory in 1940. The Second World War was already under way, sending shock waves across both oceans. The American people felt it was no time to change leadership.

WAR CLOUDS AGAIN

During the first two Roosevelt Administrations, Adolf Hitler had risen to power over Europe and made a partnership in an anticommunist axis with

World War II—A montage of photographs depicting the attack of Pearl Harbor

imperial Japan and fascist Italy. This aroused mixed reactions among Americans. Antipathy toward communism prevailed in the United States, which waited 16 years to recognize the obviously stable government of the Soviet Union. However, few Americans considered the dictators of Italy and Germany and the martial emperor of Japan champions of enlightened capitalism. They observed with distaste the ruthless treatment of Jews and dissidents in Germany, Italy's conquest of Ethiopia, the cynical participation of Italian and German troops in Spain's civil war, and the even more cynical absorption of Austria and Czechoslovakia by Hitler. On the other hand, sentiments of neutralism were strong. This caused the United States to play an ambiguous role toward Spain, to abstain from participation in the League of Nations, and to observe with aloofness the Japanese aggression against China. The Soviet Union, perhaps aware that anticommunist Europe was willing to support Hitler in an eastward drive, formed an alliance with Hitler in 1939. Most of Western Europe was overrun by the Nazis in 1940, and the United States prepared to face the imminent danger, adopting peacetime conscription for the first time in September 1940. Modest aid was tendered to Great Britain. The neutrality laws were revised. And in anticipation of the approaching Presidential campaign, Roosevelt named Republicans to the sensitive Navy and War posts in his cabinet.

SECOND WORLD WAR

Only after the Hawaiian Islands were directly attacked by the Japanese on December 7, 1941, did the United States enter the Second World War. The nation immediately became the "arsenal of democracy," and its contribution of goods and personnel undoubtedly assured the reversal of Axis aggression. Once more the entire economy was geared to a single task, this time under the Office of War Mobilization. The vast production capacity was now fully utilized, bringing an end to the Depression and even restoring prosperity to the farmers, who had languished since the end of the First World War in near-poverty. Organized labor, committed to abstain from striking for the duration, enrolled members at an accelerating pace. Among these were large numbers of women and black ex-sharecroppers who had found factory jobs in Northern cities. The prosecution of the war was conducted with enthusiasm. President Roosevelt, elected to a fourth term in 1944, maintained active leadership, attending countless conferences. These began in August 1941, with a secret meeting between Roosevelt and British Prime Minister Winston Churchill on the high seas to formulate the Atlantic Charter. This document became the basis of the United Nations Declaration of January 1942. Summit meetings of the allied leaders continued in 1943 at Casablanca, Cairo, and Teheran. The meeting at Yalta in February 1945, was

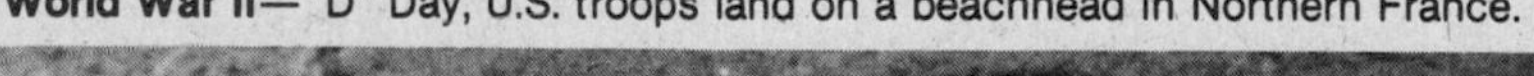
World War II—"D" Day, U.S. troops land on a beachhead in Northern France.

World War II—U.S. 3rd Infantry Division passes the shattered remains of a German convoy.

World War II—Nagasaki, Japan, following the explosion of the second U.S. atomic bomb.

World War II—Japanese Foreign Minister Mamoru Shigemitsu signs surrender terms on board the U.S.S. *Missouri.*

World War II—U.S. military personnel gather in Paris to celebrate the end of the war.

the last attended by Roosevelt, whose death in April placed his Vice-President, Harry S. Truman, in charge of the peacemaking activities.

THE BOMB AND THE UNITED NATIONS

Before the war was concluded, President Truman made the fateful decision to drop the first atomic bombs in history, over the Japanese cities of Hiroshima and Nagasaki, on August 6 and 9, 1945. This event occurred three months after the Germans had surrendered and a few days after the conclusion of the Potsdam Conference, at which the organization of the postwar world was discussed by those who would be in charge.

Meanwhile, from April to June 1945, the United States hosted a meeting in San Francisco of the nations which had signed the 1942 declaration concerning war aims. These nations now signed a charter establishing a new international organization to "maintain international peace and security," to "develop friendly relations among nations," and in general to reincarnate the League of Nations in the coming era. The United States was a charter member of this organization, the United Nations. The prospects for the international community after the Second World War seemed more promising than those for the peoples of the world after the First World War.

The Cold War (1946–1972)

Before the surrender of Japan on September 2, 1945, the friendship among the allies began to fray, revealing a schism between its communist and anticommunist members. It soon became apparent that the powers would divide into two blocs, led by the surviving superpowers, the United States and the Soviet Union. All the nations were weary of war and no power on earth would dare provoke the United States to demonstrate once more that its nuclear monopoly could bring intolerable destruction. The Soviet Union, however, chose not to relinquish this unique opportunity to establish a tier of buffer states around its heartland. Therefore, there ensued a condition between belligerency and amity between the two major powers that came to be known as "cold war."

TRUMAN DOCTRINE AND MARSHALL PLAN

Each bloc attempted to blame the other for the onset of this unwelcome atmosphere. In one version, the declaration of this "war" was attributed to Churchill, who made a speech at Fulton, Missouri, on March 5, 1946. There he described an "iron curtain" stretching across Europe from the Baltic to the Adriatic, dividing the contending camps. A year later the United States opened what may be viewed as an offensive in the contest–the proclamation of the Truman Doctrine, in the tradition of the Monroe Doctrine and the Roosevelt Corollary. President Truman declared in March 1947 (on the occasion of providing aid to the Greek government against communist insurgents) that it would be "the policy of the United States to support free peoples who are resisting attempted subjugation by armed minorities or by outside pressures." This formula was soon abbreviated to the concept of "containment" of communism. In June 1947, Secretary of State George Marshall proposed a plan to provide economic aid to the devastated countries of Europe, without discrimination. The Soviet government refused aid on behalf of its client states. Certain beneficiaries of the Marshall Plan banded together in 1949 as the North Atlantic Treaty Organization (NATO), which functioned as the military arm of the anticommunist bloc in Europe.

The first overt clash between the blocs in Europe occurred over Berlin, a disputed enclave geographically within the communist-occupied sector of

Germany. The United States supported the besieged city with an impressive airlift in 1948 and 1949. As a result, each bloc took control of a part of the former capital, and before the end of 1949 two Germanies were established as independent countries.

KOREA AND INDOCHINA

The decisive military superiority of the anticommunist camp ended when the Soviet Union demonstrated its own atomic capacity in 1949. In the same year communist power expanded with the military victory of the forces of Mao Tse-tung in China. In 1950 the communist North Koreans attacked the anticommunist South Koreans. Although the military defense of the anticommunist cause was undertaken by the United Nations (during a brief boycott of the organization by the Soviet Union), the actual conduct of the ensuing Korean War was led by the United States. China became involved and the fighting ended in a truce in 1953 that restored the lines breached in 1950.

General Dwight D. Eisenhower, supreme Allied commander in Europe during the Second World War and more recently supreme commander of the NATO forces in Europe, was elected President in 1953 to succeed Truman. One of his preelection promises was to end the war in Korea. He kept this promise. He also restrained his Secretary of State, John Foster Dulles, from providing the French in Indochina with more than economic aid in their effort to regain their colony in that area. When the French were expelled in 1954, however, Eisenhower was convinced that the Indochinese independence movement with headquarters in Hanoi was completely under communist control. During his Administration an anticommunist regime was established in Saigon with United States help. This regime proved unstable, but its maintenance as an anticommunist nucleus was considered essential. It received ever-increasing military and economic aid and finally the reinforcement of manpower. The Southeast Asia Treaty Organization was set up in 1954 in the NATO pattern. Its futility was matched only by the so-called Eisenhower Doctrine in support of any nation in the Middle East that should request aid "against armed aggression from any country controlled by international communism." In 1961 President John F. Kennedy inherited not only a bellicose policy against the communist bastion in Cuba, but also the execution of an ill-conceived military expedition against Cuba. In 1962 Kennedy compelled the Soviet Union to desist from its projected buildup of missiles in Cuba.

The Korean War—U.S. paratroopers descend on a designated location.

The Korean War—A railroad depot in North Korea minutes after being bombed by U.S. planes

BALANCE OF POWER

As the scope of the cold war widened and confrontations increased, both camps became aware of their roles. The communists, in a mirror image of the Truman Doctrine, declared that they would aid any war of "national liberation." Although nuclear war was intolerable, conventional (or "brushfire") wars could be waged. Meanwhile, both camps were subject to internal stress. Two of the anticommunist powers, France and Great Britain, joined Israel in attempting to seize the Suez Canal in 1956. The United States and the Soviet Union joined to support the United Nations' condemnation of the aggression against Egypt. On the other hand, a rift developed and widened between the Soviet and Chinese communists. Each of these major sections of the communist camp competed for goodwill within the Third World, as the uncommitted or unaligned nations–many of them liberated ex-colonies–came to be called. Finally, in the 1960s, the growing stability of China and its potential capacity to wield atomic warfare began to alter the polarity of the contest, and a triangular balance of power began to emerge. This fluid situation was of little advantage to the United States. After decades of costly effort in Indochina, the United States was left with only the certainty of defeat and diminished status.

The United Nations constantly admitted members of the Third World who tended to drift toward one of the communist groupings and almost never were attracted to the anticommunist camp. The United States found itself in the unaccustomed role of spokesman for a minority. The Nixon and Ford Administrations looked to Secretary of State Henry Kissinger as the architect of their foreign policy. They sought to adjust to the situation by establishing a détente with the Soviet Union and initiating modified diplomatic relations with China. This reversal of policy was exemplified by the admission of the People's Republic of China to the United Nations in 1971 and by an agreement with the Soviet Union in 1972 to limit the use of strategic missiles.

The Korean War—U.S. troops in action

SPACE RACE

The competition between the Soviet Union and the United States for political power on earth was paralleled by a race for the exploitation of space. The development of missiles led directly to the production of artificial satellites. The Soviet Union sent the first satellite into orbit on October 4, 1957, and less than four months later the United States sent its first satellite around the earth. The Soviet Union first made physical impact on the moon in 1959 and first sent a man into orbit in 1961, but the United States was the first to land a man on the moon's surface in 1969. The rivalry was officially terminated by a joint manned space mission in July 1975. But the competitors still covet the military and intelligence by-products that continue to accrue.

THE HOME FRONT HEATS UP

The cold war had a pronounced effect on the domestic affairs of the United States, from the Truman through the Nixon Administrations. So Under the cloak of anticommunism, dissidence of every sort was repressed. Landmark events were the "loyalty" check of government employes instituted in 1947 by Truman, the indictment of communists under the Smith Act in 1949, the enactment of the Subversive Activities Control Act and the Internal Security Act in 1950, and the series of investigations conducted or inspired by Senator Joseph McCarthy from 1950 to 1954.

Several minority groups–particularly blacks –crusaded for more civil rights in the 1950s and 1960s. The Supreme Court decision of 1954, *Brown v. Board of Education of Topeka,* reversed the 1896 ruling of *Plessy v. Ferguson* by declaring unconstitutional the segregation of blacks in public schools. This was followed by a vigorous movement to enforce and amplify the full exercise of black citizenship. The Montgomery, Alabama bus boycott began in 1955 to assert the right of blacks to equal public accommodations. It was the opening skirmish on behalf of civil rights led by the Reverend Martin Luther King, Jr., and his Southern Christian Leadership Conference. The struggle against segregation continued in its nonviolent phase as Freedom Riders tested the manner in which legal victories were translated into practice. This phase reached its climax in a mass march on Washington in 1963. A more militant phase of the movement attempted to enforce the political rights of blacks, culminating in a spectacular march from Selma to Montgomery, Alabama in 1965.

Simultaneously resistance to the war in Indochina began to peak. The antiwar and civil rights movements merged, resulting in the so-called "revolt on the campus" and the street tumult coinciding with the 1968 Democratic national convention in Chicago. Both President Lyndon Johnson and President Richard Nixon were disturbed by the rising discontent.

Astronaut Edwin E. Aldrin, Jr. stands alongside the U.S. flag deployed by him and Astronaut Neil A. Armstrong after they landed on the moon in *Apollo 11.*

The *Apollo 11* Lunar Module ascent stage on its way to a docking rendezvous prior to returning to earth.

An *Apollo 12* astronaut examines the TV camera on the surface of the moon. The Lunar Module is in the background.

Apollo 15 Astronaut James B. Irwin rides on the surface of the moon in the Lunar Rover.

The Skylab II Space Station, photographed from the Command Module.

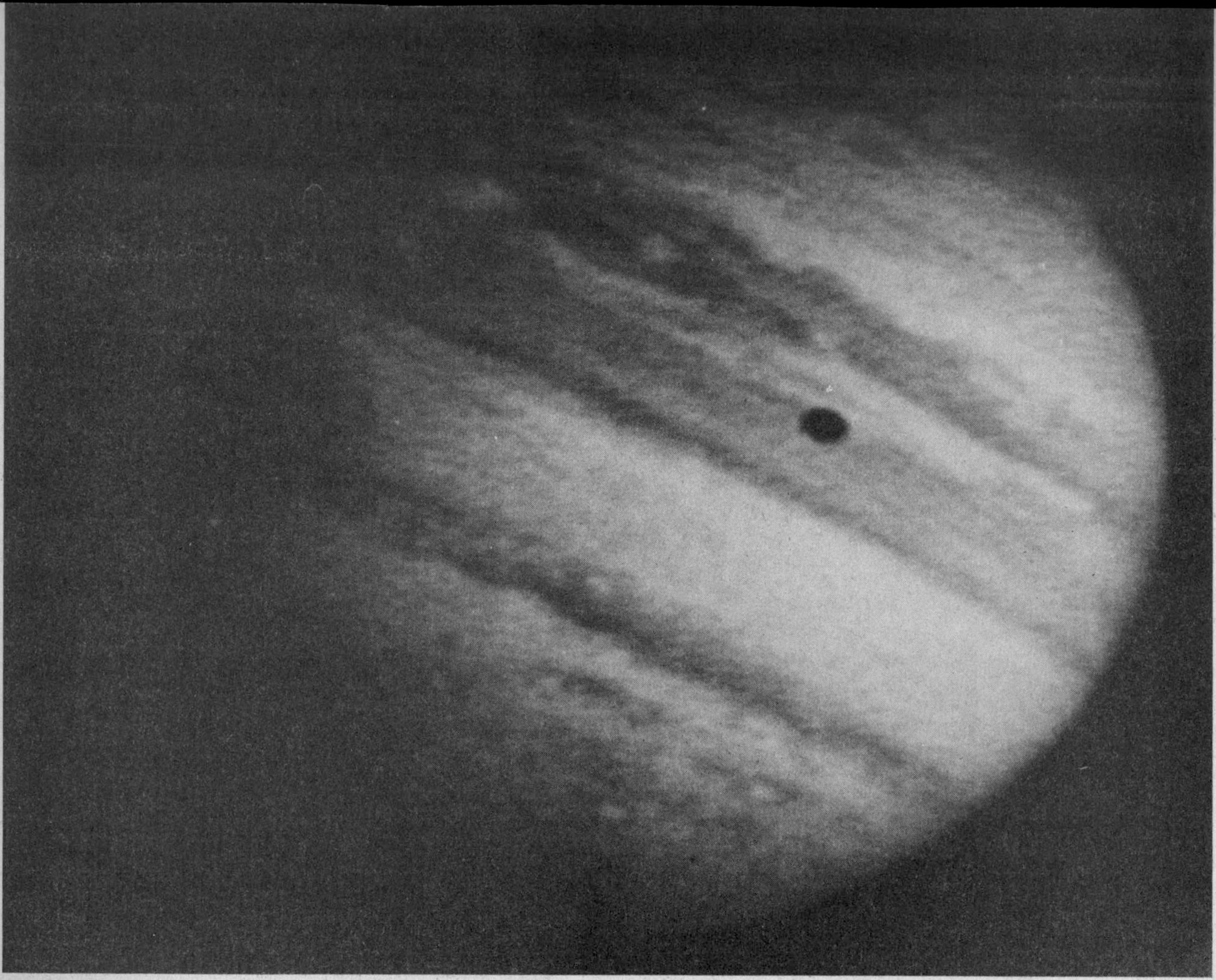

Jupiter's red spot and a shadow of the moon as photographed by *Pioneer 10*

Civil Rights Demonstration
Montgomery, Alabama, March 17, 1965

Dr. Martin Luther King, Jr.

Profile of a Superpower Since 1955

After the Second World War, the United States recovered economically far more robustly than in the period after the First World War. Following an interval of mild recession and readjustment, an upswing began during the first Eisenhower Administration with the end of the Korean War. The real gross national product in 1955 was more than twice that of 1929, and the Federal balance for fiscal 1955 and 1956 showed a surplus. Eisenhower warned of the rise of a "military-industrial complex." He was succeeded in 1961 by John F. Kennedy, whose ambitious domestic program included considerable social legislation, conservation, and accelerated space exploration. Alhough the Mercury, Gemini, and Apollo projects were virtually completed in the Kennedy and Johnson Administrations, the struggle in Indochina depleted the resources of the country at the expense of the social reforms. It so undermined the "war on poverty" declared in 1964 by President Johnson that the "great society" had to be aborted.

In November 1967, the population of the United States reached 200 million. This was double the population during the First World War, when the country first became predominantly urban. By 1967 about three-fourths of the population lived in cities. An unusually large proportion of the population were immigrants or offspring of recent immigrants, who tended to settle in urban areas. Of the 32 million immigrants who arrived in the United States by 1920, those who came before 1900 were mostly from the countries of northern Europe, but thereafter an increasing proportion came from southern and eastern Europe and were considered less capable of being assimilated. A similar attitude toward the influx of Chinese and Japanese unskilled labor in the second half of the nineteenth century resulted in discriminatory immigration laws and even total exclusion. An immigration act of 1924 restricted the proportion of south and east Europeans who could acquire permanent residence. This policy was reversed in 1965, essentially by altering the primary basis of admission from country of origin to the skill of the immigrant.

TECHNOLOGICAL INFLUENCES

At the turn of the century the highway began to take the place of the railroad as the principal mode of transport. After the Second World War, passengers and freight began to take to the air. In the aerospace age, automation was augmented by computer technology. Mobility increased and the population dispersed geographically. As manufacturing had previously gained at the expense of agriculture, now the service industries and the government bureaucracies began to draw workers away from the farms, mines, and factories. The surplus of products required new markets, either at home or abroad, while personal income failed to keep pace. Government intervention attempted to cushion the effects of inflation and a rising rate of unemployment.

POLITICAL CHANGES

The increasing role of the Federal government and tension between the executive and legislative branches of government became controversial during the third quarter of the twentieth century. The spectrum in both political parties ran from liberal to conservative; each party had a contingent favoring the reduction of government power, whether in central or local sphere. Services were expected from government, but they were costly and offered excessive opportunity for corruption. Conservatives generally proposed that the Federal Government shed its bureaucracies and allow local communities to monitor their own affairs. Liberals preferred to make sure that hard-won benefits would not be lost. Many sought a balance between laissez faire and the welfare state, and debated whether to entrust significant areas of administration to city hall, the state house, or the District of Columbia. "Strong" Presidents were somewhat out of favor, largely because of the abuse of power revealed in the aftermath of the Watergate scandal of Nixon's Administration. However, few believed that Congress could pro-

A caisson bearing the body of the assassinated black leader, Martin Luther King, Jr.

vide the world's most powerful and richest country with the leadership demanded by the contemporary situation.

CONSTITUTIONAL CHANGES

During the twentieth century, flaws in the political process were corrected several times by amendments to the Constitution, a procedure that had already rationalized the mode of Presidential elections with the Twelfth Amendment. The Seventeenth Amendment, ratified in 1913, required direct popular election of Senators instead of their selection by state legislatures. This reform was adopted after 29 of the 48 states had already passed laws compelling their legislatures to do this. In 1967 new procedures for Presidential succession in an emergency were incorporated in the Twenty-fifth Amendment. The heart attacks of President Eisenhower (during which Vice-President Nixon had tentatively assumed Executive authority) and the lingering disability of Presidents Garfield and Wilson stimulated the reform. The amendment defined the circumstances under which Presidential duties may be assumed by the Vice-President, and also prescribed the filling of a Vice-Presidential vacancy. An occasion for utilizing the Twenty-fifth Amendment occurred in 1973, when a criminal indictment forced Vice-President Spiro Agnew to resign. Nixon then appointed Congressman Gerald Ford to replace Agnew. In 1974, President Nixon also resigned and Ford succeeded to the Presidency; he in turn appointed Nelson Rockefeller to the Vice-Presidency. Thus from 1974 through 1976 the executive branch was headed by unelected but duly constituted chiefs.

TEST OF MATURITY

In general, the Constitutional procedures served well. The black population gained appropriate political power largely in the courts and by using the rights to petition, assemble, and speak freely. It took the Twenty-fourth Amendment in 1964 to eliminate the poll tax, long an instrument for denying the franchise. The threat of impeachment forced President Nixon to resign when his role in obstructing justice was established. Convictions were handed down against some of Nixon's most powerful associates in the Watergate affair. This proved to many Americans that the Constitutional process works creditably. Others, however, were so disgusted by the deeds of recent Administrations that they shunned politics altogether.

The United States entered its bicentennial year soberly, knowing that the fate of the Western world depended on the kind of example it could provide. Its economy was faltering but did not appear likely to disintegrate. Its enemies were divided; its friends were critical but could be rallied; its own population was frustrated but capable. At

Vietnam War—U.S. troops guard captured Vietcong soldiers.

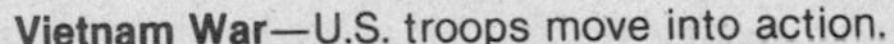

Vietnam War—U.S. troops move into action.

the nation's two-hundredth birthday the United States faced inexorable tests of its maturity.

Thus it seemed quite appropriate that 1976 should be an election year. After a hotly contested round of primaries, Georgia's Governor James Earl ("Jimmy") Carter emerged as the Democratic presidential choice. The Republicans rallied around Gerald Ford, hoping that his experience in the White House would earn official sanction at the ballot box. Carter promised to reduce unemployment and turn back the tide of inflation. He pledged to bring Washington a government that was "as good, decent, and honest as the American people themselves"–an appeal to the voters disgruntled by Watergate. On the other hand, Ford proposed to continue the policy of détente with the Soviet Union, and he predicted that the economic problems at home would take care of themselves as America developed more of its own energy resources.

Carter won the election, but soon discovered how hard it was to deliver what he'd promised. The high cost of oil, a long miners' strike in the coal industry and a series of harsh winters pushed inflation ahead. The Carter Administration created thousands of new public-service jobs, but not enough to absorb the growing number of unemployed people. Congress balked at the President's proposal to streamline the Federal government. Labor unions rejected his pleas to soften their wage demands. The public reacted skeptically to the Administration's treaty with Panamanian President Omar Trujilos, which would give the Canal Zone back to Panama by the year 2000. (The treaty passed Congress by a slim margin.) All in all, Carter fared poorly during his first year in the White House.

As time went on, Carter made better progress in foreign affairs. In a surprise move, he invited Egyptian President Anwar Sadat and Israeli Prime Minister Menachem Begin to a summit conference at Camp David in September 1978. There they drafted a "Framework for Peace in the Middle East" and vowed to sign a formal peace treaty within three months. American envoys met Soviet negotiators for a second series of Strategic Arms Limitation Talks (SALT), to hammer out an agreement on sophisticated new weapon systems.

Meanwhile, President Carter bargained with Japanese and Arab leaders in an effort to right America's balance of trade. Economic problems became a major concern of the Carter administration, in both the domestic and foreign arenas.

A group of Iranian students seized the United States embassy in Tehran on November 4, 1979, beginning one of the most tense confrontations of Carter's Administration. The students held 50 hostages for several months, ignoring the pleas of the United Nations and the new Islamic government of Iran.

Five divisions of Soviet troops invaded Afghanistan on January 3, 1980 to replace the socialist government of President Hafi-zulla Amin with leaders who would be more responsive to Russia's directives. The United States protested the invasion.

AMERICAN GOVERNMENT

The U.S. Constitution separates the powers of government as a safeguard against dictatorship. You will note that Article I of the Constitution begins with the phrase: "All legislative powers herein granted shall be vested in a Congress . . . ." Article II begins with a parallel phrase: "The executive power shall be vested in a President . . . ," while Article III states: "The judicial power of the United States shall be vested in one Supreme Court, and in . . . inferior courts. . . ." Each of these branches is independent of the others.

THE EXECUTIVE BRANCH

The office of the President has developed over the years. Many changes have taken place in the method of electing the President. The authors of the Constitution wanted to avoid having the President chosen directly by the people; they feared the public would not know the qualifications of the candidate and might choose unwisely. Consequently, they provided that every four years each state should select "electors" equal in number to the total number of the state's representatives and senators in Congress. These presidential electors would use their own judgment in electing a President and Vice-President, voting as they saw fit. Groups of electors (known as "electoral colleges") would meet in the capitals of their respective states and cast their ballots for President and Vice-President, writing two names on each ballot. The votes of the electoral colleges would then be sent to the president of the Senate, who would open and count the votes. The candidate who received a majority of all of the electoral votes cast would be declared the President-elect; the candidate with the next highest number would be the Vice-President-elect.

This system was soon changed. By 1800 two political parties had grown up, each putting forth its own candidates for office. Electors were pledged to one of these parties. They became "rubber stamps" who cast the state's electoral vote for the candidate of the party they represented. Today each party chooses a slate of electors; most voters in the state don't know them. On Election Day, voters continue to choose electors, convinced that the elector will vote for the candidate whom the voter wants. However, in the elections of 1948, 1956, 1960, 1968, and 1972 a few electors exercised their constitutional rights and voted for candidates of their own choice rather than that of the voters.

Political parties brought another important change in the method of electing the President. In 1796, John Adams became our second President because he had received the largest number of electoral college votes. Thomas Jefferson became the Vice-President, even though he and Adams were of different political parties. Furthermore, if each elector wrote on his ballot the names of the two candidates of his political party, a tie for first place might easily result. (This actually happened in 1800. The election went to the House of Representatives, where Thomas Jefferson was chosen on the thirty-sixth ballot.)

To remedy these defects, Amendment XII was added to the Constitution in 1804. It provided that the President and Vice-President be chosen on separate ballots.

Many voters dislike the electoral college system because it can elect a "minority President" who has not received even 50 percent of the popular vote. Each state's entire electoral vote goes to the candidate who polls the most votes in the state, no matter how narrow the margin of victory over his opponent. Consequently, a candidate can receive a majority of the popular vote and yet fail to win the election. This happened in 1888, when Grover Cleveland had clear majority over Benjamin Harrison, yet Harrison became President because he had more of the electoral college votes. Harrison carried the states with a large electoral vote, while Cleveland carried the states with a small electoral vote.

Reformers have often tried to make the method of electing a President more democratic. One proposal is to elect the President directly by popular vote, abolishing the electoral college. Another has been to divide each state's electoral vote among the candidates according to the popular vote.

Powers of the President

On the White House desk of President Harry S. Truman was a small sign that read, "The buck stops here." This meant that the President had to make the final decisions about a tremendous number of problems which arose each day. The Presidency has been called "the world's biggest job." As a matter of fact, it is really six different jobs:

1. The President as Chief Administrator. The Constitution states: "The executive power shall be vested in a President of the United States of America." This includes primarily the job of enforcing the laws. However, this duty is so great that the President must delegate some of this power. The President is the head of nearly two and a half million federal employees who run the approximatély 2,200 government departments, bureaus, boards, and other administrative agencies.

Directly under his command is the executive office of the President. Included in this office are several staff agencies. The White House office itself includes the President's press secretary, a legal counsel, a correspondence secretary, an appointments secretary, and a number of political, legislative, and administrative aides.

The President's chief lieutenants are the eleven members of his cabinet, who head the Departments of State; Treasury; Defense; Justice; Interior; Agriculture; Commerce; Labor; Health, Education and Welfare; Housing and Urban Development; Transportation.

Four presidential staff agencies work closely with the President:

A. *Office of Management and Budget.* The director of the budget advises the President on the fiscal requirements of the many government agencies. The Bureau advises him about legislation that concerns the costs of operating these agencies. The Office of Management and Budget has been called "Chief Housekeeper," since it tries to improve the efficiency of the Administration.

B. *Council of Economic Advisors.* This board is made up of three members who advise the President concerning economic trends. It also suggests new laws regarding the economy of the nation and helps the President prepare reports on the economic state of the nation.

C. *National Security Council.* This is an important agency concerned with national defense. It includes the Secretary of State, Secretary of Defense, director of the Central Intelligence Agency, and the director of the Office of Emergency Preparedness. It is the nation's top strategy planning body, meeting weekly with the President and Vice-President.

D. *Office of Emergency Preparedness.* This staff agency advises the President on the status of our country's raw materials, manpower, industry, military and civilian defense. It also coordinates, directs, and plans all civil and defense mobilization.

In addition to these agencies and departments, a number of others work closely with the President. These include the United States Information Agency, the Veterans' Administration, the Small Business Administration, and others.

Lastly, there are the many so-called independent agencies created by Congress. These include the Civil Aeronautics Board, the Atomic Energy Commission, the Interstate Commerce Commission, and the Federal Power Commission. These are formally part of the executive branch. (In theory, the constitution was designed to prevent executive, legislative, and judical power from being concentrated within any one of our three branches. However, these agencies do function in all three areas. They make rules, judge offenders, and execute their own laws.)

2. The President as Legislator. In spite of the separation of powers, our Chief Executive has important law-making powers. The Constitution states that the President "shall from time to time give to the Congress information on the State of the Union, and recommend to their consideration such measures as he shall judge necessary and expedient." This is how the President plays a major note in shaping national legislation. The President appears before Congress and urges legislation he considers important. The Constitution gives him the power to veto bills of which he does not approve. Congress usually cannot muster the two-thirds vote necessary to pass a bill over the President's veto. So Congress usually writes a bill to be in line with what the White House will accept.

3. The President as Chief Diplomat. In today's troubled world, the conduct of foreign relations may well be the President's most vital role. He appoints United States diplomats to their overseas posts, with the advice and consent of the Senate. The Constitution gives him also the responsibility of receiving foreign ambassadors. This involves the important power to recognize foreign governments. After the Communist revolution in 1917, Presidents Coolidge and Hoover refused to receive a Russian ambassador, thus refusing to recognize the Soviet government. Furthermore, the President has the power to make treaties, which must be approved by two-thirds of the Senate. However, he can also make executive agreements which do not require Senate approval. In 1939, for instance, President Roosevelt traded fifty United States destroyers to Great Britain for island bases without the Senate's approval.

4. The President as Chief of State. Unlike members of Congress, the President represents all Americans rather than those of a particular section. He appears at important public ceremonies. He is in a unique position to help mold public thinking, through press conferences, radio, and television. Presidents Franklin D. Roosevelt and Jimmy Carter, for example, used "fireside chats" to help gain the nation's support for their programs.

5. The President as Commander in Chief. The Constitution places the President at the head of all of the armed forces of the United States. He must approve all military promotions and is responsible for the nation's defense and military preparedness. Although the Constitution gives Congress the power to declare war, the President may determine whether or not a state of war exists. President Truman, for example, ordered United States troops into Korea in 1950, although Congress had not formally declared war. Once war comes, the President decides when, where, and how our military power will be used.

6. The President as Party Chief. Although political parties are not mentioned in the Constitution, the President is the head of his political party. He is responsible for choosing the party's national chairman. As chief executive he can award hundreds of government jobs in Washington and throughout the country, a power known as "patronage." Often, he uses these positions to reward loyal members of the party. The President often uses his prestige to support some of his party's candidates in Congressional or state elections.

Presidential Succession

John Adams, the first Vice-President of the United States, once remarked that an appropriate title for the Vice-President would be "Your Superfluous Excellency." He referred to the fact that the main responsibility of the office was to preside over the Senate. In that position, the Vice-President does not even have the privilege of voting, except in case of a tie.

Yet the constitutional qualifications for the Vice-President are the same as for the Presidency. The history of our nation has given ample evidence that this was a wise precaution. Eight of our presidents have died in office, four of them by assassination. If the President dies, the Vice-President takes office. The Constitution did not say he would necessarily become President in name. It provided that the *duties* of the chief executive would be performed by the Vice-President in case of the President's "death, resignation, or inability to discharge the duties" of his office.

While Dwight D. Eisenhower was President, he suffered two serious illnesses. The public became aware of the fact that the Constitution, in the phrase quoted above, left unanswered two important questions: (1) Who determines whether the President is incapable of serving as chief executive? (2) What happens if a President is declared unable to serve, and then recovers his health and capacities?

In 1965, Congress proposed the Twenty-fifth Amendment to the Constitution. Ratified on February 10, 1967, this amendment provides that in the event of death, resignation, or impeachment of the President, the Vice-President actually becomes the President; he does not simply perform the duties of the Chief Executive. He appoints a new Vice-President, who must be confirmed by a majority vote of Congress. Further, the amendment details the procedures to be followed if the President becomes temporarily or permanently incapacitated and unable to serve.

Presidential Tenure

How long can a President serve in office? The Constitution did not limit the number of terms of office a President might serve. Both Washington and Jefferson, however, decided that two terms were sufficient. This remained an "unwritten precedent" until 1940. In that year Franklin D. Roosevelt ran for reelection to a third term. Because he was so popular, and because World War II had broken out in Europe, the voters gave him an easy victory. In 1944, he was chosen again for a fourth term.

Many people felt that no man should be permitted to serve for so long a period. They led a movement which resulted in the adoption of the Twenty-second Amendment, which went into effect in 1951. This Amendment forbids any person from serving as President for more than two full terms. A person who has come to the Presidency from the Vice-Presidency as the result of the death of the President is considered to have had a "full term" if he holds office for over two years.

THE LEGISLATIVE BRANCH

Of the three branches of the Federal Government, the legislative branch is the only one elected *directly* by the people. The Constitution granted the power of making all federal laws to Congress, composed of the Senate and the House of Representatives.

The House of Representatives

Representation in the House is based upon population, each state being guaranteed at least one representative. There are 435 members. Most representatives are elected from a congressional district, whose area is determined by the state legislature. Some states also have Congressmen-at-large, elected by the voters of the entire state. Members of the House of Representatives serve for two years.

In addition to the law-making powers which it shares with the Senate, the House of Representatives has three special powers. It has the sole power to initiate revenue bills. It alone has the power to impeach the President or any other civil officer of the United States for "Treason, Bribery, or other high Crimes and Misdemeanors." Lastly, the House of Representatives elects the President if the electoral college fails to do so. This happened in 1800 and 1824.

The Senate

The Constitution provided that the Senate be made up of two senators from each state. Hence all states, regardless of their size or population, have an equal voice in the Senate. All senators are elected for six years. Since one-third of the Senate comes up for election every two years, the Senate never changes more than one-third of its membership at any time, as the House of Representatives may.

The Senate has three special powers, which permit it to check the power of the President. Its approval is needed for Presidential appointments to cabinet posts, ambassadorships, and other high offices. The two-thirds vote of the Senate required for ratification of treaties has given it a significant role in foreign relations. Finally, the Senate sits as a court of trial in impeachment cases, a two-thirds vote being necessary for conviction. (The Senate also has the power to elect the Vice-President when the electoral college fails to do so. However, this power has been used only once, in the election of 1836.)

The Powers of Congress

Most of the legislative powers granted to Congress are found in Article I, Section 8. In addition to granting 17 specific powers to Congress, this section also contains the so-called *elastic* clause. This provides that Congress shall have the power "to make all laws which shall be necessary and proper for carrying into execution the foregoing powers. . . ." This clause has made possible a tremendous growth of the Federal Government.

Although Congress's powers are vast, it does not have the power to legislate as it sees fit. Article I, Section 9, and the first ten Amendments (The Bill of Rights) limit the right of Congress in many ways. For example, Congress may not tax exports, appropriate money for the Army for a period of over two years, suspend the privilege of the writ of *habeas corpus,* or grant a title of nobility.

How a Bill Becomes a Law

A bill must be introduced by a member of Congress, in either one of the two houses (except for bills for the raising of revenue, which must originate in the House of Representatives). Thousands of bills are introduced in each session of Congress. Out of this number, fewer than one thousand become laws. The process by which a bill becomes a law is often long and complicated.

1. *The bill is introduced.* In the Senate, a sponsor introduces the bill from the floor, usually without discussion. In the House of Representatives, a sponsor of the bill drops it into a box known as the "hopper" at the desk of the Speaker of the House. (The Speaker is chosen at the start of each new Congress from the majority party. He ordinarily votes on issues only in case of a tie.)

2. *A committee studies the bill.* Because of the thousands of bills which are introduced during a session of Congress, the committee system was set up. In the House of Representatives there are 19 "standing" or regular committees; in the Senate there are 15. Large committees are generally broken down into subcommittees, each responsible for part of the parent committee's work. Each committee is made up of members from both political parties. Generally, the committee reflects the relative party strengths in the particular house of

Congress, so that the majority party controls each committee.

Seniority determines who will be chairman of the committee. That is, the position is usually held by a member of the majority party who has had the longest period of service on the committee.

In the House of Representatives, the Speaker assigns the bill to the appropriate committee. Senators state their choice of committee on all bills they introduce.

The committee may announce public hearings, at which supporters and opponents of the bill may appear and state their positions. At the close of the hearings, the committee decides whether to report the bill favorably or to pigeonhole it–that is, not report it at all. Over 90 percent of all bills introduced in Congress are killed in committee.

Most committee hearings are for the purpose of examining bills introduced. However, Congress also has the power to use committee hearings to "investigate," in order to see how well the laws of Congress are being executed and to find out whether new legislation is needed. In recent years, investigatory hearings into crime, Communism, and corruption have attracted widespread public attention.

3. *Bills reach the floor.* After the committee has reported a bill favorably, the bill goes on the calendar of the house to which the committee belongs. Some bills are considered more important than others. In the House of Representatives the Rules Committee may decide when a bill shall be called up. Some bills may never be reached at all if this committee places them at the bottom of the list. In the Senate, the policy committee of the majority party determines priorities.

The members debate the bill on the floor. In the House, the large membership has made it necessary to limit the time each member is allowed to speak. But in the Senate there is unlimited debate. A Senator or group of Senators can try to "talk a bill to death" to prevent its being brought to a vote. This strategy is called a "filibuster."

Each house may revise or amend the bill in the course of debate. The vote is finally taken. If a majority approves, the bill is sent to the other house for consideration. There the entire process starts all over again. The bill may be pigeonholed in committee, defeated on the floor, or approved. (Sometimes the procedure is speeded up by having similar bills start at the same time in both houses.)

4. *A conference committee may consider the bill.* In the course of its travel through both houses, the bill may have been changed considerably, so that the House version and the Senate version differ in details. In such a case, a conference committee, made up of members of both houses, meets to adjust these differences. The bill is then sent back to both houses for final approval.

5. *The bill goes to the President.* The bill becomes law after receiving the President's signature. If he holds it for a period of ten days (Sundays excepted) while Congress is in session, it also becomes law. (If Congress is not in session and the President holds the bill for ten days, it is automatically killed. This is called a "pocket veto.") If the President disapproves of the bill, he returns it to the house in which it started, with a statement of his objections, called a "veto message." If two-thirds of each house again vote for it, it becomes a law in spite of his veto.

THE JUDICIAL BRANCH

The judicial branch can be understood better if we contrast it with the legislative and executive branches. The primary function of Congress is to make laws. The primary function of the executive branch is to carry these laws into effect. The courts settle legal disputes in terms of existing law.

In the United States the courts have a particularly important role to play. Our Constitution is based upon the idea of limited government. The judicial branch has been given a major responsibility for seeing that government does not exceed the powers the people have given it.

How Federal Courts Are Organized

In Article III, Section 1, the Constitution provides for a Supreme Court and ". . . such inferior [lower] courts as the Congress may from time to time ordain and establish." In accordance with this, Congress created the Federal court system, consisting of three types of courts (and one special court, the Court of Claims).

1. *Federal District Courts.* At the base of the Federal court system are the 84 District Courts. Since these are the first to hear most cases, they are said to have *original* jurisdiction. Only one judge ordinarily sits on a case, although three may sit as a court in special circumstances. Like all other federal judges, District Court judges are appointed for life by the President, subject to the advice and consent of the Senate. In the District

Courts are tried most cases of crime against the United States and suits between individual citizens of different states.

2. *The United States Courts of Appeals.* Immediately above the District Courts are the eleven Courts of Appeals. These are ordinarily three-judge courts. Since they hear cases on appeal from the District Courts, they are said to have appellate jurisdiction. They are concerned primarily with questions of law rather than with findings of fact. Thus they relieve the Supreme Court of some of the tremendous burden of appellate work.

Usually, the decision of a Court of Appeals is final. Unless a case involves an extremely complex and important point of law, the Supreme Court would not have time to review it. Only a small fraction of cases go from the Courts of Appeals to the United States Supreme Court.

3. *The Court of Claims.* The Court of Claims was created in order to handle debt claims against the United States Government. Most of these claims arise out of government contracts. The Court of Claims has five judges.

4. *The Supreme Court of the United States.* The nation's highest tribunal consists of nine judges. Since the Constitution does not specify the number of judges, Congress decides this by law. (At first the Supreme Court had six judges. Congress has set the number at as many as ten and as few as five.)

One of the judges is designated as the chief justice. His decisions, however, have no more legal weight than those of his fellow justices. The Court ordinarily hears arguments for two weeks and then recesses for two weeks to reach decisions and write opinions. Cases are decided by a majority vote of the justices. (Many important cases have been decided by a five-to-four vote.) In addition to the majority decision, there may be a *dissenting,* or minority, opinion. In case a justice agrees with the majority decision but differs with the reasoning behind it, he may write a *concurring* opinion.

The Supreme Court has wide discretion to decide which cases it will hear on appeal from lower courts and which it will refuse to hear. In general, the Court will hear cases that have been decided differently in two or more lower courts. You will recall that unless there is a real constitutional issue or an important point of federal law involved, the Court will usually decline to hear an appeal. Thus, out of about 1,500 cases, the Court will hear only about 200.

In addition to the cases brought to the Supreme Court on appeal, the Court has original jurisdiction in certain cases. These cases are prescribed by the Constitution and are relatively rare. They include cases involving foreign diplomats and suits brought by one state against another.

Our Dual Court System

It should be noted that each of the states has its own court system. Since the United States Consitution is the supreme law of the land, any case involving federal law or the federal Constitution is heard in a United States court rather than in a state court. The Supreme Court of the United States exercises the power to void laws passed by state legislatures and to overrule decisions of state courts, when it deems these laws or decisions to be in conflict with federal law or the United States Constitution.

CHECKS AND BALANCES

We have examined the responsibilities of each of the three main branches of our government. The Constitution provided a system of checks and balances to prevent any branch from invading the rights of the others. There have been occasions in our history, however, when conflict arose because one of the branches considered that its independence was being threatened. Let us review the important checks and balances and note some of the notable instances of conflict among the three branches.

Congress and the President

As noted above, the President may check Congress by using his veto power over legislation. He may also call Congress into special session and recommend legislation to Congress. Through the prestige of his office, he can exert great influence on public opinion and on Congress.

Meanwhile, Congress can check the President by the use of its constitutional powers. The administration must depend upon Congress for money. If Congress refuses to appropriate funds the President needs to enforce a law, it can tie his hands. Furthermore, although the President is commander in chief of the armed forces, Congress determines the size and equipment of those forces. Both houses may override the President's veto by two-thirds vote. In addition, the Senate may check the President by refusing to approve his appointments or by refusing to ratify treaties. The Constitution provides that the House of Representatives may bring impeachment charges against the President, and the Senate has the power to try him on these charges.

Conflict between the executive and legislative branches has been a part of our history since the days of George Washington. In 1789, President Washington tried to hasten the Senate's ratification of an Indian treaty by going to the Senate with his advisors to answer any questions the Senators had. The Senators sat in silence, resenting what they considered to be an intrusion on their powers. Washington walked out, vowing never to set foot in the Senate chamber again. No President did, in fact, until President Wilson appeared before the Senate 130 years later. Washington's successor, John Adams, remarked that Congress and the President were "natural enemies."

During the Civil War, Abraham Lincoln not only used the constitutional powers of the President but also some that belonged to Congress. According to the Constitution, only Congress may "raise and support armies," yet Lincoln issued a call for volunteers, declared martial law, and ordered the Treasury to pay funds for military purposes. He waited until Congress had adjourned to issue his Emancipation Proclamation. He said, "I felt that measures, otherwise unconstitutional, might become lawful by becoming indispensable to the preservation of the Constitution . . ." After Lincoln's assassination, Andrew Johnson continued to insist upon the powers of the President. His conflict with Congress was climaxed by his impeachment trial, which failed of conviction by just one vote.

Woodrow Wilson believed strongly that the President must give legislative leadership to Congress. He insisted upon appearing in person before Congress on major proposals for legislation. When the Senate refused to allow the United States to join the League of Nations after World War I, he "went to the people." On a cross-country tour he urged the voters to make Congress vote for his measure.

In 1933, Franklin D. Roosevelt continued the Wilson pattern of Presidential leadership in legislation. He spoke to Congress of "building a strong and permanent tie between the legislative and executive branches of the government." When he felt that an individual Senator failed to support his program, he did not hesitate to go into the Senator's home state to campaign against his reelection.

Conficts between the legislative and executive branches have also arisen out of the activities of congressional committees. Congressional investigations have often served useful purposes, such as the uncovering of the Teapot Dome scandal during the administration of President Harding and the revelation of corruption in the Internal Revenue Department during the 1950s. However, important questions concerning the independence of each branch arise out of these hearings. How far may a committee go in requiring officials of the executive branch to appear before it and testify? The President clearly may not be so forced, but what of cabinet officers? May the President order his subordinates not to give information to a congressional committee? These and other questions arose during the hearings on the role of communism in the government and the army conducted by Senator Joseph McCarthy in 1953–1954, and the Senate investigation into campaign wrongdoings in 1973.

The Supreme Court and the Other Branches

The Constitution provides for checks by the President on the judicial branch. He has the power to appoint new Supreme Court judges and other federal judges to fill vacancies. Furthermore, he may grant pardons and reprieves, except in cases of impeachment. The Senate checks on the courts by its power to refuse to ratify Presidential appointments. Impeachment charges against federal judges are brought by the House of Representatives and tried by the Senate.

The Supreme Court, on the other hand, exercises a tremendously important check upon the other two branches. It may set aside any law passed by Congress and approved by the President if a majority of the Court's members find that the law violates any part of the Constitution. Furthermore, it may also declare any actions of the executive branch unconstitutional.

This power, known as *judicial review,* is not expressly granted to the Supreme Court by the Constitution. In 1803 Chief Justice John Marshall first declared an act of Congress unconstitutional, in the celebrated case of *Marbury* v. *Madison.* In his decision, Marshall declared: "It is emphatically the province and duty of the judicial department to say what the law is. . . . A law repugnant to the Constitution is void. . . ."

This power of judicial review has been a major

source of conflict. Thomas Jefferson strongly criticized the doctrine as making the Constitution "a mere thing of wax in the hands of the judiciary, which they might twist, and shape into any form they please." He insisted that each branch should have the authority to interpret its own powers. Andrew Jackson is reported to have said about a decision with which he disagreed: "John Marshall has made his decision, now let him enforce it!" Few decisions in our nation's history have been as unpopular as the Court's ruling in the Dred Scott case, in 1857, that Congress lacked the power to exclude slavery from the territories.

The argument over the power of judicial review reached a climax in the 1930s, when the Supreme Court held so many New Deal laws unconstitutional that President Franklin D. Roosevelt proposed to Congress that he be allowed to "pack" the Court by making as many as six new appointments to the Court. In this way, he hoped to get more favorable decisions. Congress refused to support him in his effort, however.

In 1952, President Harry S. Truman, in order to forestall a steel strike which he felt would imperil national defense at a time when the country was engaged in the war in Korea, ordered his Secretary of Commerce to seize and operate the steel mills. The Supreme Court held his action to be unconstitutional. It argued that the President normally has only those powers specifically granted to him by the Constitution and the laws. In grave emergencies, however, he may exercise powers beyond these *if Congress agrees*. Here we see a basic role of the Court: to act as the "guardian of the Constitution" by curbing the power of the other branches.

The Constitution of the United States

WE THE PEOPLE of the United States, in Order to form a more perfect Union, establish Justice, insure domestic Tranquility, provide for the common defence, promote the general Welfare, and secure the Blessings of Liberty to ourselves and our Posterity, do ordain and establish this CONSTITUTION for the United States of America.

ARTICLE I.

SECTION 1. All legislative Powers herein granted shall be vested in a Congress of the United States, which shall consist of a Senate and House of Representatives.

SECTION 2. [1] The House of Representatives shall be composed of Members chosen every second Year by the People of the several States, and the Electors in each State shall have the Qualifications requisite for Electors of the most numerous Branch of the State Legislature.

[2] No person shall be a Representative who shall not have attained to the Age of twenty five Years, and been seven Years a Citizen of the United States, and who shall not, when elected, be an Inhabitant of that State in which he shall be chosen.

[3] [*Representatives and direct Taxes shall be apportioned among the several States which may be included within this Union, according to their respective Numbers, which shall be determined by adding to the whole Number of free Persons, including those bound to Service for a Term of Years, and excluding Indians not taxed, three fifths of all other Persons.*]* The actual Enumeration shall be made within three Years after the first Meeting of the Congress of the United States, and within

NOTE.–This text of the Constitution follows the engrossed copy signed by Gen. Washington and the deputies from 12 States. The superior number preceding the paragraphs designates the number of the clause; it was not in the original. Spelling and punctuation in the Constitution are set according to copy supplied by the United States Government Printing Office; 88th Congress, 1st Session; House Document No. 112.

* The part included in heavy brackets was changed by section 2 of the fourteenth amendment.

every subsequent Term of ten Years, in such Manner as they shall by Law direct. The Number of Representatives shall not exceed one for every thirty Thousand, but each State shall have at Least one Representative; and until such enumeration shall be made, the State of New Hampshire shall be entitled to chuse three, Massachusetts eight, Rhode-Island and Providence Plantations one, Connecticut five, New-York six, New Jersey four, Pennsylvania eight, Delaware one, Maryland six, Virginia ten, North Carolina five, South Carolina five, and Georgia three.

4 When vacancies happen in the Representation from any State, the Executive Authority thereof shall issue Writs of Election to fill such Vacancies.

5 The House of Representatives shall chuse their Speaker and other Officers; and shall have the sole Power of Impeachment.

SECTION 3. 1 The Senate of the United States shall be composed of two Senators from each State, [chosen by the Legislature thereof,]* for six Years; and each Senator shall have one Vote.

2 Immediately after they shall be assembled in Consequence of the first Election, they shall be divided as equally as may be into three Classes. The Seats of the Senators of the first Class shall be vacated at the Expiration of the second Year, of the second Class at the Expiration of the fourth Year, and of the third Class at the Expiration of the sixth Year, so that one third may be chosen every second Year; [*and if Vacancies happen by Resignation, or otherwise, during the Recess of the Legislature of any State, the Executive thereof may make temporary Appointments until the next Meeting of the Legislature, which shall then fill such Vacancies*]. **

3 No Person shall be a Senator who shall not have attained to the Age of thirty Years, and been nine Years a Citizen of the United States, and who shall not, when elected, be an Inhabitant of that State for which he shall be chosen.

4 The Vice President of the United States shall be President of the Senate, but shall have no Vote, unless they be equally divided.

5 The Senate shall chuse their other Officers, and also a President pro tempore, in the Absence of the Vice President, or when he shall exercise the Office of President of the United States.

6 The Senate shall have the sole Power to try all Impeachments. When sitting for that Purpose, they shall be on Oath or Affirmation. When the President of the United States is tried, the Chief Justice shall preside: And no Person shall be convicted without the Concurrence of two thirds of the Members present.

7 Judgment in Cases of Impeachment shall not extend further than to removal from Office, and disqualification to hold and enjoy any Office of honor, Trust or Profit under the United States: but the Party convicted shall nevertheless be liable and subject to Indictment, Trial, Judgment and Punishment, according to Law.

SECTION 4. 1 The Times, Places and Manner of holding Elections for Senators and Representatives, shall be prescribed in each State by the Legislature thereof; but the Congress may at any time by Law make or alter such Regulations, except as to the Places of chusing Senators.

2 The Congress shall assemble at least once in every Year, and such Meeting shall [*be on the the first Monday in December,*]*** unless they shall by Law appoint a different Day.

SECTION 5. 1 Each House shall be the Judge of the Elections, Returns and Qualifications of its own Members, and a Majority of each shall constitute a Quorum to do Business; but a smaller Number may adjourn from day to day, and may be authorized to compel the Attendance of absent Members, in such Manner, and under such Penalties as each House may provide.

2 Each House may determine the Rules of its Proceedings, punish its Members for disorderly Behavior, and, with the Concurrence of two thirds, expel a Member.

3 Each House shall keep a Journal of its Proceedings, and from time to time publish the same, excepting such Parts as may in their Judgment require Secrecy; and the Yeas and Nays of the Members of either House on any question shall, at the Desire of one fifth of those Present, be entered on the Journal.

4 Neither House, during the Session of Congress, shall, without the Consent of the other, adjourn for more than three days, nor to any other Place than that in which the two Houses shall be sitting.

* The part included in heavy brackets was changed by section 1 of the seventeenth amendment.

** The part included in heavy brackets was changed by clause 2 of the seventeenth amendment.

*** The part included in heavy brackets was changed by section 2 of the twentieth amendment.

SECTION 6. [1] The Senators and Representatives shall receive a Compensation for their Services, to be ascertained by Law, and paid out of the Treasury of the United States. They shall in all Cases, except Treason, Felony and Breach of the Peace, be privileged from Arrest during their Attendance at the Session of their respective Houses, and in going to and returning from the same; and for any Speech or Debate in either House, they shall not be questioned in any other Place.

[2] No Senator or Representative shall, during the Time for which he was elected, be appointed to any civil Office under the Authority of the United States, which shall have been created, or the Emoluments whereof shall have been encreased during such time; and no Person holding any Office under the United States, shall be a Member of either House during his Continuance in Office.

SECTION 7. [1] All Bills for raising Revenue shall originate in the House of Representatives; but the Senate may propose or concur with Amendments as on other Bills.

[2] Every Bill which shall have passed the House of Representatives and the Senate, shall, before it become a Law, be presented to the President of the United States; If he approve he shall sign it, but if not he shall return it, with his Objections to that House in which it shall have originated, who shall enter the Objections at large on their Journal, and proceed to reconsider it. If after such Reconsideration two thirds of that House shall agree to pass the Bill, it shall be sent, together with the Objections, to the other House, by which it shall likewise be reconsidered, and if approved by two thirds of that House, it shall become a Law. But in all such Cases the Votes of both Houses shall be determined by Yeas and Nays, and the Names of the Persons voting for and against the Bill shall be entered on the Journal of each House respectively. If any Bill shall not be returned by the President within ten days (Sundays excepted) after it shall have been presented to him, the Same shall be a Law, in like Manner as if he had signed it, unless the Congress by their Adjournment prevent its Return, in which Case it shall not be a Law.

[3] Every Order, Resolution, or Vote to which the Concurrence of the Senate and House of Representatives may be necessary (except on a question of Adjournment) shall be presented to the President of the United States; and before the Same shall take Effect, shall be approved by him, or being disapproved by him, shall be repassed by two thirds of the Senate and House of Representatives, according to the Rules and Limitations prescribed in the Case of a Bill.

SECTION 8. [1] The Congress shall have Power To lay and collect Taxes, Duties, Imposts and Excises, to pay the Debts and provide for the common Defence and general Welfare of the United States; but all Duties, Imposts and Excises shall be uniform throughout the United States;

[2] To borrow Money on the credit of the United States;

[3] To regulate Commerce with foreign Nations, and among the several States, and with the Indian Tribes;

[4] To establish an uniform Rule of Naturalization, and uniform Laws on the subject of Bankruptcies throughout the United States;

[5] To coin Money, regulate the Value thereof, and of foreign Coin, and fix the Standard of Weights and Measures;

[6] To provide for the Punishment of counterfeiting the Securities and current Coin of the United States;

[7] To establish Post Offices and post Roads;

[8] To promote the Progress of Science and useful Arts, by securing for limited Times to Authors and Inventors the exclusive Right to their respective Writings and Discoveries;

[9] To constitute Tribunals inferior to the supreme Court;

[10] To define and punish Piracies and Felonies committed on the high Seas, and Offenses against the Law of Nations;

[11] To declare War, grant Letters of Marque and Reprisal, and make Rules concerning Captures on Land and Water;

[12] To raise and support Armies, but no Appropriation of Money to that Use shall be for a longer Term than two Years;

[13] To provide and maintain a Navy;

[14] To make Rules for the Government and Regulation of the land and naval Forces;

[15] To provide for calling forth the Militia to execute the Laws of the Union, suppress Insurrections and repel Invasions;

[16] To provide for organizing, arming, and disciplining the Militia, and for governing such Part of them as may be employed in the Service of the United States, reserving to the States respectively, the Appointment of the Officers, and the Authority of training the Militia according to the discipline prescribed by Congress;

[17] To exercise exclusive Legislation in all Cases whatsoever, over such District (not exceeding ten Miles square) as may, by Cession of particular States, and the Acceptance of Congress, become the Seat of the Government of the United States, and to exercise like Authority over all Places purchased by the Consent of the Legislature of the State in which the Same shall be, for the Erection of Forts, Magazines, Arsenals, dock-Yards, and other needful Buildings;–And

[18] To make all Laws which shall be necessary and proper for carrying into Execution the foregoing Powers, and all other Powers vested by this Constitution in the Government of the United States, or in any Department or Officer thereof.

SECTION 9. [1] The Migration or Importation of such Persons as any of the States now existing shall think proper to admit, shall not be prohibited by the Congress prior to the Year one thousand eight hundred and eight, but a Tax or duty may be imposed on such Importation, not exceeding ten dollars for each Person.

[2] The Privilege of the Writ of Habeas Corpus shall not be suspended, unless when in Cases of Rebellion or Invasion the public Safety may require it.

[3] No Bill of Attainder or ex post facto Law shall be passed.

*[4] No Capitation, or other direct, Tax shall be laid, unless in Proportion to the Census or Enumeration herein before directed to be taken.

[5] No Tax or Duty shall be laid on Articles exported from any State.

[6] No Preference shall be given by any Regulation of Commerce or Revenue to the Ports of one State over those of another: nor shall Vessels bound to, or from, one State be obliged to enter, clear, or pay Duties in another.

[7] No Money shall be drawn from the Treasury, but in Consequence of Appropriations made by Law; and a regular Statement and Account of the Receipts and Expenditures of all public Money shall be published from time to time.

[8] No Title of Nobility shall be granted by the United States: And no Person holding any Office of Profit or Trust under them, shall, without the Consent of the Congress, accept of any present, Emolument, Office, or Title, of any kind whatever, from any King, Prince, or foreign State.

---

*See also the sixteenth amendment.

SECTION 10. [1] No state shall enter into any Treaty, Alliance, or Confederation; grant Letters of Marque and Reprisal: coin Money; emit Bills of Credit; make any Thing but gold and silver Coin a Tender in Payment of Debts; pass any Bill of Attainder, ex post facto Law, or Law impairing the Obligation of Contracts, or grant any Title of Nobility.

[2] No State shall, without the Consent of the Congress, lay any Imposts or Duties on Imports or Exports, except what may be absolutely necessary for executing it's inspection Laws: and the net Produce of all Duties and Imposts, laid by any State on Imports or Exports, shall be for the Use of the Treasury of the United States; and all such Laws shall be subject to the Revision and Controul of the Congress.

[3] No State shall, without the Consent of Congress, lay any Duty of Tonnage, keep Troops, or Ships of War in time of Peace, enter into any Agreement or Compact with another State, or with a foreign Power, or engage in War, unless actually invaded, or in such imminent Danger as will not admit of delay.

ARTICLE II.

SECTION. 1. [1] The executive Power shall be vested in a President of the United States of America. He shall hold his Office during the Term of four Years, and, together with the Vice President, chosen for the same Term, be elected as follows

[2] Each State shall appoint, in such Manner as the Legislature thereof may direct, a Number of Electors, equal to the whole Number of Senators and Representatives to which the State may be entitled in the Congress: but no Senator or Representative, or Person holding an Office of Trust or Profit under the United States, shall be appointed an Elector.

[*The Electors shall meet in their respective States, and vote by Ballot for two Persons, of whom one at least shall not be an Inhabitant of the same State with themselves. And they shall make a List of all the Persons voted for, and of the Number of Votes for each; which List they shall sign and certify, and transmit sealed to the Seat of the Government of the United States, directed to the President of the Senate. The President of the Senate shall, in the Presence of the Senate and House of Representatives, open all the Certificates, and the Votes shall then be counted. The Person having the greatest*

Number of Votes shall be the President, if such Number be a Majority of the whole Number of Electors appointed; and if there be more than one who have such Majority, and have an equal Number of Votes, then the House of Representatives shall immediately chuse by Ballot one of them for President; and if no Person have a Majority, then from the five highest on the List the said House shall in like Manner chuse the President. But in chusing the President, the Votes shall be taken by States, the Representation from each State having one Vote; A quorum for this Purpose shall consist of a Member or Members from two thirds of the States, and a Majority of all the States shall be necessary to a Choice. In every Case, after the Choice of the President, the Person having the greatest Number of Votes of the Electors shall be the Vice President. But if there should remain two or more who have equal Votes, the Senate shall chuse from them by Ballot the Vice President.]*

[3] The Congress may determine the Time of chusing the Electors, and the Day on which they shall give their Votes; which Day shall be the same throughout the United States.

[4] No Person except a natural born Citizen, or a Citizen of the United States, at the time of the Adoption of this Constitution, shall be eligible to the Office of President; neither shall any Person be eligible to that Office who shall not have attained to the Age of thirty five Years, and been fourteen Years a Resident within the United States.

[5] In Case of the Removal of the President from Office, or of his Death, Resignation, or Inability to discharge the Powers and Duties of the said Office, the Same shall devolve on the Vice President, and the Congress may by Law provide for the Case of Removal, Death, Resignation or Inability, both of the President and Vice President, declaring what Officer shall then act as President, and such Officer shall act accordingly, until the Disability be removed, or a President shall be elected.

[6] The President shall, at stated Times, receive for his Services, a Compensation, which shall neither be encreased nor diminished during the Period for which he shall have been elected, and he shall not receive within that Period any other Emolument from the United States, or any of them.

Before he enter on the Execution of his Office, he shall take the following Oath or Affirmation:–"I do solemnly swear (or affirm) that I will faithfully execute the Office of President of the United States, and will to the best of my Ability, preserve, protect and defend the Constitution of the United States."

SECTION 2. [1] The President shall be Commander in Chief of the Army and Navy of the United States, and of the Militia of the several States, when called into the actual Service of the United States; he may require the Opinion, in writing, of the principal Officer in each of the executive Departments, upon any Subject relating to the Duties of their respective Offices, and he shall have Power to grant Reprieves and Pardons for Offences against the United States, except in Cases of Impeachment.

[2] He shall have Power, by and with the Advice and Consent of the Senate, to make Treaties, provided two thirds of the Senators present concur; and he shall nominate, and by and with the Advice and Consent of the Senate, shall appoint Ambassadors, other public Ministers and Consuls, Judges of the supreme Court, and all other Officers of the United States, whose Appointments are not herein otherwise provided for, and which shall be established by Law: but the Congress may by Law vest the Appointment of such inferior Officers, as they think proper, in the President alone, in the Courts of Law, or in the Heads of Departments.

[3] The President shall have Power to fill up all Vacancies that may happen during the Recess of the Senate, by granting Commissions which shall expire at the End of their next Session.

SECTION 3. He shall from time to time give to the Congress Information of the State of the Union, and recommend to their Consideration such Measures as he shall judge necessary and expedient; he may, on extraordinary Occasions, convene both Houses, or either of them, and in Case of Disagreement between them, with Respect to the Time of Adjournment, he may adjourn them to such Time as he shall think proper; he shall receive Ambassadors and other public Ministers; he shall take Care that the Laws be faithfully executed, and shall Commission all the Officers of the United States.

SECTION 4. The President, Vice President and all civil Officers of the United States, shall be removed from Office on Impeachment for, and Conviction of, Treason, Bribery, or other high Crimes and Misdemeanors.

---

*This paragraph has been superseded by the twelfth amendment.

ARTICLE III.

SECTION 1. The judicial Power of the United States, shall be vested in one supreme Court, and in such inferior Courts as the Congress may from time to time ordain and establish. The Judges, both of the supreme and inferior Courts, shall hold their Offices during good Behaviour, and shall, at stated Times, receive for their Services a Compensation, which shall not be diminished during their Continuance in Office.

SECTION 2. [1] The judicial Power shall extend to all Cases, in Law and Equity, arising under this Constitution, the Laws of the United States, and Treaties made, or which shall be made, under their Authority;–to all Cases affecting Ambassadors, other public Ministers and Consuls;–to all Cases of admiralty and maritime Jurisdiction;–to Controversies to which the United States shall be a Party;–to Controversies between two or more States;–between a State and Citizens of another State;*–between Citizens of different States;–between Citizens of the same State claiming Lands under Grants of different States; and between a State, or the Citizens thereof, and foreign States, Citizens or Subjects.

[2] In all Cases affecting Ambassadors, other public Ministers and Consuls, and those in which a State shall be Party, the supreme Court shall have original Jurisdiction. In all the other Cases before mentioned, the supreme Court shall have appellate Jurisdiction, both as to Law and Fact, with such Exceptions, and under such Regulations as the Congress shall make.

[3] The Trial of all Crimes, except in Cases of Impeachment shall be by Jury; and such Trial shall be held in the State where the said Crimes shall have been committed; but when not committed within any State, the Trial shall be at such Place or Places as the Congress may by Law have directed.

SECTION 3. [1] Treason against the United States, shall consist only in levying War against them, or in adhering to their Enemies, giving them Aid and Comfort. No Person shall be convicted of Treason unless on the Testimony of two Witnesses to the same overt Act, or on Confession in open Court.

[2] The Congress shall have Power to declare the Punishment of Treason, but no Attainder of Treason shall work Corruption of Blood, or Forfeiture except during the Life of the Person attainted.

ARTICLE IV.

SECTION 1. Full Faith and Credit shall be given in each State to the public Acts, Records, and judicial Proceedings of every other State. And the Congress may by general Laws prescribe the Manner in which such Acts, Records and Proceedings shall be proved, and the Effect thereof.

SECTION 2. [1] The Citizens of each State shall be entitled to all Privileges and Immunities of Citizens in the several States.

[2] A Person charged in any State with Treason, Felony, or other Crime, who shall flee from Justice, and be found in another State, shall on Demand of the executive Authority of the State from which he fled, be delivered up, to be removed to the State having Jurisdiction of the Crime.

[3] [*No Person held to Service or Labour in one State, under the Laws thereof, escaping into another, shall, in Consequence of any Law or Regulation therein, be discharged from such Service or Labour, but shall be delivered up on Claim of the Party to whom such Service or Labour may be due.*]**

SECTION 3. [1] New States may be admitted by the Congress into this Union; but no new State shall be formed or erected within the Jurisdiction of any other State; nor any State be formed by the Junction of two or more States, or Parts of States, without the Consent of the Legislatures of the States concerned as well as of the Congress.

[2] The Congress shall have Power to dispose of and make all needful Rules and Regulations respecting the Territory or other Property belonging to the United States; and nothing in this Constitution shall be so construed as to Prejudice any Claims of the United States, or of any particular State.

SECTION. 4. The United States shall guarantee to every State in this Union a Republican Form of Government, and shall protect each of them against Invasion; and on Application of the Legislature, or of the Executive (when the Legislature cannot be convened) against domestic Violence.

---

* This clause has been affected by the eleventh amendment.

** This paragraph has been superseded by the thirteenth amendment.

ARTICLE V.

The Congress, whenever two thirds of both Houses shall deem it necessary, shall propose Amendments to this Constitution, or, on the Application of the Legislatures of two thirds of the several States, shall call a Convention for proposing Amendments, which, in either Case, shall be valid to all Intents and Purposes, as Part of this Constitution, when ratified by the Legislatures of three fourths of the several States, or by Conventions in three fourths thereof, as the one or the other Mode of Ratification may be proposed by the Congress: Provided, [*that no Amendment which may be made prior to the Year One thousand eight hundred and eight shall in any Manner affect the first and fourth Clauses in the Ninth Section of the first Article; and*] * that no State, without its Consent, shall be deprived of its equal Suffrage in the Senate.

ARTICLE VI.

1 All Debts contracted and Engagements entered into, before the Adoption of this Constitution shall be as valid against the United States under this Constitution, as under the Confederation.

2 This Constitution, and the Laws of the United States which shall be made in Pursuance thereof; and all Treaties made, or which shall be made, under the Authority of the United States, shall be the supreme Law of the Land; and the Judges in every State shall be bound thereby, any Thing in the Constitution or Laws of any State to the Contrary notwithstanding.

3 The Senators and Representatives before mentioned, and the Members of the several State Legislatures, and all executive and judicial Officers, both of the United States and of the several States, shall be bound by Oath or Affirmation, to support this Constitution; but no religious Test shall ever be required as a Qualification to any Office or public Trust under the United States.

ARTICLE VII.

The Ratification of the Conventions of nine States, shall be sufficient for the Establishment of this Constitution between the States so ratifying the Same.

DONE in Convention by the Unanimous Consent of the States present the Seventeenth Day of September in the Year of our Lord one thousand seven hundred and Eighty seven and of the Independence of the United States of America the Twelfth IN WITNESS whereof We have hereto subscribed our Names,

G° WASHINGTON—
Presid[t]. and deputy from Virginia.

[Signed also by the deputies of twelve States.]

New Hampshire.
JOHN LANGDON,
NICHOLAS GILMAN.

Massachusetts.
NATHANIEL GORHAM,
RUFUS KING.

Connecticut.
WM. SAML. JOHNSON,
ROGER SHERMAN.

New York.
ALEXANDER HAMILTON.

New Jersey.
WIL: LIVINGSTON,
DAVID BREARLEY,
WM. PATERSON,
JONA: DAYTON.

Pennsylvania.
B FRANKLIN,
ROB[T] MORRIS,
THOS. FITZSIMONS,
JAMES WILSON,
THOMAS MIFFLIN,
GEO. CLYMER,
JARED INGERSOLL,
GOUV MORRIS.

Delaware.
GEO: READ,
JOHN DICKINSON,
JACO: BROOM,
GUNNING BEDFORD, jun,
RICHARD BASSETT.

Maryland.
JAMES MCHENRY,
DAN[L] CARROLL,
DAN OF S[T] THOS. JENIFER.

Virginia.
JOHN BLAIR—
JAMES MADISON Jr.

* Obsolete.

North Carolina.
Wm. Blount,
Hu Williamson,
Rich'd Dobbs Spaight.

South Carolina.
J. Rutledge,
Charles Pinckney,
Charles Cotesworth Pinckney,
Pierce Butler.

Georgia.
William Few,
Abr Baldwin,
Attest: William Jackson, *Secretary.*

ARTICLES IN ADDITION TO, AND AMENDMENT OF, THE CONSTITUTION OF THE UNITED STATES OF AMERICA, PROPOSED BY CONGRESS, AND RATIFIED BY THE LEGISLATURES OF THE SEVERAL STATES PURSUANT TO THE FIFTH ARTICLE OF THE ORIGINAL CONSTITUTION

ARTICLE [I] *

Congress shall make no law respecting an establishment of religion, or prohibiting the free exercise thereof; or abridging the freedom of speech, or of the press, or the right of the people peaceably to assemble, and to petition the Government for a redress of grievances.

ARTICLE [II]

A well regulated Militia, being necessary to the security of a free State, the right of the people to keep and bear Arms, shall not be infringed.

ARTICLE [III]

No Soldier shall, in time of peace be quartered in any house, without the consent of the Owner, nor in time of war, but in a manner to be prescribed by law.

* Only the 13th, 14th, 15th, and 16th articles of amendment had numbers assigned to them at the time of ratification. Articles of amendment that did not have numbers assigned to them at ratification are shown here in proper order with the corresponding number placed in light brackets.

ARTICLE [IV]

The right of the people to be secure in their persons, houses, papers, and effects, against unreasonable searches and seizures, shall not be violated, and no Warrants shall issue, but upon probable cause, supported by Oath or affirmation, and particularly describing the place to be searched, and the persons or things to be seized.

ARTICLE [V]

No person shall be held to answer for a capital, or otherwise infamous crime, unless on a presentment or indictment of a Grand Jury, except in cases arising in the land or naval forces, or in the Militia, when in actual service in time of War or public danger; nor shall any person be subject for the same offence to be twice put in jeopardy of life or limb, nor shall be compelled in any criminal case to be a witness against himself, nor be deprived of life, liberty, or property, without due process of law; nor shall private property be taken for public use without just compensation.

ARTICLE [VI]

In all criminal prosecutions, the accused shall enjoy the right to a speedy and public trial, by an impartial jury of the State and district wherein the crime shall have been committed; which district shall have been previously ascertained by law, and to be informed of the nature and cause of the accusation; to be confronted with the witnesses against him; to have compulsory process for obtaining Witnesses in his favor, and to have the Assistance of Counsel for his defence.

ARTICLE [VII]

In Suits at common law, where the value in controversy shall exceed twenty dollars, the right of trial by jury shall be preserved, and no fact tried by a jury shall be otherwise reexamined in any Court of the United States, than according to the rules of the common law.

ARTICLE [VIII]

Excessive bail shall not be required, nor excessive fines imposed, nor cruel and unusual punishments inflicted.

ARTICLE [IX]

The enumeration in the Constitution, of certain rights, shall not be construed to deny or disparage others retained by the people.

ARTICLE [X]

The powers not delegated to the United States by the Constitution, nor prohibited by it to the States, are reserved to the States respectively, or to the people.

ARTICLE [XI]

The Judicial power of the United States shall not be construed to extend to any suit in law or equity, commenced or prosecuted against one of the United States by Citizens of another State, or by Citizens or Subjects of any Foreign State.

ARTICLE [XII]

The electors shall meet in their respective states and vote by ballot for President and Vice-President, one of whom, at least, shall not be an inhabitant of the same state with themselves; they shall name in their ballots the person voted for as President, and in distinct ballots the person voted for as Vice-President, and they shall make distinct lists of all persons voted for as President, and of all persons voted for as Vice-President, and of the number of votes for each, which lists they shall sign and certify, and transmit sealed to the seat of the government of the United States, directed to the President of the Senate;–The President of the Senate shall, in presence of the Senate and House of Representatives, open all the certificates and the votes shall then be counted;–The person having the greatest number of votes for President, shall be the President, if such number be a majority of the whole number of Electors appointed; and if no person have such majority, then from the persons having the highest numbers not exceeding three on the list of those voted for as President, the House of Representatives shall choose immediately, by ballot, the President. But in choosing the President, the votes shall be taken by states, the representation from each state having one vote; a quorum for this purpose shall consist of a member or members from two-thirds of the states, and a majority of all the states shall be necessary to a choice. [*And if the House of Representatives shall not choose a President whenever the right of choice shall devolve upon them, before the fourth day of March next following, then the Vice-President shall act as President, as in the case of the death or other constitutional disability of the President.*]* The person having the greatest number of votes as Vice-President, shall be the Vice-President, if such number be a majority of the whole number of Electors appointed, and if no person have a majority, then from the two highest numbers on the list, the Senate shall choose the Vice-President; a quorum for the purpose shall consist of two-thirds of the whole number of Senators, and a majority of the whole number shall be necessary to a choice. But no person constitutionally ineligible to the office of President shall be eligible to that of Vice-President of the United States.

ARTICLE XIII

SECTION 1. Neither slavery nor involuntary servitude, except as a punishment for crime whereof the party shall have been duly convicted, shall exist within the United States, or any place subject to their jurisdiction.

SECTION 2. Congress shall have power to enforce this article by appropriate legislation.

ARTICLE XIV

SECTION 1. All persons born or naturalized in the United States, and subject to the jurisdiction thereof, are citizens of the United States and of the

* The part included in heavy brackets has been superseded by section 3 of the twentieth amendment.

State wherein they reside. No State shall make or enforce any law which shall abridge the privileges or immunities of citizens of the United States; nor shall any State deprive any person of life, liberty, or property, without due process of law; nor deny to any person within its jurisdiction the equal protection of the laws.

SECTION 2. Representatives shall be apportioned among the several States according to their respective numbers, counting the whole number of persons in each State, excluding Indians not taxed. But when the right to vote at any election for the choice of electors for President and Vice-President of the United States, Representatives in Congress, the Executive and Judicial officers of a State, or the members of the Legislature thereof, is denied to any of the male inhabitants of such State, being twenty-one years of age, and citizens of the United States, or in any way abridged, except for participation in rebellion, or other crime, the basis of representation therein shall be reduced in the proportion which the number of such male citizens shall bear to the whole number of male citizens twenty-one years of age in such State.

SECTION 3. No person shall be a Senator or Representative in Congress, or elector of President and Vice-President, or hold any office, civil or military, under the United States, or under any State, who, having previously taken an oath, as a member of Congress, or as an officer of the United States, or as a member of any State legislature, or as an executive or judicial officer of any State, to support the Constitution of the United States, shall have engaged in insurrection or rebellion against the same, or given aid or comfort to the enemies thereof. But Congress may by a vote of two-thirds of each House, remove such disability.

SECTION 4. The validity of the public debt of the United States, authorized by law, including debts incurred for payment of pensions and bounties for services in suppressing insurrection or rebellion, shall not be questioned. But neither the United States nor any State shall assume or pay any debt or obligation incurred in aid of insurrection or rebellion against the United States, or any claim for the loss or emancipation of any slave; but all such debts, obligations and claims shall be held illegal and void.

SECTION 5. The Congress shall have power to enforce, by appropriate legislation, the provisions of this article.

ARTICLE XV

SECTION 1. The right of citizens of the United States to vote shall not be denied or abridged by the United States or by any State on account of race, color, or previous condition of servitude.

SECTION 2. The Congress shall have power to enforce this article by appropriate legislation.

ARTICLE XVI

The Congress shall have power to lay and collect taxes on incomes, from whatever source derived, without apportionment among the several States, and without regard to any census or enumeration.

ARTICLE [XVII]

The Senate of the United States shall be composed of two Senators from each state, elected by the people thereof, for six years; and each Senator shall have one vote. The electors in each State shall have the qualifications requisite for electors of the most numerous branch of the State legislatures.

When vacancies happen in the representation of any State in the Senate, the executive authority of such State shall issue writs of election to fill such vacancies: *Provided,* That the legislature of any State may empower the executive thereof to make temporary appointments until the people fill the vacancies by election as the legislature may direct.

This amendment shall not be so construed as to affect the election or term of any Senator chosen before it becomes valid as part of the Constitution.

ARTICLE [XVIII]

[SECTION 1. After one year from the ratification of this article the manufacture, sale, or transportation of intoxicating liquors within, the importation thereof into, or the exportation thereof from the

United States and all territory subject to the jurisdiction thereof for beverage purposes is hereby prohibited.

[*SECTION 2. The Congress and the several States shall have concurrent power to enforce this article by appropriate legislation.*

[*SECTION 3. This article shall be inoperative unless it shall have been ratified as an amendment to the Constitution by the legislatures of the several States, as provided in the Constitution, within seven years from the date of the submission hereof to the States by the Congress.*]*

ARTICLE [XIX]

The right of citizens of the United States to vote shall not be denied or abridged by the United States or by any State on account of sex.

Congress shall have power to enforce this article by appropriate legislation.

ARTICLE [XX]

SECTION 1. The terms of the President and Vice-President shall end at noon on the 20th day of January, and the terms of Senators and Representatives at noon on the 3d day of January, of the years in which such terms would have ended if this article had not been ratified; and the terms of their successors shall then begin.

SECTION 2. The Congress shall assemble at least once in every year, and such meeting shall begin at noon on the 3d day of January, unless they shall by law appoint a different day.

SECTION 3. If, at the time fixed for the beginning of the term of the President, the President elect shall have died, the Vice-President elect shall become President. If a President shall not have been chosen before the time fixed for the beginning of his term, or if the President elect shall have failed to qualify, then the Vice-President elect shall act as President until a President shall have qualified; and the Congress may by law provide for the case wherein neither a President elect nor a Vice-President elect shall have qualified, declaring who shall then act as President, or the manner in which one who is to act shall be selected, and such person shall act accordingly until a President or Vice-President shall have qualified.

SECTION 4. The Congress may by law provide for the case of the death of any of the persons from whom the House of Representatives may choose a President whenever the right of choice shall have devolved upon them, and for the case of the death of any of the persons from whom the Senate may choose a Vice-President whenever the right of choice shall have devolved upon them.

SECTION 5. Sections 1 and 2 shall take effect on the 15th day of October following the ratification of this article.

SECTION 6. This article shall be inoperative unless it shall have been ratified as an amendment to the Constitution by the legislatures of three-fourths of the several States within seven years from the date of its submission.

ARTICLE [XXI]

SECTION 1. The eighteenth article of amendment to the Constitution of the United States is hereby repealed.

SECTION 2. The transportation or importation into any State, Territory, or possession of the United States for delivery or use therein of intoxicating liquors, in violation of the laws thereof, is hereby prohibited.

SECTION 3. This article shall be inoperative unless it shall have been ratified as an amendment to the Constitution by conventions in the several States, as provided in the Constitution, within seven years from the date of the submission hereof to the States by the Congress.

ARTICLE [XXII]

SECTION 1. No person shall be elected to the office of the President more than twice, and no person who has held the office of President, or acted as President, for more than two years of a term to which some other person was elected President

*Repealed by section 1 of the twenty-first amendment.

shall be elected to the office of the President more than once. But this article shall not apply to any person holding the office of President when this Article was proposed by the Congress, and shall not prevent any person who may be holding the office of President, or acting as President, during the term within which this Article becomes operative from holding the office of President or acting as President during the remainder of such term.

SECTION 2. This article shall be inoperative unless it shall have been ratified as an amendment to the Constitution by the legislatures of three-fourths of the several States within seven years from the date of its submission to the States by the Congress.

ARTICLE [XXIII]

SECTION 1. The District constituting the seat of Government of the United States shall appoint in such manner as the Congress may direct:

A number of electors of President and Vice-President equal to the whole number of Senators and Representatives in Congress to which the District would be entitled if it were a State, but in no event more than the least populous State; they shall be in addition to those appointed by the States, but they shall be considered, for the purposes of the election of President and Vice-President, to be electors appointed by a State; and they shall meet in the District and perform such duties as provided by the twelfth article of amendment.

SECTION 2. The Congress shall have power to enforce this article by appropriate legislation.

ARTICLE [XXIV]

SECTION 1. The right of citizens of the United States to vote in any primary or other election for President or Vice-President, for electors for President or Vice-President, or for Senator or Representative in Congress, shall not be denied or abridged by the United States or any State by reason of failure to pay any poll tax or other tax.

SECTION 2. The Congress shall have the power to enforce this article by appropriate legislation.

ARTICLE XXV

SECTION 1. In case of removal of the President from office or of his death or resignation, the Vice-President shall become President.

SECTION 2. Whenever there is a vacancy in the office of the Vice-President, the President shall nominate a Vice-President who shall take office upon confirmation by a majority vote of both Houses of Congress.

SECTION 3. Whenever the President transmits to the President pro tempore of the Senate and the Speaker of the House of Representatives his written declaration that he is unable to discharge the powers and duties of his office, and until he transmits to them a written declaration to the contrary, such powers and duties shall be discharged by the Vice-President as Acting President.

SECTION 4. Whenever the Vice-President and a majority of either the principal officers of the executive departments or of such other body as Congress may by law provide, transmit to the President pro tempore of the Senate and the Speaker of the House of Representatives their written declaration that the President is unable to discharge the powers and duties of his office, the Vice-President shall immediately assume the powers and duties of the office as Acting President.

Thereafter, when the President transmits to the President pro tempore of the Senate and the Speaker of the House of Representatives his written declaration that no inability exists, he shall resume the powers and duties of his office unless the Vice-President and a majority of either the principal officers of the executive department or of such other body as Congress may by law provide, transmit within four days to the President pro tempore of the Senate and the Speaker of the House of Representatives their written declaration that the President is unable to discharge the powers and duties of his office. Thereupon Congress shall decide the issue, assembling within forty-eight hours for that purpose if not in session. If the Congress, within twenty-one days after receipt of the latter written declaration, or, if Congress is not in session, within twenty-one days after Congress is required to assemble, determines by two-thirds vote of both Houses that the President is unable to discharge the powers and duties of his office, the Vice-President shall continue to discharge the same as Acting President; otherwise, the President shall resume the powers and duties of his office.

ARTICLE XXVI

SECTION 1. The right of citizens of the United States, who are eighteen years of age or older, to vote shall not be denied or abridged by the United States or by any State on account of age.

SECTION 2. The Congress shall have power to enforce this article by appropriate legislation.

ARTICLE XXVII

This Article had not completed ratification by the end of 1979, and Congress extended the term for ratification to 1982.

1. Equality of rights under the law shall not be denied or abridged by the United States or by any State on account of sex.

2. The Congress shall have the power to enforce, by appropriate legislation, the provisions of this article.

3. This amendment shall take effect two years after the date of ratification.

STATES AND COUNTRIES

The Fifty States of the United States

From the original 13 colonies, the United States has grown to the present 50 states. It is not unreasonable to assume that the number may still grow, now that the non-contiguous territories of Alaska and Hawaii have become states. Of course, this growth cannot be at the nineteenth-century rate because the possessions are now limited.

This section gives a brief history of each state including government and economy, and at the end of the next section there is a table with statistics related to the states.

ALABAMA

Alabama advertises itself as "The Heart of Dixie." It is, indeed, one of the original "Cotton Belt" states of the Old South. The first settlement in what is now Alabama was made by the French on Mobile Bay, in 1702. The French lost control of the area to the British in 1763. At the end of the War for Independence, all of the present state except the Mobile area was ceded to the United States. Mobile was then ceded to Spanish Florida, but regained by the United States in 1813.

Alabama was set up as a territory in 1817. It was then reorganized and admitted into the Union on December 14, 1819, as the twenty-second state. Alabama seceded from the Union on January 11, 1861, and joined the Confederate States of America. The first Confederate capital was located at Montgomery, Alabama. With the surrender of Mobile after the Battle of Mobile Bay in 1865, the defeat of Alabama was completed. Devastation due to the war was less severe than in other states of the South, but the economy of the state was wrecked and industry almost ceased. The state was readmitted in 1868, but federal troops were not withdrawn until four years later.

With the antebellum pattern of life destroyed, years of confusion and slow rebuilding followed. The economy revived somewhat in the eighties when steel production began in the Birmingham area. Other industries began to expand rapidly. A great industrial boom has taken place in Alabama during the twentieth century. This rapid industrial growth, combined with a revitalized agriculture that is no longer dependent solely upon cotton, has brought about vigorous change and revolutionary progress in "The Heart of Dixie."

Government. The state constitution dates from 1901. The state sends two senators and seven representatives to the U.S. Congress. The legislature consists of a senate of 35 members and a house of representatives of 106 members. The state is divided into 67 counties; in 1970 there were 35 cities with a population of more than ten thousand.

Economy. Major resources include iron, coal, limestone, and the "black soils" for agriculture. The great TVA projects that have arisen along the Tennessee River have brought extensive industrial expansion to northern Alabama. The presence of iron, coal, and limestone (all of which are major components of steel-making) in the same area of north-central Alabama has made Bir-

Alabama—Bellingrath Gardens near Mobile

mingham the leading iron and steel center of the South.

Alabama is also one of the leading lumber-producing states. Over 634,000 acres of national forests existed in Alabama in 1970. The chief crops grown in Alabama are cotton, corn, peanuts, and oats. Special crops include tung oil and pecans, both derived from nut trees. The raising of cattle and hogs is becoming significant in the state's economy.

ALASKA

Alaska was discovered in 1741 by Vitus Bering, a Danish explorer in the service of Russia. Russian fur traders and trappers followed the explorers. In 1784 they founded the Kodiak settlement and Sitka, the capital of Russian America, in 1799. On March 30, 1867, Alaska was sold to the United States by Czar Alexander II to prevent its capture by the British, with whom Russia was then at war. The United States paid $7,200,000, or less than two cents per acre!

President Andrew Johnson and Secretary William H. Seward were derided for making what was thought to be a useless purchase. The area of the present state was set up as a district and governed under the general laws of Oregon, although it was not governed by that state itself. After a series of gold discoveries in the district, Alaska was organized into a territory on August 24, 1912. The development of salmon fisheries, copper mining, and the growth of a tourist industry during the twenties and thirties strengthened the economy of the territory and generated a strong campaign for statehood. During World War II the statehood issue was set aside. The territory's strategic location and its natural wealth attracted the Japanese. They attempted an invasion in 1942 and managed to occupy Attu and Kiska islands in the Aleutian Archipelago of Alaska. The United States poured millions of dollars into Alaskan defenses, and in 1943 the Japanese were expelled.

The postwar economy was strengthened by further heavy defense spending, with the consequent expansion of industry and population. A renewed campaign for statehood resulted in victory on January 3, 1959, when Alaska entered the Union as the forty-ninth state.

Government. Alaska's executive branch consists of 20 departments under the governor's office. The legislature consists of a senate of 20 members and a house of representatives of 40 members. The state sends two senators and one representative to Congress. There are no counties in Alaska, but a system of boroughs performs the same functions. There were five cities in 1970 with a population of over 10,000.

Economy. Much economic activity centers around fishing, forestry, and the tourist industry. It is now fairly certain that Alaska's Kenai Peninsula and the Arctic Slope form two of the world's major petroleum areas, and someday may rival or even surpass production in the Middle East. An 800-mile trans-Alaska pipeline was completed in 1977 to carry oil from the North Slope to the Gulf of Alaska in the south.

Agriculture is well developed in the Matanuska Valley of southern Alaska and in the interior around Fairbanks. Hay, potatoes, wheat, and rye are the major crops. Some dairying and ranching is carried on near Anchorage, the state's largest city. Sawmills and canneries are concentrated in the panhandle.

The state's transportation system includes one railroad, 470 miles long, serving the interior between Fairbanks and Anchorage. Travel to Alaska is possible by automobile on the Alaska Highway,

Alaska—Mt. McKinley

1,523 miles long. This road lies mostly in Canada, and extends from Dawson Creek in British Columbia, to Fairbanks, Alaska, with several spur routes in both Alaska and Canada.

ARIZONA

Many of the Indians that live in Arizona today are the descendants of two highly advanced cultures that developed there in prehistoric times. Abandoned cliff-cities and other ruins scattered over Arizona belonged to the famous Basket-Maker people and their successors, the Pueblo people. A great 30-year drought during the thirteenth century is thought to be the chief cause of the abandonment of most of the cliff-cities. The descendants of the cliff-dwellers were found living in fortified towns and mesas, or near watercourses when Coronado's Spanish expedition entered the region in 1540.

Spanish settlement began in 1752, although Spanish missionaries had been active in Arizona since the end of the sixteenth century. Arizona became a part of independent Mexico in 1821. Most of the present state was ceded to the United States in 1848 by the Treaty of Guadalupe Hidalgo. That part lying south of the Gila River formed part of the Gadsden Purchase that was added in 1854 (*see also* New Mexico). Arizona was organized as a territory in 1863 and entered the Union as the forty-eighth state on February 14, 1912.

Government. The state constitution dates from 1910. The legislature consists of a senate of 30 members and a house of representatives of 60 members. The state sends to the national Congress two senators and four representatives. Arizona is divided into fourteen counties, and in 1970 there were 13 cities with a population of more than ten thousand.

Economy. The state's greatest resource is copper, and 40 to 50 percent of the entire United States production is mined in Arizona. Silver, uranium, zinc, molybdenum, gold, and other minerals are mined. Tourists, attracted by the healthful dry climate and many great natural wonders, provide a major source of revenue.

Water is always a precious mineral, and particularly so in Arizona, where it is in short supply. Four major dams on the Colorado and two on the Salt and Gila rivers provide water for irrigation and other uses. Through irrigation, deserts give way to fields of lettuce, cantaloupe, cotton, and citrus trees. Hoover Dam (formerly Boulder Dam), on the Colorado River in the northwest, is the

Arizona—Petrified Forest and Teepee Formations

highest in the U.S. and one of the highest in the world. It forms Lake Mead, which is shared with Nevada. Generators at the dam supply a large percentage of the electric power that is used in Arizona. Over one million acres of land are under irrigation in the state.

The most important crops are cotton, grain sorghums, and barley. Pasturing of sheep is heavy but diminished from earlier years.

ARKANSAS

The area of the present state of Arkansas was visited by Hernando de Soto in 1541–1542. It was claimed for France in 1682 by Sieur de La Salle as a part of the Mississippi drainage area. The French yielded the region to Spain in 1762 but it was given back to France in 1800. (French trappers established the first permanent settlement within the present state in 1686 and called it Arkansas Post. It was located at the confluence of the Arkansas River with the Mississippi River.) The region became a part of the Louisiana Purchase in 1803 and came under the American flag. Arkansas Territory was organized in 1819 from a part of Missouri Territory. It assumed its present boundaries (by excluding what is now Oklahoma) and was admitted to the Union as the twenty-fifth state on June 15, 1836.

Arkansas—Observation Tower, Hot Springs Mountain

The people of Arkansas were seriously divided on the issue of slavery and secession, but on May 6, 1861, the state voted to secede and join the Confederate States of America. Union forces won a costly battle at Pea Ridge in northwestern Arkansas in 1862, and captured Little Rock the following year. In 1868 Arkansas was readmitted to the Union.

Government. The legislature of Arkansas is called the General Assembly (*see* Colorado) and is composed of a senate of 35 members and a house of representatives of 100 members. The governor and lieutenant governor are elected for two years. Arkansas is represented in Congress by two senators and four representatives. The state is divided into 75 counties, and in 1970 there were 25 cities and towns with a population of more than ten thousand.

Economy. Arkansas is an agricultural state. Cotton is the chief crop; and rice, soybeans, wheat, fruit, and sweet potatoes are grown in significant amounts. The state ranks fifth in the production of cotton. Erosion is a serious problem in the state.

Large portions of the state's land is thought to require drastic corrective measures. Forests cover three-fifths of the state and hardwood timber forms the basis for most of the state's manufacturing.

Mineral production centers around bauxite, an ore of aluminum. Most of this (97 percent of the U.S. domestic supplies) is taken from mines just southwest of Little Rock. Titanium, lead, oil, natural gas, and coal are also mined. The tourist industry has developed greatly in recent decades. Numerous springs, caves, cool highlands, and scenic spots, along with the great many lakes, have attracted vacationers and sightseers in large numbers.

CALIFORNIA

The name *California* was first used in a book published in 1510 by Garcia Ordoñez de Montalvo. The first European known to have seen California was Juan Rodriguez Cabrillo, who passed up the coast of the present state in 1542. San Diego and Monterey were settled in 1769 and 1770, respectively, as fortified outposts and missions. It was in 1823 that Mexico achieved independence and came into possession of California. There were 21 missions in the state, strung along the coast about a day's journey apart.

San Francisco was founded in 1776 and was called Yerba Buena until 1847. Los Angeles was founded in 1781 as Neustra Señora la Reina de Los Angeles, (city of Our Lady, Queen of the Angels). By 1844 all the missions were broken up or sold by the Mexican government to private interests.

Relations with Mexico were altered in 1838 when that government recognized the separate existence of California within the Mexican Union. A final attempt to install a Mexican governor was thwarted in 1845. About this time, Americans began settling in the state, especially in the Great Central Valley, around Sacramento. In June 1846, John C. Fremont challenged Mexican authority by capturing Sonoma and setting up the famous "Bear Flag Republic." This movement was at first disavowed by the United States Government, but the onset of war between Mexico and the United States led to the recognition of Fremont's Bear Flag revolt. Fremont was persuaded to place his troops under the command of Commodore John D. Sloat, and the United States then proceeded to occupy California. In 1848 Mexico surrendered all claims to California and on September 9, 1850, California was admitted to the Union as the thirty-first state. Two years earlier, James Marshall, a lumberjack, found gold nuggets while building a sawmill for John Sutter on the American River. This started the famous "Forty-niner" gold rush and the rapid development of the state's natural resources.

Government. The legislature consists of a senate of forty members and an assembly of eighty members. The governor and lieutenant governor are elected for four years. The state sends two senators and 43 representatives to the U.S. Congress. The state is divided into 58 counties. San Bernardino County, covering 20,131 square miles, is the largest county in the United States. In 1970, there were 288 cities and towns in California with a population of more than ten thousand.

Economy. California's economic activities are as

California—San Francisco

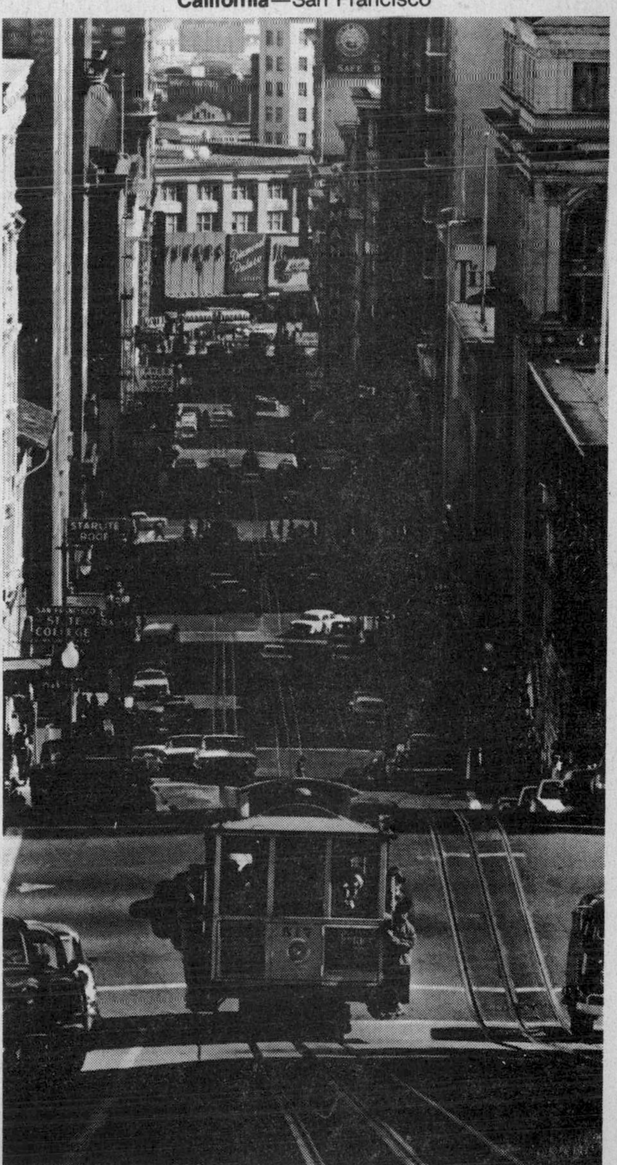

varied as are the climate and landforms. The state leads in the total value of farm products. In the agricultural picture, specialty crops and fruits are especially important. In addition, cotton, wheat, barley, rice, poultry, and vegetables are grown in large quantities. The chief specialty crops are raisin and wine grapes, plums, prunes, apricots, citrus fruits, including oranges, lemons, and grapefruit, nuts, and dates. California produces 85 percent of the nation's wine.

California ranks second in the nation in cotton production and leads all states in sugar beets, fishery products, persimmons, seed crops, lemons, walnuts, almonds, apricots, avocados, figs, grapes, olives, peaches, pears, plums, prunes, artichokes, cantaloupes, carrots, strawberries, dates, asparagus, green limas, broccoli, cauliflower, and celery. The specialty crops and fruit are grown mainly in the Great Central and the Imperial valleys, largely on irrigated lands.

The principal mineral is petroleum, in the production of which California regularly ranks third, after Louisiana and Texas. Other major minerals mined are gypsum, mercury, natural gas, tungsten, lead, zinc, copper, and iron ore. The state was fifth in the production of gold in 1960. Only Texas outranks California in total mineral production. In lumber production, California ranks second to Oregon.

However large other industries of the state are, most of California's income is derived from manufacturing. The state ranks first in slaughtering of cattle, in value of processed foods, and in the production of wine and olive oil. Iron and steel production is centered in the Los Angeles area, while shipbuilding is concentrated in San Francisco and San Diego. Palo Alto is the center of the electronics industry and of aircraft building.

Outstanding natural features such as waterfalls, canyons, and desert scenery, have been enclosed or preserved within both state and federal parks and monuments, providing the basis for a large tourist industry. In addition, sport centers, winter and summer resorts are located all over the state. Several million persons visit California every year as tourists or vacationers.

COLORADO

Spanish explorers had visited Colorado during the sixteenth and seventeenth centuries. However, it was not until 1706 that Juan de Uribarri took formal possession of the region for Spain, despite a claim by France originating with Sieur de La Salle in 1682. The eastern part of the present state eventually was included in the Louisiana Purchase and came under the American flag in 1803. The remainder of Colorado passed into United States possession in 1848 as a part of the Mexican cession.

Zebulon M. Pike explored Colorado in 1806, discovering the peak now named for him. Between 1820 and 1850 Major Stephen Long and John C. Fremont explored parts of the present state. The discovery of gold at Cherry Creek in 1858 attracted settlers; the first settlement was made at Auraria (now part of Denver). Colorado was organized as a territory in 1861. Movements for statehood failed on several occasions, but were successful in 1876 when Colorado was admitted to the Union as the thirty-eighth state. In 1906, the United States mint opened at Denver, and Mesa Verde National Park was established to preserve abandoned cliff-cities of a former Indian civilization (*see* Arizona).

Government. The state's legislative body is called the General Assembly (in other states this

Colorado—Mesa Verde National Park

name is often applied to the lower legislative chamber). It consists of a senate of 35 members and a house of representatives of 65 members. The governor and lieutenant-governor are elected for four years. The state sends two senators and five representatives to Congress. Colorado is divided into 63 counties, and in 1970 there were 26 cities and towns having a population of more than ten thousand.

Economy. More than 250 different minerals are mined in Colorado, the major ones being coal, oil, molybdenum, zinc, lead, vanadium, and uranium. Colorado has huge reserves of oil in the form of oil shales, but their mining awaits fuller development of methods to extract the oil from the shale.

Colorado is a leading sheep-raising state, and Denver is said to be the world's largest sheep-marketing center. The state's agriculture relies heavily upon irrigation and more than 20 percent of the crop lands are seriously eroded. Nevertheless, the state ranks first in the production of broomcorn, second in sugar beets, second in onions, fourth in beans, and eighth in barley. In addition, Colorado is a leading producer of celery, potatoes, wheat, peaches, cherries, and cattle feed. National forests cover nearly fourteen million acres. Tourism is a large industry, based chiefly on the big game for hunters and the Rocky Mountain scenic and ski areas.

CONNECTICUT

Connecticut is one of the 13 original states. A Dutch navigator named Adraen Block discovered and explored the Connecticut River in 1614. A Dutch trading post, established at Hartford in 1633, was replaced by an English settlement in 1635. Windsor and Wethersfield were founded in 1634. The Dutch attempted to expel the English but failed. In 1639 the three towns drew up a constitution which governed them until Charles II granted a charter in 1662. This famous charter served the colony and then the state of Connecticut until 1818. In 1687 King James II of England called upon Connecticut to surrender the charter. The colonists refused and hid it in an oak tree. However, the existing government was dissolved and the colony was despotically ruled until the overthrow of King James II in 1689. The famous Charter Oak is shown on a United States postage stamp, issued in 1935 to commemorate the three-hundreth anniversary of the state.

The charter struggle and other events in Connecticut were closely observed by other colonies and had a strong influence in arousing public opinion against England. Connecticut contributed large amounts of supplies to the Continental Army. It was the only colony in which the British governor supported the Colonists and continued in office during the Revolution. Fifteen percent of the population participated in the war. Nathan Hale, a Connecticut schoolteacher, was hanged as a spy by the British in 1776. Connecticut joined the Union as the fifth state on January 9, 1788.

Government. Our present system of representation in Congress was proposed by the Connecticut delegation to the Constitutional Convention in 1787. It was adopted and is called the Connecticut Compromise. Connecticut's legislative body is called the General Assembly (*see* Colorado); it consists of a senate of 36 members, and a house of representatives of 177 members. The governor and lieutenant-governor are elected for four years. The state sends two senators and six representatives to the U.S. Congress. County government, established in 1666, was formally abolished by the General Assembly in 1960. The eight former counties remain only as geographical subdivisions. In 1970,

Connecticut—Nathan Hale Schoolhouse, East Haddam

there were 78 cities and towns in Connecticut with a population of more than ten thousand. (For a note on New England towns, *see* Massachusetts.)

Economy. Only three minerals (mica, beryl, and feldspar) are of economic importance. The chief industry of Connecticut is manufacturing. In 1970 the state ranked thirteenth in the nation in value added by manufacturing. It was a leader in the production of hats, firearms, clocks, watches, aircraft engines, needles, pins, nails, and hardware.

A high-quality leaf tobacco is grown in Connecticut, and the Connecticut Valley is a major fruit-growing region.

DELAWARE

Delaware is one of the 13 original states. The first attempted settlement, made near Lewes by the Dutch in 1631, was destroyed by the Indians. In 1638 the Swedes established a successful colony at Fort Christina, now Wilmington. This colony, called New Sweden, prospered until it was overwhelmed by a Dutch invasion in 1655. Nine years later (1664), the Dutch were conquered by the British.

The colony was deeded to William Penn in 1682. However, the area remained a distinct unit within Penn's territory and was called the "Three Lower Counties." A long dispute between William Penn and the Baltimores (proprietors of the Maryland colony) was settled when Mason and Dixon surveyed the region in 1763.

Delaware—Caesar Rodney Statue, Rodney Square, Wilmington

The same governor and General Assembly served both colonies until 1704 when a dispute over defense caused the Three Lower Counties to form their own General Assembly. The two colonies continued to share the same governor until the War for Independence.

In 1776 the Three Lower Counties became "Delaware State," and joined with 12 other colonies to prosecute the war with the British. The first star in the American flag represents Delaware State, because it was the first to ratify the new federal constitution creating the United States, on December 7, 1787. In 1792 a new state constitution changed the name "Delaware State" to "State of Delaware." Delaware remained in the Union throughout the Civil War (1861–1865).

Government. The legislature of Delaware is called the General Assembly and consists of a senate of 19 members and a house of representatives of 39 members. The state has one representative-at-large and two senators in the U.S. Congress. The state is divided into three counties. Delaware is the only state today that subdivides the counties into "hundreds." The hundred is an ancient unit, meaning originally a piece of land that could provide 100 men for use in time of war. It was once used in Delaware as the basis for representation in the General Assembly, but today is used only for tax and other minor purposes.

Economy. Delaware is mainly an industrial state. Wilmington is one of the chief chemical manufacturing centers of the world. Textiles rank next to chemicals, followed by leather-making. Shipbuilding is also important. Wilmington is the chief industrial and urban complex. Commercial fishing centers around Lewes, a port on the Atlantic Ocean. Wilmington and New Castle are major seaports. The Chesapeake and Delaware Canal, completed in 1829 and widened in 1919, provides a shortcut between Delaware Bay and Chesapeake Bay through the Delmarva Peninsula.

Excellent highways cross Delaware in all directions. Surf bathing and harness racing attract many visitors and vacationers to the state.

FLORIDA

Florida was visited twice from 1513 to 1521 by Ponce de Leon, a Spanish adventurer. He named the country Florida. Hernando de Soto marched through the interior of the Florida Peninsula in 1539.

A settlement of French Huguenots, established in 1564 at Fort Carolina on the St. John's River, was wiped out by the Spanish in 1565. In the same year the first permanent white settlement in what is now the United States was founded at St. Augustine by Spanish colonists.

Spain ceded Florida to the English in 1763, but a fierce three-way war broke out among the English, the Indians, and the Spanish colonists. This war merged into the American Revolution. Florida was used as a base for raids on Carolina and Georgia towns. In 1783 the British gave Florida back to Spain, and in 1795 Spain sold a part of Florida on the gulf coast to France. The United States occupied that part in 1812, claiming that France had included it in the sale of Louisiana to the United States in 1803.

In the War of 1812, the British captured Pensacola but were driven out by Andrew Jackson. He abandoned it and had to recapture it in 1818. In the following year Spain sold all of Florida to the United States for five million dollars.

In 1835, war broke out between the United States and the Seminole Indians. The Seminole War was merely a more serious phase of a war that had been going on since Andrew Jackson invaded Florida in 1818.

After more than a thousand Seminoles and their allies had been rounded up and sent west of the Mississippi (*see* Oklahoma), a treaty of peace was concluded in 1839. But sporadic fighting continued until 1842. On March 3, 1845, Florida was admitted to the Union as the twenty-seventh state. Florida seceded from the Union on January 10, 1861, and was readmitted on February 6, 1868.

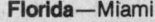

Florida—Miami

Government. The legislature of Florida consists of a senate of 48 members and a house of representatives of 119 members. The state has no lieutenant-governor. Florida sends two senators and 15 representatives to the U.S. Congress. There are 67 counties, and in 1970 there were 87 cities and towns with a population of more than ten thousand.

Economy. The great citrus fruit belt for which Florida is so famous lies in the highland section of the peninsula, among the lakes. Grapefruit and oranges are the leading citrus crops. Florida is the leading state in the production of oranges, grapefruit, and limes. Tobacco, cotton, peanuts, and sugar cane are other major crops in the state.

The state has rich mineral deposits. Three-fourths of phosphate mined in the United States comes from Florida. Fuller's earth, uranium (recovered from phosphate deposits), ilmenite and rutile (ores of titanium) are also mined in Florida.

Industrial growth has been rapid in recent years, chiefly in processed foods. The greatest industry of Florida is tourism. The long beaches, pleasant climate, and the tropical Everglades are contributing factors in the fame of Florida as a vacation land.

GEORGIA

Georgia is one of the original 13 states, and it was the last English colony to be established in what is now the United States. Before the white settlers came, Creek Indians lived on the southern plains and lowlands while the Cherokees inhabited the highlands.

Hernando de Soto visited the region in 1540 and French explorers followed a few years later. The English claimed the region in 1629 as part of the Carolina grant made by King Charles I, but did not attempt to plant a colony there until 1732. In that year, George II deeded the region to a group led by General James Oglethorpe, and Oglethorpe landed the first settlers the following year. Georgia ratified the U.S. Constitution on January 2, 1788, and in 1802 the state sold all of its claims west of the Chattahoochee River. In 1832, the Creek Indians in the state were deported westward, followed by the Cherokees in 1838. Georgia seceded from the Union on January 19, 1861.

Georgia suffered heavily in the Civil War. Several of the engagements in the state were bitterly

Georgia—Fort Pulaski Moat

fought and costly in terms of men and material. Toward the end of the war, General Sherman's troops burned Atlanta and marched toward the sea, causing such great destruction through fire and looting that the line of march is still discernible from the air. Georgia was readmitted to the Union in 1868, but expelled in 1869 and again readmitted in 1870.

Government. The constitution of 1945 is the eighth one adopted in Georgia. The Georgia legislature consists of a senate of 24 members and a house of representatives of 195 members. The minimum voting age is 18. Georgia has two senators and ten representatives in the U.S. Congress. The state is divided into 159 counties, the largest number of counties in any state except Texas. In 1970, there were 39 cities and towns with a population of more than ten thousand.

Economy. Georgia furnishes 78 percent of the nation's kaolin, or china clay. Gold was discovered in 1828 and until 1849 most of the gold in the United States came from Georgia. The quarrying of granite and marble is an important industry. Iron and coal are mined in the Appalachians. Forests cover about two-thirds of the state, and Georgia leads in the production of turpentine and resin, both derived from the sap of trees. The principal agricultural crops are cotton, peanuts, hogs, tobacco, and poultry. The state is the largest producer of sea island cotton. Georgia leads the nation in pecan and peanut production.

HAWAII

The Hawaiian Islands, formerly called the Sandwich Islands, were discovered in 1778 by Captain James Cook. Cook returned to the islands the following year after exploring the coast of North America (*see* Oregon). He was killed on the main island of Hawaii as he tried to retrieve a stolen boat.

Between 1795 and 1819, the island archipelago was united into a kingdom by Kamehameha I. Christian missionaries began working there in 1820. The kingdom adopted its first constitution in 1840. Immigration from Asia and Europe in large numbers began with Chinese in 1852, followed by Polynesians from other Pacific islands in 1859, Portuguese in 1878, Japanese in 1886, and Filipinos in 1906.

The pineapple industry was established by Captain John Kidwell in 1882, using plants imported from Jamaica. By 1893, American owners of the sugar cane and pineapple industries formed the strongest groups in the islands. The instability of the kingdom and the desire of the growers to export under more favorable conditions led to a revolt in 1893, and the establishment of a Hawaiian Republic under Sanford B. Dole.

American businessmen managed to get the islands annexed to the United States in 1898. The Territory of Hawaii was organized on June 14, 1900. A plebiscite for statehood was not held until 1940. Japanese forces attacked Pearl Harbor on December 7, 1941, forcing the United States into World War II. A constitution was adopted in 1950

Hawaii—Mauna Loa

and statehood was achieved on August 21, 1959. Thereby, Hawaii became the fiftieth state.

Government. The legislature consists of a senate of 25 members and a house of representatives of 51 members. The governor and lieutenant-governor are elected for four years. The state sends two senators and two representatives to the U.S. Congress. Hawaii is divided into five counties. There are 34 municipalities having more than 2,500 inhabitants (1970). Nine of these had a population of more than ten thousand in 1970.

Economy. The mainstays of the state's economy are military expenditures, agriculture, and tourism. Plantation agriculture is highly developed with sugar cane the most important crop. Crops vary with altitude zones. Sugar grows in the lowlands. Pineapples, the second largest crop, grow on the terraced uplands. The plantations of Hawaii are outstandingly efficient and some are highly mechanized. The people enjoy a high standard of living. Some diversified agriculture is beginning to be practiced.

IDAHO

The early history of Idaho is that of the Oregon country, especially with regard to the Oregon boundary dispute, the explorations of Lewis and Clark, and other explorations (*see* Oregon). After 1853, however, what is now Idaho became a part of the new Washington Territory. The region of Idaho became known to white men after the discovery of gold in 1859 near the present Lewiston. By 1862 there were thirty thousand white people in the region. In March 1863, Idaho was organized into a territory, with the capital at Lewiston. It included Montana until 1864, and Wyoming until 1868. These separations reduced the territorial limits to about what they are today. However, errors in earlier surveys of boundaries necessitated changes at various times.

Serious Indian troubles developed between 1877 and 1879, in which many settlers and soldiers were killed. The Snake River Valley was opened by the laying of tracks for the Oregon Short Line Railroad in 1880. Idaho was admitted to the Union on July 3, 1890 (forty-third state). Labor trouble in the Coeur d'Alene area led to rioting and the blowing up of a mill. In 1905 Governor Steunenburg was assassinated. This resulted in the famous trial of a member of the western Federation of Miners, who was sentenced to life imprisonment.

Government. Idaho is governed under its original constitution of 1889. The legislature consists of a senate of 35 members and a house of representatives of 70 members. The governor and lieutenant-governor are elected for four years. The state is represented in the U.S. Congress by two senators and two representatives. Idaho is divided into 44 counties, and in 1970 there were nine cities and towns with a population of more than ten thousand.

Economy. Silver, lead, zinc, and antimony are the chief minerals mined in Idaho. The state ranks high in the mining of antimony, lead and cobalt, and it produces 44 percent of the domestic silver. Other major minerals produced are phosphate rock, garnet, nickel, columbium, tantalum, copper, gold, and mercury. Beryllium has been recently discovered, and other minor minerals are produced.

Although large areas are arid, agriculture is a leading industry in Idaho. Irrigation is widely practiced and there are over three million acres under irrigation in the state. The most important cash crops are cereals, over 50 percent of which is wheat. The growing of hops, a new industry, is spreading. Other crops include sugar beets, potatoes, oats, barley, beans, apples, and prunes.

Idaho—Craters of the Moon National Monument

Illinois—Chicago

ILLINOIS

Illinois was discovered in 1673 by the French explorers Father Jacques Marquette and Louis Joliet.

The early history of the state is that of French exploration and settlement. Sieur de LaSalle several times crossed Illinois between Lake Michigan and the Mississippi River by using the historic portage route to the Illinois River, and thence down that river to the Mississippi. La Salle built Fort Crevecoeur near the present Peoria. In about 1700 two settlements were established near the mouth of the Illinois River. They were Kaskaskia and Kahokia. Both were settled by missionaries, traders, and Indians.

In 1717 these settlements were called the Illinois District and were annexed to the French province of Louisiana. By 1720 there were three additional villages in the district. In 1763 France ceded the district to the British, who annexed it to Quebec in 1774.

George Rogers Clark led a military expedition of Virginians into the Illinois country (1778–1779). Largely because of this expedition, the entire region was ceded to the United States in 1783. When Indiana Territory was set up in 1800 (*see* Indiana), Illinois was a part of it. In 1809 Illinois Territory was organized with the seat of government at Kaskaskia. Illinois was admitted to the Union as the twenty-first state on December 3, 1818.

Government. The Illinois legislature consists of a senate of 58 members and a house of representatives of 177 members. The governor and lieutenant-governor are elected for four years. The state sends two senators and 24 representatives to the United States Congress. The state is divided into 102 counties. In 1970 there were 147 cities and towns in Illinois with a population of more than ten thousand. Chicago is the second largest city in the United States and the thirteenth largest in the world.

Economy. Illinois is mainly an agricultural state despite the fact that it ranks fourth in value added by manufacturing. The state ranks fourth in the nation in cash receipts from farming. Nineteen percent of the total value of all farm commodities is from corn, and 16 percent of the remainder is from soybeans. Other major crops include wheat and oats. Over seven million hogs are raised every year in Illinois.

Illinois ranks eleventh among the states in mineral production; it is a leading producer of fluorspar and tripoli; and it ranks high in building stone and coal.

Chicago is the key city of the second largest manufacturing region in the United States. The Chicago area is the machinery-making center of the nation, and northern Illinois is one of the fastest growing industrial districts.

Chicago's leadership in meat-packing has been lost to such cities as Omaha and Kansas City. Some of the world's largest printing establishments and food processing plants are located in Chicago. Heavy industry, including great steel mills and oil refineries extend southeastward from Chicago and into Indiana along Lake Michigan. The great inland seaport of Indiana Harbor also serves Chicago and parts of Illinois.

INDIANA

Indiana is one of the states that formerly comprised the old Northwest Territory. The region was inhabited mainly by the Potawatomi and Miami Indians when French explorers visited there in 1679. After several unsuccessful trips, the French were able to establish a permanent settlement in 1732, at the present city of Vincennes. However, only 31 years later the entire area of the present Indiana was lost to the British. The British were driven out by Americans under George Rogers

Clark in 1779. The territory northwest of the Ohio River was organized into the Northwest Territory in 1787. Indiana Territory—an area comprising all of the present Indiana, Illinois, Wisconsin, and parts of other states—was carved out of the Northwest Territory in 1800. William Henry Harrison, later the ninth President of the United States, became the territorial governor, with his capital at Vincennes. Harrison was forced into a showdown fight with the Prophet, a famous Indian leader. At the Battle of Tippecanoe on November 7, 1811, Indian power in the Territory was broken. Congress formally admitted Indiana into the Union on December 11, 1816, as the nineteenth state. However, its area was greatly reduced from the original extent of Indiana Territory.

Government. The state's legislative body is called the General Assembly. It consists of a senate of 50 members and a house of representatives of 100 members. The state is represented in Congress by two senators and eleven representatives. Indiana is divided into 92 counties. In 1970 there were 53 cities and towns that had a population of more than ten thousand.

Economy. This is a major manufacturing state, ranking eighth in the nation; but it is also a "Corn Belt" prairie state, ranking tenth in cash income from sale of agricultural crops.

The metal industries employ six of every ten persons engaged in manufacturing. The state ranks third in steel production, provides 80 percent of all limestone used in the nation, and makes 12 percent of all household furniture. Other large industries include brick and tile making, rubber processing, the manufacture of prefabricated houses, and automotive parts.

Corn is the major farm crop, but most of it is marketed as livestock feed, mainly for hogs. Indiana is third in the nation in production of soybeans, third in corn, and third in hogs.

Indiana—St. Mary's College for Girls, South Bend

IOWA

Iowa was a part of the original Louisiana Purchase territory. Father Marquette and Louis Joliet visited the area of the present state in 1673, stopping at the mouth of the Des Moines River. The first settlement was made in 1785 by Julien Dubuque near the city that now bears his name. He was attracted by the lead deposits nearby.

In 1763, the entire region of Louisiana was ceded to Spain, and returned to France in 1800. In 1803, the United States purchased Louisiana. After the state of Louisiana took this name and entered the Union in 1812, the name of the entire region north of the new state of Louisiana was changed to Missouri. In 1821, the state of Missouri came into existence, leaving Iowa without a name or a government. In 1834, it became a part of Michigan Territory and then a part of Wisconsin Territory. Iowa was established as a territory in 1838 and separated from Wisconsin Territory. At that time it embraced the greater part of Minnesota and all of the two Dakotas. On December 28, 1846, Iowa was admitted to the Union as the twenty-ninth state. During the Civil War Iowa remained loyal to the Union and furnished nearly eighty thousand men to the federal armies.

Government. The legislature is called the General Assembly and consists of a senate of 50 members and a house of representatives of 100 members. The governor and lieutenant-governor are elected for two years. The state is represented in the U.S. Congress by two senators and six representatives.

Iowa is divided into 99 counties. Most of the county lines meet at right angles, forming tiers and rows of squares, with county seat towns nearly in the center of the square counties. These counties also contain neat rows and tiers of townships, at least twelve to a county. Nearly every community

Kansas—State House, Topeka

in Iowa is an incorporated place, but in 1970 only 27 of them had a population of more than ten thousand.

Economy. Iowa is the richest state in agriculture, with nearly 96 percent of the state under cultivation. Iowa leads all states except California in cash receipts from farming. Although it is only one-third the size of California, Iowa has almost the same amount of land as California under cultivation (36 million acres).

Corn grows on about one-third of the farm acreage of the state, and Iowa leads all other states except Illinois in corn growing. In oats Iowa leads all states. Other major crops are sugar beets, wheat, barley, buckwheat, flax, rye, alfalfa, soybeans, and red clover.

Iowa ranks thirty-first in mining, but is third in the mining of gypsum. Coal underlies large areas of the state. Meat packing leads all other manufacturing industries. Cedar Rapids has the largest cereal mill in the world.

KANSAS

The first white men to gaze upon the wide prairies of Kansas were the Spanish explorers led by Coronado in 1541. All but the southwestern section was included in the Louisiana Purchase of 1803. The southwestern area was a part of Texas until 1850 when it was turned over to the United States and became a part of the Missouri Territory. The name *Missouri* had been adopted in 1812 as the name of the remaining part of the Louisiana Purchase after the state of Louisiana had entered the Union (*see* Louisiana).

Kansas was separated from Missouri Territory and organized into a territory under provisions of the Kansas-Nebraska Bill of 1854. Immigrants from both slave and free areas further east began to pour into Kansas. Serious political conflict soon arose between pro-slavery and anti-slavery groups.

A pro-slavery government, set up in 1855, expelled anti-slavery supporters from the legislature. Free-state factions organized a new government, declaring the existing government to be illegal. Violence attended these actions. The town of Lawrence was destroyed twice, and other towns were burned in attacks and reprisals. The pro-slavery faction drew up another constitution at Lecompton and presented it to the voters, who defeated it in 1858. Thereupon the "Wyandotte" constitution, drawn up by free-state groups, was passed and adopted by large majorities. On January 29, 1861, Kansas was admitted to the Union as the thirty-fourth state. However, guerilla wárfare broke out and the conflict merged with the greater war being fought in the east. Quantrill's raiders and other groups devastated large areas of Kansas before the Confederacy was defeated in 1865.

Government. The legislature consists of a senate of 40 members and a house of representatives of 125 members. The governor and lieutenant-governor are elected for two years. Kansas sends two senators and five representatives to the United States Congress. The state is divided into 105 counties, and in 1970 there were 34 cities and

Iowa—The Capitol Building, Des Moines

towns with a population of more than ten thousand.

Economy. Kansas is the nation's number one wheat producer, and the state is primarily agricultural. Kansas is second in sorghums, and ranks fourth in the number of cattle. Corn, hay, soybeans, barley, oats, and sugar beets are also major crops. In industry, the manufacture of transportation equipment (including aircraft) has become important in recent years. This industry group is especially prominent in Wichita and Kansas City. Kansas ranks fifteenth in mining. Petroleum, natural gas, and zinc are the principal minerals.

KENTUCKY

Kentucky's recorded history began, as did that of many other states, with the journeys of great French explorers. Robert Cavelier, Sieur de La Salle (1648–1687), considered the greatest of them, passed down the Ohio River (Kentucky's northern boundary) in 1669. The French claimed the region until they released it to Spain in 1762, despite a standing British claim. France dispatched at least one expedition to the present Kentucky to police Indian attempts to reclaim the area. The English entered Kentucky as early as 1750, when it formed a part of Virginia, but were driven out by the Indians.

Kentucky—Mammoth Cave National Park

A group of settlers from Pennsylvania managed to establish Harrodsburg on the Kentucky River in 1775. In the following year, Daniel Boone led colonists through historic Cumberland Gap and founded Boonesboro as a fort and settlement. Violence began immediately, for even chance encounters between Indians and white people generally resulted in bloodshed. Boonesboro was attacked several times, but withstood the sieges.

Through the efforts of George Rogers Clark, hero of the Revolutionary War in the west, Kentucky was established as a county of Virginia in 1776. It had been divided into three counties by 1780 and a statehood movement was growing. Virginia refused to consent to statehood until after 1789. On June 1, 1792, Kentucky was admitted to the Union as the fifteenth state.

During the War of 1812, the threat to New Orleans (the chief port for Kentucky goods) aroused Kentuckians to take a leading part in Andrew Jackson's campaign to defend New Orleans against the British. Kentuckians helped explore and settle the newly acquired Louisiana region. Even the restless Daniel Boone moved westward (he died in Missouri in 1820 at the age of 86, less than a year before that state entered the Union).

Government. The legislative body of Kentucky is called the General Assembly and consists of a senate of 38 members and a house of representatives of 100 members. The governor and lieutenant-governor are elected for four years. The state sends two senators and seven representatives to the U.S. Congress. Kentucky is divided into 120 counties. In 1970 there were 37 cities and towns having a population of more than ten thousand.

Economy. Kentucky is an agricultural state. The chief crop is tobacco (the state ranks second to North Carolina). Corn, apples, strawberries, popcorn, fescue seed, bluegrass seed, hay, and soybeans are also major crops. The state is acclaimed as the home of the world's finest race horses, most of which are raised in the Bluegrass region around Lexington.

Coal is the principal mineral of Kentucky, and chiefly because of it, the state ranks ninth as a mineral producer.

LOUISIANA

Hernando De Soto entered what is now Louisiana in 1541, claiming it as a part of Spanish Florida. In 1682 the entire Mississippi and Missouri valley region was claimed for France by La Salle, and named Louisiana. In order to strengthen her claim, France sent Iberville to found the first settlement at Mobile (see Alabama). The first settlement in the present Louisiana was made at Natchitoches, on the Red River, in 1714. Bienville founded New Orleans in 1718 and in 1722 it became Louisiana's capital.

The entire region was ceded to Spain in 1762, but by the Treaty of San Iledefonso in 1800, it was returned to France. On April 30, 1803, Napoleon sold all of Louisiana to the United States for 15 million dollars, at a rate of about four cents per acre. That part lying west of the Mississippi was organized into the Territory of Orleans in 1804. Shortly afterwards the area east of the Mississippi was added and the combined areas were admitted to the Union under the name of Louisiana on April 30, 1812. The state seceded January 26, 1861. In 1862 New Orleans was captured by federal forces and occupied until the end of the war. The state was readmitted to the Union in 1868 and federal troops were withdrawn in 1877.

Government. The legislature consists of a senate of 39 members and a house of representatives of 105 members. Both governor and lieutenant-governor are elected for four years. The state sends two senators and eight representatives to the U.S. Congress. Louisiana is divided into 64 parishes that correspond to counties in other states. In 1970 there were 37 cities and towns with a population of more than ten thousand.

Louisiana—Mississippi River loading dock, Baton Rouge

Economy. About one-third of the state is composed of rich delta land. Louisiana produces most of the cane sugar and rice grown in the United States. Forests cover about 56 percent of the state and lumbering is an important industry. Louisiana is second only to Texas in petroleum output. The largest oil refinery in the United States is at Baton Rouge. The state is the second largest producer of sulphur. The port of New Orleans is second only to New York in tonnage handled. It is the chief port of entry for Latin American products. Baton Rouge and Lake Charles are also major ports. Aside from New Orleans, Shreveport in the northwest is the chief industrial and trade center.

MAINE

Giovanni da Verrazano is credited with having discovered the coast of Maine in 1524. However, it was not until a century later that systematic exploration of Maine began. One of the first explorations was that of John Smith in 1614. Temporary settlements were made in 1604 (Neutral Island), 1607 (Sabino Point), 1608 (Mount Desert Island), and 1623 (Monhegan Island). The first permanent settlement was made at Pemaquid in 1625.

Various grants of land in the region were confusing and led to disputes that lasted for two centuries. Massachusetts disputed all claims and completed the possession of Maine by 1691.

Maine's association with Canada has often been bitter. New Brunswick and Maine fought a war over their boundaries until settlement was made in 1842 by the terms of the Ashburton Treaty.

For a long time Maine was restless under the government of Massachusetts. Opportunity for separation came from the growing slavery question. Missouri had applied for admission to the Union as a slave state. This led to the famous Missouri Compromise in which a free state (in this case, Maine) was to be admitted along with Missouri, a slave state. Maine was separated from Massachusetts and entered the Union on March 15, 1820, as the twenty-third state.

Maine—Coastline at Schoodic

Government. The legislature consists of a senate of 32 members and a house of representatives of 151 members. The constitution of statehood (1820) is still in force. The governor is elected for four years. There is no office of lieutenant-governor. Maine has an Executive Council of seven members to advise the governor. Massachusetts and New Hampshire are the only other states that have executive councils. Maine sends two senators and two representatives to the U.S. Congress. The state is divided into 16 counties.

Many of the functions that are performed by counties in other states are performed by "towns" in Maine (*see* Massachusetts; Connecticut). The "town" of New England is roughly equivalent to "township" in other states except Wisconsin. The New England word "town" should *never* be confused with "town" as popularly used for any small community (as it is used in the next sentence.) In 1970, there were 18 cities and towns with a population of more than ten thousand.

Economy. Maine is a leading state in the manufacture of paper and other wood products. The chief types of trees used commercially are spruce, fir, beech, cedar, hemlock, white pine, birch, maple, and aspen. Nearly half the communities are engaged in wood products industries of one kind or another. There are numerous plants making paper, some of which are among the largest in the world. Maine is the second leading producer of potatoes in the United States. Granite is another major product of the state. Fishing is a major industry. Clams (soft-shell), lobsters, scallops, sardines, cod, haddock, and mackerel are the chief kinds of fish caught. Portland and Rockland are the chief fishing ports.

MARYLAND

Maryland is one of the 13 original states. The grant of the present state was made in 1632 by Charles I to George Calvert, first Lord Baltimore. Lord Baltimore's purpose in acquiring the grant was to establish a refuge for persons of the Catholic faith who were at that time being persecuted.

About two hundred colonists landed in Maryland in 1634, and founded the settlement of St. Mary's. The young colony experienced setbacks from several quarters and for a time (1645–1646) St. Mary's was occupied by dissident groups. In 1649 the famous Toleration Act was passed. This document guaranteed the freedom of worship to all Christians. However, several Puritan (Protestant) groups continued to be hostile, and took up separate settlements in Maryland. The Puritans revolted and held the province from 1654 to 1657. In 1657, Lord Baltimore was restored to control of Maryland. In 1692 Maryland was converted to a royal colony directly under the King of England. In 1715 the Baltimores regained possession of the

Maryland—Hampton House "Ghost Room"

colony and retained it until the Revolutionary War. A 50-year dispute with Pennsylvania was finally settled by the surveys of Mason and Dixon (the Mason-Dixon Line) from 1763 to 1767. The city of Baltimore was founded in 1730. Maryland took an active part in the struggle for independence. Congress met at Annapolis in 1783. Maryland ratified the Constitution on April 28, 1788 (seventh state).

During the War of 1812, rioting occurred in Baltimore and the city was under siege by British ships. Fort McHenry withstood the siege, an event commemorated by Francis Scott Key in our national anthem. Maryland was divided in sympathy during the Civil War, but remained loyal to the Union. In September 1862, the fierce battle of Antietam (Sharpsburg) was fought in Maryland.

Government. The legislative body is called the General Assembly and consists of a senate of 43 members and a house of delegates of 142 members. The governor is elected for four years. There is no office of lieutenant-governor. The state sends two senators and eight representatives to the U.S. Congress.The United States capital is located in the District of Columbia, which forms an enclave in Maryland and has no connection whatever with the state. Maryland is divided into 23 counties, and in 1970 there were 57 cities and towns with a population of more than ten thousand. Baltimore, the state's largest city, has the status of a county and is an enclave in Baltimore County but not a part of the county. Baltimore is the seventh largest city in the United States.

Economy. Manufacturing industries form the major part of the economy. Aluminum, chemicals, ships, missiles, clothing, rubber, and machinery are manufactured. Baltimore is a leading port, commercial and trade center. It is also a major steel center. The seafood industry is of major importance; and Maryland is a leader in its catch of striped bass, soft-shell clams, and oysters.

MASSACHUSETTS

Massachusetts is one of the 13 original states. A Protestant group in England, at first called "Separatists," and later "Pilgrims," sought refuge from religious intolerance in Holland (The Netherlands), and then set sail for North America in 1620. They established the first permanent white settlement within the present Massachusetts, at Plymouth in December 1620. They also instituted a form of democratic government in accordance with terms they had drawn up among themselves before landing—the historic Mayflower Compact. Others, seeking religious freedom, began to found settlements all along the coast, and in 1630 the Massachusetts Bay Colony was chartered to unify the settlements. Boston was settled in 1630, and Massachusetts was made a royal colony in 1691.

The people of Massachusetts were foremost in the movement that brought about a break with England and the independence of the United States. The movement began with rioting and boycotts that eventually led to the Boston Massacre of March 5, 1770, when British soldiers fired into a crowd of colonists. In 1773, cargoes of tea were dumped into Boston Harbor by a group disguised as Indians and led by Samuel Adams. In retaliation, Boston was occupied and the port closed. Patriots then called the First Continental Congress, which ordered a general boycott of all English goods. The siege of Boston followed the first engagements of the War for Independence at Lexington and at Concord Bridge. George Washington took command of the Continental Army at Cambridge on July 3, 1775. The Battle of Bunker Hill, March 17, 1776, led to the British evacuation of Boston, to which the British were never able to return. Following the end of the war, a period of economic depression set in, which lasted until Massachusetts adopted the federal Constitution on February 6, 1788.

Massachusetts—Paul Revere Statue, Boston

Government. The legislative body of the state is called the General Court of the Commonwealth and consists of a senate of 40 members and a house of representatives of 240 members. Both governor and lieutenant-governor are elected for four years. The state sends two senators and twelve representatives to the U.S. Congress in Massachusetts. As in other New England states, the "town" (roughly similar to the "township" in other states) is of greater significance in local government than is the county. There are over 300 towns within the state. In addition, there are 152 cities with a population of more than ten thousand.

Economy. Massachusetts is overwhelmingly a manufacturing state, and is the nation's oldest manufacturing region. Textiles have usually been prominent, but the state is known for the great variety of its manufactured products. Few minerals or other raw materials for industry originate within the state.

More than half of the state's population lives in the metropolitan area of Boston. The city is a major world seaport, the largest fishing port in the nation, as well as one of the leading manufacturing centers. Research is a major industry in Massachusetts. Some 338 research laboratories employing numerous scientists, engineers, and technicians are located in the state.

MICHIGAN

The French explorer Étienne Brulé (who met a tragic death as a sacrificial victim among his former friends, the Huron Indians) may have been the first white man to see what is now the state of Michigan in 1610. Jesuit missionaries and French explorers gradually opened up the region, and Father Marquette founded the first settlement at Sault Sainte Marie in 1668. Detroit was founded in 1701. After the French and Indian War, the British came into control of Michigan, annexing it to Canada in 1774. By the Treaty of Paris (1783) it was ceded to the United States. In the following years British agents stirred up Indian trouble for the settlers. Organized Indian forces defeated General Saint Clair but met disastrous defeat at the hands of General "Mad" Anthony Wayne at Fallen Timbers in 1794 (*see* Ohio).

In 1805 Michigan Territory was organized, embracing the lower peninsula and with a southern boundary farther south than at present. In 1834, the territory was expanded to include the entire region between Lake Erie and the Missouri River. The opening of the Erie Canal brought commerce and a rapid increase in population. A serious boundary dispute known as the "Toledo War" (*see* Ohio) was settled, resulting in the moving of the southern boundary northward. As compensation, Michigan was given the entire upper peninsula. The peninsula turned out to be a hidden treasure of copper, iron, and other valuable resources. Michigan was reduced to its present size by 1837 and admitted to the Union on January 26 of that year as the twenty-sixth state.

Government. The legislature consists of a senate of 38 members and a house of representatives of 109 members. The governor and lieutenant-governor are elected for four years. The state sends two senators and 19 representatives to the U.S. Congress. Michigan is divided into 83 counties. In 1970 there were 78 cities with a population of more than ten thousand. Detroit is the fifth largest city in the United States, behind Philadelphia and ahead of Houston (1970).

Economy. The state has well-diversified and highly-developed agricultural industries, including dairying. The principal crops are plums, peaches, cherries, honey (a by-product of the fruit-growing industry), apples, corn, hay, oats, winter wheat, and sugar beets.

Michigan—Isle Royale National Park

Despite its agricultural wealth, Michigan is predominantly an industrial state. The manufacture of automobiles is by far the leading industry, employing more than half the industrial workers of the state. Iron ore is the chief mineral mined in Michigan, most of it coming from the upper peninsula. Copper, petroleum, natural gas, salt, and limestone (some of the largest quarries in the world) are also mined in the state. The Great Lakes are ice-free from April to November, and they form the busiest waterway in the world. The famous Soo Canal between Lake Superior and Lake Huron handles twice as much tonnage annually as does the Panama Canal, even though the latter is open all year.

MINNESOTA

French fur traders came to Minnesota by way of the Great Lakes in about 1658. Little was known of the region until Jesuit missionaries penetrated Minnesota in 1680. Father Hennepin traveled up the Mississippi River in that year and discovered the Falls of St. Anthony, which he named (located in present-day Minneapolis). The French claimed the region east of the Mississippi River but ceded it to England in 1763. In 1783 the United States acquired this part, and the remainder of the future state was acquired as a part of the Louisiana Purchase of 1803. Zebulon Pike (*see* Colorado) traced the Mississippi's upper course to Cass Lake in 1806. Henry R. Schoolcraft traced the great river to its source in 1832, and found it to be in Lake Itasca in northcentral Minnesota.

The first settlement was made in 1819 at Fort St. Anthony (name changed to Fort Snelling in 1824). Eastern Minnesota became a part of the Northwest Territory, set up by Congress in 1787. Minnesota then became successively a part of Indiana, Illinois, Michigan, and finally Wisconsin Territories. Western Minnesota, acquired in 1803, was at first a part of Louisiana, then of Missouri, Michigan, Wisconsin, and Iowa Territories. In 1849 the two sections were at last put together to form Minnesota Territory. Minnesota became the thirty-second state on May 11, 1858.

While the Civil War was on, the Sioux Indians started a war of their own, nearly succeeding in driving white people out of southern Minnesota. Five hundred white settlers died in the Sioux War, and damage ran into millions of dollars. The war ended with the defeat of the Indians at Wood Lake (1862).

Minnesota—Minneapolis

Government. The legislature consists of a senate of 67 members and a house of representatives of 133 members. The governor and lieutenant-governor are elected for four years. The state sends two senators and eight representatives to the U.S. Congress. Minnesota is divided into 87 counties, and in 1970 there were 54 cities and towns with a population of more than ten thousand. The city of Minneapolis ranks thirty-second in the nation, while St. Paul ranks forty-sixth.

Economy. Agriculture, mining, and manufacturing are all chief industries in the state. Manufacturing is chiefly in the south and in the Duluth area around Lake Superior. The state consistently ranks first in creamery butter, oats, turkeys, and sweet corn. Other major crops are corn, soybeans, and green peas. Minnesota's principal mineral is iron ore, most of it coming from three major mining districts in the northeast. The iron is taken mainly by rail to the Lake Superior ports of Duluth and Two Harbors, where it is loaded on ore boats and sent to the great steel mills and furnaces in the lower Great Lakes region (Cleveland, Lorain, Gary, Pittsburgh, and Buffalo). The city of Duluth itself is also a steel-making center. The state supplies more than half of the nation's iron ore. The great new ore deposits of Quebec and Venezuela now pose serious competition to Minnesota iron ore.

MISSISSIPPI

Spanish explorers led by Hernando de Soto were the first white men to enter what is now Mississippi. De Soto discovered the Mississippi River in 1541. The first permanent settlement in the state was made by the French on the Gulf Coast of the future state in 1699. Natchez was settled in 1716 in an attempt by the French to secure a more firm control of the Mississippi Valley. But they lost the region to the British in 1763. After the independence of the United States, Mississippi was ceded to the United States by England. However, it was still claimed by Spain. The treaty of San Lorenzo in 1795 secured the area to legal United States control. Mississippi Territory was organized in 1798. The boundaries were extended in 1804 and in 1812 by the addition of parts of the Louisiana Purchase. On December 10, 1817, Mississippi was admitted to the Union as the twentieth state.

Mississippi seceded from the Union on January 8, 1861, the second state to do so. The chief struggle during the war that followed was for control of the Mississippi River. The siege of Vicksburg, a vital port on the river, became one of the most critical battles of the war. When Vicksburg fell on July 4, 1863, the fate of the Confederacy was sealed, although other engagements were fought in the state before the end came. Mississippi was readmitted to the Union in 1870.

Government. The legislature consists of a senate of 52 members and a house of representatives of 140 members. The governor and lieutenant-governor are elected for four years. The state is represented in the U.S. Congress by two senators and five representatives. Mississippi is divided into 82 counties. In 1970, there were 24 cities having a population of more than ten thousand.

Economy. Mississippi's greatest resources are her soils and forests. Cotton is the major crop; the state ranks third in the production of that commodity. The state leads in the output of tung-oil nuts. Other major crops include pecans, sweet potatoes, corn, rice, wheat, oats, sugar cane, and sorghum. The state ranks eighth in broiler-chicken production. It is also the tenth ranking oil producer in the nation. Mississippi is one of the major lumbering states, and about 58 percent of its area is covered by forests, including over a million acres in national forests. Shrimp fishing is important on the Gulf Coast at Biloxi and Gulfport.

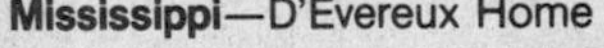

Mississippi—D'Evereux Home

MISSOURI

The Southern part of what is now the state of Missouri was visited by De Soto in 1541 when he crossed the Mississippi River near Memphis. On the basis of the explorations of Marquette, Joliet, and La Salle, the region was claimed by France. In 1705, a party of French explorers ascended the Missouri River to the present site of Kansas City. The territory, then called Louisiana, was ceded to Spain in 1763 and given back to France in 1800 (*see* Louisiana). The United States came into possession of the area in 1803 as a part of the Louisiana Purchase. When the state of Louisiana entered the Union in 1812, the name Missouri became applied to the remainder of the Purchase, which included the entire Missouri River Valley. Daniel Boone (*see* Kentucky) moved into Missouri in 1795 and was an active agent in the state's development. Under terms of the Missouri Compromise, the state of Missouri entered the Union on August 10, 1821 (*see* Maine). The boundary was much the same as today except for a small area that was added in the northwest in 1837. The remainder that was once called Missouri Territory gradually became organized into smaller units, taking on names that had already been growing in popularity or had already existed, such as Dakota, Nebraska, and Kansas.

Missouri—The climatron, Missouri Botanical Garden, St. Louis

Government. The legislative body is called the General Assembly and consists of a senate of 34 members and a house of representatives of 163 members. The governor and lieutenant-governor are elected for four years. The state sends two senators and ten representatives to the U.S. Congress. Missouri is divided into 114 counties. In 1970 there were 54 cities and towns with a population of more than ten thousand. St. Louis has the status of a county and is separate from St. Louis County (*see* Maryland for a similar condition). In 1970 St. Louis was the eighteenth largest city in the United States and Kansas City was the twenty-sixth.

Economy. Missouri is a leading livestock-raising state, ranking fourth in number of hogs and sixth in cattle. The chief crops are soybeans, wheat, corn, and clover. Missouri mines about 45 percent of the United States' lead. Other major minerals mined are barite, lime, iron, copper, and coal. Missouri's largest manufacturing industries are in transportation equipment and food processing. A unique industry in the state is the making of corncob pipes (mainly at the town of Washington). Kansas City (not to be confused with Kansas City, Kansas) and St. Louis have two-thirds of the state's total number of factories. The making of shoes and leather products are also important industries in Missouri.

MONTANA

About a third of the present Montana was included in the original Oregon country, while the remainder formed part of the Louisiana Purchase. The region was explored in 1742–1743 by Sieur de la Verendrye, a French explorer. In 1805 the Lewis and Clark expedition crossed the region. A fort was built at the mouth of the Big Horn River in 1807. The first settlements were made between 1809 and 1829. Jesuit missionaries established missions among the Flathead Indians in 1841.

The discovery of gold on Hell Gate River in 1852 and 1857 was the real beginning of Montana's modern history. Mining settlements sprang up, attracting trade, exploration, and industry.

Conflict with the Indians culminated in the disastrous battle of the Little Big Horn River on June 25, 1876, in which General George Armstrong Custer and his entire force were wiped out by Sioux Indians under Sitting Bull.

Copper and silver mining in the 1880s resulted in rapid development of the region. Montana became a state on November 8, 1889, the forty-first (six days after the two Dakotas).

Government. The Montana legislature consists of a senate of 50 members and a house of representatives of 100 members. The governor and lieutenant-governor are elected for four years. The state is

Montana—Custer's Last Stand (Marker)

represented in the U.S. Congress by two senators and two representatives. Montana is divided into 56 counties, and in 1970 there were eight cities and towns with a population of more than ten thousand.

Economy. Irrigation plays a significant part in agriculture. Montana is a major producer of wheat, barley, sugar beets, and potatoes. Cattle and sheep are also important. Forests cover nearly twenty million acres, or about one-fourth of the state.

Montana is the third-ranking copper producer, and is the number one producer of vermiculite and chromite. (Vermiculite is a form of mica and is used for heat insulation. Chromite is the ore of the metal chromium.) The state also ranks second in the mining of zinc, silver, and fluorspar. Montana is also a large producer of crude petroleum.

NEBRASKA

Nebraska's wide prairies were first seen by Europeans when Coronado reached the region in 1541. As a part of the Louisiana region, it was ceded by France to Spain in 1763. Spain returned it to France in 1800, and the area was sold by Napoleon to the United States in 1803. The explorers Lewis and Clark crossed the future state in 1804. The first settlement was made at Bellevue in 1823, although trading posts had been set up by fur traders as early as 1810. It is estimated that between 1840 and 1866 over two and one-half million people crossed Nebraska on the Overland Trail to California. Settlers began squatting on Indian lands during those years, until in 1854 the entire region (known as Missouri Territory) was opened to settlement. The Kansas-Nebraska Bill of 1854 divided Missouri Territory into Nebraska Territory and Kansas Territory.

With the breaking of ground for the Union Pacific Railroad in 1863, a period of Indian warfare ensued that lasted until the 1870s. Nebraska became a state on March 1, 1867, the thirty-seventh state. In 1882 it annexed part of Dakota Territory and in 1908 received another piece of territory from South Dakota.

Government. By an amendment to the 1875 constitution, Nebraska adopted a single-house legislature, the only state with such a body. This

Nebraska—Chimney Rock located on U.S. Highway 26

legislature consists of 49 members, elected for two years. The governor and lieutenant-governor are elected for two years. Nebraska is represented in the U.S. Congress by two senators and three representatives. Although there are a total of 536 incorporated villages and cities in the state, only 12 of them had a population of more than ten thousand in 1970.

Economy. Three-fourths of the population live in the eastern third of the state. Agriculture is the chief industry, although the processing of meats and other farm products are large industries that are dependent upon the rich farm lands. Farming provides 80 percent of the state's income. The state is third in number of cattle.

Oil and natural gas have been discovered in the western part of Nebraska. Other minerals mined include potash, pumice, gypsum, salt, shale, and clay. Omaha, on the Missouri River, is one of the largest livestock markets in the world and the largest meat-packing center in the United States. The city ranks second in frozen-food production.

NEVADA

Nevada was first visited by Europeans in 1738 when Franciscan friars crossed the state. Peter Ogden of the Hudson's Bay Company discovered the Humboldt River in 1825. John C. Fremont led an exploring party through the region (1843–1844). The first settlement was made by Mormons in 1849 in the valley of the Carson River. The area had become a part of the United States one year earlier, with the Mexican Cession. Nevada became a part of Utah Territory in 1850, but a separate government was soon established and requested annexation to California. The request was turned down, and the area was then organized into Nevada Territory (1861). The state was admitted to the Union on October 31, 1864. In 1866, a section of land was added to the state from Arizona.

The discovery of silver in the Comstock Lode region in 1859 initiated the rapid development of the state. A decline set in when the Comstock worked out, but a revival was made with the discovery of gold southeast of the Comstock region, early in the twentieth century.

Government. The legislature consists of a senate of 20 members and an assembly of 40 members. The governor and lieutenant-governor are elected for four years. Carson City, the capital, is the smallest capital city in the United States. Nevada sends two senators and one representative to the U.S. Congress. The state is divided into 17 counties. Nye County (18,064 square miles) is the third largest county in the nation. Elko (17,126 square miles) is fourth. In 1970 there were nine cities and towns with a population of more than ten thousand. (Compare this with 288 such cities and towns in California.)

Nevada—Hoover Dam

Economy. Despite its dry climate, Nevada is covered with 20 million acres of forests. However, only a small amount of this is commercial timber. Ranching is the main agricultural concern. Alfalfa is raised. Some irrigation is practiced. Other crops include wheat, barley, oats, and potatoes.

Nevada has rich mineral resources, and these form the mainstay of the state's economy. Mercury, manganese, copper, tungsten, gold, uranium, and barite are the chief minerals mined. The state currently ranks fourth in copper production. Gambling and tourism also bring dollars to the state.

NEW HAMPSHIRE

New Hampshire is one of the 13 original states. The area of the present state was first explored in 1603 by Sir Martin Pring. John Smith explored the coastline in 1604. The region was originally a part of the First Charter of Virginia of 1606, but was given to the Plymouth Company in 1620. In 1629, Captain John Mason secured a claim to all the

New Hampshire—Dartmouth College

land between the Piscataqua and the Merrimack rivers, extending northward to Lake Champlain. This he called New Hampshire, for his native district of Hampshire, England. The first permanent settlement was made at Little Harbor in 1623 by David Thompson.

Upon the death of Mason the colony was placed under the protection of Massachusetts (1641). New Hampshire was made a royal colony in 1679. Boundaries were disputed by the Mason family, and they remained to plague the colony and later the state of New Hampshire. Controversy between New Hampshire and New York developed over the land between the Connecticut River and Lake Champlain, north of Massachusetts. Eventually New York won, but the citizens of the disputed area revolted and declared themselves to be the independent state of "New Connecticut" (*see* Vermont).

Early in 1775, New Hampshire declared for independence and was the first to draw up a new constitution. In the war, a notable victory was achieved by New Hampshire and Vermont troops at Bennington (August 16, 1777). New Hampshire ratified the federal Constitution (the ninth state) in 1788.

Government. The legislature consists of a senate of 24 members and a house of representatives whose membership is restricted to from 375 to 400 members. The governor and five administrative officers (called councilors) are elected for two years. There is no office of lieutenant-governor. The state sends two senators and two representatives to the U.S. Congress. The state is divided into ten counties, but they are not as important governmentally as are the cities and towns located in them (*see* Massachusetts.) In 1970, there were 13 cities having a population of more than ten thousand.

Economy. Location, resources, and the traditions of the people have combined to make the state a land of small farms and small towns. The chief field crops are hay, potatoes, and vegetables. Granite is quarried in several places and is the chief mineral of the state. Manufacturing is concentrated in the larger cities and towns of the south and east.

NEW JERSEY

New Jersey is one of the original 13 states. It was first settled by the Dutch, who built a trading post at Bergen on the Hudson River in 1618. In 1664, the area of the present state was taken from the Dutch by the English. The Duke of York, brother of Charles II, King of England, gave the state its identity in 1664, when he granted the land between the Hudson and Delaware rivers to Lord John Berkeley and Sir George Carteret. Today, the boundaries of New Jersey are exactly those set by the Duke of York in his original deeds of lease. However, from 1674 to 1702 the state was divided into the two colonies of East New Jersey and West New Jersey. On April 17, 1702, Queen Anne reunited the two Jerseys into one royal colony.

The people were divided in feelings during the War for Independence. Those favoring independence won out when a new constitution was adopted in 1776. Because of its strategic location between New York City and Philadelphia, New Jersey became a major battleground. Washing-

New Jersey—Morven, The Executive Mansion of New Jersey at Princeton

ton's Continental Army spent a large part of its time in the state, including three winters at encampments. Nearly one hundred battles were fought by the forces of the Continental Army on New Jersey soil. New Jersey became the third state to ratify the Constitution of the United States, on December 17, 1787.

Government. The legislative body is called the Legislature and is composed of a senate of 40 members and a General Assembly of 79 members. New Jersey is represented in Congress by two senators and 15 representatives. The governor is elected for a four-year term. There is no lieutenant-governor. New Jersey is divided into 21 counties. In 1970, there were 177 cities having a population over ten thousand.

Economy. After tourism, manufacturing is the largest industry. The state ranks seventh in manufacturing in the nation. Manufacturing in the state is concentrated in a 15-mile-wide corridor between Philadelphia and New York. The state is the "core" area of research and science laboratory work in the United States, with more than four hundred research laboratories in the area. Heavy industry in the corridor is concentrated along the Delaware River and in the northeastern counties, opposite New York City.

A favorable climate and almost an unlimited market have given rise to large gardening and dairying industries. The principal farm crops are corn, wheat, potatoes, cranberries, and apples. The chief minerals of New Jersey are stone, glass sand, gravel, iron ore, and clay.

NEW MEXICO

Because of the high level of culture reached by the ancient cliff-dwellers and their descendants, the Pueblo Indians, the pre-Columbian history of New Mexico becomes a significant part of the state's heritage. Most of the larger ruined cities are enclosed within state and national parks and monuments. Many of these sites have museums and collections that portray the everyday life and cultural contributions of the past civilization in what is now New Mexico.

The earliest white explorers were Spaniards who governed the region. Cabeza de Vaca, Coronado, and Nuño de Guzman were the principal explorers. Juan de Oñate conquered the region (1588–1599) and founded the first settlement at San Gabriel. By 1630, Franciscan friars had established about fifty missions throughout New Mexico. Santa Fe was founded in 1605 or 1606 . In 1680 a great Indian revolt expelled all the Spanish from the region and it was not reconquered until 1692.

In 1821, the area became a province of the Republic of Mexico under the name of New Mexico. This entire province was ceded to the United States under terms of the Treaty of Guadalupe Hidalgo, after Mexico's defeat in the Mexican War of 1846–1848.

New Mexico—Acoma Mission

In 1850, all of the land west of Texas and east of California was organized into New Mexico Territory. These limits were changed by the addition of the Gadsden Purchase (*see* Arizona) in 1854, by the transfer of the northeastern corner to Colorado in 1861, by the transfer of the northwestern corner to Nevada in 1866, and by the organization of the western half into Arizona Territory in 1863.

Statehood was hotly debated for more than sixty years, but on January 6, 1912, New Mexico became the forty-seventh state. (Arizona followed about a month later.)

Government. The legislature consists of a senate of 42 members and a house of representatives of 70 members. The governor and lieutenant-governor are elected for four years. The state is represented in the U.S. Congress by two senators and two representatives. New Mexico is divided into 32 counties. In 1970, there were 15 cities and towns with a population of more than ten thousand.

Economy. Agriculture is a major industry in New Mexico. Irrigation is extensively practiced. The chief crops are lint cotton, cottonseed, sorghums, hay, and vegetables.

New Mexico is at present the largest domestic source of uranium, with about 66 percent of the total reserves of that metal. Petroleum, natural gas, copper, zinc, and perlite are other major minerals produced in the state. Lumbering is also important in the state's economy.

NEW YORK

New York is one of the original 13 states. Giovanni da Verazzano, sailing for France, discovered New York harbor and the lower Hudson River in 1524. In 1609, Henry Hudson explored the river that is named for him, and his voyage was the basis for the Dutch claim to all the region drained by the river. Permanent settlements were made near the present Albany in 1624, and on Manhattan Island (now a part of New York City) in the same year. The entire Dutch-settled region was called New Netherland. The chief towns were Fort Orange, now Albany, and New Amsterdam, now New York City.

Dutch rule, lasting fifty years, was notable for the famous "Patroonship" system, designed to encourage further settlement. This was the giving of feudal rights, including perpetual land tenure, to the "Patroons" who purchased land from the Indians.

In 1664, the English seized the colony. They renamed Fort Orange, Albany and changed New Amsterdam to New York, both in honor of the Duke of York and Albany.

During 110 years of British rule, many events occurred that contributed to the founding of the United States. The trial of John Peter Zenger in 1735 led to an early victory for freedom of the press in the colonies. A plan proposed in 1754 by Benjamin Franklin for the federal union of the colonies was the forerunner of the Declaration of Independence. The Stamp Act Congress, organized to protest British taxes, met in New York City in 1765.

New York's strategic location as a middle colony with a major trade route (the Hudson-Mohawk route) made it one of the most important battlegrounds during the War for Independence. In 1776 the British fleet took possession of New York City and retained it throughout the war, despite American efforts to capture the city. Washington was able, however, to draw large quantities of supplies from the free area of the colony. In 1777, a British campaign to split the 13 colonies by a three-way drive on Albany was defeated at Saratoga, in one of the world's most decisive battles. Contributing to this victory was the heroic stand made by General Herkimer at Oriskany, preventing the British from uniting their invading forces.

Washington fortified the lower Hudson in 1778, and the Iroquois Indians' alliance with the British was broken in western New York in the following year. General Washington established the Continental Army headquarters in April 1782, at Newburgh on the Hudson River, and it remained there until the end of the war. The last battle of the war was fought at Johnstown, N.Y., on October 25, 1781. After the reoccupation of New York City by the American Army in 1783, Washington bade farewell to his officers at Fraunces Tavern. Six years later he returned to the city (the first capital of the United States under the Constitution) for his inauguration as the first president of the nation. New York had entered the Union on July 26, 1788, as the eleventh state.

New York—The United Nations Building

Government. The legislative power of the state is vested in a two-house legislature. It consists of a senate of 58 members and an assembly of 150 members. Both the governor and the lieutenant-governor are elected for four years. The state sends two senators and 39 representatives to the U.S. Congress. New York is divided into 62 counties, five of which are within the city of New York. In 1970 there were 158 cities and towns with a population of more than ten thousand. New York City is the largest in the United States and third largest in the world (after Tokyo and London). Buffalo, the state's second largest city, ranks twenty-eighth in the nation.

Economy. New York has been the nation's leading state in the value of manufactured products since 1830. It also outranks all other states in the variety and extent of manufacturing.

Apparel is the largest single industry in the state. About 36 percent of all apparel produced in the nation comes from New York State. Ranking next in terms of employment are machinery, printing, and publishing. One-fourth of the printing in the United States is done in the state. The manufacture of paper, pulp, and paperboard is concentrated in the north and northwest. Instrument industries in New York employ 29 percent of the nation's workers in this field, and the photographic industry employs two-thirds of all the nation's workers in that field.

New York is not often thought of as a mineral-rich state, yet it leads the nation in the mining of industrial talc, garnet, wollastonite, emery, and titanium. It is a major producer of zinc, gypsum, salt, sand and gravel, and mines about 5 percent of the iron ore in the United States. New York leads all states in the utilization of radioactive materials in medical research, diagnosis, and treatment.

It is well to note that fully 25 percent of all the people in the United States live within a 250-mile radius of New York City, so New York State ranks unusually high as a wholesale market region. The state leads all others in both retail and wholesale activities. In banking and finance, New York is also the leader, having 518 banks with resources amounting to 78 billion dollars. This makes the state, and in particular, the city of New York, the financial center of the world (New York City is also the largest insurance center in the nation).

The Port of New York has about 600 miles of piers and handles about 24 percent of the waterborne foreign trade in the country. The Port of New

York Authority is a bi-state agency of New York and New Jersey, set up to develop and promote this port district.

The Port of Buffalo is the largest state port on the Greak Lakes, in terms of value and in tonnage. The city has 37 miles of waterfront on Lake Erie. The opening of the St. Lawrence Seaway in 1959 provided a new seacoast for ocean commerce along the river and the Great Lakes. This project stimulated plans for deep-water ports by Massena, Ogdensburg, Oswego, Rochester, and other cities in the state.

Dairying is the largest agricultural industry, and the state is second in the nation in the number of dairy cows and in the production of milk. Other major agricultural crops include grapes, apples, peaches, potatoes, maple syrup, and buckwheat. The state ranks fourth in total vegetable production and second in the production of cheese and ice cream.

North Carolina—Wright Monument in Wright Brothers National Memorial near Kitty Hawk

NORTH CAROLINA

North Carolina is one of the 13 original states. The first English attempts to establish settlements in what is now the United States were made in North Carolina in 1584, 1585, and 1587. In the year 1587, Roanoke Island became the site of a colony, established by Sir Walter Raleigh, in which the first white child was born in America. Her name was Virginia Dare. This was the famous "Lost Colony." Its disappearance was so complete that the only clues ever found were the word *Croatoan* (the name of another island) and a few pieces of armor. The state was not permanently settled until 1663.

In 1629, King Charles I of England granted what is now North and South Carolina to Sir Robert Heath. In 1663 King Charles II gave the area to a group of "proprietors." In 1710 North and South Carolina were separated. Beginning in 1712, each had a separate capital and governor. In 1729, North Carolina became a royal colony (the King having bought out the proprietors). North Carolina entered the Union on November 21, 1789, the twelfth state to ratify the new federal Constitution.

North Carolina was the last state to secede from the Union. It did so on May 20, 1861, and was readmitted in July 1868.

Government. The state legislature consists of a senate of 50 members and a house of representatives of 120 members. The governor may not succeed himself, and has no veto power. The state sends two senators and 11 representatives to the U.S. Congress. North Carolina is divided into 100 counties. In 1970 there were 41 cities and towns having a population of more than ten thousand.

Economy. The state is rich in natural resources. Its climate and soil permit a wide range of economic activities.

North Carolina's Piedmont region is dotted with the world's largest concentration of textile, tobacco, and furniture factories. The state leads the nation in all three. Value added by manufacturing is the largest in the South and fourteenth in the nation.

In agriculture, North Carolina is the number one producer of tobacco in the United States. Other major cash crops are corn, soybeans, cotton, and peanuts. Also grown extensively are wheat, oats, barley, sweet potatoes, hay, peaches, and apples. North Carolina is first in the country in farm population and eleventh in farm production. Its timber covers 20 million acres, and furnishes about 7 percent of the total value of the state's farm products.

An astounding variety of minerals are found in North Carolina. There are 300 types, leading all states in variety. The state produces 74 percent of all the sheet mica in the United States. The state is also a leading producer of feldspar, kaolin clays, talc, and stone (chiefly granite).

NORTH DAKOTA

Most of North Dakota lies in the drainage basin of the Missouri-Mississippi system which was claimed by Sieur de La Salle for France in 1682. This claim was transferred to Spain in 1762. The British obtained title to part of the state in the north and east in 1763. The United States received all but the British-claimed area in 1803, as a part of the Louisiana Purchase. In 1818, the British-claimed area was formally ceded to the United States, although French and English fur traders continued to explore the region.

Lewis and Clark crossed North Dakota on their famed journey of exploration (1804–1806). David Thompson, the great English geographer, had explored and mapped the Souris and Missouri river basins in 1797.

Attempts at settlement occurred in the early nineteenth century at Pembina in the northeast, but the present state remained virtually unoccupied except for Indians and trading posts until the 1850s. In 1829, the American Fur Company built Fort Union at the mouth of the Yellowstone River. In 1857 the first military outpost was established at Fort Abercrombie on the Red River of the North. By 1860 regular steamboat service was available on both the Missouri and Red River of the North. Dakota Territory was organized in 1861 and included both North and South Dakota, plus parts of Wyoming and Montana.

North Dakota—Theodore Roosevelt National Memorial Park

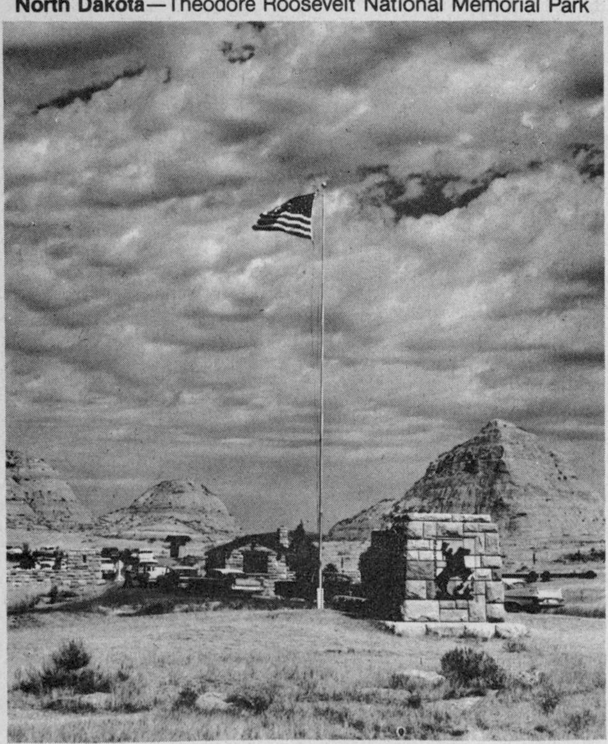

Dakota Territory was opened for homesteading in 1863. Railroads began to cross the territory in 1871. In 1889 the Dakota Territory was divided into two territories. The division was made along the seventh standard parallel. North Dakota and South Dakota were admitted to the Union on November 2, 1889. President Benjamin Harrison apparently never revealed which statehood bill he signed first, so that it will never be known which of the two sister states was the first to be admitted to the Union. North Dakota is generally given as the thirty-ninth state only because of its alphabetical position, but either state could be placed thirty-ninth or fortieth.

Government. The present constitution dates from statehood. The law-making body is called the Legislative Assembly and consists of a senate of 50 members and a house of representatives of 108 members. The governor and lieutenant-governor are elected for four years. The state is represented in the U.S. Congress by two senators and one representative. North Dakota is divided into 53 counties. There are 356 municipalities, of which 10 had a population of more than ten thousand in 1970.

Economy. Agriculture is the chief industry. Large-scale mechanized farms are common. The state leads in the production of barley, ranks second in rye, and second in wheat. Other important crops include flax seed, potatoes, hay, oats, and corn.

North Dakota is the newest oil-boom state, and petroleum is the most valuable mineral found there. The state ranks ninth in reserves. The major fields are located around Williston. Refineries are located at Dickinson, Williston, and Mandan.

OHIO

The first recorded inhabitants of Ohio were the Mound Builders, prehistoric Indians. Those living in Ohio left more than ten thousand burial and ceremonial mounds. Most of the Mound Builders of Ohio belonged to the Hopewell culture. Artifacts found in the mounds indicate advanced cultural progress and social life.

Early in the seventeenth century Jesuit priests and French explorers began entering the region.

Moravian missionaries founded a settlement which they called Schoenbrunn in eastern Ohio in 1772. This settlement was destroyed in 1776. Marietta on the Ohio River was founded in 1788, becoming the first permanent town in the future state.

After the Revolutionary War the British continued to encourage the Indians to violence in the region north of the Ohio River. The new federal Government was determined to put an end to the Indian troubles and sent General "Mad" Anthony Wayne to deal with the situation. In 1794, Wayne brought a disastrous defeat upon the Indians at Fallen Timbers, near present Toledo. In 1795, Wayne secured the Greenville Treaty, bringing about peace in Ohio.

New towns began to spring up soon after the treaty was signed. In 1796, the famous Western Reserve surveys began. Ohio became the first state to be carved out of the old Northwest Territory. It unofficially entered the Union as the seventeenth state on February 19, 1803. The entrance was made official on August 8, 1853, retroactive to the original 1803 date. A serious border dispute between Ohio and Michigan in 1835 resulted in the "Toledo War." Ohio was awarded the disputed area and Michigan was given what proved to be a tremendous bargain–the copper-rich Upper Peninsula.

Government. The legislative body of Ohio is called the General Assembly. It consists of a senate of 33 members and a house of representatives of 99 members. The governor and lieutenant-governor are elected for four years. Ohio sends two senators and 23 representatives to the U.S. Congress. The state is divided into 88 counties, and in 1970 there were 153 cities and towns with a population of more than ten thousand. Cleveland ranks tenth in the nation, and Columbus ranks twenty-first.

Economy. Although Ohio ranks third among the states in manufacturing, it is also a major farming state, ranking eighth in gross value of farm production. Agriculture in the state is varied, including even greenhouse farming, the largest such industry in the nation. Along Lake Erie is a major fruit-growing region, aided by the lake's influence on the climate. In addition, the state ranks fifth in corn, first in timothy seed, fifth in oats, third in popcorn, and sixth in hogs.

Iron and steel products are the largest group of manufactured products. Steel mills and blast furnaces are concentrated along Lake Erie, especially at Cleveland and Lorain. Ohio ranks first in business machines, clay products, electrical machinery, tires and tubes, and machine tools.

Cleveland, Toledo, Lorain, Ashtabula, and Sandusky now rank as seaports since the completion of the Great Lakes-Saint Lawrence Seaway (*see* New York). In fact, Toledo has a substantial foreign trade zone, and is the world's greatest coal-shipping port. The chief minerals mined in Ohio are coal, clay, lime, and salt.

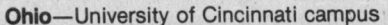

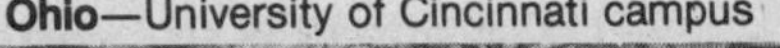
Ohio—University of Cincinnati campus

OKLAHOMA

The recorded history of Oklahoma began in 1541 when De Soto visited the eastern part of the region and the Spanish Coronado expedition crossed central Oklahoma. The section was not known as Oklahoma until 1866, and then not officially until 1890. Little was known of the area until it became a part of the Louisiana Purchase in 1803. American explorers then made maps of the region.

Oklahoma early became a refuge for Indians who were driven from east of the Mississippi, and this role shaped the destiny of the future state. Between 1820 and 1840, Indian treaties were signed with Cherokee, Choctaw, Chickasaw, Seminole, and Creek tribes. These five tribes were allotted areas for settlement and were given land by the Government. They eventually set up their

Oklahoma—Travertine Creek, Platt National Park

own governments and became autonomous areas with their own capital cities. The Five Nations were divided on the issues of the Civil War, and considerable internal strife resulted.

Cattle drives northward through the Indian country required many grazing leases on Indian lands. The railroads brought an influx of white people to the country. After the Civil War, Creek and Seminole peoples ceded large areas in the central part of the future state to the United States. These lands were opened for white settlement on April 22, 1889. On opening day, fifty thousand people were on hand. By nightfall, tent cities had sprung up and six counties had been created. The following year Oklahoma was designated a territory. By 1895 all of southwestern Oklahoma had been opened to white settlement.

The Indians struggled to remain independent of Oklahoma Territory. They attempted to become a separate state in 1905, but were defeated. In 1906 President Theodore Roosevelt joined the white and Indian territories into a single state. Oklahoma was declared the forty-sixth state on November 16, 1907.

Government. The state has a senate of 48 members and a house of representatives of from 120 to 123 members. The governor and lieutenant-governor are elected for four years. The state is represented in Congress by two senators and six representatives. Oklahoma is divided into 67 counties. In 1970, 30 cities and towns had a population of more than ten thousand.

Economy. Agriculture is the major industry of Oklahoma. However, soil erosion is a serious problem because the state lies in a region of erratic rainfall, some years being rainy and others being too dry. Farmers in the state are often faced with the problem of protecting topsoils either from severe drought or severe flooding. The most important crop is wheat and production is the second-highest in the United States. Other crops include cotton, grain, sorghums, and broomcorn.

Oklahoma ranks fourth in the production of petroleum. Natural gas, coal, gypsum, zinc, and salt are also produced. Petroleum refining is the chief nonagricultural industry.

OREGON

The name *Oregon* was originally applied to the whole region of what is now the Pacific Northwest and includes Oregon, Washington, parts of Idaho, Montana, and Canada's British Columbia. Discovery and exploration were first carried out by sea voyages along the coast. Spanish sailors from Mexico, in 1543, were the first white men to see the Oregon country. Spanish claims were challenged by the British after the visits of Sir Francis Drake in 1579, and especially after the voyages of exploration of Captain James Cook (1778), and George Vancouver (1792). The Russians, too, claimed the region as a result of their fur-trading expeditions in the latter part of the eighteenth century. American interest was stimulated by the overland expedition of Lewis and Clark in 1804–1806, and by the sea voyage to the coasts by Captain Robert Gray in 1791 and 1792.

Russian and Spanish claims lapsed by agreement, but British and American rivalry in the fur trade and between settlements brought about serious conflicts. An agreement made in 1818 for joint occupancy was finally terminated by treaty in 1846, after the so-called Oregon Question threatened to involve the United States in war with Great Britain. The original American demand was "Fifty-Four Forty or Fight," but the forty-ninth parallel of latitude was finally accepted as the boundary between the United States and British-controlled Canada.

Settlement began when the Pacific Fur Company established Astoria in 1811. In 1813 Astoria was sold to the Northwest Company. That company was then absorbed by the Hudson's Bay

Oregon—Ice Lake, Wallowa Mountain

Company, which actually governed the region of present Oregon until the treaty in 1846. Settlements were established in 1829 in the Willamette River valley. American settlers formed a provisional government in 1843 and Oregon Territory was organized in 1848. Oregon was admitted to the Union on February 14, 1859, as the thirty-third state.

Government. The present constitution of Oregon dates from statehood. The legislative body is called the Legislative Assembly and consists of a senate of 30 members and a house of representatives of 60 members. The governor is elected to a four-year term. There is no lieutenant-governor. The state is divided into 36 counties. Harney County (10,131 square miles) is the eighth largest of the more than three thousand counties in the United States. In 1970 there were 24 cities and towns with a population of more than ten thousand.

Economy. Nearly 30 million acres of standing forests blanket the state, and Oregon leads the nation in lumbering. Oregon produces annually nearly eight million board feet of lumber, or about 25 percent of the total United States' production. Agriculture is another major industry. The state is a leading producer of peppermint, filberts, black raspberries, beans, beets, lily bulbs, holly, and seedling root stocks. The most productive farm land lies in the Willamette Valley between Portland and Eugene.

Manufacturing ranges from lumber products through aluminum, textiles, and fertilizers. Mining includes gold, silver, mercury, copper, and nickel. Oregon is one of the few states with commercial deposits of quicksilver and chromite ores, and one of two states producing nickel.

Fishing is important along the coast and on the Columbia River; salmon, trawl fish, clams, crabs, and tuna are the chief kinds taken.

PENNSYLVANIA

Pennsylvania is one of the 13 original states. William Penn (1644–1718), an English Quaker, received the grant of Pennsylvania from Charles II in 1681. It has been said that the immediate purpose of Charles' act was to get rid of "the troublesome Quakers." If so, he must have been roundly satisfied, because the Quakers flocked to Pennsylvania in the first few years. Penn himself came in 1682, and Philadelphia was laid out in the same year.

Penn set about concluding a number of treaties with the Lenni-Lenape and other tribes of Indians. His work saved years of bloodshed during the opening up of the land for settlement. Penn's domain was enlarged in 1682 by the grant of the "Three Lower Counties," which were retained as a nominal part of Pennsylvania until 1776 (*see* Delaware). The constitution devised in 1701 lasted until the Revolution.

Pennsylvania was often involved in long disputes over the colony's boundaries, and later over state lines. Some of these led to violence, as in the "Pennamite" and "Yankee" wars. The last change in the boundary was the adding of a triangle in 1792 to give the state an outlet on Lake Erie in the west.

Pennsylvania took a leading part in the Revolution. The Declaration of Independence was signed at Philadelphia in 1776. During a large part of the war, Pennsylvania served as Washington's base of operations. Except for a brief period when Philadelphia was occupied by the British, the city was the seat of the Continental Congress. Winter quarters were established at Valley Forge by the Continental Army during the winter of 1777–1778. The state ratified the federal Constitution on December 12, 1787, the second state to do so (following Delaware).

Government. Pennsylvania's legislative body is called the General Assembly and consists of a senate of 46 members and a house of representatives of 202 members. The governor and lieutenant-governor are elected for four years. The state sends two senators and 25 representatives to the U.S. Congress. Pennsylvania is divided into 67 counties (including the city of Philadelphia, whose boundary includes all of Philadelphia County). Philadelphia is the fourth largest city in the United States. Pittsburgh ranks twenty-fourth in the nation. In 1970 there were 101 cities and towns with a population of more than ten thousand.

Economy. Despite a varied agriculture and some of the richest soils in the nation, Pennsylvania is predominantly an industrial state. However, the state ranks second in the nation in egg production and fifth in dairying. The chief farm crops are corn, wheat, tobacco, and potatoes. Pennsylvania ranks second (to West Virginia) in coal mining. The principal coal seams are those of hard coal (anthracite) in the northeastern counties, and soft coal (bituminous) in the southwest. Half of the world's supply of anthracite coal comes from Pennsylvania. The state also ranks fourth in kaolin and second in limestone. Petroleum and natural gas are produced in large quantities. The state leads the nation in the production of iron and steel. Heavy industry is concentrated in the Pittsburgh and Philadelphia areas. Seventeen million tons of iron and steel come from the blast furnaces of Johnstown, Pittsburgh, Morrisville, Bethlehem, Steelton, and Coatesville each year. Most of the iron ore used comes from Minnesota over the Great Lakes route. Textile manufacturing is also a large industry, concentrated mainly in Philadelphia, Allentown, and Reading. The world's largest knitting mill is located at Reading (pronounced "Redding").

Pennsylvania—Memorial Chapel, Valley Forge

RHODE ISLAND

Rhode Island is one of the 13 original states. Rhode Island and Providence Plantations (still the official name of the state) was founded by Roger Williams in 1636. Williams had been exiled from Massachusetts for his religious beliefs. He persuaded several settlers to go with him into exile, and obtained land near the present Providence by purchase from the Indians of the Narragansett Bay region. The town of Newport was founded in 1639.

The New England Confederation, which had been formed for defensive purposes in 1643, threatened the little colony along Narragansett Bay. This prompted Roger Williams to hurry off to England where he got a charter for his colony (1652). This charter remained the governing law of Rhode Island until 1842. During the colonial period Rhode Island became a principal refuge for those who were persecuted because of their political beliefs. It was one of the first colonies to resist British oppression by burning the British cruiser *Gaspée*. Nathaniel Greene, a leading hero of the war, led a thousand Rhode Island men to Boston upon the outbreak of war.

Rhode Island was suspicious of the larger states throughout the early years of independence, and was at first fearful of joining a stronger union in which the small states could be trampled upon. Threats of annexation and of cutting off trade forced Rhode Island into ratifying the federal Constitution as the thirteenth state on May 29, 1790.

Government. The legislative body is called the General Assembly and consists of a senate of 50 members and a house of representatives of 100 members. The governor and lieutenant-governor are elected for two years. Rhode Island is represented in the U.S. Congress by two senators and two representatives. The state has five counties, but they have no political functions whatever. The town and city are the major units of local government. Of the 43 towns and cities in 1970, 27 had a population of more than ten thousand.

Economy. Rhode Island's larger cities are still the stronghold of the textile industries which have been on the decline elsewhere in New England. Woolens and worsteds are the leading textiles manufactured. Machinery, fabricated metal products, and jewelry are other leading industries. Agriculture and mining in Rhode Island are not important on a national level.

Rhode Island—Kitchen of James Mitchell Varnum House, East Greenwich

South Carolina—Fort Sumter, Charleston

SOUTH CAROLINA

South Carolina is one of the original 13 states. Spanish explorers visited the area as early as 1520. However, England claimed the future South Carolina along with the entire North American coast on the basis of the voyages of discovery of John and Sebastian Cabot. In 1629, Charles I granted the region to Sir Robert Heath, who made no attempt to establish settlements. In 1663, Charles II made a second grant of the same area (which included the present North Carolina) to eight "proprietors." This colony was called Carolina. The first settlement was made in 1670 at Charlestown. This settlement was later moved and renamed Charles Town (changed to Charleston in 1783). In 1729, Carolina was divided into North Carolina and South Carolina (although actually there always had been two separate governments).

During the Revolutionary War, South Carolina contributed more money to the cause than any other state except Massachusetts. The colony had been prosperous from the very beginning, and for a time Charleston was a leading center of wealth and culture in North America. However, the state of South Carolina suffered heavily in the war. Charleston was besieged and forced to surrender. Much of the war was waged in guerrilla fashion by such leaders as Francis Marion ("Swamp Fox"), Sumter, and Pickens. South Carolina ratified the federal Constitution on May 23, 1788, the eighth state to sign.

The Civil War began in South Carolina after that state seceded from the Union on December 20, 1860. The bombardment of Fort Sumter in Charleston Harbor were the opening shots of the war (April 12–13, 1861). Tremendous damage was inflicted on the state, especially along the route of General Sherman's army in the famous march to the sea (*see* Georgia). At the close of the war a military government was imposed upon the state for twelve years. On June 25, 1868, the state was readmitted to the Union but was one of the worst sufferers during the period of Reconstruction.

Government. The legislative body is called the General Assembly. It consists of a senate of 46 members and a house of representatives of 124 members. The governor and lieutenant-governor are elected for four years. The state sends two senators and six representatives to the United States Congress. South Carolina is divided into 46 counties, and in 1970 there were 20 cities with a population of more than ten thousand.

Economy. South Carolina is an agricultural state. The principal crops are tobacco, corn, lint cotton, soybeans, and peaches. Of the minerals, large reserves of rare-earth minerals exist, although the state now ranks only forty-first in the value of minerals produced. The state ranks second in kaolin and kyanite clays. The state has a trend toward metals manufacturing, but textiles are by far the leading manufacture.

SOUTH DAKOTA

South Dakota was a part of the Louisiana Purchase of 1803. The state was first explored in 1743, mainly by the Verendrye brothers, who were French explorers from Canada. They buried a lead plate to serve as proof of their visit and of the claim of France to the region. The plate was found in 1913. The Lewis and Clark Expedition passed through the state in 1804 and 1806. Fort Teton (Fort Pierre) was established as a trading post in 1831. Steamboat service on the Missouri started the following year. Fort Pierre became a United States military post in 1855, and Sioux Falls was founded in 1857. South Dakota was successively placed under the governments of Missouri Territory (1812), Michigan Territory (1834), Wisconsin Territory (1836), Iowa Territory (1838), Minnesota Territory (1849), and then a part became part of Nebraska Territory in 1854. Dakota Territory was organized in 1861 and until 1863 included parts of Montana and Wyoming. Railroad construction initiated rapid settlement and development of the state. On November 2, 1889, South Dakota became either the thirty-ninth or the fortieth state (*see* North Dakota). A great land rush ensued when nine million acres of former Sioux Indian lands were sold in 1892.

South Dakota—Mount Rushmore

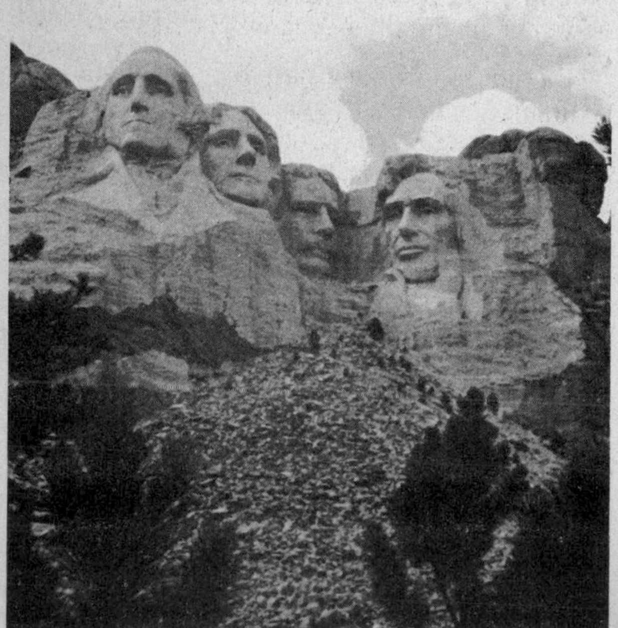

Government. The legislature consists of a senate of 35 members and a house of representatives of 75 members. The governor and lieutenant-governor are elected for two years. South Dakota is divided into 67 counties (Armstrong County was abolished in 1959). The state sends two representatives and, of course, two senators to the Congress. Three counties remain unorganized and without government functions. In 1970 there were eight cities and towns with a population of more than ten thousand.

Economy. South Dakota is a farming state, and the farms are generally large (averaging over 800 acres) and highly mechanized. The state is a major producer of wheat, barley, oats, corn, rye, and flaxseed.

The state leads in the mining of gold (the Homestake Mine), although South Dakota ranks only forty-second in the value of minerals produced. Beryllium and mica are also mined in large quantities.

TENNESSEE

In April 1541, De Soto reached the present Memphis, Tennessee area and crossed the Mississippi there into what is now Arkansas. Early in 1682 Sieur de La Salle built Fort Prud'homme. A French trading post was established near Nashville in 1714 and French settlers founded Fort Assumption. The English settled at Fort Loudoun near Knoxville in 1756. This fort was captured by the Cherokees in 1760 and the garrison was massacred. A series of permanent settlements were established in the valleys of the Holston and Watauga rivers in 1769 by colonists from Virginia and North Carolina.

A number of pioneers, including Daniel Boone, founded the state of Transylvania. They drew up a form of government in 1780 and founded a settlement at Nashville. However, Virginia refused to sanction the new state. John Sevier founded another state that was called Franklin. This time North Carolina refused to sanction the state and regained control over the territory in 1788.

After North Carolina and Virginia had given up their claims to Tennessee, the region was organized as "Territory South of the Ohio," but this did not include Kentucky (which was a Virginia County at that time). Statehood came on June 1, 1796, when Tennessee became the sixteenth state (four years after Kentucky had entered the Union).

The Tennessee people took a leading part in exploring and settling the American Southwest. In the war with Mexico, Tennessee became known as the "Volunteer State" because 30,000 soldiers volunteered for the war when only 2,800 had been called for.

Next to Virginia, Tennessee was the main battleground in the Civil War. Shiloh and the engagements around Chattanooga were bloody and crucial battles in the war. Tennessee had withdrawn from the Union on June 24, 1861, and was readmitted on July 24, 1866.

Government. The legislative body is called the General Assembly and consists of a senate of 63 members and a house of representatives of 99 members. The governor is elected for a four-year term. There is no office of lieutenant-governor. Tennessee sends two senators and eight representatives to the U.S. Congress. The state is divided into 95 counties, and in 1970 there were 32 cities and towns with a population of more than ten thousand. The largest city is Memphis, which ranks seventeenth among the United States cities in population.

Economy. The chief crops of Tennessee are cotton, tobacco, soybeans, and corn. Coal fields cover over 5,000 square miles of the state, and Tennessee is a leading producer of coal. Tennessee leads in the mining of zinc and is second in phosphate rock. The state ranks twenty-eighth in mineral production; about 30 different minerals are mined commercially. Chemicals, iron, and steel products are the chief manufactures. Memphis is Tennessee's major port. Oak Ridge was founded by the U.S. Government in 1942 for atomic energy development and research in nuclear physics.

Tennessee—Confederate Monument, Fort Donelson

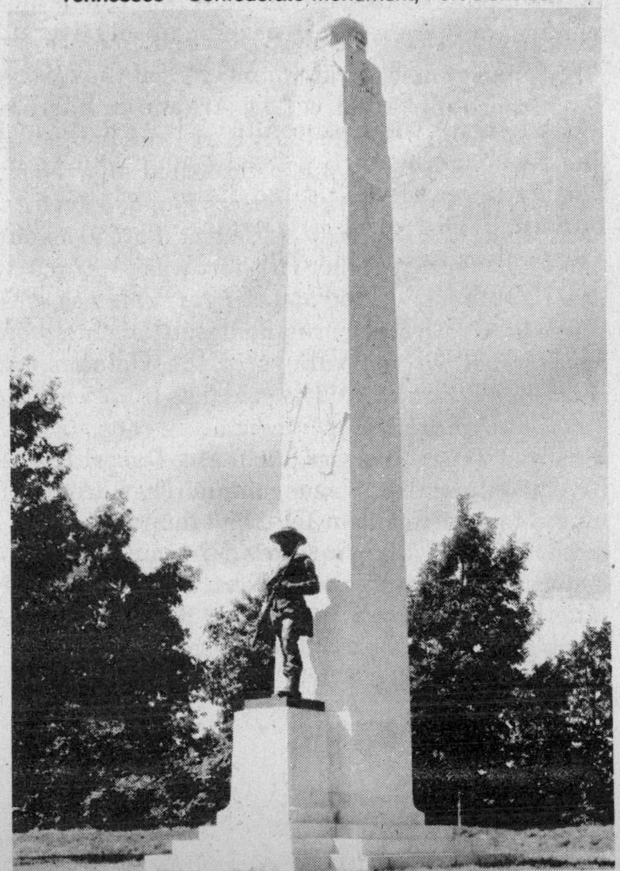

TEXAS

The Spanish initiated the exploration of Texas in 1519, when Alonso Álvarez de Peñeda was sent out to explore and map the coast along the Gulf of Mexico. Cabeza de Vaca added to European knowledge of the region by spending six years with the Indians there. In 1685, the French began exploring Texas. Thus, the claims of France and Spain overlapped until the defeat of France in 1763 by the British. Texas was then Spanish until it passed to an independent Mexico in 1821. During the Spanish period, missions and forts were established throughout the region. The first settlement in Texas dates from 1686.

American settlers, led by Moses Austin and later by his son, Stephen F. Austin, established homes in Texas while it was governed by Mexico. A flood of American settlers soon ran into conflict with Mexican sovereignty. In 1835, the colonists revolted against Mexico and set up a provisional government. Santa Anna, the Mexican general who had already overthrown his own government, set out to crush the revolt. Texans captured San Antonio in December 1835, but were crushed when Santa Anna's superior forces overwhelmed the small garrison in the Alamo, the chapel of an old Spanish mission, on March 6, 1836. There were no survivors; all died fighting, including Davy Crockett, Jim Bowie, and William Travis.

After the fall of the Alamo, Santa Anna was caught by surprise at San Jacinto. Forces under Sam Houston annihilated the Mexican Army and captured Santa Anna. This ended Mexican sovereignty over Texas. The Texas Republic came into existence on March 2, 1836 and lasted until the state entered the Union voluntarily on December 29, 1845, as the twenty-eighth state. Texas seceded from the Union in 1861 and was readmitted March 30, 1870.

Government. The present constitution dates from 1876. The Texas legislature consists of a senate of 31 members and a house of representatives of 150 members. The governor and lieutenant-governor are elected for two years. Texas sends 24 representatives besides the two senators to the Congress. Texas is divided into 254 counties, the largest number of counties in any state. In 1970 there were 125 cities and towns with a population of more than ten thousand.

Economy. Texas leads all states by a wide margin in the production of petroleum and helium. The total value of minerals is 22 percent of the United States total. More than three-fifths of all natural gas used in the country comes from Texas. Other minerals include sulphur, salt, gypsum, asphalt, and magnesium (from seawater).

Great chemical industries have grown up in the Houston area. The Port of Houston is connected to the Gulf of Mexico by the Houston Ship Canal (57.3 miles long). Houston itself is the largest inland cotton market in the world.

Texas ranks as one of the leading agricultural states. Large farms dominate the state's agriculture. Texas leads in the production of cotton and grain sorghum. Other important crops include pecans, corn, winter wheat, oats, rice, castor beans, potatoes, sweet potatoes, peanuts, and grapefruit.

Texas—The Alamo

The state also leads in the livestock industry. It has more cattle and sheep than any other state. Tourism is an important industry in southern and western Texas.

UTAH

The first white men to see Utah were Spanish explorers and the Franciscan friars. Captain James Bridger discovered Great Salt Lake in 1825. The first settlement was made at Salt Lake City in July 1847, by a group of about 150 Mormon settlers.

The Mormon Church (properly called the Church of Jesus Christ of Latter-Day Saints) was founded at Fayette, New York, in 1830 by Joseph Smith. Persecution and opposition forced the Mormons to move westward. Brigham Young joined the group after it had reached Kirtland, Ohio (near Cleveland) in 1832. They were driven from Ohio and then from Missouri. In 1840, they were at Nauvoo, Illinois; by 1844 Nauvoo had become the largest town in Illinois because of the influx of converts and settlers. Joseph Smith and his brother Hyram were jailed and then shot by a mob on June 27, 1844. The charter of Nauvoo was revoked and the Mormons were again forced to flee westward. They reached the Great Salt Lake and founded Salt Lake City in 1847. Mormons attempted to enter the Union as the State of Deseret; they were finally admitted as the Territory of Utah in 1850.

Utah early came into conflict with federal authorities over the practice of polygamy, which had been outlawed by the United States in 1862. The Edmunds Bill took citizenship away from polygamists, and in 1890 the court declared their church property forfeited. This forced the Mormons into accepting monogamist laws. Thereupon Utah was admitted to the Union as the forty-fifth state, on January 4, 1896.

Government. The Utah legislature consists of a senate of 28 members and a house of representatives of 69 members. The governor is elected for four years. There is no office of lieutenant-governor. Utah is represented in the U.S. Congress by two senators and two representatives. The state is divided into 29 counties, and in 1970 there were 15 cities and towns with a population of more than ten thousand.

Utah—Temple Square in Salt Lake City

Economy. The raising of sheep and the production of wool are a leading agricultural industry. Most farming in Utah is done by irrigation, although some dry farming is practiced. Utah is primarily a mining state, ranking sixteenth in the nation. The state is second in asphalt production, and also in copper, gold, silver, molybdenum, and vanadium; third in uranium, lead, and potassium salts; fourth in iron ore.

VERMONT

Samuel de Champlain was the first European to see Vermont. He discovered Lake Champlain in 1609. The first settlement was made by the French on La Motte Island in Lake Champlain in 1666. Fort Dummer (now Brattleboro) was the site of the first English settlement, established in 1724 by colonists from Massachusetts.

The early history of Vermont centers on the disputes over the Mason Land Grants and the earlier charter grants by both England and France. Later, the charters of both New Hampshire and Massachusetts included parts of the present Vermont. This conflict was settled in favor of New Hampshire in 1740. But the New Hampshire colony inherited a dispute with New York that had been in progress over the eastern boundary of New York. The king was asked to decide and did so—in favor of New York. The latter colony ignored the claims and rights of settlers who had purchased their lands from New Hampshire. Armed conflict resulted, especially at Bennington (now in Vermont).

In 1775, a convention met at Westminster and declared for independence, and a second convention declared for an independent state to be called New Connecticut. A third convention in 1777 changed the name of the region to Vermont. Be-

Vermont—The State House, Montpelier

cause of bitter opposition from New York and New Hampshire, Vermont was denied statehood for 14 years. The Vermonters were finally able to settle claims of both the other states and on March 4, 1791, Vermont became the first state to be admitted to the Union after the original 13 states had ratified the federal Constitution. During the War for Independence, Vermont fought independently and was for a time seeking an independent peace. But eventually it joined the other former colonies in the peace negotiations. The capture of Fort Ticonderoga (in New York) by Vermont hero Ethan Allen and his Green Mountain Boys was one of the major events of the war.

Government. The state legislature consists of a senate of 30 members and a house of representatives of 150 members. Vermont sends two senators and one representative to the U.S. Congress. The state is divided into 14 counties and 246 towns and cities (*see* Maine for a note on "town" and on New England counties). In 1970 there were eight cities with a population of more than ten thousand, and 47 cities and towns with a population of more than twenty-five hundred.

Economy. Manufacturing is the principal industry, although tourism and recreation have become much more important in recent years. Vermont leads in maple syrup production. Other crops grown are potatoes, oats, apples, and hay. Granite is the principal mineral produced, although the state is the number one producer of asbestos.

VIRGINIA

Virginia is one of the 13 original states. It was settled under a charter issued in 1606 by King James I. The first permanent settlement (at Jamestown in 1607) was established only after several unsuccessful attempts (*see* North Carolina).

The first legislative assembly in the Western Hemisphere, the House of Burgesses, convened in Jamestown in 1619. In 1622, Indians massacred nearly one-third of the settlement's inhabitants. In 1624, Virginia was made a crown colony.

After a revolution in England had overthrown the king and Cromwell had assumed the powers of government, Virginia obtained a new charter of self-government. However, the colony reverted to the crown when Charles II came to power. An era of prosperity in Virginia ensued, based mainly on the growing of tobacco on the Tidewater plantations, using slave labor.

Virginia—Houdon Statue of George Washington, in the State Capitol, Richmond

The Navigation Acts of 1660 and 1663 ushered in a period of remonstrance and protest that foreshadowed the Revolution which came a century later. The Navigation Acts imposed unwanted restrictions upon Virginia's trade. Soon after, Governor Sir William Berkeley placed drastic limitations upon democratic government and the House of Burgesses. This led to Bacon's Rebellion of 1676. Savage reprisals and brutal hangings by Berkeley ended the rebellion. In 1699, during the reign of William and Mary in England, the Virginia capital was removed to Middle Plantation, and that town's name was changed to Williamsburg. Williamsburg became one of the great social, cultural, and political centers of American life. The city declined after removal of the capital to Richmond in 1780. In 1927 the restoration of Williamsburg to its original condition was begun and has been nearly completed at a cost, so far, of more than sixty-eight million dollars.

By 1763, Virginia was moving toward revolution and independence. Virginians disputed the Hillsborough Proclamation of 1763, prohibiting settlement of Virginians beyond the crest of the Allegheny Mountains in the west. England asserted Parliament's right to legislate for the colonies. This brought a series of events that led to war.

Virginia took the lead among the colonies and provided most of the leaders in the war that resulted. The rise of Virginia politicians and farmers to the status of great American statesmen was exemplified in the careers of Jefferson, Richard Henry Lee, Patrick Henry, Madison, Pendleton, Randolph, Mason, Washington, and others. The Colonial Assembly adjourned on June 20, 1775, and never met again.

The Second Continental Congress elected George Washington commander in chief on June 14, 1775. He proceeded to Cambridge, Massachusetts, to take control of the army (*see* Massachusetts).

Virginia's second governor, Thomas Jefferson, wrote the Declaration of Independence for the colonies. George Mason drafted the Declaration of Rights—the model for the Bill of Rights that was later added to the United States Constitution. "Light Horse Harry" Lee, Daniel Morgan, John Paul Jones, George Rogers Clark, and George Washington all took leading parts in fierce battles that led to victory. Virginia became the tenth state on June 25, 1788. The state gave up its claims to the vast region west of the mountains and north of the Ohio River.

Upon the outbreak of the Civil War in 1861, Virginia decided upon secession. Again the state provided great leaders in such men as Robert E. Lee, "Stonewall" Jackson, J. E. B. Stuart, and Joseph E. Johnston. The critical battles of the war were fought in Virginia, and the capture of Richmond (the Confederate capital from April 1861) was the primary object of the boldest strikes made during the war by Union commanders. Virginia was the battlefield upon which the South's greatest victories were won. But it was also at Appomattox, Virginia that General Lee was forced to surrender, ending one of the bloodiest wars in the history of the world up to that time.

Government. In 1776, the House of Burgesses was converted into the General Assembly of two houses, the senate, presently made up of 40 members, and the house of delegates, now having 100 members. The governor and lieutenant-governor are elected for four years. The state sends two senators and 10 representatives to the U.S. Congress. As of 1963, the state was divided into 96 counties and 35 independent cities which have the status of counties. In 1970 there were 29 cities and towns having a population of more than ten thousand.

Economy. Coal is the most important mineral, including high-grade coking coal. Lead, stone, gypsum, manganese, lime, and titanium are also produced. The state has diversified agriculture, but livestock-raising and tobacco-growing are leading activities. Tobacco is the leading cash crop today, just as it was in colonial times.

WASHINGTON

The early history of Washington is that of the Oregon country (*see* Oregon). American interests grew strong and came in conflict with those of the British after the overland expedition of Lewis and Clark (1804–1806). An agreement between England and the United States in 1818 allowed both nations to occupy the region. The United States advanced its claim to the Columbia River basin during the presidential campaign of James K. Polk in 1844. The dispute was arbitrated in 1846 and a treaty was signed, establishing the boundary of Oregon on the forty-ninth parallel of latitude, which is the present international boundary. Later, a dispute over the San Juan Islands was also arbitrated and settled.

In 1848, Oregon Territory was formed, and it included the present state of Washington. In 1853, Washington Territory was separated and organized. Agitation for statehood began in 1876 and ended when Washington was admitted to the Union as the forty-second state on November 11, 1889.

Washington—Olympic National Park

Government. The legislature consists of a senate of 49 members and a house of representatives of 99 members. The governor and lieutenant-governor are elected for four-year terms. Washington sends two senators and seven representatives to the U.S. Congress. The state is divided into 39 counties, and in 1970, there were 39 cities and towns with a population of more than ten thousand. The city of Seattle, largest in the state, ranks twenty-second in the nation.

Economy. Because the state has the greatest potential power supplies, the aluminum industry was attracted there. Vast forests of principally hemlock, fir, and pine make the forestry industries among the largest in the nation. The manufacture of wood products, including paper and pulp, is the largest single industry in Washington, and the state ranks third in this field. Agriculture is also a major industry, with much of it practiced on irrigated lands. Western Washington has large dairy farms and berry fields, while in the east the growing of wheat and ranching are the chief agricultural industries. Washington leads all states in the production of apples, hops, mint; ranks second in Bartlett pears, filberts, apricots; fourth in winter wheat.

WEST VIRGINIA

West Virginia is the youngest state east of the Mississippi River. It was originally a part of Virginia. But when that state seceded from the Union in 1861, the western counties (most of the present state of West Virginia) seceded from Virginia. By a proclamation of President Lincoln on June 20, 1863, these counties were admitted to the Union as the thirty-fifth state.

West Virginia—Capitol Building, Charleston

Government. West Virginia is governed by a senate with 34 members and a house of delegates with 100 members. The state sends two senators and four representatives to the U.S. Congress and has six electoral votes in federal elections. There is no lieutenant-governor. The major unit of local government is the county. West Virginia is divided into 55 counties.

Economy. Coal underlies nearly two-thirds of the state. West Virginia has led the nation in the mining of coal since 1936. Over a hundred million tons are mined every year, accounting for 80 percent of the state's total mineral production. Other minerals produced include petroleum, natural gas, salt, and limestone.

Although there are about seven million acres of farm land, only about one million acres are in crops. Sixty-five percent of the state is in woodlands, including nearly a million acres of national forests. The chief crops grown in West Virginia include tobacco, fruit, wheat, corn, oats, and potatoes. The eastern panhandle is a noted apple-growing region.

Manufacturing in West Virginia is centered in the valley of the Kanawha River and along the Ohio River. The Kanawha Valley is one of the major chemical-producing areas of the United States.

WISCONSIN

Wisconsin was explored by the French from bases in Canada. Jean Nicolet visited eastern Wisconsin in 1534. A fuller exploration was conducted by the traders Radisson and Groseilliers (1658–1659). Father Allouez established a mission near the present Green Bay in 1665. The first permanent settlement was made near the same place in 1670. The entire state was a part of New France until the French defeat in 1763. The sympathies of the early settlers were generally with the English, and they retained this allegiance during the Revolutionary War.

The United States acquired Wisconsin as a result of the Treaty of Paris in 1783, ending the war and establishing American independence. The region was included in the Ordinance of 1787, establishing the Northwest Territory. When Indiana

Territory was separated from this in 1800, Wisconsin was included in Indiana. In 1805, it became a part of Michigan Territory, and from 1808 until 1818 it was a part of Illinois Territory. Wisconsin was again transferred to Michigan Territory after Illinois became a state in 1818, and there it remained until 1836. In that year Wisconsin Territory was organized, thus ending a complicated series of changes in government. At that time Wisconsin Territory included parts of Minnesota, Iowa, and the Dakotas. Iowa was separated in 1838. On May 29, 1848, Wisconsin became the thirtieth state and was reduced to its present boundaries.

Government. The law-making body is called the Legislature, as in most states, and consists of a senate of 32 members and an assembly of 100 members. The governor and lieutenant-governor are elected for four years. The state sends two senators and nine representatives to the U.S. Congress. Wisconsin is divided into 72 counties (Menominee became the seventy-second county in 1961). In 1970 there were 52 cities and towns with a population of more than ten thousand. Milwaukee, the state's largest city, ranks twelfth in the nation.

Economy. Wisconsin is famous for its dairy products, but agriculture has recently been surpassed in importance by the rising industrial complexes centering around Milwaukee and the southeast. Although the state has little coal, about 85 percent of the nation's iron ore is within easy reach in the Greak Lakes area and the lakes themselves form a major transportation route for incoming raw materials and outgoing finished products. The fabrication of iron and steel products is the largest industry. Textiles, footwear, furniture, chemicals, and shipbuilding are other major manufactures. In agriculture, the dairying industry is concentrated in the southern counties. In 1970 the state ranked first in milk and cheese and second in creamery butter. The principal crops are those used in feeding cattle, such as corn, oats, and hay. The best cash crop is potatoes, grown mainly in northern Wisconsin.

Wisconsin—Ancient quartzite cliffs overlooking Devils Lake, Baraboo

WYOMING

Chevalier de la Verendrye, a member of a remarkable family of Canadian explorers passed through the Wyoming Wind River region in 1743–1744. Wilson Hunt explored the Powder River on his way to Oregon in 1811. John Colter spent the winter of 1806–1807 in Wyoming, and discovered the Yellowstone region. In 1842 John C. Fremont ascended Fremont Peak in Wind River Range, accompanied by Kit Carson. The first white settlement in Wyoming was made in 1834 at Fort William (later changed to Fort Laramie) by William Sublette and Robert Campbell. This post was sold to the United States government in 1849. Part of the Mormon migration to Utah (*see* Utah) stopped in Wyoming and settled at Fort Bridger in 1853.

Wyoming came to the United States in three sections. The greater part was included in the Louisiana Purchase of 1803. More was added by the settlement of the Oregon dispute in 1846, and Mexico ceded the remainder in 1848 as a result of the Treaty of Guadalupe Hidalgo.

The discovery of gold in 1867 and the completion of the Union Pacific Railroad in Wyoming in 1868 caused a wave of settlement. The Territory of Wyoming was organized in 1868 from parts of Utah, the Dakota Territory, and Idaho Territory. The great natural wonders of the Yellowstone region were set aside as a national park in 1872 (the oldest national nature park). Wyoming became the forty-fourth state on July 10, 1890.

Government. The legislature consists of a senate of 30 members and a house of representatives of 61 members. The governor is elected for a four-year term. There is no office of lieutenant-governor in Wyoming. The Territory of Wyoming was the first government under the American flag to guarantee equal suffrage to women (in 1869). The state sends two senators and one representative to the U.S. Congress. Wyoming is divided into 23 counties, and in 1970 there were five cities with a population of more than ten thousand.

Economy. Many of the soils of the state are very fertile and produce well when water is provided. About two million acres of land are already under irrigation, and more is planned to be placed under irrigation. Wyoming's agriculture revolves around the cattle industry and sheep-raising. The chief mineral produced is oil. Natural gas is also found in large quantities and uranium has recently become a major mineral product.

Wyoming—Thousands of Oregon Trail travelers carved their names on Register Cliff near Guernsey (Inset shows actual names)

Districts, Commonwealths, Possessions, and Trust Areas Of the United States

Besides the District of Columbia and the Commonwealth of Puerto Rico, this section includes lands and peoples associated with the United States in the form of possessions, territories, or trust areas. At some time in the future these areas may become one of the United States.

DISTRICT OF COLUMBIA

The District of Columbia is the seat of government and the location of the federal capital of the United States. It is limited to the city of Washington.

Rivalry developed between northern and southern congressmen over the location of the nation's capital. The institution of slavery was one issue in the arguments. Finally, in 1790, Alexander Hamilton and Thomas Jefferson worked out a compromise.

The District of Columbia was organized from lands ceded by Maryland and Virginia. The District then was a perfect square, measuring ten miles along each of the four sides. However, in 1846 the part ceded originally by Virginia and lying across the south bank of the Potomac River was returned to Virginia, and now forms Arlington County of that State.

In 1791, President Washington chose the exact site for the Capitol Building and the city of Washington. He then commissioned Pierre L'Enfant, a French engineer, to design a layout for the city of Washington. L'Enfant's ideas for wide avenues and streets were considered wasteful by many, but Washington approved the plans himself and laid the cornerstone of the Capitol Building on September 18, 1793. President John Adams, Washington's successor, was the first President to serve the nation from the new capital. He moved from Philadelphia to Washington on June 3, 1800. The city of Washington was incorporated in 1802.

The original Capitol Building was burned (along with the White House) by the British during the War of 1812. Both the present White House and Capitol Building date from 1818. The Capitol was not actually completed until 1863.

The White House is the official residence of the President. The cornerstone of the original building was laid by Washington on October 13, 1792. Extensive alterations have been made, in 1902–1903 under President Theodore Roosevelt and in 1948–1952 under President Truman. A major redecorating project was carried out under Jacqueline Kennedy in 1963.

The Capitol is one of the chief attractions of the District of Columbia. It crowns the summit of Capitol Hill, 88 feet above the level of the Potomac River. It covers four acres and its height is 287 feet, 5.5 inches. The original plan was drawn by Dr. William Thornton of the Virgin Islands. Benjamin Latrobe and Charles Bulfinch had charge of repair and reconstruction after the British burning of the building in 1814. The present Senate and House wings were added in 1851. The bronze statue of Freedom on top of the great dome is 19.5 feet tall, and weighs 15,000 pounds. The rotunda is 180 feet high and has a diameter of 97 feet.

Government. The city of Washington (District of Columbia) is governed by a mayor, an assistant, and a 13-member city council elected by the district's voters. The district has one Delegate to the House who may vote in committees but not on the floor. Amendment Twenty-three to the Constitution of the United States gave the citizens of the District the right to vote in national elections. This amendment was ratified by the requisite number of states and became law in 1961.

Buildings and Monuments. The Lincoln Memorial in West Potomac Park was dedicated in 1922. Its famous statue of President Lincoln was the work of Daniel Chester French. The memorial is of Colorado-Yule marble. The wells are enclosed by a colonnade of 38 Doric columns. Inside are three memorials—a seated figure of Lincoln, a passage from Lincoln's Second Inaugural Address, and his Gettysburg Address.

The Thomas Jefferson Memorial was dedicated in 1943. Its central circular chamber is occupied by a huge statue of Jefferson. The building incorporates pantheonic design of Vermont and Georgia marble.

The Washington National Monument is an obelisk of white marble 555.5 feet tall. It was

District of Columbia—Capitol Building, Washington, D.C.

begun in 1848 and completed in 1885. An elevator takes visitors to the 500-foot level.

Other famous buildings and monuments in the District include the National Archives, Smithsonian Institution, the National Geographic Society, the Folger Shakespeare Library, and the National Gallery of Art. In nearby Arlington are the Pentagon, the Iwo Jima Memorial, the Tomb of the Unknown Soldier, and the Custis-Lee Mansion (the last two are in Arlington National Cemetery).

Economy. Most of the people either work for the federal Government or are in wholesale and retail businesses. There are six hundred manufacturing firms in the District. Printing and publishing is the largest single industry.

Outlying U.S. Areas

AMERICAN SAMOA

These comprise the seven eastern islands of the Samoa group in the South Pacific, 2,300 miles southwest of Hawaii. They became a United States territory in 1900. The larger islands of the Samoan group (Western Samoa) form an independent nation. Administered by the Interior Department, American Samoa elects its own governor, bicameral legislature and a non-voting delegate to Congress. Chief port is Pago Pago (pronounced "Pango Pango") but the seat of government is the nearby town of Fagatogo on the Island of Tutuila.

The islands are of volcanic origin; they have a mild climate with a distinct dry season, and are heavily forested. The people are Polynesians. The chief exports are canned fish, *copra* (dried coconut), cocoa, and handicrafts.

COMMONWEALTH OF PUERTO RICO

(Estado Libre Asociado de Puerto Rico)

The spelling *Porto Rico* is today unacceptable, having been replaced by *Puerto Rico* by an Act of Congress in 1932. Columbus discovered Puerto Rico in 1493. The famous Ponce de León (*see* Florida) founded San Juan in either 1506 or 1508. The chief purpose was to protect Mona Passage, which at that time was the principal gateway to the Spanish possessions that lay in and along the Caribbean Sea.

San Juan was fortified early because of raids and sieges by English buccaneers. Dutch warships also attacked the town and destroyed a large part of it in 1625. La Fortaleza, El Morro, and San Cristóbal are three fortresses that were built at various times as a means of defense. Puerto Rico remained a Spanish possession until 1898.

The Treaty of Paris in 1898 ended the Spanish-American War and ceded Puerto Rico (along with Guam and the Philippines) to the United States. The troops led by General Nelson Miles had captured the island without serious fighting on July 25, 1898.

The territorial status of Puerto Rico was determined by the Jones Act of 1917; this status was retained until July 25, 1952, when the Commonwealth of Puerto Rico was proclaimed.

Government. The Commonwealth form of government is defined as a "compact," establishing an association between the United States and Puerto Rico. The electorate chooses a delegate (resident commissioner) who sits in the U.S. House of Representatives, but has no vote. The citizens of Puerto Rico are citizens of the United States and subject to most of the same national laws, except the internal revenue statutes. Puerto Rico is not subject to United States taxes, including income tax.

The commonwealth is autonomous in local government. The executive power is vested in a governor, elected for four years. The Council of Secretaries (10 members) advises the governor. The legislature consists of a senate of 27 members and a house of representatives of 51 members. Spanish is the mother language, but English is widely spoken and its use is growing. All instruction below high-school level is given in Spanish.

Economy. Manufacturing is the leading industry. Textiles and apparel, plastics and chemicals, and electronic equipment are among the leading products. The processing of sugar cane is still an important industry but the income from dairy and livestock products is now greater. Tourism is also a large revenue producer.

San Juan is the chief port of entry by both air and water. The city is the governmental, cultural, and industrial heart of Puerto Rico. The chief agricultural crop is sugar cane; coffee, tobacco, and pineapples are next in importance, in that order. Eighty-seven percent of all trade is with the United States mainland.

GUAM

This is the largest and southernmost island of the Marianas group, located south of Japan and east of the Philippines. The island is not a part of the United States Trust Territory of the Pacific Islands, but serves as headquarters for the administration of that territory. One of the largest United States military installations in the Pacific is located on Guam. Under the administration of the Interior Department, Guam elects its own governor, legislature, and one delegate to the United States House of Representatives who can vote in committee but not on the floor. Residents who are American citizens cannot vote in presidential elections. It was discovered by Magellan in 1521 and acquired by the United States in 1898 as a result of the Spanish-American War. It was captured by the Japanese in 1941 but was regained after bitter fighting in 1944. It was then used as a base for the B-29 bomber raids against Japan.

NORTHERN MARIANAS

Extending in a 500-mile arc east of the Philippines and southeast of Japan, the Mariana islands (with the exception of Guam, which is separate) are in process of becoming a United States commonwealth like Puerto Rico. They were formerly part of the United States Trust Territory of the Pacific Islands but they have already elected their own governor and legislature. Military bases on the islands are important for United States defense.

TRUST TERRITORY OF THE PACIFIC ISLANDS

Assigned to United States administration by the United Nations, this group of almost 2,000 islands, 98 of them inhabited, is scattered over three million square miles in the western Pacific Ocean. Often called Micronesia, they consist of the Caroline and Marshall islands, including some noted for World War II battles (Truk, Enewetak, and Kwajalein) and as nuclear testing sites (Bikini). Negotiations are underway for full self-government, with the United States retaining responsibility for defense. When this happens the UN will end the trusteeship of the United States.

UNINCORPORATED TERRITORIES

Howland, Jarvis, and Baker Islands are south of Hawaii, uninhabited since World War II, and are under the Interior Department.

Johnston Atoll, southwest of Hawaii, is operated by the Nuclear Defense Agency. It has a population of 300 on one square mile. An atoll is an island formed by coral deposits.

The Midway islands consist of two coral atolls at the northwestern end of the Hawaiian chain of islands. They served as a "China Clipper" transoceanic flight base before World War II. During the war the Japanese were defeated in the great Battle of Midway in June 1942. Consisting of two square miles, with a population of 2,256, they are administered by the United States Navy.

Wake Island, the scene of a great World War II

battle in 1945, is on a direct route from Hawaii to Hong Kong. With its sister islands of Wilkes and Peale, it is administered by the United States Air Force.

VIRGIN ISLANDS

The United States' group comprise about 50 islands in the West Indies just east of Puerto Rico. They were discovered by Columbus in 1493, and acquired by the United States from Denmark in 1917. The people, mainly of African origin, have been United States citizens since 1927. St. Croix, the largest island, has a jet airport. St. Thomas Island is the site of the capital. Tourism is the most important industry. The making of rum, raising of cattle, and growing of sugar cane are also important. The chief export is rum. A 1972 law allows the people to elect one delegate to the United States House of Representatives who can vote in committee but not on the floor.

CANAL ZONE

The Canal Zone is no longer an outlying territory of the United States. Two treaties signed by the United States and the Republic of Panama in 1978 dealt with the operation and defense of the Canal Zone until 1999 and with the guarantee of its permanent neutrality. At that time Panama assumed general territorial jurisdiction over the former Canal Zone. The United States maintains control over the land, water and installations of the canal itself, including military bases necessary to operate and defend the zone, until December 31, 1999. Until 1990 the canal administrator is a United States citizen with a Panamanian deputy. After that, until 1999, the administrator will be a Panamanian with the deputy being a United States citizen.

The building of the Panama Canal was one of the greatest engineering projects in all history. Plans for a canal across the Isthmus of Panama had been put forward even before Columbus died. Plans were made on several occasions, down to the nineteenth century.

It remained for the French to actually begin the work. Ferdinand de Lesseps headed the construction of the Suez Canal, which opened in 1869. He was a national hero in France because of his success, and when he proposed the Panama project he received enthusiastic support.

The problems in Panama were vastly more difficult to overcome than in the Suez project. The French effort ended after an expenditure of 300 million dollars. The De Lesseps project began on New Year's Day, 1880, and ended in bankruptcy in 1888.

In 1903, the United States signed a treaty with Colombia to acquire land and construction rights in the Isthmus of Panama, which was a part of Colombia to acquire land and construction rights in the Isthmus of Panama, which was a part of Colombia at that time. However, Colombia balked at the terms of the treaty, which led to a local revolution against Colombia. A treaty with an independent Panama was then signed, granting the United States sovereignty over a Canal Zone. In 1921, Colombia accepted 25 million dollars as compensation for the loss of Panama, and established relations with the new republic in 1924 (*see* Panama).

The United States began construction in 1904, using some of the partially excavated route of the French project. However, the cost ran to almost 400 million dollars. The canal was opened to traffic on August 15, 1914.

Statistics for the United States

NAME OF STATE (ZIP CODE ABBREVIATION) NICKNAME	POPULATION RANK IN POP. AREA (SQ. MI.) RANK IN AREA	CAPITAL* LARGEST CITY	BIRD FLOWER	DESCRIPTION OF FLAG
Alabama (AL) Heart of Dixie Cotton State	3,943,000 22 51,609 29	Montgomery* 178,157 Birmingham 284,413	Yellowhammer Camellia	A crimson St. Andrew's cross on a square white field
Alaska (AK) No official nickname	438,000 50 586,412 1	Juneau* 19,528 Anchorage 173,017	Willow ptarmigan Forget-me-not	A deep blue field with seven gold stars in the shape of the Big Dipper constellation at the left and a single gold star representing Polaris in the upper right-hand corner.
Arizona (AZ) Grand Canyon State	2,860,000 29 113,909 6	Phoenix* 764,911	Cactus wren The blossom of the saguaro cactus	The lower half is a blue field; the upper half is composed of red and yellow rays, emanating from a large, copper-colored five-pointed star superimposed on the center of the flag.
Arkansas (AR) Land of Opportunity	2,291,000 33 53,104 27	Little Rock* 158,461	Mockingbird Apple blossom	A white diamond outlined in blue centered on a red field; twenty-five white stars arranged around the blue border of the diamond indicate Arkansas' position as the twenty-fifth state to enter the Union; within the white diamond are four large blue stars and the word "Arkansas"; three of these stars, placed below "Arkansas," signify the three nations of Spain, France, and the United States, to which Arkansas successively belonged; the star above "Arkansas" commemorates the Confederacy, and the diamond itself signifies that Arkansas is the only diamond-producing state in the Union.
California (CA) Golden State	24,724,000 1 158,693 3	Sacramento* 275,741 Los Angeles 2,966,763	California valley quail Golden poppy	A California grizzly bear set in the center of a white field; at the top left is a red star; below the bear the words "California Republic" appear above a broad red stripe. Known as the Bear Flag.
Colorado (CO) Centennial State	3,045,000 27 104,247 8	Denver* 491,396	Lark bunting White and lavender Rocky Mountain columbine	Three equal stripes, two of which are blue, representing the sky, and one white, representing snow-capped mountains; on the left is a red "C" encircling a disk of yellow.
Connecticut (CT) Constitution State Nutmeg State	3,153,000 26 5,009 48	Hartford* 136,392 Bridgeport 142,546	Robin Mountain laurel	A blue background with a white shield bearing the state seal in the center; beneath the shield is the state motto; the flag is bordered with a gold fringe.
Delaware (DE) First State Diamond State	602,000 47 2,057 49	Dover* 23,512 Wilmington 70,195	Blue hen chicken Peach blossom	A buff-colored diamond bearing the state seal is placed in the center of a blue field; below the diamond are the words "December 7, 1787," the date when Delaware ratified the Constitution of the United States.
Florida (FL) Sunshine State	10,416,000 7 58,560 22	Tallahassee* 81,548 Jacksonville 540,898	Mockingbird Orange blossom	The state seal lies in the center of a white field, crossed by diagonal red bars, which stand for the bars of the Confederate flag.
Georgia (GA) Empire State of the South Peach State	5,639,000 12 58,876 21	Atlanta* 425,022	Brown thrasher Cherokee rose	A combination of an earlier flag with a field of blue containing the state seal, and the battle flag of the Confederacy with its field of red containing crossed blue bars and thirteen white stars.
Hawaii (HI) The Aloha State	994,000 39 6,450 47	Honolulu* 365,048	Nene (Hawaiian goose) Hibiscus	Eight horizontal stripes which, from the top, are alternately white, red, and blue; in the upper left-hand corner is the British Union Jack.
Idaho (ID) Gem State	965,000 40 83,557 13	Boise* 102,451	Mountain bluebird Syringa	A dark-blue field bordered by a gold fringe; in the center is the state seal; below this a red band contains the words "State of Idaho" in gold.
Illinois (IL) The Inland Empire	11,448,000 5 56,400 24	Springfield* 99,637 Chicago 3,005,072	Cardinal Violet	In the center of a white field fringed in gold is a symbol based on the state seal.
Indiana (IN) Hoosier State	5,471,000 14 36,291 38	Indianapolis* 700,807	Cardinal Peony	A flaming torch in gold against a blue field surrounded by a circle of thirteen stars; below is a semicircle of five stars; above the torch is a larger star and the word "Indiana."

NAME OF STATE (ZIP CODE ABBREVIATION) NICKNAME	POPULATION RANK IN POP. AREA (SQ. MI.) RANK IN AREA	CAPITAL* LARGEST CITY	BIRD FLOWER	DESCRIPTION OF FLAG
Iowa (IA) Hawkeye State	2,905,000 28 56,290 25	Des Moines* 191,003	Eastern goldfinch Wild rose	A white field bordered on the staff end by a blue band and on the opposite end by a red band; centered in the white field is an eagle bearing the state motto.
Kansas (KS) Sunflower State	2,408,000 32 82,264 14	Topeka* 115,266 Wichita 279,272	Western meadowlark Sunflower	The flag has a wreath above the seal to represent the Louisiana Purchase. The yellow sunflower stands for the state's prairies and for the golden future.
Kentucky (KY) Bluegrass State	3,667,000 23 40,395 37	Frankfort* 25,973 Louisville 298,451	Cardinal Goldenrod	The center of the state seal on a field of blue; the words "Commonwealth of Kentucky" appear in gold around the top half of the seal, and a garland of goldenrod is below the seal; the flag is fringed in gold.
Louisiana (LA) Pelican State	4,362,000 18 48,523 31	Baton Rouge* 219,486 New Orleans 557,482	Brown pelican Magnolia	In the center of a blue field is a white pelican feeding its young; beneath the pelican is a white ribbon inscribed in blue with the state motto.
Maine (ME) Pine Tree State	1,133,000 38 32,215 39	Augusta* 21,819 Portland 61,572	Chick-a-dee Pine cone and tassel	The state seal lies in the center of a blue field.
Maryland (MD) Old Line State Free State	4,265,000 19 10,577 42	Annapolis* 31,740 Baltimore 786,775	Baltimore oriole Black-eyed Susan	Bears the coat of arms of the Calvert and Crossland families, Crossland being the maiden name of the wife of the first Lord Baltimore. The Maryland flag is the only state flag embodying recognized armorial bearings.
Massachusetts (MA) Bay State Old Colony	5,781,000 11 8,257 45	Boston* 562,994	Chick-a-dee Mayflower (ground laurel or trailing arbutus)	One side bears the state coat of arms on a white field; the reverse has a white field in the center of which is a blue shield bearing a green pine tree.
Michigan (MI) Great Lake State Wolverine State	9,109,000 8 58,216 23	Lansing* 130,414 Detroit 1,203,339	Robin Apple blossom	The symbols of the state seal appear on a dark-blue field.
Minnesota (MN) North Star State Gopher State	4,133,000 21 84,068 12	St. Paul* 270,230 Minneapolis 370,951	Loon Pink and white lady's-slipper	The state seal is placed in the center of a blue field.
Mississippi (MS) Magnolia State	2,551,000 31 47,716 32	Jackson* 202,895	Mockingbird Magnolia	In the upper left-hand corner is a Union Jack with a ground of red and saltier of blue bearing thirteen white stars; the remainder of the flag is divided into three horizontal bars of equal width, the upper blue, the center white, and the lower red.
Missouri (MO) Show Me State	4,951,000 15 69,686 19	Jefferson City* 33,619 St. Louis 453,085	Bluebird Hawthorn	Three horizontal bands of equal width, the top one of red, the center one of white, and the bottom one of blue; in the middle is the state seal surrounded by a band of blue bearing twenty-four white stars.
Montana (MT) Treasure State	801,000 44 147,138 4	Helena* 23,938 Billings 66,798	Western meadowlark Bitterroot	The state seal is centered on a bright blue field; gold fringe borders two upper and lower edges.
Nebraska (NE) Cornhusker State	1,586,000 35 77,227 15	Lincoln* 171,932 Omaha 311,681	Western meadowlark Goldenrod	The state seal is gold and silver against a blue field.
Nevada (NV) Sagebrush State Battle Born State	881,000 43 110,540 7	Carson City* 32,022 Las Vegas 164,674	No official state bird; however, the mountain bluebird is used. No official flower; however, the sagebrush is sometimes used.	Two sprays of green sagebrush with stems crossed at the bottom to form a half-wreath in the upper left-hand corner of a field of cobalt blue; above, and completing the circle, is a yellow scroll bearing the words "Battle Born"; centered in the circle is a five-pointed star surrounded by the word "Nevada."

NAME OF STATE (ZIP CODE ABBREVIATION) NICKNAME	POPULATION RANK IN POP. AREA (SQ. MI.) RANK IN AREA	CAPITAL* LARGEST CITY	BIRD FLOWER	DESCRIPTION OF FLAG
New Hampshire (NH) Granite State	951,000 42 9,304 44	Concord* 30,400 Manchester 90,936	Purple finch Purple lilac	A blue field on which is centered the state seal surrounded by laurel leaves interspersed with nine stars.
New Jersey (NJ) Garden State	7,438,000 9 7,836 46	Trenton* 92,124 Newark 329,248	Eastern goldfinch Purple violet	The state seal is centered on a buff-colored field.
New Mexico (NM) Land of Enchantment	1,359,000 37 121,666 5	Santa Fe* 48,899 Albuquerque 331,767	Roadrunner Yucca flower	A field of gold with the ancient Zia Sun symbol in red in the center.
New York (NY) Empire State	17,659,000 2 49,576 30	Albany* 101,727 New York 7,071,030	Bluebird (unofficial) Rose	The state seal lies in the center of a dark-blue field.
North Carolina (NC) Tar Heel State Old North State	6,019,000 10 52,586 28	Raleigh* 149,771 Charlotte 314,447	Cardinal Dogwood	At the right are two horizontal stripes, one red and one white; on the left is a vertical blue stripe; at the top of the vertical stripe is a gold scroll inscribed with the date "May 20 1775" commemorating the Mecklenburg Declaration of Independence; at the bottom, in another golden scroll is the date "April 12th 1776," commemorating the Halifax Resolves, which instructed North Carolina's delegates to the Continental Congress to vote for independence; in the center, between these two scrolls, are the initials "N" and "C" separated by a white star.
North Dakota (ND) Sioux State Flickertail State	670,000 46 70,665 17	Bismarck* 44,485 Fargo 61,308	Western meadowlark Wild prairie rose	On a field of blue a bald eagle with widespread wings holds a group of arrows in its left claw and an olive branch in its right claw; in its beak is a scroll that reads "*E Pluribus Unum*", beneath the eagle on a red scroll are the words, "North Dakota"; above the eagle is a double semicircle of stars representing the original thirteen states.
Ohio (OH) Buckeye State	10,791,000 6 41,222 35	Columbus* 564,871 Cleveland 573,822	Cardinal Scarlet carnation	A swallow-tailed pennant bearing three red and two white horizontal stripes; on the left is a blue union, on which seventeen stars are disposed about a white "O" centered on red.
Oklahoma (OK) Sooner State	3,177,000 25 69,919 18	Oklahoma City* 403,213	Scissor-tailed flycatcher Mistletoe	In the center of a blue field is the buckskin shield of an Osage Indiana warrior; the shield is decorated with six painted crosses; seven eagle feathers form a fringe at the bottom; a peace pipe crossed by an olive branch appears on the face of the shield.
Oregon (OR) Beaver State	2,649,000 30 96,981 10	Salem* 89,233 Portland 366,383	Western meadowlark Oregon grape	A navy blue field bearing the shield of the state seal in gold, supported by thirty-three gold stars and topped by the words "State of Oregon"; the reverse shows a gold beaver.
Pennsylvania (PA) Keystone State	11,865,000 4 45,333 33	Harrisburg* 53,264 Philadelphia 1,688,210	Ruffed grouse Mountain laurel	The state shield, with eagle and wreath, supported by two harnessed draft horses; streamers below the state motto; the field is dark blue.
Rhode Island (RI) Little Rhody Ocean State	958,000 41 1,214 50	Providence* 156,804	Rhode Island Red Violet (unofficial)	In the center of a white field is a gold anchor; beneath the anchor on a blue ribbon is the motto "Hope"; all this is surrounded by a circle of thirteen gold stars; the flag is edged with a yellow fringe.
South Carolina (SC) Palmetto State	3,203,000 24 31,055 40	Columbia* 99,296	Carolina wren Carolina jessamine	A field of blue with a white palmetto tree in the center and a white crescent in the upper corner near the staff.
South Dakota (SD) Coyote State Sunshine State	691,000 45 77,047 16	Pierre* 11,973 Sioux Falls 81,343	Ring-necked pheasant Pasqueflower	On a field of blue is a blazing sun surrounded by the words "South Dakota, The Sunshine State"; on the reverse is the state seal.
Tennessee (TN) Volunteer State	4,651,000 17 42,244 34	Nashville* 455,651 Memphis 646,356	Mockingbird Iris	In the center of a crimson field is a circle of blue with a rim of white; in the center of the circle are three white stars; on the edge are two vertical bars—one blue and one white.

NAME OF STATE (ZIP CODE ABBREVIATION) NICKNAME	POPULATION RANK IN POP. AREA (SQ. MI.) RANK IN AREA	CAPITAL* LARGEST CITY	BIRD FLOWER	DESCRIPTION OF FLAG
Texas (TX) Lone Star State	15,280,000 3 267,338 2	Austin* 345,496 Houston 1,594,086	Mockingbird Bluebonnet	A blue vertical stripe next to the staff and two horizontal stripes, the upper white and the lower red; a white star is in the center of the blue stripe.
Utah (UT) Beehive State	1,554,000 36 84,916 11	Salt Lake City* 163,033	Sea gull Sego lily	Within a gold circle in the center of a blue field is the state seal; the flag is fringed in gold.
Vermont (VT) Green Mountain State	516,000 48 9,609 43	Montpelier* 8,241 Burlington 37,712	Hermit thrush Red clover	The state coat of arms against a field of blue; the coat of arms contains a shield bearing a landscape scene with pine tree, cow, and sheaves of grain; a buck's head as the crest; a badge of crossed pine branches; and a red scroll bearing the state motto and the word "Vermont."
Virginia (VA) Old Dominion	5,491,000 13 40,817 36	Richmond* 219,214 Norfolk 266,979	Cardinal American dogwood	The state seal in the center of a deep blue field; a white fringe borders the edge farthest from the flagstaff.
Washington (WA) Evergreen State	4,245,000 20 68,192 20	Olympia* 27,447 Seattle 493,846	Willow goldfinch Rhododendron	A dark green field with the state seal in the center.
West Virginia (WV) Mountain State	1,948,000 34 24,181 41	Charleston* 63,963	Cardinal Rhododendron maximum (big laurel)	The state coat of arms (the central scene from the state seal) in a field of white bordered by a strip of blue; above the coat of arms is a ribbon bearing the words "State of West Virginia" and below is a wreath of rhododendron maximum.
Wisconsin (WI) Badger State	4,765,000 16 56,154 26	Madison* 170,616 Milwaukee 636,212	Robin Wood violet	The Wisconsin coat of arms is centered on a field of dark blue, the edges of which are trimmed with a knotted fringe of yellow silk.
Wyoming (WY) Equality State	502,000 49 97,914 9	Cheyenne* 47,283 Casper 51,016	Meadowlark Indian paintbrush	A white silhouetted buffalo in the center of the blue field with a border of white and an outer border of red; the state seal appears on the buffalo's side.
District of Columbia (DC)	631,000 67			

Statistics for Outlying United States' Areas

NAME OF OUTLYING AREA ZIP CODE ABBREVIATION	POPULATION	CAPITAL* LARGEST CITY	AREA (SQ. MI.)
American Samoa (AS)	32,297	Fagatogo* Island of Tutuila	76
Commonwealth of Puerto Rico (PR) (Estado Libre Asociado de Puerto Rico)	3,196,520	San Juan* 434,849	3,435
Guam (GU)	106,000	Agana* 4,180 Dededo 23,644	209
Johnston Atoll	300	None	1
Midway Islands	2,256	None	2
Northern Mariana Islands (CM)	16,758	None	181.9
Trust Territory of Pacific Islands (TT)	116,149	None	533
Virgin Islands (VI) (St John, St. Croix, St. Thomas)	96,569	Charlotte Amalie* on St. Thomas 11,671	133
Wake Island	300	None	3

Countries of the World

This section contains a brief history of each country of the world. Statistics will be found in the tables at the end of the section.

AFGHANISTAN

The history of Afghanistan is that of a succession of foreign conquests, by the Persians under Cyrus the Great in 516 B.C., and by Alexander the Great around 334 B.C. In the tenth century, the Turks, who brought Islamic culture with them, gained control. The Mongol hordes of Genghis Khan invaded and remained in power for two centuries. Later, another Mongol, Tamerlane, seized control.

In the seventeenth century, Afghans began a series of uprisings against foreign domination, and for centuries there was unrest in the country. An Anglo-Indian army invaded Afghanistan, precipitating the First Afghan War, lasting from 1838 to 1842, in which the Afghans were defeated. The British re-invaded the country in the Second Afghan War, in which the Afghans were again defeated. A new ruler stabilized the country, concluded treaties of demarcation with India and Russia, and curbed the power of tribal chiefs.

In 1919, while Britain was having difficulties with the liberation movement in India, Afghanistan seized the opportunity to declare war on England. Britain soon recognized Afghan independence. The country remained neutral in both world wars, and was admitted to the United Nations on November 19, 1946.

In December 1979 the U.S.S.R. invaded the country but found much guerrilla resistance. Fighting continued in 1984.

ALBANIA

Albania occupies the region that the classical Greeks called Illyria. The Greeks were never able to conquer all of Illyria, but the Romans succeeded in doing so in the second century A.D. In later centuries, their control was never firmly established. The region of present Albania fell under the control of successive invaders, including Byzantines, Bulgars, Normans, Venetians, Neapolitans, and finally the Turks. Turkish control lasted from 1479 until 1912.

Independence movements began in 1878 and ended in 1912 when, after the First Balkan War, Albania was established as a nation. After World War I, the country gradually became an Italian protectorate. A threat to partition Albania resulted in the establishment of a republic under Ahmed Zog, who proclaimed himself king in 1928. In 1939 Italy annexed Albania.

During World War II, Albania became the base for an Italian invasion of Greece. Communist-led guerrillas under Enver Hoxha freed Albania with Allied assistance. In 1946 the country was declared a People's Republic. Relations with Yugoslavia became strained and were broken in 1948.

Albania's relations with the Soviet Union deteriorated until they were broken completely in 1961. Albania was admitted to the United Nations on December 14, 1955. In 1971, the country renewed diplomatic ties with Greece and Yugoslavia.

ALGERIA

The coast of North Africa was first colonized in historic times by Phoenicians from the Mediterranean coast of Asia. Carthage, one of the Phoenician cities, controlled the entire coast until the city's destruction by Rome in 146 B.C. Romans called the region Numidia. Roman culture and economic activity progressed in Numidia until it became a wealthy cultural center of the Roman world. Invasions by Vandals and revolts by the native inhabitants (Berbers) brought an end to Roman rule in the fifth century.

The Arab conquest took place in A.D. 637, and successive waves of Arabs swept over Algeria until after the eleventh century. The Berbers gradually accepted Islam but retained their own customs and language. Spain occupied parts of the coast in the sixteenth century but a Turkish pirate named Horuk Barbarossa expelled the Spaniards. Thereafter, piracy developed along the "Barbary Coast," as the region was called after the sixteenth century. Turkish control of the region was carried out

Algeria—The Harbor, Algiers

by a series of officials known according to their rank as beylerbeys, pashas, aghas, and deys. In the seventeenth century, the city of Algiers became the chief center of piracy and the strongest state of the Barbary Coast.

Algiers began to defy even the Turkish (Ottoman) emperors in the eighteenth century and piracy thrived as never before. Early in the nineteenth century a United States fleet, and later a combined Dutch and British fleet, smashed the major strongholds along the Barbary Coast. In 1830 France invaded Algeria and took over complete control. The name Al-Jazair, the Arabic name, was changed to Algérie in French and after 1838 this became the general name for the region.

Throughout the nineteenth century movements for either independence or greater autonomy resulted in several revolts against the French. It was not until after World War II that a strong movement for independence or assimilation developed. Guerrilla warfare, initiated by an organization known as Front de Libération Nationale (FLN), eventually caused the fall of the Fourth French Republic. General Charles de Gaulle was called in to lead the Fifth Republic and to solve the Algerian crisis. He offered Algeria self-determination and a cease-fire agreement was signed in 1962.

In the meantime, many French settlers in Algeria revolted against France. The French Army in Algeria waged a heavy campaign against the rightist group among the settlers. On April 8, 1962, Algeria gained its independence, thus ending 132 years of French rule. It was admitted to the United Nations in October of the same year. Algeria's socialist government is trying to relieve the nation's deep poverty, but with only partial success.

ANDORRA

Andorra is a co-principality, and the official long form of the name is *Valls d'Andorra* ("Valleys of Andorra" in the Catalan language). The country dates from the time of Charlemagne. The counts of Foix of France and the Spanish Bishop of Urgel were the original inheritors of the principality. When Henry II of Navarre ascended the French throne, he was established along with the Bishop of Urgel as co-prince of Andorra. It has remained a co-principality to this day, except for a brief interlude of occupation by the French (1793–1806). The president of France is now co-prince with the Bishop of Urgel.

The people are mainly pastoral, but iron and lead are mined. Smuggling activities have long been associated with Andorra.

ANGOLA

The Portuguese colonized Angola in 1574. Luanda, the present capital, was founded in 1575. The Portuguese kept full possession of the huge region except for a brief occupation by the Dutch from 1641 to 1648.

Pro-independence forces have been active in Angola since World War II. In 1962 the United Nations General Assembly voted to condemn Portugal's "colonial war" against the people of Angola. In 1974 a revolution in Portugal resulted in that country's withdrawal from its African colonies. Angola was declared independent on November 11, 1975. The three main Angolan groups which had fought against the Portuguese could not agree to form a coalition government, and civil war broke out. Financial aid from Russia and about fifteen thousand Cuban troops helped the Popular Movement win most of the country in May 1977. Russian influence continued strong in 1984.

ARGENTINA

The name *Argentina* is derived from the Latin word for silver. The Spanish explorers referred to the region as *Plata,* or "silver," because they saw Indians using silver and assumed that there were rich mines in the region.

Juan Diaz de Solis was the first European to visit what is now Argentina. The first permanent settlement was made in 1553 at Santiago del Estero by colonists from Chile. Buenos Aires was founded in 1536, but was wiped out by the Indians and was reestablished in 1580.

The early settlements were ruled from Bolivia and Peru. It was not until 1776 that the huge region achieved the status of a viceroyalty in the Spanish Empire. In 1810, revolution broke out against Spanish authority. José de San Martín led the revolt that ended in independence in 1817. Soon after, San Martín collected an army and crossed the Andes to liberate Chile and Peru from Spanish rule.

The country got off to a bad start as a nation. Internal strife, combined with a series of dictatorial regimes, characterized Argentina until 1853. The War of the Triple Alliance occurred between 1856 and 1870. In this war Argentina, Brazil, and Uruguay joined to fight Paraguay.

In 1943, a pro-Axis government installed itself to prevent Argentina from joining the Allies in World War II. Colonel Juan D. Perón became president in 1946 and large-scale reforms were enacted. In 1955 Perón was overthrown by a military junta. He returned in 1973 to be elected president once again, but died 10 months later. His wife Isabel then became president. After several years of terrorism and kidnappings, the country came under the control of another military junta in 1976, when Mrs. Perón was ousted. The 1983 elections brought civilian control.

AUSTRALIA

Many Europeans believed in the existence of a great southern continent long before it was discovered. On old maps this supposed continent was named *Terra Australis Incognita* ("Unknown Southern Land").

In 1606, a Dutch navigator named Jansz sighted what is now Cape York Peninsula. Another Dutch navigator, Dirck Hartog, landed on the west coast in 1616. Dirck Hartog Island is named in his memory. In 1642 the explorer Abel Tasman discovered Tasmania (the Tasman Sea is also named for him) and New Zealand. None of the early explorers and navigators made any attempt to claim the land or even to ascertain how large it was. That was left for the greatest navigator in English history—Captain James Cook (1728–1779).

Captain Cook's first voyage (he made three to the South Pacific region) was made to observe the transit of the planet Venus from below the equator. From Tahiti (where he made the observation) he traveled westward, circled New Zealand,

Australia—Aerial view of Sydney

and then passed up the eastern coast of Australia, mapping it with remarkable precision. Cook took possession of the land for Britain. The first settlement was made in 1788 by Captain Arthur Phillip, at what is now Sydney. He landed a total of 1,030 men, of whom 736 were convicts. (Many were political prisoners with education and talent, whose offenses would today be considered misdemeanors only. All penal settlements were abolished by 1868.)

The interior grasslands beyond the great eastern mountain barrier were discovered in 1813. Settlements increased along the coasts and developed into colonies, some of which became states. The discovery of gold in 1851 made Australia famous in a short time. The population grew quickly and railroads began to open up the interior to farming. Wool and wheat were two of the commodities that helped to develop Australia. A flock of only 105 sheep in 1792 has grown to 150,000,000

The present Australian states were originally British colonies. New South Wales was founded in 1786; Tasmania in 1825; Western Australia in 1829; South Australia in 1834; Victoria in 1851; and Queensland in 1859.

On January 1, 1901, the above colonies were federated under the name Commonwealth of Australia, and the term *colony* was replaced by *state*. Northern Territory was established in 1911, the same year that the Australian Capital Territory was acquired from New South Wales. The capital was moved there in 1927. In recent times a number of dependencies were acquired. The most important of these is the Trust Territory of New Guinea which Australia first occupied in 1914. Australia was confirmed as trustee by the League of Nations in 1921 and by the United Nations in 1946. Australia became a member of the United Nations on November 1, 1945.

During World War II, Australia was threatened with invasion by the Japanese. However, the Japanese were turned back in the Solomon Islands engagements and in the famous naval battles of the Coral Sea. Japan is now Australia's most important trade partner.

AUSTRIA

The Austro-Hungarian monarchy had its origins in the eighth century under Charlemagne. After the Napoleonic Wars, the Congress of Vienna in 1815 left Austria as the dominant power on the continent. In 1919 after World War I, the monarchy was dissolved. There followed years of chaos. The Social Democrats introduced important economic reforms, which were checked by an army-supported dictatorship. After Adolf Hitler came to power in Germany, Austria was occupied by the Nazis and forcibly annexed to Germany in March 1938.

After World War II, the United States and Great Britain declared the Austrians a "liberated" people, although the country was occupied by foreign troops until 1955. Austria was admitted to the United Nations on December 14, 1955. The Socialist Party dominates Austria's government.

BAHAMA ISLANDS

The Bahama Islands, or Bahamas, are the site of Columbus' first landfall in the New World on October 12, 1492. The British have controlled the islands since the seventeenth century. At first they were merely the base for pirates; but under royal governors, appointed after 1717, the pirates were driven out. The islands became a crown colony in 1767, after many Loyalists from the Thirteen Colonies settled there. The slaves were emancipated in 1838.

In 1964, the Bahamas were granted autonomy. The population (mostly black) achieved independence on July 10, 1973, and the Commonwealth of the Bahamas was admitted to the United Nations on September 18, 1973. Banking and tourism are the major business activities.

BAHRAIN

Bahrain is one of the Persian Gulf states. It comprises several islands close to the mainland of Saudi Arabia. It is governed by an amir, whose ancestors concluded a treaty in 1882 giving the United Kingdom control over the nation's foreign affairs. On August 15, 1971, Bahrain declared its independence. On September 21, 1971, it became a member of the United Nations. Its first parliament convened in 1973.

Bahrain is one of the countries that declared an oil embargo against the United States and other nations in 1973–1974.

Austria—Ringstrasse with the Parliament, City Hall, and Votive Church, Vienna

BANGLADESH

Originally a part of British India, the territory of the present republic of Bangladesh became the eastern part of Pakistan in 1947, when the British withdrew from the subcontinent. East Pakistan was separated from West Pakistan by a thousand miles of Indian territory. Although both parts of Pakistan shared a common religion, Islam, East Pakistan, with the larger population and more advanced industry, resented the political control maintained by West Pakistan.

An independence movement, led by Sheikh Mujibur (Mujib) Rahman, culminated in a bloody revolution in December 1971. With the help of the Indian army, East Pakistan defeated the troops of West Pakistan.

The country declared its independence and adopted a parliamentary democracy on December 16, 1972, remaining part of the British Commonwealth, under the name of Bangladesh. It was admitted to the United Nations on September 17, 1974. In January 1975, Mujibur Rahman was made president of a one-party republic. He was executed during a coup on August 15, 1975. A new government came to power in 1977.

Other coups ensued, and in 1982 the Army took over and placed the country under martial law.

BARBADOS

The island of Barbados in the Caribbean Sea was occupied by the British in 1627. It remained a British crown colony for almost 340 years. In 1652, it elected its own assembly. In 1834, the slaves on Barbados were freed.

Barbados achieved autonomy in 1961, and its prime minister, Sir Grantley Adams, a black Barbadian, became prime minister of the short-lived West Indies Federation. On November 30, 1966, Barbados was made independent, and remained within the Commonwealth. The island was admitted to the United Nations on December 9, 1966.

In 1982, President Reagan became the first United States president to visit the island.

BELGIUM

The name of the country is derived from the Belgae, an ancient people who were conquered by the Romans under Julius Caesar in about 50 B.C. The present area of Belgium was a Roman province until overrun by the Germanic Franks in the fifth century A.D.

After the decline of Frankish rule under Charlemagne and his successors, the region became broken up into a series of duchies. Flanders arose as a power in the fourteenth century, united with Burgundy, and as a result of a series of princely marriages became part of the possessions of the House of Hapsburg. Charles of Hapsburg, a native of Ghent, inherited this entire region, known as the Netherlands (or Low Countries), as well as Spain and the Spanish possessions in America. In 1519 he also became Holy Roman Emperor. The

Bahamas—The Sheraton British Colonial Hotel, Nassau

present Belgium, then the southern Netherlands, was then the most prosperous part of Europe. His son, Philip II of Spain, ruled the Netherlands as a Spanish dependency. In 1568, the Netherlands revolted and in 1579 the northern provinces became the Dutch Republic.

The southern provinces remained in Hapsburg control, first ruled by Spain, after 1713 by the Austrian branch of the family. In the French revolutionary and Napoleonic periods, the Austrian Netherlands were annexed by France. From 1815 to 1830 this region was reunited with the provinces to the north as the Kingdom of the Netherlands. The southern provinces, which differed in language, religion, and culture from those in the north, revolted in 1830 and declared their independence. Prince Leopold of Saxe-Coburg became the king of the new Kingdom of Belgium.

Belgium's neutrality was guaranteed by neighboring powers. Despite this, the German armies overran Belgium during World War I. Again, during World War II, Belgium fell under German occupation.

After the war, Belgium became part of an economic union with the Netherlands and Luxembourg called Benelux. Two languages, Flemish and French, are spoken in Belgium, and the country is divided into two linguistic zones.

BELIZE

Formerly known as British Honduras, this British colony in Central America was settled by Jamaicans in the seventeenth century and was made a dependency of Jamaica in 1862. By 1884 it had become a separate colony.

British Honduras was given self-government in 1964. As an indication of its intention to seek independence, the local government changed the name of the colony to Belize, which is also the name of its largest city and former capital. Belmopan is now the capital.

Guatemala, which borders Belize to the west, has long claimed the region. The claim is based on the fact that the region was part of the Spanish captaincy-general of Guatemala when the Central American nations became independent. The inhabitants of British Honduras rejected a proposal made in 1968 by a mediator that they enter into a close relationship with Guatemala. Great Britain sent troops to Belize in 1977 to help keep peace with Guatemala.

The country achieved independence September 21, 1981.

BENIN

Formerly called Dahomey, this West African country is made up of several small native kingdoms, and its boundaries were formed through the political conflicts attending French and English territorial rivalry. However, the Portuguese were the first Europeans to explore and establish trading posts in what is now Benin. They founded Porto-Novo, the present capital. The French gradually pushed the English aside in the region, and the present boundaries took shape at the end of the nineteenth century. The area became a colony and part of the loose federation of French West Africa in 1904. In 1946 it became an overseas territory of France.

On December 4, 1958, Dahomey established its National Constituent Assembly and proclaimed the Republic of Dahomey as a member of the French Community. It became independent on August 1, 1960. It was admitted to the United Nations on September 20, 1960. The country withdrew from the French Community by agreement with France on April 24, 1961. On December 1, 1975, Dahomey changed its name to Benin.

BERMUDA

Bermuda was named for Juan de Bermúdez, who discovered the islands in 1500. Colonization began with the shipwrecked survivors of the *Sea Venture* in 1609. Until 1684 Bermuda was a part of the Virginia Company's grants. Hamilton became the capital in 1815. The United States built air and naval bases there during World War II.

Bermuda is a British dependency with semi-representative government. Its parliament, established in 1620, is the oldest British parliament outside Britain.

BHUTAN

Little is known of Bhutan before the conquest of the region by a Tibetan warlord in the sixteenth century. With Tibet, Bhutan fell under Chinese control in the eighteenth century. The British sought trade privileges in Bhutan, and by 1910 they were able to win control over Bhutan's foreign policy in return for a subsidy. India succeeded Britain in 1947 as protector of Bhutan.

Bhutan became a hereditary monarchy in 1907. The present constitutional monarchy was instituted in 1967. Bhutan was admitted to the United Nations on September 21, 1971.

BOLIVIA

Bolivia was the site of two Indian civilizations of a high level in pre-Columbian times. The first was that of the Tiahuanaco people that arose on the shores of Lake Titicaca in about A.D. 600 and lasted until A.D. 900. These people were noted for their great stone buildings, statues, and elaborate art work in pottery. The second civilization was that of the Quechua Inca Empire that spread down into Bolivia from the north. The empire developed in about A.D. 1200. Under the leaders Pachacuti and his son Topa (1471–1493) the empire expanded to include the present Ecuador, Peru, Bolivia, and part of Chile, plus other areas.

The Incas were noted for great works in stone set without mortar, and so precisely set that the blade of a knife cannot be inserted between stones. They also farmed by irrigation, built great highways with retaining walls, fabricated colorful costumes and had an elaborate government, religion, and social life. The Inca Empire was split and weakened before the coming of the Spanish. It is possible that Pizarro, the Spanish conquistador, would not have been able to conquer the empire, had not a civil war been in progress when he came in 1532.

In 1539, the town of La Plata (later changed to Sucre) was founded and became the capital of Alto Peru, the early name of the region that is now Bolivia. In 1559, it became a vice-royalty of Spanish Peru. The Indians rebelled several times in later centuries but were crushed. Spain held on to Alto Peru until 1824, when Antonio Jośe de Sucre, one of Simón Bolivar's generals, marched in and captured the region. In 1825 Bolivia declared its independence and took its name from the great South American liberator, Simón Bolivar.

A war with Chile, called the War of the Pacific, broke out over nitrate deposits, and because Bolivia was seeking an outlet to the Pacific Ocean. Bolivia was aided by Peru, but Chile defeated both and seized the province of Atatcama and part of southern Peru. Ever since, Bolivia has remained a landlocked nation. In a war with Paraguay (1932–1938), Bolivia lost additional territory.

Bolivia became a member of the United Nations on November 14, 1945. In 1967 Bolivian soldiers captured and executed Che Guevara, a naturalized Cuban Communist and guerrilla leader.

After a series of coups and revolts, a military regime took control of Bolivia in 1974 and banned all civilians from public office. The military officers resigned in October 1982, allowing a congress elected by the people to take over and elect a president.

BOTSWANA

Formerly known as Bechuanaland, this country wedged between Rhodesia and South Africa was made a British protectorate in 1885 at the request of its Bantu inhabitants, who feared the advance of the Boers from the Transvaal. In 1895, its southern part was annexed to Cape Colony (now part of South Africa), but the larger northern part of Bechuanaland remained a protectorate.

On September 30, 1966, the protectorate became the independent republic of Botswana, part of the Commonwealth. It remained economically dependent, however, on South Africa. Botswana has a one-chamber assembly, which is also advised by a council of chiefs of the principal tribes.

BRAZIL

The first European to visit Brazil was the Spanish navigator Vincent Yañez Pinzón, who landed near Recife in January 1500. By the terms of the Treaty of Tordesillas, Brazil was granted to Portugal, and Pedro Alvarez Cabral formally claimed the land for Portugal on Easter Sunday, 1500. Cargoes of dyewood called *pau brasil* had been obtained along the coast by early navigators. The name Brazil was derived from the name of this wood, although Cabral had named the region Terra de Vera Cruz.

The first settlement was made in 1532 at São Vicente. A French colony was established at Rio de Janeiro in 1555. It was abolished in 1567 with the founding of the present city of Rio de Janeiro by the Portuguese on the same spot. From 1578 to 1640, Brazil was under Spanish rule. Dutch settlements were expelled in 1654. The discovery of gold in 1693, and of diamonds in 1729, brought fresh waves of immigrants.

In 1808, the royal family of Portugal was driven out by Napoleon; they took refuge in Brazil. Dor

João VI opened Brazil to foreign commerce and removed other restrictions, which helped bring about greater prosperity and economic activity. Dom João returned to Portugal in 1821, but left his son to rule. The prince opposed his father and declared himself Dom Pedro I, Emperor of Brazil. Thereafter, Brazil's history is separate from that of Portugal.

The new empire plunged deep into internal troubles soon after independence. In 1831 Dom Pedro abdicated in favor of his son Dom Pedro II, who was not crowned until 1840 because of his youth. His reign lasted until he was desposed in 1889. The nation was then organized into the United States of Brazil with a constitution modeled after that of the United States of America.

The early years of the republic were marked by repeated revolts. However the nation adjusted nearly all its boundaries with neighboring states between 1900 and 1928. The disputed boundaries had resulted in major wars with Argentina in 1852, and with Paraguay in 1856–1870.

Brazil joined the Allies in World War I and again in World War II. In the latter war, Brazilian troops fought in Europe. The long regime of Getulio Vargas (1937–1945) improved Brazil's economic situation somewhat, but the loss of her rubber monopoly and the overproduction of coffee after World War II left Brazil with serious internal weaknesses.

Two ambitious projects were undertaken after the war. One was the building of the new capital city, Brasilia, which was begun in 1957. Three years later it was officially designated the capital, and by 1975 it had a population of more than half a million. The other project was the construction of the Trans-Amazon Highway from the Atlantic Ocean to the border of Peru, a distance of more than 3,000 miles. It was complete in 1974. Meanwhile, the phenomenal growth of the city of São Paulo occurred without plan. It is now the largest city in South America.

Brazil became a member of the United Nations on October 24, 1945.

In recent years, the country has been beset by economic troubles. In the early '80s it had huge oil debts and 95 percent inflation.

BRITISH ANTARCTIC TERRITORY

The British Antarctic Territory is a crown colony, formed in 1962 from parts of the Falkland Islands and dependencies. It comprises all British-administered, claimed, or held territories south of latitude 60° South. The chief units of the colony are South Shetland Islands (1,800 square miles) and Antarctic Peninsula.

The Falklands remain a British dependency, although Argentina, which calls them *Islas Malvinas,* claims them also. When Argentina invaded them April 2, 1982, Britain sent a task force to the area and forced an Argentine surrender.

BRITISH INDIAN OCEAN TERRITORY

A group of islands in the Indian Ocean that were formerly dependencies of Seychelles Or Mauritius were formed in 1965 into a separate British colony. They included the Chagos Archipelago and the islands of Aldabra, Farquhar, and Desroches.

Brazil—Palácio da Alvorada, Brasília

In 1973, one of the Chagos group, Diego Garcia was turned over to the United States, which two years later began building a naval base there.

BRUNEI

Brunei was once (sixteenth century) a powerful state that controlled all of the large islands of Borneo, plus parts of the Sulu and Philippine islands. But today, Brunei consists of two small enclaves on the north coast of Borneo in southeast Asia. Brunei is surrounded by the Sarawak section of the Federation of Malaysia.

The government is supported mainly by revenues from oil wells in the state. Oil production, though very large, has passed its peak. The island of Labuan lies just off the coast of Brunei but is not now a part of it. Brunei became self governing in 1971 and achieved independence January 1, 1984, becoming the world's newest nation.

BULGARIA

The Bulgars were a tribe who migrated from central Asia in A.D. 679. They mixed with the Slavic peoples already there to form the modern Bulgarians. The Bulgars founded an empire in the seventh century, but declined under pressure from the Byzantine Empire. A second empire grew up under Semeon II (893–927), but was conquered again by the Byzantines.

Bulgaria was conquered by the Turks in 1396. In 1876 the Bulgarians revolted, and with the aid of Russia, gained their independence. The Kingdom of Bulgaria that was established included all of the present Bulgaria plus Macedonia and most of what is now European Turkey. In 1885, the region of Rumelia was added.

The Bulgarian struggle to get or to keep a coastline on the Aegean Sea (and hence on the Mediterranean Sea) involved the country in the Balkan Wars, World War I, and World War II. The nation allied itself with Nazi Germany in World War II and withdrew too late to prevent a Russian invasion and an eventual Communist-backed revolution that destroyed the monarchy (1944–1946).

The country is now known as the People's Republic of Bulgaria. It was admitted to the United Nations on December 14, 1955. It is a close ally of the Soviet Union.

BURMA

Burma first became a united country in 1044 when Anawrahta founded a kingdom that was to last for two hundred years. Five hundred years of disunity followed, ending in 1754, when Alaungpaya established another kingdom over nearly all of the present Burma. British conquest began in 1824 and was completed with the annexation of Burma to the empire in 1886.

Burma gradually regained self-government, starting with a legislative council in 1897. Further steps toward political independence were taken in 1937. The long fight for independence ended in 1948 when the Union of Burma became a reality under the leadership of U Nu. In 1962, a socialist revolution deposed U Nu and General Ne Win became the head of a new government, proclaimed as the Socialist Republic of the Union of Burma in 1974. At that time Burma left the Commonwealth.

Burma was the scene of heavy fighting during World War II. The famous Burma Road led across great mountains from Lashio in Burma to southern China, and was used by the Allied armies to supply Chinese resistance forces in the war with Japan. Burma was admitted to the United Nations on April 19, 1948.

BURUNDI

The Watutsi, or Tutsi, people came to the area of the present Burundi in the fifteenth century. They gradually subjugated the Bahutu, or Hutu peoples. This was the situation when Germany, during the nineteenth century, established a zone of influence in the region.

After World War I, the League of Nations mandated the portion of German East Africa known as Ruanda-Urundi to Belgium. It was attached, for administrative purposes, to the Belgian Congo (now Zaire), but the ancient indigenous monarchies of Ruanda and Urundi were maintained.

Ruanda-Urundi became a Belgian trust territory under United Nations auspices after World War II. In 1960 separate elections were held in each of the kingdoms, and two years later they became independent as the republic of Rwanda and the kingdom of Burundi, refusing to reunite.

Both were admitted to the United Nations on September 18, 1962. In 1966 the premier of Burundi declared that country a republic and he became its president. Burundi has no constitution.

CAMBODIA

For almost a thousand years, from the sixth to the fifteenth century, the strongest power in southeastern Asia was the Khmer Empire. The magnificent ruins of Angkor are the remains of monuments that were constructed between the ninth and thirteenth centuries, at the height of that empire. It succumbed to attacks from the Thais, one of its vassal peoples, from the Annamese, and from the Mongols. After several centuries, the remnants of the Khmer Empire, the present Cambodia, became a French protectorate in 1863.

France ruled Cambodia, while maintaining its royal house in nominal authority, until after World War II. The nationalist movement that emerged under the Japanese occupation rode on the coattails of the more aggressive movement in adjoining Vietnam (Annam and Tonkin), and Cambodia was given its independence in 1949 as an "associated state of the French Union."

The Vietnamese nationalists, under the leadership of Ho Chi Minh, attempted to involve Cambodia in total repudiation of French rule, especially after the Vietnamese defeat of the French at Dien Bien Phu in 1954. The anticommunist Southeast Asia Treaty Organization, on the other hand, unilaterally guaranteed Cambodian independence.

King Norodom Sihanouk abdicated his throne in March, 1955, was elected premier in September, and withdrew Cambodia from the French Union. On December 14, 1955, Cambodia was admitted to the United Nations.

As head of state, Prince Norodom Sihanouk steered his country on a neutralist course to avoid being involved in the armed struggle under way in Vietnam.

In 1970, a pro-Western coup by Lon Nol deposed the prince, and the United States and South Vietnamese forces bombed and sent troops into Cambodia to drive out the North Vietnamese forces that were based there.

A civil war developed between the Lon Nol Government and insurgents known as the Khmer Rouge. In April 1975, Lon Nol fled from Cambodia and the Khmer Rouge forces took over the country and immediately named Norodom Sihanouk chief of state for life, although his authority was entirely honorary. He resigned in 1976.

The Khmer Rouge government kept the nation's activities a secret, but refugees said that hundreds of thousands were killed in a post-war purge. The communist regime renamed the nation "Democratic Kampuchea," but the traditional name of Cambodia is still commonly used.

In January 1979, communist troops from Vietnam seized control of the country. China protested this action, because the Soviet Union had supported the new take-over, and the Chinese feared that the Soviets would use Cambodia as a base of operations against them.

Clashes between Vietnamese and anti-Communist forces continued in 1983.

CAMEROON

The Cameroon region was visited late in the fifteenth century by the Portuguese. Trading posts were established there in the seventeenth century. From 1888 to 1914, Germany occupied Cameroons. The territory was invaded by French and British troops during World War I.

After the defeat of Germany, the region was divided into a western Cameroons under British control and a larger eastern Cameroons under French control.

The portion assigned to France obtained internal autonomy in 1959 and complete independence in 1960. The part under British control consisted of two parts. The northern part decided by plebiscite in February 1961 to join the Federation of Nigeria. At the same time a plebiscite was held in the southern part and as a result that section united with the former French area, all of which became the Federal Republic of Cameroon in 1961. In 1972 a unitary state was instituted. The republic was admitted to the United Nations on September 20, 1960.

CANADA

Both France and Great Britain based their claims to Canadian territory on the landings of explorers: that of John Cabot on Cape Breton Island for England in 1497; and that of Jacques Cartier on the Gaspé coast of Quebec for France in 1534. But neither the British nor the French tried to take permanent physical possession of any part of the territory before the seventeenth century.

The French explorer Samuel de Champlain tried unsuccessfully to establish a station in the vicinity of the Bay of Fundy in 1604 and 1605. In 1608 he was able to locate the first permanent post at

Canada—Parliament Buildings, Ottawa

Quebec. In 1610, Henry Hudson sailed into the bay named after him, still seeking a water route to Asia. On the basis of Hudson's voyage, Charles II of England granted the entire northeastern wilderness to a private trading corporation, the Hudson's Bay Company.

The French government chartered private trading companies to exploit New France for more than a half-century. Their settlements were persistently harassed by the English. A post set up by Champlain at Port Royal was destroyed by a Virginia raiding party in 1613 and twice thereafter; eventually it became British in 1713 as Annapolis Royal in Nova Scotia. Quebec was subject to a series of similar raids.

Louis XIV declared New France—the combined settlements of Acadia in the Bay of Fundy area and Canada in the St. Lawrence valley—to be a Crown colony in 1663. He appointed a governor to act as chief of state. For a century New France developed under this regime, although in the early stages of the French and Indian Wars much of Acadia was lost to the British.

The colonial wars in North America ended in 1763 with the total cession of New France to Great Britain.

But in 1774, the former New France was reorganized as an extended province called Quebec. Parliament hoped that the Quebec Act would preserve the overwhelmingly French character of the recently conquered territory, lest the French colonists find common cause with disaffected settlers

William Lyon Mackenzie.

to the south. The statute only further outraged the English-speaking colonists.

The decade following the Quebec Act was critical. English-speaking refugees from the rebellious lower colonies began to populate widely separated areas of Nova Scotia and Quebec, laying the foundation for the emerging provinces of New Brunswick, Prince Edward Island, and Upper Canada (Ontario).

In the next generation some of the ideas associated with Jacksonian democracy in the United States began to penetrate the Canadian border. Such influences inspired the uprisings of 1837, led by Louis Papineau in Lower Canada and by William Lyon Mackenzie in Upper Canada.

The Earl of Durham was sent to British North America to study the situation. He recommended the adoption of representative government for the two Canadas. Since many of the colonists were moving West, he also urged that the two provinces be reunited to guarantee a minimum French impact once the democratic regime was instituted. In 1840 Parliament created the province of Canada (in which two districts, Canada West and Canada East, were recognized). But only after Nova Scotia was granted representative government in 1848 was the same privilege extended to Canada.

The British Parliament was apprehensive of the increasing power of the United States in the second half of the nineteenth century. The British government was able to resolve several border disputes: In 1818 the forty-ninth parallel became the line of demarcation from the Lake of the Woods to the Rocky Mountains; a controversial border between Maine and New Brunswick was peaceably settled in 1842; and in 1846 the dangerous Oregon question was resolved when the forty-ninth parallel was extended almost to the Pacific Ocean. But some leaders in the United States pressed for more acquisition of British American territory. Parliament feared that British recognition of the Southern Confederacy during the American Civil War

Louis Joseph Papineau.

might serve as a pretext, following Union victory, for hostile movements across the border, and so Parliament encouraged the provinces to consolidate their powers. This was the reasoning behind Parliament's British North America Act of 1867. The Dominion of Canada was created by this act. It was a confederation of British colonies under the authority of the British Parliament. Its original members were two of the Atlantic provinces, Nova Scotia and New Brunswick, and the two sections of the province of Canada—Ontario and Quebec. The act provided for the eventual admission of all British North America.

The Hudson's Bay Company returned its holdings to Great Britain, which immediately ceded them to the Dominion of Canada. They became the Northwest Territories in 1870. The only settled district within the Territories was organized within the year as the fifth province of Canada, under the name of Manitoba. In 1871 the colony of British Columbia agreed to join the Dominion as a sixth province if a railway would be constructed to link it with the eastern provinces. Prince Edward Island became the seventh province in 1873.

The last years of the nineteenth century brought a spectacular westward shift in Canada's population. In 1898, Yukon Territory was detached from the Northwest Territories adjoining Alaska. By 1905 settled sections of the Territories between Manitoba and British Columbia were organized into the new provinces of Saskatchewan and Alberta. Except for Newfoundland (which became part of Canada in 1949), the Dominion attained its ultimate territorial extent and virtually its final political organization by 1905.

Government. The trend in Great Britain was to relax its tight control over its possessions and to encourage them to run their own affairs. The power of the Crown was vested in an appointed governor-general and in appointed lieutenant-governors of each province. Most law-making powers were assigned to a Senate, whose members were appointed for life. (Those appointed after 1965 must retire at the age of 75.) The Canadian House of Commons was, like that of the United Kingdom, elective and based on population. While the provinces have their own constitutions, which they alone may amend, they have authority only over their internal affairs to the degree authorized under the constitution. This document, the British North America Act, specifies the powers granted to the provinces. Powers not so enumerated are to be exercised by the federal government. (This is the reverse of the system in the United States, where the specified authority of the federal government is defined and residual powers are granted to the states.)

Although not quite a nation, the Dominion was admitted to the League of Nations and independently participated in foreign affairs. Great Britain called an imperial conference in 1926, at which it declared that the dominions were autonomous and equal members of a Commonwealth of Nations, headed by a single sovereign. This concept was formalized by the British Parliament in 1931 as the Statute of Westminster. Under this statute Canada formally attained sovereignty and nationhood.

Perhaps the most significant subsequent constitutional development was the ruling in 1949 that Canadian citizens could no longer appeal the decisions of the Supreme Court of Canada to the British Privy Council. In the same year the British Parliament passed the second British North America Act, which made it clear that amendments to the first British North America Act could not be made without the participation of the Canadian Parliament.

Canada's international role has been distinctive. Its national policy is independent of the United States, despite strong economic pressures. In its internal policies, however, Canada suffers from chronic controversy concerning the balance between federal and provincial authority. A cohesive and articulate French minority comprises a majority within the province of Quebec. The French nationalist movement is itself divided into factions, one of which agitates for separation and sovereignty. The use of the French language has parity throughout Canada and supersedes the English language within the province of Quebec.

Economy. Canada proved to be a late bloomer. The first years of the twentieth century saw the anticipated development of agriculture, mining, and industry. The United States had already peopled its West, and the Canadian prairies received the overflow—not only from the states, but from every part of Europe and even from the Orient. At first Canadians feared direct economic encroachment from the United States, and a policy of trade protectionism was adopted. But capital investment from the United States has become sufficiently dominant to appear as a possible menace to many Canadians.

Cape Verde Islands—Cape Verdeans display portraits of two leaders of their country.

CAPE VERDE ISLANDS

An archipelago about 375 to 525 miles west of Senegal in Africa was discovered by the Portuguese sailor Diogo Gomes in 1460. Two years later Portuguese settlers and their African slaves populated the uninhabited islands. They were transferred to the Portuguese crown in 1495 and a century later the first governor was appointed.

In modern times the Cape Verde Islands were made an overseas province of Portugal. The leaders of the independence movement in Portuguese Guinea (now Guinea-Bissau) were mostly from Cape Verde. When the Portuguese withdrew from their African colonies, both the mainland and the islands became independent. Cape Verde became a republic on July 5, 1975. On September 16, 1975, the country was admitted to the United Nations.

CAYMAN ISLANDS

These coral islands in the Caribbean Sea south of Cuba were discovered by Columbus in 1503 and were colonized from nearby Jamaica.

Until 1959, the Caymans were administered as a dependency of Jamaica. In 1962, they were given self-government as a separate colony with a partly elected legislature. The free port of Georgetown is used as a tax haven for foreign corporations and individuals.

CENTRAL AFRICAN EMPIRE

During the last decade of the nineteenth century, the French explored what is now the Central African Empire. In 1894, the Territory of Ubangi-Shari was established, and was merged in 1905 with Chad to form Ubangi-Shari-Chad. In 1910, Gabon and Middle Congo were added to this group to form French Equatorial Africa.

That loose federation came to an end when the constituent states chose to become autonomous states within the French Community of Nations in 1958. On December 1, 1958, the Ubangi-Shari section became the Central African Republic and was proclaimed an independent nation two years later. It was admitted to the United Nations on September 20, 1960. In 1976 President Jean-Bedel Bokassa changed the country's name to Central African Empire and declared himself its first emperor.

The Central African Empire exports diamonds, uranium, textiles, and other goods. It has not been able to develop many of its natural resources because it is cut off from the major trade routes.

CHAD

Arabs visited this general area in Africa many centuries ago, but it was not explored until late in the nineteenth century. Various African tribes inhabited the region, alternately warring and living in some sort of peace. Slave traders scoured the territory for their exports of human beings to Egypt and the Near East, while other traders sought ostrich feathers and ivory.

The French helped put an end to the slave trade in the Chad area, and by 1910 it had become part of French Equatorial Africa. In 1920 it was given separate administration and it became an autonomous member of the French Community in 1958. It declared its independence on August 11, 1960, and was admitted to the United Nations on September 20, 1960.

Chad suffered from conflicts between the Moslem, pro-Arab, and conservative population of the north and the black, more progressive population of the south. Years of scanty rainfall have also been destructive.

Chad has consistently tried to africanize its proper names. President François Tombalbaye change his first name to Ngarta. The capital, Fort Lamy, was renamed N'Djamema. After fifteen years in the presidency Tombalbaye was killed in a military coup in 1975.

Libya took advantage of the confusion in Chad's government to annex 37,000 square miles of territory in northern Chad in 1976. Libyan troops were withdrawn in November 1981.

CHANNEL ISLANDS

William the Conqueror, of Normandy, who invaded England in A.D. 1066 and became king of England, was already ruler of the Channel Islands. They have remained a territory of the English Crown ever since.

CHILE

In 1520, during his epic voyage around the earth, Ferdinand Magellan landed on an island near a region of South America called "Tchili" by the natives of the area. This was the first visit by Europeans to what is now called Chile. In 1535, Diego de Almagro was sent to explore the land to the south of Peru. He was not successful in the venture, but five years later Pedro Valdivia annexed the present-day Chile down to the Maipú River, near where Santiago, the capital of Chile, now stands. The chief obstacles to Spanish conquest were the fierce Araucanian Indians, who continued to resist long after Chile had become an independent nation.

In 1810, Chile declared its independence, and the war that followed with Spain was fought by Chileans under the leadership of Bernard O'Higgins and José de San Martín. The Spanish were finally driven from the country in 1818.

Chile passed through a turbulent and unstable period after independence. By 1837 the nation fought a bitter war that destroyed a Peruvian-Bolivian confederation against her. Again in 1879–1883, Chile fought the War of the Pacific against the combined armies of Peru and Bolivia, and won. In that war Bolivia lost its outlet to the sea to Chile (the Atacama region). Chile was admitted to the United Nations on October 24, 1945.

Among South American nations, Chile has a reputation for political stability. The accession by normal political processes of a Marxist president, Salvador Allende Gossens, in 1970 was unprecedented. However, the country was disunited. Foreign influence, including that of the United States, was brought to bear. In 1973, Allende was deposed by a military junta and murdered. The succeeding administration reversed Allende's policies.

The military continued control in 1983.

Chile—University of Concepcion

CHINA
(People's Republic of China)

The Chinese state has existed without interruption for over four thousand years. The Chinese were experiencing one of their periods of cultural and intellectual Golden Ages when Europe was still in the Stone Age. The original home of the Chinese people appears to have been in the valley of the Wei River in the present Shensi Province area. In about the twenty-eighth century B.C. a loose empire appeared under the Hsia dynasty. This was the first recorded state. Its successor, the Shang dynasty, left written records about the first important cultural development (1750–1122 B.C.).

The period of the Chou dynasty (1122–221 B.C.) was a great feudal period. About 770 B.C., the capital was moved from Sian to Loyang on the Yellow River. The period of the new state, called the Eastern Chou dynasty, was the time when the great philosophers Confucius and Lao-tzu lived. It was a classical age in literature and art.

From 221 to 206 B.C. one of the notable men in world history was the ruler of China. His name was Shih Huang-ti and his dynasty was known as Ch'in or Chin, from which the word *China* was derived. He was the Charlemagne of China. Although he was a "book-burner," he left the Great Wall as one of his legacies, and is the founder of modern China. The wall extends from Mongolia to the Yellow Sea, and remains as a colossal monument to Chinese ingenuity and imagination.

The Han dynasty (206 B.C.–A.D. 220) followed. The classics were restored, Buddhism was introduced, sculpturing as a fine art began, and paper was invented. The Han rulers expanded the Chinese Empire westward into the heart of Asia. They established contact with the Roman Empire in the west. The Han rulers began the system of civil service examinations that lasted to 1911.

The Grand Canal, another spectacular feat of Chinese workmanship, was begun under the Sui (A.D. 581–618) and T'ang (618–907) dynasties. The T'ang dynasty is usually considered the most splendid in Chinese history. Under Emperor Tai Tsung (627–649) China became powerful. A great system of roads was built from Sian, the capital. Handicrafts and arts flourished as never before. China reached its greatest area in 650. At that time it included all of today's China, plus southeast Asia and other areas. Printing was invented, the use of silk developed, and poetry and painting advanced. The invention of movable type, gunpowder, and the magnetic compass followed.

The Mongols crashed through the Great Wall in the thirteenth century, at the same time that they were invading western Europe. Genghis Khan established the Mongol dynasty and extended his rule as far south as the present Fukien province. Chinese civilization persisted, as was witnessed by Marco Polo who visited China during the short period of Mongol domination. During the reign of the Manchu emperors (1644–1911), the last dynasty, China declined rapidly. In the nineteenth century, rebellion weakened the ruling Manchus (Ming dynasty) and foreign interference developed. The Portuguese had reached China in 1516, the Spanish in 1557, the Dutch in 1606, and the English in 1637. Western governments supported the Manchus in the Taipeng Rebellion (1850–1864) in order to get access to Chinese commerce and trade privileges. The Boxer Rebellion (1900) was put down by foreign troops, including those of the United States. China suffered heavy losses and was further weakened in a war with Japan (1894–1895). The imperial government was finally overthrown in 1911.

Sun Yat-sen, the founder of the Republic of China (1912), lost control to a group of military chiefs or warlords. Chiang Kai-shek gained control and was for a time allied with the Communists. A split developed in 1927 between Chiang Kai-shek and the Communists. Japan, taking advantage of disunity, occupied Manchuria in 1931. The Sino-Japanese War began in 1937 and merged into World War II. During the war, American aid reached China mainly over the Burma Road and by air. By 1945 the Japanese were completely expelled. The Communist forces had been attacked by Chiang Kai-shek in 1936, and had transferred their center of power to Shensi in northern China, by means of a great land journey known as the "Long March." Their strength had been greatly reduced, but by the end of World War II, the Communist movement was again threatening Chiang Kai-shek.

Although supported by the United States, Chiang Kai-shek steadily lost ground in the civil war that erupted after World War II. By 1949 the Nationalist forces had been expelled from the mainland, and took refuge on Taiwan (Formosa).

The People's Republic of China was proclaimed in 1949 by the Communists under Mao Tse-tung. In 1950 China retrieved Tibet, which had broken away in the fall of the Manchu dynasty. For many years the Peking regime was denied membership in the United Nations, where China's seat was held by representatives of the government on Taiwan that called itself the Republic of China. In 1971 the United Nations voted to expel the dele-

U.S. President Richard M. Nixon is greeted on Feb. 21, 1972 by Chairman Mao Tse-tung of the Peoples Republic of China.

gates from Taiwan and to seat those of the People's Republic. The United States had long opposed this move, and continued to withhold full diplomatic recognition of the Peking regime. But the animosity was dissipated after President Richard Nixon visited Peking in 1972 and met with Chinese leaders Mao Tse-tung and Chou En-lai. In December 1978, President Jimmy Carter's administration announced plans to establish formal diplomatic ties with the People's Republic of China.

The Reagan administration has continued the good will policy toward both China and the Republic of China on Taiwan.

CHINA
(Republic of China)

See Taiwan

COLOMBIA

Columbus explored the northern coast of what is now Colombia in 1502 on his last voyage to the New World. The city of Bogotá, deep in the interior, was founded in 1538. Shortly after this, the region began to be called New Granada. It included the present Colombia, Panama, Ecuador, and Venezuela. The state was ranked as a viceroyalty within the Spanish American empire.

A war for independence was begun in 1810 and continued until 1819, when Bolívar and Santander won the Battle of Boyaca. From 1819 to 1830 Colombia was a part of Bolívar's Gran Colombia that included nearly the same area as did the old Spanish viceroyalty. By 1832, Ecuador and Venezuela had seceded from Gran Colombia. The remainder changed its name to Colombia and became a republic. During the turbulent nineteenth century in Colombia no less than ten different constitutions were promulgated.

In 1903, the country lost Panama to a United States-instigated revolt which established the Republic of Panama. The first seven decades of Colombia's twentieth-century history have been relatively more peaceful and accompanied by considerable economic and social progress. The nation has been experiencing severe economic and political difficulties in the past few years. Colombia became a member of the United Nations on November 5, 1945.

COMORO ISLANDS

The Comoro archipelago was acquired by France in 1886, although the island of Mayotte had been occupied since 1843. In 1912, the archipelago was declared a colony and attached to Madagascar (now the Malagasy Republic) for administration. Upon the latter's independence, the Comoro group became an overseas territory of France.

When the inhabitants voted for independence in 1974, France did nothing to impede their desire, although Mayotte had voted against independence. On July 6, 1975, the Comoro legislature declared their independence. On November 12, 1975, the country was admitted to the United Nations.

CONGO

A Portuguese navigator, Diego Cam, discovered the mouth of the Congo (Zaire) River in 1484. Thereafter, exploration was mainly done by French missionaries and slave-traders. In the nineteenth century Henry M. Stanley (in the service of Belgium) and Pierre Savorgnan de Brazza (in the service of France) opened up the country to European penetration and established claims to the region. The French claims to what is now the Republic of Congo were recognized at the Congress of Berlin in 1855. In 1903, the territory was organized into Moyen (Middle) Congo, and it became a part of French Equatorial Africa (a loose federation) in 1908. On September 28, 1958, Middle Congo became the Republic of Congo, an autonomous member of the French Community. It remained in the Community when it became an independent nation on August 15, 1960, as the Republic of Congo. It was admitted to the United Nations on September 20, 1960. In 1970, it changed its name to the People's Republic of the Congo.

This country should not be confused with Zaire, known from 1960 to 1971 as the Democratic Republic of Congo. During those years Zaire was called "Congo (Kinshasa)" to distinguish it from the country by the same name north of the Congo River, known as "Congo (Brazzaville)."

Communistic influence has been strong since 1963, and in 1981 a treaty of "friendship" was signed with the Soviets.

COSTA RICA

Costa Rica was discovered in 1502 by Christopher Columbus. It was conquered by the Spanish and made a royal province before the middle of the sixteenth century.

In 1821, Costa Rica declared its independence, but was annexed by Mexico. From 1823, when the Mexican Empire broke up, until 1839, Costa Rica was a member of a loose federation called the United Provinces of Central America.

The country became wholly independent in 1840, and proclaimed itself a republic in 1848. Many boundary disputes were settled, including one with Nicaragua and another with Panama.

Up to 1948, Costa Rica had enjoyed internal peace. In that year, a disputed presidential election resulted in new elections and a new constitution in 1949. Unrest continued to plague the country, and terrorist activity went on for several years. In 1954 Costa Rica charged Nicaragua with meddling in its internal affairs. The dispute ended in an agreement by both countries to curb terrorist activity. Costa Rica was admitted to the United Nations on November 2, 1945.

CUBA

The island of Cuba was discovered by Christopher Columbus on his first voyage in 1492. Santiago de Cuba was founded in 1514 by Diego Velásquez and was the capital until 1589. Cuba was the base for the historic expeditions of Cortés to Mexico and of De Soto to Florida. Havana was founded in 1519, captured by the British in 1762, and returned to Spanish control the following year.

Unsuccessful revolts occurred in 1868, in 1875, and in 1895. In the latter part of the nineteenth century the brilliant leader, José Marti, was mainly responsible for the development of national consciousness in Cuba.

The United States declared war against Spain after the sinking of the American battleship *Maine* in Havana harbor on February 15, 1898. The slogan, "Remember the Maine," aroused a patriotic sentiment in the United States for war against Spain. The land battles of ElCaney and San Juan Hill and the naval battle at Santiago resulted in Spain's loss of Cuba. By the terms of the Platt Amendment to the new Cuban constitution of 1901, Cuba became virtually a protectorate of the United States and was occupied by the United States Marines on three occasions. In 1934 the Platt Amendment was repealed but the United States kept its Guantanamo naval base.

A military dictatorship was inaugurated in Cuba in 1952 by Fulgencio Batista. In 1953, opposition to the Batista regime developed into a large-scale revolt. The leader of the rebel group was Fidel Castro, who operated mainly from fortified positions in the Sierra Maestra (mountains) in eastern Cuba. Several unsuccessful revolts were staged before 1958, when full civil war developed. Batista fled to exile in the Dominican Republic and Castro's rebels took over the government. At first Castro was on friendly terms with the United States, but in 1960 his government began seizing the properties of United States companies.

The United States severed diplomatic relations in 1960, and Cuba increasingly turned toward the Soviet Union for support and aid. In April 1961, a United States-sponsored invasion force landed on the Bay of Pigs at the south coast of Cuba, but was defeated in 72 hours with a loss of 1,200 prisoners. In October 1962, United States high-altitude photographs showed Soviet missiles in Cuba. The discovery nearly precipitated a war between the United States and the Soviet Union. After the United States threw up a naval blockade of Cuba, the Soviet Union withdrew the missiles and most of the troops.

Tension between the United States and the Soviet Union eased considerably, but Cuba-United States relations continued strained. Cuba has been a member of the United Nations since October 24, 1974.

Since 1975, Cuba, with considerable encouragement from the Soviets, has continually expanded its revolutionary operations in Africa and more recently in Latin America.

CYPRUS

Cyprus was famous in the ancient world for its rich copper deposits. The word *copper* is derived from the name *Cyprus*. The Egyptians occupied the island until 1450 B.C., and the Greeks came in 1400 B.C. Between 500 B.C. and A.D. 1562, Phoenicia, Egypt, Persia, Greece, Rome, the Byzantine Empire, Venice, and finally the Ottoman Empire (Turks) all held Cyprus.

The United Kingdom administered Cyprus after 1878, and in 1914 the British annexed the island. In modern times Greek Cypriots have often attempted to unite Cyprus with Greece. Although the Greeks form a majority of the population, a large Turkish minority always opposed such a move. Violence broke out in 1955 between the two groups. Civil war developed and ended only after an unexpected proposal for an independent Cyprus was suddenly accepted by the Greek Cypriots. On August 16, 1960, Cyprus became an independent republic. The country was admitted to the United Nations on September 20, 1960.

Tension between the Greek and Turkish populations of Cyprus continued to flare into open clashes, particularly in 1964. In 1974 an advocate of *enosis* (union with Greece) tried to seize control of the island. This was followed by a Turkish invasion. Finally the two groups reached a truce. The Turks maintained an enlarged sector in the northeast and refused to accept any alternative to a federal state. United Nations peace-keeping forces were sent to prevent further violence until an agreement among the Cypriots could be reached. However, the peace talks failed and fighting broke out again. The Turks enlarged the territory under their control, and on June 8, 1975, they voted to form a separate Turkish state.

Under Turkish control some 200,000 Greeks have been expelled and thousands of Turks have moved in from the Turkish mainland.

CZECHOSLOVAKIA

Czechs and Slovaks settled in the present region before the sixth century ended. The Slovaks were conquered by the Magyar people and for a thousand years had no independent existence. The Czechs, however, formed the Kingdom of Bohemia in the tenth century.

Bohemia had a golden age of cultural growth in the fourteenth century that lasted until 1620. Prague, its capital, became a great center of Latin learning. In 1526, Bohemia came under Hapsburg rule and the Czech population was subjected to German and Austrian influences. The revolt of 1618 ended disastrously at the Battle of White Hill (White Mountain) in 1620, which crushed Czech national aspirations until the mid-nineteenth century.

The breakup of the Austro-Hungarian Empire presaged a serious move for independence during World War I. A Czech state came into existence on October 28, 1918. Two days later the Slovak National Council indicated its desire to unite with the Czechs in a single state. The Republic of Czechoslovakia was declared on November 14, 1918.

Czechoslovakia became a victim of Nazi expansionist aims in 1938. The republic was dismembered and abolished in 1939. A German-sponsored Slovak state was not recognized by the Allies, who supported a government-in-exile led by Dr. Eduard Beneš in London. Czechoslovakia regained its territory in 1944, and all severed sections were eventually reunited, except for part of Ruthenia.

Czechoslovakia moved in two stages into a Communist form of government. In February 1948, Beneš had to accept Clement Gottwald, a Communist, as Prime Minister, after the Communists had taken over control of much of the machinery of government. In June 1948, President Beneš was forced to resign after an election in which the people were permitted to vote only for candidates on a slate approved by the Communists. Czechoslovakia became a member of the United Nations on October 24, 1945.

Alexander Dubček became the leader of Czechoslovakia's Party in early 1968 and announced new liberal policies for the nation. Russia and other Warsaw Pact nations invaded the country on August 20, 1968 to halt Dubček's reforms.

Despite the activity of intellectuals and liberals, Russia has continued to keep a tight rein on the country.

DENMARK

Recent excavations from Danish peat bogs have provided proof that man lived in the Jutland region of Denmark at least eleven thousand years ago.

In ancient times Jutland was colonized by Norway, which lies to the north across the Skagerrak (strait). People from Denmark invaded England in the ninth century after Christ, Harald "Bluetooth" united Denmark for the first time in the tenth century and his son Sweyn conquered England.

During these centuries the Danish Vikings took part in raids along the shores of Western Europe. During the reign of Canute the Great (1014–1035), England, Denmark, and Norway were united. During the next three centuries, Denmark continued to expand, and under the reign of Valdemar II (1202–1241) it became the leading power of northern Europe. In the reign of Margarethe (1387–1412), Denmark, Sweden, and Norway were united. This union was dissolved in 1532, but Norway remained a part of the Crown of Denmark until 1814.

Danes settled Greenland in 1721. Serfdom was abolished in 1788. In the mid-nineteenth century, Denmark lost territory on the south of the Jutland

Peninsula to Prussia. In 1918, the independence of Iceland was recognized. Germany attacked the kingdom on April 9, 1940, conquering it in a few hours. However, the conquest was costly to maintain because the Danes became expert saboteurs and the Danish fleet was scuttled by its own officers in the harbor of Copenhagen. The nation was liberated on May 5, 1945. Denmark became a member of the United Nations on October 24, 1945.

DJIBOUTI

This nation on the northeast coast of Africa was formerly French Somaliland. It was taken by France in the late nineteenth century. The country held a strategic location at the strait leading to the Suez Canal, and for many years it was Ethiopia's only link with the sea.

In 1967, the people voted to remain under French control, and the region became known as the Territory of the Afars (related to the Ethiopians) and the Issas (related to the Somalis). Immigrants from both countries kept pouring into the area and bitter fighting flared up between them. On June 27, 1977, the territory proclaimed its independence from France and adopted the name of Djibouti, the capital city. Both Ethiopia and Somalia still claim the area as their own.

Denmark—Tivoli Gardens, Copenhagen

DOMINICAN REPUBLIC

The island of Hispaniola, on which the present Dominican Republic is located, was discovered and named by Christopher Columbus during his first voyage in 1492. The city of Santo Domingo was founded by his brother, Bartholomew Columbus, in 1496. The island became a base for Spain's discovery and exploration of the New World. The Spanish lost Hispaniola to the French in 1697, but regained the eastern two-thirds of the island in 1809. The remainder of the island became the independent Haiti, now the Republic of Haiti.

A revolt by Dominicans in 1821 freed the country from the Spanish, but in 1822 Haiti occupied Santo Domingo (the name of the former Spanish-held area at that time). Haitians remained until expelled by another revolt in 1844, and the name was changed to the Dominican Republic. Independence was short-lived, however, because Spain regained the country in 1861. The Spanish withdrew in 1865.

The next half-century was one of corrupt rule, confusion, and dictatorship for Santo Domingo. In 1907, the United States undertook control of the country's finances; and in 1915, the U.S. Marines occupied the country. They remained until 1924. In 1930, Rafael Leonidas Trujillo Molina assumed power. He and members of his family maintained a tight control until he was assassinated in 1961. The Dominican Republic was admitted to the United Nations on October 24, 1945.

After Trujillo's assassination, Joaquin Balaguer resigned as president; and in 1962, the first real election in almost forty years returned Juan Bosch to the presidency. Bosch was deposed in a coup the next year, and civil turmoil continued. In 1965 the United States sent in Marines to protect American lives and property, and to prevent the possibility of a government of the Castro type. In the first election after the troops were withdrawn, Balaguer defeated Bosch, and was reelected in 1970 and 1974.

EAST GERMANY

For the history of Germany prior to the provisional partition in 1945, see West Germany (Federal Republic of Germany). The failure of the Allies to agree upon the future disposition of defeated Germany after World War II resulted in the formal division of Germany into an eastern and a western section. In June 1948, the Russians instituted a series of unilateral changes, including the use of a new currency in the eastern zone. They also blockaded Allied traffic into the western section of Berlin. That city was forced to rely upon airlifted supplies until the blockade was broken. Five months after the Federal Republic of Germany had been established in the western zone, the German Democratic Republic was organized by the Russians in the eastern zone on October 7, 1949.

The Democratic Republic was maintained largely under Soviet protection. It seemed that the unification of Germany was not imminent, and the two Germanies began to deal with one another. They finally signed their first treaty in May 1972. Both were admitted to the United Nations on the same day, September 18, 1973.

ECUADOR

The area of what is now Ecuador became a part of the great South American empire of the Inca Indians a few years before the voyages of Columbus to the New World.

The Spanish Conquistador Francisco Pizarro began the conquest of the Inca Empire in 1530. One of Pizarro's men founded Quito (the present capital of Ecuador) in 1534. Spanish colonial domination lasted until 1822. In that year the revolutionary generals Simón Bolivar and José San Martín met at Guayaquil, Ecuador, to decide on the future of the liberated regions of northern South America. The result of this meeting was the formation of Gran Colombia, which included the present states of Venezuela, Colombia, Panama, and Ecuador. This union collapsed in 1830 and Ecuador became an independent republic. Since 1830, the country has rarely been administered by a stable government. It was admitted to the United Nations on December 21, 1945.

EGYPT

The civilization of ancient Egypt arose in the lower valley of the Nile River over five thousand years ago. By 3200 B.C. the land of Egypt was unified by King Menes, who ruled as "King of Upper and Lower Egypt." The use of writing developed in Egypt at this time. From small beginnings a mighty empire and a high civilization arose, led mainly by priest-kings and kings who called themselves gods. Their civilization

Egypt—Sphinx and Pyramids

flourished for 2,500 years. The Egyptians built great cities, temples, pyramids, and statues; they opened sea and land routes of trade, and their armies commanded respect throughout the world.

In 1150 B.C., civilized peoples elsewhere discovered iron and how to use it. Egypt had no iron resources, and this contributed to the decline of its power. The history of ancient Egypt came to an end with the conquest by Alexander the Great in 332 B.C.

In 30 B.C., Roman legions entered Egypt. It became the chief source of grain in the Roman world. Byzantine (Eastern Roman Empire) rule began in A.D. 395 and lasted until the Arab conquest in A.D. 600. Egypt gradually developed into a Moslem nation with a strong Arabic culture. Arabic rule lasted to the sixteenth century and then gave way to a long period of Turkish (Ottoman Empire) rule.

In 1881, a revolution against the Turkish authorities resulted in French and British intercession. Egypt became a British protectorate in 1882. The protectorate ended in 1922, and Egypt became a self-governing kingdom in 1936. In 1951, an army junta overthrew the monarchy; and in 1956 Egypt nationalized the famous Suez Canal, over the objections of many foreign powers.

A short war between Egypt and Israel broke out in October 1956, in which the United Kingdom and France joined in attacking Egypt. It was ended when the United Nations interceded. In 1958, Egypt and Syria united to proclaim a United Arab Republic. In 1961, Syria withdrew from the union, but the name United Arab Republic was retained by Egypt as the nation's official title until 1971. Then the official designation of the country became Arab Republic of Egypt. Under one name or another, Egypt has been a member of the United Nations since it was first admitted on February 1, 1958.

Egypt sought with varying degrees of zeal to act as the spokesman of the Arab world, particularly in its relations with Israel. Hostility between Israel and Egypt developed into active warfare in June 1967. Israel emerged after six days of combat with total victory. Israel occupied Egypt's Sinai Peninsula and a truce continued until 1973. In October of that year, Egypt took the offensive, and forces of each country were able to cross the Suez Canal to establish beachheads on the other's territory. In the ensuing negotiations, Israel withdrew from the west bank of the canal and from a strip along its east bank, and Egypt reopened the canal for the first time in eight years.

El Salvador—The National Palace in the city of San Salvador

In the late '70s, Egypt's president, Anwar Sadat, emerged as a leading figure for world peace, with special attention to the Middle East. His efforts ended with his assassination October 6, 1981.

EL SALVADOR

The history of El Salvador began in 1524 with its conquest by the Spanish conquistador Pedro de Alvarado. San Salvador was founded in 1528 at its present location. Throughout the Spanish colonial period the area of the present republic formed two provinces of the captaincy-general of Guatemala.

Independence from Spain was achieved as a part of Guatemala in 1821. In 1824, the area became a part of the United Provinces of Central America, a federation of Central America that lasted until 1839. El Salvador became a separate nation on January 1, 1841. The Organization of Central American States (ODECA), formed in 1951, includes El Salvador. The capital of this loose association of states is at San Salvador. The political history of El Salvador during the past century has been marked by violence and rapid changes in government. El Salvador became a member of the United Nations on October 24, 1945.

During the early '80s, El Salvador became a battleground for competing ideologies, with the United States supporting the government (to the tune of $20 million in 1983) and Russia and Cuba backing the leftist guerrillas seeking its overthrow.

EQUATORIAL GUINEA

Equatorial Guinea is the former Spanish

Guinea. It consists of Río Muni (an enclave on the equatorial coast of West Africa) and two islands in the Gulf of Guinea. One of these islands, formerly called Fernando Póo and renamed Macias Nguema (after the first president of the country), is about 20 miles offshore. The other, formerly named Annobón and renamed Pigalu, is about four hundred miles to the southwest. All were acquired by Spain in 1778. The islands were used as stations in the slave trade. No attempt to occupy Río Muni was made until the last quarter of the nineteenth century.

In 1959, the territories were designated as two provinces of Spain. In 1963, they were granted a degree of autonomy and called Equatorial Guinea. A referendum concerning independence was held in 1968, and on October 12, 1968, full independence was granted. The country was admitted to the United Nations on November 12, 1968.

ETHIOPIA

In ancient times the power of Egypt's pharaohs extended southward into what is now Ethiopia and along the headwaters of the Nile River. By the eleventh century before Christ, Ethiopian rulers had turned the tables and ruled mighty Egypt for a few centuries. During this period of expansion the Ethiopians absorbed much Egyptian culture. Christianity was introduced in about A.D. 330.

In the following centuries Ethiopia continued as a powerful state, although it ceased to rule Egypt. Through contacts with foreign regions, trade and immigration expanded. By the fifteenth century, however, Ethiopia had become divided into many small kingdoms.

Modern Ethiopia dates from the time of Menelik I (1844–1913) who pieced the country back together again. It grew into an empire, but the former kingdoms that made up the empire now form mere provinces in modern Ethiopia.

The Italian occupation and colonization of parts of Ethiopia began in the late nineteenth century. Italian expansion culminated in a full-scale invasion and conquest of the empire in 1935.

In 1941, during World War II, British and Ethiopian troops reconquered the country. Ethiopia became a member of the United Nations on November 13, 1945. In 1952, the former Italian colony of Eritrea was made an autonomous part of Ethiopia; but in 1962, it was reduced to the status of a province. A movement for the secession of Eritrea erupted into armed clashes by 1970.

After his appearance in defense of Ethiopia before the League of Nations in 1936, the Emperor Haile Selassie became an international figure. He was deposed by a military junta in 1974, after a reign of 44 years, and the monarchy was abolished in 1975. The capital of Ethiopia, Addis Ababa, is the headquarters of the Organization of African Unity, established there in 1963. The new government signed a pact with Russia in 1977.

The following year, Cuba sent 20,000 troops in to help repulse an attack by Somali forces.

FAROE ISLANDS

About A.D. 1000, the Vikings came to the Faroe Islands from Norway. At first a Norwegian dependency, they were attached to the Danish Crown, along with Norway, in 1380. In 1709, they became a part of the Danish kingdom. In 1814, when Norway was ceded to Sweden, the Faroes remained with Denmark, along with Iceland and Greenland.

In 1940, when the Nazis invaded Denmark and the Low Countries, the British sent forces to secure the islands from German occupation; at the end of the war they withdrew. A plebiscite for self-determination resulted in such a close vote (5,660 for independence, 5,499 against) that the Danish government declared the voting indecisive. Renewed negotiations led to a degree of autonomy, especially in economic matters. The islands acquired their own currency, which had to be covered by the Danish kroner, and the right to fly their own flag at sea.

FIJI

The Fiji Islands were discovered by Abel Tasman in 1643 and were visited by Captain James Cook in 1774. Captain William Bligh was the first to describe Fiji to any extent. Missionaries came to the islands in 1835 and helped to eradicate cannibalism.

The islands were annexed by Great Britain in 1874 and were administered by the colonial office until 1970, when a parliamentary system was set up and Fiji became an independent nation. It was admitted to the United Nations on October 13, 1970.

Finland—Helsinki

FINLAND

The Finnish people came originally from the Volga region of what is now the Soviet Union. They arrived in the present area of Finland sometime during the seventh century A.D. The Swedes began to penetrate Finland in the twelfth century. Swedish invasions took the form of religious crusades to convert the people to Christianity. This struggle against pagan Finns lasted two hundred years, ending with the complete conquest of Finland by the Swedes in 1293.

Russia annexed parts of Swedish-held areas in 1721, and the remainder of Finland in 1809. Finland was a grand duchy of the Russian Empire until 1917. The revolution in Russia gave the Finns a chance to proclaim independence.

In the great civil war that followed the Bolshevik victory in November 1917, Germany intervened on behalf of Finland and secured the *de facto* separation from Russia, but intended to establish a German-controlled government. However, after Germany's defeat, Finland emerged in 1919 as a parliamentary republic.

The Aland Islands were secured from Sweden in 1921. In 1939, the Soviet Union and Finland broke relations and two short wars followed that merged with World War II. Finland was defeated and had to pay, both in money and in the loss of some territory. Finland paid her reparations by 1952 and the Soviet Union abandoned the Porkkala naval base, returning it to Finland. However, parts of Karelia and the Petsamo region are apparently permanently lost. Finland was admitted to the United Nations on December 14, 1955.

FRANCE

Classical Greek colonies were founded on the Mediterranean coast of what is now France as early as 600 B.C. However, very little was known of the region until Julius Caesar began his conquests in 58 B.C. The Celtic tribes who lived in the present France were called "Gauls" by the Romans. Gallic legends, traditions, and influence have remained an integral part of French culture. Gallic France achieved a high order of civilization. The region was richly endowed with prosperous cities, a thriving trade, and with great works of both Roman and Gallic engineering and architecture.

After A.D. 180, Gaul experienced violent invasion and wholesale destruction. Visigoths, Ostrogoths, Vandals, Lombardi, Alemanni, Burgundians, and many other invaders passed through Gaul, or conquered parts of it.

In A.D. 476 the Western Roman Empire came to an end and Gaul was left to fend for itself. The Franks, a Germanic tribe, entered Gaul and by A.D. 486 had united under Clovis, who became a convert to Christianity in 496. The Franks gradually conquered most of Gaul, but their Merovingian dynasty was unable to maintain control over large areas.

Under the later Merovingians, power passed to the mayors of the palace. Eventually these mayors took over the kingship titles, and in this way the

France—Paris

Carlovingians became the ruling dynasty of the region that was beginning to be called "France."

Charlemagne (768–814), also called Charles the Great, raised the Frankish people to the height of power in western Europe. Charlemagne ruled not only what is now France, but most of Germany and Italy as well. He had a difficult task in defending his realm from the Vikings and hundreds of other great and small groups. France became one great battlefield.

Huge castles rose over the ashes of formerly beautiful Roman cities. People locked themselves into these bastions for defense against the rising violence and lawlessness that gradually pervaded all western Europe. The population sold its freedom for protection, and serfdom became an established institution—the Age of Feudalism had come to France.

After his death the empire of Charlemagne fell apart. What was left of the once-great empire—a small area centered around Paris—went to Hugh Capet, who founded the third dynasty of French kings. His family was to rule France for 800 years.

The Capetian kings gradually expanded their authority and began to establish order in the lands they controlled. The fashioning of a new France by the Capetian kings was done at the expense of feudal elements and with the aid of a rising new middle class of merchants and nonfeudal groups.

Louis IX (1226–1270) overcame the feudal nobility by making the kingship popular to all groups—even to the peasantry. He outlawed a number of feudal practices and his capital became the intellectual center of Europe. Louis IX died while on a Crusade to the Holy Lands.

The Crusades began in 1096 and lasted until the fourteenth century. Most of the leaders in the first four Crusades were of the French nobility. France learned many lessons in warfare, and received from the Crusades the benefits of greater commerce and quickened industrial activity. These things stimulated a Renaissance in France and helped to lift Europe out of the "Dark Ages."

French power and the Capetian dynasty itself were challenged from England, first by Henry II (1154), and then by Henry's sons, Richard and John. The French kings were able to hold most of their territory in this first great encounter with English power.

In 1328, Edward III again challenged the right of the Capetian house to the French throne. The fighting began in 1337 and lasted for over one hundred years. It was during this "One Hundred Years' War" that Joan of Arc inspired French arms and helped to crown Charles VII king of France. Joan was captured and burned at the stake as a witch, but French armies advanced and by 1461 had driven the English out of France.

It should be noted that French-speaking nobility fought on both sides in this war. Yet France came out of the war more united than ever before. The next two centuries saw discord once more, but this time the conflict was a religious one.

The Protestant Reformation did not have as strong an effect on France as it did on other countries. But large areas of the population that did become Protestant were persecuted by the Catholics.

Under Louis XIV (1643–1715) kingship reached its greatest heights. The Sun King built a magnificent court and did much to make France the center of Western civilization.

The splendor of monarchial France did not last. The end came during the reign of Louis XVI, when a revolution overturned the throne in 1789. The

French Revolution abolished the divine right principle, replacing it with political authority. The bloody civil war that ensued ended only when Napoleon Bonaparte took control. Napoleon led the French nation in conquests and empire-building that ended in his defeat at Waterloo (a town in present Belgium).

The First Empire was succeeded by a monarchy (1814–1848) and the Second Republic (1848–1852). Memories of Napoleon were revived during the short Second Empire that lasted from 1852 to 1870, led by Napoleon III. After 1870, France blundered into a conflict with a newly united Germany. She was beaten, and then revolution overthrew the Empire, creating the Third Republic (1875).

A chance for revenge against German came in 1914. In that year World War I began and France became the main battlefield. Although victorious, France was greatly weakened.

World War II began in 1939 and again German armies crossed the frontiers of France. This time the nation's resistance against a large German army lasted only six weeks. A government was established to administer the German occupation. An "unoccupied" zone was governed from Vichy. Meanwhile, a government-in-exile functioned from London under the leadership of General Charles de Gaulle. French guerrilla fighters (the Resistance) worked closely with the De Gaulle headquarters and the Allies. Following the invasion by the Allies, France was liberated by October 1944.

De Gaulle retired in 1946. The Fourth Republic that governed from 1946 to 1958 lost major French colonies, including those in the Middle East, Indochina, Tunisia, and Morocco. But it made a bitter and vain effort to retain Algeria. Recalled to take the leadership of the Fifth Republic, De Gaulle granted independence to this colony in 1962. Although he resigned once more in 1969, many of his policies were continued by his successor, Georges Pompidou.

France was a charter member of the United Nations on October 24, 1945. The country also joined the North Atlantic Treaty Organization; but in that alliance French policy was independent and unpredictable.

While France has resisted communism, it has drifted toward socialism, culminating with the election May 10, 1981, of Francois Mitterrand, a socialist candidate, over Giscard D'Estaing. Mitterrand proceeded to nationalize five major industries and most banks.

FRENCH GUIANA

French Guiana was settled in 1604 and has been a French possession since 1667. It was long the site of a penal colony named Devil's Island, but the last prisoners were removed in 1945. In 1946, French Guiana became an overseas department of France. It is the last European dependency on the mainland of South America.

FRENCH POLYNESIA

The Overseas Territory of French Polynesia was formerly called French Settlements in Oceania. The major island groups that comprise the territory were made protectorates of France in 1844 and colonies in 1880. The Marquesas and Gambier groups were annexed in 1881. The entire region became a member of the French Community in 1958.

FRENCH SOUTHERN TERRITORIES

This Overseas Territory of France includes: (1) the Kerguelen Archipelago of three hundred islands, discovered in 1772 by Yves de Kerguelen. With an area of 2,700 square miles, they are located in the Indian Ocean southeast of Madagascar and used mainly in scientific research; (2) the Crozet Archipelago, discovered in 1772 by Marion-Dufressne. These 15 islands in the Indian Ocean, with an area of 193 square miles, are uninhabited; (3) St. Paul, an uninhabited island of 3 square miles south of Madagascar in the Indian Ocean; (4) New Amsterdam, an island of 19 square miles, discovered in 1522 by Magellan's ships. It is located in the south Indian Ocean and used as an administrative center; and (5) the Adelie Coast (Terre Adèlie) of the Antarctic continent, an estimated 150,000-square-mile area, discovered in 1840 by Dumont d'Urville.

In 1960, other islands were added to the territory. These include Europa, Juan de Nova (Saint-Christophe), Bassas-de-India, and the Glorioso Islands, all located in Mozambique Channel and having a total area of 23 square miles.

GABON

In the mid-nineteenth century, the region of

Gabon and the city of Libreville, together with other African republics of today, were established under French control and lumped together under the name of "French Equatorial Africa." In 1910, the colony of Gabon was officially organized as part of that region.

In 1946, the French Union was established and Gabon became an overseas territory. In 1960, it became completely independent within the French Community. Gabon was admitted to the United Nations on September 20, 1960.

GAMBIA

An enclave within Sierra Leone on the coast of West Africa is the tiny nation of Gambia, the smallest on the African mainland. It was formed out of the colony and protectorate of the same name. Great Britain acquired both in the seventeenth century and usually administered them from Sierra Leone.

In 1963, Gambia was given autonomy, and on February 18, 1965, it was made a member of the Commonwealth. On September 21, 1965, Gambia became a member of the United Nations. In 1970 the Gambians voted to become a republic, but to retain Commonwealth membership.

GHANA

The first authenticated landing of Europeans in this region of Africa was that of some Portuguese in 1470. The first British trading expedition came in 1553. Over the centuries Danes, Dutch, Germans, Portuguese, and British controlled parts of what was then called the Gold Coast.

During the eighteenth century slave trade developed, and by 1821 the British won increasing control of the region. The Crown took over the private trading-post settlements. In time the Danish forts were purchased by Britain. The Fanti chiefs approved a pact that allowed British agents to participate in administering justice.

Ghana was granted autonomy in 1951 and independence on December 12, 1956. It remained within the Commonwealth, became a member of the United Nations on March 8, 1957, and became a republic within the Commonwealth on July 1, 1960. The presidency was abolished in 1972.

GIBRALTAR

Located on a peninsula jutting out from Spain's southern coast, and guarding the Mediterranean Sea, the rock of Gibraltar was captured by England from Spain in 1704. It has been a British colony ever since, despite frequent Spanish protests. It was granted local autonomy in 1969.

GILBERT AND ELLICE ISLANDS

A group of archipelagoes in the Pacific Ocean comprise the British colony of the Gilbert and Ellice Islands, formed in 1915. It includes the Gilbert Islands on each side of the Equator, whose inhabitants are Micronesians; the Ellice Islands, south of the Equator, whose inhabitants are Melanesians; and several other islands. The colony was granted self-government in 1971. At the end of 1975, the Ellice Islands separated from the others and renamed itself the territory of Tuvalu.

GREECE

Historians regard the ancient Greeks as the founders of Western civilization. The Greeks were the first to develop the concept of democracy. They became Western civilization's first great dramatists, philosophers, scientists, doctors, geographers, orators, and poets. After two thousand years, the Greek world passed its vast heritage on to Rome. In a real sense, Greek civilization did not die; it merely moved to Rome, changed its form, and then brought forth a new civilization—that of modern times.

The recorded story of Ancient Greece began on the island of Crete, which lies on the southern limits of the Aegean Sea south of the mainland of the Greek peninsula. The Cretan civilization, also known as the Minoan, developed about 3000 B.C. It flourished until about 1600 B.C., when it was overpowered by an invasion from the mainland.

The mainland Greeks then developed the Mycenaean civilization on the mainland. By this time Greeks had entered the Bronze Age. They built fortified cities and ships that crossed the Mediterranean Sea to carry on trade with other peoples. Finally they developed a written language (deciphered in 1953). Mycenae in southern

Greece—The Acropolis, Athens

Greece was the central city of this civilization. Mycenaean civilization produced the events described in the *Iliad* and the *Odyssey*.

The Mycenaeans were eventually overwhelmed by invaders from the north. The invaders came in three separate waves, each wave displacing earlier ones. The invasions ended about 1000 B.C. All four groups (including the original Mycenaeans) settled down, intermingled, and finally created the Greek Golden Age.

About 750 B.C., Greeks began to establish colonies along the Mediterranean coast. Some of the more famous colonies were Lisbon, Marseille, Odessa, Naples, Pompeii, and Syracuse. During the Golden Age (480–399 B.C.) there were more than 150 Greek states and colonies strung along the Mediterranean and Black Seas from Spain in the West to the Caucasus, on the edge of Asia in the East.

The first coinage in the Western world appeared in Asia Minor (Kingdom of Lydia) as a result of the rise of Greek trade and commerce there. The coins of Athens became world famous for their reliability, and those of Syracuse were of unsurpassed workmanship and design.

Invasions by Persians from the east (Asia Minor) stirred the Greek world into a movement to unify the scattered states for defensive purposes. The Persian invasions were halted in a series of great battles by the Greeks. A united Greek army crushed the Persians at Platea in 479 B.C. It was at the end of the Persian Wars that the Golden Age flourished.

Athens was the center of Greek intellectual and artistic ferment during this period. The greatest works of sculpture, architecture, drama, and history were produced at Athens at that time. However, nearly all the Greek states shared in the Golden Age. As the power of Athens grew, so did the jealousies of her neighbors. In particular, Sparta became the bitter enemy of Athens. Sparta was a militaristic, highly disciplined, and regimented state. The wars that followed between Athens and her enemies were won by Sparta and the Golden Age came to an end.

Sparta was herself defeated soon after, and all Greece lay weakened by warfare—the ripe fruit for any determined conqueror. Alexander the Great seized the opportunity and in 338 B.C. conquered all of Greece.

Alexander the Great spread Greek culture and ideas throughout the known world. However, his great empire crumbled after his death in 323 B.C.

The Roman army easily conquered a divided Greece in 197 B.C. and again in 167 B.C. Greece became a mere province in the Roman Empire. It was called Achaea. The name *Greek* was first used by the Romans. The classical Greeks called themselves "Hellenes" and their land "Hellas."

After the fall of Rome, Greece became part of the Byzantine, or Eastern Empire. After A.D. 1261, a group of independent states arose and flourished until all were conquered by the Turks in 1460. Some of the islands remained in the possession of Venice until the eighteenth century.

In the nineteenth century the spirit of national independence was reawakened. Following an unsuccessful attempt in 1770, the Greeks proclaimed an independent state in 1821. Their independence was supported by Britain, France, and Russia, and was defended by those powers in 1827. The London Protocol of 1830 secured international recognition of the Greek state.

Greece became a monarchy—first under a Bavarian royal house, then under a Danish prince, who took the throne as George I in 1863. As the result of several wars, Greece acquired Crete, parts of Macedonia and Thrace, and parts of European Turkey. This led to a disastrous war with Turkey, after which some two million Greeks were exchanged for more than a million Turks living in Greece.

During World War II, Greece was under German occupation. The monarchy found exile in Cairo, while the resistance forces fought on in Greece. After the war, the resistance (which included communists) tried to seize power. But a plebiscite in 1946 accepted the monarchy.

A military junta took power in 1967 and forced Constantine, the last king, to flee. The dictatorship was overthrown in 1973, and a parliamentary republic was restored by referendum in 1974.

In 1981, Andres Papandreou of the Panhellenic Socialist Movement was elected prime minister. Greece is a member of the NATO military alliance.

GREENLAND

The huge island of Greenland was discovered and colonized at the end of the tenth century by Eric the Red. Two centuries later it was claimed by Norway, but thereafter the colony was neglected. Although many explorers passed the west coast of Greenland, only traces of the old colony remained when the island was revisited in 1721 by Danish missionaries.

Greenland was again colonized, receiving only enough aid to support the missions and provide a base for explorations.

After the Napoleonic Wars, Denmark and Norway were separated, and Greenland remained with Denmark. In 1979 it was granted home rule, electing a socialist-dominated legislature. It also translated its official name into the Greenlandic language, Kalaallit Nunaat.

GRENADA

The most southerly of the British Windward Islands, Grenada was discovered by Columbus in 1498. It was held alternately by the French and British until 1784. The Windward Islands were given autonomy in 1967, with the status of associated states in the British Commonwealth, and it declared its independence in 1974.

In 1983, acting on intelligence reports of a buildup by Soviet and Cuban operatives, the United States sent in a military detachment to secure the island. American troops were later withdrawn.

GUADELOUPE

Guadeloupe was discovered by Columbus in 1493. It was colonized in 1635 and became a French possession in 1674. It was made an overseas department of France in 1946. Its dependencies include Marie Galante, Les Saintes, Désirade, St. Barthélemy, and part of St. Martin.

GUATEMALA

The ancestors of modern-day Guatemalans were the Mayan peoples who developed a remarkable civilization between A.D. 300 and 900. The Maya were a short, stocky people who lived originally in what is now Mexico, Guatemala, Honduras, British Honduras, and El Salvador. The classic civilization (ca. A.D. 350 to 600) may have included two million people. The Maya developed mathematics, a 365-day calendar, ideographic writing, sculpture, music, and literature. Their great cities now lie abandoned, deep in the jungles of Central America. Their decline is partly a mystery. By the time the Spanish came, the cities had already been abandoned; the people had become food-gatherers and sedentary agriculturalists.

The Spanish conquest began in 1524 and was completed by 1550. The capital was established at Guatemala City in 1776. In 1821, all the Central American colonies declared their independence of Spain and joined the Mexican Empire. Soon they withdrew to form the United Provinces of Central America. This union was weak and collapsed in 1939, and Guatemala the same year became a republic. Its government has been among the least stable in Central America. Guatemala was admitted to the United Nations on November 21, 1945.

GUINEA

European penetration and exploration of what is now Guinea began in the fifteenth century under the Portuguese. France began to trade and acquire territory there early in the seventeenth century. France administered all her Guinea region as a part of Senegal until 1845. Resistance to French rule was bitterly carried out by Samory Touré, who fought the French from 1882 until he was captured in 1898. The boundaries of Guinea were established in 1882.

In 1946, Africans in Guinea became French citizens and a territorial legislature was organized. At that time it became a part of the loose federation of French West Africa. In 1958, Guinea was given the choice of becoming an independent nation, either in the French Community or outside it. Guinea chose independence without association with the Community. It was admitted to the United Nations on December 12, 1958.

GUINEA-BISSAU

Located on the West African coast between the former French colonies of Senegal and Guinea, this region belonged to Portugal since Bissau was set up as a Portuguese post in 1687. Before that, since its discovery by Nuno Tristão in 1446, this part of Guinea was active in the slave trade. Its status as a Portuguese colony was settled by an agreement with France in 1886. Initially administered from Cape Verde, Portuguese Guinea became a separate colony in 1879. In 1951, it was designated an overseas territory. Its independence was recognized by Portugal on September 7, 1974, and ten days later Guinea-Bissau was admitted to the United Nations.

GUYANA

The westernmost of the three European colonies known as the Guianas, this area was first colonized by the Dutch. It was traded to the British after the Napoleonic era.

The three settlements of Berbice, Essequibo, and Demerara were combined in 1831 to form British Guiana, and became a crown colony in 1928. Local autonomy was introduced in 1953, and a contest developed between the black and East Indian inhabitants for control. The black faction prevailed, and on May 22, 1966, the independence of the country was recognized. On September 20, 1966, Guyana was admitted to the United Nations.

HAITI

That portion of the island of Hispaniola that is now the Republic of Haiti was ceded to France in 1697. It became known as St. Domingue, while the Spanish portion of Hispaniola was called Santo Domingo.

French control was swept away by a revolution in 1803. Jean Jacques Dessalines named the country Haiti, and was proclaimed emperor. He was assassinated in 1806. From that date until 1820, Haiti was divided into a kingdom and a republic. Haiti was reunited in 1822 by Jean Pierre Boyer, who also seized Santo Domingo. He ruled the entire island of Hispaniola until 1844. The future Dominican Republic withdrew in that year.

From 1915 to 1934, Haiti was occupied by the United States. It became a member of the United Nations on October 24, 1945.

HONDURAS

In 1502, Christopher Columbus discovered the region that is now Honduras. The Spanish explorer Hernan Cortés made the first settlement there in 1524 and claimed the land for Spain.

Honduras remained under the rule of Spain until 1821, when the country revolted and was annexed to Mexico. From then on, Honduras' history includes a series of alliances and wars with neighboring countries. Starting in 1883 and continuing for twenty years, Honduras was in continuous revolt and civil disorder. In 1911 the United States intervened in the strife between Honduras and Guatemala. Civil war followed World War I. The United States intervened again in 1915, and the 1930s were turbulent.

Honduras was admitted to the United Nations on December 17, 1945.

HONG KONG

Hong Kong was occupied in 1841 by the British. In 1860, the Kowloon peninsula was added. Additional territory was added by a lease agreement in 1898. Hong Kong is a crown colony, administered by a governor assisted by an executive council. Most of the people are Chinese.

HUNGARY

Within historic times the area of the present Hungary was a part of the Roman provinces of Pannonia and Dacia. Germanic tribes displaced the Romans in the second century A.D., and were, in turn, conquered by Attila the Hun in the fifth century.

The Magyars (Hungarians) were originally located in what is now central Russia. They invaded and occupied the lands between the Tisza and Danube rivers in A.D. 895. Christianity was introduced during the reign of the first great Hungarian king, Stephen I (canonized in 1083).

The Magyars fought wars on all sides. Their greatest period of expansion was during the reign of Louis the Great (1342–1382) which was after the country had been overrun by the Mongols (1235–1270) from Asia. Hungarian power was broken by the Turks in 1526. Thereafter, the nation was split into several petty baronies and duchies.

The Hapsburg kings of Austria defeated the Turks and gradually united the Magyar people under Austrian control. Hungary was finally driven to revolt by the repressive policies of Prince Metternich in 1848. The revolt was crushed in 1849. Austria was gradually weakened by war with Prussia, and was forced to give in to Hungarian national aspirations in 1867. In that year a dual monarchy was established, called Austria-Hungary.

Austria-Hungary expanded into the Balkans in the twentieth century. By this time it was also known as the Austro-Hungarian Empire. Political annexations aimed at Turkey precipitated the Balkan Wars, and Austria-Hungary became deeply implicated in Balkan affairs. The assassination of the heir to the throne of Austria-Hungary in 1914 precipitated World War I, in

Hong Kong—General view of Victoria Island

which the dual monarchy entered on the side of Germany. After the war, the dual monarchy collapsed.

Hungary was separated from Austria and stripped of nearly two-thirds of its territory. In 1920, it became a kingdom, but without a king. In the hope of retrieving lost territory, Hungary in World War II joined the Axis powers and was again defeated along with Germany. She again lost territory, this time what had been acquired after 1937.

In 1948, the Hungarian Workers party (Communist) seized control and established the one-party (Communist) People's Republic of Hungary. A revolt occurred in 1956 which was directed against the Communist regime. After temporary success, the revolt was crushed with the aid of military forces from the U.S.S.R. Hungary was admitted to the United Nations on December 14, 1955.

By the late 1970s, Hungarian laws had relaxed to allow more personal freedoms than most other communist nations. Many Hungarians who fled the country in 1956 have returned to their homeland.

ICELAND

Iceland was settled shortly before A.D. 900, mainly by Norsemen. Christianity appeared at the beginning of the twelfth century, and with it certain reforms which helped to stablize the various fighting clans. In the mid-thirteenth century, both sides in a civil war appealed to Norway for intervention; the result was unification with that country in 1262–1264.

Then followed a succession of events which nearly wiped out the island: harsh Norwegian rule, volcanic eruptions, and bubonic plague. Iceland passed into Danish hands in 1483 when the king of Denmark came to the Norwegian throne.

With the decline of the monarchs, Iceland began its struggle for freedom, and in 1874 won limited home rule. By 1918, it had become a sovereign nation under Denmark's crown. On June 17, 1944, Iceland became a completely independent republic.

During World War II, Iceland served as an important naval station for United States warships. Iceland was admitted to the United Nations on November 19, 1946. In 1972, Iceland banned foreign fishing fleets from within 200 miles of its shores.

INDIA

The earliest civilization known to have existed on the subcontinent of India developed in the Indus River valley of what is now Pakistan about five thousand years ago. The ruins at Mohenjodaro indicate a very high degree of civilization.

Mystery surrounds the fate of that civilization. The Aryan invasions began about four thousand years ago, and their influence gradually spread throughout India. They established Hinduism, the family pattern of India, and the caste system. Alexander the Great came to India by way of the Khyber Pass in 326 B.C., but Greek influence was not felt east of the Indus valley. The Maurya Empire arose after Alexander's visit. Under Asoka (273–232 B.C.), India was finally united into one state. It included nearly all of the present India, Pakistan, and other parts of southern Asia. After Asoka, India was subdivided into many competing states. The Gupta rulers became the first Hindu kings and brought about a "golden age" of Sanskrit learning. Rich cities and great universities were founded. By about A.D. 1000, the Hindu period had reached its peak. Many of the great works of art and architecture in India that still survive date from this period.

The next age of flourishing civilization was initiated by the Moslem invaders who had gradually spread their power and influence throughout northern India from the eighth to the sixteenth century. The unification of India began again in 1526. Babar, Akbar, Shah Jahan, and Aurangzeb established the Mogul Empire and caused the rise of a new and even richer civilization in India. Aurangzeb, the last of the great emperors, tried to convert the people to Islam by force. This, together with the extravagance of the Mogul rulers, led to the downfall of Mogul power. Their demise made it easier for the Europeans to obtain a foothold on the subcontinent.

Vasco da Gama (Portuguese) reached Calicut (on the west coast of India) in 1498. Thereafter the Portuguese, English, and French began a mad scramble for spheres of trade and colonies. The British eventually won. By the middle of the nineteenth century they controlled most of India in one form or another. British withdrawal was sudden and decisive in 1947. India was then a single independent nation, but was still divided in many other ways.

The most serious division was between Hindu and Moslem. Bloodshed and civil war resulted

India—Golden Temple of Amritsar

when the Moslem state of Pakistan was proclaimed upon the date of Indian independence. Other serious problems that still plague the Indian nation are the many language and ethnic barriers; the system of caste and other religious issues; the poverty of the masses of Indians; and the lack of a genuine national tradition and spirit for the nation as a whole.

India has attempted to remain neutral between communist and capitalist nations. She tried to defend her borders against Chinese claims and invasions. India also was engaged in a serious dispute over Kashmir. Kashmir is divided between India and Pakistan, and only an armed truce prevents warfare along that frontier. India has been trying to lessen the linguistic differences and problems by establishing states on the basis of language or of national ethnic minorities. India became a member of the United Nations on October 30, 1945.

INDONESIA

According to Indonesian history, the people of the original archipelago were overwhelmed by countless migrations from the Asian mainland. Some two thousand years ago, Hindu traders introduced their religion and culture. Then followed Indian Buddhists who also greatly influenced the natives. The Islamic religion entered at the end of the fifteenth century and gained a firm foothold.

Portuguese traders came next. They were soon pushed out by the Dutch, under whom the islands became a highly important colony until World War II. From the beginning of the nineteenth century on, the Dutch rulers put down several attempts at revolution. World War II ended the Japanese occupation, and the Dutch attempted to return to power. A self-proclaimed independence followed, with both open and guerrilla warfare. At the end of 1949, the Dutch officially relinquished sovereignty. On September 28, 1950, Indonesia became a member of the United Nations.

A dispute with the Netherlands arose over the disposition of Dutch New Guinea, which Indonesia claimed as her province of West Irian. In 1963, West Irian was turned over to Indonesia by the United Nations. Meanwhile, the parliamentary system was changed to an authoritarian regime, based on the slogan of "guided democracy." A military coup in 1965 suppressed the strong communist faction of Indonesia. In 1967, it deposed President Sukarno. The leader of the junta, Suharto, became president and prime minister. Indonesia, which had been a charter member of the United Nations, withdrew from the organization in January 1965. But she resumed membership on September 28, 1966.

IRAN

Iran was called Persia until 1935. The history of Persia dates back to the time of the Medes, a people who settled in what is now Iran in 1500 B.C. The Medes dominated the Persians until the time of Cyrus the Great. In about 549, Cyrus conquered the Medes and extended his Persian kingdom. Persia conquered Babylonia, restoring Jerusalem to the Jews in 538 B.C. Persia failed to capture the Greek city-states in 490 and 480 B.C., and was itself defeated by Alexander the Great in 331 B.C.

The Parthians prevented the Romans from conquering Persia. They controlled the area until the third century A.D., and were followed by the Sassanians, who ruled for another four centuries.

The Arabs brought Islam to Persia in the seventh century A.D., and for centuries afterward religious caliphates ruled in Persia. The Mongols invaded in A.D. 1250. After the defeat of the caliphate in 1502, Persia was ruled by a shah (king). A constitution was granted in 1906. The period following was marked by attempts of foreign powers to gain spheres of influence in Persia. During World War II, Iran was occupied by the Allies to prevent German access to the rich Iranian oil fields. The sovereignty of Iran was reaffirmed by the Allies at the Tehran Conference in 1943. Iran joined the United Nations on October 24, 1945.

Iran is now one of the largest exporters of oil in the world. Its income allows the nation to invest in a wide variety of foreign enterprises. Iran is purchasing nuclear power plants from France and the United States; and in 1974, it loaned money to Great Britain to shore up the sagging British economy.

Popular protests forced the shah of Iran to leave the country in January 1979. Religious leader Ayatollah Khomeini seized control and shortly thereafter the American Embassy was stormed with 90 persons captured. Among them were 52 Americans who were held for 444 days before being released unharmed January 20, 1981.

IRAQ

Modern Iraq occupies the area the ancient Greeks called Mesopotamia, one of the cradles of modern civilization. As such, the history of Iraq extends back to the very beginning of writing, about 4000 B.C., and archaeologically even farther.

Eridu, Ur, Nineveh, and Babylon were among the earliest cities in human civilization. The Sumerian culture developed in about 3000 B.C. and later influenced the culture of Egypt, and the rising new civilizations of Greece and Crete.

The Sumerians were succeeded by Akkadians, Assyrians, Scythians, Persians, and finally Romans. The Arabs conquered Iraq in A.D. 637. Baghdad became a brilliant center of cultural and intellectual life.

The Mongol invasions of the thirteenth century ended the prosperity, destroyed the remarkable irrigation system, and turned the land of former greatness into a desert. The Ottoman Turks swept into Iraq in 1638 and maintained their control until, during World War I, British troops wrested it from them. The League of Nations established a British mandate over Iraq, and a monarchy was established in 1921. The mandate was terminated in 1932. The monarchy was overthrown in 1958, shortly after Iraq and Jordan had joined in a federation. The federation was terminated and Iraq was declared a republic.

Hostilities between Iraq and Iran flared into open warfare in September 1980. Two years later, Iraq had counted 40,000 dead and 100,000 wounded or captured.

IRELAND

Recorded Irish history begins with the arrival of St. Patrick on the Emerald Isle in the fifth century. Christianity spread rapidly thereafter and Ireland became dotted with great monasteries that were centers of learning and of Gaelic and Latin culture. The Viking invasions of the eighth century nearly put an end to Irish learning, but Viking power was finally broken at the Battle of Clontarf in 1014.

Anglo-Norman invasions began soon after. For 800 years, Ireland grappled with neighboring Britain for a separate and independent existence. Successive British monarchs attempted to control, cajole, or colonize Ireland, but usually ended up persecuting the inhabitants, either for religious or political reasons. Rebellions during the nineteenth century were fair warning that Irish nationalism was growing strong and ever more resentful of English control.

A civil war and political turmoil marked the period of 1916–1921 that ended with the establishment of the Irish Free State with dominion status in the British Commonwealth of Nations. In 1937, a further change came about when the

Ireland—Glendalough

British governor-general was replaced by a president. The name was then changed to Ireland (in Gaelic, *Eire*). In 1948, Ireland withdrew from the Commonwealth and on April 15, 1959 became a republic. The republic became a member of the United Nations on December 14, 1955.

Protestant and Catholic groups still wage a sporadic war of terrorism against one another.

ISLE OF MAN

The Isle of Man has been attached to the Crown of England since 1346. It is administered under its own laws and form of government consisting of legislative council, governor, and the Court of Tynwald. The people are Celtic in origin, and are called Manx, or Manxmen. Manx and English are spoken.

ISRAEL

Israel is the collective name that was applied to the descendants of Jacob, those Hebrew peoples who migrated under Abraham from Mesopotamia to Canaan sometime during the twentieth century before Christ.

The Israelites conquered most of the Canaanites, adopted their language and some of their culture. Later, some of the remaining Canaanites became known as Phoenicians. The land of Canaan is now called Palestine, part of which forms modern Israel.

In about 1100 B.C., the Israelites formed a loose organization of tribes. A united kingdom was established by Saul (1010 B.C.–970 B.C.). It became the heart of a great Hebrew civilization that flourished under David and his son, Solomon. After the death of Solomon, the kingdom split into two parts. In 722 B.C., northern Israel was conquered by the Assyrians. The southern part, Judea, held out until 586 B.C., when the Babylonians captured Jerusalem and exiled the Jews. Judea arose again after 538 B.C. and continued to flourish until A.D. 70, when Roman legions captured Jerusalem, bringing an end to ancient Israel.

The Arabs seized Palestine (the Roman name for Canaan) in A.D. 636. Four hundred years of Moslem rule followed, in which Christians and Jews were tolerated. The Turks seized the region in 1065, and the Crusades were begun in order to free the Holy Land of Christendom. Successive waves of invasions continued after the Crusades, and the Turks managed to recapture or retain most of Palestine until 1917. Jews began to return to Palestine in 1878. Britain occupied it from 1917 until 1948.

Zionism is the name of the national movement for the restoration of Palestine to the world's Jews. The Balfour Declaration of Britain (1917) supported the idea behind Zionism. Under the United Kingdom's mandate, Jewish immigrants arrived in large numbers, particularly under Nazi persecution of the European Jews and during World War II. Jews attempted to find refuge in Palestine, which they considered their historic homeland (Zion); their hopes collided with the aspirations of some Arabs, who wanted to establish independent Arab states in the area. Britain, caught between conflicting pressures, restricted Jewish immigration to Palestine. Eventually, Britain therefore precipitously abandoned the mandate, leaving the United Nations to provide a solution.

The solution proposed was the creation of a Jewish state and an Arab state in Palestine. On May 14, 1948, the Jews proclaimed their state, which they called Israel. The states of the Arab League immediately attacked Israel, were beaten off, and signed an armistice in 1949. However, no peace was established.

The Israeli government was forced to protect its population from constant sporadic attacks from all sides. The Palestinian Arabs either fled or accepted minority status within Israel. The issue of the displaced Palestinians became a critical factor in the Middle East question, along with the issue of Arab recognition of the state of Israel.

Warfare broke out in 1956, when Israel invaded Egypt and defeated the Egyptian army. The intervention of French and British forces on their behalf brought about a settlement by the United Nations. In 1967, Egypt took the offensive and was decisively defeated within six days. In 1973, Egypt forcibly recovered part of the territory occupied since 1967 by Israel. In all these conflicts Syria and other Arab states participated against Israel. On numerous occasions the issue was brought before the United Nations (to which Israel was admitted on May 11, 1949). After the acquisition of Arab territory in the 1967 war, most United Nations resolutions were unfavorable to Israel. The forging of peaceful relations between Israel and her Arab neighbors remained a major international problem.

ITALY

The roots of Italian history lie in the Roman period, and the history of Rome rested upon Greek and Etruscan civilizations.

Roman civilization began as an offshoot of that of the Etruscans whom the early Romans conquered about 200 B.C. Etruria (modern Tuscany) lay in the north-central part of the Italian peninsula. The Etruscan civilization spread into the Po River valley and reached its greatest development about 600 B.C. Etruscan control over Latium (Rome) lasted to about 500 B.C., and over southern Italy for another hundred years. Their influence upon Roman civilization is seen through the development of urban centers, large public works, maritime commerce, and in art forms. The Etruscans borrowed from Greece, and probably also from Lydia in Asia Minor.

When Rome conquered the Etrurian states in Southern Etruria in about 400 B.C., the Greek states and colonies in that area collapsed. By 272 B.C., the entire Italian peninsula had come under Roman rule.

The period of unification was followed by overseas expansion. Three wars were fought for control of the Mediterranean Sea with the Phoenician city of Carthage (near present-day Tunis in Africa). After one hundred years of war, Carthage was overwhelmed in 146 B.C.

Rome had been a republic since its founding, but because of the wars of conquest and expansion, an imperial form of government was established in 27 B.C. The first 200 years of the empire were marked by a golden age of peaceful development, prosperity, and progress in literature, the arts, engineering, architecture, and government. Despite the personal rule of some incompetent emperors, the Roman Empire flourished primarily through efficient administrative machinery, and through the occasional genius of such emperors as Augustus (27 B.C.–A.D. 14), Trajan (98–117), Hadrian (117–138), and Marcus Aurelius (161–180).

The empire eventually became too large and troublesome for the personal rule of one emperor. It was split in A.D. 395 into the Eastern Roman Empire with the seat of government at Constantinople (the present Istanbul) and a Western Roman Empire whose capital remained at Rome. Following the death in 337 of Emperor Constantine, who ruled both empires, open rebellions broke out. Spain, Gaul (France), and all the African territories had already been lost when

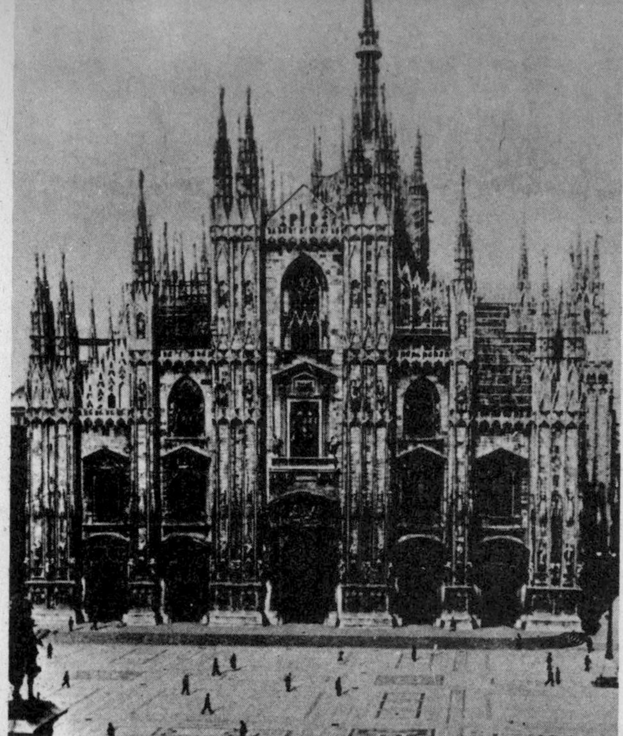

Italy—Milan Cathedral

Odoacer, a German prince, established a kingdom in the Italian peninsula in A.D. 476. The Western Roman Empire had ended. The Eastern Roman Empire survived and flourished until 1453, when the Turks overran it and captured Constantinople.

From the sixth century down to the thirteenth, Italy suffered from invasions—including those of the Lombards, Franks, Saracens, and Germans. From the tenth to the fourteenth century the Holy Roman Empire of German kings and the Christian Church, centered in Rome, became the leading contenders for power in the Italian peninsula. However, the rise of small city-states with powerful maritime interests upset the balance between papal and German rule. The south became united in the Kingdom of Naples, and the Papal States were established in central Italy; and most of the city-states were located in the north and along the coasts of both the Adriatic and Tyrrhenian seas.

Beginning in the thirteenth century, a revival of trade, commerce, and learning spread out from the main centers of both the Byzantine and the Western Christian world. This was stimulated, to a large degree, by the Crusades of Europeans against Moslem control of the Holy Lands of Christendom.

Modern Italian history dates from the rise of the new commerce, trade, and industrial centers of the Italian peninsula during and after the great Crusades. The Italian peninsula emerged as the heart of an unparalleled surge in art, music, literature, science, and philosophical movements. Industry, trade, commerce, farming, and orderly government revived. Milan, Florence, Genoa, Pisa, Lucca, Venice, and Bologna vied with one another for leadership in the Renaissance of the Western world.

In later centuries the Italian city-states were overwhelmed by other European powers. Venice, Milan, and the Kingdom of Piedmont (in the northwest) managed to keep alive ideas of national unity and their own independence.

Modern Italian national consciousness was greatly influenced and strengthened by the "Resorgimento" movement, led by Giuseppe Mazzini and Count Camillo Cavour, in the nineteenth century. The Kingdom of Piedmont and its ruling House of Savoy served as the rallying point for Italian unification. Giuseppe Garibaldi initiated a series of military adventures that helped lead to a united Italy in 1870. Rome became the capital of the kingdom in that year, but the Roman Catholic Church continued in bitter opposition to unification for another 60 years.

Italy suffered heavy losses during World War I. This setback, combined with a severe economic depression, ushered in a Fascist dictatorship led by Benito Mussolini in 1922. During World War II, Italy joined Hitler's Nazi regime in Germany. The nation became a major battlefield of the war and was devastated by land invasion and air attack. Mussolini's Fascist empire collapsed near the end of the war; and in 1945, the Italian Social Republic was set up. In 1946, this was transformed into a constitutional republic. The reign of the House of Savoy came to an end. Italy became a member of the NATO alliance in 1949 and a member of the United Nations on December 14, 1955.

The Italian constitution does not allow the reorganization of the Fascist Party, but it does allow the Communist Party to take an active role in government. Inflation and uneasy labor relations have brought down a number of Italian premiers in recent times.

IVORY COAST REPUBLIC

Portuguese navigators first landed in the late fifteenth century in what is now the Ivory Coast Republic. For the next 200 years, European traders dealt extensively in ivory and slaves taken from the region. French missionaries established themselves there in 1687, and at the beginning of the eighteenth century a trading post was set up by the French near Abidjan. Additional settlements by the French were established in the nineteenth century.

On March 10, 1893, the Ivory Coast became a French colony and later was consolidated with other French-controlled regions to form French West Africa. The colony was designated a territory within the French Union in 1946. On August 7, 1960, the Ivory Coast became an independent republic associated with the French Community. It was admitted to the United Nations on September 20, 1960.

JAMAICA

Columbus discovered Jamaica in 1494 on his second voyage. The island was colonized by the Spanish in 1523. The British captured it in 1655, and it was formally ceded by Spain in 1670. Jamaica acquired internal self-government in 1944 and cabinet government was introduced in 1953.

Jamaica joined a British-sponsored Federation of West Indies in 1958. However, the island withdrew in 1961 and became an independent nation on August 6, 1962. Jamaica was admitted to the United Nations on September 18, 1962.

In 1974, the Jamaican government took half ownership in American companies that have Jamaican mines for bauxite (aluminum ore).

In recent years, Jamaica's relations with the United States under the leadership of Prime Minister Seaga have improved. The country severed relations with Cuba in 1981 and President Reagan visited Jamaica in 1982.

JAPAN

According to legend, the Japanese Empire was founded in 660 B.C. The first capital was at Nara and was removed to Kyoto in A.D. 784. Buddhism and Chinese culture entered Japan during the Nara period. The Chinese influences were molded and changed to suit native forms. The shogunate form of government (in which real power lay not with the emperor but with military leaders called "shoguns") began in 1192 and continued until 1867.

The first contacts with the West occurred when Portuguese traders arrived in southern Japan in 1543. However, Japan remained generally sealed off to Westerners except for a few Dutch and Chinese merchants until the coming of Commodore Matthew C. Perry from the United States in 1853. The signing of a treaty of peace and friendship with the United States caused turmoil among the ruling forces and eventually led to the destruction of feudalism in Japan. In 1867, the emperor won back full control of the throne from the feudal shoguns.

The opening up of Japan to Western influence also ushered in a period of Japanese expansion. Japan defeated China in 1895, Russia in 1905, and Korea in 1910. By 1922, Japan was the third naval power of the world and one of the five "great powers." Military factions dominated Japan after 1926, and events that led up to World War II began with an invasion of China in 1931. By 1936, the military were in full control. Manchuria (a region of China) had been conquered and organized into a puppet state called Manchukuo. In 1936, Japan withdrew from the League of Nations and set up close relations with the Axis Powers (Germany and Italy).

Japan launched a full-scale invasion of China in 1937. The United States was sympathetic to China and extended her credit, placing embargoes on the shipping of aircraft and other war materials to Japan. Japan retaliated with a sneak attack on the United States Pacific naval base at Pearl Harbor, Hawaii, on December 7, 1941. This was the beginning of World War II in the Pacific area. (The war had been under way in Europe since 1939, when Germany invaded Poland.)

The Pacific war was marked by a series of great naval battles. On land it was a bitter jungle war and a series of beachhead landings from island to island. The Japanese reached the Coral Sea off Australia in May 1942, where they were stopped in the great Battle of the Coral Sea. Their eastward move was halted at Midway Island in June 1942, and in Alaska at the same time. Thereafter, the war went against Japan, as Allied strength began to build up. The most decisive battle was probably Leyte Gulf (October 23, 1944), the biggest naval battle in history. The Japanese fleet was crushed and Japanese aircraft resorted to suicide "Kamikaze" dives on American ships. By October 26, the Japanese fleet no longer existed as a force.

The final blow was an atomic bomb attack launched by the United States against Hiroshima on August 6, 1945, and against Nagasaki on August 9, 1945. Japan surrendered, signing the terms on August 14 aboard the battleship *Missouri* in Tokyo Bay. The Japanese people participated enthusiastically in the great changes that transformed Japan from a feudal militaristic empire into a progressive and democratic nation.

Japanese economic recovery was phenomenal,

Japan—Nijubashi Bridge, main entrance to Imperial Palace

but also important were the basic changes made in the life and culture of Japan. The new Japan has become a Westernized nation in many of its social patterns. Japan became a member of the United Nations on December 18, 1956.

In September 1972, Japan broke its diplomatic ties with the Chinese government-in-exile on Taiwan and restored friendly relationships with mainland China. The United States has withdrawn most of its military forces from Japan and has given virtually all of its bases there to the Japanese government.

In its rise to leadership among industrial nations of the world, Japan has become a fierce competitor to the United States in the manufacture of automobiles, electronics, computers and many other products. The rivalry has resulted in some modifications of Japan's trade policies and the imposition of some sanctions by the United States.

JORDAN

The nation is named for the famous river of Jordan whose valley forms one of the earliest sites of human civilization. Excavations at Jericho, near the Dead Sea, reveal a Neolithic culture eight thousand years old. The history of western Jordan is much the same as that of Palestine (*see* Israel). However, Jordan's history has one other chapter not included in that of Palestine. This is the era of the Nabataeans, a mysterious Arabic people who built one of the finest of all ancient cities in the desert of what is now southern Jordan. The ruins of Petra, the capital city, were discovered in A.D. 1812. The Nabataeans controlled the trade routes between the Dead Sea and Red Sea. Their empire developed an alliance with Rome that could have changed the history of the world, had it lasted. Petra developed a unique Arabic-Greco-Roman culture. The kingdom was annexed by the Romans in the second century after Christ.

The great northward invasion of the Arabs in A.D. 633 brought Islam to the region. From the twelfth century until the Ottoman conquest in 1517, the area was controlled by Christian Crusaders from Europe. The Ottoman Turks ruled this entire part of southwestern Asia until 1917, when T. E. Lawrence (known as Lawrence of Arabia) led Arab troops against the Turks to a decisive victory. As a result, an Arab state was set up in the eastern part of Britain's Palestinian mandate.

In 1921, Abdullah ibn Hussein (head of the Hashemite family of Arabia) was installed by the British as king of the new state, which was known as Transjordan because it was on the far side of the river. In 1927, it was recognized as a state under British protection. The mandatory power signed a treaty with Abdullah in 1946 recognizing him as ruler of the Hashemite Kingdom of Transjordan. Two years later the Palestinian mandate ended, Israel was formed under United Nations auspices in western Palestine, and Transjordan joined with other Arab states in a military attack on Israel. Much Palestinian territory west of the Jordan was annexed to Abdullah's kingdom, which then changed its name to Jordan. Part of the city of Jerusalem thus fell to Jordan. The state was admitted to the United Nations on December 14, 1955.

Under Abdullah's grandson, Hussein, Jordan continued to oppose Israel along with Egypt and other Arab states. During the Arab-Israeli War of 1967, Israel captured Jordan's west-bank territory. The continued occupation of the west bank became a major obstacle to peace in the Middle East. Jordan became more moderate in her relations with Israel than the Palestinians did. In fact, the Palestinians almost seized control of Jordan's kingdom, and were forced to transfer their bases to Syria in 1970. Hussein joined the other Arab states in the attack on Israel in 1973.

KENYA

Settlements of Arabs from nearby Zanzibar were established in what is now Kenya as early as the seventh century A.D. After the fifteenth century, the Portuguese competed with the Arabs for control of the coast. After 1740, the sultanate on Zanzibar Island became the ruler of most of eastern Kenya until 1887. Zanzibar then came under British influence and other opportunities, and the British East Africa Protectorate was created in 1895. Britain then induced Europeans to settle in the region, which was valued as a gateway to Uganda. Most of the usable land was occupied by Europeans, and the local tribesmen were driven to the least desirable locations. In 1920, Kenya became a colony.

A movement for African control and for independence began within the decade. The tribes organized in a guerrilla strike force known as the Mau Mau, and eventually brought self-government by stages. Jomo Kenyatta became a member of the colonial cabinet in 1962 and was prime minister when Kenya became independent on December 12, 1963. Four days later the country was admitted to the United Nations.

KUWAIT

In 1716, settlements were established in Kuwait by migrants from the neighboring Arabian Desert. The present ruling dynasty dates from 1756. British protection was extended upon the invitation of the Sheikh Mubarak al-Sabah (1896–1915), to prevent occupation by the Turks. After World War I Kuwait became independent, but remained under the protection of the British Crown. On June 19, 1961, that protection was terminated by mutual consent.

On May 14, 1963, the United Nations admitted Kuwait to membership. Kuwait exercises a great influence on Middle East and world affairs because of her enormous oil resources, which were largely developed by American companies since World War II. The country consistently supports the Arab anti-Israeli position.

LAOS

In the thirteenth century the Thai (Siamese) people migrated southward from China into Indochina, where they organized Lao tribes into a powerful kingdom that reached its peak in the seventeenth century, with its capital at Vientiane. The decline of this kingdom was complete with the fall of Vientiane to the Thais in 1827. The French, who had acquired a foothold on the Indochinese coast (in Annam and Tonkin, now North Vietnam), attached Laos to their Union of Indochina in 1893. In 1899 Laos became a French protectorate.

Japan occupied Indochina in World War II. Upon their withdrawal, resistance movements arose in all the Indochinese states. The most influential movement was that of the Vietminh, led by Ho Chi Minh in Vietnam. In 1949, a Laotian monarchy was reinstated and its government was recognized as independent within the French Union; but a dissident faction, the Pathet Lao, arose in 1953. Generally sympathetic with the Vietminh, the Pathet Lao participated at times in government with the monarchy. The kingdom of Laos became a member of the United Nations on December 14, 1955, and was assured of the protection of the anticommunist Southeast Asia Treaty Organization.

As the Pathet Lao accepted more and more aid from North Vietnam, it was inevitable that the Indochina War would involve Laos. One of the main routes used by North Vietnamese forces to reach their targets in South Vietnam passed through eastern Laos. In 1970, United States and South Vietnamese forces made a brief and unsuccessful incursion into southern Laos. With the victory of the communist forces in Indochina in 1975, the coalition and the monarchy yielded to Pathet Lao control.

LEBANON

The name *Lebanon* is derived from a great mountain range that extends through the country. The history of Lebanon has been associated with that of Syria since Phoenician times. Tyre, Sidon, and Byblos were famous Phoenician trade centers which sent colonists to found Carthage, Marsailles, Cádiz, and other cities along the Mediterranean Sea. Syria and Lebanon were united under Alexander the Great, under Rome, and later under the Arabs and Turks. Christians from Syria sought refuge in Lebanon, and the Druze sect of Islam also escaped to the Lebanese mountains and forests for protection. The Crusaders controlled parts of Lebanon in the thirteenth century, and left descendants there.

Modern Lebanon dates only from the 1860s, when France intervened in the Turkish rule of Lebanon in order to protect Maronite Christians who had revolted against the Druzes. From 1864 until World War I, the Turks ruled Lebanon under an agreement that permitted Christian freedom. During the war, France and Britain came to an agreement concerning the postwar division of the Middle East. Syria and Lebanon were allotted to France, and this change was approved by the League of Nations in 1923. At this time the state of Greater Lebanon was created, with a population about evenly divided between Moslems and Christians. The constitution of 1926 provided that the division would be reflected in the political institutions. This originated the tradition that the president should be a Christian and that he appoint a Moslem prime minister. As the Moslem population began to outnumber the Christians, this failed to be reflected in the legislature.

Plans for Lebanese independence were suspended by the conditions of World War II, when the Vichy French who controlled Lebanon were displaced in 1941 by the Free French. In 1945, the independence of Lebanon was recognized, and the country was admitted to the United Nations on October 24, 1945.

The government was fairly stable and the country was the most prosperous in the Arab world. In the conflict between the Arab states and Israel, Lebanon sided with the Arabs. The possibility of Communist influence in 1958 led President Dwight D. Eisenhower to send a large contingent of American troops to Lebanon, but they were not used in combat.

In the 1970s, the Palestinian Arabs used Lebanese soil to establish bases for raids on Israel, and this resulted in Israeli raids on Lebanon. A civil war broke out in 1975, with the Christian minority arrayed against a combination of Palestinians and Lebanese Moslems. The principal issue appeared to be the inequity of Moslem representation in Lebanese government.

The problem has been seriously exacerbated by the action of neighboring Mideast nations to protect their own interests, among them Israel and Syria. In 1982, the United States, France and Italy sent in a "peacekeeping force" that failed in its objective. In early 1984, all three nations were preparing to withdraw their forces.

LEEWARD ISLANDS

The most northerly group of islands in the Lesser Antilles of the British West Indies is called the Leeward Islands. They were discovered by Columbus in 1493, and they all have had a great degree of autonomy under British administration.

The British Virgin Islands may be considered part of this group. They were acquired in 1666 and never formed part of the West Indies Federation that existed from 1958 to 1962. All the other Leeward Islands did belong to this federation.

Antigua and Barbuda, St. Kitts-Nevis, and Anguilla are now independent nations.

LESOTHO

A small enclave within South Africa, the kingdom of Lesotho is administered under its own constitution by a hereditary monarchy. Its people, however, depend for their livelihood on the economy of the surrounding republic. The Basutos, a

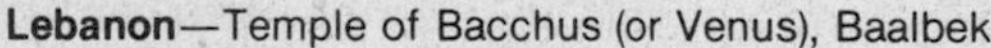

Lebanon—Temple of Bacchus (or Venus), Baalbek

Lesotho—Women building a road

Bantu people, sought British aid against the threatened encroachments of the Boers in 1867. In 1868, the area was acquired by Britain, and three years later it was annexed to Cape Colony (now Cape Province of South Africa). After a revolt of the Basutos, their territory became the crown colony of Basutoland in 1884. It was excluded from South Africa when the Union was formed in 1909.

When the Union became the Republic of South Africa in 1961, the continued separation of Basutoland was reconsidered. The British had permitted the Basuto monarchy to function, and the republic chose not to challenge the tradition. On October 4, 1966, Basutoland became the independent country of Lesotho. It was admitted to the United Nations on October 17, 1966. It chose to remain within the British Commonwealth.

After the government of Prime Minister Chief Leabua Jonathan lost an election in 1970, Jonathan suspended the constitution and parliament and the king was forced to flee from Lesotho. In 1973, Jonathan promised that a constitutional system would be reinstated.

LIBERIA

Liberia was founded in 1822 by the American Colonization Society. It was designed to promote the establishment of a country for free American blacks. The first settlement was made near the present city of Monrovia (named for James Monroe, fourth President of the United States). Immigration by blacks continued even after the American Civil War.

In 1847, the Republic of Liberia was established. Before it became well established, it lost a considerable amount of territory to French and British colonies. The United States aided in the country's finances, military organization, and in settling boundary disputes.

Liberia joined the United Nations on November 2, 1945.

LIBYA

Phoenician and Greek states competed for the control of the fertile Mediterranean coast of what is now Libya from 500 B.C. to 250 B.C. Romans replaced the Greeks in the third century before Christ. During the Phoenician, Greek, and Roman periods, some of the most prosperous and beautiful cities in the ancient world flourished along the coast.

Beginning with Vandal invasions in the fourth century A.D., Libya (the Greek name for the region) was looted and the cities were ruined. The region was then ruled in succession by the Byzantines, Arabs, and Turks (Ottoman Empire) down to the nineteenth century. It became part of the Barbary Coast of pirate strongholds, ruled by feudal deys. Between 1802 and 1805, the United States fought the pirates of Tripoli. United States Marines stormed the city in 1805. (Tripoli in Libya should not be confused with the ancient Tripoli in Lebanon).

Italy occupied Libya in 1911, but was unable to secure full control until the defeat of the Sanusi movement in 1931. In World War II, Libya became a major battlefield between the British Eighth Army and Field Marshal Rommel's German Africa Corps. Fierce tank battles developed as Rommel advanced along the coast to threaten Egypt. The battle of El Alamein in Egypt, in June 1942, was one of the critical engagements of World War II. It resulted in the defeat of Rommel, his long retreat westward back through Libya, and his final expulsion from Africa (*see* Tunisia).

Libya was not returned to Italy, which had sided with the Axis powers in the war. After a brief period of British and French control, the United Nations recognized the independence of the country under a monarchy.

With the discovery of oil in Libya and the rising resentment against remnants of British and American control, an insurrection occurred in 1969, led by a military junta. Its principal leader, Muammar al-Qadaffi, became dictator of the country.

Libya began buying jet fighters and other advanced weapons from France and the Soviet Union. In 1977, the Libyan army fought several border battles with Egypt, and Chad accused Libya of invading its northern uranium fields.

Deterioration of relations between the United States and Libya led to the closing on May 6, 1981, by the United States of the Libyan mission in Washington.

LIECHTENSTEIN

The history of Liechtenstein dates back to 1342. Its present boundaries were fixed in 1434. Liechtenstein is a sovereign European state, described as a constitutional monarchy and ranked as a principality. It consists of two counties (Vaduz and Schellenberg); it is bordered on the east by Austria, on the west by Switzerland.

LUXEMBOURG

The present Duchy of Luxembourg was originally a part of Roman-held territories called Belgica, from which the name Belgium was derived. It became a part of Charlemagne's empire from A.D. 800 until A.D. 963.

Luxembourg was founded in 963 by Count Sigefroid, a son of Charlemagne. The territory was greatly enlarged under Countess Ermesinde (1196–1247). Charles IV (1346–1378) became also emperor of the Holy Roman Empire, and it was he who made Luxembourg a duchy. After 1443, the duchy remained under foreign control for four hundred years.

The duchy was awarded to the Netherlands' king as a grand duchy in 1815; and in 1839, it lost more than half of its territory to the new Kingdom of Belgium. By the Treaty of London in 1867 Luxembourg was declared an independent state under the protection of the Great Powers.

The duchy was overrun in World Wars I and II, but in each case its territory was restored after the war. Luxembourg was admitted to the United Nations on October 24, 1945.

MACAO

Located on the coast of China southwest of Hong Kong, Macao was acquired by the Portuguese in 1557 and remained in their hands by an agree-

Libya—Theatre Sabratha near Tripoli

ment with the Chinese Empire in 1887. The Communist Chinese made no attempt to recover the peninsula and two small islands.

Macao, previously an overseas province of Portugal, was given increased autonomy in 1976 when it was redesignated a territory. Statutes passed by its assembly became as binding as laws, rather than as provisional decrees subject to Portuguese approval, and the territory was made responsible for its own defense and security.

MALAGASY REPUBLIC

The name *Madagascar* is applied generally to the large island off Africa's east coast, but it is often also used as an alternate name of the Malagasy Republic. The culture and language of the Malagasy people reveal a clear relationship with Indonesian peoples, and it has been established that the island was first colonized by Indonesians before the Christian era. Arabs, Phoenicians, and Chinese have also visited Madagascar in historic times. The Portuguese were the first Europeans to sight the island (1500). French, Dutch, and British competed in the seventeenth century for trading rights on the island.

The French gradually won out but had to deal with strong native kingdoms and were expelled for a time (1672) in an uprising of the native peoples. The French maintained a tenuous control until the twentieth century. In 1896, they made Madagascar a colony, and achieved military supremacy over the natives. National feelings continued to run high after the conquest.

France gradually permitted internal self-government. In 1947, rebellion broke out and thousands died in the year of fighting that followed. In 1958, Madagascar voted to join the new French Community of Nations. The Malagasy Republic was established in 1959 and became a sovereign state on June 26, 1960. It was admitted to the United Nations on September 20, 1960.

A coup in 1972 threw out the French-supported government in favor of a new socialist regime. The Malagasy leaders closed down French businesses and a United States satellite-tracking station. They turned to Communist China for financial aid. Several Arab business concerns have opened offices on the island.

MALAWI

Formerly known as Nyasaland, the area west and south of Lake Nyasa was crossed by David Livingstone in 1859. It became a British protectorate (British Central Africa) in 1891, and was renamed Nyasaland in 1907. In 1953, the protectorate was joined with Northern and Southern Rhodesia to form the Central African Federation, but nine years later Nyasaland withdrew from the federation, which was dissolved in 1963. On July 6, 1964, Nyasaland became the independent state of Malawi, and on December 1, 1964, it became a member of the United Nations. In 1966, Malawi decided to become a republic, although it remained within the British Commonwealth.

MALAYSIA

The Peninsula of Malaya lies across the Strait of Malacca from the island of Sumatra. For centuries it has been a land bridge between the Asian continent and the South Pacific islands. By the thirteenth century, Indian, Chinese, and Islamic cultures had reached and mingled here. Europeans entered Malaya during the fifteenth and sixteenth centuries (first the Portuguese, then the Dutch). British influences appeared in the eighteenth century, when Britain took Malacca from the Dutch. They also leased Penang Island; and in 1819, they acquired Singapore at the tip of Malaya.

The opening of the Suez Canal and the introduction of rubber trees from South America changed the economy of Malaya. By the end of the first decade of the twentieth century, Britain had treaty relationships with rulers of all the Malay states. Japan occupied the area during World War II. In 1946, these protectorates were formed into a Union and two years later into the Federation of Malaya, which also absorbed from the former crown colony of the Straits Settlements both Penang and Malacca (Singapore having been made a separate colony). The Federation of Malaya was granted independence within the British Commonwealth on August 31, 1957. And on September 17, 1957, it joined the United Nations. On September 16, 1963, two British Colonies in Borneo—Sarawak and North Borneo (renamed Sabah—and the independent state of Singapore joined the Federation, which changed its name to Malaysia. In 1965, Singapore withdrew to become an independent country once more.

Malaysia—Town of Lota Kinabalu, capital of Sabah

MALDIVE ISLANDS

This group of coral islands lies some four hundred miles south of Sri Lanka (formerly Ceylon). They were a protectorate of Ceylon after the seventeenth century; when the British acquired Ceylon, they also took over the protectorate. The islands served as a British military base until 1976.

With the independence of Ceylon in 1948, British protection was maintained. On July 26, 1965, the Maldives became independent. The country was admitted to the United Nations on September 21, 1965, and became a republic in 1968.

MALI

A great Moslem empire named Mali flourished in the western Sudan during the early part of the fourteenth century. Its ruler, Mansa Musa, conquered Timbuktu (now Tombouctou) and became legendary in African history. The empire disintegrated long before the French reached the region in the late nineteenth century. They established French West Africa in 1904, and within it the territory called French Sudan, east of Senegal.

After World War II, the French Sudan became an overseas territory; and in 1957, it was granted the right to rule itself. In 1958, the Sudanese Republic was formed within the French Union. In 1959, this republic joined with its neighbor, Senegal, as the Federation of Mali.

Senegal withdrew from the federation the next year, and the independent Republic of Mali emerged on September 22, 1960. Six days later Mali became a member of the United Nations. The constitutional regime endured until 1968, to be replaced by a military dictatorship.

MALTA

Malta has been under the rule of Phoenicians, Greeks, Carthaginians, Romans, and Arabs. In A.D. 1090, it became a part of Sicily; and in 1530, it was taken by the Knights of St. John. It was ruled by them until Napoleon captured it in 1798. After the defeat of Napoleon in 1814, the island was annexed to the British Crown.

Because of its strategic location between Sicily and North Africa, Malta has always been of great military importance. It was so useful to the British during World War II that its people were given a unique unit citation, the George Cross, for their contribution. The Maltese were accustomed to considerable local self-government, but British international policy slowed down the drive toward genuine autonomy. When the State of Malta was officially created in 1961, defense and external affairs were kept in British hands.

Following a referendum on the island, Malta acquired its independence on September 21, 1964. It remained within the Commonwealth, but chose to become a republic in 1974. It became a member of the United Nations on December 1, 1964.

MARTINIQUE

Martinique was discovered by Columbus in 1502 and colonized by the French in 1635. It has remained a French possession since 1815, first as a colony and since 1946 as an overseas department.

MAURITANIA

Like other North African countries, the territory of Mauritania derives its name from its Moorish population. However, the modern Mauritania has no other relationship to ancient Mauretania.

European traders were attracted to this barren region of northwest Africa as early as the fifteenth century, because it produced the valuable commodity called "gum arabic." The Berbers brought Islam to the region in the eleventh century, and they were in turn supplanted by Arabs. But enduring European control was imposed by the French, who set up French West Africa in 1904, including the protectorate established the preceding year over Mauritania. The colony of this name was organized in 1920, and it became an overseas territory in 1946.

On November 28, 1960, independence was granted to the Islamic Republic of Mauritania. On October 27, 1961, the country was admitted to the United Nations. In 1975, Mauritania annexed the southern part of the former Spanish Sahara, but Saharan guerrillas resisted the change.

MAURITIUS

An uninhabited island in the Indian Ocean east of Madagascar attracted Dutch colonists early in the seventeenth century. They named the island for Prince Maurice, son of William of Orange. African slaves were imported by the next owners of the land, the French; and after the British seized it in 1810, they brought in laborers from India, who became a majority of the island's dense population.

On March 12, 1968, Mauritius became an independent state within the British Commonwealth. She joined the United Nations on April 24, 1968.

MEXICO

The pre-Columbian history of Mexico is that of three related civilizations that grew up in the Valley of Mexico and the Yucatan region. Two of these civilizations were the most advanced cultures in pre-Columbia America. The first was the Mayan, described elsewhere (*see* Guatemala). The great cities of Chichen Itza, Mayapan, and Uxmil were located in present-day Mexico, in the Yucatan region. The Mayan civilization flourished from the third century B.C. until about the thirteenth century A.D. The Nahua group of people, which includes the Toltecs and the later Aztecs, developed a high culture in the Great Valley of Mexico about the tenth century A.D. The Aztecs, who conquered the Toltecs, built the brilliant culture that Cortés found and destroyed in A.D. 1519. The Spanish brought their Catholic religion, legal and economic systems, and imposed them upon the Aztecs, enslaving part of the population.

Mexico—Metropolitan Cathedral, Mexico City

The Spanish gradually extended their control outward from the Valley of Mexico until their possessions extended as far north as northern California and as far south as Guatemala. A movement for independence developed after the Napoleonic occupation of Spain had weakened the Spanish monarchy and imperial control over outlying areas. In 1810, a revolt broke out, led by a priest, Miguel Hidalgo, and later by another priest, José Maria Morelos. Finally, in 1821, Mexican independence was achieved under Vicente Guerrero and Agustin de Iturbide.

Mexico became a republic in 1823. But between 1834 and 1849 the government was controlled by dictators. Texas seceded in 1835 and joined the United States. The subsequent war between the United States and Mexico ended in defeat for Mexico and the loss of its northwestern region.

A reform government was inaugurated in 1855, but France invaded Mexico in 1861. Archduke Maximilian of Austria was placed on the throne of a French puppet state. The Mexicans revolted, executed Maximilian, and restored the republic in 1867.

In the twentieth century, Mexico has become a powerful nation, playing a leading role in Latin American affairs. Its abundant oil supply gave its economy a boost during the height of the oil shortage of the '70s but inflation and the drop in oil prices caused an economic crisis. The peso was devalued and private banks were nationalized. The U.S. maintains friendly ties with the "south of the border" country.

MONACO

Monaco dates from A.D. 1338 when the principality was established. In 1815 it was placed under the protection of the Kingdom of Sardinia (now part of Italy). It was at that time larger than it is today. It lost territory to Sardinia and France in 1848 and 1861.

In 1861, Monaco became a protectorate of France but remained otherwise independent. It is a favorite resort area.

MONGOLIA

Mongolia is an ancient land, the original center of a powerful empire that extended from the Pacific Ocean to the Danube. The most famous Mongol khan was Genghis, who led the invasion of India and Russia in the thirteenth century. More enduring empires were formed by the Golden Horde in Russia, by the Tartars in southern Asia, and by Kublai, who founded a Chinese dynasty that lasted nearly a century (1279–1368). Later, India was ruled by Mongols (known as Moguls), and Tamerland threatened Europe with a Mongol invasion.

In modern times Mongolia refers to a region north of China. The Manchus brought some of the Mongols under their control in the seventeenth century. The rest of the Mongols were not subjugated until the eighteenth century.

In 1911, the Manchu dynasty of China was overthrown, and the area known as Outer Mongolia declared its independence, while Inner Mongolia was incorporated into China. Outer Mongolia was ruled by the so-called "Living Buddha," who died in 1924. During the Russian Revolution, anticommunist ("white") Russians seized control of the region until communist forces defeated them in 1921. The communists allowed the monarchy to remain until 1924, when the Mongolian People's Republic was established in the Soviet image. This republic was not recognized by China until 1946. It was admitted to the United Nations on October 28, 1961. Treaties between Mongolia and the Soviet Union in 1966 and 1976 have brought large numbers of Russian troops to the country.

MOROCCO

The Phoenicians discovered and colonized the coast of what is now Morocco in about 1200 B.C. The Carthaginians later established control and expanded their area. Roman legions took over after the fall of Carthage in 146 B.C. The region was called Mauretania by the Romans (not to be confused with the modern republic of Mauritania).

As the Roman Empire disintegrated, northern Africa was subjected to invasions. The Vandals crossed from Spain to conquer the region early in the fifth century and were not expelled until the middle of the sixth century by the Byzantine general Belisarius. Arabs brought the religion of Islam as they swept westward across Africa in the seventh century. They united with the native Berbers in a dynasty that consolidated a great empire in what is now Morocco, Spain, Portugal, Algeria, Tunisia, and Libya. This empire flourished under the Almoravids, Almohades, Marinids, and finally the Sa'adi dynasties. The last dynasty brought about the great golden age of Moroccan history. Vast treasures in gold and ivory were amassed in the magnificent capital of Marrakech. This dynasty fought fierce wars with the Great Mali Empire and captured Timbuktu (Tombouctou) in 1591 (*see* Mali). The present dynasty of Morocco was established in 1649, and still occupies the throne.

Morocco was drawn into European conflicts chiefly because of its strategic location in Africa. France had conquered neighboring Algeria in 1832 and also became interested in Morocco. The French defeated a combined Algerian and Moroccan army in 1844. Thereafter French influence began to grow in the country.

Spain invaded northern Morocco in 1860. The next 50 years were marked by rivalry between France and Spain for control of Morocco. This rivalry almost caused a world war until the Treaty of Algeciras settled the rivalry in favor of France. Spain retained the "Rif" region of northern Morocco until expelled in the Rif War of the 1930s that helped bring on the Spanish Civil War (*see* Spain). In 1912, Morocco became officially a protectorate of France. In 1923, Tangier was separated and established as an international trading and financial zone.

In 1953, the French tried to overcome the movement toward independence by deposing the Sultan Mohammed V. On March 2, 1956, France acknowledged the independence of Morocco. On April 7, 1956, Spain followed suit. Tangiers was turned over to Morocco on October 29, 1956, and the country was admitted to the United Nations on November 12, 1956. Only the so-called Spanish presidios within Morocco remained under Spanish rule. In 1975, Spain allowed Morocco to acquire the northern part of its former colony of Spanish Sahara.

MOZAMBIQUE

Mozambique was discovered by Vasco da Gama for Portugal in 1498 and was colonized by the Portuguese in 1505. The boundaries became fixed at the end of the nineteenth century. It generally became known as Portuguese East Africa. In 1951, Mozambique was designated an overseas province of Portugal. In 1962, some inhabitants of the province formed the Mozambique Liberation Front, or *Frelimo,* to win independence. The Portuguese revolution of 1974 resulted in the victory of Frelimo in Mozambique, for independence was granted on June 25, 1975. The country became a member of the United Nations on September 16, 1975.

NAMIBIA

In 1884, Germany was given control of the region known as South-West Africa. The Germans turned the area over to South Africa in 1915, and it was governed under supervision of the League of Nations. The United Nations tried to assume this advisory role, but South Africa rejected its instructions.

In May 1968, the United Nations formed a council to plan the liberation of South-West Africa. The UN renamed the area "Namibia" and criticized South Africa for claiming the land. Marxist groups have begun raids on South African strongholds in Namibia, in an effort to force the country's independence.

NAURU

A tiny island in the Pacific Ocean, northeast of the Solomons, Nauru was annexed by Germany in 1888. After World War I, it was mandated to Australia. After World War II, Australia continued to administer Nauru under United Nations auspices. On January 31, 1968, Nauru became an independent republic with a special relationship with the British Commonwealth.

NEPAL

Little was known about the land until the fourteenth century A.D., when a Rajput ruler established a dynasty which lasted into the eighteenth. Later, Gurkhas and Chinese invaded and occupied the land.

The nineteenth century brought more conflict. As a result of border disputes, British-Nepalese relations deteriorated and the war of 1814 followed, with Britain victorious. During World War I, Nepal aided British forces and was granted independence in 1923. In World War II, Nepal was again on the Allied side.

An attempt to institute parliamentary government failed in 1959. Nepal was admitted to the United Nations on December 14, 1965. The nation has forged closer links with India and Communist China in recent years.

NETHERLANDS

Recorded history in the Netherlands began with the conquest by Julius Caesar in 55 B.C. The end of Roman rule triggered clashes between Saxon and Frankish forces over control of the region. (Christianity was introduced about A.D. 800.) Charlemagne and the Franks won control, but after his death the area of the present Netherlands became a part of the Holy Roman Empire.

The seeds of capitalism and individual enterprise were being sown at the same time. This was evident in the towns where a craftsman and merchant group began to challenge the ruling nobility, even during the Middle Ages. The country had several small, competing duchies and other feudal units.

Netherlands—Harbor of Rotterdam

In 1477, the Spanish branch of the Hapsburg family acquired control of the Netherlands. By 1549, the Netherlands, Spain, and Austria were united under Hapsburg rule.

Soon thereafter the Dutch people began to revolt. By 1581, they had established a new republic, called United Provinces. In the seventeenth century, the United Provinces became one of the world's leading maritime and commercial powers. Rivalry with Britain wore down the republic's strength, however, and it succumbed to Napoleon's great invasion of 1795. The Netherlands were reestablished by the Congress of Vienna (1815), and remained independent until they were overwhelmed by the German blitzkrieg ("lightning war") invasion of 1940. After World War II, the rich Dutch East Indies were lost in a revolt which led to the creation of the Republic of Indonesia. The Netherlands joined the United Nations on December 10, 1945.

NETHERLANDS ANTILLES

Two groups of islands in the Caribbean Sea constitute the Dutch dependency of the Netherlands Antilles.

The Leeward group, off the coast of Venezuela, comprises the islands of Curaçao, Aruba, and Bonaire, each of which is represented in the legislature. Discovered in 1499, they have been under Dutch control since 1634.

The Windward group, east of Puerto Rico, was first settled in the seventeenth century by Europeans. It is much smaller and is represented by a single legislator. The islands in this group are Saba, St. Eustachius, and Sint Maarten (the southern half of an island shared with France).

NEW CALDEDONIA

New Caledonia was discovered in 1768 by Louis Antoine de Bougainville. Captain James Cook named the island when he landed there in 1774.

New Caledonia became a French possession in 1853. It was long used as a penal colony. It became an overseas territory of France in 1946.

NEW HEBRIDES

These islands were discovered in 1606 and have been administered jointly by the United Kingdom and France. The people of the islands are mainly Melanesians.

The New Hebrides consist of 12 large islands and about 60 smaller islands. The group is located roughly 500 miles west of Fiji and 250 miles northeast of New Caledonia, in the South Pacific Ocean.

NEW ZEALAND

The Polynesian Maori people in the fourteenth century invaded the islands that now comprise modern New Zealand. The Dutch navigator Abel Tasman discovered New Zealand for Europeans in 1642. In 1769, Captain James Cook sailed around the island to determine its size. New Zealand was largely ignored thereafter until the nineteenth century when Britain took formal possession (1840).

New Zealand—Wellington City and Harbor from Tinakori Hills

Colonization resulted in conflict with the native Maoris, and war with them continued until 1864. In 1867, Maoris were granted their own representatives in government. With the introduction of refrigeration, in 1882, New Zealand became a leading world exporter of dairy produce and meat. From then on economic development became rapid.

New Zealand became a colony in 1852, a dominion in 1907, and a sovereign state within the British Commonwealth in 1947. It was admitted to the United Nations on October 24, 1945.

NICARAGUA

Columbus discovered the coast of Nicaragua and landed there in 1502. The Spanish founded Granada and León in 1524. Throughout most of the colonial period the entire region was ruled by the Spanish from bases in Guatemala. The Central American areas of the Spanish Empire declared their independence on September 15, 1821. The United Provinces of Central America, a federation, was established in 1823, and Nicaragua was a part of it. Nicaragua withdrew from the federation in 1838 and became a republic.

During the nineteenth century Nicaragua was often considered as a possible site for a transcontinental canal. In the end, the canal was built across the Isthmus of Panama. Conditions in Nicaragua became unstable, and the United States occupied the country from 1912 to 1925, and from 1926 to 1933.

Marxist rebels began a round of terrorist murders and kidnappings in the early 1970s, and President Anastasio Somoza imposed martial law. The guerrillas, led by the Marxist Sandinista, invaded Nicaragua May 29, 1979, and the Somoza government toppled seven weeks later. The United States has since actively supported the anti-Sandinista rebels and imposed trade restrictions on Nicaragua's sugar exports.

NIGER

The first European explorers to enter the region that is now the Republic of Niger arrived in the mid-nineteenth century. In 1890, the French began to settle in the area, and its status progressed from military territory in 1900, to autonomous territory in 1922, to overseas territory in 1946. On August 3, 1960, Niger became an independent country. It was admitted to the United Nations on September 20, 1960.

NIGERIA

The eastern Guinea coast of Africa was first visited by the Portuguese in 1472. All of the maritime nations of Europe participated thereafter in its lucrative slave trade.

Britain abolished this trade and began to promote trade in palm oil in its place. To protect this interest, the British seized the town of Lagos in 1851. In 1861, the surrounding area was annexed as a colony. In 1888, the Yoruba country in the interior was also brought under British protection, a claim that won international recognition.

In 1900, the protectorate of Southern Nigeria was formed; and in 1906, it became the Colony and Protectorate of Southern Nigeria. Simultaneously, Britain increased her control of the hinterland. Northern Nigeria became a protectorate and was combined with Southern Nigeria in 1914. A threefold division was made: the Lagos region became the Colony of Nigeria, while the remainder became the Eastern and Western provinces of the protectorate. In 1954, the Federation of Nigeria was formed under a single administration. The Eastern and Western regions were granted autonomy in 1957, the Northern in 1959. On October 1, 1960, the Federation of Nigeria became an independent state. It joined the United Nations six days later. In 1963, it became a republic.

The geographical divisions concealed a significant disunity within Nigeria, based on tribal allegiances—particularly involving the Hausa and Fulani in the north, the Yoruba in the west, and the Ibo in the east. This caused a savage civil war from 1967 through 1970, during which the Ibo attempted to form a separate state of Biafra. This disaster cost over a million casualties.

Calm settled over the nation with the restoration of civilian government in 1979 following 13 years of military government.

NORTH KOREA

Korea was recovered from Japanese occupation at the end of World War II. An administrative dividing line was established at the thirty-eighth parallel, pending an agreement between the Soviet Union and the United States liberation forces. Negotiations failed, but the division between the northern and southern parts of the country remained. North Korea was organized on May 1, 1948 on the Soviet model.

In 1950, North Korean forces invaded South Korea. The border war lasted three years and ended in a truce, with no territorial change. (For the history of Korea, *see* South Korea.)

NORWAY

The recorded history of Norway began during the eighth century, when a series of small kingdoms were established along the rocky coasts and deep inlets (called *fjords*) of Norway. The people who established these kingdoms were called Vikings.

The Viking period of Norwegian history lasted from about A.D. 800 to about A.D. 1050. In these years, the Vikings sailed sturdy longboats over the North Atlantic, reaching Ireland, the Hebrides, and southern Europe. They also sailed westward to Iceland, Greenland, and North America. Recent evidence has been found in Canada that proves Vikings spent some time there in about A.D. 1024. The Vikings also colonized Iceland, Greenland, and parts of western Europe. One of their most famous colonies was on the coast of northwestern France; this colony became Normandy, and the Vikings there became known as Normans. Their descendants conquered England and Ireland.

Norway was united for the first time in A.D. 860 by Harold the Fairhaired. King Olaf I introduced Christianity. After the close of the Viking period, Norway was weakened by the loss of trade to Hanseatic League cities and by internal dissension.

Norway lost its independence in 1380 when King Haakon of Denmark inherited the Norwegian kingdom. Denmark and Norway were united for more than four hundred years, and Norway was little more than a province in the Danish kingdom. Sweden was a part of this union from 1397 to 1523.

Denmark sided with Napoleon in the early years of the nineteenth century. As a result of Napoleon's defeat, Denmark was forced to give up Norway, which was then united with the Crown of Sweden. Denmark retained the former island colonies of Norway (Greenland, Iceland, and the Faroe Islands) that had come to be administered by Denmark during the union of the two countries.

Sweden and Norway remained united until 1905. Norway became a major maritime nation and selected King Haakon VII to be its king, despite Swedish opposition. The Swedes later recognized Norwegian independence.

Norway was neutral during World War I but was overrun by the Nazis during World War II. King Haakon and the government escaped to England. After the war, Norway joined NATO and abandoned her former neutral position. The kingdom was admitted to the United Nations on November 27, 1945.

OMAN

Oman is the southeastern part of the Arabian Peninsula, extending along the Arabian Sea. It is under the control of an Arab sultan whose forebears came from Yemen in 1744 and expelled the Persians. In 1798, the descendants of this Yemenite conqueror obtained protection from the British and succeeded in building an empire (called Muscat and Oman) that included Zanzibar and part of the East African coast, as well as a coastal section of Baluchistan. Only in 1958 did the small empire give its last enclave in Baluchistan back to Pakistan. In 1965, the United Nations recommended that Britain end its protectorate, but no formal action was taken. The sultan who seized the throne from his father in 1970 changed the country's name to Oman. On October 7, 1971, Oman was admitted to the United Nations.

PAKISTAN

The religion of Islam spread rapidly over southern Asia after the eighth century. In the tenth century a Moslem warrior group swept into India by way of the Khyber Pass in the west. Moslem power and influence moved eastward along the Ganges Plain and southward in the valley of the Indus River. By the sixteenth century it had reached Bengal on the far eastern edge of the Indian subcontinent and included most of the lower Ganges and Bengal regions.

Under British influence during the eighteenth and nineteenth centuries, the Moslem position was threatened by the rise of Hindu patriotism. In

1906, the All-India Moslem League was founded to help create a Moslem state.

The Moslem leader Mohammed Ali Jinnah invented the name *Pakistan* (from the first letters of "Punjab," "Afghan," and "Kashmir," and the remainder from "Baluchistan"). The Dominion of Pakistan came into existence amid riots and bloodshed in 1947. On March 3, 1956, Pakistan was proclaimed the Islamic Republic of Pakistan, but retained full membership in the British Commonwealth of Nations. The constitution proved unsatisfactory and was abolished within two years. A new constitution in 1962 provided for two provinces—West Pakistan and East Pakistan—each with its own legislature. This arrangement also proved unworkable, for the Bengalis of East Pakistan felt they were at a disadvantage. Again the constitution was abolished in 1969, and in the elections of 1971 the East Pakistan voters exerted their full powers.

When the president of Pakistan delayed convening of the legislature, East Pakistan declared itself independent. A rebellion broke out, and it was only with the aid of India that East Pakistan was able to defeat West Pakistan late in 1971. As a result, East Pakistan became the independent state of Bangladesh, and only West Pakistan remained to bear the name of the country. Once more a constitution was framed, and the country adopted the name of the Islamic Republic of Pakistan. But this time it withdrew from the Commonwealth, in which Bangladesh chose to remain.

Pakistan—Badshahi Mosque at Lahore

Pakistan's proximity to Afghanistan has made it a refuge for Afghans fleeing the Russian invasion of their country. The United States began sending economic and military aid to Pakistan in 1981.

PANAMA

The Isthmus of Panama was first seen by white men in 1501 when the Spaniard Rodrigo de Bastides landed near the present Portobelo. Columbus saw the isthmus the following year and claimed it for Spain. Balboa crossed the isthmus in 1513 and discovered the Pacific Ocean (which he named). Balboa also became the first governor of the region.

When the Spanish conquistadores began their conquest of the fabulous Inca Empire in South America, they used the Isthmus of Panama to carry supplies, soldiers, and captured treasures. British buccaneers made daring raids against strong points in Panama and against Spanish galleons that sailed to and from Panama, laden with gold and other loot from the Inca Empire.

In 1739, Panama was attached to the viceroyalty of New Granada that included the present Colombia, Panama, and Venezuela. In 1821, Panama became a part of the independent Gran Colombia, a new state that comprised the present Colombia, Venezuela, Ecuador, and Panama. Upon dissolution of Gran Colombia in 1830, Panama remained a part of Colombia. With the help of the United States, it was separated from Colombia in 1903 to facilitate the building of a projected canal across the isthmus. From time to time, Panama demanded that the zone (leased in perpetuity to the United States) be restored to Panamanian sovereignty. The United States signed a treaty to that effect in 1978.

For up-dated information on the Canal Zone, see "Outlying U.S. Areas."

PAPUA NEW GUINEA

New Guinea is an island north of Australia, also known as Papua or Irian. Its western half was once Netherlands New Guinea and was annexed in 1963 by Indonesia. The eastern half of New Guinea is itself divided into two portions, the most northerly of which was known as German New Guinea from 1884 to 1914. It was captured during World War I by Australia and became an Australian mandate, the Territory of New Guinea, in 1920. The southeastern quarter of the island was seized in 1883 by the British colony of Queensland (Australia). It was annexed by Great Britain as the colony of British New Guinea in 1888, and handed over to Australia in 1906 to become the Territory of Papua.

None of these incursions by Europeans profoundly involved the native population, which is largely Melanesian or black. The Territory of New Guinea has been administered by Australia since 1949. With the gradual increase of self-government, Papua New Guinea became capable of achieving independence, which was granted on September 16, 1975. Papua New Guinea was admitted to the United Nations on October 10, 1975.

PARAGUAY

The region of present Paraguay was first visited by Europeans in the expedition of Juan de Salazar that founded Asunción in 1537. The Jesuits came later and gathered together the Guarani Indians to build a remarkable series of prosperous Guaraní communities in the region. Spanish colonists initiated a campaign of slander against the Jesuits that led to the destruction of the mission communities. The Guaraní were eventually destroyed as a people.

The Spanish ruled Paraguay as a part of the viceroyalty of Peru and then as part of La Plata. La Plata declared independence from Spain in 1810. After the expulsion of the Spanish, Uruguay and Paraguay then fought Argentina, which was attempting to annex them.

Nearly all of Paraguay's history since that time has been concerned with wars and dictatorial rule. The War of the Triple Alliance (1865–1870) was the bloodiest in the history of Latin America. It was fought by Brazil, Uruguay, and Argentina against Paraguay. Paraguay was crushed, her economy completely ruined; she has never recovered from this disaster. In 1932, a long dispute between Paraguay and Bolivia erupted into another war that lasted until 1938. Economic difficulties and dictatorial rule have continued in the post-World War II period. Paraguay became a member of the United Nations on October 24, 1945.

Paraguay has joined its modernized neighbor, Brazil, in a series of projects to aid the economies of both. They have built a highway linking the two countries; and in 1974, they signed a pact to build the world's largest electric generator on the Paraná River.

PERU

The Inca civilization that developed in pre-Columbian Peru arose slowly from a nucleus in the Cusco Valley about A.D. 1200. In 1438 the empire began to expand under Pachacuti and his son Topa Inca. At its height, the empire had about twelve million people and included most of what is today Peru, Bolivia, Chile, Ecuador. The Incas built great palaces, irrigation works, highways, and cities. Arts, handicrafts, and agriculture were developed to a degree equalled only by the Mayan people of Mexico and Guatemala.

Francisco Pizarro brought down the empire in 1532 and 1533. In 1535, the city of Lima was founded. It became the capital of a wealthy Spanish empire in America. Treasures of gold and silver poured a veritable flood into the Spanish treasury. Indians were enslaved to work the gold mines. The Spanish treasure galleons bound from Peru became the favorite target of English "sea dogs."

Simón Bolívar and José de San Martín landed in Peru in 1820 and by 1824 (Battle of Ayacucho) had destroyed the Spanish Empire in America. Peru thereafter was a republic, but experienced harsh rule under a rigid militarist group until the twentieth century. Peru lost a nitrate-rich region to Chile, in the War of the Pacific (1879–1884). Then Peru became a relatively stable country, with a constitution. It became a member of the United Nations on October 31, 1945.

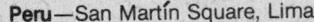

Peru—San Martín Square, Lima

PHILIPPINES

The Philippines were discovered by Ferdinand Magellan while on his epic voyage around the world in 1521. Magellan was killed in the islands by native Filipinos. Despite revolts by Filipinos, the Spanish were able to retain control over the Philippines until the end of the nineteenth century. The islands were named for Philip II, King of Spain.

Revolutions in Central and South America stimulated an independence movement in the Philippines. A Filipino doctor named Emilio Aguinaldo stirred up a revolt in 1896 which merged with the Spanish-American War.

After the war had ended, Aguinaldo demanded independence. The Americans refused, and Aguinaldo revolted against them as well. He was captured in 1901. It was not until after World War II that the Philippines finally achieved independence.

In 1941, the Japanese invaded the Philippines. The fall of the Corregidor fortress in the harbor of Manila was a major event of World War II. Americans under Douglas MacArthur returned to the Philippines with a massive invasion force on October 20, 1944. Fighting had to be waged from island to island throughout the huge archipelago.

On July 4, 1946, the Philippines were granted independence. Aguinaldo, who was nearly one hundred years old, saw his dream realized. The Philippines were admitted to the United Nations on October 24, 1946.

At first the Philippines was a republic; but in 1973, President Ferdinand Marcos instituted a parliamentary dictatorship.

Philippines—Maranao Dance by Maranao natives

PITCAIRN

Pitcairn was discovered by Philip Carteret in 1767. In 1790, the island was occupied by nine mutineers from the British ship the *Bounty,* who brought with them 12 Tahitian women. Nothing more was heard of the island until the visit of an American ship in 1808. It was learned then that all the men had killed each other, except John Adams, who ruled the colony. In 1838, Britain took formal possession of the island. In 1856, all of the colonists were removed. Forty of them later returned, but the population never exceeded one hundred. The colony is administered from New Zealand.

POLAND

Poland dates from the unification of several small Slavic states in the tenth century. In A.D. 966, Christianity was introduced. Boleslaus the Brave (992–1025) made Poland an independent kingdom.

In 1241, the Mongols invaded Poland. The Teutonic knights helped to expel the Mongols, but remained to threaten Poland's independence. For centuries Poland has contended with German pressure from the west. Poland reached the height of her power from the fourteenth to sixteenth centuries under the Jagellon dynasty of rulers. She defeated the German Tannenberg order in 1410 and annexed Lithuania in 1569.

Polish power declined under German (Prussian), Swedish, and Russian invasions. The country eventually was divided among neighboring powers.

Napoleon's Grand Duchy of Warsaw partially revived Poland, but the revival ended in 1815 when Napoleon was defeated. Revolts in 1830, 1831, and 1863 were crushed. After the Allied victory in World War I, Poland became a republic in 1918. It was divided between Germany and the Soviet Union in 1939. The Nazi invasion of Poland was the opening phase of World War II. The Poles fought fiercely, especially around Warsaw, which was nearly destroyed. After Germany's invasion of the Soviet Union, Poland's forces fought their way back into German-occupied Poland.

After World War II, Poland was reconstituted with new borders. She gained territory from Germany and yielded territory to the Soviet Union; thus the entire country shifted toward the west. As the result of an election in 1947, a procommunist government was formed, which framed a constitution of the Soviet type in 1952.

Militant labor activists led a movement that culminated in 1980 with the government's granting workers the right to form independent trade unions and to strike. Further demands by the principal trade union, Solidarity, led the government to declare martial law. The United States imposed economic sanctions, and martial law was lifted in December 1982. Meanwhile, the government arrested Lech Walesa and other Solidarity leaders, who had called for a nationwide strike that did not materialize, but they were later released.

PORTUGAL

The Iberian Peninsula was wrested from Carthage by Roman armies in about 138 B.C. The section now known as Portugal was then called Lusitania. Starting in the fifth century A.D. and continuing until 711, Portugal was overrun by a succession of invaders, including Alans, Suevi, Visigoths, and Celtic peoples. In 711, the Arabs conquered the region, but Ferdinand of Castile regained it in 1139. By the thirteenth century, the boundaries of the nation were established and Lisbon was the capital.

During the reign of John (João) I (1385–1433), the Portuguese defeated the Spanish and began a period of growth and progress. Portuguese explorations of unknown regions began under John, who founded a school for navigation. A series of brilliant navigational exploits resulted in the establishment of a Portuguese Empire by the sixteenth century. Bartholomew Diaz rounded the Cape of Good Hope in Africa (1486), discovering a new route to India. Vasco da Gama made the voyage to India in 1497, and Portuguese navigators discovered Brazil in 1500.

In 1580, Spain took over Portugal and its empire, but sovereignty was restored by a rebellion in 1640. A long war ensued. In 1668, Spain recognized Portugal's independence. Brazil was lost by Portugal in 1822, and the Bragança royal house was overthrown by a revolution in 1910. But instability plagued the nation until the rise of António de Oliveira Salazar, who became prime minister in 1932. He established a conservative dictatorship. In 1974, his successor, Marcello Caetano, was overthrown by a military junta. The administration wavered in its domestic policies, but abandoned the colonial empire that it was incapable of preserving. All the overseas territories of Africa became independent in 1974 and 1975, and Macao became an autonomous territory.

QATAR

On a peninsula jutting into the Persian Gulf, west of the United Arab Emirate is Qatar, formerly a British protectorate. It ended this relationship when it declared its independence on September 1, 1971. Admission to the United Nations followed in twenty days.

Qatar exports about one hundred seventy-eight million barrels of crude oil each year. The income from oil gives Qatar the second highest income per capita of any nation in the world.

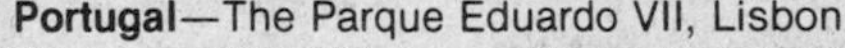

Portugal—The Parque Eduardo VII, Lisbon

RÉUNION

The largest island of the Mascarene group in the Indian Ocean was discovered by a Portuguese navigator in 1528, claimed by the French in 1638, and colonized by them in 1662. It was named Ile de Bourbon until after the French Revolution, when it was renamed La Réunion. In 1946, it became an overseas territory of France.

RHODESIA (Zimbabwe)

Cecil Rhodes, who organized the British South Africa Company in 1889, was responsible for the northward expansion of British holdings from Cape Colony at the tip of South Africa. By 1895, the Zambesi region was named Rhodesia, after Rhodes. The company administered the area under a British charter until the European settlers voted in 1923 to accept self-government, rather than join the Union of South Africa.

Meanwhile, the company had expanded its operations further north. These holdings were designated Northern Rhodesia in 1911, so the autonomous portion became known as the colony of Southern Rhodesia.

Government leaders were unable to bring the two regions together because Southern Rhodesia was controlled by its minority of white settlers, a prospect inacceptable to the black population of Northern Rhodesia. Nevertheless, the British government decided in 1953 to form a federation to include the two Rhodesias and adjoining Nyasaland. The federation was dissolved in 1963.

By this time, Southern Rhodesia had adopted a new constitution and committed itself against extending powers of government to its black majority. Great Britain disapproved this policy. So the government of Southern Rhodesia (which was renamed Rhodesia in 1964) declared its independence on November 11, 1965.

The United Nations asked all its members to impose economic sanctions against Rhodesia. Only Portugal and South Africa ignored the resolution. Rhodesia prospered as an independent nation and declared itself a republic in 1970.

Guerrilla forces began raiding government outposts to try to press the white leaders into a compromise. But peace talks failed, and the bush war spread into Mozambique. In 1977, the United States stopped buying chrome from Rhodesia to protest that government's hard line against black rule. Early in 1979, the white Rhodesians voted to relinquish their control of the government in coming years.

Elections were held and the country achieved independence on April 18, 1980.

ROMANIA

Most of the present Romania became a part of the Roman province of Dacia after Emperor Trajan conquered the Dacians in the fierce campaign of A.D. 101–106. Roman influence remained even after numerous invasions by other peoples in later centuries. The Dacians gradually emerged as the Vlachs or Wallachians who were converted to Christianity during the eleventh century.

Wallachia and another state called Moldavia developed in the region late in the thirteenth century. Wallachia was seized by the Turks in 1476 and Moldavia was taken over in 1513.

The Ottoman Empire's control over both areas was challenged from time to time by Russia. The latter took Bessarabia from Moldavia in 1812, and Austria seized Bucovina from Wallachia in 1775. The Russians invaded both areas in 1828, but released them in 1834.

The Congress of Paris established Wallachia and Moldavia as separate states, and they were united under Alexander Cuza in 1859. The resulting new nation was called Romania or Rumania.

During World War I, Romania joined the Allies, but was defeated by Germany early in 1918. Later that year Romania came back into the war on the Allied side. After the war Romania received the regions of Bucovina, Bessarabia, Transylvania, and Banat.

King Carol II, who had renounced the throne in 1925, was returned in 1930. Romania was caught in a series of threats and power moves by Russia, Germany, and Italy. King Carol abdicated and the country entered an alliance with the Axis powers on the side of Germany.

King Michael (son of Carol II) engineered a coup d'état in 1944. Romania then entered the war on the Allied side.

The communists gained election victories in 1947, and King Michael was forced to resign. Romania was then proclaimed a people's republic (in 1952 changed to "socialist republic"). It became a member of the United Nations on December 14, 1955.

RWANDA

The history of Rwanda is closely associated with the Tutsi (Watutsi) and Hutu Bahutu peoples. (The latter are a Bantu group.) The Tutsi early managed to become the ruling tribe and the Hutu became the feudal lower "caste." These conditions failed to change even when the white men came. Germany was awarded the country along with Urundi (the future Burundi) in 1884, and relations were peaceful with the native ruling Tutsi people. During World War I, Belgium occupied both Ruanda (the future Rwanda) and Urundi. The League of Nations attached both countries to the Belgian Congo in 1920. After World War II, Ruanda and Urundi (then called Ruanda-Urundi) became a single trust territory of the UN.

In 1959, clashes erupted between the Tutsi and the Hutu, the latter demanding basic freedoms. Tensions mounted until the United Nations called for popular elections, which abolished the monarchy in Ruanda. The UN hoped that the two sections would become a single independent state. However, internal differences prevented their unification. On July 1, 1962, Rwanda (with a slight change in spelling) became an independent nation. It was admitted to the United Nations on September 18, 1962.

ST. HELENA

The Portuguese discovered St. Helena in 1502. It has belonged to the United Kingdom since 1673.

St. Helena is a crown colony with several dependencies: Ascension Island, 700 miles to the northwest (administered with St. Helena since 1922), and the Tristan da Cunha archipelago, far to the south (so administered since 1938).

ST. PIERRE AND MIQUELON

These small islands lying ten miles south of Newfoundland are all that remain of the once-great French empire in North America. First settled by the French in 1604, they have been permanently French since 1816. The colony was given autonomy in 1935 and made an overseas territory in 1946.

SAMOA

This group of islands is located in the South Pacific, just east of Fiji and north of Tonga. It was a German colony from 1899 to 1914, when New Zealand landed troops on the main island and seized control. The League of Nations allowed New Zealand to administer the government of Samoa; and in 1945, the United Nations affirmed New Zealand's responsibility for the area.

The Samoans elected their own government in October 1959. The country became an independent monarchy on January 1, 1962, although New Zealand continues to give financial aid.

SAN MARINO

San Marino is the oldest republic in the world. According to tradition, it was founded in the fourth century by a Christian refugee from persecution. Its monastery has been occupied since A.D. 885. A tiny district in the midst of Italy's Apennine Mountains, San Marino preserved its independence throughout the Middle Ages and modern wars. A republic, it has a trade treaty with Italy.

SÃO TOMÉ AND PRÍNCIPE

São Tomé and Príncipe were discovered in 1471 and have been Portuguese territory since 1522. The islands became an overseas province in 1951 and were granted independence on July 12, 1975. Admission to the United Nations followed on September 16, 1975.

The country's first president, Manuel Pinto da Casta, was trained in East Germany.

SAUDI ARABIA

Saudi Arabia was founded by Abdu-l-Aziz ibn Sa'ud (1880–1953). However, the history of Saudi Arabia is closely associated with that of the Arabian peninsula, of which it occupies the greater part. (*See also* Kuwait and Yemen).

The Arabian peninsula has been inhabited throughout historic times by Semitic peoples, but unified states were not formed until the arrival of

Mohammed (A.D. 570–632), who founded Islam. Through Islam, the land of Arabia became famous throughout the world. Mohammed and his successors led the Arabians out of Arabia and spread their religion from the Atlantic Ocean to the borders of China and the Pacific Ocean. The Arabian language and culture became nearly as widespread as the religion of Islam, and remains so today.

Arabia declined soon after the Arab civilization reached other parts of the world. Little was known of life within Arabia for a thousand years thereafter.

The puritanical Islamic sect of Wahhabism was fused with the Sa'udi family in the eighteenth century, thus leading to the beginnings of the present kingdom of Saudi Arabia. By 1830, the Sa'udi family controlled Nejd, Hasa, and Oman. Setbacks occurred in the following years; but in 1901, Abdu-l-Aziz resumed his conquest of all Arabia. In 1906, he broke the power of the leading competing tribes. He captured Mecca in 1924, the Kingdom of Hejaz in 1926, and the Kingdom of Nejd in 1927. British recognition was accorded in 1927.

When Abdu-l-Aziz ibn Sa'ud died in 1953, he left a state that was largely his own creation. Arabia became a member of the United Nations on October 24, 1945.

King Faisal led the development of Saudi Arabia's crude oil reserves. The nation took control of the Arabian American Oil Company between 1973 and 1976, then launched a massive economic development program. Saudi Arabia gave financial aid to Egypt and other Arab countries in their conflict with Israel. Then King Faisal stopped oil shipments to the United States and other nations in 1973–1974 to protest American military aid to Israel.

Faisal was assassinated in March 1975, and Crown Prince Khalid became the new king.

Following Khalid's death, Fahd became king in June 1982. The United States had maintained friendly relations with the Saudis, who have exercised a moderate position in meetings of OPEC.

SÉNÉGAL

Prior to the coming of white men, Sénégal was at various times a part of the famous ancient empires of Ghana and of Mali. The Portuguese visited the present Sénégal in the fifteenth century. The French established Saint-Louis as a trading post at the mouth of the Sénégal River in 1659. From about 1870 to the end of the century, France secured Sénégal and consolidated its control.

The colony was transformed into a territory in 1946 and became autonomous in 1958. In January 1959, Sénégal and Sudan (the future Mali) joined in the Federation of Mali, but the federation broke up shortly after it became independent. Sénégal proclaimed its independence on August 20, 1960, and remained within the French Community of Nations. The country was admitted to the United Nations on September 28, 1960.

SEYCHELLES

The Seychelles archipelago was colonized by the French in the eighteenth century. The islands were captured by the British in 1794, included as a part of Mauritius in 1814, and organized as a colony in 1888. They became a crown colony in 1903, and were granted independence as of June 29, 1976.

SIERRA LEONE

Little is known of the history of Sierra Leone before its discovery by Europeans. About 1460, a Portuguese adventurer named Pedro da Cintra visited the region and gave it the present name. Some hundred years later an Englishman, Sir John Hawkins, landed an expedition to obtain slaves. Other slave traders followed.

During the seventeenth and eighteenth centuries, Sierra Leone was a pirate haunt. Around 1787, English abolitionists succeeded in having the government declare Sierra Leone to be the home for England's freed slaves.

By 1808, Sierra Leone was made a British colony with a Crown-appointed governor and advisory council. Schools were founded, frontiers with Liberia were agreed upon, and Africans were appointed to the executive council in an unofficial capacity. It was a long and slow, but orderly process.

In April 1961, Sierra Leone became independent and a member of the British Commonwealth of Nations. It maintains close ties with Great Britain. Sierra Leone was admitted to the United Nations on September 27, 1961.

SINGAPORE

A small island at the tip of the Malay Peninsula, Singapore, was founded by Sir Stamford Raffles in 1819. It was a trading post controlled by the British East India Company. Along with Penang and Malacca, it was designated as the colony of the Straits Settlements in 1867.

In 1946, Singapore became a separate crown colony and was given autonomy in 1959. Singapore joined the Federation of Malaysia in 1963, but chose to secede and become an independent republic on August 9, 1965. Shortly thereafter it joined the British Commonwealth, having already become a member of the United Nations on September 21, 1965.

SOLOMON ISLANDS

East of New Guinea is an archipelago, the Solomon Islands, that came under British protection in the last decade of the nineteenth century. They were the scene of heavy naval fighting during World War II. In the 1970s, they attained considerable self-government.

Not to be confused with this British protectorate (which includes such large islands as Guadalcanal and New Georgia) are a smaller chain of Solomon Islands to the west. This chain, including Bougainville, is part of the state of Papua New Guinea.

SOMALIA

The name *Somalia* is used here as the short form for the Somali Republic and should not be confused with the region of Somalia or Somaliland, of which it is only a part. The region includes parts of what are now Ethiopia, Kenya, and the Territory of Afars and Issas (former French Somaland).

The former Somaliland protectorate was under Egyptian control until it was acquired by Britain in 1884. It was administered as a dependency of India from Aden, until the Italians occupied it during World War II.

The colony of Italian Somaliland was established in 1889 south of the British protectorate, on a coast previously belonging to Zanzibar and to Kenya. During the war with Ethiopia in 1934, Italy added the Ethiopian province of Ogaden to its Somali colony. This colony became known as Italian East Africa; it was taken over by Britain during World War II. In 1950, the United Nations returned the former Italian Somaliland to Italy under mandate.

In June 1960, the British and Italian lands became independent and merged to form the Somali Republic on July 1. The country joined the United Nations on September 20, 1960. In 1970, a military coup changed the name to the Democratic Republic of Somalia. The new government permitted Soviet military bases to be built on Somali territory.

SOUTH AFRICA

Portuguese sailors rounded the Cape of Good Hope in 1488. One of them, Vasco da Gama, discovered the Natal coast in 1497. The first European settlement in the region was made by the Dutch at the Cape of Good Hope in 1652. Primitive Bushmen and Hottentots were the principal peoples that the white settlers found in southern Africa. They soon, however, came into contact with migrating Bantu peoples from the north. As settlement increased, conflict with Bantus arose in four separate wars, that occurred between 1779 and 1812.

The British occupied the Cape in 1795. As a result of the Napoleonic Wars, the entire colony was ceded to Great Britian in 1815. British settlers came in 1820 and slavery was abolished in 1834. The descendants of the Dutch became known as Afrikaners. Disputes with British policies led to the "Great Trek," a migration by the Afrikaners in 1836. They settled in Natal and north of the Vaal River (Transvaal). The British extended their control into those regions by the middle of the century, beginning with the annexation of Natal in 1843. By 1897, all of southern Africa, except the Orange Free State and the Transvaal, was under British rule of one form or another.

Meanwhile conflict with Africans resulted in the establishment of various *apartheid* projects, in which separate white and nonwhite settlements were developed. Nonwhite labor was essential to the economy, so *apartheid* could go only so far. The discovery of gold and diamonds brought an influx of immigrants and, with them, rising conflict between Afrikaners and the British government.

The conflict centered on the Afrikaner-controlled regions of Transvaal and the Orange

Free State. The latter had been independent since 1854, and the former since 1877.

The unsuccessful Jameson Raid of 1895 was followed by the Boer War of 1899–1902. (The descendants of the first Dutch settlers were also called Boers.) This war was between the British and an alliance of the Orange Free State and Transvaal. The two Boer republics lost their independence. In 1909 four states in southern Africa were combined to form the Union of South Africa, which was accepted as a member of the British Commonwealth of Nations (1926).

After World War II the Afrikaner segment of the population gained political control and legislated the separation of races. South Africa withdrew from the Commonwealth in 1960 and became a republic the following year.

South Africa became a member of the United Nations on November 7, 1945. Within the organization, she has been criticized by an increasing number of member states, partly because of her policy of *apartheid*.

In 1963, South Africa began setting up separate units for its black population known as *Bantustans*. Within a decade or so, most of the projected "homelands" were well under way. This did not improve the nation's image in black Africa.

SOUTH KOREA

The recorded history of Korea began with the migration of Tungusic people into northern Korea from Manchuria about four thousand years ago. At the beginning of the Christian era there were three kingdoms in Korea. One of these (the Silla dynasty) united all Korea in A.D. 669.

For many centuries thereafter, Chinese, Japanese, and Mongolians fought for possession of Korea. After the empire of Mongols fell in the thirteenth century, their power in the peninsula of Korea disappeared. In 1392, the strong Yi dynasty assumed the reins of government. A brilliant age of cultural development followed, in which the Korean alphabet was introduced and arts flourished.

A great war of survival against Japan broke out in 1592. Korea won the war but the country was left in a weakened condition.

The United States opened relations with Korea in 1882. Japan invaded Korea in 1904 and annexed the country in 1910, naming it Chosen. After the defeat of Japan in World War II, Korea was divided temporarily at the thirty-eighth parallel between Soviet and United States jurisdictions, according to agreements made at Potsdam. When the two liberating nations failed to agree, separate regimes were set up at Pyongyang and at Seoul. The former organized a procommunist government (*see* North Korea) and the latter formed the Republic of Korea, usually known as South Korea, on August 15, 1948.

On June 25, 1950, a North Korean army struck across the border without warning. Within two days, and with United Nations authorization, the United States ordered its armed forces to protect South Korea against the aggressors. Several other countries supplied small contingents to fight under the United Nations command. Seoul, the capital of South Korea, fell to the North Koreans, who advanced almost to the southern tip of the peninsula. After United States forces landed at Inchon, the North Koreans were driven back almost to their border with China. This brought the Chinese Communists into the war, and the United Nations forces retreated to the thirty-eighth parallel. In July 1953, an armistice was signed. No significant territorial change occurred.

During the intervening 30-plus years, an uneasy peace has existed between the North and South Koreans separated by a demilitarized zone (DMZ), and numerous incidents have occurred between the forces (that include American troops) on the south and those on the north.

SOUTH YEMEN

This name is generally used for an independent state that is officially called the People's Republic of Yemen. Although its population is largely Arab, it must not be confused with its neighbor to the north, the Yemen Arab Republic, generally known as Yemen.

The ancient port of Aden at the southwest corner of Arabia was acquired by Britain in 1839. Its strategic importance was increased with the opening of the Suez Canal. Long a dependency of British India, it became a crown colony in 1937. Surrounding the colony were a number of Arab sultanates that Britain loosely organized in 1937 under a protectorate. Between 1959 and 1962 the protectorate was transformed into a Federation of South Arabia, to which the colony of Aden was attached in 1963. A period of civil warfare ended when South Arabia declared its independence as the Southern Yemen People's Republic on November 30, 1967. Under that name, Southern Yemen joined the United Nations on December 14, 1967. On November 30, 1970, it assumed its present name.

SPAIN

The recorded history of Spain began about 1100 B.C. with the Phoenician colonies. The present city of Cádiz, on the southwest coast, founded by Phoenicians in 1130 B.C., may be the oldest city in Europe. Carthage also planted colonies along the coast of Spain, beginning about 500 B.C. The present city of Barcelona began as a Carthaginian colony.

Rome sought the Iberian peninsula mainly for its rich gold and silver mines. Spain was called Hispania by the Romans, who conquered it from Carthage during the Second Punic War (218–200 B.C.). Roman Hispania became a rich and prosperous center of Roman culture. Several great Roman writers (such as Seneca and Quintilian) and even some of the emperors (including Trajan and Hadrian) came from Roman Spain. Large cities, highways, aqueducts, and other great engineering works dotted the land.

In the fifth century a series of invasions ended the prosperity of Spain. The Moorish invasions from Africa, beginning in A.D. 711, had a lasting effect upon the future of the Iberian Peninsula. Moorish domination throughout most of what is now Spain continued from 711 until 1492.

Moorish Spain left a rich heritage, including prosperous cities, great philosophers, a distinctive architecture, fine craftsmanship in design and art work, and brilliant writers and physicians. The Moors introduced an efficient irrigation system that still serves Spanish farmers in some areas. The Moorish occupation left Spain with a higher civilization than that of most of Europe at the time.

In 1479, the kingdoms of Aragon and Castile were united. Granada, the last of the Moorish states, fell before the armies of King Ferdinand and Queen Isabella in 1492. This period of Spanish history was noted for the cruelty of the Inquisition, which tortured any group standing in the way of royal power. It was also the period during which Spain began her rise to world power through voyages of exploration and discovery.

The Spanish golden age came during the sixteenth century, when the treasures from her colonial empire began pouring into the country. The armies of Spain were the strongest of Europe, and on the high seas only the English pirates and buccaneers presented serious difficulties.

The beginning of decline in Spanish power dates from the defeat of the Armada that King Philip II sent in 1588 to punish England's Queen Elizabeth I. The great fleet of over one hundred thirty warships was wiped out by a combination of storm and the smaller, more maneuverable English ships. Wars sapped the strength of the empire. By the time Napoleon had come to power in France, Spain was on the verge of internal collapse. Joseph Bonaparte, brother of the Emperor, was proclaimed King of Spain. However, a Spanish revolt restored the Bourbon's throne (1816).

Spain grew still weaker, losing nearly all her American colonies to independence movements early in the nineteenth century. In 1898, the United States crushed the Spanish Empire by capturing the Philippines, Puerto Rico, and Guam, and by freeing Cuba in a short war.

Spain chose to remain neutral during World War I. The African colony of Morocco revolted in 1921 and the Spanish army was overwhelmed by Moroccan soldiers. This was the signal for a reform movement in Spain.

General Miguel Primo de Rivera made himself dictator in 1923. However, in 1930, he was overthrown and the monarchy was reestablished. In 1931, a republic was proclaimed.

In 1936, an election gave the leftist parties a strong majority. Army officers revolted later that year, setting off a violent civil war that lasted until the victory of General Francisco Franco in 1939. In the civil war, the Republican group was opposed by a rightist Nationalist group that included Fascist elements. Germany tested many of her World War II weapons by turning them over to the Nationalists while the Soviet Union contributed weapons to the Republican group.

Franco's victory resulted in the formation of a "corporative republic." Spain then proceeded to aid the Nazis during World War II, though refraining from active participation in the war. As a result of her stand, Spain was isolated diplomatically after the War. Spain was admitted to the United Nations in 1955.

The dictatorship established after the civil war endured through Franco's lifetime. He named as his successor the son of the Bourbon pretender to the throne. In November 1975, Juan Carlos de Bourbón was restored to a kingdom unlike that of his grandfather, 44 years earlier.

SRI LANKA

For nearly two thousand years, Sinhalese kings ruled Ceylon with only occasional interruptions. Many wars were fought against invaders from southern India and China. Early in the sixteenth century the Portuguese established relations with Ceylon and began a conquest of the island. By the end of the century they had gained control. The Dutch supplanted them in the middle of the seventeenth century. In 1796, the British expelled the Dutch and annexed their settlements to one of their administrations in India. In 1802, Ceylon was constituted a crown colony.

The British firmly suppressed attempted native rebellions; they introduced tea and rubber plantations, importing Tamils as coolie laborers. Internal struggles broke out between Buddhists and Moslem traders. In addition, the inhabitants strove constantly for a voice in their own government.

On February 4, 1949, Ceylon became a Dominion within the British Commonwealth. On December 14, 1955, the country became a member of the United Nations. It changed from a monarchy to a republic on May 22, 1972, and at that time also chose to use its Sinhalese name, Sri Lanka.

SUDAN

The region known as Nubia was invaded by Egyptians around 3000 B.C.; and Egypt ruled it continuously until the eighth century B.C., when the Sudanese defeated and subjugated the Egyptians.

Gradually the country became Christianized. It was invaded in the sixteenth century by Arabs from the north and Moslem blacks from the Blue Nile Valley.

In the nineteenth century, Egypt, then a Turkish province, launched a successful invasion that made Sudan an Egyptian province. The region remained under Egyptian-Turkish rule for 60 years, a period marked by native unrest. A series of revolts beginning in 1880 smashed Egyptian rule but brought little improvement in conditions. Constant wars of expansion were waged against neighboring tribes, and an attempted conquest of Egypt in 1889 ended in disaster.

Following this debacle, French influence began to spread in the Sudan. Alarmed at growing French power, Britain sent a joint British-Egyptian force into the region and won a complete victory. In 1899, Britain and Egypt assumed joint control in Sudan.

Following World War II, Egypt became dissatisfied with the joint arrangement and demanded British withdrawal. An agreement was finally reached that provided for Sudanese independence. After an election, Sudanese officials took office in 1954 and began the process of replacing all foreigners in government and military positions. On January 1, 1956, the Republic of Sudan was established, and on November 12, 1956, it was admitted to the United Nations.

Sudan has found itself in the midst of recent terrorist revolts in the Arab world. In March 1973, eight Palestinian rebels murdered the American ambassador, a Belgian diplomat, and the French *chargé d'affaires* in Khartoum. The Sudanese government released the terrorists to another revolutionary group in Egypt. Sudan also supports the Eritrean guerrillas in Ethiopia.

SURINAM

In 1667, the Dutch acquired Surinam from the British in exchange for New Netherland (an area that now includes New York) in North America. It remained a colony called Netherlands Guiana (or Dutch Guiana) until 1954, when it was given the status of a dependency of the Dutch crown. The home government was more than willing to grant this country its freedom. Most of the population of Surinam are East Indians or descendants of slaves brought over from Africa. The republic of Surinam was proclaimed on November 25, 1975, and it was admitted to the United Nations on December 4, 1975.

SWAZILAND

The Swazis, a Bantu people in southern Africa, gradually bargained away their resources to the

British and Boer colonists who were their neighbors at the end of the nineteenth century.

Sobhuza II became king of Swaziland in 1921. He remained king after Swaziland became an independent state within the British Commonwealth on September 6, 1968. Swaziland was admitted to the United Nations on September 24, 1968. A parliamentary system installed in 1967 was discarded by King Sobhuza in 1973.

SWEDEN

The first mention of the Swedes by Europeans was made by the Roman historian Tacitus in about A.D. 100. He described them as having "mighty ships and arms." Uppsala was founded about A.D. 500.

Swedes explored interior Russia. Rurik (probably a Viking from Sweden) founded the Russian State (*see* U.S.S.R.).

A long series of wars against Finland began in 1157, ending with the conquest and Christianization of Finland in 1293. In 1319, Norway and Sweden were united; and in 1397, all of Scandinavia was united under Queen Margarethe of Denmark.

Sweden broke away in 1523 and elected Gustavus Vasa (Gustaf I) as king. Gustavus freed the country from the rule of Danish nobles and the Hanseatic League cities. By 1560, Sweden was the strongest power in northern Europe. Between 1611 and 1718 Sweden expanded to be the foremost Protestant power.

Sweden declined through internal dissension and the combined efforts of Prussia, Russia, and Hanover. The last war ever fought by Sweden was against Napoleon in 1814. Norway was united to Sweden (taken from Denmark) between 1814 and 1905. Sweden gradually became a democratic nation as the king handed over more and more power to the Riksdag (Parliament). Sweden has mantained strict neutrality since 1814, but joined the United Nations on November 19, 1946.

SWITZERLAND

When Julius Caesar set about his conquest of Gaul, one of the peoples he conquered on the way were the Helvetii. Even now Switzerland calls itself by the Latin name of *Helvetia* on postage stamps. The area came under the control of various Germanic peoples in the fifth century A.D. It was part of Charlemagne's Frankish domain in the eighth century and part of the Holy Roman Empire by the eleventh century. In the thirteenth century it came under Hapsburg rule.

Oppressive rule by the Hapsburgs led to an "eternal alliance" between the cantons of Schwyz (the name from which "Switzerland" is derived), Uri, and Unterwalden in 1291. This was the first step toward a Swiss nation. In 1315, the Swiss defeated the Hapsburgs at Morgarten Pass. Thereafter the Swiss became renowned throughout Europe as great fighters and tough soldiers. Other countries hired Swiss mercenaries to do their fighting. The Swiss defeated Charles of Burgundy in 1477. The number of cantons in the alliance had grown to eight by then. Four more victories over Austria followed within a century. The country secured complete independence from the Holy Roman Empire at Basel in 1499.

The confederation had grown to 13 (plus some allied cantons) by 1513. Then the Reformation troubles began. The conflict between Catholic and Protestant in Switzerland plagued the federation until 1847. A number of rebellions occurred, but were unsuccessful. Switzerland was occupied by Napoleon's forces for a time; but it was restored with its 22 cantons in 1815 by the Congress of Vienna.

Since 1874 Switzerland has operated under an enlarged federal authority, with a constitution similar to that of the United States. The nation has managed to remain neutral in all wars since 1815. At the same time, it has been a refuge for exiles and has offered Swiss services to international organizations. Switzerland was the headquarters of the League of Nations, and the Swiss also offered the city of Geneva as the site of the United Nations. However, Switzerland is not a member of the United Nations.

SYRIA

Syria is the name of an ancient region that included the present Syria, Lebanon, Israel, and Jordan. In 1471 B.C., Egypt conquered ancient Syria. Successive invasions by Babylonia, Assyria, Persia, and Macedonia eventually destroyed the outline of Syria.

The region of the present-day Syria, centered around the city of Damascus (reputedly the oldest inhabited city in the world), became a notable trading area. Famous caravan routes between the Persian Gulf and the Mediterranean Sea passed through Palmyra and Damascus. In A.D. 105, the entire region came under Roman rule. Palmyra rose to great fame under Queen Zenobia, but was destroyed by the Roman Emperor Aurelian in A.D. 273. In A.D. 637, Damascus became the capital of a large Arab empire called the Caliphate of Omayyad, which extended all the way to India. The Christian Crusaders invaded Syria in the twelfth century. A series of small Crusaders' states grew up in Syria that lasted until the coming of the Ottoman Empire in the sixteenth century. Ottoman rule continued until after World War I. After the war, the League of Nations gave Syria the control of France. The Syrians were dissatisfied with the mandate and demanded home rule. Rebellions were crushed by the French in 1925 and 1927.

In 1941, Syria was proclaimed an independent republic. The Arab League was formed in 1945 with Syria as a member. The French withdrew in 1946, and Syria joined the Arab League to resist the formation of Israel. Syria was defeated, along with the Arab League, and an internal struggle developed. In 1958, Syria joined with Egypt to form the United Arab Republic, which was dissolved in 1961. When Syria entered the war against Israel in 1967, she lost her southwestern corner (the Golan Heights) to Israel. Syria continued to allow guerrilla units to stage raids on Israel from her territory. She refused to negotiate peace with Israel until the Golan Heights were restored and the issue of the Palestinian refugees was settled.

Syria has been the most militant of the Arab countries and has engaged in every conflict that has occurred in the Middle East over the past 30 years. In 1984, Syrian forces were in the thick of the fighting in Lebanon.

TAIWAN

This large island 110 miles east of the Chinese mainland probably received Chinese immigrants during the Tang Dynasty (A.D. 618–907), but it was not part of the Chinese Empire until the end of the seventeenth century. The Portuguese first saw the island in 1544 and named it *Formosa* ("beautiful"). By 1624, there were Dutch forts on the island; but Chinese refugees drove out the Dutch, even before others came from the mainland to conquer the island in 1662.

After the Japanese victory in her war with China in 1895, Taiwan was ceded to Japan. It remained Japanese for half a century, during which its economy was improved but its culture was blighted. It was restored to Chinese control after World War II. Within a few years, the Taiwanese began to revolt against the Chinese government. At this time, the Chinese government was being driven out of the mainland by the Chinese Communists; so the anticommunist or Nationalist governments took refuge on Taiwan, which became the official seat of administration for Nationalist China.

The Nationalist administration tried to bring peace and order to its new home, from which it expected to launch a reconquest of the mainland. It improved the economy of the island and represented China in many world capitals. It was a member of the United Nations from October 24, 1945 until 1971, when the organization voted to transfer the Chinese seat to the representatives of the People's Republic of China.

The main support of the Nationalist government was the United States. Even after 1971 the United States continued to recognize the Nationalists while negotating with the People's Republic. Both Chinese governments agreed in principle that Taiwan is part of China.

TANZANIA

The name of this republic was coined from that of its two component units, Tanganyika and Zanzibar, which had separate histories before their merger in 1964.

Vasco da Gama was the first modern European to visit the east coast of Africa in 1498. He found the Arabs entrenched there, and they remained in control as slave traders, despite Portuguese efforts to gain a foothold. In the early eighteenth century, the dominant power was that of the sultan of Muscat and Oman, whose headquarters were on the offshore island of Zanzibar (*see* Oman).

In 1884, the coast became part of German East Africa. This colony was split after World War I, and the bulk of it was mandated in 1922 to Britain under the name of the large lake on its west border, Tanganyika. It became a United Nations trust territory in 1946. After achieving local autonomy in 1960, Tanganyika became independent on December 9, 1961. Five days later it became a member of the United Nations. On its first anniversary, Tanganyika became a republic within the British Commonwealth.

Meanwhile, Zanzibar and the nearby island of Pemba acquired a population from southern Asia, and its Arab masters were supplanted by Portuguese, who dominated during the sixteenth and seventeenth centuries. In 1699, the Portuguese were driven out by Arabs from Oman. Zanzibar became one of the leading slave trading centers in eastern Africa.

British interest required the ban of this commerce with her colonies; and in 1822, the Imam of Oman signed a treaty with Britain containing this provision. Thus began an era of British protection that continued when Zanzibar was separated from Oman in 1856. The region became a colony of Great Britain during World War I. Autonomy was granted in 1963; and on June 24 of that year, the sultanate became independent. On January 12, 1964, the sultan was deposed and the People's Republic of Zanzibar was proclaimed.

Zanzibar had been admitted to the United Nations on December 16, 1963. But on April 26, 1964, Zanzibar and Tanganyika united to form a single republic. Thereafter only one membership was retained in the United Nations. The name was changed on October 29, 1964 to United Republic of Tanzania.

THAILAND

Tribes of Indochina began a migration during the sixth century B.C. into the area now called Thailand. In the middle of the fourteenth century, a unified Thai kingdom was established. It expanded over the centuries by wars of conquest against neighboring small states. It continued for 400 years. By the sixteenth century, contact with Europeans had been established, and Thailand enjoyed a flourishing trade with various Asian and European countries.

There were intermittent wars with Burma until 1764. Then Thailand was invaded by the Burmese and the Thai capital was destroyed. Shortly afterward, the Thais succeeded in driving out the Burmese and established a new capital at Bangkok.

Late in the nineteenth century, Thailand engaged in a boundary dispute with the French, who at that time controlled Indochina. France sent troops and warships that forced Thailand to give up territorial rights in Cambodia. Later, the Thais gave up additional territory to France and Great Britain.

Thailand was an absolute monarchy until 1932, when a revolt set up a representative government with universal suffrage. In 1939, the country (which had until then been known as Siam) officially changed its name to Thailand.

While France was embroiled in World War II, Thailand demanded that territory taken from it be returned. Japan mediated the dispute; this strengthened relations between Thailand and Japan. Immediately after the attack on Pearl Harbor, Japan was granted the right to move troops across Thai territory to the Malay area. In January 1942, Thailand declared war against the Allies. The pro-Japanese government was overthrown in 1944, and the new leaders expressed sympathy for the Allied cause. However, Japan remained in control of Thailand until the war ended. Thailand was admitted to the United Nations on December 16, 1946.

After World War II, the country generally sided with the anticommunist powers in the Cold War. During the war in Indochina, Thailand became a staging area for United States air forces that raided Indochina. Thailand was one of the few Asian members of the Southeast Asia Treaty Organization. Its government was overthrown by a military junta in 1971, which was in turn succeeded by a constitutional government in 1973. In 1975, the first elections ever held in Thailand returned a coalition government, but the military regained power in a coup in 1976.

TOGO

Togo should not be confused with Togoland, a term formerly used for a political unit which no longer exists. Togo was originally colonized by the Ewe people, who now form part of the population in Togo and in neighboring Ghana. The Portuguese began taking slaves from the Togo region in the fifteenth and sixteenth centuries. After competing with both France and Britain for control, Germany established a formal protectorate over the area in 1894.

The original region of which Togo now forms a part was called Togoland. It was held by the Germans until after World War I. In 1919, Togoland was divided into British-administered Togoland and French-administered Togoland, both under trusteeship. Trusteeship was continued under the United Nations after World War II. In 1956, the people of British-held Togoland voted to join the Gold Coast Colony, which became Ghana. British Togoland then ceased to exist.

In 1956, the French-held area voted to terminate trust status, but the vote was not accepted by the United Nations. In April 1958, elections were held under United Nations supervision; this time Togo was given permission to negotiate with France for independence. Full independence was granted on April 27, 1960, and the country was admitted to the United Nations on September 20, 1960.

TONGA

The archipelago of Tonga in the Pacific Ocean has been ruled by a monarchy that is at least 900 years old. The Dutch were the first Europeans to visit the islands, but it was Britain that signed a treaty establishing her protectorate in 1900. By a similar agreement, the islands regained their independence on June 4, 1970, and became a member of the British Commonwealth.

TRINIDAD AND TOBAGO

The islands of Trinidad and Tobago were discovered by Christopher Columbus in 1498, on his third voyage to the New World. The original inhabitants (Carib and Arawak Indians) were killed off or enslaved by the Spanish. The Spanish at first used both islands as centers for the expeditions of discovery and conquest in what is now Latin America.

Colonization of both islands began in the sixteenth century. Tobago was colonized by English settlers from nearby Barbados, and eventually changed hands between the Spanish and English many times before finally becoming a British colony in 1814.

Trinidad is much larger and richer in resources than Tobago. It was colonized by Spanish immigrants, who were later augmented by colonists from other lands. Slaves were introduced early to work sugar cane plantations. During the last half of the nineteenth century many people from South Asia came as laborers in the fields and forests of Trinidad. Trinidad was captured by the British in 1797.

Both islands were at first ruled as separate colonies. Trinidad became a crown colony in 1802, and Tobago was administered as a part of the Windward Islands until 1877, when it also became a crown colony. However, Trinidad and Tobago were united in 1888.

The Federation of West Indies was created in 1958 and included as one of its members a combined Trinidad and Tobago. On February 6, 1962, the British government dissolved the federation. Trinidad and Tobago were then united into an independent nation on August 31, 1962. The new nation became a member of the United Nations on September 18, 1962.

TUNISIA

The ancient city of Carthage was founded in 850 B.C., not far from the present city of Tunis. Following the destruction of Carthage in the Punic Wars, the region came under the domination of various peoples (including the Romans, Byzantines, Vandals, Arabs, Spanish, Turkish, and French). Relics of all these civilizations are still to be found throughout the country; the strongest imprint was left by the Arab-Moslem culture.

Under the Husseinite dynasty, which began early in the eighteenth century, a major source of revenue was piracy. In the nineteenth century, United States naval forces destroyed pirate bases along the so-called Barbary Coast and made the high seas safe for shipping.

In 1881, the French entered Tunisia from Algeria and forced it to become a protectorate, a status which lasted well into the twentieth century. Important World War II battles were fought in Tunisia.

After achieving autonomy, the Tunisians declared their independence on March 20, 1956. Ignoring the monarchy, they instituted a republic on July 25, 1957. Tunisia became a member of the United Nations on November 12, 1956.

TURKEY

About 1900 B.C., the Hittite people invaded Asia Minor from either Europe or Central Asia. Their language and customs persisted for 700 years in Asia Minor. Greeks from the west and Assyrians from the east eventually destroyed their empire, and they gradually disappeared from history.

From about 1000 B.C., the Greeks, Lydians, and others dominated Asia Minor. The Kingdom of Lydia is best known for minting the first coins in the Western world. The Greeks became the most influential people and established great centers of classical Greek culture at such cities as Ephesus, Pergamum, Miletus, and Halicarnassus.

The Persians overran most of Greek-controlled Asia Minor, but all of it was recaptured by Alexander the Great in 333 B.C. The Romans conquered Asia Minor in 63 B.C.

The Byzantine or Eastern Roman Empire continued Roman rule until the Seljuk Turks (a Moslem people from central Asia) invaded and conquered the area in the eleventh century. These Seljuks were the ancestors of the present-day Turks. The Crusades by Western Europeans were directed at the Seljuks. But they were conquered instead by the Mongolians of Central Asia. Turkish power revived under the Ottoman Turks after the Mongol invasions receded. The Ottoman Empire expanded at the expense of Christian and other Moslem states. Constantinople, the last Christian imperial capital in eastern Europe, fell in 1453. The city was made the Ottoman capital under the name *Istanbul.*

The history of modern Turkey begins with the decline of the Ottoman power that started in 1529, when the Ottomans failed to take Venice in a bloody siege. Throughout the later centuries, the Ottoman Empire fought defensive wars and continued to lose them. It became derisively known as the "Sick Man of Europe." The Greeks regained their independence in the 1820s. The North African territories—Egypt, Algeria—were detached. Serbia was removed from Turkish control, even after a Turkish victory in the Crimean War. The Balkans became the target of European power grabs, while Turkey was left with only a small enclave around Istanbul as a souvenir of her European holdings.

These territorial losses and the despotic domestic policy aroused patriots within the country (known as Young Turks) to force the sultan to establish a constitutional monarchy in 1909. Italy took Libya from the Turks in 1911. In a gamble to recover some power in Europe, Turkey allied herself with Germany in World War I, and lost her Middle East possessions. Out of the ruins came a revolution headed by Kemal Ataturk, who drove the Greeks out of Asia Minor and proclaimed a republic on October 29, 1923.

Turkey remained neutral throughout World War II, joining the victorious Allies only in February 1945, in time to participate as a belligerent in the peace negotiations. Turkey joined the United Nations on October 24, 1945. In 1950, Turkey sent a token contingent to fight in Korea; and in 1952, she became a signatory of the North Atlantic Treaty Organization. Relations with Greece were strained in 1974 because of the dispute over Cyprus. The Turkish invasion of Cyprus resulted in an arms embargo by the United States, and this in turn endangered Turkish membership in the North Atlantic Treaty Organization. Turkey ordered the United States to leave its Turkish military bases; but in 1976, they signed a new treaty that allowed the Americans to stay.

Turkey signed a non-aggression pact with Russia in 1978.

TURKS AND CAICOS ISLANDS

The Turks and Caicos, discovered by Ponce de León in 1512, are geographically a part of the Bahama Islands group in the West Indies. They were administered as part of Jamaica from 1848 until Jamaica became independent in 1962. After that, the Turks and Caicos became a British dependency.

UGANDA

Arab and English immigration into this region of Africa began about the middle of the nineteenth century. The British established a protectorate in 1894. Progress toward self-government was begun in 1920.

On October 9, 1962, Uganda became an independent nation within the British Commonwealth. Sixteen days later, Uganda became a member of the United Nations; and in 1967, the nation became a republic. Its government lacked stability until Idi Amin seized the presidency in 1971 and established a dictatorship. He aroused ill will in Europe and the United States by expelling the large Asian population of Uganda in 1972. The United States cut off economic aid in 1973, and Amin called for Soviet help. He was driven into exile in 1979.

UNION OF SOVIET SOCIALIST REPUBLICS

The region that now comprises the heart of the U.S.S.R. (also called the Soviet Union) was known as Scythia to the ancient Greeks. The people were called Scythians. Greek colonies were established along the northern shores of the Black Sea in Scythia about 1000 B.C.

The modern history of the Soviet Union is largely that of the Russians (also called Great Russians to distinguish them from Ukrainians, or Little Russians, and Byelorussians, or White Russians).

The first state in the region of the present European Soviet Union was founded by three Scandinavian brothers named Rurik, Sineus, and Truvor. Their seat of government became the Slavic city of Novgorod (New Town) in A.D. 862. Novgorod (also called Novgorod the Great) seems to have had a long previous association with bands of Vikings, and it is possible that the three brothers were Vikings. Rurik (from whose name the word *Russia* may have been derived) eventually became the sole ruler of Novgorod. After Rurik's death in A.D. 879, the center of political power gradually shifted southward to Kiev on the Dnieper River in the present Ukraine.

Novgorod and Kiev were growing political centers in the ninth century. They were trading posts and commercial centers on the famous trade route across Europe that has since become known as the "Water Road." The Water Road was a wilderness system of river, lake, and portage routes that connected the Baltic and Black seas through what is now the western part of European Russia.

Russia—Nevsky Prospect, Leningrad

Several princely states gradually grew up along the Water Road, but Novgorod and Kiev remained the leading centers until the coming of the Mongol invaders during the thirteenth century. Between 879 and 1242, Kiev expanded and grew to become the "mother" of Slavic culture and chief seat of learning.

The death blow to Kiev as a national center came early in the thirteenth century when the Mongol invasions began. The Mongols (called Tatars by Russians) swept over southern Russia, toppling one princely state after another. Many of the leaders, including those from Kiev, fled to the great forest where they established new cities and prepared for defense against the oncoming Mongolian armies. Kiev was overpowered and ruined by the Mongols in 1240.

Soon all the Russian states were paying tribute to the Mongols—all but Novgorod, which withstood the attacks. Alexander Nevsky, the first great Russian national hero, became the ruler of free Novgorod in 1240 and of Vladimir in 1252. In 1240, he defeated an invasion by Swedes and then crushed the Teutonic Knights on frozen Lake Peipus (Chudskoye) in 1242. However, he was no match for the "Golden Horde," and soon even Novgorod was paying taxes to the Mongol princes.

It should be noted that the Mongols did not destroy the Orthodox Church, nor did they disrupt the system of government by "Grand Princes" that had prevailed in Russia before the invasion. They simply exacted taxes from the ruling princes.

A century after the invasions, Moscow began to rise as a religious and political center. Ivan (Russian for John) Kalita, "The Purse," ruler of Moscow from 1328–1340, persuaded the head of the Christian Church to move from Vladimir to Moscow. Ivan then had himself crowned "Grand Prince of Vladimir and all Rus." This was the beginning of Muscovite expansion.

Mongol power was broken under the steady fighting of Muscovite princes. Ivan III (1462–1505) finally freed Russia from Mongol domination. Ivan also put an end to the independence of Novgorod the Great, although that city is still a prosperous industrial center of the Soviet Union.

A series of powerful rulers, including Ivan IV ("the Terrible"), continued to expand the Muscovite state. They crushed all opposition to autocratic rule and established serfdom. Peter the Great (1682–1725) founded St. Petersburg (now Leningrad) in 1703 as a glittering European capital city. After Peter, Russia began to accept Western Europe's culture, fashions, and science. The rules of Peter, Elizabeth, and Catherine the Great added Ukraine, Byelorussia (White Russia), Bessarabia, Crimea, and other areas to the growing empire. Siberia, Central Asia, and Alaska were added by Catherine the Great and Tsars Alexander I and Nicholas I.

Petty wars, heavy taxation, and repression gradually brought on a crisis in the empire. The crisis began with the Pugachev Revolt in 1773 and continued until the overthrow in 1917. Serfs had been freed in 1861 by Tsar Alexander II, who tried to stem the tide of demands by granting several reforms. (It was this Alexander who sold Alaska to the United States in 1867.) Alexander was assassinated in 1881.

World War I found Russia on the Allied side. But the war brought only defeats and privations for the Russian army. The army was finally unable to get supplies or to get clear decisions from the head of government. In March 1917, a moderate government took over upon the abdication of Tsar Nicholas II, who was no longer able to control the government. In November 1917, the moderate government was overthrown by a revolutionary Marxist group called the Bolsheviks. All authority for government was then handed over to councils of workers and peasants (the word for council in Russian is *soviet*). All major industrial and commercial activities were nationalized. A great civil war followed. Despite foreign intervention, the Bolsheviks were victorious by 1921.

The creation of the Soviet Union was the greatest act in the long career of V. I. Lenin, revolutionary leader and Marxist philosopher. After the death of Lenin in 1924, factional disputes arose. These took the form of purges and finally the redirection of state power toward the building of heavy industry. Communist leaders abandoned the idea of the world Marxist movement for immediate revolution and internal growth. Joseph Stalin ushered in a period when the Soviet Union consolidated its power internally. Heavy industry was planned and activated at the expense of consumer products and agriculture. The Stalin group laid heavy hands upon the freedom of the Russian people.

The Soviet Union was invaded by German forces in June 1941. The resulting battles on Russian soil were among the bloodiest ever fought. German armored divisions succeeded in reaching the Volga River at Stalingrad (now Volgograd), where they besieged the city for two months. This action marked the turning point in the war. United States military assistance reached the Soviet Union chiefly through the northern sea route and over the southern land route.

After the war and the death of Stalin (1953), the Soviet Union changed directions in political, social, and economic matters. A more relaxed attitude toward other nations began to appear. When Nikita Khrushchev assumed power in 1956, he denounced Stalinist excesses and tensions began to ease. The so-called Cold War between Western democracies and the Soviet Union tapered off.

The Soviets never let up, however, in their relentless effort toward world conquest. Massive military and economic help in Indo-China and aid to African and Latin American countries helped in the ideological war against the free world; and the success of their efforts is beyond question.

Khrushchev was deposed in 1964. His successor was Leonid Brezhnev who died in 1982 to be succeeded by Yuri Andropov, who died in 1984. Konstantin Chernenko was chosen his successor.

UNITED ARAB EMIRATES

Along the south coast of the Persian Gulf between Qatar and Oman are seven Arab sheikhdoms, whose main resource is oil.

In earlier times their principal activity was piracy. In the nineteenth century, they came under British influence and signed a truce to abstain from such violations of international law. This gave them the name of the Trucial States, and they became a collective British protectorate while their sheikhs maintained their local power. On December 2, 1971, the states became the United Arab Emirates and signed a treaty with Britain as an independent country. A week later the United Arab Emirates became a member of the United Nations.

UNITED KINGDOM

The full form of the name is the United Kingdom of Great Britain and Northern Ireland. This name evolved slowly, beginning in 1707. At that time the Crowns of England and Scotland were united to form the Kingdom of Great Britain. The name was correctly used for both the island and the kingdom. In 1801, the name *Ireland* was added as a result of the union of Ireland with the Crown. The last change occurred in 1927, when Ireland withdrew from the union of kingdoms, leaving behind the six counties of Ulster. These became Northern Ireland, which replaced "Ireland" in the full name of the United Kingdom.

The island of Great Britain was inhabited in pre-Roman times by Celtic peoples who lived mainly in the southern part. The chief tribe was the Briton, from which the name *Britain* is derived.

Julius Caesar was unable to conquer the island during his expedition of 54 B.C. However, the island was conquered by the Roman Emperor Claudius in A.D. 43, and Roman rule was gradually extended northward. The Romans built a great wall (part of which still stands) to mark the northern limits of their government and to keep out the warlike Picts of present-day Scotland. Roads were built. Christianity was introduced; many cities and towns were founded during the Roman period. The Romans withdrew gradually as pressure mounted from invading forces of Nordic peoples. By A.D. 410, they had left the island to the invaders.

A period of confusion and invasion followed. After the Roman departure, Danes, Saxons, Angles, and Jutes gained territory in Britain. The Celtic peoples gradually withdrew deeper into the secluded forests and uplands of what is now Wales and Scotland. The Welsh people are largely the descendants of the ancient Celts who first inhabited Britain.

England—Westminster, Big Ben, and the Houses of Parliament, also showing Westminster Abbey

Many small kingdoms developed, especially in the southern part of Britain. Some of them were united to form larger kingdoms; by the eighth century, Wessex had become the strongest. Its greatest leader was Alfred the Great (849–899), who defeated the Danes. However, Danish rule was reinstituted in 954. From 1017 to 1035, most of what is now England was united to the Crown of Denmark under King Canute.

The modern history of Britain began in 1066 when William the Conqueror, himself the descendant of Norse (Norman) invaders of France, invaded and defeated the last Saxon king at Hastings. William built a strong government. French was introduced as the language of the nobility. Under William and his descendants, the English language began to take form. This is called the Norman period (William was also king of Normandy, a region in France). In 1154, the Plantagenet family of kings introduced further refinements in government, including the jury system. Repressive taxes caused the nobility to revolt. In 1215, King John was forced to sign the Magna Charta, or Great Charter, that established several basic limits in government. The beginnings of a parliamentary system were made under Edward I (1272–1307). The "model parliament" of 1295 included clergymen and townspeople, as well as lesser nobility. It established a trend toward democracy in government.

The Hundred Years' War represented for Britain and France the final flowering of feudalism and the end of the Middle Ages. The use of gunpowder signaled the end of the armored knight on horse, as well as the great castle bastions of feudal times. A trend toward strong central government began in Britain. Trade and commerce revived, along with the beginnings of competition for markets and colonies outside Britain. As an island kingdom with a long seafaring tradition, Britain was well prepared to compete with the Dutch, Spanish, French, and others for the control of newly discovered lands.

The reign of Elizabeth I (1558–1603) initiated the golden age of British culture and history. The flowering of art, drama, and literature went hand-in-hand with expansion overseas. British power eventually gained an empire that spread over the known world and was the largest empire in history. Britain achieved supremacy in commerce and trade, as well as in naval and military power.

A period of absolute monarchy after Elizabeth I was followed by the outbreak of civil war in 1642. When monarchy was restored in 1688, it was no longer under the "divine right" concept. Parliament passed a "Bill of Rights" in 1689, which has served as a model for many other nations of the world.

After the wars with France in the seventeenth and eighteenth centuries, the British Empire had reached its greatest extent. The Industrial Revolution reached Britain and an era of political and social reform followed. The Victorian period under Queen Victoria (1837–1901) saw the rise of great parliamentarians and the beginning of the colonial movement for self-government or independence. The empire began to break up, often with violence. But in some cases, the colonies made a peaceful transition from empire to the new "commonwealth" concept. The American colonies were lost in 1783; Canada became a dominion (an associated state) in 1867; New Zealand, Australia, and South Africa, at the beginning of the twentieth century; Ireland withdrew in 1922, and Egypt in 1936. India gained her independence in 1947.

The Commonwealth of Nations, formerly called the British Commonwealth, is a loose association of Great Britain and about 35 countries which were her former colonies, although not all chose to be included. Heads of these nations meet at intervals to discuss mutual goals and problems.

The United Kingdom in the twentieth century has engaged in two world wars. The most critical of these was World War II, in which Britain was severely bombed and 360,000 British service men lost their lives.

The British of recent years have been preoccupied with problems such as the struggle in Northern Ireland, which has on occasion reached the streets of London; inflation and high unemployment; and the pesky invasion in 1982 by Argentina in the Falkland Islands. Prime Minister Margaret Thatcher's handling of that situation and her austere program to get the country back on a sound financial footing helped her win reelection in 1983. Britain has profited from huge oil discoveries in the North Sea. The United Kingdom continues as one of the United States' staunchest allies.

UNITED STATES OF AMERICA

(See Pages 1079–1134)

UPPER VOLTA

The history of Upper Volta until the end of the nineteenth century A.D. was that of the empire-building Mossi people. Their origin is somewhat obscure, but they probably came from eastern Africa sometime in the eleventh century A.D. They first established small kingdoms in the region of the present Ghana and then spread out northward along the Black, Red, and White Volta rivers.

The original empire was centered on the present city of Ouagadougou. It persisted down to modern times. The Mossi people sacked the city of Timbuktu (Tombouctou) in 1333. They also fought the Mali and Songhai peoples that were near neighbors. Mossi power declined after the eighteenth century.

By 1896, the empires of the region were weak and the French were able to establish a protectorate. In 1919, the former kingdoms were united into a territory called Upper Volta, and were added to the French West African group of colonies. In 1932, Upper Volta was dismembered and abolished. However, on September 4, 1947, the Territory of Upper Volta was reestablished with the 1932 boundaries. This was done to avoid political conflict. On December 11, 1958, Upper Volta became the autonomous Voltaic Republic. In 1959, the name was changed back to Upper Volta. Upper Volta became an independent nation on August 5, 1960. It was admitted to the United Nations on September 20, 1960.

URUGUAY

Juan de Solis discovered the Uruguay region in 1516. Colonia del Sacramento was founded by the

Uruguay—Montevideo

Portuguese as a rival to Spanish Buenos Aires, located just a few miles away (across the Río de la Plata estuary). Rivalry between the Portuguese in Uruguay and the Spanish in Argentina continued until the Uruguay region was annexed to the viceroyalty of Buenos Aires. Uruguay revolted against Spain in 1810. It had to fight not only the Spanish, but also Brazil and Argentina, both of which tried to annex the country. Independence was achieved in 1825 from Argentina and in 1828 from Brazil. Uruguay became a republic.

During the rest of the nineteenth century, Uruguay had mostly unstable governments; but in 1903, President José Batlle y Ordónez initiated a series of reforms that made Uruguay one of South America's most progressive democracies. It became a member of the United Nations on December 18, 1945.

In 1952, the presidential system was abandoned and the executive power was shared by a board of nine members—six from the majority and three from the minority party. The presidential system was restored in 1957, then again abrogated in 1973 for a military dictatorship.

VATICAN CITY

The Vatican City is an independent state located in Italy, within the city of Rome.

The state's modern history dates from February 11, 1929, when the Lateran Treaty was signed between Italy and His Holiness, the Supreme Pontiff (pope) of the Roman Catholic Church. The treaty established the boundaries and guaranteed the independence of the state. Vatican City issues its own coins and stamps and maintains diplomatic relations with about 70 nations, the United States becoming one in 1983.

VENEZUELA

Venezuela was discovered by Columbus in 1498, but until Caracas was founded in 1567 there were no important settlements. As part of New Granada (*see* Colombia) it participated in the revolt led by Simón Bolívar and Francisco de Miranda in 1810 and 1811, and after independence was won in 1821 remained part of the new state of Gran Colombia. But this state disintegrated; and in 1830, Venezuela became independent. Throughout the nineteenth century, and until the presidency of Romulo Betancourt in 1958, a succession of dictators ruled Venezuela. The constitution of 1961, and reforms of succeeding presidents, apparently made democracy work in Venezuela. The country became a member of the United Nations on December 18, 1945.

VIETNAM

The history of Vietnam can be traced back to the fourth century B.C., when a group of people called

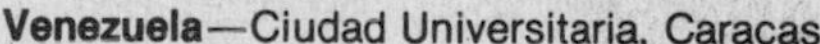

Venezuela—Ciudad Universitaria, Caracas

the Viets entered the Tonkin Gulf area of Southeast Asia. They conquered and intermarried with the local people. About 200 B.C., they set up the kingdom of Nam-Viet, which was later conquered by Chinese armies.

The Chinese ruled Nam-Viet until A.D. 938, when Viet leaders expelled them and planted the new kingdom of Vietnam. France captured Vietnam in the eighteenth century and set up a protectorate there in 1884.

Japan took control of the country in World War II and established the puppet state of Bao Dai. In 1946, Communist forces known as the Vietminh overthrew the Bao Dai. They refused to accept French rule, and France launched a full-scale attack on the country. The French forces were defeated at Dien Bien Phu in 1954.

A peace conference in Geneva divided the country into North and South Vietnam to separate the pro-communist and and anticommunists forces until elections could be held in 1956. But the elections were never held, and the two nations remained hostile toward one another.

In 1963, a guerrilla movement emerged in South Vietnam to overthrow the South Vietnamese government. A series of military chiefs held the presidency of South Vietnam, but each failed to quash the Vietcong guerrillas. The United States poured money and troops into the conflict, to no avail. South Vietnam fell to the communist forces in the spring of 1975, after more than a million Vietnamese civilians and over 200,000 Vietnamese soldiers had been killed. More than 47,000 American soldiers also died in the war.

The country was officially reunited on July 2, 1976. It adopted the flag, capital, and government of the former North Vietnam. In 1977, the United States agreed to allow Vietnam to join the United Nations. Since then, Vietnam troops have engaged troops in neighboring Cambodia and Thailand.

WALLIS AND FUTUNA

The islands were ruled by kings and as a protectorate of France from 1842 until 1961, when they became an overseas territory of France. The territory is located in the South Pacific Ocean.

WESTERN SAMOA

Western Samoa was made a German protectorate in 1900. It became a League of Nations mandated territory of New Zealand in 1920. Partial self-government was achieved in 1947. By 1961, the islands were ready for full independence, which had been pledged to them by New Zealand in 1946. Independence was granted on January 1, 1962.

WEST GERMANY

The Romans used the name *Germania* to designate an area that was almost the same as that of modern Germany. The inhabitants of Germania were described as being divided into classes of noblemen, freemen, vassals, and slaves. The Romans waged war against various tribes that came from this region, beginning with Cimbri and Teuton peoples in the second century A.D. In later centuries German peoples came over to the Roman areas peacefully and often joined up with the legions of Imperial Rome. Still later, they began to invade Roman provinces, and finally aided in the destruction of the Roman world.

The rise of Frankish power and the establishment of a Frankish empire under Merovingians marked the beginning of a long series of unification attempts in what is now Germany. Charlemagne inherited the region from the Merovingians. His Frankish empire included what is now France, Germany, and part of Italy. Upon his death the empire dissolved. Germany was again united in the Holy Roman Empire that was set up in 962. The Holy Roman Empire dominated Central Europe until the Reformation. The empire crumbled from lack of a steady central authority and from internal dissension. The rise of national kingdoms and prosperous trading cities also helped destroy the effective authority of the empire. The Thirty Years' War of 1618–1648 split Germany and the Holy Roman Empire into a maze of fragments, including over three hundred separate states and independent cities.

The rise of Prussia under Frederick II (1740–1786) once again presented an opportunity for the establishment of a German nation. German nationalism asserted itself during the French Revolution and the Napoleonic era. A successful movement for unification came into being under the leadership of Otto von Bismarck, Chancellor of Prussia. Rivalry between Prussia and Austria for the control of Germany developed into a series of wars (1864–1871) which Prussia won, assuming the position of the leading economic and military power on the Continent. An intricate system of alliances established a delicate balance of political power in Europe. This balance was finally upset in the Balkans by the 1914 murder of the heir to the throne of the Austro-Hungarian Empire, which led to World War I.

World War I ended in the defeat of Germany and the destruction of the German Empire. In the social disorder that followed, National Socialism, or Nazism, gained a powerful following under the leadership of Adolf Hitler. In 1933, Hitler converted the Weimar Republic of Germany into the German Third Reich, a Nazi dictatorship.

Expansionist policies, the persecution of political minorities, and the execution of plans to exterminate the Jewish population of Germany marked the Nazi regime. In 1938, Hitler annexed Austria and then Czechoslovakia. World War II was precipitated by the sudden German invasion of Poland on September 1, 1939. The Soviet Union had signed a nonaggression pact with Hitler and had helped in the partition of Poland. Yet German forces invaded Russia in a lightning-like stroke on June 22, 1941. On December 7, 1941, Japan, which had become allied with Germany, without warning attacked Pearl Harbor. While the Americans adopted a holding action in the Pacific, they planned, along with the Allies, an invasion of Europe. The German armies, in the meantime, pushed further into Russia and were finally halted at Stalingrad (*see* U.S.S.R.). The allied invasion began in Africa in November 1942, and continued in Sicily and Italy, gradually splitting the Axis forces and sapping German military strength. On June 1, 1944, a great Allied invasion force landed on the coast of Normandy in France. The Nazi military machine was crushed. On May 8, 1945, Germany surrendered.

On June 5, 1945, Germany was divided into four zones of occupation. The four occupation powers (the United Kingdom, France, the Soviet Union, and the United States) set up an Allied Control Council for the government of the German capital city of Berlin, which became an island in the Soviet Union's zone of occupation.

The failure of the Allies to agree upon procedures and upon the future disposition of defeated Germany ended the policy of cooperation and brought about the demise of the Allied Control Council for Berlin. In 1949, Germany was formally divided into western and eastern sections. The western part became the Federal Republic of Germany with a provisional capital at Bonn, on the Rhine River in Westphalia. Territories in the east that included East Prussia were partitioned by Poland and the Soviet Union. Berlin, originally di-

West Germany—The Lukaskirche, Protestant Church, Munich

vided into four zones of occupation, eventually consisted of only two zones—West Berlin, which was associated with the Federal Republic, and East Berlin, which was under the administration of the German Democratic Republic (the Soviet zone). The Saar region was formally united to the Federal Republic after agreement between France and the Federal Republic, after free elections had been held.

Since World War II, West Germany has become one of the leading industrial nations of the world and, like Japan, a keen competitor with U.S. auto makers. Its agreement to allow the deployment of nuclear missiles within its borders sparked huge demonstrations in 1983 but government leaders reaffirmed their determination to stick to their decision.

WINDWARD ISLANDS

The more southerly group of islands in the Lesser Antilles of the British West Indies is called the Windward Islands. They comprise, from north to south, Dominica, St. Lucia, St. Vincent, and Grenada. They were members of the West Indies Federation that existed from 1958 to 1962. Discovered by Columbus and often in dispute between the French and English, while the indigenous Carib Indians fiercely resisted conquest by Europeans, these islands were before 1958 organized as the colony of Windward Islands and in 1967 were made associated states. As such, they had maximum self-government short of independence. In 1974, Grenada declared its independence (*see* Grenada), but the others remained associated states.

Yemen—View of Sana'a, the capital

YEMEN

Yemen is the heart of the famous "Arabia Felix" of ancient times. It was the site of the Kingdom of Saba (950–115 B.C.), supposedly ruled for a time by the great Queen of Sheba.

The Yemen region was conquered by the Ottoman Turks in 1517 and remained under their loose control until they were expelled by the British in World War I (1918). Turkish control had been only nominal after 1913. Yemen became a member of the United Nations on September 30, 1947.

The ruler of Yemen was the hereditary imam until military forces proclaimed the Yemen Arab Republic on September 18, 1962.

Today two countries are recognized, North Yemen or the Yemen Arab Republic, and South Yemen or the People's Democratic Republic of Yemen.

The People's Republic of Yemen went to war with Yemen in 1979. The war was short-lived and a mutual withdrawal of forces was agreed to.

YUGOSLAVIA

The South Slavs migrated to the Balkans from the east and north during the sixth century A.D. and later. Most of them were converted to Christianity during the eighth and ninth centuries, but under later Turkish rule many became Moslems. Of the many attempts to form lasting states, only the Serbians were partially successful.

In the second half of the nineteenth century, just prior to the national liberation movements centering around Serbia, the South Slavs consisted of Serbians, Slovenes, Croatians, Bosnians, Macedonians, and Montenegrins. In 1878, Serbia achieved independence. The Balkan Wars of 1911–1913 led to a series of events that eventually became the immediate cause of World War I. After the war a unified Slavic state emerged, comprising Serbia, Croatia, Bosnia and Herzegovina, Slavonia, and Dalmatia. This new state was called the Kingdom of the Serbs, Croats, and Slovenes. The state

U.S. Secretary of State, Henry Kissinger (left) with President Josip Broz Tito of Yugoslavia (right) during the former's visit to Yugoslavia in November 1974. (With them is an interpreter.)

proved unstable, and the king declared himself dictator in 1929 and renamed the country Yugoslavia.

During World War II pressure was used by both the Axis and Allied powers to secure Yugoslav support. The Germans invaded the country in April 1941, and the king thereafter ruled from exile in London. Several resistance groups emerged within Yugoslavia, the most enduring of which was led by Tito, a communist, who was eventually supported by the Soviet Union, the British, and the Americans. Yugoslavia was a charter member of the United Nations on October 24, 1945.

On November 29, 1945, Yugoslavia was proclaimed a republic, and the constitution of 1946 made it a federal republic. The leader in the Soviet-type government was Tito, although he did not become president until 1953, when a new constitution provided for that office. By this time, relations between the Soviet Union and Yugoslavia had deteriorated. The differences between two communist countries revealed for the first time that nations could belong to the communist camp and yet not be "satellites" of the Soviet Union. Yugoslavia became a leader of the so-called unaligned bloc.

Under the constitution of 1963, the official name was changed to the Socialist Federal Republic of Yugoslavia.

Following Tito's death in 1980, a rotating system of succession was established among members representing each republic and autonomous province.

ZAIRE

This name is an African equivalent of Congo, and was adopted by the government formerly known as Republic of the Congo, with its capital at Kinshasa, both for itself and for the river. An even earlier name of this state was Belgian Congo, before independence was achieved.

The mouth of the Congo River was discovered by the Portuguese explorer Diego Cam. Exploration into the interior began when David Livingstone and Henry Stanley, in the nineteenth century, followed the Congo through the great rain forest. Stanley was in the service of Belgian King Leopold II who subsidized several of Stanley's expeditions. Conflicts between European nations over the Congo area were prevented by the Berlin Conference of 1884, which established the Belgian king's claims to the main basin of the Congo River.

The personal rule of the king ended in 1908 when the Congo region was organized into the colony of Belgian Congo. Serious movements toward independence did not occur until 1959. Belgium agreed to grant independence on June 30, 1960.

No sooner had the nation become independent than its army mutinied. The national army then became an uncertain and undisciplined force that supported various leaders at different times. Katanga province, rich in minerals, seceded from the republic. A special United Nations force tried to maintain some semblance of order but failed. The nation's first prime minister was murdered under

President Joseph Mobutu of Zaire (right) with U.S. heavyweight challenger Muhammad Ali. The latter was in Zaire for a title bout with George Foreman.

mysterious circumstances; and in 1961, the Congolese Parliament convened under United Nations auspices and protection. The central government tried to negotiate with the secessionist Katanga Province, but its leader, Moise Tshombe, refused to carry out agreements. UN Secretary-General Dag Hammarskjöld was killed in a plane crash while flying into Katanga Province in order to secure an agreement. A new constitution was drafted in 1962 but led to still another secessionist movement, in Kasai Province. By the latter part of 1963, both secessions had ended, and United Nations supervisory forces were able to leave the country by the end of June 1964.

The constitution in effect was superseded by another imposed in 1966 by President Joseph Mobutu. He remained in that office under a new constitution adopted by referendum in June 1967. As part of the africanization program, he changed his name to Mobutu Sese Seko, and that of the country to Zaire, in 1971.

Most foreign business owners sold their interests to native operators in 1974, but the government of Zaire asked them to return. Low copper prices hurt the economy of the country; and in 1977, a force of Cuban-trained guerrillas invaded Zaire from Angola. Troops and planes from Morocco, Egypt, and France helped President Mobutu repel the attack. Another invasion was attempted in 1978 but without success.

ZAMBIA

After the federation of Rhodesia and Nyasaland was dissolved on the last day of 1963, the British protectorate of Northern Rhodesia was given autonomy. (For the history of Northern Rhodesia, see Rhodesia.) On October 24, 1964, the protectorate was given its independence within the Commonwealth, as the republic of Zambia. On December 1, 1964, it joined the United Nations. Relations between black-ruled Zambia and her white-ruled neighbor, Rhodesia, continued to be unfriendly; and for a time in 1973, their borders were closed. An alternate link to the coast was provided by the building of a highway and railroad through Tasmania to the port of Dar es Salaam.

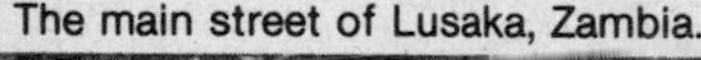

The main street of Lusaka, Zambia.

Statistics for Countries of the World

NAME OF COUNTRY	POPULATION	CAPITAL* LARGEST CITY	AREA (SQUARE MILES)	GOVERNMENT	MAJOR LANGUAGES
Afghanistan Democratic Republic of Afghanistan	15,100,000	Kabul* 891,750	251,773	Military government, U.S.S.R. control	Pushtu, Persian
Albania People's Socialist Republic of Albania	2,800,000	Tirana* 198,000	11,100	1 party, Communist state	Albanian
Algeria Democratic and Popular Republic of Algeria	20,100,000	Algiers* 2,200,000	919,595	Presidential regime	Arabic, French
Andorra Principality of Andorra	38,050 (scattered through 7 small villages)	Andorra la Vella* No population figure available	188	Co-principality, France and Spain, Council of 24 members	Catalan
Angola People's Republic of Angola	6,800,000	Luanda* 475,300	481,353	1 party, committee rule	Portuguese, Bantu
†Antigua and Barbuda	77,000	St. John's* 25,000	171	2 party, parliamentary government	English
Argentina Argentine Republic	28,438,000	Buenos Aires* 2,922,800	1,065,189	Federal republic. Long under military control, but Oct., 1983, defeat of Peronists gave civilian control.	Spanish
†Australia Commonwealth of Australia	15,000,000	Canberra* 246,100 Sydney 3,231,700	2,966,200	Multi-party, democratic federal state system, parliamentary government	English
Australian External Territories:					
Norfolk Island	1,800		13½		
Coral Sea Island			1		
Territory of Ashmore and Carter Island			2		
Cocos (Keeling) Island	3,184		5½		
Christmas Island	3,184		52		
Australian Antarctic Territory			2,472,000		
Austria Republic of Austria	7,600,000	Vienna* 1,504,200	32,374	Multi-party, federal republic	German
†The Bahamas Commonwealth of the Bahamas	260,000	Nassau* 138,000	5,380	Independent within British Commonwealth, multi-party, parliamentary government	English
Bahrain State of Bahrain	400,000	Manama* 300,000	258	No parties, traditional Emirate	Arabic
†Bangladesh People's Republic of Bangladesh	93,300,000	Dacca* 3.4 million (metropolitan area)	55,598	Military rule	Bengali, English
†Barbados	300,000	Bridgetown* 7,600	166	Independent sovereign state within British Commonwealth; multi-party, parliamentary government	English
Belgium Kingdom of Belgium	9,900,000	Brussels* 1,000,221 (metropolitan area)	11,779	Multi-party, parliamentary democracy under constitutional monarch	Flemish French
†Belize	148,300	Belmopan* 2,932 Belize City 39,887	8,867	2 party, parliamentary government	English, Spanish, Indian languages
Benin People's Republic of Benin	3,700,000	Porto-Novo* 123,000 Cotonou 215,000	43,475	No political parties, Marxist-Lenist military government	French, Fons, and Adjas

NAME OF COUNTRY	POPULATION	CAPITAL* LARGEST CITY	AREA (SQUARE MILES)	GOVERNMENT	MAJOR LANGUAGES
Bhutan Kingdom of Bhutan	1,400,000	Thimphu* 10,000	17,800	No political parties, absolute monarch	Dzong Ka, Nepali, others
Bolivia Republic of Bolivia	5,600,000	Sucre (legal)* 63,259 LaPaz (de facto)* 881,400	424,165	Multi-party, centralized republic	Spanish, Aymara Quechua
†Botswana Republic of Botswana	900,000	Gaborone* 59,000	224,600	Multi-party, parliamentary democracy	English, Tswana, and other Bantu languages
Brazil Federative Republic of Brazil	127,700,000	Brasilia* 411,305 Sao Paulo 7 million	3,286,470	2 party, military government	Portuguese
Brunei	192,832	Bandar Seri Begawan*	2,226	Sultanate	English, Malay
Bulgaria People's Republic of Bulgaria	8,900,000	Sofia* 1,056,900	42,823	Communist state	Bulgarian
Burma Socialist Republic of the Union of Burma	37,100,000	Rangoon* 2,186,000	261,288	1 party, socialist republic	Burmese, Shan, others
Burundi Republic of Burundi	4,400,000	Bujumbura* 200,000	10,759	1 party, presidential regime	Kirundi, French, others
**Cambodia (Kampuchea) Cambodian People's Republic	6,100,000	Phnom Penh* 500,000	69,900	1 party, communist state	Khmer, French Annamese
Cameroon United Republic of Cameroon	8,900,000	Yaounde* 400,000 Douala 500,000	179,558	1 party, presidential regime	French, English, others
†Canada	24,400,000	Ottawa* 695,000 Montreal 2,800,000	3,851,809	Multi-party, confederation with parliamentary democracy.	English, French
**Cape Verde Republic of Cape Verde	340,000	Praia* 36,600 Mindelo 40,000	1,557	1 party, constitutional assembly	Portuguese, Bantu
Central African Republic	2,400,000	Bangui* 367,100 (metropolitan area)	240,324	Military government	French, Sangho, others
Chad Republic of Chad	4,600,000	N'Djamena* 303,000 (metropolitan area)	495,755	1 party, military government	French, Arabic, Sara, others
Chile Republic of Chile	11,500,000	Santiago* 3,448,700	292,135	Political activity suspended, military government	Spanish
**China People's Republic of China	1,008,175,288	Peking* 8,500,000 Shanghai 12,000,000	3,691,521	1 party, communist state	Chinese
China (Taiwan) Republic of China	18,500,000	Taipei* 2,298,000 (metropolitan area)	13,814	Multi-party, presidential regime	Chinese
Colombia Republic of Colombia	25,600,000	Bogota* 4,486,200	440,831	Multi-party, parliamentary government	Spanish
Comoros Federal Islamic Republic of the Comoros	400,000	Moroni* 22,000 (metropolitan area)	838	Military rule	Malagasy, French
Congo People's Republic of the Congo	1,600,000	Brazzaville* 200,000 (metropolitan area)	132,046	1 party, military government	French, Kongo, Batéké, M'Bochi

NAME OF COUNTRY	POPULATION	CAPITAL* LARGEST CITY	AREA (SQUARE MILES)	GOVERNMENT	MAJOR LANGUAGES
Costa Rica Republic of Costa Rica	2,300,000	San Jose* 867,800	19,653	Multi-party, federal republic	Spanish
Cuba Republic of Cuba	9,800,000	Havana* 1,008,500	44,218	1 party, communist state	Spanish
**†Cyprus Republic of Cyprus	645,000	Nicosia* 121,500	3,572	Multi-party, parliamentary government	Greek, Turkish
Czechoslovakia Czechoslovak Socialist Republic	15,400,000	Prague* 1.1 million	49,365	1 party, communist state	Czech, Slovak
Denmark Kingdom of Denmark	5,100,000	Copenhagen* 654,437	16,633	Multi-party, parliamentary constitutional monarchy	Danish
Greenland (Kalaallit Nunaat*) *official name now	51,000	Nuuk* 9,717	840,000	Formerly an integral part of Denmark, it was granted home rule in 1979; has socialist-dominated legislature	Greenlandic, Danish
Djibouti Republic of Djibouti	500,000	Djibouti* 200,000 (metropolitan area)	8,996	Multi-party, parliamentary government	French, Somali
†Dominica Commonwealth of Dominica	82,000	Roseau* 20,000	290	Parliamentary	English
Dominican Republic	5,700,000	Santo Domingo* 1.3 million	18,704	Multi-party, centralized republic	Spanish
Ecuador Republic of Ecuador	8,500,000	Quito* 918,900 Guayaquil 1,278,900	108,624	Multi-party, republic	Quechau, Spanish, Jivaroan
Egypt Arab Republic of Egypt	44,000,000	Cairo* 5,084,463	385,201	Presidential regime	Arabic
El Salvador Republic of El Salvador	5,000,000	San Salvador* 400,000	8,124	Military-dominated	Spanish
Equatorial Guinea Republic of Equatorial Guinea	300,000	Malabo* 25,000	10,832	Military regime	Spanish, English, Fang
Ethiopia Socialist Ethiopia	30,500,000	Addis Ababa* 1,200,000	472,400	Military regime	Amharic, others
†Fiji Dominion of Fiji	700,000	Suva* 64,000	7,056	Parliamentary democracy	English, Fijan, Hindustani
Finland Republic of Finland	4,800,000	Helsinki* 490,204	130,119	Multi-party, parliamentary government	Finnish, Swedish
France French Republic	54,200,000	Paris* 2,296,945	210,040	Multi-party, Republic	French
French Overseas Departments:					
French Guiana	66,800		32,252		
Guadeloupe	314,800		687		
Martinique	307,700		425		
Mayotte	53,000		144		
Reunion	504,400		969		
St. Pierre and Miquelon	6,300		93		
French Overseas Territories: French Polynesia comprises 130 islands administered from Tahiti, including Society Islands, Windward and Leeward islands, Marquesas Islands, the Tuamotu Archipelago including the Gambler Islands, and the Austral Islands.	160,000		1,544		

NAME OF COUNTRY	POPULATION	CAPITAL* LARGEST CITY	AREA (SQUARE MILES)	GOVERNMENT	MAJOR LANGUAGES
France–continued French Southern and Antarctic Lands comprises Adelie Land and island groups in Indian Ocean, Kerguelen Archipelago, and Crozet Archipelago.					
New Caledonia	139,600		8,548		
Wallis and Futana Islands	11,000		106		
Gabon Gabonese Republic	700,000	Libreville* 225,200	103,347	1 party, presidential regime	French, Fange, Omyere
†The Gambia Republic of The Gambia	635,000	Banjul* 40,000	4,361	Republic	English, Mandinka, Wolof
Germany, East German Democratic Republic	16,700,000	East Berlin* 1,145,743	41,825	1 party, communist state	German
Germany, West Federal Republic of Germany	61,700,000	Bonn* 289,400 Berlin 2 million	96,011	Multi-party, federal republic	German
†Ghana Republic of Ghana	12,400,000	Accra* 998,800	92,098	Military government	English, Twi, Fanti, Ga
Greece Hellenic Republic	9,800,000	Athens* 3,300,000 (metropolitan area)	50,962	Multi-party, parliamentary government	Greek
†Grenada State of Grenada	108,000	St. George's* 30,813	133	After the U.S. invasion, Oct., 1983, government administered by a British Governor and a 9-man council until new elections could be held, presumably under a democratic constitution	English, French-African patois
**Guatemala Republic of Guatemala	7,700,000	Guatemala City* 1,307,300	42,042	Military government	Spanish, Indian languages
Guinea People's Revolutionary Republic of Guinea	5,300,000	Conakry* 575,000	94,925	1 party, presidential regime	French, Fulani
Guinea-Bissau Republic of Guinea-Bissau	800,000	Bissau* 109,500	13,948	Revolutionary council	Portuguese, Criouio
†Guyana Cooperative Republic of Guyana	900,000	Georgetown* 170,000	83,000	Multi-party, presidential regime	English, Hindi, Portuguese, Negro patois
Haiti Republic of Haiti	6,100,000	Port-au-Prince* 745,700	10,714	1 party, presidential regime	French, French-Creole
Honduras Republic of Honduras	4,000,000	Tegucigalpa* 472,700	43,277	Strong military influence	Spanish, Indian languages
Hungary Hungarian People's Republic	10,700,000	Budapest* 2,085,615	35,919	1 party, communist state	Hungarian
Iceland Republic of Iceland	232,000	Reykjavik* 84,600	39,769	Multi-party, parliamentary government	Icelandic, Danish
**India Republic of India	713,000,000	New Delhi* 5.2 million Calcutta 9.1 million	1,269,420	Multi-party, parliamentary government	Hindi, Urdu, English, and others
Indonesia Republic of Indonesia	151,000,000	Jakarta* 5,500,000	741,101	No parties, military government	Bahasa Indonesian (Malay), Javanese
Iran Islamic Republic of Iran	41,200,000	Teheran* 4,496,159	636,363	Islamic republic	Farsi Persian Kurdish
Iraq Republic of Iraq	14,000,000	Baghdad* 3,205,645	168,928	1 party, military government	Arabic, Kurdish
Ireland Irish Republic	3,500,000	Dublin* 525,360	27,137	Multi-party, parliamentary government	English, Gaelic

NAME OF COUNTRY	POPULATION	CAPITAL* LARGEST CITY	AREA (SQUARE MILES)	GOVERNMENT	MAJOR LANGUAGES
Israel State of Israel	4,100,000	Jerusalem* 398,000	8,219	Multi-party, parliamentary government	Hebrew, Arabic
Italy Italian Republic	57,400,000	Rome* 2.9 million	116,303	Multi-party, parliamentary government	Italian
Ivory Coast Republic of Ivory Coast	8,800,000	Abidjan* 1,686,100 (metropolitan area)	124,503	1 party, presidential regime	French, Mande languages
†Jamaica	2,200,000	Kingston* 671,000	4,244	2 party, parliamentary government	English
Japan	118,600,000	Tokyo* 8.2 million	145,809	2 party, parliamentary constitutional monarchy	Japanese
Jordan Hashemite Kingdom of Jordan	3,500,000	Amman* 684,600	37,297	1 party, constitutional monarchy	Arabic
Kenya Republic of Kenya	17,900,000	Nairobi* 959,000 (metropolitan area)	224,081	1 party, presidential regime	Swahili, Kikuyu, English, others
Kiribati Republic of Kiribati	60,000	Tarawa* 22,148	266	Parliamentary	English, Gilbertese, Ellice
Korea, North Democratic People's Republic of Korea	18,700,000	Pyongyang* 1,283,000	47,077	1 party, communist state	Korean
Korea, South Republic of Korea	41,000,000	Seoul* 8,000,000	38,211	Military rule	Korean
Kuwait State of Kuwait	1,500,000	Kuwait* 60,400 Hawalli 152,300	6,532	No political parties, constitutional monarchy	Arabic
Laos Lao People's Democratic Republic	3,700,000	Vientiane* 200,000	91,428	1 party, communist state	Lao, French, others
Lebanon Republic of Lebanon	2,700,000	Beirut* 1,100,000	3,950	Multi-party, parliamentary government	Arabic, French
Lesotho Kingdom of Lesotho	1,400,000	Maseru* 75,000	11,716	Multi-party, constitutional monarchy	English, Sesotho
Liberia Republic of Liberia	2,000,000	Monrovia* 306,000	38,250	Political activity suspended, military rule	English, African languages
Libya Socialist People's Libyan Arab Jamahiriya	3,200,000	Tripoli* 858,500	679,536	1 party, military government	Arabic
Liechtenstein Principality of Liechtenstein	26,000	Vaduz* 5,000	62	2 party, hereditary constitutional monarchy	German
Luxembourg Grand Duchy of Luxembourg	400,000	Luxembourg* 80,000	1,034	Multi-party, constitutional monarchy	French, German, Luxembourgian
Madagascar Democratic Republic of Madagascar	9,200,000	Antananarivo* 600,000	226,658	Political activity suspended, military government	French, Malagsy
Malawi Republic of Malawi	6,600,000	Lilongwe* 75,000 (metropolitan area)	45,747	1 party, presidential regime	English, Nyanja
Malaysia	14,700,000	Kuala Lumpur* 1,081,000 (metropolitan area)	127,316	Parliamentary democracy under a constitutional monarchy	Malay, English, Chinese, Dayak
†Maldives Republic of Maldives	155,000	Male* 32,000	115	Parliamentary government, limited democracy	Divehi
Mali Republic of Mali	7,100,000	Bamako* 620,000 (metropolitan area)	478,841	1 party, military government	French, Mande languages

NAME OF COUNTRY	POPULATION	CAPITAL* LARGEST CITY	AREA (SQUARE MILES)	GOVERNMENT	MAJOR LANGUAGES
†Malta	400,000	Valletta* 14,000	122	Multi-party, parliamentary government	Maltese, English, Italian
Mauritania Islamic Republic of Mauritania	1,700,000	Nouakchott* 250,000	398,000	Military government	Arabic, French
Mauritius	1,000,000	Port Louis* 146,884	787	Multi-party, parliamentary democracy under a constitutional monarchy (Queen Elizabeth)	English, French, Creole
**Mexico United Mexican States	71,300,000	Mexico City* 15 million	761,604	1 party, federal republic	Spanish, Indian languages
Monaco Principality of Monaco	26,000	Monaco-Ville* 1,700	0.73	1 party, constitutional monarchy	French
Mongolia Mongolian People's Republic	1,700,000	Ulaanbaatar* 435,400	604,247	1 party, communist state	Khalkha, Mongolian
Morocco Kingdom of Morocco	22,300,000	Rabat* 435,510 (Rabat-Sale) Casablanca 1,371,330	171,117	Multi-party, constitutional monarchy	Arabic, French, Spanish, Berber
Mozambique People's Republic of Mozambique	12,700,000	Maputo* 755,300	308,769	Marxist one-party state, committee rule	Portuguese, Bantu
†Nauru Republic of Nauru	8,000	Yaren* (no population figure available)	8	2 party, parliamentary government	Nauruan, English
Nepal Kingdom of Nepal	14,500,000	Kathmandu* 125,000	56,136	No political parties, monarchy	Nepali, others
Netherlands Kingdom of the Netherlands	14,300,000	Amsterdam* 712,294	16,464	Multi-party, parliamentary democracy under a constitutional monarchy	Dutch
Netherlands Antilles	246,500	Willemstad* On Curacao 50,000	385	Constitutionally on level of equality with the Netherlands within the Kingdom	
Curacao, Aruba, Bonaire, St. Eustatius, Saba, St. Maarten					
†New Zealand	3,100,000	Wellington* 342,000 Auckland 818,000	103,883	2 party, parliamentary government	English, Maori
**Nicaragua Republic of Nicaragua	2,600,000	Managua* 552,900	57,000	Five-member junta	Spanish
Niger Republic of Niger	5,800,000	Niamey* 300,000	490,100	Political activity banned, military government	French, Hausa
†Nigeria Federal Republic of Nigeria	82,300,000	Lagos* 1,404,000	356,700	Multi-party, federal republic	English, Housa, Ibo, Yoruba
Norway Kingdom of Norway	4,100,000	Oslo* 452,023	125,057	Multi-party, parliamentary constitutional monarchy	Norwegian
Oman Sultanate of Oman	948,000	Muscat* 50,000	115,800	No political parties, absolute monarchy	Arabic
Pakistan Islamic Republic of Pakistan	93,000,000	Islamabad* 201,000 Karachi 3,498,634	307,374	Military rule	Urdu, English, others
Panama Republic of Panama	1,900,000	Panama* 655,000	29,762	Military-dominated	Spanish, English
†Papua-New Guinea	3,300,000	Port Moresby* 116,900	178,704	Parliamentary government	English, Papuan

NAME OF COUNTRY	POPULATION	CAPITAL* LARGEST CITY	AREA (SQUARE MILES)	GOVERNMENT	MAJOR LANGUAGES
Paraguay Republic of Paraguay	3,300,000	Asunción 481,706	157,047	Presidential dictatorship	Spanish, Guarani
Peru Republic of Peru	18,600,000	Lima* 3.1 million	496,222	Multi-party, republic	Spanish, Quechua, Aymara
Philippines Republic of the Philippines	51,600,000	Quezon City* 1.1 million Manila is defacto capital 1.6 million	115,831	Multi-party, presidential regime	Tagalog, English, Spanish, others
Poland Polish People's Republic	36,300,000	Warsaw* 1.5 million	120,727	1 party, communist state	Polish
Portugal Republic of Portugal	9,930,000	Lisbon* 812,400	35,516	Multi-party, parliamentary government	Portuguese
Qatar State of Qatar	250,000	Doha* 190,000	4,247	No political parties, Traditional Emirate	Arabic
Romania Socialist Republic of Romania	22,600,000	Bucharest* 1,861,007	91,699	1 party, communist state	Romanian
Rwanda Republic of Rwanda	5,400,000	Kigali* 156,650	10,169	No political parties, military government	Kinyawanda, French
St. Kitts-Nevis	52,000	Basseterre* 14,725	101	Multi-party, parliamentary government	English
†Saint Lucia	124,000	Castries* 45,000	238	Parliamentary government	English
†Saint Vincent and the Grenadines	120,000	Kingstown* 23,200	150	Multi-party, parliamentary government	English
San Marino Most Serene Republic of San Marino	21,537	San Marino* 3,000	24	Multi-party, parliamentary government	Italian
Sao Tomé and Principe Democratic Republic of Sao Tome-Principe	100,000	Sao Tome 25,000	372	1 party, republic	Portuguese, Bantu
Saudi Arabia Kingdom of Saudi Arabia	11,100,000	Riyadh* 1,793,000	830,000	No political parties, absolute monarchy	Arabic
Senegambia	6,700,000	Dakar* 978,553	79,750	Multi-party, parliamentary government created in 1982 from union of Senegal and Gambia; cabinets function separately.	French, English, Wolof, Mande
†Seychelles Republic of Seychelles	67,000	Victoria* 23,000	171	Single party, republic	Creole, English, French
†Sierre Leone Republic of Sierra Leone	3,700,000	Freetown* 500,000	27,699	1 party, presidential regime	English, African languages, Creole
†Singapore* Republic of Singapore	2,500,000	Singapore* 2,334,400	239	Multi-party, parliamentary government	English, Malay, Chinese, Tamil
†Solomon Islands	240,000	Honiara* 19,200	10,640	Multi-party, parliamentary government. Within the Commonwealth of Nations	Pidgin English, English
Somalia Somali Democratic Republic	4,600,000	Mogadishu* 400,000	246,300	No political parties, military government	Somali, Italian, Arabic
South Africa Republic of South Africa	30,000,000	Cape Town* (legislative) 213,830 Pretoria* (administrative) 528,407 Bloemfontein* (judicial) 230,688	435,868	2 party, parliamentary government (limited to white adults)	English, Africaans, Shosa, Zulu, Sotho

NAME OF COUNTRY	POPULATION	CAPITAL* LARGEST CITY	AREA (SQUARE MILES)	GOVERNMENT	MAJOR LANGUAGES
Namibia (South-West Africa)	1,038,000	Windhoek* 64,095	318,827	On Jan. 18, 1983, South Africa dissolved the Namibian General Assembly and assumed direct control of the territory	
**Spain Spanish State	37,900,000	Madrid* 3,520,320	194,885	Multi-party, parliamentary monarchy	Spanish
The Balearic and the Canary Islands are provinces of Spain					
†Sri Lanka Democratic Socialist Republic of Sri Lanka	15,200,000	Colombo* 585,776	25,332	Multi-party, parliamentary government	Sinhalese, Tamil, English
Sudan Democratic Republic of the Sudan	19,900,000	Khatoum* 333,921	966,757	1 party, presidential regime	Arabic, English, African languages
Suriname	420,000	Paramaribo* 67,700	63,037	Military government	Taki-Taki, Dutch, Spanish, others
†Swaziland Kingdom of Swaziland	600,000	Mbabane* 33,000	6,704	No political parties, constitutional monarchy	English, siSwati
Sweden Kingdom of Sweden	8,310,000	Stockholm* 1,386,980	179,896	Multi-party, parliamentary constitutional monarchy	Swedish
Switzerland Swiss Confederation	6,343,000	Bern* 145,000 Zurich 375,000	15,941	Multi-party, parliamentary government	German, French, Italian, Romansch
Syria Syrian Arab Republic	9,700,000	Damascus* 1,142,000	71,498	Multi-party, presidential regime	Arabic, Kurdish, Armenian
†Tanzania United Republic of Tanzania	19,000,000	Dar-es-Salaam* 700,000	364,886	1 party, presidential regime	Swahili, English
Thailand Kingdom of Thailand	49,800,000	Bangkok* 4.7 million	198,500	Political activity suspended, military government	Thai, Chinese, English, others
Togo Republic of Togo	2,800,000	Lomé* 283,000	21,853	1 party, presidential regime	French, African languages
†Tonga Kingdom of Tonga	100,000	Nuku'alofa* 19,900	270	No political parties, constitutional monarchy	Tongan, English
†Trinidad and Tobago Republic of Trinidad and Tobago	1,100,000	Port-of-Spain* 250,000 (metropolitan area)	1,970	2 party, parliamentary government	English, Creole
Tunisia Republic of Tunisia	6,700,000	Tunis* 1,000,000	63,378	1 party, presidential regime	Arabic, French
Turkey Republic of Turkey	47,700,000	Ankara* 1,877,755 Istanbul 2,772,708	300,948	Military rule	Turkish, Kurdish, Arabic
†Tuvalu	9,000	Funafuti* 2,200	10	Parliamentary government	English, Samoan, Gilbertese
†Uganda Republic of Uganda	13,700,000	Kampala* 458,000	91,104	Presidential regime	English, African languages
Union of Soviet Socialist Republics	268,800,000	Moscow* 8.2 million	8,649,490	1 party, communist state	Russian, and other languages
United Arab Emirates	1,200,000	Abu Dhabi* 449,000	32,000	Federal system, monarchs rule member states	Arabic
United Kingdom of Great Britain and Northern Ireland	56,100,000	London* 6,696,008	94,222	Multi-party, parliamentary constitutional monarchy	English, Welsh, Gaelic
British possessions: Channel Islands	130,000		75	Separate legal existence, lieut. gov. named by Crown	
Isle of Man	61,000		227	Lieut. gov. named by Crown	

NAME OF COUNTRY	POPULATION	CAPITAL* LARGEST CITY	AREA (SQUARE MILES)	GOVERNMENT	MAJOR LANGUAGES
Gibraltar	30,000			A dependency	
British West Indies:					
Montserrat	11,600		32	Possession	
Anguilla	7,000		35	Autonomous elected government	
Cayman Islands	18,000		102	Dependency	
Turks and Caicos Islands	7,000		193	Separate possessions	
Bermuda	54,893		21 (360 small islands)	A dependency	
South Atlantic Dependencies:					
Falkland Islands	1,800		4,700		
St. Helena	5,200		47		
Tristan da Cunha	262		40		
Ascension	1,179		34		
Asia and Indian Ocean Colony					
Hong Kong	5,108,000		35½	A Crown colony	
Pacific Ocean Colony					
Pitcairn Island	54		18	A colony	
**United States of America (For information on U.S. Possessions see pp. 341-344)	232,600,000	Washington, DC* 3,060,922 (metropolitan area) New York 9,120,346 (metropolitan area)	3,628,150	2 party, federal republic	English
Upper Volta Republic of Upper Volta	6,700,000	Ouagadougou* 200,000	105,869	Military junta	French, Mande, Voltaic languages
Uruguay Oriental Republic of Uruguay	2,934,942	Montevideo* 1,260,600	68,037	Political activity banned, military government	Spanish
†Vanuatu Republic of Vanuatu	125,600	Vila* 15,100	4,707	Multi-party, parliamentary government	English, French
Vatican State of Vatican City	738	Vatican City	108.7 acres	No parties, papal state	Latin, Italian
Venezuela Republic of Venezuela	18,700,000	Caracas* 2,700,000	352,143	Multi-party, federal republic	Spanish
Vietnam Socialist Republic of Vietnam	56,600,000	Hanoi* 2 million Ho Chi Minh City 3.5 million	127,207	1 party, communist state	Annamese, Chinese, French
Western Samoa	158,000	Apia* 33,400	1,101	2 party, parliamentary constitutional monarchy	Samoan, English
Yemen, North Yemen Arab Republic	5,500,000	Sanaa* 277,800	77,200	No parties, military government	Arabic
Yemen, South People's Democratic Republic of Yemen	2,000,000	Aden* 264,326	130,541	1 party, presidential council	Arabic
Yugoslavia Socialist Federal Republic of Yugoslavia	22,600,000	Belgrade* 1,300,000	98,766	1 party, communist state	Slovene, Macedonian, Serbo-Croat
Zaire	30,300,000	Kinshasa* 3,000,000	905,063	1 party, presidential regime	French, Swahili, Lingala
†Zambia Republic of Zambia	6,000,000	Lusaka* 538,000	290,586	1 party, presidential regime	English, Bantu
†Zimbabwe	10,500,000	Harare* 657,000 (metropolitan area)	150,873	Multi-party, parliamentary government	English, Shona, Sindebele

† (Before name of country) means it belongs in the Commonwealth of Nations formerly called the British Commonwealth. Some have monarchs other than Queen Elizabeth II, some are dictatorships, etc. The Commonwealth is simply a loose association of self-governing nations plus some colonies and protectorates.

** Some countries described as one-party or two-party systems may actually have more legal political parties, but they are not viable politically, i.e. Mexico has five, but only one has governed since 1929. Also, in the U. S. other parties come and go, but there are only two major parties.

Population figures in most cases are 1982 estimates.

The United Nations

The United Nations does not represent the first attempt at world cooperation. After World War I, President Wilson and others conceived the idea of a League of Nations, an organization devoted to the settlement of disputes and the prevention of war. The main defect of the League was that it had no independent strength with which to punish aggressor nations or to enforce the peace. The League's failure during the 1930s to stop Japan from attacking Manchuria and Italy from attacking Ethiopia and its inability to stop World War II marked the demise of this well-intentioned organization.

Throughout World War II, a realization was growing that a more effective international body would have to be created. The Atlantic Charter, signed in 1941 by President Roosevelt and British Prime Minister Churchill, stressed the concept of full cooperation between nations. Later twenty-six countries signed the Declaration of the United Nations which reasserted this concept. Conferences held in 1943 at Moscow and Tehran paved the way for an organization "... for the maintenance of international peace and security." Still later, representatives of the United States, the United Kingdom, China, and the Soviet Union met at Dumbarton Oaks, near Washington, D.C., to work out a more detailed blueprint for the new world organization, which they agreed to call the United Nations.

On April 12, 1945, one of the chief architects of the United Nations, Franklin D. Roosevelt, died. Two weeks after his death the San Francisco Conference met at the Opera House in that city. After eight weeks of hard work, delegates from fifty countries approved the Charter of the United Nations. The solemn signing took eight hours.

THE BASIC STRUCTURE OF THE UNITED NATIONS

"We the peoples of the United Nations determined to save succeeding generations from the scourge of war, which twice in our lifetime has brought untold sorrow to mankind . . . do hereby establish an international organization to be known as the United Nations."

These are the words of the Preamble of the Charter of the United Nations. The Charter goes on to state the purposes of the organization and to describe its organization.

Purposes. The Charter sets forth three basic purposes:

1. To maintain international peace and security by preventing aggression and settling disputes peacefully.
2. To develop friendly relations among nations based on respect for equal rights and self-determination of peoples.
3. To achieve international cooperation in solving economic, social, cultural, and humanitarian problems and in promoting respect for human rights and fundamental freedoms for all.

In accordance with these purposes, all members agree to (1) settle disputes peacefully, (2) to refrain from threat or use of force against another state, and (3) to assist the United Nations in its undertakings and not to aid any state against which the United Nations is acting.

Bearing in mind the arguments which helped keep the United States out of the League of Nations, the Charter specifically states that there is to be no intervention in matters essentially within the domestic jurisdiction of any state.

Any amendment to the Charter must be approved by a two-thirds vote of the General Assembly and ratified by two-thirds of the members of the United Nations. The first amendments were ratified in 1965 and became effective on January 1, 1966. They increased the number of members of the Security Council and the Economic and Social Council.

Membership. The Charter provides that membership shall be "open to all . . . peace-loving states which accept the obligations contained in the present Charter and which, in the judgment of the organization, are able and willing to carry out these obligations." Members are admitted by vote of the General Assembly upon recommendation of the Security Council.

As will be explained later, the permanent members of the Security Council have a veto. During the first ten years, the Soviet Union vetoed for membership every country it considered too favorable to the West, including Italy, South Korea, and Japan. At the same time, when the Soviet Union

United Nations—The San Francisco Conference, June 26, 1945

put up Hungary, Romania, and Bulgaria for membership, the majority on the Security Council voted them down as being "satellite states" under Soviet domination. In 1955, however, a "package deal" was arranged, and sixteen nations came in together. Since then a number of other nations, including the new nations of Africa, have been admitted, making a total membership of well over 140 nations.

THE GENERAL ASSEMBLY

The central body of the United Nations is the General Assembly. All member states are members of the Assembly, each having one vote, although each nation may send up to five representatives. Often called "the Town Meeting of the World," the General Assembly meets in annual, regular sessions, although special sessions can be called by the Secretary-General at the request of the Security Council or of a majority of the members of the United Nations.

The General Assembly can discuss and make recommendations on all matters within the scope of the Charter, except that it may not discuss issues which are at that time on the agenda of the Security Council. However, at the time of the Korean conflict in November 1950, the General Assembly adopted the "Uniting for Peace" resolution. This greatly increased the power of the General Assembly. It provided that if the Security Council should, because of the use of the veto by one of its permanent members, fail to act in a situation threatening international peace, then the General Assembly might hold an emergency session within twenty-four hours and recommend collective action, including the use of armed force. You may recall that it was the failure of the Council of the League of Nations to take action to halt aggression which weakened that organization's efforts. The

United Nations—Eighteenth Regular Session of the General Assembly

"Uniting for Peace" resolution was designed to prevent a repetition of that failure.

Decisions of the General Assembly on important matters, such as those involving the maintenance of peace, the admission of members, and the election of the nonpermanent members of the Security Council, are decided by a two-thirds majority. Other less important matters are decided by a simple majority.

THE SECURITY COUNCIL

The Charter places "the primary responsibility for the maintenance of peace and security" on the Security Council. It has fifteen members including five permanent members—China, France, the Union of Soviet Socialist Republics, the United Kingdom, and the United States—and ten nonpermanent members. Each year, the General Assembly elects five nonpermanent members for a two-year term. These nonpermanent members are not eligible for immediate reelection to the Security Council.

Although the Security Council meets periodically, it is set up so as to be able to function at any time. It is said to be "in continuous session," because each member is always represented at UN Headquarters.

Each member of the Security Council has one vote. Routine, or "procedural" matters, as the Charter says, are decided by an affirmative vote of any nine of the fifteen members. However, in all other cases, the five permanent members must either cast affirmative votes or abstain. The Security Council may not take action if any permanent member casts a negative vote on a substantive matter.

The power of veto in the Security Council means that no enforcement action will be taken against any permanent member, for no nation is likely to vote against itself. The veto was written into the Charter at the insistence not only of the Soviet Union, but of the United States as well, because of the fear that otherwise the United States Senate might not ratify the Charter.

The argument against the veto power is that its abuse by the Soviet Union has weakened the ability of the United Nations to act effectively. However, the "Uniting for Peace" resolution, as we have seen, provides a method by which the General Assembly can undertake to solve a problem when a veto in the Security Council blocks action.

It is important to remember that the main aim of the United Nations is not to fight any of its members but rather to provide machinery for peaceful settlement of disputes. Hence, the Security Council may call upon disputing nations to settle their dispute by such means as negotiation or by settlement by the International Court of Justice (see below). If the dispute is not settled, the Security Council may itself recommend a settlement.

The Council is given the authority, if all attempts at a peaceful settlement fail, to call upon the members of the United Nations, who are pledged to make armed forces available to the Security Council for land, sea, and air forces to use in blockades or "other operations" against the nation whose action is threatening the peace.

THE ECONOMIC AND SOCIAL COUNCIL

The founders of the United Nations were convinced that part of the job to be done by the international organization was the improvement of living conditions all over the world. Chapter IX of the Charter states that "the United Nations shall promote higher standards of living, full employment, conditions of economic and social progress . . . international, cultural, and educational cooperation . . . universal respect for . . . human rights and fundamental freedoms for all without distinction as to sex, race, language, or religion."

In accordance with these objectives, the Economic and Social Council (ECOSOC) was provided for. ECOSOC has members, elected annually for three-year terms in groups of eighteen by the General Assembly. The Council meets as often as necessary to perform its duties, usually for two sessions a year.

The functions of the Economic and Social Council are to make studies on international health, social, economic, cultural, and educational problems, and to make recommendations to the General Assembly on the basis of these studies. It may call international conferences on matters related to these fields. In connection with these very broad areas of interest, the Council often calls upon the cooperation of private organizations and experts to help in its work. The Specialized Agencies, which will be discussed in detail later, are brought into relationship with the United Nations through the Economic and Social Council.

United Nations—Trusteeship Council concludes examination of conditions in Tanganyika, July 13, 1961.

THE TRUSTEESHIP COUNCIL

When World War I ended, Germany's colonies were taken from her and handed over to various other nations for administration as "mandates." This meant that they were no longer to be considered colonies. Instead, the administering countries promised to rule them fairly and to report regularly to the League of Nations. After World War II, most of the mandates were transferred to the United Nations, whose Charter established a Trusteeship Council to supervise the governing of trust territories. The goal is to advance these territories to the point where they will be able to govern themselves or achieve complete independence.

Trust territories include, in addition to those formerly held as mandates under the League of Nations, territories taken from Axis powers after World War II and dependent territories voluntarily turned over to trusteeship by the nations controlling them.

The Trusteeship Council is made up of those United Nations members which administer trust territories and an equal number of those which do not. Included in the number, however, must be the five permanent members of the Security Council. The Trusteeship Council holds two regular sessions a year, as well as special sessions which may be required. Decisions are made by a simple majority vote.

As the number of trust territories gaining their independence has increased, the work of the Trusteeship Council has lessened. The members are charged with taking an active part in the governing of the remaining trust territories. Each year, the administering government has to report to the Council about economic, political, and educational progress made in the trust territory during the year. Thousands of petitions and complaints are received by the Council from people in trust territories all over the world. Special missions are sent out to territories to investigate conditions. The Council reports to the General Assembly on developments in the trust territories.

THE INTERNATIONAL COURT OF JUSTICE

The principal judicial organ of the United Nations is the International Court of Justice. It is the successor of the Permanent Court of International Justice, often called the World Court. Located at The Hague, Netherlands, it has fifteen judges, no two from any one nation. They are chosen by the Security Council and the General Assembly for nine-year terms. All members of the United Nations are automatically associated with the Court. Other nations may join upon the consent of the General Assembly and the Security Council.

The function of the Court is to decide points of international law over which a dispute may arise between nations. Only nations, not individuals, may bring a case before the Court. All United Nations members undertake to obey the Court's decisions. If a nation should fail to do so, an appeal may be made to the Security Council, which may take any action it sees fit. A nation may, if it wishes, promise in advance that it will always be ready to submit to the Court's decision in certain types of cases, provided the opposing nation does the same. The United States reserved the right to decide in each specific case whether it would allow

United Nations—Security Council meets on the Cypress Question, March 3, 1964.

the matter to come before the Court. The International Court of Justice may also give advisory opinions on legal questions which the other organs of the United Nations may submit to it.

The services of the Court have been extensively used by the members of the United Nations. Cases have involved disputes between Albania and the United Kingdom over damage to British warships by mine explosions in the Corfu Channel, between the United States and France over the rights of Americans in Morocco, between Cambodia and Thailand over ownership of a holy temple, and many others.

THE SECRETARIAT

The day-to-day work of the United Nations is entrusted to a staff known as the Secretariat. About four thousand people from all over the world make up the Secretariat. They do not represent their own nations but are bound by the Charter to serve as international public servants.

Members of the Secretariat make the arrangements for conference, draft reports, and collect information for use by the delegates. Skilled interpreters sit in soundproof boxes overlooking meetings of various UN bodies and provide simultaneous translations for transmission by the language earphones that are provided at every seat on the floor. No matter what language is being spoken, a delegate can hear a translation in English, French, Spanish, Russian, or Chinese.

At the head of the Secretariat is the Secretary-General. He is elected by the General Assembly on the recommendation of the Security Council for a five-year term. As the chief administrative officer of the United Nations, he serves all the main organs of the world organization except the Court. He reports annually to the General Assembly. He supervises the staff of the Secretariat, assisted by under-secretaries and other officials.

One of the most important roles of the Secretary-General arises out of his right to go before the Security Council at any time and call its attention to a situation which he regards as a threat to world peace. This places the Secretary-General at the center of most international disputes, in a position to exercise tremendous influence in world affairs. In 1960, for example, the Security Council passed a resolution giving Secretary-General Dag Hammarskjöld, who had succeeded Trygve Lie in the post, full authority for organizing a force to secure peaceful conditions in the newly independent Congo. On September 18, 1961, while he was en route to a meeting in Africa to strengthen peace efforts, Hammarskjöld was killed when his plane crashed in flames. His successors, U Thant of Burma and Kurt Waldheim of Austria, have continued to stress the fact that the Secretary-General must take the initiative in attempting to bring about permanent peace.

SPECIALIZED AGENCIES

Associated in a close relationship with the United Nations are agencies of various kinds that are not actually part of the world organization but are related to it by special agreements through the Economic and Social Council. These agencies are called the "Specialized Agencies" because each one has a special field of work, such as education, health, or finance. Although these agencies report regularly to the United Nations through ECOSOC, they are largely independent, each having its own membership, officers, treasury, and budget. Membership in the Specialized Agencies is not dependent upon United Nations membership. Consequently, the number of nations participating is not necessarily the same as the number of nations belonging to the United Nations.

About four billion people are in the world. It has been estimated that more than half of them are ill-fed or underfed or both. These are, in the main, the people of Asia, the Middle East, much of Africa, and large areas of Latin America. Much of the problem is due to primitive and unscientific methods of farming.

Nepal—Workers at Government Forest Nursery at Thankot

The problem of food shortages is not a new one. However, it has been complicated by the so-called "population explosion." The number of people in the world is increasing faster than ever before. In 1900, the population of the world was about one and a half billion people. Today, as we have seen, it is four billion. It is estimated that by the year 2000 there will be more than six billion people in the world.

The Food and Agriculture Organization is an agency concerned with improving the production, distribution, and consumption of food from agriculture and fisheries. Its work falls into three main classes: (1) collecting and distributing information from all over the world, (2) meetings and conferences of experts to discuss ways of solving the problem of food shortages, (3) sending experts to countries whose governments ask for help in developing food resources.

FAO's varied activities have been worldwide in scope. Fishermen in Chile have been helped to discover better fishing grounds. Farmers in Ethiopia have learned to fight animal diseases and those in the Middle East, to fight desert locusts. Sri Lanka was aided in the setting-up of timber mills. Tough grasses and hardy trees have been planted in the deserts of North Africa. Israeli farmers have been taught new methods of dairy farming.

It has been estimated that fully half of the people in the world are suffering from diseases that are preventable by knowedge, skills, and techniques already at hand. The problem is to find a way of bringing the knowledge to the place where it is needed. The World Health Organization was created to direct and coordinate health work in order to raise the health standards of people all over the world.

WHO sends public health experts and demonstration teams for disease control to countries requesting this service. It helps to train health workers of all kinds and provides hundreds of fellowships for doctors and nurses to study abroad.

The results of its efforts have been very impressive. In 1950, Indonesia asked for help against yaws, a crippling disease of which there were ten million victims in Indonesia. In four years, medical teams trained by WHO had cured 1,300,000 cases. Egypt has been helped in the fight against bilharziasis, a disease which used to cause one out of every five deaths in that country. Malaria-

Peru—A census-taker in the village of Chinchera

control teams have worked in all corners of the globe and millions of people have been vaccinated against a variety of dread diseases including polio, diphtheria, and yellow fever. WHO has also worked to encourage medical research into such areas as cancer and heart disease.

World War II resulted in the destruction of schools and colleges all over Europe. Even before the war ended, representatives of various nations met to make plans for rebuilding their educational systems after the war. An agency to coordinate this effort was to be set up. However, the idea of an agency devoted only to rehabilitation gradually changed to the notion that a permanent educational and cultural organization should be set up under the United Nations.

The preamble to UNESCO's constitution expresses the basic aim of the agency: "Wars begin in the minds of men, and it is therefore in the minds of men that the defenses of peace must be constructed." The idea has been put in another way: "One idea is worth more than a hundred thousand bayonets."

At present, there are six main items in UNESCO's program: (1) compulsory primary education, (2) scientific research for the improvement of living conditions, (3) the elimination of racial and social tensions, (4) the development of mutual appreciation by peoples all over the world of the culture of other peoples, (5) the growth in freedom of information, and (6) "fundamental education," meaning learning to live properly as regards diet and health, as well as to read and write.

In recent years UNESCO has engaged in several major projects. Latin American governments have been helped to increase primary education for the children of their countries. Scientific research for the development of natural resources in the arid zone from Morocco to India has been encouraged. Appreciation of Asian and Western cultural values, primarily through international visits and exchange of ideas, literature, and art, has been promoted. Teams of experts have gone out to India, Mexico, and Egypt to set up teacher-training institutes. An extensive fellowship program has been organized to promote the exchange of students and teachers. The first committee of the International Geophysical Year was organized with the help of UNESCO. An extensive survey of the Indian Ocean has been made in an effort to provide new sources of food for much of the world's population.

The International Labor Organization was founded in 1919 as part of the League of Nations. Its aim is ". . . universal and lasting peace . . . based upon social justice." It strives to persuade nations to improve labor conditions and living standards. It is made up of representatives of employers, labor, and the governments of the member nations. Its headquarters are in Geneva, with branch offices around the world.

A major part of ILO's work is the development of "Conventions" (or treaties) dealing with such matters as safety and health for workers, minimum age for employment, collective bargaining, and equal pay for equal work. These conventions are the product of long study and debate. They are submitted to the member governments for ratification. A country that ratifies binds itself to report each year on what progress it has made toward putting into effect the laws recommended by the Convention.

ILO also conducts training courses, does research, and publishes many economic and statistical reports. It cooperates with other Specialized Agencies in the task of raising living standards through advice on how to produce more and better goods. Recent studies by ILO have dealt with automation and its effects, protection of workers against radiation, and discrimination in employment.

In 1946, a new kind of bank was ready for business. Its aim was to help nations to finance the rebuilding of areas devastated by war and to aid underdeveloped nations. It was named the International Bank for Reconstruction and Development, with headquarters in Washington, D.C. Member nations bought stock in the Bank. Each has a representative on the Board of Directors, which meets once a year, and passes on all loans. The Bank lends money to member governments or to private enterprises where payment is guaranteed by the government. It will provide funds, however, only where it is reasonably sure that the loan can be paid back with interest and where private banks will not handle the loan. The Bank obtains funds not only from the sale of its stock but also by issuing bonds, which are bought by private investors in various countries.

The effects of the Bank's activities have been felt all over the world. The Pacific Railroad of Mexico was modernized with a very large loan. Through the Bank, Colombia added 190 miles of railway and Sri Lanka was able to build hydroelectric installations. India built a power plant near Bombay. Peru was helped to irrigate 125,000 acres of land. A loan helped Israel develop the Dead Sea Potash Works.

In 1960, a new agency, affiliated with the International Bank for Reconstruction and Development, was established. It was the International Development Association, set up to help finance economic growth to the less-developed countries. Its loans are made on very flexible terms, with long periods of repayment, low rates of interest, or no interest at all.

Another agency affiliated with the Bank is the International Finance Corporation. Like IDA, it is concerned with helping less-developed countries build dams, schools, hospitals, and roads. IFC aids economic development by encouraging productive private enterprise, in association with private investors, without requiring government guarantee of repayment. It has assisted in the development of private enterprises in Brazil, Chile, Pakistan, and Australia.

The International Monetary Fund works in close association with the Bank. In fact, a government must be a member of IMF in order to join the Bank. The Fund's purpose is to help a nation which is temporarily short of gold or foreign currency because its exports are not earning enough to pay for its imports. In such a case, the nation may buy the necessary foreign money from IMF, which has available the currency of all member nations. The Fund also provides technical assistance by sending experts who advise governments on monetary questions.

The basic aim of the International Civil Aviation Organization is to make flying from one country to another safer and easier. Its headquarters are in Montreal, but it holds regional meetings all over the world.

ICAO has drafted a set of rules and regulations to standardize international air operations, and immigration, customs, and health procedures at international airports. ICAO experts make recommendations to member governments regarding suitable airport sites and the improvement of weather information and of search and rescue operations. Much of its work is directed toward meeting new requirements for jet operations. Nations with inadequate roads or railways are helped to improve air service for quick and easy transportation.

The Universal Postal Union was set up in 1874 in Berne. It is now part of the United Nations. As a result of its work, several billion pieces of mail are carried safely from one country to another. The Union guarantees the delivery of mail under the established rates throughout the world and its return to place of origin, if it cannot be delivered.

Similar to the UPU is the International Telecommunication Union, which dates back to 1865. Although in its early days it was concerned largely with improving international telegraph service, today much of its work involves radio broadcasting. If stations in different countries were to broadcast on any wave length they wished to, radio communications among nations would be extremely difficult, since there would be a great deal of interference. To prevent this, ITU records the frequency assignments made by individual nations and tries to persuade them to agree on an orderly sharing of radio frequency bands.

The scientific study of weather conditions has become increasingly important in the age of the airplane, television, and radio. The World Meteorological Organization, with headquarters in Geneva, aims to collect and exchange, among weather stations all over the world, accurate meteorological information. It also provides technical assistance to member nations to improve weather forecasting services. It has recently added to its work the spreading of information based upon the observations of weather satellites.

In 1957, the International Atomic Energy Agency was established in order to help put the power of the atom to work for peaceful uses. Its headquarters are in Vienna. Unlike the other Specialized Agencies, IAEA is an intergovernmental agency which makes an annual report directly to the General Assembly.

IAEA supplies advice to nations wishing help in establishing atomic installations for peaceful purposes, and arranges for the exchange of atomic materials.

The Intergovernmental Maritime Consultative Organization (IMCO) began operations in 1958 with headquarters in London. It seeks to promote cooperation in regard to the regulation of ocean shipping and the improvement of safety at sea.

In force since 1948, the General Agreement on Tariffs and Trade seeks to reduce barriers to international trade. To aid developing countries, GATT set up the International Trade Center in 1964.

Bangladesh—Dacca, Bengali women learning to cut cloth and sew

THE UNITED NATIONS IN ACTION

One evaluation of the work of the United Nations ended with this comment: "To measure the UN's contribution, one need only ask how much meaner and poorer, how much less touched by hope or reason, would be the world scene if it suddenly ceased to exist."

Since its establishment, the United Nations has done much to provide hope for people all over the world. In 1953, the United Nations Children's Fund, known as UNICEF, was set up as a permanent agency. It works with WHO and other Specialized Agencies to help children grow strong and healthy. UNICEF is supported by contributions from governments and from private persons and organizations.

Another program which coordinates the work of various Specialized Agencies is the Expanded Program of Technical Assistance (EPTA). A Technical Assistance Board, composed of the Secretary-General of the United Nations or his representative and the heads of the cooperating agencies, administers a special fund, which it distributes to be used for work that no agency by itself is equipped to undertake. By coordinating the work of WHO, WMO, ILO, FAO, and other agencies, TAB has provided training for doctors, nurses, and nutritionists, with the host government providing the hospitals and Specialized Agencies of the UN providing expensive equipment. Other projects have included providing engineers and other experts to help in town planning, in building dams and hydroelectric projects, and in setting up fisheries. In 1959, a new program called the Special Fund was established. It concentrates on a few large projects which are considered to be especially urgent. It is hoped that the success of these projects will open the way for investment of much larger sums by private business in countries that badly need new enterprises.

At its first meeting in 1946, the Economic and Social Council elected a Commission on Human Rights to draw up an international bill of rights for all people. On December 10, 1948, the Universal Declaration of Human Rights was unanimously adopted by the General Assembly. It proclaims that all people are born free and equal and are entitled to life, liberty, and security of person, the right to travel freely and live where they please, and freedom of speech, press, assembly, and worship.

ECOSOC has also worked for human welfare in other ways. Its Commission on the Status of Women has made a number of studies and recommendations to insure equality of rights and duties between men and women. Another commission of the Council is the Commission on Narcotic Drugs which works to strengthen control over international traffic in drugs.

A special committee of ECOSOC drafted the Genocide Convention, which the General Assembly adopted in 1958. This Convention is designed to outlaw the crime of *genocide,* defined as an attempt to destroy "a national, ethnical, racial, or religious group as such." A year later the Assembly unanimously adopted a Declaration of the Rights of the Child, which asserts the right of every child to be given proper food, shelter, medical care, and education, the right to play, and to be taught the spirit of universal brotherhood.

Another problem with which the United Nations has concerned itself has been aid to refugees. The UN Office of the High Commissioner for Refugees gives international protection to people driven out of their homelands. Refugees from Communist China, Morocco, Tunisia, Hungary, Israel, and East Germany have been given emergency relief and have been aided in finding homes and employment.

THE U.N. MEETS MANY CRISES

The United Nations has faced many serious crises, several of which could have resulted in a major war and in the destruction of the UN itself. The UN did not succeed in reaching a settlement in every one of these crises. It is important to remember, however, that a successful settlement depends upon the willingness of governments to cooperate in order to avoid war.

Math Formulas/Equivalent Measures

CIRCUMFERENCE

Circle .... $C = d\pi$, in which π is 3.1416 and d the diameter.

AREA

Circle .... $A = r^2\pi$, in which π is 3.1416 and r the radius.

Rectangle .... $A = ab$, in which a is the base and b the height.

Sphere .... $A = 4r^2\pi$, in which r is the radius.

Trapezoid .... $A = \frac{h\,(a+b)}{2}$, in which h is the height, a the longer parallel side, and b the shorter.

Triangle .... $A = \frac{ab}{2}$, in which a is the base and b the height.

VOLUME

Cone .... $V = \frac{r^2\pi h}{3}$, in which π is 3.1416, r the radius of the base, and h the height.

Cube .... $V = a^3$, in which a is one of the edges.

Cylinder .... $V = r^2\pi h$, in which π is 3.1614, r the radius of the base, and h the height.

Pyramid .... $V = \frac{Ah}{3}$, in which A is the area of the base and h the height.

Rectangular Prism .... $V = abc$, in which a is the length, b the width, and c the depth.

Sphere .... $V = \frac{4\pi r^3}{3}$, in which π is 3.1416 and r the radius.

FALLING BODIES

Speed per second acquired by falling body: $S = 32t$, in which t is the time in seconds.

Distance in feet traveled by falling body: $D = 16t$, in which t is the time in seconds.

SPEED OF SOUND

Speed of sound in feet per second through any given temperature of air: $S = \frac{1087\sqrt{273+t}}{16.52}$, in which t is the temperature in Centigrade.

ENERGY AND MATTER

Conversion of matter into energy (Einstein's theorem): $E = mc^2$, in which E is the energy in ergs, m the mass of the matter in grams, and c the speed of light in centimeters per second. ($c^2 = 9.10^{20}$).

FORMULAS USED IN SOLID GEOMETRY

LATERAL AREA

Cone of revolution	$L = \pi rs$
Cylinder of revolution	$L = 2\pi rh$
Frustum of cone of revolution	$L = \frac{1}{2}s(c + c')$
Frustum of regular pyramid	$L = \frac{1}{2}s(p + p')$
Prism	$L = ep$
Regular pyramid	$L = \frac{1}{2}sp$

TOTAL AREA

Cone of revolution	$T = \pi r(r + s)$
Cylinder of revolution	$T = 2\pi r(r + h)$
Sphere	$S = 4\pi r^2$
Zone	$S = 2\pi rh$

VOLUME

Circular cone	$V = \frac{1}{3}\pi r^2 h$
Circular cylinder	$V = Bh$
Cube	$V = e^3$
Cylinder of revolution	$V = \pi r^2 h$
Frustum of circular cone	$V = \frac{1}{3}\pi h(r^2 + r'^2 + rr')$
Frustum of pyramid	$V = \frac{1}{3}h(B + B' + \sqrt{BB'})$
Prism	$V = Bh$
Prismatoid	$V = \frac{1}{6}h(B_1 + B_2 + 4M)$
Pyramid	$V = \frac{1}{3}Bh$
Rectangular solid	$V = lwh$
Sphere	$V = \frac{4}{3}\pi r^3$
Spherical sector	$V = \frac{1}{3}rS$

PHYSICAL CONSTANTS

QUANTITY	SYMBOL	VALUE
Gravitational constant	G	$6.67 \times 10^{-11}\ n \cdot m^2/kg^2$
Acceleration of gravity at earth's surface	g	$9.81\ m/sec^2 = 32.2 ft/sec^2$
Atmospheric pressure at sea level	(none)	$14.7\ lb/in^2 = 1.01 \times 10^5\ n/m^2$
Absolute zero	$0^\circ K$	$-273^\circ C$
Boltzmann's constant	k	$1.38 \times 10^{-23}\ j/^\circ K$
Electrostatic constant	C	$9.00 \times 10^9\ n \cdot m^2/coul^2$
Electromagnetic constant	μ	$1.26 \times 10^{-6} \cdot weber/amp \cdot m$
Charge of electron	e	$1.60 \times 10^{-19}\ coul$
Electron rest mass	m_e	$9.11 \times 10^{-31}\ kg$
Proton rest mass	m_p	$1.67 \times 10^{-27}\ kg$
Neutron rest mass	m_n	$1.67 \times 10^{-27}\ kg$
Speed of light	c	$3.00 \times 10^8\ m/sec$
Planck's constant	h	$6.63 \times 10^{-34}\ j \cdot sec$

TABLES OF INTERRELATION OF UNITS OF MEASUREMENT

UNITS OF LENGTH

Units		Inches	Links	Feet
1 inch	=	1	0.126 262 6	0.083 333 33
1 link	=	7.92	1	0.66
1 foot	=	12	1.515 152	1
1 yard	=	36	4 545 45	3
1 rod	=	198	25	16.5
1 chain	=	792	100	66
1 mile	=	63 360	8000	5280
1 centimeter	=	0.393 700 8	0.049 709 70	0.032 808 40
1 meter	=	39.370 08	4.970 970	3.280 840

Units		Yards	Rods	Chains
1 inch	=	0.027 777 78	0.005 050 505	0.001 262 626
1 link	=	0.22	0.04	0.01
1 foot	=	0.333 333 3	0.060 606 06	0.015 151 52
1 yard	=	1	0.181 818 2	0.045 454 55
1 rod	=	5.5	1	0.25
1 chain	=	22	4	1
1 mile	=	1760	320	80
1 centimeter	=	0.010 936 13	0.001 988 388	0.000 497 097 0
1 meter	=	1.093 613	0.198 838 8	0.049 709 70

Units		Miles	Centimeters	Meters
1 inch	=	0.000 015 782 83	2.54	0.025 4
1 link	=	0.000 125	20.116 8	0.201 168
1 foot	=	0.000 189 393 9	30.48	0.304 8
1 yard	=	0.000 568 181 8	91.44	0.914 4
1 rod	=	0.003 125	502.92	5.029 2
1 chain	=	0.012 5	2011.68	20.116 8
1 mile	=	1	160 934.4	1609.344
1 centimeter	=	0.000 006 213 712	1	0.01
1 meter	=	0.000 621 371 2	100	1

UNITS OF VOLUME

Units		Cubic inches	Cubic feet	Cubic yards
1 cubic inch	=	1	0.000 578 703 7	0.000 021 433 47
1 cubic foot	=	1728	1	0.037 037 04
1 cubic yard	=	46 656	27	1
1 cubic centimeter	=	0.061 023 74	0.000 035 314 67	0.000 001 307 951
1 cubic decimeter	=	61.023 74	0.035 314 67	0.001 307 951
1 cubic meter	=	61 023.74	35.314 67	1.307 951

Units		Cubic Centimeters	Cubic decimeters	Cubic meters
1 cubic inch	=	16.387 064	0.016 387 064	0.000 016 387 064
1 cubic foot	=	28 316.846 592	28.316 846 592	0.028 316 846 592
1 cubic yard	=	764 554.857 984	764.554 857 984	0.764 554 857 984
1 cubic centimeter	=	1	0.001	0.000 001
1 cubic decimeter	=	1 000	1	0.001
1 cubic meter	=	1 000 000	1000	1

UNITS OF AREA

Units		Square inches	Square links	Square feet	Square yards
1 square inch	=	1	0.015 942 25	0.006 944 444	0.000 771 604 9
1 square link	=	62.726 4	1	0.435 6	0.048 4
1 square foot	=	144	2.295 684	1	0.111 111 1
1 square yard	=	1296	20.661 16	9	1
1 square rod	=	39 204	625	272.25	30.25
1 square chain	=	627 264	10 000	4356	484
1 acre	=	6 272 640	100 000	43 560	4840
1 square mile	=	4 014 489 600	64 000 000	27 878 400	3 097 600
1 square centimeter	=	0.155 000 3	0.002 471 054	0.001 076 391	0.000 119 599 0
1 square meter	=	1550.003	24.710 54	10.763 91	1.195 990
1 hectare	=	15 500 031	247 105.4	107 639.1	11 959.90

Units		Square rods	Square chains	Acres	Square miles
1 square inch	=	0.000 025 507 60	0.000 001 594 225	0.000 000 159 422 5	0.000 000 000 249 097 7
1 square link	=	0.001 6	0.000 1	0.000 01	0.000 000 015 625
1 square foot	=	0.003 673 095	0.000 229 568 4	0.000 022 956 84	0.000 000 035 870 06
1 square yard	=	0.033 057 85	0.002 066 116	0.000 206 611 6	0.000 000 322 830 6
1 square rod	=	1	0.062 5	0.006 25	0.000 009 765 625
1 square chain	=	16	1	0.1	0.000 156 25
1 acre	=	160	10	1	0.001 562 5
1 square mile	=	102 400	6400	640	1
1 square centimeter	=	0.000 003 953 686	0.000 000 247 105 4	0.000 000 024 710 54	0.000 000 000 038 610 22
1 square meter	=	0.039 536 86	0.002 471 054	0.000 247 105 4	0.000 000 386 102 2
1 hectare	=	395.368 6	24.710 54	2.471 054	0.003 861 022

Units		Square centimeters	Square meters	Hectares
1 square inch	=	6.451 6	0.000 645 16	0.000 000 064 516
1 square link	=	404.685 642 24	0.040 468 564 224	0.000 004 046 856 422 4
1 square foot	=	929.030 4	0.092 903 04	0.000 009 290 304
1 square yard	=	8 361.273 6	0.836 127 36	0.000 083 612 736
1 square rod	=	252 928.526 4	25.292 852 64	0.002 529 285 264
1 square chain	=	4 046 856.422 4	404.685 642 24	0.040 468 564 224
1 acre	=	40 468 564.224	4046.856 422 4	0.404 685 642 24
1 square mile	=	25 899 881 103.36	2 589 988.110 336	258.998 811 033 6
1 square centimeter	=	1	0.000 1	0.000 000 01
1 square meter	=	10 000	1	0.000 1
1 hectare	=	100 000 000	10 000	1

STANDARD CONVERSION FACTORS

1 m/sec = 3.28 ft/sec = 2.24 mi/hr = 3.60 km/hr

1 ft/sec = 0.305 m/sec = 0.682 mi/hr = 1.10 km/hr

1 mi/hr = 1.47 ft/sec = 0.447 m/sec = 1.61 km/hr

1 radian (rad) = 57.30° = 57°18′

1° = 0.01745 rad

1 revolution/minute (rev/min) = 0.1047 rad/sec

1 atomic mass unit (amu) = 1.66×10^{-27} kg = 1.49×10^{-10} j = 931 Mev

1 newton (n) = 0.225 lb

1 pound (lb) = 4.45 n

1 joule (j) = 0.738 ft.lb = 2.39×10^{-4} kcal = 6.24×10^{-18} ev

1 kilocalorie (kcal) = 4.186 j

1 foot-pound (ft.lb) = 1.36 j

1 electron volt (ev) = 10^{-6} Mev = 1.60×10^{-19} j = 1.18×10^{-19} ft.lb = 3.83×10^{-23} kcal

1 watt = 1 j/sec = 0.738 ft.lb/sec

UNITS OF CAPACITY LIQUID MEASURE

Units	Minims	Fluid drams	Fluid ounces
1 minim =	1	0.016 666 67	0.002 083 333
1 fluid dram =	60	1	0.125
1 fluid ounce =	480	8	1
1 gill =	1920	32	4
1 liquid pint =	7680	128	16
1 liquid quart =	15 360	256	32
1 gallon =	61 440	1024	128
1 cubic inch =	265.974 0	4.432 900	0.554 112 6
1 cubic foot =	459 603.1	7660.052	957.506 5
1 milliliter =	16.231 19	0.270 519 8	0.033 814 97
1 liter =	16 231.19	270.519 8	33.814 97

Units	Gills	Liquid pints	Liquid quarts
1 minim =	0.000 520 833 3	0.000 130 208 3	0.000 065 104 17
1 fluid dram =	0.031 25	0.007 812 5	0.003 906 25
1 fluid ounce =	0.25	0.062 5	0.031 25
1 gill =	1	0.25	0.125
1 liquid pint =	4	1	0.5
1 liquid quart =	8	2	1
1 gallon =	32	8	4
1 cubic inch =	0.138 528 1	0.034 632 03	0.017 316 02
1 cubic foot =	239.376 6	59.844 16	29.922 08
1 milliliter =	0.008 453 742	0.002 113 436	0.001 056 718
1 liter =	8.453 742	2.113 436	1.056 718

Units	Gallons	Cubic inches	Cubic feet
1 minim =	0.000 016 276 04	0.003 759 766	0.000 002 175 790
1 fluid dram =	0.000 976 562 5	0.225 585 9	0.000 130 547 4
1 fluid ounce =	0.007 812 5	1.804 687 5	0.001 044 379
1 gill =	0.031 25	7.218 75	0.004 177 517
1 liquid pint =	0.125	28.875	0.016 710 07
1 liquid quart =	0.25	57.75	0.033 420 14
1 gallon =	1	231	0.133 680 6
1 cubic inch =	0.004 329 004	1	0.000 578 703 7
1 cubic foot =	7.480 519	1728	1
1 milliliter =	0.000 264 179 4	0.061 025 45	0.000 035 315 66
1 liter =	0.264 179 4	61.025 45	0.035 315 66

Units	Milliliters	Liters
1 minim =	0.061 609 79	0.000 061 609 79
1 fluid dram =	3.696 588	0.003 696 588
1 fluid ounce =	29.572 70	0.029 572 70
1 gill =	118.290 8	0.118 290 8
1 liquid pint =	473.163 2	0.473 163 2
1 liquid quart =	946.326 4	0.946 326 4
1 gallon =	3 785.306	3.785 306
1 cubic inch =	16.386 61	0.016 386 61
1 cubic foot =	28 316.05	28.316 05
1 milliliter =	1	0.001
1 liter =	1000	1

UNITS OF CAPACITY DRY MEASURE

Units	Dry pints	Dry quarts	Pecks
1 dry pint =	1	0.5	0.062 5
1 dry quart =	2	1	0.125
1 peck =	16	8	1
1 bushel =	64	32	4
1 cubic inch =	0.029 761 6	0.014 880 8	0.001 860 10
1 cubic foot =	51.428 09	25.714 05	3.214 256
1 liter =	1.816 217	0.908 108 4	0.113 513 6
1 dekaliter =	18.162 17	9.081 084	1.135 136

Units	Bushels	Cubic inches	Cubic feet
1 dry pint =	0.015 625	33.600 312 5	0.019 444 63
1 dry quart =	0.031 25	67.200 625	0.038 889 25
1 peck =	0.25	537.605	0.311 114
1 bushel =	1	2150.42	1.244 456
1 cubic inch =	0.000 465 025	1	0.000 578 703 7
1 cubic foot =	0.803 563 95	1728	1
1 liter =	0.028 378 39	61.025 45	0.035 315 66
1 dekaliter =	0.283 783 9	610.254 5	0.353 156 6

Units	Liters	Dekaliters
1 dry pint =	0.550 595 1	0.055 059 51
1 dry quart =	1.101 190	0.110 119 0
1 peck =	8.809 521	0.880 952 1
1 bushel =	35.238 08	3.523 808
1 cubic inch =	0.016 386 61	0.001 638 661
1 cubic foot =	28.316 05	2.831 605
1 liter =	1	0.1
1 dekaliter =	10	1

UNITS OF MASS NOT LESS THAN AVOIRDUPOIS OUNCES

Units	Avoirdupois ounces	Avoirdupois pounds	Short hundred weights
1 avoirdupois ounce =	1	0.0625	0.000 625
1 avoirdupois pound =	16	1	0.01
1 short hundredweight =	1 600	100	1
1 short ton =	32 000	2 000	20
1 long ton =	35 840	2 240	22.4
1 kilogram =	35.273 96	2.204 623	0.022 046 23
1 metric ton =	35 273.96	2204.623	22.046 23

Units	Short tons	Long tons	Kilograms	Metric tons
1 avoirdupois ounce =	0.000 031 25	0.000 027 901 79	0.028 349 523 125	0.000 028 349 523 125
1 avoirdupois pound =	0.000 5	0.000 446 428 6	0.453 592 37	0.000 453 592 37
1 short hundredweight =	0.05	0.044 642 86	45.359 237	0.045 359 237
1 short ton =	1	0.892 857 1	907.184 74	0.907 184 74
1 long ton =	1.12	1	1016.046 908 8	1.016 046 908 8
1 kilogram =	0.001 102 311	0.000 984 206 5	1	0.001
1 metric ton =	1.102 311	0.984 206 5	1 000	1

SQUARE, SQUARE ROOTS, CUBES AND CUBE ROOTS OF NOS. 1 TO 100

No.	Sq.	Cube	Sq. Root	Cube Root	No.	Sq.	Cube	Sq. Root	Cube Root
1	1	1	1.000	1.000	51	2601	132651	7.141	3.708
2	4	8	1.414	1.260	52	2704	140608	7.211	3.732
3	9	27	1.732	1.442	53	2809	148877	7.280	3.756
4	16	64	2.000	1.587	54	2916	157464	7.348	3.779
5	25	125	2.236	1.710	55	3025	166375	7.416	3.803
6	36	216	2.449	1.817	56	3136	175616	7.483	3.825
7	49	343	2.646	1.913	57	3249	185193	7.550	3.848
8	64	512	2.828	2.000	58	3364	195112	7.616	3.870
9	81	729	3.000	2.080	59	3481	205379	7.681	3.893
10	100	1000	3.162	2.154	60	3600	216000	7.746	3.915
11	121	1331	3.317	2.224	61	3721	226981	7.810	3.936
12	144	1728	3.464	2.289	62	3844	238328	7.874	3.958
13	169	2197	3.605	2.351	63	3969	250047	7.937	3.979
14	196	2744	3.742	2.410	64	4096	262144	8 000	4.000
15	225	3375	3.873	2.466	65	4225	274625	8.062	4.020
16	256	4096	4.000	2.511	66	4356	287496	8.124	4.041
17	289	4913	4.123	2.571	67	4489	300763	8.185	4.062
18	324	5832	4.243	2.621	68	4624	314432	8.246	4.082
19	361	6859	4.359	2.668	69	4761	328509	8.307	4.102
20	400	8000	4.472	2.714	70	4900	343000	8.367	4.121
21	441	9261	4.583	2.759	71	5041	357911	8.426	4.140
22	484	10648	4.690	2.802	72	5184	373248	8.485	4.160
23	529	12167	4.796	2.844	73	5329	389017	8.544	4.179
24	576	13824	4.899	2.884	74	5476	405224	8.602	4.198
25	625	15625	5.000	2.924	75	5625	421875	8.660	4.217
26	676	17576	5.099	2.962	76	5776	438976	8.718	4.236
27	729	19683	5.196	3 000	77	5929	456533	8.775	4.254
28	784	21952	5.292	3.037	78	6084	474552	8.832	4.273
29	841	24389	5.385	3.072	79	6241	493039	8.888	4.291
30	900	27000	5.477	3.107	80	6400	512000	8.944	4.309
31	961	29791	5.568	3.141	81	6561	531441	9.000	4.327
32	1024	32768	5.657	3.175	82	6724	551368	9.055	4.344
33	1089	35937	5.745	3.208	83	6889	571787	9.110	4.362
34	1156	39304	5.831	3.240	84	7056	592704	9.165	4.371
35	1225	42875	5.916	3.271	85	7225	614125	9.220	4.397
36	1296	46656	6.000	3.302	86	7396	636056	9.274	4.414
37	1369	50653	6.083	3.332	87	7569	658503	9.327	4.431
38	1444	54872	6.164	3.362	88	7744	681472	9.381	4.448
39	1521	59319	6.245	3.391	89	7921	704969	9.434	4.465
40	1600	64000	6.325	3.420	90	8100	729000	9.487	4.481
41	1681	68921	6.403	3.448	91	8281	753571	9 539	4.498
42	1764	74088	6.481	3.476	92	8464	778688	9.592	4.514
43	1849	79507	6.557	3.503	93	8649	804357	9.644	4.531
44	1936	85184	6.633	3.530	94	8836	830584	9.695	4.547
45	2025	91125	6.708	3.557	95	9025	857375	9.747	4.563
46	2116	97336	6.782	3.583	96	9216	884736	9.798	4.579
47	2209	103823	6.856	3.609	97	9409	912673	9.849	4.595
48	2304	110592	6.928	3.634	98	9604	941192	9.899	4.610
49	2401	117649	7.000	3.659	99	9801	970299	9.950	4.626
50	2500	125000	7.071	3.684	100	10000	1000000	10.000	4.641

CHEMICAL ELEMENTS, ATOMIC WEIGHTS

Element	Symbol	Atomic number	Atomic weight	Element	Symbol	Atomic number	Atomic weight
Actinium	Ac	89	(1)	Mercury	Hg	80	200.61
Aluminum	Al	13	26.98	Molybdenum	Mo	42	95.95
Americium	Am	95	(1)	Neodymium	Nd	60	144.27
Antimony	Sb	51	121.76	Neon	Ne	10	20.183
Argon	Ar	18	39.944	Neptunium	Np	93	(1)
Arsenic	As	33	74.91	Nickel	Ni	28	58.71
Astatine	At	85	(1)	Niobium	Nb	41	92.91
Barium	Ba	56	137.36	Nitrogen	N	7	14.008
Berkelium	Bk	97	(1)	Nobelium	No	102	(1)
Beryllium	Be	4	9.013	Osmium	Os	76	190.2
Bismuth	Bi	83	209.00	Oxygen	O	8	[2]16
Boron	B	5	10.82	Palladium	Pd	46	106.4
Bromine	Br	35	79.916	Phosphorus	P	15	30.975
Cadmium	Cd	48	112.41	Platinum	Pt	78	195.09
Calcium	Ca	20	40.08	Plutonium	Pu	94	(1)
Californium	Cf	98	(1)	Polonium	Po	84	(1)
Carbon	C	6	12.010	Potassium	K	19	39.100
Cerium	Ce	58	140.13	Praseodymium	Pr	59	140.92
Cesium	Cs	55	132.91	Promethium	Pm	61	(1)
Chlorine	Cl	17	35.457	Protactinium	Pa	91	(1)
Chromium	Cr	24	52.01	Radium	Ra	88	(1)
Cobalt	Co	27	58.94	Radon	Rn	86	(1)
Copper	Cu	29	63.54	Rhenium	Re	75	186.22
Curium	Cm	96	(1)	Rhodium	Rh	45	102.91
Dysprosium	Dy	66	162.51	Rubidium	Rb	37	85.48
Einsteinium	Es	99	(1)	Ruthenium	Ru	44	101.1
Erbium	Er	68	167.27	Samarium	Sm	62	150.35
Europium	Eu	63	152.0	Scandium	Sc	21	44.96
Fermium	Fm	100	(1)	Selenium	Se	34	78.96
Fluorine	F	9	19.00	Silicon	Si	14	28.09
Francium	Fr	87	(1)	Silver	Ag	47	107.880
Gadolinium	Gd	64	157.26	Sodium	Na	11	22.991
Gallium	Ga	31	69.72	Strontium	Sr	38	87.63
Germanium	Ge	32	72.60	Sulfur	S	16	[3]32.066
Gold	Au	79	197.0	Tantalum	Ta	73	180.95
Hafnium	Hf	72	178.50	Technetium	Tc	43	(1)
Helium	He	2	4.003	Tellurium	Te	52	127.61
Holmium	Ho	67	164.94	Terbium	Tb	65	158.93
Hydrogen	H	1	1.0080	Thallium	TI	81	204.39
Indium	In	49	114.82	Thorium	Th	90	232.05
Iodine	I	53	126.91	Thulium	Tm	69	168.94
Iridium	Ir	77	192.2	Tin	Sn	50	118.70
Iron	Fe	26	55.85	Titanium	Ti	22	47.90
Krypton	Kr	36	83.80	Tungsten	W	74	183.86
Lanthanum	La	57	138.92	Uranium	U	92	238.07
Lawrencium	Lw	103	(1)	Vanadium	V	23	50.95
Lead	Pb	82	207.21	Xenon	Xe	54	131.30
Lithium	Li	3	6.940	Ytterbium	Yb	70	173.04
Lutetium	Lu	71	174.99	Yttrium	Y	39	88.92
Magnesium	Mg	12	24.32	Zinc	Zn	30	65.38
Manganese	Mn	25	54.94	Zirconium	Zr	40	91.22
Mendelevium	Md	101	(1)				

[1] These values are omitted because the elements do not occur in nature, and their atomic weight depends on which isotope is made.

[2] This is a defined value rather than an indicated one.

[3] Because of natural variations in the abundance ratio of the isotopes of sulfur, the atomic weight of this element has a range of ±0.003.

FOUR-PLACE LOGARITHMS

No.	0	1	2	3	4	5	6	7	8	9	No.	0	1	2	3	4	5	6	7	8	9
10	0000	0043	0086	0128	0170	0212	0253	0294	0334	0374	55	7404	7412	7419	7427	7435	7443	7451	7459	7466	7474
11	0414	0453	0492	0531	0569	0607	0645	0682	0719	0755	56	7482	7490	7497	7505	7513	7520	7528	7536	7543	7551
12	0792	0828	0864	0899	0934	0969	1004	1038	1072	1106	57	7559	7566	7574	7582	7589	7597	7604	7612	7619	7627
13	1139	1173	1206	1239	1271	1303	1335	1367	1399	1430	58	7634	7642	7649	7657	7664	7672	7679	7686	7694	7701
14	1461	1492	1523	1553	1584	1614	1644	1673	1703	1732	59	7709	7716	7723	7731	7738	7745	7752	7760	7767	7774
15	1761	1790	1818	1847	1875	1903	1931	1959	1987	2014	60	7782	7789	7796	7803	7810	7818	7825	7832	7839	7846
16	2041	2068	2095	2122	2148	2175	2201	2227	2253	2279	61	7853	7860	7868	7875	7882	7889	7896	7903	7910	7917
17	2304	2330	2355	2380	2405	2430	2455	2480	2504	2529	62	7924	7931	7938	7945	7952	7959	7966	7973	7980	7987
18	2553	2577	2601	2625	2648	2672	2695	2718	2742	2765	63	7993	8000	8007	8014	8021	8028	8035	8041	8048	8055
19	2788	2810	2833	2856	2878	2900	2923	2945	2967	2989	64	8062	8069	8075	8082	8089	8096	8102	8109	8116	8122
20	3010	3032	3054	3075	3096	3118	3139	3160	3181	3201	65	8129	8136	8142	8149	8156	8162	8169	8176	8182	8189
21	3222	3243	3263	3284	3304	3324	3345	3365	3385	3404	66	8195	8202	8209	8215	8222	8228	8235	8241	8248	8254
22	3424	3444	3464	3483	3502	3522	3541	3560	3579	3598	67	8261	8267	8274	8280	8287	8293	8299	8306	8312	8319
23	3617	3636	3655	3674	3692	3711	3729	3747	3766	3784	68	8325	8331	8338	8344	8351	8357	8363	8370	8376	8382
24	3802	3820	3838	3856	3874	3892	3909	3927	3945	3962	69	8388	8395	8401	8407	8414	8420	8426	8432	8439	8445
25	3979	3997	4014	4031	4048	4065	4082	4099	4116	4133	70	8451	8457	8463	8470	8476	8482	8488	8494	8500	8506
26	4150	4166	4183	4200	4216	4232	4249	4265	4281	4298	71	8513	8519	8525	8531	8537	8543	8549	8555	8561	8567
27	4314	4330	4346	4362	4378	4393	4409	4425	4440	4456	72	8573	8579	8585	8591	8597	8603	8609	8615	8621	8627
28	4472	4487	4502	4518	4533	4548	4564	4579	4594	4609	73	8633	8639	8645	8651	8657	8663	8669	8675	8681	8686
29	4624	4639	4654	4669	4683	4698	4713	4728	4742	4757	74	8692	8698	8704	8710	8716	8722	8727	8733	8739	8745
30	4771	4786	4800	4814	4829	4843	4857	4871	4886	4900	75	8751	8756	8762	8768	8774	8779	8785	8791	8797	8802
31	4914	4928	4942	4955	4969	4983	4997	5011	5024	5038	76	8808	8814	8820	8825	8831	8837	8842	8848	8854	8859
32	5051	5065	5079	5092	5105	5119	5132	5145	5159	5172	77	8865	8871	8876	8882	8887	8893	8899	8904	8910	8915
33	5185	5198	5211	5224	5237	5250	5263	5276	5289	5302	78	8921	8927	8932	8938	8943	8949	8954	8960	8965	8971
34	5315	5328	5340	5353	5366	5378	5391	5403	5416	5428	79	8976	8982	8987	8993	8998	9004	9009	9015	9020	9025
35	5441	5453	5465	5478	5490	5502	5514	5527	5539	5551	80	9031	9036	9042	9047	9053	9058	9063	9069	9074	9079
36	5563	5575	5587	5599	5611	5623	5635	5647	5658	5670	81	9085	9090	9096	9101	9106	9112	9117	9122	9128	9133
37	5682	5694	5705	5717	5729	5740	5752	5763	5775	5786	82	9138	9143	9149	9154	9159	9165	9170	9175	9180	9186
38	5798	5809	5821	5832	5843	5855	5866	5877	5888	5899	83	9191	9196	9201	9206	9212	9217	9222	9227	9232	9238
39	5911	5922	5933	5944	5955	5966	5977	5988	5999	6010	84	9243	9248	9253	9258	9263	9269	9274	9279	9284	9289
40	6021	6031	6042	6053	6064	6075	6085	6096	6107	6117	85	9294	9299	9304	9309	9315	9320	9325	9330	9335	9340
41	6128	6138	6149	6160	6170	6180	6191	6201	6212	6222	86	9345	9350	9355	9360	9365	9370	9375	9380	9385	9390
42	6232	6243	6253	6263	6274	6284	6294	6304	6314	6325	87	9395	9400	9405	9410	9415	9420	9425	9430	9435	9440
43	6335	6345	6355	6365	6375	6385	6395	6405	6415	6425	88	9445	9450	9455	9460	9465	9469	9474	9479	9484	9489
44	6435	6444	6454	6464	6474	6484	6493	6503	6513	6522	89	9494	9499	9504	9509	9513	9518	9523	9528	9533	9538
45	6532	6542	6551	6561	6571	6580	6590	6599	6609	6618	90	9542	9547	9552	9557	9562	9566	9571	9576	9581	9586
46	6628	6637	6646	6656	6665	6675	6684	6693	6702	6712	91	9590	9595	9600	9605	9609	9614	9619	9624	9628	9633
47	6721	6730	6739	6749	6758	6767	6776	6785	6794	6803	92	9638	9643	9647	9652	9657	9661	9666	9671	9675	9680
48	6812	6821	6830	6839	6848	6857	6866	6875	6884	6893	93	9685	9689	9694	9699	9703	9708	9713	9717	9722	9727
49	6902	6911	6920	6928	6937	6946	6955	6964	6972	6981	94	9731	9736	9741	9745	9750	9754	9759	9763	9768	9773
50	6990	6998	7007	7016	7024	7033	7042	7050	7059	7067	95	9777	9782	9786	9791	9795	9800	9805	9809	9814	9818
51	7076	7084	7093	7101	7110	7118	7126	7135	7143	7152	96	9823	9827	9832	9836	9841	9845	9850	9854	9859	9863
52	7160	7168	7177	7185	7193	7202	7210	7218	7226	7235	97	9868	9872	9877	9881	9886	9890	9894	9899	9903	9908
53	7243	7251	7259	7267	7275	7284	7292	7300	7308	7316	98	9912	9917	9921	9926	9930	9934	9939	9943	9948	9952
54	7324	7332	7340	7348	7356	7364	7372	7380	7388	7396	99	9956	9961	9965	9969	9974	9978	9983	9987	9991	9996
No.	0	1	2	3	4	5	6	7	8	9	No.	0	1	2	3	4	5	6	7	8	9

Metric Conversions

TEMPERATURE

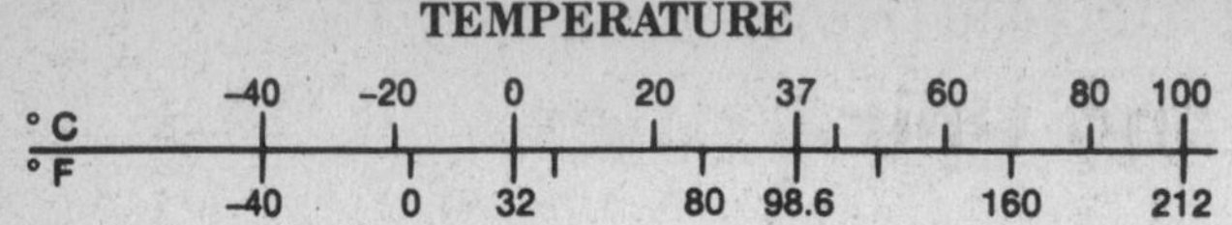

To Convert Celsius to Fahrenheit:
Multiply the Celsius temperature by 2, subtract 10%, and add 32.
Example: 25″ C x 2 = 50 – 5 = 45 + 32 = 77″ F

To Convert Fahrenheit to Celsius, Reverse the Procedure.
Example: 72″ F – 32 = 40 + 4 = 44 ÷ 2 = 22″ C

Temperatures in degrees Celsius, as in the familiar Fahrehheit system, can only be learned through experience. The following may help to orient you with regard to temperatures you normally encounter.

0″ C	Freezing point of water (32″ F)
10″ C	A warm winter day (50″ F)
20″ C	A mild spring day (68″ F)
30″ C	Quite warm — almost hot (86″ F)
37″ C	Normal body temperature (98.6″ F)
40″ C	Heat wave conditions (104″ F)
100″ C	Boiling point of water (212″ F)

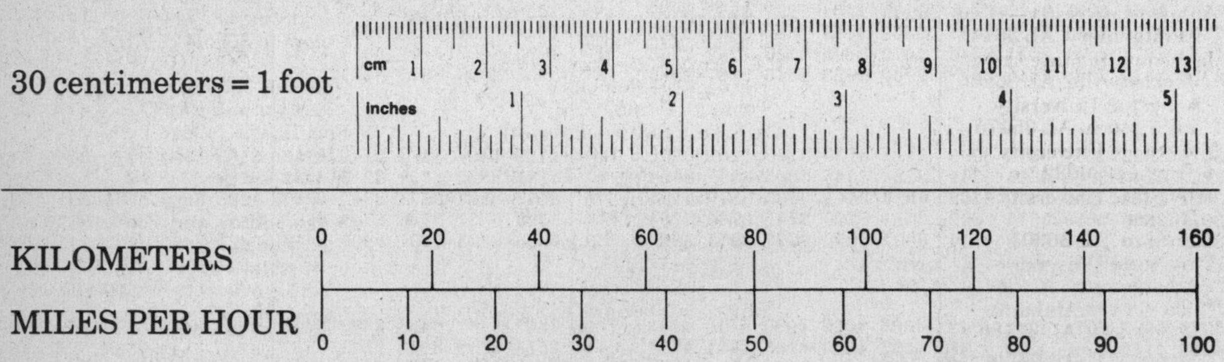

Inches	Millimeters
1/32	.79
1/16	1.59
1/8	3.175
1/4	6.35
3/8	9.53
1/2	12.7
5/8	15.88
3/4	19.05
7/8	22.3
1.0	25.4
1 1/2	38.1
2.0	50.8
2 1/2	63.5
3.0	76.2
3 1/2	88.9
4.0	101.6
4 1/2	114.3
5.0	127.0
5 1/2	139.7
6.0	152.4
6 1/2	165.1
7.0	177.8
7 1/2	190.5
8.0	203.2
8 1/2	215.9
9.0	228.6
9 1/2	241.3
10.0	254.0
10 1/2	266.7
11.0	279.4
11 1/2	292.1
12.0	304.8

Feet	Meters
1	0.3
2	0.6
3	0.9
4	1.2
5	1.5
6	1.8
7	2.1
8	2.4
9	2.7
10	3.0
15	4.6
20	6.1
25	7.6
30	9.1
35	10.7
40	12.2
45	13.7
50	15.2
55	16.8
60	18.3
65	19.8
70	21.3
75	22.9
80	24.4
85	25.9
90	27.4
95	29.0
100	30.5

Pounds	Kilograms
1	0.5
2	0.9
3	1.4
4	1.8
5	2.3
6	2.7
7	3.2
8	3.6
9	4.1
10	4.5
11	5.0
12	5.4
13	5.9
14	6.4
15	6.8
16	7.3
17	7.7
18	8.2
19	8.6
20	9.1
25	11.34
30	13.61
40	18.14
50	22.68
60	27.22
70	31.75
80	36.29
90	40.82
100	45.36

Ounces	Grams
1/4	7.1
1/2	14.2
3/2	21.3
1	28.4
2	56.7
3	85.0
4	113.4
5	141.7
6	170.1
7	198.4
8	226.8
9	255.1
10	283.5
11	311.8
12	340.2
13	368.5
14	396.9
15	425.2
16	453.6

Pints	Liters
1/2	.236
1.0	.473
1 1/2	.709
2.0	.946
2 1/2	1.183
3.0	1.419
3 1/2	1.656
4.0	1.893
4 1/2	2.129
5.0	2.366
5 1/2	2.602
6.0	2.839
6 1/2	3.075
7.0	3.312
7 1/2	3.549
8.0	3.786

Gallons	Liters
1	3.8
2	7.6
3	11.4
4	15.1
5	18.9
6	22.7
7	26.5
8	30.3
9	34.1
10	37.9
11	41.6
12	45.4
13	49.2
14	53.0
15	56.8
16	60.6
17	64.3
18	68.1
19	71.9
20	75.7
30	113.6
40	151.4
50	189.3
60	227.1
70	264.9
80	302.8
90	340.7
100	378.5

Four-Year Colleges and Universities

Four-Year Public Colleges and Universities

Alabama

Alabama A and M University
Normal, AL 35762
Alabama State University
Montgomery, AL 36195
Athens State College
Athens, AL 35611
Auburn University
Auburn University, AL 36849
Auburn University—Montgomery
Montgomery, AL 36117
Jacksonville State University
Jacksonville, AL 36265
Livingston University
Livingston, AL 35470
Troy State University
Troy, AL 36082
Troy State University—Dothan/Ft. Rucker
Dothan, AL 36301
Troy State University—Montgomery
Montgomery, AL 36104
University of Alabama
University, AL 35486
University of Alabama—Birmingham
Birmingham, AL 35294
University of Alabama—Huntsville
Huntsville, AL 35807
University of Montevallo
Montevallo, AL 35115
University of North Alabama
Florence, AL 35632
University of South Alabama
Mobile, AL 36688

Alaska

University of Alaska—Anchorage
Anchorage, AK 99504
University of Alaska—Fairbanks
Fairbanks, AK 99701
University of Alaska—Juneau
Juneau, AK 99803

Arizona

Arizona State University
Tempe, AZ 85281
Northern Arizona University
Flagstaff, AZ 86011
University of Arizona
Tucson, AZ 85721

Arkansas

Arkansas State University
State University, AR 72467
Arkansas Tech University
Russellville, AR 72801
Henderson State University
Arkadelphia, AR 71923
Southern Arkansas University
Magnolia, AR 71753
University of Arkansas
Fayetteville, AR 72701
University of Arkansas—Little Rock
Little Rock, AR 72204
University of Arkansas—Monticello
Monticello, AR 71655
University of Arkansas—Pine Bluff
Pine Bluff, AR 71601
University of Central Arkansas
Conway, AR 72032

California

California State College—Bakersfield
Bakersfield, CA 93309
California State College—San Bernadino
San Bernadino, CA 92407
California State College—Stanislaus
Turlock, CA 95380
California State Polytechnic University—Pomona
Pomona, CA 91768
California State Polytechnic University—San Luis Obispo
San Luis Obispo, CA 93407
California State University—Chico
Chico, CA 95929
California State University—Dominquez Hills
Carson, CA 90747
California State University—Fresno
Fresno, CA 93740
California State University—Fullerton
Fullerton, CA 92634
California State University—Hayward
Hayward, CA 94542
California State University—Long Beach
Long Beach, CA 90840
California State University—Los Angeles
Los Angeles, CA 90032
California State University—Northridge
Northridge, CA 91330
California State University—Sacramento
Sacramento, CA 95819
Claremont Men's College
Claremont, CA 91711
Humboldt State University
Arcata, CA 95521
National University
San Diego, CA 92108
San Diego State University
Calexico, CA 92231
San Diego State University
San Diego, CA 92182
San Francisco State University
San Francisco, CA 94132
San Jose State University
San Jose, CA 95192
Sonoma State University
Rohnert Park, CA 94928
University of California—Berkeley
Berkeley, CA 94720
University of California—Davis
Davis, CA 95616
University of California—Irvine
Irvine, CA 92717
University of California—Los Angeles
Los Angeles, CA 90024
University of California—Riverside
Riverside, CA 92521
University of California—San Diego
La Jolla, CA 92093
University of California—Santa Barbara
Santa Barbara, CA 93106
University of California—Santa Cruz
Santa Cruz, CA 95064

Colorado

Adams State College
Alamosa, CO 81102
Colorado School of Mines
Golden, CO 80401
Colorado State University
Fort Collins, CO 80523
Fort Lewis College
Durango, CO 81301
Mesa College
Grand Junction, CO 81501
Metropolitan State College
Denver, CO 80204
United States Air Force Academy
USAF Academy, CO 80840
University of Colorado
Boulder, CO 80309
University of Colorado Springs—Colorado Springs
Colorado Springs, CO 80907
University of Colorado—Denver
Denver, CO 80202
University of Northern Colorado
Greeley, CO 80639
University of Southern Colorado
Pueblo, CO 81001
Western State College of Colorado
Gunnison, CO 81230

Connecticut

Central Connecticut State College
New Britain, CT 06050
East Connecticut State College
Willimantic, CT 06226
Southern Connecticut State College
New Haven, CT 06515
United States Coast Guard Academy
New London, CT 06320
University of Connecticut
Storrs, CT 06268
Western Connecticut State College
Danbury, CT 06810

Delaware

Delaware State College
Dover, DE 19901

District Of Columbia

University of the District of Columbia
Washington, DC 20004

Florida

Florida A and M University
Tallahassee, FL 32307
Florida Atlantic University
Boca Raton, FL 33431
Florida International University
Miami, FL 33199
Florida State University
Tallahassee, FL 32306

Fort Lauderdale College
Fort Lauderdale, FL 33301
New College of the University of South Florida
Sarasota, FL 33580
Panama Canal College
APO Miami, FL 34002
University of Florida
Gainesville, FL 32611
University of North Florida
Jacksonville, FL 32216
University of South Florida
Tampa, FL 33620
University of West Florida
Pensacola, FL 32504

Georgia

Albany State College
Albany, GA 31705
Armstrong State College
Savannah, GA 31406
Augusta College
Augusta, GA 30910
Columbus College
Columbus, GA 31993
Fort Valley State College
Fort Valley, GA 31030
Georgia College
Milledgeville, GA 31601
Georgia Institute of Technology
Atlanta, GA 30332
Georgia Southern College
Statesboro, GA 30458
Georgia Southwestern College
Americus, GA 31709
Georgia State University
Athens, GA 30303
Kennesaw College
Marietta, GA 30061
Medical College of Georgia
Augusta, GA 30912
North Georgia College
Dahlonega, GA 30533
Savannah State College
Savannah, GA 31404
Southern Technical Institute
Marietta, GA 30060
University of Georgia
Athens, GA 30602
Valdosta State College
Valdosta, GA 31601
West Georgia College
Carrollton, GA 30118

Hawaii

University of Hawaii—College of Arts and Sciences
Hilo, HI 96720
University of Hawaii—Manoa
Honolulu, HI 96822
University of Hawaii—West Oahu College
Aiea, HI 96701

Idaho

Boise State University
Boise, ID 83725
Idaho State University
Pocatello, ID 83209
Lewis-Clark State College
Lewiston, ID 83501
University of Idaho
Moscow, ID 83843

Illinois

Chicago State University
Chicago, IL 60628
Eastern Illinois University
Charleston, IL 61920
Governors State University
Park Forest South, IL 60466
Illinois State University
Normal, IL 61761
National American Educational Service (s)
Chicago, IL 60640
Northeastern Illinois University
Chicago, IL 60625
Northern Illinois University
DeKalb, IL 60115
Sangamon State University
Springfield, IL 62708
Southern Illinois University
Edwardsville, IL 62026
Southern Illinois University—Carbondale
Carbondale, IL 62901
University of Illinois—Chicago Circle
Chicago, IL 60680
University of Illinois—Medical Center
Chicago, IL 60612
University of Illinois—Urbana/Champaign
Urbana, IL 61801
Western Illinois University
Macomb, IL 61455

Indiana

Ball State University
Muncie, IN 47306
Indiana State University—Evansville
Evansville, IN 47712
Indiana State University—Terre Haute
Terre Haute, IN 47809
Indiana University—Bloomington
Bloomington, IN 47405
Indiana University—Kokomo
Kokomo, IN 46901
Indiana University—Purdue University at Fort Wayne
Fort Wayne, IN 46805
Indiana University—Purdue University at Indianapolis
Indianapolis, IN 46202
Indiana University—South Bend
South Bend, IN 46615
Indiana University—Southeast
New Albany, IN 47150
Purdue University
West Lafayette, IN 47907
Purdue University—Calumet
Hammond, IN 46323
Purdue University—North Central
Westville, IN 46391

Iowa

Iowa State University
Ames, IA 50011
University of Iowa
Iowa City, IA 52242
University of Northern Iowa
Cedar Falls, IA 50613

Kansas

Emporia State University
Emporia, KS 66801
Fort Hays State University
Hays, KS 67601
Kansas State University
Manhattan, KS 66506
Pittsburg State University
Pittsburg, KS 66762
United States Army Command and General Staff College
Fort Leavenworth, KS 66027
University of Kansas
Lawrence, KS 66045
University of Kansas—College of Health Sciences and Hospital
Kansas City, KS 66103
Wichita State University
Wichita, KS 67204

Kentucky

Eastern Kentucky University
Richmond, KY 40475
Kentucky State University
Frankfort, KY 40601
Murray State University
Murray, KY 42071
Northern Kentucky University
Highland Heights, KY 41076
University of Kentucky
Lexington, KY 40506
University of Louisville
Louisville, KY 40208
Western Kentucky University
Bowling Green, KY 42101

Louisiana

Grambling State University
Grambling, LA 71245
Louisiana State University—A and M College
Baton Rouge, LA 70803
Louisiana State University—Shreveport
Shreveport, LA 71115
Louisiana Tech University
Ruston, LA 71272
McNeese State University
Lake Charles, LA 70609
Nicholls State University
Thibodaux, LA 70310
Northeast Louisiana University
Monroe, LA 71209
Northwestern State University
Natchitoches, LA 71457
Southeastern Louisiana University
Hammond, LA 70402
Southern University—Baton Rouge
Baton Rouge, LA 70813
Southern University—New Orleans
New Orleans, LA 70126
University of New Orleans
New Orleans, LA 70122
University of Southwestern Louisiana
Lafayette, LA 70504

Maine

Maine Maritime Academy
Castine, ME 04421
University of Maine—Augusta
Augusta, ME 04330
University of Maine—Farmington
Farmington, ME 04938
University of Maine—Fort Kent
Fort Kent, ME 04743
University of Maine—Machias
Machias, ME 04654

University of Maine—Orono
Orono, ME 04473
University of Maine—Presque Isle
Presque Isle, ME 04769
University of Southern Maine
Gorham, ME 04038

Maryland

Bowie State College
Bowie, MD 20715
Coppin State College
Baltimore, MD 21216
Frostburg State College
Frostburg, MD 21532
Morgan State University
Baltimore, MD 21239
Salisbury State College
Salisbury, MD 21801
St. Mary's College of Maryland
St. Mary's City, MD 20686
Towson State University
Towson, MD 21204
United States Naval Academy
Annapolis, MD 21402
University of Baltimore
Baltimore, MD 21201
University of Maryland—Baltimore County
Baltimore, MD 21228
University of Maryland—College Park
College Park, MD 20742
University of Maryland—Eastern Shore
Princess Anne, MD 28153
University of Maryland—University College
College Park, MD 20742

Massachusetts

Boston State College
Boston, MA 02115
Bridgewater State College
Bridgewater, MA 02324
Fitchburg State College
Fitchburg, MA 01420
Framingham State College
Framingham, MA 01701
Massachusetts College of Art
Boston, MA 02215
Massachusetts Maritime Academy
Buzzards Bay, MA 02532
North Adams State College
North Adams, MA 01247
Salem State College
Salem, MA 01970
Southeastern Massachusetts University
North Dartmouth, MA 02747
University of Lowell
Lowell, MA 01854
University of Massachusetts—Amherst
Amherst, MA 01003
University of Massachusetts—Boston
Boston, MA 02125
Westfield State College
Westfield, MA 01085
Worcester State College
Worcester, MA 01602

Michigan

Central Michigan University
Mount Pleasant, MI 48858
Eastern Michigan University
Ypsilanti, MI 48197
Ferris State College
Big Rapids, MI 49307
Grand Valley State Colleges
Allendale, MI 49401
Lake Superior State College
Sault Ste. Marie, MI 49783
Michigan State University
East Lansing, MI 48824
Michigan Technological University
Houghton, MI 49931
Northern Michigan University
Marquette, MI 49855
Oakland University
Rochester, MI 48063
Saginaw Valley State College
University Center, MI 48710
University of Michigan—Ann Arbor
Ann Arbor, MI 48109
University of Michigan—Dearborn
Dearborn, MI 48128
University of Michigan—Flint
Flint, MI 48503
Wayne State University
Detroit, MI 48202
Western Michigan University
Kalamazoo, MI 49008

Minnesota

Bemidji State University
Bemidji, MN 56601
Mankato State University
Mankato, MN 56001
Metropolitan State University
St. Paul, MN 55101
Moorhead State University
Moorhead, MN 56560
Southwest State University
Marshall, MN 56258
St. Cloud State University
St. Cloud, MN 56301
University of Minnesota—Duluth
Duluth, MN 55182
University of Minnesota—Morris
Morris, MN 56267
University of Minnesota—Twin Cities
Minneapolis, MN 55455
Winona State University
Winona, MN 55987

Mississippi

Alcorn State University
Lorman, MS 39096
Delta State University
Cleveland, MS 38733
Jackson State University
Jackson, MS 39217
Mississippi State University
Mississippi State, MS 39762
Mississippi University for Women
Columbus, MS 39701
Mississippi Valley State University
Itta Bena, MS 38941
University of Mississippi
University, MS 38677
University of Mississippi Medical Center
Jackson, MS 39216
University of Southern Mississippi
Hattiesburg, MS 39401

Missouri

Central Missouri State University
Warren, MO 64093
Missouri Southern State College
Joplin, MO 64801
Missouri Western State College
St. Joseph, MO 64507
Northeast Missouri State University
Kirksville, MO 63501
Northwest Missouri State University
Maryville, MO 64468
Southeast Missouri State University
Cape Girardeau, MO 63701
Southwest Missouri State University
Springfield, MO 65802
University of Missouri—Columbia
Columbia, MO 65201
University of Missouri—Kansas City
Kansas City, MO 64110
University of Missouri—Rolla
Rolla, MO 65401
University of Missouri—St. Louis
St. Louis, MO 63121

Montana

Eastern Montana College
Billings, MT 59101
Montana College of Mineral Science and Technology
Butte, MT 59701
Montana State University
Bozeman, MT 59717
Northern Montana College
Havre, MT 59501
University of Montana
Missoula, MT 59812
Western Montana College
Dillon, MT 59725

Nebraska

Chadron State College
Chadron, NE 69357
Kearney State College
Kearney, NE 68847
Peru State College
Peru, NE 68421
University of Nebraska—Lincoln
Lincoln, NE 68508
University of Nebraska—Omaha
Omaha, NE 68182
Wayne State College
Wayne, NE 68787

Nevada

University of Nevada—Las Vegas
Las Vegas, NV 89150
University of Nevada—Reno
Reno, NV 89557

New Hampshire

Keene State College
Keene, NH 03431
Plymouth State College
Plymouth, NH 03264
University of New Hampshire
Durham, NH 03824

New Jersey

Glassboro State College
Glassboro, NJ 08028
Jersey City State College
Jersey City, NJ 07305
Montclair State College
Upper Montclair, NJ 07043
New Jersey Institute of Technology
Newark, NJ 07102
Rutgers University—Camden College of Arts and Sciences
Camden, NJ 08102

Rutgers University—College of Engineering
New Brunswick, NJ 08903
Rutgers University—College of Nursing—Newark
Newark, NJ 07102
Rutgers University—College of Pharmacy
New Brunswick, NJ 08903
Rutgers University—Cook College
New Brunswick, NJ 08903
Rutgers University—Douglass College
New Brunswick, NJ 08903
Rutgers University—Livingston College
New Brunswick, NJ 08903
Rutgers University—Mason Gross School of the Arts
New Brunswick, NJ 08903
Rutgers University—Newark College of Arts and Sciences
Newark, NJ 07102
Rutgers University—Rutgers College
New Brunswick, NJ 08903
Rutgers University—University College
New Brunswick, NJ 08903
Trenton State College
Trenton, NJ 08625
William Paterson College
Wayne, NJ 07470

New Mexico

Eastern New Mexico University
Portales, NM 88130
New Mexico Highlands University
Las Vegas, NM 87701
New Mexico Institute of Mining and Technology
Socorro, NM 87801
New Mexico State University
Las Cruces, NM 88003
University of New Mexico
Albuquerque, NM 87131
Western New Mexico University
Silver City, NM 88061

New York

CUNY—Bernard Baruch College
New York, NY 10010
CUNY—Brooklyn College
Brooklyn, NY 11210
CUNY—City College
New York, NY 10031
CUNY—College of Staten Island
Staten Island, NY 10301
CUNY—Hunter College
New York, NY 10021
CUNY—John Jay College of Criminal Justice
New York, NY 10019
CUNY—Lehman College
Bronx, NY 10468
CUNY—Medgar Evers College
Brooklyn, NY 11225
CUNY—Queens College
Flushing, NY 11367
CUNY—York College
Jamaica, NY 11432
SUNY—Albany
Albany, NY 12222
SUNY—Binghamton
Binghamton, NY 13901
SUNY—Buffalo
Buffalo, NY 14214
SUNY—College at Brockport
Brockport, NY 14420
SUNY—College at Buffalo
Buffalo, NY 14222
SUNY—College at Cortland
Cortland, NY 13045
SUNY—College at Fredonia
Fredonia, NY 14063
SUNY—College at Genesco
Genesco, NY 14454
SUNY—College at New Paltz
New Paltz, NY 12561
SUNY—College at Old Westbury
Old Westbury, NY 11568
SUNY—College at Oneonta
Oneonta, NY 13820
SUNY—College at Oswego
Oswego, NY 13126
SUNY—College at Plattsburgh
Plattsburgh, NY 12901
SUNY—College at Potsdam
Potsdam, NY 13676
SUNY—College at Purchase
Purchase, NY 10577
SUNY—College of Agriculture and Life Science at Cornell
Ithaca, NY 14853
SUNY—College of Ceramics at Alfred
Alfred, NY 14802
SUNY—College of Environmental Science and Forestry
Syracuse, NY 13210
SUNY—College of Human Ecology at Cornell
Ithaca, NY 14853
SUNY—College of Technology
Utica, NY 13502
SUNY—Empire State College
Saratoga Springs, NY 12866
SUNY—Fashion Institute of Technology
New York, NY 10001
SUNY—Maritime College
Bronx, NY 10465
SUNY—School of Industrial and Labor Relations at Cornell
Ithaca, NY 14853
SUNY—Stony Brook
Stony Brook, NY 11794
SUNY—Upstate Medical Center
Syracuse, NY 13210
United States Merchant Marine Academy
Kings Point, NY 11024
United States Military Academy
West Point, NY 10996

North Carolina

Appalachian State University
Boone, NC 28608
Davidson College
Davidson, NC 28036
East Carolina University
Greenville, NC 27834
Elizabeth City State University
Elizabeth City, NC 27909
Fayetteville State University
Fayetteville, NC 28303
North Carolina Agricultural and Technical State University
Greensboro, NC 27411
North Carolina Central University
Durham, NC 27707
North Carolina School of the Arts
Winston-Salem, NC 27107
North Carolina State University—Raleigh
Raleigh, NC 27650
Pembroke State University
Pembroke, NC 28372
Salem College
Winston-Salem, NC 27108
University of North Carolina
Ashville, NC 28814
University of North Carolina—Chapel Hill
Chapel Hill, NC 27514
University of North Carolina—Charlotte
Charlotte, NC 28223
University of North Carolina—Greensboro
Greensboro, NC 27412
University of North Carolina—Wilmington
Wilmington, NC 28403
Western Carolina University
Cullowhee, NC 28723
Winston-Salem State University
Winston-Salem, NC 27102

North Dakota

Dickinson State College
Dickinson, ND 58601
Mayville State College
Mayville, ND 58257
Minot State College
Minot, ND 58701
North Dakota State University
Fargo, ND 58105
University of North Dakota
Grand Forks, ND 58202
Valley City State College
Valley City, ND 58072

Ohio

Bowling Green State University
Bowling Green, OH 43403
Central State University
Wilberforce, OH 45384
Cleveland State University
Cleveland, OH 44115
Kent State University
Kent, OH 44242
Miami University
Oxford, OH 45056
Ohio State University
Columbus, OH 43210
Ohio State University—Lima
Lima, OH 45804
Ohio State University—Mansfield
Mansfield, OH 44906
Ohio University
Athens, OH 45701
Ohio University—Lancaster
Lancaster, OH 43130
University of Akron
Akron, OH 44325
University of Cincinnati
Cincinnati, OH 45221
Write State University
Dayton, OH 45435
Youngstown State University
Youngstown, OH 44555

Oklahoma

Central State University
Edmond, OK 73034
East Central Oklahoma State University
Ada, OK 74820

Northeastern Oklahoma State University
Tahleguah, OK 74464
Northwestern Oklahoma State University
Alva, OK 73717
Oklahoma State University
Stillwater, OK 74078
Panhandle State University
Goodwell, OK 73939
Southeastern Oklahoma State University
Durant, OK 74701
Southwestern Oklahoma State University
Weatherford, OK 73096
University of Oklahoma—Health
Oklahoma City, OK 73190
University of Oklahoma—Norman
Norman, OK 73019
University of Science and Arts of Oklahoma
Chickasha, OK 73018

OREGON

Eastern Oregon State College
La Grande, OR 97850
Oregon College of Education
Monmouth, OR 97361
Oregon Institute of Technology
Klamath Falls, OR 97601
Oregon State University
Corvallis, OR 97331
Portland State University
Portland, OR 97207
Southern Oregon State College
Ashland, OR 97520
University of Oregon
Eugene, OR 97403
University of Oregon—Health
Portland, OR 97201

PENNSYLVANIA

Bloomsburg State College
Bloomsburg, PA 17815
California State College
California, PA 15419
Cheyney State College
Cheyney, PA 19319
Clarion State College
Clarion, PA 16214
East Stroudsbury State College
East Stroudsbury, PA 18301
Edinboro State College
Edinboro, PA 16412
Grove City College
Grove City, PA 16127
Indiana University of Pennsylvania
Indiana, PA 15705
Kutztown State College
Kutztown, PA 19530
Lock Haven State College
Lock Haven, PA 17745
Mansfield State College
Mansfield, PA 16933
Millersville State College
Millersville, PA 17551
Pennsylvania State University
University Park, PA 16802
Pennsylvania State University—Behrend
Erie, PA 16563
Pennsylvania State University—Capitol
Middletown, PA 17057
Shippensburg State College
Shippensburg, PA 17257
Slippery Rock State College
Slippery Rock, PA 16057
Temple University
Philadelphia, PA 19122
West Chester State College
West Chester, PA 19380

RHODE ISLAND

Rhode Island College
Providence, RI 02908
University of Rhode Island
Kingston, RI 02881

SOUTH CAROLINA

Clemson University
Clemson, SC 29631
College of Charleston
Charleston, SC 29401
Francis Marion College
Florence, SC 29501
South Carolina State College
Orangeburg, SC 29117
The Citadel
Charleston, SC 29409
University of South Carolina
Columbia, SC 29208
University of South Carolina—Aiken
Aiken, SC 29801
University of South Carolina—Coastal Carolina
Conway, SC 29526
University of South Carolina—Spartanburg
Spartanburg, SC 29303
Winthrop College
Rock Hill, SC 29733
Wofford College
Spartanburg, SC 29301

SOUTH DAKOTA

Black Hills State College
Spearfish, SD 57783
Dakota State College
Madison, SD 57042
Northern State College
Aberdeen, SD 57401
South Dakota School of Mines and Technology
Rapid City, SD 57701
South Dakota State University
Brookings, SD 57006
University of South Dakota
Vermillion, SD 57069
University of South Dakota of Springfield
Springfield, SD 57062

TENNESSEE

Austin Peay State University
Clarksville, TN 37040
East Tennessee State University
Johnson City, TN 37614
Memphis State University
Memphis, TN 38152
Middle Tennessee State University
Murfreesboro, TN 37132
Tennessee State University
Nashville, TN 37203
Tennessee Technological University
Cookeville, TN 38501
University of Tennessee—Center for the Health Sciences
Memphis, TN 38163
University of Tennessee—Chattanooga
Chattanooga, TN 37401
University of Tennessee—Knoxville
Knoxville, TN 37916
University of Tennessee—Martin
Martin, TN 38238

TEXAS

Angelo State University
San Angelo, TX 76909
Corpus Christi State University
Corpus Christi, TX 78412
East Texas State University
Commerce, TX 75428
Lamar University
Beaumont, TX 77710
Laredo State University
Laredo, TX 78040
Midwestern State University
Wichita Falls, TX 76308
North Texas State University
Denton, TX 76203
Pan American University
Edinburg, TX 78539
Prairie View A and M University
Prairie View, TX 77445
Sam Houston State University
Huntsville, TX 77340
Southwest Texas State University
San Marcos, TX 78666
Stephen F. Austin State University
Nacogdoches, TX 75962
Sul Ross State University
Alpine, TX 79830
Sul Ross State University—Uvalde Study Center
Uvalde, TX 78801
Tarleton State University
Stephenville, TX 76402
Texas A and I University—Kingsville
Kingsville, TX 78363
Texas A and M University
College Station, TX 77843
Texas A and M University at Galveston
Galveston, TX 77553
Texas Southern University
Houston, TX 77004
Texas Tech University
Lubbock, TX 79409
Texas Woman's University
Denton, TX 76204
University of Houston
Houston, TX 77004
University of Houston—Clear Lake City
Houston, TX 77058
University of Houston—Downtown
Houston, TX 77002
University of Houston—Victoria
Victoria, TX 77901
University of St. Thomas
Houston, TX 77006
University of Texas—Arlington
Arlington, TX 76019
University of Texas—Austin
Austin, TX 78712
University of Texas—Dallas
Richardson, TX 75080
University of Texas—El Paso
El Paso, TX 79968
University of Texas—Health Science Center—San Antonio
San Antonio, TX 78284

University of Texas Medical Branch—Galveston
Galveston, TX 77550
University of Texas—Permian Basin
Odessa, TX 79762
University of Texas—San Antonio
San Antonio, TX 78285
University of Texas—Tyler
Tyler, TX 75701
West Texas State University
Canyon, TX 79016

UTAH

Southern Utah State College
Cedar City, UT 84720
Utah State University
Logan, UT 84322
Weber State College
Ogden, UT 84408

VERMONT

Castleton State College
Castleton, VT 05735
Johnson State College
Johnson, VT 05656
Southern Vermont College
Bennington, VT 05201
University of Vermont
Burlington, VT 05405

VIRGINIA

Christopher Newport College
Newport News, VA 23606
College of William and Mary
Williamsburg, VA 23185
George Mason University
Fairfax, VA 22030
James Madison University
Harrisonburg, VA 22801
Norfolk State University
Norfolk, VA 23504
Old Dominion University
Norfolk, VA 23508
University of Virginia—Clinch
Wise, VA 24293
Virginia Military Institute
Lexington, VA 24450
Virginia Polytechnic Institute and State University
Blacksburg, VA 24061
Virginia State University
Petersburg, VA 23803

WASHINGTON

Central Washington University
Ellensburg, WA 98926
City College
Seattle, WA 98104
Eastern Washington University
Cheney, WA 99004
Evergreen State College
Olympia, WA 98505
University of Washington
Seattle, WA 98105
Washington State University
Pullman, WA 99164
Western Washington University
Bellingham, WA 98225

WEST VIRGINIA

Bluefield State College
Bluefield, WV 24701
Concord College
Athens, WV 24712
Fairmont State College
Fairmont, WV 26554
Glenville State College
Glenville, WV 26531
Marshall University
Huntington, WV 25705
Shepherd College
Shepherdstown, WV 25443
West Liberty State College
West Liberty, WV 26074
West Virginia Institute of Technology
Montgomery, WV 25136
West Virginia State College
Charleston, WV 25312
West Virginia University
Morgantown, WV 26506

WISCONSIN

University of Wisconsin—Eau Claire
Eau Claire, WI 54701
University of Wisconsin—Green Bay
Green Bay, WI 54302
University of Wisconsin—La Crosse
La Crosse, WI 54601
University of Wisconsin—Madison
Madison, WI 53706
University of Wisconsin—Milwaukee
Milwaukee, WI 53201
University of Wisconsin—Oshkosh
Oshkosh, WI 54901
University of Wisconsin—Parkside
Kenosha, WI 53141
University of Wisconsin—Platteville
Platteville, WI 53818
University of Wisconsin—River Falls
River Falls, WI 54022
University of Wisconsin—Stevens Point
Stevens Point, WI 54481
University of Wisconsin—Stout
Menomonie, WI 54751
University of Wisconsin—Superior
Superior, WI 54880
University of Wisconsin—Whitewater
Whitewater, WI 53190

WYOMING

University of Wyoming
Laramie, WY 82071

GUAM

University of Guam
Mangilao, Guam 96913

PUERTO RICO

Bayamon Central University
Bayamon, PR 00619

VIRGIN ISLANDS

College of the Virgin Islands
St. Thomas, VI 00801

Four-Year Private Colleges and Universities

ALABAMA

Birmingham-Southern College
Birmingham, AL 35204
Gately Christian University
Guntersville, AL 35976
Huntingdon College
Montgomery, AL 36106
International Bible College
Florence, AL 35630
Judson College
Marion, AL 36756
Miles College
Birmingham, AL 35208
Mobile College
Mobile, AL 36613
Oakwood College
Huntsville, AL 35806
Samford University
Birmingham, AL 35229
Selma University
Selma, AL 36701
Southeastern Bible College
Birmingham, AL 35256
Spring Hill College
Mobile, AL 36608
Stillman College
Tuscaloosa, AL 35401
Talladega College
Talladega, AL 35160
Tuskegee Institute
Tuskegee, AL 36088

ALASKA

Alaska Bible College
Glennallen, AK 99588
Alaska Pacific University
Anchorage, AK 99504
Sheldon Jackson College
Sitka, AK 99835

ARIZONA

Arizona College of the Bible
Phoenix, AZ 85021
Devry Institute of Technology
Phoenix, AZ 85016
Embry-Riddle Aeronautical University
Prescott, AZ 86301
Grand Canyon College
Phoenix, AZ 85017
Southwestern Baptist College
Phoenix, AZ 85032

University of Phoenix
Phoenix, AZ 85004
Western International University
Phoenix, AZ 85021

Arkansas

Arkansas Baptist College
Little Rock, AR 72202
Arkansas College
Batesville, AR 72501
Central Baptist College
Conway, AR 72032
College of the Ozarks
Clarksville, AR 72830
Harding University
Searcy, AR 72143
Hendrix College
Conway, AR 72023
John Brown University
Siloam Springs, AR 72761
Ouachita Baptist University
Arkadelphia, AR 71923
Philander Smith College
Little Rock, AR 72203

California

Ambassador College
Pasadena, CA 91123
Antioch University—West
San Francisco, CA 94108
Armstrong College
Berkeley, CA 94704
Art Center College of Design
Pasadena, CA 91103
Azusa Pacific College
Azusa, CA 91702
Bethany Bible College
Santa Cruz, CA 95066
Biola College
La Mirada, CA 90639
Brooks Institute
Santa Barbara, CA 93108
California Baptist College
Riverside, CA 92504
California Christian College
Fresno, CA 93703
California College of Arts and Crafts
Oakland, CA 94618
California College of Commerce
Long Beach, CA 90813
California Institute of Technology
Pasadena, CA 91125
California Institute of the Arts
Valencia, CA 91355
California Lutheran College
Thousand Oaks, CA 91360
California Maritime Academy
Vallejo, CA 94590
Center for Early Education
Los Angeles, CA 90048
Chapman College
Orange, CA 92666
Christ College Irvine
Irvine, CA 92715
Christian Heritage College
El Cajon, CA 92021
Cogswell College
San Francisco, CA 94108
Coleman College
La Mesa, CA 92041
College of Notre Dame
Belmont, CA 94002
Columbia College
Los Angeles, CA 90038
Dominican College of San Rafael
San Rafael, CA 94901
Dominican School of Philosophy and Theology
Berkeley, CA 95709
Fresno Pacific College
Fresno, CA 93702
Golden Gate University
San Francisco, CA 94105
Harvey Mudd College
Claremont, CA 91711
Heald Engineering College
San Francisco, CA 94109
Hebrew Union College
Los Angeles, CA 90007
Holy Family College
Fermont, CA 94538
Holy Names College
Oakland, CA 94619
John F. Kennedy University—Evenings
Orinda, CA 94563
L.I.F.E. Bible College
Los Angeles, CA 90026
Lincoln University
San Francisco, CA 94118
Loma Linda University
Loma, CA 92350
Loma Linda University—La Sierra
Riverside, CA 92515
Los Angeles Baptist College
Newhall, CA 91322
Loyola Marymount University
Los Angeles, CA 90045
Menlo College
Menlo Park, CA 94025
Mills College
Oakland, CA 94613
Monterey Institute of International Studies
Monterey, CA 93940
Mount St. Mary's College
Los Angeles, CA 90049
Music and Arts Institute of San Francisco
San Francisco, CA 94115
New College of California
San Francisco, CA 94110
Northrop University
Inglewood, CA 90306
Occidental College
Los Angeles, CA 90041
Otis Art Institute of Parsons School of Design
Los Angeles, CA 90057
Pacific Christian College
Fullerton, CA 92631
Pacific Oaks College
Pasadena, CA 91103
Pacific States University
Los Angeles, CA 90006
Pacific Union College
Angwin, CA 94508
Patten Bible College
Oakland, CA 94601
Pepperdine University
Los Angeles, CA 90044
Pepperdine University—Seaver College
Malibu, CA 90265
Pitzer College
Claremont, CA 91711
Point Loma College
San Diego, CA 92106
Pomona College
Claremont, CA 91711
San Francisco Art Institute
San Francisco, CA 94133
San Francisco Conservatory of Music
San Francisco, CA 94122
San Jose Bible College
San Jose, CA 95108
Scripps College
Claremont, CA 91711
Simpson College
San Francisco, CA 94134
Southern California College
Costa Mesa, CA 92626
Southern California Institute of Architecture
Santa Monica, CA 90404
Stanford University
Stanford, CA 94305
St. Mary's College of California
Moraga, CA 94575
St. Patrick's College
Mountain View, CA 94042
Thomas Aquinas College
Santa Paula, CA 93060
United States International University
San Diego, CA 92131
University of Judaism
Los Angeles, CA 90024
University of La Verne
La Verne, CA 91750
University of Redlands
Redlands, CA 92373
University of San Diego
San Diego, CA 92110
University of San Francisco
San Francisco, CA 94117
University of Santa Clara
Santa Clara, CA 95053
University of Southern California
Los Angeles, CA 90007
University of the Pacific
Stockton, CA 95211
University of West Los Angeles
Culver City, CA 90230
West Coast Bible College
Fresno, CA 93710
West Coast University—Evenings
Los Angeles, CA 90020
West Coast University—Orange County—Evenings
Orange, CA 92668
Western Apostolic Bible College
Stockton, CA 95205
Western States College of Engineering
Inglewood, CA 90301
Westmont College
Santa Barbara, CA 93108
Whittier College
Whittier, CA 90608
Woodbury University
Los Angeles, CA 90017
World College West
San Anselmo, CA 94960
Yeshiva University of Los Angeles
Los Angeles, CA 90035

Colorado

Baptist Bible College of Denver
Broomfield, CO 80020
Belleview College
Westminster, CO 80030
Colorado College
Colorado Springs, CO 80903
Colorado Technical College
Colorado Springs, CO 80907
Colorado Women's College
Denver, CO 80220

Intermountain Bible College
Grand Junction, CO 81501
Loretto Heights College
Denver, CO 80236
Naropa Institute
Boulder, CO 80302
Regis College
Denver, CO 80221
Rockmont College
Denver, CO 80226
University of Denver
Denver, CO 80210
Western Bible College
Morrison, CO 80465

CONNECTICUT

Albertus Magnus College
New Haven, CT 06511
Bridgeport Engineering Institute
Bridgeport, CT 06606
Connecticut College
New London, CT 06320
Fairfield University
Fairfield, CT 06430
Holy Apostles College
Cromwell, CT 06416
Post College
Waterbury, CT 06708
Quinniplac College
Hamden, CT 06518
Sacred Heart University
Bridgeport, CT 06606
St. Alphonsus College
Suffield, CT 06078
St. Basil's College
Stamford, CT 06902
St. Joseph College
West Hartford, CT 06117
Trinity College
Hartford, CT 06106
University of Bridgeport
Bridgeport, CT 06602
University of Hartford
West Hartford, CT 06117
University of New Haven
West Haven, CT 06516
Wesleyan University
Middletown, CT 06457
Yale University
New Haven, CT 06520

DELAWARE

Goldey Beacom College
Wilmington, DE 19808
University of Delaware
Newark, DE 19711
Wesley College
Dover, DE 19901
Wilmington College
New Castle, DE 19720

DISTRICT OF COLUMBIA

Beacon College
Washington, DC 20009
Benjamin Franklin University
Washington, DC 20036
Catholic University of America
Washington, DC 20064
Corcoran School of Art
Washington, DC 20006
Georgetown University
Washington, DC 20057
George Washington University
Washington, DC 20052
Howard University
Washington, DC 20059
Mount Vernon College
Washington, DC 20007
Oblate College
Washington, DC 20017
Southeastern University
Washington, DC 20024
Strayer College
Washington, DC 20005
The American University
Washington, DC 20016
Trinity College
Washington, DC 20017
Washington International College
Washington, DC 20006

FLORIDA

Barry College
Miami Shores, FL 33161
Bethune-Cookman College
Daytona Beach, FL 32015
Biscayne College
Miami, FL 33054
Clearwater Christian College
Clearwater, FL 33519
College of the Palm Beaches
West Palm Beach, FL 33402
Eckerd College
St. Petersburg, FL 33733
Edward Waters College
Jacksonville, FL 32209
Flagler College
St. Augustine, FL 32084
Florida Beacon College
Largo, FL 33541
Florida Institute of Technology
Melbourne, FL 32901
Florida Institute of Technology—School of Applied Technology
Jensen Beach, FL 33457
Florida Memorial College
Miami, FL 33054
Florida Southern College
Lakeland, FL 33802
Fort Lauderdale College
Fort Lauderdale, FL 33301
Jacksonville University
Jacksonville, FL 32211
Jones College
Orlando, FL 32803
Jones College—Jacksonville
Jacksonville, FL 32211
Miami Christian College
Miami, FL 33167
Nova University
Fort Lauderdale, FL 33314
Palm Beach Atlantic College
West Palm Beach, FL 33401
Ringling School of Art
Sarasota, FL 33580
Rollins College
Winter Park, FL 32789
Southeastern College
Lakeland, FL 33801
Stetson University
Deland, FL 32720
St. John Vianney College Seminary
Miami, FL 33165
St. Leo College
St. Leo, FL 33574
Tampa College Medical Education Center
Tampa, FL 33609
Trinity College
Dunedin, FL 33528
University of Central Florida
Orlando, FL 32816
University of Miami
Coral Gables, FL 33124
University of Sarasota
Sarasota, FL 33577
University of Tampa
Tampa, FL 33606
Warner Southern College
Lake Wales, FL 33853
Webber College
Babson Park, FL 33827

GEORGIA

Agnes Scott College
Decatur, GA 30030
Atlanta Christian College
East Point, GA 30344
Atlanta College of Art
Atlanta, GA 30309
Berry College
Mount Berry, GA 30149
Beulah Heights Bible College
Atlanta, GA 30316
Brenau College
Gainesville, GA 30501
Carver Bible Institute and College
Atlanta, GA 30313
Clark College
Atlanta, GA 30314
Emmanuel College School of Christian Ministries
Franklin Springs, GA 30639
Emory University
Atlanta, GA 30322
Georgia College
Milledgeville, GA 31601
La Grange College
La Grange, GA 30240
Mercer University—Atlanta
Atlanta, GA 30341
Mercer University School of Pharmacy
Atlanta, GA 30312
Morehouse College
Atlanta, GA 30314
Morris Brown College
Atlanta, GA 30314
Oglethorpe University
Atlanta, GA 30319
Paine College
Augusta, GA 30910
Piedmont College
Demorest, GA 30535
Shorter College
Rome, GA 30161
Spelman College
Atlanta, GA 30314
Tift College
Forsyth, GA 31029
Toccoa Falls College
Toccoa Falls, GA 30598
Wesleyan College
Macon, GA 31297

HAWAII

Brigham Young University—Hawaii
Laie Oahu, HI 96762
Chaminade University of Honolulu
Honolulu, HI 96816
Hawaii Loa College
Kaneohe, HI 96744
Hawaii Pacific College
Honolulu, HI 96744
International College
Honolulu, HI 96809

IDAHO

College of Idaho
Caldwell, ID 83605
Northwest Nazarene College
Nampa, ID 83651

ILLINOIS

Aero-Space Institute
Chicago, IL 60610
Antioch—Native American Educational Services
Chicago, IL 60640
Augustana College
Rock Island, IL 61201
Aurora College
Aurora, IL 60507
Barat College
Lake Forest, IL 60045
Blackburn College
Carlinville, IL 62626
Bradley University
Peoria, IL 61625
College of St. Francis
Joliet, IL 60435
Columbia College
Chicago, IL 60605
Concordia College
River Fores, IL 60305
De Lourdes College
Des Plaines, IL 60016
DePaul University
Chicago, IL 60604
DeVry Institute of Technology
Chicago, IL 60618
Elmhurst College
Elmhurst, IL 60126
Eureka College
Eureka, IL 61530
George Williams College
Downers Grove, IL 60515
Greenville College
Greenville, IL 62246
Hebrew Theological College
Skokie, IL 60076
Illinois Benedictine College
Lisle, IL 60532
Illinois College
Jacksonville, IL 62650
Illinois Institute of Technology
Chicago, IL 60616
Illinois Wesleyan University
Bloomington, IL 61701
Judson College
Elgin, IL 60120
Kendall College
Evanston, IL 60201
Knox College
Galesburg, IL 61401
Lake Forest College
Lake Forest, IL 60045
Lewis University
Romeoville, IL 60441
Lincoln Christian College
Lincoln, IL 62656
Loyola University of Chicago
Chicago, IL 60611
MacMurray College
Jacksonville, IL 62650
McKendree College
Lebanon, IL 62258
Midwest College of Engineering
Lombard, IL 60148
Millikin University
Decatur, IL 62522
Monmouth College
Monmouth, IL 61462
Moody Bible Institute
Chicago, IL 60610
Morrison Institute of Technology
Morrison, IL 61270
Mundelein College
Chicago, IL 60660
National American Educational Service(s)
Chicago, IL 60640
National College of Chiropractic
Lombard, IL 60148
National College of Education
Evanston, IL 60201
National College of Education—Urbana
Chicago, IL 60601
North Central College
Naperville, IL 60566
North Park College
Chicago, IL 60625
Northwestern University
Evanston, IL 60201
Olivet Nazarene College
Kankakee, IL 60901
Parks College of Aeronautical Technology of St. Louis University
Cahokia, IL 62206
Principia College
Elsah, IL 62028
Quincy College
Quincy, IL 62301
Rockford College
Rockford, IL 61101
Roosevelt University
Chicago, IL 60605
Rosary College
River Forest, IL 60305
Rush University—Colleges of Nursing and Health Sciences
Chicago, IL 60612
Sangamon State University
Springfield, IL 62708
School of the Art Institute of Chicago
Chicago, IL 60603
Sherwood Music School
Chicago, IL 60605
Shimer College
Waukegan, IL 60085
Spertus College of Judaica
Chicago, IL 60605
St. Xavier College
Chicago, IL 60655
Trinity Christian College
Palos Heights, IL 60463
Trinity College
Deerfield, IL 60015
University of Chicago—The College
Chicago, IL 60637
University of Health Sciences—Chicago Medical School
North Chicago, IL 60062
Vandercook College of Music
Chicago, IL 60616
Wheaton College
Wheaton, IL 60187

INDIANA

Anderson College
Anderson, IN 46011
Bethel College
Mishawaka, IN 46544
Butler University
Indianapolis, IN 46208
Calumet College
Whiting, IN 46394
DePauw University
Greencastle, IN 46135
Earlham College
Richmond, IN 47374
Fort Wayne Bible College
Fort Wayne, IN 46807
Franklin College
Franklin, IN 46131
Goshen College
Goshen, IN 46526
Grace College
Winona Lake, IN 46590
Hanover College
Hanover, IN 47243
Huntington College
Huntington, IN 46750
Indiana Central University
Indianapolis, IN 46227
Indiana Institute of Technology
Fort Wayne, IN 46803
Indiana University—Northwest
Gary, IN 46408
Manchester College
North Manchester, IN 46962
Marian College
Indianapolis, IN 46222
Marion College
Marion, IN 46952
Oakland City College
Oakland City, IN 47660
Rose-Hulman Institute of Technology
Terre Haute, IN 47803
St. Francis College
Fort Wayne, IN 46808
St. Joseph's College
Rensselaer, IN 47978
St. Mary-of-the-Woods College
St. Mary-of-the-Woods, IN 47876
St. Mary's College
Notre Dame, IN 46556
St. Meinrad College
St. Meinrad, IN 47577
Taylor University
Upland, IN 46989
Tri-State University
Angola, IN 46703
University of Evansville
Evansville, IN 47702
University of Notre Dame
Notre Dame, IN 46556
Valparaiso Technical Institute
Valparaiso, IN 46383
Valparaiso University
Valparaiso, IN 46383
Wabash College
Crawfordsville, IN 47933

IOWA

Briar Cliff College
Sioux City, IA 51104
Buena Vista College
Storm Lake, IA 50588
Central College
Pella, IA 50219
Clarke College
Dubuque, IA 52001
Coe College
Cedar Rapids, IA 51402
Cornell College
Mount Vernon, IA 52314
Divine Word College
Epworth, IA 52045
Dordt College
Sioux Center, IA 51250
Drake University
Des Moines, IA 50311

Faith Baptist Bible College
Ankeny, IA 50021
Graceland College
Lamoni, IA 50140
Grand View College
Des Moines, IA 50316
Grinnell College
Grinnell, IA 50112
Iowa Wesleyan College
Mt. Pleasant, IA 52641
Loras College
Dubuque, IA 52001
Luther College
Decorah, IA 52101
Meharishi International University
Fairfield, IA 52556
Marycrest College
Davenport, IA 52804
Morningside College
Sioux City, IA 51106
Mount Mercy College
Cedar Rapids, IA 52402
Mount St. Clare College
Clinton, IA 52732
Northwestern College
Orange City, IA 51041
Open Bible College
Des Moines, IA 50321
Simpson College
Indianola, IA 50125
St. Ambrose College
Davenport, IA 52803
St. Joseph Seminary College
St. Benedict, IA 70457
University of Dubuque
Dubuque, IA 52001
Upper Iowa University
Fayette, IA 52142
Vennard College
University Park, IA 52595
Wartburg College
Waverly, IA 50677
Westmar College
Le Mars, IA 51031
William Penn College
Oskaloosa, IA 52577

KANSAS

Baker University
Baldwin City, KS 66006
Benedictine College
Atchison, KS 66002
Bethany College
Lindsborg, KS 67456
Bethel College
North Newton, KS 67114
Friends Bible College
Haviland, KS 67059
Friends University
Wichita, KS 67213
Kansas City College and Bible School
Overland Park, KS 66204
Kansas Newman College
Wichita, KS 67213
Kansas Weselyan
Salina, KS 67401
Manhattan Christian College
Manhattan, KS 66502
Marymount College of Kansas
Salina, KS 67401
McPherson College
McPherson, KS 67460
Mid-America Nazarene College
Olathe, KS 66061
St. Mary College
Leavenworth, KS 66048
Ottawa University
Ottawa, KS 66067
Southwestern College
Winfield, KS 67156
Sterling College
Sterling, KS 67579
St. Mary of the Plains College
Dodge City, KS 67801
Tabor College
Hillsboro, KS 67063
Washburn University of Topeka
Topeka, KS 66621

KENTUCKY

Ashbury College
Wilmore, KY 40390
Bellarmine College
Louisville, KY 40205
Berea College
Berea, KY 40404
Brescia College
Owensboro, KY 42301
Campbellsville College
Campbellsville, KY 42718
Centre College of Kentucky
Danville, KY 40422
Cumberland College
Williamsburg, KY 40769
Georgetown College
Georgetown, KY 40324
Kentucky Christian College
Grayson, KY 41143
Kentucky Wesleyan College
Owensboro, KY 42301
Lexington Baptist College
Lexington, KY 40502
Louisville School of Art
Louisville, KY 40204
Morehead State University
Morehead, KY 40351
Pikeville College
Pikeville, KY 41501
Seminary of St. Pius X
Erlanger, KY 41018
Simmons University Bible College
Louisville, KY 40210
Spalding College
Louisville, KY 40203
Thomas More College
Fort Mitchell, KY 41017
Transylvania University
Lexington, KY 40508
Union College
Barbourville, KY 40906

LOUISIANA

Baptist Christian College
Shreveport, LA 71108
Centenary College of Louisiana
Shreveport, LA 71104
Dillard College
New Orleans, LA 70122
Louisiana College
Pineville, LA 71360
Loyola University
New Orleans, LA 70118
Our Lady of Holy Cross College
New Orleans, LA 70114
St. Mary's Dominican College
New Orleans, LA 70114
Tulane University
New Orleans, LA 70118
Xavier University of Louisiana
New Orleans, LA 70125

MAINE

Bates College
Lewiston, ME 04240
Bowdoin College
Brunswick, ME 04011
Colby College
Waterville, ME 04901
College of the Atlantic
Bar Harbor, ME 04609
Husson College
Bangor, ME 04401
Nasson College
Springvale, ME 04083
New England Baptist Bible College
Portland, ME 04101
Portland School of Art
Portland, ME 04101
St. Joseph's College
North Windham, ME 04062
Thomas College
Waterville, ME 04901
Unity College
Unity, ME 04988
University of New England—St. Francis College
Biddleford, ME 04005
Westbrook College
Portland, ME 04103

MARYLAND

Baltimore Hebrew College
Baltimore, MD 21215
Capitol Institute of Technology
Kensington, MD 20795
College of Notre Dame of Maryland
Baltimore, MD 21210
Columbia Union College
Takoma Park, MD 20012
Goucher College
Towson, MD 21204
Hood College
Frederick, MD 21701
Johns Hopkins University
Baltimore, MD 21218
Loyola College
Baltimore, MD 21210
Maryland Institute of College of Art
Baltimore, MD 21217
Mount Saint Mary's College
Emmitsburg, MD 21727
Peabody Conservatory of Music
Baltimore, MD 21202
St. John's College
Annapolis, MD 21404
St. Mary's Seminary and College
Baltimore, MD 21210
Washington Bible College
Lanham, MD 20801
Washington College
Chestertown, MD 21620
Western Maryland College
Westminster, MD 21157

MASSACHUSETTS

American International College
Springfield, MA 01109
Amherst College
Amherst, MA 01102
Anna Maria College
Paxton, MA 01612
Assumption College
Worcester, MA 01609
Atlantic Union College
South Lancaster, MA 01561

Babson College
Wellesley, MA 02157
Bentley College
Waltham, MA 02154
Berklee College of Music
Boston, MA 02215
Berkshire Christian College
Lenox, MA 01240
Boston College
Chestnut Hill, MA 02167
Boston Conservatory of Music
Boston, MA 02115
Boston University
Boston, MA 02215
Bradford College
Bradford, MA 01830
Brandeis University
Waltham, MA 02254
Central New England College of Technology
Worcester, MA 01610
Clark University
Worcester, MA 01610
College of Our Lady of the Elms
Chicopee, MA 01013
College of the Holy Cross
Worcester, MA 01610
Curry College
Milton, MA 02186
Eastern Nazarene College
Quincy, MA 02170
Emerson College
Boston, MA 02116
Emmanuel College
Boston, MA 02115
Gordon College
Wenham, MA 01984
Hampshire College
Amherst, MA 01002
Harvard and Radcliffe Colleges
Cambridge, MA 02138
Hebrew College
Brookline, MA 02146
Hellenic College
Brookline, MA 02146
Lesley College
Cambridge, MA 02238
Massachusetts College of Pharmacy and Allied Health Sciences—Hampden
Springfield, MA 01119
Massachusetts Institute of Technology
Cambridge, MA 02139
Merrimack College
North Andover, MA 01845
Mount Holyoke College
South Hadley, MA 01075
New England Conservatory of Music
Boston, MA 02115
Nichols College
Dudley, MA 01570
Northeastern University
Boston, MA 02115
Pine Manor College
Chestnut Hill, MA 02167
Regis College
Weston, MA 02193
School of the Museum of Fine Arts/ Affiliated with Tufts University
Boston, MA 02115
Simmons College
Boston, MA 02115
Simon's Rock Early College of Bard College
Great Barrington, MA 01230
Smith College
Northampton, MA 01063
Springfield College
Springfield, MA 01109
St. Hyacinth College and Seminary
Granby, MA 01033
St. John's Seminary College of Liberal Arts
Brighton, MA 02135
Stonehill College
North Easton, MA 02356
Suffolk University
Boston, MA 02114
Swain School of Design
New Bedford, MA 02740
Tufts University
Medford, MA 02155
Wellesley College
Wellesley, MA 02181
Wentworth Institute of Technology
Boston, MA 02115
Western New England College
Springfield, MA 01119
Wheaton College
Norton, MA 02766
Wheelock College
Boston, MA 02215
Williams College
Williamstown, MA 01267
Worcester Polytechnic Institute
Worcester, MA 01503

MICHIGAN

Adrian College
Adrian, MI 49221
Albion College
Albion, MI 49224
Alma College
Alma, MI 48801
Andrews University
Berrien Springs, MI 49104
Aquinas College
Grand Rapids, MI 49506
Calvin College
Grand Rapids, MI 49506
Center for Creative Studies—College of Art and Design
Detroit, MI 48202
Cleary College
Ypsilanti, MI 48197
Condordia College
Ann Arbor, MI 48105
Detroit College of Business
Dearborn, MI 48126
General Motors Institute
Flint, MI 48502
Grace Bible College
Grand Rapids, MI 49509
Grand Rapids Baptist College
Grand Rapids, MI 49505
Great Lakes Bible College
Lansing, MI 48901
Hillsdale College
Hillsdale, MI 49242
Hope College
Holland, MI 49423
Jordan College
Cedar Springs, MI 49319
Kalamazoo College
Kalamazoo, MI 49007
Kendall School of Design
Grand Rapids, MI 49503
Lawrence Institute of Technology
Southfield, MI 48075
Madonna College
Livonia, MI 48150
Marygrove College
Detroit, MI 48221
Mercy College of Detroit
Detroit, MI 48219
Nazareth College
Nazareth, MI 49074
Northwood Institute
Midland, MI 48640
Olivet College
Olivet, MI 49076
Reformed Bible College
Grand Rapids, MI 49506
Shaw College of Detroit
Detroit, MI 48202
Sacred Heart Seminary
Detroit, MI 48206
Siena Heights College
Adrian, MI 49221
Spring Arbor College
Spring Arbor, MI 49283
St. Mary's College
Orchard Lake, MI 48033
University of Detroit
Detroit, MI 48221
Walsh College of Accountancy and Business Administration
Troy, MI 48084
William Tyndale College
Farmington Hills, MI 48018

MINNESOTA

Augsburg College
Minneapolis, MN 55454
Bethel College
St. Paul, MN 55112
Carleton College
Northfield, MN 55057
College of St. Benedict
St. Joseph, MN 56374
College of St. Catherine
St. Paul, MN 55105
College of St. Scholastica
Duluth, MN 55811
College of St. Teresa
Winona, MN 55897
College of St. Thomas
St. Paul, MN 55105
Condordia College
Moorhead, MN 56560
Concordia College
St. Paul, MN 55104
Dr. Martin Luther College
New Ulm, MN 56073
Gustavus Adolphus College
St. Peter, MN 56082
Hamline University
St. Paul, MN 55104
Macalester College
St. Paul, MN 55105
Minneapolis College of Art and Design
Minneapolis, MN 55404
Minneapolis Bible College
Rochester, MN 55901
North Central Bible College
Minneapolis, MN 55404
Northwestern College
Roseville, MN 55113
Pillsbury Baptist College
Owatonna, MN 55060
St. John's University
Collegeville, MN 56321
St. Mary's College
Winona, MN 55987
St. Olaf College
Northfield, MN 55057

St. Paul Bible College
Bible College, MN 55375

MISSISSIPPI

Belhaven College
Jackson, MS 39202
Blue Mountain College
Blue Mountain, MS 38610
Millsap College
Jackson, MS 39210
Mississippi College
Clinton, MS 39058
Mississippi Industrial College
Holly Springs, MS 38635
Rust College
Holly Springs, MS 38635
Southeastern Baptist College
Laurel, MS 39440
Tougaloo College
Tougaloo, MS 39174
Wesley College
Florence, MS 39073
Whitworth Bible College
Brookhaven, MS 39601
William Carey College
Hattiesburg, MS 39401

MISSOURI

Avila College
Kansas City, MO 64145
Baptist Bible College
Springfield, MO 65803
Calvary Bible College
Kansas City, MO 64147
Cardinal Glennon College
St. Louis, MO 63119
Central Bible College
Springfield, MO 65807
Central Christian College of the Bible
Moberly, MO 65270
Central Methodist College
Fayette, MO 65248
Columbia College
Columbia, MO 65216
Conception Seminary College
Conception, MO 64433
Culver-Stockton College
Canton, MO 63435
Drury College
Springfield, MO 65802
Evangel College
Springfield, MO 65802
Finlay Engineering College
Kansas City, MO 64114
Fontbonne College
St. Louis, MO 63105
Hannibal-Le Grange College
Hannibal, MO 63401
Harris Stowe State College
St. Louis, MO 63103
Kansas City Art Institute
Kansas City, MO 64111
Lincoln University
Jefferson City, MO 65101
Lindenwood Colleges
St. Charles, MO 63301
Maryville College—St. Louis
St. Louis, MO 63141
Missouri Baptist College
St. Louis, MO 63141
Missouri Institute of Technology
Kansas City, MO 64114
Missouri Valley College
Marshall, MO 65340
Ozark Bible College
Joplin, MO 64801
Park College
Kansas City, MO 64152
Rockhurst College
Kansas City, MO 64110
School of the Ozarks
Point Lookout, MO 65726
Southwest Baptist College
Bolivar, MO 65613
Stephens College
Columbia, MO 65215
St. Louis Christian College
Florissant, MO 63033
St. Louis College of Pharmacy
St. Louis, MO 63110
St. Louis Conservatory of Music
St. Louis, MO 63130
St. Louis University
St. Louis, MO 63103
Tarkio College
Tarkio, MO 64491
Washington University
St. Louis, MO 63130
Webster College
St. Louis, MO 63119
Westminster College
Fulton, MO 65251
William Jewell College
Liberty, MO 64068
William Woods College
Fulton, MO 65251

MONTANA

Big Sky Bible College
Lewiston, MT 59457
Carroll College
Helena, MT 59601
College of Great Falls
Great Falls, MT 59405
Rocky Mountain College
Billings, MT 59102

NEBRASKA

Bellevue College
Bellevue, NE 68005
College of St. Mary
Omaha, NE 68124
Concordia Teachers College
Seward, NE 68434
Creighton University
Omaha, NE 68178
Dana College
Blair, NE 68008
Doane College
Crete, NE 68333
Grace College of the Bible
Omaha, NE 68108
Hastings College
Hastings, NE 68901
Midland Lutheran College
Fremont, NE 68025
Nebraska Christian College
Norfolk, NE 68701
Nebraska Wesleyan University
Lincoln, NE 68504
Platte Valley Bible College
Scotts Bluff, NE 69361
Union College
Lincoln, NE 68506

NEVADA

Sierra Nevada College
Incline Valley, NV 89450

NEW HAMPSHIRE

Colby-Sawyer College
New London, NH 03257
Daniel Webster College
Nashua, NH 03063
Dartmouth College
Hanover, NH 03755
Franklin Pierce College
Rindge, NH 03461
Nathaniel Hawthorne College
Antrim, NH 03440
New England College
Henniker, NH 03242
New Hampshire College
Manchester, NH 03104
Notre Dame College
Manchester, NH 03104
River College
Mashua, NH 03060
St. Anselm College
Manchester, NH 03102

NEW JERSEY

Bloomfield College
Bloomfield, NJ 07003
Centenary College
Hackettstown, NJ 07840
College of St. Elizabeth
Convent Station, NJ 07961
Don Bosco College
Newton, NJ 07860
Drew University—College of Liberal Arts
Madison, NJ 07940
Fairleigh Dickinson University—Madison
Madison, NJ 07940
Fairleigh Dickinson University—Rutherford
Rutherford, NJ 07666
Fairleigh Dickinson University—Teaneck
Teaneck, NJ 07666
Felician College
Lodi, NJ 07644
Georgian Court College
Lakewood, NJ 08701
Kean College of New Jersey
Union, NJ 07083
Monmouth College
West Long Branch, NJ 07764
Northeastern Bible College
Essex Fells, NJ 07012
Princeton University
Princeton, NJ 08544
Rabbinical College of America
Morristown, NJ 07960
Ramapo College of New Jersey
Rahway, NJ 07430
Rider College
Lawrenceville, NJ 08648
Seton Hall University
South Orange, NJ 07079
Stevens Institute of Technology
Hoboken, NJ 07030
St. Peter's College
Jersey City, NJ 07306
Thomas A. Edison College
Trenton, NJ 08625
Upsala College
East Orange, NJ 07019
Westminster Choir College
Princeton, NJ 08540

NEW MEXICO

College of Santa Fe
Santa Fe, NM 87501
College of the Southwest
Hobbs, NM 88240

National College of Business—Albuquerque
Albuquerque, NM 87108
St. John's College
Santa Fe, NM 87501
University of Albuquerque
Albuquerque, NM 87140

New York

Adelphi University
Garden City, NY 11530
Albany College of Pharmacy
Albany, NY 12208
Alfred University
Alfred, NY 14802
American University in Cairo
New York, NY 10017
Bard College
Annandale-on-Hudson, NY 12504
Barnard College of Columbia University
New York, NY 10027
Boricus College
New York, NY 10025
Canisius College
Buffalo, NY 14208
Cathedral College of the Immaculate Conception
Douglaston, NY 11362
Clarkson College
Potsdam, NY 13676
Colgate University
Hamilton, NY 13346
College of Human Services
New York, NY 10016
College of Insurance
New York, NY 10038
College of Mount St. Vincent
New York, NY 10471
College of New Rochelle—School of Arts and Sciences
New Rochelle, NY 10801
College of St. Rose
Albany, NY 12203
Columbia University—Columbia College
New York, NY 10027
Concordia College
Bronxville, NY 10708
Cooper Union
New York, NY 10003
Cornell University
Ithaca, NY 14850
Daemen College
Amherst, NY 14226
Dominican College of Blauvelt
Orangeburg, NY 10962
Dowling College
Oakdale, NY 11769
D'Youville College
Buffalo, NY 14201
Eisenhower College of Rochester Institute of Technology
Seneca Falls, NY 13148
Elmira College
Elmira, NY 14901
Fordham University—Lincoln Center
New York, NY 10023
Fordham University—Rose Hill
Bronx, NY 10458
Friends World College
Huntington, NY 11743
Hamilton College
Clinton, NY 13323
Hartwick College
Oneonta, NY 13820
Hebrew Union College
New York, NY 10023
Hobart College
Geneva, NY 14456
Hofstra University
Hempstead, NY 11550
Holy Trinity Orthodox Seminary
Jordanville, NY 13361
Houghton College
Houghton, NY 14744
Iona College
New Rochelle, NY 10801
Ithaca College
Ithaca, NY 14850
Jewish Theological Seminary of America
New York, NY 10027
Julliard School
New York, NY 10023
Keuka College
Keuka Park, NY 14478
Le Moyne College
Syracuse, NY 13224
Long Island University—Brooklyn
Brooklyn, NY 11201
Long Island University—College of Pharmacy/Health Sciences
Brooklyn, NY 11201
Long Island University—C.W. Post College
Greenvale, NY 11548
Long Island University—Southhampton College
Southhampton, NY 11968
Manhattan College
Riverdale, NY 10471
Manhattanville College
Purchase, NY 10577
Mannes College of Music
New York, NY 10021
Marist College
Poughkeepsie, NY 12601
Marymount College
Tarrytown, NY 10591
Marymount Manhattan College
New York, NY 10021
Medaille College
Buffalo, NY 14214
Mercy College
Dobbs Ferry, NY 10522
Molloy College
Rockville Centre, NY 11570
Mount Saint Mary College
Newburgh, NY 12550
Nazareth College of Rochester
Rochester, NY 14610
New School of Social Research
New York, NY 10011
New York Institute of Technology
Old Westbury, NY 11568
New York Institute of Technology—Metropolitan Center
New York, NY 10023
New York School of Interior Design
New York, NY 10022
New York University
New York, NY 10012
Niagara University
Niagara University, NY 14109
Nyack College
Nyack, NY 10960
Pace University
New York, NY 10038
Pace University—College of White Plains
White Plains, NY 10603
Pace University—Pleasant/Briarcliff
Pleasantville, NY 10570
Parsons School of Design
New York, NY 10011
Polytechnic Institute of New York
Brooklyn, NY 11201
Pratt Institute
Brooklyn, NY 11205
Rensselaer Polytechnic Institute
Troy, NY 12181
Roberts Wesleyan College
Rochester, NY 14624
Rochester Institute of Technology
Rochester, NY 14623
Russell Sage College
Troy, NY 12180
Sarah Lawrence College
Bronxville, NY 10708
School of Visual Arts
New York, NY 10010
Siena College
Loudonville, NY 12211
Skidmore College
Saratoga Springs, NY 12866
St. Bonaventure University
St. Bonaventure, NY 14778
St. Francis College
Brooklyn, NY 11201
St. John Fisher College
Rochester, NY 14618
St. John's University Jamaica/Queens/Staten Island
Jamaica, NY 11439
St. Joseph's College
Brooklyn, NY 11205
St. Joseph's College—Suffolk
Patchogue, NY 11772
St. Lawrence University
Canton, NY 13617
St. Thomas Aquinas College
Sparkill, NY 10968
Syracuse University
Syracuse, NY 13210
The King's College
Briarcliff Manor, NY 10510
Touro College
New York, NY 10036
University of Rochester
Rochester, NY 14627
Utica College of Syracuse University
Utica, NY 13421
Vassar College
Poughkeepsie, NY 12601
Wadhams Hall Seminary College
Ogdensburg, NY 13669
Wagner College
Staten Island, NY 10301
Webb Institute of Naval Architecture
Glen Cove, NY 11542
Wells College
Aurora, NY 13026
William Smith College
Geneva, NY 14456
Yeshiva College—Main Center
New York, NY 10033

North Carolina

Atlantic Christian College
Wilson, NC 27893
Barber-Scotia College
Concord, NC 28025
Belmont Abbey College
Belmont, NC 28012
Bennett College
Greensboro, NC 27420

Campbell University
Buies Creek, NC 27506
Catawba College
Salisbury, NC 28144
Duke University
Durham, NC 27706
Elon College
Elon College, NC 27244
Gardner-Webb College
Boiling Springs, NC 28017
Greensboro College
Greensboro, NC 27420
Guilford College
Greensboro, NC 27410
High Point College
High Point, NC 27262
Johnson C. Smith University
Charlotte, NC 28216
Lenoir-Rhyne College
Hickory, NC 28601
Livingstone College
Salisbury, NC 28144
Mars Hill College
Mars Hill, NC 28754
Meredith College
Raleigh, NC 27611
Methodist College
Fayetteville, NC 28301
North Carolina Wesleyan College
Rocky Mount, NC 27801
Pfeiffer College
Misenheimer, NC 28109
Piedmont Bible College
Winston-Salem, NC 27101
Queens College
Charlotte, NC 28274
Roanoke Bible College
Elizabeth City, NC 27909
Sacred Heart College
Belmont, NC 28012
Shaw University
Raleigh, NC 27611
St. Andrew's Presbyterian College
Laurinburg, NC 28352
St. Augustine's College
Raleigh, NC 27611
Wake Forest University
Winston-Salem, NC 27109
Warren Wilson College
Swannanoa, NC 28778
Winston-Salem Bible College
Winston-Salem, NC 27102

North Dakota

Jamestown College
Jamestown, ND 58401
Mary College
Bismark, ND 58501
Northwest Bible College
Minot, ND 58701
Trinity Bible Institute
Ellendale, ND 58436

Ohio

Allegheny Wesleyan College
Salem, OH 44460
Antioch College—Yellow Springs
Yellow Springs, OH 45387
Ashland College
Ashland, OH 44805
Baldwin-Wallace College
Berea, OH 44017
Bluffton College
Bluffton, OH 45817
Borromeo College of Ohio
Wickliffe, OH 44092
Capital University
Columbus, OH 43209
Case Western Reserve University
Cleveland, OH 44106
Cedarville College
Cedarville, OH 45314
Cincinnati Bible College
Cincinnati, OH 45204
Circleville Bible College
Circleville, OH 43113
Cleveland College of Jewish Studies
Beachwood, OH 44122
Cleveland Institute of Art
Cleveland, OH 44106
Cleveland Institute of Music
Cleveland, OH 44106
College of Mount St. Joseph on the Ohio
Mount St. Joseph, OH 45051
College of Wooster
Wooster, OH 44691
Columbus College of Art and Design
Columbus, OH 43215
Defiance College
Defiance, OH 43512
Denison University
Granville, OH 43023
Dyke College
Cleveland, OH 44114
Edgeclift College
Cincinnati, OH 45206
Findlay College
Findlay, OH 45840
Franklin University
Columbus, OH 43215
God's Bible School and College
Cincinnati, OH 45210
Heidelberg College
Tiffin, OH 44883
Hiram College
Hiram, OH 44234
John Carroll University
University Heights, OH 44118
Kenyon College
Gambler, OH 43022
Lake Erie College
Painesville, OH 44077
Malone College
Canton, OH 44709
Marietta College
Marietta, OH 45750
Mount Union College
Alliance, OH 44601
Mount Vernon Bible College
Mount Vernon, OH 43050
Mount Vernon Nazarene College
Mount Vernon, OH 43050
Muskingum College
New Concord, OH 43762
Notre Dame College
Cleveland, OH 44121
Oberlin College
Oberlin, OH 44074
Ohio Dominican College
Columbus, OH 43219
Ohio Institute of Technology
Columbus, OH 43209
Ohio Northern University
Ada, OH 45810
Ohio Wesleyan University
Delaware, OH 43015
Otterbein College
Westerville, OH 43081
Pontifical College Josephinum
Columbus, OH 43085
Rio Grande College/Community College
Rio Grande, OH 45674
Tiffin University
Tiffin, OH 44883
Union for Experimenting Colleges and University
Cincinnati, OH 45202
University of Dayton
Dayton, OH 45469
University of Steubenville
Steubenville, OH 43952
Urbana College
Urbana, OH 43078
Ursuline College
Pepper Pike, OH 44124
Walsh College
Canton, OH 44720
Wilberforce University
Wilberforce, OH 45384
Wilmington College of Ohio
Wilmington, OH 45177
Wittenberg University
Springfield, OH 45501
Xavier University
Cincinnati, OH 45207

Oklahoma

Bartlesville Wesleyan College
Bartlesville, OK 74003
Bethany Nazarene College
Bethany, OK 73008
Cameron University
Lawton, OK 73505
Flaming Rainbow University
Stillwell, OK 74960
Hillsdale Free Will Baptist College
Moore, OK 73153
Langston University
Langston, OK 73050
Midwest Christian College
Oklahoma City, OK 73111
Oklahoma Baptist University
Shawnee, OK 74801
Oklahoma Christian College
Oklahoma City, OK 73111
Oklahoma City University
Oklahoma City, OK 73106
Oklahoma Southwestern College
Oklahoma City, OK 73127
Oral Roberts University
Tulsa, OK 74171
Phillipe University
Enid, OK 73701
University of Tulsa
Tulsa, OK 74104

Oregon

Colegio Cesar Chavez
Mount Angel, OR 97362
Columbia Christian College
Portland, OR 97200
Concordia College
Portland, OR 97211
Eugene Bible College
Eugene, OR 97405
George Fox College
Newberg, OR 97132
Lewis and Clark College
Portland, OR 97219
Linfield College
McMinnville, OR 97128
Marylhurst College for Lifelong Learning
Marylhurst, OR 97036

Mount Angel Seminary
St. Benedict, OR 97373
Multnomah School of the Bible
Portland, OR 97220
Museum Art School
Portland, OR 97205
Northwest Christian College
Eugene, OR 97401
Pacific University
Forest Grove, OR 97116
Reed College
Portland, OR 97202
University of Portland
Portland, OR 97203
Warner Pacific College
Portland, OR 97215
Western Baptist College
Salem, OR 97302
Willamette University
Salem, OR 97301

Pennsylvania

Albright College
Reading, PA 19603
Allegheny College
Meadville, PA 16335
Allentown College of St. Francis De Sales
Center Valley, PA 18034
Alliance College
Cambridge Springs, PA 16403
Alvernia College
Reading, PA 19607
Antioch University—Philadelphia
Philadelphia, PA 19108
Baptist College of Pennsylvania
Clarks Summit, PA 18411
Beaver College
Glenside, PA 19038
Bryn Mawr College
Bryn Mawr, PA 19010
Bucknell University
Lewisburg, PA 17837
Carlow College
Pittsburgh, PA 15213
Carnegie-Mellon University
Pittsburgh, PA 15213
Cedar Crest College
Allentown, PA 18104
Chatham College
Pittsburgh, PA 15232
Chestnut Hill College
Philadelphia, PA 19118
College Misericordia
Dallas, PA 18612
College of the Academy New Church
Bryn Athyn, PA 19009
Combs College of Music
Philadelphia, PA 19119
Curtis Institute of Music
Philadelphia, PA 19103
Delaware Valley College of Science and Agriculture
Doylestown, PA 18901
Dickinson College
Carlisle, PA 17013
Drexel University
Philadelphia, PA 19104
Duquesne University
Pittsburgh, PA 15219
Eastern College
St. Davids, PA 19087
Elizabethtown College
Elizabethtown, PA 17022
Franklin and Marshall College
Lancaster, PA 17604
Gannon University
Erie, PA 16541
Geneva College
Beaver Falls, PA 15010
Gettysburg College
Gettysburg, PA 17325
Gratz College
Philadelphia, PA 19141
Gwynedd-Mercy College
Gwynedd Valley, PA 19437
Hahnemann College of Allied Health Professions
Philadelphia, PA 19102
Haverford College
Haverford, PA 19041
Holy Family College
Philadelphia, PA 19114
Immaculate College
Immaculate, PA 19345
Juniata College
Huntingdon, PA 16652
King's College
Wilkes Barre, PA 18711
Lafayette College
Easton, PA 18042
Lancaster Bible College
Lancaster, PA 17601
La Roche College
Pittsburgh, PA 15237
La Salle College
Philadelphia, PA 19141
Lebanon Valley College
Annville, PA 17003
Lehigh University
Bethlehem, PA 18015
Lincoln University
Lincoln University, PA 19352
Lycoming College
Williamsport, PA 17701
Marywood College
Scranton, PA 18509
Mercyhurst College
Erie, PA 16546
Messiah College
Grantham, PA 17027
Moore College of Art
Philadelphia, PA 19103
Moravian College
Bethlehem, PA 18018
Muhlenberg College
Allentown, PA 18104
Neumann College
Aston, PA 19014
New School of Music
Philadelphia, PA 19103
Philadelphia College of Art
Philadelphia, PA 19102
Philadelphia College of Bible
Langhorne, PA 19047
Philadelphia College of Pharmacy and Science
Philadelphia, PA 19104
Philadelphia College of Textiles and Science
Philadelphia, PA 19144
Point Park College
Pittsburgh, PA 15222
Robert Morris College
Coraopolis, PA 15108
Rosemont College
Rosemont, PA 19010
Seton Hill College
Greensburg, PA 15601
Spring Garden College
Chestnut Hill, PA 19118
St. Francis College
Loretto, PA 15940
St. Joseph's University
Philadelphia, PA 19131
St. Vincent College
Latrobe, PA 15650
Susquehanna University
Selinsgrove, PA 17870
Swarthmore College
Swarthmore, PA 19081
Thiel College
Greenville, PA 16125
Thomas Jefferson University College of Allied Health Sciences
Philadelphia, PA 19107
United Wesleyan College
Allentown, PA 18103
University of Pennsylvania
Philadelphia, PA 19104
University of Pittsburgh
Pittsburgh, PA 15620
University of Pittsburgh—Bradford
Bradford, PA 16701
University of Pittsburgh—Greensburg
Greensburg, PA 15601
University of Pittsburgh—Johnstown
Johnstown, PA 15904
University of Scranton
Scranton, PA 18510
Ursinus College
Collegeville, PA 19426
Valley Forge Christian College
Phoenixville, PA 19460
Villa Maria College
Erie, PA 16505
Villanova University
Villanova, PA 16505
Washington and Jefferson College
Washington, PA 15301
Waynesburg College
Waynesburg, PA 15370
Westminster College
New Wilmington, PA 16142
Widener College
Chester, PA 10913
Wilkes College
Wilkes-Barre, PA 18766
Wilson College
Chambersburg, PA 17201
York College of Pennsylvania
York, PA 17405

Rhode Island

Barrington College
Barrington, RI 02806
Brown University
Providence, RI 02912
Bryant College
Smithfield, RI 02917
Johnson and Wales College
Providence, RI 02903
Newport College—Salve Regina
Newport, RI 02840
Providence College
Providence, RI 02918
Rhode Island School of Design
Providence, RI 02903
Roger Williams College
Bristol, RI 02809
Roger Williams College—Providence
Providence, RI 02809

South Carolina

Allen University
Columbia, SC 29204

Baptist College at Charleston
Charleston, SC 29411
Benedict College
Columbia, SC 29204
Bob Jones University
Greenville, SC 29614
Central Wesleyan College
Central, SC 29630
Claflin College
Orangeburg, SC 29115
Coker College
Hartsville, SC 29550
Columbia Bible College
Columbia, SC 29230
Columbia College
Columbia, SC 29203
Converse College
Spartanburg, SC 29301
Erskine College
Due West, SC 29639
Friendship College
Rock Hill, SC 29730
Furman University
Greenville, SC 29163
Lander College
Greenwood, SC 29646
Limestone College
Gaffney, SC 29340
Morris College
Sumter, SC 29150
Newberry College
Newberry, SC 29108
Presbyterian College
Clinton, SC 29325
Southern Methodist College
Orangeburg, SC 29115
Voorhees College
Denmark, SC 29042
Wofford College
Spartanburg, SC 29301

South Dakota

Augustana College
Sioux Falls, SD 57197
Dakota Wesleyan University
Mitchell, SD 57301
Huron College
Huron, SD 57350
Mount Marty College
Yankton, SD 57078
National College of Business
Rapid City, SD 57709
Sinte Gleska College
Rosebud, SD 57570
Sioux Falls College
Sioux Falls, SD 57101
Yankton College
Yankton, SD 57078

Tennessee

American Baptist College
Nashville, TN 37207
Belmont College
Nashville, TN 37203
Bethel College
McKenzie, TN 38201
Bristol College
Bristol, TN 37620
Bryan College
Dayton, TN 37321
Carson-Newman College
Jefferson City, TN 37760
Christian Brothers College
Memphis, TN 38104
Covenant College
Lookout Mountain, TN 37350
David Lipscomb College
Nashville, TN 37203
Fisk University
Nashville, TN 37203
Freed-Hardeman College
Henderson, TN 38340
Free Will Baptist Bible College
Nashville, TN 37205
Johnson Bible College
Knoxville, TN 37920
Lee College
Cleveland, TN 37311
King College
Bristol, TN 37620
Knoxville College
Knoxville, TN 37921
Lambuth College
Jackson, TN 38301
Lane College
Jackson, TN 38301
Le Moyne-Owen College
Memphis, TN 38126
Lincoln Memorial University
Harrogate, TN 37752
Maryville College
Maryville, TN 37801
Memphis Academy of Arts
Memphis, TN 38112
Mid-South Bible College
Memphis, TN 38112
Milligan College
Milligan College, TN 37682
O'More College of Design
Franklin, TN 37604
Southern Missionary College
Collegedale, TN 37315
Southwestern—Memphis
Memphis, TN 38112
Steed College
Johnson City, TN 37601
Tennessee Temple University
Chattanooga, TN 37404
Tennessee Wesleyan College
Athens, TN 37303
Trevecca Nazarene College
Nashville, TN 37210
Tusculum College
Greeneville, TN 37743
Union University
Jackson, TN 38301
University of the South
Sewanee, TN 37375
Vanderbilt University
Nashville, TN 37212

Texas

Abilene Christian University
Abilene, TX 79601
Abilene Christian University—Dallas
Garland, TX 75041
American Technological University
Killeen, TX 76541
Arlington Baptist College
Arlington, TX 76012
Austin College
Sherman, TX 75090
Baylor College of Medicine
Houston, TX 77025
Baylor University
Waco, TX 76706
Bishop College
Dallas, TX 75241
Dallas Baptist College
Dallas, TX 75211
Dallas Bible College
Dallas, TX 75228
Dallas Christian College
Dallas, TX 75234
East Texas Baptist College
Marshall, TX 75670
Gulf Coast Bible College
Houston, TX 77008
Hardin-Simmons University
Abilene, TX 79601
Houston Baptist University
Houston, TX 77074
Howard Payne University
Brownwood, TX 76801
Huston-Tillotson College
Austin, TX 78702
Incarnate Word College
San Antonio, TX 78209
Jarvis Christian College
Hawkins, TX 75765
LeTourneau College (Le Tourneau Christian College)
Longview, TX 75602
Lubbock Christian College
Lubbock, TX 79407
McMurry College
Abilene, TX 79697
Our Lady of the Lake—University of San Antonio
San Antonio, TX 78285
Paul Quinn College
Waco, TX 76704
Rice University
Houston, TX 77001
Southern Bible College
Houston, TX 77015
Southern Methodist University
Dallas, TX 75275
Southwestern Adventist College
Keene, TX 76059
Southwestern Assemblies of God College
Waxahachie, TX 75165
Southwestern University
Georgetown, TX 78626
St. Edward's University
Austin, TX 78704
St. Mary's University of San Antonio
San Antonio, TX 78284
Texas Christian University
Fort Worth, TX 76129
Texas College
Tyler, TX 78155
Texas Lutheran College
Sequin, TX 78155
Texas Wesleyan College
Fort Worth, TX 76105
Trinity University
San Antonio, TX 78284
University of Dallas
Irving, TX 75061
University of Mary Hardin—Baylor
Belton, TX 76513
University of St. Thomas
Houston, TX 77006
Wayland Baptist College
Plainview, TX 79072
Wiley College
Marshall, TX 75670

Utah

Brigham Young University
Provo, UT 84602
Westminster College
Salt Lake City, UT 84105

VERMONT

Bennington College
Bennington, VT 05201
Burlington College
Burlington, VT 05401
College of St. Joseph the Provider
Rutland, VT 05701
Goddard College
Plainfield, VT 05667
Green Mountain College
Poultney, VT 05764
Lyndon State College
Lyndonville, VT 05851
Marlboro College
Marlboro, VT 05344
Middlebury College
Middlebury, VT 05753
Norwick University
Northfield, VT 05663
School for International Training
Battleboro, VT 05301
St. Michael's College
Winooski, VT 05405
Trinity College
Burlington, VT 05401
Vermont College of Norwick University
Montpelier, VT 05602

VIRGINIA

Averett College
Danville, VA 24541
Bluefield College
Bluefield, VA 24605
Bridgewater College
Bridgewater, VA 22812
Eastern Mennonite College
Harrisonburg, VA 22801
Emory and Henry College
Emory, VA 24327
Ferrum College
Ferrum, VA 24088
Hampden-Sydney College
Hampden-Sydney, VA 23943
Hampton Institute
Hampton, VA 23668
Hollins College
Hollins College, VA 24020
Liberty Baptist College
Lynchburg, VA 24506
Longwood College
Farmsville, VA 23901
Lynchburg College
Lynchburg, VA 24501
Mary Baldwin College
Staunton, VA 24401
Marymount College of Virginia
Arlington, VA 22207
Mary Washington College
Fredericksburg, VA 22401
Radford University
Radford, VA 24142
Randolph-Macon College
Ashland, VA 23005
Randolph-Macon Women's College
Lynchburg, VA 24503
Roanoke College
Salem, VA 24153
Shenandoah College and Conservatory of Music
Winchester, VA 22601
St. Paul's College
Lawrenceville, VA 23868
Sweet Briar College
Sweet Briar, VA 24595
University of Richmond
Richmond, VA 23173
Virginia Commonwealth University
Richmond, VA 23284
Virginia Intermont College
Bristol, VA 24201
Virginia Union University
Richmond, VA 23222
Virginia Wesleyan College
Norfolk, VA 23502
Washington and Lee University
Lexington, VA 24450

WASHINGTON

Cornish Institute of Allied Arts
Seattle, WA 98102
Fort Wright College
Spokane, WA 99204
Gonzaga University
Spokane, WA 99258
Lutheran Bible Institute
Issaquah, WA 98027
Northwest College
Kirkland, WA 98033
Pacific Lutheran University
Tacoma, WA 98447
Puget Sound College of the Bible
Edmonds, WA 98020
Seattle Pacific University
Seattle, WA 98119
Seattle University
Seattle, WA 98122
St. Martin's College
Lacey, WA 98503
University of Puget Sound
Tacoma, WA 98416
Walla Walla College
College Place, WA 99324
Whitman College
Walla Walla, WA 99362
Whitworth College
Spokane, WA 99251

WEST VIRGINIA

Alderson Broaddus College
Philippi, WV 26416
Appalachian Bible College
Bradley, WV 25818
Bethany College
Bethany, WV 26032
Davis and Elkins College
Elkins, WV 26241
Salem College
Salem, WV 26426
University of Charleston
Charleston, WV 25304
West Virginia Wesleyan College
Buckhannon, WV 26201
Wheeling College
Wheeling, WV 26003

WISCONSIN

Alverno College
Milwaukee, WI 53215
Beloit College
Beloit, WI 53511
Cardinal Stritch College
Milwaukee, WI 53217
Carroll College
Waukesha, WI 53186
Carthage College
Kenosha, WI 53140
Concordia College
Milwaukee, WI 53208
Edgewood College
Madison, WI 53711
Holy Redeemer College
Waterford, WI 53185
Immanuel Lutheran College
Eau Clair, WI 54701
Lakeland College
Sheboygan, WI 53081
Lawrence University
Appleton, WI 54911
Marian College
Fon Du Lac, WI 54935
Marquette University
Milwaukee, WI 53233
Milton College
Milton, WI 53563
Milwaukee Institute of Art and Design
Milwaukee, WI 53211
Milwaukee School of Engineering
Milwaukee, WI 53201
Mount Mary College
Milwaukee, WI 53222
Mount Senario College
Ladysmith, WI 54848
Northland College
Ashland, WI 54806
Ripon College
Ripon, WI 54971
Silver Lake College
Manitowoc, WI 54220
St. Norbert College
De Pere, WI 54115
Viterbo College
La Crosse, WI 54601
Wisconsin Conservatory of Music
Milwaukee, WI 53202

FRANCE

American College in Paris 75007
Paris, France

ENGLAND

New England College
Arundel, Sussex BN18 ODA, England
Richmond College
London W8 5PN, England
University of Warwick
Coventry CVA 7AL, England

WEST GERMANY

Schiller International University
6900
Heidelberg, West Germany

GREECE

Deree College
Athens, Greece

HONG KONG

Hong Kong Baptist College
Kowloon, Hong Kong

LEBANON

American University of Beirut
Beirut, Lebanon

MEXICO

University of the Americas
Puebla, Mexico

PUERTO RICO

American College of Puerto Rico
Bayamon, PR 00619
Antillian College
Mayaguez, PR 00708

Computer Science

The advancement in this century of the technology, application, and availability of computers has been remarkable. Every year computers become smaller, more efficient, and able to do more complex tasks; and every year computers become more woven into the day-to-day life of Americans. A basic knowledge of computers—how they were developed and how they work—is fast becoming a necessity in today's society.

THE HISTORICAL BACKGROUND

The earliest and most important computing device is the abacus, which has been used for over two thousand years. There are different variations of the abacus, the most common being a series of beads that can be manually positioned along a set of wires. Each wire is given to represent one position in a numerical system of notation, such as ones, tens, hundreds, thousands, etc. By manipulating the beads on the wires, complicated calculations can be performed. The abacus is still used in business and in schools in China and Japan.

Pascal. The French philosopher, physicist, and mathematician, Blaise Pascal (1623–1662), is credited to have designed and built one of the first adding and subtracting machines. This device was built in 1642 and consisted of a complex assortment of gears, rods, and dials. Pascal, who was only nineteen when he constructed his machine, gave a copy of it to Louis XIV, King of France. The use of Pascal's device, however, was not very widespread. Many clerks and accountants refused to accept the machine because they feared that it might someday eliminate their own positions as human calculators.

The first commercially practical adding machines did not appear until about 1820. By the end of the nineteenth century, a variety of manually operated machines were available for business applications. Building calculating machines capable of solving mathematical problems posed by scientists, engineers, and mathematicians developed more slowly.

Charles Babbage. In 1822 the British mathematician Charles Babbage (1792–1871) built a prototype of his "difference engine." This device was an effort to make a machine capable of solving the repetitive computations required to compile mathematical tables. In 1833, Babbage radically changed his theoretical approach to the problem of constructing a computing machine. As a result, he devised plans for a device he termed the "analytical engine." Although Babbage never completed his machine—he had envisioned an enormous array of cogged cylinders powered by a steam engine—his ideas were precursors of what would follow decades after his death.

Babbage had planned that his analytical engine would use punched cards similar to those used on the Jacquard looms of his day. These punched cards would provide the machine with the data and the instructions needed for operation. The machine would also have a primitive memory amounting to the storing of one thousand numbers of up to fifty digits each.

Lord Byron's daughter, the Countess of Lovelace, an accomplished mathematician herself, remarked that Babbage's analytical engine would weave "algebraical patterns just as the Jacquard loom weaves flowers and leaves." She even wrote what could be considered the first computer programming for Babbage's theoretical machine.

Herman Hollerith. The next important development came in 1890 with the work of Herman Hollerith (1860–1929) for the United States Census Bureau. Hollerith developed the first electric machines that could "read" census information which had been punched onto cards. Thus, the statistical work of the Bureau was more easily and quickly prepared. Hollerith's machines were also used for census work in other countries, including Canada and Czarist Russia. In 1896, Hollerith formed the Tabulating Machine Company, which was one of the companies that would join to become International Business Machines (IBM) in 1924.

In the 1920s and 1930s companies marketed computing machines that handled between 50 and 250 punched cards per minute. This is very slow when compared to today's computers and calculators, but it was an important advance over previous technology. In 1928, the astronomers Wallace J. Eckert in America and John Cromie in England devised punched card machines capable of preparing calculations for astronomical and nautical tables.

The desire to build more advanced computers increased with the requirements of World War II. Computers were needed to calculate the trajectories of artillery fire.

ENIAC. In 1943, J. Presper Eckert and John W. Mauchly, with their associates, planned a machine called an "electrical numerical integrator and calculator," which was named "ENIAC." Finally completed in 1944, this all-electric machine was an advancement that incorporated some 18,000 vacuum tubes, expended 180,000 watts of power, and took up the floor area of a two bedroom house. ENIAC would be able to solve ballistics problems in fifteen seconds that formerly would have taken twenty hours if done by a person with a desk-top manual tabulator. ENIAC was also used to perform calculations for the atomic bomb project at Los Alamos, New Mexico.

Mark I. In 1944, the Harvard Mark I was unveiled. This electromechanical machine was developed by Howard Aiken and his associates and could perform the functions Charles Babbage had planned for his analytical engine. The Mark I was eight feet tall and fifty-five feet long and contained some 750,000 parts. It could process 23-decimal place numbers, do all arithmetic operations; and this machine had the capacity to deal with logarithms and trigonometric functions.

An advance in computer design beyond the Mark I occurred in 1945, when John von Neumann proposed the idea of a stored memory capacity. This permitted the computer to store its instructions within itself. Neumann incorporated this concept in his design for the EDVAC machine (Electronic Discrete Variable Automatic Computer), which was completed in 1952.

In 1951, Eckert and Mauchly completed work on UNIVAC (Universal Automatic Computer), which the United States Census Bureau had ordered in 1947. UNIVAC, and other computers similarly designed, had delay-line memories and performed multiplication by repetitious addition.

In the late 1950s the standard for computer memories became ferrite cores, and the transistor, which had been developed in 1948, replaced the cumbersome vacuum tube.

Innovations in the programming of computers were just as important as were the technological advances. The concept of an "assembly language," which translated a computer's binary code into a more easily used set of instructions, came about in the 1950s. Higher-level languages, such as FORTRAN, ALGOL, and COBOL, more closely resembled human language or the logic of mathematics. These computer languages were developed in the late 1950s and early 1960s.

In the 1960s research focused upon building computers with expanded memories and functional capabilities. The two computers that stand out during this period were the "LARC" machine, built by the Sperry-Rand Corporation for the University of California, and "Stretch" built by IBM. Early attempts to photoprint electrical circuitry, thereby making computers smaller and faster, began about 1960.

The use of computers in the business world was also increasing. In 1963, the *Daily Oklahoman-Oklahoma City Times* was the first newspaper to set all classified and editorial text by means of computer. In 1964, American Airlines and IBM created the airlines reservation system called SABRE. The use of computers in science and engineering in the 1960s can best be illustrated by the successful Apollo lunar landing project. Without computers to calculate orbit configurations and rocket specifications, putting men on the moon would probably not have been possible.

The 1970s saw an emphasis placed on scaling down the size and cost of computers. This was especially apparent in the field of hand-held electronic calculators. Yet, the 1970s also witnessed the manufacture of huge, multimillion dollar "supercomputers" used for weather forecasting, oceanographic research, astrophysics, and nuclear engineering.

The 1980s appear to be the decade of the personal computer. Companies such as IBM, Apple, Commodore Business Machines, and the Tandy Corporation are producing microcomputers designed for use in the home or small business. The companies that profited from the home video game craze have also offered hardware that would convert their video games into modest home computers. In education, "computer literacy" is a growing concern for secondary schools; and it has become a 1980s watchword in business, science, and government.

An Alphabet Soup of Early Calculating Machines

ENIAC 1944	Electronic Numerical Integrator and Calculator
EDVAC 1952	Electronic Discrete Variable Automatic Computer
EDSAC 1949	Electronic Delay Storage Automatic Computer
SEAC 1950	Standards Eastern Automatic Computer
UNIVAC 1951	Universal Automatic Computer
MANIAC 1951	Mathematical Analyzer, Numerical Integrator and Computer

THE WAY A COMPUTER WORKS

The modern computer has two basic components: hardware and software. Hardware refers to the physical equipment of a computer system. It may include a keyboard, a video monitor, and a printer. Software refers to the programming instructions that tell the computer how to perform any given task. (The instructions for the operation of computer hardware in an owner's manual may be considered software as well.)

The most important part of a computer is the central processing unit, or CPU. The CPU is composed of an arithmetic and logic section that can perform mathematical functions, such as addition and multiplication, and logical functions, such as comparing two distinct quantities. The CPU also contains a control section that communicates with other parts of the computer system, such as output devices or a data storage disk drive. Although this vital part of the computer is called a *central* processing unit, the actual electrical circuitry that comprises the CPU may not be limited to one location within the computer.

Computers, thanks to semiconducting "chips" of silicon, can be built with two types of memory. RAM, or random-access-memory, is a temporary memory capacity that can be altered by the CPU upon the command of the user. RAM can be thought of as a kind of "scratch pad" upon which the user may write, erase, and write again.

ROM, or read-only-memory, is the computer's permanent memory. The user, through the CPU, can read the ROM, but cannot alter it. Programs that are frequently used can be entered into a computer's ROM during the manufacturing process. Many personal computers are sold with a common language, such as BASIC, already a part of the computer's ROM.

When a computer is turned on, the CPU will automatically read the instructions for it in the "boot ROM," which contains the initial directions a computer needs in order to function. These instructions will direct the CPU to the operating system program, which has been entered onto a section of the RAM so that the CPU can follow it.

But how does a computer process data? The computer must translate all data into a binary code that can be represented as a series of digits of only 0 or 1. Each digit of the binary code is termed a bit. A grouping of eight bits is termed a byte. Within the computer a continuous translation procedure occurs that changes input data into the machine's binary code—and after the data has been processed—back into a form the user can readily understand.

The keyboard is the most common device a user has to input data. When keys are hit, a keyboard processor within the computer interprets the sequence and location of the keys and a translation into machine language occurs. When the translation is completed and the desired task is performed, processed data is sent to an output device, such as a video monitor or a printer. The user may then proceed either to continue data input or to make a transfer of the data to tape or disk for storage.

COMPUTER PROGRAMS

Computers need instructions in order to operate. The central processing unit of a computer understands instructions only if translated into a machine "language" it can read. For this reason different computer languages have been developed to perform the translation process. Still other computer languages have been developed for specific functional tasks.

Languages for computers are divided into two classes: lower and higher. As a computer language more closely resembles a human language, or more closely approximates the way the task at hand is expressed, it is considered a higher-level language. Lower-level languages are more similar in form to the machine's binary code.

Assembly languages are a step more complex than is the machine's binary code. An "assembler," a program to translate assembly language into machine language was developed in the 1950s, which made programming much easier. Yet more complex is the translator program for higher-level languages, which is called a "compiler."

A query language is a popular user-access language because it closely resembles human language. It is used primarily to make computers more accessible to nonprogrammers. Query languages are very useful in business applications, such as when salesclerks need to query a computer for an inventory or price check.

FORTRAN, a higher-level language developed in the late 1950s, is a language geared for mathematical applications. For example, the algebraic expression $a^3 - 2bc$ can be expressed in FORTRAN as A***3 - 2*B*C*. Scientists and engineers find FORTRAN a very useful computer language.

BASIC, a programming language developed by John G. Kemeny and Thomas E. Kurtz of Dartmouth College, is a simplified rendition of FORTRAN and was designed especially for students. Today, BASIC is a very popular computer language for beginners and one of its variations can be found as an included component of many personal computer systems.

WHAT IS WORD PROCESSING?

Word processing is the term given when a computer and its software are designed specifically for the creation, editing, and production of written text. With a word processor typographical errors, spelling mistakes, and editorial changes can be made before a printed copy is produced. This capability saves time in the preparation of written documents because an error-free final copy can be created the first time.

In the home, word processing might be used to produce personal correspondence, school term papers, and diary entries. In business the word processor could be used to produce "personalized" advertising form letters, memoranda, project proposals, reports, and customer correspondence. The word processor would also have the ability to store on disk or tape anything that it produces. Thus, anything a word processor has created can be filed, retrieved, printed again, or revised more easily than conventional writing methods.

In addition, word processing software gives the writer control of margins, permits word, line, and paragraph deletions or insertions; and some software will check for spelling errors, or automatically construct footnotes or bibliographic citations. With such flexibility it is easy to understand why most major newspapers and book publishers, as well as professional writers, have incorporated the word processor into their business procedures. Some analysts even predict that by the year 2000 more than 60 percent of all Americans will have some form of word processing capability in their homes.

THE PERSONAL COMPUTER

Personal computers, also known as microcomputers, are quickly invading the American home and affecting the American way of life. Sales of home computers in 1983 were about $2.4 billion and this amount is expected to more than double in the next five years. Used for everything from playing video games to tax preparation and word processing, the personal computer has yet to realize its full potential as a household information processor. Many analysts expect that soon the microcomputer will be a major factor in the way the American family banks, shops, communicates long-distance, and gains access to news and reference information.

The person who wishes to buy a personal computer today, however, faces many choices. Which computer system and manufacturer is the best? Why does one system cost so much more than another? And what of all the so-called "peripherals," the devices that can be connected to the computer to expand its applications? Dot matrix versus letter-quality printers, mouses, joysticks, and modems are just a few of the options.

Perhaps the foremost idea to keep in mind, before spending the six hundred to five thousand dollars a microcomputer may cost, is to know exactly what the computer will be used for. A system used primarily for video games and itemizing the family budget need not be as expensive or complete as a system that is expected to serve as a word processor producing letter-quality text.

The prospective computer buyer should also study the software on the market before purchasing the expensive hardware. If needed software requires a large RAM capacity, then this factor will determine one of the specifications of the computer to be purchased.

Of course, it is also worth the time to find a computer retailer who is willing to let customers try out programs and equipment before buying. For example, some keyboards may not be responsive enough for speed-typing, others may be too sensitive. Some software may just be too complicated for the beginner to use. One way to be sure to get the hardware and software you can use is to try it out at the store.

Helpful store personnel will also indicate whether software and hardware are compatible with the customer's current equipment, and whether equipment purchased can be modified later to expand its applications or its memory.

FUTURE POSSIBILITIES

If the next twenty years bring as many innovations in computer science and technology as have the last twenty years, then it is very difficult indeed to foretell the extent to which computers will change our lives. However, some general observations, based on current research into new computer technology and applications, can give us a glimpse of what the future might bring.

As has been the trend for the last fifteen years, computers will become smaller, more efficient, and less costly. Computers will be more economical to use in the home, and in some areas, such as small-scale agriculture, computers will be put to work solving problems that will increase productivity and profits.

In the factory, computers will control robots designed to do the repetitive tasks of assembly line manufacturing. Already there exist automobile assembly lines in Japan, the United States, and Europe that rely almost exclusively upon the work of robots and the computers that control them.

Computers will undoubtedly play an increased role in the advancement of medical science and health care services. Research into "bionics" offers the possibility of replacing diseased or damaged body parts with computer controlled limbs or organs. One application already in operation is a computer accessed data bank of symptoms, which doctors throughout the country can use to help them diagnose disease and illness.

Computers will also change our lifestyle. Some futurists foresee the time when almost all an American family's shopping, banking, communications, and access to information will be by means of a home computer system. Sooner to come will be the wider use of magnetized plastic cards that will automatically debit the customer's bank account when presented at a grocery checkout, gasoline station, or department store. Such a situation would indeed take America closer to becoming a "cashless" society. In a scenario writer Alvin Toffler termed an "electronic cottage," more and more people will have jobs at home working at a computer terminal, rather than in an office.

Technologically, computers will incorporate synthesized voices and be able to add complex speech patterns in a variety of languages to the output capacities now available. Computers will also be able to recognize human language commands; thus, they will be able to "listen" to the user, rather than be limited to a keyboard or keypad for data and command input. The technology for these capabilities exists today. Further research and testing will make them commonplace in the future. Computers may eventually be able to project three-dimensional holograph images. Such a capacity might be used in communications, theater, and art.

Perhaps the most interesting aspect of computer research is in the field of "artificial intelligence." A number of computer scientists, Pulitzer Prize winner Douglas R. Hofstadter among them, are searching for computer programming that would create a "machine consciousness." Hofstadter believes this can be achieved only when a computer has an awareness of itself and of the method of its own problem solving routines.

With whatever the future brings, fear of computers is unjustified; rather, one should fear being ignorant of computers and their potential.

EVERYDAY USES OF COMPUTERS

How do computers affect our lives? Here are just a few of the ways computers have become a part of the American way of life:

At the store: The Universal Product Code is a code of lines and numbers printed on products and packaging. This code is read by a computer controlled sensing device and the price and product name is then printed on the customer's receipt. This system gives the consumer an itemized account of purchases, and it gives the merchant a faster, more efficient means of inventory and sales management.

At the bank: Automatic banking services are a very popular means of doing one's banking quickly and at times when regular banking services are closed. With a personalized magnetically coded plastic card a customer may make withdrawals, deposits, and transfers at any time of the day or night.

In the home: Although sales of video games and video game cartridges dropped substantially in 1983, their popularity is still very high. Video games make use of the same technology as a computer, and most video game manufacturers are offering attachments that can convert the video game into a modest home computer system.

In concert: Beginning with the era of the "moog" synthesizer of the 1970s, computer generated music has expanded to become a permanent part of the contemporary music scene.

In government: Computers are the most effective means of handling the vasts amounts of data used for purposes of Social Security management, tax collection, and military personnel records. In law enforcement, computers are used to help trace stolen property and to transfer information concerning fugitive criminals from one part of the country to another.

In the school: Computers as educational aids are increasing in numbers. Students in elementary schools are learning fundamental language and mathematic skills by interacting with a computer. In secondary schools, students are learning computer languages such as BASIC. In the university, computers are an integral part of the management of school records and the administration of business affairs. In addition, computers are a major factor in the learning experience of science and humanities students.

In the hospital: Computers play an important role in the management of health services. Insurance claims, medical histories, and other information can be stored and accessed by computer. The use of computer controlled diagnostic equipment, such as the "CAT" (Computerized Axial Tomography) scanner, has increased the medical specialist's ability to diagnose illness and disease.

Computer Glossary

Acoustic Coupler—a device that permits the transmitting of data to or from a computer by way of telephone lines. A modem can be such a device.

Address—a number that reveals the specific location of data within a computer's memory.

ALGOL—Algorithmic Oriented Language, a computer language developed in the 1960s, which is more popular in Europe than in the United States.

Artificial Intelligence—or AI, the capacity of a machine to make choices, solve problems, perceive external stimuli, and learn new tasks.

ASCII—American Standard Code for Information Interchange; this is a seven bit code that symbolizes both letters and numbers.

Assembly Language—a translation of a machine's binary language into a form easier for humans to use.

BASIC—Beginners All-purpose Symbolic Instruction Code; a computer language derivative of and interactive with FORTRAN. It is a very popular computer language, and variations are used in many personal computers.

Baud—the measure of transmission rate expressed in bits per second.

Binary System—the base-2 number system a computer uses. The only digits in base-2 are 0 and 1.

Bit—refers to binary digit, which can be only 0 or 1.

Boot—the initial program that starts the computer into action.

Bubble Memory—a computer memory capacity that uses microscopic cells or "bubbles" to store information that is not lost when the power is shut off.

Bug—a programming error, or an error caused by hardware malfunction.

Byte—a group of eight bits. A byte may represent a single letter, number, or symbol.

COBOL—Common Business Oriented Language, a computer programming language geared for business applications.

Compiler—a program that changes a high-level language into the computer's binary machine language.

CPU—or Central Processing Unit, which is the part within the computer that executes commands, such as process, store, and retrieve.

Chip—electronic circuitry that is "printed" onto a wafer of silicon. A chip may be 3/4-inch square, yet contain thousands of transistors.

Cursor—the movable indicator displayed on a computer's monitor showing the user where inputted information will appear.

Daisywheel—a mechanism in a printer that holds character symbols arrayed on spokes that originate from a common wheel.

Database—a reservoir of data contained in an organized format for easy entry, retrieval, and revision.

Disk—a magnetic plate, usually of plastic, for storage of data. The most common sizes are 5¹/₂, 3¹/₂, and 8-inch diameters.

Disk Drive—a machine that records data on disks.

Documentation—written instructions to the computer user on the operations of hardware and software.

DOS—Disk Operating System, programs that tell the CPU how to communicate with devices connected to the computer. Common DOS programs include CP/M, MS-DOS, and UNIX.

Dot Matrix—the printing of letters, numbers, or symbols using a matrix of dots. Many computer printers use this concept.

File—a block of data considered by the user as a logical grouping of information and may be handled by the computer as a single unit.

Floppy Disk—a relatively inexpensive disk used for data storage, which must be used with a disk drive.

FORTRAN—Formula Translator, a programming language used primarily for mathematical operations important to engineers and scientists.

Hard Disk—an information storage disk that is most commonly hermetically sealed. A hard disk can store much more data than a floppy disk.

Hardware—includes any of the mechanical or electrical devices of a computer system; excludes software.

Interface—the hardware or software required to couple a computer with another electronic or programming system.

I/O—input/output; refers to the possible ways information may be entered and retrieved from a computer. Common input mechanisms are keyboards, mouse, joystick, and touch-sensitive screens. Output devices include video displays, printers, and voice synthesizers.

K—or kilobyte; the symbol used to represent 1024 bytes.

Keyboard—an input device similar to a set of typewriter keys; some computer keyboards come with a numerical keypad, which is a separate arrangement of numbered keys useful for inputting digital data.

Letter-quality—a designation given to a printer that produces fine quality characters suitable for formal letter or manuscript applications.

LISP—a computer language developed in 1958 that is geared for symbols, characters, and words, rather than for numbers. Computer scientists find it useful in their study of artificial intelligence.

Load—the action of transferring data from a tape or disk into a computer.

Mainframe—the term used to designate a large computer that may be accessed by many terminals.

Menu—a menu permits the user to choose among a list of functions or commands that is displayed on the screen.

Memory—the computer's storage of data; can be "volatile" and lost when power is shut off, or "nonvolatile" and storageable for an indefinite period of time.

Microcomputers—a computer system containing a CPU, memory capacity, I/O devices; any personal computer can be considered a microcomputer.

Modem—Modulating-Demodulating; a device allowing a computer to be connected to a telephone line or a direct line, thereby permitting the transmitting or receiving of data.

Monitor—the video screen on which computer data is displayed.

Mouse—an input device that manipulates a symbol, commonly an arrow, which allows the user to select options displayed on the screen.

PASCAL—a computer language named after French mathematician Blaise Pascal.

Peripheral—a piece of hardware connected to and controlled by a computer, such as a printer, modem, etc.

Pixel—picture element; which is the smallest area of a video screen that can be affected by computer commands.

Printer—an output device that will produce a printed copy of computer generated data.

Program—a list of instructions that tells a computer to perform specified tasks.

RAM—random-access-memory; a temporary data storage capacity that must be transferred to tape, disk, or print-out before power is off, or it is lost.

Real-time processing—handling data quickly enough to influence the environment from which the data came.

ROM—read-only-memory; a memory storage capacity the user can read only and not alter.

Software—the instructions, programs, rules, etc., that make a computer work.

Terminal—a computer without a CPU that is used as an input/output station, by itself or among others, which is connected to an external CPU.

Time-sharing—a concept of handling many computer terminals so that each terminal has a satisfactory response time.

User Friendly—any computer equipment or software that is easy to understand and operate.

Windowing—the capacity of a computer to allow portions of different displays to overlap on the screen at the same time.

Word—a grouping of bits treated as a single unit by the CPU. In microcomputers a word consists of either 8 or 16 bits.

Word Processor—a computer program or system that is geared for the writing, editing, or correcting of written text.

Music Glossary

absolute music—"abstract" or "pure" music; instrumental music requiring for its appreciation neither words nor story nor any association beyond its basic statement.

absolute pitch—the capacity of identifying or singing any tone at proper pitch without the aid of an instrument.

a cappella—choral music sung without accompaniment.

accent—stress or pulse which emphasizes one note over others in a measure.

accidental—a natural, sharp, or flat not indicated by key-signature.

accompaniment—instrumental or choral support for soloists.

adagio—slow tempo; the name often given to a particular section of a musical work so characterized.

allegro—fast tempo; the name often given to a particular section of a musical work so characterized.

alto—a vocal range for a female voice which lies between soprano and contralto; sometimes mistakenly used for contralto; used to describe certain instruments like the viola.

andante—moderately slow tempo; the name often given to a particular section of a musical work so characterized.

antiphonal—the answering or alternation of two groups, choral or instrumental.

aria—a solo song or air in opera, oratorio, or cantata which often lends itself to a display of skill.

arpeggio—a chord, the notes of which are played successively in ascending or descending order.

art song—short song of high dramatic and formal value.

atonality—designating music in which there is no key center; a twentieth-century compositional style sometimes employing a twelve-tone scale.

augmentation—the repetition of a melody with changes provided by the use of proportionately longer notes.

ballet—an elaborate dance usually telling a story, with instrumental or full orchestral accompaniment for theatrical performance.

bar—a measure in musical notation.

baritone—male vocal register between tenor and bass.

baroque—musical style characteristic of composers from 1600 to 1750; includes works of Bach.

bass—deepest male voice.

beat—the rhythmic pulse of music marking time into relatively equal divisions in the measure.

bel canto—operatic singing technique used to produce a lyrical effect.

binary form—notable in music which uses two contrasting themes in a section.

bravura—great skill and expansiveness of style.

buffo—the character-comic in opera.

cadence—chords at the end of a tune, phrase, section, or movement, which have the effect of bringing the statement to a rest.

cadenza—an elaboration of the cadence, displaying the skill of a soloist.

canon—music, such as a round, in which two or more sections repeat the same melody, starting at different times but overlapping.

cantabile—emphasis upon a "singing" quality in the music.

cantata—an elaborate vocal and instrumental form with arias, recitatives, duets, and chorus, but not requiring dramatic or scenic implementation.

castrato—a eunuch with an adult male voice in the female range.

chamber music—music specifically intended for performance in a small hall, each part usually being taken by one instrument as contrasted with groups or sections of instruments in large orchestras.

chord—three or more tones sounded together.

chromatic—music with many half step intervals not in the diatonic scale.

classical music—the musical style of composers between 1750 and 1825, including the works of Mozart and Beethoven.

clef—sign on the left of each staff indicating sound or exact pitch.

coda—passage which rounds out a section or end of a composition.

coloratura—elaborate vocal passage demonstrating skill of both composer and soloist.

concert master—first violinist in orchestra, frequently also an assistant conductor.

concerto—composition for one or more instruments with orchestral accompaniment.

conductor—orchestra leader, chiefly responsible for musical interpretation.

contralto—lowest pitched female voice.

counterpoint—simultaneous use of two or more melodies.

crescendo—becoming gradually louder.

development—compositional exploration and restatement of thematic idea.

diatonic—opposite of chromatic; music confined to the use of notes in a given major or minor key.

discord—*See* dissonance.

dissonance—a combination of clashing tones requiring the addition of other tones for resolution.

divertimento—a light instrumental composition in several short movements.

dominant—fifth tone in the minor or major scale.

downbeat—first strong accent in each measure.

encore—repetition of a piece or performance of an additional one in response to applause.

enharmonic—a tone having several different forms of notation.

ensemble—combination of performers; also, overall quality of musical expression.

equal temperament—division of octave into twelve equal halftones; also characteristic method of tuning instruments.

étude—"study music" composed for practice purposes but often included in concert repertoires.

exposition—in sonata form, among others, a first section containing statement of themes to be developed.

expression—immediate personal and emotional interpretation of music by a performer.

falsetto—adult male voice used in an unnaturally high pitch.

fermata—a long pause.

finale—last section of a composition.

flat—notation indicating the lowering of a tone by a half step.

forte—loud.

fugue—a musical form similar to the canon but one in which various imitations of the melody occur in shorter phrases.

fundamental—primary note of a chord or harmonic series.

glissando—tonal effect produced by sliding finger over the strings or keys of an instrument.

grace note—an embellishing note, printed in smaller type.

Gregorian chant—early church music named for Pope Gregory I; used in Roman Catholic church services.

harmony—the simultaneous combination of tones into chords; also the study of chord functions and structure.

homophony—music composed of a melody supported by harmonic chordal accompaniment.

hymn—originally a religious song in praise of God; also used of songs with a patriotic theme.

imitation—technique of composition

which repeats theme or melody, making use of several instruments or voices as in canon, fugue, or round.

impressionism—the musical style of late nineteenth- and early twentieth-century composers, including Debussy and Ravel.

interval—the difference in pitch between two notes.

intonation—fidelity of pitch.

inversion—reversing or inverting the position of notes in chords or intervals.

-issimo—suffix meaning "very," added to many musical terms.

jazz—music of black American origin, initially called "ragtime," and characterized by syncopated rhythm.

key—scale; relating to a system of tonal relationships developed from a tonic keynote.

keynote—base or principal note from which a scale is derived.

largo—a very slow and deliberate tempo; the name often given to a particular section of a musical work so characterized.

legato—smooth transitions from note to note without breaks.

leitmotiv—thematic melody used recurrently to identify specific characters, events, places, ideas, or emotions; characteristically used by Wagner.

lento—slow tempo between andante and largo.

libretto—the entire literary text of a musical work utilizing singing and speaking.

lyrics—words set to music.

measure—a horizontally lined space between two vertical bar lines which mark off a section of a staff.

medieval music—styles of music developed during the thousand-year period beginning A.D. 500, primarily vocal; greatly influenced by church liturgy, by court and peasant life.

melodrama—scene or play in which a musical background accompanies action and dialogue.

melody—a succession of notes of varying pitch and duration having a distinct pattern.

meter—strong and weak accents in rhythmical pattern.

metronome—a clockwork pendulum invented to insure standard tempi.

mezzo—prefix meaning "half."

mezzo-soprano—female voice between soprano and alto ranges.

M.M.—letters indicating metronomic setting.

mode—general term for system(s) of arranging intervals of a scale.

moderato—moderate tempo.

modern music—styles of music developed from the beginning of the twentieth century, as distinguished from earlier styles still flourishing; among the former, works of Schoenberg and Bartok.

modulation—change of key or tonality through a succession of chords.

molto—very or much more, as in molto adagio (very slowly).

monophony—unaccompanied music composed only of a melodic line.

mordent—a grace note.

motive—a musical phrase which reappears irregularly.

movement—major division of a musical composition.

natural—symbol indicating the return of a tone to its natural pitch from a previous sharping or flatting.

notation—entire system employed for writing Western music.

obbligato—an accompaniment which is an indispensable and intrinsic part of the musical statement; by misuse, in some nineteenth-century music used in the opposite sense to refer to a part which is optional.

octave—the interval covering eight successive notes in the diatonic scale, e.g., middle C to the C above it.

opera—a form of drama set to orchestral music in which most of the dialogue is sung; generally presented in an elaborate production.

opus—a composition or set of compositions; customarily accompanied by a number to indicate its place in the chronological order of a composer's work.

oratorio—a form of drama set to orchestral music and voice; differing from opera in the absence of staging, costumes, and scenery; usually on a religious subject.

overture—introductory instrumental music to an opera or play; also now an independent form.

partita—originally, variations or a set of dances; by extension, used to mean "suite."

phrase—a short distinguishable part of a melody.

piano—softly.

pitch—degree of highness or lowness of a sound.

più—more; as in più lento (more slowly).

poco—a little.

polyphony—music composed of at least two melodies played simultaneously.

polytonality—simultaneous use of two different keys.

prelude—a short composition which can be a piece of a single movement, the beginning of a longer work, or an overture.

presto—very fast tempo; the name often given to a particular section of a musicat work so characterized.

program music—descriptive music which tells a story or describes a place; frequently employs explanatory or supportive program literature; the opposite of "absolute music."

progression—advance from one tone to another or from one chord to another.

quartet—an intimate musical form for four instruments or voices.

quintet—similar to quartet but refers to five instruments or voices.

recapitulation—repetition of a thematic statement after an intervening development and contrast.

reprise—repeat of a segment of music.

rest—musical notation indicating silence.

rhapsody—a very free musical form developed during the nineteenth century.

rhythm—recurrent pattern created by the accent and duration of notes.

rondo—a musical form in which the main theme is consistently repeated throughout.

scale—a series of consecutive tones forming an octave.

scherzo—usually the third movement of a larger composition; humorous and lively.

score—written or printed piece of music in which the different instruments or voices are entered on a separate staff, one above the other.

sharp—notation raising a tone by a half step.

signature—symbol placed at the beginning of a composition specifying key and tempo.

sonata—a composition for one or more instruments.

soprano—the highest female singing voice.

staff—the five horizontal lines and intervening spaces upon which musical notation is made.

symphonic poem—a tone poem; a form of program music.

symphony—major form of orchestral work, divided into movements.

syncopation—kind of rhythm created by altering the natural accent into a weak beat.

tempo (pl: tempi)—the rate of speed at which a piece or passage of music moves.

tenor—highest normal adult male voice; also the range of some instruments.

theme—melody used as the main musical line for development and variation.

tonality—the adherence to the keynote (tonic) as the referent of all chords and harmonies used in a composition or part of a composition.

tone—a note; sound with a fixed pitch.

tone poem—*See* symphonic poem.

transpose—changing key or pitch, leaving all other musical relationships intact.

treble—the highest register of musical sound.

upbeat—weak beat preceding a heavy accent.

variation—alteration of a melody that still retains its essential qualities.

Space Glossary*

ablation—the removal of surface material from a body by vaporization, melting, or other process; specifically the intentional removal of material from a nose cone or spacecraft during high-speed movement through a plan etary atmosphere to provide thermal protection to the underlying structure.

absolute zero—the theoretical temperature at which all molecular motion ceases.

acceleration—the rate of change of velocity.

acquisition and tracking radar—a radar set that locks onto a strong signal and tracks the object reflecting the signal.

aerodynamics—the science of the motion of air and other gaseous fluids, and of the forces acting on bodies when the bodies move through such fluids, or of the movement of such fluids against or around the bodies, as "his research in aerodynamics."

aerolite—a meteorite composed principally of stony material.

aerospace—(from aeronautics and space) of or pertaining to both the earth's atmosphere and space, as in "aerospace industries."

aerothermodynamic border—an altitude at about 100 miles, above which the atmosphere is so rarefied that the motion of an object through it at high speeds generates no significant surface heat.

aerothermodynamics—the study of the aerodynamic and thermodynamic problems connected with aerodynamic heating.

airglow—a relatively steady visible emission from the upper atmosphere, as distinguished from the sporadic emission of aurorae.

albedo—the ratio of the amount of electromagnetic radiation reflected by a body to the amount falling upon it, commonly expressed as a percentage.

angel—a radar echo caused by a physical phenomenon not discernible to the eye.

annular eclipse—an eclipse in which a thin ring of the source of light appears around the obscuring body.

aphelion—the point at which a planet or other celestial object in orbit about the sun is farthest from the sun.

apogee—in an orbit about the earth, the point at which the satellite is farthest from the earth; the highest altitude reached by a sounding rocket.

areo—combining form of Ares (Mars) as in "areography."

asteroid—one of the many small celestial bodies revolving around the sun, most of the orbits being between those of Mars and Jupiter. Also called "planetoid," "minor planet."

astroballistics—the study of the phenomena arising out of the motion of a solid through a gas at speeds high enough to cause ablation; for example, the interaction of a meteoroid with the atmosphere.

attitude—the position or orientation of an aircraft, spacecraft, etc., either in motion or at rest, as determined by the relationship between its axes and some reference line or plane such as the horizon.

aurora—the sporadic visible emission from the upper atmosphere over middle and high latitudes. Also called "northern lights."

azimuth—horizontal direction or bearing.

Baker-Nunn camera—a large camera used in tracking satellites.

ballistics—the science that deals with the motion, behavior, and effects of projectiles, especially bullets, aerial bombs, rockets, or the like; the science or art of designing and hurling projectiles so as to achieve a desired performance.

balloon-type rocket—a rocket, such as Atlas, that requires the pressure of its propellants (or other gases) within it to give it structural integrity.

beam-rider—a craft following a beam, particularly one which does so automatically, the beam providing the guidance.

bipropellant—a rocket propellant consisting of two unmixed or uncombined chemicals (fuel and oxidizer) fed to the combustion chamber separately.

blip—*See* **pip.**

boilerplate—as in "boilerplate capsule," a metal copy of the flight model, the structure or components of which are heavier than the flight model.

boiloff—the vaporization of a cold propellant, such as liquid oxygen or liquid hydrogen, as the temperature of the propellant mass rises,as in the tank of a rocket being readied for launch.

booster engine—an engine, especially a booster rocket, that adds its thrust to the thrust of the sustainer engine.

booster rocket—1. a rocket engine, either solid or liquid fuel, that assists the normal propulsive system, or sustainer engine, of a rocket or aeronautical vehicle in some phase of its flight. 2. a rocket used to set a missile vehicle in motion before another engine takes over.

boostglide vehicle—a vehicle (half aircraft, half spacecraft) designed to fly to the limits of the sensible atmosphere, then be boosted by rockets into the space above, returning to earth by gliding under aerodynamic control.

braking ellipses—a series of ellipses, decreasing in size due to aerodynamic drag, followed by a spacecraft in entering a planetary atmosphere.

breakoff phenomenon—the feeling which sometimes occurs during high altitude flight of being totally separated and detached from the earth and human society. Also called the "breakaway phenomenon."

centrifuge—specifically, a large motor-driven apparatus with a long arm at the end of which human and animal subjects or equipment can be revolved and rotated at various speeds to simulate very closely the prolonged accelerations encountered in highperformance aircraft, rockets, and spacecraft.

checkout—a sequence of actions taken to test or examine a launch vehicle or spacecraft as to its readiness to perform its intended function.

chemosphere—the vaguely defined region of the upper atmosphere in which photochemical reactions take place.

cislunar—(Latin *cis*, "on this side") of or

*The material on space exploration was selected from **Space . . . The New Frontier** and **The Challenge of Space Exploration,** prepared by The National Aeronautics and Space Administration, Washington, D.C.

pertaining to phenomena, projects, or activity in the space between the earth and moon, or between the earth and the moon's orbit.

closed ecological system—a system that provides for the maintenance of life in an isolated living chamber such as a spacecraft cabin by means of a cycle wherein exhaled carbon dioxide, urine, and other waste matter are converted chemically or by photosynthesis into oxygen, water, and food.

cold-flow test—a test of a liquid rocket without firing it to check or verify the efficiency of a propulsion subsystem, providing for the conditioning and flow of propellants (including tank pressurization, propellant loading, and propellant feeding).

companion body—a nose cone, last-stage rocket, or other body that orbits along with an earth satellite.

complex—entire area of launch site facilities. This includes blockhouse, launch pad, gantry, etc. Also referred to as a "launch complex."

composite propellant—a solid rocket propellant consisting of a fuel and an oxidizer.

conic section—a curve formed by the intersection of a plane and a right circular cone. Usually called "conic."

console—an array of controls and indicators for the monitoring and control of a particular sequence of actions, as in the checkout of a rocket, a countdown action, or a launch procedure.

control rocket—a vernier engine, retro-rocket, or other such rocket, used to guide or make small changes in the velocity of a rocket, spacecraft, or the like.

corona—the faintly luminous outer envelope of the sun. Also called "solar corona."

cosmic rays—the extremely high energy subatomic particles which bombard the atmosphere from outer space. Cosmic-ray primaries seem to be mostly protons, hydrogen nuclei, but also comprise heavier nuclei. On colliding with atmospheric particles they produce many different kinds of lower-energy secondary cosmic radiation.

cryogenic temperature—in general, a temperature range below about–50° C.; more particularly, temperatures within a few degrees of absolute zero.

deep space probes—spacecraft designed for exploring space to the vicinity of the moon and beyond. Deep space probes with specific missions may be referred to as "lunar probe," "Mars probe," "solar probe," etc.

diplexer—a device permitting an antenna system to be used simultaneously or separately by two transmitters. *Compare with* **duplexer.**

dish—a parabolic type of radio or radar antenna, roughly the shape of a soup bowl.

Doppler shift—the change in frequency with which energy reaches a receiver when the source of radiation or a reflector of the radiation and the receiver are in motion relative to each other. The Doppler shift is used in many tracking and navigation systems.

dosimeter—a device, worn by persons working around radioactive material, which indicates the amount (dose) of radiation to which they have been exposed.

Dovap—from Doppler, velocity and position, a tracking system which uses the Doppler shift caused by a target moving relative to a ground transmitter to obtain velocity and position information.

drogue parachute—a type of parachute attached to a body, used to slow it down; also called "deceleration parachute," or "drag parachute."

duplexer—a device which permits a single antenna system to be used for both transmitting and receiving.

eccentric—not having the same center; varying from a circle, as in "eccentric orbit."

ecological system—a habitable environment, either created artifically, such as in a manned space vehicle, or occurring naturally, such as the environment on the surface of the earth, in which man, animals, or other organisms can live in mutual relationship with each other.

escape velocity—the radial speed which a particle or larger body must attain in order to escape from the gravitational field of a planet or star.

extraterrestrial—from outside the earth.

film cooling—the cooling of a body or surface, such as the inner surface of a rocket combustion chamber, by maintaining a thin fluid layer over the affected area.

flashback—a reversal of flame propagation in a system, counter to the usual flow of the combustible mixture.

flux—the rate of flow of some quantity, often used in reference to the flow of some form of energy.

flying test bed—an aircraft, rocket, or other flying vehicle used to carry objects or devices being flight tested.

g or G—an acceleration equal to the acceleration of gravity, 32.2 feet per second per second at sea level; used as a unit of stress measurement for bodies undergoing acceleration.

gantry—a frame structure that spans over something, as an elevated platform that runs astride a work area, supported by wheels on each side; specifically, short for "gantry crane" or "gantry scaffold."

gas cap—the gas immediately in front of a meteoroid or reentry body as it travels through the atmosphere; the leading portion of a meteor. This gas is compressed and adiabatically heated to incandescence.

geo—a prefix meaning "earth," as in "geology," "geophysics."

geoprobe—a rocket vehicle designed to explore space near the earth at a distance of more than 4,000 miles from the earth's surface. Rocket vehicles operating lower than 4,000 miles are termed "sounding rockets."

gimbal—1. a device with two mutually perpendicular and intersecting axes of rotation, thus giving free angular movement in two directions, on which an engine or other object may be mounted. 2. in a gyro, a support which provides the spin axis with a degree of freedom.

gnotobiotics—the study of germ-free animals.

gravity—the force imparted by the earth to a mass on, or close to the earth. Since the earth is rotating, the force observed as gravity is the resultant of the force of gravitation and the centrifugal force arising from this rotation.

g-suit or G-suit—a suit that exerts pressure on the abdomen and lower parts of the body to prevent or retard the collection of blood below the chest under positive acceleration.

g-tolerance—a tolerance in a person or other animal, or in a piece of equipment, to an acceleration of a particular value.

gyro—a device which utilizes the angular momentum of a spinning rotor to sense angular motion of its base about one or two axes at right angles to the spin axis. Also called "gyroscope."

hardness—of X rays and other radiation of high energy, a measure of penetrating power. Radiation which will penetrate a 10-centimeter thickness of lead is considered "hard radiation."

hot test—a propulsion system test conducted by actually firing the propellants.

hypersonic—1. pertaining to hypersonic flow. 2. pertaining to speeds of Mach 5 or greater.

inertial guidance—guidance by means of acceleration measured and integrated within the craft.

infrared—infrared radiation; electromagnetic radiation in the wavelength interval from the red end of the visible spectrum on the lower limit to microwaves used in radar on the upper limit.

insertion—the process of putting an artificial satellite into orbit. Also the time of such action.

ionosphere—the part of the earth's outer atmosphere where ions and electrons are present in quantities sufficient to affect the propagation of radio waves.

Kepler's laws—the three empirical laws describing the motions of planets in their orbits, discovered by Johannes Kepler (1571–1630). These are: (1) The orbits of the planets are ellipses, with the sun at a common focus. (2) As a planet moves in its orbit, the line joining the planet and sun sweeps over equal areas in equal intervals of time. Also called "law of equal areas." (3) The squares of the periods of revolution of any two planets are proportional to the cubes of their mean distances from the sun.

launch ring—the metal ring on the launch pad on which a missile stands before launch.

launch vehicle—any device which propels and guides a spacecraft into orbit about the earth or into a trajectory to another celestial body. Often called "booster."

launch window—an interval of time during which a rocket can be launched to accomplish a particular purpose, as "liftoff occurred 5 minutes after the beginning of the 82-minute launch window".

lib ration—a real or apparent oscillatory motion, particularly the apparent oscillation of the moon.

Mach number—(after Ernst Mach [1838–1916], Austrian scientist) a number expressing the ratio of the speed of a body or of a point on a body with respect to the surrounding air or other fluid, or the speed of a flow, to the speed of sound in the medium; the speed represented by this number.

manometer—an instrument for measuring pressure of gases and vapors both above and below atmospheric pressure.

mass—the measure of the amount of matter in a body, thus its inertia.

mass-energy equivalence—the equivalence of a quantity of mass m and a quantity of energy E, the two quantities being related by the mass-energy relation $E = mc^2$, *where* c = the speed of light.

meteor—in particular, the light phenomenon which results from the entry into the earth's atmosphere of a solid particle from space; more generally, any physical object or phenomenon associated with such an event.

microwave region—commonly that region of the radio spectrum between approximately one thousand megacycles and three hundred thousand megacycles.

missile—any object thrown, dropped, fired, launched, or otherwise projected with the purpose of striking a target. Short for "ballistic missile," "guided missile."

mockup—a full-sized replica or dummy of something, such as a spacecraft, often made of some substitute material, such as wood, and sometimes incorporating functioning pieces of equipment, such as engines.

module—1. a self-contained unit of a launch vehicle or spacecraft which serves as a building block for the overall structure. The module is usually designated by its primary function as "command module," "lunar landing module," etc. 2. a one-package assembly of functionally associated electronic parts; usually a plug-in unit.

Newton's laws of motion—a set of three fundamental postulates forming the basis of the mechanics of rigid bodies, formulated by Newton in 1687.

The first law is concerned with the principle of inertia and states that if a body in motion is not acted upon by an external force, its momentum remains constant (law of conservation of momentum). The second law asserts that the rate of change of momentum of a body is proportional to the force acting upon the body and is in the direction of the applied force. A familiar statement of this is the equation

$$F = ma,$$

where F is vector sum of the applied forces, m the mass, and a the vector acceleration of the body. The third law is the principle of action and reaction, stating that for every force acting upon a body there exists a corresponding force of the same magnitude exerted by the body in the opposite direction.

normal shock wave—a shock wave perpendicular, or substantially so, to the direction of flow in a supersonic flow field. Sometimes shortened to "normal shock."

nozzle—specifically, the part of a rocket thrust chamber assembly in which the gases produced in the chamber are accelerated to high velocities.

orbital elements—a set of seven parameters defining the orbit of a satellite.

order of magnitude—a factor of 10.

paraglider—a flexible-winged, kite-like vehicle designed for use in a recovery system for launch vehicles or as a reentry vehicle.

passive—reflecting a signal without transmission, as "Echo is a passive satellite." Contrasted with "active."

perigee—that orbital point nearest the earth when the earth is the center of attraction.

photosphere—the intensely bright portion of the sun visible to the unaided eye.

pickoff—a sensing device, used in combination with a gyroscope in an automatic pilot or other automatic or robot apparatus, that responds to angular movement to create a signal or to effect some type of control.

pickup—a device that converts a sound, view, or other form of intelligence into corresponding electric signals (e.g., a microphone, a television camera, or a phonograph pickup).

pip—signal indication on the scope of an electronic instrument, produced by a short, sharply peaked pulse of voltage. Also called "blip."

pitchover—the programmed turn from the vertical that a rocket under power takes as it describes an arc and points in a direction other than vertical.

posigrade rocket—an auxiliary rocket which fires in the direction in which the vehicle is pointed, used for example in separating two stages of a vehicle.

precession—the change in the direction of the axis of rotation of a spinning body or of the plane of the orbit of an orbiting body when acted upon by an outside force.

prestage—a step in the action of igniting a large liquid rocket taken prior to the ignition of the full flow, and consisting of igniting a partial flow of propellants into the thrust chamber.

primary—1. short for "primary body." 2. short for "primary cosmic ray."

primary cosmic rays—high-energy particles originating outside the earth's atmosphere.

probe—any device inserted in an environment for the purpose of obtaining information about the environment, specifically, an instrumented vehicle moving through the upper atmosphere or space, or landing upon another celestial body in order to obtain information about the specific environment.

prominence—a filament-like protuberance from the visible portion of the sun.

proton—a positively charged subatomic particle of a positive charge equal to the negative charge of the electron but of 1,837 times the mass; a constituent of all atomic nuclei.

proving stand—a test stand for reaction engines, especially rocket engines.

purge—to rid a line or tank of residual fluid, especially of fuel or oxygen in the tanks or lines of a rocket after a test firing or simulated test firing.

radar astronomy—the study of celestial bodies within the solar system by means of radiation originating on earth but reflected from the body under observation.

radiosonde—a balloon-borne instrument for the simultaneous measurement and transmission of meteorological data.

reaction control system—a system of controlling the attitude of a craft when outside the atmosphere by using jets of gas in lieu of aerodynamic control surfaces.

readout—the action of a radio transmitter transmitting data either instantaneously with the acquisition of the data or by play of a magnetic tape upon which the data have been recorded.

real time—time in which reporting on events or recording of events is simultaneous with the events.

recombination—the process by which a positive and a negative ion join to form a neutral molecule or other neutral particle.

red shift—in astronomy, the displacement of observed spectral lines toward the longer wavelengths of the red end of the spectrum. *Compare* **space reddening.**

reentry—the event occurring when a spacecraft or other object comes back into the sensible atmosphere after being rocketed to altitudes above the sensible atmosphere; the action involved in this event.

regenerator—a device used in a thermo-dynamic process for capturing and returning to the process heat that would otherwise be lost.

relativity—a principle that postulates the equivalence of the description of the universe, in terms of physical laws, by various observers, or for various frames of reference.

rocket engine—a reaction engine that contains within itself, or carries along with itself, all the substances necessary for its operation or for the consumption or combustion of its fuel, not requiring intake of any outside substance and hence capable of operation in outer space. Also called "rocket motor."

rocketsonde—meteorological rocket.

rockoon—a high-altitude sounding system consisting of a small solid-propellant research rocket launched from a large plastic balloon.

roll—the rotational or oscillatory movement of an aircraft or similar body which takes place about a longitudinal axis through the body—called "roll" for any amount of such rotation.

rotation—turning of a body about an axis within the body, as the daily rotation of the earth.

rumble—a form of combustion instability, especially in a liquid-propellant rocket engine, characterized by a low-pitched, low-frequency rumbling noise; the noise made in this kind of combustion.

scrub—to cancel a scheduled rocket firing, either before or during countdown.

selenocentric—relating to the center of the moon; referring to the moon as a center.

selenographic—1. of or pertaining to the physical geography of the moon. 2. specifically, referring to positions on the moon measured in latitude from the moon's equator and in longitude from a reference meridian.

sensible atmosphere—that part of the atmosphere that offers resistance to a body passing through it.

sensor—the component of an instrument that converts an input signal into a quantity which is measured by another part of the instrument. Also called "sensing element."

service tower—*See* **gantry.**

shock tube—a relatively long tube or pipe in which very brief high-speed gas flows are produced by the sudden release of gas at very high pressure into a low-pressure portion of the tube; the high-speed flow moves into the region of low pressure behind a shock wave.

solar wind—a stream of protons constantly moving outward from the sun.

sounding—1. in geophysics, any penetration of the natural environment for scientific observation. 2. in meteorology, same as upper-air observation. However, a common connotation is that of a single complete radiosonde observation.

space—1. specifically, the part of the universe lying outside the limits of the earth's atmosphere. 2. more generally, the volume in which all spatial bodies, including the earth, move.

space reddening—the observed reddening, or absorption of shorter wavelengths, of the light from distant celestial bodies caused by scattering by small particles in interstellar space. *Compare* **red shift.**

specific impulse—a performance parameter of a rocket propellant, expressed in seconds, and equal to thrust (in pounds) divided by weight flow rate (in pounds per second). *See* **thrust.**

sunspot—a relatively dark area on the surface of the sun, consisting of a dark central umbra and a surrounding penumbra that is intermediate in brightness between the umbra and the surrounding photosphere.

sunspot cycle—a periodic variation in the number and area of sunspots with an average length of 11.1 years, but varying between about 7 and 17 years.

sustainer engine—an engine that maintains the velocity of a missile or rocket vehicle, once it has achieved its programmed velocity through use of a booster engine.

synchronous satellite—an equatorial west-to-east satellite orbiting the earth at an altitude of 22,300 statute miles, at which altitude it makes one revolution in 24 hours, synchronous with the earth's rotation.

synergic curve—a curve plotted for the ascent of a rocket, space-air vehicle, or space vehicle calculated to give the vehicle an optimum economy in fuel with an optimum velocity.

tektite—a small glassy body containing no crystals, probably of meteoritic origin, and bearing no antecedent relation to the geological formation in which it occurs.

telemetry—the science of measuring a quantity or quantities, transmitting the measured value to a distant station, and there interpreting, indicating, or recording the quantities measured.

thermodynamics—the study of the relationships between heat and other forms of energy.

thermonuclear—pertaining to a nuclear reaction that is triggered by particles of high thermal energy.

thrust—1. the pushing force developed by an aircraft engine or a rocket engine. 2. specifically, in rocketry, the product of propellant mass flow rate and exhaust velocity relative to the vehicle.

topside sounder—a satellite designed to measure ion concentration in the ionosphere from above the ionosphere.

transit—1. the passage of a celestial body across a celestial meridian; usually called "meridian transit." 2. the apparent passage of a celestial body across the face of another celestial body or across any point, area, or line.

translunar—of or pertaining to space outside the moon's orbit about the earth.

transponder—a combined receiver and transmitter whose function is to transmit signals automatically when triggered by an interrogating signal.

T-time—any specific time, minus or plus, as referenced to "zero," or "launch" time, during a countdown sequence that is intended to result in the firing of a rocket propulsion unit that launches a rocket vehicle or missile.

ullage—the amount that a container, such as a fuel tank, lacks of being full.

ultraviolet radiation—electromagnetic radiation shorter in wavelength than visible radiation but longer than X-rays; roughly, radiation in the wavelength interval between 10 and 4,000 angstroms.

umbilical cord—any of the servicing electrical or fluid lines between the ground or a tower and an upright rocket missile or vehicle before the launch. Often shortened to "umbilical."

Van Allen Belt, Van Allen Radiation Belt, Van Allen Radiation Region (for James A. Van Allen, 1914–) —the zone of high-intensity radiation surrounding the earth beginning at altitudes of approximately 500 miles.

vernier engine—a rocket engine of small thrust used primarily to obtain a fine adjustment in the velocity and trajectory of a ballistic missile or space vehicle just after the thrust cutoff of the last propulsion engine, and used secondarily to add thrust to a booster or sustainer engine. Also called "vernier rocket."

weightlessness—1. a condition in which no acceleration, whether of gravity or other force, can be detected by an observer within the system in question. 2. a condition in which gravitational and other external forces acting on a body produce no stress, either internal or external, in the body.

yaw—1. the lateral rotational or oscillatory movement of an aircraft, rocket, or the like about a transverse axis. 2. the amount of this movement; i.e., the angle of yaw.

zero g—*See* **weightlessness.**

The Shuttle Era

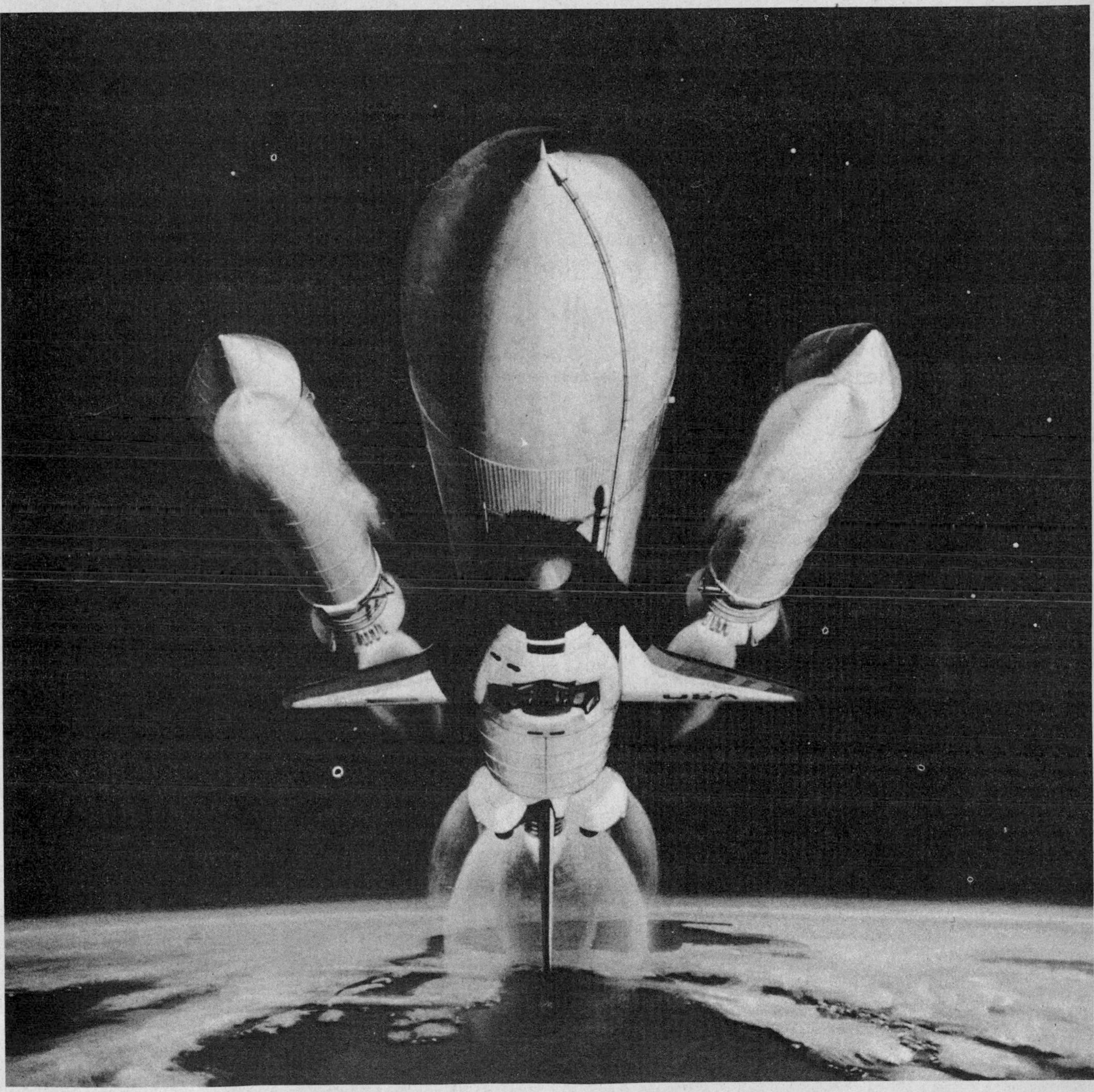

A unique high-angle view of the Space Shuttle (artist's concept). The Orbiter, still attached to the external tank as the solid rocket boosters are jettisoned, climbs upward to begin its Earth orbital mission.

The Shuttle Era

The Inertial Upper Stage (IUS) is deployed from open payload bay of Shuttle Orbiter into space by the Orbiter's remote manipulator (artist's concept). The IUS can rocket spacecraft to geosynchronous orbits or into interplanetary trajectories. The IUS is one of two expendable, low-cost propulsion vehicles that are being considered for the Space Transportation System.

On December 17, 1903, Orville and Wilbur Wright successfully achieved sustained flight in a power-driven aircraft. The first flight that day lasted only 12 seconds over a distance of 37 meters (120 feet), which is about the length of the Space Shuttle Orbiter. The fourth and final flight of the day traveled 260 meters (852 feet) in 59 seconds. The initial notification of this event to the world was a telegram to the Wrights' father.

Sixty-six years later, a man first stepped on the lunar surface and an estimated 500 million people around the world watched the event on television or listened to it on radio as it happened.

Building upon previous achievements, new plateaus in air and space transportation have been reached — military aviation, airmail, commercial passenger service, the jet age, and manned space flight. Now a new era nears. The beginning of regularly scheduled runs of NASA's Space Shuttle to and from Earth orbit in the 1980's marks the coming of age in space. The Shuttle turns formidable and costly space missions into routine and economical operations that generate maximum benefits for all people. Shuttle opens space to men and women of all nations who are reasonably healthy and have important work to do there.

A Versatile Vehicle

Space Shuttle is a true aerospace vehicle. It takes off like a rocket, maneuvers in Earth orbit like a spacecraft, and lands like an airplane. The Space Shuttle is designed to carry heavy loads into Earth orbit. Other launch vehicles have done this. But unlike the other launch vehicles which were used just once, each Space Shuttle Orbiter may be used again and again.

Moreover, Shuttle permits checkout and repair of unmanned satellites in orbit, or return of the satellites to Earth for repairs that could not be done in space. This will result in considerable savings in spacecraft costs. Satellites that the Shuttle can orbit and maintain include those involved in environmental protection, energy, weather forecasting, navigation, fishing, farming, mapping, oceanography, and many other fields useful to man.

Spacecraft destined for geosynchronous orbit will be boosted from low Earth orbit by either a Solid Spinning Upper Stage (SSUS) or by the Inertial Upper Stage (IUS) that is being developed by the United States Air Force. Interplanetary spacecraft will be propelled by a variation of the Centaur upper stage that has been used with the Atlas and Titan expendable launch vehicles.

With its manipulator arm extended, the Space Shuttle Orbiter prepares to retrieve a satellite (artist's concept).

The large Space Telescope is being designed as an optical telescope observatory to be used in Earth orbit, unhindered by atmospheric distortion. Here, it is shown being deployed in orbit by the Space Shuttle.

Unmanned satellites, such as the Space Telescope, which can multiply our view of the universe, and the Long Duration Exposure Facility (LDEF), which can demonstrate the effects on materials of long exposure to the space environment, can be placed in orbit, erected, and returned to Earth by the Space Shuttle. Shuttle crews can also perform such services as replacing the Space Telescope's film packs and lenses. The Space Telescope program is managed by NASA's Marshall Space Flight Center, Huntsville, Alabama and the LDEF is a project of the NASA Langley Research Center, Hampton, Virginia.

The Shuttle is a manned spacecraft, but unlike manned spacecraft of the past such as Mercury, Gemini, and Apollo, it touches down like an airplane on a landing strip. Thus, the Shuttle eliminates the need for the expensive sea recovery force required for Mercury, Gemini, and Apollo. In addition, unlike the previous manned spacecraft, the Shuttle is reusable. It can be refurbished and ready for another journey into space in a comparatively short turnaround time.

The Shuttle can quickly provide a vantage point in space for observations of transient astronomical events or of sudden weather, agricultural, or environmental crises. Information from Shuttle observations could contribute to sound decisions for countries dealing with such problems.

The Shuttle is scheduled to carry a complete scientific laboratory called "Spacelab" into Earth orbit. Developed by the European Space Agency (ESA), Spacelab is similar to earthbound laboratories but is adapted to operate in zero gravity (weightlessness). It provides a shirt-sleeve environment, suitable for working, eating, and sleeping without the encumbrance of special clothing or space suits.

Spacelab provides facilities for as many as four laboratory specialists to conduct experiments in such fields as medicine, manufacturing, astronomy, and pharmaceuticals. Spacelab remains attached to the Shuttle Orbiter throughout a mission. Upon return to Earth, Spacelab is removed from the Orbiter and outfitted for its next assignment. It can be reused about 50 times.

Spacelab personnel will be men and women of many nations, experts in their fields, and in reasonably good health. They will require only a few weeks of space-flight training.

Participating ESA nations are Belgium, Denmark, France, Italy, The Netherlands, Spain, Switzerland, United Kingdom, Austria, and the Federal Republic of Germany (West Germany). Spacelab is an example of international sharing of space costs and of worldwide interest in the study of science in a space environment.

Projects that only recently were considered impracticable become feasible with Space Shuttle. Shuttle can carry into orbit the building blocks for large solar power stations that would convert the abundant solar heat and sunlight of space into unlimited supplies of electricity for an energy-hungry world. These building blocks would be assembled by specialists, transported, and supported by Space Shuttle.

The Shuttle can also carry the building blocks for self-sustaining settlements into Earth orbit. Inhabitants of these settlements could be employed in such vital occupations as building and maintaining solar power stations and manufacturing drugs, metals, glass for lenses, and electronic crystals. Manufacturing in weightless space could reduce costs of certain drugs, create new alloys, produce drugs and lenses of unusual purity, and enable crystals to grow very large. Drugs, metals, glass, and electronic crystals will also be manufactured during Spacelab missions, long before the establishment of any space settlement.

A high-angle front view of the Orbiter vehicle in Earth orbit carrying Spacelab hardware as the primary cargo in its payload bay (artist's concept).
A crewmember is seen performing extravehicular operations outside the pressurized laboratory in the payload bay.

Shuttle Management Team

NASA's Lyndon B. Johnson Space Center, Houston, Texas, manages the Space Shuttle program and is also responsible for development, production, and delivery of the Orbiter.

NASA's George C. Marshall Space Flight Center, Huntsville, Alabama, is responsible for the development, production, and delivery of the solid rocket boosters, the external propellant tank, and the Orbiter main engines. Test firings of Shuttle engines are carried out at NASA's National Space Technology Laboratories, Bay St. Louis, Mississippi.

NASA's John F. Kennedy Space Center, Florida, is responsible for design and development of launch and recovery facilities and for operational missions requiring easterly launches.

Thousands of companies make up the Shuttle contractor team. They are located in nearly every state of the United States.

A head-on view of a Space Shuttle Orbiter landing at the Kennedy Space Center (artist's concept). The huge vehicle assembly building (VAB) is shown in the background.

Voyager to Saturn

From Earth, the planet Saturn appears in the predawn hours of November 12, 1980, as a steady yellowish light in the constellation Virgo, outshining all but the brightest stars in the southeastern sky, its splendid rings visible with even a good pair of binoculars. But on that same day, the first of two Voyager spacecraft sees the great Ringed Planet as no one has seen it before, when it makes a second close approach to a planet on its decade-long flyby tour of the outer Solar System.

The Voyager mission takes advantage of state-of-the-art technology as well as a rare orbital alignment of the distant planets Jupiter, Saturn, Uranus, and Neptune to extend man's sight and his imagination billions of miles to regions where the Sun is only a bright star. Having already returned a wealth of information and pictures of amazing color and clarity from their Jupiter flybys in mid-1979, Voyagers 1 and 2 now prepare for their respective encounters with Saturn in November 1980, and August 1981.

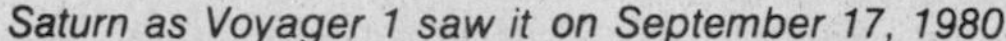
Saturn as Voyager 1 saw it on September 17, 1980.

The Voyager Spacecraft

Seemingly small for the task assigned them, the identical twin Voyagers weigh just under a ton each. The main functions of the spacecraft are clearly seen in its three-part design, beginning with the wide dish antenna for all-important radio communications to and from Earth. Underneath this dish are Voyager's "brains", the three primary and three backup computers—responsible for overall command, collection of science data, and control of the spacecraft's periodic rolls and turns. Finally, extending out from the body is a lattice-like arm, or "boom", where most of Voyager's sensors—its science instruments—are mounted.

Many of these instruments are sensors relating to different bands of the broad spectrum of electromagnetic energy that serves as a prime source of information for scientists. How a body (or a substance such as a gas) absorbs, reflects, emits, or in any way changes this energy tells much about its physical properties, especially if the energy is seen in very specific wavelengths.

And so, Voyager has four different "eyes"—TV or telemetry cameras, ultraviolet and infrared devices, and a light-analyzing photopolarimeter (no longer active on Voyager 1)—located on a scan platform which turns at almost any angle for precise targeting. Also on the boom are instruments to see cosmic rays and radio emissions from the planets.

Other science instruments supplement this spectral analysis with a search for highly energetic subatomic particles and fields. These include plasma (charged gas) detectors and magnetometers to survey the magnetic fields around planets.

Certain elements of Voyager's design, including its computer and TV systems, are adapted from the Mariner missions which have already explored the inner planets close to Earth. But in going much farther from the Sun to colder regions of space, Voyager requires special features first used by the Pioneer spacecraft, the first man-made objects to cross the asteroid belt.

Like Pioneer, Voyager is equipped with small nuclear generators to provide onboard electrical power. Earlier missions used solar panels for these energy demands, but Voyager's distance from the Sun makes this impractical, and creates an added need for small heaters and insulation against the cold.

The great distances Voyager will travel also require a giant leap in communications sophistication. Even at its highest output, the dish antenna points a narrow beam of less power than a small light bulb at a target so distant it will take nearly 1½ hours to reach Earth from Saturn.

Because we cannot yet go ourselves, Voyager goes for us. Its instruments cover the spectrum and detect charged particles and fields.

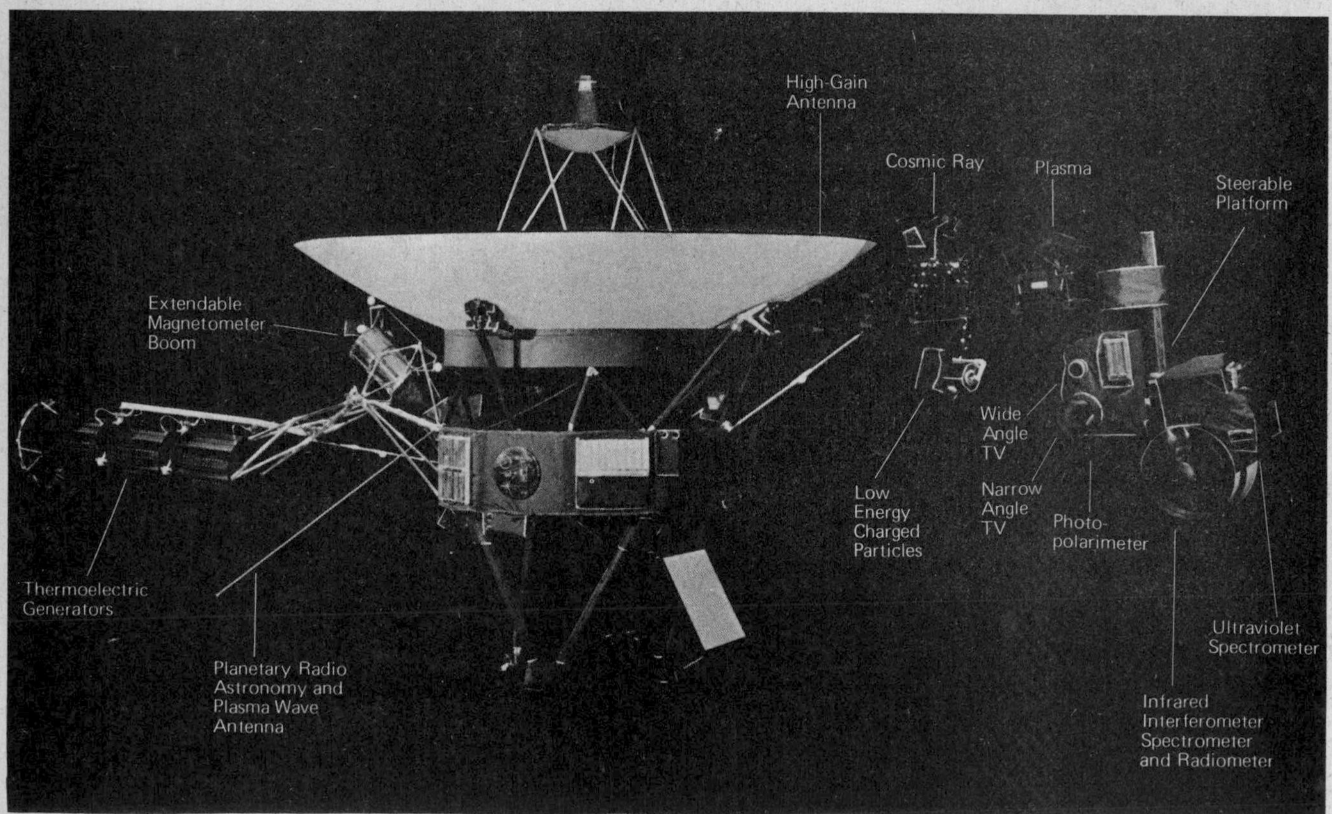

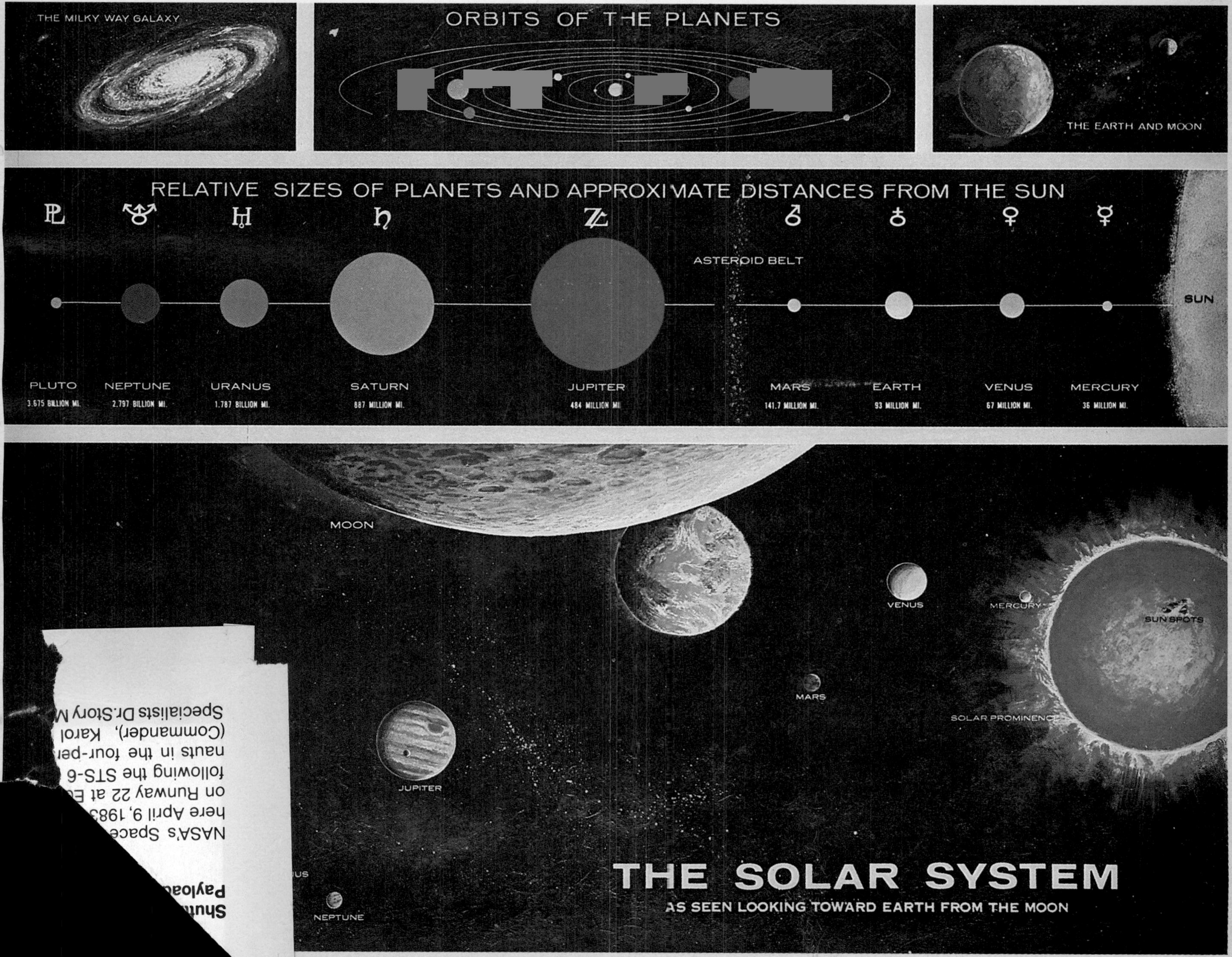

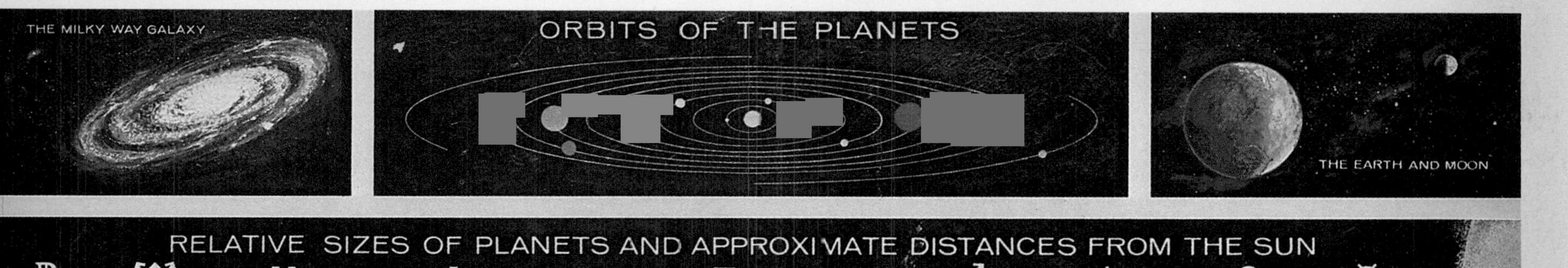

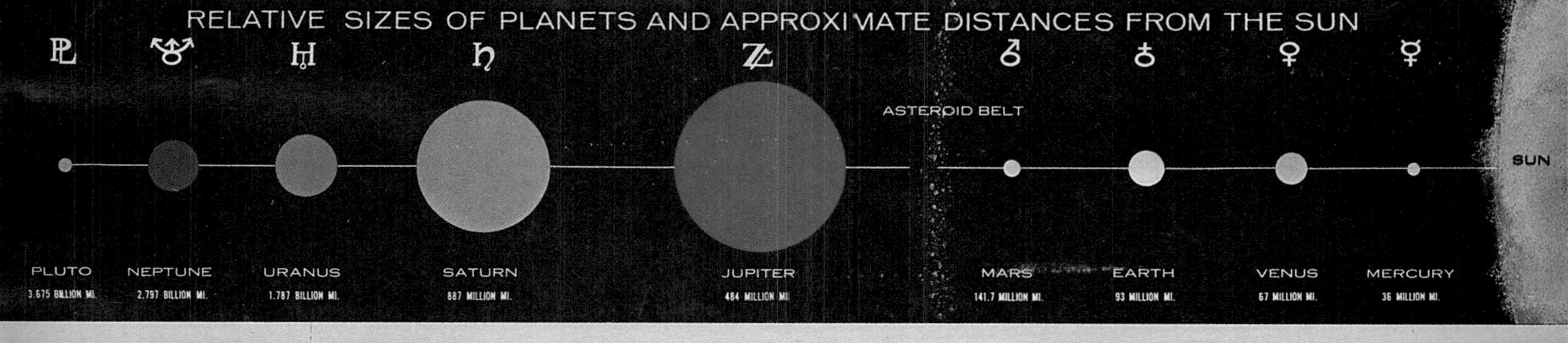

THE SOLAR SYSTEM

AS SEEN LOOKING TOWARD EARTH FROM THE MOON

MOON
VENUS
MERCURY
SUN SPOTS
MARS
SOLAR PROMINENCE
JUPITER
NEPTUNE
US

Shutt
Payloa

NASA's Space
here April 9, 198
on Runway 22 at E
following the STS-6
nauts in the four-per
(Commander), Karol
Specialists Dr. Story M

SOLAR SYSTEM — The nine known planets of the solar system can be divided into two categories: the Jovian planets and the terrestrial planets. Jupiter, Saturn, Uranus, and Neptune, the Jovian planets, are believed to consist of large cores of solid hydrogen and heavier elements surrounded by extensive atmospheres of heavy gases. As a group, the Jovian planets are less dense than the terrestrial planets and have many more satellites. Mercury, Venus, Earth, Mars, and Pluto, the terrestrial planets, are dense, solid bodies without extensive atmospheres. Between the orbits of Mars and Jupiter, the majority of asteroids, of which over 1,600 are presently known, are situated. These diminutive objects are thought to be remnants of a large planet which disintegrated. The planets travel in elliptical orbits of relatively low eccentricity around the Sun, although the eccentricity of Pluto is large enough to bring it sometimes nearer the Sun than Neptune. All the planets lie close to the plane of the earth's orbit, the ecliptic. Except for Pluto, the terrestrial planets are much nearer the Sun than the Jovian planets. For this reason, it is difficult to show in a schematic manner the relative distances of the planets, and the lithograph represents only their relative sizes, **not** their relative distance from the Sun.

EARTH AND MOON — The Earth is slightly flattened at the poles, resulting in an equatorial bulge. Energetic protons and electrons, trapped above the atmosphere by the Earth's magnetic field, form the Van Allen belts. The Moon has no atmosphere, and its cratered surface is believed caused by primordial meteorite impact and volcanic activity.

SUN — Our Sun, an incandescent body of gas, is by far the largest and most massive object in the solar system. Sunspots are large areas of cooler gas viewed against the hotter gas of the Sun's surface. Huge gaseous eruptions, know as prominences, sometimes rise several hundred thousand miles above the solar surface.

MILKY WAY — This immense aggregate of millions of stars, comprised of a flattened ellipsoid of stars with a very dense nucleus and superposed spiral arms, is 100,000 light years in diameter. The Sun, a typical star 30,000 light years from the center, is located in a spiral arm and moves with a speed of 250 miles per second around the galactic center.

...le Orbiter Challenger and Its First Spacecraft ...l

... Shuttle Orbiter *Challenger* is pictured ... on its first return to Earth from space ...dwards Air Force Base, California, ... five day mission in space. Astro- ...son crew included Paul J. Weitz ... J. Bobko (Pilot), and Mission ...usgrave and Donald H. Peterson.

Top photograph: The first of three Tracking and Data Relay Satellites (TDRS) and a portion of its Inertial Upper Stage (IUS) is shown here in the *Challenger* Space Shuttle Orbiter's open cargo bay some 10 hours after the launch of the STS-6 mission. The TDRS/IUS payload is poised on its tilt-table launch device, ready for spring ejection from the orbiter. In this view it has been raised almost 90 degrees from its stowed position. This was the heaviest payload released into orbit to date, (April 5, 1983) from a NASA Shuttle spacecraft.

Space Shuttle Orbiter OV 099 (Challenger) Crew Members

The five members for the eighth Space Shuttle flight (STS-8) are: (seated from left to right) pilot Daniel C. Brandenstein, mission specialist Dale A. Gardner, commander Richard H. Truly, mission specialists William E. Thornton and Guion S. Bluford, Jr. The STS-8 is the third flight of the Space Shuttle Challenger.

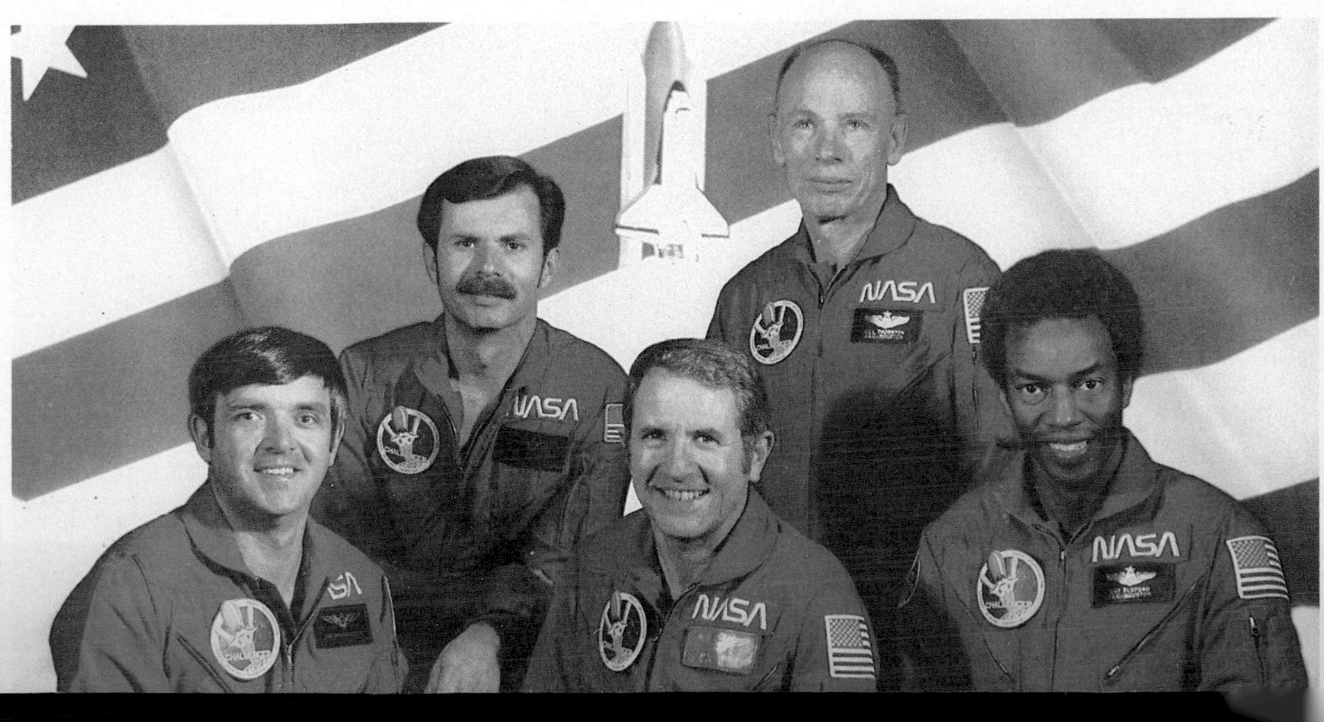

Challenger STS-6 Launch

The second reusable spacecraft in history lifts off successfully from Launch Pad 39A at NASA's Kennedy Space Center, Florida, and heads for Earth orbit. *Challenger*, its two solid rocket boosters (SRBs) and a new lightweight external fuel tank were captured on film by an automatically-tripped camera in a protected station nearer to the launch pad than human beings are able to be at launch time.

Extravehicular activity (EVA) on STS-6 Flight

Astronauts F. Story Musgrave (left) and Donald H. Peterson, STS-6 mission specialists, evaluate the handrail systems on the aft bulkhead and along the side of Challenger's open cargo bay. The activity took place during an orbital pass over a portion of Mexico's state of Jalisco, seen below. The photograph was made April 7, 1983 inside the spacecraft, with the camera looking aft from a viewing port overlooking the cargo bay.

Crew and Passenger Accommodations

The crew and passengers occupy a two-level cabin at the forward end of the Orbiter. The crew controls the launch, orbital maneuvering, atmospheric entry, and landing phases of the mission from the upper-level flight deck. Payload handling is accomplished by crewmen at the aft cabin payload station. Seating for passengers and a living area are provided on the lower deck. The cabin will have maximum utility; mission flexibility is achieved with minimal volume, complexity, and weight. Space flight will no longer be limited to intensively trained, physically perfect astronauts but will now accommodate experienced scientists and technicians.

Crewmembers and passengers will experience a designed maximum gravity load of only 3g during launch and less than 1.5g during a typical reentry. These accelerations are about one-third the levels experienced on previous manned flights. Many other features of the Space Shuttle, such as a standard sea level atmosphere, will welcome the nonastronaut space worker of the future.

Typical Shuttle Mission

The Space Shuttle mission begins with the installation of the mission payload into the Orbiter payload bay. The payload will be checked and serviced before installation and will be activated on orbit. Flight safety items for some payloads will be monitored by a caution and warning system.

In a typical Shuttle mission, which lasts from 7 to 30 days, the Orbiter's main engines and the booster ignite simultaneously to rocket the Shuttle from the launch pad. Launches are from the John F. Kennedy Space Center in Florida for east-west orbits or from Vandenberg Air Force Base in California for polar or north-south orbits.

At a predetermined point, the two unmanned solid rocket boosters separate from the Orbiter and parachute to the sea where they are recovered for reuse. The Orbiter continues into space. It jettisons its external propellant tank just before orbiting. The external tank enters the atmosphere and breaks up over a remote ocean area.

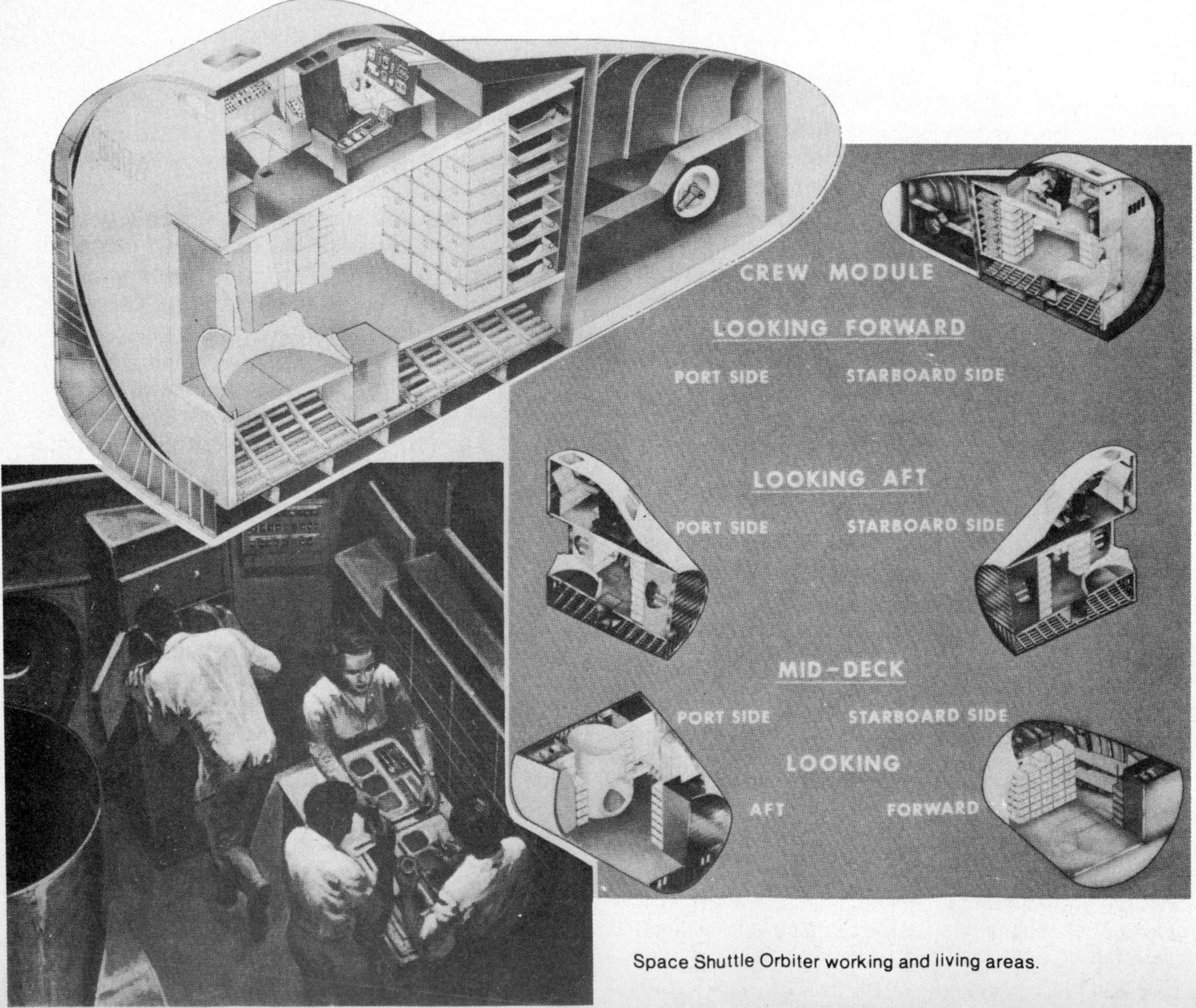

Space Shuttle Orbiter working and living areas.

Facilities on a part of the huge Edwards Air Force Base in the desertland of Southern California form the backdrop for the Shuttle Orbiter 101 "Enterprise" as it heads for a landing during the fourth Approach and Landing Test (ALT) free flight. Note that the tail cone is removed from the Enterprise for this flight, which featured a 2-minute 34-second unpowered phase after the Orbiter separated from NASA 905, a 747 carrier aircraft. Crewmen for the flight were Astronauts Joe H. Engle, commander, and Richard H. Truly, pilot.

In orbit, the Orbiter uses its orbital maneuvering subsystem (OMS) to adjust its path, for rendezvous operations, and, at the end of its mission, for slowing down so as to head back toward Earth. The orbital speed is nearly 8000 meters per second (18000 miles per hour). It takes approximately 90 minutes for an orbit of the Earth by the Space Shuttle, whether launched from NASA's Kennedy Space Center or, for some later flights, from Vandenberg Air Force Base in California. The first four orbital flight tests will be launched from Pad 39 at the Kennedy Space Center and land at Edwards Air Force Base, California

Solid rocket boosters landing at sea, where they will be picked up for reuse.

The OMS propellants are monomethyl hydrazine as the fuel and nitrogen tetroxide as the oxidizer. They ignite on contact, eliminating the need for ignition devices.

The Orbiter does not necessarily follow a ballistic path to the ground as did predecessor manned spacecraft. It has a crossrange capability (can maneuver to the right or left of its entry path) of about 2045 kilometers (1270 miles).

The Orbiter touches down like an airplane on a runway at Kennedy Space Center or Vandenberg Air Force Base. Landing speed is about 341 to 364 kilometers per hour (212 to 226 miles per hour). After refurbishing, the Shuttle is ready for another space mission.

Space Shuttle Vehicle Crew

The Shuttle crew can include as many as seven people: the commander, the pilot, the mission specialist who is responsible for management of Shuttle equipment and resources supporting payloads during the flight, and one to four payload specialists who are in charge of specific payload equipment. The commander, pilot, and mission specialist are NASA astronauts. Payload specialists conduct the experiments and may or may not be astronauts. They are nominated by the payload sponsor and certified for flight by NASA.

Space Shuttle System and Mission Profile (Principal Components)

The Space Shuttle flight system is composed of the Orbiter, an external tank (ET) that contains the ascent propellant to be used by the Orbiter main engines, and two solid rocket boosters (SRB's). Each booster rocket has a sea level thrust of 11.8 million newtons (2.65 million pounds). The Orbiter and the SRB's are reusable; the external tank is expended on each launch.

The Orbiter is the crew and payload carrying unit of the Shuttle system. It is 37 meters (122 feet) long and 17 meters (57 feet) high, has a wingspan of 24 meters (78 feet), and weighs about 68000 kilograms (150000 pounds) without fuel. It is about the size and weight of a DC-9 commercial air transport.

The direction of Earth rotation has a significant bearing on the payload launch capabilities of the Shuttle. A due east launch from the Kennedy Space Center in Florida, using the Earth's easterly rotation as a launch assist, will permit a payload of up to 29500 kilograms (65000 pounds) to be carried into orbit. A polar orbit launch from Vandenberg Air Force Base in California, where the Earth's rotation neither assists nor hinders the Shuttle's capabilities, will permit a payload of up to 18000 kilograms (40000 pounds) to be carried into orbit. The most westerly launch from Vandenberg will allow a payload up to only 14500 kilograms (32000 pounds) to be transported to orbit since the Earth's rotation is counter to the westerly launch azimuth. The Orbiter carries its cargo in a cavernous payload bay 18.3 meters (60 feet) long and 4.6 meters (15 feet) in diameter. The bay is flexible enough to provide accommodations for unmanned spacecraft in a variety of shapes and for fully equipped scientific laboratories.

Each of the Orbiter's three main liquid-rocket engines has a thrust of 2.1 million newtons (470000 pounds) at sea level. They are fed propellants from the external tank, which is 47 meters (154 feet) long and 8.7 meters (28.6 feet) in diameter.

At lift-off the tank holds 720000 kilograms (1580000 pounds) of propellants, consisting of liquid hydrogen (fuel) and liquid oxygen (oxidizer). The hydrogen and oxygen are in separate pressurized compartments of the tank. The external tank is the only part of the Shuttle system that is not reusable.

The Space Shuttle launch vehicle, with the Orbiter attached to the external tank and a pair of solid rocket boosters, climbs upward to begin its route to Earth orbit (artist's concept). This is a low- angle view indicating that the solid rocket boosters will soon be jettisoned. The external tank will also be jettisoned before the Orbiter enters an Earth-orbital configuration.

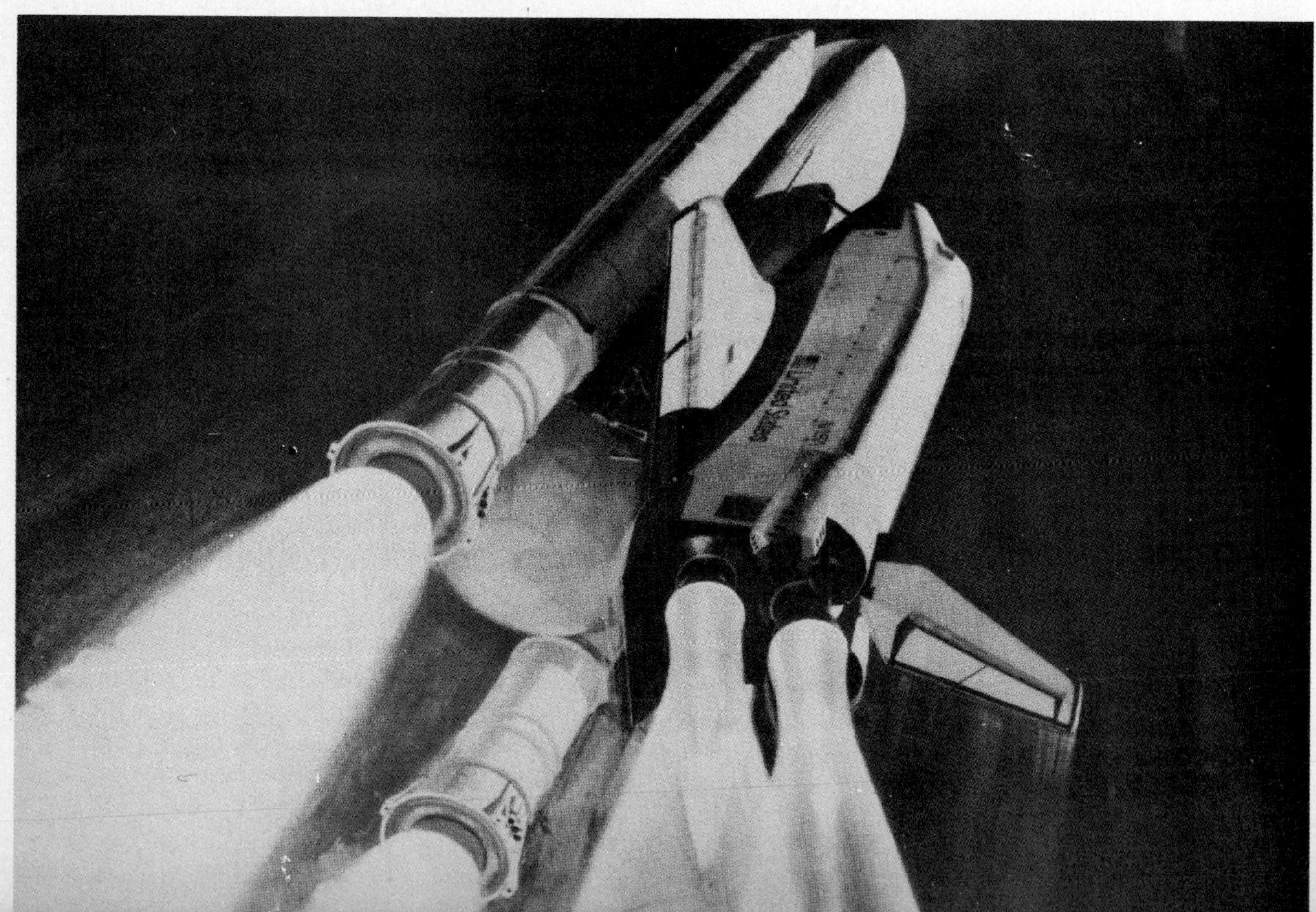

The Great Seal of the United States

Before it adjourned on July 4, 1776, the Continental Congress of the newly independent United States passed a resolution:

Resolved, that Dr. Franklin, Mr. J. Adams and Mr. Jefferson, be a committee, to bring in a device for a seal for the United States of America.

Obverse Side of the Great Seal

The most prominent feature is the American bald eagle supporting the shield, or escutcheon, which is composed of 13 red and white stripes, representing the original States, and a blue top which unites the shield and represents Congress. The motto, *E Pluribus Unum* (Out of many, one), alludes to this union. The olive branch and 13 arrows denote the power of peace and war, which is exclusively vested in Congress. The constellation of stars denotes a new State taking its place and rank among other sovereign powers.